Food & Beverage Market Place

Volume 2

2024

Twenty-third Edition

Food & Beverage Market Place

Volume 2

Equipment, Supplies & Services

Product Categories

Company Profiles

Grey House
Publishing

AMENIA, NY 12501

PUBLISHER: Leslie Mackenzie
EDITORIAL DIRECTOR: Stuart Paterson

RESEARCH ASSISTANT: Margarita Vachenkova
COMPOSITION: David Garoogian

MARKETING DIRECTOR: Jessica Moody

Grey House Publishing, Inc.
4919 Route 22
Amenia, NY 12501
518.789.8700
FAX 845.373.6390
www.greyhouse.com
e-mail: books@greyhouse.com

Copyright © 2023 Grey House Publishing, Inc.
All rights reserved
First edition published 2001
Twenty-third edition published 2023
Printed in the U.S.A.

Food & beverage market place. — 23rd ed. (2024) —
    3 v. ; 27.5 cm. Annual
  Includes index.
  ISSN: 1554-6334

1. Food industry and trade—United States—Directories. 2. Food industry and trade—Canada—Directories. 3. Beverage industry—United States—Directories. 4. Beverage industry—Canada—Directories. I. Grey House Publishing, Inc. II. Title: Food & beverage market place.

HD9003.T48
338-dc21

3-Volume Set   ISBN: 978-1-63700-542-2
Volume 1   ISBN: 978-1-63700-543-9
Volume 2   ISBN: 978-1-63700-544-6
Volume 3   ISBN: 978-1-63700-545-3

Table of Contents

VOLUME 1

VOLUME 2

VOLUME 3

Introduction

This 2024 edition of *Food & Beverage Market Place* represents the largest, most comprehensive resource of food and beverage manufacturers and service suppliers on the market today. These three volumes include over 45,000 company profiles that address all sectors of the industry-finished goods and ingredients manufacturers, equipment manufacturers, and third-party logistics providers, including transportation, warehousing, wholesalers, brokers, importers and exporters.

As the country continues to recover from the COVID-19 pandemic, the food industry is reporting a number of trends, some surprising and some not surprising at all. Predictably, there is a continued interest in health and wellness products, specifically probiotics and nutrition supplements. Sales of sustainable, plant-based, and alternative meat products continue to grow. The beverage sector sees continued growth in alcohol sales, especially wine and, at the same time, increased interest in products with no and low alcohol content.

Online shopping, food delivery, and meal kits are continuing in popularity. The shift to at-home cooking and eating also remains strong, as Americans continue to enjoy the family connections and closeness that it fosters. In terms of eating out, in-house dining is seeing a resurgence thanks to new restaurant layouts, menu items, and technological connectivity. Collaborations and multi-vendor 'ghost kitchens' are also keeping customers engaged.

Following this Introduction in Volume 1 appears *Outlook for U.S. Agricultural Trade: February 2023*, which provides an overview of American agricultural trade in the current climate, including the aftershocks of the COVID-19 pandemic.

Industry trends are likely to continue, as consumers focus on foods that encourage sustainability, foods that are convenient and healthy, foods that are processed in secure and safe environments, and foods with complex world flavors.

As the food and beverage industry adapts and pivots to a post-pandemic environment, *Food & Beverage Market Place* has adapted as well. The research for this edition focuses on healthy food options and cutting-edge food products. Manufacturers use systems that are safe and secure. Packagers are mindful of the environment. Whatever slice of the market you cater to, you will find your buyers, sellers, and users in this comprehensive, three-volume reference tool containing the complete coverage our subscribers have come to expect. Our extensive indexing makes quick work of locating exactly the company, product or service you are looking for.

Data Statistics

Each of the eight chapters in *Food & Beverage Market Place* reflects a massive update effort. This 2024 edition includes hundreds of new company profiles and thousands of updates throughout the three volumes. You will find 81,000 key executives, 23,019 web sites, and 15,103 e-mails. The volumes break down as follows:

Volume 1   Food, Beverage & Ingredient Manufacturers - 14,419

Volume 2   Equipment, Supply & Service Providers - 13,515

Volume 3   Third Party Logistics
                     Brokers - 1,287
                     Importers & Exporters - 8,819
                     Transportation Firms - 709
                     Warehouse Companies - 1,050
                     Wholesalers & Distributors - 6,019

Arrangement

The product category sections for both food and beverage products in Volume 1 and equipment and supplies in Volume 2 begin with Product Category Lists. These include over 6,000 alphabetical terms for everything from Abalone to Zinc Citrate, from Adhesive Tapes to Zipper Application Systems. Use the detailed cross-references to find the full entry in the Product Category sections that immediately follow. Here you will find up to three levels of detail, for example-*Fish & Seafood: Fish: Abalone* or *Ingredients, Flavors & Additives: Vitamins & Supplements: Zinc Citrate*-with the name, location, phone number and packaging format of companies who manufacturer/process the product you are looking for. Organic and Gluten-Free categories make it easy to locate those manufacturers who focus on these food types.

In addition to company profiles, this edition has 17 indexes, 15 chapter-specific, arranged by geographic region, product or company type, and two-All Brands and All Companies-that comprise all three volumes. See the Table of Contents for a complete list of specific indexes. Plus, chapters include User Guides that help you navigate chapter-specific data.

We are confident that this reference is the foremost research tool in the food and beverage industry. It will prove invaluable to manufacturers, buyers, specifiers, market researchers, consultants, and anyone working in food and beverage-one of the largest industries in the country.

Praise for previous editions:

> *"...This set can be used to find basic information or to track trends in a dynamic industry.... Recommended for large public or academic libraries."*

> *"...Each volume contains helpful user guides and key that describes the field of data that appear in that chapter.... This publication is essential for researchers in the food industry, and large academic and public libraries."*

—American Reference Books Annual

Online Database & Mailing Lists

Food & Beverage Market Place is also available for subscription on https://gold.greyhouse.com for even faster, easier access to this wealth of information. Subscribers can search by product category, state, sales volume, employee size, personnel name, title and much more. Plus, users can print out prospect sheets or download data into their own spreadsheet or database. This database is a must for anyone marketing a product or service to this vast industry. Visit the site, or call 800-562-2139 for a free trial.

EQUIPMENT, SUPPLIES & SERVICES

User Guide
Product Category List
Product Categories
Company Profiles
Brand Name Index
Geographic Index

Equipment User Guide

The **Equipment, Supplies and Services Chapter** of *Food & Beverage Market Place* includes companies that manufacturer equipment and supplies, or offer services, in the food and beverage industry. The chapter begins with a **Category Listing** of equipment, supplies and services that are offered by companies in this chapter. This category list is followed by a **Product Category Index**, organized first by state, then alphabetical by company. Each company listing includes packaging type, city and phone number.

Following the **Product Category Index** are the descriptive listings, which are organized alphabetically. Following the A – Z Equipment, Supplies and Services listings are two indexes: **Brand Name Index**, which lists the brand names of the equipment and supplies in this chapter, and **Geographic Index**, which lists all companies by state. These Indexes refers to listing numbers, not page numbers.

Below is a sample listing illustrating the kind of information that is or might be included in an Equipment, Supplies and Services listing. Each numbered item of information is described in the User Key on the following page.

---

1 → 245600

2 → **(HQ) A.A. A La Carte**

3 → 5600 Bloomingdale Avenue

New Berlin, WI 53151

4 → 062-789-1500

5 → 062-789-1501

6 → 888-789-1501

7 → info@AlaCarte.com

8 → www.AlaCarte.com

9 → Contract packager and exporter of hard candy in decorative tins, jars, and boxes.

10 → President: James Gold
CFO: James Filbert
COO: Gail King
Vice President: Elizabeth Timely
Marketing: Donna Paige

11 → *Estimated Sales*: $1-5 Million

12 → *Number Employees*: 35

13 → *Sq. Footage*:   25000

14 → *Parent Co.*: A.A. Special Lines

15 → *Company is also listed in the following section(s)*: Exporter

16 → Brands: Pierell, Apresa, Cocolot

Equipment Companies User Key

1 ▶ **Record Number:** Entries are listed alphabetically within each category and numbered sequentially. The entry number, rather than the page number, is used in the indexes to refer to listings.

2 ▶ **Company Name:** Formal name of company. HQ indicates headquarter location. If names are completely capitalized, the listing will appear at the beginning of the alphabetized section.

3 ▶ **Address:** Location or permanent address of the company. If the mailing address differs from the street address, it will appear second.

4 ▶ **Phone Number:** The listed phone number is usually for the main office, but may also be for the sales, marketing, or public relations office as provided.

5 ▶ **Fax Number:** This is listed when provided by the company.

6 ▶ **Toll-Free Number:** This is listed when provided by the company.

7 ▶ **E-Mail:** This is listed when provided, and is generally the main office e-mail.

8 ▶ **Web Site:** This is listed when provided by the company and is also referred to as an URL address. These web sites are accessed through the Internet by typing http:// before the URL address.

9 ▶ **Description**: This paragraph contains a brief description of the products or services that are brokered, sometimes including markets served.

10 ▶ **Key Personnel:** Names and titles of company executives.

11 ▶ **Estimated Sales:** This is listed when provided by the company.

12 ▶ **Number of Employees:** Total number of employees within the company.

13 ▶ Indicates what other section in *Food & Beverage Market Place* this company is listed: Volume 1: Manufacturers. Volume 2: Equipment, Supplies & Services; Transportation; Warehouse; Wholesalers/Distributors. Volume 3: Brokers; Importers/Exporters.

14 ▶ **Markets Served:** This further defines the company as serving one or more markers, such as Super Market Chains, Wholesale Distributors, Food Service Operators, etc. Companies are indexed by market.

15 ▶ **Primary Brands Brokered include:** A list of brand names that the company brokers.

16 ▶ **Brokered Products include**: This describes the type of product that the broker handles, such as alcoholic beverages, frozen foods, exports, ingredients, etc. Companies are indexed by product.

A

Adhesive *See Packaging Materials & Supplies: Tapes: Adhesive*

Advertising Novelties & Specialties *See Consultants & Services: Advertising Services: Advertising Novelties & Specialties*

Advertising Services *See Consultants & Services: Advertising Services*

Advertising Signs *See Foodservice Equipment & Supplies: Signs: Advertising*

Aerosol *See Equipment & Machinery: Food Processing: Aerosol*

Agglomeration *See Consultants & Services: Custom Services: Agglomeration*

Agitators *See Equipment & Machinery: Food Processing: Agitators*

Air Curtain Doors *See Building Equipment & Supplies: Doors: Air Curtain*

Air Curtains *See Building Equipment & Supplies: Air Curtains*

Air Filters *See Building Equipment & Supplies: Air Filters*

Air Knives *See Equipment & Machinery: Food Processing: Air Knives*

Airport Facilities *See Consultants & Services: Foodservice: Airport Facilities*

Alarm Systems *See Safety & Security Equipment & Supplies: Alarm Systems*

Aluminum Bottles *See Packaging Materials & Supplies: Bottles: Aluminum*

Aluminum Cans *See Packaging Materials & Supplies: Cans: Aluminum*

Aluminum Foil *See Packaging Materials & Supplies: Foil: Aluminum*

Aluminum Ware *See Food Preparation Equipment, Utensils & Cookware: Aluminum Ware*

Amino Acid, Nitrogen Analyzers *See Instrumentation & Laboratory Equipment: Analyzers: Amino Acid, Nitrogen*

Ammonia *See Sanitation Equipment & Supplies: Ammonia*

Amusement & Theme Parks *See Consultants & Services: Foodservice: Amusement & Theme Parks*

Anaerobic & Aerobic *See Sanitation Equipment & Supplies: Wastewater Treatment Systems: Anaerobic & Aerobic*

Analytical Services *See Consultants & Services: Analytical Services*

Analyzers *See Instrumentation & Laboratory Equipment: Analyzers*

Anti-Slip Flooring *See Building Equipment & Supplies: Flooring: Anti-Slip*

Aprons *See Clothing & Protective Apparel: Aprons*

Architects *See Consultants & Services: Architects*

Architectural & Engineering Designers *See Consultants & Services: Designers: Architectural & Engineering*

Aseptic Packaging *See Packaging Materials & Supplies: Packaging: Aseptic*

Augers *See Equipment & Machinery: Food Processing: Augers*

Auto Scrubbing & Burnishing Scrubbers *See Equipment & Machinery: Scrubbers: Auto Scrubbing & Burnishing*

Automated Guided Vehicles *See Transportation & Storage: Automated Guided Vehicles*

Automatic/Random Case Sealing Packaging *See Equipment & Machinery: Packaging: Automatic/Random Case Sealing*

Automation & Controls *See Instrumentation & Laboratory Equipment: Controls: Automation & Controls*

Automation *See Instrumentation & Laboratory Equipment: Automation*

Awnings *See Building Equipment & Supplies: Awnings*

B

Backers Magnetic Label *See Foodservice Equipment & Supplies: Magnetic Label: Backers*

Bag Closing *See Equipment & Machinery: Packaging: Bag Closing*

Bag Filling *See Equipment & Machinery: Packaging: Bag Filling*

Bag Holders *See Foodservice Equipment & Supplies: Holders: Bag*

Bag Opening *See Equipment & Machinery: Packaging: Bag Opening*

Bag Ties *See Packaging Materials & Supplies: Ties: Bag*

Bag, Cellophane & Pliofilm *See Equipment & Machinery: Packaging: Bag, Cellophane & Pliofilm*

Bag, Paper *See Equipment & Machinery: Packaging: Bag, Paper*

Bagel Slicer *See Food Preparation Equipment, Utensils & Cookware: Slicer: Bagel*

Bags *See Packaging Materials & Supplies: Bags*

Bakers' & Confectioners' Brushes *See Food Preparation Equipment, Utensils & Cookware: Brushes: Bakers' & Confectioners'*

Bakers' & Confectioners' Molds *See Food Preparation Equipment, Utensils & Cookware: Molds: Bakers' & Confectioners'*

Bakers' & Confectioners' Utensils *See Food Preparation Equipment, Utensils & Cookware: Utensils: Bakers' & Confectioners'*

Bakers' Boxes *See Packaging Materials & Supplies: Boxes: Bakers'*

Bakers' Gloves *See Clothing & Protective Apparel: Gloves: Bakers'*

Bakers' Mixers *See Equipment & Machinery: Food Processing: Mixers: Bakers'*

Bakers' Trays & Pans *See Food Preparation Equipment, Utensils & Cookware: Trays & Pans: Bakers'*

Bakery *See Consultants & Services: Contract Manufacturing: Bakery*

Bakery Racks *See Foodservice Equipment & Supplies: Racks: Bakery*

Baking & Roasting Pans *See Food Preparation Equipment, Utensils & Cookware: Pans: Baking & Roasting*

Baking Industry *See Equipment & Machinery: Baking Industry*

Balances *See Instrumentation & Laboratory Equipment: Balances*

Balers or Baling Presses *See Equipment & Machinery: Food Processing: Balers or Baling Presses*

Ball & Pebble Mills *See Equipment & Machinery: Food Processing: Mills: Ball & Pebble*

Bamboo Chopsticks *See Food Preparation Equipment, Utensils & Cookware: Utensils: Chopsticks: Bamboo*

Banquet Carts *See Foodservice Equipment & Supplies: Carts: Banquet*

Bar Code Devices *See Equipment & Machinery: Packaging: Bar Code Devices*

Barbecue Equipment & Supplies *See Equipment & Machinery: Barbecue Equipment & Supplies*

Barley Processing *See Equipment & Machinery: Food Processing: Barley Processing*

Barrel & Drum Draining Racks *See Transportation & Storage: Racks: Barrel & Drum Draining*

Barrel & Drum Filling *See Equipment & Machinery: Packaging: Barrel & Drum Filling*

Barrel Packers *See Equipment & Machinery: Packaging: Barrel Packers*

Bars & Bar Supplies *See Foodservice Equipment & Supplies: Bars & Bar Supplies*

Baskets *See Food Preparation Equipment, Utensils & Cookware: Baskets; Foodservice Equipment & Supplies: Baskets; Packaging Materials & Supplies: Baskets*

Batching, Blending, Weighing *See Instrumentation & Laboratory Equipment: Process Controls: Batching, Blending, Weighing*

Beam Scales *See Equipment & Machinery: Scales: Beam*

Bean & Grain Sorters *See Equipment & Machinery: Food Processing: Sorters: Bean & Grain*

Bean & Pea Hullers *See Equipment & Machinery: Food Processing: Hullers: Bean & Pea*

Bean, Pea Separators *See Equipment & Machinery: Food Processing: Separators: Bean, Pea*

Beaters *See Food Preparation Equipment, Utensils & Cookware: Beaters*

Beer & Ale Cans *See Packaging Materials & Supplies: Cans: Beer & Ale*

Beer Dispensers *See Foodservice Equipment & Supplies: Dispensers: Beer*

Beer Keg Movers *See Transportation & Storage: Beer Keg Movers*

Belt Conveyors *See Equipment & Machinery: Conveyors: Belt*

Belting *See Equipment & Machinery: Belting*

Belts *See Equipment & Machinery: Belts*

Beverage Bins *See Packaging Materials & Supplies: Bins: Beverage*

Beverage Carts *See Foodservice Equipment & Supplies: Carts: Beverage*

Beverage Coolers *See Refrigeration & Cooling Equipment: Coolers: Beverage*

Beverage Dispensers *See Foodservice Equipment & Supplies: Dispensers: Beverage*

Beverage Hoses *See Equipment & Machinery: Hoses: Beverage*

Beverage Industry *See Equipment & Machinery: Beverage Industry*

Beverages, Hot Fill Packaging *See Equipment & Machinery: Packaging: Beverages, Hot Fill*

Bins *See Packaging Materials & Supplies: Bins*

Biodegradable, Recyclable Plastic *See Packaging Materials & Supplies: Plastic: Biodegradable, Recyclable*

Biscuit & Cookie Cutters *See Food Preparation Equipment, Utensils & Cookware: Cutters: Biscuit & Cookie*

Biscuit Making *See Equipment & Machinery: Food Processing: Biscuit Making*

Blades *See Equipment & Machinery: Food Processing: Blades*

Blast Chillers *See Refrigeration & Cooling Equipment: Chillers: Blast*

Bleaches *See Sanitation Equipment & Supplies: Bleaches*

Blenders *See Equipment & Machinery: Food Processing: Blenders*

Blending & Mixing *See Consultants & Services: Contract Manufacturing: Blending & Mixing*

Blending *See Consultants & Services: Custom Services: Blending; Equipment & Machinery: Food Processing: Blending*

Blister Packaging *See Packaging Materials & Supplies: Packaging: Blister*

Blocks *See Food Preparation Equipment, Utensils & Cookware: Blocks*

Blowers *See Equipment & Machinery: Food Processing: Blowers*

Boards *See Food Preparation Equipment, Utensils & Cookware: Boards*

Boiler & Steam Controls *See Instrumentation & Laboratory Equipment: Controls: Boiler & Steam*

Boilers *See Equipment & Machinery: Food Processing: Boilers*

Borax *See Sanitation Equipment & Supplies: Borax*

Bottle & Jar Sealing *See Equipment & Machinery: Packaging: Bottle & Jar Sealing; Packaging Materials & Supplies: Seals: Bottle & Jar*

Bottle (Compounds) Cleaners *See Sanitation Equipment & Supplies: Cleaners: Bottle (Compounds)*

Bottle Brushes *See Sanitation Equipment & Supplies: Brushes: Bottle*

Bottle Cap, Plastic & Metal *See Equipment & Machinery: Packaging: Bottle Cap, Plastic & Metal*

Bottle Capping & Crowning *See Equipment & Machinery: Packaging: Bottle Capping & Crowning*

Bottle Cartoning *See Equipment & Machinery: Packaging: Bottle Cartoning*

Bottle Conveyors *See Equipment & Machinery: Conveyors: Bottle*

Bottle Corking *See Equipment & Machinery: Packaging: Bottle Corking*

Bottle Crates *See Packaging Materials & Supplies: Crates: Bottle*

Bottle Drying *See Equipment & Machinery: Packaging: Bottle Drying*

Bottle Filling *See Equipment & Machinery: Packaging: Bottle Filling*

Bottle Openers *See Equipment & Machinery: Openers: Bottle*

Bottle Racks *See Transportation & Storage: Racks: Bottle*

Bottle Sleeves *See Packaging Materials & Supplies: Sleeves: Bottle*

EXAMPLE: ‍1⎵ 2⎵ 3⎵ 4⎵ 5⎵

Dairy Cooling Vats *See Equipment & Machinery: Food Processing: Vats: Dairy Cooling*

1. Product or Service you are looking for
2. Main Category, in alphabetical order, located in the page headers starting on page 17
3. Category Description, located in black bars and in page headers
4. Product Category, located in gray bars
5. Product Type, located under gray bars, centered in bold

Bottle Sorters *See Equipment & Machinery: Packaging: Sorters: Bottle*

Bottle Washing, Soaking & Rinsing *See Equipment & Machinery: Packaging: Bottle Washing, Soaking & Rinsing*

Bottle, Can & Jar Caps *See Packaging Materials & Supplies: Caps: Bottle, Can & Jar*

Bottled for Cleaning Ammonia *See Sanitation Equipment & Supplies: Ammonia: Bottled for Cleaning*

Bottles *See Packaging Materials & Supplies: Bottles*

Bottling *See Equipment & Machinery: Packaging: Bottling*

Bowls *See Food Preparation Equipment, Utensils & Cookware: Bowls*

Box Closing *See Equipment & Machinery: Packaging: Box Closing*

Box Cutters *See Transportation & Storage: Box Cutters; Equipment & Machinery: Packaging: Box Cutting*

Box Strapping *See Equipment & Machinery: Packaging: Box Strapping; See also Packaging Materials & Supplies: Seals: Box Strapping*

Box, Carton, Case & Crate *See Packaging Materials & Supplies: Linings: Box, Carton, Case & Crate*

Box, Crate, Carton Openers *See Equipment & Machinery: Openers: Box, Crate, Carton*

Box, Paper *See Equipment & Machinery: Packaging: Box, Paper*

Boxes *See Packaging Materials & Supplies: Boxes*

Bread & Cake Slicers *See Equipment & Machinery: Food Processing: Slicers: Bread & Cake*

Bread & Pastry Bags *See Packaging Materials & Supplies: Bags: Bread & Pastry*

Bread Coolers *See Refrigeration & Cooling Equipment: Coolers: Bread*

Bread Knives *See Food Preparation Equipment, Utensils & Cookware: Knives: Bread*

Bread Slicer *See Food Preparation Equipment, Utensils & Cookware: Slicer: Bread*

Bread, Cake & Steak Wood Boards *See Food Preparation Equipment, Utensils & Cookware: Boards: Wood: Bread, Cake & Steak*

Brewery Cookers *See Equipment & Machinery: Food Processing: Cookers: Brewery; Equipment & Machinery: Food Processing: Brewery*

Brine Making Equipment *See Equipment & Machinery: Food Processing: Brine Making Equipment*

Broilers *See Equipment & Machinery: Food Processing: Broilers*

Broom Holders *See Sanitation Equipment & Supplies: Holders: Broom*

Brooms *See Sanitation Equipment & Supplies: Brooms*

Brushes *See Food Preparation Equipment, Utensils & Cookware: Brushes; See also Sanitation Equipment & Supplies: Brushes*

Bulk Bags *See Packaging Materials & Supplies: Bags: Bulk*

Bulk Grinding Grinders *See Equipment & Machinery: Food Processing: Grinders: Bulk Grinding*

Bundle, Package Ties *See Packaging Materials & Supplies: Ties: Bundle, Package*

Bussing Carts *See Foodservice Equipment & Supplies: Carts: Bussing*

Butchers' Blades *See Equipment & Machinery: Food Processing: Saws: Butchers' Blades*

Butchers' Block Scrapers *See Food Preparation Equipment, Utensils & Cookware: Scrapers: Butchers' Block*

Butchers' Blocks *See Food Preparation Equipment, Utensils & Cookware: Blocks: Butchers'*

Butchers' Cleavers *See Food Preparation Equipment, Utensils & Cookware: Cleavers: Butchers'*

Butchers' Coolers *See Refrigeration & Cooling Equipment: Coolers: Butchers'*

Butchers' Knives *See Food Preparation Equipment, Utensils & Cookware: Knives: Butchers'*

Butchers' Scales *See Equipment & Machinery: Scales: Butchers'*

Butchers' Trays *See Foodservice Equipment & Supplies: Trays: Butchers'*

Butter & Cheese Molds *See Food Preparation Equipment, Utensils & Cookware: Molds: Butter & Cheese*

C

Cabinets *See Refrigeration & Cooling Equipment: Cabinets*

Cafeteria Trays *See Foodservice Equipment & Supplies: Trays: Cafeteria*

Cafeteria, Restaurant Counters *See Foodservice Equipment & Supplies: Counters: Cafeteria, Restaurant*

Cafeteria, Restaurant, Foodservice Kitchen Tables *See Foodservice Equipment & Supplies: Tables: Cafeteria, Restaurant, Foodservice Kitchen*

Cake Cutters *See Food Preparation Equipment, Utensils & Cookware: Cutters: Cake*

Cake Knives *See Food Preparation Equipment, Utensils & Cookware: Knives: Cake*

Cake Pan Liners *See Food Preparation Equipment, Utensils & Cookware: Liners: Cake Pan*

Cake Tins *See Food Preparation Equipment, Utensils & Cookware: Tins: Cake*

Cake Turners *See Foodservice Equipment & Supplies: Cake Turners*

Can & Glass Crushers *See Equipment & Machinery: Food Processing: Crushers: Can & Glass*

Can Body Forming *See Equipment & Machinery: Packaging: Can Body Forming*

Can Capping *See Equipment & Machinery: Packaging: Can Capping*

Can Closing *See Equipment & Machinery: Packaging: Can Closing*

Can Drying *See Equipment & Machinery: Packaging: Can Drying*

Can Filling *See Equipment & Machinery: Packaging: Can Filling*

Can Openers *See Equipment & Machinery: Openers: Can*

Can Racks *See Transportation & Storage: Racks: Can*

Can Sealing *See Equipment & Machinery: Packaging: Can Sealing*

Can Seaming *See Equipment & Machinery: Packaging: Can Seaming*

Can Washing *See Equipment & Machinery: Packaging: Can Washing*

Can, Drum & Barrel Linings *See Packaging Materials & Supplies: Linings: Can, Drum & Barrel*

Candles *See Foodservice Equipment & Supplies: Candles*

Candy (Confectioners') Coolers *See Refrigeration & Cooling Equipment: Coolers: Candy (Confectioners')*

Candy Boxes *See Packaging Materials & Supplies: Boxes: Candy*

Candy Sticks *See Packaging Materials & Supplies: Sticks: Candy*

Candy Wrapping Paper *See Packaging Materials & Supplies: Paper: Candy Wrapping*

Cane Shredders *See Equipment & Machinery: Food Processing: Shredders: Cane*

Canners' & Packers' Aprons *See Clothing & Protective Apparel: Aprons: Canners' & Packers'*

Canners' Cookers *See Equipment & Machinery: Food Processing: Cookers: Canners'*

Canners' Coolers *See Refrigeration & Cooling Equipment: Coolers: Canners'*

Canners' Knives *See Food Preparation Equipment, Utensils & Cookware: Knives: Canners'*

Canners *See Consultants & Services: Canners*

Canning & Food Packing *See Equipment & Machinery: Packaging: Canning & Food Packing*

Canning & Preserving Jars *See Packaging Materials & Supplies: Jars: Canning & Preserving*

Canning & Preserving Kettles *See Food Preparation Equipment, Utensils & Cookware: Kettles: Canning & Preserving*

Canning Exhausters *See Equipment & Machinery: Packaging: Exhausters: Canning*

Canning Retorts *See Packaging Materials & Supplies: Retorts: Canning*

Cans *See Packaging Materials & Supplies: Cans*

Cap Torque Test *See Equipment & Machinery: Packaging: Cap Torque Test*

Cappers *See Equipment & Machinery: Packaging: Cappers*

Caps *See Clothing & Protective Apparel: Caps; Packaging Materials & Supplies: Caps*

Carriers *See Packaging Materials & Supplies: Carriers*

Carton *See Equipment & Machinery: Packaging: Carton*

Carton, Case, Box Sealing *See Equipment & Machinery: Packaging: Carton, Case, Box Sealing*

Cartons *See Packaging Materials & Supplies: Cartons*

Carts *See Foodservice Equipment & Supplies: Carts; Sanitation Equipment & Supplies: Carts; See also Transportation & Storage: Carts*

Carving Knives *See Food Preparation Equipment, Utensils & Cookware: Knives: Carving*

Cases *See Foodservice Equipment & Supplies: Cases*

Cash Registers *See Foodservice Equipment & Supplies: Cash Registers*

Cash, Money Drawers *See Foodservice Equipment & Supplies: Drawers: Cash, Money*

Casters *See Transportation & Storage: Casters*

Caustic Soda *See Sanitation Equipment & Supplies: Caustic Soda*

Ceiling Fans *See Building Equipment & Supplies: Fans: Ceiling*

Ceiling Surfaces & Panels *See Building Equipment & Supplies: Ceiling Surfaces & Panels*

Cellophane Bags *See Packaging Materials & Supplies: Bags: Cellophane*

Cellulose & Fiber Tags *See Packaging Materials & Supplies: Tags: Cellulose & Fiber*

Cellulose Acetate Film *See Packaging Materials & Supplies: Film: Cellulose Acetate*

Centrifuge Bags *See Packaging Materials & Supplies: Bags: Centrifuge*

Centrifuges *See Instrumentation & Laboratory Equipment: Centrifuges*

Cereal Contract Manufacturing *See Consultants & Services: Contract Manufacturing: Cereal*

Cereal Cookers *See Equipment & Machinery: Food Processing: Cookers: Cereal*

Cereal Making *See Equipment & Machinery: Food Processing: Cereal Making*

Certification *See Instrumentation & Laboratory Equipment: Certification*

Chafers *See Foodservice Equipment & Supplies: Chafers*

Chain Conveyors *See Equipment & Machinery: Conveyors: Chain*

Chairs *See Foodservice Equipment & Supplies: Chairs*

Chamois Cloths *See Sanitation Equipment & Supplies: Cloths: Chamois*

Changeable Letter Signs *See Foodservice Equipment & Supplies: Signs: Changeable Letter*

Changers *See Foodservice Equipment & Supplies: Changers*

Charcoal Briquette *See Equipment & Machinery: Food Processing: Cooking & Heating Equipment: Charcoal Briquettes*

Charcoal: Mesquite *See Equipment & Machinery: Food Processing: Cooking & Heating Equipment: Charcoal: Mesquite*

Check & Credit Card Verification Systems *See Foodservice Equipment & Supplies: Scanners: Check & Credit Card Verification Systems*

Check Weighing Systems *See Equipment & Machinery: Systems: Check Weighing*

Check, Bill & Voucher Sorters *See Foodservice Equipment & Supplies: Sorters: Check, Bill & Voucher*

Cheese Coating *See Packaging Materials & Supplies: Wax: Cheese Coating*

Cheese Cookers *See Equipment & Machinery: Food Processing: Cookers: Cheese*

Cheese Cutters *See Food Preparation Equipment, Utensils & Cookware: Cutters: Cheese*

Cheese Hoops *See Food Preparation Equipment, Utensils & Cookware: Hoops: Cheese*

Cheese Knives *See Food Preparation Equipment, Utensils & Cookware: Knives: Cheese*

Cheese Making *See Equipment & Machinery: Food Processing: Cheese Making*

Cheese Processing *See Equipment & Machinery: Food Processing: Cheese Processing*

Cheese Shredders *See Equipment & Machinery: Food Processing: Shredders: Cheese*

Cheese Vats *See Equipment & Machinery: Food Processing: Vats: Cheese; See also Transportation & Storage: Vats: Cheese*

Cheesecloth *See Equipment & Machinery: Food Processing: Cheesecloth*

Chemical Dispensing *See Equipment & Machinery: Systems: Chemical Dispensing & Feed*

Chemicals *See Instrumentation & Laboratory Equipment: Chemicals*

Chewing Gum *See Equipment & Machinery: Food Processing: Chewing Gum Processing*

Chicken, Prepared Containers *See Packaging Materials & Supplies: Containers: Chicken, Prepared*

Chillers *See Refrigeration & Cooling Equipment: Chillers*

China *See Foodservice Equipment & Supplies: China*

Chips Clear & Colored Plastic *See Foodservice Equipment & Supplies: Clear & Colored Plastic: Chips*

Chips Wood Grain Plastic *See Foodservice Equipment & Supplies: Wood Grain Plastic: Chips*

Chlorine *See Sanitation Equipment & Supplies: Chlorine*

Chocolate Grinding Mills *See Equipment & Machinery: Food Processing: Mills: Chocolate Grinding*

Chocolate Processing *See Equipment & Machinery: Food Processing: Chocolate Processing*

Chopsticks Utensils *See Food Preparation Equipment, Utensils & Cookware: Utensils: Chopsticks*

Clean Rooms *See Instrumentation & Laboratory Equipment: Laboratory Equipment: Clean Rooms*

Clean-In-Place Controls *See Instrumentation & Laboratory Equipment: Controls: Clean-In-Place*

Cleaners & Shellers *See Equipment & Machinery: Food Processing: Peanut Processing: Cleaners & Shellers*

Cleaners *See Sanitation Equipment & Supplies: Cleaners*

Cleaning & Scouring Powder *See Sanitation Equipment & Supplies: Powder: Cleaning & Scouring*

Cleaning Compound Dispensers *See Sanitation Equipment & Supplies: Dispensers: Cleaning Compound*

Cleaning Equipment & Supplies *See Sanitation Equipment & Supplies: Cleaning Equipment & Supplies*

Cleaning Oils *See Sanitation Equipment & Supplies: Oils: Cleaning*

Cleansing Tissue *See Sanitation Equipment & Supplies: Tissue: Cleansing*

Clear & Colored Plastic *See Foodservice Equipment & Supplies: Clear & Colored Plastic*

Clear Plastic *See Foodservice Equipment & Supplies: Clear Plastic*

Cleavers *See Food Preparation Equipment, Utensils & Cookware: Cleavers*

Closures & Closing Devices *See Packaging Materials & Supplies: Closures & Closing Devices*

Cloths *See Sanitation Equipment & Supplies: Cloths*

Clutches & Brakes *See Transportation & Storage: Clutches & Brakes*

Coasters *See Foodservice Equipment & Supplies: Coasters*

Cocktail Forks *See Food Preparation Equipment, Utensils & Cookware: Utensils: Forks: Cocktail*

Cocoa Processing *See Equipment & Machinery: Food Processing: Cocoa Processing*

Coding, Dating & Marking Equipment *See Equipment & Machinery: Packaging: Coding, Dating & Marking Equipment*

Coffee & Tea Urns *See Foodservice Equipment & Supplies: Urns: Coffee & Tea*

Coffee Dispensers *See Foodservice Equipment & Supplies: Dispensers: Coffee*

Coffee Filters *See Equipment & Machinery: Food Processing: Filters: Coffee*

Coffee Hoppers *See Equipment & Machinery: Food Processing: Hoppers: Coffee*

Coffee Industry *See Equipment & Machinery: Coffee Industry*

Coffee Makers *See Equipment & Machinery: Food Processing: Coffee Makers*

Coffee Pot Cleaners *See Sanitation Equipment & Supplies: Cleaners: Coffee Pot*

Coffee Pots *See Equipment & Machinery: Coffee Industry: Stainless Steel: Coffee Pots*

Coffee Processing *See Equipment & Machinery: Food Processing: Coffee Processing*

Coin Counters *See Foodservice Equipment & Supplies: Counters: Coin*

Coin Machinery *See Foodservice Equipment & Supplies: Coin Machinery*

Cold Cream *See Sanitation Equipment & Supplies: Skin Cream & Lotions: Cold Cream*

Cold Storage Doors *See Refrigeration & Cooling Equipment: Doors: Cold Storage*

Cold Storage Room Racks *See Transportation & Storage: Racks: Cold Storage Room*

Colleges & Universities *See Consultants & Services: Foodservice: Colleges & Universities*

Colloid Mills *See Equipment & Machinery: Food Processing: Mills: Colloid*

Color Measuring *See Instrumentation & Laboratory Equipment: Instrumentation: Color Measuring*

Colored Plastic *See Foodservice Equipment & Supplies: Colored Plastic*

Combination Oven/Steamers *See Equipment & Machinery: Food Processing: Combination Oven/Steamers*

Compounds *See Sanitation Equipment & Supplies: Compounds*

Compressors *See Equipment & Machinery: Food Processing: Compressors; Refrigeration & Cooling Equipment: Compressors*

Computer Software, Systems & Services *See Consultants & Services: Computer Software, Systems & Services*

Computing, Weighing *See Equipment & Machinery: Scales: Computing, Weighing*

Concession Supplies & Equipment *See Foodservice Equipment & Supplies: Concession Supplies & Equipment*

Condensed Milk *See Equipment & Machinery: Food Processing: Condensed Milk Processing*

Condensers *See Equipment & Machinery: Food Processing: Condensers*

Condiment Carts *See Foodservice Equipment & Supplies: Carts: Condiment*

Confectioners' Bags *See Packaging Materials & Supplies: Bags: Confectioners'*

Confectioners' Kettles *See Food Preparation Equipment, Utensils & Cookware: Kettles: Confectioners'*

Confectioners', Continuous Cookers *See Equipment & Machinery: Food Processing: Cookers: Confectioners', Continuous*

Confectionery *See Equipment & Machinery: Food Processing: Confectionery*

Confectionery Industry *See Equipment & Machinery: Confectionery Industry*

Construction *See Consultants & Services: Construction*

Consultants *See Consultants & Services: Consultants*

Container *See Equipment & Machinery: Packaging: Container; Packaging Materials & Supplies: Containers*

Containment Systems *See Safety & Security Equipment & Supplies: Containment Systems*

Contract Manufacturing *See Consultants & Services: Contract Manufacturing*

Contract Packaging *See Consultants & Services: Contract Packaging*

Control Panels *See Instrumentation & Laboratory Equipment: Process Controls: Control Panels*

Controls *See Instrumentation & Laboratory Equipment: Controls*

Convection Ovens *See Equipment & Machinery: Food Processing: Convection Ovens*

Convex Mirrors *See Equipment & Machinery: Mirrors: Convex*

Conveyors *See Equipment & Machinery: Conveyors*

Cookers *See Equipment & Machinery: Food Processing: Cookers*

Cookie Sheets *See Food Preparation Equipment, Utensils & Cookware: Sheets: Cookie*

Cooking & Baking Glassware *See Food Preparation Equipment, Utensils & Cookware: Glassware: Cooking & Baking*

Cooking & Heating Equipment *See Equipment & Machinery: Food Processing: Cooking & Heating Equipment*

Cookware *See Food Preparation Equipment, Utensils & Cookware: Cookware*

Coolers *See Equipment & Machinery: Water Treatment: Coolers*

Cooperage *See Equipment & Machinery: Cooperage*

Copper Kettles *See Food Preparation Equipment, Utensils & Cookware: Kettles: Copper*

Copra Grinding & Crushing Mills *See Equipment & Machinery: Food Processing: Mills: Copra Grinding & Crushing*

Cordage, Rope & Twine *See Transportation & Storage: Cordage, Rope & Twine*

Corers *See Equipment & Machinery: Food Processing: Corers*

Corks *See Packaging Materials & Supplies: Corks*

Corkscrews *See Foodservice Equipment & Supplies: Corkscrews*

Corn & Fodder Shredders *See Equipment & Machinery: Food Processing: Shredders: Corn & Fodder*

Corn Chip Processing *See Equipment & Machinery: Food Processing: Corn Chip Processing*

Corn Cob Holders *See Food Preparation Equipment, Utensils & Cookware: Holders: Corn Cob*

Corn Huskers *See Equipment & Machinery: Food Processing: Huskers: Corn*

Corn Meal & Corn Flour Mills *See Equipment & Machinery: Food Processing: Mills: Corn Meal & Corn Flour*

Corn Poppers *See Equipment & Machinery: Food Processing: Corn Poppers*

Corn Processing *See Equipment & Machinery: Food Processing: Corn Processing*

Correctional Facilities *See Consultants & Services: Foodservice: Correctional Facilities*

Corrosion Resistant Doors *See Building Equipment & Supplies: Doors: Corrosion Resistant*

Corrugated Boxes *See Packaging Materials & Supplies: Boxes: Corrugated*

Corrugated Paper *See Packaging Materials & Supplies: Paper: Corrugated*

Cost Systems *See Equipment & Machinery: Systems: Cost*

Counter Scales *See Equipment & Machinery: Scales: Counter*

Counters *See Foodservice Equipment & Supplies: Counters*

Covers *See Food Preparation Equipment, Utensils & Cookware: Covers*

Crates *See Packaging Materials & Supplies: Crates*

Creamery Cans *See Packaging Materials & Supplies: Cans: Creamery*

Creamery, Dairy Tanks *See Equipment & Machinery: Food Processing: Tanks: Creamery, Dairy*

Crown Corks *See Packaging Materials & Supplies: Corks: Crown*

Cruise Lines *See Consultants & Services: Foodservice: Cruise Lines*

Crumb Belts *See Equipment & Machinery: Belts: Crumb*

Crushers *See Equipment & Machinery: Food Processing: Crushers*

Culinary Knives *See Food Preparation Equipment, Utensils & Cookware: Knives: Culinary*

Culinary Ladles *See Food Preparation Equipment, Utensils & Cookware: Ladles: Culinary*

Culinary, Frying *See Food Preparation Equipment, Utensils & Cookware: Baskets: Culinary, Frying, Etc.*

Cup & Napkin Dispensers *See Foodservice Equipment & Supplies: Dispensers: Cup & Napkin*

Cups *See Packaging Materials & Supplies: Cups*

Curd Knives *See Food Preparation Equipment, Utensils & Cookware: Knives: Curd*

Curd Mills *See Equipment & Machinery: Food Processing: Mills: Curd*

Currency Changers *See Foodservice Equipment & Supplies: Changers: Currency*

Custom Printed Promotional Products *See Consultants & Services: Advertising Services: Custom Printed Promotional Products*

Custom Services *See Consultants & Services: Custom Services*

Cutlery *See Food Preparation Equipment, Utensils & Cookware: Cutlery*

Cutters *See Food Preparation Equipment, Utensils & Cookware: Cutters*

Cutting & Trimming Tables *See Food Preparation Equipment, Utensils & Cookware: Tables: Cutting & Trimming*

Cutting Block *See Food Preparation Equipment, Utensils & Cookware: Boards: Cutting Block*

Cylinders *See Equipment & Machinery: Cylinders*

D

Dairy & Creamery *See Equipment & Machinery: Food Processing: Dairy & Creamery*

Dairy Aprons *See Clothing & Protective Apparel: Aprons: Dairy*

Dairy Cleaners *See Sanitation Equipment & Supplies: Cleaners: Dairy*

EXAMPLE: **Dairy Cooling Vats** *See Equipment & Machinery: Food Processing: Vats: Dairy Cooling*
(1) (2) (3) (4) (5)

1. Product or Service you are looking for
2. Main Category, in alphabetical order, located in the page headers starting on page 17
3. Category Description, located in black bars and in page headers
4. Product Category, located in gray bars
5. Product Type, located under gray bars, centered in bold

Dairy Cooling *See Equipment & Machinery: Food Processing: Vats: Dairy Cooling; Refrigeration & Cooling Equipment: Vats: Dairy Cooling*

Dairy Industry *See Equipment & Machinery: Dairy Industry*

Data Loggers *See Instrumentation & Laboratory Equipment: Process Controls: Pressure: Data Loggers*

Dating & Numbering *See Packaging Materials & Supplies: Stamps: Dating & Numbering*

Deaerators *See Equipment & Machinery: Food Processing: Deaerators*

Dealers *See Consultants & Services: Dealers*

Decking *See Building Equipment & Supplies: Decking*

Decorative Items *See Foodservice Equipment & Supplies: Decorative Items*

Deep Fryer Hose *See Equipment & Machinery: Hoses: Deep Fryer*

Deep Fryers *See Equipment & Machinery: Food Processing: Deep Fryers*

Dehydration Equipment *See Equipment & Machinery: Food Processing: Dehydration Equipment*

Delivery Truck Ramps *See Transportation & Storage: Ramps: Delivery Truck*

Depositors *See Equipment & Machinery: Depositors*

Design Consultants *See Consultants & Services: Consultants: Design*

Designers *See Consultants & Services: Designers*

Dessert, Pastry Carts *See Foodservice Equipment & Supplies: Carts: Dessert, Pastry*

Detectors & Alarms *See Safety & Security Equipment & Supplies: Detectors & Alarms*

Detectors *See Equipment & Machinery: Packaging: Detectors; Safety & Security Equipment & Supplies: Detectors*

Detergents *See Sanitation Equipment & Supplies: Detergents*

Dicing Cutters *See Food Preparation Equipment, Utensils & Cookware: Cutters: Dicing*

Dish & Plate Warmers *See Foodservice Equipment & Supplies: Warmers: Dish & Plate*

Dish Cloths *See Sanitation Equipment & Supplies: Cloths: Dish*

Dish Washing Machinery *See Sanitation Equipment & Supplies: Dish Washing Machinery*

Dish, Food Display & Tray Covers *See Food Preparation Equipment, Utensils & Cookware: Covers: Dish, Food Display & Tray*

Dishes *See Foodservice Equipment & Supplies: Dishes*

Dishwasher *See Sanitation Equipment & Supplies: Dishwasher*

Dishwashing Compounds *See Sanitation Equipment & Supplies: Compounds: Dishwashing*

Disinfectants & Germicides *See Sanitation Equipment & Supplies: Disinfectants & Germicides*

Disintegrators *See Equipment & Machinery: Food Processing: Disintegrators*

Dispensers *See Foodservice Equipment & Supplies: Dispensers; Sanitation Equipment & Supplies: Dispensers*

Display Cases *See Foodservice Equipment & Supplies: Cases: Display*

Display Tables *See Foodservice Equipment & Supplies: Tables: Display*

Display, Store Hooks *See Foodservice Equipment & Supplies: Hooks: Display, Store*

Display, Store Racks *See Foodservice Equipment & Supplies: Racks: Display, Store*

Displays *See Foodservice Equipment & Supplies: Displays*

Disposable Gloves *See Clothing & Protective Apparel: Gloves: Disposable*

Disposable Towels *See Foodservice Equipment & Supplies: Towels: Disposable*

Disposable Wipers *See Sanitation Equipment & Supplies: Wipers: Disposable*

Doilies *See Foodservice Equipment & Supplies: Doilies*

Doors *See Building Equipment & Supplies: Doors; Foodservice Equipment & Supplies: Doors; Refrigeration & Cooling Equipment: Doors*

Double Acting Doors *See Building Equipment & Supplies: Doors: Double Acting*

Dough Make-up *See Equipment & Machinery: Food Processing: Dough Make-up*

Dough Sheeter *See Food Preparation Equipment, Utensils & Cookware: Sheeter: Dough*

Drawers *See Foodservice Equipment & Supplies: Drawers*

Drink Mixing *See Equipment & Machinery: Food Processing: Drink Mixing*

Drinking Glasses *See Food Preparation Equipment, Utensils & Cookware: Glasses: Drinking*

Drinking Straws *See Foodservice Equipment & Supplies: Straws: Drinking*

Drive-Thru & Pass-Thru Windows *See Building Equipment & Supplies: Windows: Drive-Thru & Pass-Thru*

Drum Mixers *See Equipment & Machinery: Food Processing: Mixers: Drum*

Drums *See Transportation & Storage: Drums*

Dry Measures *See Equipment & Machinery: Measures: Dry*

Dry Product Contract Packaging *See Consultants & Services: Contract Packaging: Dry Product*

Dry Products Filling *See Equipment & Machinery: Food Processing: Dry Products Filling*

Dryer Systems *See Sanitation Equipment & Supplies: Dryer Systems*

Dryers *See Equipment & Machinery: Food Processing: Dryers*

Drying *See Consultants & Services: Custom Services: Drying*

Drying, Evaporating Tanks *See Equipment & Machinery: Food Processing: Tanks: Drying, Evaporating*

Dumpers *See Equipment & Machinery: Food Processing: Dumpers*

Dust Collectors *See Sanitation Equipment & Supplies: Dust Collectors*

Dust Pans *See Sanitation Equipment & Supplies: Dust Pans*

Dusting Cloths *See Sanitation Equipment & Supplies: Cloths: Dusting*

E

Egg Baskets *See Packaging Materials & Supplies: Baskets: Egg*

Egg Crates *See Packaging Materials & Supplies: Crates: Egg*

Egg Processing *See Equipment & Machinery: Food Processing: Egg Processing & Cleaning*

Egg Slicers *See Equipment & Machinery: Food Processing: Slicers: Egg*

Egg, Cream, Culinary *See Food Preparation Equipment, Utensils & Cookware: Beaters: Egg, Cream, Culinary*

Electric Alarm Mats *See Safety & Security Equipment & Supplies: Mats: Electric Alarm*

Electric Heating *See Building Equipment & Supplies: Heating, Ventilation & Air Conditioning: Heating: Electric*

Electric Lighting *See Building Equipment & Supplies: Lighting Equipment: Lighting Fixtures: Electric*

Electric Signs *See Foodservice Equipment & Supplies: Signs: Electric*

Electric Steam Boilers *See Equipment & Machinery: Food Processing: Boilers: Electric Steam*

Electronic Survey *See Instrumentation & Laboratory Equipment: Process Analysis & Development: Electronic Survey*

Emergency Lighting *See Building Equipment & Supplies: Lighting Equipment: Lighting Fixtures: Emergency*

Employment Agencies *See Consultants & Services: Personnel Services: Employment Agencies*

Envelopes *See Foodservice Equipment & Supplies: Envelopes*

Equipment & Machinery *See Equipment & Machinery*

Equipment & Supplies *See Consultants & Services: Construction: Equipment & Supplies*

Equipment *See Equipment & Machinery: Food Processing: Equipment*

Equipment Packaging *See Equipment & Machinery: Packaging: Equipment*

Espresso & Cappuccino *See Equipment & Machinery: Food Processing: Espresso & Cappuccino Processing*

Ethyl Alcohol *See Instrumentation & Laboratory Equipment: Analyzers: Ethyl Alcohol*

Evaporative Condensers *See Equipment & Machinery: Food Processing: Condensers: Evaporative*

Evaporators *See Equipment & Machinery: Food Processing: Evaporators*

Exhausters *See Equipment & Machinery: Packaging: Exhausters*

Exterminators *See Sanitation Equipment & Supplies: Pest Control: Exterminators*

Extractors *See Equipment & Machinery: Food Processing: Extractors*

Extruders *See Equipment & Machinery: Food Processing: Extruders*

Extrusion *See Consultants & Services: Custom Services: Extrusion*

F

Facility Design *See Consultants & Services: Construction: Facility Design*

Factory, Warehouse, Shop & Industrial Trucks *See Transportation & Storage: Trucks: Factory, Warehouse, Shop & Industrial*

Fancy Boxes *See Packaging Materials & Supplies: Boxes: Fancy*

Fans *See Building Equipment & Supplies: Fans*

Fast Food *See Consultants & Services: Fast Food & Franchises*

Fast Food Restaurants *See Consultants & Services: Foodservice: Fast Food Restaurants*

Fats, Oils Analyzers *See Instrumentation & Laboratory Equipment: Analyzers: Fats, Oils*

Feed Mills *See Equipment & Machinery: Food Processing: Mills: Feed*

Feeders *See Equipment & Machinery: Feeders*

Fiber Boxes *See Packaging Materials & Supplies: Boxes: Fiber*

Fiber, Starch *See Instrumentation & Laboratory Equipment: Analyzers: Fiber, Starch*

Fillers *See Equipment & Machinery: Food Processing: Fillers*

Filling *See Equipment & Machinery: Packaging: Carton: Filling*

Film *See Packaging Materials & Supplies: Film*

Filters *See Equipment & Machinery: Food Processing: Filters*

Filtration and Separation *See Equipment & Machinery: Food Processing: Filtration and Separation*

Filtration Devices & Systems *See Equipment & Machinery: Filtration Devices & Systems*

Fire Alarm Systems *See Safety & Security Equipment & Supplies: Fire Alarm Systems*

Fire Extinguishers *See Safety & Security Equipment & Supplies: Fire Extinguishers*

Fire, Heat & Smoke Detectors & Alarms *See Safety & Security Equipment & Supplies: Detectors & Alarms: Fire, Heat & Smoke*

Fish Cleaning *See Equipment & Machinery: Food Processing: Fish Cleaning*

Fish Cookers *See Equipment & Machinery: Food Processing: Cookers: Fish*

Fish Scalers *See Equipment & Machinery: Food Processing: Scalers: Fish*

Fish Scaling & Slitting Knives *See Food Preparation Equipment, Utensils & Cookware: Knives: Fish Scaling & Slitting*

Fish, Meat & Produce Smokers *See Equipment & Machinery: Food Processing: Smokers: Fish, Meat & Produce*

Fittings *See Equipment & Machinery: Fittings*

Fixtures *See Foodservice Equipment & Supplies: Fixtures*

Flags, Pennants & Banners *See Consultants & Services: Advertising Services: Flags, Pennants & Banners*

Flakers or Flaking Drums *See Equipment & Machinery: Food Processing: Flakers or Flaking Drums*

Flashlights *See Safety & Security Equipment & Supplies: Flashlights*

Flexible Materials *See Packaging Materials & Supplies: Packaging: Flexible Materials*

Floor Cleaning Machinery *See Sanitation Equipment & Supplies: Floor Cleaning Machinery*

Floor Electric Alarm Mats *See Safety & Security Equipment & Supplies: Mats: Electric Alarm: Floor*

Floor Mats *See Building Equipment & Supplies: Flooring: Floor Mats*

Floor Polish *See Sanitation Equipment & Supplies: Polish: Floor*

Floor, Sweeping, Polishing & Waxing Brushes *See Sanitation Equipment & Supplies: Brushes: Floor, Sweeping, Polishing & Waxing*

Flooring *See Building Equipment & Supplies: Flooring*

Flour & Bakers' Sifters *See Food Preparation Equipment, Utensils & Cookware: Sifters: Flour & Bakers'*

Flour & Cereal Mills *See Equipment & Machinery: Food Processing: Mills: Flour & Cereal*

Flour Blending *See Equipment & Machinery: Food Processing: Blending: Flour*

Flour Hoppers *See Equipment & Machinery: Food Processing: Hoppers: Flour*

Flour Mill *See Equipment & Machinery: Food Processing: Flour Mill*

Flour, Meal & Feed Bags *See Packaging Materials & Supplies: Bags: Flour, Meal & Feed*

Flow Measurement *See Instrumentation & Laboratory Equipment: Instrumentation: Flow Measurement, Gas & Liquid*

Flow Meters *See Instrumentation & Laboratory Equipment: Meters: Flow*

Flow Regulators *See Equipment & Machinery: Flow Regulators*

Fluid, Liquid, Weighing Scales *See Equipment & Machinery: Scales: Fluid, Liquid, Weighing*

Fluorescent Lighting *See Building Equipment & Supplies: Lighting Equipment: Fluorescent*

Fluorescent Lighting Fixtures *See Building Equipment & Supplies: Lighting Equipment: Lighting Fixtures: Fluorescent*

Foil *See Packaging Materials & Supplies: Foil*

Folding Tables *See Foodservice Equipment & Supplies: Tables: Folding*

Food & Restaurant Trucks *See Transportation & Storage: Trucks: Food & Restaurant*

Food Bags *See Packaging Materials & Supplies: Bags: Food*

Food Carriers *See Packaging Materials & Supplies: Carriers: Food*

Food Certification *See Instrumentation & Laboratory Equipment: Certification: Food*

Food Closeouts *See Consultants & Services: Food Closeouts, Surplus, Salvage & Liquidators*

Food Deaerators *See Equipment & Machinery: Food Processing: Deaerators: Food*

Food Dispensers *See Foodservice Equipment & Supplies: Dispensers: Food*

Food Dryers *See Equipment & Machinery: Food Processing: Dryers: Food*

Food Filters *See Equipment & Machinery: Food Processing: Filters: Food*

Food Handlers' Protective Apparel *See Clothing & Protective Apparel: Protective Apparel: Food Handlers'*

Food Handling Hoses *See Equipment & Machinery: Hoses: Food Handling*

Food Industry Brushes *See Food Preparation Equipment, Utensils & Cookware: Brushes: Food Industry*

Food Inspection *See Instrumentation & Laboratory Equipment: Testers: Food Inspection*

Food Processing Agitators *See Equipment & Machinery: Food Processing: Agitators: Food Processing*

Food Processing *See Equipment & Machinery: Food Processing: Food Processing: Food*

Food Processing Machine Blades *See Equipment & Machinery: Food Processing: Blades: Food Processing Machine*

Food Processing Machine Knives *See Food Preparation Equipment, Utensils & Cookware: Knives: Food Processing Machine*

Food Processing Mixers *See Equipment & Machinery: Food Processing: Mixers: Food Processing*

Food Processing *See Equipment & Machinery: Food Processing: Food Processing*

Food Protective Packaging *See Packaging Materials & Supplies: Packaging: Food Protective*

Food Pumps *See Equipment & Machinery: Pumps: Food; Instrumentation & Laboratory Equipment: Pumps: Food*

Food Research *See Consultants & Services: Laboratories: Food Research & Development*

Food Storage Supplies *See Transportation & Storage: Food Storage Supplies*

Food Technology Consultants *See Consultants & Services: Consultants: Food Technology*

Food Tongs *See Food Preparation Equipment, Utensils & Cookware: Tongs: Food*

Food Trays *See Foodservice Equipment & Supplies: Trays: Food*

Food Warmers *See Foodservice Equipment & Supplies: Warmers: Food*

Food, Artificial Displays *See Foodservice Equipment & Supplies: Displays: Food, Artificial*

Food, Household, Hotel & Restaurant Mixers *See Equipment & Machinery: Food Processing: Mixers: Food, Household, Hotel & Restaurant*

Foodservice Architects *See Consultants & Services: Architects: Foodservice*

Foodservice Doors *See Foodservice Equipment & Supplies: Doors: Foodservice*

Foodservice Preparation Utensils *See Foodservice Equipment & Supplies: Utensils: Foodservice Preparation*

Foodservice *See Consultants & Services: Foodservice*

Forks *See Food Preparation Equipment, Utensils & Cookware: Utensils: Forks*

Form, Fill & Seal *See Equipment & Machinery: Packaging: Form, Fill & Seal*

Formulations *See Consultants & Services: Custom Services: Formulations*

Freeze Dryers *See Equipment & Machinery: Food Processing: Dryers: Freeze*

Freezer & Frozen Foods *See Refrigeration & Cooling Equipment: Cabinets: Freezer & Frozen Foods*

Freezer Doors *See Refrigeration & Cooling Equipment: Doors: Freezer*

Freezer Tapes *See Packaging Materials & Supplies: Tapes: Freezer*

Freezers *See Refrigeration & Cooling Equipment: Freezers*

Frozen Custard Processing *See Equipment & Machinery: Food Processing: Frozen Custard Processing*

Frozen Food Displays *See Foodservice Equipment & Supplies: Displays: Frozen Food*

Frozen Food Lockers *See Refrigeration & Cooling Equipment: Lockers: Frozen Food*

Frozen Food Wrappers *See Packaging Materials & Supplies: Wrappers: Frozen Food*

Frozen Foods Processing *See Equipment & Machinery: Food Processing: Frozen Foods Processing*

Fruit & Vegetable Bags *See Packaging Materials & Supplies: Bags: Fruit & Vegetable*

Fruit & Vegetable Baskets *See Packaging Materials & Supplies: Baskets: Fruit & Vegetable*

Fruit & Vegetable Boxes *See Packaging Materials & Supplies: Boxes: Fruit & Vegetable*

Fruit & Vegetable Corers *See Equipment & Machinery: Food Processing: Corers: Fruit & Vegetable*

Fruit & Vegetable Juice Extractors *See Equipment & Machinery: Food Processing: Extractors: Fruit & Vegetable Juice*

Fruit & Vegetable Juice Filters *See Equipment & Machinery: Food Processing: Filters: Fruit & Vegetable Juice*

Fruit & Vegetable Parers & Peelers *See Food Preparation Equipment, Utensils & Cookware: Parers & Peelers: Fruit & Vegetable*

Fruit & Vegetable Washers *See Equipment & Machinery: Food Processing: Washers: Fruit & Vegetable*

Fruit & Vegetable Waxers *See Equipment & Machinery: Food Processing: Waxers: Fruit & Vegetable*

Fruit Crushers *See Equipment & Machinery: Food Processing: Crushers: Fruit*

Fruit Dryers *See Equipment & Machinery: Food Processing: Dryers: Fruit*

Fruit Industry *See Equipment & Machinery: Fruit Industry*

Fruit Jar Openers *See Equipment & Machinery: Openers: Fruit Jar*

Fruit Juice Evaporators *See Equipment & Machinery: Food Processing: Evaporators: Fruit Juice*

Fruit Knives *See Food Preparation Equipment, Utensils & Cookware: Knives: Fruit*

Fruit Packers *See Consultants & Services: Packers: Fruit*

Fruit Processing *See Equipment & Machinery: Food Processing: Fruit Processing*

Fruit, Vegetable & Nut Graders *See Equipment & Machinery: Food Processing: Graders: Fruit, Vegetable & Nut*

Frying Pans *See Food Preparation Equipment, Utensils & Cookware: Pans: Frying*

Funnels *See Equipment & Machinery: Funnels*

Furniture Polish *See Sanitation Equipment & Supplies: Polish: Furniture*

G

Garbage & Waste *See Sanitation Equipment & Supplies: Incinerators: Garbage & Waste*

Garbage Bags *See Sanitation Equipment & Supplies: Garbage Bags*

Garbage Compactors *See Sanitation Equipment & Supplies: Garbage Compactors*

Garbage Control Units & Systems *See Sanitation Equipment & Supplies: Garbage Control Units & Systems*

Garbage Disposal Units *See Sanitation Equipment & Supplies: Garbage Disposal Units*

Gas Connectors *See Equipment & Machinery: Gas Connectors*

Gas Fired Boilers *See Equipment & Machinery: Food Processing: Boilers: Gas Fired*

Gas Leak Detectors *See Safety & Security Equipment & Supplies: Detectors: Gas Leak*

Gauges;Sanitary *See Instrumentation & Laboratory Equipment: Process Controls: Pressure: Gauges;Sanitary*

Gesticide Analyses *See Instrumentation & Laboratory Equipment: Gesticide Analyses*

Gift Baskets *See Packaging Materials & Supplies: Baskets: Gift*

Glass Bottles *See Packaging Materials & Supplies: Bottles: Glass*

Glass Dispensers *See Foodservice Equipment & Supplies: Dispensers: Glass*

Glass Jars *See Packaging Materials & Supplies: Jars: Glass*

Glass Trays *See Foodservice Equipment & Supplies: Trays: Glass*

Glasses *See Food Preparation Equipment, Utensils & Cookware: Glasses*

Glassine *See Packaging Materials & Supplies: Paper: Glassine*

Glassware *See Food Preparation Equipment, Utensils & Cookware: Glassware*

Gloves *See Clothing & Protective Apparel: Gloves*

Graders *See Equipment & Machinery: Food Processing: Graders*

Grain & Oat Crushers *See Equipment & Machinery: Food Processing: Crushers: Grain & Oat*

Grain & Seed Cleaners *See Sanitation Equipment & Supplies: Cleaners: Grain & Seed*

Grain Bags *See Packaging Materials & Supplies: Bags: Grain*

Grain Blending *See Equipment & Machinery: Food Processing: Blending: Grain*

Grain Dryers *See Equipment & Machinery: Food Processing: Dryers: Grain*

Grain Elevator *See Equipment & Machinery: Food Processing: Grain Elevator*

Grain, Flour Mill *See Equipment & Machinery: Food Processing: Separators: Grain, Flour Mill*

Grain, Rice & Seed Graders *See Equipment & Machinery: Food Processing: Graders: Grain, Rice & Seed*

Graters *See Equipment & Machinery: Food Processing: Graters*

Grating *See Building Equipment & Supplies: Grating*

Gravimetric, Volumetric, Loss-In-Weight, Etc. Feeders *See Equipment & Machinery: Feeders: Gravimetric, Volumetric, Loss-In-Weight, Etc.*

Grease & Oil Resistant Paper *See Packaging Materials & Supplies: Paper: Grease & Oil Resistant*

Grease Filters *See Equipment & Machinery: Food Processing: Filters: Grease*

Greaseproof Bags *See Packaging Materials & Supplies: Bags: Greaseproof*

Grilles *See Refrigeration & Cooling Equipment: Refrigerators: Grilles*

Grinders *See Equipment & Machinery: Food Processing: Grinders*

Grinding *See Consultants & Services: Custom Services: Grinding*

Grinding Mills *See Equipment & Machinery: Food Processing: Mills: Grinding*

```
                    1              2            3       4    5
                    ⌐‾‾‾⌐       ⌐‾‾‾⌐       ⌐‾‾⌐  ⌐‾⌐  ⌐‾⌐
EXAMPLE: Dairy Cooling Vats See Equipment & Machinery: Food Processing: Vats: Dairy Cooling
```

1. Product or Service you are looking for
2. Main Category, in alphabetical order, located in the page headers starting on page 17
3. Category Description, located in black bars and in page headers

4. Product Category, located in gray bars
5. Product Type, located under gray bars, centered in bold

Gummed Tapes See Packaging Materials & Supplies: Tapes: Gummed

H

Hair Nets See Clothing & Protective Apparel: Hair Nets

Hamburger & Meat Patty Processing See Equipment & Machinery: Food Processing: Hamburger & Meat Patty Processing

Hammer Mills See Equipment & Machinery: Food Processing: Mills: Hammer

Hand Carts See Transportation & Storage: Carts: Hand

Hand Cleaners See Sanitation Equipment & Supplies: Cleaners: Hand

Hand Trucks See Transportation & Storage: Trucks: Hand

Heat Exchangers See Equipment & Machinery: Food Processing: Heat Exchangers

Heat Resistant Glassware See Food Preparation Equipment, Utensils & Cookware: Glassware: Heat Resistant

Heat Sealed Bags See Packaging Materials & Supplies: Bags: Heat Sealed

Heat Sealers See Equipment & Machinery: Packaging: Sealers: Heat

Heat Sealing See Equipment & Machinery: Packaging: Heat Sealing

Heat Sealing Paper See Packaging Materials & Supplies: Paper: Heat Sealing

Heat Sealing Tapes See Packaging Materials & Supplies: Tapes: Heat Sealing

Heat Transfer Fluids See Equipment & Machinery: Food Processing: Heat Transfer Fluids

Heaters See Equipment & Machinery: Heaters

Heating, Ventilation & Air Conditioning See Building Equipment & Supplies: Heating, Ventilation & Air Conditioning: Heating

Hoists & Lifting Equipment See Transportation & Storage: Hoists & Lifting Equipment

Holders See Clothing & Protective Apparel: Holders; Food Preparation Equipment, Utensils & Cookware: Holders; Foodservice Equipment & Supplies: Holders; Sanitation Equipment & Supplies: Holders

Holding & Warming Equipment See Foodservice Equipment & Supplies: Holding & Warming Equipment

Holding, Storage Tanks See Transportation & Storage: Tanks: Holding, Storage

Hollowware See Food Preparation Equipment, Utensils & Cookware: Hollowware

Homogenizers See Equipment & Machinery: Food Processing: Homogenizers

Honey Processing See Equipment & Machinery: Food Processing: Honey Processing

Hoods See Building Equipment & Supplies: Hoods

Hooks See Food Preparation Equipment, Utensils & Cookware: Hooks; Foodservice Equipment & Supplies: Hooks

Hoops See Food Preparation Equipment, Utensils & Cookware: Hoops

Hoppers See Equipment & Machinery: Food Processing: Hoppers

Horizontal Form, Fill & Seal See Equipment & Machinery: Packaging: Form, Fill & Seal: Horizontal

Hose Reels See Equipment & Machinery: Hose Reels

Hoses See Equipment & Machinery: Hoses

Hospitals & Healthcare Foodservice See Consultants & Services: Foodservice: Hospitals & Healthcare

Hotel & Restaurant Glassware See Food Preparation Equipment, Utensils & Cookware: Glassware: Hotel & Restaurant

Hotel, Bar, Restaurant Interiors See Foodservice Equipment & Supplies: Interiors: Hotel, Bar, Restaurant

Household, Consumer Detergents See Sanitation Equipment & Supplies: Detergents: Household, Consumer

Household, Kitchen Utensils See Food Preparation Equipment, Utensils & Cookware: Utensils: Household, Kitchen

Housekeeping Carts See Sanitation Equipment & Supplies: Carts: Housekeeping

Hullers See Equipment & Machinery: Food Processing: Hullers

Humidity Loggers See Instrumentation & Laboratory Equipment: Process Controls: Humidity Loggers

Huskers See Equipment & Machinery: Food Processing: Huskers

I

Ice Breaking, Chipping, Crushing See Equipment & Machinery: Food Processing: Ice Breaking, Chipping, Crushing

Ice Carts See Foodservice Equipment & Supplies: Carts: Ice

Ice Coolers See Refrigeration & Cooling Equipment: Coolers: Ice

Ice Cream & Frozen Yogurt Dispensers See Foodservice Equipment & Supplies: Dispensers: Ice Cream & Frozen Yogurt

Ice Cream Cans See Packaging Materials & Supplies: Cans: Ice Cream

Ice Cream Cone, Bar, Biscuit Processing See Equipment & Machinery: Food Processing: Ice Cream Cone, Bar, Biscuit Processing

Ice Cream Coolers See Refrigeration & Cooling Equipment: Coolers: Ice Cream

Ice Cream Freezers See Refrigeration & Cooling Equipment: Freezers: Ice Cream

Ice Cream Processing See Equipment & Machinery: Food Processing: Ice Cream Processing

Ice Cream Sticks See Packaging Materials & Supplies: Sticks: Ice Cream

Ice Cubing See Equipment & Machinery: Food Processing: Ice Cubing

Ice Making Plants See Consultants & Services: Ice Making Plants

Ice Making, Refrigerating & Cooling See Equipment & Machinery: Food Processing: Ice Making, Refrigerating & Cooling

Ice Tongs See Food Preparation Equipment, Utensils & Cookware: Tongs: Ice

Incandescent Lighting See Building Equipment & Supplies: Lighting Equipment: Incandescent

Incinerators See Sanitation Equipment & Supplies: Incinerators

Incubators & Brooders See Equipment & Machinery: Incubators & Brooders

Indelible Inks See Packaging Materials & Supplies: Inks: Indelible

Indoor Sign Holders See Foodservice Equipment & Supplies: Clear & Colored Plastic: Indoor Sign Holders

Industrial Clutches & Brakes See Transportation & Storage: Clutches & Brakes: Industrial

Industrial Detergents See Sanitation Equipment & Supplies: Detergents: Industrial

Industrial Flooring See Building Equipment & Supplies: Flooring: Industrial Flooring

Industrial Lubricants See Equipment & Machinery: Lubricants: Industrial

Industrial Plant Serving See Foodservice Equipment & Supplies: Serving Equipment: Industrial Plant

Industrial Vacuum Cleaners See Sanitation Equipment & Supplies: Vacuum Cleaners: Industrial

Ingredient Water Coolers See Refrigeration & Cooling Equipment: Coolers: Ingredient Water

Inks See Packaging Materials & Supplies: Inks

Insecticides & Insect Control Systems See Sanitation Equipment & Supplies: Insecticides & Insect Control Systems

Inspection & Analysis See Instrumentation & Laboratory Equipment: Inspection & Analysis Instrumentation & Systems

Instrumentation See Instrumentation & Laboratory Equipment: Instrumentation

Insulated Bins See Packaging Materials & Supplies: Bins: Insulated

Insulated Panels See Building Equipment & Supplies: Panels: Insulated

Insulated Warehouses See Transportation & Storage: Warehouses: Insulated

Insulation See Refrigeration & Cooling Equipment: Insulation

Interchangeable Signs See Foodservice Equipment & Supplies: Signs: Interchangeable

Interior & Store Fixture Designers See Consultants & Services: Designers: Interior & Store Fixture

Interiors See Foodservice Equipment & Supplies: Interiors

Irradiation Preservation See Equipment & Machinery: Food Processing: Preservation: Irradiation

Irradiation Processing See Equipment & Machinery: Food Processing: Irradiation Processing

Isopropyl Alcohol See Sanitation Equipment & Supplies: Isopropyl Alcohol

J

Jackets See Clothing & Protective Apparel: Jackets

Jar Filling See Equipment & Machinery: Packaging: Jar Filling

Jars See Packaging Materials & Supplies: Jars

K

Kettles See Food Preparation Equipment, Utensils & Cookware: Kettles

Kiosks See Foodservice Equipment & Supplies: Kiosks

Kitchen (Commercial, Institutional, Restaurant) Designers See Consultants & Services: Designers: Kitchen (Commercial, Institutional, Restaurant)

Kitchen Racks See Transportation & Storage: Racks: Kitchen

Knife Sharpeners See Food Preparation Equipment, Utensils & Cookware: Knife Sharpeners

Knives See Food Preparation Equipment, Utensils & Cookware: Knives

Kosher Food Consultants See Consultants & Services: Consultants: Kosher Food

Kraft Paper See Packaging Materials & Supplies: Paper: Kraft

Kraut & Slaw Cutters See Food Preparation Equipment, Utensils & Cookware: Cutters: Kraut & Slaw

L

Label Holders See Foodservice Equipment & Supplies: Plastic Back Tag: Label Holders

Label Paper See Packaging Materials & Supplies: Paper: Label

Label Printing See Equipment & Machinery: Packaging: Label Printing

Labeling See Equipment & Machinery: Packaging: Labeling

Labels See Packaging Materials & Supplies: Labels

Laboratories See Consultants & Services: Laboratories

Laboratory Balances See Instrumentation & Laboratory Equipment: Balances: Laboratory

Laboratory Chemicals See Instrumentation & Laboratory Equipment: Chemicals: Laboratory

Laboratory Equipment See Instrumentation & Laboratory Equipment: Laboratory Equipment

Laboratory Testers See Instrumentation & Laboratory Equipment: Testers: Laboratory

Ladder Covers See Safety & Security Equipment & Supplies: Ladder Covers

Ladder Rungs See Safety & Security Equipment & Supplies: Ladder Rungs

Ladles See Food Preparation Equipment, Utensils & Cookware: Ladles

Laminated Bags See Packaging Materials & Supplies: Bags: Laminated

Laminated Paper See Packaging Materials & Supplies: Paper: Laminated

Lard Kettles See Food Preparation Equipment, Utensils & Cookware: Kettles: Lard

Level, Liquid & Dry Controls See Instrumentation & Laboratory Equipment: Controls: Level, Liquid & Dry

Lift Truck Pallets See Transportation & Storage: Pallets: Lift Truck

Lighting Equipment See Building Equipment & Supplies: Lighting Equipment

Lighting Fixtures See Building Equipment & Supplies: Lighting Equipment: Lighting Fixtures

Linen Goods See Foodservice Equipment & Supplies: Linen Goods

Liners See Food Preparation Equipment, Utensils & Cookware: Liners

Lining Paper See Packaging Materials & Supplies: Paper: Lining

Linings See Packaging Materials & Supplies: Linings

Liquid Chlorine See Sanitation Equipment & Supplies: Chlorine: Liquid

Liquid Product See Consultants & Services: Contract Packaging: Liquid Product

Liquid-Solid Separators See Equipment & Machinery: Food Processing: Separators: Liquid-Solid

Liquor, Wine Carts *See Foodservice Equipment & Supplies: Carts: Liquor, Wine*

Live Skid Pallets *See Transportation & Storage: Pallets: Live Skid*

Load Cells & Indicators *See Equipment & Machinery: Load Cells & Indicators*

Lockers *See Refrigeration & Cooling Equipment: Lockers*

Loin Knives *See Food Preparation Equipment, Utensils & Cookware: Knives: Loin*

Lotion *See Sanitation Equipment & Supplies: Skin Cream & Lotions: Lotion*

Lubricants *See Equipment & Machinery: Lubricants*

Luminous Tube Signs *See Foodservice Equipment & Supplies: Signs: Luminous Tube*

M

Machine Knives *See Food Preparation Equipment, Utensils & Cookware: Knives: Machine*

Magnetic Chips *See Foodservice Equipment & Supplies: Magnetic Chips*

Magnetic Label *See Foodservice Equipment & Supplies: Magnetic Label*

Magnetic Pocket *See Foodservice Equipment & Supplies: Magnetic Pocket*

Magnets *See Food Preparation Equipment, Utensils & Cookware: Magnets*

Malt Mills *See Equipment & Machinery: Food Processing: Mills: Malt*

Management *See Consultants & Services: Construction: Management*

Manufacturing Screening *See Equipment & Machinery: Screening: Manufacturing*

Markers, Pens & Pencils *See Packaging Materials & Supplies: Markers, Pens & Pencils; Foodservice Equipment & Supplies: Markers*

Marketing & Promotion Consultants *See Consultants & Services: Consultants: Marketing & Promotion*

Marking & Coding Inks *See Packaging Materials & Supplies: Inks: Marking & Coding*

Marking Tapes *See Packaging Materials & Supplies: Tapes: Marking*

Master Planning & Logistics *See Consultants & Services: Master Planning & Logistics*

Matches *See Food Preparation Equipment, Utensils & Cookware: Matches*

Material Handling & Distribution Equipment *See Transportation & Storage: Material Handling & Distribution Equipment*

Material Handling Consultants *See Consultants & Services: Consultants: Material Handling*

Materials *See Equipment & Machinery: Packaging: Equipment: Materials*

Mats & Matting Flooring *See Building Equipment & Supplies: Flooring: Mats & Matting*

Mats *See Safety & Security Equipment & Supplies: Mats*

Measurement Systems *See Instrumentation & Laboratory Equipment: Measurement Systems*

Measures *See Equipment & Machinery: Measures*

Meat Bags *See Packaging Materials & Supplies: Bags: Meat*

Meat Branding *See Packaging Materials & Supplies: Inks: Meat Branding*

Meat Curing *See Equipment & Machinery: Food Processing: Vats: Meat Curing*

Meat Cutters *See Food Preparation Equipment, Utensils & Cookware: Cutters: Meat*

Meat Dealers *See Consultants & Services: Dealers: Meat*

Meat Hooks *See Food Preparation Equipment, Utensils & Cookware: Hooks: Meat*

Meat Micer *See Food Preparation Equipment, Utensils & Cookware: Micer: Meat*

Meat Mincer *See Food Preparation Equipment, Utensils & Cookware: Mincer: Meat*

Meat Packers *See Consultants & Services: Packers: Meat*

Meat Packing Knives *See Food Preparation Equipment, Utensils & Cookware: Knives: Meat Packing*

Meat Preparation Equipment *See Equipment & Machinery: Food Processing: Meat Preparation Equipment*

Meat Slicers *See Equipment & Machinery: Food Processing: Slicers: Meat*

Meat Trucks *See Transportation & Storage: Trucks: Meat*

Menu Boards *See Foodservice Equipment & Supplies: Menu Boards*

Menus *See Foodservice Equipment & Supplies: Menus*

Mercury, High Intensity Lighting Equipment *See Building Equipment & Supplies: Lighting Equipment: Mercury, High Intensity*

Metal & Contamination Detection Systems *See Equipment & Machinery: Systems: Metal & Contamination Detection*

Metal Decking *See Building Equipment & Supplies: Decking: Metal*

Metal Detectors *See Safety & Security Equipment & Supplies: Detectors: Metal; See also Safety & Security Equipment & Supplies: Metal Detectors*

Metal Fabricators *See Consultants & Services: Construction: Metal Fabricators*

Metal Flooring *See Building Equipment & Supplies: Flooring: Metal*

Metal Grating *See Building Equipment & Supplies: Grating: Metal*

Metal Plating *See Building Equipment & Supplies: Plating: Metal*

Meters *See Instrumentation & Laboratory Equipment: Meters*

Micer *See Food Preparation Equipment, Utensils & Cookware: Micer*

Microbiology Instruments & Supplies *See Instrumentation & Laboratory Equipment: Microbiology Instruments & Supplies*

Microprocessor Controls *See Instrumentation & Laboratory Equipment: Controls: Microprocessor*

Microwave Ovens *See Equipment & Machinery: Food Processing: Microwave Ovens*

Milk & Cream Coolers *See Refrigeration & Cooling Equipment: Coolers: Milk & Cream*

Milk & Cream Regenerators *See Equipment & Machinery: Food Processing: Regenerators: Milk & Cream*

Milk & Cream Testers *See Instrumentation & Laboratory Equipment: Testers: Milk & Cream*

Milk Agitators *See Equipment & Machinery: Food Processing: Agitators: Milk*

Milk Bottle Carriers *See Packaging Materials & Supplies: Carriers: Milk Bottle*

Milk Cans *See Packaging Materials & Supplies: Cans: Milk*

Milk Evaporators *See Equipment & Machinery: Food Processing: Evaporators: Milk*

Milking *See Equipment & Machinery: Food Processing: Milking*

Mills *See Equipment & Machinery: Food Processing: Mills*

Mincer *See Food Preparation Equipment, Utensils & Cookware: Mincer*

Mirrors *See Equipment & Machinery: Mirrors*

Mist Collection *See Equipment & Machinery: Systems: Mist Collection*

Mixers *See Equipment & Machinery: Food Processing: Mixers*

Mixing Kettles *See Food Preparation Equipment, Utensils & Cookware: Kettles: Mixing*

Mobile Food Vending Carts *See Foodservice Equipment & Supplies: Carts: Mobile Food Vending*

Modular Tanks *See Transportation & Storage: Tanks: Modular*

Moldings *See Foodservice Equipment & Supplies: Plastic Store Shelf: Moldings*

Molds *See Food Preparation Equipment, Utensils & Cookware: Molds*

Mop Wringers *See Sanitation Equipment & Supplies: Mop Wringers*

Mops *See Sanitation Equipment & Supplies: Mops*

Multi-Wall Bags *See Packaging Materials & Supplies: Bags: Multi-Wall*

Mycotoxins *See Instrumentation & Laboratory Equipment: Analyzers: Mycotoxins*

N

Name Badges *See Clothing & Protective Apparel: Name Badges*

Napery *See Foodservice Equipment & Supplies: Napery*

Napkins *See Foodservice Equipment & Supplies: Napkins*

Netting, Open Mesh Bags *See Packaging Materials & Supplies: Bags: Netting, Open Mesh*

Nitrites, Nitrosamines *See Instrumentation & Laboratory Equipment: Analyzers: Nitrites, Nitrosamines*

Nozzles *See Equipment & Machinery: Nozzles*

Numerical Controls *See Instrumentation & Laboratory Equipment: Controls: Numerical*

Nut Cracking, Shelling & Salting *See Equipment & Machinery: Food Processing: Nut Cracking, Shelling & Salting*

Nut Grinding Mills *See Equipment & Machinery: Food Processing: Mills: Nut Grinding*

Nutritional Analyses & Labeling *See Consultants & Services: Nutritional Analyses & Labeling*

O

Oil Cake Grinding Mills *See Equipment & Machinery: Food Processing: Mills: Oil Cake Grinding*

Oil Extraction *See Equipment & Machinery: Food Processing: Oil Extraction*

Oil, Cottonseed & Linseed Presses *See Equipment & Machinery: Food Processing: Presses: Oil, Cottonseed & Linseed*

Oils *See Sanitation Equipment & Supplies: Oils*

Openers *See Equipment & Machinery: Openers*

Organic Acids *See Instrumentation & Laboratory Equipment: Analyzers: Organic Acids*

Outdoor Lighting *See Building Equipment & Supplies: Lighting Equipment: Outdoor*

Oven Mits *See Clothing & Protective Apparel: Oven Mits*

Ovens *See Equipment & Machinery: Food Processing: Ovens*

Oyster & Clam Knives *See Food Preparation Equipment, Utensils & Cookware: Knives: Oyster & Clam*

P

Package Tying *See Equipment & Machinery: Packaging: Package Tying*

Package, Carton & Display *See Consultants & Services: Designers: Package, Carton & Display*

Packaging & Containerizing *See Packaging Materials & Supplies: Packaging & Containerizing Products*

Packaging Consultants *See Consultants & Services: Consultants: Packaging*

Packaging Line Controls *See Instrumentation & Laboratory Equipment: Controls: Packaging Line*

Packaging Line Detectors *See Equipment & Machinery: Packaging: Detectors: Packaging Line*

Packaging Materials *See Instrumentation & Laboratory Equipment: Testers: Packaging Materials/Containers*

Packaging Services *See Consultants & Services: Packaging Services*

Packaging Systems *See Equipment & Machinery: Systems: Packaging*

Packaging *See Equipment & Machinery: Packaging; Packaging Materials & Supplies: Packaging*

Packers' & Butchers' Processing *See Equipment & Machinery: Food Processing: Packers' & Butchers'*

Packers' Glassware *See Food Preparation Equipment, Utensils & Cookware: Glassware: Packers'*

Packers *See Consultants & Services: Packers*

Packing House Racks *See Transportation & Storage: Racks: Packing House*

Packing House Supplies *See Packaging Materials & Supplies: Packing House Supplies*

Packing House Tables *See Equipment & Machinery: Packaging: Tables: Packing House*

Packing House Trucks *See Transportation & Storage: Trucks: Packing House*

Packing *See Equipment & Machinery: Packaging: Packing*

Paging Systems *See Building Equipment & Supplies: Paging Systems*

Pails *See Equipment & Machinery: Pails*

Pallet Handling Equipment *See Transportation & Storage: Pallet Handling Equipment*

EXAMPLE: **Dairy Cooling Vats** *See Equipment & Machinery: Food Processing: Vats: Dairy Cooling*

1. Product or Service you are looking for
2. Main Category, in alphabetical order, located in the page headers starting on page 17
3. Category Description, located in black bars and in page headers
4. Product Category, located in gray bars
5. Product Type, located under gray bars, centered in bold

Pallet Handling Trucks *See Transportation & Storage: Trucks: Pallet Handling*

Pallet Racks *See Transportation & Storage: Racks: Pallet*

Palletizers *See Transportation & Storage: Palletizers*

Pallets *See Transportation & Storage: Pallets; Building Equipment & Supplies: Panels*

Panomatic-Flour Collection System *See Equipment & Machinery: Food Processing: Panomatic-Flour Collection System*

Pans *See Food Preparation Equipment, Utensils & Cookware: Pans*

Paper Bags *See Packaging Materials & Supplies: Bags: Paper*

Paper Boxes *See Packaging Materials & Supplies: Boxes: Paper*

Paper Containers *See Packaging Materials & Supplies: Containers: Paper*

Paper Cups *See Packaging Materials & Supplies: Cups: Paper*

Paper Dishes *See Foodservice Equipment & Supplies: Dishes: Paper*

Paper Filters *See Equipment & Machinery: Food Processing: Filters: Paper*

Paper Lined Bags *See Packaging Materials & Supplies: Bags: Paper Lined*

Paper Napkins *See Foodservice Equipment & Supplies: Napkins: Paper*

Paper Plates *See Food Preparation Equipment, Utensils & Cookware: Plates: Paper*

Paper Towels *See Foodservice Equipment & Supplies: Towels: Paper*

Paper Wrappers *See Packaging Materials & Supplies: Wrappers: Paper*

Paper, Folding Boxes *See Packaging Materials & Supplies: Boxes: Paper, Folding*

Paper *See Foodservice Equipment & Supplies: Paper; Packaging Materials & Supplies: Paper*

Paraffin Wax *See Packaging Materials & Supplies: Wax: Paraffin*

Parers & Peelers *See Food Preparation Equipment, Utensils & Cookware: Parers & Peelers*

Parts Food Processing *See Equipment & Machinery: Food Processing: Food Processing: Parts*

Parts *See Equipment & Machinery: Parts*

Pasta Processing *See Equipment & Machinery: Food Processing: Pasta Processing*

Paste Products Mixers *See Equipment & Machinery: Food Processing: Mixers: Paste Products*

Pasteurizers *See Equipment & Machinery: Food Processing: Pasteurizers*

Peanut Butter Mills *See Equipment & Machinery: Food Processing: Mills: Peanut Butter*

Peanut Processing *See Equipment & Machinery: Food Processing: Peanut Processing*

Personnel Services *See Consultants & Services: Personnel Services*

Pest Control *See Sanitation Equipment & Supplies: Pest Control Systems & Devices; Sanitation Equipment & Supplies: Pest Control*

Pesticide Residue *See Instrumentation & Laboratory Equipment: Analyzers: Pesticide Residue, Antibiotics*

pH Loggers *See Instrumentation & Laboratory Equipment: Process Controls: pH Loggers*

pH Meters *See Instrumentation & Laboratory Equipment: Meters: pH*

Pharmaceutical Industry *See Equipment & Machinery: Pharmaceutical Industry*

Pickers *See Equipment & Machinery: Food Processing: Pickers*

Pickle Cutters *See Food Preparation Equipment, Utensils & Cookware: Cutters: Pickle*

Pie Pans *See Food Preparation Equipment, Utensils & Cookware: Pans: Pie*

Pie Plates *See Food Preparation Equipment, Utensils & Cookware: Plates: Pie*

Pizza & Pizza Products *See Equipment & Machinery: Food Processing: Pizza & Pizza Products Processing*

Place Mats *See Foodservice Equipment & Supplies: Place Mats*

Plastic Back Tag *See Foodservice Equipment & Supplies: Plastic Back Tag*

Plastic Bags *See Packaging Materials & Supplies: Bags: Plastic*

Plastic Bottles *See Packaging Materials & Supplies: Bottles: Plastic*

Plastic Boxes *See Packaging Materials & Supplies: Boxes: Plastic*

Plastic Coated Paper *See Packaging Materials & Supplies: Paper: Plastic Coated*

Plastic Containers *See Packaging Materials & Supplies: Containers: Plastic*

Plastic Cups *See Packaging Materials & Supplies: Cups: Plastic*

Plastic Doors *See Building Equipment & Supplies: Doors: Plastic*

Plastic Fabricators *See Equipment & Machinery: Plastic Fabricators*

Plastic Film *See Packaging Materials & Supplies: Film: Plastic*

Plastic Jars *See Packaging Materials & Supplies: Jars: Plastic*

Plastic Packaging *See Packaging Materials & Supplies: Packaging: Plastic*

Plastic Pallets *See Transportation & Storage: Pallets: Plastic*

Plastic Shelf Covers *See Foodservice Equipment & Supplies: Plastic Shelf Covers*

Plastic Signs *See Foodservice Equipment & Supplies: Signs: Plastic*

Plastic Store Shelf *See Foodservice Equipment & Supplies: Plastic Store Shelf*

Plastic Trays *See Foodservice Equipment & Supplies: Trays: Plastic*

Plastic Tubing *See Equipment & Machinery: Tubing: Plastic*

Plastic Utensils *See Foodservice Equipment & Supplies: Utensils: Plastic*

Plastic, Reusable Plates *See Food Preparation Equipment, Utensils & Cookware: Plates: Plastic, Reusable*

Plastic, Rubber Gloves *See Clothing & Protective Apparel: Gloves: Plastic, Rubber*

Plastic *See Packaging Materials & Supplies: Plastic*

Plastics Printing *See Equipment & Machinery: Packaging: Printing: Plastics*

Plate & Tray Dispensers *See Foodservice Equipment & Supplies: Dispensers: Plate & Tray*

Plate/Frame Exchanger *See Equipment & Machinery: Plate/Frame Exchanger*

Plates *See Food Preparation Equipment, Utensils & Cookware: Plates*

Platforms *See Building Equipment & Supplies: Platforms*

Plating *See Building Equipment & Supplies: Plating*

Platters *See Food Preparation Equipment, Utensils & Cookware: Platters*

Plumbing & Drainage *See Sanitation Equipment & Supplies: Plumbing & Drainage Equipment*

Point of Purchase Displays *See Foodservice Equipment & Supplies: Displays: Point of Purchase*

Point of Purchase Signs *See Foodservice Equipment & Supplies: Signs: Point of Purchase*

Point of Sale Systems *See Foodservice Equipment & Supplies: Point of Sale Systems*

Polarimeters *See Instrumentation & Laboratory Equipment: Measurement Systems: Polarimeters*

Polish *See Sanitation Equipment & Supplies: Polish*

Polishing, Refinishing, Sanding & Scrubbing *See Sanitation Equipment & Supplies: Floor Cleaning Machinery: Polishing, Refinishing, Sanding & Scrubbing*

Polyethylene Bags *See Packaging Materials & Supplies: Bags: Polyethylene*

Polypropylene Bags *See Packaging Materials & Supplies: Bags: Polypropylene*

Popcorn Bags *See Packaging Materials & Supplies: Bags: Popcorn*

Portion Control Equipment *See Equipment & Machinery: Packaging: Portion Control Equipment*

Pot Holders *See Clothing & Protective Apparel: Holders: Pot*

Potato & Onion Sorters *See Equipment & Machinery: Food Processing: Sorters: Potato & Onion*

Potato Chip Processing *See Equipment & Machinery: Food Processing: Potato Chip Processing*

Poultry Pickers *See Equipment & Machinery: Food Processing: Pickers: Poultry*

Poultry Processing *See Equipment & Machinery: Food Processing: Poultry Processing*

Poultry Shears *See Food Preparation Equipment, Utensils & Cookware: Shears: Poultry*

Powder Soap *See Sanitation Equipment & Supplies: Soap: Powder*

Powder *See Sanitation Equipment & Supplies: Powder*

Power Meat Cutters *See Food Preparation Equipment, Utensils & Cookware: Cutters: Meat: Power*

Powered Beer Keg Movers *See Transportation & Storage: Beer Keg Movers: Powered*

Preservation *See Equipment & Machinery: Food Processing: Preservation*

Presses *See Equipment & Machinery: Food Processing: Presses*

Pressure Cookers *See Equipment & Machinery: Food Processing: Cookers: Pressure*

Pressure Process Controls *See Instrumentation & Laboratory Equipment: Process Controls: Pressure*

Pressure Sensitive Film *See Packaging Materials & Supplies: Film: Pressure Sensitive*

Pressure Sensitive Foil *See Packaging Materials & Supplies: Foil: Pressure Sensitive*

Pressure Sensitive Labels *See Packaging Materials & Supplies: Labels: Pressure Sensitive*

Pressure Sensitive Paper *See Packaging Materials & Supplies: Paper: Pressure Sensitive*

Pressure Sensitive Seals *See Packaging Materials & Supplies: Seals: Pressure Sensitive*

Pressure Sensitive Tags *See Packaging Materials & Supplies: Tags: Pressure Sensitive*

Pressure Sensitive Tapes *See Packaging Materials & Supplies: Tapes: Pressure Sensitive*

Pressure Washers *See Sanitation Equipment & Supplies: Pressure Washers*

Pretzel Processing *See Equipment & Machinery: Food Processing: Pretzel Processing*

Price & Sign Markers *See Foodservice Equipment & Supplies: Markers: Price & Sign*

Price Card, Ticket, Etc. Holders *See Foodservice Equipment & Supplies: Holders: Price Card, Ticket, Etc.*

Price Tag Seals *See Packaging Materials & Supplies: Seals: Price Tag*

Price Tags *See Packaging Materials & Supplies: Tags: Price*

Pricer Signs *See Foodservice Equipment & Supplies: Pricer Signs*

Pricing Systems *See Equipment & Machinery: Systems: Pricing*

Primary & Secondary Schools Foodservice *See Consultants & Services: Foodservice: Primary & Secondary Schools*

Printed & Laminated Foil *See Packaging Materials & Supplies: Foil: Printed & Laminated*

Printing Carton *See Equipment & Machinery: Packaging: Carton: Printing*

Printing *See Equipment & Machinery: Packaging: Printing*

Private Label *See Packaging Materials & Supplies: Labels: Private Label*

Private Label Packaging *See Packaging Materials & Supplies: Packaging: Private Label*

Process & Production Systems *See Equipment & Machinery: Systems: Process & Production*

Process Analysis & Development *See Instrumentation & Laboratory Equipment: Process Analysis & Development*

Process Controls *See Instrumentation & Laboratory Equipment: Process Controls*

Process Vessels & Tanks *See Consultants & Services: Designers: Process Vessels & Tanks*

Programmable Process Controls *See Instrumentation & Laboratory Equipment: Process Controls: Programmable*

Project Management *See Consultants & Services: Project Management*

Protective Apparel *See Clothing & Protective Apparel: Protective Apparel*

Protective Gloves *See Clothing & Protective Apparel: Gloves: Protective*

Pulpers *See Equipment & Machinery: Food Processing: Pulpers*

Pulverizers *See Equipment & Machinery: Food Processing: Pulverizers*

Pump feeders *See Equipment & Machinery: Pump feeders*

Pumps *See Equipment & Machinery: Pumps; Foodservice Equipment & Supplies: Pumps; Instrumentation & Laboratory Equipment: Pumps*

Purifiers *See Equipment & Machinery: Water Treatment: Purifiers*

Q

Quality Control *See Consultants & Services: Quality Control*

Quick Freezing *See Refrigeration & Cooling Equipment: Freezers: Quick Freezing*

R

Racks Dishwasher *See Sanitation Equipment & Supplies: Dishwasher: Racks*

Racks Refrigerators *See Refrigeration & Cooling Equipment: Refrigerators: Racks*

Racks *See Foodservice Equipment & Supplies: Racks; Transportation & Storage: Racks*

Radios Paging Systems *See Building Equipment & Supplies: Paging Systems: Radios*

Ramps *See Transportation & Storage: Ramps*

Rat & Mouse Traps *See Sanitation Equipment & Supplies: Pest Control Systems & Devices: Traps: Rat & Mouse*

Rebuilt & Used *See Equipment & Machinery: Food Processing: Food Processing: Rebuilt & Used*

Rebuilt & Used Packaging *See Equipment & Machinery: Packaging: Rebuilt & Used*

Rechargeable Flashlights *See Safety & Security Equipment & Supplies: Flashlights: Rechargable*

Recorders *See Instrumentation & Laboratory Equipment: Process Controls: Recorders*

Refinishing *See Consultants & Services: Refinishing & Refurbishing Services*

Refractometers *See Instrumentation & Laboratory Equipment: Measurement Systems: Refractometers*

Refrigerated Display Case Doors *See Refrigeration & Cooling Equipment: Doors: Refrigerated Display Case*

Refrigerated Trailers *See Transportation & Storage: Trailers: Refrigerated*

Refrigerating & Cooling Rooms *See Refrigeration & Cooling Equipment: Refrigerating & Cooling Rooms*

Refrigerating Equipment & Machinery *See Refrigeration & Cooling Equipment: Refrigerating Equipment & Machinery*

Refrigerating Units *See Refrigeration & Cooling Equipment: Refrigerating Units*

Refrigeration & Cold Storage Insulation *See Refrigeration & Cooling Equipment: Insulation: Refrigeration & Cold Storage*

Refrigeration Systems *See Instrumentation & Laboratory Equipment: Controls: Refrigeration Systems*

Refrigeration Valves *See Refrigeration & Cooling Equipment: Valves: Refrigeration*

Refrigerator & Stove Shelves *See Equipment & Machinery: Shelves: Refrigerator & Stove*

Refrigerator Baskets *See Packaging Materials & Supplies: Baskets: Refrigerator*

Refrigerator Doors *See Refrigeration & Cooling Equipment: Doors: Refrigerator*

Refrigerators *See Refrigeration & Cooling Equipment: Refrigerators*

Regenerators *See Equipment & Machinery: Food Processing: Regenerators*

Research & Development *See Consultants & Services: Research & Development*

Resistant Flooring *See Building Equipment & Supplies: Flooring: Thermal Shock: Resistant Flooring*

Restaurant Design *See Consultants & Services: Consultants: Restaurant Design*

Restaurant Supplies & Equipment *See Foodservice Equipment & Supplies: Restaurant Supplies & Equipment*

Retail Architects *See Consultants & Services: Architects: Retail*

Retail Foodservice *See Consultants & Services: Foodservice: Retail*

Retort Pouch *See Equipment & Machinery: Packaging: Retort Pouch Processing*

Retorts *See Packaging Materials & Supplies: Retorts*

Reverse Osmosis *See Equipment & Machinery: Systems: Reverse Osmosis*

Reverse Vending *See Foodservice Equipment & Supplies: Vending Machinery: Reverse*

Rice Grinding Mills *See Equipment & Machinery: Food Processing: Mills: Rice Grinding*

Rice Processing *See Equipment & Machinery: Food Processing: Rice Processing*

Road Plates *See Equipment & Machinery: Road Plates*

Roasters *See Equipment & Machinery: Food Processing: Roasters*

Roasting *See Equipment & Machinery: Food Processing: Roasting*

Rolling Pins *See Food Preparation Equipment, Utensils & Cookware: Rolling Pins*

Room Service *See Foodservice Equipment & Supplies: Tables: Room Service*

Rotisseries *See Equipment & Machinery: Food Processing: Rotisseries*

Routing & Scheduling for Food Industry *See Consultants & Services: Computer Software, Systems & Services: Software: Routing & Scheduling for Food Industry*

Rubber Stamps *See Packaging Materials & Supplies: Stamps: Rubber*

Rubber, Bottle Stoppers *See Instrumentation & Laboratory Equipment: Stoppers: Rubber, Bottle*

S

Safety & Security *See Safety & Security Equipment & Supplies*

Safety Flooring *See Building Equipment & Supplies: Flooring: Safety*

Salad Bars *See Foodservice Equipment & Supplies: Salad Bars*

Salad Carts *See Foodservice Equipment & Supplies: Carts: Salad*

Salt & Pepper Shakers *See Packaging Materials & Supplies: Shakers: Salt & Pepper*

Salt *See Instrumentation & Laboratory Equipment: Analyzers: Salt (Sodium Chloride)*

Salt Processing *See Equipment & Machinery: Food Processing: Salt Processing*

Sampling & Testing *See Instrumentation & Laboratory Equipment: Sampling & Testing Equipment & Instrumentation*

Sandwich Bags *See Packaging Materials & Supplies: Bags: Sandwich*

Sandwich Processing *See Equipment & Machinery: Food Processing: Sandwich Processing*

Sanitary Wall *See Sanitation Equipment & Supplies: Sanitary Wall*

Sanitation Equipment & Supplies *See Sanitation Equipment & Supplies*

Sanitation, Testing & Analysis *See Consultants & Services: Consultants: Sanitation, Testing & Analysis*

Sanitizers *See Sanitation Equipment & Supplies: Sanitizers*

Sauce Pans *See Food Preparation Equipment, Utensils & Cookware: Pans: Sauce*

Sausage Meat Cutters *See Food Preparation Equipment, Utensils & Cookware: Cutters: Meat: Sausage*

Sausage Stuffers *See Equipment & Machinery: Food Processing: Stuffers: Sausage*

Sawdust Smokers *See Equipment & Machinery: Food Processing: Smokers: Sawdust*

Saws *See Equipment & Machinery: Food Processing: Saws*

Scalers *See Equipment & Machinery: Food Processing: Scalers*

Scales *See Instrumentation & Laboratory Equipment: Scales & Weighing Systems; Equipment & Machinery: Scales*

Scanners *See Foodservice Equipment & Supplies: Scanners*

Scoops, Dishers & Spades *See Food Preparation Equipment, Utensils & Cookware: Scoops, Dishers & Spades*

Scouring Pads *See Sanitation Equipment & Supplies: Scouring Pads*

Scrapers *See Food Preparation Equipment, Utensils & Cookware: Scrapers*

Screening *See Equipment & Machinery: Screening*

Scrubbers *See Equipment & Machinery: Scrubbers; See also Sanitation Equipment & Supplies: Scrubbers*

Seafood Preparation *See Equipment & Machinery: Food Processing: Seafood Preparation Equipment*

Sealers *See Equipment & Machinery: Packaging: Sealers*

Sealing Wax *See Packaging Materials & Supplies: Wax: Sealing*

Seals *See Packaging Materials & Supplies: Seals*

Sensors *See Instrumentation & Laboratory Equipment: Sensors*

Separators *See Equipment & Machinery: Food Processing: Separators*

Service Carts *See Foodservice Equipment & Supplies: Carts: Service*

Serving Equipment *See Foodservice Equipment & Supplies: Serving Equipment*

Shakers *See Packaging Materials & Supplies: Shakers*

Shears *See Food Preparation Equipment, Utensils & Cookware: Shears*

Sheeter *See Food Preparation Equipment, Utensils & Cookware: Sheeter*

Sheets *See Food Preparation Equipment, Utensils & Cookware: Sheets*

Shelf Covers *See Foodservice Equipment & Supplies: Wood Grain Plastic: Shelf Covers*

Shelf Strips Clear Plastic *See Foodservice Equipment & Supplies: Clear Plastic: Shelf Strips*

Shelf Strips Colored Plastic *See Foodservice Equipment & Supplies: Colored Plastic: Shelf Strips*

Shelves *See Equipment & Machinery: Shelves*

Shelving *See Foodservice Equipment & Supplies: Shelving; See also Transportation & Storage: Shelving*

Shirts *See Clothing & Protective Apparel: Shirts*

Shish Kebab *See Equipment & Machinery: Food Processing: Shish Kebab Systems*

Shoplifting Detectors *See Safety & Security Equipment & Supplies: Detectors: Shoplifting*

Shopping Bags *See Packaging Materials & Supplies: Bags: Shopping*

Shopping Baskets *See Foodservice Equipment & Supplies: Baskets: Shopping*

Shopping Carts *See Foodservice Equipment & Supplies: Carts: Shopping*

Shredded Paper *See Packaging Materials & Supplies: Paper: Shredded*

Shredders *See Equipment & Machinery: Food Processing: Shredders*

Shrimp Processing *See Equipment & Machinery: Food Processing: Shrimp Processing Equipment*

Shrink Packaging *See Packaging Materials & Supplies: Packaging: Shrink*

Shrinkers: Plastic *See Equipment & Machinery: Packaging: Shrinkers: Plastic Packaging*

Sieves *See Food Preparation Equipment, Utensils & Cookware: Sieves*

Sifters *See Food Preparation Equipment, Utensils & Cookware: Sifters*

Sign & Card Holders *See Foodservice Equipment & Supplies: Magnetic Pocket: Sign & Card Holders*

Signs *See Foodservice Equipment & Supplies: Signs*

Silver Cleaners *See Sanitation Equipment & Supplies: Cleaners: Silver*

Silverware Boxes *See Packaging Materials & Supplies: Boxes: Silverware*

Silverware Cleaning *See Sanitation Equipment & Supplies: Silverware Cleaning Machinery*

Sinks *See Building Equipment & Supplies: Sinks*

Sizers *See Equipment & Machinery: Sizers*

Skewers *See Food Preparation Equipment, Utensils & Cookware: Skewers*

Skids Systems *See Equipment & Machinery: Systems: Skids*

Skids *See Transportation & Storage: Skids*

Skin Cream & Lotions *See Sanitation Equipment & Supplies: Skin Cream & Lotions; Sanitation Equipment & Supplies: Skin Cream & Lotions: Skin Cream*

Skinning *See Equipment & Machinery: Food Processing: Skinning*

Sleeves *See Packaging Materials & Supplies: Sleeves*

Slicer *See Food Preparation Equipment, Utensils & Cookware: Slicer*

Slicers *See Equipment & Machinery: Food Processing: Slicers*

Slicing Knives *See Food Preparation Equipment, Utensils & Cookware: Knives: Slicing*

Smokers *See Equipment & Machinery: Food Processing: Smokers*

EXAMPLE: **Dairy Cooling Vats** *See Equipment & Machinery: Food Processing: Vats: Dairy Cooling*

1   2   3 4 5

1. Product or Service you are looking for
2. Main Category, in alphabetical order, located in the page headers starting on page 17
3. Category Description, located in black bars and in page headers
4. Product Category, located in gray bars
5. Product Type, located under gray bars, centered in bold

Snack Food *See Equipment & Machinery: Food Processing: Snack Food Processing*

Sneeze Guards *See Sanitation Equipment & Supplies: Sneeze Guards*

Soap Dispensers *See Sanitation Equipment & Supplies: Dispensers: Soap*

Soap *See Sanitation Equipment & Supplies: Soap*

Soda Fountain, Syrup & Fruit Juice Dispensers *See Foodservice Equipment & Supplies: Dispensers: Soda Fountain, Syrup & Fruit Juice*

Softeners *See Equipment & Machinery: Water Treatment: Softeners*

Software Computer *See Consultants & Services: Computer Software, Systems & Services: Software*

Software Process Controls *See Instrumentation & Laboratory Equipment: Process Controls: Software*

Sorters *See Equipment & Machinery: Food Processing: Sorters; Equipment & Machinery: Packaging: Sorters; Foodservice Equipment & Supplies: Sorters*

Soybean Processing *See Equipment & Machinery: Food Processing: Soybean Processing*

Speed Reducer *See Equipment & Machinery: Feeders: Gravimetric, Volumetric, Loss-In-Weight, Etc.: Speed Reducer*

Spice Grinding *See Equipment & Machinery: Food Processing: Mills: Spice Grinding*

Spice Racks *See Transportation & Storage: Racks: Spice*

Sponges *See Sanitation Equipment & Supplies: Sponges*

Spoons *See Food Preparation Equipment, Utensils & Cookware: Spoons*

Spray Dryers *See Equipment & Machinery: Food Processing: Dryers: Spray*

Spray Drying Services *See Consultants & Services: Spray Drying Services*

Spray Nozzles *See Equipment & Machinery: Nozzles: Spray*

Sprinkling Systems *See Sanitation Equipment & Supplies: Sprinkling Systems*

Squeegees *See Sanitation Equipment & Supplies: Squeegees*

Stacking *See Equipment & Machinery: Stacking*

Stainless Steel *See Food Preparation Equipment, Utensils & Cookware: Pans: Baking & Roasting: Stainless Steel; Equipment & Machinery: Coffee Industry: Stainless Steel*

Stainless Steel Hoods *See Building Equipment & Supplies: Hoods: Stainless Steel*

Stainless Steel Tables *See Food Preparation Equipment, Utensils & Cookware: Tables: Stainless Steel*

Stainless Steel Tanks *See Transportation & Storage: Tanks: Stainless Steel*

Stainless Steel Tubing *See Equipment & Machinery: Tubing: Stainless Steel*

Stamps *See Packaging Materials & Supplies: Stamps*

Stands *See Packaging Materials & Supplies: Stands*

Steak Knives *See Food Preparation Equipment, Utensils & Cookware: Knives: Steak*

Steam Cookers *See Equipment & Machinery: Food Processing: Cookers: Steam*

Steam Generators *See Equipment & Machinery: Steam Generators*

Steam Tables *See Equipment & Machinery: Steam Tables*

Steaming *See Food Preparation Equipment, Utensils & Cookware: Kettles: Steaming*

Steel Shelving *See Transportation & Storage: Shelving: Steel*

Stemmers *See Equipment & Machinery: Food Processing: Stemmers*

Sterilizers *See Sanitation Equipment & Supplies: Sterilizers*

Sticks *See Packaging Materials & Supplies: Sticks*

Stirrers & Picks *See Food Preparation Equipment, Utensils & Cookware: Stirrers & Picks: Cocktail, Hors D'oeuvres*

Stock Racks *See Transportation & Storage: Racks: Stock*

Stoppers *See Instrumentation & Laboratory Equipment: Stoppers*

Storage & Holding Equipment *See Transportation & Storage: Storage & Holding Equipment*

Storage Units *See Transportation & Storage: Storage Units*

Store Fixtures *See Foodservice Equipment & Supplies: Fixtures: Store*

Store Shelving *See Foodservice Equipment & Supplies: Shelving: Store*

Stoves *See Equipment & Machinery: Food Processing: Stoves*

Strainers *See Food Preparation Equipment, Utensils & Cookware: Strainers*

Straws *See Foodservice Equipment & Supplies: Straws*

Strech Sleeve *See Equipment & Machinery: Packaging: Strech Sleeve Application Equipment*

Strip Doors *See Building Equipment & Supplies: Doors: Strip*

Strips Wood Grain *See Foodservice Equipment & Supplies: Wood Grain Plastic: Strips*

Stuffers *See Equipment & Machinery: Food Processing: Stuffers*

Styrofoam Cups *See Packaging Materials & Supplies: Cups: Styrofoam*

Sub-Zero Freezers *See Refrigeration & Cooling Equipment: Freezers: Sub-Zero*

Sugar & Sugar Cane Mills *See Equipment & Machinery: Food Processing: Mills: Sugar & Sugar Cane*

Sugar & Syrup Kettles *See Food Preparation Equipment, Utensils & Cookware: Kettles: Sugar & Syrup*

Sugar & Syrup Processing *See Equipment & Machinery: Food Processing: Sugar & Syrup Processing*

Sugar Pulverizers *See Equipment & Machinery: Food Processing: Pulverizers: Sugar*

Sugars *See Instrumentation & Laboratory Equipment: Analyzers: Sugars (Dextrose, Fructose, Galactose, Lactose, Sucrose)*

Sweeping *See Sanitation Equipment & Supplies: Compounds: Sweeping*

Syrup & Soda Fountain Pumps *See Foodservice Equipment & Supplies: Pumps: Syrup & Soda Fountain*

Systems & Component *See Equipment & Machinery: Conveyors: Systems & Components*

Systems Process Controls *See Instrumentation & Laboratory Equipment: Process Controls: Systems*

Systems *See Equipment & Machinery: Systems*

T

Table Cloths *See Foodservice Equipment & Supplies: Table Cloths*

Tables *See Equipment & Machinery: Packaging: Tables; Food Preparation Equipment, Utensils & Cookware: Tables; Foodservice Equipment & Supplies: Tables*

Tabletop Supplies *See Equipment & Machinery: Tabletop Supplies*

Tags *See Packaging Materials & Supplies: Tags*

Tanks *See Equipment & Machinery: Food Processing: Tanks; Transportation & Storage: Tanks*

Tapes *See Packaging Materials & Supplies: Tapes*

Tea Bag *See Packaging Materials & Supplies: Tags: Tea Bag*

Tea Industry *See Equipment & Machinery: Tea Industry*

Tea Packaging *See Packaging Materials & Supplies: Tea Packaging Materials*

Temperature Controlled *See Transportation & Storage: Storage Units: Temperature Controlled*

Temperature Process Controls *See Instrumentation & Laboratory Equipment: Process Controls: Temperature*

Testers *See Instrumentation & Laboratory Equipment: Testers*

Testing & Sampling Services *See Consultants & Services: Testing & Sampling Services*

Thermal Shock Flooring *See Building Equipment & Supplies: Flooring: Thermal Shock*

Thermometers *See Instrumentation & Laboratory Equipment: Thermometers*

Ties *See Packaging Materials & Supplies: Ties*

Tilt Trucks *See Transportation & Storage: Trucks: Tilt*

Time Process *See Instrumentation & Laboratory Equipment: Process Controls: Time*

Timers *See Equipment & Machinery: Timers*

Tin Cans *See Packaging Materials & Supplies: Cans: Tin*

Tins *See Food Preparation Equipment, Utensils & Cookware: Tins*

Tinware *See Food Preparation Equipment, Utensils & Cookware: Tinware*

Tissue *See Sanitation Equipment & Supplies: Tissue*

Toasters *See Equipment & Machinery: Food Processing: Toasters*

Tongs *See Food Preparation Equipment, Utensils & Cookware: Tongs*

Toothpicks *See Food Preparation Equipment, Utensils & Cookware: Toothpicks*

Tortilla Making *See Equipment & Machinery: Food Processing: Tortilla Making*

Tote Bags *See Foodservice Equipment & Supplies: Tote Bags*

Towels *See Foodservice Equipment & Supplies: Towels*

Trailers *See Transportation & Storage: Trailers*

Transparent Wrappers *See Packaging Materials & Supplies: Wrappers: Transparent*

Transportation Loggers *See Instrumentation & Laboratory Equipment: Process Controls: Transportation Loggers*

Traps *See Sanitation Equipment & Supplies: Pest Control Systems & Devices: Traps*

Tray Sealers *See Equipment & Machinery: Packaging: Sealers: Tray*

Tray Stands *See Packaging Materials & Supplies: Stands: Tray*

Tray, Silverware Carts *See Foodservice Equipment & Supplies: Carts: Tray, Silverware*

Trays & Pans *See Food Preparation Equipment, Utensils & Cookware: Trays & Pans*

Trays Refrigerators *See Refrigeration & Cooling Equipment: Refrigerators: Trays*

Trays *See Foodservice Equipment & Supplies: Trays; Packaging Materials & Supplies: Trays*

Treatment Systems *See Equipment & Machinery: Water Treatment: Treatment Systems*

Truck, Trailer & Refrigerator Car *See Refrigeration & Cooling Equipment: Refrigerating Units: Truck, Trailer & Refrigerator Car*

Trucks *See Transportation & Storage: Trucks*

Tubing *See Equipment & Machinery: Tubing*

Tubularaseptic Processing *See Equipment & Machinery: Systems: Tubularaseptic Processing*

Turn Key *See Consultants & Services: Construction: Turn Key*

U

Ultrasonic Cutters *See Food Preparation Equipment, Utensils & Cookware: Cutters: Ultrasonic*

Uniforms *See Clothing & Protective Apparel: Uniforms & Special Clothing*

Unit, Packaging *See Instrumentation & Laboratory Equipment: Automation: Unit, Packaging, Bulk Handling*

Unscramblers *See Equipment & Machinery: Unscramblers*

Urns *See Foodservice Equipment & Supplies: Urns*

Utensils *See Food Preparation Equipment, Utensils & Cookware: Utensils; See also Foodservice Equipment & Supplies: Utensils*

Utility Carts *See Transportation & Storage: Carts: Utility*

Utility Vault Covers *See Transportation & Storage: Utility Vault Covers*

V

Vaccum Bags *See Sanitation Equipment & Supplies: Vaccum Bags*

Vacuum Cleaners *See Sanitation Equipment & Supplies: Vacuum Cleaners*

Vacuum Packing *See Equipment & Machinery: Packaging: Vacuum Packing*

Vacuum Process *See Instrumentation & Laboratory Equipment: Process Controls: Vacuum*

Valve Control *See Equipment & Machinery: Systems: Valve Control*

Valves *See Equipment & Machinery: Valves; Refrigeration & Cooling Equipment: Valves*

Vats *See Equipment & Machinery: Food Processing: Vats; Refrigeration & Cooling Equipment: Vats; Transportation & Storage: Vats*

Vegetable & Fruit Shredders *See Equipment & Machinery: Food Processing: Shredders: Vegetable & Fruit*

Vegetable & Fruit Slicers *See Equipment & Machinery: Food Processing: Slicers: Vegetable & Fruit*

Vegetable Cookers *See Equipment & Machinery: Food Processing: Cookers: Vegetable*

Vegetable Knives *See Food Preparation Equipment, Utensils & Cookware: Knives: Vegetable*

Vegetable Oil *See Sanitation Equipment & Supplies: Soap: Vegetable Oil*

Vegetable Preparation *See Equipment & Machinery: Food Processing: Vegetable Preparation Equipment*

Vegetable Processing *See Equipment & Machinery: Food Processing: Vegetable Processing*

Vender & Visi-Cooler Installation Systems *See Refrigeration & Cooling Equipment: Vender & Visi-Cooler Installation Systems*

Vending Carts *See Foodservice Equipment & Supplies: Vending Carts*

Vending Machinery *See Foodservice Equipment &*
Supplies: Vending Machinery
Vertical Form, Fill & Seal *See Equipment & Machinery:*
Packaging: Form, Fill & Seal: Vertical
Vibrators *See Equipment & Machinery: Food Processing:*
Vibrators
Viscous Products *See Equipment & Machinery: Pumps:*
Viscous Products
Vision Verification *See Equipment & Machinery: Systems:*
Vision Verification
Vitamin Analyzers *See Instrumentation & Laboratory*
Equipment: Analyzers: Vitamin
VOC Control *See Equipment & Machinery: Food*
Processing: VOC Control

W

Waffle Irons *See Equipment & Machinery: Food*
Processing: Waffle Irons
Walk-In Coolers *See Refrigeration & Cooling Equipment:*
Coolers: Walk-In
Walk-In Freezers *See Refrigeration & Cooling Equipment:*
Freezers: Walk-In
Warehouses *See Transportation & Storage: Warehouses*
Warmers *See Foodservice Equipment & Supplies: Warmers*
Washers & Fillers *See Equipment & Machinery: Food*
Processing: Tanks: Washers & Fillers
Washers *See Equipment & Machinery: Food Processing:*
Washers
Washing Compounds *See Sanitation Equipment &*
Supplies: Compounds: Washing
Washing Machinery *See Sanitation Equipment & Supplies:*
Washing Machinery
Washing, Drying & Polishing *See Sanitation Equipment &*
Supplies: Silverware Cleaning Machinery: Washing,
Drying & Polishing
Waste Boxes *See Packaging Materials & Supplies: Boxes:*
Waste
Waste Handling & Disposal *See Sanitation Equipment &*
Supplies: Waste Handling & Disposal Equipment

Wastewater Treatment *See Sanitation Equipment &*
Supplies: Wastewater Treatment Systems
Water Activity *See Instrumentation & Laboratory*
Equipment: Analyzers: Water Activity
Water Boilers *See Equipment & Machinery: Food*
Processing: Boilers: Water
Water Heaters *See Equipment & Machinery: Heaters:*
Water
Water Treatment *See Equipment & Machinery: Water*
Treatment
Wax *See Packaging Materials & Supplies: Wax*
Waxed Paper *See Packaging Materials & Supplies: Paper:*
Waxed
Waxers *See Equipment & Machinery: Food Processing:*
Waxers
Waxing *See Equipment & Machinery: Food Processing:*
Waxing
Webtension & Torque Controls *See Instrumentation &*
Laboratory Equipment: Controls: Webtension & Torque
Weighing *See Equipment & Machinery: Packaging:*
Weighing
Wet Strength Paper *See Packaging Materials & Supplies:*
Paper: Wet Strength
Windows *See Building Equipment & Supplies: Windows*
Wine Presses *See Equipment & Machinery: Food*
Processing: Presses: Wine
Wine Racks *See Transportation & Storage: Racks: Wine*
Wine Storage *See Transportation & Storage: Wine Storage*
Units
Wipers *See Sanitation Equipment & Supplies: Wipers*
Wire Cloths *See Sanitation Equipment & Supplies: Cloths:*
Wire
Wire Racks *See Transportation & Storage: Racks: Wire*
Wire Shelving *See Transportation & Storage: Shelving:*
Wire
Wire Stitching *See Equipment & Machinery: Packaging:*
Wire Stitching
Wirebound Boxes *See Packaging Materials & Supplies:*
Boxes: Wirebound

Wood Boards *See Food Preparation Equipment, Utensils &*
Cookware: Boards: Wood
Wood Grain Plastic *See Foodservice Equipment &*
Supplies: Wood Grain Plastic
Wooden Boxes *See Packaging Materials & Supplies: Boxes:*
Wooden
Wooden Forks *See Food Preparation Equipment, Utensils*
& Cookware: Utensils: Forks: Wooden
Wooden Pallets *See Transportation & Storage: Pallets:*
Wooden
Wooden Shipping Crates *See Packaging Materials &*
Supplies: Crates: Wooden Shipping
Work Tables *See Food Preparation Equipment, Utensils &*
Cookware: Tables: Work
Wrappers *See Packaging Materials & Supplies: Wrappers*
Wrapping *See Equipment & Machinery: Packaging:*
Wrapping
Wrapping Paper *See Packaging Materials & Supplies:*
Paper: Wrapping
Writing, Forms, Sales & Order Books *See Foodservice*
Equipment & Supplies: Paper: Writing, Forms, Sales &
Order Books

X

X-ray Contaminant Detection *See Equipment &*
Machinery: Systems: X-ray Contaminant Detection

Y

Yeast Processing *See Equipment & Machinery: Food*
Processing: Yeast Processing

Z

Zipper Application *See Equipment & Machinery: Systems:*
Zipper Application

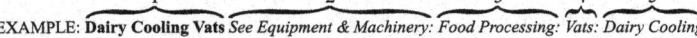

EXAMPLE: **Dairy Cooling Vats** *See Equipment & Machinery: Food Processing: Vats: Dairy Cooling*

1. Product or Service you are looking for
2. Main Category, in alphabetical order, located in the page headers starting on page 17
3. Category Description, located in black bars and in page headers
4. Product Category, located in gray bars
5. Product Type, located under gray bars, centered in bold

Building Equipment & Supplies

Air Curtains

Apollo Sheet Metal
Kennewick, WA 509-586-1104
Atlas Equipment Company
Kansas City, MO. 800-842-9188
Berner International Corp
New Castle, PA. 800-245-4455
Carnes Company
Verona, WI 608-845-6411
Chase-Doors
Cincinnati, OH 800-543-4455
Curtainaire
Los Angeles, CA. 323-753-4266
Emco Industrial Plastics
Cedar Grove, NJ 800-292-9906
Insect-O-Cutor Inc
Stone Mountain, GA. 800-966-8480
Kason
Lewis Center, OH 740-549-2100
Kason Industries
Newnan, GA. .770-254-0553
King Company
Dallas, TX. 507-451-3770
Lechler Inc
St Charles, IL 800-777-2926
Mankato Tent & Awning Co
North Mankato, MN 866-747-3524
Mars Air Products
Gardena, CA. 800-421-1266
Plas-Ties Co
Tustin, CA. 800-854-0137
Products A Curtron Div
Pittsburgh, PA. 800-888-9750
QUIKSERV Corp
Houston, TX. 800-388-8307
Ready Access
Chicago, IL 800-621-5045
Universal Jet Industries
Hialeah, FL. .305-887-4378

Air Filters

Air Quality Engineering
Minneapolis, MN 800-328-0787
Airsan Corp
Milwaukee, WI. 800-558-5494
Allergen Air Filter Corp
Houston, TX. 800-333-8880
American Ultraviolet Co
Lebanon, IN .800-288-9288
AMSOIL Inc
Superior, WI .715-392-7101
Beach Filter Products
Hanover, PA. 800-232-2485
Blue Tech
Hickory, NC .828-324-5900
CLARCOR Air Filtration Prods
Jeffersonville, IN 866-247-4827
Clyde Bergemann Eec
Halethorpe, MD 410-712-4280
Dwyer Instruments Inc
Michigan City, IN 800-872-3141
Eco-Air Products
San Diego, CA 800-284-8111
Elwood Safety Company
Buffalo, NY. .866-326-6060
Falls Filtration Technologies
Stow, OH. 330-928-4100
Flanders Corp
Washington, NC 800-637-2803
Freudenberg Nonwovens
Hopkinsville, KY 270-887-5115
G.W. Dahl Company
Greensboro, NC 800-852-4449
Gaylord Industries
Tualatin, OR .800-547-9696
Halton Company
Scottsville, KY 800-442-5866
Hunter Fan Co
Cordova, TN .901-743-1360
KETCH
Wichita, KS .800-766-3777
King Bag & Mfg Co
Cincinnati, OH 800-444-5464

King Company
Dallas, TX. 507-451-3770
King Engineering - King-Gage
Newell, WV .800-242-8871
Lamports Filter Media
Cleveland, OH 216-881-2050
Mars Air Products
Gardena, CA. 800-421-1266
Monroe Environmental Corp
Monroe, MI. .800-992-7707
Parker-Hannifin Corp
Jeffersonville, IN 866-247-4827
Refractron Technologies Corp
Newark, NY .315-331-6222
Rolfs @ Boone
Boone, IA 800-265-2010
Ultra Industries Inc
Racine, WI 800-358-5872
United Air Specialists Inc
Blue Ash, OH 800-992-4422
United States Systems Inc
Kansas City, KS 888-281-2454
Vent Master
Mississauga, ON. 800-565-2981
VMC Signs
Victoria, TX .361-575-0548

Awnings

A A A Awning Co Inc
Houston, TX. 800-281-6193
A&A International
Virginia Beach, VA. 800-252-1446
Academy Awning
Los Angeles, CA. 310-277-8383
Acme Awning
Salinas, CA. .831-424-7134
Acme Awning Co Inc
Bronx, NY. 718-409-1822
Advanced Design Awning & Sign
Cloquet, MN 800-566-8368
Allied Electric Sign & Awning
Salt Lake City, UT 801-972-6837
Alpha Canvas & Awning Co
Charlotte, NC 800-583-9179
Alpha Productions Inc
Los Angeles, CA. 800-223-0883
American Sun Control Awnings
Alpharetta, GA 800-245-6746
Anchor Industries
Evansville, IN 812-867-2421
Andgar Corp
Ferndale, WA 360-366-9900
Arrow Sign & Awning Company
East Bethel, MN 800-621-9231
Avalon Canvas & Upholstery Inc
Houston, TX. 713-607-9289
Avondale Mills
Monroe, GA .770-267-2226
Awning Co Inc
Sag Harbor, NY. 631-725-3651
Awning Enterprises
Frederick, MD. 800-735-2453
Awnings by Dee
Little Neck, NY. 516-487-6688
Awnings Plus
Addison, IL 888-627-4770
B & W Awning Co
Lexington, KY 859-252-1619
B H Awning & Tent Co
Benton Harbor, MI. 800-272-2187
Belle Isle Awning
Roseville, MI 586-294-6050
Bower's Awning & Shade
Lebanon, PA. 717-273-2351
Brock Awnings LTD
Hampton Bays, NY. 631-728-3367
C.B. Dombach & Son
Lancaster, PA 717-392-0578
Cain Awning Co Inc
Birmingham, AL. 205-323-8379
Camel Canvas Shop
Knoxville, TN 800-524-2704
Canvas Products
Grand Junction, CO 970-242-1453

Capitol Awning Co Inc
Jamaica, NY .800-241-3539
Charlotte Tent & Awning
Charlotte, NC 704-921-8743
Chattin Awning Company
Edison, NJ 800-394-3500
Chesterfield Awning Co
Chicago, IL 800-339-6522
Childres Custom Canvas Prods
Duncanville, TX 972-298-4943
Chilson's Shops Inc
Easthampton, MA 413-529-8062
City Canvas
San Jose, CA. 408-287-2688
Coastal Canvas Products
Savannah, GA. 800-476-5174
Creative Canopy Design
Hernando Beach, FL. 866-970-5200
Custom Tarpaulin Products Inc
Youngstown, OH. 888-394-5054
Dade Canvas Products Company
Silver Spring, MD. 301-680-2500
Danieli Awnings
Napa, CA 707-257-6100
Darlington Sign Awning & Neon
Warwick, RI .401-734-5800
Dean Custom Awning
Orangeburg, NY 845-425-6678
Delta Signs
Haltom City, TX 866-643-3582
Despro Manufacturing
Cedar Grove, NJ 800-292-9906
Dize Co
Winston Salem, NC. 800-583-8243
Dualite Sales & Svc Inc
Williamsburg, OH 513-724-7100
Durasol Awnings
Middletown, NY 800-444-6131
Ehmke Manufacturing
Philadelphia, PA 215-324-4200
Eide Industries Inc
Cerritos, CA .800-422-6827
Elegant Awnings
Chino, CA 800-541-9011
Encore Image Inc
Ontario, CA. .800-791-1187
Engineered Textile Products
Mobile, AL 800-222-8277
Evanston Awning Co
Evanston, IL .847-864-4520
F & S Awning & Sign Co
Edison, NJ 732-738-4110
Fort Wayne Awning
Fort Wayne, IN 800-404-1636
French Awning & Screen Co Inc
Jackson, MS .800-898-1132
Fresno Tent & Awning
Fresno, CA 559-264-4771
FTL/Happold Tensil Structure Design & Engineering
New York, NY 212-732-4691
G & J Awning & Canvas Inc
Sauk Rapids, MN 800-467-1744
Geneva Awning & Tent Works Inc
Geneva, NY. .800-789-3151
Georgia Tent & Awning
Atlanta, GA. .800-252-2391
Glawe Manufacturing Company
Fairborn, OH. 800-434-8368
Glen Raven Custom Fabrics LLC
Burlington, NC 336-227-6211
Global Canvas Products
Philadelphia, PA 267-634-6207
Goodwin-Cole Co Inc
Sacramento, CA 800-752-4477
Greeley Tent & Awning Co
Greeley, CO. .970-352-0253
Greenville Awning Company
Mauldin, SC .864-288-0063
H.B. Wall & Sons
Ozark, MO 800-373-1616
Hamilton Awning Co
Beaver, PA. 724-774-7644
Hendee Enterprises Inc
Houston, TX. 800-231-7275
Hogshire Industries
Norfolk, VA. .757-877-2297

17

J & J Window Sales Inc
Chesterfield, MO 636-532-3320
J W Hulme Co
St Paul, MN.....................800-442-8212
Jamestown Awning
Jamestown, NY 716-483-1435
Kohler Awning Inc
Buffalo, NY.....................800-875-9091
LA Graphics
Greenville, SC 864-297-1111
Lafayette Tent & Awning Co
Lafayette, IN 800-458-2955
Laggren's LLC
Monroe Twp, NJ 609-235-9883
Laurel Awning Co
Apollo, PA......................888-567-5689
Lawrence Fabric Structures
St Louis, MO...................800-527-3840
Leavitt & Parris Inc
Portland, ME....................800-833-6679
Lincoln Tent Inc
Lincoln, NE.....................800-567-4559
Lloyd's of Millville
Millville, NJ 856-825-0345
Macon Awning & Canvas Prod
Macon, GA 478-743-2684
Maple Leaf Awning & Canvas Co
Sherwood, AR...................800-947-4233
Marygrove Awnings-Toledo
Perrysburg, OH 419-241-9181
Mason City Tent & Awning Co
Mason City, IA 641-423-0044
Merrillville Awning Co
Merrillville, IN 800-781-6100
Metal Master Sales Corp
Glendale Heights, IL.............800-488-8729
Miami Awning
Miami, FL.......................800-576-0222
Mid-State Awning & Patio Co
Bellefonte, PA...................814-355-8979
Modesto Tent & Awning
Modesto, CA....................209-545-6150
Moran Canvas Products Inc
La Mesa, CA....................800-515-1130
Mt. Lebanon Awning & Tent Company
Presto, PA 412-221-2233
Muskegon Awning & Fabrication
Muskegon, MI...................800-968-3686
Neilson Canvas Company
Sandusky, OH 419-625-0581
New Haven Awnings
New Haven, CT 800-560-5650
Niantic Awning Company
Windham, NH 978-225-0108
O'Brian Tarping Systems Inc
Wilson, NC 800-334-8277
Oklahoma Neon
Tulsa, OK 888-707-6366
Omar Awnings & Signs
Johnson City, TN 800-274-6627
Ottumwa Tent & Awning Co
Ottumwa, IA 641-682-2257
Palo Alto Awning
San Jose, CA....................800-400-4270
Parasol Awnings
Memphis, TN 901-368-4477
Patio Center Inc
Lafayette, LA 337-233-9896
Pease Awning & Sunroom Co
East Providence, RI 401-438-2850
Peoria Tent & Awning
Peoria, IL.......................309-674-1128
Pike Awning Co
Portland, OR....................800-866-9172
Pride Neon Inc
Sioux Falls, SD..................605-336-3561
Quality Aluminum & Hm Imprvmt
Columbus, MS 662-329-2525
Queen City Awning
Cincinnati, OH 513-530-9660
R J Mc Cullough Co
Lancaster, PA...................717-735-8772
Reliable Tent & Awning Co
Billings, MT 800-544-1039
RHG Products Company
Castle Rock, CO.................800-553-8131
Rose City Awning Co
Portland, OR....................800-446-4104
S L Doery & Son Inc
Lawrence, NY 516-239-8090
San Jose Awnings
San Jose, CA....................800-872-9646

Shadetree Canopies
Columbus, OH 800-894-3801
Shaffer Sports & Events
Houston, TX 713-699-0088
Signtech Electrical Advg Inc
San Diego, CA..................619-527-6100
Sommer Awning Company
Indianapolis, IN 855-257-4301
South Akron Awning Co
Akron, OH......................330-848-7611
South Jersey Awning
Egg Harbor Township, NJ 609-646-2002
Southern Awning & Sign Company
Woodstock, GA..................770-516-8652
Sundance Architectural Prod
Orlando, FL.....................800-940-1337
Sunmaster of Naples Inc
Naples, FL......................239-261-3581
Taylor Made Custom Products
Gloversville, NY 518-725-0681
TCT&A Industries
Urbana, IL......................800-252-1355
The Canvas Exchange Inc
Cleveland, OH 216-749-2233
Thermal Bags By Ingrid Inc
Gilberts, IL......................800-622-5560
Total Identity Group
Cambridge, ON 877-551-5529
USA Canvas Shoppe
Dallas, TX......................877-626-8468
Van Nuys Awning Co
Van Nuys, CA...................818-345-4926
Vermont Tent Co
South Burlington, VT 800-696-8368
Vernon Plastics
Haverhill, MA 978-373-1551
Walker Engineering Inc
Sun Valley, CA..................818-252-7788
William J. Mills & Company
Greenport, NY 800-477-1535
Williams Shade & Awning Company
Memphis, TN 901-368-5055
York Tent & Awning
York, PA........................800-864-3510

Ceiling Surfaces & Panels

Arcoplast Wall & Ceiling Systems
St Peters, MO 888-736-2726

Decking

Metal

Slip Not
Detroit, MI 800-754-7668

Doors

Air Curtain

Aleco Food Svc Div
Muscle Shoals, AL...............800-633-3120
Apple-A-Day Nutritional Labeling Service
San Clemente, CA................949-855-8954
Atlas Equipment Company
Kansas City, MO.................800-842-9188
Berner International Corp
New Castle, PA..................800-245-4455
Kason Vinyl Products
Newnan, GA 800-472-7450
Products A Curtron Div
Pittsburgh, PA...................800-888-9750

Corrosion Resistant

Air-Lec Industries, Inc
Madison, WI 608-244-4754
Chem Pruf Door Co LTD
Brownsville, TX 800-444-6924

Double Acting

Carlson Products
Maize, KS 800-234-1069
Coldmatic Refrigeration
Concord, ON....................905-326-7600
Eliason Corp
Portage, MI 800-828-3655
Products A Curtron Div
Pittsburgh, PA...................800-888-9750

Super Seal ManufacturingLimited
Woodbridge, ON 800-337-3239

Plastic

Aleco Food Svc Div
Muscle Shoals, AL...............800-633-3120
Chase-Doors
Cincinnati, OH 800-543-4455
Coldmatic Refrigeration
Concord, ON....................905-326-7600
FIB-R-DOR
Cincinnati, OH 800-342-7367
Firl Industries Inc
Fond Du Lac, WI 800-558-4890
Hormann Flexan Llc
Leetsdale, PA 800-365-3667
Products A Curtron Div
Pittsburgh, PA...................800-888-9750
Reese Enterprises Inc
Rosemount, MN 800-328-0953
Seville Display Door
Temecula, CA...................800-634-0412
Trimline Corp
Elkhart Lake, WI................800-555-5895
VT Industries Inc
Holstein, IA.....................800-827-1615
Western Laminates
Omaha, NE 402-556-4600

Strip

Aleco Food Svc Div
Muscle Shoals, AL...............800-633-3120
Berner International Corp
New Castle, PA..................800-245-4455
Coastal Canvas Products
Savannah, GA...................800-476-5174
Davlynne International
Cudahy, WI.....................800-558-5208
Environmental Products Company
North Aurora, IL.................800-677-8479
Firl Industries Inc
Fond Du Lac, WI 800-558-4890
Flame Gard
Lakewood, NJ 800-526-3694
Kason Industries
Newnan, GA 770-254-0553
Kason Vinyl Products
Newnan, GA 800-472-7450
Kelley Company
Carrollton, TX...................800-558-6960
Manufacturing Warehouse
Miami, FL.......................305-635-8886
Products A Curtron Div
Pittsburgh, PA...................800-888-9750
Reese Enterprises Inc
Rosemount, MN 800-328-0953
Super Seal ManufacturingLimited
Woodbridge, ON 800-337-3239
Superior Products Company
Saint Paul, MN 800-328-9800
Tuckahoe Manufacturing Co
Vineland, NJ 800-220-3368
WORC Slitting & Mfg Co
Worcester, MA 800-356-2961

Fans

Ceiling

Acme Engineering & Mfg Corp
Muskogee, OK 918-682-7791
Airmaster Fan Co
Jackson, MI.....................800-255-3084
Canarm, Ltd.
Brockville, ON 613-342-5424
Carnes Company
Verona, WI 608-845-6411
Ceilcote Air Pollution Control
Middleburg Hts, OH..............800-554-8673
Con-tech/Conservation Technology
Northbrook, IL 800-728-0312
Fountainhead
Bensalem, PA 800-326-8998
Halton Company
Scottsville, KY 800-442-5866
Hartzell Fan Inc
Piqua, OH 800-336-3267
Hunter Fan Co
Cordova, TN 901-743-1360

Larkin Industries
  Birmingham, AL 800-322-4036
Main Lamp Corp
  Brooklyn, NY 718-436-8500
Nalge Process Technologies Group
  Rochester, NY 585-586-8800
Nu-Con Equipment
  Chanhassen, MN 877-939-0510
Panasonic Commercial Food Service
  Newark, NJ
Penn Barry
  Plano, TX 972-212-4700
SEC
  Plymouth, MI 734-455-4500
Stegall Mechanical INC
  Birmingham, AL 800-633-4373
West Metals
  London, ON 800-300-6667

Flooring

Ahlstrom Filtration LLC
  Madisonville, KY 270-821-0140
Kalman Floor Co Inc
  Evergreen, CO. 866-266-7146
Marazzi USA
  Sunnyvale, TX 972-232-3801
Stonhard
  Maple Shade, NJ 800-257-7953
VibroFloors World
  Fayetteville, GA 770-632-9701

Anti-Slip

Advanced Surfaces Corp
  Villa Rica, GA. 800-963-4632
Slip Not
  Detroit, MI 800-754-7668

Floor Mats

A&A Line & Wire Corporation
  Flushing, NY. 800-886-2657
Airomat Corp
  Fort Wayne, IN 800-348-4905
Atlantic Rubber Products
  East Wareham, MA 800-695-0446
Boardman Molded Products Inc
  Youngstown, OH. 800-233-4575
Cactus Mat ManufacturingCompany
  El Monte, CA 626-579-6287
Collins & Aikman
  Canton, OH 800-321-0244
Corson Rubber Products Inc
  Clover, SC. 803-222-7779
Durable Corp
  Norwalk, OH. 800-537-1603
Golden Star
  N Kansas City, MO. 800-821-2792
JCH International
  Rome, GA. 800-328-9203
John Rohrer Contracting Co
  Kansas City, KS 913-236-5005
Matrix Engineering
  Vero Beach, FL. 800-926-0528
R C Musson Rubber Co
  Akron, OH. 800-321-2381
Reese Enterprises Inc
  Rosemount, MN 800-328-0953
Superior Products Company
  Saint Paul, MN 800-328-9800
Tepromark International
  Osseo, MN 800-645-2622
United Textile Distribution
  Garner, NC 800-262-7624
Wearwell/Tennessee Mat Company
  Nashville, TN 615-254-8381

Industrial Flooring

Corro-Shield International Inc
  Rosemont, IL. 800-298-7637
Dura-Flex
  East Hartford, CT 877-251-5418
Grating Pacific Inc
  Los Alamitos, CA 800-321-4314
Kagetec
  Montgomery, MN 612-435-7640
Sanicrete
  Farmington Hills, MI 248-893-1000
Tufco International
  Gentry, AR 800-364-0836

VibroFloors World
  Fayetteville, GA 770-632-9701

Mats & Matting

Airomat Corp
  Fort Wayne, IN 800-348-4905
Amco Metals Indl
  City of Industry, CA 626-855-2550
Artex International
  Highland, IL 618-654-2113
Atlantic Rubber Products
  East Wareham, MA 800-695-0446
Atlas Equipment Company
  Kansas City, MO. 800-842-9188
Baker Concrete Construction
  Monroe, OH 800-539-2224
Best Brands Home Products
  New York, NY 212-684-7456
Boardman Molded Products Inc
  Youngstown, OH. 800-233-4575
C R Mfg
  Waverly, NE 877-789-5844
Cactus Mat ManufacturingCompany
  El Monte, CA 626-579-6287
Coast Scientific
  Rancho Santa Fe, CA 800-445-1544
Coburn Company
  Whitewater, WI. 800-776-7042
Collins & Aikman
  Canton, OH 800-321-0244
Conimar Corp
  Ocala, FL. 800-874-9735
Continental Identification
  Sparta, MI 800-247-2499
Continental Industrial Supply
  South Pasadena, FL. 727-341-1100
Corson Rubber Products Inc
  Clover, SC. 803-222-7779
Custom Table Pads
  St Paul, MN. 800-325-4643
Dorado Carton Company
  Dorado, PR 787-796-1670
Drehmann Paving & Flooring Company
  Pennsauken, NJ 800-523-3800
Durable Corp
  Norwalk, OH. 800-537-1603
Golden Star
  N Kansas City, MO. 800-821-2792
Gourmet Table Skirts
  Houston, TX 800-527-0440
Harsco Industrial IKG
  Garrett, IN. 800-467-2345
Have Our Plastic Inc
  Mississauga, ON. 800-263-5995
Hoffmaster Group Inc
  Oshkosh, WI. 800-327-9774
J. James
  Brooklyn, NY 718-384-6144
J.M. Rogers & Sons
  Moss Point, MS 228-475-7584
J.V. Reed & Company
  Louisville, KY 877-258-7333
Jack the Ripper Table Skirting
  Stafford, TX 800-331-7831
JCH International
  Rome, GA. 800-328-9203
John Rohrer Contracting Co
  Kansas City, KS 913-236-5005
Jr Mats
  West Chester, PA. 800-526-7763
K-C Products Company
  Van Nuys, CA 818-267-1600
Larco
  Brainerd, MN 800-523-6996
Matrix Engineering
  Vero Beach, FL. 800-926-0528
Millard Manufacturing Corp
  La Vista, NE 800-662-4263
Newell Brands
  Atlanta, GA
Northland Process Piping
  Isle, MN 320-679-2119
Paradise Products
  El Cerrito, CA. 800-227-1092
Proffitt Manufacturing Company
  Dalton, GA 800-241-4682
R C Musson Rubber Co
  Akron, OH. 800-321-2381
Reese Enterprises Inc
  Rosemount, MN 800-328-0953

Royal Paper Products
  Coatesville, PA 800-666-6655
Saunders Manufacturing Co.
  N Kansas City, MO. 800-821-2792
SCA Tissue
  Philadelphia, PA 866-722-8675
Scranton Lace Company
  Forest City, PA 800-822-1036
Smith-Lee Company
  Oshkosh, WI. 800-327-9774
Sultan Linen Inc
  New York, NY 212-689-8900
Summitville Tiles Inc
  Summitville, OH. 330-223-1511
Superior Products Company
  Saint Paul, MN 800-328-9800
Tag-Trade Associated Group
  Chicago, IL 800-621-8350
Tara Linens
  Sanford, NC 800-476-8272
Tennant Co.
  Minneapolis, MN 800-553-8033
Tepromark International
  Osseo, MN 800-645-2622
United Textile Distribution
  Garner, NC 800-262-7624
Wearwell/Tennessee Mat Company
  Nashville, TN 615-254-8381

Metal

Slip Not
  Detroit, MI 800-754-7668

Safety

Slip Not
  Detroit, MI 800-754-7668

Thermal Shock

Resistant Flooring

Dura-Flex
  East Hartford, CT 877-251-5418

Grating

Metal

Slip Not
  Detroit, MI 800-754-7668

Heating, Ventilation & Air Conditioning

A C Horn & Co Sheet Metal
  Dallas, TX. 800-657-6155
A.K. Robins
  Baltimore, MD 800-486-9656
A.O. Smith Water Products Company
  Irving, TX 800-527-1953
Acme Engineering & Mfg Corp
  Muskogee, OK 918-682-7791
ADDCHEK Coils
  Fort Mill, SC. 803-547-7566
Advanced Control Technologies
  Indianapolis, IN 800-886-2281
Aei Corp
  Irvine, CA 949-474-3070
AERCO International Inc
  Blauvelt, NY. 800-526-0288
Aerolator Systems
  Monroe, NC 800-843-8286
Aerovent Co
  Minneapolis, MN 763-551-7500
AFGO Mechanical Svc Inc
  Astoria, NY. 800-438-2346
Air Quality Engineering
  Minneapolis, MN 800-328-0787
Airmaster Fan Co
  Jackson, MI. 800-255-3084
Airsan Corp
  Milwaukee, WI. 800-558-5494
All State Fabricators Corporation
  Tampa, FL. 800-322-9925
Allergen Air Filter Corp
  Houston, TX 800-333-8880
Allied Engineering
  North Vancouver, BC 877-929-1214
Allstrong Restaurant Eqpt Inc
  South El Monte, CA 800-933-8913

ALPI Food Preparation Equipment
  Bolton, ON 800-928-2574
American Coolair Corp
  Jacksonville, FL 904-389-3646
American Radionic Co Inc
  Palm Coast, FL 800-445-6033
American Range
  Pacoima, CA 888-753-9898
American Ventilation Company
  Grafton, OH 800-854-3267
Andersen 2000
  Peachtree City, GA 800-241-5424
Anderson Snow Corp
  Schiller Park, IL 800-346-2645
Andgar Corp
  Ferndale, WA 360-366-9900
Apollo Sheet Metal
  Kennewick, WA 509-586-1104
Ari Industries Inc
  Addison, IL 800-237-6725
Armstrong International
  Three Rivers, MI 269-273-1415
Ayr King Corp
  Louisville, KY 866-266-6290
Babcock & Wilcox Power Generation Group
  Barberton, OH 800-222-2625
Baltimore Aircoil Co
  Jessup, MD 410-799-1300
Barbeque Wood Flavors Enterprises
  Ennis, TX 972-875-8391
Bbc Industries
  Pacific, MO 800-654-4205
Becker Brothers Graphite Co
  Maywood, IL 708-410-0700
Berner International Corp
  New Castle, PA 800-245-4455
Bessamaire Sales Inc
  Streetsboro, OH 800-321-5992
Betz Entec
  Horsham, PA 800-877-1940
Bioclimatic Air Systems LLC
  Delran, NJ 800-962-5594
BKI Worldwide
  Simpsonville, SC 800-927-6887
Bryan Boilers
  Peru, IN 765-473-6651
Caddy Corporation of America
  Bridgeport, NJ 856-467-4222
Canarm, Ltd.
  Brockville, ON 613-342-5424
Carnes Company
  Verona, WI 608-845-6411
Carroll Manufacturing International
  Florham Park, NJ 800-444-9696
Ceilcote Air Pollution Control
  Middleburg Hts, OH 800-554-8673
CEM Corporation
  Matthews, NC 800-726-3331
Chesmont Engineering Co Inc
  Exton, PA 610-594-9200
Chillers Solutions
  Pompton Plains, NJ 800-526-5201
Cleaver-Brooks Inc
  Thomasville, GA 800-250-5583
Climate Master Inc
  Oklahoma City, OK 877-436-0263
CMT
  Hamilton, MA 978-768-2555
Commercial Kitchen Co
  Los Angeles, CA 323-732-2291
Con-tech/Conservation Technology
  Northbrook, IL 800-728-0312
Continental Refrigerator
  Bensalem, PA 800-523-7138
Control Pak Intl
  Fenton, MI 810-735-2800
Convectronics
  Haverhill, MA 800-633-0166
Cook & Beals Inc
  Loup City, NE 308-745-0154
Cooling Products Inc
  Broken Arrow, OK 918-251-8588
Cooperheat/MQS
  Alvin, TX 800-526-4233
Crispy Lite
  St. Louis, MO 888-356-5362
Curtainaire
  Los Angeles, CA 323-753-4266
Custom Food Machinery
  Stockton, CA 209-463-4343
Delfield Co
  Mt Pleasant, MI 800-733-8821

Delta Cooling Towers Inc
  Rockaway, NJ 800-289-3358
Direct Fire Technical
  Benbrook, TX 888-920-2468
Doucette Industries
  York, PA 800-445-7511
Dreaco Products
  Elyria, OH 800-368-3267
Duke Manufacturing Co
  St Louis, MO 800-735-3853
Duo-Aire
  Winter Haven, FL 863-294-2272
Dwyer Instruments Inc
  Michigan City, IN 800-872-3141
Dynamic Cooking Systems
  Huntington Beach, CA 800-433-8466
Eclipse Innovative Ther mal Solutions
  Toledo, OH 800-662-3966
Economy Paper & Restaurant Co
  Clifton, NJ 973-279-5500
Eldorado Miranda Manufacturing Company
  Largo, FL 800-330-0708
Elmwood Sensors
  Pawtucket, RI 800-356-9663
Energymaster
  Walled Lake, MI 248-624-6900
Environmental Products Company
  North Aurora, IL 800-677-8479
Epcon Industrial Systems
  Conroe, TX 800-447-7872
ET International Technologies
  Wheat Ridge, CO 855-412-5726
Exhausto
  Atlanta, GA 800-255-2923
F.M. Corporation
  Deerfield Beach, FL 954-570-9860
Flame Gard
  Lakewood, NJ 800-526-3694
Flanders Corp
  Washington, NC 800-637-2803
Floaire
  Blue Bell, PA 800-726-5623
Fountainhead
  Bensalem, PA 800-326-8998
G W Berkheimer Co
  Fort Wayne, IN 800-535-6696
Garland Commercial Ranges
  Mississauga, ON 905-624-0260
Gaylord Industries
  Tualatin, OR 800-547-9696
Glo-Quartz Electric Heater
  Mentor, OH 800-321-3574
Governair Corp
  Oklahoma City, OK 405-525-6546
Grease Master
  Matthews, NC 704-844-6907
Greenheck Fan Corp
  Schofield, WI 715-359-6171
Greitzer
  Elizabeth City, NC 252-338-4000
Grillco Inc
  Aurora, IL 800-644-0067
Grinnell Fire ProtectionSystems Company
  Westminster, MA 800-746-7539
Gustave A Larson Co
  Pewaukee, WI 262-542-0200
Hallock Fabricating Corp
  Riverhead, NY 631-727-2441
Halton Company
  Scottsville, KY 800-442-5866
Hanson Lab Furniture Inc
  Newbury Park, CA 805-498-3121
Hartzell Fan Inc
  Piqua, OH 800-336-3267
Harvey W Hottel Inc
  Gaithersburg, MD 301-921-9599
Heatrex
  Meadville, PA 800-394-6589
Hemco Corp
  Independence, MO 800-779-4362
Hercules Food Equipment
  Weston, ON 416-742-9673
Holman Boiler Works
  Dallas, TX 800-331-1956
Hunter Fan Co
  Cordova, TN 901-743-1360
Hydro-Thermal Corp
  Waukesha, WI 800-952-0121
Ice-Cap
  Piermont, NY 888-423-2270
ICM Controls
  North Syracuse, NY 800-365-5525

Illinois Range Company
  Schiller Park, IL 800-535-7041
J L Becker Co
  Plymouth, MI 800-837-4328
Jacob Tubing LP
  Memphis, TN 901-566-1110
Jarvis-Cutter Company
  Boston, MA 617-567-7532
KEMCO
  Wareham, MA 800-231-5955
King Company
  Dallas, TX 507-451-3770
Lakewood Enginerring
  Chicago, IL 800-621-4277
Larkin Industries
  Birmingham, AL 800-322-4036
LDI Manufacturing Co
  Logansport, IN 800-366-2001
Loren Cook Co
  Springfield, MO 800-289-3267
Low Humidity Systems
  Covington, GA 770-788-6744
Ludell Manufacturing Co
  Milwaukee, WI 800-558-0800
Lumsden Flexx Flow
  Lancaster, PA 800-367-3664
Machine Ice Co
  Houston, TX 800-423-8822
Mars Air Products
  Gardena, CA 800-421-1266
Marshall Air Systems Inc
  Charlotte, NC 800-722-3474
Master Air
  Lebanon, IN 800-248-8368
MCM Fixture Co
  Hazel Park, MI 248-547-9280
Meadows Mills Inc
  North Wilkesboro, NC 800-626-2282
Met-Pro Corp
  Owosso, MI 989-725-8185
Metal Master Sales Corp
  Glendale Heights, IL 800-488-8729
Microtechnologies
  Plainville, CT 888-248-7103
Milvan Food Equipment Manufacturing
  Rexdale, ON 416-674-3456
Moll-Tron
  Lakewood, CO 800-525-9494
Monroe Environmental Corp
  Monroe, MI 800-992-7707
Monroe Extinguisher Co Inc
  Rochester, NY 585-235-3310
MovinCool/DENSO Products and Services Americas
  Long Beach, CA 800-264-9573
Muckler Industries, Inc
  Saint Louis, MO 800-444-0283
Muellermist Irrigation Company
  Broadview, IL 708-450-9595
Munters Corp
  Amesbury, MA 800-843-5360
Nalge Process Technologies Group
  Rochester, NY 585-586-8800
National FABCO Manufacturing
  St Louis, MO 314-842-4571
Newtech Inc
  Randolph, VT 800-210-2361
Noren Products Inc
  Menlo Park, CA 866-936-6736
Novar
  Cleveland, OH 800-348-1235
Nu-Con Equipment
  Chanhassen, MN 877-939-0510
NuTone
  Cincinnati, OH 888-336-3948
Omnitemp Refrigeration
  Downey, CA 800-423-9660
Pacific Steam Equipment, Inc.
  Santa Fe Springs, CA 800-321-4114
Panasonic Commercial Food Service
  Newark, NJ
Parkland
  Houston, TX 713-926-5055
Partnership Resources
  Minneapolis, MN 612-331-2075
Patterson-Kelley   Hars Company
  East Stroudsburg, PA 570-421-7500
Peerless of America
  Lincolnshire, IL 847-634-7500
Penn Barry
  Plano, TX 972-212-4700
Precision Temp Inc
  Cincinnati, OH 800-934-9690

Premium Air Systems Inc
Troy, MI 877-430-0333
Process Heating Co
Seattle, WA 866-682-1582
Process Heating Corp
Shrewsbury, MA 508-842-5200
Products A Curtron Div
Pittsburgh, PA 800-888-9750
Proheatco Manufacturing
Pomona, CA 800-423-4195
R K Electric Co Inc
Mason, OH 800-543-4936
Raypak Inc
Oxnard, CA 805-278-5300
Roberts-Gordon LLC
Buffalo, NY 800-828-7450
Ron Vallort & Associates
Oak Brook, IL 630-734-3821
Royal Prestige Health Moguls
Westbury, NY 888-802-7433
S&P USA Ventilation Systems, LLC
Jacksonville, FL 800-961-7370
Scroll Compressors LLC
Sidney, OH 937-498-3011
Seasons 4 Inc
Douglasville, GA 770-489-5405
Seattle Boiler Works Inc
Seattle, WA 206-762-0737
Sellers Engineering Division
Danville, KY 859-236-3181
South Valley Mfg Inc
Gilroy, CA 408-842-5457
Southern Metal Fabricators Inc
Albertville, AL 800-989-1330
Spencer Turbine Co
Windsor, CT 800-232-4321
Spiral Manufacturing Co Inc
Minneapolis, MN 800-426-3643
Stainless International
Rancho Cordova, CA 888-300-6196
Stainless Steel Fabricators
Tyler, TX 903-595-6625
Standex International Corp.
Salem, NH 603-893-9701
Stegall Mechanical INC
Birmingham, AL 800-633-4373
Sterling Ball & Jewel
New Berlin, WI. 800-423-3183
Storm Industrial
Shawnee Mission, KS 800-745-7483
Sturdi-Bilt Restaurant Equipment
Whitmore Lake, MI 800-521-2895
Super Radiator Coils
N Chesterfield, VA 800-229-2645
Thermalogic Corp
Hudson, MA 978-562-5974
Toronto Kitchen Equipment
North York, ON 416-745-4944
Trane Inc
Davidson, NC 704-655-4000
Tru Form Plastics
Gardena, CA 800-510-7999
Ultrafryer Systems Inc
San Antonio, TX 800-545-9189
United Fire & Safety Service
Yonkers, NY 914-968-4459
Universal Jet Industries
Hialeah, FL 305-887-4378
USECO
Murfreesboro, TN 615-893-4820
Vapor Power Intl LLC
Franklin Park, IL 888-874-9020
Vent Master
Mississauga, ON 800-565-2981
Vent-A-Hood Co
Richardson, TX 800-331-2492
Vilter Manufacturing Corporation
Cudahy, WI 414-744-0111
Vulcan Electric Co
Porter, ME 800-922-3027
Water Furnace Renewable Energy
Fort Wayne, IN 260-478-5667
Welbilt Corporation
Stamford, CT 203-325-8300
West Metals
London, ON 800-300-6667
West Star Industries
Stockton, CA 800-326-2288
Westfield Sheet Metal Works
Kenilworth, NJ 908-276-5500
Zmd International
Long Beach, CA 800-222-9674

Heating

Electric

INDEECO
St Louis, MO. 800-243-8162

Hoods

Stainless Steel

AGET Manufacturing Co
Adrian, MI. 517-263-5781

Lighting Equipment

Fluorescent

Eaton Corporation
Beachwood, OH 800-386-1911
Insect-O-Cutor Inc
Stone Mountain, GA 800-966-8480
Lumax Industries
Altoona, PA. 814-944-2537
Nemco Electric Company
Seattle, WA 206-622-1551
Oetiker Inc
Marlette, MI 800-959-0398
Trojan Inc
Mt Sterling, KY 800-264-0526
UDEC Corp
Woburn, MA 800-990-8332

Incandescent

Apex Fountain Sales Inc
Philadelphia, PA 800-523-4586
Boyd Lighting Company
Sausalito, CA 415-778-4300
Candle Lamp Company
Corona, CA 877-526-7748
Command Electronics Inc
Schoolcraft, MI 269-679-4011
Dura Electric Lamp Company
Newark, NJ 973-624-0014
G Lighting
St Louis, MO 800-331-2425
GE Lighting
Cleveland, OH 800-435-4448
Holcor
Riverdale, IL 708-841-3800
Hubbell Lighting Inc
Greenville, SC. 864-678-1000
Hybrinetics Inc
Santa Rosa, CA 800-247-6900
Indy Lighting
Fishers, IN 317-849-1233
Le Jo Enterprises
Phoenixville, PA 484-924-9187
Luxo Corporation
Elmsford, NY 800-222-5896
Mason Candlelight Company
New Albany, MS. 800-556-2766
Nova Industries
San Leandro, CA 510-357-0171
Osram Sylvania
Danvers, MA. 800-544-4828
Philips Lighting Company
Somerset, NJ 732-563-3000
Prescolite
Vallejo, CA 707-562-3500
QSR Industrial Supply
Cherry Hill, NJ 800-257-8282
Renovator's Supply
Conway, NH 800-659-0203
Sterno
Lombard, IL 630-792-0080
Strand Lighting
Dallas, TX. 214-647-7880
Super Vision International
Orlando, FL. 407-857-9900
Superior-Studio Specialties
Commerce, CA 800-354-3049
SuppliesForLess
Hampton, VA 800-235-2201
Trojan Inc
Mt Sterling, KY 800-264-0526

Lighting Fixtures

Electric

Action Lighting
Bozeman, MT 800-248-0076
ALP Lighting & Ceiling Products
Pennsauken, NJ. 800-633-7732
Apogee Translite Inc
Deer Park, NY 631-254-6975
Apollo Acme Lighting Fixture
Mount Vernon, NY 800-833-9006
Architectural Products
Highland, NY 845-691-8500
Art Craft Lighting
Champlain, NY 718-387-8000
Azz/R-A-L
Houston, TX 713-943-0340
Boyd Lighting Company
Sausalito, CA 415-778-4300
Brinkmann Corporation
Dallas, TX. 800-468-5252
C W Cole & Co
South El Monte, CA 626-443-2473
Capitol Hardware, Inc.,
Middlebury, IN 800-327-6083
Caselites
Hialeah, FL 305-819-7766
Casella Lighting
Sacramento, CA 916-363-2888
Chapman Manufacturing Co Inc
Avon, MA 508-587-7592
Claude Neon Signs
Baltimore, MD 410-685-7575
Columbia Jet/JPL
Houston, TX 800-876-4511
Columbia Lighting
Greenville, SC. 864-678-1000
Commercial Lighting Design
Memphis, TN 800-774-5799
Con-tech/Conservation Technology
Northbrook, IL 800-728-0312
Coronet Chandelier Originals
Brentwood, NY 631-273-1177
County Neon Sign Corporation
Plainview, NY. 516-349-9550
Custom Lights & Iron
National City, CA 858-274-7070
Custom Metalcraft, Architectural Lighting
Boston, MA. 617-242-0868
D'Ac Lighting
Mamaroneck, NY 914-698-5959
D'Lights
Glendale, CA 818-956-5656
E-Lite Technologies
Trumbull, CT 877-520-3951
Eclipse Electric Manufacturing
St Louis Park, MN 952-929-2500
Econo Frost Night Covers
Shawnigan Lake, BC 800-519-1222
Edison Price Lighting
Long Island City, NY 718-685-0700
EGS Electrical Group
Skokie, IL 847-679-7800
Electrodex
Bradenton, FL 800-362-1972
ESD Energy Saving Devices
St Paul, MN. 651-222-0849
Eximco Manufacturing Company
Chicago, IL 773-463-1470
Fenton Art Glass Company
Williamstown, WV 800-933-6766
Forum Lighting
Pittsburgh, PA 412-781-5970
Fredrick Ramond Company
Avon Lake, OH 800-446-5539
G Lighting
St Louis, MO. 800-331-2425
GE Lighting
Cleveland, OH 800-435-4448
Gem Electric Manufacturing Company
Hauppauge, NY 800-275-4361
GERM-O-RAY
Stone Mountain, GA 800-966-8480
Glass Industries America LLC
Wallingford, CT 203-269-6700
Greene Brothers
Brooklyn, NY 718-388-6800
Guth Lighting
Saint Louis, MO 314-533-3200
H & H Metal Fabrication Inc
Belden, MS 662-489-4626

Hanson Brass Rewd Co
Sun Valley, CA 888-841-3773
Hart Designs LLC
Ruston, LA 800-592-3500
Hub Electric Company
Crystal Lake, IL 815-455-4400
Hubbell Lighting Inc
Greenville, SC. 864-678-1000
Hydrel Corporation
Sylmar, CA .818-362-9465
Indy Lighting
Fishers, IN .317-849-1233
Insect-O-Cutor Inc
Stone Mountain, GA 800-966-8480
JDO/LNR Lighting
Live Oak, TX 800-597-1570
Jet Lite Products
Highland, IL 618-654-2217
JJI Lighting Group, Inc.
Franklin Park, IL. 847-451-0700
Kensington Lighting Corp
Greensburg, PA 800-434-5005
Kim Lighting
City of Industry, CA 626-968-5666
Kreissle Forge Ornamental
Sarasota, FL 941-355-6795
Le Jo Enterprises
Phoenixville, PA 484-924-9187
Legion Lighting Co Inc
Brooklyn, NY 800-453-4466
Light Waves Concept
Brooklyn, NY 800-670-8137
Lightolier
Fall River, MA 508-679-8131
Lights On
Yonkers, NY 914-961-0588
Linear Lighting Corp
Long Island City, NY 718-361-7552
Litecontrol
Plympton, MA. 781-294-0164
Lithonia Lighting
Conyers, GA 770-922-9000
Little Giant Pump Company
Fort Wayne, IN 260-824-2900
Louis Baldinger & Sons
New York, NY 718-204-5700
Luminiere Corporation
Bronx, NY 718-295-5450
Luxo Corporation
Elmsford, NY 800-222-5896
Main Lamp Corp
Brooklyn, NY 718-436-8500
Majestic
Bridgeport, CT 203-367-7900
Manning Lighting Inc
Sheboygan, WI 920-458-2184
Meil Electric Fixture Manufacturing Company
Philadelphia, PA 215-228-8528
Mobern Electric Corporation
Jessup, MD .800-444-9288
Modulightor Inc
New York, NY 212-371-0336
Mulholland-Harper Company
Denton, MD 800-882-3052
Natale Machine & Tool Co Inc
Carlstadt, NJ 800-883-8382
Nemco Electric Company
Seattle, WA 206-622-1551
Neo-Ray Products
Brooklyn, NY 800-221-0946
Newstamp Lighting Factory
North Easton, MA 508-238-7073
Nova Industries
San Leandro, CA. 510-357-0171
Nulco Lighting
Providence, RI 401-728-5200
Osram Sylvania
Danvers, MA. 800-544-4828
Palmer Distributors
St Clair Shores, MI 800-444-1912
Peerless Lighting Corporation
Berkeley, CA. 510-845-2760
Philadelphia Glass Bending Company
Philadelphia, PA 215-726-8468
Prescolite
Vallejo, CA .707-562-3500
Primlite Manufacturing Corporation
Freeport, NY 800-327-7583
Remcraft Lighting Products
Miami, FL 800-327-6585
Ryther-Purdy
Old Saybrook, CT 860-388-4405

Sea Gull Lighting Products, LLC
Corona, CA .800-347-5483
Standex International Corp.
Salem, NH. .603-893-9701
Sterner Lighting Systems
Greenville, SC 866-898-0131
Strand Lighting
Dallas, TX 214-647-7880
Super Vision International
Orlando, FL .407-857-9900
Swivelier Co Inc
Blauvelt, NY 845-353-1455
Tech Lighting LLC
Skokie, IL 800-323-3226
Thomas Lighting Residential
Rosemont, IL. 800-825-5844
Toronto Fabricating & Manufacturing
Mississauga, ON 905-891-2516
Troy Lighting
City of Industry, CA 800-533-8769
Tru Form Plastics
Gardena, CA 800-510-7999
U L Wholesale Lighting Fixture
Long Island City, NY 718-726-7500
UDEC Corp
Woburn, MA 800-990-8332
V&R Metal Enterprises
Brooklyn, NY 718-768-8142
Versailles Lighting
Delray Beach, FL 888-564-0240
Vimco
King of Prussia, PA 610-768-0500
Voigt Lighting Industries Inc.
Garfield, NJ .973-928-2252
Western Lighting Inc
Franklin Park, IL 847-451-7200
Weston Emergency Light Co
Weston, MA 800-649-3756
Yorkraft
York, PA 800-872-2044
Zelco Industries
Mount Vernon, NY 800-431-2486
Zumtobel Staff Lighting
Highland, NY 845-691-6262

Emergency

ALP Lighting & Ceiling Products
Pennsauken, NJ 800-633-7732
Architectural Products
Highland, NY 845-691-8500
Big Beam Emergency Systems Inc
Crystal Lake, IL 815-459-6100
Brinkmann Corporation
Dallas, TX. .800-468-5252
Carpenter Emergency Lighting
Hamilton, NJ 888-884-2270
Claude Neon Signs
Baltimore, MD 410-685-7575
Crouse-Hinds
Syracuse, NY 866-764-5454
Eaton Corporation
Beachwood, OH 800-386-1911
Gilbert Insect Light Traps
Jonesboro, AR. 800-643-0400
HD Electric Co
Park City, IL 847-473-4882
Hubbell Lighting Inc
Greenville, SC. 864-678-1000
Natale Machine & Tool Co Inc
Carlstadt, NJ 800-883-8382
Roflan Associates
Tulsa, OK 978-475-0100
UDEC Corp
Woburn, MA 800-990-8332
Weston Emergency Light Co
Weston, MA 800-649-3756

Fluorescent

ALP Lighting & Ceiling Products
Pennsauken, NJ 800-633-7732
American Louver Co
Skokie, IL 800-772-0355
Apollo Acme Lighting Fixture
Mount Vernon, NY 800-833-9006
C W Cole & Co
South El Monte, CA 626-443-2473
Claude Neon Signs
Baltimore, MD 410-685-7575
Columbia Lighting
Greenville, SC. 864-678-1000

Command Electronics Inc
Schoolcraft, MI 269-679-4011
Crownlite Manufacturing Corporation
Bohemia, NY 631-589-9100
D'Ac Lighting
Mamaroneck, NY 914-698-5959
Day-O-Lite
Warwick, RI .401-467-8232
Diversified Lighting Diffusers Inc
Copiague, NY 800-234-5464
Dura Electric Lamp Company
Newark, NJ .973-624-0014
Edison Price Lighting
Long Island City, NY 718-685-0700
ESD Energy Saving Devices
St Paul, MN. 651-222-0849
Eximco Manufacturing Company
Chicago, IL .773-463-1470
Forum Lighting
Pittsburgh, PA 412-781-5970
Garvin Industries
Franklin Park, IL. 847-451-6500
GE Lighting
Cleveland, OH 800-435-4448
GENESTA
Rockwall, TX 972-771-1653
GERM-O-RAY
Stone Mountain, GA 800-966-8480
Guth Lighting
Saint Louis, MO 314-533-3200
H & H Metal Fabrication Inc
Belden, MS .662-489-4626
Hasco Electric Corporation
Greenwich, CT 203-531-9400
Hastings Lighting Company
Los Angeles, CA. 213-622-2009
Holcor
Riverdale, IL 708-841-3800
Hybrinetics Inc
Santa Rosa, CA. 800-247-6900
Illumination Products Inc
San Juan, PR 787-754-7193
Indy Lighting
Fishers, IN. .317-849-1233
Insect-O-Cutor Inc
Stone Mountain, GA 800-966-8480
Kensington Lighting Corp
Greensburg, PA 800-434-5005
Legion Lighting Co Inc
Brooklyn, NY 800-453-4466
Lightolier
Fall River, MA 508-679-8131
Lithonia Lighting
Conyers, GA 770-922-9000
Louisville Lamp Co
Louisville, KY 502-964-4094
Lumax Industries
Altoona, PA. 814-944-2537
Luxo Corporation
Elmsford, NY 800-222-5896
Meil Electric Fixture Manufacturing Company
Philadelphia, PA 215-228-8528
Nemco Electric Company
Seattle, WA 206-622-1551
Neo-Ray Products
Brooklyn, NY 800-221-0946
Osram Sylvania
Danvers, MA. 800-544-4828
Panasonic Commercial Food Service
Newark, NJ
Paramount Industries
Croswell, MI 800-521-5405
Peerless Lighting Corporation
Berkeley, CA. 510-845-2760
Philips Lighting Company
Somerset, NJ 732-563-3000
Prudential Lighting
Vernon, CA .800-421-5483
Remcraft Lighting Products
Miami, FL 800-327-6585
Roflan Associates
Tulsa, OK 978-475-0100
Ryther-Purdy
Old Saybrook, CT 860-388-4405
Shat R Shield Inc
Salisbury, NC 800-223-0853
Shelden, Dickson, & Steven Company
Omaha, NE .402-571-4848
Steel Craft Fluorescent Company
Newark, NJ .973-349-1614
Super Vision International
Orlando, FL. 407-857-9900

Toronto Fabricating & Manufacturing
  Mississauga, ON 905-891-2516
Trojan Inc
  Mt Sterling, KY 800-264-0526
UDEC Corp
  Woburn, MA 800-990-8332
Varco Products
  Chardon, OH 216-481-6895
Versailles Lighting
  Delray Beach, FL 888-564-0240
Visual Marketing Assoc
  Santee, CA .619-258-0393
Zumtobel Staff Lighting
  Highland, NY 845-691-6262

Mercury, High Intensity

GE Lighting
  Cleveland, OH 800-435-4448
Grating Pacific Inc
  Los Alamitos, CA 800-321-4314
Guth Lighting
  Saint Louis, MO 314-533-3200
Holcor
  Riverdale, IL 708-841-3800
Hubbell Lighting Inc
  Greenville, SC 864-678-1000
J M Canty Inc E1200 Engineers
  Lockport, NY 716-625-4227
Prescolite
  Vallejo, CA .707-562-3500

Outdoor

Apollo Acme Lighting Fixture
  Mount Vernon, NY 800-833-9006
Brinkmann Corporation
  Dallas, TX .800-468-5252
Claude Neon Signs
  Baltimore, MD 410-685-7575
Crouse-Hinds
  Syracuse, NY 866-764-5454
Eaton Corporation
  Beachwood, OH 800-386-1911
Faribault Manufacturing Co
  Faribault, MN 800-447-6043
GE Lighting
  Cleveland, OH 800-435-4448
Hub Electric Company
  Crystal Lake, IL 815-455-4400
Hubbell Lighting Inc
  Greenville, SC 864-678-1000
Lightolier
  Fall River, MA 508-679-8131
Linear Lighting Corp
  Long Island City, NY 718-361-7552
Little Giant Pump Company
  Fort Wayne, IN 260-824-2900
Natale Machine & Tool Co Inc
  Carlstadt, NJ 800-883-8382
Nu-Dell Manufacturing
  Des Plaines, IL 847-803-4500
Prescolite
  Vallejo, CA .707-562-3500
Primlite Manufacturing Corporation
  Freeport, NY 800-327-7583
Progress Lighting
  Spartanburg, SC 864-599-6000
QSR Industrial Supply
  Cherry Hill, NJ 800-257-8282
Remcraft Lighting Products
  Miami, FL .800-327-6585
Sterner Lighting Systems
  Greenville, SC 866-898-0131
Thomas Lighting Residential
  Rosemont, IL 800-825-5844
Troy Lighting
  City of Industry, CA 800-533-8769
Valmont Composite Structures
  Newberry, SC 800-800-9008
Zelco Industries
  Mount Vernon, NY 800-431-2486

Paging Systems

Command Communications
  Centennial, CO 800-288-3491
Instacomm Canada
  Oakville, ON 877-426-2783
Long Range Systems
  Addison, TX 800-577-8101

NTN Wireless
  Norcross, GA 800-637-8639
UAA
  Chicago, IL 800-813-1711

Radios

Long Range Systems
  Addison, TX 800-577-8101

Panels

Insulated

Advance Energy Technologies
  Halfmoon, NY 800-724-0198
Extrutech Plastics Inc
  Manitowoc, WI 888-818-0118
Kingspan Insulated Panels, Ltd.
  Langley, BC 877-638-3266
Zeroloc
  Kirkland, WA 425-823-4888

Platforms

C&R Refrigeration Inc,
  Center, TX .800-438-6182
Delkor Systems, Inc
  Minneapolis, MN 800-328-5558
Slip Not
  Detroit, MI 800-754-7668

Plating

Metal

Slip Not
  Detroit, MI 800-754-7668

Sinks

Advance Tabco
  Edgewood, NY 800-645-3166
Aero Manufacturing Co
  Clifton, NJ 800-631-8378
All State Fabricators Corporation
  Tampa, FL .800-322-9925
Amtekco
  Columbus, OH 800-336-4677
Baker & Co
  Norfolk, VA 800-909-4325
Bar Equipment Corporation of America
  Downey, CA 888-870-2322
Baxter Manufacturing Inc
  Orting, WA 800-777-2828
Best Sanitizers Inc
  Penn Valley, CA 888-225-3267
Carts Food Equipment
  Brooklyn, NY 718-788-5540
Component Hardware Group Inc
  Lakewood, NJ 800-526-3694
Crown Steel Mfg
  San Marcos, CA 760-471-1188
D A Berther Inc
  Milwaukee, WI 877-357-9622
Den Mar Corp
  North Dartmouth, MA 508-999-3295
Duke Manufacturing Co
  St Louis, MO 800-735-3853
Duluth Sheet Metal
  Duluth, MN 218-722-2613
Dunhill Food Equipment Corporation
  Armonk, NY 800-847-4206
Eagle Foodservice Equipment
  Clayton, DE 800-441-8440
Eagle Group
  Clayton, DE 800-441-8440
Eldorado Miranda Manufacturing Company
  Largo, FL .800-330-0708
Erwin Food Service Equipment
  Fort Worth, TX 817-535-0021
Eskay Metal Fabricating
  Buffalo, NY 800-836-8015
Fab-X/Metals
  Washington, NC 800-677-3229
Fabwright Inc
  Garden Grove, CA 800-854-6464
Fisher Manufacturing Company
  Tulare, CA .800-421-6162
G K & L Inc
  Dickerson, MD 301-948-5538

Griffin Products
  Wills Point, TX 800-379-9709
Hercules Food Equipment
  Weston, ON 416-742-9673
IMC Teddy Food Service Equipment
  Amityville, NY 800-221-5644
Insinger Co
  Philadelphia, PA 800-344-4802
John Boos & Co
  Effingham, IL 888-431-2667
KEMCO
  Wareham, MA 800-231-5955
Kitchen Equipment Fabricating
  Houston, TX 713-747-3611
Kitcor Corp
  Sun Valley, CA 818-767-4800
Krowne Metal Corp
  Wayne, NJ 800-631-0442
La Crosse
  Onalaska, WI 800-345-0018
Lambertson Industries Inc
  Sparks, NV 800-548-3324
Load King Mfg
  Jacksonville, FL 800-531-4975
M-One Specialties
  Salt Lake City, UT 800-525-9223
Marlo Manufacturing
  Boonton, NJ 800-222-0450
MCM Fixture Co
  Hazel Park, MI 248-547-9280
Metal
  Columbia, SC 803-776-9252
Metal Kitchen Fabricators Inc
  Houston, TX 713-683-8375
Metal Master Sales Corp
  Glendale Heights, IL 800-488-8729
Missouri Equipment
  St Louis, MO 800-727-6326
Moli-International
  Denver, CO 800-525-8468
National Bar Systems
  Huntington Beach, CA 714-848-1688
National FABCO Manufacturing
  St Louis, MO 314-842-4571
National Scoop & Equipment Company
  Spring House, PA 215-646-2040
Polar Ware Company
  Sheboygan, WI 800-237-3655
Premium Air Systems Inc
  Troy, MI 877-430-0333
Reliable Food Service Equipment
  Concord, ON 416-738-6840
Sefi Fabricators Inc
  Amityville, NY 631-842-2200
St. Louis Stainless Service
  St Louis, MO 800-735-3853
Stainless
  La Vergne, TN 800-877-5177
Stainless Equipment Manufacturing
  Dallas, TX .800-736-2038
Stainless Fabricating Company
  Denver, CO 800-525-8966
Stainless International
  Rancho Cordova, CA 888-300-6196
Stainless Steel Fabricators
  Tyler, TX .903-595-6625
Starlite Food Service Equipment
  Detroit, MI 888-521-6603
Super Sturdy
  Weldon, NC 800-253-4833
Superior Products Company
  Saint Paul, MN 800-328-9800
Supreme Metal
  Alpharetta, GA 800-645-2526
T & S Brass & Bronze Work
  Travelers Rest, SC 800-476-4103
Terriss Consolidate
  Asbury Park, NJ 800-342-1611
Tru Form Plastics
  Gardena, CA 800-510-7999
United Fabricators
  Fort Smith, AR 800-235-4101
Universal Stainless
  Aurora, CO 800-223-8332
Universal Stainless & Alloy
  Titusville, PA 800-295-1909
Weiss Sheet Metal Inc
  Avon, MA .508-583-8300
West Metals
  London, ON 800-300-6667
West Star Industries
  Stockton, CA 800-326-2288

Windows

Drive-Thru & Pass-Thru

Ayr King Corp
  Louisville, KY 866-266-6290

Bullet Guard Corporation
  West Sacramento, CA 800-233-5632
Creative Industries Inc
  Indianapolis, IN 800-776-2068

QUIKSERV Corp
  Houston, TX 800-388-8307
Ready Access
  Chicago, IL 800-621-5045

Clothing & Protective Apparel

Aprons

A Allred Marketing
Birmingham, AL...................205-251-3700
A.D. Cowdrey Company
Modesto, CA......................209-538-4677
Adcapitol
Monroe, NC.......................800-868-7111
Adex Medical Inc
Riverside, CA....................800-873-4776
Akron Cotton Products
Akron, OH........................800-899-7173
Alex Delvecchio Enterprises
Troy, MI.........................248-619-9600
American Advertising & Shop Cap Company
Old Tappan, NJ...................800-442-8837
American Apron Inc.
Foxboro, MA......................800-262-7766
American Bag & Linen Co
Cornelia, GA.....................706-778-5377
ATD-American Co
Wyncote, PA......................800-523-2300
Atlantic Mills
Lakewood, NJ.....................800-242-7374
Bennett's Auto Inc
Neenah, WI.......................800-215-5464
Best Brands Home Products
New York, NY.....................212-684-7456
Best Manufacturing
Jersey City, NJ..................201-356-3800
Best Value Textiles
North Charleston, SC.............800-858-8589
Boss Manufacturing Co
Kewanee, IL......................800-447-4581
Bragard Professional Uniforms
New York, NY.....................800-488-2433
Carson Manufacturing Company
Petaluma, CA.....................800-423-2380
Celebrity Promotions
Remsen, IA.......................800-332-6847
Champaign Plastics Company
Champaign, IL....................800-575-0170
Charles Craft Inc
Laurinburg, NC...................910-844-3521
Christman Screenprint Inc
Springfield, MI..................800-962-9330
Coast Scientific
Rancho Santa Fe, CA..............800-445-1544
David Dobbs Enterprise Inc.
St Augustine, FL.................800-889-6368
Dove Screen Printing Co
Royston, GA......................706-245-4975
Elwood Safety Company
Buffalo, NY......................866-326-6060
Erell Manufacturing Co
Elk Grove Vlg, IL................800-622-6334
Erie Cotton Products
Erie, PA.........................800-289-4737
Fabohio Inc
Uhrichsville, OH.................740-922-4233
Fabriko
Altavista, VA....................888-203-8098
Flavor Wear
Valley Center, CA................800-647-8372
Foley's Famous Aprons
Wayne, MI........................800-634-3245
Funny Apron Co
Lake Dallas, TX..................800-835-5802
Gary Manufacturing Company
National City, CA................800-775-0804
Gourmet Table Skirts
Houston, TX......................800-527-0440
Gril-Del
Mankato, MN......................800-782-7320
Hall Safety Apparel
Uhrichsville, OH.................800-232-3671
Handgards Inc
El Paso, TX......................800-351-8161
Hank Rivera Associates
Dearborn, MI.....................313-581-8300
Hygrade Gloves
Brooklyn, NY.....................800-233-8100
Island Poly
Westbury, NY.....................800-338-4433
Jomac Products
Niles, IL........................800-566-2289

Kennedy's Specialty Sewing
Erin, ON.........................519-833-9306
Keystone Adjustable Cap Co Inc
Pennsauken, NJ...................800-663-5439
Klever Kuvers
Pasadena, CA.....................626-355-8441
LaCrosse Safety and Industrial
Portland, OR.....................800-557-7246
Landau Uniforms Inc
Olive Branch, MS.................800-238-7513
Lexidyne of Pennsylvania
Pittsburgh, PA...................800-543-2233
Liberty Ware LLC
Clearfield, UT...................888-500-5885
Locknane
Everett, WA......................800-848-9854
Mell & Co
Niles, IL........................800-262-6355
Midwest Promotional Group
Summit, IL.......................800-305-3388
Milliken & Co
Spartanburg, SC..................864-503-2020
National Embroidery Svc Inc
Portsmouth, RI...................800-227-1451
New Chief Fashion
Vernon, CA.......................800-639-2433
New Hatchwear Company
Calgary, AB......................800-661-9249
Omni Apparel
Carrollton, GA...................770-838-1008
Pacific Oasis Enterprise Inc
Santa Fe Springs, CA.............800-424-1475
PolyConversions, Inc.
Rantoul, IL......................888-893-3330
Pop Tops Co Inc
South Easton, MA.................800-647-8677
Rodes Professional Apparel
Louisville, KY...................502-584-3112
Royal Paper Products
Coatesville, PA..................800-666-6655
S & H Uniform Corp
White Plains, NY.................800-210-5295
Seven Mile Creek Corp
Eaton, OH........................800-497-6324
Shen Manufacturing Co Inc
Conshohocken, PA.................610-825-2790
ST Restaurant Supplies
Delta, BC........................888-448-4244
Sultan Linen Inc
New York, NY.....................212-689-8900
Superior Linen & Work Wear
Kansas City, MO..................800-798-7987
Superior Menus
Mankato, MN......................800-464-2182
Superior Uniform Group
Seminole, FL.....................800-727-8643
Tara Linens
Sanford, NC......................800-476-8272
Triad Products Company
Springfield, OH..................937-323-9422
Tronex Industries
Denville, NJ.....................800-833-1181
Tucker Industries
Colorado Springs, CO.............800-786-7287
Universal Overall
Chicago, IL......................800-621-3344
Vicmore Manufacturing Company
Brooklyn, NY.....................800-458-8663
Whiting & Davis
Attleboro Falls, MA..............800-876-6374
World Pride
St Petersburg, FL................800-533-2433

Canners' & Packers'

A.D. Cowdrey Company
Modesto, CA......................209-538-4677
Alabama Bag Co Inc
Talladega, AL....................800-888-4921
American Apron Inc.
Foxboro, MA......................800-262-7766
American Bag & Linen Co
Cornelia, GA.....................706-778-5377
Bennett's Auto Inc
Neenah, WI.......................800-215-5464

Champaign Plastics Company
Champaign, IL....................800-575-0170
Elwood Safety Company
Buffalo, NY......................866-326-6060
Erell Manufacturing Co
Elk Grove Vlg, IL................800-622-6334
Gary Manufacturing Company
National City, CA................800-775-0804
Hall Safety Apparel
Uhrichsville, OH.................800-232-3671
Island Poly
Westbury, NY.....................800-338-4433
Kennedy's Specialty Sewing
Erin, ON.........................519-833-9306
Locknane
Everett, WA......................800-848-9854
Seven Mile Creek Corp
Eaton, OH........................800-497-6324
Whiting & Davis
Attleboro Falls, MA..............800-876-6374

Dairy

American Apron Inc.
Foxboro, MA......................800-262-7766
Champaign Plastics Company
Champaign, IL....................800-575-0170
Erell Manufacturing Co
Elk Grove Vlg, IL................800-622-6334
Seven Mile Creek Corp
Eaton, OH........................800-497-6324

Caps

A Allred Marketing
Birmingham, AL...................205-251-3700

Gloves

Bakers'

Best Value Textiles
North Charleston, SC.............800-858-8589
Golden Needles Knitting & Glove Company
Coshocton, OH....................919-667-5102
Great Southern Corp
Memphis, TN......................800-421-7802
Hygrade Gloves
Brooklyn, NY.....................800-233-8100
Jomac Products
Niles, IL........................800-566-2289
Panhandler, Inc.
Cordova, TN......................800-654-7237

Disposable

Adex Medical Inc
Riverside, CA....................800-873-4776
AEP Industries Inc
Mankato, MN......................800-999-2374
Afassco
Minden, NV.......................775-783-3555
Alabama Bag Co Inc
Talladega, AL....................800-888-4921
Ansell Healthcare Inc
Iselin, NJ.......................800-800-0444
Bennett's Auto Inc
Neenah, WI.......................800-215-5464
Boss Manufacturing Co
Kewanee, IL......................800-447-4581
Champaign Plastics Company
Champaign, IL....................800-575-0170
Coast Scientific
Rancho Santa Fe, CA..............800-445-1544
Erie Cotton Products
Erie, PA.........................800-289-4737
Gann Manufacturing
Baltimore, MD....................800-922-9832
George Glove Company, Inc
Midland Park, NJ.................800-631-4292
Goldmax Industries
City of Industry, CA.............626-964-8820
Great Southern Corp
Memphis, TN......................800-421-7802
Handgards Inc
El Paso, TX......................800-351-8161

Hygrade Gloves
Brooklyn, NY 800-233-8100
John Plant Co
Ramseur, NC. 800-334-2711
Liberty Ware LLC
Clearfield, UT. 888-500-5885
Ontario Glove and Safety Products
Kitchener, ON 800-265-4554
Pacific Oasis Enterprise Inc
Santa Fe Springs, CA 800-424-1475
Playtex Products, LLC
New Providence, NJ 888-310-4290
Rochester Midland Corp
Rochester, NY. 800-387-7174
Royal Paper Products
Coatesville, PA 800-666-6655
Superior Products Company
Saint Paul, MN 800-328-9800
Textile Buff & Wheel
Charlestown, MA 617-241-8100
Triad Scientific
Manasquan, NJ 800-867-6690
Tronex Industries
Denville, NJ .800-833-1181
Wilkens-Anderson Co
Chicago, IL .800-847-2222
Y-Pers Inc
Philadelphia, PA 800-421-0242

Plastic, Rubber

Allied Glove Corporation
Milwaukee, WI 800-558-9263
Ansell Healthcare Inc
Iselin, NJ 800-800-0444
Boss Manufacturing Co
Kewanee, IL 800-447-4581
Carolina Glove Co
Conover, NC. 800-335-1918
Champaign Plastics Company
Champaign, IL 800-575-0170
Choctaw-Kaul Distribution Company
Detroit, MI .313-894-9494
Coast Scientific
Rancho Santa Fe, CA 800-445-1544
Comasec Safety, Inc.
Enfield, CT .800-333-0219
Eagle Home Products
Huntington, NY 631-673-3500
Erie Cotton Products
Erie, PA 800-289-4737
George Glove Company, Inc
Midland Park, NJ 800-631-4292
Glover Latex
Anaheim, CA 800-243-5110
Goldmax Industries
City of Industry, CA 626-964-8820
Great Southern Corp
Memphis, TN 800-421-7802
Hall Safety Apparel
Uhrichsville, OH. 800-232-3671
Handgards Inc
El Paso, TX 800-351-8161
Hygrade Gloves
Brooklyn, NY 800-233-8100
Island Poly
Westbury, NY 800-338-4433
Lambert Company
Chillicothe, MO 800-821-7667
Monte Glove Company
Wilkesboro, NC 662-263-5353
Ontario Glove and Safety Products
Kitchener, ON 800-265-4554
Pacific Oasis Enterprise Inc
Santa Fe Springs, CA 800-424-1475
Playtex Products, LLC
New Providence, NJ 888-310-4290
Quality Mop & Brush Manufacturers
Needham, MA. 617-884-2999
Rochester Midland Corp
Rochester, NY. 800-387-7174
Sterling Rubber
Fergus, ON .519-843-4032
Tronex Industries
Denville, NJ .800-833-1181
Wells Lamont
Niles, IL 800-323-2830
Y-Pers Inc
Philadelphia, PA 800-421-0242

Protective

Alabama Bag Co Inc
Talladega, AL 800-888-4921
Allied Glove Corporation
Milwaukee, WI 800-558-9263
Bennett's Auto Inc
Neenah, WI .800-215-5464
Carolina Glove Co
Conover, NC. 800-335-1918
Century Glove Corp
Summerville, GA 706-857-6444
Champaign Plastics Company
Champaign, IL 800-575-0170
Coast Scientific
Rancho Santa Fe, CA 800-445-1544
Comasec Safety, Inc.
Enfield, CT .800-333-0219
Fairfield Line Inc
Fairfield, IA .800-247-3383
Gann Manufacturing
Baltimore, MD 800-922-9832
George Glove Company, Inc
Midland Park, NJ 800-631-4292
Glover Latex
Anaheim, CA 800-243-5110
Golden Needles Knitting & Glove Company
Coshocton, OH 919-667-5102
Gril-Del
Mankato, MN 800-782-7320
Healthline Products
Los Angeles, CA. 800-473-4003
Island Poly
Westbury, NY 800-338-4433
Microflex Corp
Reno, NV 800-876-6866
Mid West Quality Gloves Inc
Chillicothe, MO 800-821-3028
Ontario Glove and Safety Products
Kitchener, ON 800-265-4554
Panhandler, Inc.
Cordova, TN 800-654-7237
Parvin Manufacturing Company
Los Angeles, CA. 800-648-0770
Playtex Products, LLC
New Providence, NJ 888-310-4290
Royal Paper Products
Coatesville, PA 800-666-6655
Samco Freezerwear
St Paul, MN. 651-638-3888
Showa
Menlo, GA .800-241-0323
ST Restaurant Supplies
Delta, BC. .888-448-4244
Star Glove Company
Odon, IN 800-832-7101
Superior Distributing Co
Louisville, KY 800-365-6661
Textile Buff & Wheel
Charlestown, MA 617-241-8100
Triad Scientific
Manasquan, NJ 800-867-6690
Tronex Industries
Denville, NJ .800-833-1181
Wells Lamont
Niles, IL 800-247-3295
Wells Lamont
Niles, IL 800-323-2830
Whiting & Davis
Attleboro Falls, MA 800-876-6374
Work Well Company
Gahanna, OH. 614-759-8003
Worksafe Industries
Huntington Station, NY 800-929-9000
Y-Pers Inc
Philadelphia, PA 800-421-0242

Hair Nets

Adex Medical Inc
Riverside, CA 800-873-4776
Cellucap Manufacturing Co
Philadelphia, PA 800-523-3814
Champaign Plastics Company
Champaign, IL 800-575-0170
Erie Cotton Products
Erie, PA 800-289-4737
Hairnet Corporation of America
New York, NY 212-675-5840
Hygrade Gloves
Brooklyn, NY 800-233-8100

Island Poly
Westbury, NY 800-338-4433
Joseph Titone & Sons
Burlington, NJ. 800-220-4102
Keystone Adjustable Cap Co Inc
Pennsauken, NJ 800-663-5439
Peekskill Hair Net
Peekskill, NY 914-737-1524
ST Restaurant Supplies
Delta, BC. .888-448-4244
Sta-Rite Ginnie Lou Inc
Shelbyville, IL 800-782-7483
Superior Distributing Co
Louisville, KY 800-365-6661

Holders

Pot

Arden Companies
Southfield, MI. 248-415-8500
Best Brands Home Products
New York, NY 212-684-7456
Best Value Textiles
North Charleston, SC 800-858-8589
Charles Craft Inc
Laurinburg, NC 910-844-3521
Grayline Housewares Inc
Columbus, OH 800-222-7388
Hank Rivera Associates
Dearborn, MI 313-581-8300
Healthline Products
Los Angeles, CA. 800-473-4003
Jomac Products
Niles, IL 800-566-2289
Monte Glove Company
Wilkesboro, NC 662-263-5353
Panhandler, Inc.
Cordova, TN 800-654-7237
Shen Manufacturing Co Inc
Conshohocken, PA 610-825-2790
Standard Terry Mills
Souderton, PA 215-723-8121
Stevens Linen Association
Dudley, MA. 800-772-9269

Jackets

A Allred Marketing
Birmingham, AL 205-251-3700

Name Badges

Ace Stamp & Engraving
Lakewood, WA 253-582-3322
Alex Delvecchio Enterprises
Troy, MI 248-619-9600
Artcraft Badge & Sign Company
Olney, MD. 800-739-0709
ATL-East Tag & Label Inc
West Chester, PA 866-381-8744
Atlas Labels
Montreal, QC 514-852-7000
BAW Plastics Inc
Clairton, PA. 800-783-2229
Berlekamp Plastics Inc
Fremont, OH. 419-334-4481
Cawley Co
Manitowoc, WI 800-822-9539
Central Decal
Burr Ridge, IL. 800-869-7654
Chemi-Graphic Inc
Ludlow, MA 413-589-0151
City Stamp & Seal Co
Austin, TX. 800-950-6074
Corpus Christi Stamp Works
Corpus Christi, TX 800-322-4515
Crown Marking
Minneapolis, MN 800-305-5249
Cucamonga Sign Shop LLC
Rancho Cucamonga, CA 909-945-5888
Custom ID Systems
Venice, FL. 800-242-8430
Custom Rubber Stamp Co
Crosby, MN. 888-606-4579
Custom Stamp Company
Anza, CA. .323-292-0753
Darson Corp
Detroit, MI .800-783-7781
Design-Mark Industries
Wareham, MA. 800-451-3275

Dinosaur Plastics
Houston, TX 713-923-2278
E C Shaw Co
Cincinnati, OH 866-532-7429
Economy Novelty & Printing Co
New York, NY 212-481-3022
Ed Smith's Stencil Works LTD
New Orleans, LA 504-525-2128
Ehrgott Rubber Stamp Company
Indianapolis, IN 317-353-2222
Elliot Lee
Cedarhurst, NY 516-569-9595
Emblem & Badge
Providence, RI 800-875-5444
Engraving Services Co.
Woodville South, SA
Engraving Specialists
Royal Oak, MI 248-542-2244
EPI World Graphics
Midlothian, IL 708-389-7500
Executive Line
Chatham, NY 800-333-5761
FORT Hill Sign Products Inc
Hopedale, MA. 781-321-4320
Fox Stamp Sign & Specialty
Menasha, WI. 920-725-2683
Frost Manufacturing Corp
Worcester, MA 800-462-0216
George Lauterer Corp
Chicago, IL. 312-913-1881
GM Nameplate
Seattle, WA 800-366-7668
Granite State Stamps Inc
Manchester, NH 800-937-3736
Graphics Unlimited
San Diego, CA 858-453-4031
Hartford Stamp Works
Hartford, CT 860-249-6205
IdentaBadge
Lafayette, LA 800-325-8247
Impact Awards & Promotions
Avon Park, FL 888-203-4225
ITC Systems
Toronto, ON 877-482-8326
King Badge & Button Company
Huntingtn Bch, CA 714-847-3060
Kraus & Sons
New York, NY 212-620-0408
Label Systems & Solutions
Bohemia, NY 800-811-2560
Label Systems Inc
Addison, TX 800-220-9552
Legible Signs
Loves Park, IL. 800-435-4177
Loria Awards
Yonkers, NY 800-540-2927
Martco Engravers
Fremont, NH 603-895-3561
Mastercraft Manufacturing Co
Long Island City, NY 718-729-5620
Midwest Badge & Novelty Co
Minneapolis, MN 952-927-9901
Modern Stamp Company
Baltimore, MD 800-727-3029
MTL Etching Industries
Woodmere, NY 516-295-9733
My Serenity Pond
Cold Spring, MN. 320-363-0411
N.G. Slater Corporation
New York, NY 800-848-4621
Nameplate
St Paul, MN 651-228-1522
Orber Manufacturing Co
Cranston, RI 800-761-4059
Paperweights Plus
Medford, NY 631-924-3222
Patrick & Co
Dallas, TX 214-761-0900
Photo Graphics Co
Grandview, MO 816-761-3333
Plastic Tagtrade Check
Essexville, MI 989-892-7913
Printsource Group
Wakefield, RI 401-789-9339
Pro-Ad-Co Inc
Portland, OR 800-287-5885
Rebel Stamp & Sign Co
Baton Rouge, LA 800-860-5120
Regal Plastic Supply Co
Kansas City, MO. 800-444-6390
Richardson's Stamp Works
Houston, TX 713-973-0314

Royal Label Co
Dorchester, MA. 617-825-6050
Sesame Label System
New York, NY 800-551-3020
Stoffel Seals Corp
Tallapoosa, GA 800-422-8247
Sutherland Stamp Company
San Diego, CA 858-233-7784
Volk Corp
Farmington Hills, MI 800-521-6799
Wind River Environmental
Gloucester, MA 800-332-6025
Winmark Stamp & Sign
Salt Lake City, UT 800-438-0480
Yeuell Name Plate & Label
Woburn, MA 781-933-2984

Oven Mits

Abond Plastic Corporation
Lachine, QC 800-886-7947
Arden Companies
Southfield, MI. 248-415-8500
Best Brands Home Products
New York, NY 212-684-7456
Best Value Textiles
North Charleston, SC 800-858-8589
C R Mfg
Waverly, NE 877-789-5844
Gril-Del
Mankato, MN 800-782-7320
Jomac Products
Niles, IL .800-566-2289
Monte Glove Company
Wilkesboro, NC 662-263-5353
Parvin Manufacturing Company
Los Angeles, CA. 800-648-0770
Shen Manufacturing Co Inc
Conshohocken, PA 610-825-2790
Standard Terry Mills
Souderton, PA 215-723-8121
Tucker Industries
Colorado Springs, CO. 800-786-7287
Work Well Company
Gahanna, OH 614-759-8003

Protective Apparel

Food Handlers'

Abond Plastic Corporation
Lachine, QC 800-886-7947
Adex Medical Inc
Riverside, CA 800-873-4776
AEP Industries Inc
Mankato, MN 800-999-2374
Akron Cotton Products
Akron, OH. 800-899-7173
Allied Glove Corporation
Milwaukee, WI. 800-558-9263
American Advertising & Shop Cap Company
Old Tappan, NJ 800-442-8837
American Apron Inc.
Foxboro, MA 800-262-7766
American Bag & Linen Co
Cornelia, GA. 706-778-5377
Best Brands Home Products
New York, NY 212-684-7456
Best Buy Uniforms
Homestead, PA 800-345-1924
Best Value Textiles
North Charleston, SC 800-858-8589
Boss Manufacturing Co
Kewanee, IL 800-447-4581
Bragard Professional Uniforms
New York, NY 800-488-2433
Carolina Glove Co
Conover, NC 800-335-1918
Carry-All Canvas Bag Co.
Brooklyn, NY 888-425-5224
Century Glove Corp
Summerville, GA 706-857-6444
Champaign Plastics Company
Champaign, IL 800-575-0170
Choctaw-Kaul Distribution Company
Detroit, MI 313-894-9494
Dalloz Safety
Smithfield, RI 800-977-9177
Eagle Home Products
Huntington, NY 631-673-3500
Fabohio Inc
Uhrichsville, OH. 740-922-4233

Golden Needles Knitting & Glove Company
Coshocton, OH 919-667-5102
Gourmet Gear
Los Angeles, CA 800-682-4635
Gril-Del
Mankato, MN 800-782-7320
Hall Safety Apparel
Uhrichsville, OH. 800-232-3671
Hygrade Gloves
Brooklyn, NY 800-233-8100
Island Poly
Westbury, NY 800-338-4433
John Plant Co
Ramseur, NC 800-334-2711
Jomac Products
Niles, IL .800-566-2289
Joseph Titone & Sons
Burlington, NJ. 800-220-4102
Kennedy's Specialty Sewing
Erin, ON 519-833-9306
Keystone Adjustable Cap Co Inc
Pennsauken, NJ. 800-663-5439
Kimberly-Clark Professional
Roswell, GA 800-241-3146
Knapp Shoes
Penn Yan, NY
Koch Equipment LLC
Kansas City, MO 816-931-4557
Lambert Company
Chillicothe, MO 800-821-7667
Landau Uniforms Inc
Olive Branch, MS 800-238-7513
Lexidyne of Pennsylvania
Pittsburgh, PA 800-543-2233
Microflex Corp
Reno, NV 800-876-6866
New Chief Fashion
Vernon, CA 800-639-2433
New England Overshoe Company
Williston, VT 888-289-6367
Onguard Industries LLC
Havre De Grace, MD 800-304-2282
Parvin Manufacturing Company
Los Angeles, CA. 800-648-0770
Playtex Products, LLC
New Providence, NJ 888-310-4290
PolyConversions, Inc.
Rantoul, IL 888-893-3330
Quality Mop & Brush Manufacturers
Needham, MA. 617-884-2999
Refrigiwear Inc
Dahlonega, GA. 800-645-3744
Rodes Professional Apparel
Louisville, KY 502-584-3112
Samco Freezerwear
St Paul, MN. 651-638-3888
Seven Mile Creek Corp
Eaton, OH 800-497-6324
Showa
Menlo, GA 800-241-0323
Sta-Rite Ginnie Lou Inc
Shelbyville, IL 800-782-7483
Star Glove Company
Odon, IN 800-832-7101
Sultan Linen Inc
New York, NY 212-689-8900
Superior Distributing Co
Louisville, KY 800-365-6661
Superior Linen & Work Wear
Kansas City, MO. 800-798-7987
Superior Uniform Group
Seminole, FL. 800-727-8643
Triad Scientific
Manasquan, NJ 800-867-6690
Tronex Industries
Denville, NJ 800-833-1181
Tucker Industries
Colorado Springs, CO. 800-786-7287
Universal Overall
Chicago, IL 800-621-3344
Valeo
Elmsford, Ny. 800-634-2704
Work Well Company
Gahanna, OH 614-759-8003
Worksafe Industries
Huntington Station, NY 800-929-9000
Y-Pers Inc
Philadelphia, PA 800-421-0242

Shirts

A Allred Marketing
Birmingham, AL..............205-251-3700

Uniforms & Special Clothing

A Allred Marketing
Birmingham, AL..............205-251-3700
A T Scafati Inc
New York, NY...............212-695-4944
Abond Plastic Corporation
Lachine, QC................800-886-7947
Acme Laundry Products Inc
Chatsworth, CA.............818-341-0700
Adcapitol
Monroe, NC.................800-868-7111
Adex Medical Inc
Riverside, CA..............800-873-4776
Alex Delvecchio Enterprises
Troy, MI...................248-619-9600
Allied Glove Corporation
Milwaukee, WI..............800-558-9263
American Advertising & Shop Cap Company
Old Tappan, NJ.............800-442-8837
American Design Studios
Carlsbad, CA...............800-899-7104
American Identity
Orange City, IA............800-369-2277
Ansell Healthcare Inc
Iselin, NJ.................800-800-0444
Apparel Manufacturing Co Inc
Lilburn, GA................800-366-1608
Aramark Uniform Svc
Burbank, CA................800-272-6275
ATD-American Co
Wyncote, PA................800-523-2300
Bennett's Auto Inc
Neenah, WI.................800-215-5464
Best Brands Home Products
New York, NY...............212-684-7456
Best Buy Uniforms
Homestead, PA..............800-345-1924
Best Manufacturing
Jersey City, NJ............201-356-3800
Best Value Textiles
North Charleston, SC.......800-858-8589
Big Front Uniforms
Los Angeles, CA............800-234-8383
Blue Ridge Converting
Asheville, NC..............800-438-3893
Boss Manufacturing Co
Kewanee, IL................800-447-4581
Bragard Professional Uniforms
New York, NY...............800-488-2433
Bunzl Processor Distribution LLC
Riverside, MO..............816-448-4300
Campus Collection, Inc.
Tuscaloosa, AL.............800-289-8744
Carlisle Food Svc Products Inc
Oklahoma City, OK..........800-654-8210
Carnegie Textile Co
Cleveland, OH..............800-633-4136
Carry-All Canvas Bag Co.
Brooklyn, NY...............888-425-5224
Carson Manufacturing Company
Petaluma, CA...............800-423-2380
CCP Industries, Inc.
Cleveland, OH..............800-321-2840
Celebrity Promotions
Remsen, IA.................800-332-6847
Cellucap Manufacturing Co
Philadelphia, PA...........800-523-3814
Century Glove Corp
Summerville, GA............706-857-6444
Champaign Plastics Company
Champaign, IL..............800-575-0170
Charles Craft Inc
Laurinburg, NC.............910-844-3521
Chef Revival
North Charleston, SC.......800-248-9826
Chefwear
Addison, IL................800-568-2433
Christman Screenprint Inc
Springfield, MI............800-962-9330
Cintas Corp
Cincinnati, OH.............800-864-3676
Coast Scientific
Rancho Santa Fe, CA........800-445-1544
Comasec Safety, Inc.
Enfield, CT................800-333-0219

Dalloz Safety
Smithfield, RI.............800-977-9177
David Dobbs Enterprise Inc.
St Augustine, FL...........800-889-6368
Dow Cover Co Inc
New Haven, CT..............800-735-8877
Dunrite Inc
Fremont, NE................800-782-3061
Elwood Safety Company
Buffalo, NY................866-326-6060
Erell Manufacturing Co
Elk Grove Vlg, IL..........800-622-6334
Erie Cotton Products
Erie, PA...................800-289-4737
F & F and A. Jacobs & Sons, Inc.
Baltimore, MD..............410-727-6397
Fabohio Inc
Uhrichsville, OH...........740-922-4233
Fabriko
Altavista, VA..............888-203-8098
Fairfield Line Inc
Fairfield, IA..............800-247-3383
Flavor Wear
Valley Center, CA..........800-647-8372
Foley's Famous Aprons
Wayne, MI..................800-634-3245
Franklin Uniform Corporation
Baltimore, MD..............410-235-8151
Funny Apron Co
Lake Dallas, TX............800-835-5802
Gann Manufacturing
Baltimore, MD..............800-922-9832
Gary Manufacturing Company
National City, CA..........800-775-0804
George Glove Company, Inc
Midland Park, NJ...........800-631-4292
Glover Latex
Anaheim, CA................800-243-5110
Golden Needles Knitting & Glove Company
Coshocton, OH..............919-667-5102
Goldmax Industries
City of Industry, CA.......626-964-8820
Gourmet Gear
Los Angeles, CA............800-682-4635
Gourmet Table Skirts
Houston, TX................800-527-0440
Graphic Apparel
Inniasfil, ON..............800-757-4867
Great Southern Corp
Memphis, TN................800-421-7802
Green Seams
Maple Grove, MN............612-929-3213
Gril-Del
Mankato, MN................800-782-7320
Haas Tailoring Company
Baltimore, MD..............410-732-3804
Hairnet Corporation of America
New York, NY...............212-675-5840
Hall Safety Apparel
Uhrichsville, OH...........800-232-3671
Handgards Inc
El Paso, TX................800-351-8161
Hank Rivera Associates
Dearborn, MI...............313-581-8300
Happy Chef Inc
Butler, NJ.................800-347-0288
Healthline Products
Los Angeles, CA............800-473-4003
Hygrade Gloves
Brooklyn, NY...............800-233-8100
Image Experts Uniforms
Schenectady, NY............800-789-2433
Island Poly
Westbury, NY...............800-338-4433
John Plant Co
Ramseur, NC................800-334-2711
Jomac Products
Niles, IL..................800-566-2289
Kennedy's Specialty Sewing
Erin, ON...................519-833-9306
Keystone Adjustable Cap Co Inc
Pennsauken, NJ.............800-663-5439
Kingston McKnight
Redwood City, CA...........800-900-0463
Klever Kuvers
Pasadena, CA...............626-355-8441
Knapp Shoes
Penn Yan, NY
Koch Equipment LLC
Kansas City, MO............816-931-4557
LaCrosse Safety and Industrial
Portland, OR...............800-557-7246

Lambert Company
Chillicothe, MO............800-821-7667
Landau Uniforms Inc
Olive Branch, MS...........800-238-7513
Lehigh Safety Shoe Co LLC
Nelsonville, OH............866-442-5429
Lexidyne of Pennsylvania
Pittsburgh, PA.............800-543-2233
Liberty Ware LLC
Clearfield, UT.............888-500-5885
Lion Apparel Inc
Dayton, OH.................800-548-6614
Locknane
Everett, WA................800-848-9854
Marv Holland Industries
Edmonton, AB...............800-661-7269
Metz Premiums
New York, NY...............212-315-4660
Mid West Quality Gloves Inc
Chillicothe, MO............800-821-3028
Midwest Promotional Group
Summit, IL.................800-305-3388
Monte Glove Company
Wilkesboro, NC.............662-263-5353
National Embroidery Svc Inc
Portsmouth, RI.............800-227-1451
National Scoop & Equipment Company
Spring House, PA...........215-646-2040
New Chief Fashion
Vernon, CA.................800-639-2433
New Hatchwear Company
Calgary, AB................800-661-9249
Ok Uniform Co Inc
New York, NY...............866-700-5765
Pacific Oasis Enterprise Inc
Santa Fe Springs, CA.......800-424-1475
Panhandler, Inc.
Cordova, TN................800-654-7237
Parvin Manufacturing Company
Los Angeles, CA............800-648-0770
Paul G. Gallin Company
Yonkers, NY................914-964-5800
Peekskill Hair Net
Peekskill, NY..............914-737-1524
PolyConversions, Inc.
Rantoul, IL................888-893-3330
Pop Tops Co Inc
South Easton, MA...........800-647-8677
Print Ons/Express Mark
Monroe, NC.................704-289-8261
Protexall
Greenville, IL.............800-334-8939
Put-Ons USA
Brooklyn Park, MN..........888-425-1215
Quality Mop & Brush Manufacturers
Needham, MA................617-884-2999
R&R Industries
San Clemente, CA...........800-234-1434
Radio Cap Company
San Antonio, TX............210-472-1649
Red Kap Industries
Nashville, TN..............615-565-5000
Refrigiwear Inc
Dahlonega, GA..............800-645-3744
Rocky Shoes & Boots Inc
Nelsonville, OH............866-442-4908
Rodes Professional Apparel
Louisville, KY.............502-584-3112
Royal Paper Products
Coatesville, PA............800-666-6655
S & H Uniform Corp
White Plains, NY...........800-210-5295
Samco Freezerwear
St Paul, MN................651-638-3888
Scorpio Apparel
Northbrook, IL.............800-559-3338
Seven Mile Creek Corp
Eaton, OH..................800-497-6324
Shen Manufacturing Co Inc
Conshohocken, PA...........610-825-2790
Showa
Menlo, GA..................800-241-0323
Signco Stylecraft
Cincinnati, OH.............800-733-0045
ST Restaurant Supplies
Delta, BC..................888-448-4244
Standard Terry Mills
Souderton, PA..............215-723-8121
Star Glove Company
Odon, IN...................800-832-7101
Sterling Rubber
Fergus, ON.................519-843-4032

Sultan Linen Inc
New York, NY 212-689-8900
Superior Distributing Co
Louisville, KY 800-365-6661
Superior Linen & Work Wear
Kansas City, MO 800-798-7987
Superior Uniform Group
Seminole, FL 800-727-8643
Task Footwear
Chippewa Falls, WI 800-962-0166
Terry Manufacturing Company
Birmingham, AL 205-250-0062
Textile Buff & Wheel
Charlestown, MA 617-241-8100
Todd Uniform
Saint Louis, MO 800-458-3402
Triad Products Company
Springfield, OH 937-323-9422

Tronex Industries
Denville, NJ 800-833-1181
Tru Form Plastics
Gardena, CA 800-510-7999
Tucker Industries
Colorado Springs, CO 800-786-7287
Uni First Corp
Wilmington, MA 800-455-7654
Uniforms To You
Oak Lawn, IL 800-889-6072
Uniforms To You & Co
Chicago, IL 800-864-3676
Universal Overall
Chicago, IL 800-621-3344
Valeo
Elmsford, Ny 800-634-2704
VCG Uniform
Chicago, IL 800-447-6502

Vicmore Manufacturing Company
Brooklyn, NY 800-458-8663
Weinbrenner Shoe Co
Merrill, WI 800-826-0002
Wells Lamont
Niles, IL 800-323-2830
Whiting & Davis
Attleboro Falls, MA 800-876-6374
Work Well Company
Gahanna, OH 614-759-8003
Worksafe Industries
Huntington Station, NY 800-929-9000
World Pride
St Petersburg, FL 800-533-2433
Y-Pers Inc
Philadelphia, PA 800-421-0242

Consultants & Services

Advertising Services

Advanced Process Solutions
Jeffersonville, IN..................888-294-8118

Advertising Novelties & Specialties

A Allred Marketing
Birmingham, AL..................205-251-3700
AAA Electrical Signs
Donna, TX.......................800-825-5376
Access Solutions
Knoxville, TN...................865-531-0971
Ace Signs
Little Rock, AR.................501-562-0800
Action Signs By Stubblefield
Albuquerque, NM.................505-242-9802
Adams Precision Screen
San Leandro, CA................510-632-8597
Adcapitol
Monroe, NC......................800-868-7111
Admatch Corporation
New York, NY....................800-777-9909
Alex Delvecchio Enterprises
Troy, MI........................248-619-9600
Alger Creations
Miami, FL.......................954-454-3272
Allen Signs Co
Knoxville, TN...................800-844-3524
Alliance Rubber Co
Hot Springs, AR.................800-626-5940
Altrua Marketing & Design
Tallahassee, FL.................800-443-6939
AM Graphics
Edina, MN.......................612-341-2020
American Advertising & Shop Cap Company
Old Tappan, NJ..................800-442-8837
American Identification Industries
West Chicago, IL................800-255-8890
American Identity
Orange City, IA.................800-369-2277
Ameritech Signs & Banners
Santa Monica, CA................310-829-9359
Amsterdam Printing & Litho Inc
Amsterdam, NY...................800-203-9917
Andersen Sign Company
Woodsville, NH..................603-787-6806
Apparel Manufacturing Co Inc
Lilburn, GA.....................800-366-1608
Art Poly Bag Co
Brooklyn, NY....................800-278-7659
Atlas Match Corporation
Euless, TX......................800-628-2426
Audsam Printing
Marion, OH......................740-387-6252
B.E. Industries
Stamford, CT....................203-357-8055
Baldwin/Priesmeyer
Saint Louis, MO.................314-535-2800
Bayard Kurth Company
Detroit, MI.....................313-891-0800
Betsy Ross Manufacturing Company
Paterson, NJ....................877-238-7976
Bill Carr Signs
Flint, MI.......................810-232-1569
BK Graphics
Morristown, TN..................800-581-9159
Black Horse Mfg Co
Chattanooga, TN.................423-624-0798
Blue Feather Products Inc
Ashland, OR.....................800-472-2487
Brewer-Cantelmo Inc
New York, NY....................212-244-4600
Brown's Sign & Screen Printing
Covington, GA...................800-540-3107
Bynoe Printers
New York, NY....................212-662-5041
C R Mfg
Waverly, NE.....................877-789-5844
California Toytime   Balloons
San Pedro, CA...................310-548-1234
Capital Plastics
Middlefield, OH.................440-632-5800
Caraustar
Franklin, KY....................270-586-9565

Carlton Industries
La Grange, TX...................800-231-5988
Carry-All Canvas Bag Co.
Brooklyn, NY....................888-425-5224
Cawley Co
Manitowoc, WI...................800-822-9539
CCL Label Inc
Cold Spring, KY.................800-422-6633
CCS Creative, Inc.
Toronto, ON.....................888-633-2079
Central Decal
Burr Ridge, IL..................800-869-7654
Central Missouri Sheltered Enterprises
Columbia, MO....................573-442-6935
Chain Store Graphics
Decatur, IL.....................800-443-7446
Charles E. Roberts Company
Wyckoff, NJ.....................800-237-2684
Chicago Show Inc
Buffalo Grove, IL...............847-955-0200
Christman Screenprint Inc
Springfield, MI.................800-962-9330
Chroma Tone
Saint Clair, PA.................800-878-1552
City Grafx
Eugene, OR......................800-258-2489
Classy Basket
San Diego, CA...................888-449-4901
Coast Signs & Graphics
Hermosa Beach, CA...............310-379-9921
Comm-Pak
Opelika, AL.....................334-749-6201
Commercial Printing Company
Birmingham, AL..................800-989-9203
Connecticut Laminating Co Inc
New Haven, CT...................800-753-9119
Contemporary Product Inc
Garner, NC......................919-779-4228
Continental Identification
Sparta, MI......................800-247-2499
Courtesy Signs
Amarillo, TX....................806-373-6609
Creative Enterprises
Kendall Park, NJ................732-422-0300
Creegan Animation Company
Steubenville, OH................740-283-3708
Crown Label Company
Santa Ana, CA...................800-422-3590
Cucamonga Sign Shop LLC
Rancho Cucamonga, CA............909-945-5888
Curzon Promotional Graphics
Omaha, NE.......................800-769-7446
Cyrk
Monroe, WA......................800-426-3125
Dave's Imports
Jacksonville, FL................800-553-2837
David Dobbs Enterprise Inc.
St Augustine, FL................800-889-6368
Dayton Bag & Burlap Co
Dayton, OH......................800-543-3400
Deadline Press
Kennesaw, GA....................770-419-2232
Deborah Sales LLC
Newark, NJ......................973-344-8466
Decal Techniques Inc
West Babylon, NY................800-735-3322
Design Label Manufacturing
East Lyme, CT...................800-666-1575
Design-Mark Industries
Wareham, MA.....................800-451-3275
Designers Plastics
Clearwater, FL..................727-573-1643
Diamond Packaging
Rochester, NY...................800-333-4079
Diamond Sign Co
Costa Mesa, CA..................714-545-1440
Dinosaur Plastics
Houston, TX.....................713-923-2278
Distinctive Embedments
Pawtucket, RI...................401-729-0770
DLX Industries
Pomona, NY......................845-517-2200
Dominion Regala
Toronto, ON.....................866-423-4086
Dove Screen Printing Co
Royston, GA.....................706-245-4975

Dynamic Packaging
Minneapolis, MN.................800-878-9380
E.G. Staats & Company
Mount Pleasant, IA..............800-553-1853
Ebenezer Flag Company
Newport, RI.....................401-846-1891
Eco-Bag Products
Ossining, NY....................800-720-2247
Economy Novelty & Printing Co
New York, NY....................212-481-3022
Einson Freeman
Paramus, NJ.....................201-221-2800
EIT
Elmhurst, IL....................630-279-3400
Elliot Lee
Cedarhurst, NY..................516-569-9595
Emblem & Badge
Providence, RI..................800-875-5444
Emco Industrial Plastics
Cedar Grove, NJ.................800-292-9906
Empire Screen Printing Inc
Onalaska, WI....................608-783-3301
Endurart Inc
New York, NY....................212-779-8522
Engraving Specialists
Royal Oak, MI...................248-542-2244
Erell Manufacturing Co
Elk Grove Vlg, IL...............800-622-6334
Executive Line
Chatham, NY.....................800-333-5761
Fair Publishing House
Norwalk, OH.....................419-668-3746
Flexo Transparent Inc
Buffalo, NY.....................877-993-5396
Forbes Products Corp
Rush, NY........................800-316-5235
Forest Manufacturing Co
Twinsburg, OH...................330-425-3805
Forrest Engraving Company
New Rochelle, NY................914-632-9892
Fox Stamp Sign & Specialty
Menasha, WI.....................920-725-2683
Foxfire Marketing Solutions
Newark, DE......................800-497-0512
Francis & Lusky Company
Nashville, TN...................800-251-3711
FRS Industries
Moorhead, MN....................800-747-4795
Fun-Time International
Philadelphia, PA................800-776-4386
Gallimore Industries
Lake Villa, IL..................800-927-8020
Gannett Outdoor of New Jersey
Fairfield, NJ...................973-575-6900
Garland Writing Instruments
Coventry, RI....................401-828-9582
Gary Plastic Packaging Corporation
Bronx, NY.......................800-227-4279
Geiger Bros
Lewiston, ME....................207-755-2000
General Formulations
Sparta, MI......................800-253-3664
General Methods Corporation
Peoria, IL......................309-497-3344
George Lauterer Corp
Chicago, IL.....................312-913-1881
Globe Ticket & Label Company
Warminster, PA..................800-523-5968
Gold Bond Inc
Hixson, TN......................423-842-5844
Gonterman & Associates
Saint Louis, MO.................314-771-0600
Graphic Calculator Company
Barrington, IL..................847-381-4480
Graphics Unlimited
San Diego, CA...................858-453-4031
Graydon Lettercraft
Great Neck, NY..................516-482-0531
Grays Harbor Stamp Works
Aberdeen, WA....................800-894-3830
Green Mountain Graphics
Long Island City, NY............718-472-3377
Greenfield Packaging
White Plains, NY................914-993-0233
H C Bainbridge Inc
Syracuse, NY....................315-475-5313

Harco Enterprises
Peterborough, ON 800-361-5361
HMG Worldwide
Morton Grove, IL 847-965-7100
Hughes Manufacturing Company
Giddings, TX 800-414-0765
IdentaBadge
Lafayette, LA 800-325-8247
IDL
Monroeville, PA 724-733-2234
Image Plastics
Houston, TX 800-289-2811
Imperial Plastics Inc
Lakeville, MN 952-469-4951
Inovar Packaging Group
Arlington, TX 800-285-2235
Insignia Systems Inc
Minneapolis, MN 800-874-4648
Jessup Paper Box
Brookston, IN 765-490-9043
Killion Industries Inc
Vista, CA 800-421-5352
King Badge & Button Company
Huntingtn Bch, CA 714-847-3060
Koza's Inc
Pearland, TX 800-594-5555
Kraus & Sons
New York, NY 212-620-0408
Krimstock Enterprises
Pennsauken, NJ 856-665-3676
Kuepper Favor Company, Celebrate Line
Peru, IN 800-321-5823
Label Systems & Solutions
Bohemia, NY 800-811-2560
Label Systems Inc
Addison, TX 800-220-9552
Labelprint America
Newburyport, MA 978-463-4004
Labelquest Inc
Elmhurst, IL 800-999-5301
Lake City Signs
Boulder City, NV 702-293-5805
Lane Award Manufacturing
Phoenix, AZ 800-843-2581
Legible Signs
Loves Park, IL 800-435-4177
Lewisburg Printing
Lewisburg, TN 800-559-1526
Lewtan Industries Corporation
Hartford, CT 860-278-9800
License Ad Plate Co
Cleveland, OH 216-265-4200
Lion/Circle Corp
Chicago, IL 773-284-3666
Logo Specialty Advertising Tems
Tampa, FL 800-704-0094
Lonestar Banners & Flags
Fort Worth, TX 800-288-9625
Loria Awards
Yonkers, NY 800-540-2927
M & M Display
Philadelphia, PA 800-874-7171
Maier Sign Systems
Saddle Brook, NJ 201-845-7555
Mansfield Rubber Stamp
Mansfield, OH 419-524-1442
Mar-Boro Printing & Advertising Specialties
Brooklyn, NY 718-336-4051
Martco Engravers
Fremont, NH 603-895-3561
Mastercraft Manufacturing Co
Long Island City, NY 718-729-5620
MDR International
North Miami, FL 305-944-5019
Memphis Delta Tent & Awning
Memphis, TN 901-522-1238
Merchandising Inventives
Waukegan, IL 800-367-5653
Metz Premiums
New York, NY 212-315-4660
Midwest Badge & Novelty Co
Minneapolis, MN 952-927-9901
Midwest Promotional Group
Summit, IL 800-305-3388
Minges Printing & Advg Specs
Gastonia, NC 704-867-6791
Minnesuing Acres
Lake Nebagamon, WI 715-374-2262
MODAGRAPHICS
Rolling Meadows, IL 847-392-3980
Modern Stamp Company
Baltimore, MD 800-727-3029

Moore Efficient Communication Aids
Denver, CO 303-433-8456
MTL Etching Industries
Woodmere, NY 516-295-9733
N.G. Slater Corporation
New York, NY 800-848-4621
Nameplate
St Paul, MN 651-228-1522
National Emblem
Carson, CA 800-877-5325
National Marking Products Inc
Henrico, VA 800-482-1553
Nationwide Pennant & Flag Mfg
San Antonio, TX 800-383-3524
Norgus Silk Screen Co Inc
Clifton, NJ 973-365-0600
North American Packaging Corp
New York, NY 800-499-3521
Novelty Advertising
Coshocton, OH 800-848-9163
Nutty Bavarian
Sanford, FL 800-382-4788
Orber Manufacturing Co
Cranston, RI 800-761-4059
Pak 2000 Inc
Mirror Lake, NH 603-569-3700
Paperweights Plus
Medford, NY 631-924-3222
Paradise Products
El Cerrito, CA 800-227-1092
Party Yards
Casselberry, FL 877-501-4400
Pelican Products Inc
Bronx, NY 800-552-8820
Photo Graphics Co
Grandview, MO 816-761-3333
Pierrepont Visual Graphics Inc
Rochester, NY 585-235-5620
Pilgrim Plastics
Brockton, MA 800-343-7810
Plastic Fantastics/Buck Signs
Ashland, OR 800-482-1776
Plastic Printing LLC
Dayton, KY 877-581-7748
Pop Tops Co Inc
South Easton, MA 800-647-8677
Print Ons/Express Mark
Monroe, NC 704-289-8261
Printsource Group
Wakefield, RI 401-789-9339
Pro-Ad-Co Inc
Portland, OR 800-287-5885
Process Displays
New Berlin, WI 800-533-1764
Quick Point Inc
Fenton, MO 800-638-1369
R&R Industries
San Clemente, CA 800-234-1434
Radio Cap Company
San Antonio, TX 210-472-1649
Ram Industries
Erwin, TN 800-523-3883
Ray-Craft
Cleveland, OH 216-651-3330
Rex Art Manufacturing Corp.
Lindenhurst, NY 631-884-4600
Riverside Manufacturing Company
Arlington Hts, IL 800-877-3349
Roxanne Signs Inc
Gaithersburg, MD 301-428-4911
Rutler Screen Printing
Easton, PA 610-829-2999
Samsill Corp
Fort Worth, TX 800-255-1100
Sanders Manufacturing Co
Nashville, TN 866-254-6611
Sayco Yo-Yo Molding Company
Cumberland, RI 401-724-5296
Scott Sign Systems
Sarasota, FL 800-237-9447
Screen Print Etc
Anaheim, CA 714-630-1100
Semco Plastic Co
St Louis, MO 314-487-4557
Sesame Label System
New York, NY 800-551-3020
Shild Company
New York, NY 866-435-2949
Sign Factory
Cerritos, CA 562-809-1443
Signs & Shapes Intl
Omaha, NE 800-806-6069

Sillcocks Plastics International
Hudson, MA 800-526-4919
Smyth Co LLC
St Paul, MN 800-473-3464
Source for Packaging
New York, NY 800-223-2527
Southern Tailors Flag & Banner
Atlanta, GA 877-655-2321
Spartan Flag Co
Northport, MI 231-386-5150
Special Events Supply Company
Hauppauge, NY
Steingart Associates Inc
South Fallsburg, NY 845-434-4321
Sterling Novelty Products
Northbrook, IL 847-291-0070
Stoffel Seals Corp
Tallapoosa, GA 800-422-8247
Superior-Studio Specialties
Commerce, CA 800-354-3049
SuppliesForLess
Hampton, VA 800-235-2201
Sutherland Stamp Company
San Diego, CA 858-233-7784
Thermal Bags By Ingrid Inc
Gilberts, IL 800-622-5560
Tin Box Co of America Inc
Farmingdale, NY 800-888-8467
Token Factory
La Crosse, WI 888-486-5367
Tomsed Corporation
Lillington, NC 800-334-5552
Trevor Owen Limited
Scarborough, ON 866-487-2224
Twenty/Twenty Graphics
Gaithersburg, MD 240-243-0511
Unique Manufacturing
Visalia, CA 888-737-1007
Universal Tag Inc
Dudley, MA 800-332-8247
US Magnetix
Minneapolis, MN 763-540-9497
Variant
Eden Prairie, MN 612-927-8611
Volk Corp
Farmington Hills, MI 800-521-6799
Vonco Products LLC
Lake Villa, IL 800-323-9077
Vynatex
Port Washington, NY 516-944-6130
Wendell August Forge
Grove City, PA 800-923-1390
West Hawk Industries
Ann Arbor, MI 800-678-1286
WGN Flag & Decorating Co
Chicago, IL 773-768-8076
Whirley Industries Inc
Warren, PA 800-825-5575
Willson Industries
Marmora, NJ 800-894-4169
Wishbone Utensil Tableware Line
Wheat Ridge, CO 866-266-5928
World Division
Dallas, TX 800-433-9843
WS Packaging Group Inc
Oak Creek, WI 800-837-3838
WS Packaging Group Inc
Green Bay, WI 877-977-5177

Custom Printed Promotional Products

A Allred Marketing
Birmingham, AL 205-251-3700
Eco-Bag Products
Ossining, NY 800-720-2247
Tangerine Promotion
Northbrook, IL 847-313-6000

Flags, Pennants & Banners

AAA Flag & Banner Manufacturing
Los Angeles, CA 800-266-4222
Ace Signs
Little Rock, AR 501-562-0800
Action Signs By Stubblefield
Albuquerque, NM 505-242-9802
Ad Mart Identity Group
Danville, KY 800-354-2102
Adcapitol
Monroe, NC 800-868-7111
Allen Signs Co
Knoxville, TN 800-844-3524

Altrua Marketing & Design
Tallahassee, FL 800-443-6939
AM Graphics
Edina, MN. 612-341-2020
American Flag & Banner Co Inc
Clawson, MI 800-892-5168
Ameritech Signs & Banners
Santa Monica, CA. 310-829-9359
B H Awning & Tent Co
Benton Harbor, MI 800-272-2187
Baldwin/Priesmeyer
Saint Louis, MO 314-535-2800
Baltimore Sign Company
Arnold, MD. 410-276-1500
Banner Idea
Newport Beach, CA 949-559-6600
Bannerland
Santa Fe Springs, CA 800-654-0294
Betsy Ross Manufacturing Company
Paterson, NJ 877-238-7976
Brown's Sign & Screen Printing
Covington, GA 800-540-3107
Capitol Awning Co Inc
Jamaica, NY 800-241-3539
Coast Signs & Graphics
Hermosa Beach, CA 310-379-9921
Coastal Canvas Products
Savannah, GA .800-476-5174
Collegeville Flag & Manufacturing Company
Collegeville, PA 800-523-5630
Courtesy Signs
Amarillo, TX. .806-373-6609
Creative Canopy Design
Hernando Beach, FL. 866-970-5200
Cucamonga Sign Shop LLC
Rancho Cucamonga, CA 909-945-5888
Curzon Promotional Graphics
Omaha, NE 800-769-7446
Deadline Press
Kennesaw, GA 770-419-2232
Decal Techniques Inc
West Babylon, NY 800-735-3322
Diamond Sign Co
Costa Mesa, CA 714-545-1440
Dimension Graphics Inc
Grand Rapids, MI 855-476-1281
Dinosaur Plastics
Houston, TX. .713-923-2278
Dixie Flag Mfg Co
San Antonio, TX. 800-356-4085
Dominion Regala
Toronto, ON 866-423-4086
Ebenezer Flag Company
Newport, RI. 401-846-1891
EIT
Elmhurst, IL 630-279-3400
Emedco
Williamsville, NY 877-765-8386
Flexo Transparent Inc
Buffalo, NY 877-993-5396
Florart Flock Process
North Miami, FL. 800-292-3524
Forest Manufacturing Co
Twinsburg, OH 330-425-3805
France Personalized Signs
Cleveland, OH 216-241-2198
Frost Manufacturing Corp
Worcester, MA 800-462-0216
Fuller Flag Company
Holden, MA 800-348-6723
George Lauterer Corp
Chicago, IL. 312-913-1881
Goodwin-Cole Co Inc
Sacramento, CA 800-752-4477
Graphics Unlimited
San Diego, CA 858-453-4031
Green Mountain Awning Inc
West Rutland, VT 800-479-2951
H C Bainbridge Inc
Syracuse, NY .315-475-5313
H. Arnold Wood Turning
Tarrytown, NY 888-314-0088
Hammar & Sons
Pelham, NH. 800-527-7446
Handicap Sign Inc
Grand Rapids, MI 800-690-4888
Harting Graphics
Wilmington, DE 800-848-1373
Hollywood Banners
Copiague, NY .800-691-5652
Hughes Manufacturing Company
Giddings, TX .800-414-0765

Industrial Sign Company
South El Monte, CA 800-596-3720
Inovar Packaging Group
Arlington, TX .800-285-2235
John W Keplinger & Sons
Norristown, PA 610-666-6191
KD Kanopy
Westminster, CO 800-432-4435
Kennedy's Specialty Sewing
Erin, ON 519-833-9306
Kraus & Sons
New York, NY 212-620-0408
Ladder Works
Lombard, IL 800-419-5880
Lake City Signs
Boulder City, NV 702-293-5805
Lonestar Banners & Flags
Fort Worth, TX 800-288-9625
Metropolitan Flag & Banner Co
Philadelphia, PA 215-426-2775
Nationwide Pennant & Flag Mfg
San Antonio, TX. 800-383-3524
Norgus Silk Screen Co Inc
Clifton, NJ 973-365-0600
Oates Flag Co Inc
Louisville, KY 502-267-8200
Paradise Products
El Cerrito, CA .800-227-1092
Pierrepont Visual Graphics Inc
Rochester, NY. 585-235-5620
Plasti-Clip Corp
Milford, NH 800-882-2547
Pratt Poster Company
Indianapolis, IN 800-645-1012
Radio Cap Company
San Antonio, TX. 210-472-1649
Riverside Manufacturing Company
Arlington Hts, IL 800-877-3349
Rose City Awning Co
Portland, OR 800-446-4104
Roxanne Signs Inc
Gaithersburg, MD 301-428-4911
Screen Print Etc
Anaheim, CA .714-630-1100
Sign Factory
Cerritos, CA 562-809-1443
Signet Graphic Products
St Louis, MO. .314-426-0200
Signmasters
Huntington Beach, CA 949-364-9128
Southern Tailors Flag & Banner
Atlanta, GA 877-655-2321
Spartan Flag Co
Northport, MI .231-386-5150
Special Events Supply Company
Hauppauge, NY
Sterling Novelty Products
Northbrook, IL 847-291-0070
T & M Distributing Co
Henderson, NV 702-458-1962
Timely Signs Inc
Elmont, NY 800-457-4467
Trevor Owen Limited
Scarborough, ON 866-487-2224
Us Flag & Signal
Portsmouth, VA. 757-497-8947
Volk Corp
Farmington Hills, MI 800-521-6799
Vomela/Harbor Graphics
St Paul, MN. 800-645-1012
Walker Co
Oklahoma City, OK 800-522-3015
Walker Engineering Inc
Sun Valley, CA 818-252-7788
West Hawk Industries
Ann Arbor, MI 800-678-1286
WGN Flag & Decorating Co
Chicago, IL 773-768-8076
World Division
Dallas, TX. 800-433-9843

Analytical Services

A&L Western Ag Lab
Modesto, CA. .209-529-4080
Accra Laboratory
Cleveland, OH 800-567-7200
Accu-Labs Research
Golden, CO 303-277-9514
Agriculture Consulting Services
New York City, NY. 347-709-7587

AgriTech
Columbus, OH 614-488-2772
Agspring
Leawood, KS. .913-333-3035
Airflow Sciences Corp
Livonia, MI 734-525-0300
Altek Co
Torrington, CT 860-482-7626
AM Test Laboratories
Kirkland, WA .425-885-1664
American Technical Services Group
Norcross, GA .800-893-1944
Analytical Labs
Boise, ID 800-574-5773
Anresco Laboratories
San Francisco, CA 800-359-0920
Avanti Polar Lipids
Alabaster, AL .800-227-0651
Barrow-Agee Laboratories Inc
Memphis, TN .901-332-1590
Barry-Wehmiller Design Group
St Louis, MO. .314-862-8000
BCN Research Laboratories
Rockford, TN .800-236-0505
BluMetric Environmental Inc.
Ottawa, ON 613-839-3053
Brown & Caldwell
Walnut Creek, CA 800-727-2224
Celsis Laboratory Group
Chicago, IL 800-222-8260
CERT ID LC
Fairfield, IA 641-209-1899
Coffee Enterprises
Burlington, VT 800-375-3398
Covance Inc.
Princeton, NJ. .888-268-2623
CXR Co
Warsaw, IN 800-817-5763
Deibel Laboratories Inc
Madison, WI 608-241-1177
DFL Laboratories
Chicago, IL 312-938-5151
ENSCO Inc
Springfield, VA 703-321-9000
Enviro-Test/Perry Laboratories
Woodridge, IL 630-324-6685
Environmental Systems
Culpeper, VA. .800-541-2116
Eurofins DQCI
St Paul, MN. 763-785-0484
Eurofins S-F Analytical Labs
New Berlin, WI. 800-300-6700
Eurofins Scientific Inc
Des Moines, IA 800-841-1110
Eurofins Scientific Inc.
Dayton, OH. 800-880-1038
Fettig Laboratories
Grand Rapids, MI 616-245-3000
Food & Agrosystems
Sunnyvale, CA 408-245-8450
Food Consulting Company
Del Mar, CA 800-793-2844
Food Safety Net Services Ltd
San Antonio, TX. 888-525-9788
Galbraith Laboratories Inc
Knoxville, TN .877-449-8797
Gaynes Labs Inc
Bridgeview, IL 708-233-6655
Global Product Development Group
Northbrook, IL 847-504-0464
Great Lakes Scientific
Stevensville, MI 269-429-1000
Hahn Laboratories
Columbia, SC .803-799-1614
Harold Wainess & Assoc
Arlington Hts, IL 847-722-8744
Healthy Dining
San Diego, CA 800-266-2049
Howlett Farms
Avon, NY 585-226-8340
Industrial Laboratories Co
Wheat Ridge, CO 800-456-5288
Ingman Laboratories
Minneapolis, MN 612-724-0121
International Approval Services
Cleveland, OH 877-235-9791
Irvine Analytical Labs
Irvine, CA 877-445-6554
ITS/ETL Testing Laboratories
Laguna Niguel, CA 949-448-4100
J Leek Assoc Inc
Edenton, NC 252-482-4456

JI Analytical Svc Inc
Modesto, CA 209-538-8111
Krueger Food Laboratories
Chelmsford, MA 978-256-1220
Lancaster Laboratories
Lancaster, PA 717-656-2300
Laucks' Testing Laboratories
Seattle, WA .206-767-5060
Lebensmittel Consulting
Fostoria, OH 419-435-2774
Libra Technical Center
Metuchen, NJ 732-321-5200
Mccrone Microscopes & Acces
Westmont, IL 630-288-7087
Medallion Laboratories
Minneapolis, MN 800-245-5615
Microbac Laboratories
Pittsburgh, PA 866-515-4668
Microbac-Wilson Devision
Wilson, NC .252-237-4175
Midwest Laboratories
Omaha, NE .402-334-7770
Milligan & Higgins
Johnstown, NY 518-762-4638
Minnesota Valley Testing Lab
New Ulm, MN. 800-782-3557
National Food Laboratories Inc
Livermore, CA 925-828-1440
Northeast Laboratory Svc
Winslow, ME. 866-591-7120
Northland Labs
Northbrook, IL 800-366-3522
Northview Laboratories
Spartanburg, SC 864-574-7728
Northwest Laboratories
Seattle, WA .206-763-6252
Nutrinfo Corporation
Watertown, MA 800-676-6686
Oklabs
Oklahoma City, OK 405-843-6832
Pearson Research Assoc
Santa Cruz, CA 831-429-9797
Phytopia Inc
Dallas, TX 888-750-9336
POS Pilot Plant Corporation
Saskatoon, SK. 800-230-2751
PSI
Oakbrook Terrace, IL 630-705-9290
Purity Laboratories
Lake Oswego, OR. 800-977-3636
QC
Southampton, PA 215-355-3900
Quest
San Clemente, CA. 949-643-1333
R.C. Keller & Associates
Barnegat, NJ 973-694-8810
Richardson Researches
South San Francisco, CA 510-653-4385
Rtech Laboratories
St Paul, MN. 800-328-9687
RTI Laboratories
Livonia, MI .734-422-5342
S & J Laboratories Inc
Portage, MI .269-324-7383
Sani-Pure Food Laboratories
Saddle Brook, NJ 201-843-2525
Sensory Spectrum
New Providence, NJ 908-376-7000
Shear/Kershman Laboratories
Chesterfield, MO 636-519-8900
Shuster Laboratories
Canton, MA 800-444-8705
Silliker, Inc
Chicago, IL .312-938-5151
Soyatech Inc
Bar Harbor, ME. 800-424-7692
Spencer Research Inc
Columbus, OH 800-488-3242
Strasburger & Siegel
Hanover, MD 888-726-3753
Suburban Laboratories Inc
Geneva, IL. .800-783-5227
TEI Analytical Svc Inc
Niles, IL 847-647-1345
The Good Food Institute
Washington, DC 866-849-4457
Total Quality Corporation
Branford, CT. 800-453-9729
Truesdail Corporation
Tustin, CA. .714-730-6239
Underwriters Laboratories Inc
Camas, WA .877-854-3577

VICAM
Milford, MA 800-338-4381
Warren Analytical Laboratory
Greeley, CO. 800-945-6669
Winston Laboratories Inc
Vernon Hills, IL 800-946-5229
Woodson-Tenent Laboratories
Des Moines, IA. 515-265-1461
Woodson-Tenent Laboratories
Memphis, TN 515-280-8378
Woodson-Tenent Laboratories
Dayton, OH. 937-236-5756
X-R-I Testing Inc
Troy, MI 800-973-4800
YottaMark
Redwood City, CA 866-768-7878

Architects

Foodservice

Barry Wehmiller Design Group
New London, NH 866-526-2585
Excel Engineering
Fond Du Lac, WI 920-926-9800

Retail

Mead & Hunt Inc
Madison, WI 888-364-7272

Canners

Chiquita Brands LLC.
Fort Lauderdale, FL 954-924-5700
Great Lakes Foods
Menominee, MI 800-800-7492
Hormel Foods Corp.
Austin, MN .507-437-5611
LA Monica Fine Foods
Millville, NJ
Poynette Distribution Center
Poynette, WI 608-635-4396
RDM International
North Hollywood, CA 818-985-7654
SOPAKCO Foods
Mullins, SC .800-276-9678
Sportsmen's Cannery & Smokehouse
Winchester Bay, OR 800-457-8048
Truitt Bros, Inc.
Salem, OR. .800-547-8712
Washington Frontier
Grandview, WA 509-469-7662
Whitlock Packaging Corp
Fort Gibson, OK 918-478-4300

Computer Software, Systems & Services

AC Label Company
Provo, UT 801-642-3500
Acromag Inc.
Wixom, MI .248-624-1541
Acumen Data Systems Inc
West Springfield, MA. 888-816-0933
Advance Technology Corp
Ramsey, NJ .201-934-7127
Advanced Micro Controls
Terryville, CT 860-585-1254
Advanced Software Designs
Chesterfield, MO 636-532-6021
Agilysys, Inc.
Alpharetta, GA 800-241-8768
Airflow Sciences Corp
Livonia, MI .734-525-0300
AL Systems
Rockaway, NJ 888-960-8324
Allpax Products
Covington, LA 888-893-9277
American Forms & Labels
Boise, ID. 800-388-3554
American Technical Services Group
Norcross, GA 800-893-1944
AMETEK National Controls Corp
West Chicago, IL 800-323-5293
Amplexus Corporation
Novato, CA. 800-423-8268
Ann Arbor Computer
Farmington Hills, MI 800-526-9322
Apigent Solutions
Oklahoma City, OK 800-664-8228

Asap Automation
Addison, IL. 800-409-0383
ASI Data Myte
Plymouth, MN. 800-455-4359
ASI/Restaurant Manager
Silver Spring, MD. 800-356-6037
Assembly Technology & Test
Livonia, MI .734-522-1900
At-Your-Svc Software Inc
Bronxville, NY 888-325-6937
Auto Quotes
Jacksonville, FL 904-384-2279
Automation Group
Houston, TX 713-860-5200
Batchmasters Software
Laguna Hills, CA 949-583-1646
Berg Co
Monona, WI 608-221-4281
Broadcom Inc.
San Jose, CA
BSI Instruments
Aliquippa, PA 800-274-9851
Buypass Corporation
Atlanta, GA .770-953-2664
Cache Box
Arlington, VA 800-603-4834
Camstar Systems
San Jose, CA. 800-237-2841
Catalyst International
Lemont, IL .800-236-4600
CaterMate
Ithaca, NY .800-486-2283
CBORD Group Inc
Ithaca, NY. .607-257-2410
CBORD Group Inc
Ithaca, NY. .800-982-4643
CCR Data Systems
Concord, NH 800-633-6500
Coconut Code
Lighthouse Point, FL 954-786-0252
Comalex
Van Buren, AR 866-343-2594
Command Line Corporation
Edison, NJ. .732-738-6500
Compris Technologies
Duluth, GA .800-615-3301
Computer Aid Inc
Allentown, PA. 800-327-4243
Computer Aided Marketing
Chapel Hill, NC 919-401-0996
Computer Communications Specialists
Marietta, GA. 888-231-4227
Computrition
Chatsworth, CA 800-222-4488
Comstar Printing Solutions
Streetsboro, OH 330-528-2800
Comus Restaurant Systems
Frederick, MD. 301-698-6208
Control Module
Enfield, CT. 800-722-6654
Crunch Time Information Systems
Boston, MA. 857-202-3000
Custom Business Solutions
Irvine, CA. .800-551-7674
Cycle Computer Consultants
Hicksville, NY 516-733-1892
Cyplex
Los Angeles, CA
Data Management
San Angelo, TX 800-749-8463
Data Specialists
Elkhorn, WI. 800-211-1545
Decartes Systems Group
Waterloo, ON 519-746-8110
Digital Dining
Springfield, VA 703-912-3000
Digital Dynamics Inc
Scotts Valley, CA 800-765-1288
Digital Image & Sound Corporation
Rochester, NY 585-381-0410
Domino Amjet Inc
Gurnee, IL .800-444-4512
DSA Software
Foxboro, MA 508-543-0400
E2M
Duluth, GA .800-622-4326
Eatec Corporation
Emeryville, CA. 877-374-4783
EBS
Houston, TX 713-939-1000
Ecklund-Harrison Technologies
Fort Myers, FL 239-936-6032

Economic Sciences Corp
Berkeley, CA.....510-841-6869
Edgerton Corporation
Strongsville, OH.....440-268-0000
Efficient Frontiers
Livermore, CA.....888-433-4725
Electro Cam Corp
Roscoe, IL.....800-228-5487
Electrol Specialties Co
South Beloit, IL.....815-389-2291
Elo Touch Systems
Menlo Park, CA.....800-557-1458
Elreha Controls Corporation
St Petersburg, FL.....727-327-6236
Emtrol
York, PA.....800-634-4927
EPD Technology Corporation
Elmsford, NY.....800-892-8926
ERC Parts Inc
Kennesaw, GA.....800-241-6880
Esha Research
Salem, OR.....800-659-3742
ExecuChef Software
San Anselmo, CA.....415-488-9600
First DataBank
San Bruno, CA.....800-633-3453
Fred D Pfening Co
Columbus, OH.....614-294-5361
GCA
Huntington Beach, CA.....714-379-4911
Genesis Total Solutions Inc
Fultondale, AL.....205-631-5334
Gerber Innovations
Tolland, CT.....800-331-5797
Graphic Technology
New Century, KS.....800-767-9920
Great Plains Software
Fargo, ND.....800-456-0025
GTCO CalComp
Scottsdale, AZ.....800-856-0732
Hampton-Tilley Associates
Chesterfield, MO.....813-418-3340
Heart Smart International
Scottsdale, AZ.....800-762-7819
Helm Software
Phoenix, AZ.....602-522-2999
Hope Industrial Systems
Roswell, GA.....877-762-9790
Horizon Software International
Duluth, GA.....800-741-7100
HSI
Scottsdale, AZ.....480-596-5456
Hudson Control Group Inc
Springfield, NJ.....973-376-8265
Iconics Inc
Foxboro, MA.....800-946-9679
ID Images
Brunswick, OH.....866-516-7300
Illinois Wholesale Cash Rgstr
Elgin, IL.....800-544-5493
IMAS Corporation
St. Charles, IL.....847-274-9383
Industrious Software Solutions
Inglewood, CA.....800-351-4225
InFood Corporation
Evanston, IL.....773-338-8485
Infopro Inc
Aurora, IL.....630-978-9231
Infor
New York, NY.....866-244-5479
Information Access
Cleveland, OH.....216-328-0100
Insignia Systems Inc
Minneapolis, MN.....800-874-4648
Integrated Distribution
Omaha, NE.....937-445-1936
Integrated Restaurant Software/RMS Touch
Timonium, MD.....201-461-9096
Intelligent Controls
Saco, ME.....800-872-3455
Interactive Sales Solutions
Coppell, TX.....800-352-9575
Interlake Mecalux
Chicago, IL.....708-344-9999
InterSect Business Systems Inc
Kelowna, BC.....250-860-0829
Invictus Systems Corporation
Falls Church, VA
ITC Systems
Toronto, ON.....877-482-8326
Junction Solutions
Englewood, CO.....877-502-6355

Kaye Instruments
N Billerica, MA.....800-343-4624
Kenray Associates
Greenville, IN.....812-923-9884
Kochman Consultants LTD
Morton Grove, IL.....847-470-1195
Konica Minolta Corp
Ramsey, NJ.....888-473-3637
Lablynx Inc
Atlanta, GA.....800-585-5969
LDJ Electronics
Troy, MI.....248-528-2202
Least Cost Formulations LTD
Virginia Beach, VA.....757-467-0954
Lighthouse for the Blindin New Orleans
New Orleans, LA.....504-899-4501
LIS Warehouse Systems
Charlotte, NC.....888-547-9670
Logility Transportation Group
Des Plaines, IL.....847-699-6620
Long Range Systems
Addison, TX.....800-577-8101
LPI Information Systems
Overland Park, KS.....888-729-2020
Magnetic Technologies LTD
Oxford, MA.....508-987-3303
Management Tech of America
Phoenix, AZ.....602-381-5800
MAPS Software
Columbus, MS.....662-328-6110
Menulink
Huntington Beach, CA.....714-934-6368
Microtouch Systems Inc
Methuen, MA.....978-659-9000
Microworks Pos Solutions Inc
Webster, NY.....800-787-2068
Moisture Register Products
Rancho Cucamonga, CA.....800-966-4788
Montalbano Development Inc
Ronkonkoma, NY.....800-739-9152
Murata Automated Systems
Charlotte, NC.....800-428-8469
National Computer Corporation
Greenville, SC.....866-944-5164
Newmarket Corp
Portsmouth, NH.....888-829-8871
Norback Ley & Assoc
Middleton, WI.....608-233-3814
Northwest Analytical Inc
Portland, OR.....888-692-7638
Novax Group/Point of Sales
New York, NY.....212-684-1244
Nutrition & Food Associates
Plymouth, MN.....763-550-9475
OMRON Systems LLC
Schaumburg, IL.....224-520-7650
Oracle Hospitality
Redwood, CA.....800-392-2999
Order-Matic Corporation
Oklahoma City, OK.....800-767-6733
Parity Corp
Bothell, WA.....425-487-0997
Party Perfect Catering
Houston, TX.....800-522-5440
PC/Poll Systems
Dubuque, IA.....800-670-1736
PEAK Technologies, Inc.
Columbia, MD.....800-926-9212
Preston Scientific
Anaheim, CA.....714-632-3700
Prime ProData
North Canton, OH.....877-497-2578
Prism Visual Software Inc
Port Washington, NY.....516-944-5920
Progressive Software
Charlotte, NC.....704-295-7000
ProVisions Software
Smithfield, RI.....800-422-4782
Qualtrax Inc
Christiansburg, VA.....800-277-3077
Ramco Systems Corp
Lawrence Twp, NJ.....800-472-6461
RDS of Florida
Fort Lauderdale, FL.....305-994-7756
Redi-Print
West Babylon, NY.....631-491-6373
Reflex International
Norcross, GA.....800-642-7640
Remote Equipment Systems
Alpharetta, GA.....800-803-9488
Retail Automations Products
New York, NY.....800-237-9144

Retalix
Miamisburg, OH.....877-794-7237
Rice Lake Weighing Systems
Rice Lake, WI.....800-472-6703
Robocom Systems Intl
Farmingdale, NY.....631-753-2180
Rockland Technology
Lewisville, TX.....972-221-6190
ROI Software, LLC
Knoxville, TN.....865-522-2211
Ross Computer Systems
Knoxville, TN.....865-690-3008
Round Noon Software
Dallas, TX.....972-789-5191
RTI Inc
Marietta, GA.....800-937-1290
Sable Technology Solution
St Paul, MN.....800-722-5390
Sales Partner System
Ormond Beach, FL.....800-777-2924
SalesData Software
San Jose, CA.....408-281-5811
Sanderson Computers
Worthington, OH.....614-781-2525
SBA Software
Doral, FL.....800-222-8324
SBS of Financial Industries
Washington, NJ.....908-689-5520
Scan Corporation
Brandon, FL.....800-881-7226
Schneider Electric
Foxboro, MA.....781-534-7535
Schoneman Inc
Ashtabula, OH.....800-255-4439
Schreck Software
Woodbury, MN.....651-731-6822
SEI Consultants
Slidell, LA.....800-738-1000
Shared Data Systems
Charlotte, NC.....800-622-2140
SICOM Systems
Doylestown, PA.....800-547-4266
Siemens Measurement Systems
Pittsford, NY.....800-568-7721
Simply Products
Kunkletown, PA.....610-681-6894
Squirrel Systems
Vancouver, BC.....800-388-6824
Sterling Scale Co
Southfield, MI.....800-331-9931
Stratix Corp
Peachtree Cor, GA.....800-883-8300
Success Systems
Stamford, GA.....800-653-3345
Sweetware
Oakland, CA.....800-526-7900
Swisslog Logistics Inc
Newport News, VA.....800-777-6862
SYSPRO USA
Costa Mesa, CA.....800-369-8649
System Concepts Inc
Scottsdale, AZ.....800-553-2438
Systems Comtrex
Moorestown, NJ.....800-220-2669
Tablecheck Technologies, Inc
Austin, TX.....800-522-1347
Tallygenicom
Irvine, CA.....800-665-6210
Tangible Vision
Franklin, TN.....800-763-8634
Tek Visions
Temecula, CA.....800-466-8005
Televend
Baltimore, MD.....410-532-7818
Texture Technologies Corporation
Scarsdale, NY.....914-472-0531
Tharo Systems Inc
Brunswick, OH.....800-878-6833
Tibersoft
Westborough, MA.....888-888-1969
Tinadre Inc
Tampa, FL.....813-866-0333
TMT Software Company
Mayfield Heights, OH.....800-401-6682
Touch Menus
Bellevue, WA.....800-688-6368
Tricor Systems Inc
Elgin, IL.....800-575-0161
Tricore AEA
Mt Pleasant, WI.....262-880-3630
Trola Industries Inc
York, PA.....717-848-3700

Unisoft Systems Associates
  Dublin, OH 800-448-1574
Universal Dynamics Technologies
  Richmond, BC 888-912-7246
Vande Berg SCALES/Vbs Inc
  Sioux Center, IA 712-722-1181
Venture Measurement Co LLC
  Spartanburg, SC 800-426-9010
Versatile Mobile Systems
  Lynnwood, WA 800-262-1633
Vertex Interactive
  Clifton, NJ 973-777-3500
W&H Systems
  Carlstadt, NJ 201-933-9849
Wallace Computer Services
  Chicago, IL 888-925-8324
Weber Packaging Solutions Inc
  Arlington Heights, IL 800-843-4242
X-Rite Inc
  Grand Rapids, MI 888-800-9580
Xcel Tower Controls
  Gilbertsville, NY 800-288-7362
Zebra Technologies Corporation
  Lincolnshire, IL 866-230-9494

Software

Routing & Scheduling for Food Industry

Formulator Software, LLC
  Clinton, NJ 908-735-2248
Prism Visual Software Inc
  Port Washington, NY 516-944-5920

Construction

Facility Design

Amco Mechanical
  Spring, TX...........................281-353-2171
BE&K Building Group
  Greenville, SC......................864-250-5000
Boldt Co
  Appleton, WI 920-739-6321
Dennis Engineering Group
  Springfield, MA 413-787-1785
Dennsi Group
  Springfield, MA 413-737-1353
Klinger Constructors LLC
  Albuquerque, NM 505-822-9990
Shambaugh & Son
  Fort Wayne, IN 260-487-7777
Tippmann Group
  Fort Wayne, IN 260-490-3000

Management

BE&K Building Group
  Greenville, SC......................864-250-5000
Dennis Engineering Group
  Springfield, MA 413-787-1785
Dennsi Group
  Springfield, MA 413-737-1353
Facility Group
  Smyrna, GA 770-437-2700
Stellar
  Jacksonville, FL 800-488-2900

Metal Fabricators

A & B Process Systems Corp
  Stratford, WI........................888-258-2789
A J Antunes & Co
  Carol Stream, IL 800-253-2991
A Legacy Food Svc
  Santa Fe Springs, CA 800-848-4440
A-Z Factory Supply
  Schiller Park, IL 800-323-4511
Abalon Precision Manufacturing Corporation
  Bronx, NY............................800-888-2225
ABC Letter Art
  Los Angeles, CA....................888-261-5367
ABCO Industries Limited
  Lunenburg, NS 866-634-8821
Ace Fabrication
  Mobile, AL 251-478-0401
Ace Stamp & Engraving
  Lakewood, WA 253-582-3322
Acme International
  Maplewood, NJ.....................973-416-0400
ACS Industries, Inc.
  Lincoln, RI 866-783-4838

Adam Electric Signs
  Massillon, OH 888-886-9911
Adapto Storage Products
  Hialeah, FL..........................305-499-4800
Advance Fittings Corp
  Elkhorn, WI. 262-723-6699
Advance Tabco
  Edgewood, NY 800-645-3166
Advanced Uniflo Technologies
  Wichita, KS 800-688-0400
Aero Manufacturing Co
  Clifton, NJ. 800-631-8378
AFGO Mechanical Svc Inc
  Astoria, NY...........................800-438-2346
All American Container
  Miami, FL.............................305-887-0797
All Power Inc
  Sioux City, IA 712-258-0681
All Southern Fabricators
  Clearwater, FL......................800-878-2732
All Spun Metal Products
  Des Plaines, IL 847-824-4117
All State Fabricators Corporation
  Tampa, FL............................800-322-9925
All-Clad METALCRAFTERS LLC
  Canonsburg, PA 800-255-2523
Allegheny Bradford Corp
  Bradford, PA. 800-542-0650
Alliance Products LLC
  Murfreesboro, TN...................800-522-3973
Allied Engineering
  North Vancouver, BC 877-929-1214
Alloy Products Corp
  Waukesha, WI. 800-236-6603
Allstrong Restaurant Eqpt Inc
  South El Monte, CA 800-933-8913
ALP Lighting & Ceiling Products
  Pennsauken, NJ 800-633-7732
ALPI Food Preparation Equipment
  Bolton, ON 800-928-2574
Alumaworks
  Sunny Isle Beach, FL 800-277-7267
Amco Metals Indl
  City of Industry, CA 626-855-2550
American Art Stamp
  Gardena, CA 310-965-9004
American Lifts
  Guthrie, OK. 877-360-6777
American Manufacturing-Engrng
  Cleveland, OH 800-822-9402
American Metal Door Company
  Richmond, IN 800-428-2737
American Production Co Inc
  Redwood City, CA 650-368-5334
Ametco Manufacturing Corp
  Willoughby, OH 800-321-7042
Amscor Inc
  West Babylon, NY 800-825-9800
Amtekco
  Columbus, OH 800-336-4677
Anderson-Crane Company
  Minneapolis, MN 800-314-2747
Andgar Corp
  Ferndale, WA 360-366-9900
Apache Stainless Equipment
  Beaver Dam, WI 800-444-0398
APW Wyott Food Service Equipment Company
  Cheyenne, WY 800-527-2100
ARC Specialties
  Valencia, CA 661-775-8500
Archer Wire Intl Corp
  Chicago, IL 708-563-1700
Architectural Sheet Metals LLC
  Cleveland, OH 216-361-9952
Arizona Store Equipment
  Phoenix, AZ 800-624-8395
Arkfeld Mfg & Distributing Co
  Norfolk, NE. 800-533-0676
Armbrust Paper Tubes Inc
  Chicago, IL 773-586-3232
ATD-American Co
  Wyncote, PA 800-523-2300
Atlas Tag & Label Inc
  Neenah, WI. 800-558-6418
Audrey Signs
  New York, NY 212-769-4992
Auger Fab
  Exton, PA 800-334-1529
Automatic Specialties Inc
  Marlborough, MA 800-445-2370
B C Holland Inc
  Dousman, WI 262-965-2939

Baldewein Company
  Lake Forrest, IL 800-424-5544
Ball Corp
  Broomfield, CO 303-469-3131
Ballymore Company
  West Chester, PA. 610-696-3250
Baltimore Sign Company
  Arnold, MD...........................410-276-1500
Barker Wire
  Keosauqua, IA 319-293-3176
Barn Furniture Mart
  Van Nuys, CA 888-302-2276
Bayhead Products Corp.
  Dover, NH. 800-229-4323
Beayl Weiner/Pak
  Pacific Palisades, CA 310-454-1354
Behlen Manufacturing Co.
  Columbus, NE. 402-564-3111
Bennett Manufacturing Company
  Alden, NY. 800-345-2142
Berloc Manufacturing & Sign Company
  Sun Valley, CA 818-503-9823
Berlon Industries
  Hustisford, WI 800-899-3580
Berndorf Belt Technology USA
  Gilberts, IL 800-393-8450
Bertels Can Company
  Belcamp, MD 410-272-0090
BG Industries
  Lemont, IL 800-800-5761
BMH
  City of Industry, CA 909-349-2530
Boehringer Mfg. Co. Inc.
  Felton, CA. 800-630-8665
Bohn & Dawson
  St Louis, MO. 800-225-5011
Borroughs Corp
  Kalamazoo, MI 800-748-0227
Bowers Process Equipment
  Stratford, ON. 800-567-3223
Bradford A Ducon Company
  Pewaukee, WI. 800-789-1718
Bremer Manufacturing Co Inc
  Elkhart Lake, WI. 920-894-2944
Brenner Tank LLC
  Fond Du Lac, WI. 800-558-9750
Brute Fabricators
  Castroville, TX 800-777-2788
Bulman Products Inc
  Grand Rapids, MI 616-363-4416
Burgess Mfg. - Oklahoma
  Guthrie, OK. 800-804-1913
Burrows Paper Corp
  Little Falls, NY 800-272-7122
C E Rogers Co
  Mora, MN 800-279-8081
C Nelson Mfg Co
  Oak Harbor, OH 800-922-7339
C R Mfg
  Waverly, NE 877-789-5844
C&H Store Equipment Company
  Los Angeles, CA.....................800-648-4979
Caddy Corporation of America
  Bridgeport, NJ 856-467-4222
California Caster & Handtruck
  San Francisco, CA 800-950-8750
Canton Sign Co
  Canton, OH. 330-456-7151
Caraustar Industries, Inc.
  Archdale, NC 800-223-1373
Carbis Inc
  Florence, SC 800-948-7750
Carmun International
  San Antonio, TX 800-531-7907
Carrier Vibrating Equip Inc
  Louisville, KY 502-969-3171
Carter-Hoffmann LLC
  Mundelein, IL 800-323-9793
Carton Closing Company
  Butler, PA. 724-287-7759
Carts Food Equipment
  Brooklyn, NY 718-788-5540
Central Fabricators Inc
  Cincinnati, OH 800-909-8265
Charlton & Hill
  Lethbridge, AB 403-328-3388
Chef Specialties
  Smethport, PA 800-440-2433
Chemdet Inc
  Sebastian, FL 800-645-1510
Cherry's Industrial Eqpt Corp
  Elk Grove Vlg, IL. 800-350-0011

Chester-Jensen Co., Inc.
Chester, PA 800-685-3750
Chipmaker Tooling Supply
Whittier, CA 800-659-5840
Claridge Products & Equipment
Harrison, AR
Classico Seating
Peru, IN 800-968-6655
Clawson Container Company
Clarkston, MI 800-325-8700
Clayton & Lambert Manufacturing
Buckner, KY 800-626-5819
Cleveland Metal Stamping Company
Berea, OH 440-234-0010
Cleveland Wire Cloth & Mfg Co
Cleveland, OH 800-321-3234
Cobb & Zimmer
Detroit, MI 313-923-0350
Columbian TecTank
Parsons, KS 800-421-2788
Commercial Kitchen Co
Los Angeles, CA 323-732-2291
Complex Steel & Wire Corp
Wayne, MI 734-326-1600
Consolidated Can Co
Paramount, CA 888-793-2199
Consolidated Commercial Controls
Winsted, CT 800-227-1511
Container Supply Co
Garden Grove, CA 562-594-0937
Containment Technology
St Gabriel, LA 800-388-2467
Continental-Fremont
Tiffin, OH 419-448-4045
Conveyor Components Co
Croswell, MI 800-552-3337
Corby Hall
Randolph, NJ 973-366-8300
Cotter Brothers Corp
Danvers, MA 978-777-5001
COW Industries Inc
Columbus, OH 800-542-9353
Cramer Inc
Kansas City, MO 800-366-6700
CRC Inc
Council Bluffs, IA 712-323-9477
Creative Mobile Systems Inc
Manchester, CT 800-646-8364
Crown Closures Machinery
Lancaster, OH 740-681-6593
Crown Cork & Seal Co Inc
Philadelphia, PA 215-698-5100
Crown Custom Metal Spinning
Concord, ON 800-750-1924
Crown Manufacturing Corporation
Waterford, CT 860-442-4325
Crown Metal Mfg Co
Rancho Cucamonga, CA 909-291-8585
Crown Verity
Brantford, ON 888-505-7240
Cucamonga Sign Shop LLC
Rancho Cucamonga, CA 909-945-5888
Custom Diamond Intl.
Laval, QC 800-326-5926
Custom Fabricating & Repair
Marshfield, WI 800-236-8773
D & W Fine Pack
Lake Zurich, IL 800-323-0422
D A Berther Inc
Milwaukee, WI 877-357-9622
D&D Sign Company
Wichita Falls, TX 940-692-4643
D. Picking & Company
Bucyrus, OH 419-562-6891
Damascus/Bishop Tube Company
Greenville, PA 724-646-1500
Dansk International Designs
Bristol, PA 914-697-6400
Davron Technologies Inc
Chattanooga, TN 423-870-1888
Dayco
Clearwater, FL 727-573-9330
DCI, Inc.
St Cloud, MN 320-252-8200
Den Mar Corp
North Dartmouth, MA 508-999-3295
Despro Manufacturing
Cedar Grove, NJ 800-292-9906
Dimension Graphics Inc
Grand Rapids, MI 855-476-1281
Dinosaur Plastics
Houston, TX 713-923-2278

Doering Co
Clear Lake, MN 320-743-2276
Doran Scales Inc
Batavia, IL 800-365-0084
Dormont Manufacturing Co
Export, PA 800-367-6668
Dover Parkersburg
Follansbee, WV
Dreaco Products
Elyria, OH 800-368-3267
Dubuque Steel Products Co
Dubuque, IA 563-556-6288
Duke Manufacturing Co
St Louis, MO 800-735-3853
Duluth Sheet Metal
Duluth, MN 218-722-2613
Durham Manufacturing Co
Durham, CT 800-243-3744
E C Shaw Co
Cincinnati, OH 866-532-7429
Eagle Foodservice   Equipment
Clayton, DE 800-441-8440
Eagle Group
Clayton, DE 800-441-8440
Eastern Tabletop Mfg
Brooklyn, NY 888-422-4142
Easyup Storage Systems
Tukwila, WA 800-426-9234
EB Metal Industries
Whitehall, NY 518-499-1222
Econofrost Night Covers
Shawnigan Lake, BC 800-519-1222
Economy Paper & Restaurant Co
Clifton, NJ 973-279-5500
Eldorado Miranda Manufacturing Company
Largo, FL 800-330-0708
Ellett Industries
Port Coquitlam, BC 604-941-8211
Emc Solutions
Celina, OH 419-586-2388
Emedco
Williamsville, NY 877-765-8386
Enerfab Inc.
Cincinnati, OH 513-641-0500
Engineered Products Group
Madison, WI 800-626-3111
English Manufacturing Inc
Rancho Cordova, CA 800-651-2711
Enterprise Products
Bell Gardens, CA 562-928-1918
Erwin Food Service Equipment
Fort Worth, TX 817-535-0021
Etube & Wire
Shrewsbury, PA 800-618-4720
Eugene Welding Company
Marysville, MI 810-364-7421
Eurodib
Champlain, NY 888-956-6866
Ex-Cell KAISER LLC
Franklin Park, IL 847-451-0451
F & A Fabricating Inc
Battle Creek, MI 269-965-8371
F.P. Smith Wire Cloth Company
Northlake, IL 800-323-6842
Fabricating & Welding Corp
Chicago, IL 773-928-2050
Fabwright Inc
Garden Grove, CA 800-854-6464
Falcon Fabricators Inc
Nashville, TN 615-832-0027
Fata Automation
Sterling Heights, MI 586-323-9400
Faubion Central States Tank Company
Shawnee Mission, KS 800-450-8265
Federal Heath Sign Co LLC
Oceanside, CA 800-527-9495
FEI Inc
Mansfield, TX 800-346-5908
Feldmeier Equipment Inc
Syracuse, NY 315-454-8608
Ferrer Corporation
San Juan, PR 787-761-5151
Fine Woods Manufacturing
Phoenix, AZ 800-279-2871
Finn & Son's Metal Spinning Specialists
South Lebanon, OH 513-494-2898
Fisher Manufacturing Company
Tulare, CA 800-421-6162
Fishmore
Melbourne, FL 321-723-4751
Fiskars Brands Inc.
Baldwinsville, NY 315-635-9911

Fixtur World
Cookeville, TN 800-634-9887
Flame Gard
Lakewood, NJ 800-526-3694
Flat Plate Inc
York, PA 888-854-2500
Folding Guard Co
Chicago, IL 800-622-2214
Food Warming Equipment Co
Crystal Lake, IL 800-222-4393
Forrest Engraving Company
New Rochelle, NY 914-632-9892
Forster & Son
Ada, OK 580-332-6021
Fountainhead
Bensalem, PA 800-326-8998
Frazier Industrial Co
Long Valley, NJ 800-859-1342
Frazier Signs
Decatur, IL 217-429-2349
FRC Environmental
Gainesville, GA 770-534-3681
Friskem Infinetics
Wilmington, DE 302-658-2471
Fuller Box Co
North Attleboro, MA 508-695-2525
G A Systems Inc
Huntington Beach, CA 714-848-7529
Gasser Chair Co Inc
Youngstown, OH 800-323-2234
Geerpres Inc
Muskegon, MI 231-773-3211
General Industries Inc
Goldsboro, NC 888-735-2882
Gillis Associated Industries
Prospect Heights, IL 847-541-6500
Glaro Inc
Hauppauge, NY 631-234-1717
Glo-Quartz Electric Heater
Mentor, OH 800-321-3574
GM Nameplate
Seattle, WA 800-366-7668
Goergen-Mackwirth Co Inc
Buffalo, NY 800-728-4446
Gorbel Inc
Victor, NY 585-924-6262
Graff Tank Erection
Harrisville, PA 814-385-6671
Great Lakes Brush
Centralia, MO 573-682-2128
Green Brothers
Barrington, RI 401-245-9043
Green Metal Fabricating
West Sacramento, CA 916-371-2951
Greif Inc
Delaware, OH 740-549-6000
Gribble Stamp & Stencil Co
Houston, TX 713-228-5358
Griffin Products
Wills Point, TX 800-379-9709
H & H Metal Fabrication Inc
Belden, MS 662-489-4626
Hallock Fabricating Corp
Riverhead, NY 631-727-2441
Halton Company
Scottsville, KY 800-442-5866
Hamilton Kettles
Weirton, WV 800-535-1882
Hank Rivera Associates
Dearborn, MI 313-581-8300
Hanset Stainless Inc
Portland, OR 800-360-7030
Hantover Inc
Kansas City, MO 800-821-7849
Hardware Components Inc
New Matamoras, OH 740-865-2424
Hercules Food Equipment
Weston, ON 416-742-9673
Hewitt Manufacturing Co
Waldron, IN 765-525-9829
Hillside Metal Ware Company
Union, NJ 908-964-3080
Hines III
Jacksonville, FL 904-398-5110
HMG Worldwide In-Store Marketing
New York, NY 212-736-2300
Hodge Manufacturing Company
Springfield, MA 800-262-4634
Hodges
Vienna, IL 800-444-0011
Holmco Container Manufacturing, LTD
Baltic, OH 330-897-4503

Holsman Sign Svc
Cleveland, OH 216-761-4433
Hot Food Boxes
Mooresville, IN 800-733-8073
Houston Wire Works, Inc.
South Houston, TX 800-468-9477
Howard Fabrication
City of Industry, CA 626-961-0114
Howes S Co Inc
Silver Creek, NY 888-255-2611
Hurri-Kleen Corporation
Birmingham, AL 800-455-8265
Ideal of America/Valley Rio Enterprise
Atlanta, GA 770-352-0210
Ideal Wire Works
Alhambra, CA 626-282-0886
Illinois Range Company
Schiller Park, IL 800-535-7041
IMC Teddy Food Service Equipment
Amityville, NY 800-221-5644
IMO Foods
Yarmouth, NS 902-742-3519
Imperial Schrade Corporation
Ellenville, NY 212-210-8600
Independent Can Co
Belcamp, MD 410-272-0090
Indiana Wire Company
Fremont, IN 877-786-6883
Industrial Air Conditioning Systems
Chicago, IL 773-486-4236
Industries Inc Kiefer
Random Lake, WI 920-994-2332
Institutional Equipment Inc
Bolingbrook, IL 630-771-0990
Intrex
Bethel, CT 203-792-7400
Irby
Rocky Mount, NC 252-442-0154
J L Clark Corp
Rockford, IL 815-962-8861
J.V. Reed & Company
Louisville, KY 877-258-7333
Jantec
Traverse City, MI 800-992-3303
Jarke Corporation
Prospect Hts, IL 800-722-5255
Jay-Bee Manufacturing Inc
Tyler, TX 800-445-0610
JEM Wire Products
Middletown, CT 860-347-0447
Jesco Industries
Litchfield, MI 800-455-0019
JH Display & Fixture
Greenwood, IN 317-888-0631
John Boos & Co
Effingham, IL 888-431-2667
Johnson-Rose Corporation
Lockport, NY 800-456-2055
Joyce Engraving Co Inc
Dallas, TX 214-638-1262
Jupiter Mills Corporation
Roslyn, NY 800-853-5121
JW Leser Company
Los Angeles, CA 323-731-4173
K & I Creative Plastics & Wood
Jacksonville, FL 904-387-0438
K C Booth Co
N Kansas City, MO 800-866-5226
Kaines West Michigan Co
Ludington, MI 231-845-1281
Kamflex Corp
Chicago, IL 800-323-2440
Karyall Telday Inc
Cleveland, OH 216-281-4063
Kason Central
Columbus, OH 614-885-1992
KEMCO
Wareham, MA 800-231-5955
Key Material Handling Inc
Simi Valley, CA 800-539-7225
Keystone Adjustable Cap Co Inc
Pennsauken, NJ 800-663-5439
King Sign Company
Akron, OH 330-762-7421
Kitchen Equipment Fabricating
Houston, TX 713-747-3611
Kitcor Corp
Sun Valley, CA 818-767-4800
Klinger Constructors LLC
Albuquerque, NM 505-822-9990
Kloppenberg & Co
Englewood, CO 800-346-3246

Koehler-Gibson Marking
Buffalo, NY 800-875-1562
Kofab
Algona, IA 515-295-7265
Kosempel Manufacturing Company
Philadelphia, PA 800-733-7122
L&H Wood Manufacturing Company
Farmington, MI 248-474-9000
L&L Engraving Company
Gilford, NH 888-524-3032
L&S Products
Coldwater, MI 517-279-9526
L.C. Thompson Company
Kenosha, WI 800-558-4018
La Crosse
Onalaska, WI 800-345-0018
Laidig Inc
Mishawaka, IN 574-256-0204
Lake Shore Industries Inc
Erie, PA 800-458-0463
Lakeside Manufacturing Inc
Milwaukee, WI 888-558-8565
Lakeside-Aris Manufacturing
Milwaukee, WI 800-558-8565
Lambert Material Handling
Syracuse, NY 800-253-5103
Lambertson Industries Inc
Sparks, NV 800-548-3324
Lancaster Colony Corporation
Westerville, OH 614-224-7141
Langer Manufacturing Company
Cedar Rapids, IA 800-728-6445
Lask Seating Company
Chicago, IL 888-573-2846
Laughlin Sales Corp
Fort Worth, TX 817-625-7756
Lavi Industries
Valencia, CA 800-624-6225
Lawrence Metal Products Inc
Bay Shore, NY 800-441-0019
Lazy Man Inc
Belvidere, NJ 800-475-1950
Le Smoker
Salisbury, MD 410-677-3233
Leeds Conveyor Manufacturer Company
Guilford, CT 800-724-1088
Leggett & Platt Storage
Vernon Hills, IL 847-816-6246
Legible Signs
Loves Park, IL 800-435-4177
License Ad Plate Co
Cleveland, OH 216-265-4200
Lincoln Foodservice
Cleveland, OH 800-374-3004
Linvar
Hartford, CT 800-282-5288
Little Rock Crate & Basket Co
Little Rock, AR 800-223-7823
Lloyd Disher Company
Decatur, IL 217-429-0593
Load King Mfg
Jacksonville, FL 800-531-4975
Lodge Manufacturing Company
South Pittsburg, TN 423-837-5919
Lodging By Charter
Liberty, NC 800-327-2548
Lorenz Couplings
Cobourg, ON 800-263-7782
Lorenzen's Cookie Cutters
Wantagh, NY 516-781-7116
Low Temp Industries Inc
Jonesboro, GA 678-674-1317
Loyal Manufacturing
Indianapolis, IN 317-359-3185
LPI Imports
Chicago, IL 877-389-6563
Lyco Wausau
Wausau, WI 715-845-7867
Lyon LLC
Montgomery, IL 630-892-8941
M & E Mfg Co Inc
Kingston, NY 845-331-2110
M O Industries Inc
Whippany, NJ 973-386-9228
Madsen Wire Products Inc
Orland, IN 260-829-6561
Magline Inc
Standish, MI 800-624-5463
Magsys Inc
Milwaukee, WI 414-543-2177
Malco Manufacturing Co
Los Angeles, CA 866-477-7267

Mar-Con Wire Belt
Richmond, BC 877-962-7266
Market Sign Systems
Portland, ME 800-421-1799
Marlin Steel Wire Products
Baltimore, MD 877-762-7546
Marlo Manufacturing
Boonton, NJ 800-222-0450
Marston Manufacturing
Cleveland, OH 216-587-3400
Martin/Baron
Irwindale, CA 626-960-5153
Material Storage Systems
Gadsden, AL 877-543-2467
Mcintyre Metals Inc
Thomasville, NC 800-334-0807
MCM Fixture Co
Hazel Park, MI 248-547-9280
Memphis Delta Tent & Awning
Memphis, TN 901-522-1238
Metal
Columbia, SC 803-776-9252
Metal Container Corporation
St Louis, MO 314-957-9500
Metal Equipment Company
Cleveland, OH 800-700-6326
Metal Kitchen Fabricators Inc
Houston, TX 713-683-8375
Metal Master Sales Corp
Glendale Heights, IL 800-488-8729
Metal Masters Northwest
Lynnwood, WA 425-775-4481
Metcraft
Grandview, MO 800-444-9624
Metko Inc
New Holstein, WI 920-898-4221
Mettler-Toledo, LLC
Columbus, OH 800-638-8537
Metz Premiums
New York, NY 212-315-4660
Micelli Chocolate Mold Company
West Babylon, NY 631-752-2888
Micro Wire Products Inc
Brockton, MA 508-584-0200
Micropure Filtration Inc
Mound, MN 800-654-7873
Mid-State Metal Casting & Mfg
Fresno, CA 559-445-1974
Mid-States Mfg & Engr Co Inc
Milton, IA 800-346-1792
Mid-West Wire Products
Ferndale, MI 800-989-9881
Midwest Metalcraft & Equipment
Windsor, MO 800-647-3167
Midwest Stainless
Menomonie, WI 715-235-5472
Midwest Wire Products LLC
Sturgeon Bay, WI 800-445-0225
MLS Signs Inc
Chesterfield, MI 586-948-0200
Modern Brewing & Design
Santa Rosa, CA 707-542-6620
Modern Metalcraft
Midland, MI 800-948-3182
Modern Metals Industries
El Segundo, CA 800-437-6633
Montebello Packaging
Hawkesbury, ON 613-632-7096
Mouli Manufacturing Corporation
Belleville, NJ 800-789-8285
Mouron & Co Inc
Indianapolis, IN 317-243-7955
Mulholland-Harper Company
Denton, MD 800-882-3052
Multivac
Union Grove, WI 800-640-4213
Music City Metals Inc
Nashville, TN 800-251-2674
Myers Container
Hayward, CA 510-785-8235
National Bar Systems
Huntington Beach, CA 714-848-1688
National Metal Industries
West Springfield, MA 800-628-8850
New Age Industrial
Norton, KS 800-255-0104
New Court
Texarkana, TX 903-838-0521
Nexel Industries Inc
Port Washington, NY 800-245-6682
Northern Metal Products
St Cloud, MN 800-458-5549

Northern Stainless Fabricating
Traverse City, MI 231-947-4580
Northwind Inc
Alpena, AR 877-937-2585
Novelis Foil Products
Atlanta, GA 800-776-8701
Nowakowski
Franklin, WI 800-394-5866
Ohlson Packaging
Taunton, MA 508-977-0004
Old Dominion Wood Products
Lynchburg, VA 800-245-6382
Olde Country Reproductions Inc
York, PA 800-358-3997
Olde Thompson Inc
Oxnard, CA 800-827-1565
Olive Can Company
Elgin, IL 847-468-7474
Omega Industrial Products Inc
Saukville, WI 800-279-6634
Omicron Steel Products Company
Jamaica, NY 718-805-3400
Oneida Food Service
Columbus, OH 800-828-7033
Orber Manufacturing Co
Cranston, RI 800-761-4059
OSF
Toronto, ON 800-465-4000
OTD Corporation
Hinsdale, IL 630-321-9232
Pacific Northwest Wire Works
Dupont, WA 800-222-7699
Pacific Scale Company
Clackamas, OR 800-537-1886
Packaging Aids Corporation
San Rafael, CA 415-454-4868
Padinox
Winsloe, PE. 800-263-9768
Pallet Management Systems
Lawrenceville, VA 800-446-1804
Parisi Inc
Newtown, PA 215-968-6677
Patrick & Co
Dallas, TX 214-761-0900
Paul Mueller Co Inc
Springfield, MO 800-683-5537
Paul O. Abbe
Bensenville, IL 630-350-2200
PBC
Mahwah, NJ 800-514-2739
Penasack Co Inc
Albion, NY 585-589-5873
Penco Products
Skippack, PA. 800-562-1000
Pengo Attachments Inc
Cokato, MN. 800-599-0211
Pentwater Wire Products Inc
Pentwater, MI 877-869-6911
Perfect Equipment Inc
Gurnee, IL 800-356-6301
Peter Gray Corporation
Andover, MA 978-470-0990
Peterson Manufacturing Company
Plainfield, IL 800-547-8995
Petro Moore Manufacturing Corporation
Long Island City, NY 718-784-2516
Pinquist Tool & Die Company
Brooklyn, NY 800-752-0414
Pittsburgh Tank Corp
Monongahela, PA 800-634-0243
Plasti-Line
Knoxville, TN 800-444-7446
Polar Process
Plattsville, ON. 877-896-8077
Polar Ware Company
Sheboygan, WI 800-237-3655
Pollard Brothers
Chicago, IL 773-763-6868
Polyplastic Forms Inc
Farmingdale, NY 800-428-7659
Precision Printing & Packaging
Clarksville, TN 800-500-4526
Prince Seating Corp
Brooklyn, NY 800-577-4623
Pro-Ad-Co Inc
Portland, OR 800-287-5885
Process Solutions
Riviera Beach, FL 561-840-0050
Production Equipment Co
Meriden, CT 800-758-5697
Proluxe
Paramount, CA 800-594-5528

Pronto Products Company
Arcadia, CA 800-377-6680
Pulva Corp
Valencia, PA 800-878-5828
Purolator Facet Inc
Greensboro, NC 800-852-4449
Quality Fabrication & Design
Coppell, TX 972-304-3266
Quality Industries Inc
La Vergne, TN. 615-793-3000
Quantum Storage Systems Inc
Miami, FL 800-685-4665
QUIKSERV Corp
Houston, TX. 800-388-8307
Quipco Products Inc
Sauget, IL 314-993-1442
R & D Brass
Wappingers Falls, NY 800-447-6050
R H Saw Corp
Barrington, IL 847-381-8777
R.G. Stephens Engineering
Long Beach, CA 800-499-3001
Randell Manufacturing   Unified Brands
Weidman, MI 888-994-7636
Randware Industries
Prospect Heights, IL 847-299-8884
Rath Manufacturing Company
Janesville, WI 800-367-7284
Redi-Call Inc
Reno, NV 800-648-1849
Reese Enterprises Inc
Rosemount, MN 800-328-0953
Regal Manufacturing Company
Chicago, IL 773-921-3071
Regal Ware Inc
Kewaskum, WI 262-626-2121
Reinke & Schomann
Milwaukee, WI 414-964-1100
Republic Storage Systems LLC
Canton, OH 800-477-1255
Rex Art Manufacturing Corp.
Lindenhurst, NY 631-884-4600
Richards Industries Systems
West Caldwell, NJ 973-575-7480
Rigidized Metal Corp
Buffalo, NY. 800-836-2580
Rjr Technologies
Oakland, CA 510-638-5901
Robby Vapor Systems
Sunrise, FL 800-888-8711
Robert-James Sales
Buffalo, NY. 800-777-1325
Robertson Furniture Co Inc
Toccoa, GA 800-241-0713
Romatic Manufacturing Co
Southbury, CT 203-264-3442
Rome Machine & Foundry Co
Rome, GA 800-538-7663
Ross Engineering Inc
Savannah, GA 800-524-7677
Royal Display Corporation
Middletown, CT 800-569-1295
Royal Paper Products
Coatesville, PA 800-666-6655
Royal Welding & Fabricating
Fullerton, CA 714-680-6669
Royce Rolls Ringer Co
Grand Rapids, MI 800-253-9638
RTI Shelving Systems
Elmhurst, NY 800-223-6210
Rubbermaid Commercial Products
Pottsville, PA. 800-233-0314
Rubicon Industries
Brooklyn, NY 800-662-6999
Rytec Corporation
Milwaukee, WI 888-467-9832
S & L Store Fixture
Doral, FL. 800-205-4536
S.S.I. Schaefer System International Limited
Brampton, ON. 905-458-5399
Salem China Company
Salem, OH 330-337-8771
Samuel Strapping Systems Inc
Woodridge, IL 800-323-4424
Sani-Fit
Pasadena, CA 626-395-7895
Sarasota Restaurant Equipment
Sarasota, FL 800-434-1410
Savage Brothers Company
Elk Grove Vlg, IL 800-342-0973
Scherping Systems
Winsted, MN. 320-485-4401

Schwaab, Inc
Milwaukee, WI 800-935-9877
Seating Concepts Inc
Rockdale, IL 800-421-2036
Seattle Boiler Works Inc
Seattle, WA 206-762-0737
Sefi Fabricators Inc
Amityville, NY 631-842-2200
Seneca Environmental Products
Tiffin, OH 419-447-1282
Sfb Plastics Inc
Wichita, KS. 800-343-8133
Sharpsville Container Corp
Sharpsville, PA 800-645-1248
Shaw & Slavsky Inc
Detroit, MI 800-521-7527
Sigma Industries
Elkhart, IN. 574-295-9660
Sign Systems, Inc.
Warren, MI 586-758-1600
Signet Marking Devices
Costa Mesa, CA 800-421-5150
Silgan White Cap LLC
Downers Grove, IL 800-515-1565
Sims Machinery Co Inc
Lanett, AL. 334-576-2101
Sirco Systems
Birmingham, AL 205-731-7800
Solve Needs International
White Lake, MI 800-783-2462
Sossner Steel Stamps
Elizabethton, TN. 800-828-9515
South Valley Mfg Inc
Gilroy, CA. 408-842-5457
Southern Metal Fabricators Inc
Albertville, AL 800-989-1330
Spanco Crane & Monorail Systems
Morgantown, PA 800-869-2080
Spartanburg Steel Products Inc
Spartanburg, SC 800-974-7500
Specialty Blades
Staunton, VA. 540-248-2200
Specific Mechanical Systems
Victoria, BC. 250-652-2111
Speedrack Products Group LTD
Sparta, MI 616-887-0002
Speedways Conveyors
Lancaster, NY 800-800-1022
SPG International
Covington, GA 877-503-4774
Spot Wire Works Company
Philadelphia, PA 215-627-6124
Spring USA Corp
Naperville, IL 800-535-8974
Springfield Metal Products Co
Springfield, NJ 973-379-4600
Springport Steel Wire Products
Elkhart, IN. 574-295-9660
SSW Holding Co Inc
Elizabethtown, KY 270-769-5526
Stainless
La Vergne, TN. 800-877-5177
Stainless Equipment Manufacturing
Dallas, TX 800-736-2038
Stainless Fabricating Company
Denver, CO 800-525-8966
Stainless Fabrication Inc
Springfield, MO 800-397-8265
Stainless International
Rancho Cordova, CA 888-300-6196
Stainless Products
Somers, WC 800-558-9446
Stainless Specialists Inc
Wausau, WI 800-236-4155
Stainless Steel Fabricator Inc
La Mirada, CA 714-739-9904
Stainless Steel Fabricators
Tyler, TX. 903-595-6625
Star Filters
Timmonsville, SC 800-845-5381
Starlite Food Service Equipment
Detroit, MI 888-521-6603
Steel City Corporation
Youngstown, OH. 800-321-0350
Stegall Mechanical INC
Birmingham, AL. 800-633-4373
Stello Products Inc
Spencer, IN. 800-878-2246
Sterling Process Engineering
Columbus, OH 800-783-7875
Sterling Scale Co
Southfield, MI. 800-331-9931

Stogsdill Tile Co
Huntley, IL 800-323-7504
Storm Industrial
Shawnee Mission, KS 800-745-7483
Straits Steel & Wire Co
Ludington, MI 231-843-3416
Streator Dependable Mfg
Streator, IL 800-798-0551
Stryco Wire Products
North York, ON 416-663-7000
Suburban Signs
College Park, MD 301-474-5051
Super Steel
Milwaukee, WI 414-355-4800
Super Sturdy
Weldon, NC 800-253-4833
Superior Brush Company
Cleveland, OH 216-941-6987
Supreme Fabricators
Artesia, CA 323-583-8944
Supreme Metal
Alpharetta, GA 800-645-2526
Swanson Wire Works Industries, Inc.
Mesquite, TX 972-288-7465
T & A Metal Products Inc
Deptford, NJ .856-227-1700
T & T Industries Inc
Fort Mohave, AZ 800-437-6246
Table De France: North America
New Brunswick, NJ 888-680-4616
Talbot Industries
Neosho, MO 417-451-5900
Tampa Sheet Metal Co
Tampa, FL 813-251-1845
Tar-Hong MELAMINE USA
City of Industry, CA 626-935-1612
Thermo Wisconsin
De Pere, WI 920-766-7200
Tilly Industries
St Laurent, QC 514-331-4922
Tin Box Co of America Inc
Farmingdale, NY 800-888-8467
Top Line Process Equipment Company
Bradford, PA .800-458-6095
Tops Manufacturing Co
Darien, CT 203-655-9367
Traulsen & Co
Fort Worth, TX 800-825-8220
Travelon
Elk Grove Vlg, IL 800-537-5544
Travis Manufacturing Corp
Alliance, OH .330-875-1661
Tri-Boro Shelving & Partition
Farmville, VA 800-633-3070
Triner Scale & Mfg Co
Olive Branch, MS 800-238-0152
Triple-A Manufacturing Company
Toronto, ON .800-786-2238
Tropic KOOL
Largo, FL 727-581-2824
TWM Manufacturing
Leamington, ON 888-495-4831
Ultratainer
St Jean-Sur-Richelie, QC 514-359-3651
Unifoil Corp
Fairfield, NJ .973-244-9990
United Industries Inc
Beloit, WI 608-365-8891
United Performance Metals
Northbrook, IL 888-922-0040
United Steel Products Company
East Stroudsburg, PA 570-476-1010
UniTrak Corporation
Port Hope, ON 866-883-5749
Universal Stainless
Aurora, CO 800-223-8332
Universal Stainless & Alloy
Titusville, PA 800-295-1909
Uniweb Inc
Corona, CA 800-486-4932
Update International
Vernon, CA 800-747-7124
Upham & Walsh Lumber
Hoffman Estates, IL 847-519-1010
US Can Company
Rosedale, MD 800-436-8021
US Seating Products
Ocala, FL 800-999-2589
US Standard Sign
Franklin Park, IL 800-537-4790
USECO
Murfreesboro, TN 615-893-4820

V&R Metal Enterprises
Brooklyn, NY 718-768-8142
Vacumet Corp
Wayne, NJ 973-628-1067
Vacuum Depositing Inc
Louisville, KY 502-969-4227
Valley Craft Inc
Lake City, MN 800-328-1480
Valvinox
Iberville, QC .450-346-1981
Vasconia Housewares
San Antonio, TX 800-377-6723
Venus Corp
Blytheville, AR 870-763-3830
Versailles Lighting
Delray Beach, FL 888-564-0240
Victone Manufacturing Company
Chicago, IL 312-738-3211
Viking Machine & Design Inc
De Pere, WI 888-286-2116
Vollrath Co LLC
Sheboygan, WI 800-624-2051
Vulcan Industries
Moody, AL 888-444-4417
W J Egli & Co
Alliance, OH .330-823-3666
Wahlstrom Manufacturing
Fontana, CA .909-822-4677
Walco
Utica, NY 800-879-2526
Walker Stainless Equipment Co
New Lisbon, WI 608-562-7500
Waukesha Foundry Inc
Waukesha, WI 800-727-0741
Waukesha Specialty Company
Darien, WI 262-724-3700
Wayne Industries
Clanton, AL 800-225-3148
Weavewood, Inc.
Golden Valley, MN 800-367-6460
Weiss Sheet Metal Inc
Avon, MA 508-583-8300
Wemas Metal Products
Calgary, AB 403-276-4451
Wendell August Forge
Grove City, PA 800-923-1390
West Star Industries
Stockton, CA .800-326-2288
Western Pacific Stge Solutions
San Dimas, CA 800-888-5707
Western Plastics
Calhoun, GA .800-752-4106
Westfield Sheet Metal Works
Kenilworth, NJ 908-276-5500
Wheel Tough Company
Terre Haute, IN 888-765-8833
White Rabbit Dye Inc
St Louis, MO .800-466-6588
Whiting & Davis
Attleboro Falls, MA 800-876-6374
Wilder Manufacturing Company
Port Jervis, NY 800-832-1319
Williamsburg Metal Spinning
Brooklyn, NY 888-535-5402
Winmark Stamp & Sign
Salt Lake City, UT 800-438-0480
Winston Industries
Louisville, KY 800-234-5286
Wire Belt Co of America
Londonderry, NH 603-644-2500
Wirefab Inc
Worcester, MA 877-877-4445
Wiremaid Products Div
Coral Springs, FL 800-770-4700
WITT Industries Inc
Mason, OH 800-543-7417
Woerner Wire Works
Omaha, NE 402-451-5414
Woodard
Coppell, TX 800-877-2290
Yargus Manufacturing Inc
Marshall, IL 217-826-8059
Yates Industries Inc
St Clair Shores, MI 586-778-7680
YW Yacht Basin
Easton, MD 410-822-0414
Zelco Industries
Mount Vernon, NY 800-431-2486
Zol-Mark Industries
Winnipeg, NB 204-943-7393

Turn Key

Barry Wehmiller Design Group
New London, NH 866-526-2585

Consultants

Agriculture Consulting Services
New York City, NY 347-709-7587
AgriFiber Solutions
Mundelein, IL 847-549-6002
Agworld
Windsor, CO .724-249-6753
AIB International
Manhattan, KS 800-633-5137
Austin Co
Cleveland, OH 440-544-2600
BKI
Oakland, CA .510-444-8707
Boldt Co
Appleton, WI 920-739-6321
Bridgewell Resources LLC
Clackamas, OR 800-481-3557
Burdock Group
Orlando, FL 407-802-1400
Consulting Nutritional Services
Calabasas, CA 818-880-6774
Cretel Food Equipment
Holland, MI 616-786-3980
DuPont
Wilmington, DE 800-441-7515
Excel-A-Tec Inc
Brookfield, WI 262-252-3600
Family Farms Group
Brighton, IL .877-221-3276
FoodLogiQ
Durham, NC .866-492-4468
Fresca Foods Inc.
Louisville, CO 303-996-8881
Howlett Farms
Avon, NY 585-226-8340
IFoodDecisionSciences
Kenmore, WA 206-219-3703
IMS Food Service
Shelton, CT 800-235-7072
InHarvest Inc.
Bemidji, MN .800-346-7032
J.S. Ferraro
Toronto, ON .800-278-0018
K-Coe Isom
Loveland, CO .800-461-4702
Maximus Systems
St-Bruno-de-Montarville, QC 877-445-6556
Murray Runin
Mahwah, NJ .201-512-3885
Outside the Lines, Inc
Sonoma, CA .707-933-0687
Shambaugh & Son
Fort Wayne, IN 260-487-7777
Syngenta
Greensboro, NC 800-334-9481
The Good Food Institute
Washington, DC 866-849-4457
Townsend Research Laboratories, Inc
Indianapolis, IN 317-375-0893
Trimble Agriculture
Westminster, CO
USC Consulting Group
Tampa, FL 800-888-8872
Virginia Department of Agriculture & Consumer Services
Richmond, VA 804-786-3520
WineAndHospitalityJobs.com
Sonoma, CA .707-933-0687
Zume
Mountain View, CA

Design

A & B Process Systems Corp
Stratford, WI 888-258-2789
AAMD
Liverpool, NY 800-887-4167
Accommodation Program
New York, NY 800-929-1414
Agriculture Consulting Services
New York City, NY 347-709-7587
Aidi International Hotels of America
Washington, DC 202-331-9299
Aldo Locascio
Tucson, AZ 800-488-8729
ALPI Food Preparation Equipment
Bolton, ON 800-928-2574

ALY Group of New York
  Pleasantville, NY 603-493-8088
American Agribusiness Assistance
  Alexandria, VA 202-429-0500
American Material Handling Inc
  N Little Rock, AR 800-482-5801
American Systems Associates
  Hampton Bays, NY. 800-584-3663
Anhydro Inc
  Olympia Fields, IL 708-747-7000
APA
  Omaha, NE 402-290-5597
Architectural Products
  Highland, NY 845-691-8500
Art-Tech Restaurant Design
  Rockville Centre, NY 516-593-9130
Aseptic Resources
  Overland Park, KS 913-897-4125
Aspect Engineering
  Westerville, OH. 614-638-7106
Asset Design LLC
  Mooresville, NC 888-293-1740
Awb Engineers
  Salisbury, MD 410-742-7299
B T Engineering Inc
  Bala Cynwyd, PA 610-664-9500
Baker Foodservice Design Inc
  Grand Rapids, MI 800-968-4011
Bargreen Ellingson
  Tacoma, WA .800-322-4441
Barry Wehmiller Design
  Alpharetta, GA 800-667-6250
Barry Wehmiller Design Group
  New London, NH 866-526-2585
Barry-Wehmiller Design Group
  St Louis, MO. 314-862-8000
Basic Leasing Corporation
  Kearny, NJ 973-817-7373
BEC International
  Louisville, KY 877-232-4687
Best Restaurant Equip & Design
  Columbus, OH 800-837-2378
Big-D Construction Corp
  Salt Lake City, UT 801-415-6000
Bintz Restaurant Supply Company
  Salt Lake City, UT 800-443-4746
Bresco
  Birmingham, AL. 205-252-0076
Brevard Restaurant Equipment
  Rockledge, FL. 321-631-0318
Brown/Millunzi & Associates
  Houston, TX .800-460-3387
Carmona Designs
  Chula Vista, CA 619-425-2800
Center for Packaging Education
  Somers, NY. .914-276-0425
CHL Systems
  Souderton, PA 215-723-7284
Chroust Associates International
  Woodland Hills, CA 818-348-1438
CII Food Svc Design
  Lapeer, MI. 810-667-3100
Citra-Tech
  Lefkosia, CY
Clevenger Frable Lavallee
  White Plains, NY 914-997-9660
Coastal Mechanical Svc Inc
  Stamford, CT. 203-359-3070
Cober Electronics, Inc.
  Norwalk, CT. 800-709-5948
Concepts & Design International, Ltd
  West Nyack, NY 845-358-1558
Container-Quinn Testing Lab
  Wheeling, IL. 847-537-9470
Cooper Decoration Company
  Weston, MA .315-475-1661
Crepas & Associates
  Elmhurst, IL .630-833-4880
Curtis Restaurant Equipment
  Springfield, OR. 541-746-7480
D'Addario Design Associates
  New York, NY 212-302-0059
DCS IPAL Consultants
  Laval, QC 450-973-3338
DECI Corporation
  Burgettstown, PA 724-947-3300
Dembling & Dembling Architects
  Albany, NY 518-463-8066
Dennsi Group
  Springfield, MA 413-737-1353
Design Group
  Clearwater, FL 727-441-2825

Diamond & Lappin
  Fair Lawn, NJ 877-527-7461
Digital Image & Sound Corporation
  Rochester, NY 585-381-0410
Divercon Inc
  Omaha, NE 402-571-5115
Don Walters Company
  Stanton, CA. 714-892-0275
Donalds & Associates
  Long Beach, CA 562-290-8440
Eagle-Concordia Paper Corporation
  Farmingdale, NY 212-255-3860
Fabricon Products Inc
  River Rouge, MI 313-841-8200
Fenster Consulting Inc
  Port Washington, NY 516-944-7108
First Bank of Highland P
  Northbrook, IL 847-272-1300
Fleet Wood Goldco Wyard
  Cockeysville, MD. 410-785-1934
FMB Company
  Broken Bow, OK. 580-513-5309
Food & Agrosystems
  Sunnyvale, CA 408-245-8450
Food Industry ConsultingGroup
  Dunnellon, FL. 800-443-5820
Food Technologies
  Golden Valley, MN 763-544-8586
Foodpro International
  Stockton, CA. 888-687-5797
Foodservice Design Associates
  Orlando, FL. .407-896-4115
Foster Miller Inc
  Waltham, MA 781-684-4000
Foth & Van Dyke
  Green Bay, WI. 920-497-2500
Graphic Impressions of Illinois
  River Grove, IL 708-453-1100
Group One Partners
  Boston, MA. .617-268-7000
H & H Metal Fabrication Inc
  Belden, MS 662-489-4626
Hampton-Tilley Associates
  Chesterfield, MO 813-418-3340
Hanson Lab Furniture Inc
  Newbury Park, CA 805-498-3121
Hunter Graphics
  Umatilla, FL .407-644-2060
Hy-Ten Plastics Inc
  Milford, NH .603-673-1611
Industrial Consortium
  Sulphur Springs, TX 903-885-6610
Inman Foodservices Group LLC
  Nashville, TN 615-321-5591
Innovations by Design
  Chadds Ford, PA. 610-558-0160
Innovative Space Management
  Woodside, NY. 718-278-4300
Intelplex Designers
  St Louis, MO. 314-983-9996
Interbrand Corporation
  San Francisco, CA 877-692-7263
IPG International Packaging Group
  Agoura Hills, CA 818-865-1428
Item Products
  Houston, TX .800-333-4932
J/W Design Associates
  San Francisco, CA 415-546-7707
Jacobs Engineering Group
  Dallas, TX. 214-638-0145
Janows Design Associates
  Lincolnwood, IL 847-763-0620
Jenike & Johanson Inc
  Tyngsboro, MA 978-649-3300
Joul, Engineering StaffiSolutions
  Edison, NJ 800-341-0341
Kochman Consultants LTD
  Morton Grove, IL 847-470-1195
Kohlenberger Associates Consulting Engineering
  Fullerton, CA 714-738-7733
Landmark Kitchen Design
  Chandler, AZ. 866-621-3192
Laschober & Sovich Inc
  Woodland Hills, CA 818-713-9011
Legge & Associates
  Rockwood, ON 519-856-0444
Lobsters Alive Company
  Georgetown, ME. 207-371-2990
Lockwood Greene Engineers
  Knoxville, TN 251-476-2400
Lockwood Greene Engineers
  Knoxville, TN 256-533-9907

Lockwood Greene Engineers
  Brentwood, TN 615-221-5031
Lockwood Greene Engineers
  Augusta, GA 706-724-8225
Lockwood Greene Engineers
  Somerset, NJ 732-560-5700
Lockwood Greene Engineers
  Atlanta, GA. 770-829-6500
Lockwood Greene Engineers
  Guaynabo, PR 787-781-9050
Lockwood Greene Engineers
  Knoxville, TN 865-218-5377
Lockwood Greene Engineers
  Dallas, TX. 972-991-5505
Lockwood Greene Technologies
  Augusta, GA 505-889-3831
Lorrich & Associates
  San Diego, CA 858-586-0823
Management Insight
  Malborough, MA 508-485-2100
Material Systems Engineering
  Stilesville, IN 800-634-0904
McNichols Conveyor Company
  Southfield, MI. 800-331-1926
Mead & Hunt Inc
  Madison, WI. 888-364-7272
Metcalf & Eddy
  Wakefield, MA 781-246-5200
Michael Blackman & Assoc
  Santa Monica, CA. 800-889-4925
Moseley Realty LLC
  Franklin, MA 800-667-3539
Nicosia Creative Expresso
  New York, NY 212-515-6600
Nimbus Water Systems
  Murrieta, CA. 800-451-9343
Nina Mauritz Design Service
  Libertyville, IL 847-968-4438
Northeast Box Co
  Ashtabula, OH 800-362-8100
Nutrinfo Corporation
  Watertown, MA. 800-676-6686
O.B.S. Trading
  Jackson, MO. 573-243-6999
Omega Company
  Stamford, CT. 800-848-4286
Ottenheimer Equipment Company
  Lutherville Timonium, MD 410-597-9700
PacTech Engineering
  Cincinnati, OH 513-792-1090
Patrick E. Panzarello Consulting Services
  Sunland, CA 818-353-0431
Pharmaceutical & Food Special
  San Jose, CA 408-275-0161
Phoenix & Eclectic Network
  Elmhurst, IL .630-530-4373
Premier Restaurant Equipment
  Brooklyn Park, MN. 763-544-8800
Product Solutions
  Wilkes Barre, PA. 888-776-3765
R.C. Keller & Associates
  Barnegat, NJ 973-694-8810
Raque Food Systems
  Louisville, KY 502-267-9641
Raytheon Co
  Waltham, MA 781-522-3000
RGN Developers
  New Providence, NJ
RMF Companies
  Grandview, MO. 816-839-9258
Robert C Vncek Design Assoc
  Sussex, NJ 973-702-8553
Robinett & Assoc
  Richardson, TX. 972-234-1945
ROI Software, LLC
  Knoxville, TN 865-522-2211
Ron Vallort & Associates
  Oak Brook, IL 630-734-3821
SBS of Financial Industries
  Washington, NJ 908-689-5520
Schroeder Machine
  San Marcos, CA 760-591-9733
Seattle Menu Specialists
  Kent, WA. 800-622-2826
Seiberling Associates Inc
  Beloit, WI 608-313-1235
Setter, Leach & Lindstrom
  Minneapolis, MN 612-338-8741
Shook Kelley Design Group
  Charlotte, NC 704-377-0661
Southern Store Fixtures Inc
  Bessemer, AL 800-552-6283

Sprinkman Corporation
Franksville, WI 800-816-1610
SSOE Group
Toledo, OH 419-255-3830
St Onge Ruff & Associates
Kansas City, MO. 800-800-5261
Stokes Material Handling Systs
Doylestown, PA 215-340-2200
Stratecon International Consultants
Winston Salem, NC. 336-768-6808
Sverdrup Facilities
Saint Louis, MO 800-325-7910
Syngenta
Greensboro, NC 800-334-9481
T E Ibberson Co
Hopkins, MN 952-938-7007
TDF Automation
Cedar Falls, IA 800-553-1777
Tetra Pak
Champlin, MN 763-421-2721
The Good Food Institute
Washington, DC 866-849-4457
Trimble Agriculture
Westminster, CO
Tuchenhagen
Columbia, MD 410-910-6000
Twenty First Century Design
Albany, NY 518-446-0939
UAA
Chicago, IL 800-813-1711
United Industries Group Inc
Lake Forest, CA 949-759-3200
US Magnetix
Minneapolis, MN 763-540-9497
Washington Group International
San Francisco, CA 800-877-0980
Wayne Combustion Systems
Fort Wayne, IN 800-443-4625
Webber Smith Assoc
Lancaster, PA 800-231-0392
Wesley-Kind Associates
Mineola, NY 516-747-3434
Westfield Sheet Metal Works
Kenilworth, NJ 908-276-5500
Wyssmont Co Inc
Fort Lee, NJ 201-947-4600

Food Technology

A&L Western Ag Lab
Modesto, CA. 209-529-4080
ABIC International Consultants
Fairfield, NJ 973-227-7060
ADD Testing & Research
Valley Stream, NY 516-568-9197
Agricultural Research Service
Washington, SW 202-720-3656
AgriTech
Columbus, OH 614-488-2772
AM Test Laboratories
Kirkland, WA 425-885-1664
American Style Foods
Old Hickory, TN 615-847-0410
Ameritech Laboratories
Flushing, NY. 718-461-0475
Anresco Laboratories
San Francisco, CA 800-359-0920
Arthur D Little Inc.
Boston, MA. 617-532-9550
Asi Food Safety Consultants
St Louis, MO. 800-477-0778
Aspect Engineering
Westerville, OH. 614-638-7106
Aspen Research Corporation
White Bear Lake, MN. 651-773-7961
Bedrosian & Assoc
Redwood City, CA 650-367-0259
Bernard Wolnak & Associates
Northbrook, IL 847-480-0427
BFB Consultants
Mississauga, ON 905-819-9856
Bioenergetics Inc
Madison, WI. 608-255-4028
Biovail Technologies
Chantilly, VA. 703-995-2400
Brand Specialists
Duncanville, TX 888-323-3708
Broadmoor Baker
Seattle, WA 206-624-3660
Cardinal Kitchens
London, ON 800-928-0832

Catalent Pharma Solutions Inc
Winchester, KY 859-745-8679
Chaska Chocolate
Chaska, MN 952-448-5699
Codema
Maple Grove, MN. 763-428-2266
Conatech Consulting Group, Inc
Saint Louis, MO 314-995-9767
Concepts & Design International, Ltd
West Nyack, NY 845-358-1558
Culinar
Montreal, QC 514-255-2811
Cynter Con Technology Adviser
Gaithersburg, MD. 800-287-1811
Cyntergy Corporation
Rockville, MD 800-825-5787
Damon Industries
Alliance, OH 800-362-9850
Deibel Laboratories Inc
Madison, WI 608-241-1177
EPL Technologies
Devon, PA 800-637-3743
Eurofins S-F Analytical Labs
New Berlin, WI. 800-300-6700
Food & Agrosystems
Sunnyvale, CA 408-245-8450
Food & Beverage Consultants
Cranston, RI 401-463-5784
Food Consulting Company
Del Mar, CA 800-793-2844
Food Development Centre
Portage La Prairie, NB 800-870-1044
Food Industry ConsultingGroup
Dunnellon, FL. 800-443-5820
Food Science Associates
Crugers, NY 914-739-7541
Food Science Consulting
Walnut Creek, CA 925-947-6785
Food Technologies
Golden Valley, MN. 763-544-8586
Food-Tek
Whippany, NJ 800-648-8114
Foods Research Laboratories
Boston, MA. 617-442-3322
Future Foods
Chicago, IL 312-987-9342
George G. Giddings
Randolph, NJ 973-361-4687
George Lapgley Enterpri ses
Pipersville, PA. 267-221-2426
Healthy Dining
San Diego, CA 800-266-2049
Industrial Laboratories Co
Wheat Ridge, CO 800-456-5288
Ingman Laboratories
Minneapolis, MN 612-724-0121
Innovative Food Solutions LLC
Columbus, OH 800-884-3314
Inter-Access
Etobicoke, ON 514-744-6262
J Leek Assoc Inc
Edenton, NC 252-482-4456
James V. Hurson Associates
Arlington, VA 800-642-6564
JI Analytical Svc Inc
Modesto, CA 209-538-8111
Jonessco Enterprises
Plano, TX 972-985-7961
Kashrus Technical Consultants
Lakewood, NJ 732-364-8046
Kelley Advisory Services
Northbrook, IL 847-412-9234
KOF-K Kosher Supervision
Teaneck, NJ. 201-837-0500
Landmark Kitchen Design
Chandler, AZ. 866-621-3192
Lawrence-Allen Group
San Mateo, CA 800-609-2909
Lebensmittel Consulting
Fostoria, OH 419-435-2774
Libra Technical Center
Metuchen, NJ 732-321-5200
Line of Snacks Consultants
Dallas, TX 972-484-1155
M-Tech & Associates
Downers Grove, IL 630-810-9714
Malcolm Stogo Associates
Scarsdale, NY 914-472-7255
Matrix Group Inc.
Bloomfield, NJ 973-338-5638
MC Creation
San Francisco, CA 415-775-1135

Merlin Development Inc
Minneapolis, MN 763-475-0224
Micro-Chem Laboratory
Mississauga, ON. 905-795-0490
Microbac-Wilson Devision
Wilson, NC 252-237-4175
Microwave Research Center
Eagan, MN 651-456-9190
Midwest Laboratories
Omaha, NE 402-334-7770
Miles Willard Technologies
Idaho Falls, ID 208-523-4741
Milligan & Higgins
Johnstown, NY 518-762-4638
Minnesota Valley Testing Lab
New Ulm, MN. 800-782-3557
National Food Laboratories Inc
Livermore, CA 925-828-1440
Natural Marketing Institute
Harleysville, PA 215-513-7300
NorCrest Consulting
Divide, CO 719-687-7635
Northeast Laboratory Svc
Winslow, ME. 866-591-7120
Northland Labs
Northbrook, IL 800-366-3522
Northwest Laboratories
Seattle, WA 206-763-6252
Nutrinfo Corporation
Watertown, MA. 800-676-6686
Nutrition Network
Irvine, CA 949-753-7998
Nutrition Research
Livingston, MT 406-222-3541
O.B.S. Trading
Jackson, MO 573-243-6999
Oklabs
Oklahoma City, OK 405-843-6832
Omega Company
Stamford, CT. 800-848-4286
Petal
New York, NY 212-947-3662
Peter Kalustian Associates
Boonton, NJ 973-334-3008
Phytopia Inc
Dallas, TX 888-750-9336
POS Pilot Plant Corporation
Saskatoon, SK. 800-230-2751
Positive Employment Practice
New City, NY 845-638-6442
Power Packaging Inc
Rosendale, WI. 920-872-2181
Protein Research
Livermore, CA 800-948-1991
PSI
Oakbrook Terrace, IL. 630-705-9290
Purity Laboratories
Lake Oswego, OR 800-977-3636
Q Laboratories
Cincinnati, OH 513-471-1300
Quality Bakers of America
Allentown, PA. 973-263-6970
R F Schiffmann Assoc.
New York, NY 212-362-7021
Richardson Researches
South San Francisco, CA 510-653-4385
Riverview Foods
Warsaw, KY 859-567-5211
Robin Shepherd Group
Jacksonville, FL 877-896-8774
Schiff & Co
West Caldwell, NJ. 973-227-1830
Schroeder Machine
San Marcos, CA 760-591-9733
Sensory Spectrum
New Providence, NJ 908-376-7000
Sentinel Lubricants Inc
Miami, FL 800-842-6400
Shear/Kershman Laboratories
Chesterfield, MO 636-519-8900
Simon S. Jackel Plymouth
Tarpon Springs, FL 727-942-3991
Solganik & Associates
Dayton, OH 800-253-8512
Soyatech Inc
Bar Harbor, ME. 800-424-7692
Soynut Butter Co
Glenview, IL 800-288-1012
Spencer Research Inc
Columbus, OH 800-488-3242
SSOE Group
Toledo, OH 419-255-3830

Stratecon International Consultants
Winston Salem, NC................336-768-6808
Syngenta
Greensboro, NC 800-334-9481
Thomas J Payne Market Devmnt
San Mateo, CA 650-340-8311
Tiax LLC
Lexington, MA 800-677-3000
Trans-Chemco Inc
Bristol, WI. 800-880-2498
Volumetric Technologies
Cannon Falls, MN...........507-263-0034
Warren Analytical Laboratory
Greeley, CO...............800-945-6669
Wilhelmsen Consulting
Milpitas, CA..............408-946-4525
XL Corporate & Research Services
New York, NY 800-221-2972
Zaloom Marketing Corp
South Hackensack, NJ 800-878-7609

Kosher Food

KOF-K Kosher Supervision
Teaneck, NJ................201-837-0500
Orthodox Union
New York, NY 212-563-4000
Star-K Kosher Certification
Baltimore, MD 410-484-4110

Marketing & Promotion

ABIC International Consultants
Fairfield, NJ 973-227-7060
AgriTech
Columbus, OH 614-488-2772
Aidi International Hotels of America
Washington, DC 202-331-9299
Alpert/Siegel & Associates
Los Angeles, CA...........310-571-0777
American Agribusiness Assistance
Alexandria, VA 202-429-0500
Arthur D Little Inc.
Boston, MA. 617-532-9550
Axces Systems
Westbury, NY 800-355-3534
BFB Consultants
Mississauga, ON...........905-819-9856
BlueKey Inc
Charleston, SC 843-628-6228
BNP Media
2401 W Big Beaver Rd, Su. 248-362-3700
Broadmoor Baker
Seattle, WA 206-624-3660
Calif Canning Peach Assn
Sacramento, CA 916-925-9131
Cannon Equipment Company
Cannon Falls, MN..........800-825-8501
Chain Restaurant Resolutions
Toronto, ON 416-934-4334
Coffee Enterprises
Burlington, VT............800-375-3398
Colonial Marketing Assoc
Freehold, NJ 732-462-2100
Conatech Consulting Group, Inc
Saint Louis, MO 314-995-9767
Concept Hospitality Group
Foster City, CA 650-357-1224
Connecticut Culinary Institute
Farmington, CT............860-677-7869
Container-Quinn Testing Lab
Wheeling, IL.............847-537-9470
Cooper Decoration Company
Weston, MA 315-475-1661
Cycle Computer Consultants
Hicksville, NY 516-733-1892
Dakota Valley Products, Inc.
Willow Lake, SD...........605-625-2526
Decision Analyst Inc
Arlington, TX 800-262-5974
DMG Financial Inc
Denver, CO. 888-331-3882
Dover Hospitality Consulting
Etobicoke, ON 416-622-9294
Edge Resources
Hopedale, MA. 888-849-0998
Engineering & Mgmt Consultants
Franklin Lakes, NJ 201-847-0748
Feedback Plus
Plano, TX 800-882-7467
First Bank of Highland P
Northbrook, IL. 847-272-1300

Food & Beverage Consultants
Cranston, RI 401-463-5784
Food Business Associates
Temple, ME. 207-778-2251
Food Industry ConsultingGroup
Dunnellon, FL.............800-443-5820
Food Insights
Washington, DC 202-296-6540
Food Marketing Servives
Pittsburgh, PA............412-821-8960
Food Science Consulting
Walnut Creek, CA..........925-947-6785
Food Technologies
Golden Valley, MN 763-544-8586
Foodmark, Inc
Wellesley, MA. 800-535-3447
Francorp
Olympia Fields, IL........800-327-6244
Future Foods
Chicago, IL. 312-987-9342
Graphic Promotions
Topeka, KS 785-234-6684
Grocery Products Distribution
Cedar Knolls, NJ..........973-538-1035
Groth Corp
Stafford, TX 800-354-7684
Harold M. Lincoln Company
Toledo, OH 419-255-1200
HealthFocus
Atlanta, GA. 770-645-1999
Healthy Dining
San Diego, CA 800-266-2049
Heart Smart International
Scottsdale, AZ. 800-762-7819
HMG Worldwide In-Store Marketing
New York, NY 212-736-2300
Innavision Global Marketing Consultants
Racine, WI 262-633-1000
Inter-Access
Etobicoke, ON 514-744-6262
Interbrand Corporation
San Francisco, CA 877-692-7263
Interliance
Santa Ana, CA 800-540-7917
IPG International Packaging Group
Agoura Hills, CA 818-865-1428
J.R. Ralph Marketing Company
Syracuse, NY 315-445-0255
JDG Consulting
Baulkham Hills, NS 800-243-7037
Jonessco Enterprises
Plano, TX 972-985-7961
Kelley Advisory Services
Northbrook, IL 847-412-9234
Kilcher Company
South Pasadena, FL 727-367-5839
Landmark Kitchen Design
Chandler, AZ. 866-621-3192
Line of Snacks Consultants
Dallas, TX 972-484-1155
Lorrich & Associates
San Diego, CA 858-586-0823
Main Course Consultants
Skokie, IL 847-869-7633
Malcolm Stogo Associates
Scarsdale, NY 914-472-7255
Management Insight
Malborough, MA 508-485-2100
Marketing Management Inc
Fort Worth, TX 800-433-2004
Mastio & Co
St Joseph, MO. 816-364-6200
Maui Wowi Fresh Hawaiin Blends
Greenwood Village, CO 877-849-6992
MC Creation
San Francisco, CA 415-775-1135
Mic-Ellen Associates
Collegeville, PA..........800-872-1252
Michigan Agricultural Cooperative Marketing
Association
Lansing, MI..............800-824-3779
Minnesuing Acres
Lake Nebagamon, WI 715-374-2262
Monterey Bay Food Group
Aptos, CA. 831-685-8600
Murray Runin
Mahwah, NJ 201-512-3885
National Food Laboratories Inc
Livermore, CA 925-828-1440
National Food Product Research Corporation
West Newbury, MA.............800-363-2144

Natural Marketing Institute
Harleysville, PA..........215-513-7300
NCR Counterpoint
Alpharetta, GA 800-852-5852
Nicholas Marketing Associates
Bogota, NJ 201-343-9414
Nicosia Creative Expresso
New York, NY 212-515-6600
Northland Consultants
Sault Ste. Marie, ON......705-541-8490
Nutrinfo Corporation
Watertown, MA. 800-676-6686
Partners International
Hanover, NH 603-643-8574
Pearson Research Assoc
Santa Cruz, CA 831-429-9797
Peter Kalustian Associates
Boonton, NJ 973-334-3008
Pioneer Marketing International
Los Gatos, CA. 408-356-4990
Positive Employment Practice
New City, NY 845-638-6442
Premier Restaurant Equipment
Brooklyn Park, MN.........763-544-8800
Pro Media Inc
Menomonee Falls, WI. 800-328-0439
Putnam Group
Trumbull, CT 203-452-7270
Quality Bakers of America
Allentown, PA............973-263-6970
Redwood Vintners
Novato, CA. 415-892-6949
Restaurant Development Svc
Bethesda, MD 301-263-0400
Restaurant Partners
Orlando, FL. 407-839-5070
Robert C Vncek Design Assoc
Sussex, NJ. 973-702-8553
Robin Shepherd Group
Jacksonville, FL 877-896-8774
Rqa Product Dynamics
Orland Park, IL 708-364-7055
Rtech Laboratories
St Paul, MN. 800-328-9687
Sales Building Systems
Mentor, OH. 800-435-7576
Selective Foods
Carnegie, PA.............412-458-1930
Sensors Quality Management
Toronto, ON 800-866-2624
Simonson Group
Winchester, MA 781-729-8906
SLT Group
Dayton, NJ 732-661-1030
Solganik & Associates
Dayton, OH. 800-253-8512
Sorensen Associates
Troutdale, OR 800-542-4321
Source Distribution Logistics
Batavia, IL. 630-761-1231
Southern United States Trade Association
New Orleans, LA 504-568-5986
Soynut Butter Co
Glenview, IL. 800-288-1012
Specialty Cheese Group Limited
New York, NY 212-243-7274
Stewart Marketing Services
Kirkland, WA 425-889-2455
Stratecon
Winston Salem, NC 336-768-6808
Stratecon International Consultants
Winston Salem, NC. 336-768-6808
Superior Product Pickup Services
Niles, IL 847-647-4720
Supermarket Associates
Durham, NC 919-493-0994
Swander Pace & Company
San Francisco, CA 415-477-8500
Tara Communications
Dunedin, FL. 303-417-9602
Technomic Inc
Chicago, IL. 312-876-0004
Thomas J Payne Market Devmnt
San Mateo, CA 650-340-8311
Tiax LLC
Lexington, MA 800-677-3000
TLC & Associates
Amarillo, TX. 806-353-1517
Tourtellot & Co
Warwick, RI 401-734-4200
Tragon Corp
Redwood City, CA 800-841-1177

Unity Brands Group
Saint Augustine, FL 904-940-8975
US Magnetix
Minneapolis, MN 763-540-9497
Vine Solutions
Corte Madera, CA 415-927-3308
Virginia Department of Agriculture & Consumer Services
Richmond, VA 804-786-3520
W.A. Golomski & Associates
Algoma, WI 920-487-9864
World Trade Center Harrisburg
Harrisburg, PA 717-843-1090
Zaloom Marketing Corp
South Hackensack, NJ 800-878-7609

Material Handling

California Vibratory Feeders
Anaheim, CA 800-354-0972
KLEEN Line Corp
Newburyport, MA 800-259-5973
Polyair
Toronto, ON 888-765-9847
Trimble Agriculture
Westminster, CO

Packaging

BFB Consultants
Mississauga, ON 905-819-9856
Conatech Consulting Group, Inc
Saint Louis, MO 314-995-9767
DCS IPAL Consultants
Laval, QC 450-973-3338
Food Development Centre
Portage La Prairie, NB 800-870-1044
Interbrand Corporation
San Francisco, CA 877-692-7263
Landmark Kitchen Design
Chandler, AZ 866-621-3192
Pater & Associates
Cincinnati, OH
R F Schiffmann Assoc.
New York, NY 212-362-7021
R.C. Keller & Associates
Barnegat, NJ 973-694-8810
Raque Food Systems
Louisville, KY 502-267-9641
Schroeder Machine
San Marcos, CA 760-591-9733
Stratecon International Consultants
Winston Salem, NC 336-768-6808

Restaurant Design

Top Source Industries
Addison, IL 800-362-9625

Sanitation, Testing & Analysis

A & B Process Systems Corp
Stratford, WI 888-258-2789
A&L Western Ag Lab
Modesto, CA 209-529-4080
Accra Laboratory
Cleveland, OH 800-567-7200
Accu-Labs Research
Golden, CO 303-277-9514
Accu-Ray Inspection Services
Elmhurst, IL 800-378-1226
ADD Testing & Research
Valley Stream, NY 516-568-9197
Advanced Ergonomics Inc
Frisco, TX 800-682-0169
AgriTech
Columbus, OH 614-488-2772
Airflow Sciences Corp
Livonia, MI 734-525-0300
AM Test Laboratories
Kirkland, WA 425-885-1664
American Glass Research
Maumee, OH 419-897-9000
American Services Group
Memphis, TN 800-333-6678
Ameritech Laboratories
Flushing, NY 718-461-0475
Analytical Labs
Boise, ID 800-574-5773
Anresco Laboratories
San Francisco, CA 415-822-1100
Anresco Laboratories
San Francisco, CA 800-359-0920

Applied Technologies
Brookfield, WI 262-784-7690
Arthur D Little Inc.
Boston, MA 617-532-9550
Asi Food Safety Consultants
St Louis, MO 800-477-0778
Aspect Engineering
Westerville, OH. 614-638-7106
Barrow-Agee Laboratories Inc
Memphis, TN 901-332-1590
BCN Research Laboratories
Rockford, TN 800-236-0505
Betz Entec
Horsham, PA 800-877-1940
Biological Services
Kansas City, MO 913-236-6868
Brown & Caldwell
Walnut Creek, CA 800-727-2224
Cal Western Pest Control
Arcadia, CA 800-326-2847
Cardinal Kitchens
London, ON 800-928-0832
Celsis Laboratory Group
Chicago, IL 800-222-8260
Chilton Consulting Group
Rocky Face, GA 706-694-8325
Conam Inspection
Glendale Heights, IL 630-681-0008
Container Testing Lab
Mamaroneck, NY 800-221-5170
Container-Quinn Testing Lab
Wheeling, IL 847-537-9470
Covance Inc.
Princeton, NJ. 888-268-2623
Cynter Con Technology Adviser
Gaithersburg, MD 800-287-1811
Cyntergy Corporation
Rockville, MD 800-825-5787
Dalare Associates Inc
Philadelphia, PA 215-567-1953
Deibel Laboratories Inc
Madison, WI 608-241-1177
DFL Laboratories
Chicago, IL. 312-938-5151
Engineering & Mgmt Consultants
Franklin Lakes, NJ 201-847-0748
Enviro-Test/Perry Laboratories
Woodridge, IL 630-324-6685
Environmental Consultants
Clarksville, IN. 812-282-8481
Environmental Systems
Culpeper, VA. 800-541-2116
Eurofins S-F Analytical Labs
New Berlin, WI. 800-300-6700
Eurofins Scientific Inc
Des Moines, IA 800-841-1110
Fettig Laboratories
Grand Rapids, MI 616-245-3000
Food & Beverage Consultants
Cranston, RI 401-463-5784
Food Consulting Company
Del Mar, CA 800-793-2844
Food Development Centre
Portage La Prairie, NB 800-870-1044
Food Industry ConsultingGroup
Dunnellon, FL. 800-443-5820
Food Sanitation Svc Inc
New York, NY 212-732-9540
Foodpro International
Stockton, CA. 888-687-5797
Foods Research Laboratories
Boston, MA. 617-442-3322
Foodworks
La Grange, KY 502-222-0135
Galbraith Laboratories Inc
Knoxville, TN. 877-449-8797
Gaynes Labs Inc
Bridgeview, IL 708-233-6655
Gems Sensors & Controls
Plainville, CT 860-747-3000
Genesis Nutritional Labs
Salt Lake City, UT 801-973-8824
George Lapgley Enterpri ses
Pipersville, PA. 267-221-2426
Gilbert Insect Light Traps
Jonesboro, AR. 800-643-0400
Global Product Development Group
Northbrook, IL 847-504-0464
Great Lakes Scientific
Stevensville, MI 269-429-1000
Hahn Laboratories
Columbia, SC 803-799-1614

Harold Wainess & Assoc
Arlington Hts, IL 847-722-8744
Industrial Laboratories Co
Wheat Ridge, CO 800-456-5288
Ingman Laboratories
Minneapolis, MN 612-724-0121
Innovative Food Solutions LLC
Columbus, OH 800-884-3314
Insect-O-Cutor Inc
Stone Mountain, GA 800-966-8480
International Approval Services
Cleveland, OH 877-235-9791
ITS/ETL Testing Laboratories
Laguna Niguel, CA 949-448-4100
J Leek Assoc Inc
Edenton, NC 252-482-4456
Jl Analytical Svc Inc
Modesto, CA 209-538-8111
Krueger Food Laboratories
Chelmsford, MA 978-256-1220
Labelmax Inc
Laredo, TX 956-722-6493
Lancaster Laboratories
Lancaster, PA 717-656-2300
Landmark Kitchen Design
Chandler, AZ 866-621-3192
Laucks' Testing Laboratories
Seattle, WA 206-767-5060
Lawrence-Allen Group
San Mateo, CA 800-609-2909
Lebensmittel Consulting
Fostoria, OH 419-435-2774
Libra Technical Center
Metuchen, NJ 732-321-5200
M-Tech & Associates
Downers Grove, IL 630-810-9714
Main Course Consultants
Skokie, IL 847-869-7633
Mccrone Microscopes & Acces
Westmont, IL. 630-288-7087
Medallion Laboratories
Minneapolis, MN 800-245-5615
Merieux Nutrisciences
Columbus, OH 614-486-0150
Metcalf & Eddy
Wakefield, MA 781-246-5200
Microbac Laboratories
Pittsburgh, PA 866-515-4668
Microbac-Wilson Devision
Wilson, NC 252-237-4175
Midwest Laboratories
Omaha, NE 402-334-7770
Miles Willard Technologies
Idaho Falls, ID 208-523-4741
Milligan & Higgins
Johnstown, NY 518-762-4638
Minnesota Valley Testing Lab
New Ulm, MN. 800-782-3557
Nimbus Water Systems
Murrieta, CA. 800-451-9343
Northeast Laboratory Svc
Winslow, ME. 866-591-7120
Northland Labs
Northbrook, IL 800-366-3522
Northview Laboratories
Spartanburg, SC 864-574-7728
Northview Pacific Laboratories
Northbrook, IL 847-564-8181
Nutrinfo Corporation
Watertown, MA 800-676-6686
O.D. Kurtz Associates
Palm Bay, FL. 321-723-0135
Oerlikon Balzers Coating USA
Elgin, IL 847-695-5200
Oklabs
Oklahoma City, OK 405-843-6832
Optipure
Plano, TX 972-422-1212
Orthodox Union
New York, NY 212-563-4000
Pearson Research Assoc
Santa Cruz, CA 831-429-9797
Phytopia Inc
Dallas, TX. 888-750-9336
POS Pilot Plant Corporation
Saskatoon, SK 800-230-2751
PSI
Oakbrook Terrace, IL 630-705-9290
Purity Laboratories
Lake Oswego, OR 800-977-3636
Q Laboratories
Cincinnati, OH 513-471-1300

QC
  Southampton, PA 215-355-3900
Quest
  San Clemente, CA................949-643-1333
Quick Judith & Assoc
  Hancock, MD 301-678-5737
R.C. Keller & Associates
  Barnegat, NJ 973-694-8810
Richardson Researches
  South San Francisco, CA 510-653-4385
Ron Vallort & Associates
  Oak Brook, IL 630-734-3821
Rqa Product Dynamics
  Orland Park, IL 708-364-7055
RTI Laboratories
  Livonia, MI 734-422-5342
San Diego Health & Nutrition
  Bonita, CA 619-470-3345
Sani-Pure Food Laboratories
  Saddle Brook, NJ 201-843-2525
Schiff & Co
  West Caldwell, NJ 973-227-1830
Sensory Spectrum
  New Providence, NJ 908-376-7000
SERCO Laboratories
  St. Anthony, MN 800-388-7173
Sheahan Sanitation Consulting
  Oakley, CA 800-554-4243
Shear/Kershman Laboratories
  Chesterfield, MO 636-519-8900
Shepard Brothers Co
  La Habra, CA 800-645-3594
Shuster Laboratories
  Canton, MA 800-444-8705
Silliker Laboratories of Ga
  Stone Mountain, GA 770-469-2701
Silliker Laboratories-Pa Inc
  Allentown, PA..................610-366-0264
Silliker, Inc
  Chicago, IL 312-938-5151
Simon S. Jackel Plymouth
  Tarpon Springs, FL 727-942-3991
Smith-Emery Co
  Los Angeles, CA................213-745-5333
Soynut Butter Co
  Glenview, IL 800-288-1012
Spencer Research Inc
  Columbus, OH 800-488-3242
Statex
  Montreal, QC 514-527-6039
Stay Tuned Industries
  Clinton, NJ 908-730-8455
Steritech Food Safety & Environmental Hygiene
  Charlotte, NC 800-868-0089
Strasburger & Siegel
  Hanover, MD 888-726-3753
Stratecon International Consultants
  Winston Salem, NC...............336-768-6808
Structure Probe
  West Chester, PA................800-242-4774
Suburban Laboratories Inc
  Geneva, IL....................800-783-5227
TEI Analytical Svc Inc
  Niles, IL 847-647-1345
TLC & Associates
  Amarillo, TX...................806-353-1517
Total Quality Corporation
  Branford, CT...................800-453-9729
Tragon Corp
  Redwood City, CA 800-841-1177
Trap-Zap Environmental
  Wyckoff, NJ 800-282-8727
Triad Scientific
  Manasquan, NJ 800-867-6690
Truesdail Laboratories
  Tustin, CA.....................714-730-6239
Tuchenhagen
  Columbia, MD 410-910-6000
Underwriters Laboratories Inc
  Camas, WA 877-854-3577
Universal Sanitizers & Supplies
  Rockford, TN 888-634-3196
Vivolac Cultures Corp
  Greenfield, IN 800-848-6522
Warren Analytical Laboratory
  Greeley, CO....................800-945-6669
West Agro
  Kansas City, MO................816-891-7700
Wilhelmsen Consulting
  Milpitas, CA 408-946-4525
Winston Laboratories Inc
  Vernon Hills, IL 800-946-5229

Woodson-Tenent Laboratories
  Des Moines, IA 515-265-1461
Woodson-Tenent Laboratories
  Memphis, TN 515-280-8378
Woodson-Tenent Laboratories
  Dayton, OH 937-236-5756
X-R-I Testing Inc
  Troy, MI 800-973-4800

Contract Manufacturing
Agropur MSI, LLC
  La Crosse, WI 800-359-2345
Barrington Nutritionals
  Harrison, NY 800-684-2436
Bridgewell Resources LLC
  Clackamas, OR 800-481-3557
Haven's Candies
  Westbrook, ME 800-639-6309

Bakery
Pacmoore Products
  Hammond, IN 866-610-2666

Blending & Mixing
D2 Ingredients, LP.
  De Pere, WI....................920-425-8870
Firebird Artisan Mills
  Harvey, ND 701-324-4330
Hermann Laue Spice Company
  Uxbridge, ON 905-852-5100
Pacmoore Products
  Hammond, IN 866-610-2666
Sweeteners Plus Inc
  Lakeville, NY 585-346-3193

Contract Packaging
A La Carte
  Chicago, IL 800-722-2370
Aaron Thomas Co Inc
  Garden Grove, CA 800-394-4776
All American Seasonings
  Denver, CO 303-623-2320
Ameripec
  Buena Park, CA 714-994-2990
AmeriQual Foods
  Evansville, IN 812-867-1444
Athea Laboratories
  Milwaukee, WI 800-743-6417
Baldwin Richardson Foods
  Oakbrook Terrace, IL 866-644-2732
Baron Spices Inc
  St Louis, MO 314-535-9020
Blendco Inc
  Hattiesburg, MS 888-253-6326
Bridgewell Resources LLC
  Clackamas, OR 800-481-3557
Caraustar
  Austell, GA 770-948-3101
Carton Service Co
  Shelby, OH 800-533-7744
Century Foods Intl LLC
  Sparta, WI 800-269-1901
Chem Pack Inc
  Cincinnati, OH 800-421-2700
CMS Fine Foods
  Healdsburg, CA 707-473-9561
Cobitco Inc
  Denver, CO 303-296-8575
Compact Industries Inc
  St Charles, IL 800-513-4262
Conpac
  Warminster, PA 215-322-2755
Contact Industries
  Clackamas, OR 800-345-2232
Contract Comestibles
  East Troy, WI 262-642-9400
Crest Foods Inc
  Ashton, IL 800-435-6972
Crown Chemical Products
  Mississauga, ON 905-564-0904
Cup Pac Packaging Inc
  South Beloit, IL 877-347-9725
D2 Ingredients, LP.
  De Pere, WI....................920-425-8870
Diamond Packaging
  Rochester, NY 800-333-4079
Do-It Corp
  South Haven, MI................800-426-4822

Douglas Products
  Liberty, MO 800-223-3684
EMCO Packaging
  North Chicago, IL 847-689-2200
General Methods Corporation
  Peoria, IL 309-497-3344
Ginseng Up Corp
  Worcester, MA 800-446-7364
GKI Foods
  Brighton, MI 248-486-0055
Hagerty Foods
  Orange, CA 714-628-1230
Hamilton Soap & Oil Products
  Paterson, NJ 973-225-1031
Health Products Corp
  Yonkers, NY 914-423-2900
Hearthside Food Solutions
  Downers Grove, IL 630-967-3600
Hot Mama's Foods
  Springfield, MA 413-737-6572
Hyde & Hyde Inc
  Corona, CA 951-279-5239
Impact Nutrition
  Aurora, CO 720-374-7111
Innovative Food Processors Inc
  Faribault, MN 800-997-4437
Innovative Food Solutions LLC
  Columbus, OH 800-884-3314
Inter-Pack Corporation
  Monroe, MI 734-242-7755
Jo Mar Laboratories
  Campbell, CA 800-538-4545
Kent Precision Foods Group Inc
  Muscatine, IA 800-442-5252
KETCH
  Wichita, KS...................800-766-3777
KIK Custom Products
  Denver, CO 303-728-0871
KIK Custom Products
  Concord, ON 800-276-8260
LA Monica Fine Foods
  Millville, NJ
Longhorn Packaging Inc
  San Antonio, TX................800-433-7974
LRM Packaging
  South Hackensack, NJ 201-342-2530
Max Packaging
  Attalla, AL 800-543-5369
Mcclancy Seasonings Co
  Fort Mill, SC 800-843-1968
Mid Atlantic Packaging Co
  Dover, DE 800-284-1332
Modern Packaging
  Duluth, GA 770-622-1500
Nelipak
  Phoenix, AZ 602-269-7648
New Horizon Foods
  Union City, CA 510-489-8600
Pacific Harvest Products
  Bellevue, WA 425-401-7990
Packaging Associates
  Randolph, NJ 973-252-8890
Packaging Service Co Inc
  Pearland, TX 800-826-2949
Pacmoore Products
  Hammond, IN 866-610-2666
Pak Technologies
  Milwaukee, WI 414-438-8600
Paket Corporation
  Chicago, IL 773-221-7300
Pepper Source Inc
  Metairie, LA 504-885-3223
Per Pak/Orlandi
  Farmingdale, NY...............631-756-0110
Plaze Inc
  St Clair, MO 800-986-9509
Pluto Corporation
  French Lick, IN.................812-936-9988
Power Group
  St Charles, IL 630-587-3770
Power Packaging Inc
  Rosendale, WI 920-872-2181
Proact Inc
  Eagan, MN 877-245-0405
Q & B Foods
  Irwindale, CA 626-334-8090
Rempak Industries
  Fort Lee, NJ 201-585-9007
REX Pure Foods
  New Orleans, LA 800-344-8314
Riverside Industries
  St Helens, OR 503-397-1922

Roberts Packaging Equipment
  Des Plaines, IL 888-221-0700
SOPAKCO Foods
  Mullins, SC.......................800-276-9678
Specialty Food America Inc
  Hopkinsville, KY 888-881-1633
Specialty Lubricants
  Macedonia, OH....................800-238-5823
Stage Coach Sauces
  Palatka, FL.......................386-328-6330
Techform
  Mount Airy, NC 336-789-2115
Thor Inc
  Ogden, UT........................888-846-7462
Threshold Rehabilitation Svc
  Reading, PA.......................610-777-7691
Todd's
  Des Moines, IA....................800-247-5363
Truitt Bros, Inc.
  Salem, OR.........................800-547-8712
Unette Corp
  Randolph, NJ 973-328-6800
Vita Key Packaging
  Riverside, CA 909-355-1023
Vitatech Nutritional Sciences
  Tustin, CA........................714-832-9700
W H Wildman Company
  New Hampshire, OH................419-568-7531
WePackItAll
  Duarte, CA 626-301-9214
West Penn Oil Co Inc
  Warren, PA........................814-723-9000
Westvaco Corporation
  Richmond, VA.....................804-233-9205
Whitlock Packaging Corp
  Fort Gibson, OK 918-478-4300

Dry Product

All American Seasonings
  Denver, CO.......................303-623-2320
Magic Seasoning Blends
  New Orleans, LA 800-457-2857

Liquid Product

LA Monica Fine Foods
  Millville, NJ

Custom Services

Blending

A.C. Legg
  Calera, AL........................800-422-5344
All American Seasonings
  Denver, CO.......................303-623-2320
American Pasien Co
  Burlington, NJ....................609-387-3130
Arro Corp
  Hodgkins, IL......................877-929-2776
Calhoun Bend Mill
  Libuse, LA 800-519-6455
California Blending Co
  El Monte, CA 626-448-1918
Elite Spice Inc
  Jessup, MD 800-232-3531
Invensys APV Products
  Houston, TX.......................713-329-1600
Popcorn Connection
  North Hollywood, CA 800-852-2676
Shashi Foods
  Toronto, ON 866-748-7441
Texas Spice Co
  Round Rock, TX...................800-880-8007
W H Wildman Company
  New Hampshire, OH................419-568-7531
Washington State Juice
  Pacoima, CA......................818-899-1195
Watershed Foods
  Gridley, IL........................309-747-3000

Drying

American Pasien Co
  Burlington, NJ.....................609-387-3130

Extrusion

Legacy Plastics
  Henderson, KY 270-827-1318

Formulations

American Pasien Co
  Burlington, NJ.....................609-387-3130
Apotheca Inc
  Woodbine, IA 800-736-3130
Century Foods Intl LLC
  Sparta, WI........................800-269-1901
Clofine Dairy Products Inc
  Linwood, NJ.......................800-441-1001
Compact Industries Inc
  St Charles, IL.....................800-513-4262
GKI Foods
  Brighton, MI......................248-486-0055
Innovative Food Solutions LLC
  Columbus, OH.....................800-884-3314
Jimbo's Jumbos Inc
  Edenton, NC 800-334-4771
Kline Process Systems Inc
  Reading, PA.......................610-371-0300
Magic Seasoning Blends
  New Orleans, LA 800-457-2857
Mancini Packing Co
  Zolfo Springs, FL..................800-741-1778
Old Mansion Inc
  Petersburg, VA....................800-476-1877
Solo Foods
  Countryside, IL....................800-328-7656
SOPAKCO Foods
  Mullins, SC.......................800-276-9678
Thiel Cheese & Ingredients
  Hilbert, WI.......................920-989-1440
Thor Inc
  Ogden, UT........................888-846-7462
Vita Key Packaging
  Riverside, CA 909-355-1023
W H Wildman Company
  New Hampshire, OH................419-568-7531

Grinding

Shashi Foods
  Toronto, ON 866-748-7441

Dealers

Meat

Becker Foods
  Westminster, CA 714-891-9474
Dicks Packing Plant
  New Lexington, OH 740-342-4150
ELP Inc
  Elizabeth, CO 303-688-2240
Eunice Locker Plant
  Eunice, NM.......................505-394-2060
Fresh Mark Inc.
  Massillon, OH.....................330-832-7491
Graham Ice & Locker Plant
  Graham, TX 940-549-1975
Henningsen Foods Inc
  Hopkins, MN 952-258-4000
Hormel Foods Corp.
  Austin, MN 507-437-5611
L & L Packing Co
  Chicago, IL........................773-285-5400
Marketing Management Inc
  Fort Worth, TX 800-433-2004
Moyer Packing Co.
  Elroy, PA.........................800-967-8325
Package Concepts & Materials Inc
  Greenville, SC.....................800-424-7264
Ritchie's Foods
  Piketon, OH 800-628-1290
Spencer Packing Company
  Washington, NC 252-946-4161
SugarCreek
  Washington Ct Hs, OH 800-848-8205
Weber-Stephen Products Company
  Palatine, IL.......................800-446-1071
Welch Brothers
  Bartlett, IL........................847-741-6134

Designers

Architectural & Engineering

Amherst Stainless Fabrication
  Amherst, NY......................716-691-7012
Austin Co
  Cleveland, OH 440-544-2600

Boldt Co
  Appleton, WI 920-739-6321
Concepts & Design International, Ltd
  West Nyack, NY 845-358-1558
Facility Group
  Smyrna, GA.......................770-437-2700
KLEEN Line Corp
  Newburyport, MA.................800-259-5973
Select Technologies Inc
  Belmont, MI......................616-866-6700
Stellar Group
  Jacksonville, FL...................800-488-2900
Tippmann Group
  Fort Wayne, IN 260-490-3000
Webber Smith Assoc
  Lancaster, PA.....................717-291-2266

Interior & Store Fixture

Accommodation Program
  New York, NY 800-929-1414
Acryline
  North Attleboro, MA 508-695-7124
Air Pak Products & Services
  Winter Park, FL...................800-824-7725
Aldo Locascio
  Tucson, AZ 800-488-8729
All About Furniture
  Norcross, GA 800-893-0919
Atlas Restaurant Supply
  Indianapolis, IN 877-528-5275
Bargreen Ellingson
  Tacoma, WA 800-322-4441
Big-D Construction Corp
  Salt Lake City, UT 801-415-6000
Cannon Equipment Company
  Cannon Falls, MN.................800-825-8501
Carmona Designs
  Chula Vista, CA 619-425-2800
CDI Service & Mfg Inc
  Largo, FL 727-536-2207
Citra-Tech
  Lefkosia, CY
Design Group
  Clearwater, FL 727-441-2825
Divercon Inc
  Omaha, NE 402-571-5115
Fenster Consulting Inc
  Port Washington, NY 516-944-7108
Group One Partners
  Boston, MA.......................617-268-7000
Inman Foodservices Group LLC
  Nashville, TN 615-321-5591
Innovations by Design
  Chadds Ford, PA..................610-558-0160
Intelplex Designers
  St Louis, MO......................314-983-9996
Landmark Kitchen Design
  Chandler, AZ......................866-621-3192
Legge & Associates
  Rockwood, ON 519-856-0444
Leotta Designers
  Miami, FL.........................305-371-4949
Material Systems Engineering
  Stilesville, IN 800-634-0904
Mead & Hunt Inc
  Madison, WI......................888-364-7272
Nina Mauritz Design Service
  Libertyville, IL....................847-968-4438
Oak Street Manufacturing
  Monticello, IA.....................877-465-4344
Refrigerated Warehousing
  Jasper, GA........................800-873-2008
RGN Developers
  New Providence, NJ
Ridg-U-Rak
  North East, PA....................866-479-7225
Shook Kelley Design Group
  Charlotte, NC.....................704-377-0661
Southern Express
  Saint Louis, MO 800-444-9157
Southern Store Fixtures Inc
  Bessemer, AL.....................800-552-6283
Spartan Showcase
  Union, MO 800-325-0775
SSOE Group
  Toledo, OH 419-255-3830
TKF Inc
  Cincinnati, OH 513-241-5910
Triad Scientific
  Manasquan, NJ 800-867-6690

TSG Merchandising
Perkasie, PA 215-453-9220
Twin City Wholesale
Opelika, AL........................800-344-6935
United Insulated Structures
Berkeley, IL.......................800-821-5538

Kitchen (Commercial, Institutional, Restaurant)

Andgar Corp
Ferndale, WA 360-366-9900
Atlas Restaurant Supply
Indianapolis, IN 877-528-5275
Best Restaurant Equip & Design
Columbus, OH......................800-837-2378
Carmona Designs
Chula Vista, CA 619-425-2800
G.V. Aikman Company
Indianapolis, IN 800-886-4029
Klinger Constructors LLC
Albuquerque, NM...................505-822-9990
Landmark Kitchen Design
Chandler, AZ.......................866-621-3192
St Onge Ruff & Associates
Kansas City, MO....................800-800-5261
Tiny Drumsticks
New York, NY 917-526-3263

Package, Carton & Display

Ad Mart Identity Group
Danville, KY.......................800-354-2102
Adpro
Solon, OH..........................440-542-1111
Ball Design Group
Fresno, CA.........................559-434-6100
C F Napa Brand Design
Napa, CA...........................707-265-1891
Center for Packaging Education
Somers, NY.........................914-276-0425
D'Addario Design Associates
New York, NY 212-302-0059
Dunn Woodworks
Shrewsbury, PA.....................877-835-8592
E2M
Duluth, GA.........................800-622-4326
Eagle-Concordia Paper Corporation
Farmingdale, NY 212-255-3860
FFR Merchandising Inc
Twinsburg, OH......................800-422-2547
Filet Menu
Los Angeles, CA....................310-202-8000
Gary Plastic Packaging Corporation
Bronx, NY..........................800-221-8151
Graphic Arts Center
Melbourne, FL......................888-345-7436
Graphic Impressions of Illinois
River Grove, IL....................708-453-1100
Greenfield Paper Box Co
Greenfield, MA.....................413-773-9414
HMG Worldwide In-Store Marketing
New York, NY 212-736-2300
Hunter Graphics
Umatilla, FL.......................407-644-2060
IPG International Packaging Group
Agoura Hills, CA...................818-865-1428
Krimstock Enterprises
Pennsauken, NJ.....................856-665-3676
Landmark Kitchen Design
Chandler, AZ.......................866-621-3192
LSI Industries Inc
Blue Ash, OH.......................513-793-3200
Menu Graphics
Olmsted Falls, OH..................216-696-1460
Mold-Rite Plastics LLC
Twinsburg, OH......................330-425-4206
Nottingham Spirk
Cleveland, OH......................216-231-7830
Omni Craft Inc
Hopkins, MN........................952-988-9944
PacTech Engineering
Cincinnati, OH.....................513-792-1090
Pharmaceutical & Food Special
San Jose, CA.......................408-275-0161
Presentations South
Orlando, FL........................407-657-2108
R.C. Keller & Associates
Barnegat, NJ.......................973-694-8810
Robin Shepherd Group
Jacksonville, FL...................877-896-8774

Roxanne Signs Inc
Gaithersburg, MD...................301-428-4911
Seattle Menu Specialists
Kent, WA...........................800-622-2826
THE Corporation
Terre Haute, IN 800-783-2151
Thomson-Leeds Company
New York, NY 800-535-9361
TSG Merchandising
Perkasie, PA 215-453-9220
US Magnetix
Minneapolis, MN....................763-540-9497
Wishbone Utensil Tableware Line
Wheat Ridge, CO 866-266-5928
WNA Hopple Plastics
Florence, KY.......................800-446-4622

Process Vessels & Tanks

Fourinox Inc
Green Bay, WI......................920-336-0621

Food Closeouts, Surplus, Salvage & Liquidators

All About Furniture
Norcross, GA 800-893-0919
CSV Sales
Plymouth, MI 800-886-6866
Mar-Khem Industries
Cinnaminson, NJ
Milton A. Klein Company
New York, NY 800-221-0248

Foodservice

3M
St. Paul, MN 888-364-3577
Mcclancy Seasonings Co
Fort Mill, SC......................800-843-1968
Regional Produce
Birmingham, AL.....................800-726-0711

Amusement & Theme Parks

Alkazone/Better Health Lab
Hackensack, NJ.....................800-810-1888

Branded Concepts

Hixson Architecture Engrng
Cincinnati, OH 513-241-1230

Retail

Canon Potato Company
Center, CO 719-754-3445

Supermarkets

99 Ranch Market
Hacienda Heights, CA 626-839-2899
Certified Grocers Midwest
Hodgkins, IL.......................708-579-2100
Ingles Markets, Inc.
Black Mountain, NC.................828-669-2941
Schnuck Markets, Inc.
St. Louis, MO......................800-264-4400
Sprouts Farmers Market Inc.
Phoenix, AZ
WEIS Markets Inc.
Sunbury, PA........................866-999-9347

General

Hop Growers of Washington
Moxee, WA..........................509-453-4749

Ice Making Plants

Blast It Clean
Kansas City, MO....................877-379-4233
Boise Cold Storage Co
Boise, ID..........................208-344-8477
Buck Ice & Coal Co
Columbus, GA 706-322-5451
Carbonic Reserves
San Antonio, TX....................800-880-1911
Four Corners Ice
Farmington, NM.....................505-325-3813
Girton Manufacturing Co
Millville, PA......................570-458-5521

Graham Ice & Locker Plant
Graham, TX 940-549-1975
Home City Ice Co
Cincinnati, OH 800-759-4411
Martin Electric Plants
Ephrata, PA 800-713-7968
Myers Ice Company
Garden City, KS 800-767-5751
Polar Ice
Bloomington, IN....................800-733-0423
Turbo Refrigerating Company
Denton, TX.........................940-387-4301

Laboratories

Food Research & Development

915 Labs
Centennial, CO 855-915-5227
A&L Western Ag Lab
Modesto, CA........................209-529-4080
ABC Laboratories
Columbia, MO.......................800-538-5227
Accra Laboratory
Cleveland, OH 800-567-7200
ADD Testing & Research
Valley Stream, NY 516-568-9197
Advance Energy Technologies
Halfmoon, NY.......................800-724-0198
Agricultural Research Service
Washington, SW 202-720-3656
Analytical Labs
Boise, ID..........................800-574-5773
Anresco Laboratories
San Francisco, CA..................800-359-0920
Aspen Research Corporation
White Bear Lake, MN................651-773-7961
BCN Research Laboratories
Rockford, TN.......................800-236-0505
Blendco Inc
Hattiesburg, MS....................888-253-6326
BluMetric Environmental Inc.
Ottawa, ON.........................613-839-3053
Celsis Laboratory Group
Chicago, IL........................800-222-8260
Coffee Enterprises
Burlington, VT.....................800-375-3398
CPM Roskamp Champion
Waterloo, IA.......................800-366-2563
Culinar
Montreal, QC.......................514-255-2811
Deibel Laboratories Inc
Madison, WI........................608-241-1177
ENSCO Inc
Springfield, VA....................703-321-9000
Environmental Express
Charleston, SC.....................800-343-5319
Eurofins S-F Analytical Labs
New Berlin, WI.....................800-300-6700
Eurofins Scientific Inc
Des Moines, IA.....................800-841-1110
Eurofins Scientific Inc.
Dayton, OH.........................800-880-1038
Flow International Corp.
Kent, WA...........................800-446-3569
Food Safety Net Services Ltd
San Antonio, TX....................888-525-9788
Food-Tek
Whippany, NJ 800-648-8114
Foods Research Laboratories
Boston, MA.........................617-442-3322
Global Product Development Group
Northbrook, IL.....................847-504-0464
Hahn Laboratories
Columbia, SC 803-799-1614
Hollander Horizon International
Princeton, NJ......................609-924-7577
Hydro-Thermal Corp
Waukesha, WI.......................800-952-0121
Industrial Laboratories Co
Wheat Ridge, CO....................800-456-5288
Ingman Laboratories
Minneapolis, MN....................612-724-0121
Innovative Food Solutions LLC
Columbus, OH.......................800-884-3314
Intertek USA
Boxborough, MA.....................800-967-5352
Irvine Analytical Labs
Irvine, CA.........................877-445-6554
ITS/ETL Testing Laboratories
Laguna Niguel, CA..................949-448-4100

J Leek Assoc Inc
Edenton, NC 252-482-4456
Jenike & Johanson Inc
Tyngsboro, MA.............978-649-3300
Krueger Food Laboratories
Chelmsford, MA.............978-256-1220
Lebensmittel Consulting
Fostoria, OH 419-435-2774
Libra Technical Center
Metuchen, NJ 732-321-5200
Medallion Laboratories
Minneapolis, MN 800-245-5615
Micro-Chem Laboratory
Mississauga, ON 905-795-0490
Microbac Laboratories
Pittsburgh, PA...............866-515-4668
Microbac-Wilson Devision
Wilson, NC 252-237-4175
Midwest Laboratories
Omaha, NE 402-334-7770
Miles Willard Technologies
Idaho Falls, ID 208-523-4741
National Food Laboratories Inc
Livermore, CA 925-828-1440
Northeast Laboratory Svc
Winslow, ME................866-591-7120
Northview Laboratories
Spartanburg, SC 864-574-7728
Northwest Laboratories
Seattle, WA 206-763-6252
Nutrition Research
Livingston, MT..............406-222-3541
O.D. Kurtz Associates
Palm Bay, FL................321-723-0135
Oklabs
Oklahoma City, OK 405-843-6832
Phytotherapy Research Laboratory
Lobelville, TN...............800-274-3727
POS Pilot Plant Corporation
Saskatoon, SK...............800-230-2751
Protein Research
Livermore, CA 800-948-1991
Purity Laboratories
Lake Oswego, OR............800-977-3636
Q Laboratories
Cincinnati, OH 513-471-1300
Quality Bakers of America
Allentown, PA...............973-263-6970
R F Schiffmann Assoc.
New York, NY 212-362-7021
Rqa Product Dynamics
Orland Park, IL..............708-364-7055
Rtech Laboratories
St Paul, MN.................800-328-9687
S & J Laboratories Inc
Portage, MI 269-324-7383
Sani-Pure Food Laboratories
Saddle Brook, NJ 201-843-2525
Silliker, Inc
Chicago, IL..................312-938-5151
Soyatech Inc
Bar Harbor, ME..............800-424-7692
Strasburger & Siegel
Hanover, MD................888-726-3753
Structure Probe
West Chester, PA.............800-242-4774
TEI Analytical Svc Inc
Niles, IL.....................847-647-1345
Terriss Consolidate
Asbury Park, NJ 800-342-1611
Trans-Chemco Inc
Bristol, WI...................800-880-2498
Truesdail Laboratories
Tustin, CA...................714-730-6239
USDA-NASS
Washington, DC 800-727-9540
Valley Lea Laboratories Inc
Mishawaka, IN 800-822-1283
Vivolac Cultures Corp
Greenfield, IN................800-848-6522
Warren Analytical Laboratory
Greeley, CO..................800-945-6669
Winston Laboratories Inc
Vernon Hills, IL..............800-946-5229

Master Planning & Logistics

Dennsi Group
Springfield, MA 413-737-1353

Nutritional Analyses & Labeling

Aibmr Life Sciences
Puyallup, WA 253-286-2888
BUCHI Corp
New Castle, DE...............877-692-8844
Q Laboratories
Cincinnati, OH 513-471-1300

Packaging Services

915 Labs
Centennial, CO 855-915-5227
A La Carte
Chicago, IL...................800-722-2370
Aaron Thomas Co Inc
Garden Grove, CA 800-394-4776
Baron Spices Inc
St Louis, MO..................314-535-9020
Basic Leasing Corporation
Kearny, NJ....................973-817-7373
Bluegrass Packaging Industries
Louisville, KY.................800-489-3159
Camco Chemicals
Florence, KY..................800-554-1001
Century Foods Intl LLC
Sparta, WI....................800-269-1901
Compact Industries Inc
St Charles, IL 800-513-4262
David's Goodbatter
Bausman, PA...................717-872-0652
Decko Products Inc
Sandusky, OH 800-537-6143
Diamond Packaging
Rochester, NY.................800-333-4079
Douglas Products
Liberty, MO...................800-223-3684
Faribault Foods, Inc.
Fairbault, MN 507-331-1400
Gary Plastic Packaging Corporation
Bronx, NY....................800-221-8151
Ginseng Up Corp
Worcester, MA 800-446-7364
Grace Tea Co
Acton, MA 978-635-9500
Griffin Food Co
Muskogee, OK 800-866-6311
Hamersmith, Inc.
Miami, FL....................305-685-7451
Hearthside Food Solutions
Downers Grove, IL.............630-967-3600
Hogtown Brewing Company
Mississauga, ON...............905-855-9065
IFoodDecisionSciences
Kenmore, WA 206-219-3703
Impact Nutrition
Aurora, CO....................720-374-7111
Independent Packers Corporation
Seattle, WA 206-285-6000
Innovative Food Processors Inc
Faribault, MN 800-997-4437
Jess Jones Vineyard
Dixon, CA 707-678-3839
K & L Intl
Ontario, CA...................888-598-5588
Kent Precision Foods Group Inc
Muscatine, IA 800-442-5252
Laundry Aids
Carlstadt, NJ..................201-933-3500
Linker Machines
Rockaway, NJ.................973-983-0001
LRM Packaging
South Hackensack, NJ..........201-342-2530
Luke's Almond Acres
Reedley, CA 559-638-3483
Nature Most Laboratories
Middletown, CT 800-234-2112
Pacific Spice Company Inc.
Commerce, CA.................323-726-9190
Packaging Associates
Randolph, NJ..................973-252-8890
Packaging Service Co Inc
Pearland, TX..................800-826-2949
Pak Technologies
Milwaukee, WI................414-438-8600
Pluto Corporation
French Lick, IN................812-936-9988
Power Group
St Charles, IL.................630-587-3770
Power Packaging Inc
Rosendale, WI.................920-872-2181

Proact Inc
Eagan, MN 877-245-0405
Q & B Foods
Irwindale, CA 626-334-8090
Quality Croutons
Chicago, IL...................800-334-2796
Rempak Industries
Fort Lee, NJ...................201-585-9007
REX Pure Foods
New Orleans, LA 800-344-8314
Ribble Production
Warminster, PA................215-674-1706
Roberts Packaging Equipment
Des Plaines, IL.................888-221-0700
Robin Shepherd Group
Jacksonville, FL................877-896-8774
Schroeder Machine
San Marcos, CA 760-591-9733
Sungjae Corporation
Irvine, CA 949-757-1727
Techform
Mount Airy, NC 336-789-2115
Thor Inc
Ogden, UT....................888-846-7462
Todd's
Des Moines, IA................800-247-5363
Twelve Baskets Sales & Market
Atlanta, GA...................800-420-8840
Vita Key Packaging
Riverside, CA..................909-355-1023
Welch Brothers
Bartlett, IL....................847-741-6134
WePackItAll
Duarte, CA 626-301-9214
Westvaco Corporation
Richmond, VA.................804-233-9205

Packers

Baron Spices Inc
St Louis, MO..................314-535-9020
Bluegrass Packaging Industries
Louisville, KY.................800-489-3159
Compact Industries Inc
St Charles, IL 800-513-4262
Copper Hills Fruit Sales
Fresno, CA 559-432-5400
ELP Inc
Elizabeth, CO 303-688-2240
Family Tree Farms
Reedley, CA 559-591-6280
Food Pak Corp
San Mateo, CA 650-341-6559
Ful-Flav-R Foods
Alamo, CA 925-838-0300
Grace Tea Co
Acton, MA 978-635-9500
Hamersmith, Inc.
Miami, FL....................305-685-7451
Hogtown Brewing Company
Mississauga, ON...............905-855-9065
Independent Packers Corporation
Seattle, WA 206-285-6000
Jess Jones Vineyard
Dixon, CA....................707-678-3839
Kent Precision Foods Group Inc
Muscatine, IA 800-442-5252
Luke's Almond Acres
Reedley, CA 559-638-3483
Moyer Packing Co.
Elroy, PA.....................800-967-8325
Nebraska Bean
Clearwater, NE................800-253-6502
Pacific Spice Company Inc.
Commerce, CA.................323-726-9190
Power Packaging Inc
Rosendale, WI.................920-872-2181
Q & B Foods
Irwindale, CA 626-334-8090
Quality Croutons
Chicago, IL...................800-334-2796
Rempak Industries
Fort Lee, NJ...................201-585-9007
REX Pure Foods
New Orleans, LA 800-344-8314
Robin Shepherd Group
Jacksonville, FL................877-896-8774
Signature Foods
Pendergrass, DR...............706-693-0098
Spencer Packing Company
Washington, NC 252-946-4161

Product Categories / Consultants & Services: Personnel Services

Twelve Baskets Sales & Market
Atlanta, GA 800-420-8840
Welch Brothers
Bartlett, IL 847-741-6134

Fruit

Copper Hills Fruit Sales
Fresno, CA 559-432-5400
Family Tree Farms
Reedley, CA 559-591-6280

Meat

ELP Inc
Elizabeth, CO 303-688-2240
Lynden Meat Co
Lynden, WA 360-354-2449
Spencer Packing Company
Washington, NC 252-946-4161
Welch Brothers
Bartlett, IL 847-741-6134

Personnel Services

Bristol Associates Inc
Los Angeles, CA 310-670-0525
Capitol Recruiting Group
Newport News, VA 757-812-8677
Clanton & Company
Orange, CA 714-282-7980
Cook Associates
Chicago, IL 312-329-0900
Dallas Roth Young
Richardson, TX 972-233-5000
David E. Moley & Associates
Wrightsville Beach, NC 910-256-3826
Dixie Search Associates
Dauphin Island, AL 770-675-7300
Executive Referral Services
Chicago, IL 866-466-3339
Focus
Minneapolis, MN 612-706-4444
Food Executives Network
Milwaukee, WI 414-962-7684
Fox-Morris Associates
Charlotte, NC 800-777-6503
Futures
Barrington, NH 603-664-5811
Harper Associates
Farmington Hills, MI 248-932-1170
Inter-Access
Etobicoke, ON 514-744-6262
Johnson Associates
Wheaton, IL 630-690-9200
Judge
W Conshohocken, PA 888-228-7162
Kent R Hedman & Assoc
Arlington, TX 817-277-0888
Landsman Foodservice Net
Owing Mills, MD 410-363-7038
Lawless Link
San Antonio, TX 210-342-8899
Lawrence Glaser Associates
Moorestown, NJ 856-778-9500
Management Recruiters
Philadelphia, PA 800-875-4000
McGraw Hill/London House
Park Ridge, IL 800-221-8378
Metroplex Corporation
Houston, TX 281-257-8570
Nelson & Associates Recruiting
Kirkland, WA 425-823-0956
North Company
Waupaca, WI 715-258-6104
P & A Food Ind Recruiters
Woodbury, NJ 856-384-4774
Resources in Food & FoodTeam
St Louis, MO. 800-875-1028
Riley Cole Professional Recruitment
Oakland, CA 510-336-2333
Ritt-Ritt & Associates
Rolling Meadows, IL 847-827-7771
Rjo Associates
Bradenton, FL 941-756-3001
RJR Executive Search
Houston, TX 281-368-8550
Roth Young Bellevue
Bellevue, WA 425-454-0677
Roth Young Chicago
Mount Prospect, IL 847-797-9211

Roth Young Farmington Hills
Farmington Hills, MI 248-539-9242
Roth Young Hicksville
Hicksville, NY 516-822-6000
Roth Young Minneapolis
Minneapolis, MN 800-356-6655
Roth Young Murrysville
Murrysville, PA 724-733-5900
Roth Young New York
New York, NY 212-557-8181
Roth Young of Tampa Bay
Tampa, FL 800-646-1513
Roth Young Washougal
Washougal, WA. 360-835-3136
S-H-S International of Wilkes
Wilkes Barre, PA 570-825-3411
SBB & Associates
Norcross, GA 770-449-7610
Search West
Los Angeles, CA 310-203-9797
Tom McCall & Associates
Millsboro, DE 410-539-0700
Wayne Group LTD
San Francisco, CA 415-421-2010
William Willis Worldwide
Greenwich, CT 203-532-1919

Employment Agencies

Bristol Associates Inc
Los Angeles, CA 310-670-0525
Capitol Recruiting Group
Newport News, VA 757-812-8677
Clanton & Company
Orange, CA 714-282-7980
Cook Associates
Chicago, IL 312-329-0900
Dallas Roth Young
Richardson, TX 972-233-5000
David E. Moley & Associates
Wrightsville Beach, NC 910-256-3826
Dixie Search Associates
Dauphin Island, AL 770-675-7300
Executive Referral Services
Chicago, IL 866-466-3339
Focus
Minneapolis, MN 612-706-4444
Food Executives Network
Milwaukee, WI 414-962-7684
Food Management Search
Springfield, MA 413-732-2666
Fox-Morris Associates
Charlotte, NC 800-777-6503
Futures
Barrington, NH 603-664-5811
Harper Associates
Farmington Hills, MI 248-932-1170
Inter-Access
Etobicoke, ON 514-744-6262
Johnson Associates
Wheaton, IL 630-690-9200
Judge
W Conshohocken, PA 888-228-7162
Kent R Hedman & Assoc
Arlington, TX 817-277-0888
Landsman Foodservice Net
Owing Mills, MD 410-363-7038
Lawless Link
San Antonio, TX 210-342-8899
Lawrence Glaser Associates
Moorestown, NJ 856-778-9500
Management Recruiters
Philadelphia, PA 800-875-4000
McGraw Hill/London House
Park Ridge, IL. 800-221-8378
Metroplex Corporation
Houston, TX 281-257-8570
Nelson & Associates Recruiting
Kirkland, WA 425-823-0956
North Company
Waupaca, WI. 715-258-6104
P & A Food Ind Recruiters
Woodbury, NJ 856-384-4774
Resources in Food & FoodTeam
St Louis, MO. 800-875-1028
Riley Cole Professional Recruitment
Oakland, CA 510-336-2333
Ritt-Ritt & Associates
Rolling Meadows, IL 847-827-7771
Rjo Associates
Bradenton, FL 941-756-3001

RJR Executive Search
Houston, TX 281-368-8550
Roth Young Bellevue
Bellevue, WA 425-454-0677
Roth Young Chicago
Mount Prospect, IL 847-797-9211
Roth Young Farmington Hills
Farmington Hills, MI 248-539-9242
Roth Young Hicksville
Hicksville, NY 516-822-6000
Roth Young Minneapolis
Minneapolis, MN 800-356-6655
Roth Young Murrysville
Murrysville, PA. 724-733-5900
Roth Young New York
New York, NY 212-557-8181
Roth Young of Tampa Bay
Tampa, FL 800-646-1513
Roth Young Washougal
Washougal, WA. 360-835-3136
S-H-S International of Wilkes
Wilkes Barre, PA 570-825-3411
SBB & Associates
Norcross, GA 770-449-7610
Search West
Los Angeles, CA 310-203-9797
Tom McCall & Associates
Millsboro, DE 410-539-0700
Wayne Group LTD
San Francisco, CA 415-421-2010
William Willis Worldwide
Greenwich, CT 203-532-1919

Project Management

Dennsi Group
Springfield, MA 413-737-1353

Quality Control

AIB International
Manhattan, KS 800-633-5137
Delta Trak
Pleasanton, CA 800-962-6776
FoodLogiQ
Durham, NC 866-492-4468
Haug Quality Equipment
Morgan Hill, CA. 408-465-8160
Hollander Horizon International
Princeton, NJ. 609-924-7577
J.M. Swank Company
North Liberty, IA 800-567-9265
Lixi, Inc.
Huntley, IL 847-961-6666
Orthodox Union
New York, NY 212-563-4000
Quality Chekd Dairies Inc
Lisle, IL 630-717-1110
Raque Food Systems
Louisville, KY 502-267-9641

Refinishing & Refurbishing Services

Ameriglobe LLC
Lafayette, LA 337-234-3211
B&B Neon Sign Company
Austin, TX. 800-791-6366
B.A.G. Corporation
Richardson, TX. 800-331-9200
Big State Spring Companyy
Corpus Christi, TX 800-880-0244
CDI Service & Mfg Inc
Largo, FL 727-536-2207
Cutler Brothers Box & Lumber
Fairview, NJ 201-943-2535
General Magnaplate Corp
Linden, NJ. 800-852-3301
Harrison of Texas
Houston, TX 800-245-5707
Illinois Wholesale Cash Rgstr
Elgin, IL 800-544-5493
J & L Honing
St Francis, WI. 800-747-9501
Refinishing Touch
Alpharetta, GA 800-523-9448
Sonoma Pacific Company
Montebello, CA 323-838-4374

Research & Development

Analyticon Discovery LLC
Rockville, MD 240-406-1256

Blue Diamond Growers
  Sacramento, CA 800-987-2329
Dried Ingredients, LLC.
  Miami, FL 786-999-8499
DuPont Nutrition & Biosciences
  New Century, KS 913-764-8100
Healthy Grain Foods LLC
  Northbrook, IL 847-272-5576
Island Scallops
  Qualicum Beach, BC 250-757-9811
J Rettenmaier USA LP
  Schoolcraft, MI 877-895-4099
Jagulana Herbal Products
  Badger, CA 888-465-3686
Raque Food Systems
  Louisville, KY 502-267-9641
Stratecon International Consultants
  Winston Salem, NC 336-768-6808
Terriss Consolidate
  Asbury Park, NJ 800-342-1611
Tiax LLC
  Lexington, MA 800-677-3000

Spray Drying Services

APV Americas
  Delavan, WI 800-252-5200
Brady Enterprises Inc
  East Weymouth, MA 781-337-5000
Innovative Food Processors Inc
  Faribault, MN 800-997-4437
Quality Ingredients
  Burnsville, MN 952-898-4002
Vector Corp
  Marion, IA 319-377-8263

Testing & Sampling Services

3M
  St. Paul, MN 888-364-3577
A&L Western Ag Lab
  Modesto, CA 209-529-4080
Accra Laboratory
  Cleveland, OH 800-567-7200
Accu-Labs Research
  Golden, CO 303-277-9514
Advanced Instruments Inc
  Norwood, MA 800-225-4034
AIB International
  Manhattan, KS 800-633-5137
Airflow Sciences Corp
  Livonia, MI 734-525-0300
Altek Co
  Torrington, CT 860-482-7626
AM Test Laboratories
  Kirkland, WA 425-885-1664

Barrow-Agee Laboratories Inc
  Memphis, TN 901-332-1590
Biological Services
  Kansas City, MO 913-236-6868
BluMetric Environmental Inc.
  Ottawa, ON 613-839-3053
Celsis Laboratory Group
  Chicago, IL 800-222-8260
Coffee Enterprises
  Burlington, VT 800-375-3398
Covance Inc.
  Princeton, NJ 888-268-2623
Deibel Laboratories Inc
  Madison, WI 608-241-1177
Delta Trak
  Pleasanton, CA 800-962-6776
DFL Laboratories
  Chicago, IL 312-938-5151
ENSCO Inc
  Springfield, VA 703-321-9000
Enviro-Test/Perry Laboratories
  Woodridge, IL 630-324-6685
Environmental Systems
  Culpeper, VA 800-541-2116
Eurofins DQCI
  St Paul, MN 763-785-0484
Eurofins S-F Analytical Labs
  New Berlin, WI. 800-300-6700
Eurofins Scientific Inc.
  Dayton, OH 800-880-1038
Gaynes Labs Inc
  Bridgeview, IL 708-233-6655
Global Product Development Group
  Northbrook, IL 847-504-0464
Healthy Dining
  San Diego, CA 800-266-2049
Industrial Laboratories Co
  Wheat Ridge, CO 800-456-5288
Innovative Food Solutions LLC
  Columbus, OH 800-884-3314
International Approval Services
  Cleveland, OH 877-235-9791
Intertek USA
  Boxborough, MA 800-967-5352
ITS/ETL Testing Laboratories
  Laguna Niguel, CA 949-448-4100
Jl Analytical Svc Inc
  Modesto, CA 209-538-8111
Krueger Food Laboratories
  Chelmsford, MA 978-256-1220
Libra Technical Center
  Metuchen, NJ 732-321-5200
Medallion Laboratories
  Minneapolis, MN 800-245-5615

Midwest Laboratories
  Omaha, NE 402-334-7770
Milligan & Higgins
  Johnstown, NY 518-762-4638
Minnesota Valley Testing Lab
  New Ulm, MN. 800-782-3557
Miroil
  Allentown, PA. 800-523-9844
Northland Labs
  Northbrook, IL 800-366-3522
Northview Laboratories
  Spartanburg, SC 864-574-7728
Pearson Research Assoc
  Santa Cruz, CA 831-429-9797
Phytopia Inc
  Dallas, TX. 888-750-9336
POS Pilot Plant Corporation
  Saskatoon, SK. 800-230-2751
PSI
  Oakbrook Terrace, IL 630-705-9290
Q Laboratories
  Cincinnati, OH 513-471-1300
QC
  Southampton, PA 215-355-3900
Richardson Researches
  South San Francisco, CA 510-653-4385
Rtech Laboratories
  St Paul, MN. 800-328-9687
Sani-Pure Food Laboratories
  Saddle Brook, NJ 201-843-2525
Sensory Spectrum
  New Providence, NJ. 908-376-7000
Shear/Kershman Laboratories
  Chesterfield, MO 636-519-8900
Soyatech Inc
  Bar Harbor, ME. 800-424-7692
Suburban Laboratories Inc
  Geneva, IL. 800-783-5227
TEI Analytical Svc Inc
  Niles, IL 847-647-1345
Underwriters Laboratories Inc
  Camas, WA 877-854-3577
Valley Lea Laboratories Inc
  Mishawaka, IN 800-822-1283
Vivolac Cultures Corp
  Greenfield, IN 800-848-6522
Warren Analytical Laboratory
  Greeley, CO. 800-945-6669
Woodson-Tenent Laboratories
  Des Moines, IA 515-265-1461
Woodson-Tenent Laboratories
  Memphis, TN 515-280-8378
Woodson-Tenent Laboratories
  Dayton, OH. 937-236-5756

Equipment & Machinery

Baking Industry

Allied Bakery and Food Service Equipment
Santa Fe Springs, CA 562-945-6506
Andy J. Egan Co.
Grand Rapids, MI 800-594-9244
Blendex Co
Louisville, KY 800-626-6325
C R Mfg
Waverly, NE 877-789-5844
Charles H Baldwin & Sons
West Stockbridge, MA 413-232-7785
Dunbar Co
Lemont, IL 630-257-2900
Ecs Warehouse
Buffalo, NY 716-833-7380
ENJAY Converters Limited
Cobourg, ON 800-427-5517
Exact Mixing Systems Inc
Memphis, TN 901-362-8501
FOODesign from tna
Wilsonville, OR 503-685-5030
Hcs Enterprises
Haryana,
Henry Group
Greenville, TX 903-883-2002
Lucks Food Equipment Company
Kent, WA 811-824-0696
LVO Manufacturing Inc
Rock Rapids, IA 712-472-3734
Marel Food Systems, Inc.
Lenexa, KS 913-888-9110
Nijal USA
Minneapolis, MN 651-353-6702
Oliver Packaging & Equipment Co.
Walker, MI 800-253-3893
Oshikiri Corp of America
Philadelphia, PA 215-637-8112
Ovention
Milwaukee, WI 855-298-6836
Pro Bake Inc
Twinsburg, OH 800-837-4427
Reiser
Canton, MA 734-821-1290
Render
Buffalo, NY 888-446-1010
Rheon, U.S.A.
Irvine, CA 949-768-1900
Russel T. Bundy Associates, Inc.
Urbana, OH 800-652-2151
Spray Dynamics LTD
St Clair, MO 800-260-7366
Sunset Paper Products
Simi Valley, CA 800-228-7882
Superior Products Company
Saint Paul, MN 800-328-9800
Twinkle Baker Decor USA
Daly City, CA 707-364-2740
WP Bakery Group
Shelton, CT 203-929-6530

Barbecue Equipment & Supplies

Amco Metals Indl
City of Industry, CA 626-855-2550
Archer Wire Intl Corp
Chicago, IL 708-563-1700
B R Machinery
Wedron, IL 800-310-7057
Bar-B-Q Woods
Newton, KS 800-528-0819
BBQ Pits by Klose
Houston, TX 800-487-7487
Belson Outdoors Inc
North Aurora, IL 800-323-5664
Best Brands Home Products
New York, NY 212-684-7456
Big John Corp
Pleasant Gap, PA 800-326-9575
Blodgett Oven Co
Burlington, VT 800-331-5842
Boehringer Mfg. Co. Inc.
Felton, CA 800-630-8665
Century Foods Intl LLC
Sparta, WI 800-269-1901

Cleveland Metal Stamping Company
Berea, OH 440-234-0010
Cookshack
Ponca City, OK 800-423-0698
Crown Verity
Brantford, ON 888-505-7240
Dar-B-Ques Barbecue Equipment
Minneapolis, MN 612-724-7425
Dynamic Cooking Systems
Huntington Beach, CA 800-433-8466
Esquire Mechanical Corp.
Armonk, NY 800-847-4206
F.P. Smith Wire Cloth Company
Northlake, IL 800-323-6842
GBS Foodservice Equipment, Inc.
Mississauga, ON 888-402-1242
Gril-Del
Mankato, MN 800-782-7320
Grill Greats
Saxonburg, PA 724-352-1511
Grillco Inc
Aurora, IL 800-644-0067
Grills to Go
Fresno, CA 877-869-2253
Hasty Bake Charcoal Grills
Tulsa, OK 800-426-6836
Hercules Food Equipment
Weston, ON 416-742-9673
Hickory Industries
North Bergen, NJ 800-732-9153
Holstein Manufacturing
Holstein, IA 800-368-4342
J & R Mfg Inc
Mesquite, TX 800-527-4831
Jackson Restaurant Supply
Jackson, TN 800-424-8943
Kay Home Products Inc
Antioch, IL 800-600-7009
King Packaging Co
Schenectady, NY 518-370-5464
Lazy Man Inc
Belvidere, NJ 800-475-1950
Lazzari Fuel Co LLC
Brisbane, CA 800-242-7265
Lignetics Inc
Sandpoint, ID 800-544-3834
Luhr Jensen & Sons Inc
Hood River, OR 541-386-3811
M.E. Heuck Company
Mason, OH 800-359-3200
Magi Kitch'n
Concord, NH 800-441-1492
Magnum Custom Trailer & BBQ Pits
Austin, TX 800-662-4686
Mali's All Natural Barbecue Supply Company
East Amherst, NY 800-289-6254
Masterbuilt Manufacturing Inc
Columbus, GA 706-327-5622
Mosshaim Innovations
Jacksonville, FL 888-995-7775
Music City Metals Inc
Nashville, TN 800-251-2674
Napoleon Appliance Corporation
Barrie, ON 866-820-8686
Nashville Wire Products
Nashville, TN 615-743-2480
Nature's Own
Attleboro, MA 508-399-8690
Old Mansion Inc
Petersburg, VA 800-476-1877
Ole Hickory Pits
Cape Girardeau, MO 800-223-9667
Patio King
Cutler Bay, FL 305-316-7508
Porcelain Metals Corporation
Louisville, KY 502-635-7421
Prince Castle Inc
Carol Stream, IL 800-722-7853
Profire Stainless Steel Barbecue
Miami, FL 305-665-5313
Roseville Charcoal & Mfg Co
Zanesville, OH 740-452-5473
Roto-Flex Oven Co
San Antonio, TX 877-859-1463
Smokaroma
Boley, OK 800-331-5565

Southern Pride Distributing
Alamo, TN 800-851-8180
Standex International Corp.
Salem, NH 603-893-9701
Stryco Wire Products
North York, ON 416-663-7000
Super Cooker
Lake Park, GA 800-841-7452
Superior Products Company
Saint Paul, MN 800-328-9800
Swanson Wire Works Industries, Inc.
Mesquite, TX 972-288-7465
Thermal Engineering Corp
Columbia, SC 800-331-0097
Toastmaster
Elgin, IL 847-741-3300
Townfood Equipment Corp
Brooklyn, NY 800-221-5032
West Oregon Wood Products Inc
Columbia City, OR 503-397-6707
Wilch Manufacturing
Topeka, KS 785-267-2762
Wood Stone Corp
Bellingham, WA 800-988-8103

Belting

Ace Manufacturing
Cincinnati, OH 800-653-5692
Ammeraal Beltech
Grand Rapids, MI 616-791-0292
Ammeraal Beltech Inc
Skokie, IL 800-323-4170
Andgar Corp
Ferndale, WA 360-366-9900
Asgco Manufacturing Inc
Allentown, PA 800-344-4000
Bamco Belting
Greenville, SC 800-258-2358
Belt Technologies Inc
Agawam, MA 413-786-9922
BMH
City of Industry, CA 909-349-2530
BNW Industries
Tippecanoe, IN 574-353-7855
Bowman Hollis Mfg Corp
Charlotte, NC 888-269-2358
C R Daniels Inc
Ellicott City, MD 800-933-2638
California Vibratory Feeders
Anaheim, CA 800-354-0972
Cambridge Intl. Inc.
Cambridge, MD 800-638-9560
Change Parts Inc
Ludington, MI 231-845-5107
Charles Walker North America
Fort Worth, TX 817-922-9834
Clipper Belt Lacer Company
Grand Rapids, MI 616-459-3196
Dearborn Mid-West Conveyor Co
Overland Park, KS 913-384-9950
Dresco Belting Co Inc
East Weymouth, MA 781-335-1350
Dyna-Veyor Inc
Newark, NJ 800-326-5009
Elmo Rietschle - A Gardner Denver Product
Qunicy, IL 217-222-5400
Emco Industrial Plastics
Cedar Grove, NJ 800-292-9906
Fabreeka International
Boise, ID 800-423-4469
Fenner Dunlop Americas Inc
Pittsburgh, PA 412-249-0700
Forbo Siegling LLC
Huntersville, NC 800-255-5581
Furnace Belt Company
Buffalo, NY 800-354-7213
Georgia Duck & Cordage Mill
Scottdale, GA 404-297-3170
Green Belt Industries Inc
Buffalo, NY 800-668-1114
Habasit America
Suwanee, GA 800-458-6431
Habasit America Plastic Div
Reading, PA 800-445-7898

Habasit Canada Limited
Oakville, ON.......................905-827-4131
Hoffmeyer Corp
San Leandro, CA...................888-744-1826
Home Rubber Co
Trenton, NJ.......................800-257-9441
Hudson Belting & Svc Co Inc
Worcester, MA....................508-756-0090
Intralox LLC
Harahan, LA......................800-535-8848
J L Becker Co
Plymouth, MI.....................800-837-4328
Keystone Rubber Corporation
Greenbackville, VA................800-394-5661
Lambeth Band Corporation
New Bedford, MA..................508-984-4700
LTI Boyd Corp
Modesto, CA......................888-244-6931
Lumsden Flexx Flow
Lancaster, PA.....................800-367-3664
M & R Sales & Svc Inc
Glen Ellyn, IL.....................800-736-6431
Mar-Con Wire Belt
Richmond, BC.....................877-962-7266
Maryland Wire Belts
Cleveland, OH....................800-677-2358
Mell & Co
Niles, IL..........................800-262-6355
Meriwether Industries
Bloomfield, NJ....................800-332-2358
Michigan Industrial Belting
Livonia, MI.......................800-778-1650
Midwest Rubber Svc & Supply
Minneapolis, MN..................800-537-7457
Monarch-McLaren
Weston, ON.......................416-741-9675
Northwind Inc
Alpena, AR.......................877-937-2585
Omni Metalcraft Corporation
Alpena, MI.......................989-358-7000
Our Name is Mud
New York, NY....................877-683-7867
Rademaker USA
Hudson, OH......................330-650-2345
Rahmann Belting & Industrial Rubber Products
Gastonia, NC.....................888-248-8148
Regal Power Transmission Solutions
Florence, KY......................859-342-7900
Regina USA
Oak Creek, WI....................414-571-0032
Shingle Belting
King of Prussia, PA................800-345-6294
Slip-Not Belting Corporation
Kingsport, TN.....................423-246-8141
Stiles Enterprises Inc
Rockaway, NJ.....................800-325-4232
Tecweigh
St Paul, MN.......................800-536-4880
Universal Die & Stampings
Prairie Du Sac, WI................608-643-2477
Vaughn Belting Co-Main Acct
Spartanburg, SC...................800-533-9086
Westfield Sheet Metal Works
Kenilworth, NJ....................908-276-5500
Wire Belt Co of America
Londonderry, NH..................603-644-2500

Belts

Crumb

American Conveyor Corporation
Astoria, NY.......................718-386-0480
King Bag & Mfg Co
Cincinnati, OH....................800-444-5464

Beverage Industry

Alard Equipment Corp
Williamson, NY...................315-589-4511
Bottom Line Processing Technologies, Inc.
Largo, GA........................888-834-4552
C.F.F. Stainless Steels
Hamilton, ON.....................800-263-4511
Dacam Machinery
Madison Heights, VA..............434-369-1259
Distillata
Cleveland, OH....................800-999-2906
Harrison Electropolishing
Houston, TX......................832-467-3100
Ipec
New Castle, PA...................800-377-4732

Jus-Made
Dallas, TX........................800-969-3746
Kombucha Brooklyn
Kingston, NY.....................917-261-3010
Maselli Measurements Inc
Stockton, CA......................800-964-9600
Midwest Juice
Grand Rapids, MI.................877-265-8243
Nidec Minster Corp.
Minster, OH
Primo Water Corporation
Lakeland, FL......................844-237-7466
Rocheleau Blow Molding Systems
Fitchburg, MA....................978-345-1723
Severn Trent Svc
Fort Washington, PA..............215-646-9201
SICK Inc
Bloomington, MN.................800-325-7425
Spinzer
Glen Ellyn, IL.....................630-469-7184

Coffee Industry

San Marco Coffee, Inc.
Charlotte, NC.....................800-715-9298
Stratecon International Consultants
Winston Salem, NC................336-768-6808
U Roast Em Inc
Hayward, WI......................715-634-6255
West Coast Specialty Coffee
Campbell, CA.....................650-259-9308

Stainless Steel

Coffee Pots

Castella Imports Inc
Hauppauge, NY...................631-231-5500

Confectionery Industry

A & B Process Systems Corp
Stratford, WI......................888-258-2789
Aerotech Enterprise Inc
Chesterland, OH...................440-729-2616
Aladdin Transparent Packaging
Hauppauge, NY...................631-273-4747
Andy J. Egan Co.
Grand Rapids, MI.................800-594-9244
Bakers Choice Products
Beacon Falls, CT..................203-720-1000
Braun Brush Co
Albertson, NY....................800-645-4111
Bryce Corp
Memphis, TN.....................800-238-7277
C. Cretors & Company
Chicago, IL.......................800-228-1885
Catty Inc
Harvard, IL.......................815-943-2288
Chocolate Concepts
Hartville, OH......................330-877-3322
Esterle Mold & Machine Co Inc
Stow, OH.........................800-411-4086
Hebeler Corp
Tonawanda, NY...................800-486-4709
Insect-O-Cutor Inc
Stone Mountain, GA...............800-966-8480
Kaufman Paper Box Company
Providence, RI....................401-272-7508
Liberty Engineering Co
Roscoe, IL........................877-623-9065
McCarter Corporation
Norristown, PA....................610-272-3203
Micelli Chocolate Mold Company
West Babylon, NY.................631-752-2888
Pacquet Oneida
Charlotte, NC.....................800-631-8388
Precision Brush
Cleveland, OH....................800-252-4747
Reiser
Canton, MA......................734-821-1290
Rheo-Tech
Gurnee, IL........................847-367-1557
Ribble Production
Warminster, PA...................215-674-1706
Ritz Packaging Company
Brooklyn, NY.....................718-366-2300
Saunder Brothers
Bridgton, ME.....................207-647-3331
Six Hardy Brush Manufacturing
Suffield, CT.......................860-623-8465

Stephan Machinery GmbH
Mandelein, IL.....................847-247-0182
Taconic
Petersburg, NY...................800-833-1805
Taylor Precision Products
Oak Brook, IL.....................866-843-3905
Voorhees Rubber Mfg Co
Newark, MD......................410-632-1582
West Hawk Industries
Ann Arbor, MI....................800-678-1286
Wilton Industries CanadaLtd.
Etobicoke, ON....................800-387-3300

Conveyors

Belt

A T Ferrell Co Inc
Bluffton, IN.......................800-248-8318
A.K. Robins
Baltimore, MD....................800-486-9656
ABI Limited
Concord, ON.....................800-297-8666
Advanced Uniflo Technologies
Wichita, KS.......................800-688-0400
All Power Inc
Sioux City, IA.....................712-258-0681
Amark Packaging Systems
Kansas City, MO...................816-965-9000
Anderson-Crane Company
Minneapolis, MN..................800-314-2747
Andgar Corp
Ferndale, WA.....................360-366-9900
ANDRITZ Inc
Muncy, PA.......................704-943-4343
Asgco Manufacturing Inc
Allentown, PA.....................800-344-4000
Bamco Belting
Greenville, SC.....................800-258-2358
Berkshire PPM
Litchfield, CT.....................860-567-3118
Berndorf Belt Technology USA
Gilberts, IL........................800-393-8450
Bilt-Rite Conveyors
New London, WI..................920-982-6600
BMH
City of Industry, CA...............909-349-2530
Bmh Equipment Inc
Sacramento, CA...................800-350-8828
Bowman Hollis Mfg Corp
Charlotte, NC.....................888-269-2358
BW Container Systems
Romeoville, IL....................630-759-6800
C R Daniels Inc
Ellicott City, MD..................800-933-2638
C S Bell Co
Tiffin, OH........................888-958-6381
C&R Refrigation Inc,
Center, TX........................800-438-6182
California Vibratory Feeders
Anaheim, CA.....................800-354-0972
Cambelt International Corporation
Salt Lake City, UT.................801-972-5511
Cambridge Intl. Inc.
Cambridge, MD...................800-638-9560
Chantland Company, The
Humboldt, IA.....................515-332-4040
Cleveland Vibrator Co
Cleveland, OH....................800-221-3298
Commercial Manufacturing
Fresno, CA.......................559-237-1855
Conesco Conveyor Corporation
Clifton, NJ........................973-365-1440
Conveyor Supply Inc
Deerfield, IL......................847-945-5670
Cozzini Inc
Algona, IA........................888-295-1116
Custom Conveyor & Supply Corp.
Racine, WI.......................262-634-4920
Davron Technologies Inc
Chattanooga, TN..................423-870-1888
Dearborn Mid-West Conveyor Co
Overland Park, KS.................913-384-9950
Descon EDM
Brocton, NY......................716-792-9300
Design Technology Corporation
Billerica, MA......................978-663-7000
Dorner Manufacturing Corp
Hartland, WI......................800-397-8664
Duplex Mill & Mfg Co
Springfield, OH...................937-325-5555

Dyna-Veyor Inc
Newark, NJ 800-326-5009
Dynamic Storage Systems Inc.
Brooksville, FL 800-974-8211
E-Z Lift Conveyors
Denver, CO 800-821-9966
Eckels Bilt
Fort Worth, TX 800-343-9020
Eisenmann Corp USA
Crystal Lake, IL 815-455-4100
Ermanco
Norton Shores, MI 231-798-4547
F & A Fabricating Inc
Battle Creek, MI 269-965-8371
Filling Equipment Co Inc
Flushing, NY 800-247-7127
FleetwoodGoldcoWyard
Romeoville, IL 630-759-6800
Flodin
Moses Lake, WA 509-766-2996
FreesTech
Sinking Spring, PA 717-560-7560
GEM Equipment of Oregon Inc
Woodburn, OR 503-982-9902
General Machinery Corp
Sheboygan, WI 888-243-6622
Georgia Duck & Cordage Mill
Scottdale, GA 404-297-3170
Globe Machine
Tacoma, WA 800-523-6575
Goodnature Products
Orchard Park, NY 800-875-3381
Grain Machinery Mfg Corp
Miami, FL 305-620-2525
Graybill Machines Inc
Lititz, PA 717-626-5221
Gulf Arizona Packaging
Humble, TX 800-364-3887
Gulf Systems
Brownsville, TX 800-217-4853
Gulf Systems
Humble, TX 800-364-3887
Gulf Systems
Arlington, TX 817-261-1915
Habasit Canada Limited
Oakville, ON 905-827-4131
Herche Warehouse
Denver, CO 303-371-8186
Hi Roller Enclosed Belt Conveyors
Sioux Falls, SD 800-328-1785
HMC Corp
Hopkinton, NH 603-746-4691
Hurt Conveyor Equipment Company
Los Angeles, CA 323-541-0433
ICB Greenline
Charlotte, NC 800-331-5312
Industrial Design Fab
Sioux City, IA 877-873-5858
Industrial Kinetics
Downers Grove, IL 800-655-0306
Inter-City Welding & Manufacturing
Independence, MO 816-252-1770
Intralox LLC
Harahan, LA 504-733-0463
Jantec
Traverse City, MI 800-992-3303
Kamflex Corp
Chicago, IL 800-323-2440
Kaufman Engineered Systems
Waterville, OH 419-878-9727
Keenline Conveyor Systems
Omro, WI 920-685-0365
Key Material Handling Inc
Simi Valley, CA 800-539-7225
Kinder Morgan Inc
Houston, TX 713-466-0496
Kinergy Corp
Louisville, KY 502-366-5685
Kornylak Corp
Hamilton, OH 800-837-5676
KWS Manufacturing Co LTD
Burleson, TX 800-543-6558
Laros Equipment Co Inc
Portage, MI 269-323-1441
Laughlin Sales Corp
Fort Worth, TX 817-625-7756
Le Fiell Co
Reno, NV 402-592-9993
Leeds Conveyor Manufacturer Company
Guilford, CT 800-724-1088
Lesco Design & Mfg Co
La Grange, KY 502-222-7101

Lewco Inc
Sandusky, OH 419-625-4014
Lewis M Carter Mfg Co Inc
Donalsonville, GA 800-332-8232
Magnetic Products Inc
Highland, MI 800-544-5930
Mar-Con Wire Belt
Richmond, BC 877-962-7266
Marlen International
Astoria, OR 800-862-7536
Martin Engineering
Neponset, IL 800-766-2786
Maryland Wire Belts
Cleveland, OH 800-677-2358
Matthiesen Equipment
San Antonio, TX 800-624-8635
McCormick Enterprises
Arlington Heights, IL 800-323-5201
McNichols Conveyor Company
Southfield, MI 800-331-1926
Mell & Co
Niles, IL 800-262-6355
Meyer Machine & Garroutte Products
San Antonio, TX 210-736-1811
Michigan Industrial Belting
Livonia, MI 800-778-1650
Midwest Metalcraft & Equipment
Windsor, MO 800-647-3167
Millard Manufacturing Corp
La Vista, NE 800-662-4263
Molding Automation Concepts
Woodstock, IL 800-435-6979
Monarch-McLaren
Weston, ON 416-741-9675
National Conveyor Corp
Commerce, CA 323-725-0355
Northwind Inc
Alpena, AR 877-937-2585
Ohio Conveyor & Supply Inc
Findlay, OH 419-422-3825
Omni Metalcraft Corporation
Alpena, MI 989-358-7000
OTP Industrial Solutions
Terre Haute, IN 860-953-7632
Our Name is Mud
New York, NY 877-683-7867
Overhead Conveyor Co
Ferndale, MI 800-396-2554
P & F Machine
Turlock, CA 209-667-2515
Package Conveyor Co
Fort Worth, TX 800-792-1243
Packaging & Processing Equipment
Ayr, ON 519-622-6666
Packaging Systems Intl
Denver, CO 303-244-9000
Parkson Corp
Fort Lauderdale, FL 908-464-0700
Peerless Conveyor & Mfg Corp
Kansas City, KS 913-342-2240
Portec Flowmaster
Canon City, CO 800-777-7471
Power-Pack Conveyor Co
Willoughby, OH 440-975-9955
Priority One Packaging
Waterloo, ON 800-387-9102
Prodo-Pak Corp
Garfield, NJ 973-777-7770
Psc Floturn Inc
Union, NJ 908-687-3225
Quickdraft
Canton, OH 330-477-4574
R.G. Stephens Engineering
Long Beach, CA 800-499-3001
Rapat Corp
Hawley, MN 800-325-6377
Regal Power Transmission Solutions
Florence, KY 859-342-7900
Rexnord Corporation
Milwaukee, WI 866-739-6673
San Fab Conveyor
Sandusky, OH 419-626-4465
Schneider Packaging Eqpt Co
Brewerton, NY 315-676-3035
Screw Conveyor Corp
Hammond, IN 219-931-1450
Simplex Filler Co
Napa, CA 800-796-7539
Smetco
Aurora, OR 800-253-5400
Southern Automatics
Lakeland, FL 800-441-4604

Span Tech LLC
Glasgow, KY 270-651-9166
Specialty Equipment Company
Houston, TX 713-467-1818
Speedways Conveyors
Lancaster, NY 800-800-1022
Sperling Industries
Omaha, NE 800-647-5062
Spurgeon Co
Ferndale, MI 800-396-2554
Stokes Material Handling Systs
Doylestown, PA 215-340-2200
Svedala Industries
Colorado Springs, CO 719-471-3443
Sweet Manufacturing Co
Springfield, OH 800-334-7254
The National Provisioner
Deerfield, IL 847-763-9534
Thomas L. Green & Company
Robenosia, PA 610-693-5816
Transnorm System Inc
Grand Prairie, TX 800-259-2303
Traycon Manufacturing Co
Carlstadt, NJ 201-939-5555
Tri-Pak Machinery Inc
Harlingen, TX 956-423-5140
TWM Manufacturing
Leamington, ON 888-495-4831
UniTrak Corporation
Port Hope, ON 866-883-5749
Universal Die & Stampings
Prairie Du Sac, WI 608-643-2477
Universal Industries Inc
Cedar Falls, IA 800-553-4446
Us Rubber
Brooklyn, NY 718-782-7888
Vande Berg SCALES/Vbs Inc
Sioux Center, IA 712-722-1181
Vaughn Belting Co-Main Acct
Spartanburg, SC 800-533-9086
Versa Conveyor
London, OH 740-852-5609
Viking Machine & Design Inc
De Pere, WI. 888-286-2116
Volta Belting Technology, Inc.
Pine Brook, NJ 973-276-7905
Volumetric Technologies
Cannon Falls, MN 507-263-0034
W A Powers Co
Fort Worth, TX 800-792-1243
Wall Conveyor & Manufacturing
Huntington, WV 800-456-1335
Washington Frontier
Grandview, WA. 509-469-7662
Yakima Wire Works
Reedley, CA 800-344-8951
Yargus Manufacturing Inc
Marshall, IL 217-826-8059
Ziniz
Louisville, KY 502-955-6573

Bottle

Alliance Industrial Corp
Lynchburg, VA 800-368-3556
Anderson Machine Sales
Fort Lee, NJ
Berkshire PPM
Litchfield, CT 860-567-3118
Bilt-Rite Conveyors
New London, WI 920-982-6600
Bmh Equipment Inc
Sacramento, CA 800-350-8828
California Vibratory Feeders
Anaheim, CA 800-354-0972
Climax Packaging Machinery
Hamilton, OH 513-874-1664
Conveyor Supply Inc
Deerfield, IL 847-945-5670
Ermanco
Norton Shores, MI 231-798-4547
Filling Equipment Co Inc
Flushing, NY 800-247-7127
FleetwoodGoldcoWyard
Romeoville, IL 630-759-6800
Ipec
New Castle, PA 800-377-4732
Kinsley Inc
Doylestown, PA 800-414-6664
Laughlin Sales Corp
Fort Worth, TX 817-625-7756

Lewco Inc
Sandusky, OH 419-625-4014
Ohio Conveyor & Supply Inc
Findlay, OH 419-422-3825
OnTrack Automation Inc
Waterloo, ON 519-886-9090
Priority One Packaging
Waterloo, ON 800-387-9102
Rexnord Corporation
Milwaukee, WI 866-739-6673
San Fab Conveyor
Sandusky, OH 419-626-4465
Simplex Filler Co
Napa, CA 800-796-7539

Chain

A.K. Robins
Baltimore, MD 800-486-9656
ABI Limited
Concord, ON 800-297-8666
Advanced Uniflo Technologies
Wichita, KS 800-688-0400
Airfloat LLC
Decatur, IL 800-888-0018
All Power Inc
Sioux City, IA 712-258-0681
ANDRITZ Inc
Muncy, PA 704-943-4343
Berkshire PPM
Litchfield, CT 860-567-3118
BEVCO
Canada, BC 800-663-0090
Bilt-Rite Conveyors
New London, WI 920-982-6600
Bmh Equipment Inc
Sacramento, CA 800-350-8828
BW Container Systems
Romeoville, IL 630-759-6800
California Vibratory Feeders
Anaheim, CA 800-354-0972
Cannon Equipment Company
Cannon Falls, MN 800-825-8501
Conesco Conveyor Corporation
Clifton, NJ 973-365-1440
Conveyor Supply Inc
Deerfield, IL 847-945-5670
Custom Conveyor & Supply Corp.
Racine, WI 262-634-4920
Davron Technologies Inc
Chattanooga, TN 423-870-1888
Diamond Chain
Indianapolis, IN 800-872-4246
Donahower & Company
Olathe, KS 913-829-2650
Dorner Manufacturing Corp
Hartland, WI 800-397-8664
Duplex Mill & Mfg Co
Springfield, OH 937-325-5555
Dyna-Veyor Inc
Newark, NJ 800-326-5009
Eisenmann Corp USA
Crystal Lake, IL 815-455-4100
Emc Solutions
Celina, OH 419-586-2388
Filling Equipment Co Inc
Flushing, NY 800-247-7127
Flodin
Moses Lake, WA 509-766-2996
FreesTech
Sinking Spring, PA 717-560-7560
GEM Equipment of Oregon Inc
Woodburn, OR 503-982-9902
Graybill Machines Inc
Lititz, PA 717-626-5221
Hurt Conveyor Equipment Company
Los Angeles, CA 323-541-0433
ICB Greenline
Charlotte, NC 800-331-5312
Industrial Kinetics
Downers Grove, IL 800-655-0306
Laughlin Sales Corp
Fort Worth, TX 817-625-7756
Le Fiell Co
Reno, NV 402-592-9993
Lewco Inc
Sandusky, OH 419-625-4014
Magnetic Products Inc
Highland, MI 800-544-5930
Martin Cab Div
Cleveland, OH 216-377-8200

Material Systems Engineering
Stilesville, IN 800-634-0904
McNichols Conveyor Company
Southfield, MI 800-331-1926
Mell & Co
Niles, IL 800-262-6355
Michigan Industrial Belting
Livonia, MI 800-778-1650
New London Engineering
New London, WI 800-437-1994
Ohio Conveyor & Supply Inc
Findlay, OH 419-422-3825
Omni Metalcraft Corporation
Alpena, MI 989-358-7000
Our Name is Mud
New York, NY 877-683-7867
Packaging & Processing Equipment
Ayr, ON 519-622-6666
Priority One Packaging
Waterloo, ON 800-387-9102
R.G. Stephens Engineering
Long Beach, CA 800-499-3001
Rexnord Corporation
Milwaukee, WI 866-739-6673
Richards Industries Systems
West Caldwell, NJ 973-575-7480
San Fab Conveyor
Sandusky, OH 419-626-4465
Simplex Filler Co
Napa, CA 800-796-7539
Specialty Equipment Company
Houston, TX 713-467-1818
Spurgeon Co
Ferndale, MI 800-396-2554
Sweet Manufacturing Co
Springfield, OH 800-334-7254
Tri-Pak Machinery Inc
Harlingen, TX 956-423-5140
TWM Manufacturing
Leamington, ON 888-495-4831
Versa Conveyor
London, OH 740-852-5609
Washington Frontier
Grandview, WA 509-469-7662
Wilkie Brothers Conveyor Inc
Marysville, MI 810-364-4820
Yargus Manufacturing Inc
Marshall, IL 217-826-8059
Ziniz
Louisville, KY 502-955-6573

Systems & Components

A C Horn & Co Sheet Metal
Dallas, TX 800-657-6155
A T Ferrell Co Inc
Bluffton, IN 800-248-8318
A-Z Factory Supply
Schiller Park, IL 800-323-4511
A.K. Robins
Baltimore, MD 800-486-9656
ABI Limited
Concord, ON 800-297-8666
Accutek Packaging Equipment
Vista, CA 800-989-1828
Adamation
Commerce, CA 800-383-8800
Advance Weight Systems Inc
Grafton, OH 440-926-3691
Advanced Detection Systems
Milwaukee, WI 414-672-0553
Advanced Uniflo Technologies
Wichita, KS 800-688-0400
Aerocon
Langhorne, PA 215-860-6056
Aerowerks
Mississauga, ON 888-774-1616
Airfloat LLC
Decatur, IL 800-888-0018
All Power Inc
Sioux City, IA 712-258-0681
Alliance Bakery Systems
Blythewood, SC 803-691-9227
Alliance Industrial Corp
Lynchburg, VA 800-368-3556
Alliance Products LLC
Murfreesboro, TN 800-522-3973
Allied Bakery and Food Service Equipment
Santa Fe Springs, CA 562-945-6506
Allied Uniking Corp Inc
Memphis, TN 901-365-7240

Amark Packaging Systems
Kansas City, MO 816-965-9000
American Auger & Accesories
West Chester, PA 866-219-9619
American Extrusion Intl
South Beloit, IL 815-624-6616
American Food Equipment Company
Hayward, CA 510-783-0255
Ametek Technical & Industrial Products
Kent, OH 215-256-6601
Ammeraal Beltech
Grand Rapids, MI 616-791-0292
Anderson Machine Sales
Fort Lee, NJ
Anderson-Crane Company
Minneapolis, MN 800-314-2747
Andgar Corp
Ferndale, WA 360-366-9900
ANDRITZ Inc
Muncy, PA 704-943-4343
Anver Corporation
Hudson, MA 800-654-3500
AP Dataweigh Inc
Cumming, GA 877-409-2562
Apache Inc
Cedar Rapids, IA 800-553-5455
Apache Stainless Equipment
Beaver Dam, WI 800-444-0398
Apollo Sheet Metal
Kennewick, WA 509-586-1104
APV Baker
Goldsboro, NC 919-736-4309
Asgco Manufacturing Inc
Allentown, PA 800-344-4000
Ashworth Bros Inc
Winchester, VA 800-682-4594
Atlas Equipment Company
Kansas City, MO 800-842-9188
Automated Food Systems
Waxahachie, TX 469-517-0470
Automated Production Systems Corporation
New Freedom, PA 888-345-5377
Automatic Handling Int
Erie, MI 734-847-0633
Automotion Inc
Oak Lawn, IL 708-229-3700
Baking Machines
Livermore, CA 925-449-3369
Belco Packaging Systems
Monrovia, CA 800-833-1833
Belshaw Adamatic Bakery Group
Auburn, WA 800-578-2547
Belt Technologies Inc
Agawam, MA 413-786-9922
Berndorf Belt Technology USA
Gilberts, IL 800-393-8450
Best
Brunswick, OH 800-827-9237
Best Diversified Products
Jonesboro, AR 800-327-9209
Bettendorf Stanford Inc
Salem, IL 800-548-2253
BEVCO
Canada, BC 800-663-0090
Bilt-Rite Conveyors
New London, WI 920-982-6600
Biner Ellison Packaging Systs
Vista, CA 800-733-8162
Blodgett Oven Co
Burlington, VT 800-331-5842
BMH
City of Industry, CA 909-349-2530
Bmh Equipment Inc
Sacramento, CA 800-350-8828
Bowman Hollis Mfg Corp
Charlotte, NC 888-269-2358
Brothers Metal Products
Santa Ana, CA 714-972-3008
Brush Research Mfg Co Inc
Los Angeles, CA 323-261-6162
Bryant Products Inc
Ixonia, WI 800-825-3874
Buffalo Technologies Corporation
Buffalo, NY 800-332-2419
Buhler Inc.
Plymouth, MN 763-847-9900
Bulldog Factory Svc LLC
Madison Heights, MI 248-541-3500
Bunting Magnetics Co
Newton, KS 800-835-2526
BW Container Systems
Romeoville, IL 630-759-6800

C H Babb Co Inc
Raynham, MA....................508-977-0600
C R Daniels Inc
Ellicott City, MD.................800-933-2638
C S Bell Co
Tiffin, OH.......................888-958-6381
C&R Refrigation Inc,
Center, TX......................800-438-6182
C.J. Machine
Fridley, MN.....................763-767-4630
Caddy Corporation of America
Bridgeport, NJ...................856-467-4222
California Vibratory Feeders
Anaheim, CA....................800-354-0972
Caljan America
Denver, CO......................303-321-3600
Cambelt International Corporation
Salt Lake City, UT...............801-972-5511
Can Lines Engineering Inc
Downey, CA.....................562-861-2996
Cannon Equipment Company
Cannon Falls, MN................800-825-8501
Capway Conveyor Systems Inc
York, PA.........................877-222-7929
Carman Industries Inc
Jeffersonville, IN.................800-456-7560
Carrier Vibrating Equip Inc
Louisville, KY....................502-969-3171
Carron Net Co Inc
Two Rivers, WI...................800-558-7768
Casso-Solar Corporation
Nanuet, NY......................800-988-4455
Chantland Company, The
Humboldt, IA....................515-332-4040
Charles Walker North America
Fort Worth, TX...................817-922-9834
Charlton & Hill
Lethbridge, AB...................403-328-3388
Chase-Logeman Corp
Greensboro, NC..................336-665-0754
Checker Machine
Minneapolis, MN.................888-800-5001
Chicago Conveyor Corporation
Addison, IL......................630-543-6300
CHL Systems
Souderton, PA....................215-723-7284
Chocolate Concepts
Hartville, OH.....................330-877-3322
Christianson Systems Inc
Blomkest, MN....................800-328-8896
Christy Machine Co
Fremont, OH.....................888-332-6451
CIM Bakery Equipment of USA
Arlington Heights, IL..............847-818-8121
Cincinnati Industrial Machry
Mason, OH.......................800-677-0076
Cintex of America
Carol Stream, IL..................800-424-6839
Cleveland Vibrator Co
Cleveland, OH....................800-221-3298
Climax Packaging Machinery
Hamilton, OH....................513-874-1664
Clipper Belt Lacer Company
Grand Rapids, MI.................616-459-3196
Coastline Equipment Inc
Bellingham, WA..................360-734-8509
Colborne Foodbotics
Lake Forest, IL...................847-724-5070
Columbus McKinnon Corporation
Getzville, NY.....................800-888-0985
Command Belt Cleaning Systems
Hammond, IN....................800-433-7627
Commercial Dehydrator Systems
Eugene, OR......................800-369-4283
Commercial Manufacturing
Fresno, CA.......................559-237-1855
Conesco Conveyor Corporation
Clifton, NJ.......................973-365-1440
Conveyance Technologies LLC
Cleveland, OH....................800-701-2278
Conveying Industries
Denver, CO.......................877-600-4874
Conveyor Accessories
Burr Ridge, IL....................800-323-7093
Conveyor Components Co
Croswell, MI......................800-233-3233
Conveyor Supply Inc
Deerfield, IL......................847-945-5670
Corn States Metal Fabricators
West Des Moines, IA...............515-225-7961
Coss Engineering Sales Company
Rochester Hills, MI................800-446-1365

Cozzini Inc
Algona, IA.......................888-295-1116
Crippen Manufacturing Co
St Louis, MI.....................800-872-2474
CTC
West Caldwell, NJ................973-228-2300
Cugar Machine Co
Fort Worth, TX...................817-927-0411
Currie Machinery Co
Santa Clara, CA..................408-727-0422
Custom Conveyor & Supply Corp.
Racine, WI.......................262-634-4920
Custom Food Machinery
Stockton, CA.....................209-463-4343
Custom Metal Design Inc
Oakland, FL......................800-334-1777
Custom Systems Integration Co
Carlsbad, CA.....................760-635-1099
Cyclonaire Corp
York, NE.........................800-445-0730
Davron Technologies Inc
Chattanooga, TN.................423-870-1888
Dearborn Mid-West Conveyor Co
Overland Park, KS................913-384-9950
Delavan Spray Technologies
Bamberg, SC.....................800-982-6943
Delta/Ducon
Malvern, PA......................800-238-2974
Dematic USA
Grand Rapids, MI.................877-725-7500
Descon EDM
Brocton, NY......................716-792-9300
Design Systems Inc
Farmington Hills, MI..............800-660-4374
Design Technology Corporation
Billerica, MA.....................978-663-7000
Dillin Automation Systems Corp
Perrysburg, OH...................419-666-6789
Diversified Capping Equipment
Perrysburg, OH...................419-666-2566
Diversified Metal Engineering
Charlottetown, PE.................902-628-6900
Donahower & Company
Olathe, KS.......................913-829-2650
Douglas Machine Inc
Alexandria, MN...................320-763-6587
Dresco Belting Co Inc
East Weymouth, MA...............781-335-1350
Duke Manufacturing Co
St Louis, MO.....................800-735-3853
Duluth Sheet Metal
Duluth, MN......................218-722-2613
Dunkley International Inc
Kalamazoo, MI...................800-666-1264
Dunrite Inc
Fremont, NE.....................800-782-3061
Duplex Mill & Mfg Co
Springfield, OH...................937-325-5555
Dupps Co
Germantown, OH.................937-855-0623
Durand-Wayland Inc
Lagrange, GA.....................800-241-2308
Dyco
Bloomsburg, PA..................800-545-3926
Dyna-Veyor Inc
Newark, NJ.......................800-326-5009
Dynamet
Kalamazoo, MI...................269-385-0006
Dynamic Air Inc
St Paul, MN......................651-484-2900
Dynamic Automation LTD
Simi Valley, CA...................805-584-8476
Dynamic Storage Systems Inc.
Brooksville, FL....................800-974-8211
E F Bavis & Assoc Inc
Maineville, OH...................513-677-0500
E-Z Lift Conveyors
Denver, CO.......................800-821-9966
Eckels Bilt
Fort Worth, TX...................800-343-9020
Ecs Warehouse
Buffalo, NY.......................716-833-7380
Edmeyer
Minneapolis, MN.................651-450-1210
Eisenmann Corp USA
Crystal Lake, IL...................815-455-4100
Electrical Engineering & Equip
Windsor Heights, IA...............800-955-3633
ELF Machinery
La Porte, IN......................800-328-0466
Emc Solutions
Celina, OH.......................419-586-2388

En-Hanced Products Inc
Westerville, OH...................800-783-7400
Engineered Products Corp
Greenville, SC....................800-868-0145
Equipment Outlet
Meridian, ID......................208-887-1472
Eriez Magnetics
Erie, PA..........................800-346-4946
Ermanco
Norton Shores, MI................231-798-4547
F & A Fabricating Inc
Battle Creek, MI..................269-965-8371
F N Smith Corp
Oregon, IL.......................815-732-2171
F.B. Pease Company
Rochester, NY....................585-475-1870
Fabreeka International
Boise, ID.........................800-423-4469
Fata Automation
Sterling Heights, MI...............586-323-9400
FEI Inc
Mansfield, TX.....................800-346-5908
Fenner Dunlop Americas Inc
Pittsburgh, PA....................412-249-0700
Filler Specialties
Zeeland, MI......................616-772-9235
Filling Equipment Co Inc
Flushing, NY......................800-247-7127
Fillit
Kirkland, QC......................514-694-2390
Fishmore
Melbourne, FL....................321-723-4751
Fleet Wood Goldco Wyard
Cockeysville, MD.................410-785-1934
Fleetwood Systems
Orlando, FL......................800-432-5433
FleetwoodGoldcoWyard
Romeoville, IL....................630-759-6800
Flexco
Downers Grove, IL................800-323-3444
Flexco
Downers Grove, IL................800-541-8028
Flexible Material Handling
Suwanee, GA.....................800-669-1501
Flexicell Inc
Ashland, VA......................804-550-7300
Flexicon
Bethlehem, PA....................888-353-9426
Flodin
Moses Lake, WA..................509-766-2996
Fogg Filler Co
Holland, MI......................616-786-3644
Food Engineering Unlimited
Fullerton, CA.....................714-879-8762
Food Machinery Sales
Bogart, GA.......................706-549-2207
Food Processing Equipment Co
Santa Fe Springs, CA..............562-802-3727
Forbo Siegling LLC
Huntersville, NC..................800-255-5581
FPEC Corporation
Santa Fe Springs, CA..............562-802-3727
Franz Haas Machinery-America
Henrico, VA......................804-222-6022
FreesTech
Sinking Spring, PA................717-560-7560
Frelco
Stephenville, NL..................709-643-5668
Frigoscandia Equipment
Northfield, MN...................800-426-1283
Frost Food Handling Products
Grand Rapids, MI.................800-253-9382
Garvey Corporation
Hammonton, NJ..................800-257-8581
Gates Manufacturing Company
Saint Louis, MO..................800-237-9226
Gbn Machine & Engineering
Woodford, VA....................800-446-9871
Gch Internatonal
Louisville, KY.....................502-636-1374
Gebo Conveyors, Consultants & Systems
Laval, QC........................450-973-3337
Gebo Corporation
Bradenton, FL....................941-727-1400
GEM Equipment of Oregon Inc
Woodburn, OR...................503-982-9902
Gemini Bakery Equipment
Philadelphia, PA..................800-468-9046
General Machinery Corp
Sheboygan, WI...................888-243-6622
General Tank
Berwick, PA......................800-435-8265

Georgia Duck & Cordage Mill
Scottdale, GA 404-297-3170
Globe Machine
Tacoma, WA 800-523-6575
Goergen-Mackwirth Co Inc
Buffalo, NY. 800-728-4446
Goldco Industries
Loveland, CO 970-663-4770
Gough-Econ Inc
Charlotte, NC 800-204-6844
Graco Inc
Minneapolis, MN 612-623-6000
Grain Machinery Mfg Corp
Miami, FL. 305-620-2525
Graybill Machines Inc
Lititz, PA 717-626-5221
Green Belt Industries Inc
Buffalo, NY. 800-668-1114
Greitzer
Elizabeth City, NC 252-338-4000
Griffin Automation
Buffalo, NY. 716-674-2300
Gulf Arizona Packaging
Humble, TX 800-364-3887
Gulf Systems
Brownsville, TX 800-217-4853
Gulf Systems
Humble, TX 800-364-3887
Gulf Systems
Arlington, TX 817-261-1915
H G Weber & Co
Kiel, WI. 920-894-2221
Habasit America
Suwanee, GA 800-458-6431
Habasit America Plastic Div
Reading, PA 800-445-7898
Habasit Canada Limited
Oakville, ON. 905-827-4131
Halton Packaging Systems
Oakville, ON. 905-847-9141
Hapman Conveyors
Kalamazoo, MI. 800-968-7722
Hardy Systems Corporation
Northbrook, IL 800-927-3956
Hart Design & Mfg
Green Bay, WI. 920-468-5927
Hartness International
Greenville, SC 800-845-8791
Heinzen Sales
Gilroy, CA 408-842-6678
Herche Warehouse
Denver, CO 303-371-8186
Hi Roller Enclosed Belt Conveyors
Sioux Falls, SD 800-328-1785
HMC Corp
Hopkinton, NH 603-746-4691
Hoffmeyer Corp
San Leandro, CA. 888-744-1826
Hoppmann Corporation
Elkwood, VA 800-368-3582
Howes S Co Inc
Silver Creek, NY. 888-255-2611
Hudson Belting & Svc Co Inc
Worcester, MA 508-756-0090
Hughes Co
Columbus, WI. 866-535-9303
Hurt Conveyor Equipment Company
Los Angeles, CA. 323-541-0433
I J White Corp
Farmingdale, NY. 631-293-2211
ICB Greenline
Charlotte, NC 800-331-5312
Industrial Automation Systems
Santa Clarita, CA 888-484-4427
Industrial Kinetics
Downers Grove, IL 800-655-0306
Industrial Magnetics
Boyne City, MI 800-662-4638
Inline Filling Systems
Venice, FL. 941-486-8800
Inter-City Welding & Manufacturing
Independence, MO 816-252-1770
Interlake Mecalux
Chicago, IL 708-344-9999
Interroll Corp
Wilmington, NC 800-830-9680
Intralox LLC
Harahan, LA 800-535-8848
Irby
Rocky Mount, NC 252-442-0154
J C Ford Co
La Habra, CA 714-871-7361

J L Becker Co
Plymouth, MI 800-837-4328
J.H. Thornton Company
Olathe, KS. 913-764-6550
Jantec
Traverse City, MI 800-992-3303
Jervis B WEBB Co
Novi, MI 248-553-1000
Jetstream Systems
Wichita, KN 855-861-6916
K-Tron
Salina, KS 785-825-1611
K.F. Logistics
Cincinnati, OH 800-347-9100
Kamflex Corp
Chicago, IL 800-323-2440
KAPS All Packaging
Riverhead, NY 631-727-0300
Kasel Industries Inc
Denver, CO 800-218-4417
Kaufman Engineered Systems
Waterville, OH 419-878-9727
Keenline Conveyor Systems
Omro, WI 920-685-0365
Key Material Handling Inc
Simi Valley, CA. 800-539-7225
Key Technology Inc.
Walla Walla, WA. 509-529-2161
Kinder Morgan Inc
Houston, TX 713-466-0496
Kinergy Corp
Louisville, KY 502-366-5685
Kinetic Equipment Company
Appleton, WI 806-293-4471
Kinsley Inc
Doylestown, PA 800-414-6664
Kisco Manufacturing
Port Alberni, BC 604-823-7456
KISS Packaging Systems
Vista, CA 888-522-3538
KLEEN Line Corp
Newburyport, MA. 800-259-5973
Kline Process Systems Inc
Reading, PA 610-371-0300
Klippenstein Corp
Fresno, CA 888-834-4258
Kofab
Algona, IA. 515-295-7265
Kohler Industries Inc
Lincoln, NE. 800-365-6708
Kornylak Corp
Hamilton, OH 800-837-5676
KWS Manufacturing Co LTD
Burleson, TX 800-543-6558
Laidig Inc
Mishawaka, IN 574-256-0204
Lambert Material Handling
Syracuse, NY 800-253-5103
Laros Equipment Co Inc
Portage, WI. 269-323-1441
Laughlin Sales Corp
Fort Worth, TX 817-625-7756
Le Fiell Co
Reno, NV 402-592-9993
Leeds Conveyor Manufacturer Company
Guilford, CT 800-724-1088
Lewco Inc
Sandusky, OH 419-625-4014
Lewis M Carter Mfg Co Inc
Donalsonville, GA 800-332-8232
Lock Inspection Systems
Fitchburg, MA 800-227-5539
Lorenz Couplings
Cobourg, ON. 800-263-7782
Louisville Dryer Company
Louisville, KY 800-735-3613
LPS Technology
Grafton, OH 800-586-1410
LTI Boyd Corp
Modesto, CA. 888-244-6931
Lumsden Flexx Flow
Lancaster, PA 800-367-3664
Lyco Manufacturing
Wausau, WI. 715-845-7867
Lyco Wausau
Wausau, WI. 715-845-7867
MAC Equipment
Kansas City, MO. 800-821-2476
Machine Builders & Design Inc
Shelby, NC 704-482-3456
Magnetic Products Inc
Highland, MI. 800-544-5930

Magsys Inc
Milwaukee, WI. 414-543-2177
Mar-Con Wire Belt
Richmond, BC 877-962-7266
Marlen International
Astoria, OR. 800-862-7536
Martin Engineering
Neponset, IL 800-766-2786
Martin/Baron
Irwindale, CA 626-960-5153
Maryland Wire Belts
Cleveland, OH 800-677-2358
Material Systems Engineering
Stilesville, IN 800-634-0904
Materials Transportation Co
Temple, TX 800-433-3110
Mathews Conveyor
Danville, KY 800-628-4397
Matthiesen Equipment
San Antonio, TX. 800-624-8635
McCormick Enterprises
Arlington Heights, IL 800-323-5201
McNichols Conveyor Company
Southfield, MI. 800-331-1926
MeGa Industries
Burlington, ON 800-665-6342
Mell & Co
Niles, IL 800-262-6355
Merco/Savory
Mt. Pleasant, MI 800-733-8821
Meriwether Industries
Bloomfield, NJ 800-332-2358
Metko Inc
New Holstein, WI. 920-898-4221
Metzgar Conveyors
Comstock Park, MI. 888-266-8390
Meyer Machine & Garroutte Products
San Antonio, TX. 210-736-1811
Michigan Industrial Belting
Livonia, MI 800-778-1650
Midwest Metalcraft & Equipment
Windsor, MO. 800-647-3167
Midwest Rubber Svc & Supply
Minneapolis, MN 800-537-7457
Millard Manufacturing Corp
La Vista, NE 800-662-4263
Miller Hofft Brands
Indianapolis, IN 317-638-6576
Miller Metal Fabrication
Bridgeville, DE 302-337-2291
Molding Automation Concepts
Woodstock, IL 800-435-6979
Moline Machinery LLC
Duluth, MN 800-767-5734
Monarch-McLaren
Weston, ON 416-741-9675
Mp Equip. Co.
Buford, GA 770-614-5355
Mumper Machine Corporation
Butler, WI 262-781-8908
Murata Automated Systems
Charlotte, NC 800-428-8469
National Conveyor Corp
Commerce, CA 323-725-0355
National Drying Machry Co Inc
Philadelphia, PA 215-464-6070
NECO/Nebraska Engineering
Omaha, NE 800-367-6208
Neos
Elk River, MN 888-441-6367
Nercon Engineering & Manufacturing
Oshkosh, WI. 920-233-3268
New London Engineering
New London, WI 800-437-1994
Newcastle Co Inc
New Castle, PA. 724-658-4516
Niro Inc
Hudson, WI. 715-386-9371
North American Roller Prod Inc
Glen Ellyn, IL 630-858-9161
Northwind Inc
Alpena, AR 877-937-2585
Nothum Food Processing Systems
Springfield, MO 800-435-1297
Nu-Con Equipment
Chanhassen, MN 877-939-0510
Nutec Manufacturing Inc
New Lenox, IL 815-722-5348
Ohio Magnetics Inc
Maple Heights, OH 800-486-6446
Omega Industrial Products Inc
Saukville, WI. 800-279-6634

Omicron Steel Products Company
Jamaica, NY 718-805-3400
Omni Lift Inc
Salt Lake City, UT 801-486-3776
Omni Metalcraft Corporation
Alpena, MI 989-358-7000
OnTrack Automation Inc
Waterloo, ON 519-886-9090
Optek Inc
Galena, OH 800-533-8400
Oshikiri Corp of America
Philadelphia, PA 215-637-8112
OTP Industrial Solutions
Terre Haute, IN 860-953-7632
Ouellette Machinery Systems
Fenton, MO 800-545-7619
Our Name is Mud
New York, NY 877-683-7867
Oyster Bay Pump Works Inc
Hicksville, NY 516-933-4500
Pa R Systems Inc
St Paul, MN 800-464-1320
Pacific Pneumatics
Rancho Cucamonga, CA 800-221-0961
Package Conveyor Co
Fort Worth, TX 800-792-1243
Packaging Equipment & Conveyors, Inc
Elkhart, IN. 574-266-6995
Packaging Machinery
Montgomery, AL...................334-265-9211
Packaging Progressions
Collegeville, PA 610-489-9096
Paget Equipment Co
Marshfield, WI 715-384-3158
Palace Packaging Machines Inc
Downingtown, PA. 610-873-7252
Parkson Corp
Vernon Hills, IL 847-816-3700
Parkson Corp
Fort Lauderdale, FL 908-464-0700
Paxton Products Inc
Blue Ash, OH 800-441-7475
Peerless Conveyor & Mfg Corp
Kansas City, KS 913-342-2240
Peerless Dough Mixing and Make-Up
Sidney, OH 800-999-3327
Peerless Food Equipment
Sidney, OH 937-492-4158
Peerless-Winsmith Inc
Springville, NY 716-592-9310
Pengo Attachments Inc
Cokato, MN.......................800-599-0211
Peterson Fiberglass Laminates
Shell Lake, WI 715-468-2306
Piab Vacuum Products
Hingham, MA 800-321-7422
PlexPack Corp
Toronto, ON 855-635-9238
Pneumatic Conveying Inc
Ontario, CA 800-655-4481
Polar Process
Plattsville, ON. 877-896-8077
Power-Pack Conveyor Co
Willoughby, OH 440-975-9955
Ppm Technologies LLC
Newberg, OR 800-246-2034
Precision
Miami, FL 800-762-7565
Priority One America
Oshkosh, WI 920-235-5562
Priority One Packaging
Waterloo, ON 800-387-9102
Process Engineering & Fabrication
Afton, VA 800-852-7975
Prodo-Pak Corp
Garfield, NJ....................973-777-7770
Production Systems
Marietta, GA.....................800-235-9734
Professional Engineering Assoc
Louisville, KY 502-429-0432
Psc Floturn Inc
Union, NJ 908-687-3225
PTI Packaging
Portage, WI 800-501-4077
Puritan Manufacturing Inc
Omaha, NE 800-331-0487
Quadrant Epp USA Inc
Fort Wayne, IN 800-628-7264
R.G. Stephens Engineering
Long Beach, CA 800-499-3001
Rahmann Belting & Industrial Rubber Products
Gastonia, NC 888-248-8148

Ralphs Pugh Conveyor Rollers
Benicia, CA 800-486-0021
Rapat Corp
Hawley, MN 800-325-6377
Rapid Industries Inc
Louisville, KY 800-787-4381
Raque Food Systems
Louisville, KY 502-267-9641
Reading Plastic Fabricators
Reading, PA 610-926-3245
Reese Enterprises Inc
Rosemount, MN 800-328-0953
Regal Power Transmission Solutions
Florence, KY. 859-342-7900
Regina USA
Oak Creek, WI 414-571-0032
Reinke & Schomann
Milwaukee, WI 414-964-1100
Renold Products
Westfield, NY 800-879-2529
Rexnord Corporation
Milwaukee, WI 866-739-6673
Reyco Systems Inc
Caldwell, ID 208-795-5700
Rhodes Machinery International
Louisville, KY 502-213-3865
Richards Industries Systems
West Caldwell, NJ. 973-575-7480
Rigidized Metal Corp
Buffalo, NY. 800-836-2580
Roechling Engineered Plastics
Gastonia, NC 800-541-4419
Rome Machine & Foundry Co
Rome, GA 800-538-7663
Ruiz Flour Tortillas
Riverside, CA 909-947-7811
Sadler Conveyor Systems
Montreal, QC 888-887-5129
Samuel Pressure Vessel Group
Marinette, WI 715-453-5326
San Fab Conveyor
Sandusky, OH 419-626-4465
Sardee Industries Inc
Orlando, FL 407-297-6362
Schloss Engineered Equipment
Aurora, CO 303-695-4500
Schlueter Company
Janesville, WI 800-359-1700
Schroeder Machine
San Marcos, CA 760-591-9733
Scientific Process & Research
Kendall Park, NJ 800-868-4777
Screw Conveyor Corp
Hammond, IN 219-931-1450
Servco Equipment Co
St Louis, MO.....................314-781-3189
Shelcon Inc
Ontario, CA.....................909-947-4877
Shingle Belting
King of Prussia, PA 800-345-6294
Shouldice Brothers SheetMetal
Battle Creek, MI 269-962-5579
Shuttleworth North America
Huntington, IN 800-444-7412
SI Systems Inc
Easton, PA. 800-523-9464
Sidney Manufacturing Co
Sidney, OH 800-482-3535
Simplex Filler Co
Napa, CA. 800-796-7539
Simplimatic Automation
Forest, VA 800-294-2003
Sinco
Red Wing, MN 800-243-6753
Slip-Not Belting Corporation
Kingsport, TN 423-246-8141
Smalley Manufacturing Co Inc
Knoxville, TN....................865-966-5866
Smetco
Aurora, OR 800-253-5400
Southern Ag Co Inc
Blakely, GA......................229-723-4262
Southworth Products Corp
Falmouth, ME.....................800-743-1000
Span Tech LLC
Glasgow, KY......................270-651-9166
Spanco Crane & Monorail Systems
Morgantown, PA 800-869-2080
Specialty Equipment Company
Houston, TX 713-467-1818
Speedways Conveyors
Lancaster, NY 800-800-1022

Sperling Industries
Omaha, NE 402-556-4070
Sperling Industries
Omaha, NE 800-647-5062
Spiral Manufacturing Co Inc
Minneapolis, MN 800-426-3643
Springport Steel Wire Products
Elkhart, IN. 574-295-9660
Spudnik Equipment Co
Blackfoot, ID 208-684-4120
Spurgeon Co
Ferndale, MI 800-396-2554
Stainless Specialists Inc
Wausau, WI. 800-236-4155
Stainless Steel Fabricator Inc
La Mirada, CA 714-739-9904
Steel Storage Systems Inc
Commerce City, CO 800-442-0291
Steinmetz Machine Works Inc
Stamford, CT.....................203-327-0118
Sterling Net & Twine Company
Cedar Knolls, NJ 800-342-0316
Stewart Systems Baking LLC
Plano, TX 972-422-5808
Stokes Material Handling Systs
Doylestown, PA 215-340-2200
Superior Industries
Morris, MN 800-321-1558
Svedala Industries
Colorado Springs, CO.............719-471-3443
Temp Air Inc
Burnsville, MN 800-836-7432
The National Provisioner
Deerfield, IL 847-763-9534
Thomas L. Green & Company
Robenosia, PA 610-693-5816
Titan Industries Inc
New London, WI 800-558-3616
TKF Inc
Cincinnati, OH 513-241-5910
Transnorm System Inc
Grand Prairie, TX 800-259-2303
Traycon Manufacturing Co
Carlstadt, NJ 201-939-5555
Tridyne Process Systems
South Burlington, VT 802-863-6873
Triple S Dynamics Inc
Breckenridge, TX 800-527-2116
True Manufacturing
Mexico, MO 636-240-2400
TWM Manufacturing
Leamington, ON 888-495-4831
Uhrden
Sugarcreek, OH 800-852-2411
Unex Manufacturing Inc
Lakewood, NJ 800-334-8639
United Pentek
Indianapolis, IN 800-357-9299
United Systems Inc
Kansas City, KS 888-281-2454
UniTrak Corporation
Port Hope, ON 866-883-5749
Universal Die & Stampings
Prairie Du Sac, WI 608-643-2477
Universal Industries Inc
Cedar Falls, IA 800-553-4446
Universal Labeling Systems Inc
St Petersburg, FL 877-236-0266
Universal Packaging Inc
Houston, TX 800-324-2610
Us Rubber
Brooklyn, NY 718-782-7888
Vac-U-Max
Belleville, NJ 800-822-8629
Van Der Graaf Corporation
Lithia Springs, GA 770-819-6650
Vertical Systems Intl
Lakeside Park, KY 859-485-9650
Vescom America
Henderson, NC 252-436-9067
W A Powers Co
Fort Worth, TX 800-792-1243
W.G. Durant Corporation
Whittier, CA 562-946-5555
Walker Magnetics Group Inc
Worcester, MA 800-962-4638
Wall Conveyor & Manufacturing
Huntington, WV 800-456-1335
Ward Ironworks
Welland, ON 888-441-9273
Wardcraft Conveyor & Quick Die
Spring Arbor, MI 800-782-2779

Washington Frontier
Grandview, WA..............509-469-7662
WEBB-Stiles Co
Valley City, OH..............330-273-9222
Weigh Right Automatic Scale Co
Joliet, IL..............800-571-0249
Weiler & Company
Whitewater, WI..............800-558-9507
Westfield Sheet Metal Works
Kenilworth, NJ..............908-276-5500
Whirl Air Flow
Big Lake, MN..............800-373-3461
Wilkie Brothers Conveyor Inc
Marysville, MI..............810-364-4820
Wilson Steel Products Company
Memphis, TN..............901-527-8742
Win-Holt Equipment Group
Syosset, NY..............800-444-3595
Wire Belt Co of America
Londonderry, NH..............603-644-2500
Witte Co Inc
Washington, NJ..............908-689-6500
Yakima Wire Works
Reedley, CA..............800-344-8951
Yargus Manufacturing Inc
Marshall, IL..............217-826-8059
YW Yacht Basin
Easton, MD..............410-822-0414
Ziniz
Louisville, KY..............502-955-6573

Cooperage

Brooks Barrel Company
Baltimore, MD..............800-398-2766
EGW Bradbury Enterprises
Bridgewater, ME..............800-332-6021
Fetzer Vineyards
Hopland, CA..............800-846-8637
Gibbs Brothers Cooperage
Hot Springs, AR..............501-623-8881
Oak Barrel Winecraft
Berkeley, CA..............510-849-0400
Ramoneda Bros Stave Mill
Culpeper, VA..............540-825-9166
Trilla Steel Drum Corporation
Chicago, IL..............773-847-7588
Warwick Products
Cleveland, OH..............800-535-4404

Cylinders

Catalina Cylinders
Garden Grove, CA..............714-890-0999

Dairy Industry

Cookie Kingdom
Oglesby, IL..............815-883-3331
Elmo Rietschle - A Gardner Denver Product
Qunicy, IL..............217-222-5400
GEA Niro Soavi North America
Bedford, NH..............603-606-4060
Gea Process Engineering Inc
Columbia, MD..............410-997-8700
Invensys APV Products
Houston, TX..............713-329-1600
Marel Food Systems, Inc.
Lenexa, KS..............913-888-9110
Reiser
Canton, MA..............734-821-1290
Schwartz Manufacturing Co
Two Rivers, WI..............920-793-1375
Stephan Machinery GmbH
Mandelein, IL..............847-247-0182
Stratecon International Consultants
Winston Salem, NC..............336-768-6808
Tuchenhagen North America
Portland, ME..............207-797-9500
Unitherm Food System
Bristow, OK..............918-367-0197
Wohlt Cheese Corp
New London, WI..............920-982-9000

Depositors

Alard Equipment Corp
Williamson, NY..............315-589-4511
Bogner Industries
Ronkonkoma, NY..............631-981-5123
Edhard Corp
Hackettstown, NJ..............888-334-2731

Polar Process
Plattsville, ON...............877-896-8077
Raque Food Systems
Louisville, KY..............502-267-9641
Reiser
Canton, MA..............734-821-1290

Feeders

Alard Equipment Corp
Williamson, NY..............315-589-4511
All Power Inc
Sioux City, IA..............712-258-0681
Anderson-Crane Company
Minneapolis, MN..............800-314-2747
Applied Chemical Technology
Florence, AL..............800-228-3217
Automated Flexible Conveyors
Clifton, NJ..............800-694-7271
Buffalo Technologies Corporation
Buffalo, NY..............800-332-2419
California Vibratory Feeders
Anaheim, CA..............800-354-0972
Campbell Wrapper Corporation
De Pere, WI..............920-983-7100
Carman Industries Inc
Jeffersonville, IN..............800-456-7560
Carrier Vibrating Equip Inc
Louisville, KY..............502-969-3171
Chicago Conveyor Corporation
Addison, IL..............630-543-6300
Cleveland Vibrator Co
Cleveland, OH..............800-221-3298
Creative Automation
Passaic, NJ..............973-778-0061
Custom Systems Integration Co
Carlsbad, CA..............760-635-1099
Dema Engineering Co
St Louis, MO..............800-325-3362
Eriez Magnetics
Erie, PA..............800-346-4946
Flow of Solids
Westford, MA..............978-392-0300
Fuller Weighing Systems
Columbus, OH..............614-882-8121
Gebo Corporation
Bradenton, FL..............941-727-1400
Gram Equipment of America
Tampa, FL..............813-248-1978
Graybill Machines Inc
Lititz, PA..............717-626-5221
Hart Design & Mfg
Green Bay, WI..............920-468-5927
Hoppmann Corporation
Elkwood, VA..............800-368-3582
Hyer Industries
Pembroke, MA..............781-826-8101
Ilapak Inc
Newtown, PA..............215-579-2900
Ipec
New Castle, PA..............800-377-4732
Key Technology Inc.
Walla Walla, WA..............509-529-2161
Kinergy Corp
Louisville, KY..............502-366-5685
KISS Packaging Systems
Vista, CA..............888-522-3538
Magnuson
Pueblo, CO..............719-948-9500
Martin Vibration Systems
Marine City, MI..............800-474-4538
MeGa Industries
Burlington, ON..............800-665-6342
Mell & Co
Niles, IL..............800-262-6355
MERRICK Industries Inc
Lynn Haven, FL..............800-271-7834
Meyer Machine & Garroutte Products
San Antonio, TX..............210-736-1811
Modular Packaging
Randolph, NJ..............973-970-9393
National Drying Machry Co Inc
Philadelphia, PA..............215-464-6070
Norden Inc
Branchburg, NJ..............908-252-9483
Norwalt Design Inc
Randolph, NJ..............973-927-3200
Nu-Con Equipment
Chanhassen, MN..............877-939-0510
Omega Design Corp
Exton, PA..............800-346-0191

Open Date Systems
Sunapee, NH..............877-673-6328
OTP Industrial Solutions
Terre Haute, IN..............860-953-7632
Our Name is Mud
New York, NY..............877-683-7867
Pacific Process Technology
La Jolla, CA..............858-551-3298
Palace Packaging Machines Inc
Downingtown, PA..............610-873-7252
Paramount Packaging Corp
Melville, NY..............516-333-8100
Pfankuch Machinery Corporation
Apple Valley, MN..............952-891-3311
Polar Process
Plattsville, ON..............877-896-8077
Presence From Innovation LLC
St Louis, MO..............314-423-9777
Professional Engineering Assoc
Louisville, KY..............502-429-0432
Ram Equipment Co
Waukesha, WI..............262-513-1114
Schenck Process
Whitewater, WI..............888-742-1249
Schneider Packaging Eqpt Co
Brewerton, NY..............315-676-3035
Shiffer Industries
Kihei, HI..............800-642-1774
Smalley Manufacturing Co Inc
Knoxville, TN..............865-966-5866
Summit Machine Builders Corporation
Denver, CO..............800-274-6741
Superior Food Machinery Inc
Pico Rivera, CA..............800-944-0396
Tecweigh
St Paul, MN..............800-536-4880
Universal Labeling Systems Inc
St Petersburg, FL..............877-236-0266
Vescom America
Henderson, NC..............252-436-9067
Ward Ironworks
Welland, ON..............888-441-9273
Waukesha Cherry-Burrell
Louisville, KY..............502-491-4310
Weigh Right Automatic Scale Co
Joliet, IL..............800-571-0249
Wyssmont Co Inc
Fort Lee, NJ..............201-947-4600

Gravimetric, Volumetric, Loss-In-Weight, Etc.

Applied Chemical Technology
Florence, AL..............800-228-3217
Automated Flexible Conveyors
Clifton, NJ..............800-694-7271
Chicago Conveyor Corporation
Addison, IL..............630-543-6300
Cleveland Vibrator Co
Cleveland, OH..............800-221-3298
Hyer Industries
Pembroke, MA..............781-826-8101
Ilapak Inc
Newtown, PA..............215-579-2900
MERRICK Industries Inc
Lynn Haven, FL..............800-271-7834
Polar Process
Plattsville, ON..............877-896-8077
Schenck Process
Whitewater, WI..............888-742-1249
Tecweigh
St Paul, MN..............800-536-4880
Weigh Right Automatic Scale Co
Joliet, IL..............800-571-0249

Speed Reducer

Boston Gear
Boston, MA..............888-999-9860
F R Drake Co
Waynesboro, VA..............540-949-6215

Filtration Devices & Systems

A & B Process Systems Corp
Stratford, WI..............888-258-2789
ACS Industries, Inc.
Lincoln, RI..............866-783-4838
Advance Fittings Corp
Elkhorn, WI..............262-723-6699
Air Quality Engineering
Minneapolis, MN..............800-328-0787

Airsan Corp
Milwaukee, WI 800-558-5494

Alard Equipment Corp
Williamson, NY 315-589-4511

Alexander Machinery
Spartanburg, SC 864-963-3624

Alkazone/Better Health Lab
Hackensack, NJ 800-810-1888

Allegheny Bradford Corp
Bradford, PA 800-542-0650

Allergen Air Filter Corp
Houston, TX 800-333-8880

American Ultraviolet Co
Lebanon, IN 800-288-9288

Ametek Technical & Industrial Products
Kent, OH 215-256-6601

Anguil Environmental Systems
Milwaukee, WI 800-488-0230

Applied Chemical Technology
Florence, AL 800-228-3217

APV Americas
Delavan, WI 800-252-5200

Aqua-Aerobic Systems Inc
Loves Park, IL 800-940-5008

Aquathin Corporation
Pompano Beach, FL 800-462-7634

Astro Pure Water
Deerfield Beach, FL 954-422-8966

Avery Filter Company
Westwood, NJ 201-666-9664

Avestin
Ottawa, ON 888-283-7846

Baker Hughes
Houston, TX

Beach Filter Products
Hanover, PA 800-232-2485

Berkshire PPM
Litchfield, CT 860-567-3118

Blodgett Oven Co
Burlington, VT 800-331-5842

Bloomfield Industries
St. Louis, MO 888-356-5362

Blue Tech
Hickory, NC 828-324-5900

BluMetric Environmental Inc.
Ottawa, ON 613-839-3053

Bunn-O-Matic Corp
Springfield, IL 800-352-2866

CE International Trading Corporation
Miami, FL 800-827-1169

CLARCOR Air Filtration Prods
Jeffersonville, IN 866-247-4827

Climate Master Inc
Oklahoma City, OK 877-436-0263

Complete Automation
Lake Orion, MI 248-814-4967

Corrigan Corporation of America
Gurnee, IL 800-462-6478

Crane Environmental
Norristown, PA 800-633-7435

Crispy Lite
St. Louis, MO 888-356-5362

Croll-Reynolds Engineering Company
Trumbull, CT 203-371-1983

Culligan Company
Northbrook, IL 877-530-2676

Custom Fabricating & Repair
Marshfield, WI 800-236-8773

Dallas Group of America Inc
Whitehouse, NJ 800-367-4188

Dedert Corporation
Olympia Fields, IL 708-747-7000

Delta Pure Filtration Corp
Ashland, VA 800-785-9450

Diamond Water Conditioning
Hortonville, WI. 800-236-8931

Diebolt & Co
Old Lyme, CT 800-343-2658

Durastill Export Inc
Rockland, MA 800-449-5260

Dwyer Instruments Inc
Michigan City, IN 800-872-3141

Eaton Filtration, LLC
Tinton Falls, NJ. 800-859-9212

Eco-Air Products
San Diego, CA 800-284-8111

Elwood Safety Company
Buffalo, NY. 866-326-6060

Enting Water Conditioning Inc
Moraine, OH 800-735-5100

Enviro-Clear Co
High Bridge, NJ 908-638-5507

Ertelalsop
Kingston, NY 800-553-7835

Etube & Wire
Shrewsbury, PA. 800-618-4720

Everfilt Corp
Mira Loma, CA. 800-360-8380

Everpure, LLC
Hanover Park, IL. 630-307-3000

F.P. Smith Wire Cloth Company
Northlake, IL. 800-323-6842

Falcon Fabricators Inc
Nashville, TN 615-832-0027

Falls Filtration Technologies
Stow, OH 330-928-4100

Filtercorp
Fresno, CA 800-473-4526

Filtration Systems
Sunrise, FL 954-572-2700

Filtration Systems Prods Inc
Pevely, MO 800-444-4720

Flame Gard
Lakewood, NJ 800-526-3694

Flanders Corp
Washington, NC 800-637-2803

Freudenberg Nonwovens
Hopkinsville, KY 270-887-5115

Frymaster
Shreveport, LA 800-221-4583

Fuller Ultra Violet Corp
Frankfort, IL 815-469-3301

G.W. Dahl Company
Greensboro, NC 800-852-4449

Gaylord Industries
Tualatin, OR 800-547-9696

Globe Machine
Tacoma, WA 800-523-6575

Goodnature Products
Orchard Park, NY 800-875-3381

Greig Filters Inc
Lafayette, LA 800-456-0177

Gusmer Enterprises Inc
Fresno, CA 866-213-1131

H T I Filtration
Rancho Sta Marg, CA 877-404-9372

Halton Company
Scottsville, KY 800-442-5866

Hankison International
Canonsburg, PA. 724-746-1100

Harborlite Corporation
Lompoc, CA 800-342-8667

Hayes & Stolz Indl Mfg LTD
Fort Worth, TX 800-725-7272

Hayward Industries Inc
Clemmons, NC 336-712-9900

Hemco Corp
Independence, MO 800-779-4362

Hess Machine Intl
Ephrata, PA 800-735-4377

Holland Applied Technologies
Burr Ridge, IL. 630-325-5130

Hungerford & Terry
Clayton, NJ 856-881-3200

Hunter Fan Co
Cordova, TN 901-743-1360

Hydromax Inc
Emmitsburg, MD 800-326-0602

Hydropure Water Treatment Co
Coral Springs, FL 800-753-1547

I.W. Tremont Company
Hawthorne, NJ 973-427-3800

Imperial Manufacturing Co
Corona, CA 800-343-7790

Introdel Products
Itasca, IL 800-323-4772

Kason Central
Columbus, OH 614-885-1992

Kason Industries
Newnan, GA 770-254-0553

Keating of Chicago Inc
Mc Cook, IL 800-532-8464

Kentwood Spring Water Company
Patterson, LA 985-395-9313

KETCH
Wichita, KS 800-766-3777

Kinetico
Newbury, OH 440-564-9111

King Bag & Mfg Co
Cincinnati, OH 800-444-5464

King Company
Dallas, TX 507-451-3770

King Engineering - King-Gage
Newell, WV 800-242-8871

Kiss International/Di-tech Systems
Vista, CA. 800-527-5477

Kraissl Co Inc
Hackensack, NJ 800-572-4775

L&A Process Systems
Modesto, CA. 209-581-0205

L.C. Thompson Company
Kenosha, WI 800-558-4018

Lamports Filter Media
Cleveland, OH 216-881-2050

Lenser Filtration
Lakewood, NJ. 732-370-1600

Lewis M Carter Mfg Co Inc
Donalsonville, GA 800-332-8232

Mars Air Products
Gardena, CA 800-421-1266

Melvina Can Machinery Company
Hudson Falls, NY 518-743-0606

Membrane System Specialist Inc
Wisconsin Rapids, WI 715-421-2333

Metlar Us
Riverhead, NY 631-252-5574

Micropure Filtration Inc
Mound, MN 800-654-7873

Mies Products
West Bend, WI 800-480-6437

Miroil
Allentown, PA. 800-523-9844

Moll-Tron
Lakewood, CO 800-525-9494

Mountain Safety Research
Seattle, WA 800-877-9677

Muckler Industries, Inc
Saint Louis, MO 800-444-0283

Nederman
Thomasville, NC. 800-533-5286

Netzsch Pumps North America
Exton, PA 610-363-8010

Newark Wire Cloth Co
Clifton, NJ. 800-221-0392

Newwaveenviro
Greenwood Vlg, CO. 800-592-8371

Niro
Hudson, WI 715-386-9371

Nothum Food Processing Systems
Springfield, MO 800-435-1297

Oc Lugo Co Inc
New City, NY 845-480-5121

Optipure
Plano, TX 972-422-1212

Ozotech Inc
Yreka, CA 530-842-4189

Pacific Process Technology
La Jolla, CA 858-551-3298

Pall Corp
Port Washington, NY 866-905-7255

Pall Filtron
Northborough, MA 800-345-8766

PAR-Kan
Silver Lake, IN 800-291-5487

Parker-Hannifin Corp
Cleveland, OH 800-272-7537

Parker-Hannifin Corp
Jeffersonville, IN 866-247-4827

Parkson Corp
Vernon Hills, IL 847-816-3700

Piab Vacuum Products
Hingham, MA. 800-321-7422

Prince Castle Inc
Carol Stream, IL 800-722-7853

Pro-Flo Products
Cedar Grove, NJ 800-325-1057

PURA
Sun Valley, CA 800-292-7872

Purolator Facet Inc
Greensboro, NC 800-852-4449

R F Hunter Co Inc
Dover, NH 800-332-9565

R R Street & Co
Naperville, IL 630-416-4244

Refractron Technologies Corp
Newark, NY 315-331-6222

Reynold Water Conditioning
Farmington Hills, MI 800-572-9575

Robinson/Kirshbaum Industries
Gardena, CA 800-929-3812

Rolfs @ Boone
Boone, IA 800-265-2010

Sartorius Corp
Edgewood, NY 800-635-2906

Schlueter Company
Janesville, WI 800-359-1700

Scienco Systems
Saint Louis, MO 314-621-2536
Scotsman Ice Systems
Vernon Hills, IL 800-726-8762
Selecto Scientific
Suwanee, GA 800-635-4017
Serfilco
Northbrook, IL 800-323-5431
Sermia International
Blainville, QC. 800-567-7483
Severn Trent Svc
Fort Washington, PA. 215-646-9201
Shick Esteve
Kansas City, MO. 877-744-2587
Sparkler Filters Inc
Conroe, TX 936-756-4471
Spencer Strainer Systems
Jeffersonville, IN 800-801-4977
Stainless Steel Fabricator Inc
La Mirada, CA 714-739-9904
Star Filters
Timmonsville, SC 800-845-5381
Stearns Technical Textiles Company
Cincinnati, OH 800-543-7173
Steri Technologies Inc
Bohemia, NY 800-253-7140
Straight Line Filters
Wilmington, DE 302-654-8805
Tema Systems Inc
Cincinnati, OH 513-792-2840
Therm-Tec Inc
Sherwood, OR. 800-292-9163
Thomas Technical Svc
Neillsville, WI. 715-743-4666
Trenton Mills Inc
Trenton, TN. 731-855-1323
Triad Scientific
Manasquan, NJ 800-867-6690
Ultra Industries Inc
Racine, WI 800-358-5872
Ultrafilter
Norcross, GA 800-543-3634
Ultrapar Inc.
Warren, NJ 908-647-6650
United Air Specialists Inc
Blue Ash, OH 800-992-4422
United Filters Intl
Amarillo, TX. 806-373-8386
United Industries Group Inc
Lake Forest, CA 949-759-3200
United States Systems Inc
Kansas City, KS 888-281-2454
US Filter Dewatering Systems
Holland, MI. 800-245-3006
Van Air Systems
Lake City, PA 800-840-9906
Vent Master
Mississauga, ON 800-565-2981
VMC Signs
Victoria, TX 361-575-0548
Washington Frontier
Grandview, WA. 509-469-7662
Water & Power Technologies
Salt Lake City, UT 888-271-3295
Water Sciences Services, Inc.
Jackson, TN 973-584-4131
Water System Group
Santa Clarita, CA 800-350-9283
Waterlink/Sanborn Technologies
Canton, OH 800-343-3381
Watts Premier Inc
Peoria, AZ. 800-752-5582
Whatman
Piscataway, NJ 973-245-8300
Whatman
Haverhill, MA. 978-374-7400
Williams & Mettle Company
Houston, TX 800-526-4954
Womack International Inc
Vallejo, CA 707-647-2370
Yardney Water Management Syst
Riverside, CA 800-854-4788
Zander Insurance Group
Nashville, TN 615-356-1700

Fittings

Accutek Packaging Equipment
Vista, CA. .800-989-1828
Ace Manufacturing
Cincinnati, OH 800-653-5692

Advance Fittings Corp
Elkhorn, WI. 262-723-6699
Anver Corporation
Hudson, MA 800-654-3500
Archon Industries Inc
Suffern, NY 800-554-1394
Baldewein Company
Lake Forrest, IL 800-424-5544
Bradford A Ducon Company
Pewaukee, WI. 800-789-1718
C.F.F. Stainless Steels
Hamilton, ON 800-263-4511
Carmun International
San Antonio, TX. 800-531-7907
Crown Industries
East Orange, NJ 877-747-2457
Dormont Manufacturing Co
Export, PA. 800-367-6668
Eischen Enterprises
Fresno, CA 559-834-0013
Ellett Industries
Port Coquitlam, BC. 604-941-8211
Fort, Products
Kansas City, MO. 816-741-3000
Gems Sensors & Controls
Plainville, CT 860-747-3000
General Tank
Berwick, PA 800-435-8265
Hoffmeyer Corp
San Leandro, CA. 888-744-1826
Hydra-Flex Inc
Livonia, MI. 800-234-0832
Keystone Rubber Corporation
Greenbackville, VA. 800-394-5661
Kuriyama of America Inc
Schaumburg, IL. 800-800-0320
Lake Process Systems Inc
Lake Barrington, IL 800-331-9260
Magnatech Corp
East Granby, CT 888-393-3602
Nalge Process Technologies Group
Rochester, NY. 585-586-8800
Norgren Inc.
Littleton, CO. 800-514-0129
Parker-Hannifin Corp
Cleveland, OH 800-272-7537
Pure Fit Nutrition Bars
Irvine, CA 866-787-3348
Qosina Corporation
Ronkonkoma, NY. 631-242-3000
Qualtech
Quebec, QC. 888-339-3801
Robert-James Sales
Buffalo, NY. 800-777-1325
Rolfs @ Boone
Boone, IA .800-265-2010
Rolland Machining & Fabricating
Moneta, VA. 973-827-6911
Rubber Fab Molding & Gasket
Sparta, NJ 866-442-2959
Sanitary Couplers
Springboro, OH. 513-743-0144
Southern Metal Fabricators Inc
Albertville, AL 800-989-1330
Special Products
Springfield, MO 417-881-6114
Spencer Turbine Co
Windsor, CT 800-232-4321
Spraying Systems Company
Wheaton, IL 630-655-5000
Standex International Corp.
Salem, NH. 603-893-9701
T & S Brass & Bronze Work
Travelers Rest, SC 800-476-4103
Tomlinson Industries
Cleveland, OH 800-945-4589
Top Line Process Equipment Company
Bradford, PA. 800-458-6095
Tuchenhagen
Columbia, MD 410-910-6000
Unisource Manufacturing Inc
Portland, OR. 800-234-2566
Valvinox
Iberville, QC. 450-346-1981
Waukesha Cherry-Burrell
Louisville, KY 502-491-4310
Waukesha Specialty Company
Darien, WI. 262-724-3700
WCB Ice Cream
Philadelphia, PA 215-425-4320
Windhorst Blowmold
Euless, TX. 817-540-6639

World Wide Fitting Corp
Vernon Hills, IL 800-393-9894

Flow Regulators

Alard Equipment Corp
Williamson, NY 315-589-4511
American LEWA
Holliston, MA. 888-539-2123
Boston Gear
Boston, MA. 888-999-9860
Carmun International
San Antonio, TX. 800-531-7907
Cashco Inc
Ellsworth, KS 785-472-4461
Linde North America
Murray Hill, NJ. 908-464-8100
Lumenite Control Tech Inc
Franklin Park, IL. 800-323-8510
Meltric Corporation
Franklin, WI 800-824-4031
Monitor Technologies LLC
Elburn, IL .800-601-6204
Music City Metals Inc
Nashville, TN 800-251-2674
Norgren Inc.
Littleton, CO. 800-514-0129
Samson Controls
Baytown, TX. 281-383-3677
Spraying Systems Company
Wheaton, IL. 630-655-5000
Standard Pump
Auburn, GA. 866-558-8611

Food Processing

Aerosol

John R Nalbach Engineering Co
Countryside, IL 708-579-9100
Packaging Equipment & Conveyors, Inc
Elkhart, IN. 574-266-6995

Agitators

Food Processing

A & B Process Systems Corp
Stratford, WI. 888-258-2789
APV Americas
Delavan, WI. 800-252-5200
Berkshire PPM
Litchfield, CT 860-567-3118
Bowers Process Equipment
Stratford, ON. 800-567-3223
Bush Tank Fabricators Inc
Newark, NJ. 973-596-1121
Chemineer
Dayton, OH. 937-454-3200
Coastline Equipment Inc
Bellingham, WA 360-734-8509
EKATO Corporation
St Ramsey, NJ. 201-825-4684
Et Oakes Corp
Hauppauge, NY 631-232-0002
Expert Industries Inc
Brooklyn, NY 718-434-6060
Falco Technologies
La Prairie, QC. 450-444-0566
Fernholtz Engineering
Van Nuys, CA 818-785-5800
Hamilton Kettles
Weirton, WV. 800-535-1882
National Oilwell Varco
North Andover, MA 800-643-0641
Norvell Co Inc
Fort Scott, KS 800-653-3147
Patterson Industries
Scarborough, ON 800-336-1110
Process Systems
Barrington, IL. 847-842-8618
Sonic Corp
Stratford, CT 866-493-1378
Washington Frontier
Grandview, WA. 509-469-7662

Milk

Alard Equipment Corp
Williamson, NY 315-589-4511
Bowers Process Equipment
Stratford, ON. 800-567-3223

Falco Technologies
  La Prairie, QC 450-444-0566
Liquid Scale
  New Brighton, MN 888-633-2969
National Oilwell Varco
  North Andover, MA 800-643-0641
Relco Unisystems Corp
  Willmar, MN 320-231-2210
Washington Frontier
  Grandview, WA 509-469-7662
Whey Systems
  Willmar, MN 320-905-4122

Air Knives

Ametek Technical & Industrial Products
  Kent, OH 215-256-6601
Paxton Products Inc
  Blue Ash, OH 800-441-7475
Spencer Turbine Co
  Windsor, CT 800-232-4321

Augers

A T Ferrell Co Inc
  Bluffton, IN 800-248-8318
Apollo Sheet Metal
  Kennewick, WA 509-586-1104
Auger Fab
  Exton, PA 800-334-1529
Cal-Coast Manufacturing
  Turlock, CA 209-668-9378
Polar Process
  Plattsville, ON 877-896-8077
Relco Unisystems Corp
  Willmar, MN 320-231-2210
Spee-Dee Packaging Machinery
  Sturtevant, WI 877-375-2121
TWM Manufacturing
  Leamington, ON 888-495-4831
Universal Packaging Inc
  Houston, TX 800-324-2610
Viking Machine & Design Inc
  De Pere, WI 888-286-2116
Washington Frontier
  Grandview, WA 509-469-7662
Whey Systems
  Willmar, MN 320-905-4122

Bakers'

A&J Mixing International
  Oakville, ON 800-668-3470
Aaburco Inc
  Grass Valley, CA 800-533-7437
ABI Limited
  Concord, ON 800-297-8666
Adamatic
  Auburn, WA 800-578-2547
Allied Bakery and Food Service Equipment
  Santa Fe Springs, CA 562-945-6506
American Eagle Food Machinery
  Chicago, IL 888-390-0800
AMF Bakery Systems Corp
  Richmond, VA 800-225-3771
AMF CANADA
  Sherbrooke, QC 800-255-3869
Andgar Corp
  Ferndale, WA 360-366-9900
Arcobaleno Pasta Machines
  Lancaster, PA 800-875-7096
Attias Oven Corp
  Brooklyn, NY 800-928-8427
Bakery Associates
  Setauket, NY 631-751-4156
Baking Machines
  Livermore, CA 925-449-3369
Belshaw Adamatic Bakery Group
  Auburn, WA 800-578-2547
Bettendorf Stanford Inc
  Salem, IL 800-548-2253
Bevles Company
  Dallas, TX 800-441-1601
Bolling Oven & Machine Company
  Avon, OH 440-937-6112
Breddo Likwifier
  Kansas City, MO 800-669-4092
Buss America
  Carol Stream, IL 630-933-9100
C & K Machine Co
  Holyoke, MA 413-536-8122

C H Babb Co Inc
  Raynham, MA 508-977-0600
C Palmer Mfg Co Inc
  West Newton, PA 724-872-8200
Cannon Equipment Company
  Cannon Falls, MN 800-825-8501
Christy Machine Co
  Fremont, OH 888-332-6451
Cinelli Esperia
  Woodbridge, ON 905-856-1820
Clayton Manufacturing Company
  Derby, NY 716-549-0392
CMC America Corporation
  Joliet, IL 815-726-4337
Cobatco
  Peoria, IL 800-426-2282
Comtec Industries
  Woodridge, IL 630-759-9000
Custom Diamond Intl.
  Laval, QC 800-326-5926
D.R. McClain & Son
  Commerce, CA 800-428-2263
DBE Inc
  Concord, ON 800-461-5313
Delta Machine & Maufacturing
  St Rose, LA 504-949-8304
Deluxe Equipment Company
  Bradenton, FL 800-367-8931
Don Lee
  Philadelphia, PA 760-745-0707
Doyon Equipment
  Liniere, QC 800-463-4273
Dutchess Bakers' Machinery Co
  Superior, WI 800-777-4498
Edhard Corp
  Hackettstown, NJ 888-334-2731
Empire Bakery Equipment
  Hicksville, NY 800-878-4070
Epcon Industrial Systems
  Conroe, TX 800-447-7872
Et Oakes Corp
  Hauppauge, NY 631-232-0002
Everedy Automation
  Frederick, PA 610-754-1775
Exact Mixing Systems Inc
  Memphis, TN 901-362-8501
Fish Oven & Equipment Co
  Wauconda, IL 877-526-8720
Food Engineering Unlimited
  Fullerton, CA 714-879-8762
Food Machinery Sales
  Bogart, GA 706-549-2207
Food Tools
  Santa Barbara, CA 877-836-6386
Franz Haas Machinery-America
  Henrico, VA 804-222-6022
Fred D Pfening Co
  Columbus, OH 614-294-5361
Friedrich Metal Products
  Browns Summit, NC 800-772-0326
Garland Commercial Ranges
  Mississauga, ON 905-624-0260
Good Idea
  Northampton, MA 800-462-9237
Goodway Industries Inc
  Bohemia, NY 800-943-4501
Graybill Machines Inc
  Lititz, PA 717-626-5221
Hayon Manufacturing
  Las Vegas, NV 702-562-3377
I J White Corp
  Farmingdale, NY 631-293-2211
Ika-Works Inc
  Wilmington, NC 800-733-3037
Imperial Manufacturing Co
  Corona, CA 800-343-7790
Indiana Wire Company
  Fremont, IN 877-786-6883
Industrial Air Conditioning Systems
  Chicago, IL 773-486-4236
Industrial Product Corp
  Ho Ho Kus, NJ 800-472-5913
JAS Manufacturing Company
  Carrollton, TX 972-380-1150
K B Systems Inc
  Bangor, PA 610-588-7788
Knott Slicers
  Canton, MA 781-821-0925
Lanly Co
  Cleveland, OH 216-731-1115
Latendorf Corporation
  Brielle, NJ 800-526-4057

Lawrence Equipment Inc
  South El Monte, CA 800-423-4500
Lematic Inc
  Jackson, MI 517-787-3301
Lil' Orbits
  Minneapolis, MN 800-228-8305
LVO Manufacturing Inc
  Rock Rapids, IA 712-472-3734
Maddox/Adams International
  Miami, FL 305-592-3337
Magna Machine Co
  Cincinnati, OH 800-448-3475
Merco/Savory
  Mt. Pleasant, MI 800-733-8821
Mercury Equipment Company
  Chino, CA 800-273-6688
Moffat
  San Antonio, TX 866-589-0664
Moline Machinery LLC
  Duluth, MN 800-767-5734
Motom Corporation
  Bensenville, IL 630-787-1995
Nemeth Engineering Assoc
  Crestwood, KY 502-241-1502
Nothum Food Processing Systems
  Springfield, MO 800-435-1297
Oshikiri Corp of America
  Philadelphia, PA 215-637-8112
Pavailler Distribution Company
  Northvale, NJ 201-767-0766
Peerless Food Equipment
  Sidney, OH 937-492-4158
Peerless Machinery Corporation
  Sidney, OH 800-999-3327
PMI Food Equipment Group
  Troy, OH 937-332-3000
Radio Frequency Co Inc
  Millis, MA 508-376-9555
Ram Equipment Co
  Waukesha, WI 262-513-1114
Reading Bakery Systems Inc
  Robesonia, PA 610-693-5816
Reed Oven Co
  Kansas City, MO 816-842-7446
Regal Ware Inc
  Kewaskum, WI 262-626-2121
Reiser
  Canton, MA 734-821-1290
Revent Inc
  Piscataway, NJ 732-777-9433
Rheon USA
  Irvine, CA 949-768-1900
Rhodes Bakery Equipment
  Portland, OR 800-426-3813
Rondo Inc
  Moonachie, NJ 800-882-0633
Roto-Flex Oven Co
  San Antonio, TX 877-859-1463
Ruiz Flour Tortillas
  Riverside, CA 909-947-7811
Soco System USA
  Waukesha, WI 800-441-6293
Somerset Industries
  Billerica, MA 800-772-4404
Stewart Systems Baking LLC
  Plano, TX 972-422-5808
T.K. Products
  Anaheim, CA 714-621-0267
Thomas L. Green & Company
  Robenosia, PA 610-693-5816
Thompson Bagel Machine Mfg
  Los Angeles, CA 310-836-0900
TMCo Inc.ÿ
  Houston, TX 713-465-3255
Toastmaster
  Elgin, IL 847-741-3300
Unifiller Systems
  Delta, BC 888-733-8444
United Bakery Equipment Company
  Shawnee Mission, KS 913-541-8700
US Tsubaki Holdings Inc
  Wheeling, IL 800-323-7790
Varimixer North America
  Charlotte, NC 800-221-1138
Warwick Manufacturing & Equip
  North Brunswick, NJ 732-729-0400
Wilder Manufacturing Company
  Port Jervis, NY 800-832-1319
Woody Associates Inc
  York, PA 717-843-3975
X-Press Manufacturing
  New Braunfels, TX 800-365-9440

Balers or Baling Presses

Advance Lifts Inc
  St Charles, IL 800-843-3625
Balemaster
  Crown Point, IN 219-663-4525
Consolidated Baling Machine Company
  Jacksonville, FL 800-231-9286
Enterprise Company
  Santa Ana, CA 714-835-0541
Galbreath LLC
  Winamac, IN 574-946-6631
Incinerator International Inc
  Houston, TX 713-227-1466
Load King Mfg
  Jacksonville, FL 800-531-4975
Logemann Brothers Co
  Milwaukee, WI 414-445-3005
Marathon Equipment Co
  Vernon, AL 800-269-7237
Maren Engineering Corp
  South Holland, IL 800-875-1038
Orwak
  Minneapolis, MN 800-747-0449
Ouachita Machine Works
  West Monroe, LA 318-396-1468
PTR Baler & Compactor Co
  Philadelphia, PA 800-523-3654
Schleicher & Company of America
  Sanford, NC 800-775-7570
SP Industries
  Hopkins, MI 800-592-5959
Waste Away Systems
  Newark, OH 800-223-4741
Wastequip Inc
  Charlotte, NC 704-366-7140

Barley Processing

ANDRITZ Inc
  Muncy, PA. 704-943-4343

Biscuit Making

Exact Mixing Systems Inc
  Memphis, TN 901-362-8501
Rademaker USA
  Hudson, OH 330-650-2345
Reading Bakery Systems Inc
  Robesonia, PA. 610-693-5816
Reiser
  Canton, MA 734-821-1290
Rheon USA
  Irvine, CA 949-768-1900

Blades

Food Processing Machine

Atlanta SharpTech
  Peachtree City, GA 800-462-7297
Bettendorf Stanford Inc
  Salem, IL 800-548-2253
Boehringer Mfg. Co. Inc.
  Felton, CA. 800-630-8665
CB Mfg. & Sales Co.
  Miamisburg, OH 800-543-6860
Cozzini LLC
  Chicago, IL 773-478-9700
E-Z Edge Inc
  West New York, NJ. 800-232-4470
Garvey Products
  Cincinnati, OH 513-771-8710
Good Idea
  Northampton, MA. 800-462-9237
Hansaloy Corp
  Davenport, IA. 800-553-4992
Huther Brothers
  Rochester, NY. 800-334-1115
Industrial Product Corp
  Ho Ho Kus, NJ 800-472-5913
Industrial Razorblade
  Orange, NJ 973-673-4286
KSW Corp
  Des Moines, IA 515-265-5269
Pieco
  Manchester, IA 800-334-3929
R H Saw Corp
  Barrington, IL. 847-381-8777
Ranger Blade Manufacturing Company
  Traer, IA 800-377-7860

Save-O-Seal Corporation
  Elmsford, NY 800-831-9720
Simmons Engineering Corporation
  Wheeling, IL. 800-252-3381
Simonds International
  Fitchburg, MA 800-343-1616
Specialty Blades
  Staunton, VA. 540-248-2200
Specialty Saw Inc
  Simsbury, CT 800-225-0772
TGW International
  Florence, KY 800-407-0173
Thomas Precision, Inc.
  Rice Lake, WI. 800-657-4808

Blenders

A & B Process Systems Corp
  Stratford, WI. 888-258-2789
Aaron Equipment Co Div Areco
  Bensenville, IL 630-350-2200
Acrison Inc
  Moonachie, NJ 800-422-4266
Apache Stainless Equipment
  Beaver Dam, WI 800-444-0398
APV Americas
  Delavan, WI 800-252-5200
Attias Oven Corp
  Brooklyn, NY 800-928-8427
Automated Food Systems
  Waxahachie, TX 469-517-0470
Axiflow Technologies, Inc.
  Kennesaw, GA 770-795-1195
Bepex International LLC
  Minneapolis, MN 800-607-2470
Blue Tech
  Hickory, NC 828-324-5900
Bowers Process Equipment
  Stratford, ON. 800-567-3223
Breddo Likwifier
  Kansas City, MO 800-669-4092
Bush Tank Fabricators Inc
  Newark, NJ 973-596-1121
Century Foods Intl LLC
  Sparta, WI. 800-269-1901
Charles Ross & Son Co
  Hauppauge, NY 800-243-7677
Cleveland-Eastern Mixers
  Clinton, CT 800-243-1188
CRC Inc
  Council Bluffs, IA. 712-323-9477
Dito Dean Food Prep
  Charlotte, NC 866-449-4200
Dorton Incorporated
  Arlington Hts, IL 800-299-8600
Drum-Mates Inc.
  Lumberton, NJ 800-621-3786
Ederback Corporation
  Ann Arbor, MI 800-422-2558
Eirich Machines
  Gurnee, IL. 847-336-2444
Et Oakes Corp
  Hauppauge, NY 631-232-0002
Eurodib
  Champlain, NY 888-956-6866
Expert Industries Inc
  Brooklyn, NY 718-434-6060
Falco Technologies
  La Prairie, QC 450-444-0566
Fernholtz Engineering
  Van Nuys, CA 818-785-5800
Ferrell-Ross
  Amarillo, TX. 800-299-9051
Fleet Wood Goldco Wyard
  Cockeysville, MD 410-785-1934
Flow of Solids
  Westford, MA 978-392-0300
Food Processing Equipment Co
  Santa Fe Springs, CA 562-802-3727
FPEC Corporation
  Santa Fe Springs, CA 562-802-3727
Glen Mills Inc.
  Clifton, NJ. 973-777-0777
Gold Medal Products Co
  Cincinnati, OH 800-543-0862
Hamilton Beach Brands
  Southern Pines, NC 800-851-8900
Hayes & Stolz Indl Mfg LTD
  Fort Worth, TX 800-725-7272
Hosokawa/Bepex Corporation
  Santa Rosa, CA. 707-586-6000

International Reserve Equipment Corporation
  Clarendon Hills, IL 708-531-0680
Island Oasis Frozen Cocktail
  Beloit, WI 800-777-4752
Jenike & Johanson Inc
  Tyngsboro, MA. 978-649-3300
Karl Schnell
  New London, WI 920-982-9974
Kemutec Group Inc
  Bristol, PA. 215-788-8013
Kinetic Equipment Company
  Appleton, WI 806-293-4471
Krones
  Franklin, WI 800-752-3787
M O Industries Inc
  Whippany, NJ 973-386-9228
Machanix Fabrication Inc
  Chino, CA 800-700-9701
Matcon Americas
  Elmhurst, IL 856-256-1330
Materials Transportation Co
  Temple, TX 800-433-3110
Midwest Metalcraft & Equipment
  Windsor, MO. 800-647-3167
Munson Machinery Co
  Utica, NY 800-944-6644
Paget Equipment Co
  Marshfield, WI 715-384-3158
Patterson Industries
  Scarborough, ON 800-336-1110
Patterson-Kelley   Hars Company
  East Stroudsburg, PA 570-421-7500
Paul O. Abbe
  Bensenville, IL 630-350-2200
Peerless Machinery Corporation
  Sidney, OH 800-999-3327
Polar Process
  Plattsville, ON. 877-896-8077
Pro Scientific Inc
  Oxford, CT 800-584-3776
Reiser
  Canton, MA 734-821-1290
Rubicon Industries
  Brooklyn, NY 800-662-6999
Stephan Machinery, Inc.
  Mundelein, IL 800-783-7426
Stricklin Co
  Dallas, TX. 214-637-1030
Superior Products Company
  Saint Paul, MN 800-328-9800
Swirl Freeze Corp
  Salt Lake City, UT 800-262-4275
T D Sawvel Co
  Maple Plain, MN. 877-488-1816
TSA Griddle Systems
  Kelowna, BC. 250-491-9025
VitaMinder Company
  Providence, RI 800-858-8840
Vitamix
  Olmsted Twp, OH. 800-437-4654
Waring Products
  Torrington, CT 800-492-7464
Wilch Manufacturing
  Topeka, KS 785-267-2762
Yargus Manufacturing Inc
  Marshall, IL 217-826-8059

Blending

Flour

Automated Food Systems
  Waxahachie, TX 469-517-0470
Breddo Likwifier
  Kansas City, MO. 800-669-4092
Glen Mills Inc.
  Clifton, NJ. 973-777-0777
Hosokawa/Bepex Corporation
  Santa Rosa, CA. 707-586-6000
Patterson-Kelley   Hars Company
  East Stroudsburg, PA 570-421-7500
Peerless Machinery Corporation
  Sidney, OH 800-999-3327
Tuchenhagen
  Columbia, MD 410-910-6000

Grain

ANDRITZ Inc
  Muncy, PA. 704-943-4343
Breddo Likwifier
  Kansas City, MO. 800-669-4092

Davron Technologies Inc
　Chattanooga, TN...................423-870-1888
Glen Mills Inc.
　Clifton, NJ.......................973-777-0777
Hosokawa/Bepex Corporation
　Santa Rosa, CA...................707-586-6000
M O Industries Inc
　Whippany, NJ.....................973-386-9228
Patterson-Kelley　　Hars Company
　East Stroudsburg, PA..............570-421-7500
Tuchenhagen
　Columbia, MD....................410-910-6000

Blowers

Aerovent Co
　Minneapolis, MN..................763-551-7500
Andgar Corp
　Ferndale, WA....................360-366-9900
Ceilcote Air Pollution Control
　Middleburg Hts, OH...............800-554-8673
Chicago Conveyor Corporation
　Addison, IL......................630-543-6300
Gardner Denver Inc.
　Milwaukee, WI
Hartzell Fan Inc
　Piqua, OH.......................800-336-3267
Loren Cook Co
　Springfield, MO..................800-289-3267
Nalge Process Technologies Group
　Rochester, NY...................585-586-8800
Nu-Con Equipment
　Chanhassen, MN.................877-939-0510
Palace Packaging Machines Inc
　Downingtown, PA.................610-873-7252
Paxton Products Inc
　Blue Ash, OH....................800-441-7475
Ross Cook
　Silver Spring, MD................800-233-7339
Spencer Turbine Co
　Windsor, CT.....................800-232-4321
Tuthill Vacuum & Blower Systems
　Springfield, MO..................800-825-6937
Yakima Wire Works
　Reedley, CA.....................800-344-8951

Boilers

Electric Steam

Sussman Electric Boilers
　Long Island City, NY.............800-238-3535

Gas Fired

Ecs Warehouse
　Buffalo, NY......................716-833-7380

Water

A.O. Smith Water Products Company
　Irving, TX.......................800-527-1953
Bryan Boilers
　Peru, IN........................765-473-6651
Cleaver-Brooks Inc
　Thomasville, GA.................800-250-5583
Holman Boiler Works
　Dallas, TX.......................800-331-1956
Pacific Steam Equipment, Inc.
　Santa Fe Springs, CA.............800-321-4114
PVI Industries LLC
　Fort Worth, TX..................800-784-8326
Quikwater Inc
　Sand Springs, OK................918-241-8880
Sellers Engineering Division
　Danville, KY.....................859-236-3181
Sussman Electric Boilers
　Long Island City, NY.............800-238-3535
Vanguard Technology Inc
　Eugene, OR.....................800-624-4809
Washington Frontier
　Grandview, WA..................509-469-7662

Brewery

Alfa Laval Inc
　Richmond, VA...................866-253-2528
ANDRITZ Inc
　Muncy, PA......................704-943-4343
Anver Corporation
　Hudson, MA....................800-654-3500
API Heat Transfer Inc
　Buffalo, NY......................877-274-4328

Berkshire PPM
　Litchfield, CT....................860-567-3118
BVL Controls
　Bois-Des-Filion, QC...............866-285-2668
Camerons Brewing Co.
　Oakville, ON....................905-849-8282
Chester-Jensen Co., Inc.
　Chester, PA......................800-685-3750
Criveller East
　Niagara Falls, ON................888-894-2266
Crown Holdings, Inc.
　Yardley, PA......................215-698-5100
Crown-Simplimatic
　Baltimore, MD...................410-563-6700
Diversified Metal Engineering
　Charlottetown, PE................902-628-6900
FleetwoodGoldcoWyard
　Romeoville, IL...................630-759-6800
Globe Machine
　Tacoma, WA....................800-523-6575
Goodnature Products
　Orchard Park, NY................800-875-3381
MacDonald Steel Ltd
　Cambridge, ON..................800-563-8247
MCNAB Inc
　Buena Vista, VA.................540-261-1045
Metal Master Sales Corp
　Glendale Heights, IL..............800-488-8729
Micropub Systems International
　Rochester, NY...................585-385-3990
Modern Brewing & Design
　Santa Rosa, CA..................707-542-6620
Newlands Systems
　Abbotsford, BC..................604-855-4890
Oak Barrel Winecraft
　Berkeley, CA....................510-849-0400
OI Analytical
　College Station, TX...............979-690-1711
Rahr Malting Co
　Shakopee, MN...................952-445-1431
San-Rec-Pak
　Tualatin, OR.....................503-692-5552
Simplex Filler Co
　Napa, CA.......................800-796-7539
The Pub Brewing Company
　Santa Rosa, CA
The Pub Brewing Company
　Mahwah, NJ.....................201-512-0387
Vincent Corp
　Tampa, FL......................813-248-2650
Vineco International Products
　St Catharines, ON...............905-685-9342

Brine Making Equipment

Berg Chilling Systems
　Toronto, ON.....................416-755-2221
Membrane System Specialist Inc
　Wisconsin Rapids, WI.............715-421-2333
Northland Process Piping
　Isle, MN........................320-679-2119
Peterson Fiberglass Laminates
　Shell Lake, WI...................715-468-2306
Reiser
　Canton, MA.....................734-821-1290
South Valley Mfg Inc
　Gilroy, CA.......................408-842-5457

Broilers

Amber Glo
　Chicago, IL......................866-705-0515
American Range
　Pacoima, CA....................888-753-9898
Anetsberger
　Concord, NH....................603-225-6684
APW Wyott Food Service Equipment Company
　Cheyenne, WY...................800-527-2100
Bakers Pride Oven Company
　New Rochelle, NY................800-431-2745
Broaster Co LLC
　Beloit, WI.......................800-365-8278
Comstock Castle Stove Co
　Quincy, IL.......................800-637-9188
Connerton Co
　Santa Ana, CA..................714-547-9218
CPM Wolverine Proctor LLC
　Horsham, PA....................215-443-5200
Dynamic Cooking Systems
　Huntington Beach, CA............800-433-8466
Garland Commercial Ranges
　Mississauga, ON.................905-624-0260

Garland Commercial Ranges Ltd.
　Mississauga, ON.................905-624-0260
Grande Chef Company
　Orangeville, ON 519-942-4470
Holman Cooking Equipment
　Saint Louis, MO..................888-356-5362
Imperial Manufacturing Co
　Corona, CA.....................800-343-7790
J & R Mfg Inc
　Mesquite, TX....................800-527-4831
Lang Manufacturing Co
　Everett, WA.....................800-882-6368
Leedal Inc
　Northbrook, IL...................847-498-0111
Magi Kitch'n
　Concord, NH....................800-441-1492
Marshall Air Systems Inc
　Charlotte, NC....................800-722-3474
Merco/Savory
　Mt. Pleasant, MI.................800-733-8821
Middleby Marshall Inc
　Elgin, IL.........................847-741-3300
Montague Co
　Hayward, CA....................800-345-1830
Nieco Corporation
　Windsor, CA....................800-643-2656
Optimal Automatics
　Elk Grove Village, IL..............847-439-9110
Rankin Delux
　Mira Loma, CA..................951-685-0081
Renato Specialty Product
　Garland, TX.....................866-575-6316
Stainless Steel Fabricator Inc
　La Mirada, CA...................714-739-9904
Star Manufacturing Intl Inc
　St Louis, MO....................800-264-7827
Super-Chef Manufacturing Company
　Houston, TX....................800-231-3478
Thermal Engineering Corp
　Columbia, SC...................800-331-0097
Toastmaster
　Elgin, IL.........................847-741-3300
Trimen Foodservice Equipment
　North York, ON..................877-437-1422
Vulcan Food Equipment Group
　Baltimore, MD...................800-814-2028
Welbilt Corporation
　Stamford, CT....................203-325-8300
Wells Manufacturing Company
　St. Louis, MO....................888-356-5362
Wolf Company
　Louisville, KY....................800-814-2028
Wood Stone Corp
　Bellingham, WA.................800-988-8103

Cereal Making

A & B Process Systems Corp
　Stratford, WI....................888-258-2789
Andgar Corp
　Ferndale, WA....................360-366-9900
ANDRITZ Inc
　Muncy, PA......................704-943-4343
Buffalo Technologies Corporation
　Buffalo, NY......................800-332-2419
Ferrell-Ross
　Amarillo, TX.....................800-299-9051
Lanly Co
　Cleveland, OH...................216-731-1115
Munson Machinery Co
　Utica, NY.......................800-944-6644
Pavan USA Inc
　Emigsville, PA...................717-767-4889
Polar Process
　Plattsville, ON...................877-896-8077
Puritan Manufacturing Inc
　Omaha, NE.....................800-331-0487
UniTrak Corporation
　Port Hope, ON..................866-883-5749

Cheese Making

A & B Process Systems Corp
　Stratford, WI....................888-258-2789
Breddo Likwifier
　Kansas City, MO.................800-669-4092
Custom Fabricating & Repair
　Marshfield, WI...................800-236-8773
Damrow Company
　Fond Du Lac, WI.................800-236-1501
Dito Dean Food Prep
　Charlotte, NC....................866-449-4200

Eischen Enterprises
  Fresno, CA 559-834-0013
Ivarson Inc
  Milwaukee, WI 414-351-0700
Johnson Industries Intl
  Windsor, WI 608-846-4499
Kusel Equipment Company
  Watertown, WI 920-261-4112
Midwest Stainless
  Menomonie, WI 715-235-5472
Pacific Process Technology
  La Jolla, CA 858-551-3298
Peterson Fiberglass Laminates
  Shell Lake, WI 715-468-2306
Polar Process
  Plattsville, ON. 877-896-8077
Rheo-Tech
  Gurnee, IL 847-367-1557
Rosenwach Tank Co LLC
  Long Island City, NY 212-972-4411
Scherping Systems
  Winsted, MN. 320-485-4401
Viking Machine & Design Inc
  De Pere, WI 888-286-2116
Washington Frontier
  Grandview, WA 509-469-7662
Whey Systems
  Willmar, MN. 320-905-4122

Cheese Processing

Corenco
  Santa Rosa, CA. 888-267-3626
Loos Machine
  Colby, WI 715-223-2844
Millerbernd Systems
  Winsted, MN. 320-485-2685
Reiser
  Canton, MA 734-821-1290

Cheesecloth

Ace-Tex Enterprises
  Detroit, MI 800-444-3800
Akron Cotton Products
  Akron, OH. 800-899-7173
Armaly Brands
  Commerce Twp, MI 800-772-1222
Cadie Products Corp
  Paterson, NJ 973-278-8300
Canton Sterilized Wiping Cloth
  Canton, OH 330-455-8157
Clayton L. Hagy & Son
  Philadelphia, PA 215-844-6470
De Royal Textiles
  Camden, SC 800-845-1062
Erie Cotton Products
  Erie, PA 800-289-4737
James Thompson
  New York, NY 212-686-5306
King Bag & Mfg Co
  Cincinnati, OH 800-444-5464
Lexidyne of Pennsylvania
  Pittsburgh, PA 800-543-2233
Mednik Wiping Materials Co
  St Louis, MO. 800-325-7193
Mill Wiping Rags Inc
  Bronx, NY. 718-994-7100
Nu-Tex Styles, Inc.
  Somerset, NJ 732-485-5456
Paley-Lloyd-Donohue
  Elizabeth, NJ. 908-352-5835
Textile Buff & Wheel
  Charlestown, MA 617-241-8100
Textile Products Company
  Anaheim, CA 714-761-0401
Wipe-Tex International Corp
  Bronx, NY. 800-643-9607
Y-Pers Inc
  Philadelphia, PA 800-421-0242

Chewing Gum Processing

A & B Process Systems Corp
  Stratford, WI. 888-258-2789
LIST
  Acton, MA 978-635-9521
UniTrak Corporation
  Port Hope, ON 866-883-5749

Chocolate Processing

A & B Process Systems Corp
  Stratford, WI. 888-258-2789
Buffalo Technologies Corporation
  Buffalo, NY. 800-332-2419
Chocolate Concepts
  Hartville, OH 330-877-3322
Dadant & Sons Inc
  Hamilton, IL 888-922-1293
Glen Mills Inc.
  Clifton, NJ. 973-777-0777
Hillards Chocolate System
  West Bridgewater, MA 800-258-1530
LIST
  Acton, MA 978-635-9521
Savage Brothers Company
  Elk Grove Vlg, IL 800-342-0973
Tricor Systems Inc
  Elgin, IL 800-575-0161
Union Process
  Akron, OH. 330-929-3333
UniTrak Corporation
  Port Hope, ON 866-883-5749
US Tsubaki Holdings Inc
  Wheeling, IL. 800-323-7790
Woody Associates Inc
  York, PA 717-843-3975

Cocoa Processing

A & B Process Systems Corp
  Stratford, WI. 888-258-2789
ANDRITZ Inc
  Muncy, PA. 704-943-4343
Glen Mills Inc.
  Clifton, NJ. 973-777-0777
LIST
  Acton, MA 978-635-9521
Union Process
  Akron, OH. 330-929-3333

Coffee Makers

Acorto
  Bellevue, WA 800-995-9019
Astoria General Espresso
  Greensboro, NC 336-393-0224
Bloomfield Industries
  St. Louis, MO 888-356-5362
Boyd's Coffee Co
  Portland, OR 800-735-2878
Brewmatic Company
  Torrance, CA. 800-421-6860
Bunn-O-Matic Corp
  Springfield, IL. 800-352-2866
Chemex Division/International Housewares Corporation
  Chicopee, MA. 800-243-6399
Formula Espresso
  Brooklyn, NY 718-834-8724
Gabriella Imports
  Cleveland, OH. 800-544-8117
Globex America
  Dallas, TX 214-353-0328
Grand Silver Company
  Bronx, NY. 718-585-1930
Grindmaster-Cecilware Corp
  Louisville, KY 800-695-4500
Lavazza Premium Coffees
  New York, NY 212-725-9196
Melitta North America, Inc.
  Clearwater, FL 888-635-4880
Newco Enterprises Inc
  St Charles, MO 800-325-7867
Nuova Distribution Centre
  Ferndale, WA 360-366-2226
Pasquini Espresso Co
  Los Angeles, CA. 800-724-6225
Regal Ware Inc
  Kewaskum, WI 262-626-2121
Rexcraft Fine Chafers
  Long Island City, NY 888-739-2723
Saeco
  Cleveland, OH 440-528-2000
Schaerer USA Corp
  Tustin, CA. 888-989-3004
Sheffield Platers Inc
  San Diego, CA 800-227-9242
Steel Products
  Marion, IA. 800-333-9451
Superior Products Company
  Saint Paul, MN 800-328-9800

Supramatic
  Toronto, ON 877-465-2883
T.J. Topper Company
  Redwood City, CA 650-365-6962
The Carriage Works
  Klamath Falls, OR 541-882-0700
Tops Manufacturing Co
  Darien, CT. 203-655-9367
Wells Manufacturing Company
  St. Louis, MO 888-356-5362
Wilbur Curtis Co
  Montebello, CA 800-421-6150
World Kitchen
  Elmira, NY 800-999-3436
Zelco Industries
  Mount Vernon, NY 800-431-2486

Coffee Processing

Acorto
  Bellevue, WA 800-995-9019
Alfa Laval Inc
  Richmond, VA. 866-253-2528
American Production Co Inc
  Redwood City, CA 650-368-5334
Ascaso
  Bensenville, IL 630-350-0066
Astoria General Espresso
  Greensboro, NC 336-393-0224
Astra Manufacturing Inc
  Canoga Park, CA 877-340-1800
Boyd's Coffee Co
  Portland, OR 800-735-2878
Brewmatic Company
  Torrance, CA. 800-421-6860
Bunn-O-Matic Corp
  Springfield, IL. 800-352-2866
Bunn-O-Matic Corporation
  Aurora, ON 800-263-2256
Chemex Division/International Housewares Corporation
  Chicopee, MA. 800-243-6399
Ditting USA
  Glendale, CA 800-835-5992
Eastern Tabletop Mfg
  Brooklyn, NY 888-422-4142
Eurodib
  Champlain, NY 888-956-6866
Fetco
  Lake Zurich, IL 800-338-2699
Formula Espresso
  Brooklyn, NY 718-834-8724
Gabriella Imports
  Cleveland, OH. 800-544-8117
Gensaco Marketing
  New York, NY 800-506-1935
Grindmaster-Cecilware Corp
  Louisville, KY 800-695-4500
Hamilton Beach Brands
  Southern Pines, NC. 800-851-8900
Kentwood Spring Water Company
  Patterson, LA 985-395-9313
Lavazza Premium Coffees
  New York, NY 212-725-9196
Melitta North America, Inc.
  Clearwater, FL 888-635-4880
Modern Process Equipment Inc
  Chicago, IL 773-254-3929
Newco Enterprises Inc
  St Charles, MO 800-325-7867
Pasquini Espresso Co
  Los Angeles, CA. 800-724-6225
PolyMaid Company
  Largo, FL 800-206-9188
Regal Ware Inc
  Kewaskum, WI 262-626-2121
Rexcraft Fine Chafers
  Long Island City, NY 888-739-2723
Saeco
  Cleveland, OH 440-528-2000
Schaerer USA Corp
  Tustin, CA. 888-989-3004
Sivetz Coffee
  Corvallis, OR 541-753-9713
Steel Products
  Marion, IA. 800-333-9451
Supramatic
  Toronto, ON 877-465-2883
The Carriage Works
  Klamath Falls, OR 541-882-0700
Tops Manufacturing Co
  Darien, CT. 203-655-9367

UniTrak Corporation
Port Hope, ON .866-883-5749
Wega USA
Bensenville, IL 630-350-0066
Wells Manufacturing Company
St. Louis, MO 888-356-5362
Wilbur Curtis Co
Montebello, CA 800-421-6150
Zelco Industries
Mount Vernon, NY 800-431-2486

Combination Oven/Steamers

Superior Products Company
Saint Paul, MN 800-328-9800

Compressors

Berkshire PPM
Litchfield, CT 860-567-3118
Blackmer Co
Grand Rapids, MI 616-241-1611
C&R Refrigeration
Center, TX. .800-438-6182
Cameron Intl. Corp.
Houston, TX 281-285-4376
Howe Corp
Chicago, IL .773-235-0200
Ingersoll Rand Inc
Menomonee Falls, WI. 262-232-7275
International Machinery Xchnge
Deerfield, WI 800-279-0191
Kopykake
Torrance, CA 800-999-5253
Paxton Products Inc
Blue Ash, OH 800-441-7475
Scroll Compressors LLC
Sidney, OH .937-498-3011
Seattle Refrigeration & Manufacturing
Seattle, WA .800-228-8881
Tecumseh Products Co.
Ann Arbor, MI 734-585-9500
Vilter Manufacturing Corporation
Cudahy, WI .414-744-0111
York Refrigeration Marine US
Norman, OK 877-874-7378
Zander Insurance Group
Nashville, TN 615-356-1700

Condensed Milk Processing

A & B Process Systems Corp
Stratford, WI. 888-258-2789
C E Rogers Co
Mora, MN 800-279-8081

Condensers

Evaporative

Baltimore Aircoil Co
Jessup, MD .410-799-1300
Berkshire PPM
Litchfield, CT 860-567-3118
Central Fabricators Inc
Cincinnati, OH 800-909-8265
Chil-Con Products
Brantford, ON 800-263-0086
Cooling Products Inc
Broken Arrow, OK 918-251-8588
Croll Reynolds Inc
Parsippany, NJ. 908-232-4200
Doucette Industries
York, PA 800-445-7511
EVAPCO Inc
Taneytown, MD 410-876-3782
Governair Corp
Oklahoma City, OK 405-525-6546
Howe Corp
Chicago, IL .773-235-0200
IMECO Inc
Polo, IL 815-946-2351
Industrial Piping Inc
Pineville, NC. 800-951-0988
Membrane System Specialist Inc
Wisconsin Rapids, WI 715-421-2333
Niagara Blower Company
Buffalo, NY. 800-426-5169
Paget Equipment Co
Marshfield, WI 715-384-3158
Ron Vallort & Associates
Oak Brook, IL 630-734-3821

Seattle Refrigeration & Manufacturing
Seattle, WA .800-228-8881
Vilter Manufacturing Corporation
Cudahy, WI .414-744-0111

Confectionery

A & B Process Systems Corp
Stratford, WI 888-258-2789
A&M Industries
Sioux Falls, SD 800-888-2615
Aerotech Enterprise Inc
Chesterland, OH 440-729-2616
Automated Food Systems
Waxahachie, TX 469-517-0470
C. Cretors & Company
Chicago, IL .800-228-1885
Chocolate Concepts
Hartville, OH 330-877-3322
Davron Technologies Inc
Chattanooga, TN 423-870-1888
Design Technology Corporation
Billerica, MA 978-663-7000
DT Converting Technologies - Stokes
Bristol, PA 800-635-0036
Et Oakes Corp
Hauppauge, NY 631-232-0002
Gch Internatonal
Louisville, KY 502-636-1374
Goodway Industries Inc
Bohemia, NY 800-943-4501
Graybill Machines Inc
Lititz, PA 717-626-5221
Ideal Wrapping Machine Company
Middletown, NY 845-343-7700
Matiss
St Georges, QC 888-562-8477
Munson Machinery Co
Utica, NY 800-944-6644
Polar Process
Plattsville, ON 877-896-8077
Production Techniques Limited
Auckland, NZ 649-274-3514
TSA Griddle Systems
Kelowna, BC. 250-491-9025
Unifiller Systems
Delta, BC. 888-733-8444
Union Process
Akron, OH. .330-929-3333
UniTrak Corporation
Port Hope, ON 866-883-5749
Woody Associates Inc
York, PA 717-843-3975

Convection Ovens

ALPI Food Preparation Equipment
Bolton, ON .800-928-2574
Anetsberger
Concord, NH 603-225-6684
Apollo Sheet Metal
Kennewick, WA 509-586-1104
Blodgett Oven Co
Burlington, VT 800-331-5842
Coast Scientific
Rancho Santa Fe, CA 800-445-1544
Cres Cor
Mentor, OH .877-273-7267
Davron Technologies Inc
Chattanooga, TN 423-870-1888
Dynamic Cooking Systems
Huntington Beach, CA 800-433-8466
Foster Refrigerator Corporation
Kinderhook, NY 888-828-3311
Garland Commercial Ranges
Mississauga, ON 905-624-0260
Garland Commercial Ranges Ltd.
Mississauga, ON 905-624-0260
Gehnrich Oven Sales Company
East Troy, WI 262-642-3938
Imperial Manufacturing Co
Corona, CA .800-343-7790
Lang Manufacturing Co
Everett, WA. 800-882-6368
Merco/Savory
Mt. Pleasant, MI 800-733-8821
Middleby Corp
Elgin, IL 847-741-3300
Moffat
San Antonio, TX. 866-589-0664
Montague Co
Hayward, CA 800-345-1830

Nevo Corporation
Ronkonkoma, NY 631-585-8787
Piper Products Inc
Wausau, WI. 800-544-3057
Roto-Flex Oven Co
San Antonio, TX 877-859-1463
Superior Products Company
Saint Paul, MN 800-328-9800
Welbilt Corporation
Stamford, CT. 203-325-8300

Cookers

Brewery

Custom Food Machinery
Stockton, CA. 209-463-4343
Falco Technologies
La Prairie, QC. 450-444-0566

Canners'

A.K. Robins
Baltimore, MD 800-486-9656
Custom Food Machinery
Stockton, CA. 209-463-4343
Hamilton Kettles
Weirton, WV 800-535-1882

Cereal

ANDRITZ Inc
Muncy, PA. .704-943-4343
Central Fabricators Inc
Cincinnati, OH 800-909-8265
Hamilton Kettles
Weirton, WV 800-535-1882
Lauhoff Corporation
Detroit, MI .313-259-0027

Cheese

A & B Process Systems Corp
Stratford, WI. 888-258-2789
Damrow Company
Fond Du Lac, WI 800-236-1501
Hamilton Kettles
Weirton, WV 800-535-1882
Viking Machine & Design Inc
De Pere, WI. 888-286-2116

Confectioners', Continuous

A & B Process Systems Corp
Stratford, WI. 888-258-2789
Dupps Co
Germantown, OH 937-855-0623
Hamilton Kettles
Weirton, WV 800-535-1882

Fish

Brinkmann Corporation
Dallas, TX. .800-468-5252
Coastline Equipment Inc
Bellingham, WA 360-734-8509
Diversified Metal Engineering
Charlottetown, PE. 902-628-6900
Hamilton Kettles
Weirton, WV 800-535-1882

Pressure

A & B Process Systems Corp
Stratford, WI. 888-258-2789
Hamilton Kettles
Weirton, WV 800-535-1882
Henny Penny, Inc.
Eaton, OH 800-417-8417
Littleford Day
Florence, KY 800-365-8555
Vasconia Housewares
San Antonio, TX. 800-377-6723
Winston Industries
Louisville, KY 800-234-5286

Steam

A.K. Robins
Baltimore, MD 800-486-9656
Accu Temp Products Inc
Fort Wayne, IN 800-210-5907
Alumaworks
Sunny Isle Beach, FL 800-277-7267

Amber Glo
Chicago, IL 866-705-0515
Aroma Manufacturing Company
San Diego, CA 800-276-6286
Blodgett Corp
Burlington, VT 800-331-5842
Brinkmann Corporation
Dallas, TX 800-468-5252
Cleveland Range
Concord, ON
Garland Commercial Ranges
Mississauga, ON 905-624-0260
Garvis Manufacturing Company
Des Moines, IA 515-243-8054
Hamilton Kettles
Weirton, WV 800-535-1882
Ideas Well Done LLC
Winooski, VT 877-877-1224
J C Ford Co
La Habra, CA 714-871-7361
Key Technology Inc.
Walla Walla, WA. 509-529-2161
Komline-Sanderson Engineering
Peapack, NJ. 800-225-5457
Legion Industries Inc
Waynesboro, GA. 800-887-1988
Market Forge Industries Inc
Everett, MA. 866-698-3188
Middleby Corp
Elgin, IL 847-741-3300
Sandvik Process Systems
Sweden, NJ 973-790-1600
Stellar Steam
Winooski, VT 802-654-8603
Superior Products Company
Saint Paul, MN 800-328-9800
Viatec
Victoria, BC 800-942-4702
Vulcan Food Equipment Group
Baltimore, MD 800-814-2028
Washington Frontier
Grandview, WA. 509-469-7662
Welbilt Corporation
Stamford, CT. 203-325-8300

Vegetable

A.K. Robins
Baltimore, MD 800-486-9656
Alkar Rapid Pak
Lodi, WI 608-592-3211
Amco Metals Indl
City of Industry, CA 626-855-2550
Brinkmann Corporation
Dallas, TX. 800-468-5252
Hamilton Kettles
Weirton, WV. 800-535-1882
J C Ford Co
La Habra, CA 714-871-7361
Market Forge Industries Inc
Everett, MA. 866-698-3188
Pick Heaters
West Bend, WI 800-233-9030
Washington Frontier
Grandview, WA. 509-469-7662

Cooking & Heating Equipment

A C Horn & Co Sheet Metal
Dallas, TX. 800-657-6155
A Legacy Food Svc
Santa Fe Springs, CA 800-848-4440
Abalon Precision Manufacturing Corporation
Bronx, NY. 800-888-2225
Abco International
Oneida, NY 888-263-7195
Accu Temp Products Inc
Fort Wayne, IN 800-210-5907
Acp Inc
Cedar Rapids, IA. 319-368-8198
Acra Electric Corporation
Tulsa, OK 800-223-4328
Adamatic
Auburn, WA 800-578-2547
Advance Tabco
Edgewood, NY 800-645-3166
Alkar Rapid Pak
Lodi, WI 608-592-3211
All Spun Metal Products
Des Plaines, IL 847-824-4117
All State Fabricators Corporation
Tampa, FL 800-322-9925

Alliance Products LLC
Murfreesboro, TN 800-522-3973
Allied Metal Spinning
Bronx, NY 800-615-2266
Alloy Hardfacing & Engineering
Jordan, MN 800-328-8408
Allstrong Restaurant Eqpt Inc
South El Monte, CA 800-933-8913
ALPI Food Preparation Equipment
Bolton, ON 800-928-2574
Alto-Shaam
Menomonee Falls, WI. 800-329-8744
Amber Glo
Chicago, IL 866-705-0515
American Extrusion Intl
South Beloit, IL 815-624-6616
American Housewares
Bronx, NY. 718-665-9500
American Metal Stamping
Brooklyn, NY 718-384-1500
American Range
Pacoima, CA 888-753-9898
American Systems Associates
Hampton Bays, NY. 800-584-3663
AMF CANADA
Sherbrooke, QC 800-255-3869
AMI
Richmond, CA 800-942-7466
Anchor Hocking Operating Co
Lancaster, OH 800-562-7511
Anetsberger
Concord, NH. 603-225-6684
Antrim Manufacturing Inc
Brookfield, WI 262-781-6860
Apollo Sheet Metal
Kennewick, WA 509-586-1104
APW Wyott Food Service Equipment Company
Cheyenne, WY 800-527-2100
Archer Wire Intl Corp
Chicago, IL 708-563-1700
Architectural Sheet Metals LLC
Cleveland, OH 216-361-9952
Arcobaleno Pasta Machines
Lancaster, PA 800-875-7096
Aroma Manufacturing Company
San Diego, CA 800-276-6286
Astoria General Espresso
Greensboro, NC 336-393-0224
Attias Oven Corp
Brooklyn, NY 800-928-8427
Autofry
Northborough, MA 800-348-2976
Automated Food Systems
Waxahachie, TX 469-517-0470
Automatic Specialties Inc
Marlborough, MA. 800-445-2370
Avalon Manufacturer
Corona, CA 800-676-3040
Awmco Inc
Orland Park, IL 708-478-6032
Aztec Grill
Dallas, TX. 800-346-8114
B R Machinery
Wedron, IL 800-310-7057
Bakers Pride Oven Company
New Rochelle, NY 800-431-2745
Bakery Associates
Setauket, NY. 631-751-4156
Ballantyne Food Service Equipment
Omaha, NE 800-424-1215
Bar-B-Q Woods
Newton, KS. 800-528-0819
Baxter Manufacturing Inc
Orting, WA 800-777-2828
Bbc Industries
Pacific, MO. 800-654-4205
BBQ Pits by Klose
Houston, TX 800-487-7487
Be & Sco
San Antonio, TX. 800-683-0928
Becker Brothers Graphite Co
Maywood, IL. 708-410-0700
Belshaw Adamatic Bakery Group
Auburn, WA 800-578-2547
Belson Outdoors Inc
North Aurora, IL. 800-323-5664
Benchmark Thermal
Grass Valley, CA. 800-748-6189
Benko Products
Sheffield Vlg, OH. 440-934-2180
Bethel Engineering & Equipment Inc
New Hampshire, OH. 800-889-6129

Bevles Company
Dallas, TX. 800-441-1601
Big John Corp
Pleasant Gap, PA. 800-326-9575
BKI Worldwide
Simpsonville, SC 800-927-6887
Blodgett Corp
Burlington, VT 800-331-5842
Blodgett Oven Co
Burlington, VT 800-331-5842
Bolling Oven & Machine Company
Avon, OH 440-937-6112
Brinkmann Corporation
Dallas, TX. 800-468-5252
Britt's Barbecue
Birmingham, AL. 205-612-6538
Broaster Co LLC
Beloit, WI 800-365-8278
Buhler Inc.
Plymouth, MN. 763-847-9900
C H Babb Co Inc
Raynham, MA. 508-977-0600
Carlisle Food Svc Products Inc
Oklahoma City, OK 800-654-8210
Casa Herrera
Pomona, CA 800-624-3916
Casso-Solar Corporation
Nanuet, NY 800-988-4455
Cci Industries-Cool Curtain
Costa Mesa, CA 800-854-5719
Central Fabricators Inc
Cincinnati, OH 800-909-8265
Checker Machine
Minneapolis, MN 888-800-5001
Chef's Choice Mesquite Charcoal
Carpinteria, CA. 805-684-8284
Chesmont Engineering Co Inc
Exton, PA 610-594-9200
Chester-Jensen Co., Inc.
Chester, PA 800-685-3750
Chromalox Inc
Pittsburgh, PA. 800-443-2640
Cincinnati Industrial Machry
Mason, OH 800-677-0076
Cleveland Range
Concord, ON
Coast Scientific
Rancho Santa Fe, CA 800-445-1544
Cobatco
Peoria, IL. 800-426-2282
Cober Electronics, Inc.
Norwalk, CT. 800-709-5948
Commercial Dehydrator Systems
Eugene, OR. 800-369-4283
Comstock Castle Stove Co
Quincy, IL 800-637-9188
Connerton Co
Santa Ana, CA 714-547-9218
Cooking Systems International
Redwood City, CA 650-556-6222
Cookshack
Ponca City, OK 800-423-0698
CookTek
Chicago, IL 888-266-5835
Cove Four
Freeport, NY 516-379-4232
CPM Wolverine Proctor LLC
Horsham, PA. 215-443-5200
Craft Industries
Long Island City, NY 252-753-3152
Cres Cor
Mentor, OH. 877-273-7267
Crispy Lite
St. Louis, MO 888-356-5362
Crown Verity
Brantford, ON 888-505-7240
Custom Diamond International
Laval, QC 800-363-5926
Custom Diamond Intl.
Laval, QC 800-326-5926
Cutler Industries
Morton Grove, IL 800-458-5593
D. Picking & Company
Bucyrus, OH 419-562-6891
Damrow Company
Fond Du Lac, WI 800-236-1501
Dar-B-Ques Barbecue Equipment
Minneapolis, MN 612-724-7425
Davron Technologies Inc
Chattanooga, TN 423-870-1888
DBE Inc
Concord, ON. 800-461-5313

Dean Industries
Gardena, CA 800-995-1210
Defreeze Corporation
Southborough, MA 508-485-8512
Deluxe Equipment Company
Bradenton, FL 800-367-8931
Diversified Metal Engineering
Charlottetown, PE 902-628-6900
Doyon Equipment
Liniere, QC 800-463-4273
Duke Manufacturing Co
St Louis, MO. 800-735-3853
Dupps Co
Germantown, OH 937-855-0623
Dura-Ware Company of America
Oklahoma City, OK 800-664-3872
Duralite Inc
Riverton, CT 888-432-8797
Dynamic Cooking Systems
Huntington Beach, CA 800-433-8466
Dynynstyl
Delray Beach, FL 800-774-7895
Eagle Group
Clayton, DE. 800-441-8440
Earthstone Wood-Fire Ovens
Glendale, CA 800-840-4915
Electro-Steam Generator Corp
Rancocas, NJ. 866-617-0764
Emerald City Closets Inc
Auburn, WA 800-925-1521
Empire Bakery Equipment
Hicksville, NY 800-878-4070
Epcon Industrial Systems
Conroe, TX. 800-447-7872
Equipex Limited
Providence, RI 800-649-7885
Erwin Food Service Equipment
Fort Worth, TX 817-535-0021
Esquire Mechanical Corp.
Armonk, NY 800-847-4206
Eurodib
Champlain, NY 888-956-6866
Fab-X/Metals
Washington, NC 800-677-3229
Filtercorp
Fresno, CA 800-473-4526
Fish Oven & Equipment Co
Wauconda, IL 877-526-8720
FlashBake Ovens Food Service
Fremont, CA 800-843-6836
FleetwoodGoldcoWyard
Romeoville, IL 630-759-6800
Flodin
Moses Lake, WA. 509-766-2996
Food Engineering Unlimited
Fullerton, CA 714-879-8762
FOODesign from tna
Wilsonville, OR 503-685-5030
Foster Refrigerator Corporation
Kinderhook, NY 888-828-3311
Franrica Systems
Stockton, CA 209-948-2811
Franz Haas Machinery-America
Henrico, VA 804-222-6022
Friedrich Metal Products
Browns Summit, NC 800-772-0326
Fry Tech Corporation
Dubuque, IA 319-583-1559
Frymaster
Shreveport, LA 800-221-4583
Garland Commercial Ranges
Mississauga, ON 905-624-0260
Garland Commercial Ranges Ltd.
Mississauga, ON. 905-624-0260
Garvis Manufacturing Company
Des Moines, IA 515-243-8054
GBS Foodservice Equipment, Inc.
Mississauga, ON 888-402-1242
Gehnrich Oven Sales Company
East Troy, WI 262-642-3938
GEM Equipment of Oregon Inc
Woodburn, OR 503-982-9902
General Cage
Elwood, IN 800-428-6403
Giles Enterprises Inc
Montgomery, AL 800-288-1555
Glenro Inc
Paterson, NJ 888-453-6761
Glowmaster Corporation
Clifton, NJ. 800-272-7008
Gold Medal Products Co
Cincinnati, OH 800-543-0862

Gralab Instruments
Centerville, OH. 800-876-8353
Grand Silver Company
Bronx, NY 718-585-1930
Grande Chef Company
Orangeville, ON 519-942-4470
Grill Greats
Saxonburg, PA. 724-352-1511
Grillco Inc
Aurora, IL 800-644-0067
Grills to Go
Fresno, CA 877-869-2253
GSW Jackes-Evans Manufacturing Company
Saint Louis, MO 800-325-6173
H.F. Coors China Company
New Albany, MS. 800-782-6677
Hamilton Kettles
Weirton, WV 800-535-1882
Hardt Equipment Manufacturing
Lachine, QC 888-848-4408
Hasty Bake Charcoal Grills
Tulsa, OK 800-426-6836
Hatco Corp
Milwaukee, WI 800-558-0607
Heat-It Manufacturing
San Antonio, TX 800-323-9336
Henny Penny, Inc.
Eaton, OH 800-417-8417
Hercules Food Equipment
Weston, ON. 416-742-9673
HH Controls Company
Arilington, MA 781-646-2626
Hickory Industries
North Bergen, NJ 800-732-9153
Holman Boiler Works
Dallas, TX 800-331-1956
Holman Cooking Equipment
Saint Louis, MO 888-356-5362
Holstein Manufacturing
Holstein, IA 800-368-4342
Hughes Co
Columbus, WI. 866-535-9303
Hydro-Thermal Corp
Waukesha, WI 800-952-0121
Idaho Steel Products Inc
Idaho Falls, ID 208-522-1275
Ideas Well Done LLC
Winooski, VT 877-877-1224
Illinois Range Company
Schiller Park, IL 800-535-7041
Illinois Tool Works
Glenview, IL 224-661-8870
Imperial Manufacturing Co
Corona, CA 800-343-7790
Industrial Ceramic Products
Marysville, OH 800-427-2278
Intedge Manufacturing
Woodruff, SC 866-969-9605
IR Systems
Jupiter, FL 800-893-7540
Iwatani International Corporation of America
Houston, TX 800-775-5506
J & R Mfg Inc
Mesquite, TX 800-527-4831
J C Ford Co
La Habra, CA 714-871-7361
Jackson Msc LLC
Gray, KY 888-800-5672
Jackson Restaurant Supply
Jackson, TN 800-424-8943
Jade Products Co
Brea, CA 800-884-5233
Kady International
Scarborough, ME 800-367-5239
Karl Schnell
New London, WI 920-982-9974
Kay Home Products Inc
Antioch, IL 800-600-7009
Keating of Chicago Inc
Mc Cook, IL 800-532-8464
Kelmin Products
Plymouth, FL 407-886-6079
Key Technology Inc.
Walla Walla, WA. 509-529-2161
King Packaging Co
Schenectady, NY 518-370-5464
KNOX Stove Works Inc
Knoxville, TN 865-524-4113
Komline-Sanderson Engineering
Peapack, NJ 800-225-5457
Krispy Kist Company
Chicago, IL 312-733-0900

Lancaster Colony Corporation
Westerville, OH. 614-224-7141
Lang Manufacturing Co
Everett, WA 800-882-6368
Lanly Co
Cleveland, OH. 216-731-1115
Lauhoff Corporation
Detroit, MI 313-259-0027
Lazy Man Inc
Belvidere, NJ 800-475-1950
Le Smoker
Salisbury, MD 410-677-3233
Leedal Inc
Northbrook, IL 847-498-0111
Legion Industries Inc
Waynesboro, GA 800-887-1988
Liberty Ware LLC
Clearfield, UT 888-500-5885
Lignetics Inc
Sandpoint, ID 800-544-3834
Lil' Orbits
Minneapolis, MN 800-228-8305
Lincoln Foodservice
Cleveland, OH 800-374-3004
Littleford Day
Florence, KY. 800-365-8555
LPS Technology
Grafton, OH 800-586-1410
Magi Kitch'n
Concord, NH. 800-441-1492
Market Forge Industries Inc
Everett, MA 866-698-3188
Marshall Air Systems Inc
Charlotte, NC 800-722-3474
Martin/Baron
Irwindale, CA 626-960-5153
Masterbuilt Manufacturing Inc
Columbus, GA 706-327-5622
Mastex Industries
Petersburg, VA 804-732-8300
Maytag Corporation
Benton Harbor, MI 800-344-1274
Merco/Savory
Mt. Pleasant, MI 800-733-8821
Metal Masters Northwest
Lynnwood, WA 425-775-4481
Metro Corporation
Wilkes Barre, PA. 800-992-1776
Microdry
Crestwood, KY 502-241-8933
Middleby Corp
Elgin, IL 847-741-3300
Middleby Marshall Inc
Elgin, IL 847-741-3300
Midwest Aircraft Products Co
Lexington, OH 419-884-2164
Midwest Wire Products LLC
Sturgeon Bay, WI 800-445-0225
Mies Products
West Bend, WI 800-480-6437
Miracle Exclusives
Danbury, CT 203-796-5493
Mirro Company
Lancaster, OH 800-848-7200
Moffat
San Antonio, TX 866-589-0664
Moli-International
Denver, CO 800-525-8468
Moline Machinery LLC
Duluth, MN 800-767-5734
Montague Co
Hayward, CA 800-345-1830
Mosshaim Innovations
Jacksonville, FL 888-995-7775
Motion Technologies
Northborough, MA 800-468-2976
Motom Corporation
Bensenville, IL 630-787-1995
Mouli Manufacturing Corporation
Belleville, NJ 800-789-8285
Mountain Safety Research
Seattle, WA 800-877-9677
Mr. Bar-B-Q
Winston-Salem, NC 800-333-2124
Music City Metals Inc
Nashville, TN 800-251-2674
Napoleon Appliance Corporation
Barrie, ON. 866-820-8686
National Drying Machry Co Inc
Philadelphia, PA 215-464-6070
National Hotpack
Stone Ridge, NY 800-431-8232

Nature's Own
Attleboro, MA....................508-399-8690
Nemeth Engineering Assoc
Crestwood, KY...................502-241-1502
Nevo Corporation
Ronkonkoma, NY.................631-585-8787
Nieco Corporation
Windsor, CA.....................800-643-2656
Normandie Metal Fabricators
Port Washington, NY.............800-221-2398
Northern Stainless Fabricating
Traverse City, MI...............231-947-4580
Nothum Food Processing Systems
Springfield, MO.................800-435-1297
NuTone
Cincinnati, OH..................888-336-3948
Ogden Manufacturing Company
Pittsburgh, PA..................412-967-3906
Olde Country Reproductions Inc
York, PA........................800-358-3997
Ole Hickory Pits
Cape Girardeau, MO..............800-223-9667
Otto Braun Bakery Equipment
Buffalo, NY.....................716-824-1252
Padinox
Winsloe, PE.....................800-263-9768
Panasonic Commercial Food Service
Newark, NJ
Paragon International
Nevada, IA......................800-433-0333
Patio King
Cutler Bay, FL..................305-316-7508
Peerless Ovens
Sandusky, OH....................800-548-4514
Peerless-Premier Appliance Co
Belleville, IL..................618-233-0475
Perfect Fry Company
Calgary, AB.....................800-265-7711
Peter Gray Corporation
Andover, MA.....................978-470-0990
Pick Heaters
West Bend, WI...................800-233-9030
Pier 1 Imports
Woodcliff Lake, NJ..............800-448-9993
Pino's Pasta Veloce
Staten Island, NY...............718-273-6660
Piper Products Inc
Wausau, WI......................800-544-3057
Pitco Frialator Inc
Bow, NH.........................800-258-3708
PMI Food Equipment Group
Troy, OH........................937-332-3000
Polar Ware Company
Sheboygan, WI...................800-237-3655
Porcelain Metals Corporation
Louisville, KY..................502-635-7421
Power Flame Inc
Parsons, KS.....................800-862-4256
Precision
Miami, FL.......................800-762-7565
Prince Castle Inc
Carol Stream, IL................800-722-7853
Process Heating Corp
Shrewsbury, MA..................508-842-5200
Process Systems
Barrington, IL..................847-842-8618
Profire Stainless Steel Barbecue
Miami, FL.......................305-665-5313
Proheatco Manufacturing
Pomona, CA......................800-423-4195
Proluxe
Paramount, CA...................800-594-5528
Q-Matic Technologies
Carol Stream, IL................800-880-6836
QNC Inc
Dallas, TX......................888-668-3687
Quadra-Tech
Columbus, OH....................800-443-2766
Quality Fabrication & Design
Coppell, TX.....................972-304-3266
Quantem Corp
Ewing, NJ.......................609-883-9879
Quasar Industries
Rochester Hills, MI.............248-852-0300
Randell Manufacturing   Unified Brands
Weidman, MI.....................888-994-7636
Rankin Delux
Mira Loma, CA...................951-685-0081
Rational Cooking Systems
Schaumburg, IL..................888-320-7274
Reading Bakery Systems Inc
Robesonia, PA...................610-693-5816

Reed Oven Co
Kansas City, MO.................816-842-7446
Regal Ware Inc
Kewaskum, WI....................262-626-2121
Reliable Food Service Equipment
Concord, ON.....................416-738-6840
Remco Industries International
Fort Lauderdale, FL.............800-987-3626
Renato Specialty Product
Garland, TX.....................866-575-6316
Revent Inc
Piscataway, NJ..................732-777-9433
Ricoh Technologies
Grand Prairie, TX...............800-585-9367
Rival Manufacturing Company
Kansas City, MO.................816-943-4100
Rotisol France Inc
Inglewood, CA...................800-651-5969
Roto-Flex Oven Co
San Antonio, TX.................877-859-1463
Roundup Food Equip
Carol Stream, IL................800-253-2991
Royal Oak Enterprises
Roswell, GA.....................678-461-3200
Royalton Foodservice Equip Co
North Royalton, OH..............800-662-8765
Sandvik Process Systems
Sweden, NJ......................973-790-1600
Saunder Brothers
Bridgton, ME....................207-647-3331
Savage Brothers Company
Elk Grove Vlg, IL...............800-342-0973
SCK Direct Inc
Stratford, CT...................800-327-8766
Seidman Brothers
Chelsea, MA.....................800-437-7770
Server Products Inc
Richfield, WI...................800-558-8722
Sharp Electronics Corporation
Mahwah, NJ......................800-237-4277
Sharpsville Container Corp
Sharpsville, PA.................800-645-1248
Shat R Shield Inc
Salisbury, NC...................800-223-0853
Shelcon Inc
Ontario, CA.....................909-947-4877
Shouldice Brothers SheetMetal
Battle Creek, MI................269-962-5579
Silesia Grill Machines Inc
St Petersburg, FL...............800-237-4766
Silesia Grill Machines Inc
St Petersburg, FL...............800-267-4766
Silver Weibull
Aurora, CO......................303-373-2311
Smokaroma
Boley, OK.......................800-331-5565
South Valley Mfg Inc
Gilroy, CA......................408-842-5457
Southern Pride Distributing
Alamo, TN.......................800-851-8180
Spring USA Corp
Naperville, IL..................800-535-8974
Stainless Steel Fabricator Inc
La Mirada, CA...................714-739-9904
Standex International Corp.
Salem, NH.......................603-893-9701
Star Manufacturing Intl Inc
St Louis, MO....................800-264-7827
Starkey Chemical Process Company
La Grange, IL...................800-323-3040
State Products
Long Beach, CA..................800-730-5150
Stewart Systems Baking LLC
Plano, TX.......................972-422-5808
Stricklin Co
Dallas, TX......................214-637-1030
Stryco Wire Products
North York, ON..................416-663-7000
Super Cooker
Lake Park, GA...................800-841-7452
Super-Chef Manufacturing Company
Houston, TX.....................800-231-3478
Superior Food Machinery Inc
Pico Rivera, CA.................800-944-0396
Superior Products Company
Saint Paul, MN..................800-328-9800
Svedala Industries
Colorado Springs, CO............719-471-3443
Swanson Wire Works Industries, Inc.
Mesquite, TX....................972-288-7465
Tablecraft Products Co Inc
Gurnee, IL......................800-323-8321

TEMP-TECH Company
Springfield, MA.................800-343-5579
Tempco Electric Heater Corporation
Wood Dale, IL...................888-268-6396
Texas Corn Roasters
Granbury, TX....................800-772-4345
Thermal Engineering Corp
Columbia, SC....................800-331-0097
Thermo King Corp
Bloomington, MN.................888-887-2202
Thermodyne Foodservice Prods
Fort Wayne, IN..................800-526-9182
Thermoquest
Riviera Beach, FL...............888-383-2025
Thermos Company
Schaumburg, IL..................800-243-0745
Thomas L. Green & Company
Robenosia, PA...................610-693-5816
Toastmaster
Elgin, IL.......................847-741-3300
Tolan Machinery Company
Rockaway, NJ....................973-983-7212
Tomlinson Industries
Cleveland, OH...................800-945-4589
Toronto Kitchen Equipment
North York, ON..................416-745-4944
Townfood Equipment Corp
Brooklyn, NY....................800-221-5032
Traeger Industries
Portland, OR....................800-872-3437
Trak-Air/Rair
Denver, CO......................800-688-8725
Tramontina USA
Sugar Land, TX..................800-221-7809
Trimen Foodservice Equipment
North York, ON..................877-437-1422
TruHeat Corporation
Allegan, MI.....................800-879-6199
Tupperware Brands Corporation
Orlando, FL.....................800-366-3800
TURBOCHEF Technologies
Carrollton, TX..................800-908-8726
Ultrafryer Systems Inc
San Antonio, TX.................800-545-9189
Utility Refrigerator Company
Los Angeles, CA.................800-884-5233
Valad Electric Heating Corporation
Tarrytown, NY...................914-631-4927
Vasconia Housewares
San Antonio, TX.................800-377-6723
Vimco
King of Prussia, PA.............610-768-0500
Vortron Smokehouse/Ovens
Iron Ridge, WI..................800-874-1949
Vulcan Food Equipment Group
Baltimore, MD...................800-814-2028
Wayne Combustion Systems
Fort Wayne, IN..................800-443-4625
Welbilt Corporation
Stamford, CT....................203-325-8300
Wells Manufacturing Company
St. Louis, MO...................888-356-5362
West Oregon Wood Products Inc
Columbia City, OR...............503-397-6707
Western Combustion Engineering
Carson, CA......................310-834-9389
Wheel Tough Company
Terre Haute, IN.................888-765-8833
Whitford Corporation
Frazer, PA......................610-296-3200
Wilch Manufacturing
Topeka, KS......................785-267-2762
Wilder Manufacturing Company
Port Jervis, NY.................800-832-1319
Wilton Brands LLC
Woodridge, IL...................630-963-7100
Win-Holt Equipment Group
Syosset, NY.....................800-444-3595
Winston Industries
Louisville, KY..................800-234-5286
Wisco Industries Assembly
Oregon, WI......................800-999-4726
Wittco Foodservice Equipment
Milwaukee, WI...................800-367-8413
Wittco Foodservice Equipment
Milwaukee, WI...................800-821-3912
Wolf Company
Louisville, KY..................800-814-2028
Wood Stone Corp
Bellingham, WA..................800-988-8103
World Kitchen
Elmira, NY......................800-999-3436

X-Press Manufacturing
New Braunfels, TX 800-365-9440

Charcoal Briquettes

Grill Greats
Saxonburg, PA 724-352-1511
King Packaging Co
Schenectady, NY 518-370-5464
Lazzari Fuel Co LLC
Brisbane, CA 800-242-7265
Le Smoker
Salisbury, MD 410-677-3233
Mali's All Natural Barbecue Supply Company
East Amherst, NY 800-289-6254
Mex-Char
Douglas, AZ 520-364-2138
Music City Metals Inc
Nashville, TN 800-251-2674
Nature's Own
Attleboro, MA 508-399-8690
Roseville Charcoal & Mfg Co
Zanesville, OH 740-452-5473
Royal Oak Enterprises
Roswell, GA 678-461-3200

Charcoal: Mesquite

Chef's Choice Mesquite Charcoal
Carpinteria, CA 805-684-8284
Lazzari Fuel Co LLC
Brisbane, CA 800-242-7265
Le Smoker
Salisbury, MD 410-677-3233
Lignetics Inc
Sandpoint, ID 800-544-3834
Mali's All Natural Barbecue Supply Company
East Amherst, NY 800-289-6254
Mex-Char
Douglas, AZ 520-364-2138
Music City Metals Inc
Nashville, TN 800-251-2674

Corers

Fruit & Vegetable

A.D. Cowdrey Company
Modesto, CA 209-538-4677
Amco Metals Indl
City of Industry, CA 626-855-2550
F.B. Pease Company
Rochester, NY 585-475-1870
Globe Machine
Tacoma, WA 800-523-6575
Goodnature Products
Orchard Park, NY 800-875-3381

Corn Chip Processing

A C Horn & Co Sheet Metal
Dallas, TX 800-657-6155
Casa Herrera
Pomona, CA 800-624-3916
Graybill Machines Inc
Lititz, PA 717-626-5221
J C Ford Co
La Habra, CA 714-871-7361
Krispy Kist Company
Chicago, IL 312-733-0900
Maddox/Adams International
Miami, FL 305-592-3337
Pavan USA Inc
Emigsville, PA 717-767-4889
Polar Process
Plattsville, ON 877-896-8077

Corn Poppers

A C Horn & Co Sheet Metal
Dallas, TX 800-657-6155
C. Cretors & Company
Chicago, IL 800-228-1885
Dunbar Manufacturing Co
South Elgin, IL 847-741-6394
Fun City Popcorn
Las Vegas, NV 800-423-1710
Gold Medal Products Co
Cincinnati, OH 800-543-0862
Great Western Co LLC
Hollywood, AL 256-259-3578
Maddox/Adams International
Miami, FL 305-592-3337

Paragon International
Nevada, IA 800-433-0333
Server Products Inc
Richfield, WI 800-558-8722
Star Manufacturing Intl Inc
St Louis, MO 800-264-7827
Treier Popcorn Farms
Bloomdale, OH 419-454-2811

Corn Processing

ANDRITZ Inc
Muncy, PA 704-943-4343
Automated Food Systems
Waxahachie, TX 469-517-0470
Custom Millers Supply Co
Monmouth, IL 309-734-6312
Hughes Co
Columbus, WI 866-535-9303
J C Ford Co
La Habra, CA 714-871-7361
Lee Financial Corporation
Dallas, TX 972-960-1001
Oxbo International Corp
Clear Lake, WI 800-628-6196
Texas Corn Roasters
Granbury, TX 800-772-4345

Crushers

Can & Glass

A T Ferrell Co Inc
Bluffton, IN 800-248-8318
Berkshire PPM
Litchfield, CT 860-567-3118
C S Bell Co
Tiffin, OH 888-958-6381
Compactors Inc
Hilton Head Isle, SC 800-423-4003
Consolidated Baling Machine Company
Jacksonville, FL 800-231-9286
Ertelalsop
Kingston, NY 800-553-7835
Glen Mills Inc.
Clifton, NJ 973-777-0777
Langsenkamp Manufacturing
Indianapolis, IN 877-585-1950
Maren Engineering Corp
South Holland, IL 800-875-1038
Waring Products
Torrington, CT 800-492-7464

Fruit

A.K. Robins
Baltimore, MD 800-486-9656
Globe Machine
Tacoma, WA 800-523-6575
Goodnature Products
Orchard Park, NY 800-875-3381
Healdsburg Machine Company
Santa Rosa, CA 707-433-3348
Oak Barrel Winecraft
Berkeley, CA 510-849-0400

Grain & Oat

C S Bell Co
Tiffin, OH 888-958-6381
CPM Roskamp Champion
Waterloo, IA 800-366-2563
Glen Mills Inc.
Clifton, NJ 973-777-0777
M O Industries Inc
Whippany, NJ 973-386-9228
Schutte Buffalo Hammermill
Buffalo, NY 800-447-4634

Dairy & Creamery

A & B Process Systems Corp
Stratford, WI 888-258-2789
Advance Energy Technologies
Halfmoon, NY 800-724-0198
Apex Packing & Rubber Co
Farmingdale, NY 800-645-9110
Aw Sheepscot Holding Co Inc
Franksville, WI 800-850-6110
B T Engineering Inc
Bala Cynwyd, PA 610-664-9500
Ben H. Anderson Manufacturers
Morrisonville, WI 608-846-5474

Berlon Industries
Hustisford, WI 800-899-3580
Bowers Process Equipment
Stratford, ON. 800-567-3223
C E Rogers Co
Mora, MN 800-279-8081
C&R Refrigation Inc,
Center, TX. 800-438-6182
Cal-Coast Manufacturing
Turlock, CA 209-668-9378
Cannon Equipment Company
Cannon Falls, MN 800-825-8501
Chester-Jensen Co., Inc.
Chester, PA 800-685-3750
Coburn Company
Whitewater, WI. 800-776-7042
Custom Fabricating & Repair
Marshfield, WI 800-236-8773
Custom Food Machinery
Stockton, CA. 209-463-4343
Damrow Company
Fond Du Lac, WI 800-236-1501
Dipwell Co
Northampton, MA. 413-587-4673
Diversified Metal Engineering
Charlottetown, PE. 902-628-6900
Doering Machines Inc
San Francisco, CA 415-526-2131
Dyna-Veyor Inc
Newark, NJ 800-326-5009
Dynamic Automation LTD
Simi Valley, CA. 805-584-8476
Eischen Enterprises
Fresno, CA 559-834-0013
Equipment Specialists Inc
Manassas, VA 703-361-2227
Food Resources International
Concord, ON. 905-482-8967
GEA North America
Naperville, IL 630-369-8100
Gea Us
Galesville, WI. 608-582-3081
General Machinery Corp
Sheboygan, WI. 888-243-6622
Girton Manufacturing Co
Millville, PA 570-458-5521
Globe Food Equipment Co
Moraine, OH 800-347-5423
Gruenewald ManufacturingCompany
Danvers, MA. 800-229-9447
Ika-Works Inc
Wilmington, NC 800-733-3037
Ivarson Inc
Milwaukee, WI 414-351-0700
Johnson Industries Intl
Windsor, WI 608-846-4499
Kusel Equipment Company
Watertown, WI 920-261-4112
Leland Limited Inc
South Plainfield, NJ 800-984-9793
Lyco Manufacturing
Wausau, WI. 715-845-7867
Lyco Wausau
Wausau, WI. 715-845-7867
Master-Bilt
New Albany, MS. 800-647-1284
Membrane System Specialist Inc
Wisconsin Rapids, WI 715-421-2333
Millbernd Systems
Winsted, MN. 320-485-2685
Nicholas Machine and Grinding
Houston, TX 800-747-1256
Omni International
Kennesaw, GA 800-776-4431
Opal Manufacturing Ltd
Toronto, ON 416-646-5232
Pacific Process Technology
La Jolla, CA 858-551-3298
Papertech
North Vancouver, BC 877-787-2737
Paradigm Technologies
Eugene, OR. 541-345-5543
Peterson Fiberglass Laminates
Shell Lake, WI 715-468-2306
Polar Process
Plattsville, ON. 877-896-8077
Pro Scientific Inc
Oxford, CT 800-584-3776
Reiser
Canton, MA 734-821-1290
Relco Unisystems Corp
Willmar, MN 320-231-2210

Rheo-Tech
  Gurnee, IL......................847-367-1557
Sanchelima International
  Miami, FL......................305-591-4343
Scherping Systems
  Winsted, MN....................320-485-4401
Schlueter Company
  Janesville, WI.................800-359-1700
Sepragen Corp
  Hayward, CA....................510-475-0650
Sonic Corp
  Stratford, CT..................866-493-1378
Stanfos
  Edmonton, AB...................800-661-5648
Superflex Limited
  Brooklyn, NY...................800-394-3665
Swirl Freeze Corp
  Salt Lake City, UT.............800-262-4275
T D Sawvel Co
  Maple Plain, MN................877-488-1816
Tetra Pak
  Denton, TX.....................940-380-4630
Tindall Packaging
  Vicksburg, MI..................269-649-1163
Tuchenhagen North America
  Portland, ME...................207-797-9500
WCB Ice Cream
  Philadelphia, PA...............215-425-4320
Whey Systems
  Willmar, MN....................320-905-4122

Deaerators

Food

B.A.G. Corporation
  Richardson, TX.................800-331-9200
Bryan Boilers
  Peru, IN.......................765-473-6651
Cornell Machine Co
  Springfield, NJ...............973-379-6860
Hebeler Corp
  Tonawanda, NY..................800-486-4709
Sellers Engineering Division
  Danville, KY...................859-236-3181
South Valley Mfg Inc
  Gilroy, CA.....................408-842-5457

Deep Fryers

Abalon Precision Manufacturing Corporation
  Bronx, NY......................800-888-2225
All State Fabricators Corporation
  Tampa, FL......................800-322-9925
Alumaworks
  Sunny Isle Beach, FL...........800-277-7267
American Extrusion Intl
  South Beloit, IL...............815-624-6616
Apollo Sheet Metal
  Kennewick, WA..................509-586-1104
Autofry
  Northborough, MA...............800-348-2976
Automated Food Systems
  Waxahachie, TX.................469-517-0470
Ballantyne Food Service Equipment
  Omaha, NE......................800-424-1215
Baxter Manufacturing Inc
  Orting, WA.....................800-777-2828
Belshaw Adamatic Bakery Group
  Auburn, WA.....................800-578-2547
Blodgett Oven Co
  Burlington, VT.................800-331-5842
Broaster Co LLC
  Beloit, WI.....................800-365-8278
Comstock Castle Stove Co
  Quincy, IL.....................800-637-9188
Crispy Lite
  St. Louis, MO..................888-356-5362
Davron Technologies Inc
  Chattanooga, TN................423-870-1888
Dean Industries
  Gardena, CA....................800-995-1210
FOODesign from tna
  Wilsonville, OR................503-685-5030
Fry Tech Corporation
  Dubuque, IA....................319-583-1559
Frymaster
  Shreveport, LA.................800-221-4583
Garland Commercial Ranges
  Mississauga, ON................905-624-0260
GEM Equipment of Oregon Inc
  Woodburn, OR...................503-982-9902

Giles Enterprises Inc
  Montgomery, AL.................800-288-1555
Gold Medal Products Co
  Cincinnati, OH.................800-543-0862
Imperial Manufacturing Co
  Corona, CA.....................800-343-7790
Keating of Chicago Inc
  Mc Cook, IL....................800-532-8464
Krispy Kist Company
  Chicago, IL....................312-733-0900
Lang Manufacturing Co
  Everett, WA....................800-882-6368
Lucks Food Equipment Company
  Kent, WA.......................811-824-0696
Market Forge Industries Inc
  Everett, MA....................866-698-3188
Masterbuilt Manufacturing Inc
  Columbus, GA...................706-327-5622
Meyer Machine & Garroutte Products
  San Antonio, TX................210-736-1811
Middleby Corp
  Elgin, IL......................847-741-3300
Mies Products
  West Bend, WI..................800-480-6437
Moline Machinery LLC
  Duluth, MN.....................800-767-5734
Motion Technologies
  Northborough, MA...............800-468-2976
Nothum Food Processing Systems
  Springfield, MO................800-435-1297
Otto Braun Bakery Equipment
  Buffalo, NY....................716-824-1252
Perfect Fry Company
  Calgary, AB....................800-265-7711
Pitco Frialator Inc
  Bow, NH........................800-258-3708
Ricoh Technologies
  Grand Prairie, TX..............800-585-9367
Stafford-Smith Inc
  Kalamazoo, MI..................800-968-2442
Stainless Steel Fabricator Inc
  La Mirada, CA..................714-739-9904
Star Manufacturing Intl Inc
  St Louis, MO...................800-264-7827
Super-Chef Manufacturing Company
  Houston, TX....................800-231-3478
Superior Products Company
  Saint Paul, MN.................800-328-9800
Toastmaster
  Elgin, IL......................847-741-3300
Trak-Air/Rair
  Denver, CO.....................800-688-8725
TWM Manufacturing
  Leamington, ON.................888-495-4831
Ultrafryer Systems Inc
  San Antonio, TX................800-545-9189
Vulcan Food Equipment Group
  Baltimore, MD..................800-814-2028
Welbilt Corporation
  Stamford, CT...................203-325-8300
Wells Manufacturing Company
  St. Louis, MO..................888-356-5362
Western Combustion Engineering
  Carson, CA.....................310-834-9389
Wheel Tough Company
  Terre Haute, IN................888-765-8833
Wolf Company
  Louisville, KY.................800-814-2028

Dehydration Equipment

A&J Mixing International
  Oakville, ON...................800-668-3470
ANDRITZ Inc
  Muncy, PA......................704-943-4343
B.A.G. Corporation
  Richardson, TX.................800-331-9200
BNW Industries
  Tippecanoe, IN.................574-353-7855
Brothers Metal Products
  Santa Ana, CA..................714-972-3008
Brown International Corp LLC
  Winter Haven, FL...............863-299-2111
Buhler Inc.
  Plymouth, MN...................763-847-9900
C E Rogers Co
  Mora, MN.......................800-279-8081
Commercial Dehydrator Systems
  Eugene, OR.....................800-369-4283
Davenport Machine
  Rock Island, IL................309-786-1500

Davron Technologies Inc
  Chattanooga, TN................423-870-1888
Dito Dean Food Prep
  Charlotte, NC..................866-449-4200
EnWave Corporation
  Vancouver, BC..................604-806-6110
Evaporator Dryer Technologies
  Hammond, WI....................715-796-2313
Flodin
  Moses Lake, WA.................509-766-2996
Fluid Air Inc
  Aurora, IL.....................630-665-5001
Fluid Energy Processing & Eqpt
  Hatfield, PA...................215-368-2510
French Oil Mill Machinery Co
  Piqua, OH......................937-773-3420
Globe Machine
  Tacoma, WA.....................800-523-6575
Goodnature Products
  Orchard Park, NY...............800-875-3381
H. Gartenberg & Company
  Buffalo Grove, IL..............847-821-7590
Joneca Corp
  Anaheim, CA....................714-993-5997
Lanly Co
  Cleveland, OH..................216-731-1115
Littleford Day
  Florence, KY...................800-365-8555
Low Humidity Systems
  Covington, GA..................770-788-6744
M-E-C Co
  Neodesha, KS...................620-325-2673
Muth Associates
  Springfield, MA................800-388-0157
National Drying Machry Co Inc
  Philadelphia, PA...............215-464-6070
P & F Machine
  Turlock, CA....................209-667-2515
Patterson Industries
  Scarborough, ON................800-336-1110
Raytheon Co
  Waltham, MA....................781-522-3000
SP Industries Inc
  Warminster, PA.................800-523-2327
Thermex Thermatron
  Louisville, KY.................502-493-1299
Thoreson Mc Cosh Inc
  Troy, MI.......................800-959-0805
United Mc Gill Corp
  Groveport, OH..................614-829-1200
Van Air Systems
  Lake City, PA..................800-840-9906
Wittemann Company
  Palm Coast, FL.................386-445-4200

Disintegrators

Schutte Buffalo Hammermill
  Buffalo, NY....................800-447-4634

Dough Make-up

Benier
  Lithia Springs, GA.............770-745-2200
La Poblana Food Machines
  Mesa, AZ.......................480-258-2091
Rheon, U.S.A.
  Irvine, CA.....................949-768-1900

Drink Mixing

A & B Process Systems Corp
  Stratford, WI..................888-258-2789
Component Hardware Group Inc
  Lakewood, NJ...................800-526-3694
Nuova Distribution Centre
  Ferndale, WA...................360-366-2226
Polar Beer Systems
  Sun City, CA...................951-928-8174
Vitamix
  Olmsted Twp, OH................800-437-4654

Dry Products Filling

Inspired Automation Inc
  Agoura Hills, CA...............818-991-4598
Tuchenhagen North America
  Portland, ME...................207-797-9500

Dryers

Gea Processing
  Hudson, WI.....................800-376-6476

Relco Unisystems Corp
Willmar, MN 320-231-2210
Spiral Systems
Fair Oaks, CA 800-998-6111

Food

A & B Process Systems Corp
Stratford, WI 888-258-2789
Ametek Technical & Industrial Products
Kent, OH 215-256-6601
Anhydro Inc
Olympia Fields, IL 708-747-7000
Apollo Sheet Metal
Kennewick, WA 509-586-1104
Applied Chemical Technology
Florence, AL 800-228-3217
APV Americas
Delavan, WI 800-252-5200
Berg Chilling Systems
Toronto, ON, ON 416-755-2221
BNW Industries
Tippecanoe, IN 574-353-7855
Brothers Metal Products
Santa Ana, CA 714-972-3008
Buffalo Technologies Corporation
Buffalo, NY 800-332-2419
Buhler Inc.
Plymouth, MN 763-847-9900
C E Rogers Co
Mora, MN .800-279-8081
Carrier Vibrating Equip Inc
Louisville, KY 502-969-3171
Casso-Solar Corporation
Nanuet, NY 800-988-4455
Columbus Instruments
Columbus, OH 800-669-5011
Commercial Dehydrator Systems
Eugene, OR 800-369-4283
Davron Technologies Inc
Chattanooga, TN 423-870-1888
Delux Manufacturing Co
Kearney, NE 800-658-3240
Dito Dean Food Prep
Charlotte, NC 866-449-4200
Dupps Co
Germantown, OH 937-855-0623
Fernholtz Engineering
Van Nuys, CA 818-785-5800
FFI Corporation
Baltimore, MD 908-810-7100
Fitzpatrick Co
Elmhurst, IL 630-592-4425
Fluid Air Inc
Aurora, IL .630-665-5001
Fluid Energy Processing & Eqpt
Hatfield, PA 215-368-2510
French Oil Mill Machinery Co
Piqua, OH .937-773-3420
Gaston County Dyeing Mach Co
Mt Holly, NC 704-822-5000
Glatt Air Techniques Inc
Ramsey, NJ 201-825-8700
Hebeler Corp
Tonawanda, NY 800-486-4709
Heinzen Sales
Gilroy, CA .408-842-6678
Idaho Steel Products Inc
Idaho Falls, ID 208-522-1275
International Reserve Equipment Corporation
Clarendon Hills, IL 708-531-0680
K & L Intl
Ontario, CA 888-598-5588
Komline-Sanderson Engineering
Peapack, NJ 800-225-5457
Lanly Co
Cleveland, OH 216-731-1115
LIST
Acton, MA 978-635-9521
Littleford Day
Florence, KY 800-365-8555
M-E-C Co
Neodesha, KS 620-325-2673
Mannhart
Fort Worth, TX 817-421-0100
Marriott Walker Corporation
Bingham Farms, MI 248-644-6868
MCD Technologies
Tacoma, WA 253-476-0968
National Drying Machry Co Inc
Philadelphia, PA 215-464-6070

Nemeth Engineering Assoc
Crestwood, KY 502-241-1502
Paget Equipment Co
Marshfield, WI 715-384-3158
Patterson Industries
Scarborough, ON 800-336-1110
Patterson-Kelley   Hars Company
East Stroudsburg, PA 570-421-7500
Paul O. Abbe
Bensenville, IL 630-350-2200
Paxton Products Inc
Blue Ash, OH 800-441-7475
Plainview Milk Products
Plainview, MN 800-356-5606
Procedyne Corp
New Brunswick, NJ 732-249-8347
Radio Frequency Co Inc
Millis, MA 508-376-9555
Raytheon Co
Waltham, MA 781-522-3000
Sandvik Process Systems
Sweden, NJ 973-790-1600
Shanzer Grain Dryer
Sioux Falls, SD 800-843-9887
Shivvers
Corydon, IA 641-872-1007
SP Industries Inc
Warminster, PA 800-523-2327
Spray Drying
Sykesville, MD 410-549-8090
Steri Technologies Inc
Bohemia, NY 800-253-7140
Thermex Thermatron
Louisville, KY 502-493-1299
Ultrafilter
Norcross, GA 800-543-3634
United Mc Gill Corp
Groveport, OH 614-829-1200
Van Air Systems
Lake City, PA 800-840-9906
Vector Corp
Marion, IA 319-377-8263
Vortron Smokehouse/Ovens
Iron Ridge, WI 800-874-1949
Witte Co Inc
Washington, NJ 908-689-6500
Wittemann Company
Palm Coast, FL 386-445-4200
Wyssmont Co Inc
Fort Lee, NJ 201-947-4600
Zeeco Inc
Broken Arrow, OK 918-258-8551

Freeze

Apollo Sheet Metal
Kennewick, WA 509-586-1104
Berg Chilling Systems
Toronto, ON, ON 416-755-2221
Berndorf Belt Technology USA
Gilberts, IL 800-393-8450
SP Industries Inc
Warminster, PA 800-523-2327

Fruit

Ametek Technical & Industrial Products
Kent, OH 215-256-6601
Apollo Sheet Metal
Kennewick, WA 509-586-1104
BNW Industries
Tippecanoe, IN 574-353-7855
Davron Technologies Inc
Chattanooga, TN 423-870-1888
Globe Machine
Tacoma, WA 800-523-6575
Goodnature Products
Orchard Park, NY 800-875-3381
Paxton Products Inc
Blue Ash, OH 800-441-7475
Sandvik Process Systems
Sweden, NJ 973-790-1600

Grain

Apollo Sheet Metal
Kennewick, WA 509-586-1104
Chief Industries
Kearney, NE 800-359-8833
Davenport Machine
Rock Island, IL 309-786-1500
Davron Technologies Inc
Chattanooga, TN 423-870-1888

Delux Manufacturing Co
Kearney, NE 800-658-3240
DMC-David Manufacturing Company
Mason City, IA 641-424-7010
Driall Inc
Attica, IN. .765-295-2255
FFI Corporation
Baltimore, MD 908-810-7100
Forster & Son
Ada, OK 580-332-6021
Grain Machinery Mfg Corp
Miami, FL .305-620-2525
NECO/Nebraska Engineering
Omaha, NE 800-367-6208
Patterson-Kelley   Hars Company
East Stroudsburg, PA 570-421-7500
Sandvik Process Systems
Sweden, NJ 973-790-1600
Shanzer Grain Dryer
Sioux Falls, SD 800-843-9887
Shivvers
Corydon, IA 641-872-1007

Spray

A & B Process Systems Corp
Stratford, WI 888-258-2789
Davron Technologies Inc
Chattanooga, TN 423-870-1888
Evaporator Dryer Technologies
Hammond, WI. 715-796-2313
Food Resources International
Concord, ON. 905-482-8967
Gardner Denver Inc.
Milwaukee, WI
Marriott Walker Corporation
Bingham Farms, MI 248-644-6868
Niro
Hudson, WI. 715-386-9371
Paget Equipment Co
Marshfield, WI 715-384-3158
Spray Drying
Sykesville, MD 410-549-8090
Spraying Systems Company
Wheaton, IL 630-655-5000
Stainless Fabrication Inc
Springfield, MO 800-397-8265

Dumpers

American Food Equipment Company
Hayward, CA 510-783-0255
Andgar Corp
Ferndale, WA 360-366-9900
Apache Stainless Equipment
Beaver Dam, WI 800-444-0398
Automated Flexible Conveyors
Clifton, NJ 800-694-7271
Bridge Machine Company
Palmyra, NJ 877-754-1800
Cecor
Verona, WI 800-356-9042
Cleasby Manufacturing Co
San Francisco, CA 800-253-2729
Coastline Equipment Inc
Bellingham, WA 360-734-8509
Cozzini Inc
Algona, IA 888-295-1116
Cugar Machine Co
Fort Worth, TX 817-927-0411
Custom Food Machinery
Stockton, CA 209-463-4343
Dynamet
Kalamazoo, MI 269-385-0006
Flodin
Moses Lake, WA. 509-766-2996
Food Processing Equipment Co
Santa Fe Springs, CA 562-802-3727
GEM Equipment of Oregon Inc
Woodburn, OR 503-982-9902
Heinzen Sales
Gilroy, CA. 408-842-6678
Jesco Industries
Litchfield, MI 800-455-0019
Kinetic Equipment Company
Appleton, WI 806-293-4471
MAF Industries Inc
Traver, CA. 559-897-2905
Materials Transportation Co
Temple, TX 800-433-3110
Midwest Metalcraft & Equipment
Windsor, MO. 800-647-3167

Palace Packaging Machines Inc
  Downingtown, PA 610-873-7252
Phelps Industries
  Little Rock, AR 501-568-5550
Pucel Enterprises Inc
  Cleveland, OH 800-336-4986
Reiser
  Canton, MA 734-821-1290
Screw Conveyor Corp
  Hammond, IN 219-931-1450
SP Industries
  Hopkins, MI 800-592-5959
TWM Manufacturing
  Leamington, ON 888-495-4831
Uhrden
  Sugarcreek, OH 800-852-2411
Vanmark Equipment
  Creston, IA 800-523-6261
Vertical Systems Intl
  Lakeside Park, KY 859-485-9650

Egg Processing & Cleaning

A & B Process Systems Corp
  Stratford, WI 888-258-2789
ADSI Inc
  Durant, OK 580-924-4461
Behrens Manufacturing LLC
  Winona, MN 507-454-4664
Brush Research Mfg Co Inc
  Los Angeles, CA 323-261-6162
Davidson's Safest Choice Eggs
  Lansing, IL 800-410-7619
Diamond Automation
  Farmington Hills, MI 248-426-9394
Eggboxes Inc
  Deerfield Beach, FL 800-326-6667
H. Gartenberg & Company
  Buffalo Grove, IL 847-821-7590
Hayon Manufacturing
  Las Vegas, NV 702-562-3377
KL Products, Ltd.
  London, ON 800-388-5744
Kuhl Corporation
  Flemington, NJ 908-782-5696

Equipment

Advance Energy Technologies
  Halfmoon, NY 800-724-0198
Ashcroft Inc
  Stratford, CT 800-328-8258
Eirich Machines
  Gurnee, IL 847-336-2444
Ever Extruder Co
  Festus, MO 636-937-8830
Famco Automatic Sausage Linkers
  Pittsburgh, PA 412-241-6410
Gea Process Engineering Inc
  Columbia, MD 410-997-8700
Graybill Machines Inc
  Lititz, PA 717-626-5221
Gridpath, Inc.
  Stony Creek, ON 905-643-0955
I. Fm Usa Inc.
  Franklin Park, IL 866-643-6872
Lyco Manufacturing
  Wausau, WI 715-845-7867
Lyco Manufacturing Inc
  Columbus, WI 920-623-4152
M-Vac Systems Inc
  Bluffdale, UT 801-523-3962
Marlen Research Corporation
  Shawnee Mission, KS 913-888-3333
MPS North America, Inc.
  Lenexa, KS 913-310-0055
Murzan Inc
  Peachtree Cor, GA 770-448-0583
Paramount Packaging Corp
  Melville, NY 516-333-8100
Reiser
  Canton, MA 734-821-1290
Rheon, U.S.A.
  Irvine, CA 949-768-1900
Risco USA Corp
  South Easton, MA 888-474-7267
Ross Industries Inc
  Midland, VA 540-439-3271
Ryowa Company America
  Elk Grove Village, IL 800-700-9692
Stephan Machinery GmbH
  Mandelein, IL 847-247-0182

Sympak, Inc.
  Mundelein, IL 847-247-0182
Terlet USA
  Swedesboro, NJ 856-241-9970

Espresso & Cappuccino Processing

Acorto
  Bellevue, WA 800-995-9019
Ascaso
  Bensenville, IL 630-350-0066
Astoria General Espresso
  Greensboro, NC 336-393-0224
Boston's Best Coffee Roasters
  South Easton, MA 800-898-8393
Espresso Roma
  Emeryville, CA 800-437-1668
Formula Espresso
  Brooklyn, NY 718-834-8724
Gabriella Imports
  Cleveland, OH 800-544-8117
Gensaco Marketing
  New York, NY 800-506-1935
Grindmaster-Cecilware Corp
  Louisville, KY 800-695-4500
Lavazza Premium Coffees
  New York, NY 212-725-9196
Michaelo Espresso
  Seattle, WA 800-545-2883
Nuova Distribution Centre
  Ferndale, WA 360-366-2226
Pasquini Espresso Co
  Los Angeles, CA 800-724-6225
Pier 1 Imports
  Woodcliff Lake, NJ 800-448-9993
Saeco
  Cleveland, OH 440-528-2000
Schaerer USA Corp
  Tustin, CA 888-989-3004
Steel Products
  Marion, IA 800-333-9451
Supramatic
  Toronto, ON 877-465-2883
The Carriage Works
  Klamath Falls, OR 541-882-0700
Wega USA
  Bensenville, IL 630-350-0066
Wells Manufacturing Company
  St. Louis, MO 888-356-5362

Evaporators

Fruit Juice

A & B Process Systems Corp
  Stratford, WI 888-258-2789
Berkshire PPM
  Litchfield, CT 860-567-3118
Central Fabricators Inc
  Cincinnati, OH 800-909-8265
Custom Food Machinery
  Stockton, CA 209-463-4343
Dedert Corporation
  Olympia Fields, IL 708-747-7000
Globe Machine
  Tacoma, WA 800-523-6575
Goodnature Products
  Orchard Park, NY 800-875-3381
L&A Process Systems
  Modesto, CA 209-581-0205
South Valley Mfg Inc
  Gilroy, CA 408-842-5457
Washington Frontier
  Grandview, WA 509-469-7662

Milk

A & B Process Systems Corp
  Stratford, WI 888-258-2789
Central Fabricators Inc
  Cincinnati, OH 800-909-8265
LIST
  Acton, MA 978-635-9521
Marriott Walker Corporation
  Bingham Farms, MI 248-644-6868
Membrane System Specialist Inc
  Wisconsin Rapids, WI 715-421-2333
Niro
  Hudson, WI 715-386-9371

Extractors

Fruit & Vegetable Juice

A.K. Robins
  Baltimore, MD 800-486-9656
Berkshire PPM
  Litchfield, CT 860-567-3118
Brown International Corp LLC
  Winter Haven, FL 863-299-2111
Chop-Rite Two Inc
  Harleysville, PA 800-683-5858
Custom Food Machinery
  Stockton, CA 209-463-4343
Dorton Incorporated
  Arlington Hts, IL 800-299-8600
Eurodib
  Champlain, NY 888-956-6866
French Oil Mill Machinery Co
  Piqua, OH 937-773-3420
Globe Machine
  Tacoma, WA 800-523-6575
Goodnature Products
  Orchard Park, NY 800-875-3381
Hollymatic Corp
  Countryside, IL 708-579-3700
JBT Food Tech
  Lakeland, FL 863-683-5411
Juice Tree
  Omaha, NE 714-891-4425
Mandeville Company
  Minneapolis, MN 800-328-8490
Mulligan Associates
  Mequon, WI 800-627-2886
Nutrifaster Inc
  Seattle, WA 800-800-2641
Omega Products Inc
  Harrisburg, PA 800-633-3401
Ruby Manufacturing & Sales
  South El Monte, CA 626-443-1171
Technium
  Medford, NJ 609-702-5910
Waring Products
  Torrington, CT 800-492-7464
Washington Frontier
  Grandview, WA 509-469-7662

Extruders

Bogner Industries
  Ronkonkoma, NY 631-981-5123
Polar Process
  Plattsville, ON 877-896-8077
Reiser
  Canton, MA 734-821-1290

Fillers

Bogner Industries
  Ronkonkoma, NY 631-981-5123
Edhard Corp
  Hackettstown, NJ 888-334-2731
Fogg Filler Co
  Holland, MI 616-786-3644
G & F Mfg
  Oak Lawn, IL 800-282-1574
HAMBA USA, Inc
  Saint Peters, MO
Handtmann Inc
  Lake Forest, IL 800-477-3585
Innovative Foods, Inc.
  South San Francisco, CA 650-871-8912
Niro Inc
  Hudson, WI 715-386-9371
Raque Food Systems
  Louisville, KY 502-267-9641
Reiser
  Canton, MA 734-821-1290
Risco USA Corp
  South Easton, MA 888-474-7267
SeamTech
  Acampo, CA 209-464-4610
Statco Engineering
  Huntington Beach, CA 800-421-0362
T D Sawvel Co
  Maple Plain, MN 877-488-1816
Terlet USA
  Swedesboro, NJ 856-241-9970

Filters

Coffee

Andex Corp
Rochester, NY 585-328-3790
Boston's Best Coffee Roasters
South Easton, MA. 800-898-8393
Bunn-O-Matic Corp
Springfield, IL. 800-352-2866
Chemex Division/International Housewares Corporation
Chicopee, MA 800-243-6399
Coffee Sock Company
Eugene, OR. .541-344-7698
Kennedy's Specialty Sewing
Erin, ON 519-833-9306
Keurig Dr Pepper
Burlington, MA. 877-208-9991
Lamports Filter Media
Cleveland, OH 216-881-2050
Melitta Canada
Vaughan, ON. 800-565-4882
Melitta North America, Inc.
Clearwater, FL 888-635-4880
Rockline Industries
Sheboygan, WI 800-558-7790
Superior Products Company
Saint Paul, MN 800-328-9800
Tops Manufacturing Co
Darien, CT. 203-655-9367
UniPro Foodservice, Inc.
Atlanta, GA. .770-952-0871

Food

Alexander Machinery
Spartanburg, SC 864-963-3624
Avalon Manufacturer
Corona, CA 800-676-3040
Baker Hughes
Houston, TX
Cambridge Intl. Inc.
Cambridge, MD 800-638-9560
Crispy Lite
St. Louis, MO 888-356-5362
Eaton Filtration, LLC
Tinton Falls, NJ. 800-859-9212
Ertelalsop
Kingston, NY 800-553-7835
Falcon Fabricators Inc
Nashville, TN 615-832-0027
Filtercorp
Fresno, CA 800-473-4526
Globe Machine
Tacoma, WA .800-523-6575
Goodnature Products
Orchard Park, NY 800-875-3381
Greig Filters Inc
Lafayette, LA 800-456-0177
Gusmer Enterprises Inc
Fresno, CA 866-213-1131
International Reserve Equipment Corporation
Clarendon Hills, IL. 708-531-0680
Komline-Sanderson Engineering
Peapack, NJ. .800-225-5457
L.C. Thompson Company
Kenosha, WI .800-558-4018
Micropure Filtration Inc
Mound, MN .800-654-7873
Mies Products
West Bend, WI 800-480-6437
Pall Filtron
Northborough, MA 800-345-8766
Piab Vacuum Products
Hingham, MA 800-321-7422
Prince Castle Inc
Carol Stream, IL 800-722-7853
Purolator Facet Inc
Greensboro, NC 800-852-4449
Refractron Technologies Corp
Newark, NY .315-331-6222
Sparkler Filters Inc
Conroe, TX 936-756-4471
Steri Technologies Inc
Bohemia, NY 800-253-7140
Ultrafilter
Norcross, GA 800-543-3634
Ultrafryer Systems Inc
San Antonio, TX. 800-545-9189
Williams & Mettle Company
Houston, TX .800-526-4954

Womack International Inc
Vallejo, CA 707-647-2370

Fruit & Vegetable Juice

Berkshire PPM
Litchfield, CT 860-567-3118
Conwed Global Netting Sltns
Roanoke, VA 800-368-3610
Delta Pure Filtration Corp
Ashland, VA .800-785-9450
F.P. Smith Wire Cloth Company
Northlake, IL. 800-323-6842
Filtration Systems
Sunrise, FL 954-572-2700
Globe Machine
Tacoma, WA .800-523-6575
Goodnature Products
Orchard Park, NY 800-875-3381
Komline-Sanderson Engineering
Peapack, NJ. .800-225-5457
Lenser Filtration
Lakewood, NJ 732-370-1600
Metlar Us
Riverhead, NY 631-252-5574
Refractron Technologies Corp
Newark, NY .315-331-6222
Washington Frontier
Grandview, WA 509-469-7662

Grease

Component Hardware Group Inc
Lakewood, NJ 800-526-3694
Flame Gard
Lakewood, NJ 800-526-3694
Trine Rolled Moulding Corp
Bronx, NY 800-223-8075

Paper

Andex Corp
Rochester, NY 585-328-3790
Avery Filter Company
Westwood, NJ 201-666-9664

Filtration and Separation

Wes Tech Engineering Inc
Salt Lake City, UT 801-265-1000

Fish Cleaning

Coastline Equipment Inc
Bellingham, WA 360-734-8509
Crane Research & Engineering
Hampton, VA 757-826-1707
Design Technology Corporation
Billerica, MA 978-663-7000
Diversified Metal Engineering
Charlottetown, PE 902-628-6900
Fishmore
Melbourne, FL 321-723-4751
Skrmetta Machinery Corporation
New Orleans, LA 504-488-4413
Steamway Corporation
Scottsburg, IN 800-259-8171
TWM Manufacturing
Leamington, ON 888-495-4831

Flakers or Flaking Drums

Biro Manufacturing Co
Lakeside Marblhd, OH 419-798-4451
Buffalo Technologies Corporation
Buffalo, NY .800-332-2419
CPM Roskamp Champion
Waterloo, IA .800-366-2563
Ferrell-Ross
Amarillo, TX. 800-299-9051
General Machinery Corp
Sheboygan, WI 888-243-6622
Hoshizaki America Inc
Peachtree City, GA 800-438-6087
Lauhoff Corporation
Detroit, MI 313-259-0027

Flour Mill

Buffalo Technologies Corporation
Buffalo, NY .800-332-2419
Commodity Traders International
Trilla, IL 217-235-4322

Forster & Son
Ada, OK 580-332-6021

Food Processing

915 Labs
Centennial, CO 855-915-5227
Advance Energy Technologies
Halfmoon, NY. 800-724-0198
Alard Equipment Corp
Williamson, NY 315-589-4511
Amfec Inc
Hayward, CA 510-780-0134
Anderson Chemical Co
Litchfield, MN 320-693-2477
Anritsu Industrial Solutions
Elk Grove Vlg, IL 847-419-9729
Axiflow Technologies, Inc.
Kennesaw, GA 770-795-1195
Bizerba USA
Piscataway, NJ 732-565-6000
Bogner Industries
Ronkonkoma, NY 631-981-5123
CPM Century Extrusion
Traverse City, MI 231-947-6400
CPM Roskamp Champion
Waterloo, IA .800-366-2563
CPM Wolverine Proctor LLC
Horsham, PA 215-443-5200
Cresco Food Technologies
Cresco, IA 563-547-4241
Eischen Enterprises
Fresno, CA 559-834-0013
Ennio International
Aurora, IL. 630-851-5808
Evonik Corporation   North America
Parsippany, NJ. 973-929-8000
F R Drake Co
Waynesboro, VA 540-949-6215
Fourinox Inc
Green Bay, WI. 920-336-0621
Frost ET Inc
Grand Rapids, MI 800-253-9382
Gea Process Engineering Inc
Columbia, MD 410-997-8700
Gridpath, Inc.
Stony Creek, ON. 905-643-0955
Hughes Co
Columbus, WI. 920-623-2000
Incomec-Cerex Industries
Fairfield, CT .203-335-1050
Insect-O-Cutor Inc
Stone Mountain, GA 800-966-8480
JCS Controls, Inc.
Rochester, NY. 585-227-5910
Kasel Engineering
Dayton, OH. .937-854-8875
KL Products, Ltd.
London, ON .800-388-5744
Lechler Inc
St Charles, IL 800-777-2926
Libra Technical Center
Metuchen, NJ 732-321-5200
Loeb Equipment
Chicago, IL 773-496-5720
Loos Machine
Colby, WI 715-223-2844
Lyco Manufacturing
Wausau, WI. .715-845-7867
Marel Food Systems, Inc.
Lenexa, KS 913-888-9110
Marlen
Riverside, MO. 913-888-3333
Microthermics
Raleigh, NC .919-878-8045
Mtc Food Equipment
Poulsbo, WA 360-697-6319
Qualtech
Quebec, QC. .888-339-3801
Raque Food Systems
Louisville, KY 502-267-9641
Reiser
Canton, MA .734-821-1290
Ripon Manufacturing Co Inc
Ripon, CA 800-800-1232
Risco USA Corp
South Easton, MA. 888-474-7267
Scott Process Equipment & Controls
Guelph, ON. .888-343-5421
SICK Inc
Bloomington, MN. 800-325-7425

Simply Manufacturing
Prairie Du Sac, WI 608-643-6656
Sperling Boss
Sperling, MB. 877-626-3401
Statco Engineering
Huntington Beach, CA 800-421-0362
Stone Enterprises Inc.
Omaha, NE 877-653-0500
Superior Products Company
Saint Paul, MN 800-328-9800
Thunderbird Food Machinery
Blaine, WA 866-875-6868
Ultra Process Systems
Oak Ridge, TN 865-483-2772
Warren Rupp Inc
Mansfield, OH 419-524-8388
Washington Frontier
Grandview, WA 509-469-7662
Weiler Equipment
Whitewater, WI. 800-558-9507
Young & Associates
Kenosha, WI 262-657-6394

Food

A & B Process Systems Corp
Stratford, WI 888-258-2789
A C Horn & Co Sheet Metal
Dallas, TX. 800-657-6155
A C Tool & Machine Co
Louisville, KY 502-447-5505
A T Ferrell Co Inc
Bluffton, IN. 800-248-8318
A&J Mixing International
Oakville, ON. 800-668-3470
A&M Industries
Sioux Falls, SD 800-888-2615
A&M Process Equipment
Ajax, ON. 905-619-8001
A.K. Robins
Baltimore, MD 800-486-9656
Aaburco Inc
Grass Valley, CA. 800-533-7437
Aaron Equipment Co Div Areco
Bensenville, IL 630-350-2200
ABCO Industries Limited
Lunenburg, NS 866-634-8821
Abel Pumps
Sewickley, PA 412-741-3222
ABI Limited
Concord, ON. 800-297-8666
ABO Industries
San Diego, CA 858-566-9750
Acra Electric Corporation
Tulsa, OK 800-223-4328
Acraloc Corp
Oak Ridge, TN 865-483-1368
Acrison Inc
Moonachie, NJ 800-422-4266
ADMIX
Manchester, NH 800-466-2369
ADSI Inc
Durant, OK 580-924-4461
Aerotech Enterprise Inc
Chesterland, OH 440-729-2616
AEW Thurne
Lake Zurich, IL. 800-239-7297
Agricultural Data Systems
Laguna Niguel, CA. 800-328-2246
Albion Machine & Tool Co
Albion, MI 517-629-9135
Alfa Laval Ashbrook Simon-Hartley
Houston, TX. 713-934-3160
Alfa Laval Inc
Richmond, VA. 866-253-2528
Alkar Rapid Pak
Lodi, WI 608-592-3211
Allegheny Bradford Corp
Bradford, PA 800-542-0650
Allen Gauge & Tool Co
Pittsburgh, PA. 412-241-6410
Alloy Hardfacing & Engineering
Jordan, MN 800-328-8408
Allpax Products
Covington, LA 888-893-9277
Alpha Omega Technology
Cedar Knolls, NJ. 800-442-1969
ALPI Food Preparation Equipment
Bolton, ON 800-928-2574
Altman Industries
Gray, GA. 478-986-3116

AM-Mac
Fairfield, NJ 800-829-2018
American Extrusion Intl
South Beloit, IL 815-624-6616
American Food Equipment Company
Hayward, CA 510-783-0255
American Housewares
Bronx, NY. 718-665-9500
American Manufacturing-Engrng
Cleveland, OH 800-822-9402
American Metal Stamping
Brooklyn, NY. 718-384-1500
Ametek Technical & Industrial Products
Kent, OH 215-256-6601
AMF Bakery Systems Corp
Richmond, VA. 800-225-3771
AMF CANADA
Sherbrooke, QC 800-255-3869
Anderson International Corp
Stow, OH. 800-336-4730
Andgar Corp
Ferndale, WA 360-366-9900
ANDRITZ Inc
Muncy, PA. 704-943-4343
Anhydro Inc
Olympia Fields, IL 708-747-7000
Apache Stainless Equipment
Beaver Dam, WI. 800-444-0398
APEC
Lake Odessa, MI. 616-374-1000
API Heat Transfer Inc
Buffalo, NY. 877-274-4328
Apollo Sheet Metal
Kennewick, WA 509-586-1104
Applied Chemical Technology
Florence, AL. 800-228-3217
APV Americas
Delavan, WI. 800-252-5200
Architectural Sheet Metals LLC
Cleveland, OH 216-361-9952
Arcobaleno Pasta Machines
Lancaster, PA 800-875-7096
Arde Inc
Carlstadt, NJ 800-909-6070
Arrow Tank Co
Buffalo, NY. 716-893-7200
Artisan Controls Corp
Randolph, NJ 800-457-4950
Artisan Industries
Waltham, MA 781-893-6800
Ashlock Co
San Leandro, CA. 510-351-0560
Astoria General Espresso
Greensboro, NC 336-393-0224
Atlanta SharpTech
Peachtree City, GA 800-462-7297
Atlas Minerals & Chemicals Inc
Mertztown, PA 800-523-8269
Atlas Pacific Engineering
Pueblo, CO 719-948-3040
Auger Fab
Exton, PA 800-334-1529
Automated Food Systems
Waxahachie, TX 469-517-0470
Avestin
Ottawa, ON 888-283-7846
Ay Machine Company
Ephrata, PA 717-733-0335
Ayr King Corp
Louisville, KY 866-266-6290
B & P Process Equipment
Saginaw, MI 989-757-1300
B C Holland Inc
Dousman, WI 262-965-2939
B T Engineering Inc
Bala Cynwyd, PA 610-664-9500
B.A.G. Corporation
Richardson, TX. 800-331-9200
Backwoods Smoker Inc
Shreveport, LA 318-220-0380
Bake Star
Somerset, WI. 763-427-7611
Baker Hughes
Houston, TX
Bakery Machinery Dealers
Holbrook, NY. 631-567-6666
Baking Machines
Livermore, CA 925-449-3369
Baldewein Company
Lake Forrest, IL 800-424-5544
Be & Sco
San Antonio, TX. 800-683-0928

Bean Machines
Sonoma, CA 707-996-0706
BEI
South Haven, MI. 800-364-7425
Belshaw Adamatic Bakery Group
Auburn, WA 800-578-2547
Bematek Systems Inc
Salem, MA 877-236-2835
Ben H. Anderson Manufacturers
Morrisonville, WI 608-846-5474
Bepex International LLC
Minneapolis, MN 800-607-2470
Berg Chilling Systems
Toronto, ON 416-755-2221
Berkshire PPM
Litchfield, CT 860-567-3118
Bermar America
Malvern, PA 888-289-5838
Best & Donovan
Blue Ash, OH 800-553-2378
Bete Fog Nozzle Inc
Greenfield, MA. 800-235-0049
Bettcher Industries Inc
Wakeman, OH. 800-321-8763
Bettendorf Stanford Inc
Salem, IL 800-548-2253
BFM Equipment Sales
Fall River, WI 920-484-3341
Bijur Lubricating Corporation
Morrisville, NC. 800-631-0168
Billington Welding & Mfg Inc
Modesto, CA. 800-932-9312
Biomerieux Inc
Durham, NC 800-682-2666
Biro Manufacturing Co
Lakeside Marblhd, OH 419-798-4451
Blackmer Co
Grand Rapids, MI 616-241-1611
Blakeslee, Inc.
Addison, IL 630-532-5021
Bloomfield Industries
St. Louis, MO 888-356-5362
Blue Tech
Hickory, NC 828-324-5900
BluMetric Environmental Inc.
Ottawa, ON 613-839-3053
Bmh Equipment Inc
Sacramento, CA 800-350-8828
Boehringer Mfg. Co. Inc.
Felton, CA 800-630-8665
Bonnot Co
Akron, OH. 330-896-6544
Bowers Process Equipment
Stratford, ON. 800-567-3223
Branson Ultrasonics Corp
Danbury, CT 203-796-0400
Breddo Likwifier
Kansas City, MO. 800-669-4092
Bridge Machine Company
Palmyra, NJ. 877-754-1800
Brothers Metal Products
Santa Ana, CA 714-972-3008
Brower
Houghton, IA 800-553-1791
Brown International Corp LLC
Winter Haven, FL 863-299-2111
Buffalo Technologies Corporation
Buffalo, NY. 800-332-2419
Buhler Inc.
Plymouth, MN. 763-847-9900
Bulldog Factory Svc LLC
Madison Heights, MI 248-541-3500
Bunting Magnetics Co
Newton, KS. 800-835-2526
Buss America
Carol Stream, IL 630-933-9100
BVL Controls
Bois-Des-Filion, QC 866-285-2668
C E Rogers Co
Mora, MN 800-279-8081
C H Babb Co Inc
Raynham, MA. 508-977-0600
C S Bell Co
Tiffin, OH 888-958-6381
C. Cretors & Company
Chicago, IL 800-228-1885
Cal-Coast Manufacturing
Turlock, CA 209-668-9378
Cameron Intl. Corp.
Houston, TX. 281-285-4376
Camerons Brewing Co.
Oakville, ON. 905-849-8282

Capway Conveyor Systems Inc
York, PA...................877-222-7929
Carolina Knife
Asheville, NC................800-520-5030
Carrier Vibrating Equip Inc
Louisville, KY...............502-969-3171
Carter-Day International Inc
Minneapolis, MN.............763-571-1000
Casa Herrera
Pomona, CA.................800-624-3916
Casso-Solar Corporation
Nanuet, NY.................800-988-4455
Champion Trading Corporation
Marlboro, NJ................732-780-4200
Charles Ross & Son Co
Hauppauge, NY..............800-243-7677
Chart Inc
New Prague, MN.............800-428-3777
Chemicolloid Laboratories, Inc.
New Hyde Park, NY...........516-747-2666
Chester-Jensen Co., Inc.
Chester, PA.................800-685-3750
Chicago Stainless Eqpt Inc
Palm City, FL...............800-927-8575
Chil-Con Products
Brantford, ON...............800-263-0086
Chocolate Concepts
Hartville, OH...............330-877-3322
Chop-Rite Two Inc
Harleysville, PA.............800-683-5858
Cleveland-Eastern Mixers
Clinton, CT.................800-243-1188
Clextral USA
Tampa, FL..................813-854-4434
CMC America Corporation
Joliet, IL...................815-726-4337
Coastline Equipment Inc
Bellingham, WA..............360-734-8509
Cobatco
Peoria, IL...................800-426-2282
Coburn Company
Whitewater, WI..............800-776-7042
Codema
Maple Grove, MN.............763-428-2266
Columbus Instruments
Columbus, OH...............800-669-5011
Commercial Dehydrator Systems
Eugene, OR.................800-369-4283
Commercial Manufacturing
Fresno, CA.................559-237-1855
Commodity Traders International
Trilla, IL...................217-235-4322
Computer Controlled Machines
Pueblo, CO.................719-948-9500
Convay Systems
Minnetonka, MN.............800-334-1099
Cook & Beals Inc
Loup City, NE...............308-745-0154
Corenco
Santa Rosa, CA..............888-267-3626
Cornell Machine Co
Springfield, NJ..............973-379-6860
Cornell Pump Company
Portland, OR................503-653-0330
Cozzini Inc
Algona, IA..................888-295-1116
Cozzini LLC
Chicago, IL.................773-478-9700
CPM Roskamp Champion
Waterloo, IA................800-366-2563
Crane Pumps & Systems
Piqua, OH..................937-778-8947
Crane Research & Engineering
Hampton, VA................757-826-1707
CRC Inc
Council Bluffs, IA............712-323-9477
Croll Reynolds Inc
Parsippany, NJ...............908-232-4200
Crown Controls Inc.
Charlotte, NC...............800-541-7874
Crown Iron Works Company
Roseville, MN...............888-703-7500
Cugar Machine Co
Fort Worth, TX..............817-927-0411
Custom Fabricating & Repair
Marshfield, WI..............800-236-8773
Custom Food Machinery
Stockton, CA................209-463-4343
Custom Metal Crafts
Springfield, MO.............417-862-9324
Custom Pools Inc
Portsmouth, NH.............800-323-9509

Cutrite Company
Fremont, OH................800-928-8748
D & S Mfg
Auburn, MA.................508-799-7812
D A Berther Inc
Milwaukee, WI..............877-357-9622
D.R. McClain & Son
Commerce, CA...............800-428-2263
Dadant & Sons Inc
Hamilton, IL................888-922-1293
Daily Printing Inc
Plymouth, MN...............800-622-6596
Daleco
West Chester, PA.............610-429-0181
Damrow Company
Fond Du Lac, WI.............800-236-1501
Davenport Machine
Rock Island, IL..............309-786-1500
Davron Technologies Inc
Chattanooga, TN.............423-870-1888
DBE Inc
Concord, ON................800-461-5313
DCI, Inc.
St Cloud, MN...............320-252-8200
Dedert Corporation
Olympia Fields, IL............708-747-7000
Defreeze Corporation
Southborough, MA............508-485-8512
Dehyco Company
Memphis, TN...............901-774-3322
Delta Machine & Maufacturing
St Rose, LA.................504-949-8304
Delux Manufacturing Co
Kearney, NE................800-658-3240
Demaco
Ridgewood, NY
Design Technology Corporation
Billerica, MA................978-663-7000
Designpro Engineering
Clearwater, MN..............800-221-4144
Diamond Automation
Farmington Hills, MI...........248-426-9394
Dipwell Co
Northampton, MA............413-587-4673
Direct South
Macon, GA.................478-746-3518
Dito Dean Food Prep
Charlotte, NC...............866-449-4200
Diversified Metal Engineering
Charlottetown, PE............902-628-6900
Dixie Canner Machine Shop
Athens, GA.................706-549-0592
Doering Co
Clear Lake, MN..............320-743-2276
Doering Machines Inc
San Francisco, CA............415-526-2131
Dole Refrigerating Co
Lewisburg, TN...............800-251-8990
Dorton Incorporated
Arlington Hts, IL.............800-299-8600
Driall Inc
Attica, IN..................765-295-2255
Drum-Mates Inc.
Lumberton, NJ..............800-621-3786
DSW Converting Knives
Birmingham, AL.............205-322-2021
DT Converting Technologies - Stokes
Bristol, PA..................800-635-0036
Dunbar Manufacturing Co
South Elgin, IL...............847-741-6394
Dunkley International Inc
Kalamazoo, MI..............800-666-1264
Duplex Mill & Mfg Co
Springfield, OH..............937-325-5555
Dupps Co
Germantown, OH.............937-855-0623
Duralite Inc
Riverton, CT................888-432-8797
Dutchess Bakers' Machinery Co
Superior, WI................800-777-4498
Dynamic Automation LTD
Simi Valley, CA..............805-584-8476
Eaton Sales & Service
Denver, CO.................800-208-2657
Ecklund-Harrison Technologies
Fort Myers, FL...............239-936-6032
Eclipse Systems Inc
Milpitas, CA................408-263-2201
Edhard Co
Hackettstown, NJ............888-334-2731
Edlund Co
Burlington, VT...............800-772-2126

Eirich Machines
Gurnee, IL..................847-336-2444
EKATO Corporation
St Ramsey, NJ...............201-825-4684
Electro Cam Corp
Roscoe, IL..................800-228-5487
Elliott Manufacturing Co Inc
Fresno, CA.................559-233-6235
Emerald City Closets Inc
Auburn, WA.................800-925-1521
Emery Thompson Machine &Supply Company
Brooksville, FL..............718-588-7300
Empire Bakery Equipment
Hicksville, NY...............800-878-4070
Engineered Products Group
Madison, WI................800-626-3111
Equipment Specialists Inc
Manassas, VA...............703-361-2227
Ertelalsop
Kingston, NY................800-553-7835
Esco Products Inc
Houston, TX................800-966-5514
Et Oakes Corp
Hauppauge, NY..............631-232-0002
Eurodib
Champlain, NY..............888-956-6866
Evaporator Dryer Technologies
Hammond, WI...............715-796-2313
Everedy Automation
Frederick, PA...............610-754-1775
Exact Mixing Systems Inc
Memphis, TN...............901-362-8501
Expert Industries Inc
Brooklyn, NY...............718-434-6060
F N Smith Corp
Oregon, IL..................815-732-2171
F.B. Pease Company
Rochester, NY...............585-475-1870
Falcon Fabricators Inc
Nashville, TN...............615-832-0027
Feldmeier Equipment Inc
Syracuse, NY...............315-454-8608
Fernholtz Engineering
Van Nuys, CA...............818-785-5800
Fish Oven & Equipment Co
Wauconda, IL...............877-526-8720
Fishmore
Melbourne, FL..............321-723-4751
Fitzpatrick Co
Elmhurst, IL................630-592-4425
Fleet Wood Goldco Wyard
Cockeysville, MD.............410-785-1934
FleetwoodGoldcoWyard
Romeoville, IL...............630-759-6800
Flex-Hose Co Inc
East Syracuse, NY............315-437-1611
Flodin
Moses Lake, WA.............509-766-2996
Flow Aerospace
Jeffersonville, IN.............812-283-7888
Flow International Corp.
Kent, WA...................800-446-3569
Flow of Solids
Westford, MA...............978-392-0300
Fluid Air Inc
Aurora, IL..................630-665-5001
Fluid Energy Processing & Eqpt
Hatfield, PA.................215-368-2510
Fluid Metering Inc
Syosset, NY.................800-223-3388
Flux Pumps Corporation
Atlanta, GA.................800-367-3589
Food Engineering Unlimited
Fullerton, CA................714-879-8762
Food Processing Equipment Co
Santa Fe Springs, CA..........562-802-3727
Food Resources International
Concord, ON................905-482-8967
Food Service Equipment Corporation
Cape Coral, FL..............941-574-7767
Food Tools
Santa Barbara, CA............877-836-6386
Forster & Son
Ada, OK...................580-332-6021
Foster Miller Inc
Waltham, MA...............781-684-4000
FPEC Corporation
Santa Fe Springs, CA..........562-802-3727
Franrica Systems
Stockton, CA................209-948-2811
Frelco
Stephenville, NL.............709-643-5668

French Oil Mill Machinery Co
Piqua, OH.....................937-773-3420
Friedr Dick Corp
Farmingdale, NY.................800-554-3425
Frosty Factory of America Inc
Ruston, LA.....................800-544-4071
Gabriella Imports
Cleveland, OH..................800-544-8117
Garroutte
San Antonio, TX................888-457-4997
Gch Internatonal
Louisville, KY.................502-636-1374
GEA North America
Naperville, IL.................630-369-8100
Gea Us
Galesville, WI.................608-582-3081
GEM Equipment of Oregon Inc
Woodburn, OR...................503-982-9902
General Machinery Corp
Sheboygan, WI..................888-243-6622
General, Inc
Weston, FL.....................954-202-7419
Giles Enterprises Inc
Montgomery, AL.................800-288-1555
Gilson Co Inc
Lewis Center, OH...............800-444-1508
Glatt Air Techniques Inc
Ramsey, NJ.....................201-825-8700
Global Manufacturing
Little Rock, AR................800-551-3569
Globe Food Equipment Co
Moraine, OH....................800-347-5423
Goodnature Products
Orchard Park, NY...............800-875-3381
Goodway Industries Inc
Bohemia, NY....................800-943-4501
Grain Machinery Mfg Corp
Miami, FL......................305-620-2525
Gram Equipment of America
Tampa, FL......................813-248-1978
Granco Manufacturing Inc
San Ramon, CA..................510-652-8847
Grant-Letchworth
Tonawanda, NY..................716-692-1000
Graybill Machines Inc
Lititz, PA.....................717-626-5221
Great Western Manufacturing Company
Leavenworth, KS................800-682-3121
Green Belt Industries Inc
Buffalo, NY....................800-668-1114
Gregor Jonsson Inc
Lake Forest, IL................847-247-4200
Grote Co
Columbus, OH...................888-534-7683
H. Gartenberg & Company
Buffalo Grove, IL..............847-821-7590
Hamilton Beach Brands
Southern Pines, NC.............800-851-8900
Hamilton Kettles
Weirton, WV....................800-535-1882
Hayes & Stolz Indl Mfg LTD
Fort Worth, TX.................800-725-7272
HBD Industries
Salisbury, NC..................800-438-2312
Healdsburg Machine Company
Santa Rosa, CA.................707-433-3348
Health Star
Randolph, MA...................800-545-3639
Helken Equipment Co
Crystal Lake, IL...............847-697-3690
Hinds-Bock Corp
Bothell, WA....................425-885-1183
Hollymatic Corp
Countryside, IL................708-579-3700
Hosokawa/Bepex Corporation
Santa Rosa, CA.................707-586-6000
Howard Fabrication
City of Industry, CA...........626-961-0114
Hughes Co
Columbus, WI...................866-535-9303
Hydro-Miser
San Marcos, CA.................800-736-5083
Hydro-Thermal Corp
Waukesha, WI...................800-952-0121
Hyer Industries
Pembroke, MA...................781-826-8101
IBA Food Safety
Memphis, TN....................800-777-9012
Idaho Steel Products Inc
Idaho Falls, ID................208-522-1275
Ika-Works Inc
Wilmington, NC.................800-733-3037

Indiana Wire Company
Fremont, IN....................877-786-6883
Industrial Automation Systems
Santa Clarita, CA..............888-484-4427
Industrial Piping Inc
Pineville, NC..................800-951-0988
Insta-Pro International
Urbandale, IA..................800-383-4524
International Knife & Saw
Florence, SC...................800-354-9872
International Machinery Xchnge
Deerfield, WI..................800-279-0191
International Reserve Equipment Corporation
Clarendon Hills, IL............708-531-0680
Ivarson Inc
Milwaukee, WI..................414-351-0700
J C Ford Co
La Habra, CA...................714-871-7361
Jarvis Products Corp
Middletown, CT.................860-347-7271
Jay-Bee Manufacturing Inc
Tyler, TX......................800-445-0610
Jayhawk Manufacturing Co Inc
Hutchinson, KS.................866-886-8269
JBT Food Tech
Lakeland, FL...................863-683-5411
Jenike & Johanson Inc
Tyngsboro, MA..................978-649-3300
Jescorp
Des Plaines, IL................847-299-7800
Johnson Food Equipment Inc
Kansas City, KS................800-288-3434
Johnson Industries Intl
Windsor, WI....................608-846-4499
Johnson Pump of America
Hanover Park, IL...............847-671-7867
Juice Tree
Omaha, NE......................714-891-4425
JW Leser Company
Los Angeles, CA................323-731-4173
Kady International
Scarborough, ME................800-367-5239
Karl Schnell
New London, WI.................920-982-9974
Kasel Industries Inc
Denver, CO.....................800-218-4417
Kemutec Group Inc
Bristol, PA....................215-788-8013
Kerian Machines Inc
Grafton, ND....................701-352-0480
Key Technology Inc.
Walla Walla, WA................509-529-2161
Kinetic Equipment Company
Appleton, WI...................806-293-4471
King Company
Dallas, TX.....................507-451-3770
Kirkco Corp
Monroe, NC.....................704-289-7090
Kitcor Corp
Sun Valley, CA.................818-767-4800
Knott Slicers
Canton, MA.....................781-821-0925
Koch Equipment LLC
Kansas City, MO................816-931-4557
Kofab
Algona, IA.....................515-295-7265
Kohler Industries Inc
Lincoln, NE....................800-365-6708
Krispy Kist Company
Chicago, IL....................312-733-0900
Krogh Pump Co
Benicia, CA....................800-225-7644
Krones
Franklin, WI...................800-752-3787
Kuest Enterprise
Filer, ID......................208-326-4084
Kusel Equipment Company
Watertown, WI..................920-261-4112
L&A Process Systems
Modesto, CA....................209-581-0205
Laciny Brothers Inc
St Louis, MO...................314-862-8330
Langsenkamp Manufacturing
Indianapolis, IN...............877-585-1950
Latendorf Corporation
Brielle, NJ....................800-526-4057
Lauhoff Corporation
Detroit, MI....................313-259-0027
Le Jo Enterprises
Phoenixville, PA...............484-924-9187
Lee Financial Corporation
Dallas, TX.....................972-960-1001

Leland Limited Inc
South Plainfield, NJ...........800-984-9793
Leland Limited Inc
South Plainfield, NJ...........908-561-2000
Lematic Inc
Jackson, MI....................517-787-3301
Letrah International Corp
Fort Atkinson, WI..............920-563-6597
Lewis M Carter Mfg Co Inc
Donalsonville, GA..............800-332-8232
Liberty Engineering Co
Roscoe, IL.....................877-623-9065
Lil' Orbits
Minneapolis, MN................800-228-8305
Lima Sheet Metal
Lima, OH.......................419-229-1161
LineSource
Springfield, MA................413-747-9488
Linker Machines
Rockaway, NJ...................973-983-0001
Liquid Controls LLC
Lake Bluff, IL.................800-458-5262
Liquid Scale
New Brighton, MN...............888-633-2969
LIST
Acton, MA......................978-635-9521
Littleford Day
Florence, KY...................800-365-8555
Louisville Dryer Company
Louisville, KY.................800-735-3613
Luhr Jensen & Sons Inc
Hood River, OR.................541-386-3811
Lumenite Control Tech Inc
Franklin Park, IL..............800-323-8510
Luthi Machinery Company, Inc.
Pueblo, CO.....................719-948-1110
Lyco Wausau
Wausau, WI.....................715-845-7867
M O Industries Inc
Whippany, NJ...................973-386-9228
M-One Specialties
Salt Lake City, UT.............800-525-9223
Machanix Fabrication Inc
Chino, CA......................800-700-9701
Maddox/Adams International
Miami, FL......................305-592-3337
Magna Machine Co
Cincinnati, OH.................800-448-3475
Magnetool Inc
Troy, MI.......................248-588-5400
Magnuson
Pueblo, CO.....................719-948-9500
Maja Equipment Company
Omaha, NE......................402-346-6252
Mandeville Company
Minneapolis, MN................800-328-8490
Mar-Con Wire Belt
Richmond, BC...................877-962-7266
Marel Stork Poultry Processing
Gainesville, GA................770-532-7041
Market Forge Industries Inc
Everett, MA....................866-698-3188
Marlen International
Astoria, OR....................800-862-7536
Marlo Manufacturing
Boonton, NJ....................800-222-0450
Marriott Walker Corporation
Bingham Farms, MI..............248-644-6868
Martin Engineering
Neponset, IL...................800-766-2786
Martin/Baron
Irwindale, CA..................626-960-5153
Matcon Americas
Elmhurst, IL...................856-256-1330
Materials Transportation Co
Temple, TX.....................800-433-3110
Matfer Inc
Van Nuys, CA...................800-766-0333
Matiss
St Georges, QC.................888-562-8477
Maurer North America
Kansas City, MO................816-914-3518
May-Wes Manufacturing Inc
Hutchinson, MN.................800-788-6483
MBC Food Machinery Corp
Hackensack, NJ.................201-489-7000
McCarter Corporation
Norristown, PA.................610-272-3203
McCormick Enterprises
Arlington Heights, IL..........800-323-5201
MCD Technologies
Tacoma, WA.....................253-476-0968

MDS Nordion
Ottawa, ON 800-465-3666
Meadows Mills Inc
North Wilkesboro, NC 800-626-2282
Membrane System Specialist Inc
Wisconsin Rapids, WI 715-421-2333
Mepsco
Batavia, IL 800-323-8535
Mercury Equipment Company
Chino, CA 800-273-6688
Merlin Process Equipment
Houston, TX 713-221-1651
Mesa Laboratories Inc
Lakewood, CO 800-525-1215
Met-Pro Corp
Owosso, MI 800-392-7621
Metal Master Sales Corp
Glendale Heights, IL 800-488-8729
Metcraft
Grandview, MO 800-444-9624
Meyer & Garroutte Systems
San Antonio, TX 210-736-1811
Microdry
Crestwood, KY 502-241-8933
Microfluidics International
Westwood, MA 800-370-5452
Micropub Systems International
Rochester, NY 585-385-3990
MicroThermics, Inc.
Raleigh, NC 919-878-8045
Middleby Corp
Elgin, IL 847-741-3300
Midwest Metalcraft & Equipment
Windsor, MO 800-647-3167
Midwest Stainless
Menomonie, WI 715-235-5472
Millard Manufacturing Corp
La Vista, NE 800-662-4263
Miller Technical Svc
Plymouth, MI 734-414-1769
Modern Electronics Inc
Grand Cane, LA 318-872-4764
Modern Process Equipment Inc
Chicago, IL 773-254-3929
Moline Machinery LLC
Duluth, MN 800-767-5734
Monroe Environmental Corp
Monroe, MI 800-992-7707
Morris & Associates
Garner, NC 919-582-9200
Motom Corporation
Bensenville, IL 630-787-1995
Mouli Manufacturing Corporation
Belleville, NJ 800-789-8285
Moyno
Springfield, OH 937-327-3111
Mulligan Associates
Mequon, WI 800-627-2886
Mumper Machine Corporation
Butler, WI 262-781-8908
Munson Machinery Co
Utica, NY 800-944-6644
Murotech
St Marys, OH 800-565-6876
National Band Saw Co
Santa Clarita, CA 800-851-5050
National Drying Machry Co Inc
Philadelphia, PA 215-464-6070
National Equipment Corporation
Bronx, NY 800-237-8873
National Oilwell Varco
North Andover, MA 800-643-0641
NECO/Nebraska Engineering
Omaha, NE 800-367-6208
Nederman
Thomasville, NC 800-533-5286
Nemeth Engineering Assoc
Crestwood, KY 502-241-1502
Netzsch Pumps North America
Exton, PA 610-363-8010
Newlands Systems
Abbotsford, BC 604-855-4890
Niro
Hudson, WI 715-386-9371
Northwind Inc
Alpena, AR 877-937-2585
Norvell Co Inc
Fort Scott, KS 800-653-3147
Nothum Food Processing Systems
Springfield, MO 800-435-1297
Nowakowski
Franklin, WI 800-394-5866

NST Metals
Louisville, KY 502-584-5846
Nu CO2 LLC
Stuart, FL 800-472-2855
Nutec Manufacturing Inc
New Lenox, IL 815-722-5348
Nutrifaster Inc
Seattle, WA 800-800-2641
Nydree Flooring
Forest, VA 800-682-5698
Oak Barrel Winecraft
Berkeley, CA 510-849-0400
Oden Machinery
Tonawanda, NY 800-658-3622
Odenberg Engineering
West Sacramento, CA 800-688-8396
Omcan Inc.
Mississauga, ON 800-465-0234
Omega Products Inc
Harrisburg, PA 800-633-3401
Omni International
Kennesaw, GA 800-776-4431
Oxbo International Corp
Clear Lake, WI 800-628-6196
P & F Machine
Turlock, CA 209-667-2515
Pacific Process Technology
La Jolla, CA 858-551-3298
Pacific Tank
Adelanto, CA 800-449-5838
Packaging & Processing Equipment
Ayr, ON 519-622-6666
Packaging Progressions
Collegeville, PA 610-489-9096
Paget Equipment Co
Marshfield, WI 715-384-3158
Paoli Properties
Rockford, IL 815-965-0621
Paradigm Technologies
Eugene, OR 541-345-5543
Paragon Group USA
St Petersburg, FL 800-835-6962
Parkson Corporation
Fort Lauderdale, FL 954-974-6610
Patterson Industries
Scarborough, ON 800-336-1110
Patterson-Kelley   Hars Company
East Stroudsburg, PA 570-421-7500
Paul O. Abbe
Bensenville, IL 630-350-2200
Pavailler Distribution Company
Northvale, NJ 201-767-0766
Pavan USA Inc
Emigsville, PA 717-767-4889
Paxton Corp
Bristol, RI 401-396-9062
Peerless Food Equipment
Sidney, OH 937-492-4158
Peerless Machinery Corporation
Sidney, OH 800-999-3327
Peerless-Winsmith Inc
Springville, NY 716-592-9310
Peterson Fiberglass Laminates
Shell Lake, WI 715-468-2306
Phase II Pasta Machine Inc
Farmingdale, NY 800-457-5070
Piab Vacuum Products
Hingham, MA 800-321-7422
Pickwick Manufacturing Svc
Cedar Rapids, IA 800-397-9797
Pier 1 Imports
Woodcliff Lake, NJ 800-448-9993
Planet Products Corp
Blue Ash, OH 513-984-5544
Polar Process
Plattsville, ON 877-896-8077
PolyMaid Company
Largo, FL 800-206-9188
Prawnto Systems
Caddo Mills, TX 800-426-7254
Preferred Machining Corporation
Englewood, CO 303-761-1535
Pressure Pack
Williamsburg, VA 757-220-3693
Prince Castle Inc
Carol Stream, IL 800-722-7853
Prince Industries Inc
Murrayville, GA 800-441-3303
Pro Scientific Inc
Oxford, CT 800-584-3776
Procedyne Corp
New Brunswick, NJ 732-249-8347

Process Engineering & Fabrication
Afton, VA 800-852-7975
Process Systems
Barrington, IL 847-842-8618
Production Packaging & Processing Equipment
Company
Savannah, GA 912-856-4281
Professional Engineering Assoc
Louisville, KY 502-429-0432
Pulva Corp
Valencia, PA 800-878-5828
Puritan Manufacturing Inc
Omaha, NE 800-331-0487
Putsch & Co Inc
Fletcher, NC 800-847-8427
Quality Fabrication & Design
Coppell, TX 972-304-3266
Quality Industries
Cleveland, OH 216-961-5566
Quantum Topping Systems Quantum Technical Services
Inc
Frankfort, IL 888-464-1540
R Murphy Co Inc
Ayer, MA 888-772-3481
R.G. Stephens Engineering
Long Beach, CA 800-499-3001
Ram Equipment Co
Waukesha, WI 262-513-1114
Ranger Blade Manufacturing Company
Traer, IA 800-377-7860
Raque Food Systems
Louisville, KY 502-267-9641
RAS Process Equipment Inc
Trenton, NJ 609-371-1220
Raytheon Co
Waltham, MA 781-522-3000
RBS Fab Inc
Hummelstown, PA 717-566-9513
Readco Kurimoto LLC
York, PA 800-395-4959
Reading Bakery Systems Inc
Robesonia, PA 610-693-5816
Regal Ware Inc
Kewaskum, WI 262-626-2121
Renard Machine Company
Green Bay, WI 920-432-8412
Respirometry Plus, LLC
Fond Du Lac, WI 800-328-7518
Rheo-Tech
Gurnee, IL 847-367-1557
Rheon USA
Irvine, CA 949-768-1900
Rhodes Bakery Equipment
Portland, OR 800-426-3813
RMF Companies
Grandview, MO 816-839-9258
Robot Coupe
Ridgeland, MS 800-824-1646
Rome Machine & Foundry Co
Rome, GA 800-538-7663
Rondo Inc
Moonachie, NJ 800-882-0633
Rosenwach Tank Co LLC
Long Island City, NY 212-972-4411
Ross Cook
Silver Spring, MD 800-233-7339
Ross Engineering Inc
Savannah, GA 800-524-7677
Ruiz Flour Tortillas
Riverside, CA 909-947-7811
S J Controls Inc
Signal Hill, CA 562-494-1400
Samson Controls
Baytown, TX 281-383-3677
Samuel Pressure Vessel Group
Marinette, WI 715-453-5326
Samuel Underberg Food Store
Brooklyn, NY 718-363-0787
San-Rec-Pak
Tualatin, OR 503-692-5552
Sanchelima International
Miami, FL 305-591-4343
Sandvik Process Systems
Sweden, NJ 973-790-1600
Sanford Redmond Company
Stamford, CT 203-351-9800
SaniServ
Mooresville, IN 800-733-8073
Sasib Beverage & Food North America
Plano, TX 800-558-3814
Satake USA
Stafford, TX 281-276-3600

Savage Brothers Company
Elk Grove Vlg, IL 800-342-0973
Scherping Systems
Winsted, MN 320-485-4401
Schlagel Inc
Cambridge, MN 800-328-8002
Schlueter Company
Janesville, WI 800-359-1700
Schutte Buffalo Hammermill
Buffalo, NY 800-447-4634
Scientific Process & Research
Kendall Park, NJ 800-868-4777
Scott Turbon Mixer
Adelanto, CA 800-285-8512
Seepex Inc
Enon, OH 800-695-3659
Sellers Engineering Division
Danville, KY 859-236-3181
Semi-Bulk Systems Inc
Fenton, MO 800-732-8769
Separators Inc
Indianapolis, IN 800-233-9022
Sepragen Corp
Hayward, CA 510-475-0650
Shanzer Grain Dryer
Sioux Falls, SD 800-843-9887
Sharp Brothers
Bayonne, NJ 201-339-0404
Sharpsville Container Corp
Sharpsville, PA 800-645-1248
Silver Weibull
Aurora, CO 303-373-2311
Silverson Machines Inc
East Longmeadow, MA 800-204-6400
Simmons Engineering Corporation
Wheeling, IL 800-252-3381
Simplimatic Automation
Forest, VA 800-294-2003
Sine Pump
Arvada, CO 888-504-8301
Smico Manufacturing Co Inc
Oklahoma City, OK 800-351-9088
Smith-Berger Marine
Seattle, WA 206-764-4650
Solbern Corp
Fairfield, NJ 973-227-3030
Somerset Industries
Billerica, MA 800-772-4404
Sonic Corp
Stratford, CT 866-493-1378
Sonics & Materials Inc
Newtown, CT 800-745-1105
Sortex
Fremont, CA 510-797-5000
South River Machine
Hackensack, NJ 201-487-1736
South Shore Controls Inc
Perry, OH 440-259-2500
Southern Ag Co Inc
Blakely, GA 229-723-4262
SP Industries Inc
Warminster, PA 800-523-2327
Sperling Industries
Omaha, NE 402-556-4070
Sperling Industries
Omaha, NE 800-647-5062
Spray Dynamics LTD
St Clair, MO 800-260-7366
SPX Flow Inc
Charlotte, NC 800-252-5200
Stainless Fabrication Inc
Springfield, MO 800-397-8265
Stainless Specialists Inc
Wausau, WI 800-236-4155
Stainless Steel Fabricator Inc
La Mirada, CA 714-739-9904
Standard Casing Company
Lyndhurst, NJ 800-847-4141
Stanfos
Edmonton, AB 800-661-5648
STARMIX srl
Marano, VI 044- 57- 659
Stephan Machinery, Inc.
Mundelein, IL 800-783-7426
Steri Technologies Inc
Bohemia, NY 800-253-7140
Stock America Inc
Grafton, WI 262-375-4100
Stork Townsend Inc.
Des Moines, IA 800-247-8609
Straight Line Filters
Wilmington, DE 302-654-8805

Strategic Equipment & Supply
Scottsdale, AZ 480-905-5530
Straub Designs Co
St Louis Park, MN 952-546-6686
Stricklin Co
Dallas, TX 214-637-1030
Sturdi-Bilt Restaurant Equipment
Whitmore Lake, MI 800-521-2895
Stutz Products Corp
Hartford City, IN 765-348-2510
Superior Food Machinery Inc
Pico Rivera, CA 800-944-0396
Sweco Inc
Florence, KY 800-807-9326
Swirl Freeze Corp
Salt Lake City, UT 800-262-4275
T & S Perfection Chain Prods
Cullman, AL 888-856-4864
T D Sawvel Co
Maple Plain, MN 877-488-1816
T.K. Products
Anaheim, CA 714-621-0267
Taylor Manufacturing Co
Moultrie, GA 229-985-5445
TDH
Sand Springs, OK 888-251-7961
Techno-Design
Union, KY 800-641-1822
Tema Systems Inc
Cincinnati, OH 513-792-2840
Tetra Pak
Vernon Hills, IL 847-955-6000
Tetra Pak
Denton, TX 940-380-4630
TGW International
Florence, KY 800-407-0173
Thomas L. Green & Company
Robenosia, PA 610-693-5816
Thoreson Mc Cosh Inc
Troy, MI 800-959-0805
Tindall Packaging
Vicksburg, MI 269-649-1163
Todd's
Des Moines, IA 800-247-5363
Tolan Machinery Company
Rockaway, NJ 973-983-7212
Torpac Capsules
Fairfield, NJ 973-244-1125
Tranter INC
Wichita Falls, TX 940-723-7125
Tri-Pak Machinery Inc
Harlingen, TX 956-423-5140
Triple S Dynamics Inc
Breckenridge, TX 800-527-2116
Tru Form Plastics
Gardena, CA 800-510-7999
TSA Griddle Systems
Kelowna, BC 250-491-9025
Tuthill Vacuum & Blower Systems
Springfield, MO 800-825-6937
TWM Manufacturing
Leamington, ON 888-495-4831
Unifiller Systems
Delta, BC 888-733-8444
Union Process
Akron, OH 330-929-3333
United Mc Gill Corp
Groveport, OH 614-829-1200
United Performance Metals
Northbrook, IL 888-922-0040
UniTrak Corporation
Port Hope, ON 866-883-5749
Univex Corp
Salem, NH 800-258-6358
Vacuum Barrier Corp
Woburn, MA 781-933-3570
Van Air Systems
Lake City, PA 800-840-9906
Vanmark Equipment
Creston, IA 800-523-6261
Varimixer North America
Charlotte, NC 800-221-1138
Vector Corp
Marion, IA 319-377-8263
Viatec
Victoria, BC 800-942-4702
Viking Machine & Design Inc
De Pere, WI 888-286-2116
Vincent Corp
Tampa, FL 813-248-2650
Vineco International Products
St Catharines, ON 905-685-9342

Virginia Industrial Services
Waynesboro, VA 800-825-3050
VitaMinder Company
Providence, RI 800-858-8840
Vitamix
Olmsted Twp, OH 800-437-4654
Vortron Smokehouse/Ovens
Iron Ridge, WI 800-874-1949
Vulcan Food Equipment Group
Baltimore, MD 800-814-2028
Walton's Inc
Wichita, KS 800-835-2832
Waring Products
Torrington, CT 800-492-7464
Warwick Manufacturing & Equip
North Brunswick, NJ 732-729-0400
Washington Frontier
Grandview, WA 509-469-7662
Waukesha Cherry-Burrell
Louisville, KY 502-491-4310
Waukesha Cherry-Burrell
Louisville, KY 800-252-5200
WCB Ice Cream
Philadelphia, PA 215-425-4320
Webb's Machine Design
Clearwater, FL 727-799-1768
Weiler & Company
Whitewater, WI 800-558-9507
Welbilt Corporation
Stamford, CT 203-325-8300
Welliver Metal Products Corporation
Salem, OR 503-362-1568
Wemas Metal Products
Calgary, AB 403-276-4451
Western Polymer Corp
Moses Lake, WA 800-362-6845
Westfalia Separator
Northvale, NJ 800-722-6622
White Mountain Freezer
Kansas City, MO 816-943-4100
Wilch Manufacturing
Topeka, KS 785-267-2762
Wilevco Inc
Billerica, MA 978-667-0400
Wyssmont Co Inc
Fort Lee, NJ 201-947-4600
X-Press Manufacturing
New Braunfels, TX 800-365-9440
Yargus Manufacturing Inc
Marshall, IL 217-826-8059
York Saw & Knife
York, PA 800-233-1969
Zenith Cutter
Loves Park, IL. 800-223-5202
Zitropack Limited
Addison, IL 630-543-1016

Parts

A C Tool & Machine Co
Louisville, KY 502-447-5505
A-L-L Magnetics Inc
Anaheim, CA 800-262-4638
ABB
Cary, NC 800-435-7365
Accuflex Industrial Hose LTD
Romulus, MI 734-713-4100
Action Technology
Prussia, PA 217-935-8311
AFT Advanced Fiber Technologies
Sherbrooke, QC 800-668-7273
AGC
Bristow, VA 800-825-8820
Alard Equipment Corp
Williamson, NY 315-589-4511
All Weather Energy Systems
Plymouth, MI 888-636-8324
American Extrusion Intl
South Beloit, IL 815-624-6616
American Manufacturing-Engrng
Cleveland, OH 800-822-9402
Andgar Corp
Ferndale, WA 360-366-9900
Apex Packing & Rubber Co
Farmingdale, NY 800-645-9110
APV Americas
Delavan, WI 800-252-5200
Artisan Controls Corp
Randolph, NJ 800-457-4950
Automatic Specialties Inc
Marlborough, MA 800-445-2370

Ay Machine Company
Ephrata, PA .717-733-0335
Baader-Linco
Kansas City, KS 800-288-3434
Baker Hughes
Houston, TX
Baldewein Company
Lake Forrest, IL 800-424-5544
Baldor Electric Co
Fort Smith, AR 479-646-4711
Bardo Abrasives
Ridgewood, NY 718-456-6400
Beacon Specialties
New York, NY 800-221-9405
Becker Brothers Graphite Co
Maywood, IL. 708-410-0700
Bert Manufacturing
Gardnerville, NV 775-265-3900
Bodine Electric Co
Northfield, IL 773-478-3515
Boston Gear
Boston, MA. 888-999-9860
Bradford A Ducon Company
Pewaukee, WI. 800-789-1718
Cal Controls
Gurnee, IL. .800-866-6659
Candy Manufacturing Co
Niles, IL 847-588-2639
Chicago Stainless Eqpt Inc
Palm City, FL 800-927-8575
Chipmaker Tooling Supply
Whittier, CA 800-659-5840
Continental Disc Corp
Liberty, MO. 816-792-1500
Conxall Corporation
Villa Park, IL. 630-834-7504
Corenco
Santa Rosa, CA 888-267-3626
Cornell Pump Company
Portland, OR 503-653-0330
Crouzet Corporation
Carrollton, TX. 800-677-5311
Debbie Wright Sales
Fort Worth, TX 800-935-7883
Duralite Inc
Riverton, CT. 888-432-8797
Dyna-Veyor Inc
Newark, NJ 800-326-5009
Electro Cam Corp
Roscoe, IL. 800-228-5487
Esco Products Inc
Houston, TX 800-966-5514
Fabreeka International
Boise, ID 800-423-4469
Falcon Fabricators Inc
Nashville, TN 615-832-0027
Florida Knife Co
Sarasota, FL 800-966-5643
Gary W. Pritchard Engineer
Huntington Beach, CA 714-893-5441
GED, LLC
Laurel, DE .302-856-1756
General Grinding Inc
Oakland, CA 800-806-6037
Glo-Quartz Electric Heater
Mentor, OH. 800-321-3574
Good Idea
Northampton, MA. 800-462-9237
Granco Manufacturing Inc
San Ramon, CA 510-652-8847
Graphite Metalizing Corp
Yonkers, NY 914-968-8400
Green Belt Industries Inc
Buffalo, NY. 800-668-1114
Greenbridge
Mentor, OH. 440-357-1500
Gridpath, Inc.
Stony Creek, ON. 905-643-0955
H. Yamamoto
Port Washington, NY 718-821-7700
Habasit Canada Limited
Oakville, ON. 905-827-4131
Hansaloy Corp
Davenport, IA 800-553-4992
Harrington's Equipment Co
Fairfield, PA 800-468-8467
Hayes & Stolz Indl Mfg LTD
Fort Worth, TX 800-725-7272
Hi-Temp Inc
Tuscumbia, AL 800-239-5066
Home Rubber Co
Trenton, NJ 800-257-9441

Hydra-Flex Inc
Livonia, MI. 800-234-0832
Industrial Product Corp
Ho Ho Kus, NJ 800-472-5913
Infitec Inc
East Syracuse, NY 800-334-0837
International Tank & Pipe Co
Clackamas, OR 888-988-0011
Introdel Products
Itasca, IL 800-323-4772
Ivarson Inc
Milwaukee, WI. 414-351-0700
Jokamsco Group
Waterford,, NY 518-237-6416
Keystone Rubber Corporation
Greenbackville, VA. 800-394-5661
Kinetic Equipment Company
Appleton, WI 806-293-4471
King Company
Dallas, TX .507-451-3770
Knobs Unlimited
Bowling Green, OH 419-353-8215
L.C. Thompson Company
Kenosha, WI. 800-558-4018
Lako Tool & Mfg Inc
Perrysburg, OH. 800-228-2982
Lambeth Band Corporation
New Bedford, MA 508-984-4700
LEESON Electric Corp
Grafton, WI. 262-377-8810
Lil' Orbits
Minneapolis, MN 800-228-8305
Lucas Industrial
Cedar Hill, TX 800-877-1720
M-One Specialties
Salt Lake City, UT 800-525-9223
Master Magnetics
Castle Rock, CO 800-525-3536
Mckey Perforating Co Inc
New Berlin, WI. 800-345-7373
Meadows Mills Inc
North Wilkesboro, NC 800-626-2282
Metal Master Sales Corp
Glendale Heights, IL. 800-488-8729
Miller Technical Svc
Plymouth, MI 734-414-1769
Modern Process Equipment Inc
Chicago, IL. 773-254-3929
Moyno
Springfield, OH. 937-327-3111
Nalge Process Technologies Group
Rochester, NY. 585-586-8800
National Band Saw Co
Santa Clarita, CA 800-851-5050
National Metal Industries
West Springfield, MA 800-628-8850
Newman Sanitary Gasket Co
Lebanon, OH. 513-932-7379
Northland Process Piping
Isle, MN 320-679-2119
Oerlikon Leybold Vacuum
Export, PA. 724-327-5700
Pacer Pumps
Lancaster, PA 800-233-3861
Paramount Packing & Rubber Inc
Baltimore, MD 866-727-7225
Paul Mueller Co Inc
Springfield, MO 800-683-5537
Payne Controls Co
Scott Depot, WV 800-331-1345
Piab Vacuum Products
Hingham, MA 800-321-7422
Pres-Air-Trol Corporation
Altoona, WI. 800-431-2625
Pure Fit Nutrition Bars
Irvine, CA 866-787-3348
Qosina Corporation
Ronkonkoma, NY 631-242-3000
Quadrant Epp USA Inc
Fort Wayne, IN 800-628-7264
Quality Industries
Cleveland, OH 216-961-5566
Rath Manufacturing Company
Janesville, WI 800-367-7284
Rigidized Metal Corp
Buffalo, NY. 800-836-2580
Robert-James Sales
Buffalo, NY. 800-777-1325
Salem-Republic Rubber Co
Sebring, OH 800-425-5079
Sanchelima International
Miami, FL .305-591-4343

Sani-Fit
Pasadena, CA 626-395-7895
Sanitary Couplers
Springboro, OH. 513-743-0144
Schwartz Manufacturing Co
Two Rivers, WI. 920-793-1375
Sellers Engineering Division
Danville, KY. 859-236-3181
Senior Flexonics
Bartlett, IL. .800-473-0474
Sew-Eurodrive Inc
Lyman, SC. 864-439-8792
Sharon Manufacturing Inc
Deer Park, NY. 800-424-6455
Simolex Rubber Corp
Plymouth, MI 734-453-4500
Simply Manufacturing
Prairie Du Sac, WI. 608-643-6656
Sine Pump
Arvada, CO 888-504-8301
Specialty Blades
Staunton, VA 540-248-2200
STD Precision Gear
West Bridgewater, MA 888-783-4327
Strahman Valves Inc
Bethlehem, PA 877-787-2462
Stutz Products Corp
Hartford City, IN. 765-348-2510
Thomas Precision, Inc.
Rice Lake, WI. 800-657-4808
Top Line Process Equipment Company
Bradford, PA 800-458-6095
TWM Manufacturing
Leamington, ON. 888-495-4831
Union Cord Products Company
Schaumburg, IL. 847-240-1500
United Performance Metals
Northbrook, IL 888-922-0040
US Tsubaki Holdings Inc
Wheeling, IL. 800-323-7790
Valvinox
Iberville, QC 450-346-1981
Vaughn Belting Co-Main Acct
Spartanburg, SC 800-533-9086
Viking Machine & Design Inc
De Pere, WI. 888-286-2116
Warner Electric Inc
South Beloit, IL 800-234-3369
Washington Frontier
Grandview, WA. 509-469-7662
Waukesha Cherry-Burrell
Louisville, KY 800-252-5200
Wilden Pump & Engineering LLC
Grand Terrace, CA 909-422-1700
Wire Belt Co of America
Londonderry, NH 603-644-2500
Womack International Inc
Vallejo, CA .707-647-2370
World Wide Fitting Corp
Vernon Hills, IL 800-393-9894
Yates Industries Inc
St Clair Shores, MI 586-778-7680
Zenith Cutter
Loves Park, IL. 800-223-5202

Rebuilt & Used

A C Tool & Machine Co
Louisville, KY 502-447-5505
A&M Industries
Sioux Falls, SD 800-888-2615
Alard Equipment Corp
Williamson, NY 315-589-4511
Albion Machine & Tool Co
Albion, MI. .517-629-9135
Alpha Resources Inc
Stevensville, MI 800-833-3083
Ay Machine Company
Ephrata, PA 717-733-0335
Berkshire PPM
Litchfield, CT 860-567-3118
Big State Spring Companyy
Corpus Christi, TX 800-880-0244
Buffalo Wire Works Co Inc
Buffalo, NY. 800-828-7028
Champion Trading Corporation
Marlboro, NJ 732-780-4200
Commodity Traders International
Trilla, IL 217-235-4322
Custom Food Machinery
Stockton, CA. 209-463-4343

Delphi Food Machinery
  Tempe, AZ .480-483-8361
Denman Equipment
  Memphis, TN 901-755-7135
Equipment Specialists Inc
  Manassas, VA 703-361-2227
Esco Products Inc
  Houston, TX 800-966-5514
Food Resources International
  Concord, ON. 905-482-8967
GED, LLC
  Laurel, DE .302-856-1756
Hallmark Equipment Inc
  Morgan Hill, CA 408-782-2600
Harrington's Equipment Co
  Fairfield, PA 800-468-8467
Health Star
  Randolph, MA 800-545-3639
Helken Equipment Co
  Crystal Lake, IL 847-697-3690
International Machinery Xchnge
  Deerfield, WI 800-279-0191
Jarboe Equipment
  Georgetown, DE 800-699-7988
Lehman Sales Associates
  Sun Prairie, WI 608-575-7712
Machinery Corporation ofAmerica
  Capitola, CA 831-479-9901
Mandeville Company
  Minneapolis, MN 800-328-8490
Mba Suppliers Inc.
  Bellevue, NE. 800-467-1201
McNeil Food Machinery
  Stockton, CA. 209-463-4343
Miller Technical Svc
  Plymouth, MI 734-414-1769
National Equipment Corporation
  Bronx, NY. .800-237-8873
Naughton Equipment Sales
  Fort Calhoun, NE 866-858-4682
Pacific Process Machinery
  Santa Rosa, CA. 707-523-4122
Packaging & Processing Equipment
  Ayr, ON 519-622-6666
Paxton Corp
  Bristol, RI 401-396-9062
Peerless Machinery Corporation
  Sidney, OH .800-999-3327
Polar Process
  Plattsville, ON. 877-896-8077
Regal Equipment Inc
  Ravenna, OH 330-325-9000
Separators Inc
  Indianapolis, IN 800-233-9022
Stone Enterprises Inc.
  Omaha, NE .877-653-0500
Thomas Precision, Inc.
  Rice Lake, WI 800-657-4808
Warwick Manufacturing & Equip
  North Brunswick, NJ 732-729-0400
Wohl Associates Inc
  Bohemia, NY 631-244-7979
Zitropack Limited
  Addison, IL. 630-543-1016

Frozen Custard Processing

Emery Thompson Machine &Supply Company
  Brooksville, FL. 718-588-7300

Frozen Foods Processing

Automated Food Systems
  Waxahachie, TX 469-517-0470
Chart Inc
  New Prague, MN 800-428-3777
Design Technology Corporation
  Billerica, MA 978-663-7000
Dipwell Co
  Northampton, MA. 413-587-4673
Dole Refrigerating Co
  Lewisburg, TN 800-251-8990
Emery Thompson Machine &Supply Company
  Brooksville, FL. 718-588-7300
Flodin
  Moses Lake, WA. 509-766-2996
Food Engineering Unlimited
  Fullerton, CA 714-879-8762
Frazier & Son
  Conroe, TX .800-365-5438
Gabriella Imports
  Cleveland, OH. 800-544-8117

MBC Food Machinery Corp
  Hackensack, NJ. 201-489-7000
Millard Manufacturing Corp
  La Vista, NE 800-662-4263
Multi-Fill Inc
  West Jordan, UT 801-280-1570
Raque Food Systems
  Louisville, KY 502-267-9641
Techno-Design
  Union, KY. .800-641-1822
TWM Manufacturing
  Leamington, ON 888-495-4831
UniTrak Corporation
  Port Hope, ON 866-883-5749

Fruit Processing

A.K. Robins
  Baltimore, MD 800-486-9656
ABCO Industries Limited
  Lunenburg, NS 866-634-8821
Advance Energy Technologies
  Halfmoon, NY. 800-724-0198
Altman Industries
  Gray, GA. 478-986-3116
Ametek Technical & Industrial Products
  Kent, OH. 215-256-6601
Andgar Corp
  Ferndale, WA 360-366-9900
Ashlock Co
  San Leandro, CA. 510-351-0560
Atlas Pacific Engineering
  Pueblo, CO .719-948-3040
Autoline
  Reedley, CA 559-638-5432
Automated Food Systems
  Waxahachie, TX 469-517-0470
Bake Star
  Somerset, WI. 763-427-7611
BEI
  South Haven, MI. 800-364-7425
Bmh Equipment Inc
  Sacramento, CA 800-350-8828
BNW Industries
  Tippecanoe, IN 574-353-7855
Branson Ultrasonics Corp
  Danbury, CT 203-796-0400
Brown International Corp LLC
  Winter Haven, FL 863-299-2111
Chop-Rite Two Inc
  Harleysville, PA 800-683-5858
Citra-Tech
  Lefkosia, CY
Coastline Equipment Inc
  Bellingham, WA 360-734-8509
Commercial Dehydrator Systems
  Eugene, OR. 800-369-4283
Corenco
  Santa Rosa, CA 888-267-3626
Custom Food Machinery
  Stockton, CA. 209-463-4343
Dixie Canner Machine Shop
  Athens, GA .706-549-0592
Dunkley International Inc
  Kalamazoo, MI 800-666-1264
Durand-Wayland Inc
  Lagrange, GA 800-241-2308
Elliott Manufacturing Co Inc
  Fresno, CA .559-233-6235
Eveready Automation
  Frederick, PA 610-754-1775
F.B. Pease Company
  Rochester, NY. 585-475-1870
Globe Machine
  Tacoma, WA 800-523-6575
Goodnature Products
  Orchard Park, NY 800-875-3381
Healdsburg Machine Company
  Santa Rosa, CA 707-433-3348
JBT Food Tech
  Lakeland, FL. 863-683-5411
Juice Tree
  Omaha, NE .714-891-4425
Kerian Machines Inc
  Grafton, ND 701-352-0480
Key Technology Inc.
  Walla Walla, WA. 509-529-2161
Lyco Wausau
  Wausau, WI. 715-845-7867
Mulligan Associates
  Mequon, WI 800-627-2886

Murotech
  St Marys, OH 800-565-6876
Odenberg Engineering
  West Sacramento, CA. 800-688-8396
Paxton Corp
  Bristol, RI 401-396-9062
Paxton Products Inc
  Blue Ash, OH 800-441-7475
Pick Heaters
  West Bend, WI 800-233-9030
Tew Manufacturing Corp
  Penfield, NY 800-380-5839
Tri-Pak Machinery Inc
  Harlingen, TX. 956-423-5140
TWM Manufacturing
  Leamington, ON. 888-495-4831
UniTrak Corporation
  Port Hope, ON 866-883-5749
Vanmark Equipment
  Creston, IA .800-523-6261
Vincent Corp
  Tampa, FL 813-248-2650
Webb's Machine Design
  Clearwater, FL 727-799-1768
White Mountain Freezer
  Kansas City, MO. 816-943-4100

Graders

Fruit, Vegetable & Nut

A.K. Robins
  Baltimore, MD 800-486-9656
Berkshire PPM
  Litchfield, CT 860-567-3118
Commercial Manufacturing
  Fresno, CA .559-237-1855
Descon EDM
  Brocton, NY 716-792-9300
Durand-Wayland Inc
  Lagrange, GA 800-241-2308
Hughes Co
  Columbus, WI 866-535-9303
Kerian Machines Inc
  Grafton, ND 701-352-0480
Key Technology Inc.
  Walla Walla, WA. 509-529-2161
Sortex
  Fremont, CA 510-797-5000
Tri-Pak Machinery Inc
  Harlingen, TX. 956-423-5140
Welliver Metal Products Corporation
  Salem, OR. .503-362-1568

Grain, Rice & Seed

ANDRITZ Inc
  Muncy, PA. .704-943-4343
Commercial Manufacturing
  Fresno, CA .559-237-1855
Commodity Traders International
  Trilla, IL. 217-235-4322
Crippen Manufacturing Co
  St Louis, MI 800-872-2474
Grain Machinery Mfg Corp
  Miami, FL. .305-620-2525
Sortex
  Fremont, CA 510-797-5000
Welliver Metal Products Corporation
  Salem, OR. .503-362-1568

Grain Elevator

ANDRITZ Inc
  Muncy, PA. .704-943-4343
Chief Industries
  Kearney, NE 800-359-8833
Dunrite Inc
  Fremont, NE 800-782-3061
NECO/Nebraska Engineering
  Omaha, NE .800-367-6208
Schlagel Inc
  Cambridge, MN 800-328-8002
Screw Conveyor Corp
  Hammond, IN 219-931-1450
Universal Industries Inc
  Cedar Falls, IA 800-553-4446
Yargus Manufacturing Inc
  Marshall, IL 217-826-8059

Graters

Acme International
Maplewood, NJ 973-416-0400
Amco Metals Indl
City of Industry, CA 626-855-2550
Browne & Company
Markham, ON 905-475-6104
Corenco
Santa Rosa, CA 888-267-3626
Giunta Brothers
Philadelphia, PA 215-389-9670
Leggett & Platt Storage
Vernon Hills, IL 847-816-6246
Polar Process
Plattsville, ON. 877-896-8077
Samuel Underberg Food Store
Brooklyn, NY 718-363-0787

Grinders

Bulk Grinding

Ditting USA
Glendale, CA 800-835-5992
La Poblana Food Machines
Mesa, AZ. .480-258-2091
Marlen Research Corporation
Shawnee Mission, KS. 913-888-3333
Reiser
Canton, MA 734-821-1290
Risco USA Corp
South Easton, MA. 888-474-7267
Weiler Equipment
Whitewater, WI. 800-558-9507

Hamburger & Meat Patty Processing

Bridge Machine Company
Palmyra, NJ. 877-754-1800
Daleco
West Chester, PA. 610-429-0181
Design Technology Corporation
Billerica, MA 978-663-7000
Hollymatic Corp
Countryside, IL. 708-579-3700
Nieco Corporation
Windsor, CA 800-643-2656
Nutec Manufacturing Inc
New Lenox, IL 815-722-5348
Reiser
Canton, MA 734-821-1290

Heat Exchangers

A & B Process Systems Corp
Stratford, WI. 888-258-2789
AFGO Mechanical Svc Inc
Astoria, NY. 800-438-2346
AGC
Bristow, VA. 800-825-8820
Allegheny Bradford Corp
Bradford, PA. 800-542-0650
Allied Engineering
North Vancouver, BC 877-929-1214
Alloy Hardfacing & Engineering
Jordan, MN 800-328-8408
Andgar Corp
Ferndale, WA 360-366-9900
API Heat Transfer Inc
Buffalo, NY. 877-274-4328
Apollo Sheet Metal
Kennewick, WA 509-586-1104
APV Americas
Delavan, WI 800-252-5200
Baltimore Aircoil Co
Jessup, MD 410-799-1300
Bimetalix
Sullivan, WI 262-593-8066
Buffalo Technologies Corporation
Buffalo, NY. 800-332-2419
Carmel Engineering
Kirklin, IN. 888-427-0497
Carnes Company
Verona, WI 608-845-6411
Central Fabricators Inc
Cincinnati, OH 800-909-8265
Chester-Jensen Co., Inc.
Chester, PA. 800-685-3750
Chil-Con Products
Brantford, ON. 800-263-0086

Cooling Products Inc
Broken Arrow, OK 918-251-8588
Doucette Industries
York, PA 800-445-7511
E.L. Nickell Company
Constantine, MI 269-435-2475
Eclipse Innovative Ther mal Solutions
Toledo, OH 800-662-3966
Eischen Enterprises
Fresno, CA 559-834-0013
Ellett Industries
Port Coquitlam, BC. 604-941-8211
Enerquip Inc
Medford, WI 715-748-5888
EVAPCO Inc
Taneytown, MD 410-876-3782
Feldmeier Equipment Inc
Syracuse, NY 315-454-8608
Flat Plate Inc
York, PA 888-854-2500
Franrica Systems
Stockton, CA 209-948-2811
Gaston County Dyeing Mach Co
Mt Holly, NC 704-822-5000
GEA Refrigeration North America
York, PA 800-888-4337
Gram Equipment of America
Tampa, FL 813-248-1978
Harris Equipment Corp
Melrose Park, IL 800-365-0315
Hebeler Corp
Tonawanda, NY 800-486-4709
International Machinery Xchnge
Deerfield, WI 800-279-0191
Lake Process Systems Inc
Lake Barrington, IL 800-331-9260
Louisville Dryer Company
Louisville, KY 800-735-3613
Ludell Manufacturing Co
Milwaukee, WI 800-558-0800
M G Newell Corp
Greensboro, NC 800-334-0231
MadgeTech, Inc.
Contoocook, NH 603-456-2011
Midwest Stainless
Menomonie, WI 715-235-5472
National Oilwell Varco
North Andover, MA 800-643-0641
Noren Products Inc
Menlo Park, CA 866-936-6736
Patterson Industries
Scarborough, ON 800-336-1110
Pick Heaters
West Bend, WI 800-233-9030
RAS Process Equipment Inc
Trenton, NJ 609-371-1220
Samuel Pressure Vessel Group
Marinette, WI 715-453-5326
Seattle Boiler Works Inc
Seattle, WA 206-762-0737
Seattle Refrigeration & Manufacturing
Seattle, WA 800-228-8881
Standard Refrigeration Co
Wood Dale, IL. 708-345-5400
Statco Engineering
Huntington Beach, CA 800-421-0362
Svedala Industries
Colorado Springs, CO. 719-471-3443
Tolan Machinery Company
Rockaway, NJ 973-983-7212
Tranter INC
Wichita Falls, TX 940-723-7125
Ultra Process Systems
Oak Ridge, TN 865-483-2772
Vilter Manufacturing Corporation
Cudahy, WI 414-744-0111
Washington Frontier
Grandview, WA 509-469-7662
Waukesha Cherry-Burrell
Louisville, KY 800-252-5200
Wilevco Inc
Billerica, MA 978-667-0400

Heat Transfer Fluids

Brown Fired Heater
Elyria, OH. 440-323-3291
Paratherm Corporation
Conshohocken, PA 800-222-3611
Quikwater Inc
Sand Springs, OK 918-241-8880

Washington Frontier
Grandview, WA. 509-469-7662

Homogenizers

APV Americas
Delavan, WI 800-252-5200
Avestin
Ottawa, ON. 888-283-7846
Bematek Systems Inc
Salem, MA 877-236-2835
Berkshire PPM
Litchfield, CT 860-567-3118
Cornell Machine Co
Springfield, NJ 973-379-6860
Ederback Corporation
Ann Arbor, MI 800-422-2558
Eischen Enterprises
Fresno, CA 559-834-0013
Et Oakes Corp
Hauppauge, NY 631-232-0002
GEA Niro Soavi North America
Bedford, NH 603-606-4060
Glen Mills Inc.
Clifton, NJ. 973-777-0777
Goodway Industries Inc
Bohemia, NY 800-943-4501
Ika-Works Inc
Wilmington, NC 800-733-3037
JW Leser Company
Los Angeles, CA. 323-731-4173
National Oilwell Varco
North Andover, MA 800-643-0641
Omni International
Kennesaw, GA 800-776-4431
Pro Scientific Inc
Oxford, CT 800-584-3776
Sanchelima International
Miami, FL 305-591-4343
Silverson Machines Inc
East Longmeadow, MA 800-204-6400
Sonic Corp
Stratford, CT 866-493-1378
Special Products
Springfield, MO 417-881-6114
Statco Engineering
Huntington Beach, CA 800-421-0362
Stephan Machinery, Inc.
Mundelein, IL 800-783-7426
WCB Ice Cream
Philadelphia, PA 215-425-4320

Honey Processing

Cook & Beals Inc
Loup City, NE 308-745-0154
Dadant & Sons Inc
Hamilton, IL 888-922-1293

Hoppers

Anderson-Crane Company
Minneapolis, MN 800-314-2747
Andgar Corp
Ferndale, WA 360-366-9900
ANDRITZ Inc
Muncy, PA. 704-943-4343
Bonar Plastics
West Chicago, IL 800-295-3725
COW Industries Inc
Columbus, OH 800-542-9353
Food Processing Equipment Co
Santa Fe Springs, CA 562-802-3727
Galbreath LLC
Winamac, IN. 574-946-6631
Jesco Industries
Litchfield, MI 800-455-0019
Midwest Metalcraft & Equipment
Windsor, MO. 800-647-3167
Our Name is Mud
New York, NY 877-683-7867
Palace Packaging Machines Inc
Downington, PA. 610-873-7252
Pittsburgh Tank Corp
Monongahela, PA 800-634-0243
Puritan Manufacturing Inc
Omaha, NE 800-331-0487
Schlueter Company
Janesville, WI 800-359-1700
Sharpsville Container Corp
Sharpsville, PA 800-645-1248

Shick Esteve
  Kansas City, MO................877-744-2587
TWM Manufacturing
  Leamington, ON................888-495-4831
UniTrak Corporation
  Port Hope, ON.................866-883-5749
Wilson Steel Products Company
  Memphis, TN..................901-527-8742

Coffee

Bonar Plastics
  West Chicago, IL...............800-295-3725
Pittsburgh Tank Corp
  Monongahela, PA...............800-634-0243
Sharpsville Container Corp
  Sharpsville, PA................800-645-1248
Shick Esteve
  Kansas City, MO................877-744-2587
TWM Manufacturing
  Leamington, ON................888-495-4831
UniTrak Corporation
  Port Hope, ON.................866-883-5749

Flour

Anderson-Crane Company
  Minneapolis, MN...............800-314-2747
ANDRITZ Inc
  Muncy, PA....................704-943-4343
Bonar Plastics
  West Chicago, IL...............800-295-3725
COW Industries Inc
  Columbus, OH.................800-542-9353
Food Processing Equipment Co
  Santa Fe Springs, CA............562-802-3727
Galbreath LLC
  Winamac, IN..................574-946-6631
Midwest Metalcraft & Equipment
  Windsor, MO..................800-647-3167
Pittsburgh Tank Corp
  Monongahela, PA...............800-634-0243
Puritan Manufacturing Inc
  Omaha, NE...................800-331-0487
Schlueter Company
  Janesville, WI.................800-359-1700
Sharpsville Container Corp
  Sharpsville, PA................800-645-1248
Shick Esteve
  Kansas City, MO................877-744-2587
TWM Manufacturing
  Leamington, ON................888-495-4831
Wilson Steel Products Company
  Memphis, TN..................901-527-8742

Hullers

Bean & Pea

A C Horn & Co Sheet Metal
  Dallas, TX....................800-657-6155
A.K. Robins
  Baltimore, MD.................800-486-9656
Grain Machinery Mfg Corp
  Miami, FL....................305-620-2525
Lee Financial Corporation
  Dallas, TX....................972-960-1001

Huskers

Corn

Berkshire PPM
  Litchfield, CT.................860-567-3118
Hughes Co
  Columbus, WI.................866-535-9303

Ice Breaking, Chipping, Crushing

Clawson Machine Co Inc
  Franklin, NJ..................800-828-4088
Flodin
  Moses Lake, WA...............509-766-2996
Hoshizaki America Inc
  Peachtree City, GA..............800-438-6087
Howe Corp
  Chicago, IL...................773-235-0200
International Cooling Systems
  Richmond Hill, ON..............888-213-5566
Island Oasis Frozen Cocktail
  Beloit, WI....................800-777-4752
Machine Ice Co
  Houston, TX..................800-423-8822

Swing-A-Way Manufacturing Company
  St Louis, MO..................314-773-1488
Vitamix
  Olmsted Twp, OH...............800-437-4654
Vogt Tube Ice
  Louisville, KY.................800-853-8648
Waring Products
  Torrington, CT................800-492-7464
Welbilt Corporation
  Stamford, CT..................203-325-8300

Ice Cream Cone, Bar, Biscuit Processing

Darfill
  Westerville, OH................614-890-3274
Eischen Enterprises
  Fresno, CA...................559-834-0013
Norse Dairy Systems
  Columbus, OH.................800-338-7465
Schroeder Machine
  San Marcos, CA................760-591-9733

Ice Cream Processing

A & B Process Systems Corp
  Stratford, WI.................888-258-2789
Advance Energy Technologies
  Halfmoon, NY.................800-724-0198
Carpigiani Corporation of America
  Winston Salem, NC..............800-648-4389
Dipwell Co
  Northampton, MA...............413-587-4673
Emery Thompson Machine &Supply Company
  Brooksville, FL................718-588-7300
Frosty Factory of America Inc
  Ruston, LA...................800-544-4071
Gram Equipment of America
  Tampa, FL...................813-248-1978
H C Duke & Son Inc
  East Moline, IL................309-755-4553
Master-Bilt
  New Albany, MS...............800-647-1284
Norse Dairy Systems
  Columbus, OH.................800-338-7465
Swirl Freeze Corp
  Salt Lake City, UT..............800-262-4275
Tetra Pak
  Vernon Hills, IL...............847-955-6000
Tindall Packaging
  Vicksburg, MI.................269-649-1163
Vitamix
  Olmsted Twp, OH...............800-437-4654
White Mountain Freezer
  Kansas City, MO...............816-943-4100

Ice Cubing

Hoshizaki America Inc
  Peachtree City, GA..............800-438-6087
Iceomatic
  Denver, CO...................800-423-3367
Machine Ice Co
  Houston, TX..................800-423-8822
Morris & Associates
  Garner, NC...................919-582-9200
Scotsman Ice Systems
  Vernon Hills, IL...............800-726-8762
SerVend International
  Sellersburg, IN................800-367-4233
Vogt Tube Ice
  Louisville, KY.................800-853-8648
Water Sciences Services, Inc.
  Jackson, TN..................973-584-4131
Welbilt Corporation
  Stamford, CT..................203-325-8300

Ice Making, Refrigerating & Cooling

A-1 Refrigeration Co
  Ontario, CA...................800-669-4423
Advance Energy Technologies
  Halfmoon, NY.................800-724-0198
American Food Equipment
  Miami, FL....................305-377-8991
Applied Chemical Technology
  Florence, AL..................800-228-3217
Arctic Glacier Premium Ice
  Winnepeg, MB.................888-783-9857
Attias Oven Corp
  Brooklyn, NY.................800-928-8427
Berg Chilling Systems
  Toronto, ON, ON...............416-755-2221

BVL Controls
  Bois-Des-Filion, QC.............866-285-2668
C&R Refrigeration
  Center, TX...................800-438-6182
Carbonic Machines Inc
  Minneapolis, MN...............612-824-0745
Cooling Technology Inc
  Charlotte, NC.................800-872-1448
Cornelius
  Mason City, IA................800-238-3600
Cornelius Inc.
  Osseo, MN...................800-238-3600
Cornelius Wilshire Corporation
  Schaumburg; IL................847-397-4600
Delta Cooling Towers Inc
  Rockaway, NJ.................800-289-3358
Dole Refrigerating Co
  Lewisburg, TN.................800-251-8990
Flakice Corporation
  Everett, WA..................800-654-4630
Follett Corp
  Easton, PA...................800-523-9361
Hoshizaki America Inc
  Peachtree City, GA..............800-438-6087
Howe Corp
  Chicago, IL...................773-235-0200
Iceomatic
  Denver, CO...................800-423-3367
IMI Cornelius
  Schaumburg, IL................800-323-4789
International Cooling Systems
  Richmond Hill, ON..............888-213-5566
Kloppenberg & Co
  Englewood, CO................800-346-3246
Leer Inc
  New Lisbon, WI...............800-237-8350
Louisville Dryer Company
  Louisville, KY.................800-735-3613
Machine Ice Co
  Houston, TX..................800-423-8822
Maja Equipment Company
  Omaha, NE...................402-346-6252
Mannhardt Inc
  Sheboygan Falls, WI.............800-423-2327
Master-Bilt
  New Albany, MS...............800-647-1284
Matthiesen Equipment
  San Antonio, TX...............800-624-8635
Maximicer
  Georgetown, TX...............800-289-9098
McCormack Manufacturing Company
  Lake Oswego, OR..............800-395-1593
Morris & Associates
  Garner, NC...................919-582-9200
North Star Ice EquipmentCorporation
  Seattle, WA..................800-321-1381
Scotsman Ice Systems
  Vernon Hills, IL...............800-726-8762
Seattle Refrigeration & Manufacturing
  Seattle, WA..................800-228-8881
Semco Manufacturing Company
  Pharr, TX....................956-787-4203
SerVend International
  Sellersburg, IN................800-367-4233
Superior Products Company
  Saint Paul, MN................800-328-9800
Tom Lockerbie
  Edmeston, NY.................315-737-5612
Turbo Refrigerating Company
  Denton, TX...................940-387-4301
U-Line Corporation
  Milwaukee, WI................800-779-2547
Vilter Manufacturing Corporation
  Cudahy, WI...................414-744-0111
Welbilt Corporation
  Stamford, CT..................203-325-8300
Welbilt Inc.
  New Port Richey, FL.............877-375-9300
Wittemann Company
  Palm Coast, FL................386-445-4200

Irradiation Processing

Alpha Omega Technology
  Cedar Knolls, NJ...............800-442-1969
IBA Food Safety
  Memphis, TN.................800-777-9012
Insect-O-Cutor Inc
  Stone Mountain, GA.............800-966-8480
MDS Nordion
  Ottawa, ON...................800-465-3666

New Horizon Technologies
Richland, WA 509-372-4868

Meat Preparation Equipment

A C Tool & Machine Co
Louisville, KY 502-447-5505
AEW Thurne
Lake Zurich, IL 800-239-7297
Alfa Laval Inc
Richmond, VA. 866-253-2528
Allen Gauge & Tool Co
Pittsburgh, PA 412-241-6410
AM-Mac
Fairfield, NJ 800-829-2018
Andgar Corp
Ferndale, WA 360-366-9900
ANKOM Technology
Macedon, NY 315-986-8090
Ashcroft Inc
Stratford, CT 800-328-8258
Atlanta SharpTech
Peachtree City, GA 800-462-7297
Automated Food Systems
Waxahachie, TX 469-517-0470
B H Bunn Co
Lakeland, FL 800-222-2866
Beacon Inc
Chicago, IL 800-445-4203
Biro Manufacturing Co
Lakeside Marblhd, OH 419-798-4451
Blakeslee, Inc.
Addison, IL 630-532-5021
Boehringer Mfg. Co. Inc.
Felton, CA 800-630-8665
Bridge Machine Company
Palmyra, NJ 877-754-1800
Chop-Rite Two Inc
Harleysville, PA 800-683-5858
Cozzini Inc
Algona, IA 888-295-1116
Cozzini LLC
Chicago, IL 773-478-9700
Cutrite Company
Fremont, OH. 800-928-8748
Daleco
West Chester, PA. 610-429-0181
Dc Tech
Kansas City, MO. 877-742-9090
Design Technology Corporation
Billerica, MA 978-663-7000
E-Z Edge Inc
West New York, NJ. 800-232-4470
EZE-Lap Diamond Products
Carson City, NV 800-843-4815
Friedr Dick Corp
Farmingdale, NY 800-554-3425
Friedrich Metal Products
Browns Summit, NC. 800-772-0326
G.F. Frank & Sons
Fairfield, OH. 513-870-9075
General Machinery Corp
Sheboygan, WI 888-243-6622
General, Inc
Weston, FL 954-202-7419
Globe Food Equipment Co
Moraine, OH. 800-347-5423
Haban Saw Company
St.Louis, MO. 314-968-3991
Handtmann Inc
Lake Forest, IL 800-477-3585
Hansaloy Corp
Davenport, IA 800-553-4992
Hoegger Food Technology
Minneapolis, MN 877-789-5400
Hollingsworth Custom Wood Products
Sault Ste. Marie, ON. 705-759-1756
Hollymatic Corp
Countryside, IL 708-579-3700
I. Fm Usa Inc.
Franklin Park, IL. 866-643-6872
ICB Greenline
Charlotte, NC 800-331-5312
Indeco Products Inc
San Marcos, TX 888-246-3326
Jarvis Products Corp
Middletown, CT 860-347-7271
Kasel Industries Inc
Denver, CO 800-218-4417
Kentmaster Manufacturing Co
Monrovia, CA 800-421-1477

Key Technology Inc.
Walla Walla, WA. 509-529-2161
Koch Equipment LLC
Kansas City, MO. 816-931-4557
Le Fiell Co
Reno, NV 402-592-9993
Linker Machines
Rockaway, NJ 973-983-0001
Loos Machine
Colby, WI 715-223-2844
Luthi Machinery Company, Inc.
Pueblo, CO 719-948-1110
M-One Specialties
Salt Lake City, UT 800-525-9223
Maja Equipment Company
Omaha, NE 402-346-6252
Mandeville Company
Minneapolis, MN 800-328-8490
Marlen
Riverside, MO. 913-888-3333
Marlen International
Astoria, OR. 800-862-7536
Mba Suppliers Inc.
Bellevue, NE 800-467-1201
Mepsco
Batavia, IL. 800-323-8535
Michigan Maple Block Co
Petoskey, MI 800-447-7975
Mp Equip. Co.
Buford, GA 770-614-5355
MPS North America, Inc.
Lenexa, KS 913-310-0055
National Band Saw Co
Santa Clarita, CA 800-851-5050
Nieco Corporation
Windsor, CA 800-643-2656
Nutec Manufacturing Inc
New Lenox, IL 815-722-5348
Packaging Progressions
Collegeville, PA 610-489-9096
Paoli Properties
Rockford, IL 815-965-0621
Paragon Group USA
St Petersburg, FL 800-835-6962
Patty O Matic Machinery
Farmingdale, NJ 877-938-5244
Pemberton & Associates
Brooklyn, NY 800-736-2664
Planet Products Corp
Blue Ash, OH 513-984-5544
Prince Castle Inc
Carol Stream, IL 800-722-7853
Prince Industries Inc
Murrayville, GA 800-441-3303
Quickdraft
Canton, OH 330-477-4574
R Murphy Co Inc
Ayer, MA. 888-772-3481
Ranger Tool Co Inc
Memphis, TN 800-737-9999
Reiser
Canton, MA 734-821-1290
Rheo-Tech
Gurnee, IL. 847-367-1557
Rollstock Inc
Kansas City, MO. 800-954-6020
SFK Danfotech, Inc.
Kansas City, MO. 816-891-7357
Simmons Engineering Corporation
Wheeling, IL 800-252-3381
Simonds International
Fitchburg, MA 978-345-7521
Sperling Industries
Omaha, NE 402-556-4070
Sperling Industries
Omaha, NE 800-647-5062
Standard Casing Company
Lyndhurst, NJ 800-847-4141
Stanfos
Edmonton, AB 800-661-5648
Stephan Machinery GmbH
Mandelein, IL 847-247-0182
Stone Enterprises Inc.
Omaha, NE 877-653-0500
Stork Townsend Inc.
Des Moines, IA. 800-247-8609
Superior Distributing Co
Louisville, KY 800-365-6661
Tech-Roll Inc
Blaine, WA 888-946-3929
TGW International
Florence, KY. 800-407-0173

Tni Packaging Inc
West Chicago, IL 800-383-0990
Trenton Mills Inc
Trenton, TN. 731-855-1323
Unitherm Food System
Bristow, OK 918-367-0197
Univex Corp
Salem, NH. 800-258-6358
Walton's Inc
Wichita, KS 800-835-2832
Weber Inc
Kansas City, MO. 816-891-8397

Microwave Ovens

Accu Temp Products Inc
Fort Wayne, IN 800-210-5907
Acp Inc
Cedar Rapids, IA. 319-368-8198
Cober Electronics, Inc.
Norwalk, CT 800-709-5948
Defreeze Corporation
Southborough, MA 508-485-8512
Hickory Industries
North Bergen, NJ 800-732-9153
Kreative Koncepts
Marquette, MI 800-638-2019
Microdry
Crestwood, KY 502-241-8933
Panasonic Commercial Food Service
Newark, NJ
Quasar Industries
Rochester Hills, MI. 248-852-0300
R F Schiffmann Assoc.
New York, NY 212-362-7021
Sharp Electronics Corporation
Mahwah, NJ 800-237-4277

Milking

Ben H. Anderson Manufacturers
Morrisonville, WI 608-846-5474
Coburn Company
Whitewater, WI. 800-776-7042
Lyco Wausau
Wausau, WI. 715-845-7867
Schlueter Company
Janesville, WI 800-359-1700

Mills

Ball & Pebble

Fernholtz Engineering
Van Nuys, CA 818-785-5800
Glen Mills Inc.
Clifton, NJ. 973-777-0777
NaraKom
Peapack, NJ. 908-234-1776
Paul O. Abbe
Bensenville, IL 630-350-2200
Union Process
Akron, OH. 330-929-3333

Chocolate Grinding

Glen Mills Inc.
Clifton, NJ. 973-777-0777
Union Process
Akron, OH. 330-929-3333

Colloid

Bematek Systems Inc
Salem, MA 877-236-2835
Berkshire PPM
Litchfield, CT 860-567-3118
Chemicolloid Laboratories, Inc.
New Hyde Park, NY 516-747-2666
Glen Mills Inc.
Clifton, NJ. 973-777-0777
National Oilwell Varco
North Andover, MA 800-643-0641
Silverson Machines Inc
East Longmeadow, MA 800-204-6400
Sonic Corp
Stratford, CT 866-493-1378
Waukesha Cherry-Burrell
Louisville, KY 502-491-4310

Copra Grinding & Crushing

ANDRITZ Inc
Muncy, PA. 704-943-4343

Corenco
Santa Rosa, CA 888-267-3626

Corn Meal & Corn Flour

C S Bell Co
Tiffin, OH 888-958-6381
Glen Mills Inc.
Clifton, NJ 973-777-0777
International Reserve Equipment Corporation
Clarendon Hills, IL 708-531-0680
La Poblana Food Machines
Mesa, AZ. 480-258-2091
M O Industries Inc
Whippany, NJ 973-386-9228

Curd

Damrow Company
Fond Du Lac, WI 800-236-1501

Feed

A T Ferrell Co Inc
Bluffton, IN. 800-248-8318
Amherst Milling Co
Amherst, VA 434-946-7601
ANDRITZ Inc
Muncy, PA. 704-943-4343
C S Bell Co
Tiffin, OH 888-958-6381
Custom Millers Supply Co
Monmouth, IL 309-734-6312
Forster & Son
Ada, OK 580-332-6021
Germantown Milling Company
Germantown, KY 606-728-5857
Meadows Mills Inc
North Wilkesboro, NC 800-626-2282
Summit Machine Builders Corporation
Denver, CO 800-274-6741

Flour & Cereal

CHS Inc.
Inver Grove Hts., MN 800-328-6539
Fernholtz Engineering
Van Nuys, CA 818-785-5800
Ferrell-Ross
Amarillo, TX. 800-299-9051
Germantown Milling Company
Germantown, KY 606-728-5857
International Reserve Equipment Corporation
Clarendon Hills, IL 708-531-0680
Lauhoff Corporation
Detroit, MI 313-259-0027
Lehi Mills
Lehi, UT 877-311-3566
Meadows Mills Inc
North Wilkesboro, NC 800-626-2282
Mill Engineering & Machinery Company
Oakland, CA 510-562-1832
Norvell Co Inc
Fort Scott, KS 800-653-3147
Satake USA
Stafford, TX 281-276-3600

Grinding

A C Horn & Co Sheet Metal
Dallas, TX 800-657-6155
ANDRITZ Inc
Muncy, PA. 704-943-4343
Autio Co
Astoria, OR. 800-483-8884
C S Bell Co
Tiffin, OH 888-958-6381
Corenco
Santa Rosa, CA 888-267-3626
Daily Printing Inc
Plymouth, MN. 800-622-6596
Ferrell-Ross
Amarillo, TX. 800-299-9051
Fitzpatrick Co
Elmhurst, IL 630-592-4425
Fluid Air Inc
Aurora, IL 630-665-5001
Fluid Energy Processing & Eqpt
Hatfield, PA. 215-368-2510
Gilson Co Inc
Lewis Center, OH 800-444-1508
Glen Mills Inc.
Clifton, NJ 973-777-0777

Globe Machine
Tacoma, WA 800-523-6575
Goodnature Products
Orchard Park, NY 800-875-3381
Jayhawk Manufacturing Co Inc
Hutchinson, KS. 866-886-8269
Kemutec Group Inc
Bristol, PA. 215-788-8013
Lasermation Inc
Philadelphia, PA 800-523-2759
M O Industries Inc
Whippany, NJ 973-386-9228
Modern Process Equipment Inc
Chicago, IL 773-254-3929
NaraKom
Peapack, NJ. 908-234-1776
Nederman
Thomasville, NC. 800-533-5286
Netzsch Pumps North America
Exton, PA 610-363-8010
Straub Designs Co
St Louis Park, MN 952-546-6686
Union Process
Akron, OH. 330-929-3333

Hammer

A C Horn & Co Sheet Metal
Dallas, TX. 800-657-6155
A T Ferrell Co Inc
Bluffton, IN. 800-248-8318
ANDRITZ Inc
Muncy, PA. 704-943-4343
Berkshire PPM
Litchfield, CT 860-567-3118
C S Bell Co
Tiffin, OH 888-958-6381
Corenco
Santa Rosa, CA 888-267-3626
CPM Roskamp Champion
Waterloo, IA 800-366-2563
Dehyco Company
Memphis, TN 901-774-3322
Duplex Mill & Mfg Co
Springfield, OH 937-325-5555
Fernholtz Engineering
Van Nuys, CA 818-785-5800
Fitzpatrick Co
Elmhurst, IL 630-592-4425
Forster & Son
Ada, OK 580-332-6021
Glen Mills Inc.
Clifton, NJ. 973-777-0777
Globe Machine
Tacoma, WA 800-523-6575
Goodnature Products
Orchard Park, NY 800-875-3381
Jay-Bee Manufacturing Inc
Tyler, TX 800-445-0610
Meadows Mills Inc
North Wilkesboro, NC 800-626-2282
NaraKom
Peapack, NJ. 908-234-1776
Schutte Buffalo Hammermill
Buffalo, NY. 800-447-4634

Malt

ANDRITZ Inc
Muncy, PA. 704-943-4343

Nut Grinding

A C Horn & Co Sheet Metal
Dallas, TX. 800-657-6155
ANDRITZ Inc
Muncy, PA. 704-943-4343
Corenco
Santa Rosa, CA 888-267-3626
Straub Designs Co
St Louis Park, MN 952-546-6686

Oil Cake Grinding

ANDRITZ Inc
Muncy, PA. 704-943-4343
Corenco
Santa Rosa, CA 888-267-3626

Peanut Butter

A C Horn & Co Sheet Metal
Dallas, TX. 800-657-6155

Berkshire PPM
Litchfield, CT 860-567-3118
Glen Mills Inc.
Clifton, NJ. 973-777-0777

Rice Grinding

ANDRITZ Inc
Muncy, PA. 704-943-4343
Satake USA
Stafford, TX 281-276-3600

Spice Grinding

ANDRITZ Inc
Muncy, PA. 704-943-4343
Berkshire PPM
Litchfield, CT 860-567-3118
Browne & Company
Markham, ON 905-475-6104
C S Bell Co
Tiffin, OH 888-958-6381
Chef Specialties
Smethport, PA. 800-440-2433
Corenco
Santa Rosa, CA 888-267-3626
Ferrell-Ross
Amarillo, TX. 800-299-9051
Glen Mills Inc.
Clifton, NJ. 973-777-0777

Sugar & Sugar Cane

Silver Weibull
Aurora, CO 303-373-2311

Mixers

Eirich Machines
Gurnee, IL 847-336-2444
G & F Mfg
Oak Lawn, IL 800-282-1574
Hamilton Beach Brands
Southern Pines, NC. 800-851-8900
Quadro Engineering
Waterloo, ON 519-884-9660
Reiser
Canton, MA 734-821-1290
Thunderbird Food Machinery
Blaine, WA 866-875-6868

Bakers'

A&J Mixing International
Oakville, ON. 800-668-3470
ABI Limited
Concord, ON. 800-297-8666
Adamatic
Auburn, WA 800-578-2547
Alliance Bakery Systems
Blythewood, SC 803-691-9227
American Eagle Food Machinery
Chicago, IL 888-390-0800
AMF CANADA
Sherbrooke, QC 800-255-3869
Arcobaleno Pasta Machines
Lancaster, PA 800-875-7096
Arde Inc
Carlstadt, NJ 800-909-6070
Benier USA
Lithia Springs, GA 770-745-2200
Blakeslee, Inc.
Addison, IL. 630-532-5021
Breddo Likwifier
Kansas City, MO. 800-669-4092
CMC America Corporation
Joliet, IL 815-726-4337
DBE Inc
Concord, ON. 800-461-5313
Empire Bakery Equipment
Hicksville, NY. 800-878-4070
Exact Mixing Systems Inc
Memphis, TN 901-362-8501
Excellent Bakery Equipment Co
Fairfield, NJ 973-244-1664
Food Engineering Unlimited
Fullerton, CA 714-879-8762
Gemini Bakery Equipment
Philadelphia, PA 800-468-9046
Goodway Industries Inc
Bohemia, NY 800-943-4501
Hayes & Stolz Indl Mfg LTD
Fort Worth, TX 800-725-7272

Hebeler Corp
Tonawanda, NY 800-486-4709
International Reserve Equipment Corporation
Clarendon Hills, IL 708-531-0680
Kemper Bakery Systems
Rockaway, NJ 973-625-1566
Leland Limited Inc
South Plainfield, NJ 908-561-2000
Magna Machine Co
Cincinnati, OH 800-448-3475
Moline Machinery LLC
Duluth, MN 800-767-5734
Packaging & Processing Equipment
Ayr, ON 519-622-6666
Pavailler Distribution Company
Northvale, NJ 201-767-0766
Peerless Dough Mixing and Make-Up
Sidney, OH 800-999-3327
Peerless Food Equipment
Sidney, OH 937-492-4158
Peerless Machinery Corporation
Sidney, OH 800-999-3327
Pro Bake Inc
Twinsburg, OH 800-837-4427
Rondo Inc
Moonachie, NJ 800-882-0633
T.K. Products
Anaheim, CA 714-621-0267
Thomas L. Green & Company
Robenosia, PA 610-693-5816
TMCo Inc.ÿ
Houston, TX 713-465-3255
Varimixer North America
Charlotte, NC 800-221-1138

Drum

Arde Inc
Carlstadt, NJ 800-909-6070
Custom Food Machinery
Stockton, CA 209-463-4343
Drum-Mates Inc.
Lumberton, NJ 800-621-3786
Eclipse Systems Inc
Milpitas, CA 408-263-2201
Glen Mills Inc.
Clifton, NJ 973-777-0777
Munson Machinery Co
Utica, NY 800-944-6644
National Oilwell Varco
North Andover, MA 800-643-0641
Packaging & Processing Equipment
Ayr, ON 519-622-6666
Scott Turbon Mixer
Adelanto, CA 800-285-8512

Food Processing

A & B Process Systems Corp
Stratford, WI 888-258-2789
A&J Mixing International
Oakville, ON 800-668-3470
A&M Process Equipment
Ajax, ON 905-619-8001
ADMIX
Manchester, NH 800-466-2369
AM-Mac
Fairfield, NJ 800-829-2018
American Extrusion Intl
South Beloit, IL 815-624-6616
American Food Equipment Company
Hayward, CA 510-783-0255
American Manufacturing-Engrng
Cleveland, OH 800-822-9402
AMF CANADA
Sherbrooke, QC 800-255-3869
Apache Stainless Equipment
Beaver Dam, WI 800-444-0398
APEC
Lake Odessa, MI 616-374-1000
APV Americas
Delavan, WI 800-252-5200
Arcobaleno Pasta Machines
Lancaster, PA 800-875-7096
Arde Inc
Carlstadt, NJ 800-909-6070
Automated Food Systems
Waxahachie, TX 469-517-0470
AZO Food
Memphis, TN 901-794-9480
B C Holland Inc
Dousman, WI 262-965-2939

Baldewein Company
Lake Forrest, IL 800-424-5544
Bematek Systems Inc
Salem, MA 877-236-2835
Bepex International LLC
Minneapolis, MN 800-607-2470
Berkshire PPM
Litchfield, CT 860-567-3118
Biro Manufacturing Co
Lakeside Marblhd, OH 419-798-4451
Blakeslee, Inc.
Addison, IL 630-532-5021
Blue Tech
Hickory, NC 828-324-5900
Bowers Process Equipment
Stratford, ON 800-567-3223
Breddo Likwifier
Kansas City, MO 800-669-4092
Bulldog Factory Svc LLC
Madison Heights, MI 248-541-3500
Bush Tank Fabricators Inc
Newark, NJ 973-596-1121
California Vibratory Feeders
Anaheim, CA 800-354-0972
Carlisle Food Svc Products Inc
Oklahoma City, OK 800-654-8210
Charles Ross & Son Co
Hauppauge, NY 800-243-7677
Cinelli Esperia
Woodbridge, ON 905-856-1820
Cleveland-Eastern Mixers
Clinton, CT 800-243-1188
CMC America Corporation
Joliet, IL 815-726-4337
Coastline Equipment Inc
Bellingham, WA 360-734-8509
Columbus Instruments
Columbus, OH 800-669-5011
Cornell Machine Co
Springfield, NJ 973-379-6860
CRC Inc
Council Bluffs, IA 712-323-9477
Custom Food Machinery
Stockton, CA 209-463-4343
Davron Technologies Inc
Chattanooga, TN 423-870-1888
Dito Dean Food Prep
Charlotte, NC 866-449-4200
Dorton Incorporated
Arlington Hts, IL 800-299-8600
Drum-Mates Inc.
Lumberton, NJ 800-621-3786
Duplex Mill & Mfg Co
Springfield, OH 937-325-5555
Eclipse Systems Inc
Milpitas, CA 408-263-2201
Eirich Machines
Gurnee, IL 847-336-2444
EKATO Corporation
St Ramsey, NJ 201-825-4684
Empire Bakery Equipment
Hicksville, NY 800-878-4070
Ertelalsop
Kingston, NY 800-553-7835
Et Oakes Corp
Hauppauge, NY 631-232-0002
Exact Mixing Systems Inc
Memphis, TN 901-362-8501
Expert Industries Inc
Brooklyn, NY 718-434-6060
Falco Technologies
La Prairie, QC 450-444-0566
Fernholtz Engineering
Van Nuys, CA 818-785-5800
Fish Oven & Equipment Co
Wauconda, IL 877-526-8720
Fitzpatrick Co
Elmhurst, IL 630-592-4425
Food Engineering Unlimited
Fullerton, CA 714-879-8762
Food Processing Equipment Co
Santa Fe Springs, CA 562-802-3727
GEM Equipment of Oregon Inc
Woodburn, OR 503-982-9902
General, Inc
Weston, FL 954-202-7419
Glen Mills Inc.
Clifton, NJ 973-777-0777
Goodway Industries Inc
Bohemia, NY 800-943-4501
Grant-Letchworth
Tonawanda, NY 716-692-1000

Hamilton Beach Brands
Southern Pines, NC 800-851-8900
Hayes & Stolz Indl Mfg LTD
Fort Worth, TX 800-725-7272
Hebeler Corp
Tonawanda, NY 800-486-4709
Hollymatic Corp
Countryside, IL 708-579-3700
Hosokawa/Bepex Corporation
Santa Rosa, CA 707-586-6000
Howard Fabrication
City of Industry, CA 626-961-0114
Howes S Co Inc
Silver Creek, NY 888-255-2611
International Reserve Equipment Corporation
Clarendon Hills, IL 708-531-0680
JW Leser Company
Los Angeles, CA 323-731-4173
Kady International
Scarborough, ME 800-367-5239
Karl Schnell
New London, WI 920-982-9974
Kelmin Products
Plymouth, FL 407-886-6079
Kemutec Group Inc
Bristol, PA 215-788-8013
Kinetic Equipment Company
Appleton, WI 806-293-4471
KOFLO Corp
Cary, IL 800-782-8427
Leland Limited Inc
South Plainfield, NJ 908-561-2000
LIST
Acton, MA 978-635-9521
Littleford Day
Florence, KY 800-365-8555
Machanix Fabrication Inc
Chino, CA 800-700-9701
Mandeville Company
Minneapolis, MN 800-328-8490
Marel Food Systems, Inc.
Lenexa, KS 913-888-9110
Matcon Americas
Elmhurst, IL 856-256-1330
Matfer Inc
Van Nuys, CA 800-766-0333
McCarter Corporation
Norristown, PA 610-272-3203
Merlin Process Equipment
Houston, TX 713-221-1651
Microfluidics International
Westwood, MA 800-370-5452
Midwest Metalcraft & Equipment
Windsor, MO 800-647-3167
Modern Process Equipment Inc
Chicago, IL 773-254-3929
Munson Machinery Co
Utica, NY 800-944-6644
Nalge Process Technologies Group
Rochester, NY 585-586-8800
National Oilwell Varco
North Andover, MA 800-643-0641
Pacific Process Technology
La Jolla, CA 858-551-3298
Package Concepts & Materials Inc
Greenville, SC 800-424-7264
Packaging & Processing Equipment
Ayr, ON 519-622-6666
Patterson-Kelley   Hars Company
East Stroudsburg, PA 570-421-7500
Paul Mueller Co Inc
Springfield, MO 800-683-5537
Paul O. Abbe
Bensenville, IL 630-350-2200
Paxton Corp
Bristol, RI 401-396-9062
Peerless Machinery Corporation
Sidney, OH 800-999-3327
Polar Process
Plattsville, ON 877-896-8077
PolyMaid Company
Largo, FL 800-206-9188
Prince Castle Inc
Carol Stream, IL 800-722-7853
Process Systems
Barrington, IL 847-842-8618
Production Packaging & Processing Equipment
Company
Savannah, GA 912-856-4281
Provisur Technologies, Inc.
Mokena, IL 708-479-3500

Puritan Manufacturing Inc
Omaha, NE 800-331-0487
Readco Kurimoto LLC
York, PA 800-395-4959
Reading Bakery Systems Inc
Robesonia, PA 610-693-5816
Reiser
Canton, MA 734-821-1290
Ross Engineering Inc
Savannah, GA 800-524-7677
Savage Brothers Company
Elk Grove Vlg, IL 800-342-0973
Scott Turbon Mixer
Adelanto, CA 800-285-8512
Semi-Bulk Systems Inc
Fenton, MO 800-732-8769
Silverson Machines Inc
East Longmeadow, MA 800-204-6400
Sonic Corp
Stratford, CT 866-493-1378
South River Machine
Hackensack, NJ 201-487-1736
Specific Mechanical Systems
Victoria, BC 250-652-2111
Stainless Fabrication Inc
Springfield, MO 800-397-8265
Stephan Machinery, Inc.
Mundelein, IL 800-783-7426
Stricklin Co
Dallas, TX 214-637-1030
Superior Products Company
Saint Paul, MN 800-328-9800
T.K. Products
Anaheim, CA 714-621-0267
TDH
Sand Springs, OK 888-251-7961
Thomas L. Green & Company
Robenosia, PA 610-693-5816
TSA Griddle Systems
Kelowna, BC 250-491-9025
Varimixer North America
Charlotte, NC 800-221-1138
Viatec
Victoria, BC 800-942-4702
Vitamix
Olmsted Twp, OH 800-437-4654
Waring Products
Torrington, CT 800-492-7464
Washington Frontier
Grandview, WA 509-469-7662
Weiler & Company
Whitewater, WI 800-558-9507
Welbilt Corporation
Stamford, CT 203-325-8300
Wilevco Inc
Billerica, MA 978-667-0400

Food, Household, Hotel & Restaurant

Arcobaleno Pasta Machines
Lancaster, PA 800-875-7096
Attias Oven Corp
Brooklyn, NY 800-928-8427
Blakeslee, Inc.
Addison, IL 630-532-5021
CRC Inc
Council Bluffs, IA 712-323-9477
Custom Food Machinery
Stockton, CA 209-463-4343
Dorton Incorporated
Arlington Hts, IL 800-299-8600
General, Inc
Weston, FL 954-202-7419
Island Oasis Frozen Cocktail
Beloit, WI 800-777-4752
Jiffy Mixer Co Inc
Corona, CA 800-560-2903
Leland Limited Inc
South Plainfield, NJ 908-561-2000
Mandeville Company
Minneapolis, MN 800-328-8490
Matfer Inc
Van Nuys, CA 800-766-0333
Nalge Process Technologies Group
Rochester, NY 585-586-8800
Packaging & Processing Equipment
Ayr, ON 519-622-6666
Paul Mueller Co Inc
Springfield, MO 800-683-5537
Paxton Corp
Bristol, RI 401-396-9062

Prince Castle Inc
Carol Stream, IL 800-722-7853
Puritan Manufacturing Inc
Omaha, NE 800-331-0487
Superior Products Company
Saint Paul, MN 800-328-9800
T.K. Products
Anaheim, CA 714-621-0267
Toronto Kitchen Equipment
North York, ON 416-745-4944
Univex Corp
Salem, NH 800-258-6358
Varimixer North America
Charlotte, NC 800-221-1138
VitaMinder Company
Providence, RI 800-858-8840
Welbilt Corporation
Stamford, CT 203-325-8300

Paste Products

A & B Process Systems Corp
Stratford, WI 888-258-2789
Breddo Likwifier
Kansas City, MO 800-669-4092
Kelmin Products
Plymouth, FL 407-886-6079
McCarter Corporation
Norristown, PA 610-272-3203
National Oilwell Varco
North Andover, MA 800-643-0641
Packaging & Processing Equipment
Ayr, ON 519-622-6666
Paxton Corp
Bristol, RI 401-396-9062
Polar Process
Plattsville, ON 877-896-8077
Reiser
Canton, MA 734-821-1290

Nut Cracking, Shelling & Salting

A C Horn & Co Sheet Metal
Dallas, TX 800-657-6155
Carolina Cracker
Garner, NC 919-779-6899
Design Technology Corporation
Billerica, MA 978-663-7000
Key Technology Inc.
Walla Walla, WA 509-529-2161
Krispy Kist Company
Chicago, IL 312-733-0900
Lewis M Carter Mfg Co Inc
Donalsonville, GA 800-332-8232
Maddox/Adams International
Miami, FL 305-592-3337
Modern Electronics Inc
Grand Cane, LA 318-872-4764
Nutty Bavarian
Sanford, FL 800-382-4788
Satake USA
Stafford, TX 281-276-3600

Oil Extraction

Abanaki Corp
Chagrin Falls, OH 800-358-7546
Alfa Laval Inc
Richmond, VA 866-253-2528
Anderson International Corp
Stow, OH 800-336-4730
Caron Products & Svc Inc
Marietta, OH 800-648-3042
Crown Iron Works Company
Roseville, MN 888-703-7500
French Oil Mill Machinery Co
Piqua, OH 937-773-3420

Ovens

A C Horn & Co Sheet Metal
Dallas, TX 800-657-6155
ABI Limited
Concord, ON 800-297-8666
Accu Temp Products Inc
Fort Wayne, IN 800-210-5907
Acp Inc
Cedar Rapids, IA 319-368-8198
Adamatic
Auburn, WA 800-578-2547
Allied Bakery and Food Service Equipment
Santa Fe Springs, CA 562-945-6506

ALPI Food Preparation Equipment
Bolton, ON 800-928-2574
Alto-Shaam
Menomonee Falls, WI. 800-329-8744
American Extrusion Intl
South Beloit, IL 815-624-6616
American Range
Pacoima, CA 888-753-9898
AMF CANADA
Sherbrooke, QC 800-255-3869
Anetsberger
Concord, NH 603-225-6684
Antrim Manufacturing Inc
Brookfield, WI 262-781-6860
Apollo Sheet Metal
Kennewick, WA 509-586-1104
Attias Oven Corp
Brooklyn, NY 800-928-8427
Bakers Pride Oven Company
New Rochelle, NY 800-431-2745
Bakery Associates
Setauket, NY 631-751-4156
Ballantyne Food Service Equipment
Omaha, NE 800-424-1215
Baxter Manufacturing Inc
Orting, WA 800-777-2828
Bbc Industries
Pacific, MO 800-654-4205
Benier USA
Lithia Springs, GA 770-745-2200
Benko Products
Sheffield Vlg, OH 440-934-2180
Bethel Engineering & Equipment Inc
New Hampshire, OH. 800-889-6129
Bevles Company
Dallas, TX. 800-441-1601
BKI Worldwide
Simpsonville, SC 800-927-6887
Blodgett Corp
Burlington, VT 800-331-5842
Blodgett Oven Co
Burlington, VT 800-331-5842
Bolling Oven & Machine Company
Avon, OH 440-937-6112
C H Babb Co Inc
Raynham, MA. 508-977-0600
Casso-Solar Corporation
Nanuet, NY 800-988-4455
Chase Industries Inc
West Chester, OH 800-543-4455
Checker Machine
Minneapolis, MN 888-800-5001
Chesmont Engineering Co Inc
Exton, PA 610-594-9200
Cincinnati Industrial Machry
Mason, OH 800-677-0076
Cinelli Esperia
Woodbridge, ON 905-856-1820
Cleveland Range
Concord, ON
Coast Scientific
Rancho Santa Fe, CA 800-445-1544
Cober Electronics, Inc.
Norwalk, CT 800-709-5948
Comstock Castle Stove Co
Quincy, IL 800-637-9188
Cookshack
Ponca City, OK 800-423-0698
Custom Diamond International
Laval, QC 800-363-5926
Cutler Industries
Morton Grove, IL 800-458-5593
Davron Technologies Inc
Chattanooga, TN. 423-870-1888
DBE Inc
Concord, ON 800-461-5313
Defreeze Corporation
Southborough, MA 508-485-8512
Deluxe Equipment Company
Bradenton, FL 800-367-8931
Doyon Equipment
Liniere, QC 800-463-4273
Duke Manufacturing Co
St Louis, MO. 800-735-3853
Dynamic Cooking Systems
Huntington Beach, CA 800-433-8466
Earthstone Wood-Fire Ovens
Glendale, CA 800-840-4915
Empire Bakery Equipment
Hicksville, NY 800-878-4070
Ensign Ribbon Burners LLC
Pelham, NY. 914-813-0815

Epcon Industrial Systems
Conroe, TX 800-447-7872
Equipex Limited
Providence, RI 800-649-7885
Excellent Bakery Equipment Co
Fairfield, NJ 973-244-1664
Fab-X/Metals
Washington, NC 800-677-3229
FBM/Baking Machines Inc
Cranbury, NJ 800-449-0433
FECO/MOCO
Warren, OH 800-547-1527
Fish Oven & Equipment Co
Wauconda, IL 877-526-8720
FlashBake Ovens Food Service
Fremont, CA 800-843-6836
Food Engineering Unlimited
Fullerton, CA 714-879-8762
FOODesign from tna
Wilsonville, OR 503-685-5030
Foster Refrigerator Corporation
Kinderhook, NY 888-828-3311
Franz Haas Machinery-America
Henrico, VA 804-222-6022
Friedrich Metal Products
Browns Summit, NC 800-772-0326
Garland Commercial Ranges
Mississauga, ON 905-624-0260
Garland Commercial Ranges Ltd.
Mississauga, ON 905-624-0260
Gehnrich Oven Sales Company
East Troy, WI 262-642-3938
Gemini Bakery Equipment
Philadelphia, PA 800-468-9046
Glenro Inc
Paterson, NJ 888-453-6761
Grande Chef Company
Orangeville, ON 519-942-4470
Hardt Equipment Manufacturing
Lachine, QC 888-848-4408
Hasty Bake Charcoal Grills
Tulsa, OK 800-426-6836
Hatco Corp
Milwaukee, WI 800-558-0607
Henry Group
Greenville, TX 903-883-2002
Hercules Food Equipment
Weston, ON 416-742-9673
Hickory Industries
North Bergen, NJ 800-732-9153
Holman Cooking Equipment
Saint Louis, MO 888-356-5362
Illinois Range Company
Schiller Park, IL 800-535-7041
Imperial Manufacturing Co
Corona, CA 800-343-7790
Industronics Service Co
South Windsor, CT 800-878-1551
IR Systems
Jupiter, FL 800-893-7540
J C Ford Co
La Habra, CA 714-871-7361
Jackson Msc LLC
Gray, KY 888-800-5672
K B Systems Inc
Bangor, PA 610-588-7788
Kemper Bakery Systems
Rockaway, NJ 973-625-1566
La Poblana Food Machines
Mesa, AZ 480-258-2091
Laboratory Devices
Holliston, MA 508-429-1716
Lang Manufacturing Co
Everett, WA 800-882-6368
Lanly Co
Cleveland, OH 216-731-1115
Legion Industries Inc
Waynesboro, GA 800-887-1988
LPS Technology
Grafton, OH 800-586-1410
Ltg Inc
Spartanburg, SC 864-599-6340
Lucks Food Equipment Company
Kent, WA 811-824-0696
M F & B Restaurant Systems Inc
Dunbar, PA 724-628-3050
Market Forge Industries Inc
Everett, MA 866-698-3188
Martin/Baron
Irwindale, CA 626-960-5153
Mayekawa USA, Inc.
Chicago, IL 773-516-5070

Merco/Savory
Mt. Pleasant, MI 800-733-8821
Meyer Machine & Garroutte Products
San Antonio, TX 210-736-1811
Microdry
Crestwood, KY 502-241-8933
Middleby Corp
Elgin, IL 847-741-3300
Middleby Marshall Inc
Elgin, IL 847-741-3300
Moffat
San Antonio, TX 866-589-0664
Montague Co
Hayward, CA 800-345-1830
Mosshaim Innovations
Jacksonville, FL 888-995-7775
Motom Corporation
Bensenville, IL 630-787-1995
Mugnaini Imports
Watsonville, CA 888-887-7206
National Drying Machry Co Inc
Philadelphia, PA 215-464-6070
National Hotpack
Stone Ridge, NY 800-431-8232
Nevo Corporation
Ronkonkoma, NY 631-585-8787
Normandie Metal Fabricators
Port Washington, NY 800-221-2398
Nothum Food Processing Systems
Springfield, MO 800-435-1297
Nu-Vu Food Service Systems
Menominee, MI 800-338-9886
Packotronics
Glenview, IL 947-487-1281
Panasonic Commercial Food Service
Newark, NJ
Pavailler Distribution Company
Northvale, NJ 201-767-0766
Peerless Gouet LLC
Lafayette, CO 720-890-7306
Peerless Ovens
Sandusky, OH 800-548-4514
Peerless-Premier Appliance Co
Belleville, IL 618-233-0475
Pier 1 Imports
Woodcliff Lake, NJ 800-448-9993
Piper Products Inc
Wausau, WI 800-544-3057
PMI Food Equipment Group
Troy, OH 937-332-3000
Pro Scientific Inc
Oxford, CT 800-584-3776
Process Heating Corp
Shrewsbury, MA 508-842-5200
Proheatco Manufacturing
Pomona, CA 800-423-4195
Proluxe
Paramount, CA 800-594-5528
Q-Matic Technologies
Carol Stream, IL 800-880-6836
QNC Inc
Dallas, TX 888-668-3687
Quasar Industries
Rochester Hills, MI 248-852-0300
Randell Manufacturing   Unified Brands
Weidman, MI 888-994-7636
Rankin Delux
Mira Loma, CA 951-685-0081
Rational Cooking Systems
Schaumburg, IL 888-320-7274
Reading Bakery Systems Inc
Robesonia, PA 610-693-5816
Reed Oven Co
Kansas City, MO 816-842-7446
Reliable Food Service Equipment
Concord, ON 416-738-6840
Remco Industries International
Fort Lauderdale, FL 800-987-3626
Renato Specialty Product
Garland, TX 866-575-6316
Revent Inc
Piscataway, NJ 732-777-9433
Rotisol France Inc
Inglewood, CA 800-651-5969
Roto-Flex Oven Co
San Antonio, TX 877-859-1463
Royalton Foodservice Equip Co
North Royalton, OH 800-662-8765
Ruiz Flour Tortillas
Riverside, CA 909-947-7811
Server Products Inc
Richfield, WI 800-558-8722

Sharp Electronics Corporation
Mahwah, NJ 800-237-4277
Shouldice Brothers SheetMetal
Battle Creek, MI 269-962-5579
Solbern Corp
Fairfield, NJ 973-227-3030
Southern Pride Distributing
Alamo, TN 800-851-8180
Stafford-Smith Inc
Kalamazoo, MI 800-968-2442
Stainless Steel Fabricator Inc
La Mirada, CA 714-739-9904
Standex International Corp.
Salem, NH 603-893-9701
Stewart Systems Baking LLC
Plano, TX 972-422-5808
Super-Chef Manufacturing Company
Houston, TX 800-231-3478
Superior Products Company
Saint Paul, MN 800-328-9800
Thermodyne Foodservice Prods
Fort Wayne, IN 800-526-9182
Thomas L. Green & Company
Robenosia, PA 610-693-5816
Toastmaster
Elgin, IL 847-741-3300
Toronto Kitchen Equipment
North York, ON 416-745-4944
Townfood Equipment Corp
Brooklyn, NY 800-221-5032
Trak-Air/Rair
Denver, CO 800-688-8725
Triad Scientific
Manasquan, NJ 800-867-6690
Trimen Foodservice Equipment
North York, ON 877-437-1422
TURBOCHEF Technologies
Carrollton, TX. 800-908-8726
Valad Electric Heating Corporation
Tarrytown, NY 914-631-4927
Vortron Smokehouse/Ovens
Iron Ridge, WI 800-874-1949
Vulcan Food Equipment Group
Baltimore, MD 800-814-2028
Welbilt Corporation
Stamford, CT. 203-325-8300
Western Combustion Engineering
Carson, CA 310-834-9389
Win-Holt Equipment Group
Syosset, NY. 800-444-3595
Winston Industries
Louisville, KY 800-234-5286
Wisco Industries Assembly
Oregon, WI 800-999-4726
Wittco Foodservice Equipment
Milwaukee, WI 800-367-8413
Wolf Company
Louisville, KY 800-814-2028
Wood Stone Corp
Bellingham, WA 800-988-8103

Packers' & Butchers'

Aaron Equipment Co Div Areco
Bensenville, IL 630-350-2200
Allen Gauge & Tool Co
Pittsburgh, PA 412-241-6410
AM-Mac
Fairfield, NJ 800-829-2018
Architecture Plus Intl Inc
Rocky Point, FL 813-281-9299
Automated Food Systems
Waxahachie, TX 469-517-0470
B H Bunn Co
Lakeland, FL 800-222-2866
Best & Donovan
Blue Ash, OH 800-553-2378
Biro Manufacturing Co
Lakeside Marblhd, OH 419-798-4451
Chop-Rite Two Inc
Harleysville, PA 800-683-5858
CMC America Corporation
Joliet, IL 815-726-4337
Compacker Systems LLC
Davenport, IA 563-391-2751
Customized Equipment SE
Tucker, GA 770-934-9300
Dc Tech
Kansas City, MO 877-742-9090
Doering Co
Clear Lake, MN 320-743-2276

Durable Packaging Corporation
Countryside, IL 800-700-5677
Ennio International
Aurora, IL 630-851-5808
Friedr Dick Corp
Farmingdale, NY 800-554-3425
Globe Food Equipment Co
Moraine, OH 800-347-5423
Grant-Letchworth
Tonawanda, NY 716-692-1000
Hollymatic Corp
Countryside, IL 708-579-3700
Indeco Products Inc
San Marcos, TX 888-246-3326
Kasel Industries Inc
Denver, CO 800-218-4417
Kohler Industries Inc
Lincoln, NE 800-365-6708
Linker Machines
Rockaway, NJ 973-983-0001
Marlen International
Astoria, OR 800-862-7536
Molins/Sandiacre Richmond
Richmond, VA 864-486-4000
Pemberton & Associates
Brooklyn, NY 800-736-2664
Pickwick Manufacturing Svc
Cedar Rapids, IA 800-397-9797
Preferred Machining Corporation
Englewood, CO 303-761-1535
Pressure Pack
Williamsburg, VA 757-220-3693
Professional Marketing Group
Seattle, WA 800-227-3769
Ranger Tool Co Inc
Memphis, TN 800-737-9999
Schroeder Machine
San Marcos, CA 760-591-9733
Sperling Industries
Omaha, NE 402-556-4070
Stork Townsend Inc.
Des Moines, IA 800-247-8609
Walsroder Packaging
Willowbrook, IL 800-882-9987

Panomatic-Flour Collection System

AGET Manufacturing Co
Adrian, MI 517-263-5781

Pasta Processing

A.K. Robins
Baltimore, MD 800-486-9656
ALPI Food Preparation Equipment
Bolton, ON 800-928-2574
APV Baker
Goldsboro, NC 919-736-4309
Arcobaleno Pasta Machines
Lancaster, PA 800-875-7096
Demaco
Ridgewood, NY
Design Technology Corporation
Billerica, MA 978-663-7000
Exact Mixing Systems Inc
Memphis, TN 901-362-8501
Gemini Bakery Equipment
Philadelphia, PA 800-468-9046
I J White Corp
Farmingdale, NY 631-293-2211
Industrial Product Corp
Ho Ho Kus, NJ 800-472-5913
Kemper Bakery Systems
Rockaway, NJ 973-625-1566
Lawrence Equipment Inc
South El Monte, CA 800-423-4500
Lyco Manufacturing
Wausau, WI 715-845-7867
MBC Food Machinery Corp
Hackensack, NJ 201-489-7000
Molded Fiber Glass Tray Company
Linesville, PA 800-458-6050
Mouli Manufacturing Corporation
Belleville, NJ 800-789-8285
Multi-Fill Inc
West Jordan, UT 801-280-1570
Oshikiri Corp of America
Philadelphia, PA 215-637-8112
Pavan USA Inc
Emigsville, PA 717-767-4889
Peerless Dough Mixing and Make-Up
Sidney, OH 800-999-3327

Phase II Pasta Machine Inc
Farmingdale, NY 800-457-5070
Pier 1 Imports
Woodcliff Lake, NJ 800-448-9993
Pro Bake Inc
Twinsburg, OH 800-837-4427
Rademaker USA
Hudson, OH 330-650-2345
Reiser
Canton, MA 734-821-1290
Rheon USA
Irvine, CA 949-768-1900
Shick Esteve
Kansas City, MO 877-744-2587
South River Machine
Hackensack, NJ 201-487-1736
Spraying Systems Company
Wheaton, IL 630-655-5000
Stephan Machinery, Inc.
Mundelein, IL 800-783-7426
Techno-Design
Union, KY 800-641-1822
TWM Manufacturing
Leamington, ON 888-495-4831
UniTrak Corporation
Port Hope, ON 866-883-5749
US Tsubaki Holdings Inc
Wheeling, IL 800-323-7790
Wohl Associates Inc
Bohemia, NY 631-244-7979

Pasteurizers

AGC
Bristow, VA 800-825-8820
API Heat Transfer Inc
Buffalo, NY 877-274-4328
Arcobaleno Pasta Machines
Lancaster, PA 800-875-7096
B T Engineering Inc
Bala Cynwyd, PA 610-664-9500
Chad Co Inc
Olathe, KS 800-444-8360
Chester-Jensen Co., Inc.
Chester, PA 800-685-3750
Convay Systems
Minnetonka, MN 800-334-1099
Eischen Enterprises
Fresno, CA 559-834-0013
Feldmeier Equipment Inc
Syracuse, NY 315-454-8608
FleetwoodGoldcoWyard
Romeoville, IL 630-759-6800
Frigoscandia
Redmond, WA 800-423-1743
Globe Machine
Tacoma, WA 800-523-6575
Goodnature Products
Orchard Park, NY 800-875-3381
Krones
Franklin, WI 800-752-3787
MicroThermics, Inc.
Raleigh, NC 919-878-8045
Pacific Process Technology
La Jolla, CA 858-551-3298
Packaging & Processing Equipment
Ayr, ON 519-622-6666
Pneumatic Scale Angelus
Cuyahoga Falls, OH 330-923-0491
Relco Unisystems Corp
Willmar, MN 320-231-2210
Sanchelima International
Miami, FL 305-591-4343
Schlueter Company
Janesville, WI 800-359-1700
South Valley Mfg Inc
Gilroy, CA 408-842-5457
Stanfos
Edmonton, AB 800-661-5648
Stephan Machinery, Inc.
Mundelein, IL 800-783-7426
Unitherm Food System
Bristow, OK 918-367-0197
Whey Systems
Willmar, MN 320-905-4122

Peanut Processing

A C Horn & Co Sheet Metal
Dallas, TX 800-657-6155
ANDRITZ Inc
Muncy, PA 704-943-4343

Krispy Kist Company
Chicago, IL 312-733-0900
Lewis M Carter Mfg Co Inc
Donalsonville, GA 800-332-8232
Star Manufacturing Intl Inc
St Louis, MO 800-264-7827
Straub Designs Co
St Louis Park, MN 952-546-6686
Suffolk Iron Works Inc
Suffolk, VA 757-539-2353
UniTrak Corporation
Port Hope, ON 866-883-5749

Cleaners & Shellers

Southern Ag Co Inc
Blakely, GA 229-723-4262

Pickers

Poultry

Brower
Houghton, IA 800-553-1791
M & M Poultry Equipment Inc
Hollister, MO 800-872-9687
MSSH
Greensburg, IN 812-663-2180
Pickwick Manufacturing Svc
Cedar Rapids, IA 800-397-9797

Pizza & Pizza Products Processing

ABI Limited
Concord, ON 800-297-8666
AC Dispensing Equipment
Lower Sackville, NS 888-777-9990
ALPI Food Preparation Equipment
Bolton, ON 800-928-2574
APV Baker
Goldsboro, NC 919-736-4309
Bakers Pride Oven Company
New Rochelle, NY 800-431-2745
Benier USA
Lithia Springs, GA 770-745-2200
C H Babb Co Inc
Raynham, MA 508-977-0600
Christy Machine Co
Fremont, OH 888-332-6451
CIM Bakery Equipment of USA
Arlington Heights, IL 847-818-8121
Comtec Industries
Woodridge, IL 630-759-9000
DBE Inc
Concord, ON 800-461-5313
Doughpro
Perris, CA 800-594-5528
DoughXpress
Pittsburg, KS 800-835-0606
Doyon Equipment
Liniere, QC 800-463-4273
Dutchess Bakers' Machinery Co
Superior, WI 800-777-4498
Exact Mixing Systems Inc
Memphis, TN 901-362-8501
Fritsch USA
San Antonio, TX 210-491-9309
Garland Commercial Ranges
Mississauga, ON 905-624-0260
Garland Commercial Ranges Ltd.
Mississauga, ON 905-624-0260
Gemini Bakery Equipment
Philadelphia, PA 800-468-9046
Grote Co
Columbus, OH 888-534-7683
I J White Corp
Farmingdale, NY 631-293-2211
Industrial Ceramic Products
Marysville, OH 800-427-2278
Kemper Bakery Systems
Rockaway, NJ 973-625-1566
Lanly Co
Cleveland, OH 216-731-1115
Lawrence Equipment Inc
South El Monte, CA 800-423-4500
Martin/Baron
Irwindale, CA 626-960-5153
Matiss
St Georges, QC 888-562-8477
Merco/Savory
Mt. Pleasant, MI 800-733-8821
Molded Fiber Glass Tray Company
Linesville, PA 800-458-6050

Normandie Metal Fabricators
Port Washington, NY 800-221-2398
Oshikiri Corp of America
Philadelphia, PA 215-637-8112
Paxton Corp
Bristol, RI 401-396-9062
Peerless Dough Mixing and Make-Up
Sidney, OH 800-999-3327
Peerless Food Equipment
Sidney, OH 937-492-4158
Peerless Ovens
Sandusky, OH 800-548-4514
Piper Products Inc
Wausau, WI 800-544-3057
Pizzamatic USA
South Holland, IL 888-749-9279
Pro Bake Inc
Twinsburg, OH 800-837-4427
Proluxe
Paramount, CA 800-594-5528
Rademaker USA
Hudson, OH 330-650-2345
Raque Food Systems
Louisville, KY 502-267-9641
Reiser
Canton, MA 734-821-1290
Remco Industries International
Fort Lauderdale, FL 800-987-3626
Renato Specialty Product
Garland, TX 866-575-6316
Rheon USA
Irvine, CA 949-768-1900
Roto-Flex Oven Co
San Antonio, TX 877-859-1463
Server Products Inc
Richfield, WI 800-558-8722
Shick Esteve
Kansas City, MO 877-744-2587
Stephan Machinery, Inc.
Mundelein, IL 800-783-7426
Trak-Air/Rair
Denver, CO 800-688-8725
US Tsubaki Holdings Inc
Wheeling, IL 800-323-7790
Vulcan Food Equipment Group
Baltimore, MD 800-814-2028
Wood Stone Corp
Bellingham, WA 800-988-8103

Potato Chip Processing

Graybill Machines Inc
Lititz, PA 717-626-5221
Krispy Kist Company
Chicago, IL 312-733-0900
Pavan USA Inc
Emigsville, PA 717-767-4889
Paxton Corp
Bristol, RI 401-396-9062
Polar Process
Plattsville, ON 877-896-8077

Poultry Processing

Advance Energy Technologies
Halfmoon, NY 800-724-0198
Automated Food Systems
Waxahachie, TX 469-517-0470
Bluffton Motor Works
Bluffton, IN 800-579-8527
Brower
Houghton, IA 800-553-1791
Designpro Engineering
Clearwater, MN 800-221-4144
Doering Co
Clear Lake, MN 320-743-2276
Ennio International
Aurora, IL 630-851-5808
Falcon Fabricators Inc
Nashville, TN 615-832-0027
Gainco Inc
Gainesville, GA 800-467-2828
ICB Greenline
Charlotte, NC 800-331-5312
Johnson Food Equipment Inc
Kansas City, KS 800-288-3434
Kent Co
North Miami, FL 800-521-4886
Lyco Wausau
Wausau, WI 715-845-7867
Maja Equipment Company
Omaha, NE 402-346-6252

Marel Stork Poultry Processing
Gainesville, GA 770-532-7041
Marlen International
Astoria, OR 800-862-7536
Mepsco
Batavia, IL 800-323-8535
Millard Manufacturing Corp
La Vista, NE 800-662-4263
Miller Metal Fabrication
Bridgeville, DE 302-337-2291
Morris & Associates
Garner, NC 919-582-9200
Mp Equip. Co.
Buford, GA 770-614-5355
MSSH
Greensburg, IN 812-663-2180
P & F Machine
Turlock, CA 209-667-2515
Paoli Properties
Rockford, IL 815-965-0621
Pemberton & Associates
Brooklyn, NY 800-736-2664
Pickwick Manufacturing Svc
Cedar Rapids, IA 800-397-9797
Polar Process
Plattsville, ON 877-896-8077
Preferred Machining Corporation
Englewood, CO 303-761-1535
Prince Industries Inc
Murrayville, GA 800-441-3303
Reiser
Canton, MA 734-821-1290
Stork Townsend Inc.
Des Moines, IA 800-247-8609
Tech-Roll Inc
Blaine, WA 888-946-3929

Preservation

Irradiation

Nydree Flooring
Forest, VA 800-682-5698
Paragon Group USA
St Petersburg, FL 800-835-6962

Presses

Oil, Cottonseed & Linseed

Alfa Laval Ashbrook Simon-Hartley
Houston, TX 713-934-3160
Anderson International Corp
Stow, OH 800-336-4730
Davenport Machine
Rock Island, IL 309-786-1500
French Oil Mill Machinery Co
Piqua, OH 937-773-3420
Packaging & Processing Equipment
Ayr, ON 519-622-6666

Wine

Alfa Laval Ashbrook Simon-Hartley
Houston, TX 713-934-3160
Globe Machine
Tacoma, WA 800-523-6575
Goodnature Products
Orchard Park, NY 800-875-3381
Oak Barrel Winecraft
Berkeley, CA 510-849-0400
P & F Machine
Turlock, CA 209-667-2515

Pretzel Processing

Design Technology Corporation
Billerica, MA 978-663-7000
Exact Mixing Systems Inc
Memphis, TN 901-362-8501
Graybill Machines Inc
Lititz, PA 717-626-5221
I J White Corp
Farmingdale, NY 631-293-2211
Industrial Product Corp
Ho Ho Kus, NJ 800-472-5913
Krispy Kist Company
Chicago, IL 312-733-0900
Lanly Co
Cleveland, OH 216-731-1115
Peerless Dough Mixing and Make-Up
Sidney, OH 800-999-3327

Rademaker USA
Hudson, OH 330-650-2345
Rheon USA
Irvine, CA 949-768-1900
Shick Esteve
Kansas City, MO 877-744-2587
Stephan Machinery, Inc.
Mundelein, IL 800-783-7426
UniTrak Corporation
Port Hope, ON 866-883-5749
US Tsubaki Holdings Inc
Wheeling, IL 800-323-7790

Pulpers

Brown International Corp LLC
Winter Haven, FL 863-299-2111
Corenco
Santa Rosa, CA 888-267-3626
Corp Somat
Lancaster, PA 800-237-6628
Custom Food Machinery
Stockton, CA 209-463-4343
Dixie Canner Machine Shop
Athens, GA 706-549-0592

Pulverizers

Sugar

Glen Mills Inc.
Clifton, NJ 973-777-0777
Pro Scientific Inc
Oxford, CT 800-584-3776

Regenerators

Milk & Cream

Chester-Jensen Co., Inc.
Chester, PA 800-685-3750

Rice Processing

ANDRITZ Inc
Muncy, PA 704-943-4343
Grain Machinery Mfg Corp
Miami, FL 305-620-2525
Multi-Fill Inc
West Jordan, UT 801-280-1570

Roasters

A C Horn & Co Sheet Metal
Dallas, TX 800-657-6155
Alumaworks
Sunny Isle Beach, FL 800-277-7267
Amco Metals Indl
City of Industry, CA 626-855-2550
Browne & Company
Markham, ON 905-475-6104
Commercial Dehydrator Systems
Eugene, OR 800-369-4283
Davron Technologies Inc
Chattanooga, TN 423-870-1888
Gourmet COFFEE Roasters
Wixom, MI 866-933-6300
Imperial Manufacturing Co
Corona, CA 800-343-7790
Krispy Kist Company
Chicago, IL 312-733-0900
National Drying Machry Co Inc
Philadelphia, PA 215-464-6070
Star Manufacturing Intl Inc
St Louis, MO 800-264-7827
Superior Products Company
Saint Paul, MN 800-328-9800
Sweet Manufacturing Co
Springfield, OH 800-334-7254
Texas Corn Roasters
Granbury, TX 800-772-4345
Unitherm Food System
Bristow, OK 918-367-0197

Roasting

A C Horn & Co Sheet Metal
Dallas, TX 800-657-6155
Gourmet COFFEE Roasters
Wixom, MI 866-933-6300
Imperial Manufacturing Co
Corona, CA 800-343-7790

Krispy Kist Company
Chicago, IL 312-733-0900
Renato Specialty Product
Garland, TX 866-575-6316
Sivetz Coffee
Corvallis, OR 541-753-9713

Rotisseries

American Range
Pacoima, CA 888-753-9898
Attias Oven Corp
Brooklyn, NY 800-928-8427
Aztec Grill
Dallas, TX 800-346-8114
Ballantyne Food Service Equipment
Omaha, NE 800-424-1215
Belson Outdoors Inc
North Aurora, IL 800-323-5664
BKI Worldwide
Simpsonville, SC 800-927-6887
Broaster Co LLC
Beloit, WI 800-365-8278
Esquire Mechanical Corp.
Armonk, NY 800-847-4206
Friedrich Metal Products
Browns Summit, NC 800-772-0326
Grillco Inc
Aurora, IL 800-644-0067
Hardt Equipment Manufacturing
Lachine, QC 888-848-4408
Henny Penny, Inc.
Eaton, OH 800-417-8417
Hickory Industries
North Bergen, NJ 800-732-9153
J & R Mfg Inc
Mesquite, TX 800-527-4831
Merco/Savory
Mt. Pleasant, MI 800-733-8821
Music City Metals Inc
Nashville, TN 800-251-2674
Remco Industries International
Fort Lauderdale, FL 800-987-3626
Renato Specialty Product
Garland, TX 866-575-6316
Roto-Flex Oven Co
San Antonio, TX 877-859-1463
Shelcon Inc
Ontario, CA 909-947-4877
Southern Pride Distributing
Alamo, TN 800-851-8180
Superior Products Company
Saint Paul, MN 800-328-9800
Toastmaster
Elgin, IL 847-741-3300
Welbilt Corporation
Stamford, CT 203-325-8300
Win-Holt Equipment Group
Syosset, NY 800-444-3595
Wood Stone Corp
Bellingham, WA 800-988-8103

Salt Processing

A C Horn & Co Sheet Metal
Dallas, TX 800-657-6155
Viking Machine & Design Inc
De Pere, WI 888-286-2116

Sandwich Processing

APV Baker
Goldsboro, NC 919-736-4309
Design Technology Corporation
Billerica, MA 978-663-7000
Machine Builders & Design Inc
Shelby, NC 704-482-3456
Nuova Distribution Centre
Ferndale, WA 360-366-2226
Peerless Food Equipment
Sidney, OH 937-492-4158
Polar Process
Plattsville, ON 877-896-8077

Saws

Butchers' Blades

Acraloc Corp
Oak Ridge, TN 865-483-1368
AEW Thurne
Lake Zurich, IL 800-239-7297

Atlanta SharpTech
Peachtree City, GA 800-462-7297
Best & Donovan
Blue Ash, OH 800-553-2378
Biro Manufacturing Co
Lakeside Marblhd, OH 419-798-4451
California Saw & Knife Works
San Francisco, CA 888-729-6533
Carter Products
Grand Rapids, MI 888-622-7837
Cass Saw & Tool   Sharpening
Westmont, IL 630-968-1617
EZE-Lap Diamond Products
Carson City, NV 800-843-4815
Haban Saw Company
St.Louis, MO. 314-968-3991
Hollymatic Corp
Countryside, IL 708-579-3700
Jarvis Products Corp
Middletown, CT 860-347-7271
Kentmaster Manufacturing Co
Monrovia, CA. 800-421-1477
Mandeville Company
Minneapolis, MN 800-328-8490
Pieco
Manchester, IA 800-334-3929
Simmons Engineering Corporation
Wheeling, IL 800-252-3381
Simonds International
Fitchburg, MA 800-343-1616
Specialty Saw Inc
Simsbury, CT 800-225-0772

Scalers

Fish

Cretel Food Equipment
Holland, MI. 616-786-3980
Fishmore
Melbourne, FL 321-723-4751
Samuel Underberg Food Store
Brooklyn, NY 718-363-0787

Seafood Preparation Equipment

Alfa Laval Inc
Richmond, VA. 866-253-2528
Buck Knives
Post Falls, ID. 800-326-2825
Crane Research & Engineering
Hampton, VA 757-826-1707
Defreeze Corporation
Southborough, MA 508-485-8512
Design Technology Corporation
Billerica, MA 978-663-7000
E-Z Edge Inc
West New York, NJ 800-232-4470
Fishmore
Melbourne, FL 321-723-4751
Gregor Jonsson Inc
Lake Forest, IL 847-247-4200
Key Technology Inc.
Walla Walla, WA. 509-529-2161
Mp Equip. Co.
Buford, GA 770-614-5355
Nieco Corporation
Windsor, CA 800-643-2656
Paoli Properties
Rockford, IL 815-965-0621
Patty O Matic Machinery
Farmingdale, NJ 877-938-5244
Prawnto Systems
Caddo Mills, TX. 800-426-7254
R Murphy Co Inc
Ayer, MA. 888-772-3481
Simmons Engineering Corporation
Wheeling, IL 800-252-3381
Skrmetta Machinery Corporation
New Orleans, LA 504-488-4413
Smith-Berger Marine
Seattle, WA 206-764-4650
Steamway Corporation
Scottsburg, IN 800-259-8171
Stork Townsend Inc.
Des Moines, IA 800-247-8609
Superior Products Company
Saint Paul, MN 800-328-9800
Universal Stainless
Aurora, CO 800-223-8332
Universal Stainless & Alloy
Titusville, PA 800-295-1909

Separators

Bean, Pea

A C Horn & Co Sheet Metal
Dallas, TX. 800-657-6155
A.K. Robins
Baltimore, MD 800-486-9656
ANDRITZ Inc
Muncy, PA. 704-943-4343
Crippen Manufacturing Co
St Louis, MI 800-872-2474
Hebeler Corp
Tonawanda, NY 800-486-4709
Lewis M Carter Mfg Co Inc
Donalsonville, GA 800-332-8232
Lyco Manufacturing Inc
Columbus, WI. 920-623-4152
Magnetool Inc
Troy, MI 248-588-5400
Pro Scientific Inc
Oxford, CT 800-584-3776
Thomas Precision, Inc.
Rice Lake, WI. 800-657-4808
TWM Manufacturing
Leamington, ON 888-495-4831

Grain, Flour Mill

A T Ferrell Co Inc
Bluffton, IN. 800-248-8318
Alfa Laval Inc
Richmond, VA. 866-253-2528
ANDRITZ Inc
Muncy, PA. 704-943-4343
Cleland Manufacturing Company
Columbia Heights, MN. 763-571-4606
Crippen Manufacturing Co
St Louis, MI 800-872-2474
Dehyco Company
Memphis, TN 901-774-3322
Eischen Enterprises
Fresno, CA 559-834-0013
Hebeler Corp
Tonawanda, NY 800-486-4709
International Reserve Equipment Corporation
Clarendon Hills, IL. 708-531-0680
Magnetic Products Inc
Highland, MI. 800-544-5930
Magnetool Inc
Troy, MI 248-588-5400
Meadows Mills Inc
North Wilkesboro, NC 800-626-2282
Pro Scientific Inc
Oxford, CT 800-584-3776
Southern Ag Co Inc
Blakely, GA. 229-723-4262
TWM Manufacturing
Leamington, ON 888-495-4831

Liquid-Solid

Abanaki Corp
Chagrin Falls, OH. 800-358-7546
AFL Industries
West Palm Beach, FL 800-807-2709
Alfa Laval Inc
Richmond, VA. 866-253-2528
Alkota Cleaning Systems Inc
Alcester, SD 800-255-6823
Baker Hughes
Houston, TX
Bunting Magnetics Co
Newton, KS. 800-835-2526
Chil-Con Products
Brantford, ON 800-263-0086
Compatible Components Corporation
Houston, TX 713-688-2008
Cook & Beals Inc
Loup City, NE 308-745-0154
Dedert Corporation
Olympia Fields, IL 708-747-7000
Dings Co Magnetic Group
Milwaukee, WI 414-672-7830
Enviro-Clear Co
High Bridge, NJ 908-638-5507
Everfilt Corp
Mira Loma, CA. 800-360-8380
Fernholtz Engineering
Van Nuys, CA 818-785-5800
Filtration Systems
Sunrise, FL 954-572-2700

French Oil Mill Machinery Co
Piqua, OH 937-773-3420
General Industries Inc
Goldsboro, NC 888-735-2882
Globe Machine
Tacoma, WA 800-523-6575
Goodnature Products
Orchard Park, NY 800-875-3381
Hebeler Corp
Tonawanda, NY 800-486-4709
Hosokawa/Bepex Corporation
Santa Rosa, CA 707-586-6000
Jay R Smith Mfg Co
Montgomery, AL 334-277-8520
Lyco Manufacturing Inc
Columbus, WI 920-623-4152
Membrane Process & Controls
Edgar, WI 715-352-3206
Membrane System Specialist Inc
Wisconsin Rapids, WI 715-421-2333
Monroe Environmental Corp
Monroe, MI 800-992-7707
Pacific Process Technology
La Jolla, CA 858-551-3298
Pall Filtron
Northborough, MA 800-345-8766
Pro Scientific Inc
Oxford, CT 800-584-3776
Provisur Technologies, Inc.
Mokena, IL 708-479-3500
Relco Unisystems Corp
Willmar, MN 320-231-2210
Scienco Systems
Saint Louis, MO 314-621-2536
Sermia International
Blainville, QC 800-567-7483
Statco Engineering
Huntington Beach, CA 800-421-0362
Sweco Inc
Florence, KY 800-807-9326
Tema Systems Inc
Cincinnati, OH 513-792-2840
TWM Manufacturing
Leamington, ON 888-495-4831
Ultrafilter
Norcross, GA 800-543-3634
Van Air Systems
Lake City, PA 800-840-9906
Vincent Corp
Tampa, FL 813-248-2650
Waterlink/Sanborn Technologies
Canton, OH 800-343-3381
Welliver Metal Products Corporation
Salem, OR 503-362-1568
Westfalia Separator
Northvale, NJ 800-722-6622

Shish Kebab Systems

Automated Food Systems
Waxahachie, TX 469-517-0470
Wishbone Utensil Tableware Line
Wheat Ridge, CO 866-266-5928

Shredders

Cane

Silver Weibull
Aurora, CO 303-373-2311

Cheese

Corenco
Santa Rosa, CA 888-267-3626
Deville Technologies
St Laurent, QC 866-404-4545
Reiser
Canton, MA 734-821-1290

Corn & Fodder

Dito Dean Food Prep
Charlotte, NC 866-449-4200
Grote Co
Columbus, OH 888-534-7683

Vegetable & Fruit

Corenco
Santa Rosa, CA 888-267-3626
Globe Machine
Tacoma, WA 800-523-6575

Goodnature Products
Orchard Park, NY 800-875-3381
Paxton Corp
Bristol, RI 401-396-9062
Reiser
Canton, MA 734-821-1290
Rival Manufacturing Company
Kansas City, MO 816-943-4100
Superior Products Company
Saint Paul, MN 800-328-9800
Univex Corp
Salem, NH. 800-258-6358

Shrimp Processing Equipment

Steamway Corporation
Scottsburg, IN 800-259-8171
Tri-Pak Machinery Inc
Harlingen, TX 956-423-5140

Skinning

Cretel Food Equipment
Holland, MI 616-786-3980
Mtc Food Equipment
Poulsbo, WA 360-697-6319

Slicers

Bread & Cake

ABI Limited
Concord, ON........................800-297-8666
AM-Mac
Fairfield, NJ 800-829-2018
American Eagle Food Machinery
Chicago, IL 888-390-0800
AMF CANADA
Sherbrooke, QC 800-255-3869
Bettendorf Stanford Inc
Salem, IL. 800-548-2253
C & K Machine Co
Holyoke, MA 413-536-8122
Chicago Scale & Slicer Company
Franklin Park, IL................847-455-3400
Clayton Manufacturing Company
Derby, NY 716-549-0392
Deluxe Equipment Company
Bradenton, FL 800-367-8931
DoughXpress
Pittsburg, KS......................800-835-0606
Empire Bakery Equipment
Hicksville, NY 800-878-4070
Food Tools
Santa Barbara, CA 877-836-6386
Good Idea
Northampton, MA................800-462-9237
Grote Co
Columbus, OH 888-534-7683
Hansaloy Corp
Davenport, IA 800-553-4992
Knott Slicers
Canton, MA 781-821-0925
Lematic Inc
Jackson, MI........................517-787-3301
Soco System USA
Waukesha, WI. 800-441-6293
Solbern Corp
Fairfield, NJ 973-227-3030
Steinmetz Machine Works Inc
Stamford, CT......................203-327-0118
Toronto Kitchen Equipment
North York, ON. 416-745-4944
United Bakery Equipment Company
Shawnee Mission, KS..........913-541-8700
Waring Products
Torrington, CT 800-492-7464

Egg

Acme International
Maplewood, NJ 973-416-0400
Amco Metals Indl
City of Industry, CA 626-855-2550
Grote Co
Columbus, OH 888-534-7683
Polar Process
Plattsville, ON....................877-896-8077
Superior Products Company
Saint Paul, MN 800-328-9800

Meat

AEW Thurne
Lake Zurich, IL. 800-239-7297
AM-Mac
Fairfield, NJ 800-829-2018
Automated Food Systems
Waxahachie, TX 469-517-0470
Bettcher Industries Inc
Wakeman, OH. 800-321-8763
Biro Manufacturing Co
Lakeside Marblhd, OH........419-798-4451
Bizerba USA
Piscataway, NJ 732-565-6000
Blakeslee, Inc.
Addison, IL 630-532-5021
Bridge Machine Company
Palmyra, NJ 877-754-1800
Browne & Company
Markham, ON 905-475-6104
Chicago Scale & Slicer Company
Franklin Park, IL................847-455-3400
Edlund Co
Burlington, VT 800-772-2126
General Machinery Corp
Sheboygan, WI 888-243-6622
General, Inc
Weston, FL 954-202-7419
Globe Food Equipment Co
Moraine, OH 800-347-5423
Grote Co
Columbus, OH 888-534-7683
Handtmann Inc
Lake Forest, IL 800-477-3585
I. Fm Usa Inc.
Franklin Park, IL. 866-643-6872
Kasel Industries Inc
Denver, CO 800-218-4417
Machanix Fabrication Inc
Chino, CA 800-700-9701
Mandeville Company
Minneapolis, MN 800-328-8490
Marlen International
Astoria, OR 800-862-7536
Mtc Food Equipment
Poulsbo, WA 360-697-6319
Planet Products Corp
Blue Ash, OH 513-984-5544
Prince Castle Inc
Carol Stream, IL 800-722-7853
Quantum Topping Systems Quantum Technical Services Inc
Frankfort, IL......................888-464-1540
Reiser
Canton, MA 734-821-1290
Ross Industries Inc
Midland, VA 540-439-3271
Spiral Slices Ham Market
Detroit, MI 313-259-6262
Spiro-Cut Equipment Co
Fort Worth, TX 888-887-4267
Standex International Corp.
Salem, NH. 603-893-9701
STARMIX srl
Marano, VI 044- 57- 659
Superior Products Company
Saint Paul, MN 800-328-9800
Toronto Kitchen Equipment
North York, ON. 416-745-4944
TWM Manufacturing
Leamington, ON 888-495-4831
Univex Corp
Salem, NH. 800-258-6358
Waring Products
Torrington, CT 800-492-7464
Weber Inc
Kansas City, MO. 800-505-9591
Weber Inc
Kansas City, MO. 816-891-8397

Vegetable & Fruit

A.K. Robins
Baltimore, MD 800-486-9656
AM-Mac
Fairfield, NJ 800-829-2018
Ashlock Co
San Leandro, CA. 510-351-0560
Atlas Pacific Engineering
Pueblo, CO 719-948-3040
Automated Food Systems
Waxahachie, TX 469-517-0470

Blakeslee, Inc.
Addison, IL........................630-532-5021
Bluffton Slaw Cutter Company
Bluffton, OH.....................419-358-9840
Brothers Metal Products
Santa Ana, CA 714-972-3008
Chicago Scale & Slicer Company
Franklin Park, IL.................847-455-3400
Dito Dean Food Prep
Charlotte, NC.....................866-449-4200
Edlund Co
Burlington, VT....................800-772-2126
F.B. Pease Company
Rochester, NY.....................585-475-1870
General, Inc
Weston, FL........................954-202-7419
Goodnature Products
Orchard Park, NY..................800-875-3381
Grote Co
Columbus, OH......................888-534-7683
Insinger Co
Philadelphia, PA..................800-344-4802
International Knife & Saw
Florence, SC......................800-354-9872
Keen Kutter
Torrance, CA......................310-370-6941
Knott Slicers
Canton, MA........................781-821-0925
Lincoln Foodservice
Cleveland, OH.....................800-374-3004
Machanix Fabrication Inc
Chino, CA.........................800-700-9701
Mandeville Company
Minneapolis, MN...................800-328-8490
Mannhart
Fort Worth, TX....................817-421-0100
Matfer Inc
Van Nuys, CA......................800-766-0333
Nemco Food Equipment
Hicksville, OH....................800-782-6761
Paxton Corp
Bristol, RI.......................401-396-9062
Prince Castle Inc
Carol Stream, IL..................800-722-7853
Reiser
Canton, MA........................734-821-1290
Rival Manufacturing Company
Kansas City, MO...................816-943-4100
Slicechief Co
Toledo, OH........................419-241-7647
South Valley Mfg Inc
Gilroy, CA........................408-842-5457
Stafford-Smith Inc
Kalamazoo, MI.....................800-968-2442
Superior Products Company
Saint Paul, MN....................800-328-9800
Toronto Kitchen Equipment
North York, ON....................416-745-4944
TWM Manufacturing
Leamington, ON....................888-495-4831
Univex Corp
Salem, NH.........................800-258-6358
Urschel Laboratories
Valparaiso, IN....................219-464-4811
Waring Products
Torrington, CT....................800-492-7464

Smokers

Fish, Meat & Produce

Alto-Shaam
Menomonee Falls, WI...............800-329-8744
Backwoods Smoker Inc
Shreveport, LA....................318-220-0380
Ballantyne Food Service Equipment
Omaha, NE.........................800-424-1215
BBQ Pits by Klose
Houston, TX.......................800-487-7487
Brinkmann Corporation
Dallas, TX........................800-468-5252
Britt's Barbecue
Birmingham, AL....................205-612-6538
Cookshack
Ponca City, OK....................800-423-0698
Custom Diamond Intl.
Laval, QC.........................800-326-5926
Friedrich Metal Products
Browns Summit, NC.................800-772-0326
Gregg Industries Inc
Waunakee, WI......................608-846-5143

Le Smoker
Salisbury, MD.....................410-677-3233
Luhr Jensen & Sons Inc
Hood River, OR....................541-386-3811
Masterbuilt Manufacturing Inc
Columbus, GA......................706-327-5622
Reiser
Canton, MA........................734-821-1290
Roto-Flex Oven Co
San Antonio, TX...................877-859-1463
Seven B Plus
Sandy, OR.........................503-668-5079
Smokaroma
Boley, OK.........................800-331-5565
Southern Pride Distributing
Alamo, TN.........................800-851-8180
Super Cooker
Lake Park, GA.....................800-841-7452
Superior Products Company
Saint Paul, MN....................800-328-9800
Townfood Equipment Corp
Brooklyn, NY......................800-221-5032
Traeger Industries
Portland, OR......................800-872-3437
Unitherm Food System
Bristow, OK.......................918-367-0197
Vortron Smokehouse/Ovens
Iron Ridge, WI....................800-874-1949
Win-Holt Equipment Group
Syosset, NY.......................800-444-3595

Sawdust

American Wood Fibers
Columbia, MD......................800-624-9663
Northeastern Products Corp
Warrensburg, NY...................800-873-8233
West Oregon Wood Products Inc
Columbia City, OR.................503-397-6707

Snack Food Processing

A & B Process Systems Corp
Stratford, WI.....................888-258-2789
A C Horn & Co Sheet Metal
Dallas, TX........................800-657-6155
Automated Food Systems
Waxahachie, TX....................469-517-0470
Berkshire PPM
Litchfield, CT....................860-567-3118
Design Technology Corporation
Billerica, MA.....................978-663-7000
Et Oakes Corp
Hauppauge, NY.....................631-232-0002
Exact Mixing Systems Inc
Memphis, TN.......................901-362-8501
Food Machinery Sales
Bogart, GA........................706-549-2207
Formost Packaging Machines
Woodinville, WA...................425-483-9090
Fritsch USA
San Antonio, TX...................210-491-9309
Graybill Machines Inc
Lititz, PA........................717-626-5221
Industrial Product Corp
Ho Ho Kus, NJ.....................800-472-5913
J C Ford Co
La Habra, CA......................714-871-7361
Krispy Kist Company
Chicago, IL.......................312-733-0900
Lanly Co
Cleveland, OH.....................216-731-1115
Oshikiri Corp of America
Philadelphia, PA..................215-637-8112
Pavan USA Inc
Emigsville, PA....................717-767-4889
Peerless Dough Mixing and Make-Up
Sidney, OH........................800-999-3327
Polar Process
Plattsville, ON...................877-896-8077
Pro Bake Inc
Twinsburg, OH.....................800-837-4427
Reading Bakery Systems Inc
Robesonia, PA.....................610-693-5816
Reiser
Canton, MA........................734-821-1290
Stephan Machinery, Inc.
Mundelein, IL.....................800-783-7426
Superior Food Machinery Inc
Pico Rivera, CA...................800-944-0396
UniTrak Corporation
Port Hope, ON.....................866-883-5749

US Tsubaki Holdings Inc
Wheeling, IL......................800-323-7790
Woody Associates Inc
York, PA..........................717-843-3975

Sorters

Bean & Grain

A.K. Robins
Baltimore, MD.....................800-486-9656
Oxbo International Corp
Clear Lake, WI....................800-628-6196
Sortex
Fremont, CA.......................510-797-5000
Welliver Metal Products Corporation
Salem, OR.........................503-362-1568

Potato & Onion

A.K. Robins
Baltimore, MD.....................800-486-9656
Andgar Corp
Ferndale, WA......................360-366-9900
Atlas Pacific Engineering
Pueblo, CO........................719-948-3040
Odenberg Engineering
West Sacramento, CA...............800-688-8396
Southern Automatics
Lakeland, FL......................800-441-4604
Welliver Metal Products Corporation
Salem, OR.........................503-362-1568

Soybean Processing

A.K. Robins
Baltimore, MD.....................800-486-9656
ANDRITZ Inc
Muncy, PA.........................704-943-4343
Bean Machines
Sonoma, CA........................707-996-0706
Corenco
Santa Rosa, CA....................888-267-3626
Insta-Pro International
Urbandale, IA.....................800-383-4524

Stemmers

Healdsburg Machine Company
Santa Rosa, CA....................707-433-3348

Stoves

American Range
Pacoima, CA.......................888-753-9898
Connerton Co
Santa Ana, CA.....................714-547-9218
Dynamic Cooking Systems
Huntington Beach, CA..............800-433-8466
Gold Star Products
Oak Park, MI......................800-800-0205
Imperial Manufacturing Co
Corona, CA........................800-343-7790
Iwatani International Corporation of America
Houston, TX.......................800-775-5506
Krispy Kist Company
Chicago, IL.......................312-733-0900
Maytag Corporation
Benton Harbor, MI.................800-344-1274
Mosshaim Innovations
Jacksonville, FL..................888-995-7775
Mountain Safety Research
Seattle, WA.......................800-877-9677
Mr. Bar-B-Q
Winston-Salem, NC.................800-333-2124
Savage Brothers Company
Elk Grove Vlg, IL.................800-342-0973
Seidman Brothers
Chelsea, MA.......................800-437-7770
Superior Products Company
Saint Paul, MN....................800-328-9800
Toronto Kitchen Equipment
North York, ON....................416-745-4944
Townfood Equipment Corp
Brooklyn, NY......................800-221-5032

Stuffers

Sausage

Biro Manufacturing Co
Lakeside Marblhd, OH..............419-798-4451

Famco Automatic Sausage Linkers
Pittsburgh, PA .412-241-6410
Friedr Dick Corp
Farmingdale, NY 800-554-3425
Handtmann Inc
Lake Forest, IL 800-477-3585
Hitec Food Equipment
Wood Dale, IL. 630-521-9460
Marlen
Riverside, MO. 913-888-3333
Polar Process
Plattsville, ON. 877-896-8077
Reiser
Canton, MA 734-821-1290
Stork Townsend Inc.
Des Moines, IA 800-247-8609

Sugar & Syrup Processing

Alfa Laval Inc
Richmond, VA. 866-253-2528
Custom Food Machinery
Stockton, CA. 209-463-4343
Honiron Corp
Jeanerette, LA 337-276-6314
Mulligan Associates
Mequon, WI 800-627-2886
Progressive Tractor & Implement Co.
Parks, LA 337-845-5080
Putsch & Co Inc
Fletcher, NC 800-847-8427
Raytheon Co
Waltham, MA 781-522-3000
Silver Weibull
Aurora, CO 303-373-2311
Vendome Copper & Brass Works
Louisville, KY 888-384-5161

Tanks

Creamery, Dairy

A & B Process Systems Corp
Stratford, WI. 888-258-2789
Bowers Process Equipment
Stratford, ON. 800-567-3223
C E Rogers Co
Mora, MN 800-279-8081
Chester-Jensen Co., Inc.
Chester, PA 800-685-3750
DCI, Inc.
St Cloud, MN 320-252-8200
Diversified Metal Engineering
Charlottetown, PE. 902-628-6900
Eischen Enterprises
Fresno, CA 559-834-0013
Electrol Specialties Co
South Beloit, IL 815-389-2291
Enerfab Inc.
Cincinnati, OH 513-641-0500
Falco Technologies
La Prairie, QC. 450-444-0566
Feldmeier Equipment Inc
Syracuse, NY 315-454-8608
Howard Fabrication
City of Industry, CA 626-961-0114
Midwest Stainless
Menomonie, WI 715-235-5472
Northland Process Piping
Isle, MN .320-679-2119
Packaging & Processing Equipment
Ayr, ON. .519-622-6666
Paul Mueller Co Inc
Springfield, MO 800-683-5537
Puritan Manufacturing Inc
Omaha, NE 800-331-0487
Rosenwach Tank Co LLC
Long Island City, NY 212-972-4411
Sanchelima International
Miami, FL. 305-591-4343
Scherping Systems
Winsted, MN. 320-485-4401
Schlueter Company
Janesville, WI 800-359-1700
Sharpsville Container Corp
Sharpsville, PA 800-645-1248
Stainless Fabrication Inc
Springfield, MO 800-397-8265
Viatec
Victoria, BC 800-942-4702
Walker Stainless Equipment Co
New Lisbon, WI 608-562-7500

Drying, Evaporating

A & B Process Systems Corp
Stratford, WI. 888-258-2789
Behlen Manufacturing Co.
Columbus, NE. 402-564-3111
DCI, Inc.
St Cloud, MN 320-252-8200
Electrol Specialties Co
South Beloit, IL 815-389-2291
Ellett Industries
Port Coquitlam, BC. 604-941-8211
Falco Technologies
La Prairie, QC. 450-444-0566
Gaston County Dyeing Mach Co
Mt Holly, NC 704-822-5000
Northland Process Piping
Isle, MN .320-679-2119
Packaging & Processing Equipment
Ayr, ON. .519-622-6666
Paget Equipment Co
Marshfield, WI 715-384-3158
Pittsburgh Tank Corp
Monongahela, PA 800-634-0243
Sharpsville Container Corp
Sharpsville, PA 800-645-1248
Stainless Fabrication Inc
Springfield, MO 800-397-8265

Washers & Fillers

Abco Automation
Browns Summit, NC. 336-375-6400

Toasters

APW Wyott Food Service Equipment Company
Cheyenne, WY 800-527-2100
Attias Oven Corp
Brooklyn, NY 800-928-8427
Hatco Corp
Milwaukee, WI. 800-558-0607
Holman Cooking Equipment
Saint Louis, MO 888-356-5362
Machanix Fabrication Inc
Chino, CA. 800-700-9701
Merco/Savory
Mt. Pleasant, MI 800-733-8821
Middleby Corp
Elgin, IL .847-741-3300
Middleby Marshall Inc
Elgin, IL .847-741-3300
Prince Castle Inc
Carol Stream, IL 800-722-7853
Roundup Food Equip
Carol Stream, IL 800-253-2991
Superior Products Company
Saint Paul, MN 800-328-9800
Toastmaster
Elgin, IL .847-741-3300
Welbilt Corporation
Stamford, CT. 203-325-8300

Tortilla Making

Alliance Bakery Systems
Blythewood, SC 803-691-9227
Baking Machines
Livermore, CA 925-449-3369
Be & Sco
San Antonio, TX 800-683-0928
Bettendorf Stanford Inc
Salem, IL .800-548-2253
Burford Corp
Maysville, OK. 877-287-3673
Casa Herrera
Pomona, CA 800-624-3916
Christy Machine Co
Fremont, OH. 888-332-6451
Design Technology Corporation
Billerica, MA 978-663-7000
Dutchess Bakers' Machinery Co
Superior, WI. 800-777-4498
Exact Mixing Systems Inc
Memphis, TN 901-362-8501
Food Tools
Santa Barbara, CA 877-836-6386
Formost Packaging Machines
Woodinville, WA. 425-483-9090
Fritsch USA
San Antonio, TX 210-491-9309
Gemini Bakery Equipment
Philadelphia, PA 800-468-9046

I J White Corp
Farmingdale, NY. 631-293-2211
J C Ford Co
La Habra, CA 714-871-7361
K B Systems Inc
Bangor, PA 610-588-7788
Lanly Co
Cleveland, OH. 216-731-1115
Lawrence Equipment Inc
South El Monte, CA 800-423-4500
Maddox/Adams International
Miami, FL 305-592-3337
Peerless Dough Mixing and Make-Up
Sidney, OH. 800-999-3327
Peerless Food Equipment
Sidney, OH. 937-492-4158
Pinckney Molded Plastics
Howell, MI 800-854-2920
Proluxe
Paramount, CA 800-594-5528
Rademaker USA
Hudson, OH 330-650-2345
Rheon USA
Irvine, CA 949-768-1900
Shick Esteve
Kansas City, MO. 877-744-2587
Soco System USA
Waukesha, WI. 800-441-6293
Stephan Machinery, Inc.
Mundelein, IL 800-783-7426
Superior Food Machinery Inc
Pico Rivera, CA 800-944-0396
X-Press Manufacturing
New Braunfels, TX. 800-365-9440

VOC Control

Anguil Environmental Systems
Milwaukee, WI. 800-488-0230
Dennsi Group
Springfield, MA 413-737-1353
Lyco Manufacturing
Wausau, WI. 715-845-7867

Vats

Cheese

Relco Unisystems Corp
Willmar, MN 320-231-2210

Dairy Cooling

Relco Unisystems Corp
Willmar, MN 320-231-2210

Meat Curing

Dc Tech
Kansas City, MO. 877-742-9090
Dubuque Steel Products Co
Dubuque, IA 563-556-6288

Vegetable Preparation Equipment

A.K. Robins
Baltimore, MD 800-486-9656
Altman Industries
Gray, GA. 478-986-3116
Berkshire PPM
Litchfield, CT 860-567-3118
Bluffton Slaw Cutter Company
Bluffton, OH. 419-358-9840
Brothers Metal Products
Santa Ana, CA 714-972-3008
Brown International Corp LLC
Winter Haven, FL 863-299-2111
Computer Controlled Machines
Pueblo, CO 719-948-9500
Design Technology Corporation
Billerica, MA 978-663-7000
Diversified Metal Engineering
Charlottetown, PE. 902-628-6900
Eurodib
Champlain, NY 888-956-6866
French Oil Mill Machinery Co
Piqua, OH. 937-773-3420
General, Inc
Weston, FL 954-202-7419
Globe Machine
Tacoma, WA 800-523-6575
Goodnature Products
Orchard Park, NY 800-875-3381

Harold F Haines Manufacturing Inc
  Presque Isle, ME 207-762-1411
Hughes Co
  Columbus, WI. 866-535-9303
Keen Kutter
  Torrance, CA. 310-370-6941
Kerian Machines Inc
  Grafton, ND 701-352-0480
Key Technology Inc.
  Walla Walla, WA. 509-529-2161
Knott Slicers
  Canton, MA 781-821-0925
Kusel Equipment Company
  Watertown, WI 920-261-4112
Lee Financial Corporation
  Dallas, TX. 972-960-1001
Mannhart
  Fort Worth, TX 817-421-0100
Matfer Inc
  Van Nuys, CA 800-766-0333
Mumper Machine Corporation
  Butler, WI .262-781-8908
Murotech
  St Marys, OH 800-565-6876
Nemco Food Equipment
  Hicksville, OH 800-782-6761
Odenberg Engineering
  West Sacramento, CA 800-688-8396
OXO International
  New York, NY 212-242-3333
Patty O Matic Machinery
  Farmingdale, NJ 877-938-5244
Paxton Corp
  Bristol, RI .401-396-9062
Pick Heaters
  West Bend, WI 800-233-9030
Power Brushes
  Toledo, OH 800-968-9600
Prince Castle Inc
  Carol Stream, IL 800-722-7853
Reiser
  Canton, MA 734-821-1290
Simmons Engineering Corporation
  Wheeling, IL 800-252-3381
South Valley Mfg Inc
  Gilroy, CA .408-842-5457
Superior Products Company
  Saint Paul, MN 800-328-9800
Taylor Manufacturing Co
  Moultrie, GA. 229-985-5445
Univex Corp
  Salem, NH. 800-258-6358
Urschel Laboratories
  Valparaiso, IN 219-464-4811
Vanmark Equipment
  Creston, IA .800-523-6261

Vegetable Processing

A.K. Robins
  Baltimore, MD 800-486-9656
ABCO Industries Limited
  Lunenburg, NS 866-634-8821
Altman Industries
  Gray, GA. .478-986-3116
AM-Mac
  Fairfield, NJ 800-829-2018
Ametek Technical & Industrial Products
  Kent, OH. .215-256-6601
Andgar Corp
  Ferndale, WA 360-366-9900
Berkshire PPM
  Litchfield, CT 860-567-3118
Brown International Corp LLC
  Winter Haven, FL 863-299-2111
Computer Controlled Machines
  Pueblo, CO 719-948-9500
Corenco
  Santa Rosa, CA. 888-267-3626
Custom Food Machinery
  Stockton, CA. 209-463-4343
Dipwell Co
  Northampton, MA. 413-587-4673
Dito Dean Food Prep
  Charlotte, NC 866-449-4200
Diversified Metal Engineering
  Charlottetown, PE. 902-628-6900
Dixie Canner Machine Shop
  Athens, GA. 706-549-0592
F.B. Pease Company
  Rochester, NY. 585-475-1870

Franrica Systems
  Stockton, CA. 209-948-2811
Globe Machine
  Tacoma, WA 800-523-6575
Goodnature Products
  Orchard Park, NY 800-875-3381
Harold F Haines Manufacturing Inc
  Presque Isle, ME 207-762-1411
Hughes Co
  Columbus, WI. 866-535-9303
Kerian Machines Inc
  Grafton, ND 701-352-0480
Key Technology Inc.
  Walla Walla, WA. 509-529-2161
Kusel Equipment Company
  Watertown, WI 920-261-4112
Lyco Wausau
  Wausau, WI. 715-845-7867
Mannhart
  Fort Worth, TX 817-421-0100
Mouli Manufacturing Corporation
  Belleville, NJ 800-789-8285
Multi-Fill Inc
  West Jordan, UT 801-280-1570
Mumper Machine Corporation
  Butler, WI .262-781-8908
Murotech
  St Marys, OH 800-565-6876
Nemco Food Equipment
  Hicksville, OH 800-782-6761
Paxton Corp
  Bristol, RI .401-396-9062
Paxton Products Inc
  Blue Ash, OH 800-441-7475
Reiser
  Canton, MA 734-821-1290
Semco Manufacturing Company
  Pharr, TX. .956-787-4203
Slicechief Co
  Toledo, OH 419-241-7647
Taylor Manufacturing Co
  Moultrie, GA. 229-985-5445
Tew Manufacturing Corp
  Penfield, NY 800-380-5839
UniTrak Corporation
  Port Hope, ON 866-883-5749
Urschel Laboratories
  Valparaiso, IN 219-464-4811
Vanmark Equipment
  Creston, IA .800-523-6261

Vibrators

MeGa Industries
  Burlington, ON 800-665-6342

Waffle Irons

Superior Products Company
  Saint Paul, MN 800-328-9800

Washers

Fruit & Vegetable

A.K. Robins
  Baltimore, MD 800-486-9656
Atlas Pacific Engineering
  Pueblo, CO 719-948-3040
Berkshire PPM
  Litchfield, CT 860-567-3118
Brogdex Company
  Pomona, CA 909-622-1021
Davron Technologies Inc
  Chattanooga, TN. 423-870-1888
Globe Machine
  Tacoma, WA 800-523-6575
Goodnature Products
  Orchard Park, NY 800-875-3381
Harold F Haines Manufacturing Inc
  Presque Isle, ME 207-762-1411
Hughes Co
  Columbus, WI. 866-535-9303
Key Technology Inc.
  Walla Walla, WA. 509-529-2161
Leon C. Osborn Company
  Houston, TX 281-488-0755
N & A Mfg
  Mallard, IA .712-425-3512
Tew Manufacturing Corp
  Penfield, NY 800-380-5839

Tri-Pak Machinery Inc
  Harlingen, TX 956-423-5140
Vanmark Equipment
  Creston, IA .800-523-6261

Waxers

International Wax Refining Company
  Warren, NJ 908-561-2500
Sandvik Process Systems
  Sweden, NJ 973-790-1600

Waxing

Kent Co
  North Miami, FL. 800-521-4886
MAF Industries Inc
  Traver, CA .559-897-2905
Tri-Pak Machinery Inc
  Harlingen, TX. 956-423-5140

Yeast Processing

Alfa Laval Inc
  Richmond, VA. 866-253-2528
Sharp Brothers
  Bayonne, NJ 201-339-0404
Tuchenhagen
  Columbia, MD 410-910-6000
Vendome Copper & Brass Works
  Louisville, KY 888-384-5161

Fruit Industry

Alard Equipment Corp
  Williamson, NY 315-589-4511
Ocs Checkweighers, Inc.
  Snellville, GA. 678-344-8030

Funnels

American Metalcraft Inc
  Franklin Park, IL. 708-345-1177
Behrens Manufacturing LLC
  Winona, MN 507-454-4664
Jacob Tubing LP
  Memphis, TN 901-566-1110
Kosempel Manufacturing Company
  Philadelphia, PA 800-733-7122
M O Industries Inc
  Whippany, NJ 973-386-9228
Southern Metal Fabricators Inc
  Albertville, AL 800-989-1330
Superior Products Company
  Saint Paul, MN 800-328-9800
Tolco Corp
  Toledo, OH 800-537-4786
Wilks Precision Instr Co Inc
  Union Bridge, MD 410-775-7917
World Kitchen
  Elmira, NY .800-999-3436
Zeier Plastic & Mfg Inc
  Madison, WI 608-244-5782

Gas Connectors

Dormont Manufacturing Co
  Export, PA. 800-367-6668
Hose Master Inc
  Euclid, OH .216-481-2020
Linde North America
  Murray Hill, NJ. 908-464-8100
Spraying Systems Company
  Wheaton, IL 630-655-5000
Superior Products Company
  Saint Paul, MN 800-328-9800

General

915 Labs
  Centennial, CO 855-915-5227
AgroFresh
  Philadelphia, PA 866-850-6846
Alard Equipment Corp
  Williamson, NY 315-589-4511
ALLCAMS Machine Company
  Folsom, PA 610-534-9004
Allied Purchasing Co
  Mason City, IA 800-247-5956
Altra Industrial Motion Corp
  Braintree, MA 781-917-0600
American Conveyor Corporation
  Astoria, NY. 718-386-0480

Amerivap Systems Inc
Dawsonville, GA..........................800-763-7687
Amsler Equipment Inc
Richmond Hill, ON, ON...........877-738-2569
Annie's Frozen Yogurt
Minneapolis, MN.....................800-969-9648
Automation Ideas Inc
Rockford, MI...........................877-254-3327
Baldor Electric Co
Fort Smith, AR........................479-646-4711
Bison Gear & Engineering Corp.
St. Charles, IL........................800-282-4766
Blentech Corp
Santa Rosa, CA.......................707-523-5949
Boston Gear
Boston, MA.............................888-999-9860
Bunzl Processor Distribution LLC
Riverside, MO.........................816-448-4300
Butler Winery
Bloomington, IN......................812-332-6660
Carmel Engineering
Kirklin, IN..............................888-427-0497
Cipriani
Rancho Sta Marg, CA...............949-589-3978
Cold Jet, LLC
Loveland, OH..........................800-337-9423
Control Concepts, Inc.
Putnam, CT.............................860-928-6551
Control Techniques
Eden Prairie, MN.....................800-893-2321
Coperion Corp
Sewell, NJ..............................854-253-3265
Culinary Depot
Monsey, NY............................888-845-8200
Ecolab Inc
St. Paul, MN...........................800-352-5326
Emerson Industrial Automation
Eden Prairie, MN.....................800-893-2321
Euchner-USA
East Syracuse, NY...................315-701-0315
Gates Mectrol Inc
Salem, NH..............................800-394-4844
Ickler Co Inc
St Cloud, MN..........................800-243-8382
Illinois Tool Works
Glenview, IL............................224-661-8870
Kastalon, Inc.
Alsip, IL.................................800-527-8566
KION North America
Summerville, SC.....................843-875-8000
La Poblana Food Machines
Mesa, AZ................................480-258-2091
Lenze Americas
Uxbridge, MA..........................800-217-9100
Lepel Corp
Waukesha, WI.........................800-231-6008
Liburdi Group of Companies
Mooresville, NC.......................800-533-9353
Lumaco Inc
Hackensack, NJ.......................800-735-8258
Material Handling Technology, Inc
Morrisville, NC........................800-779-2475
Meltric Corporation
Franklin, WI...........................800-824-4031
Motoman
West Carrollton, OH.................937-847-6200
Mountain States Processing
Fort Lupton, CO.......................303-857-0380
Nigrelli Systems Purchasing
Kiel, WI.................................800-693-3144
Nijal USA
Minneapolis, MN.....................651-353-6702
PCM Delasco Inc
Houston, TX...........................713-896-4888
Plymouth Tube Company
East Troy, WI..........................262-642-8201
Precision Plus
Sanborn, NY...........................800-526-2707
Quadro Engineering
Waterloo, ON..........................519-884-9660
Reiser
Canton, MA.............................734-821-1290
Rocheleau Blow Molding Systems
Fitchburg, MA.........................978-345-1723
Rockwell Automation Inc
Milwaukee, WI........................414-382-2000
Ryowa Company America
Elk Grove Village, IL................800-700-9692
Schneider Packaging Eqpt Co
Brewerton, NY.........................315-676-3035
Scrivner Equipment Co Inc
Carthage, MS..........................601-267-7614

Septimatech Group
Waterloo, ON..........................888-777-6775
Serac Inc
Carol Stream, IL......................630-510-9343
SICK Inc
Bloomington, MN.....................800-325-7425
Specialty Food America Inc
Hopkinsville, KY......................888-881-1633
Spencer Strainer Systems
Jeffersonville, IN.....................800-801-4977
Stainless Motors Inc
Rio Rancho, NM.......................505-867-0224
Standard Pump
Auburn, GA.............................866-558-8611
Sterling Electric Inc
Indianapolis, IN......................800-654-6220
Strongarm
Horsham, PA...........................215-443-3400
Sundyne Corp
Arvada, CO.............................303-425-0800
Superior Menus
Mankato, MN..........................800-464-2182
T-Drill Industries Inc
Norcross, GA...........................800-554-2730
Technical Tool Solutions Inc.
Lake Forest, IL........................847-235-5551
Tente Casters Inc
Hebron, KY.............................800-783-2470
Uhrden
Sugarcreek, OH.......................800-852-2411
Ultra Process Systems
Oak Ridge, TN.........................865-483-2772
Unisource Manufacturing Inc
Portland, OR...........................800-234-2566
Volumetric Technologies
Cannon Falls, MN....................507-263-0034
W.Y. International
Los Angeles, CA......................323-726-8733
World Water Works
Elmsford, NY..........................800-607-7873
Young & Associates
Kenosha, WI...........................262-657-6394

Heaters

Water

Alard Equipment Corp
Williamson, NY.......................315-589-4511
Andgar Corp
Ferndale, WA..........................360-366-9900
Hatco Corp
Milwaukee, WI........................800-558-0607
Hubbell Electric Heater Co
Stratford, CT...........................800-647-3165
PVI Industries LLC
Fort Worth, TX........................800-784-8326
Quikwater Inc
Sand Springs, OK....................918-241-8880
ScanTech Sciences
Norcross, GA...........................470-359-3660
Vanguard Technology Inc
Eugene, OR.............................800-624-4809

Hose Reels

Hannay Reels
Westerlo, NY...........................877-467-3357
Kuriyama of America Inc
Schaumburg, IL.......................800-800-0320
Reelcraft Industries Inc
Columbia City, IN....................800-444-3134
Unisource Manufacturing Inc
Portland, OR...........................800-234-2566

Hoses

Beverage

Accuflex Industrial Hose LTD
Romulus, MI...........................734-713-4100
Action Technology
Prussia, PA.............................217-935-8311
Alard Equipment Corp
Williamson, NY.......................315-589-4511
Associated Industrial Rubber
Magna, UT..............................800-526-6288
Cardinal Rubber & Seal Inc
Roanoke, VA............................800-542-5737
Emco Industrial Plastics
Cedar Grove, NJ......................800-292-9906

Nalge Process Technologies Group
Rochester, NY.........................585-586-8800
Parker-Hannifin Corp
Wickliffe, OH..........................440-943-5700
Simolex Rubber Corp
Plymouth, MI..........................734-453-4500
Superflex Limited
Brooklyn, NY...........................800-394-3665
Superior Products Company
Saint Paul, MN........................800-328-9800
Union Plastics Co
Marshville, NC........................704-624-2112

Deep Fryer

Diebolt & Co
Old Lyme, CT...........................800-343-2658

Food Handling

Accuflex Industrial Hose LTD
Romulus, MI...........................734-713-4100
Action Technology
Prussia, PA.............................217-935-8311
Baldewein Company
Lake Forrest, IL.......................800-424-5544
Cardinal Rubber & Seal Inc
Roanoke, VA............................800-542-5737
Emco Industrial Plastics
Cedar Grove, NJ......................800-292-9906
Fabwright Inc
Garden Grove, CA....................800-854-6464
Flex-Hose Co Inc
East Syracuse, NY...................315-437-1611
HBD Industries
Salisbury, NC..........................800-438-2312
Hoffmeyer Corp
San Leandro, CA......................888-744-1826
Home Rubber Co
Trenton, NJ.............................800-257-9441
Hydra-Flex Inc
Livonia, MI.............................800-234-0832
Keystone Rubber Corporation
Greenbackville, VA..................800-394-5661
L.C. Thompson Company
Kenosha, WI...........................800-558-4018
Marlow Watson Inc
Wilmington, MA.......................800-282-8823
Nalge Process Technologies Group
Rochester, NY.........................585-586-8800
Parker-Hannifin Corp
Wickliffe, OH..........................440-943-5700
Pure Fit Nutrition Bars
Irvine, CA...............................866-787-3348
Salem-Republic Rubber Co
Sebring, OH............................800-425-5079
Sanitary Couplers
Springboro, OH.......................513-743-0144
Strahman Valves Inc
Bethlehem, PA.........................877-787-2462
Superflex Limited
Brooklyn, NY...........................800-394-3665
Union Plastics Co
Marshville, NC........................704-624-2112
Us Rubber
Brooklyn, NY...........................718-782-7888
Vaughn Belting Co-Main Acct
Spartanburg, SC......................800-533-9086

Incubators & Brooders

Kuhl Corporation
Flemington, NJ........................908-782-5696
National Hotpack
Stone Ridge, NY......................800-431-8232
Pro Scientific Inc
Oxford, CT..............................800-584-3776
Triad Scientific
Manasquan, NJ.......................800-867-6690

Load Cells & Indicators

Tedea-Huntliegh
Chatsworth, CA........................800-423-5483

Lubricants

Industrial

Alex E Fergusson Co Inc
Chambersburg, PA...................800-345-1329

AMSOIL Inc
  Superior, WI 715-392-7101
Bel-Ray Co LLC
  Wall Township, NJ 732-938-2421
Boyer Corporation
  La Grange, IL 800-323-3040
Cantol
  Markham, ON 800-387-9773
Cellier Corporation
  Taunton, MA 508-655-5906
Crc Industries Inc
  Warminster, PA 800-556-5074
DT Industrials
  Holland, OH 567-703-8550
Graco Inc
  Minneapolis, MN 612-623-6000
Haynes Manufacturing Co
  Westlake, OH 800-992-2166
Huskey Specialty Lubricants
  Norco, CA 888-448-7539
Kluber Lubrication N America
  Londonderry, NH 800-447-2238
Kurtz Oil Company
  Winston Salem, NC 336-768-1515
LANXESS Corp.
  Pittsburgh, PA 800-526-9377
Linker Machines
  Rockaway, NJ 973-983-0001
Lubriplate Lubricants
  Newark, NJ 800-733-4755
Lubriquip
  Minneapolis, MN 612-623-6000
Moly-XL Company
  Westville, NJ 856-848-2880
Momar
  Atlanta, GA 800-556-3967
National Purity LLC
  Brooklyn Center, MN 612-672-0022
Orelube Corp
  Bellport, NY 800-645-9124
Rock Valley Oil & Chemical Co
  Loves Park, IL 815-654-2401
Sentinel Lubricants Inc
  Miami, FL 800-842-6400
Specialty Lubricants
  Macedonia, OH 800-238-5823
Stoner
  Quarryville, PA 800-227-5538
Thermoil Corporation
  Brooklyn, NY 718-855-0544
Tribology Tech Lube
  Yaphank, NY 800-569-1757
US Industrial Lubricants
  Cincinnati, OH 800-562-5454

Measures

Dry

Alard Equipment Corp
  Williamson, NY 315-589-4511
Frye's Measure Mill
  Wilton, NH 603-654-6581
Optek-Danulat
  Germantown, WI. 888-551-4288

Mirrors

Convex

American Louver Co
  Skokie, IL 800-772-0355
American Store Fixtures
  Skokie, IL
Emco Industrial Plastics
  Cedar Grove, NJ 800-292-9906
Emedco
  Williamsville, NY 877-765-8386
Mirror Tech Mfg Co Inc
  Yonkers, NY 914-423-1600
Rosco Inc
  Jamaica, NY 800-227-2095
Se Kure Controls Inc
  Franklin Park, IL 800-250-9260

Nozzles

Spray

Arthur Products Co
  Medina, OH. 800-322-0510

Bete Fog Nozzle Inc
  Greenfield, MA 800-235-0049
California Vibratory Feeders
  Anaheim, CA 800-354-0972
Delavan Spray Technologies
  Charlotte, NC 704-423-7000
Greenfield Packaging
  White Plains, NY 914-993-0233
Lechler Inc
  St Charles, IL 800-777-2926
Sani-Matic
  Madison, WI 800-356-3300
Spraying Systems Company
  Wheaton, IL 630-655-5000
Superior Products Company
  Saint Paul, MN 800-328-9800
Viking Corp
  Hastings, MI 800-968-9501

Openers

Bottle

Amco Metals Indl
  City of Industry, CA 626-855-2550
Brown Manufacturing Company
  Decatur, GA 404-378-8311
Browne & Company
  Markham, ON 905-475-6104
C R Mfg
  Waverly, NE 877-789-5844
Cleveland Metal Stamping Company
  Berea, OH 440-234-0010
G.G. Greene Enterprises
  West Warren, PA 814-723-5700
Superior Products Company
  Saint Paul, MN 800-328-9800

Box, Crate, Carton

Climax Packaging Machinery
  Hamilton, OH 513-874-1664
Edson Packaging Machinery
  Hamilton, ON 800-493-3766
Gulf Arizona Packaging
  Humble, TX 800-364-3887
Innovative Marketing
  Riverside, CA 800-438-4627
Listo Pencil Corp
  Alameda, CA. 800-547-8648
Samuel Underberg Food Store
  Brooklyn, NY 718-363-0787
Seal-O-Matic Corp
  Jacksonville, OR. 800-631-2072
Thiele Technologies-Reedley
  Reedley, CA 800-344-8951

Can

Berkshire PPM
  Litchfield, CT 860-567-3118
C R Mfg
  Waverly, NE 877-789-5844
CanPacific Engineering
  Delta, BC. 604-946-1680
Dorton Incorporated
  Arlington Hts, IL 800-299-8600
Edlund Co
  Burlington, VT 800-772-2126
G.G. Greene Enterprises
  West Warren, PA 814-723-5700
Langsenkamp Manufacturing
  Indianapolis, IN 877-585-1950
Lincoln Foodservice
  Cleveland, OH 800-374-3004
Morrison Timing Screw Co
  Glenwood, IL 708-331-6600
Rival Manufacturing Company
  Kansas City, MO. 816-943-4100
Swing-A-Way Manufacturing Company
  St Louis, MO. 314-773-1488
T & S Perfection Chain Prods
  Cullman, AL 888-856-4864

Fruit Jar

Swing-A-Way Manufacturing Company
  St Louis, MO. 314-773-1488

Packaging

A M S Filling Systems
  Glenmoore, PA 800-647-5390
A Snow Craft Co Inc
  New Hyde Park, NY 516-739-1399
A&M Industries
  Sioux Falls, SD 800-888-2615
A-A1 Aaction Bag
  Denver, CO 800-783-1224
A-B-C Packaging Machine Corp
  Tarpon Springs, FL 800-237-5975
A.B. Sealer, Inc.
  Beaver Dam, WI. 877-885-9299
A.K. Robins
  Baltimore, MD 800-486-9656
Aabbitt Adhesives
  Chicago, IL 800-222-2488
AAMD
  Liverpool, NY. 800-887-4167
Aaron Equipment Co Div Areco
  Bensenville, IL 630-350-2200
About Packaging Robotics
  Thornton, CO 303-449-2559
Accu-Pak
  Akron, OH
Accurate Paper Box Co Inc
  Knoxville, TN 865-690-0311
Accutek Packaging Equipment
  Vista, CA. 800-989-1828
Ace Technical Plastics Inc
  East Hartford, CT 860-278-2444
Achilles USA
  Everett, WA. 425-353-7000
ACMA/GD
  Richmond, VA. 800-525-2735
Acraloc Corp
  Oak Ridge, TN 865-483-1368
Actionpac Scales Automation
  Oxnard, CA. 800-394-0154
ADCO Manufacturing Inc
  Sanger, CA 559-875-5563
Adhesive Products Inc
  Vernon, CA. 800-669-5516
Adhesive Technologies Inc
  Hampton, NH 800-458-3486
Adpro
  Solon, OH 440-542-1111
Advance Engineering Co
  Canton, MI 800-497-6388
Advance Weight Systems Inc
  Grafton, OH 440-926-3691
Advanced Poly-Packaging Inc
  Akron, OH. 800-754-4403
AEP Industries
  South Hackensack, NJ 800-999-2374
Ag-Pak
  Gasport, NY 716-772-2651
Air Products & Chemicals Inc
  Allentown, PA. 800-224-2724
Air Technical Industries
  Mentor, OH. 888-857-6265
Aladdin Transparent Packaging
  Hauppauge, NY 631-273-4747
Alard Equipment Corp
  Williamson, NY 315-589-4511
Alcoa - Lake Charles Carbon Plant
  Lake Charles, LA 337-480-7600
Alcoa - Massena Operations
  Massena, NY
Alcoa - Warrick Operations
  Newburgh, IN 812-853-6111
Alcon Packaging
  Weston, ON. 416-742-8910
Alfa Systems Inc
  Westfield, NJ 908-654-0255
Aline Heat Seal Corporation
  Los Angeles, CA. 888-285-3917
All American Poly
  Piscataway, NJ 800-526-3551
All Fill Inc
  Exton, PA 866-255-4455
All Packaging Machinery Corp
  Ronkonkoma, NY. 800-637-8808
All Sorts Premium Packaging
  Buffalo, NY. 888-565-9727
Alliance Rubber Co
  Hot Springs, AR 800-626-5940
ALLIED Graphics Inc
  St Michael, MN. 800-490-9931
Alloyd Brands
  Dekalb, IL 800-756-7639

Allpac
  Dallas, TX 214-630-8804
Amark Packaging Systems
  Kansas City, MO 816-965-9000
Amco Products Co
  Fort Smith, AR 479-646-8949
Amcor
  Oshkosh, WI 800-544-4672
American Bag & Burlap Company
  Chelsea, MA 617-884-7600
American Excelsior Co
  Arlington, TX 800-777-7645
American Glass Research
  Butler, PA 724-482-2163
American Labelmark Co
  Chicago, IL 800-621-5808
American Manufacturing-Engrng
  Cleveland, OH 800-822-9402
American Printpak Inc
  Sussex, WI 800-441-8003
American Renolit Corp LA
  Commerce, CA 323-721-2720
Ameripak Packaging Equipment
  Warrington, PA 215-343-1530
Amerivacs
  San Diego, CA 619-498-8227
AMF Bakery Systems Corp
  Richmond, VA 804-225-3771
AMF CANADA
  Sherbrooke, QC 800-255-3869
Ampak
  Cleveland, OH 800-342-6329
Anderson Machine Sales
  Fort Lee, NJ
Anderson Tool & Engineering Company
  Anderson, IN 765-643-6691
Andy Printed Products
  Lagrangeville, NY 845-223-5101
Anver Corporation
  Hudson, MA 800-654-3500
Applied Product Sales
  Lilburn, GA 650-218-3104
APS Packaging Systems
  San Jose, CA 800-526-2276
Archer Daniels Midland Company
  Chicago, IL 312-634-8100
Architecture Plus Intl Inc
  Rocky Point, FL 813-281-9299
Arthur G Russell Co Inc
  Bristol, CT 860-583-4109
Artistic Packaging Concepts
  Massapequa Pk, NY 516-797-4020
ARY
  Kansas City, MO 800-821-7849
ASCENT Technics Corporation
  Brick, NJ 800-774-7077
Associated Packaging Equipment Corporation
  Markham, ON 905-475-6647
Astoria Laminations
  St Clair Shores, MI 800-526-7325
Atlantic Foam & Packaging Company
  Sanford, FL 407-328-9444
Atlas Packaging Inc
  Opa Locka, FL 800-662-0630
Atlas Tag & Label Inc
  Neenah, WI 800-558-6418
Audion Automation
  Carrollton, TX 972-389-0777
Auger Fab
  Exton, PA 800-334-1529
Automated Packaging Systems
  Streetsboro, OH 800-527-0733
Automated Production Systems Corporation
  New Freedom, PA 888-345-5377
Autoprod
  Davenport, IA 563-391-1100
Avon Tape
  Chestnut Hill, MA 508-584-8273
B H Bunn Co
  Lakeland, FL 800-222-2866
B T Engineering Inc
  Bala Cynwyd, PA 610-664-9500
B.A.G. Corporation
  Richardson, TX 800-331-9200
Bagcraft Papercon
  Chicago, IL 800-621-8468
Balemaster
  Crown Point, IN 219-663-4525
Barnes Machine Company
  Saint Petersburg, FL 727-327-9452
Barrette Outdoor Living
  Cleveland, OH 800-336-2383

Batching Systems
  Prince Frederick, MD 800-311-0851
Baur Tape & Label Co
  San Antonio, TX 877-738-3222
Bedford Industries
  Worthington, MN 800-533-5314
BEI
  Goleta, GA 800-350-2727
BEI
  South Haven, MI 800-364-7425
Berlin Foundry & Mach Co
  Berlin, NH 603-752-4550
Bernal Technology
  Rochester Hills, MI 800-237-6251
Berry Global
  Evansville, IN 800-343-1295
Bertek Systems Inc
  Fairfax, VT 800-367-0210
Bettendorf Stanford Inc
  Salem, IL 800-548-2253
Better Packages
  Ansonia, CT 800-237-9151
Biner Ellison Packaging Systs
  Vista, CA 800-733-8162
Bivac Enterprise
  Brick, NJ 732-920-0080
Black Brothers
  Mendota, IL 800-252-2568
Blako Industries
  Dunbridge, OH 419-833-4491
Blodgett Co
  Houston, TX 281-933-6195
Blue Print Automation
  S Chesterfield, VA 804-520-5400
Bosch Packaging Technology
  New Richmond, WI 715-246-6511
BP
  Houston, TX 281-366-2000
Bradman Lake Inc
  Rock Hill, SC 803-366-3688
Branson Ultrasonics Corp
  Danbury, CT 203-796-0400
Brechteen
  Chesterfield, MI 586-949-2240
Brenton Engineering Co
  Alexandria, MN 800-535-2730
Brentwood Plastics In
  St Louis, MO 314-968-1135
Brothers Metal Products
  Santa Ana, CA 714-972-3008
Brown Machine LLC
  Beaverton, MI 877-702-4142
Bulman Products Inc
  Grand Rapids, MI 616-363-4416
Burghof Engineering & Mfg Co
  Prairie View, IL 847-634-0737
BW Container Systems
  Romeoville, IL 630-759-6800
C & K Machine Co
  Holyoke, MA 413-536-8122
C.J. Machine
  Fridley, MN 763-767-4630
California Vibratory Feeders
  Anaheim, CA 800-354-0972
Campbell Wrapper Corporation
  De Pere, WI 920-983-7100
Can Creations
  Pembroke Pines, FL 954-581-3312
Cannon Equipment Company
  Cannon Falls, MN 800-825-8501
Cantech Industries Inc
  Johnson City, TN 800-654-3947
Capmatic, Ltd.
  Monreal North, QC 514-332-0062
Carando Technologies Inc
  Stockton, CA 209-948-6500
Care Controls, Inc.
  Mill Creek, WA 800-593-6050
Carlisle Plastics
  Minneapolis, MN 952-884-1309
Carpenter-Hayes Paper Box Company
  East Hampton, CT 203-267-4436
Carroll Co
  Garland, TX 800-527-5722
Carroll Packaging
  Dearborn, MI 313-584-0400
Carton Closing Company
  Butler, PA 724-287-7759
Cartpac Inc
  Carol Stream, IL 630-510-1100
Catty Inc
  Harvard, IL 815-943-2288

Cellotape, Inc.
  Newark, CA 510-651-5551
Central Coated Products Inc
  Alliance, OH 330-821-9830
Central Fine Pack Inc
  Fort Wayne, IN 260-432-3027
Central Ohio Bag & Burlap
  Columbus, OH 800-798-9405
Chaffee Co
  Rocklin, CA 916-630-3980
Chambers Container Company
  Gastonia, NC 704-377-6317
Champion Trading Corporation
  Marlboro, NJ 732-780-4200
Change Parts Inc
  Ludington, MI 231-845-5107
Charles Beck Machine Corporation
  King of Prussia, PA 610-265-0500
Chase Industries Inc
  West Chester, OH 800-543-4455
Chase-Logeman Corp
  Greensboro, NC 336-665-0754
Chroma Color Corp
  McHenry, IL 877-385-8777
Circle Packaging Machinery Inc
  De Pere, WI 920-983-3420
City Box Company
  Aurora, IL 773-277-5500
CL&D Graphics
  Oconomowoc, WI 800-777-1114
Clamco Corporation
  Berea, OH 216-267-1911
Clayton Corp.
  Fenton, MO 800-729-8220
Clearwater Packaging Inc
  Clearwater, FL 800-299-2596
Cleveland Plastic Films
  Elyria, OH 800-832-6799
Cleveland Wire Cloth & Mfg Co
  Cleveland, OH 800-321-3234
Climax Packaging Machinery
  Hamilton, OH 513-874-1664
CMD Corp
  Appleton, WI 920-730-6888
Collectors Gallery
  St Charles, IL 800-346-3063
Colonial Transparent Products Company
  Hicksville, NY 516-822-4430
Colter & Peterson
  Paterson, NJ 973-684-0901
Columbia Labeling Machinery
  Benton City, WA 888-791-9590
Combi Packaging Systems LLC
  Canton, OH 866-472-5236
Compacker Systems LLC
  Davenport, IA 563-391-2751
Conflex, Inc.
  Germantown, WI 800-225-4296
Constantia Colmar
  Colmar, PA 215-997-6222
Continental Packaging Corporation
  Elgin, IL 847-289-6400
Contour Products
  Kansas City, KS 800-638-3626
Control & Metering
  Mississauga, ON 800-736-5739
CoolBrands International
  Ronkonkoma, NY 631-737-9700
Corfab
  Chicago, IL 708-458-8750
Corrugated Inner-Pak Corporation
  Conshohocken, PA 610-825-0200
Corrugated Packaging
  Sarasota, FL 941-371-0000
Cortec Aero
  St Paul, MN 800-426-7832
Cozzoli Machine Co
  Somerset, NJ 732-564-0400
Crandall Filling Machinery
  Buffalo, NY 800-280-8551
Crayex Corp
  Piqua, OH 800-837-1747
Creative Automation
  Passaic, NJ 973-778-0061
Creative Coatings Corporation
  Nashua, NH 800-229-1957
Creative Foam Corp
  Fenton, MI 810-629-4149
Crystal Creative Products
  Middletown, OH 800-776-6762
Crystal-Flex Packaging Corporation
  Rockville Centre, NY 888-246-7325

Crystal-Vision Packaging Systems
Torrance, CA 800-331-3240
CSS International Corp
Philadelphia, PA 800-278-8107
CTK Plastics
Moose Jaw, SK 800-667-8847
Cup Pac Packaging Inc
South Beloit, IL 877-347-9725
Custom Card & Label Corporation
Lincoln Park, NJ 973-492-0022
Custom Foam Molders
Foristell, MO 636-441-2307
Custom Food Machinery
Stockton, CA 209-463-4343
Custom Metal Design Inc
Oakland, FL 800-334-1777
Customized Equipment SE
Tucker, GA 770-934-9300
CVP Systems Inc
Downers Grove, IL 800-422-4720
Cyro Industries/Degussa
Parsippany, NJ 800-631-5384
D & L Manufacturing
Milwaukee, WI 414-256-8160
Dacam Corporation
Madison Heights, VA 434-929-4001
Dacam Machinery
Madison Heights, VA 434-369-1259
Dalemark Industries
Lakewood, NJ 732-367-3100
Danafilms Inc
Westborough, MA 508-366-8884
Data Scale
Fremont, CA 800-651-7350
Davis Core & Pa
Cave Spring, GA 800-235-7483
Decker Plastics
Council Bluffs, IA 866-869-6293
Decko Products Inc
Sandusky, OH 800-537-6143
Dehyco Company
Memphis, TN 901-774-3322
Delta Cyklop Orga Pac
Charlotte, NC 800-446-4347
Delta Engineering Corporation
Walpole, MA 781-729-8650
Desert Box & Supply Corporation
Thermal, CA 760-399-5161
Design Packaging Company
Glencoe, IL 800-321-7659
Design Plastics Inc
Omaha, NE 800-491-0786
Design Technology Corporation
Billerica, MA 978-663-7000
Design-Mark Industries
Wareham, MA 800-451-3275
Developak Corporation
Vista, CA 760-598-7404
Diamond Automation
Farmington Hills, MI 248-426-9394
Diversified Capping Equipment
Perrysburg, OH 419-666-2566
Diversified Metal Engineering
Charlottetown, PE 902-628-6900
Dixie Canner Machine Shop
Athens, GA 706-549-0592
Dolco Packaging Co
Decatur, IN 260-728-2161
DomainMarket
Potomac, MD 888-694-6735
Donahower & Company
Olathe, KS 913-829-2650
Dorell Equipment Inc
Somerset, NJ 732-247-5400
Douglas Machine Inc
Alexandria, MN 320-763-6587
DT Converting Technologies - Stokes
Bristol, PA 800-635-0036
Durable Engravers
Franklin Park, IL 800-869-9565
Durable Packaging Corporation
Countryside, IL 800-700-5677
Durand-Wayland Inc
Lagrange, GA 800-241-2308
Durango-Georgia Paper
Tampa, FL 813-286-2718
Dyco
Bloomsburg, PA 800-545-3926
Dynaclear Packaging
Wyckoff, NJ 201-337-1001
Dynamic Packaging
Minneapolis, MN 800-878-9380

Dynamic Pak LLC
Syracuse, NY 315-474-8593
Dynaric Inc
Virginia Beach, VA 800-526-0827
East Coast Group New York
Springfield Gardens, NY 718-527-8464
Eastern Machine
Middlebury, CT................203-598-0066
Ebel Tape & Label
Cincinnati, OH 513-471-1067
Econocorp Inc
Randolph, MA 781-986-7500
Edl Packaging Engineers
Green Bay, WI.................920-336-7744
Edmeyer
Minneapolis, MN 651-450-1210
Edson Packaging Machinery
Hamilton, ON 800-493-3766
Electro Cam Corp
Roscoe, IL....................800-228-5487
ELF Machinery
La Porte, IN...................800-328-0466
Ellehammer Industries
Langley, BC 604-882-9326
Elliott Manufacturing Co Inc
Fresno, CA 559-233-6235
Elmar Worldwide
Depew, NY 800-433-3562
Elmark Packaging Inc
West Chester, PA..............800-670-9688
Elopak Americas
Wixom, MI 248-486-4600
Emerald Packaging Inc
Union City, CA................510-429-5700
Energy Sciences Inc
Wilmington, MA...............978-658-3731
Engineered Automation
Biddeford, MI 207-200-8301
Enhance Packaging Technologies
Whitby, ON 905-668-5811
Ensinger Inc
Washington, PA...............800-243-3221
Enviropak Corp
Earth City, MO 314-739-1202
Equipment Outlet
Meridian, ID 208-887-1472
Esselte Meto
Morris Plains, NJ 800-645-3290
Evergreen Packaging
Memphis, TN 901-821-5350
Exact Equipment Corporation
Morrisville, PA.................215-295-2000
Excelsior Transparent Bag Manufacturing
Yonkers, NY 914-968-1300
F N Smith Corp
Oregon, IL....................815-732-2171
Fabricon Products Inc
River Rouge, MI...............313-841-8200
Fairchild Industrial Products
Winston Salem, NC.............800-334-8422
Fallas Automation Inc.
Waco, TX 254-772-9524
Farnell Packaging
Dartmouth, NS 800-565-9378
Fawema Packaging Machinery
Palmetto, FL 941-351-9597
Federal Label Systems
Elmhurst, NY 800-238-0015
Fehlig Brothers Box & Lbr Co
St Louis, MO..................314-241-6900
Felco Packaging Specialist
Baltimore, MD 800-673-8488
Felins USA Inc
Milwaukee, WI 800-343-5667
Fibre Converters Inc
Constantine, MI 269-279-1700
Fibre Leather Manufacturing Company
New Bedford, MA 800-358-6012
Fiedler Technology
Maple, ON....................905-832-0493
Filler Specialties
Zeeland, MI...................616-772-9235
Filling Equipment Co Inc
Flushing, NY..................800-247-7127
Film-Pak Inc
Crowley, TX 800-526-1838
Filmco Inc
Aurora, OH 800-545-8457
Fischbein LLC
Statesville, NC 704-838-4600
Fitec International Inc
Memphis, TN 800-332-6387

Flexicell Inc
Ashland, VA 804-550-7300
Flojet
Foothill Ranch, CA.............800-235-6538
Florida Knife Co
Sarasota, FL 800-966-5643
Foam Concepts Inc
Uxbridge, MA 508-278-7255
Foam Pack Industries
Springfield, NJ 973-376-3700
Fogg Filler Co
Holland, MI...................616-786-3644
Folding Carton/Flexible Packaging
North Hollywood, CA 818-896-3449
Food Equipment Manufacturing Company
Bedford Heights, OH 216-672-5859
Food Pak Corp
San Mateo, CA 650-341-6559
Formflex
Bloomingdale, IN 800-255-7659
Formost Packaging Machines
Woodinville, WA...............425-483-9090
Four M Manufacturing Group
San Jose, CA 408-998-1141
Fowler Products Co LLC
Athens, GA 877-549-3301
Framarx Corp
S Chicago Hts, IL 800-336-3936
Frazier & Son
Conroe, TX 800-365-5438
Free Flow Packaging Corporation
Redwood City, CA 800-888-3725
Fremont Die Cut Products
Fremont, OH 800-223-3177
Friendly City Box Co Inc
Johnstown, PA.................814-266-6287
Frontier Bag
Kansas City, MO...............816-765-4811
Fuller Weighing Systems
Columbus, OH 614-882-8121
Fulton-Denver Co
Denver, CO 800-521-1414
Future Commodities Intl Inc
Rancho Cucamonga, CA 888-588-2378
Gallo
Racine, WI 262-752-9950
Ganz Brothers
Paramus, NJ 201-845-6010
Garvey Products
Cincinnati, OH 513-771-8710
Gbs
North Canton, OH..............800-552-2427
GCA
Huntington Beach, CA 714-379-4911
GE Appliances
Louisville, KY 877-959-8688
GEI Autowrappers
Exton, PA 610-321-1115
GEI Turbo
Exton, PA 800-345-1308
Gemini Plastic Films Corporation
Garfield, NJ...................800-789-4732
General Bag Corporation
Cleveland, OH 800-837-9396
General Corrugated Machinery Company
Palisades Park, NJ..............201-944-0644
General Formulations
Sparta, MI 800-253-3664
General Methods Corporation
Peoria, IL.....................309-497-3344
General Packaging Equipment Co
Houston, TX 713-686-4331
General Processing Systems
Holland, MI...................800-547-9370
Genpak
Peterborough, ON..............800-461-1995
GHM Industries Inc
Charlton, MA 800-793-7013
Giltron Inc
Norwood, MA.................781-762-4310
Gleason Industries
Roseville, CA 916-784-1302
Glenmarc Manufacturing
Chicago, IL 800-323-5350
Glopak
St Leonard, QC 800-361-6994
Goex Corporation
Janesville, WI 608-754-3303
Goldco Industries
Loveland, CO 970-663-4770
Goodwrappers Inc
Halethorpe, MD 800-638-1127

Gram Equipment of America
Tampa, FL.....................813-248-1978
Grand Valley Labels
Grand Rapids, MI
Graphic Impressions of Illinois
River Grove, IL..................708-453-1100
Graybill Machines Inc
Lititz, PA......................717-626-5221
Great Southern Corp
Memphis, TN 800-421-7802
Green Tek
Janesville, WI 800-747-6440
Greenbush Tape & Label Inc
Albany, NY 518-465-2389
Greenfield Packaging
White Plains, NY 914-993-0233
Greif Inc
Delaware, OH 740-549-6000
GTI
Arvada, CO 303-420-6699
Gulf Arizona Packaging
Humble, TX 800-364-3887
Gulf Packaging Company
Safety Harbor, FL 800-749-3466
Gulf Systems
Brownsville, TX 800-217-4853
Gulf Systems
Humble, TX 800-364-3887
Gulf Systems
Arlington, TX 817-261-1915
H B Fuller Co
St. Paul, MN 651-236-5900
H G Weber & Co
Kiel, WI.......................920-894-2221
H&H Lumber Company
Amarillo, TX...................806-335-1813
Halpak Plastics
Deer Park, NY..................800-442-5725
Halton Packaging Systems
Oakville, ON...................905-847-9141
Hampden Papers Inc
Holyoke, MA 413-536-1000
Hamrick Manufacturing & Svc
Mogadore, OH 800-321-9590
Handy Wacks Corp
Sparta, MI 800-445-4434
Hannan Products
Corona, CA.....................800-954-4266
Hantover Inc
Kansas City, MO................800-821-7849
Harbro Packaging Co
Chicago, IL....................877-428-5812
Harpak-ULMA Packaging LLC
Ball Ground, GA................770-345-5300
Hart Design & Mfg
Green Bay, WI..................920-468-5927
Hartford Containers
Terryville, CT.................860-584-1194
Hartness International
Greenville, SC.................800-845-8791
Harwil Corp
Oxnard, CA.....................800-562-2447
Haumiller Engineering Co
Elgin, IL......................847-695-9111
Hayes Machine Co Inc
Des Moines, IA.................800-860-6224
Hayssen Flexible Systems
Duncan, SC.....................864-486-4000
Health Star
Randolph, MA...................800-545-3639
Heisler Machine & Tool Co
Fairfield, NJ..................973-227-6300
Henkel Consumer Adhesive
Avon, OH.......................800-321-0253
Henley Paper Company
Greensboro, NC.................336-668-0081
Henschel Coating & Laminating
New Berlin, WI.................800-866-5683
Herche Warehouse
Denver, CO.....................303-371-8186
Highland Plastics Inc
Mira Loma, CA..................800-368-0491
Highland Supply Corp
Highland, IL...................800-472-3645
Highlight Industries
Wyoming, MI....................800-531-2465
Hinchcliff Products Company
Strongsville, OH...............440-238-5200
Holland Applied Technologies
Burr Ridge, IL.................630-325-5130
Hollymatic Corp
Countryside, IL................708-579-3700

Hoppmann Corporation
Elkwood, VA....................800-368-3582
Hudson Control Group Inc
Springfield, NJ................973-376-8265
Hudson Poly Bag Inc
Hudson, MA.....................800-229-7566
Hudson-Sharp Machine Co
Green Bay, WI..................800-950-4362
Hudson-Sharp Machine Company
Green Bay, WI..................920-494-4571
Huhtamaki Food Service Plastics
Lake Forest, IL................800-244-6382
Hurst Corp
Wayne, PA......................610-687-2404
IBC Shell Packaging
New Hyde Park, NY..............516-352-5138
ID Images
Brunswick, OH..................866-516-7300
Ideal of America
Charlotte, NC..................704-523-1604
Ideal of America/Valley Rio Enterprise
Atlanta, GA....................770-352-0210
Ideal Wrapping Machine Company
Middletown, NY.................845-343-7700
Ilapak Inc
Newtown, PA....................215-579-2900
Iman Pack
Westland, MI...................800-810-4626
Imar
Miami Beach, FL................305-531-5757
In-Line Corporation
Hopkins, MN....................952-938-0046
Indeco Products Inc
San Marcos, TX.................888-246-3326
Indiana Carton Co Inc
Bremen, IN.....................800-348-2390
Industrial Automation Systems
Santa Clarita, CA..............888-484-4427
Industrial Devices Corporation
Petaluma, CA...................707-789-1000
Industrial Machine Manufacturing
Richmond, VA...................804-271-6979
Industrial Magnetics
Boyne City, MI.................800-662-4638
Inland Paperboard & Packaging
Rock Hill, SC..................803-366-4103
Inline Filling Systems
Venice, FL.....................941-486-8800
Innovative Packaging Solution
Martin, MI.....................616-656-2100
Inspired Automation Inc
Agoura Hills, CA...............818-991-4598
Instabox
Calgary, AB....................800-482-6173
Inter-Pack Corporation
Monroe, MI.....................734-242-7755
International Adhesive Coating
Windham, NH....................800-253-4450
International Omni-Pac Corporation
La Verne, CA...................909-593-2833
International Packaging Machinery
Naples, FL.....................800-237-6496
International Paper Box Machine Company
Nashua, NH.....................603-889-6651
Interstate Packaging
White Bluff, TN................800-251-1072
Intertape Polymer Group
Menasha, WI....................800-558-5006
ITW United Silicone
Lancaster, NY..................716-681-8222
Ivarson Inc
Milwaukee, WI..................414-351-0700
Ives-Way Products
Round Lake Beach, IL...........847-740-0658
Jagenberg
Enfield, CT....................860-741-2501
January & Wood Company
Maysville, KY..................606-564-3301
Jarisch Paper Box Company
North Adams, MA................413-663-5396
Jay Packaging Group Inc
Warwick, RI....................401-244-1300
Jeb Plastics
Wilmington, DE.................800-556-2247
Jescorp
Des Plaines, IL................847-299-7800
Jetstream Systems
Wichita, KN....................855-861-6916
Jif-Pak Manufacturing
Vista, CA......................800-777-6613
Jilson Group
Lodi, NJ.......................800-969-5400

JMC Packaging Equipment
Burlington, ON.................800-263-5252
John E. Ruggles & Company
New Bedford, MA................508-992-9766
John R Nalbach Engineering Co
Countryside, IL................708-579-9100
Johnson Corrugated Products Corporation
Thompson, CT...................860-923-9563
Jones Packaging Machinery
Ooltewah, TN...................423-238-4558
JW Aluminum
Mt Holly, SC...................800-568-1100
JW Leser Company
Los Angeles, CA................323-731-4173
K & L Intl
Ontario, CA....................888-598-5588
Kammann Machine
Portsmouth, NH.................978-463-0050
Kapak Corporation
Minneapolis, MN................952-541-0730
KAPCO
Kent, OH.......................800-843-5368
KAPS All Packaging
Riverhead, NY..................631-727-0300
Karolina Polymers
Hickory, NC....................828-328-2247
Kaufman Engineered Systems
Waterville, OH.................419-878-9727
Kennedy Group
Willoughby, OH.................440-951-7660
Key Automation
Eagan, MN......................651-455-0547
Keystone Packaging Svc Inc
Phillipsburg, NJ...............800-473-8567
KHL Engineered Packaging
Montebello, CA.................323-721-5300
Khs USA Inc
Sarasota, FL...................877-227-8358
Kinsley Inc
Doylestown, PA.................800-414-6664
Kirkco Corp
Monroe, NC.....................704-289-7090
Kisters Kayat
Sarasota, FL...................386-424-0101
Kliklok-Woodman
Decatur, GA....................770-981-5200
Klippenstein Corp
Fresno, CA.....................888-834-4258
Klockner Pentaplast of America
Gordonsville, VA...............540-832-3600
Kloppenberg & Co
Englewood, CO..................800-346-3246
KM International Corp
Kenton, TN.....................731-749-8700
Knapp Container
Beacon Falls, CT...............203-888-0511
Koch Equipment LLC
Kansas City, MO................816-931-4557
Kohler Industries Inc
Lincoln, NE....................800-365-6708
Korab Engineering Company
Los Angeles, CA................310-670-7710
Kord Products Inc.
Brantford, ON..................800-452-9070
Krones
Franklin, WI...................800-752-3787
KWIK Lok Corp
Yakima, WA.....................800-688-5945
L&H Wood Manufacturing Company
Farmington, MI.................248-474-9000
LAB Equipment
Skaneateles, NY................800-522-5781
Label Makers
Pleasant Prairie, WI...........800-208-3331
Label Technology Inc
Merced, CA.....................800-388-1990
Lako Tool & Mfg Inc
Perrysburg, OH.................800-228-2982
Lamcraft Inc
Lees Summit, MO................800-821-1333
Langen Packaging
Mississauga, ON................905-670-7200
Laub-Hunt Packaging Systems
Norwalk, CA....................888-671-9338
Lawrence Schiff Silk Mills
New York, NY...................800-272-4433
Leader Engineering-Fab Inc
Napoleon, OH...................419-592-0008
Leal True Form Corporation
Freeport, NY...................516-379-2008
Leco Plastic Inc
Hackensack, NJ.................201-343-3330

Lematic Inc
Jackson, MI......................517-787-3301
Lenkay Sani Products Corporation
Brooklyn, NY....................718-927-9260
Lester Box & Mfg Div
Long Beach, CA..................562-437-5123
Letrah International Corp
Fort Atkinson, WI...............920-563-6597
Levin Brothers Paper
Cicero, IL......................800-545-6200
Liqui-Box Corp
Richmond, VA....................804-325-1400
Livingston-Wilbor Corporation
Edison, NJ......................908-322-8403
Lockwood Packaging
Woburn, MA......................800-641-3100
Loeb Equipment
Chicago, IL.....................773-496-5720
Longford Equipment US
Glastonbury, CT.................416-298-6622
Longhorn Packaging Inc
San Antonio, TX.................800-433-7974
Longview Fibre Co
Longview, WA....................800-929-8111
Los Angeles Paper Box & Board Mills
Los Angeles, CA.................323-685-8900
Loveshaw Corp
South Canaan, PA................800-572-3434
Luetzow Industries
South Milwaukee, WI.............800-558-6055
Lunn Industries
Glen Cove, NY...................516-671-9000
Lyco Wausau
Wausau, WI......................715-845-7867
Lydall
Doswell, VA.....................804-266-9611
Lynch Corp
Greenwich, CT...................203-340-2590
M & G Packaging Corp
Floral Park, NY.................800-240-5288
M & Q Packaging Corp
North Wales, PA.................267-498-4000
M S Plastics & Packaging Inc
Butler, NJ......................800-593-1802
M S Willett Inc
Cockeysville, MD................410-771-0460
M&R Flexible Packaging
Springboro, OH..................800-543-3380
MAC Tac LLC
Stow, OH........................866-262-2822
Machine Electronics Company
Brooklyn, NY....................718-384-3211
Madison County Wood Products
Fredericktown, MO...............314-584-1802
MAF Industries Inc
Traver, CA......................559-897-2905
Magnuson
Pueblo, CO......................719-948-9500
Mail-Well Label
Sparks, NV......................775-359-1703
Malnove of Nebraska
Omaha, NE.......................800-228-9877
Malo Inc
Tulsa, OK.......................918-583-2743
Manchester Tool & Die Inc
North Manchester, IN............260-982-8524
Maren Engineering Corp
South Holland, IL...............800-875-1038
Mark Products Company
Denville, NJ....................973-983-8818
Markwell Manufacturing Company
Norwood, MA.....................800-666-1123
Marlen International
Astoria, OR.....................800-862-7536
Maro Paper Products Company
Bellwood, IL....................708-649-9982
Marq Packaging Systems Inc
Yakima, WA......................800-998-4301
Marshall Paper Products
East Norwich, NY
Marshall Plastic Film Inc
Martin, MI......................269-672-5511
Maryland Packaging Corporation
Elkridge, MD....................410-540-9700
Massachusetts Container Corporation
North Haven, CT.................203-248-2161
Mastercraft International
Charlotte, NC...................704-392-7436
Material Handling Technology, Inc
Morrisville, NC.................800-779-2475
Matiss
St Georges, QC..................888-562-8477

Matrix Packaging Machinery
Saukville, WI...................888-628-7491
Matthiesen Equipment
San Antonio, TX.................800-624-8635
Maull-Baker Box Company
Brookfield, WI..................414-463-1290
Maxco Supply
Parlier, CA.....................559-646-6700
Maypak Inc
Wayne, NJ.......................973-696-0780
Measurex/S&L Plastics
Nazareth, PA....................800-752-0650
Medical Packaging Corporation
Camarillo, CA...................805-388-2383
Merix Chemical Company
Chicago, IL.....................312-573-1400
Merryweather Foam Inc
Sylacauga, AL...................256-249-8546
Micro Solutions Ent Tech & Dev
Van Nuys, CA....................800-673-4968
Mid Cities Paper Box Company
Downey, CA......................877-277-6272
Miller Technical Svc
Plymouth, MI....................734-414-1769
Milprint
Oshkosh, WI.....................920-303-8600
Milwaukee Tool & MachineCompany
Okauchee, WI....................262-821-0160
Minipack
Orange, CA......................714-283-4200
Mitsubishi Polyester Film, Inc.
Greer, SC.......................864-879-5000
Modern Packaging Inc
Deer Park, NY...................631-595-2437
Modular Packaging
Randolph, NJ....................973-970-9393
Moen Industries
Santa Fe Springs, CA............800-732-7766
Mold-Rite Plastics LLC
Twinsburg, OH...................330-425-4206
Molins/Sandiacre Richmond
Richmond, VA....................864-486-4000
Monument Industries Inc
Bennington, VT..................802-442-8187
Moore Production Tool Spec Inc
Farmington Hills, MI............248-476-1200
Morphy Container Company
Brantford, ON...................519-752-5428
Mount Hope Machinery Company
Westborough, MA.................508-616-9458
Mount Vernon Plastics
Mamaroneck, NY..................914-698-1122
Multi-Plastics Extrusions Inc
Hazleton, PA....................570-455-2021
Multisorb Technologies Inc
Buffalo, NY.....................800-445-9890
Muth Associates
Springfield, MA.................800-388-0157
Namco Controls Corporation
Cleveland, OH...................800-626-8324
NAP Industries
Brooklyn, NY....................877-635-4948
Nashua Corporation
Nashua, NH......................603-661-2004
National Equipment Corporation
Bronx, NY.......................800-237-8873
National Instruments
Baltimore, MD...................866-258-1914
National Package SealingCompany
Santa Ana, CA...................714-630-1505
National Packaging
Rumford, RI.....................401-434-1070
National Poly Bag Manufacturing Corporation
Brooklyn, NY....................718-629-9800
National Velour Corp
Warwick, RI.....................800-556-6523
Neos
Elk River, MN...................888-441-6367
New England Machinery Inc
Bradenton, FL...................941-755-5550
New Jersey Wire Stitching Machine Company
Cherry Hill, NJ.................856-428-2572
Nichols Specialty Products
Southborough, MA................508-481-4367
Nigrelli Systems Purchasing
Kiel, WI........................800-693-3144
Niro
Hudson, WI......................715-386-9371
Nitech
Columbus, NE....................800-237-6496
NJM/CLI
Pointe Claire, QC...............514-630-6990

Norden Inc
Branchburg, NJ..................908-252-9483
Nordson Corp
Duluth, GA......................800-683-2314
Nordson Sealant Equipment
Plymouth, MI....................734-459-8600
Norpak Corp
Newark, NJ......................800-631-6970
North American Container Corp
Marietta, GA....................800-929-0610
Northeast Packaging Materials
Monsey, NY......................845-426-2900
Norwalt Design Inc
Randolph, NJ....................973-927-3200
Norwood Paper Inc
Chicago, IL.....................773-788-1528
Novelis Foil Products
Atlanta, GA.....................800-776-8701
Now Plastics Inc
East Longmeadow, MA.............413-525-1010
Nu-Con Equipment
Chanhassen, MN..................877-939-0510
Nu-Trend Plastics Thermoformer
Jacksonville, FL................904-353-5936
NYP
Leola, PA.......................800-541-0961
Ocme America Corporation
York, PA........................717-843-6263
OCS Checkweighers Inc
Snellville, GA..................678-344-8300
Oden Machinery
Tonawanda, NY...................800-658-3622
Oerlikon Leybold Vacuum
Export, PA......................724-327-5700
Old Dominion Box Company
Burlington, NC..................336-226-4491
Oliver Packaging & Equipment Co.
Walker, MI......................800-253-3893
Olney Machinery
Westernville, NY................315-827-4208
Omega Design Corp
Exton, PA.......................800-346-0191
Omnitech International
Midland, MI.....................989-631-3377
OMNOVA Solutions
Fairlawn, OH....................330-869-4200
OnTrack Automation Inc
Waterloo, ON....................519-886-9090
Orange Plastics
Compton, CA.....................310-609-2121
Orics Industries
Farmingdale, NY.................718-461-8613
Orion Packaging Systems Inc
Alexandria, MN..................800-333-6556
Osgood Industries
Oldsmar, FL.....................813-855-7337
Ossid Corp
Battleboro, NC..................800-334-8369
Ouachita Machine Works
West Monroe, LA.................318-396-1468
Outlook Packaging
Neenah, WI......................920-722-1666
Oystar North America
Edison, NJ......................732-343-7600
Pa R Systems Inc
St Paul, MN.....................800-464-1320
Pacemaker Packaging Corp
Woodside, NY....................718-458-1188
Pack Line Corporation
Racine, WI......................800-248-6868
Pack Rite Machine Mettler
Mt Pleasant, WI.................800-248-6868
Pack West Machinery
Baldwin Park, CA................626-814-4766
Package Machinery Co Inc
Holyoke, MA.....................413-315-3801
Package Service Company of Colorado
Northmoor, MO...................800-748-7799
Package Systems Corporation
Danielson, CT...................800-522-3548
Packaging & Processing Equipment
Ayr, ON.........................519-622-6666
Packaging Aids Corporation
San Rafael, CA..................415-454-4868
Packaging Associates
Randolph, NJ....................973-252-8890
Packaging By Design of Il
Elgin, IL.......................847-741-5600
Packaging Dynamics
Walnut Creek, CA................925-938-2711
Packaging Dynamics Corp
Chicago, IL.....................773-843-8000

Packaging Dynamics International
Caldwell, OH 740-732-5665

Packaging Enterprises
Rockledge, PA..................800-453-6213

Packaging Equipment & Conveyors, Inc
Elkhart, IN...................574-266-6995

Packaging Machinery & Equipment
West Orange, NJ...............973-325-2418

Packaging Machinery International
Elk Grove Village, IL...........800-871-4764

Packaging Materials Inc
Cambridge, OH.................800-565-8550

Packaging Products Corp
Mission, KS...................913-262-3033

Packaging Progressions
Collegeville, PA...............610-489-9096

Packing Material Company
Southfield, MI.................248-489-7000

Packotronics
Glenview, IL..................947-487-1281

Packrite Packaging
Archdale, NC.................336-431-1111

Packworld USA
Nazareth, PA.................610-746-2765

Paco Manufacturing
Clarksville, IN................812-283-7963

Pacur
Oshkosh, WI.................920-236-2888

Page Slotting Saw Co Inc
Toledo, OH..................419-476-7475

Pak-Rapid
Conshohocken, PA.............610-828-3511

Pakmark
Chesterfield, MO..............800-423-1379

Palmetto Canning
Palmetto, FL.................941-722-1100

Paper Box & Specialty Co
Sheboygan, WI...............888-240-3756

Paper Converting MachineCompany
Green Bay, WI................920-494-5601

Paper Machinery Corp
Milwaukee, WI...............414-354-8050

Paper Pak Industries
La Verne, CA.................909-392-1750

Paper Service
Hinsdale, NH.................603-239-6344

Paragon Films Inc
Broken Arrow, OK.............800-274-9727

PASCO
St Louis, MO.................800-489-3300

Pater & Associates
Cincinnati, OH

PDC International
Austin, TX...................512-302-0194

PDMP
Leesburg, VA.................703-777-8400

Pearson Packaging Systems
Spokane, WA.................800-732-7766

Peco Controls Corporation
Modesto, CA.................800-732-6285

Peerless Food Equipment
Sidney, OH..................937-492-4158

Peerless-Winsmith Inc
Springville, NY................716-592-9310

Penny Plate
Haddonfield, NJ...............856-429-7583

Pepperell Paper Company
Lawrence, MA................978-433-6951

Per-Fil Industries Inc
Riverside, NJ.................856-461-5700

Performance Packaging
Trail Creek, IN................219-874-6226

Perl Packaging Systems
Middlebury, CT...............800-864-2853

Pfankuch Machinery Corporation
Apple Valley, MN.............952-891-3311

PFM Packaging Machinery Corporation
Newmarket, ON...............905-836-6709

Phase Fire Systems
Vista, CA...................888-741-2341

Phoenix Closures Inc
Naperville, IL.................630-544-3475

Plastech Corp
Atlanta, GA..................404-355-9682

Plasti-Mach Corporation
Valley Cottage, NY.............800-394-1128

Plastic Suppliers Inc
Columbus, OH................800-722-5577

PlexPack Corp
Toronto, ON.................855-635-9238

Pneumatic Scale Angelus
Cuyahoga Falls, OH............330-923-0491

Polar Tech Industries Inc
Genoa, IL...................800-423-2749

Poly Plastic Products Inc
Delano, PA..................570-467-3000

Poly Shapes Corporation
Elyria, OH...................800-605-9359

Polypack Inc
Pinellas Park, FL...............727-578-5000

Polyplastics
Austin, TX...................800-753-7659

Portco Corporation
Vancouver, WA...............800-426-1794

Powertex Inc
Rouses Point, NY..............800-769-3783

Praxair Inc
Danbury, CT.................800-772-9247

Preferred Packaging Systems
San Dimas, CA...............800-378-4777

Premier Plastics Inc
Omaha, NE..................866-446-2998

Premium Foil Products Company
Louisville, KY................502-459-2820

Pres-On Products
Addison, IL..................800-323-7467

Pressure Pack
Williamsburg, VA..............757-220-3693

Prestige Label Company
Burgaw, NC.................800-969-4449

Print & Peel
New York, NY................800-451-0807

Printpack Inc.
Atlanta, GA..................404-460-7000

Priority One America
Oshkosh, WI.................920-235-5562

Priority One Packaging
Waterloo, ON................800-387-9102

Prodo-Pak Corp
Garfield, NJ.................973-777-7770

Production Packaging & Processing Equipment
Company
Savannah, GA................912-856-4281

Production Systems
Marietta, GA.................800-235-9734

Professional Marketing Group
Seattle, WA..................800-227-3769

Progressive Packaging Inc
Minneapolis, MN..............800-844-7889

Propac Marketing Inc
Addison, TX..................972-733-3199

Prototype Equipment Corporation
Libertyville, IL................847-680-4433

PTI Packaging
Portage, WI..................800-501-4077

Pure & Secure LLC-Cust Svc
Lincoln, NE..................800-875-5915

Quality Films
Three Rivers, MI...............269-679-5263

Quality Industries
Cleveland, OH................216-961-5566

Quantum Performance Films
Streamwood, IL...............800-323-6963

R R Donnelley
Chicago, IL..................800-742-4455

Racine Paper Box Manufacturing
Chicago, IL..................773-227-3900

RAM Center
Red Wing, MN...............800-309-5431

Ramoneda Bros Stave Mill
Culpeper, VA.................540-825-9166

Ranger Blade Manufacturing Company
Traer, IA....................800-377-7860

Raque Food Systems
Louisville, KY................502-267-9641

Ray C. Sprosty Bag Company
Wooster, OH.................330-264-8559

Refrigiwear Inc
Dahlonega, GA...............800-645-3744

Reggie Balls Cajun Foods
Lake Charles, LA..............337-436-0291

Reilly Foam Corporation
Conshohocken, PA.............610-834-1900

Reiser
Canton, MA.................734-821-1290

Remcon Plastics Inc
Reading, PA..................800-360-3636

Renard Machine Company
Green Bay, WI................920-432-8412

Rennco LLC
Homer, MI..................800-409-5225

Republic Foil
Danbury, CT.................800-722-3645

Rer Services
Northridge, CA................818-993-1826

Resina
Temecula, CA................800-207-4804

Restaurant Data
Irvington, NY.................800-346-9390

Rexford Paper Company
Racine, WI..................262-886-9100

Rico Packaging Company
Chicago, IL..................773-523-9190

Rigidized Metal Corp
Buffalo, NY..................800-836-2580

Riverwood International
Atlanta, GA..................770-984-5477

Robert Bosch LLC
Farmington, MI...............917-421-7209

Roberts Packaging Equipment
Des Plaines, IL................888-221-0700

Roberts Poly Pro Inc
Charlotte, NC................800-269-7409

Rockford-Midland Corporation
Rockford, IL..................800-327-7908

Rohrer Corp.
Wadsworth, OH...............800-243-6640

Rollprint Packaging Prods Inc
Addison, IL..................800-276-7629

Romanow Container
Westwood, MA...............781-320-9200

Rondo of America
Naugatuck, CT...............203-723-7474

Ropak Manufacturing Co Inc
Decatur, AL..................256-350-4241

Roplast Industries Inc
Oroville, CA..................800-767-5278

Rose City Awning Co
Portland, OR.................800-446-4104

Rose Forgrove
Saint Charles, IL..............630-443-1317

Ross Industries Inc
Midland, VA.................540-439-3271

Rowland Technologies
Wallingford, CT...............203-269-9500

Royal Label Co
Dorchester, MA...............617-825-6050

RTS Packaging
Scarborough, ME..............207-883-8921

RTS Packaging
Hillside, IL..................708-338-2800

Rudd Container Corp
Chicago, IL..................773-847-7600

Ruffino Paper Box Co
Hackensack, NJ...............201-487-1260

Rutan Poly Industries Inc
Mahwah, NJ.................800-872-1474

Rutherford Engineering
Rockford, IL..................815-623-2141

S L Sanderson & Co
Berry Creek, CA...............800-763-7845

S.V. Dice Designers
Rowland Heights, CA...........888-478-3423

Sabel Engineering Corporation
Villard, MN..................320-554-3611

Salinas Valley Wax Paper Co
Salinas, CA..................831-424-2747

Samuel P. Harris
Rumford, RI.................401-438-4020

Samuel Strapping Systems Inc
Woodridge, IL................800-323-4424

San Fab Conveyor
Sandusky, OH................419-626-4465

Sanchelima International
Miami, FL...................305-591-4343

Sanford Redmond Company
Stamford, CT.................203-351-9800

Sasib Beverage & Food North America
Plano, TX...................800-558-3814

Scandia Packaging Machinery Co
Fairfield, NJ.................973-473-6100

Schaefer Machine Co Inc
Deep River, CT...............800-243-5143

Schneider Packaging Eqpt Co
Brewerton, NY................315-676-3035

Schroeder Machine
San Marcos, CA..............760-591-9733

Seal-O-Matic Corp
Jacksonville, OR..............800-631-2072

Sealstrip Corporation
Boyertown, PA...............610-367-6282

Seepex Inc
Enon, OH...................800-695-3659

Seiler Plastics
St Louis, MO.................888-673-4537

Sekisui TA Industries
Brea, CA 800-258-8273
Serac Inc
Carol Stream, IL 630-510-9343
Serpa Packaging Solutions
Visalia, CA 800-348-5453
Sertapak Packaging Corporation
Woodstock, ON. 800-265-1162
Servpak Corp
Hollywood, FL 800-782-0840
Seville Flexpack Corp
Oak Creek, WI 414-761-2751
Shamrock Paper Company
Saint Louis, MO 314-241-2370
Shawano Specialty Papers
Shawano, WI. 800-543-5554
Sherwood Tool
Owings Mills, MD 860-828-4161
Shields Bag & Printing Co
Yakima, WA 800-541-8630
Shields Products Inc
West Pittston, PA. 570-655-4596
Shippers Supply
Saskatoon, SK. 800-661-5639
Shippers Supply, Labelgraphic
Calgary, AB. 800-661-5639
ShockWatch
Dallas, TX 800-393-7920
Shrinkfast Marketing
Newport, NH. 800-867-4746
Sierra Dawn Products
Santa Rosa, CA 707-535-0172
SIG Combibloc USA, Inc.
Chester, PA 610-546-4200
Sig Pack
Oakland, CA 800-824-3245
Signature Packaging
West Orange, NJ 800-376-2299
Signode Industrial Group LLC
Glenview, IL 800-323-2464
Silgan Plastic Closure Sltns
Downers Grove, IL 800-727-8652
Silgan Plastic Closure Sltns
Downers Grove, IL 800-767-8652
Silgan White Cap LLC
Downers Grove, IL 800-515-1565
Silver Spur Corp
Cerritos, CA 562-921-6880
Simolex Rubber Corp
Plymouth, MI 734-453-4500
Simplex Filler Co
Napa, CA. 800-796-7539
Simplimatic Automation
Forest, VA 800-294-2003
Sitma USA
Spilamberto, MO 800-728-1254
SKW Gelatin & Specialties
Waukesha, WI. 800-654-2396
Slautterback Corporation
Duluth, GA 800-827-3308
Snapware
Fullerton, CA 800-334-3062
Sohn Manufacturing
Elkhart Lake, WI. 920-876-3361
Somerville Packaging
Toronto, ON 416-754-7228
Somerville Packaging
Mississauga, ON 905-678-8211
Soudal Accumetric
Elizabethtown, KY 800-928-2677
Southern Automatics
Lakeland, FL 800-441-4604
Southern Container Corporation
Deer Park, NY 631-586-6006
Southern Film Extruders
High Point, NC 800-334-6101
Southern Packaging Machinery
Athens, GA 706-208-0814
Southern Pallet
Christchurch, NZ 901-942-4603
Southern Tool
West Monroe, LA 800-458-3687
Spartec Plastics
Conneaut, OH. 800-325-5176
Spartech Plastics
Wichita, KS. 316-722-8621
Spartech Plastics
Portage, WI. 800-998-7123
Spartech Poly Com
Clayton, MI 888-721-4242
Specialty Films & Associates
Hebron, KY 800-984-3346

Specialty Packaging Inc
Fort Worth, TX 800-284-7722
Spee-Dee Packaging Machinery
Sturtevant, WI. 877-375-2121
St. Clair Pakwell
Bellwood, IL 800-323-1922
St. Pierre Box & Lumber Company
Canton, CT 860-693-2089
Stainless Specialists Inc
Wausau, WI. 800-236-4155
Standard-Knapp Inc
Portland, CT 800-628-9565
Staplex Co Inc
Brooklyn, NY 800-221-0822
Star Poly Bag Inc
Brooklyn, NY 718-384-7034
Starview Packaging Machinery
Dorval, QC 888-278-5555
Stewart Mechanical Seals
Bakersfield, CA 661-391-9332
Stiles Enterprises Inc
Rockaway, NJ 800-325-4232
Stock America Inc
Grafton, WI. 262-375-4100
Stone Container
Chicago, IL 312-346-6600
Stormax International
Concord, NH. 800-874-7629
Straub Designs Co
St Louis Park, MN 800-959-3708
Stretch-Vent Packaging System
Ontario, CA. 800-822-8368
Sungjae Corporation
Irvine, CA 949-757-1727
Superior Distributing Co
Louisville, KY 800-365-6661
Superior Packaging Equipment Corporation
Fairfield, NJ 973-575-8818
Surekap Inc
Winder, GA 770-867-5793
SWF Co
Reedley, CA 800-344-8951
SWF McDowell
Orlando, FL. 800-877-7971
Sycamore Containers
Sycamore, IL. 815-895-2343
Systems Technology Inc
San Bernardino, CA 909-799-9950
T & T Industries Inc
Fort Mohave, AZ 800-437-6246
T D Sawvel Co
Maple Plain, MN. 877-488-1816
T.O. Plastics
Minneapolis, MN 952-854-2131
Taconic
Petersburg, NY 800-833-1805
Target Industries
North Salt Lake, UT 866-617-2253
Taylor Products Co
Parsons, KS. 888-882-9567
TDF Automation
Cedar Falls, IA 800-553-1777
Technistar Corporation
Denver, CO 303-651-0188
Tecweigh
St Paul, MN. 800-536-4880
Telesonic Packaging
Wilmington, DE 302-658-6945
Temco
Oakland, CA 707-746-5966
Templock Corporation
Santa Barbara, CA 800-777-1715
TEQ
Huntley, IL 800-874-7113
Terkelsen Machine Company
Hyannis, MA. 508-775-6229
Terphane Inc
Bloomfield, NY 800-724-3456
THARCO
San Lorenzo, CA. 800-772-2332
Tharo Systems Inc
Brunswick, OH 800-878-6833
Thiele Engineering Company
Fergus Falls, MN 218-739-3321
Thiele Technologies Inc
Minneapolis, MN 612-782-1200
Thiele Technologies-Reedley
Reedley, CA 800-344-8951
Thomas Tape & Supply Co Inc
Springfield, OH 937-325-6414
Tieco-Unadilla Corporation
Unadilla, NY 877-889-6540

Tilly Industries
St Laurent, QC 514-331-4922
Tisma Machinery Corporation
Elk Grove Village, IL 847-427-9525
TMT Vacuum Filters
Danville, IL 217-446-0742
TNA Packaging Solutions
Coppell, TX 972-462-6500
Tolas Health Care Packaging
Feasterville Trevose, PA 215-322-7900
Tomac Packaging
Woburn, MA 800-641-3100
Trans World Services
Melrose, MA. 800-882-2105
Trenton Mills Inc
Trenton, TN. 731-855-1323
Tri-Sterling
Altamonte Spgs, FL 407-260-0330
Triangle Package Machinery Co
Chicago, IL 800-621-4170
Trico Converting Inc
Fullerton, CA 714-563-0701
Tridyne Process Systems
South Burlington, VT 802-863-6873
Trinity Packaging
Cheektowaga, NY 800-778-3111
True Pac
New Castle, DE. 800-825-7890
Tucson Container Corp
Tucson, AZ 520-746-3171
Tyco Plastics
Lakeville, MN. 800-328-4080
UCB Inc
Smyrna, GA 770-970-8338
Ultrapak
Dunkirk, NY 800-228-6030
Unifoil Corp
Fairfield, NJ 973-244-9990
Unique Boxes
Chicago, IL 800-281-1670
United Desiccants
Reno, NE. 888-659-1377
United Flexible
Westbury, NY 516-222-2150
United States Systems Inc
Kansas City, KS 888-281-2454
UniTrak Corporation
Port Hope, ON 866-883-5749
Universal Labeling Systems Inc
St Petersburg, FL 877-236-0266
Universal Packaging Inc
Houston, TX 800-324-2610
Universal Paper Box
Seattle, WA 800-228-1045
UPACO Adhesives
Richmond, VA. 800-446-9984
US Label Corporation
Greensboro, NC 336-332-7000
US Line Company
Westfield, MA. 413-562-3629
V C 999 Packaging Systems
Kansas City, MO. 800-728-2999
Vacumet Corp
Wayne, NJ 973-628-1067
Vacumet Corporation
Austell, GA 800-776-0865
Vacuum Depositing Inc
Louisville, KY 502-969-4227
Valco Melton
West Chester, OH 513-874-6550
VIFAN Canada
Lanoraie, QC. 800-557-0192
Viking Industries
New Smyrna Beach, FL 888-605-5560
Viking Packaging & Display
San Jose, CA 408-998-1000
Virginia Plastics Co
Roanoke, VA. 800-777-8541
Vista International Packaging
Kenosha, WI. 800-558-4058
Volk Corp
Farmington Hills, MI 800-521-6799
Volumetric Technologies
Cannon Falls, MN. 507-263-0034
W.G. Durant Corporation
Whittier, CA 562-946-5555
Warwick Manufacturing & Equip
North Brunswick, NJ 732-729-0400
Washington Frontier
Grandview, WA. 509-469-7662
Wasserman Bag Company
Center Moriches, NY 631-909-8656

Water Sciences Services, Inc.
Jackson, TN 973-584-4131
Waukesha Cherry-Burrell
Louisville, KY 502-491-4310
Wayne Automation Corp
Eagleville, PA 610-630-8900
WCB Ice Cream
Philadelphia, PA 215-425-4320
WE Killam Enterprises
Waterford, ON. 519-443-7421
Weber Display & Packaging Inc
Philadelphia, PA 215-426-3500
Weigh Right Automatic Scale Co
Joliet, IL 800-571-0249
WeighPack Systems/Paxiom Group
Montreal, QC 888-934-4472
Welliver Metal Products Corporation
Salem, OR. 503-362-1568
Wepackit
Orangeville, ON 519-942-1700
West-Pak
Dallas, TX. 214-337-8984
Western Plastics
Portland, TN 615-325-7331
Western Plastics
Calhoun, GA. 800-752-4106
Westervelt Co Inc
Tuscaloosa, AL 205-562-5000
Wexxar Corporation
Chicago, IL 630-983-6666
Wexxar Packaging Inc
Richmond, BC 888-565-3219
Whirley Industries Inc
Warren, PA 800-825-5575
Wick's Packaging Service
Cutler, IN 574-967-3104
Wilks Precision Instr Co Inc
Union Bridge, MD 410-775-7917
Williamson & Co
Greer, SC 800-849-3263
Winpak Portion Packaging
San Bernardino, CA 800-804-4224
Winpak Technologies
Toronto, ON 416-421-1700
Winzen Film
Taylor, TX 800-779-7595
Wisconsin Film & Bag Inc
Shawano, WI. 800-765-9224
Witt Plastics
Greenville, OH 800-227-9181
Woodstock Line Co
Putnam, CT 860-928-6557
Woodward Manufacturing
Paramus, NJ 201-262-6700
Wrap Pack
Yakima, WA 800-879-9727
Wrapade Packaging Systems
Fairfield, NJ 888-815-8564
Wraps
East Orange, NJ 973-673-7873
WS Packaging Group Inc
Green Bay, WI. 877-977-5177
Y-Z Sponge & Foam Products
Delta, BC. 604-525-1665
Yakima Wire Works
Reedley, CA 800-344-8951
Yohay Baking Co
Lindenhurst, NY 631-225-0300
Zed Industries
Vandalia, OH. 937-667-8407
Zepf Technologies
Clearwater, FL 727-535-4100
Zerand Corp
New Berlin, WI. 262-827-3800
Zimmer Custom-Made Packaging
Indianapolis, IN 317-263-3436
Zitropack Limited
Addison, IL. 630-543-1016
Zume Manufacturing
Mountain View, CA

Automatic/Random Case Sealing

Alard Equipment Corp
Williamson, NY 315-589-4511
Reiser
Canton, MA 734-821-1290
S&R Machinery
Olyphant, PA 800-229-4896
Tetra Pak
Champlin, MN 763-421-2721

Bag Closing

About Packaging Robotics
Thornton, CO 303-449-2559
Alard Equipment Corp
Williamson, NY 315-589-4511
Aline Heat Seal Corporation
Los Angeles, CA 888-285-3917
Amark Packaging Systems
Kansas City, MO. 816-965-9000
American Bag & Burlap Company
Chelsea, MA 617-884-7600
Andgar Corp
Ferndale, WA 360-366-9900
Automated Packaging Systems
Streetsboro, OH 800-527-0733
Bosch Packaging Technology
New Richmond, WI 715-246-6511
Branson Ultrasonics Corp
Danbury, CT 203-796-0400
Chaffee Co
Rocklin, CA 916-630-3980
Clamco Corporation
Berea, OH 216-267-1911
Crystal-Vision Packaging Systems
Torrance, CA. 800-331-3240
Custom Food Machinery
Stockton, CA. 209-463-4343
Customized Equipment SE
Tucker, GA 770-934-9300
Dynamic Automation LTD
Simi Valley, CA. 805-584-8476
Fawema Packaging Machinery
Palmetto, FL 941-351-9597
Fischbein LLC
Statesville, NC 704-838-4600
Gulf Arizona Packaging
Humble, TX 800-364-3887
Gulf Systems
Brownsville, TX 800-217-4853
Gulf Systems
Humble, TX 800-364-3887
Gulf Systems
Arlington, TX 817-261-1915
Harwil Corp
Oxnard, CA. 800-562-2447
Herche Warehouse
Denver, CO 303-371-8186
Herrmann Ultrasonics
Bartlett, IL 630-626-1626
ID Images
Brunswick, OH 866-516-7300
Iman Pack
Westland, MI. 800-810-4626
Industrial Automation Systems
Santa Clarita, CA 888-484-4427
JMC Packaging Equipment
Burlington, ON 800-263-5252
KWIK Lok Corp
Yakima, WA 800-688-5945
Lockwood Packaging
Woburn, MA 800-641-3100
Matthiesen Equipment
San Antonio, TX. 800-624-8635
New Jersey Wire Stitching Machine Company
Cherry Hill, NJ 856-428-2572
Pacemaker Packaging Corp
Woodside, NY. 718-458-1188
Pack Rite Machine Mettler
Mt Pleasant, WI 800-248-6868
Packaging Systems Intl
Denver, CO 303-244-9000
Pacmac Inc
Fayetteville, AR 800-834-1544
PlexPack Corp
Toronto, ON 855-635-9238
Prodo-Pak Corp
Garfield, NJ. 973-777-7770
Save-O-Seal Corporation
Elmsford, NY 800-831-9720
Staplex Co Inc
Brooklyn, NY 800-221-0822
Tomac Packaging
Woburn, MA 800-641-3100
Triangle Package Machinery Co
Chicago, IL 800-621-4170
Weigh Right Automatic Scale Co
Joliet, IL 800-571-0249

Bag Filling

About Packaging Robotics
Thornton, CO 303-449-2559
Actionpac Scales Automation
Oxnard, CA. 800-394-0154
Ag-Pak
Gasport, NY 716-772-2651
Alard Equipment Corp
Williamson, NY 315-589-4511
Amark Packaging Systems
Kansas City, MO. 816-965-9000
American Bag & Burlap Company
Chelsea, MA 617-884-7600
Ameriglobe LLC
Lafayette, LA 337-234-3211
Andgar Corp
Ferndale, WA 360-366-9900
Audion Automation
Carrollton, TX. 972-389-0777
Automated Packaging Systems
Streetsboro, OH 800-527-0733
Batching Systems
Prince Frederick, MD 800-311-0851
Bettendorf Stanford Inc
Salem, IL 800-548-2253
California Vibratory Feeders
Anaheim, CA 800-354-0972
Chantland Company, The
Humboldt, IA 515-332-4040
Circle Packaging Machinery Inc
De Pere, WI. 920-983-3420
Control & Metering
Mississauga, ON 800-736-5739
Crystal-Vision Packaging Systems
Torrance, CA. 800-331-3240
Custom Food Machinery
Stockton, CA. 209-463-4343
Custom Metal Design Inc
Oakland, FL 800-334-1777
Customized Equipment SE
Tucker, GA 770-934-9300
Enhance Packaging Technologies
Whitby, ON. 905-668-5811
Fawema Packaging Machinery
Palmetto, FL 941-351-9597
Franrica Systems
Stockton, CA. 209-948-2811
Glopak
St Leonard, QC 800-361-6994
Hudson-Sharp Machine Co
Green Bay, WI. 800-950-4362
ID Images
Brunswick, OH 866-516-7300
Ideal of America
Charlotte, NC 704-523-1604
Iman Pack
Westland, MI. 800-810-4626
JMC Packaging Equipment
Burlington, ON 800-263-5252
Khs USA Inc
Sarasota, FL 877-227-8358
Kloppenberg & Co
Englewood, CO. 800-346-3246
Liqui-Box
Richmond, VA. 804-325-1400
Liqui-Box Corp
Richmond, VA. 804-325-1400
Lockwood Packaging
Woburn, MA 800-641-3100
Machine Electronics Company
Brooklyn, NY 718-384-3211
Multi-Fill Inc
West Jordan, UT 801-280-1570
Oden Machinery
Tonawanda, NY 800-658-3622
Pacemaker Packaging Corp
Woodside, NY. 718-458-1188
Packaging Enterprises
Rockledge, PA 800-453-6213
Packaging Systems Intl
Denver, CO 303-244-9000
Pacmac Inc
Fayetteville, AR 800-834-1544
Palace Packaging Machines Inc
Downingtown, PA. 610-873-7252
PlexPack Corp
Toronto, ON 855-635-9238
Pneumatic Scale Angelus
Cuyahoga Falls, OH 330-923-0491
Prodo-Pak Corp
Garfield, NJ. 973-777-7770

Prototype Equipment Corporation
Libertyville, IL 847-680-4433
Reiser
Canton, MA 734-821-1290
Save-O-Seal Corporation
Elmsford, NY 800-831-9720
Simplex Filler Co
Napa, CA 800-796-7539
Summit Machine Builders Corporation
Denver, CO 800-274-6741
Taylor Products Co
Parsons, KS 888-882-9567
Telesonic Packaging
Wilmington, DE 302-658-6945
Temco
Oakland, CA 707-746-5966
TMT Vacuum Filters
Danville, IL 217-446-0742
Triangle Package Machinery Co
Chicago, IL 800-621-4170
Tridyne Process Systems
South Burlington, VT 802-863-6873
United States Systems Inc
Kansas City, KS 888-281-2454
UniTrak Corporation
Port Hope, ON 866-883-5749
V C 999 Packaging Systems
Kansas City, MO 800-728-2999
Water Sciences Services, Inc.
Jackson, TN 973-584-4131
WCB Ice Cream
Philadelphia, PA 215-425-4320
Weigh Right Automatic Scale Co
Joliet, IL 800-571-0249

Bag Opening

About Packaging Robotics
Thornton, CO 303-449-2559
Alard Equipment Corp
Williamson, NY 315-589-4511
Audion Automation
Carrollton, TX 972-389-0777
Automated Packaging Systems
Streetsboro, OH 800-527-0733
General Processing Systems
Holland, MI 800-547-9370
Gulf Arizona Packaging
Humble, TX 800-364-3887
Gulf Systems
Brownsville, TX 800-217-4853
Gulf Systems
Humble, TX 800-364-3887
Gulf Systems
Arlington, TX 817-261-1915
Herche Warehouse
Denver, CO 303-371-8186
Lockwood Packaging
Woburn, MA 800-641-3100
Our Name is Mud
New York, NY 877-683-7867
Packaging Systems Intl
Denver, CO 303-244-9000
Pacmac Inc
Fayetteville, AR 800-834-1544
Temco
Oakland, CA 707-746-5966

Bag, Cellophane & Pliofilm

Alard Equipment Corp
Williamson, NY 315-589-4511
Automated Packaging Systems
Streetsboro, OH 800-527-0733
Batching Systems
Prince Frederick, MD 800-311-0851
Dynaclear Packaging
Wyckoff, NJ 201-337-1001
Fawema Packaging Machinery
Palmetto, FL 941-351-9597
Hudson-Sharp Machine Co
Green Bay, WI 800-950-4362
Hudson-Sharp Machine Company
Green Bay, WI 920-494-4571
Liqui-Box Corp
Richmond, VA 804-325-1400
M & Q Packaging Corp
North Wales, PA 267-498-4000

Bag, Paper

About Packaging Robotics
Thornton, CO 303-449-2559
Alard Equipment Corp
Williamson, NY 315-589-4511
H G Weber & Co
Kiel, WI. 920-894-2221
New Jersey Wire Stitching Machine Company
Cherry Hill, NJ 856-428-2572
PlexPack Corp
Toronto, ON 855-635-9238
V C 999 Packaging Systems
Kansas City, MO 800-728-2999

Bar Code Devices

Accu-Sort Systems
Telford, PA 800-227-2633
Alard Equipment Corp
Williamson, NY 315-589-4511
Alfa Systems Inc
Westfield, NJ 908-654-0255
American Forms & Labels
Boise, ID 800-388-3554
Baublys Control Laser
Orlando, FL 866-612-8619
Cognitive
Golden, CO 800-765-6600
Columbia Labeling Machinery
Benton City, WA 888-791-9590
Command Line Corporation
Edison, NJ 732-738-6500
Computype Inc
St Paul, MN 800-328-0852
Comstar Printing Solutions
Streetsboro, OH 330-528-2800
Control Module
Enfield, CT 800-722-6654
Creative Automation
Passaic, NJ 973-778-0061
CRS Marking Systems
Portland, OR 800-547-7158
Durable Engravers
Franklin Park, IL 800-869-9565
Esselte Meto
Morris Plains, NJ 800-645-3290
Exact Equipment Corporation
Morrisville, PA 215-295-2000
Fairbanks Scales
Overland Park, KS 800-451-4107
Fernqvist Labeling Solutions
Mountain View, CA 800-426-8215
Formulator Software, LLC
Clinton, NJ 908-735-2248
Fotel
Lombard, IL 800-834-4920
GCA
Huntington Beach, CA 714-379-4911
Graphic Technology
New Century, KS 800-767-9920
Herche Warehouse
Denver, CO 303-371-8186
ID Images
Brunswick, OH 866-516-7300
Imaging Technologies
Cookeville, TN 800-488-2804
Imaje
Kennesaw, GA 678-594-7153
InterSect Business Systems Inc
Kelowna, BC. 250-860-0829
ITW Diagraph
St Charles, MO 800-722-1125
L G I Intl Inc
Portland, OR 800-345-0534
Label Products Inc
Burnsville, MN 877-370-0688
Los Angeles Label Company
Commerce, CA 800-606-5223
Marsh Company
Belleville, IL 800-527-6275
Microscan Systems Inc
Renton, WA 800-762-1149
Qsx Labels
Everett, MA. 800-225-3496
Sato America
Charlotte, NC 888-871-8741
Southern Atlantic Label Co
Chesapeake, VA 800-456-5999
Stratix Corp
Peachtree Cor, GA 800-883-8300

Tallygenicom
Irvine, CA 800-665-6210
Tharo Systems Inc
Brunswick, OH 800-878-6833
Trident
Brookfield, CT 203-740-9333
Vertex Interactive
Clifton, NJ 973-777-3500
Videx Inc
Corvallis, OR 541-738-5500
Wallace Computer Services
Chicago, IL 888-925-8324
Zebra Technologies Corporation
Lincolnshire, IL 866-230-9494

Barrel & Drum Filling

Alard Equipment Corp
Williamson, NY 315-589-4511
Custom Food Machinery
Stockton, CA. 209-463-4343
Data Scale
Fremont, CA 800-651-7350
J.G. Machine Works
Holmdel, NJ 732-203-2077
Washington Frontier
Grandview, WA. 509-469-7662

Barrel Packers

Alard Equipment Corp
Williamson, NY 315-589-4511
Buffalo Technologies Corporation
Buffalo, NY. 800-332-2419
Centennial Moldings
Hastings, NE. 888-883-2189

Beverages, Hot Fill

Alard Equipment Corp
Williamson, NY 315-589-4511
Innovative Food Solutions LLC
Columbus, OH 800-884-3314
Power Packaging Inc
Rosendale, WI. 920-872-2181
Promens
St. John, NB 800-295-3725
Washington Frontier
Grandview, WA. 509-469-7662

Bottle & Jar Sealing

AAMD
Liverpool, NY. 800-887-4167
Alard Equipment Corp
Williamson, NY 315-589-4511
Anderson Machine Sales
Fort Lee, NJ
Arkansas Poly
N Little Rock, AR. 800-342-7659
Crown Closures Machinery
Lancaster, OH 740-681-6593
Custom Food Machinery
Stockton, CA. 209-463-4343
Giltron Inc
Norwood, MA 781-762-4310
Herrmann Ultrasonics
Bartlett, IL. 630-626-1626
Lyco Wausau
Wausau, WI. 715-845-7867
New England Machinery Inc
Bradenton, FL 941-755-5550
Pack Line Corporation
Racine, WI 800-248-6868
Packaging & Processing Equipment
Ayr, ON. 519-622-6666
Promens
St. John, NB 800-295-3725
Resina
Temecula, CA. 800-207-4804
Sanchelima International
Miami, FL. 305-591-4343

Bottle Cap, Plastic & Metal

AAMD
Liverpool, NY. 800-887-4167
Alard Equipment Corp
Williamson, NY 315-589-4511
Anderson Machine Sales
Fort Lee, NJ
Auto-Mate Technologies
Riverhead, NY 631-727-8886

Berkshire PPM
Litchfield, CT 860-567-3118
California Vibratory Feeders
Anaheim, CA 800-354-0972
Crown Closures Machinery
Lancaster, OH 740-681-6593
Custom Food Machinery
Stockton, CA 209-463-4343
Maverick Enterprises Inc
Ukiah, CA 707-463-5591
Silgan Plastic Closure Sltns
New Castle, PA 724-658-3004
Silgan Plastic Closure Sltns
Downers Grove, IL 800-727-8652
Surekap Inc
Winder, GA 770-867-5793

Bottle Capping & Crowning

AAMD
Liverpool, NY 800-887-4167
Accutek Packaging Equipment
Vista, CA 800-989-1828
Alard Equipment Corp
Williamson, NY 315-589-4511
Alcoa - Massena Operations
Massena, NY
Anderson Machine Sales
Fort Lee, NJ
Automated Production Systems Corporation
New Freedom, PA 888-345-5377
Berkshire PPM
Litchfield, CT 860-567-3118
Biner Ellison Packaging Systs
Vista, CA 800-733-8162
California Vibratory Feeders
Anaheim, CA 800-354-0972
Chase-Logeman Corp
Greensboro, NC 336-665-0754
Closure Systems Intl Inc
Indianapolis, IN 800-311-2740
Cozzoli Machine Co
Somerset, NJ 732-564-0400
Crown Closures Machinery
Lancaster, OH 740-681-6593
Custom Food Machinery
Stockton, CA 209-463-4343
Diversified Capping Equipment
Perrysburg, OH 419-666-2566
Donahower & Company
Olathe, KS 913-829-2650
Dynamic Automation LTD
Simi Valley, CA 805-584-8476
Eastern Machine
Middlebury, CT 203-598-0066
ELF Machinery
La Porte, IN 800-328-0466
Elmar Worldwide
Depew, NY 800-433-3562
Filler Specialties
Zeeland, MI 616-772-9235
Filling Equipment Co Inc
Flushing, NY 800-247-7127
Fillit
Kirkland, QC 514-694-2390
Fogg Filler Co
Holland, MI 616-786-3644
Fowler Products Co LLC
Athens, GA 877-549-3301
Giltron Inc
Norwood, MA 781-762-4310
Haumiller Engineering Co
Elgin, IL 847-695-9111
Horix Manufacturing Co
Mc Kees Rocks, PA 412-771-1111
Inline Filling Systems
Venice, FL 941-486-8800
KAPS All Packaging
Riverhead, NY 631-727-0300
Kinsley Inc
Doylestown, PA 800-414-6664
KISS Packaging Systems
Vista, CA 888-522-3538
Lake Eyelet Manufacturing Company
Weatogue, CT 860-628-5543
National Instruments
Baltimore, MD 866-258-1914
New England Machinery Inc
Bradenton, FL 941-755-5550
Nichols Specialty Products
Southborough, MA 508-481-4367

NJM/CLI
Pointe Claire, QC 514-630-6990
Norwalt Design Inc
Randolph, NJ 973-927-3200
Packaging & Processing Equipment
Ayr, ON 519-622-6666
Palace Packaging Machines Inc
Downingtown, PA 610-873-7252
Perl Packaging Systems
Middlebury, CT 800-864-2853
Production Packaging & Processing Equipment
Company
Savannah, GA 912-856-4281
Resina
Temecula, CA 800-207-4804
Silgan Containers LLC
Woodland Hills, CA 818-710-3700
Silgan Plastic Closure Sltns
New Castle, PA 724-658-3004
Silgan Plastic Closure Sltns
Downers Grove, IL 800-767-8652
Silgan White Cap LLC
Downers Grove, IL 800-515-1565
Simplex Filler Co
Napa, CA 800-796-7539
Surekap Inc
Winder, GA 770-867-5793
Universal Labeling Systems Inc
St Petersburg, FL 877-236-0266
Us Bottlers Machinery Co Inc
Charlotte, NC 704-588-4750

Bottle Cartoning

Alard Equipment Corp
Williamson, NY 315-589-4511
Berkshire PPM
Litchfield, CT 860-567-3118
Cannon Equipment Company
Cannon Falls, MN 800-825-8501
Packaging & Processing Equipment
Ayr, ON 519-622-6666
Sasib Beverage & Food North America
Plano, TX 800-558-3814

Bottle Corking

Alard Equipment Corp
Williamson, NY 315-589-4511
Power Packaging Inc
Rosendale, WI 920-872-2181

Bottle Drying

Alard Equipment Corp
Williamson, NY 315-589-4511
Ametek Technical & Industrial Products
Kent, OH 215-256-6601
Custom Food Machinery
Stockton, CA 209-463-4343
Gardner Denver Inc.
Milwaukee, WI
Paxton Products Inc
Blue Ash, OH 800-441-7475

Bottle Filling

A.K. Robins
Baltimore, MD 800-486-9656
Accutek Packaging Equipment
Vista, CA 800-989-1828
Alard Equipment Corp
Williamson, NY 315-589-4511
B T Engineering Inc
Bala Cynwyd, PA 610-664-9500
Berkshire PPM
Litchfield, CT 860-567-3118
Biner Ellison Packaging Systs
Vista, CA 800-733-8162
California Vibratory Feeders
Anaheim, CA 800-354-0972
Chase-Logeman Corp
Greensboro, NC 336-665-0754
Cozzoli Machine Co
Somerset, NJ 732-564-0400
Custom Food Machinery
Stockton, CA 209-463-4343
E2M
Duluth, GA 800-622-4326
Eischen Enterprises
Fresno, CA 559-834-0013

Elmar Worldwide
Depew, NY 800-433-3562
Federal Mfg Co
Milwaukee, WI 414-384-3200
Filler Specialties
Zeeland, MI 616-772-9235
Fogg Filler Co
Holland, MI 616-786-3644
Globe Machine
Tacoma, WA 800-523-6575
Goodnature Products
Orchard Park, NY 800-875-3381
Horix Manufacturing Co
Mc Kees Rocks, PA 412-771-1111
J.G. Machine Works
Holmdel, NJ 732-203-2077
Jetstream Systems
Wichita, KN 855-861-6916
John R Nalbach Engineering Co
Countryside, IL 708-579-9100
KAPS All Packaging
Riverhead, NY 631-727-0300
Kinsley Inc
Doylestown, PA 800-414-6664
KISS Packaging Systems
Vista, CA 888-522-3538
Liqui-Box
Richmond, VA 804-325-1400
Lyco Wausau
Wausau, WI 715-845-7867
Morrison Timing Screw Co
Glenwood, IL 708-331-6600
Multi-Fill Inc
West Jordan, UT 801-280-1570
National Instruments
Baltimore, MD 866-258-1914
Oden Machinery
Tonawanda, NY 800-658-3622
Packaging & Processing Equipment
Ayr, ON 519-622-6666
Packaging Dynamics
Walnut Creek, CA 925-938-2711
Packaging Enterprises
Rockledge, PA 800-453-6213
Per-Fil Industries Inc
Riverside, NJ 856-461-5700
Perl Packaging Systems
Middlebury, CT 800-864-2853
Pneumatic Scale Angelus
Cuyahoga Falls, OH 330-923-0491
Power Packaging Inc
Rosendale, WI 920-872-2181
Sanchelima International
Miami, FL 305-591-4343
Sasib Beverage & Food North America
Plano, TX 800-558-3814
Simplex Filler Co
Napa, CA 800-796-7539
Tindall Packaging
Vicksburg, MI 269-649-1163
Universal Labeling Systems Inc
St Petersburg, FL 877-236-0266
Us Bottlers Machinery Co Inc
Charlotte, NC 704-588-4750
Volckening Inc
Brooklyn, NY 800-221-0276

Bottle Washing, Soaking & Rinsing

Alard Equipment Corp
Williamson, NY 315-589-4511
Alliance Industrial Corp
Lynchburg, VA 800-368-3556
Berkshire PPM
Litchfield, CT 860-567-3118
BEVCO
Canada, BC 800-663-0090
Custom Food Machinery
Stockton, CA 209-463-4343
Davron Technologies Inc
Chattanooga, TN 423-870-1888
Horix Manufacturing Co
Mc Kees Rocks, PA 412-771-1111
Jetstream Systems
Wichita, KN 855-861-6916
Krones
Franklin, WI 800-752-3787
Mcbrady Engineering Co
Rockdale, IL 815-744-8900
Metal Equipment Company
Cleveland, OH 800-700-6326

Namco Machinery
Maspeth, NY
National Hotpack
Stone Ridge, NY 800-431-8232
Palace Packaging Machines Inc
Downingtown, PA. 610-873-7252
Priority One Packaging
Waterloo, ON 800-387-9102
Sasib Beverage & Food North America
Plano, TX .800-558-3814
Us Bottlers Machinery Co Inc
Charlotte, NC 704-588-4750

Bottling

AC Label Company
Provo, UT .801-642-3500
Alard Equipment Corp
Williamson, NY 315-589-4511
Amco Products Co
Fort Smith, AR 479-646-8949
Ametek Technical & Industrial Products
Kent, OH. .215-256-6601
Anver Corporation
Hudson, MA 800-654-3500
Berkshire PPM
Litchfield, CT 860-567-3118
Capmatic, Ltd.
Monreal North, QC. 514-332-0062
Crown Holdings, Inc.
Yardley, PA 215-698-5100
Custom Food Machinery
Stockton, CA 209-463-4343
Filling Equipment Co Inc
Flushing, NY 800-247-7127
Fowler Products Co LLC
Athens, GA 877-549-3301
Horix Manufacturing Co
Mc Kees Rocks, PA. 412-771-1111
Improved Blow Molding
Hollis, NH .800-256-1766
KAPS All Packaging
Riverhead, NY 631-727-0300
Kinsley Inc
Doylestown, PA 800-414-6664
Krones
Franklin, WI 800-752-3787
New England Machinery Inc
Bradenton, FL. 941-755-5550
Oak Barrel Winecraft
Berkeley, CA. 510-849-0400
OnTrack Automation Inc
Waterloo, ON 519-886-9090
Pace Packaging Corp
Fairfield, NJ 800-867-2726
Packaging & Processing Equipment
Ayr, ON 519-622-6666
Packaging Dynamics
Walnut Creek, CA. 925-938-2711
Palace Packaging Machines Inc
Downingtown, PA. 610-873-7252
Paxton Products Inc
Blue Ash, OH 800-441-7475
Pearson Packaging Systems
Spokane, WA. 800-732-7766
Peerless-Winsmith Inc
Springville, NY 716-592-9310
Pneumatic Scale Angelus
Cuyahoga Falls, OH 330-923-0491
Pure & Secure LLC-Cust Svc
Lincoln, NE. 800-875-5915
Rocheleau Blow Molding Systems
Fitchburg, MA 978-345-1723
Silver Spur Corp
Cerritos, CA. 562-921-6880
Simplex Filler Co
Napa, CA. 800-796-7539
Universal Aqua Technologies
Torrance, CA. 800-777-6939

Box Closing

Berkshire PPM
Litchfield, CT 860-567-3118
Charles Beck Machine Corporation
King of Prussia, PA. 610-265-0500
Custom Food Machinery
Stockton, CA. 209-463-4343
Gulf Arizona Packaging
Humble, TX 800-364-3887
Gulf Systems
Brownsville, TX 800-217-4853

Gulf Systems
Humble, TX 800-364-3887
Gulf Systems
Arlington, TX 817-261-1915
Herche Warehouse
Denver, CO 303-371-8186
Iman Pack
Westland, MI 800-810-4626
Moen Industries
Santa Fe Springs, CA 800-732-7766
Nordson Sealant Equipment
Plymouth, MI 734-459-8600
Thiele Technologies-Reedley
Reedley, CA. 800-344-8951
WE Killam Enterprises
Waterford, ON. 519-443-7421
Weigh Right Automatic Scale Co
Joliet, IL 800-571-0249

Box Cutting

Accurate Paper Box Co Inc
Knoxville, TN. 865-690-0311
Charles Beck Machine Corporation
King of Prussia, PA. 610-265-0500
D & L Manufacturing
Milwaukee, WI 414-256-8160
Premier Packages
Saint Louis, MO 800-466-6588

Box Strapping

Delta Cyklop Orga Pac
Charlotte, NC 800-446-4347
Dynaric Inc
Virginia Beach, VA. 800-526-0827
Gulf Arizona Packaging
Humble, TX 800-364-3887
Gulf Systems
Brownsville, TX 800-217-4853
Gulf Systems
Humble, TX 800-364-3887
Gulf Systems
Arlington, TX 817-261-1915
Herche Warehouse
Denver, CO 303-371-8186

Box, Paper

Accurate Paper Box Co Inc
Knoxville, TN. 865-690-0311
Ameripak Packaging Equipment
Warrington, PA 215-343-1530
Barnes Machine Company
Saint Petersburg, FL 727-327-9452
Colter & Peterson
Paterson, NJ 973-684-0901
D & L Manufacturing
Milwaukee, WI 414-256-8160
Fuller Box Co
North Attleboro, MA 508-695-2525
General Corrugated Machinery Company
Palisades Park, NJ. 201-944-0644
Gram Equipment of America
Tampa, FL. 813-248-1978
International Paper Box Machine Company
Nashua, NH. 603-889-6651
Marquip Ward United
Phillips, WI 715-339-2191
Moen Industries
Santa Fe Springs, CA 800-732-7766
New Jersey Wire Stitching Machine Company
Cherry Hill, NJ 856-428-2572
Standard Paper Box Mach Co Inc
Bronx, NY. 800-367-8755
Superior Packaging Equipment Corporation
Fairfield, NJ 973-575-8818
Thiele Technologies-Reedley
Reedley, CA. 800-344-8951

Can Body Forming

Custom Food Machinery
Stockton, CA. 209-463-4343
Dietzco
Hudson, MA 508-481-4000
M S Willett Inc
Cockeysville, MD 410-771-0460
Melvina Can Machinery Company
Hudson Falls, NY 518-743-0606
Omnitech International
Midland, MI 989-631-3377

Precision Component Industries
Canton, OH. 330-477-6287

Can Capping

Accutek Packaging Equipment
Vista, CA .800-989-1828
Alcoa - Massena Operations
Massena, NY
Anderson Machine Sales
Fort Lee, NJ
Berkshire PPM
Litchfield, CT 860-567-3118
BW Container Systems
Romeoville, IL 630-759-6800
Custom Food Machinery
Stockton, CA. 209-463-4343
Filling Equipment Co Inc
Flushing, NY 800-247-7127
Nichols Specialty Products
Southborough, MA 508-481-4367
Pack Line Corporation
Racine, WI 800-248-6868
Pneumatic Scale Angelus
Cuyahoga Falls, OH 330-923-0491
Production Packaging & Processing Equipment
Company
Savannah, GA 912-856-4281
Resina
Temecula, CA. 800-207-4804
Silgan Containers LLC
Woodland Hills, CA 818-710-3700

Can Closing

Berkshire PPM
Litchfield, CT 860-567-3118
Custom Food Machinery
Stockton, CA. 209-463-4343
Dixie Canner Machine Shop
Athens, GA 706-549-0592
Heisler Machine & Tool Co
Fairfield, NJ 973-227-6300
Herrmann Ultrasonics
Bartlett, IL. 630-626-1626
Schroeder Machine
San Marcos, CA 760-591-9733

Can Drying

Ametek Technical & Industrial Products
Kent, OH. 215-256-6601
BFM Equipment Sales
Fall River, WI 920-484-3341
Custom Food Machinery
Stockton, CA. 209-463-4343
Gardner Denver Inc.
Milwaukee, WI
Mountaingate Engineering
Campbell, CA. 408-866-5100
Paxton Products Inc
Blue Ash, OH 800-441-7475

Can Filling

A.K. Robins
Baltimore, MD 800-486-9656
Berkshire PPM
Litchfield, CT 860-567-3118
Custom Food Machinery
Stockton, CA. 209-463-4343
E2M
Duluth, GA 800-622-4326
Elmar Worldwide
Depew, NY 800-433-3562
Horix Manufacturing Co
Mc Kees Rocks, PA. 412-771-1111
J.G. Machine Works
Holmdel, NJ 732-203-2077
Jetstream Systems
Wichita, KN 855-861-6916
John R Nalbach Engineering Co
Countryside, IL. 708-579-9100
KISS Packaging Systems
Vista, CA .888-522-3538
Luthi Machinery Company, Inc.
Pueblo, CO 719-948-1110
Marlen International
Astoria, OR. 800-862-7536
Multi-Fill Inc
West Jordan, UT 801-280-1570

Nu-Con Equipment
  Chanhassen, MN 877-939-0510
Oden Machinery
  Tonawanda, NY 800-658-3622
Per-Fil Industries Inc
  Riverside, NJ 856-461-5700
Pneumatic Scale Angelus
  Cuyahoga Falls, OH 330-923-0491
Pressure Pack
  Williamsburg, VA 757-220-3693
Rutherford Engineering
  Rockford, IL 815-623-2141
Sasib Beverage & Food North America
  Plano, TX 800-558-3814
SeamTech
  Acampo, CA 209-464-4610
SICK Inc
  Bloomington, MN 800-325-7425
Simplex Filler Co
  Napa, CA 800-796-7539
Temco
  Oakland, CA 707-746-5966
Tindall Packaging
  Vicksburg, MI 269-649-1163
Weigh Right Automatic Scale Co
  Joliet, IL 800-571-0249

Can Sealing

AAMD
  Liverpool, NY 800-887-4167
Alcoa - Massena Operations
  Massena, NY
Anderson Machine Sales
  Fort Lee, NJ
Berkshire PPM
  Litchfield, CT 860-567-3118
BW Container Systems
  Romeoville, IL 630-759-6800
Custom Food Machinery
  Stockton, CA 209-463-4343
Herrmann Ultrasonics
  Bartlett, IL .630-626-1626
Ives-Way Products
  Round Lake Beach, IL 847-740-0658
Nu-Con Equipment
  Chanhassen, MN 877-939-0510

Can Seaming

Berkshire PPM
  Litchfield, CT 860-567-3118
BW Container Systems
  Romeoville, IL 630-759-6800
Custom Food Machinery
  Stockton, CA 209-463-4343
Jescorp
  Des Plaines, IL 847-299-7800
Melvina Can Machinery Company
  Hudson Falls, NY 518-743-0606
Pneumatic Scale Angelus
  Cuyahoga Falls, OH 330-923-0491
SeamTech
  Acampo, CA 209-464-4610

Can Washing

A.K. Robins
  Baltimore, MD 800-486-9656
BFM Equipment Sales
  Fall River, WI 920-484-3341
Cincinnati Industrial Machry
  Mason, OH .800-677-0076
Custom Food Machinery
  Stockton, CA 209-463-4343
Davron Technologies Inc
  Chattanooga, TN 423-870-1888
IMC Teddy Food Service Equipment
  Amityville, NY 800-221-5644

Canning & Food Packing

A.K. Robins
  Baltimore, MD 800-486-9656
ABCO Industries Limited
  Lunenburg, NS 866-634-8821
Acraloc Corp
  Oak Ridge, TN 865-483-1368
Ametek Technical & Industrial Products
  Kent, OH 215-256-6601
Apollo Sheet Metal
  Kennewick, WA 509-586-1104

Berkshire PPM
  Litchfield, CT 860-567-3118
Blue Print Automation
  S Chesterfield, VA 804-520-5400
BW Container Systems
  Romeoville, IL 630-759-6800
Custom Food Machinery
  Stockton, CA 209-463-4343
Dixie Canner Machine Shop
  Athens, GA 706-549-0592
Douglas Machine Inc
  Alexandria, MN 320-763-6587
E2M
  Duluth, GA .800-622-4326
Et Oakes Corp
  Hauppauge, NY 631-232-0002
Horix Manufacturing Co
  Mc Kees Rocks, PA 412-771-1111
Hughes Co
  Columbus, WI 866-535-9303
JBT Food Tech
  Lakeland, FL 863-683-5411
Krones
  Franklin, WI 800-752-3787
Langsenkamp Manufacturing
  Indianapolis, IN 877-585-1950
Leader Engineering-Fab Inc
  Napoleon, OH 419-592-0008
Lima Sheet Metal
  Lima, OH 419-229-1161
M S Willett Inc
  Cockeysville, MD 410-771-0460
Magnuson
  Pueblo, CO 719-948-9500
Melco Steel Inc
  Azusa, CA .626-334-7875
Millard Manufacturing Corp
  La Vista, NE 800-662-4263
Muskogee Rubber Stamp & Seal Company
  Fort Gibson, OK 918-478-3046
Olney Machinery
  Westernville, NY 315-827-4208
Paxton Products Inc
  Blue Ash, OH 800-441-7475
Reid Boiler Works
  Bellingham, WA 360-714-6157
Riverwood International
  Atlanta, GA 770-984-5477
T D Sawvel Co
  Maple Plain, MN 877-488-1816
Techno-Design
  Union, KY .800-641-1822
Welliver Metal Products Corporation
  Salem, OR .503-362-1568

Cap Torque Test

Vibrac LLC-Fax
  Amherst, NH 603-886-3857

Cappers

G & F Mfg
  Oak Lawn, IL 800-282-1574

Carton

ADCO Manufacturing Inc
  Sanger, CA .559-875-5563
Berkshire PPM
  Litchfield, CT 860-567-3118
Bradman Lake Inc
  Rock Hill, SC 803-366-3688
C & K Machine Co
  Holyoke, MA 413-536-8122
Combi Packaging Systems LLC
  Canton, OH 866-472-5236
Custom Food Machinery
  Stockton, CA 209-463-4343
D & L Manufacturing
  Milwaukee, WI 414-256-8160
Delkor Systems, Inc
  Minneapolis, MN 800-328-5558
Douglas Machine Inc
  Alexandria, MN 320-763-6587
Econocorp Inc
  Randolph, MA 781-986-7500
F N Smith Corp
  Oregon, IL .815-732-2171
Future Commodities Intl Inc
  Rancho Cucamonga, CA 888-588-2378

Gram Equipment of America
  Tampa, FL .813-248-1978
Hayes Machine Co Inc
  Des Moines, IA 800-860-6224
Heisler Machine & Tool Co
  Fairfield, NJ 973-227-6300
International Paper Box Machine Company
  Nashua, NH 603-889-6651
Micro Solutions Ent Tech & Dev
  Van Nuys, CA 800-673-4968
Packaging Machinery & Equipment
  West Orange, NJ 973-325-2418
Prototype Equipment Corporation
  Libertyville, IL 847-680-4433
San Fab Conveyor
  Sandusky, OH 419-626-4465
Scandia Packaging Machinery Co
  Fairfield, NJ 973-473-6100
Serpa Packaging Solutions
  Visalia, CA 800-348-5453
TDF Automation
  Cedar Falls, IA 800-553-1777
Thiele Technologies-Reedley
  Reedley, CA 800-344-8951
Tisma Machinery Corporation
  Elk Grove Village, IL 847-427-9525

Filling

ADCO Manufacturing Inc
  Sanger, CA .559-875-5563
Bradman Lake Inc
  Rock Hill, SC 803-366-3688
C & K Machine Co
  Holyoke, MA 413-536-8122
Cannon Equipment Company
  Cannon Falls, MN 800-825-8501
Crystal-Vision Packaging Systems
  Torrance, CA 800-331-3240
Custom Food Machinery
  Stockton, CA 209-463-4343
Design Technology Corporation
  Billerica, MA 978-663-7000
Doering Machines Inc
  San Francisco, CA 415-526-2131
Eischen Enterprises
  Fresno, CA 559-834-0013
Elliott Manufacturing Co Inc
  Fresno, CA 559-233-6235
Iman Pack
  Westland, MI 800-810-4626
Key Automation
  Eagan, MN 651-455-0547
Khs USA Inc
  Sarasota, FL 877-227-8358
MAF Industries Inc
  Traver, CA .559-897-2905
Multi-Fill Inc
  West Jordan, UT 801-280-1570
Optek Inc
  Galena, OH 800-533-8400
Packaging Dynamics
  Walnut Creek, CA 925-938-2711
Pomona Service & Pkgng Co LA
  Yakima, WA 509-452-7121
R A Jones & Co Inc
  Ft Mitchell, KY 859-341-1807
Simplex Filler Co
  Napa, CA 800-796-7539
Summit Machine Builders Corporation
  Denver, CO 800-274-6741
TDF Automation
  Cedar Falls, IA 800-553-1777
Temco
  Oakland, CA 707-746-5966
Thiele Engineering Company
  Fergus Falls, MN 218-739-3321
Tindall Packaging
  Vicksburg, MI 269-649-1163
Tisma Machinery Corporation
  Elk Grove Village, IL 847-427-9525
Tridyne Process Systems
  South Burlington, VT 802-863-6873
Universal Labeling Systems Inc
  St Petersburg, FL 877-236-0266
Weigh Right Automatic Scale Co
  Joliet, IL 800-571-0249

Printing

Algene Marking Equipment Company
  Garfield, NJ 973-478-9041

Custom Food Machinery
   Stockton, CA.............209-463-4343
Matthews Marking Systems Div
   Pittsburgh, PA.............412-665-2500
Trident
   Brookfield, CT.............203-740-9333
WE Killam Enterprises
   Waterford, ON.............519-443-7421

Carton, Case, Box Sealing

A.B. Sealer, Inc.
   Beaver Dam, WI.............877-885-9299
Accutek Packaging Equipment
   Vista, CA.............800-989-1828
ADCO Manufacturing Inc
   Sanger, CA.............559-875-5563
Barnes Machine Company
   Saint Petersburg, FL.............727-327-9452
Belco Packaging Systems
   Monrovia, CA.............800-833-1833
Berkshire PPM
   Litchfield, CT.............860-567-3118
Better Packages
   Ansonia, CT.............800-237-9151
Bradman Lake Inc
   Rock Hill, SC.............803-366-3688
Brenton Engineering Co
   Alexandria, MN.............800-535-2730
C.J. Machine
   Fridley, MN.............763-767-4630
Charles Beck Machine Corporation
   King of Prussia, PA.............610-265-0500
Combi Packaging Systems LLC
   Canton, OH.............866-472-5236
Compacker Systems LLC
   Davenport, IA.............563-391-2751
Custom Food Machinery
   Stockton, CA.............209-463-4343
Customized Equipment SE
   Tucker, GA.............770-934-9300
Douglas Machine Inc
   Alexandria, MN.............320-763-6587
Durable Packaging Corporation
   Countryside, IL.............800-700-5677
Econocorp Inc
   Randolph, MA.............781-986-7500
Elliott Manufacturing Co Inc
   Fresno, CA.............559-233-6235
Future Commodities Intl Inc
   Rancho Cucamonga, CA.............888-588-2378
General Corrugated Machinery Company
   Palisades Park, NJ.............201-944-0644
Gulf Arizona Packaging
   Humble, TX.............800-364-3887
Gulf Systems
   Brownsville, TX.............800-217-4853
Gulf Systems
   Humble, TX.............800-364-3887
Gulf Systems
   Arlington, TX.............817-261-1915
Hayes Machine Co Inc
   Des Moines, IA.............800-860-6224
Heisler Machine & Tool Co
   Fairfield, NJ.............973-227-6300
Herche Warehouse
   Denver, CO.............303-371-8186
Herrmann Ultrasonics
   Bartlett, IL.............630-626-1626
Iman Pack
   Westland, MI.............800-810-4626
Intertape Polymer Group
   Menasha, WI.............800-558-5006
Kirkco Corp
   Monroe, NC.............704-289-7090
Kisters Kayat
   Sarasota, FL.............386-424-0101
Klippenstein Corp
   Fresno, CA.............888-834-4258
Liqui-Box
   Richmond, VA.............804-325-1400
Loveshaw Corp
   South Canaan, PA.............800-572-3434
Markwell Manufacturing Company
   Norwood, MA.............800-666-1123
Marq Packaging Systems Inc
   Yakima, WA.............800-998-4301
Mastercraft International
   Charlotte, NC.............704-392-7436
Moen Industries
   Santa Fe Springs, CA.............800-732-7766

On-Hand Adhesives
   Lake Zurich, IL.............800-323-5158
Packaging & Processing Equipment
   Ayr, ON.............519-622-6666
Peace Industries
   Rolling Meadows, IL.............800-873-2239
Pearson Packaging Systems
   Spokane, WA.............800-732-7766
Prototype Equipment Corporation
   Libertyville, IL.............847-680-4433
Rockford-Midland Corporation
   Rockford, IL.............800-327-7908
S.V. Dice Designers
   Rowland Heights, CA.............888-478-3423
Sabel Engineering Corporation
   Villard, MN.............320-554-3611
Samuel Strapping Systems Inc
   Woodridge, IL.............800-323-4424
San Fab Conveyor
   Sandusky, OH.............419-626-4465
Scandia Packaging Machinery Co
   Fairfield, NJ.............973-473-6100
Sekisui TA Industries
   Brea, CA.............800-258-8273
Staplex Co Inc
   Brooklyn, NY.............800-221-0822
Superior Packaging Equipment Corporation
   Fairfield, NJ.............973-575-8818
SWF McDowell
   Orlando, FL.............800-877-7971
TDF Automation
   Cedar Falls, IA.............800-553-1777
Technistar Corporation
   Denver, CO.............303-651-0188
Temco
   Oakland, CA.............707-746-5966
Thiele Engineering Company
   Fergus Falls, MN.............218-739-3321
Thiele Technologies-Reedley
   Reedley, CA.............800-344-8951
Triangle Package Machinery Co
   Chicago, IL.............800-621-4170
WE Killam Enterprises
   Waterford, ON.............519-443-7421
Weigh Right Automatic Scale Co
   Joliet, IL.............800-571-0249
Wepackit
   Orangeville, ON.............519-942-1700
Wexxar Corporation
   Chicago, IL.............630-983-6666
Wexxar Packaging Inc
   Richmond, BC.............888-565-3219
Zed Industries
   Vandalia, OH.............937-667-8407

Coding, Dating & Marking Equipment

A.D. Johnson Engraving Company
   Kalamazoo, MI.............269-342-5500
A.D. Joslin Manufacturing Company
   Manistee, MI.............231-723-2908
ABC Stamp Signs & Awards
   Boise, ID.............208-375-4470
ABM Marking
   Belleville, IL.............800-626-9012
Accent Mark
   Palmdale, CA.............661-274-8191
Accu-Sort Systems
   Telford, PA.............800-227-2633
Ace Stamp & Engraving
   Lakewood, WA.............253-582-3322
Allmark Impressions LTD
   Fort Worth, TX.............817-834-0080
American Art Stamp
   Gardena, CA.............310-965-9004
American Forms & Labels
   Boise, ID.............800-388-3554
Ameristamp/Sign-A-Rama
   Evansville, IN.............800-543-6693
Applied Products Co
   El Segundo, CA.............888-551-0447
Astoria Laminations
   St Clair Shores, MI.............800-526-7325
Atlas Rubber Stamp & Printing
   York, PA.............717-751-0459
Authentic Biocode Corp
   Addison, TX.............866-434-1402
Axiohm USA
   Myrtle Beach, SC.............843-443-3155
Baublys Control Laser
   Orlando, FL.............866-612-8619

Bell-Mark Corporation
   Pine Brook, NJ.............973-882-0202
Bishop Machine Shop
   Zanesville, OH.............740-453-8818
Bren Instruments
   Franklin, TN.............615-794-6825
Chattanooga Rubber Stamp & Stencil Works
   Sale Creek, TN.............800-894-1164
City Stamp & Seal Co
   Austin, TX.............800-950-6074
Cognitive
   Golden, CO.............800-765-6600
Columbia Labeling Machinery
   Benton City, WA.............888-791-9590
Computype Inc
   St Paul, MN.............800-328-0852
Comstar Printing Solutions
   Streetsboro, OH.............330-528-2800
Control Module
   Enfield, CT.............800-722-6654
Corpus Christi Stamp Works
   Corpus Christi, TX.............800-322-4515
Crown Marking
   Minneapolis, MN.............800-305-5249
CRS Marking Systems
   Portland, OR.............800-547-7158
Cup Pac Packaging Inc
   South Beloit, IL.............877-347-9725
Custom Food Machinery
   Stockton, CA.............209-463-4343
Custom Rubber Stamp Co
   Crosby, MN.............888-606-4579
Custom Stamp Company
   Anza, CA.............323-292-0753
Custom Stamping & Manufacturing
   Portland, OR.............503-238-3700
D & L Manufacturing
   Milwaukee, WI.............414-256-8160
Dalemark Industries
   Lakewood, NJ.............732-367-3100
Daymark Safety Systems
   Bowling Green, OH.............419-353-2458
Dayton Marking Devices Company
   Dayton, OH.............937-432-0285
Design Technology Corporation
   Billerica, MA.............978-663-7000
Detroit Marking Products
   Detroit, MI.............800-833-8222
Dixie Rubber Stamp & Seal Company
   Atlanta, GA.............404-875-8883
Domino Amjet Inc
   Gurnee, IL.............800-444-4512
Dorell Equipment Inc
   Somerset, NJ.............732-247-5400
Drs Designs
   Bethel, CT.............888-792-3740
Durable Engravers
   Franklin Park, IL.............800-869-9565
E C Shaw Co
   Cincinnati, OH.............866-532-7429
E2M
   Duluth, GA.............800-622-4326
East Memphis Rubber Stamp Company
   Bartlett, TN.............901-384-0887
Easterday Fluid Technologies
   Saint Francis, WI.............414-482-4488
Ed Smith's Stencil Works LTD
   New Orleans, LA.............504-525-2128
Ehrgott Rubber Stamp Company
   Indianapolis, IN.............317-353-2222
ELF Machinery
   La Porte, IN.............800-328-0466
Elmark Packaging Inc
   West Chester, PA.............800-670-9688
EMCO
   Miamisburg, OH.............800-722-3626
Everett Rubber Stamp
   Everett, WA.............425-258-6747
Fairbanks Scales
   Overland Park, KS.............800-451-4107
Fas-Co Coders
   Lithia Springs, GA.............800-478-0685
Federal Stamp & Seal Manufacturing Company
   Atlanta, GA.............800-333-7726
Fleming Packaging Corporation
   Peoria, IL.............309-676-7657
Flint Rubber Stamp Works
   Flint, MI.............810-235-2341
Fox Stamp Sign & Specialty
   Menasha, WI.............920-725-2683
Franklin Rubber Stamp Co
   Wilmington, DE.............302-654-8841

Fraser Stamp & Seal
Chicago, IL 800-540-8565
Frost Manufacturing Corp
Worcester, MA 800-462-0216
Fuller Box Co
North Attleboro, MA 508-695-2525
G&R Graphics
West Orange, NJ 813-503-8592
Garvey Products
Cincinnati, OH 513-771-8710
Garvey Products
West Chester, OH 800-543-1908
GCA
Huntington Beach, CA 714-379-4911
Glover Rubber Stamp & Crafts
Wills Point, TX 214-824-6900
Gotham Pen Co Inc
Bronx, NY 800-334-7970
Granite State Stamps Inc
Manchester, NH 800-937-3736
Graphic Impressions of Illinois
River Grove, IL 708-453-1100
Graphic Technology
New Century, KS 800-767-9920
Grays Harbor Stamp Works
Aberdeen, WA 800-894-3830
Gribble Stamp & Stencil Co
Houston, TX 713-228-5358
Grueny's Rubber Stamps
Little Rock, AR 501-376-0393
Gulf Systems
Humble, TX 800-364-3887
Gulf Systems
Arlington, TX 817-261-1915
H G Weber & Co
Kiel, WI 920-894-2221
Hartford Stamp Works
Hartford, CT 860-249-6205
Hathaway Stamps
Cincinnati, OH 513-621-1052
Herche Warehouse
Denver, CO 303-371-8186
House Stamp Works
Chicago, IL 312-939-7177
Houston Label
Pasadena, TX 800-477-6995
Houston Stamp & Stencil Company
Houston, TX 713-869-4337
Howard Imprinting Machine Company
Houston, TX 800-334-6943
Hub Pen Company
Quincy, MA 617-471-9900
Huntington Park Rbr Stamp Co
Huntington Park, CA 800-882-0029
ID Images
Brunswick, OH 866-516-7300
Ideal Stencil Machine & Tape Company
Marion, IL 800-388-0162
Imaging Technologies
Cookeville, TN 800-488-2804
Imaje
Kennesaw, GA 678-594-7153
Independent Ink
Gardena, CA 800-446-5538
Innovative Ceramic Corp
East Liverpool, OH 330-385-6515
Irby
Rocky Mount, NC 252-442-0154
ITW Diagraph
St Charles, MO 800-722-1125
Jim Lake Companies
Dallas, TX 214-741-5018
Joyce Engraving Co Inc
Dallas, TX 214-638-1262
Justrite Rubber Stamp & Seal
Kansas City, MO 800-229-5010
Kirkco Corp
Monroe, NC 704-289-7090
Koehler-Gibson Marking
Buffalo, NY 800-875-1562
Kwikprint Manufacturing Inc
Jacksonville, FL 800-940-5945
L&L Engraving Company
Gilford, NH 888-524-3032
Label Art
Tucker, GA 800-652-1072
Label-Aire Inc
Fullerton, CA 714-441-0700
Labelprint America
Newburyport, MA 978-463-4004
Lake Eyelet Manufacturing Company
Weatogue, CT 860-628-5543

Lakeland Rubber Stamp Company
Lakeland, FL 863-682-5111
Lakeview Rubber Stamp Co
Chicago, IL 773-539-1525
Larry B Newman Printing
Knoxville, TN 888-835-4566
Lasertechnics Marking Corporation
Nepean, ON. 613-749-4895
Listo Pencil Corp
Alameda, CA. 800-547-8648
Long Island Stamp Corporation
Flushing, NY 800-547-8267
Lord Label Machine Systems
Charlotte, NC 704-644-1650
Loveshaw Corp
South Canaan, PA 800-572-3434
Mankuta Bros Rubber Stamp Co
Bohemia, NY 800-223-4481
Mansfield Rubber Stamp
Mansfield, OH 419-524-1442
Mark-It Rubber Stamp & Label Company
Stamford, CT. 203-348-3204
Marking Devices Inc
Cleveland, OH 216-861-4498
Marking Methods Inc
Alhambra, CA. 626-308-5800
Marsh Company
Belleville, IL 800-527-6275
Mastermark
Kent, WA. 206-762-9610
Matthews Marking Systems Div
Pittsburgh, PA 412-665-2500
Mecco Marking & Traceability
Cranberry Township, PA. 888-369-9190
Menke Marking Devices
Santa Fe Springs, CA 800-231-6023
Mettler-Toledo, LLC
Columbus, OH 800-638-8537
Modern Stamp Company
Baltimore, MD 800-727-3029
Moore Efficient Communication Aids
Denver, CO 303-433-8456
Muskogee Rubber Stamp & Seal Company
Fort Gibson, OK 918-478-3046
My Serenity Pond
Cold Spring, MN 320-363-0411
National Metal Industries
West Springfield, MA 800-628-8850
National Pen Co
San Diego, CA 858-675-3000
NCR Corp
Atlanta, GA 800-225-5627
Newstamp Lighting Factory
North Easton, MA 508-238-7073
Northern Berkshire Tourist
North Adams, MA 413-663-9204
Norwood Marking Systems
Downers Grove, IL 800-626-3464
O.K. Marking Devices
Regina, SK 306-522-2856
Oak International
Sturgis, MI 269-651-9790
OK Stamp & Seal Company
Oklahoma City, OK 405-235-7853
Open Date Systems
Sunapee, NH 877-673-6328
Oration Rubber Stamp Company
Columbus, NJ 908-496-4161
Organic Products Co
Irving, TX 972-438-7321
Oshikiri Corp of America
Philadelphia, PA 215-637-8112
Packaging & Processing Equipment
Ayr, ON 519-622-6666
Packaging Machinery & Equipment
West Orange, NJ 973-325-2418
Plastimatic Arts Corporation
Mishawaka, IN 800-442-3593
Printcraft Marking Devices Inc
Buffalo, NY 716-873-8181
Pulse Systems
Los Alamos, NM 505-662-7599
Qsx Labels
Everett, MA 800-225-3496
Quick Stamp & Sign Mfg
Lafayette, LA 337-232-2171
R R Donnelley
Chicago, IL 800-742-4455
R.P. Childs Stamp Company
Ludlow, MA 413-733-1211
Rebel Stamp & Sign Co
Baton Rouge, LA 800-860-5120

Richardson's Stamp Works
Houston, TX 713-973-0314
Rubber Stamp Shop
Accokeek, MD 800-835-0839
Sancoa International
Lumberton, NJ 609-953-5050
Sato America
Charlotte, NC 888-871-8741
Schwaab, Inc
Milwaukee, WI 800-935-9877
Signet Marking Devices
Costa Mesa, CA 800-421-5150
Sioux Falls Rbr Stamp Works
Sioux Falls, SD 855-334-5990
Smyth Co LLC
St Paul, MN. 800-473-3464
Sossner Steel Stamps
Elizabethton, TN 800-828-9515
Southern Rubber Stamp
Tulsa, OK 888-826-4304
Spectrum Enterprises
Evansville, IN 812-425-1771
Spencer Business Form Company
Spencer, WV 304-372-8877
Sprinter Marking Inc
Zanesville, OH 740-453-1000
Stratix Corp
Peachtree Cor, GA 800-883-8300
Sutherland Stamp Company
San Diego, CA 858-233-7784
Tallygenicom
Irvine, CA 800-665-6210
Tharo Systems Inc
Brunswick, OH 800-878-6833
TNA Packaging Solutions
Coppell, TX 972-462-6500
Trident
Brookfield, CT 203-740-9333
United Ribtype Co
Fort Wayne, IN 800-473-4039
Universal Die & Stampings
Prairie Du Sac, WI 608-643-2477
Universal Packaging Inc
Houston, TX 800-324-2610
Vande Berg SCALES/Vbs Inc
Sioux Center, IA 712-722-1181
Varitronic Systems
Brooklyn Park, MN. 763-536-6400
Videojet Technologies Inc
Wood Dale, IL 800-843-3610
Videx Inc
Corvallis, OR 541-738-5500
Volk Corp
Farmington Hills, MI 800-521-6799
Walker Co
Oklahoma City, OK 800-522-3015
Wallace Computer Services
Chicago, IL 888-925-8324
WE Killam Enterprises
Waterford, ON. 519-443-7421
Weber Packaging Solutions Inc
Arlington Heights, IL 800-843-4242
Wichita Stamp & Seal Inc
Wichita, KS. 316-263-4223
Wildes Printing Co Inc
White Plains, MD 301-870-4141
Willett America
Wood Dale, IL. 800-259-2600
Winmark Stamp & Sign
Salt Lake City, UT 800-438-0480
Zanasi USA
Brooklyn Park, MN. 800-627-2633
Zerand Corp
New Berlin, WI 262-827-3800

Coding, Marking, Dating

A.D. Johnson Engraving Company
Kalamazoo, MI 269-342-5500
A.D. Joslin Manufacturing Company
Manistee, MI 231-723-2908
Algene Marking Equipment Company
Garfield, NJ. 973-478-9041
American Art Stamp
Gardena, CA 310-965-9004
American Forms & Labels
Boise, ID 800-388-3554
Ameristamp/Sign-A-Rama
Evansville, IN 800-543-6693
Astoria Laminations
St Clair Shores, MI 800-526-7325

Baublys Control Laser
Orlando, FL.....................866-612-8619
Bell-Mark Corporation
Pine Brook, NJ.................973-882-0202
Berkshire PPM
Litchfield, CT...................860-567-3118
Bishop Machine Shop
Zanesville, OH..................740-453-8818
Bren Instruments
Franklin, TN.....................615-794-6825
Century Rubber Stamp Company
New York, NY...................212-962-6165
Cognitive
Golden, CO......................800-765-6600
Columbia Labeling Machinery
Benton City, WA................888-791-9590
Computype Inc
St Paul, MN.....................800-328-0852
Crown Marking
Minneapolis, MN................800-305-5249
Cup Pac Packaging Inc
South Beloit, IL.................877-347-9725
Custom Food Machinery
Stockton, CA....................209-463-4343
D & L Manufacturing
Milwaukee, WI..................414-256-8160
Dalemark Industries
Lakewood, NJ...................732-367-3100
Daymark Safety Systems
Bowling Green, OH..............419-353-2458
Dayton Marking Devices Company
Dayton, OH......................937-432-0285
Dorell Equipment Inc
Somerset, NJ....................732-247-5400
E C Shaw Co
Cincinnati, OH..................866-532-7429
E2M
Duluth, GA......................800-622-4326
Easterday Fluid Technologies
Saint Francis, WI...............414-482-4488
Ed Smith's Stencil Works LTD
New Orleans, LA.................504-525-2128
ELF Machinery
La Porte, IN.....................800-328-0466
Elmark Packaging Inc
West Chester, PA................800-670-9688
Esselte Meto
Morris Plains, NJ................800-645-3290
Everett Rubber Stamp
Everett, WA......................425-258-6747
Fairbanks Scales
Overland Park, KS...............800-451-4107
Fas-Co Coders
Lithia Springs, GA..............800-478-0685
Federal Stamp & Seal Manufacturing Company
Atlanta, GA......................800-333-7726
Franklin Rubber Stamp Co
Wilmington, DE..................302-654-8841
Fsi Technologies
Lombard, IL......................800-468-6009
Fuller Box Co
North Attleboro, MA.............508-695-2525
Garvey Products
Cincinnati, OH..................513-771-8710
GCA
Huntington Beach, CA...........714-379-4911
Glover Rubber Stamp & Crafts
Wills Point, TX..................214-824-6900
Granite State Stamps Inc
Manchester, NH..................800-937-3736
Graphic Technology
New Century, KS.................800-767-9920
Gulf Arizona Packaging
Humble, TX......................800-364-3887
Gulf Systems
Brownsville, TX..................800-217-4853
Gulf Systems
Humble, TX......................800-364-3887
Gulf Systems
Arlington, TX....................817-261-1915
H G Weber & Co
Kiel, WI..........................920-894-2221
Herche Warehouse
Denver, CO.......................303-371-8186
Howard Imprinting Machine Company
Houston, TX......................800-334-6943
Huntington Park Rbr Stamp Co
Huntington Park, CA.............800-882-0029
ID Images
Brunswick, OH...................866-516-7300
Ideal Stencil Machine & Tape Company
Marion, IL........................800-388-0162

Imaje
Kennesaw, GA....................678-594-7153
Independent Ink
Gardena, CA......................800-446-5538
Irby
Rocky Mount, NC................252-442-0154
ITW Diagraph
St Charles, MO...................800-722-1125
Joyce Engraving Co Inc
Dallas, TX........................214-638-1262
Kirkco Corp
Monroe, NC......................704-289-7090
Koehler-Gibson Marking
Buffalo, NY.......................800-875-1562
Kwikprint Manufacturing Inc
Jacksonville, FL..................800-940-5945
Labelprint America
Newburyport, MA................978-463-4004
Lake Eyelet Manufacturing Company
Weatogue, CT....................860-628-5543
Lasertechnics Marking Corporation
Nepean, ON.......................613-749-4895
Loveshaw Corp
South Canaan, PA................800-572-3434
Marking Methods Inc
Alhambra, CA....................626-308-5800
Marsh Company
Belleville, IL.....................800-527-6275
Matthews Marking Systems Div
Pittsburgh, PA....................412-665-2500
Mecco Marking & Traceability
Cranberry Township, PA.........888-369-9190
Menke Marking Devices
Santa Fe Springs, CA.............800-231-6023
Moore Efficient Communication Aids
Denver, CO.......................303-433-8456
Muskogee Rubber Stamp & Seal Company
Fort Gibson, OK..................918-478-3046
National Metal Industries
West Springfield, MA.............800-628-8850
Newstamp Lighting Factory
North Easton, MA................508-238-7073
Norwood Marking Systems
Downers Grove, IL...............800-626-3464
Oration Rubber Stamp Company
Columbus, NJ....................908-496-4161
Packaging & Processing Equipment
Ayr, ON..........................519-622-6666
Precision Component Industries
Canton, OH.......................330-477-6287
Pulse Systems
Los Alamos, NM..................505-662-7599
R.P. Childs Stamp Company
Ludlow, MA.......................413-733-1211
Rebel Stamp & Sign Co
Baton Rouge, LA.................800-860-5120
Rubber Stamp Shop
Accokeek, MD....................800-835-0839
Schwaab, Inc
Milwaukee, WI...................800-935-9877
Shiffer Industries
Kihei, HI..........................800-642-1774
Signet Marking Devices
Costa Mesa, CA...................800-421-5150
Sossner Steel Stamps
Elizabethton, TN.................800-828-9515
Southern Rubber Stamp
Tulsa, OK.........................888-826-4304
Sprinter Marking Inc
Zanesville, OH....................740-453-1000
Tallygenicom
Irvine, CA........................800-665-6210
Tharo Systems Inc
Brunswick, OH...................800-878-6833
Trident
Brookfield, CT....................203-740-9333
Universal Die & Stampings
Prairie Du Sac, WI...............608-643-2477
Vande Berg SCALES/Vbs Inc
Sioux Center, IA..................712-722-1181
Varitronic Systems
Brooklyn Park, MN...............763-536-6400
Videojet Technologies Inc
Wood Dale, IL....................800-843-3610
Videx Inc
Corvallis, OR.....................541-738-5500
Volk Corp
Farmington Hills, MI.............800-521-6799
WE Killam Enterprises
Waterford, ON....................519-443-7421
Weber Packaging Solutions Inc
Arlington Heights, IL.............800-843-4242

Wichita Stamp & Seal Inc
Wichita, KS.......................316-263-4223
Willett America
Wood Dale, IL....................800-259-2600
Zanasi USA
Brooklyn Park, MN...............800-627-2633
Zerand Corp
New Berlin, WI...................262-827-3800

Container

About Packaging Robotics
Thornton, CO....................303-449-2559
Barnes Machine Company
Saint Petersburg, FL.............727-327-9452
Berry Global
Evansville, IN....................800-343-1295
Burd & Fletcher
Independence, MO................800-821-2776
Carando Technologies Inc
Stockton, CA.....................209-948-6500
Carleton Helical Technologies
Doylestown, PA...................215-230-8900
Dietzco
Hudson, MA......................508-481-4000
Heisler Machine & Tool Co
Fairfield, NJ......................973-227-6300
Heuft USA Inc
Downers Grove, IL...............630-968-9011
Hoegger Food Technology
Minneapolis, MN.................877-789-5400
Marquip Ward United
Phillips, WI.......................715-339-2191
Neos
Elk River, MN....................888-441-6367
Osgood Industries
Oldsmar, FL......................813-855-7337
Paradise Inc.
Tampa, FL........................813-752-1155
Peco Controls Corporation
Modesto, CA......................800-732-6285
Plastic Ingenuity
Cross Plains, WI..................608-798-3071
Plastipak Industries
La Prairie, QC....................800-387-7452
Promens
St. John, NB......................800-295-3725
Quick Label Systems
West Warwick, RI.................877-757-7978
Rotonics Manufacturing
Gardena, CA......................310-327-5401
Silver Spur Corp
Cerritos, CA......................562-921-6880
Solbern Corp
Fairfield, NJ......................973-227-3030
Southworth Products Corp
Falmouth, ME....................800-743-1000
Stormax International
Concord, NH......................800-874-7629
Tindall Packaging
Vicksburg, MI....................269-649-1163
V C 999 Packaging Systems
Kansas City, MO.................800-728-2999

Detectors

Packaging Line

Aw Sheepscot Holding Co Inc
Franksville, WI...................800-850-6110
Axelrod, Norman N
New York, NY....................212-369-2885
Binks Industries Inc
Montgomery, IL..................630-801-1100
Care Controls, Inc.
Mill Creek, WA...................800-593-6050
Carter Products
Grand Rapids, MI................888-622-7837
Daystar
Glen Arm, MD....................800-494-6537
Eriez Magnetics
Erie, PA...........................800-346-4946
FILTEC-Inspection Systems
Torrance, CA......................888-434-5832
LDJ Electronics
Troy, MI..........................248-528-2202
Lixi Inc
Carpentersville, IL...............847-961-6666
Lock Inspection Systems
Fitchburg, MA....................800-227-5539
Mettler-Toledo Safeline Inc
Lutz, FL...........................800-638-8537

Mocon Inc
Minneapolis, MN 763-493-7229
Nikka Densok
Lakewood, CO 800-806-4587
Ohio Magnetics Inc
Maple Heights, OH. 800-486-6446
Peco Controls Corporation
Modesto, CA. 800-732-6285
ShockWatch
Dallas, TX 800-393-7920
Tec5USA
Plainview, NY 516-653-2000
Vande Berg SCALES/Vbs Inc
Sioux Center, IA 712-722-1181

Equipment

Materials

Loeb Equipment
Chicago, IL. 773-496-5720
Lyco Manufacturing
Wausau, WI. 715-845-7867
Priority One Packaging
Waterloo, ON 800-387-9102

Exhausters

Canning

A.K. Robins
Baltimore, MD 800-486-9656
Dixie Canner Machine Shop
Athens, GA 706-549-0592
Ross Cook
Silver Spring, MD. 800-233-7339

Form, Fill & Seal

Horizontal

ACMA/GD
Richmond, VA. 800-525-2735
Bradman Lake Inc
Rock Hill, SC 803-366-3688
Campbell Wrapper Corporation
De Pere, WI. 920-983-7100
Circle Packaging Machinery Inc
De Pere, WI. 920-983-3420
Elopak Americas
Wixom, MI 248-486-4600
Enhance Packaging Technologies
Whitby, ON 905-668-5811
Equipment Outlet
Meridian, ID 208-887-1472
Formost Packaging Machines
Woodinville, WA. 425-483-9090
Herrmann Ultrasonics
Bartlett, IL. 630-626-1626
Ilapak Inc
Newtown, PA 215-579-2900
Iman Pack
Westland, MI. 800-810-4626
Maryland Packaging Corporation
Elkridge, MD 410-540-9700
Ossid Corp
Battleboro, NC 800-334-8369
Packaging Dynamics
Walnut Creek, CA. 925-938-2711
Prodo-Pak Corp
Garfield, NJ. 973-777-7770
Reiser
Canton, MA 734-821-1290
Sitma USA
Spilamberto, MO 800-728-1254
Southern Packaging Machinery
Athens, GA 706-208-0814
Zed Industries
Vandalia, OH. 937-667-8407

Vertical

Accu-Pak
Akron, OH
ACMA/GD
Richmond, VA. 800-525-2735
Amark Packaging Systems
Kansas City, MO. 816-965-9000
Blodgett Co
Houston, TX. 281-933-6195
Bradman Lake Inc
Rock Hill, SC 803-366-3688

Circle Packaging Machinery Inc
De Pere, WI. 920-983-3420
Elopak Americas
Wixom, MI 248-486-4600
Enhance Packaging Technologies
Whitby, ON 905-668-5811
Equipment Outlet
Meridian, ID 208-887-1472
Formost Packaging Machines
Woodinville, WA. 425-483-9090
General Packaging Equipment Co
Houston, TX 713-686-4331
Hayssen Flexible Systems
Duncan, SC 864-486-4000
Herrmann Ultrasonics
Bartlett, IL. 630-626-1626
Ilapak Inc
Newtown, PA 215-579-2900
Iman Pack
Westland, MI. 800-810-4626
Key-Pak Machines
Lebanon, NJ 908-236-2111
Korab Engineering Company
Los Angeles, CA. 310-670-7710
Longhorn Packaging Inc
San Antonio, TX 800-433-7974
Matrix Packaging Machinery
Saukville, WI 888-628-7491
Ossid Corp
Battleboro, NC 800-334-8369
Packaging Dynamics
Walnut Creek, CA. 925-938-2711
Pacmac Inc
Fayetteville, AR 800-834-1544
PFM Packaging Machinery Corporation
Newmarket, ON 905-836-6709
Prodo-Pak Corp
Garfield, NJ. 973-777-7770
TNA Packaging Solutions
Coppell, TX 972-462-6500
Universal Packaging Inc
Houston, TX 800-324-2610
Wick's Packaging Service
Cutler, IN 574-967-3104
Zed Industries
Vandalia, OH. 937-667-8407

Heat Sealing

AAMD
Liverpool, NY. 800-887-4167
Audion Automation
Carrollton, TX. 972-389-0777
Bosch Packaging Technology
New Richmond, WI 715-246-6511
Branson Ultrasonics Corp
Danbury, CT 203-796-0400
Chaffee Co
Rocklin, CA 916-630-3980
Chase Industries Inc
West Chester, OH 800-543-4455
Circle Packaging Machinery Inc
De Pere, WI. 920-983-3420
Custom Food Machinery
Stockton, CA. 209-463-4343
Design Technology Corporation
Billerica, MA 978-663-7000
Edson Packaging Machinery
Hamilton, ON 800-493-3766
Food Equipment Manufacturing Company
Bedford Heights, OH 216-672-5859
Giltron Inc
Norwood, MA. 781-762-4310
Green Tek
Janesville, WI 800-747-6440
Harwil Corp
Oxnard, CA. 800-562-2447
Key-Pak Machines
Lebanon, NJ 908-236-2111
Kliklok-Woodman
Decatur, GA 770-981-5200
On-Hand Adhesives
Lake Zurich, IL. 800-323-5158
PlexPack Corp
Toronto, ON 855-635-9238
Pressure Pack
Williamsburg, VA 757-220-3693
Reiser
Canton, MA 734-821-1290
Rockford-Midland Corporation
Rockford, IL. 800-327-7908

Save-O-Seal Corporation
Elmsford, NY 800-831-9720
Servpak Corp
Hollywood, FL 800-782-0840
Stock America Inc
Grafton, WI 262-375-4100
Wraps
East Orange, NJ 973-673-7873
Zed Industries
Vandalia, OH. 937-667-8407

Jar Filling

A.K. Robins
Baltimore, MD 800-486-9656
Berkshire PPM
Litchfield, CT 860-567-3118
Custom Food Machinery
Stockton, CA. 209-463-4343
Dana Labels
Beaverton, OR 800-255-1492
Delta Plastics
Hot Springs, AR 501-760-3000
Elmar Worldwide
Depew, NY 800-433-3562
J.G. Machine Works
Holmdel, NJ 732-203-2077
Morrison Timing Screw Co
Glenwood, IL 708-331-6600
Multi-Fill Inc
West Jordan, UT 801-280-1570
Oden Machinery
Tonawanda, NY 800-658-3622
Packaging Enterprises
Rockledge, PA. 800-453-6213
SICK Inc
Bloomington, MN 800-325-7425
Simplex Filler Co
Napa, CA. 800-796-7539
Tindall Packaging
Vicksburg, MI 269-649-1163
Weigh Right Automatic Scale Co
Joliet, IL 800-571-0249

Label Printing

Advent Machine Co
Commerce, CA 800-846-7716
Apex Machine Company
Oakland Park, FL 954-566-1572
Auto Labe
Fort Pierce, FL 800-634-5376
Cam Tron Systems
Addison, IL 630-543-2884
Comstar Printing Solutions
Streetsboro, OH 330-528-2800
Dana Labels
Beaverton, OR 800-255-1492
Dorell Equipment Inc
Somerset, NJ 732-247-5400
Dynic USA Corp
Hillsboro, OR 800-326-1249
Fairbanks Scales
Overland Park, KS 800-451-4107
Fernqvist Labeling Solutions
Mountain View, CA 800-426-8215
Grand Valley Labels
Grand Rapids, MI
ID Images
Brunswick, OH 866-516-7300
Labelprint America
Newburyport, MA 978-463-4004
Lord Label Group
Charlotte, NC 800-341-5225
Mateer Burt
Exton, PA 800-345-1308
Matthews Marking Systems Div
Pittsburgh, PA 412-665-2500
MPI Label Systems
Sebring, OH 800-837-2134
Paper Converting Machine Company
Green Bay, WI. 920-494-5601
PEAK Technologies, Inc.
Columbia, MD 800-926-9212
Reliable Label
Downers Grove, IL 800-323-7265
Robbie Manufacturing Inc
Lenexa, KS 800-255-6328
Sohn Manufacturing
Elkhart Lake, WI. 920-876-3361
Start International
Addison, TX 800-259-1986

StickerYou
  Toronto, ON 416-532-7373
Tharo Systems Inc
  Brunswick, OH 800-878-6833
Virginia Artesian Bottling Company
  Mechanicsville, VA 804-779-7500
Wishbone Utensil Tableware Line
  Wheat Ridge, CO 866-266-5928
WS Packaging Group Inc
  Rochester, NY 800-836-8186
Wt Nickell Co
  Batavia, OH 888-899-1991

Labeling

A.D. Joslin Manufacturing Company
  Manistee, MI .231-723-2908
About Packaging Robotics
  Thornton, CO .303-449-2559
AC Label Company
  Provo, UT 801-642-3500
Accraply/Trine
  Burlington Ontario, ON 800-387-6742
Accu Place
  Plantation, FL 954-791-1500
Accutek Packaging Equipment
  Vista, CA 800-989-1828
ASCENT Technics Corporation
  Brick, NJ 800-774-7077
Associated Packaging Equipment Corporation
  Markham, ON 905-475-6647
Auto Labe
  Fort Pierce, FL 800-634-5376
Automated Packaging Systems
  Streetsboro, OH 800-527-0733
Bell & Howell Company
  Lincolnwood, IL 800-647-2290
Berkshire PPM
  Litchfield, CT .860-567-3118
C-P Flexible Packaging
  Newtown, PA .800-448-8183
Cam Tron Systems
  Addison, IL 630-543-2884
Cognitive
  Golden, CO 800-765-6600
Columbia Labeling Machinery
  Benton City, WA 888-791-9590
Convergent Label Technology
  Tampa, FL 800-252-6111
CRS Marking Systems
  Portland, OR .800-547-7158
Custom Food Machinery
  Stockton, CA .209-463-4343
CVP Systems Inc
  Downers Grove, IL 800-422-4720
D & L Manufacturing
  Milwaukee, WI 414-256-8160
Dalemark Industries
  Lakewood, NJ 732-367-3100
Daymark Safety Systems
  Bowling Green, OH 419-353-2458
Dispensa-Matic Label Dispense
  Rocky Mount, MO 800-325-7303
Dorell Equipment Inc
  Somerset, NJ .732-247-5400
Dow Industries
  Wilmington, MA 800-776-1201
ELF Machinery
  La Porte, IN. .800-328-0466
Elmark Packaging Inc
  West Chester, PA 800-670-9688
EMCO
  Miamisburg, OH 800-722-3626
EPI Labelers
  New Freedom, PA 800-755-8344
Esselte Meto
  Morris Plains, NJ 800-645-3290
Exact Equipment Corporation
  Morrisville, PA 215-295-2000
Fairbanks Scales
  Overland Park, KS 800-451-4107
Fast Industries
  Fort Lauderdale, FL 800-775-5345
Fernqvist Labeling Solutions
  Mountain View, CA 800-426-8215
Garvey Products
  West Chester, OH 800-543-1908
GCA
  Huntington Beach, CA 714-379-4911
GEI PPM
  Exton, PA 800-345-1308

Glen Mills Inc.
  Clifton, NJ. 973-777-0777
Gluemaster
  Kenosha, WI .262-857-7212
Gulf Arizona Packaging
  Humble, TX .800-364-3887
Gulf Systems
  Brownsville, TX 800-217-4853
Gulf Systems
  Humble, TX .800-364-3887
Gulf Systems
  Arlington, TX 817-261-1915
Heisler Machine & Tool Co
  Fairfield, NJ .973-227-6300
Herche Warehouse
  Denver, CO .303-371-8186
Horix Manufacturing Co
  Mc Kees Rocks, PA 412-771-1111
Houston Label
  Pasadena, TX 800-477-6995
Hurst Corp
  Wayne, PA 610-687-2404
Hurst Labeling Systems
  Chatsworth, CA 800-969-1705
Industrial Automation Systems
  Santa Clarita, CA 888-484-4427
Innovative Packaging Solution
  Martin, MI 616-656-2100
ITW Diagraph
  St Charles, MO 800-722-1125
KISS Packaging Systems
  Vista, CA 888-522-3538
Krones
  Franklin, WI .800-752-3787
Label Technology Inc
  Merced, CA .800-388-1990
Label-Aire Inc
  Fullerton, CA 714-441-0700
Labelette Company
  Forest Park, IL 708-366-2010
Labelprint America
  Newburyport, MA 978-463-4004
Livingston-Wilbor Corporation
  Edison, NJ 908-322-8403
Lord Label Group
  Charlotte, NC 800-341-5225
Lord Label Machine Systems
  Charlotte, NC 704-644-1650
Loveshaw Corp
  South Canaan, PA 800-572-3434
Marking Methods Inc
  Alhambra, CA 626-308-5800
Master Magnetics
  Castle Rock, CO 800-525-3536
Mateer Burt
  Exton, PA 800-345-1308
Matthews Marking Systems Div
  Pittsburgh, PA 412-665-2500
Miken Cosmpanies
  Buffalo, NY .716-668-6311
Modular Packaging
  Randolph, NJ 973-970-9393
MPI Label Systems
  Sebring, OH .800-837-2134
National Label Co
  Lafayette Hill, PA 610-825-3250
National Package SealingCompany
  Santa Ana, CA 714-630-1505
Nercon Engineering & Manufacturing
  Oshkosh, WI 920-233-3268
New Way Packaging Machinery
  Hanover, PA .800-522-3537
NJM/CLI
  Pointe Claire, QC 514-630-6990
Nordson Corp
  Duluth, GA .800-683-2314
OnTrack Automation Inc
  Waterloo, ON 519-886-9090
Package Systems Corporation
  Danielson, CT 800-522-3548
Packaging & Processing Equipment
  Ayr, ON 519-622-6666
Paragon Labeling
  St Paul, MN .800-429-7722
PDC International
  Austin, TX. .512-302-0194
PEAK Technologies, Inc.
  Columbia, MD 800-926-9212
Perl Packaging Systems
  Middlebury, CT. 800-864-2853
PMI Food Equipment Group
  Troy, OH 937-332-3000

Priority One Packaging
  Waterloo, ON 800-387-9102
Production Packaging & Processing Equipment
  Company
  Savannah, GA 912-856-4281
Qsx Labels
  Everett, MA. 800-225-3496
Quadrel Labeling Systems
  Mentor, OH .800-321-8509
Renard Machine Company
  Green Bay, WI. 920-432-8412
Roberts Poly Pro Inc
  Charlotte, NC 800-269-7409
Sasib Beverage & Food North America
  Plano, TX 800-558-3814
Schaefer Machine Co Inc
  Deep River, CT 800-243-5143
Seal-O-Matic Corp
  Jacksonville, OR 800-631-2072
Smyth Co LLC
  St Paul, MN. 800-473-3464
Tamarack Products Inc
  Wauconda, IL 847-526-9333
Tharo Systems Inc
  Brunswick, OH 800-878-6833
Universal Labeling Systems Inc
  St Petersburg, FL 877-236-0266
Vande Berg SCALES/Vbs Inc
  Sioux Center, IA 712-722-1181
Varitronic Systems
  Brooklyn Park, MN. 763-536-6400
Wallace Computer Services
  Chicago, IL .888-925-8324
WE Killam Enterprises
  Waterford, ON. 519-443-7421
Weber Packaging Solutions Inc
  Arlington Heights, IL 800-843-4242
WS Packaging Group Inc
  Rochester, NY 800-836-8186
Zebra Technologies Corporation
  Lincolnshire, IL 866-230-9494

Package Tying

B H Bunn Co
  Lakeland, FL 800-222-2866
Delta Cyklop Orga Pac
  Charlotte, NC 800-446-4347
Felins USA Inc
  Milwaukee, WI 800-343-5667
Gulf Arizona Packaging
  Humble, TX 800-364-3887
Gulf Systems
  Brownsville, TX 800-217-4853
Gulf Systems
  Humble, TX 800-364-3887
Gulf Systems
  Arlington, TX 817-261-1915
Herche Warehouse
  Denver, CO 303-371-8186
KWIK Lok Corp
  Yakima, WA 800-688-5945
Machine Electronics Company
  Brooklyn, NY 718-384-3211
Steinmetz Machine Works Inc
  Stamford, CT 203-327-0118

Packing

A.K. Robins
  Baltimore, MD 800-486-9656
Aaron Equipment Co Div Areco
  Bensenville, IL 630-350-2200
About Packaging Robotics
  Thornton, CO 303-449-2559
ADCO Manufacturing Inc
  Sanger, CA .559-875-5563
Amark Packaging Systems
  Kansas City, MO 816-965-9000
Architecture Plus Intl Inc
  Rocky Point, FL 813-281-9299
Arthur G Russell Co Inc
  Bristol, CT .860-583-4109
Automated Production Systems Corporation
  New Freedom, PA 888-345-5377
B H Bunn Co
  Lakeland, FL 800-222-2866
B T Engineering Inc
  Bala Cynwyd, PA 610-664-9500
BEI
  South Haven, MI. 800-364-7425

Belco Packaging Systems
Monrovia, CA 800-833-1833
Blue Print Automation
S Chesterfield, VA 804-520-5400
Bradman Lake Inc
Rock Hill, SC 803-366-3688
Branson Ultrasonics Corp
Danbury, CT 203-796-0400
Brechteen
Chesterfield, MI 586-949-2240
BW Container Systems
Romeoville, IL 630-759-6800
C.J. Machine
Fridley, MN 763-767-4630
Clamco Corporation
Berea, OH .216-267-1911
Cleveland Vibrator Co
Cleveland, OH 800-221-3298
Climax Packaging Machinery
Hamilton, OH 513-874-1664
Coastline Equipment Inc
Bellingham, WA 360-734-8509
Combi Packaging Systems LLC
Canton, OH 866-472-5236
Compacker Systems LLC
Davenport, IA 563-391-2751
Custom Food Machinery
Stockton, CA 209-463-4343
CVP Systems Inc
Downers Grove, IL 800-422-4720
Data Scale
Fremont, CA 800-651-7350
Design Technology Corporation
Billerica, MA 978-663-7000
Diversified Metal Engineering
Charlottetown, PE 902-628-6900
Dorell Equipment Inc
Somerset, NJ 732-247-5400
Douglas Machine Inc
Alexandria, MN 320-763-6587
Durable Packaging Corporation
Countryside, IL 800-700-5677
Durand-Wayland Inc
Lagrange, GA 800-241-2308
Eastern Machine
Middlebury, CT 203-598-0066
Edl Packaging Engineers
Green Bay, WI 920-336-7744
Edmeyer
Minneapolis, MN 651-450-1210
Edson Packaging Machinery
Hamilton, ON 800-493-3766
Elliott Manufacturing Co Inc
Fresno, CA 559-233-6235
Fillit
Kirkland, QC 514-694-2390
Fogg Filler Co
Holland, MI 616-786-3644
Fox Iv Technologies
Export, PA 877-436-2434
Gainco Inc
Gainesville, GA 800-467-2828
GEI Autowrappers
Exton, PA .610-321-1115
General Bag Corporation
Cleveland, OH 800-837-9396
General Processing Systems
Holland, MI 800-547-9370
Gram Equipment of America
Tampa, FL 813-248-1978
Grigg Box Company
Detroit, MI 313-273-9000
GTI
Arvada, CO 303-420-6699
Halton Packaging Systems
Oakville, ON 905-847-9141
Hamrick Manufacturing & Svc
Mogadore, OH 800-321-9590
Harpak-ULMA Packaging LLC
Taunton, MA 508-238-8884
Hart Design & Mfg
Green Bay, WI 920-468-5927
Hartness International
Greenville, SC 800-845-8791
Herrmann Ultrasonics
Bartlett, IL 630-626-1626
Hoegger Food Technology
Minneapolis, MN 877-789-5400
Hudson Control Group Inc
Springfield, NJ 973-376-8265
ID Images
Brunswick, OH 866-516-7300

Ideal of America
Charlotte, NC 704-523-1604
Ilapak Inc
Newtown, PA 215-579-2900
Iman Pack
Westland, MI 800-810-4626
Industrial Magnetics
Boyne City, MI 800-662-4638
International Omni-Pac Corporation
La Verne, CA 909-593-2833
Jagenberg
Enfield, CT 860-741-2501
Jeb Plastics
Wilmington, DE 800-556-2247
Jetstream Systems
Wichita, KN 855-861-6916
Kisters Kayat
Sarasota, FL 386-424-0101
Kohler Industries Inc
Lincoln, NE 800-365-6708
Krones
Franklin, WI 800-752-3787
L&H Wood Manufacturing Company
Farmington, MI 248-474-9000
Lako Tool & Mfg Inc
Perrysburg, OH 800-228-2982
Langen Packaging
Mississauga, ON 905-670-7200
Longford Equipment US
Glastonbury, CT 416-298-6622
Machine Builders & Design Inc
Shelby, NC 704-482-3456
Malo Inc
Tulsa, OK .918-583-2743
Maren Engineering Corp
South Holland, IL 800-875-1038
Marq Packaging Systems Inc
Yakima, WA 800-998-4301
Mateer Burt
Exton, PA .800-345-1308
Matthiesen Equipment
San Antonio, TX 800-624-8635
Melco Steel Inc
Azusa, CA .626-334-7875
Molins/Sandiacre Richmond
Richmond, VA 864-486-4000
Newcastle Co Inc
New Castle, PA 724-658-4516
Nigrelli Systems Purchasing
Kiel, WI 800-693-3144
Nu-Con Equipment
Chanhassen, MN 877-939-0510
Olney Machinery
Westernville, NY 315-827-4208
Pacemaker Packaging Corp
Woodside, NY 718-458-1188
Package Systems Corporation
Danielson, CT 800-522-3548
Peco Controls Corporation
Modesto, CA 800-732-6285
Per-Fil Industries Inc
Riverside, NJ 856-461-5700
Pneumatic Scale Angelus
Cuyahoga Falls, OH 330-923-0491
Pressure Pack
Williamsburg, VA 757-220-3693
Priority One America
Oshkosh, WI 920-235-5562
Professional Marketing Group
Seattle, WA 800-227-3769
Promarks
Ontario, CA 909-923-3888
Prototype Equipment Corporation
Libertyville, IL 847-680-4433
PTI Packaging
Portage, WI 800-501-4077
RAM Center
Red Wing, MN 800-309-5431
Reiser
Canton, MA 734-821-1290
Remcon Plastics Inc
Reading, PA 800-360-3636
Rennco LLC
Homer, MI 800-409-5225
Riverwood International
Atlanta, GA 770-984-5477
Rockford-Midland Corporation
Rockford, IL 800-327-7908
Ropak Manufacturing Co Inc
Decatur, AL 256-350-4241
Rose Forgrove
Saint Charles, IL 630-443-1317

Sabel Engineering Corporation
Villard, MN 320-554-3611
Schroeder Machine
San Marcos, CA 760-591-9733
Semco Manufacturing Company
Pharr, TX .956-787-4203
Serpa Packaging Solutions
Visalia, CA 800-348-5453
Southern Automatics
Lakeland, FL 800-441-4604
Standard-Knapp Inc
Portland, CT 800-628-9565
T D Sawvel Co
Maple Plain, MN 877-488-1816
TDF Automation
Cedar Falls, IA 800-553-1777
Thiele Engineering Company
Fergus Falls, MN 218-739-3321
Thiele Technologies-Reedley
Reedley, CA 800-344-8951
Trio Packaging Corp
Ronkonkoma, NY 800-331-0492
Universal Packaging Inc
Houston, TX 800-324-2610
W.G. Durant Corporation
Whittier, CA 562-946-5555
Wayne Automation Corp
Eagleville, PA 610-630-8900
WE Killam Enterprises
Waterford, ON 519-443-7421
WeighPack Systems/Paxiom Group
Montreal, QC 888-934-4472
Wick's Packaging Service
Cutler, IN .574-967-3104
Wrapade Packaging Systems
Fairfield, NJ 888-815-8564
Zepf Technologies
Clearwater, FL 727-535-4100

Portion Control Equipment

AC Dispensing Equipment
Lower Sackville, NS 888-777-9990
Acme Scale Co
San Leandro, CA 888-638-5040
AEW Thurne
Lake Zurich, IL 800-239-7297
AM-Mac
Fairfield, NJ 800-829-2018
Avery Weigh-Tronix LLC
Fairmont, MN 800-368-2039
Beer Magic Devices
Hamilton, ON 905-522-3081
BVL Controls
Bois-Des-Filion, QC 866-285-2668
CCi Scale Company
Clovis, CA 800-900-0224
Crestware
North Salt Lake, UT 800-345-0513
Daleco
West Chester, PA 610-429-0181
Design Technology Corporation
Billerica, MA 978-663-7000
Detecto Scale Co
Webb City, MO 800-641-2008
Diversified Metal Engineering
Charlottetown, PE 902-628-6900
Doering Machines Inc
San Francisco, CA 415-526-2131
Edlund Co
Burlington, VT 800-772-2126
Genpak
Peterborough, ON 800-461-1995
Hoegger Food Technology
Minneapolis, MN 877-789-5400
Hollymatic Corp
Countryside, IL 708-579-3700
Industrial Laboratory Eqpt Co
Charlotte, NC 704-357-3930
Label Makers
Pleasant Prairie, WI 800-208-3331
Liberty Ware LLC
Clearfield, UT 888-500-5885
Little Squirt
Toronto, ON 416-665-6605
Magnuson Industries
Rockford, IL 800-435-2816
Opal Manufacturing Ltd
Toronto, ON 416-646-5232
Packaging Progressions
Collegeville, PA 610-489-9096

Patty O Matic Machinery
Farmingdale, NJ 877-938-5244
Pelouze Scale Company
Bridgeview, IL 800-323-8363
Pino's Pasta Veloce
Staten Island, NY 718-273-6660
Plastic Fantastics/Buck Signs
Ashland, OR 800-482-1776
Proluxe
Paramount, CA 800-594-5528
Quantum Topping Systems Quantum Technical Services Inc
Frankfort, IL 888-464-1540
Reiser
Canton, MA 734-821-1290
Superior Products Company
Saint Paul, MN 800-328-9800
Traex
Dane, WI 800-356-8006
TWM Manufacturing
Leamington, ON 888-495-4831
Unifiller Systems
Delta, BC 888-733-8444
Weiler & Company
Whitewater, WI 800-558-9507
Zeroll Company
Fort Pierce, FL 800-872-5000

Printing

ABM Marking
Belleville, IL 800-626-9012
Accurate Paper Box Co Inc
Knoxville, TN 865-690-0311
Advanced Poly-Packaging Inc
Akron, OH 800-754-4403
Algene Marking Equipment Company
Garfield, NJ 973-478-9041
Apex Machine Company
Oakland Park, FL 954-566-1572
Axiohm USA
Myrtle Beach, SC 843-443-3155
Bell-Mark Corporation
Pine Brook, NJ 973-882-0202
Bren Instruments
Franklin, TN 615-794-6825
Carl Strutz & Company
Mars, PA 724-625-1501
Cognitive
Golden, CO 800-765-6600
Columbia Labeling Machinery
Benton City, WA 888-791-9590
Computype Inc
St Paul, MN 800-328-0852
Comstar Printing Solutions
Streetsboro, OH 330-528-2800
D & L Manufacturing
Milwaukee, WI 414-256-8160
Dana Labels
Beaverton, OR 800-255-1492
Dependable Machine, Inc.
d'Alene, ID 866-967-0146
Desco Equipment Corporation
Twinsburg, OH 330-405-1581
Domino Amjet Inc
Gurnee, IL 800-444-4512
Donnick Label Systems
Jacksonville, FL 800-334-7849
Dorell Equipment Inc
Somerset, NJ 732-247-5400
Durable Engravers
Franklin Park, IL 800-869-9565
EMCO
Miamisburg, OH 800-722-3626
Esselte Meto
Morris Plains, NJ 800-645-3290
Exact Equipment Corporation
Morrisville, PA 215-295-2000
Fernqvist Labeling Solutions
Mountain View, CA 800-426-8215
GCA
Huntington Beach, CA 714-379-4911
GM Nameplate
Seattle, WA 800-366-7668
GTCO CalComp
Scottsdale, AZ 800-856-0732
H G Weber & Co
Kiel, WI 920-894-2221
Howard Imprinting Machine Company
Houston, TX 800-334-6943
ID Images
Brunswick, OH 866-516-7300

Imaging Technologies
Cookeville, TN 800-488-2804
Kammann Machine
Portsmouth, NH 978-463-0050
KASE Equipment
Cleveland, OH 216-642-9040
Kurz Transfer Products LP
Huntersville, NC 800-950-3645
Kwikprint Manufacturing Inc
Jacksonville, FL 800-940-5945
Label Systems & Solutions
Bohemia, NY 800-811-2560
Labelmart
Maple Grove, MN 888-577-0141
Loveshaw Corp
South Canaan, PA 800-572-3434
Marsh Company
Belleville, IL 800-527-6275
Mettler-Toledo, LLC
Columbus, OH 800-638-8537
MPI Label Systems
Sebring, OH 800-837-2134
Norwood Marking Systems
Downers Grove, IL 800-626-3464
Packaging Machinery & Equipment
West Orange, NJ 973-325-2418
Paper Converting Machine Company
Green Bay, WI 920-494-5601
Paper Converting MachineCompany
Green Bay, WI 920-494-5601
Paragon Labeling
St Paul, MN 800-429-7722
Reflex International
Norcross, GA 800-642-7640
Service Stamp Works
Chicago, IL 312-666-8839
Sohn Manufacturing
Elkhart Lake, WI 920-876-3361
Star Micronics
Edison, NJ 800-782-7636
Stratix Corp
Peachtree Cor, GA 800-883-8300
Tallygenicom
Irvine, CA 800-665-6210
Tamarack Products Inc
Wauconda, IL 847-526-9333
Tharo Systems Inc
Brunswick, OH 800-878-6833
Trident
Brookfield, CT 203-740-9333
Varitronic Systems
Brooklyn Park, MN 763-536-6400
Videojet Technologies Inc
Wood Dale, IL 800-843-3610
Wallace Computer Services
Chicago, IL 888-925-8324
Wichita Stamp & Seal Inc
Wichita, KS 316-263-4223
Wt Nickell Co
Batavia, OH 888-899-1991
Yamato Corporation
Colorado Springs, CO 800-538-1762
Zebra Technologies Corporation
Lincolnshire, IL 866-230-9494
Zerand Corp
New Berlin, WI 262-827-3800

Plastics

Carl Strutz & Company
Mars, PA 724-625-1501
Desco Equipment Corporation
Twinsburg, OH 330-405-1581
Trident
Brookfield, CT 203-740-9333
Uniloy Milacron
Tecumseh, MI 517-424-8900
WE Killam Enterprises
Waterford, ON 519-443-7421

Rebuilt & Used

A&M Industries
Sioux Falls, SD 800-888-2615
American Equipment Co
Aberdeen, MD 410-272-2626
Ameripak Packaging Equipment
Warrington, PA 215-343-1530
Automated Packaging Systems
Streetsboro, OH 800-527-0733
Berkshire PPM
Litchfield, CT 860-567-3118

Cartpac Inc
Carol Stream, IL 630-510-1100
Champion Trading Corporation
Marlboro, NJ 732-780-4200
Change Parts Inc
Ludington, MI 231-845-5107
Circle Packaging Machinery Inc
De Pere, WI 920-983-3420
Colter & Peterson
Paterson, NJ 973-684-0901
Custom Food Machinery
Stockton, CA 209-463-4343
Eischen Enterprises
Fresno, CA 559-834-0013
Equipment Specialists Inc
Manassas, VA 703-361-2227
Gulf Systems
Humble, TX 800-364-3887
Gulf Systems
Arlington, TX 817-261-1915
Hallmark Equipment Inc
Morgan Hill, CA 408-782-2600
Health Star
Randolph, MA 800-545-3639
Ilapak Inc
Newtown, PA 215-579-2900
Lehman Sales Associates
Sun Prairie, WI 608-575-7712
Madison County Wood Products
Fredericktown, MO 314-584-1802
McNeil Food Machinery
Stockton, CA 209-463-4343
Miller Technical Svc
Plymouth, MI 734-414-1769
National Equipment Corporation
Bronx, NY 800-237-8873
Package Machinery Co Inc
Holyoke, MA 413-315-3801
Packaging & Processing Equipment
Ayr, ON 519-622-6666
Packaging Machinery & Equipment
West Orange, NJ 973-325-2418
Palace Packaging Machines Inc
Downingtown, PA 610-873-7252
Plasti-Mach Corporation
Valley Cottage, NY 800-394-1128
Production Packaging & Processing Equipment Company
Savannah, GA 912-856-4281
Professional Marketing Group
Seattle, WA 800-227-3769
QMS International, Inc.
Mississauga, Ontario, ON 905-820-7225
Schroeder Machine
San Marcos, CA 760-591-9733
Warwick Manufacturing & Equip
North Brunswick, NJ 732-729-0400
Wick's Packaging Service
Cutler, IN 574-967-3104

Retort Pouch Processing

AmeriQual Foods
Evansville, IN 812-867-1444
SOPAKCO Foods
Mullins, SC 800-276-9678
Stock America Inc
Grafton, WI 262-375-4100
Sungjae Corporation
Irvine, CA 949-757-1727

Sealers

Heat

AAMD
Liverpool, NY 800-887-4167
Audion Automation
Carrollton, TX 972-389-0777
Branson Ultrasonics Corp
Danbury, CT 203-796-0400
Carson Manufacturing Company
Petaluma, CA 800-423-2380
Chaffee Corp
Rocklin, CA 916-630-3980
Chase Industries Inc
West Chester, OH 800-543-4455
Durable Packaging Corporation
Countryside, IL 800-700-5677
Giltron Inc
Norwood, MA 781-762-4310

Gulf Arizona Packaging
Humble, TX 800-364-3887
Herche Warehouse
Denver, CO 303-371-8186
ITW United Silicone
Lancaster, NY 716-681-8222
Jeb Plastics
Wilmington, DE 800-556-2247
Korab Engineering Company
Los Angeles, CA 310-670-7710
Lako Tool & Mfg Inc
Perrysburg, OH 800-228-2982
Matthiesen Equipment
San Antonio, TX 800-624-8635
Moen Industries
Santa Fe Springs, CA 800-732-7766
Nordson Corp
Duluth, GA 800-683-2314
Osgood Industries
Oldsmar, FL 813-855-7337
Pack Rite Machine Mettler
Mt Pleasant, WI 800-248-6868
Packaging & Processing Equipment
Ayr, ON 519-622-6666
Packaging Aids Corporation
San Rafael, CA 415-454-4868
Packworld USA
Nazareth, PA 610-746-2765
Plasti-Mach Corporation
Valley Cottage, NY 800-394-1128
PlexPack Corp
Toronto, ON 855-635-9238
Pressure Pack
Williamsburg, VA 757-220-3693
Reiser
Canton, MA 734-821-1290
Rockford-Midland Corporation
Rockford, IL 800-327-7908
Seal-O-Matic Corp
Jacksonville, OR 800-631-2072
Servpak Corp
Hollywood, FL 800-782-0840
Wraps
East Orange, NJ 973-673-7873
Zed Industries
Vandalia, OH 937-667-8407

Tray

K & L Intl
Ontario, CA 888-598-5588
Reiser
Canton, MA 734-821-1290

Shrinkers: Plastic Packaging

Adex Medical Inc
Riverside, CA 800-873-4776
AEP Industries Inc
Mankato, MN 800-999-2374
Alfa Systems Inc
Westfield, NJ 908-654-0255
Aline Heat Seal Corporation
Los Angeles, CA 888-285-3917
Architecture Plus Intl Inc
Rocky Point, FL 813-281-9299
Arkansas Poly
N Little Rock, AR 800-342-7659
Audion Automation
Carrollton, TX 972-389-0777
Bollore Inc
Dayville, CT 860-774-2930
Brenton Engineering Co
Alexandria, MN 800-535-2730
Chase Industries Inc
West Chester, OH 800-543-4455
CiMa-Pak Corp.
Dorval, QC 877-631-2462
Clamco Corporation
Berea, OH 216-267-1911
Conflex, Inc.
Germantown, WI. 800-225-4296
Douglas Machine Inc
Alexandria, MN 320-763-6587
Ideal of America
Charlotte, NC 704-523-1604
Ideal of America/Valley Rio Enterprise
Atlanta, GA. 770-352-0210
Iman Pack
Westland, MI. 800-810-4626
L&H Wood Manufacturing Company
Farmington, MI. 248-474-9000

M & Q Packaging Corp
North Wales, PA 267-498-4000
M S Plastics & Packaging Inc
Butler, NJ .800-593-1802
Packaging Machinery International
Elk Grove Village, IL 800-871-4764
Phase Fire Systems
Vista, CA. .888-741-2341
Polypack Inc
Pinellas Park, FL 727-578-5000
Reiser
Canton, MA 734-821-1290
Rennco LLC
Homer, MI 800-409-5225
Robbie Manufacturing Inc
Lenexa, KS 800-255-6328
Triune Enterprises
Gardena, CA 310-719-1600
V C 999 Packaging Systems
Kansas City, MO 800-728-2999
Vector Packaging
Oak Brook, IL 800-435-9100
Zepf Technologies
Clearwater, FL 727-535-4100

Sorters

Bottle

California Vibratory Feeders
Anaheim, CA 800-354-0972
Heuft USA Inc
Downers Grove, IL 630-968-9011
Kinsley Inc
Doylestown, PA 800-414-6664
Packaging & Processing Equipment
Ayr, ON 519-622-6666
Palace Packaging Machines Inc
Downingtown, PA. 610-873-7252

Tables

Packing House

A.K. Robins
Baltimore, MD 800-486-9656
Atlas Equipment Company
Kansas City, MO. 800-842-9188
Belco Packaging Systems
Monrovia, CA 800-833-1833
Brothers Metal Products
Santa Ana, CA 714-972-3008
Cleveland Vibrator Co
Cleveland, OH 800-221-3298
Columbus McKinnon Corporation
Getzville, NY 800-888-0985
Cozzini Inc
Algona, IA 888-295-1116
Dc Tech
Kansas City, MO. 877-742-9090
Key Material Handling Inc
Simi Valley, CA. 800-539-7225
MeGa Industries
Burlington, ON 800-665-6342
MSSH
Greensburg, IN 812-663-2180
Packaging & Processing Equipment
Ayr, ON 519-622-6666
Sperling Industries
Omaha, NE 800-647-5062

Vacuum Packing

Cretel Food Equipment
Holland, MI. 616-786-3980
Elmo Rietschle - A Gardner Denver Product
Quincy, IL. 217-222-5400
Market Sales Company
Newton, MA 617-232-0239
Promarks
Ontario, CA. 909-923-3888
Reiser
Canton, MA 734-821-1290
RMF Companies
Grandview, MO. 816-839-9258
Rollstock Inc
Kansas City, MO. 800-954-6020

Weighing

A&D Weighing
San Jose, CA. 800-726-3364

Abel Manufacturing Co
Appleton, WI 920-734-4443
Accu-Pak
Akron, OH
Acme Scale Co
San Leandro, CA. 888-638-5040
Action Packaging Automation
Roosevelt, NJ 800-241-2724
Actionpac Scales Automation
Oxnard, CA 800-394-0154
Ag-Pak
Gasport, NY 716-772-2651
All Fill Inc
Exton, PA .866-255-4455
Amark Packaging Systems
Kansas City, MO. 816-965-9000
American Bag & Burlap Company
Chelsea, MA 617-884-7600
Ameriglobe LLC
Lafayette, LA 337-234-3211
Andgar Corp
Ferndale, WA 360-366-9900
AP Dataweigh Inc
Cumming, GA 877-409-2562
APEC
Lake Odessa, MI. 616-374-1000
Arkfeld Mfg & Distributing Co
Norfolk, NE. 800-533-0676
Avery Weigh-Tronix
Fairmont, MN 877-368-2039
Bell & Howell Company
Lincolnwood, IL 800-647-2290
BLH Electronics
Canton, MA 781-821-2000
Blodgett Co
Houston, TX 281-933-6195
Cardinal Scale Mfg Co
Webb City, MO 800-441-4237
Care Controls, Inc.
Mill Creek, WA. 800-593-6050
CCi Scale Company
Clovis, CA 800-900-0224
Chemi-Graphic Inc
Ludlow, MA 413-589-0151
Chlorinators Inc
Stuart, FL .800-327-9761
Cintex of America
Carol Stream, IL 800-424-6839
Convergent Label Technology
Tampa, FL. 800-252-6111
Crestware
North Salt Lake, UT 800-345-0513
Crystal-Vision Packaging Systems
Torrance, CA. 800-331-3240
Delta Engineering Corporation
Walpole, MA. 781-729-8650
Detecto Scale Co
Webb City, MO 800-641-2008
Doran Scales Inc
Batavia, IL. 800-365-0084
Edlund Co
Burlington, VT 800-772-2126
Emery Winslow Scale Co
Seymour, CT 203-881-9333
Equipment Outlet
Meridian, ID 208-887-1472
Exact Equipment Corporation
Morrisville, PA 215-295-2000
Fairbanks Scales
Overland Park, KS 800-451-4107
Fawema Packaging Machinery
Palmetto, FL 941-351-9597
Fuller Weighing Systems
Columbus, OH 614-882-8121
Gainco Inc
Gainesville, GA 800-467-2828
General Packaging Equipment Co
Houston, TX 713-686-4331
Grain Machinery Mfg Corp
Miami, FL .305-620-2525
Hardy Systems Corporation
Northbrook, IL 800-927-3956
Howes S Co Inc
Silver Creek, NY. 888-255-2611
Hyer Industries
Pembroke, MA 781-826-8101
IEW
Niles, OH .330-652-0113
Ilapak Inc
Newtown, PA 215-579-2900
Iman Pack
Westland, MI. 800-810-4626

Industrial Laboratory Eqpt Co
Charlotte, NC 704-357-3930
Inspired Automation Inc
Agoura Hills, CA 818-991-4598
IWS Scales
San Diego, CA 800-881-9755
Key Material Handling Inc
Simi Valley, CA. 800-539-7225
Kliklok-Woodman
Decatur, GA 770-981-5200
Lock Inspection Systems
Fitchburg, MA 800-227-5539
Lockwood Packaging
Woburn, MA. 800-641-3100
Loma International
Carol Stream, IL 800-872-5662
Mandeville Company
Minneapolis, MN 800-328-8490
MERRICK Industries Inc
Lynn Haven, FL 800-271-7834
Mettler-Toledo, LLC
Columbus, OH 800-638-8537
Micro-Strain
Spring City, PA 610-948-4550
Mortec Industries Inc
Brush, CO 800-541-9983
National Scoop & Equipment Company
Spring House, PA 215-646-2040
Newton OA & Son Co
Bridgeville, DE 800-726-5745
Ocs Checkweighers, Inc.
Snellville, GA 678-344-8030
Ohaus Corp
Parsippany, NJ. 800-672-7722
Ohlson Packaging
Taunton, MA 508-977-0004
Pacific Scale Company
Clackamas, OR 800-537-1886
Peco Controls Corporation
Modesto, CA. 800-732-6285
Pelouze Scale Company
Bridgeview, IL 800-323-8363
PMI Food Equipment Group
Troy, OH 937-332-3000
Pomona Service & Pkgng Co LA
Yakima, WA 509-452-7121
Quest Corp
North Royalton, OH 440-230-9400
Renard Machine Company
Green Bay, WI. 920-432-8412
Rice Lake Weighing Systems
Rice Lake, WI 800-472-6703
Sartorius Corp
Edgewood, NY 800-635-2906
Schaffer Poidometer Company
Pittsburgh, PA 412-281-9031
Scientech, Inc
Boulder, CO 800-525-0522
Si-Lodec
Tukwila, WA 800-255-8274
Sig Pack
Oakland, CA 800-824-3245
Sterling Scale Co
Southfield, MI. 800-331-9931
Sterling Systems & Controls
Sterling, IL 800-257-7214
Taylor Precision Products
Oak Brook, IL. 866-843-3905
Taylor Products Co
Parsons, KS 888-882-9567
Tecweigh
St Paul, MN. 800-536-4880
Temco
Oakland, CA 707-746-5966
Tomac Packaging
Woburn, MA. 800-641-3100
Toroid Corp
Huntsville, AL 256-837-7510
Triangle Package Machinery Co
Chicago, IL 800-621-4170
Tridyne Process Systems
South Burlington, VT 802-863-6873
Triner Scale & Mfg Co
Olive Branch, MS 800-238-0152
Vande Berg SCALES/Vbs Inc
Sioux Center, IA 712-722-1181
Venture Measurement Co LLC
Spartanburg, SC 800-426-9010
VitaMinder Company
Providence, RI 800-858-8840
Water Sciences Services, Inc.
Jackson, TN 973-584-4131

Weigh Right Automatic Scale Co
Joliet, IL 800-571-0249
WeighPack Systems/Paxiom Group
Montreal, QC 888-934-4472
Yakima Wire Works
Reedley, CA 800-344-8951
Yargus Manufacturing Inc
Marshall, IL 217-826-8059

Wire Stitching

New Jersey Wire Stitching Machine Company
Cherry Hill, NJ 856-428-2572

Wrapping

Air Technical Industries
Mentor, OH. 888-857-6265
Aline Heat Seal Corporation
Los Angeles, CA. 888-285-3917
Allpac
Dallas, TX. 214-630-8804
Ampak
Cleveland, OH 800-342-6329
APS Packaging Systems
San Jose, CA. 800-526-2276
Architecture Plus Intl Inc
Rocky Point, FL 813-281-9299
Audion Automation
Carrollton, TX. 972-389-0777
Automatic Electronic Machines Company
Brooklyn, NY 718-384-3211
B W Cooney & Associates
Bolton, Ontario, ON 905-857-7880
Berkshire PPM
Litchfield, CT 860-567-3118
Berlin Foundry & Mach Co
Berlin, NH. 603-752-4550
Brenton Engineering Co
Alexandria, MN 800-535-2730
C & K Machine Co
Holyoke, MA 413-536-8122
Campbell Wrapper Corporation
De Pere, WI. 920-983-7100
Charles Beseler Company
Stroudsburg, PA 800-237-3537
Chase Industries Inc
West Chester, OH 800-543-4455
Circle Packaging Machinery Inc
De Pere, WI. 920-983-3420
Conflex, Inc.
Germantown, WI. 800-225-4296
Crystal-Vision Packaging Systems
Torrance, CA. 800-331-3240
Delkor Systems, Inc
Minneapolis, MN 800-328-5558
Design Technology Corporation
Billerica, MA 978-663-7000
Doering Machines Inc
San Francisco, CA 415-526-2131
Dorell Equipment Inc
Somerset, NJ 732-247-5400
Edl Packaging Engineers
Green Bay, WI. 920-336-7744
Exact Equipment Corporation
Morrisville, PA 215-295-2000
Felins USA Inc
Milwaukee, WI 800-343-5667
Formost Packaging Machines
Woodinville, WA. 425-483-9090
Ganz Brothers
Paramus, NJ 201-845-6010
GEI Autowrappers
Exton, PA. 610-321-1115
Goodwrappers Inc
Halethorpe, MD 800-638-1127
Halton Packaging Systems
Oakville, ON. 905-847-9141
Hart Design & Mfg
Green Bay, WI. 920-468-5927
Hayssen Flexible Systems
Duncan, SC 864-486-4000
Highlight Industries
Wyoming, MI 800-531-2465
Ideal of America
Charlotte, NC 704-523-1604
Ideal of America/Valley Rio Enterprise
Atlanta, GA. 770-352-0210
Ideal Wrapping Machine Company
Middletown, NY 845-343-7700
Ilapak Inc
Newtown, PA 215-579-2900

Illinois Tool Works
Glenview, IL 224-661-8870
International Packaging Machinery
Naples, FL. 800-237-6496
Kisters Kayat
Sarasota, FL 386-424-0101
Machine Electronics Company
Brooklyn, NY 718-384-3211
Mark Products Company
Denville, NJ 973-983-8818
Maryland Packaging Corporation
Elkridge, MD 410-540-9700
Nitech
Columbus, NE. 800-237-6496
Orion Packaging Systems Inc
Alexandria, MN 800-333-6556
Ossid Corp
Battleboro, NC 800-334-8369
Pack Line Corporation
Racine, WI 800-248-6868
Packaging & Processing Equipment
Ayr, ON 519-622-6666
Packaging Dynamics
Walnut Creek, CA 925-938-2711
Peerless Food Equipment
Sidney, OH 937-492-4158
Pfankuch Machinery Corporation
Apple Valley, MN 952-891-3311
PMI Food Equipment Group
Troy, OH 937-332-3000
Polypack Inc
Pinellas Park, FL 727-578-5000
Renard Machine Company
Green Bay, WI. 920-432-8412
Rose Forgrove
Saint Charles, IL 630-443-1317
Sanford Redmond Company
Stamford, CT. 203-351-9800
Scan Coin
Ashburn, VA 800-336-3311
Scandia Packaging Machinery Co
Fairfield, NJ 973-473-6100
Seal-O-Matic Corp
Jacksonville, OR 800-631-2072
Shrinkfast Marketing
Newport, NH. 800-867-4746
Sitma USA
Spilamberto, MO 800-728-1254
Telesonic Packaging
Wilmington, DE 302-658-6945

Pails

Acra Electric Corporation
Tulsa, OK 800-223-4328
All American Container
Miami, FL 305-887-0797
Container Supply Co
Garden Grove, CA 562-594-0937
Greenfield Packaging
White Plains, NY 914-993-0233
Hedwin Division
Baltimore, MD 800-638-1012
Indianapolis Container Company
Indianapolis, IN 800-760-3318
IPL Inc
Saint-Damien, QC. 800-463-4755
Landis Plastics
Alsip, IL 708-396-1470
Louisville Container Company
Indianapolis, IN 888-539-7225
National Scoop & Equipment Company
Spring House, PA 215-646-2040
Poly One Corp
Avon Lake, OH. 866-765-9663
Prolon
Port Gibson, MS 888-480-9828
Reliance Product
Winnipeg, MB. 800-665-0258

Parts

A C Tool & Machine Co
Louisville, KY 502-447-5505
ABB
Cary, NC 800-435-7365
Accuflex Industrial Hose LTD
Romulus, MI 734-713-4100
Acromag Inc.
Wixom, MI 248-624-1541
Action Technology
Prussia, PA 217-935-8311

Advance Fittings Corp
Elkhorn, WI............262-723-6699
Advanced Control Technologies
Indianapolis, IN........800-886-2281
AFT Advanced Fiber Technologies
Sherbrooke, QC.........800-668-7273
AGC
Bristow, VA............800-825-8820
Air Quality Engineering
Minneapolis, MN........800-328-0787
Alkota Cleaning Systems Inc
Alcester, SD...........800-255-6823
All Packaging Machinery Corp
Ronkonkoma, NY.........800-637-8808
AllPoints Foodservice
Mt. Prospect, IL
American Extrusion Intl
South Beloit, IL.......815-624-6616
American Radionic Co Inc
Palm Coast, FL.........800-445-6033
Ampco Pumps Co Inc
Milwaukee, WI..........800-737-8671
Andantex USA Inc
Ocean, NJ.............800-713-6170
ANVER Corporation
Hudson, MA............800-654-3500
Apex Packing & Rubber Co
Farmingdale, NY........800-645-9110
APV Americas
Delavan, WI...........800-252-5200
Arc Machines Inc
Pacoima, CA...........818-896-9556
Architecture Plus Intl Inc
Rocky Point, FL........813-281-9299
Arctic Seal & Gasket
Palm City, FL..........800-881-4663
Armstrong Hot Water
Three Rivers, MI.......269-279-3602
Arthur Products Co
Medina, OH............800-322-0510
Artisan Controls Corp
Randolph, NJ..........800-457-4950
Automatic Specialties Inc
Marlborough, MA........800-445-2370
Bal Seal Engineering Inc
Foothill Ranch, CA.....800-366-1006
Baldewein Company
Lake Forrest, IL.......800-424-5544
Banner Equipment Co
Morris, IL............800-621-4625
Bardo Abrasives
Ridgewood, NY..........718-456-6400
Basiloid Products Corp
Elnora, IN............866-692-5511
Bayside Motion Group
Port Washington, NY....800-305-4555
Beacon Specialties
New York, NY...........800-221-9405
Beam Industries
Webster City, IA.......800-369-2326
Becker Brothers Graphite Co
Maywood, IL...........708-410-0700
Benchmark Thermal
Grass Valley, CA.......800-748-6189
Bert Manufacturing
Gardnerville, NV.......775-265-3900
Bettendorf Stanford Inc
Salem, IL.............800-548-2253
BFM Equipment Sales
Fall River, WI.........920-484-3341
Bodine Electric Co
Northfield, IL.........773-478-3515
Bohn & Dawson
St Louis, MO..........800-225-5011
Bolzoni Auramo
Homewood, IL..........800-358-5438
Boston Gear
Boston, MA............888-999-9860
Bradford A Ducon Company
Pewaukee, WI..........800-789-1718
C & D Valve Mfg Co
Oklahoma City, OK......800-654-9233
Cal Controls
Gurnee, IL............800-866-6659
Caldwell Group
Rockford, IL..........800-628-4263
Caloritech
Greensburg, IN.........800-473-2403
Carmun International
San Antonio, TX........800-531-7907
Carter Products
Grand Rapids, MI.......888-622-7837

Cashco Inc
Ellsworth, KS..........785-472-4461
Cat Pumps
Minneapolis, MN........763-780-5440
Change Parts Inc
Ludington, MI..........231-845-5107
Chicago Stainless Eqpt Inc
Palm City, FL..........800-927-8575
Chipmaker Tooling Supply
Whittier, CA..........800-659-5840
Chromalox Inc
Pittsburgh, PA.........800-443-2640
Clark-Cooper Division   Magnatrol Valve Corporation
Cinnaminson, NJ........856-829-4580
Clean Water Systems
Klamath Falls, OR......866-273-9993
Consolidated Commercial Controls
Winsted, CT...........800-227-1511
Continental Disc Corp
Liberty, MO...........816-792-1500
Conveyor Accessories
Burr Ridge, IL.........800-323-7093
Conxall Corporation
Villa Park, IL.........630-834-7504
Cornell Pump Company
Portland, OR..........503-653-0330
Cramer Company
South Windsor, CT......877-684-6464
Crown Battery Mfg
Fremont, OH...........800-487-2879
CSS International Corp
Philadelphia, PA.......800-278-8107
Delavan Spray Technologies
Charlotte, NC..........704-423-7000
Doering Co
Clear Lake, MN.........320-743-2276
Dormont Manufacturing Co
Export, PA............800-367-6668
Dyna-Veyor Inc
Newark, NJ............800-326-5009
Electro Cam Corp
Roscoe, IL............800-228-5487
Elite Forming Design Solutions
Rome, GA..............706-232-3021
Ellett Industries
Port Coquitlam, BC.....604-941-8211
Ernst Timing Screw Co
Bensalem, PA..........215-639-1438
Esco Products Inc
Houston, TX...........800-966-5514
Fabreeka International
Boise, ID.............800-423-4469
Falcon Fabricators Inc
Nashville, TN.........615-832-0027
Faribault Manufacturing Co
Faribault, MN.........800-447-6043
Federal Machine Corp
Clive, IA.............800-247-2446
FEI Inc
Mansfield, TX.........800-346-5908
Fleetwood Systems
Orlando, FL...........800-432-5433
Flomatic International
Sellersburg, IN........800-367-4233
Florida Knife Co
Sarasota, FL..........800-966-5643
Fluid Metering Inc
Syosset, NY...........800-223-3388
Frost Food Handling Products
Grand Rapids, MI.......800-253-9382
Furnace Belt Company
Buffalo, NY...........800-354-7213
G.W. Dahl Company
Greensboro, NC........800-852-4449
Garvey Products
West Chester, OH.......800-543-1908
GE Interlogix Industrial
Tualatin, OR..........800-247-9447
Gems Sensors & Controls
Plainville, CT.........860-747-3000
Glo-Quartz Electric Heater
Mentor, OH............800-321-3574
Globe Fire Sprinkler Corp
Standish, MI..........800-248-0278
Good Idea
Northampton, MA........800-462-9237
Granco Manufacturing Inc
San Ramon, CA.........510-652-8847
Graphite Metalizing Corp
Yonkers, NY...........914-968-8400
Green Belt Industries Inc
Buffalo, NY...........800-668-1114

Greenbridge
Mentor, OH............440-357-1500
H & H Metal Fabrication Inc
Belden, MS............662-489-4626
H A Phillips & Co
Dekalb, IL............630-377-0050
Habasit Canada Limited
Oakville, ON..........905-827-4131
Hansaloy Corp
Davenport, IA.........800-553-4992
Haumiller Engineering Co
Elgin, IL.............847-695-9111
Hayes & Stolz Indl Mfg LTD
Fort Worth, TX.........800-725-7272
Hi-Temp Inc
Tuscumbia, AL.........800-239-5066
Hoffmeyer Corp
San Leandro, CA.......888-744-1826
Home Rubber Co
Trenton, NJ...........800-257-9441
Hose Master Inc
Euclid, OH............216-481-2020
Ika-Works Inc
Wilmington, NC........800-733-3037
IMI Precision Engineering
Brookville, OH........937-833-4033
Indemax Inc
Vernon, NJ............800-345-7185
Industrial Product Corp
Ho Ho Kus, NJ.........800-472-5913
Infitec Inc
East Syracuse, NY......800-334-0837
International Tank & Pipe Co
Clackamas, OR.........888-988-0011
Introdel Products
Itasca, IL............800-323-4772
Irby
Rocky Mount, NC.......252-442-0154
Ivarson Inc
Milwaukee, WI.........414-351-0700
J & J Industries Inc
Bensenville, IL.......630-595-8878
Jilson Group
Lodi, NJ.............800-969-5400
Jokamsco Group
Waterford,, NY........518-237-6416
Kason Central
Columbus, OH..........614-885-1992
Kinetic Equipment Company
Appleton, WI..........806-293-4471
King Company
Dallas, TX............507-451-3770
Kinsley Inc
Doylestown, PA........800-414-6664
Knobs Unlimited
Bowling Green, OH......419-353-8215
Kraissl Co Inc
Hackensack, NJ........800-572-4775
KWS Manufacturing Co LTD
Burleson, TX..........800-543-6558
L.C. Thompson Company
Kenosha, WI...........800-558-4018
Lake Process Systems Inc
Lake Barrington, IL....800-331-9260
Lakeside Manufacturing Inc
Milwaukee, WI.........888-558-8565
Lako Tool & Mfg Inc
Perrysburg, OH........800-228-2982
Lambeth Band Corporation
New Bedford, MA.......508-984-4700
Liburdi Group of Companies
Mooresville, NC.......800-533-9353
Lil' Orbits
Minneapolis, MN.......800-228-8305
Livingston-Wilbor Corporation
Edison, NJ............908-322-8403
Lorenz Couplings
Cobourg, ON...........800-263-7782
Lucas Industrial
Cedar Hill, TX........800-877-1720
Lumsden Flexx Flow
Lancaster, PA.........800-367-3664
M & R Sales & Svc Inc
Glen Ellyn, IL........800-736-6431
M O Industries Inc
Whippany, NJ..........973-386-9228
M.H. Rhodes Cramer
South Windsor, CT......877-684-6464
Master Magnetics
Castle Rock, CO.......800-525-3536
Mastercraft Industries Inc
Newburgh, NY..........800-835-7812

McCormack Manufacturing Company
Lake Oswego, OR..................800-395-1593
Mckey Perforating Co Inc
New Berlin, WI..................800-345-7373
Meadows Mills Inc
North Wilkesboro, NC.............800-626-2282
Membrane Process & Controls
Edgar, WI.......................715-352-3206
Metal Master Sales Corp
Glendale Heights, IL.............800-488-8729
Micro Solutions Ent Tech & Dev
Van Nuys, CA....................800-673-4968
Midwest Rubber Svc & Supply
Minneapolis, MN.................800-537-7457
Midwest Stainless
Menomonie, WI...................715-235-5472
Miller Metal Fabrication
Bridgeville, DE.................302-337-2291
Miller Technical Svc
Plymouth, MI....................734-414-1769
Mollenberg-Betz Inc
Buffalo, NY.....................716-614-7473
Monarch-McLaren
Weston, ON......................416-741-9675
Morse Manufacturing Co Inc
East Syracuse, NY...............315-437-8475
Motion Industries Inc
Birmingham, AL..................877-609-7975
Moyno
Springfield, OH.................937-327-3111
Murtech Manufacturing
Kenilworth, NJ..................908-245-1556
Nalge Process Technologies Group
Rochester, NY...................585-586-8800
National Band Saw Co
Santa Clarita, CA...............800-851-5050
National Metal Industries
West Springfield, MA............800-628-8850
Nelles Automation
Houston, TX.....................713-939-9399
Newman Sanitary Gasket Co
Lebanon, OH.....................513-932-7379
Norgren Inc.
Littleton, CO...................800-514-0129
Northland Process Piping
Isle, MN........................320-679-2119
Ogden Manufacturing Company
Pittsburgh, PA..................412-967-3906
Pacer Pumps
Lancaster, PA...................800-233-3861
Package Machinery Co Inc
Holyoke, MA.....................413-315-3801
Parker-Hannifin Corp
Cleveland, OH...................800-272-7537
Partex Corporation
Flint, MI.......................810-736-5656
Pengo Attachments Inc
Cokato, MN......................800-599-0211
Piab Vacuum Products
Hingham, MA.....................800-321-7422
Plasti-Clip Corp
Milford, NH.....................800-882-2547
Pres-Air-Trol Corporation
Altoona, WI.....................800-431-2625
Pure Fit Nutrition Bars
Irvine, CA......................866-787-3348
Pyromation Inc
Fort Wayne, IN..................260-484-2580
Qosina Corporation
Ronkonkoma, NY..................631-242-3000
Quadrant Epp USA Inc
Fort Wayne, IN..................800-628-7264
Quality Industries
Cleveland, OH...................216-961-5566
R K Electric Co Inc
Mason, OH.......................800-543-4936
R.H. Chandler Company
Saint Louis, MO.................314-962-9353
Ralphs Pugh Conveyor Rollers
Benicia, CA.....................800-486-0021
Ranger Blade Manufacturing Company
Traer, IA.......................800-377-7860
Rath Manufacturing Company
Janesville, WI..................800-367-7284
Reading Plastic Fabricators
Reading, PA.....................610-926-3245
Rees Inc
Fremont, IN.....................260-495-9811
Refrigeration Research
Brighton, MI....................810-227-1151
Reid Boiler Works
Bellingham, WA..................360-714-6157

Rigidized Metal Corp
Buffalo, NY.....................800-836-2580
RM Waite Inc
Clintonville, WI................715-823-4327
Robert-James Sales
Buffalo, NY.....................800-777-1325
Rolland Machining & Fabricating
Moneta, VA......................973-827-6911
Salem-Republic Rubber Co
Sebring, OH.....................800-425-5079
Sanchelima International
Miami, FL.......................305-591-4343
Sani-Fit
Pasadena, CA....................626-395-7895
Sanitary Couplers
Springboro, OH..................513-743-0144
Seattle Refrigeration & Manufacturing
Seattle, WA.....................800-228-8881
Sellers Engineering Division
Danville, KY....................859-236-3181
Senior Flexonics
Bartlett, IL....................800-473-0474
Sew-Eurodrive Inc
Lyman, SC.......................864-439-8792
Sharon Manufacturing Inc
Deer Park, NY...................800-424-6455
Shingle Belting
King of Prussia, PA.............800-345-6294
Shivvers
Corydon, IA.....................641-872-1007
Simolex Rubber Corp
Plymouth, MI....................734-453-4500
Sine Pump
Arvada, CO......................888-504-8301
Smokehouse Limited
Franklinville, NC...............800-554-8385
Southern Metal Fabricators Inc
Albertville, AL.................800-989-1330
Special Products
Springfield, MO.................417-881-6114
Specialty Blades
Staunton, VA....................540-248-2200
Spot Wire Works Company
Philadelphia, PA................215-627-6124
Stainless Products
Somers, WC......................800-558-9446
Standex International Corp.
Salem, NH.......................603-893-9701
STD Precision Gear
West Bridgewater, MA............888-783-4327
Step Products
Round Rock, TX..................800-777-7837
Storm Industrial
Shawnee Mission, KS.............800-745-7483
Strahman Valves Inc
Bethlehem, PA...................877-787-2462
Stroter Inc
Freeport, IL....................815-616-2506
Stutz Products Corp
Hartford City, IN...............765-348-2510
Super Radiator Coils
N Chesterfield, VA..............800-229-2645
Super Steel
Milwaukee, WI...................414-355-4800
Svedala Industries
Colorado Springs, CO............719-471-3443
T & S Brass & Bronze Work
Travelers Rest, SC..............800-476-4103
Tema Systems Inc
Cincinnati, OH..................513-792-2840
Tente Casters Inc
Hebron, KY......................800-783-2470
Top Line Process Equipment Company
Bradford, PA....................800-458-6095
Travis Manufacturing Corp
Alliance, OH....................330-875-1661
Tropic KOOL
Largo, FL.......................727-581-2824
TruHeat Corporation
Allegan, MI.....................800-879-6199
Tuchenhagen
Columbia, MD....................410-910-6000
Unifiller Systems
Delta, BC.......................888-733-8444
United Performance Metals
Northbrook, IL..................888-922-0040
US Tsubaki Holdings Inc
Wheeling, IL....................800-323-7790
Valvinox
Iberville, QC...................450-346-1981
Vaughn Belting Co-Main Acct
Spartanburg, SC.................800-533-9086

Vilter Manufacturing Corporation
Cudahy, WI......................414-744-0111
Wade Manufacturing Company
Tigard, OR......................800-222-7246
Warner Electric Inc
South Beloit, IL................800-234-3369
Waukesha Cherry-Burrell
Louisville, KY..................502-491-4310
Waukesha Cherry-Burrell
Louisville, KY..................800-252-5200
Waukesha Foundry Inc
Waukesha, WI....................800-727-0741
Waukesha Specialty Company
Darien, WI......................262-724-3700
Wico Corporation
Niles, IL.......................800-367-9426
Wiegmann & Rose Thermxchanger
Oakland, CA.....................510-632-8828
Wilden Pump & Engineering LLC
Grand Terrace, CA...............909-422-1700
Windhorst Blowmold
Euless, TX......................817-540-6639
Wire Belt Co of America
Londonderry, NH.................603-644-2500
Womack International Inc
Vallejo, CA.....................707-647-2370
World Wide Fitting Corp
Vernon Hills, IL................800-393-9894
Wright Metal Products Crates
Greenville, SC..................864-297-6610
Wt Nickell Co
Batavia, OH.....................888-899-1991
Yates Industries Inc
St Clair Shores, MI.............586-778-7680

Pharmaceutical Industry

Arro Corp
Hodgkins, IL....................877-929-2776
Decagon Devices Inc
Pullman, WA.....................800-755-2751
Medical Packaging Corporation
Camarillo, CA...................805-388-2383

Plastic Fabricators

A Allred Marketing
Birmingham, AL..................205-251-3700
A La Carte
Chicago, IL.....................800-722-2370
A-A1 Aaction Bag
Denver, CO......................800-783-1224
Abbott Industries
Paterson, NJ
ABC Letter Art
Los Angeles, CA.................888-261-5367
ABI Limited
Concord, ON.....................800-297-8666
Abond Plastic Corporation
Lachine, QC.....................800-886-7947
Ace Stamp & Engraving
Lakewood, WA....................253-582-3322
Ace Technical Plastics Inc
East Hartford, CT...............860-278-2444
Achilles USA
Everett, WA.....................425-353-7000
Acme Bag Co
Chula Vista, CA.................800-275-2263
Aco Container Systems
Pickering, ON...................800-542-9942
Adam Electric Signs
Massillon, OH...................888-886-9911
Advance Engineering Co
Canton, MI......................800-497-6388
Advantage Puck Technologies
Corry, PA.......................814-664-4810
AEP Industries
South Hackensack, NJ............800-999-2374
AEP Industries Inc
Mankato, MN.....................800-999-2374
Aero Housewares
Fayetteville, GA................770-914-4240
Aero Manufacturing Co
Clifton, NJ.....................800-631-8378
Aeromat Plastics Inc
Burnsville, MN..................888-286-8729
Alger Creations
Miami, FL.......................954-454-3272
All American Container
Miami, FL.......................305-887-0797
All American Poly
Piscataway, NJ..................800-526-3551

Alouf Plastics
Orangeburg, NY 800-394-2247
ALP Lighting & Ceiling Products
Pennsauken, NJ 800-633-7732
Alpack
Centerville, NA 774-994-8086
Altira Inc
Miami, FL 305-687-8074
Amcel
Watertown, MA 800-225-7992
Amco Metals Indl
City of Industry, CA 626-855-2550
American Bag & Burlap Company
Chelsea, MA 617-884-7600
American Identification Industries
West Chicago, IL 800-255-8890
American Renolit Corp LA
Commerce, CA 323-721-2720
Ameriglobe LLC
Lafayette, LA 337-234-3211
Ametco Manufacturing Corp
Willoughby, OH 800-321-7042
Archer Daniels Midland Company
Chicago, IL 312-634-8100
Arena Products
Rochester, NY 844-762-0127
Art Poly Bag Co
Brooklyn, NY 800-278-7659
Artcraft Badge & Sign Company
Olney, MD 800-739-0709
Artistic Packaging Concepts
Massapequa Pk, NY 516-797-4020
Atlantis Industries Inc
Milton, DE 302-684-8542
Audrey Signs
New York, NY 212-769-4992
B&B Neon Sign Company
Austin, TX 800-791-6366
Bag Company
Kennesaw, GA 800-533-1931
Bag Masters
St Petersburg, FL 800-330-2247
Bagcraft Papercon
Chicago, IL 800-621-8468
Baltimore Sign Company
Arnold, MD 410-276-1500
Bardes Plastics Inc
Milwaukee, WI 800-558-5161
Barrette Outdoor Living
Cleveland, OH 800-336-2383
BAW Plastics Inc
Clairton, PA 800-783-2229
Bayhead Products Corp.
Dover, NH 800-229-4323
Beayl Weiner/Pak
Pacific Palisades, CA 310-454-1354
Bel-Art Products
Wayne, NJ 800-423-5278
Belleview
Brookline, NH 603-878-1583
Bergen Barrel & Drum Company
Kearny, NJ 201-998-3500
Berloc Manufacturing & Sign Company
Sun Valley, CA 818-503-9823
Berry Global
Evansville, IN 800-343-1295
BG Industries
Lemont, IL 800-800-5761
Blako Industries
Dunbridge, OH 419-833-4491
Bloomfield Industries
St. Louis, MO 888-356-5362
BOC Plastics Inc
Winston Salem, NC 800-334-8687
Bonar Plastics
West Chicago, IL 800-295-3725
Boss Manufacturing Co
Kewanee, IL 800-447-4581
Brechteen
Chesterfield, MI 586-949-2240
Brentwood Plastics In
St Louis, MO 314-968-1135
Brown International Corp LLC
Winter Haven, FL 863-299-2111
Brown Paper Goods Co
Waukegan, IL 847-688-1450
Buckhorn Inc
Milford, OH 800-543-4454
Budget Blinds Inc
Orange, CA 800-800-9250
Bulk Lift International, LLC
Carpentersville, IL 800-879-2247

Burgess Mfg. - Oklahoma
Guthrie, OK. 800-804-1913
C R Daniels Inc
Ellicott City, MD. 800-933-2638
C R Mfg
Waverly, NE 877-789-5844
C-P Flexible Packaging
Newtown, PA 800-448-8183
Canton Sign Co
Canton, OH. 330-456-7151
Caraustar
Franklin, KY 270-586-9565
Caraustar Industries, Inc.
Archdale, NC 800-223-1373
Cardinal Packaging
Evansville, IN 800-343-1295
Cardinal Rubber & Seal Inc
Roanoke, VA 800-542-5737
Carlisle Food Svc Products Inc
Oklahoma City, OK 800-654-8210
Carlisle Plastics
Minneapolis, MN 952-884-1309
Carolina Glove Co
Conover, NC 800-335-1918
Carroll Co
Garland, TX 800-527-5722
Carson Industries
Pomona, CA 800-735-5566
Cash Caddy
Palm Desert, CA 888-522-2221
Castle Bag Co.
Wilmington, DE 302-656-1001
Cayne Industrial Sales Corp
Bronx, NY 718-993-5800
Ccw Products
Arvada, CO 303-427-9663
CDF Corp
Plymouth, MA. 800-443-1920
Cell-O-Core Company
Sharon Center, OH 800-239-4370
Cello Bag Company
Bowling Green, KY 800-347-0338
Central Bag Co
Leavenworth, KS 913-250-0325
Central Fine Pack Inc
Fort Wayne, IN 260-432-3027
Central Package & Display
Minneapolis, MN 763-425-7444
Chalmur Bag Company, LLC
Philadelphia, PA 800-349-2247
Champion Plastics
Clifton, NJ 800-526-1230
Chase-Doors
Cincinnati, OH 800-543-4455
Checker Bag Co
St Louis, MO. 800-489-3130
Chem-Tainer Industries Inc
West Babylon, NY 800-275-2436
Chem-Tainer Industries Inc
West Babylon, NY 800-938-8896
Chester Plastics
Chester, NS 902-275-3522
Chili Plastics
Rochester, NY. 585-889-4680
Chinet Company
Laguna Niguel, CA 949-348-1711
Chipmaker Tooling Supply
Whittier, CA 800-659-5840
Chocolate Concepts
Hartville, OH 330-877-3322
Choctaw-Kaul Distribution Company
Detroit, MI 313-894-9494
Choklit Molds LTD
Lincoln, RI 800-777-6653
City Signs LLC
Jackson, TN 877-248-9744
CKS Packaging
Atlanta, GA 800-800-4257
Clawson Container Company
Clarkston, MI 800-325-8700
Clear View Bag Co Inc of Nc
Albany, NY 800-458-7153
Clear View Bag Company
Thomasville, NC 336-885-8131
Cleveland Plastic Films
Elyria, OH 800-832-6799
Cleveland Specialties Co
Loveland, OH 513-677-9787
CMD Corporation
Appleton, WI 920-730-6888
Coast Scientific
Rancho Santa Fe, CA 800-445-1544

Collins & Aikman
Canton, OH. 800-321-0244
Colonial Transparent Products Company
Hicksville, NY 516-822-4430
Conn Container Corp
North Haven, CT. 203-248-0241
Connecticut Laminating Co Inc
New Haven, CT. 800-753-9119
Consolidated Container Co LLC
Atlanta, GA 888-831-2184
Consolidated Plastics Co Inc
Stow, OH 800-858-5001
Container Specialties
Melrose Park, IL 800-548-7513
Container Supply Co
Garden Grove, CA 562-594-0937
Contico Container
Norwalk, CA 562-921-9967
Continental Commercial Products
Bridgeton, MO 800-325-1051
Continental Packaging Corporation
Elgin, IL 847-289-6400
Continental Products
Mexico, MO 800-325-0216
Contour Packaging
Philadelphia, PA 215-457-1600
Convoy
Canton, OH 800-899-1583
Cope Plastics Inc
Alton, IL 800-851-5510
Cork Specialties
Miami, FL 305-477-1506
Covestro LLC
Sheffield, MA 800-628-5084
Crayex Corp
Piqua, OH 800-837-1747
Creative Essentials
Ronkonkoma, NY 800-355-5891
Creative Forming
Ripon, WI 920-748-7285
Creative Packaging
Hayward, CA 510-785-6500
Crespac Incorporated
Tucker, GA 800-438-1900
Crystal-Flex Packaging Corporation
Rockville Centre, NY 888-246-7325
CTK Plastics
Moose Jaw, SK 800-667-8847
Custom Bottle of Connecticut
Naugatuck, CT 203-723-6661
Custom Foam Molders
Foristell, MO 636-441-2307
Custom ID Systems
Venice, FL 800-242-8430
Custom Molders
Rocky Mount, NC 919-688-8061
Custom Plastics Inc
Decatur, GA 404-373-1691
Custom Poly Packaging
Fort Wayne, IN 800-548-6603
Dadant & Sons Inc
Hamilton, IL 888-922-1293
Danafilms Inc
Westborough, MA. 508-366-8884
Danbury Plastics
Cumming, GA. 678-455-7391
Dansk International Designs
Bristol, PA. 914-697-6400
Dart Canada Inc.
Toronto, ON 800-465-9696
Dart Container Corp.
Mason, MI 800-248-5960
Dashco
Gloucester, ON 613-834-6825
Davron Technologies Inc
Chattanooga, TN. 423-870-1888
Dayton Bag & Burlap Co
Dayton, OH. 800-543-3400
De Ster Corporation
Atlanta, GA 800-237-8270
Decker Plastics
Council Bluffs, IA. 866-869-6293
DEFCO
Landenberg, PA. 215-274-8245
DEL-Tec Packaging Inc
Greer, SC. 800-747-8683
Delfin Design & Mfg
Rancho Sta Marg, CA 800-354-7919
Delta Cooling Towers Inc
Rockaway, NJ 800-289-3358
Den Ray Sign Company
Jackson, TN 800-530-7291

Design Packaging Company
Glencoe, IL .800-321-7659
Design Plastics Inc
Omaha, NE .800-491-0786
Design Specialties Inc
Hamden, CT .800-999-1584
Designers Plastics
Clearwater, FL 727-573-1643
Detroit Forming
Southfield, MI 248-440-1317
Development Workshop Inc
Idaho Falls, ID 800-657-5597
Dimension Graphics Inc
Grand Rapids, MI 855-476-1281
Dinosaur Plastics
Houston, TX .713-923-2278
Display Tray
Mont-Royal, QC 800-782-8861
Dispoz-O Plastics
Fountain Inn, SC 864-862-4004
Diversified Lighting Diffusers Inc
Copiague, NY 800-234-5464
Dixie Poly Packaging
Greenville, SC 864-268-3751
Do-It Corp
South Haven, MI 800-426-4822
Donoco Industries
Huntington Beach, CA 888-822-8763
Dordan Manufacturing Co
Woodstock, IL 800-663-5460
Douglas Stephen Plastics Inc
Paterson, NJ .973-523-3030
Dow Packaging
Midland, MI .800-331-6451
Dowling Signs Inc
Fredericksburg, VA 800-572-2100
Dub Harris Corporation
Pomona, CA .909-596-6300
Dwinell's Central Neon
Yakima, WA .800-932-8832
Dyna-Veyor Inc
Newark, NJ 800-326-5009
East Coast Group New York
Springfield Gardens, NY 718-527-8464
Eastern Poly Packaging Company
Brooklyn, NY 800-421-6006
Eaton Manufacturing Co
Houston, TX .800-328-6610
Eaton Quade Plastics & Sign Co
Oklahoma City, OK 405-236-4475
Economy Label Sales Company
Daytona Beach, FL 386-253-4741
Ed Smith's Stencil Works LTD
New Orleans, LA 504-525-2128
Edco Industries
Bridgeport, CT 203-333-8982
Ellehammer Industries
Langley, BC .604-882-9326
Elliot Lee
Cedarhurst, NY 516-569-9595
Elopak Americas
Wixom, MI 248-486-4600
Elrene Home Fashions
New York, NY 212-213-0425
Emco Industrial Plastics
Cedar Grove, NJ 800-292-9906
Emedco
Williamsville, NY 877-765-8386
Encore Plastics
Huntington Beach, CA 888-822-8763
Engineered Plastics Inc
Gibsonville, NC 800-711-1740
Engraving Services Co.
Woodville South, SA
Erell Manufacturing Co
Elk Grove Vlg, IL 800-622-6334
ES Robbins Corp
Muscle Shoals, AL 800-633-3325
Esterle Mold & Machine Co Inc
Stow, OH 800-411-4086
Everett Rubber Stamp
Everett, WA .425-258-6747
Exhibitron Co
Grants Pass, OR 800-437-4571
Fabohio Inc
Uhrichsville, OH 740-922-4233
Fabreeka International
Boise, ID 800-423-4469
Fabri-Kal Corp
Kalamazoo, MI 800-888-5054
Fan Bag Company
Chicago, IL 773-342-2752

Faribault Manufacturing Co
Faribault, MN 800-447-6043
Farnell Packaging
Dartmouth, NS 800-565-9378
Fast Bags
Fort Worth, TX 800-321-3687
Fato Industries
Kankakee, IL .815-932-3015
Federal Heath Sign Co LLC
Oceanside, CA 800-527-9495
Ferrer Corporation
San Juan, PR .787-761-5151
Field Manufacturing Corporation
Torrance, CA 310-781-9292
Film X
Dayville, CT .800-628-6128
Film-Pak Inc
Crowley, TX .800-526-1838
Filmco Inc
Aurora, OH 800-545-8457
Filmpack Plastic Corporation
Dayton, NJ 732-329-6523
Finn Industries
Ontario, CA .909-930-1500
Firl Industries Inc
Fond Du Lac, WI 800-558-4890
First Plastics Co Inc
Leominster, MA 978-840-6908
Five-M Plastics Company
Allentown, PA 610-628-4291
Flex Products
Carlstadt, NJ .800-526-6273
FLEXcon Company
Spencer, MA .508-885-8200
Flexible Foam Products
Elkhart, IN 800-678-3626
FMI Display
Elkins Park, PA 215-663-1998
Foamex
Cornelius, NC 704-892-8081
Formflex
Bloomingdale, IN 800-255-7659
Forrest Engraving Company
New Rochelle, NY 914-632-9892
FORT Hill Sign Products Inc
Hopedale, MA 781-321-4320
Fort James Canada
Toronto, ON .416-784-1621
Fortune Plastics, Inc
Old Saybrook, CT 800-243-0306
France Personalized Signs
Cleveland, OH 216-241-2198
Franklin Rubber Stamp Co
Wilmington, DE 302-654-8841
Frankston Paper Box Company of Texas
Frankston, TX 903-876-2550
Fredman Bag Co
Milwaukee, WI 800-945-5686
Freeman Electric Co Inc
Panama City, FL 850-785-7448
Fremont Die Cut Products
Fremont, OH .800-223-3177
Fresno Pallet, Inc.
Sultana, CA 559-591-4111
Frontier Bag
Kansas City, MO 816-765-4811
Fuller Industries LLC
Great Bend, KS 800-522-0499
Fulton-Denver Co
Denver, CO 800-521-1414
Gary Manufacturing Company
National City, CA 800-775-0804
Gary Plastic Packaging Corporation
Bronx, NY 800-221-8151
Gary Plastic Packaging Corporation
Bronx, NY 800-227-4279
Gastro-Gnomes
West Hartford, CT 800-747-4666
GE Appliances
Louisville, KY 877-959-8688
Geerpres Inc
Muskegon, MI 231-773-3211
Gelberg Signs
Washington, DC 800-443-5237
Gemini Plastic Films Corporation
Garfield, NJ .800-789-4732
General Films Inc
Covington, OH 888-436-3456
General Neon Sign Co
San Antonio, TX 210-227-1203
GENESTA
Rockwall, TX 972-771-1653

Genpak
Peterborough, ON 800-461-1995
Genpak LLC
Lakeville, MN 800-328-4556
Genpak LLC
Charlotte, NC 800-626-6695
Gessner Products
Ambler, PA 800-874-7808
Gibraltar Packaging Group Inc
Hastings, NE .402-463-1366
Glover Latex
Anaheim, CA 800-243-5110
GM Nameplate
Seattle, WA 800-366-7668
Goebel Fixture Co
Hutchinson, MN 888-339-0509
Goex Corporation
Janesville, WI 608-754-3303
Golden West Packaging Concept
Lake Forest, CA 949-855-9646
Goldmax Industries
City of Industry, CA 626-964-8820
Graham Engineering Corp
York, PA 717-848-3755
Gralab Instruments
Centerville, OH 800-876-8353
Grande Ronde Sign Company
La Grande, OR 541-963-5841
Great Northern Corp.
Appleton, WI 800-236-3671
Great Southern Corp
Memphis, TN 800-421-7802
Green Tek
Janesville, WI 800-747-6440
Greif Inc
Delaware, OH 740-549-6000
Gulf Arizona Packaging
Humble, TX .800-364-3887
Gulf Coast Plastics
Tampa, FL 800-277-7491
Gulf Packaging Company
Safety Harbor, FL 800-749-3466
H P Mfg Co
Cleveland, OH 216-361-6500
H&H Lumber Company
Amarillo, TX 806-335-1813
Habasit America Plastic Div
Reading, PA .800-445-7898
Hal-One Plastics
Olathe, KS 800-626-5784
Hall Manufacturing Co
Ringwood, NJ 973-962-6022
Hall Safety Apparel
Uhrichsville, OH 800-232-3671
Handgards Inc
El Paso, TX 800-351-8161
Handy Wacks Corp
Sparta, MI 800-445-4434
Hank Rivera Associates
Dearborn, MI 313-581-8300
Harbor Pallet Company
Anaheim, CA 714-871-0932
Harco Enterprises
Peterborough, ON 800-361-5361
Hardin Signs Inc
Peoria, IL 309-688-4111
Have Our Plastic Inc
Mississauga, ON 800-263-5995
Hayward Industries Inc
Clemmons, NC 336-712-9900
Heath & Company
Roswell, GA .770-650-2724
Hedwin Division
Baltimore, MD 800-638-1012
Herche Warehouse
Denver, CO 303-371-8186
Heritage Bag Co
Roanoke, TX .800-527-2247
Highland Plastics Inc
Mira Loma, CA 800-368-0491
Himolene
Carrollton, TX 800-777-4411
HMG Worldwide In-Store Marketing
New York, NY 212-736-2300
Hoarel Sign Co
Amarillo, TX 806-373-2175
Hoffmaster Group Inc
Oshkosh, WI .800-367-2877
Hoffmaster Group Inc.
Oshkosh, WI .800-558-9300
Hollywood Banners
Copiague, NY 800-691-5652

119

Holsman Sign Svc
Cleveland, OH 216-761-4433
Home Plastics Inc
Des Moines, IA....................515-265-2562
Hood Packaging
Burlington, ON 877-462-6627
HPI North America/ Plastics
Eagan, MN 800-752-7462
HPI North America/Plastics
Chicago, IL 800-327-3534
Hubco Inc
Hutchinson, KS 800-563-1867
Hudson Poly Bag Inc
Hudson, MA 800-229-7566
Hughes Manufacturing Company
Giddings, TX 800-414-0765
Huntsman Packaging Corporation
Birmingham, Bi....................205-328-4720
Ideal Office Supply & Rubber Stamp Company
Kingsport, TN 423-246-7371
Image Plastics
Houston, TX 800-289-2811
Indeco Products Inc
San Marcos, TX 888-246-3326
Indian Valley Industries
Johnson City, NY 800-659-5111
Indiana Bottle Co
Scottsburg, IN 800-752-8702
Indiana Vac Form Inc
Warsaw, IN 574-269-1725
Indianapolis Container Company
Indianapolis, IN 800-760-3318
Industrial Nameplate Inc
Warminster, PA 800-878-6263
Inland Showcase & Fixture Company
Fresno, CA 559-237-4158
Inline Plastic Corp
McDonough, GA 678-466-3467
Innovative Molding
Sebastopol, CA 707-829-2666
Innovative Plastics Corp
Orangeburg, NY 845-359-7500
Insulair
Vernalis, CA 800-343-3402
Inteplast Bags & Films Corporation
Delta, BC 604-946-5431
Intermold Corporation
Greenville, SC 864-627-0300
International Polymers Corp
Allentown, PA.....................800-526-0953
Interplast
Troy, OH 937-332-1110
Interstate Packaging
White Bluff, TN 800-251-1072
Intralox LLC
Harahan, LA 800-535-8848
Intrex
Bethel, CT........................203-792-7400
IPL Plastics
Edmundston, NB. 800-739-9595
Island Poly
Westbury, NY 800-338-4433
J A Heilferty & Co
Teaneck, NJ.......................201-836-5060
J L Clark Corp
Rockford, IL 815-962-8861
J.E. Roy
St Claire, QC......................418-883-2711
James River Canada
North York, ON. 416-789-5151
Jamison Plastic Corporation
Allentown, PA.....................610-391-1400
Jarden Home Brands
Cloquet, MN 218-879-6700
Jarden Home Brands
Daleville, IN 800-392-2575
Jarisch Paper Box Company
North Adams, MA 413-663-5396
Jeb Plastics
Wilmington, DE 800-556-2247
Jeffcoat Signs
Gainesville, FL 877-377-4248
Jescorp
Des Plaines, IL 847-299-7800
Jet Plastica Industries
Hatfield, PA
Jewell Bag Company
Dallas, TX 214-749-1223
JH Display & Fixture
Greenwood, IN 317-888-0631
Jilson Group
Lodi, NJ 800-969-5400

Jim Scharf Holdings
Perdue, SK 800-667-9727
Johnson Refrigerated Truck
Rice Lake, WI 800-922-8360
Johnstown Manufacturing
Columbus, OH 614-236-8853
Jomar Corp
Egg Harbor Twp, NJ 609-646-8000
Jomar Plastics Industry
Nanty Glo, PA 800-681-4039
Jones-Zylon Co
West Lafayette, OH................800-848-8160
Joseph Struhl Co Inc
New Hyde Park, NY 800-552-0023
Juice Merchandising Corp
Kansas City, MO 800-950-1998
Juice Tree
Omaha, NE 714-891-4425
Jupiter Mills Corporation
Roslyn, NY 800-853-5121
Just Plastics Inc
New York, NY 212-569-8500
K & I Creative Plastics & Wood
Jacksonville, FL 904-387-0438
K-C Products Company
Van Nuys, CA.....................818-267-1600
Kadon Corporation
Milford, OH 937-299-0088
Kal Pac Corp
Montgomery, NY 800-852-5722
Keena Corporation
Newton, MA 617-244-9800
Kendrick Johnson & Assoc Inc
Minneapolis, MN 800-826-1271
Kenro
Fredonia, WI......................262-692-2411
Key Packaging Co
Sarasota, FL 941-355-2728
KHM Plastics Inc
Gurnee, IL 847-249-4910
Kimball Companies
East Longmeadow, MA 413-525-1881
King Plastic Corp
North Port, FL 800-780-5502
Kitchener Plastics
Kitchener, ON 800-429-5633
Klever Kuvers
Pasadena, CA 626-355-8441
Klockner Pentaplast of America
Gordonsville, VA 540-832-3600
KM International Corp
Kenton, TN 731-749-8700
Knobs Unlimited
Bowling Green, OH 419-353-8215
Kord Products Inc.
Brantford, ON 800-452-9070
Kornylak Corp
Hamilton, OH 800-837-5676
Kuriyama of America Inc
Schaumburg, IL 800-800-0320
L & C Plastic Bags
Covington, OH 937-473-2968
L T Hampel Corp
Germantown, WI..................800-681-6979
L&H Wood Manufacturing Company
Farmington, MI 248-474-9000
L&L Engraving Company
Gilford, NH 888-524-3032
Lafayette Sign Company
Little Falls, NJ 800-343-5366
Lakeside Manufacturing Inc
Milwaukee, WI 888-558-8565
Lakeside-Aris Manufacturing
Milwaukee, WI 800-558-8565
Lamb Sign
Manassas, VA 703-791-7960
Lambert Company
Chillicothe, MO 800-821-7667
Lamcraft Inc
Lees Summit, MO.................800-821-1333
Landis Plastics
Alsip, IL 708-396-1470
Laughlin Sales Corp
Fort Worth, TX 817-625-7756
Laydon Company
Brown City, MI 810-346-2952
Leathertone
Findlay, OH 419-429-0188
Leeds Conveyor Manufacturer Company
Guilford, CT 800-724-1088
Legible Signs
Loves Park, IL.....................800-435-4177

Letica Corp
Rochester Hills, MI.................800-538-4221
Lexington Logistics LLC
Portage, WI 800-356-8150
Linvar
Hartford, CT 800-282-5288
Liqui-Box Corp
Richmond, VA.....................804-325-1400
Liquitane
Berwick, PA 570-759-6200
LMK Containers
Centerville, UT 626-821-9984
Locknane
Everett, WA. 800-848-9854
Long Island Stamp Corporation
Flushing, NY......................800-547-8267
Longhorn Packaging Inc
San Antonio, TX...................800-433-7974
LoTech Industries
Lakewood, CO 800-295-0199
LPI Imports
Chicago, IL 877-389-6563
Luetzow Industries
South Milwaukee, WI..............800-558-6055
Lynn Sign Inc
Andover, MA 800-225-5764
M & E Mfg Co Inc
Kingston, NY 845-331-2110
M & G Packaging Corp
Floral Park, NY 800-240-5288
M S Plastics & Packaging Inc
Butler, NJ 800-593-1802
M&R Flexible Packaging
Springboro, OH...................800-543-3380
Maco Bag Corp
Newark, NY 315-226-1000
Majestic
Bridgeport, CT 203-367-7900
Malpack Polybag
Ajax, ON 905-428-3751
Marco Products
Adrian, MI 517-265-3333
Marpac Industries
Philmont, NY 888-462-7722
Marshall Plastic Film Inc
Martin, MI 269-672-5511
Martin/Baron
Irwindale, CA 626-960-5153
Mason Transparent Package Company
Armonk, NY 718-792-6000
Max Packaging
Attalla, AL 800-543-5369
May-Wes Manufacturing Inc
Hutchinson, MN 800-788-6483
Maypak Inc
Wayne, NJ 973-696-0780
MBX Packaging Specialists
Wausau, WI 715-845-1171
Mcbride Sign Co
Madison Heights, VA 434-847-4151
McQueen Sign & Lighting
Canton, OH 330-452-5769
MDR International
North Miami, FL 305-944-5019
Measurex/S&L Plastics
Nazareth, PA 800-752-0650
Melmat Inc
Huntington Beach, CA 800-635-6289
Merchandising Inventives
Waukegan, IL 800-367-5653
Merryweather Foam Inc
Sylacauga, AL.....................256-249-8546
Micelli Chocolate Mold Company
West Babylon, NY 631-752-2888
Micro Qwik
Cross Plains, WI 608-798-3071
Microplas Industries
Dunwoody, GA 800-952-4528
Midco Plastics
Enterprise, KS 800-235-2729
Midland Manufacturing Co
Monroe, IA 800-394-2625
Millhiser
Richmond, VA.....................800-446-2247
Mimi et Cie
Seattle, WA 206-545-1850
Mini-Bag Company
Farmingdale, NY 631-694-3325
MIT Poly-Cart Corp
New York, NY 800-234-7659
Mohawk Northern Plastics
Auburn, WA 800-426-1100

Mold-Rite Plastics LLC
Twinsburg, OH 330-425-4206
Molded Container Corporation
Portland, OR 503-233-8601
Monument Industries Inc
Bennington, VT 802-442-8187
Moser Bag & Paper Company
Cleveland, OH 800-433-6638
Mount Vernon Plastics
Mamaroneck, NY 914-698-1122
Mr Ice Bucket
New Brunswick, NJ 732-545-0420
Mulholland-Harper Company
Denton, MD 800-882-3052
Mullnix Packages Inc
Fort Wayne, IN 260-747-3149
Multi-Plastics Extrusions Inc
Hazleton, PA 570-455-2021
Naltex
Austin, TX 800-531-5112
NAP Industries
Brooklyn, NY 877-635-4948
National Marker Co Inc
North Smithfield, RI 800-453-2727
National Poly Bag Manufacturing Corporation
Brooklyn, NY 718-629-9800
National Sign Corporation
Seattle, WA 206-282-0700
NCC
Groveland, FL 800-429-9037
Neokraft Signs Inc
Lewiston, ME 800-339-2258
Net Pack Systems
Oakland, ME 207-465-4531
Newell Brands
Atlanta, GA
Newman Sanitary Gasket Co
Lebanon, OH 513-932-7379
Nolon Industries
Mantua, OH 330-274-2283
Norgus Silk Screen Co Inc
Clifton, NJ 973-365-0600
North American Packaging Corp
New York, NY 800-499-3521
North American Plastic Manufacturing Company
Bethel, CT 800-934-7752
Northeast Packaging Materials
Monsey, NY 845-426-2900
Northwind Inc
Alpena, AR 877-937-2585
Noteworthy Company
Amsterdam, NY 800-696-7849
Novelty Crystal
Long Island City, NY 800-622-0250
Now Plastics Inc
East Longmeadow, MA 413-525-1010
Nu-Trend Plastics Thermoformer
Jacksonville, FL 904-353-5936
Nucon Corporation
Deerfield, IL 877-545-0070
Nutty Bavarian
Sanford, FL 800-382-4788
Nyman Manufacturing Company
Rumford, RI 401-438-3410
NYP
Leola, PA 800-541-0961
Occidental Chemical Corporation
Dallas, TX 800-733-3665
Ockerlund Industries
Addison, IL 708-771-7707
Oklahoma Neon
Tulsa, OK 888-707-6366
Olcott Plastics
St Charles, IL 888-313-5277
Olde Thompson Inc
Oxnard, CA 800-827-1565
OMNOVA Solutions
Fairlawn, OH 330-869-4200
Ontario Glove and Safety Products
Kitchener, ON 800-265-4554
ORBIS
Oconomowoc, WI 262-560-5000
ORBIS
Oconomowoc, WI 800-890-7292
Orbis Corp.
Rexdale, ON 800-890-7292
OWD
Tupper Lake, NY 800-836-1693
Owens-Illinois Inc
Perrysburg, OH 567-336-5000
P M Plastics
Pewaukee, WI 262-691-1700

Pace Packaging Corp
Fairfield, NJ 800-867-2726
Pacific Oasis Enterprise Inc
Santa Fe Springs, CA 800-424-1475
Pacific Paper Box Co
Cudahy, CA 323-771-7733
Packaging Associates
Randolph, NJ 973-252-8890
Packing Material Company
Southfield, MI 248-489-7000
Pactiv LLC
Lake Forest, IL 800-476-4300
Pak 2000 Inc
Mirror Lake, NH 603-569-3700
Pak-Sak Industries I
Sparta, MI 800-748-0431
Pallet Management Systems
Lawrenceville, VA 800-446-1804
Palmer Snyder
Brookfield, WI 800-762-0415
Pan Pacific Plastics Inc
Hayward, CA 888-475-6888
Papelera Puertorriquena
Utuado, PR 787-894-2098
Par-Pak
Houston, TX 713-686-6700
Par-Pak
Houston, TX 888-727-7252
Parade Packaging
Mundelein, IL 847-566-6264
Paradigm Packaging Inc
Upland, CA 909-985-2750
Paragon Packaging
Ferndale, CA 888-615-0065
Parisian Novelty Company
Homewood, IL 773-847-1212
Park Custom Molding
Linden, NJ 908-486-8882
Parkway Plastic Inc
Piscataway, NJ 800-881-4996
Parsons Manufacturing Corp.
Menlo Park, CA 650-324-4726
Parta
Kent, OH 800-543-5781
Party Yards
Casselberry, FL 877-501-4400
Peerless Packages
Cleveland, OH 216-464-3620
Pelco Packaging Corporation
Stirling, NJ 908-647-3500
Pelican Displays
Homer, IL 800-627-1517
Pelican Products Inc
Bronx, NY 800-552-8820
Penda Form Corp
New Concord, OH 800-837-2574
Penley Corporation
West Paris, ME 800-368-6449
Penn Bottle & Supply Company
Philadelphia, PA 215-365-5700
Penn Products
Portland, CT 800-490-7366
Perfex Corporation
Poland, NY 800-848-8483
Peter Gray Corporation
Andover, MA 978-470-0990
Pexco Packaging Corporation
Toledo, OH 800-227-9950
Pfeil & Holding Inc
Woodside, NY 800-247-7955
Phoenix Sign Company
Aberdeen, WA 360-532-1111
Pilant Corp
Bloomington, IN 800-366-3525
Pilgrim Plastics
Brockton, MA 800-343-7810
Pioneer Plastics Inc
Dixon, KY 800-951-1551
Plascal Corp
Farmingdale, NY 800-899-7527
Plastech Corp
Atlanta, GA 404-355-9682
Plasti Print Inc
Burlingame, CA 650-652-4950
Plasti-Clip Corp
Milford, NH 800-882-2547
Plasti-Line
Knoxville, TN 800-444-7446
Plastic Assembly Corporation
Ayer, MA
Plastic Craft Products Corp
West Nyack, NY 800-627-3010

Plastic Fantastics/Buck Signs
Ashland, OR 800-482-1776
Plastic Suppliers Inc
Columbus, OH 800-722-5577
Plastic Tagtrade Check
Essexville, MI 989-892-7913
Plastic Turning Company
Leominster, MA 978-534-8326
Plastican Corporation
Fairfield, NJ 973-227-7817
Plastics Industries
Athens, TN 800-894-4876
Plastipak Packaging
Plymouth, MI 734-354-3510
Plastipro
Los Angeles, CA 800-779-0561
Plastiques Cascades Group
Montreal, QC 888-703-6515
Plaxall Inc
Long Island City, NY 800-876-5706
Podnar Plastics Inc
Kent, OH 800-673-5277
Polar Plastics
St Laurent, QC 514-331-0207
Poliplastic
Granby, QC 450-378-8417
Poly Processing Co
French Camp, CA 877-325-3142
Poly Shapes Corporation
Elyria, OH 800-605-9359
Polybottle Group
Surrey, BC 604-594-4999
PolyConversions, Inc.
Rantoul, IL 888-893-3330
Polyplastic Forms Inc
Farmingdale, NY 800-428-7659
Port Erie Plastics Inc
Harborcreek, PA 814-899-7602
Portco Corporation
Vancouver, WA 800-426-1794
Prairie Packaging Inc
Mooresville, NC 704-660-6600
Pretium Packaging
Chesterfield, MO 314-727-8673
Pretium Packaging
Hazle Twp, PA 570-459-1800
Printpack Inc.
Atlanta, GA. 404-460-7000
Priority Plastics Inc
Grinnell, IA. 800-798-3512
Pro-Gram Plastics Inc
Geneva, OH. 440-466-8080
Progressive Plastics
Cleveland, OH 800-252-0053
Prolon
Port Gibson, MS 888-480-9828
Quality Container Company
Ypsilanti, MI 734-481-1373
Quality Films
Three Rivers, MI. 269-679-5263
Quality Plastic Bag Corporation
Flushing, NY. 800-532-2247
Quantum Performance Films
Streamwood, IL. 800-323-6963
Quantum Storage Systems Inc
Miami, FL 800-685-4665
Quintex Corp
Nampa, ID 208-467-1113
Qyk Syn Industries
Miami, FL 800-354-5640
R C Molding Inc
Greer, SC 864-879-7279
R H Saw Corp
Barrington, IL 847-381-8777
Rainbow Neon Sign Company
Houston, TX 713-923-2759
Ram Industries
Erwin, TN 800-523-3883
Rand-Whitney Group LLC
Worcester, MA 508-791-2301
RAPAC Inc
Oakland, TN 800-280-6333
Ray C. Sprosty Bag Company
Wooster, OH 330-264-8559
Rayne Sign Co
Rayne, LA 337-334-4276
Reading Plastic Fabricators
Reading, PA 610-926-3245
Redi-Call Inc
Reno, NV 800-648-1849
Reese Enterprises Inc
Rosemount, MN 800-328-0953

Regal Plastic Company
Mission, KS 800-852-1556
Regal Plastic Supply Co
Kansas City, MO. 800-444-6390
Regina USA
Oak Creek, WI 414-571-0032
Reidler Decal Corporation
Saint Clair, PA................800-628-7770
Reilly Foam Corporation
Conshohocken, PA..............610-834-1900
Reliance Product
Winnipeg, MB..................800-665-0258
Rez-Tech Corp
Kent, OH.....................800-673-5277
Richard Read Construction Company
Arcadia, CA..................888-450-7343
Richards Packaging
Memphis, TN 800-583-0327
Riverside Manufacturing Company
Arlington Hts, IL 800-877-3349
Rjr Technologies
Oakland, CA 510-638-5901
RMI-C/Rotonics Manaufacturing
Bensenville, IL 630-773-9510
Roberts Poly Pro Inc
Charlotte, NC 800-269-7409
Robinson Industries Inc
Coleman, MI 989-465-6111
Rochester Midland Corp
Rochester, NY................800-387-7174
Roechling Engineered Plastics
Gastonia, NC.................800-541-4419
Roll-O-Sheets Canada
Barrie, ON...................888-767-3456
Rolland Machining & Fabricating
Moneta, VA...................973-827-6911
Ropak
Oak Brook, IL................800-527-2267
Roplast Industries Inc
Oroville, CA 800-767-5278
Ross & Wallace Inc
Hammond, LA 800-854-2300
Rosson Sign Co
Macon, GA 478-788-3905
Roth Sign Systems
Petaluma, CA 800-585-7446
Rowland Technologies
Wallingford, CT 203-269-9500
Royal Ecoproducts
Vaughan, ON..................800-465-7670
RubaTex Polymer
Middlefield, OH 440-632-1691
Rutan Poly Industries Inc
Mahwah, NJ..................800-872-1474
RXI Silgan Specialty Plastics
Triadelphia, WV 304-547-9100
Rytec Corporation
Milwaukee, WI 888-467-9832
Sabert Corp
Sayreville, NJ 800-722-3781
Sacramento Bag Manufacturing
Woodland, CA. 530-662-6130
Saeplast Canada
St John, NB 800-567-3966
Samuel P. Harris
Rumford, RI 401-438-4020
Samuel Strapping Systems Inc
Woodridge, IL.................800-323-4424
San Miguel Label Manufacturing
Ciales, PR 787-871-3120
Sani-Top Products
De Leon Springs, FL. 800-874-6094
Schlueter Company
Janesville, WI 800-359-1700
Schoeneck Containers Inc
New Berlin, WI................262-786-9360
Scott Sign Systems
Sarasota, FL 800-237-9447
Sealed Air Corp
Charlotte, NC 800-391-5645
Seiler Plastics
St Louis, MO.................888-673-4537
Selby Sign Co Inc
Pocomoke City, MD 410-742-0095
Semco Plastic Co
St Louis, MO.................314-487-4557
Senior Housing Options Inc
Denver, CO...................800-659-2656
Sertapak Packaging Corporation
Woodstock, ON................800-265-1162
Service Neon Signs
Springfield, VA...............703-354-3000

Setco
Monroe Twp, NJ 609-655-4600
Setco
Anaheim, CA 714-777-5200
Seton Indentification Products
Branford, CT..................800-571-2596
Seville Display Door
Temecula, CA.................800-634-0412
Sfb Plastics Inc
Wichita, KS...................800-343-8133
Shamrock Plastics
Mt Vernon, OH................800-765-1611
Sharpsville Container Corp
Sharpsville, PA 800-645-1248
Shaw-Clayton Corporation
San Rafael, CA................800-537-6712
Sheboygan Paper Box Co
Sheboygan, WI................800-458-8373
Shields Bag & Printing Co
Yakima, WA..................800-541-8630
Shingle Belting
King of Prussia, PA............800-345-6294
Ship Rite Packaging
Bergenfield, NJ 800-721-7447
Shippers Supply
Saskatoon, SK................800-661-5639
Sign Graphics
Evansville, IN 812-476-9151
Sign Systems, Inc.
Warren, MI 586-758-1600
SignArt Advertising
Van Buren, AR................479-474-8581
Signature Packaging
West Orange, NJ 800-376-2299
Silgan Plastics Canada
Chesterfield, MO 800-274-5426
Silgan Plastics LLC
Chesterfield, MO 800-274-5426
Silgan White Cap LLC
Downers Grove, IL.............800-515-1565
Skd Distribution Corp
Jamaica, NY..................800-458-8753
Snapware
Fullerton, CA.................800-334-3062
Snyder Crown
Marked Tree, AR 870-358-3400
Snyder Industries Inc.
Lincoln, NE..................800-351-1363
Sommers Plastic Product Co Inc
Clifton, NJ...................800-225-7677
Soodhalter Plastics
Los Angeles, CA...............213-747-0231
Southern Film Extruders
High Point, NC................800-334-6101
Spartanburg Steel Products Inc
Spartanburg, SC...............800-974-7500
Spartec Plastics
Conneaut, OH.................800-325-5176
Spartech Plastics
Portage, WI..................800-998-7123
Spartech Poly Com
Clayton, MI..................888-721-4242
Specialty Films & Associates
Hebron, KY...................800-984-3346
Spectrum Plastics
Las Vegas, NV 702-876-8650
Spir-It/Zoo Piks
Andover, MA 800-343-0996
Spirit Foodservice, Inc.
Andover, MA 800-343-0996
SQP
Schenectady, NY...............800-724-1129
Star Container Company
Phoenix, AZ..................480-281-4200
Star Filters
Timmonsville, SC..............800-845-5381
Steel City Corporation
Youngstown, OH...............800-321-0350
Stelray Plastic Products Inc
Ansonia, CT..................800-735-2331
Step Products
Round Rock, TX...............800-777-7837
Sterling Net & Twine Company
Cedar Knolls, NJ..............800-342-0316
Sterling Novelty Products
Northbrook, IL 847-291-0070
Stoffel Seals Corp
Tallapoosa, GA................800-422-8247
Storm Industrial
Shawnee Mission, KS...........800-745-7483
Stratis Plastic Pallets
Indianapolis, IN 800-725-5387

Straubel Company
De Pere, WI...................888-336-1412
Stripper Bags
Henderson, NV.................800-354-2247
Suburban Sign Company
Anoka, MN...................763-753-8849
Suburban Signs
College Park, MD..............301-474-5051
Sun Plastics
Clearwater, MN................800-862-1673
Sunland Manufacturing Company
Minneapolis, MN...............800-790-1905
Superfos Packaging Inc
Cumberland, MD 800-537-9242
Sutherland Stamp Company
San Diego, CA................858-233-7784
T & T Industries Inc
Fort Mohave, AZ...............800-437-6246
T&S Blow Molding
Scarborough, ON 416-752-8330
T.O. Plastics
Minneapolis, MN...............952-854-2131
Tablet & Ticket Co
West Chicago, IL...............800-438-4959
Tar-Hong MELAMINE USA
City of Industry, CA............626-935-1612
Target Industries
North Salt Lake, UT............866-617-2253
Taymar Industries
Palm Desert, CA...............800-624-1972
Techform
Mount Airy, NC................336-789-2115
TEMP-TECH Company
Springfield, MA...............800-343-5579
Templock Corporation
Santa Barbara, CA.............800-777-1715
TEQ
Huntley, IL...................800-874-7113
Terphane Inc
Bloomfield, NY................800-724-3456
Thermo Service
Dallas, TX...................800-635-5559
Thermodynamics
Commerce City, CO 800-627-9037
Thermodyne International LTD
Ontario, CA...................909-923-9945
Thombert
Newton, IA 800-433-3572
Thornton Plastics
Salt Lake City, UT.............800-248-3434
Three P
Salt Lake City, UT.............801-486-7407
Tolas Health Care Packaging
Feasterville Trevose, PA.........215-322-7900
Tolco Corp
Toledo, OH...................800-537-4786
Toledo Sign Co Inc
Toledo, OH...................419-244-4444
Toscarora
Sandusky, OH.................419-625-7343
Total Identity Group
Cambridge, ON................877-551-5529
Trans Flex Packagers Inc
Unionville, CT.................860-673-2531
Tray-Pak Corp
Reading, PA..................610-926-5800
Trevor Industries
Eden, NY....................716-992-4775
Tri-State Plastics
Henderson, KY................270-826-8361
Tri-State Plastics
Glenwillard, PA................724-457-6900
Triad Scientific
Manasquan, NJ................800-867-6690
Trident Plastics
Ivyland, PA...................800-222-2318
Trinity Packaging
Cheektowaga, NY..............800-778-3111
Triple Dot Corp
Santa Ana, CA................714-241-0888
Triple-A Manufacturing Company
Toronto, ON..................800-786-2238
Tru Form Plastics
Gardena, CA..................800-510-7999
Tuckahoe Manufacturing Co
Vineland, NJ..................800-220-3368
Tulsa Plastics Co
Tulsa, OK....................888-273-5303
Tupperware Brands Corporation
Orlando, FL..................800-366-3800
Tyco Plastics
Lakeville, MN.................800-328-4080

UCB Inc
 Smyrna, GA 770-970-8338
Uniloy Milacron
 Tecumseh, MI 517-424-8900
Union Industries
 Providence, RI 800-556-6454
Uniplast Films
 Palmer, MA 800-343-1295
Unique Manufacturing
 Visalia, CA 888-737-1007
Unique Plastics
 Rio Rico, AZ. 800-658-5946
United Bags Inc
 St Louis, MO. 800-550-2247
United Commercial Corporation
 Shrewsbury, NJ................800-498-7147
United Flexible
 Westbury, NY 516-222-2150
United Seal & Tag Corporation
 Port Charlotte, FL 800-211-9552
Universal Container Corporation
 Odessa, FL 800-582-7477
Universal Paper Box
 Seattle, WA 800-228-1045
Universal Sign Company and Manufacturing Company
 Lafayette, LA 337-234-1466
Upham & Walsh Lumber
 Hoffman Estates, IL 847-519-1010
Vacumet Corporation
 Austell, GA. 800-776-0865
Valley City Sign Co
 Comstock Park, MI.............616-784-5711
Valley Packaging Supply Co
 Green Bay, WI. 920-336-9012
Vermont Bag & Film
 Bennington, VT 802-442-3166
Vicmore Manufacturing Company
 Brooklyn, NY 800-458-8663
VIFAN Canada
 Lanoraie, QC. 800-557-0192
Virginia Plastics Co
 Roanoke, VA..................800-777-8541
Visual Packaging Corp
 Haskell, NJ 973-835-7055
Volk Corp
 Farmington Hills, MI 800-521-6799
Vollrath Co LLC
 Sheboygan, WI 800-624-2051
Vonco Products LLC
 Lake Villa, IL 800-323-9077
VPI Manufacturing
 Draper, UT 801-495-2310
Vulcan Industries
 Moody, AL 888-444-4417
Waddington North America
 Chelmsford, MA 888-962-2877
Wasserman Bag Company
 Center Moriches, NY 631-909-8656
Wedlock Paper ConvertersLtd.
 Mississauga, ON...............800-388-0447
Wells Lamont
 Niles, IL 800-323-2830
West Rock
 Atlanta, GA. 770-448-2193
Western Plastics
 Portland, TN 615-325-7331
Western Plastics
 Calhoun, GA..................800-752-4106
Wilks Precision Instr Co Inc
 Union Bridge, MD 410-775-7917
Winmark Stamp & Sign
 Salt Lake City, UT 800-438-0480
Winnebago Sign Company
 Fond Du Lac, WI 920-922-5930
Winpak Portion Packaging
 San Bernardino, CA 800-804-4224
Winzen Film
 Taylor, TX....................800-779-7595
Wisconsin Film & Bag Inc
 Shawano, WI..................800-765-9224
Witt Plastics
 Greenville, OH 800-227-9181
WNA
 Lancaster, TX 800-334-2877
WNA
 Chattanooga, TN..............800-404-9318
Wna Comet West Inc
 City of Industry, CA 800-225-0939
Wolens Company
 Dallas, TX....................214-634-0800
Woodstock Plastics Co Inc
 Marengo, IL 815-568-5281

WORC Slitting & Mfg Co
 Worcester, MA 800-356-2961
Wright Plastics Company
 Prattville, AL 800-874-7659
Zeier Plastic & Mfg Inc
 Madison, WI..................608-244-5782
Zimmer Custom-Made Packaging
 Indianapolis, IN 317-263-3436
Zip-Pak
 Manteno, IL 800-488-6973

Plate/Frame Exchanger

Harris Equipment Corp
 Melrose Park, IL 800-365-0315

Pump Feeders

John Crane Mechanical Sealing Devices
 Chicago, IL
Polar Process
 Plattsville, ON..................877-896-8077
Warren Rupp Inc
 Mansfield, OH 419-524-8388

Pumps

Food

A.K. Robins
 Baltimore, MD 800-486-9656
Abel Pumps
 Sewickley, PA 412-741-3222
ABO Industries
 San Diego, CA 858-566-9750
Alloy Hardfacing & Engineering
 Jordan, MN 800-328-8408
American LEWA
 Holliston, MA 888-539-2123
APV Americas
 Delavan, WI 800-252-5200
Arcobaleno Pasta Machines
 Lancaster, PA 800-875-7096
Autio Co
 Astoria, OR...................800-483-8884
Automated Food Systems
 Waxahachie, TX 469-517-0470
Axiflow Technologies, Inc.
 Kennesaw, GA 770-795-1195
Baldewein Company
 Lake Forrest, IL 800-424-5544
Blackmer Co
 Grand Rapids, MI 616-241-1611
Bran & Luebbe
 Schaumburg, IL...............847-882-8116
Chocolate Concepts
 Hartville, OH 330-877-3322
Commercial Manufacturing
 Fresno, CA 559-237-1855
Cook & Beals Inc
 Loup City, NE 308-745-0154
Cornell Pump Company
 Portland, OR..................503-653-0330
Crane Pumps & Systems
 Piqua, OH 937-778-8947
Custom Food Machinery
 Stockton, CA..................209-463-4343
Doering Machines Inc
 San Francisco, CA 415-526-2131
Dupps Co
 Germantown, OH 937-855-0623
Eirich Machines
 Gurnee, IL 847-336-2444
Eischen Enterprises
 Fresno, CA 559-834-0013
Esco Products Inc
 Houston, TX 800-966-5514
Flojet
 Foothill Ranch, CA 800-235-6538
Flow of Solids
 Westford, MA 978-392-0300
Flux Pumps Corporation
 Atlanta, GA...................800-367-3589
Franrica Systems
 Stockton, CA..................209-948-2811
Fristam Pumps USA LLP
 Middleton, WI. 608-831-5001
Fristam Pumps USA LLP
 Middleton, WI. 800-841-5001
GEA Niro Soavi North America
 Bedford, NH 603-606-4060

General Tank
 Berwick, PA 800-435-8265
Granco Manufacturing Inc
 San Ramon, CA 510-652-8847
Greenfield Packaging
 White Plains, NY 914-993-0233
Handtmann Inc
 Lake Forest, IL 800-477-3585
Healdsburg Machine Company
 Santa Rosa, CA................707-433-3348
Hinds-Bock Corp
 Bothell, WA...................425-885-1183
John Crane Mechanical Sealing Devices
 Chicago, IL
Johnson Pump of America
 Hanover Park, IL..............847-671-7867
Karl Schnell
 New London, WI 920-982-9974
Kelmin Products
 Plymouth, FL 407-886-6079
Key Technology Inc.
 Walla Walla, WA 509-529-2161
Kinetic Equipment Company
 Appleton, WI 806-293-4471
Krogh Pump Co
 Benicia, CA. 800-225-7644
L.C. Thompson Company
 Kenosha, WI 800-558-4018
Langsenkamp Manufacturing
 Indianapolis, IN 877-585-1950
Lear Romec
 Elyria, OH....................440-323-3211
Liberty Engineering Co
 Roscoe, IL....................877-623-9065
Lyco Manufacturing
 Wausau, WI...................715-845-7867
Lyco Wausau
 Wausau, WI...................715-845-7867
Marlen
 Riverside, MO.................913-888-3333
Marlow Watson Inc
 Wilmington, MA...............800-282-8823
MBC Food Machinery Corp
 Hackensack, NJ 201-489-7000
Met-Pro Corp
 Owosso, MI. 800-392-7621
Midwest Stainless
 Menomonie, WI 715-235-5472
Moyno
 Springfield, OH................937-327-3111
Murzan Inc
 Peachtree Cor, GA 770-448-0583
Oerlikon Leybold Vacuum
 Export, PA....................724-327-5700
Pacer Pumps
 Lancaster, PA 800-233-3861
Pacific Pneumatics
 Rancho Cucamonga, CA 800-221-0961
Pacific Process Technology
 La Jolla, CA 858-551-3298
Piab Vacuum Products
 Hingham, MA.................800-321-7422
Polar Process
 Plattsville, ON.................877-896-8077
Preferred Machining Corporation
 Englewood, CO. 303-761-1535
Prince Industries Inc
 Murrayville, GA 800-441-3303
Raque Food Systems
 Louisville, KY 502-267-9641
Redi-Call Inc
 Reno, NV 800-648-1849
Reiser
 Canton, MA 734-821-1290
Rheo-Tech
 Gurnee, IL 847-367-1557
Rieke Packaging Systems
 Auburn, IN 260-925-3700
Roto-Jet Pump
 Salt Lake City, UT 801-359-8731
Seepex Inc
 Enon, OH 800-695-3659
Server Products Inc
 Richfield, WI 800-558-8722
SHURflo
 Costa Mesa, CA 800-854-3218
Sine Pump
 Arvada, CO...................888-504-8301
Special Products
 Springfield, MO 417-881-6114
Stainless Products
 Somers, WC 800-558-9446

TDH
Sand Springs, OK 888-251-7961
Top Line Process Equipment Company
Bradford, PA 800-458-6095
Tuchenhagen North America
Portland, ME 207-797-9500
Valvinox
Iberville, QC 450-346-1981
Walton's Inc
Wichita, KS 800-835-2832
Waukesha Cherry-Burrell
Louisville, KY 502-491-4310
Waukesha Cherry-Burrell
Louisville, KY 800-252-5200
WCB Ice Cream
Philadelphia, PA 215-425-4320
Wilden Pump & Engineering LLC
Grand Terrace, CA 909-422-1700

Viscous Products

Invensys APV Products
Houston, TX 713-329-1600
John Crane Mechanical Sealing Devices
Chicago, IL
Murzan Inc
Peachtree Cor, GA 770-448-0583
PCM Delasco Inc
Houston, TX 713-896-4888
Polar Process
Plattsville, ON 877-896-8077
Precision Plus
Sanborn, NY 800-526-2707
Qualtech
Quebec, QC 888-339-3801
Raque Food Systems
Louisville, KY 502-267-9641
Reiser
Canton, MA 734-821-1290
Standard Pump
Auburn, GA 866-558-8611
Sundyne Corp
Arvada, CO 303-425-0800
Warren Rupp Inc
Mansfield, OH 419-524-8388

Road Plates

Slip Not
Detroit, MI .800-754-7668

Scales

Beam

Fairbanks Scales
Overland Park, KS 800-451-4107
Q A Supplies LLC
Norfolk, VA 800-472-7205
Vande Berg SCALES/Vbs Inc
Sioux Center, IA 712-722-1181

Butchers'

Acme Scale Co
San Leandro, CA 888-638-5040
Arkfeld Mfg & Distributing Co
Norfolk, NE 800-533-0676
Exact Equipment Corporation
Morrisville, PA 215-295-2000
Fairbanks Scales
Overland Park, KS 800-451-4107
Mandeville Company
Minneapolis, MN 800-328-8490
Marel Food Systems, Inc.
Lenexa, KS .913-888-9110
Q A Supplies LLC
Norfolk, VA 800-472-7205
Vande Berg SCALES/Vbs Inc
Sioux Center, IA 712-722-1181

Computing, Weighing

Acme Scale Co
San Leandro, CA 888-638-5040
Automated Packaging Systems
Streetsboro, OH 800-527-0733
Avery Weigh-Tronix
Fairmont, MN 877-368-2039
Avery Weigh-Tronix LLC
Fairmont, MN 800-368-2039

Bizerba USA
Piscataway, NJ 732-565-6000
Brechbuhler Scales
Canton, OH 330-453-2424
Browne & Company
Markham, ON 905-475-6104
Bunzl Processor Distribution LLC
Riverside, MO 816-448-4300
Cardinal Scale Mfg Co
Webb City, MO 800-441-4237
Detecto Scale Co
Webb City, MO 800-641-2008
Emery Winslow Scale Co
Seymour, CT 203-881-9333
Exact Equipment Corporation
Morrisville, PA 215-295-2000
Fairbanks Scales
Overland Park, KS 800-451-4107
Gainco Inc
Gainesville, GA 800-467-2828
Ilapak Inc
Newtown, PA 215-579-2900
Iman Pack
Westland, MI 800-810-4626
Industrial Laboratory Eqpt Co
Charlotte, NC 704-357-3930
Intercomp
Hamel, MN 800-328-3336
IWS Scales
San Diego, CA 800-881-9755
Key-Pak Machines
Lebanon, NJ 908-236-2111
Kisco Manufacturing
Port Alberni, BC 604-823-7456
Mandeville Company
Minneapolis, MN 800-328-8490
Mettler-Toledo, LLC
Columbus, OH 800-638-8537
Q A Supplies LLC
Norfolk, VA 800-472-7205
Si-Lodec
Tukwila, WA 800-255-8274
Sig Pack
Oakland, CA 800-824-3245
Sterling Scale Co
Southfield, MI 800-331-9931
Taylor Precision Products
Oak Brook, IL 866-843-3905
Thermo BLH
Canton, MA 781-821-2000
Tridyne Process Systems
South Burlington, VT 802-863-6873
Vande Berg SCALES/Vbs Inc
Sioux Center, IA 712-722-1181
Weigh Right Automatic Scale Co
Joliet, IL 800-571-0249
Yamato Corporation
Colorado Springs, CO. 800-538-1762

Counter

Acme Scale Co
San Leandro, CA. 888-638-5040
Action Packaging Automation
Roosevelt, NJ 800-241-2724
Automated Packaging Systems
Streetsboro, OH 800-527-0733
Detecto Scale Co
Webb City, MO 800-641-2008
Fairbanks Scales
Overland Park, KS 800-451-4107
Iman Pack
Westland, MI. 800-810-4626
Industrial Laboratory Eqpt Co
Charlotte, NC 704-357-3930
Mettler-Toledo, LLC
Columbus, OH 800-638-8537
NJM/CLI
Pointe Claire, QC 514-630-6990
Q A Supplies LLC
Norfolk, VA. 800-472-7205
Vande Berg SCALES/Vbs Inc
Sioux Center, IA 712-722-1181
Yamato Corporation
Colorado Springs, CO. 800-538-1762

Fluid, Liquid, Weighing

APEC
Lake Odessa, MI. 616-374-1000
Fairbanks Scales
Overland Park, KS 800-451-4107

Fuller Weighing Systems
Columbus, OH 614-882-8121
Industrial Laboratory Eqpt Co
Charlotte, NC 704-357-3930
Magnetic Products Inc
Highland, MI. 800-544-5930
Sartorius Corp
Edgewood, NY 800-635-2906
Thermo BLH
Canton, MA 781-821-2000
Vande Berg SCALES/Vbs Inc
Sioux Center, IA 712-722-1181
Yamato Corporation
Colorado Springs, CO. 800-538-1762

Screening

Manufacturing

ANKOM Technology
Macedon, NY 315-986-8090
Buffalo Wire Works Co Inc
Buffalo, NY. 800-828-7028

Scrubbers

Auto Scrubbing & Burnishing

Surtec Inc
Tracy, CA .800-877-6330

Shelves

Refrigerator & Stove

Bmh Equipment Inc
Sacramento, CA 800-350-8828
E-Z Shelving Systems Inc
Shawnee, KS. 800-353-1331
FFR Merchandising Inc
Twinsburg, OH 800-422-2547
G.F. Frank & Sons
Fairfield, OH. 513-870-9075
Grillco Inc
Aurora, IL .800-644-0067
Kaines West Michigan Co
Ludington, MI. 231-845-1281
Kason Industries
Newnan, GA 770-254-0553
Marlin Steel Wire Products
Baltimore, MD 877-762-7546
Metro Corporation
Wilkes Barre, PA. 800-992-1776
Midwest Wire Specialties
Chicago, IL 800-238-0228
Olson Wire Products Co
Baltimore, MD 410-242-7900
Pacific Northwest Wire Works
Dupont, WA 800-222-7699
Princeton Shelving
Cedar Rapids, IA. 319-369-0355
SSW Holding Co Inc
Elizabethtown, KY 270-769-5526
Straits Steel & Wire Co
Ludington, MI. 231-843-3416
Superior Products Company
Saint Paul, MN 800-328-9800
Triple-A Manufacturing Company
Toronto, ON 800-786-2238
Wald Wire & Mfg Co
Oshkosh, WI 800-236-0053

Sizers

Andgar Corp
Ferndale, WA 360-366-9900
Bepex International LLC
Minneapolis, MN 800-607-2470
Brown International Corp LLC
Winter Haven, FL 863-299-2111
Carter-Day International Inc
Minneapolis, MN 763-571-1000
Durand-Wayland Inc
Lagrange, GA 800-241-2308
Glen Mills Inc.
Clifton, NJ. 973-777-0777
Harold F Haines Manufacturing Inc
Presque Isle, ME 207-762-1411
Hosokawa/Bepex Corporation
Santa Rosa, CA 707-586-6000

Kerian Machines Inc
  Grafton, ND 701-352-0480
Lewis M Carter Mfg Co Inc
  Donalsonville, GA 800-332-8232
MAF Industries Inc
  Traver, CA 559-897-2905
Southern Ag Co Inc
  Blakely, GA...................229-723-4262
Southern Automatics
  Lakeland, FL..................800-441-4604
Suffolk Iron Works Inc
  Suffolk, VA...................757-539-2353
Tri-Pak Machinery Inc
  Harlingen, TX.................956-423-5140

Stacking

Anver Corporation
  Hudson, MA 800-654-3500
Architecture Plus Intl Inc
  Rocky Point, FL...............813-281-9299
Bmh Equipment Inc
  Sacramento, CA...............800-350-8828
C.J. Machine
  Fridley, MN...................763-767-4630
Food Equipment Manufacturing Company
  Bedford Heights, OH..........216-672-5859
Gbn Machine & Engineering
  Woodford, VA.................800-446-9871
Graybill Machines Inc
  Lititz, PA....................717-626-5221
Kisters Kayat
  Sarasota, FL..................386-424-0101
Lift Rite
  Mississauga, ON..............905-456-2603
Packaging Systems Intl
  Denver, CO...................303-244-9000
Peerless Food Equipment
  Sidney, OH...................937-492-4158
Planet Products Corp
  Blue Ash, OH.................513-984-5544
Roberts Poly Pro Inc
  Charlotte, NC.................800-269-7409
Vertical Systems Intl
  Lakeside Park, KY.............859-485-9650

Steam Generators

AERCO International Inc
  Blauvelt, NY..................800-526-0288
Direct Fire Technical
  Benbrook, TX.................888-920-2468
Electro-Steam Generator Corp
  Rancocas, NJ.................866-617-0764
PVI Industries LLC
  Fort Worth, TX...............800-784-8326
Vapor Power Intl LLC
  Franklin Park, IL.............888-874-9020

Steam Tables

Allstrong Restaurant Eqpt Inc
  South El Monte, CA...........800-933-8913
Caselites
  Hialeah, FL...................305-819-7766
Craig Manufacturing
  Irvington, NJ.................800-631-7936
Custom Diamond Intl.
  Laval, QC....................800-326-5926
Delfield Co
  Mt Pleasant, MI..............800-733-8821
Den Mar Corp
  North Dartmouth, MA.........508-999-3295
Duke Manufacturing Co
  St Louis, MO.................800-735-3853
Dunhill Food Equipment Corporation
  Armonk, NY..................800-847-4206
Habco
  Concord, CA.................925-682-6203
Hot Food Boxes
  Mooresville, IN..............800-733-8073
Institutional Equipment Inc
  Bolingbrook, IL..............630-771-0990
LA Rosa Refrigeration & Equip
  Detroit, MI..................800-527-6723
Lambertson Industries Inc
  Sparks, NV..................800-548-3324
Lazy Man Inc
  Belvidere, NJ................800-475-1950
Leedal Inc
  Northbrook, IL...............847-498-0111

M&S Manufacturing
  Arnold, MO..................636-464-2739
Mayekawa USA, Inc.
  Chicago, IL..................773-516-5070
Newell Brands
  Atlanta, GA
Professional Bakeware Company
  Willis, TX....................800-440-9547
Randell Manufacturing Unified Brands
  Weidman, MI.................888-994-7636
Reliable Food Service Equipment
  Concord, ON.................416-738-6840
Rexcraft Fine Chafers
  Long Island City, NY..........888-739-2723
Superior Products Company
  Saint Paul, MN...............800-328-9800
Supreme Metal
  Alpharetta, GA...............800-645-2526
Update International
  Vernon, CA...................800-747-7124
West Metals
  London, ON..................800-300-6667

Systems

Check Weighing

Cintex of America
  Carol Stream, IL..............800-424-6839
Gainco Inc
  Gainesville, GA...............800-467-2828
New-Ma Co. Llc
  Grand Rapids, MI.............616-942-5500
SICK Inc
  Bloomington, MN.............800-325-7425
Thompson Scale Co
  Houston, TX..................713-932-9071

Chemical Dispensing & Feed

Solvox Manufacturing Company
  Milwaukee, WI...............414-774-5664

Cost

Berg Co
  Monona, WI..................608-221-4281
InFood Corporation
  Evanston, IL..................773-338-8485

Metal & Contamination Detection

Cintex of America
  Carol Stream, IL..............800-424-6839
Loma Systems
  Carol Stream, IL..............800-872-5662

Mist Collection

AGET Manufacturing Co
  Adrian, MI...................517-263-5781

Packaging

Advance Weight Systems Inc
  Grafton, OH..................440-926-3691
AGA Gas
  Cleveland, OH...............216-642-6600
Alfa Systems Inc
  Westfield, NJ.................908-654-0255
Bradman Lake Inc
  Rock Hill, SC.................803-366-3688
California Vibratory Feeders
  Anaheim, CA.................800-354-0972
Campbell Wrapper Corporation
  De Pere, WI..................920-983-7100
Creative Foam Corp
  Fenton, MI...................810-629-4149
Indeco Products Inc
  San Marcos, TX..............888-246-3326
New-Ma Co. Llc
  Grand Rapids, MI.............616-942-5500
Niro
  Hudson, WI..................715-386-9371
Pa R Systems Inc
  St Paul, MN..................800-464-1320
Palace Packaging Machines Inc
  Downingtown, PA.............610-873-7252
Parish Manufacturing Inc
  Indianapolis, IN..............800-592-2268
Promarks
  Ontario, CA..................909-923-3888

Raque Food Systems
  Louisville, KY................502-267-9641
Reiser
  Canton, MA..................734-821-1290
Schroeder Machine
  San Marcos, CA..............760-591-9733
Sertapak Packaging Corporation
  Woodstock, ON...............800-265-1162
SIG Combibloc USA, Inc.
  Chester, PA..................610-546-4200
Simplimatic Automation
  Forest, VA...................800-294-2003
Somerville Packaging
  Toronto, ON.................416-754-7228
Stock America Inc
  Grafton, WI..................262-375-4100
TNA Packaging Solutions
  Coppell, TX..................972-462-6500

Pricing

Astoria Laminations
  St Clair Shores, MI...........800-526-7325
Garvey Products
  West Chester, OH............800-543-1908
L.A. Darling Co., LLC
  Paragould, AR................800-682-5730
Stratecon International Consultants
  Winston Salem, NC...........336-768-6808

Process & Production

Ace Manufacturing
  Cincinnati, OH...............800-653-5692
All Fill Inc
  Exton, PA....................800-334-1529
ANKOM Technology
  Macedon, NY................315-986-8090
Cog-Veyor Systems, Inc.
  Woodbridge, Ontario, ON......888-337-2358
Dennsi Group
  Springfield, MA..............413-737-1353
F R Drake Co
  Waynesboro, VA..............540-949-6215
Gainco Inc
  Gainesville, GA...............800-467-2828
Newtech Inc
  Randolph, VT................800-210-2361
Reiser
  Canton, MA..................734-821-1290
Spray Dynamics LTD
  St Clair, MO..................800-260-7366
Strongarm
  Horsham, PA................215-443-3400

Reverse Osmosis

Aquathin Corporation
  Pompano Beach, FL...........800-462-7634
Culligan Company
  Northbrook, IL...............877-530-2676
Ecodyne Water Treatment, LLC
  Naperville, IL................800-228-9326
Enting Water Conditioning Inc
  Moraine, OH.................800-735-5100
Hungerford & Terry
  Clayton, NJ..................856-881-3200
Hydropure Water Treatment Co
  Coral Springs, FL.............800-753-1547
Kiss International/Di-tech Systems
  Vista, CA....................800-527-5477
Multiplex Co Inc
  Sellersburg, IN...............800-787-8880
Pacific Process Technology
  La Jolla, CA..................858-551-3298
Thomas Technical Svc
  Neillsville, WI................715-743-4666
Water & Power Technologies
  Salt Lake City, UT............888-271-3295
Waterlink/Sanborn Technologies
  Canton, OH..................800-343-3381

Skids

Relco Unisystems Corp
  Willmar, MN.................320-231-2210

Tubularaseptic Processing

Excel-A-Tec Inc
  Brookfield, WI...............262-252-3600

Valve Control

Andersen 2000
Peachtree City, GA 800-241-5424

Vision Verification

Cintex of America
Carol Stream, IL 800-424-6839
Cotton Goods Mfg Co
Chicago, IL 773-265-0088
SICK Inc
Bloomington, MN 800-325-7425

X-ray Contaminant Detection

Cintex of America
Carol Stream, IL 800-424-6839

Zipper Application

Com-Pac International Inc
Carbondale, IL 888-297-2824
Zip-Pak
Manteno, IL 815-468-6500

Tabletop Supplies

A1 Tablecloth Co
South Hackensack, NJ 800-727-8987
Abco International
Melville, NY 866-240-2226
Adcapitol
Monroe, NC. 800-868-7111
AJM Packaging Corporation
Bloomfield Hills, MI 248-901-0040
Amcel
Watertown, MA. 800-225-7992
Anchor Hocking Operating Co
Lancaster, OH 800-562-7511
Artex International
Highland, IL 618-654-2113
Arthur Corporation
Huron, OH. 419-433-7202
Atlantis Industries Inc
Milton, DE 302-684-8542
AWP Butcher Block Inc
Horse Cave, KY 800-764-7840
Babco International, Inc
Tucson, AZ 520-628-7596
Benner China & Glassware Inc
Jacksonville, FL 904-733-4620
Best Buy Uniforms
Homestead, PA 800-345-1924
Bib Pak
Racine, WI 262-633-5803
Bright of America
Summersville, WV 304-872-3000
Brooklace
Oshkosh, WI. 800-572-4552
Browne & Company
Markham, ON 905-475-6104
Buffalo China
Buffalo, NY. 716-824-8515
C R Mfg
Waverly, NE 877-789-5844
Carnegie Textile Co
Cleveland, OH 800-633-4136
Carthage Cup Company
Longview, TX. 903-238-9833
Ceramica De Espana
Doral, FL. 305-597-9161
Chef Specialties
Smethport, PA. 800-440-2433
China Lenox Incorporated
Bristol, PA. 267-525-7800
Chinet Company
Winter Springs, FL 800-539-3726
Chinet Company
Laguna Niguel, CA 949-348-1711
City Grafx
Eugene, OR. 800-258-2489
Colonial Paper Company
Silver Springs, FL. 352-622-4171
Creative Converting Inc
Clintonville, WI 800-826-0418
Custom Table Pads
St Paul, MN. 800-325-4643
Cyclamen Collection
Oakland, CA 510-434-7620
Dansk International Designs
Bristol, PA. 914-697-6400

Dart Canada Inc.
Toronto, ON 800-465-9696
Dart Container Corp.
Mason, MI. 800-248-5960
De Ster Corporation
Atlanta, GA 800-237-8270
Delco Tableware
Port Washington, NY 800-221-9557
Delfin Design & Mfg
Rancho Sta Marg, CA. 800-354-7919
Design Specialties Inc
Hamden, CT 800-999-1584
Dorado Carton Company
Dorado, PR 787-796-1670
Drapes 4 Show
Sylmar, CA 800-525-7469
Durango-Georgia Paper
Tampa, FL 813-286-2718
Dynynstyl
Delray Beach, FL 800-774-7895
Eastern Tabletop Mfg
Brooklyn, NY 888-422-4142
Eide Industries Inc
Cerritos, CA 800-422-6827
Elrene Home Fashions
New York, NY 212-213-0425
Erving Industries
Erving, MA 413-422-2700
Fabri-Kal Corp
Kalamazoo, MI 800-888-5054
Fenton Art Glass Company
Williamstown, WV 800-933-6766
Filet Menu
Los Angeles, CA. 310-202-8000
Filmpack Plastic Corporation
Dayton, NJ 732-329-6523
Flamingo Food Service Products
Hialeah, FL 800-432-8269
Fonda Group
Goshen, IN 574-534-2515
Fort James Canada
Toronto, ON 416-784-1621
Four M Manufacturing Group
San Jose, CA 408-998-1141
Gaetano America
El Monte, CA 626-442-2858
Genpak
Peterborough, ON 800-461-1995
Genpak LLC
Charlotte, NC 800-626-6695
Georgia Pacific
Green Bay, WI. 920-435-8821
Gourmet Table Skirts
Houston, TX 800-527-0440
Grand Silver Company
Bronx, NY. 718-585-1930
H.F. Coors China Company
New Albany, MS. 800-782-6677
Hal-One Plastics
Olathe, KS. 800-626-5784
Hall China Co
East Liverpool, OH 800-445-4255
Hartstone Pottery Inc
Zanesville, OH 740-452-9999
Have Our Plastic Inc
Mississauga, ON 800-263-5995
Hilden Halifax
South Boston, VA 800-431-2514
Hoffman & Levy Inc Tasseldepot
Deerfield Beach, FL 954-698-0001
Hoffmaster Group Inc
Oshkosh, WI 800-327-9774
Hoffmaster Group Inc
Oshkosh, WI 800-367-2877
Hoffmaster Group Inc.
Oshkosh, WI 800-558-9300
Hollowick Inc
Manlius, NY 800-367-3015
Homer Laughlin China Co
Newell, WV 800-452-4462
HPI North America/ Plastics
Eagan, MN 800-752-7462
HPI North America/Plastics
Chicago, IL 800-327-3534
Image Plastics
Houston, TX 800-289-2811
International Paper Co.
Memphis, TN
J. James
Brooklyn, NY 718-384-6144
Jack the Ripper Table Skirting
Stafford, TX 800-331-7831

Jarden Home Brands
Cloquet, MN 218-879-6700
JBC Plastics
St Louis, MO. 877-834-5526
Jet Plastica Industries
Hatfield, PA
Jones-Zylon Co
West Lafayette, OH. 800-848-8160
K-C Products Company
Van Nuys, CA 818-267-1600
Kenro
Fredonia, WI 262-692-2411
Klever Kuvers
Pasadena, CA 626-355-8441
Kuepper Favor Company, Celebrate Line
Peru, IN 800-321-5823
Libbey Inc.
Toledo, OH 419-325-2100
Libby Canada
Mississauga, ON 905-607-8280
Liberty Ware LLC
Clearfield, UT 888-500-5885
Louis Jacobs & Son
Brooklyn, NY 718-782-3500
Mack-Chicago Corporation
Chicago, IL 800-992-6225
Majestic
Bridgeport, CT 203-367-7900
Marston Manufacturing
Cleveland, OH 216-587-3400
Mason Candlelight Company
New Albany, MS. 800-556-2766
Mastercraft
Appleton, WI 800-242-6602
Masterpiece Crystal
Jane Lew, WV. 304-884-7841
Metal Master Sales Corp
Glendale Heights, IL. 800-488-8729
Michael Leson Dinnerware
Youngstown, OH 800-821-3541
Milliken & Co
Spartanburg, SC 864-503-2020
Mr Ice Bucket
New Brunswick, NJ 732-545-0420
Novelty Crystal
Long Island City, NY 800-622-0250
Olde Country Reproductions Inc
York, PA 800-358-3997
Oneida Food Service
Columbus, OH 800-828-7033
Oneida LTD Silversmiths
Oneida, NY 888-263-7195
OWD
Tupper Lake, NY 800-836-1693
Palmland Paper Company
Fort Lauderdale, FL 800-266-9067
Paradise Products
El Cerrito, CA 800-227-1092
Party Linens
Chicago, IL 800-281-0003
Party Yards
Casselberry, FL 877-501-4400
Penley Corporation
West Paris, ME 800-368-6449
Philmont Manufacturing Co.
Englewood, NJ 888-379-6483
Placemat Printers
Fogelsville, PA 800-628-7746
Plastiques Cascades Group
Montreal, QC 888-703-6515
Potlatch Corp
Spokane, WA. 509-835-1500
Prairie Packaging Inc
Mooresville, NC 704-660-6600
Premier
Cincinnati, OH 800-354-9817
Premier Skirting Products
Lawrence, NY. 800-544-2516
Prestige Skirting & Tablecloths
Orangeburg, NY 800-635-3313
Racket Group
Kansas City, MO. 816-283-0490
Resource One/Resource Two
Reseda, CA 818-343-3451
Rixie Paper Products Inc
Pottstown, PA 800-377-2692
Ronnie's Ceramic Company
San Francisco, CA 800-888-8218
Royal Paper Products
Coatesville, PA 800-666-6655
Royal Prestige Health Moguls
Westbury, NY 888-802-7433

Rubbermaid Canada
Oakville, ON 905-279-1010
Sabert Corp
Sayreville, NJ 800-722-3781
Salem China Company
Salem, OH .330-337-8771
Sani-Top Products
De Leon Springs, FL 800-874-6094
SCA Tissue
Philadelphia, PA 866-722-8675
Scan Group
Appleton, WI 920-730-9150
Sims Superior Seating
Locust Grove, GA 800-729-9178
Smith-Lee Company
Oshkosh, WI 800-327-9774
Snap Drape Inc
Carrollton, TX 800-527-5147
Solo Cup Company
Lake Forest, IL
Something Different Linen
Clifton, NJ 800-422-2180
Spir-It/Zoo Piks
Andover, MA 800-343-0996
Spirit Foodservice, Inc.
Andover, MA 800-343-0996
Stanley Roberts
Piscataway, NJ 973-778-5900
Sterling Paper Company
Ohio, PA 800-282-1124
Stevens Linen Association
Dudley, MA .800-772-9269
Straubel Company
De Pere, WI 888-336-1412
Superior Linen & Work Wear
Kansas City, MO 800-798-7987
Superior Products Company
Saint Paul, MN 800-328-9800
Table De France: North America
New Brunswick, NJ 888-680-4616
Tag-Trade Associated Group
Chicago, IL .800-621-8350
Tango Shatterproof Drinkware
Walpole, MA 888-898-2646
Tar-Hong MELAMINE USA
City of Industry, CA 626-935-1612
TEMP-TECH Company
Springfield, MA 800-343-5579
Townfood Equipment Corp
Brooklyn, NY 800-221-5032
Tradeco International Corp
Addison, IL .800-628-3738
Traex
Dane, WI 800-356-8006
Uhtamaki Foods Services
Waterville, ME 207-873-3351
Ullman, Shapiro & UllmanLLP
New York, NY 212-755-0299
Ultimate Textile
Paterson, NJ 973-523-5866
Vertex China
Pomona, CA 800-483-7839
Vicmore Manufacturing Company
Brooklyn, NY 800-458-8663
Victoria Porcelain
Miami, FL 888-593-2353
Waddington North America
Chelmsford, MA 888-962-2877
Wiltec
Leominster, MA 978-537-1497
Wilton Armetale
Mt Joy, PA 800-779-4586
Wishbone Utensil Tableware Line
Wheat Ridge, CO 866-266-5928
WNA
Chattanooga, TN 800-404-9318
Wna Comet West Inc
City of Industry, CA 800-225-0939
Xtreme Beverages, LLC
Dana Point, CA 949-495-7929

Tea Industry

Washington Frontier
Grandview, WA 509-469-7662

Timers

Alarm Controls Corp
Deer Park, NY 800-645-5538
Amco Metals Indl
City of Industry, CA 626-855-2550

American Time & Signal Co
Dassel, MN .800-328-8996
AMETEK National Controls Corp
West Chicago, IL 800-323-5293
Automatic Timing & Controls
Newell, WV .800-727-5646
Chaney Instrument Co
Lake Geneva, WI 800-777-0565
Coley Industries
Wayland, NY 716-728-2390
Control Products Inc
Chanhassen, MN 800-947-9098
Cramer Company
South Windsor, CT 877-684-6464
Dayton Marking Devices Company
Dayton, OH .937-432-0285
Elreha Controls Corporation
St Petersburg, FL 727-327-6236
ERC Parts Inc
Kennesaw, GA 800-241-6880
Gralab Instruments
Centerville, OH 800-876-8353
M.H. Rhodes Cramer
South Windsor, CT 877-684-6464
National Time Recording Eqpt
New York, NY 212-227-3310
Pelouze Scale Company
Bridgeview, IL 800-323-8363
Prince Castle Inc
Carol Stream, IL 800-722-7853
R.P. Childs Stamp Company
Ludlow, MA .413-733-1211
SCK Direct Inc
Stratford, CT 800-327-8766
Superior Products Company
Saint Paul, MN 800-328-9800
Wilkens-Anderson Co
Chicago, IL .800-847-2222

Tubing

Plastic

Arbee Transparent Inc
Elk Grove Vlg, IL 800-642-2247
Emco Industrial Plastics
Cedar Grove, NJ 800-292-9906
Flexo Transparent Inc
Buffalo, NY .877-993-5396
Hall Manufacturing Co
Ringwood, NJ 973-962-6022
Home Plastics Inc
Des Moines, IA 515-265-2562
Legacy Plastics
Henderson, KY 270-827-1318
M S Plastics & Packaging Inc
Butler, NJ 800-593-1802
Roechling Engineered Plastics
Gastonia, NC 800-541-4419
Rubber Fab Molding & Gasket
Sparta, NJ .866-442-2959
Target Industries
North Salt Lake, UT 866-617-2253
Trident Plastics
Ivyland, PA .800-222-2318
Wilkens-Anderson Co
Chicago, IL .800-847-2222

Stainless Steel

Accutek Packaging Equipment
Vista, CA 800-989-1828
Arc Machines Inc
Pacoima, CA 818-896-9556
Baldewein Company
Lake Forrest, IL 800-424-5544
Damascus/Bishop Tube Company
Greenville, PA 724-646-1500
J & L Honing
St Francis, WI 800-747-9501
Jacob Tubing LP
Memphis, TN 901-566-1110
L&S Products
Coldwater, MI 517-279-9526
L.C. Thompson Company
Kenosha, WI 800-558-4018
Liburdi Group of Companies
Mooresville, NC 800-533-9353
Melrose Displays
Passaic, NJ .973-471-7700
Northland Process Piping
Isle, MN 320-679-2119

Pinquist Tool & Die Company
Brooklyn, NY 800-752-0414
Plymouth Tube Company
East Troy, WI 262-642-8201
Rath Manufacturing Company
Janesville, WI 800-367-7284
Robert-James Sales
Buffalo, NY .800-777-1325
Spencer Turbine Co
Windsor, CT 800-232-4321
Sterling Process Engineering
Columbus, OH 800-783-7875
Sudmo North America, Inc
Machesney Park, IL 800-218-3915
T-Drill Industries Inc
Norcross, GA 800-554-2730
Top Line Process Equipment Company
Bradford, PA 800-458-6095
United Industries Inc
Beloit, WI 608-365-8891
Valvinox
Iberville, QC 450-346-1981

Unscramblers

A.K. Robins
Baltimore, MD 800-486-9656
BEVCO
Canada, BC 800-663-0090
Chase-Logeman Corp
Greensboro, NC 336-665-0754
ELF Machinery
La Porte, IN .800-328-0466
Fogg Filler Co
Holland, MI .616-786-3644
Inline Filling Systems
Venice, FL 941-486-8800
John R Nalbach Engineering Co
Countryside, IL 708-579-9100
JW Leser Company
Los Angeles, CA 323-731-4173
KAPS All Packaging
Riverhead, NY 631-727-0300
Kinsley Inc
Doylestown, PA 800-414-6664
Leader Engineering-Fab Inc
Napoleon, OH 419-592-0008
Leeds Conveyor Manufacturer Company
Guilford, CT .800-724-1088
Mcbrady Engineering Co
Rockdale, IL 815-744-8900
New England Machinery Inc
Bradenton, FL 941-755-5550
Norwalt Design Inc
Randolph, NJ 973-927-3200
Omega Design Corp
Exton, PA 800-346-0191
Pace Packaging Corp
Fairfield, NJ .800-867-2726
Palace Packaging Machines Inc
Downingtown, PA 610-873-7252
Pearson Packaging Systems
Spokane, WA 800-732-7766
Perl Packaging Systems
Middlebury, CT 800-864-2853
Simplex Filler Co
Napa, CA 800-796-7539
Spurgeon Co
Ferndale, MI 800-396-2554
Stiles Enterprises Inc
Rockaway, NJ 800-325-4232
Weigh Right Automatic Scale Co
Joliet, IL 800-571-0249

Valves

Advance Fittings Corp
Elkhorn, WI .262-723-6699
Anver Corporation
Hudson, MA 800-654-3500
APV Americas
Delavan, WI 800-252-5200
Archon Industries Inc
Suffern, NY .800-554-1394
Armstrong Hot Water
Three Rivers, MI 269-279-3602
Baldewein Company
Lake Forrest, IL 800-424-5544
Boston Gear
Boston, MA .888-999-9860
Bradford A Ducon Company
Pewaukee, WI 800-789-1718

C & D Valve Mfg Co
Oklahoma City, OK 800-654-9233
C&R Refrigation Inc,
Center, TX. 800-438-6182
C.F.F. Stainless Steels
Hamilton, ON 800-263-4511
Cashco Inc
Ellsworth, KS 785-472-4461
Chlorinators Inc
Stuart, FL 800-327-9761
Cincinnati Industrial Machry
Mason, OH. 800-677-0076
Cipriani
Rancho Sta Marg, CA 949-589-3978
Clark-Cooper Division   Magnatrol Valve Corporation
Cinnaminson, NJ. 856-829-4580
Conbraco Industries Inc
Matthews, NC 704-841-6000
Delavan Spray Technologies
Bamberg, SC 800-982-6943
Doering Co
Clear Lake, MN 320-743-2276
Dormont Manufacturing Co
Export, PA. 800-367-6668
Duplex Mill & Mfg Co
Springfield, OH. 937-325-5555
EVAPCO Inc
Taneytown, MD 410-876-3782
Firematic Sprinkler Devices
Shrewsbury, MA 800-225-7288
Flomatic International
Sellersburg, IN 800-367-4233
Flynn Burner Corporation
New Rochelle, NY 800-643-8910
General Tank
Berwick, PA 800-435-8265
Globe Fire Sprinkler Corp
Standish, MI 800-248-0278
Harris Equipment Corp
Melrose Park, IL 800-365-0315
Hayes & Stolz Indl Mfg LTD
Fort Worth, TX 800-725-7272
Hayward Industries Inc
Clemmons, NC 336-712-9900
Heuft USA Inc
Downers Grove, IL 630-968-9011
Hi-Temp Inc
Tuscumbia, AL 800-239-5066
Hilliard Corp
Elmira, NY 607-733-7121
Holland Applied Technologies
Burr Ridge, IL. 630-325-5130
Hydra-Flex Inc
Livonia, MI 800-234-0832
IMI Precision Engineering
Brookville, OH 937-833-4033
Invensys APV Products
Houston, TX 713-329-1600
Josam Co
Michigan City, IN 800-365-6726
K-Tron
Salina, KS 785-825-1611
Kemutec Group Inc
Bristol, PA. 215-788-8013
Kraissl Co Inc
Hackensack, NJ. 800-572-4775
L.C. Thompson Company
Kenosha, WI 800-558-4018
Lumaco Inc
Hackensack, NJ. 800-735-8258
M O Industries Inc
Whippany, NJ 973-386-9228
M-One Specialties
Salt Lake City, UT 800-525-9223
Matcon Americas
Elmhurst, IL. 856-256-1330
Midwest Stainless
Menomonie, WI 715-235-5472
Moyno
Springfield, OH. 937-327-3111
Norgren Inc.
Littleton, CO. 800-514-0129
Northland Process Piping
Isle, MN 320-679-2119
Numatics Inc
Novi, MI 248-596-3200
Parker-Hannifin Corp
Cleveland, OH 800-272-7537
Paxton Corp
Bristol, RI 401-396-9062
PBM Inc
Irwin, PA. 800-967-4PBM

Plast-O-Matic Valves Inc
Cedar Grove, NJ 973-256-9344
Qosina Corporation
Ronkonkoma, NY 631-242-3000
Qualtech
Quebec, QC 888-339-3801
Robert-James Sales
Buffalo, NY. 800-777-1325
Rubber Fab Molding & Gasket
Sparta, NJ 866-442-2959
Rutherford Engineering
Rockford, IL 815-623-2141
Samson Controls
Baytown, TX. 281-383-3677
Sanchelima International
Miami, FL 305-591-4343
SerVend International
Sellersburg, IN 800-367-4233
Shick Esteve
Kansas City, MO 877-744-2587
Special Products
Springfield, MO 417-881-6114
Spraying Systems Company
Wheaton, IL 630-655-5000
Stainless Products
Somers, WC 800-558-9446
Storm Industrial
Shawnee Mission, KS 800-745-7483
Strahman Valves Inc
Bethlehem, PA 877-787-2462
Sudmo North America, Inc
Machesney Park, IL 800-218-3915
TechnipFMC
Houston, TX 218-591-4000
Top Line Process Equipment Company
Bradford, PA 800-458-6095
Tuchenhagen
Columbia, MD 410-910-6000
Tuchenhagen North America
Portland, ME. 207-797-9500
Valvinox
Iberville, QC 450-346-1981
Van Air Systems
Lake City, PA 800-840-9906
Viatec
Victoria, BC 800-942-4702
Viking Corp
Hastings, MI 800-968-9501
Vilter Manufacturing Corporation
Cudahy, WI 414-744-0111
Watts Regulator Co
North Andover, MA 978-688-1811
Waukesha Cherry-Burrell
Louisville, KY 800-252-5200
Waukesha Specialty Company
Darien, WI. 262-724-3700

Water Treatment

Alar Engineering Corp
Mokena, IL 708-479-6100
Alkazone/Better Health Lab
Hackensack, NJ. 800-810-1888
American Ultraviolet Co
Lebanon, IN 800-288-9288
AMSOIL Inc
Superior, WI 715-392-7101
Anderson Chemical Co
Litchfield, MN 320-693-2477
Astro Pure Water
Deerfield Beach, FL 954-422-8966
Babcock & Wilcox MEGTEC
De Pere, WI. 920-336-5715
Bloomfield Industries
St. Louis, MO 888-356-5362
Crane Environmental
Norristown, PA 800-633-7435
Croll-Reynolds Engineering Company
Trumbull, CT 203-371-1983
Culligan Company
Northbrook, IL 877-530-2676
Delta Pure Filtration Corp
Ashland, VA 800-785-9450
Diamond Water Conditioning
Hortonville, WI. 800-236-8931
Eaton Filtration, LLC
Tinton Falls, NJ. 800-859-9212
Enting Water Conditioning Inc
Moraine, OH. 800-735-5100
Everpure, LLC
Hanover Park, IL. 630-307-3000

Filtrine Manufacturing
Keene, NH. 800-930-3367
Freudenberg Nonwovens
Hopkinsville, KY 270-887-5115
G.W. Dahl Company
Greensboro, NC 800-852-4449
Gusmer Enterprises Inc
Fresno, CA 866-213-1131
Hess Machine Intl
Ephrata, PA 800-735-4377
Holland Applied Technologies
Burr Ridge, IL. 630-325-5130
Hungerford & Terry
Clayton, NJ 856-881-3200
Hydromax Inc
Emmitsburg, MD 800-326-0602
Hydropure Water Treatment Co
Coral Springs, FL 800-753-1547
Introdel Products
Itasca, IL 800-323-4772
Jamieson Wellness Inc.
Toronto, ON 800-265-5088
Kinetico
Newbury, OH 440-564-9111
King Bag & Mfg Co
Cincinnati, OH 800-444-5464
Lamports Filter Media
Cleveland, OH 216-881-2050
Miura Boilers
Atlanta, GA 770-916-1695
Moll-Tron
Lakewood, CO 800-525-9494
Optipure
Plano, TX 972-422-1212
Our Name is Mud
New York, NY 877-683-7867
Parkson Corp
Vernon Hills, IL 847-816-3700
PURA
Sun Valley, CA 800-292-7872
RainSoft Water Treatment System
Elk Grove Vlg, IL. 847-437-9400
Refractron Technologies Corp
Newark, NY 315-331-6222
Reynold Water Conditioning
Farmington Hills, MI 800-572-9575
Selecto Scientific
Suwanee, GA 800-635-4017
Sermia International
Blainville, QC 800-567-7483
Star Filters
Timmonsville, SC 800-845-5381
Trisep Corporation
Goleta, CA 805-964-8003
VMC Signs
Victoria, TX 361-575-0548
Water Management Resources
Overton, NV 800-552-5797
Water Sciences Services, Inc.
Jackson, TN 973-584-4131
Watts Premier Inc
Peoria, AZ. 800-752-5582

Coolers

Allied Bakery and Food Service Equipment
Santa Fe Springs, CA 562-945-6506
Baxter Manufacturing Inc
Orting, WA 800-777-2828
DBE Inc
Concord, ON. 800-461-5313
Distillata
Cleveland, OH 800-999-2906
Fred D Pfening Co
Columbus, OH 614-294-5361
Girard Spring Water
North Providence, RI 800-477-9287
Hoshizaki
Worthington, OH. 800-642-1140
Lucks Food Equipment Company
Kent, WA 811-824-0696
Moli-International
Denver, CO 800-525-8468
Oshikiri Corp of America
Philadelphia, PA 215-637-8112
Pavailler Distribution Company
Northvale, NJ 201-767-0766
Perfect Equipment Inc
Gurnee, IL. 800-356-6301
Pro Bake Inc
Twinsburg, OH 800-837-4427

Pro-Flo Products
Cedar Grove, NJ 800-325-1057
Sunroc Corporation
Columbus, OH 800-478-6762

Purifiers

Aquathin Corporation
Pompano Beach, FL 800-462-7634
Astro Pure Water
Deerfield Beach, FL 954-422-8966
Bestech Inc
Pompano Beach, FL 800-977-2378
Diamond Water Conditioning
Hortonville, WI 800-236-8931
Distillata
Cleveland, OH 800-999-2906
Durastill Export Inc
Rockland, MA 800-449-5260
Enting Water Conditioning Inc
Moraine, OH 800-735-5100
Fuller Ultra Violet Corp
Frankfort, IL 815-469-3301
Hydromax Inc
Emmitsburg, MD 800-326-0602
Hydropure Water Treatment Co
Coral Springs, FL 800-753-1547
Joneca Corp
Anaheim, CA 714-993-5997
Kinetico
Newbury, OH 440-564-9111
Kiss International/Di-tech Systems
Vista, CA 800-527-5477
Manhattan Truck Lines
Paterson, NJ 800-370-7627
RainSoft Water Treatment System
Elk Grove Vlg, IL 847-437-9400
Reynold Water Conditioning
Farmington Hills, MI 800-572-9575
Royal Prestige Health Moguls
Westbury, NY 888-802-7433
Ulcra Dynamics
Colmar, PA 800-727-6931
United Industries Group Inc
Lake Forest, CA 949-759-3200
Water & Power Technologies
Salt Lake City, UT 888-271-3295
Watts Premier Inc
Peoria, AZ 800-752-5582

Softeners

Aquathin Corporation
Pompano Beach, FL 800-462-7634
Culligan Company
Northbrook, IL 877-530-2676
Diamond Water Conditioning
Hortonville, WI 800-236-8931
Ecodyne Water Treatment, LLC
Naperville, IL 800-228-9326
Enting Water Conditioning Inc
Moraine, OH 800-735-5100
Hungerford & Terry
Clayton, NJ 856-881-3200
Reynold Water Conditioning
Farmington Hills, MI 800-572-9575

Treatment Systems

A-L-L Magnetics Inc
Anaheim, CA 800-262-4638
ABJ/Sanitaire Corporation
Milwaukee, WI 414-365-2200
Action Engineering
Liburn, GA 800-228-4668
ADI Systems Inc
Fredericton, NB 800-561-2831
Aeration Industries Intl LLC
Chaska, MN 800-328-8287
Aeromix Systems
Minneapolis, MN 800-879-3677
AERTEC
North Andover, MA 978-475-6385
AFL Industries
West Palm Beach, FL 800-807-2709
Alar Engineering Corp
Mokena, IL 708-479-6100
ALCO Designs
Gardena, CA 800-228-2346
Alkazone/Better Health Lab
Hackensack, NJ 800-810-1888

Alkota Cleaning Systems Inc
Alcester, SD 800-255-6823
Alloy Hardfacing & Engineering
Jordan, MN 800-328-8408
American Ultraviolet Co
Lebanon, IN 800-288-9288
Andco Environmental Processes
Amherst, NY 716-691-2100
API Industries
Tulsa, OK 918-664-4010
Applied Membranes
Vista, CA 800-321-9321
Aqua-Aerobic Systems Inc
Loves Park, IL 800-940-5008
Aquathin Corporation
Pompano Beach, FL 800-462-7634
Astro Pure Water
Deerfield Beach, FL 954-422-8966
Atlantic Ultraviolet Corp
Hauppauge, NY 866-958-9085
Ayer Sales Inc
Woburn, MA 800-225-5736
Bestech Inc
Pompano Beach, FL 800-977-2378
Betz Entec
Horsham, PA 800-877-1940
Bio Cide Intl Inc
Norman, OK 800-323-1398
Bioionix Inc
Mc Farland, WI 608-838-0300
Biothane Corporation
Camden, NJ 856-541-3500
BluMetric Environmental Inc.
Ottawa, ON 613-839-3053
Centrisys
Kenosha, WI 262-654-6006
ChemTreat, Inc.
Glen Allen, VA 800-648-4579
Chicago Conveyor Corporation
Addison, IL 630-543-6300
Chlorinators Inc
Stuart, FL 800-327-9761
Clean Water Systems
Klamath Falls, OR 866-273-9993
Clean Water Technology
Los Angeles, CA. 310-380-4658
Conquest International LLC
Plainville, KS 785-434-2483
Continental Industrial Supply
South Pasadena, FL. 727-341-1100
Corp Somat
Lancaster, PA 800-237-6628
Crane Environmental
Norristown, PA 800-633-7435
Culligan Company
Northbrook, IL 877-530-2676
Diamond Water Conditioning
Hortonville, WI. 800-236-8931
Discovery Chemical
Marietta, GA 800-973-9881
Durastill Export Inc
Rockland, MA. 800-449-5260
Eaton Filtration, LLC
Tinton Falls, NJ 800-859-9212
Ecodyne Water Treatment, LLC
Naperville, IL 800-228-9326
Enting Water Conditioning Inc
Moraine, OH. 800-735-5100
Equipment Enterprises
Charlotte, NC 800-221-3681
ESD Waste2water Inc
Ocala, FL. 800-277-3279
Eutek Systems
Hillsboro, OR 503-601-0843
Everfilt Corp
Mira Loma, CA. 800-360-8380
Evoqua Water Technologies
Thomasville, GA. 800-841-1550
Filtrine Manufacturing
Keene, NH. 800-930-3367
FRC Environmental
Gainesville, GA 770-534-3681
Global Water Group Inc
Dallas, TX. 214-678-9866
Greenbridge
Mentor, OH. 440-357-1500
Hess Machine Intl
Ephrata, PA 800-735-4377
Hibrett Puratex
Pennsauken, NJ 800-260-5124
Hoshizaki
Worthington, OH. 800-642-1140

Hubbell Electric Heater Co
Stratford, CT. 800-647-3165
Hungerford & Terry
Clayton, NJ 856-881-3200
Hydrite Chemical Co
Brookfield, WI 262-792-1450
HydroCal
Laguna Hills, CA 800-877-0765
Hydromax Inc
Emmitsburg, MD 800-326-0602
Hydropure Water Treatment Co
Coral Springs, FL 800-753-1547
Innova-Tech
Paoli, PA. 800-523-7299
Interlab
The Woodlands, TX 888-876-2844
International Reserve Equipment Corporation
Clarendon Hills, IL. 708-531-0680
Introdel Products
Itasca, IL 800-323-4772
Jamieson Wellness Inc.
Toronto, ON 800-265-5088
Jemolo Enterprises
Porterville, CA 559-784-5566
Kinetico
Newbury, OH 440-564-9111
Kiss International/Di-tech Systems
Vista, CA 800-527-5477
KMT Aqua-Dyne Inc
Baxter Springs, KS 800-826-9274
Komline-Sanderson Engineering
Peapack, NJ. 800-225-5457
Lechler Inc
St Charles, IL 800-777-2926
Little Giant Pump Company
Fort Wayne, IN 260-824-2900
Loprest Co
Rodeo, CA. 888-228-5982
Ludell Manufacturing Co
Milwaukee, WI 800-558-0800
Manhattan Truck Lines
Paterson, NJ 800-370-7627
Membrane System Specialist Inc
Wisconsin Rapids, WI 715-421-2333
Midbrook Inc
Jackson, MI. 800-966-9274
Moll-Tron
Lakewood, CO 800-525-9494
Momar
Atlanta, GA. 800-556-3967
Mountain Safety Research
Seattle, WA. 800-877-9677
Multiplex Co Inc
Sellersburg, IN 800-787-8880
Navy Brand
St Louis, MO. 800-325-3312
Newco Enterprises Inc
St Charles, MO. 800-325-7867
Newtech Inc
Randolph, VT. 800-210-2361
Nijhuis Water Technology
Chicago, IL. 312-466-9900
Nimbus Water Systems
Murrieta, CA. 800-451-9343
Otterbine Barebo Inc
Emmaus, PA. 800-237-8837
Ozotech Inc
Yreka, CA. 530-842-4189
Parkson Corp
Vernon Hills, IL 847-816-3700
Parkson Corporation
Fort Lauderdale, FL 954-974-6610
Pro-Flo Products
Cedar Grove, NJ 800-325-1057
PURA
Sun Valley, CA 800-292-7872
Pure & Secure LLC-Cust Svc
Lincoln, NE. 800-875-5915
Puronics Water Systems Inc
Livermore, CA 925-456-7000
Quality Control Equipment Co
Des Moines, IA. 515-266-2268
RainSoft Water Treatment System
Elk Grove Vlg, IL. 847-437-9400
Reynold Water Conditioning
Farmington Hills, MI 800-572-9575
Rochester Midland Corp
Rochester, NY. 800-836-1627
Ryter Corporation
Saint James, MN. 800-643-2184
Scaltrol Inc
Suwanee, GA. 800-868-0629

Scienco Systems
  Saint Louis, MO 314-621-2536
Sermia International
  Blainville, QC 800-567-7483
Severn Trent Svc
  Fort Washington, PA 215-646-9201
Severn Trent Svc
  Colmar, PA 215-822-2901
Shepard Brothers Co
  La Habra, CA 800-645-3594
Southeastern Filtration Systs
  Canton, GA 800-935-8500
Star Filters
  Timmonsville, SC 800-845-5381
SUEZ Water Technologies & Solutions
  Trevose, PA 866-439-2837

Systems IV
  Chandler, AZ 800-852-4221
Telechem Corp
  Atlanta, GA 800-637-0495
TLB Corporation
  Ellicott, MD 410-773-9443
TRITEN Corporation
  Houston, TX 832-214-5000
Ulcra Dynamics
  Colmar, PA 800-727-6931
United Industries Group Inc
  Lake Forest, CA 949-759-3200
US Filter
  Palm Desert, CA 760-340-0098
US Filter/Continental Water
  San Antonio, TX 800-426-3426

Vulcan Materials Co
  Vestavia, AL 205-298-3000
Wade Manufacturing Company
  Tigard, OR 800-222-7246
Water & Power Technologies
  Salt Lake City, UT 888-271-3295
Water System Group
  Santa Clarita, CA 800-350-9283
Waterlink/Sanborn Technologies
  Canton, OH 800-343-3381
Watts Premier Inc
  Peoria, AZ 800-752-5582
World Water Works
  Elmsford, NY 800-607-7873
Yardney Water Management Syst
  Riverside, CA 800-854-4788

Food Preparation Equipment, Utensils & Cookware

Aluminum Ware

A Legacy Food Svc
Santa Fe Springs, CA 800-848-4440
Advance Tabco
Edgewood, NY 800-645-3166
Alumaworks
Sunny Isle Beach, FL 800-277-7267
C R Mfg
Waverly, NE 877-789-5844
Culinary Depot
Monsey, NY 888-845-8200
Dur-Able Aluminum Corporation
Hoffman Estates, IL 847-843-1100
Econofrost Night Covers
Shawnigan Lake, BC 800-519-1222
H. Yamamoto
Port Washington, NY 718-821-7700
Handi-Foil Corp
Wheeling, IL 847-520-8347
Hillside Metal Ware Company
Union, NJ 908-964-3080
Johnson-Rose Corporation
Lockport, NY 800-456-2055
Lloyd Disher Company
Decatur, IL 217-429-0593
Montebello Packaging
Hawkesbury, ON................. 613-632-7096
Regal Ware Inc
Kewaskum, WI................... 262-626-2121
Vasconia Housewares
San Antonio, TX.................. 800-377-6723
Weavewood, Inc.
Golden Valley, MN 800-367-6460
Wilkinson Manufacturing Company
Fort Calhoun, NE 402-468-5511
Williamsburg Metal Spinning
Brooklyn, NY 888-535-5402

Baskets

Culinary, Frying, Etc.

Archer Wire Intl Corp
Chicago, IL 708-563-1700
Atlanta Burning Bush
Newnan, GA 800-665-5611
Automatic Specialties Inc
Marlborough, MA................. 800-445-2370
Barker Wire
Keosauqua, IA 319-293-3176
Bluebird Manufacturing
Montreal, QC 800-406-2505
Dean Industries
Gardena, CA 800-995-1210
Etube & Wire
Shrewsbury, PA.................. 800-618-4720
F.P. Smith Wire Cloth Company
Northlake, IL.................... 800-323-6842
J.C. Products Inc.
Haddam, CT 860-267-5516
Jesco Industries
Litchfield, MI 800-455-0019
Keating of Chicago Inc
Mc Cook, IL 800-532-8464
Madsen Wire Products Inc
Orland, IN 260-829-6561
Mid-West Wire Products
Ferndale, MI 800-989-9881
Midwest Wire Products LLC
Sturgeon Bay, WI................ 800-445-0225
Mouli Manufacturing Corporation
Belleville, NJ 800-789-8285
Music City Metals Inc
Nashville, TN 800-251-2674
Pitco Frialator Inc
Bow, NH 800-258-3708
Prince Castle Inc
Carol Stream, IL 800-722-7853
Pronto Products Company
Arcadia, CA 800-377-6680
Quadra-Tech
Columbus, OH 800-443-2766
SSW Holding Co Inc
Elizabethtown, KY 270-769-5526

Stryco Wire Products
North York, ON................... 416-663-7000
Technibilt/Cari-All
Newton, NC 800-233-3972
Wirefab Inc
Worcester, MA 877-877-4445

Blocks

Butchers'

Anderson Wood Products
Louisville, KY 502-778-5591
Bally Block Co
Bally, PA 610-845-7511
Canada Goose Wood Produc
Gloucester, ON 888-890-6506
Emco Industrial Plastics
Cedar Grove, NJ 800-292-9906
Greensburg Manufacturing Company
Greensburg, KY 270-932-5511
Hollingsworth Custom Wood Products
Sault Ste. Marie, ON 705-759-1756
John Boos & Co
Effingham, IL 888-431-2667
M & E Mfg Co Inc
Kingston, NY 845-331-2110
Michigan Maple Block Co
Petoskey, MI.................... 800-447-7975
Perfect Plank Co
Oroville, CA 800-327-1961

Boards

Cutting Block

Arrow Plastic Mfg Co
Elk Grove Vlg, IL................. 847-595-9000
Bally Block Co
Bally, PA 610-845-7511
Browne & Company
Markham, ON.................... 905-475-6104
C R Mfg
Waverly, NE 877-789-5844
Canada Goose Wood Produc
Gloucester, ON 888-890-6506
Capital Plastics
Middlefield, OH 440-632-5800
Catskill Craftsmen Inc
Stamford, NY 607-652-7321
Chef Specialties
Smethport, PA 800-440-2433
Ellingers Agatized Wood Inc
Sheboygan, WI 888-287-8906
Emco Industrial Plastics
Cedar Grove, NJ 800-292-9906
Goebel Fixture Co
Hutchinson, MN 888-339-0509
Greensburg Manufacturing Company
Greensburg, KY 270-932-5511
Hollingsworth Custom Wood Products
Sault Ste. Marie, ON 705-759-1756
John Boos & Co
Effingham, IL 888-431-2667
KTG
Cincinnati, OH 888-533-6900
M & E Mfg Co Inc
Kingston, NY 845-331-2110
Michigan Maple Block Co
Petoskey, MI.................... 800-447-7975
Newell Brands
Atlanta, GA
Read Products Inc
Seattle, WA 800-445-3416
Spartec Plastics
Conneaut, OH................... 800-325-5176
Superior Products Company
Saint Paul, MN 800-328-9800
Vermillion Flooring
Springfield, MO 417-862-3785
Wolf Works
Arroyo Grande, CA............... 800-549-3806
Wooster Novelty Company
Brooklyn, NY 718-852-8934

Wood

Bread, Cake & Steak

Enjay Converters Ltd.
Cobourg, ON..................... 800-427-5517
H A Stiles
Westbrook, ME 800-447-8537
Lady Mary
Rockingham, NC 910-997-7321
Lillsun Manufacturing Co
Huntington, IN 260-356-6514
Marston Manufacturing
Cleveland, OH 216-587-3400
Michigan Maple Block Co
Petoskey, MI.................... 800-447-7975
Sunset Paper Products
Simi Valley, CA.................. 800-228-7882
Wooster Novelty Company
Brooklyn, NY 718-852-8934

Bowls

AJM Packaging Corporation
Bloomfield Hills, MI 248-901-0040
Amco Metals Indl
City of Industry, CA 626-855-2550
Apex Fountain Sales Inc
Philadelphia, PA 800-523-4586
Atlantis Industries Inc
Milton, DE 302-684-8542
BG Industries
Lemont, IL 800-800-5761
C R Mfg
Waverly, NE 877-789-5844
Cal-Mil Plastic Products Inc
Oceanside, CA 800-321-9069
Carlisle Food Svc Products Inc
Oklahoma City, OK 800-654-8210
Carthage Cup Company
Longview, TX.................... 903-238-9833
Chef Specialties
Smethport, PA 800-440-2433
Cleveland Metal Stamping Company
Berea, OH 440-234-0010
Coley Industries
Wayland, NY.................... 716-728-2390
Cyclamen Collection
Oakland, CA 510-434-7620
Delfin Design & Mfg
Rancho Sta Marg, CA............. 800-354-7919
Design Specialties Inc
Hamden, CT 800-999-1584
Dover Parkersburg
Follansbee, WV
Eastern Tabletop Mfg
Brooklyn, NY 888-422-4142
Ellingers Agatized Wood Inc
Sheboygan, WI 888-287-8906
Engineered Plastics Inc
Gibsonville, NC 800-711-1740
Finn & Son's Metal Spinning Specialists
South Lebanon, OH 513-494-2898
Gaetano America
El Monte, CA 626-442-2858
Genpak LLC
Charlotte, NC 800-626-6695
Grand Silver Company
Bronx, NY...................... 718-585-1930
Granville Manufacturing Co
Granville, VT 800-828-1005
Hoffmaster Group Inc.
Oshkosh, WI.................... 800-558-9300
HPI North America/Plastics
Chicago, IL 800-327-3534
Jones-Zylon Co
West Lafayette, OH............... 800-848-8160
Kendrick Johnson & Assoc Inc
Minneapolis, MN 800-826-1271
Kosempel Manufacturing Company
Philadelphia, PA 800-733-7122
Leggett & Platt Storage
Vernon Hills, IL 847-816-6246
Majestic
Bridgeport, CT 203-367-7900

NCC
Groveland, FL.....................800-429-9037
Novelty Crystal
Long Island City, NY 800-622-0250
Olde Country Reproductions Inc
York, PA.........................800-358-3997
Palmer Distributors
St Clair Shores, MI................800-444-1912
Polar Ware Company
Sheboygan, WI...................800-237-3655
Prairie Packaging Inc
Mooresville, NC..................704-660-6600
Prolon
Port Gibson, MS..................888-480-9828
Sani-Top Products
De Leon Springs, FL...............800-874-6094
Savage Brothers Company
Elk Grove Vlg, IL.................800-342-0973
Service Ideas
Woodbury, MN....................800-328-4493
Superior Products Company
Saint Paul, MN....................800-328-9800
Tablecraft Products Co Inc
Gurnee, IL........................800-323-8321
Techform
Mount Airy, NC...................336-789-2115
Ullman, Shapiro & UllmanLLP
New York, NY.....................212-755-0299
Vertex China
Pomona, CA......................800-483-7839
Victoria Porcelain
Miami, FL.........................888-593-2353
Weavewood, Inc.
Golden Valley, MN................800-367-6460
Western Stoneware
Monmouth, IL....................309-734-2161
Wiltec
Leominster, MA...................978-537-1497
WNA
Chattanooga, TN.................800-404-9318
Wna Comet West Inc
City of Industry, CA..............800-225-0939

Brushes

Bakers' & Confectioners'

Amco Metals Indl
City of Industry, CA...............626-855-2550
Braun Brush Co
Albertson, NY.....................800-645-4111
Carlisle Food Svc Products Inc
Oklahoma City, OK 800-654-8210
Kiefer Brushes, Inc
Franklin, NJ 800-526-2905
Kopykake
Torrance, CA.....................800-999-5253
Linzer Products Corp
West Babylon, NY 800-423-3254
Music City Metals Inc
Nashville, TN.....................800-251-2674
Opie Brush Company
Independence, MO 800-877-6743
Precision Brush
Cleveland, OH 800-252-4747
Six Hardy Brush Manufacturing
Suffield, CT.......................860-623-8465
Tucel Industries, Inc.
Forestdale, VT 800-558-8235

Food Industry

Abco Products
Miami, FL.........................888-694-2226
Akron Cotton Products
Akron, OH........................800-899-7173
All Weather Energy Systems
Plymouth, MI.....................888-636-8324
Amco Metals Indl
City of Industry, CA...............626-855-2550
American Brush Company
Portland, OR.....................800-826-8492
Anderson Products
Cresco, PA.......................800-729-4694
Baldewein Company
Lake Forrest, IL...................800-424-5544
Bouras Mop Manufacturing Company
Saint Louis, MO...................800-634-9153
Braun Brush Co
Albertson, NY.....................800-645-4111
Brush Research Mfg Co Inc
Los Angeles, CA..................323-261-6162

Carlisle Food Svc Products Inc
Oklahoma City, OK 800-654-8210
Carlisle Sanitary Mntnc Prods
Oklahoma City, OK 800-654-8210
Cosgrove Enterprises Inc
Miami Lakes, FL...................800-888-3396
Detroit Quality Brush Mfg Co
Livonia, MI.......................800-722-3037
Furgale Industries Ltd.
Winnipeg, NB.....................800-665-0506
Great Lakes Brush
Centralia, MO.....................573-682-2128
Greenwood Mop & Broom Inc
Greenwood, SC...................800-635-6849
Harper Brush Works Inc
Fairfield, IA.......................800-223-7894
Hoge Brush Company
New Knoxville, OH 800-494-4643
Hub City Brush Co
Petal, MS.........................800-278-7452
Ideal Stencil Machine & Tape Company
Marion, IL........................800-388-0162
Industries For the Blind
Milwaukee, WI....................800-642-8778
Justman Brush Co
Omaha, NE.......................800-800-6940
Keating of Chicago Inc
Mc Cook, IL.......................800-532-8464
Kiefer Brushes, Inc
Franklin, NJ 800-526-2905
Labpride Chemicals
Bronx, NY........................800-467-1255
Libman Co
Arcola, IL.........................877-818-3380
Messina Brothers Manufacturing Company
Brooklyn, NY.....................800-924-6454
Mill-Rose Co
Mentor, OH......................800-321-3598
Murk Brush Company
New Britain, CT...................860-249-2550
Music City Metals Inc
Nashville, TN.....................800-251-2674
Nation/Ruskin
Montgomeryville, PA 800-523-2489
National Novelty Brush Co
Lancaster, PA.....................717-299-5681
Nationwide Wire & Brush Manufacturing
Lodi, CA..........................209-334-9660
Newell Brands
Atlanta, GA
Newton Broom Co
Newton, IL........................618-783-4424
O'Dell Corp
Ware Shoals, SC..................800-342-2843
O-Cedar
Aurora, IL.........................800-543-8105
Opie Brush Company
Independence, MO 800-877-6743
Pepper Mill
Mobile, AL........................800-669-5175
Power Brushes
Toledo, OH.......................800-968-9600
Precision Brush
Cleveland, OH 800-252-4747
Quality Mop & Brush Manufacturers
Needham, MA....................617-884-2999
Quickie Manufacturing Corp
Cinnaminson, NJ..................856-829-7900
Remco Products Corp
Zionsville, IN......................800-585-8619
RidgeView Products LLC
La Crosse, WI.....................888-782-1221
Six Hardy Brush Manufacturing
Suffield, CT.......................860-623-8465
Special Products
Springfield, MO...................417-881-6114
Superior Products Company
Saint Paul, MN....................800-328-9800
TRC
Middlefield, OH...................440-834-0078
Tucel Industries, Inc.
Forestdale, VT 800-558-8235
Urnex Brands Inc
Elmsford, NY.....................800-222-2826
Volckening Inc
Brooklyn, NY.....................800-221-0276
Walker Brush Inc
Webster, NY......................585-545-4748
Warren E. Conley Corporation
Carmel, IN........................800-367-7875
Wilen Professional Cleaning Products
Atlanta, GA.......................800-241-7371

Young & Swartz Inc
Buffalo, NY.......................800-466-7682
Zephyr Manufacturing Co
Sedalia, MO......................660-827-0352
Zoia Banquetier Co
Cleveland, OH....................216-631-6414

Cleavers

Butchers'

Lamson & Goodnow
Shelburne Falls, MA...............800-872-6564

Cookware

A Legacy Food Svc
Santa Fe Springs, CA 800-848-4440
Alegacy
Santa Fe Springs, CA 800-848-4440
All-Clad METALCRAFTERS LLC
Canonsburg, PA..................800-255-2523
Alumaworks
Sunny Isle Beach, FL..............800-277-7267
Amber Glo
Chicago, IL.......................866-705-0515
American Griddle Corp.
Fort Wayne, IN...................800-428-6550
APW Wyott Food Service Equipment Company
Cheyenne, WY....................800-527-2100
Baking Machines
Livermore, CA....................925-449-3369
Bluebird Manufacturing
Montreal, QC.....................800-406-2505
Browne & Company
Markham, ON....................905-475-6104
CookTek
Chicago, IL.......................888-266-5835
Crown Custom Metal Spinning
Concord, ON.....................800-750-1924
Cyclamen Collection
Oakland, CA......................510-434-7620
Danger Men Cooking
Highland, NY.....................845-691-7029
Dover Parkersburg
Follansbee, WV
Dura-Ware Company of America
Oklahoma City, OK 800-664-3872
Eagleware Manufacturing
Compton, CA.....................310-604-0404
Esterle Mold & Machine Co Inc
Stow, OH.........................800-411-4086
Eurodib
Champlain, NY....................888-956-6866
Finn & Son's Metal Spinning Specialists
South Lebanon, OH 513-494-2898
Floaire
Blue Bell, PA......................800-726-5623
H.F. Coors China Company
New Albany, MS..................800-782-6677
Harold Leonard Southwest Corporation
Houston, TX......................800-245-8105
Hartstone Pottery Inc
Zanesville, OH....................740-452-9999
Hillside Metal Ware Company
Union, NJ.........................908-964-3080
Johnson-Rose Corporation
Lockport, NY 800-456-2055
Lancaster Colony Corporation
Westerville, OH...................614-224-7141
Legion Industries Inc
Waynesboro, GA..................800-887-1988
Liberty Ware LLC
Clearfield, UT.....................888-500-5885
Lincoln Foodservice
Cleveland, OH....................800-374-3004
Lodge Manufacturing Company
South Pittsburg, TN...............423-837-5919
Marston Manufacturing
Cleveland, OH....................216-587-3400
Mirro Company
Lancaster, OH....................800-848-7200
Padinox
Winsloe, PE.......................800-263-9768
Professional Bakeware Company
Willis, TX.........................800-440-9547
Regal Ware Inc
Kewaskum, WI....................262-626-2121
Ricoh Technologies
Grand Prairie, TX..................800-585-9367
Royal Prestige Health Moguls
Westbury, NY.....................888-802-7433

Spring USA Corp
Naperville, IL 800-535-8974
Superior Products Company
Saint Paul, MN 800-328-9800
Thermoquest
Riviera Beach, FL. 888-383-2025
Thermos Company
Schaumburg, IL. 800-243-0745
Tomlinson Industries
Cleveland, OH 800-945-4589
Tramontina USA
Sugar Land, TX. 800-221-7809
Tufty Ceramics Inc
Andover, NY. 607-478-5150
Tupperware Brands Corporation
Orlando, FL. 800-366-3800
United Performance Metals
Northbrook, IL 888-922-0040
Vasconia Housewares
San Antonio, TX. 800-377-6723
Vorwerk
Thousand Oaks, CA 888-867-9375
WaffleWaffle
Nutley, NJ 201-559-1286
World Kitchen
Elmira, NY 800-999-3436
Xtreme Beverages, LLC
Dana Point, CA. 949-495-7929

Covers

Dish, Food Display & Tray

A1 Tablecloth Co
South Hackensack, NJ 800-727-8987
Acryline
North Attleboro, MA 508-695-7124
Amco Metals Indl
City of Industry, CA 626-855-2550
American Metalcraft Inc
Franklin Park, IL. 708-345-1177
Apple-A-Day Nutritional Labeling Service
San Clemente, CA. 949-855-8954
Arden Companies
Southfield, MI. 248-415-8500
Bardes Plastics Inc
Milwaukee, WI 800-558-5161
Brooklace
Oshkosh, WI 800-572-4552
C-Through Covers
San Diego, CA 619-286-0671
Carlisle Food Svc Products Inc
Oklahoma City, OK 800-654-8210
Davlynne International
Cudahy, WI 800-558-5208
Delfin Design & Mfg
Rancho Sta Marg, CA 800-354-7919
Delta Plastics
Hot Springs, AR 501-760-3000
Dilley Manufacturing Co
Des Moines, IA. 800-247-5087
Dow Cover Co Inc
New Haven, CT 800-735-8877
Dynynstyl
Delray Beach, FL 800-774-7895
Eaton Quade Plastics & Sign Co
Oklahoma City, OK 405-236-4475
Econofrost Night Covers
Shawnigan Lake, BC 800-519-1222
Eide Industries Inc
Cerritos, CA 800-422-6827
Eliason Corp
Portage, MI 800-828-3655
Erving Industries
Erving, MA. 413-422-2700
Fato Industries
Kankakee, IL. 815-932-3015
Goldenwest Sales
Cerritos, CA 800-827-6175
Highland Supply Corp
Highland, IL 800-472-3645
Hoffmaster Group Inc
Oshkosh, WI 800-327-9774
J. James
Brooklyn, NY 718-384-6144
J.V. Reed & Company
Louisville, KY 877-258-7333
Jordan Specialty Company
Brooklyn, NY 877-567-3265
K & L Intl
Ontario, CA. 888-598-5588

K-C Products Company
Van Nuys, CA 818-267-1600
Kendrick Johnson & Assoc Inc
Minneapolis, MN 800-826-1271
Lakeside Manufacturing Inc
Milwaukee, WI 888-558-8565
Michael Leson Dinnerware
Youngstown, OH. 800-821-3541
Midco Plastics
Enterprise, KS 800-235-2729
Morris Transparent Box Co
East Providence, RI. 401-438-6116
MultiFab Plastics
Boston, MA. 888-293-5754
Nyman Manufacturing Company
Rumford, RI 401-438-3410
Palmer Distributors
St Clair Shores, MI 800-444-1912
Penda Form Corp
New Concord, OH 800-837-2574
Polar Plastics
St Laurent, QC 514-331-0207
Polar Ware Company
Sheboygan, WI 800-237-3655
Products A Curtron Div
Pittsburgh, PA 800-888-9750
Reading Plastic Fabricators
Reading, PA 610-926-3245
Samsill Corp
Fort Worth, TX 800-255-1100
Sani-Top Products
De Leon Springs, FL. 800-874-6094
Sims Superior Seating
Locust Grove, GA. 800-729-9178
Springprint Medallion
Augusta, GA 800-543-5990
Standard Terry Mills
Souderton, PA 215-723-8121
Steril-Sil Company
Bowmansville, PA. 800-784-5537
Superior Linen & Work Wear
Kansas City, MO. 800-798-7987
Superior Products Company
Saint Paul, MN 800-328-9800
Tara Linens
Sanford, NC 800-476-8272
TEMP-TECH Company
Springfield, MA 800-343-5579
Thermal Bags By Ingrid Inc
Gilberts, IL 800-622-5560
Tri-State Plastics
Glenwillard, PA. 724-457-6900
WORC Slitting & Mfg Co
Worcester, MA 800-356-2961
Zoia Banquetier Co
Cleveland, OH 216-631-6414

Cutlery

A G Russell Knives
Rogers, AR 800-255-9034
Ace Co Precision Mfg
Boise, ID 800-359-7012
Acme International
Maplewood, NJ 973-416-0400
Amcel
Watertown, MA. 800-225-7992
American Housewares
Bronx, NY. 718-665-9500
Babco International, Inc
Tucson, AZ 520-628-7596
Bettendorf Stanford Inc
Salem, IL. 800-548-2253
BOC Plastics Inc
Winston Salem, NC. 800-334-8687
Boehringer Mfg. Co. Inc.
Felton, CA. 800-630-8665
Brooklyn Boys Pizza & Pasta
Boca Raton, FL. 561-477-3663
Browne & Company
Markham, ON 905-475-6104
Buck Knives
Post Falls, ID. 800-326-2825
Burrell Cutlery Company
Ellicottville, NY 716-699-2343
C R Mfg
Waverly, NE 877-789-5844
CB Mfg. & Sales Co.
Miamisburg, OH 800-543-6860
Chef Revival
North Charleston, SC 800-248-9826

Chicago Scale & Slicer Company
Franklin Park, IL. 847-455-3400
Chuppa Knife Manufacturing
Jackson, TN 731-424-1212
Conimar Corp
Ocala, FL. 800-874-9735
CUTCO Corp
Olean, NY 716-372-3111
Cutrite Company
Fremont, OH 800-928-8748
Dart Container Corp.
Mason, MI. 800-248-5960
De Ster Corporation
Atlanta, GA 800-237-8270
Delco Tableware
Port Washington, NY 800-221-9557
Dexter Russell Inc
Southbridge, MA 800-343-6042
Dispoz-O Plastics
Fountain Inn, SC. 864-862-4004
E K Lay Co
Philadelphia, PA 800-523-3220
E-Z Edge Inc
West New York, NJ 800-232-4470
Edge Resources
Hopedale, MA 888-849-0998
Edgecraft Corp
Avondale, PA 800-342-3255
F N Smith Corp
Oregon, IL. 815-732-2171
Fioriware
Zanesville, OH 740-454-7400
Florida Knife Co
Sarasota, FL 800-966-5643
Friedr Dick Corp
Farmingdale, NY 800-554-3425
General Cutlery Co
Fremont, OH 419-332-2316
Gerber Legendary Blades
Portland, OR 800-950-6161
Gril-Del
Mankato, MN 800-782-7320
Hansaloy Corp
Davenport, IA 800-553-4992
Hantover Inc
Kansas City, MO. 800-821-7849
Hoffmaster Group Inc
Oshkosh, WI 800-367-2877
Hollymatic Corp
Countryside, IL. 708-579-3700
Imperial Schrade Corporation
Ellenville, NY 212-210-8600
Izabel Lam International
Brooklyn, NY 718-797-3983
James River Canada
North York, ON. 416-789-5151
Jarden Home Brands
Cloquet, MN 218-879-6700
Jet Plastica Industries
Hatfield, PA
Jim Scharf Holdings
Perdue, SK 800-667-9727
John J. Adams Die Corporation
Worcester, MA 508-757-3894
Kinetic Co
Greendale, WI. 414-425-8221
KSW Corp
Des Moines, IA. 515-265-5269
Lamson & Goodnow
Shelburne Falls, MA. 800-872-6564
Les Industries Touch Inc
Sherbrooke, QC 800-267-4140
Lifetime Brands Inc
Garden City, NY 516-683-6000
Mandeville Company
Minneapolis, MN 800-328-8490
Max Packaging
Attalla, AL 800-543-5369
Mundial
Norwood, MA. 800-487-2224
Omcan Manufacturing & Distributing Company
Mississauga, ON. 800-465-0234
Oneida Food Service
Columbus, OH 800-828-7033
Penley Corporation
West Paris, ME 800-368-6449
Polar Plastics
St Laurent, QC 514-331-0207
Prairie Packaging Inc
Mooresville, NC 704-660-6600
R H Saw Corp
Barrington, IL. 847-381-8777

R Murphy Co Inc
Ayer, MA 888-772-3481
Ranger Blade Manufacturing Company
Traer, IA 800-377-7860
Replacements LTD
Mc Leansville, NC 800-737-5223
Rhineland Cutlery
Melbourne, FL 321-725-2101
Royal Prestige Health Moguls
Westbury, NY 888-802-7433
Royal Silver Mfg Co Inc
Norfolk, VA .757-855-6004
Safe-T-Cut Inc
Monson, MA 413-267-9984
Salem China Company
Salem, OH. .330-337-8771
Simmons Engineering Corporation
Wheeling, IL 800-252-3381
Spir-It/Zoo Piks
Andover, MA 800-343-0996
Superior Products Company
Saint Paul, MN 800-328-9800
Tramontina USA
Sugar Land, TX. 800-221-7809
Utica Cutlery Co
Utica, NY 800-879-2526
Waddington North America
Chelmsford, MA. 888-962-2877
Walco
Utica, NY 800-879-2526
Warther Museum
Dover, OH. .330-343-7513
Wishbone Utensil Tableware Line
Wheat Ridge, CO 866-266-5928
Wna Comet West Inc
City of Industry, CA 800-225-0939
Zelco Industries
Mount Vernon, NY 800-431-2486

Cutters

Biscuit & Cookie

Amco Metals Indl
City of Industry, CA 626-855-2550
Ann Clark, LTD
Rutland, VT .800-252-6798
Arcobaleno Pasta Machines
Lancaster, PA 800-875-7096
Boehringer Mfg. Co. Inc.
Felton, CA. .800-630-8665
Browne & Company
Markham, ON 905-475-6104
Dito Dean Food Prep
Charlotte, NC 866-449-4200
Don Lee
Philadelphia, PA 760-745-0707
Educational Products Company
Hope, NJ 800-272-3822
Irresistible Cookie Jar
Hayden Lake, ID. 208-664-1261
Lee Financial Corporation
Dallas, TX. .972-960-1001
Lorenzen's Cookie Cutters
Wantagh, NY. 516-781-7116
LoTech Industries
Lakewood, CO 800-295-0199
Moline Machinery LLC
Duluth, MN. 800-767-5734
Parrish's Cake Decorating
Gardena, CA. 800-736-8443
Polar Process
Plattsville, ON. 877-896-8077
Pro Bake Inc
Twinsburg, OH 800-837-4427
Rademaker USA
Hudson, OH 330-650-2345
Reading Bakery Systems Inc
Robesonia, PA. 610-693-5816
Rhodes Bakery Equipment
Portland, OR. 800-426-3813
Soco System USA
Waukesha, WI. 800-441-6293
Superior Products Company
Saint Paul, MN 800-328-9800

Cake

Belshaw Adamatic Bakery Group
Auburn, WA 800-578-2547
Colborne Foodbotics
Lake Forest, IL 847-724-5070

Hinds-Bock Corp
Bothell, WA. 425-885-1183
Matiss
St Georges, QC 888-562-8477
Polar Process
Plattsville, ON. 877-896-8077

Cheese

Amco Metals Indl
City of Industry, CA 626-855-2550
Berkshire PPM
Litchfield, CT 860-567-3118
Bluffton Slaw Cutter Company
Bluffton, OH. 419-358-9840
C&R Refrigation Inc,
Center, TX. .800-438-6182
General Machinery Corp
Sheboygan, WI. 888-243-6622
Globe Food Equipment Co
Moraine, OH 800-347-5423
Hart Design & Mfg
Green Bay, WI. 920-468-5927
Lincoln Foodservice
Cleveland, OH 800-374-3004
Mouli Manufacturing Corporation
Belleville, NJ 800-789-8285
Polar Process
Plattsville, ON. 877-896-8077
Samuel Underberg Food Store
Brooklyn, NY 718-363-0787
Superior Products Company
Saint Paul, MN 800-328-9800
TGW International
Florence, KY 800-407-0173

Dicing

Berkshire PPM
Litchfield, CT 860-567-3118
Custom Food Machinery
Stockton, CA. 209-463-4343
D & S Mfg
Auburn, MA 508-799-7812
General Machinery Corp
Sheboygan, WI. 888-243-6622
Insinger Co
Philadelphia, PA 800-344-4802
Luthi Machinery Company, Inc.
Pueblo, CO .719-948-1110
Paxton Corp
Bristol, RI 401-396-9062
Slicechief Co
Toledo, OH .419-241-7647
Superior Products Company
Saint Paul, MN 800-328-9800
Urschel Laboratories
Valparaiso, IN 219-464-4811

Kraut & Slaw

A.K. Robins
Baltimore, MD 800-486-9656
Bluffton Slaw Cutter Company
Bluffton, OH. 419-358-9840
Clawson Machine Co Inc
Franklin, NJ 800-828-4088
Paxton Corp
Bristol, RI 401-396-9062

Meat

Power

AEW Thurne
Lake Zurich, IL. 800-239-7297
Berkshire PPM
Litchfield, CT 860-567-3118
Biro Manufacturing Co
Lakeside Marblhd, OH 419-798-4451
Globe Food Equipment Co
Moraine, OH 800-347-5423
Jarvis Products Corp
Middletown, CT 860-347-7271
Prince Castle Inc
Carol Stream, IL 800-722-7853
Superior Products Company
Saint Paul, MN 800-328-9800
TGW International
Florence, KY 800-407-0173
Urschel Laboratories
Valparaiso, IN 219-464-4811

Sausage

Automated Food Systems
Waxahachie, TX 469-517-0470
Cozzini LLC
Chicago, IL .773-478-9700
General Machinery Corp
Sheboygan, WI. 888-243-6622
Handtmann Inc
Lake Forest, IL 800-477-3585
Linker Machines
Rockaway, NJ 973-983-0001
Marlen International
Astoria, OR. 800-862-7536
Sperling Industries
Omaha, NE .402-556-4070
TGW International
Florence, KY 800-407-0173

Pickle

A.K. Robins
Baltimore, MD 800-486-9656
Berkshire PPM
Litchfield, CT 860-567-3118
Custom Food Machinery
Stockton, CA. 209-463-4343

Ultrasonic

Polar Process
Plattsville, ON. 877-896-8077

Glasses

Drinking

Anchor Hocking Operating Co
Lancaster, OH 800-562-7511
ATAGO USA Inc
Bellevue, WA 877-282-4687
Atlantis Industries Inc
Milton, DE .302-684-8542
Babco International, Inc
Tucson, AZ .520-628-7596
Benner China & Glassware Inc
Jacksonville, FL 904-733-4620
Browne & Company
Markham, ON 905-475-6104
Carlisle Food Svc Products Inc
Oklahoma City, OK 800-654-8210
Design Specialties Inc
Hamden, CT 800-999-1584
Donoco Industries
Huntington Beach, CA 888-822-8763
Edco Industries
Bridgeport, CT 203-333-8982
Encore Plastics
Huntington Beach, CA 888-822-8763
Epic Products
Santa Ana, CA 800-548-9791
HPI North America/Plastics
Chicago, IL .800-327-3534
Ideas Etc Inc
Louisville, KY 800-733-0337
Image Plastics
Houston, TX 800-289-2811
Indiana Glass Company
Columbus, OH 800-543-0357
Izabel Lam International
Brooklyn, NY 718-797-3983
Jet Plastica Industries
Hatfield, PA
Jones-Zylon Co
West Lafayette, OH. 800-848-8160
Judel Products
Elmsford, NY 800-583-3526
Libby Canada
Mississauga, ON 905-607-8280
Loria Awards
Yonkers, NY 800-540-2927
Majestic
Bridgeport, CT 203-367-7900
MDR International
North Miami, FL 305-944-5019
Michael Leson Dinnerware
Youngstown, OH. 800-821-3541
Mikasa Hotelware
Secaucus, NJ. 866-645-2721
Novelty Crystal
Long Island City, NY 800-622-0250

Prairie Packaging Inc
  Mooresville, NC 704-660-6600
Prolon
  Port Gibson, MS 888-480-9828
Royal Prestige Health Moguls
  Westbury, NY 888-802-7433
Spirit Foodservice, Inc.
  Andover, MA 800-343-0996
Superior Products Company
  Saint Paul, MN 800-328-9800
Tango Shatterproof Drinkware
  Walpole, MA 888-898-2646
Tar-Hong MELAMINE USA
  City of Industry, CA 626-935-1612
Ullman, Shapiro & UllmanLLP
  New York, NY 212-755-0299
Wiltec
  Leominster, MA 978-537-1497
Xtreme Beverages, LLC
  Dana Point, CA 949-495-7929

Glassware

Cooking & Baking

Anchor Hocking Operating Co
  Lancaster, OH 800-562-7511
Judel Products
  Elmsford, NY 800-583-3526
Oneida LTD Silversmiths
  Oneida, NY 888-263-7195
World Kitchen
  Elmira, NY 800-999-3436

Heat Resistant

Automated Packaging Systems
  Streetsboro, OH 800-527-0733
Corning Life Sciences
  Tewksbury, MA 800-492-1110
Hartstone Pottery Inc
  Zanesville, OH 740-452-9999
Judel Products
  Elmsford, NY 800-583-3526
Triad Scientific
  Manasquan, NJ 800-867-6690
World Kitchen
  Elmira, NY 800-999-3436

Hotel & Restaurant

Abco International
  Oneida, NY 888-263-7195
Anchor Hocking Operating Co
  Lancaster, OH 800-562-7511
ATAGO USA Inc
  Bellevue, WA 877-282-4687
Browne & Company
  Markham, ON 905-475-6104
Epic Products
  Santa Ana, CA 800-548-9791
Fenton Art Glass Company
  Williamstown, WV 800-933-6766
Judel Products
  Elmsford, NY 800-583-3526
Lancaster Colony Corporation
  Westerville, OH. 614-224-7141
Libbey Inc.
  Toledo, OH 419-325-2100
Libby Canada
  Mississauga, ON. 905-607-8280
Masterpiece Crystal
  Jane Lew, WV 304-884-7841
Mikasa Hotelware
  Secaucus, NJ. 866-645-2721
Minners Designs   Inc.
  New York, NY 212-688-7441
Mr Ice Bucket
  New Brunswick, NJ 732-545-0420
Novelty Crystal
  Long Island City, NY 800-622-0250
Oneida Food Service
  Columbus, OH 800-828-7033
Royal Prestige Health Moguls
  Westbury, NY 888-802-7433
Superior Products Company
  Saint Paul, MN 800-328-9800
Tango Shatterproof Drinkware
  Walpole, MA 888-898-2646
Variety Glass Inc
  Cambridge, OH 740-432-3643

World Kitchen
  Elmira, NY 800-999-3436
Xtreme Beverages, LLC
  Dana Point, CA 949-495-7929

Packers'

All American Container
  Miami, FL 305-887-0797
Indianapolis Container Company
  Indianapolis, IN 800-760-3318

Holders

Corn Cob

Jarden Home Brands
  Daleville, IN 800-392-2575

Hollowware

Abco International
  Oneida, NY 888-263-7195
Americana Marketing
  Newbury Park, CA 800-742-7520
Browne & Company
  Markham, ON 905-475-6104
Corby Hall
  Randolph, NJ 973-366-8300
Delco Tableware
  Port Washington, NY 800-221-9557
Dynynstyl
  Delray Beach, FL 800-774-7895
Grand Silver Company
  Bronx, NY. 718-585-1930
Lenox Corp
  Bristol, PA. 800-223-4311
Libby Canada
  Mississauga, ON 905-607-8280
Oneida Food Service
  Columbus, OH 800-828-7033
Oneida LTD Silversmiths
  Oneida, NY 888-263-7195
Rexcraft Fine Chafers
  Long Island City, NY 888-739-2723
Superior Products Company
  Saint Paul, MN 800-328-9800
Tradeco International Corp
  Addison, IL 800-628-3738
Walco
  Utica, NY 800-879-2526
Xtreme Beverages, LLC
  Dana Point, CA 949-495-7929

Hooks

Meat

Boehringer Mfg. Co. Inc.
  Felton, CA 800-630-8665
G.F. Frank & Sons
  Fairfield, OH 513-870-9075
Le Fiell Co
  Reno, NV 402-592-9993
Samuel Underberg Food Store
  Brooklyn, NY 718-363-0787

Hoops

Cheese

Damrow Company
  Fond Du Lac, WI 800-236-1501
Viking Machine & Design Inc
  De Pere, WI. 888-286-2116

Kettles

G & F Mfg
  Oak Lawn, IL 800-282-1574

Canning & Preserving

A.K. Robins
  Baltimore, MD 800-486-9656
Berkshire PPM
  Litchfield, CT 860-567-3118
Central Fabricators Inc
  Cincinnati, OH 800-909-8265
Custom Food Machinery
  Stockton, CA 209-463-4343

El Cerrito Steel
  El Cerrito, CA 510-230-4709
Hamilton Kettles
  Weirton, WV 800-535-1882
Packaging & Processing Equipment
  Ayr, ON 519-622-6666
Production Packaging & Processing Equipment
  Company
  Savannah, GA 912-856-4281

Confectioners'

A & B Process Systems Corp
  Stratford, WI 888-258-2789
Berkshire PPM
  Litchfield, CT 860-567-3118
Chocolate Concepts
  Hartville, OH 330-877-3322
D. Picking & Company
  Bucyrus, OH 419-562-6891
Hamilton Kettles
  Weirton, WV 800-535-1882
Packaging & Processing Equipment
  Ayr, ON 519-622-6666
Vendome Copper & Brass Works
  Louisville, KY 888-384-5161

Copper

All Spun Metal Products
  Des Plaines, IL 847-824-4117
D. Picking & Company
  Bucyrus, OH 419-562-6891
Packaging & Processing Equipment
  Ayr, ON 519-622-6666
Savage Brothers Company
  Elk Grove Vlg, IL 800-342-0973
Vendome Copper & Brass Works
  Louisville, KY 888-384-5161

Lard

A & B Process Systems Corp
  Stratford, WI. 888-258-2789
Hamilton Kettles
  Weirton, WV 800-535-1882
Packaging & Processing Equipment
  Ayr, ON 519-622-6666

Mixing

A & B Process Systems Corp
  Stratford, WI 888-258-2789
Berkshire PPM
  Litchfield, CT 860-567-3118
Bowers Process Equipment
  Stratford, ON. 800-567-3223
Chocolate Concepts
  Hartville, OH 330-877-3322
Custom Food Machinery
  Stockton, CA. 209-463-4343
DCI, Inc.
  St Cloud, MN 320-252-8200
Eischen Enterprises
  Fresno, CA 559-834-0013
Hamilton Kettles
  Weirton, WV 800-535-1882
Packaging & Processing Equipment
  Ayr, ON 519-622-6666
Savage Brothers Company
  Elk Grove Vlg, IL 800-342-0973
Sharpsville Container Corp
  Sharpsville, PA 800-645-1248
South Valley Mfg Inc
  Gilroy, CA. 408-842-5457
Stainless Fabrication Inc
  Springfield, MO 800-397-8265

Steaming

Berkshire PPM
  Litchfield, CT 860-567-3118
Chester-Jensen Co., Inc.
  Chester, PA 800-685-3750
Cleasby Manufacturing Co
  San Francisco, CA 800-253-2729
Cleveland Range
  Concord, ON
Eischen Enterprises
  Fresno, CA 559-834-0013
Electro-Steam Generator Corp
  Rancocas, NJ. 866-617-0764

Hamilton Kettles
Weirton, WV............................800-535-1882
Legion Industries Inc
Waynesboro, GA....................800-887-1988
Packaging & Processing Equipment
Ayr, ON...............................519-622-6666
Process Systems
Barrington, IL.......................847-842-8618
Sharpsville Container Corp
Sharpsville, PA.....................800-645-1248
South Valley Mfg Inc
Gilroy, CA...........................408-842-5457
Welbilt Corporation
Stamford, CT........................203-325-8300
Welliver Metal Products Corporation
Salem, OR...........................503-362-1568

Sugar & Syrup

A & B Process Systems Corp
Stratford, WI........................888-258-2789
Hamilton Kettles
Weirton, WV.........................800-535-1882
Packaging & Processing Equipment
Ayr, ON...............................519-622-6666

Knife Sharpeners

Browne & Company
Markham, ON.......................905-475-6104
Cass Saw & Tool   Sharpening
Westmont, IL........................630-968-1617
Diamond Machining Technology
Marlborough, MA...................800-666-4368
Edgecraft Corp
Avondale, PA........................800-342-3255
EZE-Lap Diamond Products
Carson City, NV....................800-843-4815
Fortune Products Inc
Cedar Park, TX.....................512-249-0334
Friedr Dick Corp
Farmingdale, NY...................800-554-3425
General Grinding Inc
Oakland, CA.........................800-806-6037
Imperial Schrade Corporation
Ellenville, NY.......................212-210-8600
R X Honing Machine Corp
Mishawaka, IN......................800-346-6464
Serr-Edge Machine Company
Cleveland, Cl........................800-443-8097
Superior Products Company
Saint Paul, MN......................800-328-9800
Tru Hone Corp
Ocala, FL............................800-237-4663

Knives

Bread

Brooklyn Boys Pizza & Pasta
Boca Raton, FL.....................561-477-3663
Lamson & Goodnow
Shelburne Falls, MA...............800-872-6564
Mundial
Norwood, MA.......................800-487-2224
Simmons Engineering Corporation
Wheeling, IL.........................800-252-3381
Superior Products Company
Saint Paul, MN......................800-328-9800

Butchers'

Atlanta SharpTech
Peachtree City, GA.................800-462-7297
Boehringer Mfg. Co. Inc.
Felton, CA...........................800-630-8665
Chicago Scale & Slicer Company
Franklin Park, IL....................847-455-3400
General Cutlery Co
Fremont, OH........................419-332-2316
Jarvis Products Corp
Middletown, CT.....................860-347-7271
Lamson & Goodnow
Shelburne Falls, MA...............800-872-6564
Mandeville Company
Minneapolis, MN...................800-328-8490
Mundial
Norwood, MA.......................800-487-2224
R Murphy Co Inc
Ayer, MA............................888-772-3481
Simmons Engineering Corporation
Wheeling, IL.........................800-252-3381

Superior Products Company
Saint Paul, MN......................800-328-9800

Cake

C R Mfg
Waverly, NE.........................877-789-5844
Mundial
Norwood, MA.......................800-487-2224
Polar Process
Plattsville, ON.......................877-896-8077
Simmons Engineering Corporation
Wheeling, IL.........................800-252-3381

Canners'

A.D. Cowdrey Company
Modesto, CA.........................209-538-4677
A.K. Robins
Baltimore, MD.......................800-486-9656
General Cutlery Co
Fremont, OH........................419-332-2316

Carving

Browne & Company
Markham, ON.......................905-475-6104
Burrell Cutlery Company
Ellicottville, NY....................716-699-2343
CUTCO Corp
Olean, NY...........................716-372-3111
Dexter Russell Inc
Southbridge, MA...................800-343-6042
General Cutlery Co
Fremont, OH........................419-332-2316
Gerber Legendary Blades
Portland, OR........................800-950-6161
Imperial Schrade Corporation
Ellenville, NY.......................212-210-8600
Mandeville Company
Minneapolis, MN...................800-328-8490
Mundial
Norwood, MA.......................800-487-2224
R Murphy Co Inc
Ayer, MA............................888-772-3481
Superior Products Company
Saint Paul, MN......................800-328-9800

Cheese

Browne & Company
Markham, ON.......................905-475-6104
General Cutlery Co
Fremont, OH........................419-332-2316
Lamson & Goodnow
Shelburne Falls, MA...............800-872-6564
Mundial
Norwood, MA.......................800-487-2224
Polar Process
Plattsville, ON.......................877-896-8077
TGW International
Florence, KY........................800-407-0173

Culinary

Browne & Company
Markham, ON.......................905-475-6104
Buck Knives
Post Falls, ID........................800-326-2825
Burrell Cutlery Company
Ellicottville, NY....................716-699-2343
Dexter Russell Inc
Southbridge, MA...................800-343-6042
Gerber Legendary Blades
Portland, OR........................800-950-6161
Gunter Wilhelm Cutlery
Fair Lawn, NJ.......................201-569-6866
Imperial Schrade Corporation
Ellenville, NY.......................212-210-8600
John J. Adams Die Corporation
Worcester, MA......................508-757-3894
Lamson & Goodnow
Shelburne Falls, MA...............800-872-6564
Lifetime Brands Inc
Garden City, NY....................516-683-6000
Mundial
Norwood, MA.......................800-487-2224
OWD
Tupper Lake, NY...................800-836-1693
Superior Products Company
Saint Paul, MN......................800-328-9800

Curd

Damrow Company
Fond Du Lac, WI...................800-236-1501
Engineered Products Corp
Greenville, SC......................800-868-0145

Fish Scaling & Slitting

Buck Knives
Post Falls, ID........................800-326-2825
Dexter Russell Inc
Southbridge, MA...................800-343-6042
E-Z Edge Inc
West New York, NJ................800-232-4470
General Cutlery Co
Fremont, OH........................419-332-2316
Imperial Schrade Corporation
Ellenville, NY.......................212-210-8600
R Murphy Co Inc
Ayer, MA............................888-772-3481
Simmons Engineering Corporation
Wheeling, IL.........................800-252-3381
Steamway Corporation
Scottsburg, IN......................800-259-8171
TGW International
Florence, KY........................800-407-0173

Food Processing Machine

Ace Co Precision Mfg
Boise, ID.............................800-359-7012
AM-Mac
Fairfield, NJ.........................800-829-2018
Branson Ultrasonics Corp
Danbury, CT.........................203-796-0400
Brooklyn Boys Pizza & Pasta
Boca Raton, FL.....................561-477-3663
California Saw & Knife Works
San Francisco, CA.................888-729-6533
Carolina Knife
Asheville, NC.......................800-520-5030
Chapman Corp
St Louis, MO........................800-843-1404
Dexter Russell Inc
Southbridge, MA...................800-343-6042
DSW Converting Knives
Birmingham, AL....................205-322-2021
Florida Knife Co
Sarasota, FL........................800-966-5643
Huther Brothers
Rochester, NY......................800-334-1115
International Knife & Saw
Florence, SC........................800-354-9872
KSW Corp
Des Moines, IA.....................515-265-5269
Lako Tool & Mfg Inc
Perrysburg, OH.....................800-228-2982
Pappas Inc.
Detroit, MI...........................800-521-0888
R H Saw Corp
Barrington, IL.......................847-381-8777
Simmons Engineering Corporation
Wheeling, IL.........................800-252-3381
Simonds International
Fitchburg, MA......................800-343-1616
Simonds International
Fitchburg, MA......................978-345-7521
Specialty Blades
Staunton, VA........................540-248-2200
Stutz Products Corp
Hartford City, IN...................765-348-2510
TGW International
Florence, KY........................800-407-0173
York Saw & Knife
York, PA.............................800-233-1969
Zenith Cutter
Loves Park, IL......................800-223-5202

Fruit

Amco Metals Indl
City of Industry, CA...............626-855-2550
Burrell Cutlery Company
Ellicottville, NY....................716-699-2343
Globe Machine
Tacoma, WA........................800-523-6575
Goodnature Products
Orchard Park, NY..................800-875-3381
International Knife & Saw
Florence, SC........................800-354-9872
Mundial
Norwood, MA.......................800-487-2224

Q A Supplies LLC
Norfolk, VA....................800-472-7205
Simmons Engineering Corporation
Wheeling, IL...................800-252-3381
TGW International
Florence, KY..................800-407-0173

Loin

Mound Tool Co
St Louis, MO..................314-968-3991

Machine

Ace Co Precision Mfg
Boise, ID.....................800-359-7012
Bettendorf Stanford Inc
Salem, IL.....................800-548-2253
California Saw & Knife Works
San Francisco, CA.............888-729-6533
Carolina Knife
Asheville, NC.................800-520-5030
D & S Mfg
Auburn, MA...................508-799-7812
DSW Converting Knives
Birmingham, AL...............205-322-2021
Florida Knife Co
Sarasota, FL.................800-966-5643
Greenfield Disston
Greensboro, NC...............336-855-4200
Huther Brothers
Rochester, NY................800-334-1115
International Knife & Saw
Florence, SC.................800-354-9872
Kinetic Co
Greendale, WI................414-425-8221
KSW Corp
Des Moines, IA...............515-265-5269
Lako Tool & Mfg Inc
Perrysburg, OH...............800-228-2982
Moore Production Tool Spec Inc
Farmington Hills, MI.........248-476-1200
Nitsch Tool Co Inc
Syracuse, NY.................315-472-4044
Page Slotting Saw Co Inc
Toledo, OH...................419-476-7475
Polar Process
Plattsville, ON..............877-896-8077
Rudolph Industries
Mississauga, ON..............905-564-6160
Simonds International
Fitchburg, MA................800-343-1616
Simonds International
Fitchburg, MA................978-345-7521
Specialty Blades
Staunton, VA.................540-248-2200
Stutz Products Corp
Hartford City, IN............765-348-2510
TGW International
Florence, KY.................800-407-0173
York Saw & Knife
York, PA.....................800-233-1969
Zenith Cutter
Loves Park, IL...............800-223-5202

Meat Packing

Cutrite Company
Fremont, OH..................800-928-8748
E-Z Edge Inc
West New York, NJ............800-232-4470
General Cutlery Co
Fremont, OH..................419-332-2316
Lamson & Goodnow
Shelburne Falls, MA..........800-872-6564
Mandeville Company
Minneapolis, MN..............800-328-8490
Omcan Manufacturing & Distributing Company
Mississauga, ON..............800-465-0234
Specialty Blades
Staunton, VA.................540-248-2200
TGW International
Florence, KY.................800-407-0173

Oyster & Clam

Mundial
Norwood, MA..................800-487-2224
Superior Products Company
Saint Paul, MN...............800-328-9800
TGW International
Florence, KY.................800-407-0173

Slicing

Bettendorf Stanford Inc
Salem, IL.....................800-548-2253
Browne & Company
Markham, ON..................905-475-6104
Burrell Cutlery Company
Ellicottville, NY............716-699-2343
Dexter Russell Inc
Southbridge, MA..............800-343-6042
Friedr Dick Corp
Farmingdale, NY..............800-554-3425
Gerber Legendary Blades
Portland, OR.................800-950-6161
Gril-Del
Mankato, MN..................800-782-7320
Huther Brothers
Rochester, NY................800-334-1115
Industrial Razorblade
Orange, NJ...................973-673-4286
International Knife & Saw
Florence, SC.................800-354-9872
Lamson & Goodnow
Shelburne Falls, MA..........800-872-6564
Mundial
Norwood, MA..................800-487-2224
Pappas Inc.
Detroit, MI..................800-521-0888
R H Saw Corp
Barrington, IL...............847-381-8777
Rudolph Industries
Mississauga, ON..............905-564-6160
Simmons Engineering Corporation
Wheeling, IL.................800-252-3381
Stutz Products Corp
Hartford City, IN............765-348-2510
TGW International
Florence, KY.................800-407-0173

Steak

Browne & Company
Markham, ON..................905-475-6104
Burrell Cutlery Company
Ellicottville, NY............716-699-2343
Delco Tableware
Port Washington, NY..........800-221-9557
General Cutlery Co
Fremont, OH..................419-332-2316
Gerber Legendary Blades
Portland, OR.................800-950-6161
Lamson & Goodnow
Shelburne Falls, MA..........800-872-6564
Mundial
Norwood, MA..................800-487-2224
Superior Products Company
Saint Paul, MN...............800-328-9800
Walco
Utica, NY....................800-879-2526

Vegetable

AM-Mac
Fairfield, NJ................800-829-2018
Brooklyn Boys Pizza & Pasta
Boca Raton, FL...............561-477-3663
Browne & Company
Markham, ON..................905-475-6104
International Knife & Saw
Florence, SC.................800-354-9872
Jim Scharf Holdings
Perdue, SK...................800-667-9727
Mundial
Norwood, MA..................800-487-2224
Simmons Engineering Corporation
Wheeling, IL.................800-252-3381
Superior Products Company
Saint Paul, MN...............800-328-9800
TGW International
Florence, KY.................800-407-0173

Ladles

Culinary

Amco Metals Indl
City of Industry, CA.........626-855-2550
Browne & Company
Markham, ON..................905-475-6104
Carlisle Food Svc Products Inc
Oklahoma City, OK............800-654-8210

Eastern Tabletop Mfg
Brooklyn, NY.................888-422-4142
Leggett & Platt Storage
Vernon Hills, IL.............847-816-6246
Liberty Ware LLC
Clearfield, UT...............888-500-5885
Olde Country Reproductions Inc
York, PA.....................800-358-3997
Superior Products Company
Saint Paul, MN...............800-328-9800
Vollrath Co LLC
Sheboygan, WI................800-624-2051
Wiltec
Leominster, MA...............978-537-1497

Liners

Cake Pan

Brown Paper Goods Co
Waukegan, IL.................847-688-1450
M S Plastics & Packaging Inc
Butler, NJ...................800-593-1802
Norpak Corp
Newark, NJ...................800-631-6970
State Products
Long Beach, CA...............800-730-5150
Taconic
Petersburg, NY...............800-833-1805
Zenith Specialty Bag Co
City of Industry, CA.........800-962-2247

Magnets

Industrial Magnetics
Boyne City, MI...............800-662-4638

Matches

Admatch Corporation
New York, NY.................800-777-9909
Atlas Match Company
Toronto, ON..................888-285-2783
Atlas Match Corporation
Euless, TX...................800-628-2426
Bradley Industries
Westchester, IL..............815-469-2314
D D Bean & Sons Co
Jaffrey, NH..................800-326-8311
Jarden Home Brands
Cloquet, MN..................218-879-6700
K & L Intl
Ontario, CA..................888-598-5588
Palmland Paper Company
Fort Lauderdale, FL..........800-266-9067
Penley Corporation
West Paris, ME...............800-368-6449

Micer

Meat

Thunderbird Food Machinery
Blaine, WA...................866-875-6868

Mincer

Thunderbird Food Machinery
Blaine, WA...................866-875-6868

Molds

Bakers' & Confectioners'

Amco Metals Indl
City of Industry, CA.........626-855-2550
Carnegie Manufacturing Company
Fairfield, NJ................973-575-3449
Chocolate Concepts
Hartville, OH................330-877-3322
Choklit Molds LTD
Lincoln, RI..................800-777-6653
D.R. McClain & Son
Commerce, CA.................800-428-2263
Edhard Corp
Hackettstown, NJ.............888-334-2731
Hartstone Pottery Inc
Zanesville, OH...............740-452-9999
Hillside Metal Ware Company
Union, NJ....................908-964-3080
Intermold Corporation
Greenville, SC...............864-627-0300

Liberty Engineering Co
Roscoe, IL 877-623-9065
Matfer Inc
Van Nuys, CA 800-766-0333
Micelli Chocolate Mold Company
West Babylon, NY 631-752-2888
Moline Machinery LLC
Duluth, MN 800-767-5734
Parrish's Cake Decorating
Gardena, CA 800-736-8443
Somerset Industries
Billerica, MA 800-772-4404
Voorhees Rubber Mfg Co
Newark, MD 410-632-1582

Butter & Cheese

Carnegie Manufacturing Company
Fairfield, NJ 973-575-3449
Lancaster Colony Corporation
Westerville, OH. 614-224-7141
Roaring Brook Dairy
Chappaqua, NY 646-559-9330
Sanchelima International
Miami, FL 305-591-4343
Viking Machine & Design Inc
De Pere, WI 888-286-2116

Pans

Baking & Roasting

ABI Limited
Concord, ON 800-297-8666
Advance Tabco
Edgewood, NY 800-645-3166
Allied Metal Spinning
Bronx, NY 800-615-2266
Alumaworks
Sunny Isle Beach, FL 800-277-7267
American Metal Stamping
Brooklyn, NY 718-384-1500
APW Wyott Food Service Equipment Company
Cheyenne, WY 800-527-2100
Baking Machines
Livermore, CA 925-449-3369
Bluebird Manufacturing
Montreal, QC 800-406-2505
Browne & Company
Markham, ON 905-475-6104
Cambro Manufacturing Co
Huntington Beach, CA 800-833-3003
Carlson Products
Maize, KS 800-234-1069
Crestware
North Salt Lake, UT 800-345-0513
Crown Custom Metal Spinning
Concord, ON. 800-750-1924
D & W Fine Pack
Lake Zurich, IL. 800-323-0422
Dur-Able Aluminum Corporation
Hoffman Estates, IL 847-843-1100
Dura-Ware Company of America
Oklahoma City, OK 800-664-3872
G & S Metal Products Co Inc
Cleveland, OH 216-441-0700
Hillside Metal Ware Company
Union, NJ 908-964-3080
Kosempel Manufacturing Company
Philadelphia, PA 800-733-7122
Legion Industries Inc
Waynesboro, GA. 800-887-1988
Lincoln Foodservice
Cleveland, OH 800-374-3004
Magna Industries Inc
Lakewood, NJ 800-510-9856
Matfer Inc
Van Nuys, CA 800-766-0333
Mouli Manufacturing Corporation
Belleville, NJ 800-789-8285
National Cart Co
St Charles, MO 636-947-3800
Parrish's Cake Decorating
Gardena, CA 800-736-8443
Pfeil & Holding Inc
Woodside, NY 800-247-7955
Piper Products Inc
Wausau, WI 800-544-3057
State Products
Long Beach, CA 800-730-5150
Superior Products Company
Saint Paul, MN 800-328-9800

Vollrath Co LLC
Sheboygan, WI 800-624-2051
Williamsburg Metal Spinning
Brooklyn, NY 888-535-5402
World Kitchen
Elmira, NY 800-999-3436

Stainless Steel

Castella Imports Inc
Hauppauge, NY 631-231-5500

Frying

Adcraft
Hicksville, NY 800-223-7750
Alumaworks
Sunny Isle Beach, FL 800-277-7267
Bluebird Manufacturing
Montreal, QC 800-406-2505
Browne & Company
Markham, ON 905-475-6104
Crown Custom Metal Spinning
Concord, ON 800-750-1924
Dura-Ware Company of America
Oklahoma City, OK 800-664-3872
Imperial Manufacturing Co
Corona, CA 800-343-7790
Liberty Ware LLC
Clearfield, UT 888-500-5885
Market Forge Industries Inc
Everett, MA. 866-698-3188
Matfer Inc
Van Nuys, CA 800-766-0333
Olde Country Reproductions Inc
York, PA 800-358-3997
Regal Ware Inc
Kewaskum, WI 262-626-2121
Superior Products Company
Saint Paul, MN 800-328-9800
Vollrath Co LLC
Sheboygan, WI 800-624-2051

Pie

ABI Limited
Concord, ON 800-297-8666
Allied Metal Spinning
Bronx, NY 800-615-2266
Browne & Company
Markham, ON 905-475-6104
Carlson Products
Maize, KS 800-234-1069
Crown Custom Metal Spinning
Concord, ON. 800-750-1924
D & W Fine Pack
Lake Zurich, IL. 800-323-0422
Lincoln Foodservice
Cleveland, OH 800-374-3004
Malco Manufacturing Co
Los Angeles, CA. 866-477-7267
Revere Packaging
Shelbyville, KY 800-626-2668
Superior Products Company
Saint Paul, MN 800-328-9800
V&R Metal Enterprises
Brooklyn, NY 718-768-8142

Sauce

Alumaworks
Sunny Isle Beach, FL 800-277-7267
Bluebird Manufacturing
Montreal, QC 800-406-2505
Dover Parkersburg
Follansbee, WV
Dura-Ware Company of America
Oklahoma City, OK 800-664-3872
Lincoln Foodservice
Cleveland, OH 800-374-3004
Regal Ware Inc
Kewaskum, WI 262-626-2121
Superior Products Company
Saint Paul, MN 800-328-9800

Parers & Peelers

Fruit & Vegetable

A.K. Robins
Baltimore, MD 800-486-9656
Amco Metals Indl
City of Industry, CA 626-855-2550

Atlas Pacific Engineering
Pueblo, CO 719-948-3040
Blakeslee, Inc.
Addison, IL 630-532-5021
Browne & Company
Markham, ON. 905-475-6104
Conimar Corp
Ocala, FL. 800-874-9735
F.B. Pease Company
Rochester, NY. 585-475-1870
Insinger Co
Philadelphia, PA 800-344-4802
Juice Tree
Omaha, NE 714-891-4425
Magnuson
Pueblo, CO 719-948-9500
Mouli Manufacturing Corporation
Belleville, NJ 800-789-8285
Murotech
St Marys, OH 800-565-6876
Odenberg Engineering
West Sacramento, CA. 800-688-8396
Superior Products Company
Saint Paul, MN 800-328-9800
Univex Corp
Salem, NH. 800-258-6358
Vanmark Equipment
Creston, IA 800-523-6261
White Mountain Freezer
Kansas City, MO 816-943-4100

Plates

Paper

AJM Packaging Corporation
Bloomfield Hills, MI 248-901-0040
Bergschrond
Seattle, WA 206-763-3502
Carthage Cup Company
Longview, TX 903-238-9833
Chinet Company
Laguna Niguel, CA 949-348-1711
Creative Converting Inc
Clintonville, WI 800-826-0418
Dart Canada Inc.
Toronto, ON 800-465-9696
Durango-Georgia Paper
Tampa, FL 813-286-2718
E K Lay Co
Philadelphia, PA 800-523-3220
Enviro-Ware
Pittsburgh, PA 888-233-7857
Fonda Group
Goshen, IN 574-534-2515
Four M Manufacturing Group
San Jose, CA 408-998-1141
Genpak LLC
Charlotte, NC 800-626-6695
Hoffmaster Group Inc.
Oshkosh, WI 800-558-9300
James River Canada
North York, ON. 416-789-5151
Jones-Zylon Co
West Lafayette, OH. 800-848-8160
Premier
Cincinnati, OH 800-354-9817
Primary Liquidation
Bohemia, NY 631-244-1410
Scan Group
Appleton, WI 920-730-9150
Smith-Lee Company
Oshkosh, WI 800-327-9774
Solo Cup Company
Lake Forest, IL
Sterling Paper Company
Ohio, PA 800-282-1124
Westervelt Co Inc
Tuscaloosa, AL 205-562-5000

Pie

Carlisle Food Svc Products Inc
Oklahoma City, OK 800-654-8210
Norand Aluminum
Franklin, TX 615-771-5700

Plastic, Reusable

Dart Canada Inc.
Toronto, ON 800-465-9696

De Ster Corporation
Atlanta, GA.........................800-237-8270
Hoffmaster Group Inc
Oshkosh, WI.......................800-367-2877
HPI North America/Plastics
Chicago, IL........................800-327-3534
K & L Intl
Ontario, CA........................888-598-5588
Kendrick Johnson & Assoc Inc
Minneapolis, MN..................800-826-1271
OWD
Tupper Lake, NY..................800-836-1693
Plastiques Cascades Group
Montreal, QC......................888-703-6515
Wiltec
Leominster, MA...................978-537-1497

Platters

Bon Chef
Lafayette, NJ......................800-331-0177
Browne & Company
Markham, ON......................905-475-6104
Cal-Mil Plastic Products Inc
Oceanside, CA.....................800-321-9069
Carlisle Food Svc Products Inc
Oklahoma City, OK...............800-654-8210
Cyclamen Collection
Oakland, CA........................510-434-7620
Delfin Design & Mfg
Rancho Sta Marg, CA............800-354-7919
First Plastics Co Inc
Leominster, MA...................978-840-6908
Gaetano America
El Monte, CA.......................626-442-2858
Gril-Del
Mankato, MN......................800-782-7320
M & E Mfg Co Inc
Kingston, NY.......................845-331-2110
Michael Leson Dinnerware
Youngstown, OH..................800-821-3541
Olde Country Reproductions Inc
York, PA............................800-358-3997
Olde Thompson Inc
Oxnard, CA.........................800-827-1565
Prolon
Port Gibson, MS...................888-480-9828
Ronnie's Ceramic Company
San Francisco, CA................800-888-8218
Sabert Corp
Sayreville, NJ......................800-722-3781
Sims Superior Seating
Locust Grove, GA.................800-729-9178
Superior Products Company
Saint Paul, MN....................800-328-9800
Tomlinson Industries
Cleveland, OH.....................800-945-4589
Ullman, Shapiro & UllmanLLP
New York, NY.....................212-755-0299
Vertex China
Pomona, CA........................800-483-7839
Weavewood, Inc.
Golden Valley, MN...............800-367-6460
WNA
Chattanooga, TN..................800-404-9318

Rolling Pins

H. Arnold Wood Turning
Tarrytown, NY.....................888-314-0088
Read Products Inc
Seattle, WA........................800-445-3416
Superior Products Company
Saint Paul, MN....................800-328-9800
Thorpe Rolling Pin Co
Hamden, CT........................800-344-6966

Scoops, Dishers & Spades

Amco Metals Indl
City of Industry, CA..............626-855-2550
Bremer Manufacturing Co Inc
Elkhart Lake, WI..................920-894-2944
C R Mfg
Waverly, NE.......................877-789-5844
Carlisle Food Svc Products Inc
Oklahoma City, OK...............800-654-8210
E-Z Dip
Frankfort, IN.......................866-347-3279
Landis Plastics
Alsip, IL.............................708-396-1470

Lloyd Disher Company
Decatur, IL.........................217-429-0593
Measurex/S&L Plastics
Nazareth, PA.......................800-752-0650
National Scoop & Equipment Company
Spring House, PA..................215-646-2040
Penn Scale ManufacturingCompany
Philadelphia, PA...................215-739-9644
Prolon
Port Gibson, MS...................888-480-9828
Superior Products Company
Saint Paul, MN....................800-328-9800
Tolco Corp
Toledo, OH.........................800-537-4786
Zeroll Company
Fort Pierce, FL.....................800-872-5000

Scrapers

Butchers' Block

Boehringer Mfg. Co. Inc.
Felton, CA..........................800-630-8665
C R Mfg
Waverly, NE.......................877-789-5844
Goodell Tools
New Hope, MN....................800-542-3906

Shears

Poultry

Amco Metals Indl
City of Industry, CA..............626-855-2550
Cutrite Company
Fremont, OH.......................800-928-8748
E-Z Edge Inc
West New York, NJ...............800-232-4470
Imperial Schrade Corporation
Ellenville, NY......................212-210-8600
Mundial
Norwood, MA......................800-487-2224
Superior Products Company
Saint Paul, MN....................800-328-9800

Sheeter

Dough

Thunderbird Food Machinery
Blaine, WA.........................866-875-6868

Sheets

Cookie

Browne & Company
Markham, ON......................905-475-6104
Dover Parkersburg
Follansbee, WV
Lincoln Foodservice
Cleveland, OH.....................800-374-3004
Matfer Inc
Van Nuys, CA......................800-766-0333
State Products
Long Beach, CA...................800-730-5150
Superior Products Company
Saint Paul, MN....................800-328-9800

Sieves

ANDRITZ Inc
Muncy, PA..........................704-943-4343
ATM Corporation
New Berlin, WI.....................800-511-2096
Browne & Company
Markham, ON......................905-475-6104
Cleveland Vibrator Co
Cleveland, OH.....................800-221-3298
CSC Scientific Co Inc
Fairfax, VA.........................800-621-4778
Gilson Co Inc
Lewis Center, OH.................800-444-1508
Glen Mills Inc.
Clifton, NJ..........................973-777-0777
Great Western Manufacturing Company
Leavenworth, KS..................800-682-3121
Newark Wire Cloth Co
Clifton, NJ..........................800-221-0392
Norvell Co Inc
Fort Scott, KS......................800-653-3147

Vorti-Siv
Salem, OH..........................800-227-7487

Sifters

Flour & Bakers'

Amco Metals Indl
City of Industry, CA..............626-855-2550
Ayr King Corp
Louisville, KY......................866-266-6290
B & P Process Equipment
Saginaw, MI........................989-757-1300
Browne & Company
Markham, ON......................905-475-6104
Buffalo Technologies Corporation
Buffalo, NY.........................800-332-2419
F.P. Smith Wire Cloth Company
Northlake, IL.......................800-323-6842
Fred D Pfening Co
Columbus, OH.....................614-294-5361
Great Western Manufacturing Company
Leavenworth, KS..................800-682-3121
Howes S Co Inc
Silver Creek, NY..................888-255-2611
K B Systems Inc
Bangor, PA.........................610-588-7788
Kemutec Group Inc
Bristol, PA..........................215-788-8013
Meadows Mills Inc
North Wilkesboro, NC............800-626-2282
Norvell Co Inc
Fort Scott, KS......................800-653-3147
Shick Esteve
Kansas City, MO..................877-744-2587
Sifter Parts & Svc
Wesley Chapel, FL................800-367-3591
Smico Manufacturing Co Inc
Oklahoma City, OK...............800-351-9088
Stewart Systems Baking LLC
Plano, TX...........................972-422-5808

Skewers

Amco Metals Indl
City of Industry, CA..............626-855-2550
Automated Food Systems
Waxahachie, TX...................469-517-0470
C R Mfg
Waverly, NE.......................877-789-5844
Chicago Dowel Co Inc
Chicago, IL.........................800-333-6935
Coastline Equipment Inc
Bellingham, WA...................360-734-8509
G.F. Frank & Sons
Fairfield, OH.......................513-870-9075
H. Arnold Wood Turning
Tarrytown, NY.....................888-314-0088
Hardwood Products Co LP
Guilford, ME.......................800-289-3340
Jarden Home Brands
Daleville, IN........................800-392-2575
K & L Intl
Ontario, CA........................888-598-5588
Les Industries Touch Inc
Sherbrooke, QC...................800-267-4140
Lynch-Jamentz Company
Lakewood, CA.....................800-828-6217
Royal Paper Products
Coatesville, PA....................800-666-6655
Saunder Brothers
Bridgton, ME......................207-647-3331
Trepte's Wire & Metal Works
Bellflower, CA.....................800-828-6217

Slicer

Bagel

Larien Products
Northampton, MA.................800-462-9237

Bread

Paramount Packaging Corp
Melville, NY........................516-333-8100
Thunderbird Food Machinery
Blaine, WA.........................866-875-6868

Spoons

Abco International
Oneida, NY 888-263-7195
Amco Metals Indl
City of Industry, CA 626-855-2550
American Housewares
Bronx, NY 718-665-9500
C R Mfg
Waverly, NE 877-789-5844
Carlisle Food Svc Products Inc
Oklahoma City, OK 800-654-8210
CUTCO Corp
Olean, NY 716-372-3111
Dart Canada Inc.
Toronto, ON 800-465-9696
Design Specialties Inc
Hamden, CT 800-999-1584
Fab-X/Metals
Washington, NC 800-677-3229
Fioriware
Zanesville, OH 740-454-7400
Hal-One Plastics
Olathe, KS 800-626-5784
Harco Enterprises
Peterborough, ON 800-361-5361
Hardwood Products Co LP
Guilford, ME. 800-289-3340
Imperial Schrade Corporation
Ellenville, NY 212-210-8600
Jarden Home Brands
Daleville, IN 800-392-2575
Jones-Zylon Co
West Lafayette, OH 800-848-8160
Lifetime Brands Inc
Garden City, NY 516-683-6000
LoTech Industries
Lakewood, CO 800-295-0199
Lynch-Jamentz Company
Lakewood, CA 800-828-6217
OWD
Tupper Lake, NY 800-836-1693
Polar Plastics
St Laurent, QC 514-331-0207
Polar Ware Company
Sheboygan, WI 800-237-3655
Solon Manufacturing Company
North Haven, CT. 800-341-6640
Superior Products Company
Saint Paul, MN 800-328-9800
Tops Manufacturing Co
Darien, CT. 203-655-9367
Trepte's Wire & Metal Works
Bellflower, CA 800-828-6217
Vollrath Co LLC
Sheboygan, WI 800-624-2051
Weavewood, Inc.
Golden Valley, MN 800-367-6460
Wiltec
Leominster, MA 978-537-1497

Stirrers & Picks: Cocktail, Hors D'oeuvres

C R Mfg
Waverly, NE 877-789-5844
Cell-O-Core Company
Sharon Center, OH 800-239-4370
Epic Products
Santa Ana, CA 800-548-9791
Goldmax Industries
City of Industry, CA 626-964-8820
Harco Enterprises
Peterborough, ON 800-361-5361
Hardwood Products Co LP
Guilford, ME. 800-289-3340
Jarden Home Brands
Daleville, IN 800-392-2575
Johnstown Manufacturing
Columbus, OH 614-236-8853
Pelican Products Inc
Bronx, NY. 800-552-8820
Royal Paper Products
Coatesville, PA 800-666-6655
Soodhalter Plastics
Los Angeles, CA 213-747-0231
Spinzer
Glen Ellyn, IL 630-469-7184
Spir-It/Zoo Piks
Andover, MA 800-343-0996
Spirit Foodservice, Inc.
Andover, MA 800-343-0996

SQP
Schenectady, NY 800-724-1129
Superior Products Company
Saint Paul, MN 800-328-9800
Token Factory
La Crosse, WI 888-486-5367
Tops Manufacturing Co
Darien, CT. 203-655-9367
Trevor Industries
Eden, NY. 716-992-4775
Ursini Plastics
Bracebridge, ON 705-646-2701
Waddington North America
Chelmsford, MA 888-962-2877

Strainers

Amco Metals Indl
City of Industry, CA 626-855-2550
American Metal Stamping
Brooklyn, NY 718-384-1500
C R Mfg
Waverly, NE 877-789-5844
Eaton Filtration, LLC
Tinton Falls, NJ 800-859-9212
Feldmeier Equipment Inc
Syracuse, NY 315-454-8608
Giunta Brothers
Philadelphia, PA 215-389-9670
Globe Machine
Tacoma, WA 800-523-6575
Goodnature Products
Orchard Park, NY 800-875-3381
L.C. Thompson Company
Kenosha, WI 800-558-4018
Lincoln Foodservice
Cleveland, OH 800-374-3004
Mouli Manufacturing Corporation
Belleville, NJ 800-789-8285
Schlueter Company
Janesville, WI 800-359-1700
South Valley Mfg Inc
Gilroy, CA 408-842-5457
Superior Products Company
Saint Paul, MN 800-328-9800

Tables

Cutting & Trimming

Bally Block Co
Bally, PA 610-845-7511
Bmh Equipment Inc
Sacramento, CA 800-350-8828
Catskill Craftsmen Inc
Stamford, NY 607-652-7321
Dunhill Food Equipment Corporation
Armonk, NY 800-847-4206
Fishmore
Melbourne, FL 321-723-4751
Frelco
Stephenville, NL 709-643-5668
Michigan Maple Block Co
Petoskey, MI 800-447-7975
MSSH
Greensburg, IN 812-663-2180
Rheon USA
Irvine, CA 949-768-1900
Triple-A Manufacturing Company
Toronto, ON 800-786-2238
Ultrafryer Systems Inc
San Antonio, TX 800-545-9189

Stainless Steel

A J Antunes & Co
Carol Stream, IL 800-253-2991
A-1 Booth Manufacturing
Burley, ID 800-820-3285
Advance Tabco
Edgewood, NY 800-645-3166
All State Fabricators Corporation
Tampa, FL. 800-322-9925
Allstrong Restaurant Eqpt Inc
South El Monte, CA 800-933-8913
Amtekco
Columbus, OH 800-336-4677
Andgar Corp
Ferndale, WA 360-366-9900
ARC Specialties
Valencia, CA 661-775-8500

Atlas Equipment Company
Kansas City, MO. 800-842-9188
Avalon Manufacturer
Corona, CA 800-676-3040
California Vibratory Feeders
Anaheim, CA 800-354-0972
Carts Food Equipment
Brooklyn, NY 718-788-5540
Cobb & Zimmer
Detroit, MI 313-923-0350
Commercial Kitchen Co
Los Angeles, CA 323-732-2291
Custom Diamond Intl.
Laval, QC 800-326-5926
D A Berther Inc
Milwaukee, WI 877-357-9622
Dayco
Clearwater, FL 727-573-9330
Den Mar Corp
North Dartmouth, MA 508-999-3295
Duluth Sheet Metal
Duluth, MN 218-722-2613
Eagle Group
Clayton, DE. 800-441-8440
Eldorado Miranda Manufacturing Company
Largo, FL. 800-330-0708
Erwin Food Service Equipment
Fort Worth, TX 817-535-0021
Fabwright Inc
Garden Grove, CA 800-854-6464
Falcon Fabricators Inc
Nashville, TN 615-832-0027
Fixtur World
Cookeville, TN 800-634-9887
Gasser Chair Co Inc
Youngstown, OH. 800-323-2234
Griffin Products
Wills Point, TX 800-379-9709
Hot Food Boxes
Mooresville, IN. 800-733-8073
IMC Teddy Food Service Equipment
Amityville, NY 800-221-5644
Industries Inc Kiefer
Random Lake, WI. 920-994-2332
Institutional Equipment Inc
Bolingbrook, IL 630-771-0990
John Boos & Co
Effingham, IL 888-431-2667
KEMCO
Wareham, MA. 800-231-5955
Kitchen Equipment Fabricating
Houston, TX 713-747-3611
Lakeside Manufacturing Inc
Milwaukee, WI 888-558-8565
Load King Mfg
Jacksonville, FL 800-531-4975
M & E Mfg Co Inc
Kingston, NY 845-331-2110
Marlo Manufacturing
Boonton, NJ 800-222-0450
MCM Fixture Co
Hazel Park, MI 248-547-9280
Metal
Columbia, SC 803-776-9252
Metal Master Sales Corp
Glendale Heights, IL. 800-488-8729
Miami Metal
Miami, FL 305-576-3600
Midwest Folding Products
Chicago, IL 800-344-2864
Mouron & Co Inc
Indianapolis, IN 317-243-7955
New Age Industrial
Norton, KS 800-255-0104
Northern Stainless Fabricating
Traverse City, MI 231-947-4580
Omicron Steel Products Company
Jamaica, NY 718-805-3400
Pollard Brothers
Chicago, IL 773-763-6868
Premium Air Systems Inc
Troy, MI 877-430-0333
Quipco Products Inc
Sauget, IL 314-993-1442
Randell Manufacturing   Unified Brands
Weidman, MI 888-994-7636
Sarasota Restaurant Equipment
Sarasota, FL 800-434-1410
Savage Brothers Company
Elk Grove Vlg, IL. 800-342-0973
Schlueter Company
Janesville, WI 800-359-1700

Sefi Fabricators Inc
Amityville, NY 631-842-2200
South Valley Mfg Inc
Gilroy, CA 408-842-5457
Southwestern Porcelain Steel
Sand Springs, OK 918-245-1375
Stainless
La Vergne, TN. 800-877-5177
Stainless Fabricating Company
Denver, CO 800-525-8966
Stainless International
Rancho Cordova, CA 888-300-6196
Stainless Steel Fabricators
Tyler, TX 903-595-6625
Starlite Food Service Equipment
Detroit, MI 888-521-6603
Super Sturdy
Weldon, NC. 800-253-4833
Superior Products Company
Saint Paul, MN 800-328-9800
Supreme Metal
Alpharetta, GA 800-645-2526
Travis Manufacturing Corp
Alliance, OH 330-875-1661
Unarco Industries LLC
Wagoner, OK. 800-654-4100
Universal Stainless
Aurora, CO 800-223-8332
Universal Stainless & Alloy
Titusville, PA 800-295-1909
Vande Berg SCALES/Vbs Inc
Sioux Center, IA .712-722-1181
Weiss Sheet Metal Inc
Avon, MA 508-583-8300
West Star Industries
Stockton, CA 800-326-2288
Wilder Manufacturing Company
Port Jervis, NY 800-832-1319
Zol-Mark Industries
Winnipeg, NB 204-943-7393

Work

Advance Tabco
Edgewood, NY 800-645-3166
Allstrong Restaurant Eqpt Inc
South El Monte, CA 800-933-8913
Bmh Equipment Inc
Sacramento, CA .800-350-8828
Carts Food Equipment
Brooklyn, NY 718-788-5540
Eldorado Miranda Manufacturing Company
Largo, FL 800-330-0708
Falcon Fabricators Inc
Nashville, TN 615-832-0027
John Boos & Co
Effingham, IL 888-431-2667
Lakeside Manufacturing Inc
Milwaukee, WI 888-558-8565
MCM Fixture Co
Hazel Park, MI 248-547-9280
Metro Corporation
Wilkes Barre, PA. 800-992-1776
National Bar Systems
Huntington Beach, CA 714-848-1688
Stainless Equipment Manufacturing
Dallas, TX. 800-736-2038
Superior Products Company
Saint Paul, MN 800-328-9800
Weiss Sheet Metal Inc
Avon, MA 508-583-8300

Tins

Cake

Browne & Company
Markham, ON. 905-475-6104
Dover Parkersburg
Follansbee, WV
Independent Can Co
Belcamp, MD 410-272-0090
Olive Can Company
Elgin, IL 847-468-7474

Tinware

Dover Parkersburg
Follansbee, WV
Greenfield Packaging
White Plains, NY 914-993-0233

Independent Can Co
Belcamp, MD 410-272-0090
Xtreme Beverages, LLC
Dana Point, CA .949-495-7929

Tongs

Food

Amco Metals Indl
City of Industry, CA 626-855-2550
Atlanta Burning Bush
Newnan, GA 800-665-5611
Browne & Company
Markham, ON 905-475-6104
C R Mfg
Waverly, NE 877-789-5844
Carlisle Food Svc Products Inc
Oklahoma City, OK 800-654-8210
First Plastics Co Inc
Leominster, MA .978-840-6908
Gril-Del
Mankato, MN 800-782-7320
Liberty Ware LLC
Clearfield, UT 888-500-5885
LoTech Industries
Lakewood, CO 800-295-0199
Music City Metals Inc
Nashville, TN 800-251-2674
Superior Products Company
Saint Paul, MN 800-328-9800
Vollrath Co LLC
Sheboygan, WI 800-624-2051
Weavewood, Inc.
Golden Valley, MN 800-367-6460
Wiltec
Leominster, MA .978-537-1497
Wishbone Utensil Tableware Line
Wheat Ridge, CO 866-266-5928

Ice

Browne & Company
Markham, ON 905-475-6104
C R Mfg
Waverly, NE 877-789-5844
Superior Products Company
Saint Paul, MN 800-328-9800
Weavewood, Inc.
Golden Valley, MN 800-367-6460
Wiltec
Leominster, MA .978-537-1497

Toothpicks

Admatch Corporation
New York, NY 800-777-9909
Atlas Match Company
Toronto, ON 888-285-2783
C R Mfg
Waverly, NE 877-789-5844
Cell-O-Core Company
Sharon Center, OH 800-239-4370
Goldmax Industries
City of Industry, CA 626-964-8820
H A Stiles
Westbrook, ME .800-447-8537
Jarden Home Brands
Cloquet, MN 218-879-6700
Jarden Home Brands
Daleville, IN 800-392-2575
K & L Intl
Ontario, CA. 888-598-5588
Les Industries Touch Inc
Sherbrooke, QC 800-267-4140
Penley Corporation
West Paris, ME .800-368-6449
Royal Paper Products
Coatesville, PA .800-666-6655
Unique Manufacturing
Visalia, CA 888-737-1007
Z 2000 the Pick of the Millenium
Bartlesville, OK 800-654-7311

Trays & Pans

Bakers'

Aeromat Plastics Inc
Burnsville, MN .888-286-8729
Allied Bakery and Food Service Equipment
Santa Fe Springs, CA 562-945-6506

Allied Metal Spinning
Bronx, NY. 800-615-2266
American Metal Stamping
Brooklyn, NY 718-384-1500
American Metalcraft Inc
Franklin Park, IL 708-345-1177
Browne & Company
Markham, ON. 905-475-6104
Buckhorn Inc
Milford, OH 800-543-4454
COW Industries Inc
Columbus, OH 800-542-9353
D & W Fine Pack
Lake Zurich, IL. .800-323-0422
Dur-Able Aluminum Corporation
Hoffman Estates, IL 847-843-1100
Green Tek
Janesville, WI 800-747-6440
Music City Metals Inc
Nashville, TN 800-251-2674
National Cart Co
St Charles, MO .636-947-3800
Omega Industries
St Louis, MO. 314-961-1668
Paper Products Company
Cincinnati, OH .513-921-4717
Polar Ware Company
Sheboygan, WI .800-237-3655
Superior Products Company
Saint Paul, MN .800-328-9800
Toscarora
Sandusky, OH 419-625-7343
Unique Plastics
Rio Rico, AZ. 800-658-5946

Utensils

Bakers' & Confectioners'

Allied Metal Spinning
Bronx, NY. 800-615-2266
Amco Metals Indl
City of Industry, CA 626-855-2550
August Thomsen Corp
Glen Cove, NY 800-645-7170
Automated Food Systems
Waxahachie, TX 469-517-0470
Belshaw Adamatic Bakery Group
Auburn, WA 800-578-2547
Browne & Company
Markham, ON. 905-475-6104
Dur-Able Aluminum Corporation
Hoffman Estates, IL 847-843-1100
Esterle Mold & Machine Co Inc
Stow, OH. 800-411-4086
Florida Knife Co
Sarasota, FL 800-966-5643
H. Arnold Wood Turning
Tarrytown, NY .888-314-0088
Hodges
Vienna, IL. 800-444-0011
Johnson Corrugated Products Corporation
Thompson, CT .860-923-9563
Kosempel Manufacturing Company
Philadelphia, PA 800-733-7122
Lady Mary
Rockingham, NC 910-997-7321
Leggett & Platt Storage
Vernon Hills, IL 847-816-6246
Leon Bush Manufacturer
Glenview, IL 847-657-8888
Measurex/S&L Plastics
Nazareth, PA 800-752-0650
Parrish's Cake Decorating
Gardena, CA 800-736-8443
Pfeil & Holding Inc
Woodside, NY .800-247-7955
Saunder Brothers
Bridgton, ME 207-647-3331
State Products
Long Beach, CA 800-730-5150
T & S Perfection Chain Prods
Cullman, AL 888-856-4864
Unifiller Systems
Delta, BC. 888-733-8444
Wishbone Utensil Tableware Line
Wheat Ridge, CO 866-266-5928
Zeier Plastic & Mfg Inc
Madison, WI 608-244-5782

Chopsticks

Bamboo

K & L Intl
Ontario, CA....................888-598-5588

Forks

Cocktail

Amco Metals Indl
City of Industry, CA..............626-855-2550
C R Mfg
Waverly, NE....................877-789-5844
Jarden Home Brands
Daleville, IN...................800-392-2575
Pelican Products Inc
Bronx, NY.....................800-552-8820
Soodhalter Plastics
Los Angeles, CA.................213-747-0231
Wishbone Utensil Tableware Line
Wheat Ridge, CO.................866-266-5928

Wooden

Coley Industries
Wayland, NY....................716-728-2390
Jarden Home Brands
Daleville, IN...................800-392-2575
Weavewood, Inc.
Golden Valley, MN...............800-367-6460

Household, Kitchen

A G Russell Knives
Rogers, AR.....................800-255-9034
Abco International
Oneida, NY.....................888-263-7195
Abond Plastic Corporation
Lachine, QC....................800-886-7947
Ace Fabrication
Mobile, AL.....................251-478-0401
Acme International
Maplewood, NJ..................973-416-0400
All-Clad METALCRAFTERS LLC
Canonsburg, PA.................800-255-2523
Amco Metals Indl
City of Industry, CA.............626-855-2550
American Housewares
Bronx, NY.....................718-665-9500
American Time & Signal Co
Dassel, MN....................800-328-8996
Bally Block Co
Bally, PA......................610-845-7511
Best Manufacturers
Portland, OR...................800-500-1528
Bluffton Slaw Cutter Company
Bluffton, OH...................419-358-9840
Bremer Manufacturing Co Inc
Elkhart Lake, WI................920-894-2944
Brown Manufacturing Company
Decatur, GA....................404-378-8311
Browne & Company
Markham, ON....................905-475-6104
Buck Knives
Post Falls, ID...................800-326-2825
Burrell Cutlery Company
Ellicottville, NY.................716-699-2343
C R Mfg
Waverly, NE....................877-789-5844
Carlisle Food Svc Products Inc
Oklahoma City, OK...............800-654-8210
Carolina Cracker
Garner, NC.....................919-779-6899
Chef Revival
North Charleston, SC.............800-248-9826
Chef Specialties
Smethport, PA..................800-440-2433
Chicago Scale & Slicer Company
Franklin Park, IL................847-455-3400
Cleveland Metal Stamping Company
Berea, OH.....................440-234-0010
Coley Industries
Wayland, NY....................716-728-2390
Conimar Corp
Ocala, FL.....................800-874-9735
Corby Hall
Randolph, NJ...................973-366-8300
CUTCO Corp
Olean, NY.....................716-372-3111
Cyclamen Collection
Oakland, CA....................510-434-7620

Dart Container Corp.
Mason, MI.....................800-248-5960
Dexter Russell Inc
Southbridge, MA................800-343-6042
Diamond Machining Technology
Marlborough, MA................800-666-4368
Dorton Incorporated
Arlington Hts, IL...............800-299-8600
Dynynstyl
Delray Beach, FL...............800-774-7895
E K Lay Co
Philadelphia, PA................800-523-3220
Edco Industries
Bridgeport, CT..................203-333-8982
Educational Products Company
Hope, NJ......................800-272-3822
Fab-X/Metals
Washington, NC.................800-677-3229
Fioriware
Zanesville, OH..................740-454-7400
Fortune Products Inc
Cedar Park, TX..................512-249-0334
Fun-Time International
Philadelphia, PA................800-776-4386
G & S Metal Products Co Inc
Cleveland, OH..................216-441-0700
G.G. Greene Enterprises
West Warren, PA................814-723-5700
Giunta Brothers
Philadelphia, PA................215-389-9670
Goebel Fixture Co
Hutchinson, MN.................888-339-0509
Gold Star Products
Oak Park, MI...................800-800-0205
Good Idea
Northampton, MA................800-462-9237
Goodell Tools
New Hope, MN..................800-542-3906
Grand Silver Company
Bronx, NY.....................718-585-1930
Gril-Del
Mankato, MN...................800-782-7320
H A Stiles
Westbrook, ME..................800-447-8537
H. Arnold Wood Turning
Tarrytown, NY..................888-314-0088
Hardwood Products Co LP
Guilford, ME...................800-289-3340
Harold Leonard Southwest Corporation
Houston, TX....................800-245-8105
Hillside Metal Ware Company
Union, NJ......................908-964-3080
Insinger Co
Philadelphia, PA................800-344-4802
James River Canada
North York, ON..................416-789-5151
Jim Scharf Holdings
Perdue, SK.....................800-667-9727
Kosempel Manufacturing Company
Philadelphia, PA................800-733-7122
Lady Mary
Rockingham, NC.................910-997-7321
Lamson & Goodnow
Shelburne Falls, MA.............800-872-6564
Lancaster Colony Corporation
Westerville, OH.................614-224-7141
Leggett & Platt Storage
Vernon Hills, IL.................847-816-6246
Lenox Corp
Bristol, PA.....................800-223-4311
Libby Canada
Mississauga, ON.................905-607-8280
Liberty Ware LLC
Clearfield, UT..................888-500-5885
Lifetime Brands Inc
Garden City, NY................516-683-6000
Lincoln Foodservice
Cleveland, OH..................800-374-3004
Lloyd Disher Company
Decatur, IL....................217-429-0593
Lodge Manufacturing Company
South Pittsburg, TN.............423-837-5919
Lorenzen's Cookie Cutters
Wantagh, NY...................516-781-7116
Luce Corp
Hamden, CT....................800-344-6966
Lynch-Jamentz Company
Lakewood, NJ..................800-828-6217
M & E Mfg Co Inc
Kingston, NY...................845-331-2110
M.E. Heuck Company
Mason, OH.....................800-359-3200

Majestic
Bridgeport, CT..................203-367-7900
Mastex Industries
Petersburg, VA.................804-732-8300
Measurex/S&L Plastics
Nazareth, PA...................800-752-0650
Michael Leson Dinnerware
Youngstown, OH................800-821-3541
Michigan Maple Block Co
Petoskey, MI...................800-447-7975
Mid-West Wire Products
Ferndale, MI...................800-989-9881
Mundial
Norwood, MA...................800-487-2224
Music City Metals Inc
Nashville, TN...................800-251-2674
National Novelty Brush Co
Lancaster, PA..................717-299-5681
New Age Industrial
Norton, KS.....................800-255-0104
Novelty Crystal
Long Island City, NY............800-622-0250
Olde Country Reproductions Inc
York, PA......................800-358-3997
Olde Thompson Inc
Oxnard, CA....................800-827-1565
Oneida Food Service
Columbus, OH..................800-828-7033
Oneida LTD Silversmiths
Oneida, NY....................888-263-7195
OWD
Tupper Lake, NY................800-836-1693
OXO International
New York, NY..................212-242-3333
Penley Corporation
West Paris, ME.................800-368-6449
Pinn Pack Packaging LLC
Oxnard, CA....................805-385-4100
Polar Ware Company
Sheboygan, WI.................800-237-3655
Prairie Packaging Inc
Mooresville, NC................704-660-6600
Ranger Blade Manufacturing Company
Traer, IA......................800-377-7860
Regal Ware Inc
Kewaskum, WI..................262-626-2121
Reiner Products
Waterbury, CT..................800-345-6775
Replacements LTD
Mc Leansville, NC...............800-737-5223
Rival Manufacturing Company
Kansas City, MO................816-943-4100
RubaTex Polymer
Middlefield, OH.................440-632-1691
Samuel Underberg Food Store
Brooklyn, NY...................718-363-0787
Saunder Brothers
Bridgton, ME...................207-647-3331
Serr-Edge Machine Company
Cleveland, CI...................800-443-8097
Slicechief Co
Toledo, OH.....................419-241-7647
Spir-It/Zoo Piks
Andover, MA...................800-343-0996
ST Restaurant Supplies
Delta, BC......................888-448-4244
Stanley Roberts
Piscataway, NJ.................973-778-5900
Sturdi-Bilt Restaurant Equipment
Whitmore Lake, MI..............800-521-2895
Swing-A-Way Manufacturing Company
St Louis, MO...................314-773-1488
T & A Metal Products Inc
Deptford, NJ...................856-227-1700
T & S Perfection Chain Prods
Cullman, AL....................888-856-4864
Table De France: North America
New Brunswick, NJ..............888-680-4616
Tar-Hong MELAMINE USA
City of Industry, CA.............626-935-1612
Techform
Mount Airy, NC.................336-789-2115
Thorpe Rolling Pin Co
Hamden, CT....................800-344-6966
Tops Manufacturing Co
Darien, CT.....................203-655-9367
Traeger Industries
Portland, OR...................800-872-3437
TRC
Middlefield, OH.................440-834-0078
Trepte's Wire & Metal Works
Bellflower, CA..................800-828-6217

Tru Hone Corp
Ocala, FL.......................800-237-4663
Ultrafryer Systems Inc
San Antonio, TX..................800-545-9189
Unique Manufacturing
Visalia, CA 888-737-1007
United Performance Metals
Northbrook, IL 888-922-0040
United Showcase Company
Wood Ridge, NJ 800-526-6382
Utica Cutlery Co
Utica, NY 800-879-2526
Vermillion Flooring
Springfield, MO 417-862-3785
Vita Craft Corp
Shawnee, KS....................800-359-3444

Vollrath Co LLC
Sheboygan, WI 800-624-2051
Waddington North America
Chelmsford, MA..................888-962-2877
Walco
Utica, NY 800-879-2526
Warren E. Conley Corporation
Carmel, IN......................800-367-7875
Warther Museum
Dover, OH.......................330-343-7513
Waukesha Cherry-Burrell
Louisville, KY...................502-491-4310
Weavewood, Inc.
Golden Valley, MN...............800-367-6460
Western Stoneware
Monmouth, IL....................309-734-2161

Wiltec
Leominster, MA 978-537-1497
Wilton Brands LLC
Woodridge, IL...................630-963-7100
Wishbone Utensil Tableware Line
Wheat Ridge, CO 866-266-5928
World Kitchen
Elmira, NY 800-999-3436
York Saw & Knife
York, PA 800-233-1969
Zelco Industries
Mount Vernon, NY...............800-431-2486
Zeroll Company
Fort Pierce, FL 800-872-5000

Foodservice Equipment & Supplies

Bars & Bar Supplies

Admatch Corporation
New York, NY 800-777-9909
Advanced Design Mfg
Concord, CA .800-690-0002
Alegacy
Santa Fe Springs, CA 800-848-4440
Alluserv
West Milwaukee, WI 800-558-8565
Alpine Store Equipment Corporation
Long Island City, NY 718-361-1213
Alvarado Manufacturing Co Inc
Chino, CA 800-423-4143
AMC Industries
Palmetto, FL .941-479-7834
Amco Metals Indl
City of Industry, CA 626-855-2550
American Coaster Company
Sanborn, NY .888-423-8628
American Metalcraft Inc
Franklin Park, IL 708-345-1177
AMI
Richmond, CA 800-942-7466
Amtekco
Columbus, OH 800-336-4677
Anchor Hocking Operating Co
Lancaster, OH 800-562-7511
Atlas Match Company
Toronto, ON .888-285-2783
Atlas Match Corporation
Euless, TX 800-628-2426
Automatic Bar Controls Inc
Vacaville, CA .800-722-6738
Ballantyne Food Service Equipment
Omaha, NE 800-424-1215
Bar Equipment Corporation of America
Downey, CA .888-870-2322
Bar-Maid Corp
Garfield, NJ .800-227-6243
Berg Co
Monona, WI .608-221-4281
Best Brands Home Products
New York, NY 212-684-7456
Best Buy Uniforms
Homestead, PA 800-345-1924
Booth
Dallas, TX 800-497-2958
Bradley Industries
Westchester, IL 815-469-2314
Brass Smith
Denver, CO 800-662-9595
Brown Manufacturing Company
Decatur, GA .404-378-8311
Browne & Company
Markham, ON 905-475-6104
C R Mfg
Waverly, NE .877-789-5844
Carlisle Food Svc Products Inc
Oklahoma City, OK 800-654-8210
Carnegie Textile Co
Cleveland, OH 800-633-4136
Carpigiani Corporation of America
Winston Salem, NC. 800-648-4389
Carroll Chair Company
Onalaska, WI. 800-331-4704
Carts Food Equipment
Brooklyn, NY .718-788-5540
CCS Stone, Inc.
Moonachie, NJ 800-227-7785
CDI Service & Mfg Inc
Largo, FL 727-536-2207
Cell-O-Core Company
Sharon Center, OH 800-239-4370
Chaircraft
Hickory, NC .828-326-8458
Classico Seating
Peru, IN 800-968-6655
Co-Rect Products Inc
Golden Valley, MN 800-328-5702
Coastal Canvas Products
Savannah, GA 800-476-5174
Cobb & Zimmer
Detroit, MI 313-923-0350
Commercial Seating Specialists
Santa Clara, CA 408-453-8983

Conimar Corp
Ocala, FL. 800-874-9735
Control Beverage
Adelanto, CA 330-549-5376
Cork Specialties
Miami, FL 305-477-1506
Cove Woodworking
Gloucester, MA. 800-273-0037
Craig Manufacturing
Irvington, NJ 800-631-7936
Cruvinet Winebar Co LLC
Sparks, NV 800-278-8463
Culinary Depot
Monsey, NY .888-845-8200
D D Bean & Sons Co
Jaffrey, NH 800-326-8311
De Felsko Corp
Ogdensburg, NY 800-448-3835
Dometic Mini Bar
Elkhart, IN. .800-301-8118
Dorado Carton Company
Dorado, PR .787-796-1670
Eagle Group
Clayton, DE. 800-441-8440
Eagle Products Company
Houston, TX .713-690-1161
Edco Industries
Bridgeport, CT 203-333-8982
Electric Contract Furniture
New York, NY 888-311-6272
Ellingers Agatized Wood Inc
Sheboygan, WI 888-287-8906
English Manufacturing Inc
Rancho Cordova, CA 800-651-2711
Epic Products
Santa Ana, CA 800-548-9791
Erie Cotton Products
Erie, PA 800-289-4737
Ex-Cell KAISER LLC
Franklin Park, IL 847-451-0451
Felix Storch Inc
Bronx, NY. 800-932-4267
Flojet
Foothill Ranch, CA 800-235-6538
Fun-Time International
Philadelphia, PA 800-776-4386
Gar Products
Lakewood, NJ. 800-424-2477
Gasser Chair Co Inc
Youngstown, OH. 800-323-2234
Gensaco Marketing
New York, NY 800-506-1935
Glastender
Saginaw, MI .800-748-0423
Goldmax Industries
City of Industry, CA 626-964-8820
GSW Jackes-Evans Manufacturing Company
Saint Louis, MO 800-325-6173
H A Stiles
Westbrook, ME. 800-447-8537
Harbour House Bar Crafting
Stamford, CT. 800-755-1227
Harco Enterprises
Peterborough, ON 800-361-5361
Hardwood Products Co LP
Guilford, ME. 800-289-3340
Hines III
Jacksonville, FL 904-398-5110
Hoshizaki America Inc
Peachtree City, GA 800-438-6087
Ideas Etc Inc
Louisville, KY 800-733-0337
Ilc Dover
Frederica, DE 800-631-9567
IMI Cornelius
Schaumburg, IL. 800-323-4789
Infra Corp
Waterford, MI 888-434-6372
J.H. Carr & Sons
Seattle, WA .800-523-8842
Jarden Home Brands
Cloquet, MN .218-879-6700
Jarden Home Brands
Daleville, IN .800-392-2575
Jarlan Manufacturing
Los Angeles, CA 323-752-1211

Johnstown Manufacturing
Columbus, OH 614-236-8853
K & I Creative Plastics & Wood
Jacksonville, FL 904-387-0438
K-Way Products
Mount Carroll, IL 800-622-9163
Karma
Watertown, WI 800-558-9565
Kings River Casting
Sanger, CA 888-545-5157
Krowne Metal Corp
Wayne, NJ 800-631-0442
La Crosse
Onalaska, WI. 800-345-0018
Lakeside Manufacturing Inc
Milwaukee, WI. 888-558-8565
Lask Seating Company
Chicago, IL .888-573-2846
Lauritzen Makin Inc
Fort Worth, TX 817-921-0218
Lavi Industries
Valencia, CA 800-624-6225
Lawrence Metal Products Inc
Bay Shore, NY 800-441-0019
Leggett & Platt Storage
Vernon Hills, IL 847-816-6246
Les Industries Touch Inc
Sherbrooke, QC 800-267-4140
Lodging By Charter
Liberty, NC .800-327-2548
Long Range Systems
Addison, TX .800-577-8101
Magnuson Industries
Rockford, IL .800-435-2816
Majestic
Bridgeport, CT 203-367-7900
Manitowoc Foodservice
Sellersburg, IN 800-367-4233
Marcal Paper Mills
Elmwood Park, NJ 800-631-8451
Mars Systems
Dallas, TX. .214-634-7441
Metal Master Sales Corp
Glendale Heights, IL. 800-488-8729
Milvan Food Equipment Manufacturing
Rexdale, ON .416-674-3456
Mts Seating
Temperance, MI 734-847-3875
National Bar Systems
Huntington Beach, CA 714-848-1688
National Plastics Co
Santa Fe Springs, CA 800-221-9149
Newell Brands
Atlanta, GA
Northwest Art Glass
Redmond, WA. 800-888-9444
Omicron Steel Products Company
Jamaica, NY .718-805-3400
OWD
Tupper Lake, NY 800-836-1693
Palmland Paper Company
Fort Lauderdale, FL 800-266-9067
Parisi Inc
Newtown, PA 215-968-6677
Pelican Products Inc
Bronx, NY. 800-552-8820
Penley Corporation
West Paris, ME 800-368-6449
Perfect Equipment Inc
Gurnee, IL. .800-356-6301
Perlick Corp
Milwaukee, WI. 800-558-5592
Peter Gray Corporation
Andover, MA 978-470-0990
Placemat Printers
Fogelsville, PA 800-628-7746
Polar Hospitality Products
Philadelphia, PA 800-831-7823
Polar Ware Company
Sheboygan, WI 800-237-3655
Precision Pours
Minneapolis, MN 800-549-4491
Prince Seating Corp
Brooklyn, NY 800-577-4623
ProBar Systems Inc.
Barrie, ON 800-521-7294

Redi-Call Inc
Reno, NV 800-648-1849
Regal Manufacturing Company
Chicago, IL 773-921-3071
Richardson Seating Corp
Chicago, IL 800-522-1883
Rixie Paper Products Inc
Pottstown, PA 800-377-2692
Rodo Industries
London, ON 519-668-3711
Royal Oak Enterprises
Roswell, GA 678-461-3200
Royal Paper Products
Coatesville, PA 800-666-6655
S & R Products
Bronson, MI 800-328-3887
Salem China Company
Salem, OH. 330-337-8771
San Jamar
Elkhorn, WI. 800-248-9826
SaniServ
Mooresville, IN. 800-733-8073
Scheb International
North Barrington, IL. 847-381-2573
Semco Plastic Co
St Louis, MO. 314-487-4557
Sentry/Bevcon North America
Adelanto, CA 800-661-3003
Servco Equipment Co
St Louis, MO. 314-781-3189
Server Products Inc
Richfield, WI 800-558-8722
Sipco Products
Peoria Heights, IL 309-682-5400
Smith-Lee Company
Oshkosh, WI. 800-327-9774
Smoke Right
Chicago, IL 888-375-8885
Sneezeguard Solutions
Columbia, MO 800-569-2056
Soodhalter Plastics
Los Angeles, CA. 213-747-0231
Spir-It/Zoo Piks
Andover, MA 800-343-0996
Spirit Foodservice, Inc.
Andover, MA 800-343-0996
Springprint Medallion
Augusta, GA 800-543-5990
SQP
Schenectady, NY 800-724-1129
Stainless International
Rancho Cordova, CA 888-300-6196
Summit Commercial
Bronx, NY. 800-932-4267
Superior Menus
Mankato, MN 800-464-2182
Supreme Metal
Alpharetta, GA 800-645-2526
Token Factory
La Crosse, WI. 888-486-5367
Tops Manufacturing Co
Darien, CT. 203-655-9367
Toronto Fabricating & Manufacturing
Mississauga, ON. 905-891-2516
Trevor Industries
Eden, NY 716-992-4775
True Food Service Equipment, Inc.
O Fallon, MO 800-325-6152
U B KLEM Furniture Co Inc
St Anthony, IN 800-264-1995
United Showcase Company
Wood Ridge, NJ 800-526-6382
Ursini Plastics
Bracebridge, ON. 705-646-2701
Valley Fixtures
Sparks, NV 775-331-1050
Vintage
Jasper, IN 800-992-3491
Vitro Seating Products
St Louis, MO. 800-325-7093
Vynatex
Port Washington, NY 516-944-6130
Waddington North America
Chelmsford, MA. 888-962-2877
Wag Industries
Skokie, IL 800-621-3305
Wallace & Hinz
Blue Lake, CA 800-831-8282
Walsh & Simmons Seating
Saint Louis, MO 800-727-0364
Weavewood, Inc.
Golden Valley, MN 800-367-6460

West Metals
London, ON 800-300-6667
Wind River Environmental
Gloucester, MA. 800-332-6025
Wood & Laminates
Lodi, NJ. 973-773-7475
Wylie Systems
Mississauga, ON. 800-525-6609
Yorkraft
York, PA 800-872-2044
Z 2000 the Pick of the Millenium
Bartlesville, OK 800-654-7311
Zol-Mark Industries
Winnipeg, NB 204-943-7393

Baskets

Shopping

American Louver Co
Skokie, IL 800-772-0355
American Store Fixtures
Skokie, IL
Clamp Swing Pricing Co Inc
Oakland, CA. 800-227-7615
Day Basket Factory
North East, MD. 410-398-5150
Pentwater Wire Products Inc
Pentwater, MI 877-869-6911
Peterboro Basket Co
Peterborough, NH 603-924-3861
Southern Imperial Inc
Rockford, IL 800-747-4665

Cake Turners

American Housewares
Bronx, NY. 718-665-9500
Dexter Russell Inc
Southbridge, MA 800-343-6042

Candles

Amco Metals Indl
City of Industry, CA 626-855-2550
Culinart Inc
Cincinnati, OH 800-333-5678
Empire Candle Mfg LLC
Kansas City, KS 800-231-9398
General Wax & Candle Co
North Hollywood, CA 800-929-7867
Hollowick Inc
Manlius, NY 800-367-3015
Jarden Home Brands
Cloquet, MN 218-879-6700
Mason Candlelight Company
New Albany, MS. 800-556-2766
Neo-Image Candle Light
Mississauga, ON. 800-375-8023
Spin-Tech Corporation
Hoboken, NJ 800-977-4692
Sterno
Lombard, IL 630-792-0080
Will & Baumer
Syracuse, NY 315-451-1000
Xtreme Beverages, LLC
Dana Point, CA. 949-495-7929

Carts

Banquet

Amco Metals Indl
City of Industry, CA 626-855-2550
Bmh Equipment Inc
Sacramento, CA 800-350-8828
Carter-Hoffmann LLC
Mundelein, IL 800-323-9793
Duke Manufacturing Co
St Louis, MO. 800-735-3853
EPCO
Murfreesboro, TN 800-251-3398
Forbes Industries
Ontario, CA. 909-923-4549
Hot Food Boxes
Mooresville, IN. 800-733-8073
Lakeside Manufacturing Inc
Milwaukee, WI. 888-558-8565
Leggett & Platt Storage
Vernon Hills, IL 847-816-6246
Shammi Industries
Corona, CA. 800-417-9260

Superior Products Company
Saint Paul, MN 800-328-9800
Wilder Manufacturing Company
Port Jervis, NY 800-832-1319

Beverage

ARC Specialties
Valencia, CA. 661-775-8500
Bmh Equipment Inc
Sacramento, CA 800-350-8828
Cannon Equipment Company
Cannon Falls, MN. 800-825-8501
Carlisle Food Svc Products Inc
Oklahoma City, OK 800-654-8210
Custom Sales & Svc Inc
Hammonton, NJ 800-257-7855
Duke Manufacturing Co
St Louis, MO. 800-735-3853
Espresso Carts and Supplies
Lindenwold, NJ. 856-782-1775
Hot Food Boxes
Mooresville, IN. 800-733-8073
Lakeside Manufacturing Inc
Milwaukee, WI. 888-558-8565
Midwest Aircraft Products Co
Lexington, OH 419-884-2164
Prestige Metal Products Inc
Antioch, IL 847-395-0775
Superior Products Company
Saint Paul, MN 800-328-9800
The Carriage Works
Klamath Falls, OR 541-882-0700

Bussing

Amco Metals Indl
City of Industry, CA 626-855-2550
Bmh Equipment Inc
Sacramento, CA 800-350-8828
Forbes Industries
Ontario, CA. 909-923-4549
Lakeside Manufacturing Inc
Milwaukee, WI. 888-558-8565
Leggett & Platt Storage
Vernon Hills, IL 847-816-6246
Paxton Corp
Bristol, RI 401-396-9062
Shammi Industries
Corona, CA. 800-417-9260
Sneezeguard Solutions
Columbia, MO 800-569-2056
Superior Products Company
Saint Paul, MN 800-328-9800

Condiment

Bmh Equipment Inc
Sacramento, CA 800-350-8828
Lakeside Manufacturing Inc
Milwaukee, WI. 888-558-8565

Dessert, Pastry

ARC Specialties
Valencia, CA. 661-775-8500
Bmh Equipment Inc
Sacramento, CA 800-350-8828
Lakeside Manufacturing Inc
Milwaukee, WI. 888-558-8565
Merchandising Frontiers Inc
Winterset, IA. 800-421-2278
Superior Products Company
Saint Paul, MN 800-328-9800

Ice

Bmh Equipment Inc
Sacramento, CA 800-350-8828
Cannon Equipment Company
Cannon Falls, MN. 800-825-8501
Kloppenberg & Co
Englewood, CO. 800-346-3246
Lakeside Manufacturing Inc
Milwaukee, WI. 888-558-8565
Tooterville Trolley Company
Newburgh, IN. 812-858-8585

Liquor, Wine

Amco Metals Indl
City of Industry, CA 626-855-2550

Bmh Equipment Inc
Sacramento, CA 800-350-8828
Cannon Equipment Company
Cannon Falls, MN 800-825-8501
La Crosse
Onalaska, WI. 800-345-0018
Lakeside Manufacturing Inc
Milwaukee, WI 888-558-8565
Leggett & Platt Storage
Vernon Hills, IL 847-816-6246

Mobile Food Vending

All A Cart Custom Mfg
Columbus, OH 800-695-2278
All Star Carts & Vehicles
Bay Shore, NY 800-831-3166
All State Fabricators Corporation
Tampa, FL 800-322-9925
Alliance Products LLC
Murfreesboro, TN 800-522-3973
Alto-Shaam
Menomonee Falls, WI. 800-329-8744
Amco Metals Indl
City of Industry, CA 626-855-2550
AMI
Richmond, CA 800-942-7466
ARC Specialties
Valencia, CA. 661-775-8500
Automated Food Systems
Waxahachie, TX 469-517-0470
B R Machinery
Wedron, IL 800-310-7057
Barrette Outdoor Living
Cleveland, OH 800-336-2383
BBQ Pits by Klose
Houston, TX 800-487-7487
Blodgett Oven Co
Burlington, VT 800-331-5842
Boyd's Coffee Co
Portland, OR 800-735-2878
Burgess Enterprises, Inc
Renton, WA. 800-927-3286
C Nelson Mfg Co
Oak Harbor, OH 800-922-7339
Caddy Corporation of America
Bridgeport, NJ 856-467-4222
Carlin Manufacturing
Fresno, CA 888-212-0801
Carlisle Food Svc Products Inc
Oklahoma City, OK 800-654-8210
Carts of Colorado Inc
Greenwood Vlg, CO 800-227-8634
Continental Cart by Kullman Industries
Lebanon, NJ 888-882-2278
Corsair Display Systems
Canandalgua, NY 800-347-5245
Creative Mobile Systems Inc
Manchester, CT. 800-646-8364
Custom Diamond Intl.
Laval, QC 800-326-5926
Custom Sales & Svc Inc
Hammonton, NJ 800-257-7855
Delfield Co
Mt Pleasant, MI. 800-733-8821
Dometic Mini Bar
Elkhart, IN. 800-301-8118
Duke Manufacturing Co
St Louis, MO. 800-735-3853
Embee Sunshade Co
Brooklyn, NY. 718-387-8566
EPCO
Murfreesboro, TN 800-251-3398
Eskay Metal Fabricating
Buffalo, NY. 800-836-8015
Ex-Cell KAISER LLC
Franklin Park, IL. 847-451-0451
Fetco
Lake Zurich, IL. 800-338-2699
Gensaco Marketing
New York, NY 800-506-1935
Global Carts and Equipment
Jackson, NJ 800-653-0881
Gold Medal Products Co
Cincinnati, OH 800-543-0862
Hot Food Boxes
Mooresville, IN. 800-733-8073
Hotshot Delivery System
Bloomingdale, IL 630-924-8817
InterMetro Industries
Wilkes-Barre, PA 570-825-2741

International Thermal Dispensers
Boston, MA. 617-239-3600
King Arthur
Statesville, NC 800-257-7244
Lakeside Manufacturing Inc
Milwaukee, WI. 888-558-8565
Lakeside-Aris Manufacturing
Milwaukee, WI. 800-558-8565
Leggett & Platt Storage
Vernon Hills, IL 847-816-6246
Lil' Orbits
Minneapolis, MN 800-228-8305
Magnum Custom Trailer & BBQ Pits
Austin, TX. 800-662-4686
Merchandising Frontiers Inc
Winterset, IA 800-421-2278
Metal Master Sales Corp
Glendale Heights, IL. 800-488-8729
Metro Corporation
Wilkes Barre, PA 800-992-1776
Michaelo Espresso
Seattle, WA 800-545-2883
Midwest Aircraft Products Co
Lexington, OH 419-884-2164
National FABCO Manufacturing
St Louis, MO 314-842-4571
New Age Industrial
Norton, KS 800-255-0104
Palmer Snyder
Brookfield, WI 800-762-0415
Paragon International
Nevada, IA 800-433-0333
Plastocon
Oconomowoc, WI. 800-966-0103
Precision
Miami, FL. 800-762-7565
Prestige Metal Products Inc
Antioch, IL 847-395-0775
Proluxe
Paramount, CA 800-594-5528
Quantum Storage Systems Inc
Miami, FL 800-685-4665
Sico Inc
Minneapolis, MN 800-328-6138
Sopralco
Plantation, FL 954-584-2225
Sould Manufacturing
Winnepeg, NB. 204-339-3499
Southern Express
Saint Louis, MO 800-444-9157
SPG International
Covington, GA 877-503-4774
Star Manufacturing Intl Inc
St Louis, MO. 800-264-7827
Steamway Corporation
Scottsburg, IN 800-259-8171
Super Sturdy
Weldon, NC. 800-253-4833
Super-Chef Manufacturing Company
Houston, TX 800-231-3478
Supreme Products
Waco, TX 254-799-4941
Technibilt/Cari-All
Newton, NC 800-233-3972
The Carriage Works
Klamath Falls, OR 541-882-0700
Tooterville Trolley Company
Newburgh, IN 812-858-8585
USECO
Murfreesboro, TN 615-893-4820
Vollrath Co LLC
Sheboygan, WI 800-624-2051
Wag Industries
Skokie, IL 800-621-3305
Wittco Foodservice Equipment
Milwaukee, WI. 800-821-3912
Worksman 800 Buy Cart
Ozone Park, NY 800-289-2278
WR Key
Scarborough, ON 416-291-6246
Yorkraft
York, PA 800-872-2044

Salad

Bmh Equipment Inc
Sacramento, CA 800-350-8828
Lakeside Manufacturing Inc
Milwaukee, WI. 888-558-8565
Steamway Corporation
Scottsburg, IN 800-259-8171

Tooterville Trolley Company
Newburgh, IN 812-858-8585

Service

Amco Metals Indl
City of Industry, CA 626-855-2550
ARC Specialties
Valencia, CA 661-775-8500
Blodgett Oven Co
Burlington, VT 800-331-5842
Bmh Equipment Inc
Sacramento, CA 800-350-8828
Cannon Equipment Company
Cannon Falls, MN. 800-825-8501
Duke Manufacturing Co
St Louis, MO. 800-735-3853
Gillis Associated Industries
Prospect Heights, IL. 847-541-6500
Glowmaster Corporation
Clifton, NJ 800-272-7008
Hanson Brass Rewd Co
Sun Valley, CA 888-841-3773
Hot Food Boxes
Mooresville, IN 800-733-8073
Infanti International
Staten Island, NY 800-874-8590
King Arthur
Statesville, NC 800-257-7244
Lakeside Manufacturing Inc
Milwaukee, WI 888-558-8565
Leggett & Platt Storage
Vernon Hills, IL 847-816-6246
Marlen
Riverside, MO. 913-888-3333
Moli-International
Denver, CO 800-525-8468
Paxton Corp
Bristol, RI 401-396-9062
Princeton Shelving
Cedar Rapids, IA. 319-369-0355
Shammi Industries
Corona, CA 800-417-9260
Sico Inc
Minneapolis, MN 800-328-6138
Superior Products Company
Saint Paul, MN 800-328-9800
Tri-Boro Shelving & Partition
Farmville, VA 800-633-3070
USECO
Murfreesboro, TN 615-893-4820

Shopping

Assembled Products Corp
Rogers, AR 800-548-3373
Seymour Housewares
Seymour, IN 800-457-9881
Technibilt/Cari-All
Newton, NC 800-233-3972
Unarco Industries LLC
Wagoner, OK. 800-654-4100

Tray, Silverware

Alliance Products LLC
Murfreesboro, TN. 800-522-3973
Duke Manufacturing Co
St Louis, MO. 800-735-3853
EPCO
Murfreesboro, TN 800-251-3398
Hot Food Boxes
Mooresville, IN 800-733-8073
Lakeside Manufacturing Inc
Milwaukee, WI 888-558-8565
National Cart Co
St Charles, MO 636-947-3800
Paramount Packaging Corp
Melville, NY. 516-333-8100
Traycon Manufacturing Co
Carlstadt, NJ 201-939-5555
Wilder Manufacturing Company
Port Jervis, NY 800-832-1319

Cases

Display

Accent Store Fixtures
Kenosha, WI. 800-545-1144
Acme Display Fixture Company
Los Angeles, CA. 800-959-5657

ALCO Designs
Gardena, CA 800-228-2346
All State Fabricators Corporation
Tampa, FL 800-322-9925
Allstate Manufacturing Company
Manchester, OH 800-262-2340
Alto-Shaam
Menomonee Falls, WI. 800-329-8744
Arctica Showcase Company
Cayuga, ON. 800-839-5536
Arizona Store Equipment
Phoenix, AZ 800-624-8395
Arneg LLC
Lexington, NC 800-276-3487
Bailly Showcase & Fixture Company
Las Vegas, NV 702-947-6885
Barker Company
Keosauqua, IA 319-293-3777
BKI Worldwide
Simpsonville, SC 800-927-6887
Bon Chef
Lafayette, NJ. 800-331-0177
Brass Smith
Denver, CO 800-662-9595
C&H Store Equipment Company
Los Angeles, CA. 800-648-4979
Carman And Company
Burlington, MA. 781-221-3500
Caselites
Hialeah, FL 305-819-7766
Claridge Products & Equipment
Harrison, AR
Coldstream Products Corporation
Crossfield, AB 888-946-4097
Corsair Display Systems
Canandalgua, NY 800-347-5245
Craig Manufacturing
Irvington, NJ. 800-631-7936
Crispy Lite
St. Louis, MO. 888-356-5362
Crown Metal Manufacturing Company
Elmhurst, IL 630-279-9800
Cruvinet Winebar Co LLC
Sparks, NV 800-278-8463
CSC Worldwide
Columbus, OH 800-848-3573
Delfield Co
Mt Pleasant, MI. 800-733-8821
Display Creations
Brooklyn, NY 718-257-2300
Dunhill Food Equipment Corporation
Armonk, NY 800-847-4206
Dunn Woodworks
Shrewsbury, PA 877-835-8592
Empire Bakery Equipment
Hicksville, NY 800-878-4070
Esquire Mechanical Corp.
Armonk, NY 800-847-4206
Federal Industries
Belleville, WI 800-356-4206
Fogel Jordon Commercial Refrigeration Company
Philadelphia, PA 800-523-0171
Forbes Industries
Ontario, CA. 909-923-4549
Greene Industries
East Greenwich, RI 401-884-7530
Handy Manufacturing Co Inc
Newark, NJ 800-631-4280
Hardt Equipment Manufacturing
Lachine, QC 888-848-4408
Hercules Food Equipment
Weston, ON 416-742-9673
Hoshizaki America Inc
Peachtree City, GA 800-438-6087
Interstate Showcase & Fixture Company
West Orange, NJ 973-483-5555
Jordan Specialty Company
Brooklyn, NY 877-567-3265
Kedco Wine Storage Systems
Farmingdale, NY 800-654-9988
Langer Manufacturing Company
Cedar Rapids, IA. 800-728-6445
Leggett & Platt Inc
Carthage, MO 417-358-8131
Lynn Sign Inc
Andover, MA 800-225-5764
Madix Inc
Goodwater, AL 256-839-6354
Mayworth Showcase Works Inc
Tampa, FL. 813-251-1558
Merco/Savory
Mt. Pleasant, MI 800-733-8821

Mercury Equipment Company
Chino, CA. 800-273-6688
Merix Chemical Company
Chicago, IL 312-573-1400
Modar
Benton Harbor, MI 800-253-6186
Modern Store Fixtures Company
Dallas, TX. 800-634-7777
Moli-International
Denver, CO 800-525-8468
MultiFab Plastics
Boston, MA. 888-293-5754
Nor-Lake
Hudson, WI. 715-386-2323
Northwestern
Van Nuys, CA 818-786-1581
Omega Industries
St Louis, MO. 314-961-1668
Omnitemp Refrigeration
Downey, CA 800-423-9660
Oscartek
Burlingame, CA 855-885-2400
OSF
Toronto, ON 800-465-4000
Palmer Distributors
St Clair Shores, MI 800-444-1912
Parisi Inc
Newtown, PA 215-968-6677
Plastic Supply Inc
Londonderry, NH 800-752-7759
Poblocki Sign Co
Milwaukee, WI 414-453-4010
Premier Brass
Atlanta, GA 800-251-5800
Process Displays
New Berlin, WI. 800-533-1764
QBD Modular Systems
Santa Clara, CA 800-663-3005
Rathe Productions
New York, NY 212-242-9000
Refcon
Medford, NJ 609-714-2330
Refrigeration Engineering
Grand Rapids, MI 800-968-3227
Regal Custom Fixture Company
Westampton, NJ 800-525-3092
Retail Decor
Ironton, OH. 800-726-3402
Robelan Displays Inc
Hempstead, NY. 865-564-8600
RW Products
Edgewood, NY 800-345-1022
Sani-Top Products
De Leon Springs, FL. 800-874-6094
Seattle Plastics
Seattle, WA 800-441-0679
Silver King Refrigeration Inc
Minneapolis, MN 800-328-3329
Sitka Store Fixtures
Kansas City, MO. 800-821-7558
Southern Store Fixtures Inc
Bessemer, AL 800-552-6283
Spartan Showcase
Union, MO 800-325-0775
Standex International Corp.
Salem, NH. 603-893-9701
Taymar Industries
Palm Desert, CA 800-624-1972
Top Source Industries
Addison, IL 800-362-9625
True Food Service Equipment, Inc.
O Fallon, MO. 800-325-6152
United Showcase Company
Wood Ridge, NJ 800-526-6382
Universal Folding Box
East Orange, NJ 973-482-4300
West Metals
London, ON 800-300-6667
William Hecht
Philadelphia, PA 215-925-6223

Cash Registers

Data Visible Corporation
Charlottesville, VA 800-368-3494
Kelmin Products
Plymouth, FL 407-886-6079
OMRON Systems LLC
Schaumburg, IL. 224-520-7650
PAR Tech Inc
New Hartford, NY 800-448-6505

Superior Products Company
Saint Paul, MN 800-328-9800

Chafers

Apex Fountain Sales Inc
Philadelphia, PA 800-523-4586
ARC Specialties
Valencia, CA. 661-775-8500
Bon Chef
Lafayette, NJ. 800-331-0177
Browne & Company
Markham, ON. 905-475-6104
Candle Lamp Company
Corona, CA. 877-526-7748
Crestware
North Salt Lake, UT 800-345-0513
Dura-Ware Company of America
Oklahoma City, OK 800-664-3872
Dynynstyl
Delray Beach, FL 800-774-7895
Eastern Tabletop Mfg
Brooklyn, NY 888-422-4142
Glowmaster Corporation
Clifton, NJ. 800-272-7008
Kelmin Products
Plymouth, FL 407-886-6079
King Arthur
Statesville, NC 800-257-7244
Mack-Chicago Corporation
Chicago, IL 800-992-6225
Mosshaim Innovations
Jacksonville, FL 888-995-7775
Polar Ware Company
Sheboygan, WI 800-237-3655
Randware Industries
Prospect Heights, IL 847-299-8884
Rexcraft Fine Chafers
Long Island City, NY 888-739-2723
Superior Products Company
Saint Paul, MN 800-328-9800

Chairs

A-1 Booth Manufacturing
Burley, ID 800-820-3285
AMC Industries
Palmetto, FL 941-479-7834
Barn Furniture Mart
Van Nuys, CA 888-302-2276
Beaufurn
Advance, NC. 888-766-7706
Beka Furniture
Concord, ON. 905-669-4255
Bennington Furniture Corporation
Bennington, PA 802-447-3212
Brill Manufacturing Co
Ludington, MI. 866-896-6420
Carroll Chair Company
Onalaska, WI. 800-331-4704
CCS Stone, Inc.
Moonachie, NJ 800-227-7785
Chaircraft
Hickory, NC 828-326-8458
Classico Seating
Peru, IN. 800-968-6655
Commercial Furniture Group Inc
Newport, TN. 800-873-3252
Commercial Seating Specialists
Santa Clara, CA 408-453-8983
Cosco Home & Office Products
Columbus, IN 800-628-8321
Cramer Inc
Kansas City, MO. 800-366-6700
Eagle Products Company
Houston, TX 713-690-1161
Electric Contract Furniture
New York, NY. 888-311-6272
Fab-X/Metals
Washington, NC 800-677-3229
FDL/Flair Designs
Kokomo, IN 765-452-6000
Fiskars Brands Inc.
Baldwinsville, NY 315-635-9911
Fixtur World
Cookeville, TN 800-634-9887
Fixtures Furniture
Florence, AL 855-321-4999
Fred Beesley's Booth & Upholstery
Centerville, UT 801-364-8189
Furniturelab
Carrboro, NC 800-449-8677

Gar Products
Lakewood, NJ......................800-424-2477
Gasser Chair Co Inc
Youngstown, OH..................800-323-2234
Gaychrome Division of CSL
Crystal Lake, IL..................800-873-4370
Hines III
Jacksonville, FL...................904-398-5110
Imperial
Carlstadt, NJ......................800-526-6261
Infanti International
Staten Island, NY................800-874-8590
International Patterns, Inc.
Bay Shore, NY....................631-952-2000
J.A. Thurston Company
Rumford, ME......................207-364-7921
J.H. Carr & Sons
Seattle, WA.......................800-523-8842
John Boos & Co
Effingham, IL.....................888-431-2667
K C Booth Co
N Kansas City, MO...............800-866-5226
Ken Coat
Bardstown, KY....................888-536-2628
Kings River Casting
Sanger, CA........................888-545-5157
Krueger International Holding
Green Bay, WI....................800-424-2432
Lask Seating Company
Chicago, IL.......................888-573-2846
Lauritzen Makin Inc
Fort Worth, TX...................817-921-0218
LB Furniture Industries
Hudson, NY.......................800-221-8752
Line-Master Products
Cocolalla, ID......................208-265-4743
Lodging By Charter
Liberty, NC.......................800-327-2548
Marston Manufacturing
Cleveland, OH....................216-587-3400
Merric
Bridgeton, MO....................314-770-9944
Miami Metal
Miami, FL..........................305-576-3600
Mity Lite Inc
Orem, UT..........................800-909-8034
Mlp Seating
Elk Grove Vlg, IL.................800-723-3030
Mts Seating
Temperance, MI..................734-847-3875
Old Dominion Wood Products
Lynchburg, VA....................800-245-6382
Omicron Steel Products Company
Jamaica, NY.......................718-805-3400
Palmer Snyder
Brookfield, WI....................800-762-0415
Pinnacle Furnishing
Aberdeen, NC.....................866-229-5704
Plymold
Kenyon, MN......................800-759-6653
Prince Castle Inc
Carol Stream, IL..................800-722-7853
Prince Seating Corp
Brooklyn, NY......................800-577-4623
Quality Highchairs
Pacoima, CA.......................800-969-9635
Quality Seating Co
Youngstown, OH..................800-323-2234
Regal Manufacturing Company
Chicago, IL.......................773-921-3071
Richardson Seating Corp
Chicago, IL.......................800-522-1883
Robertson Furniture Co Inc
Toccoa, GA........................800-241-0713
Rodo Industries
London, ON.......................519-668-3711
Rollhaus Seating Products Inc
Long Island City, NY.............800-822-6684
Rosenwach Tank Co LLC
Long Island City, NY.............212-972-4411
Sandler Seating
Atlanta, GA.......................404-982-9000
Sauvagnat Inc
Huntersville, NC..................800-258-5619
Seating Concepts Inc
Rockdale, IL......................800-421-2036
Shafer Commercial Seating
Denver, CO.......................303-322-7792
Shelby Williams Industries Inc
Newport, TN......................800-873-3252
Sims Superior Seating
Locust Grove, GA.................800-729-9178

Superior Products Company
Saint Paul, MN....................800-328-9800
Thorpe & Associates
Siler City, NC.....................919-742-5516
Toronto Fabricating & Manufacturing
Mississauga, ON..................905-891-2516
Trojan Commercial Furni ture Inc.
Montereal, QC....................877-271-3878
U B KLEM Furniture Co Inc
St Anthony, IN....................800-264-1995
US Seating Products
Ocala, FL..........................800-999-2589
Vintage
Jasper, IN........................800-992-3491
Vitro Seating Products
St Louis, MO......................800-325-7093
Walsh & Simmons Seating
Saint Louis, MO...................800-727-0364
Waymar Industries
Burnsville, MN....................888-474-1112
Wheel Tough Company
Terre Haute, IN...................888-765-8833
Woodard
Coppell, TX.......................800-877-2290
World Wide Hospitality Furn
Paramount, CA....................800-728-8262
Xiaoping Design
New York, NY.....................800-891-9896
Zol-Mark Industries
Winnipeg, NB.....................204-943-7393

Changers

Currency

Advantus Corp.
Jacksonville, FL...................904-482-0091
Automated Business Products
Hackensack, NJ...................800-334-1440
Giesecke & Devrient America
Dulles, VA.........................800-856-7712
Hamilton Manufacturing Corp
Holland, OH.......................888-723-4858
Rowe International
Grand Rapids, MI.................616-246-0483

China

Abco International
Oneida, NY.......................888-263-7195
Americana Art China Company
Sebring, FL.......................800-233-6133
Babco International, Inc
Tucson, AZ........................520-628-7596
Bel-Terr China
Warren, OH.......................800-900-2371
Benner China & Glassware Inc
Jacksonville, FL...................904-733-4620
Brooklyn Boys Pizza & Pasta
Boca Raton, FL...................561-477-3663
Buffalo China
Buffalo, NY.......................716-824-8515
China Lenox Incorporated
Bristol, PA........................267-525-7800
Crestware
North Salt Lake, UT..............800-345-0513
Dansk International Designs
Bristol, PA........................914-697-6400
Delco Tableware
Port Washington, NY.............800-221-9557
Dynynstyl
Delray Beach, FL.................800-774-7895
H.F. Coors China Company
New Albany, MS..................800-782-6677
Hall China Co
East Liverpool, OH...............800-445-4255
Hartstone Pottery Inc
Zanesville, OH....................740-452-9999
Homer Laughlin China Co
Newell, WV.......................800-452-4462
Izabel Lam International
Brooklyn, NY......................718-797-3983
Lenox Corp
Bristol, PA........................800-223-4311
Libby Canada
Mississauga, ON..................905-607-8280
Michael Leson Dinnerware
Youngstown, OH..................800-821-3541
Mikasa Hotelware
Secaucus, NJ......................866-645-2721
Minners Designs   Inc.
New York, NY.....................212-688-7441

Oneida Food Service
Columbus, OH....................800-828-7033
Oneida LTD Silversmiths
Oneida, NY.......................888-263-7195
Pickard China
Antioch, IL........................847-395-3800
Prolon
Port Gibson, MS..................888-480-9828
Rego China Corporation
Melville, NY.......................800-221-1707
Rexcraft Fine Chafers
Long Island City, NY.............888-739-2723
Royal Prestige Health Moguls
Westbury, NY.....................888-802-7433
Salem China Company
Salem, OH.........................330-337-8771
Sterling China Company
Wellsville, OH.....................800-682-7628
Superior Products Company
Saint Paul, MN....................800-328-9800
Syracuse China Company
Syracuse, NY......................800-448-5711
Townfood Equipment Corp
Brooklyn, NY......................800-221-5032
Tradeco International Corp
Addison, IL........................800-628-3738
Vertex China
Pomona, CA.......................800-483-7839
Victoria Porcelain
Miami, FL..........................888-593-2353
Wedgwood USA
Wall Township, NJ................800-999-9936
Xtreme Beverages, LLC
Dana Point, CA....................949-495-7929

Clear & Colored Plastic

Chips

Hopp Co Inc
New Hyde Park, NY..............800-889-8425

Indoor Sign Holders

Hopp Co Inc
New Hyde Park, NY..............800-889-8425

Clear Plastic

Shelf Strips

Hopp Co Inc
New Hyde Park, NY..............800-889-8425

Coasters

Admatch Corporation
New York, NY.....................800-777-9909
Amco Metals Indl
City of Industry, CA..............626-855-2550
American Coaster Company
Sanborn, NY......................888-423-8628
Atlas Match Company
Toronto, ON.......................888-285-2783
Best Brands Home Products
New York, NY.....................212-684-7456
Conimar Corp
Ocala, FL..........................800-874-9735
Edco Industries
Bridgeport, CT....................203-333-8982
Gessner Products
Ambler, PA........................800-874-7808
Harco Enterprises
Peterborough, ON................800-361-5361
IB Concepts
Elizabeth, NJ......................888-671-0800
Majestic
Bridgeport, CT....................203-367-7900
Pelican Products Inc
Bronx, NY.........................800-552-8820
Polar Hospitality Products
Philadelphia, PA..................800-831-7823
Rixie Paper Products Inc
Pottstown, PA.....................800-377-2692
Royal Paper Products
Coatesville, PA....................800-666-6655
Springprint Medallion
Augusta, GA......................800-543-5990
Tops Manufacturing Co
Darien, CT.........................203-655-9367
Unique Manufacturing
Visalia, CA........................888-737-1007

Weavewood, Inc.
  Golden Valley, MN 800-367-6460

Coin Machinery

Giesecke & Devrient America
  Dulles, VA. 800-856-7712
Scan Coin
  Ashburn, VA 800-336-3311
Wico Corporation
  Niles, IL 800-367-9426

Colored Plastic

Shelf Strips

Hopp Co Inc
  New Hyde Park, NY 800-889-8425

Concession Supplies & Equipment

All Star Carts & Vehicles
  Bay Shore, NY 800-831-3166
Alliance Products LLC
  Murfreesboro, TN 800-522-3973
Automated Food Systems
  Waxahachie, TX 469-517-0470
Carlin Manufacturing
  Fresno, CA 888-212-0801
Century Industries Inc
  Sellersburg, IN 800-248-3371
Creative Mobile Systems Inc
  Manchester, CT. 800-646-8364
Delfield Co
  Mt Pleasant, MI. 800-733-8821
Fun City Popcorn
  Las Vegas, NV 800-423-1710
Gold Medal Products Co
  Cincinnati, OH 800-543-0862
Great Western Co LLC
  Hollywood, AL 256-259-3578
Holstein Manufacturing
  Holstein, IA 800-368-4342
International Thermal Dispensers
  Boston, MA. 617-239-3600
Karma
  Watertown, WI 800-558-9565
Kloss Manufacturing Co Inc
  Allentown, PA 800-445-7100
Lazy Man Inc
  Belvidere, NJ 800-475-1950
Magnum Custom Trailer & BBQ Pits
  Austin, TX. 800-662-4686
Marston Manufacturing
  Cleveland, OH 216-587-3400
New Centennial
  Columbus, GA 800-241-7541
Rio Syrup Co
  St Louis, MO. 800-325-7666
Server Products Inc
  Richfield, WI 800-558-8722
Steamway Corporation
  Scottsburg, IN 800-259-8171
Supreme Products
  Waco, TX 254-799-4941
Texas Corn Roasters
  Granbury, TX 800-772-4345
The Carriage Works
  Klamath Falls, OR 541-882-0700
Thermal Bags By Ingrid Inc
  Gilberts, IL 800-622-5560
Yorkraft
  York, PA 800-872-2044

Corkscrews

Amco Metals Indl
  City of Industry, CA 626-855-2550
C R Mfg
  Waverly, NE 877-789-5844
Cove Four
  Freeport, NY 516-379-4232
Pelican Products Inc
  Bronx, NY 800-552-8820
Superior Products Company
  Saint Paul, MN 800-328-9800
Swing-A-Way Manufacturing Company
  St Louis, MO. 314-773-1488

Counters

Cafeteria, Restaurant

Accent Store Fixtures
  Kenosha, WI 800-545-1144
Ace Fabrication
  Mobile, AL 251-478-0401
All State Fabricators Corporation
  Tampa, FL. 800-322-9925
Alpine Store Equipment Corporation
  Long Island City, NY 718-361-1213
American Creative Solutions
  Matthews, NC. 877-925-4406
Atlas Metal Industries
  Miami, FL. 800-762-7565
Baker & Co
  Norfolk, VA. 800-909-4325
Barn Furniture Mart
  Van Nuys, CA 888-302-2276
Borroughs Corp
  Kalamazoo, MI 800-748-0227
Cara Products Company
  Jonesboro, GA 770-478-9802
Carman And Company
  Burlington, MA. 781-221-3500
Catskill Craftsmen Inc
  Stamford, NY 607-652-7321
Cobb & Zimmer
  Detroit, MI 313-923-0350
Custom Diamond Intl.
  Laval, QC 800-326-5926
Delfield Co
  Mt Pleasant, MI. 800-733-8821
Duke Manufacturing Co
  St Louis, MO. 800-735-3853
Duluth Sheet Metal
  Duluth, MN. 218-722-2613
Dunhill Food Equipment Corporation
  Armonk, NY 800-847-4206
Economy Paper & Restaurant Co
  Clifton, NJ. 973-279-5500
Erwin Food Service Equipment
  Fort Worth, TX 817-535-0021
Eskay Metal Fabricating
  Buffalo, NY 800-836-8015
Fixtur World
  Cookeville, TN 800-634-9887
Fred Beesley's Booth & Upholstery
  Centerville, UT 801-364-8189
Gervasi Wood Products
  Madison, WI 608-274-6752
Habco
  Concord, CA 925-682-6203
Hallock Fabricating Corp
  Riverhead, NY 631-727-2441
Hercules Food Equipment
  Weston, ON. 416-742-9673
IGS Store Fixtures
  Peabody, MA. 978-532-0010
Inland Showcase & Fixture Company
  Fresno, CA. 559-237-4158
Institutional Equipment Inc
  Bolingbrook, IL 630-771-0990
Kitchen Equipment Fabricating
  Houston, TX 713-747-3611
Kitcor Corp
  Sun Valley, CA 818-767-4800
Lauritzen Makin Inc
  Fort Worth, TX 817-921-0218
Load King Mfg
  Jacksonville, FL 800-531-4975
Low Temp Industries Inc
  Jonesboro, GA 678-674-1317
Marlo Manufacturing
  Boonton, NJ 800-222-0450
MCM Fixture Co
  Hazel Park, MI 248-547-9280
Mcroyal Industries Inc
  Youngstown, OH. 800-785-2556
Merric
  Bridgeton, MO 314-770-9944
Metal Kitchen Fabricators Inc
  Houston, TX 713-683-8375
Metal Master Sales Corp
  Glendale Heights, IL. 800-488-8729
Missouri Equipment
  St Louis, MO. 800-727-6326
Monroe Extinguisher Co Inc
  Rochester, NY 585-235-3310

Mouron & Co Inc
  Indianapolis, IN 317-243-7955
National FABCO Manufacturing
  St Louis, MO. 314-842-4571
Omicron Steel Products Company
  Jamaica, NY 718-805-3400
Oscartek
  Burlingame, CA 855-885-2400
Paramount Manufacturing Company
  Wilmington, MA. 978-657-4300
Parisi Inc
  Newtown, PA 215-968-6677
Perfect Plank Co
  Oroville, CA 800-327-1961
Pierce Laminated Products Inc
  Rockford, IL 815-968-9651
PMI Food Equipment Group
  Troy, OH 937-332-3000
Quipco Products Inc
  Sauget, IL 314-993-1442
Sarasota Restaurant Equipment
  Sarasota, FL 800-434-1410
Seating Concepts Inc
  Rockdale, IL 800-421-2036
Sefi Fabricators Inc
  Amityville, NY 631-842-2200
Shelley Cabinet Company
  Shelley, ID. 208-357-3700
Solid Surface Acrylics
  North Tonawanda, NY 888-595-4114
Southwestern Porcelain Steel
  Sand Springs, OK 918-245-1375
Spartan Showcase
  Union, MO 800-325-0775
St. Louis Stainless Service
  St Louis, MO. 800-735-3853
Stainless Equipment Manufacturing
  Dallas, TX. 800-736-2038
Stainless Fabricating Company
  Denver, CO 800-525-8966
Stainless International
  Rancho Cordova, CA 888-300-6196
Stainless Steel Fabricators
  Tyler, TX. 903-595-6625
Top Source Industries
  Addison, IL 800-362-9625
Trojan Commercial Furniture Inc.
  Montereal, QC 877-271-3878
United Fabricators
  Fort Smith, AR 800-235-4101
Universal Stainless
  Aurora, CO 800-223-8332
Universal Stainless & Alloy
  Titusville, PA 800-295-1909
Walsh & Simmons Seating
  Saint Louis, MO 800-727-0364
Weiss Sheet Metal Inc
  Avon, MA 508-583-8300
West Coast Industries Inc
  San Francisco, CA 800-243-3150
Western Laminates
  Omaha, NE 402-556-4600

Coin

Automated Business Products
  Hackensack, NJ. 800-334-1440
Giesecke & Devrient America
  Dulles, VA. 800-856-7712
Scan Coin
  Ashburn, VA 800-336-3311

Decorative Items

Hollowick Inc
  Manlius, NY 800-367-3015
Irresistible Cookie Jar
  Hayden Lake, ID. 208-664-1261
Stanpac, Inc.
  Smithville, ON 905-957-3326
Xtreme Beverages, LLC
  Dana Point, CA. 949-495-7929

Dishes

Paper

Design Specialties Inc
  Hamden, CT 800-999-1584
Hoffmaster Group Inc.
  Oshkosh, WI 800-558-9300

Primary Liquidation
Bohemia, NY 631-244-1410

Dispensers

Beer

Autobar Systems
Asbury Park, NJ 732-922-3355
Automatic Bar Controls Inc
Vacaville, CA 800-722-6738
Banner Equipment Co
Morris, IL 800-621-4625
Beer Magic Devices
Hamilton, ON 905-522-3081
Berg Co
Monona, WI 608-221-4281
Bijur Lubricating Corporation
Morrisville, NC 800-631-0168
Carbonic Machines Inc
Minneapolis, MN 612-824-0745
Carmun International
San Antonio, TX 800-531-7907
Custom Diamond International
Laval, QC 800-363-5926
Easybar Corp
Tualatin, OR 888-294-7405
Felix Storch Inc
Bronx, NY 800-932-4267
Flojet
Foothill Ranch, CA 800-235-6538
IMI Cornelius
Schaumburg, IL 800-323-4789
K-Way Products
Mount Carroll, IL 800-622-9163
Multiplex Co Inc
Sellersburg, IN 800-787-8880
Perlick Corp
Milwaukee, WI 800-558-5592
Sentry/Bevcon North America
Adelanto, CA 800-661-3003
Stainless One DispensingSystem
Vacaville, CA 888-723-3827
Summit Commercial
Bronx, NY 800-932-4267
Superior Products Company
Saint Paul, MN 800-328-9800
True Food Service Equipment, Inc.
O Fallon, MO 800-325-6152

Beverage

Action Technology
Prussia, PA 217-935-8311
American Manufacturing-Engrng
Cleveland, OH 800-822-9402
Apex Fountain Sales Inc
Philadelphia, PA 800-523-4586
Autobar Systems
Asbury Park, NJ 732-922-3355
Automatic Bar Controls Inc
Vacaville, CA 800-722-6738
Automatic Products
Williston, SC 800-523-8363
Azbar Plus
Qu,bec, QC 418-687-3672
Banner Equipment Co
Morris, IL 800-621-4625
Beer Magic Devices
Hamilton, ON 905-522-3081
Berg Co
Monona, WI 608-221-4281
Bevistar
Oswego, IL 877-238-7827
BG Industries
Lemont, IL 800-800-5761
Bijur Lubricating Corporation
Morrisville, NC 800-631-0168
Booth
Dallas, TX 800-497-2958
C R Mfg
Waverly, NE 877-789-5844
Carbonic Machines Inc
Minneapolis, MN 612-824-0745
Carlisle Food Svc Products Inc
Oklahoma City, OK 800-654-8210
Carmun International
San Antonio, TX 800-531-7907
Carpigiani Corporation of America
Winston Salem, NC 800-648-4389
Chill Rite Mfg
Slidell, LA 800-256-2190

Cleland Sales Corp
Los Alamitos, CA 562-598-6616
Commercial Refrigeration Service, Inc.
Phoenix, AZ 623-869-8881
Control Beverage
Adelanto, CA 330-549-5376
Cornelius Inc.
Osseo, MN 800-238-3600
Cornelius Wilshire Corporation
Schaumburg, IL 847-397-4600
Cruvinet Winebar Co LLC
Sparks, NV 800-278-8463
Custom Diamond International
Laval, QC 800-363-5926
Delfield Co
Mt Pleasant, MI 800-733-8821
Easybar Corp
Tualatin, OR 888-294-7405
Elmeco SRL
Bartlett, TN 901-385-0490
Eurodib
Champlain, NY 888-956-6866
Federal Machine Corp
Clive, IA 800-247-2446
Felix Storch Inc
Bronx, NY 800-932-4267
Fetco
Lake Zurich, IL 800-338-2699
Flojet
Foothill Ranch, CA 800-235-6538
Fountainhead
Bensalem, PA 800-326-8998
Grindmaster-Cecilware Corp
Louisville, KY 800-695-4500
Hedwin Division
Baltimore, MD 800-638-1012
Hoshizaki America Inc
Peachtree City, GA 800-438-6087
Icee-USA Corporation
Ontario, CA 800-426-4233
Igloo Products Corp
Katy, TX 866-509-3503
IMI Cornelius
Schaumburg, IL 800-323-4789
In Sink Erator
Racine, WI 800-558-5700
Juicy Whip Inc
La Verne, CA 909-392-7500
K-Way Products
Mount Carroll, IL 800-622-9163
Karma
Watertown, WI 800-558-9565
Lancaster Colony Corporation
Westerville, OH 614-224-7141
Lancer Corp
Roselle, IL 877-814-2271
Lancer Corp
San Antonio, TX 888-676-5196
Leland Limited Inc
South Plainfield, NJ 800-984-9793
Little Squirt
Toronto, ON 416-665-6605
Magnuson Industries
Rockford, IL 800-435-2816
Manitowoc Foodservice
Sellersburg, IN 800-367-4233
Moli-International
Denver, CO 800-525-8468
Mulligan Associates
Mequon, WI 800-627-2886
Multiplex Co Inc
Sellersburg, IN 800-787-8880
Perfect Equipment Inc
Gurnee, IL 800-356-6301
Perlick Corp
Milwaukee, WI 800-558-5592
Polar Beer Systems
Sun City, CA 951-928-8174
Precision Pours
Minneapolis, MN 800-549-4491
Pro-Flo Products
Cedar Grove, NJ 800-325-1057
ProBar Systems Inc.
Barrie, ON 800-521-7294
PROCON Products
Smyrna, TN 615-355-8000
Prolon
Port Gibson, MS 888-480-9828
Regal Ware Inc
Kewaskum, WI 262-626-2121
Remco Products Corp
Zionsville, IN 800-585-8619

Rieke Packaging Systems
Auburn, IN 260-925-3700
Robinson/Kirshbaum Industries
Gardena, CA 800-929-3812
Rocket Man
Louisville, KY 800-365-6661
S & R Products
Bronson, MI 800-328-3887
SaniServ
Mooresville, IN 800-733-8073
Scotsman Ice Systems
Vernon Hills, IL 800-726-8762
Sea Breeze Fruit Flavors
Towaco, NJ 800-732-2733
Sentry/Bevcon North America
Adelanto, CA 800-661-3003
SerVend International
Sellersburg, IN 800-367-4233
Server Products Inc
Richfield, WI 800-558-8722
Silver King Refrigeration Inc
Minneapolis, MN 800-328-3329
Sopralco
Plantation, FL 954-584-2225
Spin-Tech Corporation
Hoboken, NJ 800-977-4692
Spinco Metal Products Inc
Newark, NY 315-331-6285
Stainless One DispensingSystem
Vacaville, CA 888-723-3827
Star Manufacturing Intl Inc
St Louis, MO 800-264-7827
Steel Products
Marion, IA 800-333-9451
Summit Commercial
Bronx, NY 800-932-4267
Sunroc Corporation
Columbus, OH 800-478-6762
Superflex Limited
Brooklyn, NY 800-394-3665
Superior Products Company
Saint Paul, MN 800-328-9800
Tablecraft Products Co Inc
Gurnee, IL 800-323-8321
Technium
Medford, NJ 609-702-5910
Thermos Company
Schaumburg, IL 800-243-0745
Tops Manufacturing Co
Darien, CT 203-655-9367
True Food Service Equipment, Inc.
O Fallon, MO 800-325-6152
Wells Manufacturing Company
St. Louis, MO 888-356-5362
Wilch Manufacturing
Topeka, KS 785-267-2762
Wine Chillers of California
Santa Ana, CA 800-331-4274
Winekeeper
Santa Barbara, CA 805-963-3451

Coffee

American Production Co Inc
Redwood City, CA 650-368-5334
Bevistar
Oswego, IL 877-238-7827
Custom Diamond International
Laval, QC 800-363-5926
Fetco
Lake Zurich, IL 800-338-2699
Franke Americas
Hatfield, PA 215-822-6590
K-Way Products
Mount Carroll, IL 800-622-9163
Karma
Watertown, WI 800-558-9565
Midwest Juice
Grand Rapids, MI 877-265-8243
Red Diamond Coffee & Tea
Moody, AL 800-292-4651
Regal Ware Inc
Kewaskum, WI 262-626-2121
Sopralco
Plantation, FL 954-584-2225
Steel Products
Marion, IA 800-333-9451
Superior Products Company
Saint Paul, MN 800-328-9800
Thermos Company
Schaumburg, IL 800-243-0745

Tops Manufacturing Co
Darien, CT. 203-655-9367
Wells Manufacturing Company
St. Louis, MO 888-356-5362

Cup & Napkin

Atlas Metal Industries
Miami, FL. .800-762-7565
Browne & Company
Markham, ON. 905-475-6104
C R Mfg
Waverly, NE. 877-789-5844
Component Hardware Group Inc
Lakewood, NJ. 800-526-3694
Custom Diamond International
Laval, QC 800-363-5926
Dispense Rite
Northbrook, IL 800-772-2877
Diversified Metal Products Inc
Northbrook, IL 800-772-2877
Georgia Pacific
Green Bay, WI. 920-435-8821
Igloo Products Corp
Katy, TX 866-509-3503
K & L Intl
Ontario, CA. 888-598-5588
Levelmatic
Miami, FL. .800-762-7565
M-One Specialties
Salt Lake City, UT 800-525-9223
Palmer Fixture Company
Green Bay, WI. 800-558-8678
Plastic Fantastics/Buck Signs
Ashland, OR 800-482-1776
Pronto Products Company
Arcadia, CA .800-377-6680
Redi-Call Inc
Reno, NV 800-648-1849
San Jamar
Elkhorn, WI. 800-248-9826
Sanitor Manufacturing Co
Portage, MI. 800-379-5314
SerVend International
Sellersburg, IN 800-367-4233
Superior Products Company
Saint Paul, MN 800-328-9800
Tomlinson Industries
Cleveland, OH 800-945-4589
Tops Manufacturing Co
Darien, CT. .203-655-9367
Traex
Dane, WI. 800-356-8006

Food

AC Dispensing Equipment
Lower Sackville, NS. 888-777-9990
Action Technology
Prussia, PA .217-935-8311
American Production Co Inc
Redwood City, CA 650-368-5334
Automatic Bar Controls Inc
Vacaville, CA 800-722-6738
Belshaw Adamatic Bakery Group
Auburn, WA 800-578-2547
Bijur Lubricating Corporation
Morrisville, NC. 800-631-0168
Carlisle Food Svc Products Inc
Oklahoma City, OK 800-654-8210
Carpigiani Corporation of America
Winston Salem, NC. 800-648-4389
Cornelius Wilshire Corporation
Schaumburg, IL. 847-397-4600
Creamery Plastics Products, Ltd
Chilliwack, BC 604-792-0232
Custom Diamond International
Laval, QC 800-363-5926
Design Technology Corporation
Billerica, MA 978-663-7000
Dispense Rite
Northbrook, IL 800-772-2877
Diversified Metal Products Inc
Northbrook, IL 800-772-2877
Drum-Mates Inc.
Lumberton, NJ 800-621-3786
Dunkin' Brands, Inc.
Canton, MA 800-859-5339
Eurodispenser
Decatur, IL .217-864-4061
Federal Machine Corp
Clive, IA 800-247-2446

Gruenewald ManufacturingCompany
Danvers, MA. 800-229-9447
Hoshizaki America Inc
Peachtree City, GA 800-438-6087
K & L Intl
Ontario, CA. 888-598-5588
Karma
Watertown, WI. 800-558-9565
Lakeside Manufacturing Inc
Milwaukee, WI. 888-558-8565
LBP Manufacturing LLC
Cicero, IL 708-652-5600
Lincoln Foodservice
Cleveland, OH 800-374-3004
Mid-Southwest Marketing
Edmond, OK 405-341-3962
National Scoop & Equipment Company
Spring House, PA 215-646-2040
Neos
Elk River, MN 888-441-6367
Nuova Distribution Centre
Ferndale, WA 360-366-2226
Opal Manufacturing Ltd
Toronto, ON 416-646-5232
Perfect Equipment Inc
Gurnee, IL. .800-356-6301
Pez Candy Inc
Orange, CT .203-795-0531
Plastic Fantastics/Buck Signs
Ashland, OR 800-482-1776
Precision Pours
Minneapolis, MN 800-549-4491
Prestige Metal Products Inc
Antioch, IL .847-395-0775
Prince Castle Inc
Carol Stream, IL 800-722-7853
Pro-Flo Products
Cedar Grove, NJ 800-325-1057
Ragtime
Ceres, CA 209-667-5525
Rieke Packaging Systems
Auburn, IN .260-925-3700
San Jamar
Elkhorn, WI. 800-248-9826
SaniServ
Mooresville, IN. 800-733-8073
Server Products Inc
Richfield, WI 800-558-8722
Silver King Refrigeration Inc
Minneapolis, MN 800-328-3329
Steril-Sil Company
Bowmansville, PA. 800-784-5537
Summit Machine Builders Corporation
Denver, CO .800-274-6741
Tablecraft Products Co Inc
Gurnee, IL. .800-323-8321
Texican Specialty Products
Houston, TX 800-869-5918
Thermos Company
Schaumburg, IL. 800-243-0745
Tomlinson Industries
Cleveland, OH 800-945-4589
Traex
Dane, WI. 800-356-8006
Viking Industries
New Smyrna Beach, FL 888-605-5560
Wells Manufacturing Company
St. Louis, MO 888-356-5362
Wilch Manufacturing
Topeka, KS .785-267-2762

Glass

Lakeside Manufacturing Inc
Milwaukee, WI. 888-558-8565

Ice Cream & Frozen Yogurt

Carpigiani Corporation of America
Winston Salem, NC. 800-648-4389
Custom Diamond International
Laval, QC 800-363-5926
Delfield Co
Mt Pleasant, MI. 800-733-8821
Dispense Rite
Northbrook, IL 800-772-2877
Diversified Metal Products Inc
Northbrook, IL 800-772-2877
Dunkin' Brands, Inc.
Canton, MA 800-859-5339
Federal Machine Corp
Clive, IA 800-247-2446

Flavor Burst
Danville, IN 800-264-3528
Frosty Factory of America Inc
Ruston, LA .800-544-4071
Gruenewald ManufacturingCompany
Danvers, MA. 800-229-9447
H C Duke & Son Inc
East Moline, IL 309-755-4553
Oceanpower America
Leesburg, VA 305-721-7823
SaniServ
Mooresville, IN. 800-733-8073
Superior Products Company
Saint Paul, MN 800-328-9800
Wilch Manufacturing
Topeka, KS .785-267-2762

Plate & Tray

APW Wyott Food Service Equipment Company
Cheyenne, WY 800-527-2100
Atlas Metal Industries
Miami, FL. .800-762-7565
Custom Diamond International
Laval, QC 800-363-5926
Delfield Co
Mt Pleasant, MI. 800-733-8821
K & L Intl
Ontario, CA. 888-598-5588
Lakeside Manufacturing Inc
Milwaukee, WI. 888-558-8565

Soda Fountain, Syrup & Fruit Juice

Automatic Bar Controls Inc
Vacaville, CA 800-722-6738
Bevistar
Oswego, IL .877-238-7827
Carbonic Machines Inc
Minneapolis, MN 612-824-0745
Commercial Refrigeration Service, Inc.
Phoenix, AZ 623-869-8881
Control Beverage
Adelanto, CA 330-549-5376
Custom Diamond International
Laval, QC 800-363-5926
Easybar Corp
Tualatin, OR 888-294-7405
Eurodispenser
Decatur, IL .217-864-4061
Follett Corp
Easton, PA. .800-523-9361
IMI Cornelius
Schaumburg, IL. 800-323-4789
K-Way Products
Mount Carroll, IL 800-622-9163
Karma
Watertown, WI. 800-558-9565
Leland Limited Inc
South Plainfield, NJ 800-984-9793
Manitowoc Foodservice
Sellersburg, IN 800-367-4233
Sentry/Bevcon North America
Adelanto, CA 800-661-3003
Server Products Inc
Richfield, WI 800-558-8722

Displays

Food, Artificial

Accent Store Fixtures
Kenosha, WI 800-545-1144
Buffet Enhancements Intl
Point Clear, AL 251-990-6119
Cal-Mil Plastic Products Inc
Oceanside, CA 800-321-9069
Consolidated Display Co Inc
Oswego, IL .888-851-7669
Despro Manufacturing
Cedar Grove, NJ 800-292-9906
Display Studios Inc
Kansas City, KS 800-648-8479
Dufeck Manufacturing Co
Denmark, WI. 888-603-9663
Fax Foods
Vista, CA. 760-599-6030
GCJ Mattei Company
Louisville, KY 502-583-4774
Hiclay Studios
St Louis, MO. 314-533-8393

Madix Inc
Goodwater, AL 256-839-6354
Marineland Commercial Aquariums
Blacksburg, VA 800-322-1266
Merchandising Frontiers Inc
Winterset, IA 800-421-2278
Rathe Productions
New York, NY 212-242-9000
Schmidt Progressive
Lebanon, OH 800-272-3706
Trade Fixtures
Little Rock, AR 800-872-3490
Vomela/Harbor Graphics
St Paul, MN 800-645-1012

Frozen Food

Arneg LLC
Lexington, NC 800-276-3487
Coldstream Products Corporation
Crossfield, AB 888-946-4097
Display Studios Inc
Kansas City, KS 800-648-8479
G A Systems Inc
Huntington Beach, CA 714-848-7529
GCJ Mattei Company
Louisville, KY 502-583-4774
Hercules Food Equipment
Weston, ON 416-742-9673
Hiclay Studios
St Louis, MO 314-533-8393
Novelty Baskets
Hurst, TX 817-268-5426
Oscartek
Burlingame, CA 855-885-2400
Oscartielle Equipment Company
Burlingame, CA 800-672-2784
Refcon
Medford, NJ 609-714-2330
Retail Decor
Ironton, OH 800-726-3402
Vomela/Harbor Graphics
St Paul, MN 800-645-1012

Point of Purchase

ABC Letter Art
Los Angeles, CA 888-261-5367
Accent Store Fixtures
Kenosha, WI 800-545-1144
ALCO Designs
Gardena, CA 800-228-2346
Alger Creations
Miami, FL 954-454-3272
Alphabet Signs
Gap, PA 800-582-6366
American Led-Gible
Columbus, OH 614-851-1100
AMI
Richmond, CA 800-942-7466
Archer Wire Intl Corp
Chicago, IL 708-563-1700
Arlington Display Industries
Detroit, MI 313-837-1212
Art Wire Works Co
Chicago, IL 708-458-3993
Art-Phyl Creations
Hialeah, FL 800-327-8318
Atlas Packaging Inc
Opa Locka, FL 800-662-0630
B S C Signs
Broomfield, CO 866-223-0101
B&B Neon Sign Company
Austin, TX 800-791-6366
Baltimore Sign Company
Arnold, MD 410-276-1500
Barrette Outdoor Living
Cleveland, OH 800-336-2383
Beemak-IDL Display
La Mirada, CA 800-421-4393
Better Bilt Products
Addison, IL 800-544-4550
Bill Carr Signs
Flint, MI 810-232-1569
Blue Ridge Signs
Weatherford, TX 800-659-5645
Boston Retail
Medford, MA 800-225-1633
Boxes.com
Livingston, NJ 201-646-9050
Cannon Equipment Company
Cannon Falls, MN 800-825-8501

Canton Sign Co
Canton, OH 330-456-7151
Capitol Hardware, Inc.,
Middlebury, IN 800-327-6083
Ccw Products
Arvada, CO 303-427-9663
Cellox Corp
Reedsburg, WI 608-524-2316
Chicago Show Inc
Buffalo Grove, IL 847-955-0200
Chroma Tone
Saint Clair, PA 800-878-1552
Clearr Corporation
Minneapolis, MN 800-548-3269
Collegeville Flag & Manufacturing Company
Collegeville, PA 800-523-5630
Comm-Pak
Opelika, AL 334-749-6201
Commercial Corrugated Co Inc
Baltimore, MD 800-242-8861
Conn Container Corp
North Haven, CT 203-248-0241
Containair Packaging Corporation
Paterson, NJ 888-276-6500
Corfab
Chicago, IL 708-458-8750
Corman & Assoc Inc
Lexington, KY 859-233-0544
Corr Pak Corp
Mc Cook, IL 708-442-7806
Courtesy Signs
Amarillo, TX 806-373-6609
Creative Enterprises
Kendall Park, NJ 732-422-0300
Cucamonga Sign Shop LLC
Rancho Cucamonga, CA 909-945-5888
Curry Enterprises
Atlanta, GA 800-241-7308
Curzon Promotional Graphics
Omaha, NE 800-769-7446
Custom ID Systems
Venice, FL 800-242-8430
Custom Packaging Inc
Richmond, VA 804-232-3299
Daytech Limited
Toronto, ON 877-329-1907
Derse Inc
Milwaukee, WI 800-562-2300
Designers Plastics
Clearwater, FL 727-573-1643
Despro Manufacturing
Cedar Grove, NJ 800-292-9906
Diamond Packaging
Rochester, NY 800-333-4079
Dinosaur Plastics
Houston, TX 713-923-2278
Display Concepts
Trenton, ME 800-446-0033
Display Studios Inc
Kansas City, KS 800-648-8479
Drake Co
Houston, TX 800-299-5644
Dunn Woodworks
Shrewsbury, PA 877-835-8592
Eastern Container Corporation
Mansfield, MA 508-337-0400
Eastern Plastics
Pawtucket, RI 800-442-8585
Eaton Quade Plastics & Sign Co
Oklahoma City, OK 405-236-4475
EGW Bradbury Enterprises
Bridgewater, ME 800-332-6021
Einson Freeman
Paramus, NJ 201-221-2800
Embro Manufacturing Company
East Canton, OH 330-489-3500
Emco Industrial Plastics
Cedar Grove, NJ 800-292-9906
Enterprise Products
Bell Gardens, CA 562-928-1918
ERC Parts Inc
Kennesaw, GA 800-241-6880
ERS International
Norwalk, CT 800-377-4685
Esco Manufacturing Inc
Watertown, SD 800-843-3726
Everbrite LLC
Greenfield, WI 800-558-3888
Exhibitron Co
Grants Pass, OR 800-437-4571
Expo Displays
Birmingham, AL 800-367-3976

FFR Merchandising Inc
Twinsburg, OH 800-422-2547
Filet Menu
Los Angeles, CA 310-202-8000
First Bank of Highland P
Northbrook, IL 847-272-1300
Fitzpatrick Container Company
North Wales, PA 215-699-3515
Five-M Plastics Company
Allentown, PA 610-628-4291
Fleetwood International Paper
Vernon, CA 323-588-7121
Florida Plastics Intl
Evergreen Park, IL 800-499-0400
FMI Display
Elkins Park, PA 215-663-1998
Foxfire Marketing Solutions
Newark, DE 800-497-0512
France Personalized Signs
Cleveland, OH 216-241-2198
Freely Display
Cleveland, OH 216-721-6056
Fresno Neon Sign Co Inc
Fresno, CA 559-292-2944
Fuller Packaging Inc
Central Falls, RI 401-725-4300
Garvin Industries
Franklin Park, IL 847-451-6500
GCJ Mattei Company
Louisville, KY 502-583-4774
Gelberg Signs
Washington, DC 800-443-5237
GENESTA
Rockwall, TX 972-771-1653
Great Northern Corp
Chippewa Falls, WI 800-472-1800
Greif Inc
Delaware, OH 800-476-1635
Hager Containers Inc
Carrollton, TX 972-416-7660
Handicap Sign Inc
Grand Rapids, MI 800-690-4888
Hanley Sign Company
Latham, NY 518-783-6183
Harmar
Sarasota, FL 800-833-0478
Harting Graphics
Wilmington, DE 800-848-1373
Hiclay Studios
St Louis, MO 314-533-8393
HMG Worldwide
Morton Grove, IL 847-965-7100
HMG Worldwide In-Store Marketing
New York, NY 212-736-2300
Hoarel Sign Co
Amarillo, TX 806-373-2175
Hunter Packaging Corporation
South Elgin, IL 800-428-4747
IBC Shell Packaging
New Hyde Park, NY 516-352-5138
Icee-USA Corporation
Ontario, CA 800-426-4233
Illuma Display
Brookfield, WI 800-501-0128
Industrial Nameplate Inc
Warminster, PA 800-878-6263
Industrial Sign Company
South El Monte, CA 800-596-3720
Innovative Space Management
Woodside, NY 718-278-4300
International Patterns, Inc.
Bay Shore, NY 631-952-2000
J.C. Products Inc.
Haddam, CT 860-267-5516
Jay Packaging Group Inc
Warwick, RI 401-244-1300
JBC Plastics
St Louis, MO 877-834-5526
JEM Wire Products
Middletown, CT 860-347-0447
Jesse Jones Box Corporation
Philadelphia, PA 215-425-6600
Just Plastics Inc
New York, NY 212-569-8500
K & I Creative Plastics & Wood
Jacksonville, FL 904-387-0438
Kehr-Buffalo Wire Frame Co Inc
Buffalo, NY 800-875-4212
King Products
Mississauga, ON 866-454-6757
Koch Container
Victor, NY 585-924-1600

Krimstock Enterprises
Pennsauken, NJ..................856-665-3676
L.A. Darling Co., LLC
Paragould, AR...................800-682-5730
LBP Manufacturing LLC
Cicero, IL.......................708-652-5600
Lil' Orbits
Minneapolis, MN................800-228-8305
Lorac Union Tool Co
Providence, RI...................888-680-3236
Loy Lange Box Co
St Louis, MO....................800-886-4712
LSI Industries Inc
Blue Ash, OH...................513-793-3200
M & M Display
Philadelphia, PA................800-874-7171
Mack-Chicago Corporation
Chicago, IL.....................800-992-6225
Madsen Wire Products Inc
Orland, IN......................260-829-6561
Mainstreet Menu Systems
Brookfield, WI..................800-782-6222
Mall City Containers Inc
Kalamazoo, MI..................800-643-6721
Mannkraft Corporation
Newark, NJ.....................973-589-7400
Mark Slade ManufacturingCompany
Seymour, WI....................920-833-6557
Market Sign Systems
Portland, ME....................800-421-1799
Mcintyre Metals Inc
Thomasville, NC.................800-334-0807
Mcroyal Industries Inc
Youngstown, OH.................800-785-2556
MDI Worldwide
Farmington Hills, MI............800-228-8925
Meilahn Manufacturing Co
Chicago, IL.....................773-581-5204
Melrose Displays
Passaic, NJ.....................973-471-7700
Merchandising Inventives
Waukegan, IL...................800-367-5653
Merric
Bridgeton, MO..................314-770-9944
Metaline Products Co Inc
South Amboy, NJ................732-721-1373
Michigan Box Co
Detroit, MI.....................888-642-4269
Micro Wire Products Inc
Brockton, MA...................508-584-0200
Mid Cities Paper Box Company
Downey, CA.....................877-277-6272
Mid-West Wire Products
Ferndale, MI....................800-989-9881
Midwest Wire Specialties
Chicago, IL.....................800-238-0228
Miller Group Multiplex
Dupo, IL........................800-325-3350
Mirro Products Company
High Point, NC..................336-885-4166
Modar
Benton Harbor, MI...............800-253-6186
Modern Metalcraft
Midland, MI.....................800-948-3182
Morrissey Displays & Models
Port Washington, NY.............516-883-6944
Moseley Realty LLC
Franklin, MA....................800-667-3539
Multi-Panel Display Corporation
Brooklyn, NY....................800-439-0879
MultiFab Plastics
Boston, MA......................888-293-5754
Nashville Display Manufacturing Company
Lebanon, TN....................888-743-2572
Neal Walters Poster Corporation
Bentonville, AR..................501-273-2489
Nelipak
Phoenix, AZ.....................602-269-7648
North American Plastic Manufacturing Company
Bethel, CT......................800-934-7752
Northeast Box Co
Ashtabula, OH...................800-362-8100
Northern Metal Products
St Cloud, MN....................800-458-5549
Northwestern
Van Nuys, CA....................818-786-1581
Nu-Dell Manufacturing
Des Plaines, IL..................847-803-4500
Omega Industries
St Louis, MO....................314-961-1668
Omni Craft Inc
Hopkins, MN....................952-988-9944

OSF
Toronto, ON.....................800-465-4000
P M Plastics
Pewaukee, WI...................262-691-1700
Pacific Store Designs Inc
Garden Grove, CA................800-772-5661
Pentwater Wire Products Inc
Pentwater, MI...................877-869-6911
Peter Pepper Products Inc
Compton, CA....................310-639-0390
PFI Displays Inc
Rittman, OH.....................800-925-9075
Philipp Lithographing Co
Grafton, WI.....................800-657-0871
Pilgrim Plastics
Brockton, MA....................800-343-7810
Plastech
Monrovia, CA....................626-358-9306
Plasti-Clip Corp
Milford, NH.....................800-882-2547
Plasti-Line
Knoxville, TN....................800-444-7446
Plastic Fantastics/Buck Signs
Ashland, OR.....................800-482-1776
PMI Food Equipment Group
Troy, OH........................937-332-3000
Prengler Products
Sherman, TX.....................903-892-9791
Presentations South
Orlando, FL......................407-657-2108
Prestige Plastics Corporation
Delta, BC.......................604-930-2931
Princeton Shelving
Cedar Rapids, IA.................319-369-0355
Pro-Ad-Co Inc
Portland, OR....................800-287-5885
Process Displays
New Berlin, WI..................800-533-1764
Propak
Burlington, ON..................800-263-4872
R R Donnelley
Chicago, IL.....................800-742-4455
R T C
Rolling Meadows, IL.............847-640-2400
R Wireworks Inc
Elmira, NY......................800-550-4009
Racks
San Diego, CA...................619-661-0987
Rairdon Dodge Chrysler Jeep
Kirkland, WA....................425-821-1777
Rand-Whitney Group LLC
Worcester, MA...................508-791-2301
Randware Industries
Prospect Heights, IL.............847-299-8884
Rapid Displays Inc
Chicago, IL.....................800-356-5775
Rathe Productions
New York, NY....................212-242-9000
Reading Plastic Fabricators
Reading, PA.....................610-926-3245
Reeve Store Equipment Co
Pico Rivera, CA..................800-927-3383
Refcon
Medford, NJ.....................609-714-2330
Reflex International
Norcross, GA....................800-642-7640
Render
Buffalo, NY.....................888-446-1010
Retail Decor
Ironton, OH.....................800-726-3402
Rex Art Manufacturing Corp.
Lindenhurst, NY.................631-884-4600
Rice Packaging Inc
Ellington, CT....................800-367-6725
Robelan Displays Inc
Hempstead, NY..................865-564-8600
Royal Display Corporation
Middletown, CT..................800-569-1295
Royce Corp
Glendale, AZ.....................602-256-0006
RPA Process Technologies
Marblehead, MA.................800-631-9707
Rudd Container Corp
Chicago, IL.....................773-847-7600
Russell-William
Odenton, MD....................410-551-3602
Rutler Screen Printing
Easton, PA......................610-829-2999
Sam Pievac Company
Santa Fe Springs, CA.............800-742-8585
San Juan Signs Inc
Farmington, NM.................505-326-5511

Schiffenhaus Industries
Newark, NJ.....................973-484-5000
SEMCO
Ocala, FL.......................800-749-6894
Smurfit Kappa
Carson, CA......................310-537-8190
Smurfit Stone
Norcross, GA....................314-656-5300
Smurfit-Stone Container Corp
Santa Fe Springs, CA.............714-523-3550
Smyth Co LLC
St Paul, MN.....................800-473-3464
Source Packaging Inc
Mahwah, NJ.....................888-665-9768
Southern Container Corporation
Deer Park, NY...................631-586-6006
Southern Imperial Inc
Rockford, IL.....................800-747-4665
Special Events Supply Company
Hauppauge, NY
St Joseph Packaging Inc
St Joseph, MO...................800-383-3000
St. Elizabeth Street Display Corporation
Hackensack, NJ..................201-883-0333
Standex International Corp.
Salem, NH.......................603-893-9701
Steel City Corporation
Youngstown, OH.................800-321-0350
Stoffel Seals Corp
Tallapoosa, GA..................800-422-8247
Stout Sign Company
Saint Louis, MO..................800-325-8530
Stricker & Co
La Plata, MD.....................301-934-8346
Stylmark Inc
Minneapolis, MN................800-328-2495
Sutton Designs
Ithaca, NY......................800-326-8119
Talbot Industries
Neosho, MO.....................417-451-5900
THARCO
San Lorenzo, CA.................800-772-2332
Thomson-Leeds Company
New York, NY....................800-535-9361
TMCo Inc.ÿ
Houston, TX.....................713-465-3255
Top Source Industries
Addison, IL......................800-362-9625
Traitech Industries
Vaughan, ON....................877-872-4835
Traub Container Corporation
Cleveland, OH...................216-475-5100
Travelon
Elk Grove Vlg, IL................800-537-5544
Trinkle Sign & Display
Youngstown, OH.................330-747-9712
Tru Form Plastics
Gardena, CA.....................800-510-7999
Twenty/Twenty Graphics
Gaithersburg, MD................240-243-0511
Universal Folding Box
East Orange, NJ..................973-482-4300
Uniweb Inc
Corona, CA......................800-486-4932
US Magnetix
Minneapolis, MN................763-540-9497
Vacuform Inc.
Sebring, OH.....................330-938-9674
Vega Mfg Ltd.
Port Coquitlam, BC...............800-224-8342
Viking Packaging & Display
San Jose, CA.....................408-998-1000
VIP Real Estate LTD
Chicago, IL.....................773-376-5000
Visual Marketing Assoc
Santee, CA......................619-258-0393
Vomela/Harbor Graphics
St Paul, MN.....................800-645-1012
VPC Gordon Sign
Denver, CO......................303-629-6121
Vulcan Industries
Moody, AL.......................888-444-4417
Wahlstrom Manufacturing
Fontana, CA.....................909-822-4677
Warwick Products
Cleveland, OH...................800-535-4404
Wayne Industries
Clanton, AL.....................800-225-3148
Webster Packaging Corporation
Loveland, OH....................513-683-5666
Welbilt Corporation
Stamford, CT....................203-325-8300

West Rock
  Atlanta, GA.................770-448-2193
White Way Sign & Maintenance
  Mt Prospect, IL.............800-621-4122
Willamette Industries
  Beaverton, OR..............503-641-1131
Willson Industries
  Marmora, NJ...............800-894-4169
Wiremaid Products Div
  Coral Springs, FL............800-770-4700
Woodstock Plastics Co Inc
  Marengo, IL................815-568-5281
WS Packaging Group Inc
  Neenah, WI................888-532-3334

Doilies

American Pan Co
  Urbana, OH................800-652-2151
Brooklace
  Oshkosh, WI...............800-572-4552
Cannon Equipment Company
  Cannon Falls, MN...........800-825-8501
Dorado Carton Company
  Dorado, PR................787-796-1670
Frost ET Inc
  Grand Rapids, MI...........800-253-9382
Hoffmaster Group Inc
  Oshkosh, WI...............800-327-9774
IB Concepts
  Elizabeth, NJ..............888-671-0800
Pinckney Molded Plastics
  Howell, MI................800-854-2920
Pro Bake Inc
  Twinsburg, OH.............800-837-4427
Smith-Lee Company
  Oshkosh, WI...............800-327-9774
Stein-DSI
  Northfield, MN.............507-645-9546
Sunset Paper Products
  Simi Valley, CA.............800-228-7882

Doors

Foodservice

Aleco Food Svc Div
  Muscle Shoals, AL...........800-633-3120
American Metal Door Company
  Richmond, IN..............800-428-2737
Andgar Corp
  Ferndale, WA..............360-366-9900
Beta Screen Corp
  Carlstadt, NJ..............800-272-7336
Eliason Corp
  Portage, MI...............800-828-3655
FIB-R-DOR
  Cincinnati, OH.............800-342-7367
Hoffman Co
  Corpus Christi, TX..........361-882-9281
Hormann Flexan Llc
  Leetsdale, PA..............800-365-3667
Kedco Wine Storage Systems
  Farmingdale, NY............800-654-9988
Marlite
  Dover, OH................800-377-1221
Plas-Ties Co
  Tustin, CA................800-854-0137
Products A Curtron Div
  Pittsburgh, PA.............800-888-9750
Rasco Industries
  Hamel, MN................800-537-3802
Stanley Access Technologies
  Farmington, CT.............800-722-2377
Super Seal ManufacturingLimited
  Woodbridge, ON............800-337-3239
Trimline Corp
  Elkhart Lake, WI............800-555-5895
Woodfold-Marco Manufacturing
  Forest Grove, OR...........503-357-7181

Drawers

Cash, Money

APG Cash Drawer
  Fridley, MN................763-571-5000
E F Bavis & Assoc Inc
  Maineville, OH.............513-677-0500
Leggett & Platt Inc
  Carthage, MO..............417-358-8131

Loyal Manufacturing
  Indianapolis, IN............317-359-3185
Superior Products Company
  Saint Paul, MN.............800-328-9800

Envelopes

Appleson Press
  Syosset, NY...............800-888-2775
Archer Daniels Midland Company
  Chicago, IL................312-634-8100
Artistic Packaging Concepts
  Massapequa Pk, NY..........516-797-4020
Barkley Filing Supplies
  Hattiesburg, MS............800-647-3070
BAW Plastics Inc
  Clairton, PA...............800-783-2229
Cenveo Inc
  Chicago, IL................800-388-8406
Check Savers Inc
  Garland, TX...............800-276-8315
Coleman Resources
  Greensboro, NC............336-852-4006
Commercial Envelope Manufacturing Company
  Hauppauge, NY
Continental Envelope
  Geneva, IL................800-621-8155
Dagher Printing
  Jacksonville, FL............904-998-0921
Double Envelope Corp
  Roanoke, VA..............540-362-3311
Eastern Envelope
  Flanders, NJ...............973-584-3311
Eaton Manufacturing Co
  Houston, TX...............800-328-6610
Enterprise Box Company
  Montclair, NJ..............973-509-2200
Enterprise Envelope Inc
  Grand Rapids, MI...........800-422-4255
Excelsior Transparent Bag Manufacturing
  Yonkers, NY...............914-968-1300
Flexo Transparent Inc
  Buffalo, NY...............877-993-5396
Forbes Products Corp
  Rush, NY.................800-316-5235
Grand Valley Labels
  Grand Rapids, MI
Heinrich Envelope Corp
  Minneapolis, MN............800-346-7957
Innova Envelopes
  La Salle, QC...............514-595-0555
International Envelope Company
  Exton, PA.................610-363-0900
Mac Papers Inc
  Jacksonville, FL............800-334-7026
Miami Systems Corporation
  Blue Ash, OH..............800-543-4540
Murray Envelope Corporation
  Hattiesburg, MS............601-583-8292
North American Packaging Corp
  New York, NY..............800-499-3521
Oles De Puerto Rico Inc
  Bayamon, PR..............787-786-1700
Poser Envelope
  Oakland, CA...............800-208-6100
Steingart Associates Inc
  South Fallsburg, NY.........845-434-4321
Stone Container
  Chicago, IL................312-346-6600
Volk Corp
  Farmington Hills, MI.........800-521-6799
Westrick Paper Co
  Jacksonville, FL............904-737-2122
Worcester Envelope Co
  Auburn, MA...............508-832-5397

Fixtures

Store

A.T. Foote Woodworking Company
  Hartford, CT...............860-249-6821
AAA Mill
  Austin, TX................512-385-2215
Acme Display Fixture Company
  Los Angeles, CA............800-959-5657
Acme Fixture Company
  Los Angeles, CA............888-379-9566
Acraloc Corp
  Oak Ridge, TN.............865-483-1368
ALCO Designs
  Gardena, CA...............800-228-2346

Amscor Inc
  West Babylon, NY...........800-825-9800
Amtekco
  Columbus, OH.............800-336-4677
Andrew's Fixture Co
  Tacoma, WA...............253-627-8388
Architectural Sheet Metals LLC
  Cleveland, OH.............216-361-9952
Arizona Store Equipment
  Phoenix, AZ...............800-624-8395
Art-Phyl Creations
  Hialeah, FL................800-327-8318
B J Wood Products Inc
  Ladysmith, WI.............715-532-6626
Bailly Showcase & Fixture Company
  Las Vegas, NV.............702-947-6885
Baker Cabinet Co
  Costa Mesa, CA............714-540-5515
Blue Ridge Signs
  Weatherford, TX............800-659-5645
Boston Retail
  Medford, MA..............800-225-1633
C&H Store Equipment Company
  Los Angeles, CA............800-648-4979
Cannon Equipment Company
  Cannon Falls, MN...........800-825-8501
Capitol Hardware, Inc.,
  Middlebury, IN.............800-327-6083
Chicago Show Inc
  Buffalo Grove, IL...........847-955-0200
Clearr Corporation
  Minneapolis, MN............800-548-3269
Corman & Assoc Inc
  Lexington, KY..............859-233-0544
Crown Metal Manufacturing Company
  Elmhurst, IL...............630-279-9800
Crown Metal Mfg Co
  Rancho Cucamonga, CA.......909-291-8585
CSC Worldwide
  Columbus, OH.............800-848-3573
Custom Business Interiors
  Henderson, NV.............702-564-6661
Custom Craft Laminates
  Tampa, FL................800-486-4367
Display Craft Mfg Co
  Halethorpe, MD............410-242-0400
Display Creations
  Brooklyn, NY..............718-257-2300
Dunn Woodworks
  Shrewsbury, PA............877-835-8592
East Bay Fixture Co
  Emeryville, CA.............800-995-4521
EGW Bradbury Enterprises
  Bridgewater, ME............800-332-6021
Emco Industrial Plastics
  Cedar Grove, NJ............800-292-9906
Enterprise Products
  Bell Gardens, CA............562-928-1918
Exhibits & More Shopworks
  Liverpool, NY..............888-326-9100
Fab-X/Metals
  Washington, NC............800-677-3229
FFR Merchandising Inc
  Twinsburg, OH.............800-422-2547
Field Manufacturing Corporation
  Torrance, CA..............310-781-9292
Fine Woods Manufacturing
  Phoenix, AZ...............800-279-2871
Freely Display
  Cleveland, OH.............216-721-6056
Garvey Products
  West Chester, OH...........800-543-1908
GDM Concepts
  Paramount, CA.............562-633-0195
General Cage
  Elwood, IN................800-428-6403
Handy Manufacturing Co Inc
  Newark, NJ...............800-631-4280
Heartwood
  Montclair, CA..............909-626-8104
Henry Hanger & Fixture Corporation of America
  New York City, NY..........877-279-0852
Hoffman Co
  Corpus Christi, TX..........361-882-9281
Huck Store Fixture Company
  Quincy, IL................800-680-4823
Hurlingham Company
  San Pedro, CA.............310-538-0236
IGS Store Fixtures
  Peabody, MA..............978-532-0010
Inland Showcase & Fixture Company
  Fresno, CA................559-237-4158

Interior Systems Inc
   Milwaukee, WI 800-837-8373
Interstate Showcase & Fixture Company
   West Orange, NJ 973-483-5555
Ironwood Displays
   Niles, MI 231-683-8500
J.K. Harman, Inc.
   Hamden, CT 800-248-1627
Kedco Wine Storage Systems
   Farmingdale, NY 800-654-9988
Kehr-Buffalo Wire Frame Co Inc
   Buffalo, NY 800-875-4212
Kent Corp
   Birmingham, AL 800-252-5368
Killion Industries Inc
   Vista, CA 800-421-5352
L A Cabinet & Finishing Co
   Los Angeles, CA 323-233-7245
L&S Products
   Coldwater, MI 517-279-9526
L.A. Darling Co., LLC
   Paragould, AR 800-682-5730
Lauritzen Makin Inc
   Fort Worth, TX 817-921-0218
Leggett & Platt Inc
   Carthage, MO 417-358-8131
Lozier Corp
   Omaha, NE 800-228-9882
Madix Inc
   Goodwater, AL 256-839-6354
Mark Slade ManufacturingCompany
   Seymour, WI 920-833-6557
Melrose Displays
   Passaic, NJ 973-471-7700
Merchandising Systems Manufacturing
   Union City, CA 800-523-1468
Metal Master Sales Corp
   Glendale Heights, IL 800-488-8729
Micro Wire Products Inc
   Brockton, MA 508-584-0200
Modar
   Benton Harbor, MI 800-253-6186
Modern Store Fixtures Company
   Dallas, TX 800-634-7777
New Court
   Texarkana, TX 903-838-0521
Northern Metal Products
   St Cloud, MN 800-458-5549
Northwestern
   Van Nuys, CA 818-786-1581
Omaha Fixture Mfg
   Omaha, NE 800-637-2257
Omicron Steel Products Company
   Jamaica, NY 718-805-3400
Omni Craft Inc
   Hopkins, MN 952-988-9944
Oscartek
   Burlingame, CA 855-885-2400
OSF
   Toronto, ON 800-465-4000
Pacific Store Designs Inc
   Garden Grove, CA 800-772-5661
Paramount Manufacturing Company
   Wilmington, MA 978-657-4300
Peacock Crate Factory
   Jacksonville, TX 800-657-2200
Pentwater Wire Products Inc
   Pentwater, MI 877-869-6911
Peter Pepper Products Inc
   Compton, CA 310-639-0390
PFI Displays Inc
   Rittman, OH 800-925-9075
Pierce Laminated Products Inc
   Rockford, IL 815-968-9651
Premier Brass
   Atlanta, GA 800-251-5800
Primlite Manufacturing Corporation
   Freeport, NY 800-327-7583
Quality Cabinet & Fixture Co
   San Diego, CA 619-266-1011
R C Smith Co
   Burnsville, MN 800-747-7648
R Wireworks Inc
   Elmira, NY 800-550-4009
Rairdon Dodge Chrysler Jeep
   Kirkland, WA 425-821-1777
Reeve Store Equipment Co
   Pico Rivera, CA 800-927-3383
Reeves Enterprises
   La Verne, CA 909-392-9999
Regal Plastic Supply Co
   Kansas City, MO 800-444-6390

Russell-William
   Odenton, MD 410-551-3602
RW Products
   Edgewood, NY 800-345-1022
S & L Store Fixture
   Doral, FL 800-205-4536
Sam Pievac Company
   Santa Fe Springs, CA 800-742-8585
SEMCO
   Ocala, FL 800-749-6894
Shelley Cabinet Company
   Shelley, ID 208-357-3700
Sinicrope & Sons Inc
   Alhambra, CA 323-283-5131
Sitka Store Fixtures
   Kansas City, MO 800-821-7558
Southern Store Fixtures Inc
   Bessemer, AL 800-552-6283
Spartan Showcase
   Union, MO 800-325-0775
Specialty Wood Products
   Clanton, AL 800-322-5343
Stanly Fixtures Co Inc
   Norwood, NC 704-474-3184
Streater Inc
   Albert Lea, MN 800-527-4197
Tables Cubed
   Chesterfield, MO 800-878-3001
Talbert Display
   Fort Worth, TX 817-429-4504
Thomson-Leeds Company
   New York, NY 800-535-9361
Thorco Industries LLC
   Lamar, MO 800-445-3375
Tulsa Plastics Co
   Tulsa, OK 888-273-5303
Unarco Industries LLC
   Wagoner, OK 800-654-4100
Uniweb Inc
   Corona, CA 800-486-4932
Valley Fixtures
   Sparks, NV 775-331-1050
Van Dereems Mfg Co
   Hawthorne, NJ 973-427-2355
View-Rite Manufacturing
   Daly City, CA 415-468-3856
Vulcan Industries
   Moody, AL 888-444-4417
Warwick Products
   Cleveland, OH 800-535-4404
William Hecht
   Philadelphia, PA 215-925-6223

Holders

Bag

Eastern Plastics
   Pawtucket, RI 800-442-8585
Grayline Housewares Inc
   Columbus, OH 800-222-7388
Seattle Plastics
   Seattle, WA 800-441-0679
Sipco Products
   Peoria Heights, IL 309-682-5400
Thorco Industries LLC
   Lamar, MO 800-445-3375
UniTrak Corporation
   Port Hope, ON 866-883-5749

Price Card, Ticket, Etc.

Amco Metals Indl
   City of Industry, CA 626-855-2550
BAW Plastics Inc
   Clairton, PA 800-783-2229
Beemak-IDL Display
   La Mirada, CA 800-421-4393
C R Mfg
   Waverly, NE 877-789-5844
Cannon Equipment Company
   Cannon Falls, MN 800-825-8501
Clamp Swing Pricing Co Inc
   Oakland, CA 800-227-7615
Cleveland Menu Printing
   Cleveland, OH 800-356-6368
Creative Essentials
   Ronkonkoma, NY 800-355-5891
Crown Metal Mfg Co
   Rancho Cucamonga, CA 909-291-8585
Fast Industries
   Fort Lauderdale, FL 800-775-5345

FFR Merchandising Inc
   Twinsburg, OH 800-422-2547
Forbes Industries
   Ontario, CA 909-923-4549
Gastro-Gnomes
   West Hartford, CT 800-747-4666
Illuma Display
   Brookfield, WI 800-501-0128
JBC Plastics
   St Louis, MO 877-834-5526
Jordan Specialty Company
   Brooklyn, NY 877-567-3265
Just Plastics Inc
   New York, NY 212-569-8500
Lorac Union Tool Co
   Providence, RI 888-680-3236
Lynn Sign Inc
   Andover, MA 800-225-5764
Market Sign Systems
   Portland, ME 800-421-1799
Menu Men
   Palm Harbor, FL 727-934-7191
MultiFab Plastics
   Boston, MA 888-293-5754
National Plastics Co
   Santa Fe Springs, CA 800-221-9149
Plasti-Clip Corp
   Milford, NH 800-882-2547
Ram Industries
   Erwin, TN 800-523-3883
Redi-Call Inc
   Reno, NV 800-648-1849
Reeve Store Equipment Co
   Pico Rivera, CA 800-927-3383
RPA Process Technologies
   Marblehead, MA 800-631-9707
Spirit Foodservice, Inc.
   Andover, MA 800-343-0996
Sutton Designs
   Ithaca, NY 800-326-8119
US Magnetix
   Minneapolis, MN 763-540-9497

Holding & Warming Equipment

Acra Electric Corporation
   Tulsa, OK 800-223-4328
Aladdin Temp-Rite, LLC
   Hendersonville, TN 800-888-8018
Alliance Products LLC
   Murfreesboro, TN 800-522-3973
Alto-Shaam
   Menomonee Falls, WI 800-329-8744
American Creative Solutions
   Matthews, NC 877-925-4406
American Metalcraft Inc
   Franklin Park, IL 708-345-1177
American Production Co Inc
   Redwood City, CA 650-368-5334
Antrim Manufacturing Inc
   Brookfield, WI 262-781-6860
Apex Fountain Sales Inc
   Philadelphia, PA 800-523-4586
APW Wyott Food Service Equipment Company
   Cheyenne, WY 800-527-2100
ARC Specialties
   Valencia, CA 661-775-8500
Arctica Showcase Company
   Cayuga, ON 800-839-5536
Aroma Manufacturing Company
   San Diego, CA 800-276-6286
Ballantyne Food Service Equipment
   Omaha, NE 800-424-1215
BEVCO
   Canada, BC 800-663-0090
Bevles Company
   Dallas, TX 800-441-1601
BG Industries
   Lemont, IL 800-800-5761
BKI Worldwide
   Simpsonville, SC 800-927-6887
Bon Chef
   Lafayette, NJ 800-331-0177
Brass Smith
   Denver, CO 800-662-9595
Brewmatic Company
   Torrance, CA 800-421-6860
Broaster Co LLC
   Beloit, WI 800-365-8278
Canadian Display Systems
   Concord, ON 800-895-5862

Candle Lamp Company
Corona, CA 877-526-7748
Carlisle Food Svc Products Inc
Oklahoma City, OK 800-654-8210
Carter-Hoffmann LLC
Mundelein, IL 800-323-9793
Caselites
Hialeah, FL 305-819-7766
Convay Systems
Minnetonka, MN..............800-334-1099
Craig Manufacturing
Irvington, NJ 800-631-7936
Creative Mobile Systems Inc
Manchester, CT...............800-646-8364
Cres Cor
Mentor, OH 877-273-7267
Crispy Lite
St. Louis, MO 888-356-5362
Custom Diamond Intl.
Laval, QC 800-326-5926
D'Lights
Glendale, CA 818-956-5656
Delfield Co
Mt Pleasant, MI. 800-733-8821
Deluxe Equipment Company
Bradenton, FL. 800-367-8931
Duke Manufacturing Co
St Louis, MO..................800-735-3853
Dynynstyl
Delray Beach, FL 800-774-7895
Eagle Foodservice   Equipment
Clayton, DE. 800-441-8440
Eagle Group
Clayton, DE. 800-441-8440
EPCO
Murfreesboro, TN 800-251-3398
Esquire Mechanical Corp.
Armonk, NY 800-847-4206
Faubion Central States Tank Company
Shawnee Mission, KS 800-450-8265
Fixtur World
Cookeville, TN 800-634-9887
FleetwoodGoldcoWyard
Romeoville, IL 630-759-6800
Food Warming Equipment Co
Crystal Lake, IL 800-222-4393
Fred D Pfening Co
Columbus, OH 614-294-5361
Galley
Jupiter, FL 800-537-2772
Garland Commercial Ranges
Mississauga, ON...............905-624-0260
Gold Medal Products Co
Cincinnati, OH 800-543-0862
Habco
Concord, CA 925-682-6203
Hatco Corp
Milwaukee, WI................800-558-0607
Heat-It Manufacturing
San Antonio, TX..............800-323-9336
Henny Penny, Inc.
Eaton, OH 800-417-8417
Hickory Industries
North Bergen, NJ 800-732-9153
Hot Food Boxes
Mooresville, IN................800-733-8073
InfraTech Corporation
Azusa, CA....................800-955-2476
Intedge Manufacturing
Woodruff, SC 866-969-9605
J.V. Reed & Company
Louisville, KY 877-258-7333
Karma
Watertown, WI 800-558-9565
Keating of Chicago Inc
Mc Cook, IL 800-532-8464
Kelmin Products
Plymouth, FL 407-886-6079
King Arthur
Statesville, NC 800-257-7244
LA Rosa Refrigeration & Equip
Detroit, MI 800-527-6723
Lakeside Manufacturing Inc
Milwaukee, WI................888-558-8565
Lambertson Industries Inc
Sparks, NV 800-548-3324
Lazy Man Inc
Belvidere, NJ 800-475-1950
Leedal Inc
Northbrook, IL 847-498-0111
Lewco Inc
Sandusky, OH 419-625-4014

Lincoln Foodservice
Cleveland, OH 800-374-3004
Low Temp Industries Inc
Jonesboro, GA 678-674-1317
M&S Manufacturing
Arnold, MO. 636-464-2739
Marshall Air Systems Inc
Charlotte, NC 800-722-3474
Mastex Industries
Petersburg, VA................804-732-8300
Merco/Savory
Mt. Pleasant, MI 800-733-8821
Metal Masters Northwest
Lynnwood, WA 425-775-4481
Metro Corporation
Wilkes Barre, PA...............800-992-1776
Mies Products
West Bend, WI 800-480-6437
Moffat
San Antonio, TX..............866-589-0664
Monroe Extinguisher Co Inc
Rochester, NY. 585-235-3310
Mosshaim Innovations
Jacksonville, FL 888-995-7775
Mr. Bar-B-Q
Winston-Salem, NC 800-333-2124
Nutty Bavarian
Sanford, FL 800-382-4788
Parvin Manufacturing Company
Los Angeles, CA...............800-648-0770
Piper Products Inc
Wausau, WI..................800-544-3057
Plastocon
Oconomowoc, WI. 800-966-0103
Prince Castle Inc
Carol Stream, IL 800-722-7853
Products A Curtron Div
Pittsburgh, PA. 800-888-9750
Proluxe
Paramount, CA 800-594-5528
Randell Manufacturing   Unified Brands
Weidman, MI 888-994-7636
Randware Industries
Prospect Heights, IL 847-299-8884
Reliable Food Service Equipment
Concord, ON..................416-738-6840
Remco Industries International
Fort Lauderdale, FL 800-987-3626
Rexcraft Fine Chafers
Long Island City, NY 888-739-2723
Royalton Foodservice Equip Co
North Royalton, OH 800-662-8765
Server Products Inc
Richfield, WI 800-558-8722
Sheffield Platers Inc
San Diego, CA 800-227-9242
Sico Inc
Minneapolis, MN 800-328-6138
Sould Manufacturing
Winnepeg, NB. 204-339-3499
Southern Pride Distributing
Alamo, TN 800-851-8180
Super-Chef Manufacturing Company
Houston, TX 800-231-3478
Superior Products Company
Saint Paul, MN 800-328-9800
Tempco Electric Heater Corporation
Wood Dale, IL. 888-268-6396
Texican Specialty Products
Houston, TX 800-869-5918
Thermal Bags By Ingrid Inc
Gilberts, IL 800-622-5560
Tomlinson Industries
Cleveland, OH 800-945-4589
Tranter INC
Wichita Falls, TX 940-723-7125
Ultrafryer Systems Inc
San Antonio, TX..............800-545-9189
Update International
Vernon, CA 800-747-7124
Valad Electric Heating Corporation
Tarrytown, NY 914-631-4927
Vimco
King of Prussia, PA............610-768-0500
Vollrath Co LLC
Sheboygan, WI...............800-624-2051
Vulcan Food Equipment Group
Baltimore, MD 800-814-2028
Welbilt Corporation
Stamford, CT.................203-325-8300
Wells Manufacturing Company
St. Louis, MO 888-356-5362

West Metals
London, ON 800-300-6667
Wilder Manufacturing Company
Port Jervis, NY 800-832-1319
Will & Baumer
Syracuse, NY.................315-451-1000
Williamsburg Metal Spinning
Brooklyn, NY 888-535-5402
Win-Holt Equipment Group
Syosset, NY...................800-444-3595
Wisco Industries Assembly
Oregon, WI..................800-999-4726
Wittco Foodservice Equipment
Milwaukee, WI...............800-367-8413
Wittco Foodservice Equipment
Milwaukee, WI...............800-821-3912
Zoia Banquetier Co
Cleveland, OH 216-631-6414

Hooks

Display, Store

Cannon Equipment Company
Cannon Falls, MN............800-825-8501
Clamp Swing Pricing Co Inc
Oakland, CA 800-227-7615
Etube & Wire
Shrewsbury, PA...............800-618-4720
FFR Merchandising Inc
Twinsburg, OH 800-422-2547
Mark Slade ManufacturingCompany
Seymour, WI. 920-833-6557
Merchandising Inventives
Waukegan, IL 800-367-5653
SEMCO
Ocala, FL. 800-749-6894
Southern Imperial Inc
Rockford, IL 800-747-4665

Interiors

Hotel, Bar, Restaurant

American Creative Solutions
Matthews, NC.................877-925-4406
Commercial Furniture Group Inc
Newport, TN. 800-873-3252
Original Wood Seating
Atlanta, GA...................678-966-0406

Kiosks

All A Cart Custom Mfg
Columbus, OH 800-695-2278
Burgess Enterprises, Inc
Renton, WA. 800-927-3286
Carts of Colorado Inc
Greenwood Vlg, CO 800-227-8634
Corsair Display Systems
Canandalgua, NY 800-347-5245
Daytech Limited
Toronto, ON 877-329-1907
Lakeside Manufacturing Inc
Milwaukee, WI 888-558-8565
Landmark Kitchen Design
Chandler, AZ. 866-621-3192
Mcroyal Industries Inc
Youngstown, OH. 800-785-2556
Merchandising Frontiers Inc
Winterset, IA..................800-421-2278
Michaelo Espresso
Seattle, WA 800-545-2883
Moseley Realty LLC
Franklin, MA 800-667-3539
Reflex International
Norcross, GA 800-642-7640
Southern Express
Saint Louis, MO...............800-444-9157
Steamway Corporation
Scottsburg, IN.................800-259-8171
The Carriage Works
Klamath Falls, OR 541-882-0700

Linen Goods

A1 Tablecloth Co
South Hackensack, NJ 800-727-8987
Artex International
Highland, IL 618-654-2113
ATD-American Co
Wyncote, PA 800-523-2300

Babco International, Inc
  Tucson, AZ 520-628-7596
Best Brands Home Products
  New York, NY 212-684-7456
Best Buy Uniforms
  Homestead, PA 800-345-1924
Bragard Professional Uniforms
  New York, NY 800-488-2433
Cotton Goods Mfg Co
  Chicago, IL 773-265-0088
Drapes 4 Show
  Sylmar, CA 800-525-7469
Gary Manufacturing Company
  National City, CA 800-775-0804
Gourmet Table Skirts
  Houston, TX 800-527-0440
Happy Chef Inc
  Butler, NJ 800-347-0288
Hilden Halifax
  South Boston, VA 800-431-2514
Jack the Ripper Table Skirting
  Stafford, TX 800-331-7831
Jones-Zylon Co
  West Lafayette, OH 800-848-8160
K Katen & Company
  Rahway, NJ 732-381-0220
Marko Inc
  Spartanburg, SC 866-466-2756
Party Linens
  Chicago, IL 800-281-0003
Philmont Manufacturing Co.
  Englewood, NJ 888-379-6483
Premier Skirting Products
  Lawrence, NY 800-544-2516
Prestige Skirting & Tablecloths
  Orangeburg, NY 800-635-3313
Radius Display Products
  Dallas, TX 888-322-7429
Stevens Linen Association
  Dudley, MA 800-772-9269
Sultan Linen Inc
  New York, NY 212-689-8900
Tara Linens
  Sanford, NC 800-476-8272

Magnetic Chips

Hopp Co Inc
  New Hyde Park, NY 800-889-8425

Magnetic Label

Backers

Hopp Co Inc
  New Hyde Park, NY 800-889-8425

Magnetic Pocket

Sign & Card Holders

Hopp Co Inc
  New Hyde Park, NY 800-889-8425

Markers

Price & Sign

Atlas Rubber Stamp & Printing
  York, PA 717-751-0459
Century Rubber Stamp Company
  New York, NY 212-962-6165
Courtesy Signs
  Amarillo, TX 806-373-6609
Display Concepts
  Trenton, ME 800-446-0033
Ed Smith's Stencil Works LTD
  New Orleans, LA 504-525-2128
FFR Merchandising Inc
  Twinsburg, OH 800-422-2547
Garvey Products
  Cincinnati, OH 513-771-8710
Grueny's Rubber Stamps
  Little Rock, AR 501-376-0393
Lamb Sign
  Manassas, VA 703-791-7960
Muskogee Rubber Stamp & Seal Company
  Fort Gibson, OK 918-478-3046
Neal Walters Poster Corporation
  Bentonville, AR 501-273-2489

Plastimatic Arts Corporation
  Mishawaka, IN 800-442-3593
Quick Stamp & Sign Mfg
  Lafayette, LA 337-232-2171
US Magnetix
  Minneapolis, MN 763-540-9497
Wildes Printing Co Inc
  White Plains, MD 301-870-4141

Menu Boards

Qyk Syn Industries
  Miami, FL 800-354-5640

Menus

A Allred Marketing
  Birmingham, AL 205-251-3700
Ad Art Litho.
  Cleveland, OH 800-875-6368
Beaverite Corporation
  Croghan, NY 800-424-6337
Brass Smith
  Denver, CO 800-662-9595
Charles Mayer Studios
  Akron, OH. 330-535-6121
City Grafx
  Eugene, OR. 800-258-2489
Cleveland Menu Printing
  Cleveland, OH 800-356-6368
Corsair Display Systems
  Canandalgua, NY 800-347-5245
Creative Essentials
  Ronkonkoma, NY 800-355-5891
Creative Impressions
  Buena Park, CA 800-524-5278
Creative Printing Co
  Burr Ridge, IL 630-734-3244
Custom Color Corp
  Lenexa, KS 888-605-4050
David Dobbs Enterprise Inc.
  St Augustine, FL 800-889-6368
Dilley Manufacturing Co
  Des Moines, IA 800-247-5087
Encore Image Inc
  Ontario, CA. 800-791-1187
Ennis Inc.
  Midlothian, TX 800-972-1069
Everbrite LLC
  Greenfield, WI 800-558-3888
Filet Menu
  Los Angeles, CA. 310-202-8000
Florida Plastics Intl
  Evergreen Park, IL 800-499-0400
Forbes Industries
  Ontario, CA. 909-923-4549
Frost Manufacturing Corp
  Worcester, MA 800-462-0216
Futura 2000 Corporation
  Miami, FL 305-256-5877
GA Design Menu Company
  Wixom, MI 313-561-2530
Gastro-Gnomes
  West Hartford, CT. 800-747-4666
Have Our Plastic Inc
  Mississauga, ON 800-263-5995
Impulse Signs
  Toronto, ON 866-636-8273
International Patterns, Inc.
  Bay Shore, NY 631-952-2000
Jordan Specialty Company
  Brooklyn, NY 877-567-3265
Kenyon Press
  Signal Hill, CA 800-752-9395
Landmark Kitchen Design
  Chandler, AZ. 866-621-3192
Legible Signs
  Loves Park, IL. 800-435-4177
Lynn Sign Inc
  Andover, MA 800-225-5764
Maier Sign Systems
  Saddle Brook, NJ 201-845-7555
Mainstreet Menu Systems
  Brookfield, WI 800-782-6222
Mastercraft
  Appleton, WI 800-242-6602
MDI Worldwide
  Farmington Hills, MI 800-228-8925
Menu Graphics
  Olmsted Falls, OH 216-696-1460
Menu Men
  Palm Harbor, FL 727-934-7191

Menu Promotions
  Bronx, NY. 718-324-3800
Milwaukee Sign Company
  Grafton, WI 262-375-5740
National Menuboard
  Auburn, WA 800-800-5237
National Plastics Co
  Santa Fe Springs, CA 800-221-9149
National Sign Systems
  Hilliard, OH 800-544-6726
Placemat Printers
  Fogelsville, PA 800-628-7746
Polar Hospitality Products
  Philadelphia, PA 800-831-7823
Posterloid Corporation
  Long Island City, NY 800-651-5000
Ram Industries
  Erwin, TN 800-523-3883
RAO Contract Sales Inc
  Paterson, NJ 888-324-0020
Redi-Print
  West Babylon, NY 631-491-6373
Retail Decor
  Ironton, OH. 800-726-3402
Roxanne Signs Inc
  Gaithersburg, MD 301-428-4911
Samsill Corp
  Fort Worth, TX 800-255-1100
School Marketing Partners
  San Juan Cpstrno, CA. 800-565-7778
Seattle Menu Specialists
  Kent, WA. 800-622-2826
Signets/Menu-Quik
  Mentor, OH. 800-775-6368
Spokane House of Hose Inc
  Spokane Valley, WA 800-541-6351
Sutton Designs
  Ithaca, NY 800-326-8119
Tablet & Ticket Co
  West Chicago, IL 800-438-4959
Unique Manufacturing
  Visalia, CA 888-737-1007
Vacuform Inc.
  Sebring, OH 330-938-9674
VC Menus
  Eastland, TX 800-826-3687
Visual Marketing Assoc
  Santee, CA 619-258-0393
Visual Planning Corp
  Champlain, NY 800-361-1192
VMC Signs
  Victoria, TX 361-575-0548
Vynatex
  Port Washington, NY 516-944-6130
Wayne Industries
  Clanton, AL 800-225-3148
Western Textile & Manufacturing Inc.
  Sausalito, CA 800-734-8683
Wind River Environmental
  Gloucester, MA 800-332-6025
Your Place Menu Systems
  Carson City, NV 800-321-8105

Napery

A1 Tablecloth Co
  South Hackensack, NJ 800-727-8987
Adcapitol
  Monroe, NC. 800-868-7111
Americo
  West Memphis, AR. 800-626-2350
Artex International
  Highland, IL 618-654-2113
Best Brands Home Products
  New York, NY 212-684-7456
Best Buy Uniforms
  Homestead, PA 800-345-1924
Carnegie Textile Co
  Cleveland, OH 800-633-4136
Connecticut Laminating Co Inc
  New Haven, CT. 800-753-9119
Cotton Goods Mfg Co
  Chicago, IL 773-265-0088
Drapes 4 Show
  Sylmar, CA 800-525-7469
Erving Industries
  Erving, MA. 413-422-2700
Filet Menu
  Los Angeles, CA. 310-202-8000
Gary Manufacturing Company
  National City, CA 800-775-0804

Gourmet Table Skirts
Houston, TX .800-527-0440
Happy Chef Inc
Butler, NJ 800-347-0288
Hilden Halifax
South Boston, VA 800-431-2514
Jack the Ripper Table Skirting
Stafford, TX .800-331-7831
Jones-Zylon Co
West Lafayette, OH. 800-848-8160
K Katen & Company
Rahway, NJ 732-381-0220
K-C Products Company
Van Nuys, CA 818-267-1600
Marcal Paper Mills
Elmwood Park, NJ 800-631-8451
Marko Inc
Spartanburg, SC 866-466-2756
Palmland Paper Company
Fort Lauderdale, FL 800-266-9067
Paper Service
Hinsdale, NH 603-239-6344
Party Linens
Chicago, IL 800-281-0003
Premier Skirting Products
Lawrence, NY 800-544-2516
Prestige Skirting & Tablecloths
Orangeburg, NY 800-635-3313
Resource One/Resource Two
Reseda, CA 818-343-3451
Scan Group
Appleton, WI 920-730-9150
Scranton Lace Company
Forest City, PA 800-822-1036
Shen Manufacturing Co Inc
Conshohocken, PA 610-825-2790
Showeray Corporation
Brooklyn, NY 718-965-3633
Smith-Lee Company
Oshkosh, WI .800-327-9774
Something Different Linen
Clifton, NJ. 800-422-2180
Springprint Medallion
Augusta, GA .800-543-5990
Sultan Linen Inc
New York, NY 212-689-8900
Tag-Trade Associated Group
Chicago, IL 800-621-8350
Tara Linens
Sanford, NC .800-476-8272
Ultimate Textile
Paterson, NJ .973-523-5866

Napkins

Paper

Admatch Corporation
New York, NY 800-777-9909
Alex Delvecchio Enterprises
Troy, MI 248-619-9600
Atlas Match Company
Toronto, ON .888-285-2783
Chinet Company
Laguna Niguel, CA. 949-348-1711
Creative Converting Inc
Clintonville, WI 800-826-0418
Erving Industries
Erving, MA 413-422-2700
Flamingo Food Service Products
Hialeah, FL 800-432-8269
Georgia Pacific
Green Bay, WI. 920-435-8821
Gold Star Products
Oak Park, MI. 800-800-0205
Hoffmaster Group Inc
Oshkosh, WI .800-367-2877
Hoffmaster Group Inc.
Oshkosh, WI .800-558-9300
K & L Intl
Ontario, CA. .888-598-5588
Kentfield's
Greenbrae, CA 888-461-7454
Kimberly-Clark Professional
Roswell, GA .800-241-3146
Lasermation Inc
Philadelphia, PA 800-523-2759
Marcal Paper Mills
Elmwood Park, NJ 800-631-8451
Palmland Paper Company
Fort Lauderdale, FL 800-266-9067

Paper Service
Hinsdale, NH 603-239-6344
Paradise Products
El Cerrito, CA. 800-227-1092
Potlatch Corp
Spokane, WA. 509-835-1500
Primary Liquidation
Bohemia, NY 631-244-1410
SCA Tissue
Philadelphia, PA 866-722-8675
SCA Tissue North America
S Glens Falls, NY 518-743-0240
Scan Group
Appleton, WI 920-730-9150
Schroeder Machine
San Marcos, CA 760-591-9733
Sorg Paper Company
Middletown, OH 513-420-5300
Spirit Foodservice, Inc.
Andover, MA 800-343-0996
Springprint Medallion
Augusta, GA .800-543-5990
SQP
Schenectady, NY. 800-724-1129

Paper

Writing, Forms, Sales & Order Books

Access Solutions
Knoxville, TN. 865-531-0971
Appleson Press
Syosset, NY. .800-888-2775
Atlas Match Corporation
Euless, TX. 800-628-2426
Conimar Corp
Ocala, FL. 800-874-9735
Dagher Printing
Jacksonville, FL 904-998-0921
Double Envelope Corp
Roanoke, VA. 540-362-3311
Durango-Georgia Paper
Tampa, FL 813-286-2718
Ennis Inc.
Midlothian, TX 800-972-1069
Fay Paper Products
Foxboro, MA 800-765-4620
Graydon Lettercraft
Great Neck, NY 516-482-0531
Hazen Paper Co
Holyoke, MA 413-538-8204
Holden Graphic Services
Minneapolis, MN 612-339-0241
Larry B Newman Printing
Knoxville, TN. 888-835-4566
Miami Systems Corporation
Blue Ash, OH 800-543-4540
Mohawk Paper Mills
Clifton Park, NY. 518-371-6700
Monadnock Paper Mills Inc
Bennington, NH 603-588-3311
Neal Walters Poster Corporation
Bentonville, AR 501-273-2489
North American Packaging Corp
New York, NY 800-499-3521
Old English Printing & Label Company
Delray Beach, FL 561-997-9990
Pan American Papers Inc
Miami, FL. 305-635-2534
Patrick & Co
Dallas, TX. 214-761-0900
Randall Printing
Brockton, MA 508-588-3830
Salinas Valley Wax Paper Co
Salinas, CA 831-424-2747
Steingart Associates Inc
South Fallsburg, NY 845-434-4321
Tops Business Forms
Covington, TN 800-762-7283
Visual Planning Corp
Champlain, NY 800-361-1192
Westrick Paper Co
Jacksonville, FL 904-737-2122

Place Mats

Abond Plastic Corporation
Lachine, QC .800-886-7947
Admatch Corporation
New York, NY 800-777-9909
Artex International
Highland, IL .618-654-2113

Bright of America
Summersville, WV 304-872-3000
Brooklace
Oshkosh, WI. 800-572-4552
Conimar Corp
Ocala, FL. 800-874-9735
Connecticut Laminating Co Inc
New Haven, CT. 800-753-9119
Creative Essentials
Ronkonkoma, NY 800-355-5891
Custom Table Pads
St Paul, MN. .800-325-4643
Decolin
Montreal, QC 514-384-2910
Dorado Carton Company
Dorado, PR 787-796-1670
Elrene Home Fashions
New York, NY 212-213-0425
Ennis Inc.
Midlothian, TX 800-972-1069
Erving Industries
Erving, MA 413-422-2700
Filet Menu
Los Angeles, CA. 310-202-8000
Gourmet Table Skirts
Houston, TX .800-527-0440
Have Our Plastic Inc
Mississauga, ON 800-263-5995
Hoffmaster Group Inc
Oshkosh, WI. 800-327-9774
Hoffmaster Group Inc
Oshkosh, WI. 800-367-2877
J. James
Brooklyn, NY 718-384-6144
Jack the Ripper Table Skirting
Stafford, TX .800-331-7831
K-C Products Company
Van Nuys, CA 818-267-1600
Louisville Bedding Co Inc.
Louisville, KY 502-813-8059
Marko Inc
Spartanburg, SC 866-466-2756
Mastercraft
Appleton, WI 800-242-6602
Milliken & Co
Spartanburg, SC 864-503-2020
Palmland Paper Company
Fort Lauderdale, FL 800-266-9067
Paradise Products
El Cerrito, CA. 800-227-1092
Placemat Printers
Fogelsville, PA 800-628-7746
Premier Skirting Products
Lawrence, NY 800-544-2516
Process Displays
New Berlin, WI. 800-533-1764
Rixie Paper Products Inc
Pottstown, PA 800-377-2692
Royal Paper Products
Coatesville, PA 800-666-6655
SCA Tissue
Philadelphia, PA 866-722-8675
Scranton Lace Company
Forest City, PA 800-822-1036
Seattle Menu Specialists
Kent, WA. 800-622-2826
Shen Manufacturing Co Inc
Conshohocken, PA 610-825-2790
Smith-Lee Company
Oshkosh, WI. 800-327-9774
Springprint Medallion
Augusta, GA .800-543-5990
Stevens Linen Association
Dudley, MA. .800-772-9269
Sultan Linen Inc
New York, NY 212-689-8900
Tag-Trade Associated Group
Chicago, IL 800-621-8350
Tara Linens
Sanford, NC .800-476-8272

Plastic Back Tag

Label Holders

Hopp Co Inc
New Hyde Park, NY. 800-889-8425

Plastic Shelf Covers

Hopp Co Inc
New Hyde Park, NY. 800-889-8425

Plastic Store Shelf

Moldings

Hopp Co Inc
New Hyde Park, NY 800-889-8425

Point of Sale Systems

APG Cash Drawer
Fridley, MN. 763-571-5000
ASI/Restaurant Manager
Silver Spring, MD. 800-356-6037
Astoria Laminations
St Clair Shores, MI 800-526-7325
Business Control Systems
Iselin, NJ. 800-233-5876
Cache Box
Arlington, VA 800-603-4834
CDI Service & Mfg Inc
Largo, FL 727-536-2207
Compris Technologies
Duluth, GA 800-615-3301
Comtek Systems
San Antonio, TX. 210-340-8253
Comus Restaurant Systems
Frederick, MD. 301-698-6208
Custom Business Solutions
Irvine, CA 800-551-7674
Cyplex
Los Angeles, CA
Data Management
San Angelo, TX 800-749-8463
Digital Dining
Springfield, VA. 703-912-3000
Elo Touch Systems
Menlo Park, CA 800-557-1458
FFR Merchandising Inc
Twinsburg, OH 800-422-2547
Illinois Wholesale Cash Rgstr
Elgin, IL 800-544-5493
ITC Systems
Toronto, ON 877-482-8326
Lowen Color Graphics
Hutchinson, KS. 800-545-5505
Loyal Manufacturing
Indianapolis, IN 317-359-3185
MAPS Software
Columbus, MS 662-328-6110
Metro Corporation
Wilkes Barre, PA. 800-992-1776
Microcheck Solutions
Humble, TX 800-647-4524
Microtouch Systems Inc
Methuen, MA 978-659-9000
National Computer Corporation
Greenville, SC. 866-944-5164
Novax Group/Point of Sales
New York, NY 212-684-1244
OMRON Systems LLC
Schaumburg, IL. 224-520-7650
Order-Matic Corporation
Oklahoma City, OK 800-767-6733
PAR Tech Inc
New Hartford, NY 800-448-6505
PC/Poll Systems
Dubuque, IA 800-670-1736
RDS of Florida
Fort Lauderdale, FL 305-994-7756
Reflex International
Norcross, GA 800-642-7640
Retail Automations Products
New York, NY 800-237-9144
Retail Decor
Ironton, OH. 800-726-3402
Retalix
Miamisburg, OH 877-794-7237
Sable Technology Solution
St Paul, MN. 800-722-5390
SalesData Software
San Jose, CA 408-281-5811
Scan Corporation
Brandon, FL 800-881-7226
SICOM Systems
Doylestown, PA 800-547-4266
Simply Products
Kunkletown, PA 610-681-6894
Southern Atlantic Label Co
Chesapeake, VA 800-456-5999
Squirrel Systems
Vancouver, BC 800-388-6824

Star Micronics
Edison, NJ. 800-782-7636
Stoffel Seals Corp
Tallapoosa, GA 800-422-8247
Systems Comtrex
Moorestown, NJ. 800-220-2669
Tinadre Inc
Tampa, FL. 813-866-0333
Touch Menus
Bellevue, WA 800-688-6368
US Magnetix
Minneapolis, MN 763-540-9497
Veri Fone Inc
Alpharetta, GA 770-663-0196

Pricer Signs

Dualite Sales & Svc Inc
Williamsburg, OH. 513-724-7100

Pumps

Syrup & Soda Fountain

Fristam Pumps USA LLP
Middleton, WI. 800-841-5001
John Crane Mechanical Sealing Devices
Chicago, IL
Manitowoc Foodservice
Sellersburg, IN 800-367-4233
PROCON Products
Smyrna, TN. 615-355-8000
Rio Syrup Co
St Louis, MO. 800-325-7666
Server Products Inc
Richfield, WI 800-558-8722
SHURflo
Costa Mesa, CA 800-854-3218
Standex International Corp.
Salem, NH. 603-893-9701
Superflex Limited
Brooklyn, NY 800-394-3665

Racks

Bakery

AFCO Manufacturing
Cincinnati, OH 800-747-7332
Allied Bakery and Food Service Equipment
Santa Fe Springs, CA 562-945-6506
Amco Metals Indl
City of Industry, CA 626-855-2550
ARC Specialties
Valencia, CA 661-775-8500
Better Bilt Products
Addison, IL. 800-544-4550
Bmh Equipment Inc
Sacramento, CA 800-350-8828
California Caster & Handtruck
San Francisco, CA 800-950-8750
Cannon Equipment Company
Cannon Falls, MN. 800-825-8501
Crown Custom Metal Spinning
Concord, ON. 800-750-1924
DBE Inc
Concord, ON. 800-461-5313
Dubuque Steel Products Co
Dubuque, IA 563-556-6288
EPCO
Murfreesboro, TN 800-251-3398
Esterle Mold & Machine Co Inc
Stow, OH. 800-411-4086
Hodges
Vienna, IL 800-444-0011
Lakeside Manufacturing Inc
Milwaukee, WI. 888-558-8565
Langer Manufacturing Company
Cedar Rapids, IA. 800-728-6445
Leggett & Platt Storage
Vernon Hills, IL 847-816-6246
Lynch-Jamentz Company
Lakewood, CA 800-828-6217
M & E Mfg Co Inc
Kingston, NY 845-331-2110
Magna Industries Inc
Lakewood, NJ. 800-510-9856
Malco Manufacturing Co
Los Angeles, CA. 866-477-7267
Market Forge Industries Inc
Everett, MA. 866-698-3188

Marlin Steel Wire Products
Baltimore, MD 877-762-7546
Metro Corporation
Wilkes Barre, PA. 800-992-1776
Micro Wire Products Inc
Brockton, MA 508-584-0200
National Cart Co
St Charles, MO 636-947-3800
Olson Wire Products Co
Baltimore, MD 410-242-7900
Omega Industries
St Louis, MO. 314-961-1668
Otto Braun Bakery Equipment
Buffalo, NY. 716-824-1252
Piper Products Inc
Wausau, WI. 800-544-3057
Products A Curtron Div
Pittsburgh, PA 800-888-9750
Proluxe
Paramount, CA 800-594-5528
Sitka Store Fixtures
Kansas City, MO. 800-821-7558
SPG International
Covington, GA 877-503-4774
Stein-DSI
Northfield, MN. 507-645-9546
Storage Unlimited
Nixa, MO 800-478-6642
Straits Steel & Wire Co
Ludington, MI. 231-843-3416
Superior Products Company
Saint Paul, MN. 800-328-9800
Trepte's Wire & Metal Works
Bellflower, CA 800-828-6217
Wirefab Inc
Worcester, MA 877-877-4445

Display, Store

Abalon Precision Manufacturing Corporation
Bronx, NY. 800-888-2225
Acryline
North Attleboro, MA 508-695-7124
ARC Specialties
Valencia, CA. 661-775-8500
Arlington Display Industries
Detroit, MI 313-837-1212
Art Wire Works Co
Chicago, IL 708-458-3993
Art-Phyl Creations
Hialeah, FL 800-327-8318
Beemak-IDL Display
La Mirada, CA 800-421-4393
Best Brands Home Products
New York, NY 212-684-7456
Better Bilt Products
Addison, IL. 800-544-4550
Bmh Equipment Inc
Sacramento, CA 800-350-8828
Cannon Equipment Company
Cannon Falls, MN. 800-825-8501
Chroma Tone
Saint Clair, PA. 800-878-1552
Dayton Wire Products
Dayton, OH. 888-265-1711
Despro Manufacturing
Cedar Grove, NJ. 800-292-9906
Display Creations
Brooklyn, NY 718-257-2300
Dubuque Steel Products Co
Dubuque, IA 563-556-6288
Dunn Woodworks
Shrewsbury, PA. 877-835-8592
E-Z Shelving Systems Inc
Shawnee, KS. 800-353-1331
Eastern Plastics
Pawtucket, RI 800-442-8585
Emco Industrial Plastics
Cedar Grove, NJ. 800-292-9906
Enterprise Products
Bell Gardens, CA 562-928-1918
Fab-X/Metals
Washington, NC 800-677-3229
General Cage
Elwood, IN 800-428-6403
Harmar
Sarasota, FL 800-833-0478
Hewitt Manufacturing Co
Waldron, IN. 765-525-9829
HMG Worldwide In-Store Marketing
New York, NY 212-736-2300

Hodges
Vienna, IL 800-444-0011
Houston Wire Works, Inc.
South Houston, TX 800-468-9477
Ideal Wire Works
Alhambra, CA 626-282-0886
InterMetro Industries
Wilkes-Barre, PA 570-825-2741
Ironwood Displays
Niles, MI 231-683-8500
JEM Wire Products
Middletown, CT 860-347-0447
Kaines West Michigan Co
Ludington, MI 231-845-1281
Key Material Handling Inc
Simi Valley, CA 800-539-7225
L&S Products
Coldwater, MI 517-279-9526
L.A. Darling Co., LLC
Paragould, AR 800-682-5730
Langer Manufacturing Company
Cedar Rapids, IA 800-728-6445
Load King Mfg
Jacksonville, FL 800-531-4975
Loyal Manufacturing
Indianapolis, IN 317-359-3185
Marlin Steel Wire Products
Baltimore, MD 877-762-7546
McMillin Manufacturing Corporation
Los Angeles, CA 323-268-1900
Melrose Displays
Passaic, NJ 973-471-7700
Merchandising Systems Manufacturing
Union City, CA 800-523-1468
Metaline Products Co Inc
South Amboy, NJ 732-721-1373
Metro Corporation
Wilkes Barre, PA 800-992-1776
Midwest Wire Products LLC
Sturgeon Bay, WI 800-445-0225
Mirro Products Company
High Point, NC 336-885-4166
Multi-Panel Display Corporation
Brooklyn, NY 800-439-0879
Olson Wire Products Co
Baltimore, MD 410-242-7900
Omega Industries
St Louis, MO 314-961-1668
Peterson Manufacturing Company
Plainfield, IL 800-547-8995
Pinquist Tool & Die Company
Brooklyn, NY 800-752-0414
Piper Products Inc
Wausau, WI 800-544-3057
Princeton Shelving
Cedar Rapids, IA 319-369-0355
Quality Industries Inc
La Vergne, TN 615-793-3000
R & D Brass
Wappingers Falls, NY 800-447-6050
R.I. Enterprises
Hernando, MS 662-429-7863
Racks
San Diego, CA 619-661-0987
Rex Art Manufacturing Corp.
Lindenhurst, NY 631-884-4600
Ridg-U-Rak
North East, PA 866-479-7225
Riverside Wire & Metal Co.
Ionia, MI 616-527-3500
Royal Display Corporation
Middletown, CT 800-569-1295
Royce Corp
Glendale, AZ 602-256-0006
Selma Wire Products Company
Selma, IN 765-282-3532
SEMCO
Ocala, FL 800-749-6894
Southern Imperial Inc
Rockford, IL 800-747-4665
Southwest Fixture
Dallas, TX 214-634-2800
Spot Wire Works Company
Philadelphia, PA 215-627-6124
Steel City Corporation
Youngstown, OH 800-321-0350
Straits Steel & Wire Co
Ludington, MI 231-843-3416
Superior Products Company
Saint Paul, MN 800-328-9800
Swanson Wire Works Industries, Inc.
Mesquite, TX 972-288-7465

Technibilt/Cari-All
Newton, NC 800-233-3972
Thorco Industries LLC
Lamar, MO 800-445-3375
Toledo Wire Products
Toledo, OH 888-430-7445
Vomela/Harbor Graphics
St Paul, MN 800-645-1012
Vulcan Industries
Moody, AL 888-444-4417
W J Egli & Co
Alliance, OH 330-823-3666
Wahlstrom Manufacturing
Fontana, CA 909-822-4677
Wald Wire & Mfg Co
Oshkosh, WI 800-236-0053
Wire Products Mfg
Merrill, WI 715-536-7884
Wiremaid Products Div
Coral Springs, FL 800-770-4700
Woerner Wire Works
Omaha, NE 402-451-5414
Xtreme Beverages, LLC
Dana Point, CA 949-495-7929
Yeager Wire Works
Berwick, PA 570-752-2769

Restaurant Supplies & Equipment

A Legacy Food Svc
Santa Fe Springs, CA 800-848-4440
Action Lighting
Bozeman, MT 800-248-0076
Advance Energy Technologies
Halfmoon, NY 800-724-0198
AMC Industries
Palmetto, FL 941-479-7834
Anderson Wood Products
Louisville, KY 502-778-5591
Architectural Sheet Metals LLC
Cleveland, OH 216-361-9952
ASI/Restaurant Manager
Silver Spring, MD 800-356-6037
Bargreen Ellingson
Tacoma, WA 800-322-4441
Bargreen Ellingson
Fife, WA 866-722-2665
Best Buy Uniforms
Homestead, PA 800-345-1924
Blue Line Foodservice Distr
Farmington Hills, MI 800-892-8272
Browne & Company
Markham, ON 905-475-6104
Carroll Chair Company
Onalaska, WI. 800-331-4704
Charles Mayer Studios
Akron, OH 330-535-6121
Co-Rect Products Inc
Golden Valley, MN 800-328-5702
Coastal Canvas Products
Savannah, GA 800-476-5174
Cove Woodworking
Gloucester, MA 800-273-0037
Daga Restaurant Ware
Honolulu, HI 808-847-3100
Dorado Carton Company
Dorado, PR 787-796-1670
Electro-Steam Generator Corp
Rancocas, NJ 866-617-0764
Ex-Cell KAISER LLC
Franklin Park, IL 847-451-0451
Green Metal Fabricating
West Sacramento, CA 916-371-2951
H A Sparke Co
Shreveport, LA 318-222-0927
Inland Showcase & Fixture Company
Fresno, CA 559-237-4158
Instacomm Canada
Oakville, ON 877-426-2783
K & L Intl
Ontario, CA 888-598-5588
Kessenich's Limited
Madison, WI 800-248-0555
Lauritzen Makin Inc
Fort Worth, TX 817-921-0218
Libra Technical Center
Metuchen, NJ 732-321-5200
Lockwood Manufacturing
Livonia, MI 800-521-0238
Menu Graphics
Olmsted Falls, OH 216-696-1460

Metal Masters Northwest
Lynnwood, WA 425-775-4481
Metro Corporation
Wilkes Barre, PA 800-992-1776
Mosshaim Innovations
Jacksonville, FL 888-995-7775
NTN Wireless
Norcross, GA 800-637-8639
Order-Matic Corporation
Oklahoma City, OK 800-767-6733
Original Wood Seating
Atlanta, GA 678-966-0406
Pinnacle Furnishing
Aberdeen, NC 866-229-5704
Products A Curtron Div
Pittsburgh, PA 800-888-9750
R X Honing Machine Corp
Mishawaka, IN 800-346-6464
RDS of Florida
Fort Lauderdale, FL 305-994-7756
Sable Technology Solution
St Paul, MN 800-722-5390
Sandler Seating
Atlanta, GA 404-982-9000
Sarasota Restaurant Equipment
Sarasota, FL 800-434-1410
Shanker Industries
Deer Park, NY 877-742-6561
Sign Classics
San Jose, CA 408-298-1600
Sign Products
Sheridan, WY 800-532-4753
Sims Superior Seating
Locust Grove, GA 800-729-9178
Standex International Corp.
Salem, NH 603-893-9701
Sturdi-Bilt Restaurant Equipment
Whitmore Lake, MI 800-521-2895
Superior Products Company
Saint Paul, MN 800-328-9800
Superior Uniform Group
Seminole, FL 800-727-8643
Tango Shatterproof Drinkware
Walpole, MA 888-898-2646
Tec Art Industries Inc
Wixom, MI 800-886-6615
Trojan Commercial Furniture Inc.
Montereal, QC 877-271-3878
Valley Fixtures
Sparks, NV 775-331-1050
Waymar Industries
Burnsville, MN 888-474-1112
Wheel Tough Company
Terre Haute, IN 888-765-8833
Woodard
Coppell, TX 800-877-2290

Salad Bars

Advanced Design Mfg
Concord, CA 800-690-0002
Atlas Metal Industries
Miami, FL 800-762-7565
Brass Smith
Denver, CO 800-662-9595
Craig Manufacturing
Irvington, NJ 800-631-7936
Custom Plastics Inc
Decatur, GA 404-373-1691
Delfield Co
Mt Pleasant, MI 800-733-8821
Duke Manufacturing Co
St Louis, MO 800-735-3853
Forbes Industries
Ontario, CA 909-923-4549
Galley
Jupiter, FL 800-537-2772
Just Plastics Inc
New York, NY 212-569-8500
LA Rosa Refrigeration & Equip
Detroit, MI 800-527-6723
Lavi Industries
Valencia, CA 800-624-6225
Load King Mfg
Jacksonville, FL 800-531-4975
Northern Stainless Fabricating
Traverse City, MI 231-947-4580
Northwest Art Glass
Redmond, WA 800-888-9444
Plymold
Kenyon, MN 800-759-6653

PMI Food Equipment Group
Troy, OH 937-332-3000
R & D Brass
Wappingers Falls, NY 800-447-6050
Steamway Corporation
Scottsburg, IN 800-259-8171
Stryco Wire Products
North York, ON. 416-663-7000
Superior Products Company
Saint Paul, MN 800-328-9800
Tables Cubed
Chesterfield, MO 800-878-3001
United Showcase Company
Wood Ridge, NJ 800-526-6382
Wylie Systems
Mississauga, ON 800-525-6609
Yorkraft
York, PA 800-872-2044

Scanners

Check & Credit Card Verification Systems

Axiohm USA
Myrtle Beach, SC 843-443-3155
Bruins Instruments
Salem, NH. 603-898-6527
CSPI
Billerica, MA 978-663-7598
Intercard Inc
St Louis, MO. 314-275-8066
NCR Corp
Atlanta, GA. 800-225-5627
Reflex International
Norcross, GA 800-642-7640
Retalix
Miamisburg, OH 877-794-7237
Scan Corporation
Brandon, FL 800-881-7226

Serving Equipment

A J Antunes & Co
Carol Stream, IL 800-253-2991
Ace Fabrication
Mobile, AL 251-478-0401
Advance Engineering Co
Canton, MI 800-497-6388
Advanced Plastic Coating Svc
Parsons, KS 620-421-1660
Aero Manufacturing Co
Clifton, NJ. 800-631-8378
Aladdin Temp-Rite, LLC
Hendersonville, TN. 800-888-8018
All State Fabricators Corporation
Tampa, FL 800-322-9925
Amco Metals Indl
City of Industry, CA 626-855-2550
AMI
Richmond, CA 800-942-7466
Apex Fountain Sales Inc
Philadelphia, PA 800-523-4586
ARC Specialties
Valencia, CA. 661-775-8500
Art Wire Works Co
Chicago, IL 708-458-3993
Aurora Design Associates, Inc.
Salt Lake City, UT. 801-588-0111
Automatic Specialties Inc
Marlborough, MA 800-445-2370
Bakers Choice Products
Beacon Falls, CT. 203-720-1000
Bardes Plastics Inc
Milwaukee, WI. 800-558-5161
Bloomfield Industries
St. Louis, MO 888-356-5362
Bon Chef
Lafayette, NJ 800-331-0177
Boyd's Coffee Co
Portland, OR 800-735-2878
Brooklace
Oshkosh, WI 800-572-4552
C R Mfg
Waverly, NE 877-789-5844
Cal-Mil Plastic Products Inc
Oceanside, CA 800-321-9069
California Vibratory Feeders
Anaheim, CA 800-354-0972
Carlisle Food Svc Products Inc
Oklahoma City, OK 800-654-8210

Carter-Hoffmann LLC
Mundelein, IL 800-323-9793
Component Hardware Group Inc
Lakewood, NJ. 800-526-3694
Creative Forming
Ripon, WI 920-748-7285
Crespac Incorporated
Tucker, GA 800-438-1900
Crestware
North Salt Lake, UT 800-345-0513
Custom Diamond International
Laval, QC 800-363-5926
Custom Molders
Rocky Mount, NC. 919-688-8061
Cyclamen Collection
Oakland, CA 510-434-7620
Dart Container Corp.
Mason, MI. 800-248-5960
De Ster Corporation
Atlanta, GA. 800-237-8270
Delco Tableware
Port Washington, NY 800-221-9557
Delfin Design & Mfg
Rancho Sta Marg, CA 800-354-7919
Detroit Forming
Southfield, MI. 248-440-1317
Douglas Stephen Plastics Inc
Paterson, NJ 973-523-3030
Duke Manufacturing Co
St Louis, MO. 800-735-3853
Dura-Ware Company of America
Oklahoma City, OK 800-664-3872
Dynynstyl
Delray Beach, FL 800-774-7895
Eastern Tabletop Mfg
Brooklyn, NY 888-422-4142
Edco Industries
Bridgeport, CT 203-333-8982
Ellingers Agatized Wood Inc
Sheboygan, WI 888-287-8906
Engineered Plastics Inc
Gibsonville, NC 800-711-1740
EPCO
Murfreesboro, TN. 800-251-3398
Epic Products
Santa Ana, CA 800-548-9791
Eskay Metal Fabricating
Buffalo, NY. 800-836-8015
Fetco
Lake Zurich, IL 800-338-2699
Fold-Pak South
Columbus, GA 706-689-2924
Food Warming Equipment Co
Crystal Lake, IL 800-222-4393
Gaetano America
El Monte, CA 626-442-2858
Galley
Jupiter, FL. 800-537-2772
Gaychrome Division of CSL
Crystal Lake, IL 800-873-4370
Gessner Products
Ambler, PA 800-874-7808
Glaro Inc
Hauppauge, NY 631-234-1717
Gourmet Display
Kent, WA. 800-767-4711
Grand Silver Company
Bronx, NY. 718-585-1930
Gril-Del
Mankato, MN 800-782-7320
Hal-One Plastics
Olathe, KS. 800-626-5784
Hot Food Boxes
Mooresville, IN. 800-733-8073
HPI North America/ Plastics
Eagan, MN 800-752-7462
HPI North America/Plastics
Chicago, IL. 800-327-3534
Infanti International
Staten Island, NY 800-874-8590
Innovative Plastics Corp
Orangeburg, NY 845-359-7500
Institutional & Supermarket
Plantation, FL 954-584-3100
International Patterns, Inc.
Bay Shore, NY 631-952-2000
Jack Stack
Inwood, NY. 800-999-9840
Jones-Zylon Co
West Lafayette, OH. 800-848-8160
K & I Creative Plastics & Wood
Jacksonville, FL 904-387-0438

K & L Intl
Ontario, CA. 888-598-5588
Keating of Chicago Inc
Mc Cook, IL 800-532-8464
Kelmin Products
Plymouth, FL 407-886-6079
Key Packaging Co
Sarasota, FL 941-355-2728
King Arthur
Statesville, NC 800-257-7244
Lakeside Manufacturing Inc
Milwaukee, WI 888-558-8565
Lambertson Industries Inc
Sparks, NV 800-548-3324
Lancaster Colony Corporation
Westerville, OH. 614-224-7141
Leggett & Platt Storage
Vernon Hills, IL 847-816-6246
Leon Bush Manufacturer
Glenview, IL 847-657-8888
Lincoln Foodservice
Cleveland, OH 800-374-3004
Lodge Manufacturing Company
South Pittsburg, TN 423-837-5919
LoTech Industries
Lakewood, CO 800-295-0199
Low Temp Industries Inc
Jonesboro, GA 678-674-1317
M & E Mfg Co Inc
Kingston, NY 845-331-2110
Mack-Chicago Corporation
Chicago, IL 800-992-6225
Madsen Wire Products Inc
Orland, IN 260-829-6561
Majestic
Bridgeport, CT 203-367-7900
Metal Master Sales Corp
Glendale Heights, IL. 800-488-8729
Metal Masters Northwest
Lynnwood, WA 425-775-4481
Mid-West Wire Products
Ferndale, MI 800-989-9881
Moli-International
Denver, CO 800-525-8468
Mosshaim Innovations
Jacksonville, FL 888-995-7775
Mr Ice Bucket
New Brunswick, NJ 732-545-0420
National Scoop & Equipment Company
Spring House, PA 215-646-2040
NCC
Groveland, FL. 800-429-9037
Normandie Metal Fabricators
Port Washington, NY 800-221-2398
Novelty Crystal
Long Island City, NY 800-622-0250
Olde Country Reproductions Inc
York, PA 800-358-3997
Olde Thompson Inc
Oxnard, CA. 800-827-1565
Olive Can Company
Elgin, IL 847-468-7474
Orbis Corp.
Rexdale, ON 800-890-7292
PacknWood
New York, NY 201-604-3840
Palmer Distributors
St Clair Shores, MI. 800-444-1912
Par-Pak
Houston, TX 888-727-7252
Plastocon
Oconomowoc, WI. 800-966-0103
PMC Global Inc.
Sun Valley, CA 818-896-1101
Polar Beer Systems
Sun City, CA. 951-928-8174
Polar Ware Company
Sheboygan, WI 800-237-3655
Precision
Miami, FL. 800-762-7565
Process Displays
New Berlin, WI. 800-533-1764
Prolon
Port Gibson, MS 888-480-9828
Quipco Products Inc
Sauget, IL 314-993-1442
Rexcraft Fine Chafers
Long Island City, NY 888-739-2723
Robinson Industries Inc
Coleman, MI 989-465-6111
Rolland Machining & Fabricating
Moneta, VA 973-827-6911

Ronnie's Ceramic Company
San Francisco, CA 800-888-8218
Sani-Top Products
De Leon Springs, FL.............800-874-6094
Server Products Inc
Richfield, WI 800-558-8722
Service Ideas
Woodbury, MN 800-328-4493
Shammi Industries
Corona, CA 800-417-9260
Sheffield Platers Inc
San Diego, CA 800-227-9242
Sico Inc
Minneapolis, MN 800-328-6138
Sonofresco
Burlington, WA.................360-757-2800
Spin-Tech Corporation
Hoboken, NJ 800-977-4692
Superior Products Company
Saint Paul, MN 800-328-9800
Techform
Mount Airy, NC 336-789-2115
TEMP-TECH Company
Springfield, MA 800-343-5579
Thermo Service
Dallas, TX......................800-635-5559
Thermodynamics
Commerce City, CO 800-627-9037
Thermos Company
Schaumburg, IL 800-243-0745
Tomlinson Industries
Cleveland, OH 800-945-4589
Tops Manufacturing Co
Darien, CT......................203-655-9367
Toscarora
Sandusky, OH 419-625-7343
Toska Foodservice Systems
Lannon, WI 262-253-4782
Tramontina USA
Sugar Land, TX.................800-221-7809
Tray-Pak Corp
Reading, PA 610-926-5800
Tri-State Plastics
Glenwillard, PA.................724-457-6900
Ullman, Shapiro & UllmanLLP
New York, NY 212-755-0299
Unique Plastics
Rio Rico, AZ 800-658-5946
Update International
Vernon, CA 800-747-7124
Vermillion Flooring
Springfield, MO 417-862-3785
Vollrath Co LLC
Sheboygan, WI 800-624-2051
Waddington North America
Chelmsford, MA................888-962-2877
Weavewood, Inc.
Golden Valley, MN 800-367-6460
Wells Manufacturing Company
St. Louis, MO 888-356-5362
Wilton Armetale
Mt Joy, PA......................800-779-4586
WR Key
Scarborough, ON 416-291-6246
Yorkraft
York, PA........................800-872-2044
Zeier Plastic & Mfg Inc
Madison, WI 608-244-5782
Zeroll Company
Fort Pierce, FL 800-872-5000
Zoia Banquetier Co
Cleveland, OH 216-631-6414

Industrial Plant

Andgar Corp
Ferndale, WA 360-366-9900
Ashcroft Inc
Stratford, CT....................800-328-8258
Bmh Equipment Inc
Sacramento, CA 800-350-8828
Institutional & Supermarket
Plantation, FL 954-584-3100
National Scoop & Equipment Company
Spring House, PA 215-646-2040
Quipco Products Inc
Sauget, IL 314-993-1442
Standex International Corp.
Salem, NH......................603-893-9701

Shelving

Store

Accent Store Fixtures
Kenosha, WI 800-545-1144
Amscor Inc
West Babylon, NY 800-825-9800
Arizona Store Equipment
Phoenix, AZ 800-624-8395
Bmh Equipment Inc
Sacramento, CA 800-350-8828
Borroughs Corp
Kalamazoo, MI..................800-748-0227
Cannon Equipment Company
Cannon Falls, MN...............800-825-8501
Continental Commercial Products
Bridgeton, MO 800-325-1051
Despro Manufacturing
Cedar Grove, NJ 800-292-9906
E-Z Shelving Systems Inc
Shawnee, KS 800-353-1331
Easyup Storage Systems
Tukwila, WA....................800-426-9234
Handy Manufacturing Co Inc
Newark, NJ 800-631-4280
Hodge Manufacturing Company
Springfield, MA 800-262-4634
Hodges
Vienna, IL 800-444-0011
InterMetro Industries
Wilkes-Barre, PA 570-825-2741
Kent Corp
Birmingham, AL................800-252-5368
L.A. Darling Co., LLC
Paragould, AR..................800-682-5730
Leggett & Platt Inc
Carthage, MO 417-358-8131
LPI Imports
Chicago, IL 877-389-6563
Lyon LLC
Montgomery, IL 630-892-8941
Madsen Wire Products Inc
Orland, IN......................260-829-6561
Metro Corporation
Wilkes Barre, PA................800-992-1776
Modar
Benton Harbor, MI 800-253-6186
Newcourt, Inc.
Madison, IN 800-933-0006
Pacific Store Designs Inc
Garden Grove, CA 800-772-5661
Princeton Shelving
Cedar Rapids, IA................319-369-0355
Quantum Storage Systems Inc
Miami, FL 800-685-4665
RTI Shelving Systems
Elmhurst, NY 800-223-6210
S & L Store Fixture
Doral, FL 800-205-4536
Sefi Fabricators Inc
Amityville, NY 631-842-2200
SPG International
Covington, GA 877-503-4774
Strong Hold Products
Louisville, KY 800-880-2625
Teilhaber Manufacturing Corp
Broomfield, CO 800-358-7225
Tennsco Corp
Dickson, TN 800-251-8184
Triple-A Manufacturing Company
Toronto, ON 800-786-2238
Western Pacific Stge Solutions
San Dimas, CA 800-888-5707

Signs

Advertising

A Allred Marketing
Birmingham, AL.................205-251-3700
AAA Electrical Signs
Donna, TX......................800-825-5376
AAA Flag & Banner Manufacturing
Los Angeles, CA.................800-266-4222
ABC Letter Art
Los Angeles, CA.................888-261-5367
Ace Signs
Little Rock, AR..................501-562-0800
Ace Stamp & Engraving
Lakewood, WA..................253-582-3322

ACME Sign Corp
Peabody, MA....................978-535-6600
Ad Mart Identity Group
Danville, KY.....................800-354-2102
Adam Electric Signs
Massillon, OH...................888-886-9911
Affiliated Resource Inc
Chicago, IL......................800-366-9336
Alex Delvecchio Enterprises
Troy, MI 248-619-9600
Allen Industries Inc
Greensboro, NC.................800-967-2553
Allen Signs Co
Knoxville, TN....................800-844-3524
Altrua Marketing & Design
Tallahassee, FL 800-443-6939
AM Graphics
Edina, MN 612-341-2020
American Art Stamp
Gardena, CA....................310-965-9004
American Labelmark Co
Chicago, IL......................800-621-5808
American Led-Gible
Columbus, OH 614-851-1100
American Menu Displays
Long Island City, NY 877-544-8046
Ameritech Signs & Banners
Santa Monica, CA..............310-829-9359
Andersen Sign Company
Woodsville, NH.................603-787-6806
Andrew H Lawson Co
Philadelphia, PA 800-411-6628
Andrew W Nissly Inc
Lancaster, PA 717-393-3841
Arrow Sign & Awning Company
East Bethel, MN 800-621-9231
Artcraft Badge & Sign Company
Olney, MD......................800-739-0709
Artkraft Strauss LLC
New York, NY 212-265-5156
Audrey Signs
New York, NY 212-769-4992
B S C Signs
Broomfield, CO 866-223-0101
B&B Neon Sign Company
Austin, TX.......................800-791-6366
Baltimore Sign Company
Arnold, MD 410-276-1500
Banner Idea
Newport Beach, CA.............949-559-6600
Barlo Signs
Hudson, NH 800-227-5674
Berloc Manufacturing & Sign Company
Sun Valley, CA..................818-503-9823
Blue Ridge Signs
Weatherford, TX................800-659-5645
Brown's Sign & Screen Printing
Covington, GA 800-540-3107
Cal-Mil Plastic Products Inc
Oceanside, CA..................800-321-9069
Canton Sign Co
Canton, OH 330-456-7151
Capital City Signs
Monona, WI 608-222-1881
Cascade Signs & Neon
Salem, OR.......................503-378-0012
Century Sign Company
Fargo, ND 701-235-5323
Chain Store Graphics
Decatur, IL 800-443-7446
Chapman Sign
Warren, MI 586-758-1600
Charles Mayer Studios
Akron, OH.......................330-535-6121
Chatelain Plastics
Findlay, OH......................866-421-4323
Chicago Show Inc
Buffalo Grove, IL................847-955-0200
Christman Screenprint Inc
Springfield, MI 800-962-9330
Chroma Tone
Saint Clair, PA...................800-878-1552
City Grafx
Eugene, OR......................800-258-2489
City Neon Sign Company
Spokane, WA...................509-483-5171
City Sign Svc Inc
Dallas, TX.......................214-826-4475
City Signs LLC
Jackson, TN 877-248-9744
City Stamp & Seal Co
Austin, TX.......................800-950-6074

Classic Signs Inc
  Amherst, NH 800-734-7446
Clearr Corporation
  Minneapolis, MN 800-548-3269
Coleman Rubber Stamps
  Daytona Beach, FL 386-252-8597
Color Ad Tech Signs
  Amarillo, TX 806-374-8117
Comco Signs
  Charlotte, NC 704-375-2338
Comet Signs
  San Antonio, TX 210-341-7244
Command Packaging
  Vernon, CA 800-996-2247
Connecticut Laminating Co Inc
  New Haven, CT. 800-753-9119
Cook Neon Signs
  Tullahoma, TN 800-488-0944
Corsair Display Systems
  Canandalgua, NY 800-347-5245
Couch & Philippi
  Stanton, CA 800-854-3360
Courtesy Signs
  Amarillo, TX. 806-373-6609
Creative Signage System,
  College Park, MD 800-220-7446
Crown Marking
  Minneapolis, MN 800-305-5249
Cucamonga Sign Shop LLC
  Rancho Cucamonga, CA 909-945-5888
Cuerden Sign Co
  Conway, AR 501-375-7705
Cummings
  Nashville, TN .615-673-8999
Curzon Promotional Graphics
  Omaha, NE 800-769-7446
Custom Color Corp
  Lenexa, KS 888-605-4050
Custom ID Systems
  Venice, FL 800-242-8430
D&D Sign Company
  Wichita Falls, TX 940-692-4643
Darlington Sign Awning & Neon
  Warwick, RI 401-734-5800
Day Nite Neon Signs
  Dartmouth, NS 902-469-7095
Daytech Limited
  Toronto, ON 877-329-1907
Delta Signs
  Haltom City, TX 866-643-3582
Derse Inc
  Milwaukee, WI. 800-562-2300
Dewey & Wilson Displays
  Lincoln, NE 402-489-0868
Diamond Sign Co
  Costa Mesa, CA 714-545-1440
Dimension Graphics Inc
  Grand Rapids, MI 855-476-1281
Dinosaur Plastics
  Houston, TX 713-923-2278
Display Concepts
  Trenton, ME 800-446-0033
Dixie Neon Company
  Tampa, FL. 813-248-2531
Dixie Signs Inc
  Lakeland, FL. 863-644-3521
Dove Screen Printing Co
  Royston, GA. 706-245-4975
Dowling Signs Inc
  Fredericksburg, VA. 800-572-2100
Doyle Signs Inc
  Addison, IL 630-543-9490
Drs Designs
  Bethel, CT. 888-792-3740
Dualite Sales & Svc Inc
  Williamsburg, OH. 513-724-7100
Dwinell's Central Neon
  Yakima, WA 800-932-8832
Dynamic Packaging
  Minneapolis, MN 800-878-9380
Ehrgott Rubber Stamp Company
  Indianapolis, IN 317-353-2222
Electric City Signs & Neon Inc.
  Anderson, SC .800-270-5851
Elro Signs
  Gardena, CA 800-927-4555
Empire Screen Printing Inc
  Onalaska, WI. .608-783-3301
Encore Image Inc
  Ontario, CA. 800-791-1187
Engraving Specialists
  Royal Oak, MI 248-542-2244

Esco Manufacturing Inc
  Watertown, SD 800-843-3726
Everett Rubber Stamp
  Everett, WA. 425-258-6747
Exhibitron Co
  Grants Pass, OR 800-437-4571
Fair Publishing House
  Norwalk, OH. .419-668-3746
Federal Heath Sign Co LLC
  Oceanside, CA 800-527-9495
Federal Sign
  Providence, RI 401-421-9643
Ferrer Corporation
  San Juan, PR .787-761-5151
Fiber Does
  San Jose, CA .408-453-5533
First Choice Sign & Lighting
  Escondido, CA 800-659-0629
Flexlume Sign Corp
  Buffalo, NY. 716-884-2020
FMI Display
  Elkins Park, PA 215-663-1998
Foley Sign Co
  Seattle, WA 206-324-3040
Formflex
  Bloomingdale, IN 800-255-7659
FORT Hill Sign Products Inc
  Hopedale, MA. 781-321-4320
Fox Stamp Sign & Specialty
  Menasha, WI. 920-725-2683
France Personalized Signs
  Cleveland, OH 216-241-2198
Frank O Carlson & Co
  Chicago, IL 773-847-6900
Franklin Rubber Stamp Co
  Wilmington, DE 302-654-8841
Frazier Signs
  Decatur, IL 217-429-2349
Frost Manufacturing Corp
  Worcester, MA 800-462-0216
Futura 2000 Corporation
  Miami, FL. 305-256-5877
Gannett Outdoor of New   Jersey
  Fairfield, NJ 973-575-6900
Gardenville Signs
  Baltimore, MD 410-485-4800
Gary Sign Co
  Merrillville, IN 219-942-3191
Gelberg Signs
  Washington, DC 800-443-5237
General Neon Sign Co
  San Antonio, TX. 210-227-1203
General Sign Co
  Sheffield, AL. 256-383-3176
Gessner Products
  Ambler, PA 800-874-7808
Glaro Inc
  Hauppauge, NY 631-234-1717
Glover Rubber Stamp & Crafts
  Wills Point, TX 214-824-6900
Grays Harbor Stamp Works
  Aberdeen, WA. 800-894-3830
Green Mountain Graphics
  Long Island City, NY 718-472-3377
Gribble Stamp & Stencil Co
  Houston, TX .713-228-5358
Gulf Coast Sign Company
  Pensacola, FL 800-768-3549
Haden Signs of Texas
  Lubbock, TX. 806-744-4404
Hammar & Sons
  Pelham, NH .800-527-7446
Handicap Sign Inc
  Grand Rapids, MI 800-690-4888
Hanley Sign Company
  Latham, NY 518-783-6183
Hardin Signs Inc
  Peoria, IL 309-688-4111
Harlan Laws Corp
  Durham, NC .800-596-7602
Harting Graphics
  Wilmington, DE 800-848-1373
Heath & Company
  Roswell, GA .770-650-2724
Hiclay Studios
  St Louis, MO. 314-533-8393
HMG Worldwide In-Store Marketing
  New York, NY 212-736-2300
Hoarel Sign Co
  Amarillo, TX. 806-373-2175
Holsman Sign Svc
  Cleveland, OH 216-761-4433

Horn & Todak
  Fairfax, VA 703-352-7330
Hutz Sign & Awning
  Youngstown, OH. 330-743-5168
IdentaBadge
  Lafayette, LA .800-325-8247
Image National Inc
  Nampa, ID. 208-345-4020
Imperial Plastics Inc
  Lakeville, MN. 952-469-4951
Imperial Signs & Manufacturing
  Rapid City, SD 605-348-2511
Industrial Sign Company
  South El Monte, CA 800-596-3720
Industrial Signs
  Elmwood, LA 504-736-0600
Inovar Packaging Group
  Arlington, TX 800-285-2235
Insignia Systems Inc
  Minneapolis, MN 800-874-4648
Interior Systems Inc
  Milwaukee, WI 800-837-8373
International Patterns, Inc.
  Bay Shore, NY 631-952-2000
J.V. Reed & Company
  Louisville, KY 877-258-7333
Jack Stone Lighting & Electrical
  Landover, MD 301-322-3323
Janedy Sign Company
  Everett, MA .617-776-5700
JBC Plastics
  St Louis, MO. 877-834-5526
Jeffcoat Signs
  Gainesville, FL 877-377-4248
Johnson Brothers Sign Co Inc
  South Whitley, IN 800-477-7516
Joseph Struhl Co Inc
  New Hyde Park, NY 800-552-0023
Jutras Signs & Flags
  Manchester, NH 800-924-3524
K & I Creative Plastics & Wood
  Jacksonville, FL 904-387-0438
K & M Intl Inc
  Twinsburg, OH 330-425-2550
Kessler Sign Co
  Zanesville, OH 800-686-1870
King Electric Sign Co
  Nampa, ID. 208-466-2000
King Sign Company
  Akron, OH. 330-762-7421
Krimstock Enterprises
  Pennsauken, NJ. 856-665-3676
Krusoe Sign Co
  Cleveland, OH. 216-447-1177
L&L Engraving Company
  Gilford, NH. 888-524-3032
La Crosse Sign Co.
  Eau Claire, WI 715-835-6189
Lake Shore Industries Inc
  Erie, PA 800-458-0463
Lamar Advertising Co
  Baton Rouge, LA 225-926-1000
Lamar Advertising Co
  Pearl, MS. 800-893-2560
Lasermation Inc
  Philadelphia, PA 800-523-2759
Lawrence Sign
  St Paul, MN. 800-998-8901
Leathertone
  Findlay, OH. 419-429-0188
License Ad Plate Co
  Cleveland, OH 216-265-4200
Lion Labels Inc
  South Easton, MA. 800-875-5300
Little Rock Sign
  Conway, AR .501-372-7403
Lonestar Banners & Flags
  Fort Worth, TX 800-288-9625
Long Island Stamp Corporation
  Flushing, NY. 800-547-8267
LSI Industries Inc
  Blue Ash, OH 513-793-3200
Lynn Sign Inc
  Andover, MA 800-225-5764
M & M Display
  Philadelphia, PA 800-874-7171
Macdonald Signs & Advertising
  Edinburg, TX 956-787-0016
Maier Sign Systems
  Saddle Brook, NJ 201-845-7555
Maltese Signs
  Norcross, GA 770-368-0911

Mankuta Bros Rubber Stamp Co
  Bohemia, NY 800-223-4481
Mansfield Rubber Stamp
  Mansfield, OH 419-524-1442
Master Printers
  Canon City, CO 719-275-8608
Master Signs-Div of Masterco
  Dallas, TX 214-381-6207
Mastermark
  Kent, WA 206-762-9610
Mcbride Sign Co
  Madison Heights, VA 434-847-4151
Mcneill Signs Inc
  Pompano Beach, FL 954-946-3474
MDI Worldwide
  Farmington Hills, MI 800-228-8925
Metro Signs
  N Las Vegas, NV 702-649-9333
Milwaukee Sign Company
  Grafton, WI 262-375-5740
Mirro Products Company
  High Point, NC 336-885-4166
MLS Signs Inc
  Chesterfield, MI 586-948-0200
MODAGRAPHICS
  Rolling Meadows, IL 847-392-3980
Modern Stamp Company
  Baltimore, MD 800-727-3029
Morrow Technologies Corporation
  St Petersburg, FL 877-526-8711
Mulholland-Harper Company
  Denton, MD 800-882-3052
Muskogee Rubber Stamp & Seal Company
  Fort Gibson, OK 918-478-3046
Nameplate
  St Paul, MN 651-228-1522
National Sign Corporation
  Seattle, WA 206-282-0700
National Sign Systems
  Hilliard, OH 800-544-6726
National Stock Sign Co
  Santa Cruz, CA 800-462-7726
Neal Walters Poster Corporation
  Bentonville, AR 501-273-2489
Nebraska Neon Sign Co
  Lincoln, NE 402-476-6563
Nelson Custom Signs
  Plymouth, MI 734-455-0500
Neon Design-a-Sign
  Laguna Niguel, CA 888-636-6327
Norgus Silk Screen Co Inc
  Clifton, NJ 973-365-0600
North American Signs
  South Bend, IN 800-348-5000
Nu-Dell Manufacturing
  Des Plaines, IL 847-803-4500
O.K. Marking Devices
  Regina, SK 306-522-2856
Parisian Novelty Company
  Homewood, IL 773-847-1212
Patrick & Co
  Dallas, TX 214-761-0900
Patrick Signs
  Rockville, MD 301-770-6200
Pearson Signs Service
  Hampstead, MD 410-239-3838
Perfect Plank Co
  Oroville, CA 800-327-1961
Peterson Sign Co
  Honolulu, HI 808-521-6785
Phoenix Sign Company
  Aberdeen, WA 360-532-1111
Pierrepont Visual Graphics Inc
  Rochester, NY 585-235-5620
Pioneer Sign Company
  Lewiston, ID 208-743-1275
Plasti-Line
  Knoxville, TN 800-444-7446
Plastic Craft Products Corp
  West Nyack, NY 800-627-3010
Plastic Fantastics/Buck Signs
  Ashland, OR 800-482-1776
Plastic Turning Company
  Leominster, MA 978-534-8326
Poblocki Sign Co
  Milwaukee, WI 414-453-4010
Polyplastic Forms Inc
  Farmingdale, NY 800-428-7659
Posterloid Corporation
  Long Island City, NY 800-651-5000
Pratt Poster Company
  Indianapolis, IN 800-645-1012

Pride Neon Inc
  Sioux Falls, SD 605-336-3561
Printsource Group
  Wakefield, RI 401-789-9339
Pro-Ad-Co Inc
  Portland, OR 800-287-5885
Process Displays
  New Berlin, WI. 800-533-1764
Qyk Syn Industries
  Miami, FL 800-354-5640
R R Donnelley
  Chicago, IL 800-742-4455
R T C
  Rolling Meadows, IL 847-640-2400
R Wireworks Inc
  Elmira, NY 800-550-4009
Radding Signs
  Springfield, MA 413-736-5400
Rainbow Neon Sign Company
  Houston, TX 713-923-2759
Ramsay Signs Inc
  Portland, OR 206-623-3100
Rapid Displays Inc
  Chicago, IL 800-356-5775
Rayne Sign Co
  Rayne, LA 337-334-4276
Reading Plastic Fabricators
  Reading, PA 610-926-3245
Regal Plastic Supply Co
  Kansas City, MO 800-444-6390
Reinhold Sign Svc Inc
  Green Bay, WI. 920-494-7161
Retail Decor
  Ironton, OH 800-726-3402
Rex Art Manufacturing Corp.
  Lindenhurst, NY 631-884-4600
Rosson Sign Co
  Macon, GA 478-788-3905
Roth Sign Systems
  Petaluma, CA 800-585-7446
Roxanne Signs Inc
  Gaithersburg, MD 301-428-4911
RPA Process Technologies
  Marblehead, MA 800-631-9707
Rueff Sign Co Inc
  Louisville, KY 502-582-1714
Rutler Screen Printing
  Easton, PA 610-829-2999
S & S Metal & Plastics Inc
  Jacksonville, FL 904-730-4655
San Juan Signs Inc
  Farmington, NM 505-326-5511
Scott Sign Systems
  Sarasota, FL 800-237-9447
Screen Print Etc
  Anaheim, CA 714-630-1100
Seiz Sign Co Inc
  Hot Spgs Natl Pk, AR. 501-623-3181
Selby Sign Co Inc
  Pocomoke City, MD 410-742-0095
Service Neon Signs
  Springfield, VA 703-354-3000
Seton Indentification Products
  Branford, CT. 800-571-2596
Sexton Sign
  Anderson, SC 864-226-6071
Shaw & Slavsky Inc
  Detroit, MI 800-521-7527
Shelby Co
  Westlake, OH 800-842-1650
Sheridan Sign Company
  Salisbury, MD 410-749-7441
Sign Classics
  San Jose, CA 408-298-1600
Sign Expert
  Pacific, MO 800-874-9942
Sign Factory
  Cerritos, CA 562-809-1443
Sign Graphics
  Evansville, IN 812-476-9151
Sign Products
  Sheridan, WY 800-532-4753
Sign Systems, Inc.
  Warren, MI 586-758-1600
Sign Warehouse
  Denison, TX 800-699-5512
SignArt Advertising
  Van Buren, AR 479-474-8581
Signco Inc
  Kansas City, KS 913-722-1377
Signet Graphic Products
  St Louis, MO. 314-426-0200

Signmasters
  Huntington Beach, CA 949-364-9128
Signs & Designs
  Palmdale, CA 888-480-7446
Signs & Shapes Intl
  Omaha, NE 800-806-6069
Signs O' Life
  Avon, MA 800-750-1475
Southwest Neon Signs
  San Antonio, TX 800-927-3221
Southwestern Porcelain Steel
  Sand Springs, OK 918-245-1375
Steel Art Co
  Norwood, MA 800-322-2828
Steingart Associates Inc
  South Fallsburg, NY 845-434-4321
Stello Products Inc
  Spencer, IN 800-878-2246
Stoffel Seals Corp
  Tallapoosa, GA 800-422-8247
Stout Sign Company
  Saint Louis, MO 800-325-8530
Stricker & Co
  La Plata, MD. 301-934-8346
Stylmark Inc
  Minneapolis, MN 800-328-2495
Suburban Sign Company
  Anoka, MN 763-753-8849
Suburban Signs
  College Park, MD 301-474-5051
Sun Ray Sign Group Inc
  Holland, MI 616-392-2824
Super Vision International
  Orlando, FL 407-857-9900
Superior Neon Signs Inc
  Oklahoma City, OK 405-528-5515
SuppliesForLess
  Hampton, VA 800-235-2201
Sutherland Stamp Company
  San Diego, CA 858-233-7784
Symmetry Products Group
  Lincoln, RI 401-365-6272
Tec Art Industries Inc
  Wixom, MI 800-886-6615
Timely Signs Inc
  Elmont, NY 800-457-4467
Toledo Sign Co Inc
  Toledo, OH 419-244-4444
Total Identity Group
  Cambridge, ON 877-551-5529
Triangle Sign & Svc
  Halethorpe, MD 410-247-5300
Trident Plastics
  Ivyland, PA 800-222-2318
Trinkle Sign & Display
  Youngstown, OH. 330-747-9712
Trumbull Nameplates
  New Smyrna Beach, FL 386-423-1105
Twenty/Twenty Graphics
  Gaithersburg, MD 240-243-0511
Twin State Signs
  Essex Junction, VT 802-872-8949
Universal Sign Company and Manufacturing Company
  Lafayette, LA 337-234-1466
University-Brink
  Foxboro, MA 617-926-4400
US Magnetix
  Minneapolis, MN 763-540-9497
US Standard Sign
  Franklin Park, IL. 800-537-4790
Vacuform Inc.
  Sebring, OH 330-938-9674
Valley City Sign Co
  Comstock Park, MI 616-784-5711
Varco Products
  Chardon, OH 216-481-6895
Visual Marketing Assoc
  Santee, CA 619-258-0393
VMC Signs
  Victoria, TX 361-575-0548
Volk Corp
  Farmington Hills, MI 800-521-6799
Vomela/Harbor Graphics
  St Paul, MN. 800-645-1012
VPC Gordon Sign
  Denver, CO 303-629-6121
Walker Co
  Oklahoma City, OK 800-522-3015
Walker Engineering Inc
  Sun Valley, CA 818-252-7788
Wayne Industries
  Clanton, AL 800-225-3148

Webster Packaging Corporation
Loveland, OH 513-683-5666
Wedlock Paper ConvertersLtd.
Mississauga, ON 800-388-0447
Welch Stencil Company
Scarborough, ME 800-635-3506
West Hawk Industries
Ann Arbor, MI 800-678-1286
Western Lighting Inc
Franklin Park, IL 847-451-7200
WGN Flag & Decorating Co
Chicago, IL 773-768-8076
Winmark Stamp & Sign
Salt Lake City, UT 800-438-0480
Winnebago Sign Company
Fond Du Lac, WI 920-922-5930
World Division
Dallas, TX 800-433-9843
YESCO
Salt Lake City, UT 800-444-3847

Changeable Letter

AAA Electrical Signs
Donna, TX 800-825-5376
ABC Letter Art
Los Angeles, CA 888-261-5367
ACME Sign Corp
Peabody, MA 978-535-6600
Ad Mart Identity Group
Danville, KY 800-354-2102
Alex Delvecchio Enterprises
Troy, MI 248-619-9600
Arrow Sign & Awning Company
East Bethel, MN 800-621-9231
Audrey Signs
New York, NY 212-769-4992
Charles Mayer Studios
Akron, OH 330-535-6121
Claridge Products & Equipment
Harrison, AR
Classic Signs Inc
Amherst, NH 800-734-7446
Comco Signs
Charlotte, NC 704-375-2338
Exhibitron Co
Grants Pass, OR 800-437-4571
FFR Merchandising Inc
Twinsburg, OH 800-422-2547
Gelberg Signs
Washington, DC 800-443-5237
Hardin Signs Inc
Peoria, IL 309-688-4111
Heath & Company
Roswell, GA 770-650-2724
Hiclay Studios
St Louis, MO 314-533-8393
Hoarel Sign Co
Amarillo, TX 806-373-2175
International Patterns, Inc.
Bay Shore, NY 631-952-2000
Lamb Sign
Manassas, VA 703-791-7960
Lynn Sign Inc
Andover, MA 800-225-5764
Mcbride Sign Co
Madison Heights, VA 434-847-4151
MDI Worldwide
Farmington Hills, MI 800-228-8925
Neon Design-a-Sign
Laguna Niguel, CA 888-636-6327
Nu-Dell Manufacturing
Des Plaines, IL 847-803-4500
Omaha Neon Sign Co
Omaha, NE 800-786-6366
Poblocki Sign Co
Milwaukee, WI 414-453-4010
Roth Sign Systems
Petaluma, CA 800-585-7446
Selby Sign Co Inc
Pocomoke City, MD 410-742-0095
Seton Indentification Products
Branford, CT 800-571-2596
Signets/Menu-Quik
Mentor, OH 800-775-6368
Signs O' Life
Avon, MA 800-750-1475
Super Vision International
Orlando, FL 407-857-9900
Tablet & Ticket Co
West Chicago, IL 800-438-4959

Toledo Sign Co Inc
Toledo, OH 419-244-4444
Total Identity Group
Cambridge, ON 877-551-5529
Vomela/Harbor Graphics
St Paul, MN 800-645-1012

Electric

A Allred Marketing
Birmingham, AL 205-251-3700
AAA Electrical Signs
Donna, TX 800-825-5376
ACME Sign Corp
Peabody, MA 978-535-6600
Ad Mart Identity Group
Danville, KY 800-354-2102
Adam Electric Signs
Massillon, OH 888-886-9911
Affiliated Resource Inc
Chicago, IL 800-366-9336
Allen Industries Inc
Greensboro, NC 800-967-2553
Allen Signs Co
Knoxville, TN 800-844-3524
Alphabet Signs
Gap, PA 800-582-6366
American Led-Gible
Columbus, OH 614-851-1100
Attracta Sign
Rogers, MN 763-428-6377
B S C Signs
Broomfield, CO 866-223-0101
Barlo Signs
Hudson, NH 800-227-5674
Big Beam Emergency Systems Inc
Crystal Lake, IL 815-459-6100
Canton Sign Co
Canton, OH 330-456-7151
Cascade Signs & Neon
Salem, OR 503-378-0012
Chapman Sign
Warren, MI 586-758-1600
City Neon Sign Company
Spokane, WA 509-483-5171
City Sign Svc Inc
Dallas, TX 214-826-4475
City Signs LLC
Jackson, TN 877-248-9744
Classic Signs Inc
Amherst, NH 800-734-7446
Claude Neon Signs
Baltimore, MD 410-685-7575
Clearr Corporation
Minneapolis, MN 800-548-3269
Comco Signs
Charlotte, NC 704-375-2338
Comet Signs
San Antonio, TX 210-341-7244
Cook Neon Signs
Tullahoma, TN 800-488-0944
Corsair Display Systems
Canandalgua, NY 800-347-5245
County Neon Sign Corporation
Plainview, NY 516-349-9550
Cuerden Sign Co
Conway, AR 501-375-7705
Cummings
Nashville, TN 615-673-8999
Custom ID Systems
Venice, FL 800-242-8430
Darlington Sign Awning & Neon
Warwick, RI 401-734-5800
Day Nite Neon Signs
Dartmouth, NS 902-469-7095
Delta Signs
Haltom City, TX 866-643-3582
Den Ray Sign Company
Jackson, TN 800-530-7291
Dixie Neon Company
Tampa, FL 813-248-2531
Dowling Signs Inc
Fredericksburg, VA 800-572-2100
Doyle Signs Inc
Addison, IL 630-543-9490
Dualite Sales & Svc Inc
Williamsburg, OH 513-724-7100
Dwinell's Central Neon
Yakima, WA 800-932-8832
Electric City Signs & Neon Inc.
Anderson, SC 800-270-5851

Electro-Lite Signs
Rancho Cucamonga, CA 909-945-3555
Elro Signs
Gardena, CA 800-927-4555
Encore Image Inc
Ontario, CA 800-791-1187
Engraving Services Co.
Woodville South, SA
Esco Manufacturing Inc
Watertown, SD 800-843-3726
Everbrite LLC
Greenfield, WI 800-558-3888
Federal Sign
Providence, RI 401-421-9643
Ferrer Corporation
San Juan, PR 787-761-5151
Fiber Does
San Jose, CA 408-453-5533
First Choice Sign & Lighting
Escondido, CA 800-659-0629
Frank Torrone & Sons
Staten Island, NY 718-273-7600
Frazier Signs
Decatur, IL 217-429-2349
Freeman Electric Co Inc
Panama City, FL 850-785-7448
Fresno Neon Sign Co Inc
Fresno, CA 559-292-2944
Frohling Sign Co
Nanuet, NY 845-623-2258
Gainesville Neon & Signs
Gainesville, FL 800-852-1407
Gelberg Signs
Washington, DC 800-443-5237
General Neon Sign Co
San Antonio, TX 210-227-1203
General Sign Co
Sheffield, AL 256-383-3176
Gilbert Insect Light Traps
Jonesboro, AR 800-643-0400
Grande Ronde Sign Company
La Grande, OR 541-963-5841
Gulf Coast Sign Company
Pensacola, FL 800-768-3549
Haden Signs of Texas
Lubbock, TX 806-744-4404
Hammar & Sons
Pelham, NH 800-527-7446
Harlan Laws Corp
Durham, NC 800-596-7602
Heath & Company
Roswell, GA 770-650-2724
Heath Signs
Reno, NV 775-359-9007
Hiclay Studios
St Louis, MO 314-533-8393
Hoarel Sign Co
Amarillo, TX 806-373-2175
Holsman Sign Svc
Cleveland, OH 216-761-4433
Houser Neon Sign Company
Houston, TX 713-691-5765
Image National Inc
Nampa, ID 208-345-4020
Industrial Neon Sign Corp
Houston, TX 713-748-6600
Industrial Sign Company
South El Monte, CA 800-596-3720
Industrial Signs
Elmwood, LA 504-736-0600
International Patterns, Inc.
Bay Shore, NY 631-952-2000
Jack Stone Lighting & Electrical
Landover, MD 301-322-3323
Johnson Brothers Sign Co Inc
South Whitley, IN 800-477-7516
Jutras Signs & Flags
Manchester, NH 800-924-3524
K & M Intl Inc
Twinsburg, OH 330-425-2550
King Electric Sign Co
Nampa, ID 208-466-2000
La Crosse Sign Co.
Eau Claire, WI 715-835-6189
Lafayette Sign Company
Little Falls, NJ 800-343-5366
Lake City Signs
Boulder City, NV 702-293-5805
Leroy Signs, Inc.
Brooklyn Park, MN 763-535-0080
Little Rock Sign
Conway, AR 501-372-7403

Master Signs-Div of Masterco
Dallas, TX.....................214-381-6207
Mcbride Sign Co
Madison Heights, VA.............434-847-4151
Mcneill Signs Inc
Pompano Beach, FL.............954-946-3474
McQueen Sign & Lighting
Canton, OH...................330-452-5769
MDI Worldwide
Farmington Hills, MI............800-228-8925
Milwaukee Sign Company
Grafton, WI..................262-375-5740
Mirro Products Company
High Point, NC...............336-885-4166
MLS Signs Inc
Chesterfield, MI...............586-948-0200
Mt Vernon Neon Inc
Mt Vernon, IL................618-242-0645
Mulholland-Harper Company
Denton, MD..................800-882-3052
MultiMedia Electronic Displays
Rancho Cordova, CA............800-888-3007
National Menuboard
Auburn, WA..................800-800-5237
National Sign Corporation
Seattle, WA..................206-282-0700
National Sign Systems
Hilliard, OH..................800-544-6726
Nelson Custom Signs
Plymouth, MI.................734-455-0500
Neon Design-a-Sign
Laguna Niguel, CA.............888-636-6327
North American Signs
South Bend, IN...............800-348-5000
Nu-Dell Manufacturing
Des Plaines, IL................847-803-4500
Oklahoma Neon
Tulsa, OK...................888-707-6366
Omaha Neon Sign Co
Omaha, NE..................800-786-6366
Pearson Signs Service
Hampstead, MD...............410-239-3838
Phoenix Sign Company
Aberdeen, WA................360-532-1111
Plastic Art Signs
Pensacola, FL................866-662-7060
Poblocki Sign Co
Milwaukee, WI...............414-453-4010
Pride Neon Inc
Sioux Falls, SD...............605-336-3561
Radding Signs
Springfield, MA...............413-736-5400
Rainbow Neon Sign Company
Houston, TX.................713-923-2759
Ramsay Signs Inc
Portland, OR.................206-623-3100
Rosson Sign Co
Macon, GA..................478-788-3905
Roth Sign Systems
Petaluma, CA................800-585-7446
Roxanne Signs Inc
Gaithersburg, MD.............301-428-4911
Rueff Sign Co Inc
Louisville, KY................502-582-1714
Sasser Signs
Danville, VA..................800-752-6091
Selby Sign Co Inc
Pocomoke City, MD............410-742-0095
Service Neon Signs
Springfield, VA...............703-354-3000
Sexton Sign
Anderson, SC................864-226-6071
Sheridan Sign Company
Salisbury, MD................410-749-7441
Sign Art
Charlotte, NC................800-929-3521
SignArt Advertising
Van Buren, AR...............479-474-8581
Signs & Designs
Palmdale, CA................888-480-7446
Signs O' Life
Avon, MA...................800-750-1475
Southwest Neon Signs
San Antonio, TX..............800-927-3221
Spann Sign Company
Kenosha, WI.................262-658-1288
Steel Art Signs
Markham, ON................800-771-6971
Stylmark Inc
Minneapolis, MN..............800-328-2495
Super Vision International
Orlando, FL..................407-857-9900

Superior Neon Signs Inc
Oklahoma City, OK............405-528-5515
Superior Products Company
Saint Paul, MN...............800-328-9800
Tec Art Industries Inc
Wixom, MI..................800-886-6615
Texas Neon Advertising Inc
San Antonio, TX..............210-734-6694
Thomson-Leeds Company
New York, NY................800-535-9361
Toledo Sign Co Inc
Toledo, OH..................419-244-4444
Total Identity Group
Cambridge, ON...............877-551-5529
Triple A Neon Company
Valley Village, CA.............323-877-5381
Twin State Signs
Essex Junction, VT.............802-872-8949
United Sign Corp
Kansas City, MO..............816-923-9512
Universal Sign Company and Manufacturing Company
Lafayette, LA.................337-234-1466
University-Brink
Foxboro, MA.................617-926-4400
Valley City Sign Co
Comstock Park, MI.............616-784-5711
Varco Products
Chardon, OH.................216-481-6895
Visual Marketing Assoc
Santee, CA...................619-258-0393
VMC Signs
Victoria, TX..................361-575-0548
VPC Gordon Sign
Denver, CO..................303-629-6121
Western Lighting Inc
Franklin Park, IL..............847-451-7200
Weston Emergency Light Co
Weston, MA..................800-649-3756
White Way Sign & Maintenance
Mt Prospect, IL...............800-621-4122
Wilhite Sign Company
Joplin, MO..................417-623-1411
Winnebago Sign Company
Fond Du Lac, WI..............920-922-5930
YESCO
Salt Lake City, UT.............800-444-3847

Interchangeable

ACME Sign Corp
Peabody, MA.................978-535-6600
Ad Mart Identity Group
Danville, KY.................800-354-2102
Allen Industries Inc
Greensboro, NC...............800-967-2553
American Menu Displays
Long Island City, NY...........877-544-8046
Audrey Signs
New York, NY................212-769-4992
Claridge Products & Equipment
Harrison, AR
Comco Signs
Charlotte, NC................704-375-2338
Diskey Architectural Signs
Fort Wayne, IN...............260-424-0233
Display Concepts
Trenton, ME.................800-446-0033
Everbrite LLC
Greenfield, WI...............800-558-3888
Exhibitron Co
Grants Pass, OR..............800-437-4571
Forbes Industries
Ontario, CA.................909-923-4549
Frost Manufacturing Corp
Worcester, MA...............800-462-0216
Gelberg Signs
Washington, DC..............800-443-5237
Heath & Company
Roswell, GA.................770-650-2724
Hoarel Sign Co
Amarillo, TX.................806-373-2175
Impulse Signs
Toronto, ON.................866-636-8273
Lynn Sign Inc
Andover, MA.................800-225-5764
Maier Sign Systems
Saddle Brook, NJ.............201-845-7555
Mainstreet Menu Systems
Brookfield, WI...............800-782-6222
Mcbride Sign Co
Madison Heights, VA...........434-847-4151

McQueen Sign & Lighting
Canton, OH..................330-452-5769
MDI Worldwide
Farmington Hills, MI...........800-228-8925
Menu Men
Palm Harbor, FL..............727-934-7191
Norgus Silk Screen Co Inc
Clifton, NJ...................973-365-0600
Plasti-Line
Knoxville, TN................800-444-7446
Roth Sign Systems
Petaluma, CA................800-585-7446
Screen Print Etc
Anaheim, CA.................714-630-1100
Tablet & Ticket Co
West Chicago, IL..............800-438-4959
Toledo Sign Co Inc
Toledo, OH..................419-244-4444
Total Identity Group
Cambridge, ON...............877-551-5529
US Magnetix
Minneapolis, MN..............763-540-9497
Vomela/Harbor Graphics
St Paul, MN..................800-645-1012
VPC Gordon Sign
Denver, CO..................303-629-6121
Wayne Industries
Clanton, AL..................800-225-3148
Your Place Menu Systems
Carson City, NV..............800-321-8105

Luminous Tube

A Allred Marketing
Birmingham, AL...............205-251-3700
AAA Electrical Signs
Donna, TX...................800-825-5376
ACME Sign Corp
Peabody, MA.................978-535-6600
Adam Electric Signs
Massillon, OH................888-886-9911
Alphabet Signs
Gap, PA....................800-582-6366
Arrow Sign & Awning Company
East Bethel, MN..............800-621-9231
Audrey Signs
New York, NY................212-769-4992
B S C Signs
Broomfield, CO...............866-223-0101
B&B Neon Sign Company
Austin, TX...................800-791-6366
Capital City Signs
Monona, WI.................608-222-1881
Cascade Signs & Neon
Salem, OR...................503-378-0012
Century Sign Company
Fargo, ND...................701-235-5323
Cheshire Signs
Keene, NH..................603-352-5985
City Neon Sign Company
Spokane, WA................509-483-5171
City Signs LLC
Jackson, TN.................877-248-9744
Claude Neon Signs
Baltimore, MD...............410-685-7575
Cobb Sign Co Inc
Burlington, NC...............336-227-0181
Comco Signs
Charlotte, NC................704-375-2338
Cook Neon Signs
Tullahoma, TN...............800-488-0944
County Neon Sign Corporation
Plainview, NY................516-349-9550
Custom ID Systems
Venice, FL..................800-242-8430
D&D Sign Company
Wichita Falls, TX.............940-692-4643
Darlington Sign Awning & Neon
Warwick, RI.................401-734-5800
Day Nite Neon Signs
Dartmouth, NS...............902-469-7095
Den Ray Sign Company
Jackson, TN.................800-530-7291
Display Concepts
Trenton, ME.................800-446-0033
Dowling Signs Inc
Fredericksburg, VA............800-572-2100
Dualite Sales & Svc Inc
Williamsburg, OH.............513-724-7100
Dwinell's Central Neon
Yakima, WA.................800-932-8832

Electric City Signs & Neon Inc.
Anderson, SC 800-270-5851
Elro Signs
Gardena, CA .800-927-4555
Encore Image Inc
Ontario, CA 800-791-1187
Esco Manufacturing Inc
Watertown, SD 800-843-3726
Everbrite LLC
Greenfield, WI 800-558-3888
Federal Sign
Providence, RI 401-421-9643
Ferrer Corporation
San Juan, PR .787-761-5151
Frazier Signs
Decatur, IL 217-429-2349
Freeman Electric Co Inc
Panama City, FL 850-785-7448
Fresno Neon Sign Co Inc
Fresno, CA 559-292-2944
Frohling Sign Co
Nanuet, NY 845-623-2258
Gainesville Neon & Signs
Gainesville, FL 800-852-1407
General Neon Sign Co
San Antonio, TX 210-227-1203
Grande Ronde Sign Company
La Grande, OR 541-963-5841
Gulf Coast Sign Company
Pensacola, FL .800-768-3549
Haden Signs of Texas
Lubbock, TX 806-744-4404
Hammar & Sons
Pelham, NH 800-527-7446
Hardin Signs Inc
Peoria, IL 309-688-4111
Harlan Laws Corp
Durham, NC 800-596-7602
Heath & Company
Roswell, GA 770-650-2724
Heath Signs
Reno, NV 775-359-9007
Hedges Neon Sales
Salina, KS 785-827-9341
Hoarel Sign Co
Amarillo, TX 806-373-2175
Holsman Sign Svc
Cleveland, OH 216-761-4433
Houser Neon Sign Company
Houston, TX 713-691-5765
Imperial Signs & Manufacturing
Rapid City, SD 605-348-2511
Industrial Signs
Elmwood, LA .504-736-0600
Jeffcoat Signs
Gainesville, FL 877-377-4248
Jenkins Sign Co
Youngstown, OH 330-799-3205
Jet Lite Products
Highland, IL 618-654-2217
Jim Did It Sign Company
Allston, MA 617-782-2410
Johnson Brothers Sign Co Inc
South Whitley, IN 800-477-7516
Jutras Signs & Flags
Manchester, NH 800-924-3524
K & M Intl Inc
Twinsburg, OH 330-425-2550
King Electric Sign Co
Nampa, ID 208-466-2000
La Crosse Sign Co.
Eau Claire, WI 715-835-6189
Lafayette Sign Company
Little Falls, NJ 800-343-5366
Leroy Signs, Inc.
Brooklyn Park, MN 763-535-0080
Maier Sign Systems
Saddle Brook, NJ 201-845-7555
Master Signs-Div of Masterco
Dallas, TX 214-381-6207
Mcbride Sign Co
Madison Heights, VA 434-847-4151
Mcneill Signs Inc
Pompano Beach, FL 954-946-3474
McQueen Sign & Lighting
Canton, OH 330-452-5769
MDI Worldwide
Farmington Hills, MI 800-228-8925
Mt Vernon Neon Inc
Mt Vernon, IL 618-242-0645
National Sign Corporation
Seattle, WA 206-282-0700

National Sign Systems
Hilliard, OH 800-544-6726
Nebraska Neon Sign Co
Lincoln, NE 402-476-6563
Neokraft Signs Inc
Lewiston, ME .800-339-2258
Neonetics Inc
Hampstead, MD 410-374-8057
North American Signs
South Bend, IN 800-348-5000
Oklahoma Neon
Tulsa, OK 888-707-6366
Omaha Neon Sign Co
Omaha, NE 800-786-6366
Pacific Sign Construction
Poway, CA 858-486-8006
Pearson Signs Service
Hampstead, MD 410-239-3838
Peskin Sign Co
Youngstown, OH 330-783-2470
Phoenix Sign Company
Aberdeen, WA 360-532-1111
Plastic Art Signs
Pensacola, FL .866-662-7060
Poblocki Sign Co
Milwaukee, WI 414-453-4010
Porter Bowers Signs
Des Moines, IA 515-253-9622
Pride Neon Inc
Sioux Falls, SD 605-336-3561
Qyk Syn Industries
Miami, FL 800-354-5640
R R Donnelley
Chicago, IL 800-742-4455
Rainbow Neon Sign Company
Houston, TX 713-923-2759
Rainbow Sign Co
Salt Lake City, UT 801-466-7856
Ramsay Signs Inc
Portland, OR 206-623-3100
Rosson Sign Co
Macon, GA 478-788-3905
Roth Sign Systems
Petaluma, CA .800-585-7446
Roxanne Signs Inc
Gaithersburg, MD 301-428-4911
Ruggles Sign Company
Versailles, KY .859-879-1199
Safety Light Corporation
Bloomsburg, PA 570-784-4344
Sasser Signs
Danville, VA 800-752-6091
Selby Sign Co Inc
Pocomoke City, MD 410-742-0095
Service Neon Signs
Springfield, VA 703-354-3000
Sheridan Sign Company
Salisbury, MD 410-749-7441
Sign Products
Sheridan, WY .800-532-4753
SignArt Advertising
Van Buren, AR 479-474-8581
Signs & Designs
Palmdale, CA .888-480-7446
Signs O' Life
Avon, MA 800-750-1475
Spann Sign Company
Kenosha, WI 262-658-1288
Stylmark Inc
Minneapolis, MN 800-328-2495
Super Vision International
Orlando, FL 407-857-9900
SuppliesForLess
Hampton, VA .800-235-2201
Tablet & Ticket Co
West Chicago, IL 800-438-4959
Tec Art Industries Inc
Wixom, MI 800-886-6615
Texas Neon Advertising Inc
San Antonio, TX 210-734-6694
Toledo Sign Co Inc
Toledo, OH 419-244-4444
Total Identity Group
Cambridge, ON 877-551-5529
Triangle Sign & Svc
Halethorpe, MD 410-247-5300
Twin State Signs
Essex Junction, VT 802-872-8949
United Sign Corp
Kansas City, MO 816-923-9512
Universal Sign Company and Manufacturing Company
Lafayette, LA .337-234-1466

University-Brink
Foxboro, MA .617-926-4400
VMC Signs
Victoria, TX 361-575-0548
Western Lighting Inc
Franklin Park, IL 847-451-7200
Wilhite Sign Company
Joplin, MO 417-623-1411
Winnebago Sign Company
Fond Du Lac, WI 920-922-5930
Your Place Menu Systems
Carson City, NV 800-321-8105

Plastic

A Allred Marketing
Birmingham, AL 205-251-3700
ABC Letter Art
Los Angeles, CA 888-261-5367
Ace Stamp & Engraving
Lakewood, WA 253-582-3322
Ad Mart Identity Group
Danville, KY 800-354-2102
Adam Electric Signs
Massillon, OH 888-886-9911
Andrew W Nissly Inc
Lancaster, PA .717-393-3841
Audrey Signs
New York, NY 212-769-4992
B&B Neon Sign Company
Austin, TX 800-791-6366
Baltimore Sign Company
Arnold, MD 410-276-1500
Berlekamp Plastics Inc
Fremont, OH .419-334-4481
Berryhill Signs
Memphis, TN .901-324-1730
Canton Sign Co
Canton, OH 330-456-7151
Capital City Signs
Monona, WI 608-222-1881
Century Sign Company
Fargo, ND 701-235-5323
Chain Store Graphics
Decatur, IL 800-443-7446
Chatelain Plastics
Findlay, OH 866-421-4323
Cheshire Signs
Keene, NH 603-352-5985
Chroma Tone
Saint Clair, PA 800-878-1552
City Neon Sign Company
Spokane, WA .509-483-5171
City Signs LLC
Jackson, TN 877-248-9744
City Stamp & Seal Co
Austin, TX 800-950-6074
Clearr Corporation
Minneapolis, MN 800-548-3269
Cobb Sign Co Inc
Burlington, NC 336-227-0181
Comco Signs
Charlotte, NC .704-375-2338
Continental Commercial Products
Bridgeton, MO 800-325-1051
Creative Signage System,
College Park, MD 800-220-7446
Custom ID Systems
Venice, FL 800-242-8430
Custom Plastics Inc
Decatur, GA 404-373-1691
Custom Rubber Stamp Co
Crosby, MN 888-606-4579
Den Ray Sign Company
Jackson, TN 800-530-7291
Dimension Graphics Inc
Grand Rapids, MI 855-476-1281
Dinosaur Plastics
Houston, TX 713-923-2278
Diskey Architectural Signs
Fort Wayne, IN 260-424-0233
Dixie Neon Company
Tampa, FL 813-248-2531
Dowling Signs Inc
Fredericksburg, VA 800-572-2100
Dwinell's Central Neon
Yakima, WA 800-932-8832
Eaton Quade Plastics & Sign Co
Oklahoma City, OK 405-236-4475
Ed Smith's Stencil Works LTD
New Orleans, LA 504-525-2128

Electric City Signs & Neon Inc.
Anderson, SC .800-270-5851
Elro Signs
Gardena, CA 800-927-4555
Emco Industrial Plastics
Cedar Grove, NJ 800-292-9906
Emedco
Williamsville, NY 877-765-8386
Engraving Services Co.
Woodville South, SA
Engraving Specialists
Royal Oak, MI 248-542-2244
Everett Rubber Stamp
Everett, WA 425-258-6747
Exhibitron Co
Grants Pass, OR 800-437-4571
Federal Heath Sign Co LLC
Oceanside, CA 800-527-9495
Ferrer Corporation
San Juan, PR 787-761-5151
Five-M Plastics Company
Allentown, PA 610-628-4291
Forrest Engraving Company
New Rochelle, NY 914-632-9892
FORT Hill Sign Products Inc
Hopedale, MA 781-321-4320
France Personalized Signs
Cleveland, OH 216-241-2198
Franklin Rubber Stamp Co
Wilmington, DE 302-654-8841
Frazier Signs
Decatur, IL .217-429-2349
Freeman Electric Co Inc
Panama City, FL 850-785-7448
Fresno Neon Sign Co Inc
Fresno, CA .559-292-2944
Frohling Sign Co
Nanuet, NY 845-623-2258
Gelberg Signs
Washington, DC 800-443-5237
General Neon Sign Co
San Antonio, TX 210-227-1203
Grande Ronde Sign Company
La Grande, OR 541-963-5841
Gulf Coast Sign Company
Pensacola, FL 800-768-3549
Hardin Signs Inc
Peoria, IL 309-688-4111
Heath & Company
Roswell, GA 770-650-2724
HMG Worldwide In-Store Marketing
New York, NY 212-736-2300
Hoarel Sign Co
Amarillo, TX 806-373-2175
Holsman Sign Svc
Cleveland, OH 216-761-4433
Houser Neon Sign Company
Houston, TX 713-691-5765
Houston Stamp & Stencil Company
Houston, TX 713-869-4337
Ideal Office Supply & Rubber Stamp Company
Kingsport, TN 423-246-7371
Impact Awards & Promotions
Avon Park, FL 888-203-4225
Imperial Plastics Inc
Lakeville, MN 952-469-4951
Imperial Signs & Manufacturing
Rapid City, SD 605-348-2511
Industrial Neon Sign Corp
Houston, TX 713-748-6600
Jeffcoat Signs
Gainesville, FL 877-377-4248
Jenkins Sign Co
Youngstown, OH 330-799-3205
Jim Did It Sign Company
Allston, MA 617-782-2410
Johnson Brothers Sign Co Inc
South Whitley, IN 800-477-7516
Joseph Struhl Co Inc
New Hyde Park, NY 800-552-0023
Just Plastics Inc
New York, NY 212-569-8500
K & I Creative Plastics & Wood
Jacksonville, FL 904-387-0438
King Electric Sign Co
Nampa, ID. 208-466-2000
King Products
Mississauga, ON 866-454-6757
King Sign Company
Akron, OH. 330-762-7421
Kitchener Plastics
Kitchener, ON. 800-429-5633

Krusoe Sign Co
Cleveland, OH. 216-447-1177
L&L Engraving Company
Gilford, NH 888-524-3032
La Crosse Sign Co.
Eau Claire, WI 715-835-6189
Lafayette Sign Company
Little Falls, NJ 800-343-5366
Lamb Sign
Manassas, VA 703-791-7960
Leathertone
Findlay, OH. 419-429-0188
Legacy Plastics
Henderson, KY 270-827-1318
Legible Signs
Loves Park, IL. 800-435-4177
Leroy Signs, Inc.
Brooklyn Park, MN 763-535-0080
License Ad Plate Co
Cleveland, OH 216-265-4200
Little Rock Sign
Conway, AR 501-372-7403
Lynn Sign Inc
Andover, MA 800-225-5764
Maier Sign Systems
Saddle Brook, NJ 201-845-7555
Mansfield Rubber Stamp
Mansfield, OH. 419-524-1442
Master Signs-Div of Masterco
Dallas, TX. 214-381-6207
Mcbride Sign Co
Madison Heights, VA 434-847-4151
Mcneill Signs Inc
Pompano Beach, FL 954-946-3474
McQueen Sign & Lighting
Canton, OH 330-452-5769
MDI Worldwide
Farmington Hills, MI 800-228-8925
Mirro Products Company
High Point, NC 336-885-4166
Mulholland Co
Fort Worth, TX 817-624-1153
Mulholland-Harper Company
Denton, MD 800-882-3052
National Marker Co Inc
North Smithfield, RI 800-453-2727
National Marking Products Inc
Henrico, VA 800-482-1553
National Sign Corporation
Seattle, WA 206-282-0700
National Stock Sign Co
Santa Cruz, CA. 800-462-7726
Neokraft Signs Inc
Lewiston, ME 800-339-2258
Norgus Silk Screen Co Inc
Clifton, NJ. 973-365-0600
Oklahoma Neon
Tulsa, OK 888-707-6366
Omaha Neon Sign Co
Omaha, NE 800-786-6366
P M Plastics
Pewaukee, WI. 262-691-1700
Parisian Novelty Company
Homewood, IL 773-847-1212
Pearson Signs Service
Hampstead, MD 410-239-3838
Peskin Sign Co
Youngstown, OH. 330-783-2470
Phoenix Sign Company
Aberdeen, WA 360-532-1111
Plastech Corp
Atlanta, GA. 404-355-9682
Plasti-Line
Knoxville, TN 800-444-7446
Plastic Art Signs
Pensacola, FL 866-662-7060
Plastic Craft Products Corp
West Nyack, NY 800-627-3010
Plastic Turning Company
Leominster, MA 978-534-8326
Plastimatic Arts Corporation
Mishawaka, IN 800-442-3593
Printsource Group
Wakefield, RI 401-789-9339
Qyk Syn Industries
Miami, FL 800-354-5640
R R Donnelley
Chicago, IL 800-742-4455
Rainbow Neon Sign Company
Houston, TX 713-923-2759
Rayne Sign Co
Rayne, LA 337-334-4276

Regal Plastic Supply Co
Kansas City, MO. 800-444-6390
Reidler Decal Corporation
Saint Clair, PA. 800-628-7770
Reinhold Sign Svc Inc
Green Bay, WI. 920-494-7161
Richardson's Stamp Works
Houston, TX 713-973-0314
Rosson Sign Co
Macon, GA 478-788-3905
Roth Sign Systems
Petaluma, CA 800-585-7446
Rueff Sign Co Inc
Louisville, KY 502-582-1714
Ruggles Sign Company
Versailles, KY 859-879-1199
S & S Metal & Plastics Inc
Jacksonville, FL 904-730-4655
Scott Sign Systems
Sarasota, FL 800-237-9447
Service Neon Signs
Springfield, VA 703-354-3000
Seton Indentification Products
Branford, CT 800-571-2596
Sign Graphics
Evansville, IN 812-476-9151
Sign Systems, Inc.
Warren, MI 586-758-1600
SignArt Advertising
Van Buren, AR 479-474-8581
Signet Graphic Products
St Louis, MO. 314-426-0200
Signs & Designs
Palmdale, CA 888-480-7446
Spann Sign Company
Kenosha, WI. 262-658-1288
Stoffel Seals Corp
Tallapoosa, GA 800-422-8247
Suburban Sign Company
Anoka, MN 763-753-8849
Suburban Signs
College Park, MD 301-474-5051
Superior Neon Signs Inc
Oklahoma City, OK 405-528-5515
Sutherland Stamp Company
San Diego, CA 858-233-7784
Tablet & Ticket Co
West Chicago, IL 800-438-4959
Three P
Salt Lake City, UT 801-486-7407
Toledo Sign Co Inc
Toledo, OH 419-244-4444
Total Identity Group
Cambridge, ON 877-551-5529
Triangle Sign & Svc
Halethorpe, MD 410-247-5300
Trident Plastics
Ivyland, PA 800-222-2318
Tulsa Plastics Co
Tulsa, OK .888-273-5303
United Sign Corp
Kansas City, MO. 816-923-9512
Universal Sign Company and Manufacturing Company
Lafayette, LA 337-234-1466
University-Brink
Foxboro, MA 617-926-4400
Valley City Sign Co
Comstock Park, MI. 616-784-5711
Volk Corp
Farmington Hills, MI 800-521-6799
Vomela/Harbor Graphics
St Paul, MN. 800-645-1012
Wilhite Sign Company
Joplin, MO 417-623-1411
Winnebago Sign Company
Fond Du Lac, WI 920-922-5930
Wolens Company
Dallas, TX. 214-634-0800

Point of Purchase

A Allred Marketing
Birmingham, AL. 205-251-3700
ACME Sign Corp
Peabody, MA. 978-535-6600
Arlington Display Industries
Detroit, MI 313-837-1212
B&B Neon Sign Company
Austin, TX 800-791-6366
Barlo Signs
Hudson, NH 800-227-5674

Blanc Industries
  Dover, NJ 888-332-5262
Carlton Industries
  La Grange, TX 800-231-5988
Chicago Show Inc
  Buffalo Grove, IL 847-955-0200
City Signs LLC
  Jackson, TN 877-248-9744
Clearr Corporation
  Minneapolis, MN 800-548-3269
Comco Signs
  Charlotte, NC 704-375-2338
Curzon Promotional Graphics
  Omaha, NE 800-769-7446
Daytech Limited
  Toronto, ON 877-329-1907
Dimension Graphics Inc
  Grand Rapids, MI 855-476-1281
Dunn Woodworks
  Shrewsbury, PA 877-835-8592
Emco Industrial Plastics
  Cedar Grove, NJ 800-292-9906
Empire Screen Printing Inc
  Onalaska, WI 608-783-3301
Federal Stamp & Seal Manufacturing Company
  Atlanta, GA 800-333-7726
FFR Merchandising Inc
  Twinsburg, OH 800-422-2547
Florida Plastics Intl
  Evergreen Park, IL 800-499-0400
FMI Display
  Elkins Park, PA 215-663-1998
Futura 2000 Corporation
  Miami, FL 305-256-5877
Gelberg Signs
  Washington, DC 800-443-5237
Greif Inc
  Delaware, OH 800-476-1635
Hammar & Sons
  Pelham, NH 800-527-7446
Harting Graphics
  Wilmington, DE 800-848-1373
Heath & Company
  Roswell, GA 770-650-2724
Hoarel Sign Co
  Amarillo, TX 806-373-2175
Impulse Signs
  Toronto, ON 866-636-8273
Insignia Systems Inc
  Minneapolis, MN 800-874-4648
JBC Plastics
  St Louis, MO 877-834-5526
Mcbride Sign Co
  Madison Heights, VA 434-847-4151
MDI Worldwide
  Farmington Hills, MI 800-228-8925
National Sign Systems
  Hilliard, OH 800-544-6726
Neal Walters Poster Corporation
  Bentonville, AR 501-273-2489
Norgus Silk Screen Co Inc
  Clifton, NJ 973-365-0600
Pilgrim Plastics
  Brockton, MA 800-343-7810
Plasti-Line
  Knoxville, TN 800-444-7446
Pratt Poster Company
  Indianapolis, IN 800-645-1012
Prestige Plastics Corporation
  Delta, BC 604-930-2931
Rex Art Manufacturing Corp.
  Lindenhurst, NY 631-884-4600
Royal Display Corporation
  Middletown, CT 800-569-1295
RPA Process Technologies
  Marblehead, MA 800-631-9707
Shelby Co
  Westlake, OH 800-842-1650
Stoffel Seals Corp
  Tallapoosa, GA 800-422-8247
Toledo Sign Co Inc
  Toledo, OH 419-244-4444
Total Identity Group
  Cambridge, ON 877-551-5529
Trident Plastics
  Ivyland, PA 800-222-2318
Twin State Signs
  Essex Junction, VT 802-872-8949
US Magnetix
  Minneapolis, MN 763-540-9497
Vomela/Harbor Graphics
  St Paul, MN 800-645-1012

Wayne Industries
  Clanton, AL 800-225-3148
Welch Stencil Company
  Scarborough, ME 800-635-3506
Wichita Stamp & Seal Inc
  Wichita, KS 316-263-4223
Willson Industries
  Marmora, NJ 800-894-4169

Sorters

Check, Bill & Voucher

Automated Business Products
  Hackensack, NJ 800-334-1440
Bell & Howell Company
  Lincolnwood, IL 800-647-2290
C R Mfg
  Waverly, NE 877-789-5844
Savasort Inc
  Riviera Beach, FL 800-255-8744
Scan Coin
  Ashburn, VA 800-336-3311
Sortie/Kohlhaas
  Monee, IL 708-534-3940

Straws

Drinking

C R Mfg
  Waverly, NE 877-789-5844
Cell-O-Core Company
  Sharon Center, OH 800-239-4370
Fun-Time International
  Philadelphia, PA 800-776-4386
Goldmax Industries
  City of Industry, CA 626-964-8820
Jet Plastica Industries
  Hatfield, PA
Johnstown Manufacturing
  Columbus, OH 614-236-8853
K & L Intl
  Ontario, CA 888-598-5588
OWD
  Tupper Lake, NY 800-836-1693
Penley Corporation
  West Paris, ME 800-368-6449
RubaTex Polymer
  Middlefield, OH 440-632-1691
Semco Plastic Co
  St Louis, MO 314-487-4557
Spinzer
  Glen Ellyn, IL 630-469-7184
Spir-It/Zoo Piks
  Andover, MA 800-343-0996
Spirit Foodservice, Inc.
  Andover, MA 800-343-0996
SQP
  Schenectady, NY 800-724-1129
Superior Products Company
  Saint Paul, MN 800-328-9800
Trevor Industries
  Eden, NY 716-992-4775
Waddington North America
  Chelmsford, MA 888-962-2877

Table Cloths

A1 Tablecloth Co
  South Hackensack, NJ 800-727-8987
Abond Plastic Corporation
  Lachine, QC 800-886-7947
Adcapitol
  Monroe, NC 800-868-7111
AEP Industries Inc
  Mankato, MN 800-999-2374
Americo
  West Memphis, AR 800-626-2350
Artex International
  Highland, IL 618-654-2113
Best Brands Home Products
  New York, NY 212-684-7456
Best Buy Uniforms
  Homestead, PA 800-345-1924
Best Value Textiles
  North Charleston, SC 800-858-8589
Carnegie Textile Co
  Cleveland, OH 800-633-4136
Cotton Goods Mfg Co
  Chicago, IL 773-265-0088

Creative Converting Inc
  Clintonville, WI 800-826-0418
Custom Table Pads
  St Paul, MN 800-325-4643
Decolin
  Montreal, QC 514-384-2910
Drapes 4 Show
  Sylmar, CA 800-525-7469
Elrene Home Fashions
  New York, NY 212-213-0425
Erving Industries
  Erving, MA 413-422-2700
Gary Manufacturing Company
  National City, CA 800-775-0804
Gourmet Table Skirts
  Houston, TX 800-527-0440
Hilden Halifax
  South Boston, VA 800-431-2514
Hoffmaster Group Inc.
  Oshkosh, WI 800-558-9300
Jack the Ripper Table Skirting
  Stafford, TX 800-331-7831
K Katen & Company
  Rahway, NJ 732-381-0220
K-C Products Company
  Van Nuys, CA 818-267-1600
Klever Kuvers
  Pasadena, CA 626-355-8441
Louis Jacobs & Son
  Brooklyn, NY 718-782-3500
Louisville Bedding Co Inc.
  Louisville, KY 502-813-8059
Marko Inc
  Spartanburg, SC 866-466-2756
Milliken & Co
  Spartanburg, SC 864-503-2020
Party Linens
  Chicago, IL 800-281-0003
Philmont Manufacturing Co.
  Englewood, NJ 888-379-6483
Premier Skirting Products
  Lawrence, NY 800-544-2516
Radius Display Products
  Dallas, TX 888-322-7429
Resource One/Resource Two
  Reseda, CA 818-343-3451
SCA Tissue
  Philadelphia, PA 866-722-8675
Showeray Corporation
  Brooklyn, NY 718-965-3633
Something Different Linen
  Clifton, NJ 800-422-2180
Straubel Company
  De Pere, WI 888-336-1412
Sultan Linen Inc
  New York, NY 212-689-8900
Superior Products Company
  Saint Paul, MN 800-328-9800
Tag-Trade Associated Group
  Chicago, IL 800-621-8350
Tara Linens
  Sanford, NC 800-476-8272
Ultimate Textile
  Paterson, NJ 973-523-5866
Vicmore Manufacturing Company
  Brooklyn, NY 800-458-8663

Tables

Cafeteria, Restaurant, Foodservice Kitchen

A J Antunes & Co
  Carol Stream, IL 800-253-2991
A-1 Booth Manufacturing
  Burley, ID 800-820-3285
Advance Tabco
  Edgewood, NY 800-645-3166
Aero Manufacturing Co
  Clifton, NJ 800-631-8378
All State Fabricators Corporation
  Tampa, FL 800-322-9925
Allstrong Restaurant Eqpt Inc
  South El Monte, CA 800-933-8913
AMC Industries
  Palmetto, FL 941-479-7834
AMI
  Richmond, CA 800-942-7466
Amtab Manufacturing Corp
  Aurora, IL 800-878-2257

Anderson Wood Products
Louisville, KY 502-778-5591
ARC Specialties
Valencia, CA .661-775-8500
ATD-American Co
Wyncote, PA .800-523-2300
Atlas Metal Industries
Miami, FL 800-762-7565
AWP Butcher Block Inc
Horse Cave, KY 800-764-7840
Barn Furniture Mart
Van Nuys, CA 888-302-2276
Barrette Outdoor Living
Cleveland, OH 800-336-2383
Beaufurn
Advance, NC .888-766-7706
Beka Furniture
Concord, ON .905-669-4255
Berco
St Louis, MO .888-772-4788
Bessco Tube Bending & Pipe Fabricating
Thornton, IL .800-337-3977
Brill Manufacturing Co
Ludington, MI 866-896-6420
Carts Food Equipment
Brooklyn, NY .718-788-5540
Catskill Craftsmen Inc
Stamford, NY .607-652-7321
CCS Stone, Inc.
Moonachie, NJ 800-227-7785
CDI Service & Mfg Inc
Largo, FL 727-536-2207
Charter House
Zeeland, MI 800-314-7659
Chocolate Concepts
Hartville, OH .330-877-3322
Classico Seating
Peru, IN 800-968-6655
Cobb & Zimmer
Detroit, MI 313-923-0350
Colecraft Commercial Furnishings
Jamestown, NY 800-622-2777
Commercial Furniture Group Inc
Newport, TN .800-873-3252
Commercial Seating Specialists
Santa Clara, CA 408-453-8983
Component Hardware Group Inc
Lakewood, NJ 800-526-3694
Cove Woodworking
Gloucester, MA 800-273-0037
Crown Industries
East Orange, NJ 877-747-2457
Crown Steel Mfg
San Marcos, CA 760-471-1188
Custom Diamond International
Laval, QC 800-363-5926
Custom Diamond Intl.
Laval, QC 800-326-5926
Dayco
Clearwater, FL 727-573-9330
Delfield Co
Mt Pleasant, MI. 800-733-8821
Den Mar Corp
North Dartmouth, MA 508-999-3295
Duke Manufacturing Co
St Louis, MO. 800-735-3853
Duluth Sheet Metal
Duluth, MN. .218-722-2613
Dunhill Food Equipment Corporation
Armonk, NY .800-847-4206
Eagle Foodservice   Equipment
Clayton, DE. .800-441-8440
Eagle Group
Clayton, DE. .800-441-8440
Eagle Products Company
Houston, TX .713-690-1161
Eash Industries
Elkhart, IN. .574-295-4450
Economy Paper & Restaurant Co
Clifton, NJ. .973-279-5500
Edgemold Products
Oconomowoc, WI. 800-450-0051
Eldorado Miranda Manufacturing Company
Largo, FL 800-330-0708
Electric Contract Furniture
New York, NY. 888-311-6272
Empire Bakery Equipment
Hicksville, NY 800-878-4070
Erwin Food Service Equipment
Fort Worth, TX 817-535-0021
Eskay Metal Fabricating
Buffalo, NY. .800-836-8015

Fab-X/Metals
Washington, NC 800-677-3229
FCD Tabletops
Brooklyn, NY 800-822-5399
Fiskars Brands Inc.
Baldwinsville, NY 315-635-9911
Fixtur World
Cookeville, TN 800-634-9887
Fixtures Furniture
Florence, AL. 855-321-4999
Forbes Industries
Ontario, CA .909-923-4549
Fred Beesley's Booth & Upholstery
Centerville, UT 801-364-8189
Furniturelab
Carrboro, NC 800-449-8677
Gar Products
Lakewood, NJ 800-424-2477
Gasser Chair Co Inc
Youngstown, OH. 800-323-2234
Gates Manufacturing Company
Saint Louis, MO 800-237-9226
Harbour House Bar Crafting
Stamford, CT. 800-755-1227
Hines III
Jacksonville, FL 904-398-5110
Hot Food Boxes
Mooresville, IN 800-733-8073
Industrial Plastics Company
Fort Smith, AR 800-850-0916
Industries Inc Kiefer
Random Lake, WI. 920-994-2332
J.H. Carr & Sons
Seattle, WA .800-523-8842
John Boos & Co
Effingham, IL 888-431-2667
K C Booth Co
N Kansas City, MO 800-866-5226
KaiRak
Anaheim, CA 714-870-8661
Kamran & Co
Santa Barbara, CA 800-480-9418
Kay Home Products Inc
Antioch, IL 800-600-7009
Ken Coat
Bardstown, KY 888-536-2628
Kings River Casting
Sanger, CA 888-545-5157
Krueger International Holding
Green Bay, WI. 800-424-2432
Lakeside Manufacturing Inc
Milwaukee, WI. 888-558-8565
Lambertson Industries Inc
Sparks, NV 800-548-3324
Lask Seating Company
Chicago, IL 888-573-2846
LB Furniture Industries
Hudson, NY .800-221-8752
Load King Mfg
Jacksonville, FL 800-531-4975
Lodging By Charter
Liberty, NC 800-327-2548
Lumacurve Airfield Signs
Macedonia, OH. 800-258-1997
M & E Mfg Co Inc
Kingston, NY 845-331-2110
M&S Manufacturing
Arnold, MO. 636-464-2739
MCM Fixture Co
Hazel Park, MI. 248-547-9280
Mcroyal Industries Inc
Youngstown, OH. 800-785-2556
Merric
Bridgeton, MO 314-770-9944
Metal
Columbia, SC 803-776-9252
Metal Master Sales Corp
Glendale Heights, IL. 800-488-8729
Metro Corporation
Wilkes Barre, PA. 800-992-1776
Miami Metal
Miami, FL 305-576-3600
Michigan Maple Block Co
Petoskey, MI 800-447-7975
Midwest Folding Products
Chicago, IL 800-344-2864
Migali Industries
Camden, NJ .800-852-5292
Milvan Food Equipment Manufacturing
Rexdale, ON .416-674-3456
Missouri Equipment
St Louis, MO .800-727-6326

Mity Lite Inc
Orem, UT 800-909-8034
Mlp Seating
Elk Grove Vlg, IL. 800-723-3030
Monroe Extinguisher Co Inc
Rochester, NY. 585-235-3310
Mosshaim Innovations
Jacksonville, FL 888-995-7775
Mouron & Co Inc
Indianapolis, IN 317-243-7955
Mts Seating
Temperance, MI 734-847-3875
National Bar Systems
Huntington Beach, CA 714-848-1688
National FABCO Manufacturing
St Louis, MO. 314-842-4571
Nor-Lake
Hudson, WI. 715-386-2323
Normandie Metal Fabricators
Port Washington, NY 800-221-2398
Northern Stainless Fabricating
Traverse City, MI 231-947-4580
Old Dominion Wood Products
Lynchburg, VA 800-245-6382
Palmer Snyder
Brookfield, WI 800-762-0415
Paramount Manufacturing Company
Wilmington, MA. 978-657-4300
Parisi Inc
Newtown, PA 215-968-6677
Peter Pepper Products Inc
Compton, CA 310-639-0390
Petro Moore Manufacturing Corporation
Long Island City, NY 718-784-2516
Pinnacle Furnishing
Aberdeen, NC. 866-229-5704
Plymold
Kenyon, MN .800-759-6653
PMI Food Equipment Group
Troy, OH 937-332-3000
Pollard Brothers
Chicago, IL 773-763-6868
Prince Seating Corp
Brooklyn, NY 800-577-4623
Quadra-Tech
Columbus, OH 800-443-2766
Quality Seating Co
Youngstown, OH. 800-323-2234
Quipco Products Inc
Sauget, IL 314-993-1442
R.R. Scheibe Company
Newton Center, MA 508-584-4900
Robertson Furniture Co Inc
Toccoa, GA 800-241-0713
Rodo Industries
London, ON .519-668-3711
Rollhaus Seating Products Inc
Long Island City, NY 800-822-6684
Sandler Seating
Atlanta, GA .404-982-9000
Sarasota Restaurant Equipment
Sarasota, FL .800-434-1410
Sauvagnat Inc
Huntersville, NC. 800-258-5619
Seating Concepts Inc
Rockdale, IL .800-421-2036
Sefi Fabricators Inc
Amityville, NY. 631-842-2200
Shafer Commercial Seating
Denver, CO. .303-322-7792
Shammi Industries
Corona, CA .800-417-9260
Sico Inc
Minneapolis, MN 800-328-6138
Silver King Refrigeration Inc
Minneapolis, MN 800-328-3329
Solid Surface Acrylics
North Tonawanda, NY 888-595-4114
St. Louis Stainless Service
St Louis, MO. 800-735-3853
Stainless
La Vergne, TN. 800-877-5177
Stainless Equipment Manufacturing
Dallas, TX. 800-736-2038
Stainless Steel Fabricators
Tyler, TX. 903-595-6625
Starlite Food Service Equipment
Detroit, MI 888-521-6603
Straubel Company
De Pere, WI. .888-336-1412
Super Sturdy
Weldon, NC .800-253-4833

Superior Products Company
Saint Paul, MN 800-328-9800
Supreme Metal
Alpharetta, GA 800-645-2526
Thorpe & Associates
Siler City, NC 919-742-5516
Toronto Fabricating & Manufacturing
Mississauga, ON 905-891-2516
Trimen Foodservice Equipment
North York, ON. 877-437-1422
Trojan Commercial Furni ture Inc.
Montereal, QC 877-271-3878
True Food Service Equipment, Inc.
O Fallon, MO 800-325-6152
U B KLEM Furniture Co Inc
St Anthony, IN 800-264-1995
United Fabricators
Fort Smith, AR 800-235-4101
Universal Stainless
Aurora, CO 800-223-8332
Universal Stainless & Alloy
Titusville, PA 800-295-1909
US Seating Products
Ocala, FL. 800-999-2589
Versailles Lighting
Delray Beach, FL 888-564-0240
Vintage
Jasper, IN 800-992-3491
Vitro Seating Products
St Louis, MO. 800-325-7093
Walsh & Simmons Seating
Saint Louis, MO 800-727-0364
Waymar Industries
Burnsville, MN 888-474-1112
Weiss Sheet Metal Inc
Avon, MA 508-583-8300
West Coast Industries Inc
San Francisco, CA 800-243-3150
West Metals
London, ON 800-300-6667
Wheel Tough Company
Terre Haute, IN 888-765-8833
Wilder Manufacturing Company
Port Jervis, NY 800-832-1319
Wood Goods Industries
Luck, WI. 715-472-2226
Woodard
Coppell, TX 800-877-2290
World Wide Hospitality Furn
Paramount, CA 800-728-8262
Xiaoping Design
New York, NY 800-891-9896
Zol-Mark Industries
Winnipeg, NB 204-943-7393

Display

Altrua Marketing & Design
Tallahassee, FL 800-443-6939
Bmh Equipment Inc
Sacramento, CA 800-350-8828
Cal-Mil Plastic Products Inc
Oceanside, CA 800-321-9069
Dunn Woodworks
Shrewsbury, PA. 877-835-8592
Eskay Metal Fabricating
Buffalo, NY 800-836-8015
Juice Tree
Omaha, NE 714-891-4425
Kehr-Buffalo Wire Frame Co Inc
Buffalo, NY. 800-875-4212
Schmidt Progressive
Lebanon, OH 800-272-3706
Southern Store Fixtures Inc
Bessemer, AL 800-552-6283

Folding

Amtab Manufacturing Corp
Aurora, IL. 800-878-2257
Mity Lite Inc
Orem, UT 800-909-8034
Palmer Snyder
Brookfield, WI 800-762-0415
Rheon USA
Irvine, CA 949-768-1900
Rollhaus Seating Products Inc
Long Island City, NY 800-822-6684
Superior Products Company
Saint Paul, MN 800-328-9800

Room Service

Forbes Industries
Ontario, CA. 909-923-4549
Lakeside Manufacturing Inc
Milwaukee, WI. 888-558-8565

Tote Bags

Eco-Bag Products
Ossining, NY 800-720-2247

Towels

Disposable

Adex Medical Inc
Riverside, CA 800-873-4776
Akron Cotton Products
Akron, OH. 800-899-7173
American Textile Mills Inc
Kansas City, MO. 816-842-2909
Atlantic Mills
Lakewood, NJ 800-242-7374
Best Brands Home Products
New York, NY 212-684-7456
Blue Ridge Converting
Asheville, NC 800-438-3893
Browne & Company
Markham, ON 905-475-6104
C R Mfg
Waverly, NE 877-789-5844
Diamond Wipes Intl Inc
Chino, CA 800-454-1077
Erie Cotton Products
Erie, PA 800-289-4737
Georgia Pacific
Green Bay, WI. 920-435-8821
Healthline Products
Los Angeles, CA. 800-473-4003
IFC Disposables Inc
Brownsville, TN 800-432-9473
Kimberly-Clark Professional
Roswell, GA 800-241-3146
Lexidyne of Pennsylvania
Pittsburgh, PA. 800-543-2233
Mainline Industries Inc
Springfield, MA 800-527-7917
Mednik Wiping Materials Co
St Louis, MO. 800-325-7193
National Towelette
Bensalem, PA 215-245-7300
Nosaj Disposables
Paterson, NJ 800-631-3809
Nu-Towel Co
Kansas City, MO 800-800-7247
Rockline Industries
Sheboygan, WI 800-558-7790
SCA Tissue
Philadelphia, PA 866-722-8675
Superior Linen & Work Wear
Kansas City, MO 800-798-7987
Wipeco Inc
Hillside, IL 708-544-7247

Paper

Bro-Tex Inc
St Paul, MN. 800-328-2282
Diamond Wipes Intl Inc
Chino, CA 800-454-1077
Erie Cotton Products
Erie, PA 800-289-4737
Georgia Pacific
Green Bay, WI. 920-435-8821
Goodman Wiper & Paper Co
Auburn, ME 207-784-5779
K & L Intl
Ontario, CA. 888-598-5588
Kentfield's
Greenbrae, CA 888-461-7454
Kimberly-Clark Corporation
Irving, TX 972-281-1200
Marcal Paper Mills
Elmwood Park, NJ 800-631-8451
Mednik Wiping Materials Co
St Louis, MO. 800-325-7193
Nice-Pak Products Inc
Orangeburg, NY 800-444-6725
Nosaj Disposables
Paterson, NJ 800-631-3809

Potlatch Corp
Spokane, WA. 509-835-1500
SCA Hygiene Paper
San Ramon, CA 800-992-8675
SCA Tissue
Philadelphia, PA 866-722-8675
SCA Tissue North America
S Glens Falls, NY 518-743-0240
Sorg Paper Company
Middletown, OH 513-420-5300
United Textile Distribution
Garner, NC 800-262-7624
Wipeco Inc
Hillside, IL 708-544-7247

Trays

Butchers'

Buckhorn Inc
Milford, OH 800-543-4454
COW Industries Inc
Columbus, OH 800-542-9353
Quality Industries Inc
La Vergne, TN 615-793-3000
Tenneco Specialty Packaging
Smyrna, GA 800-241-4402

Cafeteria

Browne & Company
Markham, ON 905-475-6104
Carlisle Food Svc Products Inc
Oklahoma City, OK 800-654-8210
Central Fine Pack Inc
Fort Wayne, IN 260-432-3027
Hoffmaster Group Inc.
Oshkosh, WI 800-558-9300
Innovative Plastics Corp
Orangeburg, NY 845-359-7500
Kendrick Johnson & Assoc Inc
Minneapolis, MN 800-826-1271
Lincoln Foodservice
Cleveland, OH 800-374-3004
Polar Ware Company
Sheboygan, WI 800-237-3655
Prolon
Port Gibson, MS 888-480-9828
Superior Products Company
Saint Paul, MN 800-328-9800
Traex
Dane, WI. 800-356-8006
Wiltec
Leominster, MA 978-537-1497
Xtreme Beverages, LLC
Dana Point, CA. 949-495-7929

Food

Advance Engineering Co
Canton, MI 800-497-6388
Advanced Plastic Coating Svc
Parsons, KS 620-421-1660
ALCO Designs
Gardena, CA 800-228-2346
Allied Metal Spinning
Bronx, NY 800-615-2266
Ample Industries
Franklin, OH 888-818-9700
Art Wire Works Co
Chicago, IL 708-458-3993
Automatic Specialties Inc
Marlborough, MA 800-445-2370
Bakers Choice Products
Beacon Falls, CT. 203-720-1000
Bardes Plastics Inc
Milwaukee, WI. 800-558-5161
Brooklace
Oshkosh, WI 800-572-4552
Browne & Company
Markham, ON 905-475-6104
Buckhorn Inc
Milford, OH 800-543-4454
Cal-Mil Plastic Products Inc
Oceanside, CA 800-321-9069
Canada Goose Wood Produc
Gloucester, ON 888-890-6506
Carlisle Food Svc Products Inc
Oklahoma City, OK 800-654-8210
Delfin Design & Mfg
Rancho Sta Marg, CA. 800-354-7919

Designers Folding Box Corp
Buffalo, NY 716-853-5141
Detroit Forming
Southfield, MI 248-440-1317
Display Tray
Mont-Royal, QC 800-782-8861
Dynynstyl
Delray Beach, FL 800-774-7895
Eastern Tabletop Mfg
Brooklyn, NY 888-422-4142
Ellingers Agatized Wood Inc
Sheboygan, WI 888-287-8906
Engineered Plastics Inc
Gibsonville, NC 800-711-1740
Esterle Mold & Machine Co Inc
Stow, OH 800-411-4086
Ex-Cell KAISER LLC
Franklin Park, IL 847-451-0451
Foam Packaging Inc
Vicksburg, MS 800-962-2655
Fold-Pak South
Columbus, GA 706-689-2924
Handy Wacks Corp
Sparta, MI 800-445-4434
Hoffmaster Group Inc.
Oshkosh, WI 800-558-9300
K & I Creative Plastics & Wood
Jacksonville, FL 904-387-0438
K & L Intl
Ontario, CA 888-598-5588
Kay Home Products Inc
Antioch, IL 800-600-7009
Kendrick Johnson & Assoc Inc
Minneapolis, MN 800-826-1271
Key Packaging Co
Sarasota, FL 941-355-2728
Lakeside Manufacturing Inc
Milwaukee, WI 888-558-8565
Lancaster Colony Corporation
Westerville, OH. 614-224-7141
Lin Pac Plastics
Roswell, GA 770-751-6006
Newell Brands
Atlanta, GA
Olive Can Company
Elgin, IL 847-468-7474
Par-Pak
Houston, TX 888-727-7252
Pinn Pack Packaging LLC
Oxnard, CA 805-385-4100
Plastiques Cascades Group
Montreal, QC 888-703-6515
Plastocon
Oconomowoc, WI. 800-966-0103
Polar Ware Company
Sheboygan, WI 800-237-3655
Premier
Cincinnati, OH 800-354-9817
Process Displays
New Berlin, WI. 800-533-1764
Promens
St. John, NB 800-295-3725
R.R. Scheibe Company
Newton Center, MA 508-584-4900
Sani-Top Products
De Leon Springs, FL. 800-874-6094
Spin-Tech Corporation
Hoboken, NJ 800-977-4692
SQP
Schenectady, NY 800-724-1129
Sterling Paper Company
Ohio, PA 800-282-1124
Stock America Inc
Grafton, WI. 262-375-4100
Superior Products Company
Saint Paul, MN 800-328-9800
Tenneco Inc
Lake Forest, IL 800-403-3393
Tenneco Specialty Packaging
Smyrna, GA 800-241-4402
Toscarora
Sandusky, OH 419-625-7343
Traex
Dane, WI. 800-356-8006
Traitech Industries
Vaughan, ON. 877-872-4835
Unique Plastics
Rio Rico, AZ 800-658-5946
Vermillion Flooring
Springfield, MO 417-862-3785
Westervelt Co Inc
Tuscaloosa, AL 205-562-5000

Wiltec
Leominster, MA 978-537-1497
WNA Hopple Plastics
Florence, KY. 800-446-4622
Xtreme Beverages, LLC
Dana Point, CA. 949-495-7929

Glass

Browne & Company
Markham, ON 905-475-6104
Superior Products Company
Saint Paul, MN 800-328-9800
World Kitchen
Elmira, NY 800-999-3436

Plastic

ACO
Moore, OK 405-794-7662
Advance Engineering Co
Canton, MI 800-497-6388
Aeromat Plastics Inc
Burnsville, MN 888-286-8729
Anchor Packaging
Ballwin, MO 800-467-3900
Arthur Corporation
Huron, OH. 419-433-7202
Bardes Plastics Inc
Milwaukee, WI 800-558-5161
Barrette Outdoor Living
Cleveland, OH 800-336-2383
Buckhorn Inc
Milford, OH 800-543-4454
C R Mfg
Waverly, NE 877-789-5844
Cambro Manufacturing Co
Huntington Beach, CA 800-833-3003
Carlisle Food Svc Products Inc
Oklahoma City, OK 800-654-8210
Cash Caddy
Palm Desert, CA. 888-522-2221
Central Fine Pack Inc
Fort Wayne, IN 260-432-3027
Creative Forming
Ripon, WI 920-748-7285
Crespac Incorporated
Tucker, GA 800-438-1900
Custom Molders
Rocky Mount, NC 919-688-8061
Dart Container Corp.
Mason, MI. 800-248-5960
De Ster Corporation
Atlanta, GA. 800-237-8270
DEL-Tec Packaging Inc
Greer, SC. 800-747-8683
Delfin Design & Mfg
Rancho Sta Marg, CA. 800-354-7919
Design Specialties Inc
Hamden, CT 800-999-1584
Detroit Forming
Southfield, MI. 248-440-1317
Display Tray
Mont-Royal, QC 800-782-8861
Douglas Stephen Plastics Inc
Paterson, NJ 973-523-3030
Edco Industries
Bridgeport, CT 203-333-8982
Engineered Plastics Inc
Gibsonville, NC 800-711-1740
Esterle Mold & Machine Co Inc
Stow, OH. 800-411-4086
Fato Industries
Kankakee, IL. 815-932-3015
Gateway Plastics Inc
Mequon, WI 262-242-2020
Gessner Products
Ambler, PA 800-874-7808
Hal-One Plastics
Olathe, KS. 800-626-5784
Hoffmaster Group Inc.
Oshkosh, WI. 800-558-9300
HPI North America/   Plastics
Eagan, MN 800-752-7462
Imperial Plastics Inc
Lakeville, MN. 952-469-4951
Inline Plastic Corp
McDonough, GA 678-466-3467
Innovative Plastics Corp
Orangeburg, NY 845-359-7500
IVEX Packaging Corporation
Longueuil, QC 450-651-8887

Kendrick Johnson & Assoc Inc
Minneapolis, MN 800-826-1271
Kenro
Fredonia, WI 262-692-2411
Key Packaging Co
Sarasota, FL 941-355-2728
Majestic
Bridgeport, CT 203-367-7900
Mr Ice Bucket
New Brunswick, NJ 732-545-0420
Novelty Crystal
Long Island City, NY 800-622-0250
Nu-Trend Plastics Thermoformer
Jacksonville, FL 904-353-5936
Orbis Corp.
Rexdale, ON 800-890-7292
Penda Form Corp
New Concord, OH 800-837-2574
Plastech Corp
Atlanta, GA. 404-355-9682
Plaxall Inc
Long Island City, NY 800-876-5706
Prolon
Port Gibson, MS 888-480-9828
Promens
St. John, NB 800-295-3725
Robinson Industries Inc
Coleman, MI 989-465-6111
Rolland Machining & Fabricating
Moneta, VA 973-827-6911
Sani-Top Products
De Leon Springs, FL 800-874-6094
Snapware
Fullerton, CA 800-334-3062
Spirit Foodservice, Inc.
Andover, MA 800-343-0996
Stock America Inc
Grafton, WI 262-375-4100
Techform
Mount Airy, NC 336-789-2115
TEMP-TECH Company
Springfield, MA 800-343-5579
Thermodynamics
Commerce City, CO 800-627-9037
Toscarora
Sandusky, OH 419-625-7343
Tray-Pak Corp
Reading, PA 610-926-5800
Tri-State Plastics
Glenwillard, PA. 724-457-6900
Tulip Molded Plastics Corp
Milwaukee, WI 414-963-3120
Unique Plastics
Rio Rico, AZ 800-658-5946
Wilks Precision Instr Co Inc
Union Bridge, MD 410-775-7917
Wiltec
Leominster, MA 978-537-1497
WNA Hopple Plastics
Florence, KY. 800-446-4622
Zeier Plastic & Mfg Inc
Madison, WI 608-244-5782

Urns

Coffee & Tea

BG Industries
Lemont, IL 800-800-5761
Bon Chef
Lafayette, NJ. 800-331-0177
Bunn-O-Matic Corp
Springfield, IL. 800-352-2866
Eastern Tabletop Mfg
Brooklyn, NY 888-422-4142
Grindmaster-Cecilware Corp
Louisville, KY 800-695-4500
Kelmin Products
Plymouth, FL 407-886-6079
Lancaster Colony Corporation
Westerville, OH. 614-224-7141
Lazy Man Inc
Belvidere, NJ 800-475-1950
Red Diamond Coffee & Tea
Moody, AL 800-292-4651
Regal Ware Inc
Kewaskum, WI 262-626-2121
Rexcraft Fine Chafers
Long Island City, NY 888-739-2723
Sheffield Platers Inc
San Diego, CA 800-227-9242

T.J. Topper Company
Redwood City, CA 650-365-6962
Wells Manufacturing Company
St. Louis, MO 888-356-5362
World Kitchen
Elmira, NY 800-999-3436
Xtreme Beverages, LLC
Dana Point, CA 949-495-7929

Utensils

Foodservice Preparation

Abond Plastic Corporation
Lachine, QC 800-886-7947
Ace Fabrication
Mobile, AL 251-478-0401
All Southern Fabricators
Clearwater, FL 800-878-2732
Amco Metals Indl
City of Industry, CA 626-855-2550
American Metal Stamping
Brooklyn, NY 718-384-1500
Browne & Company
Markham, ON 905-475-6104
C R Mfg
Waverly, NE 877-789-5844
Carlisle Food Svc Products Inc
Oklahoma City, OK 800-654-8210
Chef Revival
North Charleston, SC 800-248-9826
Chef Specialties
Smethport, PA 800-440-2433
Chuppa Knife Manufacturing
Jackson, TN 731-424-1212
Crestware
North Salt Lake, UT 800-345-0513
Cugar Machine Co
Fort Worth, TX 817-927-0411
Cutrite Company
Fremont, OH 800-928-8748
Cyclamen Collection
Oakland, CA 510-434-7620
Delco Tableware
Port Washington, NY 800-221-9557
Dur-Able Aluminum Corporation
Hoffman Estates, IL 847-843-1100
E-Z Dip
Frankfort, IN 866-347-3279
E-Z Edge Inc
West New York, NJ 800-232-4470
Eagleware Manufacturing
Compton, CA 310-604-0404
Edge Resources
Hopedale, MA 888-849-0998
Edgecraft Corp
Avondale, PA 800-342-3255
Ellingers Agatized Wood Inc
Sheboygan, WI 888-287-8906
Fab-X/Metals
Washington, NC 800-677-3229
Fioriware
Zanesville, OH 740-454-7400
Fortune Products Inc
Cedar Park, TX 512-249-0334
Franke Americas
Hatfield, PA 215-822-6590
Gerber Legendary Blades
Portland, OR 800-950-6161
Goebel Fixture Co
Hutchinson, MN 888-339-0509
Good Idea
Northampton, MA 800-462-9237
Goodell Tools
New Hope, MN 800-542-3906
Grand Silver Company
Bronx, NY 718-585-1930
Greensburg Manufacturing Company
Greensburg, KY 270-932-5511
H. Arnold Wood Turning
Tarrytown, NY 888-314-0088
Hank Rivera Associates
Dearborn, MI 313-581-8300
Hantover Inc
Kansas City, MO 800-821-7849
Hodges
Vienna, IL 800-444-0011
Hollingsworth Custom Wood Products
Sault Ste. Marie, ON. 705-759-1756
Imperial Schrade Corporation
Ellenville, NY 212-210-8600

Industrial Razorblade
Orange, NJ 973-673-4286
John Boos & Co
Effingham, IL 888-431-2667
John J. Adams Die Corporation
Worcester, MA 508-757-3894
Keen Kutter
Torrance, CA 310-370-6941
Kosempel Manufacturing Company
Philadelphia, PA 800-733-7122
KTG
Cincinnati, OH 888-533-6900
Lady Mary
Rockingham, NC 910-997-7321
Lamson & Goodnow
Shelburne Falls, MA. 800-872-6564
Leggett & Platt Storage
Vernon Hills, IL 847-816-6246
Leon Bush Manufacturer
Glenview, IL 847-657-8888
Lillsun Manufacturing Co
Huntington, IN 260-356-6514
Lodge Manufacturing Company
South Pittsburg, TN 423-837-5919
LoTech Industries
Lakewood, CO 800-295-0199
M & E Mfg Co Inc
Kingston, NY 845-331-2110
Matfer Inc
Van Nuys, CA 800-766-0333
Mill-Rose Co
Mentor, OH 800-321-3598
Mosshaim Innovations
Jacksonville, FL 888-995-7775
Mouli Manufacturing Corporation
Belleville, NJ 800-789-8285
Mulligan Associates
Mequon, WI 800-627-2886
Mundial
Norwood, MA. 800-487-2224
National Novelty Brush Co
Lancaster, PA 717-299-5681
Nemco Food Equipment
Hicksville, OH 800-782-6761
Novelty Crystal
Long Island City, NY 800-622-0250
Olde Thompson Inc
Oxnard, CA. 800-827-1565
Pepper Mill
Mobile, AL 800-669-5175
Polar Ware Company
Sheboygan, WI 800-237-3655
Proluxe
Paramount, CA 800-594-5528
R H Saw Corp
Barrington, IL 847-381-8777
R Murphy Co Inc
Ayer, MA. 888-772-3481
R X Honing Machine Corp
Mishawaka, IN 800-346-6464
Read Products Inc
Seattle, WA 800-445-3416
Royal Paper Products
Coatesville, PA 800-666-6655
Samuel Underberg Food Store
Brooklyn, NY 718-363-0787
Slicechief Co
Toledo, OH 419-241-7647
Spartec Plastics
Conneaut, OH 800-325-5176
Sturdi-Bilt Restaurant Equipment
Whitmore Lake, MI 800-521-2895
Superior Products Company
Saint Paul, MN 800-328-9800
T & A Metal Products Inc
Deptford, NJ 856-227-1700
T & S Perfection Chain Prods
Cullman, AL 888-856-4864
Tablecraft Products Co Inc
Gurnee, IL 800-323-8321
Thorpe Rolling Pin Co
Hamden, CT 800-344-6966
Toronto Kitchen Equipment
North York, ON. 416-745-4944
Townfood Equipment Corp
Brooklyn, NY 800-221-5032
Update International
Vernon, CA. 800-747-7124
Varimixer North America
Charlotte, NC 800-221-1138
Vermillion Flooring
Springfield, MO 417-862-3785

Vita Craft Corp
Shawnee, KS 800-359-3444
Vollrath Co LLC
Sheboygan, WI 800-624-2051
Wilton Armetale
Mt Joy, PA 800-779-4586
Wishbone Utensil Tableware Line
Wheat Ridge, CO 866-266-5928
Zeroll Company
Fort Pierce, FL 800-872-5000

Plastic

Action Technology
Prussia, PA 217-935-8311
BOC Plastics Inc
Winston Salem, NC. 800-334-8687
C R Mfg
Waverly, NE 877-789-5844
Carlisle Food Svc Products Inc
Oklahoma City, OK 800-654-8210
Chinet Company
Laguna Niguel, CA 949-348-1711
Dart Canada Inc.
Toronto, ON 800-465-9696
Design Specialties Inc
Hamden, CT 800-999-1584
Dispoz-O Plastics
Fountain Inn, SC 864-862-4004
First Plastics Co Inc
Leominster, MA 978-840-6908
Hal-One Plastics
Olathe, KS. 800-626-5784
Harold Leonard Southwest Corporation
Houston, TX 800-245-8105
Hoffmaster Group Inc
Oshkosh, WI 800-367-2877
HPI North America/Plastics
Chicago, IL 800-327-3534
James River Canada
North York, ON. 416-789-5151
Jarden Home Brands
Daleville, IN 800-392-2575
Jet Plastica Industries
Hatfield, PA
Jones-Zylon Co
West Lafayette, OH. 800-848-8160
LoTech Industries
Lakewood, CO 800-295-0199
Max Packaging
Attalla, AL 800-543-5369
Measurex/S&L Plastics
Nazareth, PA 800-752-0650
Novelty Crystal
Long Island City, NY 800-622-0250
Nyman Manufacturing Company
Rumford, RI 401-438-3410
Olde Thompson Inc
Oxnard, CA. 800-827-1565
OWD
Tupper Lake, NY 800-836-1693
Penley Corporation
West Paris, ME 800-368-6449
Polar Plastics
St Laurent, QC 514-331-0207
Prairie Packaging Inc
Mooresville, NC 704-660-6600
R H Saw Corp
Barrington, IL 847-381-8777
Spir-It/Zoo Piks
Andover, MA 800-343-0996
Tenneco Specialty Packaging
Smyrna, GA 800-241-4402
Waddington North America
Chelmsford, MA. 888-962-2877
Wiltec
Leominster, MA 978-537-1497
Wishbone Utensil Tableware Line
Wheat Ridge, CO 866-266-5928
WNA
Chattanooga, TN. 800-404-9318

Vending Carts

All Star Carts & Vehicles
Bay Shore, NY 800-831-3166
All State Fabricators Corporation
Tampa, FL. 800-322-9925
Alliance Products LLC
Murfreesboro, TN. 800-522-3973
Alto-Shaam
Menomonee Falls, WI. 800-329-8744

Amco Metals Indl
  City of Industry, CA 626-855-2550
ARC Specialties
  Valencia, CA 661-775-8500
Automated Food Systems
  Waxahachie, TX 469-517-0470
BBQ Pits by Klose
  Houston, TX 800-487-7487
Corsair Display Systems
  Canandalgua, NY 800-347-5245
Custom Sales & Svc Inc
  Hammonton, NJ 800-257-7855
Eskay Metal Fabricating
  Buffalo, NY 800-836-8015
Hackney Brothers
  Washington, NC 800-763-0700
Hot Food Boxes
  Mooresville, IN 800-733-8073
Hotshot Delivery System
  Bloomingdale, IL 630-924-8817
International Thermal Dispensers
  Boston, MA 617-239-3600
Lakeside Manufacturing Inc
  Milwaukee, WI 888-558-8565
Leggett & Platt Storage
  Vernon Hills, IL 847-816-6246
Magnum Custom Trailer & BBQ Pits
  Austin, TX 800-662-4686
Merchandising Frontiers Inc
  Winterset, IA 800-421-2278
Metal Master Sales Corp
  Glendale Heights, IL 800-488-8729
Michaelo Espresso
  Seattle, WA 800-545-2883
Moseley Realty LLC
  Franklin, MA 800-667-3539
Paragon International
  Nevada, IA 800-433-0333
Prestige Metal Products Inc
  Antioch, IL 847-395-0775
Proluxe
  Paramount, CA 800-594-5528
Southern Express
  Saint Louis, MO 800-444-9157
Steamway Corporation
  Scottsburg, IN 800-259-8171
Super Sturdy
  Weldon, NC 800-253-4833
Super-Chef Manufacturing Company
  Houston, TX 800-231-3478
Supreme Products
  Waco, TX 254-799-4941
The Carriage Works
  Klamath Falls, OR 541-882-0700
Tooterville Trolley Company
  Newburgh, IN 812-858-8585
Vollrath Co LLC
  Sheboygan, WI 800-624-2051
Wag Industries
  Skokie, IL 800-621-3305
Worksman 800 Buy Cart
  Ozone Park, NY 800-289-2278

Vending Machinery

Reverse

Can & Bottle Systems, Inc.
  Milwaukie, OR 866-302-2636
Environmental Products Corp
  Naugatuck, CT 800-275-3861

Warmers

Dish & Plate

Bloomfield Industries
  St. Louis, MO 888-356-5362
Convay Systems
  Minnetonka, MN 800-334-1099
Cyclamen Collection
  Oakland, CA 510-434-7620
Kelmin Products
  Plymouth, FL 407-886-6079
Mastex Industries
  Petersburg, VA 804-732-8300
Metro Corporation
  Wilkes Barre, PA. 800-992-1776
Monroe Extinguisher Co Inc
  Rochester, NY 585-235-3310
Super-Chef Manufacturing Company
  Houston, TX 800-231-3478
Wells Manufacturing Company
  St. Louis, MO 888-356-5362

Food

Aroma Manufacturing Company
  San Diego, CA 800-276-6286
BG Industries
  Lemont, IL 800-800-5761
BKI Worldwide
  Simpsonville, SC 800-927-6887
Bon Chef
  Lafayette, NJ 800-331-0177
Broaster Co LLC
  Beloit, WI 800-365-8278
Canadian Display Systems
  Concord, ON 800-895-5862
Cres Cor
  Mentor, OH 877-273-7267
Crispy Lite
  St. Louis, MO 888-356-5362
D'Lights
  Glendale, CA 818-956-5656
Deluxe Equipment Company
  Bradenton, FL 800-367-8931
Duke Manufacturing Co
  St Louis, MO. 800-735-3853
Dynynstyl
  Delray Beach, FL 800-774-7895
Eagle Foodservice   Equipment
  Clayton, DE. 800-441-8440
Eagle Group
  Clayton, DE. 800-441-8440
Esquire Mechanical Corp.
  Armonk, NY 800-847-4206
Garland Commercial Ranges
  Mississauga, ON 905-624-0260
Gold Medal Products Co
  Cincinnati, OH 800-543-0862
Hatco Corp
  Milwaukee, WI 800-558-0607
Henny Penny, Inc.
  Eaton, OH 800-417-8417
Hot Food Boxes
  Mooresville, IN 800-733-8073
InfraTech Corporation
  Azusa, CA. 800-955-2476
Keating of Chicago Inc
  Mc Cook, IL 800-532-8464
Lincoln Foodservice
  Cleveland, OH 800-374-3004

Merco/Savory
  Mt. Pleasant, MI 800-733-8821
Metro Corporation
  Wilkes Barre, PA. 800-992-1776
Middleby Marshall Inc
  Elgin, IL 847-741-3300
Mies Products
  West Bend, WI 800-480-6437
Monroe Extinguisher Co Inc
  Rochester, NY. 585-235-3310
Mosshaim Innovations
  Jacksonville, FL 888-995-7775
Prince Castle Inc
  Carol Stream, IL 800-722-7853
Remco Industries International
  Fort Lauderdale, FL 800-987-3626
Rexcraft Fine Chafers
  Long Island City, NY 888-739-2723
Server Products Inc
  Richfield, WI 800-558-8722
Sico Inc
  Minneapolis, MN 800-328-6138
Southern Pride Distributing
  Alamo, TN 800-851-8180
Star Manufacturing Intl Inc
  St Louis, MO. 800-264-7827
Super-Chef Manufacturing Company
  Houston, TX 800-231-3478
Tomlinson Industries
  Cleveland, OH 800-945-4589
Ultrafryer Systems Inc
  San Antonio, TX. 800-545-9189
Vulcan Food Equipment Group
  Baltimore, MD 800-814-2028
Welbilt Corporation
  Stamford, CT. 203-325-8300
Wells Manufacturing Company
  St. Louis, MO 888-356-5362
Wilder Manufacturing Company
  Port Jervis, NY 800-832-1319
Win-Holt Equipment Group
  Syosset, NY. 800-444-3595
Wisco Industries Assembly
  Oregon, WI 800-999-4726
Zoia Banquetier Co
  Cleveland, OH 216-631-6414

Wood Grain Plastic

Chips

Hopp Co Inc
  New Hyde Park, NY 800-889-8425

Shelf Covers

Hopp Co Inc
  New Hyde Park, NY 800-889-8425

Strips

Hopp Co Inc
  New Hyde Park, NY 800-889-8425

Instrumentation & Laboratory Equipment

Analyzers

Entech Instruments Inc.
Simi Valley, CA 805-527-5939

Amino Acid, Nitrogen

Bran & Luebbe
Schaumburg, IL. 847-882-8116
Petroleum Analyzer Co LP
Houston, TX 800-444-8378

Ethyl Alcohol

Greer's Ferry Glass Work
Dubuque, IA 501-589-2947
NDC Infrared EngineeringInc
Irwindale, CA 626-960-3300
YSI Inc
Yellow Springs, OH 800-765-4974

Fats, Oils

Ashcroft Inc
Stratford, CT 800-328-8258
Bran & Luebbe
Schaumburg, IL. 847-882-8116
CEM Corporation
Matthews, NC 800-726-3331
Columbus Instruments
Columbus, OH 800-669-5011
Foss Nirsystems
Silver Spring, MD. 301-755-5200
Industrial Laboratories Co
Wheat Ridge, CO 800-456-5288
Libra Technical Center
Metuchen, NJ 732-321-5200
NDC Infrared EngineeringInc
Irwindale, CA 626-960-3300
Univex Corp
Salem, NH. 800-258-6358

Fiber, Starch

Supelco Inc
Bellefonte, PA. 800-247-6628
Texture Technologies Corporation
Scarsdale, NY 914-472-0531

Mycotoxins

R-Biopharm Inc
Washington, MO. 269-789-3033
Supelco Inc
Bellefonte, PA. 800-247-6628
VICAM
Milford, MA 800-338-4381

Nitrites, Nitrosamines

Supelco Inc
Bellefonte, PA. 800-247-6628

Organic Acids

YSI Inc
Yellow Springs, OH 800-765-4974

Pesticide Residue, Antibiotics

Charm Sciences Inc
Lawrence, MA 978-687-9200
R-Biopharm Inc
Washington, MO. 269-789-3033
Supelco Inc
Bellefonte, PA. 800-247-6628

Salt (Sodium Chloride)

Ashcroft Inc
Stratford, CT 800-328-8258
Greer's Ferry Glass Work
Dubuque, IA 501-589-2947
Hanna Instruments
Woonsocket, RI. 800-426-6287
Newport Electronics Inc
Santa Ana, CA 800-639-7678

Q A Supplies LLC
Norfolk, VA. 800-472-7205

Sugars (Dextrose, Fructose, Galactose, Lactose, Su

Foss Nirsystems
Silver Spring, MD. 301-755-5200
Greer's Ferry Glass Work
Dubuque, IA 501-589-2947
MISCO Refractometer
Cleveland, OH 866-831-1999
YSI Inc
Yellow Springs, OH 800-765-4974

Vitamin

Industrial Laboratories Co
Wheat Ridge, CO 800-456-5288

Water Activity

Arizona Instrument LLC
Chandler, AZ. 800-528-7411
Astro/Polymetron Zellweger
League City, TX 281-332-2484
Biopath
West Palm Beach, FL 800-645-2302
Burkert Fluid Control
Irvine, CA 800-325-1405
CEM Corporation
Matthews, NC 800-726-3331
Chemetrics Inc
Midland, VA 800-356-3072
CSC Scientific Co Inc
Fairfax, VA 800-621-4778
Forte Technology
South Easton, MA 508-297-2363
Foss Nirsystems
Silver Spring, MD. 301-755-5200
Machine Applications Corp
Sandusky, OH 419-621-2322
Mocon Inc
Minneapolis, MN 763-493-7229
NDC Infrared EngineeringInc
Irwindale, CA 626-960-3300
Onset Computer Corp
Bourne, MA 800-564-4377
Orion Research
Beverly, MA 978-232-6000
Precision Systems Inc
Natick, MA 508-655-7010
Rosemount Analytical Inc
Irvine, CA 800-543-8257
Rotronic Instrument Corp Inc
Hauppauge, NY 800-628-7101
Severn Trent Svc
Colmar, PA 215-822-2901
Suburban Laboratories Inc
Geneva, IL. 800-783-5227
Thermo Detection
Franklin, MA 866-269-0070
Troxler Electronic Lab Inc
Durham, NC 877-876-9537

Automation

Unit, Packaging, Bulk Handling

Andgar Corp
Ferndale, WA 360-366-9900
Barclay & Assoc PC
Ames, IA 515-292-3023
California Vibratory Feeders
Anaheim, CA 800-354-0972
Falco Technologies
La Prairie, QC. 450-444-0566
Hampton-Tilley Associates
Chesterfield, MO 813-418-3340
Jacobs Engineering Group
Dallas, TX. 214-638-0145
Lockwood Greene Engineers
Knoxville, TN. 251-476-2400
Lockwood Greene Engineers
Knoxville, TN. 256-533-9907

Lockwood Greene Engineers
Brentwood, TN 615-221-5031
Lockwood Greene Engineers
Augusta, GA 706-724-8225
Lockwood Greene Engineers
Somerset, NJ 732-560-5700
Lockwood Greene Engineers
Atlanta, GA 770-829-6500
Lockwood Greene Engineers
Guaynabo, PR. 787-781-9050
Lockwood Greene Engineers
Knoxville, TN. 865-218-5377
Lockwood Greene Engineers
Dallas, TX. 972-991-5505
Lockwood Greene Technologies
Augusta, GA 505-889-3831
Priority One Packaging
Waterloo, ON 800-387-9102
Schroeder Machine
San Marcos, CA 760-591-9733
Stock America Inc
Grafton, WI. 262-375-4100
Vande Berg SCALES/Vbs Inc
Sioux Center, IA 712-722-1181
Washington Frontier
Grandview, WA. 509-469-7662

Balances

Laboratory

A&D Weighing
San Jose, CA 800-726-3364
Denver Instrument Company
Bohemia, NY 800-321-1135
Fairbanks Scales
Overland Park, KS 800-451-4107
Precision Solutions Inc
Quakertown, PA 215-536-4400
Q A Supplies LLC
Norfolk, VA. 800-472-7205
Sartorius Corp
Edgewood, NY 800-635-2906
Vande Berg SCALES/Vbs Inc
Sioux Center, IA 712-722-1181
Vertex Interactive
Clifton, NJ. 973-777-3500
Wilkens-Anderson Co
Chicago, IL 800-847-2222

Centrifuges

Alfa Laval Inc
Richmond, VA. 866-253-2528
Ampco Pumps Co Inc
Milwaukee, WI. 800-737-8671
Baker Hughes
Houston, TX
C&R Refrigation Inc,
Center, TX. 800-438-6182
Cameron Intl. Corp.
Houston, TX 281-285-4376
Centrisys
Kenosha, WI 262-654-6006
Commercial Manufacturing
Fresno, CA 559-237-1855
Dedert Corporation
Olympia Fields, IL 708-747-7000
International Machinery Xchnge
Deerfield, WI 800-279-0191
International Reserve Equipment Corporation
Clarendon Hills, IL. 708-531-0680
Pacer Pumps
Lancaster, PA 800-233-3861
Pacific Process Technology
La Jolla, CA 858-551-3298
Pro Scientific Inc
Oxford, CT 800-584-3776
Ross Cook
Silver Spring, MD. 800-233-7339
Separators Inc
Indianapolis, IN 800-233-9022
Silver Weibull
Aurora, CO 303-373-2311
Tecumseh Products Co.
Ann Arbor, MI 734-585-9500

Tema Systems Inc
Cincinnati, OH 513-792-2840

Certification

Food

International Kosher Supervision
Keller, TX 817-337-4700
KOF-K Kosher Supervision
Teaneck, NJ 201-837-0500
Lloyd's Register QualityAssurance
Houston, TX 888-877-8001
Ok Kosher Certification
Brooklyn, NY 718-756-7500
Orthodox Union
New York, NY 212-563-4000
Star-K Kosher Certification
Baltimore, MD 410-484-4110

Chemicals

Laboratory

Advance Energy Technologies
Halfmoon, NY 800-724-0198
CFS North America
Urbandale, IA 844-808-2063
Exaxol Chemical Corp
Clearwater, FL 800-739-2965
Fisher Scientific Company
Pittsburgh, PA 412-490-8300
Ricca Chemical Co
Batesville, IN 888-467-4222
S & J Laboratories Inc
Portage, MI 269-324-7383
Solvox Manufacturing Company
Milwaukee, WI 414-774-5664
Wilkens-Anderson Co
Chicago, IL 800-847-2222

Controls

Automation & Controls

Dennsi Group
Springfield, MA 413-737-1353
Eaton Electrical Sector
Moon Township, PA 877-386-2273
M G Newell Corp
Greensboro, NC 800-334-0231
Red Lion Controls Inc
York, PA 717-767-6511
SICK Inc
Bloomington, MN........... 800-325-7425
Sterling Electric Inc
Indianapolis, IN 800-654-6220

Boiler & Steam

Acme Control Svc Inc
Chicago, IL 800-621-6427
Heatrex
Meadville, PA 800-394-6589
Paxton Corp
Bristol, RI 401-396-9062
Sellers Engineering Division
Danville, KY................ 859-236-3181
Vega Americas Inc
Cincinnati, OH 800-367-5383
Washington Frontier
Grandview, WA 509-469-7662

Clean-In-Place

A & B Process Systems Corp
Stratford, WI 888-258-2789
Ashcroft Inc
Stratford, CT............... 800-328-8258
Debelak Technical Systems
Greenville, WI 800-888-4207
Electrol Specialties Co
South Beloit, IL 815-389-2291
Lake Process Systems Inc
Lake Barrington, IL 800-331-9260
Letrah International Corp
Fort Atkinson, WI.......... 920-563-6597
Northland Process Piping
Isle, MN 320-679-2119
Papertech
North Vancouver, BC 877-787-2737

Scherping Systems
Winsted, MN 320-485-4401
Stainless Products
Somers, WC 800-558-9446
Sterling Process Engineering
Columbus, OH 800-783-7875
West Agro
Kansas City, MO............. 816-891-7700

Level, Liquid & Dry

A & B Process Systems Corp
Stratford, WI 888-258-2789
Anderson-Negele
Fultonville, NY 800-833-0081
ASI Electronics Inc
Cypress, TX 800-231-6066
Azbar Plus
Qu,bec, QC 418-687-3672
Banner Engineering Corp
Minneapolis, MN 888-373-6767
Berthold Technologies
Oak Ridge, TN 865-483-1488
Clean Water Systems
Klamath Falls, OR 866-273-9993
Conveyor Components Co
Croswell, MI 800-233-3233
Crown Controls Inc.
Charlotte, NC 800-541-7874
Distaview Corp
Bowling Green, OH 800-795-9970
Gems Sensors & Controls
Plainville, CT 860-747-3000
Heuft USA Inc
Downers Grove, IL 630-968-9011
Honeywell Sensing & Internet of Things
DE 800-537-6945
Infitec Inc
East Syracuse, NY 800-334-0837
Innovative Components
Southington, CT 800-789-2851
Intelligent Controls
Saco, ME 800-872-3455
King Engineering - King-Gage
Newell, WV 800-242-8871
Knight Equipment International
Lake Forest, CA 800-854-3764
Letrah International Corp
Fort Atkinson, WI.......... 920-563-6597
Liquid Scale
New Brighton, MN 888-633-2969
Lumenite Control Tech Inc
Franklin Park, IL 800-323-8510
Peco Controls Corporation
Modesto, CA 800-732-6285
SICK Inc
Bloomington, MN........... 800-325-7425
Tokheim Co
Marion, IA................. 800-747-3442
Vega Americas Inc
Cincinnati, OH 800-367-5383
Washington Frontier
Grandview, WA 509-469-7662

Microprocessor

GEA Refrigeration North America
York, PA 800-888-4337

Numerical

American Autogard Corporation
Rockford, IL 815-229-3190
Candy Manufacturing Co
Niles, IL 847-588-2639
ENM Co
Chicago, IL 773-775-8400

Packaging Line

Alfa Systems Inc
Westfield, NJ 908-654-0255
Andantex USA Inc
Ocean, NJ 800-713-6170
ASI Electronics Inc
Cypress, TX 800-231-6066
Aw Sheepscot Holding Co Inc
Franksville, WI 800-850-6110
Banner Engineering Corp
Minneapolis, MN 888-373-6767
Blodgett Co
Houston, TX 281-933-6195

Cal Controls
Gurnee, IL................. 800-866-6659
Candy Manufacturing Co
Niles, IL 847-588-2639
Centent Co
Santa Ana, CA 714-979-6491
Container Machinery Corporation
Albany, NY 518-694-3310
Contrex Inc
Maple Grove, MN 763-424-7800
Control & Metering
Mississauga, ON 800-736-5739
Conveyor Components Co
Croswell, MI 800-233-3233
Electro Cam Corp
Roscoe, IL................. 800-228-5487
Fairchild Industrial Products
Winston Salem, NC 800-334-8422
Gebo Conveyors, Consultants & Systems
Laval, QC 450-973-3337
Harland Simon Control Systems USA
Oakbrook, IL............... 630-572-7650
Honeywell Sensing & Internet of Things
DE 800-537-6945
Hoppmann Corporation
Elkwood, VA............... 800-368-3582
Hudson Control Group Inc
Springfield, NJ 973-376-8265
Industrial Devices Corporation
Petaluma, CA 707-789-1000
Industrial Magnetics
Boyne City, MI 800-662-4638
Kinematics & Controls Corporation
Brooksville, FL 800-833-8103
Letrah International Corp
Fort Atkinson, WI........... 920-563-6597
Moeller Electric
Houston, TX 800-394-5687
Namco Controls Corporation
Cleveland, OH 800-626-8324
OMRON Systems LLC
Schaumburg, IL............. 800-556-6766
Optek Inc
Galena, OH 800-533-8400
Payne Controls Co
Scott Depot, WV 800-331-1345
Peco Controls Corporation
Modesto, CA 800-732-6285
Rexroth Corporation
Hoffman Estates, IL 847-645-3600
Schroeder Machine
San Marcos, CA 760-591-9733
Sure Torque
Lakewood, CO 800-387-6572
Tri-Tronics
Tampa, FL 800-237-0946
W.G. Durant Corporation
Whittier, CA 562-946-5555
Washington Frontier
Grandview, WA............. 509-469-7662

Refrigeration Systems

Andgar Corp
Ferndale, WA 360-366-9900
Apollo Sheet Metal
Kennewick, WA 509-586-1104
Chillers Solutions
Pompton Plains, NJ......... 800-526-5201
Cooling Technology Inc
Charlotte, NC 800-872-1448
Frigoscandia
Redmond, WA.............. 800-423-1743
H A Phillips & Co
Dekalb, IL 630-377-0050
Hansen Technologies Corporation
Bolingbrook, IL 800-426-7368
Johnson Controls Inc
Milwaukee, WI 414-524-1200
Letrah International Corp
Fort Atkinson, WI.......... 920-563-6597
Novar
Cleveland, OH 800-348-1235
Paragon Electric Company
Two Rivers, WI 920-793-1161
Quantem Corp
Ewing, NJ 609-883-9879
Ron Vallort & Associates
Oak Brook, IL.............. 630-734-3821
Selco Products Company
Anaheim, CA 800-257-3526

WA Brown & Son
Salisbury, NC 704-636-5131

Webtension & Torque

Magpowr
Fenton, MO 800-624-7697

General

Alpha MOS America
Hanover, MD 800-257-4249
Bio-Rad Laboratories Inc.
Hercules, CA.......................510-724-7000
EMD Performance Materials
Philadelphia, PA 888-367-3275
FactoryTalk
Milwaukee, WI.......................414-382-2000
Shimadzu Scientific Instrs
Columbia, MD 800-477-1227

Inspection & Analysis Instrumentation & Systems

Abbeon Cal Inc
Santa Barbara, CA 800-922-0977
Accu-Ray Inspection Services
Elmhurst, IL 800-378-1226
ACR Systems
Surrey, BC.......................800-663-7845
Acrison Inc
Moonachie, NJ 800-422-4266
Advanced Detection Systems
Milwaukee, WI.......................414-672-0553
Advanced Instruments Inc
Norwood, MA.......................800-225-4034
Agricultural Data Systems
Laguna Niguel, CA...................800-328-2246
Agtron Inc
Reno, NV.......................775-850-4600
Air Logic Power Systems
Milwaukee, WI.......................800-325-8717
Altek Co
Torrington, CT 860-482-7626
American Gas & Chemical Co LTD
Northvale, NJ 800-288-3647
American Glass Research
Butler, PA.......................724-482-2163
AMETEK Brookfield
Middleboro, MA.......................800-628-8139
Analytical Development
Dahlonega, GA.......................770-237-2330
Analytical Measurements
Chester, NJ 800-635-5580
Aqua Measure
Rancho Cucamonga, CA 800-966-4788
Arizona Instrument LLC
Chandler, AZ.......................800-528-7411
Aromascan PLC
Hollis, NH.......................603-598-2922
Arthur G Russell Co Inc
Bristol, CT 860-583-4109
Ashcroft Inc
Stratford, CT.......................800-328-8258
Astro/Polymetron Zellweger
League City, TX 281-332-2484
Atkins Technical
Gainesville, FL 800-284-2842
ATS Rheosystems
Bordentown, NJ 609-298-2522
Automation Service
Earth City, MO 800-325-4808
Baltimore Aircoil Co
Jessup, MD 410-799-1300
Banner Engineering Corp
Minneapolis, MN 888-373-6767
Barco Inc
Duluth, GA.......................678-475-8000
Becton Dickinson & Co.
Franklin Lakes, NJ 201-847-6800
Bel-Art Products
Wayne, NJ.......................800-423-5278
Bentley Instruments Inc
Chaska, MN 952-448-7600
Berthold Technologies
Oak Ridge, TN.......................865-483-1488
Bia Diagnostics
Colchester, VT 802-540-0148
Binks Industries Inc
Montgomery, IL 630-801-1100
Biocontrol Systems Inc
Bellevue, WA 800-245-0113

Biolog Inc
Hayward, CA 800-284-4949
Biological Services
Kansas City, MO.......................913-236-6868
Biomerieux Inc
Durham, NC 800-682-2666
Bioscience International Inc
Rockville, MD.......................301-231-7400
Biotest Diagnostics Corporation
Rockaway, NJ.......................800-522-0090
Bran & Luebbe
Schaumburg, IL.......................847-882-8116
Brooks Instrument LLC
Hatfield, PA.......................888-554-3569
C.W. Brabender Instruments
South Hackensack, NJ 201-343-8425
CanPacific Engineering
Delta, BC.......................604-946-1680
Care Controls, Inc.
Mill Creek, WA.......................800-593-6050
Carleton Technologies Inc
Orchard Park, NY 716-662-0006
Caron Products & Svc Inc
Marietta, OH.......................800-648-3042
Carter Products
Grand Rapids, MI.......................888-622-7837
CEA Instrument Inc
Westwood, NJ 888-893-9640
CEM Corporation
Matthews, NC.......................800-726-3331
Charm Sciences Inc
Lawrence, MA.......................978-687-9200
Chicago Stainless Eqpt Inc
Palm City, FL.......................800-927-8575
Chord Engineering
Niwot, CO.......................303-449-5812
Cintex of America
Carol Stream, IL 800-424-6839
Clean Water Systems
Klamath Falls, OR 866-273-9993
Columbus Instruments
Columbus, OH 800-669-5011
Comark Instruments
Everett, WA.......................800-555-6658
Container Machinery Corporation
Albany, NY.......................518-694-3310
Control Instruments Corp
Fairfield, NJ 973-575-9114
Cooperheat/MQS
Alvin, TX.......................800-526-4233
Crown Controls Inc.
Charlotte, NC 800-541-7874
Crystal Chem Inc.
Downers Grove, IL 630-889-9003
CSC Scientific Co Inc
Fairfax, VA 800-621-4778
CSPI
Billerica, MA 978-663-7598
Custom Pools Inc
Portsmouth, NH 800-323-9509
CXR Co
Warsaw, IN.......................800-817-5763
Datapaq
Wilmington, MA.......................800-326-5270
Debelak Technical Systems
Greenville, WI 800-888-4207
Delavan-Delta
Naugatuck, CT 203-720-5610
Delta F Corporation
Woburn, MA.......................781-935-4600
Design Technology Corporation
Billerica, MA.......................978-663-7000
Devar Inc
Bridgeport, CT 800-566-6822
Dipix Technologies
Ottawa, ON.......................613-596-4942
Dunkley International Inc
Kalamazoo, MI.......................800-666-1264
Dupps Co
Germantown, OH 937-855-0623
Ecklund-Harrison Technologies
Fort Myers, FL.......................239-936-6032
Endress & Hauser
Greenwood, IN 800-428-4344
ENSCO Inc
Springfield, VA.......................703-321-9000
EPD Technology Corporation
Elmsford, NY 800-892-8926
Eurotherm
Ashburn, VA.......................703-726-0138
FILTEC-Inspection Systems
Torrance, CA.......................888-434-5832

Food Instrument Corp
Federalsburg, MD.......................800-542-5688
Food Technology Corporation
Sterling, VA.......................703-444-1870
Forte Technology
South Easton, MA.......................508-297-2363
Foss Nirsystems
Silver Spring, MD.......................301-755-5200
Fsi Technologies
Lombard, IL 800-468-6009
Garver Manufacturing Inc
Union City, IN.......................765-964-5828
Gems Sensors & Controls
Plainville, CT 860-747-3000
Geo. Olcott Company
Scottsboro, AL 800-634-2769
Gerstel Inc
Linthicum Hts, MD.......................800-413-8160
Grace Instrument Co
Houston, TX 800-304-5859
Gralab Instruments
Centerville, OH 800-876-8353
Greer's Ferry Glass Work
Dubuque, IA 501-589-2947
Haake
Paramus, NJ 800-631-1369
Hanna Instruments
Woonsocket, RI.......................800-426-6287
Heuft USA Inc
Downers Grove, IL 630-968-9011
High-Purity Standards
North Charleston, SC 866-767-4771
Hoffer Flow Controls Inc
Elizabeth City, NC 800-628-4584
Hygiena LLC
Camarillo, CA.......................805-388-8007
I.W. Tremont Company
Hawthorne, NJ 973-427-3800
Idexx Laboratories Inc
Westbrook, ME.......................800-548-6733
IMC Instruments
Menomonee Falls, WI.......................262-252-4620
Innovative Components
Southington, CT 800-789-2851
International Equipment Trading
Vernon Hills, IL 800-438-4522
International Tank & Pipe Co
Clackamas, OR 888-988-0011
Interstate Monroe Machinery
Seattle, WA.......................206-682-4870
IQ Scientific Instruments
Loveland, CO 800-227-4224
J M Canty Inc E1200 Engineers
Lockport, NY 716-625-4227
Kodex Inc
Nutley, NJ 800-325-6339
Koehler Instrument Co Inc
Bohemia, NY 800-878-9070
Konica Minolta Corp
Ramsey, NJ 888-473-3637
Labconco Corp
Kansas City, MO.......................800-821-5525
Labvantage Solutions Inc
Somerset, NJ.......................888-346-5467
Leeman Labs Inc
Hudson, NH 800-634-9942
Leica Microsystems
Depew, NY 800-346-4560
Light Technology Ind
Gaithersburg, MD.......................301-990-4050
Lixi Inc
Carpentersville, IL 847-961-6666
Lock Inspection Systems
Fitchburg, MA.......................800-227-5539
Loma International
Carol Stream, IL 800-872-5662
Lumenite Control Tech Inc
Franklin Park, IL.......................800-323-8510
Machine Applications Corp
Sandusky, OH 419-621-2322
Malthus Diagnostics
North Ridgeville, OH 800-346-7202
MAP Tech Packaging Inc
Hilton Head Isle, SC.......................843-342-5900
Maselli Measurements Inc
Stockton, CA.......................800-964-9600
MDS-Vet Inc
Valrico, FL 813-653-1180
Mesa Laboratories Inc
Lakewood, CO 800-525-1215
Mettler-Toledo Process Analytics, Inc
Billerica, MA.......................800-352-8763

Mettler-Toledo Safeline Inc
Lutz, FL 800-638-8537
Miroil
Allentown, PA 800-523-9844
MISCO Refractometer
Cleveland, OH 866-831-1999
Mocon Inc
Minneapolis, MN 763-493-7229
Moisture Register Products
Rancho Cucamonga, CA 800-966-4788
Namco Controls Corporation
Cleveland, OH 800-626-8324
National Hotpack
Stone Ridge, NY 800-431-8232
NDC Infrared EngineeringInc
Irwindale, CA 626-960-3300
Neogen Corp
Lansing, MI 800-234-5333
Noral
Natick, MA 800-348-2345
Ohio Magnetics Inc
Maple Heights, OH 800-486-6446
Omni Controls Inc
Tampa, FL 800-783-6664
Omnion
Rockland, MA 781-878-7200
OMRON Systems LLC
Schaumburg, IL 800-556-6766
Onevision Corp
Westerville, OH 614-794-1144
Optel Vision
Quebec, QC 866-688-0334
Orion Research
Beverly, MA 978-232-6000
Pacific Scientific Instrument
Grants Pass, OR 800-866-7889
Paktronics Controls
Southfield, MI 248-356-1400
Peco Controls Corporation
Modesto, CA 800-732-6285
Perten Instruments
Springfield, IL 888-773-7836
Petroleum Analyzer Co LP
Houston, TX 800-444-8378
Polyscience
Niles, IL 800-229-7569
Process Sensors Corp
Milford, MA 508-473-9901
Promega
Madison, WI 800-356-9526
Pyrometer Instrument Co Inc
Windsor, NJ 800-468-7976
Q A Supplies LLC
Norfolk, VA 800-472-7205
QMI
St Paul, MN 651-501-2337
Quality Control Equipment Co
Des Moines, IA 515-266-2268
Quest Corp
North Royalton, OH 440-230-9400
Reotemp Instrument Corp
San Diego, CA 800-648-7737
Rexroth Corporation
Hoffman Estates, IL 847-645-3600
Rheometric Scientific
New Castle, DE. 732-560-8550
Rosemount Analytical Inc
Irvine, CA 800-543-8257
Rotronic Instrument Corp Inc
Hauppauge, NY 800-628-7101
SDIX
Newark, DE. 800-544-8881
Sensidyne
St. Petersburg, FL 800-451-9444
Sensitech Inc
Beverly, MA 800-843-8367
Sensitech Inc
Redmond, WA. 800-999-7926
Sensor Systems
Chatsworth, CA 818-341-5366
Sentry Equipment Corp
Oconomowoc, WI. 262-567-7256
ShockWatch
Dallas, TX 800-393-7920
SIGHTech Vision Systems
Santa Clara, CA 408-282-3770
Spectro
Marble Falls, TX. 800-580-6608
Spiral Biotech Inc
Norwood, MA 800-554-1620
Sure Torque
Lakewood, CO 800-387-6572

Tangent Systems
Charlotte, NC 800-992-7577
Technistar Corporation
Denver, CO 303-651-0188
Teledyne Benthos Inc
North Falmouth, MA 508-563-1000
Teledyne TEKMAR
Mason, OH 800-874-2004
Testing Machines Inc
New Castle, DE. 800-678-3221
Texture Technologies Corporation
Scarsdale, NY 914-472-0531
Thermedics Detection
Chelmsford, MA 888-846-7226
Thermo Detection
Franklin, MA 866-269-0070
Thermo Fisher Scientific
Waltham, MA 800-678-5599
Theta Sciences
San Diego, CA 760-745-3311
Thorn Smith Laboratories
Beulah, MI 231-882-4672
Tricor Systems Inc
Elgin, IL 800-575-0161
Troxler Electronic Lab Inc
Durham, NC 877-876-9537
TVC Systems
Portsmouth, NH 888-431-5251
Tyco Fire Protection Products
Marinette, WI 800-862-6785
Univex Corp
Salem, NH. 800-258-6358
Vee Gee Scientific Inc
Kirkland, WA 800-423-8842
Venture Measurement Co LLC
Spartanburg, SC 864-574-8960
VICAM
Milford, MA 800-338-4381
Washington Frontier
Grandview, WA 509-469-7662
Whatman
Haverhill, MA 978-374-7400
Wilkens-Anderson Co
Chicago, IL 800-847-2222
X-R-I Testing Inc
Troy, MI 800-973-4800
Xylem Inc
Rye Brook, NY 914-323-5700
YSI Inc
Yellow Springs, OH 800-765-4974
Zeltex
Hagerstown, MD 800-732-1950

Instrumentation

Color Measuring

BYK Gardner Inc
Columbia, MD 301-483-6500
Hunter Lab
Reston, VA 703-471-6870
Konica Minolta Corp
Ramsey, NJ 888-473-3637
SICK Inc
Bloomington, MN 800-325-7425
Wilkens-Anderson Co
Chicago, IL 800-847-2222

Flow Measurement, Gas & Liquid

ACR Systems
Surrey, BC. 800-663-7845
Auburn Systems LLC
Danvers, MA 800-255-5008
Berthold Technologies
Oak Ridge, TN 865-483-1488
Brooks Instrument LLC
Hatfield, PA. 888-554-3569
CEA Instrument Inc
Westwood, NJ 888-893-9640
CEM Corporation
Matthews, NC 800-726-3331
Columbus Instruments
Columbus, OH 800-669-5011
Endress & Hauser
Greenwood, IN 800-428-4344
Hardy Systems Corporation
Northbrook, IL 800-927-3956
Hoffer Flow Controls Inc
Elizabeth City, NC 800-628-4584
IMC Instruments
Menomonee Falls, WI. 262-252-4620

Interstate Monroe Machinery
Seattle, WA 206-682-4870
Labconco Corp
Kansas City, MO. 800-821-5525
MAP Tech Packaging Inc
Hilton Head Isle, SC. 843-342-5900
Mocon Inc
Minneapolis, MN 763-493-7229
Omni Controls Inc
Tampa, FL. 800-783-6664
Optek Inc
Galena, OH 800-533-8400
Rotronic Instrument Corp Inc
Hauppauge, NY 800-628-7101
Tuchenhagen
Columbia, MD 410-910-6000
Washington Frontier
Grandview, WA. 509-469-7662

Laboratory Equipment

Acme Scale Co
San Leandro, CA. 888-638-5040
Advance Energy Technologies
Halfmoon, NY. 800-724-0198
Advance Technology Corp
Ramsey, NJ 201-934-7127
Agri-Equipment International
Longs, SC 877-550-4709
AMETEK Brookfield
Middleboro, MA 800-628-8139
Analytical Measurements
Chester, NJ 800-635-5580
Arizona Instrument LLC
Chandler, AZ. 800-528-7411
Ashcroft Inc
Stratford, CT. 800-328-8258
Atkins Technical
Gainesville, FL 800-284-2842
Bahnson Environmental Specs
Raleigh, NC 800-688-5859
Barnant Company
Lake Barrington, IL 800-637-3739
Becton Dickinson & Co.
Franklin Lakes, NJ 201-847-6800
Bel-Art Products
Wayne, NJ 800-423-5278
Bematek Systems Inc
Salem, MA 877-236-2835
Bentley Instruments Inc
Chaska, MN 952-448-7600
Biocontrol Systems Inc
Bellevue, WA 800-245-0113
Bioscience International Inc
Rockville, MD 301-231-7400
Bran & Luebbe
Schaumburg, IL. 847-882-8116
Brimrose Corporation of America
Sparks Glencoe, MD. 410-472-7070
C.W. Brabender Instruments
South Hackensack, NJ 201-343-8425
Caron Products & Svc Inc
Marietta, OH 800-648-3042
Charm Sciences Inc
Lawrence, MA 978-687-9200
Chemindustrial Systems Inc
Cedarburg, WI. 262-375-8570
Clark-Cooper Division   Magnatrol Valve Corporation
Cinnaminson, NJ. 856-829-4580
Cleveland Vibrator Co
Cleveland, OH 800-221-3298
Corning Life Sciences
Tewksbury, MA 800-492-1110
Crown Controls Inc.
Charlotte, NC 800-541-7874
Custom Poly Packaging
Fort Wayne, IN 800-548-6603
E & E Process Instrumentation
Concord, Ontario, ON. 905-669-4857
Ederback Corporation
Ann Arbor, MI 800-422-2558
ENSCO Inc
Springfield, VA 703-321-9000
Fluid Imaging Technologies Inc
Scarborough, ME 207-846-6100
Food Technology Corporation
Sterling, VA. 703-444-1870
Foss Nirsystems
Silver Spring, MD. 301-755-5200
Gerstel Inc
Linthicum Hts, MD. 800-413-8160

Glen Mills Inc.
Clifton, NJ 973-777-0777
Grace Instrument Co
Houston, TX 800-304-5859
Gralab Instruments
Centerville, OH 800-876-8353
Greer's Ferry Glass Work
Dubuque, IA 501-589-2947
Haake
Paramus, NJ 800-631-1369
Hanna Instruments
Woonsocket, RI. 800-426-6287
Hanson Lab Furniture Inc
Newbury Park, CA 805-498-3121
Hemco Corp
Independence, MO 800-779-4362
Henry Troemner LLC
West Deptford, NJ. 856-686-1600
Hunter Lab
Reston, VA .703-471-6870
Idexx Laboratories Inc
Westbrook, ME 800-548-6733
Ika-Works Inc
Wilmington, NC 800-733-3037
IMC Instruments
Menomonee Falls, WI. 262-252-4620
IQ Scientific Instruments
Loveland, CO 800-227-4224
Labconco Corp
Kansas City, MO. 800-821-5525
Laboratory Devices
Holliston, MA. 508-429-1716
Labvantage Solutions Inc
Somerset, NJ 888-346-5467
Lauhoff Corporation
Detroit, MI 313-259-0027
Leeman Labs Inc
Hudson, NH 800-634-9942
Leica Microsystems
Depew, NY 800-346-4560
Libra Technical Center
Metuchen, NJ 732-321-5200
Maselli Measurements Inc
Stockton, CA. 800-964-9600
MicroThermics, Inc.
Raleigh, NC 919-878-8045
National Hotpack
Stone Ridge, NY. 800-431-8232
National Oilwell Varco
North Andover, MA 800-643-0641
NDC Infrared EngineeringInc
Irwindale, CA 626-960-3300
Netzsch Pumps North America
Exton, PA .610-363-8010
Noral
Natick, MA 800-348-2345
Omnion
Rockland, MA. 781-878-7200
Pa R Systems Inc
St Paul, MN 800-464-1320
Pacific Scientific Instrument
Grants Pass, OR 800-866-7889
Patterson-Kelley   Hars Company
East Stroudsburg, PA 570-421-7500
Perten Instruments
Springfield, IL. 888-773-7836
Polyscience
Niles, IL .800-229-7569
Pro Line Co
Haverhill, MA. 978-521-2600
Pro Scientific Inc
Oxford, CT 800-584-3776
Q A Supplies LLC
Norfolk, VA. 800-472-7205
Radiation Processing Division
Parsippany, NJ. 800-442-1969
Rosemount Analytical Inc
Irvine, CA 800-543-8257
Schlueter Company
Janesville, WI 800-359-1700
Scott Turbon Mixer
Adelanto, CA 800-285-8512
Sefi Fabricators Inc
Amityville, NY 631-842-2200
Silverson Machines Inc
East Longmeadow, MA 800-204-6400
Spiral Biotech Inc
Norwood, MA. 800-554-1620
Stewart Laboratories
Strattanville, PA 800-640-7869
Straub Designs Co
St Louis Park, MN 952-546-6686

Texture Technologies Corporation
Scarsdale, NY 914-472-0531
Thermex Thermatron
Louisville, KY 502-493-1299
TMCo Inc.ÿ
Houston, TX 713-465-3255
Triad Scientific
Manasquan, NJ 800-867-6690
Tricor Systems Inc
Elgin, IL .800-575-0161
Variety Glass Inc
Cambridge, OH 740-432-3643
Vee Gee Scientific Inc
Kirkland, WA 800-423-8842
VICAM
Milford, MA 800-338-4381
Weber Scientific Inc
Trenton, NJ 800-328-8378
Whatman
Piscataway, NJ 973-245-8300
Whatman
Haverhill, MA. 978-374-7400
Wilkens-Anderson Co
Chicago, IL 800-847-2222
X-R-I Testing Inc
Troy, MI .800-973-4800
X-Rite Inc
Grand Rapids, MI 888-800-9580
YSI Inc
Yellow Springs, OH 800-765-4974

Clean Rooms

Advance Energy Technologies
Halfmoon, NY. 800-724-0198

Laboratory Sample Testing

Great Lakes Scientific
Stevensville, MI 269-429-1000
Kerry, Inc
Beloit, WI 608-363-1200
Promega
Madison, WI 800-356-9526

Measurement Systems

A&D Weighing
San Jose, CA. 800-726-3364
A&M Thermometer Corporation
Asheville, NC 800-685-9211
Abbeon Cal Inc
Santa Barbara, CA 800-922-0977
Abel Manufacturing Co
Appleton, WI 920-734-4443
Acme Scale Co
San Leandro, CA. 888-638-5040
Acrison Inc
Moonachie, NJ 800-422-4266
Action Packaging Automation
Roosevelt, NJ 800-241-2724
Advanced Instruments Inc
Norwood, MA. 800-225-4034
Agri-Equipment International
Longs, SC 877-550-4709
Agtron Inc
Reno, NV 775-850-4600
Alnor Instrument Company
Skokie, IL 800-424-7427
Ametek
Sellersville, PA 215-257-6531
AMETEK Brookfield
Middleboro, MA. 800-628-8139
Analytical Measurements
Chester, NJ 800-635-5580
Anderson-Negele
Fultonville, NY 800-833-0081
Aqua Measure
Rancho Cucamonga, CA 800-966-4788
Arkfeld Mfg & Distributing Co
Norfolk, NE. 800-533-0676
ASI Electronics Inc
Cypress, TX 800-231-6066
Athena Controls Inc
Plymouth Meeting, PA 800-782-6776
Atkins Technical
Gainesville, FL 800-284-2842
ATM Corporation
New Berlin, WI. 800-511-2096
ATS Rheosystems
Bordentown, NJ 609-298-2522

Aw Sheepscot Holding Co Inc
Franksville, WI 800-850-6110
Badger Meter Inc
Milwaukee, WI 800-876-3837
Banner Engineering Corp
Minneapolis, MN 888-373-6767
Barnant Company
Lake Barrington, IL 800-637-3739
Berthold Technologies
Oak Ridge, TN 865-483-1488
Blancett
Racine, WI 800-235-1638
BLH Electronics
Canton, MA 781-821-2000
Blodgett Co
Houston, TX 281-933-6195
Bowtemp
Mont-Royal, QC. 514-735-5551
Brooks Instrument LLC
Hatfield, PA. 888-554-3569
Brown Fired Heater
Elyria, OH 440-323-3291
Bry-Air Inc
Sunbury, OH 877-379-2479
BYK Gardner Inc
Columbia, MD 301-483-6500
Cambridge Viscosity, Inc.
Medford, MA 800-554-4639
CEA Instrument Inc
Westwood, NJ 888-893-9640
Chaney Instrument Co
Lake Geneva, WI 800-777-0565
Chemindustrial Systems Inc
Cedarburg, WI. 262-375-8570
Chocolate Concepts
Hartville, OH 330-877-3322
Clark-Cooper Division   Magnatrol Valve Corporation
Cinnaminson, NJ. 856-829-4580
Clayton Industries
City of Industry, CA 800-423-4585
CMT
Hamilton, MA. 978-768-2555
Columbus Instruments
Columbus, OH 800-669-5011
Comark Instruments
Everett, WA. 800-555-6658
Conax Buffalo Technologies
Buffalo, NY. 800-223-2389
Control Products Inc
Chanhassen, MN. 800-947-9098
Crystal-Vision Packaging Systems
Torrance, CA. 800-331-3240
Cyvex Nutrition
Irvine, CA 888-992-9839
Datapaq
Wilmington, MA. 800-326-5270
Debelak Technical Systems
Greenville, WI 800-888-4207
Delavan-Delta
Naugatuck, CT 203-720-5610
Devar Inc
Bridgeport, CT 800-566-6822
Dwyer Instruments Inc
Michigan City, IN 800-872-3141
E & E Process Instrumentation
Concord, Ontario, ON. 905-669-4857
Electronic Weighing Systems
Opa Locka, FL 305-685-8067
ELISA Technologies, Inc.
Gainesville, FL 352-337-3929
Endress & Hauser
Greenwood, IN 800-428-4344
ENM Co
Chicago, IL 773-775-8400
EPD Technology Corporation
Elmsford, NY 800-892-8926
Esco Products Inc
Houston, TX 800-966-5514
Exact Mixing Systems Inc
Memphis, TN 901-362-8501
Flow Technology Inc
Tempe, AZ 800-833-2448
Food Technology Corporation
Sterling, VA. 703-444-1870
Forte Technology
South Easton, MA. 508-297-2363
Frazier Precision Instr Co
Hagerstown, MD. 301-790-2585
Frye's Measure Mill
Wilton, NH 603-654-6581
Gea Us
Galesville, WI 608-582-3081

Grace Instrument Co
Houston, TX 800-304-5859
Greer's Ferry Glass Work
Dubuque, IA 501-589-2947
Haake
Paramus, NJ 800-631-1369
Hanna Instruments
Woonsocket, RI 800-426-6287
HD Electric Co
Park City, IL 847-473-4882
Hoffer Flow Controls Inc
Elizabeth City, NC 800-628-4584
Hunter Lab
Reston, VA 703-471-6870
Hyer Industries
Pembroke, MA 781-826-8101
IMC Instruments
Menomonee Falls, WI. 262-252-4620
Industrial Automation Specs
Hampton, VA 800-916-4272
Industrial Laboratory Eqpt Co
Charlotte, NC 704-357-3930
Inspired Automation Inc
Agoura Hills, CA 818-991-4598
Intelligent Controls
Saco, ME. 800-872-3455
IQ Scientific Instruments
Loveland, CO 800-227-4224
IVEK Corp
N Springfield, VT 800-356-4746
Kason Central
Columbus, OH 614-885-1992
Kason Industries
Newnan, GA 770-254-0553
King Engineering - King-Gage
Newell, WV 800-242-8871
Konica Minolta Corp
Ramsey, NJ 888-473-3637
L.C. Thompson Company
Kenosha, WI. 800-558-4018
Leica Microsystems
Depew, NY 800-346-4560
Liquid Controls LLC
Lake Bluff, IL 800-458-5262
Liquid Scale
New Brighton, MN 888-633-2969
Liquid Solids Control Inc
Upton, MA 508-529-3377
Lockwood Packaging
Woburn, MA 800-641-3100
Loma International
Carol Stream, IL 800-872-5662
Loma Systems
Carol Stream, IL 800-872-5662
Lumenite Control Tech Inc
Franklin Park, IL. 800-323-8510
M.H. Rhodes Cramer
South Windsor, CT 877-684-6464
Machine Applications Corp
Sandusky, OH 419-621-2322
Maselli Measurements Inc
Stockton, CA. 800-964-9600
Mesa Laboratories Inc
Lakewood, CO 800-525-1215
Micro-Strain
Spring City, PA 610-948-4550
Miljoco Corp
Mt Clemens, MI 888-888-1498
Moisture Register Products
Rancho Cucamonga, CA 800-966-4788
Monitor Company
Modesto, CA 800-537-3201
Monitor Technologies LLC
Elburn, IL 800-601-6204
MTL Etching Industries
Woodmere, NY 516-295-9733
Munters Corp
Amesbury, MA 800-843-5360
Music City Metals Inc
Nashville, TN 800-251-2674
National Time Recording Eqpt
New York, NY 212-227-3310
NDC Infrared EngineeringInc
Irwindale, CA 626-960-3300
Nicol Scales & Measurement LP
Dallas, TX. 800-225-8181
Noral
Natick, MA 800-348-2345
Ogden Manufacturing Company
Pittsburgh, PA 412-967-3906
Optek-Danulat
Germantown, WI. 888-551-4288

Orion Research
Beverly, MA 978-232-6000
Oyster Bay Pump Works Inc
Hicksville, NY 516-933-4500
Pacific Scale Company
Clackamas, OR 800-537-1886
Pacific Scientific Instrument
Grants Pass, OR 800-866-7889
Paktronics Controls
Southfield, MI. 248-356-1400
Paratherm Corporation
Conshohocken, PA 800-222-3611
Peco Controls Corporation
Modesto, CA. 800-732-6285
Pelouze Scale Company
Bridgeview, IL 800-323-8363
Perten Instruments
Springfield, IL. 888-773-7836
Prince Castle Inc
Carol Stream, IL 800-722-7853
Process Sensors Corp
Milford, MA 508-473-9901
Reotemp Instrument Corp
San Diego, CA 800-648-7737
Rheometric Scientific
New Castle, DE. 732-560-8550
Rosemount Analytical Inc
Irvine, CA 800-543-8257
Rotronic Instrument Corp Inc
Hauppauge, NY 800-628-7101
S J Controls Inc
Signal Hill, CA 562-494-1400
Samson Controls
Baytown, TX. 281-383-3677
Scientech, Inc
Boulder, CO 800-525-0522
Sensitech Inc
Beverly, MA 800-843-8367
Sensor Systems
Chatsworth, CA 818-341-5366
Sentron
Gig Harbor, WA 800-472-4361
Siko Products Inc
Dexter, MI. 800-447-7456
Spinco Metal Products Inc
Newark, NY 315-331-6285
Sure Torque
Lakewood, CO 800-387-6572
Tangent Systems
Charlotte, NC 800-992-7577
Taylor Precision Products
Oak Brook, IL 866-843-3905
TechnipFMC
Houston, TX 218-591-4000
Tel-Tru Manufacturing Co
Rochester, NY. 800-232-5335
Testing Machines Inc
New Castle, DE. 800-678-3221
Texture Technologies Corporation
Scarsdale, NY 914-472-0531
Thermalogic Corp
Hudson, MA 978-562-5974
Thermo Detection
Franklin, MA 866-269-0070
Thermo Instruments
Yaphank, NY. 631-924-0880
Thermo King Corp
Bloomington, MN 888-887-2202
Triad Scientific
Manasquan, NJ 800-867-6690
Tuchenhagen
Columbia, MD 410-910-6000
Venture Measurement Co LLC
Spartanburg, SC 800-426-9010
Venture Measurement Co LLC
Spartanburg, SC 864-574-8960
VitaMinder Company
Providence, RI 800-858-8840
Water Sciences Services, Inc.
Jackson, TN 973-584-4131
Weiss Instruments Inc
Holtsville, NY. 631-207-1200
Wescor
Logan, UT. 800-453-2725
Whatman
Haverhill, MA 978-374-7400
Wika Instrument LP
Lawrenceville, GA 800-645-0606
X-Rite Inc
Grand Rapids, MI 888-800-9580
YSI Inc
Yellow Springs, OH 800-765-4974

Polarimeters

Bellingham + Stanley
Suwanee, GA 800-678-8573
Cyvex Nutrition
Irvine, CA 888-992-9839

Refractometers

Bellingham + Stanley
Suwanee, GA 800-678-8573
Cyvex Nutrition
Irvine, CA 888-992-9839

Meters

Flow

Ametek
Sellersville, PA 215-257-6531
Anderson-Negele
Fultonville, NY 800-833-0081
Auburn Systems LLC
Danvers, MA. 800-255-5008
Aw Sheepscot Holding Co Inc
Franksville, WI 800-850-6110
Badger Meter Inc
Milwaukee, WI 800-876-3837
Barnant Company
Lake Barrington, IL 800-637-3739
Blancett
Racine, WI 800-235-1638
Chemindustrial Systems Inc
Cedarburg, WI. 262-375-8570
Conflow Technologies, Inc.
Brampton, ON. 800-275-9887
Crown Controls Inc.
Charlotte, NC 800-541-7874
DMC-David Manufacturing Company
Mason City, IA 641-424-7010
Flow Technology Inc
Tempe, AZ 800-833-2448
Hayward Industries Inc
Clemmons, NC 336-712-9900
Hoffer Flow Controls Inc
Elizabeth City, NC 800-628-4584
Kisco Manufacturing
Port Alberni, BC. 604-823-7456
Liquid Controls LLC
Lake Bluff, IL 800-458-5262
Lumenite Control Tech Inc
Franklin Park, IL. 800-323-8510
Machine Applications Corp
Sandusky, OH 419-621-2322
Mesa Laboratories Inc
Lakewood, CO 800-525-1215
Monitor Technologies LLC
Elburn, IL 800-601-6204
Music City Metals Inc
Nashville, TN 800-251-2674
Quality Control Equipment Co
Des Moines, IA 515-266-2268
S J Controls Inc
Signal Hill, CA 562-494-1400
Samson Controls
Baytown, TX. 281-383-3677
Schenck Process
Whitewater, WI. 888-742-1249
Special Products
Springfield, MO 417-881-6114
Spinco Metal Products Inc
Newark, NY 315-331-6285
TechnipFMC
Houston, TX 218-591-4000
TWM Manufacturing
Leamington, ON 888-495-4831

pH

Analytical Measurements
Chester, NJ 800-635-5580
Ashcroft Inc
Stratford, CT 800-328-8258
BYK Gardner Inc
Columbia, MD 301-483-6500
Chemindustrial Systems Inc
Cedarburg, WI. 262-375-8570
Cyvex Nutrition
Irvine, CA 888-992-9839
DeltaTrak
Pleasanton, CA 800-962-6776

Devar Inc
   Bridgeport, CT 800-566-6822
E & E Process Instrumentation
   Concord, Ontario, ON. 905-669-4857
Hanna Instruments
   Woonsocket, RI. 800-426-6287
IQ Scientific Instruments
   Loveland, CO 800-227-4224
Q A Supplies LLC
   Norfolk, VA. 800-472-7205
Tricor Systems Inc
   Elgin, IL 800-575-0161
Wilkens-Anderson Co
   Chicago, IL 800-847-2222
X-Rite Inc
   Grand Rapids, MI 888-800-9580
YSI Inc
   Yellow Springs, OH 800-765-4974

Microbiology Instruments & Supplies

Baltimore Aircoil Co
   Jessup, MD 410-799-1300
Becton Dickinson & Co.
   Franklin Lakes, NJ 201-847-6800
Biolog Inc
   Hayward, CA 800-284-4949
Biomerieux Inc
   Durham, NC 800-682-2666
Malthus Diagnostics
   North Ridgeville, OH 800-346-7202
Microbiologics Inc
   St Cloud, MN 800-599-2847
Neutec Group
   Farmingdale, NY 888-810-5179
Q A Supplies LLC
   Norfolk, VA. 800-472-7205
VICAM
   Milford, MA 800-338-4381
Whatman
   Piscataway, NJ 973-245-8300
Wilkens-Anderson Co
   Chicago, IL 800-847-2222

Process Analysis & Development

A & B Process Systems Corp
   Stratford, WI. 888-258-2789
Asset Design LLC
   Mooresville, NC 888-293-1740
Datapaq
   Wilmington, MA. 800-326-5270
Emerson Process Management
   Boulder, CO 800-522-6277
Food & Agrosystems
   Sunnyvale, CA 408-245-8450
J M Canty Inc E1200 Engineers
   Lockport, NY 716-625-4227
Vee Gee Scientific Inc
   Kirkland, WA 800-423-8842

Electronic Survey

Innovative Food Solutions LLC
   Columbus, OH 800-884-3314
Libra Technical Center
   Metuchen, NJ 732-321-5200
Long Range Systems
   Addison, TX 800-577-8101

Process Controls

Batching, Blending, Weighing

A & B Process Systems Corp
   Stratford, WI. 888-258-2789
Abel Manufacturing Co
   Appleton, WI 920-734-4443
APEC
   Lake Odessa, MI 616-374-1000
ASI Electronics Inc
   Cypress, TX 800-231-6066
Autocon Mixing Systems
   St Helena, CA 800-225-6192
AZO Food
   Memphis, TN 901-794-9480
Batching Systems
   Prince Frederick, MD 800-311-0851
BLH Electronics
   Canton, MA 781-821-2000
Chicago Conveyor Corporation
   Addison, IL 630-543-6300

Coastline Equipment Inc
   Bellingham, WA 360-734-8509
Conflow Technologies, Inc.
   Brampton, ON. 800-275-9887
Digital Dynamics Inc
   Scotts Valley, CA 800-765-1288
Hoffer Flow Controls Inc
   Elizabeth City, NC 800-628-4584
JCS Controls, Inc.
   Rochester, NY. 585-227-5910
Letrah International Corp
   Fort Atkinson, WI 920-563-6597
Liquid Solids Control Inc
   Upton, MA 508-529-3377
Matiss
   St Georges, QC 888-562-8477
MERRICK Industries Inc
   Lynn Haven, FL 800-271-7834
Nu-Con Equipment
   Chanhassen, MN. 877-939-0510
Pickwick Manufacturing Svc
   Cedar Rapids, IA. 800-397-9797
Pro Scientific Inc
   Oxford, CT 800-584-3776
Quest Corp
   North Royalton, OH 440-230-9400
Schaffer Poidometer Company
   Pittsburgh, PA 412-281-9031
Schenck Process
   Whitewater, WI. 888-742-1249
Silverson Machines Inc
   East Longmeadow, MA 800-204-6400
Sterling Systems & Controls
   Sterling, IL 800-257-7214
T D Sawvel Co
   Maple Plain, MN. 877-488-1816
Tecweigh
   St Paul, MN. 800-536-4880
Thermedics Detection
   Chelmsford, MA. 888-846-7226
Trola Industries Inc
   York, PA 717-848-3700

Control Panels

A & B Process Systems Corp
   Stratford, WI. 888-258-2789
Asap Automation
   Addison, IL 800-409-0383
Digital Dynamics Inc
   Scotts Valley, CA 800-765-1288
Letrah International Corp
   Fort Atkinson, WI 920-563-6597
Novar
   Cleveland, OH 800-348-1235
Our Name is Mud
   New York, NY 877-683-7867
Pro Controls Inc
   Yakima, WA 800-488-3386
Process Solutions
   Riviera Beach, FL. 561-840-0050
Red Lion Controls Inc
   York, PA 717-767-6511
South Shore Controls Inc
   Perry, OH 440-259-2500
Trola Industries Inc
   York, PA 717-848-3700
Viatran Corporation
   North Tonawanda, NY 800-688-0030
Washington Frontier
   Grandview, WA. 509-469-7662

Humidity Loggers

Ashcroft Inc
   Stratford, CT 800-328-8258

Pressure

ACR Systems
   Surrey, BC. 800-663-7845
Acromag Inc.
   Wixom, MI 248-624-1541
Alnor Instrument Company
   Skokie, IL 800-424-7427
Ashcroft Inc
   Stratford, CT 800-328-8258
Chicago Stainless Eqpt Inc
   Palm City, FL 800-927-8575
Control Products Inc
   Chanhassen, MN. 800-947-9098

Endress & Hauser
   Greenwood, IN 800-428-4344
IMC Instruments
   Menomonee Falls, WI. 262-252-4620
Omni Controls Inc
   Tampa, FL. 800-783-6664
Peco Controls Corporation
   Modesto, CA. 800-732-6285
Samson Controls
   Baytown, TX. 281-383-3677
United Electric Controls Co
   Watertown, MA. 617-926-1000
Washington Frontier
   Grandview, WA. 509-469-7662
Weiss Instruments Inc
   Holtsville, NY. 631-207-1200

Data Loggers

Ashcroft Inc
   Stratford, CT 800-328-8258
JUMO Process Control Inc
   East Syracuse, NY 800-554-5866

Gauges; Sanitary

Ashcroft Inc
   Stratford, CT. 800-328-8258

Programmable

ACR Systems
   Surrey, BC. 800-663-7845
Allpax Products
   Covington, LA 888-893-9277
American Autogard Corporation
   Rockford, IL 815-229-3190
Ashcroft Inc
   Stratford, CT 800-328-8258
Boston Gear
   Boston, MA. 888-999-9860
Chicago Conveyor Corporation
   Addison, IL 630-543-6300
Intelligent Controls
   Saco, ME. 800-872-3455
Pro Scientific Inc
   Oxford, CT 800-584-3776
Selco Products Company
   Anaheim, CA 800-257-3526
Sterling Systems & Controls
   Sterling, IL 800-257-7214
Thermex Thermatron
   Louisville, KY 502-493-1299
Theta Sciences
   San Diego, CA 760-745-3311

Recorders

Ashcroft Inc
   Stratford, CT 800-328-8258
Datapaq
   Wilmington, MA. 800-326-5270
Delta Trak
   Pleasanton, CA 800-962-6776
Devar Inc
   Bridgeport, CT 800-566-6822
Hanna Instruments
   Woonsocket, RI. 800-426-6287
Industrial Automation Specs
   Hampton, VA 800-916-4272
Mesa Laboratories Inc
   Lakewood, CO 800-525-1215
Pyrometer Instrument Co Inc
   Windsor, NJ. 800-468-7976
Sensitech Inc
   Redmond, WA. 800-999-7926
Simplex Time Recorder Company
   Santa Ana, CA 949-724-5000

Software

Iconics Inc
   Foxboro, MA 800-946-9679
Loma Systems
   Carol Stream, IL 800-872-5662

Systems

A & B Process Systems Corp
   Stratford, WI. 888-258-2789
Abel Manufacturing Co
   Appleton, WI 920-734-4443
Ace Specialty Mfg Co Inc
   Rosemead, CA 626-444-3867

Acrison Inc
Moonachie, NJ 800-422-4266
Acromag Inc.
Wixom, MI 248-624-1541
Advanced Instruments Inc
Norwood, MA 800-225-4034
AL Systems
Rockaway, NJ 888-960-8324
Allegheny Bradford Corp
Bradford, PA 800-542-0650
Allpax Products
Covington, LA 888-893-9277
Alnor Instrument Company
Skokie, IL 800-424-7427
American Autogard Corporation
Rockford, IL 815-229-3190
American LEWA
Holliston, MA 888-539-2123
American Metal Door Company
Richmond, IN 800-428-2737
Analite
Plainview, NY 800-229-3357
Andantex USA Inc
Ocean, NJ 800-713-6170
Anderson-Negele
Fultonville, NY 800-833-0081
Applexion
Chicago, IL 773-243-0454
APV Americas
Delavan, WI 800-252-5200
Artisan Controls Corp
Randolph, NJ 800-457-4950
Asap Automation
Addison, IL 800-409-0383
ASI Electronics Inc
Cypress, TX 800-231-6066
Athena Controls Inc
Plymouth Meeting, PA 800-782-6776
Auburn Systems LLC
Danvers, MA. 800-255-5008
Autocon Mixing Systems
St Helena, CA 800-225-6192
Automation Service
Earth City, MO 800-325-4808
Autotron
Oak Creek, WI 800-527-7500
Axelrod, Norman N
New York, NY 212-369-2885
AZO Food
Memphis, TN 901-794-9480
B T Engineering Inc
Bala Cynwyd, PA 610-664-9500
Batching Systems
Prince Frederick, MD 800-311-0851
Bentley Instruments Inc
Chaska, MN 952-448-7600
BLH Electronics
Canton, MA 781-821-2000
Blue Tech
Hickory, NC 828-324-5900
Brown Fired Heater
Elyria, OH 440-323-3291
Bry-Air Inc
Sunbury, OH 877-379-2479
BSI Instruments
Aliquippa, PA 800-274-9851
Burling Instrument Inc
Chatham, NJ 800-635-2526
Burns Engineering Inc
Hopkins, MN 800-328-3871
Cal Controls
Gurnee, IL 800-866-6659
Cashco Inc
Ellsworth, KS 785-472-4461
Centent Co
Santa Ana, CA 714-979-6491
Chil-Con Products
Brantford, ON 800-263-0086
Chillers Solutions
Pompton Plains, NJ. 800-526-5201
Cleveland Motion Controls
Cleveland, OH 800-321-8072
Coastline Equipment Inc
Bellingham, WA 360-734-8509
Conflow Technologies, Inc.
Brampton, ON. 800-275-9887
Contrex Inc
Maple Grove, MN. 763-424-7800
Control Concepts Inc.
Chanhassen, MN 800-765-2799
Control Pak Intl
Fenton, MI 810-735-2800

Control Products Inc
Chanhassen, MN 800-947-9098
Control Systems Design
Forest Hill, MD 410-296-0466
Control Technology Corp
Hopkinton, MA 800-282-5008
Conveyor Components Co
Croswell, MI 800-233-3233
Cotter Brothers Corp
Danvers, MA. 978-777-5001
Cramer Company
South Windsor, CT 877-684-6464
Crouzet Corporation
Carrollton, TX. 800-677-5311
Damrow Company
Fond Du Lac, WI 800-236-1501
Debelak Technical Systems
Greenville, WI 800-888-4207
DEFCO
Landenberg, PA. 215-274-8245
Delavan-Delta
Naugatuck, CT 203-720-5610
Design Technology Corporation
Lexington, MA 800-597-7063
Devar Inc
Bridgeport, CT 800-566-6822
Diamond Automation
Farmington Hills, MI 248-426-9394
Dickson
Addison, IL 800-757-3747
Digital Dynamics Inc
Scotts Valley, CA 800-765-1288
Dipix Technologies
Ottawa, ON 613-596-4942
Distaview Corp
Bowling Green, OH 800-795-9970
Dwyer Instruments Inc
Michigan City, IN 800-872-3141
Ecklund-Harrison Technologies
Fort Myers, FL 239-936-6032
Electro Cam Corp
Roscoe, IL 800-228-5487
Electrol Specialties Co
South Beloit, IL 815-389-2291
Endress & Hauser
Greenwood, IN 800-428-4344
ESE, Inc
Marshfield, WI 800-236-4778
Eurotherm
Ashburn, VA 703-726-0138
Fata Automation
Sterling Heights, MI 586-323-9400
Flow Aerospace
Jeffersonville, IN 812-283-7888
Forte Technology
South Easton, MA 508-297-2363
Foxboro Company
Houston, TX 888-369-2676
Gems Sensors & Controls
Plainville, CT 860-747-3000
Glatt Air Techniques Inc
Ramsey, NJ 201-825-8700
Gralab Instruments
Centerville, OH 800-876-8353
Hanna Instruments
Woonsocket, RI 800-426-6287
Harland Simon Control Systems USA
Oakbrook, IL. 630-572-7650
Hectronic
Oklahoma City, OK 405-946-3574
Hoffer Flow Controls Inc
Elizabeth City, NC 800-628-4584
Hudson Control Group Inc
Springfield, NJ 973-376-8265
Innovative Components
Southington, CT 800-789-2851
Intelligent Controls
Saco, ME 800-872-3455
Interstate Monroe Machinery
Seattle, WA 206-682-4870
ITW Engineered Polymers
Oxford, MI 248-628-2587
Kinematics & Controls Corporation
Brooksville, FL. 800-833-8103
L.C. Thompson Company
Kenosha, WI 800-558-4018
Lake Process Systems Inc
Lake Barrington, IL 800-331-9260
LDJ Electronics
Troy, MI 248-528-2202
Letrah International Corp
Fort Atkinson, WI. 920-563-6597

Light Technology Ind
Gaithersburg, MD. 301-990-4050
Liquid Controls LLC
Lake Bluff, IL 800-458-5262
Liquid Solids Control Inc
Upton, MA 508-529-3377
Lumenite Control Tech Inc
Franklin Park, IL. 800-323-8510
Maselli Measurements Inc
Stockton, CA. 800-964-9600
MeGa Industries
Burlington, ON 800-665-6342
Membrane Process & Controls
Edgar, WI 715-352-3206
MERRICK Industries Inc
Lynn Haven, FL 800-271-7834
Micromeritics
Norcross, GA 770-638-7569
Midwest Stainless
Menomonie, WI 715-235-5472
Monitor Technologies LLC
Elburn, IL 800-601-6204
Murata Automated Systems
Charlotte, NC 800-428-8469
Murzan Inc
Peachtree Cor, GA 770-448-0583
Namco Controls Corporation
Cleveland, OH 800-626-8324
Napco Security Systems Inc
Amityville, NY 631-842-0253
Nelles Automation
Houston, TX 713-939-9399
Novar
Cleveland, OH 800-348-1235
Nu-Con Equipment
Chanhassen, MN. 877-939-0510
Omni Controls Inc
Tampa, FL 800-783-6664
OMRON Systems LLC
Schaumburg, IL. 800-556-6766
Onset Computer Corp
Bourne, MA 800-564-4377
Optek Inc
Galena, OH 800-533-8400
Paktronics Controls
Southfield, MI. 248-356-1400
Papertech
North Vancouver, BC 877-787-2737
Partnership Resources
Minneapolis, MN 612-331-2075
Payne Controls Co
Scott Depot, WV. 800-331-1345
Peco Controls Corporation
Modesto, CA. 800-732-6285
Pro Controls Inc
Yakima, WA 800-488-3386
Process Automation
Hurst, TX 800-460-9546
Process Solutions
Riviera Beach, FL 561-840-0050
Process Systems
Barrington, IL 847-842-8618
Production Systems
Marietta, GA 800-235-9734
Professional Engineering Assoc
Louisville, KY 502-429-0432
Pyrometer Instrument Co Inc
Windsor, NJ. 800-468-7976
Quest Corp
North Royalton, OH 440-230-9400
R.G. Stephens Engineering
Long Beach, CA 800-499-3001
Ram Equipment Co
Waukesha, WI 262-513-1114
Relco Unisystems Corp
Willmar, MN. 320-231-2210
Rexroth Corporation
Hoffman Estates, IL 847-645-3600
Rheometric Scientific
New Castle, DE. 732-560-8550
Roberts-Gordon LLC
Buffalo, NY. 800-828-7450
S J Controls Inc
Signal Hill, CA 562-494-1400
Samson Controls
Baytown, TX 281-383-3677
Schneider Electric
Foxboro, MA 781-534-7535
Scientech, Inc
Boulder, CO 800-525-0522
SCK Direct Inc
Stratford, CT 800-327-8766

Seneca Environmental Products
Tiffin, OH 419-447-1282
Sepragen Corp
Hayward, CA 510-475-0650
Simpson Electric
Elgin, IL 847-697-2260
South Shore Controls Inc
Perry, OH 440-259-2500
Spinco Metal Products Inc
Newark, NY 315-331-6285
Stainless Products
Somers, WC 800-558-9446
Sterling Ball & Jewel
New Berlin, WI 800-423-3183
Sterling Systems & Controls
Sterling, IL 800-257-7214
T D Sawvel Co
Maple Plain, MN 877-488-1816
Tecweigh
St Paul, MN 800-536-4880
Thermedics Detection
Chelmsford, MA 888-846-7226
Thermo Detection
Franklin, MA 866-269-0070
Thermo King Corp
Bloomington, MN 888-887-2202
Theta Sciences
San Diego, CA 760-745-3311
Transbotics Corp
Charlotte, NC 704-362-1115
Trola Industries Inc
York, PA 717-848-3700
Tuchenhagen
Columbia, MD 410-910-6000
TVC Systems
Portsmouth, NH 888-431-5251
TWM Manufacturing
Leamington, ON 888-495-4831
Vee Gee Scientific Inc
Kirkland, WA 800-423-8842
Videx Inc
Corvallis, OR 541-738-5500
Vulcan Electric Co
Porter, ME 800-922-3027
W.G. Durant Corporation
Whittier, CA 562-946-5555
Watlow Electric
San Jose, CA
Watlow Electric
St Louis, MO 314-878-4600
Waukesha Cherry-Burrell
Louisville, KY 800-252-5200
Webb-Triax Company
Farmington Hills, MI 248-553-1000
WeighPack Systems/Paxiom Group
Montreal, QC 888-934-4472
Williamson & Co
Greer, SC 800-849-3263
Xcel Tower Controls
Gilbertsville, NY 800-288-7362

Temperature

ACR Systems
Surrey, BC 800-663-7845
Acromag Inc.
Wixom, MI 248-624-1541
Advance Energy Technologies
Halfmoon, NY 800-724-0198
Alnor Instrument Company
Skokie, IL 800-424-7427
Analite
Plainview, NY 800-229-3357
Ari Industries Inc
Addison, IL 800-237-6725
Artisan Controls Corp
Randolph, NJ 800-457-4950
Athena Controls Inc
Plymouth Meeting, PA 800-782-6776
Automatic Timing & Controls
Newell, WV 800-727-5646
Brown Fired Heater
Elyria, OH 440-323-3291
Bry-Air Inc
Sunbury, OH 877-379-2479
Burling Instrument Inc
Chatham, NJ 800-635-2526
Burns Engineering Inc
Hopkins, MN 800-328-3871
Chicago Stainless Eqpt Inc
Palm City, FL 800-927-8575

CMT
Hamilton, MA 978-768-2555
Control Concepts Inc.
Chanhassen, MN 800-765-2799
Control Pak Intl
Fenton, MI 810-735-2800
Control Products Inc
Chanhassen, MN 800-947-9098
Cooling Technology Inc
Charlotte, NC 800-872-1448
Crouzet Corporation
Carrollton, TX 800-677-5311
Debelak Technical Systems
Greenville, WI 800-888-4207
Dwyer Instruments Inc
Michigan City, IN 800-872-3141
Eurotherm
Ashburn, VA 703-726-0138
Glo-Quartz Electric Heater
Mentor, OH 800-321-3574
Hanna Instruments
Woonsocket, RI 800-426-6287
Heatrex
Meadville, PA 800-394-6589
IMC Instruments
Menomonee Falls, WI 262-252-4620
Kaye Instruments
N Billerica, MA 800-343-4624
L.C. Thompson Company
Kenosha, WI 800-558-4018
Laboratory Devices
Holliston, MA 508-429-1716
Lumenite Control Tech Inc
Franklin Park, IL 800-323-8510
Munters Corp
Amesbury, MA 800-843-5360
Novar
Cleveland, OH 800-348-1235
Ogden Manufacturing Company
Pittsburgh, PA 412-967-3906
Omni Controls Inc
Tampa, FL 800-783-6664
OMRON Systems LLC
Schaumburg, IL 800-556-6766
Paktronics Controls
Southfield, MI 248-356-1400
Paratherm Corporation
Conshohocken, PA 800-222-3611
Payne Controls Co
Scott Depot, WV 800-331-1345
Polyscience
Niles, IL 800-229-7569
Pyrometer Instrument Co Inc
Windsor, NJ 800-468-7976
Quantem Corp
Ewing, NJ 609-883-9879
Selco Products Company
Anaheim, CA 800-257-3526
Sterling Ball & Jewel
New Berlin, WI 800-423-3183
Thermalogic Corp
Hudson, MA 978-562-5974
Thermo King Corp
Bloomington, MN 888-887-2202
United Electric Controls Co
Watertown, MA 617-926-1000
Vulcan Electric Co
Porter, ME 800-922-3027
Weiss Instruments Inc
Holtsville, NY 631-207-1200

Data Loggers

Ashcroft Inc
Stratford, CT 800-328-8258

Time

Artisan Controls Corp
Randolph, NJ 800-457-4950
Ashcroft Inc
Stratford, CT 800-328-8258
Automatic Timing & Controls
Newell, WV 800-727-5646
Control Products Inc
Chanhassen, MN 800-947-9098
Dayton Marking Devices Company
Dayton, OH 937-432-0285
M.H. Rhodes Cramer
South Windsor, CT 877-684-6464
Pro Scientific Inc
Oxford, CT 800-584-3776

Transportation Loggers

Ashcroft Inc
Stratford, CT 800-328-8258

Vacuum

Ashcroft Inc
Stratford, CT 800-328-8258
BUCHI Corp
New Castle, DE 877-692-8244
Lyco Wausau
Wausau, WI 715-845-7867

pH Loggers

Ashcroft Inc
Stratford, CT 800-328-8258

Pumps

Food

Barnant Company
Lake Barrington, IL 800-637-3739
Clark-Cooper Division   Magnatrol Valve Corporation
Cinnaminson, NJ 856-829-4580
Fluid Metering Inc
Syosset, NY 800-223-3388
Glen Mills Inc.
Clifton, NJ 973-777-0777
Kelmin Products
Plymouth, FL 407-886-6079
Lyco Wausau
Wausau, WI 715-845-7867
Marlow Watson Inc
Wilmington, MA 800-282-8823
Netzsch Pumps North America
Exton, PA 610-363-8010
Northland Process Piping
Isle, MN 320-679-2119
Pump Solutions Group
Oakbrook Terrace, IL 630-487-2240
Roto-Jet Pump
Salt Lake City, UT 801-359-8731
Savage Brothers Company
Elk Grove Vlg, IL 800-342-0973
Waukesha Cherry-Burrell
Louisville, KY 800-252-5200

Sampling & Testing Equipment & Instrumentation

ACR Systems
Surrey, BC 800-663-7845
Advance Fittings Corp
Elkhorn, WI 262-723-6699
Advanced Instruments Inc
Norwood, MA 800-225-4034
Air Logic Power Systems
Milwaukee, WI 800-325-8717
Atkins Technical
Gainesville, FL 800-284-2842
Barco Inc
Duluth, GA 678-475-8000
Binks Industries Inc
Montgomery, IL 630-801-1100
Biocontrol Systems Inc
Bellevue, WA 800-245-0113
Bioscience International Inc
Rockville, MD 301-231-7400
Biotest Diagnostics Corporation
Rockaway, NJ 800-522-0090
Bran & Luebbe
Schaumburg, IL 847-882-8116
Charm Sciences Inc
Lawrence, MA 978-687-9200
Comark Instruments
Everett, WA 800-555-6658
DeltaTrak
Pleasanton, CA 800-962-6776
Elwood Safety Company
Buffalo, NY 866-326-6060
ENSCO Inc
Springfield, VA 703-321-9000
FILTEC-Inspection Systems
Torrance, CA 888-434-5832
Gerstel Inc
Linthicum Hts, MD 800-413-8160
Glen Mills Inc.
Clifton, NJ 973-777-0777

Grace Instrument Co
Houston, TX 800-304-5859
HD Electric Co
Park City, IL 847-473-4882
I.W. Tremont Company
Hawthorne, NJ 973-427-3800
Idexx Laboratories Inc
Westbrook, ME 800-548-6733
IQ Scientific Instruments
Loveland, CO 800-227-4224
Kodex Inc
Nutley, NJ 800-325-6339
Konica Minolta Corp
Ramsey, NJ 888-473-3637
Labvantage Solutions Inc
Somerset, NJ 888-346-5467
Light Technology Ind
Gaithersburg, MD 301-990-4050
Machine Applications Corp
Sandusky, OH 419-621-2322
Maselli Measurements Inc
Stockton, CA 800-964-9600
Mosshaim Innovations
Jacksonville, FL 888-995-7775
National Hotpack
Stone Ridge, NY 800-431-8232
Neogen Corp
Lansing, MI 800-234-5333
Noral
Natick, MA 800-348-2345
Ohio Magnetics Inc
Maple Heights, OH 800-486-6446
Orion Research
Beverly, MA 978-232-6000
Paul N. Gardner Company
Pompano Beach, FL 800-762-2478
Peco Controls Corporation
Modesto, CA 800-732-6285
Perten Instruments
Springfield, IL 888-773-7836
Polyscience
Niles, IL 800-229-7569
Promega
Madison, WI 800-356-9526
QMI
St Paul, MN 651-501-2337
Quality Control Equipment Co
Des Moines, IA 515-266-2268
Remel
Lenexa, KS 800-255-6730
SDIX
Newark, DE 800-544-8881
Sensidyne
St. Petersburg, FL 800-451-9444
Sentry Equipment Corp
Oconomowoc, WI 262-567-7256
Spiral Biotech Inc
Norwood, MA 800-554-1620
Staplex Co Inc
Brooklyn, NY 800-221-0822
Tricor Systems Inc
Elgin, IL 800-575-0161
Troxler Electronic Lab Inc
Durham, NC 877-876-9537
Univex Corp
Salem, NH 800-258-6358
Vee Gee Scientific Inc
Kirkland, WA 800-423-8842
Weber Scientific Inc
Trenton, NJ 800-328-8378
Whatman
Haverhill, MA 978-374-7400

Scales & Weighing Systems

A&D Weighing
San Jose, CA 800-726-3364
Abel Manufacturing Co
Appleton, WI 920-734-4443
Accu-Pak
Akron, OH
Acme Scale Co
San Leandro, CA 888-638-5040
Action Packaging Automation
Roosevelt, NJ 800-241-2724
Actionpac Scales Automation
Oxnard, CA 800-394-0154
Adamatic
Auburn, WA 800-578-2547
Advance Weight Systems Inc
Grafton, OH 440-926-3691

Ag-Pak
Gasport, NY 716-772-2651
All Fill Inc
Exton, PA 866-255-4455
Amark Packaging Systems
Kansas City, MO 816-965-9000
American Bag & Burlap Company
Chelsea, MA 617-884-7600
Andgar Corp
Ferndale, WA 360-366-9900
AP Dataweigh Inc
Cumming, GA 877-409-2562
APEC
Lake Odessa, MI 616-374-1000
Arkfeld Mfg & Distributing Co
Norfolk, NE 800-533-0676
ASI Electronics Inc
Cypress, TX 800-231-6066
Atlas Equipment Company
Kansas City, MO 800-842-9188
Automated Packaging Systems
Streetsboro, OH 800-527-0733
Avery Weigh-Tronix
Fairmont, MN 877-368-2039
Avery Weigh-Tronix LLC
Fairmont, MN 800-368-2039
AZO Food
Memphis, TN 901-794-9480
B & P Process Equipment
Saginaw, MI 989-757-1300
BLH Electronics
Canton, MA 781-821-2000
Blodgett Co
Houston, TX 281-933-6195
Brechbuhler Scales
Canton, OH 330-453-2424
Cardinal Scale Mfg Co
Webb City, MO 800-441-4237
CCi Scale Company
Clovis, CA 800-900-0224
Chemi-Graphic Inc
Ludlow, MA 413-589-0151
Chlorinators Inc
Stuart, FL 800-327-9761
Cintex of America
Carol Stream, IL 800-424-6839
Circuits & Systems Inc
East Rockaway, NY 800-645-4301
Crestware
North Salt Lake, UT 800-345-0513
Crystal-Vision Packaging Systems
Torrance, CA 800-331-3240
DBE Inc
Concord, ON 800-461-5313
Delavan Spray Technologies
Bamberg, SC 800-982-6943
Detecto Scale Co
Webb City, MO 800-641-2008
Dipix Technologies
Ottawa, ON 613-596-4942
Doran Scales Inc
Batavia, IL 800-365-0084
Edlund Co
Burlington, VT 800-772-2126
Electronic Weighing Systems
Opa Locka, FL 305-685-8067
Emery Winslow Scale Co
Seymour, CT 203-881-9333
Equipment Outlet
Meridian, ID 208-887-1472
Exact Equipment Corporation
Morrisville, PA 215-295-2000
Fairbanks Scales
Overland Park, KS 800-451-4107
Fawema Packaging Machinery
Palmetto, FL 941-351-9597
Frazier Precision Instr Co
Hagerstown, MD 301-790-2585
Fred D Pfening Co
Columbus, OH 614-294-5361
Fuller Weighing Systems
Columbus, OH 614-882-8121
General Bag Corporation
Cleveland, OH 800-837-9396
General Packaging Equipment Co
Houston, TX 713-686-4331
Grain Machinery Mfg Corp
Miami, FL 305-620-2525
Hardy Systems Corporation
Northbrook, IL 800-927-3956
Howes S Co Inc
Silver Creek, NY 888-255-2611

Hyer Industries
Pembroke, MA 781-826-8101
IEW
Niles, OH 330-652-0113
Ilapak Inc
Newtown, PA 215-579-2900
Iman Pack
Westland, MI 800-810-4626
Industrial Laboratory Eqpt Co
Charlotte, NC 704-357-3930
Inspired Automation Inc
Agoura Hills, CA 818-991-4598
Intercomp
Hamel, MN 800-328-3336
IWS Scales
San Diego, CA 800-881-9755
Key Material Handling Inc
Simi Valley, CA 800-539-7225
Key-Pak Machines
Lebanon, NJ 908-236-2111
Kisco Manufacturing
Port Alberni, BC 604-823-7456
Kliklok-Woodman
Decatur, GA 770-981-5200
Lock Inspection Systems
Fitchburg, MA 800-227-5539
Lockwood Packaging
Woburn, MA 800-641-3100
MAC Equipment
Kansas City, MO 800-821-2476
Mandeville Company
Minneapolis, MN 800-328-8490
Measurement Systems Intl
Tukwila, WA 800-874-4320
MERRICK Industries Inc
Lynn Haven, FL 800-271-7834
Micro-Strain
Spring City, PA 610-948-4550
MTL Etching Industries
Woodmere, NY 516-295-9733
National Scoop & Equipment Company
Spring House, PA 215-646-2040
Nicol Scales & Measurement LP
Dallas, TX 800-225-8181
Ohaus Corp
Parsippany, NJ 800-672-7722
Pacific Scale Company
Clackamas, OR 800-537-1886
Peco Controls Corporation
Modesto, CA 800-732-6285
Pelouze Scale Company
Bridgeview, IL 800-323-8363
Penn Scale ManufacturingCompany
Philadelphia, PA 215-739-9644
Precision Solutions Inc
Quakertown, PA 215-536-4400
Q A Supplies LLC
Norfolk, VA 800-472-7205
Quest Corp
North Royalton, OH 440-230-9400
Renard Machine Company
Green Bay, WI 920-432-8412
Renold Products
Westfield, NY 800-879-2529
Rice Lake Weighing Systems
Rice Lake, WI 800-472-6703
Sartorius Corp
Edgewood, NY 800-635-2906
Schaffer Poidometer Company
Pittsburgh, PA 412-281-9031
Scientech, Inc
Boulder, CO 800-525-0522
Si-Lodec
Tukwila, WA 800-255-8274
Sig Pack
Oakland, CA 800-824-3245
Sterling Scale Co
Southfield, MI 800-331-9931
Sterling Systems & Controls
Sterling, IL 800-257-7214
Summit Machine Builders Corporation
Denver, CO 800-274-6741
Superior Products Company
Saint Paul, MN 800-328-9800
Taylor Products Co
Parsons, KS 888-882-9537
Tecweigh
St Paul, MN 800-536-4880
Temco
Oakland, CA 707-746-5966
Thermo BLH
Canton, MA 781-821-2000

Thurman Scale
Groveport, OH .800-688-9741
Tomac Packaging
Woburn, MA 800-641-3100
Toroid Corp
Huntsville, AL .256-837-7510
Triangle Package Machinery Co
Chicago, IL 800-621-4170
Tridyne Process Systems
South Burlington, VT 802-863-6873
Triner Scale & Mfg Co
Olive Branch, MS 800-238-0152
Vande Berg SCALES/Vbs Inc
Sioux Center, IA 712-722-1181
Vega Americas Inc
Cincinnati, OH .800-367-5383
Vertex Interactive
Clifton, NJ 973-777-3500
VitaMinder Company
Providence, RI .800-858-8840
Weigh Right Automatic Scale Co
Joliet, IL 800-571-0249
WeighPack Systems/Paxiom Group
Montreal, QC 888-934-4472
Yakima Wire Works
Reedley, CA 800-344-8951
Yamato Corporation
Colorado Springs, CO. 800-538-1762
Yargus Manufacturing Inc
Marshall, IL 217-826-8059

Sensors

Applied Robotics Inc
Schenectady, NY 800-309-3475
Ari Industries Inc
Addison, IL 800-237-6725
Ashcroft Inc
Stratford, CT 800-328-8258
Automatic Timing & Controls
Newell, WV 800-727-5646
Aw Sheepscot Holding Co Inc
Franksville, WI .800-850-6110
Axelrod, Norman N
New York, NY .212-369-2885
Banner Engineering Corp
Minneapolis, MN 888-373-6767
Burns Engineering Inc
Hopkins, MN 800-328-3871
Clean Water Systems
Klamath Falls, OR 866-273-9993
Conax Buffalo Technologies
Buffalo, NY 800-223-2389
Eurotherm
Ashburn, VA 703-726-0138
Fsi Technologies
Lombard, IL 800-468-6009
GE Interlogix Industrial
Tualatin, OR 800-247-9447
Honeywell Sensing & Internet of Things
DE 800-537-6945
Industrial Devices Corporation
Petaluma, CA 707-789-1000
Infitec Inc
East Syracuse, NY 800-334-0837
Kinematics & Controls Corporation
Brooksville, FL .800-833-8103
Light Technology Ind
Gaithersburg, MD 301-990-4050
Magpowr
Fenton, MO 800-624-7697
Mesa Laboratories Inc
Lakewood, CO .800-525-1215
Migatron Corp
Woodstock, IL .888-644-2876
Monitor Technologies LLC
Elburn, IL 800-601-6204
Namco Controls Corporation
Cleveland, OH .800-626-8324
OMRON Systems LLC
Schaumburg, IL. 800-556-6766
Ozotech Inc
Yreka, CA 530-842-4189
Prominent Fluid Controls Inc
Pittsburgh, PA .412-787-2484
Pyrometer Instrument Co Inc
Windsor, NJ. 800-468-7976
Quantem Corp
Ewing, NJ 609-883-9879
Raytek Corporation
Santa Cruz, CA .800-866-5478

Reflectronics
Lexington, KY .888-415-0441
SICK Inc
Bloomington, MN. 800-325-7425
Tri-Tronics
Tampa, FL. 800-237-0946
United Electric Controls Co
Watertown, MA. 617-926-1000
Vega Americas Inc
Cincinnati, OH .800-367-5383
Venture Measurement Co LLC
Spartanburg, SC 864-574-8960
Viatran Corporation
North Tonawanda, NY 800-688-0030
Vulcan Electric Co
Porter, ME. 800-922-3027
Watlow Electric
Richmond, IL

Stoppers

Rubber, Bottle

Crown Holdings, Inc.
Yardley, PA 215-698-5100
Imperial Plastics Inc
Lakeville, MN. .952-469-4951
Oak Barrel Winecraft
Berkeley, CA. 510-849-0400
Qualiform, Inc
Wadsworth, OH. 330-336-6777
RubaTex Polymer
Middlefield, OH 440-632-1691
Simolex Rubber Corp
Plymouth, MI 734-453-4500
Wilkens-Anderson Co
Chicago, IL. 800-847-2222

Testers

Food Inspection

Advanced Instruments Inc
Norwood, MA. .800-225-4034
Ameritech Laboratories
Flushing, NY. 718-461-0475
Ashcroft Inc
Stratford, CT 800-328-8258
Biotek Instruments Inc
Winooski, VT 802-655-4040
Charm Sciences Inc
Lawrence, MA .978-687-9200
DeltaTrak
Pleasanton, CA 800-962-6776
Eurofins Scientific Inc.
Dayton, OH. 800-880-1038
Fettig Laboratories
Grand Rapids, MI 616-245-3000
Industrial Laboratories Co
Wheat Ridge, CO 800-456-5288
Kodex Inc
Nutley, NJ 800-325-6339
Libra Technical Center
Metuchen, NJ .732-321-5200
Loma Systems
Carol Stream, IL 800-872-5662
Marshfield Food Safety
Marshfield, WI .888-780-9897
MISCO Refractometer
Cleveland, OH .866-831-1999
Neogen Corp
Lansing, MI. 800-234-5333
Northwest Laboratories
Seattle, WA 206-763-6252
Pacific Scientific Instrument
Grants Pass, OR 800-866-7889
Q A Supplies LLC
Norfolk, VA. 800-472-7205
Radiation Processing Division
Parsippany, NJ. 800-442-1969
Raytek Corporation
Santa Cruz, CA 800-866-5478
Reichert Analytical Instruments
Depew, NY 716-686-4500
SDIX
Newark, DE. 800-544-8881
Supelco Inc
Bellefonte, PA. .800-247-6628
Total Quality Corporation
Branford, CT. 800-453-9729

Woodson-Tenent Laboratories
Des Moines, IA 515-265-1461
Woodson-Tenent Laboratories
Memphis, TN .515-280-8378
Woodson-Tenent Laboratories
Dayton, OH 937-236-5756

Laboratory

Aerotech Laboratories
Phoenix, AZ 800-651-4802
Analytical Measurements
Chester, NJ 800-635-5580
Ashcroft Inc
Stratford, CT 800-328-8258
Beckman Coulter Inc.
Brea, CA 800-526-3821
Biocontrol Systems Inc
Bellevue, WA 800-245-0113
BluMetric Environmental Inc.
Ottawa, ON 613-839-3053
C.W. Brabender Instruments
South Hackensack, NJ 201-343-8425
Charm Sciences Inc
Lawrence, MA .978-687-9200
Chestnut Labs
Springfield, MO 417-829-3788
CSC Scientific Co Inc
Fairfax, VA 800-621-4778
Enviro-Test/Perry Laboratories
Woodridge, IL .630-324-6685
Eurofins Scientific Inc
Des Moines, IA 800-841-1110
Eurofins Scientific Inc.
Dayton, OH. 800-880-1038
Industrial Laboratories Co
Wheat Ridge, CO 800-456-5288
Libra Technical Center
Metuchen, NJ .732-321-5200
Northwest Laboratories
Seattle, WA 206-763-6252
Oxoid
Nepean, ON. 800-567-8378
Perten Instruments
Springfield, IL. .888-773-7836
Radiation Processing Division
Parsippany, NJ. 800-442-1969
Remel
Lenexa, KS 800-255-6730
Spiral Biotech Inc
Norwood, MA. .800-554-1620
Teledyne TEKMAR
Mason, OH 800-874-2004
Texture Technologies Corporation
Scarsdale, NY .914-472-0531
Troxler Electronic Lab Inc
Durham, NC 877-876-9537
Vee Gee Scientific Inc
Kirkland, WA 800-423-8842
VICAM
Milford, MA 800-338-4381
Wilkens-Anderson Co
Chicago, IL 800-847-2222
Woodson-Tenent Laboratories
Des Moines, IA 515-265-1461
Woodson-Tenent Laboratories
Memphis, TN .515-280-8378
Woodson-Tenent Laboratories
Dayton, OH 937-236-5756

Milk & Cream

Advanced Instruments Inc
Norwood, MA. .800-225-4034

Packaging Materials/Containers

Air Logic Power Systems
Milwaukee, WI. 800-325-8717
Altek Co
Torrington, CT .860-482-7626
Carleton Technologies Inc
Orchard Park, NY 716-662-0006
Daystar
Glen Arm, MD .800-494-6537
Food Instrument Corp
Federalsburg, MD 800-542-5688
Kodex Inc
Nutley, NJ 800-325-6339
Libra Technical Center
Metuchen, NJ .732-321-5200

Mocon Inc
Minneapolis, MN 763-493-7229
NDC Infrared EngineeringInc
Irwindale, CA 626-960-3300
United Desiccants
Reno, NE 888-659-1377

Thermometers

A&M Thermometer Corporation
Asheville, NC 800-685-9211
Agri-Equipment International
Longs, SC 877-550-4709
Alnor Instrument Company
Skokie, IL 800-424-7427
Ametek
Sellersville, PA 215-257-6531
AMETEK National Controls Corp
West Chicago, IL 800-323-5293
Ashcroft Inc
Stratford, CT 800-328-8258
Atkins Technical
Gainesville, FL 800-284-2842
Barnant Company
Lake Barrington, IL 800-637-3739
Bowtemp
Mont-Royal, QC 514-735-5551
Browne & Company
Markham, ON 905-475-6104
Chaney Instrument Co
Lake Geneva, WI 800-777-0565
Chicago Stainless Eqpt Inc
Palm City, FL 800-927-8575
Comark Instruments
Everett, WA 800-555-6658
Crestware
North Salt Lake, UT 800-345-0513
Datapaq
Wilmington, MA 800-326-5270
Delta Trak
Pleasanton, CA 800-962-6776
DeltaTrak
Pleasanton, CA 800-962-6776

Dynasys Technologies
Clearwater, FL 800-867-5968
E & E Process Instrumentation
Concord, Ontario, ON 905-669-4857
Elreha Controls Corporation
St Petersburg, FL 727-327-6236
EPD Technology Corporation
Elmsford, NY 800-892-8926
Esco Products Inc
Houston, TX 800-966-5514
Eurotherm
Ashburn, VA 703-726-0138
Grace Instrument Co
Houston, TX 800-304-5859
Greer's Ferry Glass Work
Dubuque, IA 501-589-2947
Hanna Instruments
Woonsocket, RI 800-426-6287
Kason Central
Columbus, OH 614-885-1992
Kason Industries
Newnan, GA 770-254-0553
L.C. Thompson Company
Kenosha, WI 800-558-4018
Liberty Ware LLC
Clearfield, UT 888-500-5885
Luma Sense Technologies Inc
Santa Clara, CA 800-631-0176
Marshall Instruments Inc
Anaheim, CA 800-222-8476
Matfer Inc
Van Nuys, CA 800-766-0333
Mesa Laboratories Inc
Lakewood, CO 800-525-1215
Miljoco Corp
Mt Clemens, MI 888-888-1498
Music City Metals Inc
Nashville, TN 800-251-2674
National Time Recording Eqpt
New York, NY 212-227-3310
Noral
Natick, MA 800-348-2345

Pelouze Scale Company
Bridgeview, IL 800-323-8363
Q A Supplies LLC
Norfolk, VA 800-472-7205
Raytek Corporation
Santa Cruz, CA 800-866-5478
Reotemp Instrument Corp
San Diego, CA 800-648-7737
Sensitech Inc
Beverly, MA 800-843-8367
Sensitech Inc
Redmond, WA 800-999-7926
Special Products
Springfield, MO 417-881-6114
Superior Products Company
Saint Paul, MN 800-328-9800
Taylor Precision Products
Oak Brook, IL
Taylor Precision Products
Oak Brook, IL 866-843-3905
Tel-Tru Manufacturing Co
Rochester, NY 800-232-5335
TESTO
Sparta, NJ 800-227-0729
Thermo Instruments
Yaphank, NY 631-924-0880
Trans World Services
Melrose, MA 800-882-2105
United Electric Controls Co
Watertown, MA 617-926-1000
Weiss Instruments Inc
Holtsville, NY 631-207-1200
Wescor
Logan, UT 800-453-2725
Wika Instrument LP
Lawrenceville, GA 800-645-0606
Wilkens-Anderson Co
Chicago, IL 800-847-2222

Packaging Materials & Supplies

Bags

Ampac Packaging, LLC
Cincinnati, OH 800-543-7030
Bella Vita
Phoenix, AZ 877-827-3638
Can Creations
Pembroke Pines, FL 800-272-0235
Clear Lam Packaging
Elk Grove Village, IL 847-439-8570
Clorox Company
Oakland, CA 800-227-1860
Dura-Pack Inc.
Taylor, MI 313-299-9600
Grayling Industries
Alpharetta, GA 800-635-1551
Libra Technical Center
Metuchen, NJ 732-321-5200
Nashville Wraps LLC
Hendersonville, TN 800-547-9727
Novolex
Hartsville, SC 800-845-6051
Polytarp Products
Toronto, ON 800-606-2231
Revere Group
Seattle, WA 206-545-1850
S Walter Packaging Corp
Philadelphia, PA 888-429-5673
Temkin International
Payson, UT 800-235-5263
Tenka Flexible Packaging
Chino, CA 888-836-5255
Vista International Packaging
Kenosha, WI 800-558-4058

Bread & Pastry

Aladdin Transparent Packaging
Hauppauge, NY 631-273-4747
All American Poly
Piscataway, NJ 800-526-3551
Arbee Transparent Inc
Elk Grove Vlg, IL 800-642-2247
Checker Bag Co
St Louis, MO. 800-489-3130
Flexo Transparent Inc
Buffalo, NY. 877-993-5396
Jomar Plastics Industry
Nanty Glo, PA. 800-681-4039
Malpack Polybag
Ajax, ON. 905-428-3751
Mini-Bag Company
Farmingdale, NY 631-694-3325
Moser Bag & Paper Company
Cleveland, OH 800-433-6638
Pactiv LLC
Lake Forest, IL 800-476-4300
Pak-Sher
Kilgore, TX. 903-984-8596
Pater & Associates
Cincinnati, OH
Pexco Packaging Corporation
Toledo, OH 800-227-9950
Pfeil & Holding Inc
Woodside, NY. 800-247-7955
Seal-Tite Bag Company
Philadelphia, PA 717-917-1949
Specialty Paper Bag Company
City of Industry, CA 800-962-2247
Star Poly Bag Inc
Brooklyn, NY 718-384-7034
Stewart Sutherland Inc
Vicksburg, MI 269-649-0530

Bulk

King Bag & Mfg Co
Cincinnati, OH 800-444-5464

Cellophane

Arbee Transparent Inc
Elk Grove Vlg, IL. 800-642-2247
Beayl Weiner/Pak
Pacific Palisades, CA 310-454-1354
Chalmur Bag Company, LLC
Philadelphia, PA 800-349-2247

Checker Bag Co
St Louis, MO. 800-489-3130
Collectors Gallery
St Charles, IL 800-346-3063
Formel Industries
Franklin Park, IL 800-373-3300
Milprint
Oshkosh, WI. 920-303-8600
Pater & Associates
Cincinnati, OH
Ultrapak
Dunkirk, NY 800-228-6030

Centrifuge

King Bag & Mfg Co
Cincinnati, OH 800-444-5464

Confectioners'

Accurate Flannel Bag Company
Paterson, NJ 800-234-9200
Arbee Transparent Inc
Elk Grove Vlg, IL 800-642-2247
August Thomsen Corp
Glen Cove, NY 800-645-7170
Checker Bag Co
St Louis, MO. 800-489-3130
Collectors Gallery
St Charles, IL 800-346-3063
Colonial Transparent Products Company
Hicksville, NY 516-822-4430
Flexo Transparent Inc
Buffalo, NY. 877-993-5396
Milprint
Oshkosh, WI. 920-303-8600
Mimi et Cie
Seattle, WA 206-545-1850
Star Poly Bag Inc
Brooklyn, NY 718-384-7034
Stewart Sutherland Inc
Vicksburg, MI 269-649-0530
Wisconsin Converting Inc
Green Bay, WI. 800-544-1935

Flour, Meal & Feed

Accurate Flannel Bag Company
Paterson, NJ 800-234-9200
Chatfield & Woods Sack Company
Harrison, OH. 513-202-9700
Coveris
Excelsior Springs, MO
Dayton Bag & Burlap Co
Dayton, OH. 800-543-3400
Flexo Transparent Inc
Buffalo, NY. 877-993-5396
Frontier Bag Co Inc
Omaha, NE 800-278-2247
Fulton-Denver Co
Denver, CO. 800-521-1414
Hubco Inc
Hutchinson, KS. 800-563-1867
Indian Valley Industries
Johnson City, NY 800-659-5111
Set Point Paper Company
Mansfield, MA 800-225-0501
Star Poly Bag Inc
Brooklyn, NY 718-384-7034

Food

Accurate Flannel Bag Company
Paterson, NJ 800-234-9200
Aladdin Transparent Packaging
Hauppauge, NY 631-273-4747
All American Poly
Piscataway, NJ 800-526-3551
Arbee Transparent Inc
Elk Grove Vlg, IL. 800-642-2247
Automated Packaging Systems
Streetsboro, OH 800-527-0733
Bag Masters
St Petersburg, FL 800-330-2247
Bagcraft Papercon
Chicago, IL. 800-621-8468

Brown Paper Goods Co
Waukegan, IL 847-688-1450
Bryce Corp
Memphis, TN 800-238-7277
Cadie Products Corp
Paterson, NJ 973-278-8300
Castle Bag Co.
Wilmington, DE 302-656-1001
Checker Bag Co
St Louis, MO. 800-489-3130
Cincinnati Convertors Inc
Cincinnati, OH 513-731-6600
Cleveland Plastic Films
Elyria, OH. 800-832-6799
Collectors Gallery
St Charles, IL 800-346-3063
Conwed Global Netting Sltns
Roanoke, VA. 800-368-3610
COVERIS
Tomah, WI 608-372-2153
David Dobbs Enterprise Inc.
St Augustine, FL. 800-889-6368
Development Workshop Inc
Idaho Falls, ID 800-657-5597
Dixie Poly Packaging
Greenville, SC. 864-268-3751
Eco-Bag Products
Ossining, NY 800-720-2247
Emoshun
Rancho Cucamonga, CA 909-484-9559
Fabriko
Altavista, VA. 888-203-8098
Fischer Paper Products Inc
Antioch, IL. 800-323-9093
Flexo Transparent Inc
Buffalo, NY. 877-993-5396
Food Pak Corp
San Mateo, CA 650-341-6559
Fulton-Denver Co
Denver, CO. 800-521-1414
Glopak
St Leonard, QC 800-361-6994
GP Plastics Corporation
Medley, FL 305-888-3555
Gulf Arizona Packaging
Humble, TX 800-364-3887
Gulf Systems
Brownsville, TX 800-217-4853
Gulf Systems
Humble, TX 800-364-3887
Gulf Systems
Arlington, TX 817-261-1915
Hank Rivera Associates
Dearborn, MI 313-581-8300
Herche Warehouse
Denver, CO. 303-371-8186
Hubco Inc
Hutchinson, KS. 800-563-1867
Jomar Plastics Industry
Nanty Glo, PA. 800-681-4039
K & L Intl
Ontario, CA. 888-598-5588
Keeper Thermal Bag Co
Bartlett, IL. 800-765-9244
Liqui-Box
Richmond, VA. 804-325-1400
Masternet, Ltd
Mississauga, ON. 800-216-2536
McDowell Industries
Memphis, TN 800-622-3695
Millhiser
Richmond, VA. 800-446-2247
Mimi et Cie
Seattle, WA 206-545-1850
Mini-Bag Company
Farmingdale, NY 631-694-3325
Morgan Brothers Bag Company
Richmond, VA. 804-355-9107
Moser Bag & Paper Company
Cleveland, OH 800-433-6638
Naltex
Austin, TX. 800-531-5112
Net Pack Systems
Oakland, ME. 207-465-4531
Noteworthy Company
Amsterdam, NY 800-696-7849

NOVOLEX
  Glendale, AZ............800-243-0306
Orange Plastics
  Compton, CA............310-609-2121
Pactiv LLC
  Lake Forest, IL..........800-476-4300
Pak-Sher
  Kilgore, TX.............903-984-8596
Pan Pacific Plastics Inc
  Hayward, CA............888-475-6888
Parvin Manufacturing Company
  Los Angeles, CA.........800-648-0770
Pater & Associates
  Cincinnati, OH
Petoskey Plastics
  Morristown, TN..........423-586-8917
Pexco Packaging Corporation
  Toledo, OH.............800-227-9950
Poly Plastic Products Inc
  Delano, PA.............570-467-3000
Portco Corporation
  Vancouver, WA..........800-426-1794
Rapak
  Romeoville, IL..........815-372-3670
Ray C. Sprosty Bag Company
  Wooster, OH............330-264-8559
Roplast Industries Inc
  Oroville, CA............800-767-5278
Ross & Wallace Inc
  Hammond, LA...........800-854-2300
Rutan Poly Industries Inc
  Mahwah, NJ............800-872-1474
Scholle IPN
  Merced, CA.............209-384-3100
Service Manufacturing
  Aurora, IL..............888-325-2788
Sheboygan Paper Box Co
  Sheboygan, WI..........800-458-8373
Signature Packaging
  West Orange, NJ.........800-376-2299
Specialty Paper Bag Company
  City of Industry, CA......800-962-2247
Star Poly Bag Inc
  Brooklyn, NY...........718-384-7034
Sterling Net & Twine Company
  Cedar Knolls, NJ.........800-342-0316
Sterling Novelty Products
  Northbrook, IL..........847-291-0070
Stewart Sutherland Inc
  Vicksburg, MI...........269-649-0530
Storsack Inc
  Houston, TX............800-841-4982
Stretch-Vent Packaging System
  Ontario, CA............800-822-8368
TEMP-TECH Company
  Springfield, MA..........800-343-5579
Tenka Flexible Packaging
  Chino, CA.............888-836-5255
Thermal Bags By Ingrid Inc
  Gilberts, IL............800-622-5560
Trevor Owen Limited
  Scarborough, ON........866-487-2224
Urnex Brands Inc
  Elmsford, NY...........800-222-2826
Valley Packaging Supply Co
  Green Bay, WI..........920-336-9012
Vonco Products LLC
  Lake Villa, IL...........800-323-9077
Walnut Packaging Inc
  Farmingdale, NY.........631-293-3836
Wins Paper Products
  Springtown, TX.........800-733-2420
Wisconsin Converting Inc
  Green Bay, WI..........800-544-1935

Fruit & Vegetable

Accurate Flannel Bag Company
  Paterson, NJ...........800-234-9200
Arbee Transparent Inc
  Elk Grove Vlg, IL........800-642-2247
Conwed Global Netting Sltns
  Roanoke, VA...........800-368-3610
Eco-Bag Products
  Ossining, NY...........800-720-2247
Flexo Transparent Inc
  Buffalo, NY............877-993-5396
Frontier Bag Co Inc
  Omaha, NE............800-278-2247
Fulton-Denver Co
  Denver, CO............800-521-1414

Gulf Arizona Packaging
  Humble, TX............800-364-3887
Gulf Systems
  Brownsville, TX.........800-217-4853
Gulf Systems
  Humble, TX............800-364-3887
Gulf Systems
  Arlington, TX...........817-261-1915
Herche Warehouse
  Denver, CO............303-371-8186
Indian Valley Industries
  Johnson City, NY........800-659-5111
Inteplast Bags & Films Corporation
  Delta, BC.............604-946-5431
Langston Co Inc
  Memphis, TN...........901-774-4440
Masternet, Ltd
  Mississauga, ON.........800-216-2536
McDowell Industries
  Memphis, TN...........800-622-3695
Mini-Bag Company
  Farmingdale, NY.........631-694-3325
Morgan Brothers Bag Company
  Richmond, VA..........804-355-9107
Naltex
  Austin, TX.............800-531-5112
Net Pack Systems
  Oakland, ME...........207-465-4531
Orange Plastics
  Compton, CA...........310-609-2121
Pan Pacific Plastics Inc
  Hayward, CA...........888-475-6888
Pater & Associates
  Cincinnati, OH
Portco Corporation
  Vancouver, WA.........800-426-1794
Roplast Industries Inc
  Oroville, CA...........800-767-5278
Signature Packaging
  West Orange, NJ........800-376-2299
Sterling Net & Twine Company
  Cedar Knolls, NJ........800-342-0316
Urnex Brands Inc
  Elmsford, NY...........800-222-2826

Grain

Coveris
  Excelsior Springs, MO
Dayton Bag & Burlap Co
  Dayton, OH............800-543-3400
Development Workshop Inc
  Idaho Falls, ID..........800-657-5597
Flexo Transparent Inc
  Buffalo, NY............877-993-5396
Indian Valley Industries
  Johnson City, NY........800-659-5111
McDowell Industries
  Memphis, TN...........800-622-3695
Portco Corporation
  Vancouver, WA.........800-426-1794
Storsack Inc
  Houston, TX...........800-841-4982

Greaseproof

Arbee Transparent Inc
  Elk Grove Vlg, IL........800-642-2247
Brown Paper Goods Co
  Waukegan, IL...........847-688-1450
Cincinnati Convertors Inc
  Cincinnati, OH..........513-731-6600
COVERIS
  Tomah, WI............608-372-2153
Coveris
  Excelsior Springs, MO
Dayton Bag & Burlap Co
  Dayton, OH............800-543-3400
Mini-Bag Company
  Farmingdale, NY.........631-694-3325

Heat Sealed

Aladdin Transparent Packaging
  Hauppauge, NY.........631-273-4747
Arbee Transparent Inc
  Elk Grove Vlg, IL........800-642-2247
Atlas Tag & Label Inc
  Neenah, WI............800-558-6418
Automated Packaging Systems
  Streetsboro, OH.........800-527-0733

Beayl Weiner/Pak
  Pacific Palisades, CA......310-454-1354
Chalmur Bag Company, LLC
  Philadelphia, PA.........800-349-2247
Cincinnati Convertors Inc
  Cincinnati, OH..........513-731-6600
COVERIS
  Tomah, WI............608-372-2153
Coveris
  Excelsior Springs, MO
Flexo Transparent Inc
  Buffalo, NY............877-993-5396
Gulf Arizona Packaging
  Humble, TX............800-364-3887
Gulf Systems
  Humble, TX............800-364-3887
Gulf Systems
  Arlington, TX...........817-261-1915
Herche Warehouse
  Denver, CO............303-371-8186
Home Plastics Inc
  Des Moines, IA..........515-265-2562
Keystone Packaging Svc Inc
  Phillipsburg, NJ.........800-473-8567
Liqui-Box
  Richmond, VA..........804-325-1400
Mini-Bag Company
  Farmingdale, NY.........631-694-3325
NAP Industries
  Brooklyn, NY...........877-635-4948
Net Pack Systems
  Oakland, ME...........207-465-4531
Pater & Associates
  Cincinnati, OH
Ram Industries
  Erwin, TN.............800-523-3883
Seal-Tite Bag Company
  Philadelphia, PA.........717-917-1949
Servin Company
  New Baltimore, MI.......800-824-0962
Set Point Paper Company
  Mansfield, MA..........800-225-0501
Star Poly Bag Inc
  Brooklyn, NY...........718-384-7034
Thermal Bags By Ingrid Inc
  Gilberts, IL............800-622-5560
Ultrapak
  Dunkirk, NY...........800-228-6030
Urnex Brands Inc
  Elmsford, NY...........800-222-2826

Laminated

Arbee Transparent Inc
  Elk Grove Vlg, IL........800-642-2247
BAW Plastics Inc
  Clairton, PA............800-783-2229
Cincinnati Convertors Inc
  Cincinnati, OH..........513-731-6600
Coveris
  Excelsior Springs, MO
Gulf Arizona Packaging
  Humble, TX............800-364-3887
Gulf Systems
  Humble, TX............800-364-3887
Gulf Systems
  Arlington, TX...........817-261-1915
Herche Warehouse
  Denver, CO............303-371-8186
Pater & Associates
  Cincinnati, OH
Sheboygan Paper Box Co
  Sheboygan, WI..........800-458-8373
Sungjae Corporation
  Irvine, CA.............949-757-1727
Vonco Products LLC
  Lake Villa, IL...........800-323-9077
Workman Packaging Inc.
  Saint-Laurent, QC.......800-252-5208

Meat

Accurate Flannel Bag Company
  Paterson, NJ...........800-234-9200
All American Poly
  Piscataway, NJ..........800-526-3551
Arbee Transparent Inc
  Elk Grove Vlg, IL........800-642-2247
Flexo Transparent Inc
  Buffalo, NY............877-993-5396
Frontier Bag
  Kansas City, MO........816-765-4811

Jomar Plastics Industry
Nanty Glo, PA..............800-681-4039
Morgan Brothers Bag Company
Richmond, VA..............804-355-9107
NAP Industries
Brooklyn, NY..............877-635-4948
Net Pack Systems
Oakland, ME..............207-465-4531
Pan Pacific Plastics Inc
Hayward, CA..............888-475-6888
VPI Manufacturing
Draper, UT..............801-495-2310

Multi-Wall

Central Bag Co
Leavenworth, KS..............913-250-0325
Colonial Transparent Products Company
Hicksville, NY..............516-822-4430
Coveris
Excelsior Springs, MO
Durango-Georgia Paper
Tampa, FL..............813-286-2718
First Midwest of Iowa Corporation
Des Moines, IA..............800-247-8411
Flexo Transparent Inc
Buffalo, NY..............877-993-5396
Hood Packaging
Madison, MS..............800-321-8115
Indian Valley Industries
Johnson City, NY..............800-659-5111
Langston Co Inc
Memphis, TN..............901-774-4440
Northeast Packaging Co
Presque Isle, ME..............207-764-6271
NYP
Leola, PA..............800-541-0961
Ray C. Sprosty Bag Company
Wooster, OH..............330-264-8559
Santa Fe Bag Company
Vernon, CA..............323-585-7225
Stone Container
Chicago, IL..............312-346-6600
United Bags Inc
St Louis, MO..............800-550-2247

Netting, Open Mesh

Alabama Bag Co Inc
Talladega, AL..............800-888-4921
Conwed Global Netting Sltns
Roanoke, VA..............800-368-3610
Fitec International Inc
Memphis, TN..............800-332-6387
Friedman Bag Company
Manhattan Beach, CA..............213-628-2341
Fulton-Denver Co
Denver, CO..............800-521-1414
General Bag Corporation
Cleveland, OH..............800-837-9396
Indian Valley Industries
Johnson City, NY..............800-659-5111
Jif-Pak Manufacturing
Vista, CA..............800-777-6613
Langston Co Inc
Memphis, TN..............901-774-4440
Masternet, Ltd
Mississauga, ON..............800-216-2536
Naltex
Austin, TX..............800-531-5112
Net Pack Systems
Oakland, ME..............207-465-4531
NYP
Leola, PA..............800-541-0961
Sterling Net & Twine Company
Cedar Knolls, NJ..............800-342-0316
Tni Packaging Inc
West Chicago, IL..............800-383-0990
Tree Saver
Englewood, CO..............800-676-7741
United Bags Inc
St Louis, MO..............800-550-2247
Wasserman Bag Company
Center Moriches, NY..............631-909-8656

Paper

A-A1 Aaction Bag
Denver, CO..............800-783-1224
Acme Bag Co
Chula Vista, CA..............800-275-2263

AJM Packaging Corporation
Bloomfield Hills, MI..............248-901-0040
American Bag & Burlap Company
Chelsea, MA..............617-884-7600
Bancroft Bag Inc
West Monroe, LA..............318-387-2550
Brown Paper Goods Co
Waukegan, IL..............847-688-1450
Burrows Paper Corp
Little Falls, NY..............800-272-7122
Clearwater Paper Corporation
Spokane, WA..............877-847-7831
Coveris
Excelsior Springs, MO
Custom Poly Packaging
Fort Wayne, IN..............800-548-6603
Dayton Bag & Burlap Co
Dayton, OH..............800-543-3400
El Dorado Packaging Inc
El Dorado, AR..............870-862-4977
F&G Packaging
Yulee, FL..............904-225-5121
Fabricon Products Inc
River Rouge, MI..............313-841-8200
Fast Bags
Fort Worth, TX..............800-321-3687
Felco Packaging Specialist
Baltimore, MD..............800-673-8488
First Midwest of Iowa Corporation
Des Moines, IA..............800-247-8411
Fischer Paper Products Inc
Antioch, IL..............800-323-9093
Fortifiber Building Systs Grp
Fernley, NV..............800-773-4777
Fulton-Denver Co
Denver, CO..............800-521-1414
Gateway Packaging Co
Kansas City, MO..............816-483-9800
General Bag Corporation
Cleveland, OH..............800-837-9396
Gilchrist Bag Co Inc
Camden, AR..............800-643-1513
Hood Packaging
Madison, MS..............800-321-8115
Indian Valley Industries
Johnson City, NY..............800-659-5111
Keystone Packaging Svc Inc
Phillipsburg, NJ..............800-473-8567
Langston Co Inc
Memphis, TN..............901-774-4440
Milprint
Oshkosh, WI..............920-303-8600
Mimi et Cie
Seattle, WA..............206-545-1850
Moser Bag & Paper Company
Cleveland, OH..............800-433-6638
North American Packaging Corp
New York, NY..............800-499-3521
Northeast Packaging Co
Presque Isle, ME..............207-764-6271
NYP
Leola, PA..............800-541-0961
Package Containers Inc
Canby, OR..............800-266-5806
Pak 2000 Inc
Mirror Lake, NH..............603-569-3700
Pak-Sher
Kilgore, TX..............903-984-8596
Papelera Puertorriquena
Utuado, PR..............787-894-2098
Peerless Packages
Cleveland, OH..............216-464-3620
Portco Corporation
Vancouver, WA..............800-426-1794
Ray C. Sprosty Bag Company
Wooster, OH..............330-264-8559
Ross & Wallace Inc
Hammond, LA..............800-854-2300
Samuels Products Inc
Blue Ash, OH..............800-543-7155
Santa Fe Bag Company
Vernon, CA..............323-585-7225
Seaboard Bag Corporation
Richmond, VA
Shippers Paper Products Co
Sheridan, AR..............800-468-1230
Solo Cup Company
Lake Forest, IL
Specialty Packaging Inc
Fort Worth, TX..............800-284-7722
Specialty Paper Bag Company
City of Industry, CA..............800-962-2247

Stone Container
Chicago, IL..............312-346-6600
Surfine Central Corporation
Pine Bluff, AR..............870-247-2387
TULSACK
Tulsa, OK..............800-228-1936
United Bags Inc
St Louis, MO..............800-550-2247
Walker Bag Mfg Co
Louisville, KY..............800-642-4949
Wasserman Bag Company
Center Moriches, NY..............631-909-8656
Wedlock Paper ConvertersLtd.
Mississauga, ON..............800-388-0447
Wins Paper Products
Springtown, TX..............800-733-2420
Wisconsin Converting Inc
Green Bay, WI..............800-544-1935
Zenith Specialty Bag Co
City of Industry, CA..............800-962-2247

Paper Lined

Coveris
Excelsior Springs, MO
Dayton Bag & Burlap Co
Dayton, OH..............800-543-3400

Plastic

A La Carte
Chicago, IL..............800-722-2370
A-A1 Aaction Bag
Denver, CO..............800-783-1224
Abond Plastic Corporation
Lachine, QC..............800-886-7947
Acme Bag Co
Chula Vista, CA..............800-275-2263
Alabama Bag Co Inc
Talladega, AL..............800-888-4921
Alger Creations
Miami, FL..............954-454-3272
All American Poly
Piscataway, NJ..............800-526-3551
Alouf Plastics
Orangeburg, NY..............800-394-2247
Amcel
Watertown, MA..............800-225-7992
American Bag & Burlap Company
Chelsea, MA..............617-884-7600
Ameriglobe LLC
Lafayette, LA..............337-234-3211
Arbee Transparent Inc
Elk Grove Vlg, IL..............800-642-2247
Archer Daniels Midland Company
Chicago, IL..............312-634-8100
Art Poly Bag Co
Brooklyn, NY..............800-278-7659
Artistic Packaging Concepts
Massapequa Pk, NY..............516-797-4020
Automated Packaging Systems
Streetsboro, OH..............800-527-0733
Avantage Group Inc
Redondo Beach, CA..............310-379-3933
Bag Company
Kennesaw, GA..............800-533-1931
Bag Masters
St Petersburg, FL..............800-330-2247
Beayl Weiner/Pak
Pacific Palisades, CA..............310-454-1354
Bennett's Auto Inc
Neenah, WI..............800-215-5464
Blako Industries
Dunbridge, OH..............419-833-4491
Brown Paper Goods Co
Waukegan, IL..............847-688-1450
Bulk Lift International, LLC
Carpentersville, IL..............800-879-2247
C-P Flexible Packaging
Newtown, PA..............800-448-8183
Carlisle Plastics
Minneapolis, MN..............952-884-1309
Carroll Co
Garland, TX..............800-527-5722
Castle Bag Co.
Wilmington, DE..............302-656-1001
Cello Bag Company
Bowling Green, KY..............800-347-0338
Central Bag Co
Leavenworth, KS..............913-250-0325
Central Package & Display
Minneapolis, MN..............763-425-7444

Chalmur Bag Company, LLC
Philadelphia, PA 800-349-2247
Champion Plastics
Clifton, NJ 800-526-1230
Checker Bag Co
St Louis, MO 800-489-3130
Clear View Bag Co Inc of Nc
Albany, NY 800-458-7153
Clear View Bag Company
Thomasville, NC 336-885-8131
Cleveland Plastic Films
Elyria, OH 800-832-6799
Coast Scientific
Rancho Santa Fe, CA 800-445-1544
Colonial Transparent Products Company
Hicksville, NY 516-822-4430
Command Packaging
Vernon, CA 800-996-2247
Continental Extrusion Corporation
Cedar Grove, NJ 800-822-4748
Continental Packaging Corporation
Elgin, IL 847-289-6400
Continental Products
Mexico, MO 800-325-0216
Conwed Global Netting Sltns
Roanoke, VA 800-368-3610
Cortec Aero
St Paul, MN 800-426-7832
COVERIS
Tomah, WI 608-372-2153
Coveris
Excelsior Springs, MO
Crayex Corp
Piqua, OH 800-837-1747
Crystal-Flex Packaging Corporation
Rockville Centre, NY 888-246-7325
Custom Poly Packaging
Fort Wayne, IN 800-548-6603
Dairyland Plastics Company
Colfax, WI 715-962-3425
Dashco
Gloucester, ON 613-834-6825
Dayton Bag & Burlap Co
Dayton, OH 800-543-3400
Decker Plastics
Council Bluffs, IA 866-869-6293
Design Packaging Company
Glencoe, IL 800-321-7659
Development Workshop Inc
Idaho Falls, ID 800-657-5597
Dixie Poly Packaging
Greenville, SC 864-268-3751
Dub Harris Corporation
Pomona, CA 909-596-6300
Dynamic Packaging
Minneapolis, MN 800-878-9380
East Coast Group New York
Springfield Gardens, NY 718-527-8464
Eastern Poly Packaging Company
Brooklyn, NY 800-421-6006
Eaton Manufacturing Co
Houston, TX 800-328-6610
Ellehammer Industries
Langley, BC 604-882-9326
Elliot Lee
Cedarhurst, NY 516-569-9595
Fabohio Inc
Uhrichsville, OH 740-922-4233
Fan Bag Company
Chicago, IL 773-342-2752
Fast Bags
Fort Worth, TX 800-321-3687
Flexo Transparent Inc
Buffalo, NY 877-993-5396
Fortune Plastics, Inc
Old Saybrook, CT 800-243-0306
Fredman Bag Co
Milwaukee, WI 800-945-5686
Friedman Bag Company
Manhattan Beach, CA 213-628-2341
Frontier Bag
Kansas City, MO 816-765-4811
Fulton-Denver Co
Denver, CO 800-521-1414
Garvey Products
West Chester, OH 800-543-1908
Gemini Plastic Films Corporation
Garfield, NJ 800-789-4732
General Bag Corporation
Cleveland, OH 800-837-9396
General Films Inc
Covington, OH 888-436-3456

Genpak LLC
Lakeville, MN 800-328-4556
Gibraltar Packaging Group Inc
Hastings, NE 402-463-1366
Goldmax Industries
City of Industry, CA 626-964-8820
GP Plastics Corporation
Medley, FL 305-888-3555
Gulf Arizona Packaging
Humble, TX 800-364-3887
Gulf Coast Plastics
Tampa, FL 800-277-7491
Gulf Systems
Brownsville, TX 800-217-4853
Gulf Systems
Humble, TX 800-364-3887
Gulf Systems
Arlington, TX 817-261-1915
Handgards Inc
El Paso, TX 800-351-8161
Hedwin Division
Baltimore, MD 800-638-1012
Herche Warehouse
Denver, CO 303-371-8186
Heritage Bag Co
Roanoke, TX 800-527-2247
Himolene
Carrollton, TX 800-777-4411
Hubco Inc
Hutchinson, KS 800-563-1867
Hudson Poly Bag Inc
Hudson, MA 800-229-7566
INA Co
San Carlos, CA 650-631-7066
Indian Valley Industries
Johnson City, NY 800-659-5111
Interstate Packaging
White Bluff, TN 800-251-1072
J A Heilferty & Co
Teaneck, NJ 201-836-5060
Jeb Plastics
Wilmington, DE 800-556-2247
Jomar Plastics Industry
Nanty Glo, PA 800-681-4039
Jupiter Mills Corporation
Roslyn, NY 800-853-5121
K & L Intl
Ontario, CA 888-598-5588
K-C Products Company
Van Nuys, CA 818-267-1600
Kal Pac Corp
Montgomery, NY 800-852-5722
KANE Bag Supply Co
Baltimore, MD 410-732-5800
KM International Corp
Kenton, TN 731-749-8700
L & C Plastic Bags
Covington, OH 937-473-2968
Luetzow Industries
South Milwaukee, WI 800-558-6055
M & G Packaging Corp
Floral Park, NY 800-240-5288
M S Plastics & Packaging Inc
Butler, NJ 800-593-1802
M&R Flexible Packaging
Springboro, OH 800-543-3380
Maco Bag Corp
Newark, NY 315-226-1000
Malpack Polybag
Ajax, ON 905-428-3751
Marshall Plastic Film Inc
Martin, MI 269-672-5511
Mason Transparent Package Company
Armonk, NY 718-792-6000
Mercury Plastic Bag Company
Passaic, NJ 973-778-7200
Microplas Industries
Dunwoody, GA 800-952-4528
Midco Plastics
Enterprise, KS 800-235-2729
Millhiser
Richmond, VA 800-446-2247
Mini-Bag Company
Farmingdale, NY 631-694-3325
Mohawk Northern Plastics
Auburn, WA 800-426-1100
Mohawk Western Plastics Inc
La Verne, CA 909-593-7547
Mount Vernon Plastics
Mamaroneck, NY 914-698-1122
Naltex
Austin, TX 800-531-5112

NAP Industries
Brooklyn, NY 877-635-4948
National Poly Bag Manufacturing Corporation
Brooklyn, NY 718-629-9800
Net Pack Systems
Oakland, ME 207-465-4531
North American Packaging Corp
New York, NY 800-499-3521
Noteworthy Company
Amsterdam, NY 800-696-7849
NOVOLEX
Glendale, AZ 800-243-0306
Now Plastics Inc
East Longmeadow, MA 413-525-1010
NYP
Leola, PA 800-541-0961
Osterneck Company
Lumberton, NC 800-682-2416
Packaging Enterprises
Rockledge, PA 800-453-6213
Packaging Materials Inc
Cambridge, OH 800-565-8550
Pactiv LLC
Lake Forest, IL 800-476-4300
Pak 2000 Inc
Mirror Lake, NH 603-569-3700
Pak-Sak Industries I
Sparta, MI 800-748-0431
Pak-Sher
Kilgore, TX 903-984-8596
Pan Pacific Plastics Inc
Hayward, CA 888-475-6888
Papelera Puertorriquena
Utuado, PR 787-894-2098
Parade Packaging
Mundelein, IL 847-566-6264
Paradise Plastics
Brooklyn, NY 718-788-3733
Pater & Associates
Cincinnati, OH
Peerless Packages
Cleveland, OH 216-464-3620
Pexco Packaging Corporation
Toledo, OH 800-227-9950
Pilant Corp
Bloomington, IN 800-366-3525
Poliplastic
Granby, QC 450-378-8417
Poly Plastic Products Inc
Delano, PA 570-467-3000
Poly Shapes Corporation
Elyria, OH 800-605-9359
Portco Corporation
Vancouver, WA 800-426-1794
ProAmpac
Cincinnati, OH 800-543-7030
Quality Plastic Bag Corporation
Flushing, NY 800-532-2247
Quality Transparent Bag Co
Bay City, MI 989-893-3561
Ram Industries
Erwin, TN 800-523-3883
Ray C. Sprosty Bag Company
Wooster, OH 330-264-8559
Roplast Industries Inc
Oroville, CA 800-767-5278
Ross & Wallace Inc
Hammond, LA 800-854-2300
Rutan Poly Industries Inc
Mahwah, NJ 800-872-1474
Sacramento Bag Manufacturing
Woodland, CA 530-662-6130
San Miguel Label Manufacturing
Ciales, PR 787-871-3120
Seal-Tite Bag Company
Philadelphia, PA 717-917-1949
Seattle-Tacoma Box Co
Kent, WA 253-854-9700
Senior Housing Options Inc
Denver, CO 800-659-2656
Servin Company
New Baltimore, MI 800-824-0962
Shamrock Plastics
Mt Vernon, OH 800-765-1611
Sheboygan Paper Box Co
Sheboygan, WI 800-458-8373
Shields Bag & Printing Co
Yakima, WA 800-541-8630
Ship Rite Packaging
Bergenfield, NJ 800-721-7447
Shippers Paper Products Co
Sheridan, AR 800-468-1230

Signature Packaging
West Orange, NJ.................800-376-2299
Silver State Plastics Inc
Greeley, CO.................970-346-8667
Specialty Films & Associates
Hebron, KY.................800-984-3346
Specialty Paper Bag Company
City of Industry, CA.................800-962-2247
Spectrum Plastics
Las Vegas, NV.................702-876-8650
Star Poly Bag Inc
Brooklyn, NY.................718-384-7034
Steel City Corporation
Youngstown, OH.................800-321-0350
Sterling Net & Twine Company
Cedar Knolls, NJ.................800-342-0316
Sterling Novelty Products
Northbrook, IL.................847-291-0070
Stone Container
Chicago, IL.................312-346-6600
Stretch-Vent Packaging System
Ontario, CA.................800-822-8368
Stripper Bags
Henderson, NV.................800-354-2247
Sungjae Corporation
Irvine, CA.................949-757-1727
Sunland Manufacturing Company
Minneapolis, MN.................800-790-1905
Target Industries
North Salt Lake, UT.................866-617-2253
Thermal Bags By Ingrid Inc
Gilberts, IL.................800-622-5560
Trans Flex Packagers Inc
Unionville, CT.................860-673-2531
Trinity Packaging
Cheektowaga, NY.................800-778-3111
Tyco Plastics
Lakeville, MN.................800-328-4080
United Bags Inc
St Louis, MO.................800-550-2247
United Flexible
Westbury, NY.................516-222-2150
Universal Plastics
Holyoke, MA.................800-553-0120
US Plastic Corporation
Swampscott, MA.................781-595-1030
Valley Packaging Supply Co
Green Bay, WI.................920-336-9012
Vermont Bag & Film
Bennington, VT.................802-442-3166
Vonco Products LLC
Lake Villa, IL.................800-323-9077
VPI Manufacturing
Draper, UT.................801-495-2310
Walker Bag Mfg Co
Louisville, KY.................800-642-4949
Walnut Packaging Inc
Farmingdale, NY.................631-293-3836
Wasserman Bag Company
Center Moriches, NY.................631-909-8656
Wisconsin Film & Bag Inc
Shawano, WI.................800-765-9224
Wright Plastics Company
Prattville, AL.................800-874-7659
Zip-Pak
Manteno, IL.................800-488-6973

Polyethylene

AEP Industries
South Hackensack, NJ.................800-999-2374
Alabama Bag Co Inc
Talladega, AL.................800-888-4921
All American Poly
Piscataway, NJ.................800-526-3551
Alouf Plastics
Orangeburg, NY.................800-394-2247
Arbee Transparent Inc
Elk Grove Vlg, IL.................800-642-2247
Art Poly Bag Co
Brooklyn, NY.................800-278-7659
Automated Packaging Systems
Streetsboro, OH.................800-527-0733
Bag Company
Kennesaw, GA.................800-533-1931
Bag Masters
St Petersburg, FL.................800-330-2247
Beayl Weiner/Pak
Pacific Palisades, CA.................310-454-1354
Bennett's Auto Inc
Neenah, WI.................800-215-5464

Blako Industries
Dunbridge, OH.................419-833-4491
C-P Flexible Packaging
Newtown, PA.................800-448-8183
Carlisle Plastics
Minneapolis, MN.................952-884-1309
Castle Bag Co.
Wilmington, DE.................302-656-1001
Central Package & Display
Minneapolis, MN.................763-425-7444
Chalmur Bag Company, LLC
Philadelphia, PA.................800-349-2247
Champion Plastics
Clifton, NJ.................800-526-1230
Checker Bag Co
St Louis, MO.................800-489-3130
Cleveland Plastic Films
Elyria, OH.................800-832-6799
Coast Scientific
Rancho Santa Fe, CA.................800-445-1544
Collectors Gallery
St Charles, IL.................800-346-3063
Command Packaging
Vernon, CA.................800-996-2247
Continental Packaging Corporation
Elgin, IL.................847-289-6400
Cortec Aero
St Paul, MN.................800-426-7832
Coveris
Excelsior Springs, MO
Crayex Corp
Piqua, OH.................800-837-1747
Crystal-Flex Packaging Corporation
Rockville Centre, NY.................888-246-7325
Custom Poly Packaging
Fort Wayne, IN.................800-548-6603
Decker Plastics
Council Bluffs, IA.................866-869-6293
Dixie Poly Packaging
Greenville, SC.................864-268-3751
Dynamic Packaging
Minneapolis, MN.................800-878-9380
Eastern Poly Packaging Company
Brooklyn, NY.................800-421-6006
Eaton Manufacturing Co
Houston, TX.................800-328-6610
Emerald Packaging Inc
Union City, CA.................510-429-5700
Film-Pak Inc
Crowley, TX.................800-526-1838
Flexo Transparent Inc
Buffalo, NY.................877-993-5396
Fortune Plastics, Inc
Old Saybrook, CT.................800-243-0306
Fredman Bag Co
Milwaukee, WI.................800-945-5686
Friedman Bag Company
Manhattan Beach, CA.................213-628-2341
Frontier Bag
Kansas City, MO.................816-765-4811
Fulton-Denver Co
Denver, CO.................800-521-1414
Gemini Plastic Films Corporation
Garfield, NJ.................800-789-4732
Genpak LLC
Lakeville, MN.................800-328-4556
Gibraltar Packaging Group Inc
Hastings, NE.................402-463-1366
GP Plastics Corporation
Medley, FL.................305-888-3555
Gulf Arizona Packaging
Humble, TX.................800-364-3887
Gulf Systems
Brownsville, TX.................800-217-4853
Gulf Systems
Humble, TX.................800-364-3887
Gulf Systems
Arlington, TX.................817-261-1915
Herche Warehouse
Denver, CO.................303-371-8186
Home Plastics Inc
Des Moines, IA.................515-265-2562
Hudson Poly Bag Inc
Hudson, MA.................800-229-7566
Indian Valley Industries
Johnson City, NY.................800-659-5111
Inteplast Bags & Films Corporation
Delta, BC.................604-946-5431
Interstate Packaging
White Bluff, TN.................800-251-1072
J A Heilferty & Co
Teaneck, NJ.................201-836-5060

Jewell Bag Company
Dallas, TX.................214-749-1223
King Bag & Mfg Co
Cincinnati, OH.................800-444-5464
KM International Corp
Kenton, TN.................731-749-8700
L & C Plastic Bags
Covington, OH.................937-473-2968
Luetzow Industries
South Milwaukee, WI.................800-558-6055
M S Plastics & Packaging Inc
Butler, NJ.................800-593-1802
Malpack Polybag
Ajax, ON.................905-428-3751
Mason Transparent Package Company
Armonk, NY.................718-792-6000
Microplas Industries
Dunwoody, GA.................800-952-4528
Millhiser
Richmond, VA.................800-446-2247
Mini-Bag Company
Farmingdale, NY.................631-694-3325
Mohawk Northern Plastics
Auburn, WA.................800-426-1100
Mohawk Western Plastics Inc
La Verne, CA.................909-593-7547
Monument Industries Inc
Bennington, VT.................802-442-8187
NAP Industries
Brooklyn, NY.................877-635-4948
Net Pack Systems
Oakland, ME.................207-465-4531
Noteworthy Company
Amsterdam, NY.................800-696-7849
NOVOLEX
Glendale, AZ.................800-243-0306
NYP
Leola, PA.................800-541-0961
Packaging Materials Inc
Cambridge, OH.................800-565-8550
Pactiv LLC
Lake Forest, IL.................800-476-4300
Pak-Sak Industries I
Sparta, MI.................800-748-0431
Pater & Associates
Cincinnati, OH
Pexco Packaging Corporation
Toledo, OH.................800-227-9950
Pilant Corp
Bloomington, IN.................800-366-3525
Portco Corporation
Vancouver, WA.................800-426-1794
ProAmpac
Cincinnati, OH.................800-543-7030
Quality Transparent Bag Co
Bay City, MI.................989-893-3561
Rutan Poly Industries Inc
Mahwah, NJ.................800-872-1474
Sacramento Bag Manufacturing
Woodland, CA.................530-662-6130
Shields Bag & Printing Co
Yakima, WA.................800-541-8630
Ship Rite Packaging
Bergenfield, NJ.................800-721-7447
Signature Packaging
West Orange, NJ.................800-376-2299
Silver State Plastics Inc
Greeley, CO.................970-346-8667
Sungjae Corporation
Irvine, CA.................949-757-1727
Sunland Manufacturing Company
Minneapolis, MN.................800-790-1905
Superior Distributing Co
Louisville, KY.................800-365-6661
Target Industries
North Salt Lake, UT.................866-617-2253
Trans Flex Packagers Inc
Unionville, CT.................860-673-2531
Trinity Packaging
Cheektowaga, NY.................800-778-3111
United Flexible
Westbury, NY.................516-222-2150
US Plastic Corporation
Swampscott, MA.................781-595-1030
VPI Manufacturing
Draper, UT.................801-495-2310
Walnut Packaging Inc
Farmingdale, NY.................631-293-3836
Wasserman Bag Company
Center Moriches, NY.................631-909-8656
Workman Packaging Inc.
Saint-Laurent, QC.................800-252-5208

Wright Plastics Company
Prattville, AL 800-874-7659
Zip-Pak
Manteno, IL 800-488-6973

Polypropylene

Arbee Transparent Inc
Elk Grove Vlg, IL 800-642-2247
Astro Plastics
Oakland, NJ 201-337-8170
Automated Packaging Systems
Streetsboro, OH 800-527-0733
Bag Company
Kennesaw, GA 800-533-1931
Bag Masters
St Petersburg, FL 800-330-2247
Beayl Weiner/Pak
Pacific Palisades, CA 310-454-1354
Bulk Lift International, LLC
Carpentersville, IL 800-879-2247
Central Bag Co
Leavenworth, KS 913-250-0325
Checker Bag Co
St Louis, MO......................800-489-3130
Custom Poly Packaging
Fort Wayne, IN 800-548-6603
Dayton Bag & Burlap Co
Dayton, OH........................800-543-3400
Design Packaging Company
Glencoe, IL 800-321-7659
Eastern Poly Packaging   Company
Brooklyn, NY 800-421-6006
Eaton Manufacturing Co
Houston, TX 800-328-6610
Flexo Transparent Inc
Buffalo, NY.......................877-993-5396
Gibraltar Packaging Group Inc
Hastings, NE 402-463-1366
Gulf Arizona Packaging
Humble, TX 800-364-3887
Gulf Systems
Brownsville, TX...................800-217-4853
Gulf Systems
Humble, TX 800-364-3887
Gulf Systems
Arlington, TX 817-261-1915
Herche Warehouse
Denver, CO 303-371-8186
Hubco Inc
Hutchinson, KS....................800-563-1867
Indian Valley Industries
Johnson City, NY 800-659-5111
Mason Transparent Package Company
Armonk, NY 718-792-6000
Masternet, Ltd
Mississauga, ON...................800-216-2536
Mercury Plastic Bag Company
Passaic, NJ 973-778-7200
Millhiser
Richmond, VA......................800-446-2247
Mimi et Cie
Seattle, WA 206-545-1850
NYP
Leola, PA.........................800-541-0961
Pater & Associates
Cincinnati, OH
Pexco Packaging Corporation
Toledo, OH........................800-227-9950
Ray C. Sprosty Bag Company
Wooster, OH 330-264-8559
Sacramento Bag Manufacturing
Woodland, CA......................530-662-6130
Shields Bag & Printing Co
Yakima, WA 800-541-8630
Sterling Net & Twine Company
Cedar Knolls, NJ 800-342-0316
Storsack Inc
Houston, TX 800-841-4982
Target Industries
North Salt Lake, UT 866-617-2253
Trans Flex Packagers Inc
Unionville, CT 860-673-2531
United Bags Inc
St Louis, MO......................800-550-2247
Walker Bag Mfg Co
Louisville, KY 800-642-4949
Wasserman Bag Company
Center Moriches, NY 631-909-8656
Workman Packaging Inc.
Saint-Laurent, QC.................800-252-5208

Popcorn

Arbee Transparent Inc
Elk Grove Vlg, IL 800-642-2247
Coveris
Excelsior Springs, MO
Flexo Transparent Inc
Buffalo, NY.......................877-993-5396
Hubco Inc
Hutchinson, KS....................800-563-1867
Stewart Sutherland Inc
Vicksburg, MI.....................269-649-0530

Sandwich

Aladdin Transparent Packaging
Hauppauge, NY 631-273-4747
Arbee Transparent Inc
Elk Grove Vlg, IL 800-642-2247
Brown Paper Goods Co
Waukegan, IL 847-688-1450
Castle Bag Co.
Wilmington, DE 302-656-1001
Colonial Transparent Products Company
Hicksville, NY 516-822-4430
Food Pak Corp
San Mateo, CA 650-341-6559
Pater & Associates
Cincinnati, OH
Stewart Sutherland Inc
Vicksburg, MI.....................269-649-0530
Vermont Bag & Film
Bennington, VT 802-442-3166

Shopping

All American Poly
Piscataway, NJ 800-526-3551
American Advertising & Shop Cap Company
Old Tappan, NJ 800-442-8837
Arbee Transparent Inc
Elk Grove Vlg, IL 800-642-2247
Celebrity Promotions
Remsen, IA 800-332-6847
Colonial Transparent Products Company
Hicksville, NY 516-822-4430
Continental Extrusion Corporation
Cedar Grove, NJ 800-822-4748
Continental Products
Mexico, MO 800-325-0216
Custom Poly Packaging
Fort Wayne, IN 800-548-6603
David Dobbs Enterprise Inc.
St Augustine, FL 800-889-6368
Eco-Bag Products
Ossining, NY 800-720-2247
Excelsior Transparent Bag Manufacturing
Yonkers, NY 914-968-1300
Fabriko
Altavista, VA.....................888-203-8098
Fischer Paper Products Inc
Antioch, IL 800-323-9093
Fitec International Inc
Memphis, TN 800-332-6387
Genpak LLC
Lakeville, MN.....................800-328-4556
Green Seams
Maple Grove, MN...................612-929-3213
Hall Manufacturing Company
Henderson, TX 903-657-4501
J A Heilferty & Co
Teaneck, NJ.......................201-836-5060
Memphis Delta Tent & Awning
Memphis, TN 901-522-1238
Millhiser
Richmond, VA......................800-446-2247
Moser Bag & Paper Company
Cleveland, OH 800-433-6638
NAP Industries
Brooklyn, NY 877-635-4948
North American Packaging Corp
New York, NY 800-499-3521
Pater & Associates
Cincinnati, OH
Pexco Packaging Corporation
Toledo, OH........................800-227-9950
Poliplastic
Granby, QC 450-378-8417
Save-A-Tree
Berkeley, CA......................510-843-5233
Shamrock Plastics
Mt Vernon, OH 800-765-1611

Sheboygan Paper Box Co
Sheboygan, WI.....................800-458-8373
Source for Packaging
New York, NY 800-223-2527
Star Poly Bag Inc
Brooklyn, NY 718-384-7034
Tree Saver
Englewood, CO.....................800-676-7741
Vermont Bag & Film
Bennington, VT 802-442-3166
Walker Bag Mfg Co
Louisville, KY 800-642-4949
Wisconsin Converting Inc
Green Bay, WI.....................800-544-1935

Baskets

Egg

Langer Manufacturing Company
Cedar Rapids, IA..................800-728-6445
Xtreme Beverages, LLC
Dana Point, CA....................949-495-7929

Fruit & Vegetable

Berlin Fruit Box Company
Berlin Heights, OH 800-877-7721
Classy Basket
San Diego, CA 888-449-4901
Collectors Gallery
St Charles, IL 800-346-3063
Day Basket Factory
North East, MD 410-398-5150
Farmer's Co-Op Elevator Co
Hudsonville, MI 800-439-9859
Frobisher Industries
Waterborough, NB 506-362-2198
Fruit Growers Package Company
Grandville, MI 616-724-1400
Harvey's Indian River Groves
Rockledge, FL.....................800-327-9312
Langer Manufacturing Company
Cedar Rapids, IA..................800-728-6445
Little Rock Crate & Basket Co
Little Rock, AR 800-223-7823
Longaberger Basket Company
Dresden, OH 740-518-8018
Peacock Crate Factory
Jacksonville, TX 800-657-2200
Peterboro Basket Co
Peterborough, NH 603-924-3861
Shipley Basket Mfg Co
Dayton, TN 800-251-0806
Smalley Package Company
Berryville, VA....................540-955-2550
Specialty Wood Products
Clanton, AL 800-322-5343
Straits Steel & Wire Co
Ludington, MI.....................231-843-3416
Thorco Industries LLC
Lamar, MO 800-445-3375
Traitech Industries
Vaughan, ON.......................877-872-4835
Xtreme Beverages, LLC
Dana Point, CA....................949-495-7929

Gift

All Sorts Premium Packaging
Buffalo, NY.......................888-565-9727
Andrea Basket
Bohemia, NY 888-272-8826
Baskets Extraordinaires
Westbury, NY 800-666-1685
Classy Basket
San Diego, CA 888-449-4901
Coe & Dru Inc
San Dimas, CA 800-722-7538
Collectors Gallery
St Charles, IL 800-346-3063
Dufeck Manufacturing Co
Denmark, WI.......................888-603-9663
Gril-Del
Mankato, MN 800-782-7320
Harvey's Indian River Groves
Rockledge, FL.....................800-327-9312
Houdini Inc
Fullerton, CA.....................714-525-0325
Mar-Boro Printing & Advertising Specialties
Brooklyn, NY 718-336-4051

Metrovock Snacks
Maywood, CA.....................800-428-0522
Peacock Crate Factory
Jacksonville, TX..................800-657-2200
Roofian
Sun Valley, CA...................800-431-3886
Seymour Woodenware Company
Seymour, WI.....................920-833-6551
United Basket Co Inc
Maspeth, NY.....................718-894-5454
Xtreme Beverages, LLC
Dana Point, CA..................949-495-7929

Refrigerator

Coastline Equipment Inc
Bellingham, WA..................360-734-8509
Langer Manufacturing Company
Cedar Rapids, IA................800-728-6445
Straits Steel & Wire Co
Ludington, MI...................231-843-3416

Bins

A-Z Factory Supply
Schiller Park, IL.................800-323-4511
ABI Limited
Concord, ON.....................800-297-8666
American Pallet Inc
Oakdale, CA.....................209-847-6122
Anderson-Crane Company
Minneapolis, MN................800-314-2747
Andgar Corp
Ferndale, WA....................360-366-9900
Atlas Equipment Company
Kansas City, MO.................800-842-9188
AZO Food
Memphis, TN....................901-794-9480
BestBins Corporation
Chaska, MN......................866-448-3114
Bonar Plastics
West Chicago, IL.................800-295-3725
Bonar Plastics
Ridgefield, WA...................800-972-5252
Bowers Process Equipment
Stratford, ON....................800-567-3223
Buhler Inc.
Plymouth, MN...................763-847-9900
Cecor
Verona, WI.......................800-356-9042
Centennial Moldings
Hastings, NE.....................888-883-2189
Chief Industries
Kearney, NE......................800-359-8833
Clayton & Lambert Manufacturing
Buckner, KY......................800-626-5819
Containair Packaging Corporation
Paterson, NJ.....................888-276-6500
Continental-Fremont
Tiffin, OH........................419-448-4045
Corbox-Meyers Inc
Cleveland, OH...................800-321-7286
Davron Technologies Inc
Chattanooga, TN................423-870-1888
DBE Inc
Concord, ON.....................800-461-5313
DEL-Tec Packaging Inc
Greer, SC.........................800-747-8683
Despro Manufacturing
Cedar Grove, NJ.................800-292-9906
Duke Manufacturing Co
St Louis, MO.....................800-735-3853
Earl Soesbe Company
Romeoville, IL...................219-866-4191
Eastern Plastics
Pawtucket, RI....................800-442-8585
Electrical Engineering & Equip
Windsor Heights, IA.............800-955-3633
Emco Industrial Plastics
Cedar Grove, NJ.................800-292-9906
Expert Industries Inc
Brooklyn, NY.....................718-434-6060
F N Smith Corp
Oregon, IL.......................815-732-2171
F.E. Wood & Sons
West Baldwin, ME...............207-286-5003
Falco Technologies
La Prairie, QC....................450-444-0566
Faribault Manufacturing Co
Faribault, MN....................800-447-6043
Flow of Solids
Westford, MA....................978-392-0300

Follett Corp
Easton, PA.......................800-523-9361
Forbes Industries
Ontario, CA......................909-923-4549
Fred D Pfening Co
Columbus, OH...................614-294-5361
Frem Corporation
Worcester, MA...................508-791-3152
Fresno Pallet, Inc.
Sultana, CA......................559-591-4111
Gates Manufacturing Company
Saint Louis, MO..................800-237-9226
Gch Internatonal
Louisville, KY....................502-636-1374
Goergen-Mackwirth Co Inc
Buffalo, NY.......................800-728-4446
Goldenwest Sales
Cerritos, CA......................800-827-6175
Graff Tank Erection
Harrisville, PA...................814-385-6671
Hardy Systems Corporation
Northbrook, IL...................800-927-3956
Hedstrom Corporation
Ashland, OH.....................700-765-9665
Hodge Manufacturing Company
Springfield, MA..................800-262-4634
Hoshizaki America Inc
Peachtree City, GA...............800-438-6087
Imperial Industries Inc
Rothschild, WI...................800-558-2945
International Wood Industries
Snohomish, WA..................800-922-6141
Jacksonville Box & Woodwork Co
Jacksonville, FL..................800-683-2699
Jarlan Manufacturing
Los Angeles, CA..................323-752-1211
Jenike & Johanson Inc
Tyngsboro, MA..................978-649-3300
K & I Creative Plastics & Wood
Jacksonville, FL..................904-387-0438
K-Tron
Salina, KS........................785-825-1611
Kason
Lewis Center, OH................740-549-2100
KHM Plastics Inc
Gurnee, IL.......................847-249-4910
Kimball Companies
East Longmeadow, MA..........413-525-1881
Lakeside Manufacturing Inc
Milwaukee, WI...................888-558-8565
Longview Fibre Company
Beaverton, OR...................503-350-1600
Machine Ice Co
Houston, TX......................800-423-8822
Mannhardt Inc
Sheboygan Falls, WI.............800-423-2327
Material Storage Systems
Gadsden, AL.....................877-543-2467
Matthiesen Equipment
San Antonio, TX.................800-624-8635
MeGa Industries
Burlington, ON..................800-665-6342
Mell & Co
Niles, IL..........................800-262-6355
Melmat Inc
Huntington Beach, CA..........800-635-6289
Michiana Box & Crate
Niles, MI.........................800-677-6372
Miller Hofft Brands
Indianapolis, IN.................317-638-6576
Moli-International
Denver, CO......................800-525-8468
Mt Valley Farms & Lumber Prods
Biglerville, PA...................717-677-6166
MultiFab Plastics
Boston, MA......................888-293-5754
NEPA Pallet & Container Co
Snohomish, WA..................360-568-3185
Newell Brands
Atlanta, GA
NST Metals
Louisville, KY....................502-584-5846
Omega Industries
St Louis, MO.....................314-961-1668
Our Name is Mud
New York, NY....................877-683-7867
Pallet One Inc
Bartow, FL........................800-771-1148
Pelican Displays
Homer, IL........................800-627-1517
Pittsburgh Tank Corp
Monongahela, PA................800-634-0243

Precision Plastics Inc
Beltsville, MD....................800-922-1317
Prestige Plastics Corporation
Delta, BC.........................604-930-2931
Prince Castle Inc
Carol Stream, IL.................800-722-7853
Pro Bake Inc
Twinsburg, OH...................800-837-4427
Process Solutions
Riviera Beach, FL.................561-840-0050
Pruitt's Packaging Services
Grand Rapids, MI................800-878-0553
Quantum Storage Systems Inc
Miami, FL........................800-685-4665
Ram Equipment Co
Waukesha, WI...................262-513-1114
Remcon Plastics Inc
Reading, PA......................800-360-3636
Render
Buffalo, NY.......................888-446-1010
RMI-C/Rotonics Manaufacturing
Bensenville, IL...................630-773-9510
Rotonics Manufacturing
Gardena, CA.....................310-327-5401
Schenck Process
Whitewater, WI..................888-742-1249
Scotsman Ice Systems
Vernon Hills, IL..................800-726-8762
Seattle Plastics
Seattle, WA......................800-441-0679
SEMCO
Ocala, FL.........................800-749-6894
SerVend International
Sellersburg, IN...................800-367-4233
Shouldice Brothers SheetMetal
Battle Creek, MI.................269-962-5579
Snyder Crown
Marked Tree, AR.................870-358-3400
Solve Needs International
White Lake, MI...................800-783-2462
Southern Ag Co Inc
Blakely, GA......................229-723-4262
Spudnik Equipment Co
Blackfoot, ID.....................208-684-4120
Stainless Fabrication Inc
Springfield, MO..................800-397-8265
Stearnswood Inc
Hutchinson, MN.................800-657-0144
Supreme Metal
Alpharetta, GA...................800-645-2526
Thermodynamics
Commerce City, CO.............800-627-9037
Tolan Machinery Company
Rockaway, NJ....................973-983-7212
Trade Fixtures
Little Rock, AR...................800-872-3490
Tri-Boro Shelving & Partition
Farmville, VA.....................800-633-3070
Triple-A Manufacturing Company
Toronto, ON.....................800-786-2238
Tulip Molded Plastics Corp
Milwaukee, WI...................414-963-3120
Upham & Walsh Lumber
Hoffman Estates, IL..............847-519-1010
Vande Berg SCALES/Vbs Inc
Sioux Center, IA..................712-722-1181
Vanmark Equipment
Creston, IA.......................800-523-6261
Warwick Products
Cleveland, OH...................800-535-4404
Welbilt Inc.
New Port Richey, FL.............877-375-9300
Westeel
Saskatoon, SK...................306-931-2855
Westfield Sheet Metal Works
Kenilworth, NJ...................908-276-5500
Wilder Manufacturing Company
Port Jervis, NY...................800-832-1319
Wilson Steel Products Company
Memphis, TN....................901-527-8742
Woodstock Plastics Co Inc
Marengo, IL......................815-568-5281

Beverage

Crown Plastics Inc
Minneapolis, MN................800-423-2769
Falco Technologies
La Prairie, QC....................450-444-0566
Lakeside Manufacturing Inc
Milwaukee, WI...................888-558-8565

Insulated

ABI Limited
Concord, ON 800-297-8666
Falco Technologies
La Prairie, QC 450-444-0566
Lakeside Manufacturing Inc
Milwaukee, WI 888-558-8565
Melmat Inc
Huntington Beach, CA 800-635-6289
Promens
St. John, NB 800-295-3725

Bottles

Aluminum

California Vibratory Feeders
Anaheim, CA 800-354-0972
Elemental Containers
Union, NJ 800-577-7624
Mountain Safety Research
Seattle, WA 800-877-9677

Glass

Ameripec
Buena Park, CA 714-994-2990
Arkansas Glass Container Corp
Jonesboro, AR. 800-527-4527
Bal/Foster Glass Container Company
Port Allegany, PA 814-642-2521
Ball Foster Glass Container Company
Sapulpa, OK 918-224-1440
Ball Glass Container Corporation
El Monte, CA 626-448-9831
California Vibratory Feeders
Anaheim, CA 800-354-0972
Foster-Forbes Glass Company
Vernon, CA 800-767-4527
Greenfield Packaging
White Plains, NY 914-993-0233
Indiana Glass Company
Columbus, OH 800-543-0357
Indianapolis Container Company
Indianapolis, IN 800-760-3318
LMK Containers
Centerville, UT 626-821-9984
Louisville Container Company
Indianapolis, IN 888-539-7225
Oak Barrel Winecraft
Berkeley, CA 510-849-0400
Palmer Distributors
St Clair Shores, MI 800-444-1912
Penn Bottle & Supply Company
Philadelphia, PA 215-365-5700
Richards Packaging
Memphis, TN 800-583-0327
Saint-Gobain Containers
Malvern, PA
Stanpac, Inc.
Smithville, ON 905-957-3326
World Kitchen
Elmira, NY 800-999-3436
Xtreme Beverages, LLC
Dana Point, CA. 949-495-7929

Plastic

Abbott Industries
Paterson, NJ
Alpack
Centerville, NA. 774-994-8086
Altira Inc
Miami, FL 305-687-8074
Brown International Corp LLC
Winter Haven, FL 863-299-2111
California Vibratory Feeders
Anaheim, CA 800-354-0972
CapSnap Equipment
Jackson, MI 517-787-3481
Chester Plastics
Chester, NS 902-275-3522
CMD Corporation
Appleton, WI 920-730-6888
Consolidated Container Co LLC
Atlanta, GA. 888-831-2184
Consolidated Plastics Co Inc
Stow, OH. 800-858-5001
Constar International
Plymouth, MI 734-455-3600

Container Specialties
Melrose Park, IL 800-548-7513
Continental Plastic Container
Dallas, TX 972-303-1825
Contour Packaging
Philadelphia, PA 215-457-1600
CTK Plastics
Moose Jaw, SK 800-667-8847
Custom Bottle of Connecticut
Naugatuck, CT 203-723-6661
Flexo Transparent Inc
Buffalo, NY. 877-993-5396
Fuller Industries LLC
Great Bend, KS 800-522-0499
Graham Engineering Corp
York, PA 717-848-3755
Greenfield Packaging
White Plains, NY 914-993-0233
Hartford Plastics
Omaha, NE
Hedwin Division
Baltimore, MD 800-638-1012
Indiana Bottle Co
Scottsburg, IN 800-752-8702
Indianapolis Container Company
Indianapolis, IN 800-760-3318
Intertech Corp
Greensboro, NC 800-364-2255
J.E. Roy
St Claire, QC 418-883-2711
Juice Merchandising Corp
Kansas City, MO. 800-950-1998
Jupiter Mills Corporation
Roslyn, NY 800-853-5121
Liqui-Box
Richmond, VA. 804-325-1400
Liquitane
Berwick, PA 570-759-6200
LMK Containers
Centerville, UT 626-821-9984
Louisville Container Company
Indianapolis, IN 888-539-7225
Marpac Industries
Philmont, NY 888-462-7722
Owens-Illinois Inc
Perrysburg, OH 567-336-5000
Packaging Associates
Randolph, NJ 973-252-8890
Parkway Plastic Inc
Piscataway, NJ 800-881-4996
Penn Bottle & Supply Company
Philadelphia, PA 215-365-5700
Plastics Industries
Athens, TN 800-894-4876
Plastipak Packaging
Plymouth, MI 734-354-3510
Podnar Plastics Inc
Kent, OH. 800-673-5277
Polycon Industries
Chicago, IL 773-374-5500
Pretium Packaging
Chesterfield, MO 314-727-8673
Pretium Packaging
Hazle Twp, PA 570-459-1800
Pretium Packaging
Hermann, MO 573-486-2811
Pretium Packaging, LLC.
Chesterfield, MO 314-727-8200
Priority Plastics Inc
Grinnell, IA. 800-798-3512
Pro-Gram Plastics Inc
Geneva, OH. 440-466-8080
Progressive Plastics
Cleveland, OH 800-252-0053
Q Pak Inc
Newark, NJ 973-483-4404
Quintex Corp
Nampa, ID. 208-467-1113
RAPAC Inc
Oakland, TN 800-280-6333
Redi-Call Inc
Reno, NV 800-648-1849
Reliance Product
Winnipeg, MB. 800-665-0258
Richard Read Construction Company
Arcadia, CA. 888-450-7343
Richards Packaging
Memphis, TN 800-583-0327
RXI Silgan Specialty Plastics
Triadelphia, WV 304-547-9100
Sailor Plastics
Adrian, MN 800-380-7429

Schoeneck Containers Inc
New Berlin, WI. 262-786-9360
Setco
Monroe Twp, NJ 609-655-4600
Setco
Anaheim, CA 714-777-5200
Silgan Plastics Canada
Chesterfield, MO 800-274-5426
Silgan Plastics LLC
Chesterfield, MO 800-274-5426
Snapware
Fullerton, CA 800-334-3062
T&S Blow Molding
Scarborough, ON 416-752-8330
Thornton Plastics
Salt Lake City, UT 800-248-3434
Tolco Corp
Toledo, OH 800-537-4786
Wheaton Plastic Containers
Millville, NJ 856-825-1400

Boxes

Bakers'

International Paper Co.
Memphis, TN
Morris Transparent Box Co
East Providence, RI. 401-438-6116
Pater & Associates
Cincinnati, OH
Piper Products Inc
Wausau, WI. 800-544-3057
Premier Packages
Saint Louis, MO 800-466-6588
Reliable Container Corporation
Downey, CA 562-745-0200
Ritz Packaging Company
Brooklyn, NY 718-366-2300
Schiefer Packaging Corporation
Syracuse, NY 315-422-0615
Schroeder Machine
San Marcos, CA 760-591-9733
Smyrna Container Co
Atlanta, GA 800-868-4305
Xtreme Beverages, LLC
Dana Point, CA. 949-495-7929

Candy

A La Carte
Chicago, IL 800-722-2370
Cardinal Packaging Prod LLC
Crystal Lake, IL 866-216-4942
Central Paper Box
Kansas City, MO. 816-753-3126
Collectors Gallery
St Charles, IL 800-346-3063
Creative Cookie
Easton, MD. 800-451-4005
Elegant Packaging
Cicero, IL 800-367-5493
Friend Box Co
Danvers, MA. 978-774-0240
Gary Plastic Packaging Corporation
Bronx, NY. 800-227-4279
H.P. Neun
Fairport, NY 585-388-1360
Impress Industries
Emmaus, PA 610-967-6027
Kaufman Paper Box Company
Providence, RI 401-272-7508
Lengsfield Brothers
New Orleans, LA 504-529-2235
Nashville Wraps LLC
Hendersonville, TN. 800-547-9727
Pater & Associates
Cincinnati, OH
Ritz Packaging Company
Brooklyn, NY 718-366-2300
Schiefer Packaging Corporation
Syracuse, NY 315-422-0615
Taylor Box Co
Warren, RI 800-304-6361
Visual Packaging Corp
Haskell, NJ 973-835-7055
Xtreme Beverages, LLC
Dana Point, CA. 949-495-7929

Corrugated

Adpro
Solon, OH 440-542-1111
American Containers Inc
Plymouth, IN. 574-936-4068
Atlas Packaging Inc
Opa Locka, FL 800-662-0630
Bell Container
Newark, NJ .973-344-6997
Bell Packaging Corporation
Marion, IN. .800-382-0153
Boxes.com
Livingston, NJ. 201-646-9050
Cantwell-Cleary Co Inc
Elkridge, MD 301-773-9800
Cantwell-Cleary Co Inc
Richmond, VA. 804-329-9800
Capital City Container Corporation
Buda, TX. 512-312-1222
Capitol Carton Company
Sacramento, CA 916-388-7848
Capitol City Container Corp
Indianapolis, IN 800-233-5145
Cardinal Container Corp
Indianapolis, IN 800-899-2715
Cardinal Packaging Prod LLC
Crystal Lake, IL 866-216-4942
Carolina Container
High Point, NC 800-627-0825
Carpet City Paper Box Company
Amsterdam, NY 518-842-5430
Cedar Box Co
Minneapolis, MN 612-332-4287
Central Package & Display
Minneapolis, MN 763-425-7444
Chambers Container Company
Gastonia, NC. 704-377-6317
Champlin Co
Hartford, CT 800-458-5261
City Box Company
Aurora, IL 773-277-5500
Color Carton Corp
Bronx, NY. .718-665-0840
Columbus Paperbox Company
Columbus, OH 800-968-0797
Commencement Bay Corrugated
Orting, WA .253-845-3100
Commercial Corrugated Co Inc
Baltimore, MD 800-242-8861
Complete Packaging & Shipping
Freeport, NY 877-269-3236
Conn Container Corp
North Haven, CT. 203-248-0241
Corbox-Meyers Inc
Cleveland, OH 800-321-7286
Corfab
Chicago, IL 708-458-8750
Corr Pak Corp
Mc Cook, IL 708-442-7806
Corrugated Packaging
Sarasota, FL 941-371-0000
Corrugated Specialties
Plainwell, MI 269-685-9821
Craft Corrugated Box Inc
New Bedford, MA 508-998-2115
Creative Packaging
Hayward, CA 510-785-6500
Cush-Pak Container Corporation
Henderson, TX 903-657-0555
Custom Packaging Inc
Richmond, VA. 804-232-3299
Dakota Corrugated Box
Sioux Falls, SD. 605-332-3501
Deline Box Co
Denver, CO 303-376-1283
Desert Box & Supply Corporation
Thermal, CA 760-399-5161
Diamond Packaging
Rochester, NY. 800-333-4079
Die Cut Specialties Inc
Savage, MN. 952-890-7590
Display One
Hartford, WI 262-673-5880
Dixie Printing & Packaging
Glen Burnie, MD 800-433-4943
Dorado Carton Company
Dorado, PR 787-796-1670
Drake Co
Houston, TX 800-299-5644
Drescher Paper Box Inc
Buffalo, NY. 716-854-0288

Dusobox Company
Haverhill, MA. 978-372-7192
Duval Container Co
Jacksonville, FL 800-342-8194
Dzignpak LLC Englander
Waco, TX. .888-314-5259
E-Cooler
Chicago, IL 866-955-3266
Eagle Box Company
Farmingdale, NY 212-255-3860
EB Box Company
Richmond Hill, ON. 800-513-2269
Felco Packaging Specialist
Baltimore, MD 800-673-8488
Ferguson Containers
Phillipsburg, NJ 908-454-9755
Fitzpatrick Container Company
North Wales, PA 215-699-3515
Fleetwood International Paper
Vernon, CA 323-588-7121
Flint Boxmakers Inc
Flint, MI 810-743-0400
Four M Manufacturing Group
San Jose, CA 408-998-1141
Frankston Paper Box Company of Texas
Frankston, TX. 903-876-2550
Fuller Box Co
North Attleboro, MA 508-695-2525
Gateway Packaging Corp
Export, PA .888-289-2693
Gaylord Container Corporation
Tampa, FL .813-621-3591
General Bag Corporation
Cleveland, OH 800-837-9396
Genesee Corrugated
Flint, MI 810-228-3702
Georgia-Pacific LLC
Atlanta, GA 800-283-5547
Goldman Manufacturing Company
Detroit, MI .313-834-5535
Graphic Packaging Intl
Elk Grove Vlg, IL 847-437-1700
Great Lakes-Triad Package Corporation
Grand Rapids, MI 616-241-6441
Great Northern Corp
Chippewa Falls, WI 800-472-1800
Great Northern Corp
Racine, WI .800-558-4711
Green Bay Packaging Inc.
Tulsa, OK .918-446-3341
Green Bay Packaging Inc.
Green Bay, WI. 920-433-5111
Greenfield Packaging
White Plains, NY 914-993-0233
Greif Inc
Delaware, OH 740-549-6000
Gulf Arizona Packaging
Humble, TX 800-364-3887
Gulf Systems
Brownsville, TX 800-217-4853
Gulf Systems
Humble, TX 800-364-3887
Gulf Systems
Arlington, TX 817-261-1915
H.P. Neun
Fairport, NY 585-388-1360
Hager Containers Inc
Carrollton, TX. 972-416-7660
Hawkeye Corrugated Box
Cedar Falls, IA 319-268-0407
Herche Warehouse
Denver, CO 303-371-8186
Hinkle Manufacturing
Perrysburg, OH 419-666-5367
Hope Paper Box Company
Pawtucket, RI 401-724-5700
Hunter Packaging Corporation
South Elgin, IL 800-428-4747
Il Valley Container Inc
Peru, IL 815-223-7200
Imperial Containers
City of Industry, CA 626-333-6363
Imperial Packaging Corporation
Pawtucket, RI 401-753-7778
Impress Industries
Emmaus, PA 610-967-6027
Industrial Container Corp
High Point, NC 336-886-7031
Industrial Crating & Packing
Tukwila, WA. 800-942-0499
Inland Consumer Packaging
Harrington, DE 302-398-4211

Inland Paper Company
Ontario, CA. 909-923-4505
Inland Paperboard & Packaging
Rock Hill, SC 803-366-4103
Instabox
Calgary, AB. 800-482-6173
Ivarson Inc
Milwaukee, WI. 414-351-0700
J&J Corrugated Box Corporation
Franklin, MA 508-528-6200
J&J Mid-South Container Corporation
Augusta, GA 800-395-1025
Jamestown Container Corporation
Buffalo, NY. 855-234-4054
Jayhawk Boxes
Fremont, NE 800-642-8363
Jesse Jones Box Corporation
Philadelphia, PA 215-425-6600
Jessup Paper Box
Brookston, IN 765-490-9043
Jet Box Co
Troy, MI 248-362-1260
Johnson Corrugated Products Corporation
Thompson, CT 860-923-9563
Jupiter Mills Corporation
Roslyn, NY 800-853-5121
K & H Corrugated Corp
Walden, NY. 845-778-3555
K&H Container
Wallingford, CT 203-265-1547
Kelly Box & Packaging Corp
Fort Wayne, IN 260-432-4570
Kendel
Countryside, IL 800-323-1100
Kerrigan Paper Products Inc
Haverhill, MA. 978-374-4797
Kimball Companies
East Longmeadow, MA 413-525-1881
Knapp Container
Beacon Falls, CT. 203-888-0511
Koch Container
Victor, NY. 585-924-1600
Kole Industries
Miami, FL .305-633-2556
Lakeside Container Corp
Plattsburgh, NY 518-561-6150
Lansing Corrugated Products
Lansing, MI. 517-323-2752
Laval Paper Box
Pointe Claire, QC 450-669-3551
Lawrence Paper Co
Lawrence, KS 785-843-8111
Leaman Container
Fort Worth, TX 817-429-2660
Levin Brothers Paper
Cicero, IL .800-545-6200
Liberty Carton Co.
Golden Valley, MN 800-328-1784
LinPac
San Angelo, TX 800-453-7393
Lone Star Container Corp
Irving, TX. 800-552-6937
Loy Lange Box Co
St Louis, MO. 800-886-4712
Mack-Chicago Corporation
Chicago, IL 800-992-6225
MacMillan Bloedel Packaging
Montgomery, AL. 800-239-4464
Mall City Containers Inc
Kalamazoo, MI. 800-643-6721
Mannkraft Corporation
Newark, NJ 973-589-7400
Manufacturers Corrugate Box
Flushing, NY. 718-894-7200
Marfred Industries
Sun Valley, CA 800-529-5156
Mark Container Corporation
San Leandro, CA. 510-483-4440
Maro Paper Products Company
Bellwood, IL 708-649-9982
Massachusetts Container Corporation
North Haven, CT. 203-248-2161
Menasha Corp
Neenah, WI. 800-558-5073
Michiana Corrugate Products
Sturgis, MI. 269-651-5225
Michigan Box Co
Detroit, MI 888-642-4269
Midwest Box Co
Cleveland, OH 216-281-3980
Midwest Fibre Products Inc
Viola, IL 309-596-2955

Midwest Paper Products Company
Louisville, KY 502-636-2741
Morphy Container Company
Brantford, ON 519-752-5428
Muth Associates
Springfield, MA 800-388-0157
Neff Packaging
Simpsonville, KY 800-445-4383
Nelson Container Corp
Germantown, WI 262-250-5000
New England Wooden Ware
Gardner, MA 800-252-9214
New York Corugated Box Co
Paterson, NJ 973-742-5000
Northeast Box Co
Ashtabula, OH 800-362-8100
Northeast Container Corporation
Dumont, NJ 201-385-6200
Northern Box Co Inc
Elkhart, IN 574-264-2161
Northern Package Corporation
Minneapolis, MN 952-881-5861
Ockerlund Industries
Addison, IL 708-771-7707
Old Dominion Box Co Inc
Madison Heights, VA 434-929-6701
Packaging Design Corp
Burr Ridge, IL 630-323-1354
Palmetto Packaging
Florence, SC 843-662-5800
Parlor City Paper Box Co Inc
Binghamton, NY 607-772-0600
Pel-Pak Container
Pell City, AL 800-239-2699
Performance Packaging
Trail Creek, IN 219-874-6226
Phoenix Industries Corp
Madison, WI 888-241-7482
Pratt Industries
Conyers, GA 800-428-9269
Pratt Industries
Raleigh, NC 919-334-7400
Premier Packages
Saint Louis, MO 800-466-6588
President Container Inc
Moonachie, NJ 212-244-0345
Propak
Burlington, ON 800-263-4872
Providence Packaging
Mooresville, NC 866-779-4945
Quality Packaging Inc
Fond Du Lac, WI 800-923-3633
R&R Corrugated Container
Terryville, CT 860-584-1194
Rand-Whitney Group LLC
Worcester, MA 508-791-2301
Rand-Whitney Packaging Corp
Portsmouth, NH 508-791-2301
RDA Container Corp
Gates, NY 585-247-2323
Regal Box Corp
Milwaukee, WI 414-562-5890
Reliable Container Corporation
Downey, CA 562-745-0200
Reliance-Paragon
Philadelphia, PA 215-743-1231
Rex Carton Co Inc
Chicago, IL 773-581-4115
Richmond Corrugated Box Company
Richmond, VA 804-222-1300
Romanow Container
Westwood, MA 781-320-9200
Royal Group
Cicero, IL 708-656-2020
Rudd Container Corp
Chicago, IL 773-847-7600
Ruffino Paper Box Co
Hackensack, NJ 201-487-1260
Rusken Packaging
Cullman, AL 256-775-0014
Schermerhorn Inc
Chicopee, IL 413-598-8348
Schiffenhaus Industries
Newark, NJ 973-484-5000
Scope Packaging
Orange, CA 714-998-4411
Seattle-Tacoma Box Co
Kent, WA 253-854-9700
Sebring Container Corporation
Salem, OH 330-332-1533
Security Packaging
North Bergen, NJ 201-854-1955

Sheboygan Paper Box Co
Sheboygan, WI 800-458-8373
Shillington Box Co LLC
St Louis, MO 636-825-6471
Shippers Supply
Saskatoon, SK 800-661-5639
Shippers Supply, Labelgraphic
Calgary, AB 800-661-5639
Simkins Industries Inc
East Haven, CT 203-787-7171
Smith Packaging
Mississauga, ON 905-564-6640
Smurfit Stone
Norcross, GA 314-656-5300
Smurfit-Stone Container Corp
Santa Fe Springs, CA 714-523-3550
Solve Needs International
White Lake, MI 800-783-2462
Somerville Packaging
Toronto, ON 416-754-7228
Southern Missouri Containers
Springfield, MO 800-999-7666
Southern Packaging Machinery
Athens, GA 706-208-0814
Spring Cove Container Div
Roaring Spring, PA 814-224-5141
SQP
Schenectady, NY 800-724-1129
St Joseph Packaging Inc
St Joseph, MO 800-383-3000
Stand Fast Pkgng Prods Inc
Addison, IL 630-543-6390
Star Container Corporation
Leominster, MA 978-537-1676
Stearnswood Inc
Hutchinson, MN 800-657-0144
Stone Container
Moss Point, MS 502-491-4870
Stronghaven Containers Co
Matthews, NC 800-222-7919
Suburban Corrugated Box Company
Indianhead Park, IL 630-920-1230
Supply One Inc
Tulsa, OK
Tampa Corrugated Carton Company
Tampa, FL 813-623-5115
Taylor Box Co
Warren, RI 800-304-6361
Tenneco Packaging
Westmont, IL 630-850-7034
Tennessee Packaging
Loudon, TN 800-968-6894
THARCO
San Lorenzo, CA 800-772-2332
Traub Container Corporation
Cleveland, OH 216-475-5100
Trent Corp
Trenton, NJ 609-587-7515
Triple A Containers
Buena Park, CA 714-521-2820
Tucson Container Corp
Tucson, AZ 520-746-3171
Union Camp Corporation
Denver, CO 303-371-0760
Unique Boxes
Chicago, IL 800-281-1670
Universal Folding Box
East Orange, NJ 973-482-4300
Valley Container Corporation
Saint Louis, MO 314-652-8050
Valley Container Inc
Bridgeport, CT 203-368-6546
Vermont Container Corp
Bennington, VT 802-442-5455
Victory Box Corp
Roselle, NJ 908-245-5100
Victory Packaging, Inc.
Houston, TX 800-486-5606
Volk Packaging Corp
Biddeford, ME 207-282-6151
Wagner Brothers Containers
Baltimore, MD 410-354-0044
Wasserman Bag Company
Center Moriches, NY 631-909-8656
Weber Display & Packaging Inc
Philadelphia, PA 215-426-3500
Webster Packaging Corporation
Loveland, OH 513-683-5666
Welch Packaging Group Inc
Elkhart, IN 574-295-2460
Westvaco Corporation
Newark, DE 302-453-7200

Weyerhaeuser Co
Seattle, WA 800-525-5440
Willamette Industries
Beaverton, OR 503-641-1131
Willard Packaging Co
Gaithersburg, MD 301-948-7700
Woodson Pallet Co
Anmoore, WV 304-623-2858
Xtreme Beverages, LLC
Dana Point, CA 949-495-7929
York Container Co
York, PA 717-757-7611

Fancy

Can Creations
Pembroke Pines, FL 954-581-3312
Central Paper Box
Kansas City, MO 816-753-3126
Colbert Packaging Corp
Lake Forest, IL 847-367-5990
Collectors Gallery
St Charles, IL 800-346-3063
Elegant Packaging
Cicero, IL 800-367-5493
Gates
West Peterborough, NH 888-543-6316
Godshall Paper Box Company
Oshkosh, WI 920-235-4040
H.P. Neun
Fairport, NY 585-388-1360
McGraw Box Company
Mc Graw, NY 607-836-6465
Nordic Printing & Packaging
New Hope, MN 763-535-6440
North American Packaging Corp
New York, NY 800-499-3521
Paragon Packaging
Ferndale, CA 888-615-0065
Pater & Associates
Cincinnati, OH
Paul T. Freund Corporation
Palmyra, NY 800-333-0091
Racine Paper Box Manufacturing
Chicago, IL 773-227-3900
Smurfit Stone
Norcross, GA 314-656-5300
Xtreme Beverages, LLC
Dana Point, CA 949-495-7929

Fiber

Goldman Manufacturing Company
Detroit, MI 313-834-5535
Greenfield Packaging
White Plains, NY 914-993-0233
Jupiter Mills Corporation
Roslyn, NY 800-853-5121
Lansing Corrugated Products
Lansing, MI 517-323-2752
North American Container Corp
Marietta, GA 800-929-0610
Palmetto Packaging
Florence, SC 843-662-5800
Romanow Container
Westwood, MA 781-320-9200
Round Paper Packages Inc
Erlanger, KY 859-331-7200
Smith Packaging
Mississauga, ON 905-564-6640
Solve Needs International
White Lake, MI 800-783-2462
Tucson Container Corp
Tucson, AZ 520-746-3171
Union Camp Corporation
Denver, CO 303-371-0760
Volk Packaging Corp
Biddeford, ME 207-282-6151

Fruit & Vegetable

Franklin Crates
Micanopy, FL 352-466-3141
Frobisher Industries
Waterborough, NB 506-362-2198
Jacksonville Box & Woodwork Co
Jacksonville, FL 800-683-2699
Luke's Almond Acres
Reedley, CA 559-638-3483
Remmey Wood Products
Southampton, PA 215-355-3335

Schiefer Packaging Corporation
Syracuse, NY .315-422-0615
Supply One Inc
Tulsa, OK
Upham & Walsh Lumber
Hoffman Estates, IL 847-519-1010
Wnc Pallet & Forest Pdts Co
Candler, NC .828-667-5426
Xtreme Beverages, LLC
Dana Point, CA 949-495-7929

Paper

Accurate Paper Box Co Inc
Knoxville, TN 865-690-0311
Adpro
Solon, OH 440-542-1111
Alcan Packaging
Baie D'Urfe, QC 514-457-4555
Ample Industries
Franklin, OH 888-818-9700
Artistic Carton
Auburn, IN 800-735-7225
Artistic Carton Co
Elgin, IL 847-741-0247
Bancroft Bag Inc
West Monroe, LA 318-387-2550
Bell Packaging Corporation
Marion, IN. 800-382-0153
Boxes.com
Livingston, NJ. 201-646-9050
Brewer-Cantelmo Inc
New York, NY 212-244-4600
Burrows Paper Corp
Little Falls, NY 800-272-7122
Capitol Carton Company
Sacramento, CA 916-388-7848
Cardinal Packaging Prod LLC
Crystal Lake, IL 866-216-4942
Carpenter-Hayes Paper Box Company
East Hampton, CT. 203-267-4436
Carpet City Paper Box Company
Amsterdam, NY 518-842-5430
Cedar Box Co
Minneapolis, MN 612-332-4287
Central Paper Box
Kansas City, MO. 816-753-3126
Chambers Container Company
Gastonia, NC 704-377-6317
Cleveland Specialties Co
Loveland, OH 513-677-9787
Coast Paper Box Company
San Bernardino, CA 909-382-3475
Colbert Packaging Corp
Lake Forest, IL 847-367-5990
Color Box
Richmond, IN 765-966-7588
Color Carton Corp
Bronx, NY 718-665-0840
Columbus Paperbox Company
Columbus, OH 800-968-0797
Commencement Bay Corrugated
Orting, WA 253-845-3100
Commercial Corrugated Co Inc
Baltimore, MD 800-242-8861
Complete Packaging & Shipping
Freeport, NY 877-269-3236
Conn Container Corp
North Haven, CT. 203-248-0241
Corbox-Meyers Inc
Cleveland, OH 800-321-7286
Corfab
Chicago, IL 708-458-8750
Corpak
San Juan, PR 787-787-9085
Corr Pak Corp
Mc Cook, IL .708-442-7806
Corrobilt Container Company
Livermore, CA 925-373-0880
Corrugated Packaging
Sarasota, FL .941-371-0000
Corson Manufacturing Company
Lockport, NY 716-434-8871
Crane Carton Corporation
Chicago, IL 773-722-0555
Creative Packaging
Hayward, CA 510-785-6500
Curtis Packaging
Sandy Hook, CT 203-426-5861
Custom Packaging Inc
Richmond, VA. 804-232-3299

Day Manufacturing Company
Sherman, TX 903-893-1138
Designers Folding Box Corp
Buffalo, NY. .716-853-5141
Diamond Packaging
Rochester, NY 800-333-4079
Dixie Printing & Packaging
Glen Burnie, MD 800-433-4943
Dorado Carton Company
Dorado, PR .787-796-1670
Drescher Paper Box Inc
Buffalo, NY. .716-854-0288
Dusobox Company
Haverhill, MA 978-372-7192
Duval Container Co
Jacksonville, FL 800-342-8194
Eagle Box Company
Farmingdale, NY 212-255-3860
EB Box Company
Richmond Hill, ON. 800-513-2269
Economy Folding Box Corporation
Chicago, IL 800-771-1053
Elegant Packaging
Cicero, IL 800-367-5493
Enterprise Box Company
Montclair, NJ 973-509-2200
Eureka Paper Box Company
Williamsport, PA. 570-326-9147
F C MEYER Packaging LLC
Jeannette, PA. 724-523-5565
Felco Packaging Specialist
Baltimore, MD 800-673-8488
Finn Industries
Ontario, CA. .909-930-1500
Fitzpatrick Container Company
North Wales, PA 215-699-3515
Flashfold Carton Inc
Fort Wayne, IN 260-423-9431
Flour City Press-Pack Company
Minneapolis, MN 952-831-1265
Folding Carton/Flexible Packaging
North Hollywood, CA 818-896-3449
Food Pak Corp
San Mateo, CA 650-341-6559
Four M Manufacturing Group
San Jose, CA 408-998-1141
Frankston Paper Box Company of Texas
Frankston, TX 903-876-2550
Friend Box Co
Danvers, MA. 978-774-0240
Friendly City Box Co Inc
Johnstown, PA. 814-266-6287
Fuller Box Co
North Attleboro, MA 508-695-2525
Fuller Packaging Inc
Central Falls, RI 401-725-4300
Gateway Packaging Corp
Export, PA. .888-289-2693
Godshall Paper Box Company
Oshkosh, WI. 920-235-4040
Goldman Manufacturing Company
Detroit, MI .313-834-5535
Graphic Packaging Intl
Elk Grove Vlg, IL 847-437-1700
Great Northern Corp
Chippewa Falls, WI 800-472-1800
Green Bay Packaging Inc.
Tulsa, OK 918-446-3341
Green Bay Packaging Inc.
Green Bay, WI. 920-433-5111
Green Brothers
Barrington, RI 401-245-9043
Greenfield Paper Box Co
Greenfield, MA 413-773-9414
Greif Inc
Delaware, OH 740-549-6000
Grigsby Brothers Paper Box Manufacturers
Portland, OR 866-233-4690
Gulf Packaging Company
Safety Harbor, FL 800-749-3466
H.P. Neun
Fairport, NY 585-388-1360
Hager Containers Inc
Carrollton, TX. 972-416-7660
Harvard Folding Box Company
Lynn, MA 781-598-1600
Henry Ira L Co
Watertown, WI 920-261-0648
Hope Paper Box Company
Pawtucket, RI 401-724-5700
Hub Folding Box Co
Mansfield, MA 508-339-0102

Hunter Packaging Corporation
South Elgin, IL 800-428-4747
Imperial Packaging Corporation
Pawtucket, RI 401-753-7778
Impress Industries
Emmaus, PA 610-967-6027
Industrial Nameplate Inc
Warminster, PA. 800-878-6263
Inland Consumer Packaging
Harrington, DE 302-398-4211
Inland Paper Company
Ontario, CA. 909-923-4505
Inland Paperboard & Packaging
Rock Hill, SC 803-366-4103
Ivarson Inc
Milwaukee, WI 414-351-0700
Jamestown Container Corporation
Buffalo, NY. 855-234-4054
Jarisch Paper Box Company
North Adams, MA 413-663-5396
Jesse Jones Box Corporation
Philadelphia, PA 215-425-6600
Jessup Paper Box
Brookston, IN 765-490-9043
Johnson Corrugated Products Corporation
Thompson, CT 860-923-9563
Jordan Box Co
Syracuse, NY 315-422-3419
Jordan Paper Box Co
Chicago, IL .773-287-5362
Jupiter Mills Corporation
Roslyn, NY .800-853-5121
K & H Corrugated Corp
Walden, NY. 845-778-3555
K & L Intl
Ontario, CA. 888-598-5588
K&H Container
Wallingford, CT 203-265-1547
Kaufman Paper Box Company
Providence, RI 401-272-7508
Kendel
Countryside, IL 800-323-1100
Knight Paper Box Company
Chicago, IL .773-585-2035
Koch Container
Victor, NY 585-924-1600
Lakeside Container Corp
Plattsburgh, NY 518-561-6150
Levin Brothers Paper
Cicero, IL 800-545-6200
Liberty Carton Co.
Golden Valley, MN 800-328-1784
LinPac
San Angelo, TX 800-453-7393
Lone Star Container Corp
Irving, TX 800-552-6937
Los Angeles Paper Box & Board Mills
Los Angeles, CA. 323-685-8900
Lowell Paper Box Company
Nashua, NH 603-595-0700
Loy Lange Box Co
St Louis, MO. 800-886-4712
Mack-Chicago Corporation
Chicago, IL .800-992-6225
MacMillan Bloedel Packaging
Montgomery, AL. 800-239-4464
Mall City Containers Inc
Kalamazoo, MI 800-643-6721
Malnove of Nebraska
Omaha, NE .800-228-9877
Marcus Carton Company
Melville, NY 631-752-4200
Marfred Industries
Sun Valley, CA 800-529-5156
Marion Paper Box Co
Marion, IN. .765-664-6435
Maro Paper Products Company
Bellwood, IL. 708-649-9982
Master Paper Box Co
Chicago, IL .877-927-0252
Maypak Inc
Wayne, NJ .973-696-0780
Menasha Corp
Neenah, WI. 800-558-5073
Merchants Publishing Company
Kalamazoo, MI 269-345-1175
Meyer Packaging
Palmyra, PA. 717-838-6300
Michiana Corrugate Products
Sturgis, MI .269-651-5225
Michigan Box Co
Detroit, MI .888-642-4269

Mid Cities Paper Box Company
Downey, CA 877-277-6272
Midwest Fibre Products Inc
Viola, IL 309-596-2955
Modern Paper Box Company
Providence, RI 401-861-7357
Moore Paper Boxes Inc
Dayton, OH 937-278-7327
Morphy Container Company
Brantford, ON 519-752-5428
Mt Vernon Packaging Inc
Mt Vernon, OH 888-397-3221
Muth Associates
Springfield, MA 800-388-0157
Nagel Paper & Box Company
Saginaw, MI .800-292-3654
Neff Packaging
Simpsonville, KY 800-445-4383
New England Wooden Ware
Gardner, MA .800-252-9214
New York Corugated Box Co
Paterson, NJ .973-742-5000
New York Folding Box Co Inc
Stanhope, NJ 973-347-6932
Norristown Box Company
Norristown, PA 610-275-5540
Northeast Box Co
Ashtabula, OH 800-362-8100
Northeast Container Corporation
Dumont, NJ .201-385-6200
Northern Package Corporation
Minneapolis, MN 952-881-5861
Oakes Carton Co
Kalamazoo, MI 269-381-6022
Ockerlund Industries
Addison, IL 708-771-7707
Old Dominion Box Co Inc
Madison Heights, VA 434-929-6701
Old Dominion Box Company
Burlington, NC 336-226-4491
Oracle Packaging
Winston Salem, NC 800-952-9536
Original Packaging & Display Company
Saint Louis, MO 314-772-7797
Ott Packagings
Selinsgrove, PA 570-374-2811
Pacific Paper Box Co
Cudahy, CA .323-771-7733
Packaging Corporation of America
Lake Forest, IL 800-456-4725
Packaging Design Corp
Burr Ridge, IL 630-323-1354
Packrite Packaging
Archdale, NC 336-431-1111
Paddington Corporation
Fort Lee, NJ .201-461-7800
Paper Box & Specialty Co
Sheboygan, WI 888-240-3756
Paper Works Industries Inc
Baldwinsville, NY 800-847-5677
Paragon Packaging
Ferndale, MI .888-615-0065
Parlor City Paper Box Co Inc
Binghamton, NY 607-772-0600
Parta
Kent, OH 800-543-5781
Pater & Associates
Cincinnati, OH
Paul T. Freund Corporation
Palmyra, NY .800-333-0091
Peerless Packages
Cleveland, OH 216-464-3620
Pell Paper Box Company
Elizabeth City, NC 252-335-4361
Performance Packaging
Trail Creek, IN 219-874-6226
Pioneer Packaging
Chicopee, MA 413-378-6930
Pioneer Packaging & Printing
Anoka, MN 800-708-1705
Piqua Paper Box Co
Piqua, OH 800-536-2136
Pohlig Brothers
N Chesterfield, VA 804-275-9000
Portland Paper Box Company
Portland, OR 800-547-2571
Premier Packages
Saint Louis, MO 800-466-6588
Quality Packaging Inc
Fond Du Lac, WI 800-923-3633
Rand-Whitney Group LLC
Worcester, MA 508-791-2301

Rand-Whitney Packaging Corp
Portsmouth, NH 508-791-2301
RDA Container Corp
Gates, NY 585-247-2323
Reliable Container Corporation
Downey, CA .562-745-0200
Reliance-Paragon
Philadelphia, PA 215-743-1231
Rhoades Paper Box Corporation
Springfield, OH 800-441-6494
Rice Paper Box Company
Colorado Springs, CO 303-733-1000
Ritz Packaging Company
Brooklyn, NY 718-366-2300
Rock-Tenn Company
Norcross, GA 608-223-6272
Romanow Container
Westwood, MA 781-320-9200
Round Paper Packages Inc
Erlanger, KY .859-331-7200
Roy's Folding Box
Cleveland, OH 216-464-1191
Royal Paper Box Co
Montebello, CA 323-728-7041
Ruffino Paper Box Co
Hackensack, NJ 201-487-1260
Rusken Packaging
Cullman, AL .256-775-0014
Schermerhorn Inc
Chicopee, MA 413-598-8348
Schwarz Supply Source
Morton Grove, IL 800-323-4903
Scope Packaging
Orange, CA .714-998-4411
Seaboard Carton Company
Downers Grove, IL 708-344-0575
Seaboard Folding Box Corp
Fitchburg, MA 800-255-6313
Seattle-Tacoma Box Co
Kent, WA 253-854-9700
Sebring Container Corporation
Salem, OH 330-332-1533
Security Packaging
North Bergen, NJ 201-854-1955
Sheboygan Paper Box Co
Sheboygan, WI 800-458-8373
Shillington Box Co LLC
St Louis, MO 636-825-6471
Shippers Supply
Saskatoon, SK 800-661-5639
Shippers Supply, Labelgraphic
Calgary, AB .800-661-5639
Shore Paper Box Co
Mardela Springs, MD 410-749-7125
Shorewood Packaging
Carlstadt, NJ 201-933-3203
Simkins Industries Inc
East Haven, CT 203-787-7171
Smith-Lustig Paper Box Manufacturing
Cleveland, OH 216-621-0454
Smurfit Stone
Norcross, GA 314-656-5300
Smurfit-Stone Container Corp
Santa Fe Springs, CA 714-523-3550
Smyrna Container Co
Atlanta, GA .800-868-4305
Solve Needs International
White Lake, MI 800-783-2462
Somerville Packaging
Toronto, ON .416-754-7228
Sonderen Packaging
Spokane, WA 800-727-9139
Southern Champion Tray LP
Chattanooga, TN 800-468-2222
Southern Missouri Containers
Springfield, MO 800-999-7666
Southern Packaging Machinery
Athens, GA .706-208-0814
Specialized Packaging London
London, ON .519-659-7011
Spring Cove Container Div
Roaring Spring, PA 814-224-5141
SQP
Schenectady, NY 800-724-1129
St Joseph Packaging Inc
St Joseph, MO 800-383-3000
St. Louis Carton Company
Saint Louis, MO 314-241-0990
Stand Fast Pkgng Prods Inc
Addison, IL .630-543-6390
Stearnswood Inc
Hutchinson, MN 800-657-0144

Sterling Paper Company
Ohio, PA 800-282-1124
Stone Container
Moss Point, MS 502-491-4870
Stronghaven Containers Co
Matthews, NC 800-222-7919
Suburban Corrugated Box Company
Indianhead Park, IL 630-920-1230
T J Smith Box Co
Fort Smith, AR 877-540-7933
Tampa Corrugated Carton Company
Tampa, FL 813-623-5115
Taylor Box Co
Warren, RI 800-304-6361
THARCO
San Lorenzo, CA 800-772-2332
Traub Container Corporation
Cleveland, OH 216-475-5100
Trent Corp
Trenton, NJ .609-587-7515
Unipak Inc
West Chester, PA 610-436-6600
Unique Boxes
Chicago, IL .800-281-1670
Universal Folding Box
East Orange, NJ 973-482-4300
Universal Folding Box Company
Hoboken, NJ 201-659-7373
Universal Paper Box
Seattle, WA .800-228-1045
Utah PaperBox Company
Salt Lake City, UT 801-363-0093
Victory Box Corp
Roselle, NJ .908-245-5100
Victory Packaging, Inc.
Houston, TX 800-486-5606
VIP Real Estate LTD
Chicago, IL .773-376-5000
Volk Packaging Corp
Biddeford, ME 207-282-6151
Wasserman Bag Company
Center Moriches, NY 631-909-8656
West Rock
Atlanta, GA .770-448-2193
Western Container Company
Kansas City, MO 816-924-5700
Westvaco Corporation
Newark, DE .302-453-7200
Willamette Industries
Beaverton, OR 503-641-1131
Winchester Carton
Eutaw, AL 205-372-3337
Woodson Pallet Co
Anmoore, WV 304-623-2858
Wright Brothers Paper Box Company
Fond Du Lac, WI 920-921-8270
Xtreme Beverages, LLC
Dana Point, CA 949-495-7929
York Container Co
York, PA 717-757-7611

Paper, Folding

Adpro
Solon, OH 440-542-1111
Alcan Packaging
Baie D'Urfe, QC 514-457-4555
Ample Industries
Franklin, OH 888-818-9700
Artistic Carton
Auburn, IN 800-735-7225
Artistic Carton Co
Elgin, IL 847-741-0247
Bell Packaging Corporation
Marion, IN 800-382-0153
Boxes.com
Livingston, NJ 201-646-9050
Brewer-Cantelmo Inc
New York, NY 212-244-4600
Burrows Paper Corp
Little Falls, NY 800-272-7122
Capitol Carton Company
Sacramento, CA 916-388-7848
Cardinal Packaging Prod LLC
Crystal Lake, IL 866-216-4942
Carpet City Paper Box Company
Amsterdam, NY 518-842-5430
Carton Service Co
Shelby, OH .800-533-7744
Cedar Box Co
Minneapolis, MN 612-332-4287

Central Paper Box
Kansas City, MO 816-753-3126
Chambers Container Company
Gastonia, NC 704-377-6317
Cleveland Specialties Co
Loveland, OH 513-677-9787
Coast Paper Box Company
San Bernardino, CA 909-382-3475
Collectors Gallery
St Charles, IL 800-346-3063
Color Carton Corp
Bronx, NY 718-665-0840
Columbus Paperbox Company
Columbus, OH 800-968-0797
Commencement Bay Corrugated
Orting, WA 253-845-3100
Commercial Corrugated Co Inc
Baltimore, MD 800-242-8861
Complete Packaging & Shipping
Freeport, NY 877-269-3236
Conn Container Corp
North Haven, CT 203-248-0241
Corbox-Meyers Inc
Cleveland, OH 800-321-7286
Corfab
Chicago, IL 708-458-8750
Corr Pak Corp
Mc Cook, IL 708-442-7806
Corrobilt Container Company
Livermore, CA 925-373-0880
Corrugated Packaging
Sarasota, FL 941-371-0000
Corson Manufacturing Company
Lockport, NY 716-434-8871
Crane Carton Corporation
Chicago, IL 773-722-0555
Creative Packaging
Hayward, CA 510-785-6500
Curtis Packaging
Sandy Hook, CT 203-426-5861
Day Manufacturing Company
Sherman, TX 903-893-1138
Designers Folding Box Corp
Buffalo, NY 716-853-5141
Diamond Packaging
Rochester, NY 800-333-4079
Dixie Printing & Packaging
Glen Burnie, MD 800-433-4943
Dorado Carton Company
Dorado, PR 787-796-1670
Drescher Paper Box Inc
Buffalo, NY 716-854-0288
Dusobox Company
Haverhill, MA 978-372-7192
Duval Container Co
Jacksonville, FL 800-342-8194
Eagle Box Company
Farmingdale, NY 212-255-3860
EB Box Company
Richmond Hill, ON 800-513-2269
Eureka Paper Box Company
Williamsport, PA 570-326-9147
F C MEYER Packaging LLC
Jeannette, PA 724-523-5565
Felco Packaging Specialist
Baltimore, MD 800-673-8488
Finn Industries
Ontario, CA 909-930-1500
Fitzpatrick Container Company
North Wales, PA 215-699-3515
Flashfold Carton Inc
Fort Wayne, IN 260-423-9431
Flour City Press-Pack Company
Minneapolis, MN 952-831-1265
Folding Carton/Flexible Packaging
North Hollywood, CA 818-896-3449
Food Pak Corp
San Mateo, CA 650-341-6559
Four M Manufacturing Group
San Jose, CA 408-998-1141
Frankston Paper Box Company of Texas
Frankston, TX 903-876-2550
Friendly City Box Co Inc
Johnstown, PA 814-266-6287
Goldman Manufacturing Company
Detroit, MI 313-834-5535
Graphic Packaging Intl
Elk Grove Vlg, IL 847-437-1700
Great Northern Corp
Chippewa Falls, WI 800-472-1800
Green Bay Packaging Inc.
Tulsa, OK 918-446-3341

Green Bay Packaging Inc.
Green Bay, WI 920-433-5111
Greenfield Packaging
White Plains, NY 914-993-0233
Greenfield Paper Box Co
Greenfield, MA 413-773-9414
Greif Inc
Delaware, OH 740-549-6000
Grigsby Brothers Paper Box Manufacturers
Portland, OR 866-233-4690
Gulf Packaging Company
Safety Harbor, FL 800-749-3466
H.P. Neun
Fairport, NY 585-388-1360
Hager Containers Inc
Carrollton, TX 972-416-7660
Harvard Folding Box Company
Lynn, MA 781-598-1600
Heritage Corrugated Box Corporation
Brooklyn, NY 718-495-1500
Hope Paper Box Company
Pawtucket, RI 401-724-5700
Hub Folding Box Co
Mansfield, MA 508-339-0102
Hunter Packaging Corporation
South Elgin, IL 800-428-4747
Imperial Packaging Corporation
Pawtucket, RI 401-753-7778
Impress Industries
Emmaus, PA 610-967-6027
Indiana Carton Co Inc
Bremen, IN 800-348-2390
Industrial Nameplate Inc
Warminster, PA 800-878-6263
Inland Consumer Packaging
Harrington, DE 302-398-4211
Inland Paper Company
Ontario, CA 909-923-4505
Inland Paperboard & Packaging
Rock Hill, SC 803-366-4103
International Paper Co.
Memphis, TN
Ivarson Inc
Milwaukee, WI 414-351-0700
Jamestown Container Corporation
Buffalo, NY 855-234-4054
Jarisch Paper Box Company
North Adams, MA 413-663-5396
Jesse Jones Box Corporation
Philadelphia, PA 215-425-6600
Jessup Paper Box
Brookston, IN 765-490-9043
Jupiter Mills Corporation
Roslyn, NY 800-853-5121
Kendel
Countryside, IL 800-323-1100
Knight Paper Box Company
Chicago, IL 773-585-2035
Koch
Victor, NY 585-924-1600
Lakeside Container Corp
Plattsburgh, NY 518-561-6150
Levin Brothers Paper
Cicero, IL 800-545-6200
Lone Star Container Corp
Irving, TX 800-552-6937
Los Angeles Paper Box & Board Mills
Los Angeles, CA 323-685-8900
Lowell Paper Box Company
Nashua, NH 603-595-0700
Loy Lange Box Co
St Louis, MO 800-886-4712
MacMillan Bloedel Packaging
Montgomery, AL 800-239-4464
Malnove of Nebraska
Omaha, NE 800-228-9877
Marcus Carton Company
Melville, NY 631-752-4200
Marfred Industries
Sun Valley, CA 800-529-5156
Marion Paper Box Co
Marion, IN 765-664-6435
Maro Paper Products Company
Bellwood, IL 708-649-9982
Master Paper Box Co
Chicago, IL 877-927-0252
Menasha Corp
Neenah, WI 800-558-5073
Merchants Publishing Company
Kalamazoo, MI 269-345-1175
Meyer Packaging
Palmyra, PA 717-838-6300

Michigan Box Co
Detroit, MI 888-642-4269
Mid Cities Paper Box Company
Downey, CA 877-277-6272
Midvale Paper Box
Wilkes Barre, PA 570-824-3577
Midwest Fibre Products Inc
Viola, IL 309-596-2955
Nagel Paper & Box Company
Saginaw, MI 800-292-3654
Neff Packaging
Simpsonville, KY 800-445-4383
New England Wooden Ware
Gardner, MA 800-252-9214
New York Corrugated Box Co
Paterson, NJ 973-742-5000
New York Folding Box Co Inc
Stanhope, NJ 973-347-6932
Norristown Box Company
Norristown, PA 610-275-5540
Northeast Box Co
Ashtabula, OH 800-362-8100
Northeast Container Corporation
Dumont, NJ 201-385-6200
Oakes Carton Co
Kalamazoo, MI 269-381-6022
Ockerlund Industries
Addison, IL 708-771-7707
Old Dominion Box Co Inc
Madison Heights, VA 434-929-6701
Old Dominion Box Company
Burlington, NC 336-226-4491
Oracle Packaging
Winston Salem, NC. 800-952-9536
Original Packaging & Display Company
Saint Louis, MO 314-772-7797
Ott Packagings
Selinsgrove, PA 570-374-2811
Packaging Design Corp
Burr Ridge, IL. 630-323-1354
Packrite Packaging
Archdale, NC. 336-431-1111
Paper Works Industries Inc
Baldwinsville, NY 800-847-5677
Paragon Packaging
Ferndale, CA 888-615-0065
Parlor City Paper Box Co Inc
Binghamton, NY. 607-772-0600
Parta
Kent, OH 800-543-5781
Pater & Associates
Cincinnati, OH
Peerless Cartons
Bartlett, IL. 312-226-7952
Peerless Packages
Cleveland, OH 216-464-3620
Pell Paper Box Company
Elizabeth City, NC 252-335-4361
Performance Packaging
Trail Creek, IN 219-874-6226
Pioneer Packaging
Chicopee, MA 413-378-6930
Pioneer Packaging & Printing
Anoka, MN 800-708-1705
Piqua Paper Box Co
Piqua, OH 800-536-2136
Pohlig Brothers
N Chesterfield, VA 804-275-9000
Portland Paper Box Company
Portland, OR 800-547-2571
Premier Packages
Saint Louis, MO 800-466-6588
Prystup Packaging Products
Livingston, AL 205-652-9583
Quality Packaging Inc
Fond Du Lac, WI 800-923-3633
Racine Paper Box Manufacturing
Chicago, IL 773-227-3900
Rand-Whitney Group LLC
Worcester, MA 508-791-2301
Rand-Whitney Packaging Corp
Portsmouth, NH 508-791-2301
RDA Container Corp
Gates, NY 585-247-2323
Reliable Container Corporation
Downey, CA 562-745-0200
Reliance-Paragon
Philadelphia, PA 215-743-1231
Rhoades Paper Box Corporation
Springfield, OH 800-441-6494
Rice Paper Box Company
Colorado Springs, CO. 303-733-1000

199

Ritz Packaging Company
Brooklyn, NY .718-366-2300
Rock-Tenn Company
Norcross, GA 608-223-6272
Romanow Container
Westwood, MA 781-320-9200
Rondo of America
Naugatuck, CT 203-723-7474
Roy's Folding Box
Cleveland, OH. 216-464-1191
Royal Paper Box Co
Montebello, CA 323-728-7041
Ruffino Paper Box Co
Hackensack, NJ. 201-487-1260
Rusken Packaging
Cullman, AL 256-775-0014
San Diego Paper Box Company
Spring Valley, CA 619-660-9566
Schermerhorn Inc
Chicopee, MA. 413-598-8348
Schiefer Packaging Corporation
Syracuse, NY 315-422-0615
Schwarz Supply Source
Morton Grove, IL 800-323-4903
Scope Packaging
Orange, CA 714-998-4411
Scott & Daniells
Portland, CT 860-342-1932
Seaboard Carton Company
Downers Grove, IL 708-344-0575
Seaboard Folding Box Corp
Fitchburg, MA 800-255-6313
Seattle-Tacoma Box Co
Kent, WA .253-854-9700
Sebring Container Corporation
Salem, OH. 330-332-1533
Security Packaging
North Bergen, NJ 201-854-1955
SFBC, LLC dba Seaboard Folding Box
Fitchburg, MA 800-225-6313
Sheboygan Paper Box Co
Sheboygan, WI 800-458-8373
Shelby Co
Westlake, OH 800-842-1650
Shillington Box Co LLC
St Louis, MO. 636-825-6471
Shippers Supply
Saskatoon, SK 800-661-5639
Shippers Supply, Labelgraphic
Calgary, AB. 800-661-5639
Shore Paper Box Co
Mardela Springs, MD 410-749-7125
Shorewood Packaging
Carlstadt, NJ 201-933-3203
Simkins Industries Inc
East Haven, CT. 203-787-7171
Smurfit-Stone Container Corp
Santa Fe Springs, CA 714-523-3550
Smyrna Container Co
Atlanta, GA 800-868-4305
Somerville Packaging
Toronto, ON 416-754-7228
Sonderen Packaging
Spokane, WA. 800-727-9139
SoOPAK
Mississauga, ON 905-677-9666
Southern Champion Tray LP
Chattanooga, TN. 800-468-2222
Southern Missouri Containers
Springfield, MO 800-999-7666
Southern Packaging Machinery
Athens, GA 706-208-0814
Spring Cove Container Div
Roaring Spring, PA 814-224-5141
SQP
Schenectady, NY 800-724-1129
St Joseph Packaging Inc
St Joseph, MO 800-383-3000
St. Louis Carton Company
Saint Louis, MO 314-241-0990
Stand Fast Pkgng Prods Inc
Addison, IL 630-543-6390
Stearnswood Inc
Hutchinson, MN 800-657-0144
Stone Container
Moss Point, MS 502-491-4870
Stoneway Carton Company
Mercer Island, WA 800-498-2185
Suburban Corrugated Box Company
Indianhead Park, IL 630-920-1230
T J Smith Box Co
Fort Smith, AR 877-540-7933

Tampa Corrugated Carton Company
Tampa, FL 813-623-5115
Taylor Box Co
Warren, RI. 800-304-6361
THARCO
San Lorenzo, CA. 800-772-2332
Traub Container Corporation
Cleveland, OH 216-475-5100
Trent Corp
Trenton, NJ 609-587-7515
Unique Boxes
Chicago, IL 800-281-1670
Universal Folding Box
East Orange, NJ 973-482-4300
Universal Folding Box Company
Hoboken, NJ 201-659-7373
Utah PaperBox Company
Salt Lake City, UT 801-363-0093
Victory Box Corp
Roselle, NJ 908-245-5100
Victory Packaging, Inc.
Houston, TX 800-486-5606
VIP Real Estate LTD
Chicago, IL. 773-376-5000
Volk Packaging Corp
Biddeford, ME 207-282-6151
Warren Packaging
San Bernardino, CA 909-888-7008
West Rock
Atlanta, GA 770-448-2193
Western Container Company
Kansas City, MO. 816-924-5700
Westvaco Corporation
Newark, DE. 302-453-7200
Willamette Industries
Beaverton, OR. 503-641-1131
Woodson Pallet Co
Anmoore, WV. 304-623-2858
Wright Brothers Paper Box Company
Fond Du Lac, WI 920-921-8270
Xtreme Beverages, LLC
Dana Point, CA 949-495-7929
York Container Co
York, PA 717-757-7611

Plastic

ACO
Moore, OK 405-794-7662
Alpack
Centerville, NA. 774-994-8086
Bardes Plastics Inc
Milwaukee, WI 800-558-5161
Billie-Ann Plastics Packaging
Brooklyn, NY 888-245-5432
Buckhorn Canada
Brampton, ON. 800-461-7579
Buckhorn Inc
Milford, OH 800-543-4454
Cambro Manufacturing Co
Huntington Beach, CA 800-833-3003
CKS Packaging
Atlanta, GA 800-800-4257
Convoy
Canton, OH. 800-899-1583
DEL-Tec Packaging Inc
Greer, SC. .800-747-8683
Emco Industrial Plastics
Cedar Grove, NJ 800-292-9906
Finn Industries
Ontario, CA. 909-930-1500
Frankston Paper Box Company of Texas
Frankston, TX 903-876-2550
Fremont Die Cut Products
Fremont, OH 800-223-3177
Gary Plastic Packaging Corporation
Bronx, NY. 800-221-8151
Georg Fischer Central Plastics
Shawnee, OK 800-654-3872
Great Northern Corp.
Appleton, WI 800-236-3671
Gulf Packaging Company
Safety Harbor, FL 800-749-3466
Imperial Plastics Inc
Lakeville, MN. 952-469-4951
Jarisch Paper Box Company
North Adams, MA 413-663-5396
Jupiter Mills Corporation
Roslyn, NY 800-853-5121
K & L Intl
Ontario, CA. 888-598-5588

Kimball Companies
East Longmeadow, MA 413-525-1881
Midland Manufacturing Co
Monroe, IA 800-394-2625
Morris Transparent Box Co
East Providence, RI. 401-438-6116
Nolon Industries
Mantua, OH. 330-274-2283
Ockerlund Industries
Addison, IL 708-771-7707
Pacific Paper Box Co
Cudahy, CA. 323-771-7733
Paragon Packaging
Ferndale, CA. 888-615-0065
Parkway Plastic Inc
Piscataway, NJ. 800-881-4996
Parsons Manufacturing Corp.
Menlo Park, CA 650-324-4726
Peerless Packages
Cleveland, OH 216-464-3620
Pelco Packaging Corporation
Stirling, NJ 908-647-3500
Penn Products
Portland, CT 800-490-7366
Piqua Paper Box Co
Piqua, OH .800-536-2136
Prestige Plastics Corporation
Delta, BC. .604-930-2931
Prolon
Port Gibson, MS 888-480-9828
Quantum Storage Systems Inc
Miami, FL .800-685-4665
R C Molding Inc
Greer, SC. .864-879-7279
Regal Plastic Company
Mission, KS 800-852-1556
Reliance-Paragon
Philadelphia, PA 215-743-1231
Ropak
Oak Brook, IL. 800-527-2267
Saeplast Canada
St John, NB 800-567-3966
Semco Plastic Co
St Louis, MO. 314-487-4557
Sharpsville Container Corp
Sharpsville, PA 800-645-1248
Snyder Industries Inc.
Lincoln, NE. 800-351-1363
Spartech Plastics
Portage, WI 800-998-7123
Tectonics
Westmoreland, NH 603-352-8894
Thermodynamics
Commerce City, CO 800-627-9037
Thermodyne International LTD
Ontario, CA. 909-923-9945
Tri-State Plastics
Henderson, KY 270-826-8361
Tulip Molded Plastics Corp
Milwaukee, WI 414-963-3120
Visual Packaging Corp
Haskell, NJ 973-835-7055
WES Plastics
Richmond Hill, ON. 905-508-1546
Wilks Precision Instr Co Inc
Union Bridge, MD 410-775-7917
Wiltec
Leominster, MA 978-537-1497
Zero Manufacturing Inc
North Salt Lake, UT 800-959-5050

Silverware

Gates Manufacturing Company
Saint Louis, MO 800-237-9226
Lakeside Manufacturing Inc
Milwaukee, WI 888-558-8565
McGraw Box Company
Mc Graw, NY 607-836-6465
Newell Brands
Atlanta, GA
Supreme Metal
Alpharetta, GA 800-645-2526

Waste

Anova
St Louis, MO. 800-231-1327
Bennett Manufacturing Company
Alden, NY. 800-345-2142
Continental Commercial Products
Bridgeton, MO 800-325-1051

Erwyn Products Inc
Morganville, NJ 800-331-9208
Ex-Cell KAISER LLC
Franklin Park, IL. 847-451-0451
Frem Corporation
Worcester, MA 508-791-3152
Glaro Inc
Hauppauge, NY 631-234-1717
Hodge Manufacturing Company
Springfield, MA 800-262-4634
Intrex
Bethel, CT. 203-792-7400
J.V. Reed & Company
Louisville, KY 877-258-7333
Lakeside Manufacturing Inc
Milwaukee, WI 888-558-8565
Rubbermaid Commercial Products
Pottsville, PA. 800-233-0314

Wirebound

Corbett Timber Co
Wilmington, NC 800-334-0684
Elberta Crate & Box Company
Carpentersville, IL 888-672-9260
Franklin Crates
Micanopy, FL 352-466-3141
Gulf Arizona Packaging
Humble, TX 800-364-3887
Gulf Systems
Brownsville, TX 800-217-4853
Gulf Systems
Humble, TX 800-364-3887
Gulf Systems
Arlington, TX 817-261-1915
Herche Warehouse
Denver, CO 303-371-8186
L&H Wood Manufacturing Company
Farmington, MI. 248-474-9000
Milan Box Corporation
Milan, TN .800-225-8057
Wisconsin Box Co
Wausau, WI. 800-876-6658

Wooden

A.M. Loveman Lumber & Box Company
Nashville, TN 615-297-1397
American Box Corporation
Lisbon, OH 330-424-8055
Auto Pallets-Boxes
Lathrup Village, MI 800-875-2699
Babcock Co
Bath, NY 607-776-3341
Buckeye Group
South Charleston, OH. 937-462-8361
Burgess Mfg. - Oklahoma
Guthrie, OK. 800-804-1913
Caravan Packaging Inc
Brookpark, OH 440-243-4100
Cassel Box & Lumber Co Inc
Grafton, WI. 262-377-9503
Cedar Box Co
Minneapolis, MN 612-332-4287
Century Box Company
Chicago, IL. 773-847-7070
Champlin Co
Hartford, CT 800-458-5261
Coastal Pallet Corp
Bridgeport, CT 203-333-6222
Corinth Products
Corinth, ME 207-285-3387
Corrugated Inner-Pak Corporation
Conshohocken, PA 610-825-0200
Cush-Pak Container Corporation
Henderson, TX 903-657-0555
D&M Pallet Company
Neshkoro, WI 920-293-4616
Davis Brothers Produce Boxes
Evergreen, NC 910-654-4913
Denver Reel & Pallet Company
Denver, CO 303-321-1920
Desert Box & Supply Corporation
Thermal, CA 760-399-5161
Die Cut Specialties Inc
Savage, MN. 952-890-7590
Donnelly Industries, Inc
Wayne, NJ 973-672-1800
Dufeck Manufacturing Co
Denmark, WI. 888-603-9663
Eichler Wood Products
Laurys Station, PA 610-262-6749

Farmer's Co-Op Elevator Co
Hudsonville, MI 800-439-9859
Fehlig Brothers Box & Lbr Co
St Louis, MO. 314-241-6900
Fox Valley Wood Products Inc
Kaukauna, WI 920-766-4069
Frobisher Industries
Waterborough, NB 506-362-2198
Frye's Measure Mill
Wilton, NH 603-654-6581
Gates
West Peterborough, NH 888-543-6316
Gatewood Products LLC
Parkersburg, WV. 800-827-5461
H. Arnold Wood Turning
Tarrytown, NY 888-314-0088
Hampton Roads Box Company
Suffolk, VA. 757-934-2355
Hanson Box & Lumber Company
Wakefield, MA 617-245-0358
Harbor Pallet Company
Anaheim, CA 714-871-0932
Heritage Packaging
Victor, NY .585-742-3310
Herkimer Pallet & Wood Products Company
Herkimer, NY 315-866-4591
Hinchcliff Products Company
Strongsville, OH 440-238-5200
Hunter Woodworks
Carson, CA 800-966-4751
Industrial Contracting & Rggng
Mahwah, NJ 888-427-7444
Industrial Hardwood
Perrysburg, OH 419-666-2503
Industrial Lumber & Packaging
Spring Lake, MI 616-842-1457
Industrial Woodfab & Packaging
Riverview, MI 734-284-4808
Jacksonville Box & Woodwork Co
Jacksonville, FL 800-683-2699
Jupiter Mills Corporation
Roslyn, NY 800-853-5121
Kelley Wood Products
Fitchburg, MA 978-345-7531
Kelly Box & Packaging Corp
Fort Wayne, IN 260-432-4570
KETCH
Wichita, KS 800-766-3777
Killington Wood ProductsCompany
Rutland, VT. 802-773-9111
Kimball Companies
East Longmeadow, MA 413-525-1881
Kontane
Charleston, SC 843-352-0011
L&H Wood Manufacturing Company
Farmington, MI. 248-474-9000
Lester Box & Mfg Div
Long Beach, CA 562-437-5123
Longhorn Imports Inc
Irving, TX .800-641-8348
Luke's Almond Acres
Reedley, CA 559-638-3483
Lumber & Things
Keyser, WV. 800-296-5656
Manufacturers Wood Supply Company
Cleveland, OH 216-771-7848
Marshall Boxes Inc
Rochester, NY. 585-458-7432
Maull-Baker Box Company
Brookfield, WI 414-463-1290
Maypak Inc
Wayne, NJ 973-696-0780
McGraw Box Company
Mc Graw, NY 607-836-6465
Mcintosh Box & Pallet Co
East Syracuse, NY 800-219-9552
Meriden Box Company
Southington, CT 860-621-7141
Michiana Box & Crate
Niles, MI 800-677-6372
Michigan Pallet Inc
St Charles, MI. 989-865-9915
Milan Box Corporation
Milan, TN .800-225-8057
Moorecraft Box & Crate
Tarboro, NC 252-823-2510
Nefab Packaging, Inc.
Coppell, TX. 800-322-4425
New Mexico Products Inc
Albuquerque, NM 877-345-7864
Oak Creek Pallet Company
Milwaukee, WI 414-762-7170

Ockerlund Industries
Addison, IL 708-771-7707
Original Lincoln Logs
Chestertown, NY 800-833-2461
Pack-Rite
Newington, CT 860-953-0120
Packing Material Company
Southfield, MI. 248-489-7000
Pallox Incorporated
Onsted, MI 517-456-4101
PPC Perfect Packaging Co
Perrysburg, OH 419-874-3167
Precision Wood of Hawaii
Vancouver, WA 808-682-2055
Pruitt's Packaging Services
Grand Rapids, MI 800-878-0553
Rand-Whitney Group LLC
Worcester, MA 508-791-2301
Reading Box Co Inc
Reading, PA. 610-372-7411
Red River Lumber Company
Saint Helena, CA 707-963-1251
Remmey Wood Products
Southampton, PA 215-355-3335
Roddy Products Pkgng Co Inc
Aldan, PA .610-623-7040
Romanow Container
Westwood, MA 781-320-9200
Seattle-Tacoma Box Co
Kent, WA. .253-854-9700
Seymour Woodenware Company
Seymour, WI. 920-833-6551
Smalley Package Company
Berryville, VA. 540-955-2550
Smith Packaging
Mississauga, ON. 905-564-6640
Smith Box Co Inc
Hatfield, AR 870-389-6184
Southern Pallet
Christchurch, NZ 901-942-4603
Spring Wood Products
Geneva, OH 440-466-1135
St. Pierre Box & Lumber Company
Canton, CT 860-693-2089
Stearnswood Inc
Hutchinson, MN 800-657-0144
Tampa Pallet Co
Tampa, FL .813-626-5700
Technipac
Le Sueur, MN 507-665-6658
Thunder Pallet Inc
Theresa, WI 800-354-0643
Treen Box & Pallet Inc
Bensalem, PA 215-639-5100
Van Dereems Mfg Co
Hawthorne, NJ 973-427-2355
Volk Packaging Corp
Biddeford, ME 207-282-6151
Wisconsin Box Co
Wausau, WI. 800-876-6658
Wnc Pallet & Forest Pdts Co
Candler, NC 828-667-5426
Xtreme Beverages, LLC
Dana Point, CA. 949-495-7929

Cans

Aluminum

Ball Corp
Broomfield, CO 303-469-3131
Can Corp of America Inc
Blandon, PA 610-926-3044
CCL Container
Toronto, ON 416-756-8500
IMO Foods
Yarmouth, NS 902-742-3519
Impress USA Inc
San Pedro, CA. 310-519-2400
Metal Container Corporation
St Louis, MO. 314-957-9500
Montebello Packaging
Hawkesbury, ON. 613-632-7096
Schroeder Machine
San Marcos, CA 760-591-9733
US Can Company
Rosedale, MD 800-436-8021

Beer & Ale

Crown Holdings, Inc.
Yardley, PA 215-698-5100

201

Metal Container Corporation
St Louis, MO.....................314-957-9500

Creamery

Schroeder Machine
San Marcos, CA..................760-591-9733

Ice Cream

Armbrust Paper Tubes Inc
Chicago, IL.....................773-586-3232
Independent Can Co
Belcamp, MD....................410-272-0090
Phoenix Industries Corp
Madison, WI....................888-241-7482

Milk

Schroeder Machine
San Marcos, CA..................760-591-9733

Tin

Bertels Can Company
Belcamp, MD....................410-272-0090
Consolidated Can Co
Paramount, CA..................888-793-2199
Container Supply Co
Garden Grove, CA...............562-594-0937
Crown Cork & Seal Co Inc
Philadelphia, PA...............215-698-5100
Crown Holdings, Inc.
Yardley, PA....................215-698-5100
GED, LLC
Laurel, DE.....................302-856-1756
Independent Can Co
Belcamp, MD....................410-272-0090
J L Clark Corp
Rockford, IL...................815-962-8861
Jupiter Mills Corporation
Roslyn, NY.....................800-853-5121
Quality Containers
Weston, ON.....................416-749-6247
Schroeder Machine
San Marcos, CA.................760-591-9733
US Can Company
Rosedale, MD...................800-436-8021
Xtreme Beverages, LLC
Dana Point, CA.................949-495-7929

Caps

Bottle, Can & Jar

All American Container
Miami, FL......................305-887-0797
Alpha Packaging
St Louis, MO...................800-421-4772
California Vibratory Feeders
Anaheim, CA....................800-354-0972
Clayton Corp.
Fenton, MO.....................800-729-8220
Consolidated Can Co
Paramount, CA..................888-793-2199
Crown Closures Machinery
Lancaster, OH..................740-681-6593
Crown Holdings, Inc.
Yardley, PA....................215-698-5100
Danbury Plastics
Cumming, GA....................678-455-7391
Eastern Cap & Closure Company
Baltimore, MD..................410-327-5640
ES Robbins Corp
Muscle Shoals, AL..............800-633-3325
Greenfield Packaging
White Plains, NY...............914-993-0233
Ideal Wire Works
Alhambra, CA...................626-282-0886
Innovative Molding
Sebastopol, CA.................707-829-2666
Keystone Adjustable Cap Co Inc
Pennsauken, NJ.................800-663-5439
Label Makers
Pleasant Prairie, WI...........800-208-3331
Landis Plastics
Alsip, IL......................708-396-1470
LMK Containers
Centerville, UT................626-821-9984
Metal Container Corporation
St Louis, MO...................314-957-9500

Nagel Paper & Box Company
Saginaw, MI....................800-292-3654
National Novelty Brush Co
Lancaster, PA..................717-299-5681
Nyman Manufacturing Company
Rumford, RI....................401-438-3410
Olcott Plastics
St Charles, IL.................888-313-5277
Orca Inc
New Britain, CT................860-223-4180
Parkway Plastic Inc
Piscataway, NJ.................800-881-4996
Phoenix Closures Inc
Naperville, IL.................630-544-3475
Romatic Manufacturing Co
Southbury, CT..................203-264-3442
RXI Silgan Specialty Plastics
Triadelphia, WV................304-547-9100
Silgan Containers LLC
Woodland Hills, CA.............818-710-3700
Silgan Plastic Closure Sltns
Downers Grove, IL..............800-727-8652
Silgan Plastics Canada
Chesterfield, WV...............800-274-5426
Smith-Lee Company
Oshkosh, WI....................800-327-9774
Snapware
Fullerton, CA..................800-334-3062
Sonoco Paperboard Specialties
Norcross, GA...................800-264-7494
Tecnocap
Glen Dale, WV..................800-999-2567
Van Blarcom Closures Inc
Brooklyn, NY...................718-855-3810
Wheaton Plastic Containers
Millville, NJ..................856-825-1400

Carriers

Food

B&H Labeling Systems
Ceres, CA......................209-537-5785
Cambro Manufacturing Co
Huntington Beach, CA...........800-833-3003
Carlisle Food Svc Products Inc
Oklahoma City, OK..............800-654-8210
Fold-Pak Corporation
Newark, NY.....................315-331-3159
Hank Rivera Associates
Dearborn, MI...................313-581-8300
Igloo Products Corp
Katy, TX.......................866-509-3503
ITW Hi-Cone
Itasca, IL.....................630-438-5300
K & L Intl
Ontario, CA....................888-598-5588
Keeper Thermal Bag Co
Bartlett, IL...................800-765-9244
Naltex
Austin, TX.....................800-531-5112
Newell Brands
Atlanta, GA
Owens-Illinois Inc
Perrysburg, OH.................567-336-5000
Paper Works Industries Inc
Baldwinsville, NY..............800-847-5677
Plastocon
Oconomowoc, WI.................800-966-0103
Service Manufacturing
Aurora, IL.....................888-325-2788
Sterling Paper Company
Ohio, PA.......................800-282-1124
Thermal Bags By Ingrid Inc
Gilberts, IL...................800-622-5560
Vollrath Co LLC
Sheboygan, WI..................800-624-2051

Milk Bottle

B&H Labeling Systems
Ceres, CA......................209-537-5785
Graphic Packaging Corporation
Golden, CO.....................800-677-2886
Paper Works Industries Inc
Baldwinsville, NY..............800-847-5677

Cartons

A La Carte
Chicago, IL....................800-722-2370

Accurate Paper Box Co Inc
Knoxville, TN..................865-690-0311
Adpro
Solon, OH......................440-542-1111
Alcan Packaging
Baie D'Urfe, QC................514-457-4555
Americraft Carton Inc
St Paul, MN....................651-227-6655
Americraft Carton Inc
Prairie Village, KS............913-387-3700
Artistic Carton
Auburn, IN.....................800-735-7225
Artistic Carton Co
Elgin, IL......................847-741-0247
Atlas Packaging Inc
Opa Locka, FL..................800-662-0630
B F Nelson Cartons Inc
Savage, MN.....................800-328-2380
Boelter Industries
Winona, MN.....................507-452-2315
Cardinal Container Corp
Indianapolis, IN...............800-899-2715
Cardinal Packaging Prod LLC
Crystal Lake, IL...............866-216-4942
Carpenter-Hayes Paper Box Company
East Hampton, CT...............203-267-4436
Carton Service Co
Shelby, OH.....................800-533-7744
Central Paper Box
Kansas City, MO................816-753-3126
City Box Company
Aurora, IL.....................773-277-5500
CKS Packaging
Atlanta, GA....................800-800-4257
Cleveland Specialties Co
Loveland, OH...................513-677-9787
Coast Paper Box Company
San Bernardino, CA.............909-382-3475
Color Box
Richmond, IN...................765-966-7588
Columbus Paperbox Company
Columbus, OH...................800-968-0797
Commencement Bay Corrugated
Orting, WA.....................253-845-3100
Commercial Corrugated Co Inc
Baltimore, MD..................800-242-8861
Complete Packaging & Shipping
Freeport, NY...................877-269-3236
Conn Container Corp
North Haven, CT................203-248-0241
Containair Packaging Corporation
Paterson, NJ...................888-276-6500
Corrobilt Container Company
Livermore, CA..................925-373-0880
Corson Manufacturing Company
Lockport, NY...................716-434-8871
Curtis Packaging
Sandy Hook, CT.................203-426-5861
Cush-Pak Container Corporation
Henderson, TX..................903-657-0555
Day Manufacturing Company
Sherman, TX....................903-893-1138
Diamond Packaging
Rochester, NY..................800-333-4079
Donnelly Industries, Inc
Wayne, NJ......................973-672-1800
Dorado Carton Company
Dorado, PR.....................787-796-1670
Eagle Box Company
Farmingdale, NY................212-255-3860
EB Box Company
Richmond Hill, ON..............800-513-2269
Elopak Americas
Wixom, MI......................248-486-4600
Eureka Paper Box Company
Williamsport, PA...............570-326-9147
Farmer's Co-Op Elevator Co
Hudsonville, MI................800-439-9859
Finn Industries
Ontario, CA....................909-930-1500
Flashfold Carton Inc
Fort Wayne, IN.................260-423-9431
Flour City Press-Pack Company
Minneapolis, MN................952-831-1265
Foam Packaging Inc
Vicksburg, MS..................800-962-2655
Fold-Pak Corporation
Newark, NY.....................315-331-3159
Folding Carton/Flexible Packaging
North Hollywood, CA............818-896-3449
Food Pak Corp
San Mateo, CA..................650-341-6559

Four M Manufacturing Group
San Jose, CA 408-998-1141
Friendly City Box Co Inc
Johnstown, PA....................814-266-6287
Fulton-Denver Co
Denver, CO 800-521-1414
Gaylord Container Corporation
Tampa, FL 813-621-3591
Georg Fischer Central Plastics
Shawnee, OK 800-654-3872
Gibraltar Packaging Group Inc
Hastings, NE 402-463-1366
Goldman Manufacturing Company
Detroit, MI 313-834-5535
Graphic Packaging Corporation
Golden, CO 800-677-2886
Graphic Packaging Intl
Elk Grove Vlg, IL 847-437-1700
Green Bay Packaging Inc.
Green Bay, WI.....................920-433-5111
Greenfield Packaging
White Plains, NY 914-993-0233
Greif Brothers Corporation
Cleveland, OH 800-424-0342
Grigsby Brothers Paper Box Manufacturers
Portland, OR 866-233-4690
Gulf Arizona Packaging
Humble, TX 800-364-3887
Gulf Systems
Brownsville, TX 800-217-4853
Gulf Systems
Humble, TX 800-364-3887
Gulf Systems
Arlington, TX 817-261-1915
H.J. Jones & Sons
London, ON 800-667-0476
Hager Containers Inc
Carrollton, TX.....................972-416-7660
Herche Warehouse
Denver, CO 303-371-8186
Hope Paper Box Company
Pawtucket, RI 401-724-5700
Hunter Packaging Corporation
South Elgin, IL 800-428-4747
Impress Industries
Emmaus, PA 610-967-6027
Indiana Carton Co Inc
Bremen, IN 800-348-2390
Inland Consumer Packaging
Harrington, DE 302-398-4211
Innovative Folding Carton Company
South Plainfield, NJ 908-757-0205
Instabox
Calgary, AB.......................800-482-6173
International Paper Co.
Memphis, TN
Jamestown Container Corporation
Buffalo, NY.......................855-234-4054
Jarisch Paper Box Company
North Adams, MA 413-663-5396
Jordan Paper Box Co
Chicago, IL.......................773-287-5362
Jupiter Mills Corporation
Roslyn, NY 800-853-5121
Kelly Box & Packaging Corp
Fort Wayne, IN 260-432-4570
Kendel
Countryside, IL 800-323-1100
Laminated Paper Products
San Jose, CA 408-888-0880
Lawrence Paper Co
Lawrence, KS 785-843-8111
Lexel
Fort Worth, TX 817-332-4061
Liberty Carton Co.
Golden Valley, MN 800-328-1784
Lin Pac Plastics
Roswell, GA 770-751-6006
Lowell Paper Box Company
Nashua, NH.......................603-595-0700
Loy Lange Box Co
St Louis, MO......................800-886-4712
LTI Printing Inc
Sturgis, MI 269-651-7574
M & G Packaging Corp
Floral Park, NY....................800-240-5288
Malnove of Nebraska
Omaha, NE 800-228-9877
Mannkraft Corporation
Newark, NJ.......................973-589-7400
Marcus Carton Company
Melville, NY.......................631-752-4200

Marfred Industries
Sun Valley, CA 800-529-5156
Marion Paper Box Co
Marion, IN........................765-664-6435
Maro Paper Products Company
Bellwood, IL 708-649-9982
Massachusetts Container Corporation
North Haven, CT...................203-248-2161
Maull-Baker Box Company
Brookfield, WI 414-463-1290
Maypak Inc
Wayne, NJ 973-696-0780
Melville Plastics
Haw River, NC 336-578-5800
Merchants Publishing Company
Kalamazoo, MI 269-345-1175
Mid Cities Paper Box Company
Downey, CA 877-277-6272
Midlands Packaging Corp
Lincoln, NE 402-464-9124
Muth Associates
Springfield, MA 800-388-0157
Neff Packaging
Simpsonville, KY 800-445-4383
New York Corrugated Box Co
Paterson, NJ......................973-742-5000
Northeast Container Corporation
Dumont, NJ.......................201-385-6200
Nosco
Waukegan, IL 847-360-4806
Oakes Carton Co
Kalamazoo, MI 269-381-6022
Old Dominion Box Co Inc
Madison Heights, VA 434-929-6701
Old Dominion Box Company
Burlington, NC 336-226-4491
Oracle Packaging
Winston Salem, NC.................800-952-9536
Packaging Solutions
Los Altos Hills, CA 650-917-1022
Packrite Packaging
Archdale, NC......................336-431-1111
Pactiv LLC
Lake Forest, IL 800-476-4300
Paper Products Company
Cincinnati, OH 513-921-4717
Paper Works Industries Inc
Baldwinsville, NY 800-847-5677
Parta
Kent, OH.........................800-543-5781
Pater & Associates
Cincinnati, OH
Peerless Cartons
Bartlett, IL 312-226-7952
Piqua Paper Box Co
Piqua, OH 800-536-2136
Premier Packages
Saint Louis, MO 800-466-6588
Prestige Plastics Corporation
Delta, BC.........................604-930-2931
Quantum Storage Systems Inc
Miami, FL 800-685-4665
Rand-Whitney Group LLC
Worcester, MA 508-791-2301
Reliance-Paragon
Philadelphia, PA...................215-743-1231
Rex Carton Co Inc
Chicago, IL.......................773-581-4115
Rice Packaging Inc
Ellington, CT 800-367-6725
Rjr Technologies
Oakland, CA 510-638-5901
Rock-Tenn Company
Norcross, GA 608-223-6272
Rose City Printing & Packaging
Vancouver, WA 800-704-8693
Rudd Container Corp
Chicago, IL.......................773-847-7600
Rusken Packaging
Cullman, AL.......................256-775-0014
San Diego Paper Box Company
Spring Valley, CA 619-660-9566
Schroeder Machine
San Marcos, CA 760-591-9733
Scott & Daniells
Portland, CT 860-342-1932
Seaboard Carton Company
Downers Grove, IL 708-344-0575
Security Packaging
North Bergen, NJ...................201-854-1955
Set Point Paper Company
Mansfield, MA 800-225-0501

Sheboygan Paper Box Co
Sheboygan, WI 800-458-8373
Shelby Co
Westlake, OH 800-842-1650
Shippers Supply
Winnipeg, NB 800-661-5639
Shore Paper Box Co
Mardela Springs, MD 410-749-7125
Smith Packaging
Mississauga, ON...................905-564-6640
Smurfit Stone Container
St Louis, MO......................314-679-2300
Smurfit-Stone Container Corp
Santa Fe Springs, CA 714-523-3550
Somerville Packaging
Toronto, ON 416-754-7228
Somerville Packaging
Mississauga, ON...................905-678-8211
SoOPAK
Mississauga, ON...................905-677-9666
Southern Champion Tray LP
Chattanooga, TN...................800-468-2222
Southern Missouri Containers
Springfield, MO 800-999-7666
Southern Packaging Machinery
Athens, GA 706-208-0814
Specialized Packaging London
London, ON 519-659-7011
Spring Cove Container Div
Roaring Spring, PA.................814-224-5141
SQP
Schenectady, NY 800-724-1129
St Joseph Packaging Inc
St Joseph, MO 800-383-3000
St. Louis Carton Company
Saint Louis, MO 314-241-0990
St. Pierre Box & Lumber Company
Canton, CT 860-693-2089
Standard Folding Cartons Inc
Flushing, NY......................718-396-4522
Stearnswood Inc
Hutchinson, MN 800-657-0144
Sterling Paper Company
Ohio, PA 800-282-1124
Stoneway Carton Company
Mercer Island, WA 800-498-2185
Suburban Corrugated Box Company
Indianhead Park, IL 630-920-1230
Tampa Corrugated Carton Company
Tampa, FL 813-623-5115
Thermodyne International LTD
Ontario, CA.......................909-923-9945
Traub Container Corporation
Cleveland, OH 216-475-5100
Unipak Inc
West Chester, PA..................610-436-6600
Unique Boxes
Chicago, IL 800-281-1670
Universal Folding Box
East Orange, NJ 973-482-4300
Universal Folding Box Company
Hoboken, NJ......................201-659-7373
Utah PaperBox Company
Salt Lake City, UT 801-363-0093
Victory Packaging, Inc.
Houston, TX 800-486-5606
VIP Real Estate LTD
Chicago, IL.......................773-376-5000
Volk Packaging Corp
Biddeford, ME 207-282-6151
Warren Packaging
San Bernardino, CA 909-888-7008
Weber Display & Packaging Inc
Philadelphia, PA 215-426-3500
Welch Packaging Group Inc
Elkhart, IN........................574-295-2460
West Rock
Atlanta, GA.......................770-448-2193
Western Container Company
Kansas City, MO...................816-924-5700
Westervelt Co Inc
Tuscaloosa, AL....................205-562-5000
Westvaco Corporation
Newark, DE.......................302-453-7200
Willamette Industries
Beaverton, OR.....................503-641-1131
Willard Packaging Co
Gaithersburg, MD..................301-948-7700
Winchester Carton
Eutaw, AL 205-372-3337
Woodson Pallet Co
Anmoore, WV 304-623-2858

Wright Brothers Paper Box Company
Fond Du Lac, WI 920-921-8270
WS Packaging Group Inc
Green Bay, WI. 877-977-5177
York Container Co
York, PA 717-757-7611

Closures & Closing Devices

AAMD
Liverpool, NY 800-887-4167
All American Container
Miami, FL 305-887-0797
Allendale Cork Company
Rye, NY 800-816-2675
Alliance Rubber Co
Hot Springs, AR 800-626-5940
Alpha Packaging
St Louis, MO. 800-421-4772
American National Rubber
Ceredo, WV 304-453-1311
American Printpak Inc
Sussex, WI 800-441-8003
American Star Cork Company
Woodside, NY 800-338-3581
Autoprod
Davenport, IA 563-391-1100
Bal Seal Engineering Inc
Foothill Ranch, CA 800-366-1006
Ball Corp
Broomfield, CO 303-469-3131
Bedford Industries
Worthington, MN 800-533-5314
Bericap North America, Inc.
CDN-Burlington, ON 905-634-2248
Berry Global
Evansville, IN 800-343-1295
Bettag & Associates
O Fallon, MO 800-325-0959
Blackhawk Molding Co Inc
Addison, IL 630-458-2100
Brown International Corp LLC
Winter Haven, FL 863-299-2111
Cameo Metal Products Inc
Brooklyn, NY 718-788-1106
Caraustar
Franklin, KY 270-586-9565
Carton Closing Company
Butler, PA 724-287-7759
Chaffee Co
Rocklin, CA 916-630-3980
Chase-Logeman Corp
Greensboro, NC 336-665-0754
Clayton Corp.
Fenton, MO 800-729-8220
Cleveland Specialties Co
Loveland, OH 513-677-9787
Conax Buffalo Technologies
Buffalo, NY. 800-223-2389
Consolidated Can Co
Paramount, CA 888-793-2199
Constantia Colmar
Colmar, PA 215-997-6222
Cork Specialties
Miami, FL 305-477-1506
Crandall Filling Machinery
Buffalo, NY. 800-280-8551
Creative Packaging Corporation
Buffalo Grove, IL 847-459-1001
Cresthill Industries
Yonkers, NY 914-965-9510
Crown Closures Machinery
Lancaster, OH 740-681-6593
Crown Holdings, Inc.
Yardley, PA 215-698-5100
Cup Pac Packaging Inc
South Beloit, IL 877-347-9725
Danbury Plastics
Cumming, GA. 678-455-7391
Dickey Manufacturing Company
St Charles, IL 630-584-2918
Diversified Capping Equipment
Perrysburg, OH 419-666-2566
Eastern Cap & Closure Company
Baltimore, MD 410-327-5640
Et Oakes Corp
Hauppauge, NY 631-232-0002
Filler Specialties
Zeeland, MI. 616-772-9235
Flex Products
Carlstadt, NJ 800-526-6273

Gallo
Racine, WI 262-752-9950
Gateway Plastics Inc
Mequon, WI 262-242-2020
Gemini Plastic Films Corporation
Garfield, NJ. 800-789-4732
General Press Corp
Natrona Heights, PA 724-224-3500
Genpak
Peterborough, ON 800-461-1995
Greenfield Packaging
White Plains, NY 914-993-0233
Gulf Arizona Packaging
Humble, TX 800-364-3887
Gulf Systems
Brownsville, TX 800-217-4853
Gulf Systems
Humble, TX 800-364-3887
Gulf Systems
Arlington, TX 817-261-1915
Herche Warehouse
Denver, CO 303-371-8186
Highland Plastics Inc
Mira Loma, CA. 800-368-0491
Innovative Molding
Sebastopol, CA 707-829-2666
IPEC
New Castle, PA 800-377-4732
Ipec
New Castle, PA 800-377-4732
Ives-Way Products
Round Lake Beach, IL 847-740-0658
J L Clark Corp
Rockford, IL 815-962-8861
J.E. Roy
St Claire, QC. 418-883-2711
Kapak Corporation
Minneapolis, MN 952-541-0730
Keystone Adjustable Cap Co Inc
Pennsauken, NJ 800-663-5439
KWIK Lok Corp
Yakima, WA 800-688-5945
L&H Wood Manufacturing Company
Farmington, MI 248-474-9000
Label Makers
Pleasant Prairie, WI 800-208-3331
Landis Plastics
Alsip, IL 708-396-1470
Leco Plastic Inc
Hackensack, NJ. 201-343-3330
LMK Containers
Centerville, UT 626-821-9984
Metal Container Corporation
St Louis, MO. 314-957-9500
Mold-Rite Plastics LLC
Twinsburg, OH 330-425-4206
Molded Container Corporation
Portland, OR 503-233-8601
Montebello Packaging
Hawkesbury, ON. 613-632-7096
National Novelty Brush Co
Lancaster, PA 717-299-5681
New Jersey Wire Stitching Machine Company
Cherry Hill, NJ. 856-428-2572
Nyman Manufacturing Company
Rumford, RI 401-438-3410
Olcott Plastics
St Charles, IL 888-313-5277
On-Hand Adhesives
Lake Zurich, IL. 800-323-5158
Orca Inc
New Britain, CT 860-223-4180
Owens-Illinois Inc
Perrysburg, OH 567-336-5000
Package Containers Inc
Canby, OR. 800-266-5806
Packaging Associates
Randolph, NJ 973-252-8890
PAR-Kan
Silver Lake, IN 800-291-5487
Paradigm Packaging Inc
Upland, CA. 909-985-2750
Parkway Plastic Inc
Piscataway, NJ 800-881-4996
Parta
Kent, OH 800-543-5781
Perl Packaging Systems
Middlebury, CT. 800-864-2853
Phoenix Closures Inc
Naperville, IL 630-544-3475
Qosina Corporation
Ronkonkoma, NY. 631-242-3000

Reotemp Instrument Corp
San Diego, CA 800-648-7737
Richards Packaging
Memphis, TN 800-583-0327
Rieke Packaging Systems
Auburn, IN 260-925-3700
Romatic Manufacturing Co
Southbury, CT. 203-264-3442
Scheidegger
Yorktown Heights, NY 914-245-7850
Schiffmayer Plastics Corp.
Algonquin, IL 847-658-8140
Signature Packaging
West Orange, NJ 800-376-2299
Silgan Plastic Closure Sltns
Downers Grove, IL 800-727-8652
Silgan Plastic Closure Sltns
Downers Grove, IL 800-767-8652
Silgan Plastics Canada
Chesterfield, MO 800-274-5426
Silgan White Cap LLC
Downers Grove, IL 800-515-1565
Smith-Lee Company
Oshkosh, WI 800-327-9774
Sonoco Paperboard Specialties
Norcross, GA 800-264-7494
Staplex Co Inc
Brooklyn, NY 800-221-0822
Stoffel Seals Corp
Tallapoosa, GA 800-422-8247
Stormax International
Concord, NH. 800-874-7629
T & T Industries Inc
Fort Mohave, AZ 800-437-6246
Techform
Mount Airy, NC 336-789-2115
Tipper Tie Inc
Apex, NC 919-362-8811
Trent Corp
Trenton, NJ 609-587-7515
Ultrapak
Dunkirk, NY 800-228-6030
Us Bottlers Machinery Co Inc
Charlotte, NC 704-588-4750
Van Blarcom Closures Inc
Brooklyn, NY 718-855-3810
Wheaton Plastic Containers
Millville, NJ 856-825-1400
Zero Manufacturing Inc
North Salt Lake, UT 800-959-5050

Containers

A La Carte
Chicago, IL 800-722-2370
A Snow Craft Co Inc
New Hyde Park, NY 516-739-1399
A-A1 Aaction Bag
Denver, CO. 800-783-1224
A-Z Factory Supply
Schiller Park, IL 800-323-4511
Abbott Industries
Paterson, NJ
Accurate Paper Box Co Inc
Knoxville, TN. 865-690-0311
Ace Manufacturing & Parts Co
Sullivan, MO. 800-325-6138
Aco Container Systems
Pickering, ON 800-542-9942
Acryline
North Attleboro, MA 508-695-7124
Adpro
Solon, OH. 440-542-1111
Aero Tec Laboratories/ATL
Ramsey, NJ 800-526-5330
Alcan Packaging
Baie D'Urfe, QC. 514-457-4555
All American Container
Miami, FL 305-887-0797
All American Poly
Piscataway, NJ 800-526-3551
Allflex Packaging Products
Ambler, PA 800-448-2467
Alpack
Centerville, NA. 774-994-8086
Althor Products
Bethel, CT. 800-688-2693
Amco Metals Indl
City of Industry, CA. 626-855-2550
American Box Corporation
Lisbon, OH 330-424-8055

American Production Co Inc
Redwood City, CA 650-368-5334
Americraft Carton Inc
St Paul, MN 651-227-6655
Ample Industries
Franklin, OH 888-818-9700
Anchor Packaging
Ballwin, MO 800-467-3900
Anova
St Louis, MO 800-231-1327
Arena Products
Rochester, NY 844-762-0127
Arkansas Glass Container Corp
Jonesboro, AR 800-527-4527
Armbrust Paper Tubes Inc
Chicago, IL 773-586-3232
Arthur Corporation
Huron, OH 419-433-7202
Artistic Carton
Auburn, IN 800-735-7225
Artistic Carton Co
Elgin, IL 847-741-0247
ATD-American Co
Wyncote, PA 800-523-2300
Atlas Case Inc
Denver, CO 888-325-2199
Atlas Equipment Company
Kansas City, MO 800-842-9188
Atlas Packaging Inc
Opa Locka, FL 800-662-0630
Auto Pallets-Boxes
Lathrup Village, MI 800-875-2699
B C Holland Inc
Dousman, WI 262-965-2939
B F Nelson Cartons Inc
Savage, MN 800-328-2380
B.A.G Corporation
Richardson, TX 800-331-9200
Bakers Choice Products
Beacon Falls, CT 203-720-1000
Bal/Foster Glass Container Company
Port Allegany, PA 814-642-2521
Ball Corp
Broomfield, CO 303-469-3131
Ball Foster Glass Container Company
Sapulpa, OK 918-224-1440
Ball Glass Container Corporation
El Monte, CA 626-448-9831
Bardes Plastics Inc
Milwaukee, WI 800-558-5161
Bayhead Products Corp.
Dover, NH 800-229-4323
Bell Packaging Corporation
Marion, IN 800-382-0153
Belleview
Brookline, NH 603-878-1583
Bennett Manufacturing Company
Alden, NY 800-345-2142
Berenz Packaging Corp
Menomonee Falls, WI 262-251-8787
Bergen Barrel & Drum Company
Kearny, NJ 201-998-3500
Berlin Fruit Box Company
Berlin Heights, OH 800-877-7721
Berlon Industries
Hustisford, WI 800-899-3580
Berry Global
Evansville, IN 800-343-1295
Bertels Can Company
Belcamp, MD 410-272-0090
Best
Brunswick, OH 800-827-9237
Boelter Industries
Winona, MN 507-452-2315
Boise Cascade Corporation
Burley, ID 208-678-3531
Bonar Plastics
West Chicago, IL 800-295-3725
Boxes.com
Livingston, NJ 201-646-9050
Brenner Tank LLC
Fond Du Lac, WI 800-558-9750
Brewer-Cantelmo Inc
New York, NY 212-244-4600
Brooks Barrel Company
Baltimore, MD 800-398-2766
Brown International Corp LLC
Winter Haven, FL 863-299-2111
Bruni Glass Packaging
Lachine Montreal, QC 877-771-7856
Buckhorn Canada
Brampton, ON 800-461-7579

Buckhorn Inc
Milford, OH 800-543-4454
Buffet Enhancements Intl
Point Clear, AL 251-990-6119
Bulk Lift International, LLC
Carpentersville, IL 800-879-2247
Bulk Pack
Monroe, LA. 800-498-4215
Bulk Sak Intl Inc
Malvern, AR 501-332-8745
Burd & Fletcher
Independence, MO 800-821-2776
Burgess Mfg. - Oklahoma
Guthrie, OK. 800-804-1913
Burrows Paper Corp
Little Falls, NY 800-272-7122
C & L Wood Products Inc
Hartselle, AL. 800-483-2035
Calzone Case Co
Bridgeport, CT 800-243-5152
Cambro Manufacturing Co
Huntington Beach, CA 800-833-3003
Can Corp of America Inc
Blandon, PA 610-926-3044
Cantwell-Cleary Co Inc
Elkridge, MD 301-773-9800
Cantwell-Cleary Co Inc
Richmond, VA. 804-329-9800
Capital City Container Corporation
Buda, TX. 512-312-1222
Capitol Carton Company
Sacramento, CA 916-388-7848
Capitol City Container Corp
Indianapolis, IN 800-233-5145
Cardinal Packaging
Evansville, IN 800-343-1295
Cardinal Packaging Prod LLC
Crystal Lake, IL 866-216-4942
Carlisle Food Svc Products Inc
Oklahoma City, OK 800-654-8210
Carolina Container
High Point, NC 800-627-0825
Carpet City Paper Box Company
Amsterdam, NY 518-842-5430
Carrier Corp
Farmington, CT. 800-227-7437
Carson Industries
Pomona, CA 800-735-5566
Carton Service Co
Shelby, OH 800-533-7744
Ccw Products
Arvada, CO 303-427-9663
Cecor
Verona, WI 800-356-9042
Cedar Box Co
Minneapolis, MN 612-332-4287
Century Box Company
Chicago, IL 773-847-7070
Chambers Container Company
Gastonia, NC. 704-377-6317
Champlin Co
Hartford, CT 800-458-5261
Charles Engineering & Service
Belcamp, MD 410-272-1090
Chem-Tainer Industries Inc
West Babylon, NY 800-275-2436
Chem-Tainer Industries Inc
West Babylon, NY 800-938-8896
Cherry's Industrial Eqpt Corp
Elk Grove Vlg, IL 800-350-0011
Chili Plastics
Rochester, NY 585-889-4680
Cin-Made Packaging Group
Norcross, GA 800-264-7494
Cincinnati Foam Products
Cincinnati, OH 513-741-7722
City Box Company
Aurora, IL 773-277-5500
CKS Packaging
Atlanta, GA. 800-800-4257
Clawson Container Company
Clarkston, MI 800-325-8700
Clearwater Paper Corporation
Spokane, WA. 877-847-7831
Cleveland Canvas Goods Mfg Co
Cleveland, OH 216-361-4567
Clorox Company
Oakland, CA. 800-227-1860
Coast Paper Box Company
San Bernardino, CA 909-382-3475
Coastal Pallet Corp
Bridgeport, CT 203-333-6222

Colbert Packaging Corp
Lake Forest, IL 847-367-5990
Cold Chain Technologies
Holliston, MA. 800-370-8566
Collectors Gallery
St Charles, IL 800-346-3063
Color Box
Richmond, IN 765-966-7588
Color Carton Corp
Bronx, NY 718-665-0840
Columbus Paperbox Company
Columbus, OH 800-968-0797
Commencement Bay Corrugated
Orting, WA 253-845-3100
Commercial Corrugated Co Inc
Baltimore, MD 800-242-8861
Complete Packaging & Shipping
Freeport, NY 877-269-3236
Conductive Containers Inc
Minneapolis, MN 800-327-2329
Conn Container Corp
North Haven, CT. 203-248-0241
Consolidated Container Co
New Castle, PA 724-658-0549
Constar International
Plymouth, MI 734-455-3600
Containair Packaging Corporation
Paterson, NJ 888-276-6500
Container Specialties
Melrose Park, IL 800-548-7513
Container Supply Co
Garden Grove, CA 562-594-0937
Containment Technology
St Gabriel, LA. 800-388-2467
Contico Container
Norwalk, CA. 562-921-9967
Continental Plastic Container
Dallas, TX. 972-303-1825
Contour Packaging
Philadelphia, PA 215-457-1600
Convoy
Canton, OH 800-899-1583
Corbett Timber Co
Wilmington, NC 800-334-0684
Corbox-Meyers Inc
Cleveland, OH 800-321-7286
Cornish Containers
Maumee, OH 419-893-7911
Corpak
San Juan, PR 787-787-9085
Corr Pak Corp
Mc Cook, IL 708-442-7806
Corrobilt Container Company
Livermore, CA 925-373-0880
Corrugated Inner-Pak Corporation
Conshohocken, PA 610-825-0200
Corrugated Packaging
Sarasota, FL 941-371-0000
Corson Manufacturing Company
Lockport, NY 716-434-8871
Craft Corrugated Box Inc
New Bedford, MA 508-998-2115
Crate Ideas by Wilderness House
Cave Junction, OR 800-592-2206
Cream of the Valley Plastics
Arvada, CO 303-425-5499
Creative Packaging
Hayward, CA 510-785-6500
Crespac Incorporated
Tucker, GA 800-438-1900
Crown Manufacturing Corporation
Waterford, CT. 860-442-4325
CTK Plastics
Moose Jaw, SK 800-667-8847
Cumberland Container Corp
Monterey, TN 931-839-2227
Curtis Packaging
Sandy Hook, CT 203-426-5861
Cush-Pak Container Corporation
Henderson, TX 903-657-0555
Custom Bottle of Connecticut
Naugatuck, CT. 203-723-6661
Custom Stamping & Manufacturing
Portland, OR. 503-238-3700
D & W Fine Pack
San Bernardino, CA 800-232-5959
D & W Fine Pack
Lake Zurich, IL 800-323-0422
Dakota Corrugated Box
Sioux Falls, SD 605-332-3501
Dallas Container Corp
Dallas, TX. 800-381-7148

Dart Container Corp.
Mason, MI 800-248-5960
Davis Brothers Produce Boxes
Evergreen, NC 910-654-4913
Davis Core & Pa
Cave Spring, GA 800-235-7483
Day Lumber Company
Westfield, MA 413-568-3511
Day Manufacturing Company
Sherman, TX 903-893-1138
De Ster Corporation
Atlanta, GA 800-237-8270
DEL-Tec Packaging Inc
Greer, SC 800-747-8683
Deline Box Co
Denver, CO 303-376-1283
Delta Container Corporation
New Orleans, LA 800-752-7292
Delta Wire And Mfg.
Harrow, ON 800-221-3794
Design Plastics Inc
Omaha, NE 800-491-0786
Designers Folding Box Corp
Buffalo, NY 716-853-5141
Despro Manufacturing
Cedar Grove, NJ 800-292-9906
Diamond Packaging
Rochester, NY 800-333-4079
Display One
Hartford, WI 262-673-5880
Dixie Printing & Packaging
Glen Burnie, MD 800-433-4943
Donnelly Industries, Inc
Wayne, NJ 973-672-1800
Dorado Carton Company
Dorado, PR 787-796-1670
Douglas Stephen Plastics Inc
Paterson, NJ 973-523-3030
Drescher Paper Box Inc
Buffalo, NY 716-854-0288
Dufeck Manufacturing Co
Denmark, WI 888-603-9663
Dusobox Company
Haverhill, MA 978-372-7192
Duval Container Co
Jacksonville, FL 800-342-8194
Dynabilt Products
Readville, MA 800-443-1008
E K Lay Co
Philadelphia, PA 800-523-3220
Eagle Box Company
Farmingdale, NY 212-255-3860
Eastern Container Corporation
Mansfield, MA 508-337-0400
EB Box Company
Richmond Hill, ON 800-513-2269
Economy Folding Box Corporation
Chicago, IL 800-771-1053
Edco Industries
Bridgeport, CT 203-333-8982
EGA Products Inc
Brookfield, WI 800-937-3427
EGW Bradbury Enterprises
Bridgewater, ME 800-332-6021
Eichler Wood Products
Laurys Station, PA 610-262-6749
Elberta Crate & Box Company
Carpentersville, IL 888-672-9260
Elm Packaging Company
Memphis, TN 901-795-2711
Elopak Americas
Wixom, MI 248-486-4600
Emco Industrial Plastics
Cedar Grove, NJ 800-292-9906
Enterprise Box Company
Montclair, NJ 973-509-2200
Erie Container
Cleveland, OH 216-631-1650
ERO/Goodrich Forest Products
Tualatin, OR 800-458-5545
Erwyn Products Inc
Morganville, NJ 800-331-9208
ES Robbins Corp
Muscle Shoals, AL 800-633-3325
Eureka Paper Box Company
Williamsport, PA 570-326-9147
Expert Industries Inc
Brooklyn, NY 718-434-6060
F G Products Inc
Rice Lake, WI 800-247-3854
F N Smith Corp
Oregon, IL 815-732-2171

F.E. Wood & Sons
West Baldwin, ME 207-286-5003
Fabri-Kal Corp
Kalamazoo, MI 800-888-5054
Fabricated Components Inc
Stroudsburg, PA 800-233-8163
Fabricon Products Inc
River Rouge, MI 313-841-8200
Faribault Manufacturing Co
Faribault, MN 800-447-6043
Farmer's Co-Op Elevator Co
Hudsonville, MI 800-439-9859
Faubion Central States Tank Company
Shawnee Mission, KS 800-450-8265
Felco Packaging Specialist
Baltimore, MD 800-673-8488
Ferguson Containers
Phillipsburg, NJ 908-454-9755
Fibre Containers Inc
City of Industry, CA 626-968-5897
Finn Industries
Ontario, CA 909-930-1500
Fitzpatrick Container Company
North Wales, PA 215-699-3515
Flashfold Carton Inc
Fort Wayne, IN 260-423-9431
Fleetwood International Paper
Vernon, CA 323-588-7121
Flex Products
Carlstadt, NJ 800-526-6273
Flexible Foam Products
Elkhart, IN 800-678-3626
Flow of Solids
Westford, MA 978-392-0300
Foam Concepts Inc
Uxbridge, MA 508-278-7255
Foam Pack Industries
Springfield, NJ 973-376-3700
Foam Packaging Inc
Vicksburg, MS 800-962-2655
Fold-Pak Corporation
Newark, NY 315-331-3159
Fold-Pak South
Columbus, GA 706-689-2924
Folding Carton/Flexible Packaging
North Hollywood, CA 818-896-3449
Food Pak Corp
San Mateo, CA 650-341-6559
Foster Forbes Glass
Marion, IN 765-668-1200
Four M Manufacturing Group
San Jose, CA 408-998-1141
Franklin Crates
Micanopy, FL 352-466-3141
Frankston Paper Box Company of Texas
Frankston, TX 903-876-2550
Frem Corporation
Worcester, MA 508-791-3152
Fremont Die Cut Products
Fremont, OH 800-223-3177
Fresno Pallet, Inc.
Sultana, CA 559-591-4111
Friend Box Co
Danvers, MA 978-774-0240
Friendly City Box Co Inc
Johnstown, PA 814-266-6287
Fruit Growers Package Company
Grandville, MI 616-724-1400
Frye's Measure Mill
Wilton, NH 603-654-6581
Fuller Box Co
North Attleboro, MA 508-695-2525
Fuller Industries LLC
Great Bend, KS 800-522-0499
Fuller Packaging Inc
Central Falls, RI 401-725-4300
Fulton-Denver Co
Denver, CO 800-521-1414
Fun-Time International
Philadelphia, PA 800-776-4386
Gabriel Container Co
Santa Fe Springs, CA 323-685-8844
Galbreath LLC
Winamac, IN 574-946-6631
Gatewood Products LLC
Parkersburg, WV 800-827-5461
Gaylord Container Corporation
Tampa, FL 813-621-3591
Geerpres Inc
Muskegon, MI 231-773-3211
General Bag Corporation
Cleveland, OH 800-837-9396

General Industries Inc
Goldsboro, NC 888-735-2882
Genesee Corrugated
Flint, MI 810-228-3702
Genpak
Peterborough, ON 800-461-1995
Genpak LLC
Charlotte, NC 800-626-6695
Georg Fischer Central Plastics
Shawnee, OK 800-654-3872
Georgia-Pacific LLC
Atlanta, GA 800-283-5547
Gibbs Brothers Cooperage
Hot Springs, AR 501-623-8881
Gibraltar Packaging Group Inc
Hastings, NE 402-463-1366
Gillis Associated Industries
Prospect Heights, IL 847-541-6500
Glaro Inc
Hauppauge, NY 631-234-1717
Glasko Plastics
Santa Ana, CA 714-751-7830
Global Equipment Co Inc
Port Washington, NY 888-628-3466
Goldenwest Sales
Cerritos, CA 800-827-6175
Goldman Manufacturing Company
Detroit, MI 313-834-5535
Graff Tank Erection
Harrisville, PA 814-385-6671
Graham Engineering Corp
York, PA 717-848-3755
GranPac
Wetaskiwin, AB 780-352-3324
Graphic Packaging Corporation
Golden, CO 800-677-2886
Graphic Packaging International
Atlanta, GA 770-240-7200
Graphic Packaging Intl
Elk Grove Vlg, IL 847-437-1700
Great Lakes-Triad Package Corporation
Grand Rapids, MI 616-241-6441
Great Northern Corp
Chippewa Falls, WI 800-472-1800
Great Northern Corp.
Appleton, WI 800-236-3671
Great Southern Industries
Jackson, MS 877-638-3667
Green Bay Packaging Inc.
Kalamazoo, MI 269-552-1000
Green Bay Packaging Inc.
Tulsa, OK 918-446-3341
Green Bay Packaging Inc.
Green Bay, WI 920-433-5111
Green Brothers
Barrington, RI 401-245-9043
Greenfield Packaging
White Plains, NY 914-993-0233
Greenfield Paper Box Co
Greenfield, MA 413-773-9414
Greif Brothers Corporation
Cleveland, OH 800-424-0342
Greif Inc
Delaware, OH 740-549-6000
Grigsby Brothers Paper Box Manufacturers
Portland, OR 866-233-4690
Gulf Arizona Packaging
Humble, TX 800-364-3887
Gulf Packaging Company
Safety Harbor, FL 800-749-3466
Gulf Systems
Brownsville, TX 800-217-4853
Gulf Systems
Humble, TX 800-364-3887
Gulf Systems
Arlington, TX 817-261-1915
H S Inc
Oklahoma City, OK 800-238-1240
H. Arnold Wood Turning
Tarrytown, NY 888-314-0088
Hager Containers Inc
Carrollton, TX 972-416-7660
Hampton Roads Box Company
Suffolk, VA 757-934-2355
Hanson Box & Lumber Company
Wakefield, MA 617-245-0358
Harbor Pallet Company
Anaheim, CA 714-871-0932
Hardi-Tainer
South Deerfield, MA 800-882-9878
Hardy Systems Corporation
Northbrook, IL 800-927-3956

Harpak-ULMA Packaging LLC
Ball Ground, GA.....................770-345-5300
Hartford Containers
Terryville, CT 860-584-1194
Hartford Plastics
Omaha, NE
Harvard Folding Box Company
Lynn, MA 781-598-1600
Hedstrom Corporation
Ashland, OH 700-765-9665
Hedwin Division
Baltimore, MD 800-638-1012
Henry Ira L Co
Watertown, WI 920-261-0648
Herche Warehouse
Denver, CO 303-371-8186
Heritage Packaging
Victor, NY 585-742-3310
Herkimer Pallet & Wood Products Company
Herkimer, NY 315-866-4591
Highland Plastics Inc
Mira Loma, CA 800-368-0491
Hinchcliff Products Company
Strongsville, OH 440-238-5200
Hinkle Manufacturing
Perrysburg, OH 419-666-5367
Hodge Manufacturing Company
Springfield, MA 800-262-4634
Hodges
Vienna, IL 800-444-0011
Hoffmaster Group Inc.
Oshkosh, WI 800-558-9300
Holmco Container Manufacturing, LTD
Baltic, OH 330-897-4503
Hood Packaging
Madison, MS 800-321-8115
Hoover Materials Handling Group
Houston, TX 800-844-8683
Hope Paper Box Company
Pawtucket, RI 401-724-5700
Hot Food Boxes
Mooresville, IN....................800-733-8073
Hunter Packaging Corporation
South Elgin, IL 800-428-4747
Hunter Woodworks
Carson, CA 800-966-4751
Hurri-Kleen Corporation
Birmingham, AL...................800-455-8265
IBC Shell Packaging
New Hyde Park, NY 516-352-5138
Ideas Etc Inc
Louisville, KY 800-733-0337
Il Valley Container Inc
Peru, IL 815-223-7200
IMO Foods
Yarmouth, NS 902-742-3519
Imperial Containers
City of Industry, CA 626-333-6363
Imperial Industries Inc
Rothschild, WI 800-558-2945
Imperial Packaging Corporation
Pawtucket, RI 401-753-7778
Impress Industries
Emmaus, PA 610-967-6027
Incinerator International Inc
Houston, TX 713-227-1466
Independent Can Co
Belcamp, MD 410-272-0090
Indiana Bottle Co
Scottsburg, IN.....................800-752-8702
Indiana Vac Form Inc
Warsaw, IN 574-269-1725
Indianapolis Container Company
Indianapolis, IN 800-760-3318
Industrial Container Corp
High Point, NC 336-886-7031
Industrial Contracting & Rggng
Mahwah, NJ 888-427-7444
Industrial Hardwood
Perrysburg, OH 419-666-2503
Industrial Lumber & Packaging
Spring Lake, MI 616-842-1457
Industrial Nameplate Inc
Warminster, PA 800-878-6263
Industrial Woodfab & Packaging
Riverview, MI 734-284-4808
Inland Consumer Packaging
Harrington, DE 302-398-4211
Inland Paper Company
Ontario, CA 909-923-4505
Inland Paperboard & Packaging
Rock Hill, SC 803-366-4103

Innovative Folding Carton Company
South Plainfield, NJ 908-757-0205
Instabox
Calgary, AB.......................800-482-6173
Inter-Pack Corporation
Monroe, MI 734-242-7755
International Wood Industries
Snohomish, WA 800-922-6141
IPL Plastics
Edmundston, NB...................800-739-9595
IPS International
Snohomish, WA 360-668-5050
Ivarson Inc
Milwaukee, WI 414-351-0700
J&J Corrugated Box Corporation
Franklin, MA 508-528-6200
J&J Mid-South Container Corporation
Augusta, GA 800-395-1025
Jackson Corrugated Container
Middletown, CT 860-346-9671
Jacksonville Box & Woodwork Co
Jacksonville, FL 800-683-2699
Jamestown Container Corporation
Buffalo, NY 855-234-4054
Jarisch Paper Box Company
North Adams, MA 413-663-5396
Jenike & Johanson Inc
Tyngsboro, MA....................978-649-3300
Jescorp
Des Plaines, IL 847-299-7800
Jesse Jones Box Corporation
Philadelphia, PA 215-425-6600
Jessup Paper Box
Brookston, IN 765-490-9043
John Henry Packaging
Penngrove, CA 800-327-5997
Jordan Box Co
Syracuse, NY 315-422-3419
Jordan Paper Box Co
Chicago, IL........................773-287-5362
Juice Merchandising Corp
Kansas City, MO...................800-950-1998
Juice Tree
Omaha, NE 714-891-4425
Jupiter Mills Corporation
Roslyn, NY 800-853-5121
Just Plastics Inc
New York, NY 212-569-8500
K & L Intl
Ontario, CA.......................888-598-5588
K B Systems Inc
Bangor, PA 610-588-7788
K&H Container
Wallingford, CT 203-265-1547
Kadon Corporation
Milford, OH 937-299-0088
Karyall Telday Inc
Cleveland, OH 216-281-4063
Kaufman Paper Box Company
Providence, RI 401-272-7508
Kelley Wood Products
Fitchburg, MA 978-345-7531
Kendel
Countryside, IL 800-323-1100
Key Container Company
South Gate, CA....................323-564-4211
Key Material Handling Inc
Simi Valley, CA....................800-539-7225
Key Packaging Co
Sarasota, FL 941-355-2728
KHM Plastics Inc
Gurnee, IL.........................847-249-4910
Killington Wood ProductsCompany
Rutland, VT 802-773-9111
Kimball Companies
East Longmeadow, MA 413-525-1881
King Bag & Mfg Co
Cincinnati, OH 800-444-5464
King Plastic Corp
North Port, FL.....................800-780-5502
Knapp Container
Beacon Falls, CT...................203-888-0511
Knight Paper Box Company
Chicago, IL........................773-585-2035
Koch Container
Victor, NY.........................585-924-1600
Kontane
Charleston, SC 843-352-0011
Konz Wood Products Co
Appleton, WI......................877-610-5145
Label Makers
Pleasant Prairie, WI 800-208-3331

Lakeside Container Corp
Plattsburgh, NY 518-561-6150
Lakeside Manufacturing Inc
Milwaukee, WI 888-558-8565
Laminated Paper Products
San Jose, CA 408-888-0880
Landis Plastics
Alsip, IL 708-396-1470
Larose & Fils Lte
Laval, QC 877-382-7001
Laval Paper Box
Pointe Claire, QC..................450-669-3551
Lawrence Paper Co
Lawrence, KS 785-843-8111
LBP Manufacturing LLC
Cicero, IL 708-652-5600
Leclaire Packaging Corp
Ixonia, WI 920-206-9902
Leggett & Platt Storage
Vernon Hills, IL 847-816-6246
Lester Box & Mfg Div
Long Beach, CA 562-437-5123
Letica Corp
Rochester Hills, MI................800-538-4221
Levin Brothers Paper
Cicero, IL 800-545-6200
Lewis Steel Works Inc
Wrens, GA. 800-521-5239
Lewisburg Container Co
Lewisburg, OH 937-962-0101
Lexel
Fort Worth, TX 817-332-4061
Lima Barrel & Drum Company
Lima, OH 419-224-8916
Lin Pac Plastics
Roswell, GA.......................770-751-6006
LinPac
San Angelo, TX....................800-453-7393
Linpac Materials Handling
Dallas, TX.........................214-599-9023
Linvar
Hartford, CT 800-282-5288
Liquitane
Berwick, PA 570-759-6200
Little Rock Crate & Basket Co
Little Rock, AR.....................800-223-7823
LMK Containers
Centerville, UT 626-821-9984
Lone Star Container Corp
Irving, TX 800-552-6937
Longview Fibre Co
Longview, WA. 800-929-8111
Longview Fibre Company
Beaverton, OR 503-350-1600
Lowell Paper Box Company
Nashua, NH. 603-595-0700
Loy Lange Box Co
St Louis, MO. 800-886-4712
LTI Printing Inc
Sturgis, MI 269-651-7574
Luce Corp
Hamden, CT 800-344-6966
Luke's Almond Acres
Reedley, CA 559-638-3483
Lunn Industries
Glen Cove, NY 516-671-9000
M & G Packaging Corp
Floral Park, NY....................800-240-5288
M & H Crate Inc
Jacksonville, TX....................903-683-5351
M&L Plastics
Easthampton, MA..................413-527-1330
Mack-Chicago Corporation
Chicago, IL........................800-992-6225
MacMillan Bloedel Packaging
Montgomery, AL...................800-239-4464
Madsen Wire Products Inc
Orland, IN.........................260-829-6561
Malco Manufacturing Co
Los Angeles, CA...................866-477-7267
Mall City Containers Inc
Kalamazoo, MI....................800-643-6721
Mannkraft Corporation
Newark, NJ 973-589-7400
Marco Products
Adrian, MI. 517-265-3333
Marcus Carton Company
Melville, NY.......................631-752-4200
Marfred Industries
Sun Valley, CA 800-529-5156
Marion Paper Box Co
Marion, IN. 765-664-6435

Maro Paper Products Company
Bellwood, IL 708-649-9982
Marpac Industries
Philmont, NY 888-462-7722
Marshall Boxes Inc
Rochester, NY 585-458-7432
Massachusetts Container Corporation
North Haven, CT 203-248-2161
Massillon Container Co
Navarre, OH 330-879-5653
Master Containers
Mulberry, FL 800-881-6847
Master Package Corporation
Menomonie, WI 800-347-4144
Maull-Baker Box Company
Brookfield, WI 414-463-1290
Maypak Inc
Wayne, NJ 973-696-0780
Measurex/S&L Plastics
Nazareth, PA 800-752-0650
MeGa Industries
Burlington, ON 800-665-6342
Mello Smello LLC
Minneapolis, MN 888-574-2964
Melmat Inc
Huntington Beach, CA 800-635-6289
Melville Plastics
Haw River, NC 336-578-5800
Menasha Corp
Neenah, WI 800-558-5073
Merchants Publishing Company
Kalamazoo, MI 269-345-1175
Meyer Packaging
Palmyra, PA 717-838-6300
Michael Leson Dinnerware
Youngstown, OH 800-821-3541
Michiana Corrugate Products
Sturgis, MI 269-651-5225
Michigan Box Co
Detroit, MI 888-642-4269
Michigan Pallet Inc
St Charles, MI 989-865-9915
Micro Qwik
Cross Plains, WI 608-798-3071
Micro Wire Products Inc
Brockton, MA 508-584-0200
Mid Cities Paper Box Company
Downey, CA 877-277-6272
Mid-States Mfg & Engr Co Inc
Milton, IA 800-346-1792
Midland Manufacturing Co
Monroe, IA 800-394-2625
Midwest Aircraft Products Co
Lexington, OH 419-884-2164
Midwest Box Co
Cleveland, OH 216-281-3980
Midwest Paper Products Company
Louisville, KY 502-636-2741
Midwest Paper Tube & CanCorporation
New Berlin, WI 262-782-7300
Midwest Rubber Svc & Supply
Minneapolis, MN 800-537-7457
Milan Box Corporation
Milan, TN 800-225-8057
Miller Hofft Brands
Indianapolis, IN 317-638-6576
Modern Paper Box Company
Providence, RI 401-861-7357
Molded Container Corporation
Portland, OR 503-233-8601
Moli-International
Denver, CO 800-525-8468
Montebello Container Corp
La Mirada, CA 714-994-2351
Montebello Packaging
Hawkesbury, ON 613-632-7096
Morphy Container Company
Brantford, ON 519-752-5428
Morris Transparent Box Co
East Providence, RI 401-438-6116
Mountain Safety Research
Seattle, WA 800-877-9677
Mt Vernon Packaging Inc
Mt Vernon, OH 888-397-3221
Mullnix Packages Inc
Fort Wayne, IN 260-747-3149
Multibulk Systems International
Wendell, NC 919-366-2100
MultiFab Plastics
Boston, MA 888-293-5754
Muth Associates
Springfield, MA 800-388-0157

Nagel Paper & Box Company
Saginaw, MI 800-292-3654
Nefab Packaging Inc.
Coppell, TX 800-322-4425
Nefab Packaging, Inc.
Coppell, TX 800-322-4425
Neff Packaging
Simpsonville, KY 800-445-4383
Nelson Container Corp
Germantown, WI. 262-250-5000
NEPA Pallet & Container Co
Snohomish, WA 360-568-3185
New England Wooden Ware
Gardner, MA 800-252-9214
New Lisbon Wood ProductsManufacturing Company
New Lisbon, WI 608-562-3122
New Mexico Products Inc
Albuquerque, NM 877-345-7864
New York Corugated Box Co
Paterson, NJ 973-742-5000
North American Container Corp
Marietta, GA 800-929-0610
North American Packaging Corp
New York, NY 800-499-3521
Northeast Box Co
Ashtabula, OH 800-362-8100
Northeast Container Corporation
Dumont, NJ 201-385-6200
Nosco
Waukegan, IL 847-360-4806
Novelis Foil Products
Atlanta, GA 800-776-8701
NPC Display Group
Newark, NJ 973-589-2155
Nu-Trend Plastics Thermoformer
Jacksonville, FL 904-353-5936
Oak Barrel Winecraft
Berkeley, CA 510-849-0400
Oakes Carton Co
Kalamazoo, MI 269-381-6022
Ockerlund Industries
Addison, IL. 708-771-7707
Olcott Plastics
St Charles, IL 888-313-5277
Old Dominion Box Co Inc
Madison Heights, VA 434-929-6701
Old Dominion Box Company
Burlington, NC 336-226-4491
Oracle Packaging
Winston Salem, NC. 800-952-9536
ORBIS
Oconomowoc, WI. 262-560-5000
ORBIS
Oconomowoc, WI. 800-890-7292
Original Packaging & Display Company
Saint Louis, MO 314-772-7797
OTD Corporation
Hinsdale, IL 630-321-9232
Ott Packagings
Selinsgrove, PA 570-374-2811
Owens-Illinois Inc
Perrysburg, OH 567-336-5000
Pacific Paper Box Co
Cudahy, CA 323-771-7733
Pack-Rite
Newington, CT 860-953-0120
Packaging Associates
Randolph, NJ 973-252-8890
Packaging Corporation of America
Lake Forest, IL 800-456-4725
Packaging Design Corp
Burr Ridge, IL 630-323-1354
Packaging Dynamics International
Caldwell, OH 740-732-5665
Packaging Solutions
Los Altos Hills, CA 650-917-1022
Packing Material Company
Southfield, MI. 248-489-7000
Packing Specialities
Warren, MI 586-758-5240
Packrite Packaging
Archdale, NC. 336-431-1111
Pactiv LLC
Lake Forest, IL 800-476-4300
Pak-Sher
Kilgore, TX 903-984-8596
Pallet One Inc
Bartow, FL. 800-771-1148
Palmer Distributors
St Clair Shores, MI 800-444-1912
Pan Pacific Plastics Inc
Hayward, CA 888-475-6888

Paper Systems Inc
Des Moines, IA 800-342-2855
Paper Works Industries Inc
Baldwinsville, NY 800-847-5677
PAR-Kan
Silver Lake, IN 800-291-5487
Par-Pak
Houston, TX 713-686-6700
Par-Pak
Houston, TX 888-727-7252
Paradigm Packaging Inc
Upland, CA 909-985-2750
Paragon Packaging
Ferndale, CA 888-615-0065
Parkway Plastic Inc
Piscataway, NJ 800-881-4996
Parlor City Paper Box Co Inc
Binghamton, NY 607-772-0600
Parta
Kent, OH 800-543-5781
Paul T. Freund Corporation
Palmyra, NY 800-333-0091
Pelco Packaging Corporation
Stirling, NJ 908-647-3500
Pell Paper Box Company
Elizabeth City, NC 252-335-4361
Penn Bottle & Supply Company
Philadelphia, PA 215-365-5700
Penn Products
Portland, CT 800-490-7366
Penny Plate
Haddonfield, NJ 856-429-7583
Pentwater Wire Products Inc
Pentwater, MI 877-869-6911
Performance Packaging
Trail Creek, IN 219-874-6226
Peter Pepper Products Inc
Compton, CA 310-639-0390
Phoenix Industries Corp
Madison, WI 888-241-7482
Pine Point Wood Products Inc
Osseo, MN 763-428-4301
Pinn Pack Packaging LLC
Oxnard, CA 805-385-4100
Pioneer Packaging & Printing
Anoka, MN 800-708-1705
Pioneer Plastics Inc
Dixon, KY 800-951-1551
Pittsburgh Tank Corp
Monongahela, PA 800-634-0243
Plastic Assembly Corporation
Ayer, MA
Plastican Corporation
Fairfield, NJ 973-227-7817
Plastics Inc
Greensboro, AL 334-624-8801
Plastics Industries
Athens, TN 800-894-4876
Plastipak Packaging
Plymouth, MI 734-354-3510
Plastiques Cascades Group
Montreal, QC 888-703-6515
Plaxall Inc
Long Island City, NY 800-876-5706
Podnar Plastics Inc
Kent, OH 800-673-5277
Pohlig Brothers
N Chesterfield, VA 804-275-9000
Polar Tech Industries Inc
Genoa, IL 800-423-2749
Polar Ware Company
Sheboygan, WI 800-237-3655
Poliplastic
Granby, QC 450-378-8417
Poly One Corp
Avon Lake, OH 866-765-9663
Poly Processing Co
French Camp, CA 877-325-3142
Polybottle Group
Surrey, BC. 604-594-4999
Polycon Industries
Chicago, IL 773-374-5500
Portland Paper Box Company
Portland, OR 800-547-2571
PPC Perfect Packaging Co
Perrysburg, OH 419-874-3167
Prairie Packaging Inc
Mooresville, NC 704-660-6600
Precision Wood of Hawaii
Vancouver, WA 808-682-2055
Precision Wood Products
Vancouver, WA 360-694-8322

Premier Packages
Saint Louis, MO 800-466-6588
Premium Foil Products Company
Louisville, KY 502-459-2820
President Container Inc
Moonachie, NJ 212-244-0345
Prestige Plastics Corporation
Delta, BC .604-930-2931
Pretium Packaging
Chesterfield, MO 314-727-8673
Pretium Packaging
Hazle Twp, PA 570-459-1800
Pride Container Corporation
Chicago, IL 773-227-6000
Princeton Shelving
Cedar Rapids, IA 319-369-0355
Priority Plastics Inc
Grinnell, IA 800-798-3512
Progressive Plastics
Cleveland, OH 800-252-0053
Prolon
Port Gibson, MS 888-480-9828
Propak
Burlington, ON 800-263-4872
Pruitt's Packaging Services
Grand Rapids, MI 800-878-0553
Quality Container Company
Ypsilanti, MI 734-481-1373
Quality Containers
Weston, ON 416-749-6247
Quality Packaging Inc
Fond Du Lac, WI 800-923-3633
Quantum Storage Systems Inc
Miami, FL .800-685-4665
Quintex Corp
Nampa, ID 208-467-1113
R C Molding Inc
Greer, SC .864-879-7279
Ram Equipment Co
Waukesha, WI 262-513-1114
Rand-Whitney Group LLC
Worcester, MA 508-791-2301
Rand-Whitney Packaging Corp
Portsmouth, NH 508-791-2301
RAPAC Inc
Oakland, TN 800-280-6333
RDA Container Corp
Gates, NY .585-247-2323
Regal Plastic Company
Mission, KS 800-852-1556
Regal Plastic Supply Co
Kansas City, MO 800-444-6390
Reliable Container Corporation
Downey, CA 562-745-0200
Reliance Product
Winnipeg, MB 800-665-0258
Reliance-Paragon
Philadelphia, PA 215-743-1231
Remcon Plastics Inc
Reading, PA 800-360-3636
Revere Packaging
Shelbyville, KY 800-626-2668
Rez-Tech Corp
Kent, OH .800-673-5277
Rhoades Paper Box Corporation
Springfield, OH 800-441-6494
Rice Packaging Inc
Ellington, CT 800-367-6725
Richard Read Construction Company
Arcadia, CA 888-450-7343
Ritz Packaging Company
Brooklyn, NY 718-366-2300
Rjr Technologies
Oakland, CA 510-638-5901
RMI-C/Rotonics Manufacturing
Bensenville, IL 630-773-9510
Romanow Container
Westwood, MA 781-320-9200
Ronnie's Ceramic Company
San Francisco, CA 800-888-8218
Ropak
Oak Brook, IL 800-527-2267
Round Paper Packages Inc
Erlanger, KY 859-331-7200
Rownd & Son
Dillon, SC .803-774-8264
Roy's Folding Box
Cleveland, OH 216-464-1191
Royal Group
Cicero, IL .708-656-2020
Rubbermaid
High Point, NC 888-895-2110

Rudd Container Corp
Chicago, IL 773-847-7600
Ruffino Paper Box Co
Hackensack, NJ 201-487-1260
Rusken Packaging
Cullman, AL 256-775-0014
S.S.I. Schaefer System International Limited
Brampton, ON 905-458-5399
Sabert Corp
Sayreville, NJ 732-721-5546
Sabert Corp
Sayreville, NJ 800-722-3781
Saeplast Canada
St John, NB 800-567-3966
Saint-Gobain Containers
Malvern, PA
Sanchelima International
Miami, FL .305-591-4343
Schermerhorn Inc
Chicopee, MA 413-598-8348
Schiefer Packaging Corporation
Syracuse, NY 315-422-0615
Schwarz Supply Source
Morton Grove, IL 800-323-4903
Scope Packaging
Orange, CA 714-998-4411
Scott & Daniells
Portland, CT 860-342-1932
Seaboard Carton Company
Downers Grove, IL 708-344-0575
Seattle-Tacoma Box Co
Kent, WA .253-854-9700
Sebring Container Corporation
Salem, OH 330-332-1533
Security Packaging
North Bergen, NJ 201-854-1955
Semco Plastic Co
St Louis, MO 314-487-4557
Sertapak Packaging Corporation
Woodstock, ON 800-265-1162
Set Point Paper Company
Mansfield, MA 800-225-0501
Setco
Monroe Twp, NJ 609-655-4600
Setco
Anaheim, CA 714-777-5200
Seville Flexpack Corp
Oak Creek, WI 414-761-2751
Seymour Woodenware Company
Seymour, WI 920-833-6551
Sfb Plastics Inc
Wichita, KS 800-343-8133
SFBC, LLC dba Seaboard Folding Box
Fitchburg, MA 800-225-6313
Sharpsville Container Corp
Sharpsville, PA 800-645-1248
Shaw-Clayton Corporation
San Rafael, CA 800-537-6712
Sheboygan Paper Box Co
Sheboygan, WI 800-458-8373
Shelby Co
Westlake, OH 800-842-1650
Shillington Box Co LLC
St Louis, MO 636-825-6471
Shipmaster Containers Ltd.
Markham, ON 416-493-9193
Shippers Supply
Saskatoon, SK 800-661-5639
Shippers Supply, Labelgraphic
Calgary, AB 800-661-5639
Shore Paper Box Co
Mardela Springs, MD 410-749-7125
Shorewood Packaging
Carlstadt, NJ 201-933-3203
Sigma Industries
Elkhart, IN 574-295-9660
Silgan Plastics Canada
Chesterfield, MO 800-274-5426
Simkins Industries Inc
East Haven, CT 203-787-7171
Sirco Systems
Birmingham, AL 205-731-7800
Smith Packaging
Mississauga, ON 905-564-6640
Smurfit Kappa
Carson, CA 310-537-8190
Smurfit Stone
Norcross, GA 314-656-5300
Smurfit Stone Container
St Louis, MO 314-679-2300
Smurfit-Stone Container Corp
Santa Fe Springs, CA 714-523-3550

Smyrna Container Co
Atlanta, GA 800-868-4305
Snapware
Fullerton, CA 800-334-3062
Snyder Crown
Marked Tree, AR 870-358-3400
Snyder Industries Inc.
Lincoln, NE 800-351-1363
Sobel Corrugated Containers
Cleveland, OH 216-475-2100
Somerville Packaging
Toronto, ON 416-754-7228
Somerville Packaging
Mississauga, ON 905-678-8211
Sonderen Packaging
Spokane, WA 800-727-9139
Sonoco ThermoSafe
Arlington Heights, IL 800-323-7442
SOPAKCO Foods
Mullins, SC 800-276-9678
Southern Champion Tray LP
Chattanooga, TN 800-468-2222
Southern Metal Fabricators Inc
Albertville, AL 800-989-1330
Southern Missouri Containers
Springfield, MO 800-999-7666
Southern Packaging Machinery
Athens, GA 706-208-0814
Spartanburg Steel Products Inc
Spartanburg, SC 800-974-7500
Spartech Plastics
Portage, WI 800-998-7123
Spring Cove Container Div
Roaring Spring, PA 814-224-5141
Spring Wood Products
Geneva, OH 440-466-1135
Springport Steel Wire Products
Elkhart, IN 574-295-9660
SQP
Schenectady, NY 800-724-1129
St Joseph Packaging Inc
St Joseph, MO 800-383-3000
Stand Fast Pkgng Prods Inc
Addison, IL 630-543-6390
Standard Folding Cartons Inc
Flushing, NY 718-396-4522
Star Container Company
Phoenix, AZ 480-281-4200
Star Container Corporation
Leominster, MA 978-537-1676
Stearnswood Inc
Hutchinson, MN 800-657-0144
Step Products
Round Rock, TX 800-777-7837
Steril-Sil Company
Bowmansville, PA 800-784-5537
Stone Container
Moss Point, MS 502-491-4870
Streator Dependable Mfg
Streator, IL 800-798-0551
Stronghaven Containers Co
Matthews, NC 800-222-7919
Suburban Corrugated Box Company
Indianhead Park, IL 630-920-1230
Superfos Packaging Inc
Cumberland, MD 800-537-9242
T J Smith Box Co
Fort Smith, AR 877-540-7933
T&S Blow Molding
Scarborough, ON 416-752-8330
Tap Packaging Solutions
Cleveland, OH 800-827-5679
Taylor Box Co
Warren, RI 800-304-6361
Technibilt/Cari-All
Newton, NC 800-233-3972
Technipac
Le Sueur, MN 507-665-6658
TEMP-TECH Company
Springfield, MA 800-343-5579
Temple-Inland
Memphis, TN 901-419-9000
Tenneco Packaging
Westmont, IL 630-850-7034
TEQ
Huntley, IL 800-874-7113
TGR Container Sales
San Leandro, CA 800-273-6887
THARCO
San Lorenzo, CA 800-772-2332
Thermo Wisconsin
De Pere, WI 920-766-7200

Thermodynamics
Commerce City, CO 800-627-9037
Thermodyne International LTD
Ontario, CA 909-923-9945
Thornton Plastics
Salt Lake City, UT 800-248-3434
Tinwerks Packaging Co
Addison, IL 630-628-8600
Titan Plastics
East Rutherford, NJ 201-935-7700
TMS
San Francisco, CA 800-447-7223
Tolco Corp
Toledo, OH 800-537-4786
Trade Fixtures
Little Rock, AR 800-872-3490
Traex
Dane, WI 800-356-8006
Transparent Container Co
Addison, IL 630-458-9031
Traub Container Corporation
Cleveland, OH 216-475-5100
Treen Box & Pallet Inc
Bensalem, PA 215-639-5100
Trent Corp
Trenton, NJ 609-587-7515
Tri-State Plastics
Henderson, KY 270-826-8361
Trilla Steel Drum Corporation
Chicago, IL 773-847-7588
Triple A Containers
Buena Park, CA 714-521-2820
Triple Dot Corp
Santa Ana, CA 714-241-0888
True Pac
New Castle, DE 800-825-7890
Tucson Container Corp
Tucson, AZ 520-746-3171
Tupperware Brands Corporation
Orlando, FL 800-366-3800
Ultratainer
St Jean-Sur-Richelie, QC 514-359-3651
Unarco Industries LLC
Wagoner, OK 800-654-4100
Unipak Inc
West Chester, PA 610-436-6600
Unique Boxes
Chicago, IL 800-281-1670
Universal Container Corporation
Odessa, FL 800-582-7477
Universal Folding Box
East Orange, NJ 973-482-4300
Universal Folding Box Company
Hoboken, NJ 201-659-7373
Universal Paper Box
Seattle, WA 800-228-1045
US Can Company
Rosedale, MD 800-436-8021
Utah PaperBox Company
Salt Lake City, UT 801-363-0093
Valley Container Inc
Bridgeport, CT 203-368-6546
Van Dereems Mfg Co
Hawthorne, NJ 973-427-2355
Victory Box Corp
Roselle, NJ 908-245-5100
Victory Packaging, Inc.
Houston, TX 800-486-5606
Viking Packaging & Display
San Jose, CA 408-998-1000
VIP Real Estate LTD
Chicago, IL 773-376-5000
Visual Packaging Corp
Haskell, NJ 973-835-7055
VitaMinder Company
Providence, RI 800-858-8840
Volk Packaging Corp
Biddeford, ME 207-282-6151
Wald Imports
Kirkland, WA 800-426-2822
Wastequip Teem
Charlotte, NC 877-468-9278
Waymar Industries
Burnsville, MN 888-474-1112
Weber Display & Packaging Inc
Philadelphia, PA 215-426-3500
Webster Packaging Corporation
Loveland, OH 513-683-5666
Welbilt Inc.
New Port Richey, FL 877-375-9300
WES Plastics
Richmond Hill, ON 905-508-1546

West Rock
Atlanta, GA 770-448-2193
Westeel
Saskatoon, SK 306-931-2855
Wheaton Plastic Containers
Millville, NJ 856-825-1400
Willamette Industries
Beaverton, OR 503-641-1131
Willamette Industries
Louisville, KY 800-465-3065
Willard Packaging Co
Gaithersburg, MD 301-948-7700
Winchester Carton
Eutaw, AL 205-372-3337
Winzen Film
Taylor, TX 800-779-7595
Wisconsin Box Co
Wausau, WI 715-842-2248
Wisconsin Box Co
Wausau, WI 800-876-6658
WNA Hopple Plastics
Florence, KY 800-446-4622
Woodson Pallet Co
Anmoore, WV 304-623-2858
Woodstock Plastics Co Inc
Marengo, IL 815-568-5281
World Kitchen
Rosemont, IL 847-678-8600
Wright Brothers Paper Box Company
Fond Du Lac, WI 920-921-8270
Xtreme Beverages, LLC
Dana Point, CA 949-495-7929
York Container Co
York, PA 717-757-7611
Zero Manufacturing Inc
North Salt Lake, UT 800-959-5050

Chicken, Prepared

Flexo Transparent Inc
Buffalo, NY 877-993-5396
Foam Packaging Inc
Vicksburg, MS 800-962-2655

Paper

Accurate Paper Box Co Inc
Knoxville, TN 865-690-0311
Adpro
Solon, OH 440-542-1111
Alcan Packaging
Baie D'Urfe, QC 514-457-4555
Ample Industries
Franklin, OH 888-818-9700
Apache Inc
Cedar Rapids, IA 800-553-5455
Armbrust Paper Tubes Inc
Chicago, IL 773-586-3232
Artistic Carton
Auburn, IN 800-735-7225
Artistic Carton Co
Elgin, IL 847-741-0247
Bell Packaging Corporation
Marion, IN 800-382-0153
Boelter Industries
Winona, MN 507-452-2315
Boxes.com
Livingston, NJ 201-646-9050
Brewer-Cantelmo Inc
New York, NY 212-244-4600
Burrows Paper Corp
Little Falls, NY 800-272-7122
Capitol Carton Company
Sacramento, CA 916-388-7848
Cardinal Packaging Prod LLC
Crystal Lake, IL 866-216-4942
Carpet City Paper Box Company
Amsterdam, NY 518-842-5430
Cedar Box Co
Minneapolis, MN 612-332-4287
Chambers Container Company
Gastonia, NC 704-377-6317
Cin-Made Packaging Group
Norcross, GA 800-264-7494
Coast Paper Box Company
San Bernardino, CA 909-382-3475
Colbert Packaging Corp
Lake Forest, IL 847-367-5990
Collectors Gallery
St Charles, IL 800-346-3063
Color Box
Richmond, IN 765-966-7588

Color Carton Corp
Bronx, NY 718-665-0840
Columbus Paperbox Company
Columbus, OH 800-968-0797
Commencement Bay Corrugated
Orting, WA 253-845-3100
Commercial Corrugated Co Inc
Baltimore, MD 800-242-8861
Complete Packaging & Shipping
Freeport, NY 877-269-3236
Conn Container Corp
North Haven, CT 203-248-0241
Corbox-Meyers Inc
Cleveland, OH 800-321-7286
Corpak
San Juan, PR 787-787-9085
Corr Pak Corp
Mc Cook, IL 708-442-7806
Corrobilt Container Company
Livermore, CA 925-373-0880
Corrugated Packaging
Sarasota, FL 941-371-0000
Creative Packaging
Hayward, CA 510-785-6500
Cumberland Container Corp
Monterey, TN 931-839-2227
Curtis Packaging
Sandy Hook, CT 203-426-5861
Dallas Container Corp
Dallas, TX 800-381-7148
Day Manufacturing Company
Sherman, TX 903-893-1138
Designers Folding Box Corp
Buffalo, NY 716-853-5141
Diamond Packaging
Rochester, NY 800-333-4079
Dixie Printing & Packaging
Glen Burnie, MD 800-433-4943
Dorado Carton Company
Dorado, PR 787-796-1670
Drescher Paper Box Inc
Buffalo, NY 716-854-0288
Dusobox Company
Haverhill, MA 978-372-7192
Duval Container Co
Jacksonville, FL 800-342-8194
Eagle Box Company
Farmingdale, NY 212-255-3860
Eastern Container Corporation
Mansfield, MA 508-337-0400
EB Box Company
Richmond Hill, ON 800-513-2269
Economy Folding Box Corporation
Chicago, IL 800-771-1053
Enterprise Box Company
Montclair, NJ 973-509-2200
Erie Container
Cleveland, OH 216-631-1650
Eureka Paper Box Company
Williamsport, PA 570-326-9147
Fabricon Products Inc
River Rouge, MI 313-841-8200
Felco Packaging Specialist
Baltimore, MD 800-673-8488
Fibre Containers Inc
City of Industry, CA 626-968-5897
Finn Industries
Ontario, CA 909-930-1500
Fitzpatrick Container Company
North Wales, PA 215-699-3515
Flashfold Carton Inc
Fort Wayne, IN 260-423-9431
Folding Carton/Flexible Packaging
North Hollywood, CA 818-896-3449
Food Pak Corp
San Mateo, CA 650-341-6559
Four M Manufacturing Group
San Jose, CA 408-998-1141
Frankston Paper Box Company of Texas
Frankston, TX 903-876-2550
Friend Box Co
Danvers, MA 978-774-0240
Friendly City Box Co Inc
Johnstown, PA 814-266-6287
Fuller Box Co
North Attleboro, MA 508-695-2525
Fuller Packaging Inc
Central Falls, RI 401-725-4300
Gabriel Container Co
Santa Fe Springs, CA 323-685-8844
Goldman Manufacturing Company
Detroit, MI 313-834-5535

Graphic Packaging International
Atlanta, GA..................770-240-7200
Graphic Packaging Intl
Elk Grove Vlg, IL..............847-437-1700
Great Northern Corp
Chippewa Falls, WI............800-472-1800
Green Bay Packaging Inc.
Tulsa, OK.....................918-446-3341
Green Bay Packaging Inc.
Green Bay, WI.................920-433-5111
Green Brothers
Barrington, RI................401-245-9043
Greenfield Paper Box Co
Greenfield, MA................413-773-9414
Greif Brothers Corporation
Cleveland, OH................800-424-0342
Greif Inc
Delaware, OH.................740-549-6000
Grigsby Brothers Paper Box Manufacturers
Portland, OR..................866-233-4690
Gulf Packaging Company
Safety Harbor, FL.............800-749-3466
Hager Containers Inc
Carrollton, TX...............972-416-7660
Harvard Folding Box Company
Lynn, MA.....................781-598-1600
Henry Ira L Co
Watertown, WI................920-261-0648
Hoffmaster Group Inc.
Oshkosh, WI..................800-558-9300
Hood Packaging
Madison, MS..................800-321-8115
Hope Paper Box Company
Pawtucket, RI.................401-724-5700
Hunter Packaging Corporation
South Elgin, IL...............800-428-4747
Il Valley Container Inc
Peru, IL......................815-223-7200
Imperial Containers
City of Industry, CA...........626-333-6363
Imperial Packaging Corporation
Pawtucket, RI.................401-753-7778
Impress Industries
Emmaus, PA...................610-967-6027
Industrial Container Corp
High Point, NC................336-886-7031
Industrial Nameplate Inc
Warminster, PA...............800-878-6263
Inland Consumer Packaging
Harrington, DE................302-398-4211
Inland Paper Company
Ontario, CA...................909-923-4505
Inland Paperboard & Packaging
Rock Hill, SC.................803-366-4103
Instabox
Calgary, AB...................800-482-6173
Ivarson Inc
Milwaukee, WI................414-351-0700
J&J Mid-South Container Corporation
Augusta, GA..................800-395-1025
Jamestown Container Corporation
Buffalo, NY...................855-234-4054
Jarisch Paper Box Company
North Adams, MA..............413-663-5396
Jesse Jones Box Corporation
Philadelphia, PA..............215-425-6600
Jessup Paper Box
Brookston, IN.................765-490-9043
Jordan Box Co
Syracuse, NY..................315-422-3419
Jupiter Mills Corporation
Roslyn, NY....................800-853-5121
K&H Container
Wallingford, CT...............203-265-1547
Kaufman Paper Box Company
Providence, RI................401-272-7508
Kendel
Countryside, IL...............800-323-1100
Knight Paper Box Company
Chicago, IL...................773-585-2035
Koch Container
Victor, NY....................585-924-1600
Lakeside Container Corp
Plattsburgh, NY...............518-561-6150
Levin Brothers Paper
Cicero, IL....................800-545-6200
Lewisburg Container Co
Lewisburg, OH.................937-962-0101
Lone Star Container Corp
Irving, TX....................800-552-6937
Longview Fibre Co
Longview, WA.................800-929-8111

Lowell Paper Box Company
Nashua, NH...................603-595-0700
Loy Lange Box Co
St Louis, MO..................800-886-4712
Mack-Chicago Corporation
Chicago, IL...................800-992-6225
MacMillan Bloedel Packaging
Montgomery, AL...............800-239-4464
Mall City Containers Inc
Kalamazoo, MI................800-643-6721
Marcus Carton Company
Melville, NY..................631-752-4200
Marfred Industries
Sun Valley, CA................800-529-5156
Marion Paper Box Co
Marion, IN...................765-664-6435
Maro Paper Products Company
Bellwood, IL..................708-649-9982
Maypak Inc
Wayne, NJ....................973-696-0780
Merchants Publishing Company
Kalamazoo, MI................269-345-1175
Meyer Packaging
Palmyra, PA..................717-838-6300
Michiana Corrugate Products
Sturgis, MI...................269-651-5225
Michigan Box Co
Detroit, MI...................888-642-4269
Mid Cities Paper Box Company
Downey, CA...................877-277-6272
Midwest Paper Tube & CanCorporation
New Berlin, WI................262-782-7300
Modern Paper Box Company
Providence, RI................401-861-7357
Morphy Container Company
Brantford, ON.................519-752-5428
Mt Vernon Packaging Inc
Mt Vernon, OH................888-397-3221
Muth Associates
Springfield, MA...............800-388-0157
Nagel Paper & Box Company
Saginaw, MI..................800-292-3654
Neff Packaging
Simpsonville, KY..............800-445-4383
New England Wooden Ware
Gardner, MA..................800-252-9214
New York Corugated Box Co
Paterson, NJ..................973-742-5000
North American Packaging Corp
New York, NY.................800-499-3521
Northeast Box Co
Ashtabula, OH................800-362-8100
Northeast Container Corporation
Dumont, NJ...................201-385-6200
NPC Display Group
Newark, NJ...................973-589-2155
Oakes Carton Co
Kalamazoo, MI................269-381-6022
Ockerlund Industries
Addison, IL...................708-771-7707
Old Dominion Box Co Inc
Madison Heights, VA...........434-929-6701
Oracle Packaging
Winston Salem, NC............800-952-9536
Original Packaging & Display Company
Saint Louis, MO...............314-772-7797
Ott Packagings
Selinsgrove, PA...............570-374-2811
Pacific Paper Box Co
Cudahy, CA...................323-771-7733
Packaging Corporation of America
Lake Forest, IL...............800-456-4725
Packaging Design Corp
Burr Ridge, IL................630-323-1354
Packing Material Company
Southfield, MI................248-489-7000
Packrite Packaging
Archdale, NC.................336-431-1111
Paper Works Industries Inc
Baldwinsville, NY.............800-847-5677
Paragon Packaging
Ferndale, MI.................888-615-0065
Parlor City Paper Box Co Inc
Binghamton, NY...............607-772-0600
Parta
Kent, OH.....................800-543-5781
Paul T. Freund Corporation
Palmyra, NY..................800-333-0091
Pell Paper Box Company
Elizabeth City, NC............252-335-4361
Performance Packaging
Trail Creek, IN...............219-874-6226

Phoenix Industries Corp
Madison, WI..................888-241-7482
Pioneer Packaging & Printing
Anoka, MN...................800-708-1705
Pohlig Brothers
N Chesterfield, VA.............804-275-9000
Portland Paper Box Company
Portland, OR..................800-547-2571
Premier Packages
Saint Louis, MO...............800-466-6588
Pride Container Corporation
Chicago, IL...................773-227-6000
Quality Packaging Inc
Fond Du Lac, WI...............800-923-3633
R.N.C. Industries
Lawrenceville, GA.............888-844-3864
Rand-Whitney Group LLC
Worcester, MA................508-791-2301
Rand-Whitney Packaging Corp
Portsmouth, NH...............508-791-2301
RDA Container Corp
Gates, NY....................585-247-2323
Reliable Container Corporation
Downey, CA...................562-745-0200
Reliance-Paragon
Philadelphia, PA..............215-743-1231
Rhoades Paper Box Corporation
Springfield, OH...............800-441-6494
Rice Packaging Inc
Ellington, CT.................800-367-6725
Ritz Packaging Company
Brooklyn, NY.................718-366-2300
Rjr Technologies
Oakland, CA..................510-638-5901
Romanow Container
Westwood, MA................781-320-9200
Round Paper Packages Inc
Erlanger, KY..................859-331-7200
Roy's Folding Box
Cleveland, OH................216-464-1191
Ruffino Paper Box Co
Hackensack, NJ...............201-487-1260
Rusken Packaging
Cullman, AL..................256-775-0014
Schermerhorn Inc
Chicopee, MA.................413-598-8348
Schwarz Supply Source
Morton Grove, IL..............800-323-4903
Scope Packaging
Orange, CA...................714-998-4411
Scott & Daniells
Portland, CT..................860-342-1932
Seaboard Carton Company
Downers Grove, IL.............708-344-0575
Sebring Container Corporation
Salem, OH....................330-332-1533
Security Packaging
North Bergen, NJ..............201-854-1955
Set Point Paper Company
Mansfield, MA................800-225-0501
SFBC, LLC dba Seaboard Folding Box
Fitchburg, MA................800-225-6313
Shelby Co
Westlake, OH.................800-842-1650
Shillington Box Co LLC
St Louis, MO..................636-825-6471
Shippers Supply
Saskatoon, SK................800-661-5639
Shippers Supply, Labelgraphic
Calgary, AB...................800-661-5639
Shore Paper Box Co
Mardela Springs, MD..........410-749-7125
Shorewood Packaging
Carlstadt, NJ.................201-933-3203
Simkins Industries Inc
East Haven, CT...............203-787-7171
Smurfit Kappa
Carson, CA...................310-537-8190
Smurfit Stone
Norcross, GA.................314-656-5300
Smurfit-Stone Container Corp
Santa Fe Springs, CA..........714-523-3550
Smyrna Container Co
Atlanta, GA..................800-868-4305
Somerville Packaging
Toronto, ON..................416-754-7228
Sonderen Packaging
Spokane, WA.................800-727-9139
Southern Champion Tray LP
Chattanooga, TN..............800-468-2222
Southern Missouri Containers
Springfield, MO...............800-999-7666

Southern Packaging Machinery
  Athens, GA 706-208-0814
Spring Cove Container Div
  Roaring Spring, PA 814-224-5141
SQP
  Schenectady, NY 800-724-1129
St Joseph Packaging Inc
  St Joseph, MO. 800-383-3000
Stand Fast Pkgng Prods Inc
  Addison, IL 630-543-6390
Standard Folding Cartons Inc
  Flushing, NY. 718-396-4522
Stearnswood Inc
  Hutchinson, MN 800-657-0144
Stone Container
  Moss Point, MS 502-491-4870
Stronghaven Containers Co
  Matthews, NC. 800-222-7919
Suburban Corrugated Box Company
  Indianhead Park, IL 630-920-1230
T J Smith Box Co
  Fort Smith, AR 877-540-7933
Taylor Box Co
  Warren, RI. 800-304-6361
Tenneco Packaging
  Westmont, IL. 630-850-7034
THARCO
  San Lorenzo, CA. 800-772-2332
Traub Container Corporation
  Cleveland, OH 216-475-5100
Trent Corp
  Trenton, NJ 609-587-7515
Tucson Container Corp
  Tucson, AZ. 520-746-3171
Unipak Inc
  West Chester, PA. 610-436-6600
Unique Boxes
  Chicago, IL 800-281-1670
Universal Folding Box
  East Orange, NJ 973-482-4300
Universal Folding Box Company
  Hoboken, NJ 201-659-7373
Universal Paper Box
  Seattle, WA 800-228-1045
Utah PaperBox Company
  Salt Lake City, UT 801-363-0093
Victory Box Corp
  Roselle, NJ 908-245-5100
Victory Packaging, Inc.
  Houston, TX 800-486-5606
Viking Packaging & Display
  San Jose, CA. 408-998-1000
VIP Real Estate LTD
  Chicago, IL 773-376-5000
Volk Packaging Corp
  Biddeford, ME 207-282-6151
West Rock
  Atlanta, GA. 770-448-2193
Willamette Industries
  Beaverton, OR. 503-641-1131
Winchester Carton
  Eutaw, AL 205-372-3337
Woodson Pallet Co
  Anmoore, WV. 304-623-2858
Wright Brothers Paper Box Company
  Fond Du Lac, WI 920-921-8270
York Container Co
  York, PA 717-757-7611

Plastic

Abbott Industries
  Paterson, NJ
Aco Container Systems
  Pickering, ON 800-542-9942
All American Container
  Miami, FL. 305-887-0797
All American Poly
  Piscataway, NJ 800-526-3551
Alpack
  Centerville, NA. 774-994-8086
Anchor Packaging
  Ballwin, MO. 800-467-3900
Arena Products
  Rochester, NY. 844-762-0127
Arthur Corporation
  Huron, OH. 419-433-7202
Atlas Equipment Company
  Kansas City, MO. 800-842-9188
Bardes Plastics Inc
  Milwaukee, WI 800-558-5161

Belleview
  Brookline, NH. 603-878-1583
Bergen Barrel & Drum Company
  Kearny, NJ 201-998-3500
Berry Global
  Evansville, IN 800-343-1295
Bonar Plastics
  West Chicago, IL 800-295-3725
Brown International Corp LLC
  Winter Haven, FL 863-299-2111
Buckhorn Canada
  Brampton, ON. 800-461-7579
Buckhorn Inc
  Milford, OH 800-543-4454
Bulk Lift International, LLC
  Carpentersville, IL 800-879-2247
Cardinal Packaging
  Evansville, IN 800-343-1295
Carson Industries
  Pomona, CA 800-735-5566
Ccw Products
  Arvada, CO. 303-427-9663
Chem-Tainer Industries Inc
  West Babylon, NY 800-275-2436
Chem-Tainer Industries Inc
  West Babylon, NY 800-938-8896
Chili Plastics
  Rochester, NY. 585-889-4680
CKS Packaging
  Atlanta, GA. 800-800-4257
Clawson Container Company
  Clarkston, MI 800-325-8700
Conductive Containers Inc
  Minneapolis, MN 800-327-2329
Consolidated Container Co
  New Castle, PA. 724-658-0549
Constar International
  Plymouth, MI 734-455-3600
Container Specialties
  Melrose Park, IL. 800-548-7513
Container Supply Co
  Garden Grove, CA 562-594-0937
Continental Plastic Container
  Dallas, TX. 972-303-1825
Contour Packaging
  Philadelphia, PA 215-457-1600
Convoy
  Canton, OH. 800-899-1583
Creative Packaging
  Hayward, CA 510-785-6500
Crespac Incorporated
  Tucker, GA. 800-438-1900
CTK Plastics
  Moose Jaw, SK 800-667-8847
Cube Plastics
  Concord, Ontario, ON. 877-260-2823
Custom Bottle of Connecticut
  Naugatuck, CT 203-723-6661
Dahl-Tech Inc
  Stillwater, MN. 800-626-5812
Dart Container Corp.
  Mason, MI. 800-248-5960
De Ster Corporation
  Atlanta, GA. 800-237-8270
DEL-Tec Packaging Inc
  Greer, SC. 800-747-8683
Design Plastics Inc
  Omaha, NE 800-491-0786
Douglas Stephen Plastics Inc
  Paterson, NJ 973-523-3030
Edco Industries
  Bridgeport, CT 203-333-8982
Emco Industrial Plastics
  Cedar Grove, NJ 800-292-9906
Engineered Products
  Hazelwood, MO 314-731-5744
ES Robbins Corp
  Muscle Shoals, AL 800-633-3325
Fabri-Kal Corp
  Kalamazoo, MI 800-888-5054
Finn Industries
  Ontario, CA. 909-930-1500
Flex Products
  Carlstadt, NJ 800-526-6273
Frankston Paper Box Company of Texas
  Frankston, TX 903-876-2550
Fuller Industries LLC
  Great Bend, KS. 800-522-0499
Gary Plastic Packaging Corporation
  Bronx, NY. 800-221-8151
Genpak
  Peterborough, ON. 800-461-1995

Genpak LLC
  Charlotte, NC 800-626-6695
Georg Fischer Central Plastics
  Shawnee, OK. 800-654-3872
Glasko Plastics
  Santa Ana, CA 714-751-7830
Graham Engineering Corp
  York, PA 717-848-3755
GranPac
  Wetaskiwin, AB 780-352-3324
Greenfield Packaging
  White Plains, NY 914-993-0233
Gulf Packaging Company
  Safety Harbor, FL 800-749-3466
Hartford Plastics
  Omaha, NE
Hedstrom Corporation
  Ashland, OH. 700-765-9665
Hedwin Division
  Baltimore, MD 800-638-1012
Highland Plastics Inc
  Mira Loma, CA. 800-368-0491
Indiana Bottle Co
  Scottsburg, IN. 800-752-8702
Indiana Vac Form Inc
  Warsaw, IN 574-269-1725
Indianapolis Container Company
  Indianapolis, IN 800-760-3318
Inmark, Inc
  Austell, GA 800-646-6275
Intertech Corp
  Greensboro, NC 800-364-2255
IPL Plastics
  Edmundston, NB. 800-739-9595
Jarisch Paper Box Company
  North Adams, MA 413-663-5396
Jescorp
  Des Plaines, IL 847-299-7800
Juice Merchandising Corp
  Kansas City, MO. 800-950-1998
Juice Tree
  Omaha, NE 714-891-4425
Jupiter Mills Corporation
  Roslyn, NY. 800-853-5121
Just Plastics Inc
  New York, NY 212-569-8500
K & L Intl
  Ontario, CA. 888-598-5588
Kadon Corporation
  Milford, OH 937-299-0088
Key Packaging Co
  Sarasota, FL 941-355-2728
KHM Plastics Inc
  Gurnee, IL. 847-249-4910
Kimball Companies
  East Longmeadow, MA 413-525-1881
King Plastic Corp
  North Port, FL. 800-780-5502
Landis Plastics
  Alsip, IL 708-396-1470
Letica Corp
  Rochester Hills, MI. 800-538-4221
Lin Pac Plastics
  Roswell, GA 770-751-6006
Linvar
  Hartford, CT 800-282-5288
Liquitane
  Berwick, PA 570-759-6200
LMK Containers
  Centerville, UT 626-821-9984
Lunn Industries
  Glen Cove, NY 516-671-9000
M&L Plastics
  Easthampton, MA 413-527-1330
Marco Products
  Adrian, MI. 517-265-3333
Marpac Industries
  Philmont, NY 888-462-7722
Melmat Inc
  Huntington Beach, CA 800-635-6289
Melville Plastics
  Haw River, NC 336-578-5800
Micro Qwik
  Cross Plains, WI 608-798-3071
Midland Manufacturing Co
  Monroe, IA 800-394-2625
Molded Container Corporation
  Portland, OR. 503-233-8601
Morris Transparent Box Co
  East Providence, RI. 401-438-6116
Mullnix Packages Inc
  Fort Wayne, IN 260-747-3149

North American Packaging Corp
New York, NY 800-499-3521
Nu-Trend Plastics Thermoformer
Jacksonville, FL 904-353-5936
Ockerlund Industries
Addison, IL 708-771-7707
Olcott Plastics
St Charles, IL 888-313-5277
ORBIS
Oconomowoc, WI.................262-560-5000
ORBIS
Oconomowoc, WI.................800-890-7292
Owens-Illinois Inc
Perrysburg, OH...................567-336-5000
Pacific Paper Box Co
Cudahy, CA 323-771-7733
Packaging Associates
Randolph, NJ 973-252-8890
Pactiv LLC
Lake Forest, IL 800-476-4300
Pan Pacific Plastics Inc
Hayward, CA 888-475-6888
Par-Pak
Houston, TX 713-686-6700
Par-Pak
Houston, TX 888-727-7252
Paradigm Packaging Inc
Upland, CA 909-985-2750
Paragon Packaging
Ferndale, CA 888-615-0065
Pelco Packaging Corporation
Stirling, NJ 908-647-3500
Penn Bottle & Supply Company
Philadelphia, PA 215-365-5700
Penn Products
Portland, CT 800-490-7366
Pinckney Molded Plastics
Howell, MI 800-854-2920
Pioneer Plastics Inc
Dixon, KY..........................800-951-1551
Plastic Assembly Corporation
Ayer, MA
Plastics Inc
Greensboro, AL 334-624-8801
Plastics Industries
Athens, TN 800-894-4876
Plastipak Packaging
Plymouth, MI 734-354-3510
Plastiques Cascades Group
Montreal, QC 888-703-6515
Podnar Plastics Inc
Kent, OH............................800-673-5277
Poliplastic
Granby, QC........................450-378-8417
Poly Plastic Products Inc
Delano, PA 570-467-3000
Poly Processing Co
French Camp, CA.................877-325-3142
Polybottle Group
Surrey, BC.........................604-594-4999
Polycon Industries
Chicago, IL........................773-374-5500
Prairie Packaging Inc
Mooresville, NC 704-660-6600
Prestige Plastics Corporation
Delta, BC...........................604-930-2931
Pretium Packaging
Chesterfield, MO 314-727-8673
Pretium Packaging
Hazle Twp, PA 570-459-1800
Pretium Packaging, LLC.
Chesterfield, MO..................314-727-8200
Printsource Group
Wakefield, RI 401-789-9339
Priority Plastics Inc
Grinnell, IA 800-798-3512
Progressive Plastics
Cleveland, OH 800-252-0053
Prolon
Port Gibson, MS 888-480-9828
Promens
St. John, NB 800-295-3725
Quality Container Company
Ypsilanti, MI 734-481-1373
Quantum Storage Systems Inc
Miami, FL 800-685-4665
Quintex Corp
Nampa, ID..........................208-467-1113
R C Molding Inc
Greer, SC...........................864-879-7279
RAPAC Inc
Oakland, TN 800-280-6333

Regal Plastic Company
Mission, KS 800-852-1556
Reliance Product
Winnipeg, MB......................800-665-0258
Reliance-Paragon
Philadelphia, PA 215-743-1231
Rez-Tech Corp
Kent, OH............................800-673-5277
Richard Read Construction Company
Arcadia, CA 888-450-7343
RMI-C/Rotonics Manaufacturing
Bensenville, IL 630-773-9510
Ropak
Oak Brook, IL 800-527-2267
S.S.I. Schaefer System International Limited
Brampton, ON.....................905-458-5399
Sabert Corp
Sayreville, NJ 800-722-3781
Saeplast Canada
St John, NB 800-567-3966
Semco Plastic Co
St Louis, MO.......................314-487-4557
Set Point Paper Company
Mansfield, MA 800-225-0501
Setco
Monroe Twp, NJ 609-655-4600
Setco
Anaheim, CA 714-777-5200
Sfb Plastics Inc
Wichita, KS.........................800-343-8133
Sharpsville Container Corp
Sharpsville, PA 800-645-1248
Shaw-Clayton Corporation
San Rafael, CA 800-537-6712
Sheboygan Paper Box Co
Sheboygan, WI.....................800-458-8373
Silgan Plastics Canada
Chesterfield, MO 800-274-5426
Snapware
Fullerton, CA 800-334-3062
Snyder Industries Inc.
Lincoln, NE.........................800-351-1363
Spartanburg Steel Products Inc
Spartanburg, SC...................800-974-7500
Spartech Plastics
Portage, WI.........................800-998-7123
Star Container Company
Phoenix, AZ 480-281-4200
Step Products
Round Rock, TX 800-777-7837
Stock America Inc
Grafton, WI.........................262-375-4100
Superfos Packaging Inc
Cumberland, MD 800-537-9242
T&S Blow Molding
Scarborough, ON 416-752-8330
TEQ
Huntley, IL 800-874-7113
Thermodynamics
Commerce City, CO 800-627-9037
Thermodyne International LTD
Ontario, CA.........................909-923-9945
Thornton Plastics
Salt Lake City, UT 800-248-3434
Titan Plastics
East Rutherford, NJ 201-935-7700
Tri-State Plastics
Henderson, KY 270-826-8361
Triple Dot Corp
Santa Ana, CA 714-241-0888
Tupperware Brands Corporation
Orlando, FL.........................800-366-3800
Universal Container Corporation
Odessa, FL 800-582-7477
Visual Packaging Corp
Haskell, NJ 973-835-7055
WES Plastics
Richmond Hill, ON...............905-508-1546
Willamette Industries
Louisville, KY 800-465-3065
Wiltec
Leominster, MA 978-537-1497
Winzen Film
Taylor, TX 800-779-7595
WNA
Lancaster, TX 800-334-2877
WNA Hopple Plastics
Florence, KY.......................800-446-4622
Woodstock Plastics Co Inc
Marengo, IL 815-568-5281
World Kitchen
Rosemont, IL.......................847-678-8600

Zero Manufacturing Inc
North Salt Lake, UT 800-959-5050

Corks

Crown

Cork Specialties
Miami, FL 305-477-1506
Fetzer Vineyards
Hopland, CA.......................800-846-8637
Palace Packaging Machines Inc
Downingtown, PA.................610-873-7252

Crates

Bottle

Langer Manufacturing Company
Cedar Rapids, IA..................800-728-6445
Tulip Molded Plastics Corp
Milwaukee, WI.....................414-963-3120

Egg

Eggboxes Inc
Deerfield Beach, FL 800-326-6667
Jacksonville Box & Woodwork Co
Jacksonville, FL 800-683-2699

Wooden Shipping

American Box Corporation
Lisbon, OH.........................330-424-8055
American Pallet Inc
Oakdale, CA 209-847-6122
Babcock Co
Bath, NY 607-776-3341
Brooks Barrel Company
Baltimore, MD 800-398-2766
Burgess Mfg. - Oklahoma
Guthrie, OK........................800-804-1913
C & L Wood Products Inc
Hartselle, AL 800-483-2035
Cassel Box & Lumber Co Inc
Grafton, WI........................262-377-9503
Corbett Timber Co
Wilmington, NC 800-334-0684
Corrugated Inner-Pak Corporation
Conshohocken, PA 610-825-0200
Creative Packaging
Hayward, CA 510-785-6500
Denver Reel & Pallet Company
Denver, CO 303-321-1920
Eichler Wood Products
Laurys Station, PA 610-262-6749
Elberta Crate & Box Company
Carpentersville, IL 888-672-9260
Farmer's Co-Op Elevator Co
Hudsonville, MI 800-439-9859
Fehlig Brothers Box & Lbr Co
St Louis, MO.......................314-241-6900
Fox Valley Wood Products Inc
Kaukauna, WI......................920-766-4069
Franklin Crates
Micanopy, FL 352-466-3141
Fruit Growers Package Company
Grandville, MI 616-724-1400
Gatewood Products LLC
Parkersburg, WV..................800-827-5461
Goeman's Wood Products
Hartford, WI 262-673-6090
Greene Industries
East Greenwich, RI...............401-884-7530
H. Arnold Wood Turning
Tarrytown, NY.....................888-314-0088
Hampton Roads Box Company
Suffolk, VA.........................757-934-2355
Heritage Packaging
Victor, NY..........................585-742-3310
Herkimer Pallet & Wood Products Company
Herkimer, NY 315-866-4591
Hinchcliff Products Company
Strongsville, OH...................440-238-5200
Hunter Woodworks
Carson, CA 800-966-4751
Industrial Contracting & Rggng
Mahwah, NJ 888-427-7444
Industrial Crating & Packing
Tukwila, WA........................800-942-0499
Industrial Lumber & Packaging
Spring Lake, MI 616-842-1457

Industrial Woodfab & Packaging
Riverview, MI 734-284-4808
Jacksonville Box & Woodwork Co
Jacksonville, FL 800-683-2699
Killington Wood ProductsCompany
Rutland, VT 802-773-9111
Kontane
Charleston, SC 843-352-0011
Konz Wood Products Co
Appleton, WI 877-610-5145
Lawson Industries
Holden, MO 816-732-4347
Lester Box & Mfg Div
Long Beach, CA 562-437-5123
Lexel
Fort Worth, TX 817-332-4061
Little Rock Crate & Basket Co
Little Rock, AR 800-223-7823
Luke's Almond Acres
Reedley, CA 559-638-3483
Lumber & Things
Keyser, WV 800-296-5656
M & H Crate Inc
Jacksonville, TX 903-683-5351
Maull-Baker Box Company
Brookfield, WI 414-463-1290
Michiana Box & Crate
Niles, MI 800-677-6372
Michigan Box Co
Detroit, MI 888-642-4269
Milan Box Corporation
Milan, TN 800-225-8057
Moorecraft Box & Crate
Tarboro, NC 252-823-2510
Nefab Packaging Inc.
Coppell, TX 800-322-4425
Nefab Packaging, Inc.
Coppell, TX 800-322-4425
New Lisbon Wood ProductsManufacturing Company
New Lisbon, WI 608-562-3122
New Mexico Products Inc
Albuquerque, NM 877-345-7864
Oak Creek Pallet Company
Milwaukee, WI 414-762-7170
Original Lincoln Logs
Chestertown, NY 800-833-2461
Packing Material Company
Southfield, MI 248-489-7000
Pallets Inc
Fort Edward, NY 518-747-4177
Pine Point Wood Products Inc
Osseo, MN 763-428-4301
PPC Perfect Packaging Co
Perrysburg, OH 419-874-3167
Precision Wood of Hawaii
Vancouver, WA 808-682-2055
Precision Wood Products
Vancouver, WA 360-694-8322
Rand-Whitney Group LLC
Worcester, MA 508-791-2301
Remmey Wood Products
Southampton, PA 215-355-3335
Roddy Products Pkgng Co Inc
Aldan, PA 610-623-7040
Royal Group
Cicero, IL 708-656-2020
Seattle-Tacoma Box Co
Kent, WA 253-854-9700
Smith Pallet Co Inc
Hatfield, AR 870-389-6184
Southern Pallet
Christchurch, NZ 901-942-4603
Spring Wood Products
Geneva, OH 440-466-1135
Stearnswood Inc
Hutchinson, MN 800-657-0144
Tampa Pallet Co
Tampa, FL 813-626-5700
Thunder Pallet Inc
Theresa, WI 800-354-0643
Wisconsin Box Co
Wausau, WI 715-842-2248
Wisconsin Box Co
Wausau, WI 800-876-6658
Wnc Pallet & Forest Pdts Co
Candler, NC 828-667-5426
Xtreme Beverages, LLC
Dana Point, CA 949-495-7929

Cups

Paper

A-A1 Aaction Bag
Denver, CO 800-783-1224
Acme International
Maplewood, NJ 973-416-0400
AJM Packaging Corporation
Bloomfield Hills, MI 248-901-0040
Bynoe Printers
New York, NY 212-662-5041
Chinet Company
Laguna Niguel, CA 949-348-1711
Creative Converting Inc
Clintonville, WI 800-826-0418
Dart Canada Inc.
Toronto, ON 800-465-9696
Dart Container Corp.
Mason, MI 800-248-5960
Durango-Georgia Paper
Tampa, FL 813-286-2718
Fort James Canada
Toronto, ON 416-784-1621
Four M Manufacturing Group
San Jose, CA 408-998-1141
Hoffmaster Group Inc.
Oshkosh, WI 800-558-9300
Insulair
Vernalis, CA 800-343-3402
International Paper Co.
Memphis, TN
James River Canada
North York, ON. 416-789-5151
Jones-Zylon Co
West Lafayette, OH. 800-848-8160
Letica Corp
Rochester Hills, MI. 800-538-4221
Nyman Manufacturing Company
Rumford, RI 401-438-3410
Primary Liquidation
Bohemia, NY 631-244-1410
Rockline Industries
Sheboygan, WI 800-558-7790
Scan Group
Appleton, WI 920-730-9150
Solo Cup Company
Lake Forest, IL
Tenneco Specialty Packaging
Smyrna, GA 800-241-4402

Plastic

A-A1 Aaction Bag
Denver, CO 800-783-1224
Arthur Corporation
Huron, OH. 419-433-7202
C R Mfg
Waverly, NE 877-789-5844
Carlisle Food Svc Products Inc
Oklahoma City, OK 800-654-8210
Carthage Cup Company
Longview, TX 903-238-9833
Chinet Company
Laguna Niguel, CA 949-348-1711
Creative Converting Inc
Clintonville, WI 800-826-0418
Dart Canada Inc.
Toronto, ON 800-465-9696
Dart Container Corp.
Mason, MI 800-248-5960
De Ster Corporation
Atlanta, GA 800-237-8270
Design Specialties Inc
Hamden, CT 800-999-1584
Donoco Industries
Huntington Beach, CA 888-822-8763
Elliot Lee
Cedarhurst, NY 516-569-9595
Fabri-Kal Corp
Kalamazoo, MI 800-888-5054
Filmpack Plastic Corporation
Dayton, NJ 732-329-6523
Fort James Canada
Toronto, ON 416-784-1621
Genpak
Peterborough, ON. 800-461-1995
Highland Plastics Inc
Mira Loma, CA. 800-368-0491
Hoffmaster Group Inc.
Oshkosh, WI 800-558-9300

HPI North America/ Plastics
Eagan, MN 800-752-7462
Huhtamaki Food Service Plastics
Lake Forest, IL 800-244-6382
Image Plastics
Houston, TX 800-289-2811
James River Canada
North York, ON. 416-789-5151
Jones-Zylon Co
West Lafayette, OH. 800-848-8160
Kendrick Johnson & Assoc Inc
Minneapolis, MN 800-826-1271
King Plastic Corp
North Port, FL 800-780-5502
Letica Corp
Rochester Hills, MI. 800-538-4221
Master Containers
Mulberry, FL 800-881-6847
MDR International
North Miami, FL. 305-944-5019
NCC
Groveland, FL. 800-429-9037
Nyman Manufacturing Company
Rumford, RI 401-438-3410
OWD
Tupper Lake, NY 800-836-1693
Party Yards
Casselberry, FL 877-501-4400
Peter Gray Corporation
Andover, MA 978-470-0990
Plaxall Inc
Long Island City, NY 800-876-5706
Polar Plastics
St Laurent, QC 514-331-0207
Prairie Packaging Inc
Mooresville, NC 704-660-6600
Set Point Paper Company
Mansfield, MA 800-225-0501
Spirit Foodservice, Inc.
Andover, MA 800-343-0996
Techform
Mount Airy, NC 336-789-2115
Tenneco Specialty Packaging
Smyrna, GA 800-241-4402
Thermo Service
Dallas, TX 800-635-5559
Ullman, Shapiro & UllmanLLP
New York, NY 212-755-0299
Whirley Industries Inc
Warren, PA 800-825-5575
Wiltec
Leominster, MA 978-537-1497
WNA
Lancaster, TX 800-334-2877
Wna Comet West Inc
City of Industry, CA 800-225-0939

Film

Cellulose Acetate

Emco Industrial Plastics
Cedar Grove, NJ 800-292-9906
Modern Plastics
Shelton, CT. 800-243-9696
Pater & Associates
Cincinnati, OH
Star Poly Bag Inc
Brooklyn, NY 718-384-7034
Teepak LLC
Lisle, IL. 800-621-0264
UCB Inc
Smyrna, GA 770-970-8338

Plastic

A-A1 Aaction Bag
Denver, CO 800-783-1224
Achilles USA
Everett, WA. 425-353-7000
AEP Industries
South Hackensack, NJ 800-999-2374
AEP Industries Inc
Mankato, MN 800-999-2374
Aep Industries Inc.
South Hackensack, NJ 800-999-2374
American Renolit Corp LA
Commerce, CA 323-721-2720
Anchor Packaging
Ballwin, MO 800-467-3900
Atlantis Plastics Linear Film
Tulsa, OK 800-324-9727

Bagcraft Papercon
Chicago, IL 800-621-8468
Beayl Weiner/Pak
Pacific Palisades, CA 310-454-1354
Blako Industries
Dunbridge, OH 419-833-4491
Bollore Inc
Dayville, CT 860-774-2930
Brentwood Plastics In
St Louis, MO...........................314-968-1135
Carlisle Plastics
Minneapolis, MN 952-884-1309
Cello Bag Company
Bowling Green, KY 800-347-0338
Champion Plastics
Clifton, NJ 800-526-1230
Cincinnati Convertors Inc
Cincinnati, OH 513-731-6600
Cleveland Plastic Films
Elyria, OH...............................800-832-6799
Cleveland Specialties Co
Loveland, OH..........................513-677-9787
Colonial Transparent Products Company
Hicksville, NY 516-822-4430
Command Packaging
Vernon, CA 800-996-2247
Cortec Aero
St Paul, MN............................800-426-7832
COVERIS
Tomah, WI 608-372-2153
Coveris
Excelsior Springs, MO
Crayex Corp
Piqua, OH 800-837-1747
Crystal-Flex Packaging Corporation
Rockville Centre, NY 888-246-7325
Danafilms Inc
Westborough, MA....................508-366-8884
Dynamic Packaging
Minneapolis, MN 800-878-9380
Ellehammer Industries
Langley, BC 604-882-9326
Farnell Packaging
Dartmouth, NS 800-565-9378
Film X
Dayville, CT 800-628-6128
Film-Pak Inc
Crowley, TX 800-526-1838
Filmco Inc
Aurora, OH 800-545-8457
FLEXcon Company
Spencer, MA 508-885-8200
Flexo Transparent Inc
Buffalo, NY.............................877-993-5396
Formflex
Bloomingdale, IN 800-255-7659
Fredman Bag Co
Milwaukee, WI 800-945-5686
Gbs
North Canton, OH....................800-552-2427
Gemini Plastic Films Corporation
Garfield, NJ 800-789-4732
General Films Inc
Covington, OH 888-436-3456
Gloucester Engineering
Gloucester, MA 978-281-1800
Goodwrappers Inc
Halethorpe, MD 800-638-1127
Greenfield Packaging
White Plains, NY 914-993-0233
Gulf Arizona Packaging
Humble, TX 800-364-3887
Gulf Systems
Brownsville, TX 800-217-4853
Gulf Systems
Humble, TX 800-364-3887
Harpak-ULMA Packaging LLC
Ball Ground, GA......................770-345-5300
Hedwin Division
Baltimore, MD 800-638-1012
Herche Warehouse
Denver, CO 303-371-8186
Holo-Source Corporation
Livonia, MI 888-995-7799
Home Plastics Inc
Des Moines, IA........................515-265-2562
Hudson Poly Bag Inc
Hudson, MA 800-229-7566
Huntsman Packaging Corporation
Birmingham, Bi.......................205-328-4720
Inmark, Inc
Austell, GA 800-646-6275

Inteplast Bags & Films Corporation
Delta, BC. 604-946-5431
Jescorp
Des Plaines, IL 847-299-7800
Karolina Polymers
Hickory, NC 828-328-2247
Klockner Pentaplast of America
Gordonsville, VA 540-832-3600
KM International Corp
Kenton, TN 731-749-8700
Kurz Transfer Products LP
Huntersville, NC 800-950-3645
L&H Wood Manufacturing Company
Farmington, MI........................248-474-9000
Longhorn Packaging Inc
San Antonio, TX.......................800-433-7974
Luetzow Industries
South Milwaukee, WI...............800-558-6055
M S Plastics & Packaging Inc
Butler, NJ 800-593-1802
Mark Products Company
Denville, NJ 973-983-8818
Marshall Plastic Film Inc
Martin, MI 269-672-5511
Mason Transparent Package Company
Armonk, NY 718-792-6000
Merix Chemical Company
Chicago, IL 312-573-1400
Microplas Industries
Dunwoody, GA 800-952-4528
Mitsubishi Polyester Film, Inc.
Greer, SC. 864-879-5000
Modern Plastics
Shelton, CT 800-243-9696
Mohawk Northern Plastics
Auburn, WA 800-426-1100
Multi-Plastics Extrusions Inc
Hazleton, PA 570-455-2021
National Poly Bag Manufacturing Corporation
Brooklyn, NY 718-629-9800
Northeast Packaging Materials
Monsey, NY 845-426-2900
Now Plastics Inc
East Longmeadow, MA 413-525-1010
Occidental Chemical Corporation
Dallas, TX 800-733-3665
OMNOVA Solutions
Fairlawn, OH...........................330-869-4200
Packaging Materials Inc
Cambridge, OH 800-565-8550
Packing Material Company
Southfield, MI 248-489-7000
Pactiv LLC
Lake Forest, IL 800-476-4300
Pak-Sak Industries I
Sparta, MI 800-748-0431
Parade Packaging
Mundelein, IL 847-566-6264
Pater & Associates
Cincinnati, OH
Plascal Corp
Farmingdale, NY 800-899-7527
Plastic Craft Products Corp
West Nyack, NY 800-627-3010
Plastic Suppliers Inc
Columbus, OH 800-722-5577
Poly Plastic Products Inc
Delano, PA 570-467-3000
Portco Corporation
Vancouver, WA 800-426-1794
Printpack Inc.
Atlanta, GA 404-460-7000
Quality Films
Three Rivers, MI......................269-679-5263
Quantum Performance Films
Streamwood, IL........................800-323-6963
Rjr Technologies
Oakland, CA 510-638-5901
Robbie Manufacturing Inc
Lenexa, KS 800-255-6328
Roll-O-Sheets Canada
Barrie, ON. 888-767-3456
Roplast Industries Inc
Oroville, CA 800-767-5278
Rowland Technologies
Wallingford, CT 203-269-9500
Rutan Poly Industries Inc
Mahwah, NJ 800-872-1474
Seal-Tite Bag Company
Philadelphia, PA 717-917-1949
Sealed Air Corp
Charlotte, NC 800-391-5645

Senior Housing Options Inc
Denver, CO 800-659-2656
Shields Bag & Printing Co
Yakima, WA 800-541-8630
Ship Rite Packaging
Bergenfield, NJ 800-721-7447
Shippers Supply
Saskatoon, SK 800-661-5639
Sommers Plastic Product Co Inc
Clifton, NJ. 800-225-7677
Southern Film Extruders
High Point, NC 800-334-6101
Spartech Plastics
Wichita, KS.............................316-722-8621
Spartech Plastics
Portage, WI 800-998-7123
Spartech Poly Com
Clayton, MI 888-721-4242
Specialty Films & Associates
Hebron, KY 800-984-3346
Star Poly Bag Inc
Brooklyn, NY 718-384-7034
Stone Container
Chicago, IL 312-346-6600
Sungjae Corporation
Irvine, CA 949-757-1727
Teknor Apex Co
City of Industry, CA 800-556-3864
Terphane Inc
Bloomfield, NY 800-724-3456
Trident Plastics
Ivyland, PA 800-222-2318
Trinity Packaging
Cheektowaga, NY 800-778-3111
Trio Packaging Corp
Ronkonkoma, NY.....................800-331-0492
Triune Enterprises
Gardena, CA 310-719-1600
Tyco Plastics
Lakeville, MN 800-328-4080
UCB Inc
Smyrna, GA 770-970-8338
Ultrapak
Dunkirk, NY 800-228-6030
Uniplast Films
Palmer, MA 800-343-1295
V C 999 Packaging Systems
Kansas City, MO......................800-728-2999
Vacumet Corporation
Austell, GA 800-776-0865
VIFAN Canada
Lanoraie, QC. 800-557-0192
Virginia Plastics Co
Roanoke, VA 800-777-8541
Viskase Co Inc
Darien, IL 800-323-8562
Western Plastics
Portland, TN 615-325-7331
Western Plastics
Calhoun, GA 800-752-4106
Wisconsin Film & Bag Inc
Shawano, WI...........................800-765-9224
Wright Plastics Company
Prattville, AL 800-874-7659
Zimmer Custom-Made Packaging
Indianapolis, IN 317-263-3436

Pressure Sensitive

Amcor
Oshkosh, WI 800-544-4672
CL&D Graphics
Oconomowoc, WI.....................800-777-1114
Creative Coatings Corporation
Nashua, NH. 800-229-1957
FLEXcon Company
Spencer, MA............................508-885-8200
General Formulations
Sparta, MI 800-253-3664
MAC Tac LLC
Stow, OH 866-262-2822
Multi-Color Corp
Green Bay, WI. 800-236-8208
Shippers Supply
Winnipeg, NB 800-661-5639
Tyco Plastics
Lakeville, MN..........................800-328-4080

Foil

Aluminum

All Foils Inc
Strongsville, OH 800-521-0054
Alufoil Products Co Inc
Hauppauge, NY 631-231-4141
Burrows Paper Corp
Little Falls, NY 800-272-7122
Holo-Source Corporation
Livonia, MI 888-995-7799
JW Aluminum
Mt Holly, SC 800-568-1100
Norand Aluminum
Franklin, TX 615-771-5700
Novelis Foil Products
Atlanta, GA 800-776-8701
Packaging Dynamics International
Caldwell, OH 740-732-5665
Republic Foil
Danbury, CT 800-722-3645
Rjr Technologies
Oakland, CA 510-638-5901
Somerville Packaging
Mississauga, ON 905-678-8211
Source for Packaging
New York, NY 800-223-2527
Tilly Industries
St Laurent, QC 514-331-4922
Trinidad Benham Corporation
Denver, CO 303-220-1400
Unifoil Corp
Fairfield, NJ 973-244-9990
Western Plastics
Portland, TN 615-325-7331
Western Plastics
Calhoun, GA 800-752-4106

Pressure Sensitive

Advanced Labelworx
Anderson, SC 865-966-8711
MAC Tac LLC
Stow, OH .866-262-2822

Printed & Laminated

Advanced Labelworx
Anderson, SC 865-966-8711
All Foils Inc
Strongsville, OH 800-521-0054
Alufoil Products Co Inc
Hauppauge, NY 631-231-4141
Bagcraft Papercon
Chicago, IL 800-621-8468
Catty Inc
Harvard, IL 815-943-2288
Cincinnati Convertors Inc
Cincinnati, OH 513-731-6600
Clearwater Paper Corporation
Spokane, WA 877-847-7831
Formflex
Bloomingdale, IN 800-255-7659
Hampden Papers Inc
Holyoke, MA 413-536-1000
Kurz Transfer Products LP
Huntersville, NC 800-950-3645
Label Makers
Pleasant Prairie, WI 800-208-3331
Milprint
Oshkosh, WI 920-303-8600
Norand Aluminum
Franklin, TX 615-771-5700
Pakmark
Chesterfield, MO 800-423-1379
Paper Products Company
Cincinnati, OH 513-921-4717
Pater & Associates
Cincinnati, OH
Tolas Health Care Packaging
Feasterville Trevose, PA 215-322-7900
Unifoil Corp
Fairfield, NJ 973-244-9990

General

A & G Foods
Chicago, IL 773-783-1672
Americasia International
Hillsborough, NJ 609-608-6886

Barrington Packaging Systems Group
Harrison, NY 888-814-7999
Carmi Flavor & Fragrance Company
Commerce, CA 800-421-9647
CFC International, Inc.
Chicago Heights, IL 708-891-3456
CHEP Pallecon Solutions
Livonia, MI 888-873-2277
Cougar Packaging Concepts, Inc.
St. Charles, IL 630-689-4050
Cougar Packaging Solutions
Lemont, IL 630-231-7800
DuPont
Wilmington, DE 800-441-7515
Groeb Farms
Onsted, MI 800-530-9969
Harpak-Ulma
Taunton, MA 800-813-6644
Horton Fruit Co Inc
Louisville, KY 800-626-2245
Jowat Corp.
High Point, NC 800-322-4583
Kalle USA Inc
Gurnee, IL 847-775-0781
Khs USA Inc
Waukesha, WI 262-797-7200
MonoSol
Merrillville, IN 219-762-3165
ProMach
Covington, KY 866-776-6224
Tecnocap
Glen Dale, WV 800-999-2567
Weyauwega Star Dairy
Weyauwega, WI 888-813-9720

Inks

Indelible

Chicago Ink & Research Co
Antioch, IL 847-395-1078
Ideal Stencil Machine & Tape Company
Marion, IL 800-388-0162
Organic Products Co
Irving, TX .972-438-7321
Trident
Brookfield, CT 203-740-9333
Volk Corp
Farmington Hills, MI 800-521-6799
Wichita Stamp & Seal Inc
Wichita, KS 316-263-4223

Marking & Coding

ABM Marking
Belleville, IL 800-626-9012
Carteret Coding Inc
Clark, NJ .732-574-0900
Chicago Ink & Research Co
Antioch, IL 847-395-1078
Colorcon Inc
Harleysville, PA 215-256-7700
Custom Rubber Stamp Co
Crosby, MN 888-606-4579
Dixie Rubber Stamp & Seal Company
Atlanta, GA 404-875-8883
Domino Amjet Inc
Gurnee, IL 800-444-4512
Easterday Fluid Technologies
Saint Francis, WI 414-482-4488
Federal Stamp & Seal Manufacturing Company
Atlanta, GA 800-333-7726
Ferro Corporation
Mayfield Heights, OH 216-875-5600
Fox Stamp Sign & Specialty
Menasha, WI 920-725-2683
Fraser Stamp & Seal
Chicago, IL 800-540-8565
Frost Manufacturing Corp
Worcester, MA 800-462-0216
Garvey Products
Cincinnati, OH 513-771-8710
Graphic Impressions of Illinois
River Grove, IL 708-453-1100
Hartford Stamp Works
Hartford, CT 860-249-6205
Hiss Stamp Company
Columbus, OH 614-224-5119
Ideal Stencil Machine & Tape Company
Marion, IL 800-388-0162
Imaje
Kennesaw, GA 678-594-7153

Independent Ink
Gardena, CA 800-446-5538
Innovative Ceramic Corp
East Liverpool, OH 330-385-6515
Koehler-Gibson Marking
Buffalo, NY 800-875-1562
Marsh Company
Belleville, IL 800-527-6275
Mastermark
Kent, WA .206-762-9610
Modern Stamp Company
Baltimore, MD 800-727-3029
Muskogee Rubber Stamp & Seal Company
Fort Gibson, OK 918-478-3046
Organic Products Co
Irving, TX .972-438-7321
Quick Stamp & Sign Mfg
Lafayette, LA 337-232-2171
Richardson's Stamp Works
Houston, TX 713-973-0314
Sohn Manufacturing
Elkhart Lake, WI 920-876-3361
Southern Rubber Stamp
Tulsa, OK .888-826-4304
Starkey Chemical Process Company
La Grange, IL 800-323-3040
Tharo Systems Inc
Brunswick, OH 800-878-6833
Trident
Brookfield, CT 203-740-9333
Videojet Technologies Inc
Wood Dale, IL 800-843-3610
Volk Corp
Farmington Hills, MI 800-521-6799

Meat Branding

Ideal Stencil Machine & Tape Company
Marion, IL 800-388-0162
Service Stamp Works
Chicago, IL 312-666-8839

Jars

Canning & Preserving

Alcoa - Massena Operations
Massena, NY
Delta Plastics
Hot Springs, AR 501-760-3000

Glass

All American Container
Miami, FL .305-887-0797
Arkansas Glass Container Corp
Jonesboro, AR 800-527-4527
Bal/Foster Glass Container Company
Port Allegany, PA 814-642-2521
Ball Glass Container Corporation
El Monte, CA 626-448-9831
Gessner Products
Ambler, PA 800-874-7808
Greenfield Packaging
White Plains, NY 914-993-0233
Indiana Glass Company
Columbus, OH 800-543-0357
Indianapolis Container Company
Indianapolis, IN 800-760-3318
LMK Containers
Centerville, UT 626-821-9984
Louisville Container Company
Indianapolis, IN 888-539-7225
Olcott Plastics
St Charles, IL 888-313-5277
Promens
St. John, NB 800-295-3725
Richards Packaging
Memphis, TN 800-583-0327
World Kitchen
Elmira, NY 800-999-3436

Plastic

Delta Plastics
Hot Springs, AR 501-760-3000

Labels

A-1 Business Supplies Inc
Dover, NJ .800-631-3421

Aabbitt Adhesives
Chicago, IL . . . 800-222-2488
About Packaging Robotics
Thornton, CO . . . 303-449-2559
AC Label Company
Provo, UT . . . 801-642-3500
Accuform Manufacturing, Inc.
Vacaville, CA . . . 800-233-3352
Ad Mart Identity Group
Danville, KY . . . 800-354-2102
Adhesive Label
Minneapolis, MN . . . 763-546-1182
Adhesive Products Inc
Vernon, CA . . . 800-669-5516
Adhesives Research
Glen Rock, PA. . . . 800-445-6240
Adstick Custom Labels Inc
Denver, CO . . . 800-255-7314
Advanced Labelworx
Anderson, SC . . . 865-966-8711
Advanced Labelworx Inc
Oak Ridge, TN . . . 864-224-2122
Ahlstrom Filtration LLC
Madisonville, KY . . . 270-821-0140
Aigner Index
New Windsor, NY. . . . 800-242-3919
ALLIED Graphics Inc
St Michael, MN. . . . 800-490-9931
Altrua Marketing & Design
Tallahassee, FL . . . 800-443-6939
AM Graphics
Edina, MN. . . . 612-341-2020
American Forms & Labels
Boise, ID . . . 800-388-3554
American Labelmark Co
Chicago, IL . . . 800-621-5808
Andrew H Lawson Co
Philadelphia, PA . . . 800-411-6628
Andy Printed Products
Lagrangeville, NY . . . 845-223-5101
Appleson Press
Syosset, NY. . . . 800-888-2775
Artistic Packaging Concepts
Massapequa Pk, NY . . . 516-797-4020
ASCENT Technics Corporation
Brick, NJ. . . . 800-774-7077
ATK
Chicago, IL . . . 800-522-3582
ATL-East Tag & Label Inc
West Chester, PA. . . . 866-381-8744
Atlas Labels
Montreal, QC . . . 514-852-7000
Atlas Packaging Inc
Opa Locka, FL . . . 800-662-0630
Atlas Tag & Label Inc
Neenah, WI. . . . 800-558-6418
Auburn Label & Tag Company
New York, NY . . . 212-971-0338
Avery Dennison Corporation
Mentor, OH. . . . 440-534-6000
Axon Styrotech
Raleigh, NC . . . 800-598-8601
Baltimore Tape Products Inc
Sykesville, MD . . . 410-795-0063
Barkley Filing Supplies
Hattiesburg, MS . . . 800-647-3070
Baur Tape & Label Co
San Antonio, TX. . . . 877-738-3222
Bedford Industries
Worthington, MN . . . 800-533-5314
Bertek Systems Inc
Fairfax, VT . . . 800-367-0210
Born Printing Company
Baltimore, MD . . . 410-646-7768
Burford Corp
Maysville, OK. . . . 877-287-3673
Bynoe Printers
New York, NY . . . 212-662-5041
C-P Flexible Packaging
Newtown, PA . . . 800-448-8183
Carlton Industries
La Grange, TX . . . 800-231-5988
CCL Label Inc
Cold Spring, KY. . . . 800-422-6633
Cellotape, Inc.
Newark, CA . . . 510-651-5551
Central Decal
Burr Ridge, IL. . . . 800-869-7654
Central Package & Display
Minneapolis, MN . . . 763-425-7444
Christman Screenprint Inc
Springfield, MI . . . 800-962-9330
Church Offset Printing Inc
Albert Lea, MN. . . . 800-345-2116
CL&D Graphics
Oconomowoc, WI. . . . 800-777-1114
Coast Label Co
Fountain Valley, CA . . . 800-995-0483
Colonial Transparent Products Company
Hicksville, NY . . . 516-822-4430
Comm-Pak
Opelika, AL. . . . 334-749-6201
Computerized Machinery Systs
Maple Grove, MN. . . . 763-493-0099
Computype Inc
St Paul, MN. . . . 800-328-0852
Conimar Corp
Ocala, FL. . . . 800-874-9735
Consolidated Label Company
Longwood, FL . . . 800-475-2235
Continental Identification
Sparta, MI . . . 800-247-2499
Covergent Label Technology
Tampa, FL . . . 800-252-6111
Creative Label Designers
Lees Summit, MO. . . . 816-537-8757
Crown Label Company
Santa Ana, CA . . . 800-422-3590
Cucamonga Sign Shop LLC
Rancho Cucamonga, CA . . . 909-945-5888
Cummins Label Co
Kalamazoo, MI . . . 800-280-7589
Curtis 1000
Duluth, GA . . . 877-287-8715
Curzon Promotional Graphics
Omaha, NE . . . 800-769-7446
Custom Card & Label Corporation
Lincoln Park, NJ. . . . 973-492-0022
Custom Stamp Company
Anza, CA. . . . 323-292-0753
D A C Labels & Graphic
Dallas, TX . . . 800-483-1700
Dana Labels
Beaverton, OR . . . 800-255-1492
Darson Corp
Detroit, MI . . . 800-783-7781
Data Visible Corporation
Charlottesville, VA . . . 800-368-3494
Daydots
Fort Worth, TX . . . 800-321-3687
Daymark Safety Systems
Bowling Green, OH . . . 419-353-2458
De Leone Corp
Redmond, OR . . . 541-504-8311
Deadline Press
Kennesaw, GA . . . 770-419-2232
Decal Techniques Inc
West Babylon, NY . . . 800-735-3322
Deco Labels & Tags
Toronto, ON . . . 888-496-9029
Decorated Products Company
Westfield, MA. . . . 413-568-0944
Design Label Manufacturing
East Lyme, CT. . . . 800-666-1575
Design-Mark Industries
Wareham, MA. . . . 800-451-3275
Donnick Label Systems
Jacksonville, FL . . . 800-334-7849
Dot-It Food Safety Products
Arlington, TX . . . 800-642-3687
Double Envelope Corp
Roanoke, VA. . . . 540-362-3311
Dow Industries
Wilmington, MA. . . . 800-776-1201
Drs Designs
Bethel, CT. . . . 888-792-3740
Eaton Manufacturing Co
Houston, TX . . . 800-328-6610
Ebel Tape & Label
Cincinnati, OH . . . 513-471-1067
Economy Label Sales Company
Daytona Beach, FL. . . . 386-253-4741
Emedco
Williamsville, NY . . . 877-765-8386
Engraving Services Co.
Woodville South, SA
EPI World Graphics
Midlothian, IL. . . . 708-389-7500
Epsen Hillmer Graphics Co
Omaha, NE . . . 800-228-9940
ERS International
Norwalk, CT . . . 800-377-4685
Esselte Meto
Morris Plains, NJ . . . 800-645-3290
Farnell Packaging
Dartmouth, NS . . . 800-565-9378
Fast Bags
Fort Worth, TX . . . 800-321-3687
Federal Label Systems
Elmhurst, NY . . . 800-238-0015
Fernqvist Labeling Solutions
Mountain View, CA . . . 800-426-8215
Ferro Corporation
Mayfield Heights, OH . . . 216-875-5600
FFR Merchandising Inc
Twinsburg, OH . . . 800-422-2547
Fleming Packaging Corporation
Peoria, IL. . . . 309-676-7657
FLEXcon Company
Spencer, MA . . . 508-885-8200
Flexible Tape & Label Co
Memphis, TN . . . 901-522-1410
Flexo Graphics
Amarillo, TX. . . . 866-533-5396
Forest Manufacturing Co
Twinsburg, OH . . . 330-425-3805
Fort Dearborn Company
Elk Grove, IL . . . 847-357-9500
Fotel
Lombard, IL . . . 800-834-4920
Foxon Co
Providence, RI . . . 800-556-6943
France Personalized Signs
Cleveland, OH . . . 216-241-2198
Frost Manufacturing Corp
Worcester, MA . . . 800-462-0216
Garvey Products
Cincinnati, OH . . . 513-771-8710
Garvey Products
West Chester, OH . . . 800-543-1908
Gbs
North Canton, OH. . . . 800-552-2427
GCA
Huntington Beach, CA . . . 714-379-4911
General Press Corp
Natrona Heights, PA . . . 724-224-3500
General Tape & Supply
Wixom, MI . . . 800-490-3633
General Trade Mark Labelcraft
Staten Island, NY . . . 718-448-9800
Gintzler Graphics Inc
Buffalo, NY. . . . 716-631-9700
Globe Ticket & Label Company
Warminster, PA . . . 800-523-5968
GM Nameplate
Seattle, WA . . . 800-366-7668
Grand Rapids Label
Grand Rapids, MI . . . 616-776-2778
Grand Valley Labels
Grand Rapids, MI
Graphic Impressions of Illinois
River Grove, IL. . . . 708-453-1100
Graphic Packaging Corporation
Golden, CO . . . 800-677-2886
Graphic Technology
New Century, KS . . . 800-767-9920
Graphics Unlimited
San Diego, CA . . . 858-453-4031
Green Bay Packaging Inc.
Green Bay, WI. . . . 920-433-5111
Greenbush Tape & Label Inc
Albany, NY . . . 518-465-2389
Gulf Arizona Packaging
Humble, TX . . . 800-364-3887
H B Fuller Co
St. Paul, MN . . . 651-236-5900
Hal Mather & Sons
Woodstock, IL. . . . 800-338-4007
Halpak Plastics
Deer Park, NY. . . . 800-442-5725
Hano Business Forms
Wilbraham, MA . . . 413-781-7800
Harris & Company
Salem, OH. . . . 330-332-4127
Herche Warehouse
Denver, CO . . . 303-371-8186
Holo-Source Corporation
Livonia, MI. . . . 888-995-7799
Home Plastics Inc
Des Moines, IA. . . . 515-265-2562
Hub Labels Inc
Hagerstown, MD. . . . 800-433-4532
Hurst Labeling Systems
Chatsworth, CA . . . 800-969-1705
Imprinting Systems Specialty
Charlotte, NC . . . 800-497-1403

Industrial Nameplate Inc
Warminster, PA 800-878-6263
Inland Label & Marketing Svc
La Crosse, WI 800-657-4413
Innovative Folding Carton Company
South Plainfield, NJ 908-757-0205
Innovative Packaging Solution
Martin, MI. 616-656-2100
Inovar Packaging Group
Arlington, TX 800-285-2235
Intermec Technologies Corporation
Everett, WA 425-348-2600
Interstate Packaging
White Bluff, TN 800-251-1072
Itac Label & Tag Corp
Brooklyn, NY 718-625-2148
J M Packaging Co
Warren, MI 586-771-7800
J.V. Reed & Company
Louisville, KY 877-258-7333
John Henry Packaging
Penngrove, CA 800-327-5997
KAPCO
Kent, OH 800-843-5368
Kemex Meat Brands
Washington, DC 301-277-2444
Kennedy Group
Willoughby, OH 440-951-7660
KHS Co
West Simsbury, CT 860-658-9454
KWIK Lok Corp
Yakima, WA 800-688-5945
L & N Label Co
Clearwater, FL 800-944-5401
L G I Intl Inc
Portland, OR 800-345-0534
Label Art
Tucker, GA 800-652-1072
Label House
Fullerton, CA 800-499-5858
Label Products Inc
Burnsville, MN 877-370-0688
Label Specialties Inc
Placentia, CA 800-635-2386
Label Systems
Bridgeport, CT 203-333-5503
Label Systems
Newmarket, ON 905-836-7844
Label Systems & Solutions
Bohemia, NY 800-811-2560
Label Systems Inc
Addison, TX 800-220-9552
Label Technology Inc
Merced, CA. 800-388-1990
Labelmart
Maple Grove, MN 888-577-0141
Labelmax Inc
Laredo, TX 956-722-6493
Labelprint America
Newburyport, MA 978-463-4004
Labelquest Inc
Elmhurst, IL 800-999-5301
Labels By Pulizzi Inc
Williamsport, PA. 570-326-1244
Lacroix Packaging
St-Placide, Quebec, QC 450-258-2262
Lawrence Schiff Silk Mills
New York, NY 800-272-4433
Leathertone
Findlay, OH. 419-429-0188
Lewis Label Products Corporation
Fort Worth, TX 800-772-7728
Lewisburg Printing
Lewisburg, TN 800-559-1526
Liberty Label
Liberty, MO. 800-783-5285
License Ad Plate Co
Cleveland, OH 216-265-4200
Lifeline Technology Inc
Morris Plains, NJ 973-984-0525
Lion Labels Inc
South Easton, MA. 800-875-5300
Lone Peak Labeling Systems
West Valley City, UT 800-658-8599
Long Island Stamp Corporation
Flushing, NY. 800-547-8267
Lord Label Group
Charlotte, NC 800-341-5225
Los Angeles Label Company
Commerce, CA 800-606-5223
Louis Roesch Company
Foster City, CA 415-621-4700

LPI Imports
Chicago, IL 877-389-6563
LTI Printing Inc
Sturgis, MI 269-651-7574
Lustrecal
Lodi, CA 800-234-6264
Mail-Well Label
Sparks, NV 775-359-1703
Mail-Well Label
Baltimore, MD 800-637-4879
Mar-Boro Printing & Advertising Specialties
Brooklyn, NY 718-336-4051
Mark-It Rubber Stamp & Label Company
Stamford, CT. 203-348-3204
Marklite Line
Bellwood, IL 708-668-4900
Master Tape & Label Printers
Chicago, IL 800-621-5801
Mateer Burt
Exton, PA 800-345-1308
Mc Court Label Co
Lewis Run, PA 800-458-2390
Merchants Publishing Company
Kalamazoo, MI 269-345-1175
Meyer Label Company
Fort Myers, FL 239-489-0342
Meyers Printing Co
Minneapolis, MN 763-533-9730
Miami Systems Corporation
Blue Ash, OH 800-543-4540
Mid South Graphics
Nashville, TN 615-331-4210
Middleton Printing & Label Co
Grand Rapids, MI 800-952-0076
Mister Label, Inc
Bluffton, SC 800-732-0439
Modern Stamp Company
Baltimore, MD 800-727-3029
Morris Industries
Forestville, MD. 301-568-5005
Moss Inc
Elk Grove Vlg, IL 800-341-1557
Multi-Color Corp
Green Bay, WI. 800-236-8208
Nameplate
St Paul, MN. 651-228-1522
Nashua Corporation
Nashua, NH. 603-661-2004
Nashua Corporation
Park Ridge, IL 800-323-4265
National Emblem
Carson, CA 800-877-5325
National Label Co
Lafayette Hill, PA 610-825-3250
National Marking Products Inc
Henrico, VA 800-482-1553
National Printing Converters
Encino, CA 818-906-7936
National Tape Corporation
New Orleans, LA 800-535-8846
Nationwide Pennant & Flag Mfg
San Antonio, TX. 800-383-3524
Neal Walters Poster Corporation
Bentonville, AR 501-273-2489
New England Label
Barre, VT 800-368-3932
New Era Label Corporation
Belleville, NJ 973-759-2444
North American Packaging Corp
New York, NY 800-499-3521
Northern Berkshire Tourist
North Adams, MA 413-663-9204
Nosco
Waukegan, IL 847-360-4806
Old English Printing & Label Company
Delray Beach, FL 561-997-9990
Ozark Tape & Label Co
Springfield, MO 417-831-1444
Pace Labels Inc
Williamston, SC 800-789-1592
Package Containers Inc
Canby, OR. 800-266-5806
Package Service Company of Colorado
Northmoor, MO 800-748-7799
Package Systems Corporation
Danielson, CT. 800-522-3548
Packaging Materials Co
El Paso, TX. 800-325-4195
Packaging Solutions
Los Altos Hills, CA 650-917-1022
Paco Label Systems Inc
Tyler, TX. 800-346-4185

Pakmark
Chesterfield, MO 800-423-1379
Pamco Label Co Inc
Des Plaines, IL 847-803-2200
Panther Industries Inc
Highlands Ranch, CO 800-530-6018
Paper Product Specialties
Waukesha, WI 262-549-1730
Parisian Novelty Company
Homewood, IL 773-847-1212
Paxar
Paterson, NJ 973-684-6564
Pharmaceutic Litho & Label Co.
Simi Valley, CA. 800-882-9743
Phenix Label Co
Olathe, KS. 800-274-3649
Philipp Lithographing Co
Grafton, WI. 800-657-0871
Photo Graphics Co
Grandview, MO. 816-761-3333
Pierrepont Visual Graphics Inc
Rochester, NY 585-235-5620
Pioneer Labels Inc
Denver, CO 877-744-1606
Pittsfield Weaving Company
Pittsfield, NH 603-435-8301
Plasti Print Inc
Burlingame, CA 650-652-4950
Precision Printing & Packaging
Clarksville, TN 800-500-4526
Premier Southern Ticket Co
Cincinnati, OH 800-331-2283
Prestige Label Company
Burgaw, NC 800-969-4449
Prestolabels.Com
Tipp City, OH 800-201-7120
Primera Technology
Plymouth, MN. 800-797-2772
Print & Peel
New York, NY 800-451-0807
Print-O-Tape Inc
Mundelein, IL 800-346-6311
Printsource Group
Wakefield, RI 401-789-9339
Pro-Ad-Co Inc
Portland, OR 800-287-5885
Promo Edge
Wall Township, NJ 732-938-4242
Qsx Labels
Everett, MA 800-225-3496
Quali-Tech Tape & Label
Denver, CO
R R Donnelley
Chicago, IL 800-742-4455
Racine County Court Cmmssnr
Racine, WI 800-242-4202
Randall Printing
Brockton, MA. 508-588-3830
Raypress Corp
Hoover, AL 800-423-3731
Recco International
West Columbia, SC 800-334-3008
Regency Label Corporation
Wood Ridge, NJ 201-342-2288
Reid Graphics Inc
Andover, MA 800-887-7461
Reidler Decal Corporation
Saint Clair, PA. 800-628-7770
Rhode Island Label Work Inc
West Warwick, RI 401-828-6400
Rice Packaging Inc
Ellington, CT 800-367-6725
Richmond Printed Tape & Label
Hatfield, PA. 800-522-3525
Robinson Tape & Label
Branford, CT 800-433-7102
Rose City Label
Portland, OR 800-547-9920
Rothchild Printing Company
Flushing, NY. 800-238-0015
Royal Label Co
Dorchester, MA. 617-825-6050
RSI ID Technologies
St. Paul, MN. 888-364-3577
S Walter Packaging Corp
Philadelphia, PA 888-429-5673
Samuels Products Inc
Blue Ash, OH 800-543-7155
San Miguel Label Manufacturing
Ciales, PR 787-871-3120
Sancoa International
Lumberton, NJ 609-953-5050

Seal-Tite Bag Company
Philadelphia, PA 717-917-1949
Seneca Tape & Label
Cleveland, OH 800-251-0514
Sesame Label System
New York, NY 800-551-3020
Seton Indentification Products
Branford, CT 800-571-2596
SFBC, LLC dba Seaboard Folding Box
Fitchburg, MA 800-225-6313
Shippers Supply
Saskatoon, SK. 800-661-5639
Shippers Supply, Labelgraphic
Calgary, AB. 800-661-5639
Signature Packaging
West Orange, NJ 800-376-2299
Smurfit Stone Container
St Louis, MO. 314-679-2300
Smyth Co
Bedford, VA 800-950-7011
Smyth Co LLC
St Paul, MN. 800-473-3464
Sohn Manufacturing
Elkhart Lake, WI. 920-876-3361
Source for Packaging
New York, NY 800-223-2527
Southern Atlantic Label Co
Chesapeake, VA 800-456-5999
Southern Imperial Inc
Rockford, IL 800-747-4665
Steven Label Corp
Santa Fe Springs, CA 800-752-4968
Stoffel Seals Corp
Tallapoosa, GA 800-422-8247
Storad Tape Company
Marion, OH. 740-382-6440
Stratix Corp
Peachtree Cor, GA 800-883-8300
Stricker & Co
La Plata, MD. 301-934-8346
Stripper Bags
Henderson, NV 800-354-2247
Superior Products Company
Saint Paul, MN 800-328-9800
Swan Label & Tag Co
Coraopolis, PA 412-264-9000
Syracuse Label Co
Liverpool, NY. 315-422-1037
System Graphics Inc
St Louis, MO. 800-221-7858
T & T Industries Inc
Fort Mohave, AZ 800-437-6246
TAC-PAD
Irvine, CA. 800-947-1609
Tape & Label Converters
Santa Fe Springs, CA 888-285-2462
Tape & Label Engineering
St Petersburg, FL 800-237-8955
Tarason Packaging, LLC.
Conover, NC 828-464-4743
TeleTech Label Company
Fort Collins, CO 888-403-8253
Tharo Systems Inc
Brunswick, OH 800-878-6833
Three P
Salt Lake City, UT 801-486-7407
Thunderbird Label Corportion
Fairfield, NJ 973-575-6677
Timely Signs Inc
Elmont, NY. 800-457-4467
Timemed Labeling Systems
Valencia, CA 818-897-1111
Toledo Ticket Co
Toledo, OH 800-533-6620
Trident
Brookfield, CT 203-740-9333
Trumbull Nameplates
New Smyrna Beach, FL 386-423-1105
Twin City Pricing & Label
Minneapolis, MN 800-328-5076
Typecraft Wood & Jones
Pasadena, CA 626-795-8093
United Ad Label
Downers Grove, IL. 800-423-4643
United Label Corp
Newark, NJ 800-252-0917
United Seal & Tag Corporation
Port Charlotte, FL 800-211-9552
Universal Tag Inc
Dudley, MA. 800-332-8247
University Products
Holyoke, MA 800-628-9281

US Label Corporation
Greensboro, NC 336-332-7000
Vacumet Corp
Wayne, NJ 973-628-1067
Varitronic Systems
Brooklyn Park, MN. 763-536-6400
Vetter Vineyards Winery
Westfield, NY 716-326-3100
Viking Identification Product
Hopkins, MN 952-935-5245
Viking Label Inc
Nisswa, MN 800-247-6573
Vomela/Harbor Graphics
St Paul, MN. 800-645-1012
Wallace Computer Services
Chicago, IL 888-925-8324
Walle Corp
New Orleans, LA 800-942-6761
Wishbone Utensil Tableware Line
Wheat Ridge, CO 866-266-5928
Worthen Industries Inc
Nashua, NH. 603-888-5443
WS Packaging Group Inc
Dallas, TX. 214-330-7770
WS Packaging Group Inc
Algoma, WI. 800-236-3424
WS Packaging Group Inc
Rochester, NY 800-836-8186
WS Packaging Group Inc
Oak Creek, WI 800-837-3838
WS Packaging Group Inc
Green Bay, WI. 877-977-5177
WS Packaging Group Inc
Neenah, WI. 888-532-3334
Wt Nickell Co
Batavia, OH. 888-899-1991
Yerecic Label Co
New Kensington, PA. 724-334-3300
Yeuell Name Plate & Label
Woburn, MA 781-933-2984

Pressure Sensitive

AC Label Company
Provo, UT 801-642-3500
Accuform Manufacturing, Inc.
Vacaville, CA 800-233-3352
Ad Mart Identity Group
Danville, KY. 800-354-2102
Adhesive Products Inc
Vernon, CA 800-669-5516
Adstick Custom Labels Inc
Denver, CO 800-255-7314
Advanced Labelworx
Anderson, SC 865-966-8711
Advanced Labelworx Inc
Oak Ridge, TN 864-224-2122
ALLIED Graphics Inc
St Michael, MN. 800-490-9931
AM Graphics
Edina, MN. 612-341-2020
American Forms & Labels
Boise, ID 800-388-3554
American Labelmark Co
Chicago, IL 800-621-5808
Andy Printed Products
Lagrangeville, NY 845-223-5101
Appleson Press
Syosset, NY. 800-888-2775
ATL-East Tag & Label Inc
West Chester, PA. 866-381-8744
Atlas Tag & Label Inc
Neenah, WI. 800-558-6418
Auburn Label & Tag Company
New York, NY 212-971-0338
Avery Dennison Corporation
Mentor, OH 440-534-6000
Baltimore Tape Products Inc
Sykesville, MD 410-795-0063
Barkley Filing Supplies
Hattiesburg, MS 800-647-3070
Bertek Systems Inc
Fairfax, VT 800-367-0210
CCL Label Inc
Cold Spring, KY 800-422-6633
Cellotape, Inc.
Newark, CA 510-651-5551
Central Decal
Burr Ridge, IL. 800-869-7654
CL&D Graphics
Oconomowoc, WI 800-777-1114

Comm-Pak
Opelika, AL. 334-749-6201
Computerized Machinery Systs
Maple Grove, MN. 763-493-0099
Consolidated Label Company
Longwood, FL 800-475-2235
Creative Label Designers
Lees Summit, MO. 816-537-8757
Cucamonga Sign Shop LLC
Rancho Cucamonga, CA 909-945-5888
Cummins Label Co
Kalamazoo, MI. 800-280-7589
Custom Card & Label Corporation
Lincoln Park, NJ. 973-492-0022
Custom Stamp Company
Anza, CA. 323-292-0753
D A C Labels & Graphic
Dallas, TX. 800-483-1700
Dana Labels
Beaverton, OR 800-255-1492
De Leone Corp
Redmond, OR 541-504-8311
Deadline Press
Kennesaw, GA 770-419-2232
Deco Labels & Tags
Toronto, ON 888-496-9029
Design Label Manufacturing
East Lyme, CT. 800-666-1575
Double Envelope Corp
Roanoke, VA. 540-362-3311
Dow Industries
Wilmington, MA 800-776-1201
Drs Designs
Bethel, CT. 888-792-3740
Eagles Printing & Label
Eau Claire, WI 715-835-6631
Ebel Tape & Label
Cincinnati, OH 513-471-1067
Economy Label Sales Company
Daytona Beach, FL 386-253-4741
Elmark Packaging Inc
West Chester, PA. 800-670-9688
Emedco
Williamsville, NY 877-765-8386
Epsen Hillmer Graphics Co
Omaha, NE 800-228-9940
Farnell Packaging
Dartmouth, NS 800-565-9378
Federal Label Systems
Elmhurst, NY 800-238-0015
FLEXcon Company
Spencer, MA. 508-885-8200
Flexible Tape & Label Co
Memphis, TN 901-522-1410
Flexo Graphics
Amarillo, TX. 866-533-5396
Forest Manufacturing Co
Twinsburg, OH 330-425-3805
Foxon Co
Providence, RI 800-556-6943
Garvey Products
Cincinnati, OH 513-771-8710
Garvey Products
West Chester, OH 800-543-1908
Gbs
North Canton, OH. 800-552-2427
General Tape & Supply
Wixom, MI 800-490-3633
General Trade Mark Labelcraft
Staten Island, NY 718-448-9800
Gintzler Graphics Inc
Buffalo, NY. 716-631-9700
Globe Ticket & Label Company
Warminster, PA 800-523-5968
Grand Rapids Label
Grand Rapids, MI 616-776-2778
Grand Valley Labels
Grand Rapids, MI
Graphic Impressions of Illinois
River Grove, IL 708-453-1100
Graphic Technology
New Century, KS 800-767-9920
Greenbush Tape & Label Inc
Albany, NY. 518-465-2389
Greenfield Packaging
White Plains, NY 914-993-0233
Gulf Arizona Packaging
Humble, TX 800-364-3887
Herche Warehouse
Denver, CO. 303-371-8186
Houston Label
Pasadena, TX 800-477-6995

Hub Labels Inc
Hagerstown, MD. 800-433-4532
Hurst Labeling Systems
Chatsworth, CA 800-969-1705
Imprinting Systems Specialty
Charlotte, NC 800-497-1403
Innovative Folding Carton Company
South Plainfield, NJ 908-757-0205
Innovative Packaging Solution
Martin, MI. 616-656-2100
Interstate Packaging
White Bluff, TN 800-251-1072
Itac Label & Tag Corp
Brooklyn, NY 718-625-2148
KAPCO
Kent, OH. .800-843-5368
KHS Co
West Simsbury, CT 860-658-9454
L & N Label Co
Clearwater, FL 800-944-5401
L G I Intl Inc
Portland, OR 800-345-0534
Label House
Fullerton, CA 800-499-5858
Label Products Inc
Burnsville, MN 877-370-0688
Label Specialties Inc
Placentia, CA 800-635-2386
Label Systems
Bridgeport, CT 203-333-5503
Label Systems
Newmarket, ON 905-836-7844
Label Systems & Solutions
Bohemia, NY 800-811-2560
Label Systems Inc
Addison, TX 800-220-9552
Label Technology Inc
Merced, CA. 800-388-1990
Label-Aire Inc
Fullerton, CA 714-441-0700
Labelmart
Maple Grove, MN 888-577-0141
Labelmax Inc
Laredo, TX 956-722-6493
Labelprint America
Newburyport, MA 978-463-4004
Labels By Pulizzi Inc
Williamsport, PA. 570-326-1244
Lewis Label Products Corporation
Fort Worth, TX 800-772-7728
Liberty Label
Liberty, MO. 800-783-5285
License Ad Plate Co
Cleveland, OH 216-265-4200
Lion Labels Inc
South Easton, MA. 800-875-5300
Long Island Stamp Corporation
Flushing, NY. 800-547-8267
M & M Display
Philadelphia, PA 800-874-7171
Marklite Line
Bellwood, IL 708-668-4900
Master Tape & Label Printers
Chicago, IL 800-621-5801
Mc Court Label Co
Lewis Run, PA 800-458-2390
Metspeed Labels
Levittown, PA. 888-886-0638
Meyer Label Company
Fort Myers, FL 239-489-0342
Meyers Printing Co
Minneapolis, MN 763-533-9730
Mid South Graphics
Nashville, TN 615-331-4210
Middleton Printing & Label Co
Grand Rapids, MI 800-952-0076
Mister Label, Inc
Bluffton, SC 800-732-0439
Morris Industries
Forestville, MD. 301-568-5005
Moss Inc
Elk Grove Vlg, IL. 800-341-1557
MPI Label Systems
Sebring, OH 800-837-2134
Multi-Color Corp
Green Bay, WI. 800-236-8208
Nashua Corporation
Nashua, NH. 603-661-2004
Nashua Corporation
Park Ridge, IL. 800-323-4265
National Printing Converters
Encino, CA 818-906-7936

National Tape Corporation
New Orleans, LA 800-535-8846
Neal Walters Poster Corporation
Bentonville, AR 501-273-2489
New England Label
Barre, VT .800-368-3932
New Era Label Corporation
Belleville, NJ 973-759-2444
NJM Packaging
Lebanon, NH. 800-432-2990
Ozark Tape & Label Co
Springfield, MO 417-831-1444
Pace Labels Inc
Williamston, SC 800-789-1592
Package Service Company of Colorado
Northmoor, MO 800-748-7799
Package Systems Corporation
Danielson, CT. 800-522-3548
Packaging Materials Co
El Paso, TX. 800-325-4195
Pakmark
Chesterfield, MO 800-423-1379
Pamco Label Co Inc
Des Plaines, IL 847-803-2200
Paper Product Specialties
Waukesha, WI. 262-549-1730
Pierrepont Visual Graphics Inc
Rochester, NY. 585-235-5620
Plasti Print Inc
Burlingame, CA 650-652-4950
Premier Southern Ticket Co
Cincinnati, OH 800-331-2283
Print & Peel
New York, NY 800-451-0807
Print-O-Tape Inc
Mundelein, IL 800-346-6311
Printsource Group
Wakefield, RI 401-789-9339
Promo Edge
Wall Township, NJ 732-938-4242
Quali-Tech Tape & Label
Denver, CO
R R Donnelley
Chicago, IL 800-742-4455
Racine County Court Cmmssnr
Racine, WI 800-242-4202
Raypress Corp
Hoover, AL 800-423-3731
Regency Label Corporation
Wood Ridge, NJ 201-342-2288
Rhode Island Label Work Inc
West Warwick, RI 401-828-6400
Rice Packaging Inc
Ellington, CT 800-367-6725
Richmond Printed Tape & Label
Hatfield, PA. 800-522-3525
Robinson Tape & Label
Branford, CT 800-433-7102
Rose City Label
Portland, OR 800-547-9920
Royal Label Co
Dorchester, MA. 617-825-6050
Samuels Products Inc
Blue Ash, OH 800-543-7155
Sancoa International
Lumberton, NJ 609-953-5050
Seneca Tape & Label
Cleveland, OH 800-251-0514
Seton Indentification Products
Branford, CT. 800-571-2596
Smyth Co
Bedford, VA 800-950-7011
Smyth Co LLC
St Paul, MN. 800-473-3464
Source for Packaging
New York, NY 800-223-2527
Southern Atlantic Label Co
Chesapeake, VA 800-456-5999
Steven Label Corp
Santa Fe Springs, CA 800-752-4968
Stoffel Seals Corp
Tallapoosa, GA 800-422-8247
Storad Tape Company
Marion, OH. 740-382-6440
Stratix Group
Peachtree Cor, GA 800-883-8300
Stripper Bags
Henderson, NV 800-354-2247
Swan Label & Tag Co
Coraopolis, PA 412-264-9000
Syracuse Label Co
Liverpool, NY 315-422-1037

System Graphics Inc
St Louis, MO. 800-221-7858
TAC-PAD
Irvine, CA .800-947-1609
Tape & Label Converters
Santa Fe Springs, CA 888-285-2462
Tape & Label Engineering
St Petersburg, FL 800-237-8955
Tarason Packaging, LLC.
Conover, NC 828-464-4743
TeleTech Label Company
Fort Collins, CO 888-403-8253
Tharo Systems Inc
Brunswick, OH 800-878-6833
Three P
Salt Lake City, UT 801-486-7407
Thunderbird Label Corportion
Fairfield, NJ 973-575-6677
Timemed Labeling Systems
Valencia, CA 818-897-1111
Trident
Brookfield, CT 203-740-9333
Trumbull Nameplates
New Smyrna Beach, FL 386-423-1105
United Ad Label
Downers Grove, IL 800-423-4643
United Seal & Tag Corporation
Port Charlotte, FL 800-211-9552
Universal Tag Inc
Dudley, MA. 800-332-8247
University Products
Holyoke, MA 800-628-9281
Viking Identification Product
Hopkins, MN 952-935-5245
Vomela/Harbor Graphics
St Paul, MN. 800-645-1012
Wallace Computer Services
Chicago, IL 888-925-8324
Wishbone Utensil Tableware Line
Wheat Ridge, CO 866-266-5928
WS Packaging Group Inc
Dallas, TX. 214-330-7770
WS Packaging Group Inc
Algoma, WI. 800-236-3424
WS Packaging Group Inc
Rochester, NY. 800-836-8186
WS Packaging Group Inc
Oak Creek, WI. 800-837-3838
Wt Nickell Co
Batavia, OH. 888-899-1991
Yerecic Label Co
New Kensington, PA. 724-334-3300

Private Label

Adrienne's Gourmet Foods
Santa Barbara, CA 800-937-7010
Alewel's Country Meats
Warrensburg, MO 800-353-8553
Baldwin Richardson Foods
Oakbrook Terrace, IL 866-644-2732
Bunzl Distribution USA
St. Louis, MO. 888-997-5959
Century Foods Intl LLC
Sparta, WI. 800-269-1901
Old Mansion Inc
Petersburg, VA 800-476-1877
Treofan America LLC
Winston Salem, NC. 800-424-6273

Linings

Box, Carton, Case & Crate

Atlantic Foam & Packaging Company
Sanford, FL 407-328-9444
Chalmur Bag Company, LLC
Philadelphia, PA 800-349-2247
Conwed Global Netting Sltns
Roanoke, VA 800-368-3610
Grayling Industries
Alpharetta, GA 800-635-1551
Greenfield Packaging
White Plains, NY 914-993-0233
Gulf Arizona Packaging
Humble, TX 800-364-3887
Herche Warehouse
Denver, CO 303-371-8186
IB Concepts
Elizabeth, NJ 888-671-0800
J A Heilferty & Co
Teaneck, NJ. 201-836-5060

Midco Plastics
Enterprise, KS................800-235-2729
Naltex
Austin, TX.................800-531-5112
Paper Pak Industries
La Verne, CA...............909-392-1750
Powertex Inc
Rouses Point, NY...........800-769-3783
Target Industries
North Salt Lake, UT........866-617-2253
Weyerhaeuser Co
Seattle, WA................800-525-5440

Can, Drum & Barrel

Carson Manufacturing Company
Petaluma, CA...............800-423-2380
CDF Corp
Plymouth, MA...............800-443-1920
Chalmur Bag Company, LLC
Philadelphia, PA...........800-349-2247
Enerfab Inc.
Cincinnati, OH.............513-641-0500
Fabohio Inc
Uhrichsville, OH...........740-922-4233
Fortifiber Building Systs Grp
Fernley, NV................800-773-4777
Greenfield Packaging
White Plains, NY...........914-993-0233
Gulf Arizona Packaging
Humble, TX.................800-364-3887
Hedwin Division
Baltimore, MD..............800-638-1012
Herche Warehouse
Denver, CO.................303-371-8186
Home Plastics Inc
Des Moines, IA.............515-265-2562
Indiana Vac Form Inc
Warsaw, IN.................574-269-1725
Inteplast Bags & Films Corporation
Delta, BC..................604-946-5431
J A Heilferty & Co
Teaneck, NJ................201-836-5060
Mello Smello LLC
Minneapolis, MN............888-574-2964
Midco Plastics
Enterprise, KS.............800-235-2729
Nosaj Disposables
Paterson, NJ...............800-631-3809
Packaging Dynamics International
Caldwell, OH...............740-732-5665
Powertex Inc
Rouses Point, NY...........800-769-3783
Pres-On Products
Addison, IL................800-323-7467
Scholle IPN
Merced, CA.................209-384-3100
Target Industries
North Salt Lake, UT........866-617-2253
Tri-Seal
Blauvelt, NY...............845-353-3300

Markers, Pens & Pencils

Amsterdam Printing & Litho Inc
Amsterdam, NY..............800-203-9917
Dri Mark Products
Port Washington, NY........800-645-9118
Elliot Lee
Cedarhurst, NY.............516-569-9595
Garland Writing Instruments
Coventry, RI...............401-828-9582
Gold Bond Inc
Hixson, TN.................423-842-5844
Gotham Pen Co Inc
Bronx, NY..................800-334-7970
Hub Pen Company
Quincy, MA.................617-471-9900
Industries of the Blind
Greensboro, NC.............336-274-1591
Listo Pencil Corp
Alameda, CA................800-547-8648
Markwell Manufacturing Company
Norwood, MA................800-666-1123
Micropoint
Mountain View, CA..........650-969-3097
National Pen Co
San Diego, CA..............858-675-3000
Pelican Products Inc
Bronx, NY..................800-552-8820
Visual Planning Corp
Champlain, NY..............800-361-1192

Volk Corp
Farmington Hills, MI.......800-521-6799

Packaging

Aseptic

Century Foods Intl LLC
Sparta, WI.................800-269-1901
Elopak Americas
Wixom, MI..................248-486-4600
Green Spot Packaging
Claremont, CA..............800-456-3210
Innovative Food Solutions LLC
Columbus, OH...............800-884-3314
JCS Controls, Inc.
Rochester, NY..............585-227-5910
Power Packaging Inc
Rosendale, WI..............920-872-2181
Pressure Pack
Williamsburg, VA...........757-220-3693
Professional Marketing Group
Seattle, WA................800-227-3769
Scholle IPN
Merced, CA.................209-384-3100

Blister

Accurate Paper Box Co Inc
Knoxville, TN..............865-690-0311
Ace Technical Plastics Inc
East Hartford, CT..........860-278-2444
Artistic Packaging Concepts
Massapequa Pk, NY..........516-797-4020
California Vibratory Feeders
Anaheim, CA................800-354-0972
Dynamic Pak LLC
Syracuse, NY...............315-474-8593
Gulf Arizona Packaging
Humble, TX.................800-364-3887
Gulf Packaging Company
Safety Harbor, FL..........800-749-3466
Gulf Systems
Brownsville, TX............800-217-4853
Gulf Systems
Humble, TX.................800-364-3887
Gulf Systems
Arlington, TX..............817-261-1915
H.J. Jones & Sons
London, ON.................800-667-0476
Hannan Products
Corona, CA.................800-954-4266
Harpak-ULMA Packaging LLC
Ball Ground, GA............770-345-5300
Herche Warehouse
Denver, CO.................303-371-8186
In-Touch Products
North Salt Lake, UT........801-298-4466
Jay Packaging Group Inc
Warwick, RI................401-244-1300
Key Packaging Co
Sarasota, FL...............941-355-2728
Kord Products Inc.
Brantford, ON..............800-452-9070
Leal True Form Corporation
Freeport, NY...............516-379-2008
Maro Paper Products Company
Bellwood, IL...............708-649-9982
Packaging & Processing Equipment
Ayr, ON....................519-622-6666
Pinn Pack Packaging LLC
Oxnard, CA.................805-385-4100
Plastech Corp
Atlanta, GA................404-355-9682
Power Packaging Inc
Rosendale, WI..............920-872-2181
Professional Marketing Group
Seattle, WA................800-227-3769
Rohrer Corp.
Wadsworth, OH..............800-243-6640
Rose City Printing & Packaging
Vancouver, WA..............800-704-8693
Scott Packaging Corporation
Philadelphia, PA...........215-925-5595
Sheboygan Paper Box Co
Sheboygan, WI..............800-458-8373
TEQ
Huntley, IL................800-874-7113
Thermex Thermatron
Louisville, KY.............502-493-1299
Woodstock Plastics Co Inc
Marengo, IL................815-568-5281

Flexible Materials

A-A1 Aaction Bag
Denver, CO.................800-783-1224
Ace Technical Plastics Inc
East Hartford, CT..........860-278-2444
Achilles USA
Everett, WA................425-353-7000
Aladdin Transparent Packaging
Hauppauge, NY..............631-273-4747
Alcon Packaging
Weston, ON.................416-742-8910
All Foils Inc
Strongsville, OH...........800-521-0054
All Sorts Premium Packaging
Buffalo, NY................888-565-9727
Alufoil Products Co Inc
Hauppauge, NY..............631-231-4141
Amcor
Oshkosh, WI................800-544-4672
American Printpak Inc
Sussex, WI.................800-441-8003
American Renolit Corp LA
Commerce, CA...............323-721-2720
Anchor Packaging
Ballwin, MO................800-467-3900
Arbee Transparent Inc
Elk Grove Vlg, IL..........800-642-2247
Archer Daniels Midland Company
Chicago, IL................312-634-8100
Atlantis Plastics Linear Film
Tulsa, OK..................800-324-9727
B.A.G. Corporation
Richardson, TX.............800-331-9200
Bagcraft Papercon
Chicago, IL................800-621-8468
Beayl Weiner/Pak
Pacific Palisades, CA......310-454-1354
Blako Industries
Dunbridge, OH..............419-833-4491
Brentwood Plastics In
St Louis, MO...............314-968-1135
Bryce Corp
Memphis, TN................800-238-7277
Burrows Paper Corp
Little Falls, NY...........800-272-7122
Can Creations
Pembroke Pines, FL.........954-581-3312
Carlisle Plastics
Minneapolis, MN............952-884-1309
Catty Inc
Harvard, IL................815-943-2288
Cello Bag Company
Bowling Green, KY..........800-347-0338
Central Bag Co
Leavenworth, KS............913-250-0325
Champion Plastics
Clifton, NJ................800-526-1230
Cincinnati Convertors Inc
Cincinnati, OH.............513-731-6600
Circle Packaging Machinery Inc
De Pere, WI................920-983-3420
CL&D Graphics
Oconomowoc, WI.............800-777-1114
Clear Lam Packaging
Elk Grove Village, IL......847-439-8570
Cleveland Plastic Films
Elyria, OH.................800-832-6799
Cleveland Specialties Co
Loveland, OH...............513-677-9787
Conn Container Corp
North Haven, CT............203-248-0241
Continental Packaging Corporation
Elgin, IL..................847-289-6400
Continental Products
Mexico, MO.................800-325-0216
CoolBrands International
Ronkonkoma, NY.............631-737-9700
Coveris
Excelsior Springs, MO
Crystal-Flex Packaging Corporation
Rockville Centre, NY.......888-246-7325
Danafilms Inc
Westborough, MA............508-366-8884
Design Packaging Company
Glencoe, IL................800-321-7659
Dynamic Packaging
Minneapolis, MN............800-878-9380
Ensinger Inc
Washington, PA.............800-243-3221
Excelsior Transparent Bag Manufacturing
Yonkers, NY................914-968-1300

Fabricon Products Inc
  River Rouge, MI.....................313-841-8200
Farnell Packaging
  Dartmouth, NS.....................800-565-9378
Film X
  Dayville, CT.....................800-628-6128
Filmco Inc
  Aurora, OH.....................800-545-8457
Flexicon
  Cary, IL.....................847-639-3530
Flexo Transparent Inc
  Buffalo, NY.....................877-993-5396
Foam Pack Industries
  Springfield, NJ.....................973-376-3700
Food Pak Corp
  San Mateo, CA.....................650-341-6559
Formflex
  Bloomingdale, IN.....................800-255-7659
Gemini Plastic Films Corporation
  Garfield, NJ.....................800-789-4732
General Films Inc
  Covington, OH.....................888-436-3456
Gibraltar Packaging Group Inc
  Hastings, NE.....................402-463-1366
Glopak
  St Leonard, QC.....................800-361-6994
Gulf Arizona Packaging
  Humble, TX.....................800-364-3887
Gulf Systems
  Brownsville, TX.....................800-217-4853
Gulf Systems
  Humble, TX.....................800-364-3887
Gulf Systems
  Arlington, TX.....................817-261-1915
H&H Lumber Company
  Amarillo, TX.....................806-335-1813
Hedwin Division
  Baltimore, MD.....................800-638-1012
Herche Warehouse
  Denver, CO.....................303-371-8186
Home Plastics Inc
  Des Moines, IA.....................515-265-2562
Hudson Poly Bag Inc
  Hudson, MA.....................800-229-7566
Huntsman Packaging Corporation
  Birmingham, Bi.....................205-328-4720
In-Line Corporation
  Hopkins, MN.....................952-938-0046
Interstate Packaging
  White Bluff, TN.....................800-251-1072
J A Heilferty & Co
  Teaneck, NJ.....................201-836-5060
Jif-Pak Manufacturing
  Vista, CA.....................800-777-6613
JW Aluminum
  Mt Holly, SC.....................800-568-1100
Kapak Corporation
  Minneapolis, MN.....................952-541-0730
KAPCO
  Kent, OH.....................800-843-5368
Karolina Polymers
  Hickory, NC.....................828-328-2247
KHL Engineered Packaging
  Montebello, CA.....................323-721-5300
Klockner Pentaplast of America
  Gordonsville, VA.....................540-832-3600
KM International Corp
  Kenton, TN.....................731-749-8700
Label Technology Inc
  Merced, CA.....................800-388-1990
Longhorn Packaging Inc
  San Antonio, TX.....................800-433-7974
LPS Industries
  Moonachie, NJ.....................800-275-4577
Luetzow Industries
  South Milwaukee, WI.....................800-558-6055
M&R Flexible Packaging
  Springboro, OH.....................800-543-3380
MAC Tac LLC
  Stow, OH.....................866-262-2822
Maco Bag Corp
  Newark, NY.....................315-226-1000
Mark Products Company
  Denville, NJ.....................973-983-8818
Marshall Plastic Film Inc
  Martin, MI.....................269-672-5511
Masternet, Ltd
  Mississauga, ON.....................800-216-2536
Microplas Industries
  Dunwoody, GA.....................800-952-4528
Milprint
  Oshkosh, WI.....................920-303-8600

Mimi et Cie
  Seattle, WA.....................206-545-1850
Mohawk Northern Plastics
  Auburn, WA.....................800-426-1100
Mohawk Western Plastics Inc
  La Verne, CA.....................909-593-7547
Morris Industries
  Forestville, MD.....................301-568-5005
Multi-Plastics Extrusions Inc
  Hazleton, PA.....................570-455-2021
Multibulk Systems International
  Wendell, NC.....................919-366-2100
National Poly Bag Manufacturing Corporation
  Brooklyn, NY.....................718-629-9800
Net Pack Systems
  Oakland, ME.....................207-465-4531
Northeast Packaging Materials
  Monsey, NY.....................845-426-2900
Now Plastics Inc
  East Longmeadow, MA.....................413-525-1010
OMNOVA Solutions
  Fairlawn, OH.....................330-869-4200
Outlook Packaging
  Neenah, WI.....................920-722-1666
Packaging Enterprises
  Rockledge, PA.....................800-453-6213
Packaging Products Corp
  Mission, KS.....................913-262-3033
Paco Manufacturing
  Clarksville, IN.....................812-283-7963
Pak-Sak Industries I
  Sparta, MI.....................800-748-0431
Pater & Associates
  Cincinnati, OH
PDMP
  Leesburg, VA.....................703-777-8400
Phoenix Closures Inc
  Naperville, IL.....................630-544-3475
Plascal Corp
  Farmingdale, NY.....................800-899-7527
Plastic Craft Products Corp
  West Nyack, NY.....................800-627-3010
Plastic Packaging Technologies
  Kansas City, KS.....................800-468-0029
Plastic Suppliers Inc
  Columbus, OH.....................800-722-5577
Poly Shapes Corporation
  Elyria, OH.....................800-605-9359
Polyplastics
  Austin, TX.....................800-753-7659
Portco Corporation
  Vancouver, WA.....................800-426-1794
Power Packaging Inc
  Rosendale, WI.....................920-872-2181
Print & Peel
  New York, NY.....................800-451-0807
Printpack Inc.
  Atlanta, GA.....................404-460-7000
Professional Marketing Group
  Seattle, WA.....................800-227-3769
Quality Films
  Three Rivers, MI.....................269-679-5263
Quantum Performance Films
  Streamwood, IL.....................800-323-6963
Ray C. Sprosty Bag Company
  Wooster, OH.....................330-264-8559
Rico Packaging Company
  Chicago, IL.....................773-523-9190
Rjr Technologies
  Oakland, CA.....................510-638-5901
Rohrer Corp.
  Wadsworth, OH.....................800-243-6640
Roll-O-Sheets Canada
  Barrie, ON.....................888-767-3456
Rollprint Packaging Prods Inc
  Addison, IL.....................800-276-7629
Roplast Industries Inc
  Oroville, CA.....................800-767-5278
Rowland Technologies
  Wallingford, CT.....................203-269-9500
Rutan Poly Industries Inc
  Mahwah, NJ.....................800-872-1474
Schwab Paper Products Co
  Romeoville, IL.....................800-837-7225
Seal-Tite Bag Company
  Philadelphia, PA.....................717-917-1949
Sealed Air Corp
  Charlotte, NC.....................800-391-5645
Seiler Plastics
  St Louis, MO.....................888-673-4537
Seville Flexpack Corp
  Oak Creek, WI.....................414-761-2751

Shields Bag & Printing Co
  Yakima, WA.....................800-541-8630
Shields Products Inc
  West Pittston, PA.....................570-655-4596
Ship Rite Packaging
  Bergenfield, NJ.....................800-721-7447
Shippers Supply
  Saskatoon, SK.....................800-661-5639
Shippers Supply, Labelgraphic
  Calgary, AB.....................800-661-5639
Southern Film Extruders
  High Point, NC.....................800-334-6101
Spartech Poly Com
  Clayton, MI.....................888-721-4242
Specialty Films & Associates
  Hebron, KY.....................800-984-3346
Star Poly Bag Inc
  Brooklyn, NY.....................718-384-7034
Sterling Novelty Products
  Northbrook, IL.....................847-291-0070
Stock America Inc
  Grafton, WI.....................262-375-4100
Sungjae Corporation
  Irvine, CA.....................949-757-1727
Sunland Manufacturing Company
  Minneapolis, MN.....................800-790-1905
Terphane Inc
  Bloomfield, NY.....................800-724-3456
Trans Flex Packagers Inc
  Unionville, CT.....................860-673-2531
Trico Converting Inc
  Fullerton, CA.....................714-563-0701
Trident Plastics
  Ivyland, PA.....................800-222-2318
Trinity Packaging
  Cheektowaga, NY.....................800-778-3111
Trio Packaging Corp
  Ronkonkoma, NY.....................800-331-0492
Tyco Plastics
  Lakeville, MN.....................800-328-4080
UCB Inc
  Smyrna, GA.....................770-970-8338
Ultrapak
  Dunkirk, NY.....................800-228-6030
Unifoil Corp
  Fairfield, NJ.....................973-244-9990
Union Industries
  Providence, RI.....................800-556-6454
Uniplast Films
  Palmer, MA.....................800-343-1295
United Flexible
  Westbury, NY.....................516-222-2150
Vacumet Corp
  Wayne, NJ.....................973-628-1067
Vacumet Corporation
  Austell, GA.....................800-776-0865
Vacuum Depositing Inc
  Louisville, KY.....................502-969-4227
VIFAN Canada
  Lanoraie, QC.....................800-557-0192
Viskase Co Inc
  Darien, IL.....................800-323-8562
Western Plastics
  Portland, TN.....................615-325-7331
Western Plastics
  Calhoun, GA.....................800-752-4106
Winpak Technologies
  Toronto, ON.....................416-421-1700
Witt Plastics
  Greenville, OH.....................800-227-9181
Wraps
  East Orange, NJ.....................973-673-7873
Zimmer Custom-Made Packaging
  Indianapolis, IN.....................317-263-3436

Food Protective

A-A1 Aaction Bag
  Denver, CO.....................800-783-1224
Accurate Flannel Bag Company
  Paterson, NJ.....................800-234-9200
Alkar Rapid Pak
  Lodi, WI.....................608-592-3211
Allflex Packaging Products
  Ambler, PA.....................800-448-2467
American Excelsior Co
  Arlington, TX.....................800-777-7645
Ample Industries
  Franklin, OH.....................888-818-9700
Anchor Packaging
  Ballwin, MO.....................800-467-3900

Arbee Transparent Inc
Elk Grove Vlg, IL................800-642-2247
Bag Masters
St Petersburg, FL................800-330-2247
BEI
Goleta, GA.....................800-350-2727
Bryce Corp
Memphis, TN...................800-238-7277
Burrows Paper Corp
Little Falls, NY.................800-272-7122
Catty Inc
Harvard, IL....................815-943-2288
Ccw Products
Arvada, CO....................303-427-9663
Central Coated Products Inc
Alliance, OH...................330-821-9830
Central Fine Pack Inc
Fort Wayne, IN.................260-432-3027
Cincinnati Convertors Inc
Cincinnati, OH.................513-731-6600
Colbert Packaging Corp
Lake Forest, IL.................847-367-5990
Collectors Gallery
St Charles, IL..................800-346-3063
Crystal-Flex Packaging Corporation
Rockville Centre, NY............888-246-7325
Curwood Specialty Films
Oshkosh, WI...................800-544-4672
Custom Foam Molders
Foristell, MO..................636-441-2307
Design Plastics Inc
Omaha, NE....................800-491-0786
Elmo Rietschle - A Gardner Denver Product
Quincy, IL.....................217-222-5400
Ensinger Inc
Washington, PA................800-243-3221
Fabri-Kal Corp
Kalamazoo, MI.................800-888-5054
Flexo Transparent Inc
Buffalo, NY....................877-993-5396
Foam Concepts Inc
Uxbridge, MA..................508-278-7255
Free Flow Packaging Corporation
Redwood City, CA..............800-888-3725
Glopak
St Leonard, QC.................800-361-6994
Greenfield Paper Box Co
Greenfield, MA.................413-773-9414
Gulf Arizona Packaging
Humble, TX....................800-364-3887
Gulf Systems
Brownsville, TX.................800-217-4853
Gulf Systems
Humble, TX....................800-364-3887
Gulf Systems
Arlington, TX...................817-261-1915
Handy Wacks Corp
Sparta, MI.....................800-445-4434
Harpak-ULMA Packaging LLC
Ball Ground, GA................770-345-5300
Herche Warehouse
Denver, CO....................303-371-8186
Hubco Inc
Hutchinson, KS.................800-563-1867
Indian Valley Industries
Johnson City, NY...............800-659-5111
Jewel Case Corp
Cranston, RI...................800-441-4447
K & L Intl
Ontario, CA....................888-598-5588
Kalco Enterprises
New York, NY..................800-396-6600
King Plastic Corp
North Port, FL..................800-780-5502
Lenkay Sani Products Corporation
Brooklyn, NY...................718-927-9260
Letica Corp
Rochester Hills, MI..............800-538-4221
Maco Bag Corp
Newark, NY....................315-226-1000
Mullnix Packages Inc
Fort Wayne, IN.................260-747-3149
Multisorb Technologies Inc
Buffalo, NY....................800-445-9890
Norpak Corp
Newark, NJ....................800-631-6970
ORBIS
Oconomowoc, WI...............800-890-7292
Osgood Industries
Oldsmar, FL....................813-855-7337
Packaging Progressions
Collegeville, PA.................610-489-9096

Packing Material Company
Southfield, MI..................248-489-7000
Pacquet Oneida
Charlotte, NC..................800-631-8388
Pater & Associates
Cincinnati, OH
Patty Paper Inc
Plymouth, IN...................800-782-1703
Plastilite Corporation
Omaha, NE....................800-228-9506
Polytainers
Toronto, ON...................800-268-2424
Professional Marketing Group
Seattle, WA....................800-227-3769
Promarks
Ontario, CA....................909-923-3888
Roll-O-Sheets Canada
Barrie, ON.....................888-767-3456
Roplast Industries Inc
Oroville, CA....................800-767-5278
Rownd & Son
Dillon, SC.....................803-774-8264
Rutan Poly Industries Inc
Mahwah, NJ...................800-872-1474
Saeplast Canada
St John, NB....................800-567-3966
Salinas Valley Wax Paper Co
Salinas, CA....................831-424-2747
Schroeder Machine
San Marcos, CA................760-591-9733
Schwab Paper Products Co
Romeoville, IL..................800-837-7225
Schwarz Supply Source
Morton Grove, IL...............800-323-4903
Shields Products Inc
West Pittston, PA...............570-655-4596
SIG Combibloc USA, Inc.
Chester, PA....................610-546-4200
Southern Film Extruders
High Point, NC.................800-334-6101
Sun Plastics
Clearwater, MN................800-862-1673
T D Sawvel Co
Maple Plain, MN...............877-488-1816
TEMP-TECH Company
Springfield, MA.................800-343-5579
Tenneco Packaging
Westmont, IL...................630-850-7034
Trans World Services
Melrose, MA...................800-882-2105
Trevor Owen Limited
Scarborough, ON...............866-487-2224
Tri-State Plastics
Henderson, KY.................270-826-8361
Triune Enterprises
Gardena, CA...................310-719-1600
Union Industries
Providence, RI..................800-556-6454
Unipac Shipping
Jamaica, NY...................800-586-2711
United Desiccants
Reno, NE......................888-659-1377
Urnex Brands Inc
Elmsford, NY..................800-222-2826
Valley Packaging Supply Co
Green Bay, WI.................920-336-9012
Viscofan USA Inc
Montgomery, AL...............800-521-3577
Vista International Packaging
Kenosha, WI...................800-558-4058
West-Pak
Dallas, TX.....................214-337-8984
Wisconsin Converting Inc
Green Bay, WI.................800-544-1935

Plastic

A-A1 Aaction Bag
Denver, CO....................800-783-1224
Ace Technical Plastics Inc
East Hartford, CT...............860-278-2444
Acme Bag Co
Chula Vista, CA................800-275-2263
AEP Industries
South Hackensack, NJ...........800-999-2374
AEP Industries Inc
Mankato, MN..................800-999-2374
Alcoa - Massena Operations
Massena, NY
Alkar Rapid Pak
Lodi, WI.......................608-592-3211

Anchor Packaging
Ballwin, MO...................800-467-3900
Arbee Transparent Inc
Elk Grove Vlg, IL................800-642-2247
Atlantis Plastics Linear Film
Tulsa, OK.....................800-324-9727
Automated Packaging Systems
Streetsboro, OH................800-527-0733
Beayl Weiner/Pak
Pacific Palisades, CA............310-454-1354
Blako Industries
Dunbridge, OH.................419-833-4491
Brechteen
Chesterfield, MI................586-949-2240
Brentwood Plastics In
St Louis, MO...................314-968-1135
Buckhorn Inc
Milford, OH....................800-543-4454
Bunzl Distribution USA
St. Louis, MO...................888-997-5959
C-P Flexible Packaging
Newtown, PA...................800-448-8183
Ccw Products
Arvada, CO....................303-427-9663
CDF Corp
Plymouth, MA..................800-443-1920
Central Fine Pack Inc
Fort Wayne, IN.................260-432-3027
Century Foods Intl LLC
Sparta, WI.....................800-269-1901
Champion Plastics
Clifton, NJ.....................800-526-1230
Chem-Tainer Industries Inc
West Babylon, NY..............800-275-2436
Chester Plastics
Chester, NS....................902-275-3522
Cincinnati Convertors Inc
Cincinnati, OH.................513-731-6600
Clawson Container Company
Clarkston, MI...................800-325-8700
Clorox Company
Oakland, CA...................800-227-1860
Conn Container Corp
North Haven, CT................203-248-0241
Consolidated Container Co LLC
Atlanta, GA....................888-831-2184
Contour Packaging
Philadelphia, PA................215-457-1600
Covestro LLC
Sheffield, MA...................800-628-5084
Crayex Corp
Piqua, OH.....................800-837-1747
Creative Packaging
Hayward, CA...................510-785-6500
CTK Plastics
Moose Jaw, SK.................800-667-8847
Custom Foam Molders
Foristell, MO..................636-441-2307
Danafilms Inc
Westborough, MA...............508-366-8884
Davis Core & Pa
Cave Spring, GA................800-235-7483
Decker Plastics
Council Bluffs, IA...............866-869-6293
Denice & Filice LLC
Hollister, CA...................831-637-7492
Design Packaging Company
Glencoe, IL....................800-321-7659
Design Plastics Inc
Omaha, NE....................800-491-0786
Dub Harris Corporation
Pomona, CA...................909-596-6300
Eaton Manufacturing Co
Houston, TX...................800-328-6610
Fabri-Kal Corp
Kalamazoo, MI.................800-888-5054
Farnell Packaging
Dartmouth, NS.................800-565-9378
Film X
Dayville, CT....................800-628-6128
Flexo Transparent Inc
Buffalo, NY....................877-993-5396
Fredman Bag Co
Milwaukee, WI.................800-945-5686
Fremont Die Cut Products
Fremont, OH...................800-223-3177
Fulton-Denver Co
Denver, CO....................800-521-1414
Gary Plastic Packaging Corporation
Bronx, NY.....................800-221-8151
Gary Plastic Packaging Corporation
Bronx, NY.....................800-227-4279

Gateway Plastics Inc
Mequon, WI 262-242-2020
Genpak LLC
Lakeville, MN. 800-328-4556
Gibraltar Packaging Group Inc
Hastings, NE 402-463-1366
Goex Corporation
Janesville, WI 608-754-3303
Golden West Packaging Concept
Lake Forest, CA 949-855-9646
Goodwrappers Inc
Halethorpe, MD 800-638-1127
Greif Inc
Delaware, OH 740-549-6000
Gulf Arizona Packaging
Humble, TX 800-364-3887
Gulf Coast Plastics
Tampa, FL 800-277-7491
Gulf Systems
Brownsville, TX 800-217-4853
Gulf Systems
Humble, TX 800-364-3887
Gulf Systems
Arlington, TX 817-261-1915
H&H Lumber Company
Amarillo, TX. 806-335-1813
Handy Wacks Corp
Sparta, MI 800-445-4434
Herche Warehouse
Denver, CO 303-371-8186
Hinkle Manufacturing
Perrysburg, OH 419-666-5367
Hood Packaging
Burlington, ON 877-462-6627
Hubco Inc
Hutchinson, KS 800-563-1867
Hudson Poly Bag Inc
Hudson, MA 800-229-7566
Indianapolis Container Company
Indianapolis, IN 800-760-3318
Inline Plastic Corp
McDonough, GA 678-466-3467
Inline Plastic Corp
Shelton, CT 800-826-5567
Interstate Packaging
White Bluff, TN 800-251-1072
IPL Plastics
Edmundston, NB. 800-739-9595
IVEX Packaging Corporation
Longueuil, QC 450-651-8887
J A Heilferty & Co
Teaneck, NJ. 201-836-5060
Jomar Plastics Industry
Nanty Glo, PA 800-681-4039
K & L Intl
Ontario, CA. 888-598-5588
Kimball Companies
East Longmeadow, MA 413-525-1881
Klockner Pentaplast of America
Gordonsville, VA 540-832-3600
KM International Corp
Kenton, TN 731-749-8700
Kord Products Inc.
Brantford, ON 800-452-9070
L&H Wood Manufacturing Company
Farmington, MI. 248-474-9000
Letica Corp
Rochester Hills, MI. 800-538-4221
Luetzow Industries
South Milwaukee, WI. 800-558-6055
M S Plastics & Packaging Inc
Butler, NJ 800-593-1802
Maco Bag Corp
Newark, NY 315-226-1000
Marpac Industries
Philmont, NY 888-462-7722
Marshall Plastic Film Inc
Martin, MI 269-672-5511
Mason Transparent Package Company
Armonk, NY 718-792-6000
Masternet, Ltd
Mississauga, ON 800-216-2536
Maypak Inc
Wayne, NJ 973-696-0780
Melville Plastics
Haw River, NC 336-578-5800
Microplas Industries
Dunwoody, GA 800-952-4528
Midco Plastics
Enterprise, KS 800-235-2729
Mohawk Western Plastics Inc
La Verne, CA 909-593-7547

Mullnix Packages Inc
Fort Wayne, IN 260-747-3149
National Poly Bag Manufacturing Corporation
Brooklyn, NY 718-629-9800
Net Pack Systems
Oakland, ME 207-465-4531
Nolon Industries
Mantua, OH 330-274-2283
North American Packaging Corp
New York, NY 800-499-3521
Noteworthy Company
Amsterdam, NY 800-696-7849
ORBIS RPM
Madison, WI 608-852-8840
Packaging Materials Inc
Cambridge, OH. 800-565-8550
Packing Material Company
Southfield, MI 248-489-7000
Papelera Puertorriquena
Utuado, PR 787-894-2098
Par-Pak
Houston, TX 713-686-6700
Pater & Associates
Cincinnati, OH
Pelco Packaging Corporation
Stirling, NJ 908-647-3500
Pilant Corp
Bloomington, IN 800-366-3525
Pioneer Plastics Inc
Dixon, KY 800-951-1551
Plascal Corp
Farmingdale, NY 800-899-7527
Plastic Suppliers Inc
Columbus, OH 800-722-5577
Plastipak Packaging
Plymouth, MI 734-354-3510
Poly Plastic Products Inc
Delano, PA 570-467-3000
Portco Corporation
Vancouver, WA 800-426-1794
Power Packaging Inc
Rosendale, WI. 920-872-2181
Prairie Packaging Inc
Mooresville, NC 704-660-6600
Pretium Packaging
Hazle Twp, PA 570-459-1800
Printpack Inc.
Atlanta, GA 404-460-7000
Professional Marketing Group
Seattle, WA 800-227-3769
Quality Transparent Bag Co
Bay City, MI 989-893-3561
Quantum Performance Films
Streamwood, IL. 800-323-6963
Quintex Corp
Nampa, ID 208-467-1113
Reliance Product
Winnipeg, MB. 800-665-0258
Ropak
Oak Brook, IL 800-527-2267
Roplast Industries Inc
Oroville, CA 800-767-5278
Ross & Wallace Inc
Hammond, LA 800-854-2300
Rowland Technologies
Wallingford, CT 203-269-9500
Rutan Poly Industries Inc
Mahwah, NJ 800-872-1474
Saeplast Canada
St John, NB 800-567-3966
Samuel Strapping Systems Inc
Woodridge, IL 800-323-4424
San Miguel Label Manufacturing
Ciales, PR 787-871-3120
Sealed Air Corp
Charlotte, NC 800-391-5645
Shamrock Plastics
Mt Vernon, OH 800-765-1611
Shields Bag & Printing Co
Yakima, WA 800-541-8630
Shields Products Inc
West Pittston, PA. 570-655-4596
Ship Rite Packaging
Bergenfield, NJ 800-721-7447
Shippers Supply
Saskatoon, SK. 800-661-5639
Snapware
Fullerton, CA 800-334-3062
Spartec Plastics
Conneaut, OH 800-325-5176
Star Container Company
Phoenix, AZ 480-281-4200

Steel City Corporation
Youngstown, OH. 800-321-0350
Stock America Inc
Grafton, WI 262-375-4100
Stripper Bags
Henderson, NV 800-354-2247
Sun Plastics
Clearwater, MN. 800-862-1673
Sungjae Corporation
Irvine, CA 949-757-1727
T&S Blow Molding
Scarborough, ON 416-752-8330
Target Industries
North Salt Lake, UT 866-617-2253
Templock Corporation
Santa Barbara, CA 800-777-1715
Terphane Inc
Bloomfield, NY 800-724-3456
Tolas Health Care Packaging
Feasterville Trevose, PA 215-322-7900
Trans Flex Packagers Inc
Unionville, CT 860-673-2531
Trident Plastics
Ivyland, PA 800-222-2318
Trio Products
Elyria, OH 440-323-5457
Ultrapak
Dunkirk, NY 800-228-6030
Union Industries
Providence, RI 800-556-6454
Uniplast Films
Palmer, MA 800-343-1295
United Flexible
Westbury, NY 516-222-2150
United Seal & Tag Corporation
Port Charlotte, FL 800-211-9552
Vacumet Corporation
Austell, GA 800-776-0865
VIFAN Canada
Lanorale, QC 800-557-0192
Virginia Plastics Co
Roanoke, VA 800-777-8541
Western Plastics
Calhoun, GA 800-752-4106
Witt Plastics
Greenville, OH 800-227-9181
Woodstock Plastics Co Inc
Marengo, IL 815-568-5281
Zimmer Custom-Made Packaging
Indianapolis, IN 317-263-3436

Private Label

Agropur MSI, LLC
La Crosse, WI 800-359-2345
Bridgewell Resources LLC
Clackamas, OR 800-481-3557
C-P Flexible Packaging
Newtown, PA 800-448-8183
Cache Creek Foods LLC
Woodland, CA. 530-662-1764
Calhoun Bend Mill
Libuse, LA 800-519-6455
Century Foods Intl LLC
Sparta, WI 800-269-1901
Couprie Fenton
Augusta, GA 706-650-7017
Penguin Natural Foods, Inc.
Vernon, CA 323-727-7980
Professional Image
Tulsa, OK 800-722-8550
The Rubin Family of Wines
Sebastopol, CA 707-887-8130
TRFG Inc
Springfield, OH. 937-322-2040
Tri-Connect
Oak Park, IL 708-660-8190
Truitt Bros. Inc.
Salem, OR. 800-547-8712
Vetter Vineyards Winery
Westfield, NY 716-326-3100

Shrink

Adpro
Solon, OH 440-542-1111
AEP Industries Inc
Mankato, MN 800-999-2374
Audion Automation
Carrollton, TX. 972-389-0777
Campbell Wrapper Corporation
De Pere, WI. 920-983-7100

Can Creations
  Pembroke Pines, FL 800-272-0235
Can Creations
  Pembroke Pines, FL 954-581-3312
Central Bag Co
  Leavenworth, KS 913-250-0325
Chem Pack Inc
  Cincinnati, OH 800-421-2700
CiMa-Pak Corp.
  Dorval, QC 877-631-2462
Collectors Gallery
  St Charles, IL 800-346-3063
Coveris
  Excelsior Springs, MO
Crayex Corp
  Piqua, OH 800-837-1747
ESS Technologies
  Blacksburg, VA 540-961-5716
Flexo Transparent Inc
  Buffalo, NY 877-993-5396
Gulf Arizona Packaging
  Humble, TX 800-364-3887
Gulf Systems
  Humble, TX 800-364-3887
Gulf Systems
  Arlington, TX 817-261-1915
Halpak Plastics
  Deer Park, NY 800-442-5725
Herche Warehouse
  Denver, CO 303-371-8186
Ilapak Inc
  Newtown, PA 215-579-2900
M S Plastics & Packaging Inc
  Butler, NJ 800-593-1802
Mark Products Company
  Denville, NJ 973-983-8818
Marshall Plastic Film Inc
  Martin, MI 269-672-5511
Mimi et Cie
  Seattle, WA 206-545-1850
Oaklee International
  Ronkonkoma, NY 800-333-7250
Pack Line Corporation
  Racine, WI 800-248-6868
Packaging Materials Inc
  Cambridge, OH 800-565-8550
Power Packaging Inc
  Rosendale, WI. 920-872-2181
Preferred Packaging Systems
  San Dimas, CA 800-378-4777
Quantum Performance Films
  Streamwood, IL. 800-323-6963
Seal-O-Matic Corp
  Jacksonville, OR 800-631-2072
Shippers Supply
  Saskatoon, SK. 800-661-5639
Shrinkfast Marketing
  Newport, NH. 800-867-4746
Sungjae Corporation
  Irvine, CA 949-757-1727
Templock Corporation
  Santa Barbara, CA 800-777-1715
Tri-Sterling
  Altamonte Spgs, FL 407-260-0330
Ultrapak
  Dunkirk, NY 800-228-6030
United Flexible
  Westbury, NY 516-222-2150
Willow Specialties
  Batavia, NY 800-724-7300

Packaging & Containerizing Products

A La Carte
  Chicago, IL 800-722-2370
A-A1 Aaction Bag
  Denver, CO 800-783-1224
A-Z Factory Supply
  Schiller Park, IL 800-323-4511
Aabbitt Adhesives
  Chicago, IL 800-222-2488
Abbott Industries
  Paterson, NJ
Abond Plastic Corporation
  Lachine, QC 800-886-7947
AC Label Company
  Provo, UT 801-642-3500
Accurate Flannel Bag Company
  Paterson, NJ 800-234-9200
Accurate Paper Box Co Inc
  Knoxville, TN 865-690-0311

Ace Manufacturing & Parts Co
  Sullivan, MO. 800-325-6138
Ace Technical Plastics Inc
  East Hartford, CT 860-278-2444
Acme Bag Co
  Chula Vista, CA 800-275-2263
Aco Container Systems
  Pickering, ON 800-542-9942
Adcapitol
  Monroe, NC. 800-868-7111
Adhesive Applications
  Easthampton, MA 800-356-3572
Adpro
  Solon, OH 440-542-1111
Adstick Custom Labels Inc
  Denver, CO 800-255-7314
Advanced Poly-Packaging Inc
  Akron, OH 800-754-4403
Advantage Puck Technologies
  Corry, PA 814-664-4810
AEP Industries Inc
  Mankato, MN 800-999-2374
Aero Tec Laboratories/ATL
  Ramsey, NJ 800-526-5330
AJM Packaging Corporation
  Bloomfield Hills, MI 248-901-0040
Aladdin Transparent Packaging
  Hauppauge, NY 631-273-4747
Alcan Packaging
  Baie D'Urfe, QC 514-457-4555
Alcoa - Massena Operations
  Massena, NY
Alger Creations
  Miami, FL 954-454-3272
All American Container
  Miami, FL 305-887-0797
All American Poly
  Piscataway, NJ 800-526-3551
All Foils Inc
  Strongsville, OH 800-521-0054
All Sorts Premium Packaging
  Buffalo, NY. 888-565-9727
Allflex Packaging Products
  Ambler, PA 800-448-2467
Alpack
  Centerville, NA 774-994-8086
Alpha Packaging
  St Louis, MO. 800-421-4772
Althor Products
  Bethel, CT 800-688-2693
Altira Inc
  Miami, FL 305-687-8074
Amcel
  Watertown, MA. 800-225-7992
Amco Metals Indl
  City of Industry, CA 626-855-2550
American Advertising & Shop Cap Company
  Old Tappan, NJ 800-442-8837
American Bag & Burlap Company
  Chelsea, MA 617-884-7600
American Box Corporation
  Lisbon, OH 330-424-8055
American Containers Inc
  Plymouth, IN. 574-936-4068
American Labelmark Co
  Chicago, IL. 800-621-5808
American Pallet Inc
  Oakdale, CA 209-847-6122
American Production Co Inc
  Redwood City, CA 650-368-5334
Americraft Carton Inc
  St Paul, MN. 651-227-6655
Americraft Carton Inc
  Prairie Village, KS 913-387-3700
Ameriglobe LLC
  Lafayette, LA. 337-234-3211
Ample Industries
  Franklin, OH 888-818-9700
Anchor Packaging
  Ballwin, MO 800-467-3900
Appleson Press
  Syosset, NY. 800-888-2775
Archer Daniels Midland Company
  Chicago, IL 312-634-8100
Arena Products
  Rochester, NY. 844-762-0127
Arkansas Glass Container Corp
  Jonesboro, AR. 800-527-4527
Armbrust Paper Tubes Inc
  Chicago, IL. 773-586-3232
Art Poly Bag Co
  Brooklyn, NY 800-278-7659

Artistic Carton
  Auburn, IN 800-735-7225
Artistic Carton Co
  Elgin, IL 847-741-0247
Artistic Packaging Concepts
  Massapequa Pk, NY 516-797-4020
Atlantis Plastics Linear Film
  Tulsa, OK 800-324-9727
Atlas Case Inc
  Denver, CO 888-325-2199
Atlas Packaging Inc
  Opa Locka, FL 800-662-0630
Atlas Tag & Label Inc
  Neenah, WI. 800-558-6418
Aurora Design Associates, Inc.
  Salt Lake City, UT. 801-588-0111
Auto Pallets-Boxes
  Lathrup Village, MI 800-875-2699
Automatic Electronic Machines Company
  Brooklyn, NY 718-384-3211
Automatic Liquid Packaging Solutions
  Arlington Heights, IL 847-264-5349
Automatic Specialties Inc
  Marlborough, MA 800-445-2370
Avantage Group Inc
  Redondo Beach, CA 310-379-3933
Avon Tape
  Chestnut Hill, MA 508-584-8273
B F Nelson Cartons Inc
  Savage, MN. 800-328-2380
B.A.G. Corporation
  Richardson, TX 800-331-9200
Babcock Co
  Bath, NY 607-776-3341
Bag Company
  Kennesaw, GA 800-533-1931
Bag Masters
  St Petersburg, FL 800-330-2247
Bagcraft Papercon
  Chicago, IL. 800-621-8468
Bakers Choice Products
  Beacon Falls, CT. 203-720-1000
Bal/Foster Glass Container Company
  Port Allegany, PA 814-642-2521
Ball Corp
  Broomfield, CO 303-469-3131
Ball Foster Glass Container Company
  Sapulpa, OK 918-224-1440
Bancroft Bag Inc
  West Monroe, LA 318-387-2550
Barbour Threads
  Anniston, AL 256-237-9461
Bardes Plastics Inc
  Milwaukee, WI. 800-558-5161
Baskets Extraordinaires
  Westbury, NY 800-666-1685
Bayard Kurth Company
  Detroit, MI 313-891-0800
Beayl Weiner/Pak
  Pacific Palisades, CA 310-454-1354
BEI
  Goleta, GA 800-350-2727
Bell Container
  Newark, NJ 973-344-6997
Bell Packaging Corporation
  Marion, IN. 800-382-0153
Belleview
  Brookline, NH. 603-878-1583
Bennett's Auto Inc
  Neenah, WI. 800-215-5464
Berenz Packaging Corp
  Menomonee Falls, WI. 262-251-8787
Bergen Barrel & Drum Company
  Kearny, NJ. 201-998-3500
Berlin Fruit Box Company
  Berlin Heights, OH. 800-877-7721
Berlon Industries
  Hustisford, WI 800-899-3580
Berry Global
  Evansville, IN. 800-343-1295
Bertels Can Company
  Belcamp, MD 410-272-0090
Blackhawk Molding Co Inc
  Addison, IL. 630-458-2100
Blako Industries
  Dunbridge, OH 419-833-4491
Boelter Industries
  Winona, MN 507-452-2315
Boise Cascade Corporation
  Burley, ID 208-678-3531
Bonar Plastics
  West Chicago, IL 800-295-3725

225

Bonar Plastics
Ridgefield, WA 800-972-5252
Boxes.com
Livingston, NJ. 201-646-9050
Brechteen
Chesterfield, MI 586-949-2240
Brewer-Cantelmo Inc
New York, NY 212-244-4600
Brooks Barrel Company
Baltimore, MD 800-398-2766
Brown International Corp LLC
Winter Haven, FL 863-299-2111
Brown Paper Goods Co
Waukegan, IL 847-688-1450
Bryce Corp
Memphis, TN 800-238-7277
Buckeye Group
South Charleston, OH. 937-462-8361
Buckhorn Canada
Brampton, ON. 800-461-7579
Buckhorn Inc
Milford, OH .800-543-4454
Bulk Lift International, LLC
Carpentersville, IL 800-879-2247
Bulk Pack
Monroe, LA. .800-498-4215
Bulk Sak Intl Inc
Malvern, AR .501-332-8745
Burgess Mfg. - Oklahoma
Guthrie, OK. .800-804-1913
Burrows Paper Corp
Little Falls, NY 800-272-7122
C & L Wood Products Inc
Hartselle, AL. 800-483-2035
C R Daniels Inc
Ellicott City, MD. 800-933-2638
C-P Flexible Packaging
Newtown, PA 800-448-8183
Calzone Case Co
Bridgeport, CT 800-243-5152
Cambro Manufacturing Co
Huntington Beach, CA 800-833-3003
Can Corp of America Inc
Blandon, PA .610-926-3044
Can Creations
Pembroke Pines, FL 954-581-3312
Cannon Equipment Company
Cannon Falls, MN. 800-825-8501
Cantwell-Cleary Co Inc
Elkridge, MD 301-773-9800
Cantwell-Cleary Co Inc
Richmond, VA. 804-329-9800
Capital City Container Corporation
Buda, TX. 512-312-1222
Capitol Carton Company
Sacramento, CA 916-388-7848
Capitol City Container Corp
Indianapolis, IN 800-233-5145
Caraustar Industries, Inc.
Archdale, NC 800-223-1373
Caravan Packaging Inc
Brookpark, OH 440-243-4100
Cardinal Container Corp
Indianapolis, IN 800-899-2715
Cardinal Packaging
Evansville, IN 800-343-1295
Cardinal Packaging Prod LLC
Crystal Lake, IL 866-216-4942
Caristrap International
Laval, QC 800-361-9466
Carlisle Food Svc Products Inc
Oklahoma City, OK 800-654-8210
Carlisle Plastics
Minneapolis, MN 952-884-1309
Carpenter-Hayes Paper Box Company
East Hampton, CT. 203-267-4436
Carpet City Paper Box Company
Amsterdam, NY 518-842-5430
Carrier Corp
Farmington, CT. 800-227-7437
Carroll Co
Garland, TX .800-527-5722
Carson Industries
Pomona, CA .800-735-5566
Carton Service Co
Shelby, OH 800-533-7744
Castle Bag Co.
Wilmington, DE 302-656-1001
CCL Container
Toronto, ON .416-756-8500
Ccw Products
Arvada, CO 303-427-9663

CDF Corp
Plymouth, MA. 800-443-1920
Cedar Box Co
Minneapolis, MN 612-332-4287
Cello Bag Company
Bowling Green, KY 800-347-0338
Centennial Moldings
Hastings, NE 888-883-2189
Central Bag Co
Leavenworth, KS 913-250-0325
Central Missouri Sheltered Enterprises
Columbia, MO 573-442-6935
Central Ohio Bag & Burlap
Columbus, OH 800-798-9405
Central Package & Display
Minneapolis, MN 763-425-7444
Central Paper Box
Kansas City, MO 816-753-3126
Century Foods Intl LLC
Sparta, WI 800-269-1901
Chalmur Bag Company, LLC
Philadelphia, PA 800-349-2247
Chambers Container Company
Gastonia, NC 704-377-6317
Champion Plastics
Clifton, NJ 800-526-1230
Checker Bag Co
St Louis, MO. 800-489-3130
Chem-Tainer Industries Inc
West Babylon, NY 800-275-2436
Chem-Tainer Industries Inc
West Babylon, NY 800-938-8896
Cherry's Industrial Eqpt Corp
Elk Grove Vlg, IL 800-350-0011
Chester Plastics
Chester, NS .902-275-3522
Chili Plastics
Rochester, NY. 585-889-4680
Cin-Made Packaging Group
Norcross, GA 800-264-7494
Cincinnati Foam Products
Cincinnati, OH 513-741-7722
City Box Company
Aurora, IL 773-277-5500
CKS Packaging
Atlanta, GA .800-800-4257
Clawson Container Company
Clarkston, MI 800-325-8700
Clayton L. Hagy & Son
Philadelphia, PA 215-844-6470
Clear Lam Packaging
Elk Grove Village, IL 847-439-8570
Clear View Bag Co Inc of Nc
Albany, NY 800-458-7153
Clear View Bag Company
Thomasville, NC. 336-885-8131
Clearwater Paper Corporation
Spokane, WA. 877-847-7831
Cleveland Canvas Goods Mfg Co
Cleveland, OH 216-361-4567
Cleveland Plastic Films
Elyria, OH 800-832-6799
Cleveland Specialties Co
Loveland, OH 513-677-9787
CMD Corporation
Appleton, WI 920-730-6888
Coast Label Co
Fountain Valley, CA 800-995-0483
Coast Paper Box Company
San Bernardino, CA 909-382-3475
Coast Scientific
Rancho Santa Fe, CA 800-445-1544
Coastal Pallet Corp
Bridgeport, CT. 203-333-6222
Coffee Sock Company
Eugene, OR. .541-344-7698
Colbert Packaging Corp
Lake Forest, IL 847-367-5990
Cold Chain Technologies
Holliston, MA 800-370-8566
Collectors Gallery
St Charles, IL 800-346-3063
Colonial Transparent Products Company
Hicksville, NY 516-822-4430
Color Box
Richmond, IN 765-966-7588
Color Carton Corp
Bronx, NY. 718-665-0840
Columbus Paperbox Company
Columbus, OH 800-968-0797
Commencement Bay Corrugated
Orting, WA .253-845-3100

Commercial Corrugated Co Inc
Baltimore, MD 800-242-8861
Complete Packaging & Shipping
Freeport, NY 877-269-3236
Conductive Containers Inc
Minneapolis, MN 800-327-2329
Conn Container Corp
North Haven, CT. 203-248-0241
Consolidated Can Co
Paramount, CA 888-793-2199
Consolidated Container Co
New Castle, PA 724-658-0549
Consolidated Container Co LLC
Atlanta, GA .888-831-2184
Consolidated Plastics Co Inc
Stow, OH. 800-858-5001
Consolidated Thread Mills, Inc.
Fall River, MA 508-672-0032
Constar International
Plymouth, MI 734-455-3600
Containair Packaging Corporation
Paterson, NJ 888-276-6500
Container Specialties
Melrose Park, IL 800-548-7513
Container Supply Co
Garden Grove, CA 562-594-0937
Containment Technology
St Gabriel, LA 800-388-2467
Contico Container
Norwalk, CA. 562-921-9967
Continental Extrusion Corporation
Cedar Grove, NJ 800-822-4748
Continental Packaging Corporation
Elgin, IL 847-289-6400
Continental Plastic Container
Dallas, TX 972-303-1825
Continental Products
Mexico, MO .800-325-0216
Continental-Fremont
Tiffin, OH 419-448-4045
Contour Packaging
Philadelphia, PA 215-457-1600
Convoy
Canton, OH .800-899-1583
Conwed Global Netting Sltns
Roanoke, VA. 800-368-3610
Corbett Timber Co
Wilmington, NC 800-334-0684
Corbox-Meyers Inc
Cleveland, OH 800-321-7286
Corfab
Chicago, IL 708-458-8750
Corinth Products
Corinth, ME .207-285-3387
Cornish Containers
Maumee, OH. 419-893-7911
Corpak
San Juan, PR 787-787-9085
Corr Pak Corp
Mc Cook, IL .708-442-7806
Corrobilt Container Company
Livermore, CA 925-373-0880
Corrugated Inner-Pak Corporation
Conshohocken, PA 610-825-0200
Corrugated Packaging
Sarasota, FL .941-371-0000
Corrugated Specialties
Plainwell, MI 269-685-9821
Corrugated Supplies Co.
Bedford, IL 888-826-2738
Corson Manufacturing Company
Lockport, NY 716-434-8871
Cortec Aero
St Paul, MN. .800-426-7832
COVERIS
Tomah, WI 608-372-2153
Covestro LLC
Sheffield, MA 800-628-5084
Craft Corrugated Box Inc
New Bedford, MA 508-998-2115
Crane Carton Corporation
Chicago, IL 773-722-0555
Crate Ideas by Wilderness House
Cave Junction, OR 800-592-2206
Crayex Corp
Piqua, OH 800-837-1747
Cream of the Valley Plastics
Arvada, CO 303-425-5499
Creative Packaging
Hayward, CA 510-785-6500
Creative Packaging Corporation
Buffalo Grove, IL 847-459-1001

Creative Techniques
Auburn Hills, MI 800-473-0284
Crespac Incorporated
Tucker, GA 800-438-1900
Cresthill Industries
Yonkers, NY 914-965-9510
Crown Cork & Seal Co Inc
Philadelphia, PA 215-698-5100
Crystal-Flex Packaging Corporation
Rockville Centre, NY 888-246-7325
CTK Plastics
Moose Jaw, SK 800-667-8847
Cumberland Container Corp
Monterey, TN 931-839-2227
Curtis Packaging
Sandy Hook, CT 203-426-5861
Cush-Pak Container Corporation
Henderson, TX 903-657-0555
Custom Bottle of Connecticut
Naugatuck, CT 203-723-6661
Custom Card & Label Corporation
Lincoln Park, NJ 973-492-0022
Custom Foam Molders
Foristell, MO. 636-441-2307
Custom Pack Inc
Exton, PA 800-722-7005
Custom Packaging Inc
Richmond, VA. 804-232-3299
Custom Poly Packaging
Fort Wayne, IN 800-548-6603
Custom Stamping & Manufacturing
Portland, OR 503-238-3700
D & W Fine Pack
San Bernardino, CA 800-232-5959
D & W Fine Pack
Lake Zurich, IL. 800-323-0422
D&M Pallet Company
Neshkoro, WI 920-293-4616
Dahl-Tech Inc
Stillwater, MN. 800-626-5812
Dairyland Plastics Company
Colfax, WI. 715-962-3425
Dakota Corrugated Box
Sioux Falls, SD. 605-332-3501
Dallas Container Corp
Dallas, TX. 800-381-7148
Dart Container Corp.
Mason, MI 800-248-5960
Dashco
Gloucester, ON 613-834-6825
Davis Brothers Produce Boxes
Evergreen, NC. 910-654-4913
Davis Core & Pa
Cave Spring, GA. 800-235-7483
Davron Technologies Inc
Chattanooga, TN. 423-870-1888
Day Lumber Company
Westfield, MA. 413-568-3511
Day Manufacturing Company
Sherman, TX 903-893-1138
Dayton Bag & Burlap Co
Dayton, OH. 800-543-3400
DBE Inc
Concord, ON. 800-461-5313
De Ster Corporation
Atlanta, GA. 800-237-8270
Deccofelt Corp
Glendora, CA 800-543-3226
Decker Plastics
Council Bluffs, IA. 866-869-6293
Deco Labels & Tags
Toronto, ON 888-496-9029
Decorated Products Company
Westfield, MA. 413-568-0944
DEL-Tec Packaging Inc
Greer, SC. 800-747-8683
Deline Box Co
Denver, CO 303-376-1283
Delta Container Corporation
New Orleans, LA 800-752-7292
Delta Plastics
Hot Springs, AR 501-760-3000
Delta Wire And Mfg.
Harrow, ON. 800-221-3794
Denver Reel & Pallet Company
Denver, CO 303-321-1920
Desert Box & Supply Corporation
Thermal, CA 760-399-5161
Design Plastics Inc
Omaha, NE 800-491-0786
Designers Folding Box Corp
Buffalo, NY. 716-853-5141

Despro Manufacturing
Cedar Grove, NJ 800-292-9906
Detroit Forming
Southfield, MI. 248-440-1317
Development Workshop Inc
Idaho Falls, ID 800-657-5597
Diamond Packaging
Rochester, NY 800-333-4079
Die Cut Specialties Inc
Savage, MN. 952-890-7590
Display One
Hartford, WI 262-673-5880
Dixie Poly Packaging
Greenville, SC. 864-268-3751
Dixie Printing & Packaging
Glen Burnie, MD 800-433-4943
Donnelly Industries, Inc
Wayne, NJ 973-672-1800
Dorado Carton Company
Dorado, PR 787-796-1670
Dordan Manufacturing Co
Woodstock, IL 800-663-5460
Douglas Stephen Plastics Inc
Paterson, NJ 973-523-3030
Drake Co
Houston, TX 800-299-5644
Drescher Paper Box Inc
Buffalo, NY. 716-854-0288
Dub Harris Corporation
Pomona, CA 909-596-6300
Dubuque Steel Products Co
Dubuque, IA 563-556-6288
Dufeck Manufacturing Co
Denmark, WI. 888-603-9663
Durango-Georgia Paper
Tampa, FL. 813-286-2718
Dusobox Company
Haverhill, MA. 978-372-7192
Duval Container Co
Jacksonville, FL 800-342-8194
Dynamic Packaging
Minneapolis, MN 800-878-9380
Dynamic Pak LLC
Syracuse, NY 315-474-8593
Dzignpak LLC Englander
Waco, TX 888-314-5259
E K Lay Co
Philadelphia, PA 800-523-3220
E2M
Duluth, GA 800-622-4326
Eagle Box Company
Farmingdale, NY 212-255-3860
Eastern Container Corporation
Mansfield, MA 508-337-0400
Eastern Plastics
Pawtucket, RI 800-442-8585
Eastern Poly Packaging   Company
Brooklyn, NY 800-421-6006
Eaton Manufacturing Co
Houston, TX 800-328-6610
EB Box Company
Richmond Hill, ON. 800-513-2269
EB Eddy Paper
Port Huron, MI 810-982-0191
Eco-Bag Products
Ossining, NY 800-720-2247
Economy Folding Box Corporation
Chicago, IL 800-771-1053
EGA Products Inc
Brookfield, WI 800-937-3427
EGW Bradbury Enterprises
Bridgewater, ME. 800-332-6021
Eichler Wood Products
Laurys Station, PA 610-262-6749
El Dorado Packaging Inc
El Dorado, AR 870-862-4977
Elberta Crate & Box Company
Carpentersville, IL 888-672-9260
Electrol Specialties Co
South Beloit, IL 815-389-2291
Elegant Packaging
Cicero, IL 800-367-5493
Ellehammer Industries
Langley, BC 604-882-9326
Elm Packaging Company
Memphis, TN 901-795-2711
Elopak Americas
Wixom, MI 248-486-4600
Emoshun
Rancho Cucamonga, CA 909-484-9559
Engineered Products
Hazelwood, MO 314-731-5744

Ensinger Inc
Washington, PA. 800-243-3221
Enterprise Box Company
Montclair, NJ 973-509-2200
Epsen Hillmer Graphics Co
Omaha, NE 800-228-9940
Erie Container
Cleveland, OH 216-631-1650
ERO/Goodrich Forest Products
Tualatin, OR 800-458-5545
Erwyn Products Inc
Morganville, NJ 800-331-9208
ES Robbins Corp
Muscle Shoals, AL 800-633-3325
Eureka Paper Box Company
Williamsport, PA. 570-326-9147
Excelsior Transparent Bag Manufacturing
Yonkers, NY 914-968-1300
Expert Industries Inc
Brooklyn, NY 718-434-6060
F C MEYER Packaging LLC
Jeannette, PA 724-523-5565
F G Products Inc
Rice Lake, WI 800-247-3854
F N Smith Corp
Oregon, IL 815-732-2171
F&G Packaging
Yulee, FL. 904-225-5121
F.E. Wood & Sons
West Baldwin, ME 207-286-5003
Fabohio Inc
Uhrichsville, OH. 740-922-4233
Fabri-Kal Corp
Kalamazoo, MI 800-888-5054
Fabricated Components Inc
Stroudsburg, PA 800-233-8163
Fabriko
Altavista, VA. 888-203-8098
Fan Bag Company
Chicago, IL 773-342-2752
Faribault Manufacturing Co
Faribault, MN 800-447-6043
Farmer's Co-Op Elevator Co
Hudsonville, MI 800-439-9859
Fast Bags
Fort Worth, TX 800-321-3687
Fehlig Brothers Box & Lbr Co
St Louis, MO. 314-241-6900
Felco Packaging Specialist
Baltimore, MD 800-673-8488
Ferguson Containers
Phillipsburg, NJ 908-454-9755
Fibre Containers Inc
City of Industry, CA 626-968-5897
Film X
Dayville, CT 800-628-6128
Film-Pak Inc
Crowley, TX 800-526-1838
Finn Industries
Ontario, CA. 909-930-1500
First Midwest of Iowa Corporation
Des Moines, IA 800-247-8411
Fischer Paper Products Inc
Antioch, IL 800-323-9093
Fitec International Inc
Memphis, TN 800-332-6387
Fitzpatrick Container Company
North Wales, PA 215-699-3515
Flashfold Carton Inc
Fort Wayne, IN 260-423-9431
Flex Products
Carlstadt, NJ 800-526-6273
FLEXcon Company
Spencer, MA 508-885-8200
Flexible Foam Products
Elkhart, IN. 800-678-3626
Flexicon
Cary, IL. 847-639-3530
Flexo Transparent Inc
Buffalo, NY. 877-993-5396
Flint Boxmakers Inc
Flint, MI 810-743-0400
Flour City Press-Pack Company
Minneapolis, MN 952-831-1265
Foam Concepts Inc
Uxbridge, MA. 508-278-7255
Foam Pack Industries
Springfield, NJ 973-376-3700
Foam Packaging Inc
Vicksburg, MS 800-962-2655
Foamex
Cornelius, NC 704-892-8081

Foamold Corporation
Oneida, NY 315-363-5350
Fold-Pak Corporation
Newark, NY 315-331-3159
Fold-Pak South
Columbus, GA 706-689-2924
Folding Carton/Flexible Packaging
North Hollywood, CA 818-896-3449
Food Pak Corp
San Mateo, CA 650-341-6559
Formel Industries
Franklin Park, IL. 800-373-3300
Fortune Plastics, Inc
Old Saybrook, CT 800-243-0306
Four M Manufacturing Group
San Jose, CA 408-998-1141
Franklin Crates
Micanopy, FL 352-466-3141
Frankston Paper Box Company of Texas
Frankston, TX. 903-876-2550
Fredman Bag Co
Milwaukee, WI 800-945-5686
Freedom Packaging
Watsonville, CA 831-722-3565
Frem Corporation
Worcester, MA 508-791-3152
Fremont Die Cut Products
Fremont, OH 800-223-3177
Fresno Pallet, Inc.
Sultana, CA 559-591-4111
Friedman Bag Company
Manhattan Beach, CA. 213-628-2341
Friend Box Co
Danvers, MA. 978-774-0240
Friendly City Box Co Inc
Johnstown, PA. 814-266-6287
Frobisher Industries
Waterborough, NB 506-362-2198
Frontier Bag
Kansas City, MO 816-765-4811
Frontier Bag Co Inc
Omaha, NE 800-278-2247
Fruit Growers Package Company
Grandville, MI 616-724-1400
Frye's Measure Mill
Wilton, NH 603-654-6581
Fuller Box Co
North Attleboro, MA 508-695-2525
Fuller Industries LLC
Great Bend, KS 800-522-0499
Fuller Packaging Inc
Central Falls, RI 401-725-4300
Fulton-Denver Co
Denver, CO 800-521-1414
Gabriel Container Co
Santa Fe Springs, CA 323-685-8844
Garvey Products
Cincinnati, OH 513-771-8710
Gary Plastic Packaging Corporation
Bronx, NY 800-221-8151
Gates
West Peterborough, NH 888-543-6316
Gateway Packaging Co
Kansas City, MO. 816-483-9800
Gateway Packaging Corp
Export, PA. 888-289-2693
Gatewood Products LLC
Parkersburg, WV. 800-827-5461
Gaylord Container Corporation
Tampa, FL 813-621-3591
Gemini Plastic Films Corporation
Garfield, NJ 800-789-4732
General Bag Corporation
Cleveland, OH 800-837-9396
General Films Inc
Covington, OH 888-436-3456
General Press Corp
Natrona Heights, PA 724-224-3500
Genesee Corrugated
Flint, MI .810-228-3702
Genpak
Peterborough, ON 800-461-1995
Genpak LLC
Lakeville, MN. 800-328-4556
Genpak LLC
Charlotte, NC 800-626-6695
Georg Fischer Central Plastics
Shawnee, OK 800-654-3872
Georgia-Pacific LLC
Atlanta, GA 800-283-5547
Gessner Products
Ambler, PA 800-874-7808

Gibbs Brothers Cooperage
Hot Springs, AR 501-623-8881
Gibraltar Packaging Group Inc
Hastings, NE 402-463-1366
Gilchrist Bag Co Inc
Camden, AR 800-643-1513
Glasko Plastics
Santa Ana, CA 714-751-7830
Glopak
St Leonard, QC 800-361-6994
Goeman's Wood Products
Hartford, WI 262-673-6090
Goergen-Mackwirth Co Inc
Buffalo, NY. 800-728-4446
Golden West Packaging Concept
Lake Forest, CA 949-855-9646
Goldenwest Sales
Cerritos, CA 800-827-6175
Goldman Manufacturing Company
Detroit, MI 313-834-5535
Goldmax Industries
City of Industry, CA 626-964-8820
GP Plastics Corporation
Medley, FL 305-888-3555
Graff Tank Erection
Harrisville, PA. 814-385-6671
Graham Engineering Corp
York, PA .717-848-3755
Grand Valley Labels
Grand Rapids, MI
GranPac
Wetaskiwin, AB 780-352-3324
Graphic Impressions of Illinois
River Grove, IL 708-453-1100
Graphic Packaging Corporation
Golden, CO 800-677-2886
Graphic Packaging International
Atlanta, GA 770-240-7200
Graphic Packaging Intl
Elk Grove Vlg, IL 847-437-1700
Great Lakes-Triad Package Corporation
Grand Rapids, MI 616-241-6441
Great Northern Corp
Chippewa Falls, WI 800-472-1800
Great Northern Corp
Racine, WI 800-558-4711
Great Northern Corp.
Appleton, WI 800-236-3671
Great Southern Industries
Jackson, MS 877-638-3667
Green Bay Packaging Inc.
Kalamazoo, MI 269-552-1000
Green Bay Packaging Inc.
Tulsa, OK 918-446-3341
Green Bay Packaging Inc.
Green Bay, WI 920-433-5111
Green Brothers
Barrington, RI. 401-245-9043
Green Seams
Maple Grove, MN 612-929-3213
Greenfield Packaging
White Plains, NY 914-993-0233
Greenfield Paper Box Co
Greenfield, MA. 413-773-9414
Greif Brothers Corporation
Cleveland, OH 800-424-0342
Greif Inc
Delaware, OH 740-549-6000
Greif Inc
Delaware, OH 800-476-1635
Gribble Stamp & Stencil Co
Houston, TX 713-228-5358
Grigsby Brothers Paper Box Manufacturers
Portland, OR 866-233-4690
Gulf Coast Plastics
Tampa, FL 800-277-7491
Gulf Packaging Company
Safety Harbor, FL 800-749-3466
H S Inc
Oklahoma City, OK 800-238-1240
H. Arnold Wood Turning
Tarrytown, NY 888-314-0088
H.J. Jones & Sons
London, ON 800-667-0476
H.P. Neun
Fairport, NY 585-388-1360
Hager Containers Inc
Carrollton, TX 972-416-7660
Hampton Roads Box Company
Suffolk, VA 757-934-2355
Handgards Inc
El Paso, TX 800-351-8161

Hank Rivera Associates
Dearborn, MI 313-581-8300
Hanson Box & Lumber Company
Wakefield, MA 617-245-0358
Harbor Pallet Company
Anaheim, CA 714-871-0932
Hardi-Tainer
South Deerfield, MA 800-882-9878
Hardy Systems Corporation
Northbrook, IL 800-927-3956
Harpak-ULMA Packaging LLC
Ball Ground, GA. 770-345-5300
Hartford Containers
Terryville, CT 860-584-1194
Hartford Plastics
Omaha, NE
Harvard Folding Box Company
Lynn, MA 781-598-1600
Hawkeye Corrugated Box
Cedar Falls, IA 319-268-0407
Hedstrom Corporation
Ashland, OH 700-765-9665
Hedwin Division
Baltimore, MD 800-638-1012
Henry Ira L Co
Watertown, WI 920-261-0648
Heritage Bag Co
Roanoke, TX 800-527-2247
Heritage Packaging
Victor, NY 585-742-3310
Herkimer Pallet & Wood Products Company
Herkimer, NY 315-866-4591
Hibco Plastics
Yadkinville, NC 800-849-8683
Highland Plastics Inc
Mira Loma, CA. 800-368-0491
Hinchcliff Products Company
Strongsville, OH 440-238-5200
Hinkle Manufacturing
Perrysburg, OH 419-666-5367
Hodge Manufacturing Company
Springfield, MA 800-262-4634
Hodges
Vienna, IL 800-444-0011
Holmco Container Manufacturing, LTD
Baltic, OH 330-897-4503
Home Plastics Inc
Des Moines, IA 515-265-2562
Hood Packaging
Madison, MS. 800-321-8115
Hood Packaging
Burlington, ON 877-462-6627
Hoover Materials Handling Group
Houston, TX 800-844-8683
Hope Paper Box Company
Pawtucket, RI 401-724-5700
Hub Folding Box Co
Mansfield, MA 508-339-0102
Hubco Inc
Hutchinson, KS 800-563-1867
Hudson Poly Bag Inc
Hudson, MA 800-229-7566
Hunter Packaging Corporation
South Elgin, IL 800-428-4747
Huntsman Packaging Corporation
Birmingham, Bi. 205-328-4720
Hurri-Kleen Corporation
Birmingham, AL. 800-455-8265
IB Concepts
Elizabeth, NJ. 888-671-0800
IBC Shell Packaging
New Hyde Park, NY. 516-352-5138
Ideal Wire Works
Alhambra, CA. 626-282-0886
Il Valley Container Inc
Peru, IL 815-223-7200
Imperial Containers
City of Industry, CA 626-333-6363
Imperial Industries Inc
Rothschild, WI 800-558-2945
Imperial Packaging Corporation
Pawtucket, RI 401-753-7778
Impress Industries
Emmaus, PA 610-967-6027
In-Touch Products
North Salt Lake, UT 801-298-4466
Incinerator International Inc
Houston, TX 713-227-1466
Independent Can Co
Belcamp, MD 410-272-0090
Indian Valley Industries
Johnson City, NY 800-659-5111

Indiana Bottle Co
Scottsburg, IN 800-752-8702
Indiana Carton Co Inc
Bremen, IN 800-348-2390
Indiana Vac Form Inc
Warsaw, IN 574-269-1725
Indianapolis Container Company
Indianapolis, IN 800-760-3318
Industrial Container Corp
High Point, NC 336-886-7031
Industrial Contracting & Rggng
Mahwah, NJ 888-427-7444
Industrial Crating & Packing
Tukwila, WA 800-942-0499
Industrial Hardwood
Perrysburg, OH 419-666-2503
Industrial Lumber & Packaging
Spring Lake, MI 616-842-1457
Industrial Nameplate Inc
Warminster, PA 800-878-6263
Industrial Woodfab & Packaging
Riverview, MI 734-284-4808
Inland Consumer Packaging
Harrington, DE 302-398-4211
Inland Paper Company
Ontario, CA 909-923-4505
Inland Paperboard & Packaging
Rock Hill, SC 803-366-4103
Inline Plastic Corp
McDonough, GA 678-466-3467
Innova Envelopes
La Salle, QC 514-595-0555
Innovative Folding Carton Company
South Plainfield, NJ 908-757-0205
Instabox
Calgary, AB 800-482-6173
Inteplast Bags & Films Corporation
Delta, BC 604-946-5431
International Wood Industries
Snohomish, WA 800-922-6141
Interstate Packaging
White Bluff, TN 800-251-1072
Intertape Polymer Group
Sarasota, FL 888-898-7834
Intertech Corp
Greensboro, NC 800-364-2255
IPL Inc
Saint-Damien, QC 800-463-4755
IPL Plastics
Edmundston, NB. 800-739-9595
IPS International
Snohomish, WA 360-668-5050
ITW Angleboard
Villa Rica, GA 770-459-5747
ITW Hi-Cone
Itasca, IL 630-438-5300
Ivarson Inc
Milwaukee, WI 414-351-0700
IVEX Packaging Corporation
Longueuil, QC 450-651-8887
J A Heilferty & Co
Teaneck, NJ 201-836-5060
J L Clark Corp
Rockford, IL 815-962-8861
J M Packaging Co
Warren, MI 586-771-7800
J&J Corrugated Box Corporation
Franklin, MA 508-528-6200
J&J Mid-South Container Corporation
Augusta, GA 800-395-1025
J.C. Products Inc.
Haddam, CT 860-267-5516
J.V. Reed & Company
Louisville, KY 877-258-7333
Jackson Corrugated Container
Middletown, CT 860-346-9671
Jacksonville Box & Woodwork Co
Jacksonville, FL 800-683-2699
James Thompson
New York, NY 212-686-5306
Jamestown Container Corporation
Buffalo, NY. 855-234-4054
Jamison Plastic Corporation
Allentown, PA 610-391-1400
Jarisch Paper Box Company
North Adams, MA 413-663-5396
Java Jacket
Portland, OR 800-208-4128
Jayhawk Boxes
Fremont, NE 800-642-8363
Jeb Plastics
Wilmington, DE 800-556-2247

Jeco Plastic Products LLC
Plainfield, IN. 800-593-5326
JEM Wire Products
Middletown, CT 860-347-0447
Jesco Industries
Litchfield, MI 800-455-0019
Jescorp
Des Plaines, IL 847-299-7800
Jesse Jones Box Corporation
Philadelphia, PA 215-425-6600
Jessup Paper Box
Brookston, IN 765-490-9043
Jewel Case Corp
Cranston, RI 800-441-4447
Jewell Bag Company
Dallas, TX 214-749-1223
Johnson Corrugated Products Corporation
Thompson, CT 860-923-9563
Jomar Plastics Industry
Nanty Glo, PA 800-681-4039
Jordan Box Co
Syracuse, NY 315-422-3419
Jordan Paper Box Co
Chicago, IL 773-287-5362
JP Plastics, Inc.
Foxboro, MA 508-203-2420
Juice Tree
Omaha, NE 714-891-4425
Jupiter Mills Corporation
Roslyn, NY 800-853-5121
K & H Corrugated Corp
Walden, NY. 845-778-3555
K&H Container
Wallingford, CT 203-265-1547
K-C Products Company
Van Nuys, CA 818-267-1600
Kadon Corporation
Milford, OH 937-299-0088
Kal Pac Corp
Montgomery, NY 800-852-5722
KANE Bag Supply Co
Baltimore, MD 410-732-5800
KAPCO
Kent, OH 800-843-5368
Karyall Telday Inc
Cleveland, OH 216-281-4063
Kaufman Paper Box Company
Providence, RI 401-272-7508
Keeper Thermal Bag Co
Bartlett, IL 800-765-9244
Kelley Wood Products
Fitchburg, MA 978-345-7531
Kelly Box & Packaging Corp
Fort Wayne, IN 260-432-4570
Kendel
Countryside, IL 800-323-1100
Kerrigan Paper Products Inc
Haverhill, MA 978-374-4797
KETCH
Wichita, KS 800-766-3777
Key Container Company
South Gate, CA 323-564-4211
Key Packaging Co
Sarasota, FL 941-355-2728
Keystone Packaging Svc Inc
Phillipsburg, NJ 800-473-8567
KHM Plastics Inc
Gurnee, IL. 847-249-4910
Killington Wood ProductsCompany
Rutland, VT 802-773-9111
Kimball Companies
East Longmeadow, MA 413-525-1881
King Plastic Corp
North Port, FL 800-780-5502
KM International Corp
Kenton, TN 731-749-8700
Knapp Container
Beacon Falls, CT. 203-888-0511
Knight Paper Box Company
Chicago, IL 773-585-2035
Koch Container
Victor, NY 585-924-1600
Koch Equipment LLC
Kansas City, MO. 816-931-4557
Kole Industries
Miami, FL 305-633-2556
Kontane
Charleston, SC 843-352-0011
Konz Wood Products Co
Appleton, WI 877-610-5145
L & C Plastic Bags
Covington, OH 937-473-2968

L&H Wood Manufacturing Company
Farmington, MI 248-474-9000
Label Makers
Pleasant Prairie, WI 800-208-3331
Label Systems Inc
Addison, TX 800-220-9552
Lakeside Container Corp
Plattsburgh, NY 518-561-6150
Lakeside Manufacturing Inc
Milwaukee, WI 888-558-8565
Laminated Paper Products
San Jose, CA 408-888-0880
Landis Plastics
Alsip, IL .708-396-1470
Langer Manufacturing Company
Cedar Rapids, IA. 800-728-6445
Langston Co Inc
Memphis, TN 901-774-4440
Lansing Corrugated Products
Lansing, MI 517-323-2752
Laval Paper Box
Pointe Claire, QC 450-669-3551
Lawrence Paper Co
Lawrence, KS 785-843-8111
Lawrence Schiff Silk Mills
New York, NY 800-272-4433
LBP Manufacturing LLC
Cicero, IL 708-652-5600
Leaman Container
Fort Worth, TX 817-429-2660
Leclaire Packaging Corp
Ixonia, WI 920-206-9902
Leggett & Platt Storage
Vernon Hills, IL 847-816-6246
Lengsfield Brothers
New Orleans, LA 504-529-2235
Lenkay Sani Products Corporation
Brooklyn, NY 718-927-9260
Lester Box & Mfg Div
Long Beach, CA 562-437-5123
Letica Corp
Rochester Hills, MI 800-538-4221
Levin Brothers Paper
Cicero, IL 800-545-6200
Lewis Steel Works Inc
Wrens, GA. 800-521-5239
Lewisburg Container Co
Lewisburg, OH 937-962-0101
Lexel
Fort Worth, TX 817-332-4061
Liberty Carton Co.
Golden Valley, MN 800-328-1784
Lima Barrel & Drum Company
Lima, OH 419-224-8916
Lin Pac Plastics
Roswell, GA 770-751-6006
LinPac
San Angelo, TX 800-453-7393
Linvar
Hartford, CT 800-282-5288
Liqui-Box
Richmond, VA. 804-325-1400
Liquitane
Berwick, PA 570-759-6200
Little Rock Crate & Basket Co
Little Rock, AR. 800-223-7823
LMK Containers
Centerville, UT 626-821-9984
Lone Star Container Corp
Irving, TX 800-552-6937
Longview Fibre Co
Longview, WA. 800-929-8111
Longview Fibre Company
Beaverton, OR 503-350-1600
Los Angeles Paper Box & Board Mills
Los Angeles, CA. 323-685-8900
Lowell Paper Box Company
Nashua, NH. 603-595-0700
Loy Lange Box Co
St Louis, MO. 800-886-4712
LPS Industries
Moonachie, NJ 800-275-4577
LTI Printing Inc
Sturgis, MI 269-651-7574
Luce Corp
Hamden, CT 800-344-6966
Luetzow Industries
South Milwaukee, WI. 800-558-6055
Luke's Almond Acres
Reedley, CA 559-638-3483
Lunn Industries
Glen Cove, NY 516-671-9000

Lustrecal
Lodi, CA 800-234-6264
M & G Packaging Corp
Floral Park, NY 800-240-5288
M & H Crate Inc
Jacksonville, TX 903-683-5351
M O Industries Inc
Whippany, NJ 973-386-9228
M&L Plastics
Easthampton, MA 413-527-1330
M&R Flexible Packaging
Springboro, OH 800-543-3380
Mack-Chicago Corporation
Chicago, IL 800-992-6225
MacMillan Bloedel Packaging
Montgomery, AL 800-239-4464
Maco Bag Corp
Newark, NY 315-226-1000
Madsen Wire Products Inc
Orland, IN .260-829-6561
Malco Manufacturing Co
Los Angeles, CA 866-477-7267
Mall City Containers Inc
Kalamazoo, MI 800-643-6721
Malnove of Nebraska
Omaha, NE 800-228-9877
Malpack Polybag
Ajax, ON 905-428-3751
Mannkraft Corporation
Newark, NJ 973-589-7400
Manufacturers Corrugate Box
Flushing, NY 718-894-7200
Manufacturers Wood Supply Company
Cleveland, OH 216-771-7848
Mar-Boro Printing & Advertising Specialties
Brooklyn, NY 718-336-4051
Marco Products
Adrian, MI. 517-265-3333
Marcus Carton Company
Melville, NY 631-752-4200
Marden Edwards
Antioch, CA 800-332-1838
Marfred Industries
Sun Valley, CA 800-529-5156
Marion Paper Box Co
Marion, IN. 765-664-6435
Mark Container Corporation
San Leandro, CA 510-483-4440
Maro Paper Products Company
Bellwood, IL 708-649-9982
Marpac Industries
Philmont, NY 888-462-7722
Marshall Boxes Inc
Rochester, NY 585-458-7432
Marshall Plastic Film Inc
Martin, MI. 269-672-5511
Mason Transparent Package Company
Armonk, NY 718-792-6000
Massachusetts Container Corporation
North Haven, CT. 203-248-2161
Massillon Container Co
Navarre, OH 330-879-5653
Master Containers
Mulberry, FL 800-881-6847
Master Package Corporation
Menomonie, WI 800-347-4144
Master Paper Box Co
Chicago, IL 877-927-0252
Maull-Baker Box Company
Brookfield, WI 414-463-1290
Maypak Inc
Wayne, NJ 973-696-0780
McDowell Industries
Memphis, TN 800-622-3695
McGraw Box Company
Mc Graw, NY 607-836-6465
Meadwestvaco Corp
Richmond, VA. 804-444-1000
MeGa Industries
Burlington, ON 800-665-6342
Mello Smello LLC
Minneapolis, MN 888-574-2964
Melmat Inc
Huntington Beach, CA 800-635-6289
Melville Plastics
Haw River, NC 336-578-5800
Memphis Delta Tent & Awning
Memphis, TN 901-522-1238
Menasha Corp
Neenah, WI. 800-558-5073
Merchants Publishing Company
Kalamazoo, MI 269-345-1175

Meriden Box Company
Southington, CT 860-621-7141
Metal Container Corporation
St Louis, MO. 314-957-9500
Meyer Packaging
Palmyra, PA. 717-838-6300
Michiana Box & Crate
Niles, MI. .800-677-6372
Michiana Corrugate Products
Sturgis, MI 269-651-5225
Michigan Box Co
Detroit, MI. 888-642-4269
Michigan Pallet Inc
St Charles, MI. 989-865-9915
Micro Qwik
Cross Plains, WI 608-798-3071
Micro Wire Products Inc
Brockton, MA 508-584-0200
Microplas Industries
Dunwoody, GA. 800-952-4528
Mid Cities Paper Box Company
Downey, CA 877-277-6272
Mid-States Mfg & Engr Co Inc
Milton, IA .800-346-1792
Midco Plastics
Enterprise, KS 800-235-2729
Midland Manufacturing Co
Monroe, IA 800-394-2625
Midlands Packaging Corp
Lincoln, NE. 402-464-9124
Midvale Paper Box
Wilkes Barre, PA. 570-824-3577
Midwest Aircraft Products Co
Lexington, OH 419-884-2164
Midwest Box Co
Cleveland, OH 216-281-3980
Midwest Fibre Products Inc
Viola, IL 309-596-2955
Midwest Paper Products Company
Louisville, KY 502-636-2741
Midwest Paper Tube & CanCorporation
New Berlin, WI. 262-782-7300
Midwest Rubber Svc & Supply
Minneapolis, MN 800-537-7457
Midwest Wire Specialties
Chicago, IL 800-238-0228
Milan Box Corporation
Milan, TN .800-225-8057
Millhiser
Richmond, VA. 800-446-2247
Milprint
Oshkosh, WI 920-303-8600
Mimi et Cie
Seattle, WA 206-545-1850
Mini-Bag Company
Farmingdale, NY 631-694-3325
Mmi Engineered Soultions Inc
Saline, MI. 800-825-2566
Modern Packaging Inc
Deer Park, NY 631-595-2437
Modern Paper Box Company
Providence, RI 401-861-7357
Mohawk Northern Plastics
Auburn, WA 800-426-1100
Mohawk Western Plastics Inc
La Verne, CA 909-593-7547
Molded Container Corporation
Portland, OR 503-233-8601
Monte Package Co
Riverside, MI 800-653-2807
Montebello Container Corp
La Mirada, CA 714-994-2351
Montebello Packaging
Hawkesbury, ON. 613-632-7096
Moore Paper Boxes Inc
Dayton, OH 937-278-7327
Moorecraft Box & Crate
Tarboro, NC 252-823-2510
Morgan Brothers Bag Company
Richmond, VA. 804-355-9107
Morphy Container Company
Brantford, ON 519-752-5428
Morris Industries
Forestville, MD. 301-568-5005
Morris Transparent Box Co
East Providence, RI. 401-438-6116
Moser Bag & Paper Company
Cleveland, OH 800-433-6638
Mountain Safety Research
Seattle, WA 800-877-9677
Mt Vernon Packaging Inc
Mt Vernon, OH 888-397-3221

Mullnix Packages Inc
Fort Wayne, IN 260-747-3149
Multibulk Systems International
Wendell, NC 919-366-2100
MultiFab Plastics
Boston, MA 888-293-5754
Murray Envelope Corporation
Hattiesburg, MS 601-583-8292
Muth Associates
Springfield, MA 800-388-0157
Nagel Paper & Box Company
Saginaw, MI 800-292-3654
Naltex
Austin, TX. 800-531-5112
Nameplate
St Paul, MN. 651-228-1522
NAP Industries
Brooklyn, NY 877-635-4948
Nashua Corporation
Nashua, NH. 603-661-2004
National Marking Products Inc
Henrico, VA 800-482-1553
National Poly Bag Manufacturing Corporation
Brooklyn, NY 718-629-9800
Neal Walters Poster Corporation
Bentonville, AR 501-273-2489
Nefab Packaging Inc
Elk Grove Vlg, IL 847-787-0340
Nefab Packaging Inc.
Coppell, TX 800-322-4425
Nefab Packaging, Inc.
Coppell, TX 800-322-4425
Neff Packaging
Simpsonville, KY 800-445-4383
Nelson Container Corp
Germantown, WI. 262-250-5000
Neos
Elk River, MN. 888-441-6367
Net Pack Systems
Oakland, ME. 207-465-4531
New England Wooden Ware
Gardner, MA 800-252-9214
New Era Label Corporation
Belleville, NJ 973-759-2444
New Lisbon Wood ProductsManufacturing Company
New Lisbon, WI 608-562-3122
New Mexico Products Inc
Albuquerque, NM 877-345-7864
New York Corugated Box Co
Paterson, NJ 973-742-5000
New York Folding Box Co Inc
Stanhope, NJ. 973-347-6932
Nolon Industries
Mantua, OH. 330-274-2283
Nordic Printing & Packaging
New Hope, MN. 763-535-6440
North American Container Corp
Marietta, GA 800-929-0610
North American Packaging Corp
New York, NY 800-499-3521
Northeast Box Co
Ashtabula, OH 800-362-8100
Northeast Container Corporation
Dumont, NJ 201-385-6200
Northeast Packaging Co
Presque Isle, ME 207-764-6271
Northeast Packaging Materials
Monsey, NY 845-426-2900
Northern Box Co Inc
Elkhart, IN. 574-264-2161
Northern Package Corporation
Minneapolis, MN 952-881-5861
Nosco
Waukegan, IL 847-360-4806
Noteworthy Company
Amsterdam, NY 800-696-7849
Nottingham Spirk
Cleveland, OH 216-231-7830
Novelis Foil Products
Atlanta, GA. 800-776-8701
NOVOLEX
Glendale, AZ. 800-243-0306
Now Plastics Inc
East Longmeadow, MA 413-525-1010
NPC Display Group
Newark, NJ 973-589-2155
Nu-Trend Plastics Thermoformer
Jacksonville, FL 904-353-5936
O.C. Adhesives Corporation
Ridgefield, NJ 800-662-1595
Oak Barrel Winecraft
Berkeley, CA. 510-849-0400

Oak Creek Pallet Company
Milwaukee, WI 414-762-7170
Oakes Carton Co
Kalamazoo, MI 269-381-6022
Occidental Chemical Corporation
Dallas, TX 800-733-3665
Ockerlund Industries
Addison, IL 708-771-7707
Okura USA Inc
Lenexa, KS 800-772-1187
Olcott Plastics
St Charles, IL 888-313-5277
Old Dominion Box Co Inc
Madison Heights, VA 434-929-6701
Old Dominion Box Company
Burlington, NC 336-226-4491
Old English Printing & Label Company
Delray Beach, FL 561-997-9990
Olive Can Company
Elgin, IL 847-468-7474
Oracle Packaging
Winston Salem, NC 800-952-9536
Orange Plastics
Compton, CA 310-609-2121
Oration Rubber Stamp Company
Columbus, NJ 908-496-4161
ORBIS
Oconomowoc, WI 262-560-5000
ORBIS
Oconomowoc, WI 800-890-7292
Original Lincoln Logs
Chestertown, NY 800-833-2461
Original Packaging & Display Company
Saint Louis, MO 314-772-7797
Osterneck Company
Lumberton, NC 800-682-2416
OTD Corporation
Hinsdale, IL 630-321-9232
Owens-Illinois Inc
Perrysburg, OH 567-336-5000
P M Plastics
Pewaukee, WI 262-691-1700
P&E
Altamonte Spgs, FL 800-438-0674
Pacific Paper Box Co
Cudahy, CA 323-771-7733
Pack-Rite
Newington, CT 860-953-0120
Package Containers Inc
Canby, OR 800-266-5806
Packaging Associates
Randolph, NJ 973-252-8890
Packaging Corporation of America
Lake Forest, IL 800-456-4725
Packaging Design Corp
Burr Ridge, IL 630-323-1354
Packaging Dynamics International
Caldwell, OH 740-732-5665
Packaging Enterprises
Rockledge, PA 800-453-6213
Packaging Solutions
Los Altos Hills, CA 650-917-1022
Packaging Technologies
Tuckahoe, NY 914-337-2005
Packing Material Company
Southfield, MI 248-489-7000
Packing Specialties
Warren, MI 586-758-5240
Packrite Packaging
Archdale, NC 336-431-1111
Pacquet Oneida
Charlotte, NC 800-631-8388
Pactiv LLC
Lake Forest, IL 800-476-4300
Pak-Sak Industries I
Sparta, MI 800-748-0431
Pak-Sher
Kilgore, TX 903-984-8596
Pakmark
Chesterfield, MO 800-423-1379
Pallet One Inc
Bartow, FL 800-771-1148
Pallets Inc
Fort Edward, NY 518-747-4177
Pallox Incorporated
Onsted, MI 517-456-4101
Palmer Distributors
St Clair Shores, MI 800-444-1912
Palmetto Packaging
Florence, SC 843-662-5800
Pan Pacific Plastics Inc
Hayward, CA 888-475-6888

Papelera Puertorriquena
Utuado, PR 787-894-2098
Paper Box & Specialty Co
Sheboygan, WI 888-240-3756
Paper Products Company
Cincinnati, OH 513-921-4717
Paper Systems Inc
Des Moines, IA 800-342-2855
Paper Works Industries Inc
Baldwinsville, NY 800-847-5677
PAR-Kan
Silver Lake, IN 800-291-5487
Par-Pak
Houston, TX 713-686-6700
Par-Pak
Houston, TX 888-727-7252
Parade Packaging
Mundelein, IL 847-566-6264
Paradigm Packaging Inc
Upland, CA 909-985-2750
Paragon Packaging
Ferndale, CA 888-615-0065
Parisian Novelty Company
Homewood, IL 773-847-1212
Park Custom Molding
Linden, NJ 908-486-8882
Parkway Plastic Inc
Piscataway, NJ 800-881-4996
Parlor City Paper Box Co Inc
Binghamton, NY 607-772-0600
Parsons Manufacturing Corp.
Menlo Park, CA 650-324-4726
Parta
Kent, OH 800-543-5781
Parvin Manufacturing Company
Los Angeles, CA 800-648-0770
Paul T. Freund Corporation
Palmyra, NY 800-333-0091
PBC
Mahwah, NJ 800-514-2739
Peace Industries
Rolling Meadows, IL 800-873-2239
Peacock Crate Factory
Jacksonville, TX 800-657-2200
Peerless Cartons
Bartlett, IL 312-226-7952
Peerless Packages
Cleveland, OH 216-464-3620
Pel-Pak Container
Pell City, AL 800-239-2699
Pelco Packaging Corporation
Stirling, NJ 908-647-3500
Pelican Displays
Homer, IL 800-627-1517
Pell Paper Box Company
Elizabeth City, NC 252-335-4361
Peninsula Plastics
Auburn Hills, MI 800-394-8698
Penn Bottle & Supply Company
Philadelphia, PA 215-365-5700
Penn Products
Portland, CT 800-490-7366
Penny Plate
Haddonfield, NJ 856-429-7583
Pentwater Wire Products Inc
Pentwater, MI 877-869-6911
Performance Packaging
Trail Creek, IN 219-874-6226
Peter Dudgeon International
Honolulu, HI 808-841-8211
Peter Pepper Products Inc
Compton, CA 310-639-0390
Peterboro Basket Co
Peterborough, NH 603-924-3861
Petoskey Plastics
Morristown, TN 423-586-8917
Pexco Packaging Corporation
Toledo, OH 800-227-9950
Pfeil & Holding Inc
Woodside, NY 800-247-7955
Phoenix Closures Inc
Naperville, IL 630-544-3475
Phoenix Industries Corp
Madison, WI 888-241-7482
Pilant Corp
Bloomington, IN 800-366-3525
Pine Point Wood Products Inc
Osseo, MN 763-428-4301
Pinn Pack Packaging LLC
Oxnard, CA 805-385-4100
Pioneer Packaging
Chicopee, MA 413-378-6930

Pioneer Packaging & Printing
Anoka, MN 800-708-1705
Pioneer Plastics Inc
Dixon, KY 800-951-1551
Pittsburgh Tank Corp
Monongahela, PA 800-634-0243
Plastic Assembly Corporation
Ayer, MA
Plastican Corporation
Fairfield, NJ 973-227-7817
Plastics Inc
Greensboro, AL 334-624-8801
Plastics Industries
Athens, TN 800-894-4876
Plastilite Corporation
Omaha, NE 800-228-9506
Plastipak Packaging
Plymouth, MI 734-354-3510
Plastiques Cascades Group
Montreal, QC 888-703-6515
Plaxall Inc
Long Island City, NY 800-876-5706
Pohlig Brothers
N Chesterfield, VA 804-275-9000
Polar Tech Industries Inc
Genoa, IL 800-423-2749
Poly One Corp
Avon Lake, OH 866-765-9663
Poly Plastic Products Inc
Delano, PA 570-467-3000
Poly Processing Co
French Camp, CA 877-325-3142
Poly Shapes Corporation
Elyria, OH 800-605-9359
Polybottle Group
Surrey, BC 604-594-4999
Polycon Industries
Chicago, IL 773-374-5500
Polyplastics
Austin, TX 800-753-7659
Polytainers
Toronto, ON 800-268-2424
Pop Tops Co Inc
South Easton, MA 800-647-8677
Portco Corporation
Vancouver, WA 800-426-1794
Portland Paper Box Company
Portland, OR 800-547-2571
Power Packaging Inc
Rosendale, WI 920-872-2181
PPC Perfect Packaging Co
Perrysburg, OH 419-874-3167
PPI
Baton Rouge, LA 225-330-4602
Prairie Packaging Inc
Mooresville, NC 704-660-6600
Pratt Industries
New Orleans, LA 504-733-7292
Pratt Industries
Conyers, GA 800-428-9269
Pratt Industries
Raleigh, NC 919-334-7400
Precision Printing & Packaging
Clarksville, TN 800-500-4526
Precision Wood of Hawaii
Vancouver, WA 808-682-2055
Precision Wood Products
Vancouver, WA 360-694-8322
Premier Packages
Saint Louis, MO 800-466-6588
Premium Foil Products Company
Louisville, KY 502-459-2820
President Container Inc
Moonachie, NJ 212-244-0345
Prestige Plastics Corporation
Delta, BC 604-930-2931
Pretium Packaging
Chesterfield, MO 314-727-8673
Pretium Packaging
Hazle Twp, PA 570-459-1800
Pretium Packaging
Hermann, MO 573-486-2811
Pride Container Corporation
Chicago, IL 773-227-6000
Priority Plastics Inc
Grinnell, IA 800-798-3512
Pro-Gram Plastics Inc
Geneva, OH 440-466-8080
ProAmpac
Cincinnati, OH 800-543-7030
Process Solutions
Riviera Beach, FL 561-840-0050

Professional Marketing Group
Seattle, WA .800-227-3769
Progressive Plastics
Cleveland, OH 800-252-0053
Promo Edge
Wall Township, NJ 732-938-4242
Propac Marketing Inc
Addison, TX 972-733-3199
Propak
Burlington, ON 800-263-4872
Pruitt's Packaging Services
Grand Rapids, MI 800-878-0553
Prystup Packaging Products
Livingston, AL 205-652-9583
Q Pak Inc
Newark, NJ .973-483-4404
Quality Container Company
Ypsilanti, MI 734-481-1373
Quality Containers
Weston, ON 416-749-6247
Quality Containers of New England
Yarmouth, ME 800-639-1550
Quality Packaging Inc
Fond Du Lac, WI 800-923-3633
Quality Plastic Bag Corporation
Flushing, NY 800-532-2247
Quality Transparent Bag Co
Bay City, MI 989-893-3561
Quantum Storage Systems Inc
Miami, FL 800-685-4665
Quintex Corp
Nampa, ID .208-467-1113
R C Molding Inc
Greer, SC 864-879-7279
R&R Corrugated Container
Terryville, CT 860-584-1194
R.N.C. Industries
Lawrenceville, GA 888-844-3864
Racine Paper Box Manufacturing
Chicago, IL 773-227-3900
Ram Equipment Co
Waukesha, WI 262-513-1114
Rand-Whitney Group LLC
Worcester, MA 508-791-2301
Rand-Whitney Packaging Corp
Portsmouth, NH 508-791-2301
RAPAC Inc
Oakland, TN 800-280-6333
Ray C. Sprosty Bag Company
Wooster, OH 330-264-8559
RDA Container Corp
Gates, NY .585-247-2323
Reading Box Co Inc
Reading, PA. 610-372-7411
Red River Lumber Company
Saint Helena, CA 707-963-1251
Regal Box Corp
Milwaukee, WI 414-562-5890
Regal Plastic Company
Mission, KS 800-852-1556
Regal Plastic Supply Co
Kansas City, MO 800-444-6390
Regency Label Corporation
Wood Ridge, NJ 201-342-2288
Reliable Container Corporation
Downey, CA 562-745-0200
Reliance Product
Winnipeg, MB. 800-665-0258
Reliance-Paragon
Philadelphia, PA 215-743-1231
Remcon Plastics Inc
Reading, PA 800-360-3636
Remmey Wood Products
Southampton, PA 215-355-3335
Rex Carton Co Inc
Chicago, IL 773-581-4115
Rez-Tech Corp
Kent, OH 800-673-5277
Rhoades Paper Box Corporation
Springfield, OH. 800-441-6494
Rice Packaging Inc
Ellington, CT 800-367-6725
Rice Paper Box Company
Colorado Springs, CO. 303-733-1000
Richard Read Construction Company
Arcadia, CA 888-450-7343
Richards Packaging
Memphis, TN 800-583-0327
Richmond Corrugated Box Company
Richmond, VA. 804-222-1300
Ritz Packaging Company
Brooklyn, NY 718-366-2300

Rjr Technologies
Oakland, CA 510-638-5901
RMI-C/Rotonics Manaufacturing
Bensenville, IL 630-773-9510
Robinette Co
Bristol, TN .423-968-7800
Robinson Industries Inc
Coleman, MI 989-465-6111
Rock-Tenn Company
Norcross, GA 608-223-6272
Roddy Products Pkgng Co
Aldan, PA .610-623-7040
Roll-O-Sheets Canada
Barrie, ON. 888-767-3456
Romanow Container
Westwood, MA 781-320-9200
Rondo of America
Naugatuck, CT 203-723-7474
Ropak
Oak Brook, IL 800-527-2267
Roplast Industries Inc
Oroville, CA 800-767-5278
Rose City Printing & Packaging
Vancouver, WA 800-704-8693
Ross & Wallace Inc
Hammond, LA 800-854-2300
Round Paper Packages Inc
Erlanger, KY 859-331-7200
Rownd & Son
Dillon, SC .803-774-8264
Roy's Folding Box
Cleveland, OH 216-464-1191
Royal Group
Cicero, IL .708-656-2020
Royal Paper Box Co
Montebello, CA 323-728-7041
RubaTex Polymer
Middlefield, OH 440-632-1691
Rudd Container Corp
Chicago, IL 773-847-7600
Ruffino Paper Box Co
Hackensack, NJ. 201-487-1260
Rusken Packaging
Cullman, AL 256-775-0014
RXI Silgan Specialty Plastics
Triadelphia, WV 304-547-9100
S.S.I. Schaefer System International Limited
Brampton, ON. 905-458-5399
Sabert Corp
Sayreville, NJ 800-722-3781
Sacramento Bag Manufacturing
Woodland, CA. 530-662-6130
Saeplast Canada
St John, NB. 800-567-3966
Saint-Gobain Containers
Malvern, PA
San Diego Paper Box Company
Spring Valley, CA 619-660-9566
San Miguel Label Manufacturing
Ciales, PR .787-871-3120
Sanchelima International
Miami, FL .305-591-4343
Santa Fe Bag Company
Vernon, CA 323-585-7225
Saunders West
Azusa, CA .888-932-8836
Save-A-Tree
Berkeley, CA. 510-843-5233
Scheb International
North Barrington, IL 847-381-2573
Schermerhorn Inc
Chicopee, MA. 413-598-8348
Schiefer Packaging Corporation
Syracuse, NY 315-422-0615
Schiffenhaus Industries
Newark, NJ 973-484-5000
Schiffmayer Plastics Corp.
Algonquin, IL 847-658-8140
Schoeneck Containers Inc
New Berlin, WI. 262-786-9360
Scholle IPN
Merced, CA. 209-384-3100
Schroeder Machine
San Marcos, CA 760-591-9733
Schwab Paper Products Co
Romeoville, IL 800-837-7225
Schwarz Supply Source
Morton Grove, IL 800-323-4903
Scope Packaging
Orange, CA 714-998-4411
Scott & Daniells
Portland, CT 860-342-1932

Scott Packaging Corporation
Philadelphia, PA 215-925-5595
Seaboard Bag Corporation
Richmond, VA
Seaboard Carton Company
Downers Grove, IL 708-344-0575
Seaboard Folding Box Corp
Fitchburg, MA 800-255-6313
Seal-Tite Bag Company
Philadelphia, PA 717-917-1949
Sealed Air Corp
Charlotte, NC 800-391-5645
Sealstrip Corporation
Boyertown, PA 610-367-6282
Seattle Plastics
Seattle, WA 800-441-0679
Seattle-Tacoma Box Co
Kent, WA 253-854-9700
Sebring Container Corporation
Salem, OH. 330-332-1533
Seco Industries
Commerce, CA 323-726-9721
Security Packaging
North Bergen, NJ 201-854-1955
Sekisui TA Industries
Brea, CA 800-258-8273
Semco Plastic Co
St Louis, MO. 314-487-4557
Sertapak Packaging Corporation
Woodstock, ON 800-265-1162
SerVend International
Sellersburg, IN 800-367-4233
Service Manufacturing
Aurora, IL .888-325-2788
Servin Company
New Baltimore, MI. 800-824-0962
Set Point Paper Company
Mansfield, MA 800-225-0501
Setco
Monroe Twp, NJ 609-655-4600
Setco
Anaheim, CA 714-777-5200
Seton Indentification Products
Branford, CT. 800-571-2596
Setterstix Corp
Cattaraugus, NY 716-257-3451
Seville Flexpack Corp
Oak Creek, WI 414-761-2751
Seymour Woodenware Company
Seymour, WI. 920-833-6551
Sfb Plastics Inc
Wichita, KS 800-343-8133
SFBC, LLC dba Seaboard Folding Box
Fitchburg, MA 800-225-6313
Shamrock Plastics
Mt Vernon, OH 800-765-1611
Sharpsville Container Corp
Sharpsville, PA 800-645-1248
Shaw-Clayton Corporation
San Rafael, CA 800-537-6712
Sheboygan Paper Box Co
Sheboygan, WI 800-458-8373
Shelby Co
Westlake, OH 800-842-1650
Shields Bag & Printing Co
Yakima, WA 800-541-8630
Shillington Box Co LLC
St Louis, MO. 636-825-6471
Ship Rite Packaging
Bergenfield, NJ 800-721-7447
Shipley Basket Mfg Co
Dayton, TN 800-251-0806
Shipmaster Containers Ltd.
Markham, ON. 416-493-9193
Shippers Paper Products Co
Sheridan, AR. 800-468-1230
Shippers Supply
Saskatoon, SK. 800-661-5639
Shippers Supply, Labelgraphic
Calgary, AB. 800-661-5639
Shore Paper Box Co
Mardela Springs, MD 410-749-7125
Shorewood Packaging
Carlstadt, NJ 201-933-3203
Shouldice Brothers SheetMetal
Battle Creek, MI 269-962-5579
Sicht-Pack Hagner
Dornstetten/ Hallwangen, QC 800-454-5269
SIG Combibloc USA, Inc.
Chester, PA 610-546-4200
Sigma Industries
Elkhart, IN. 574-295-9660

Signature Packaging
West Orange, NJ.....................800-376-2299
Silgan Plastic Closure Sltns
Downers Grove, IL.................800-727-8652
Silgan Plastics Canada
Chesterfield, MO....................800-274-5426
Silgan Plastics LLC
Chesterfield, MO....................800-274-5426
Silver State Plastics Inc
Greeley, CO.........................970-346-8667
Simkins Industries Inc
East Haven, CT......................203-787-7171
Sirco Systems
Birmingham, AL.....................205-731-7800
Skd Distribution Corp
Jamaica, NY........................800-458-8753
Smalley Package Company
Berryville, VA......................540-955-2550
Smith Pallet Co Inc
Hatfield, AR.......................870-389-6184
Smith-Lee Company
Oshkosh, WI........................800-327-9774
Smith-Lustig Paper Box Manufacturing
Cleveland, OH......................216-621-0454
Smurfit Kappa
Carson, CA.........................310-537-8190
Smurfit Stone
Norcross, GA.......................314-656-5300
Smurfit Stone Container
St Louis, MO.......................314-679-2300
Smurfit-Stone Container Corp
Santa Fe Springs, CA...............714-523-3550
Smyrna Container Co
Atlanta, GA........................800-868-4305
Smyth Co
Bedford, VA........................800-950-7011
Snapware
Fullerton, CA......................800-334-3062
Snyder Crown
Marked Tree, AR....................870-358-3400
Snyder Industries Inc.
Lincoln, NE........................800-351-1363
Sobel Corrugated Containers
Cleveland, OH......................216-475-2100
Solve Needs International
White Lake, MI.....................800-783-2462
Somerville Packaging
Toronto, ON........................416-754-7228
Somerville Packaging
Mississauga, ON....................905-678-8211
Sommers Plastic Product Co Inc
Clifton, NJ........................800-225-7677
Sonderen Packaging
Spokane, WA........................800-727-9139
Sonoco ThermoSafe
Arlington Heights, IL..............800-323-7442
SOPAKCO Foods
Mullins, SC........................800-276-9678
Source for Packaging
New York, NY.......................800-223-2527
Source Packaging Inc
Mahwah, NJ.........................888-665-9768
Southern Champion Tray LP
Chattanooga, TN....................800-468-2222
Southern Film Extruders
High Point, NC.....................800-334-6101
Southern Metal Fabricators Inc
Albertville, AL....................800-989-1330
Southern Missouri Containers
Springfield, MO....................800-999-7666
Southern Packaging Machinery
Athens, GA.........................706-208-0814
Southern Pallet
Christchurch, NZ...................901-942-4603
Spartanburg Steel Products Inc
Spartanburg, SC....................800-974-7500
Spartech Plastics
Portage, WI........................800-998-7123
Specialized Packaging London
London, ON.........................519-659-7011
Specialty Films & Associates
Hebron, KY.........................800-984-3346
Specialty Packaging Inc
Fort Worth, TX.....................800-284-7722
Specialty Paper Bag Company
City of Industry, CA...............800-962-2247
Spectape Inc
Erlanger, KY.......................859-283-2044
Spectrum Plastics
Las Vegas, NV......................702-876-8650
Spring Cove Container Div
Roaring Spring, PA.................814-224-5141

Spring Wood Products
Geneva, OH.........................440-466-1135
SQP
Schenectady, NY....................800-724-1129
Squire Corrugated Container Company
South Plainfield, NJ...............908-561-8550
SSW Holding Co Inc
Elizabethtown, KY..................270-769-5526
St Joseph Packaging Inc
St Joseph, MO......................800-383-3000
St. Louis Carton Company
Saint Louis, MO....................314-241-0990
St. Pierre Box & Lumber Company
Canton, CT.........................860-693-2089
Stand Fast Pkgng Prods Inc
Addison, IL........................630-543-6390
Standard Folding Cartons Inc
Flushing, NY.......................718-396-4522
Star Container Company
Phoenix, AZ........................480-281-4200
Star Container Corporation
Leominster, MA.....................978-537-1676
Star Poly Bag Inc
Brooklyn, NY.......................718-384-7034
Steel City Corporation
Youngstown, OH.....................800-321-0350
Step Products
Round Rock, TX.....................800-777-7837
Steril-Sil Company
Bowmansville, PA...................800-784-5537
Sterling Net & Twine Company
Cedar Knolls, NJ...................800-342-0316
Sterling Novelty Products
Northbrook, IL.....................847-291-0070
Sterling Paper Company
Ohio, PA...........................800-282-1124
Stewart Sutherland Inc
Vicksburg, MI......................269-649-0530
Stock America Inc
Grafton, WI........................262-375-4100
Stoffel Seals Corp
Tallapoosa, GA.....................800-422-8247
Stone Container
Chicago, IL........................312-346-6600
Stone Container
Moss Point, MS.....................502-491-4870
Stoneway Carton Company
Mercer Island, WA..................800-498-2185
Streator Dependable Mfg
Streator, IL.......................800-798-0551
Stretch-Vent Packaging System
Ontario, CA........................800-822-8368
Stripper Bags
Henderson, NV......................800-354-2247
Stronghaven Containers Co
Matthews, NC.......................800-222-7919
Stryco Wire Products
North York, ON.....................416-663-7000
Suburban Corrugated Box Company
Indianhead Park, IL................630-920-1230
Sun Plastics
Clearwater, MN.....................800-862-1673
Sunland Manufacturing Company
Minneapolis, MN....................800-790-1905
Superfos Packaging Inc
Cumberland, MD.....................800-537-9242
Superior Uniform Group
Seminole, FL.......................800-727-8643
Supply One Inc
Tulsa, OK
Surfine Central Corporation
Pine Bluff, AR.....................870-247-2387
T & T Industries Inc
Fort Mohave, AZ....................800-437-6246
T J Smith Box Co
Fort Smith, AR.....................877-540-7933
T&S Blow Molding
Scarborough, ON....................416-752-8330
Tampa Corrugated Carton Company
Tampa, FL..........................813-623-5115
Tampa Pallet Co
Tampa, FL..........................813-626-5700
Tampa Sheet Metal Co
Tampa, FL..........................813-251-1845
Target Industries
North Salt Lake, UT................866-617-2253
Taylor Box Co
Warren, RI.........................800-304-6361
Technipac
Le Sueur, MN.......................507-665-6658
TEMP-TECH Company
Springfield, MA....................800-343-5579

Temple-Inland
Memphis, TN........................901-419-9000
Tenneco Inc
Lake Forest, IL....................800-403-3393
Tenneco Packaging
Westmont, IL.......................630-850-7034
Tenneco Specialty Packaging
Smyrna, GA.........................800-241-4402
TEQ
Huntley, IL........................800-874-7113
Tesa Tape Inc
Charlotte, NC......................800-429-8273
TGR Container Sales
San Leandro, CA....................800-273-6887
THARCO
San Lorenzo, CA....................800-772-2332
Thermal Bags By Ingrid Inc
Gilberts, IL.......................800-622-5560
Thermodynamics
Commerce City, CO..................800-627-9037
Thermodyne International LTD
Ontario, CA........................909-923-9945
Thermos Company
Schaumburg, IL.....................800-243-0745
Thomas Tape & Supply Co Inc
Springfield, OH....................937-325-6414
Thornton Plastics
Salt Lake City, UT.................800-248-3434
Thunder Pallet Inc
Theresa, WI........................800-354-0643
Tin Box Co of America Inc
Farmingdale, NY....................800-888-8467
Tipper Tie Inc
Apex, NC...........................919-362-8811
TMS
San Francisco, CA..................800-447-7223
Tni Packaging Inc
West Chicago, IL...................800-383-0990
Tolan Machinery Company
Rockaway, NJ.......................973-983-7212
Tolco Corp
Toledo, OH.........................800-537-4786
Trade Fixtures
Little Rock, AR....................800-872-3490
Trans Flex Packagers Inc
Unionville, CT.....................860-673-2531
Trans World Services
Melrose, MA........................800-882-2105
Transparent Container Co
Addison, IL........................630-458-9031
Traub Container Corporation
Cleveland, OH......................216-475-5100
Tree Saver
Englewood, CO......................800-676-7741
Treen Box & Pallet Inc
Bensalem, PA.......................215-639-5100
Trent Corp
Trenton, NJ........................609-587-7515
Trevor Owen Limited
Scarborough, ON....................866-487-2224
Tri-Seal
Blauvelt, NY.......................845-353-3300
Tri-State Plastics
Henderson, KY......................270-826-8361
Tri-Sterling
Altamonte Spgs, FL.................407-260-0330
Trident Plastics
Ivyland, PA........................800-222-2318
Trinidad Benham Corporation
Denver, CO.........................303-220-1400
Trinity Packaging
Cheektowaga, NY....................800-778-3111
Trio Packaging Corp
Ronkonkoma, NY.....................800-331-0492
Trio Products
Elyria, OH.........................440-323-5457
Triple A Containers
Buena Park, CA.....................714-521-2820
Triple Dot Corp
Santa Ana, CA......................714-241-0888
True Pac
New Castle, DE.....................800-825-7890
Tucson Container Corp
Tucson, AZ.........................520-746-3171
Tudor Pulp & Paper Corporation
Prospect, CT.......................203-758-4494
TULSACK
Tulsa, OK..........................800-228-1936
Tupperware Brands Corporation
Orlando, FL........................800-366-3800
Tyco Plastics
Lakeville, MN......................800-328-4080

Ultratainer
St Jean-Sur-Richelie, QC 514-359-3651
Union Camp Corporation
Denver, CO 303-371-0760
Union Industries
Providence, RI 800-556-6454
Unipac Shipping
Jamaica, NY 800-586-2711
Unipak Inc
West Chester, PA................ 610-436-6600
Uniplast Films
Palmer, MA 800-343-1295
Unique Boxes
Chicago, IL 800-281-1670
United Bags Inc
St Louis, MO 800-550-2247
United Flexible
Westbury, NY 516-222-2150
United Seal & Tag Corporation
Port Charlotte, FL 800-211-9552
Universal Container Corporation
Odessa, FL 800-582-7477
Universal Folding Box
East Orange, NJ 973-482-4300
Universal Folding Box Company
Hoboken, NJ 201-659-7373
Universal Paper Box
Seattle, WA 800-228-1045
Universal Plastics
Holyoke, MA 800-553-0120
Upham & Walsh Lumber
Hoffman Estates, IL 847-519-1010
Urnex Brands Inc
Elmsford, NY 800-222-2826
US Can Company
Rosedale, MD 800-436-8021
US Plastic Corporation
Swampscott, MA 781-595-1030
US Tsubaki Holdings Inc
Wheeling, IL 800-323-7790
Utah PaperBox Company
Salt Lake City, UT 801-363-0093
Vacumet Corporation
Austell, GA 800-776-0865
Valley Container Corporation
Saint Louis, MO 314-652-8050
Valley Container Inc
Bridgeport, CT 203-368-6546
Valley Packaging Supply Co
Green Bay, WI. 920-336-9012
Van Dereems Mfg Co
Hawthorne, NJ 973-427-2355
Vermont Bag & Film
Bennington, VT 802-442-3166
Vermont Container Corp
Bennington, VT 802-442-5455
Victory Box Corp
Roselle, NJ 908-245-5100
Victory Packaging, Inc.
Houston, TX 800-486-5606
VIFAN Canada
Lanoraie, QC 800-557-0192
Viking Packaging & Display
San Jose, CA 408-998-1000
VIP Real Estate LTD
Chicago, IL 773-376-5000
Virginia Plastics Co
Roanoke, VA.................. 800-777-8541
Visual Packaging Corp
Haskell, NJ 973-835-7055
VitaMinder Company
Providence, RI 800-858-8840
Volk Packaging Corp
Biddeford, ME 207-282-6151
Vonco Products LLC
Lake Villa, IL 800-323-9077
VPI Manufacturing
Draper, UT 801-495-2310
Wagner Brothers Containers
Baltimore, MD 410-354-0044
Walker Bag Mfg Co
Louisville, KY 800-642-4949
Warner Electric Inc
South Beloit, IL 800-234-3369
Warren Packaging
San Bernardino, CA 909-888-7008
Wasserman Bag Company
Center Moriches, NY 631-909-8656
Wastequip Teem
Charlotte, NC 877-468-9278
Waymar Industries
Burnsville, MN 888-474-1112

WCB Ice Cream
Philadelphia, PA 215-425-4320
Weber Display & Packaging Inc
Philadelphia, PA 215-426-3500
Webster Packaging Corporation
Loveland, OH 513-683-5666
Wedlock Paper ConvertersLtd.
Mississauga, ON 800-388-0447
Welch Packaging Group Inc
Elkhart, IN. 574-295-2460
West Rock
Atlanta, GA 770-448-2193
Westeel
Saskatoon, SK. 306-931-2855
Western Container Company
Kansas City, MO. 816-924-5700
Westvaco Corporation
Newark, DE. 302-453-7200
Weyerhaeuser Co
Seattle, WA 800-525-5440
Wilks Precision Instr Co Inc
Union Bridge, MD 410-775-7917
Willamette Industries
Beaverton, OR. 503-641-1131
Willamette Industries
Louisville, KY 800-465-3065
Willard Packaging Co
Gaithersburg, MD 301-948-7700
Winchester Carton
Eutaw, AL 205-372-3337
Wins Paper Products
Springtown, TX 800-733-2420
Winzen Film
Taylor, TX..................... 800-779-7595
Wisconsin Box Co
Wausau, WI. 800-876-6658
Wisconsin Converting Inc
Green Bay, WI. 800-544-1935
Wisconsin Film & Bag Inc
Shawano, WI. 800-765-9224
WNA
Lancaster, TX 800-334-2877
WNA Hopple Plastics
Florence, KY 800-446-4622
Wnc Pallet & Forest Pdts Co
Candler, NC 828-667-5426
Woodson Pallet Co
Anmoore, WV. 304-623-2858
Woodstock Plastics Co Inc
Marengo, IL. 815-568-5281
Workman Packaging Inc.
Saint-Laurent, QC............. 800-252-5208
World Kitchen
Rosemont, IL. 847-678-8600
Wrap Pack
Yakima, WA 800-879-9727
Wright Brothers Paper Box Company
Fond Du Lac, WI 920-921-8270
WS Packaging Group Inc
Green Bay, WI. 877-977-5177
Yerecic Label Co
New Kensington, PA. 724-334-3300
Yeuell Name Plate & Label
Woburn, MA 781-933-2984
York Container Co
York, PA 717-757-7611
Zenith Specialty Bag Co
City of Industry, CA 800-962-2247
Zero Manufacturing Inc
North Salt Lake, UT 800-959-5050
Zip-Pak
Manteno, IL 800-488-6973

Packing House Supplies

Acme Scale Co
San Leandro, CA................. 888-638-5040
Actionpac Scales Automation
Oxnard, CA 800-394-0154
All Power Inc
Sioux City, IA 712-258-0681
Allflex Packaging Products
Ambler, PA 800-448-2467
Auto Pallets-Boxes
Lathrup Village, MI 800-875-2699
Barrette Outdoor Living
Cleveland, OH 800-336-2383
Belco Packaging Systems
Monrovia, CA 800-833-1833
Bennett Box & Pallet Company
Winston, NC 800-334-8741

C.J. Machine
Fridley, MN..................... 763-767-4630
Carton Closing Company
Butler, PA 724-287-7759
Cincinnati Foam Products
Cincinnati, OH 513-741-7722
Columbia Machine Inc
Vancouver, WA 800-628-4065
Columbus McKinnon Corporation
Getzville, NY 800-888-0985
Cozzini Inc
Algona, IA 888-295-1116
Crown Equipment Corp.
New Bremen, OH 419-629-2311
Cutler Brothers Box & Lumber
Fairview, NJ 201-943-2535
Dearborn Mid-West Conveyor Co
Overland Park, KS 913-384-9950
Dorell Equipment Inc
Somerset, NJ 732-247-5400
Douglas Machine Inc
Alexandria, MN 320-763-6587
Dynabilt Products
Readville, MA. 800-443-1008
Edson Packaging Machinery
Hamilton, ON 800-493-3766
Elite Storage Solutions Inc
Monroe, GA 800-367-0572
Elliott Manufacturing Co Inc
Fresno, CA 559-233-6235
Exact Equipment Corporation
Morrisville, PA 215-295-2000
F.E. Wood & Sons
West Baldwin, ME 207-286-5003
Fabricating & Welding Corp
Chicago, IL 773-928-2050
Fabrication Specialties
Centerville, TN 931-729-2283
Florida Knife Co
Sarasota, FL 800-966-5643
Food Equipment Manufacturing Company
Bedford Heights, OH 216-672-5859
Frazier Industrial Co
Long Valley, NJ. 800-859-1342
FreesTech
Sinking Spring, PA 717-560-7560
Fresno Pallet, Inc.
Sultana, CA 559-591-4111
Gemini Plastic Films Corporation
Garfield, NJ. 800-789-4732
Genesee Corrugated
Flint, MI 810-228-3702
Girard Wood Products Inc
Puyallup, WA 800-532-0505
Goldco Industries
Loveland, CO 970-663-4770
Goldman Manufacturing Company
Detroit, MI 313-834-5535
Gram Equipment of America
Tampa, FL 813-248-1978
H.J. Jones & Sons
London, ON 800-667-0476
Halpak Plastics
Deer Park, NY. 800-442-5725
Halton Packaging Systems
Oakville, ON. 905-847-9141
Hanson Box & Lumber Company
Wakefield, MA 617-245-0358
Hudson Control Group Inc
Springfield, NJ 973-376-8265
Iman Pack
Westland, MI. 800-810-4626
Industrial Hardwood
Perrysburg, OH. 419-666-2503
Industrial Lumber & Packaging
Spring Lake, MI 616-842-1457
International Paper Box Machine Company
Nashua, NH. 603-889-6651
J.M. Rogers & Sons
Moss Point, MS 228-475-7584
Jetstream Systems
Wichita, KN 855-861-6916
Kimball Companies
East Longmeadow, MA 413-525-1881
Kisters Kayat
Sarasota, FL 386-424-0101
Konz Wood Products Co
Appleton, WI 877-610-5145
Krones
Franklin, WI 800-752-3787
L&H Wood Manufacturing Company
Farmington, MI. 248-474-9000

Landis Plastics
  Alsip, IL 708-396-1470
Le Fiell Co
  Reno, NV 402-592-9993
Load King Mfg
  Jacksonville, FL 800-531-4975
Longford Equipment US
  Glastonbury, CT 416-298-6622
M&R Flexible Packaging
  Springboro, OH.....................800-543-3380
Market Forge Industries Inc
  Everett, MA........................866-698-3188
Matthiesen Equipment
  San Antonio, TX....................800-624-8635
Michiana Box & Crate
  Niles, MI..........................800-677-6372
Millwood Inc
  Vienna, OH.........................330-393-4400
New Age Industrial
  Norton, KS 800-255-0104
New Jersey Wire Stitching Machine Company
  Cherry Hill, NJ 856-428-2572
Old English Printing & Label Company
  Delray Beach, FL 561-997-9990
Packaging & Processing Equipment
  Ayr, ON 519-622-6666
Packaging Dynamics
  Walnut Creek, CA...................925-938-2711
Pallet Pro
  Moss, TN...........................800-489-3661
PDC International
  Austin, TX.........................512-302-0194
Pneumatic Scale Angelus
  Cuyahoga Falls, OH.................330-923-0491
Precision Printing & Packaging
  Clarksville, TN 800-500-4526
Premier Packages
  Saint Louis, MO 800-466-6588
Premium Pallet
  Philadelphia, PA 800-648-7347
Priority One America
  Oshkosh, WI 920-235-5562
Production Systems
  Marietta, GA.......................800-235-9734
PTI Packaging
  Portage, WI 800-501-4077
RAM Center
  Red Wing, MN 800-309-5431
Ratcliff Hoist Company
  San Carlos, CA.....................650-595-3840
Refrigiwear Inc
  Dahlonega, GA......................800-645-3744
Remcon Plastics Inc
  Reading, PA 800-360-3636
Rennco LLC
  Homer, MI..........................800-409-5225
Rockford-Midland Corporation
  Rockford, IL 800-327-7908
Saeplast Canada
  St John, NB 800-567-3966
Sapac International
  Fond Du Lac, WI 800-257-2722
Seal-O-Matic Corp
  Jacksonville, OR...................800-631-2072
Seattle-Tacoma Box Co
  Kent, WA...........................253-854-9700
Sekisui TA Industries
  Brea, CA...........................800-258-8273
Shields Products Inc
  West Pittston, PA..................570-655-4596
Shippers Supply
  Saskatoon, SK......................800-661-5639
Sinco
  Red Wing, MN 800-243-6753
Solve Needs International
  White Lake, MI.....................800-783-2462
Sonoma Pacific Company
  Montebello, CA 323-838-4374
Sperling Industries
  Omaha, NE 800-647-5062
Standard-Knapp Inc
  Portland, CT 800-628-9565
Steel King Industries
  Stevens Point, WI 800-553-3096
Studd & Whipple Company
  Conewango Valley, NY...............716-287-3791
Swift Creek Forest Products
  Jetersville, VA....................804-561-4498
Technibilt/Cari-All
  Newton, NC 800-233-3972
Thiele Technologies-Reedley
  Reedley, CA 800-344-8951

Tier-Rack Corp
  Ballwin, MO 800-325-7869
Trenton Mills Inc
  Trenton, TN........................731-855-1323
Trident Plastics
  Ivyland, PA 800-222-2318
Triple-A Manufacturing Company
  Toronto, ON 800-786-2238
Unirak Storage Systems
  Taylor, MI 800-348-7225
UPACO Adhesives
  Richmond, VA.......................800-446-9984
Upham & Walsh Lumber
  Hoffman Estates, IL 847-519-1010
UPN Pallet Company
  Penns Grove, NJ 856-299-1192
Vertical Systems Intl
  Lakeside Park, KY 859-485-9650
Viking Pallet Corp
  Maple Grove, MN....................763-425-6707
W.G. Durant Corporation
  Whittier, CA 562-946-5555
WE Killam Enterprises
  Waterford, ON 519-443-7421
Western Plastics
  Portland, TN 615-325-7331
Whallon Machinery Inc
  Royal Center, IN 574-643-9561
Williamsburg Millwork
  Ruther Glen, VA 804-994-2151
Woodson Pallet Co
  Anmoore, WV 304-623-2858
Wrap Pack
  Yakima, WA 800-879-9727
Zed Industries
  Vandalia, OH.......................937-667-8407

Paper

Candy Wrapping

Alufoil Products Co Inc
  Hauppauge, NY 631-231-4141
ESS Technologies
  Blacksburg, VA.....................540-961-5716
IB Concepts
  Elizabeth, NJ 888-671-0800

Corrugated

Clearwater Paper Corporation
  Spokane, WA........................877-847-7831
Corfab
  Chicago, IL 708-458-8750
Corrugated Specialties
  Plainwell, MI 269-685-9821
Corrugated Supplies Co.
  Bedford, IL 888-826-2738
Graphic Packaging Intl
  Elk Grove Vlg, IL 847-437-1700
Inter-Pack Corporation
  Monroe, MI 734-242-7755
IVEX Packaging Corporation
  Longueuil, QC 450-651-8887
Lumber & Things
  Keyser, WV 800-296-5656
Marshall Paper Products
  East Norwich, NY
National Packaging
  Rumford, RI 401-434-1070
RTS Packaging
  Hillside, IL 708-338-2800
Shipmaster Containers Ltd.
  Markham, ON 416-493-9193

Glassine

Brooklace
  Oshkosh, WI 800-572-4552
Simkins Industries Inc
  East Haven, CT.....................203-787-7171

Grease & Oil Resistant

Brooklace
  Oshkosh, WI 800-572-4552
Central Coated Products Inc
  Alliance, OH.......................330-821-9830
Pepperell Paper Company
  Lawrence, MA 978-433-6951
Printpack Inc.
  Atlanta, GA 404-460-7000

Simkins Industries Inc
  East Haven, CT.....................203-787-7171
Sorg Paper Company
  Middletown, OH.....................513-420-5300
Tudor Pulp & Paper Corporation
  Prospect, CT.......................203-758-4494

Heat Sealing

Hazen Paper Co
  Holyoke, MA 413-538-8204
Paper Product Specialties
  Waukesha, WI.......................262-549-1730
Printpack Inc.
  Atlanta, GA........................404-460-7000

Kraft

Durango-Georgia Paper
  Tampa, FL..........................813-286-2718
Lumber & Things
  Keyser, WV.........................800-296-5656
Meadwestvaco Corp
  Richmond, VA.......................804-444-1000
Pepperell Paper Company
  Lawrence, MA 978-433-6951
Salinas Valley Wax Paper Co
  Salinas, CA........................831-424-2747
Shamrock Paper Company
  Saint Louis, MO 314-241-2370

Label

Graphic Impressions of Illinois
  River Grove, IL....................708-453-1100
Harris & Company
  Salem, OH..........................330-332-4127
Print & Peel
  New York, NY 800-451-0807
Southern Imperial Inc
  Rockford, IL 800-747-4665
Vande Berg SCALES/Vbs Inc
  Sioux Center, IA 712-722-1181

Laminated

Alufoil Products Co Inc
  Hauppauge, NY 631-231-4141
Burrows Paper Corp
  Little Falls, NY...................800-272-7122
Fibre Converters Inc
  Constantine, MI 269-279-1700
Fortifiber Building Systs Grp
  Fernley, NV........................800-773-4777
Hampden Papers Inc
  Holyoke, MA 413-536-1000
Hazen Paper Co
  Holyoke, MA 413-538-8204
Henschel Coating & Laminating
  New Berlin, WI.....................800-866-5683
Lamcraft Inc
  Lees Summit, MO....................800-821-1333
Laminated Papers
  Holyoke, MA 413-533-3906
Mail-Well Label
  Baltimore, MD 800-637-4879
Norpak Corp
  Newark, NJ 800-631-6970
Packaging Dynamics International
  Caldwell, OH 740-732-5665
Salinas Valley Wax Paper Co
  Salinas, CA........................831-424-2747
Sorg Paper Company
  Middletown, OH.....................513-420-5300
Trinity Packaging
  Cheektowaga, NY....................800-778-3111
West Rock
  Atlanta, GA........................770-448-2193
Zimmer Custom-Made Packaging
  Indianapolis, IN 317-263-3436

Lining

Cellier Corporation
  Taunton, MA........................508-655-5906
Gardiner Paperboard
  Gardiner, ME.......................207-582-3230
International Tray Pads
  Aberdeen, NC.......................910-944-1800
Salinas Valley Wax Paper Co
  Salinas, CA........................831-424-2747

Plastic Coated

Central Coated Products Inc
  Alliance, OH 330-821-9830
Fibre Leather Manufacturing Company
  New Bedford, MA 800-358-6012
Henschel Coating & Laminating
  New Berlin, WI. 800-866-5683
International Tray Pads
  Aberdeen, NC 910-944-1800
Jen-Coat, Inc.
  Westfield, MA. 877-536-2628
Salinas Valley Wax Paper Co
  Salinas, CA 831-424-2747
Zimmer Custom-Made Packaging
  Indianapolis, IN 317-263-3436

Pressure Sensitive

KAPCO
  Kent, OH .800-843-5368
MAC Tac LLC
  Stow, OH. 866-262-2822
Print & Peel
  New York, NY 800-451-0807

Waxed

Burrows Paper Corp
  Little Falls, NY. 800-272-7122
Clearwater Paper Corporation
  Spokane, WA. 877-847-7831
Fabricon Products Inc
  River Rouge, MI. 313-841-8200
Framarx Corp
  S Chicago Hts, IL 800-336-3936
Handy Wacks Corp
  Sparta, MI 800-445-4434
Norpak Corp
  Newark, NJ. 800-631-6970
Patty Paper Inc
  Plymouth, IN. 800-782-1703
Rochester Midland Corp
  Rochester, NY. 800-387-7174
Salinas Valley Wax Paper Co
  Salinas, CA 831-424-2747
Schwab Paper Products Co
  Romeoville, IL 800-837-7225
Shields Products Inc
  West Pittston, PA. 570-655-4596

Wet Strength

SCA Hygiene Paper
  San Ramon, CA 800-992-8675
Shawano Specialty Papers
  Shawano, WI. 800-543-5554
Sorg Paper Company
  Middletown, OH. 513-420-5300

Wrapping

Alufoil Products Co Inc
  Hauppauge, NY 631-231-4141
Dorado Carton Company
  Dorado, PR 787-796-1670
ESS Technologies
  Blacksburg, VA. 540-961-5716
Hampden Papers Inc
  Holyoke, MA 413-536-1000
Jupiter Mills Corporation
  Roslyn, NY. 800-853-5121
Mimi et Cie
  Seattle, WA 206-545-1850
Norpak Corp
  Newark, NJ. 800-631-6970
North American Packaging Corp
  New York, NY 800-499-3521
Paper Service
  Hinsdale, NH 603-239-6344
Patty Paper Inc
  Plymouth, IN. 800-782-1703
Pepperell Paper Company
  Lawrence, MA 978-433-6951
Robinette Co
  Bristol, TN 423-968-7800
Salinas Valley Wax Paper Co
  Salinas, CA 831-424-2747
Shamrock Paper Company
  Saint Louis, MO 314-241-2370
Sorg Paper Company
  Middletown, OH. 513-420-5300

St. Clair Pakwell
  Bellwood, IL 800-323-1922

Plastic

Alcoa Corp
  Pittsburgh, PA 412-315-2900

Biodegradable, Recyclable

Arbee Transparent Inc
  Elk Grove Vlg, IL. 800-642-2247
Gateway Plastics Inc
  Mequon, WI 262-242-2020
Hinkle Manufacturing
  Perrysburg, OH. 419-666-5367
International Polymers Corp
  Allentown, PA. 800-526-0953
Stock America Inc
  Grafton, WI. 262-375-4100
Tectonics
  Westmoreland, NH 603-352-8894
Tolas Health Care Packaging
  Feasterville Trevose, PA. 215-322-7900

Retorts

Canning

A.K. Robins
  Baltimore, MD 800-486-9656
Allpax Products
  Covington, LA 888-893-9277
Dixie Canner Machine Shop
  Athens, GA 706-549-0592
Innovative Food Solutions LLC
  Columbus, OH 800-884-3314
Melco Steel Inc
  Azusa, CA. 626-334-7875
Reid Boiler Works
  Bellingham, WA 360-714-6157
Stock America Inc
  Grafton, WI. 262-375-4100

Seals

Bottle & Jar

American National Rubber
  Ceredo, WV 304-453-1311
Crown Closures Machinery
  Lancaster, OH. 740-681-6593
Crown Holdings, Inc.
  Yardley, PA 215-698-5100
Dickey Manufacturing Company
  St Charles, IL 630-584-2918
Greenfield Packaging
  White Plains, NY 914-993-0233
Pack Line Corporation
  Racine, WI 800-248-6868
Phoenix Closures Inc
  Naperville, IL 630-544-3475
Romatic Manufacturing Co
  Southbury, CT. 203-264-3442
Simolex Rubber Corp
  Plymouth, MI 734-453-4500
Tri-Seal
  Blauvelt, NY. 845-353-3300
Ultrapak
  Dunkirk, NY 800-228-6030

Box Strapping

Gulf Arizona Packaging
  Humble, TX 800-364-3887
Herche Warehouse
  Denver, CO. 303-371-8186
L&H Wood Manufacturing Company
  Farmington, MI. 248-474-9000

Pressure Sensitive

Cantech Industries Inc
  Johnson City, TN 800-654-3947
City Stamp & Seal Co
  Austin, TX. 800-950-6074
Coleman Rubber Stamps
  Daytona Beach, FL 386-252-8597
Cummins Label Co
  Kalamazoo, MI 800-280-7589
Deco Labels & Tags
  Toronto, ON 888-496-9029

Grand Rapids Label
  Grand Rapids, MI 616-776-2778
Innovative Packaging Solution
  Martin, MI. 616-656-2100
Long Island Stamp Corporation
  Flushing, NY 800-547-8267
M & M Display
  Philadelphia, PA 800-874-7171
New Era Label Corporation
  Belleville, NJ 973-759-2444
Reotemp Instrument Corp
  San Diego, CA 800-648-7737
Rhode Island Label Work Inc
  West Warwick, RI 401-828-6400
Schwaab, Inc
  Milwaukee, WI 800-935-9877
Stoffel Seals Corp
  Tallapoosa, GA 800-422-8247
Timemed Labeling Systems
  Valencia, CA 818-897-1111

Price Tag

General Trade Mark Labelcraft
  Staten Island, NY 718-448-9800
House Stamp Works
  Chicago, IL 312-939-7177
Muskogee Rubber Stamp & Seal Company
  Fort Gibson, OK 918-478-3046
Stoffel Seals Corp
  Tallapoosa, GA 800-422-8247

Shakers

Salt & Pepper

Amco Metals Indl
  City of Industry, CA 626-855-2550
Browne & Company
  Markham, ON 905-475-6104
C R Mfg
  Waverly, NE 877-789-5844
Carlisle Food Svc Products Inc
  Oklahoma City, OK 800-654-8210
Coley Industries
  Wayland, NY. 716-728-2390
Gril-Del
  Mankato, MN 800-782-7320
Liberty Ware LLC
  Clearfield, UT 888-500-5885
Michael Leson Dinnerware
  Youngstown, OH. 800-821-3541
Reiner Products
  Waterbury, CT. 800-345-6775
Superior Products Company
  Saint Paul, MN 800-328-9800
Tablecraft Products Co Inc
  Gurnee, IL. 800-323-8321
Traex
  Dane, WI. 800-356-8006

Sleeves

Bottle

Flexo Transparent Inc
  Buffalo, NY. 877-993-5396
Ultrapak
  Dunkirk, NY 800-228-6030
Wilkens-Anderson Co
  Chicago, IL 800-847-2222

Stamps

Dating & Numbering

A.D. Johnson Engraving Company
  Kalamazoo, MI 269-342-5500
A.D. Joslin Manufacturing Company
  Manistee, MI. 231-723-2908
ABC Stamp Signs & Awards
  Boise, ID. 208-375-4470
Accent Mark
  Palmdale, CA 661-274-8191
American Art Stamp
  Gardena, CA 310-965-9004
Century Rubber Stamp Company
  New York, NY 212-962-6165
City Stamp & Seal Co
  Austin, TX. 800-950-6074

Des Moines Stamp Mfg Co
Des Moines, IA.............888-236-7739
Drs Designs
Bethel, CT.................888-792-3740
Durable Engravers
Franklin Park, IL............800-869-9565
E C Shaw Co
Cincinnati, OH..............866-532-7429
Fleming Packaging Corporation
Peoria, IL.................309-676-7657
Fraser Stamp & Seal
Chicago, IL................800-540-8565
G&R Graphics
West Orange, NJ............813-503-8592
Hartford Stamp Works
Hartford, CT...............860-249-6205
Hiss Stamp Company
Columbus, OH..............614-224-5119
Innovative Ceramic Corp
East Liverpool, OH..........330-385-6515
Joyce Engraving Co Inc
Dallas, TX.................214-638-1262
L&L Engraving Company
Gilford, NH................888-524-3032
Mecco Marking & Traceability
Cranberry Township, PA......888-369-9190
Modern Stamp Company
Baltimore, MD..............800-727-3029
Nameplate
St Paul, MN................651-228-1522
National Metal Industries
West Springfield, MA........800-628-8850
Pinquist Tool & Die Company
Brooklyn, NY...............800-752-0414
Plastimatic Arts Corporation
Mishawaka, IN..............800-442-3593
R.P. Childs Stamp Company
Ludlow, MA.................413-733-1211
Schwaab, Inc
Milwaukee, WI..............800-935-9877
South Well Co
San Antonio, TX.............210-223-1831
Southern Atlantic Label Co
Chesapeake, VA.............800-456-5999
United Ribtype Co
Fort Wayne, IN.............800-473-4039
Volk Corp
Farmington Hills, MI.........800-521-6799

Rubber

ABC Stamp Signs & Awards
Boise, ID..................208-375-4470
Accent Mark
Palmdale, CA...............661-274-8191
Ace Stamp & Engraving
Lakewood, WA..............253-582-3322
Allmark Impressions LTD
Fort Worth, TX.............817-834-0080
American Art Stamp
Gardena, CA................310-965-9004
Ameristamp/Sign-A-Rama
Evansville, IN..............800-543-6693
Atlas Rubber Stamp & Printing
York, PA..................717-751-0459
Century Rubber Stamp Company
New York, NY...............212-962-6165
Chattanooga Rubber Stamp & Stencil Works
Sale Creek, TN.............800-894-1164
City Stamp & Seal Co
Austin, TX.................800-950-6074
Coleman Rubber Stamps
Daytona Beach, FL...........386-252-8597
Corpus Christi Stamp Works
Corpus Christi, TX..........800-322-4515
Crown Marking
Minneapolis, MN.............800-305-5249
Custom Rubber Stamp Co
Crosby, MN.................888-606-4579
Custom Stamp Company
Anza, CA..................323-292-0753
Dayton Marking Devices Company
Dayton, OH.................937-432-0285
Des Moines Stamp Mfg Co
Des Moines, IA.............888-236-7739
Detroit Marking Products
Detroit, MI................800-833-8222
Dixie Rubber Stamp & Seal Company
Atlanta, GA................404-875-8883
Drs Designs
Bethel, CT.................888-792-3740

East Memphis Rubber Stamp Company
Bartlett, TN................901-384-0887
Ed Smith's Stencil Works LTD
New Orleans, LA.............504-525-2128
Ehrgott Rubber Stamp Company
Indianapolis, IN............317-353-2222
Everett Rubber Stamp
Everett, WA................425-258-6747
Federal Stamp & Seal Manufacturing Company
Atlanta, GA................800-333-7726
Fleming Packaging Corporation
Peoria, IL.................309-676-7657
Flint Rubber Stamp Works
Flint, MI..................810-235-2341
Fox Stamp Sign & Specialty
Menasha, WI................920-725-2683
Franklin Rubber Stamp Co
Wilmington, DE.............302-654-8841
Fraser Stamp & Seal
Chicago, IL................800-540-8565
Frost Manufacturing Corp
Worcester, MA..............800-462-0216
G&R Graphics
West Orange, NJ............813-503-8592
Glover Rubber Stamp & Crafts
Wills Point, TX.............214-824-6900
Granite State Stamps Inc
Manchester, NH.............800-937-3736
Grays Harbor Stamp Works
Aberdeen, WA...............800-894-3830
Gribble Stamp & Stencil Co
Houston, TX................713-228-5358
Gruney's Rubber Stamps
Little Rock, AR.............501-376-0393
Hartford Stamp Works
Hartford, CT...............860-249-6205
Hathaway Stamps
Cincinnati, OH..............513-621-1052
Hiss Stamp Company
Columbus, OH..............614-224-5119
House Stamp Works
Chicago, IL................312-939-7177
Houston Stamp & Stencil Company
Houston, TX................713-869-4337
Huntington Park Rbr Stamp Co
Huntington Park, CA.........800-882-0029
Ideal Office Supply & Rubber Stamp Company
Kingsport, TN...............423-246-7371
Innovative Ceramic Corp
East Liverpool, OH..........330-385-6515
Jim Lake Companies
Dallas, TX.................214-741-5018
Justrite Rubber Stamp & Seal
Kansas City, MO.............800-229-5010
JVC Rubber Stamp Company
Elkhart, IN................574-293-0113
L&L Engraving Company
Gilford, NH................888-524-3032
Lakeland Rubber Stamp Company
Lakeland, FL...............863-682-5111
Lakeview Rubber Stamp Co
Chicago, IL................773-539-1525
Larry B Newman Printing
Knoxville, TN...............888-835-4566
Lobue's Rubber Stamp Co
Houston, TX................713-652-0031
Long Island Stamp Corporation
Flushing, NY...............800-547-8267
Mankuta Bros Rubber Stamp Co
Bohemia, NY................800-223-4481
Mansfield Rubber Stamp
Mansfield, OH..............419-524-1442
Mark-It Rubber Stamp & Label Company
Stamford, CT...............203-348-3204
Marking Devices Inc
Cleveland, OH..............216-861-4498
Martco Engravers
Fremont, NH................603-895-3561
Mastermark
Kent, WA..................206-762-9610
Modern Stamp Company
Baltimore, MD..............800-727-3029
Moore Efficient Communication Aids
Denver, CO.................303-433-8456
Muskogee Rubber Stamp & Seal Company
Fort Gibson, OK.............918-478-3046
My Serenity Pond
Cold Spring, MN.............320-363-0411
Nameplate
St Paul, MN................651-228-1522
National Marking Products Inc
Henrico, VA................800-482-1553

Northern Berkshire Tourist
North Adams, MA............413-663-9204
O.K. Marking Devices
Regina, SK.................306-522-2856
OK Stamp & Seal Company
Oklahoma City, OK...........405-235-7853
Oration Rubber Stamp Company
Columbus, NJ...............908-496-4161
Plastimatic Arts Corporation
Mishawaka, IN..............800-442-3593
Printcraft Marking Devices Inc
Buffalo, NY................716-873-8181
Quick Stamp & Sign Mfg
Lafayette, LA...............337-232-2171
R.P. Childs Stamp Company
Ludlow, MA.................413-733-1211
Rebel Stamp & Sign Co
Baton Rouge, LA............800-860-5120
Richardson's Stamp Works
Houston, TX................713-973-0314
Royal ACME
Cleveland, OH..............216-241-1477
Rubber Stamp Shop
Accokeek, MD...............800-835-0839
Schwaab, Inc
Milwaukee, WI..............800-935-9877
Service Stamp Works
Chicago, IL................312-666-8839
Sioux Falls Rbr Stamp Works
Sioux Falls, SD.............855-334-5990
South Well Co
San Antonio, TX.............210-223-1831
Southern Rubber Stamp
Tulsa, OK..................888-826-4304
Spectrum Enterprises
Evansville, IN..............812-425-1771
Spencer Business Form Company
Spencer, WV................304-372-8877
Sutherland Stamp Company
San Diego, CA..............858-233-7784
United Ribtype Co
Fort Wayne, IN.............800-473-4039
Volk Corp
Farmington Hills, MI.........800-521-6799
Walker Co
Oklahoma City, OK...........800-522-3015
Welch Stencil Company
Scarborough, ME............800-635-3506
Wichita Stamp & Seal Inc
Wichita, KS................316-263-4223
Wildes Printing Co Inc
White Plains, MD............301-870-4141
Winmark Stamp & Sign
Salt Lake City, UT..........800-438-0480

Stands

Tray

C R Mfg
Waverly, NE................877-789-5844
Carlisle Food Svc Products Inc
Oklahoma City, OK...........800-654-8210
Creative Essentials
Ronkonkoma, NY.............800-355-5891
Duke Manufacturing Co
St Louis, MO...............800-735-3853
Ex-Cell KAISER LLC
Franklin Park, IL............847-451-0451
Fixtur World
Cookeville, TN..............800-634-9887
Gaychrome Division of CSL
Crystal Lake, IL.............800-873-4370
Glaro Inc
Hauppauge, NY..............631-234-1717
International Patterns, Inc.
Bay Shore, NY..............631-952-2000
Marston Manufacturing
Cleveland, OH..............216-587-3400
MLS Signs Inc
Chesterfield, MI............586-948-0200
Quality Highchairs
Pacoima, CA................800-969-9635
R.R. Scheibe Company
Newton Center, MA..........508-584-4900
Superior Products Company
Saint Paul, MN.............800-328-9800
US Seating Products
Ocala, FL..................800-999-2589
WES Plastics
Richmond Hill, ON...........905-508-1546

Sticks

Candy

Automated Food Systems
Waxahachie, TX 469-517-0470
Jarden Home Brands
Daleville, IN 800-392-2575
Saunder Brothers
Bridgton, ME 207-647-3331
Setterstix Corp
Cattaraugus, NY 716-257-3451

Ice Cream

Global Sticks, Inc.
Surrey, BC 866-433-5770
Hardwood Products Co LP
Guilford, ME 800-289-3340
Jarden Home Brands
Cloquet, MN 218-879-6700
Norse Dairy Systems
Columbus, OH 800-338-7465
Solon Manufacturing Company
North Haven, CT 800-341-6640

Tags

Cellulose & Fiber

Atlas Tag & Label Inc
Neenah, WI .800-558-6418
Connecticut Laminating Co Inc
New Haven, CT 800-753-9119
Labelprint America
Newburyport, MA 978-463-4004

Pressure Sensitive

Advanced Labelworx
Anderson, SC 865-966-8711
ATL-East Tag & Label Inc
West Chester, PA 866-381-8744
Carlton Industries
La Grange, TX 800-231-5988
D A C Labels & Graphic
Dallas, TX .800-483-1700
Deco Labels & Tags
Toronto, ON 888-496-9029
Emedco
Williamsville, NY 877-765-8386
Gbs
North Canton, OH 800-552-2427
Grand Valley Labels
Grand Rapids, MI
Itac Label & Tag Corp
Brooklyn, NY 718-625-2148
Label House
Fullerton, CA 800-499-5858
Label Technology Inc
Merced, CA .800-388-1990
Labelmart
Maple Grove, MN 888-577-0141
Labelprint America
Newburyport, MA 978-463-4004
Metspeed Labels
Levittown, PA 888-886-0638
Mid South Graphics
Nashville, TN 615-331-4210
Multi-Color Corp
Green Bay, WI 800-236-8208
Nameplate
St Paul, MN .651-228-1522
Ozark Tape & Label Co
Springfield, MO 417-831-1444
Paper Product Specialties
Waukesha, WI 262-549-1730
Royal Label Co
Dorchester, MA 617-825-6050
Seton Indentification Products
Branford, CT 800-571-2596
Southern Atlantic Label Co
Chesapeake, VA 800-456-5999
Stoffel Seals Corp
Tallapoosa, GA 800-422-8247
Swan Label & Tag Co
Coraopolis, PA 412-264-9000
TAC-PAD
Irvine, CA 800-947-1609
Three P
Salt Lake City, UT 801-486-7407

Universal Tag Inc
Dudley, MA .800-332-8247

Price

Andrew H Lawson Co
Philadelphia, PA 800-411-6628
Bedford Industries
Worthington, MN 800-533-5314
Clamp Swing Pricing Co Inc
Oakland, CA 800-227-7615
Esselte Meto
Morris Plains, NJ 800-645-3290
Federal Label Systems
Elmhurst, NY 800-238-0015
General Trade Mark Labelcraft
Staten Island, NY 718-448-9800
Intermec Technologies Corporation
Everett, WA 425-348-2600
KHS Co
West Simsbury, CT 860-658-9454
Labelprint America
Newburyport, MA 978-463-4004
Los Angeles Label Company
Commerce, CA 800-606-5223
National Marking Products Inc
Henrico, VA .800-482-1553
Plasti-Clip Corp
Milford, NH .800-882-2547
Plastic Tagtrade Check
Essexville, MI 989-892-7913
Reeve Store Equipment Co
Pico Rivera, CA 800-927-3383
Rothchild Printing Company
Flushing, NY 800-238-0015
Royal Label Co
Dorchester, MA 617-825-6050
SFBC, LLC dba Seaboard Folding Box
Fitchburg, MA 800-225-6313
Stoffel Seals Corp
Tallapoosa, GA 800-422-8247
United Seal & Tag Corporation
Port Charlotte, FL 800-211-9552

Tea Bag

Cincinnati Convertors Inc
Cincinnati, OH 513-731-6600
Stoffel Seals Corp
Tallapoosa, GA 800-422-8247

Tapes

Adhesive

Adhesive Applications
Easthampton, MA 800-356-3572
Afassco
Minden, NV .775-783-3555
Cantech Industries Inc
Johnson City, TN 800-654-3947
Deccofelt Corp
Glendora, CA 800-543-3226
Dunrite Inc
Fremont, NE 800-782-3061
Felco Packaging Specialist
Baltimore, MD 800-673-8488
FFR Merchandising Inc
Twinsburg, OH 800-422-2547
Glue Dots International
New Berlin, WI 888-688-7131
Gulf Arizona Packaging
Humble, TX .800-364-3887
Herche Warehouse
Denver, CO .303-371-8186
International Adhesive Coating
Windham, NH 800-253-4450
Jupiter Mills Corporation
Roslyn, NY .800-853-5121
Label Systems & Solutions
Bohemia, NY 800-811-2560
Levin Brothers Paper
Cicero, IL 800-545-6200
Master Tape & Label Printers
Chicago, IL .800-621-5801
Miller Studio
New Philadelphia, OH 800-332-0050
Nashua Corporation
Nashua, NH .603-661-2004
National Tape Corporation
New Orleans, LA 800-535-8846

O.C. Adhesives Corporation
Ridgefield, NJ 800-662-1595
On-Hand Adhesives
Lake Zurich, IL 800-323-5158
Quali-Tech Tape & Label
Denver, CO
Recco International
West Columbia, SC 800-334-3008
Saunders West
Azusa, CA 888-932-8836
Sekisui TA Industries
Brea, CA 800-258-8273
Spectape Inc
Erlanger, KY 859-283-2044
Tesa Tape Inc
Charlotte, NC 800-429-8273
Thomas Tape & Supply Co Inc
Springfield, OH 937-325-6414
US Label Corporation
Greensboro, NC 336-332-7000
Wasserman Bag Company
Center Moriches, NY 631-909-8656
Worthen Industries Inc
Nashua, NH .603-888-5443
WS Packaging Group Inc
Green Bay, WI 877-977-5177

Freezer

Gulf Arizona Packaging
Humble, TX .800-364-3887
Herche Warehouse
Denver, CO .303-371-8186
Verilon Products Co
Wheeling, IL 800-323-1056

Gummed

Adhesive Products Inc
Vernon, CA .800-669-5516
Cantech Industries Inc
Johnson City, TN 800-654-3947
Ebel Tape & Label
Cincinnati, OH 513-471-1067
Gulf Arizona Packaging
Humble, TX .800-364-3887
Herche Warehouse
Denver, CO .303-371-8186
Intertape Polymer Group
Menasha, WI 800-558-5006
Keena Corporation
Newton, MA 617-244-9800
Master Tape & Label Printers
Chicago, IL .800-621-5801
Rexford Paper Company
Racine, WI .262-886-9100
Rudd Container Corp
Chicago, IL .773-847-7600
Thomas Tape & Supply Co Inc
Springfield, OH 937-325-6414
Timemed Labeling Systems
Valencia, CA 818-897-1111
Volk Corp
Farmington Hills, MI 800-521-6799

Heat Sealing

International Adhesive Coating
Windham, NH 800-253-4450
National Tape Corporation
New Orleans, LA 800-535-8846
Rexford Paper Company
Racine, WI .262-886-9100

Marking

Carlton Industries
La Grange, TX 800-231-5988
Felco Packaging Specialist
Baltimore, MD 800-673-8488
Master Tape & Label Printers
Chicago, IL .800-621-5801
National Tape Corporation
New Orleans, LA 800-535-8846

Pressure Sensitive

Adhesive Products Inc
Vernon, CA .800-669-5516
Adstick Custom Labels Inc
Denver, CO .800-255-7314
Advanced Labelworx
Anderson, SC 865-966-8711

Advanced Labelworx Inc
  Oak Ridge, TN 864-224-2122
Avon Tape
  Chestnut Hill, MA 508-584-8273
Baltimore Tape Products Inc
  Sykesville, MD 410-795-0063
Cantech Industries Inc
  Johnson City, TN 800-654-3947
D A C Labels & Graphic
  Dallas, TX....................800-483-1700
Deccofelt Corp
  Glendora, CA 800-543-3226
Ebel Tape & Label
  Cincinnati, OH 513-471-1067
Emco Industrial Plastics
  Cedar Grove, NJ 800-292-9906
Fibre Leather Manufacturing Company
  New Bedford, MA 800-358-6012
Gulf Arizona Packaging
  Humble, TX 800-364-3887
Henkel Consumer Adhesive
  Avon, OH 800-321-0253
Herche Warehouse
  Denver, CO 303-371-8186
International Adhesive Coating
  Windham, NH 800-253-4450
Intertape Polymer Group
  Menasha, WI 800-558-5006
J M Packaging Co
  Warren, MI 586-771-7800
Jupiter Mills Corporation
  Roslyn, NY 800-853-5121
KAPCO
  Kent, OH 800-843-5368
Label Systems & Solutions
  Bohemia, NY 800-811-2560
Marklite Line
  Bellwood, IL 708-668-4900
Master Tape & Label Printers
  Chicago, IL 800-621-5801
Merryweather Foam Inc
  Sylacauga, AL.................256-249-8546
Miller Studio
  New Philadelphia, OH 800-332-0050
NAP Industries
  Brooklyn, NY 877-635-4948
National Tape Corporation
  New Orleans, LA 800-535-8846
Ozark Tape & Label Co
  Springfield, MO 417-831-1444
Pakmark
  Chesterfield, MO 800-423-1379
Pamco Label Co Inc
  Des Plaines, IL 847-803-2200
Print-O-Tape Inc
  Mundelein, IL 800-346-6311
Raypress Corp
  Hoover, AL...................800-423-3731
Rexford Paper Company
  Racine, WI 262-886-9100
Richmond Printed Tape & Label
  Hatfield, PA..................800-522-3525
Robinson Tape & Label
  Branford, CT..................800-433-7102
Saunders West
  Azusa, CA 888-932-8836
Sekisui TA Industries
  Brea, CA 800-258-8273
Shippers Supply
  Saskatoon, SK................800-661-5639
Shippers Supply, Labelgraphic
  Calgary, AB..................800-661-5639
Source for Packaging
  New York, NY 800-223-2527
Spectape Inc
  Erlanger, KY 859-283-2044
Tape & Label Engineering
  St Petersburg, FL 800-237-8955
Tesa Tape Inc
  Charlotte, NC 800-429-8273
Thomas Tape & Supply Co Inc
  Springfield, OH................937-325-6414
Volk Corp
  Farmington Hills, MI 800-521-6799

Tea Packaging Materials

Cin-Made Packaging Group
  Norcross, GA 800-264-7494
Packaging Dynamics
  Walnut Creek, CA..............925-938-2711

PPI
  Baton Rouge, LA 225-330-4602
Xtreme Beverages, LLC
  Dana Point, CA................949-495-7929

Ties

Bag

Arbee Transparent Inc
  Elk Grove Vlg, IL...............800-642-2247
Bedford Industries
  Worthington, MN 800-533-5314
Cavert Wire Co
  Rural Hall, NC 800-245-4042
Gulf Arizona Packaging
  Humble, TX 800-364-3887
Herche Warehouse
  Denver, CO 303-371-8186
Leco Plastic Inc
  Hackensack, NJ 201-343-3330
Package Containers Inc
  Canby, OR...................800-266-5806
Superior Products Company
  Saint Paul, MN 800-328-9800
T & T Industries Inc
  Fort Mohave, AZ 800-437-6246

Bundle, Package

Bedford Industries
  Worthington, MN 800-533-5314
Cavert Wire Co
  Rural Hall, NC 800-245-4042
Emco Industrial Plastics
  Cedar Grove, NJ 800-292-9906
Gulf Arizona Packaging
  Humble, TX 800-364-3887
Herche Warehouse
  Denver, CO 303-371-8186
Indeco Products Inc
  San Marcos, TX 888-246-3326
Jilson Group
  Lodi, NJ.....................800-969-5400
Leco Plastic Inc
  Hackensack, NJ...............201-343-3330
Package Containers Inc
  Canby, OR...................800-266-5806
QMS International, Inc.
  Mississauga, Ontario, ON.......905-820-7225
T & T Industries Inc
  Fort Mohave, AZ 800-437-6246

Trays

Ace Technical Plastics Inc
  East Hartford, CT 860-278-2444
Bayhead Products Corp.
  Dover, NH...................800-229-4323
Collectors Gallery
  St Charles, IL 800-346-3063
DEL-Tec Packaging Inc
  Greer, SC....................800-747-8683
Douglas Stephen Plastics Inc
  Paterson, NJ 973-523-3030
In-Touch Products
  North Salt Lake, UT 801-298-4466
IVEX Packaging Corporation
  Longueuil, QC 450-651-8887
Jay Packaging Group Inc
  Warwick, RI 401-244-1300
K & L Intl
  Ontario, CA..................888-598-5588
Key Packaging Co
  Sarasota, FL 941-355-2728
Leal True Form Corporation
  Freeport, NY 516-379-2008
Madsen Wire Products Inc
  Orland, IN...................260-829-6561
Mmi Engineered Soultions Inc
  Saline, MI 800-825-2566
Nelipak
  Phoenix, AZ 602-269-7648
Nu-Trend Plastics Thermoformer
  Jacksonville, FL 904-353-5936
Olive Can Company
  Elgin, IL.....................847-468-7474
Packaging Solutions
  Los Altos Hills, CA 650-917-1022
Pactiv LLC
  Lake Forest, IL 800-476-4300

Palace Packaging Machines Inc
  Downingtown, PA..............610-873-7252
Parlor City Paper Box Co Inc
  Binghamton, NY...............607-772-0600
Pinn Pack Packaging LLC
  Oxnard, CA..................805-385-4100
Revere Group
  Seattle, WA 206-545-1850
Schroeder Machine
  San Marcos, CA 760-591-9733
Scott Packaging Corporation
  Philadelphia, PA 215-925-5595
Seal Pac USA
  Richmond, VA.................804-261-0580
Tenneco Inc
  Lake Forest, IL 800-403-3393
Tenneco Specialty Packaging
  Smyrna, GA 800-241-4402
V C 999 Packaging Systems
  Kansas City, MO...............800-728-2999
WNA Hopple Plastics
  Florence, KY 800-446-4622
Xtreme Beverages, LLC
  Dana Point, CA................949-495-7929

Wax

Cheese Coating

Frank B Ross Co Inc
  Rahway, NJ 732-669-0810
International Group Inc
  Oshkosh, WI 920-233-5500

Paraffin

Hollowick Inc
  Manlius, NY 800-367-3015

Sealing

Frank B Ross Co Inc
  Rahway, NJ 732-669-0810
Stevenson-Cooper Inc
  Philadelphia, PA 215-223-2600

Wrappers

Frozen Food

Campbell Wrapper Corporation
  De Pere, WI..................920-983-7100
Schwab Paper Products Co
  Romeoville, IL 800-837-7225

Paper

Alufoil Products Co Inc
  Hauppauge, NY 631-231-4141
Burrows Paper Corp
  Little Falls, NY 800-272-7122
Campbell Wrapper Corporation
  De Pere, WI..................920-983-7100
Gardiner Paperboard
  Gardiner, ME 207-582-3230
Handy Wacks Corp
  Sparta, MI 800-445-4434
Patty Paper Inc
  Plymouth, IN.................800-782-1703
Printpack Inc.
  Atlanta, GA 404-460-7000
Ross & Wallace Inc
  Hammond, LA 800-854-2300
Salinas Valley Wax Paper Co
  Salinas, CA..................831-424-2747
Schwab Paper Products Co
  Romeoville, IL 800-837-7225
Signature Packaging
  West Orange, NJ 800-376-2299
Stewart Sutherland Inc
  Vicksburg, MI.................269-649-0530
Wrap Pack
  Yakima, WA 800-879-9727

Transparent

Arbee Transparent Inc
  Elk Grove Vlg, IL...............800-642-2247
Campbell Wrapper Corporation
  De Pere, WI..................920-983-7100
Flexo Transparent Inc
  Buffalo, NY 877-993-5396

Goodwrappers Inc
Halethorpe, MD 800-638-1127
M S Plastics & Packaging Inc
Butler, NJ 800-593-1802

MSK Covertech
Marietta, GA 770-928-1099
Trans World Services
Melrose, MA 800-882-2105

Refrigeration & Cooling Equipment

Cabinets

Freezer & Frozen Foods

AAA Mill
Austin, TX......512-385-2215
Andgar Corp
Ferndale, WA......360-366-9900
Arkfeld Mfg & Distributing Co
Norfolk, NE......800-533-0676
Bacchus Wine Cellars
Houston, TX......800-487-8812
Bettag & Associates
O Fallon, MO......800-325-0959
Bevles Company
Dallas, TX......800-441-1601
C Nelson Mfg Co
Oak Harbor, OH......800-922-7339
Crown Manufacturing Corporation
Waterford, CT......860-442-4325
Cryochem
St Simons Island, GA......800-237-4001
Delfield Co
Mt Pleasant, MI......800-733-8821
Duke Manufacturing Co
St Louis, MO......800-735-3853
EPCO
Murfreesboro, TN......800-251-3398
Eskay Metal Fabricating
Buffalo, NY......800-836-8015
Everidge
Plymouth, MN......888-227-1629
Fogel Jordon Commercial Refrigeration Company
Philadelphia, PA......800-523-0171
Food Warming Equipment Co
Crystal Lake, IL......800-222-4393
Foster Refrigerator Corporation
Kinderhook, NY......888-828-3311
G A Systems Inc
Huntington Beach, CA......714-848-7529
Habco
Concord, CA......925-682-6203
Hoshizaki America Inc
Peachtree City, GA......800-438-6087
IMC Teddy Food Service Equipment
Amityville, NY......800-221-5644
J.H. Carr & Sons
Seattle, WA......800-523-8842
Kedco Wine Storage Systems
Farmingdale, NY......800-654-9988
LA Rosa Refrigeration & Equip
Detroit, MI......800-527-6723
Lauritzen Makin Inc
Fort Worth, TX......817-921-0218
Lyon LLC
Montgomery, IL......630-892-8941
Master-Bilt
New Albany, MS......800-647-1284
Merric
Bridgeton, MO......314-770-9944
Metal Master Sales Corp
Glendale Heights, IL......800-488-8729
Normandie Metal Fabricators
Port Washington, NY......800-221-2398
Ojeda USA
Spartanburg, SC......864-574-6004
Omicron Steel Products Company
Jamaica, NY......718-805-3400
Piper Products Inc
Wausau, WI......800-544-3057
Sefi Fabricators Inc
Amityville, NY......631-842-2200
Shammi Industries
Corona, CA......800-417-9260
Silver King Refrigeration Inc
Minneapolis, MN......800-328-3329
St. Louis Stainless Service
St Louis, MO......800-735-3853
Super Sturdy
Weldon, NC......800-253-4833
Talbert Display
Fort Worth, TX......817-429-4504
Texican Specialty Products
Houston, TX......800-869-5918
Valad Electric Heating Corporation
Tarrytown, NY......914-631-4927

Welbilt Corporation
Stamford, CT......203-325-8300
Western Laminates
Omaha, NE......402-556-4600
Wine Chillers of California
Santa Ana, CA......800-331-4274
Zero Manufacturing Inc
North Salt Lake, UT......800-959-5050

Chillers

Blast

Advance Energy Technologies
Halfmoon, NY......800-724-0198
Alkar Rapid Pak
Lodi, WI......608-592-3211
Chillers Solutions
Pompton Plains, NJ......800-526-5201
Elliott-Williams Company
Indianapolis, IN......800-428-9303
Gea Intec, Llc
Durham, NC......919-433-0131
Glastender
Saginaw, MI......800-748-0423
Henny Penny, Inc.
Eaton, OH......800-417-8417
Pacific Pneumatics
Rancho Cucamonga, CA......800-221-0961
Superior Products Company
Saint Paul, MN......800-328-9800
USECO
Murfreesboro, TN......615-893-4820
Williams Refrigeration
Hillsdale, NJ......800-445-9979

Compressors

GEA FES, Inc.
York, PA......025-119-1051
GEA Refrigeration North America
York, PA......800-888-4337
Tecumseh Products Co.
Ann Arbor, MI......734-585-9500

Coolers

Beverage

Advance Energy Technologies
Halfmoon, NY......800-724-0198
Alkar Rapid Pak
Lodi, WI......608-592-3211
Aurora Design Associates, Inc.
Salt Lake City, UT......801-588-0111
Bar Equipment Corporation of America
Downey, CA......888-870-2322
Berkshire PPM
Litchfield, CT......860-567-3118
Beverage Air
Winston Salem, NC......800-845-9800
Chester-Jensen Co., Inc.
Chester, PA......800-685-3750
Cleland Sales Corp
Los Alamitos, CA......562-598-6616
Convay Systems
Minnetonka, MN......800-334-1099
Cool-Pitch Co
Jacksonville, FL......800-938-0128
Cramer Products
New York, NY......212-645-2368
Duke Manufacturing Co
St Louis, MO......800-735-3853
Elwood Safety Company
Buffalo, NY......866-326-6060
Felix Storch Inc
Bronx, NY......800-932-4267
FleetwoodGoldcoWyard
Romeoville, IL......630-759-6800
Fogel Jordon Commercial Refrigeration Company
Philadelphia, PA......800-523-0171
Foster Refrigerator Corporation
Kinderhook, NY......888-828-3311
Girard Spring Water
North Providence, RI......800-477-9287

Glastender
Saginaw, MI......800-748-0423
Hebeler Corp
Tonawanda, NY......800-486-4709
Hoshizaki America Inc
Peachtree City, GA......800-438-6087
Ilc Dover
Frederica, DE......800-631-9567
International Patterns, Inc.
Bay Shore, NY......631-952-2000
Ojeda USA
Spartanburg, SC......864-574-6004
Perlick Corp
Milwaukee, WI......800-558-5592
Pro-Flo Products
Cedar Grove, NJ......800-325-1057
QBD Modular Systems
Santa Clara, CA......800-663-3005
RubaTex Polymer
Middlefield, OH......440-632-1691
Rubbermaid
High Point, NC......888-895-2110
Summit Commercial
Bronx, NY......800-932-4267
Superior Products Company
Saint Paul, MN......800-328-9800
True Food Service Equipment, Inc.
O Fallon, MO......800-325-6152
Wine Chillers of California
Santa Ana, CA......800-331-4274
Wine Well Chiller Co
Milford, CT......203-878-2465

Bread

Advance Energy Technologies
Halfmoon, NY......800-724-0198
Fred D Pfening Co
Columbus, OH......614-294-5361
I J White Corp
Farmingdale, NY......631-293-2211
Industrial Air Conditioning Systems
Chicago, IL......773-486-4236
Peerless Food Equipment
Sidney, OH......937-492-4158

Butchers'

Advance Energy Technologies
Halfmoon, NY......800-724-0198

Candy (Confectioners')

Advance Energy Technologies
Halfmoon, NY......800-724-0198
Applied Thermal Technologies
San Marcos, CA......800-736-5083
Hebeler Corp
Tonawanda, NY......800-486-4709
Komline-Sanderson Engineering
Peapack, NJ......800-225-5457

Canners'

Advance Energy Technologies
Halfmoon, NY......800-724-0198
Berkshire PPM
Litchfield, CT......860-567-3118
Custom Food Machinery
Stockton, CA......209-463-4343
Hebeler Corp
Tonawanda, NY......800-486-4709
Horix Manufacturing Co
Mc Kees Rocks, PA......412-771-1111
Nercon Engineering & Manufacturing
Oshkosh, WI......920-233-3268
South Valley Mfg Inc
Gilroy, CA......408-842-5457

Ice

Eskay Metal Fabricating
Buffalo, NY......800-836-8015
Hoshizaki America Inc
Peachtree City, GA......800-438-6087
Igloo Products Corp
Katy, TX......866-509-3503

241

Majestic
  Bridgeport, CT 203-367-7900
Mid-Lands Chemical Company
  Omaha, NE 800-642-5263
Midwest Aircraft Products Co
  Lexington, OH 419-884-2164
Northfield Freezing Systems
  Northfield, MN 800-426-1283
Olde Country Reproductions Inc
  York, PA 800-358-3997
Plastilite Corporation
  Omaha, NE 800-228-9506
Presence From Innovation LLC
  St Louis, MO 314-423-9777
Rubbermaid
  High Point, NC 888-895-2110
Semco Manufacturing Company
  Pharr, TX 956-787-4203
Superior Products Company
  Saint Paul, MN 800-328-9800

Ice Cream

Advance Energy Technologies
  Halfmoon, NY 800-724-0198
Jack Langston Manufacturing Company
  Dallas, TX 214-821-9844
Manufacturing Warehouse
  Miami, FL 305-635-8886
Superior Products Company
  Saint Paul, MN 800-328-9800
WA Brown & Son
  Salisbury, NC 704-636-5131

Ingredient Water

Advance Energy Technologies
  Halfmoon, NY 800-724-0198
Applied Thermal Technologies
  San Marcos, CA 800-736-5083
Bevistar
  Oswego, IL 877-238-7827
Filtrine Manufacturing
  Keene, NH 800-930-3367
Girard Spring Water
  North Providence, RI 800-477-9287
Komline-Sanderson Engineering
  Peapack, NJ 800-225-5457
Koolant Koolers
  Kalamazoo, MI 800-968-5665
Perfect Equipment Inc
  Gurnee, IL 800-356-6301
Wine Well Chiller Co
  Milford, CT 203-878-2465

Milk & Cream

Advance Energy Technologies
  Halfmoon, NY 800-724-0198
Applied Thermal Technologies
  San Marcos, CA 800-736-5083
Beverage Air
  Winston Salem, NC 800-845-9800
C E Rogers Co
  Mora, MN 800-279-8081
Carrier Vibrating Equip Inc
  Louisville, KY 502-969-3171
Chester-Jensen Co., Inc.
  Chester, PA 800-685-3750
Foster Refrigerator Corporation
  Kinderhook, NY 888-828-3311
Gea Us
  Galesville, WI 608-582-3081
Hebeler Corp
  Tonawanda, NY 800-486-4709
Precision
  Miami, FL 800-762-7565
Viatec
  Victoria, BC 800-942-4702

Walk-In

Advance Energy Technologies
  Halfmoon, NY 800-724-0198
American Panel Corp
  Ocala, FL 800-327-3015
Arctic Industries
  Medley, FL 800-325-0123
Bally Refrigerated Boxes Inc
  Morehead City, NC 800-242-2559
C.M. Lingle Company
  Henderson, TX 800-256-6963

Crown Tonka Walk-Ins
  Minneapolis, MN 800-523-7337
Dade Engineering
  Tampa, FL 800-321-2112
David A Lingle & Son Mfg
  Russellville, AR 479-968-2500
Elliott-Williams Company
  Indianapolis, IN 800-428-9303
Emjac
  Hialeah, FL 305-883-2194
Erickson Industries
  River Falls, WI 800-729-9941
Everidge
  Plymouth, MN 888-227-1629
FleetwoodGoldcoWyard
  Romeoville, IL 630-759-6800
Flo-Cold
  Wixom, MI 248-348-6666
Harford Duracool LLC
  Aberdeen, MD 410-272-9999
Heatcraft Worldwide Refrig
  Columbus, GA 800-866-5596
International Cold Storage
  Andover, KS 800-835-0001
Jack Langston Manufacturing Company
  Dallas, TX 214-821-9844
KEMCO
  Wareham, MA 800-231-5955
Kolpak
  Parsons, TN 800-826-7036
Kolpak Walk-ins
  Parsons, TN 800-826-7036
Kysor Panel Systems
  Fort Worth, TX 800-633-3426
Kysor/Kalt
  Portland, OR 503-235-0776
M&S Manufacturing
  Arnold, MO 636-464-2739
Manufacturing Warehouse
  Miami, FL 305-635-8886
Marquis Products
  Concord, ON 800-268-1282
Mollenberg-Betz Inc
  Buffalo, NY 716-614-7473
Nor-Lake
  Hudson, WI 715-386-2323
Pacific Refrigerator Company
  San Bernardino, CA 909-381-5669
Penn Refrigeration Service Corporation
  Wilkes Barre, PA 800-233-8354
Perley-Halladay Assoc
  West Chester, PA 800-248-5800
Polar King Transportation
  Fort Wayne, IN 888-541-8330
Portable Cold Storage
  Edison, NJ 800-535-2445
QBD Modular Systems
  Santa Clara, CA 800-663-3005
Refrigeration Engineering
  Grand Rapids, MI 800-968-3227
Superior Products Company
  Saint Paul, MN 800-328-9800
Tafco Inc
  Hyde, PA 800-233-1954
US Cooler Company
  Quincy, IL 800-521-2665
WA Brown & Son
  Salisbury, NC 704-636-5131
Zero Temp
  Santa Ana, CA 714-538-3177

Doors

Cold Storage

Advance Energy Technologies
  Halfmoon, NY 800-724-0198
Advanced Insulation Concepts
  Florence, KY 800-826-3100
Air-Lec Industries, Inc
  Madison, WI 608-244-4754
Aleco Food Svc Div
  Muscle Shoals, AL 800-633-3120
Aluma Shield
  Deland, FL 877-638-3266
Andgar Corp
  Ferndale, WA 360-366-9900
Apple-A-Day Nutritional Labeling Service
  San Clemente, CA 949-855-8954
Berner International Corp
  New Castle, PA 800-245-4455

C.M. Lingle Company
  Henderson, TX 800-256-6963
Carlson Products
  Maize, KS 800-234-1069
Chase Doors
  Cincinnati, OH 800-543-4455
Coldmatic Refrigeration
  Concord, ON 905-326-7600
Dade Engineering
  Tampa, FL 800-321-2112
David A Lingle & Son Mfg
  Russellville, AR 479-968-2500
Dole Refrigerating Co
  Lewisburg, TN 800-251-8990
Kingspan Insulated Panels, Ltd.
  Langley, BC 877-638-3266
Manufacturing Warehouse
  Miami, FL 305-635-8886
Products A Curtron Div
  Pittsburgh, PA 800-888-9750
Rytec Corporation
  Milwaukee, WI 888-467-9832
Therm L Tec Building Systems
  Basehor, KS 913-728-2662

Freezer

Advance Energy Technologies
  Halfmoon, NY 800-724-0198
Advanced Insulation Concepts
  Florence, KY 800-826-3100
Air-Lec Industries, Inc
  Madison, WI 608-244-4754
Aleco Food Svc Div
  Muscle Shoals, AL 800-633-3120
Berner International Corp
  New Castle, PA 800-245-4455
Chase Doors
  Cincinnati, OH 800-543-4455
Dole Refrigerating Co
  Lewisburg, TN 800-251-8990
Jamison Door Co
  Hagerstown, MD 800-532-3667
Kingspan Insulated Panels, Ltd.
  Langley, BC 877-638-3266
Products A Curtron Div
  Pittsburgh, PA 800-888-9750
Rytec Corporation
  Milwaukee, WI 888-467-9832
Superior Products Company
  Saint Paul, MN 800-328-9800

Refrigerated Display Case

Advance Energy Technologies
  Halfmoon, NY 800-724-0198
Kedco Wine Storage Systems
  Farmingdale, NY 800-654-9988
Ojeda USA
  Spartanburg, SC 864-574-6004
Seville Display Door
  Temecula, CA 800-634-0412
Superior Products Company
  Saint Paul, MN 800-328-9800

Refrigerator

Advance Energy Technologies
  Halfmoon, NY 800-724-0198
Advanced Insulation Concepts
  Florence, KY 800-826-3100
Aleco Food Svc Div
  Muscle Shoals, AL 800-633-3120
Berner International Corp
  New Castle, PA 800-245-4455
Carlson Products
  Maize, KS 800-234-1069
Chase Doors
  Cincinnati, OH 800-543-4455
Coldmatic Refrigeration
  Concord, ON 905-326-7600
Dole Refrigerating Co
  Lewisburg, TN 800-251-8990
Illinois Tool Works
  Glenview, IL 224-661-8870
JUMO Process Control Inc
  East Syracuse, NY 800-554-5866
Kason Industries
  Newnan, GA 770-254-0553
Pro Refrigeration
  Auburn, WA 253-735-1189

Products A Curtron Div
Pittsburgh, PA 800-888-9750
Seville Display Door
Temecula, CA 800-634-0412
Therm L Tec Building Systems
Basehor, KS 913-728-2662

Freezers

Advance Energy Technologies
Halfmoon, NY 800-724-0198
Advanced Equipment
Richmond, BC 604-276-8989
American Food Equipment
Miami, FL 305-377-8991
APV Americas
Delavan, WI 800-252-5200
Arctic Air
Eden Prairie, MN 800-853-3508
Arctic Industries
Medley, FL 800-325-0123
Attias Oven Corp
Brooklyn, NY 800-928-8427
Bally Refrigerated Boxes Inc
Morehead City, NC 800-242-2559
Berndorf Belt Technology USA
Gilberts, IL 800-393-8450
C Nelson Mfg Co
Oak Harbor, OH 800-922-7339
C.M. Lingle Company
Henderson, TX 800-256-6963
Carbonic Reserves
San Antonio, TX 800-880-1911
Carpigiani Corporation of America
Winston Salem, NC 800-648-4389
Cci Industries-Cool Curtain
Costa Mesa, CA 800-854-5719
Checker Machine
Minneapolis, MN 888-800-5001
Chrysler & Koppin Co
Detroit, MI 800-441-0038
Cloudy & Britton
Mountlake Ter, WA 425-775-7424
Coldstream Products Corporation
Crossfield, AB 888-946-4097
Crown Tonka Walk-Ins
Minneapolis, MN 800-523-7337
Cryochem
St Simons Island, GA 800-237-4001
Dade Engineering
Tampa, FL 800-321-2112
David A Lingle & Son Mfg
Russellville, AR 479-968-2500
Delfield Co
Mt Pleasant, MI 800-733-8821
Dole Refrigerating Co
Lewisburg, TN 800-251-8990
Duke Manufacturing Co
St Louis, MO 800-735-3853
Elliott-Williams Company
Indianapolis, IN 800-428-9303
Emjac
Hialeah, FL 305-883-2194
Empire Bakery Equipment
Hicksville, NY 800-878-4070
Erickson Industries
River Falls, WI 800-729-9941
Esco Products Inc
Houston, TX 800-966-5514
Everidge
Plymouth, MN 888-227-1629
Felix Storch Inc
Bronx, NY 800-932-4267
Flo-Cold
Wixom, MI 248-348-6666
Fogel Jordon Commercial Refrigeration Company
Philadelphia, PA 800-523-0171
Food Engineering Unlimited
Fullerton, CA 714-879-8762
Foster Refrigerator Corporation
Kinderhook, NY 888-828-3311
FreesTech
Sinking Spring, PA 717-560-7560
Frigidaire Co.
Charlotte, NC 866-449-4200
Frigoscandia
Redmond, WA 800-423-1743
Frigoscandia Equipment
Northfield, MN 800-426-1283
Galley
Jupiter, FL 800-537-2772

Gch Internatonal
Louisville, KY 502-636-1374
Gem Refrigerator Company
Philadelphia, PA 215-426-8700
General Electric Company
Fairfield, CT 203-373-2211
Glastender
Saginaw, MI 800-748-0423
Gold Star Products
Oak Park, MI 800-800-0205
Gram Equipment of America
Tampa, FL 813-248-1978
HABCO Beverage Systems
Toronto, ON 800-448-0244
Heatcraft Worldwide Refrig
Columbus, GA 800-866-5596
Howard-Mccray
Philadelphia, PA 800-344-8222
I J White Corp
Farmingdale, NY 631-293-2211
IMECO Inc
Polo, IL 815-946-2351
International Cold Storage
Andover, KS 800-835-0001
Jack Langston Manufacturing Company
Dallas, TX 214-821-9844
JBT Food Tech
Lakeland, FL 863-683-5411
Jordon Commercial Refrigerator
Philadelphia, PA 800-523-0171
KEMCO
Wareham, MA 800-231-5955
Kold Pack
Jackson, MI 800-824-2661
Kolpak
Parsons, TN 800-826-7036
Kolpak Walk-ins
Parsons, TN 800-826-7036
Kysor/Kalt
Portland, OR 503-235-0776
LA Rosa Refrigeration & Equip
Detroit, MI 800-527-6723
Manufacturing Warehouse
Miami, FL 305-635-8886
Mar-Con Wire Belt
Richmond, BC 877-962-7266
Marc Refrigeration Mfg Inc
Miami, FL 305-691-0500
Marquis Products
Concord, ON 800-268-1282
Martin Cab Div
Cleveland, OH 216-377-8200
Martin/Baron
Irwindale, CA 626-960-5153
Master-Bilt
New Albany, MS 800-647-1284
McCormack Manufacturing Company
Lake Oswego, OR 800-395-1593
Migali Industries
Camden, NJ 800-852-5292
Mollenberg-Betz Inc
Buffalo, NY 716-614-7473
National Hotpack
Stone Ridge, NY 800-431-8232
Nor-Lake
Hudson, WI 715-386-2323
Northfield Freezing Systems
Northfield, MN 800-426-1283
Northland Corp
Greenville, MI 800-223-3900
Nothum Food Processing Systems
Springfield, MO 800-435-1297
Odenberg Engineering
West Sacramento, CA 800-688-8396
Ojeda USA
Spartanburg, SC 864-574-6004
Pacific Refrigerator Company
San Bernardino, CA 909-381-5669
Penn Refrigeration Service Corporation
Wilkes Barre, PA 800-233-8354
Perley-Halladay Assoc
West Chester, PA 800-248-5800
Polar King Transportation
Fort Wayne, IN 888-541-8330
Praxair Inc
Danbury, CT 800-772-9247
Ransco Industries
Ventura, CA 805-487-7777
Refrigerated Warehousing
Jasper, GA 800-873-2008
Reliable Food Service Equipment
Concord, ON 416-738-6840

Rival Manufacturing Company
Kansas City, MO 816-943-4100
Ron Vallort & Associates
Oak Brook, IL 630-734-3821
Ross Industries Inc
Midland, VA 540-439-3271
Russell
Scottsboro, AL 800-288-9488
Sandvik Process Systems
Sweden, NJ 973-790-1600
SaniServ
Mooresville, IN 800-733-8073
Seattle Refrigeration & Manufacturing
Seattle, WA 800-228-8881
Semco Manufacturing Company
Pharr, TX 956-787-4203
Silver King Refrigeration Inc
Minneapolis, MN 800-328-3329
SP Industries Inc
Warminster, PA 800-523-2327
Stafford-Smith Inc
Kalamazoo, MI 800-968-2442
Starlite Food Service Equipment
Detroit, MI 888-521-6603
Summit Commercial
Bronx, NY 800-932-4267
Superior Products Company
Saint Paul, MN 800-328-9800
Supreme Corporation
Goshen, IN 800-642-4889
Systemate Numafa
Canton, GA 800-240-3770
Tafco Inc
Hyde, PA 800-233-1954
Thermo King Corp
Bloomington, MN 888-887-2202
Traulsen & Co
Fort Worth, TX 800-825-8220
True Food Service Equipment, Inc.
O Fallon, MO 800-325-6152
U-Line Corporation
Milwaukee, WI 800-779-2547
US Cooler Company
Quincy, IL 800-521-2665
Utility Refrigerator Company
Los Angeles, CA 800-884-5233
Victory Refrigeration
Cherry Hill, NJ 856-428-4200
WA Brown & Son
Salisbury, NC 704-636-5131
Waukesha Cherry-Burrell
Louisville, KY 502-491-4310
WCB Ice Cream
Philadelphia, PA 215-425-4320
Welbilt Inc.
New Port Richey, FL 877-375-9300
White Mountain Freezer
Kansas City, MO 816-943-4100
Wilch Manufacturing
Topeka, KS 785-267-2762
Zero Temp
Santa Ana, CA 714-538-3177

Ice Cream

Advance Energy Technologies
Halfmoon, NY 800-724-0198
C Nelson Mfg Co
Oak Harbor, OH 800-922-7339
Carpigiani Corporation of America
Winston Salem, NC 800-648-4389
Delfield Co
Mt Pleasant, MI 800-733-8821
Eischen Enterprises
Fresno, CA 559-834-0013
Felix Storch Inc
Bronx, NY 800-932-4267
FreesTech
Sinking Spring, PA 717-560-7560
Glastender
Saginaw, MI 800-748-0423
Howard-Mccray
Philadelphia, PA 800-344-8222
LA Rosa Refrigeration & Equip
Detroit, MI 800-527-6723
Manufacturing Warehouse
Miami, FL 305-635-8886
Marc Refrigeration Mfg Inc
Miami, FL 305-691-0500
Rival Manufacturing Company
Kansas City, MO 816-943-4100

SaniServ
Mooresville, IN.............................800-733-8073
Schroeder Machine
San Marcos, CA 760-591-9733
Stainless Fabrication Inc
Springfield, MO............................800-397-8265
Summit Commercial
Bronx, NY.................................800-932-4267
White Mountain Freezer
Kansas City, MO...........................816-943-4100
Wilch Manufacturing
Topeka, KS................................785-267-2762

Quick Freezing

Advance Energy Technologies
Halfmoon, NY..............................800-724-0198
Advanced Equipment
Richmond, BC..............................604-276-8989
Carbonic Reserves
San Antonio, TX...........................800-880-1911
Dole Refrigerating Co
Lewisburg, TN.............................800-251-8990
Foster Refrigerator Corporation
Kinderhook, NY............................888-828-3311
FreesTech
Sinking Spring, PA........................717-560-7560
Frigoscandia
Redmond, WA..............................800-423-1743
Gch Internatonal
Louisville, KY.............................502-636-1374
Manufacturing Warehouse
Miami, FL.................................305-635-8886
Mar-Con Wire Belt
Richmond, BC..............................877-962-7266
Mayekawa USA, Inc.
Chicago, IL...............................773-516-5070
McCormack Manufacturing Company
Lake Oswego, OR...........................800-395-1593
Stainless Fabrication Inc
Springfield, MO............................800-397-8265
Witte Brothers Exchange Inc
Troy, MO..................................800-325-8151

Sub-Zero

Advance Energy Technologies
Halfmoon, NY..............................800-724-0198
C.M. Lingle Company
Henderson, TX.............................800-256-6963
Cryochem
St Simons Island, GA......................800-237-4001
Fogel Jordon Commercial Refrigeration Company
Philadelphia, PA..........................800-523-0171
Foster Refrigerator Corporation
Kinderhook, NY............................888-828-3311
Frigidaire Co.
Charlotte, NC.............................866-449-4200
Hoshizaki America Inc
Peachtree City, GA........................800-438-6087
Howard-Mccray
Philadelphia, PA..........................800-344-8222
IMECO Inc
Polo, IL..................................815-946-2351
Martin/Baron
Irwindale, CA.............................626-960-5153
McCormack Manufacturing Company
Lake Oswego, OR...........................800-395-1593
Portable Cold Storage
Edison, NJ................................800-535-2445
Ransco Industries
Ventura, CA...............................805-487-7777
Ron Vallort & Associates
Oak Brook, IL.............................630-734-3821
Semco Manufacturing Company
Pharr, TX.................................956-787-4203
SP Industries Inc
Warminster, PA............................800-523-2327

Walk-In

Advance Energy Technologies
Halfmoon, NY..............................800-724-0198
Arctic Industries
Medley, FL................................800-325-0123
Bally Refrigerated Boxes Inc
Morehead City, NC.........................800-242-2559
C.M. Lingle Company
Henderson, TX.............................800-256-6963
Chrysler & Koppin Co
Detroit, MI...............................800-441-0038

Coldstream Products Corporation
Crossfield, AB............................888-946-4097
Crown Tonka Walk-Ins
Minneapolis, MN...........................800-523-7337
Dade Engineering
Tampa, FL.................................800-321-2112
David A Lingle & Son Mfg
Russellville, AR..........................479-968-2500
Elliott-Williams Company
Indianapolis, IN..........................800-428-9303
Emjac
Hialeah, FL...............................305-883-2194
Foster Refrigerator Corporation
Kinderhook, NY............................888-828-3311
Gem Refrigerator Company
Philadelphia, PA..........................215-426-8700
HABCO Beverage Systems
Toronto, ON...............................800-448-0244
Howard-Mccray
Philadelphia, PA..........................800-344-8222
International Cold Storage
Andover, KS...............................800-835-0001
Jack Langston Manufacturing Company
Dallas, TX................................214-821-9844
Jordon Commercial Refrigerator
Philadelphia, PA..........................800-523-0171
KEMCO
Wareham, MA...............................800-231-5955
Kolpak
Parsons, TN...............................800-826-7036
Kolpak Walk-ins
Parsons, TN...............................800-826-7036
Kysor/Kalt
Portland, OR..............................503-235-0776
Manufacturing Warehouse
Miami, FL.................................305-635-8886
Martin Cab Div
Cleveland, OH.............................216-377-8200
Nor-Lake
Hudson, WI................................715-386-2323
Pacific Refrigerator Company
San Bernardino, CA........................909-381-5669
Penn Refrigeration Service Corporation
Wilkes Barre, PA..........................800-233-8354
Polar King Transportation
Fort Wayne, IN............................888-541-8330
Portable Cold Storage
Edison, NJ................................800-535-2445
Russell
Scottsboro, AL............................800-288-9488
Semco Manufacturing Company
Pharr, TX.................................956-787-4203
Superior Products Company
Saint Paul, MN............................800-328-9800
Tafco Inc
Hyde, PA..................................800-233-1954
US Cooler Company
Quincy, IL................................800-521-2665
WA Brown & Son
Salisbury, NC.............................704-636-5131
Zero Temp
Santa Ana, CA.............................714-538-3177

Insulation

Refrigeration & Cold Storage

Advanced Insulation Concepts
Florence, KY..............................800-826-3100
Andgar Corp
Ferndale, WA..............................360-366-9900
Cellofoam North America
Conyers, GA...............................800-241-3634
David A Lingle & Son Mfg
Russellville, AR..........................479-968-2500
Foam Pack Industries
Springfield, NJ...........................973-376-3700
Modular Panel Company
New Bedford, MA...........................508-993-9955
Reilly Foam Corporation
Conshohocken, PA..........................610-834-1900
Republic Refrigeration Inc
Monroe, NC................................704-225-0410
Ron Vallort & Associates
Oak Brook, IL.............................630-734-3821
Therm L Tec Building Systems
Basehor, KS...............................913-728-2662
WA Brown & Son
Salisbury, NC.............................704-636-5131

Lockers

Frozen Food

Cayne Industrial Sales Corp
Bronx, NY.................................718-993-5800
Remcon Plastics Inc
Reading, PA...............................800-360-3636
Welch Brothers
Bartlett, IL..............................847-741-6134

Refrigerating & Cooling Rooms

Advance Energy Technologies
Halfmoon, NY..............................800-724-0198
AeroFreeze, Inc.
Richmond, BC, BC..........................604-278-4118
American Panel Corp
Ocala, FL.................................800-327-3015
Arctic Industries
Medley, FL................................800-325-0123
Bakery Refrigeration & Services
Lake Park, FL.............................561-882-1655
C.M. Lingle Company
Henderson, TX.............................800-256-6963
Cool Care
Boynton Beach, FL.........................561-364-5711
David A Lingle & Son Mfg
Russellville, AR..........................479-968-2500
Elliott-Williams Company
Indianapolis, IN..........................800-428-9303
Erickson Industries
River Falls, WI...........................800-729-9941
Fogel Jordon Commercial Refrigeration Company
Philadelphia, PA..........................800-523-0171
Heatcraft Worldwide Refrig
Columbus, GA..............................800-866-5596
Kysor Panel Systems
Fort Worth, TX............................800-633-3426
Kysor/Kalt
Portland, OR..............................503-235-0776
M&S Manufacturing
Arnold, MO................................636-464-2739
Master-Bilt
New Albany, MS............................800-647-1284
Mollenberg-Betz Inc
Buffalo, NY...............................716-614-7473
National Hotpack
Stone Ridge, NY...........................800-431-8232
Pacific Refrigerator Company
San Bernardino, CA........................909-381-5669
Perley-Halladay Assoc
West Chester, PA..........................800-248-5800
QBD Modular Systems
Santa Clara, CA...........................800-663-3005
Ransco Industries
Ventura, CA...............................805-487-7777
Refrigerated Warehousing
Jasper, GA................................800-873-2008
Refrigerator Manufacturers LLC
Cerritos, CA..............................562-926-2006
RMF Companies
Grandview, MO.............................816-839-9258
Ron Vallort & Associates
Oak Brook, IL.............................630-734-3821
Tafco Inc
Hyde, PA..................................800-233-1954
Thermal Technologies
Broomall, PA..............................610-353-8887
US Cooler Company
Quincy, IL................................800-521-2665
Zero Temp
Santa Ana, CA.............................714-538-3177

Refrigerating Equipment & Machinery

ABCO Industries Limited
Lunenburg, NS.............................866-634-8821
Advance Energy Technologies
Halfmoon, NY..............................800-724-0198
Advanced Equipment
Richmond, BC..............................604-276-8989
Advanced Insulation Concepts
Florence, KY..............................800-826-3100
AeroFreeze, Inc.
Richmond, BC, BC..........................604-278-4118
AGA Gas
Cleveland, OH.............................216-642-6600
Aleco Food Svc Div
Muscle Shoals, AL.........................800-633-3120

Alkar Rapid Pak
Lodi, WI 608-592-3211
Alto-Shaam
Menomonee Falls, WI. 800-329-8744
Aluma Shield
Deland, FL 877-638-3266
American Food Equipment
Miami, FL 305-377-8991
American Panel Corp
Ocala, FL. 800-327-3015
American Systems Associates
Hampton Bays, NY 800-584-3663
Applied Thermal Technologies
San Marcos, CA 800-736-5083
Arctic Air
Eden Prairie, MN 800-853-3508
Arctic Industries
Medley, FL 800-325-0123
Arctica Showcase Company
Cayuga, ON. 800-839-5536
Attias Oven Corp
Brooklyn, NY 800-928-8427
Baltimore Aircoil Co
Jessup, MD 410-799-1300
Bar Equipment Corporation of America
Downey, CA 888-870-2322
Bar-Maid Corp
Garfield, NJ. 800-227-6243
Barker Company
Keosauqua, IA 319-293-3777
Beacon Specialties
New York, NY 800-221-9405
Benko Products
Sheffield Vlg, OH. 440-934-2180
Berg Chilling Systems
Toronto, ON, ON 416-755-2221
Berner International Corp
New Castle, PA 800-245-4455
Beverage Air
Winston Salem, NC. 800-845-9800
BNW Industries
Tippecanoe, IN 574-353-7855
Buffalo Technologies Corporation
Buffalo, NY. 800-332-2419
Buhler Inc.
Plymouth, MN. 763-847-9900
Bush Refrigeration Inc
Pennsauken, NJ 800-220-2874
C&R Refrigeration
Center, TX. 800-438-6182
C.M. Lingle Company
Henderson, TX 800-256-6963
Caddy Corporation of America
Bridgeport, NJ. 856-467-4222
Carbonic Reserves
San Antonio, TX 800-880-1911
Carpigiani Corporation of America
Winston Salem, NC. 800-648-4389
Carrier Corp
Farmington, CT. 800-227-7437
Carter-Hoffmann LLC
Mundelein, IL. 800-323-9793
Carts Food Equipment
Brooklyn, NY 718-788-5540
Cci Industries-Cool Curtain
Costa Mesa, CA 800-854-5719
Century Refrigeration
Pryor, OK 918-825-6363
Checker Machine
Minneapolis, MN 888-800-5001
Chrysler & Koppin Co
Detroit, MI 800-441-0038
Cloudy & Britton
Mountlake Ter, WA. 425-775-7424
Coldmatic Refrigeration
Concord, ON. 905-326-7600
Coldstream Products Corporation
Crossfield, AB 888-946-4097
ColdZone
Anaheim, CA
Continental Refrigerator
Bensalem, PA 800-523-7138
Control Beverage
Adelanto, CA 330-549-5376
Cool Care
Boynton Beach, FL 561-364-5711
Cornelius Inc.
Osseo, MN 800-238-3600
Cornell Pump Company
Portland, OR 503-653-0330
Craig Manufacturing
Irvington, NJ 800-631-7936

Cramer Products
New York, NY 212-645-2368
Cres Cor
Mentor, OH. 877-273-7267
Crown Tonka Walk-Ins
Minneapolis, MN 800-523-7337
Cryochem
St Simons Island, GA 800-237-4001
Custom Diamond International
Laval, QC 800-363-5926
Davenport Machine
Rock Island, IL. 309-786-1500
David A Lingle & Son Mfg
Russellville, AR 479-968-2500
Dole Refrigerating Co
Lewisburg, TN 800-251-8990
Doucette Industries
York, PA 800-445-7511
Duke Manufacturing Co
St Louis, MO. 800-735-3853
Econofrost Night Covers
Shawnigan Lake, BC 800-519-1222
Eliason Corp
Portage, MI 800-828-3655
Elliott-Williams Company
Indianapolis, IN 800-428-9303
Elwood Safety Company
Buffalo, NY 866-326-6060
Emjac
Hialeah, FL 305-883-2194
Empire Bakery Equipment
Hicksville, NY 800-878-4070
EPCO
Murfreesboro, TN 800-251-3398
Erickson Industries
River Falls, WI 800-729-9941
EVAPCO Inc
Taneytown, MD 410-876-3782
F G Products Inc
Rice Lake, WI. 800-247-3854
Federal Industries
Belleville, WI 800-356-4206
Felix Storch Inc
Bronx, NY. 800-932-4267
Flakice Corporation
Everett, WA. 800-654-4630
Flat Plate Inc
York, PA 888-854-2500
FleetwoodGoldcoWyard
Romeoville, IL 630-759-6800
Flo-Cold
Wixom, MI 248-348-6666
Food Engineering Unlimited
Fullerton, CA 714-879-8762
Food Warming Equipment Co
Crystal Lake, IL 800-222-4393
FreesTech
Sinking Spring, PA 717-560-7560
FRICK by Johnson Controls
Milwaukee, WI. 855-270-5546
Frigidaire Co.
Charlotte, NC 866-449-4200
Frigoscandia
Redmond, WA. 800-423-1743
Galley
Jupiter, FL. 800-537-2772
Gates Manufacturing Company
Saint Louis, MO 800-237-9226
Gch Internatonal
Louisville, KY 502-636-1374
Gem Refrigerator Company
Philadelphia, PA 215-426-8700
Gold Star Products
Oak Park, MI. 800-800-0205
Governair Corp
Oklahoma City, OK 405-525-6546
H A Phillips & Co
Dekalb, IL 630-377-0050
Hackney Brothers
Washington, NC 800-763-0700
Hall Manufacturing Co
Ringwood, NJ 973-962-6022
Hansen Technologies Corporation
Bolingbrook, IL 800-426-7368
Harford Duracool LLC
Aberdeen, MD 410-272-9999
Harford Systems Inc
Havre De Grace, MD 800-638-7620
Harvey W Hottel Inc
Gaithersburg, MD. 301-921-9599
Heatcraft Refrigeration Prods
Stone Mountain, GA. 770-465-5600

Heatcraft Worldwide Refrig
Columbus, GA 800-866-5596
Hoshizaki America Inc
Peachtree City, GA 800-438-6087
Howard-Mccray
Philadelphia, PA 800-344-8222
Howe Corp
Chicago, IL 773-235-0200
Hussmann Corp
Bridgeton, MO 314-291-2000
Hydro-Miser
San Marcos, CA 800-736-5083
IMECO Inc
Polo, IL 815-946-2351
International Cold Storage
Andover, KS 800-835-0001
International Cooling Systems
Richmond Hill, ON. 888-213-5566
Interstate Showcase & Fixture Company
West Orange, NJ 973-483-5555
Jack Langston Manufacturing Company
Dallas, TX. 214-821-9844
Jade Products Co
Brea, CA 800-884-5233
Johnson Refrigerated Truck
Rice Lake, WI 800-922-8360
Jordon Commercial Refrigerator
Philadelphia, PA 800-523-0171
KaiRak
Anaheim, CA 714-870-8661
Kason Central
Columbus, OH 614-885-1992
Kason Industries
Newnan, GA 770-254-0553
Kedco Wine Storage Systems
Farmingdale, NY 800-654-9988
KEMCO
Wareham, MA. 800-231-5955
Kold Pack
Jackson, MI 800-824-2661
Kold-Hold
Edgefield, SC 803-637-3166
Kolpak
Parsons, TN. 800-826-7036
Kolpak Walk-ins
Parsons, TN. 800-826-7036
Koolant Koolers
Kalamazoo, MI 800-968-5665
Krewson Enterprises
Cleveland, OH 800-521-2282
Kysor Panel Systems
Fort Worth, TX. 800-633-3426
Kysor/Kalt
Portland, OR 503-235-0776
LA Rosa Refrigeration & Equip
Detroit, MI 800-527-6723
Letrah International Corp
Fort Atkinson, WI. 920-563-6597
Liberty Machine Company
York, PA 800-745-8152
Little Squirt
Toronto, ON 416-665-6605
M&S Manufacturing
Arnold, MO. 636-464-2739
Mannhardt Inc
Sheboygan Falls, WI. 800-423-2327
Manufacturing Warehouse
Miami, FL 305-635-8886
Marc Refrigeration Mfg Inc
Miami, FL. 305-691-0500
Marquis Products
Concord, ON. 800-268-1282
Martin Cab Div
Cleveland, OH 216-377-8200
Martin/Baron
Irwindale, CA 626-960-5153
Master-Bilt
New Albany, MS. 800-647-1284
McCormack Manufacturing Company
Lake Oswego, OR. 800-395-1593
MCM Fixture Co
Hazel Park, MI 248-547-9280
Migali Industries
Camden, NJ. 800-852-5292
MMR Technologies
Mountain View, CA 855-962-9620
Mollenberg-Betz Inc
Buffalo, NY. 716-614-7473
Mycom Group
Richmond, BC 604-270-1544
National Drying Machry Co Inc
Philadelphia, PA 215-464-6070

Niagara Blower Company
Buffalo, NY 800-426-5169
Nor-Lake
Hudson, WI 715-386-2323
Noren Products Inc
Menlo Park, CA 866-936-6736
Northfield Freezing Systems
Northfield, MN 800-426-1283
Northland Corp
Greenville, MI 800-223-3900
Odenberg Engineering
West Sacramento, CA 800-688-8396
Omnitemp Refrigeration
Downey, CA 800-423-9660
Pacific Refrigerator Company
San Bernardino, CA 909-381-5669
Paragon Electric Company
Two Rivers, WI 920-793-1161
Parkland
Houston, TX 713-926-5055
Peerless of America
Lincolnshire, IL 847-634-7500
Penn Refrigeration Service Corporation
Wilkes Barre, PA 800-233-8354
Perley-Halladay Assoc
West Chester, PA 800-248-5800
Perlick Corp
Milwaukee, WI 800-558-5592
Pioneer Manufacturing Co Inc
Cleveland, OH 800-877-1500
Pittsburgh Corning Corp
Pittsburgh, PA 724-327-6100
PMI Food Equipment Group
Troy, OH 937-332-3000
Polar King Transportation
Fort Wayne, IN 888-541-8330
Praxair Inc
Danbury, CT 800-772-9247
Precision
Miami, FL 800-762-7565
Premium Air Systems Inc
Troy, MI 877-430-0333
Presence From Innovation LLC
St Louis, MO. 314-423-9777
Pro-Flo Products
Cedar Grove, NJ 800-325-1057
Process Engineering & Fabrication
Afton, VA 800-852-7975
R T C
Rolling Meadows, IL 847-640-2400
Randall Manufacturing Inc
Elmhurst, IL 800-323-7424
Randell Manufacturing   Unified Brands
Weidman, MI 888-994-7636
Ransco Industries
Ventura, CA 805-487-7777
Refrigerated Design Tech
Waxahachie, TX 800-736-9518
Refrigerated Warehousing
Jasper, GA 800-873-2008
Refrigeration Engineering
Grand Rapids, MI 800-968-3227
Refrigeration Research
Brighton, MI 810-227-1151
Reliable Food Service Equipment
Concord, ON. 416-738-6840
Ron Vallort & Associates
Oak Brook, IL 630-734-3821
Rubbermaid
High Point, NC 888-895-2110
Sandvik Process Systems
Sweden, NJ 973-790-1600
Schmidt Progressive
Lebanon, OH. 800-272-3706
Scroll Compressors LLC
Sidney, OH 937-498-3011
Seattle Refrigeration & Manufacturing
Seattle, WA 800-228-8881
Seidman Brothers
Chelsea, MA 800-437-7770
Semco Manufacturing Company
Pharr, TX. 956-787-4203
Servco Equipment Co
St Louis, MO. 314-781-3189
Silver King Refrigeration Inc
Minneapolis, MN 800-328-3329
South Shore Controls Inc
Perry, OH 440-259-2500
SP Industries Inc
Warminster, PA 800-523-2327
Spartan Showcase
Union, MO 800-325-0775

Spinco Metal Products Inc
Newark, NY 315-331-6285
Standard Refrigeration Co
Wood Dale, IL. 708-345-5400
Starlite Food Service Equipment
Detroit, MI 888-521-6603
Summit Commercial
Bronx, NY. 800-932-4267
Superflex Limited
Brooklyn, NY 800-394-3665
Supreme Corporation
Goshen, IN 800-642-4889
Sure Kol Refrigerator
Brooklyn, NY 718-625-0601
Tecumseh Products Co.
Ann Arbor, MI 734-585-9500
Tetra Pak
Vernon Hills, IL 847-955-6000
Therm L Tec Building Systems
Basehor, KS 913-728-2662
Thermo King Corp
Bloomington, MN. 888-887-2202
Thermo-KOOL/Mid-South Ind Inc
Laurel, MS 601-649-4600
Toromont Process Systems
North Salt Lake, UT 801-292-1747
Tranter INC
Wichita Falls, TX 940-723-7125
Traulsen & Co
Fort Worth, TX 800-825-8220
Trimen Foodservice Equipment
North York, ON. 877-437-1422
True Food Service Equipment, Inc.
O Fallon, MO 800-325-6152
US Cooler Company
Quincy, IL 800-521-2665
USECO
Murfreesboro, TN. 615-893-4820
Utility Refrigerator Company
Los Angeles, CA. 800-884-5233
Victory Refrigeration
Cherry Hill, NJ 856-428-4200
Vilter Manufacturing Corporation
Cudahy, WI 414-744-0111
VT Kidron
Washington, NC 800-763-0700
WA Brown & Son
Salisbury, NC 704-636-5131
Welbilt Inc.
New Port Richey, FL. 877-375-9300
West Star Industries
Stockton, CA 800-326-2288
Wilevco Inc
Billerica, MA 978-667-0400
Williams Refrigeration
Hillsdale, NJ 800-445-9979
Wine Chillers of California
Santa Ana, CA 800-331-4274
Wine Well Chiller Co
Milford, CT. 203-878-2465
Wittemann Company
Palm Coast, FL 386-445-4200
York Refrigeration Marine US
Norman, OK 877-874-7378

Refrigerating Units

Truck, Trailer & Refrigerator Car

Advance Distribution Svc
Louisville, KY 502-449-1720
American Food Equipment
Miami, FL 305-377-8991
Carrier Corp
Farmington, CT. 800-227-7437
Collins Manufacturing Company Ltd
Langley, BC 800-663-6761
Dole Refrigerating Co
Lewisburg, TN 800-251-8990
Hackney Brothers
Washington, NC 800-763-0700
Johnson Refrigerated Truck
Rice Lake, WI 800-922-8360
Kold-Hold
Edgefield, SC 803-637-3166
Martin Cab Div
Cleveland, OH 216-377-8200
National FABCO Manufacturing
St Louis, MO. 314-842-4571
New Centennial
Columbus, GA 800-241-7541

Portable Cold Storage
Edison, NJ 800-535-2445
Supreme Corporation
Goshen, IN 800-642-4889
Thermo King Corp
Bloomington, MN. 888-887-2202
VT Kidron
Washington, NC 800-763-0700

Refrigerators

Adamatic
Auburn, WA 800-578-2547
Advance Energy Technologies
Halfmoon, NY 800-724-0198
Arctic Air
Eden Prairie, MN 800-853-3508
Arctic Industries
Medley, FL 800-325-0123
Attias Oven Corp
Brooklyn, NY 800-928-8427
Bally Refrigerated Boxes Inc
Morehead City, NC. 800-242-2559
Bar Equipment Corporation of America
Downey, CA 888-870-2322
Bar-Maid Corp
Garfield, NJ 800-227-6243
Benko Products
Sheffield Vlg, OH 440-934-2180
C.M. Lingle Company
Henderson, TX 800-256-6963
Carts Food Equipment
Brooklyn, NY 718-788-5540
Caselites
Hialeah, FL 305-819-7766
Chrysler & Koppin Co
Detroit, MI 800-441-0038
Cloudy & Britton
Mountlake Ter, WA. 425-775-7424
Coldstream Products Corporation
Crossfield, AB 888-946-4097
Continental Refrigerator
Bensalem, PA 800-523-7138
Craig Manufacturing
Irvington, NJ 800-631-7936
Custom Diamond International
Laval, QC 800-363-5926
Delfield Co
Mt Pleasant, MI. 800-733-8821
Duke Manufacturing Co
St Louis, MO. 800-735-3853
Elliott-Williams Company
Indianapolis, IN 800-428-9303
Empire Bakery Equipment
Hicksville, NY 800-878-4070
EPCO
Murfreesboro, TN. 800-251-3398
Erickson Industries
River Falls, WI 800-729-9941
Eskay Metal Fabricating
Buffalo, NY. 800-836-8015
Everidge
Plymouth, MN. 888-227-1629
Felix Storch Inc
Bronx, NY. 800-932-4267
Fogel Jordon Commercial Refrigeration Company
Philadelphia, PA 800-523-0171
Follett Corp
Easton, PA 800-523-9361
Foster Refrigerator Corporation
Kinderhook, NY 888-828-3311
Gates Manufacturing Company
Saint Louis, MO 800-237-9226
Gem Refrigerator Company
Philadelphia, PA 215-426-8700
HABCO Beverage Systems
Toronto, ON 800-448-0244
Helmer
Noblesville, IN 317-773-9082
Hoshizaki America Inc
Peachtree City, GA 800-438-6087
Howard-Mccray
Philadelphia, PA 800-344-8222
Hussmann Corp
Bridgeton, MO 314-291-2000
International Cold Storage
Andover, KS 800-835-0001
Jack Langston Manufacturing Company
Dallas, TX. 214-821-9844
Jade Products Co
Brea, CA 800-884-5233

Jordon Commercial Refrigerator
Philadelphia, PA 800-523-0171
Kolpak Walk-ins
Parsons, TN. 800-826-7036
Lockwood Manufacturing
Livonia, MI 800-521-0238
Marc Refrigeration Mfg Inc
Miami, FL 305-691-0500
Master-Bilt
New Albany, MS. 800-647-1284
Mayekawa USA, Inc.
Chicago, IL 773-516-5070
MCM Fixture Co
Hazel Park, MI 248-547-9280
National Hotpack
Stone Ridge, NY 800-431-8232
Nor-Lake
Hudson, WI. .715-386-2323
Northland Corp
Greenville, MI. 800-223-3900
Parkland
Houston, TX .713-926-5055
Polar King Transportation
Fort Wayne, IN 888-541-8330
Portable Cold Storage
Edison, NJ. 800-535-2445
QBD Modular Systems
Santa Clara, CA 800-663-3005
Randell Manufacturing   Unified Brands
Weidman, MI .888-994-7636
Ransco Industries
Ventura, CA. .805-487-7777
Seidman Brothers
Chelsea, MA .800-437-7770
Servco Equipment Co
St Louis, MO. 314-781-3189
Silver King Refrigeration Inc
Minneapolis, MN 800-328-3329
Spartan Showcase
Union, MO 800-325-0775
Springer-Penguin
Mount Vernon, NY 800-835-8500
Stafford-Smith Inc
Kalamazoo, MI 800-968-2442
Summit Commercial
Bronx, NY. 800-932-4267
Superior Products Company
Saint Paul, MN 800-328-9800
Sure Kol Refrigerator
Brooklyn, NY .718-625-0601
Tafco Inc
Hyde, PA 800-233-1954
Thermo-KOOL/Mid-South Ind Inc
Laurel, MS 601-649-4600

Toromont Process Systems
North Salt Lake, UT 801-292-1747
Traulsen & Co
Fort Worth, TX 800-825-8220
Triad Scientific
Manasquan, NJ 800-867-6690
Tru Form Plastics
Gardena, CA .800-510-7999
True Food Service Equipment, Inc.
O Fallon, MO 800-325-6152
U-Line Corporation
Milwaukee, WI 800-779-2547
USECO
Murfreesboro, TN 615-893-4820
Utility Refrigerator Company
Los Angeles, CA 800-884-5233
Victory Refrigeration
Cherry Hill, NJ 856-428-4200
Welbilt Inc.
New Port Richey, FL. 877-375-9300
Williams Refrigeration
Hillsdale, NJ .800-445-9979

Grilles

Gea Intec, Llc
Durham, NC .919-433-0131
Liberty Machine Company
York, PA 800-745-8152

Racks

ABI Limited
Concord, ON. 800-297-8666
Caddy Corporation of America
Bridgeport, NJ. 856-467-4222
ColdZone
Anaheim, CA
Dubuque Steel Products Co
Dubuque, IA .563-556-6288
Eagle Wire Works
Cleveland, OH 216-341-8550
Hewitt Manufacturing Co
Waldron, IN. .765-525-9829
Houston Wire Works, Inc.
South Houston, TX 800-468-9477
Kedco Wine Storage Systems
Farmingdale, NY 800-654-9988
Metro Corporation
Wilkes Barre, PA. 800-992-1776
Olson Wire Products Co
Baltimore, MD 410-242-7900
Straits Steel & Wire Co
Ludington, MI. 231-843-3416

Unirak Storage Systems
Taylor, MI 800-348-7225
Universal Coatings
Twinsburg, OH 330-963-6776
Wald Wire & Mfg Co
Oshkosh, WI .800-236-0053

Trays

Kaines West Michigan Co
Ludington, MI. 231-845-1281
Nelipak
Phoenix, AZ .602-269-7648
Olson Wire Products Co
Baltimore, MD 410-242-7900
Spot Wire Works Company
Philadelphia, PA 215-627-6124
World Kitchen
Elmira, NY 800-999-3436

Valves

Refrigeration

C & D Valve Mfg Co
Oklahoma City, OK 800-654-9233
Doering Co
Clear Lake, MN 320-743-2276
EVAPCO Inc
Taneytown, MD 410-876-3782
H A Phillips & Co
Dekalb, IL 630-377-0050
Hansen Technologies Corporation
Bolingbrook, IL 800-426-7368
Parker-Hannifin Corp
Cleveland, OH 800-272-7537
Vilter Manufacturing Corporation
Cudahy, WI 414-744-0111

Vats

Dairy Cooling

Dubuque Steel Products Co
Dubuque, IA .563-556-6288
Falco Technologies
La Prairie, QC 450-444-0566

Vender & Visi-Cooler Installation Systems

Ultra Lift Corp
San Jose, CA .800-346-3057

Safety & Security Equipment & Supplies

Alarm Systems

Acromag Inc.
Wixom, MI 248-624-1541
Alarm Controls Corp
Deer Park, NY 800-645-5538
AMSECO
Carson, CA 800-421-1096
Christy Industries Inc
Brooklyn, NY 800-472-2078
CMT
Hamilton, MA 978-768-2555
Control Products Inc
Chanhassen, MN 800-947-9098
Electro Alarms
Tiffin, OH 800-261-9174
Ellenco
Brentwood, MD 301-927-4370
Faraday
Tecumseh, MI 517-423-2111
Flair Electronics
Pomona, CA 800-532-3492
Gamewell Corporation
Northborough, MA 888-347-3269
George Risk Industries Inc
Kimball, NE 800-445-5218
Globe Fire Sprinkler Corp
Standish, MI 800-248-0278
Gralab Instruments
Centerville, OH 800-876-8353
Harford Systems Inc
Havre De Grace, MD 800-638-7620
Honeywell International
Charlotte, NC 877-841-2840
Iconics Inc
Foxboro, MA 800-946-9679
King Research Laboratory
Maywood, IL 708-344-7877
Krewson Enterprises
Cleveland, OH 800-521-2282
Liquid Scale
New Brighton, MN 888-633-2969
Long Range Systems
Addison, TX 800-577-8101
Napco Security Systems Inc
Amityville, NY 631-842-0253
Optex
Chino, CA 800-966-7839
Permaloc Security Devices
Silver Spring, MD 301-681-6300
Quantis Secure Systems
Hanover, MD 800-325-6124
Raco Mfg & Engineering Co
Emeryville, CA 800-722-6999
Sargent & Greenleaf
Nicholasville, KY 800-826-7652
Security Link
Danville, IL 217-446-4871
Sensidyne
St. Petersburg, FL 800-451-9444
Silent Watchman Security Services LLC
Danbury, CT 800-932-3822
Simplex Time Recorder Company
Santa Ana, CA 800-746-7539
Star Micronics
Edison, NJ 800-782-7636
Sterling Corp
Glendora, CA 800-932-9561
Ultrak
Westminster, CO 303-428-9480
Viking Corp
Hastings, MI 800-968-9501
W L Jenkins Co
Canton, OH 330-477-3407

Containment Systems

Arcoplast Wall & Ceiling Systems
St Peters, MO 888-736-2726
Blome International
O Fallon, MO 636-379-9119
Modutank Inc
Long Island City, NY 800-245-6964

Detectors

Detectamet Inc
Richmond, VA 844-820-7244

Gas Leak

Amerex
Trussville, AL 205-655-3271
American Gas & Chemical Co LTD
Northvale, NJ 800-288-3647
Chlorinators Inc
Stuart, FL 800-327-9761
Control Instruments Corp
Fairfield, NJ 973-575-9114
Gems Sensors & Controls
Plainville, CT 860-747-3000
Q A Supplies LLC
Norfolk, VA. 800-472-7205
Rosemount Analytical Inc
Irvine, CA 800-543-8257
Sensidyne
St. Petersburg, FL 800-451-9444
Teledyne Benthos Inc
North Falmouth, MA 508-563-1000

Metal

Accu-Pak
Akron, OH
Accu-Ray Inspection Services
Elmhurst, IL 800-378-1226
Advanced Detection Systems
Milwaukee, WI 414-672-0553
Andgar Corp
Ferndale, WA 360-366-9900
Berkshire PPM
Litchfield, CT 860-567-3118
Bunting Magnetics Co
Newton, KS. 800-835-2526
Cintex of America
Carol Stream, IL 800-424-6839
Eriez Magnetics
Erie, PA 800-346-4946
Friskem Infinetics
Wilmington, DE 302-658-2471
Geo. Olcott Company
Scottsboro, AL 800-634-2769
Leeman Labs Inc
Hudson, NH 800-634-9942
Lock Inspection Systems
Fitchburg, MA 800-227-5539
Loma International
Carol Stream, IL 800-872-5662
Magnetic Products Inc
Highland, MI. 800-544-5930
Mettler-Toledo Safeline Inc
Lutz, FL. 800-638-8537
Ohio Magnetics Inc
Maple Heights, OH 800-486-6446
TNA Packaging Solutions
Coppell, TX 972-462-6500
Vande Berg SCALES/Vbs Inc
Sioux Center, IA 712-722-1181

Shoplifting

Engineered Security System Inc
Towaco, NJ 800-742-1263
Friskem Infinetics
Wilmington, DE 302-658-2471
King Research Laboratory
Maywood, IL. 708-344-7877
Protex International Corp.
Bohemia, NY 800-835-3580
Se Kure Controls Inc
Franklin Park, IL. 800-250-9260
Silent Watchman Security Services LLC
Danbury, CT 800-932-3822

Detectors & Alarms

Fire, Heat & Smoke

Alarm Controls Corp
Deer Park, NY. 800-645-5538

Amerex
Trussville, AL 205-655-3271
CMT
Hamilton, MA 978-768-2555
Krewson Enterprises
Cleveland, OH 800-521-2282
Migatron Corp
Woodstock, IL 888-644-2876
Napco Security Systems Inc
Amityville, NY 631-842-0253
Protectowire Co Inc
Pembroke, MA 781-924-5384
Silent Watchman Security Services LLC
Danbury, CT 800-932-3822
Simplex Time Recorder Company
Santa Ana, CA 800-746-7539
Sterling Corp
Glendora, CA 800-932-9561

Fire Alarm Systems

Carroll Manufacturing International
Florham Park, NJ 800-444-9696
Charles Gratz Fire Protection
Philadelphia, PA 215-235-5800
Christy Industries Inc
Brooklyn, NY 800-472-2078
Duke Manufacturing Co
St Louis, MO. 800-735-3853
Ellenco
Brentwood, MD 301-927-4370
Faraday
Tecumseh, MI 517-423-2111
Gamewell Corporation
Northborough, MA 888-347-3269
Globe Fire Sprinkler Corp
Standish, MI 800-248-0278
Grinnell Fire ProtectionSystems Company
Sauk Rapids, MN 320-253-8665
Honeywell International
Charlotte, NC 877-841-2840
Monroe Extinguisher Co Inc
Rochester, NY. 585-235-3310
Napco Security Systems Inc
Amityville, NY 631-842-0253
Protectowire Co Inc
Pembroke, MA 781-924-5384
Quantis Secure Systems
Hanover, MD 800-325-6124
Scientific Fire Prevention
Long Island City, NY 718-433-3880
Signal Equipment
Seattle, WA 800-542-0884
Silent Watchman Security Services LLC
Danbury, CT 800-932-3822
Simplex Time Recorder Company
Santa Ana, CA 800-746-7539
Simplex Time Recorder Company
Santa Ana, CA 949-724-5000
Sterling Corp
Glendora, CA 800-932-9561
Tyco Fire Protection Products
Marinette, WI 800-862-6785
Viking Corp
Hastings, MI 800-968-9501
W L Jenkins Co
Canton, OH 330-477-3407

Fire Extinguishers

Amerex
Trussville, AL 205-655-3271
Charles Gratz Fire Protection
Philadelphia, PA 215-235-5800
Greenheck Fan Corp
Schofield, WI 715-359-6171
Grinnell Fire ProtectionSystems Company
Westminster, MA 800-746-7539
Kidde Residential & Commercial
Mebane, NC 919-563-5911
National Foam
Exton, PA 610-363-1400
Pyro-Chem
Marinette, WI 800-526-1079
Scientific Fire Prevention
Long Island City, NY 718-433-3880

Tyco Fire Protection Products
Marinette, WI 800-862-6785
United Fire & Safety Service
Yonkers, NY 914-968-4459

Flashlights

Rechargable

Natale Machine & Tool Co Inc
Carlstadt, NJ 800-883-8382

General

A&B Safe Corporation
Glassboro, NJ 800-253-1267
Accuform Manufacturing, Inc.
Vacaville, CA 800-233-3352
Afassco
Minden, NV 775-783-3555
AIB International
Manhattan, KS 800-633-5137
Alarm Controls Corp
Deer Park, NY 800-645-5538
Alvarado Manufacturing Co Inc
Chino, CA 800-423-4143
Amerex
Trussville, AL 205-655-3271
American Louver Co
Skokie, IL 800-772-0355
American Store Fixtures
Skokie, IL
AMSECO
Carson, CA 800-421-1096
Analogic Corp.
Peabody, MA 978-326-4000
Applied Robotics Inc
Schenectady, NY 800-309-3475
Ashcroft Inc
Stratford, CT 800-328-8258
Atlantic Rubber Products
East Wareham, MA 800-695-0446
Atlas Equipment Company
Kansas City, MO 800-842-9188
Ballymore Company
West Chester, PA 610-696-3250
Banner Engineering Corp
Minneapolis, MN 888-373-6767
Best Value Textiles
North Charleston, SC 800-858-8589
Bmh Equipment Inc
Sacramento, CA 800-350-8828
Boston Retail
Medford, MA 800-225-1633
Bullet Guard Corporation
West Sacramento, CA 800-233-5632
CCP Industries, Inc.
Cleveland, OH 800-321-2840
Cesco Magnetics
Rohnert Park, CA 877-624-8727
Charles Gratz Fire Protection
Philadelphia, PA 215-235-5800
Christy Industries Inc
Brooklyn, NY 800-472-2078
Cintex of America
Carol Stream, IL 800-424-6839
Claude Neon Signs
Baltimore, MD 410-685-7575
Continental Commercial Products
Bridgeton, MO 800-325-1051
Control Instruments Corp
Fairfield, NJ 973-575-9114
Conveyor Components Co
Croswell, MI 800-233-3233
Conveyor Components Co
Croswell, MI 800-552-3337
Corporate Safe Specialists
Posen, IL 800-342-3033
Creative Industries Inc
Indianapolis, IN 800-776-2068
Dalloz Safety
Smithfield, RI 800-977-9177
Detex Corp
New Braunfels, TX 830-629-2900
Diamond Electronics
Lancaster, OH 800-443-6680
Dickey Manufacturing Company
St Charles, IL 630-584-2918
Diversified Lighting Diffusers Inc
Copiague, NY 800-234-5464
Dometic Mini Bar
Elkhart, IN 800-301-8118

Dri Mark Products
Port Washington, NY 800-645-9118
Duke Manufacturing Co
St Louis, MO 800-735-3853
Durable Corp
Norwalk, OH 800-537-1603
Dynamic Storage Systems Inc.
Brooksville, FL 800-974-8211
EJ Brooks Company
Atlanta, GE 800-458-7325
Ellenco
Brentwood, MD 301-927-4370
Elwood Safety Company
Buffalo, NY 866-326-6060
Emedco
Williamsville, NY 877-765-8386
Empire Safe Company
New York, NY 212-226-2255
Engineered Security System Inc
Towaco, NJ 800-742-1263
Etube & Wire
Shrewsbury, PA 800-618-4720
Firematic Sprinkler Devices
Shrewsbury, MA 800-225-7288
Flair Electronics
Pomona, CA 800-532-3492
Flame Gard
Lakewood, NJ 800-526-3694
Folding Guard Co
Chicago, IL 800-622-2214
Friskem Infinetics
Wilmington, DE 302-658-2471
Gamewell Corporation
Northborough, MA 888-347-3269
Gaylord Industries
Tualatin, OR 800-547-9696
George Risk Industries Inc
Kimball, NE 800-445-5218
Gilbert Insect Light Traps
Jonesboro, AR 800-643-0400
Glaro Inc
Hauppauge, NY 631-234-1717
Globe Fire Sprinkler Corp
Standish, MI 800-248-0278
Grecon
Tigard, OR 503-641-7731
Grinnell Fire ProtectionSystems Company
Sauk Rapids, MN 320-253-8665
Grinnell Fire ProtectionSystems Company
Westminster, MA 800-746-7539
Halton Company
Scottsville, KY 800-442-5866
Harford Systems Inc
Havre De Grace, MD 800-638-7620
HD Electric Co
Park City, IL 847-473-4882
Hodge Manufacturing Company
Springfield, MA 800-262-4634
Honeywell International
Charlotte, NC 877-841-2840
Iconics Inc
Foxboro, MA 800-946-9679
Idesco Corp
New York, NY 800-336-1383
Inficon
East Syracuse, NY 315-434-1100
Jesco Industries
Litchfield, MI 800-455-0019
JL Industries Inc
Bloomington, MN 800-554-6077
Kason
Lewis Center, OH 740-549-2100
Kidde Residential & Commercial
Mebane, NC 919-563-5911
King Research Laboratory
Maywood, IL 708-344-7877
Koke Inc
Queensbury, NY 800-535-5303
Krewson Enterprises
Cleveland, OH 800-521-2282
KTG
Cincinnati, OH 888-533-6900
Larco
Brainerd, MN 800-523-6996
Lavi Industries
Valencia, CA 800-624-6225
LDJ Electronics
Troy, MI 248-528-2202
Lima Sheet Metal
Lima, OH 419-229-1161
Linde North America
Murray Hill, NJ 908-464-8100

Lixi, Inc.
Huntley, IL 847-961-6666
Locknetics
Carmel, IN
Lomont IMT
Mt. Pleasant, IA 800-776-0380
Long Range Systems
Addison, TX 800-577-8101
Loyal Manufacturing
Indianapolis, IN 317-359-3185
McGunn Safe Company
Chicago, IL 800-621-2816
Metro Corporation
Wilkes Barre, PA 800-992-1776
Mettler-Toledo Safeline Inc
Lutz, FL 800-638-8537
Micro Affiliates
Fairfax, VA 800-430-1099
Mirror Tech Mfg Co Inc
Yonkers, NY 914-423-1600
Monroe Extinguisher Co Inc
Rochester, NY 585-235-3310
Nalge Process Technologies Group
Rochester, NY 585-586-8800
Napco Security Systems Inc
Amityville, NY 631-842-0253
National Foam
Exton, PA 610-363-1400
National Marker Co Inc
North Smithfield, RI 800-453-2727
National Stock Sign Co
Santa Cruz, CA 800-462-7726
Nelson-Jameson Inc
Marshfield, WI 800-826-8302
New Pig Corp
Tipton, PA 800-468-4647
Newstamp Lighting Factory
North Easton, MA 508-238-7073
Niroflex, USA
Deerfield, IL 847-400-2638
Nrd LLC
Grand Island, NY 800-525-8076
O'Brien Bros Inc
West Springfield, MA 800-343-0949
Omicron Steel Products Company
Jamaica, NY 718-805-3400
Optex
Chino, CA 800-966-7839
Our Name is Mud
New York, NY 877-683-7867
Pak 2000 Inc
Mirror Lake, NH 603-569-3700
Patlite Corp
Torrance, CA 888-214-2580
Penco Products
Skippack, PA 800-562-1000
Permaloc Security Devices
Silver Spring, MD 301-681-6300
Plasticard-Locktech Intl
Asheville, NC 800-752-1017
Pro-Com Security Systems
Lehi, UT 877-776-2669
Protectowire Co Inc
Pembroke, MA 781-924-5384
Protex International Corp.
Bohemia, NY 800-835-3580
QUIKSERV Corp
Houston, TX 800-388-8307
R & D Brass
Wappingers Falls, NY 800-447-6050
Raco Mfg & Engineering Co
Emeryville, CA 800-722-6999
Reidler Decal Corporation
Saint Clair, PA 800-628-7770
Remcon Plastics Inc
Reading, PA 800-360-3636
Rocky Shoes & Boots Inc
Nelsonville, OH 866-442-4908
Roni LLC
Charlotte, NC 866-543-8635
Rosco Inc
Jamaica, NY 800-227-2095
Safety Light Corporation
Bloomsburg, PA 570-784-4344
Sargent & Greenleaf
Nicholasville, KY 800-826-7652
Scientific Fire Prevention
Long Island City, NY 718-433-3880
Se Kure Controls Inc
Franklin Park, IL 800-250-9260
Security Link
Danville, IL 217-446-4871

Sensidyne
St. Petersburg, FL 800-451-9444
Server Products Inc
Richfield, WI 800-558-8722
Seton Indentification Products
Branford, CT 800-571-2596
Shelden, Dickson, & Steven Company
Omaha, NE .402-571-4848
SICK Inc
Bloomington, MN 800-325-7425
Signal Equipment
Seattle, WA .800-542-0884
Silent Watchman Security Services LLC
Danbury, CT 800-932-3822
Simplex Time Recorder Company
Santa Ana, CA 800-746-7539
Simplex Time Recorder Company
Santa Ana, CA 949-724-5000
Sinco
Red Wing, MN 800-243-6753
Sipco Products
Peoria Heights, IL 309-682-5400
Slip Not
Detroit, MI .800-754-7668
Stanley Access Technologies
Farmington, CT 800-722-2377
Star Micronics
Edison, NJ 800-782-7636
Steel King Industries
Stevens Point, WI 800-553-3096
Sterling Corp
Glendora, CA 800-932-9561
Stoffel Seals Corp
Tallapoosa, GA 800-422-8247

Technibilt/Cari-All
Newton, NC .800-233-3972
Tepromark International
Osseo, MN .800-645-2622
Theta Sciences
San Diego, CA 760-745-3311
Tomsed Corporation
Lillington, NC 800-334-5552
Torbeck Industries
Harrison, OH 800-333-0080
Tucker Industries
Colorado Springs, CO 800-786-7287
Tyco Fire Protection Products
Lansdale, PA 800-558-5236
Tyco Fire Protection Products
Marinette, WI 800-862-6785
UAA
Chicago, IL .800-813-1711
Ultrak
Westminster, CO 303-428-9480
United Fire & Safety Service
Yonkers, NY 914-968-4459
Valeo
Elmsford, Ny. 800-634-2704
Vent Master
Mississauga, ON 800-565-2981
Viking Corp
Hastings, MI 800-968-9501
W L Jenkins Co
Canton, OH 330-477-3407
Wearwell/Tennessee Mat Company
Nashville, TN 615-254-8381
Weinbrenner Shoe Co
Merrill, WI .800-826-0002

Wiginton Corp
Sanford, FL .407-585-3200
World Wide Safe Brokers
Woodbury, NJ 800-593-2893
Wylie Systems
Mississauga, ON 800-525-6609
YottaMark
Redwood City, CA 866-768-7878

Ladder Covers

Slip Not
Detroit, MI .800-754-7668

Ladder Rungs

Slip Not
Detroit, MI .800-754-7668

Mats

Electric Alarm

Floor

Larco
Brainerd, MN 800-523-6996

Metal Detectors

Industrial Magnetics
Boyne City, MI 800-662-4638

Sanitation Equipment & Supplies

Ammonia

Bottled for Cleaning

James Austin Co
Mars, PA 724-625-1535
KIK Custom Products
Salem, VA 540-389-5401
Laundry Aids
Carlstadt, NJ 201-933-3500
Patterson Laboratories
Detroit, MI 313-843-4500
Rooto Corp
Howell, MI 517-546-8330

Bleaches

Bio Pac Inc
Incline Village, NV 800-225-2855
Blue Cross Laboratories
Santa Clarita, CA
Country Save Products Corp
Arlington, WA 360-435-9868
Delta Chemical Corporation
Baltimore, MD 800-282-5322
Diamond Chemical Co Inc
East Rutherford, NJ 800-654-7627
Dover Chemical Corp
Dover, OH 800-321-8805
Hilex Company
Eagan, MN 651-454-1160
Hydrite Chemical Co
Brookfield, WI 262-792-1450
James Austin Co
Mars, PA 724-625-1535
KIK Custom Products
Salem, VA 540-389-5401
Kuehne Chemical
Kearny, NJ 973-589-0700
Patterson Laboratories
Detroit, MI 313-843-4500
Rooto Corp
Howell, MI 517-546-8330
Venturetech Corporation
Knoxville, TN 800-826-4095

Borax

Ceramic Color & Chemical Mfg
New Brighton, PA 724-846-4000

Brooms

Abco Products
Miami, FL 888-694-2226
Amarillo Mop & Broom Company
Amarillo, TX 800-955-8596
American Broom Co
Mattoon, IL 217-235-1992
American Brush Company
Portland, OR 800-826-8492
American Water Broom
Doraville, GA 800-241-6565
Anderson Products
Cresco, PA 800-729-4694
Birmingham Mop Manufacturing Company
Birmingham, AL 205-942-6101
Bouras Mop Manufacturing Company
Saint Louis, MO 800-634-9153
Bruske Products
Tinley Park, IL 708-532-3800
Carlisle Food Svc Products Inc
Oklahoma City, OK 800-654-8210
Carolina Mop
Anderson, SC 800-845-9725
Chickasaw Broom Mfg Co Inc
Little Rock, AR 501-562-0311
Cleveland Mop Manufacturing Company
Cleveland, OH 800-767-9934
Cornelia Broom Company
Cornelia, GA 800-228-2551
Cosgrove Enterprises Inc
Miami Lakes, FL 800-888-3396
Costa Broom Works
Tampa, FL 813-385-1722

Crystal Lake Mfg Inc
Autaugaville, AL 800-633-8720
Culicover & Shapiro
Bay Shore, NY 631-918-4560
Detroit Quality Brush Mfg Co
Livonia, MI 800-722-3037
Fuller Industries LLC
Great Bend, KS 800-522-0499
Furgale Industries Ltd.
Winnipeg, NB 800-665-0506
Greenwood Mop & Broom Inc
Greenwood, SC 800-635-6849
H. Arnold Wood Turning
Tarrytown, NY 888-314-0088
Harper Brush Works Inc
Fairfield, IA 800-223-7894
Hoge Brush Company
New Knoxville, OH 800-494-4643
Howard Overman & Sons
Baltimore, MD 410-276-8445
Hub City Brush Co
Petal, MS 800-278-7452
Imperial Broom Company
Richmond, VA 888-353-7840
Industries For the Blind
Milwaukee, WI 800-642-8778
Industries of the Blind
Greensboro, NC 336-274-1591
J.I. Holcomb Manufacturing
Independence, OH 800-458-3222
John L. Denning & Company
Wichita, KS 316-264-2357
Labpride Chemicals
Bronx, NY 800-467-1255
Libman Co
Arcola, IL 877-818-3380
Lighthouse for the Blindin New Orleans
New Orleans, LA 504-899-4501
Little Rock Broom Works
Little Rock, AR 501-562-0311
LMCO
Rosenberg, TX 281-342-8888
Luco Mop Co
St Louis, MO. 800-522-5826
Messina Brothers Manufacturing Company
Brooklyn, NY 800-924-6454
Michigan Brush Mfg Co
Detroit, MI 800-642-7874
Milwaukee Dustless Brush Co
Delavan, WI 323-724-7777
Minuteman Power Boss
Aberdeen, NC 800-323-9420
Nationwide Wire & Brush Manufacturing
Lodi, CA 209-334-9660
Newton Broom Co
Newton, IL 618-783-4424
O'Dell Corp
Ware Shoals, SC 800-342-2843
O-Cedar
Aurora, IL 800-543-8105
Perfex Corporation
Poland, NY 800-848-8483
Quality Mop & Brush Manufacturers
Needham, MA 617-884-2999
Quickie Manufacturing Corp
Cinnaminson, NJ 856-829-7900
Reit-Price ManufacturingCompany
Union City, IN. 800-521-5343
RidgeView Products LLC
La Crosse, WI 888-782-1221
Royal Broom & Mop Factory Inc
New Orleans, LA 800-537-6925
S&M Manufacturing Company
Cisco, TX 800-772-8532
Tucel Industries, Inc.
Forestdale, VT 800-558-8235
Waco Broom & Mop Factory
Waco, TX 800-548-7716
Warren E. Conley Corporation
Carmel, IN. 800-367-7875
Whitley Manufacturing Company
Midland, NC 704-888-2625
Young & Swartz Inc
Buffalo, NY 800-466-7682

Brushes

Bottle

Braun Brush Co
Albertson, NY 800-645-4111
Carlisle Food Svc Products Inc
Oklahoma City, OK 800-654-8210
Justman Brush Co
Omaha, NE 800-800-6940
Volckening Inc
Brooklyn, NY 800-221-0276

Floor, Sweeping, Polishing & Waxing

Abco Products
Miami, FL 888-694-2226
Anderson Products
Cresco, PA 800-729-4694
Braun Brush Co
Albertson, NY 800-645-4111
Bruske Products
Tinley Park, IL 708-532-3800
Carlisle Food Svc Products Inc
Oklahoma City, OK 800-654-8210
Carlisle Sanitary Mntnc Prods
Oklahoma City, OK 800-654-8210
Cornelia Broom Company
Cornelia, GA 800-228-2551
Costa Broom Works
Tampa, FL 813-385-1722
Culicover & Shapiro
Bay Shore, NY 631-918-4560
Detroit Quality Brush Mfg Co
Livonia, MI 800-722-3037
Fox Brush Company
Oxford, ME 207-539-2208
Fuller Industries LLC
Great Bend, KS 800-522-0499
Harper Brush Works Inc
Fairfield, IA 800-223-7894
Hoge Brush Company
New Knoxville, OH 800-494-4643
Kiefer Brushes, Inc
Franklin, NJ 800-526-2905
Labpride Chemicals
Bronx, NY 800-467-1255
Lighthouse for the Blindin New Orleans
New Orleans, LA 504-899-4501
Michigan Brush Mfg Co
Detroit, MI 800-642-7874
Microtron Abrasives
Pineville, NC 800-476-7237
Milwaukee Dustless Brush Co
Delavan, WI 323-724-7777
O'Dell Corp
Ware Shoals, SC 800-342-2843
O-Cedar
Aurora, IL 800-543-8105
Perfex Corporation
Poland, NY 800-848-8483
Reit-Price ManufacturingCompany
Union City, IN. 800-521-5343
Superior Brush Company
Cleveland, OH 216-941-6987
Tucel Industries, Inc.
Forestdale, VT 800-558-8235
Walker Brush Inc
Webster, NY 585-545-4748
Wilen Professional Cleaning Products
Atlanta, GA. 800-241-7371
Young & Swartz Inc
Buffalo, NY 800-466-7682
Zephyr Manufacturing Co
Sedalia, MO 660-827-0352

Carts

Housekeeping

Amco Metals Indl
City of Industry, CA 626-855-2550
Bmh Equipment Inc
Sacramento, CA 800-350-8828
Geerpres Inc
Muskegon, MI. 231-773-3211

James Varley & Sons
Saint Louis, MO 800-325-8891
Lakeside Manufacturing Inc
Milwaukee, WI 888-558-8565
Princeton Shelving
Cedar Rapids, IA. 319-369-0355

Caustic Soda

ATOFINA Chemicals
Philadelphia, PA 800-225-7788

Chlorine

Liquid

ATOFINA Chemicals
Philadelphia, PA 800-225-7788
Delta Chemical Corporation
Baltimore, MD 800-282-5322
Selig Chemical Industries
Atlanta, GA 404-876-5511

Cleaners

Bottle (Compounds)

American Formula
Atlanta, GA. 800-282-1215
American Municipal Chemical
Milwaukee, WI 800-598-3106
APR Associates Inc
Memphis, TN 800-238-5150
Champion Chemical Co
Whittier, CA 800-621-7868
Church & Dwight Co., Inc.
Ewing, NJ 800-833-9532
Diamond Chemical Co Inc
East Rutherford, NJ 800-654-7627
ELF Machinery
La Porte, IN. 800-328-0466
Essential Industries Inc
Merton, WI 800-551-9679
Hy-Trous/Flash Sales
Woburn, MA. 781-933-5772
James Varley & Sons
Saint Louis, MO 800-325-8891
Lubar Chemical
Kansas City, MO. 816-471-2560
Magnuson Products
Clifton, NJ 973-472-9292
Mertz L. Carlton Company
Bedford Park, IL 708-594-1050
National Interchem Corporation
Blue Island, IL 800-638-6688
Oakite Products
New Providence, NJ 800-526-4473
Occidental Chemical Corporation
Houston, TX 713-215-7000
Pneumatic Scale Angelus
Cuyahoga Falls, OH 330-923-0491
Seatex Ltd
Rosenberg, TX 800-829-3020
Shepard Brothers Co
La Habra, CA 800-645-3594
Warren E. Conley Corporation
Carmel, IN. 800-367-7875
Warsaw Chemical Co Inc
Warsaw, IN 800-548-3396

Coffee Pot

Urnex Brands Inc
Elmsford, NY 800-222-2826

Dairy

GEA North America
Naperville, IL 630-369-8100
Hoge Brush Company
New Knoxville, OH 800-494-4643
Hy-Ko Enviro-MaintenanceProducts
Salt Lake City, UT 801-973-6099
Lechler Inc
St Charles, IL 800-777-2926
Magnuson Products
Clifton, NJ. 973-472-9292
Winn-Sol Products
Oshkosh, WI. 920-231-2031

Grain & Seed

A C Horn & Co Sheet Metal
Dallas, TX. 800-657-6155
A T Ferrell Co Inc
Bluffton, IN. 800-248-8318
A.K. Robins
Baltimore, MD 800-486-9656
Carter-Day International Inc
Minneapolis, MN 763-571-1000
Cleland Manufacturing Company
Columbia Heights, MN. 763-571-4606
Crippen Manufacturing Co
St Louis, MI 800-872-2474
DMC-David Manufacturing Company
Mason City, IA 641-424-7010
En-Hanced Products Inc
Westerville, OH. 800-783-7400
Forster & Son
Ada, OK 580-332-6021
Grain Machinery Mfg Corp
Miami, FL 305-620-2525
Lewis M Carter Mfg Co Inc
Donalsonville, GA 800-332-8232
NECO/Nebraska Engineering
Omaha, NE 800-367-6208

Hand

Afassco
Minden, NV 775-783-3555
Amodex Products
Bridgeport, CT 877-866-1255
Athea Laboratories
Milwaukee, WI. 800-743-6417
Buckeye International
Maryland Heights, MO. 314-291-1900
CCP Industries, Inc.
Cleveland, OH 800-321-2840
Chef Revival
North Charleston, SC 800-248-9826
Coleman Manufacturing Co Inc
Everett, MA. 617-389-0380
Concord Chemical Co Inc
Camden, NJ. 800-282-2436
Crc Industries Inc
Warminster, PA 800-556-5074
Cresset Chemical Company
Weston, OH. 800-367-2020
Critzas Industries Inc
St Louis, MO. 800-537-1418
Crown Chemical Products
Mississauga, ON 905-564-0904
DCL Solutions LLC
Philadelphia, PA 800-426-1127
Deb Canada
Waterford, ON. 888-332-7627
Development Workshop Inc
Idaho Falls, ID 800-657-5597
Diamond Wipes Intl Inc
Chino, CA 800-454-1077
Dober Chemical Corporation
Midlothian, IL. 800-323-4983
Dreumex USA
York, PA 800-233-9382
Du-Good Chemical Laboratory & Manufacturing
Company
Saint Louis, MO 314-773-5007
Emulso
Tonawanda, NY 716-854-2889
Essential Industries Inc
Merton, WI 800-551-9679
Fishers Investment
Cincinnati, OH 800-833-5916
Galaxy Chemical Corp
Sarasota, FL 941-755-8545
GOJO Industries Inc
Akron, OH. 800-321-9647
Hallberg Manufacturing Corporation
Tampa, FL. 800-633-7627
Hewitt Soap Company
Dayton, OH. 800-543-2245
Hill Manufacturing Co Inc
Atlanta, GA. 404-522-8364
Hy-Ko Enviro-MaintenanceProducts
Salt Lake City, UT 801-973-6099
Hy-Trous/Flash Sales
Woburn, MA. 781-933-5772
Industrial EnvironmentalPollution Control
Bronx, NY. 718-585-2410
Inksolv 30, LLC.
Emerson, NE 515-537-5344

ITW Dymon
Olathe, KS. 800-443-9536
J C Whitlam Mfg Co
Wadsworth, OH. 800-321-8358
J.I. Holcomb Manufacturing
Independence, OH 800-458-3222
James Austin Co
Mars, PA 724-625-1535
James Varley & Sons
Saint Louis, MO 800-325-8891
Kildon Manufacturing
Ingersoll, ON 800-485-4930
Kleen Products Inc
Oklahoma City, OK 800-392-1792
L&M Chemicals
Tampa, FL. 800-362-3331
Lee Products Co
Minneapolis, MN 952-300-2908
Man-O Products
Cincinnati, OH 888-210-6266
Martin Laboratories
Owensboro, KY 800-345-9352
Micro-Brush Pro Soap
Rockwall, TX 800-776-7627
Milburn Company
Detroit, MI 313-259-3410
Mione Manufacturing Company
Mickleton, NJ 800-257-0497
Mission Laboratories
Los Angeles, CA 888-201-8866
Nice-Pak Products Inc
Orangeburg, NY 800-444-6725
Nosaj Disposables
Paterson, NJ 800-631-3809
Nuance Solutions Inc
Chicago, IL 800-621-8553
R&C Pro Brands
Wayne, NJ 973-633-7374
Rochester Midland Corp
Rochester, NY 800-535-5053
Rochester Midland Corp
Rochester, NY 800-836-1627
S & S Soap Co
Bronx, NY 718-585-2900
Sanitek Products Inc
Los Angeles, CA 818-242-1071
Savogran Co
Norwood, MA. 800-225-9872
SCA Hygiene Paper
San Ramon, CA 800-992-8675
Simoniz USA Inc
Bolton, CT 800-227-5536
Starkey Chemical Process Company
La Grange, IL 800-323-3040
Steiner Company
Holland, IL 800-222-4638
Steiner Industries Inc
Chicago, IL 800-621-4515
Stone Soap Co Inc
Sylvan Lake, MI 800-952-7627
Sunbeam Products Co LLC
Toledo, OH 419-691-1551
Telechem Corp
Atlanta, GA. 800-637-0495
Tropical Soap Company
Carrollton, TX. 800-527-2368
Verax Chemical Co
Snohomish, WA 800-637-7771
W.M. Barr & Co Inc.
Memphis, TN 901-775-0100
Whisk Products Inc
Wentzville, MO. 800-204-7627

Silver

Burnishine Products
Gurnee, IL. 800-818-8275
Casabar
Morristown, NJ 877-745-8700
Copper Clad
Reading, PA 610-375-4596
Dynynstyl
Delray Beach, FL 800-774-7895
George Basch Company
Freeport, NY 516-378-8100
Swisher Hygiene
Charlotte, NC 800-444-4138

Cleaning Equipment & Supplies

9-12 Corporation
Caguas, PR 787-747-0405

A J Funk & Co
Elgin, IL 877-225-3865
A&L Laboratories
Minneapolis, MN 800-225-3832
A.K. Robins
Baltimore, MD. 800-486-9656
Abco Products
Miami, FL 888-694-2226
Abicor Binzel
Frederick, MD. 800-542-4867
Absorbco
Walterboro, SC 888-335-6439
Ace-Tex Enterprises
Detroit, MI 800-444-3800
Acme Sponge & Chamois Co Inc
Tarpon Springs, FL. 727-937-3222
Acro Dishwashing Svc Co
Kansas City, KS 913-342-4282
ACS Industries, Inc.
Lincoln, RI 866-783-4838
Activon Products
Beaver Dam, WI. 800-841-0410
Adamation
Commerce, CA 800-383-8800
ADCO
Albany, GA 800-821-7556
Advance Cleaning Products
Milwaukee, WI 800-925-5326
Air-Scent International
Pittsburgh, PA. 800-247-0770
Airosol Co Inc
Neodesha, KS 800-633-9576
Akron Cotton Products
Akron, OH. 800-899-7173
Alconox Inc
White Plains, NY 914-437-7585
Alex E Fergusson Co Inc
Chambersburg, PA 800-345-1329
Alkota Cleaning Systems Inc
Alcester, SD 800-255-6823
All American Container
Miami, FL 305-887-0797
Alumin-Nu Corporation
Lyndhurst, OH 800-899-7097
Amarillo Mop & Broom Company
Amarillo, TX 800-955-8596
Amco Metals Indl
City of Industry, CA 626-855-2550
Ameri-Khem
Port Orange, FL 800-224-9950
American Broom Co
Mattoon, IL 217-235-1992
American Brush Company
Portland, OR. 800-826-8492
American Formula
Atlanta, GA 800-282-1215
American Municipal Chemical
Milwaukee, WI. 800-598-3106
American Textile Mills Inc
Kansas City, MO 816-842-2909
American Water Broom
Doraville, GA 800-241-6565
American Wax Co Inc
Long Island City, NY 718-361-4820
Ametek Technical & Industrial Products
Kent, OH. 215-256-6601
Amodex Products
Bridgeport, CT 877-866-1255
Andersen 2000
Peachtree City, GA 800-241-5424
Anderson Products
Cresco, PA. 800-729-4694
APR Associates Inc
Memphis, TN 800-238-5150
Aquafine Corp
Valencia, CA 800-423-3015
Aquionics Inc
Erlanger, KY 800-925-0440
ARC Specialties
Valencia, CA 661-775-8500
Arden Companies
Southfield, MI. 248-415-8500
Argo & Company
Spartanburg, SC 864-583-9766
Armaly Brands
Commerce Twp, MI 800-772-1222
Armstrong Hot Water
Three Rivers, MI. 269-279-3602
Armstrong Manufacturing
Mississauga, ON 866-627-6588
Arrow-Magnolia Intl Inc
Dallas, TX. 800-527-2101

Assembled Products Corp
Rogers, AR 800-548-3373
Associated Products Inc
Glenshaw, PA 800-243-5689
Athea Laboratories
Milwaukee, WI 800-743-6417
Atlantic Mills
Lakewood, NJ 800-242-7374
ATOFINA Chemicals
Philadelphia, PA 800-225-7788
Auto Chlor Systems
Memphis, TN 800-477-3693
Banner Chemical Co
Orange, NJ 973-676-0105
Bar Keepers Friend Cleanser
Indianapolis, IN 800-433-5818
Bar Maid Corp
Pompano Beach, FL 954-960-1468
Beam Industries
Webster City, IA 800-369-2326
Beaumont Products
Kennesaw, GA 800-451-7096
Bel-Art Products
Wayne, NJ 800-423-5278
Bete Fog Nozzle Inc
Greenfield, MA 800-235-0049
Bethel Engineering & Equipment Inc
New Hampshire, OH. 800-889-6129
BEX Inc
Ann Arbor, MI 734-464-8282
Bi-O-Kleen Industries
Portland, OR 503-224-6246
Bio Cide Intl Inc
Norman, OK 800-323-1398
Bio Industries
Luxemburg, WI. 920-845-2355
Bio Pac Inc
Incline Village, NV 800-225-2855
Bio Zapp Laboratories
Sarasota, FL 941-922-9199
Birko Corporation
Olathe, KS 800-444-8360
Birmingham Mop Manufacturing Company
Birmingham, AL. 205-942-6101
Black Bear Corp
Roanoke, VA. 800-223-1284
Black's Products of HighPoint
High Point, NC 336-886-5011
Blue Cross Laboratories
Santa Clarita, CA
Blue Feather Products Inc
Ashland, OR 800-472-2487
Blue Ridge Converting
Asheville, NC 800-438-3893
Bouras Mop Manufacturing Company
Saint Louis, MO 800-634-9153
Boyer Corporation
La Grange, IL 800-323-3040
Bradford Soap Works Inc
West Warwick, RI 401-821-2141
Branson Ultrasonics Corp
Danbury, CT 203-796-0400
Braun Brush Co
Albertson, NY 800-645-4111
Bro-Tex Inc
St Paul, MN. 800-328-2282
Brulin & Company
Indianapolis, IN 800-776-7149
Bruske Products
Tinley Park, IL 708-532-3800
Buckeye International
Maryland Heights, MO. 314-291-1900
Bunzl Distribution USA
St. Louis, MO 888-997-5959
Burnishine Products
Gurnee, IL 800-818-8275
Butterworth Inc
Houston, TX 281-821-7300
C P Industries
Salt Lake City, UT 800-453-4931
C&H Chemical
St Paul, MN. 651-227-4343
C&R Refrigation Inc,
Center, TX. 800-438-6182
Cadie Products Corp
Paterson, NJ 973-278-8300
Cal Ben Soap Co
Oakland, CA 800-340-7091
Cam Spray
Iowa Falls, IA 800-648-5011
Candy & Company/Peck's Products Company
Chicago, IL 800-837-9189

Cantol
Markham, ON. 800-387-9773
Canton Sterilized Wiping Cloth
Canton, OH 330-455-8157
Carbon Clean Industries Inc
Kingston, PA 570-288-1155
Carhoff Company
Cleveland, OH 216-541-4835
Carlisle Food Svc Products Inc
Oklahoma City, OK 800-654-8210
Carlisle Sanitary Mntnc Prods
Oklahoma City, OK 800-654-8210
Carnegie Textile Co
Cleveland, OH 800-633-4136
Carolina Mop
Anderson, SC 800-845-9725
Carroll Co
Garland, TX 800-527-5722
Casabar
Morristown, NJ. 877-745-8700
CC Custom Technology Corporation
Cleveland, OH 216-662-5500
CCP Industries, Inc.
Cleveland, OH 800-321-2840
Central Solutions Inc
Kansas City, KS 800-255-0262
Century Chemical Corp
Elkhart, IN. 800-348-3505
Ceramic Color & Chemical Mfg
New Brighton, PA. 724-846-4000
Chad Co Inc
Olathe, KS. 800-444-8360
Champion Chemical Co
Whittier, CA 800-621-7868
Champion Industries Inc
Winston Salem, NC. 800-532-8591
Chef Revival
North Charleston, SC 800-248-9826
Chemclean Corp
Jamaica, NY 800-538-2436
Chemdet Inc
Sebastian, FL 800-645-1510
Chemifax
Santa Fe Springs, CA 800-527-5722
Chickasaw Broom Mfg Co Inc
Little Rock, AR. 501-562-0311
Cincinnati Industrial Machry
Mason, OH 800-677-0076
Claire Manufacturing Company
Addison, IL 800-252-4731
Clarke American Sanders
Minneapolis, MN 800-253-0367
Clarkson Supply
Williamsport, PA. 800-326-9457
Clayton L. Hagy & Son
Philadelphia, PA 215-844-6470
Clean-All Pool Svc
Syracuse, NY 315-472-7665
Cleanfreak
Appleton, WI 888-722-5508
Cleveland Mop Manufacturing Company
Cleveland, OH 800-767-9934
Clorox Company
Oakland, CA. 800-227-1860
Cloud Inc
San Luis Obispo, CA 800-234-5650
Clyde Bergemann Eec
Halethorpe, MD 410-712-4280
Cma Dishmachines
Garden Grove, CA 800-854-6417
Coast Scientific
Rancho Santa Fe, CA 800-445-1544
Cobitco Inc
Denver, CO 303-296-8575
Coburn Company
Whitewater, WI. 800-776-7042
Coleman Manufacturing Co Inc
Everett, MA. 617-389-0380
Colgate-Palmolive Professional Products Group
North York, ON. 800-468-6502
Colonial Paper Company
Silver Springs, FL. 352-622-4171
Command Belt Cleaning Systems
Hammond, IN 800-433-7627
Common Sense Natural Soap & Bodycare Products
Rutland, VT 802-773-0582
Compliance Control Inc
Hyattsville, MD 800-810-4000
Composition Materials Co Inc
Milford, CT. 800-262-7763
Concord Chemical Co Inc
Camden, NJ. 800-282-2436

Continental Commercial Products
Bridgeton, MO 800-325-1051
Continental Equipment Corporation
Milwaukee, WI 414-463-0500
Continental Girbau Inc
Oshkosh, WI 800-256-1073
Conveyor Components Co
Croswell, MI 800-233-3233
Copper Brite
Santa Barbara, CA 805-565-1566
Copper Clad
Reading, PA 610-375-4596
Core Products Co
Canton, TX 800-825-2673
Cornelia Broom Company
Cornelia, GA 800-228-2551
Cosgrove Enterprises Inc
Miami Lakes, FL 800-888-3396
Costa Broom Works
Tampa, FL 813-385-1722
Cougar Packaging Concepts, Inc.
St. Charles, IL 630-689-4050
Country Save Products Corp
Arlington, WA 360-435-9868
Crc Industries Inc
Warminster, PA 800-556-5074
Cresset Chemical Company
Weston, OH 800-367-2020
Critzas Industries Inc
St Louis, MO 800-537-1418
Crown Chemical Products
Mississauga, ON 905-564-0904
Crystal Lake Mfg Inc
Autaugaville, AL 800-633-8720
Culicover & Shapiro
Bay Shore, NY 631-918-4560
D R Technology Inc
Freehold, NJ 732-780-4664
D W Davies & Co
Racine, WI 800-888-6133
D&M Products
Santa Monica, CA 800-245-0485
Damas Corporation
Trenton, NJ 609-695-9121
Damon Industries
Alliance, OH 800-362-9850
Damp Rid
Memphis, TN 888-326-7743
DCL Solutions LLC
Philadelphia, PA 800-426-1127
De Laval
Kansas City, MO 816-891-7700
De Royal Textiles
Camden, SC 800-845-1062
Deb Canada
Waterford, ON 888-332-7627
Delta Carbona
Fairfield, NJ 888-746-5599
Delta Chemical Corporation
Baltimore, MD 800-282-5322
Dema Engineering Co
St Louis, MO 800-325-3362
Detroit Quality Brush Mfg Co
Livonia, MI 800-722-3037
Development Workshop Inc
Idaho Falls, ID 800-657-5597
Diablo Chemical
Kingston, PA 800-548-1384
Dial Corporation
Scottsdale, AZ 480-754-3425
Diamond Chemical Co Inc
East Rutherford, NJ 800-654-7627
Diamond Wipes Intl Inc
Chino, CA 800-454-1077
Dirt Killer Pressure Washer
Gwynn Oak, MD 800-544-1188
Distribution Results
Akron, OH 800-737-9671
DL Enterprises
Etters, PA 717-938-1292
Dober Chemical Corporation
Midlothian, IL 800-323-4983
Donaldson Co Inc
Bloomington, MN 952-887-3131
Dorden & Co
Detroit, MI 313-834-7910
Douglas Machines Corp.
Clearwater, FL 800-331-6870
Dover Chemical Corp
Dover, OH 800-321-8805
Dover Parkersburg
Follansbee, WV

Downeast Chemical
Westbrook, ME 800-287-2225
DPC
Norristown, PA 800-220-9473
Drackett Professional
Cincinnati, OH 513-583-3900
Dreumex USA
York, PA 800-233-9382
Du-Good Chemical Laboratory & Manufacturing
Company
Saint Louis, MO 314-773-5007
Dynablast Manufacturing
Mississauga, ON 888-242-8597
Dynynstyl
Delray Beach, FL 800-774-7895
Eagle Home Products
Huntington, NY 631-673-3500
Ecolo Odor Control Systems Worldwide
North York, ON 800-667-6355
Economy Paper & Restaurant Co
Clifton, NJ 973-279-5500
Ecover
Los Angeles, CA 323-720-5730
Electro-Steam Generator Corp
Rancocas, NJ 866-617-0764
ELF Machinery
La Porte, IN 800-328-0466
Elgene
Hamden, CT 800-922-4623
Emulso
Tonawanda, NY 716-854-2889
Erie Cotton Products
Erie, PA 800-289-4737
Essential Industries Inc
Merton, WI 800-551-9679
Ettore
Alameda, CA 510-748-4130
Eureka Company
Bloomington, IL 800-282-2886
Ex-Cell KAISER LLC
Franklin Park, IL 847-451-0451
Excel Chemical Company
Jacksonville, FL 904-356-0446
Faciltec Corporation
Elgin, IL 800-284-8273
Falls Chemical Products
Oconto Falls, WI 920-846-3561
Fast Industries
Fort Lauderdale, FL 800-775-5345
Feather Duster Corporation
Amsterdam, NY 800-967-8659
Fiebing Co
Milwaukee, WI 800-558-1033
Fishers Investment
Cincinnati, OH 800-833-5916
Fitzpatrick Brothers
Pleasant Prairie, WI 800-233-8064
FleetwoodGoldcoWyard
Romeoville, IL 630-759-6800
Flo-Matic Corporation
Belvidere, IL 800-959-1179
Floor Master Inc
Chattanooga, TN 423-867-4525
Flow International Corp.
Kent, WA 800-446-3569
Fuller Industries LLC
Great Bend, KS 800-522-0499
Furgale Industries Ltd.
Winnipeg, NB 800-665-0506
FX-Lab Company
Union, NJ 908-810-1212
Galaxy Chemical Corp
Sarasota, FL 941-755-8545
Gamajet Cleaning Systems
Exton, PA 800-289-5387
Gamecock Chemical Co Inc
Sumter, SC 803-773-7391
Gardner Denver Inc.
Milwaukee, WI
Garman Co Inc
Valley Park, MO 800-466-5150
Geerpres Inc
Muskegon, MI 231-773-3211
Gemtek Products LLC
Phoenix, AZ 800-331-7022
General Floor Craft
Little Silver, NJ 973-742-7400
General Steel Fabricators
Joplin, MO 800-820-8644
General, Inc
Weston, FL 954-202-7419

Geo. Olcott Company
Scottsboro, AL 800-634-2769
George Basch Company
Freeport, NY 516-378-8100
Georgia Pacific
Green Bay, WI 920-435-8821
Ghibli North American
Wilmington, DE 302-654-5908
Girton Manufacturing Co
Millville, PA 570-458-5521
Glass Pro
Addison, IL 888-641-8919
Glastender
Saginaw, MI 800-748-0423
Glit Microtron
Bridgetown, MO 800-325-1051
Glover Latex
Anaheim, CA 800-243-5110
GOJO Industries Inc
Akron, OH 800-321-9647
Golden Star
N Kansas City, MO 800-821-2792
Goodman Wiper & Paper Co
Auburn, ME 207-784-5779
Goodway Technologies Corp
Stamford, CT 800-333-7467
Goodwin Co
Garden Grove, CA 714-894-0531
Grace-Lee Products
Minneapolis, MN 612-379-2711
Graco Inc
Minneapolis, MN 877-844-7226
Great Western Chemical Company
Portland, OR 800-547-1400
Greenwood Mop & Broom Inc
Greenwood, SC 800-635-6849
Griffin Bros Inc
Salem, OR 800-456-4743
Guardsman
Grand Rapids, MI 616-940-2900
Guest Supply
Monmouth Jct, NJ 800-448-3787
H F Staples & Co Inc
Merrimack, NH 800-682-0034
H. Arnold Wood Turning
Tarrytown, NY 888-314-0088
H.L. Diehl Company
South Windham, CT 860-423-7741
Hallberg Manufacturing Corporation
Tampa, FL 800-633-7627
Hamilton Soap & Oil Products
Paterson, NJ 973-225-1031
Hanco Manufacturing Company
Memphis, TN 800-530-7364
Hardt Equipment Manufacturing
Lachine, QC 888-848-4408
Hardwood Products Co LP
Guilford, ME 800-289-3340
Harper Brush Works Inc
Fairfield, IA 800-223-7894
Haviland Enterprises Inc
Grand Rapids, MI 800-456-1134
Hedgetree Chemical Manufacturing
Savannah, GA 912-691-0408
Hewitt Soap Company
Dayton, OH 800-543-2245
Hibrett Puratex
Pennsauken, NJ 800-260-5124
Hilex Company
Eagan, MN 651-454-1160
Hill Manufacturing Co Inc
Atlanta, GA 404-522-8364
Hillyard Inc
St Joseph, MO 800-365-1555
Hodges
Vienna, IL 800-444-0011
Hoge Brush Company
New Knoxville, OH 800-494-4643
Hohn Manufacturing Company
Fenton, MO 800-878-1440
Holland Applied Technologies
Burr Ridge, IL 630-325-5130
Holland Chemicals Company
Windsor, ON 519-948-4373
Hollowell Products Corporation
Wyandotte, MI 734-282-8200
Hoover Company
Glenwillow, OH 330-499-9499
Hope Chemical Corporation
Pawtucket, RI 401-724-8000
Hosch Properties
Oakdale, PA 800-695-3310

Howard Overman & Sons
Baltimore, MD .410-276-8445
Howell Brothers Chemical Laboratories
Philadelphia, PA 215-477-0260
Hub City Brush Co
Petal, MS 800-278-7452
Hy-Ko Enviro-MaintenanceProducts
Salt Lake City, UT 801-973-6099
Hy-Trous/Flash Sales
Woburn, MA .781-933-5772
Hydrite Chemical Co
Brookfield, WI 262-792-1450
Idexx Laboratories Inc
Westbrook, ME 800-548-6733
IFC Disposables Inc
Brownsville, TN 800-432-9473
Imperial Broom Company
Richmond, VA 888-353-7840
Indian Valley Industries
Johnson City, NY 800-659-5111
Indiana Wiping Cloth
Mishawaka, IN 800-446-9645
Industries For the Blind
Milwaukee, WI 800-642-8778
Industries of the Blind
Greensboro, NC 336-274-1591
Insect-O-Cutor Inc
Stone Mountain, GA 800-966-8480
Interlab
The Woodlands, TX 888-876-2844
International Environmental Solutions
South Pasadena, FL 800-972-8348
Iron Out
Fort Wayne, IN 888-476-6688
ITW Dymon
Olathe, KS 800-443-9536
J C Whitlam Mfg Co
Wadsworth, OH 800-321-8358
J.I. Holcomb Manufacturing
Independence, OH 800-458-3222
J.V. Reed & Company
Louisville, KY 877-258-7333
Jacks Manufacturing Company
Mendota, MN 800-821-2089
James Austin Co
Mars, PA 724-625-1535
James Varley & Sons
Saint Louis, MO 800-325-8891
JAS Manufacturing Company
Carrollton, TX 972-380-1150
John L. Denning & Company
Wichita, KS .316-264-2357
Johnson International Materials
Brownsville, TX 956-541-6364
Justman Brush Co
Omaha, NE 800-800-6940
Kafko International LTD
Skokie, IL 800-528-0334
Kent Co
North Miami, FL 800-521-4886
Kiefer Brushes, Inc
Franklin, NJ .800-526-2905
KIK Custom Products
Salem, VA 540-389-5401
Kilgore Chemical Corporation
Layton, UT 801-546-9909
Kimberly-Clark Corporation
Irving, TX 972-281-1200
King of All Manufacturing
Clio, MI 810-564-0139
Kleen Products Inc
Oklahoma City, OK 800-392-1792
KMT Aqua-Dyne Inc
Baxter Springs, KS 800-826-9274
Knapp Manufacturing
Fresno, CA 559-251-8254
Knight Equipment International
Lake Forest, CA 800-854-3764
Kuehne Chemical
Kearny, NJ 973-589-0700
L&M Chemicals
Tampa, FL 800-362-3331
Labpride Chemicals
Bronx, NY 800-467-1255
Labtech Industries
Detroit, MI 800-525-8667
Lake Process Systems Inc
Lake Barrington, IL 800-331-9260
Lakeside Manufacturing Inc
Milwaukee, WI 888-558-8565
Lamco Chemical Co Inc
Chelsea, MA .617-884-8470

Larose & Fils Lte
Laval, QC 877-382-7001
Laundry Aids
Carlstadt, NJ .201-933-3500
Laundrylux
Inwood, NY .800-645-2205
Lavo Company
Milwaukee, WI 414-353-2140
Layflat Products
Shreveport, LA 800-551-8515
Lechler Inc
St Charles, IL 800-777-2926
Lee Products Co
Minneapolis, MN 952-300-2908
Lee Soap Company
Commerce City, CO 800-888-1896
Leedal Inc
Northbrook, IL 847-498-0111
Leggett & Platt Storage
Vernon Hills, IL 847-816-6246
Letraw Manufacturing Company
Rockford, IL .815-987-9670
Lexidyne of Pennsylvania
Pittsburgh, PA 800-543-2233
Libman Co
Arcola, IL 877-818-3380
Lighthouse for the Blindin New Orleans
New Orleans, LA 504-899-4501
Lite-Weight Tool & Mfg Co
Sun Valley, CA 800-859-3529
Little Rock Broom Works
Little Rock, AR 501-562-0311
LMCO
Rosenberg, TX 281-342-8888
LPI Imports
Chicago, IL 877-389-6563
Lubar Chemical
Kansas City, MO 816-471-2560
Luco Mop Co
St Louis, MO 800-522-5826
Luseaux Labs Inc
Gardena, CA .800-266-1555
M D Stetson Co
Randolph, MA 800-255-8651
Machem Industries
Delta, BC 604-526-5655
Magic American Corporation
Cleveland, OH 800-321-6330
Magnuson Products
Clifton, NJ 973-472-9292
Mahoney Environmental
Joliet, IL 800-892-9392
Mainline Industries Inc
Springfield, MA 800-527-7917
Majestic Industries Inc
Macomb, IL .586-786-9100
Manhattan Truck Lines
Paterson, NJ .800-370-7627
Mar-Len Supply Inc
Hayward, CA 510-782-3555
Marcal Paper Mills
Elmwood Park, NJ 800-631-8451
Marko Inc
Spartanburg, SC 866-466-2726
Martin Laboratories
Owensboro, KY 800-345-9352
Mastercraft Industries Inc
Newburgh, NY 800-835-7812
Maxi-Vac Inc.
Dundee, IL 855-629-4538
Mba Suppliers Inc.
Bellevue, NE 800-467-1201
Mcbrady Engineering Co
Rockdale, IL .815-744-8900
Mednik Wiping Materials Co
St Louis, MO 800-325-7193
Meguiar's Inc
Irvine, CA 949-752-8000
Mercury Floor Machines Inc
Englewood, NJ 888-568-4606
Meritech
Golden, CO .800-932-7707
Mertz L. Carlton Company
Bedford Park, IL 708-594-1050
Messina Brothers Manufacturing Company
Brooklyn, NY 800-924-6454
Metalloid Corp
Huntington, IN 800-686-3201
Metcraft
Grandview, MO 800-444-9624
MGF.com
Atlanta, GA .770-444-9686

Mia Rose Products
Newport Beach, CA 800-615-2767
Michigan Brush Mfg Co
Detroit, MI 800-642-7874
Micro-Brush Pro Soap
Rockwall, TX 800-776-7627
Microbest Inc
Waterbury, CT 800-426-4246
Microtron Abrasives
Pineville, NC 800-476-7237
MIFAB Inc
Chicago, IL 800-465-2736
Mil-Du-Gas Company/Star Brite
Fort Lauderdale, FL 800-327-8583
Mill Wiping Rags Inc
Bronx, NY 718-994-7100
Milsek Furniture Polish Inc.
North Lima, OH 330-542-2700
Milwaukee Dustless Brush Co
Delavan, WI .323-724-7777
Minuteman Power Boss
Aberdeen, NC 800-323-9420
Mione Manufacturing Company
Mickleton, NJ 800-257-0497
Mission Laboratories
Los Angeles, CA 888-201-8866
Moly-XL Company
Westville, NJ 856-848-2880
Momar
Atlanta, GA .800-556-3967
Motom Corporation
Bensenville, IL 630-787-1995
Moyer Diebel
Winston Salem, NC 336-661-1992
Murk Brush Company
New Britain, CT 860-249-2550
Murnell Wax Company
Springfield, MA 781-395-1323
N & A Mfg
Mallard, IA 712-425-3512
Nation/Ruskin
Montgomeryville, PA 800-523-2489
National Conveyor Corp
Commerce, CA 323-725-0355
National Interchem Corporation
Blue Island, IL 800-638-6688
National Purity LLC
Brooklyn Center, MN 612-672-0022
National Scoop & Equipment Company
Spring House, PA 215-646-2040
National Towelette
Bensalem, PA 215-245-7300
Nationwide Wire & Brush Manufacturing
Lodi, CA 209-334-9660
Navy Brand
St Louis, MO 800-325-3312
New Klix Corporation
South San Francisco, CA 800-522-5544
New Pig Corp
Tipton, PA 800-468-4647
Newell Brands
Atlanta, GA
Newton Broom Co
Newton, IL 618-783-4424
Newton OA & Son Co
Bridgeville, DE 800-726-5745
Nice-Pak Products Inc
Orangeburg, NY 800-444-6725
Northwind Inc
Alpena, AR 877-937-2585
Nosaj Disposables
Paterson, NJ .800-631-3809
Nova Hand Dryers
Herndon, VA .703-615-3636
Novus
St. Paul, MN .800-328-1117
Nu-Tex Styles, Inc.
Somerset, NJ .732-485-5456
Nu-Towel Co
Kansas City, MO 800-800-7247
Nuance Solutions Inc
Chicago, IL 800-621-8553
NuTone
Cincinnati, OH 888-336-3948
Nyco Products Co
Countryside, IL 800-752-4754
O'Dell Corp
Ware Shoals, SC 800-342-2843
O-Cedar
Aurora, IL 800-543-8105
Occidental Chemical Corporation
Houston, TX .713-215-7000

Oerlikon Balzers Coating USA
Elgin, IL 847-695-5200
Ohio Soap Products Company
Wickliffe, OH 440-585-1100
Omni Lift Inc
Salt Lake City, UT 801-486-3776
Opie Brush Company
Independence, MO 800-877-6743
Oreck Manufacturing Co
Cookeville, TN 800-989-3535
Ostrem Chemical Co. Ltd
Edmonton, AB 780-440-1911
Pacific Oasis Enterprise Inc
Santa Fe Springs, CA 800-424-1475
Packaging & Processing Equipment
Ayr, ON 519-622-6666
Packaging Distribution Svc
Des Moines, IA 515-243-3156
Pagoda Industries Inc
Reading, PA 610-678-8096
Paley-Lloyd-Donohue
Elizabeth, NJ 908-352-5835
Panasonic Commercial Food Service
Newark, NJ
Paper Pak Industries
La Verne, CA 909-392-1750
Parachem Corporation
Des Moines, IA 515-280-9445
Paragon Group USA
St Petersburg, FL 800-835-6962
Patterson Laboratories
Detroit, MI 313-843-4500
Paxton Products Inc
Blue Ash, OH 800-441-7475
PCI Inc
St Louis, MO. 800-752-7657
Pepper Mill
Mobile, AL 800-669-5175
Perfex Corporation
Poland, NY 800-848-8483
Pioneer Chemical Co
Gardena, CA 310-366-7393
Pioneer Manufacturing Co Inc
Cleveland, OH 800-877-1500
PM Chemical Company
San Diego, CA 619-296-0191
Portion-Pac Chemical Corp.
Chicago, IL 312-226-0400
Potlatch Corp
Spokane, WA. 509-835-1500
Pretty Products
Wauconda, IL 800-726-4849
Pro-Tex-All Co
Evansville, IN 800-755-5458
Productos Familia
Santurce, PR 787-268-5929
Proffitt Manufacturing Company
Dalton, GA 800-241-4682
ProRestore Products
Pittsburgh, PA 800-332-6037
ProTeam
Boise, ID 800-541-1456
Puritan/Churchill Chemical Company
Marietta, GA. 800-275-8914
Purity Products
Plainview, NY 800-256-6102
Quaker Chemical Company
Columbia, SC 800-849-9520
Quality Mop & Brush Manufacturers
Needham, MA 617-884-2999
Quickie Manufacturing Corp
Cinnaminson, NJ. 856-829-7900
R R Street & Co
Naperville, IL 630-416-4244
R&C Pro Brands
Wayne, NJ 973-633-7374
Ready White
Holyoke, MA 413-534-4864
Rebel Green
Mequon, WI 262-240-9992
Reeno Detergent & Soap Company
Saint Louis, MO. 314-429-6078
Reit-Price ManufacturingCompany
Union City, IN. 800-521-5343
REM Ohio Inc
Cincinnati, OH 513-381-3700
Remco Products Corp
Zionsville, IN 800-585-8619
Rex Chemical Corporation
Miami, FL 877-634-5539
RHG Products Company
Castle Rock, CO 800-553-8131

Rjs Carter Co Inc
New Brighton, MN 651-636-8818
Robby Vapor Systems
Sunrise, FL 800-888-8711
Rochester Midland Corp
Rochester, NY. 800-535-5053
Rochester Midland Corp
Rochester, NY. 800-836-1627
Rockford Chemical Co
Belvidere, IL 815-544-3476
Rockline Industries
Sheboygan, WI 800-558-7790
Ronell Industries
Roselle, NJ 908-245-5255
Rooto Corp
Howell, MI 517-546-8330
Roxide International
Larchmont, NY 800-431-5500
Royal Broom & Mop Factory Inc
New Orleans, LA 800-537-6925
Royal Chemical Co Inc
Albemarle, NC 800-650-6346
Royal Paper Products
Coatesville, PA 800-666-6655
Royal Welding & Fabricating
Fullerton, CA 714-680-6669
Royce Rolls Ringer Co
Grand Rapids, MI 800-253-9638
Rubbermaid Commercial Products
Cleveland, TN 423-476-4544
S & S Soap Co
Bronx, NY. 718-585-2900
S&M Manufacturing Company
Cisco, TX 800-772-8532
San Aire Industries
Fort Worth, TX 800-757-1912
San Joaquin Pool Svc & Supply
Stockton, CA. 209-952-0680
Sangamon Mills
Cohoes, NY 518-237-5321
Sani-Matic
Madison, WI 800-356-3300
Sanitech Inc
Lorton, VA 800-486-4321
Sanitek Products Inc
Los Angeles, CA. 818-242-1071
Sasib Beverage & Food North America
Plano, TX 800-558-3814
Saunders Manufacturing Co.
N Kansas City, MO. 800-821-2792
Savogran Co
Norwood, MA. 800-225-9872
SCA Hygiene Paper
San Ramon, CA 800-992-8675
SCA Tissue
Philadelphia, PA 866-722-8675
SCA Tissue North America
S Glens Falls, NY 518-743-0240
Schlueter Company
Janesville, WI 800-359-1700
Scot Young Research LTD
St Joseph, MO. 816-233-4898
Scott's Liquid Gold-Inc
Denver, CO 800-447-1919
Seatex Ltd
Rosenberg, TX 800-829-3020
Sedalia Janitorial & Paper Supplies
Sedalia, MO 660-826-9899
Selig Chemical Industries
Atlanta, GA 404-876-5511
Seneca Environmental Products
Tiffin, OH 419-447-1282
Shen Manufacturing Co Inc
Conshohocken, PA 610-825-2790
Shepard Brothers Co
La Habra, CA 800-645-3594
Sierra Dawn Products
Santa Rosa, CA 707-535-0172
Sioux Corp
Beresford, SD 888-763-8833
Snee Chemical Co
New Orleans, LA 800-489-7633
Solvit
Monona, WI 888-314-1072
Solvox Manufacturing Company
Milwaukee, WI. 414-774-5664
Sonicor
West Babylon, NY 800-864-5022
Southend Janitorial Supply
Los Angeles, CA. 323-754-2842
Spartan Tool LLC
Mendota, IL 800-435-3866

Specialty Equipment Company
Mendota Heights, MN 651-452-7909
Spencer Turbine Co
Windsor, CT 800-232-4321
Spontex
Columbia, TN 800-251-4222
Sprayway Inc
Addison, IL 800-332-9000
Spurrier Chemical Companies
Atlanta, GA 800-795-9222
SQP
Schenectady, NY 800-724-1129
Squar-Buff
Oakland, CA 800-525-6955
ST Restaurant Supplies
Delta, BC. 888-448-4244
Stampendous
Anaheim, CA 800-869-0474
Stanford Chemicals
Dallas, TX 972-682-5600
Star Pacific Inc
Union City, CA 800-227-0760
Starkey Chemical Process Company
La Grange, IL 800-323-3040
State Industrial Products Corp
Mayfield Heights, OH 877-747-6986
Stearns Packaging Corp
Madison, WI 608-246-5150
Stearns Technical Textiles Company
Cincinnati, OH 800-543-7173
Steiner Company
Holland, IL 800-222-4638
Steiner Industries Inc
Chicago, IL 800-621-4515
Sterling Novelty Products
Northbrook, IL 847-291-0070
Stero Co
Petaluma, CA 800-762-7600
Stewart Laboratories
Strattanville, PA 800-640-7869
Stone Soap Co Inc
Sylvan Lake, MI 800-952-7627
Stoner
Quarryville, PA 800-227-5538
Strahman Valves Inc
Bethlehem, PA 877-787-2462
Sun Paints & Coatings
Tampa, FL 800-247-9691
Sunbeam Products Co LLC
Toledo, OH 419-691-1551
Sunpoint Products
Lawrence, MA 978-794-3100
Superior Brush Company
Cleveland, OH 216-941-6987
Superior Distributing Co
Louisville, KY 800-365-6661
Superior Linen & Work Wear
Kansas City, MO. 800-798-7987
Surco Products
Pittsburgh, PA 800-556-0111
Sure Clean Corporation
Two Rivers, WI. 920-793-3838
Surtec Inc
Tracy, CA 800-877-6330
Swisher Hygiene
Charlotte, NC 800-444-4138
Swissh Commercial Equipment
Montreal, QC 888-794-7749
Synthron Inc.
Morganton, NC 828-437-8611
T & S Brass & Bronze Work
Travelers Rest, SC 800-476-4103
Tate Western
Goleta, CA 800-903-0200
Techni-Chem
Boise, ID 800-635-8930
Telechem Corp
Atlanta, GA 800-637-0495
Tennant Co.
Minneapolis, MN 800-553-8033
Texas Refinery Corp
Fort Worth, TX 817-332-1161
Textile Buff & Wheel
Charlestown, MA 617-241-8100
Textile Products Company
Anaheim, CA 714-761-0401
Thamesville Metal Products Ltd
Thamesville, ON. 519-692-3963
The Procter & Gamble Company
Cincinnati, OH 800-692-0132
Theochem Laboratories Inc
Tampa, FL 800-237-2591

Therma Kleen
Plainfield, IL.............800-999-3120
Thermaco Inc
Asheboro, NC.............800-633-4204
Time Products
Atlanta, GA.............800-241-6681
Tolco Corp
Toledo, OH.............800-537-4786
Trap-Zap Environmental
Wyckoff, NJ.............800-282-8727
TRC
Middlefield, OH.............440-834-0078
TRITEN Corporation
Houston, TX.............832-214-5000
Tropical Soap Company
Carrollton, TX.............800-527-2368
Tucel Industries, Inc.
Forestdale, VT.............800-558-8235
Tuchenhagen
Columbia, MD.............410-910-6000
Turtle Wax
Westmont, IL.............905-470-6665
Tuway American Group
Rockford, OH.............800-537-3750
Twi Laq
Bronx, NY.............800-950-7627
U B KLEM Furniture Co Inc
St Anthony, IN.............800-264-1995
Ulmer Pharmacal
Park Rapids, MN.............800-848-5637
United Floor Machine Co
Chicago, IL.............800-288-0848
United Textile Distribution
Garner, NC.............800-262-7624
Universal Stainless
Aurora, CO.............800-223-8332
Universal Stainless & Alloy
Titusville, PA.............800-295-1909
Upright
St Louis, MO.............800-248-7007
Urnex Brands Inc
Elmsford, NY.............800-222-2826
US Chemical
Watertown, WI.............800-558-9566
US Industrial Lubricants
Cincinnati, OH.............800-562-5454
Valspar Paint
Cleveland, OH.............877-825-7727
Vector Technologies
Milwaukee, WI.............800-832-4010
Venturetech Corporation
Knoxville, TN.............800-826-4095
Verax Chemical Co
Snohomish, WA.............800-637-7771
Vulcan Materials Co
Vestavia, AL.............205-298-3000
W.M. Barr & Co Inc.
Memphis, TN.............901-775-0100
Waco Broom & Mop Factory
Waco, TX.............800-548-7716
Wal-Vac
Wyoming, MI.............616-241-6717
Warren E. Conley Corporation
Carmel, IN.............800-367-7875
Warsaw Chemical Co Inc
Warsaw, IN.............800-548-3396
Waste Minimization/Containment
Cleveland, OH.............216-696-8797
Wave Chemical Company
New York, NY.............973-243-5852
Waxine
Bow, NH.............603-228-8241
WCS Corp
Hayward, CA.............510-782-8727
West Agro
Kansas City, MO.............816-891-7700
Whisk Products Inc
Wentzville, MO.............800-204-7627
White Mop Wringer Company
Tampa, FL.............800-237-7582
Whitley Manufacturing Company
Midland, NC.............704-888-2625
Wilen Professional Cleaning Products
Atlanta, GA.............800-241-7371
Wilson AL Chemical Co
Kearny, NJ.............800-526-1188
Windsor Wax Co Inc
Charlestown, RI.............800-243-8929
Winn-Sol Products
Oshkosh, WI.............920-231-2031
Wipe-Tex International Corp
Bronx, NY.............800-643-9607

Wipeco Inc
Hillside, IL.............708-544-7247
World Dryer Corp
Berkeley, IL.............800-323-0701
Y-Pers Inc
Philadelphia, PA.............800-421-0242
Young & Swartz Inc
Buffalo, NY.............800-466-7682
Zealco Industries
Calvert City, KY.............800-759-5531
Zephyr Manufacturing Co
Sedalia, MO.............660-827-0352
Zipskin
Dexter, MI.............734-426-5559

Cloths

Chamois

Acme Sponge & Chamois Co Inc
Tarpon Springs, FL.............727-937-3222
Blue Feather Products Inc
Ashland, OR.............800-472-2487
Clayton L. Hagy & Son
Philadelphia, PA.............215-844-6470

Dish

Arden Companies
Southfield, MI.............248-415-8500
Bro-Tex Inc
St Paul, MN.............800-328-2282
Charles Craft Inc
Laurinburg, NC.............910-844-3521
Letraw Manufacturing Company
Rockford, IL.............815-987-9670
Mednik Wiping Materials Co
St Louis, MO.............800-325-7193
Nu-Tex Styles, Inc.
Somerset, NJ.............732-485-5456
Sangamon Mills
Cohoes, NY.............518-237-5321
Shen Manufacturing Co Inc
Conshohocken, PA.............610-825-2790
Standard Terry Mills
Souderton, PA.............215-723-8121
Wipe-Tex International Corp
Bronx, NY.............800-643-9607

Dusting

Cadie Products Corp
Paterson, NJ.............973-278-8300
CCP Industries, Inc.
Cleveland, OH.............800-321-2840
Clayton L. Hagy & Son
Philadelphia, PA.............215-844-6470
Lexidyne of Pennsylvania
Pittsburgh, PA.............800-543-2233
Majestic Industries Inc
Macomb, MI.............586-786-9100
Mednik Wiping Materials Co
St Louis, MO.............800-325-7193
Mill Wiping Rags Inc
Bronx, NY.............718-994-7100
Nu-Tex Styles, Inc.
Somerset, NJ.............732-485-5456
Ready White
Holyoke, MA.............413-534-4864
Shen Manufacturing Co Inc
Conshohocken, PA.............610-825-2790
Superior Distributing Co
Louisville, KY.............800-365-6661
Tuway American Group
Rockford, OH.............800-537-3750
Wipe-Tex International Corp
Bronx, NY.............800-643-9607

Wire

Cleveland Wire Cloth & Mfg Co
Cleveland, OH.............800-321-3234
F.P. Smith Wire Cloth Company
Northlake, IL.............800-323-6842
Newark Wire Cloth Co
Clifton, NJ.............800-221-0392

Compounds

Dishwashing

American Municipal Chemical
Milwaukee, WI.............800-598-3106
Cal Ben Soap Co
Oakland, CA.............800-340-7091
Clarkson Supply
Williamsport, PA.............800-326-9457
D W Davies & Co
Racine, WI.............800-888-6133
Emulso
Tonawanda, NY.............716-854-2889
Essential Industries Inc
Merton, WI.............800-551-9679
Falls Chemical Products
Oconto Falls, WI.............920-846-3561
Fishers Investment
Cincinnati, OH.............800-833-5916
J.I. Holcomb Manufacturing
Independence, OH.............800-458-3222
Labpride Chemicals
Bronx, NY.............800-467-1255
Magnuson Products
Clifton, NJ.............973-472-9292
Rochester Midland Corp
Rochester, NY.............800-535-5053
Simoniz USA Inc
Bolton, CT.............800-227-5536
Swisher Hygiene
Charlotte, NC.............800-444-4138
Texas Refinery Corp
Fort Worth, TX.............817-332-1161

Sweeping

American Municipal Chemical
Milwaukee, WI.............800-598-3106
APR Associates Inc
Memphis, TN.............800-238-5150
Floor Master Inc
Chattanooga, TN.............423-867-4525
Gamecock Chemical Co Inc
Sumter, SC.............803-773-7391
Grayling Industries
Alpharetta, GA.............800-635-1551
Mission Laboratories
Los Angeles, CA.............888-201-8866
Waxine
Bow, NH.............603-228-8241
Windsor Wax Co Inc
Charlestown, RI.............800-243-8929

Washing

American Municipal Chemical
Milwaukee, WI.............800-598-3106
C&H Chemical
St Paul, MN.............651-227-4343
Candy & Company/Peck's Products Company
Chicago, IL.............800-837-9189
Elgene
Hamden, CT.............800-922-4623
Essential Industries Inc
Merton, WI.............800-551-9679
Fishers Investment
Cincinnati, OH.............800-833-5916
Garman Co Inc
Valley Park, MO.............800-466-5150
Hibrett Puratex
Pennsauken, NJ.............800-260-5124
Hill Manufacturing Co Inc
Atlanta, GA.............404-522-8364
Hohn Manufacturing Company
Fenton, MO.............800-878-1440
Hy-Ko Enviro-MaintenanceProducts
Salt Lake City, UT.............801-973-6099
J.I. Holcomb Manufacturing
Independence, OH.............800-458-3222
KIK Custom Products
Salem, VA.............540-389-5401
Labpride Chemicals
Bronx, NY.............800-467-1255
Magnuson Products
Clifton, NJ.............973-472-9292
Manhattan Truck Lines
Paterson, NJ.............800-370-7627
Ostrem Chemical Co. Ltd
Edmonton, AB.............780-440-1911
R&C Pro Brands
Wayne, NJ.............973-633-7374

Solvit
Monona, WI 888-314-1072
Stanford Chemicals
Dallas, TX 972-682-5600
Swisher Hygiene
Charlotte, NC 800-444-4138
Techni-Chem
Boise, ID 800-635-8930
Windsor Wax Co Inc
Charlestown, RI 800-243-8929

Detergents

Household, Consumer

9-12 Corporation
Caguas, PR 787-747-0405
A&L Laboratories
Minneapolis, MN 800-225-3832
Abicor Binzel
Frederick, MD. 800-542-4867
American Wax Co Inc
Long Island City, NY 718-361-4820
APR Associates Inc
Memphis, TN 800-238-5150
Auto Chlor Systems
Memphis, TN 800-477-3693
Bar Maid Corp
Pompano Beach, FL 954-960-1468
Bio Industries
Luxemburg, WI. 920-845-2355
C P Industries
Salt Lake City, UT 800-453-4931
Cal Ben Soap Co
Oakland, CA 800-340-7091
Cantol
Markham, ON 800-387-9773
Chef Revival
North Charleston, SC 800-248-9826
Chemifax
Santa Fe Springs, CA 800-527-5722
Clarkson Supply
Williamsport, PA 800-326-9457
Clorox Company
Oakland, CA 800-227-1860
Cobitco Inc
Denver, CO 303-296-8575
Concord Chemical Co Inc
Camden, NJ. 800-282-2436
Country Save Products Corp
Arlington, WA. 360-435-9868
DCL Solutions LLC
Philadelphia, PA 800-426-1127
De Vere Co Inc
Janesville, WI 800-833-8373
Diablo Chemical
Kingston, PA 800-548-1384
Diamond Chemical Co Inc
East Rutherford, NJ 800-654-7627
Downeast Chemical
Westbrook, ME 800-287-2225
Du-Good Chemical Laboratory & Manufacturing
Company
Saint Louis, MO 314-773-5007
Essential Industries Inc
Merton, WI 800-551-9679
Falls Chemical Products
Oconto Falls, WI. 920-846-3561
Fitzpatrick Brothers
Pleasant Prairie, WI 800-233-8064
Fuller Industries LLC
Great Bend, KS. 800-522-0499
Goodwin Co
Garden Grove, CA 714-894-0531
Grace-Lee Products
Minneapolis, MN 612-379-2711
Griffin Bros Inc
Salem, OR. 800-456-4743
Hamilton Soap & Oil Products
Paterson, NJ 973-225-1031
Hanco Manufacturing Company
Memphis, TN 800-530-7364
Hohn Manufacturing Company
Fenton, MO. 800-878-1440
Holland Chemicals Company
Windsor, ON 519-948-4373
James Austin Co
Mars, PA 724-625-1535
Knapp Manufacturing
Fresno, CA 559-251-8254
L&M Chemicals
Tampa, FL. 800-362-3331

Labpride Chemicals
Bronx, NY. 800-467-1255
Laundry Aids
Carlstadt, NJ 201-933-3500
Lee Soap Company
Commerce City, CO 800-888-1896
Lubar Chemical
Kansas City, MO. 816-471-2560
MGF.com
Atlanta, GA. 770-444-9686
Mione Manufacturing Company
Mickleton, NJ 800-257-0497
National Purity LLC
Brooklyn Center, MN 612-672-0022
New Klix Corporation
South San Francisco, CA 800-522-5544
Nyco Products Co
Countryside, IL 800-752-4754
Ostrem Chemical Co. Ltd
Edmonton, AB 780-440-1911
Portion-Pac Chemical Corp.
Chicago, IL 312-226-0400
Reeno Detergent & Soap Company
Saint Louis, MO 314-429-6078
REM Ohio Inc
Cincinnati, OH 513-381-3700
Rochester Midland Corp
Rochester, NY. 800-535-5053
S & S Soap Co
Bronx, NY. 718-585-2900
Snee Chemical Co
New Orleans, LA 800-489-7633
Star Pacific Inc
Union City, CA 800-227-0760
Stearns Packaging Corp
Madison, WI 608-246-5150
Stone Soap Co Inc
Sylvan Lake, MI 800-952-7627
Sunbeam Products Co LLC
Toledo, OH 419-691-1551
Sure Clean Corporation
Two Rivers, WI. 920-793-3838
Swisher Hygiene
Charlotte, NC 800-444-4138
Synthron Inc.
Morganton, NC 828-437-8611
Telechem Corp
Atlanta, GA. 800-637-0495
Texas Refinery Corp
Fort Worth, TX 817-332-1161
The Procter & Gamble Company
Cincinnati, OH 800-692-0132
Theochem Laboratories Inc
Tampa, FL. 800-237-2591
Twi Laq
Bronx, NY. 800-950-7627
Ulmer Pharmacal
Park Rapids, MN. 800-848-5637
US Industrial Lubricants
Cincinnati, OH 800-562-5454
Venturetech Corporation
Knoxville, TN 800-826-4095
Wave Chemical Company
New York, NY 973-243-5852
West Chemical Products
Princeton, NJ. 609-921-0501
Wilson AL Chemical Co
Kearny, NJ. 800-526-1188

Industrial

9-12 Corporation
Caguas, PR 787-747-0405
A&L Laboratories
Minneapolis, MN 800-225-3832
Abicor Binzel
Frederick, MD. 800-542-4867
Alconox Inc
White Plains, NY 914-437-7585
American Wax Co Inc
Long Island City, NY 718-361-4820
Auto Chlor Systems
Memphis, TN 800-477-3693
Bio Industries
Luxemburg, WI. 920-845-2355
Bradford Soap Works Inc
West Warwick, RI. 401-821-2141
Church & Dwight Co., Inc.
Ewing, NJ 800-833-9532
Clarkson Supply
Williamsport, PA 800-326-9457

Colgate-Palmolive Professional Products Group
North York, ON. 800-468-6502
Country Save Products Corp
Arlington, WA. 360-435-9868
Diablo Chemical
Kingston, PA 800-548-1384
Dial Corporation
Scottsdale, AZ. 480-754-3425
Falls Chemical Products
Oconto Falls, WI. 920-846-3561
Fitzpatrick Brothers
Pleasant Prairie, WI 800-233-8064
Hope Chemical Corporation
Pawtucket, RI 401-724-8000
Hydrite Chemical Co
Brookfield, WI 262-792-1450
King of All Manufacturing
Clio, MI. 810-564-0139
Knapp Manufacturing
Fresno, CA 559-251-8254
Labpride Chemicals
Bronx, NY. 800-467-1255
Lubar Chemical
Kansas City, MO. 816-471-2560
Luseaux Labs Inc
Gardena, CA 800-266-1555
Manhattan Truck Lines
Paterson, NJ 800-370-7627
Mione Manufacturing Company
Mickleton, NJ 800-257-0497
Pagoda Industries Inc
Reading, PA 610-678-8096
Patterson Laboratories
Detroit, MI 313-843-4500
PM Chemical Company
San Diego, CA 619-296-0191
Reeno Detergent & Soap Company
Saint Louis, MO 314-429-6078
Seatex Ltd
Rosenberg, TX 800-829-3020
Snee Chemical Co
New Orleans, LA 800-489-7633
Spurrier Chemical Companies
Atlanta, GA. 800-795-9222
Stewart Laboratories
Strattanville, PA 800-640-7869
Swisher Hygiene
Charlotte, NC 800-444-4138
US Industrial Lubricants
Cincinnati, OH 800-562-5454
Whisk Products Inc
Wentzville, MO 800-204-7627

Dish Washing Machinery

Acro Dishwashing Svc Co
Kansas City, KS 913-342-4282
Adamation
Commerce, CA 800-383-8800
Ali Group
Winston Salem, NC 800-532-8591
American Dish Service
Edwardsville, KS 800-922-2178
Attias Oven Corp
Brooklyn, NY 800-928-8427
Blakeslee, Inc.
Addison, IL 630-532-5021
Burns Chemical Systems
Cleveland, OH 724-327-7600
Champion Industries Inc
Winston Salem, NC. 800-532-8591
Cma Dishmachines
Garden Grove, CA 800-854-6417
Colonial Paper Company
Silver Springs, FL. 352-622-4171
Convay Systems
Minnetonka, MN. 800-334-1099
Custom Diamond International
Laval, QC 800-363-5926
Douglas Machines Corp.
Clearwater, FL 800-331-6870
Hartstone Pottery Inc
Zanesville, OH 740-452-9999
Insinger Co
Philadelphia, PA 800-344-4802
Jackson Msc LLC
Gray, KY 888-800-5672
Knight Equipment Canada
Mississauga, ON 800-854-3764
Knight Equipment International
Lake Forest, CA 800-854-3764

Moyer Diebel
    Winston Salem, NC..............336-661-1992
National Hotpack
    Stone Ridge, NY..............800-431-8232
Stero Co
    Petaluma, CA................800-762-7600
Swissh Commercial Equipment
    Montreal, QC...............888-794-7749
The Procter & Gamble Company
    Cincinnati, OH.............800-692-0132
TNN-Jeros, Inc.
    Byron, IL..................815-978-2210
Vanguard Technology Inc
    Eugene, OR................800-624-4809

Dishwasher

Racks

Amco Metals Indl
    City of Industry, CA........626-855-2550
Blakeslee, Inc.
    Addison, IL................630-532-5021
Carlisle Food Svc Products Inc
    Oklahoma City, OK.........800-654-8210
Duke Manufacturing Co
    St Louis, MO..............800-735-3853
Marlin Steel Wire Products
    Baltimore, MD.............877-762-7546
Metro Corporation
    Wilkes Barre, PA..........800-992-1776
Micro Wire Products Inc
    Brockton, MA..............508-584-0200
Straits Steel & Wire Co
    Ludington, MI.............231-843-3416
Superior Products Company
    Saint Paul, MN............800-328-9800
Traex
    Dane, WI..................800-356-8006

Disinfectants & Germicides

Accommodation Mollen
    Philadelphia, PA..........800-872-6268
ADCO
    Albany, GA................800-821-7556
Afassco
    Minden, NV................775-783-3555
American Wax Co Inc
    Long Island City, NY......718-361-4820
Bio Cide Intl Inc
    Norman, OK................800-323-1398
Burnishine Products
    Gurnee, IL................800-818-8275
Candy & Company/Peck's Products Company
    Chicago, IL...............800-837-9189
Carroll Co
    Garland, TX...............800-527-5722
Central Solutions Inc
    Kansas City, KS...........800-255-0262
Chemifax
    Santa Fe Springs, CA......800-527-5722
Church & Dwight Co., Inc.
    Ewing, NJ.................800-833-9532
Claire Manufacturing Company
    Addison, IL...............800-252-4731
Cobitco Inc
    Denver, CO................303-296-8575
Colgate-Palmolive Professional Products Group
    North York, ON............800-468-6502
Concord Chemical Co Inc
    Camden, NJ................800-282-2436
Crown Chemical Products
    Mississauga, ON...........905-564-0904
Damon Industries
    Alliance, OH..............800-362-9850
DCL Solutions LLC
    Philadelphia, PA..........800-426-1127
De Vere Co Inc
    Janesville, WI............800-833-8373
Diamond Chemical Co Inc
    East Rutherford, NJ.......800-654-7627
Emulso
    Tonawanda, NY.............716-854-2889
GERM-O-RAY
    Stone Mountain, GA........800-966-8480
Griffin Bros Inc
    Salem, OR.................800-456-4743
Hanco Manufacturing Company
    Memphis, TN...............800-530-7364
Hilex Company
    Eagan, MN.................651-454-1160

Hill Manufacturing Co Inc
    Atlanta, GA...............404-522-8364
Hy-Ko Enviro-MaintenanceProducts
    Salt Lake City, UT........801-973-6099
Hydrite Chemical Co
    Brookfield, WI............262-792-1450
Insect-O-Cutor Inc
    Stone Mountain, GA........800-966-8480
ITW Dymon
    Olathe, KS................800-443-9536
J.I. Holcomb Manufacturing
    Independence, OH..........800-458-3222
James Austin Co
    Mars, PA..................724-625-1535
Knapp Manufacturing
    Fresno, CA................559-251-8254
L&M Chemicals
    Tampa, FL.................800-362-3331
Labpride Chemicals
    Bronx, NY.................800-467-1255
Larose & Fils Lte
    Laval, QC.................877-382-7001
Lubar Chemical
    Kansas City, MO...........816-471-2560
Marko Inc
    Spartanburg, SC...........866-466-2726
MGF.com
    Atlanta, GA...............770-444-9686
Mission Laboratories
    Los Angeles, CA...........888-201-8866
Nuance Solutions Inc
    Chicago, IL...............800-621-8553
Paley-Lloyd-Donohue
    Elizabeth, NJ.............908-352-5835
Pioneer Chemical Co
    Gardena, CA...............310-366-7393
ProRestore Products
    Pittsburgh, PA............800-332-6037
Puritan/Churchill Chemical Company
    Marietta, GA..............800-275-8914
R&C Pro Brands
    Wayne, NJ.................973-633-7374
Rochester Midland Corp
    Rochester, NY.............800-535-5053
Rochester Midland Corp
    Rochester, NY.............800-836-1627
San Joaquin Pool Svc & Supply
    Stockton, CA..............209-952-0680
Sanco Products Co Inc
    Greenville, OH............937-548-2225
Seatex Ltd
    Rosenberg, TX.............800-829-3020
Selig Chemical Industries
    Atlanta, GA...............404-876-5511
Simoniz USA Inc
    Bolton, CT................800-227-5536
State Industrial Products Corp
    Mayfield Heights, OH......877-747-6986
Sunpoint Products
    Lawrence, MA..............978-794-3100
Swisher Hygiene
    Charlotte, NC.............800-444-4138
The Procter & Gamble Company
    Cincinnati, OH............800-692-0132
Ulmer Pharmacal
    Park Rapids, MN...........800-848-5637
Verax Chemical Co
    Snohomish, WA.............800-637-7771
Vulcan Materials Co
    Vestavia, AL..............205-298-3000
West Chemical Products
    Princeton, NJ.............609-921-0501
Whisk Products Inc
    Wentzville, MO............800-204-7627

Dispensers

Cleaning Compound

Auto Chlor Systems
    Memphis, TN...............800-477-3693
Carbon Clean Industries Inc
    Kingston, PA..............570-288-1155
Crc Industries Inc
    Warminster, PA............800-556-5074
Eurodispenser
    Decatur, IL...............217-864-4061
GOJO Industries Inc
    Akron, OH.................800-321-9647
Graco Inc
    Minneapolis, MN...........877-844-7226

Hygiene-Technik
    Beamsville, ON............905-563-4987
Knight Equipment Canada
    Mississauga, ON...........800-854-3764
Knight Equipment International
    Lake Forest, CA...........800-854-3764
Labpride Chemicals
    Bronx, NY.................800-467-1255
Steiner Industries Inc
    Chicago, IL...............800-621-4515
Tate Western
    Goleta, CA................800-903-0200

Soap

Best Sanitizers Inc
    Penn Valley, CA...........888-225-3267
Deb Canada
    Waterford, ON.............888-332-7627
Dema Engineering Co
    St Louis, MO..............800-325-3362
Dreumex USA
    York, PA..................800-233-9382
Eurodispenser
    Decatur, IL...............217-864-4061
GOJO Industries Inc
    Akron, OH.................800-321-9647
Hygiene-Technik
    Beamsville, ON............905-563-4987
Micro-Brush Pro Soap
    Rockwall, TX..............800-776-7627
Milburn Company
    Detroit, MI...............313-259-3410
Parachem Corporation
    Des Moines, IA............515-280-9445
Steiner Company
    Holland, IL...............800-222-4638
Steiner Industries Inc
    Chicago, IL...............800-621-4515
Superior Products Company
    Saint Paul, MN............800-328-9800
Tate Western
    Goleta, CA................800-903-0200
Tolco Corp
    Toledo, OH................800-537-4786
Whisk Products Inc
    Wentzville, MO............800-204-7627
World Dryer Corp
    Berkeley, IL..............800-323-0701

Dryer Systems

A & B Process Systems Corp
    Stratford, WI.............888-258-2789
A&J Mixing International
    Oakville, ON..............800-668-3470
Amerivap Systems Inc
    Dawsonville, GA...........800-763-7687
Ametek Technical & Industrial Products
    Kent, OH..................215-256-6601
Applied Chemical Technology
    Florence, AL..............800-228-3217
Bepex International LLC
    Minneapolis, MN...........800-607-2470
BFM Equipment Sales
    Fall River, WI............920-484-3341
Brothers Metal Products
    Santa Ana, CA.............714-972-3008
Buffalo Technologies Corporation
    Buffalo, NY...............800-332-2419
Carman Industries Inc
    Jeffersonville, IN........800-456-7560
Casso-Solar Corporation
    Nanuet, NY................800-988-4455
Chief Industries
    Kearney, NE...............800-359-8833
Convay Systems
    Minnetonka, MN............800-334-1099
Crown Iron Works Company
    Roseville, MN.............888-703-7500
Damas Corporation
    Trenton, NJ...............609-695-9121
Davenport Machine
    Rock Island, IL...........309-786-1500
Davron Technologies Inc
    Chattanooga, TN...........423-870-1888
Dito Dean Food Prep
    Charlotte, NC.............866-449-4200
Evaporator Dryer Technologies
    Hammond, WI...............715-796-2313
Fitzpatrick Co
    Elmhurst, IL..............630-592-4425

Flodin
Moses Lake, WA.....................509-766-2996
Fluid Energy Processing & Eqpt
Hatfield, PA........................215-368-2510
Gardner Denver Inc.
Milwaukee, WI
Gaston County Dyeing Mach Co
Mt Holly, NC.......................704-822-5000
Glatt Air Techniques Inc
Ramsey, NJ........................201-825-8700
Grain Machinery Mfg Corp
Miami, FL..........................305-620-2525
Hankison International
Canonsburg, PA....................724-746-1100
Hoyt Corporation
Westport, MA.......................508-636-8811
Insinger Co
Philadelphia, PA...................800-344-4802
International Reserve Equipment Corporation
Clarendon Hills, IL................708-531-0680
Kinergy Corp
Louisville, KY.....................502-366-5685
Laundrylux
Inwood, NY.........................800-645-2205
LIST
Acton, MA..........................978-635-9521
Littleford Day
Florence, KY.......................800-365-8555
Louisville Dryer Company
Louisville, KY.....................800-735-3613
M-E-C Co
Neodesha, KS.......................620-325-2673
Midbrook Inc
Jackson, MI........................800-966-9274
National Drying Machry Co Inc
Philadelphia, PA...................215-464-6070
National Hotpack
Stone Ridge, NY....................800-431-8232
NECO/Nebraska Engineering
Omaha, NE..........................800-367-6208
Nemeth Engineering Assoc
Crestwood, KY......................502-241-1502
Niro
Hudson, WI.........................715-386-9371
Paget Equipment Co
Marshfield, WI.....................715-384-3158
Patterson Industries
Scarborough, ON....................800-336-1110
Patterson-Kelley   Hars Company
East Stroudsburg, PA...............570-421-7500
Paul O. Abbe
Bensenville, IL....................630-350-2200
Paxton Products Inc
Blue Ash, OH.......................800-441-7475
Procedyne Corp
New Brunswick, NJ..................732-249-8347
Professional Engineering Assoc
Louisville, KY.....................502-429-0432
Radio Frequency Co Inc
Millis, MA.........................508-376-9555
San Aire Industries
Fort Worth, TX.....................800-757-1912
Shanzer Grain Dryer
Sioux Falls, SD....................800-843-9887
Spencer Turbine Co
Windsor, CT........................800-232-4321
Spray Drying
Sykesville, MD.....................410-549-8090
Steri Technologies Inc
Bohemia, NY........................800-253-7140
Tuthill Vacuum & Blower Systems
Springfield, MO....................800-825-6937
United Mc Gill Corp
Groveport, OH......................614-829-1200
Vector Corp
Marion, IA.........................319-377-8263
Vortron Smokehouse/Ovens
Iron Ridge, WI.....................800-874-1949
Wittemann Company
Palm Coast, FL.....................386-445-4200
World Dryer Corp
Berkeley, IL.......................800-323-0701
Zeeco Inc
Broken Arrow, OK...................918-258-8551

Dust Collectors

Chicago Conveyor Corporation
Addison, IL........................630-543-6300
Paget Equipment Co
Marshfield, WI.....................715-384-3158

Spencer Turbine Co
Windsor, CT........................800-232-4321
Temp Air Inc
Burnsville, MN.....................800-836-7432

Dust Pans

Carlisle Food Svc Products Inc
Oklahoma City, OK..................800-654-8210
Ex-Cell KAISER LLC
Franklin Park, IL..................847-451-0451
J.V. Reed & Company
Louisville, KY.....................877-258-7333
Superior Products Company
Saint Paul, MN.....................800-328-9800

Floor Cleaning Machinery

Polishing, Refinishing, Sanding & Scrubbing

Clarke American Sanders
Minneapolis, MN....................800-253-0367
Cleanfreak
Appleton, WI.......................888-722-5508
Dynamic Coatings Inc
Fresno, CA.........................559-225-4605
Larose & Fils Lte
Laval, QC..........................877-382-7001
Mercury Floor Machines Inc
Englewood, NJ......................888-568-4606
Microtron Abrasives
Pineville, NC......................800-476-7237
Squar-Buff
Oakland, CA........................800-525-6955
Surtec Inc
Tracy, CA..........................800-877-6330
United Floor Machine Co
Chicago, IL........................800-288-0848

Garbage Bags

All American Poly
Piscataway, NJ.....................800-526-3551
Arbee Transparent Inc
Elk Grove Vlg, IL..................800-642-2247
Brown Paper Goods Co
Waukegan, IL.......................847-688-1450
Carlisle Plastics
Minneapolis, MN....................952-884-1309
COVERIS
Tomah, WI..........................608-372-2153
Custom Poly Packaging
Fort Wayne, IN.....................800-548-6603
Dashco
Gloucester, ON.....................613-834-6825
Development Workshop Inc
Idaho Falls, ID....................800-657-5597
East Coast Group New York
Springfield Gardens, NY............718-527-8464
GP Plastics Corporation
Medley, FL.........................305-888-3555
Himolene
Carrollton, TX.....................800-777-4411
J A Heilferty & Co
Teaneck, NJ........................201-836-5060
KM International Corp
Kenton, TN.........................731-749-8700
Lakeside Manufacturing Inc
Milwaukee, WI......................888-558-8565
Luetzow Industries
South Milwaukee, WI................800-558-6055
Marshall Plastic Film Inc
Martin, MI.........................269-672-5511
Nosaj Disposables
Paterson, NJ.......................800-631-3809
NOVOLEX
Glendale, AZ.......................800-243-0306
Package Containers Inc
Canby, OR..........................800-266-5806
Pactiv LLC
Lake Forest, IL....................800-476-4300
Pan Pacific Plastics Inc
Hayward, CA........................888-475-6888
Paradise Plastics
Brooklyn, NY.......................718-788-3733
S&O Corporation
Gallaway, MD.......................800-624-7858
Schroeder Machine
San Marcos, CA.....................760-591-9733
Servin Company
New Baltimore, MI..................800-824-0962

Star Poly Bag Inc
Brooklyn, NY.......................718-384-7034
Tree Saver
Englewood, CO......................800-676-7741
Valley Packaging Supply Co
Green Bay, WI......................920-336-9012
Wisconsin Converting Inc
Green Bay, WI......................800-544-1935

Garbage Compactors

Chicago Trashpacker Corporation
Marengo, IL........................800-635-5745
Compactors Inc
Hilton Head Isle, SC...............800-423-4003
Consolidated Baling Machine Company
Jacksonville, FL...................800-231-9286
Dempster Systems
Toccoa, GA.........................706-886-2327
Enterprise Company
Santa Ana, CA......................714-835-0541
Galbreath LLC
Winamac, IN........................574-946-6631
Incinerator International Inc
Houston, TX........................713-227-1466
Logemann Brothers Co
Milwaukee, WI......................414-445-3005
Marathon Equipment Co
Vernon, AL.........................800-269-7237
Maren Engineering Corp
South Holland, IL..................800-875-1038
Multi-Pak
Hackensack, NJ.....................201-342-7474
Orwak
Minneapolis, MN....................800-747-0449
PAC Equipment Company
Garfield, NJ.......................973-478-1008
PTR Baler & Compactor Co
Philadelphia, PA...................800-523-3654
Robar International Inc
Milwaukee, WI......................800-279-7750
Schleicher & Company of America
Sanford, NC........................800-775-7570
Schloss Engineered Equipment
Aurora, CO.........................303-695-4500
SP Industries
Hopkins, MI........................800-592-5959
Universal Handling Equipment
Hamilton, ON.......................877-843-1122
Waste Away Systems
Newark, OH.........................800-223-4741
Wastequip Inc
Charlotte, NC......................704-366-7140
Wayne Engineering
Cedar Falls, IA....................319-266-1721

Garbage Control Units & Systems

Chicago Trashpacker Corporation
Marengo, IL........................800-635-5745
Compactors Inc
Hilton Head Isle, SC...............800-423-4003
Consolidated Baling Machine Company
Jacksonville, FL...................800-231-9286
Convay Systems
Minnetonka, MN.....................800-334-1099
Fabwright Inc
Garden Grove, CA...................800-854-6464
Harmony Enterprises
Harmony, MN........................800-658-2320
Jwc Environmental
Costa Mesa, CA.....................800-331-2277
Lodal Inc
Kingsford, MI......................800-435-3500
Maren Engineering Corp
South Holland, IL..................800-875-1038
Mell & Co
Niles, IL..........................800-262-6355
Multi-Pak
Hackensack, NJ.....................201-342-7474
Our Name is Mud
New York, NY.......................877-683-7867
PAC Equipment Company
Garfield, NJ.......................973-478-1008
PTR Baler & Compactor Co
Philadelphia, PA...................800-523-3654
Robar International Inc
Milwaukee, WI......................800-279-7750
Tema Systems Inc
Cincinnati, OH.....................513-792-2840
U B KLEM Furniture Co Inc
St Anthony, IN.....................800-264-1995

Universal Handling Equipment
Hamilton, ON 877-843-1122
Wastequip Inc
Charlotte, NC 704-366-7140
Wayne Engineering
Cedar Falls, IA 319-266-1721

Garbage Disposal Units

Anaheim Manufacturing Company
Anaheim, CA 800-767-6293
Anova
St Louis, MO. 800-231-1327
Blower Application Co Inc
Germantown, WI. 800-959-0880
Consolidated Baling Machine Company
Jacksonville, FL 800-231-9286
Convay Systems
Minnetonka, MN. 800-334-1099
Dempster Systems
Toccoa, GA 706-886-2327
Dover Parkersburg
Follansbee, WV
Dynabilt Products
Readville, MA. 800-443-1008
Fabwright Inc
Garden Grove, CA 800-854-6464
General Electric Company
Fairfield, CT 203-373-2211
Harmony Enterprises
Harmony, MN. 800-658-2320
In Sink Erator
Racine, WI 800-558-5700
Insinger Co
Philadelphia, PA 800-344-4802
Ken Coat
Bardstown, KY 888-536-2628
Larose & Fils Lte
Laval, QC 877-382-7001
Lewis Steel Works Inc
Wrens, GA. 800-521-5239
Maren Engineering Corp
South Holland, IL 800-875-1038
Old Dominion Wood Products
Lynchburg, VA 800-245-6382
PAC Equipment Company
Garfield, NJ 973-478-1008
Pack-A-Drum
Satellite Beach, FL 800-694-6163
Robar International Inc
Milwaukee, WI. 800-279-7750
Salvajor Co
Kansas City, MO 800-SAL-AJOR
Tema Systems Inc
Cincinnati, OH 513-792-2840
U B KLEM Furniture Co Inc
St Anthony, IN 800-264-1995
Universal Handling Equipment
Hamilton, ON 877-843-1122
Wastequip Inc
Charlotte, NC 704-366-7140
White Mop Wringer Company
Tampa, FL. 800-237-7582

General

9-12 Corporation
Caguas, PR 787-747-0405
A & B Process Systems Corp
Stratford, WI. 888-258-2789
A.K. Robins
Baltimore, MD 800-486-9656
Activon Products
Beaver Dam, WI 800-841-0410
Air-Scent International
Pittsburgh, PA 800-247-0770
Airosol Co Inc
Neodesha, KS 800-633-9576
Alconox Inc
White Plains, NY 914-437-7585
All American Container
Miami, FL. 305-887-0797
Alumin-Nu Corporation
Lyndhurst, OH 800-899-7097
Ameri-Khem
Port Orange, FL 800-224-9950
Amerivap Systems Inc
Dawsonville, GA 800-763-7687
Ampco Pumps Co Inc
Milwaukee, WI. 800-737-8671
Andco Environmental Processes
Amherst, NY. 716-691-2100

Aquafine Corp
Valencia, CA. 800-423-3015
Aquionics Inc
Erlanger, KY. 800-925-0440
Archon Industries Inc
Suffern, NY. 800-554-1394
Ashcroft Inc
Stratford, CT. 800-328-8258
Atlantic Ultraviolet Corp
Hauppauge, NY 866-958-9085
ATOFINA Chemicals
Philadelphia, PA 800-225-7788
Bake Star
Somerset, WI. 763-427-7611
Bar Maid Corp
Pompano Beach, FL 954-960-1468
Bennett Manufacturing Company
Alden, NY. 800-345-2142
Bio Cide Intl Inc
Norman, OK 800-323-1398
Bio Zapp Laboratories
Sarasota, FL 941-922-9199
Birko Corporation
Olathe, KS. 800-444-8360
Black Bear Corp
Roanoke, VA. 800-223-1284
C&R Refrigation Inc,
Center, TX. 800-438-6182
Cadie Products Corp
Paterson, NJ 973-278-8300
Candy & Company/Peck's Products Company
Chicago, IL 800-837-9189
Carroll Co
Garland, TX 800-527-5722
Cashco Inc
Ellsworth, KS 785-472-4461
Century Chemical Corp
Elkhart, IN. 800-348-3505
Cesco Magnetics
Rohnert Park, CA 877-624-8727
Champion Chemical Co
Whittier, CA 800-621-7868
Chore-Boy Corporation
Centerville, IN 765-855-5434
Clean Water Systems
Klamath Falls, OR 866-273-9993
Coburn Company
Whitewater, WI. 800-776-7042
Colgate-Palmolive Professional Products Group
North York, ON. 800-468-6502
Compliance Control Inc
Hyattsville, MD 800-810-4000
Contec, Inc.
Spartenburg, SC 800-289-5762
Control Beverage
Adelanto, CA 330-549-5376
Cosgrove Enterprises Inc
Miami Lakes, FL. 800-888-3396
Crown Chemical Products
Mississauga, ON 905-564-0904
Culinary Depot
Monsey, NY 888-845-8200
D R Technology Inc
Freehold, NJ 732-780-4664
Damon Industries
Alliance, OH 800-362-9850
Damrow Company
Fond Du Lac, WI 800-236-1501
DH/Sureflow
Portland, OR 800-654-2548
Diamond Wipes Intl Inc
Chino, CA 800-454-1077
Dipwell Co
Northampton, MA. 413-587-4673
Discovery Chemical
Marietta, GA. 800-973-9881
DL Enterprises
Etters, PA 717-938-1292
Donaldson Co Inc
Bloomington, MN. 952-887-3131
Dorden & Co
Detroit, MI 313-834-7910
Driall Inc
Attica, IN. 765-295-2255
Ecolo Odor Control Systems Worldwide
North York, ON. 800-667-6355
Electro-Steam Generator Corp
Rancocas, NJ. 866-617-0764
Electrol Specialties Co
South Beloit, IL 815-389-2291
Elgene
Hamden, CT 800-922-4623

Encompass Supply
Kalispell, MT 888-852-7590
Essential Industries Inc
Merton, WI 800-551-9679
Faciltec Corporation
Elgin, IL 800-284-8273
Falls Chemical Products
Oconto Falls, WI. 920-846-3561
FX-Lab Company
Union, NJ 908-810-1212
Gamajet Cleaning Systems
Exton, PA 800-289-5387
Geerpres Inc
Muskegon, MI. 231-773-3211
Graco Inc
Minneapolis, MN 877-844-7226
Gralab Instruments
Centerville, OH 800-876-8353
Great Western Chemical Company
Portland, OR 800-547-1400
Haviland Enterprises Inc
Grand Rapids, MI 800-456-1134
Hill Brush, Inc.
Baltimore, MD 800-998-1515
Hoge Brush Company
New Knoxville, OH 800-494-4643
Hubbell Electric Heater Co
Stratford, CT 800-647-3165
Hydrite Chemical Co
Brookfield, WI 262-792-1450
Insect-O-Cutor Inc
Stone Mountain, GA. 800-966-8480
Interlab
The Woodlands, TX 888-876-2844
ITW Dymon
Olathe, KS. 800-443-9536
James Varley & Sons
Saint Louis, MO 800-325-8891
Joneca Corp
Anaheim, CA 714-993-5997
Justman Brush Co
Omaha, NE 800-800-6940
KES Science & Technology Inc
Kennesaw, GA 800-627-4913
Kimberly-Clark Corporation
Irving, TX 972-281-1200
Knapp Manufacturing
Fresno, CA 559-251-8254
Labpride Chemicals
Bronx, NY. 800-467-1255
Lake Process Systems Inc
Lake Barrington, IL 800-331-9260
Laundry Aids
Carlstadt, NJ. 201-933-3500
Lechler Inc
St Charles, IL 800-777-2926
Little Giant Pump Company
Fort Wayne, IN 260-824-2900
Luseaux Labs Inc
Gardena, CA 800-266-1555
M D Stetson Co
Randolph, MA 800-255-8651
Manhattan Truck Lines
Paterson, NJ 800-370-7627
Metcraft
Grandview, MO. 800-444-9624
Midbrook Inc
Jackson, MI. 800-966-9274
Mil-Du-Gas Company/Star Brite
Fort Lauderdale, FL 800-327-8583
Milsek Furniture Polish Inc.
North Lima, OH 330-542-2700
Mission Laboratories
Los Angeles, CA. 888-201-8866
Moly-XL Company
Westville, NJ 856-848-2880
Navy Brand
St Louis, MO. 800-325-3312
Netzsch Pumps North America
Exton, PA 610-363-8010
Nilfisk, Inc.
Morgantown, PA 800-645-3475
Northwind Inc
Alpena, AR 877-937-2585
Nuance Solutions Inc
Chicago, IL 800-621-8553
Oakite Products
New Providence, NJ 800-526-4473
Omni Controls Inc
Tampa, FL 800-783-6664
Orwak
Minneapolis, MN 800-747-0449

PAC Equipment Company
Garfield, NJ .973-478-1008
Parachem Corporation
Des Moines, IA. 515-280-9445
Paragon Group USA
St Petersburg, FL 800-835-6962
Paramount Packaging Corp
Melville, NY. .516-333-8100
Paxton Corp
Bristol, RI 401-396-9062
Pioneer Chemical Co
Gardena, CA. 310-366-7393
Pioneer Manufacturing Co Inc
Cleveland, OH 800-877-1500
Portion-Pac Chemical Corp.
Chicago, IL 312-226-0400
Potlatch Corp
Spokane, WA. 509-835-1500
Pretty Products
Wauconda, IL 800-726-4849
ProRestore Products
Pittsburgh, PA 800-332-6037
Purolator Facet Inc
Greensboro, NC 800-852-4449
PVI Industries LLC
Fort Worth, TX 800-784-8326
Quikwater Inc
Sand Springs, OK 918-241-8880
Radiation Processing Division
Parsippany, NJ. 800-442-1969
Rea UltraVapor
Ancaster, ON. 800-323-3865
RHG Products Company
Castle Rock, CO 800-553-8131
Rochester Midland Corp
Rochester, NY. 800-535-5053
Rochester Midland Corp
Rochester, NY. 800-836-1627
Ronell Industries
Roselle, NJ 908-245-5255
Royal Paper Products
Coatesville, PA 800-666-6655
Royce Rolls Ringer Co
Grand Rapids, MI 800-253-9638
Ryter Corporation
Saint James, MN 800-643-2184
Sanitech Inc
Lorton, VA 800-486-4321
Sanitor Manufacturing Co
Portage, MI .800-379-5314
SCA Tissue
Philadelphia, PA 866-722-8675
SCA Tissue North America
S Glens Falls, NY 518-743-0240
Sedalia Janitorial & Paper Supplies
Sedalia, MO .660-826-9899
Selig Chemical Industries
Atlanta, GA. .404-876-5511
Seneca Environmental Products
Tiffin, OH 419-447-1282
Shamrock Foods Co
Phoenix, AZ .877-228-9030
Sigma Engineering Corporation
White Plains, NY 914-682-1820
Snee Chemical Co
New Orleans, LA 800-489-7633
Southend Janitorial Supply
Los Angeles, CA. 323-754-2842
Spartan Tool LLC
Mendota, IL .800-435-3866
Spurrier Chemical Companies
Atlanta, GA. .800-795-9222
Sterling Novelty Products
Northbrook, IL 847-291-0070
Swisher Hygiene
Charlotte, NC 800-444-4138
T & S Brass & Bronze Work
Travelers Rest, SC 800-476-4103
Telechem Corp
Atlanta, GA. .800-637-0495
Tennant Co.
Minneapolis, MN 800-553-8033
Thermaco Inc
Asheboro, NC 800-633-4204
TRITEN Corporation
Houston, TX .832-214-5000
Tuchenhagen
Columbia, MD 410-910-6000
Uni First Corp
Wilmington, MA. 800-455-7654
United Electric Controls Co
Watertown, MA. 617-926-1000

United Floor Machine Co
Chicago, IL 800-288-0848
Upright
St Louis, MO. 800-248-7007
US Industrial Lubricants
Cincinnati, OH 800-562-5454
Waco Broom & Mop Factory
Waco, TX 800-548-7716
Warren E. Conley Corporation
Carmel, IN. 800-367-7875
Warsaw Chemical Co Inc
Warsaw, IN 800-548-3396
Waste Away Systems
Newark, OH .800-223-4741
Water Sciences Services, Inc.
Jackson, TN .973-584-4131
Water System Group
Santa Clarita, CA 800-350-9283
West Chemical Products
Princeton, NJ. 609-921-0501
Zipskin
Dexter, MI. 734-426-5559

Holders

Broom

Geerpres Inc
Muskegon, MI. 231-773-3211

Incinerators

Garbage & Waste

Andersen 2000
Peachtree City, GA 800-241-5424
Brown Fired Heater
Elyria, OH 440-323-3291
Chesmont Engineering Co Inc
Exton, PA 610-594-9200
Driall Inc
Attica, IN. 765-295-2255
Incinerator International Inc
Houston, TX .713-227-1466
Incinerator Specialty Company
Houston, TX .713-681-4207
Industronics Service Co
South Windsor, CT 800-878-1551
Jarvis-Cutter Company
Boston, MA. .617-567-7532
Outotec USA Inc
Jessup, MD 301-543-1200
Process Heating Corp
Shrewsbury, MA 508-842-5200
Therm-Tec Inc
Sherwood, OR. 800-292-9163
Zeeco Inc
Broken Arrow, OK 918-258-8551

Insecticides & Insect Control Systems

Accommodation Mollen
Philadelphia, PA 800-872-6268
Actron
Tarzana, CA .800-866-8887
Air-Scent International
Pittsburgh, PA 800-247-0770
Airosol Co Inc
Neodesha, KS 800-633-9576
All Weather Energy Systems
Plymouth, MI 888-636-8324
APR Associates Inc
Memphis, TN 800-238-5150
Arrow-Magnolia Intl Inc
Dallas, TX. 800-527-2101
Atlas Equipment Company
Kansas City, MO. 800-842-9188
Bacon Products Corp
Chattanooga, TN. 800-251-6238
Bell Laboratories Inc
Madison, WI .608-241-0202
Berner International Corp
New Castle, PA 800-245-4455
Cantol
Markham, ON 800-387-9773
Cardinal Professional Products
Woodland, CA. 800-548-2223
Cci Industries-Cool Curtain
Costa Mesa, CA 800-854-5719
Claire Manufacturing Company
Addison, IL. .800-252-4731

Commercial Dehydrator Systems
Eugene, OR. .800-369-4283
Contech Enterprises Inc
Grand Rapids, MI 800-767-8658
Copper Brite
Santa Barbara, CA 805-565-1566
Discovery Chemical
Marietta, GA 800-973-9881
Entech Systems Corp
Kenner, LA 800-783-6561
Envirolights Manufacturing
Concord, ON. 905-738-0357
Gardner Manufacturing Inc
Horicon, WI .800-242-5513
Gilbert Industries, Inc
Jonesboro, AR. 800-643-0400
Gilbert Insect Light Traps
Jonesboro, AR. 800-643-0400
Grant Laboratories
San Leandro, CA. 510-483-6070
Hanco Manufacturing Company
Memphis, TN 800-530-7364
Insect-O-Cutor Inc
Stone Mountain, GA. 800-966-8480
Insects Limited Inc
Westfield, IN. 800-992-1991
J.I. Holcomb Manufacturing
Independence, OH 800-458-3222
Kincaid Enterprises
Nitro, WV 800-951-3377
L ChemCo Distribution
Louisville, KY 800-292-1977
Mars Air Products
Gardena, CA. 800-421-1266
Matson LLC
North Bend, WA 800-308-3723
Mclaughlin Gormley King Co
Minneapolis, MN 800-645-6466
Nozzle Nolen Inc
Palm Springs, FL 800-226-6536
P.F. Harris Manufacturing Company
Alpharetta, GA 800-637-0317
Paraclipse
Columbus, NE 800-854-6379
Pioneer Manufacturing Co Inc
Cleveland, OH 800-877-1500
Prentiss
Alpharetta, GA 770-552-8072
Research Products Co
Salina, KS 785-825-2181
Rochester Midland Corp
Rochester, NY. 800-535-5053
Rochester Midland Corp
Rochester, NY. 800-836-1627
Roxide International
Larchmont, NY. 800-431-5500
Safety Fumigant Co
Hingham, MA 800-244-1199
Sanco Products Co Inc
Greenville, OH 937-548-2225
Selig Chemical Industries
Atlanta, GA. .404-876-5511
Solvit
Monona, WI .888-314-1072
Sprayway Inc
Addison, IL. .800-332-9000
Surco Products
Pittsburgh, PA 800-556-0111
Temp Air Inc
Burnsville, MN 800-836-7432
Terminix
Flushing, NY. 866-319-6528
Venturetech Corporation
Knoxville, TN. 800-826-4095
Walco-Linck Company
Bellingham, WA 800-338-2329
Warren E. Conley Corporation
Carmel, IN. 800-367-7875
West Chemical Products
Princeton, NJ. 609-921-0501
Western Exterminator Co
Irvine, CA 949-954-8023
Whitmire Microgen Research Lab
St Louis, MO. 800-777-8570

Isopropyl Alcohol

Afassco
Minden, NV .775-783-3555
Dow Packaging
Midland, MI .800-331-6451

Hydrite Chemical Co
Brookfield, WI 262-792-1450

Maintenance

Bunzl Processor Distribution LLC
Riverside, MO. 816-448-4300

Mop Wringers

Geerpres Inc
Muskegon, MI. 231-773-3211
Royce Rolls Ringer Co
Grand Rapids, MI 800-253-9638
Superior Products Company
Saint Paul, MN 800-328-9800

Mops

Abco Products
Miami, FL. .888-694-2226
Amarillo Mop & Broom Company
Amarillo, TX. 800-955-8596
Argo & Company
Spartanburg, SC 864-583-9766
Birmingham Mop Manufacturing Company
Birmingham, AL. 205-942-6101
Bouras Mop Manufacturing Company
Saint Louis, MO 800-634-9153
Bro-Tex Inc
St Paul, MN. 800-328-2282
Carlisle Food Svc Products Inc
Oklahoma City, OK 800-654-8210
Carnegie Textile Co
Cleveland, OH 800-633-4136
Carolina Mop
Anderson, SC 800-845-9725
Chickasaw Broom Mfg Co Inc
Little Rock, AR. 501-562-0311
Cleveland Mop Manufacturing Company
Cleveland, OH 800-767-9934
Continental Commercial Products
Bridgeton, MO 800-325-1051
Cornelia Broom Company
Cornelia, GA. 800-228-2551
Cosgrove Enterprises Inc
Miami Lakes, FL. 800-888-3396
Costa Broom Works
Tampa, FL. 813-385-1722
Crystal Lake Mfg Inc
Autaugaville, AL 800-633-8720
Dover Parkersburg
Follansbee, WV
Drackett Professional
Cincinnati, OH 513-583-3900
Fuller Industries LLC
Great Bend, KS. 800-522-0499
Furgale Industries Ltd.
Winnipeg, NB. 800-665-0506
Golden Star
N Kansas City, MO. 800-821-2792
Greenwood Mop & Broom Inc
Greenwood, SC. 800-635-6849
H. Arnold Wood Turning
Tarrytown, NY 888-314-0088
Harper Brush Works Inc
Fairfield, IA 800-223-7894
Hub City Brush Co
Petal, MS. .800-278-7452
Industries of the Blind
Greensboro, NC 336-274-1591
J.I. Holcomb Manufacturing
Independence, OH 800-458-3222
Kiefer Brushes, Inc
Franklin, NJ 800-526-2905
Labpride Chemicals
Bronx, NY. 800-467-1255
Layflat Products
Shreveport, LA 800-551-8515
Libman Co
Arcola, IL .877-818-3380
Lighthouse for the Blindin New Orleans
New Orleans, LA 504-899-4501
Little Rock Broom Works
Little Rock, AR. 501-562-0311
LMCO
Rosenberg, TX 281-342-8888
Luco Mop Co
St Louis, MO. 800-522-5826
Majestic Industries Inc
Macomb, MI 586-786-9100

Messina Brothers Manufacturing Company
Brooklyn, NY 800-924-6454
Milwaukee Dustless Brush Co
Delavan, WI 323-724-7777
Newton Broom Co
Newton, IL 618-783-4424
O'Dell Corp
Ware Shoals, SC 800-342-2843
Perfex Corporation
Poland, NY 800-848-8483
Pioneer Manufacturing Co Inc
Cleveland, OH 800-877-1500
Quaker Chemical Company
Columbia, SC 800-849-9520
Quality Mop & Brush Manufacturers
Needham, MA. 617-884-2999
Quickie Manufacturing Corp
Cinnaminson, NJ. 856-829-7900
Reit-Price ManufacturingCompany
Union City, NJ. 800-521-5343
Royal Broom & Mop Factory Inc
New Orleans, LA 800-537-6925
Rubbermaid Commercial Products
Cleveland, TN. 423-476-4544
S&M Manufacturing Company
Cisco, TX .800-772-8532
Saunders Manufacturing Co.
N Kansas City, MO. 800-821-2792
Shen Manufacturing Co Inc
Conshohocken, PA 610-825-2790
Superior Products Company
Saint Paul, MN 800-328-9800
Tuway American Group
Rockford, OH 800-537-3750
Uni First Corp
Wilmington, MA. 800-455-7654
Verax Chemical Co
Snohomish, WA 800-637-7771
Waco Broom & Mop Factory
Waco, TX .800-548-7716
Whitley Manufacturing Company
Midland, NC 704-888-2625

Oils

Cleaning

Gemtek Products LLC
Phoenix, AZ 800-331-7022
Labpride Chemicals
Bronx, NY. 800-467-1255
Moly-XL Company
Westville, NJ. 856-848-2880
Oak International
Sturgis, MI 269-651-9790
Stoner
Quarryville, PA. 800-227-5538
US Industrial Lubricants
Cincinnati, OH 800-562-5454

Pest Control

Exterminators

Nozzle Nolen Inc
Palm Springs, FL 800-226-6536
Western Exterminator Co
Irvine, CA .949-954-8023

Pest Control Systems & Devices

Actron
Tarzana, CA 800-866-8887
Air-Scent International
Pittsburgh, PA 800-247-0770
All Weather Energy Systems
Plymouth, MI 888-636-8324
Bacon Products Corp
Chattanooga, TN. 800-251-6238
Bell Laboratories Inc
Madison, WI. 608-241-0202
Cardinal Professional Products
Woodland, CA. 800-548-2223
Claire Manufacturing Company
Addison, IL. 800-252-4731
Contech Enterprises Inc
Grand Rapids, MI 800-767-8658
Copesan
Menomonee Falls, WI. 800-267-3726
Envirolights Manufacturing
Concord, ON. 905-738-0357

Gardner Manufacturing Inc
Horicon, WI 800-242-5513
Gilbert Insect Light Traps
Jonesboro, AR. 800-643-0400
Grant Laboratories
San Leandro, CA. 510-483-6070
Insect-O-Cutor Inc
Stone Mountain, GA. 800-966-8480
Insects Limited Inc
Westfield, IN. 800-992-1991
Kincaid Enterprises
Nitro, WV .800-951-3377
L ChemCo Distribution
Louisville, KY 800-292-1977
Matson LLC
North Bend, WA 800-308-3723
Mclaughlin Gormley King Co
Minneapolis, MN 800-645-6466
Nozzle Nolen Inc
Palm Springs, FL 800-226-6536
P.F. Harris Manufacturing Company
Alpharetta, GA 800-637-0317
Paraclipse
Columbus, NE. 800-854-6379
Pioneer Manufacturing Co Inc
Cleveland, OH 800-877-1500
Prentiss
Alpharetta, GA 770-552-8072
Q A Supplies LLC
Norfolk, VA. 800-472-7205
Rochester Midland Corp
Rochester, NY 800-535-5053
Roxide International
Larchmont, NY 800-431-5500
Selig Chemical Industries
Atlanta, GA 404-876-5511
Sprayway Inc
Addison, IL 800-332-9000
Superior Products Company
Saint Paul, MN 800-328-9800
Surco Products
Pittsburgh, PA 800-556-0111
Temp Air Inc
Burnsville, MN 800-836-7432
Terminix
Flushing, NY. 866-319-6528
Truly Nolen Pest Control
Tucson, AZ 877-977-1553
Walco-Linck Company
Bellingham, WA 800-338-2329
Warren E. Conley Corporation
Carmel, IN. 800-367-7875
Western Exterminator Co
Irvine, CA .949-954-8023
Whitmire Microgen Research Lab
St Louis, MO. 800-777-8570

Traps

Rat & Mouse

Bell Laboratories Inc
Madison, WI. 608-241-0202
Nozzle Nolen Inc
Palm Springs, FL 800-226-6536
Roxide International
Larchmont, NY. 800-431-5500

Plumbing & Drainage Equipment

A B T Inc
Troutman, NC. 800-438-6057
Advanced Detection Systems
Milwaukee, WI. 414-672-0553
Alkota Cleaning Systems Inc
Alcester, SD 800-255-6823
All Power Inc
Sioux City, IA. 712-258-0681
Alumin-Nu Corporation
Lyndhurst, OH 800-899-7097
Ampco Pumps Co Inc
Milwaukee, WI. 800-737-8671
Andco Environmental Processes
Amherst, NY. 716-691-2100
Athea Laboratories
Milwaukee, WI. 800-743-6417
Atlas Minerals & Chemicals Inc
Mertztown, PA. 800-523-8269
Beacon Specialties
New York, NY 800-221-9405
Boyer Corporation
La Grange, IL 800-323-3040

Browne & Company
Markham, ON 905-475-6104
Carts Food Equipment
Brooklyn, NY 718-788-5540
Continental Industrial Supply
South Pasadena, FL 727-341-1100
Corp Somat
Lancaster, PA 800-237-6628
Croll-Reynolds Engineering Company
Trumbull, CT 203-371-1983
DH/Sureflow
Portland, OR 800-654-2548
Drehmann Paving & Flooring Company
Pennsauken, NJ 800-523-3800
Enpoco
Richmond, VA. 800-338-2581
FX-Lab Company
Union, NJ 908-810-1212
G K & L Inc
Dickerson, MD 301-948-5538
Hankison International
Canonsburg, PA 724-746-1100
Hi-Temp Inc
Tuscumbia, AL 800-239-5066
Hydrite Chemical Co
Brookfield, WI 262-792-1450
IMC Teddy Food Service Equipment
Amityville, NY 800-221-5644
Interlab
The Woodlands, TX 888-876-2844
Josam Co
Michigan City, IN 800-365-6726
Kason Central
Columbus, OH 614-885-1992
King of All Manufacturing
Clio, MI. .810-564-0139
Kraissl Co Inc
Hackensack, NJ. 800-572-4775
Krogh Pump Co
Benicia, CA. 800-225-7644
M-One Specialties
Salt Lake City, UT 800-525-9223
Metcraft
Grandview, MO. 800-444-9624
MIFAB Inc
Chicago, IL 800-465-2736
Netzsch Pumps North America
Exton, PA 610-363-8010
Newstamp Lighting Factory
North Easton, MA 508-238-7073
Northland Process Piping
Isle, MN .320-679-2119
PCI Inc
St Louis, MO. 800-752-7657
Plastipro
Los Angeles, CA. 800-779-0561
Rochester Midland Corp
Rochester, NY. 800-836-1627
Rockford Sanitary Systems
Rockford, IL 800-747-5077
Sefi Fabricators Inc
Amityville, NY 631-842-2200
StainlessDrains.com
Greenville, TX 888-785-2345
Stogsdill Tile Co
Huntley, IL 800-323-7504
Trap-Zap Environmental
Wyckoff, NJ 800-282-8727
Van Air Systems
Lake City, PA 800-840-9906
Vaughan Co Inc
Montesano, WA 888-249-2467
Viking Corp
Hastings, MI 800-968-9501
Warren E. Conley Corporation
Carmel, IN. 800-367-7875
Watts Regulator Co
North Andover, MA 978-688-1811
World Dryer Corp
Berkeley, IL. 800-323-0701
Zurn Industries LLC
Erie, PA 855-663-9876

Polish

Floor

ADCO
Albany, GA 800-821-7556
Advance Cleaning Products
Milwaukee, WI 800-925-5326

American Wax Co Inc
Long Island City, NY 718-361-4820
Bar Keepers Friend Cleanser
Indianapolis, IN 800-433-5818
Boyer Corporation
La Grange, IL 800-323-3040
Brulin & Company
Indianapolis, IN 800-776-7149
Buckeye International
Maryland Heights, MO. 314-291-1900
Cantol
Markham, ON 800-387-9773
Chemifax
Santa Fe Springs, CA 800-527-5722
Claire Manufacturing Company
Addison, IL. 800-252-4731
Cobitco Inc
Denver, CO 303-296-8575
Concord Chemical Co Inc
Camden, NJ. 800-282-2436
D W Davies & Co
Racine, WI 800-888-6133
Dial Corporation
Scottsdale, AZ. 480-754-3425
Emulso
Tonawanda, NY 716-854-2889
Essential Industries Inc
Merton, WI 800-551-9679
Fuller Industries LLC
Great Bend, KS 800-522-0499
Golden Star
N Kansas City, MO. 800-821-2792
Griffin Bros Inc
Salem, OR. 800-456-4743
H F Staples & Co Inc
Merrimack, NH. 800-682-0034
Hill Manufacturing Co Inc
Atlanta, GA 404-522-8364
Hillyard Inc
St Joseph, MO. 800-365-1555
Holland Chemicals Company
Windsor, ON 519-948-4373
Hy-Ko Enviro-MaintenanceProducts
Salt Lake City, UT 801-973-6099
J.I. Holcomb Manufacturing
Independence, OH 800-458-3222
James Varley & Sons
Saint Louis, MO 800-325-8891
Knapp Manufacturing
Fresno, CA 559-251-8254
Lamco Chemical Co Inc
Chelsea, MA 617-884-8470
Larose & Fils Lte
Laval, QC 877-382-7001
Lavo Company
Milwaukee, WI 414-353-2140
Lubar Chemical
Kansas City, MO. 816-471-2560
M D Stetson Co
Randolph, MA 800-255-8651
Magic American Corporation
Cleveland, OH 800-321-6330
Marko Inc
Spartanburg, SC 866-466-2726
Meguiar's Inc
Irvine, CA 949-752-8000
Microbest Inc
Waterbury, CT. 800-426-4246
Mission Laboratories
Los Angeles, CA. 888-201-8866
Murnell Wax Company
Springfield, MA 781-395-1323
Pioneer Manufacturing Co Inc
Cleveland, OH 800-877-1500
Portion-Pac Chemical Corp.
Chicago, IL 312-226-0400
Quaker Chemical Company
Columbia, SC 800-849-9520
R&C Pro Brands
Wayne, NJ 973-633-7374
Rochester Midland Corp
Rochester, NY. 800-535-5053
Rochester Midland Corp
Rochester, NY. 800-836-1627
Sanitek Products Inc
Los Angeles, CA. 818-242-1071
Selig Chemical Industries
Atlanta, GA 404-876-5511
Twi Laq
Bronx, NY. 800-950-7627
Valspar Paint
Cleveland, OH 877-825-7727

Verax Chemical Co
Snohomish, WA 800-637-7771
Warren E. Conley Corporation
Carmel, IN. 800-367-7875
West Chemical Products
Princeton, NJ. 609-921-0501
Windsor Wax Co Inc
Charlestown, RI 800-243-8929

Furniture

ADCO
Albany, GA 800-821-7556
Bar Keepers Friend Cleanser
Indianapolis, IN 800-433-5818
Black's Products of HighPoint
High Point, NC 336-886-5011
Burnishine Products
Gurnee, IL. 800-818-8275
Claire Manufacturing Company
Addison, IL. 800-252-4731
Golden Star
N Kansas City, MO. 800-821-2792
H F Staples & Co Inc
Merrimack, NH. 800-682-0034
Hohn Manufacturing Company
Fenton, MO. 800-878-1440
M D Stetson Co
Randolph, MA 800-255-8651
Meguiar's Inc
Irvine, CA 949-752-8000
Milsek Furniture Polish Inc.
North Lima, OH 330-542-2700
Novus
St. Paul, MN 800-328-1117
Scott's Liquid Gold-Inc
Denver, CO 800-447-1919

Powder

Cleaning & Scouring

Bar Keepers Friend Cleanser
Indianapolis, IN 800-433-5818
Church & Dwight Co., Inc.
Ewing, NJ 800-833-9532
Fitzpatrick Brothers
Pleasant Prairie, WI 800-233-8064
Hill Manufacturing Co Inc
Atlanta, GA 404-522-8364
J.I. Holcomb Manufacturing
Independence, OH 800-458-3222
Rochester Midland Corp
Rochester, NY. 800-836-1627
Savogran Co
Norwood, MA 800-225-9872

Pressure Washers

Aaladin Industries Inc
Elk Point, SD 800-356-3325
Alkota Cleaning Systems Inc
Alcester, SD 800-255-6823
Cam Spray
Iowa Falls, IA 800-648-5011
Clarke American Sanders
Minneapolis, MN 800-253-0367
D&M Products
Santa Monica, CA. 800-245-0485
Davron Technologies Inc
Chattanooga, TN 423-870-1888
Dirt Killer Pressure Washer
Gwynn Oak, MD. 800-544-1188
General Tank
Berwick, PA 800-435-8265
Goodway Technologies Corp
Stamford, CT. 800-333-7467
Hector Delorme & Sons
Farnham, QC 450-293-5310
Industrial Washing Machine Corporation
Jackson, NJ 732-304-9203
Kew Cleaning Systems
Clearwater, FL 800-942-1690
Kewanee Washer Corporaton
Findlay, OH. 419-435-8269
Larose & Fils Lte
Laval, QC 877-382-7001
Lechler Inc
St Charles, IL 800-777-2926
Mart CART-Smt
Rogers, AR 800-548-3373

Maxi-Vac Inc.
Dundee, IL 855-629-4538
N & A Mfg
Mallard, IA 712-425-3512
Pro Scientific Inc
Oxford, CT 800-584-3776
Sani-Matic
Madison, WI 800-356-3300
Sioux Corp
Beresford, SD 888-763-8833
Therma Kleen
Plainfield, IL 800-999-3120

Sanitary Wall

AlphaBio Inc
Rancho Santa Maragarita, CA . 800-966-0716
Arcoplast Wall & Ceiling Systems
St Peters, MO 888-736-2726
Zeroloc
Kirkland, WA 425-823-4888

Sanitizers

A&L Laboratories
Minneapolis, MN 800-225-3832
Activon Products
Beaver Dam, WI.................800-841-0410
Air-Scent International
Pittsburgh, PA 800-247-0770
Atlantic Mills
Lakewood, NJ.................800-242-7374
Bar Maid Corp
Pompano Beach, FL 954-960-1468
Best Sanitizers Inc
Penn Valley, CA 888-225-3267
Birko Corporation
Olathe, KS.................800-444-8360
Burnishine Products
Gurnee, IL.................800-818-8275
Candy & Company/Peck's Products Company
Chicago, IL.................800-837-9189
Century Chemical Corp
Elkhart, IN.................800-348-3505
Colgate-Palmolive Professional Products Group
North York, ON.................800-468-6502
Discovery Chemical
Marietta, GA 800-973-9881
Electro-Steam Generator Corp
Rancocas, NJ.................866-617-0764
Falls Chemical Products
Oconto Falls, WI.................920-846-3561
Glass Pro
Addison, IL.................888-641-8919
Hilex Company
Eagan, MN 651-454-1160
Hydrite Chemical Co
Brookfield, WI 262-792-1450
James Varley & Sons
Saint Louis, MO 800-325-8891
Labpride Chemicals
Bronx, NY.................800-467-1255
Lee Industries
Philipsburg, PA 814-342-0461
Luseaux Labs Inc
Gardena, CA.................800-266-1555
M D Stetson Co
Randolph, MA 800-255-8651
Machem Industries
Delta, BC.................604-526-5655
Meritech
Golden, CO.................800-932-7707
Nelson-Jameson Inc
Marshfield, WI 800-826-8302
Nice-Pak Products Inc
Orangeburg, NY 800-444-6725
Nuance Solutions Inc
Chicago, IL.................800-621-8553
Oakite Products
New Providence, NJ 800-526-4473
Paxton Corp
Bristol, RI 401-396-9062
Portion-Pac Chemical Corp.
Chicago, IL.................312-226-0400
Pretty Products
Wauconda, IL 800-726-4849
ProRestore Products
Pittsburgh, PA 800-332-6037
REM Ohio Inc
Cincinnati, OH 513-381-3700
Rochester Midland Corp
Rochester, NY.................800-836-1627

Shepard Brothers Co
La Habra, CA 800-645-3594
Vulcan Materials Co
Vestavia, AL 205-298-3000
Water Sciences Services, Inc.
Jackson, TN 973-584-4131

Scouring Pads

ACS Industries, Inc.
Lincoln, RI 866-783-4838
Arden Companies
Southfield, MI.................248-415-8500
Argo & Company
Spartanburg, SC 864-583-9766
Armaly Brands
Commerce Twp, MI 800-772-1222
Banner Chemical Co
Orange, NJ.................973-676-0105
Carlisle Food Svc Products Inc
Oklahoma City, OK 800-654-8210
Glit Microtron
Bridgetown, MO.................800-325-1051
Mainline Industries Inc
Springfield, MA 800-527-7917
Microtron Abrasives
Pineville, NC.................800-476-7237
Pacific Oasis Enterprise Inc
Santa Fe Springs, CA 800-424-1475
Quickie Manufacturing Corp
Cinnaminson, NJ.................856-829-7900
Royal Paper Products
Coatesville, PA 800-666-6655
Stearns Technical Textiles Company
Cincinnati, OH 800-543-7173
Thamesville Metal Products Ltd
Thamesville, ON.................519-692-3963
Tucel Industries, Inc.
Forestdale, VT 800-558-8235
Tuway American Group
Rockford, OH 800-537-3750
Wilen Professional Cleaning Products
Atlanta, GA.................800-241-7371

Scrubbers

Andersen 2000
Peachtree City, GA 800-241-5424

Silverware Cleaning Machinery

Washing, Drying & Polishing

Adamation
Commerce, CA.................800-383-8800
Vanguard Technology Inc
Eugene, OR.................800-624-4809

Skin Cream & Lotions

Cold Cream

Milburn Company
Detroit, MI 313-259-3410

Lotion

Milburn Company
Detroit, MI 313-259-3410

Skin Cream

Milburn Company
Detroit, MI 313-259-3410
The Procter & Gamble Company
Cincinnati, OH 800-692-0132

Sneeze Guards

Advanced Design Mfg
Concord, CA.................800-690-0002
Brass Smith
Denver, CO.................800-662-9595
Carlisle Food Svc Products Inc
Oklahoma City, OK 800-654-8210
Custom Plastics Inc
Decatur, GA.................404-373-1691
Duke Manufacturing Co
St Louis, MO.................800-735-3853
Emco Industrial Plastics
Cedar Grove, NJ 800-292-9906

English Manufacturing Inc
Rancho Cordova, CA 800-651-2711
Hanson Brass Rewd Co
Sun Valley, CA.................888-841-3773
K & I Creative Plastics & Wood
Jacksonville, FL.................904-387-0438
Lavi Industries
Valencia, CA.................800-624-6225
Precision Plastics Inc
Beltsville, MD.................800-922-1317
R & D Brass
Wappingers Falls, NY 800-447-6050
Sneezeguard Solutions
Columbia, MO 800-569-2056
Superior Products Company
Saint Paul, MN 800-328-9800

Soap

Advance Cleaning Products
Milwaukee, WI.................800-925-5326
Akron Cotton Products
Akron, OH.................800-899-7173
American Wax Co Inc
Long Island City, NY 718-361-4820
APR Associates Inc
Memphis, TN 800-238-5150
Beaumont Products
Kennesaw, GA 800-451-7096
Bi-O-Kleen Industries
Portland, OR.................503-224-6246
Bio Pac Inc
Incline Village, NV.................800-225-2855
Blue Cross Laboratories
Santa Clarita, CA
Bradford Soap Works Inc
West Warwick, RI 401-821-2141
Buckeye International
Maryland Heights, MO.................314-291-1900
Cal Ben Soap Co
Oakland, CA 800-340-7091
Cantol
Markham, ON.................800-387-9773
Carroll Co
Garland, TX 800-527-5722
Chef Revival
North Charleston, SC 800-248-9826
Colgate-Palmolive Professional Products Group
North York, ON.................800-468-6502
Common Sense Natural Soap & Bodycare Products
Rutland, VT 802-773-0582
Concord Chemical Co Inc
Camden, NJ.................800-282-2436
Crc Industries Inc
Warminster, PA 800-556-5074
Critzas Industries Inc
St Louis, MO.................800-537-1418
Crown Chemical Products
Mississauga, ON 905-564-0904
DCL Solutions LLC
Philadelphia, PA 800-426-1127
Deb Canada
Waterford, ON.................888-332-7627
Diablo Chemical
Kingston, PA.................800-548-1384
Dial Corporation
Scottsdale, AZ.................480-754-3425
Dirt Killer Pressure Washer
Gwynn Oak, MD.................800-544-1188
Dober Chemical Corporation
Midlothian, IL.................800-323-4983
Dreumex USA
York, PA 800-233-9382
Economy Paper & Restaurant Co
Clifton, NJ.................973-279-5500
Emulso
Tonawanda, NY 716-854-2889
Essential Industries Inc
Merton, WI.................800-551-9679
Falls Chemical Products
Oconto Falls, WI.................920-846-3561
Fiebing Co
Milwaukee, WI.................800-558-1033
Fishers Investment
Cincinnati, OH 800-833-5916
GOJO Industries Inc
Akron, OH.................800-321-9647
Hallberg Manufacturing Corporation
Tampa, FL.................800-633-7627
Hamilton Soap & Oil Products
Paterson, NJ 973-225-1031

Hanco Manufacturing Company
Memphis, TN 800-530-7364
Hewitt Soap Company
Dayton, OH. 800-543-2245
Hohn Manufacturing Company
Fenton, MO. 800-878-1440
Hy-Trous/Flash Sales
Woburn, MA 781-933-5772
Inksolv 30, LLC.
Emerson, NE 515-537-5344
J.I. Holcomb Manufacturing
Independence, OH 800-458-3222
James Austin Co
Mars, PA 724-625-1535
James Varley & Sons
Saint Louis, MO 800-325-8891
Kildon Manufacturing
Ingersoll, ON 800-485-4930
Larose & Fils Lte
Laval, QC. 877-382-7001
Lavo Company
Milwaukee, WI. 414-353-2140
Lee Soap Company
Commerce City, CO 800-888-1896
M D Stetson Co
Randolph, MA. 800-255-8651
Man-O Products
Cincinnati, OH 888-210-6266
Martin Laboratories
Owensboro, KY. 800-345-9352
Meritech
Golden, CO .800-932-7707
Micro-Brush Pro Soap
Rockwall, TX 800-776-7627
Milburn Company
Detroit, MI 313-259-3410
Mione Manufacturing Company
Mickleton, NJ 800-257-0497
Mission Laboratories
Los Angeles, CA. 888-201-8866
National Purity LLC
Brooklyn Center, MN 612-672-0022
Nuance Solutions Inc
Chicago, IL .800-621-8553
Ohio Soap Products Company
Wickliffe, OH 440-585-1100
Parachem Corporation
Des Moines, IA. 515-280-9445
Pioneer Chemical Co
Gardena, CA 310-366-7393
PM Chemical Company
San Diego, CA 619-296-0191
R R Street & Co
Naperville, IL 630-416-4244
Rochester Midland Corp
Rochester, NY 800-535-5053
Rochester Midland Corp
Rochester, NY 800-836-1627
Rooto Corp
Howell, MI 517-546-8330
S & S Soap Co
Bronx, NY. 718-585-2900
San Joaquin Pool Svc & Supply
Stockton, CA. 209-952-0680
Sanitek Products Inc
Los Angeles, CA. 818-242-1071
SCA Hygiene Paper
San Ramon, CA 800-992-8675
Selig Chemical Industries
Atlanta, GA .404-876-5511
Sierra Dawn Products
Santa Rosa, CA 707-535-0172
Simoniz USA Inc
Bolton, CT 800-227-5536
Snee Chemical Co
New Orleans, LA 800-489-7633
State Industrial Products Corp
Mayfield Heights, OH 877-747-6986
Steiner Company
Holland, IL 800-222-4638
Steiner Industries Inc
Chicago, IL .800-621-4515
Stone Soap Co Inc
Sylvan Lake, MI 800-952-7627
Sunbeam Products Co LLC
Toledo, OH .419-691-1551
Sunpoint Products
Lawrence, MA 978-794-3100
Sure Clean Corporation
Two Rivers, WI. 920-793-3838
The Procter & Gamble Company
Cincinnati, OH 800-692-0132

Tropical Soap Company
Carrollton, TX. 800-527-2368
Twi Laq
Bronx, NY. 800-950-7627
Ulmer Pharmacal
Park Rapids, MN. 800-848-5637
Uni First Corp
Wilmington, MA 800-455-7654
US Industrial Lubricants
Cincinnati, OH 800-562-5454
Venturetech Corporation
Knoxville, TN. 800-826-4095
Verax Chemical Co
Snohomish, WA 800-637-7771
Whisk Products Inc
Wentzville, MO 800-204-7627

Powder

Hallberg Manufacturing Corporation
Tampa, FL. .800-633-7627

Vegetable Oil

National Purity LLC
Brooklyn Center, MN 612-672-0022
US Industrial Lubricants
Cincinnati, OH 800-562-5454

Sponges

Acme Sponge & Chamois Co Inc
Tarpon Springs, FL. 727-937-3222
ACS Industries, Inc.
Lincoln, RI 866-783-4838
Armaly Brands
Commerce Twp, MI 800-772-1222
Carlisle Food Svc Products Inc
Oklahoma City, OK 800-654-8210
Distribution Results
Akron, OH. .800-737-9671
Glit Microtron
Bridgetown, MO. 800-325-1051
Labpride Chemicals
Bronx, NY. 800-467-1255
Nation/Ruskin
Montgomeryville, PA 800-523-2489
Quickie Manufacturing Corp
Cinnaminson, NJ. 856-829-7900
Royal Paper Products
Coatesville, PA 800-666-6655
Spontex
Columbia, TN 800-251-4222
Tee-Jay Corporation
Shelton, CT .203-924-4767
Tucel Industries, Inc.
Forestdale, VT 800-558-8235

Sprinkling Systems

American Fire Sprinkler Services, Inc
Hialeah, FL. .305-628-0100
APEC
Lake Odessa, MI. 616-374-1000
Corrigan Corporation of America
Gurnee, IL. .800-462-6478
Doering Co
Clear Lake, MN 320-743-2276
Fire Protection Industries
Bensalem, PA 215-245-1830
Firematic Sprinkler Devices
Shrewsbury, MA. 800-225-7288
Globe Fire Sprinkler Corp
Standish, MI 800-248-0278
Grinnell Fire ProtectionSystems Company
Sauk Rapids, MN 320-253-8665
Muellermist Irrigation Company
Broadview, IL. 708-450-9595
Storm Industrial
Shawnee Mission, KS 800-745-7483
Tyco Fire Protection Products
Lansdale, PA. 800-558-5236
Viking Corp
Hastings, MI 800-968-9501
Wiginton Corp
Sanford, FL .407-585-3200

Squeegees

Carlisle Food Svc Products Inc
Oklahoma City, OK 800-654-8210
Continental Commercial Products
Bridgeton, MO 800-325-1051

Dorden & Co
Detroit, MI 313-834-7910
Ettore
Alameda, CA. 510-748-4130
Harper Brush Works Inc
Fairfield, IA .800-223-7894
Kiefer Brushes, Inc
Franklin, NJ .800-526-2905
Labpride Chemicals
Bronx, NY. 800-467-1255
Lite-Weight Tool & Mfg Co
Sun Valley, CA 800-859-3529
Milwaukee Dustless Brush Co
Delavan, WI .323-724-7777
Perfex Corporation
Poland, NY .800-848-8483
Reit-Price ManufacturingCompany
Union City, IN. 800-521-5343
Superior Products Company
Saint Paul, MN 800-328-9800
Warren E. Conley Corporation
Carmel, IN. .800-367-7875

Sterilizers

A.K. Robins
Baltimore, MD 800-486-9656
Allpax Products
Covington, LA 888-893-9277
American Ultraviolet Co
Lebanon, IN .800-288-9288
API Heat Transfer Inc
Buffalo, NY. .877-274-4328
Atlantic Ultraviolet Corp
Hauppauge, NY 866-958-9085
Burnishine Products
Gurnee, IL 800-818-8275
Cleaver-Brooks Inc
Thomasville, GA. 800-250-5583
Electro-Steam Generator Corp
Rancocas, NJ 866-617-0764
GERM-O-RAY
Stone Mountain, GA 800-966-8480
Hess Machine Intl
Ephrata, PA. 800-735-4377
Littleford Day
Florence, KY. 800-365-8555
Market Forge Industries Inc
Everett, MA. 866-698-3188
Melco Steel Inc
Azusa, CA. .626-334-7875
National Hotpack
Stone Ridge, NY 800-431-8232
San Joaquin Pool Svc & Supply
Stockton, CA. 209-952-0680
Schlueter Company
Janesville, WI. 800-359-1700
Severn Trent Svc
Colmar, PA. 215-822-2901
South Valley Mfg Inc
Gilroy, CA. .408-842-5457
SP Industries Inc
Warminster, PA 800-523-2327
TMI-USA
Reston, VA .703-668-0114
Triad Scientific
Manasquan, NJ 800-867-6690

Tissue

Cleansing

Carhoff Company
Cleveland, OH 216-541-4835
Georgia Pacific
Green Bay, WI. 920-435-8821
Kimberly-Clark Professional
Roswell, GA .800-241-3146
Marcal Paper Mills
Elmwood Park, NJ 800-631-8451
Potlatch Corp
Spokane, WA. 509-835-1500
Productos Familia
Santurce, PR 787-268-5929
SCA Hygiene Paper
San Ramon, CA 800-992-8675
SCA Tissue
Philadelphia, PA 866-722-8675
Sorg Paper Company
Middletown, OH 513-420-5300
SQP
Schenectady, NY 800-724-1129

The Procter & Gamble Company
Cincinnati, OH 800-692-0132
Vermont Tissue Paper Company
North Bennington, VT 802-447-7558

Vaccuum Bags

Cretel Food Equipment
Holland, MI........................616-786-3980

Vacuum Cleaners

Industrial

Beam Industries
Webster City, IA 800-369-2326
Clarke American Sanders
Minneapolis, MN 800-253-0367
DL Enterprises
Etters, PA 717-938-1292
Eureka Company
Bloomington, IL 800-282-2886
Gardner Denver Inc.
Milwaukee, WI
General Floor Craft
Little Silver, NJ...................973-742-7400
Goodway Technologies Corp
Stamford, CT......................800-333-7467
H.L. Diehl Company
South Windham, CT 860-423-7741
Hollowell Products Corporation
Wyandotte, MI 734-282-8200
Hoover Company
Glenwillow, OH 330-499-9499
Mastercraft Industries Inc
Newburgh, NY 800-835-7812
Mercury Floor Machines Inc
Englewood, NJ 888-568-4606
Multivac
Union Grove, WI 800-640-4213
Oreck Manufacturing Co
Cookeville, TN 800-989-3535
ProTeam
Boise, ID 800-541-1456
Spencer Turbine Co
Windsor, CT 800-232-4321
Superior Products Company
Saint Paul, MN 800-328-9800
United Floor Machine Co
Chicago, IL 800-288-0848
Vector Technologies
Milwaukee, WI....................800-832-4010

Washing Machinery

A.K. Robins
Baltimore, MD 800-486-9656
Aaladin Industries Inc
Elk Point, SD 800-356-3325
Adamation
Commerce, CA.....................800-383-8800
Ali Group
Winston Salem, NC................800-532-8591
Alkota Cleaning Systems Inc
Alcester, SD 800-255-6823
Ametek Technical & Industrial Products
Kent, OH..........................215-256-6601
Andgar Corp
Ferndale, WA 360-366-9900
Assembled Products Corp
Rogers, AR 800-548-3373
Atlas Pacific Engineering
Pueblo, CO 719-948-3040
Attias Oven Corp
Brooklyn, NY 800-928-8427
Bar Maid Corp
Pompano Beach, FL 954-960-1468
Bete Fog Nozzle Inc
Greenfield, MA....................800-235-0049
Bethel Engineering & Equipment Inc
New Hampshire, OH...............800-889-6129
BFM Equipment Sales
Fall River, WI.....................920-484-3341
Burns Chemical Systems
Cleveland, OH 724-327-7600
Cam Spray
Iowa Falls, IA 800-648-5011
Cannon Equipment Company
Cannon Falls, MN 800-825-8501
Chad Co Inc
Olathe, KS.........................800-444-8360

Champion Industries Inc
Winston Salem, NC.................800-532-8591
Chemdet Inc
Sebastian, FL 800-645-1510
Cincinnati Industrial Machry
Mason, OH 800-677-0076
Cloud Inc
San Luis Obispo, CA 800-234-5650
Cma Dishmachines
Garden Grove, CA 800-854-6417
Colonial Paper Company
Silver Springs, FL.................352-622-4171
Commercial Dehydrator Systems
Eugene, OR........................800-369-4283
Commercial Manufacturing
Fresno, CA.........................559-237-1855
Component Hardware Group Inc
Lakewood, NJ......................800-526-3694
Continental Equipment Corporation
Milwaukee, WI.....................414-463-0500
Continental Girbau Inc
Oshkosh, WI.......................800-256-1073
Convay Systems
Minnetonka, MN...................800-334-1099
Cugar Machine Co
Fort Worth, TX 817-927-0411
Custom Diamond International
Laval, QC 800-363-5926
Custom Food Machinery
Stockton, CA.......................209-463-4343
D&M Products
Santa Monica, CA 800-245-0485
Damas Corporation
Trenton, NJ 609-695-9121
Davron Technologies Inc
Chattanooga, TN...................423-870-1888
Dirt Killer Pressure Washer
Gwynn Oak, MD...................800-544-1188
Diversified Metal Engineering
Charlottetown, PE.................902-628-6900
Douglas Machines Corp.
Clearwater, FL 800-331-6870
Dynablast Manufacturing
Mississauga, ON...................888-242-8597
FleetwoodGoldcoWyard
Romeoville, IL 630-759-6800
Flo-Matic Corporation
Belvidere, IL 800-959-1179
Gamajet Cleaning Systems
Exton, PA 800-289-5387
Geo. Olcott Company
Scottsboro, AL 800-634-2769
Ghibli North American
Wilmington, DE 302-654-5908
Girton Manufacturing Co
Millville, PA 570-458-5521
Glass Pro
Addison, IL 888-641-8919
Glastender
Saginaw, MI 800-748-0423
Harold F Haines Manufacturing Inc
Presque Isle, ME...................207-762-1411
Hector Delorme & Sons
Farnham, QC......................450-293-5310
Horix Manufacturing Co
Mc Kees Rocks, PA.................412-771-1111
Hoyt Corporation
Westport, MA 508-636-8811
Hughes Co
Columbus, WI.....................866-535-9303
IMC Teddy Food Service Equipment
Amityville, NY.....................800-221-5644
Industrial Washing Machine Corporation
Jackson, NJ 732-304-9203
Kew Cleaning Systems
Clearwater, FL 800-942-1690
Kewanee Washer Corporaton
Findlay, OH.......................419-435-8269
Key Technology Inc.
Walla Walla, WA..................509-529-2161
Knight Equipment International
Lake Forest, CA 800-854-3764
Krones
Franklin, WI.......................800-752-3787
Krowne Metal Corp
Wayne, NJ 800-631-0442
Kuhl Corporation
Flemington, NJ 908-782-5696
Larose & Fils Lte
Laval, QC 877-382-7001
Laundrylux
Inwood, NY.......................800-645-2205

Lechler Inc
St Charles, IL 800-777-2926
Leedal Inc
Northbrook, IL 847-498-0111
Leon C. Osborn Company
Houston, TX.......................281-488-0755
LPS Technology
Grafton, OH 800-586-1410
Ltg Inc
Spartanburg, SC 864-599-6340
Magnuson
Pueblo, CO 719-948-9500
Mart CART-Smt
Rogers, AR 800-548-3373
Matcon Americas
Elmhurst, IL 856-256-1330
Maxi-Vac Inc.
Dundee, IL 855-629-4538
Mcbrady Engineering Co
Rockdale, IL 815-744-8900
Meritech
Golden, CO 800-932-7707
Metal Equipment Company
Cleveland, OH 800-700-6326
Metcraft
Grandview, MO....................800-444-9624
Midbrook Inc
Jackson, MI........................800-966-9274
Moyer Diebel
Winston Salem, NC................336-661-1992
N & A Mfg
Mallard, IA 712-425-3512
Namco Machinery
Maspeth, NY
National Conveyor Corp
Commerce, CA.....................323-725-0355
Paxton Products Inc
Blue Ash, OH 800-441-7475
Pellerin Milnor Corporation
Kenner, LA 800-469-8780
PMI Food Equipment Group
Troy, OH 937-332-3000
Pneumatic Scale Angelus
Cuyahoga Falls, OH 330-923-0491
Puritan/Churchill Chemical Company
Marietta, GA 800-275-8914
Roto-Jet Pump
Salt Lake City, UT 801-359-8731
Sani-Matic
Madison, WI 800-356-3300
Sanitech Inc
Lorton, VA 800-486-4321
Sasib Beverage & Food North America
Plano, TX 800-558-3814
Schlueter Company
Janesville, WI 800-359-1700
Sioux Corp
Beresford, SD 888-763-8833
Sonicor
West Babylon, NY 800-864-5022
Specialty Equipment Company
Mendota Heights, MN 651-452-7909
Spraying Systems Company
Wheaton, IL 630-655-5000
Stero Co
Petaluma, CA 800-762-7600
Superior Food Machinery Inc
Pico Rivera, CA 800-944-0396
Swissh Commercial Equipment
Montreal, QC 888-794-7749
Therma Kleen
Plainfield, IL.......................800-999-3120
Tri-Pak Machinery Inc
Harlingen, TX 956-423-5140
Us Bottlers Machinery Co Inc
Charlotte, NC 704-588-4750
Waring Products
Torrington, CT 800-492-7464
Washing Systems
Loveland, OH 800-272-1974
Zealco Industries
Calvert City, KY 800-759-5531

Waste Handling & Disposal Equipment

Abel Pumps
Sewickley, PA 412-741-3222
Adamation
Commerce, CA.....................800-383-8800

Aeration Industries Intl LLC
Chaska, MN 800-328-8287
Aeromix Systems
Minneapolis, MN 800-879-3677
Ali Group
Winston Salem, NC. 800-532-8591
Alkota Cleaning Systems Inc
Alcester, SD 800-255-6823
Alloy Hardfacing & Engineering
Jordan, MN 800-328-8408
Ameri-Khem
Port Orange, FL 800-224-9950
Ampco Pumps Co Inc
Milwaukee, WI 800-737-8671
Anaheim Manufacturing Company
Anaheim, CA .800-767-6293
Andco Environmental Processes
Amherst, NY. .716-691-2100
Anova
St Louis, MO. .800-231-1327
Apache Stainless Equipment
Beaver Dam, WI 800-444-0398
API Industries
Tulsa, OK 918-664-4010
Armstrong International
Three Rivers, MI. 269-273-1415
Athea Laboratories
Milwaukee, WI 800-743-6417
Bennett Manufacturing Company
Alden, NY 800-345-2142
Betz Entec
Horsham, PA. .800-877-1940
Biothane Corporation
Camden, NJ. 856-541-3500
Blower Application Co Inc
Germantown, WI. 800-959-0880
Brown Fired Heater
Elyria, OH 440-323-3291
C E Rogers Co
Mora, MN 800-279-8081
C S Bell Co
Tiffin, OH 888-958-6381
Can & Bottle Systems, Inc.
Milwaukie, OR 866-302-2636
Cavert Wire Co
Rural Hall, NC 800-245-4042
Chesmont Engineering Co Inc
Exton, PA 610-594-9200
Chicago Trashpacker Corporation
Marengo, IL 800-635-5745
Clean Water Systems
Klamath Falls, OR 866-273-9993
Compactors Inc
Hilton Head Isle, SC 800-423-4003
Consolidated Baling Machine Company
Jacksonville, FL 800-231-9286
Continental Commercial Products
Bridgeton, MO 800-325-1051
Convay Systems
Minnetonka, MN. 800-334-1099
Corenco
Santa Rosa, CA. 888-267-3626
Cornell Pump Company
Portland, OR 503-653-0330
Corp Somat
Lancaster, PA .800-237-6628
Dempster Systems
Toccoa, GA 706-886-2327
Driall Inc
Attica, IN. 765-295-2255
Ertelalsop
Kingston, NY .800-553-7835
Erwyn Products Inc
Morganville, NJ 800-331-9208
Evoqua Water Technologies
Thomasville, GA. 800-841-1550
Fabwright Inc
Garden Grove, CA 800-854-6464
Foremost Machine Builders Inc
Fairfield, NJ 973-227-0700
Frem Corporation
Worcester, MA 508-791-3152
Galbreath LLC
Winamac, IN. .574-946-6631
Garb-El Products Co
Lockport, NY .716-434-6010
General Electric Company
Fairfield, CT 203-373-2211
General, Inc.
Weston, FL 954-202-7419
Glaro Inc
Hauppauge, NY 631-234-1717

Harmony Enterprises
Harmony, MN. 800-658-2320
Himolene
Carrollton, TX. 800-777-4411
Hines III
Jacksonville, FL 904-398-5110
Hodge Manufacturing Company
Springfield, MA 800-262-4634
Hygiene-Technik
Beamsville, ON 905-563-4987
In Sink Erator
Racine, WI 800-558-5700
Incinerator International Inc
Houston, TX 713-227-1466
Incinerator Specialty Company
Houston, TX 713-681-4207
Industronics Service Co
South Windsor, CT 800-878-1551
Insect-O-Cutor Inc
Stone Mountain, GA. 800-966-8480
Insinger Co
Philadelphia, PA 800-344-4802
International Reserve Equipment Corporation
Clarendon Hills, IL 708-531-0680
Intrex
Bethel, CT. 203-792-7400
J C Industries Inc
West Babylon, NY 800-322-1189
J.V. Reed & Company
Louisville, KY .877-258-7333
Joneca Corp
Anaheim, CA .714-993-5997
Jones Environmental
Fullerton, CA .714-449-9937
Jwc Environmental
Costa Mesa, CA 800-331-2277
Kew Cleaning Systems
Clearwater, FL 800-942-1690
Komline-Sanderson Engineering
Peapack, NJ 800-225-5457
Krogh Pump Co
Benicia, CA. 800-225-7644
Lenser Filtration
Lakewood, NJ. 732-370-1600
Lewis Steel Works Inc
Wrens, GA. 800-521-5239
Load King Mfg
Jacksonville, FL 800-531-4975
Lodal Inc
Kingsford, MI .800-435-3500
Logemann Brothers Co
Milwaukee, WI 414-445-3005
Ludell Manufacturing Co
Milwaukee, WI 800-558-0800
Mahoney Environmental
Joliet, IL 800-892-9392
Marathon Equipment Co
Vernon, AL 800-269-7237
Maren Engineering Corp
South Holland, IL 800-875-1038
Mell & Co
Niles, IL 800-262-6355
Metal Industrial Company
Cleveland, OH 800-700-6326
Midbrook Inc
Jackson, MI. 800-966-9274
Miller Manufacturing Co
Turlock, CA 209-632-3846
Multi-Pak
Hackensack, NJ. 201-342-7474
National Conveyor Corp
Commerce, CA 323-725-0355
Netzsch Pumps North America
Exton, PA 610-363-8010
Oil Skimmers Inc
Cleveland, OH 800-200-4603
Old Dominion Wood Products
Lynchburg, VA 800-245-6382
Orwak
Minneapolis, MN 800-747-0449
Our Name is Mud
New York, NY .877-683-7867
Outotec USA Inc
Jessup, MD 301-543-1200
PAC Equipment Company
Garfield, NJ. 973-478-1008
Pack-A-Drum
Satellite Beach, FL 800-694-6163
Paradise Plastics
Brooklyn, NY .718-788-3733
Parallel Products Inc
Louisville, KY .800-883-9100

Parkson Corp
Vernon Hills, IL 847-816-3700
Peter Pepper Products Inc
Compton, CA .310-639-0390
Plymold
Kenyon, MN 800-759-6653
PMI Food Equipment Group
Troy, OH 937-332-3000
PTR Baler & Compactor Co
Philadelphia, PA 800-523-3654
R.G. Stephens Engineering
Long Beach, CA 800-499-3001
Respirometry Plus, LLC
Fond Du Lac, WI 800-328-7518
Reyco Systems Inc
Caldwell, ID 208-795-5700
Robar International Inc
Milwaukee, WI 800-279-7750
Rubbermaid Commercial Products
Pottsville, PA. .800-233-0314
Salvajor Co
Kansas City, MO 800-SAL-AJOR
Schleicher & Company of America
Sanford, NC 800-775-7570
Schloss Engineered Equipment
Aurora, CO 303-695-4500
Scienco Systems
Saint Louis, MO 314-621-2536
Seating Concepts Inc
Rockdale, IL 800-421-2036
Serfilco
Northbrook, IL 800-323-5431
Shepard Brothers Co
La Habra, CA .800-645-3594
SP Industries
Hopkins, MI 800-592-5959
Star Industries
Timmonsville, SC 800-845-5381
Tema Systems Inc
Cincinnati, OH 513-792-2840
Terminix
Flushing, NY. .866-319-6528
Therm-Tec Inc
Sherwood, OR. 800-292-9163
TLB Corporation
Ellicott, MD 410-773-9443
U B KLEM Furniture Co Inc
St Anthony, IN 800-264-1995
Universal Handling Equipment
Hamilton, ON .877-843-1122
US Filter
Palm Desert, CA. 760-340-0098
US Filter Dewatering Systems
Holland, MI 800-245-3006
V-Ram Solids
Albert Lea, MN. 888-373-3996
Vaughan Co Inc
Montesano, WA 888-249-2467
Vescom America
Henderson, NC 252-436-9067
Waste Away Systems
Newark, OH 800-223-4741
Wastequip Inc
Charlotte, NC .704-366-7140
Waterlink/Sanborn Technologies
Canton, OH 800-343-3381
Waymar Industries
Burnsville, MN 888-474-1112
Wayne Engineering
Cedar Falls, IA 319-266-1721
White Mop Wringer Company
Tampa, FL 800-237-7582
WITT Industries Inc
Mason, OH 800-543-7417
Worcester Industrial Products
Worcester, MA 800-533-5711
Zeeco Inc
Broken Arrow, OK 918-258-8551

Wastewater Treatment Systems

Anaerobic & Aerobic

ADI Systems Inc
Fredericton, NB 800-561-2831
AERTEC
North Andover, MA 978-475-6385
Biothane Corporation
Camden, NJ. 856-541-3500
FRC Systems International
Roswell, GA 770-534-3681

GW&E Global Water & Energy
Austin, TX.....................512-697-1930
Hach Co.
Loveland, CO....................800-227-4224
M-Vac Systems Inc
Bluffdale, UT....................801-523-3962
Oakite Products
New Providence, NJ..............800-526-4473
Radiant Industrial Solutions
Houston, TX....................713-972-0196
SPX Flow Inc
Rochester, NY...................585-436-5550
World Water Works
Oklahoma City, OK..............800-607-7973

Wipers

Disposable

Absorbco
Walterboro, SC..................888-335-6439
Akron Cotton Products
Akron, OH.......................800-899-7173
Atlantic Mills
Lakewood, NJ....................800-242-7374

Blue Ridge Converting
Asheville, NC....................800-438-3893
Bro-Tex Inc
St Paul, MN.....................800-328-2282
Casabar
Morristown, NJ..................877-745-8700
CCP Industries, Inc.
Cleveland, OH...................800-321-2840
Coast Scientific
Rancho Santa Fe, CA.............800-445-1544
De Royal Textiles
Camden, SC.....................800-845-1062
DPC
Norristown, PA..................800-220-9473
Georgia Pacific
Green Bay, WI...................920-435-8821
Goodman Wiper & Paper Co
Auburn, ME.....................207-784-5779
ITW Dymon
Olathe, KS......................800-443-9536
Johnson International Materials
Brownsville, TX..................956-541-6364
Lexidyne of Pennsylvania
Pittsburgh, PA...................800-543-2233
Mainline Industries Inc
Springfield, MA..................800-527-7917

Mednik Wiping Materials Co
St Louis, MO....................800-325-7193
Mill Wiping Rags Inc
Bronx, NY......................718-994-7100
Nosaj Disposables
Paterson, NJ....................800-631-3809
Nu-Towel Co
Kansas City, MO.................800-800-7247
Packaging Distribution Svc
Des Moines, IA..................515-243-3156
Rockline Industries
Sheboygan, WI..................800-558-7790
SCA Hygiene Paper
San Ramon, CA..................800-992-8675
Textile Products Company
Anaheim, CA....................714-761-0401
United Textile Distribution
Garner, NC.....................800-262-7624
Wipeco Inc
Hillside, IL.....................708-544-7247

Transportation & Storage

Automated Guided Vehicles

John Bean Technologies Corp
Chalfont, PA 888-362-3622

Beer Keg Movers

Powered

Ultra Lift Corp
San Jose, CA 800-346-3057

Box Cutters

Charles Beck Machine Corporation
King of Prussia, PA 610-265-0500
Garvey Products
West Chester, OH 800-543-1908
Handy Roll Company
San Marcos, CA 760-471-6214
Listo Pencil Corp
Alameda, CA 800-547-8648
Safe-T-Cut Inc
Monson, MA 413-267-9984

Carts

Hand

Alliance Products LLC
Murfreesboro, TN 800-522-3973
Amco Metals Indl
City of Industry, CA 626-855-2550
ARC Specialties
Valencia, CA 661-775-8500
Art Wire Works Co
Chicago, IL 708-458-3993
Atlas Equipment Company
Kansas City, MO 800-842-9188
Baking Machines
Livermore, CA 925-449-3369
Barrette Outdoor Living
Cleveland, OH 800-336-2383
Bennett Manufacturing Company
Alden, NY 800-345-2142
Bessco Tube Bending & Pipe Fabricating
Thornton, IL 800-337-3977
Bmh Equipment Inc
Sacramento, CA 800-350-8828
Burgess Enterprises, Inc
Renton, WA 800-927-3286
C Nelson Mfg Co
Oak Harbor, OH 800-922-7339
C R Daniels Inc
Ellicott City, MD 800-933-2638
Caddy Corporation of America
Bridgeport, NJ 856-467-4222
California Caster & Handtruck
San Francisco, CA 800-950-8750
Cambro Manufacturing Co
Huntington Beach, CA 800-833-3003
Cannon Equipment Company
Cannon Falls, MN 800-825-8501
Carlisle Food Svc Products Inc
Oklahoma City, OK 800-654-8210
Clark Caster Company
Cave in Rock, IL 800-538-0765
Conveyance Technologies LLC
Cleveland, OH 800-701-2278
Corsair Display Systems
Canandalgua, NY 800-347-5245
Custom Diamond Intl.
Laval, QC 800-326-5926
Decoren Equipment
Willowbrook, IL 708-789-3367
Dubuque Steel Products Co
Dubuque, IA 563-556-6288
Dutro Co
Logan, UT 866-388-7660
EPCO
Murfreesboro, TN 800-251-3398
Equipment Design & Fabrication
Charlotte, NC 800-949-0165
Exel
Lincolnton, NC 704-735-6535

Fabricated Components Inc
Stroudsburg, PA 800-233-8163
Fetco
Lake Zurich, IL 800-338-2699
Forbes Industries
Ontario, CA 909-923-4549
Galbreath LLC
Winamac, IN 574-946-6631
Galley
Jupiter, FL 800-537-2772
Gillis Associated Industries
Prospect Heights, IL 847-541-6500
Glowmaster Corporation
Clifton, NJ 800-272-7008
Hodges
Vienna, IL 800-444-0011
Houston Wire Works, Inc.
South Houston, TX 800-468-9477
Item Products
Houston, TX 800-333-4932
Jesco Industries
Litchfield, MI 800-455-0019
KEMCO
Wareham, MA 800-231-5955
Key Material Handling Inc
Simi Valley, CA 800-539-7225
Lakeside Manufacturing Inc
Milwaukee, WI 888-558-8565
Lambertson Industries Inc
Sparks, NV 800-548-3324
Leggett & Platt Storage
Vernon Hills, IL 847-816-6246
Line-Master Products
Cocolalla, ID 208-265-4743
Linett Company
Blawnox, PA 800-565-2165
Load King Mfg
Jacksonville, FL 800-531-4975
M & E Mfg Co Inc
Kingston, NY 845-331-2110
Metal Equipment Company
Cleveland, OH 800-700-6326
Metal Master Sales Corp
Glendale Heights, IL 800-488-8729
Metro Corporation
Wilkes Barre, PA 800-992-1776
Mid-States Mfg & Engr Co Inc
Milton, IA 800-346-1792
Midwest Aircraft Products Co
Lexington, OH 419-884-2164
Miller Metal Fabrication
Bridgeville, DE 302-337-2291
MIT Poly-Cart Corp
New York, NY 800-234-7659
Moseley Realty LLC
Franklin, MA 800-667-3539
Mosshaim Innovations
Jacksonville, FL 888-995-7775
New Age Industrial
Norton, KS 800-255-0104
Newell Brands
Atlanta, GA
Nexel Industries Inc
Port Washington, NY 800-245-6682
Normandie Metal Fabricators
Port Washington, NY 800-221-2398
Norris Products Corp   oration
Cincinnati, OH 877-543-2278
Nu-Star Inc
Shakopee, MN 800-800-9274
Omicron Steel Products Company
Jamaica, NY 718-805-3400
Ortmayer Materials Handling
Brooklyn, NY 718-875-7995
Palmer Snyder
Brookfield, WI 800-762-0415
Piper Products Inc
Wausau, WI 800-544-3057
Polar Beer Systems
Sun City, CA 951-928-8174
Princeton Shelving
Cedar Rapids, IA 319-369-0355
Pucel Enterprises Inc
Cleveland, OH 800-336-4986
Reelcraft Industries Inc
Columbia City, IN 800-444-3134

Royce Rolls Ringer Co
Grand Rapids, MI 800-253-9638
Schlueter Company
Janesville, WI 800-359-1700
Shammi Industries
Corona, CA 800-417-9260
Sharpsville Container Corp
Sharpsville, PA 800-645-1248
Shouldice Brothers SheetMetal
Battle Creek, MI 269-962-5579
Solve Needs International
White Lake, MI 800-783-2462
Super Sturdy
Weldon, NC 800-253-4833
Superior Products Company
Saint Paul, MN 800-328-9800
Technibilt/Cari-All
Newton, NC 800-233-3972
Travelon
Elk Grove Vlg, IL 800-537-5544
Traycon Manufacturing Co
Carlstadt, NJ 201-939-5555
Tri-Boro Shelving & Partition
Farmville, VA 800-633-3070
Westfield Sheet Metal Works
Kenilworth, NJ 908-276-5500
White Mop Wringer Company
Tampa, FL 800-237-7582
Wilder Manufacturing Company
Port Jervis, NY 800-832-1319

Utility

Amco Metals Indl
City of Industry, CA 626-855-2550
Antrim Manufacturing Inc
Brookfield, WI 262-781-6860
ARC Specialties
Valencia, CA 661-775-8500
Bmh Equipment Inc
Sacramento, CA 800-350-8828
Caddy Corporation of America
Bridgeport, NJ 856-467-4222
Cannon Equipment Company
Cannon Falls, MN 800-825-8501
Continental Commercial Products
Bridgeton, MO 800-325-1051
Duke Manufacturing Co
St Louis, MO 800-735-3853
Food Warming Equipment Co
Crystal Lake, IL 800-222-4393
Galley
Jupiter, FL 800-537-2772
Hodge Manufacturing Company
Springfield, MA 800-262-4634
Hot Food Boxes
Mooresville, IN 800-733-8073
InterMetro Industries
Wilkes-Barre, PA 570-825-2741
Lakeside Manufacturing Inc
Milwaukee, WI 888-558-8565
Leggett & Platt Storage
Vernon Hills, IL 847-816-6246
Linett Company
Blawnox, PA 800-565-2165
Princeton Shelving
Cedar Rapids, IA 319-369-0355
Technibilt/Cari-All
Newton, NC 800-233-3972

Casters

Albion Industries Inc
Albion, MI 800-835-8911
Atlas Equipment Company
Kansas City, MO 800-842-9188
Beacon Specialties
New York, NY 800-221-9405
Berlon Industries
Hustisford, WI 800-899-3580
Bmh Equipment Inc
Sacramento, CA 800-350-8828
California Caster & Handtruck
San Francisco, CA 800-950-8750
Clark Caster Company
Cave in Rock, IL 800-538-0765

Colson Caster Corp
Jonesboro, AR.............................800-643-5515
Component Hardware Group Inc
Lakewood, NJ...........................800-526-3694
Darcor Casters
Toronto, ON............................800-387-7206
Faultless Caster
Evansville, IN..........................800-322-7359
FFR Merchandising Inc
Twinsburg, OH..........................800-422-2547
Hamilton Caster
Hamilton, OH...........................888-699-7164
Jarvis Caster Company
Jackson, TN............................800-995-9876
Jilson Group
Lodi, NJ................................800-969-5400
Lakeside Manufacturing Inc
Milwaukee, WI.........................888-558-8565
LPI Imports
Chicago, IL............................877-389-6563
Metro Corporation
Wilkes Barre, PA.......................800-992-1776
Mid-State Metal Casting & Mfg
Fresno, CA.............................559-445-1974
Monarch-McLaren
Weston, ON............................416-741-9675
PAR-Kan
Silver Lake, IN.........................800-291-5487
Roll Rite Corp
Hayward, CA...........................800-345-9305
Solve Needs International
White Lake, MI.........................800-783-2462
Standex International Corp.
Salem, NH.............................603-893-9701
Tente Casters Inc
Hebron, KY............................800-783-2470

Clutches & Brakes

Industrial

Warner Electric Inc
South Beloit, IL........................800-234-3369

Cordage, Rope & Twine

A&A Line & Wire Corporation
Flushing, NY...........................800-886-2657
Barbour Threads
Anniston, AL...........................256-237-9461
Caristrap International
Laval, QC..............................800-361-9466
Consolidated Thread Mills, Inc.
Fall River, MA.........................508-672-0032
Crown Industries
East Orange, NJ........................877-747-2457
Fitec International Inc
Memphis, TN...........................800-332-6387
Fulton-Denver Co
Denver, CO............................800-521-1414
James Thompson
New York, NY..........................212-686-5306
January & Wood Company
Maysville, KY..........................606-564-3301
John E. Ruggles & Company
New Bedford, MA.......................508-992-9766
Pensacola Rope Company
Slidell, LA..............................850-968-9760
Rose City Awning Co
Portland, OR...........................800-446-4104
Terkelsen Machine Company
Hyannis, MA...........................508-775-6229
US Line Company
Westfield, MA..........................413-562-3629
Woodstock Line Co
Putnam, CT............................860-928-6557

Drums

Acra Electric Corporation
Tulsa, OK..............................800-223-4328
Bergen Barrel & Drum Company
Kearny, NJ.............................201-998-3500
Centennial Moldings
Hastings, NE...........................888-883-2189
Containair Packaging Corporation
Paterson, NJ...........................888-276-6500
Dubuque Steel Products Co
Dubuque, IA...........................563-556-6288
Greenfield Packaging
White Plains, NY.......................914-993-0233

Greif Inc
Delaware, OH..........................740-549-6000
Independent Stave Co
Lebanon, MO..........................417-588-4151
Jupiter Mills Corporation
Roslyn, NY.............................800-853-5121
Lima Barrel & Drum Company
Lima, OH..............................419-224-8916
M O Industries Inc
Whippany, NJ..........................973-386-9228
Munson Machinery Co
Utica, NY..............................800-944-6644
Myers Container
Hayward, CA...........................510-785-8235
Process Solutions
Riviera Beach, FL......................561-840-0050
Pucel Enterprises Inc
Cleveland, OH..........................800-336-4986
Remcon Plastics Inc
Reading, PA............................800-360-3636
RMI-C/Rotonics Manaufacturing
Bensenville, IL.........................630-773-9510
Sharpsville Container Corp
Sharpsville, PA.........................800-645-1248
Sirco Systems
Birmingham, AL........................205-731-7800
Trilla Steel Drum Corporation
Chicago, IL.............................773-847-7588

Food Storage Supplies

Abel Manufacturing Co
Appleton, WI...........................920-734-4443
Accent Store Fixtures
Kenosha, WI...........................800-545-1144
Acrison Inc
Moonachie, NJ.........................800-422-4266
Advance Energy Technologies
Halfmoon, NY..........................800-724-0198
Aero Tec Laboratories/ATL
Ramsey, NJ............................800-526-5330
AFGO Mechanical Svc Inc
Astoria, NY............................800-438-2346
Alliance Products LLC
Murfreesboro, TN......................800-522-3973
Allied Engineering
North Vancouver, BC...................877-929-1214
Althor Products
Bethel, CT.............................800-688-2693
Amco Metals Indl
City of Industry, CA....................626-855-2550
Anderson-Crane Company
Minneapolis, MN.......................800-314-2747
Apache Stainless Equipment
Beaver Dam, WI........................800-444-0398
ARC Specialties
Valencia, CA...........................661-775-8500
Avalon Manufacturer
Corona, CA............................800-676-3040
Barker Company
Keosauqua, IA.........................319-293-3777
Barker Wire
Keosauqua, IA.........................319-293-3176
Bennett Manufacturing Company
Alden, NY..............................800-345-2142
Bergen Barrel & Drum Company
Kearny, NJ.............................201-998-3500
Bertels Can Company
Belcamp, MD...........................410-272-0090
Bowers Process Equipment
Stratford, ON...........................800-567-3223
Brenner Tank LLC
Fond Du Lac, WI.......................800-558-9750
Brisker Dry Food Crisper
Oldsmar, FL............................800-356-9080
Buckhorn Canada
Brampton, ON..........................800-461-7579
Buckhorn Inc
Milford, OH............................800-543-4454
Bulk Pack
Monroe, LA............................800-498-4215
C Nelson Mfg Co
Oak Harbor, OH........................800-922-7339
Cal-Mil Plastic Products Inc
Oceanside, CA..........................800-321-9069
Cambro Manufacturing Co
Huntington Beach, CA..................800-833-3003
Cardinal Packaging
Evansville, IN...........................800-343-1295
Carlisle Food Svc Products Inc
Oklahoma City, OK.....................800-654-8210

Carter-Hoffmann LLC
Mundelein, IL..........................800-323-9793
Ccw Products
Arvada, CO............................303-427-9663
Central Fabricators Inc
Cincinnati, OH.........................800-909-8265
Chem-Tainer Industries Inc
West Babylon, NY......................800-275-2436
Chem-Tainer Industries Inc
West Babylon, NY......................800-938-8896
Clayton & Lambert Manufacturing
Buckner, KY............................800-626-5819
Columbian TecTank
Parsons, KS............................800-421-2788
Commercial Kitchen Co
Los Angeles, CA........................323-732-2291
Containair Packaging Corporation
Paterson, NJ...........................888-276-6500
Containment Technology
St Gabriel, LA..........................800-388-2467
Continental Commercial Products
Bridgeton, MO.........................800-325-1051
Continental-Fremont
Tiffin, OH..............................419-448-4045
Conwed Global Netting Sltns
Roanoke, VA...........................800-368-3610
Cozzini Inc
Algona, IA.............................888-295-1116
Cramer Products
New York, NY..........................212-645-2368
Cres Cor
Mentor, OH............................877-273-7267
Crown Custom Metal Spinning
Concord, ON...........................800-750-1924
Cruvinet Winebar Co LLC
Sparks, NV.............................800-278-8463
Culinary Depot
Monsey, NY............................888-845-8200
Custom Diamond Intl.
Laval, QC..............................800-326-5926
Custom Metal Crafts
Springfield, MO........................417-862-9324
Custom Systems Integration Co
Carlsbad, CA...........................760-635-1099
Den Mar Corp
North Dartmouth, MA..................508-999-3295
Denstor Mobile Storage Systems
Walker, MI.............................800-234-7477
Design Plastics Inc
Omaha, NE............................800-491-0786
Despro Manufacturing
Cedar Grove, NJ.......................800-292-9906
Dubuque Steel Products Co
Dubuque, IA...........................563-556-6288
Duke Manufacturing Co
St Louis, MO...........................800-735-3853
E-Z Shelving Systems Inc
Shawnee, KS...........................800-353-1331
Easyup Storage Systems
Tukwila, WA...........................800-426-9234
Eaton Sales & Service
Denver, CO............................800-208-2657
Edwards Fiberglass
Sedalia, MO............................660-826-3915
Eldorado Miranda Manufacturing Company
Largo, FL...............................800-330-0708
Electrol Specialties Co
South Beloit, IL........................815-389-2291
Eliason Corp
Portage, MI............................800-828-3655
Ellett Industries
Port Coquitlam, BC.....................604-941-8211
Enerfab Inc.
Cincinnati, OH.........................513-641-0500
Engineered Products Corp
Greenville, SC..........................800-868-0145
EPCO
Murfreesboro, TN......................800-251-3398
Epic Products
Santa Ana, CA.........................800-548-9791
ES Robbins Corp
Muscle Shoals, AL......................800-633-3325
Fab-X/Metals
Washington, NC........................800-677-3229
Fabricated Components Inc
Stroudsburg, PA........................800-233-8163
Faribault Manufacturing Co
Faribault, MN..........................800-447-6043
Fato Industries
Kankakee, IL...........................815-932-3015
Faubion Central States Tank Company
Shawnee Mission, KS...................800-450-8265

271

Federal Industries
Belleville, WI 800-356-4206
First Plastics Co Inc
Leominster, MA 978-840-6908
Flexible Material Handling
Suwanee, GA 800-669-1501
Flow of Solids
Westford, MA 978-392-0300
Forbes Industries
Ontario, CA. 909-923-4549
FreesTech
Sinking Spring, PA 717-560-7560
G.F. Frank & Sons
Fairfield, OH. 513-870-9075
Gates Manufacturing Company
Saint Louis, MO 800-237-9226
General Industries Inc
Goldsboro, NC 888-735-2882
Gillis Associated Industries
Prospect Heights, IL 847-541-6500
Grayline Housewares Inc
Columbus, OH 800-222-7388
H S Inc
Oklahoma City, OK 800-238-1240
Hall-Woolford Wood Tank Co Inc
Philadelphia, PA 215-329-9022
Harmar
Sarasota, FL 800-833-0478
Hedstrom Corporation
Ashland, OH 700-765-9665
Hewitt Manufacturing Co
Waldron, IN. 765-525-9829
Hodges
Vienna, IL 800-444-0011
Hoover Materials Handling Group
Houston, TX 800-844-8683
Houston Wire Works, Inc.
South Houston, TX 800-468-9477
Howard Fabrication
City of Industry, CA 626-961-0114
Hughes Co
Columbus, WI. 866-535-9303
IMC Teddy Food Service Equipment
Amityville, NY 800-221-5644
Industrial Air Conditioning Systems
Chicago, IL 773-486-4236
International Machinery Xchnge
Deerfield, WI 800-279-0191
IPL Plastics
Edmundston, NB. 800-739-9595
Irby
Rocky Mount, NC. 252-442-0154
Item Products
Houston, TX 800-333-4932
J.H. Carr & Sons
Seattle, WA 800-523-8842
Jack Stack
Inwood, NY. 800-999-9840
Jenike & Johanson Inc
Tyngsboro, MA 978-649-3300
Jesco Industries
Litchfield, MI 800-455-0019
JH Display & Fixture
Greenwood, IN 317-888-0631
K & I Creative Plastics & Wood
Jacksonville, FL 904-387-0438
Kason
Lewis Center, OH 740-549-2100
Kedco Wine Storage Systems
Farmingdale, NY 800-654-9988
KHM Plastics Inc
Gurnee, IL 847-249-4910
Kisco Manufacturing
Port Alberni, BC. 604-823-7456
Kold-Hold
Edgefield, SC 803-637-3166
LA Rosa Refrigeration & Equip
Detroit, MI 800-527-6723
Lakeside Manufacturing Inc
Milwaukee, WI. 888-558-8565
Langer Manufacturing Company
Cedar Rapids, IA. 800-728-6445
Langsenkamp Manufacturing
Indianapolis, IN 877-585-1950
Leggett & Platt Storage
Vernon Hills, IL 847-816-6246
Liberty Machine Company
York, PA 800-745-8152
Lodi Metal Tech
Lodi, CA 800-359-5999
Loyal Manufacturing
Indianapolis, IN 317-359-3185

LPI Imports
Chicago, IL 877-389-6563
Luce Corp
Hamden, CT 800-344-6966
Lyon LLC
Montgomery, IL 630-892-8941
M & E Mfg Co Inc
Kingston, NY. 845-331-2110
Machine Ice Co
Houston, TX 800-423-8822
Madsen Wire Products Inc
Orland, IN. 260-829-6561
Marineland Commercial Aquariums
Blacksburg, VA. 800-322-1266
Material Storage Systems
Gadsden, AL 877-543-2467
McMillin Manufacturing Corporation
Los Angeles, CA. 323-268-1900
Melville Plastics
Haw River, NC 336-578-5800
Metal Equipment Company
Cleveland, OH 800-700-6326
Metal Master Sales Corp
Glendale Heights, IL. 800-488-8729
Metaline Products Co Inc
South Amboy, NJ 732-721-1373
Metro Corporation
Wilkes Barre, PA. 800-992-1776
Meyer Machine & Garroutte Products
San Antonio, TX 210-736-1811
Michiana Box & Crate
Niles, MI 800-677-6372
Midwest Aircraft Products Co
Lexington, MI 419-884-2164
Miller Metal Fabrication
Bridgeville, DE. 302-337-2291
MultiFab Plastics
Boston, MA. 888-293-5754
Myers Container
Hayward, CA 510-785-8235
Nalge Process Technologies Group
Rochester, NY. 585-586-8800
Nelipak
Phoenix, AZ 602-269-7648
New Age Industrial
Norton, KS 800-255-0104
Newell Brands
Atlanta, GA
Nexel Industries Inc
Port Washington, NY 800-245-6682
Normandie Metal Fabricators
Port Washington, NY 800-221-2398
NST Metals
Louisville, KY 502-584-5846
Oak Barrel Winecraft
Berkeley, CA. 510-849-0400
Omega Industries
St Louis, MO. 314-961-1668
Omicron Steel Products Company
Jamaica, NY 718-805-3400
Overhead Conveyor Co
Ferndale, MI 800-396-2554
Pallet One Inc
Bartow, FL. 800-771-1148
Paltier
Michigan City, IN 800-348-3201
Paul Mueller Co Inc
Springfield, MO 800-683-5537
PBC
Mahwah, NJ 800-514-2739
Peterboro Basket Co
Peterborough, NH 603-924-3861
Peterson Manufacturing Company
Plainfield, IL. 800-547-8995
Piper Products Inc
Wausau, WI. 800-544-3057
Plastic Supply Inc
Londonderry, NH 800-752-7759
Plastilite Corporation
Omaha, NE 800-228-9506
Plastocon
Oconomowoc, WI. 800-966-0103
Polar Ware Company
Sheboygan, WI. 800-237-3655
Precision
Miami, FL 800-762-7565
Process Solutions
Riviera Beach, FL 561-840-0050
Prolon
Port Gibson, MS 888-480-9828
Pruitt's Packaging Services
Grand Rapids, MI 800-878-0553

QBD Modular Systems
Santa Clara, CA 800-663-3005
RAS Process Equipment Inc
Trenton, NJ 609-371-1220
Ridg-U-Rak
North East, PA. 866-479-7225
Rose City Awning Co
Portland, OR 800-446-4104
Royal Display Corporation
Middletown, CT 800-569-1295
Royce Corp
Glendale, AZ. 602-256-0006
S.S.I. Schaefer System International Limited
Brampton, ON. 905-458-5399
Saeplast Canada
St John, NB 800-567-3966
Scheb International
North Barrington, IL. 847-381-2573
Scherping Systems
Winsted, MN. 320-485-4401
Schiefer Packaging Corporation
Syracuse, NY. 315-422-0615
Schlueter Company
Janesville, WI. 800-359-1700
Seattle Plastics
Seattle, WA 800-441-0679
Sefi Fabricators Inc
Amityville, NY 631-842-2200
Shammi Industries
Corona, CA 800-417-9260
Shelley Cabinet Company
Shelley, ID. 208-357-3700
Silver King Refrigeration Inc
Minneapolis, MN 800-328-3329
Sims Machinery Co Inc
Lanett, AL. 334-576-2101
Southern Ag Co Inc
Blakely, GA. 229-723-4262
Spartan Showcase
Union, MO 800-325-0775
Specific Mechanical Systems
Victoria, BC. 250-652-2111
SPG International
Covington, GA 877-503-4774
SSW Holding Co Inc
Elizabethtown, KY 270-769-5526
St. Louis Stainless Service
St Louis, MO. 800-735-3853
Stainless Steel Fabricators
Tyler, TX. 903-595-6625
Stearnswood Inc
Hutchinson, MN 800-657-0144
Steel City Corporation
Youngstown, OH. 800-321-0350
Steelmaster Material Handling
Marietta, GA 800-875-9900
Stock America Inc
Grafton, WI. 262-375-4100
Storage Unlimited
Nixa, MO 800-478-6642
Stryco Wire Products
North York, ON. 416-663-7000
Super Sturdy
Weldon, NC. 800-253-4833
Superior Products Company
Saint Paul, MN 800-328-9800
Supreme Metal
Alpharetta, GA 800-645-2526
Tag-Trade Associated Group
Chicago, IL 800-621-8350
Teilhaber Manufacturing Corp
Broomfield, CO 800-358-7225
Tennsco Corp
Dickson, TN 800-251-8184
Thermal Bags By Ingrid Inc
Gilberts, IL 800-622-5560
Tosca Ltd
Green Bay, WI. 920-617-4000
Traex
Dane, WI. 800-356-8006
Triple-A Manufacturing Company
Toronto, ON 800-786-2238
Tupperware Brands Corporation
Orlando, FL. 800-366-3800
United States Systems Inc
Kansas City, KS 888-281-2454
Universal Stainless
Aurora, CO 800-223-8332
Universal Stainless & Alloy
Titusville, PA 800-295-1909
Upham & Walsh Lumber
Hoffman Estates, IL 847-519-1010

Valad Electric Heating Corporation
Tarrytown, NY 914-631-4927
Vermillion Flooring
Springfield, MO 417-862-3785
Viatec
Victoria, BC 800-942-4702
Vollrath Co LLC
Sheboygan, WI 800-624-2051
Wag Industries
Skokie, IL 800-621-3305
Walker Stainless Equipment Co
New Lisbon, WI 608-562-7500
Weiss Sheet Metal Inc
Avon, MA 508-583-8300
Welbilt Corporation
Stamford, CT 203-325-8300
Welbilt Inc.
New Port Richey, FL 877-375-9300
Westfield Sheet Metal Works
Kenilworth, NJ 908-276-5500
Wilder Manufacturing Company
Port Jervis, NY 800-832-1319
Wine Chillers of California
Santa Ana, CA 800-331-4274
Wire Products Mfg
Merrill, WI 715-536-7884
Woerner Wire Works
Omaha, NE 402-451-5414
WR Key
Scarborough, ON 416-291-6246
Yorkraft
York, PA 800-872-2044
Zero Manufacturing Inc
North Salt Lake, UT 800-959-5050

Hoists & Lifting Equipment

A C Horn & Co Sheet Metal
Dallas, TX 800-657-6155
A-Z Factory Supply
Schiller Park, IL 800-323-4511
Abell-Howe Crane
Amherst, NY 800-888-0985
Ace Engineering Company
Fort Worth, TX 800-431-4223
Advance Lifts Inc
St Charles, IL 800-843-3625
Air Technical Industries
Mentor, OH 888-857-6265
Airfloat LLC
Decatur, IL 800-888-0018
American Crane & Equip Corp
Douglassville, PA 610-385-6061
American Lifts
Guthrie, OK 877-360-6777
American Solving Inc.
Brook Park, OH 800-822-2285
AMF CANADA
Sherbrooke, QC 800-255-3869
Anchor Crane & Hoist Service Company
Houston, TX 800-835-2223
Anderson Crane Company
Minneapolis, MN 800-314-2747
ANVER Corporation
Hudson, MA 800-654-3500
Anver Corporation
Hudson, MA 800-654-3500
Apache Stainless Equipment
Beaver Dam, WI 800-444-0398
Atlas Equipment Company
Kansas City, MO 800-842-9188
Autoquip Corp
Guthrie, OK 877-360-6777
Baking Machines
Livermore, CA 925-449-3369
Ballymore Company
West Chester, PA 610-696-3250
Basiloid Products Corp
Elnora, IN 866-692-5511
Benko Products
Sheffield Vlg, OH 440-934-2180
BEVCO
Canada, BC 800-663-0090
Bishamon Industry Corp
Ontario, CA. 800-358-8833
Bmh Equipment Inc
Sacramento, CA 800-350-8828
Bolzoni Auramo
Homewood, IL 800-358-5438
Bradley Lifting
York, PA 717-848-3121

Buffalo Technologies Corporation
Buffalo, NY. 800-332-2419
Burns Industries
Line Lexington, PA. 800-223-6430
Bushman Equipment Inc
Menomonee Falls, WI. 800-338-7810
C.J. Machine
Fridley, MN. 763-767-4630
Caldwell Group
Rockford, IL 800-628-4263
Century Crane & Hoist
Dravosburg, PA. 888-601-8801
Chester Hoist
Lisbon, OH 800-424-7248
Cleasby Manufacturing Co
San Francisco, CA 800-253-2729
Columbus McKinnon Corporation
Getzville, NY 800-888-0985
Commercial Manufacturing
Fresno, CA 559-237-1855
Conveyance Technologies LLC
Cleveland, OH 800-701-2278
Conveyor Components Co
Croswell, MI 800-552-3337
Corn States Metal Fabricators
West Des Moines, IA 515-225-7961
Crown Equipment Corp.
New Bremen, OH 419-629-2311
Currie Machinery Co
Santa Clara, CA 408-727-0422
Custom Conveyor & Supply Corp.
Racine, WI. 262-634-4920
Custom Metal Design Inc
Oakland, FL 800-334-1777
Delta Machine & Maufacturing
St Rose, LA. 504-949-8304
Demag Cranes & Components Corp
Cleveland, OH 440-248-2400
Deshazo Crane Company
Alabaster, AL 205-664-2006
Downs Crane & Hoist Co Inc
Los Angeles, CA. 800-748-5994
Duplex Mill & Mfg Co
Springfield, OH. 937-325-5555
Electro Lift Inc
Clifton, NJ 973-471-0204
En-Hanced Products Inc
Westerville, OH. 800-783-7400
Equipment Outlet
Meridian, ID 208-887-1472
Frazier & Son
Conroe, TX 800-365-5438
GEM Equipment of Oregon Inc
Woodburn, OR 503-982-9902
Gorbel Inc
Victor, NY. 585-924-6262
Gough-Econ Inc
Charlotte, NC 800-204-6844
Grain Machinery Mfg Corp
Miami, FL. 305-620-2525
Harrington Hoists Inc
Manheim, PA 800-233-3010
Hayes & Stolz Indl Mfg LTD
Fort Worth, TX 800-725-7272
Howes S Co Inc
Silver Creek, NY. 888-255-2611
Industrial Hoist Service
Angleton, TX 800-766-7077
Innovation Moving Systems
Oostburg, WI. 800-619-0625
Joyce Dayton Corp
Moraine, OH 800-523-5204
Keenline Conveyor Systems
Omro, WI. 920-685-0365
Key Material Handling Inc
Simi Valley, CA. 800-539-7225
Knight Ind
Auburn Hills, MI 248-377-4950
Komatsu Forklift USA
Rolling Meadows, IL 847-437-5800
KWS Manufacturing Co LTD
Burleson, TX. 800-543-6558
Landoo Corporation
Horsham, PA 785-562-5381
Lift Rite
Mississauga, ON 905-456-2603
Liftomatic Material Handling
Buffalo Grove, IL 800-837-6540
Matot - Commercial GradeLift Solutions
Bellwood, IL. 800-369-1070
Meyer Machine & Garroutte Products
San Antonio, TX. 210-736-1811

NACCO Industries Inc.
Cleveland, OH 440-229-5151
O'Brien Installations
Ontario, CA. 905-336-8245
OTP Industrial Solutions
Terre Haute, IN 860-953-7632
Pa R Systems Inc
St Paul, MN. 800-464-1320
Parkson Corp
Fort Lauderdale, FL 908-464-0700
Pucel Enterprises Inc
Cleveland, OH 800-336-4986
Quality Corporation
Denver, CO 800-383-3018
R.G. Stephens Engineering
Long Beach, CA 800-499-3001
Ratcliff Hoist Company
San Carlos, CA 650-595-3840
Raymond Corp
Greene, NY 800-235-7200
Remstar International
Westbrook, ME 800-639-5805
Richards Industries Systems
West Caldwell, NJ. 973-575-7480
Sackett Systems
Bensenville, IL 800-323-8332
Saturn Overhead Equipment
Somerset, NJ 800-631-4473
Screw Conveyor Corp
Hammond, IN 219-931-1450
Shepard Niles Parts
Montour Falls, NY 800-727-8774
Sidney Manufacturing Co
Sidney, OH 800-482-3535
SIT Indeva Inc
Charlotte, NC 704-357-8811
Smetco
Aurora, OR 800-253-5400
Solve Needs International
White Lake, MI 800-783-2462
Southern Ag Co Inc
Blakely, GA 229-723-4262
Southworth Products Corp
Falmouth, ME 800-743-1000
Spanco Crane & Monorail Systems
Morgantown, PA 800-869-2080
Sperling Industries
Omaha, NE 800-647-5062
Stertil Alm Corp
Streator, IL 800-544-5438
TC/American Monorail
Saint Michael, MN 763-497-7000
Theimeg
Sharpsville, PA 724-962-3571
Toter Inc
Statesville, NC 800-772-0071
Unidex
Warsaw, NY 800-724-1302
Unimove LLC
Palmerton, PA 610-826-7855
UniTrak Corporation
Port Hope, ON 866-883-5749
Valley Craft Inc
Lake City, MN 800-328-1480
Vertical Systems Intl
Lakeside Park, KY 859-485-9650
Ward Ironworks
Welland, ON 888-441-9273
Wastequip Inc
Charlotte, NC 704-366-7140
Weigh Right Automatic Scale Co
Joliet, IL 800-571-0249
Whit-Log Trailers Inc
Wilbur, OR 800-452-1234
Yargus Manufacturing Inc
Marshall, IL 217-826-8059
Zenar Corp
Oak Creek, WI 414-764-1800
Zimmerman Handling Systems
Madison Heights, MI 800-347-7047

Material Handling & Distribution Equipment

A C Horn & Co Sheet Metal
Dallas, TX. 800-657-6155
A T Ferrell Co Inc
Bluffton, IN. 800-248-8318
A-Z Factory Supply
Schiller Park, IL 800-323-4511

273

A.K. Robins
  Baltimore, MD 800-486-9656
A.M. Loveman Lumber & Box Company
  Nashville, TN 615-297-1397
AAMD
  Liverpool, NY 800-887-4167
Abel Manufacturing Co
  Appleton, WI 920-734-4443
Abel Pumps
  Sewickley, PA 412-741-3222
Abell-Howe Crane
  Amherst, NY 800-888-0985
ACCO Systems
  Warren, MI 800-342-2226
Accutek Packaging Equipment
  Vista, CA 800-989-1828
Ace Engineering Company
  Fort Worth, TX 800-431-4223
Ace Specialty Mfg Co Inc
  Rosemead, CA 626-444-3867
ACLAUSA Inc
  Cranberry Twp, PA 724-776-0099
ACO
  Moore, OK 405-794-7662
Acrison Inc
  Moonachie, NJ 800-422-4266
Action Engineering
  Liburn, GA 800-228-4668
Adamation
  Commerce, CA 800-383-8800
Advance Engineering Co
  Canton, MI 800-497-6388
Advance Lifts Inc
  St Charles, IL 800-843-3625
Advance Weight Systems Inc
  Grafton, OH 440-926-3691
Advanced Detection Systems
  Milwaukee, WI 414-672-0553
Advanced Uniflo Technologies
  Wichita, KS 800-688-0400
Aerocon
  Langhorne, PA 215-860-6056
Aerowerks
  Mississauga, ON 888-774-1616
AFCO Manufacturing
  Cincinnati, OH 800-747-7332
Air Technical Industries
  Mentor, OH 888-857-6265
Airfloat LLC
  Decatur, IL 800-888-0018
Albion Industries Inc
  Albion, MI 800-835-8911
All Power Inc
  Sioux City, IA 712-258-0681
All Star Carts & Vehicles
  Bay Shore, NY 800-831-3166
Allflex Packaging Products
  Ambler, PA 800-448-2467
Alliance Industrial Corp
  Lynchburg, VA 800-368-3556
Alliance Products LLC
  Murfreesboro, TN 800-522-3973
Allied Uniking Corp Inc
  Memphis, TN 901-365-7240
Alloy Products Corp
  Waukesha, WI 800-236-6603
Amark Packaging Systems
  Kansas City, MO 816-965-9000
Amco Metals Indl
  City of Industry, CA 626-855-2550
American Box Corporation
  Lisbon, OH 330-424-8055
American Crane & Equip Corp
  Douglassville, PA 610-385-6061
American Extrusion Intl
  South Beloit, IL 815-624-6616
American Food Equipment Company
  Hayward, CA 510-783-0255
American Lifts
  Guthrie, OK 877-360-6777
American Pallet Inc
  Oakdale, CA 209-847-6122
American Solving Inc.
  Brook Park, OH 800-822-2285
Ametek Technical & Industrial Products
  Kent, OH 215-256-6601
AMF CANADA
  Sherbrooke, QC 800-255-3869
Ampco Pumps Co Inc
  Milwaukee, WI 800-737-8671
Anchor Crane & Hoist Service Company
  Houston, TX 800-835-2223

Anderson Machine Sales
  Fort Lee, NJ
Anderson Tool & Engineering Company
  Anderson, IN. 765-643-6691
Anderson-Crane Company
  Minneapolis, MN 800-314-2747
ANDRITZ Inc
  Muncy, PA 704-943-4343
Ann Arbor Computer
  Farmington Hills, MI 800-526-9322
Antrim Manufacturing Inc
  Brookfield, WI 262-781-6860
ANVER Corporation
  Hudson, MA 800-654-3500
Anver Corporation
  Hudson, MA 800-654-3500
AP Dataweigh Inc
  Cumming, GA 877-409-2562
Apache Stainless Equipment
  Beaver Dam, WI 800-444-0398
Apollo Sheet Metal
  Kennewick, WA 509-586-1104
Applied Chemical Technology
  Florence, AL 800-228-3217
ARC Specialties
  Valencia, CA 661-775-8500
Arpac LP
  Schiller Park, IL 847-678-9034
Art Wire Works Co
  Chicago, IL 708-458-3993
Asgco Manufacturing Inc
  Allentown, PA 800-344-4000
Ashworth Bros Inc
  Winchester, VA 800-682-4594
Assembly Technology & Test
  Livonia, MI 734-522-1900
Atlas Equipment Company
  Kansas City, MO 800-842-9188
Auto Pallets-Boxes
  Lathrup Village, MI 800-875-2699
Automated Flexible Conveyors
  Clifton, NJ 800-694-7271
Automated Production Systems Corporation
  New Freedom, PA 888-345-5377
Automatic Handling Int
  Erie, MI 734-847-0633
Automotion Inc
  Oak Lawn, IL 708-229-3700
Autoquip Corp
  Guthrie, OK 877-360-6777
AZO Food
  Memphis, TN 901-794-9480
Baking Machines
  Livermore, CA 925-449-3369
Balemaster
  Crown Point, IN 219-663-4525
Ballymore Company
  West Chester, PA 610-696-3250
Bamco Belting
  Greenville, SC 800-258-2358
Barrette Outdoor Living
  Cleveland, OH 800-336-2383
Basiloid Products Corp
  Elnora, IN 866-692-5511
Bay Area Pallet Company/IFCO Systems
  Houston, TX 877-430-4326
Bayhead Products Corp.
  Dover, NH 800-229-4323
Bc Wood Products
  Ashland, VA 804-798-9154
Bedford Enterprises Inc
  Santa Maria, CA 800-242-8884
Beech Engineering
  Ashland, OH 419-281-0894
Belco Packaging Systems
  Monrovia, CA 800-833-1833
Bell Packaging Corporation
  Marion, IN 800-382-0153
Belt Technologies Inc
  Agawam, MA 413-786-9922
Benko Products
  Sheffield Vlg, OH 440-934-2180
Bennett Box & Pallet Company
  Winston, NC 800-334-8741
Bergen Barrel & Drum Company
  Kearny, NJ 201-998-3500
Berndorf Belt Technology USA
  Gilberts, IL 800-393-8450
Bessco Tube Bending & Pipe Fabricating
  Thornton, IL 800-337-3977
Best
  Brunswick, OH 800-827-9237

Best Diversified Products
  Jonesboro, AR. 800-327-9209
Bettendorf Stanford Inc
  Salem, IL 800-548-2253
BEUMER Corp
  Somerset, NJ 732-893-2800
BEVCO
  Canada, BC 800-663-0090
Bevles Company
  Dallas, TX. 800-441-1601
Bilt-Rite Conveyors
  New London, WI 920-982-6600
Biner Ellison Packaging Systs
  Vista, CA 800-733-8162
Bishamon Industry Corp
  Ontario, CA 800-358-8833
Black River Pallet Co
  Zeeland, MI. 800-427-6515
Blue Giant Equipment Corporation
  Brampton, ON. 800-668-7078
Bluff Manufacturing Inc
  Fort Worth, TX 800-433-2212
BMH
  City of Industry, CA 909-349-2530
Bmh Equipment Inc
  Sacramento, CA 800-350-8828
Bolzoni Auramo
  Homewood, IL 800-358-5438
Bowman Hollis Mfg Corp
  Charlotte, NC 888-269-2358
Bradley Lifting
  York, PA 717-848-3121
Branford Vibrator Company
  Peru, IL 800-262-2106
Brothers Metal Products
  Santa Ana, CA 714-972-3008
Brute Fabricators
  Castroville, TX 800-777-2788
Bryant Products Inc
  Ixonia, WI 800-825-3874
Buckhorn Canada
  Brampton, ON. 800-461-7579
Buffalo Technologies Corporation
  Buffalo, NY. 800-332-2419
Buhler Inc.
  Plymouth, MN. 763-847-9900
Bulldog Factory Svc LLC
  Madison Heights, MI 248-541-3500
Bunting Magnetics Co
  Newton, KS. 800-835-2526
Burgess Enterprises, Inc
  Renton, WA. 800-927-3286
Burgess Mfg. - Oklahoma
  Guthrie, OK. 800-804-1913
Burns Industries
  Line Lexington, PA 800-223-6430
Bushman Equipment Inc
  Menomonee Falls, WI. 800-338-7810
Busse/SJI Corp
  Randolph, WI 800-882-4995
BW Container Systems
  Romeoville, IL 630-759-6800
C & L Wood Products Inc
  Hartselle, AL. 800-483-2035
C H Babb Co Inc
  Raynham, MA. 508-977-0600
C Nelson Mfg Co
  Oak Harbor, OH 800-922-7339
C R Daniels Inc
  Ellicott City, MD. 800-933-2638
C S Bell Co
  Tiffin, OH 888-958-6381
C&R Refrigation Inc,
  Center, TX. 800-438-6182
C.J. Machine
  Fridley, MN. 763-767-4630
Caddy Corporation of America
  Bridgeport, NJ. 856-467-4222
Caldwell Group
  Rockford, IL 800-628-4263
California Caster & Handtruck
  San Francisco, CA 800-950-8750
Caljan America
  Denver, CO 303-321-3600
Cambelt International Corporation
  Salt Lake City, UT 801-972-5511
Can Lines Engineering Inc
  Downey, CA 562-861-2996
Cannon Equipment Company
  Cannon Falls, MN 800-825-8501
Cantley-Ellis Manufacturing Company
  Kingsport, TN 423-246-4671

Carbis Inc
Florence, SC 800-948-7750
Carleton Helical Technologies
Doylestown, PA 215-230-8900
Carman Industries Inc
Jeffersonville, IN 800-456-7560
Carrier Vibrating Equip Inc
Louisville, KY 502-969-3171
Carron Net Co Inc
Two Rivers, WI 800-558-7768
Carson Industries
Pomona, CA 800-735-5566
Cassel Box & Lumber Co Inc
Grafton, WI 262-377-9503
Casso-Solar Corporation
Nanuet, NY 800-988-4455
Cattron Group International
Sharpsville, PA 724-962-1629
Cayne Industrial Sales Corp
Bronx, NY 718-993-5800
Cedar Box Co
Minneapolis, MN 612-332-4287
Century Crane & Hoist
Dravosburg, PA 888-601-8801
Century Industries Inc
Sellersburg, IN 800-248-3371
Challenger Pallet & Supply Inc
Idaho Falls, ID 800-733-0205
Chantland Company, The
Humboldt, IA 515-332-4040
Charles Tirschman Pallet Co
Dundalk, MD 410-282-6199
Charlton & Hill
Lethbridge, AB 403-328-3388
Chase-Logeman Corp
Greensboro, NC 336-665-0754
Checker Machine
Minneapolis, MN 888-800-5001
Chem-Tainer Industries Inc
West Babylon, NY 800-938-8896
Cherry's Industrial Eqpt Corp
Elk Grove Vlg, IL 800-350-0011
Chester Hoist
Lisbon, OH 800-424-7248
Chicago Conveyor Corporation
Addison, IL 630-543-6300
Chief Industries
Kearney, NE 800-359-8833
CHL Systems
Souderton, PA 215-723-7284
Chocolate Concepts
Hartville, OH 330-877-3322
Christianson Systems Inc
Blomkest, MN 800-328-8896
Christy Machine Co
Fremont, OH 888-332-6451
Cimino Box & Pallet Co
Cleveland, OH 216-961-7377
Cintex of America
Carol Stream, IL 800-424-6839
Citra-Tech
Lefkosia, CY
Clamp Swing Pricing Co Inc
Oakland, CA 800-227-7615
Clark Caster Company
Cave in Rock, IL 800-538-0765
Cleasby Manufacturing Co
San Francisco, CA 800-253-2729
CLECO Systems
Marietta, GA 770-392-0330
Cleveland Vibrator Co
Cleveland, OH 800-221-3298
Climax Packaging Machinery
Hamilton, OH 513-874-1664
Clipper Belt Lacer Company
Grand Rapids, MI 616-459-3196
Coastal Pallet Corp
Bridgeport, CT 203-333-6222
Coblentz Brothers Inc
Apple Creek, OH 330-857-7211
Coddington Lumber Co
Frostburg, MD 301-689-8816
Collins Manufacturing Company Ltd
Langley, BC 800-663-6761
Colson Caster Corp
Jonesboro, AR 800-643-5515
Columbia Machine Inc
Vancouver, WA 800-628-4065
Columbus McKinnon Corporation
Getzville, NY 800-888-0985
Commercial Manufacturing
Fresno, CA 559-237-1855

Conesco Conveyor Corporation
Clifton, NJ 973-365-1440
Continental Commercial Products
Bridgeton, MO 800-325-1051
Control & Metering
Mississauga, ON 800-736-5739
Control Chief Holdings Inc
Bradford, PA 814-362-6811
Conveyance Technologies LLC
Cleveland, OH 800-701-2278
Conveying Industries
Denver, CO 877-600-4874
Conveyor Accessories
Burr Ridge, IL 800-323-7093
Conveyor Components Co
Croswell, MI 800-233-3233
Conveyor Components Co
Croswell, MI 800-552-3337
Conveyor Dynamics Corp
St Peters, MO 636-279-1111
Conveyor Supply Inc
Deerfield, IL 847-945-5670
Corinth Products
Corinth, ME 207-285-3387
Corn States Metal Fabricators
West Des Moines, IA 515-225-7961
Coss Engineering Sales Company
Rochester Hills, MI 800-446-1365
Cotter Brothers Corp
Danvers, MA 978-777-5001
Cozzini Inc
Algona, IA 888-295-1116
Craft Industries
Long Island City, NY 252-753-3152
Creative Foam Corp
Fenton, MI 810-629-4149
Creative Techniques
Auburn Hills, MI 800-473-0284
Crippen Manufacturing Co
St Louis, MI 800-872-2474
Crown Equipment Corp.
New Bremen, OH 419-629-2311
Cryovac
Charlotte, NC 800-391-5645
CSS International Corp
Philadelphia, PA 800-278-8107
Cugar Machine Co
Fort Worth, TX 817-927-0411
Cumberland Box & Mill Co
Cumberland, MD 301-724-1010
Currie Machinery Co
Santa Clara, CA 408-727-0422
Custom Conveyor & Supply Corp.
Racine, WI 262-634-4920
Custom Diamond Intl.
Laval, QC 800-326-5926
Custom Food Machinery
Stockton, CA 209-463-4343
Custom Metal Crafts
Springfield, MO 417-862-9324
Custom Metal Design Inc
Oakland, FL 800-334-1777
Custom Millers Supply Co
Monmouth, IL 309-734-6312
Custom Systems Integration Co
Carlsbad, CA 760-635-1099
Cutler Brothers Box & Lumber
Fairview, NJ 201-943-2535
Cutter Lumber Products
Livermore, CA 925-443-5959
Cyclonaire Corp
York, NE 800-445-0730
D&M Pallet Company
Neshkoro, WI 920-293-4616
Dairy Conveyor Corp
Brewster, NY 845-278-7878
Damrow Company
Fond Du Lac, WI 800-236-1501
Daniel Boone Lumber Industries
Morehead, KY 606-784-7586
Darcor Casters
Toronto, ON 800-387-7206
Darnell-Rose Inc
City of Industry, CA 800-327-6355
Davis Core & Pa
Cave Spring, GA 800-235-7483
Davron Technologies Inc
Chattanooga, TN 423-870-1888
Day Lumber Company
Westfield, MA 413-568-3511
Dearborn Mid-West Conveyor Co
Taylor, MI 734-288-4400

Dearborn Mid-West Conveyor Co
Overland Park, KS 913-384-9950
Decoren Equipment
Willowbrook, IL 708-789-3367
DEL-Tec Packaging Inc
Greer, SC 800-747-8683
Delta Machine & Maufacturing
St Rose, LA 504-949-8304
Delta Wire And Mfg.
Harrow, ON 800-221-3794
Delta/Ducon
Malvern, PA 800-238-2974
Demag Cranes & Components Corp
Cleveland, OH 440-248-2400
Dematic USA
Grand Rapids, MI 877-725-7500
Dempster Systems
Toccoa, GA 706-886-2327
Denver Reel & Pallet Company
Denver, CO 303-321-1920
Descon EDM
Brocton, NY 716-792-9300
Deshazo Crane Company
Alabaster, AL 205-664-2006
Design Systems Inc
Farmington Hills, MI 800-660-4374
Design Technology Corporation
Lexington, MA 800-597-7063
Development Workshop Inc
Idaho Falls, ID 800-657-5597
Dillin Automation Systems Corp
Perrysburg, OH 419-666-6789
Diversified Capping Equipment
Perrysburg, OH 419-666-2566
Diversified Metal Engineering
Charlottetown, PE 902-628-6900
DMC-David Manufacturing Company
Mason City, IA 641-424-7010
Dominion Pallet Inc
Mineral, VA 800-227-5321
Donahower & Company
Olathe, KS 913-829-2650
Doosan Industrial Vehicle America Corp
Buford, GA 678-745-2200
Douglas Machine Inc
Alexandria, MN 320-763-6587
Douglas Machines Corp.
Clearwater, FL 800-331-6870
Downs Crane & Hoist Co Inc
Los Angeles, CA 800-748-5994
Dubuque Steel Products Co
Dubuque, IA 563-556-6288
Dufeck Manufacturing Co
Denmark, WI 888-603-9663
Duke Manufacturing Co
St Louis, MO 800-735-3853
Dunkley International Inc
Kalamazoo, MI 800-666-1264
Dunrite Inc
Fremont, NE 800-782-3061
Duplex Mill & Mfg Co
Springfield, OH 937-325-5555
Dupps Co
Germantown, OH 937-855-0623
Durable Corp
Norwalk, OH 800-537-1603
Durand-Wayland Inc
Lagrange, GA 800-241-2308
Durant Box Factory
Durant, OK 580-924-4035
Dutro Co
Logan, UT 866-388-7660
Dyco
Bloomsburg, PA 800-545-3926
Dyna-Veyor Inc
Newark, NJ 800-326-5009
Dynabilt Products
Readville, MA 800-443-1008
Dynamet
Kalamazoo, MI 269-385-0006
Dynamic Air Inc
St Paul, MN 651-484-2900
Dynamic Automation LTD
Simi Valley, CA 805-584-8476
Dynamic Storage Systems Inc.
Brooksville, FL 800-974-8211
E F Bavis & Assoc Inc
Maineville, OH 513-677-0500
E-Z Lift Conveyors
Denver, CO 800-821-9966
E2M
Duluth, GA 800-622-4326

Earl Soesbe Company
Romeoville, IL 219-866-4191
Eckels Bilt
Fort Worth, TX 800-343-9020
Edmeyer
Minneapolis, MN 651-450-1210
Edson Packaging Machinery
Hamilton, ON 800-493-3766
Edwards Products
Cincinnati, OH 800-543-1835
EGA Products Inc
Brookfield, WI 800-937-3427
Eichler Wood Products
Laurys Station, PA 610-262-6749
Eisenmann Corp USA
Crystal Lake, IL 815-455-4100
Elba Pallets Company
Elba, AL 334-897-6034
Elberta Crate & Box Company
Carpentersville, IL 888-672-9260
Electrical Engineering & Equip
Windsor Heights, IA 800-955-3633
Electro Lift Inc
Clifton, NJ 973-471-0204
ELF Machinery
La Porte, IN .800-328-0466
Elite Storage Solutions Inc
Monroe, GA .800-367-0572
Elwell Parker
Coraopolis, PA 800-272-9953
Emc Solutions
Celina, OH 419-586-2388
Emtrol
York, PA 800-634-4927
En-Hanced Products Inc
Westerville, OH 800-783-7400
Engineered Products Corp
Greenville, SC 800-868-0145
Enrick Co
Zumbrota, MN 507-732-5215
Equipment Design & Fabrication
Charlotte, NC 800-949-0165
Equipment Outlet
Meridian, ID .208-887-1472
Eriez Magnetics
Erie, PA 800-346-4946
Ermanco
Norton Shores, MI 231-798-4547
ERO/Goodrich Forest Products
Tualatin, OR .800-458-5545
Eugene Welding Company
Marysville, MI 810-364-7421
Excalibur Miretti Group LLC
Fairfield, NJ .973-808-8399
Exel
Lincolnton, NC 704-735-6535
F & A Fabricating Inc
Battle Creek, MI 269-965-8371
F N Smith Corp
Oregon, IL 815-732-2171
F.E. Wood & Sons
West Baldwin, ME 207-286-5003
Fabreeka International
Boise, ID 800-423-4469
Fabricated Components Inc
Stroudsburg, PA 800-233-8163
Fabricating & Welding Corp
Chicago, IL 773-928-2050
Fabrication Specialties
Centerville, TN 931-729-2283
Fairborn USA Inc
Upper Sandusky, OH 800-262-1188
Fata Automation
Sterling Heights, MI 586-323-9400
Faultless Caster
Evansville, IN 800-322-7359
Fehlig Brothers Box & Lbr Co
St Louis, MO 314-241-6900
FEI Inc
Mansfield, TX 800-346-5908
Felco Packaging Specialist
Baltimore, MD 800-673-8488
Fenner Dunlop Americas Inc
Pittsburgh, PA 412-249-0700
Fetco
Lake Zurich, IL 800-338-2699
Fibre Converters Inc
Constantine, MI 269-279-1700
Filler Specialties
Zeeland, MI .616-772-9235
Filling Equipment Co Inc
Flushing, NY 800-247-7127

Fillit
Kirkland, QC .514-694-2390
Fishmore
Melbourne, FL 321-723-4751
Fleet Wood Goldco Wyard
Cockeysville, MD 410-785-1934
Fleetwood Systems
Orlando, FL .800-432-5433
FleetwoodGoldcoWyard
Romeoville, IL 630-759-6800
Flexco
Downers Grove, IL 800-323-3444
Flexible Material Handling
Suwanee, GA 800-669-1501
Flexicon
Bethlehem, PA 888-353-9426
Flodin
Moses Lake, WA 509-766-2996
Flow of Solids
Westford, MA 978-392-0300
Fogg Filler Co
Holland, MI 616-786-3644
Food Engineering Unlimited
Fullerton, CA 714-879-8762
Food Machinery Sales
Bogart, GA 706-549-2207
Food Processing Equipment Co
Santa Fe Springs, CA 562-802-3727
Forbo Siegling LLC
Huntersville, NC 800-255-5581
Foremost Machine Builders Inc
Fairfield, NJ .973-227-0700
Fox Valley Wood Products Inc
Kaukauna, WI 920-766-4069
FPEC Corporation
Santa Fe Springs, CA 562-802-3727
Frazier & Son
Conroe, TX 800-365-5438
Frazier Industrial Co
Long Valley, NJ 800-859-1342
Fred D Pfening Co
Columbus, OH 614-294-5361
FreesTech
Sinking Spring, PA 717-560-7560
Frelco
Stephenville, NL 709-643-5668
Fresno Pallet, Inc.
Sultana, CA .559-591-4111
Frost Food Handling Products
Grand Rapids, MI 800-253-9382
G L Packaging Products Inc
West Chicago, IL 866-935-8755
G.F. Frank & Sons
Fairfield, OH .513-870-9075
Galbreath LLC
Winamac, IN .574-946-6631
Garvey Corp
Hammonton, NJ 800-257-8581
Gates Manufacturing Company
Saint Louis, MO 800-237-9226
Gatewood Products LLC
Parkersburg, WV 800-827-5461
Gbn Machine & Engineering
Woodford, VA 800-446-9871
Gch Internatonal
Louisville, KY 502-636-1374
GE Appliances
Louisville, KY 877-959-8688
Gebo Conveyors, Consultants & Systems
Laval, QC 450-973-3337
Gebo Corporation
Bradenton, FL 941-727-1400
GEM Equipment of Oregon Inc
Woodburn, OR 503-982-9902
General Corrugated Machinery Company
Palisades Park, NJ 201-944-0644
General Machinery Corp
Sheboygan, WI 888-243-6622
General Steel Fabricators
Joplin, MO 800-820-8644
General Tank
Berwick, PA .800-435-8265
Georgia Duck & Cordage Mill
Scottdale, GA 404-297-3170
Gerrity Industries
Monmouth, ME 877-933-2804
Gillis Associated Industries
Prospect Heights, IL 847-541-6500
Girard Wood Products Inc
Puyallup, WA 800-532-0505
Glatt Air Techniques Inc
Ramsey, NJ .201-825-8700

Goeman's Wood Products
Hartford, WI .262-673-6090
Goergen-Mackwirth Co Inc
Buffalo, NY 800-728-4446
Goldco Industries
Loveland, CO 970-663-4770
Gorbel Inc
Victor, NY 585-924-6262
Gough-Econ Inc
Charlotte, NC 800-204-6844
Graco Inc
Minneapolis, MN 612-623-6000
Graham Pallet Co Inc
Tompkinsville, KY 888-525-0694
Grain Machinery Mfg Corp
Miami, FL 305-620-2525
Gram Equipment of America
Tampa, FL 813-248-1978
Gray Woodproducts
Tacoma, WA .253-752-7000
Graybill Machines Inc
Lititz, PA 717-626-5221
Green Belt Industries Inc
Buffalo, NY 800-668-1114
Green Tek
Janesville, WI 800-747-6440
Greitzer
Elizabeth City, NC 252-338-4000
H G Weber & Co
Kiel, WI 920-894-2221
H&H Lumber Company
Amarillo, TX .806-335-1813
H&H Wood Products
Hamburg, NY 716-648-5600
Habasit America
Suwanee, GA 800-458-6431
Habasit America Plastic Div
Reading, PA .800-445-7898
Hackney Brothers
Washington, NC 800-763-0700
Halton Packaging Systems
Oakville, ON .905-847-9141
Hamilton Caster
Hamilton, OH 888-699-7164
Hampton Roads Box Company
Suffolk, VA 757-934-2355
Handling Specialty
Niagara Falls, NY 800-559-8366
Hanel Storage Systems
Pittsburgh, PA 412-787-3444
Hannay Reels
Westerlo, NY 877-467-3357
Hanson Box & Lumber Company
Wakefield, MA 617-245-0358
Hapman Conveyors
Kalamazoo, MI 800-968-7722
Harbor Pallet Company
Anaheim, CA 714-871-0932
Hardy Systems Corporation
Northbrook, IL 800-927-3956
Harold F Haines Manufacturing Inc
Presque Isle, ME 207-762-1411
Harper Trucks Inc
Wichita, KS 800-835-4099
Harrington Hoists Inc
Manheim, PA 800-233-3010
Hart Design & Mfg
Green Bay, WI 920-468-5927
Hartness International
Greenville, SC 800-845-8791
Hawkeye Pallet Co
Johnston, IA .515-276-0409
Hayes & Stolz Indl Mfg LTD
Fort Worth, TX 800-725-7272
HDT Manufacturing
Salem, OH 800-968-7438
Hectronic
Oklahoma City, OK 405-946-3574
Herkimer Pallet & Wood Products Company
Herkimer, NY 315-866-4591
Hevi-Haul International LTD
Menomonee Falls, WI 800-558-0577
HHP Inc
Henniker, NH 603-428-3298
Hi Roller Enclosed Belt Conveyors
Sioux Falls, SD 800-328-1785
Hildreth Wood Products Inc
Wadesboro, NC 704-826-8326
Hinchcliff Products Company
Strongsville, OH 440-238-5200
Hodge Manufacturing Company
Springfield, MA 800-262-4634

Hodges
Vienna, IL....................800-444-0011
Hoffmeyer Corp
San Leandro, CA.............888-744-1826
Hoppmann Corporation
Elkwood, VA.................800-368-3582
Hormann Flexan Llc
Leetsdale, PA...............800-365-3667
Hot Food Boxes
Mooresville, IN.............800-733-8073
Hotshot Delivery System
Bloomingdale, IL............630-924-8817
Houston Wire Works, Inc.
South Houston, TX...........800-468-9477
Hovair Systems Inc
Kent, WA....................800-237-4518
Howes S Co Inc
Silver Creek, NY............888-255-2611
Hunter Woodworks
Carson, CA..................800-966-4751
Hurt Conveyor Equipment Company
Los Angeles, CA.............323-541-0433
Hyster Company
San Diego, CA...............855-804-2118
ICB Greenline
Charlotte, NC...............800-331-5312
IEW
Niles, OH...................330-652-0113
Iman Pack
Westland, MI................800-810-4626
Incinerator International Inc
Houston, TX.................713-227-1466
Industrial Automation Systems
Santa Clarita, CA...........888-484-4427
Industrial Hardwood
Perrysburg, OH..............419-666-2503
Industrial Kinetics
Downers Grove, IL...........800-655-0306
Industrial Lumber & Packaging
Spring Lake, MI.............616-842-1457
Industrial Woodfab & Packaging
Riverview, MI...............734-284-4808
Innovation Moving Systems
Oostburg, WI................800-619-0625
Inter-City Welding & Manufacturing
Independence, MO............816-252-1770
Interlake Mecalux
Chicago, IL.................708-344-9999
InterMetro Industries
Wilkes-Barre, PA............570-825-2741
International Wood Industries
Snohomish, WA...............800-922-6141
Interroll Corp
Wilmington, NC..............800-830-9680
Intralox LLC
Harahan, LA.................800-535-8848
Irby
Rocky Mount, NC.............252-442-0154
Item Products
Houston, TX.................800-333-4932
J C Ford Co
La Habra, CA................714-871-7361
J L Becker Co
Plymouth, MI................800-837-4328
J.H. Thornton Company
Olathe, KS..................913-764-6550
J.M. Rogers & Sons
Moss Point, MS..............228-475-7584
Jantec
Traverse City, MI...........800-992-3303
Jarke Corporation
Prospect Hts, IL............800-722-5255
Jarvis Caster Company
Jackson, TN.................800-995-9876
Jervis B WEBB Co
Novi, MI....................248-553-1000
Jesco Industries
Litchfield, MI..............800-455-0019
Jetstream Systems
Wichita, KN.................855-861-6916
Jilson Group
Lodi, NJ....................800-969-5400
John Rock Inc
Coatesville, PA.............610-857-4809
Johnston Equipment
Delta, BC...................800-237-5159
Joyce Dayton Corp
Moraine, OH.................800-523-5204
K-Tron
Salina, KS..................785-825-1611
K.F. Logistics
Cincinnati, OH..............800-347-9100

Kadon Corporation
Milford, OH.................937-299-0088
Kamflex Corp
Chicago, IL.................800-323-2440
KAPS All Packaging
Riverhead, NY...............631-727-0300
Kasel Industries Inc
Denver, CO..................800-218-4417
Kaufman Engineered Systems
Waterville, OH..............419-878-9727
Kauling Wood Products Company
Beckemeyer, IL..............618-594-2901
Keenline Conveyor Systems
Omro, WI....................920-685-0365
Kelley Wood Products
Fitchburg, MA...............978-345-7531
Kelly Dock Systems
Milwaukee, WI...............414-352-1000
Kent District Library System
Comstock Park, MI...........616-784-2007
KETCH
Wichita, KS.................800-766-3777
Key Material Handling Inc
Simi Valley, CA.............800-539-7225
Key Technology Inc.
Walla Walla, WA.............509-529-2161
Killington Wood ProductsCompany
Rutland, VT.................802-773-9111
Kimball Companies
East Longmeadow, MA.........413-525-1881
Kinder Morgan Inc
Houston, TX.................713-466-0496
Kinergy Corp
Louisville, KY..............502-366-5685
Kinetic Equipment Company
Appleton, WI................806-293-4471
Kinsley Inc
Doylestown, PA..............800-414-6664
Kisco Manufacturing
Port Alberni, BC............604-823-7456
KISS Packaging Systems
Vista, CA...................888-522-3538
Klippenstein Corp
Fresno, CA..................888-834-4258
Knight Ind
Auburn Hills, MI............248-377-4950
Koke Inc
Queensbury, NY..............800-535-5303
Komatsu Forklift USA
Rolling Meadows, IL.........847-437-5800
Konz Wood Products Co
Appleton, WI................877-610-5145
Kornylak Corp
Hamilton, OH................800-837-5676
Krones
Franklin, WI................800-752-3787
KUKA Robotics Corp
Shelby Township, MI.........800-459-6691
Kusel Equipment Company
Watertown, WI...............920-261-4112
KWS Manufacturing Co LTD
Burleson, TX................800-543-6558
L T Hampel Corp
Germantown, WI..............800-681-6979
L&H Wood Manufacturing Company
Farmington, MI..............248-474-9000
L&S Pallet Company
Houston, TX.................281-443-6537
La Crosse
Onalaska, WI................800-345-0018
LA Marche Mfg Co
Des Plaines, IL.............847-299-1193
La Menuiserie East Angus
East Angus, QC..............819-832-2746
Laidig Inc
Mishawaka, IN...............574-256-0204
Lake Michigan Hardwood Company
Leland, MI..................231-256-9811
Lakeside Manufacturing Inc
Milwaukee, WI...............888-558-8565
Lakeside-Aris Manufacturing
Milwaukee, WI...............800-558-8565
Lambert Material Handling
Syracuse, NY................800-253-5103
Landoo Corporation
Horsham, PA.................785-562-5381
Laros Equipment Co Inc
Portage, MI.................269-323-1441
Larson Pallet Company
Ogema, WI...................715-767-5131
Laughlin Sales Corp
Fort Worth, TX..............817-625-7756

Lawson Industries
Holden, MO..................816-732-4347
Le Fiell Co
Reno, NV....................402-592-9993
Lear Romec
Elyria, OH..................440-323-3211
Lee Engineering Company
Pawtucket, RI...............401-725-6100
Leeds Conveyor Manufacturer Company
Guilford, CT................800-724-1088
Leggett & Platt Storage
Vernon Hills, IL............847-816-6246
Lesco Design & Mfg Co
La Grange, KY...............502-222-7101
Lester Box & Mfg Div
Long Beach, CA..............562-437-5123
Lewco Inc
Sandusky, OH................419-625-4014
Lewis M Carter Mfg Co Inc
Donalsonville, GA...........800-332-8232
Lexington Logistics LLC
Portage, WI.................800-356-8150
Leyman Manufacturing   Corporation
Cincinnati, OH..............866-539-6261
Liberty Machine Company
York, PA....................800-745-8152
Lift Rite
Mississauga, ON.............905-456-2603
Liftomatic Material Handling
Buffalo Grove, IL...........800-837-6540
Line-Master Products
Cocolalla, ID...............208-265-4743
Linett Company
Blawnox, PA.................800-565-2165
Lista International Corp
Holliston, MA...............800-722-3020
Load King Mfg
Jacksonville, FL............800-531-4975
LoadBank International
Orlando, FL.................800-458-9010
Lock Inspection Systems
Fitchburg, MA...............800-227-5539
Logemann Brothers Co
Milwaukee, WI...............414-445-3005
Long Reach ManufacturingCompany
Westport, CT................800-285-7000
Longford Equipment US
Glastonbury, CT.............416-298-6622
Longview Fibre Co
Longview, WA................800-929-8111
Lorenz Couplings
Cobourg, ON.................800-263-7782
Louisville Dryer Company
Louisville, KY..............800-735-3613
LPI Imports
Chicago, IL.................877-389-6563
LPS Technology
Grafton, OH.................800-586-1410
Lumsden Flexx Flow
Lancaster, PA...............800-367-3664
M & E Mfg Co Inc
Kingston, NY................845-331-2110
M & H Crate Inc
Jacksonville, TX............903-683-5351
M G Newell Corp
Greensboro, NC..............800-334-0231
M O Industries Inc
Whippany, NJ................973-386-9228
Madison County Wood Products
Fredericktown, MO...........314-584-1802
Madsen Wire Products Inc
Orland, IN..................260-829-6561
Magline Inc
Standish, MI................800-624-5463
Magna Power Controls
Milwaukee, WI...............800-288-8178
Magnuson
Pueblo, CO..................719-948-9500
Magsys Inc
Milwaukee, WI...............414-543-2177
Manufacturers Wood Supply Company
Cleveland, OH...............216-771-7848
Mar-Con Wire Belt
Richmond, BC................877-962-7266
Marion Body Works Inc
Marion, WI..................715-754-5261
Marion Pallet Company
Marion, OH..................800-432-4117
Mark Slade ManufacturingCompany
Seymour, WI.................920-833-6557
Marlen International
Astoria, OR.................800-862-7536

Marshall Boxes Inc
Rochester, NY 585-458-7432
Martin Cab Div
Cleveland, OH 216-377-8200
Martin Engineering
Neponset, IL 800-766-2786
Martin/Baron
Irwindale, CA 626-960-5153
Matcon Americas
Elmhurst, IL 856-256-1330
Material Storage Systems
Humble, TX 800-881-6750
Material Systems Engineering
Stilesville, IN 800-634-0904
Materials Transportation Co
Temple, TX 800-433-3110
Mathews Conveyor
Danville, KY 800-628-4397
Matot - Commercial GradeLift Solutions
Bellwood, IL 800-369-1070
Matthiesen Equipment
San Antonio, TX 800-624-8635
Maull-Baker Box Company
Brookfield, WI 414-463-1290
May-Wes Manufacturing Inc
Hutchinson, MN 800-788-6483
MBX Packaging Specialists
Wausau, WI 715-845-1171
McCormick Enterprises
Arlington Heights, IL 800-323-5201
Mccullough Industries Inc
Kenton, OH 800-245-9490
Mcintosh Box & Pallet Co
East Syracuse, NY 800-219-9552
Mcneilly Wood Products Inc
Campbell Hall, NY 845-457-9651
McNichols Conveyor Company
Southfield, MI 800-331-1926
MeGa Industries
Burlington, ON 800-665-6342
Melcher Manufacturing Co
Spokane Valley, WA 800-541-4227
Merco/Savory
Mt. Pleasant, MI 800-733-8821
Meriden Box Company
Southington, CT 860-621-7141
Meriwether Industries
Bloomfield, NJ 800-332-2358
MERRICK Industries Inc
Lynn Haven, FL 800-271-7834
Metal Equipment Company
Cleveland, OH 800-700-6326
Metko Inc
New Holstein, WI 920-898-4221
Metro Corporation
Wilkes Barre, PA 800-992-1776
Metzgar Conveyors
Comstock Park, MI 888-266-8390
Meyer Machine & Garroutte Products
San Antonio, TX 210-736-1811
Michaelo Espresso
Seattle, WA 800-545-2883
Michiana Box & Crate
Niles, MI 800-677-6372
Michigan Box Co
Detroit, MI 888-642-4269
Michigan Industrial Belting
Livonia, MI 800-778-1650
Michigan Pallet Inc
St Charles, MI 989-865-9915
Micro Solutions Ent Tech & Dev
Van Nuys, CA 800-673-4968
Mid-States Mfg & Engr Co Inc
Milton, IA 800-346-1792
Mid-West Wire Products
Ferndale, MI 800-989-9881
Midwest Metalcraft & Equipment
Windsor, MO. 800-647-3167
Midwest Wire Specialties
Chicago, IL 800-238-0228
Milan Box Corporation
Milan, TN 800-225-8057
Millard Manufacturing Corp
La Vista, NE 800-662-4263
Miller Hofft Brands
Indianapolis, IN 317-638-6576
Miller Metal Fabrication
Bridgeville, DE. 302-337-2291
Millwood Inc
Vienna, OH 330-393-4400
MIT Poly-Cart Corp
New York, NY 800-234-7659

Modern Metals Industries
El Segundo, CA 800-437-6633
Molding Automation Concepts
Woodstock, IL. 800-435-6979
Moline Machinery LLC
Duluth, MN. 800-767-5734
Momence Pallet Corp
Momence, IL 815-472-6451
Monarch-McLaren
Weston, ON 416-741-9675
Moorecraft Box & Crate
Tarboro, NC 252-823-2510
Morse Manufacturing Co Inc
East Syracuse, NY 315-437-8475
Moseley Realty LLC
Franklin, MA 800-667-3539
Motom Corporation
Bensenville, IL 630-787-1995
Mt Valley Farms & Lumber Prods
Biglerville, PA. 717-677-6166
Multivac
Union Grove, WI 800-640-4213
Mumper Machine Corporation
Butler, WI 262-781-8908
Murata Automated Systems
Charlotte, NC 800-428-8469
NACCO Industries Inc.
Cleveland, OH 440-229-5151
Namco Controls Corporation
Cleveland, OH 800-626-8324
National Conveyor Corp
Commerce, CA 323-725-0355
National Distributor Services
Aurora, CO 303-755-4411
National Drying Machry Co Inc
Philadelphia, PA 215-464-6070
National Scrap & Equipment Company
Spring House, PA 215-646-2040
Native Lumber Company
Wallingford, CT 203-269-2625
Navco
Houston, TX 800-231-0164
Necedah Pallet Co Inc
Necedah, WI 800-672-5538
NECO/Nebraska Engineering
Omaha, NE 800-367-6208
Nefab Packaging Inc.
Coppell, TX 800-322-4425
Nefab Packaging, Inc.
Coppell, TX 800-322-4425
Nelson Co
Sparrows Point, MD 410-477-3000
Neos
Elk River, MN. 888-441-6367
NEPA Pallet & Container Co
Snohomish, WA 360-568-3185
Nercon Engineering & Manufacturing
Oshkosh, WI 920-233-3268
Net Material Handling
Milwaukee, WI 800-558-7260
Nevlen Co. 2, Inc.
Wakefield, MA 800-562-7225
New Age Industrial
Norton, KS 800-255-0104
New England Machinery Inc
Bradenton, FL 941-755-5550
New England Pallets & Skids
Ludlow, MA 413-583-6628
New Lisbon Wood ProductsManufacturing Company
New Lisbon, WI 608-562-3122
New London Engineering
New London, WI 800-437-1994
New Mexico Products Inc
Albuquerque, NM 877-345-7864
New Pig Corp
Tipton, PA 800-468-4647
Newcastle Co Inc
New Castle, PA 724-658-4516
Newell Brands
Atlanta, GA
Newton OA & Son Co
Bridgeville, DE. 800-726-5745
Nexel Industries Inc
Port Washington, NY 800-245-6682
Norris Products Corp   oration
Cincinnati, OH 877-543-2278
North Star Ice EquipmentCorporation
Seattle, WA 800-321-1381
Northwest Products
Archbold, OH 419-445-1950
Northwind Inc
Alpena, AR 877-937-2585

Norwalt Design Inc
Randolph, NJ 973-927-3200
Nothum Food Processing Systems
Springfield, MO 800-435-1297
NST Metals
Louisville, KY 502-584-5846
Nu-Con Equipment
Chanhassen, MN 877-939-0510
Nu-Star Inc
Shakopee, MN 800-800-9274
Nucon Corporation
Deerfield, IL 877-545-0070
Nutec Manufacturing Inc
New Lenox, IL 815-722-5348
O'Brien Installations
Ontario, CA. 905-336-8245
Oak Creek Pallet Company
Milwaukee, WI 414-762-7170
Occidental Chemical Corporation
Dallas, TX. 800-733-3665
Ohio Magnetics Inc
Maple Heights, OH 800-486-6446
Ohio Rack Inc
Alliance, OH 800-344-4164
Omega Design Corp
Exton, PA 800-346-0191
Omicron Steel Products Company
Jamaica, NY 718-805-3400
Omni Lift Inc
Salt Lake City, UT 801-486-3776
Omni Metalcraft Corporation
Alpena, MI 989-358-7000
OnTrack Automation Inc
Waterloo, ON 519-886-9090
ORBIS
Oconomowoc, WI. 262-560-5000
ORBIS
Oconomowoc, WI. 800-890-7292
Original Lincoln Logs
Chestertown, NY 800-833-2461
Orion Packaging Systems Inc
Alexandria, MN 800-333-6556
Ortmayer Materials Handling
Brooklyn, NY 718-875-7995
OTD Corporation
Hinsdale, IL 630-321-9232
OTP Industrial Solutions
Terre Haute, IN 860-953-7632
Otto Braun Bakery Equipment
Buffalo, NY. 716-824-1252
Ouellette Machinery Systems
Fenton, MO. 800-545-7619
Our Name is Mud
New York, NY 877-683-7867
Overhead Conveyor Co
Ferndale, MI 800-396-2554
Pa R Systems Inc
St Paul, MN. 800-464-1320
Pacific Pneumatics
Rancho Cucamonga, CA 800-221-0961
Pacific Process Technology
La Jolla, CA 858-551-3298
Pacific Tank
Adelanto, CA 800-449-5838
Package Conveyor Co
Fort Worth, TX 800-792-1243
Packaging & Processing Equipment
Ayr, ON 519-622-6666
Packaging Equipment & Conveyors, Inc
Elkhart, IN. 574-266-6995
Packaging Machinery
Montgomery, AL. 334-265-9211
Packaging Systems Intl
Denver, CO 303-244-9000
Packing Material Company
Southfield, MI. 248-489-7000
Paco Manufacturing
Clarksville, IN. 812-283-7963
Paget Equipment Co
Marshfield, WI 715-384-3158
Palace Packaging Machines Inc
Downingtown, PA. 610-873-7252
Pallet Management Systems
Lawrenceville, VA 800-446-1804
Pallet Masters
Los Angeles, CA. 800-675-2579
Pallet One Inc
Mocksville, NC 336-492-5565
Pallet One Inc
Bartow, FL. 800-771-1148
Pallet Pro
Moss, TN. 800-489-3661

Pallet Service Corp
Maple Grove, MN 888-391-8020
Pallets Inc
Fort Edward, NY 518-747-4177
Pallister Pallet
Wapello, IA 319-523-8161
Pallox Incorporated
Onsted, MI 517-456-4101
Paltier
Michigan City, IN 800-348-3201
Paper Systems Inc
Des Moines, IA 800-342-2855
Paradigm Technologies
Eugene, OR 541-345-5543
Parkson Corp
Vernon Hills, IL 847-816-3700
Parkson Corp
Fort Lauderdale, FL 908-464-0700
Paul Hawkins Lumber Company
Mannington, WV 304-986-2230
Paxton Products Inc
Blue Ash, OH 800-441-7475
Payne Controls Co
Scott Depot, WV 800-331-1345
Peerless Conveyor & Mfg Corp
Kansas City, KS 913-342-2240
Peerless Food Equipment
Sidney, OH 937-492-4158
Peerless-Winsmith Inc
Springville, NY 716-592-9310
Pelco Packaging Corporation
Stirling, NJ 908-647-3500
Penda Form Corp
New Concord, OH 800-837-2574
Pengo Attachments Inc
Cokato, MN 800-599-0211
Peregrine Inc
Lincoln, NE 800-777-3433
Peterson Fiberglass Laminates
Shell Lake, WI 715-468-2306
Phelps Industries
Little Rock, AR 501-568-5550
Piab Vacuum Products
Hingham, MA 800-321-7422
Pine Bluff Crating & Pallet
Pine Bluff, AR 866-415-1075
Pine Point Wood Products Inc
Osseo, MN 763-428-4301
Piper Products Inc
Wausau, WI 800-544-3057
PlexPack Corp
Toronto, ON 855-635-9238
Pneumatic Conveying Inc
Ontario, CA 800-655-4481
Polar Beer Systems
Sun City, CA 951-928-8174
Pomona Service & Pkgng Co LA
Yakima, WA 509-452-7121
Port Erie Plastics Inc
Harborcreek, PA 814-899-7602
Portec Flowmaster
Canon City, CO 800-777-7471
Porter & Porter Lumber
Fort Gay, WV 304-648-5133
Positech Corp
Laurens, IA 800-831-6026
Power Electronics Intl Inc
East Dundee, IL 800-362-7959
Power-Pack Conveyor Co
Willoughby, OH 440-975-9955
Poweramp
Germantown, WI 800-643-5424
Ppm Technologies LLC
Newberg, OR 800-246-2034
Prater Industries
Bolingbrook, IL 877-247-5625
Precision Wood of Hawaii
Vancouver, WA 808-682-2055
Precision Wood Products
Vancouver, WA 360-694-8322
Premium Pallet
Philadelphia, PA 800-648-7347
Presence From Innovation LLC
St Louis, MO 314-423-9777
Priority One America
Oshkosh, WI 920-235-5562
Priority One Packaging
Waterloo, ON 800-387-9102
Pro Line Co
Haverhill, MA 978-521-2600
Process Engineering & Fabrication
Afton, VA 800-852-7975

Process Solutions
Riviera Beach, FL 561-840-0050
Prodo-Pak Corp
Garfield, NJ 973-777-7770
Production Equipment Co
Meriden, CT 800-758-5697
Production Systems
Marietta, GA 800-235-9734
Professional Engineering Assoc
Louisville, KY 502-429-0432
Progressive Tractor & Implement Co.
Parks, LA 337-845-5080
Pruitt's Packaging Services
Grand Rapids, MI 800-878-0553
Psc Floturn Inc
Union, NJ 908-687-3225
PTI Packaging
Portage, WI 800-501-4077
PTR Baler & Compactor Co
Philadelphia, PA 800-523-3654
Pucel Enterprises Inc
Cleveland, OH 800-336-4986
Puritan Manufacturing Inc
Omaha, NE 800-331-0487
Quality Corporation
Denver, CO 800-383-3018
Quality Fabrication & Design
Coppell, TX 972-304-3266
R.G. Stephens Engineering
Long Beach, CA 800-499-3001
Rahmann Belting & Industrial Rubber Products
Gastonia, NC 888-248-8148
Ralph L. Mason,
Newark, MD 410-632-1766
Ralphs Pugh Conveyor Rollers
Benicia, CA 800-486-0021
RAM Center
Red Wing, MN 800-309-5431
Rand-Whitney Group LLC
Worcester, MA 508-791-2301
Rapat Corp
Hawley, MN 800-325-6377
Rapid Industries Inc
Louisville, KY 800-787-4381
Rapid Pallet
Jermyn, PA 570-876-4000
Rapid Rack Industries
City of Industry, CA 800-736-7225
Ratcliff Hoist Company
San Carlos, CA 650-595-3840
Raymond Corp
Greene, NY 800-235-7200
Reading Plastic Fabricators
Reading, PA 610-926-3245
Redding Pallet Inc
Redding, CA 530-241-6321
Reelcraft Industries Inc
Columbia City, IN 800-444-3134
Reese Enterprises Inc
Rosemount, MN 800-328-0953
Regina USA
Oak Creek, WI 414-571-0032
Reinke & Schomann
Milwaukee, WI 414-964-1100
Reis Robotics
Carpentersville, IL 847-741-9500
Remco Products Corp
Zionsville, IN 800-585-8619
Remcon Plastics Inc
Reading, PA 800-360-3636
Remmey Wood Products
Southampton, PA 215-355-3335
Remstar International
Westbrook, ME 800-639-5805
Renold Products
Westfield, NY 800-879-2529
RETROTECH, Inc
West Henrietta, NY 866-915-2777
Rexnord Corporation
Milwaukee, WI 866-739-6673
Reyco Systems Inc
Caldwell, ID 208-795-5700
Rhodes Machinery International
Louisville, KY 502-213-3865
Richards Industries Systems
West Caldwell, NJ 973-575-7480
Rigidized Metal Corp
Buffalo, NY 800-836-2580
RMI-C/Rotonics Manaufacturing
Bensenville, IL 630-773-9510
Roberts Pallet Co
Ellington, MO 573-663-7877

Robinson Industries Inc
Coleman, MI 989-465-6111
Roechling Engineered Plastics
Gastonia, NC 800-541-4419
Roll Rite Corp
Hayward, CA 800-345-9305
Rome Machine & Foundry Co
Rome, GA 800-538-7663
Ron Vallort & Associates
Oak Brook, IL 630-734-3821
Ross Technology Corp
Leola, PA 800-345-8170
Roto-Jet Pump
Salt Lake City, UT 801-359-8731
Royal Ecoproducts
Vaughan, ON 800-465-7670
Royce Corp
Glendale, AZ 602-256-0006
Royce Rolls Ringer Co
Grand Rapids, MI 800-253-9638
Ruiz Flour Tortillas
Riverside, CA 909-947-7811
S & W Pallet Co
Camden, TN 800-640-0522
Sackett Systems
Bensenville, IL 800-323-8332
Sadler Conveyor Systems
Montreal, QC 888-887-5129
Saeplast Canada
St John, NB 800-567-3966
Samuel Pressure Vessel Group
Marinette, WI 715-453-5326
San Fab Conveyor
Sandusky, OH 419-626-4465
Sapac International
Fond Du Lac, WI 800-257-2722
Sardee Industries Inc
Orlando, FL 407-297-6362
Sardee Industries Inc
Lisle, IL 630-824-4200
Sasib Beverage & Food North America
Plano, TX 800-558-3814
Saturn Overhead Equipment
Somerset, NJ 800-631-4473
Savanna Pallets
McGregor, MN 218-768-2077
Savanna Pallets
Cloquet, MN 218-879-8553
Schaeff
Bridgeview, IL 888-436-7867
Scheb International
North Barrington, IL 847-381-2573
Schenck Process
Whitewater, WI 888-742-1249
Schloss Engineered Equipment
Aurora, CO 303-695-4500
Schlueter Company
Janesville, WI 800-359-1700
Schroeder Machine
San Marcos, CA 760-591-9733
Scientific Process & Research
Kendall Park, NJ 800-868-4777
Scott Pallets Inc
Amelia Court Hse, VA 800-394-2514
Screw Conveyor Corp
Hammond, IN 219-931-1450
Semco Manufacturing Company
Pharr, TX 956-787-4203
Sencorp White
Hyannis, MA 508-771-9400
Sertapak Packaging Corporation
Woodstock, ON 800-265-1162
Servco Equipment Co
St Louis, MO 314-781-3189
Sfb Plastics Inc
Wichita, KS 800-343-8133
Shammi Industries
Corona, CA 800-417-9260
Shelby Pallet & Box Company
Shelby, MI 231-861-4214
Shelcon Inc
Ontario, CA 909-947-4877
Sheldon Wood Products
Toano, VA 757-566-8880
Shepard Niles Parts
Montour Falls, NY 800-727-8774
Shick Esteve
Kansas City, MO 877-744-2587
Shiffer Industries
Kihei, HI 800-642-1774
Shingle Belting
King of Prussia, PA 800-345-6294

Shippers Supply
Saskatoon, SK 800-661-5639
Shippers Supply, Labelgraphic
Calgary, AB .800-661-5639
Shouldice Brothers SheetMetal
Battle Creek, MI 269-962-5579
Shuttleworth North America
Huntington, IN 800-444-7412
SI Systems Inc
Easton, PA 800-523-9464
Sidney Manufacturing Co
Sidney, OH .800-482-3535
Sigma Industries
Elkhart, IN. .574-295-9660
Simplex Filler Co
Napa, CA 800-796-7539
Simplimatic Automation
Forest, VA 800-294-2003
Sinco
Red Wing, MN 800-243-6753
SIT Indeva Inc
Charlotte, NC 704-357-8811
Slip-Not Belting Corporation
Kingsport, TN 423-246-8141
Smalley Manufacturing Co Inc
Knoxville, TN 865-966-5866
Smalley Package Company
Berryville, VA 540-955-2550
Smetco
Aurora, OR .800-253-5400
Smith Pallet Co Inc
Hatfield, AR 870-389-6184
Solve Needs International
White Lake, MI 800-783-2462
Sonoma Pacific Company
Montebello, CA 323-838-4374
Sould Manufacturing
Winnepeg, NB 204-339-3499
South Shore Controls Inc
Perry, OH 440-259-2500
Southern Ag Co Inc
Blakely, GA .229-723-4262
Southern Pallet
Christchurch, NZ 901-942-4603
Southworth Products Corp
Falmouth, ME 800-743-1000
SP Industries
Hopkins, MI 800-592-5959
Span Tech LLC
Glasgow, KY 270-651-9166
Spanco Crane & Monorail Systems
Morgantown, PA 800-869-2080
Sparks Belting Co
Grand Rapids, MI 800-451-4537
Speedways Conveyors
Lancaster, NY 800-800-1022
Spencer Turbine Co
Windsor, CT 800-232-4321
Sperling Industries
Omaha, NE .402-556-4070
SPG International
Covington, GA 877-503-4774
Spring Wood Products
Geneva, OH 440-466-1135
Springport Steel Wire Products
Elkhart, IN. .574-295-9660
Spudnik Equipment Co
Blackfoot, ID 208-684-4120
Spurgeon Co
Ferndale, MI 800-396-2554
St. Pierre Box & Lumber Company
Canton, CT .860-693-2089
Stainless Specialists Inc
Wausau, WI. 800-236-4155
Stainless Steel Fabricator Inc
La Mirada, CA 714-739-9904
Stearnswood Inc
Hutchinson, MN 800-657-0144
Steel King Industries
Stevens Point, WI 800-553-3096
Steel Storage Systems Inc
Commerce City, CO 800-442-0291
Steinmetz Machine Works Inc
Stamford, CT. 203-327-0118
Sterling Net & Twine Company
Cedar Knolls, NJ. 800-342-0316
Stewart Systems Baking LLC
Plano, TX 972-422-5808
Stiles Enterprises Inc
Rockaway, NJ 800-325-4232
Stokes Material Handling Systs
Doylestown, PA 215-340-2200

Storax
Bromsgrove, UK. 845-130-3090
Stratis Plastic Pallets
Indianapolis, IN 800-725-5387
Streator Dependable Mfg
Streator, IL .800-798-0551
Studd & Whipple Company
Conewango Valley, NY. 716-287-3791
Suffolk Iron Works Inc
Suffolk, VA. .757-539-2353
Summit Machine Builders Corporation
Denver, CO .800-274-6741
Super Sturdy
Weldon, NC. 800-253-4833
Superior Industries
Morris, MN .800-321-1558
Svedala Industries
Colorado Springs, CO. 719-471-3443
Sweet Manufacturing Co
Springfield, OH. 800-334-7254
SWF Co
Reedley, CA 800-344-8951
Swift Creek Forest Products
Jetersville, VA. 804-561-4498
Swisslog Logistics Inc
Newport News, VA 800-777-6862
Tampa Pallet Co
Tampa, FL 813-626-5700
Tasler Inc
Webster City, IA 515-832-5200
TC/American Monorail
Saint Michael, MN 763-497-7000
TDF Automation
Cedar Falls, IA 800-553-1777
Technibilt/Cari-All
Newton, NC 800-233-3972
Technipac
Le Sueur, MN 507-665-6658
Technistar Corporation
Denver, CO .303-651-0188
Tecweigh
St Paul, MN. 800-536-4880
Tennessee Mills
Red Boiling Springs, TN 615-699-2253
The National Provisioner
Deerfield, IL 847-763-9534
Theimeg
Sharpsville, PA 724-962-3571
Thermodynamics
Commerce City, CO 800-627-9037
Thiele Technologies Inc
Minneapolis, MN 612-782-1200
Thomas L. Green & Company
Robenosia, PA. 610-693-5816
Thombert
Newton, IA .800-433-3572
Thorco Industries LLC
Lamar, MO .800-445-3375
Thoreson Mc Cosh Inc
Troy, MI 800-959-0805
Thunder Pallet Inc
Theresa, WI. 800-354-0643
Timbertech Company
Milton, NH .800-572-5538
Titan Industries Inc
New London, WI 800-558-3616
TKF Inc
Cincinnati, OH 513-241-5910
Torbeck Industries
Harrison, OH. 800-333-0080
Toter Inc
Statesville, NC 800-772-0071
Tower Pallet Co Inc
De Pere, WI. 920-336-3495
Transbotics Corp
Charlotte, NC 704-362-1115
Transnorm System Inc
Grand Prairie, TX 800-259-2303
Travelon
Elk Grove Vlg., IL 800-537-5544
Traycon Manufacturing Co
Carlstadt, NJ 201-939-5555
Treen Box & Pallet Inc
Bensalem, PA 215-639-5100
Tri-Pak Machinery Inc
Harlingen, TX 956-423-5140
Tri-State Plastics
Glenwillard, PA 724-457-6900
Tri-Tronics
Tampa, FL 800-237-0946
Triad Pallet Co Inc
Greensboro, NC 336-292-8175

Tridyne Process Systems
South Burlington, VT 802-863-6873
Triple S Dynamics Inc
Breckenridge, TX 800-527-2116
Triple-A Manufacturing Company
Toronto, ON 800-786-2238
TWM Manufacturing
Leamington, ON 888-495-4831
Uhrden
Sugarcreek, OH. 800-852-2411
Unarco Material Handling Inc
Pandora, OH 800-448-0784
Unex Manufacturing Inc
Lakewood, NJ. 800-334-8639
Uni Carriers Americas Corp
Marengo, IL 800-871-5438
Unidex
Warsaw, NY 800-724-1302
United Pentek
Indianapolis, IN 800-357-9299
United States Systems Inc
Kansas City, KS 888-281-2454
UniTrak Corporation
Port Hope, ON 866-883-5749
Universal Die & Stampings
Prairie Du Sac, WI 608-643-2477
Universal Industries Inc
Cedar Falls, IA 800-553-4446
Universal Labeling Systems Inc
St Petersburg, FL 877-236-0266
Universal Packaging Inc
Houston, TX 800-324-2610
Upham & Walsh Lumber
Hoffman Estates, IL 847-519-1010
UPN Pallet Company
Penns Grove, NJ 856-299-1192
Us Rubber
Brooklyn, NY 718-782-7888
USECO
Murfreesboro, TN 615-893-4820
V-Ram Solids
Albert Lea, MN 888-373-3996
Vac-U-Max
Belleville, NJ 800-822-8629
Van Dereems Mfg Co
Hawthorne, NJ 973-427-2355
Vancouver Manufacturing
Washougal, WA. 360-835-8519
Vande Berg SCALES/Vbs Inc
Sioux Center, IA 712-722-1181
Vaughn Belting Co-Main Acct
Spartanburg, SC 800-533-9086
Versa Conveyor
London, OH 740-852-5609
Vertical Systems Intl
Lakeside Park, KY 859-485-9650
Vescom America
Henderson, NC 252-436-9067
Videojet Technologies Inc
Wood Dale, IL. 800-843-3610
W A Powers Co
Fort Worth, TX 800-792-1243
W.G. Durant Corporation
Whittier, CA 562-946-5555
Waldon Manufacturing LLC
Fairview, OK. 800-486-0023
Walker Magnetics Group Inc
Worcester, MA 800-962-4638
Wall Conveyor & Manufacturing
Huntington, WV 800-456-1335
Walters Brothers
Radisson, WI. 715-945-2646
Ward Ironworks
Welland, ON 888-441-9273
Wardcraft Conveyor & Quick Die
Spring Arbor, MI 800-782-2779
Warren Pallet Co Inc
Bloomsbury, NJ. 908-995-7172
Wastequip Inc
Charlotte, NC 704-366-7140
Wayne Engineering
Cedar Falls, IA 319-266-1721
WEBB-Stiles Co
Valley City, OH 330-273-9222
Weigh Right Automatic Scale Co
Joliet, IL 800-571-0249
Welch Packaging Group Inc
Elkhart, IN. .574-295-2460
Wesley International Corp
Scottdale, GA 800-241-8649
Westfield Sheet Metal Works
Kenilworth, NJ 908-276-5500

Wetterau Wood Products
Burlington, MA..................800-986-0958
Whallon Machinery Inc
Royal Center, IN.................574-643-9561
Whirl Air Flow
Big Lake, MN....................800-373-3461
Whit-Log Trailers Inc
Wilbur, OR......................800-452-1234
White Mop Wringer Company
Tampa, FL.......................800-237-7582
White Mountain Lumber Co
Berlin, NH......................603-752-1000
Wilder Manufacturing Company
Port Jervis, NY.................800-832-1319
Wilkie Brothers Conveyor Inc
Marysville, MI..................810-364-4820
Williams Pallet
West Chester, OH................513-874-4014
Williamsburg Millwork
Ruther Glen, VA.................804-994-2151
Williamson & Co
Greer, SC.......................864-849-3263
Wilson Steel Products Company
Memphis, TN.....................901-527-8742
Win-Holt Equipment Group
Syosset, NY.....................800-444-3595
Wire Belt Co of America
Londonderry, NH.................603-644-2500
Wireway Husky Corp
Denver, NC......................800-438-5629
Wittco Foodservice Equipment
Milwaukee, WI...................800-821-3912
Witte Co Inc
Washington, NJ..................908-689-6500
Wnc Pallet & Forest Pdts Co
Candler, NC.....................828-667-5426
Woodson Pallet Co
Anmoore, WV.....................304-623-2858
Yakima Wire Works
Reedley, CA.....................800-344-8951
Yargus Manufacturing Inc
Marshall, IL....................217-826-8059
Yerger Wood Products
East Greenville, PA.............215-679-4413
York River Pallet Corporation
Shacklefords, VA................804-785-5811
YW Yacht Basin
Easton, MD......................410-822-0414
Z-Loda Systems Engineering Inc
Stamford, CT....................203-325-8001
Zenar Corp
Oak Creek, WI...................414-764-1800
Zimmerman Handling Systems
Madison Heights, MI.............800-347-7047
Ziniz
Louisville, KY..................502-955-6573
Zoia Banquetier Co
Cleveland, OH...................216-631-6414

Pallet Handling Equipment

Advanced Uniflo Technologies
Wichita, KS.....................800-688-0400
Air Technical Industries
Mentor, OH......................888-857-6265
Anver Corporation
Hudson, MA......................800-654-3500
Automated Production Systems Corporation
New Freedom, PA.................888-345-5377
Bayhead Products Corp.
Dover, NH.......................800-229-4323
Bmh Equipment Inc
Sacramento, CA..................800-350-8828
Burgess Mfg. - Oklahoma
Guthrie, OK.....................800-804-1913
Bushman Equipment Inc
Menomonee Falls, WI.............800-338-7810
Cannon Equipment Company
Cannon Falls, MN................800-825-8501
Cherry's Industrial Eqpt Corp
Elk Grove Vlg, IL...............800-350-0011
CLECO Systems
Marietta, GA....................770-392-0330
Conveyance Technologies LLC
Cleveland, OH...................800-701-2278
Currie Machinery Co
Santa Clara, CA.................408-727-0422
Douglas Machine Inc
Alexandria, MN..................320-763-6587
Dynabilt Products
Readville, MA...................800-443-1008

Edson Packaging Machinery
Hamilton, ON....................800-493-3766
Equipment Design & Fabrication
Charlotte, NC...................800-949-0165
Eugene Welding Company
Marysville, MI..................810-364-7421
Fibre Converters Inc
Constantine, MI.................269-279-1700
FreesTech
Sinking Spring, PA..............717-560-7560
Goldco Industries
Loveland, CO....................970-663-4770
Halton Packaging Systems
Oakville, ON....................905-847-9141
Johnston Equipment
Delta, BC.......................800-237-5159
Krones
Franklin, WI....................800-752-3787
KUKA Robotics Corp
Shelby Township, MI.............800-459-6691
Lexington Logistics LLC
Portage, WI.....................800-356-8150
Load King Mfg
Jacksonville, FL................800-531-4975
Long Reach ManufacturingCompany
Westport, CT....................800-285-7000
Metal Equipment Company
Cleveland, OH...................800-700-6326
Metzgar Conveyors
Comstock Park, MI...............888-266-8390
Mitsubishi Caterpillar Mcfa
Houston, TX.....................800-228-5438
Ohio Rack Inc
Alliance, OH....................800-344-4164
Priority One Packaging
Waterloo, ON....................800-387-9102
PTI Packaging
Portage, WI.....................800-501-4077
RAM Center
Red Wing, MN....................800-309-5431
Reis Robotics
Carpentersville, IL.............847-741-9500
Sadler Conveyor Systems
Montreal, QC....................888-887-5129
San Fab Conveyor
Sandusky, OH....................419-626-4465
Sfb Plastics Inc
Wichita, KS.....................800-343-8133
Shrinkfast Marketing
Newport, NH.....................800-867-4746
Sigma Industries
Elkhart, IN.....................574-295-9660
Smetco
Aurora, OR......................800-253-5400
Solve Needs International
White Lake, MI..................800-783-2462
Springport Steel Wire Products
Elkhart, IN.....................574-295-9660
Steel King Industries
Stevens Point, WI...............800-553-3096
Unarco Material Handling Inc
Pandora, OH.....................800-448-0784
WEBB-Stiles Co
Valley City, OH.................330-273-9222
Wesley International Corp
Scottdale, GA...................800-241-8649
Wireway Husky Corp
Denver, NC......................800-438-5629

Palletizers

Automated Production Systems Corporation
New Freedom, PA.................888-345-5377
Bell Packaging Corporation
Marion, IN......................800-382-0153
Berkshire PPM
Litchfield, CT..................860-567-3118
BEUMER Corp
Somerset, NJ....................732-893-2800
Busse/SJI Corp
Randolph, WI....................800-882-4995
Cannon Equipment Company
Cannon Falls, MN................800-825-8501
Chantland Company, The
Humboldt, IA....................515-332-4040
Columbia Machine Inc
Vancouver, WA...................800-628-4065
Conveying Industries
Denver, CO......................877-600-4874
Currie Machinery Co
Santa Clara, CA.................408-727-0422

Custom Metal Design Inc
Oakland, FL.....................800-334-1777
Dearborn Mid-West Conveyor Co
Overland Park, KS...............913-384-9950
Douglas Machine Inc
Alexandria, MN..................320-763-6587
Edmeyer
Minneapolis, MN.................651-450-1210
FleetwoodGoldcoWyard
Romeoville, IL..................630-759-6800
FreesTech
Sinking Spring, PA..............717-560-7560
General Corrugated Machinery Company
Palisades Park, NJ..............201-944-0644
Goldco Industries
Loveland, CO....................970-663-4770
Halton Packaging Systems
Oakville, ON....................905-847-9141
Iman Pack
Westland, MI....................800-810-4626
ITW Angleboard
Villa Rica, GA..................770-459-5747
Jetstream Systems
Wichita, KN.....................855-861-6916
Krones
Franklin, WI....................800-752-3787
KUKA Robotics Corp
Shelby Township, MI.............800-459-6691
Kusel Equipment Company
Watertown, WI...................920-261-4112
Lambert Material Handling
Syracuse, NY....................800-253-5103
Lexington Logistics LLC
Portage, WI.....................800-356-8150
Magnuson
Pueblo, CO......................719-948-9500
Mathews Conveyor
Danville, KY....................800-628-4397
Newcastle Co Inc
New Castle, PA..................724-658-4516
Nitech
Columbus, NE....................800-237-6496
Ocme America Corporation
York, PA........................717-843-6263
Ouellette Machinery Systems
Fenton, MO......................800-545-7619
Packaging & Processing Equipment
Ayr, ON.........................519-622-6666
Packaging Systems Intl
Denver, CO......................303-244-9000
PASCO
St Louis, MO....................800-489-3300
Priority One America
Oshkosh, WI.....................920-235-5562
Priority One Packaging
Waterloo, ON....................800-387-9102
Production Systems
Marietta, GA....................800-235-9734
PTI Packaging
Portage, WI.....................800-501-4077
R.G. Stephens Engineering
Long Beach, CA..................800-499-3001
RAM Center
Red Wing, MN....................800-309-5431
Reis Robotics
Carpentersville, IL.............847-741-9500
Sapac International
Fond Du Lac, WI.................800-257-2722
Sardee Industries Inc
Orlando, FL.....................407-297-6362
Sardee Industries Inc
Lisle, IL.......................630-824-4200
Sasib Beverage & Food North America
Plano, TX.......................800-558-3814
Simplimatic Automation
Forest, VA......................800-294-2003
Southworth Products Corp
Falmouth, ME....................800-743-1000
Technistar Corporation
Denver, CO......................303-651-0188
Thiele Technologies Inc
Minneapolis, MN.................612-782-1200
W.G. Durant Corporation
Whittier, CA....................562-946-5555
Whallon Machinery Inc
Royal Center, IN................574-643-9561

Pallets

A.M. Loveman Lumber & Box Company
Nashville, TN...................615-297-1397

Advance Engineering Co
Canton, MI 800-497-6388
Allflex Packaging Products
Ambler, PA 800-448-2467
American Box Corporation
Lisbon, OH 330-424-8055
American Pallet Inc
Oakdale, CA 209-847-6122
Auto Pallets-Boxes
Lathrup Village, MI 800-875-2699
Barrette Outdoor Living
Cleveland, OH 800-336-2383
Bay Area Pallet Company/IFCO Systems
Houston, TX 877-430-4326
Bc Wood Products
Ashland, VA 804-798-9154
Bell Packaging Corporation
Marion, IN. 800-382-0153
Bennett Box & Pallet Company
Winston, NC 800-334-8741
Bergen Barrel & Drum Company
Kearny, NJ 201-998-3500
Black River Pallet Co
Zeeland, MI 800-427-6515
Buckhorn Canada
Brampton, ON. 800-461-7579
Buckhorn Inc
Milford, OH 800-543-4454
Burgess Mfg. - Oklahoma
Guthrie, OK 800-804-1913
C & L Wood Products Inc
Hartselle, AL. 800-483-2035
Cantley-Ellis Manufacturing Company
Kingsport, TN. 423-246-4671
Carson Industries
Pomona, CA 800-735-5566
Cascade Wood Components
Cascade Locks, OR. 541-374-8413
Cassel Box & Lumber Co Inc
Grafton, WI. 262-377-9503
Cedar Box Co
Minneapolis, MN 612-332-4287
Challenger Pallet & Supply Inc
Idaho Falls, ID 800-733-0205
Charles Tirschman Pallet Co
Dundalk, MD 410-282-6199
Cimino Box & Pallet Co
Cleveland, OH 216-961-7377
Coblentz Brothers Inc
Apple Creek, OH 330-857-7211
Coddington Lumber Co
Frostburg, MD 301-689-8816
Corinth Products
Corinth, ME 207-285-3387
Cutler Brothers Box & Lumber
Fairview, NJ 201-943-2535
Cutter Lumber Products
Livermore, CA 925-443-5959
D&M Pallet Company
Neshkoro, WI 920-293-4616
Daniel Boone Lumber Industries
Morehead, KY 606-784-7586
Davis Core & Pa
Cave Spring, GA. 800-235-7483
Day Lumber Company
Westfield, MA. 413-568-3511
Denver Reel & Pallet Company
Denver, CO 303-321-1920
Development Workshop Inc
Idaho Falls, ID 800-657-5597
Dufeck Manufacturing Co
Denmark, WI. 888-603-9663
Durant Box Factory
Durant, OK 580-924-4035
Eichler Wood Products
Laurys Station, PA 610-262-6749
Elba Pallets Company
Elba, AL. 334-897-6034
Elberta Crate & Box Company
Carpentersville, IL 888-672-9260
ERO/Goodrich Forest Products
Tualatin, OR 800-458-5545
F.E. Wood & Sons
West Baldwin, ME 207-286-5003
Fabricated Components Inc
Stroudsburg, PA 800-233-8163
Fabrication Specialties
Centerville, TN 931-729-2283
Fehlig Brothers Box & Lbr Co
St Louis, MO. 314-241-6900
Felco Packaging Specialist
Baltimore, MD 800-673-8488

Fresno Pallet, Inc.
Sultana, CA 559-591-4111
G L Packaging Products Inc
West Chicago, IL 866-935-8755
Gatewood Products LLC
Parkersburg, WV 800-827-5461
Gbn Machine & Engineering
Woodford, VA. 800-446-9871
Gemini Plastic Films Corporation
Garfield, NJ. 800-789-4732
Gerrity Industries
Monmouth, ME. 877-933-2804
Girard Wood Products Inc
Puyallup, WA. 800-532-0505
Goeman's Wood Products
Hartford, WI 262-673-6090
Graham Pallet Co Inc
Tompkinsville, KY 888-525-0694
Gray Woodproducts
Tacoma, WA 253-752-7000
Green Tek
Janesville, WI 800-747-6440
H&H Lumber Company
Amarillo, TX. 806-335-1813
H&H Wood Products
Hamburg, NY 716-648-5600
Hampton Roads Box Company
Suffolk, VA 757-934-2355
Hanson Box & Lumber Company
Wakefield, MA 617-245-0358
Harbor Pallet Company
Anaheim, CA 714-871-0932
Hawkeye Pallet Co
Johnston, IA 515-276-0409
Herkimer Pallet & Wood Products Company
Herkimer, NY 315-866-4591
HHP Inc
Henniker, NH 603-428-3298
Hildreth Wood Products Inc
Wadesboro, NC 704-826-8326
Hinchcliff Products Company
Strongsville, OH 440-238-5200
Hunter Woodworks
Carson, CA 800-966-4751
Industrial Hardwood
Perrysburg, OH 419-666-2503
Industrial Lumber & Packaging
Spring Lake, MI 616-842-1457
Industrial Woodfab & Packaging
Riverview, MI 734-284-4808
International Wood Industries
Snohomish, WA 800-922-6141
ITW Plastic Packaging
Denver, CO 303-316-6816
J.M. Rogers & Sons
Moss Point, MS 228-475-7584
Jarke Corporation
Prospect Hts, IL 800-722-5255
Jeco Plastic Products LLC
Plainfield, IN. 800-593-5326
John Rock Inc
Coatesville, PA 610-857-4809
Kadon Corporation
Milford, OH 937-299-0088
Kauling Wood Products Company
Beckemeyer, IL 618-594-2901
Kelley Wood Products
Fitchburg, MA 978-345-7531
KETCH
Wichita, KS. 800-766-3777
Killington Wood ProductsCompany
Rutland, VT. 802-773-9111
Kimball Companies
East Longmeadow, MA 413-525-1881
Konz Wood Products Co
Appleton, WI 877-610-5145
L T Hampel Corp
Germantown, WI. 800-681-6979
L&H Wood Manufacturing Company
Farmington, MI 248-474-9000
L&S Pallet Company
Houston, TX 281-443-6537
La Menuiserie East Angus
East Angus, QC 819-832-2746
Lake Michigan Hardwood Company
Leland, MI. 231-256-9811
Larson Pallet Company
Ogema, WI 715-767-5131
Lawson Industries
Holden, MO 816-732-4347
Lester Box & Mfg Div
Long Beach, CA 562-437-5123

Lexington Logistics LLC
Portage, WI 800-356-8150
Load King Mfg
Jacksonville, FL 800-531-4975
Longview Fibre Co
Longview, WA. 800-929-8111
Lumber & Things
Keyser, WV. 800-296-5656
Lydall
Doswell, VA. 804-266-9611
M & H Crate Inc
Jacksonville, TX 903-683-5351
M O Industries Inc
Whippany, NJ 973-386-9228
Madison County Wood Products
Fredericktown, MO. 314-584-1802
Marion Pallet Company
Marion, OH 800-432-4117
Mark Slade ManufacturingCompany
Seymour, WI 920-833-6557
Marshall Boxes Inc
Rochester, NY 585-458-7432
Mason Ways Indestructible
West Palm Beach, FL 800-837-2881
Maull-Baker Box Company
Brookfield, WI 414-463-1290
Mayco Inc
Dallas, TX. 214-638-4848
MBX Packaging Specialists
Wausau, WI. 715-845-1171
Mcintosh Box & Pallet Co
East Syracuse, NY 800-219-9552
Mcneilly Wood Products Inc
Campbell Hall, NY 845-457-9651
Meriden Box Company
Southington, CT 860-621-7141
Michiana Box & Crate
Niles, MI. 800-677-6372
Michigan Box Co
Detroit, MI 888-642-4269
Michigan Pallet Inc
St Charles, MI. 989-865-9915
Millwood Inc
Vienna, OH 330-393-4400
Momence Pallet Corp
Momence, IL. 815-472-6451
Moorecraft Box & Crate
Tarboro, NC 252-823-2510
Mt Valley Farms & Lumber Prods
Biglerville, PA. 717-677-6166
Native Lumber Company
Wallingford, CT 203-269-2625
Necedah Pallet Co Inc
Necedah, WI. 800-672-5538
Nefab Packaging Inc.
Coppell, TX 800-322-4425
Nefab Packaging, Inc.
Coppell, TX 800-322-4425
Nelson Co
Sparrows Point, MD 410-477-3000
NEPA Pallet & Container Co
Snohomish, WA 360-568-3185
New England Pallets & Skids
Ludlow, MA 413-583-6628
New Lisbon Wood ProductsManufacturing Company
New Lisbon, WI 608-562-3122
New Mexico Products Inc
Albuquerque, NM. 877-345-7864
Newcourt, Inc.
Madison, IN 800-933-0006
Northwest Products
Archbold, OH 419-445-1950
Nucon Corporation
Deerfield, IL 877-545-0070
Oak Creek Pallet Company
Milwaukee, WI 414-762-7170
Occidental Chemical Corporation
Dallas, TX. 800-733-3665
ORBIS
Oconomowoc, WI. 262-560-5000
ORBIS
Oconomowoc, WI. 800-890-7292
Original Lincoln Logs
Chestertown, NY 800-833-2461
OTD Corporation
Hinsdale, IL 630-321-9232
Packing Material Company
Southfield, MI. 248-489-7000
Pallet Management Systems
Lawrenceville, VA 800-446-1804
Pallet Masters
Los Angeles, CA. 800-675-2579

Pallet One Inc
Bartow, FL.............................800-771-1148
Pallet Pro
Moss, TN..............................800-489-3661
Pallet Service Corp
Maple Grove, MN...................888-391-8020
Pallets Inc
Fort Edward, NY....................518-747-4177
Pallister Pallet
Wapello, IA..........................319-523-8161
Pallox Incorporated
Onsted, MI...........................517-456-4101
Paper Systems Inc
Des Moines, IA......................800-342-2855
Paul Hawkins Lumber Company
Mannington, WV....................304-986-2230
Penda Form Corp
New Concord, OH..................800-837-2574
Pinckney Molded Plastics
Howell, MI...........................800-854-2920
Pine Bluff Crating & Pallet
Pine Bluff, AR.......................866-415-1075
Pine Point Wood Products Inc
Osseo, MN............................763-428-4301
Port Erie Plastics Inc
Harborcreek, PA.....................814-899-7602
Porter & Porter Lumber
Fort Gay, WV........................304-648-5133
Precision Wood of Hawaii
Vancouver, WA......................808-682-2055
Precision Wood Products
Vancouver, WA......................360-694-8322
Premium Pallet
Philadelphia, PA....................800-648-7347
Pruitt's Packaging Services
Grand Rapids, MI...................800-878-0553
Ralph L. Mason,
Newark, MD.........................410-632-1766
Rapid Pallet
Jermyn, PA...........................570-876-4000
Redding Pallet Inc
Redding, CA..........................530-241-6321
Remcon Plastics Inc
Reading, PA..........................800-360-3636
Remmey Wood Products
Southampton, PA...................215-355-3335
Roberts Pallet Co
Ellington, MO.......................573-663-7877
Robinson Industries Inc
Coleman, MI.........................989-465-6111
Rotonics Manufacturing
Gardena, CA..........................310-327-5401
Royal Ecoproducts
Vaughan, ON.........................800-465-7670
S & W Pallet Co
Camden, TN..........................800-640-0522
Saeplast Canada
St John, NB...........................800-567-3966
Savanna Pallets
McGregor, MN......................218-768-2077
Savanna Pallets
Cloquet, MN..........................218-879-8553
Scott Pallets Inc
Amelia Court Hse, VA..............800-394-2514
Sertapak Packaging Corporation
Woodstock, ON......................800-265-1162
Sfb Plastics Inc
Wichita, KS...........................800-343-8133
Shelby Pallet & Box Company
Shelby, MI............................231-861-4214
Sheldon Wood Products
Toano, VA.............................757-566-8880
Sigma Industries
Elkhart, IN............................574-295-9660
Smalley Package Company
Berryville, VA........................540-955-2550
Smith Pallet Co Inc
Hatfield, AR..........................870-389-6184
Sonoma Pacific Company
Montebello, CA......................323-838-4374
Southern Pallet
Christchurch, NZ....................901-942-4603
Spring Wood Products
Geneva, OH..........................440-466-1135
Springport Steel Wire Products
Elkhart, IN............................574-295-9660
St. Pierre Box & Lumber Company
Canton, CT............................860-693-2089
Stearnswood Inc
Hutchinson, MN.....................800-657-0144
Sterling Net & Twine Company
Cedar Knolls, NJ....................800-342-0316

Stratis Plastic Pallets
Indianapolis, IN.....................800-725-5387
Streator Dependable Mfg
Streator, IL............................800-798-0551
Studd & Whipple Company
Conewango Valley, NY............716-287-3791
Swift Creek Forest Products
Jetersville, VA........................804-561-4498
Tampa Pallet Co
Tampa, FL.............................813-626-5700
Tasler Inc
Webster City, IA.....................515-832-5200
Technipac
Le Sueur, MN.........................507-665-6658
Thermodynamics
Commerce City, CO................800-627-9037
Thunder Pallet Inc
Theresa, WI...........................800-354-0643
Timbertech Company
Milton, NH...........................800-572-5538
Tower Pallet Co Inc
De Pere, WI...........................920-336-3495
Treen Box & Pallet Inc
Bensalem, PA.........................215-639-5100
Triad Pallet Co Inc
Greensboro, NC.....................336-292-8175
Upham & Walsh Lumber
Hoffman Estates, IL................847-519-1010
UPN Pallet Company
Penns Grove, NJ.....................856-299-1192
Vancouver Manufacturing
Washougal, WA......................360-835-8519
Viking Pallet Corp
Maple Grove, MN...................763-425-6707
Walters Brothers
Radisson, WI.........................715-945-2646
Warren Pallet Co Inc
Bloomsbury, NJ......................908-995-7172
Welch Packaging Group Inc
Elkhart, IN............................574-295-2460
Wetterau Wood Products
Burlington, MA......................800-986-0958
White Mountain Lumber Co
Berlin, NH............................603-752-1000
Williams Pallet
West Chester, OH...................513-874-4014
Williamsburg Millwork
Ruther Glen, VA.....................804-994-2151
Wnc Pallet & Forest Pdts Co
Candler, NC...........................828-667-5426
Woodson Pallet Co
Anmoore, WV........................304-623-2858
Yerger Wood Products
East Greenville, PA.................215-679-4413
York River Pallet Corporation
Shacklefords, VA....................804-785-5811

Lift Truck

Bmh Equipment Inc
Sacramento, CA......................800-350-8828
Cantley-Ellis Manufacturing Company
Kingsport, TN........................423-246-4671
Central Pallet Mills Inc
Central City, KY.....................270-754-2900
Dominion Pallet Inc
Mineral, VA...........................800-227-5321
Hanson Box & Lumber Company
Wakefield, MA.......................617-245-0358
L T Hampel Corp
Germantown, WI....................800-681-6979
Paul Hawkins Lumber Company
Mannington, WV....................304-986-2230

Live Skid

L T Hampel Corp
Germantown, WI....................800-681-6979
Load King Mfg
Jacksonville, FL......................800-531-4975

Plastic

Barrette Outdoor Living
Cleveland, OH........................800-336-2383
Buckhorn Inc
Milford, OH..........................800-543-4454
Burgess Mfg. - Oklahoma
Guthrie, OK...........................800-804-1913
Emco Industrial Plastics
Cedar Grove, NJ.....................800-292-9906

Fresno Pallet, Inc.
Sultana, CA...........................559-591-4111
Green Tek
Janesville, WI........................800-747-6440
Gulf Arizona Packaging
Humble, TX...........................800-364-3887
Gulf Systems
Oklahoma City, OK.................800-364-3887
Harbor Pallet Company
Anaheim, CA.........................714-871-0932
Herche Warehouse
Denver, CO...........................303-371-8186
Kadon Corporation
Milford, OH..........................937-299-0088
Kimball Companies
East Longmeadow, MA.............413-525-1881
L T Hampel Corp
Germantown, WI....................800-681-6979
Lexington Logistics LLC
Portage, WI...........................800-356-8150
Lumber & Things
Keyser, WV............................800-296-5656
MBX Packaging Specialists
Wausau, WI...........................715-845-1171
Nucon Corporation
Deerfield, IL..........................877-545-0070
Occidental Chemical Corporation
Dallas, TX.............................800-733-3665
ORBIS
Oconomowoc, WI...................262-560-5000
ORBIS
Oconomowoc, WI...................800-890-7292
Pallet Management Systems
Lawrenceville, VA...................800-446-1804
PDQ Plastics Inc
Bayonne, NJ...........................800-447-7141
Penda Form Corp
New Concord, OH..................800-837-2574
Port Erie Plastics Inc
Harborcreek, PA.....................814-899-7602
Robinson Industries Inc
Coleman, MI.........................989-465-6111
Royal Ecoproducts
Vaughan, ON.........................800-465-7670
Saeplast Canada
St John, NB...........................800-567-3966
Sfb Plastics Inc
Wichita, KS...........................800-343-8133
Stearnswood Inc
Hutchinson, MN.....................800-657-0144
Stratis Plastic Pallets
Indianapolis, IN.....................800-725-5387
Thermodynamics
Commerce City, CO................800-627-9037
TMF Corporation
Havertown, PA.......................610-853-3080
Upham & Walsh Lumber
Hoffman Estates, IL................847-519-1010

Wooden

A.M. Loveman Lumber & Box Company
Nashville, TN........................615-297-1397
American Box Corporation
Lisbon, OH............................330-424-8055
Auto Pallets-Boxes
Lathrup Village, MI.................800-875-2699
Bay Area Pallet Company/IFCO Systems
Houston, TX..........................877-430-4326
Bc Wood Products
Ashland, VA..........................804-798-9154
Burgess Mfg. - Oklahoma
Guthrie, OK...........................800-804-1913
C & L Wood Products Inc
Hartselle, AL.........................800-483-2035
Cantley-Ellis Manufacturing Company
Kingsport, TN........................423-246-4671
Cascade Wood Components
Cascade Locks, OR..................541-374-8413
Cedar Box Co
Minneapolis, MN....................612-332-4287
Coastal Pallet Corp
Bridgeport, CT.......................203-333-6222
Coblentz Brothers Inc
Apple Creek, OH....................330-857-7211
Corinth Products
Corinth, ME..........................207-285-3387
Cutler Brothers Box & Lumber
Fairview, NJ..........................201-943-2535
D&M Pallet Company
Neshkoro, WI........................920-293-4616

Daniel Boone Lumber Industries
Morehead, KY 606-784-7586
Day Lumber Company
Westfield, MA 413-568-3511
Development Workshop Inc
Idaho Falls, ID 800-657-5597
Dufeck Manufacturing Co
Denmark, WI. 888-603-9663
Durant Box Factory
Durant, OK 580-924-4035
Eichler Wood Products
Laurys Station, PA 610-262-6749
Elba Pallets Company
Elba, AL 334-897-6034
ERO/Goodrich Forest Products
Tualatin, OR 800-458-5545
F.E. Wood & Sons
West Baldwin, ME 207-286-5003
Fabrication Specialties
Centerville, TN 931-729-2283
Fehlig Brothers Box & Lbr Co
St Louis, MO. 314-241-6900
Fox Valley Wood Products Inc
Kaukauna, WI. 920-766-4069
Fresno Pallet, Inc.
Sultana, CA 559-591-4111
G L Packaging Products Inc
West Chicago, IL 866-935-8755
Girard Wood Products Inc
Puyallup, WA 800-532-0505
Goeman's Wood Products
Hartford, WI. 262-673-6090
Graham Pallet Co Inc
Tompkinsville, KY 888-525-0694
H&H Lumber Company
Amarillo, TX. 806-335-1813
H&H Wood Products
Hamburg, NY 716-648-5600
Hanson Box & Lumber Company
Wakefield, MA 617-245-0358
Harbor Pallet Company
Anaheim, CA 714-871-0932
Hawkeye Pallet Co
Johnston, IA 515-276-0409
Herkimer Pallet & Wood Products Company
Herkimer, NY. 315-866-4591
HHP Inc
Henniker, NH 603-428-3298
Hildreth Wood Products Inc
Wadesboro, NC. 704-826-8326
Hinchcliff Products Company
Strongsville, OH 440-238-5200
Hunter Woodworks
Carson, CA 800-966-4751
Industrial Hardwood
Perrysburg, OH 419-666-2503
Industrial Woodfab & Packaging
Riverview, MI. 734-284-4808
International Wood Industries
Snohomish, WA 800-922-6141
John Rock Inc
Coatesville, PA 610-857-4809
Kauling Wood Products Company
Beckemeyer, IL. 618-594-2901
Kelley Wood Products
Fitchburg, MA 978-345-7531
KETCH
Wichita, KS. 800-766-3777
Killington Wood ProductsCompany
Rutland, VT. 802-773-9111
L&S Pallet Company
Houston, TX. 281-443-6537
La Menuiserie East Angus
East Angus, QC. 819-832-2746
Lake Michigan Hardwood Company
Leland, MI. 231-256-9811
Lumber & Things
Keyser, WV. 800-296-5656
Lydall
Doswell, VA 804-266-9611
M & H Crate Inc
Jacksonville, TX. 903-683-5351
Madison County Wood Products
Fredericktown, MO. 314-584-1802
Marion Pallet Company
Marion, OH 800-432-4117
Mark Slade ManufacturingCompany
Seymour, WI. 920-833-6557
Marshall Boxes Inc
Rochester, NY. 585-458-7432
Maull-Baker Box Company
Brookfield, WI. 414-463-1290

Mayco Inc
Dallas, TX. 214-638-4848
Mcintosh Box & Pallet Co
East Syracuse, NY 800-219-9552
Mcneilly Wood Products Inc
Campbell Hall, NY 845-457-9651
Meriden Box Company
Southington, CT 860-621-7141
Michigan Pallet Inc
St Charles, MI. 989-865-9915
Millwood Inc
Vienna, OH 330-393-4400
Momence Pallet Corp
Momence, IL. 815-472-6451
Moorecraft Box & Crate
Tarboro, NC 252-823-2510
Mt Valley Farms & Lumber Prods
Biglerville, PA. 717-677-6166
Native Lumber Company
Wallingford, CT 203-269-2625
Nefab Packaging, Inc.
Coppell, TX 800-322-4425
Nelson Co
Sparrows Point, MD 410-477-3000
New England Pallets & Skids
Ludlow, MA 413-583-6628
New Lisbon Wood ProductsManufacturing Company
New Lisbon, WI. 608-562-3122
New Mexico Products Inc
Albuquerque, NM 877-345-7864
Northwest Products
Archbold, OH 419-445-1950
Oak Creek Pallet Company
Milwaukee, WI. 414-762-7170
Original Lincoln Logs
Chestertown, NY 800-833-2461
Packing Material Company
Southfield, MI. 248-489-7000
Pallet Management Systems
Lawrenceville, VA 800-446-1804
Pallet One Inc
Mocksville, NC. 336-492-5565
Pallet One Inc
Bartow, FL. 800-771-1148
Pallets Inc
Fort Edward, NY. 518-747-4177
Pallister Pallet
Wapello, IA. 319-523-8161
Pallox Incorporated
Onsted, MI 517-456-4101
Paul Hawkins Lumber Company
Mannington, WV 304-986-2230
Pine Bluff Crating & Pallet
Pine Bluff, AR. 866-415-1075
Pine Point Wood Products Inc
Osseo, MN 763-428-4301
Porter & Porter Lumber
Fort Gay, WV 304-648-5133
Precision Wood of Hawaii
Vancouver, WA 808-682-2055
Precision Wood Products
Vancouver, WA 360-694-8322
Pruitt's Packaging Services
Grand Rapids, MI 800-878-0553
Ralph L. Mason,
Newark, MD 410-632-1766
Redding Pallet Inc
Redding, CA 530-241-6321
Remmey Wood Products
Southampton, PA 215-355-3335
Roberts Pallet Co
Ellington, MO 573-663-7877
S & W Pallet Co
Camden, TN 800-640-0522
Scott Pallets Inc
Amelia Court Hse, VA 800-394-2514
Sheldon Wood Products
Toano, VA 757-566-8880
Smith Pallet Co Inc
Hatfield, AR. 870-389-6184
Sonoma Pacific Company
Montebello, CA 323-838-4374
Southern Pallet
Christchurch, NZ 901-942-4603
Spring Wood Products
Geneva, OH 440-466-1135
St. Pierre Box & Lumber Company
Canton, CT 860-693-2089
Stearnswood Inc
Hutchinson, MN 800-657-0144
Studd & Whipple Company
Conewango Valley, NY. 716-287-3791

Tampa Pallet Co
Tampa, FL. 813-626-5700
Tasler Inc
Webster City, IA 515-832-5200
Technipac
Le Sueur, MN 507-665-6658
Tennessee Mills
Red Boiling Springs, TN 615-699-2253
Thunder Pallet Inc
Theresa, WI. 800-354-0643
Treen Box & Pallet Inc
Bensalem, PA. 215-639-5100
Triad Pallet Co Inc
Greensboro, NC 336-292-8175
Upham & Walsh Lumber
Hoffman Estates, IL. 847-519-1010
UPN Pallet Company
Penns Grove, NJ 856-299-1192
Vancouver Manufacturing
Washougal, WA. 360-835-8519
Viking Pallet Corp
Maple Grove, MN. 763-425-6707
Warren Pallet Co Inc
Bloomsbury, NJ. 908-995-7172
White Mountain Lumber Co
Berlin, NH. 603-752-1000
Williams Pallet
West Chester, OH 513-874-4014
Williamsburg Millwork
Ruther Glen, VA 804-994-2151
Wnc Pallet & Forest Pdts Co
Candler, NC 828-667-5426
Yerger Wood Products
East Greenville, PA. 215-679-4413
York River Pallet Corporation
Shacklefords, VA 804-785-5811

Racks

Barrel & Drum Draining

Bmh Equipment Inc
Sacramento, CA 800-350-8828
Key Material Handling Inc
Simi Valley, CA. 800-539-7225
Triple-A Manufacturing Company
Toronto, ON 800-786-2238

Bottle

Cannon Equipment Company
Cannon Falls, MN. 800-825-8501
Dunn Woodworks
Shrewsbury, PA 877-835-8592
Houston Wire Works, Inc.
South Houston, TX 800-468-9477
Metro Corporation
Wilkes Barre, PA. 800-992-1776
Olson Wire Products Co
Baltimore, MD 410-242-7900
Polymer Solutions International
Newtown Square, PA 877-444-7225
Supreme Metal
Alpharetta, GA 800-645-2526
Triple-A Manufacturing Company
Toronto, ON 800-786-2238
Vermillion Flooring
Springfield, MO 417-862-3785
Western Square Industries
Stockton, CA. 800-367-8383
Xtreme Beverages, LLC
Dana Point, CA. 949-495-7929

Can

Amco Metals Indl
City of Industry, CA 626-855-2550
ARC Specialties
Valencia, CA. 661-775-8500
EPCO
Murfreesboro, TN. 800-251-3398
Grayline Housewares Inc
Columbus, OH 800-222-7388
Lakeside Manufacturing Inc
Milwaukee, WI 888-558-8565
Leggett & Platt Storage
Vernon Hills, IL 847-816-6246
Metro Corporation
Wilkes Barre, PA. 800-992-1776
New Age Industrial
Norton, KS 800-255-0104

Storage Unlimited
Nixa, MO 800-478-6642
Superior Products Company
Saint Paul, MN 800-328-9800
Triple-A Manufacturing Company
Toronto, ON 800-786-2238
Xtreme Beverages, LLC
Dana Point, CA 949-495-7929

Cold Storage Room

ABI Limited
Concord, ON 800-297-8666
Ace Manufacturing & Parts Co
Sullivan, MO 800-325-6138
Bmh Equipment Inc
Sacramento, CA 800-350-8828
Carlisle Food Svc Products Inc
Oklahoma City, OK 800-654-8210
ColdZone
Anaheim, CA
Jarke Corporation
Prospect Hts, IL 800-722-5255
Kaines West Michigan Co
Ludington, MI 231-845-1281
Marlin Steel Wire Products
Baltimore, MD 877-762-7546
Metal Equipment Company
Cleveland, OH 800-700-6326
Metro Corporation
Wilkes Barre, PA 800-992-1776
Ridg-U-Rak
North East, PA 866-479-7225
Ron Vallort & Associates
Oak Brook, IL 630-734-3821
RTI Shelving Systems
Elmhurst, NY 800-223-6210
Superior Products Company
Saint Paul, MN 800-328-9800
Triple-A Manufacturing Company
Toronto, ON 800-786-2238

Kitchen

Advance Tabco
Edgewood, NY 800-645-3166
Amco Metals Indl
City of Industry, CA 626-855-2550
American Housewares
Bronx, NY 718-665-9500
ARC Specialties
Valencia, CA 661-775-8500
Archer Wire Intl Corp
Chicago, IL 708-563-1700
Bevles Company
Dallas, TX 800-441-1601
Bmh Equipment Inc
Sacramento, CA 800-350-8828
California Caster & Handtruck
San Francisco, CA 800-950-8750
Dubuque Steel Products Co
Dubuque, IA 563-556-6288
Grayline Housewares Inc
Columbus, OH 800-222-7388
H A Sparke Co
Shreveport, LA 318-222-0927
Hodges
Vienna, IL 800-444-0011
Jack Stack
Inwood, NY 800-999-9840
Lavi Industries
Valencia, CA 800-624-6225
LPI Imports
Chicago, IL 877-389-6563
M & E Mfg Co Inc
Kingston, NY 845-331-2110
Metro Corporation
Wilkes Barre, PA 800-992-1776
New Age Industrial
Norton, KS 800-255-0104
Princeton Shelving
Cedar Rapids, IA 319-369-0355
Quipco Products Inc
Sauget, IL 314-993-1442
Storage Unlimited
Nixa, MO 800-478-6642
Thermal Bags By Ingrid Inc
Gilberts, IL 800-622-5560
United Showcase Company
Wood Ridge, NJ 800-526-6382
Universal Stainless
Aurora, CO 800-223-8332

Universal Stainless & Alloy
Titusville, PA 800-295-1909
Vermillion Flooring
Springfield, MO 417-862-3785
Westfield Sheet Metal Works
Kenilworth, NJ 908-276-5500
Wilder Manufacturing Company
Port Jervis, NY 800-832-1319

Packing House

Bmh Equipment Inc
Sacramento, CA 800-350-8828
Cannon Equipment Company
Cannon Falls, MN 800-825-8501
Cozzini Inc
Algona, IA 888-295-1116
Market Forge Industries Inc
Everett, MA 866-698-3188
New Age Industrial
Norton, KS 800-255-0104
Tier-Rack Corp
Ballwin, MO 800-325-7869
Unirak Storage Systems
Taylor, MI 800-348-7225
United Steel Products Company
East Stroudsburg, PA 570-476-1010
Westfield Sheet Metal Works
Kenilworth, NJ 908-276-5500
Xtreme Beverages, LLC
Dana Point, CA 949-495-7929

Pallet

Ace Manufacturing & Parts Co
Sullivan, MO 800-325-6138
Atlas Equipment Company
Kansas City, MO 800-842-9188
Bmh Equipment Inc
Sacramento, CA 800-350-8828
Brute Fabricators
Castroville, TX 800-777-2788
Delta Wire And Mfg.
Harrow, ON 800-221-3794
Durham Manufacturing Co
Durham, CT 800-243-3744
Dynamic Storage Systems Inc.
Brooksville, FL 800-974-8211
Elite Storage Solutions Inc
Monroe, GA 800-367-0572
Engineered Products Corp
Greenville, SC 800-868-0145
Equipment Design & Fabrication
Charlotte, NC 800-949-0165
Eugene Welding Company
Marysville, MI 810-364-7421
Frazier Industrial Co
Long Valley, NJ 800-859-1342
Global Equipment Co Inc
Port Washington, NY 888-628-3466
Key Material Handling Inc
Simi Valley, CA 800-539-7225
Lumber & Things
Keyser, WV 800-296-5656
Mason Ways Indestructible
West Palm Beach, FL 800-837-2881
Material Storage Systems
Humble, TX 800-881-6750
Omicron Steel Products Company
Jamaica, NY 718-805-3400
Penco Products
Skippack, PA 800-562-1000
Princeton Shelving
Cedar Rapids, IA 319-369-0355
Ross Technology Corp
Leola, PA 800-345-8170
Sackett Systems
Bensenville, IL 800-323-8332
Sigma Industries
Elkhart, IN 574-295-9660
Solve Needs International
White Lake, MI 800-783-2462
Steel King Industries
Stevens Point, WI 800-553-3096
Steelmaster Material Handling
Marietta, GA 800-875-9900
Teilhaber Manufacturing Corp
Broomfield, CO 800-358-7225
Triple-A Manufacturing Company
Toronto, ON 800-786-2238
Unirak Storage Systems
Taylor, MI 800-348-7225

Wireway Husky Corp
Denver, NC 800-438-5629

Spice

Metro Corporation
Wilkes Barre, PA 800-992-1776
Storage Unlimited
Nixa, MO 800-478-6642
Xtreme Beverages, LLC
Dana Point, CA 949-495-7929

Stock

Acme Display Fixture Company
Los Angeles, CA 800-959-5657
Advance Storage Products
Garden Grove, CA 888-478-7422
ARC Specialties
Valencia, CA 661-775-8500
Bayhead Products Corp.
Dover, NH 800-229-4323
Bennett Manufacturing Company
Alden, NY 800-345-2142
Bmh Equipment Inc
Sacramento, CA 800-350-8828
Cres Cor
Mentor, OH 877-273-7267
Edwards Products
Cincinnati, OH 800-543-1835
Faribault Manufacturing Co
Faribault, MN 800-447-6043
Flexible Material Handling
Suwanee, GA 800-669-1501
Hodge Manufacturing Company
Springfield, MA 800-262-4634
Hodges
Vienna, IL 800-444-0011
Interlake Mecalux
Chicago, IL 708-344-9999
Irby
Rocky Mount, NC 252-442-0154
Item Products
Houston, TX 800-333-4932
Lodi Metal Tech
Lodi, CA 800-359-5999
Metro Corporation
Wilkes Barre, PA 800-992-1776
Omicron Steel Products Company
Jamaica, NY 718-805-3400
Paltier
Michigan City, IN 800-348-3201
Princeton Shelving
Cedar Rapids, IA 319-369-0355
Pucel Enterprises Inc
Cleveland, OH 800-336-4986
Rapid Rack Industries
City of Industry, CA 800-736-7225
RW Products
Edgewood, NY 800-345-1022
Southern Metal Fabricators Inc
Albertville, AL 800-989-1330
Speedrack Products Group LTD
Sparta, MI 616-887-0002
SPG International
Covington, GA 877-503-4774
Tier-Rack Corp
Ballwin, MO 800-325-7869
Unirak Storage Systems
Taylor, MI 800-348-7225
United Steel Products Company
East Stroudsburg, PA 570-476-1010
W.A. Schmidt Company
Oaks, PA 800-523-6719
Wirefab Inc
Worcester, MA 877-877-4445

Wine

Amco Metals Indl
City of Industry, CA 626-855-2550
Cannon Equipment Company
Cannon Falls, MN 800-825-8501
Cramer Products
New York, NY 212-645-2368
Dunn Woodworks
Shrewsbury, PA 877-835-8592
Epic Products
Santa Ana, CA 800-548-9791
Harmar
Sarasota, FL 800-833-0478

Houston Wire Works, Inc.
South Houston, TX 800-468-9477
Kedco Wine Storage Systems
Farmingdale, NY 800-654-9988
Leggett & Platt Storage
Vernon Hills, IL 847-816-6246
Metro Corporation
Wilkes Barre, PA. 800-992-1776
Tag-Trade Associated Group
Chicago, IL 800-621-8350
Triple-A Manufacturing Company
Toronto, ON 800-786-2238
Vermillion Flooring
Springfield, MO 417-862-3785
Wine Chillers of California
Santa Ana, CA 800-331-4274
Wineracks by Marcus
Costa Mesa, CA 714-546-4922
Xtreme Beverages, LLC
Dana Point, CA. 949-495-7929

Wire

Ace Manufacturing & Parts Co
Sullivan, MO. 800-325-6138
Advanced Plastic Coating Svc
Parsons, KS. 620-421-1660
Aero Manufacturing Co
Clifton, NJ. 800-631-8378
Amco Metals Indl
City of Industry, CA 626-855-2550
American Housewares
Bronx, NY. 718-665-9500
Automatic Specialties Inc
Marlborough, MA. 800-445-2370
Avalon Manufacturer
Corona, CA 800-676-3040
Barker Wire
Keosauqua, IA 319-293-3176
Better Bilt Products
Addison, IL 800-544-4550
Complex Steel & Wire Corp
Wayne, MI. 734-326-1600
Cramer Products
New York, NY 212-645-2368
Dubuque Steel Products Co
Dubuque, IA 563-556-6288
Eagle Wire Works
Cleveland, OH 216-341-8550
Embro Manufacturing Company
East Canton, OH. 330-489-3500
Emco Industrial Plastics
Cedar Grove, NJ 800-292-9906
FMI Display
Elkins Park, PA 215-663-1998
Gillis Associated Industries
Prospect Heights, IL 847-541-6500
Grayline Housewares Inc
Columbus, OH 800-222-7388
Harmar
Sarasota, FL 800-833-0478
Hewitt Manufacturing Co
Waldron, IN. 765-525-9829
HMG Worldwide In-Store Marketing
New York, NY 212-736-2300
Hodges
Vienna, IL 800-444-0011
Houston Wire Works, Inc.
South Houston, TX 800-468-9477
Indiana Wire Company
Fremont, IN. 877-786-6883
J.C. Products Inc.
Haddam, CT 860-267-5516
Jarke Corporation
Prospect Hts, IL 800-722-5255
JEM Wire Products
Middletown, CT 860-347-0447
Kaines West Michigan Co
Ludington, MI. 231-845-1281
Key Material Handling Inc
Simi Valley, CA. 800-539-7225
Leggett & Platt Storage
Vernon Hills, IL 847-816-6246
Liberty Machine Company
York, PA 800-745-8152
Load King Mfg
Jacksonville, FL 800-531-4975
LPI Imports
Chicago, IL 877-389-6563
Lynch-Jamentz Company
Lakewood, CA 800-828-6217

Marlin Steel Wire Products
Baltimore, MD 877-762-7546
McMillin Manufacturing Corporation
Los Angeles, CA. 323-268-1900
Metaline Products Co Inc
South Amboy, NJ 732-721-1373
Metro Corporation
Wilkes Barre, PA. 800-992-1776
Micro Wire Products Inc
Brockton, MA. 508-584-0200
Midwest Wire Products LLC
Sturgeon Bay, WI 800-445-0225
Midwest Wire Specialties
Chicago, IL 800-238-0228
Nashville Wire Products
Nashville, TN 615-743-2480
New Age Industrial
Norton, KS 800-255-0104
Northern Metal Products
St Cloud, MN 800-458-5549
Olson Wire Products Co
Baltimore, MD 410-242-7900
Pentwater Wire Products Inc
Pentwater, MI 877-869-6911
Pinquist Tool & Die Company
Brooklyn, NY 800-752-0414
Princeton Shelving
Cedar Rapids, IA 319-369-0355
R.I. Enterprises
Hernando, MS 662-429-7863
Racks
San Diego, CA 619-661-0987
Randware Industries
Prospect Heights, IL 847-299-8884
Riverside Wire & Metal Co.
Ionia, MI 616-527-3500
Royal Display Corporation
Middletown, CT 800-569-1295
Schlueter Company
Janesville, WI 800-359-1700
Selma Wire Products Company
Selma, IN 765-282-3532
SEMCO
Ocala, FL. 800-749-6894
Sipco Products
Peoria Heights, IL 309-682-5400
Spot Wire Works Company
Philadelphia, PA 215-627-6124
SSW Holding Co Inc
Elizabethtown, KY 270-769-5526
Steel City Corporation
Youngstown, OH. 800-321-0350
Straits Steel & Wire Co
Ludington, MI. 231-843-3416
Superior Products Company
Saint Paul, MN 800-328-9800
Tennsco Corp
Dickson, TN 800-251-8184
Toledo Wire Products
Toledo, OH 888-430-7445
Trepte's Wire & Metal Works
Bellflower, CA 800-828-6217
Triple-A Manufacturing Company
Toronto, ON 800-786-2238
Victone Manufacturing Company
Chicago, IL 312-738-3211
W J Egli & Co
Alliance, OH 330-823-3666
Wahlstrom Manufacturing
Fontana, CA 909-822-4677
Wald Wire & Mfg Co
Oshkosh, WI 800-236-0053
Wire Products Mfg
Merrill, WI 715-536-7884
Wirefab Inc
Worcester, MA. 877-877-4445
Wiremaid Products Div
Coral Springs, FL 800-770-4700
Woerner Wire Works
Omaha, NE 402-451-5414
Yeager Wire Works
Berwick, PA 570-752-2769

Ramps

Delivery Truck

Hormann Flexan Llc
Leetsdale, PA 800-365-3667
Melcher Manufacturing Co
Spokane Valley, WA 800-541-4227

Shelving

Steel

Ace Manufacturing & Parts Co
Sullivan, MO. 800-325-6138
Advance Tabco
Edgewood, NY 800-645-3166
Allied Engineering
North Vancouver, BC 877-929-1214
Amco Metals Indl
City of Industry, CA 626-855-2550
Amscor Inc
West Babylon, NY 800-825-9800
ARC Specialties
Valencia, CA 661-775-8500
ATD-American Co
Wyncote, PA 800-523-2300
Atlas Equipment Company
Kansas City, MO. 800-842-9188
Bmh Equipment Inc
Sacramento, CA 800-350-8828
Borroughs Corp
Kalamazoo, MI 800-748-0227
Cleveland Metal Stamping Company
Berea, OH 440-234-0010
Commercial Kitchen Co
Los Angeles, CA. 323-732-2291
Custom Diamond Intl.
Laval, QC 800-326-5926
Den Mar Corp
North Dartmouth, MA 508-999-3295
Despro Manufacturing
Cedar Grove, NJ 800-292-9906
Duluth Sheet Metal
Duluth, MN. 218-722-2613
Durham Manufacturing Co
Durham, CT 800-243-3744
E-Z Shelving Systems Inc
Shawnee, KS 800-353-1331
Eagle Group
Clayton, DE. 800-441-8440
Easyup Storage Systems
Tukwila, WA 800-426-9234
Eldorado Miranda Manufacturing Company
Largo, FL 800-330-0708
Emco Industrial Plastics
Cedar Grove, NJ 800-292-9906
Global Equipment Co Inc
Port Washington, NY 888-628-3466
Hodges
Vienna, IL 800-444-0011
IMC Teddy Food Service Equipment
Amityville, NY 800-221-5644
Infra Corp
Waterford, MI 888-434-6372
Institutional Equipment Inc
Bolingbrook, IL 630-771-0990
InterMetro Industries
Wilkes-Barre, PA 570-825-2741
Jarke Corporation
Prospect Hts, IL 800-722-5255
Kent Corp
Birmingham, AL. 800-252-5368
Key Material Handling Inc
Simi Valley, CA. 800-539-7225
Lambertson Industries Inc
Sparks, NV 800-548-3324
Leggett & Platt Storage
Vernon Hills, IL 847-816-6246
Linvar
Hartford, CT 800-282-5288
Lista International Corp
Holliston, MA. 800-722-3020
Loyal Manufacturing
Indianapolis, IN 317-359-3185
LPI Imports
Chicago, IL 877-389-6563
Lyon LLC
Montgomery, IL 630-892-8941
M & E Mfg Co Inc
Kingston, NY 845-331-2110
Market Forge Industries Inc
Everett, MA. 866-698-3188
Marlin Steel Wire Products
Baltimore, MD 877-762-7546
Metal Kitchen Fabricators Inc
Houston, TX 713-683-8375
Metro Corporation
Wilkes Barre, PA. 800-992-1776

New Age Industrial
  Norton, KS 800-255-0104
Nexel Industries Inc
  Port Washington, NY 800-245-6682
Omicron Steel Products Company
  Jamaica, NY 718-805-3400
OSF
  Toronto, ON 800-465-4000
Princeton Shelving
  Cedar Rapids, IA..................319-369-0355
Pucel Enterprises Inc
  Cleveland, OH 800-336-4986
Quantum Storage Systems Inc
  Miami, FL.........................800-685-4665
Republic Storage Systems LLC
  Canton, OH 800-477-1255
Royce Corp
  Glendale, AZ......................602-256-0006
RTI Shelving Systems
  Elmhurst, NY 800-223-6210
Sefi Fabricators Inc
  Amityville, NY 631-842-2200
Solve Needs International
  White Lake, MI....................800-783-2462
Spot Wire Works Company
  Philadelphia, PA 215-627-6124
Stainless Fabricating Company
  Denver, CO 800-525-8966
Stainless Steel Fabricators
  Tyler, TX.........................903-595-6625
Starlite Food Service Equipment
  Detroit, MI.......................888-521-6603
Steelmaster Material Handling
  Marietta, GA......................800-875-9900
Streater Inc
  Albert Lea, MN....................800-527-4197
Stryco Wire Products
  North York, ON....................416-663-7000
Travis Manufacturing Corp
  Alliance, OH......................330-875-1661
Tri-Boro Shelving & Partition
  Farmville, VA.....................800-633-3070
Triple-A Manufacturing Company
  Toronto, ON.......................800-786-2238
Universal Stainless
  Aurora, CO 800-223-8332
Universal Stainless & Alloy
  Titusville, PA 800-295-1909
Weiss Sheet Metal Inc
  Avon, MA 508-583-8300
Western Pacific Stge Solutions
  San Dimas, CA 800-888-5707

Wire

Ace Manufacturing & Parts Co
  Sullivan, MO......................800-325-6138
Advance Tabco
  Edgewood, NY......................800-645-3166
Amco Metals Indl
  City of Industry, CA 626-855-2550
Atlas Equipment Company
  Kansas City, MO...................800-842-9188
Barker Wire
  Keosauqua, IA 319-293-3176
Bettag & Associates
  O Fallon, MO 800-325-0959
Bmh Equipment Inc
  Sacramento, CA 800-350-8828
Coast Scientific
  Rancho Santa Fe, CA 800-445-1544
Despro Manufacturing
  Cedar Grove, NJ 800-292-9906
Enterprise Products
  Bell Gardens, CA 562-928-1918
Etube & Wire
  Shrewsbury, PA....................800-618-4720
Gillis Associated Industries
  Prospect Heights, IL 847-541-6500
Global Equipment Co Inc
  Port Washington, NY 888-628-3466
Hodge Manufacturing Company
  Springfield, MA 800-262-4634
Hodges
  Vienna, IL........................800-444-0011
Indiana Wire Company
  Fremont, IN.......................877-786-6883
JEM Wire Products
  Middletown, CT....................860-347-0447
Kaines West Michigan Co
  Ludington, MI.....................231-845-1281

Kotoff & Company
  San Dimas, CA.....................626-443-7115
Langer Manufacturing Company
  Cedar Rapids, IA..................800-728-6445
Leggett & Platt Storage
  Vernon Hills, IL 847-816-6246
LPI Imports
  Chicago, IL.......................877-389-6563
Luckner Steel Shelving
  Flushing, NY......................800-888-4212
Madsen Wire Products Inc
  Orland, IN........................260-829-6561
Marlin Steel Wire Products
  Baltimore, MD.....................877-762-7546
McMillin Manufacturing Corporation
  Los Angeles, CA...................323-268-1900
Metaline Products Co Inc
  South Amboy, NJ 732-721-1373
Metro Corporation
  Wilkes Barre, PA..................800-992-1776
Midwest Wire Products LLC
  Sturgeon Bay, WI..................800-445-0225
Nexel Industries Inc
  Port Washington, NY 800-245-6682
Ortmayer Materials Handling
  Brooklyn, NY 718-875-7995
Pacific Northwest Wire Works
  Dupont, WA 800-222-7699
Pentwater Wire Products Inc
  Pentwater, MI 877-869-6911
Princeton Shelving
  Cedar Rapids, IA..................319-369-0355
Riverside Wire & Metal Co.
  Ionia, MI.........................616-527-3500
Royal Display Corporation
  Middletown, CT 800-569-1295
Royce Corp
  Glendale, AZ......................602-256-0006
RTI Shelving Systems
  Elmhurst, NY 800-223-6210
Sefi Fabricators Inc
  Amityville, NY 631-842-2200
Spaceguard Products
  Seymour, IN 800-841-0680
Spot Wire Works Company
  Philadelphia, PA 215-627-6124
Springport Steel Wire Products
  Elkhart, IN.......................574-295-9660
Straits Steel & Wire Co
  Ludington, MI.....................231-843-3416
Stryco Wire Products
  North York, ON....................416-663-7000
Superior Products Company
  Saint Paul, MN 800-328-9800
Swanson Wire Works Industries, Inc.
  Mesquite, TX 972-288-7465
Technibilt/Cari-All
  Newton, NC 800-233-3972
Tennsco Corp
  Dickson, TN 800-251-8184
Triad Scientific
  Manasquan, NJ 800-867-6690
Triple-A Manufacturing Company
  Toronto, ON 800-786-2238
Wirefab Inc
  Worcester, MA 877-877-4445
Wiremaid Products Div
  Coral Springs, FL 800-770-4700

Skids

American Box Corporation
  Lisbon, OH 330-424-8055
American Pallet Inc
  Oakdale, CA 209-847-6122
Bay Area Pallet Company/IFCO Systems
  Houston, TX 877-430-4326
Bennett Box & Pallet Company
  Winston, NC 800-334-8741
Black River Pallet Co
  Zeeland, MI.......................800-427-6515
Burgess Mfg. - Oklahoma
  Guthrie, OK.......................800-804-1913
Cassel Box & Lumber Co Inc
  Grafton, WI.......................262-377-9503
Cedar Box Co
  Minneapolis, MN 612-332-4287
Charles Tirschman Pallet Co
  Dundalk, MD 410-282-6199
Cotter Brothers Corp
  Danvers, MA 978-777-5001

Cumberland Box & Mill Co
  Cumberland, MD 301-724-1010
Cutter Lumber Products
  Livermore, CA 925-443-5959
D&M Pallet Company
  Neshkoro, WI......................920-293-4616
Daniel Boone Lumber Industries
  Morehead, KY 606-784-7586
Day Lumber Company
  Westfield, MA.....................413-568-3511
Denver Reel & Pallet Company
  Denver, CO 303-321-1920
Durant Box Factory
  Durant, OK 580-924-4035
Eichler Wood Products
  Laurys Station, PA 610-262-6749
F.E. Wood & Sons
  West Baldwin, ME 207-286-5003
Fabricating & Welding Corp
  Chicago, IL.......................773-928-2050
Fabrication Specialties
  Centerville, TN 931-729-2283
Fresno Pallet, Inc.
  Sultana, CA 559-591-4111
Gatewood Products LLC
  Parkersburg, WV...................800-827-5461
Gerrity Industries
  Monmouth, ME......................877-933-2804
Girard Wood Products Inc
  Puyallup, WA 800-532-0505
Global Equipment Co Inc
  Port Washington, NY 888-628-3466
Goeman's Wood Products
  Hartford, WI 262-673-6090
Graham Pallet Co Inc
  Tompkinsville, KY 888-525-0694
Gray Woodproducts
  Tacoma, WA 253-752-7000
Hanson Box & Lumber Company
  Wakefield, MA 617-245-0358
Harbor Pallet Company
  Anaheim, CA 714-871-0932
Hildreth Wood Products Inc
  Wadesboro, NC 704-826-8326
Hinchcliff Products Company
  Strongsville, OH 440-238-5200
Industrial Hardwood
  Perrysburg, OH 419-666-2503
Industrial Lumber & Packaging
  Spring Lake, MI 616-842-1457
International Wood Industries
  Snohomish, WA 800-922-6141
J.M. Rogers & Sons
  Moss Point, MS 228-475-7584
Jarke Corporation
  Prospect Hts, IL 800-722-5255
Kauling Wood Products Company
  Beckemeyer, IL....................618-594-2901
Kelley Wood Products
  Fitchburg, MA 978-345-7531
Kent District Library System
  Comstock Park, MI.................616-784-2007
Kimball Companies
  East Longmeadow, MA 413-525-1881
Konz Wood Products Co
  Appleton, WI 877-610-5145
L&H Wood Manufacturing Company
  Farmington, MI....................248-474-9000
Lester Box & Mfg Div
  Long Beach, CA 562-437-5123
Load King Mfg
  Jacksonville, FL 800-531-4975
Lumber & Things
  Keyser, WV........................800-296-5656
Maull-Baker Box Company
  Brookfield, WI 414-463-1290
May-Wes Manufacturing Inc
  Hutchinson, MN 800-788-6483
Mcintosh Box & Pallet Co
  East Syracuse, NY 800-219-9552
Mcneilly Wood Products Inc
  Campbell Hall, NY 845-457-9651
Michiana Box & Crate
  Niles, MI.........................800-677-6372
Michigan Pallet Inc
  St Charles, MI....................989-865-9915
Mt Valley Farms & Lumber Prods
  Biglerville, PA..................717-677-6166
Necedah Pallet Co Inc
  Necedah, WI.......................800-672-5538
Nefab Packaging, Inc.
  Coppell, TX 800-322-4425

Nelson Co
Sparrows Point, MD 410-477-3000
New England Pallets & Skids
Ludlow, MA 413-583-6628
New Lisbon Wood ProductsManufacturing Company
New Lisbon, WI 608-562-3122
Original Lincoln Logs
Chestertown, NY 800-833-2461
Ortmayer Materials Handling
Brooklyn, NY 718-875-7995
Packing Material Company
Southfield, MI 248-489-7000
Pallet One Inc
Mocksville, NC 336-492-5565
Pallets Inc
Fort Edward, NY 518-747-4177
Pallox Incorporated
Onsted, MI 517-456-4101
Pine Bluff Crating & Pallet
Pine Bluff, AR 866-415-1075
Pine Point Wood Products Inc
Osseo, MN 763-428-4301
Porter & Porter Lumber
Fort Gay, WV 304-648-5133
Premium Pallet
Philadelphia, PA 800-648-7347
Pruitt's Packaging Services
Grand Rapids, MI 800-878-0553
Rand-Whitney Group LLC
Worcester, MA 508-791-2301
Remmey Wood Products
Southampton, PA 215-355-3335
S & W Pallet Co
Camden, TN 800-640-0522
Savanna Pallets
McGregor, MN 218-768-2077
Shelby Pallet & Box Company
Shelby, MI 231-861-4214
Sheldon Wood Products
Toano, VA 757-566-8880
Smith Pallet Co Inc
Hatfield, AR 870-389-6184
Sonoma Pacific Company
Montebello, CA 323-838-4374
St. Pierre Box & Lumber Company
Canton, CT 860-693-2089
Streator Dependable Mfg
Streator, IL 800-798-0551
Swift Creek Forest Products
Jetersville, VA 804-561-4498
Technipac
Le Sueur, MN 507-665-6658
Thunder Pallet Inc
Theresa, WI 800-354-0643
Tower Pallet Co Inc
De Pere, WI 920-336-3495
Treen Box & Pallet Inc
Bensalem, PA 215-639-5100
Triad Pallet Co Inc
Greensboro, NC 336-292-8175
Upham & Walsh Lumber
Hoffman Estates, IL 847-519-1010
Van Dereems Mfg Co
Hawthorne, NJ 973-427-2355
Westfield Sheet Metal Works
Kenilworth, NJ 908-276-5500
Wetterau Wood Products
Burlington, MA 800-986-0958
Williams Pallet
West Chester, OH 513-874-4014
Wnc Pallet & Forest Pdts Co
Candler, NC 828-667-5426

Storage & Holding Equipment

A&B Safe Corporation
Glassboro, NJ 800-253-1267
A-Z Factory Supply
Schiller Park, IL 800-323-4511
Accent Store Fixtures
Kenosha, WI 800-545-1144
Acme Display Fixture Company
Los Angeles, CA 800-959-5657
Aco Container Systems
Pickering, ON 800-542-9942
Acrison Inc
Moonachie, NJ 800-422-4266
Adapto Storage Products
Hialeah, FL 305-499-4800
Advance Fittings Corp
Elkhorn, WI 262-723-6699

Advance Storage Products
Garden Grove, CA 888-478-7422
Advance Tabco
Edgewood, NY 800-645-3166
Aero Manufacturing Co
Clifton, NJ 800-631-8378
AFGO Mechanical Svc Inc
Astoria, NY 800-438-2346
Agspring
Leawood, KS 913-333-3035
Allegheny Bradford Corp
Bradford, PA 800-542-0650
Alliance Products LLC
Murfreesboro, TN 800-522-3973
Allied Engineering
North Vancouver, BC 877-929-1214
Alloy Products Corp
Waukesha, WI 800-236-6603
Althor Products
Bethel, CT 800-688-2693
Amco Metals Indl
City of Industry, CA 626-855-2550
Amscor Inc
West Babylon, NY 800-825-9800
Anderson-Crane Company
Minneapolis, MN 800-314-2747
ANDRITZ Inc
Muncy, PA 704-943-4343
Apache Stainless Equipment
Beaver Dam, WI 800-444-0398
Apollo Sheet Metal
Kennewick, WA 509-586-1104
APV Americas
Delavan, WI 800-252-5200
ARC Specialties
Valencia, CA 661-775-8500
Arizona Store Equipment
Phoenix, AZ 800-624-8395
Arkfeld Mfg & Distributing Co
Norfolk, NE. 800-533-0676
Art Wire Works Co
Chicago, IL 708-458-3993
Art-Phyl Creations
Hialeah, FL 800-327-8318
ATD-American Co
Wyncote, PA 800-523-2300
Atlas Equipment Company
Kansas City, MO 800-842-9188
Atlas Minerals & Chemicals Inc
Mertztown, PA 800-523-8269
Automatic Specialties Inc
Marlborough, MA 800-445-2370
B C Holland Inc
Dousman, WI 262-965-2939
Bacchus Wine Cellars
Houston, TX 800-487-8812
Bailly Showcase & Fixture Company
Las Vegas, NV 702-947-6885
Baldewein Company
Lake Forrest, IL 800-424-5544
Barker Company
Keosauqua, IA 319-293-3777
Barker Wire
Keosauqua, IA 319-293-3176
Baxter Manufacturing Inc
Orting, WA 800-777-2828
Bayhead Products Corp.
Dover, NH 800-229-4323
Bennett Manufacturing Company
Alden, NY 800-345-2142
Bergen Barrel & Drum Company
Kearny, NJ 201-998-3500
Best
Brunswick, OH 800-827-9237
Bevles Company
Dallas, TX 800-441-1601
BMH
City of Industry, CA 909-349-2530
Bonar Plastics
West Chicago, IL 800-295-3725
Bonar Plastics
Ridgefield, WA 800-972-5252
Borroughs Corp
Kalamazoo, MI 800-748-0227
Bowers Process Equipment
Stratford, ON. 800-567-3223
Brenner Tank LLC
Fond Du Lac, WI 800-558-9750
Brisker Dry Food Crisper
Oldsmar, FL 800-356-9080
Brothers Manufacturing
Hermansville, MI 888-277-6117

Buckhorn Inc
Milford, OH 800-543-4454
Buhler Inc.
Plymouth, MN. 763-847-9900
Bulk Pack
Monroe, LA. 800-498-4215
Bulk Sak Intl Inc
Malvern, AR 501-332-8745
Bush Tank Fabricators Inc
Newark, NJ 973-596-1121
C E Rogers Co
Mora, MN 800-279-8081
C Nelson Mfg Co
Oak Harbor, OH 800-922-7339
C&H Store Equipment Company
Los Angeles, CA 800-648-4979
C&R Refrigation Inc,
Center, TX. 800-438-6182
Cal-Coast Manufacturing
Turlock, CA 209-668-9378
Calzone Case Co
Bridgeport, CT 800-243-5152
Carter-Hoffmann LLC
Mundelein, IL 800-323-9793
Cayne Industrial Sales Corp
Bronx, NY. 718-993-5800
Central Fabricators Inc
Cincinnati, OH 800-909-8265
Chart Industries Inc
Cleveland, OH 800-247-4446
Chem-Tainer Industries Inc
West Babylon, NY 800-938-8896
Chester-Jensen Co., Inc.
Chester, PA 800-685-3750
Chicago Conveyor Corporation
Addison, IL. 630-543-6300
Clayton & Lambert Manufacturing
Buckner, KY 800-626-5819
Coast Scientific
Rancho Santa Fe, CA 800-445-1544
Columbian TecTank
Parsons, KS 800-421-2788
Commercial Kitchen Co
Los Angeles, CA 323-732-2291
Complex Steel & Wire Corp
Wayne, MI. 734-326-1600
Containair Packaging Corporation
Paterson, NJ 888-276-6500
Containment Technology
St Gabriel, LA 800-388-2467
Continental Commercial Products
Bridgeton, MO 800-325-1051
Continental-Fremont
Tiffin, OH 419-448-4045
Corbox-Meyers Inc
Cleveland, OH 800-321-7286
Coss Engineering Sales Company
Rochester Hills, MI. 800-446-1365
COW Industries Inc
Columbus, OH 800-542-9353
Cozzini Inc
Algona, IA 888-295-1116
Cres Cor
Mentor, OH. 877-273-7267
Crown Custom Metal Spinning
Concord, ON 800-750-1924
Cruvinet Winebar Co LLC
Sparks, NV 800-278-8463
Custom Diamond Intl.
Laval, QC 800-326-5926
Custom Metal Crafts
Springfield, MO 417-862-9324
DBE Inc
Concord, ON 800-461-5313
DCI, Inc.
St Cloud, MN 320-252-8200
Dematic USA
Grand Rapids, MI 877-725-7500
Denstor Mobile Storage Systems
Walker, MI 800-234-7477
Despro Manufacturing
Cedar Grove, NJ 800-292-9906
Dubuque Steel Products Co
Dubuque, IA 563-556-6288
Duke Manufacturing Co
St Louis, MO. 800-735-3853
Dunn Woodworks
Shrewsbury, PA. 877-835-8592
Durham Manufacturing Co
Durham, CT 800-243-3744
Dynamic Storage Systems Inc.
Brooksville, FL 800-974-8211

E2M
Duluth, GA 800-622-4326
Eagle Group
Clayton, DE. .800-441-8440
Earl Soesbe Company
Romeoville, IL 219-866-4191
Eastern Plastics
Pawtucket, RI 800-442-8585
Easyup Storage Systems
Tukwila, WA .800-426-9234
Eaton Sales & Service
Denver, CO 800-208-2657
Edwards Fiberglass
Sedalia, MO .660-826-3915
Edwards Products
Cincinnati, OH 800-543-1835
EGA Products Inc
Brookfield, WI 800-937-3427
Eldorado Miranda Manufacturing Company
Largo, FL 800-330-0708
Electrol Specialties Co
South Beloit, IL 815-389-2291
Ellett Industries
Port Coquitlam, BC. 604-941-8211
Enerfab Inc.
Cincinnati, OH 513-641-0500
Engineered Products Group
Madison, WI .800-626-3111
Eskay Metal Fabricating
Buffalo, NY .800-836-8015
Etube & Wire
Shrewsbury, PA 800-618-4720
Eugene Welding Company
Marysville, MI 810-364-7421
Expert Industries Inc
Brooklyn, NY 718-434-6060
F.E. Wood & Sons
West Baldwin, ME 207-286-5003
Fab-X/Metals
Washington, NC 800-677-3229
Fabricated Components Inc
Stroudsburg, PA 800-233-8163
Faribault Manufacturing Co
Faribault, MN 800-447-6043
Feldmeier Equipment Inc
Syracuse, NY 315-454-8608
Flexible Material Handling
Suwanee, GA 800-669-1501
Flow of Solids
Westford, MA 978-392-0300
Follett Corp
Easton, PA. 800-523-9361
Foster Forbes Glass
Marion, IN. 765-668-1200
Fourinox Inc
Green Bay, WI. 920-336-0621
Frazier Industrial Co
Long Valley, NJ. 800-859-1342
Frelco
Stephenville, NL 709-643-5668
G A Systems Inc
Huntington Beach, CA 714-848-7529
G.F. Frank & Sons
Fairfield, OH 513-870-9075
Gch Internatonal
Louisville, KY 502-636-1374
Geerpres Inc
Muskegon, MI. 231-773-3211
General Industries Inc
Goldsboro, NC 888-735-2882
General Steel Fabricators
Joplin, MO 800-820-8644
Gibbs Brothers Cooperage
Hot Springs, AR 501-623-8881
Goldenwest Sales
Cerritos, CA .800-827-6175
Graff Tank Erection
Harrisville, PA. 814-385-6671
Greene Industries
East Greenwich, RI 401-884-7530
Greif Inc
Delaware, OH 740-549-6000
Hall-Woolford Wood Tank Co Inc
Philadelphia, PA 215-329-9022
Handy Manufacturing Co Inc
Newark, NJ 800-631-4280
Hanel Storage Systems
Pittsburgh, PA. 412-787-3444
Hardware Components Inc
New Matamoras, OH 740-865-2424
Hardy Systems Corporation
Northbrook, IL 800-927-3956

Hedstrom Corporation
Ashland, OH .700-765-9665
Hewitt Manufacturing Co
Waldron, IN. .765-525-9829
Hodge Manufacturing Company
Springfield, MA 800-262-4634
Hodges
Vienna, IL 800-444-0011
Hoover Materials Handling Group
Houston, TX .800-844-8683
Houston Wire Works, Inc.
South Houston, TX 800-468-9477
Howard Fabrication
City of Industry, CA 626-961-0114
Hughes Co
Columbus, WI. 866-535-9303
Hydro-Miser
San Marcos, CA 800-736-5083
Hyster Company
San Diego, CA 855-804-2118
Ideal Wire Works
Alhambra, CA. 626-282-0886
IMC Teddy Food Service Equipment
Amityville, NY 800-221-5644
Imperial Industries Inc
Rothschild, WI 800-558-2945
Indeco Products Inc
San Marcos, TX 888-246-3326
Indiana Wire Company
Fremont, IN. .877-786-6883
Interlake Mecalux
Chicago, IL 708-344-9999
InterMetro Industries
Wilkes-Barre, PA 570-825-2741
International Machinery Xchnge
Deerfield, WI 800-279-0191
International Tank & Pipe Co
Clackamas, OR 888-988-0011
Interroll Corp
Wilmington, NC 800-830-9680
Item Products
Houston, TX .800-333-4932
J.H. Carr & Sons
Seattle, WA .800-523-8842
JBC Plastics
St Louis, MO. 877-834-5526
JEM Wire Products
Middletown, CT 860-347-0447
Jenike & Johanson Inc
Tyngsboro, MA. 978-649-3300
Jesco Industries
Litchfield, MI 800-455-0019
JH Display & Fixture
Greenwood, IN 317-888-0631
Jupiter Mills Corporation
Roslyn, NY 800-853-5121
JW Leser Company
Los Angeles, CA. 323-731-4173
K & I Creative Plastics & Wood
Jacksonville, FL 904-387-0438
Kadon Corporation
Milford, OH .937-299-0088
Kedco Wire Storage Systems
Farmingdale, NY 800-654-9988
Key Material Handling Inc
Simi Valley, CA. 800-539-7225
KHM Plastics Inc
Gurnee, IL. 847-249-4910
Kisco Manufacturing
Port Alberni, BC. 604-823-7456
La Crosse
Onalaska, WI. 800-345-0018
Laidig Inc
Mishawaka, IN 574-256-0204
Lakeside Manufacturing Inc
Milwaukee, WI 888-558-8565
Lambertson Industries Inc
Sparks, NV 800-548-3324
Langsenkamp Manufacturing
Indianapolis, IN 877-585-1950
Leggett & Platt Storage
Vernon Hills, IL 847-816-6246
Liberty Machine Company
York, PA 800-745-8152
Linvar
Hartford, CT .800-282-5288
LoadBank International
Orlando, FL. .800-458-9010
Lodi Metal Tech
Lodi, CA 800-359-5999
Longview Fibre Company
Beaverton, OR 503-350-1600

Loyal Manufacturing
Indianapolis, IN 317-359-3185
LPI Imports
Chicago, IL 877-389-6563
Luckner Steel Shelving
Flushing, NY. 800-888-4212
Ludell Manufacturing Co
Milwaukee, WI. 800-558-0800
Lyon LLC
Montgomery, IL 630-892-8941
M & E Mfg Co Inc
Kingston, NY 845-331-2110
M O Industries Inc
Whippany, NJ 973-386-9228
Madsen Wire Products Inc
Orland, IN 260-829-6561
Mannhardt Inc
Sheboygan Falls, WI. 800-423-2327
Marineland Commercial Aquariums
Blacksburg, VA. 800-322-1266
Marlin Steel Wire Products
Baltimore, MD 877-762-7546
Material Storage Systems
Humble, TX .800-881-6750
Material Storage Systems
Gadsden, AL .877-543-2467
Mccullough Industries Inc
Kenton, OH. .800-245-9490
MeGa Industries
Burlington, ON 800-665-6342
Melmat Inc
Huntington Beach, CA 800-635-6289
Merric
Bridgeton, MO 314-770-9944
Metal Equipment Company
Cleveland, OH 800-700-6326
Metal Master Sales Corp
Glendale Heights, IL. 800-488-8729
Metro Corporation
Wilkes Barre, PA. 800-992-1776
Meyer Machine & Garroutte Products
San Antonio, TX. 210-736-1811
Michiana Box & Crate
Niles, MI 800-677-6372
Micro Wire Products Inc
Brockton, MA 508-584-0200
Midwest Aircraft Products Co
Lexington, OH 419-884-2164
Midwest Stainless
Menomonie, WI 715-235-5472
Miller Hofft Brands
Indianapolis, IN 317-638-6576
Miller Metal Fabrication
Bridgeville, DE. 302-337-2291
Modar
Benton Harbor, MI 800-253-6186
Modern Brewing & Design
Santa Rosa, CA 707-542-6620
Modern Metals Industries
El Segundo, CA 800-437-6633
MultiFab Plastics
Boston, MA. .888-293-5754
Murata Automated Systems
Charlotte, NC 800-428-8469
Myers Container
Hayward, CA 510-785-8235
Nalge Process Technologies Group
Rochester, NY 585-586-8800
National Bar Systems
Huntington Beach, CA 714-848-1688
Nefab Packaging Inc
Elk Grove Vlg, IL. 847-787-0340
Nelipak
Phoenix, AZ .602-269-7648
NEPA Pallet & Container Co
Snohomish, WA 360-568-3185
New Pig Corp
Tipton, PA. 800-468-4647
Newell Brands
Atlanta, GA
Nexel Industries Inc
Port Washington, NY 800-245-6682
Oak Barrel Winecraft
Berkeley, CA. 510-849-0400
Omicron Steel Products Company
Jamaica, NY .718-805-3400
Pacific Store Designs Inc
Garden Grove, CA 800-772-5661
Pacific Tank
Adelanto, CA 800-449-5838
Pallet One Inc
Bartow, FL. 800-771-1148

Paltier
Michigan City, IN 800-348-3201
Paramount Manufacturing Company
Wilmington, MA. 978-657-4300
PBC
Mahwah, NJ 800-514-2739
Pelican Displays
Homer, IL 800-627-1517
Penco Products
Skippack, PA. 800-562-1000
Pentwater Wire Products Inc
Pentwater, MI 877-869-6911
Peter Gray Corporation
Andover, MA 978-470-0990
Peterson Manufacturing Company
Plainfield, IL 800-547-8995
Piper Products Inc
Wausau, WI. 800-544-3057
Pittsburgh Tank Corp
Monongahela, PA 800-634-0243
Plastic Supply Inc
Londonderry, NH 800-752-7759
Plastilite Corporation
Omaha, NE 800-228-9506
Plastocon
Oconomowoc, WI. 800-966-0103
Ppm Technologies LLC
Newberg, OR 800-246-2034
Prestige Skirting & Tablecloths
Orangeburg, NY 800-635-3313
Prince Castle Inc
Carol Stream, IL 800-722-7853
Princeton Shelving
Cedar Rapids, IA. 319-369-0355
Process Solutions
Riviera Beach, FL 561-840-0050
Production Packaging & Processing Equipment
Company
Savannah, GA 912-856-4281
Proluxe
Paramount, CA 800-594-5528
Pucel Enterprises Inc
Cleveland, OH 800-336-4986
QBD Modular Systems
Santa Clara, CA 800-663-3005
Quantum Storage Systems Inc
Miami, FL 800-685-4665
R & D Brass
Wappingers Falls, NY 800-447-6050
Ram Equipment Co
Waukesha, WI. 262-513-1114
Ransco Industries
Ventura, CA. 805-487-7777
Rapid Rack Industries
City of Industry, CA 800-736-7225
Reflex International
Norcross, GA 800-642-7640
Remcon Plastics Inc
Reading, PA 800-360-3636
Remstar International
Westbrook, ME 800-639-5805
Republic Storage Systems LLC
Canton, OH 800-477-1255
RETROTECH, Inc
West Henrietta, NY. 866-915-2777
Ridg-U-Rak
North East, PA. 866-479-7225
Rolland Machining & Fabricating
Moneta, VA. 973-827-6911
Rosenwach Tank Co LLC
Long Island City, NY 212-972-4411
Ross Technology Corp
Leola, PA. 800-345-8170
Royal Welding & Fabricating
Fullerton, CA 714-680-6669
RTI Shelving Systems
Elmhurst, NY. 800-223-6210
Rubicon Industries
Brooklyn, NY 800-662-6999
Saeplast Canada
St John, NB 800-567-3966
Sanchelima International
Miami, FL. 305-591-4343
Scheb International
North Barrington, IL. 847-381-2573
Seattle Plastics
Seattle, WA 800-441-0679
Sefi Fabricators Inc
Amityville, NY 631-842-2200
SEMCO
Ocala, FL. 800-749-6894

SerVend International
Sellersburg, IN 800-367-4233
Sharpsville Container Corp
Sharpsville, PA 800-645-1248
Shelley Cabinet Company
Shelley, ID. 208-357-3700
Silver King Refrigeration Inc
Minneapolis, MN 800-328-3329
Sirco Systems
Birmingham, AL. 205-731-7800
Smalley Manufacturing Co Inc
Knoxville, TN 865-966-5866
Snyder Crown
Marked Tree, AR 870-358-3400
Solve Needs International
White Lake, MI 800-783-2462
Southern Imperial Inc
Rockford, IL 800-747-4665
Spacesaver Corp
Fort Atkinson, WI. 800-492-3434
Spartanburg Steel Products Inc
Spartanburg, SC 800-974-7500
Specific Mechanical Systems
Victoria, BC. 250-652-2111
Speedrack Products Group LTD
Sparta, MI 616-887-0002
SPG International
Covington, GA 877-503-4774
Spirit Foodservice, Inc.
Andover, MA 800-343-0996
Springport Steel Wire Products
Elkhart, IN. 574-295-9660
SSW Holding Co Inc
Elizabethtown, KY 270-769-5526
St. Louis Stainless Service
St Louis, MO. 800-735-3853
Stackbin Corp
Lincoln, RI 800-333-1603
Stainless Fabrication Inc
Springfield, MO 800-397-8265
Stainless Specialists Inc
Wausau, WI. 800-236-4155
Stainless Steel Fabricators
Tyler, TX 903-595-6625
Starlite Food Service Equipment
Detroit, MI 888-521-6603
Stearnswood Inc
Hutchinson, MN 800-657-0144
Steel King Industries
Stevens Point, WI 800-553-3096
Stor-Loc
Kankakee, IL. 800-786-7562
Storage Unlimited
Nixa, MO. 800-478-6642
Strong Hold Products
Louisville, KY 800-880-2625
Summit Commercial
Bronx, NY. 800-932-4267
Super Sturdy
Weldon, NC. 800-253-4833
Supreme Fabricators
Artesia, CA 323-583-8944
Supreme Metal
Alpharetta, GA 800-645-2526
Tag-Trade Associated Group
Chicago, IL. 800-621-8350
Tampa Sheet Metal Co
Tampa, FL. 813-251-1845
Technibilt/Cari-All
Newton, NC 800-233-3972
Tennsco Corp
Dickson, TN 800-251-8184
TGR Container Sales
San Leandro, CA. 800-273-6887
Thermal Bags By Ingrid Inc
Gilberts, IL. 800-622-5560
Thermo Wisconsin
De Pere, WI. 920-766-7200
Thermodynamics
Commerce City, CO 800-627-9037
Tier-Rack Corp
Ballwin, MO. 800-325-7869
TMS
San Francisco, CA 800-447-7223
Traex
Dane, WI. 800-356-8006
Travis Manufacturing Corp
Alliance, OH. 330-875-1661
Tri-Boro Shelving & Partition
Farmville, VA 800-633-3070
Triad Scientific
Manasquan, NJ 800-867-6690

Tupperware Brands Corporation
Orlando, FL. 800-366-3800
Turbo Refrigerating Company
Denton, TX 940-387-4301
Unex Manufacturing Inc
Lakewood, NJ 800-334-8639
Unirak Storage Systems
Taylor, MI 800-348-7225
United Industries Group Inc
Lake Forest, CA 949-759-3200
United Showcase Company
Wood Ridge, NJ 800-526-6382
United States Systems Inc
Kansas City, KS 888-281-2454
United Steel Products Company
East Stroudsburg, PA 570-476-1010
Universal Stainless
Aurora, CO 800-223-8332
Universal Stainless & Alloy
Titusville, PA 800-295-1909
Upham & Walsh Lumber
Hoffman Estates, IL 847-519-1010
Vac-U-Max
Belleville, NJ 800-822-8629
Valad Electric Heating Corporation
Tarrytown, NY 914-631-4927
Valley Fixtures
Sparks, NV 775-331-1050
Victone Manufacturing Company
Chicago, IL. 312-738-3211
Vorti-Siv
Salem, OH. 800-227-7487
W.A. Schmidt Company
Oaks, PA. 800-523-6719
Walker Stainless Equipment Co
New Lisbon, WI 608-562-7500
Waukesha Cherry-Burrell
Louisville, KY 502-491-4310
WCB Ice Cream
Philadelphia, PA 215-425-4320
Welbilt Corporation
Stamford, CT. 203-325-8300
Welbilt Inc.
New Port Richey, FL. 877-375-9300
Welliver Metal Products Corporation
Salem, OR. 503-362-1568
Westeel
Saskatoon, SK. 306-931-2855
Western Pacific Stge Solutions
San Dimas, CA 800-888-5707
Westfield Sheet Metal Works
Kenilworth, NJ 908-276-5500
Wilder Manufacturing Company
Port Jervis, NY 800-832-1319
Wiltec
Leominster, MA 978-537-1497
Wine Chillers of California
Santa Ana, CA 800-331-4274
Winekeeper
Santa Barbara, CA 805-963-3451
Winston Industries
Louisville, KY 800-234-5286
Wirefab Inc
Worcester, MA 877-877-4445
Woerner Wire Works
Omaha, NE 402-451-5414
Workman Packaging Inc.
Saint-Laurent, QC. 800-252-5208

Storage Units

Temperature Controlled

Advance Energy Technologies
Halfmoon, NY. 800-724-0198
Agspring
Leawood, KS. 913-333-3035
American Panel Corp
Ocala, FL. 800-327-3015
B C Holland Inc
Dousman, WI. 262-965-2939
Bacchus Wine Cellars
Houston, TX 800-487-8812
Baltimore Aircoil Co
Jessup, MD 410-799-1300
Bmh Equipment Inc
Sacramento, CA 800-350-8828
Cool Care
Boynton Beach, FL. 561-364-5711
Cramer Products
New York, NY 212-645-2368

Creative Mobile Systems Inc
Manchester, CT.................800-646-8364
Cruvinet Winebar Co LLC
Sparks, NV....................800-278-8463
Dade Engineering
Tampa, FL.....................800-321-2112
Davis Core & Pa
Cave Spring, GA...............800-235-7483
Edwards Fiberglass
Sedalia, MO...................660-826-3915
Elliott-Williams Company
Indianapolis, IN..............800-428-9303
Eskay Metal Fabricating
Buffalo, NY...................800-836-8015
Faubion Central States Tank Company
Shawnee Mission, KS...........800-450-8265
Graff Tank Erection
Harrisville, PA...............814-385-6671
HABCO Beverage Systems
Toronto, ON...................800-448-0244
Hoshizaki America Inc
Peachtree City, GA............800-438-6087
Interstate Showcase & Fixture Company
West Orange, NJ...............973-483-5555
Johanson Transportation Svc
Fresno, CA....................800-742-2053
Kold-Hold
Edgefield, SC.................803-637-3166
La Crosse
Onalaska, WI..................800-345-0018
National Bar Systems
Huntington Beach, CA..........714-848-1688
Portable Cold Storage
Edison, NJ....................800-535-2445
Refrigerator Manufacturers LLC
Cerritos, CA..................562-926-2006
Starlite Food Service Equipment
Detroit, MI...................888-521-6603
Superior Products Company
Saint Paul, MN................800-328-9800
TMS
San Francisco, CA.............800-447-7223
Tolan Machinery Company
Rockaway, NJ..................973-983-7212
Tranter INC
Wichita Falls, TX.............940-723-7125
Winekeeper
Santa Barbara, CA.............805-963-3451
Zero Temp
Santa Ana, CA.................714-538-3177

Tanks

Holding, Storage

A & B Process Systems Corp
Stratford, WI.................888-258-2789
Abalon Precision Manufacturing Corporation
Bronx, NY.....................800-888-2225
Aco Container Systems
Pickering, ON.................800-542-9942
Advance Fittings Corp
Elkhorn, WI...................262-723-6699
AFGO Mechanical Svc Inc
Astoria, NY...................800-438-2346
Allegheny Bradford Corp
Bradford, PA..................800-542-0650
Alloy Products Corp
Waukesha, WI..................800-236-6603
Anderson-Crane Company
Minneapolis, MN...............800-314-2747
Andgar Corp
Ferndale, WA..................360-366-9900
Apache Stainless Equipment
Beaver Dam, WI................800-444-0398
Apollo Sheet Metal
Kennewick, WA.................509-586-1104
APV Americas
Delavan, WI...................800-252-5200
Arrow Tank Co
Buffalo, NY...................716-893-7200
Atlas Minerals & Chemicals Inc
Mertztown, PA.................800-523-8269
Baldewein Company
Lake Forrest, IL..............800-424-5544
Bayhead Products Corp.
Dover, NH.....................800-229-4323
Berkshire PPM
Litchfield, CT................860-567-3118
Bonar Plastics
Ridgefield, WA................800-972-5252

Bowers Process Equipment
Stratford, ON.................800-567-3223
Brenner Tank LLC
Fond Du Lac, WI...............800-558-9750
Brothers Manufacturing
Hermansville, MI..............888-277-6117
Bush Tank Fabricators Inc
Newark, NJ....................973-596-1121
C&R Refrigation Inc,
Center, TX....................800-438-6182
Cal-Coast Manufacturing
Turlock, CA...................209-668-9378
Centennial Moldings
Hastings, NE..................888-883-2189
Central Fabricators Inc
Cincinnati, OH................800-909-8265
Chart Industries Inc
Cleveland, OH.................800-247-4446
Chem-Tainer Industries Inc
West Babylon, NY..............800-275-2436
Chem-Tainer Industries Inc
West Babylon, NY..............800-938-8896
Chester-Jensen Co., Inc.
Chester, PA...................800-685-3750
Clayton & Lambert Manufacturing
Buckner, KY...................800-626-5819
Coastline Equipment Inc
Bellingham, WA................360-734-8509
Columbian TecTank
Parsons, KS...................800-421-2788
Cozzini Inc
Algona, IA....................888-295-1116
Davron Technologies Inc
Chattanooga, TN...............423-870-1888
DCI, Inc.
St Cloud, MN..................320-252-8200
Eaton Sales & Service
Denver, CO....................800-208-2657
Electrol Specialties Co
South Beloit, IL..............815-389-2291
Emco Industrial Plastics
Cedar Grove, NJ...............800-292-9906
Enerfab Inc.
Cincinnati, OH................513-641-0500
Engineered Products Group
Madison, WI...................800-626-3111
Expert Industries Inc
Brooklyn, NY..................718-434-6060
Falco Technologies
La Prairie, QC................450-444-0566
General Industries Inc
Goldsboro, NC.................888-735-2882
General Tank
Berwick, PA...................800-435-8265
Graff Tank Erection
Harrisville, PA...............814-385-6671
Howard Fabrication
City of Industry, CA..........626-961-0114
Hughes Co
Columbus, WI..................866-535-9303
Imperial Industries Inc
Rothschild, WI................800-558-2945
International Tank & Pipe Co
Clackamas, OR.................888-988-0011
JW Leser Company
Los Angeles, CA...............323-731-4173
Langsenkamp Manufacturing
Indianapolis, IN..............877-585-1950
Melmat Inc
Huntington Beach, CA..........800-635-6289
Miller Metal Fabrication
Bridgeville, DE...............302-337-2291
Modern Brewing & Design
Santa Rosa, CA................707-542-6620
Nalge Process Technologies Group
Rochester, NY.................585-586-8800
Northland Process Piping
Isle, MN......................320-679-2119
Northwind Inc
Alpena, AR....................877-937-2585
Pacific Tank
Adelanto, CA..................800-449-5838
PBC
Mahwah, NJ....................800-514-2739
Pittsburgh Tank Corp
Monongahela, PA...............800-634-0243
Polar Process
Plattsville, ON...............877-896-8077
Poly Processing Co
French Camp, CA...............877-325-3142
Process Solutions
Riviera Beach, FL.............561-840-0050

Production Packaging & Processing Equipment
Company
Savannah, GA..................912-856-4281
PVI Industries LLC
Fort Worth, TX................800-784-8326
RAS Process Equipment Inc
Trenton, NJ...................609-371-1220
Remcon Plastics Inc
Reading, PA...................800-360-3636
Rolland Machining & Fabricating
Moneta, VA....................973-827-6911
Rosenwach Tank Co LLC
Long Island City, NY..........212-972-4411
Royal Welding & Fabricating
Fullerton, CA.................714-680-6669
Rubicon Industries
Brooklyn, NY..................800-662-6999
Sanchelima International
Miami, FL.....................305-591-4343
Scherping Systems
Winsted, MN...................320-485-4401
Sharpsville Container Corp
Sharpsville, PA...............800-645-1248
Sims Machinery Co Inc
Lanett, AL....................334-576-2101
Snyder Crown
Marked Tree, AR...............870-358-3400
Southern Metal Fabricators Inc
Albertville, AL...............800-989-1330
Specific Mechanical Systems
Victoria, BC..................250-652-2111
Stainless Specialists Inc
Wausau, WI....................800-236-4155
Sterling Process Engineering
Columbus, OH..................800-783-7875
Supreme Fabricators
Artesia, CA...................323-583-8944
Tampa Sheet Metal Co
Tampa, FL.....................813-251-1845
Thermo Wisconsin
De Pere, WI...................920-766-7200
Tolan Machinery Company
Rockaway, NJ..................973-983-7212
United Industries Group Inc
Lake Forest, CA...............949-759-3200
Vorti-Siv
Salem, OH.....................800-227-7487
Waukesha Cherry-Burrell
Louisville, KY................502-491-4310
WCB Ice Cream
Philadelphia, PA..............215-425-4320
Welliver Metal Products Corporation
Salem, OR.....................503-362-1568

Modular

Modutank Inc
Long Island City, NY..........800-245-6964

Stainless Steel

G & F Mfg
Oak Lawn, IL..................800-282-1574

Trailers

Refrigerated

All A Cart Custom Mfg
Columbus, OH..................800-695-2278
Fruehauf Trailer Services
St Louis, MO..................314-822-1113
Great Dane LP
Chicago, IL...................773-254-5533
Manufacturers Railway Company
Saint Louis, MO...............314-577-1775
New Centennial
Columbus, GA..................800-241-7541
Portable Cold Storage
Edison, NJ....................800-535-2445
Texas Corn Roasters
Granbury, TX..................800-772-4345

Trucks

Factory, Warehouse, Shop & Industrial

A-Z Factory Supply
Schiller Park, IL.............800-323-4511
Ace Engineering Company
Fort Worth, TX................800-431-4223

AFCO Manufacturing
Cincinnati, OH 800-747-7332
All Power Inc
Sioux City, IA 712-258-0681
Bell & Howell Company
Lincolnwood, IL 800-647-2290
Bessco Tube Bending & Pipe Fabricating
Thornton, IL 800-337-3977
Bishamon Industry Corp
Ontario, CA 800-358-8833
C R Daniels Inc
Ellicott City, MD 800-933-2638
Caddy Corporation of America
Bridgeport, NJ 856-467-4222
California Caster & Handtruck
San Francisco, CA 800-950-8750
Cannon Equipment Company
Cannon Falls, MN 800-825-8501
Cayne Industrial Sales Corp
Bronx, NY 718-993-5800
Collins Manufacturing Company Ltd
Langley, BC 800-663-6761
Continental Commercial Products
Bridgeton, MO 800-325-1051
Conveyance Technologies LLC
Cleveland, OH 800-701-2278
Crown Equipment Corp.
New Bremen, OH 419-629-2311
Doosan Industrial Vehicle America Corp
Buford, GA 678-745-2200
Dubuque Steel Products Co
Dubuque, IA 563-556-6288
Dutro Co
Logan, UT 866-388-7660
Dynabilt Products
Readville, MA 800-443-1008
Edwards Products
Cincinnati, OH 800-543-1835
Elwell Parker
Coraopolis, PA 800-272-9953
Excalibur Miretti Group LLC
Fairfield, NJ 973-808-8399
Exel
Lincolnton, NC 704-735-6535
General Truck Body Mfg
Houston, TX 800-395-8585
Hackney Brothers
Washington, NC 800-763-0700
Hamilton Caster
Hamilton, OH 888-699-7164
Harper Trucks Inc
Wichita, KS 800-835-4099
HDT Manufacturing
Salem, OH 800-968-7438
Hotshot Delivery System
Bloomingdale, IL 630-924-8817
Hyster Company
San Diego, CA 855-804-2118
Incinerator International Inc
Houston, TX 713-227-1466
Industrial Equipment Company
Derry, NH 603-432-2037
Jarke Corporation
Prospect Hts, IL 800-722-5255
Jesco Industries
Litchfield, MI 800-455-0019
John Bean Technologies Corp
Chalfont, PA 888-362-3622
Johnston Equipment
Delta, BC 800-237-5159
Kent District Library System
Comstock Park, MI 616-784-2007
Komatsu Forklift USA
Rolling Meadows, IL 847-437-5800
Lakeside Manufacturing Inc
Milwaukee, WI 888-558-8565
Landoo Corporation
Horsham, PA 785-562-5381
Leyman Manufacturing Corporation
Cincinnati, OH 866-539-6261
Load King Mfg
Jacksonville, FL 800-531-4975
Long Reach ManufacturingCompany
Westport, CT 800-285-7000
Marion Body Works Inc
Marion, WI 715-754-5261
Metal Equipment Company
Cleveland, OH 800-700-6326
Mid-States Mfg & Engr Co Inc
Milton, IA 800-346-1792
Mitsubishi Caterpillar Mcfa
Houston, TX 800-228-5438

NACCO Industries Inc.
Cleveland, OH 440-229-5151
National Scoop & Equipment Company
Spring House, PA 215-646-2040
Net Material Handling
Milwaukee, WI 800-558-7260
Nevlen Co. 2, Inc.
Wakefield, MA 800-562-7225
New Age Industrial
Norton, KS 800-255-0104
Nexel Industries Inc
Port Washington, NY 800-245-6682
Ortmayer Materials Handling
Brooklyn, NY 718-875-7995
Peregrine Inc
Lincoln, NE 800-777-3433
Pucel Enterprises Inc
Cleveland, OH 800-336-4986
Raymond Corp
Greene, NY 800-235-7200
Royce Corp
Glendale, AZ 602-256-0006
Schaeff
Bridgeview, IL 888-436-7867
Solve Needs International
White Lake, MI 800-783-2462
Technibilt/Cari-All
Newton, NC 800-233-3972
Thermo King Corp
Bloomington, MN 888-887-2202
Thombert
Newton, IA 800-433-3572
Uni Carriers Americas Corp
Marengo, IL 800-871-5438
Valley Craft Inc
Lake City, MN 800-328-1480
Waldon Manufacturing LLC
Fairview, OK 800-486-0023
Wesley International Corp
Scottdale, GA 800-241-8649

Food & Restaurant

All A Cart Custom Mfg
Columbus, OH 800-695-2278
All Star Carts & Vehicles
Bay Shore, NY 800-831-3166
Alliance Products LLC
Murfreesboro, TN 800-522-3973
Amco Metals Indl
City of Industry, CA 626-855-2550
ARC Specialties
Valencia, CA 661-775-8500
Bmh Equipment Inc
Sacramento, CA 800-350-8828
Century Industries Inc
Sellersburg, IN 800-248-3371
Creative Mobile Systems Inc
Manchester, CT 800-646-8364
Custom Sales & Svc Inc
Hammonton, NJ 800-257-7855
Hackney Brothers
Washington, NC 800-763-0700
Holstein Manufacturing
Holstein, IA 800-368-4342
Lakeside Manufacturing Inc
Milwaukee, WI 888-558-8565
Lakeside-Aris Manufacturing
Milwaukee, WI 800-558-8565
Leggett & Platt Storage
Vernon Hills, IL 847-816-6246
M & E Mfg Co Inc
Kingston, NY 845-331-2110
Metro Corporation
Wilkes Barre, PA 800-992-1776
Technibilt/Cari-All
Newton, NC 800-233-3972
Wag Industries
Skokie, IL 800-621-3305
Worksman 800 Buy Cart
Ozone Park, NY 800-289-2278

Hand

ARC Specialties
Valencia, CA 661-775-8500
Bmh Equipment Inc
Sacramento, CA 800-350-8828
California Caster & Handtruck
San Francisco, CA 800-950-8750
Clamp Swing Pricing Co Inc
Oakland, CA 800-227-7615

Clark Caster Company
Cave in Rock, IL 800-538-0765
Enrick Co
Zumbrota, MN 507-732-5215
Hamilton Caster
Hamilton, OH 888-699-7164
Hodge Manufacturing Company
Springfield, MA 800-262-4634
Innovation Moving Systems
Oostburg, WI 800-619-0625
Magline Inc
Standish, MI 800-624-5463
Net Material Handling
Milwaukee, WI 800-558-7260
Otto Braun Bakery Equipment
Buffalo, NY 716-824-1252
Roll Rite Corp
Hayward, CA 800-345-9305
Ultra Lift Corp
San Jose, CA 800-346-3057
Valley Craft Inc
Lake City, MN 800-328-1480

Meat

Dubuque Steel Products Co
Dubuque, IA 563-556-6288
Techform
Mount Airy, NC 336-789-2115

Packing House

Bessco Tube Bending & Pipe Fabricating
Thornton, IL 800-337-3977
Bmh Equipment Inc
Sacramento, CA 800-350-8828
Cannon Equipment Company
Cannon Falls, MN 800-825-8501
Dc Tech
Kansas City, MO 877-742-9090
Elwell Parker
Coraopolis, PA 800-272-9953
Key Material Handling Inc
Simi Valley, CA 800-539-7225
Le Fiell Co
Reno, NV 402-592-9993
Wesley International Corp
Scottdale, GA 800-241-8649

Pallet Handling

Bishamon Industry Corp
Ontario, CA 800-358-8833
Bmh Equipment Inc
Sacramento, CA 800-350-8828
Cannon Equipment Company
Cannon Falls, MN 800-825-8501
Elwell Parker
Coraopolis, PA 800-272-9953
Key Material Handling Inc
Simi Valley, CA 800-539-7225
Landoll Corp
Marysville, KS 785-562-5381
Lift Rite
Mississauga, ON 905-456-2603
Long Reach ManufacturingCompany
Westport, CT 800-285-7000
Lumber & Things
Keyser, WV 800-296-5656
NACCO Industries Inc.
Cleveland, OH 440-229-5151
Net Material Handling
Milwaukee, WI 800-558-7260
Sackett Systems
Bensenville, IL 800-323-8332
Wesley International Corp
Scottdale, GA 800-241-8649

Tilt

Bayhead Products Corp.
Dover, NH 800-229-4323
Bmh Equipment Inc
Sacramento, CA 800-350-8828
Pucel Enterprises Inc
Cleveland, OH 800-336-4986
RMI-C/Rotonics Manaufacturing
Bensenville, IL 630-773-9510

Utility Vault Covers

Slip Not
Detroit, MI 800-754-7668

Vats

Cheese

A & B Process Systems Corp
Stratford, WI......................888-258-2789
Damrow Company
Fond Du Lac, WI 800-236-1501
DCI, Inc.
St Cloud, MN 320-252-8200
Dubuque Steel Products Co
Dubuque, IA......................563-556-6288
Peterson Fiberglass Laminates
Shell Lake, WI 715-468-2306
Rosenwach Tank Co LLC
Long Island City, NY 212-972-4411

Warehouses

Insulated

Advance Energy Technologies
Halfmoon, NY.....................800-724-0198

Wine Storage Units

Advance Energy Technologies
Halfmoon, NY.....................800-724-0198
Bacchus Wine Cellars
Houston, TX 800-487-8812
Cramer Products
New York, NY 212-645-2368
Cruvinet Winebar Co LLC
Sparks, NV 800-278-8463
Dufeck Manufacturing Co
Denmark, WI.....................888-603-9663

Falco Technologies
La Prairie, QC....................450-444-0566
International Patterns, Inc.
Bay Shore, NY 631-952-2000
Kedco Wine Storage Systems
Farmingdale, NY 800-654-9988
Lockwood Manufacturing
Livonia, MI.......................800-521-0238
Metro Corporation
Wilkes Barre, PA..................800-992-1776
PBC
Mahwah, NJ 800-514-2739
Summit Commercial
Bronx, NY........................800-932-4267
Winekeeper
Santa Barbara, CA 805-963-3451
Wineracks by Marcus
Costa Mesa, CA 714-546-4922

18000 1515 Design & Manufacturing
405 N. Oak Street
Inglewood, CA 90302
310-671-0345
Fax: 310-689-2879 888-671-0360
info@1515design.com www.1515design.com
Rotisseries and display cases.
Co-Founder, President & CEO: Francis Delpech
Co-Founder: Eric Maurice *Year Founded:* 1963

18001 3D Instruments LLC
2900 E White Star Ave
Anaheim, CA 92806-2627
714-399-9200
Fax: 714-399-9221 www.3dinstruments.com
Quality Control: Charlene L Lah
VP: Garey Cooper
Manager: Felix Brockmeyer
fbrockmeyer@3dinstruments.com
Estimated Sales: $50 - 100 Million
Number Employees: 100-249

18002 3DT, LLC
N114 W18850 Clinton Dr
Germantown, WI 53022
262-253-6700
Fax: 262-253-6977 888-326-7662
sales@3dtllc.com www.3dtllc.com
Corona treaters
President: Morten Jorgensen
Sales/Marketing Manager: S. Erik Kiel
Estimated Sales: $2.5 - 5 Million
Number Employees: 20-49

18003 3Greenmoms LLC
Po Box 59033
Potomac, MD 20859-9033
301-802-9390
Fax: 888-236-9043 kirsten@3greenmoms.com
www.lunchskins.com
Maker of reuseable decorative sandwich bags.

18004 (HQ)3M
3M Center
St. Paul, MN 55144-1000
888-364-3577
www.3m.com
Food safety products
Chairman & CEO: Michael Roman
SVP, Innovation & CTO: John Banovetz
EVP, Safety & Industrial Business Group: Michael Vale
EVP, Enterprise Operations: Eric Hammes
EVP, Consumer Business Group: Paul Keel
SVP & General Counsel: Ivan Fong
SVP & Chief Financial Officer: Nicholas Gangestad
SVP, Corporate Affairs: Denise Rutherford
Year Founded: 1902
Estimated Sales: $32.7 Billion
Number Employees: 93,516
Other Locations:
    3M Indianapolis
    Indianapolis IN
    3M Medina
    Medina OH
Brands:
    3M Littman
    ACE
    Command
    FUTURO
    Filtrete
    Nexcare
    Post-it
    Scotch
    Scotch Painter's Tape
    Scotch-Brite

18005 4front Entrematic
1612 Hutton Dr # 140
Suite 140
Carrollton, TX 75006-6642
972-236-2400
Fax: 972-389-4752 sales@sercocompany.com
www.4frontes.com
President: Keith Moore
keith.moore@4frontes.com
Estimated Sales: $1,000,000 - $2,499,999
Number Employees: 100-249

18006 5 Star Foods International LLC (5 Star Organic Foods)
844-645-7827
info@5star-foods.com www.5star-foods.com
Organic supplier specializing in sourcing, processing and packaging of natural, non-GMO and gluten-free certified organic food. Products include grains, seeds, nuts, flours, vegetables, fruits, juices & purees, cocoa productssweeteners, dairy, and culinary herbs.
Owner: Ron Orlowski *Year Founded:* 2019
Type of Packaging: Food Service

18007 518 Corporation
518 Martin Luther King Jr.
Savannah, GA 31401-4881
912-232-1141
Fax: 912-236-7969
President: Louis C Mathews III
Estimated Sales: $5 - 10 Million
Number Employees: 10-19

18008 7 Seas Submarine
11216 S Michigan Ave
Chicago, IL 60628-4910
773-785-0550
Fax: 312-942-0236
Owner: Natibad Cortez
natibadcortez@hrblock.com
Estimated Sales: Less Than $500,000
Number Employees: 1-4

18009 9-12 Corporation
HC-1 Box 29030
Department 388
Caguas, PR 00725
787-747-0405
Fax: 787-747-0318
Manufacturers of elevate enhanced fiber water beverages.
President/CEO: Joe Lazoff
Estimated Sales: $1-5 Million
Number Employees: 10
Square Footage: 40000
Type of Packaging: Consumer, Food Service, Private Label
Brands:
    Apres
    Pirel

18010 915 Labs
9200 E Mineral Ave.
Centennial, CO 80112
855-915-5227
info@915Labs.com www.915labs.com
Offers microwave food processing technology to the food industry.
CEO: Michael Locatis
Year Founded: 2014
Number Employees: 10-20

18011 99 Ranch Market
1625 S Azusa Ave
Hacienda Heights, CA 91745-3832
626-839-2899
Fax: 626-839-2127 www.99ranch.com
Asian American groceries
Founder/CEO: Roger Chen
Year Founded: 1984
Estimated Sales: $500,000
Number Employees: 50-99
Other Locations:
    Manufacturing Facility - Sugarland
    Sugarland TX

18012 A & B Process Systems Corp
201 S Wisconsin Ave
P.O. Box 86
Stratford, WI 54484
715-687-4332
Fax: 715-687-3225 888-258-2789
www.abprocess.com
Manufacturer and exporter of ASME U stamps, process systems, tanks, vessels and custom components.
Chief Executive Officer: Paul Kinate
Health & Safety Manager: Bill Thompson
Year Founded: 1973
Estimated Sales: $120 Million
Number Employees: 50-99
Square Footage: 175000
Type of Packaging: Food Service, Bulk
Brands:
    Oc Guide Bearing
    Vacushear

18013 A & D Sales
145 E Colt Dr
Fayetteville, AR 72703-2847
479-521-8665
Fax: 479-521-0841
President: Jim Stockland
jim@adchicken.com
Treasurer: Pam Stockland
Estimated Sales: $5 - 10 Million
Number Employees: 5-9

18014 A & E Conveyor Systems Inc
121 P Rickman Industrial Dr
Canton, GA 30115-9099
770-345-7300
Fax: 770-345-7391 info@ae-conveyor.com
www.ae-conveyor.com
Waterless container cleaning systems, container handling, conveying systems
President: Raymond Young
ryoung@ae-conveyor.com
Estimated Sales: Below $5 000,000
Number Employees: 10-19

18015 A & G Foods
6945 S State St
Chicago, IL 60637-4528
773-783-1672
Fax: 773-994-9623
Owner: Sam Johnson
Estimated Sales: $3 - 5 Million
Number Employees: 10-19

18016 A & K Development Co
410 Chambers St
Eugene, OR 97402-4375
541-686-0012
Fax: 541-485-2892 akdco@akdco.net
Sweet corn processing equipment: power huskers, power orienter, vibratory receiving conveyors, steam wilters, elevators, distribution systems, automatic feeding and lubrication systems, roll washers, short piece graders, scalpers, andsilage choppers
President and R&D: Ronald L Anderson
akdevelop@akdco.com
CFO: Bob King
Marketing Director: Zack Zachemtmayer
Office Manager: Darla Vicksie
Estimated Sales: $1 - 2.5 000,000
Number Employees: 20-49

18017 A A A Awning Co Inc
8810 Madie Dr
Houston, TX 77022-2617
800-281-6193
Fax: 713-694-0863 800-281-6193
www.aaaawning.net
Commercial awnings
Owner: Paul Yee
VP: Randy Deaton
Estimated Sales: $2.5-5 Million
Number Employees: 5-9

18018 A A Label Co
350 Stevenson Blvd # 2
New Kensington, PA 15068-5944
USA
724-335-5505
888-290-6012
customerservice@aalabel.com www.aalabel.com
Print and design of labels, gift wrap, boxes, containers
President: Mark Fisher
mfisher@aalabel.com
Estimated Sales: 700,000
Number Employees: 10-19

18019 A Allred Marketing
401 Graymont Ave W
Birmingham, AL 35204-4007
205-251-3700
Fax: 205-251-3706 allredpromos@gmail.com
Advertising specialties, signs, uniforms, shirts, caps, jackets, menus, flag poles and promotional items; also, custom printing and embroidery available.
President: Larry Allred
allredpromos@gmail.com
Estimated Sales: $500,000-$1 Million
Number Employees: 5-9
Parent Co: Promotional Products

18020 A B T Inc
259 Murdock Rd
Troutman, NC 28166-9695
704-528-9806
Fax: 704-528-5478 800-438-6057
sales@abtdrains.com
Pre-engineered drainage systems
President: Ralph Brafford
National Sales Manager: Jim DelRe
Estimated Sales: $2.5-5 Million
Number Employees: 50-99
Other Locations:
    ABT
    Lexington KY
Brands:
    Polydrain
    Polyduct
    Trench Former System

18021 A C Birox
200 Centennial Ave # 209
Piscataway, NJ 08854-3950
732-457-0015
Fax: 732-457-0016 800-242-2599
Biosensor-based instrument: quantifying folic acid
and biotin levels
President: Jerry Williamson
CFO: George Hogan
National Account Manager: Thomas Grace
Contact: Anders Felt
    anders.falt@biacore.com
Estimated Sales: $3 - 5 Million
Number Employees: 10-19

18022 A C Horn & Co Sheet Metal
1269 Majesty Dr
Dallas, TX 75247-3917
214-630-3311
Fax: 214-905-1365 800-657-6155
www.achornco.com
Food processing, packaging, and material handling
equipment.
President: Doug Horn
CEO: Ricardo Pounds
    rpounds@achornmfg.com
Vice President: Mark Ritter
Research/Development: Paul Lima
Quality Control: Paul Lima
Director Marketing/Sales: Mark Ritter
Public Relations: Michael Horn, Jr
Plant/Production Manager: Tommy Galloway
Purchasing: Elizabeth Durban
Estimated Sales: $10-20 Million
Number Employees: 50-99
Square Footage: 240000
Parent Co: A.C. Horn & Company
Brands:
    Radiant Ray
    Ray-O-Matic

18023 A C Tool & Machine Co
3711 Nobel Ct
Louisville, KY 40216-4113
502-447-5505
Fax: 502-447-2305 www.actoolandmachine.com
Sausage processing and packaging equipment; re-
building of food processing equipment and replace-
ment parts.
President: Matthew Thoben
    mthoben@actoolandmachine.com
Estimated Sales: $1-2.5 Million
Number Employees: 10-19
Square Footage: 48000
Type of Packaging: Food Service
Brands:
    Ac Slit & Trim

18024 A G Russell Knives
2900 S 26th St
Rogers, AR 72758-8571
479-631-0130
Fax: 479-631-8734 800-255-9034
ag@agrussell.com www.agrussell.com
Manufacturer and exporter of household knives
Owner: A G Russell
    goldie@agrussell.com
CFO: Michael Donnovan
Sales Exec: Goldie Russell
Estimated Sales: $20-50 Million
Number Employees: 20-49
Brands:
    Camillus Classic Cartridge
    Cartridge
    Dura-Tool

Promaster
Silver Sword
Sword
Western
Woodcraft
Yello-Jacket

18025 (HQ)A J Antunes & Co
180 Kehoe Blvd
Carol Stream, IL 60188-1814
630-784-1000
Fax: 630-784-1650 800-253-2991
scott.march@antunes.com antunes.com
Manufacturer and exporter of stainless steel food
service equipment for restaurants and concession
operations including tables and serving equipment in
addition to filtration products that remove
particulates, bacteria, and virusesfrom water.
President & CEO: Glenn Bullock
Estimated Sales: $50 - 100 Million
Number Employees: 100-249
Type of Packaging: Food Service
Brands:
    Antunes Control
    Roundup

18026 A J Funk & Co
1471 Timber Dr
Elgin, IL 60123-1898
847-741-6760
Fax: 847-741-6767 877-225-3865
info@glasscleaner.com
www.sparkle-glasscleaner.com
Glass cleaner. Also supply product and service to
distributors and end-users
President: Patrick Funk
Director of Sales: Lou Carlotti
Estimated Sales: $4 Million
Number Employees: 5-9
Square Footage: 48000
Type of Packaging: Consumer, Food Service
Brands:
    Sparkle

18027 A La Carte
5610 W Bloomingdale Ave
Chicago, IL 60639-4110
773-237-3000
Fax: 773-237-3075 800-722-2370
service@alacarteline.com
Custom promotional products including hard candy
and popcorn in decorative tins, jars, boxes, etc.
President: Michael Shulkin
CEO: Adam Robins
Sales Director: James Janowski
Purchasing: Marly Robins
Estimated Sales: $10 - 20 Million
Number Employees: 50-99
Parent Co: David Scott Industries
Type of Packaging: Food Service, Private Label,
Bulk

18028 A Legacy Food Svc
12683 Corral Pl
Santa Fe Springs, CA 90670-4748
562-320-3100
Fax: 888-604-1066 800-848-4440
info@alegacy.com www.alegacy.com
Manufacturer and exporter of top-of-range alumi-
num cookware. Also, restaurant supplies and
equipment
President: Brett Gross
Sales Director: Eric Gross
Manager: Eric Gross
    egross@alegacy.com
Estimated Sales: $1 - 5 Million
Number Employees: 5-9
Square Footage: 320000
Other Locations:
    Leonard, Harold, & Co.
    Chicago IL
Brands:
    Alegacy
    Eagleware

18029 A Line Corporation
5410 Powerhouse Court
Concord, NC 28027
704-793-1602
Fax: 704-793-1603 sales@aline1.com
www.aline1.com
Top-Load Carton Forming and Closing machinery
President: Maria Naas
Marketing: Jan Stull

Estimated Sales: $5 - 10 Million
Number Employees: 5-9

18030 A M S Filling Systems
2500 Chestnut Tree Rd
Glenmoore, PA 19343
610-942-3056
Fax: 610-942-7123 800-647-5390
sales@amsfilling.com www.amsfilling.com
Auger filling equipment for powder, granules, liq-
uids and pastes
President/CEO: Andy Baker
Sales: Mark Pezone
Estimated Sales: $3,000,000
Number Employees: 20-49
Square Footage: 140000
Brands:
    Ams

18031 A M Source Inc
261 Narragansett Park Dr
Rumford, RI 02916-1043
401-431-4080
Fax: 401-431-0606 800-556-6254
info@ajksales.com
Manufacturers' representative for disposable paper
and plastic food service products and packaging;
serving all markets
President: Arthur Kaufman
    spritchard@amsourcellc.com
Controller: H John Madden
VP: Allan Kaufman
Marketing Sales Manager: Kenneth McAuliffe
Sales Exec: Scott Prichard
Estimated Sales: $20-50 Million
Number Employees: 50-99
Type of Packaging: Food Service
Brands:
    Aep Institutional Products
    Austins
    Cascades
    Cascades Ifc Disposables
    Destiny Plastics
    Disposable Products Company
    Dopaco
    Fabri-Kal Corporation
    Fold Pak Company
    Genpak
    Handi-Foil of America
    Johnsondiversey
    McNarin Packaging
    Morgro
    Plastirun Corporation
    Poliback Plastics America
    Quality Paper Products
    Stewart Sutherland
    Tradex International

18032 A O A C Intl
481 N Frederick Ave
Suite 500
Gaithersburg, MD 20877-2417
301-924-7087
Fax: 301-924-7089 800-379-2622
aoac@aoac.org www.aoac.org
CFO: Joyce Schumacher
Executive Director: James Bradford
Contact: Don Bark
    dbark@aoac.org
Estimated Sales: $1 - 5 Million
Number Employees: 20-49

18033 A One Mfg Co
549 Evergreen Rd
Strafford, MO 65757-8810
417-736-2195
Fax: 417-736-2833 www.a-onemfg.com
Conveyors and accessories, pressure washers, blend-
ers, massagers and tumblers
President: David Cobb
    d.cobb@a-onemfg.com
Estimated Sales: $5-10 000,000
Number Employees: 50-99

18034 A Snow Craft Co Inc
200 Fulton Ave
PO Box 829
New Hyde Park, NY 11040-5306
516-739-1399
Fax: 516-739-1637 snowcraft1@aol.com
www.snowcraft.com
Insulated shipping containers

President: Ron Pelesko
rpelesko@skydyne.com
Secretary: William Hess
Estimated Sales: $5-10 Million
Number Employees: 20-49

18035 A T C Inc
4037 Guion Ln
Indianapolis, IN 46268-2564
317-429-1099
Fax: 317-328-2686 hsagi@atcinc.net
www.atcinc.net
President: Hemi Sagi
Estimated Sales: Less Than $500,000
Number Employees: 1-4

18036 A T Ferrell Co Inc
1440 S Adams St
Bluffton, IN 46714-9793
260-824-3400
Fax: 260-824-5463 800-248-8318
www.atferrell.com
Manufacturer and exporter of automatic electric feed mills, augers, pneumatic feed conveyors and aluminum beverage can crushers
President: Steve Stuller
bsstuller@atferrell.com
Estimated Sales: $1-2.5 Million
Number Employees: 50-99
Number of Brands: 2
Brands:
Modern Mill
Monarch Can Crushers

18037 A T Ferrell Co Inc
1440 S Adams St
Bluffton, IN 46714-9793
260-824-3400
Fax: 260-824-5463 800-248-8318
info@atferrell.com www.atferrell.com
Manufacturer and exporter of grain and seed cleaners and separators, hammer and roller mills, grain and feed coolers and vibrator and air conveyors
President: Steve Stuller
bsstuller@atferrell.com
CFO: Roger Stackhouse
Vice President: Phillip Petrakos
Research & Development: Dan Johnson
Sales Director: John Hay
Plant Manager: Howard Vaughn
Purchasing Manager: Brian Dynes
Estimated Sales: $5 - 10 Million
Number Employees: 50-99
Square Footage: 100000
Other Locations:
Clipper Separation Technologies
Bluffton IN
Ferrell-Ross Division
Amarillo TX
Brands:
Clipper
Ferrell-Ross
Mix-Mill

18038 A T Information Products Inc
575 Corporate Dr # 401
Mahwah, NJ 07430-3703
201-529-0202
Fax: 201-529-5603 www.atip-usa.com
Ink jet printing systems
President: Joseph Traut
joseph.traut@atip-usa.com
Estimated Sales: Below $5 000,000
Number Employees: 10-19

18039 A T Scafati Inc
417 W 44th St # A
New York, NY 10036-4402
212-695-4944
Fax: 212-695-4944
Doorman, bellboy, waiter uniforms
President: Joe Scafati
Estimated Sales: Below $5 Million
Number Employees: 10-19

18040 A Tec Technologic
5335 Progress Boulevard
Bethel Park, PA 15102-2545
412-835-6270
Fax: 412-835-6205
President: Philip Bochicchio

18041 A&A International
544 Central Dr Ste 110
Virginia Beach, VA 23454
757-463-1446
Fax: 757-463-4917 800-252-1446
info@aaawnings.com www.aaawnings.com
Commercial awnings
Manager: Rhonda Yarborough
Estimated Sales: $1-2,500,000
Number Employees: 20-49

18042 A&A Line & Wire Corporation
5118 Grand Ave Ste 10
Flushing, NY 11378
718-456-2657
Fax: 718-366-8284 800-886-2657
jlach@aalinewire.com
Manufacturer, importer and exporter of rope, twine and doormats, also sausage and pastella twine
President: Wally Greenburg
Treasurer: F Lach
Contact: Robert Giragosian
rgiragosian@aalinewire.com
Estimated Sales: Below $5 Million
Number Employees: 10-19
Square Footage: 32000
Parent Co: Long Island Import Center
Brands:
Coco
Crown
Queen O Mat

18043 A&A Manufacturing Company
2300 S Calhoun Rd
New Berlin, WI 53151-2708
414-906-4200
Fax: 262-786-3280 sales@gortite.com
www.gortite.com
Protective walk-on covers
President: Jim O'Rourke
CEO: Jerry O'Rourke
CFO: Larry Kean
VP: Tom Schanover
Quality Control: Darol Varter
Marketing Manager: Ken Sczyzkwski
Contact: Mike Adler
mike.adler@aaman.com
Estimated Sales: $20-50 Million
Number Employees: 100-249
Parent Co: Standalone

18044 A&B Safe Corporation
114 Delsea Dr S
Glassboro, NJ 08028
856-863-1186
Fax: 856-863-1208 800-253-1267
www.a-bsafecorp.com
Manufacturer, importer and exporter of depository, burglary and insulated safes and chests; also, insulated filing cabinets, safes and locks
President: Edward Dornisch
Sales Director: Edward C Dornisch
Operations Manager: Mildred Dornisch
Estimated Sales: $.5 - 1 million
Number Employees: 1-4
Number of Brands: 20
Square Footage: 10000
Brands:
A&B

18045 A&D Weighing
1756 Automation Pkwy
San Jose, CA 95131-1873
408-263-5333
Fax: 408-263-0119 800-726-3364
scales@andweighing.com www.andonline.com
Manufacturer and exporter of balances, scales and indicators
President: Paul Huber
President, Chief Executive Officer: Teruhisa Moriya
CEO: Peru Moriya
Marketing Communications Coordinator: Regina Starzyk
Director Sales: Dan Ashton
dashton@andweighing.com
Estimated Sales: $20-50 Million
Number Employees: 20-49
Square Footage: 3000

18046 A&D Weighing
1756 Automation Pkwy
San Jose, CA 95131-1873
408-263-5333
Fax: 408-263-0119 scales@andweighing.com
www.andonline.com
President: Paul Huver
President, Chief Executive Officer: Teruhisa Moriya
Quality Control: Maggie Tan
CEO: Peru Moriya
Contact: Dan Ashton
dashton@andweighing.com
Estimated Sales: $20 - 50 Million
Number Employees: 20-49

18047 A&F
5355 115th Avenue N
Clearwater, FL 33760-4840
727-572-7753
Fax: 727-573-0367
Filling and sealing machinery
President: Paul Desocio
Contact: Paul De Socio
paul@autoprodinc.com
Estimated Sales: $10-20 Million
Number Employees: 50-100
Parent Co: Jagenberg

18048 A&F Automation
1210 Campus Dr
Morganville, NJ 07751-1262
732-536-8770
Fax: 732-536-8850 www.oystarusa.com
President: Charles Ravalli
Estimated Sales: $3 - 5 Million
Number Employees: 10-19
Parent Co: IWKA Company

18049 A&G Machine Company
50 Dunnell Lane
Pawtucket, RI 02860-5828
401-726-4180
Fax: 401-723-2333
Aerators, candy making equipment including stringers and cookers, batch and continuous cooking equipment, cream machines, heat exchangers, kettle lifters and marshmallow equipment
President: Paul Desocio
Estimated Sales: $300,000-500,000
Number Employees: 1-4

18050 A&J Mixing International
8-2345 Wyecroft Road
Oakville, ON L6L 6L8
Canada
905-827-7288
Fax: 905-827-5045 800-668-3470
www.ajmixing.com
Manufacturer and exporter of food dry ingredient mixers, mixing sytems, vacuum coaters, dryers and continuous mixers.
President: A Flower
Sales: Lyndon Flower
Estimated Sales: $2.5 Million
Square Footage: 5000
Other Locations:
Sycamore IL
Brands:
Phlauer High Performance Mixers

18051 A&K Automation
1010 N Ashland Avenue
Aurora, ON L4G4R6
Canada
905-713-3429
Fax: 920-432-4356 www.akautomation.ca
Bakery products and pizza crust equipment
President: Randy Charles
CFO: Jim Charles
R & D: Dennis Dolski
Estimated Sales: Below $5 Million
Number Employees: 10
Square Footage: 1600

18052 A&L Laboratories
1001 Glenwood Ave
Minneapolis, MN 55405
612-374-9141
Fax: 612-374-5426 800-225-3832
Detergents and sanitizers
President: Guy Pochard
VP: Gabreiele Wittenburg
Contact: Roger Beers
beers@aandl-labs.com

Estimated Sales: $20-50 Million
Number Employees: 20-49

18053 A&L Western Ag Lab

1311 Woodland Avenue
Suite 1
Modesto, CA 95351-1221
　209-529-4080
　Fax: 209-529-4736 www.al-labs-west.com
Testing laboratory providing sanitation and nutritional analysis for product labeling
President and Laboratory Director: Robert Butterfield
Estimated Sales: $1-2.5 Million
Number Employees: 10-19
Square Footage: 26000

18054 A&M Industries

3610 North Cliff Avenue
Sioux Falls, SD 57104
　605-332-4877
　Fax: 605-338-6015 800-888-2615
　amindustries@amindustries.com
　www.amindustries.com
Manufacturer and exporter of rebuilt packaging, food processing and confectionery machinery, carton over-wrappers and specialty tooling
Owner: Richard Miller
Estimated Sales: Below $5 Million
Number Employees: 1-4
Square Footage: 20000
Type of Packaging: Consumer, Food Service, Private Label

18055 A&M Process Equipment

487 Westney Rd.
S., Unit #1
Ajax, ON L1S 6W7
Canada
　905-619-8001
　Fax: 905-619-8816
Food processing equipment including powder mixing and size reduction; exporter of ribbon, conical and twin shell blenders
President: John Lang
Number Employees: 4
Square Footage: 8000

18056 A&M Thermometer Corporation

17 Piney Park Road
Asheville, NC 28806-1727
　828-251-9092
　Fax: 828-254-5611 800-685-9211
Manufacturer and exporter of glass thermometers
President: M Pflaumbaum
R&D: Armin Pflaumbaum
Marketing: Kathy Toomey
Production: Armin Pflaumbaum
Purchasing Director: M Pflaumbaun
Estimated Sales: $2.5-5 Million
Number Employees: 10-19
Type of Packaging: Private Label, Bulk
Brands:
　Accutest
　Asico

18057 A&R Ceka North America

1755 North Brown Road
Suite 200
Lawrenceville, GA 30043-8196
　770-623-8235
　Fax: 770-623-8236 www.ar-carton.com
Supplier of carton packaging solutions.
President, Chief Executive Officer: Harald Schulz
Vice President, Chief Financial Officer: Niclas Nystrom
Senior Vice President of Sales and Marke: Jean-Francois Roche

18058 A-1 Booth Manufacturing

375 S 250 E
Burley, ID 83318-3718
　208-678-2877
　Fax: 800-952-3285 800-820-3285
　sales@a1booth.com www.a1booth.com
Manufacturer and exporter of tables, chairs and seats
President: Robert Silcock
Estimated Sales: $1-2.5 Million
Number Employees: 5-9
Type of Packaging: Food Service
Brands:
　Patriot Plus
　Patriot Series

18059 A-1 Business Supplies Inc

158 W Clinton St # N
Dover, NJ 07801-3411
　973-366-3690
　800-631-3421
Tags, price tags, day dots and labels including inventory control
Manager: Janet Larkin
VP: Janet Larkin
Sales Manager: Dick Burbaum
Estimated Sales: $1-2,500,000
Number Employees: 5-9

18060 A-1 Refrigeration Co

1720 E Monticello Ct
Ontario, CA 91761-7740
　909-930-9910
　Fax: 909-930-9026 800-669-4423
　custserv@a1flakeice.com www.a1flakeice.com
Ice machines.
Plant Manager: Tony Gallinucci
Estimated Sales: Less Than $500,000
Number Employees: 1-4
Number of Products: 10
Brands:
　A-1

18061 A-A1 Aaction Bag

5601 Logan St
Denver, CO 80216-1301
　303-297-9955
　Fax: 303-297-9960 800-783-1224
　www.centralbag.com
Manufacturer and wholesaler/distributor of packaging materials including paper and plastic bags, deli containers, cups and packaging for meats and seafood; also, custom printed and plain bags available
President: Esther Seaman
CEO: Elly Zussman
　elly@centralbag.com
CFO: David Fine
Vice President: Morton Zussman
VP, Marketing: Morty Zussman
Sales: Chuck Fine
Operations Manager: David Zussman
Estimated Sales: $5 Million
Number Employees: 10-19
Square Footage: 70000
Parent Co: Al-AAction Bag Company
Type of Packaging: Consumer, Food Service, Private Label, Bulk

18062 A-A1 Aaction Bag

5601 Logan St
Denver, CO 80216-1301
　303-297-9955
　Fax: 303-297-9960 800-783-1224
　searichcorp@aol.com www.centralbag.com
Manufacturer and exporter of bags including plastic, burlap and cotton; also, plastic film; importer of burlap and woven polypropylene bags
President: Esther Seaman
Partner: Elly Zussman
　elly@centralbag.com
VP: Lewis Bradford
Sales Director: Morton Seaman
Estimated Sales: $500,000 - $1 Million
Number Employees: 10-19
Square Footage: 48000
Parent Co: Sea-Rich Corporation
Type of Packaging: Bulk

18063 A-B-C Packaging MachineCorp

811 Live Oak St
Tarpon Springs, FL 34689-4199
　727-937-5144
　Fax: 727-938-1239 800-237-5975
　sales@abcpackaging.com
　www.abcpackaging.com
Manufacturer and exporter of packaging machinery
President: Donald G Reichert
Director Sales/Marketing: Bryan Sinicrope
Estimated Sales: $10-20 Million
Number Employees: 50-99
Square Footage: 200000

18064 A-L-L Magnetics Inc

2831 E Via Martens
Anaheim, CA 92806-1751
　714-632-1754
　Fax: 714-632-1757 800-262-4638
　sales@allmagnetics.com www.allmagnetics.com
Manufacturer, exporter and importer of magnets used for holding, separating and water treatment

President: John Nellessen
　john@allmagnetics.com
CFO: John Nellessen
Sales: Rosemary Kute
Estimated Sales: Below $5 Million
Number Employees: 10-19
Square Footage: 80000
Brands:
　Magnet Source, The

18065 A-Z Factory Supply

10512 United Pkwy
Schiller Park, IL 60176-1716
　847-261-0620
　Fax: 800-233-4512 800-323-4511
　sales@azsupply.com www.azsupply.com
Manufacturer and exporter of material handling and storage equipment, shelving, carts, shelf trucks, boxes, bins, hoppers, corrugated steel containers, conveyors, lifts, hoists, etc
Manager: Henry Bolden
　henry@azsupply.com
VP: R Hannesson
Sales Manager: B Spurling
Estimated Sales: Below $5,000,000
Number Employees: 10-19

18066 A. Klein & Company

P.O. Box 670
Claremont, NC 28610
　828-459-9261
　Fax: 828-459-9608
Custom made boxes for the confectionery industry
President: Jesse Salwen
Estimated Sales: $50-100 Million
Number Employees: 100-249

18067 A.A. Pesce Glass Company

216 Birch St
Kennett Square, PA 19348-3606
　610-444-5065
　Fax: 610-444-3358
Scientific and laboratory glassware
Manager: Mike Carroll
Estimated Sales: $1-2.5 Million
Number Employees: 5-9

18068 A.B. Sealer, Inc.

N 7212 Farwell Road
PO Box 635
Beaver Dam, WI 53916-0635
　920-885-9299
　Fax: 920-885-0288 877-885-9299
　sales@absealer.com www.absealer.com
Manufacturer and exporter of packaging machinery including portable case erectors and sealers and custom equipment systems
Owner: Lou Stikowsky
CEO: Russell Quandt
Estimated Sales: $1-2.5 Million
Number Employees: 50-99
Brands:
　Aantek
　Series 9000

18069 A.C. Legg

P.O. Box 709
Calera, AL 35040
　Fax: 205-668-7835 800-422-5344
　sales@aclegg.com www.aclegg.com
Processor of custom-blended seasonings for meat, poultry, seafood and snack foods.
President/CEO: James Purvis
EVP: Charles Purvis
Year Founded: 1923
Estimated Sales: $20-50 Million
Number Employees: 100-249
Number of Brands: 1
Square Footage: 131000
Type of Packaging: Food Service, Private Label, Bulk
Brands:
　Legg's Old Plantation

18070 A.D. Cowdrey Company

1442 Angie Avenue
Modesto, CA 95351-4952
　209-538-4677
　Fax: 209-538-6087 cvpsdp@aol.com
　www.adcowdrey.com
Canners' and packers' knives, aprons and corers

President: David Racher
VP: John Hassapakis
Contact: Dave Racher
  d.racher@adcowdrey.com
Estimated Sales: Below $5 Million
Number Employees: 20
Parent Co: Central Valley Professional Service

18071 A.D. Johnson Engraving Company
229 Woodward Ave
Kalamazoo, MI 49007-3221

269-342-5500
Fax: 269-342-5511
Engraving and embossing dies and stamps; also, engraving for premium goods and advertising novelties
President: Donovan J Kindle
Estimated Sales: $500,000-$1 Million
Number Employees: 1-4

18072 A.D. Joslin Manufacturing Company
33 Artic St
Manistee, MI 49660

231-723-2908
Fax: 231-723-2908 www.manistee.com/joslin
Manufacturer and exporter of handheld and electric seal embossing machinery, dating machinery, steel code marking stamps, ticket validators and handheld case numbering machines
General Manager: Norman Ware
Office Manager: Carol Westberg
Estimated Sales: $3 - 5 Million
Number Employees: 10-19
Parent Co: Cosco Industries

18073 A.K. Robins
4100 Pistorio Road
Baltimore, MD 21229-5509

410-247-4000
Fax: 410-247-9165 800-486-9656
Manufacturer and exporter of cleaners, conveyors, cookers, cutters, exhausters, extractors, etc.; also, CAD engineering and design and USDA services available
Sales Manager: Steve Ward
Operations Manager: Ken Vogel
Number Employees: 50

18074 A.M. Loveman Lumber & Box Company
PO Box 40123
Nashville, TN 37204-0123

615-297-1397
Wooden boxes and pallets
President: Andrew M Loveman
Estimated Sales: $500,000-$1 Million
Number Employees: 8
Square Footage: 24000

18075 A.M. Manufacturing
14151 Irving Ave
Dolton, IL 60419

708-841-0959
Fax: 708-841-0975 800-342-6744
www.ammfg.com
Baking equipment
Owner: Claudia Kunis
Co-owner: Holly Rentner
Contact: Wojciechows Mentz
  wojo2424@aol.com
Estimated Sales: $5 - 10 Million
Number Employees: 20-49
Square Footage: 28000

18076 A.O. Smith Water Products Company
600 E John Carpenter Fwy # 200
Irving, TX 75062-3985

972-792-4371
Fax: 972-719-5967 800-527-1953
techctr@hotwater.com www.hotwater.com
Manufacturer and exporter of tank-type water heaters and boilers and booster heaters
Chairman, Chief Executive Officer: Paul Jones
Vice President, Controller: Daniel Kempken
President, Chief Operating Officer: Ajita Rajendra
Project Manager: Will Harris
Number Employees: 50-99
Square Footage: 4000000
Parent Co: A.O. Smith Corporation

Brands:
  Burkay
  Cyclone Xhe
  Dura-Max
  Legend
  Master Fit

18077 A.P.M.
1500 Hillcrest Rd
Norcross, GA 30093-2617

770-921-6300
Fax: 770-925-7801 800-226-5557
www.apminc.org
President: James R Sabourin
Estimated Sales: $3 - 5 Million
Number Employees: 10-19

18078 A.T. Foote Woodworking Company
726 Windsor Street
Hartford, CT 06120

860-249-6821
Fax: 860-249-6192
Store fixtures
President: Arthur Foote, Sr.
VP: Arthur Foote, Jr.
Estimated Sales: $20-50 Million
Number Employees: 4

18079 A1 Tablecloth Co
450 Huyler St # 102
South Hackensack, NJ 07606-1563

201-727-4364
Fax: 201-727-8988 800-727-8987
a1@a1tablecloth.com www.a1tablecloth.com
Manufacturer and exporter of tablecloths, napkins, table skirting, chair covers and drapes
Owner: Robert Fox
Contact: Pearle Adam
  ap@a-1tablecloth.com
Estimated Sales: $10 - 50,000,000
Number Employees: 1-4

18080 AAA Electrical Signs
2407 E Business Highway 83
Donna, TX 78537-3545

956-546-2735
Fax: 956-464-2408 800-825-5376
www.3asigns.com
Custom electrical signs, brass plaques, illuminated letters and time and temperature units; also, electronic message centers and color elcetronic signs, we sell and lease.
President: Paul Sullivan
  paulsullivan@3asigns.com
General Manager: Steve Smith
Plant Manager: Ken Bailey
Estimated Sales: $4 Million
Number Employees: 20-49
Square Footage: 20000
Parent Co: Tesoro Corporation

18081 AAA Flag & Banner Manufacturing
8955 National Blvd
Los Angeles, CA 90034-3307

310-836-3341
Fax: 310-836-7253 800-266-4222
www.aaaflag.com
Flags, pennants, banners and signs
Controller: Carol Hettiger
CEO: Howard Furst
Estimated Sales: $20 - 50 Million
Number Employees: 500-999

18082 AAA Mill
812 Airport Blvd
Austin, TX 78702-4106

512-385-2215
Fax: 512-385-0860
Wood and plastic laminated freezer cabinets and store fixtures
President: David Bockhorn
General Manager: David Bockhorn
Estimated Sales: Below $5 Million
Number Employees: 5 to 9
Square Footage: 20000

18083 AAMD
7342 Tomwood Dr
Liverpool, NY 13090-3747

315-451-0951
Fax: 315-451-8740 800-887-4167

Manufacturer, importer and exporter of packaging machinery including tamper evident sealing equipment, closure lining equipment, assembly machines, metal closure threaders, tamper evident cap slitting machines, etc.; also, consultingservices available
VP Sales/Marketing: Eugene Orr
Estimated Sales: $1 - 3 Million
Number Employees: 1-4
Square Footage: 52000

18084 AANTEC
3116 N Pointer Rd
Appleton, WI 54911

920-830-9723
Fax: 920-830-9840
Packaging equipment; case packers, palletizers, tray packers/formers, case erectors/sealers, napkin folders, towel and tissue interfolders, tissue rewinders, napkin wrappers and bundlers, roll wrappers, conveyors, grip per elevatorsand lowerators, high-speed case-packers
President: Robert Schuh
VP: Corben Hoffman
Sales: Jeffrey Aissen
Public Relations: Julia Kirsch
Operations: Paul Tassoul
Estimated Sales: $5 - 10 Million
Number Employees: 10-19
Type of Packaging: Consumer, Food Service, Private Label, Bulk
Brands:
  Involvo
  Tmc

18085 AB McLauchlan Company
P.O. Box 12006
Salem, OR 97309-0006

503-363-8611
Fax: 503-364-5546
Blenders, food processing, conveying, size grading, cleaning, slicing, sorting, filling, and mixing equipment, mixers
President: John Layton
Estimated Sales: $1-2.5 Million
Number Employees: 5-9

18086 AB6
17190 Grant Road
Cypress, TX 77429

713-824-7275
Fax: 775-366-0516 john@ab6.net
www.ab6.net
President: John de Penne rouge

18087 ABB
North American Headquarters
305 Gregson Dr
Cary, NC 27511

440-585-7804
Fax: 919-666-1377 800-435-7365
contact.center@us.abb.com new.abb.com
Manufacturer and exporter of presses and drives for high-pressure food processing equipment for pasteurization and sterilization, generators, control systems, drives, motors, instrumentation and metering.
CEO: Peter Voser
Managing Director, U.S.: Maryrose Sylvester
CFO, U.S.: Michael Gray
Year Founded: 1891
Estimated Sales: $27.9 Billion
Number Employees: 147,000
Parent Co: ABB Group

18088 (HQ)ABC Laboratories
7200 E. ABC Lane
Columbia, MO 65202

573-443-9000
Fax: 573-777-6033 800-538-5227
www.abclabs.com
Laboratory offering analysis, testing and field research to the food service industry
President/CEO: John D Bucksath
R&D: Eric Lawerence
VP: Kristein King
VP, Business Dev.: Amy Mize
Contact: Ambroise Akue
  akuea@abclabs.com
Estimated Sales: $10 - 20 Million
Number Employees: 100-249
Square Footage: 300000

18089 ABC Letter Art
1623 S Vermont Ave
Los Angeles, CA 90006

323-733-0191
Fax: 323-733-6505 888-261-5367
Displays and signs including interior and exterior
graphics, wood, metal, plastic and 3-D letters; also,
installation services available
CEO: Mark Shear
Sales Director: Jerry Eckert
Estimated Sales: $1-2.5 Million
Number Employees: 10-19
Brands:
  A Sign of Good Taste

18090 ABC Research Corp
3437 SW 24th Ave
Gainesville, FL 32607-4599

352-372-0436
Fax: 352-378-6483 866-233-5883
info@abcr.com
Certified, third-party, independent contract food lab-
oratory specializing in microbiological and chemical
analyses of commercial food products.
President: William Brown
CEO: George Baker
  george.baker@abcr.com
VP: James Kennedy
Marketing Director: Larry Clement
COO/Executive Director: Gillian Folkes
Estimated Sales: $5 Million
Number Employees: 100-249
Square Footage: 99000

18091 ABC Scales
240 Boone Ave
Marion, OH 43302-3356

740-382-0551
Fax: 740-387-4869
Estimated Sales: $1 - 3 Million
Number Employees: 1-4
Parent Co: Fairfield Engineering Company

18092 ABC Stamp Signs & Awards
407 N Orchard St
Boise, ID 83706-1976

208-375-4470
Fax: 208-377-3509 abcstamp@abcstamp.com
www.abcstamp.com
Rubber stamps
President: Richard Paulson
  abcstamp@abcstamp.com
Estimated Sales: Below $5 Million
Number Employees: 10-19
Square Footage: 12800

18093 ABCO Industries
2675 E Us Highway 80
Abilene, TX 79601

915-677-2011
Fax: 915-677-1420 800-530-4060
Estimated Sales: Below $500,000
Number Employees: 20-49

18094 ABCO Industries Limited
PO Box 1120
Lunenburg, NS B0J 2C0
Canada

902-634-8821
Fax: 902-634-8583 866-634-8821
www.abco.ca
Manufacturer and exporter of aluminum and stain-
less steel food processing equipment including
steam blanchers evaporative coolers
President: John Meisner
CEO: J Eisenhauer
Marketing Director: Graham Gerhardt
Sales Director: Dan Croft
Number Employees: 50-99
Square Footage: 120000
Brands:
  Abco

18095 ABCO Laboratories Inc
2450 S Watney Way
Fairfield, CA 94533-6730

707-432-2200
Fax: 707-432-2240 800-678-2226
www.abcolabs.com
Nutraceutical products-liquids, tablets, capsules,
powder blends. Foods-spices, dry blends, seasonings, functional food blends.

President: David Baron
Founder: Allen Baron
  abaron@abcolabs.com
R&D: Dr Muhammed Al-Nasassrah
Quality Control: Rich Hale
Marketing: Greg Northam
Sales: Victoria Gonzales
Operations: Richard Snowden
Plant Manager: Dick Snowden
Purchasing Director: Carl Falcone
Number Employees: 100-249
Number of Brands: 10
Number of Products: 5000
Square Footage: 800000
Type of Packaging: Consumer, Food Service, Pri-
vate Label, Bulk
Brands:
  Nutra Naturally Essentials

18096 ABG Industries
1051 Clinton St
Buffalo, NY 14206-2823

716-853-6132
Fax: 905-479-9752 www.abgindustries.com
Owner: Martin Malthouse
CFO: Ken Pice
Manager: Richard Dipchon
Estimated Sales: Below $5 Million
Number Employees: 5-9

18097 ABI Limited
8900 Keele Street, Unit 1
Concord, ON L4K 2N2
Canada

905-738-6070
Fax: 905-738-6085 800-297-8666
info@abiltd.com
ABI Ltd. manufacturers automated food processing
equipment with the emphasis on performance, dura-
bility, reliability and simplicity in maintenance.
President: Alex Kuperman
Marketing: Regine Kuperman
Production VP: Mike Kuperman
Number Employees: 20
Square Footage: 60000
Brands:
  Belt Saver 2000
  Bpl 10000
  Bpl 12000
  Bpl 24000
  Bpl 6000
  Bpl 8600
  Df 5000
  Superformer

18098 ABIC International Consultants
24 Spielman Rd
Fairfield, NJ 07004-3412

973-227-7060
Fax: 973-227-0172 www.abic-consulting.com
Consultant providing product development, evalua-
tion and improvement of current products and pro-
cessing and implementation of cost efficiencies;
also, expertise in food science, process engineering
and sensory evaluation
President: Abraham Bakal
CEO: Penny Cash
Contact: Fifi Bakal
  fbakal@abic-consulting.com
Estimated Sales: Less Than $500,000
Number Employees: 1-4
Square Footage: 32000

18099 ABJ/Sanitaire Corporation
9333 N 49th St
Milwaukee, WI 53223-1472

414-365-2200
Fax: 414-365-2210 www.sanitaire.com
Manufacturer and exporter of anaerobic wastewater
systems including sequencing batch reactors
Estimated Sales: $50 Million
Number Employees: 100-249
Square Footage: 7000
Parent Co: Xylem
Brands:
  Iceas

18100 ABLOY Security Inc
6005 Commerce Dr # 330
Irving, TX 75063-2664

972-753-1127
Fax: 972-753-0792 800-367-4598
info@abloyusa.com www.abloyusa.com

High security locks, T-handle cylinders, padlocks,
key-ring padlocks, cam locks
President: Martha Bartley
  mbartley@abloy.com
CFO and QC and R&D: Jeff Carpenter
Sales Manager: Martha Bartley
Estimated Sales: $1 - 2.5 Million
Number Employees: 10-19
Parent Co: Assa Abloy

18101 ABM Marking
2799 S Belt W
Belleville, IL 62226-6777

618-277-3773
Fax: 618-277-3782 800-626-9012
abmmarking@aol.com www.abmmarking.com
Manufacturer and exporter of ink jet printers and
coding inks for porous and nonporous surfaces in-
cluding coated, plastic and polyethylene; importer of
tape dispensers and machines
Owner: Al Merchiori
Sales Manager: Alberto Merchiori
  abmmarking@aol.com
Operations: Roger Schaefer
Estimated Sales: $3 - 5 Million
Number Employees: 5-9
Square Footage: 24000
Brands:
  Abm
  Abm's Safemark

18102 ABO Industries
13620 Lindamere Ln
San Diego, CA 92128

858-566-9750
Fax: 858-566-9590
Manufacturer, exporter and importer of industrial
progressive cavity, peristaltic, gear, metering and air
operated diaphragm pumps
President: Joseph Schulman
VP: Ming Li
Estimated Sales: $1 - 5 Million
Number Employees: 5-9
Square Footage: 5000
Brands:
  Carmine
  Carminic Acid

18103 AC Dispensing Equipment
100 Dispensing Way
Lower Sackville, NS B4C 4H2
Canada

902-865-9602
Fax: 902-865-9604 888-777-9990
sales@sureshotdispensing.com
www.sureshotdispensing.com
Electronic portion controlled dispensers for cream,
sugar, milk and oil
President: Michel Duck
R&D: Ian Maclen
CFO: Ian Tramble
Director Sales/Marketing: W William Morris
Number Employees: 80
Brands:
  Sureshot

18104 AC Label Company
2101 Eest VallyVistaWay
Provo, UT 84606

801-642-3500
Fax: 801-642-3510
Bottling equipment and supplies, computer software,
labeling and packaging machinery and packaging
materials; also, printer, bar code, pressure sensitive
and security labels
Manager: Matt Schwanbeck
VP: Jim DiBona
Estimated Sales: $10 - 20,000,000
Number Employees: 50-99
Parent Co: Impaxx

18105 ACCO Systems
12755 E 9 Mile Rd
Warren, MI 48089

845-456-2236
Fax: 586-758-1901 800-342-2226
www.accosystems.co.uk
Manufacturer and exporter of material handling sys-
tems and equipment
President: Anthony Gore
Director Sales/Marketing: Mark Murray
Contact: Glenn Clannell
  gclannell@andek.com

Number Employees: 250-499
Parent Co: Durr GmbH

18106 ACH Rice Specialties
7171 Goodlett Farms Pkwy
Cordova, TN 38016-4909

901-381-3000
Fax: 901-381-2968 800-691-1106
information@achfood.com
President: Dan Antonelli
CFO: Jeff Atkins
R&D and Quality Control: Pete Sriedman
Estimated Sales: $20 - 30 Million
Number Employees: 1,000-4,999

18107 ACI
3731b San Gabriel River Pkwy
Pico Rivera, CA 90660-1404

562-699-4999
Fax: 562-699-0919
Industrial ink jet printers

18108 ACLAUSA Inc
509 Thomson Park Dr
Cranberry Twp, PA 16066-6425

724-776-0099
Fax: 724-776-0477
Manufacturer and exporter of material handling
equipment including rollers, tires, wheels, bumpers
and seals
President: Andy Mc Intyre
andym@aclausa.com
Estimated Sales: $1-2.5 Million
Number Employees: 1-4
Parent Co: ACLA

18109 ACMA/GD
501 Southlake Blvd
Richmond, VA 23236-3078

804-794-6688
Fax: 804-379-2199 800-525-2735
paul.smith@gidi.it www.acmavolpak.com
Manufacturer, importer and exporter of liquid filling
machinery and vertical and horizontal form/fill/seal
equipment
CEO: Guiseppe Venturi
Marketing: Glen Coater
Estimated Sales: Below $500,000
Number Employees: 250-499
Square Footage: 800000

18110 ACME Sign Corp
3 Lakeland Park Dr
Peabody, MA 01960-3835

978-535-6600
Fax: 978-536-5051 info@acmesigncorp.com
www.acmesigncorp.com
Custom sign manufacturer and supplier
President: Darius Aleksas
darius@acmesigncorp.com
Estimated Sales: $1 Million
Number Employees: 1-4
Square Footage: 16000

18111 ACME-McClain & Son
4759 Durfee Avenue
Pico Rivera, CA 90660-2037

562-692-0026
Fax: 800-428-2263

18112 ACO
501 SW 19th St
Moore, OK 73160-5427

405-794-7662
Fax: 405-236-4014 www.mcdonalds.com
Manufacturer and exporter of material handling
boxes, trays and racks
Founder: Ray Kroc
Estimated Sales: $1-2.5 Million
Number Employees: 10-19

18113 ACO Polymer Products
12080 Ravenna Road
Chardon, OH 44024-7008

440-285-7000
Fax: 440-285-7005
President: Derek Humphries
Contact: Ben Aulick
baulick@aco-online.com
Number Employees: 50-99

18114 ACR Systems
#210-15110 54A Avenue
Surrey, BC V3S 5X7
Canada

604-591-1128
Fax: 604-591-2252 800-663-7845
sales@acrsystems.com www.acrsystems.com
Data loggers-measure and record temperature and
humidity, current, power quality, pressure, process
signals and more
President: Albert C Rock
CFO: David McDougall
Director of Operations: Wayne Thompson
Number Employees: 30
Type of Packaging: Private Label
Brands:
Acr Jr.
Acr Powerwatch
Owl
Smartreader
Smartreader Plus
Smartvision
Trendreader

18115 ACS Industries, Inc.
One New England Way
Lincoln, RI 02865

866-783-4838
Fax: 401-333-2294 acsind@acsind.com
www.acsindustries.com
Stainless steel sponges, nylon scouring pads,
screens, filter cones and grill cleaning systems; also,
nonsulphate antioxidants
President: Steven N Buckler
Contact: Ryan Abranovic
rabranovic@acsind.com
Estimated Sales: $5 - 10 Million
Number Employees: 1,000-4,999
Square Footage: 1200000
Brands:
Acs Industries, Inc. Scrubble

18116 ACUair/York Refrigeration
5757 N. Green Bay Ave
P.O. Box 591
Milwaukee, WI 53201

414-524-1200
Fax: 305-887-7853 414-524-1200
www.johnsoncontrols.com
Chairman, President and Chief Executive: Alex A.
Molinaroli
EVP and Chief Financial Officer: R. Bruce
McDonald
Human Resources: William Hyland
VP and Chief Marketing Officer: Kim
Metcalf-Kupres
Estimated Sales: Below $500,000
Parent Co: Johnson Controls, Inc.

18117 AD Products
2919 Industrial Park Dr
Finksburg, MD 21048

800-743-8815
Fax: 410-833-8817 800-743-8815
www.adprods.com
Material handling equipment - dollies, racks, carts,
baskets, trays (stock and custom)
Manager: Nick Hailston
CFO: Ami Markle
R & D: William Fauntleroy
Sales: Nick Hailstone
Estimated Sales: Below $5 000,000
Number Employees: 10-19

18118 ADCO
P.O. Box 999
Sedalia, MO 65302-0999

660-826-3300
Fax: 660-826-1361 sales@adco-inc.com
www.adco-inc.com
President: Charles M Van Dyne
Quality Control: Archie Shrieman
Contact: Juanita Salmons
salmons@adco-inc.com
Estimated Sales: $10 - 20 Million
Number Employees: 50-99
Parent Co: AlliedSignal Company

18119 ADCO
1909 West Oakridge
Albany, GA 31707

660-826-3300
Fax: 660-826-1361 800-821-7556
sales@adco-inc.com www.adco-inc.com

Disinfectants, polishes and dry cleaning compounds
Chief Executive Officer: Mark Grimaldi
EVP/Business Operations: Yalda Harris
Quality/Compliance Manager: Scott Stanfill
Chief Products/Technology Officer: Jim Schreiner
National Sales Manager: Greg Reinhardt
Contact: James Schreiner
schreiner@adco-inc.com
Estimated Sales: $5-10 Million
Number Employees: 50-99

18120 ADCO Manufacturing Inc
2170 Academy Ave
Sanger, CA 93657-3795

559-875-5563
Fax: 559-875-7665 sales@adcomfg.com
www.adcomfg.com
Manufacturer and exporter of packaging machinery
for cartons
President: Frank Hoffman
CEO: Kate King
kking@adcomfg.com
VP Marketing: Scott Reed
VP Sales: Paul Kessock
Human Resources Manager: Maureen Say
Operations/Plant Manager: Dale Kingen
Purchasing Director: Juanita Johnson
Estimated Sales: $24 Million
Number Employees: 100-249
Square Footage: 76000
Type of Packaging: Consumer, Food Service, Pri-
vate Label

18121 ADCO Manufacturing Inc
2170 Academy Ave
Sanger, CA 93657-3795

559-875-5563
Fax: 559-875-7665 sales@adcomfg.com
www.adcomfg.com
Packaging machinery
President: Frank Hoffman
CEO: Kate King
kking@adcomfg.com
CFO: Kate King
CEO: Kate King
Estimated Sales: $20 - 50 Million
Number Employees: 100-249

18122 ADD Testing & Research
19 Addison Pl
Valley Stream, NY 11580

516-568-9197
Fax: 516-568-3147 info@addtestinglab.com
www.addtestinglab.com
Laboratory providing research, development, food
testing, spice analysis, sanitation testing, etc
President: Michael Schenoude
Owner: Aida Shenouga
Estimated Sales: Below 1 Million
Number Employees: 1-4
Square Footage: 6000

18123 ADDCHEK Coils
1285 Jim Wilson Rd
Fort Mill, SC 29715-7605

803-547-7566
Fax: 803-547-5250
Heat transfer equipment using aluminum, copper,
cupro nickel and stainless steel
President: Anna D Wood
Corporate Secretary: Helen Wood
Estimated Sales: $5-10 Million
Number Employees: 10-19

18124 ADE Inc
1430 E 130th St
Chicago, IL 60633-2399

773-646-3400
Fax: 773-646-3919 800-222-0221
info@ade-usa.com www.ade-usa.com
Protective packaging alternatives, package designs
using elastomeric film
Manager: Lewis Lofgren
CEO: L Lofgren
llotgren@ade-usa.com
Estimated Sales: $5-10 000,000
Number Employees: 20-49

18125 ADI Systems
370 Wilsey Rd
Fredericton, NB E3B 6E9
Canada

506-452-7307
Fax: 506-452-7308 800-561-2831
www.adisystemsinc.com
Wastewater treatment and water reuse.
President: Graham Brown
CFO: Hazen Hawker

18126 ADI Systems Inc
370 Wilsey Road
Fredericton, NB E3B 6E9
Canada

506-452-7307
Fax: 506-452-7308 800-561-2831
systems@adi.ca www.adisystemsinc.com
ADI offers proprietary anaerobic and aerobic industrial wastewater treatment and waste-to-energy technologies, biogas cleaning and utilization, plus complete design-build services. ADI also conducts treatability studies, pilot testingbench-scale studies, operator training, and aftercare services to customers who need to anaerobically or aerobically treat industrial wastewater.
President: Graham Brown
CEO: Hazen Hawker
VP Technology: Shannon Grant
Marketing Assistant: Connie Smith
Manager Business Development: Scott Christian
Marketing & Communications Manager: Sarah Brown
Estimated Sales: $10-20 Million
Number Employees: 25
Square Footage: 4000
Parent Co: ADI Group
Other Locations:
Wolfeboro NH
Brands:
Adi-Anmbr
Adi-Bvf Digester
Adi-Hybrid
Adi-Mbr
Adi-Sbr

18127 ADM/Matsutani LLC
4666 Faries Pkwy
Decatur, IL 62526

847-418-1615
Manufacturer of soluable dietary fiber ingredients, specifically Fibersol.
Senior Sales Manager: Barbara Brojack
Contact: Bob Heard
bheard97@aol.com
General Manager: George Perujo
Number Employees: 3
Parent Co: ADM
Brands:
Fibersol 2

18128 ADMIX
234 Abby Rd
Manchester, NH 03103-3332

603-627-2340
Fax: 603-627-2019 800-466-2369
mixing@admix.com www.admix.com
Sanitary mixing and dispersion, and particle size reduction equipment
General Manager: L Beaudette
President: Louis Beaudette
Sales Manager: P Leitner
Contact: Jerry Baresich
jbaresich@admix.com
Operations Manager: P Foskitt
Estimated Sales: Below $5 Million
Number Employees: 20-49
Square Footage: 60000
Brands:
Admixer
Boston Shearpump
Dynashear
Oprishear
Optifeed
Rotomixx
Rotosolver
Rotostat
Vacushear

18129 ADSI Inc
22971 State Road 78
Durant, OK 74701-1130

580-924-4461
Fax: 580-924-7375 adsi@adsiinc.com
www.adsiinc.com
Manufacturer & exporter of commercial egg breaking machinery, egg washing & sanitizing machines.
President, Sales, & Operations: Mike Maynard
VP, Sales, Production & Plant Mgr.: Steve Maynard
Estimated Sales: Below $5 Million
Number Employees: 10-19
Type of Packaging: Food Service
Brands:
Centri-Matic Iii
Egg Valet
Sew 400
Sew 800

18130 ADT Inc
1501 NW 51st St
Boca Raton, FL 33431-4438

800-521-1734
www.adt.com
Wholesaler/distributor of general merchandise including burglar and fire alarm systems, access control systems, security equipment and closed circuit TV.
Chief Executive Officer: Jim DeVries
Chief Financial Officer: Jeff Likosar
Chief Administration Officer: Dan Bresingham
Chief Legal Officer: P. Gray Finney
Chief Customer Officer: Jamie Rosand Haenggi
Chief Information Officer: Donald Young
Year Founded: 1874
Estimated Sales: Over $1 Billion
Number Employees: 18,000
Parent Co: Apollo Global Management

18131 AEP Industries
125 Phillips Ave
South Hackensack, NJ 07606

201-641-6600
Fax: 201-807-2567 800-999-2374
info@aepinc.com www.aepinc.com
Plastic sheeting, stretch films and liners and polyethylene products including bags, packaging and film
President & CEO: John Powers
Estimated Sales: $75 Million - 1 Billion
Number Employees: 2900

18132 AEP Industries Inc
1970 Excel Dr
Mankato, MN 56001-5903

507-386-4420
Fax: 507-388-4420 800-999-2374
www.aepinc.com
Manufacturer and exporter of disposable gloves, aprons, bibs, table covers, specialty bags and films including cling, polyethylene, stretch and shrink
President: Jenny Pherson
Research & Development: Thea Ellingson
Marketing Director: Mike Sauer
Sales Director: Ken Christensen
Operations/Purchasing: Mike Ellis
Estimated Sales: $20 - 50 Million
Number Employees: 100-249
Parent Co: Atlantis Plastics
Type of Packaging: Consumer, Food Service, Bulk
Other Locations:
Mankato-Institutional Operations
Mankato MN
Brands:
Linear
Sta-Dri

18133 AEP Texas
539 N Carancahua
Corpus Christi, TX 78478

877-373-4858
www.aeptexas.com
Electric utility systems.
President & COO: Judith Talavera
VP, Regulatory & Finance: Leigh Anne Strahler
VP, External Affairs: Julio Reyes
Year Founded: 1906
Estimated Sales: $1,000,000,000+
Parent Co: American Electric Power

18134 AERCO International Inc
100 Oritani Dr
Blauvelt, NY 10913-1022

845-580-8000
Fax: 845-580-8090 800-526-0288
www.aerco.com
Water heaters, condensing boilers and steam generators
President: Fred Depuy
CEO: Patricia Abrahamsen
pabrahamsen@aerco.com
VP: Fred F Campagna
Marketing Director: Mark Croche
Estimated Sales: $10-20 Million
Number Employees: 10-19

18135 AERTEC
P.O. Box 488
North Andover, MA 01845-0488

978-475-6385
Fax: 978-475-6387 info@aertec.com
www.aertec.com
Waste and water aeration
President: R Gary Gilbert
Estimated Sales: $1 - 5 Million
Number Employees: 5-9

18136 AES Corp
3412 Center Point Rd NE
Suite A
Cedar Rapids, IA 52402-5529

319-432-7365
Fax: 319-395-7693 info@aescorp.com
www.aescorp.com
Design and installation of aseptic processing and packaging systems specialize in fruit and vegetables; dairy; pharmaceuticals
Manager: David Garrelts
Estimated Sales: $1 - 5 Million
Number Employees: 50-99

18137 AET Films
15 Reads Way
New Castle, DE 19720-1648

302-326-5500
Fax: 302-326-5501 800-688-2044
ODP film for flexible packaging and labeling
President: David Terhuna
CFO: Bryan Crescenzo
CEO: Thomas Mohr
Contact: Mike Demchinski
mdemchinski@aetinc.com
Estimated Sales: $20 - 50 Million
Number Employees: 500-999

18138 AEW Thurne
1148 Ensell Road
Lake Zurich, IL 60047-1539

847-726-8000
Fax: 847-726-1600 800-239-7297
chicago@aewdelford.com www.aewdelford.com
Manufacturer and exporter of high-speed bandsaws and automated portion control slicing systems
President: Chris Mason
Chief Operating Officer, Chief Executive: Sigsteinn Gretarsson
Regional Sales Manager: David Bertelsen
Estimated Sales: $300,000-500,000
Number Employees: 9
Square Footage: 32000
Brands:
Aew

18139 AFA Systems
8 Tilbury Court.
Brampton
Ontario, CA L6T 3T4

905-456-8700
Fax: 905-456-2343 info@afasystemsinc.com
www.afasystemsinc.com
Liquid fillers, software
Estimated Sales: $.5 - 1 million
Number Employees: 1-4

18140 AFCO
5121 Coffey Ave
Chambersburg, PA 17201-4127

813-684-6362
Fax: 610-644-8240 800-345-1329
sourcethree@afco.net www.afcocare.com
Cleaning and sanitizing soaps and chemicals
President: Michael Hinkle
Estimated Sales: Below $5 Million
Number Employees: 10-19

18141 AFCO Manufacturing
7007 Valley Lane
Cincinnati, OH 45244-3031
859-261-3585
Fax: 859-261-3590 800-747-7332
www.afcomanufacturing.com
Baking equipment including bakery pan racks, pan trucks, dough troughs, custom dollies and flow racks
President: Frank Eberle
CEO: Peter Sullivan
Sales Manager: Brion Walter
Estimated Sales: Below $5 Million
Number Employees: 25
Square Footage: 100000

18142 AFGO Mechanical Svc Inc
3614 32nd St
Astoria, NY 11106-2325
718-389-2354
Fax: 718-476-2222 800-438-2346
info@afgo.com www.afgo.com
Heaters, heat exchangers and stainless steel tanks; also, repair services available
President/COO: Blaine Udell
blaine@afgo.com
CEO: Glenn S. Udell
Vice President: Gregory Oro
Director of Operations: Michael McGuire
Estimated Sales: $5 - 10 Million
Number Employees: 20-49
Square Footage: 280000
Parent Co: Heat Transfer

18143 AFL Industries
1751 W 10th St
West Palm Beach, FL 33404-6431
561-844-5200
Fax: 561-844-5246 800-807-2709
www.rwlwater.com
Manufacturer and exporter of oil and water separators for wastewater treatment systems
CEO: Tom Bieneman
CEO: Thomas Bieneman
tbieneman@aflindustries.com
Sales Manager: Ray Lopez
Administrative VP: Beverly Willcox
Estimated Sales: $1 - 2.5 Million
Number Employees: 10-19
Square Footage: 80000

18144 AFT Advanced Fiber Technologies
72 Queen Street
Sherbrooke, QC J1M 2C3
Canada
819-562-4754
Fax: 819-562-6064 800-668-7273
info@aikawagroup.com www.aft-global.com
Manufacturer, importer and exporter of custom made screen and extraction plates
President: Roch Leblanc
CFO: Norman Pogdin
R&D: Robert Gooding
Quality Control: Serge Turcotte
Sales Manager: Jean Marc Brousseau
Number Employees: 175
Square Footage: 436560
Parent Co: CAE
Brands:
Cae Profile
Cae Select
Durachrome

18145 AG Beverage
7031 Cahill Rd
Minneapolis, MN 55439
952-943-8148
Markets beverages for the food and beverage industy
Estimated Sales: $2.5-5 000,000
Number Employees: 9

18146 AGA Gas
P.O. Box 94737
Cleveland, OH 44101-4737
216-642-6600
Fax: 216-642-6625 www.airgas.com
Cryogenic gas packaging and freezing equipment; also, industrial gases including oxygen, nitrogen, argon and carbon dioxide for the food industry

President: Bob Bradshaw
Applications Engineer: Keith Davis
Vice President of HR: Ann Rice
Sales Manager: Jay Loo
Vice President of Operations: Don Goldschmidt
Estimated Sales: $1 - 5 Million
Number Employees: 100-249
Parent Co: AGA Gas AB

18147 AGC
10129 Piper Ln
Bristow, VA 20136-1418
703-257-1660
Fax: 703-330-7940 800-825-8820
info@agcengineering.com
www.agcheattransfer.com
Manufacturer and exporter sanitary plate heat exchangers and replacement parts
President: Tamika Carter
cartert@agc.org
Director, Resaerch & Development: George Tholl
Director, Sales & Marketing: John C. Bohn
Office Manager - Western Factory: Jill Davis
Estimated Sales: $3-$5 Million
Number Employees: 20-49
Square Footage: 160000
Type of Packaging: Bulk

18148 AGC Engineering Portland
9109 SE 64th Avenue
Portland, OR 97206-9505
503-774-7342
Fax: 503-774-2550 800-715-8820
wadec@agcengineering.com
www.agcengineering.com
Manufacturers of heat exchangers
President: Robert Bohn
Plant Manager: Patrick Palmer
Estimated Sales: $2.5-5 Million
Number Employees: 20-49

18149 AGET Manufacturing Co
1408 E Church St
PO Box 248
Adrian, MI 49221-3437
517-263-5781
Fax: 517-263-7154 sales@agetmfg.com
www.agetmfg.com
Cleaners and dust and mist collectors
President: Ray Wakefield
rwakefield@agetmfg.com
CFO: Chuck Morrow
VP/Owner: Rich Olsaver
Sales: Rich Olsaver
Estimated Sales: $5-10 Million
Number Employees: 20-49
Square Footage: 200000
Brands:
Dustkop
Mistkup

18150 AGM Container Controls Inc
3526 E Fort Lowell Rd
Tucson, AZ 85716-1705
520-881-2130
Fax: 520-881-4983 800-995-5590
sales@agmcontainer.com
Container breather valves, tie-down straps and shelving and portable wheelchair lifts
President: Howard Stewart
IT: Ellen Howlett
sales@custompowersystems.us
Estimated Sales: Less Than $500,000
Number Employees: 1-4

18151 AIB International
P.O. Box 3999
1213 Bakers Way
Manhattan, KS 66505-3999
785-537-4750
Fax: 785-537-1493 800-633-5137
info@aibonline.org www.aibinternational.com
Offers various food quality and safety services including inspections and business consultations. Offers training programs.
President & CEO: Andre Biane
CFO: Tom Ogle
VP, Global Sales: Steve Robert
VP, Operations, America: Stephanie Lopez
Year Founded: 1919
Number Employees: 300-500

18152 AIB International, Inc.
1213 Bakers Way
P.O. Box 3999
Manhattan, KS 66505-3999
785-537-4750
Fax: 785-537-1493 800-633-5137
info@aibonline.org www.aibonline.org
Food safety education guides and classes for the packaging, distribution and food service operations industries
President: Virgil Smail
Contact: Leslie Ackerman
lackerman@aibonline.org
Estimated Sales: $10 - 20 Million
Number Employees: 100-249

18153 AIDCO International
P.O. Box 15339
Cincinnati, OH 45215-339
Fax: 517-265-2131 www.aidcoint.com
Palletizers, depalletizers
Estimated Sales: $5-10 000,000
Number Employees: 10-19

18154 AIM
One Landmark North
20399 Route 19, Suite 203
Cranberry Township, PA 16066
724-742-4473
Fax: 724-742-4476 info@aim-na.org
President: Dan Mullen
COO: Mary Bosco
Number Employees: 6

18155 AIMCAL
201 Springs St
Fort Mill, SC 29715-1723
803-802-7820
Fax: 803-948-9471 aimcal@aimcal.org
www.aimcal.org
Executive Director: Craig Sheppard
aimcal@aimcal.org
Number Employees: 5-9

18156 AIS Container Handling
7000 Dutton Ind Pk Dr SE
Dutton, MI 49316
616-554-1000
Fax: 616-554-1008 800-253-4621
Manufacturer and exporter of bagging and debagging equipment, conveyor, insepction and analysis systems for plastic containers
President: Jerry Pollard
Sales Manager: Jim McDonald
Production Manager: Gary Shaw
Purchasing Manager: Mark Luebs
Estimated Sales: $5-10 000,000
Number Employees: 20-49
Square Footage: 25000

18157 AJM Packaging Corporation
E-4111 Andover Rd
Bloomfield Hills, MI 48302
248-901-0040
Fax: 248-901-0062 sales@ajmpack.com
www.ajmpack.com
Paper plates, cups, bowls and bags.
President: Robert Epstein
Chief Financial Officer: Terry Jackson
VP, Sales & Marketing: Michael Pickman
Year Founded: 1957
Estimated Sales: $111 Million
Number Employees: 1,000
Square Footage: 12000
Brands:
Designer's Choice
Green Label
Original Heavyweight
Penthouse

18158 AK Robbins
4030 Benson Avenue
Baltimore, MD 21227-1408
410-247-4000
Fax: 410-247-9165 800-486-9656
www.akrobins.com
Meat slicers, cooling tank elevators, tramp metal eliminators, length and diameter grading equipment, cutting equipment, vibratory and belt conveyors, pack-off tables, hydrators, jar washers, chemical peelers, laminar-flo liquidfiller, washers, cleaners
Estimated Sales: $2.5-5 Million
Number Employees: 19

18159 AK Steel Corp
9227 Centre Pointe Dr
West Chester, OH 45069
> 513-425-5000
> 833-505-1899
> www.aksteel.com

Manufacturer of carbon, stainless steel, electrial products, mechanical tubing, and steel stamping.
President & Chief Operating Officer: Kirk Reich
Chief Executive Officer: Roger Newport
  roger_newport@aksteel.com
Interim Chief Financial Officer: Christopher Ross
VP/General Counsel/Secretary: Joseph Alter
Year Founded: 1899
Estimated Sales: $6.8 Billion
Number Employees: 9,500
Parent Co: Cleveland-Cliffs, Inc

18160 AL Systems
385 Franklin Ave
Suite C
Rockaway, NJ 07866
> 973-586-8500
> Fax: 973-586-8865 888-960-8324

Manufacturer and exporter of automated control systems and software
President: Paul Lightfoot
Contact: Hilary Galt
  hilary@cardiomedicalproducts.com
Director Operations: Gary Oriani
Director of Product Management: Gary Clemens
Estimated Sales: $1 - 5 Million
Number Employees: 20-49

18161 (HQ)ALCO Designs
407 E Redondo Beach Blvd
Gardena, CA 90248
> 310-353-2300
> Fax: 310-353-2301 800-228-2346
> www.alcodesigns.com

Manufacturer and exporter of water treatment systems including outdoor fogging and standard and reverse osmosis misting, fogging and humidification
President: Samuel Cohen
Owner: Sam Cohen
CFO: Sam Cohen
VP: Issac Cohen
Marketing: Dick Wardlaw
Administrator: Liz Luna
Estimated Sales: $3 - 5 Million
Number Employees: 20-49
Square Footage: 5000
Other Locations:
  Vege Mist
  Tucker GA

18162 ALCO Designs
407 E Redondo Beach Blvd
Gardena, CA 90248
> 310-353-2300
> Fax: 310-353-2301 800-228-2346
> www.alcodesigns.com

Vacuum-molded risers, step-ups, trays and extenders for produce, meat and deli/dairy cases and dry tables; also, wooden display items available
President: Sam Cohen
Quality Control: Carlos Sanchez
Director Marketing: Bob Matsie
Estimated Sales: Below $5 Million
Number Employees: 20-49
Parent Co: Vege Mist

18163 ALL-CON World Systems
P.O. Box 647
Seaford, DE 19973
> 302-628-3380
> Fax: 302-628-3390 sales@all-con.com
> www.all-con.com

Feeding, weighing and conveying of dry powder ingredients for food and baking industries
President: G Barry Slater
Sales Director: Mark Allen
Estimated Sales: Below $5 Million
Number Employees: 10

18164 ALLCAMS Machine Company
116 Sycamore Ave
Folsom, PA 19033
> 610-534-9004
> Fax: 610-534-7517 sales@allcams.net
> www.allcams.net

Manufactures and designs CAMs for automated industrial machinery
Number Employees: 10

18165 ALLIED Graphics Inc
16290 54th St NE
St Michael, MN 55376-3471
> 763-428-8365
> Fax: 763-428-8366 800-490-9931
> sales@allied-graphics.com
> www.allied-graphics.com

Pressure sensitive decals
President: Patrick Kohler
Estimated Sales: $1-2.5 Million
Number Employees: 10-19
Square Footage: 40000

18166 ALP Lighting & Ceiling Products
6965 Airport Highway Ln
Pennsauken, NJ 08109
> 856-663-0095
> Fax: 856-661-0870 800-633-7732
> www.alplighting.com

Manufacturer, importer and exporter of lighting fixtures including louvers, lens, fluorescent fixture diffusers and components
VP: Steven Dix
Contact: William Foley
  b.foley@alplighting.com
Estimated Sales: $1 - 5,000,000
Number Employees: 100-249
Square Footage: 120000

18167 (HQ)ALPI Food Preparation Equipment
511 Piercey Road
Bolton, ON L7E 5B8
Canada
> 905-951-1067
> Fax: 905-951-1608 800-928-2574
> www.alpiinc.com

Manufacturer, exporter and importer of stainless steel convection/steam ovens, pasta cookers, pizza equipment, exhaust hoods, etc; consultant specializing in restaurant equipment design services
President: Pier Luigi Odorico
VP: Gian Paolo O'Dorico
National Sales Manager: Nazareno Cavallaro
Number Employees: 2
Square Footage: 28000
Type of Packaging: Food Service
Other Locations:
  ALPI Food Preparation Equipme
  Fort Lauderdale FL

18168 ALY Group of New York
70 Memorial Plaza
Pleasantville, NY 10570-2931
> 603-493-8088
> Fax: 603-428-4280 alygroup@comcast.net
> www.alygroup.com

Consultant and designer of restaurant interiors; also, space planning available.
President: Dolores Jones
CEO: A Eric Arctandfer
Estimated Sales: Less than $500,000
Number Employees: 5
Square Footage: 125000

18169 AM Graphics
5249 W. 73rd St.
Edina, MN 55439
> 612-341-2020
> Fax: 612-333-3295
> AMGraphics@AMGraphicsInc.com
> www.amgraphicsinc.com

Pressure sensitive labels and promotional items including banners, decals and shirts
President: Craig Nygaard
Estimated Sales: Less than $500,000
Number Employees: 1-4

18170 AM Test Laboratories
13600 NE 126th Pl # C
Suite C
Kirkland, WA 98034-8720
> 425-885-1664
> Fax: 425-820-0245
> customerservice@amtestlab.com
> www.amtestlab.com

Laboratory providing environmental testing, microbial and chemical food analysis and industrial hygiene services

President: Kathy Fugiel
  kathyf@amtestlab.com
QA/QC Manager: Heidi Limmer
Vice President/Lab Manager: Aaron Young
Food Lab Director: Jim Pratt
General Manager: Mark Fugiel
Estimated Sales: Below $5 Million
Number Employees: 10-19
Square Footage: 80000

18171 AM-Mac
311 US Highway 46 # C
Fairfield, NJ 07004-2419
> 973-575-7567
> Fax: 973-575-1956 800-829-2018
> ammac1@aol.com www.am-mac.com

Manufacturer and exporter of meat and bread slicers, mixers, vegetable cutters and meat grinders; wholesaler/distributor of food handling and storage equipment, wire shelving and ovens
President: Judith Spritzer
  ammac1@aol.com
Vice President: Jon Spritzer
Estimated Sales: $10-20,000,000
Number Employees: 10-19
Brands:
  Arimex
  Lan Elec

18172 AMAC Plastic Products Corp
740 Southpoint Blvd
Petaluma, CA 94954-7494
> 415-332-2170
> Fax: 707-763-9500 800-852-7158
> info@amacplastics.com www.catechiphoto.com

Rigid plastic containers for fine packaging; production and shopping of AMAC boxes to retail and manufacturing outlets worldwide
President: Jone Catechi
Contact: Gus Catechi
  gcatechi@amacplastics.com
Estimated Sales: $2.5-5 Million
Number Employees: 10-19

18173 AMC Chemicals
93 Main St
Woodbridge, NJ 07095-2863
> 732-636-8720
> Fax: 732-636-8727 www.amcchemical.com

Essential oils, aroma chemicals
Owner: Jerry Bozio
Estimated Sales: $1 - 5 Million
Number Employees: 1-4

18174 AMC Industries
12291 US 41 N
Palmetto, FL 33675-5006
> 941-479-7834
> Fax: 941-981-3830

Restaurant furniture including bars, tables and booths; custom manufacturing available
President: Don Walstad
CEO: Gene Cornish
Accounting Controller: Richard Lee
Sales Director: John Ogden
Contact: Graham Bradford
  gbradford@amcindustries.com
Estimated Sales: $10 - 20 Million
Number Employees: 50-99

18175 AME Engineering
209 Gateway Rd
Bensenville, IL 60106-1952
> 630-694-1828
> Fax: 630-694-1827 www.ameengineering.com

Packaging systems for meat
Owner: M Epstein
  ame1948@aol.com
Estimated Sales: $.5 - 1 000,000
Number Employees: 1-4

18176 AMEC
800 Marquett Ave
McGladrey Plaza Building, Suite 1200
Minneapolis, MN 55402
> 612-332-8326
> Fax: 612-332-2423 iain.mcnerlin@amec.com
> www.amec.com

Supplier of full service consulting, engineering and project management services to the following sectors: natural resources, clean energy, water and environmental.
Contact: Iain Mcnerlin
  i_mcnerlin@amec.com

Estimated Sales: $1 - 5 Million
Number Employees: 22,000

18177 AMETEK Brookfield

11 Commerce Blvd
Middleboro, MA 02346-1031

      508-946-6200
Fax: 508-946-6262 800-628-8139
MA-MID.websales@ametek.com
www.brookfieldengineering.com
Manufacturer and supplier of rotational viscometers
and rheometers and also Texture Analyzers and
powder flow testers.
CEO: David Zapico
Parent Co: AMETEK

18178 AMETEK Inc

1100 Cassatt Rd
PO Box 1764
Berwyn, PA 19312-1177

      610-647-2121
Fax: 215-323-9337 800-473-1286
webmaster@ametek.com www.ametek.com
Controls, meters, transducers, temperature and chart
recorders, calibrating devices, temperature and pres-
sure transmitters
President: Frank Hermance
CEO: David A Zapico
  david.zapico@ametek.com
Estimated Sales: Over $1 Billion
Number Employees: 10000+

18179 AMETEK Inc

8600 Somerset Dr
Largo, FL 33773-2700

      727-536-7831
Fax: 727-538-2400 www.ametek.com
Force gauges, mechanical and motorized test stands,
material test systems, packaging testers, puncture
testers, peel strength testers, grips, fixtures and
accessories
Manager: Mike Kern
  mike.kern@ametek.com
Estimated Sales: $20 - 50 Million
Number Employees: 50-99

18180 AMETEK Inc

1100 Cassatt Rd
Berwyn, PA 19312-1177

      610-647-2121
Fax: 215-323-9337 chatillon.fl-lar@ametek.com
www.ametek.com
Test and calibration instruments
President/GM: Timothy Jones
CEO: David A Zapico
  david.zapico@ametek.com
VP: Tom Marecic
R&D: Mark Coppler
Quality Control: Dennis Petro
Estimated Sales: Over $1 Billion
Number Employees: 10000+

18181 AMETEK National Controls Corp

1725 Western Dr
West Chicago, IL 60185-1877

      630-231-5900
Fax: 630-231-1377 800-323-5293
webmaster@ametek.com www.ameteknccc.com
Manufacturer and exporter of cooking computers,
electronic timers and thermometers
COO: Tim Croal
  tim.croal@ametek.com
VP: Tim Croal
General Manager: Nick Hoilds
Sales/Marketing Executive: John Meggesin
Sales Manager: Gerald Brown
Purchasing Manager: Cathy Porch
Number Employees: 20-49
Parent Co: Ametek
Brands:
  Ncc

18182 AMF Bakery Systems Corp

2115 W Laburnum Ave
Richmond, VA 23227-4315

      804-355-7961
Fax: 804-355-1074 800-225-3771
service-us@amfbakery.com www.amfbakery.com
Manufacturer and exporter of bakery and packaging
equipment
President: Ken Newsome
CFO: Margaret Shaia
Director Product Marketing: Larry Gore
Sales Director: Richard MacArthur

Number Employees: 100-249
Square Footage: 400000
Parent Co: Bakery Holding
Type of Packaging: Consumer, Food Service, Pri-
vate Label, Bulk
Other Locations:
  AMF Bakery Systems
  Sherbrooke, Quebec

18183 AMF CANADA

1025 Cabana Street
Sherbrooke, QC J1K 2M4
Canada

      819-563-3111
Fax: 819-821-2832 800-255-3869
mbissonnette@amfcanada.com
www.amfbakery.com
Manufacturer and exporter of mixers, ovens,
troughs, trough elevators, fermentation rooms, di-
viders, rounders, moulders, panners, final proofers,
slicers and baggers for the baking industry
CFO: Manon Bissonnette
Vice President Sales & Marketing: Jason Ward
Research & Development: Alain Lemieux
Director of Sales & Marketing: Larry Gore
Public Relations: Marie-Eve Raqieot
Operations Manager: Claude La Jeunesse
Production Manager: Danny Morin
Purchasing Manager: Jean-Pierre Rosa
Number Employees: 180
Square Footage: 500000
Brands:
  Etm
  Etmw
  Supermix
  Supertilt
  Versatilt

18184 AMI

PO Box 70520
Richmond, CA 94807-0520

      510-234-5050
Fax: 510-234-5055 800-942-7466
www.amiincorporated.com
Manufacturer and exporter of food service serving
carts, portable bars, mirror display products, cooking
carts, maitre d' desks, etc
President: Kent Brown
CEO: Josh Yarrington
Sales: Lois Kitiuk
Plant Manager: Dang Nuygen
Number Employees: 10-19
Square Footage: 32000
Brands:
  Ami

18185 AMI/RECPRO

4250 Northeast Expy
Atlanta, GA 30340-3304

      770-458-9189
Fax: 770-454-7350 800-241-1833
www.ami-recpro.com

18186 AMISTCO Separation Products

23147 Highway 6 Alvin
Friendswood, TX 77512

      281-331-5956
Fax: 281-585-1780 800-839-6374
amistco@amistco.com www.amistco.com
Owner: Mia Romar
Estimated Sales: $1 - 5 Million
Number Employees: 50-99
Square Footage: 210

18187 AMSECO

228 E. Star of India Lane
236
Carson, CA 90746-1418

      310-538-4670
Fax: 310-538-9932 800-421-1096
Manufacturer and exporter of burglar and fire
alarms, closed circuit televisions, annunciator sys-
tems and security equipment
President: Yukata Odawara
VP Sales: Tom Galvez
Advertising Manager: Sergio Galvez
Estimated Sales: $10-20 Million
Number Employees: 10-19
Parent Co: AMSECO
Brands:
  Audeocam
  Crimeshield
  E2 D2
  Pal

Select-A-Horn/Strobe
Select-A-Strobe
Shadow
Supershield

18188 AMSOIL Inc

925 Tower Ave
Superior, WI 54880-1582

      715-392-7101
Fax: 715-392-5225 www.amsoil.com
Manufacturer and exporter of lubricating oils and
greases, vitamins and filters including air and water
President: Albert Amatuzio
  aamatuzio@amsoil.com
COO: Alan Amatuzio
Estimated Sales: $20,000,000 - $49,999,999
Number Employees: 100-249

18189 ANDRITZ Inc

35 Sherman St
Muncy, PA 17756-1227

      704-943-4343
www.andritz.com
Manufacturer and exporter of size reduction, screen-
ing, mixing, pelleting, material handling, conveyor,
cereal cooking, dehydration, grading, barley, blend-
ing, milling, crushing, grinding, separating and
storage equipment
President & CEO, USA: Mark Staton
Estimated Sales: $90 Million
Number Employees: 500-999
Square Footage: 400000
Parent Co: Andritz Maschinenfabrik AG
Brands:
  Dynestene
  Hydrasieve
  Roto Shaker
  Sonisift

18190 ANGUS Chemical Co

1500 E Lake Cook Rd
Buffalo Grove, IL 60089-6556

      847-215-8600
Fax: 989-832-1465 www.angus.com
CEO: Kola Ajala
  kola@angus.com
CEO: Mark Henning
Number Employees: 100-249

18191 ANHYDRA - Dried Foods

1878 Rue Power
Drummondville, QC J2C 5X5
Canada

      819-870-2001
www.anhydra.ca
Supplier of dried fruits and vegetables.
Co-Founder/Dir., Quality and R&D: Marie-Eve
Gaudet
Co-Founder/Dir., Business Development: Martin
Gibeault
Year Founded: 2012
Number Employees: 2-10

18192 ANKOM Technology

2052 Oneil Rd
Macedon, NY 14502-8953

      315-986-8090
Fax: 315-986-8091 info@ankom.com
www.ankom.com
Instrumentation for the meat processing and food
manufacturing industry.
President: Andrew Komarek
  akomarek@ankom.com
Vice President, Manufacturing Operations: Shawn
Ritchie
Vice President, Research and Development: Ronald
Komarek
Director, Strategic Marketing: Greg Coutant
Technical Sales Manager: Nick Tedesche
Office Manager/Accounting: Scott Giali
Production Coordinator-Extraction System: Tom
Bopp
Domestic Administrator: Mary Lou Williams
Number Employees: 50-99

18193 ANKOM Technology

2052 Oneil Rd
Macedon, NY 14502-8953

      315-986-8090
Fax: 315-986-8091 info@ankom.com
www.ankom.com
Analytical instruments for analyzing foods,
determinine solubility of dietary fiber contents, and
increasing employee outputs.

President: Andrew Komarek
 akomarek@ankom.com
Production Coordinator, RF Systems: Dave Lauber
VP Research & Development: Ronald Komarek
Quality Control Testing: Kurt Ouwenga
VP Marketing & Sales: Christopher Kelley
Technical Sales Manager: Nick Tedesche
Director, Strategic Marketing: Greg Coutant
VP Manufacturing Operations: Shawn Ritchie
Sr Design Engineer: Rick Giannetti
Estimated Sales: $3.3 Million
Number Employees: 50-99
Square Footage: 100000

18194 (HQ)ANVER Corporation
36 Parmenter Rd
Hudson, MA 1749

978-568-0221
Fax: 978-568-1570 800-654-3500
rfq13@anver.com www.anver.com
Manufacturer and exporter of FDA approved vac-
uum lifting equipment and parts including compo-
nents, pumps and cups
President: Frank Vernooy
Contact: Anver Anderson
 anver@anver.com
Estimated Sales: $10 - 20 Million
Number Employees: 50-99
Square Footage: 120000
Brands:
 Anver
 Vacu-Lift
 Veribor

18195 (HQ)AP Dataweigh Inc
2730 Northgate Ct
Cumming, GA 30041-6482

678-679-8000
Fax: 678-679-8001 877-409-2562
www.checkweigh.com
Manufacturer and exporter of check weighers,
in-motion conveyor scales and checkweighers.
President: Myrna Stanczak
 myrnastanczak@apdataweigh.com
Operations Manager: Scott Gibson
Estimated Sales: $1 Million
Number Employees: 10-19
Number of Brands: 2
Number of Products: 14
Brands:
 Ap Checkweigers

18196 APA
14536 Monroe Circle
Omaha, NE 68137-3962

402-290-5597
Fax: 402-390-2005
kathryn.a.hanson@ue.corp.com
www.apaleagues.com
Consultant specializing in conceptual and final de-
sign, scheduling and cost estimating, specification
development, contract awards and construction
oversight for food industry
CEO: Eddie Barvan
CFO: Ken Everett
VP: Bud Dose
VP: Ivan Vrtiska
Marketing Director: Kathryn Hanson
Contact: Russell East
 russ@omahapoolplayers.com
Estimated Sales: $10 Million
Number Employees: 50-99
Square Footage: 30000
Other Locations:
 APA
 Dublin CA

18197 APEC
1201 4th Ave
Lake Odessa, MI 48849-1301

616-374-1000
Fax: 616-374-1010 sales@apecusa.com
www.apecusa.com
Process equipment including liquid scales, weighing
and discharging systems, powder applicators, batch
mixers, etc
President: Kendall Wilcox
 kendallw@apecusa.com
Sales Director: Terry Stemler
Operations Manager: Garrett Billmire
Estimated Sales: $4,500,000
Number Employees: 50-99

18198 APG Cash Drawer
5250 Industrial Blvd NE
Fridley, MN 55421

763-571-5000
Fax: 763-571-5771 apginfo@apgcd.com
Heavy duty and standard duty cash draw for point of
sales systems.
President: Mark Olson
Research & Development: Bob Daugs
Quality Control: Jan Leathers
Marketing Director: Bob Daugs
Sales Director: John Meilahn
Operations/Production: Dale Dahlberg
Plant Manager: Wally Szulga
Purchasing Manager: Sheila Weber
Estimated Sales: $22 Million
Number Employees: 100-249
Number of Brands: 12
Number of Products: 12
Square Footage: 60000
Parent Co: Upper Midwest Industries
Type of Packaging: Private Label
Brands:
 Caddy
 Series100
 Series4000
 Series6000c
 Vasario

18199 API Foils
3841 Greenway Cir
Lawrence, KS 66046-5444

785-842-7674
Fax: 785-842-9748 800-255-4605
marketing@api-foils.com www.api-foils.com
Coding and marking foils
Estimated Sales: $50 Million
Number Employees: 50-99

18200 API Heat Transfer Inc
2777 Walden Ave # 1
Buffalo, NY 14225-4788

716-684-6700
Fax: 716-684-2155 877-274-4328
sales@apiheattransfer.com
www.apiheattransfer.com
Manufacturer and exporter of thermal processing
equipment and systems including plate heat
exchangers, pasteurizers, evaporators, sterilizers and
de-alcoholization systems
President: Joseph Cordosi
CEO: Mike Laisure
 mlaisure@apiheattransfer.com
CFO: Jeff Lennox
Quality Control: Barry Kent
R&D: David Sijas
Marketing Director: Gary Trumpfheller
General Manager: David Parrott
Estimated Sales: $50 - 100 Million
Number Employees: 500-999
Brands:
 Advance Aroma System
 Sigma Plates
 Sigmastar
 Sigmatec
 Sigmatherm

18201 API Industries
6590 E 40th St
Tulsa, OK 74145

918-664-4010
Fax: 918-664-8741
Waste water pre-treatment systems
President: David Plumb
VP: John Roberds
Estimated Sales: $1-2.5 Million
Number Employees: 10-19
Square Footage: 10000
Brands:
 Ech20
 Point

18202 API Industries
560 Sylvan Avenue
Englewood Cliffs, NJ 07632-3119

201-569-1700
Fax: 201-569-8907 800-229-7659
Estimated Sales: $300,000-500,000
Number Employees: 1-4

18203 APIUM Apparel
5060 Fairview St
Burlington, ON L7L 0B4
Canada

416-737-5763
customer.service@apiumapparel.com
www.apium.ca
Manufacturer of uniforms.
President: Andrew Frank *Year Founded:* 2008

18204 APM
7661 NW 68th Street
Miami, FL 33166-2850

305-888-0161
Estimated Sales: $1 - 3 Million
Number Employees: 10

18205 APM
441 Industrial Way
Benicia, CA 94510-1119

707-399-8706
Fax: 707-745-0371 800-487-7555
www.apmglobal.com
Packaging supplies, plastic lids, closures, metal and
plastic capsules, wine corks, and imported and do-
mestic specialty glass
Contact: Bert Loughmiller
 b.loughmiller@lairdtech.com
Estimated Sales: $20-50 Million
Number Employees: 50-100

18206 APM/NNZ Industrial Packaging
805 Marathon Pkwy # 170
Lawrenceville, GA 30045-2890

770-921-9210
Fax: 770-682-7340 www.nnzusa.com
President: Marco Boot

18207 APN Inc
921 Industry Rd
Caledonia, MN 55921-1838

507-725-3392
Fax: 507-725-2073
Batch control systems, filtration equipment, piping,
fittings and tubing
President: Richard Bever
 rbever@apn-inc.net
Vice President: Neil Goetzinger
Estimated Sales: $2.5-5 000,000
Number Employees: 20-49

18208 APR Associates Inc
3915 Air Park St
Memphis, TN 38118-6007

901-363-5904
Fax: 901-375-3600 800-238-5150
sales@deltaforemost.com www.deltaforemost.com
Cleaning compounds, insecticides, germicidal soap,
aerosols, etc
President: Ronald Cooper
 rcooper@deltaforemost.com
CFO: John Trobaugh
R & D: Steve Cooper
Quality Control: Charles Autks
Director Sales: George Foust
VP Sales Administrator: Steven Cole
Plant Manager: Tim Martin
Estimated Sales: $10-20 Million
Number Employees: 50-99
Square Footage: 200000

18209 APS Packaging Systems
499 Parrot St.
San Jose, CA 95112-4118

408-286-7770
Fax: 408-286-3800 800-526-2276
aps@apspackaging.com www.apspackaging.com
Manual and automatic shrink wrap machinery
VP Sales: Eric Verbeke
Contact: Aron Blaustein
 ablaustein@apspackaging.com
Estimated Sales: $2.5-5 Million
Number Employees: 10-19
Square Footage: 40000

18210 APS Plastic Systems
3 Bowerwalls Place
Crossmill Business Park, Gl G78 1BF

141-880-6688
info@apssafetysystems.com
www.apssafetysystems.com
Specialises in design and installation of fall protection systems and roof access systems.

President: Joe Carr
VP: Rick Roberts
Estimated Sales: $1-2.5 Million
Number Employees: 19

18211 APV Americas
611 Sugar Creek Road
Delavan, WI 53115

847-678-4300
Fax: 800-252-5012 800-252-5200
apvproducts.us@apv.com www.apv.com
Manufacturer and exporter of automation, process
systems, heat exchangers, dryers, evaporizers, mem-
brane filtration systems, tanks, mixers, blenders,
evaporators, etc.; spray drying available
Marketing Director: Richard Johnston
Project Sales Manager: Enrique Hinojosa
Contact: Dick Powner
  dick.powner@apv.com
Estimated Sales: $1 - 5 Million
Number Employees: 50-100
Square Footage: 1800000
Parent Co: Invensys

18212 APV Baker
1200 W Ash St
Goldsboro, NC 27530

919-736-4309
Fax: 919-735-5275 www.apvbaker.com
Manufacturer and exporter of baking equipment:
conveyors, ovens and mixers
VP Sales Bakery Machinery: Ricahrd Kirkland
Contact: Cindi Congdon
  cindi.congdon@apv.com
Estimated Sales: $50-100 Million
Number Employees: 2800
Brands:
  Powerpro

18213 APV Engineered Systems
105 CrossPoint Pkwy
Getzville, NY 14068

800-462-6893
Fax: 716-692-6416 800-369-2782
apvservicena@apv.com www.apv.com
Agglomerators, custom fabrication, dryers, fluid
bed, spray filtration equipment, processing and
packaging
Project Sales Manager: Enrique Hinojosa
Contact: Maureen Ansell
  ansell@apv.com
Estimated Sales: $1 - 5 Million

18214 APV Fluid Handling
100 S Cp Ave
Lake Mills, WI 53551-1726

920-648-8311
Fax: 920-648-1441 800-369-2782
www.apv.com
Sanitary and industrial rotary and centrifugal pumps,
pumping assemblies, sanitary valves, stainless steel
or rubber rotor pumps, W+ Series high efficiency
centrifugal pumps, mixproof double seat or single
seat, butterfly, diaphragmand control valves
Executive Director: Jim Keene
General Manager: Frank Wheelwright
Project Sales Manager: Enrique Hinojosa
Contact: Paul Beduze
  pbeduze@apv.com
Estimated Sales: $50-100 Million
Number Employees: 100-249

18215 APV Heat Transfer
P.O. Box 1718
Goldsboro, NC 27533-1718

919-735-4570
Fax: 919-735-5275 800-369-2787
infous@apvbaker.com
Aseptic heat processing equipment
CEO: John Lucas
Contact: Kirt Jarrett
  kirt.jarrett@apv.com
Estimated Sales: $10-25 Million
Number Employees: 250-499

18216 APV Mixing & Blending
100 S Cp Ave
Lake Mills, WI 53551-1726

920-648-8311
Fax: 920-648-1441 800-369-2782
ekiessli@apv.com
Mixing and blending equipment

Executive Director: Jim Keene
Marketing Communications Manager: Antonella
Crimi
Contact: Paul Beduze
  pbeduze@apv.com
Estimated Sales: $20 - 50 Million
Number Employees: 100-249

18217 APV Systems
9525w Bryn Mawr Avenue
Rosemont, IL 60018-5205

847-678-4300
Fax: 847-678-4313 888-278-9087
answers@apv.com www.apv.com
Process to boardroom automation and systems for
food, dairy, beverage, brewery
Project Sales Manager: Enrique Hinojosa
Estimated Sales: $1 - 5 Million
Number Employees: 500

18218 APV Tanks & Fabricated Products
100 S Cp Ave
Lake Mills, WI 53551-1726

920-648-8311
Fax: 920-648-1441 888-278-4321
Auger feed units, food blenders, dual ribbon blend-
ers, pumping assemblies for viscous products and
the multiverter that chops, mixes, heats and cools, in
one tank
Executive Director: Jim Keene
Marketing Communications Manager: Antonella
Crimi
Contact: Paul Beduze
  pbeduze@apv.com
Estimated Sales: $20 - 50 Million
Number Employees: 100-249

18219 (HQ)APW Wyott Food Service Equipment Company
1938 Wyott Dr
Cheyenne, WY 82007-2102

307-634-5801
Fax: 307-637-8071 800-527-2100
www.apwwyott.com
Manufacturer and exporter of hardware, stainless
steel kitchen pans, bun toasters, hot plates, food
wells, broiling grills, dish dispensers and commer-
cial food warming equipment
President: Lawrence Rosenbloom
Director National Accounts: Bruce Deckard
VP: Jim Humphrey
VP Marketing: Jeff King
Estimated Sales: $20-50 Million
Number Employees: 100-249
Type of Packaging: Food Service
Other Locations:
  APW/WYOTT Food Service Equipment
  New Rochelle NY
Brands:
  Lowerraters

18220 ARBO Engineering
3 White Horse Road
Unit 5
Toronto, ON M3J 3G8
Canada

416-636-7057
Fax: 416-630-9135 800-689-2726
sgicza@arbo-feeders.com www.arbo-feeders.com
Manufacturer of feeding and closing equipment
President: Shlomo Gicza
Product Manager: David Gicza
Sales Manager: David Gicza
Estimated Sales: Below $5 Million
Number Employees: 10

18221 ARC Specialties
29120 Commerce Center Dr
Valencia, CA 91355-5404

661-775-8500
Fax: 661-775-1499 www.arc-specialties.com
Tables, racks, mobile storage equipment, cabinets,
dollies, hand trucks, carts, chafers, chafing dishes
and shelving
President: Jay Lateko
President, Chief Executive Officer: Steven DarnelL
Vice President of Business Development: Dave
Mack
VP Sales: Bill Gage
  bgage@arcspecialties.com
Vice President of Operations: Bob Buehler
Estimated Sales: $10 - 20 Million
Number Employees: 20-49

Square Footage: 40000
Parent Co: Leggett & Platt

18222 ARPAC Group
9511 River St
Schiller Park, IL 60176

847-678-9034
Fax: 847-678-2109 info@arpac.com
www.arpac.com
Shrink wrap and pallett stretch wrappers
President: Michael Levy
Sales Manager: Greg Levy
Contact: Armando Agguire
  aaguirre@arpac.com
Number Employees: 230
Square Footage: 180
Type of Packaging: Consumer, Food Service, Pri-
vate Label, Bulk

18223 ARY
10301 Hickman Mills Dr Ste 200
Kansas City, MO 64137

816-761-2900
Fax: 816-761-0055 800-821-7849
Commercial manufacturer of Professional Cutlery
and Vacuum Packaging Equipment for the Food Pro-
cessing and Food Service Industries
Administrator: David Philgreen
Marketing: Tracey Edwards
Sales: Gary Ralstin
Contact: Bernard Huff
  ary@aryinc.com
General Manager: David Philgreen
Estimated Sales: $3 - 5 000,000
Number Employees: 5-9

18224 ASC Industries Inc
2100 International Pkwy
Canton, OH 44720-1373

330-899-0340
Fax: 330-899-0345 800-253-6009
www.asc-ind.com
President: Ted Swaldo
Contact: Alfred Cardoza
  acardoza@ascind.com
Number Employees: 100-249

18225 ASCENT Technics Corporation
PO Box 981
Brick, NJ 08723-0981

732-279-0144
Fax: 732-255-3152 800-774-7077
Manufacturer and exporter of pressure sensitive la-
bel applicators including automatic, semi-automatic
and handheld, also; labels and packaging systems
President: Ched Greenhill
Estimated Sales: Below $5 Million
Number Employees: 15
Number of Products: 6
Square Footage: 20000
Brands:
  Air-Ply
  Atc
  Sharpshooter
  Smart 300

18226 ASI Data Myte
2800 Campus Dr # 60
Plymouth, MN 55441-2669

763-553-1040
Fax: 763-553-1041 800-455-4359
info@asidatamyte.com www.asidatamyte.com
Manufacturer and exporter of packaging and quality
control software
Chairman: Joel Ronning
President: Rick Bump
  rickbump@asidatamyte.com
Global Financial Controller: Dave Nelson
CTO & VP Engineering: Raj Chauhan
R&D: Cecil Nelson
Quality Control: Douglas Stohr
VP Global Marketing: Mary Braunwarth
VP Sales: Rudiger Laabs
Customer Manager: Mike McCalley
Sr. Director, Global Operations: John Cullinane
Number Employees: 50-99
Brands:
  Applied Stats
  M-Ware

18227 ASI Electronics Inc
13006 Cricket Hollow Ln
Cypress, TX 77429-2262

281-373-3835
Fax: 281-256-1406 800-231-6066
www.asielectronics.com
Manufacturer, exporter and importer of process controllers including level, weight and gate
Owner: William Jackson
Vice President: Alice Jackson
Sales: Bill Jackson
bjackson54@aol.com
Estimated Sales: $150,000
Number Employees: 1-4
Square Footage: 1000
Type of Packaging: Food Service, Bulk
Brands:
Kasi-Weigh

18228 (HQ)ASI International Inc
10 Shawnee Dr # M
Suite B5
Watchung, NJ 07069-5803

908-753-4448
Fax: 908-753-1917 sales@info-asi.net
www.info-asi.net
Importer and distributor of bulk raw material ingredients to the nutritional, food, beverage and cosmetic industries.
Owner: Joseph Campis
joseph@info-asi.net
VP: Joseph Campis
Operations: John Wyckoff
Number Employees: 1-4
Type of Packaging: Bulk
Other Locations:
Padre Warehouse - California
Anaheim CA
Arco Warehouse - New Jersey
Passaic NJ

18229 ASI MeltPro Systems
PO Box 1085
Auburn, GA 30011-1085

800-366-0568
Fax: 770-339-1308
Hot melt tanks, heads, hoses and nozzles compatible with Nordson, Itw, slautterback at 50 % savings. M-Series applicator head modular that allows end user to adapt 1-2-3-4 modules and types, for carton, case sealing, non wovenapplication, replace all heads with one. Module types extrusion, spray, reduced cavity, zero cavity, and air on air off
Research & Development: Merk Morriseette
Sales Director: Steve Wages
Plant Manager: Jesse Owens
Estimated Sales: $1-2.5 Million
Number Employees: 19

18230 ASI Technologies
5848 N 95th Ct
Milwaukee, WI 53225

414-464-6200
Fax: 414-464-9863 800-558-7068
info@asidoors.com www.asidoors.com
Maunfacturer and exporter of cold storsge and industrial refrigerator doors including manual, powered, fiberglass and stainless steel
President: George C Balbach
CFO: Steve Contrucci
Estimated Sales: $5 - 10 000,000
Number Employees: 100-249
Square Footage: 60000

18231 ASI/Restaurant Manager
1734 Elton Rd Ste 219
Silver Spring, MD 20903

800-356-6037
Fax: 301-445-6104 800-356-6037
sales@actionsystems.com
the most compreensive and user-friendly POS system available. Improve service, reduce labor costs and makes faster, more informed decisions to boost your bottom line with powerful backoffice tracking. Choose the traditional touchscreen POS or give your servers the Write-On Handheld for the ultimate in imporved tableside service.
Owner: Smiley Shu
VP: Lisa Wilson
Sales/Marketing Director: Craig Bednarovsky
Contact: Rm Asi
asi.rm@rmpos.com

Estimated Sales: $1-3 Million
Number Employees: 10-19
Square Footage: 12000
Type of Packaging: Food Service
Brands:
Restaurant Manager

18232 ATAGO USA Inc
11811 NE First Street
Suite 101
Bellevue, WA 98005

425-637-2107
Fax: 425-637-2110 877-282-4687
customerservice@atago-usa.com www.atago.net
Suppliers of manufacturing equipment.
President: Yusuke Amamiya
Technical Sales Supervisor: Emerson Carillo
Marketing Director: Frank Young
Sales Director: Wesley LeMay, Jr.
Estimated Sales: Under $500,000
Number Employees: 1-4

18233 ATD-American Co
135 Greenwood Ave
Wyncote, PA 19095-1396

215-576-1000
Fax: 215-576-1827 800-523-2300
american@atd.com www.atdamerican.com
Furniture, steel shelving, cabinets, bins, table linens and chef aprons; exporter of furniture, linens and food service equipment
President: Janet Wischnia
janet@atd.com
VP: S Zaslow
VP: A Zaslow
R&D: Eric Wischnia
Estimated Sales: $65Million
Number Employees: 100-249

18234 ATK
847 N Troy St
Chicago, IL 60622

Fax: 773-826-0696 800-522-3582
www.andysthaikitchen.com
Labels
Estimated Sales: $500,000-$1 Million
Number Employees: 1-4

18235 ATL-East Tag & Label Inc
1244 W Chester Pike # 407
Suite 407, PO Box 3551
West Chester, PA 19382-5687

610-692-2999
Fax: 610-692-3044 866-381-8744
www.atl-east.com
Roll, pressure sensitive and continuous self-adhesive labels; also, shipping and multiport tags, nameplates and seals
President: James W Gordon
jgordon@atlas-tag.com
Estimated Sales: Less Than $500,000
Number Employees: 1-4
Parent Co: Bissell Corporation

18236 ATM Corporation
2450 S Commerce Dr
New Berlin, WI 53151

414-453-1100
Fax: 262-786-5074 800-511-2096
atm@execpc.com
Manufacturer and exporter of testing sieves and particle size measurement equipment
President: James Lang
VP: Stephen Kohl
VP of Marketing: Tony Romano
Contact: Eduardo Bolognesi
e.bolognesi@advantechmfg.com
Estimated Sales: $5-10,000,000
Number Employees: 20-49

18237 ATOFINA Chemicals
2000 Market St
Philadelphia, PA 19103-3231

215-419-7000
Fax: 215-419-7591 800-225-7788
Manufacturer, importer and exporter of cleaning equipment and supplies including liquid chlorine and caustic soda
President: Doug Sharp
CFO: Larry Hartnett
R&D: Louis Hegedus
Contact: Francois Girin
francois.girin@atofina.com

Number Employees: 500-999

18238 ATS
5025-C N. Royal Atlanta Dr.
Tucker, GA 30084

770-270-1688
Fax: 770-270-5919 800-358-0212
Info@ATSfurniture.com www.atsfurniture.com
Tables and seating manufacturer
President: Sandra Xing
Estimated Sales: $10,000,000 - $20,000,000
Number Employees: 50 - 90

18239 ATS Rheosystems
231 Crosswicks Rd # 7
Bordentown, NJ 08505-2602

609-298-2522
Fax: 609-298-2795 www.cannoninstrument.com
A comprehensive analytical instrumentation, rheological consulting and materials testing, technical support and services company. Rheometer and viscometer design, viscometers and viscosity measurements, research level rheometers andrheology measurements, capillary rheometers, dynamic shear rheometers for asphalt testing, and dynamic mechanical thermal analysis. Other materials characterization techniques are also available, including thermal analysis, surface tension, andcontact angle.
President/CEO: Steven Colo
Manager: Louise Colo
lc@atsrheosystems.com
Estimated Sales: Less Than $500,000
Number Employees: 1-4
Brands:
Dynalyser
Stresstech
Viscoanalyser

18240 ATW Manufacturing Company
4065 W. 11th Ave
Eugene, OR 97402-0029

800-759-3388
Fax: 541-484-1493 800-759-3388
sales@atwmfg.com www.atwmfg.com
Shrink-wrapping, shrink banding, labeling and heat sealing, shrink tunnels, vacuum packaging.
President and CEO: Thomas Drew
Sales: Jeff Spencer
Contact: Luminita Burmaster
luminita.burmaster@atwmfg.com
Operations: James Warren
Estimated Sales: $1-2.5 Million
Number Employees: 7

18241 ATZ Natural
7800 River Road
North Bergen, NJ 07047-6245

888-569-6449
Fax: 201-869-5655
Row materials for nutrition, health food and botanical industries

18242 AVC Industries Inc
20311 Valley Blvd
Suite H
Walnut, CA 91789

909-839-1188
Fax: 909-839-1060 info@avcfilms.com
www.avcfilms.com
POF Shrink Film and Cross Linked POF Film applications and uses of which include that of the food and beverage industry.
Owner: Bill Pan
Vice President Sales: Bill Pan

18243 AVG Automation
4140 Utica Ridge Rd
Bettendorf, IA 52722-1632

563-359-7501
Fax: 630-668-4676 800-TEC-ENGR
www.avg.net
Microprocessor based PLS, programmable limit switches, and revolver decoders for packaging machines
Plant Manager: Hyder Khan
Number Employees: 100-249

18244 AWP Butcher Block Inc
320 Cherry St
Horse Cave, KY 42749

270-786-2319
Fax: 270-786-2321 800-764-7840

Laminated butcher block tops including kitchen counter and island tops, table tops for restaurant, institutional and home use
Owner: Marcia Baugh
 marciabaugh@awpbutcherblock.com
Estimated Sales: $1-2.5 Million
Number Employees: 20-49
Type of Packaging: Consumer

18245 AZO Food
4445 Malone Road
P.O. Box 181070
Memphis, TN 38181-1070
901-794-9480
Fax: 901-794-9934 info@azo.com
www.azo-inc.com
Pneumatic and automated handling equipment and systems for ingredients; also, mixers, hoppers, bins, batching and mixing controls and process control and weighing systems
President: Robert Moore
CFO: Jack Kerwin
Executive VP: Jim Cavender
Sales Manager: Kevin Pecha
Contact: Karl-Heinz Bubbach
 bkh@azo.de
Estimated Sales: $10 - 20 Million
Number Employees: 50-99
Brands:
 Componenter
 Dositainer
 Flexitainer
 Ruberg

18246 Aabbitt Adhesives
2403 N Oakley Ave
Chicago, IL 60647-2093
773-227-2700
Fax: 773-227-2103 800-222-2488
info@aabbitt.com www.aabbitt.com
Manufacturer and exporter of hot melt and water based labeling adhesives, casein-based ice proof label glue and resin emulsion systems
President: Benjamin Sarmas
 ben@aabbitt.com
VP: Daniel Sarmas
Sales Manager: Greg Sarmas
General Manager/VP Sales: David Sarmas
Purchasing Director: Donna Hendrickson
Estimated Sales: $20-50 Million
Number Employees: 5-9
Square Footage: 150000

18247 (HQ)Aaburco Inc
17745 Atwater Ln
Grass Valley, CA 95949-7416
530-268-2734
Fax: 530-273-9312 800-533-7437
support@piemaster.com www.piemaster.com
Manufacturer, exporter and wholesaler/distributor of food processing equipment including manually operated, semi-automatic and electro-pneumatic machines and dough rollers for calzones, empanadas and pierogies
President: Edward Downs
 aaburco@piemaster.com
CFO: F Burgard
Estimated Sales: Less Than $500,000
Number Employees: 1-4
Square Footage: 40000
Type of Packaging: Consumer, Food Service
Brands:
 Mt20
 Piemaster
 Sa21

18248 Aaladin Industries Inc
32584 477th Ave
Elk Point, SD 57025-6700
605-356-3325
Fax: 605-356-2330 800-356-3325
info@aaladin.com www.aaladin.com
Manufacturer and exporter of portable, stationary pressure and aqueous parts washers
President of Systems: Pat Wingen
 pwingen@aaladin.com
Purchasing Manager: Don Klunder
Estimated Sales: $10-20 Million
Number Employees: 50-99
Square Footage: 450000
Brands:
 Aaladin

18249 Aalint Fluid Measure Solutions
150 Venture Boulevard
Spartanburg, SC 29306-3805
864-574-8960
Fax: 864-578-7308 sales@venturemeas.com
www.venturemeas.com
President: Mark Earl
Number Employees: 50-99

18250 Aaron Equipment Co Div Areco
735 E Green St
P.O. Box 80
Bensenville, IL 60106-2549
630-350-2200
Fax: 630-350-9047 sales@aaronequipment.com
www.aaronequipment.com
Provider of new, used and reconditioned process equipment and asset management services to the chemical, plastics, pharmaceutical, food, mining and related industries.
President: Jerrold V Cohen
Vice President of Business Development: Bruce Baird
Estimated Sales: $20-50 Million
Number Employees: 5-9
Square Footage: 250000

18251 Aaron Fink Group
501 Mulberry Street
Newark, NJ 07114-2740
973-824-1414
President: Aaron Fink
Estimated Sales: Below $500,000
Number Employees: 2

18252 Aaron Thomas Co Inc
7421 Chapman Ave
Garden Grove, CA 92841-2115
714-894-4468
Fax: 714-373-8633 800-394-4776
www.packaging.com
Contract packager of promotional on-pack samples and coupons; shrink wrapping, over wrappings and display assemblies on pallets or racks available
President: Thomas Bacon
VP: Bob Cassens
CFO: James Chang
Quality Control: Danny Bacarrelaq
Sales Executive: Aaron Bacon
Purchasing Executive: Linda Bacon
Estimated Sales: $10-20 Million
Number Employees: 100-249
Square Footage: 700000

18253 Abacus Label Applications
20120 115a Avenue
Maple Ridge, BC V2X 0Z4
Canada
604-465-8633
Fax: 604-465-0818 888-595-8633
President: Roy Ashworth
Number Employees: 9

18254 Abalon Precision Manufacturing Corporation
1040 Home Street
Bronx, NY 10459
718-589-5682
Fax: 718-589-0300 800-888-2225
Manufacturer and exporter of fryer tanks, display store racks and metal fabricated rack parts
President: Norman Orent
Estimated Sales: $2.5 Million
Number Employees: 25
Square Footage: 160000
Parent Co: Abalon Precision Manufacturing Corporation

18255 Abanaki Corp
17387 Munn Rd
Chagrin Falls, OH 44023-5400
440-543-7400
Fax: 440-543-7404 800-358-7546
skimmers@abanaki.com www.abanaki.com
Manufacturer and exporter of oil and grease skimming equipment including portable models and multi-belt systems
President/Owner: Tom Hobson
 tom@abanaki.com
Estimated Sales: $1 - 2.5 Million
Number Employees: 10-19
Square Footage: 20000
Brands:
 Abanaki Concentrators

 Abanaki Mighty Minn
 Abanaki Oil Grabber
 Abanaki Petro Extractor
 Abanaki Tote-Its
 Grease Grabber
 Mighty Mini
 Oil Concentrator
 Oil Grabber
 Oil Grabber Multi-Belt
 Petroxtractor
 Tote-It

18256 Abanda
PO Box 2028
Decatur, AL 35602-2028
205-340-1400
Fax: 205-340-5777

18257 Abatron Inc
5501 95th Ave
Kenosha, WI 53144-7499
262-653-2000
Fax: 262-653-2019 800-445-1754
www.abatron.com
Epoxy and plastic compounds, molds, adhesives, protective coatings, sealants, wood and concrete restoration products
Owner: Marsha Caporaso
 marsha.caporaso@abatron.com
Estimated Sales: $10-25 000,000
Number Employees: 20-49
Type of Packaging: Consumer, Bulk

18258 Abb Labels
1010 E 18th St
Los Angeles, CA 90021-3008
213-748-7480
Fax: 213-748-5838 888-22 -5 22
sales@abblabels.com www.abblabels.com
Labels and tags specialized in quick turnaround at competitive prices
President: Pedram Fararooy
Owner: Albert Khoshbin
 sales@abblabels.com
Sales: Pedram Fararooy
Estimated Sales: $10 - 20 Million
Number Employees: 50-99

18259 Abbeon Cal Inc
123 Gray Ave
Santa Barbara, CA 93101-1895
805-966-0810
Fax: 805-966-7659 800-922-0977
abbeoncal@abbeon.com www.abbeon.com
Manufacturer, exporter and importer of temperature, humidity and moisture measurement instruments and plastic cutting, bending & welding tools.
President: Alice Wertheim
CEO: Mark Tubbs
 mtubbs@abbeon.com
CFO: Karen Barros
VP: Mara Hassenbein
Quality Control: Robyn Ramirez
Mktg/Sales/Pub Relations/Operations: Bob Brunsman
Estimated Sales: $2.5 - 5 Million
Number Employees: 5-9
Square Footage: 40000

18260 Abbey Specialty Foods LLC
18 Spielman Road
Fairfield, NJ 07004
862-210-8150
info@abbeyspecialty.com
www.abbeyspecialty.com
Importer and distributor of specialty cheese.
CEO: Tom Slattery
Manager: Jim Robinson
Year Founded: 1999
Number Employees: 2-10
Number of Brands: 17
Brands:
 Abbey Farms
 Abbey Farms England
 Abbey Farms Holland
 Belletoile
 Bergader
 Carrigaline
 Castillo Espanol
 Glenstal
 Henri Hutin
 Kase Rebellen
 Knockanore
 Lye Cross

Sorella
Swiss Castle
Tipperary
Wicklow
Zijerveld

18261 Abbotsford Farms
301 Carlson Parkway
Suite 400
Abbotsford, WI 54405

877-203-7620
888-300-3447
nfo@abbotsfordfarms.com

Supplier of organic and cage free liquid eggs to the
food service industry.

18262 Abbott Industries
1-11 Morris St
Paterson, NJ 07501

Fax: 973-345-9154 abbott.harold@verizon.net
www.abbottind.com

Plastic bottles including extrusion, blow molded and
decoration
President: Leonard Grossman
Owner: Harold Sheck
VP: John Klandt
Operations Manager: Richard Lowe
Estimated Sales: $5-10 Million
Number Employees: 20-49
Square Footage: 19000
Brands:
  Similac Toddler's Best

18263 Abbott Plastics & Supply Co
3302 Lonergan Dr
Rockford, IL 61109-2670

815-874-8500
Fax: 815-874-6297 800-850-8551
Sales@abbottplastics.com
www.abbottplastics.com

Abbott Plastics is a plastics distributor the product
line of which includes sheets, rods, tubes or machined plastic parts that are applicable to a variety of
industries including dairy and food processing.
President: Roger Becknell
  roger@abbottplastics.com
Sales Representative: Steve Forberg
Number Employees: 20-49

18264 Abco Automation
6202 Technology Dr
Browns Summit, NC 27214-9702

336-375-6400
Fax: 336-375-0090 contact@goabco.com
www.goabco.com

Serving industry since 1977. Our extensive experi-
ence, broad capabilities and strong technical aptitude
make ABCO a most capable supplier of automated
solutions
President: W Graham Ricks
Marketing: Terry Love
Sales: Paul Game
Purchasing: Tammy Murphy
Estimated Sales: $5-10 000,000
Number Employees: 100-249
Type of Packaging: Consumer

18265 Abco International
200 Broadhollow Rd # 400
Suite 400
Melville, NY 11747-4806

631-427-9000
Fax: 631-427-9001 866-240-2226

Tableware for the airline, cruise, and railroad indus-
try
Manager: Bill Grannis
Estimated Sales: Below $500,000
Number Employees: 10-19
Parent Co: Oneida

18266 Abco International
163 Kenwood Ave
Oneida, NY 13421

631-427-9000
Fax: 631-427-9001 888-263-7195
www.oneida.com

Manufacturer and exporter of dinnerware, flatware,
glassware, hollowware and ovenware
Manager: Bill Grannis
Managing Director: Peter Kranes
Estimated Sales: Below $500,000
Number Employees: 10-19
Parent Co: Delco Tableware International

Type of Packaging: Food Service
Brands:
  Abco International

18267 Abco Products
6800 NW 36th Ave
Miami, FL 33147-6504

305-694-9465
Fax: 305-694-0451 888-694-2226

Manufacturer and exporter of mops, brooms,
brushes and dust control treatment systems
President: Mark Gray
  m.gray@jea.com
VP of Sales: Jonathan Clark
Quality Control Manager: Bill Scheler
VP Sales/Marketing: Christopher Meaney
Customer Service Coordinator: Tiff Vereen
Estimated Sales: Below $500,000
Number Employees: 20-49
Type of Packaging: Food Service
Brands:
  Abco

18268 Abel Manufacturing Co
1100 N Mayflower Dr
Appleton, WI 54913-9656

920-734-4443
Fax: 920-734-1084 www.abelusa.com

Manufacturer and exporter of material handling
equipment and batch weighing and bulk storage
systems
President: Donald Abel
  abel@abelusa.com
Estimated Sales: $5 - 10 Million
Number Employees: 10-19
Type of Packaging: Bulk

18269 Abel Pumps
79 N Industrial Park # 207
Sewickley, PA 15143

412-741-3222
Fax: 412-741-2599 mail@abelpumps.com
www.abelpumps.com

Food processing pumps including solids handling,
sanitary stainless steel centrifugal and positive dis-
placement diaphragm
Manager: Carl Dawson
Manager Sales Support: Mark Neiderhauser
Contact: Ken Silay
  jknight@abelpumps.com
Estimated Sales: $1-2.5 Million
Number Employees: 5-9
Square Footage: 96000
Parent Co: ABEL-Twiete 1
Brands:
  Abel

18270 Abell-Howe Crane
140 John James Audubon Parkway
Amherst, NY 14228-1197

716-689-5400
Fax: 630-972-0897 800-888-0985
gree.rodriguez@ces-cranes.com
www.cmworks.com

Overhead and stainless steel jib cranes
Sales: Eric Vach
Sales/Marketing Manager: Eric Vack
Number Employees: 50-99

18271 Abicor Binzel
650 Medimmune Ct # 110
Suite 110
Frederick, MD 21703-2602

301-846-4196
Fax: 301-846-4497 800-542-4867
customerservice@abicorusa.com
www.binzel-abicor.com

Dishwashing and laundry detergents
President: Gerry Anderson
  andersongerry@binzel-abicor.com
VP, Finance & Administration: John R. Kuhn
Marketing Specialist: Megan Ensminger
Director of Sales/ Marketing: Paul Pfingston
VP Operations: Jutilda Binzel
Estimated Sales: Below $5 Million
Number Employees: 50-99

18272 Able Brands Inc
10540 72nd St
Largo, FL 33777-1500

727-547-5222
Fax: 727-541-3182 800-854-5019
nutritionsale@hotmail.com

Owner: David Mc Cabe

Estimated Sales: $5 - 10 Million
Number Employees: 5-9

18273 Abond Plastic Corporation
10050 Chemin Cote de Liesse
Lachine, QC H8T 1A3
Canada

514-636-7979
Fax: 514-273-3155 800-886-7947
info@abondcorp.com

Manufacturer and importer of tablecloths, oven
mitts, place mats and vinyl bags
Sales Manager: R Katz
Estimated Sales: Below $500,000
Number Employees: 20

18274 About Packaging Robotics
2131 E 99th Pl
Thornton, CO 80229-2483

303-449-2559
Fax: 303-449-3420 aboutpr@apris.com
www.apris.com

Open/fill/seal systems for pouches and bags; also,
labeling machinery and applicators
President: Sal Beltrami
  aboutpr@apris.com
CFO: Lynda Muhlbauer
Estimated Sales: $5 - 10 Million
Number Employees: 5-9
Square Footage: 5000
Brands:
  Labelmaster Applicator
  Pal Labelmaster
  Pouchmaster Abs System
  Pouchmaster Pac's System
  Pouchmaster Xii
  Thermal Printmaster
  Twin Abs Poucher

18275 Abresist Kalenborn Corp
5541 N State Road 13
Urbana, IN 46990-9548

260-774-3327
Fax: 260-774-8188 800-348-0717
info@abresist.com www.abresist.com

Wear resistant linings to extend equipment life
President: Joe Acceta
CEO: Joe Accetta
Estimated Sales: $5-10 000,000
Number Employees: 20-49

18276 Absolute Custom Extrusions Inc
3868 N Fratney St
Milwaukee, WI 53212-1341

414-332-8133
Fax: 414-332-1827 info@ace-extrusions.com
www.ace-extrusions.com

Cocktail stirrers and straws including custom size
and color
President: Barbara Cupertino
IT Executive: Anthony Johnson
  tony@ace-extrusions.com
Engineering/Technical: Mark Winiger
IT Executive: Anthony Johnson
  tony@ace-extrusions.com
Estimated Sales: $500,000 - $1 Million
Number Employees: 20-49
Type of Packaging: Food Service, Private Label,
  Bulk
Brands:
  Ace
  Rainbow of New Colors

18277 Absolute Green
P.O. Box 4342
Metuchen, NJ 08840

732-225-5353
sales@absolutegreen.com
absolutegreen.com

Natural cleaning products.
Founder: Karen Halo
Year Founded: 2008
Number Employees: 2-10

18278 Absolute Process Instruments
1220 American Way
Libertyville, IL 60048-3936

847-918-3510
Fax: 800-942-7502 800-942-0315
tgrimes@api-usa.com

Signal conditioners
President: William Sawyer
  wsawyer@api-cecomp.net

Estimated Sales: $5-10 000,000
Number Employees: 20-49

18279 Absorbco
68 Anderson Road
Walterboro, SC 29488

Fax: 843-538-8678 888-335-6439
www.absorbco.com
Manufacturer and exporter of disposable wipers
VP: Scott Brown
Director Marketing: Randy Schubert
Number Employees: 107
Type of Packaging: Consumer, Food Service, Private Label, Bulk
Brands:
Mighty Wipe

18280 Abundant Earth Corporation
495 Fernwood Dr
Ashland, OR 97520-1611
President: Brian Hoffman
Estimated Sales: $300,000-500,000
Number Employees: 1-4
Brands:
Abundant

18281 Academy Awning
2080 Century Park E # 803
Los Angeles, CA 90067-2011

310-277-8383
Fax: 323-277-8370
Commercial awnings
President: James D Richman
Estimated Sales: $2,500,000-5,000,000
Number Employees: 10-19

18282 Accent Mark
345 Morningside Terrace
Palmdale, CA 93551-4445

661-274-8191
Rubber date and number stamps including plastic and inspection
Owner: Mark Evans
Estimated Sales: Less than $500,000
Number Employees: 4
Brands:
Baselock
Cosco
Ideal
Just-Rite
Pullman
Ribtype
X-Stamper

18283 Accent Store Fixtures
9629 58th Place
Kenosha, WI 53144

262-857-9450
Fax: 262-857-6620 800-545-1144
sales@accentind.com
Checkout counters, displays, shelving and self-service displays; equipment service and installation available
Owner/President: Dave Shaw
Sales Executive: Chris Osborn
Estimated Sales: $5-10 Million
Number Employees: 55
Square Footage: 60000
Brands:
Accent

18284 Access Solutions
8705 Unicorn Dr Ste C302
Knoxville, TN 37923

865-531-0971
Fax: 865-531-3547 www.accesssolutionsinc.com
Manufacturer and exporter of advertising specialties and forms; also, embroidery available
Owner: Randy Philipps
Estimated Sales: Below $5,000,000
Number Employees: 10-19

18285 Accessible Products Co
2122 W 5th Pl
Tempe, AZ 85281-7281

480-967-8888
Fax: 480-894-6255 800-922-5252
info@TechLite.net www.djtags.com
Foam insulation
Manager: Sean Pummer
seanp@techlite.net
Estimated Sales: $5,000,000 - $10,000,000
Number Employees: 20-49

18286 Acco Systems
12755 E 9 Mile Rd
Warren, MI 48089

586-755-7501
Fax: 586-758-1901
Industrial conveyors, automated storage and retrieval systems and electrified monorail systems
President: Anthony Gore
Contact: Glenn Clannell
gclannell@andek.com
Estimated Sales: $10-25 000,000
Number Employees: 200
Parent Co: FKI Company

18287 Accommodation Mollen
2150 Kubach Road
Philadelphia, PA 19116-4203

215-739-2115
Fax: 215-739-4571 800-872-6268
sales@accommodation-mollen.com
Disinfectants and insecticides
President: Dave Potack
CFO: Sara Botoss
Quality Control: Ray Brand
Contact: Mark Berger
mberger@accommodation-mollen.com
General Manager: Dave Potack
Estimated Sales: Below $5 Million
Number Employees: 20-49
Brands:
3m
Buckeye
Chemspec
Taski

18288 Accommodation Program
120 Park Avenue
New York, NY 10017-5577

917-663-4048
Fax: 917-663-5544 800-929-1414
www.120parkhq.com
Consultant specializing in providing plans for designated and nondesignated smoking seats in food service establishments
President: Tara Carraro
Senior Vice President: Diana L Biasotti
Number Employees: 20
Parent Co: Phillip Morris

18289 Accra Laboratory
2686 Lisbon Road
Cleveland, OH 44104-3145

216-721-4747
Fax: 216-721-8715 800-567-7200
Laboratory performing bacterial and nutritional analysis on food and water, shelf-life studies, FDA labeling, sanitation consulting and plant inspections
President: G Lancaster
Senior Microbiologist: Monique Panzeter
Estimated Sales: Below $500,000
Number Employees: 4
Square Footage: 15000
Parent Co: CWC Industries

18290 Accraply/Trine
3070 Mainway
Units 16-19
Burlington Ontario, ON L7M 3X1
Canada

905-336-8880
Fax: 905-335-5988 800-387-6742
sales@accraply.com www.accraply.com
Supplier of product identification and decorating systems, offering pressure sensitive labeling systems, stand-alone label applicators, print and apply labeling systems, trine roll-fed labeling systems, shrink sleeve applicators andRFID solutions.
Manager: Peter Nicholson
Vice President: Rob Leonard
Sales Director: Stuart Moss
Operations Manager: Peter Nicholson
Number Employees: 100-249
Number of Brands: 5
Square Footage: 88000
Parent Co: Barry-Wehmiller Companies Inc
Brands:
Avery Dennison
Ccl Label
Collamat
Graham Sleeving
Mateer Burt
Novexx
Sato
Trine Labeling
Zebra

18291 Accro-Seal
316 Briggs St
Vicksburg, MI 49097-1162

269-649-1014
Fax: 269-649-1067 sales@accroseal.com
www.accroseal.com
Gaskets, seals, O-rings and machinery parts
President: Joe Messer
Sales/Marketing: Neil Patten
Estimated Sales: Below $5 000,000
Number Employees: 20-49

18292 Accu Place
1800 NW 69th Ave # 102
Plantation, FL 33313-4583

954-791-1500
Fax: 954-791-1501 www.accuplace.com
Labeling equipment
Owner: Jamie Schlinkmann
IT: Sharon Humphries
sharon.humphries@accuplace.com
Estimated Sales: $10 - 20 Million
Number Employees: 20-49

18293 Accu Seal Corp
225 Bingham Dr # B
San Marcos, CA 92069-1418

760-591-9800
Fax: 760-591-9117 800-452-6040
info@accu-seal.com www.accu-seal.com
Vacuum, modified-atmosphere, medical, validatable, long-line, tube and hand-held sealers
Manager: Lesley Jensen
info@accu-seal.com
R&D: Chris Moore
General Manager: Roger Ricky
Estimated Sales: $1 - 2.5 000,000
Number Employees: 10-19

18294 Accu Temp Products Inc
8415 Clinton Park Dr
Fort Wayne, IN 46825-3197

260-490-5870
Fax: 260-493-0318 800-210-5907
sswogger@accutemp.net www.accutemp.net
Manufacturer and exporter of vacuum steam cookers and flat top grills and griddles.
President/CEO: Scott Swogger
sswogger@accutemp.com
CFO: Dave Ogram
Research & Development: Dean Stanley
Estimated Sales: $20 Million
Number Employees: 50-99
Square Footage: 45000
Brands:
Flipper the Robocook
Steam 'n' Hold
World's Best Griddle

18295 Accu-Labs Research
4663 Table Mountain Drive
Golden, CO 80403-1650

303-277-9514
Fax: 303-277-9512
Laboratory specializing in chemical and environmental analysis
President: William Gilgren
Lab Manager: Christopher Shugarts
Marketing Director: Thomas Balka
Estimated Sales: $2.5-5 Million
Number Employees: 20-49
Square Footage: 108000

18296 Accu-Pak
2422 Prikel Rd
Akron, OH 44312

www.accu-pak.com
Vertical form/fill/seal packaging and metal detection systems
President: Bill Frievalt
Vice President: Roy Allen
Operations Manager: Richard Camps
Production Manager: Curt Frievalt
Purchasing Manager: Ron Rendessy
Estimated Sales: $10-20,000,000
Number Employees: 50-99
Type of Packaging: Food Service

18297 Accu-Ray Inspection Services
211 Spangler Avenue
Elmhurst, IL 60126-1129

630-833-4027
800-378-1226
www.accu-ray.com
X-ray inspection services, X-ray rentals, metal detector rentals, manufaturers of metal detection equipment;, X-ray inspection services available
Manager: Doug Bierma
Contact: Fred Deruiter
  fderuiter@accu-ray.com
Estimated Sales: Less than $500,000
Number Employees: 1-4
Brands:
  Fortress Technology

18298 Accu-Sort Systems
511 School House Rd
Telford, PA 18969

Fax: 215-996-8249 800-227-2633
info@accusort.com www.accusort.com
Manufacturer and exporter of bar code scanners, CCD cameras, RFID solutions, integrated solutions, and data collection systems for material handling applications
President: Bob Joyce
CFO: Greg Banning
Marketing: Mark Verheyden
Sales: Don De Lash
Contact: Melissa Barsuhn
  melissa.barsuhn@accusort.com
Production: John Broderick
Estimated Sales: $50-100 Million
Type of Packaging: Bulk

18299 AccuLife
PO Box 218
Blanchester, OH 45107-0218

937-783-5565
Fax: 937-783-5574 acculift@compuserve.com

18300 Accubar
PO Box 6013
Suite 5
Newport News, VA 23606

757-873-9394
Fax: 757-873-8311
Distributor of Easy Bar
President: David Epps

18301 Accuflex Industrial Hose LTD
36663 Van Born Rd # 300
Romulus, MI 48174-4160

734-713-4100
Fax: 734-713-4190 sales@accuflex.com
www.accuflex.com
Manufacturer, exporter and importer of food and beverage pressure and vacuum hoses and tubing; NSF, FDA and USDA approved
President: Les Kraska
Estimated Sales: $5 - 10 Million
Number Employees: 10-19
Brands:
  Accu-Clear
  Accu-Flo
  Accu-Poly
  Bev-Flex
  Bev-Seal
  Bevlex
  Kuni-Tec

18302 Accuform Manufacturing,Inc.
PO Box 6299
Vacaville, CA 95696-6299

707-452-1430
Fax: 707-452-1636 800-233-3352
www.accuform.com
Safety signs and pressure sensitive labels
Director of Product Development: Matt Johnson
Number Employees: 10

18303 Accura Tool & Mold
101 W Terra Cotta Ave
Crystal Lake, IL 60014-3507

815-459-5520
Fax: 815-459-4434
Die cast molds
Estimated Sales: $5-10 000,000
Number Employees: 50-99

18304 Accurate Flannel Bag Company
468 Totowa Ave. Ste 3
Paterson, NJ 07522-1573

973-720-1800
Fax: 973-689-6774 800-234-9200
Custom designed bags for ham, sea salt, spices, flour, beverage mixes, candy, coffee beans, fruits and vegetables
Executive VP: Fred Baron
Marketing Manager: Wanda Morales
Estimated Sales: $1 - 3 Million
Number Employees: 100
Square Footage: 50000
Brands:
  Silverpak

18305 Accurate Paper Box Co Inc
2635 Byington Solway Rd
Knoxville, TN 37931-3253

865-690-0311
Fax: 865-690-0312 www.accuratepaperbox.com
Paper boxes, cartons, containers, blister packaging and machinery including box making, cutting, folding, gluing, printing and sheeting
President: Carl B Hutchison
  carl@accuratepaperbox.com
Chairman: Virgil Lawson
Sales Manager: Michael Cox
Estimated Sales: $1-2,500,000
Number Employees: 10-19

18306 Accutek Packaging Equipment
1399 Specialty Dr
Vista, CA 92081-8521

760-734-4177
Fax: 760-734-4188 800-989-1828
sales@accutekpackaging.com
Manufacturer of turnkey packaging solutions.
President: Edward Chocholek
  ed@accutekpackagingequipment.com
VP: Darren Chocholek
Estimated Sales: $3-5 Million
Number Employees: 50-99
Square Footage: 80000
Brands:
  Accucap
  Accucapper
  Accuvac
  Auto Pinch-25
  Auto Pinch-50
  Auto-Mini
  Handle Capper
  Mini-6
  Mini-Pinch
  Mini-Punch
  Pinch-25

18307 Ace Co Precision Mfg
4419 S Federal Way
Boise, ID 83716-5528

208-343-7712
Fax: 208-343-1237 800-359-7012
info@aceco.com www.aceco.com
Manufacturer and exporter of industrial knives and water knife assemblies; also, custom cutting assemblies available
President: Sheng Vang
  svang@acecosemicon.com
CFO: Sid Sullivan
VP: William Moynihan
Sales/Marketing: Joe Jensen
Technical Support: Larry Rupe
Estimated Sales: $10 - 20,000,000
Number Employees: 50-99
Brands:
  Strapslicer System

18308 Ace Co Precision Mfg
4419 S Federal Way
Boise, ID 83716-5528

208-343-7712
Fax: 208-343-1237 800-359-7012
cut@aceco.com www.aceco.com
President: Brian Barber
  bbarber@acecosemicon.com
CFO: Syd Sullivan
Estimated Sales: $10 - 20 Million
Number Employees: 50-99

18309 Ace Engineering Company
10200 Jacksboro Hwy
Fort Worth, TX 76135

817-237-7700
Fax: 817-237-2777 800-431-4223
tchapman@aceworldcompanies.com
www.aceworldcompanies.com
Manufacturer and exporter of hoists, load blocks and end trucks
President: John Watson
CFO: Mike Harris
Vice President: Rick Reeves
Contact: Ellen Bellamy
  ellen.bellamy@aceworldcompanies.com
Estimated Sales: $20 - 50 Million
Number Employees: 50-99

18310 Ace Fabrication
2715 Dauphin St
Mobile, AL 36606-4899

251-478-0401
Fax: 251-479-8080 acefab@bellsouth.com
Custom built stainless steel food serving equipment
President: Bill Stewart
  bill@acefab.com
Estimated Sales: Below $5 Million
Number Employees: 20-49
Square Footage: 60000
Parent Co: Ace Fabrication
Type of Packaging: Food Service
Brands:
  Design Series Counters

18311 Ace Manufacturing
5031 Winton Rd
Cincinnati, OH 45232-1506

513-541-2490
Fax: 513-541-2492 800-653-5692
Precision machining services
President: Linda Fullbeck
Contact: Mark Hess
  mark.hess@acemanco.com
Number Employees: 10-19

18312 Ace Manufacturing & Parts Co
300 Ramsey Dr
Sullivan, MO 63080-1456

573-468-4181
Fax: 573-468-1711 800-325-6138
acesrmv@pacbell.net www.ace-mfg.com
Manufacturer and exporter of wire containers and decks, shelving and racks:cantilever, pallet, drive-in and push-back; also, repair services available
President: Richard Vartanian
HR Executive: Tina Cook
  tcook@ace-mfg.com
Estimated Sales: $2.5-5 Million
Number Employees: 50-99
Square Footage: 92000

18313 Ace Signs
5512 Patterson Road
Little Rock, AR 72209-2450

501-562-0800
Fax: 501-423-2407 www.ace-sign.com
Decals, posters and banners
President: Sam Peters
Estimated Sales: $2.5 - 5 Million
Number Employees: 10

18314 Ace Specialty Mfg Co Inc
9616 Valley Blvd
Rosemead, CA 91770-1510

626-444-3867
Fax: 626-444-6395
Manufacturer and exporter of can ejectors.
President: Karl Anderson
Secretary/Treasurer: Keith Anderson
Estimated Sales: Less Than $500,000
Number Employees: 1-4
Square Footage: 12000
Brands:
  Ace

18315 Ace Stamp & Engraving
10510 Bridgeport Way SW # 6
Lakewood, WA 98499-4846

253-582-3322
Fax: 253-582-1955
Corporate and recognition awards, medals, plaques, seals, rubber stamps, signs, ID and name tags, seals.
Owner: Thomas Joseph

Estimated Sales: Less Than $500,000
Number Employees: 1-4
Square Footage: 2400

18316 Ace Technical Plastics Inc
150 Park Ave
East Hartford, CT 06108-4011
860-278-2444
Fax: 860-525-7000 www.acetechnicalplastics.com
Manufacturer, importer and exporter of packaging
materials including skin, blister, shrink, trays, etc
President: Robert Pomerantz
Estimated Sales: Below $5 Million
Number Employees: 5-9
Square Footage: 24000

18317 Ace-Tex Enterprises
7601 Central St
Detroit, MI 48210
313-834-4000
Fax: 313-834-0260 800-444-3800
info@ace-tex.com www.ace-tex.com
Wiping, lint free disposable and polyester cheese-
cloths.
President: Martin Laker
Year Founded: 1946
Estimated Sales: $23 Million
Number Employees: 75
Other Locations:
Ace Wiping Cloth
Detroit MI
Cross Wiping Cloth
Baltimore MD
Hamilton Wiping Cloth
Hamilton OH
Indiana Wiping Cloth
Mishawaka IN
Sanitary Wiping Cloth
Jamestown NY
Casselman Global
Toronto, Canada
Manufacturers Resource Group
St. Thomas, Canada
Windsor Wiping Cloth
Windsor, Canada

18318 Acebright Inc.
13-15 Deangelo Dr
Bedford, MA 01730
484-919-8980
deana.wang@acebright.com
Supplier and marketer of nutraceutical products such
as vitamin B2, B6, H; L-Lactic acid, Oxytetracycline
and Griseofulvin, etc.
President: Ying Kan
Estimated Sales: $700 Thousand
Number Employees: 7
Parent Co: Hegno Corporation
Type of Packaging: Bulk

18319 Achem Industry AmericaInc.
938 Hatcher Ave
City of Industry, CA 91748
626-839-0800
Fax: 562-802-5069 800-442-8273
www.achem-usa.com
Polyvinyl Chloride (PVC) and double-sided Pres-
sure Sensitive Tapes
Estimated Sales: $50 - 100 Million
Number Employees: 50-100
Other Locations:
ANCHEM Industry America
Chicago IL
ANCHEM Industry America
Charlotte NC
ANCHEM
China
ANCHEM
Taiwan
ANCHEM
South Asia
ANCHEM
Europe

18320 Achilles USA
1407 80th St SW
Everett, WA 98203-6295
425-353-7000
Fax: 425-348-6683 www.achillesusa.com
Manufacturer and exporter of flexible and semi-rigid
polyvinyl chloride film and sheeting
President: Chad Turner
VP, Operations & Finance: Jestin Fought
Estimated Sales: $34 Million
Number Employees: 50-99

Square Footage: 14910
Parent Co: Achilles Corporation
Type of Packaging: Bulk

18321 Acme
8563 Whittier Blvd
Pico Rivera, CA 90660
323-821-3930
Fax: 562-696-0026
Manufaturers of bakery and restaurant equipment
President: Mario Labat

18322 Acme Awning
210 N Main St
Salinas, CA 93901-2816
831-424-7134
Fax: 831-424-0328 info@acmeawn.com
www.acmeawnings.com
Commercial awnings, canopies and fabric products
Owner: Gale Rawitzer
grawitzer@gmail.com
Purchasing Manager: Jay Loiacono
Estimated Sales: Less Than $500,000
Number Employees: 5-9
Square Footage: 32000

18323 Acme Awning Co Inc
435 Van Nest Ave
Bronx, NY 10460-2876
718-409-1822
Fax: 718-824-3571 info@acmeawn.com
www.acmeawn.com
Commercial awnings
President: Julio Escalera
j.escalera@acmeawn.com
Estimated Sales: $1-2,500,000
Number Employees: 10-19
Square Footage: 50000

18324 Acme Bag Co
1031 Bay Blvd # T
Suite J
Chula Vista, CA 91911-1625
619-429-9800
Fax: 619-429-0969 800-275-2263
info@acmebag.com www.acmebag.com
Paper and plastic bags, also burlap and polypropy-
lene bags
President: Steve Short
acmebag@aol.com
Estimated Sales: $5-10 Million
Number Employees: 1-4

18325 Acme Control Svc Inc
6140 W Higgins Ave
Chicago, IL 60630-1845
773-774-9191
Fax: 773-774-3737 800-621-6427
info@acmecontrols.com www.acmecontrol.com
Reconditioner of boiler and burner controls
President: Steven R Huening
stevenh@acmecontrol.com
Estimated Sales: $5-10,000,000
Number Employees: 10-19

18326 Acme Display Fixture Company
1057 S Olive St
Los Angeles, CA 90015
800-379-9566
Fax: 213-749-9822 800-959-5657
sales@acmedisplay.com www.acmedisplay.com
Store fixtures including racks, display cases and
store buildouts
President: Lewis J Berenzweig
Director Marketing: Mitch Blumenfeld
Contact: Lindsay Berenzweig
lindsay.berenzweig@acmedisplay.com
Estimated Sales: $10-20,000,000
Number Employees: 50-99

18327 Acme Engineering & Mfg Corp
1820 N York St
Muskogee, OK 74403-1451
918-682-7791
Fax: 918-682-0134 marketing@acmefan.com
www.acmefan.com
Manufacturer and exporter of kitchen ventilation
systems and fans.
EVP, Sales & Marketing: Doug Yamashita
Year Founded: 1938
Estimated Sales: $50-100 Million
Number Employees: 500-999
Square Footage: 500000

Other Locations:
Acme Engineering & Manufacture
Fort Smith AR
Brands:
Centrimaster
Dynamaster
Propmaster
Sky Master
Tube Mastervent
Windmaster

18328 Acme Equipment Corporation
2202 Vondron Road
Madison, WI 53718-6732
608-222-6302
Fax: 608-222-2940 tmartin@mailbag.com
Agitation systems, milk and tank, continuous cook-
ers, fine savers, forks, cheese equipment, agitators,
custom fabrication, heat exchangers, plates, scraped
surface, tubular, piping, fittings and tubing
President: Todd Martin
Estimated Sales: $1-5 000,000
Number Employees: 30

18329 Acme Fixture Company
1057 S Olive Street
Los Angeles, CA 90015
888-388-2263
Fax: 213-749-9822 888-379-9566
www.acmedisplay.com
Store fixtures
Estimated Sales: Below $500,000
Number Employees: 20-50

18330 Acme International
1006 Chancellor Avenue
Maplewood, NJ 07040-3015
973-416-0400
Fax: 973-416-0499
Household kitchen gadgets and utensils including
baking cups, cutlery, cheese graters, egg slicers, gar-
lic presses, etc
President: Emil Gillotti
CEO: K Fischer
Contact: Alex Coutino
acoutino@acme-usa.com
Estimated Sales: $20-50 Million
Number Employees: 50-100
Square Footage: 150000

18331 Acme International Limited
115 West Avenue
Jenkintown, PA 19046-2031
215-885-7750
Fax: 215-885-5182 acmeintusa@aol.com
Estimated Sales: Below $500,000

18332 Acme Laundry Products Inc
21600 Lassen St
Chatsworth, CA 91311-4121
818-341-0700
Fax: 818-341-1546 www.hi-tecgarments.com
Uniforms
President: Chris Collins
chris@peerless-acme.com
Estimated Sales: $5 - 10 Million
Number Employees: 100-249

18333 Acme Scale Co
1801 Adams Ave
PO Box 1922
San Leandro, CA 94577-1069
510-638-5040
Fax: 510-638-5619 888-638-5040
www.acmescales.com
Manufacturer, importer and exporter of scales in-
cluding butchers', counting, portable, portion con-
trol, warehouse, educational and laboratory
Owner: Lou Buran
CFO: Lou Buran
VP: Lou Buran
Quality Control: Ron Widgren
Sales Manager: Barbara Byrd
Manager: Jerry Anderson
janderson@acmescales.com
Estimated Sales: Below $5 Million
Number Employees: 20-49
Square Footage: 52000
Parent Co: Buran & Reed
Other Locations:
Acme Scale Co.
Santa Fe Springs CA
Brands:
Chatillon
Detecto

Homs
Ohaus
Toledo

18334 Acme Sponge & Chamois Co Inc
855 Pine St
Tarpon Springs, FL 34689-5902
727-937-3222
Fax: 727-942-3064
www.acmespongeandchamoisonline.com
Manufacturer, distributor and exporter of chamois
and natural sponges
President: James Cantonis
CEO: George Cantonis
gcantonis@acmesponge.com
VP of Sales/Marketing: Steve Heller
Sales Manager: Nancy Troio
Estimated Sales: $5-10 Million
Number Employees: 50-99
Square Footage: 200000
Type of Packaging: Consumer, Food Service, Private Label, Bulk
Brands:
Aqua
Careware
Duro
Tanners Select
Thenatura;

18335 Acme Wire Products Company
1 Broadway Ave
Mystic, CT 06355
860-572-0511
Fax: 860-572-9456 800-723-7015
www.acmewire.com
President: Mary Fitzgerald
Vice-President: Michael Planeta
VP Sales: Edward Planeta
Contact: John Montalbano
montalbanoj@bc-egan.com
Estimated Sales: $10 - 20 Million
Number Employees: 50-99

18336 Aco Container Systems
794 McKay Road
Pickering, ON L1W 2Y4
Canada
905-683-8222
Fax: 905-683-2969 800-542-9942
custserv@acotainers.com www.acotainers.com
Manufacturer and exporter of polyethylene tanks including full draining, transportable and semi-bulk;
also, custom fabricator of liquid dispensing systems
President and CFO: Stefan Assmann
Order Desk: Kevin Wentzell
Quality Control: Dave Marsden
General Manager: Stephan Assman
Plant Manager: Mike Banas
Number Employees: 30
Square Footage: 50000

18337 Acorto
1287 120th Ave NE
Bellevue, WA 98005
425-453-2800
Fax: 425-453-2167 800-995-9019
contactus@concordiacoffee.com
www.concordiacoffee.com
Manufacturer and exporter of fully automatic
espresso, cappuccino and latte machines
President: David Isett
CFO: Ann Dimond
VP: Mike McLaughlin
Sales Director: Robin Mooney
Contact: Tony Grossi
tgrossi@acorto.com
VP, Operation: Wayne Stearns
Estimated Sales: $10-20 Million
Number Employees: 20-49
Square Footage: 32000
Brands:
Acorto

18338 Acoustical Systems Inc
59 N Dixie Dr # C
Vandalia, OH 45377-2067
937-898-3198
Fax: 937-898-5043 info@acousticalsystems.com
www.acousticalsystems.com
President: Rick Seitz
rseitz@acousticalsystems.com
Estimated Sales: Below 1 Million
Number Employees: 1-4

18339 Acp Inc
225 49th Avenue Dr SW
Cedar Rapids, IA 52404-4772
319-368-8120
Fax: 319-622-8589 319-368-8198
commercialservice@acpsolutions.com
www.acpsolutions.com
Manufacturer and exporter of commercial microwave and combination ovens.
Cio/Cto: Steve Gimse
sgimse@acp.com
Marketing Communications Manager: Wendy
Roltgen
Estimated Sales: $1 - 5 Million
Number Employees: 10-19
Square Footage: 7200000
Parent Co: Maytag Corporation
Type of Packaging: Food Service
Brands:
Amana
Menumaster
Radarange
Radarline

18340 Acra Electric Corporation
P. O. Box 9889
Tulsa, OK 74157
918-224-6755
Fax: 918-224-6866 800-223-4328
www.acraelectric.com
Manufacturer and exporter of electric heating elements for soup pots, food warmers, dispensers, popcorn machines and coffee brewing equipment; also,
drum and pail heaters
President: Robert Browne
Sales Director: Gary Marschke
Estimated Sales: $10 - 20 Million
Number Employees: 85
Brands:
Acrawatt
Wrap-It-Heat

18341 (HQ)Acraloc Corp
113 Flint Rd
Oak Ridge, TN 37830-7033
865-483-1368
Fax: 865-483-3500 acraloc@comcast.net
www.acraloc.com
Manufacturer and exporter of food processing
equipment, vacuum packaging equipment, robotic
saws, fixtures, etc
President: George Andre
CFO: Kent Park
R&D: Scott Andre
Quality Control: David Dyer
Director Corporate Development: Scott Andre
VP Engineering: Harry Ailey
Estimated Sales: $5 - 10 Million
Number Employees: 50-99
Square Footage: 100000

18342 (HQ)Acrison Inc
20 Empire Blvd
Moonachie, NJ 07074-1382
201-440-8301
Fax: 201-440-4939 800-422-4266
informail@acrison.com www.acrison.com
Manufacturer and exporter of metering equipment,
hoppers, blenders and microprocessor controls and
control systems.
Estimated Sales: $50 - 100 Million
Number Employees: 100-249
Square Footage: 130000
Other Locations:
Acrison
Manchester, England
Brands:
Acrason
Acri Lok
Acrison
Batch Lok
Md-Ii
Md-Ii-200

18343 Acro Dishwashing Svc Co
940 Miami Ave
Kansas City, KS 66105-1840
913-342-4282
Fax: 913-342-8006
Commercial low-temperature dishwashers

Manager: Scott Nelson
acroman940@gmail.com
Manager: Lisa Zane
Manager: Scott Nelson
acroman940@gmail.com
Estimated Sales: $1-2.5 Million
Number Employees: 5-9
Parent Co: Acro Manufacturing & Chemical
Company

18344 Acro Plastics
8630 Airport Hwy
Holland, OH 43528-8639
419-865-0256
Fax: 419-865-0256 wjllmi@megsinet.net
Plastic molds and products
President: William J Lowry
VP: Larry Lowry
Estimated Sales: $10 - 20 000,000
Number Employees: 5-9

18345 Acromag Inc.
30765 S Wixom Rd
P.O. Box 437
Wixom, MI 48393-2417
248-624-1541
Fax: 248-624-9234 sales@acromag.com
www.acromag.com
Manufactures measurement and control instrumentation, signal conditioning products, network I/O modules, VMEbus, PCI, and CompactPCI Bus Boards as
well as industry pack and PMC mezzanine modules
President: David Wolfe
Quality Control: Chuck Smith
Marketing: Robert Greenfield
Sales Director: Donald Lupo
Contact: Debbie Baron
dbaron@acromag.com
Plant Manager: Bret Stephenson
Purchasing Agent: Reg Crawford
Estimated Sales: $10-20 Million
Number Employees: 50-99
Brands:
Intelli Pack

18346 Acrotech
4770 Chino Ave Ste E
Chino, CA 91710
909-465-0610
Fax: 909-465-0403
Industrial electronics for force, weight, pressure
management and control
President: Dan Blessum
d-b@acrotechinc.com
Estimated Sales: $1-2.5 000,000
Number Employees: 8

18347 Acryline
PO Box 872
North Attleboro, MA 2761
508-695-7124
Fax: 508-699-5636 rbaker@acryline.com
www.acryline.com
Merchandising displays
President: Russell Baker
Estimated Sales: $5 - 10 Million
Number Employees: 20-49

18348 Acta Health Products
380 N Pastoria Avenue
Sunnyvale, CA 94085-4108
408-732-6830
Fax: 408-732-0208 www.actaproducts.com
Processor and exporter of vitamins, minerals, herbal
extracts and other dietary supplements; importer of
raw materials
President: David Chang
david.chang@actaproducts.com
VP: K Y Chang
Director Quality Control: Michael Chang
Director Marketing/Sales: Cal Bewicke
Director Purchasing: Leo Liu
Estimated Sales: $3 Million
Number Employees: 30
Square Footage: 124000
Type of Packaging: Private Label, Bulk

18349 Acta Products Corporation
1131 N Fairoaks Avenue
Sunnyvale, CA 94089-2102
408-732-6830
Fax: 408-732-0208

18350 Action Engineering
4373 Lilburn Industrial Way
P.O. Box 505
Liburn, GA 30047
770-717-1000
Fax: 770-717-3000 800-228-4668
www.actionengineering.com
Manufacturer and exporter of oil skimmers, separators, wastewater equipment, corn bins, mixers, heavy-duty, low-profile dollies and flexible tank liners
President: Amos Broughton
CFO: Patricia Broughton
Estimated Sales: $.5 - 1 million
Number Employees: 5-9
Number of Brands: 3
Brands:
Hi-Rise Lls Liquid Separator
Hunter Oil Skimmer
Tred-Ties Adjustable Railroad Ties

18351 Action Instruments Company
741 Miller Drive SE
Suite F1
Leesburg, VA 20175-8994
703-443-0000
Fax: 858-279-6290
Modules for measurement and control, electronic instrumentation
President: William Perry
Estimated Sales: $10-20 000,000
Number Employees: 100-250

18352 Action Lighting
310 Ice Pond Rd
Bozeman, MT 59715-5380
406-586-5105
Fax: 406-585-3078 800-248-0076
action@actionlighting.com
www.actionlighting.com
Manufacturer and exporter of lighting for restaurants, bars, casinos, etc
Owner: Jeff Buckley
jeff@actionlighting.com
CFO: Hubert Reid
General Manager: Robert Stone
Sales & Marketing: Allan Kottwitz
Manager: Dan Corthes
Estimated Sales: $5 - 10,000,000
Number Employees: 10-19
Type of Packaging: Food Service

18353 Action Packaging Automation
15 Oscar Dr
P.O. Box 190
Roosevelt, NJ 08555-7010
609-448-9210
Fax: 609-448-8116 800-241-2724
sales@apaiusa.com www.apaiusa.com
Manufacturer, exporter and importer of automatic packaging machinery for recloseable pouches including counters, scales and support equipment, high speed counting systems, blister packaging machines
Owner: John Wojnicki
Marketing Administrative Assistant: Robin Carroll
Sales Manager: John Wojnicki
Office Manager: Robin Carroll
robin.carroll@apai-usa.com
Estimated Sales: $2.5-5 Million
Number Employees: 20-49

18354 Action Signs By Stubblefield
2323 1st St NW
Albuquerque, NM 87102-1064
505-242-9802
Fax: 505-243-4187 ana@stubblefieldprint.com
www.stubblefieldprint.com
Emblems and decals
Owner: Patrick Segura
patrick@stubblefieldprint.com
Estimated Sales: Less Than $500,000
Number Employees: 5-9

18355 Action Technology
1150 First Avenue
Suite 500
Prussia, PA 19406
217-935-8311
Fax: 217-935-9132 Info@tekni-plex.com
www.tekni-plex.com
Manufacturer and exporter of extruded tubing for beverage dispensing and food handling, extruded coffee stirrers, cheese spreader applicators, sticks and tubing for frozen foods, etc
Sales Manager: Frank Lofrano
Plant Manager: Jason Gribbins
Number Employees: 100-249
Square Footage: 240000
Parent Co: Tekni-Plex
Other Locations:
Action Technology
City of Industry CA
Brands:
Ablex

18356 Actionpac Scales Automation
1300 Yarnell Pl
Oxnard, CA 93033-2457
805-486-5754
Fax: 805-487-0719 800-394-0154
info@actionpacscales.com
www.actionpacscales.com
Manufacturer and exporter of packaging machinery including automated bag filling; also, weighing machinery
President: John Dishion
john@actionpacscales.com
Sales & Services Manager: Johnathan Cantalupo
Sales Assistant: Jennifer Taylor
Purchasing Manager: Justin Pence
Estimated Sales: $500,000-$1 Million
Number Employees: 20-49
Square Footage: 8000

18357 Activon Products
123 Commercial Drive
Beaver Dam, WI 53916-1160
970-484-5560
Fax: 970-482-6184 800-841-0410
www.activon.com
Biodegradable sanitizers in tablet form
President: Todd Howe
Marketing Director: Jim Heeren
Parent Co: PR Pharmacuticals

18358 Actron
PO Box 572244
Tarzana, CA 91357-2244
818-654-9744
Fax: 818-654-9788 800-866-8887
flymaster@actroninc.com
Manufacturer and exporter of flying-insect control systems and washable and decorative insect light and glue traps
Director Marketing: Abe Thomas
Estimated Sales: Below $500,000
Brands:
Actron
Efk
G-T 200/100 Ilt
Gardner
Haccp
Industrial
Wall Sconce
Ws-50/Ws-50 Bl

18359 Acuair
1700 Cannon Road
Northfield, MN 55057-1680
952-707-1286
Fax: 952-707-0914
Parent Co: York International

18360 Acumen Data Systems Inc
2223 Westfield St
West Springfield, MA 01089-2000
413-737-4800
Fax: 413-737-5544 888-816-0933
info@acumendatasystems.com
Manufacturer and exporter of computer software for bakery management including order, production, formulation, delivery, billing, etc
Owner: Edward W Squires
edward.squires@acumendatasystems.com
VP: Dan Coffey
Estimated Sales: $2.5 - 5,000,000
Number Employees: 10-19
Brands:
Clockview
Inview
Laborview
Opmview
Proview

18361 Ad Art Litho.
3133 Chester Ave
Cleveland, OH 44114
216-696-1460
Fax: 216-696-1463 800-875-6368
Menus and menu covers; also, printing and silk screening available
President: Felicia West
CFO: Felicia West
Director Operations: Felicia West
Estimated Sales: $1 - 2,500,000
Number Employees: 10

18362 (HQ)Ad Mart Identity Group
124 Daniel Dr
Danville, KY 40422-2527
859-236-7600
Fax: 859-236-9050 800-354-2102
www.admart.com
Flags, pennants, banners, labels and signs; also, design services available
President: Ed Cahoon
edcahoon@admart.com
Regional Sales Manager: Ed Cahoon
Office Manager: Dana Sheets
Estimated Sales: Less Than $500,000
Number Employees: 1-4
Square Footage: 10000

18363 Ad-Pak Systems Co
3545 North Pkwy
Cumming, GA 30040-5871
770-889-0033
Fax: 770-889-0189 www.adpaksystems.com
Labeling equipment
President: Ray Hawkins
r.hawkins@adpaksystems.com
Estimated Sales: $1 - 3 Million
Number Employees: 5-9

18364 Adam Electric Signs
1100 Industrial Ave SW
Massillon, OH 44647-7608
330-832-9844
Fax: 330-832-6999 888-886-9911
clevelandeast@adamsigns.com
www.adamsigns.com
Electric, neon, plastic and aluminum signs; also, interior graphics available, also message centers and reimaging
Owner: Kristal Dadisman
dadismankristal@adamsigns.com
Estimated Sales: $10-15 Million
Number Employees: 20-49
Square Footage: 140000

18365 Adamatic
814 44th St NW Ste 103
Auburn, WA 98001
206-322-5474
Fax: 206-322-5425 800-578-2547
info@adamatic.com www.adamatic.com
Manufacturer and exporter of bakers' equipment including ovens and machinery; also, refrigerators
General manager and Controller: Michael Hartnett
R&D: Walter Kopp
Quality Control: Michael Liberatore
Contact: Scott Ummel
scottu@belshaw-adamatic.com
General Manager: John Muldowney
Estimated Sales: $10 - 20 Million
Number Employees: 55
Parent Co: PMI Food Equipment Group
Type of Packaging: Consumer, Food Service

18366 Adamation
7039 E Slauson Ave
Commerce, CA 90040-3620
323-722-7900
Fax: 323-726-4700 800-383-8800
www.adamationinc.com
Manufacturer and exporter of dish washing and silver burnishing machinery, tray conveyors and food waste shredder disposal systems
Owner: Jeff Branstein
CEO: Hubert Perry, Jr.
CFO: Joe Braver
Operations Manager: John Onu
Plant Manager: Cliff Bergland
Purchasing Manager: Mike Schulng
Estimated Sales: $5 Million
Number Employees: 50-99
Square Footage: 84000
Parent Co: Winbro Group

Brands:
  Adamation
  Lusterator

18367 Adams Inc
2131 16th St N # C
Fargo, ND 58102-1840

701-277-9422
Fax: 701-277-9411 800-342-4748
info@adamsfargo.com www.adamsfargo.com
A leading maufacturers representative for hundreds
of material handling and storage products.
Owner: Al Hagger
  al@adamsfargo.com
Manager: Al Hager
Estimated Sales: $2.5-5 Million
Number Employees: 5-9
Square Footage: 12000
Type of Packaging: Consumer, Food Service, Private Label

18368 Adams Precision Screen
704 Whitney St
San Leandro, CA 94577-1118

510-632-8597
Fax: 510-632-1545 www.adamsscreenprint.com
Decals and screen printing and metal finishing available
Owner: Mark Adams
  mark@adamsscreenprint.com
Estimated Sales: Less Than $500,000
Number Employees: 1-4
Square Footage: 12000

18369 Adapto Storage Products
PO Box 111600
Hialeah, FL 33011-1600

305-499-4800
Fax: 305-885-8677

Steel storage equipment
President: Joe Carignan
Quality Control: Elisa Hannna
Plant Manager: Ernie Ignaza
Purchasing: Jim Shutes
Number Employees: 70
Square Footage: 320000

18370 Adcapitol
1400 Goldmire Road
Monroe, NC 28111-5017

704-283-2147
Fax: 704-289-6857 800-868-7111
sales@adcapitol.com www.adcapitol.com
Cut and sew uniforms and promotional printed
aprons, tote bags, tablecloths, napkins, lunch bags,
banners and caps
President: Lance Dunn
Estimated Sales: $50-100 Million
Number Employees: 300
Square Footage: 100000
Parent Co: Dunn Manufacturing
Type of Packaging: Bulk

18371 Adcraft
940 S Oyster Bay Rd
Hicksville, NY 11801

516-433-4534
Fax: 800-447-7751 800-223-7750
Sales@Hdsheldon.com www.admiralcraft.com
Equipment, utensils and supplies
President: Matthew Lobman
  m.lobman@admiralcraft.com
Owner: Brett Ashley
EVP: Richard Powers
Estimated Sales: $
Number Employees: 44
Square Footage: 100000
Type of Packaging: Food Service
Brands:
  Atlas
  Hercules

18372 Adenna Inc
201 S Milliken Ave
Ontario, CA 91761-7832

909-510-6999
Fax: 909-510-8999 888-323-3662
info@adenna.com
Adenna markets and distributes a variety of hand
protection products including disposable polyethylene gloves for the food industry.
President: Maxwell Lee
Marketing Manager: Evangelene Cheng
Sales: Kevin Toshima

Estimated Sales: $3 - 5 Million
Number Employees: 10-19
Other Locations:
  San Marc Liquidators
  Philadelphia PA

18373 Adept Solutions, Inc.
990 Klamath Lane
Suite 6
Yuba City, CA 95993

530-751-5100
Fax: 530-313-5447 help@adept-solutions.net
  www.adept-solutions.net
Specialty ingredients and technical services
President: Bud Sanchez
Owner: Jason Neukirchner
Contact: Kris Granger
  kris@adept-solutions.net
Operations Manager: Geoffrey Granger
Estimated Sales: $370,000
Number Employees: 4
Square Footage: 2852
Type of Packaging: Consumer, Food Service

18374 Adept Technology
5960 Inglewood Dr Ste 300
Pleasanton, CA 94588

925-245-3400
Fax: 925-960-0452 www.adept.com
CEO: John Dulchinos
Contact: Jeffery Baird
  jeff.baird@adeptechno.com
Estimated Sales: $50,000,000 - $99,999,999
Number Employees: 100-249

18375 Adex Medical Inc
6101 Quail Valley Ct # D
Riverside, CA 92507-0764

951-653-9122
Fax: 951-653-9133 800-873-4776
info@adexmed.com www.adexmed.com
Manufacturer, wholesaler/distributor, importer and
exporter of disposable apparel including gloves,
goggles, aprons, hair nets, caps, masks, shoe covers,
etc.; also, towels, industrial safety products, emergency preparednessproducts
President/CEO: Michael Ghafouri
  mmg@adexmed.com
Estimated Sales: $5 Million
Number Employees: 20-49
Number of Brands: 3
Number of Products: 200
Square Footage: 44000
Type of Packaging: Consumer, Food Service, Private Label
Brands:
  Adex
  Dispomed

18376 Adheron Coatings Corporation
16420 Kilbourne Ave
Oak Forest, IL 60452

708-687-0010

18377 Adhesive Applications
41 Oneil St
Easthampton, MA 01027-1103

413-527-7120
Fax: 413-527-7249 800-356-3572
Manufacturer and exporter of pressure sensitive
foam cloth adhesive tapes
President: Michael Schaefer
  mschaefer@stikiiproducts.com
Sales Manager: David Premo
Sales Specialist: Judette Savino
Estimated Sales: $10 - 20 Million
Number Employees: 20-49
Parent Co: October Company

18378 Adhesive Label
2916 Nevada Ave N # 1
Minneapolis, MN 55427-2887

763-546-1182
Fax: 763-546-1182 www.adhesivelabelinc.com
Labels
President: Steve Ericcson
VP: Diane Hurley
Estimated Sales: $4 Million
Number Employees: 100-249
Square Footage: 14000

18379 Adhesive Products Inc
4727 E 48th St
Vernon, CA 90058-2799

323-589-5516
Fax: 323-589-6460 800-669-5516
www.adhesiveproductsinc.com
Resin emulsion, starch based and hot melt adhesives, water activated paper and reinforced gummed
tapes and custom printed self adhesive labels and
tapes
President: Paul Shattuck
  paul@ashesiveproducts.com
VP: W Shattuck
Operations Manager: William Almas
Estimated Sales: $2.5-5 Million
Number Employees: 5-9
Square Footage: 56000
Type of Packaging: Consumer, Bulk

18380 Adhesive Products Inc
945 S Doris St
Seattle, WA 98108-2729

206-762-7459
Fax: 206-762-9852 www.atwoodadhesives.com
Manager: Laurel Mangan
Estimated Sales: $5 - 10 Million
Number Employees: 10-19
Parent Co: Adhesive Products

18381 Adhesive Technologies Inc
3 Merrill Industrial Dr
Hampton, NH 03842-1995

603-929-5300
Fax: 603-926-1780 800-458-3486
marketing@adhesivetech.com
  www.adhesivetech.com
Manufacturer, importer and exporter of application-based systems: hot melts, sprays, solids, 2-part
reactives and a wide range of applicators (glue guns)
from craft to industrial.
Chief Executive Officer, Founder: Peter Melendy
  pmelendy@adhesivetech.com
Marketing Director: Laura Scaccia
VP Sales: John Starer
Public Relations: Laura Scaccia
Estimated Sales: $20-50 Million
Number Employees: 20-49
Brands:
  Crafty
  Floralpro
  Magic Melt

18382 Adhesives Research
400 Seaks Run Rd
Glen Rock, PA 17327

717-235-7979
800-445-6240
www.adhesivesresearch.com
High-performance, pressure-sensitive adhesives,
tapes, coatings, films and laminates
President/Owner: Richard Widden
Marketing: Deepak Hariharan
Sales: Dave Koppenhaver
Operations: Cameron Sterner
Year Founded: 1961
Number Employees: 300
Square Footage: 240000
Type of Packaging: Consumer

18383 Adhesives Research Inc
400 Seaks Run Rd
Glen Rock, PA 17327-9500

717-235-7979
Fax: 717-235-8320 800-445-6240
gandrews@arglobal.com
Armark Authentication Technologies develops custom authentication systems for use across a wide variety of brand owner applications. ARmark's covert
markers aid in brand protection, product surety and
risk mitigation to fight globalcounterfeiting and can
be combined with custom-developed delivery systems for application to a variety of goods, including
pharmaceuticals, packaging, food, apparel, currency,
bonds and documents.

President: Geoff Bennett
Vice President & General Manager: George Stolakis
Vice President & General Manager: Bill Stratton
Vice President of Sales: Rick Alexander
Vice President & General Manager: Beth Vondrak
Director & General Manager: Jeff Robertson
Marketing Manager: Greg Andrews
Vice President Commercial Development: George Cramer
General Counsel & Secretary: Lynne Durbin
Controller: Gary Messersmith
Vice President Human Resources: Robert Valenti
Number Employees: 250-499

18384 Admatch Corporation
36 W 25th St
Fl 8
New York, NY 10010
212-696-2600
Fax: 212-696-0620 800-777-9909
ask@admatch.com www.admatch.com
Manufacturer, exporter and importer of wood and paper matches with custom printed boxes and books, wood toothpicks, paper napkins, place mats, coasters and tissues
President: Mark Nackman
Sales Manager: Agatha Laura
Contact: King Chau
king@admatch.com
Estimated Sales: $10-20 Million
Number Employees: 10-19
Type of Packaging: Consumer, Food Service, Private Label, Bulk
Brands:
Admatch
Promotissues

18385 Admix Inc.
234 Abby Rd
Manchester, NH 03103
603-627-2340
Fax: 603-627-2019 800-466-2369
mixing@admix.com www.admix.com
President: Louis Beaudette
Contact: Jerry Baresich
jbaresich@admix.com
Estimated Sales: $5-10 Million
Number Employees: 20-49

18386 Adolph Gottscho
835 Lehigh Ave
Union, NJ 07083-7631
908-688-2400
Fax: 908-687-9250 sales@gottscho.com
www.gottscho.com
President: Eva Gottscho
Contact: Paul Jancek
paul@gottscho.com
Estimated Sales: $5 - 10 Million
Number Employees: 20-49

18387 Adpro
30500 Solon Industrial Pkwy
Solon, OH 44139-4330
440-542-1111
www.ad-pro.net
Manufacturer and importer of boxes including folding, set-up and corrugated; shrink packaging available; also, designer of sales promotion and marketing materials
VP: Stephen Lebby
Estimated Sales: $2.5-5 Million
Number Employees: 20-49
Square Footage: 130000
Parent Co: ADPRO

18388 Adrienne's Gourmet Foods
849 Ward Dr
Santa Barbara, CA 93111
805-964-6848
Fax: 805-964-8698 800-937-7010
Organic and kosher cookies, crackers and high protein pastas.
President: John O'Donnell
Vice President: Adrienne O'Donnell
Contact: Sarah Guiginano
sarah@adriennes.com
Estimated Sales: $5-10 Million
Number Employees: 20-49
Type of Packaging: Consumer, Food Service, Private Label, Bulk
Brands:
Appeteasers
California Crisps

Courtney's
Courtney's Organic Water Crackers
Darcia's Organic Crostini
Lavosh Hawaii
Papadina Pasta
Papadini Hi-Protein

18389 Adstick Custom Labels Inc
11000 E 53rd Ave
Denver, CO 80239-2111
303-388-5821
Fax: 303-321-4536 800-255-7314
info@adstick.com www.adstick.com
Pressure sensitive tapes and labels
Owner: Daryl Leeson
dcleeson@adstick.com
CEO: R Stillahn
CEO: Brad Stillahn
General Manager: Robert Morland
Estimated Sales: $3 - 5 Million
Number Employees: 10-19
Square Footage: 28000

18390 Adstick Custom Labels Inc
3845 Forest St
Denver, CO 80207-1120
303-388-5821
Fax: 303-321-4536 brad@adstick.com
www.adstick.com
Labels
Owner: John Kiernan
jkiernan@adstick.com
Estimated Sales: $5 - 10 Million
Number Employees: 5-9

18391 Advance Adhesives
2403 N Oakley Ave
Chicago, IL 60647-2093
773-278-3988
Fax: 773-227-2103 www.aabbitt.com
President: Benjamin B Sarmas
Estimated Sales: $50 - 100 Million
Number Employees: 50-99

18392 Advance Automated Systems Inc
3775 14 Mile Rd NW
PO Box 476
Sparta, MI 49345-9362
616-887-0316
Fax: 616-887-8407
dale@advanceautomatedsystems.com
www.advanceautomatedsystems.com
Supplier of automated systems.
President: Dale Montgomery
dale@advanceautomatedsystems.com
Estimated Sales: $1 - 2.5 000,000
Number Employees: 1-4

18393 Advance Cleaning Products
PO Box 170950
Milwaukee, WI 53217-8086
414-937-8181
Fax: 414-344-3458 800-925-5326
Self-polishing floor polish and cleaners including all purpose, toilet bowl and liquid soap
President: Mark Halaska
Estimated Sales: Less than $1 Million
Number Employees: 10-19
Square Footage: 120000
Brands:
Easy Strip
Floor Suds
Perma Shine
Scrub 'n Shine
Shine-Off
Snappy
Ultrashine

18394 Advance Distribution Svc
2349 Millers Ln
Louisville, KY 40216-5329
502-449-1720
Fax: 502-778-1718
contactADS@advancedistribution.com
www.advancedistribution.com
A packaging, warehouse and distributor company for the food industry
President: Brian Johnson
bjohnson@advancedistribution.com
R&D: J Perrier
Quality Control: L Defaint
Sales: Judy Jaedine
Operations: Aldo Dagnino
Plant Manager: Jorge Monge

Estimated Sales: $300,000-500,000
Number Employees: 50-99
Square Footage: 2400000
Type of Packaging: Consumer, Food Service

18395 Advance Energy Technologies
1 Solar Dr
Halfmoon, NY 12065-3402
518-371-2140
Fax: 518-371-0737 800-724-0198
sales@advanceet.com www.advanceet.com
Manufacturer and exporter of walk-in coolers and freezers, refrigerated warehouses, foam injected insulated panels, clean rooms and environmental chambers.
President: Timothy Carlo
sales@advanceet.com
General Manager: Dan Carlo
Estimated Sales: $10-20 Million
Number Employees: 20-49
Square Footage: 60000
Type of Packaging: Bulk

18396 Advance Engineering Co
7505 Baron Dr
Canton, MI 48187-2494
313-537-3500
Fax: 313-537-7389 800-497-6388
www.adveng.net
Plastic trays, pallets and packaging
President: Mike Baran
mbaran@adveng.net
Customer Service: Angela Frasher
General Manager: Gene Cook
Estimated Sales: $10-20,000,000
Number Employees: 50-99
Parent Co: L&W Engineering

18397 Advance Fittings Corp
218 W Centralia St
Elkhorn, WI 53121-1606
262-723-6699
Fax: 262-723-6643 advance@genevaonline.com
Manufacturer, importer and exporter of filtration equipment, fittings, clamps, tanks, sampling devices, tube and pipe supports, tubes and valves; also, custom fabrications available
President: Edward W Mentzer
ementzer@advancefittingscorp.com
VP: Roger Klemp
Marketing/Sales: Jeffery Klemp
VP of Sales: Peter Mentzer
Estimated Sales: $5-10 Million
Number Employees: 20-49

18398 Advance Grower Solutions
3343 Locke Ave
Suite 107
Fort Worth, TX 76107
503-646-5581
Fax: 503-646-0622 800-367-7082
sales@advgrower.com www.advgrower.com
Wine industry computer software
Owner: Dan Harris
Contact: Lucci Altman
lucci@advgrower.com
Estimated Sales: $3 - 5 Million
Number Employees: 10-19

18399 Advance Lifts Inc
701 Kirk Rd
St Charles, IL 60174-3428
630-584-9881
Fax: 630-584-9405 800-843-3625
sales@advancelifts.com www.advancelifts.com
Hydraulic scissor lifts and recycling equipment
President: Henry Renken
hank@advancelifts.com
VP Sales: David Ferguson
Estimated Sales: $20-50 Million
Number Employees: 50-99
Square Footage: 120000

18400 Advance Storage Products
7341 Lincoln Way
Garden Grove, CA 92841-1428
714-902-9000
Fax: 714-902-9001 888-478-7422
asp@advstore.com
www.advancestorageproducts.com

Technology-driven company dedicated to developing the most efficient and economical solution to our customers' material storage needs. State-of-the-art engineering-providing turnkey systems. in business over 40 years
President: John Krummell
asp@advstore.com
CFO: Rick Callow
R&D: T J Imholte
Marketing/Public Relations: Judy Pugh
Sales Director: Adel Santner
Operations Manager: T Imholte
Purchasing Manager: Lisa Ramirez
Estimated Sales: $20 - 50 Million
Number Employees: 20-49
Brands:
    Pushback

18401 (HQ)Advance Tabco
200 Heartland Blvd
Edgewood, NY 11717-8379
631-242-8270
Fax: 631-242-6900 800-645-3166
www.advancetabco.com
Stainless steel sinks, worktables, shelving and dish tables; also, aluminum and racks and wire shelving
President: Penny Hutner
VP: Danny Schwartz
Estimated Sales: $50-100 Million
Number Employees: 250-499
Brands:
    Advance Tabco

18402 Advance Technology Corp
79 N Franklin Tpke
Suite 103
Ramsey, NJ 07446-2035
201-934-7127
Fax: 201-236-1891 sales@vetstar.com
www.vetstar.com
Manufacturer and exporter of laboratory information management system software
President: John Cummins
Sales Manager: Susan Cummins
IT: Eileen Costello
eeaston@vetstar.com
Number Employees: 10-19
Brands:
    V-Lims
    Vetstar

18403 Advance Weight Systems Inc
409 Main St
PO Box 6
Grafton, OH 44044-1205
440-926-3691
sales@advancew8.com
www.advancew8.com
Scales, weighers and conveyors for food packaging systems
President: Martha Noel
martha.noel@advancew8.com
VP Sales: John Koliha
Estimated Sales: Below $5 Million
Number Employees: 10-19

18404 Advanced Coating & Converting
1229 S Dickerson Rd
Goodlettsville, TN 37072-2802
615-851-2000
Fax: 615-851-5683 advancedcoating1@aol.com
Hot melt applicators and replacement parts, packaging
Owner: Gary Faulkner
advancedcoating1@aol.com
Estimated Sales: $1 - 3 Million
Number Employees: 10-19

18405 Advanced Coating & Converting
1229 S Dickerson Rd
Goodlettsville, TN 37072-2802
615-851-2000
Fax: 615-851-5683 advancedcoating1@aol.com
Owner: Gary Faulkner
advancedcoating1@aol.com
Number Employees: 10-19

18406 Advanced Control Technologies
6805 Hillsdale Ct
Indianapolis, IN 46250-2039
317-806-2750
Fax: 317-806-2770 800-886-2281
info@act-solutions.com
Manufacturer and exporter of HVAC controls

President: Gary Colip
gcolip@act-solutions.com
Estimated Sales: $5-10,000,000
Number Employees: 10-19

18407 Advanced Design Awning & Sign
1600 29th St
Cloquet, MN 55720-2886
612-870-7634
Fax: 218-879-2936 800-566-8368
www.advancedawning.com
Commercial awnings
Owner: Chris Mathews
camathews@advancedawning.com
Estimated Sales: Below $5 Million
Number Employees: 10-19

18408 Advanced Design Mfg
1281 Franquette Ave
Concord, CA 94520-5378
925-680-8764
Fax: 925-680-7252 800-690-0002
sales@sneezeguard.com www.sneezeguard.com
Stock and custom sneeze guards
Owner: David Murry
david@adc9001.com
CFO: Richard Harris
R & D: Peter Otool
Sales Director: Jeff Bigby
Production Director: Andy McGrath
Estimated Sales: $5-10 Million
Number Employees: 10-19
Square Footage: 88000

18409 Advanced Detection Systems
4740 W Electric Ave
Milwaukee, WI 53219-1626
414-672-0553
Fax: 414-672-5354 dsmith@adsdetection.com
www.adsdetection.com
Manufacturer and exporter of electronic metal detectors with reject devices, conveyors and pipeline systems; also, washdown severe-duty models
CFO: Matt Nagel
mnagel@adsdetection.com
Human Resources: Sue Medbed
Sales Manager: Dave Smith
Production Manager: Chuck Morgan
Estimated Sales: $10-20,000,000
Number Employees: 50-99
Parent Co: Venturedyne

18410 Advanced Equipment
2411 Vauxhall Place
Richmond, BC V6V 1Z5
Canada
604-276-8989
Fax: 604-276-8962 info@advancedfreezer.com
www.advancedfreezer.com
Manufacturer and exporter of freezers
President: Peter Pao
Purchasing Agent: Thomas Leung
Estimated Sales: Below $5 Million
Number Employees: 40
Square Footage: 80000
Brands:
    Advanced Equipment

18411 Advanced Ergonomics Inc
7460 Warren Pkwy # 265
Suite 265
Frisco, TX 75034-4279
972-294-7506
Fax: 972-294-7620 800-682-0169
aei@advancedergonomics.com
www.advancedergonomics.com
Consultant providing pre-employment testing services and job site analysis
President: Harry Broxson
CEO: Terry Broxson
Manager: Mary Selan
mary.selan@advancedergonomics.com
Estimated Sales: Below $5,000,000
Number Employees: 5-9

18412 Advanced Food Equipment LLC
PO Box 470
Mt Vernon, OH 43050-0470
814-772-6396
Fax: 740-392-4785
Package spiral freezers and steam cookers, site-built spiral freezers, fluidized belt and tray freezers, car/dolley freezers, contact belt freezers, pouch water and prine chillers, case/box freezers and chillers

President: Michael Webber
R&D: John Webber
Estimated Sales: $1 - 5 000,000
Number Employees: 1-4

18413 Advanced Food Systems
2141 E Highland Ave # 10
Phoenix, AZ 85016-4736
602-522-8282
Fax: 602-522-1856 877-821-3007
ninad@afsi.com www.afsi.com
Equipment
CEO: Kurien Jacob
Number Employees: 50-99

18414 Advanced Food Systems
133 Lake Bluff Drive
Columbus, OH 43235
888-871-9885
Fax: 888-807-9632 sendmeinfo@afsusa.net
www.advancedfoodsys.com
President: Denny Vincent
Contact: Richelle Goldilla
rg@rvin.net
Estimated Sales: $300,000-500,000
Number Employees: 1-4

18415 Advanced Industrial Systems
21068 Bake Pkwy
Suite 200
Lake Forest, CA 92630-2185
208-237-2222
Fax: 949-597-9898 800-658-3850
www.advancedindustrial.com
Real-time process control systems, human-machine interfaces, supervisory and cell control - SCADA systems, statistical process control
President: Gene Kaplan
Estimated Sales: Below $500,000

18416 Advanced Ingredients, Inc.
401 N 3rd St
Suite 400
Minneapolis, MN 55401
Fax: 763-201-5820 888-238-4647
info@advancedingredients.com
www.advancedingredients.com
Specialty ingredients
President: Fred Greenland
Estimated Sales: $1 - 3 Million
Number Employees: 5-9
Brands:
    Bakesmart
    Energysmart
    Energysource
    Fruitrim
    Fruitsavr
    Fruitsource
    Moisturlok
    Plus and Moisturlok

18417 (HQ)Advanced Instruments Inc
2 Technology Way # 1
Norwood, MA 02062-2630
781-320-9000
Fax: 781-320-8181 800-225-4034
info@aicompanies.com www.aicompanies.com
Manufacturer and exporter of clinical, industrial laboratory and food and dairy quality control equipment.
CEO: John Coughlin
CFO: Jim Noris
jimn@aicompanies.com
Marketing Manager: Kristen Vuotto
Sales: John Ryder
Plant Manager: Mike Graham
Estimated Sales: $10-20 Million
Number Employees: 50-99
Number of Brands: 4
Number of Products: 6
Square Footage: 80000
Other Locations:
    Advanced Instruments
    Bethesda MD
Brands:
    Advanced
    Fiske
    Fiske Associates
    Fluorophos Test System

18418 Advanced Instruments Inc
2 Technology Way # 1
Norwood, MA 02062-2630
781-320-9000
Fax: 781-320-8181 800-225-4034
info@aicompanies.com www.aicompanies.com
Equipment for the dairy and food industry.
Director: Blanton Wiggin
CFO: Jim Noris
jimn@aicompanies.com
Vice President: Pierre Emond
Vice President Sales: John Ryder
Number Employees: 50-99

18419 Advanced Insulation Concepts
8055 Production Dr
Florence, KY 41042-3094
859-342-8550
Fax: 859-342-5445 800-826-3100
info@aicinsulate.com
www.advancedinsulationconcepts.com
Manufacturer and exporter of insulated panels and
doors for refrigerated and other atmosphere-con-
trolled rooms including horizontal sliding, bi-part-
ing, vertical lift and swing. Also insulated fire wall
panels
President: W Burton Lloyd
VP: Michael Lloyd
Sales: Michael Lloyd
Estimated Sales: $6-10 Million
Number Employees: 30
Square Footage: 124000
Brands:
Insulrock
Isowall
Regent

18420 Advanced Labelworx
2800 W Whitner St
Anderson, SC 29626-1035
865-966-8711
Fax: 865-813-9918
marketing@advancedlabelworx.com
www.advancedlabelworx.com
Pressure sensitive roll labels and printed tape, foils
and tags
President: Gabrina Kelly
gkelly@tagandlabel.com
VP Marketing: Dennis Burt
VP Sales: Paul Neerhof
Plant Manager: John Kaser
Estimated Sales: $10-20 Million
Number Employees: 50-99
Square Footage: 125000

18421 (HQ)Advanced Labelworx Inc
1006 Larson Dr
Oak Ridge, TN 37830-8013
864-224-2122
Fax: 865-813-9918 www.advancedlabelworx.com
Manufacturer and exporter of pressure sensitive pa-
per labels and tapes
President: Lana Sellers
CFO: Clyde Duncan
HR Executive: Dan Piper
dpiper@advancedlabelworx.com
Quality Control: Gabrina Kelly
Number Employees: 50-99
Square Footage: 120000
Type of Packaging: Bulk

18422 Advanced Micro Controls
20 Gear Dr
Terryville, CT 06786
860-585-1254
Fax: 860-584-1973 sales@amci.com
www.amci.com
Hardware and software for packaging machinery
President: William Herbs
VP: Peter Serv
Contact: Laureen Archer
larcher@amci.com
Estimated Sales: $20 - 50 Million
Number Employees: 20-49
Brands:
Ez Pack

18423 Advanced Organics
701 W Johnson St
Upper Sandusky, OH 43351
419-209-0216
Fax: 419-209-5010
Organic waste disposal service, sanitation
President: Doug Craig

Estimated Sales: $2.5-5 000,000
Number Employees: 20-49
Type of Packaging: Bulk

**18424 Advanced Packaging Techniques
Corporation**
393 Bentley Place
Buffalo Grove, IL 60089-2500
847-808-9227
Fax: 630-887-0771
Packaging machinery soces consultants
President: Barbara Bloom
Number Employees: 2

18425 Advanced Plastic Coating Svc
1407 Corporate Dr
Parsons, KS 67357-4964
620-421-1660
Fax: 620-421-1662 adpowdergreg@par1.net
Custom manufacturer of plastic coated wire products
including trays, ice cream cup holders and condi-
ment holders for drive-in car service
President: Don Alexander
CFO: Don Alexander
R&D: Don Alexander
Quality Control: Don Alexander
Number Employees: 10-19
Square Footage: 40000
Brands:
Serv-A-Car
Wire Rite

18426 Advanced Poly-PackagingInc
1331 Emmitt Rd
Akron, OH 44306-3807
330-785-4000
Fax: 330-785-4010 800-754-4403
sales@advancedpoly.com
www.advancedpoly.com
Bags including pre-opened and printed polyfilm and
printers, ribbon and packaging equipment including
automatic bagging
President: Stewart Baker
stewart@advancedpoly.com
VP of Sales: Stuart Baker
National Sales Manager: Dan Moute
Estimated Sales: $20-50 Million
Number Employees: 100-249
Brands:
Advanced Polybagger

18427 Advanced Process Solutions
914 Springdale Dr
Jeffersonville, IN 47130
812-280-7450
888-294-8118
info@gotoaps.com
Provide food and beverage manufacturers with process engineering designs for aspetic, extended shelf
life, pasteurization, hot fill, batching, blending and
CIP equipment.

**18428 Advanced Separation
Technologies**
5315 Great Oak Drive
Lakeland, FL 33815-3113
863-687-4460
Fax: 863-687-9362
Ion exchange, biotechnology, chromatography, fer-
mentation, separators
President: Robert O'Brian
Estimated Sales: $5-10 Million
Number Employees: 60

**18429 Advanced Separations andProcess
Systems**
6111 Pepsi Way
Windsor, WI 53598-9642
608-846-1130
Fax: 608-846-1144 800-879-8461
Software, systems integrator, membrane systems, re-
source recovery, separation equipment
Number Employees: 120

18430 Advanced Software Designs
1350 Elbridge Payne Rd Ste 150
Chesterfield, MO 63017
636-532-6021
Fax: 636-532-2935 info@asdsoftware.com
www.asdsoftware.com
Formula management software for nutritional labeling, production assistance and quality control
measures

President: Ray Cook
Marketing Director: Stephanie Hanebrink
Account Executive: Ted Pliakos
Contact: Tom Galczynski
tom_galczynski@asdsoftware.com
Estimated Sales: $5-10 Million
Number Employees: 10-19
Brands:
Product Vision

18431 Advanced Surfaces Corp
3355 Liberty Rd
Villa Rica, GA 30180
800-963-4632
www.advancedsurfacescorp.com
Specializing in flooring for the food and beverage
industries.
President: Paul Patuka
paul@advancedsurfacescorp.com
Owner: Kerry Patuka
Year Founded: 1997
Estimated Sales: $5.67 million

18432 Advanced Uniflo Technologies
1850 N Ohio Ave
Wichita, KS 67214-1530
316-688-0000
Fax: 316-267-3387 800-688-0400
uniflo@gplains.com
Conveyor systems including small package, pallet
handling, belt, chain, live roller and accumulation;
also, steel fabrication services available
CEO: Steve Nulty
Sales Manager: Chuck Driskell
Marketing Technical Specialist: Brenda Salvati
Estimated Sales: $10-20 Million
Number Employees: 50-99
Square Footage: 160000
Brands:
Uniflo

18433 Advantage Puck Technologies
1 Plastics Rd # 6
Corry, PA 16407-8538
814-664-4810
Fax: 814-663-6081 sales@advantagepuck.com
www.advantagepuck.com
Manufacturer and exporter of plastic product carri-
ers for assembly line filling
President: Kurt Sieber
Estimated Sales: $1-2.5 Million
Number Employees: 1-4
Brands:
Puck

18434 Advantage Puck Technologies
1 Plastics Rd # 6
Corry, PA 16407-8538
814-664-4810
Fax: 814-663-6081 800-396-7825
Sales@AdvantagePuck.com
www.advantagepuck.com
Pucks and puck handling machinery
Number Employees: 1-4

18435 Advantec Process Systems
95 Wyngate Dr
Newnan, GA 30265
770-253-1021
Fax: 770-251-3437
www.advantecprocesssystems.com
Supplier of process instrumentation for the food industry.
President: James Camp

18436 Advantek
7900 West 78th Street
Suite 180
Eden Prairie, MN 55439
952-746-9850
Fax: 952-938-1800 www.advantek.com
President: Bruce Bratten
CEO: Bruce Batten
CFO: Mike Eggers
Owner: Jared Koll
Quality Control: Mike Miller
Contact: Elena Nemirovsky
elena.nemirovsky@advantek.com
Number Employees: 250-499

18437 Advantus Corp.
12276 San Jose Blvd
Building 618
Jacksonville, FL 32223
904-482-0091
Fax: 904-482-0099 www.mcgillinc.com
Manufacturer and exporter of coin changers
President: Wayne Schwartzman
R&D: Becky McDaniel
VP Sales: Jim Booth
Estimated Sales: $5 - 10 Million
Number Employees: 10-19
Square Footage: 260000

18438 Advent Machine Co
6815 E Washington Blvd
Commerce, CA 90040-1905
323-728-5367
Fax: 323-728-2443 800-846-7716
info@adventmachine.net www.adventmachine.net
Pressure-sensitive or plain paper labels
Owner: Richard G Ealy
rgealy@fjsmith.com
Estimated Sales: $1 - 3 Million
Number Employees: 5-9

18439 Adwest Technologies
151 Trapping Brook Rd
Wellsville, NY 14895
585-593-1405
Fax: 585-593-6614
Air pollution control systems
President: Jack Preston
Sales: Brian Cannon
Number Employees: 50-100
Parent Co: Adwest Technologies

18440 Aei Corp
2641 Du Bridge Ave
Irvine, CA 92606-5001
949-474-3070
Fax: 949-474-0559 www.patio-comfort.com
Outdoor and infrared patio heaters and outdoor heating equipment
Owner: Pete Arnold
p.arnold@aeicorporation.com
CFO: Fred Speicher
Estimated Sales: $5-10 Million
Number Employees: 10-19
Brands:
 Ducane
 Infratech
 Pgs
 Profire
 Sunglo
 Sunpak

18441 Aep Industries Inc.
125 Phillips Ave
South Hackensack, NJ 07606
201-641-6600
Fax: 201-807-6801 800-999-2374
www.aepinc.com
Plastic packaging film.
President/CEO/Chairman of the Board: J. Brendan Barba
Managing Principal: Kenneth Avia
Executive VP/Finance/CFO: Paul M. Feeney
Vice President-Finance: Richard E. Davis
Vice President and Treasurer: James B. Rafferty
Executive Vice President, Sales/Marketin: John J. Powers
Contact: Glenny Adames
adamesg@aepinc.com
Executive Vice President, Operations: Paul C. Vegliante
Senior Vice President-Manufacturing: David J. Cron

18442 Aeration Industries Intl LLC
4100 Peavey Rd
Chaska, MN 55318-2353
952-448-6789
Fax: 952-448-7293 800-328-8287
aii@aireo2.com www.aireo2.com
Manufactures waste water treatment systems & equipment, including the dual-process Triton aerator and mixer to provide solutions for challenging wastewater needs.
President: Daniel Durda
aiii@aireo2.com
VP: Brian Cohen
Estimated Sales: $10-20 Million
Number Employees: 20-49
Square Footage: 500000

Brands:
 Aire-02
 Aire-02 Triton
 Microfloat
 Turbo
 Unisystem

18443 Aeration Technologies Inc
11 Bartlet St
Andover, MA 01810-3655
978-475-6385
Fax: 978-475-6387 info@aertec.com
www.aertec.com
Wastewater aeration systems
Owner: R Gilbert
Office Manager: Linda Corners
Estimated Sales: Less Than $500,000
Number Employees: 1-4

18444 Aercology
8 Custom Drive
Old Saybrook, CT 06475-4009
860-399-7941
Fax: 860-399-7049 800-826-6123
www.aercology.com
Air filtration
Chairman, President, Chief Executive Off: Bill Cook
Estimated Sales: $5-10 Million
Number Employees: 50-100

18445 Aero Company
90 Mechanic St
Southbridge, MA 01550-2555
508-764-5500
Fax: 508-764-3350 800-678-4163
Manufactures and distributes safety equipment
President: Mike Mc Clain
Plant Manager: Earl Vancelette
Estimated Sales: $5 - 10 Million
Number Employees: 20-49
Parent Co: Aearo Company

18446 Aero Housewares
Ste C
600 Glynn St N
Fayetteville, GA 30214-6716
770-914-4240
Fax: 770-914-4236 www.aeroplastics.com
Injection molded plastic products including storage containers, bowls, tableware, plates, tumblers, microwave containers, snack trays, etc
President: Jeffry Goldberg
CFO: Andrew Rice
Director Marketing/Sales: Heather Plaster
National Sales Manager: Steven Waugh
Regional Sales Manager: Keith Gouin
Estimated Sales: $20-50 Million
Number Employees: 20

18447 Aero Manufacturing Co
310 Allwood Rd
PO Box 1250
Clifton, NJ 07012-1786
973-473-5300
Fax: 973-473-3794 800-631-8378
sales@aeromfg.com www.aeromfg.com
Stainless steel sinks, tables, dishtables, cabinets, shelving, and custom fabrication.
President/CEO: Wayne Phillips
kkreiss@aeromfg.com
Sales Exec: Ken Kreiss
Number Employees: 50-99
Square Footage: 600000
Brands:
 Aerospec

18448 (HQ)Aero Tec Laboratories/ATL
45 Spear Rd Industrial Park
Ramsey, NJ 07446-1251
201-825-1400
Fax: 201-825-1962 800-526-5330
atl@atlinc.com www.atlinc.com
Collapsible pillow-style storage tanks
President: Peter J Regna
VP, Contracts: I. Janeiro
VP, R&D: R. Clark
VP of Sales: David Dack
VP, Operations: L. Damico
Estimated Sales: $3 - 5 Million
Number Employees: 50-99
Square Footage: 280000
Other Locations:
 Aero Tec Laboratories/ATL
 Bletchley, Milton Keynes

18449 Aero-Motive Company
333 Knightsbridge Pkwy
Suite 200
Lincolnshire, IL 60069
847-353-2500
Fax: 847-353-2500 800-999-8559
wctechsup@molex.com
President: Micheal Gies
Number Employees: 100-249
Parent Co: Woodhead Industries

18450 Aero-Power Unitized Fueler
103 Smithtown Blvd
Smithtown, NY 11787
631-366-4362
Fax: 631-366-0905 info@areotank.com
www.areotank.com
Owner: Rudy Benit
Contact: Lou Benit
sales@areotank.com
Estimated Sales: $1 - 3 Million
Number Employees: 1-4

18451 AeroFreeze, Inc.
2551 Viking Way
Richmond, BC, BC V6V 1N4
Canada
604-278-4118
Fax: 604-278-4847 www.aerofreeze.com
Manufacturers of freezers, chillers and air cooling products.

18452 Aerocon
1707 Langhorne Newtown Rd # 1
Langhorne, PA 19047
215-860-6056
Fax: 215-860-8606
Owner: Rosemary Caligiuri
Parent Co: Vac-U-Max

18453 Aerofreeze
P.O. Box 2439
Redmond, WA 98073
425-869-8889
Fax: 425-869-8839 www.aerofreeze.com
Freezing units, plate and belt freezers
Manager: Lars Johansson
Estimated Sales: $.5 - 1 000,000
Number Employees: 5-9

18454 Aerolator Systems
2716 Chamber Dr
Monroe, NC 28110
704-289-9585
Fax: 704-289-9580 800-843-8286
Hood systems; wholesaler/distributor of exhaust fans; serving the food service market
President: Janet Griffen
Sales Manager: Steve Surratt
Estimated Sales: $10-20 Million
Number Employees: 50-99
Square Footage: 80000
Brands:
 Aerolator

18455 Aeromat Plastics Inc
801 Cliff Rd E # 104
Suite 104
Burnsville, MN 55337-1534
952-890-4697
Fax: 952-890-1814 888-286-8729
www.aero-mat.com
Manufacturer and exporter of plastic proofer trays and machined plastic parts
President: Bruce Dahlke
bruce@aeromatplastics.com
Estimated Sales: $2.5 Million
Number Employees: 10-19
Square Footage: 34000

18456 Aeromix Systems
7135 Madison Ave W
Minneapolis, MN 55427
763-746-8400
Fax: 763-746-8408 800-879-3677
www.aeromix.com
Water and wastewater treatment equipment for the municipal, industrial and freshwater markets. Also offers a line of eco-friendly equipment that is completely powered by solar energy
President and CEO: Henry J. Charrabe
Contact: Limor Amar
lamar@nirosoft.com
Operations: Peter Gross

Estimated Sales: $5-10 Million
Number Employees: 25
Brands:
   Cyclone
   Hurricane
   Tornado
   Zephyr

18457 Aerotech Enterprise Inc
8511 Mulberry Rd
Chesterland, OH 44026

440-729-2616
Fax: 440-729-1620 amatic@aerotechcnc.com
www.aerotechcnc.com
Confectionery machinery
Owner: Andrea Maticci
Contact: Nicholas Tadic
ntadic@aerotechcnc.com
Office Manager: Elizabeth Krukowski
Estimated Sales: $500,000-$1 Million
Number Employees: 5-9

18458 Aerotech Laboratories
1501 W Knudsen Dr
Phoenix, AZ 85027

623-780-4800
Fax: 623-780-7695 800-651-4802
www.aerotechpk.com
Contact: Lori Thompson
al.yankulov@coat.com
Manager: Ben Sublasky

18459 (HQ)Aerovent Co
5959 Trenton Ln N
Minneapolis, MN 55442-3237

763-551-7500
Fax: 763-551-7501 aerovent_sales@aerovent.com
www.tcf.com
Industrial air handling equipment, fans and blowers
President: Zika Srejovic
CEO: Chuck Barry
Estimated Sales: $50-100 Million
Number Employees: 100-249
Brands:
   Axiad II
   Axico
   Axipal

18460 Aerovent Co
5959 Trenton Ln N
Minneapolis, MN 55442-3237

763-551-7500
Fax: 763-551-7501 aerovent_sales@aerovent.com
www.tcf.com
Manufacturer and exporter of fans
President: Charles Barry
CEO: Chuck Barry
cbarry@tcf.com
CFO: Julie Dale
VP Sales: Dave Laclerc
Estimated Sales: $50 - 75 Million
Number Employees: 100-249
Parent Co: Twin City Fan Company

18461 Aerowerks
6625 millcreek drive
Mississauga, ON L5M 5M4
Canada

905-363-6999
Fax: 905-363-6998 888-774-1616
aman@aero-werks.com www.aero-werks.com
Manufacturer and exporter of conveyors
President: Balbir Singh
Sales Manager: Aman Singh
Number Employees: 35
Parent Co: Aerotool
Brands:
   K-Flex Systems

18462 Aerzen USA Corp
108 Independence Way
Coatesville, PA 19320-1653

610-380-0244
Fax: 610-380-0278 800-444-1692
inquiries@aerzenusa.com www.aerzenusa.com
150 year old manufacturer of oil-free rotary lobe
blower packages and screw compressor packages
President: Michelle Abney
mabney@aerzenusa.com
CFO: Keith Rolfe
Marketing Manager: Ralph Wilton
Sales Manager: Darrel Hill
Production Manager: Steve Wark

Number Employees: 50-99
Square Footage: 60000
Parent Co: Aerzener/Maschinenfabrik

18463 Afassco
2244 Park Pl # C
Suite C
Minden, NV 89423-8632

775-783-3555
Fax: 775-783-3555 www.afassco.com
CEO: Don Schumaker
afassco@intercomm.com
Number Employees: 10-19

18464 Afeco
4300 West Bryn Mawr Ave
Chicago, IL 60646

773-478-9700
Fax: 773-478-8689 sales@cozzini.com
Contact: Bruce Keith
bkeith@afeco.com

18465 Affiliated Resource Inc
3839 N Western Ave
Chicago, IL 60618-3733

773-509-9300
Fax: 773-509-9929 800-366-9336
info@4ledsigns.com www.forledsigns.com
Manufacturer, wholesaler/distributor of indoor and
outdoor electronic signs
President: Stephen Stillman
stephen@yledsigns.com
National Sales Manager: Rick Markle
Regional Sales Manager: Pam Zayas
Estimated Sales: $1 - 3 Million
Number Employees: 1-4
Square Footage: 4000

18466 Aftermarket Specialties Inc
980 Cobb Place Blvd NW # 100
Kennesaw, GA 30144-4804

678-819-2274
Fax: 678-819-2275 800-438-5931
Vending compressors, refrigeration compressors
President: Dallas Rohrer
CFO: Dallas Rohrer
Vice President: Dion Rohrer
Estimated Sales: $1 - 2.5 Million
Number Employees: 1-4

18467 Ag-Pak
8416 State Street
PO Box 304
Gasport, NY 14067

716-772-2651
Fax: 716-772-2555 info@agpak.com
www.agpak.com
Manufacturer and exporter of produce weighers and
bag fillers
President: Andy Currie
VP, Technical Support: Joe Gabree
Sales Manager: Greg Lureman
Plant Manager/ Engineering: Warren Farewell
Estimated Sales: Below $5 Million
Number Employees: 10-19

18468 AgTracker
2335 81st Ter
Vero Beach, FL 32966-1329

772-770-3293
Fax: 303-440-6162
Computer systems and software and weight control
systems
Estimated Sales: $1 - 5 000,000
Number Employees: 3

18469 Aggreko Rental
15600 J F Kennedy Blvd # 200
Houston, TX 77032-2343

281-848-1400
Fax: 713-852-4590 877-244-7356
aggreko@aggreko.com
As the world leader in temporary utility services we
are ready to satisfy your power, temperature and oil-
free compressed air needs. Our unique fleet of
equipment is custom designed and built for the rig-
ors of the diverse anddemanding temporary utility
industry
Manager: Gary Meador
gary.meador@aggreko.com
Estimated Sales: $.5 - 1 000,000
Number Employees: 20-49

18470 Agilysys, Inc.
1000 Windward Concourse
Suite 250
Alpharetta, GA 30005

770-810-7800
800-241-8768
sales@agilysys.com www.agilysys.com
A leading developer and marketer of proprietary enterprise software, services and solutions to the hospitality and retail industries. Specializes in
market-leading point-of-sale, property managerment,
inventory & procurement and mobile& wireless so-
lutions that are designed to streamline operations,
improve efficiency and enhance the consumer's
experience.
President & CEO: James Dennedy
Sr. VP, General Counsel & Secretary: Kyle C.
Badger
Senior Vice President, Chief Financial O: Janine
Seebeck
Senior Vice President, General Counsel a: Kyle C.
Badger
Senior Vice President and Chief Technolo: Larry
Steinberg
Sr. Vice President & General Manager: Paul Civils
Senior Vice President of Sales and Marke: Michael
Buckham-White
VP of Sales: Tony Ross
Estimated Sales: $5 - 10 Million
Number Employees: 50-99
Square Footage: 80000
Parent Co: Agilysys/Alpharetta GA
Brands:
   Infogenesis Gsa
   Infogenesis Hospitality
   Infogenesis Iqs
   Infogenesis Its
   Infogenesis Ticketing

18471 Agrana Fruit US Inc
6850 Southpointe Pkwy
Cleveland, OH 44141-3260

440-546-1199
Fax: 440-546-0038 800-477-3788
www.agrana.us
Sugar; starch; and processed fruits.
President/CEO: Johann Marihart
Board Member: Fritz Gattermeyer
Estimated Sales: $10-20 Million
Number Employees: 50-99
Parent Co: SIAS MPA
Type of Packaging: Food Service, Private Label,
Bulk

18472 Agri-Business Services
PO Box 1237
Lakeville, MN 55044-1237

952-469-6767

18473 Agri-Equipment International
493 Colonial Trace Dr
Longs, SC 29568

843-283-2583
Fax: 864-343-0076 877-550-4709
www.agri-equipmentonline.com
Manufacturer and wholesaler/distributor of release
(interleaver) sheets, thermometers, temperature data
loggers and probes
President: Tom Gaffney
VP Sales: Gary Gaffney
Estimated Sales: $1-2.5,000,000
Number Employees: 1-4

18474 Agri-Northwest
PO Box 230
Hope, AR 71802-0230

870-777-7105
Equipment Supply
Estimated Sales: Under $500,000
Number Employees: 20-49
Parent Co: Agri-Northwest

18475 Agri-Sales Assoc Inc
209 Louise Ave
Nashville, TN 37203-1811

615-329-1141
Fax: 615-329-2770 800-251-1141
info@agri-sales.com www.agri-sales.com
Manufacturer's Representative Group
President/Founder: Jerry Bellar
president@agri-sales.com
VP: Phillip Ferrell
Estimated Sales: Less than $500,000
Number Employees: 5-9

18476 AgriFiber Solutions
1011 Campus Dr.
Mundelein, IL 60060
847-549-6002
Fax: 847-549-6028 sales@agrfbr.com
www.agrifibersolutions.com
Offers agriculture solutions for corn and oat fiber,
including cost reduction, moisture retention, nutritional value, gluten-free options, and more.
Senior Managing Partner: Jonathan Kahn
Type of Packaging: Food Service

18477 AgriTech
1989 W 5th Avenue
Columbus, OH 43212-1912
614-488-2772
Fax: 715-335-4390 agritech@iwaynet.net
Consultation firm offering market research and assessment, operations analysis, technology transfer
and planning; specializing in food processing, agricultural development, grains, dairy products and
foreign markets
President: William Riddle
Estimated Sales: less than $500,000
Number Employees: 1

18478 Agribuys Incorporated
3625 Del Amo Blvd
Suite 210
Torrance, CA 90503
310-944-9655
Fax: 310-944-9665 877-499-3052
Online supply chain integrator for the food industry
Quality Control: Le Vu
Manager: B J Asneck
Number Employees: 20-49

18479 Agricultural Data Systems
24331 Los Arboles Dr
Laguna Niguel, CA 92677-2196
949-363-5353
Fax: 949-495-7066 800-328-2246
sales@touchmemory.com www.touchmemory.com
Automatic harvesting and data collection equipment
President: Carl Gennaro
boss@touchmemory.com
VP: Carl Gennaro
National Sales Manager/Marketing: Paul Geisterfer
Estimated Sales: $3 - 5,000,000
Number Employees: 10-19

18480 Agricultural Research Service
Jamie L. Whitten Building
Washington, SW 20250
202-720-3656
Fax: 202-720-5427 www.ars.usda.gov
Government research center for fresh and processed
foods; food development services available
Manager: Wendy H Kramer
Technical Transfer Coordinator: C Crawford
Director: John Cherry
Number Employees: 250-499
Parent Co: Agricultural Research Service/US De-
partment of Agriculture

18481 Agriculture Consulting Services
New York City, NY
347-709-7587
jeffrey@agritecture.com
www.agritecture.com
Services include farm design, economic analysis,
market research, techical assessment, and more.
Managing Director: Henry Gordon-Smith
Director of Business Development: Jeffrey Landau
Director of Operations: Yara Nagi *Year Founded:*
2014

18482 Agripac
PO Box 5110
Denver, CO 80217-5110
503-363-9255
Fax: 503-371-5666
Packaging of canned and frozen vegetables and fruit
products
Number Employees: 150

18483 AgroFresh
510-513 Walnut St.
Ste. 1350
Philadelphia, PA 19106
866-850-6846
fusafna@agrofresh.com www.agrofresh.com

Offers technologies and solutions that support grow-
ers, packers, retailers, exporters and marketers. Fo-
cus is on fruits and vegetables.
CEO: Jordi Ferre
VP & General Counsel: Thomas Ermi
CFO: Graham Miao
Year Founded: 1996
Number Employees: 200-500

18484 Agropur MSI, LLC
2340 Enterprise Ave
La Crosse, WI 54603
800-359-2345
ingredients@agropur.com
www.agropuringredients.com
Supply the food, beverage and nutritional industries
with contract manufacturing and private labelling
services. Manufacture ingredients and additives:
anticaking agents, dairy ingredients, egg replacers,
gums, gydrocolloidsstabilizers, nutraceuticals, organic ingredients, proteins, whey and whey
products.
Marketing & Communications Manager: Corrie
Drellack

18485 Agspring
5101 College Blvd.
Leawood, KS 66211
913-333-3035
inquiry@agspring.com
agspring.com
Services include storage & handling, marketing &
distribution, light processing, logistics, and risk
management. Market focus is on grains & oilseeds,
livestock feed ingredients, and food ingredients.
CEO: Mark Beemer
CFO: Bruce Chapin
VP, Merchandising: Brian Aust
VP, Marketing & Customer Engagement: Bradford
Warner
VP, Sales: Mike Hallman
Director of Corporate Safety: Chris Stanger
AVP, Transportation & Supply Chain: Josh
Skatvold
Plant Manager: Brady Eckart
Year Founded: 2012
Number Employees: 200-500

18486 Agtron Inc
9395 Double R Blvd
Reno, NV 89521-5919
775-850-4600
Fax: 775-850-4611 agtron@aol.com
www.agtron.net
Manufacturer and exporter of spectrophotometers
used in the food industry to measure the degree of
roasted, baked or fried goods or color grading of
most food products.
President: Carl Staub
agtron@aol.com
CEO: Mike Rowley
CFO: Mike Rowley
Sales/Marketing: Kim Franke
Estimated Sales: $1 - 2.5 Million
Number Employees: 5-9
Square Footage: 80000
Brands:
Agtron

18487 Agworld
1601 Pelican Lakes Pt.
Windsor, CO 80550
724-249-6753
www.agworld.com
Offers solutions and consultation concerning crops,
farming staff, operation management, pre-season
planning and more.
Co-Founder & President: Zach Sheely
Co-Founder & CEO: Doug Fitch
Year Founded: 2007
Number Employees: 65-100

18488 Ahlstrom Filtration LLC
215 Nebo Rd
P.O. Box 1708
Madisonville, KY 42431
270-821-0140
Fax: 270-326-3290 www.ahlstrom-munksjo.com
Filters, wallcovers, wipes, flooring, labels and food
packaging.

President & CEO: Hans Sohlstrom
Deputy CEO & CFO: Sakari Ahdekivi
EVP, Filtration & Performance: Daniele Borlatto
EVP, Legal & General Counsel: Andreas Elving
EVP, People & Safety: Tarja Takko
Year Founded: 1851
Estimated Sales: $2.2 Billion
Number Employees: 6,000
Square Footage: 5000
Parent Co: Ahlstrom-Munksjo
Type of Packaging: Food Service

18489 Ahlstrom Nonwovens LLC
2 Elm St
Windsor Locks, CT 06096-2335
860-654-8300
Fax: 860-654-8301 www.ahlstrom.com
Tea and coffee industry filters (paper), pouch materi-
als (cellophane, paper, films), teabag paper
Estimated Sales: $1,000,000,000+
Number Employees: 5000-9999
Parent Co: Ahlstrom-Munksjo

18490 Aibmr Life Sciences
4117 S Meridian
#202
Puyallup, WA 98373-3697
253-286-2888
Fax: 253-286-2451 info@aibmr.com
www.aibmr.com
Consulting firm specializing in nutraceutical re-
search and product development.
Vice President: Connie Knapp
connie@aibmr.com
Chief Scientific Officer: John Endres
Vice President: Connie Knapp
connie@aibmr.com
Senior Director of Research: Alexander Schauss
Chief Operating/Financial Officer: Laura Schauss
Number Employees: 10-19

18491 Aidco International
P.O. Box 15339
Cincinnati, OH 45215-339
Fax: 517-265-2131 www.aidcoint.com
President: Salh Khan
Estimated Sales: $5 - 10000,000
Number Employees: 45

**18492 Aidi International Hotels of
America**
1050-17th Street NW
Suite 600
Washington, DC 20036-
202-331-9299
Fax: 202-478-0367 www.royalregencyhotels.com
Engineering and marketing consultant specializing
in construction, management, decoration and opera-
tions in overseas hotels; wholesaler/distributor and
exporter of equipment, furniture and food
President: Ghassane Aidi
Chairman: Adnan Aidi
VP: Samia Aidi
Number Employees: 200
Square Footage: 28000
Parent Co: Aidi Group

18493 Aigner Index
P.O. Box 4084
New Windsor, NY 12553-0084
845-562-4510
Fax: 845-562-2638 800-242-3919
holdex@frontiernet.net
High quality plastic insertable label holders
President: Mark Aigner
maigner@aignerindex.com
Estimated Sales: $5 - 10 Million
Number Employees: 10-19

18494 Aim Blending Technologies Inc
4196 Suffolk Way
Pleasanton, CA 94588
925-484-5000
Fax: 925-484-5007 800-328-6060
pahelman@comcast.net www.aimblending.com
Premium quality dry powder blending equipment,
ribbon, paddle, fluidicers, continuous, V, cone and
numerous other dry powder blender.
President: Phil Helman
Marketing Director: Kassandra Cunningham
Sales Director: Phil Helman
Contact: Jesse Dornan
jdornan@aimblending.com

Estimated Sales: $5 - 10 000,000
Number Employees: 20-49
Square Footage: 20000

18495 Air Barge Company
26807 Springcreek Rd
Rancho Palos Verdes, CA 90275

310-378-2928

President: Carol Vaughen
R & D: Jack Vaughen
Estimated Sales: $5-10 Million
Number Employees: 1-4

18496 Air Economy Corporation
PO Box 29
Flemington, NJ 08822-0029

908-782-8888

18497 Air Liquide USA, LLC
9811 Katy Freeway
Houston, TX 77024

713-624-8000
www.airliquide.com

Complete line of industrial gases, develops custom freezing, chilling, or gas packaging systems.
Chairman & CEO: Benoit Pottier
Executive Vice President: Michael Graff
Executive Vice President: Guy Salzgeber
Executive Vice President: Fabienne Lecorvaisier
Executive Vice President: Francois Jackow
CEO, Air Liquide USA, LLC: Sue Ellerbusch
Director, Marketing Supply Chain: Genevieve Matte
Chief Customer Officer: Rich Jahr
Year Founded: 1902
Estimated Sales: Over $1 Billion
Number Employees: 67,000
Parent Co: Air Liquide S.A.
Other Locations:
San Francisco CA
Los Angeles CA
Dallas TX
Chicago IL
Baton Rouge LA
Philadelphia PA

18498 Air Locke Dock Seal
549 W Indianola Ave
Youngstown, OH 44511-2460

330-788-6504
Fax: 330-788-6705 800-538-2388
www.airlocke.com

President: Larry O Neal
Marketing: Marijo Rischar
Estimated Sales: $1 - 5 Million
Number Employees: 5-9
Parent Co: O'Neal Tarpaulin & Awning Company

18499 Air Logic Power Systems
1745 S. 38th Street
Suite 100
Milwaukee, WI 53215

414-671-3332
Fax: 414-671-6645 800-325-8717
info@alpsleak.com www.alpsleak.com

On-line leak detection equipment for the plastic container manufacturing industry.
President: Roger Tambling
Sales Manager: Scott Heins
Contact: Pierre Aterianus
pierrea@alpsleak.com
Estimated Sales: $5-10 Million
Number Employees: 20-49
Square Footage: 80000
Brands:
Alps Model 7385
Alps Smart Test Module
Alps Sx-Flex
Alps Vision Plus

18500 Air Pak Products & Services
2976 Forsyth Road
Winter Park, FL 32792-6628

407-678-1847
Fax: 407-679-5655 800-824-7725
www.air-pakpsi.com

Designer/builder providing restaurant remodeling, renovation, cabinetry, millwork and HVAC services
President: David W McLeod
VP: Robert Nippes
Purchasing Manager: Sulyn McLeod
Estimated Sales: $20-50 Million
Number Employees: 100-249

18501 Air Products & Chemicals Inc
7201 Hamilton Blvd
Allentown, PA 18195-1501

610-481-4911
Fax: 610-481-5900 800-224-2724
www.airproducts.com

Gas production, storage, and handling equipment, including food freezers, oxy-fuel burners, and heat exchangers.
Chairman/President/CEO: Seifi Ghasemi
Executive Vice President: Dr. Samir Serhan
serhansj@airproducts.com
EVP/Chief Financial Officer: M. Scott Crocco
SVP/Chief Human Resources Officer: Victoria Brifo
EVP/General Counsel/Secretary: Sean Major
Year Founded: 1940
Estimated Sales: $9.8 Billion
Number Employees: 15,500
Other Locations:
Air Products and Chemicals Inc
Tempe AZ
Air Products and Chemicals Inc
Geismar LA
Air Products and Chemicals Inc
Carlsbad CA
Air Products and Chemicals Inc
Austin TX
Air Products and Chemicals Inc
Fountain Valley CA
Air Products and Chemicals Inc
Houston TX
Air Products and Chemicals Inc
Santa Clara CA
Air Products and Chemicals Inc
Irving TX
Brands:
Crustplus
Cryo Batch
Cryo Dip
Cryo Quick
Cyro Rotary
Freshpak
Vt Tune

18502 Air Quality Engineering
7140 Northland Dr N
Minneapolis, MN 55428-1520

888-883-3273
Fax: 763-531-9900 800-328-0787
info@air-quality-eng.com
www.air-quality-eng.com

Manufacturer and exporter of electronic and media air cleaners, parts and accessories
President & CEO: Heidi Oas
VP, Sales: Ira Golden
Estimated Sales: $5 - 10 Million
Number Employees: 50-75
Square Footage: 142800
Brands:
Smokemaster

18503 Air System Components Inc
605 Shiloh Rd
Plano, TX 75074

972-212-4888
www.airsysco.com

Market-leading supplier of heating, air conditioning and ventilation system components for commercial, industrial, and residential applications.
Estimated Sales: $212 Million
Number Employees: 1000-4999
Parent Co: Air Distribution Technologies Inc.
Brands:
Koch Filter
Krueger
Pennbarry
Superior Rex
Titus
Trion Indoor Air Quality
Tuttle & Bailey

18504 Air Technical Industries
7501 Clover Ave.
Mentor, OH 44060

440-951-5191
Fax: 440-953-9237 888-857-6265
ati@airtechnical.com www.airtechnical.com

Manufacturer and exporter of material handling equipment including floor cranes, fork lifts and pallet inverters and handlers; also, automatic wrappers and hydraulic lift tables
President: Pero Novak
VP: Jane Goff
Contact: Chad Aschbacher
chad@airtechnical.com

Estimated Sales: $10-20 Million
Number Employees: 50-99
Square Footage: 240000
Brands:
Articularm
Econo-Verter
Husky Master
Low Profile E-Z Wrap
Universal-Lift
V-Master

18505 Air-Knife Systems/PaxtonProducts Corporation
10125 Carver Rd
Cincinnati, OH 45242

513-891-7485
Fax: 513-891-4092 800-441-7475
sales@paxtonproducts.com
www.paxtonproducts.com

We off custom designed, complete air knife drying and blow-off cleaning systems.
General Manager: Barbara Stefl
Engineering Manager: Steve Pucciani
Sales Engineer: Jeem Newland
Operations Manager: Stan Coley
Number Employees: 30

18506 Air-Lec Industries, Inc
3300 Commercial Ave
Madison, WI 53714

608-244-4754
Fax: 608-246-7676 info@air-lec.com
www.air-lec.com

Quality door operating devices, track systems and door hardware, providing industry with reliable, productivity enhancing products since 1921.
President: John Lunenschloss
Contact: John Ganahl
john.ganahl@air-lec.com
Estimated Sales: $10 - 20,000,000
Number Employees: 10-19
Square Footage: 30000
Brands:
Air-Lec
Zephyr

18507 (HQ)Air-Scent International
290 Alpha Drive RIDC Industrial Park
Pittsburgh, PA 15238

412-252-2000
Fax: 412-252-1010 800-247-0770
www.airscent.com

Manufacturer and exporter of air fresheners, sanitizers and odor control systems including aerosol dispensers and refills; also, aerosol insecticides
President: Arnold Zlotnik
Estimated Sales: Below $5 Million
Number Employees: 50-99
Square Footage: 160000
Brands:
Air-Scent
Ch
Nature Scent
Scent Flo
Surcotta

18508 Air/Tak Inc
107 W Main St
Worthington, PA 16262-2303

724-297-3416
Fax: 724-297-5189 airtak@airtak.com
www.airtak.com

President: Donald Burk
Manager: Gary Byers
gbyers@airtak.com
Estimated Sales: $3-5 Million
Number Employees: 10-19

18509 Airblast
2050 Pepper St
Alhambra, CA 91801-3162

626-576-0144
Fax: 626-289-2548 866-424-7252
sales@airblastinc.com www.airblastinc.com

President: Carl Von Wolffradt
Estimated Sales: Below 1 Million
Number Employees: 5-9

18510 Aire-Mate
17335 Us 31 N
Westfield, IN 46074-9119
317-896-2561
Fax: 317-896-3788 www.airemate.com
President: Conrad Mc Ginnis
Estimated Sales: $3 - 5 Million
Number Employees: 5-9

18511 Airflex
9919 Clinton Rd
Cleveland, OH 44144-1077
216-281-2211
Fax: 216-281-3890 edlunder@eaton.com
www.airflex.com
President: Alexander M Cutler
Executive: Ed Luehring
Estimated Sales: $20 - 50 Million
Number Employees: 100-249
Parent Co: Eaton Corporation

18512 Airfloat LLC
2230 N Brush College Rd
Decatur, IL 62526-5522
217-423-6001
Fax: 217-422-1049 800-888-0018
sales@airfloat.com www.airfloat.com
Manufacturer and designer of bulk handling machinery, conveyors and bucket elevators for the food industry
President: Jason Stoecker
Marketing Manager: Gary Mollohan
Director of Sales: Ken Adkins
Estimated Sales: $10-20 Million
Number Employees: 20-49

18513 Airfloat LLC
2230 N Brush College Rd
Decatur, IL 62526-5522
217-423-6001
Fax: 217-422-1049 800-888-0018
sales@alignprod.com
Manufacturer and exporter of lift, tilt and turn tables
President: Jason Stoecker
Marketing Manager: Kara Demarjian
Estimated Sales: $10-20 Million
Number Employees: 20-49

18514 Airflow Sciences Corp
12190 Hubbard St
Livonia, MI 48150-1737
734-525-0300
Fax: 734-525-0303 asc@airflowsciences.com
www.airflowsciences.com
Consultant specializing in product development testing, process trouble shooting, dryer, mixer, cooking, chilling and freezing reactions and computer simulations of heat transfer, fluid flow and chemical reactions
Manager: James C Paul
paul@ricardo.com
CEO: Robert Nelson
VP Western Office: James Paul
Manager: James Paul
paul@ricardo.com
Estimated Sales: $2.5-5 Million
Number Employees: 10-19
Square Footage: 16000
Parent Co: Airflow Science Corporation

18515 Airgas Carbonic
6340 Sugarloaf Pkwy Ste 300
Duluth, GA 30097
770-717-2200
Fax: 770-717-2222 800-241-5882
www.airgas.com
Water treatment, temperature controls, gas packaging, refrigeration systems
President: Phil Filer
Contact: John Cochran
john.cochran@airgas.com
Estimated Sales: $50 Million
Number Employees: 50-99

18516 Airgas Carbonic Inc
2530 Sever Rd # 300
Suite 300
Lawrenceville, GA 30043-4022
770-717-2200
Fax: 770-717-2222 www.airgas.com
Water pollution treatment and monitoring systems, cryogenics, carbon dioxide and nitrogen refrigeration systems, dry ice, blocks or pellets, freeze tunnels, refrigeration supplies, trucks and trailers

President: Philip J Filer
philip.filer@airgas.com
Estimated Sales: $.5 - 1 million
Number Employees: 50-99

18517 Airlite Plastics Co
P.O. Box 8400
Omaha, NE 68108-0400
402-341-7300
888-228-3506
info@airliteplastics.com www.airliteplastics.com
Plastic injection molding and printing manufacturer product line; includes drink cups, polystyrene coolers, ICF (Insulating Concrete Form) building blocks, and customized plastic products. Also, in-mold labeling, shrink sleeving andoffset printing.
President & CEO: Brad Crosby
CFO: Steve Kane
Estimated Sales: $100-125 Million
Number Employees: 1000-4999
Square Footage: 325000

18518 (HQ)Airmaster Fan Co
1300 Falahee Rd # 5
Jackson, MI 49203-3548
517-764-2300
Fax: 517-764-3838 800-255-3084
sales@airmasterfan.com www.airmasterfan.com
Industrial and commercial fans, stainless steel fan guards, aluminum air circulator blades and explosion proof fans
President: Richard Stone
CEO: Robert Lazebrick
CFO: Ronald Johnson
Marketing: Maryann Talbot
Director of Sales: Mike Pignataro
Product Manager: Mike Hemer
Estimated Sales: $10-20 Million
Number Employees: 20-49
Square Footage: 1500000
Brands:
  Airmaster
  Chelsea
  Nova
  Powerline

18519 Airomat Corp
2916 Engle Rd
Fort Wayne, IN 46809-1198
260-747-7408
Fax: 260-747-7409 800-348-4905
airomat@airomat.com
Manufacturer and exporter of safety and fatigue relief matting
President: Joanne K Feasel
VP: Jody Feasel
Marketing/Sales: Claudia Logan
Operations Manager: Pam Peters
Plant Manager: John Solga
Estimated Sales: $1 - 3,000,000
Number Employees: 5-9
Square Footage: 6000
Brands:
  Airomat

18520 Airosol Co Inc
1206 Illinois St
Neodesha, KS 66757-1483
620-325-2666
Fax: 620-325-2602 800-633-9576
www.airosol.com
Aerosol propelled drain opener
Owner: Carl Stratemeier
Sales Coordinator: Linda Cushman
carls@airosol.com
Estimated Sales: $20 - 50 Million
Number Employees: 20-49
Parent Co: Airosol Company
Brands:
  Power Plumber

18521 (HQ)Airosol Co Inc
1101 Illinois St
Neodesha, KS 66757-1475
620-325-2666
Fax: 620-325-2602 800-633-9576
www.airosol.com
Manufacturer and exporter of insecticides and counter cleaners
President: Carl G Stratemeier
Marketing Specialist: Jim Leiker
VP Sales/Marketing: Don Gillen
Contact: Tim Bell
tbell@airosol.com

Estimated Sales: $20-50 Million
Number Employees: 10-19
Square Footage: 80000
Brands:
  Aero-Counter
  Blacknight

18522 Airsan Corp
4554 W Woolworth Ave
Milwaukee, WI 53218-1497
414-353-5800
Fax: 414-353-8402 800-558-5494
Manufacturer and exporter of filters including air and restaurant grease extractor
Owner: Randy Perry
Quality Control: Kurt Gleisner
VP Sales: Kurt Glaisner
randyperry@airsan.com
Estimated Sales: $5-10 Million
Number Employees: 10-19
Type of Packaging: Food Service
Brands:
  Airsan

18523 Ajinomoto Heartland Inc
8430 W Bryn Mawr Ave
Suite 650
Chicago, IL 60631-3421
773-380-7000
Fax: 773-380-7006 www.lysine.com
Feed-grade amino acids
President: Daniel Bercovici
Number Employees: 10-19
Parent Co: Ajinomoto Co., Inc.
Type of Packaging: Bulk
Brands:
  AjiLys
  AjiPro-L
  L-Lysine
  L-Threonine
  L-Tryptophan
  L-Valine

18524 Akers Group
1450 East North Blvd.
Suite 8
Leesburg, FL 34748
352-787-4112
Fax: 201-475-7667 877-253-7744
kendra@akersmediagroup.com
www.akersmediagroup.com
Computerized software for flavor and fragrance formula
Manager: Robert Sobel

18525 Akicorp
20145 NE 21st CT
N Miami Beach, FL 33179
786-426-5750
ysaac@akinin.com
Oilseeds
Manager: Ysaac Akinin
yakinin@akinin.com

18526 Akro-Mils
P.O. Box 989
Akron, OH 44309
330-848-3773
Fax: 330-761-6133 www.myersindustries.com
Molded plastic bins, cabinets and trays
President: John Orr
CFO: Gregory Stodnick
Quality Control: Guy Lyon
Marketing Director: Joseph Gluzyn
Estimated Sales: $75-100 Million
Number Employees: 1,000-4,999

18527 (HQ)Akron Cotton Products
437 W Cedar St
Akron, OH 44307-2321
330-434-7171
Fax: 330-434-7150 800-899-7173
akroncotton@akroncotton.com
www.akroncotton.com
Manufacturer filter bags: beer and winemaking
President: Michael L Zwick
mike@akroncotton.com
VP: Shawn Zwick
Estimated Sales: $1 - 3 Million
Number Employees: 10-19
Square Footage: 52000

18528 Alabama Bag Co Inc
230 Broadway Ave
Talledega, AL 35160-3659
256-362-4921
Fax: 256-362-1801 800-888-4921
www.alabamabag.com
Manufacturer and exporter of food bags, twine, uniforms, aprons, butcher frocks, disposable wipers, stockinettes, elastic netting, knit gloves, ham tubings, shrouds, money bags, courier bags, transit bags, locking bags and coin andcurrency bags, Poly money bags, coin wrappers, bill straps, tags, security seals.
President: Larkin Coker
wc@alabamabag.com
Number Employees: 10-19
Brands:
U.S. Bag

18529 Alabama Power Company
PO Box 242
Birmingham, AL 35292
888-430-5787
www.alabamapower.com
Provides electricity to parts of Alabama and operates appliance stores.
Chairman/President/CEO: Mark Crosswhite
EVP/CFO: Philip Raymond
Customer Services: Gregory Barker
EVP, External Affairs: Zeke Smith
Year Founded: 1906
Estimated Sales: $6.1 Billion
Number Employees: 6,613
Parent Co: Southern Company

18530 Aladdin Label Inc
11301 W Forest Home Ave
Franklin, WI 53132-1402
USA
262-544-4455
Fax: 414-425-2384 www.aladdinlabel.com
Display fixtures, specialty food packaging: giftwrap, label, boxes, containers
President: Tony Heinl
Vice President: Rick Lichter
rickl@aladdinlabe.com
Sales Representative: Samantha Forster
Plant Manager: Aaron Dumke
Number Employees: 50-99

18531 Aladdin Temp-Rite, LLC
250 East Main Street
Hendersonville, TN 37075-2521
615-537-3600
Fax: 615-537-3634 800-888-8018
info@aladdin-atr.com www.aladdintemprite.com
Manufacturer and exporter of serving and heating equipment
President: Martin A. Rothshchild
VP Marketing: Marty Rothchild
VP Sales: Steve Avery
Contact: Kimmie Biggs
kbiggs@aladdin-atr.com
Estimated Sales: $300,000-500,000
Number Employees: 1-4
Parent Co: ENOCIS
Type of Packaging: Food Service
Brands:
Heat on Demand
Insul-Plus
Temp-Rite Excel Ii

18532 Aladdin Transparent Packaging
115 Engineers Rd # 100
Hauppauge, NY 11788-4005
631-273-4747
Fax: 631-273-2523 www.aladdinpackaging.com
Cellophane, polyethylene and polypropylene bags, rolls and sheets; also, baking and candy cups/padding
Owner: Abe Mandel
abe@aladdinpackaging.com
Product Manager: Donny Uccellini
Plant Manager: Larry O'Connell
Estimated Sales: $10-20 Million
Number Employees: 20-49
Square Footage: 80000
Parent Co: Bleyer Industries
Other Locations:
Aladdin Transparent Packaging
Peoria IL
Brands:
Pantry Bakers

18533 Alar Engineering Corp
9651 196th St
Mokena, IL 60448-9307
708-479-6100
Fax: 708-479-9059 info@alarcorp.com
www.alarcorp.com
Manufacturer and exporter of water pollution control equipment including filters for dewatering sludges, clarifiers, separators, carbon columns, drum compactors and holding tanks
President: Paula Jackfert
paulaj@alarcorp.com
CEO: Vickey Hassen
Estimated Sales: $5-10 Million
Number Employees: 20-49
Square Footage: 78000
Brands:
Alar
Auto-Vac
Clar-O-Floc
Flero Star
Microklear
Spiral Flow

18534 Alard Equipment Corp
6483 Lake Ave
PO Box 57
Williamson, NY 14589-9504
315-589-4511
Fax: 315-589-3871 sales@alard.com
www.alard.com
Buy, sell and refurbish food processing machinery and food packaging equipment for industrial fruit and vegetable canning, freezing, juice, bottling, and fresh cut applications, as well as all related packaging and labeling equipmentfor cans, jars, bottles, bags, etc.
President: Alvin E Shults
diane@alard.com
CEO: Susan Laird
VP: Edward Shults
Marketing Director: Michael Shults
Sales: Daryl Hoffman & Christopher Weigel
Purchasing: Diane Jenkins
Estimated Sales: $3 Million
Number Employees: 10-19
Square Footage: 40000

18535 Alarm Controls Corp
19 Brandywine Dr
Deer Park, NY 11729-5721
631-586-4220
Fax: 631-586-6500 800-645-5538
info@alarmcontrols.com www.alarmcontrols.com
Manufacturer and exporter of electronic burglar and smoke alarm systems and timers
President: Howard Berger
info@alarmcontrols.com
Sales Manager: John Benedetto
Estimated Sales: $5-10 Million
Number Employees: 10-19

18536 Albany International
975 Old Norcross Rd # A
Lawrenceville, GA 30045-4321
770-338-5000
Fax: 770-338-5024 800-252-2691
Contact: Joe Aiken
j.aiken@albanydoors.com
Plant Manager: Dan Garrau
Estimated Sales: $20 - 50 Million
Number Employees: 100-249

18537 Alberici Constructors Inc
8800 Page Ave
Overland, MO 63114-6106
314-733-2000
Fax: 314-733-2001 800-261-2611
gkozicz@alberici.com www.alberici.com
President/CEO: Gregory J. Kozicz
gkozicz@alberici.com
Vice President: Mark W. Okroy
Quality Control: Ron Rogge
Marketing Leader: Donald C. Oberlies
Estimated Sales: Over $1 Billion
Number Employees: 250-499

18538 Albion Industries Inc
800 N Clark St
Albion, MI 49224-1455
517-629-9441
Fax: 517-629-9501 800-835-8911
email@albioninc.com www.albioncasters.com
Casters and wheels.

President: Bill Winslow
CFO: Leanne Harbaugh
lharbaugh@albioninc.com
R&D: Rob Jorden
Sales: Mike Thorne
Estimated Sales: $35-45 Million
Number Employees: 50-99
Number of Brands: 10
Square Footage: 165000
Brands:
Contender
Prevenz
Shockmaster
Trionix

18539 Albion Machine & Tool Co
1001 Industrial Blvd
Albion, MI 49224-8551
517-629-9135
Fax: 517-629-6888
customercentral@casterconcepts.com
www.albionmachine.com
Manufacturer and exporter of specialty and reworked food processing equipment; repair services available
President: Robert Herwarth
CEO/Chairman: William Stoffer
wstoffer@albionmachine.com
VP: James Herwarth
Estimated Sales: $3 - 5 Million
Number Employees: 10-19

18540 Alburt Labeling Systems
3130 Pintail Ln
Signal Mountain, TN 37377
423-886-1664
Fax: 423-886-1676
Rollfed labeling, machines; foam labels
Owner: Alan Jones
*Estimated Sales:*less than $500,000
Number Employees: 1-4

18541 Alcan Foil Products
191 Evans Avenue
Etobicoke, ON M8Z 1J5
Canada
416-503-6709
Fax: 416-503-6720
President: Kevin Kindllan
Quality Control: Pierre Achim
Number Employees: 150

18542 Alcan Packaging
19701 Clark Graham Boulevard
Baie D'Urfe, QC H9X 3T1
Canada
514-457-4555
www.alcanpackaging.com
Folding cartons and paper boxes
President: Michael Rubensteil
CFO: Marcel Hetu
Research & Development: Martin Fogel
Plant Manager: Gilles Neron
Number Employees: 10
Square Footage: 300000
Parent Co: Algroup Wheaton Margo

18543 Alcoa - Lake Charles Carbon Plant
Lake Charles, LA 70605
337-480-7600
www.alcoa.com
Manufacturer of carbon.
Number Employees: 50

18544 Alcoa - Massena Operations
45 County Route 42
P.O. Box 5278
Massena, NY 13662
www.alcoa.com
Rod, billet, sow.
Number Employees: 480

18545 Alcoa - Warrick Operations
4400 State Route 66
P.O. Box 10
Newburgh, IN 47629-0010
812-853-6111
www.alcoa.com
Aluminum & sheet (litho and packaging)

18546 (HQ)Alcoa Corp

201 Isabella St
Suite 500
Pittsburgh, PA 15212-5858

412-315-2900
www.alcoa.com

Production and conversion of flexible packaging, including plastic films and laminates and printed foils used by manufacturers within the pharmaceutical, tobacco, and food and beverage industries.
President & CEO: Roy Harvey
EVP & Chief Financial Officer: Bill Oplinger
EVP & Chief Operations Officer: John Slaven
EVP/General Counsel/Secretary: Jeff Heeter
EVP & Chief HR Officer: Tammi Jones
EVP & Chief Innovation Officer: Ben Kahrs
EVP & Chief Commercial Officer: Timothy Reyes
Year Founded: 1888
Estimated Sales: $11.6 Billion
Number Employees: 14,600
Brands:
    Mansi

18547 Alcon Packaging

130 Arrow Road
Weston, ON M9M 2M1
Canada

416-742-8910
Fax: 416-742-7118 www.alcon.com

Rotogravure printed flexible packaging laminations for food, beverage and personal care products
Technical Director: Don Iwacha
Number Employees: 10
Parent Co: Lawson Mardon Group
Brands:
    Mixpap

18548 Alconox Inc

30 Glenn St # 309
Suite 309
White Plains, NY 10603-3252

914-437-7585
Fax: 914-948-4088 cleaning@alconox.com
www.alconox.biz

Manufacturer and exporter of USDA approved detergents for critical cleaning applications including food preparation surfaces
President: Stewart Katz
    skatz@alconox.com
CFO: Elliot Lebowitz
CEO: Elliot M Lebowitz
General Manager: Malcolm McLaughlin
Estimated Sales: $3 - 5 Million
Number Employees: 5-9
Type of Packaging: Food Service
Brands:
    Alco Tabs
    Alcojet
    Alconox
    Citranox
    Det-O-Jet
    Detergent 8
    Liqui-Nox
    Terg-A-Zyme

18549 Alconox Inc

30 Glenn St # 309
White Plains, NY 10603-3252

914-437-7585
Fax: 914-948-4088 cleaning@alconox.com

Cleaning detergents
President: Stewart Katz
    skatz@alconox.com
CEO: Elliot M Lebowitz
Estimated Sales: $1-2.5 000,000
Number Employees: 5-9

18550 Alcor PMC

3730 S Kalamath Street
Englewood, CO 80110-3460

303-761-1535
Fax: 303-789-9300 www.pmc1.net

End liner technology for the food, beer and beverage packaging industry as well as its line of food equipment, which include stuffers, formers and portioners
President and Owner: David Groetsch
Sales: Tom Hoffmann
Contact: Jeff Isaacs
    isaacs@stollemachinery.com
General Manager: Bob Geoffroy
Number Employees: 75
Number of Products: 20
Square Footage: 64000

18551 Aldo Locascio

1440 S Alvernon Way
Tucson, AZ 85711-5604

520-270-3059
Fax: 520-325-6776 800-488-8729

Consultant specializing in industrial design of commercial kitchens, concept dining rooms and food service operations, BBQ's, tabletop accessories
President: John Richards
Number Employees: 36
Number of Brands: 2
Number of Products: 40
Square Footage: 24000
Parent Co: Richards Manufacturing Company

18552 Aldon Co Inc

3410 Sunset Ave
Waukegan, IL 60087-3295

847-623-8800
Fax: 847-623-6139 e-rail@aldonco.com
www.aldonco.com

President: Joseph Ornig
    e-rail@aldonco.com
CFO: Ralph V Switzer
Estimated Sales: $1 - 5 Million
Number Employees: 10-19

18553 Aleco Food Svc Div

2802 Avalon Ave
Muscle Shoals, AL 35661-2708

256-248-2400
Fax: 800-750-9616 800-633-3120
info@aleco.com www.aleco.com

PVC vinyl strip and impact-type doors for walk-in coolers, freezers; also, traffic doors
CEO: Edward Robbins III
VP Sales/Marketing: Stan Denton
Estimated Sales: $1 - 3 Million
Number Employees: 20-49
Type of Packaging: Food Service
Brands:
    Clear-Flex Ii
    Impacdor

18554 Aleco Food Svc Div

2802 Avalon Ave
Muscle Shoals, AL 35661-2708

256-248-2400
800-633-3120
info@aleco.com www.aleco.com

PVC door strips or walk-in coolers and freezers, impact doors for restaurants, insect control doors, air curtain doors.
Vice President: Stan Denton
    rsdenton@aleco.com
CFO: Doug Sledge
Vice President: John Saylor
R&D/Quality Control: Steve Bacon
Marketing Director: Kelli Bush
Regional Account Manager: John Keddie
Public Relations: Bill May
Operations Manager: Ronald White
Production Manager: Jessie Hall
Plant Manager: Keith Rhodes
Purchasing Manager: Nancy Hamilton
Estimated Sales: $30,000,000
Number Employees: 20-49
Number of Brands: 10
Number of Products: 10
Square Footage: 100000
Parent Co: ER Robbins Corp
Type of Packaging: Food Service, Bulk
Brands:
    Air Pro
    Airflex
    Clear-Flex Ii
    Impacdoors
    Maxbullet
    Maxslide
    Scratch-Guard

18555 Alef Custom Packaging

204 E Pennsylvania Blvd
Feastervl Trvs, PA 19053-7845

215-355-5200
Fax: 215-355-2577 800-453-2212
info@alefcustom.com www.alefcustom.com

President: Jeffrey Gottlieb
    j.gottlieb@subway.com
Estimated Sales: $1 - 3 Million
Number Employees: 1-4

18556 Alegacy

12683 Corral Place
Santa Fe Springs, CA 90670

Fax: 888-604-1066 800-848-4440
info@alegacy.com www.alegacy.com

Cookware and small wares*Year Founded:* 1947
Brands:
    EAGLEWARE

18557 Alewel's Country Meats

911 N Simpson Dr
Junction 13 & 50
Warrensburg, MO 64093-9277

660-747-8261
Fax: 660-747-1857 800-353-8553
ralewel@alewels.com www.country-meats.com

Dry, shelf stable, game and summer sausage, and game jerky including deer and buffalo.
Owner: Randy Alewel
    alewels@sprintmail.com
Estimated Sales: $2.5-5 Million
Number Employees: 5-9
Square Footage: 20000
Type of Packaging: Consumer, Food Service, Private Label, Bulk
Brands:
    Alewel's Country Meats
    Grandpa A'S

18558 Alex Delvecchio Enterprises

PO Box 516
Troy, MI 48099-516

248-619-9600
Fax: 248-619-9688 sales@theimprintshop.com
www.theimprintshop.com

Promotional products including changeable letter bulletin boards, plaques, name plates, signs, matches and napkins; also, special clothing and uniforms
President: Alex Delvecchio Sr
CFO: Alex Delvecchio Jr
Estimated Sales: $5-10 Million
Number Employees: 10-19

18559 Alex E Fergusson Co Inc

800 Development Ave
Chambersburg, PA 17201

717-263-3132
Fax: 717-264-9182 800-345-1329
www.afcocare.info

Sanitizing and cleaning products including pressure cleaners, cleaning compounds and lubricants
President: Brett Bailey
    brettbailey@afco.net
VP Sales: Joseph Woodring
Estimated Sales: $20-50 Million
Number Employees: 20-49
Square Footage: 80000
Brands:
    Afco

18560 Alexander Machinery

P.O. Box 6446
Spartanburg, SC 29304

864-963-3624
Fax: 864-963-7018 alexcoair@aol.com

Manufacturer and exporter of pneumatic coalescer filters and system drainage equipment
President: Martin Cornelson
VP: W Spearman
Pneumatic Systems Design: Cliff Troutman
Estimated Sales: $20-50 Million
Number Employees: 20-49
Square Footage: 400000
Brands:
    Alexco

18561 Alfa Chem

2 Harbor Way
Kings Point, NY 11024-2117

516-504-0059
Fax: 516-504-0039 800-375-6869
alfachem@gmail.com www.alfachem1.com

Provides raw materials to industries such as manufacturing, repackaging, research, pharmaceutical, food and cosmetics, as well as Universities and Hospitals.
President: Alfred Khalily
    alfredkhalily@yahoo.com
Estimated Sales: $2.5 000,000
Number Employees: 1-4
Number of Products: 300
Square Footage: 7500
Type of Packaging: Private Label, Bulk

18562 Alfa Food Service
231 Millway Ave
Concord, ON L4K 3W7
Canada
905-660-2750
alfafoodservice.com
Espresso machines, coffee grinders, and pizza ovens.
Number of Brands: 5
Brands:
Fiamma
Fiorenzano
Gaggia
Pizzamaster
Quality Espresso

18563 Alfa Laval Ashbrook Simon-Hartley
10470 Deer Trail Dr
Houston, TX 77038
713-934-3160
ashbrook.sales@alfalaval.com
Manufacturer and exporter of liquid solid separation
equipment (presses) and thickeners
Project Manager: Carl Boyd
Estimated Sales: $20-50 Million
Number Employees: 250-499
Parent Co: Alfa Laval Inc
Brands:
Aquabelt
Klampress
Winklepress

18564 Alfa Laval Inc
5400 International Trade Dr
Richmond, VA 23231
Fax: 804-236-3276 866-253-2528
customerservice.usa@alfalaval.com
www.alfalaval.us
Manufacturer and exporter of centrifuges including
liquid/liquid and liquid/solid separators for edible
oil, fish, meat, starch, protein, grain, yeast, wine,
beer, coffee and sugar processing.
President & CEO: Tom Erixon
CFO: Jan Allde
Corporate Social Responsibility: Catarina Paulson
Senior VP, Communications: Peter Torstensson
Corporate General Counsel: Emma Adlerton
Executive VP, Global Sales & Service: Joakim
Vilson
President, Operations: Mikael Tyden
Year Founded: 1883
Estimated Sales: $28 Billion
Number Employees: 17,000
Parent Co: Alfa Laval AB
Brands:
Sharples

18565 Alfa Systems Inc
522 Boulevard
Westfield, NJ 07090-3208
908-654-0255
Fax: 908-654-0256 www.alfasystems.biz
Manufacturer and exporter of custom automation
equipment and packaging systems including tamper
evident packaging, print registration systems, sealer
mounted shrink tunnels, fragile product automatic
infeeders, random product bar codescanning, etc
Owner: Steve Williams
Vice President: Chuck Holata
Estimated Sales: $1.25 Million
Number Employees: 10-19
Square Footage: 6000

18566 Alfacel
20w201 101st Street
Lemont, IL 60439-9674
630-783-9702
Fax: 630-783-9780
Casings, films, laminates, flexible packages, and
shrink packaging materials
Estimated Sales: $1-2.5 000,000
Number Employees: 20-49

18567 Algene Marking Equipment Company
P.O. Box 410
Garfield, NJ 7026
973-478-9041
Fax: 973-473-3847
Manufacturer, importer and exporter of marking and
printing equipment, coders, hand marking tools, air
feed systems and indenters.

President: Milton Mann
VP/Production: Garry Mann
Plant Manager: Garry Mann
Estimated Sales: $1-1.5 Million
Number Employees: 5-9
Number of Brands: 19
Number of Products: 15
Square Footage: 10000
Brands:
Algene

18568 Alger Creations
P.O. Box 800604
Miami, FL 32380
954-454-3272
Fax: 954-239-5773
Manufacturer and exporter of plastic bags, advertis-
ing specialties, displays and exhibits; importer of in-
flatable displays.
President: Alvin Brenner
Sales/Marketing: Ogden Farray
Contact: Luisa Maichel
luisa@algercreations.com
Estimated Sales: $2.5-5 Million
Number Employees: 20-49
Number of Brands: 1
Number of Products: 100
Square Footage: 40000
Type of Packaging: Private Label

18569 Algroup
17-17 State Route 208
Fair Lawn, NJ 07410-2820
201-794-2409
Fax: 201-794-2685 800-777-1875
www.algroupint.com
Chemicals, chemical manufacturing
CEO: Sergio Marchionne
CFO: Markus Hofer
VP: Michael Newman
Number Employees: 15
Parent Co: Algroup
Type of Packaging: Bulk

18570 Algus Packaging Inc
1212 E Taylor St
Dekalb, IL 60115-4507
815-756-1881
Fax: 815-758-2281 800-266-8581
algus@algus.com www.algus.com
Packaging service providing equipment and materi-
als
Founder, President: Art Gustafson
CFO: Pat Stoner
pstoner@algus.com
Estimated Sales: $5-10 Million
Number Employees: 100-249

18571 (HQ)Ali Group
P.O. Box 4149
Winston Salem, NC 27115-4149
336-661-1556
Fax: 336-661-1979 800-532-8591
champion@championindustries.com
www.championindustries.com
Manufacturer and exporter of dishwashers, dish ta-
bles, manual and powered glass washers, pot and
pan washers and waste disposal systems
President: Dexter Laughlin
CFO: Christian Miller
CEO: Hank Holt
Estimated Sales: $20 - 50 Million
Number Employees: 100-249
Brands:
Champion
Coldelite
Moyer Diebel

18572 Aliments LUDA Foods
6200 Trans-Canadienne
Pointe-Claire, QC H9R 1B9
Canada
514-695-3333
Fax: 514-695-0281 800-267-3333
www.luda.ca
Gluten-free, vegetarian, sodium-reduced, Halal, and
Kosher soups, sauces, and custom blends.
President: Robert Eiser
Year Founded: 1951
Estimated Sales: $30 Million
Square Footage: 45000
Type of Packaging: Consumer, Food Service, Pri-
vate Label, Bulk

18573 Aline Heat Seal Corporation
13700 South Broadway
Los Angeles, CA 90061
310-715-6600
Fax: 310-715-6606 888-285-3917
alineinfo@sorbentsystems.com www.alinesys.com
Manufacturer and exporter of packaging machinery
including shrink wrap, bundling, tube, bag and blis-
ter sealing and custom heat sealers for plastic films
President: Charles Schapira
Controller: Susanna Cano
VP: John Rydgren
Marketing and Sales: Charles Schapira
Customer Service: Pat Almanza
Plant Supervisor: Domingo Ayala
Estimated Sales: $5 - 10 Million
Number Employees: 10-19
Square Footage: 20000
Brands:
Aline

18574 Aline Systems Corporation
13700 South Broadway
Los Angeles, CA 90061
310-715-6600
Fax: 310-715-6606 888-825-3917
alineinfo@sorbentsystems.com www.alinesys.com
Semi and automatic binders, shrink wrappers, heat
sealing, blister sealing and custom machinery
President: Charles Schapira
charles@alinesys.com
Controller: Susanna Cano
Vice President of Manufacturing: Julio Gonzalez
Estimated Sales: Below $5 Million
Number Employees: 10-19

18575 Alipack Americas
525 S Shore Dr
Osprey, FL 34229-9620
847-607-0591
Fax: 847-607-0592 www.alipack.it

18576 Alkar Rapid Pak
932 Development Dr
Lodi, WI 53555-1300
608-592-3211
Fax: 608-592-4039 marketing@alkar.com
www.alkar.com
Manufacturer and exporter of chillers including air
blast, brine and glycol; also, smokehouses and con-
tinuous cook/chill systems.
President: Magdy Albert
Estimated Sales: $50-100 Million
Number Employees: 20-49
Square Footage: 80000

18577 Alkar Rapid Pak
932 Development Dr
PO Box 260
Lodi, WI 53555-1300
608-592-3211
Fax: 608-592-4039
daryl.shackelford@rapidpak.com
www.alkar.com
Form/fill/seal horizontal packaging equipment,
rollstock machines
President: Jim Peterson
jim.peterson@rapidpak.com
CFO: Dave Smith
R&D: Bob Hanson
Quality Control: Dave Brathorst
Regional Sales Manager: Mike McCann
Estimated Sales: $5 - 10 Million
Number Employees: 20-49

18578 Alkar Rapid Pak
932 Development Dr
Lodi, WI 53555-1300
608-592-3211
Fax: 608-592-4039 www.alkar.com
Manufacturers of cooking and chilling systems for
the food service industry.
President: Vic Addotta
addottavic@alkar1.com
Vice President/Sales: Timothy Moskal
Number Employees: 20-49

18579 Alkar Rapid Pak
932 Development Dr
PO Box 260
Lodi, WI 53555-1300
608-592-3211
Fax: 608-592-4039
Daryl.Shackelford@rapidpak.com
www.alkar.com
Food packaging machines for cook-in turkeys, hot
dogs and string cheese.
President: Vic Addotta
addottavic@alkar1.com
Chief Financial Officer: Mary Jane Hansen
Research/Development: Seth Pulsfus
Marketing: Keith Shackleford
Plant Manager: Nick Cable
Number Employees: 20-49
Parent Co: Middleby Corporation

18580 Alkazone/Better Health Lab
200 S Newman St
Hackensack, NJ 07601-3124
201-880-7966
Fax: 201-880-7967 800-810-1888
contactus@alkazone.com www.alkazone.com
Manufacturer and exporter of antioxidant water and
alkaline mineral supplement and water ionizers.
President: Robert Kim
Estimated Sales: $5-10 Million
Number Employees: 8
Square Footage: 80000
Type of Packaging: Consumer
Brands:
Alkaline
Alkazone
Alkazone Alkaline Booster Drops
Alkazone Antioxidant Water Ionizer
Alkazone Vitamins & Herbs
Antioxidant
Better Health Lab
Bhl

18581 Alkota Cleaning SystemsInc
105 Broad St
PO Box 288
Alcester, SD 57001-2120
605-934-2222
Fax: 605-934-1808 800-255-6823
info@alkota.com www.alkota.com
Manufacturer and exporter of high-pressure washers
and parts, steam cleaners, water reclaim units and
waste water/oil separators
President: Gary Scott
CEO: Jeff Burros
burrosjeff@spellcapital.com
CEO: Joseph Bjorkman
Head of Engineering: Roger Walz
Marketing Manager: Jim Scott
VP Sales: Jeff Burros
Estimated Sales: $10-20 Million
Number Employees: 50-99
Square Footage: 50000
Brands:
Alkota

18582 All A Cart Custom Mfg
2001 Courtright Rd
Columbus, OH 43232-4216
614-443-5544
Fax: 614-443-4248 800-695-2278
jjmorris@allacart.com
Manufacturer and exporter of vending carts, kiosks,
trucks, mobile kitchens, catering vehicles and
trailers
Owner: Jeff Morris
jjmorris@allacart.com
Estimated Sales: $5 - 10 Million
Number Employees: 20-49
Square Footage: 120000
Brands:
All a Cart

18583 All About Furniture
6702 Jimmy Carter Blvd
Norcross, GA 30071
Fax: 678-916-8383 800-893-0919
www.aafllc.com
Seating products for the hospitality industry

18584 All American Container
9330 NW 110th Ave
Miami, FL 33178
305-887-0797
Fax: 305-888-4133
sales@americancontainers.com
www.allamericancontainers.com
Supplier of glass, plastic bottles and jars, can,
pumps, sprayers and atomizers.
President: Remedios Diaz-Oliver
sales@americancontainers.com
CEO: Fausto Diaz-Oliver
Estimated Sales: $120 Million
Number Employees: 100-249
Square Footage: 100000
Other Locations:
All American Containers
Tampa FL

18585 All American Poly
40 Turner Pl
Piscataway, NJ 08854-3839
732-752-2305
Fax: 732-752-5570 800-526-3551
steveb@allampoly.com www.allampoly.com
Extruders, converters and polyethylene bags includ-
ing food, meat, shopping, plastic, shrink, liners and
compactor
President: Jack Klein
jack@allampoly.com
Sales Manager: Joe Friedman
Estimated Sales: $20-50 Million
Number Employees: 50-99

18586 All American Seasonings
10600 E 54th Ave
Suite B
Denver, CO 80239-2132
303-623-2320
Fax: 303-623-1920
www.allamericanseasonings.com
Baking mixes for bread, cakes, other pasteries; as-
sorted seasoned snacks including: chips, popcorn,
nuts, & pretzels; sauces; variety of hot and cold bev-
erages, energy drinks, and mixers.
Chairman: Andy Rodriguez
Director of Quality Assurance: Mary Davis
Marketing Director: Joseph Gallagher
Year Founded: 1968
Estimated Sales: $12 Million
Number Employees: 20-49
Square Footage: 70000
Type of Packaging: Consumer, Food Service, Pri-
vate Label, Bulk
Brands:
All American

18587 All Bake Technologies
1930 Heck Avenue, Build 1
Suite 4
Neptune, NJ 07753
732-988-0060
Fax: 732-776-6418 info@allbaketech.com
www.allbaketech.com
Mixing, proofing, baking, makeup equipment, re-
tarding
President: Robert Hassell
Number Employees: 20-49

18588 All Fill Inc
418 Creamery Way
Exton, PA 19341-2536
610-524-1918
Fax: 610-524-7346 866-255-4455
info@all-fill.com www.all-fill.com
Manufacturer and exporter of auger and Liouis fill-
ing and check weighing machinery
President/CEO: Ryan Edginton
ryane@allfill.com
CFO: Bill Egan
Executive VP/General Manager: Raymond Arra Jr
VP of Sales & Marketing: Kyle Edginton
Regional Sales Manager: Raymond Arra
All-Fill Operations Manager: Rick Brennecke
Purchasing Manager: Nick Dienno
Estimated Sales: $10-20 Million
Number Employees: 20-49
Square Footage: 110000

18589 All Fill Inc
418 Creamery Way
Exton, PA 19341-2536
610-524-1918
Fax: 610-524-7346 800-334-1529
sales@all-fill.com www.all-fill.com
Powder and liquid filling machines and packaging
equipment.
President: Ryan Edginton
ryane@allfill.com
Number Employees: 20-49
Square Footage: 55000

18590 All Foils Inc
16100 Imperial Pkwy
Strongsville, OH 44149-0600
440-572-3645
Fax: 440-378-0161 800-521-0054
www.allfoils.com
Manufacturer and exporter of aluminum, foil and
sheet gauges; importer of aluminum and copper;
also, printing and laminating services available
President: Robert B Papp
rpapp@allfoils.com
Estimated Sales: $20-50 Million
Number Employees: 50-99
Square Footage: 140000
Brands:
Metalix

18591 All Packaging MachineryCorp
90 13th Ave # 11
Unit 11
Ronkonkoma, NY 11779-6818
631-588-7310
Fax: 631-467-4690 800-637-8808
sales@apmpackaging.com
www.allpackagingmachinery.com
Manufacturer and exporter of packaging machinery
and parts
President: Daniel Wood
Corp Comms: Lynn Miranda
lynn@allpackagingmachinery.com
Marketing/Sales: Lynn Miranda
Plant Manager: Dan Wood
Number Employees: 20-49
Square Footage: 80000
Parent Co: All Packaging Machinery & Supplies
Corporation
Brands:
Speedy Bag Packager

18592 All Power Inc
2228 Murray St
Sioux City, IA 51111-1148
712-258-0681
Fax: 712-258-6561 info@allpowerinc.com
www.allpowerinc.com
Manufacturer and wholesaler/distributor of packing
house equipment, trolleys, shackles and stainless
steel conveyors; also, sludge pumps, pressure ves-
sels, indexers, auto feeders and drives including
electric motor, gear boxeshydraulics and line
shafting
President: Eugene Anderson
General Manager: Gene Anderson, Jr.
Purchasing Manager: Jim Tucker
Estimated Sales: $10-20 Million
Number Employees: 50-99
Square Footage: 70000

18593 All Sorts Premium Packaging
2495 Main Street
Suite 548
Buffalo, NY 14214-2154
716-831-1622
Fax: 716-831-1630 888-565-9727
Gift basket wrap and bags
VP: Penny Duke
Estimated Sales: less than $500,000
Number Employees: 1-4
Brands:
All Sorts

18594 All Southern Fabricators
5010 126th Ave N
Clearwater, FL 33760-4607
727-571-1147
Fax: 727-573-2360 800-878-2732
asf@allsouthern.com
www.allsouthernfabricators.com
Custom stainless steel food service equipment

President: Bernie Auer
 bauer@allsouthern.com
CFO: Pav Willis
VP: Pavilyn Willis
Quality Control: Tom Richardson
Operations Manager: Tom Richardson
Estimated Sales: $10 - 20 Million
Number Employees: 50-99

18595 All Spun Metal Products
1877 Busse Hwy
Des Plaines, IL 60016

847-824-4117
Fax: 847-824-0419
Copper and stainless steel kettles; stainless steel
sheet metal fabrication services available
President: Gianfranco Isaia
General Manager: Douglas Reed
Estimated Sales: $1-2.5 Million
Number Employees: 5-9
Parent Co: Spectracrafts

18596 All Star Carts & Vehicles
1565 5th Industrial Ct # B
Bay Shore, NY 11706-3434

631-666-5581
Fax: 631-666-1319 800-831-3166
info@allstarcarts.com www.allstarcarts.com
Quality carts, kiosks, trailers and trucks for the food
service and general merchandise industries
President: Stephen Kronrad
 info@allstarcarts.com
Sales Director: Mark Weiner
VP: Robert Kronrad
Sales Executive: Michael Clark
Estimated Sales: $5 - 10 Million
Number Employees: 20-49
Square Footage: 50000

18597 All Star Dairy Foods
620 New Ludlow Rd
South Hadley, MA 01075-2669

413-538-5240
Fax: 413-532-4093 800-462-1129
www.allstardairyfoods.com
Dairy products
Owner: Russ Sawyer
Inside Sales Manager: Lynne Sawyer
 rsawyer@allstardairyfoods.com
Office Manager: Lynn Rivest
Estimated Sales: $7.5 Million
Number Employees: 20-49
Square Footage: 10400
Type of Packaging: Consumer
Other Locations:
 Schenkel's Dairy
 Fort Wayne IN

18598 All State Fabricators Corporation
1316 Tech Blvd
Tampa, FL 33619

813-626-3166
Fax: 800-867-3609 800-322-9925
www.emiindustries.com
Stainless steel food service equipment including
counters, hoods, tables, sinks, dishtables, display
cases, mobile food carts and ventless fryers
Manager: Steven Rooney
General Manager: Steven Rooney
Estimated Sales: $10 - 20 Million
Number Employees: 50-99
Square Footage: 140000
Brands:
 Auto Fry

18599 All States Caster/F.I.R
Neils Thompson Drive
Suite 113
Austin, TX 78758-7653

512-832-9821
Fax: 512-832-9834 800-234-3882
daves@allstatescasters.com
www.allstatesequip.com
President: Dave Spencer
Estimated Sales: $5 - 10 Million
Number Employees: 10-19

18600 All Valley Packaging
PO Box 63201
Colorado Springs, CO 80962-3201

Fax: 425-650-5090
Printed boxes, labels, bags, pouches, food service
containers, pallets, janitorial maintenance supply

President: Cheryl Mikel
VP/Sales: Steve Hobden
Purchasing Manager: Cheryl Mikel
Number Employees: 5
Number of Brands: 100+
Number of Products: 1000
Type of Packaging: Food Service, Private Label
Brands:
 3m
 Clorox
 Dixie
 Dow
 Dupont
 Reynolds
 Rubbermaid
 Solo

18601 All Weather Energy Systems
PO Box 701064
Plymouth, MI 48170-0958

888-636-8324
Fax: 888-636-8304 escheatzle@aol.com
Door and dock leveler sealing systems, brushes, gas-
kets, containment seals, dust and infiltration control
systems and pest control devices; design and instal-
lation services available
Owner/President: Elizabeth Scheatzle
Sales/Marketing Executive: Molly McCarville
Purchasing Agent: Mario Derrick
Number Employees: 5
Square Footage: 5000

18602 All-Clad METALCRAFTERS LLC
424 Morganza Rd
Canonsburg, PA 15317-5716

724-745-8300
Fax: 724-746-5035 800-255-2523
www.all-clad.com
Manufacturer and exporter of stainless steel, alumi-
num and copper cookware and utensils.
CEO: Peter Cameron
Manager: Hideyuki Nishizawa
 hnishizawa@tubecityims.com
Estimated Sales: $20-50 Million
Number Employees: 100-249
Parent Co: Clad Metals
Brands:
 Cop*R*Chef
 Master Chef Ltd.
 Stainless

18603 All-Right Enterprises
2307 Conciliation Lane
Green Cove Springs, FL 32043-8240
Canada

904-400-1245
Fax: 604-528-6103 lallright@aol.com
Principal: Vern Smith

18604 All-State Industries Inc
520 S 18th St
West Des Moines, IA 50265-6449

515-223-5843
Fax: 515-223-8305 800-247-4178
dsmsales@all-statebelting.com
www.all-stateind.com
Wholesaler/distributor of food handling belting for
conveyors
President: Doug Berner
 dberner@all-statebelting.com
Vice President: Casey Price
Research & Development: Doug Tibkin
Quality Control: Sherry Wilkinson
Estimated Sales: $20 - 50 Million
Number Employees: 10-19
Parent Co: All-State Industries

18605 All-State Industries Inc
520 S 18th St
West Des Moines, IA 50265-6449

515-223-5843
Fax: 515-223-8305 info@all-stateind.com
www.all-stateind.com
Food handling belting for conveyors and pulleys
President: Doug Berner
 dberner@all-statebelting.com
Estimated Sales: $20 - 50 Million
Number Employees: 10-19
Square Footage: 120000

18606 AllPoints Foodservice
607 W Dempster St
Mt. Prospect, IL 60056

www.allpointsfps.com
Replacement parts and supplies for commercial
cooking and refrigeration equipment
VP, Sales: Eric Trelstad
Year Founded: 1983
Number Employees: 51-200

18607 Alleghany Highlands Economic Development Authority
322 W Riverside St
Covington, VA 24426

540-862-6673
Fax: 540-962-8425 www.heartofva.org
Owner: Steve Bowers
Estimated Sales: $1 - 3 Million
Number Employees: 5-9

18608 Allegheny Bradford Corp
P.O. Box 200
Bradford, PA 16701

814-362-2590
Fax: 814-362-2574 800-542-0650
sales@alleghenybradford.com
www.alleghenybradford.com
Manufacturer and exporter of sanitary stainless steel
heat exchangers, filter housings, tanks, pressure vessels, manifolds and modular process systems; custom fabrication available
President & CEO: Dan McCune
 dmccune@alleghenybradford.com
Estimated Sales: $50 - 100 Million
Number Employees: 50-99
Square Footage: 40000

18609 Allegheny Technologies Inc
1000 Six PPG Place
Pittsburgh, PA 15222

412-394-2800
800-289-7454
www.atimetals.com
Manufacturer of titanium, nickle, cobalt and other
materials; also, machine components.
Chair: Diane Creel
President & CEO: Robert Wetherbee
SVP, Finance & Chief Financial Officer: Don
Newman
SVP & Chief Commercial/Marketing Officer: Kevin
Kramer
EVP, High Performance Materials Segment: John
Sims
VP, Environmental Affairs: Lauren McAndrews
VP, Investor Relations: Scott Minder
Year Founded: 1996
Estimated Sales: $4 Billion
Number Employees: 8,600

18610 Allen Coding & Marking Systems
501 90th Avenue NW
Minneapolis, MN 55433-8005

763-783-2734
Fax: 763-783-2580 877-611-1711
www.allencoding.com
Coding and marking equipment, hot stamp and ther-
mal processes
Estimated Sales: $500,000-$1 Million
Number Employees: 10

18611 Allen Gauge & Tool Co
421 N Braddock Ave
Pittsburgh, PA 15208-2514

412-241-6410
Fax: 412-242-8877 info@allengauges.com
www.allengauges.com
Manufacturer and exporter of sausage linking ma-
chinery and other meat processing equipment
Owner: Charles Allen
Manager: C Moekle
Number Employees: 10-19
Parent Co: Allen Gauge & Tool Company

18612 (HQ)Allen Industries Inc
6434 Burnt Poplar Rd
Greensboro, NC 27409-9712

336-668-2791
Fax: 336-668-7875 800-967-2553
info@allenindustries.com
www.allenindustries.com
Menu boards, advertising and electric signs
President: Tom Allen
 jenny.seamster@allenindustires.com
VP: John Allen

Estimated Sales: $10-20 Million
Number Employees: 250-499
Other Locations:
   Allen Industries
   Clearwater FL

18613 Allen Signs Co
2408 Chapman Hwy
Knoxville, TN 37920-1910

865-579-1683
Fax: 865-579-0356 800-844-3524
www.allensign.com
Manufacturer and exporter of advertising specialties,
flags, pennants, banners, electric signs, lighting and
flag poles, etc.; also, sign painting services available
Owner: Tom Allen
  tom@allensign.com
CFO: Tom Allen
Public Relations: Scott Marshall
Operations Manager: Benjamin Booker
Plant Manager: Andrew Asbury
Estimated Sales: Below $5,000,000
Number Employees: 10-19
Square Footage: 7500

18614 Allenair Corp
255 E 2nd St
Mineola, NY 11501-3524

516-747-5450
Fax: 516-747-5481 info@allenair.com
All stainless steel air cylinders
Owner: John Allen
CFO: Linda Johanson
  linda@allenair.com
Research Manager: Wayne Butner
Quality Control Director: Daniel Palladino
Sales Manager: Waler Scheid
Marketing Manager: Steve Santoriello
Human Resources Manager: Virginia Amato
Plant Manager: Stephen Werlinitsch
Purchasing Manager: Tin Byrnes
Estimated Sales: $12 Million
Number Employees: 100-249
Square Footage: 150000

18615 Allendale Cork Company
4 Walnut St
Rye, NY 10579

914-921-2787
Fax: 914-967-9605 800-816-2675
Manufacturer and exporter of wine and tapered cork
stoppers and champagne corks; importer of cork
President: Dale Balun
Vice President: Ken Queen
Contact: Ken Queen
  ken12564@aol.com
Estimated Sales: $1-2,500,000
Number Employees: 10-19

18616 Allergen Air Filter Corp
5205 Ashbrook Dr
Houston, TX 77081-2903

713-668-2371
Fax: 713-668-6815 800-333-8880
Air filters
President: Michael Horan
Estimated Sales: Below $5 Million
Number Employees: 5-9

18617 Allflex Packaging Products
105 Race St
Ambler, PA 19002-4423

215-542-9200
Fax: 215-643-3339 800-448-2467
sales@allflex.com www.allflex.com
Promotional sales kits, material handling totes, trays
and bins, cases, insulated and hazardous material
containers and protective packaging
President: Joel Cohen
Marketing Director: Kristine Koelzer
Purchasing Manager: Joy Rudegeair
Estimated Sales: $3 - 5 Million
Number Employees: 10-19

18618 Alliance Bakery Systems
130 Northpoint Court
Blythewood, SC 29016-8875

803-691-9227
Fax: 803-691-9239
Equipment: baking systems, dough handling, trans-
port and sheeting lines
President: Cory Bolkestein
Estimated Sales: $10-20 Million
Number Employees: 19

18619 Alliance Industrial Corp
208 Tomahawk Industrial Park
Lynchburg, VA 24502-4153

434-239-2642
Fax: 434-239-5692 800-368-3556
www.allianceindustrial.com
Designer and manufacturer of conveying systems,
material handling machinery, and controls. Spiral
Conveyers for bulk and case, Depalletisers, Eleva-
tors, and Lowerators for can, bottle and case, rinsers,
case switches, bulk case, andair conveyer systems
and much more.
President: Bob Abbott
  babbott@allianceindustrial.com
Marketing/Sales: David Loyd
Sales Manager: Wayne Walker
Purhasing: Todd Farrar
Estimated Sales: $20-50 Million
Number Employees: 100-249
Square Footage: 80000

18620 Alliance Knife Inc
124 May Dr
Harrison, OH 45030-2024

513-367-9000
Fax: 513-367-2233 800-852-7447
contactus@allianceknife.com
www.allianceknife.com
Produces and markets paper trimming knives, press
knives, sheeters, slitter, granulator blades,
woodworking knives, and packaging knives, as well
as knives for the metal converting industry.
Owner: Lonnie Keith
  akiknife@aol.com
Estimated Sales: $5 - 10 000,000
Number Employees: 20-49

18621 Alliance Products LLC
820 Esther Ln
Murfreesboro, TN 37129-5536

615-895-5333
Fax: 615-895-5334 800-522-3973
jparker@allianceproducts.net
www.allianceproducts.net
Custom and stock metal carts, nonpowered convey-
ors, heated cabinets, racks, heaters and proofers
President: Scott Marshall
  smarshall@allianceproducts.net
Marketing Manager: Donna Sikes
Engineering Manager: Scott Marshall
Estimated Sales: $5 - 10 Million
Number Employees: 20-49
Square Footage: 80000
Parent Co: Win-Holt Equipment
Brands:
  Alliance

18622 Alliance Rubber Co
210 Carpenter Dam Rd
Hot Springs, AR 71901-8219

501-262-2700
Fax: 501-262-5268 800-626-5940
sales@alliance-rubber.com www.rubberband.com
Manufacturer and exporter of imprinted rubber
bands for brand identification, logos, produce, etc.;
also, UPC imprinted tape for produce
Owner: Lance Gyldenege
Marketing Manager: Jason Risa
Sales Manager: Rachel Atkinson
  lance_gyldenege@msn.com
Operations Manager: Brandon Hughes
Estimated Sales: $50 - 100 Million
Number Employees: 100-249
Number of Brands: 10
Number of Products: 4500
Square Footage: 160000
Type of Packaging: Consumer, Food Service, Pri-
vate Label, Bulk
Brands:
  Advantage
  Alliance
  Eco
  Pale Crepe Gold
  Protape
  Sterling

18623 Alliance Shippers Inc
516 Sylvan Ave
Englewood Cliffs, NJ 07632-3022

201-227-0400
Fax: 201-227-1212 800-222-0451
www.alliance.com
President: Leona Allen
  leona_allen@alliance.com

Estimated Sales: $10 - 20 Million
Number Employees: 20-49

18624 Alliance/PMS
267 Livingston St
Northvale, NJ 07647-1901

201-784-1101
Fax: 201-784-1116 www.wcbicecream.com
Encapsulation equipment, qualification, validation
and rebuilding services
Owner: Neal White
Estimated Sales: $10 - 20 Million
Number Employees: 50-99
Square Footage: 34000
Parent Co: SBX

18625 Allied Adhesive Corporation
P.O. Box 1866
Baldwin, NY 11510-8566

718-846-3200
President: Steve Pollack
Estimated Sales: $1 - 3 Million
Number Employees: 5-9

18626 Allied Bakery and Food Service Equipment
12015 E. Slauson Ave
Suite K
Santa Fe Springs, CA 90670-8542

562-945-6506
Fax: 562-945-4282 info@alliedbake.com
www.alliedbake.com
Supplier of bakery equipment and systems
President: Roger Harsted
CFO: Phillis Markle
Estimated Sales: $5 - 10 Million
Number Employees: 10-19

18627 Allied Electric Sign & Awning
1920 S 900 W
Salt Lake City, UT 84104-1723

801-972-6837
Fax: 801-972-5670 www.allied-sign.com
Commercial awnings
President: Chris Blake
  chris@allied-sign.com
Estimated Sales: Below $5 Million
Number Employees: 20-49

18628 (HQ)Allied Engineering
94 Riverside Drive
North Vancouver, BC V7H 2M6
Canada

604-929-1214
Fax: 604-929-5184 877-929-1214
sales@alliedboilers.com www.alliedboilers.com
Manufacturers of gas and electric boilers, tankless
coils and electric boosters.
President: George Gilbert
Quality Control: Brad Gilbert
Marketing Director: Garry Epstein
Sales Director: T Weaver
Operations Manager: Urbano Pandin
Plant Manager: Howard Larlee
Purchasing Manager: Harry Bowker
Number Employees: 60
Square Footage: 340000
Brands:
  Aae Series
  E-Z-Rect
  Mini-Gas Series
  Saturn Series
  Super Hot
  Trim-Line
  Type 1

18629 Allied Gear & Machine Company
1101 Research Blvd.
St Louis, MO 63132

314-991-5900
Fax: 314-991-5911 800-896-1989
Sales@alliedgear.com www.alliedgear.com
General Manager: Skip Liu
Technical Manager: Amy Zhang
Regional Sales Manager: Dan Jahn
Contact: Tom Serra
  tom@alliedgear.com
Estimated Sales: $1 - 5 Million

18630 Allied Glove Corporation
433 E Stewart St
Milwaukee, WI 53207

414-481-0900
Fax: 414-481-0700 800-558-9263

Manufacturer, importer and exporter of safety products and disposable wear for food handlers including industrial gloves and X-ray protective materials
Manager: Sarah Cunningham
VP: Ray Sroka
Plant Manager: Dan Sroka
Estimated Sales: $1 - 3 Million
Number Employees: 10-19
Square Footage: 300000
Brands:
  Security
  Superguard
  White Hawk

18631 Allied Metal Spinning
1290 Viele Ave
Bronx, NY 10474-7133
718-893-3300
Fax: 718-589-5780 800-615-2266
www.alliedmetalusa.com
Woks, cake rings, pizza screens, trays, cutters and bakery, pizza and chinese cooking utensils; also, pans including cake, pie, pizza, black nonstick, anodized, sheet extenders, etc. Importer of 2000 items to complement manufacturedline
Owner: Arlene Saunders
  alliedsteam@aol.com
Plant Manager: Carlos Heredia
Purchasing Manager: Arlene Saunders
Number Employees: 20-49
Type of Packaging: Food Service, Private Label, Bulk

18632 Allied Purchasing Co
1334 18th St SW
Mason City, IA 50401-5602
641-423-1824
Fax: 641-423-2346 800-247-5956
brian@alliedpurchasing.com
www.alliedpurchasing.com
Equipment, supplies, ingredients and services for the dairy, soft drink, bottled water, water treatment and brewery industries.
President/CFO: Brian Janssen
  brian@alliedpurchasing.com
EVP: Steve Husome
Customer Service: Angela Stadtlander
Senior Account Manager - Bottled Water: Kari Mondt
Number Employees: 10-19
Square Footage: 10500
Type of Packaging: Food Service

18633 Allied Trades of the Baking Industry
PO Box 1853
Sonoma, CA 95476-1853
847-920-9885
Fax: 847-920-9886 www.atbi.org

18634 Allied Uniking Corp Inc
4750 Cromwell Ave
Memphis, TN 38118-6367
901-365-7240
Fax: 901-365-7306
Conveyors including overhead monorail, overhead power and free and inverted power and free
President: Kenneth Anderson
CFO: Mike Baker
VP: Dolph Stritzel
Quality Control: Sharron Dean
IT Executive: Mark Coward
  mcoward@allieduniking.com
Estimated Sales: $20 - 50 Million
Number Employees: 10-19
Square Footage: 100000

18635 Allione Agrifood USA
10390 Wilshire Boulevard
Apt 608
Los Angeles, CA 90024-6409
310-271-3663
Fax: 310-271-3664
Fruit processing, preparations, aromatic herbs, customized products, technology, quality control

18636 Allison Systems Inc
245 Regency Ct # L120
Suite 210
Brookfield, WI 53045-6157
262-522-9800
Fax: 262-522-9600 800-536-9077
info@allisonsystems.com

Owner: John Travares
  j_travares@allisonblades.com
Estimated Sales: $1 - 5 Million
Number Employees: 5-9

18637 Allmark Impressions LTD
823 N Riverside Dr
Fort Worth, TX 76111-4249
817-834-0080
Fax: 817-838-2315 allmark7@aol.com
www.allmarkimpressions.com
Rubber stamps
President: Nancy Menchaca
  allmark7@aol.com
Estimated Sales: $1-2.5 Million
Number Employees: 10-19

18638 Alloy Cast Products Inc
700 Swenson Dr
Kenilworth, NJ 07033-1326
908-245-2255
Fax: 908-245-3267 rexalloy@aol.com
www.alloycastproducts.com
President: Frank Panico
  fpanico@alloycastproducts.com
Estimated Sales: $3 - 5 Million
Number Employees: 10-19

18639 Alloy Fab
200 Ryan St.
South Plainfield, NJ 07080-4208
908-753-9393
President: Larry Schillings
Estimated Sales: $10 - 20 Million
Number Employees: 50-99

18640 Alloy Hardfacing & Engineering
20425 Johnson Memorial Dr
Jordan, MN 55352-9518
952-492-5569
Fax: 952-492-3100 800-328-8408
juliek@alloyhardfacing.net
www.alloyhardfacing.com
Manufacturer and exporter of primary waste water equipment, CIP-option pumps, heat exchangers and custom cooking vessels
President: Mark Aulik
  paulr@alloyhardfacing.net
Sales Director: Paul Rothenberger
Estimated Sales: $5-10 Million
Number Employees: 20-49

18641 Alloy Products Corp
1045 Perkins Ave
Waukesha, WI 53186-5249
262-542-6603
Fax: 262-542-5421 800-236-6603
info@alloyproductscorp.com
www.alloyproductscorp.com
Stainless steel pharmaceutical, bio-tech, specialty chemicals and hygenic tanks; also, UN transport and ASME portable pressure vessels
President: Joseph E. Vick
  jvick@alloyproductscorp.com
CFO: Robert Rosenkranz
Executive VP: Betsy Bear Hoff
Engineering & Quality Assurance: Ray Woo
Sales & Customer Service: Pat Pajerski
Customer Service Representative: Matt Gamble
Estimated Sales: $10-20 Million
Number Employees: 100-249
Square Footage: 200000

18642 Alloy Wire Belt Company
2318 Tenaya Dr
Modesto, CA 95354
410-901-2660
Fax: 410-901-2680 877-649-7492
sales@cambridge-es.com www.alloywirebelt.com
Market Sales Manager: Cory Bloodsworth
Market Sales Manager: Melissa Lewis
Contact: Gene Ford
  gene@alloywirebelt.com
Plant Manager: Gene Ford
Estimated Sales: $1 - 5 Million
Number Employees: 10-19

18643 Alloyd Brands
1401 Pleasant St
Dekalb, IL 60115-2663
815-756-8452
Fax: 815-756-5187 800-756-7639
info@alloyd.com www.tegrant.com

Formerly SCA Consumer Packaging, manufacturers of light-gauge custom thermoformed retail packaging.
President: Ron Leach
Vice President of Business Development: Prakash Mahesh
Marketing: Rob VanGilse
Contact: Joy Butzke
  jbutzke@alloyd.com
Estimated Sales: $20 - 50 Million
Number Employees: 1-4
Type of Packaging: Bulk

18644 Allpac
P.O. Box 565685
Dallas, TX 75356-5685
214-630-8804
Fax: 214-630-3912
Horizontal fin seal wrapping machines
President: Lawrence D Lakey
VP of Sales/Marketing: Cheryl DiMarzio
Estimated Sales: $2.5-5 Million
Number Employees: 20-49

18645 Allpax Products
13510 Seymour Meyers Blvd
Covington, LA 70433-6879
985-893-9277
Fax: 985-893-9477 888-893-9277
info@allpax.com
Manufacturer and exporter of loading, unloading and shuttle systems, retorts, autoclaves and control software. Equipment manufactured for the following products: dairy, meat, produce, seafood, and beverages.
VP & General Manager: Greg Jacob
  steveh@allpax.com
VP, Sales: Scott Williams
Estimated Sales: $30-40 Million
Number Employees: 50-99
Type of Packaging: Consumer, Food Service
Brands:
  2404
  Monitor
  Paxware
  Rotopax
  Stillpax

18646 Allsorts Premium Packaging
2495 Main St Ste 548
Buffalo, NY 14214
716-831-1622
Fax: 800-301-5301 888-565-9727
Gift basket packaging specialists, basket bags, candy bags, tissue paper
Business Manager: Rosemarie Duke
Estimated Sales: Less than $500,000
Number Employees: 1-4

18647 Allstate Can Corporation
1 Woodhollow Rd
Parsippany, NJ 07054-2821
973-560-9030
Fax: 973-560-9217 tincans@allstatecan.com
www.allstatecan.com
Decorative stock tins, to include round, square and rectangular shapes
President: Joseph Papera
CEO: Dave West
Estimated Sales: $5 - 10 Million
Number Employees: 50-99

18648 Allstate Food & Marketing Inc
2251 Lynx Lane
Suie 10
Orlando, FL 32804
321-400-5779
Foodservice sales and marketing agency focused on manufacturers who sell to the restaurant and hospitality industries.
Year Founded: 1986
Estimated Sales: $50-100 Million
Number Employees: 100
Square Footage: 13400
Type of Packaging: Food Service

18649 Allstate Manufacturing Company
20 East Seventh Street
PO Box 326
Manchester, OH 45144
937-549-3133
Fax: 937-549-2709 800-262-2340
sales@allstatemfgco.com www.allstatemfgco.com
Portable display cases

President: Joel Birnbaum
Contact: Contactfirs Contactlastnam
  jeff@solterra.us
Estimated Sales: $500,000-$1 Million
Number Employees: 5-9

18650 (HQ)Allstrong Restaurant Eqpt Inc

1839 Durfee Ave
South El Monte, CA 91733-3708

626-448-7878
Fax: 626-448-7838 800-933-8913
www.allstrong.com

Manufacturer and exporter of Chinese woks, exhaust systems and stainless steel work and steam tables
President: Yuancansing Situ
Manager: Yuan Situ
  yuan.situ@allstronginc.com
General Manager: Ken Situ
Estimated Sales: Less than $500,000
Number Employees: 20-49
Other Locations:
  Allstrong Restaurant Equipmen
  Alhambra CA
Brands:
  Allstrong

18651 Alltech Inc

3031 Catnip Hill Rd
Nicholasville, KY 40356-9765

859-885-9613
Fax: 859-887-3223 globalfoods@alltech.com
www.alltech.com

Bulk supplier and manufacture natural, safe, and environmental products that enhance crop production
President: T Pearse Lyons
Cmo: Elizabeth Bagby
  ebagby@alltech.com
Product Manager: Elizabeth Graves
Estimated Sales: $20-50 Million
Number Employees: 500-999
Type of Packaging: Bulk

18652 Alluserv

4900 W Electric Ave
West Milwaukee, WI 53219

414-902-6400
Fax: 414-902-6446 800-558-8565
info@elakeside.com alluserv.com

Equipment for healthcare food service meal assembly and delivery
President/Owner: Joe Carlson
Principal: Larry Moon
General Manager: Tony Yenzer

18653 Allylix Inc

7220 Trade St
Suite 209
San Diego, CA 92121

858-909-0595
Fax: 858-909-0695 info@allylix.com
www.allylix.com

Terpene products and derivatives; food ingredients.
President & CEO: Carolyn Fritz
VP Business Development: Seth Goldblum
VP Research & Development: Richard Burlingame
  sgoldblum@allylix.com
VP Sales & Marketing: Leandro Nonino
Contact: Seth Goldblum
  sgoldblum@allylix.com
Estimated Sales: $280,000
Number Employees: 5-9

18654 Alnor Instrument Company

7555 Linder Avenue
Skokie, IL 60077-3223

800-424-7427
Fax: 847-677-3539 www.alnor-usa.com

Measuring equipment including air volume, air velocity, humidity, pressure and temperature
Marketing Communications Manager: Danielle Kenney
National Sales Manager: John Rose
General Manager: Alan Traylor
Number Employees: 50-99
Parent Co: TSI

18655 Aloe Hi-Tech

7921 NW South River Drive
Medley, FL 33166-2515

305-884-0399
Fax: 305-884-0365

Aloe vera raw materials
Estimated Sales: $1 - 5 000,000

18656 Alouf Plastics

4 Glenshaw St
Orangeburg, NY 10962-1207

845-512-8864
Fax: 845-365-2294 800-394-2247
ron.s@alufplastics.com www.alufplastics.com

Plastic and polyethylene bags
President: Reuven Rosenberg
Estimated Sales: $20 - 50 Million
Number Employees: 10-19
Parent Co: API Industries
Brands:
  Commander

18657 Alpack

69 Holly Point Rd
Centerville, NA 2632

774-994-8086
Fax: 774-994-8170 www.alpackplastics.com

Plastic boxes, bottles, jars and packaging components
President: Joseph Kopelman
Type of Packaging: Consumer

18658 Alpert/Siegel & Associates

3272 Motor Ave
Suite J
Los Angeles, CA 90034

310-571-0777
Fax: 310-826-8311 www.asaproperty.com

Consultant providing site selection for restaurants
Co Founder/ Chief Property Manager: Abe Skaletzky
Estimated Sales: $500,000 - $1,000,000
Number Employees: 1-4

18659 Alpha Associates

2 Amboy Avenue
Woodbridge, NJ 07095-2699

732-634-5700
Fax: 732-634-1430 800-631-5399
ranton@alphainc.com www.alphainc.com

Industrial, coated, laminated and fiberglass insulation materials
President: Christopher Avallone
Contact: Kevin Burton
  kburton@alphainc.com
Estimated Sales: $20-50 Million
Number Employees: 50-99

18660 Alpha Associates Inc

145 Lehigh Ave
Lakewood, NJ 08701-4527

732-634-5700
Fax: 732-634-1430 800-631-5399
www.alphainc.com

President: Christopher Avallone
  cavallone@alphainc.com
Estimated Sales: $1 - 5 Million
Number Employees: 50-99

18661 Alpha Canvas & Awning Co

411 E 13th St
Charlotte, NC 28206-3310

704-333-1581
Fax: 704-333-1599 800-583-9179
www.alphacanvas.com

Commercial awnings
Owner: Angela Riggins
Quality Control: Eric Regans
VP: Brian Regans
Secretary: Jane Riggins
Estimated Sales: $1 - 2,500,000
Number Employees: 10-19
Square Footage: 8800

18662 Alpha Checkweigher

418 Creamery Way
Exton, PA 19341-2536

610-524-7350
Fax: 610-524-7346 www.all-fill.com

President: Glenn Edginton
Contact: Brian Jones
  brianj@alphacheckweighers.com
Estimated Sales: $20 - 50 Million
Number Employees: 50-99

18663 Alpha Gear Drives Inc

1249 Humbracht Cir
Bartlett, IL 60103-1606

630-540-5300
Fax: 847-439-0755 888-534-1222
info@wittenstein-us.com

Motion control products and planetary gear reducers

President: Karl Heinz Schwarz
General Manager/VP: Tim Herbst
Marketing: Ronald Larsen
National Sales Manager: Ray Hamilton
Contact: Mike Anselmo
  manselmo@alphagear.com
Estimated Sales: $15 000,000
Number Employees: 35

18664 Alpha MOS America

7502 Connelley Drive
Suite 110
Hanover, MD 21076-1075

410-553-9736
Fax: 410-553-9871 800-257-4249
www.alpha-mos.com

Importer of inspection and analysis instrumentation and systems including electronic nose for testing shelf life, spoilage & mishandling.
CEO: Jean-Paul Ansel
General Manager: Andrew Cowell
Estimated Sales: $1-2.5 Million
Number Employees: 5-9
Parent Co: Alpha MOS Sa

18665 (HQ)Alpha Omega Technology

14 Ridgedale Avenue #110
Cedar Knolls, NJ 07927-1106

973-537-0073
Fax: 973-292-4999 800-442-1969
info@karibafarms.com www.karibafarms.com

Designer, builder and wholesaler/distributor of turn-key facilities; also, irradiation processing facility for the sanitation and sterilization of food ingredients
CEO: Martin Welt
Office Manager: Ruth Welt
Estimated Sales: $500,000-$1 Million
Number Employees: 5-9
Square Footage: 120000

18666 Alpha Packaging

1555 Page Industrial Blvd
St Louis, MO 63132-1309

314-427-4300
Fax: 314-427-5445 800-421-4772
www.alphap.com

Manufacturer and exporter of jars, bottles and caps
CEO: David Spence
  ds@alphaplastic.com
CFO: Jim Flower
VP: Dan Creston
R&D: Robert Wilson
Quality Control: Shane Vorden
Sales: Paul Bonastia
Operations Manager: Roy Allen
Plant Manager: Darren Viernes
Estimated Sales: $20-50 Million
Number Employees: 100-249
Square Footage: 210000

18667 Alpha Productions Inc

5800 W Jefferson Blvd
Los Angeles, CA 90016-3109

310-559-1364
Fax: 310-559-2151 800-223-0883
john@alphaproductions.com
www.alphaproductions.com

Retractable awnings
President: Missak Azirian
  service@alphaproductions.com
Sales Manager: Howard Goldstein
Estimated Sales: $2.5-5 Million
Number Employees: 20-49

18668 Alpha Resources Inc

3090 Johnson Rd
Stevensville, MI 49127-1270

269-465-3629
Fax: 269-465-3629 800-833-3083
sales@alpharesources.com
www.alpharesources.com

Aftermarket parts Perkin Elmer, Leco & Specto machinery.
President: Phil Lunsford
  alphares@aol.com
Number Employees: 20-49

18669 AlphaBio Inc

29816 Avenida De Las Banderas
Rancho Santa Maragarita, CA 92688

949-858-4999
Fax: 949-858-4994 800-966-0716

Sanitary pumps

Account Manager: Sean Pursaid
Estimated Sales: $25 Million
Number Employees: 100

18670 Alphabet Signs
91 Newport Rd # 102
Gap, PA 17527-9579

610-979-0174
Fax: 610-979-0066 800-582-6366
info@alphabetsigns.com www.alphabetsigns.com
Retailer of restaurant signs
President: Daniel Keane
Contact: Dan Keane
dan@alphabetsigns.com
Estimated Sales: Less Than $500,000
Number Employees: 1-4
Square Footage: 5000

18671 Alphasonics
15 Cottondale Rd
The Hills, TX 78738-1513

512-837-8088
Estimated Sales: $3 - 5 Million
Number Employees: 5-9

18672 Alpine Store Equipment Corporation
3710 10th St
Long Island City, NY 11101-6005

718-361-1213
Fax: 718-786-1220
Self-service food bars, restaurant counters and equipment
Estimated Sales: $2.5-5 Million
Number Employees: 20-49

18673 Alro Plastics
3100 E High St
Jackson, MI 49203-3467

517-787-5500
Fax: 517-787-6390 800-877-2576
aglick@alro.com www.alro.com
Engineering plastics parts and shapes, delrin, teflon, UHMW, nylon, polycarbonate, Ertalyte Pet - P & TX, fiberglass grating and structurals
President: Dean Davis
CEO: Al Glick
aglick@alro.com
Quality Control: Mike Mraz
CEO: Al Glick
Estimated Sales: $20 Million
Number Employees: 20-49
Parent Co: Alro Steel Corporation
Type of Packaging: Bulk

18674 Alstor America
PO Box 98
Stockbridge, WI 53088-0098

920-439-1777
Fax: 920-439-1002 pekaty1@fox.tds.net
Stainless steel, galvanized and epoxy coated bolted tanks, silos and bins for processing and storage of liquids, solids and semi-solids

Type of Packaging: Bulk

18675 Alta Refrigeration Inc
403 Dividend Dr
Peachtree City, GA 30269-1905

678-554-1100
Fax: 678-554-1111 alexg@cold4u.com
www.altarefrigeration.com
Owner: Rex Brown
alta@cold4you.com
Estimated Sales: $10 - 20 Million
Number Employees: 50-99

18676 Alteca Limited
731 Mccall Rd
Manhattan, KS 66502-5037

785-537-9773
Fax: 785-537-1800 alteca@alteca.com
Food and beverage research and inspection
President: Lynn Bates
info@alteca.com
Marketing/Advertising: Lisa Bardmment
Estimated Sales: $500,000
Number Employees: 5-9

18677 Altech
888 Gilbert Highway
Fairfield, CT 06824-1645

203-259-1525
Fax: 203-259-1527 www.altech.co.jp

Anti-microbial materials, long term anto-mite solution and anti-static agent for thermoplastic materials
President: Hirokazu Yuri

18678 Altech Packaging Company
330 Himrod St
Brooklyn, NY 11237

718-386-8800
Fax: 718-366-2398 800-362-2247
mitchell@altechpackaging.com
www.altechpackaging.com
Company is a wholesaler of packaging/recycling management.
President: Mitchell Lomazow
chicoman57@aol.com
Estimated Sales: $4 000,000
Number Employees: 10-19
Number of Brands: 50
Number of Products: 300
Square Footage: 45000

18679 Altek Co
245 E Elm St
Torrington, CT 06790-5059

860-482-7626
Fax: 860-496-7113 info@altekcompany.com
www.altekcompany.com
Manufacturer and exporter of can testing equipment; also, food and beverage can and bottle testing services available
President: Stephen Altschuler
steve@altekcompany.com
Marketing: Brian Mazurkivich
Office Manager: David Altschuler
Estimated Sales: $10-20,000,000
Number Employees: 100-249
Square Footage: 46000
Brands:
Tech

18680 Altek Industries Corporation
35 Vantage Point Drive
Rochester, NY 14624-1142

716-349-3500
Contact: John Devoldre
jdevoldre@altekcalibrators.com

18681 Alternative Air & StoreFixtures Company
30 Echo Lane
Willingboro, NJ 08046

609-267-5870
Fax: 609-261-5531 aainfo@aafixtures.com
www.aafixtures.com
Display Fixtures
Contact: Mike Banks
mbanks@airalternative.com

18682 Althor Products
2 Turnage Lane
Bethel, CT 06801-2853

203-830-6060
Fax: 203-830-6064 800-688-2693
althor640@aol.com www.althor.com
FDA approved containers
President: Harold Shupack
Sales Manager: Judy Vivone
Estimated Sales: $1-2.5 Million
Number Employees: 5-9
Square Footage: 48000
Parent Co: American Hinge Corporation

18683 Altira Inc
3225 NW 112th St
Miami, FL 33167-3330

305-687-8074
Fax: 305-688-8029 sales@altira.com
www.altira.com
Manufacturer and exporter of blow molded plastic bottles; also, silk screening, pressure sensitive labeling and hot stamping available
President: Ramon Poo
Vice President: Concepcion Alonso
alonso@altira.com
General Manager: Art Hammel
Estimated Sales: $10-20 Million
Number Employees: 100-249

18684 Altman Industries
699 Altman Road
Gray, GA 31032-3431

478-986-3116
Fax: 478-986-1699

Manufacturer and exporter of processing machinery for peppers, citrus fruits, cabbage, cauliflower, carrots, celery, etc
President: James E Altman
OFC Administrator: Jeri Hastings
Secretary: Gwen Jones
Estimated Sales: Below $5 Million
Number Employees: 10
Square Footage: 40000

18685 Alto-Shaam
W164n9221 Water St
P.O. Box 450
Menomonee Falls, WI 53052

262-251-7067
800-329-8744
www.alto-shaam.com
Warming ovens, low temperature cook and holding equipment, hot deli display cases, smokers, combination oven/steamers, quick chillers, fryers and convection ovens.
President: Steve Maahs
stevem@alto-shaam.com
Director, Finance: Kevin Noonan
Vice President, Marketing: John Muldowney
Year Founded: 1950
Estimated Sales: $29 Million
Number Employees: 250-499
Number of Brands: 3
Number of Products: 200
Square Footage: 350000
Type of Packaging: Food Service
Brands:
Combitherm
Frytech
Halo Heat
Quickchiller

18686 Altra Industrial Motion Corp
300 Granite St.
Suite 201
Braintree, MA 02184

781-917-0600
Fax: 781-843-0709 info@altramotion.com
www.altramotion.com
Wide range of mechanical power transmission products.
Chairman/CEO: Carl Christenson
Vice President/CFO: Christian Storch
EVP, Legal & HR: Glenn Deegan
VP, Marketing & Business Development: Craig Schuele
Year Founded: 2004
Estimated Sales: $1.8 Billion
Number Employees: 9,500
Number of Brands: 27
Brands:
Ameridrives
Bauer Gear Motor
Bibby Turboflex
Boston Gear
Delroyd Worm Gear
Formsprag Clutch
Guardian Couplings
Huco
Industrial Clutch
Inertia Dynamics
Jacobs Vehicle Systems
Kilian
Kollmorgen
Lamiflex Couplings
Marland Clutch
Matrix
Nuttall Gear
Portescap
Stieber
Stromag
Svendborg Brakes
TB Wood's
Thomson
Twiflex
Warner Electric
Warner Linear
Wichita Clutch

18687 Altrafilters
200 Wanaque Ave # 401
Pompton Lakes, NJ 07442-2130

973-831-1010
Fax: 973-831-8181
Executive Director: Elaine Gordon

18688 Altrua Marketing & Design
3225 Hartsfield Rd
Tallahassee, FL 32303-3153
850-562-4564
Fax: 850-562-8511 800-443-6939
mfloyd@altrua.com www.wave94.com
Manufacturer and wholesaler/distributor of signs, banners, flags, pennants, table displays, decals and other printed promotional materials
President: Michael Floyd
msmelko@altrua.com
Sales Exec: Melode Smelko
Estimated Sales: $6 Million
Number Employees: 20-49
Square Footage: 160000

18689 Alturdyne Power Systems LLC
660 Steele St
El Cajon, CA 92020-1630
619-440-5531
Fax: 619-442-0481 info@alturdyne.com
www.alturdyne.com
President: Frank Dverbeke
CEO: James Eggert
Estimated Sales: $5,000,000 - $9,999,999
Number Employees: 100-249

18690 Alufoil Products Co Inc
135 Oser Ave # 3
Hauppauge, NY 11788-3722
631-231-4141
Fax: 631-231-1435 sales@alufoil.com
www.alufoil.com
A supplier of aluminum foil, paper foil and foil board for food packaging and laminating. Uses include ham & turkey wrap, confectioners foil and general food service
President: Howard Lent
elliot@alufoil.com
VP: Elliot Lent
Estimated Sales: $3-5 000,000
Number Employees: 10-19
Square Footage: 40000
Type of Packaging: Food Service

18691 Aluma Shield
725 Summerhill Drive
Deland, FL 32724-2024
386-626-6789
877-638-3266
Manufacturer and exporter of cold storage panels and doors
President: John Peters
Sales Director: Allen Rockafellow
Estimated Sales: $20-50 Million
Number Employees: 10

18692 Alumar
4809 N Armenia Avenue
Suite 05
Tampa, FL 33603-1447
813-870-0998
Fax: 813-870-0590
Food processing and can closing machinery
Estimated Sales: Below 1 Million
Number Employees: 1
Square Footage: 8000
Type of Packaging: Bulk
Brands:
    Canco

18693 Alumaworks
16850-112 Collins Avenue #185
Sunny Isle Beach, FL 33160
305-635-6100
Fax: 866-790-2153 800-277-7267
rod@alumaworks.com www.alumaworks.com
Manufacturer and exporter of aluminum bakeware and cookware including frying, sauce, saute, cake and pizza pans, stock pots, deep fryers, pasta cookers, roasters, steamers, etc
President: Rod Haber
Sales Manager: Rod Haber
Number Employees: 14
Square Footage: 40000
Brands:
    Alumaworks

18694 Alumaworks
16850-112 Collins Avenue #185
Sunny Isles Bch, FL 33160-4238
305-635-6100
Fax: 866-790-2153 800-277-7267
sales@alumaworks.com www.alumaworks.com

Bakeware, cookware, pizza pans and accessories
President: Rod Haber
Estimated Sales: $2.5-5 Million
Number Employees: 5-9

18695 Alumin-Nu Corporation
PO Box 24359
Lyndhurst, OH 44124
216-421-2116
Fax: 216-791-8018 800-899-7097
aluminnu@aol.com www.aluminnu.com
Cleaners for drains, septics, ponds, lakes, fish, bird bath cleaner, aluminum and vinyl doors, window, gutters, siding and boats.
President/Purchasing Director: Howard Kaufman
aluminnu@aol.com
Plant Manager: Charles Moon
Number Employees: 3
Number of Products: 11
Square Footage: 30000
Type of Packaging: Consumer, Private Label, Bulk
Brands:
    Alumin-Nu
    Nice N Easy
    Power

18696 Alusett Precision Manufacturing
3 Cecilia Ln
Pleasantville, NY 10570
914-769-4900
alusett@alusett-usa.com
www.alusett-usa.com
Estimated Sales: $1 - 3 Million
Number Employees: 1-4

18697 Alvarado Manufacturing Co Inc
12660 Colony Ct
Chino, CA 91710-2975
909-591-8431
Fax: 909-628-1403 800-423-4143
information@alvaradomfg.com
www.alvaradomfg.com
railings including ornamental, metal, brass, chrome and color; also, bar railings and glass partitions and stair and ramp rails
President: Jack Horener
CEO: Bret Armatas
barmatas@alvaradomfg.com
Chairman: James P Armatas
CEO: Bret Armatas
VP Sales/Marketing: Bret Armatas
Estimated Sales: $10-20 Million
Number Employees: 50-99
Brands:
    Escort

18698 Amagic Holographics
1652 Deere Avenue
Irvine, CA 92606-4813
877-693-6457
Fax: 949-474-3979 800-262-4421
sales@amagicholo.com www.amagicholo.com
Vertically integrated holographic images including holographic security labels, pressure sensitive stickers, PET/PVC/OPP film and hot stamping foil
President: Howard Chen
Marketing Manager: Susan Chiang

18699 Amano Artisan Chocolate
496 S 1325 W
Orem, UT 84058-5877
801-655-1996
amano@amanochocolate.com
www.amanochocolate.com
Chocolates
Owner: Art Pollard
Pastry Chef: Rebecca Millican
Number Employees: 20-49
Type of Packaging: Private Label
Brands:
    Amano Jenbrana
    Amano Ocumare

18700 Amarillo Mop & Broom Company
801 S Fillmore
Suite 205
Amarillo, TX 79101
806-372-8596
Fax: 806-379-8724 800-955-8596
Mop manufacturer
President: E Bryan
VP: Sue Ann Bryan

Estimated Sales: $2.5-5 Million
Number Employees: 10-19
Square Footage: 96000
Type of Packaging: Private Label, Bulk
Brands:
    Amco
    Trouble Shooter

18701 Amark Packaging Systems
4717 E. 119th Street
PO Box 9824
Kansas City, MO 64134
816-965-9000
Fax: 816-965-9003 amarkpkg@sprintmail.com
www.amarkpackaging.com
Manufacturer, exporter of conveyors, bag closers, sewing machines, heat sealers, scales, and pinch closers; custom fabrications available.
Owner: Bob Mc Cullough
Plant Manager: Jack Groblebe
Estimated Sales: $2.5-5 Million
Number Employees: 10
Number of Products: 15
Square Footage: 80000
Brands:
    Amark/Simionato
    Dura-Pak

18702 Amax Nutrasource Inc
1770 Prairie Rd
Eugene, OR 97402-9734
541-688-4944
Fax: 541-688-4866 800-893-5306
www.amaxnutrasource.com
Manufacturer and distributor of herbal extracts and nutritional ingredients.
President: Larry Martinez
lm@amaxnutrasource.com
CFO: Daniel Rothwell
Business Development Manager: Steve Light
Production Manager: Charles Lofton
Number Employees: 10-19

18703 Ambaflex
2202 113th Street
Suite 112
Grand Prairie, TX 75050-1200
877-800-1634
Fax: 877-800-1635 877-800-1634
info@ambaflex.com www.ambaflex.com
Contact: Phil Miller
bcallanan@businessreadysolutions.net

18704 Amber Glo
4140 W Victoria St
Chicago, IL 60646-6727
773-604-8700
Fax: 773-604-4070 866-705-0515
info@emberglo.com www.emberglo.com
Manufacturer and exporter of commercial cooking equipment including gas broilers and steam cookers
President: Teryl A Stanger
Marketing Director: J Kelderhouse
National Sales Manager: Karen Trice
Contact: Joseph Hrabovecky
karent@emberglo.com
Estimated Sales: $3,000,000
Number Employees: 100-249
Number of Brands: 1
Square Footage: 320000
Parent Co: Midco International
Type of Packaging: Food Service
Brands:
    Ember-Glo

18705 Ambient Engineering Co
5 Crescent Ave # A-1
Rocky Hill, NJ 8553
609-279-6888
Fax: 609-279-9444 john@ambienteng.com
www.hydronics-env.com
President: Bruce Bruns
Estimated Sales: $.5 - 1 million
Number Employees: 1-4

18706 Ambitech Engineering Corp
1411 Opus Pl # 200
Downers Grove, IL 60515-1060
630-963-5800
Fax: 630-963-8099 www.ambitech.com
President: Alan Koenig
akoenig@ambitech.com
CFO: Christopher Hunt

Estimated Sales: $10 - 20 Million
Number Employees: 500-999

18707 Ambrose CM Co
2919 Fulton St
Everett, WA 98201-3733

425-317-9818
Fax: 425-317-8597
Manufacturer and exporter of liquid packaging
equipment including turnkey systems, pail denesters,
fillers, check weighters, conveyors, palletizers, con-
trols and engineering services
President: John Bowman
CFO: Cindy Annyas
Vice President: Jeff Bowman
Sales Director: John Bowman
Operations Manager: Jeff Bowman
Estimated Sales: $1.5 Million
Number Employees: 1-4
Number of Products: 12
Square Footage: 24000
Brands:
Ambrose

18708 Amcel
1 Galen Street
Watertown, MA 02472-4501

617-924-0800
Fax: 617-924-2931 800-225-7992
www.amcel.com
Producers of linear low density and high density
polyethylene liners, and stock-size polyethylene
bags for food packaging applications; also a leading
supplier of disposable plastic cutlery
President: Brad Gordon
Sales Manager: Mike Milich
Customer Service Manager: Laura Ott
Estimated Sales: $50-100 Million
Number Employees: 20-49
Square Footage: 18000
Brands:
Amcel

18709 Amco Mechanical
25915 Aldine Westfield Rd
Spring, TX 77373

281-353-2171
Fax: 281-353-2171 www.theamcogroup.com
Commercial contractor
President/Owner: Harold Herridge
VP: Kim Gabehart

18710 Amco Metals Indl
461 S 7th Ave
City of Industry, CA 91746-3119

626-855-2550
Fax: 626-855-2551 info@amcocorporation.com
www.amcocorporation.com
Manufacturer and exporter of racks, utensils, carts,
dollies, trucks, mobile storage equipment, shelving,
etc
Owner: Fank Ko
amcocorporation@aol.com
Sales Director: Dennis Dominic
Estimated Sales: $20-50 Million
Number Employees: 10-19
Square Footage: 240000
Parent Co: Leggett & Platt Storage Products Group
Brands:
Amco
Amcoat
Amcoll
Amtrax
Challenger
Magic Wall
Mod-A-Flex
Plasteel
Plastic Plus
Polygard
Shelving By the Inch
Take 10
Ultra Density

18711 Amco Products Co
501 S Phoenix Ave
Fort Smith, AR 72916-8008

479-646-8949
Fax: 479-648-1032 www.amcoprod.com
Bottling machinery
President: Wendell Martin
Estimated Sales: $20-50 Million
Number Employees: 20-49
Square Footage: 65000

**18712 Amco Warehouse &
Transportation**
1210 Kona Drive
Suite B
Compton, CA 90220-5405

310-635-1885
Fax: 310-604-9762
Samplers and weighing machinery

18713 Amcor
2200 Badger Ave
P.O. Box 2968
Oshkosh, WI 54904

920-527-7300
800-544-4672
NorthAmericaFlexibles@amcor.com
www.amcor.com
Major manufacturer of flexible packaging, rigid con-
tainers, specialty cartons, closures and other services
Managing Director/CEO: Ron Delia
President, Amcor Speciality Cartons: Jerzy Czubak
EVP & Chief Financial Officer: Michael Casamento
President, Amcor Rigid Packaging: Eric Roegner
President, Flexibles North America: Fred Stephan
Year Founded: 1860
Estimated Sales: $13 Billion
Number Employees: 50,000
Parent Co: Amcor plc
Brands:
Bemistape
Tension-Master Ii

18714 Amcor Group Limited
539 46th Avenue
Long Island City, NY 11101-5230

718-361-2700
Fax: 718-706-6058

18715 Ameranth Inc
5820 Oberlin Dr # 202
San Diego, CA 92121-3744

858-362-0150
Fax: 858-362-0151 888-263-7268
www.ameranth.net
Wireless provider
CEO: Keith McNally
Contact: Steve Brooks
sbrooks@ameranth.com
Estimated Sales: $20 - 50 Million
Number Employees: 20-49

18716 Amerex
7595 Gadsden Hwy
Trussville, AL 35173

205-655-3271
Fax: 800-654-5980 www.amerex-fire.com
Fire protection
Executive VP: Harrison Bishop
Year Founded: 1971
Estimated Sales: $100 Million
Number Employees: 500
Parent Co: McWane, Inc.

18717 Ameri Quest Transportation Svc
457 Haddonfield Rd # 220
Cherry Hill, NJ 08002-2201

800-608-0809
Fax: 856-773-0609 888-999-6957
feedback@fleetxchange.com
www.ameriquestcorp.com
President: Doug Clarck
CFO: Rich Spotts
CEO: Douglas W Clark
Estimated Sales: $50 - 75 Million
Number Employees: 10-19

18718 Ameri-Khem
530 New Town Road
PO Box 291907
Port Orange, FL 32129-1907

386-756-9950
800-224-9950
www.truckcompaniesin.com
Anti-bacterial drain cleaner and waste reduction
equipment
President: George Huth
Number Employees: 1-4
Brands:
Nature's Best Liquid Live

18719 AmeriQual Foods
18200 Highway 41 N
Evansville, IN 47725

812-867-1444
Fax: 812-867-0278 www.ameriqual.com
Processor and contract packager of shelf stable en-
trees using retort processing
President: Dennis Straub
CEO: Dan Hermann
Estimated Sales: $50-100 Million
Number Employees: 100-249
Square Footage: 100000

18720 America's Electric Cooperatives
4301 Wilson Boulevard
Arlington, VA 22203-1867

703-907-5707
Fax: 703-907-5531 nreca@nreca.coop
www.nreca.org
President: James Baker
Senior Vice President of Programs: Vivek Talvadkar

18721 American & Efird
24 American St
Mount Holly, NC 28120

704-827-4311
Fax: 704-861-8579
Industrial yarns
Contact: Melissa Carpenter
melissa.carpenter@amefird.com
Plant Manager: Chris McGuret
Estimated Sales: $20 - 50 Million
Number Employees: 100-249

18722 American Adhesives
1730 Evergreen St
Duarte, CA 91010

626-256-4417
Fax: 626-256-4427 800-557-4747
President: John S. Sepulveda
Owner: Tim Thornton
Estimated Sales: $1 - 5 Million
Number Employees: 1-4

**18723 American Advertising & Shop
Cap Company**
48 Bi State Plaza
Suite 231
Old Tappan, NJ 07675-7003

845-639-1596
Fax: 845-639-1597 800-442-8837
Men's work headwear, imprinted painters' caps,
aprons, cloth bags, baseball caps, t-shirts, tote bags
sunvisors, golf shirts, sweatshirts and engineer caps.
President: Ronnie Ehrlich
Number Employees: 50

18724 American Agribusiness Assistance
2916 Dartmouth Road
Alexandria, VA 22314-4822

202-429-0500
Fax: 202-429-0525 agequip@aol.com
www.agribusiness.org.pk
Export broker of processing and packaging equip-
ment for baked goods, sausage, vegetables, fruits,
cheese, dairy products, etc.; consultant offering plant
design and equipment installation
President: James Roberts
VP: Dick Verga
Number Employees: 1-4

18725 American Air Filter
4800 Hockaday Rd
Four Oaks, NC 27524

919-207-1376
Fax: 704-365-1975 800-600-5546
info@aafintl.com www.aafintl.com
Heating, cooling, ventilating, noise pollution control
and air cleaning products and systems
Manager: Sam C Price
Sales/Marketing Director: Bob Sturges
APC Sales Manager: Chris O'Connor
Estimated Sales: Below 1 Million
Number Employees: 50-99

18726 American Apron Inc.
P.O. Box 318
Foxboro, MA 02035-0318

508-384-9600
Fax: 508-384-9601 800-262-7766
Aprons, safety vests and screen printing
President: James Holicker
VP: Connie Holicker

Estimated Sales: Less than $500,000
Number Employees: 1-4

18727 American Art Stamp
17803 South Harvard Street
Suite B
Gardena, CA 90248

310-965-9004
amartstamp@aol.com

Rubber, number, pre-inked and self-inking stamps; also, marking devices, signage and metal marking devices
Co-Owner: Robert Tepper
Estimated Sales: $300,000-500,000
Number Employees: 1-4
Square Footage: 6800

18728 American Association-Meat
1 Meating Pl
Elizabethtown, PA 17022-2883

717-367-1168
Fax: 717-367-9096 aamp@aamp.com
www.aamp.com

AAMP is a meat trade association which provides quality service, knowledge through education to it's members.
Manager: Jody Bartlett
jodi@aamp.com
Secretary: Marty Manion
Number Employees: 5-9

18729 American Auger & Accesories
325 Westtown Rd
Suite 8
West Chester, PA 19382

610-692-7811
Fax: 610-692-7886 866-219-9619
www.americanauger.com

Replacement augers and funnels for all make model of auger filling machines. We also make augers for conveyors and horizontal feeders
President: Jack Treptow
Estimated Sales: $.5 - 1 million
Number Employees: 1-4

18730 American Autoclaves Co
PO Box 430
Sumner, WA 98390-0080

253-863-5000
Fax: 253-863-1770 info@americanautoclave.com
President: Patty Stack
aautoclave@aol.com
Estimated Sales: Below $5 Million
Number Employees: 5-9

18731 American Autogard Corporation
5173 26th Avenue
Rockford, IL 61109

815-229-3190
Fax: 815-229-4615 www.autogard.com
Mechanical and pneumatic torque limiting/overload release clutches and monitors
Manager: Thomas Johnson
Contact: Bill Kuchler
autogarde@gmail.com
Operations Ex: Les Wodecki

18732 American Bag & Burlap Company
36 Arlington St
Chelsea, MA 2150

617-884-7600
Fax: 617-437-7917 info@cormanbag.com
www.cormanbag.com

Manufacturer and importer of bags including burlap, paper and plastic; also, weighing, filling and closing machinery
President: Elliot Corman
VP: Barry Corman
VP: Julie Corman
Estimated Sales: $12 Million
Number Employees: 10-19
Square Footage: 50000
Type of Packaging: Private Label

18733 American Bag & Linen Co
339 Airport Rd W
PO Box 8
Cornelia, GA 30531-5928

706-778-5377
Fax: 706-778-9118 abl@abl-sewing.com
www.abl-sewing.com

Aprons

Owner: Jim Harris
abl@windstream.net
Office Manager: Judy Porter
Plant Manager: Ramona Holt
Estimated Sales: $5-10 Million
Number Employees: 100-249

18734 American Bakery Equipment Company
435 Johnston St # B
PO Box 3135
Half Moon Bay, CA 94019

650-560-9970
Fax: 650-560-9971 800-341-5581
www.americanbakeryequipment.biz

Wholesaler/distributor of new and used bakery equipment for pastries, muffins, cookies, cakes, breads, pizzas, bagels, etc.; installation services available
Manager: John Candelori Jr
CEO: Ken Skelton
CFO: Norman Gwinn
VP: John Candelori, Jr.
Research & Development: Polly Vandersyde
CFO: Sabatino Compi
Estimated Sales: Below $5,000,000
Number Employees: 5-9
Number of Brands: 200
Number of Products: 1000
Square Footage: 4750

18735 American Box Corporation
PO Box 112
Lisbon, OH 44432-0112

330-424-8055
Fax: 330-424-7441 amboxcorp@aol.com
Custom, new and reconditioned wooden pallets, skids, boxes and crates
Estimated Sales: less than $500,000
Number Employees: 10

18736 American Broom Co
1200 Moultrie Ave
Mattoon, IL 61938-3123

217-235-1992
Fax: 217-234-9180 www.lucomop.com

Brooms
Manager: Clarence Gillispie
Manager: Clarence Gillespie
c.gillespie@lucomop.com
Manager: Clarence Gillespie
Estimated Sales: $1 - 2.5 Million
Number Employees: 5-9
Parent Co: Luco Mop Company

18737 American Brush Company
3150 NW 31st Avenue
Suite 3
Portland, OR 97210

503-234-5064
Fax: 503-234-1270 800-826-8492
www.americanbrush.com

Manufacturer and exporter of industrial and commercial brooms and brushes
President: Laddie M. Wirth, Sr.
CEO: John S. Martin
Vice President: Janine M. Wirth
Contact: Gladys Doern
gladys@americanbrush.com
Estimated Sales: $2.5-5 Million
Number Employees: 10-19
Square Footage: 40000

18738 American Cart Company
12 Eccleston Avenue
North Kingstown, RI 02852-7406

401-885-5055
Fax: 401-885-5057

Coffee and espresso carts

18739 American Casting & Mfg Corp
51 Commercial St
Plainview, NY 11803-2490

516-349-8389
Fax: 516-349-8389 800-342-0333
info@americancasting.com www.seals.com

Seals, security seals, cargo seals, ctpat seals, truch seals
President: Norman Wenk Iii
Cmo: Jim Wenk
jimwenk@americancasting.com
Number Employees: 50-99

18740 American Chocolate Mould Co.
1401 Church St
Suite 5
Bohemia, NY 11716-5016

631-589-5080
Fax: 516-908-3660 amerchoc@mindspring.com
www.americanchocolatemould.com

Chocolate equipment chocolate moulds, plain and printed aluminum foils, foil wrapping machines
President: Raymond J. Cote Jr.
amerchoc@mindspring.com
Sales Director: David Cote
Public Relations: Katie Cote
Estimated Sales: $500,000-$1,000,000
Number Employees: 5-9
Square Footage: 1700
Type of Packaging: Private Label, Bulk

18741 American Coaster Company
3685 Lockport Rd
Sanborn, NY 14132-9404

716-731-9193
Fax: 716-731-4138 888-423-8628

Custom designed beverage coasters
President: Tom Muraca
Sales Manager: Tammy Gorzka
Contact: Kristin Kinney
kkinney@katzamericas.com
Estimated Sales: $10-20 Million
Number Employees: 50-99
Parent Co: Gardei

18742 American Containers Inc
2526 Western Ave
Plymouth, IN 46563-1050

574-936-4068
Fax: 574-936-4036 info@acontainers.com
www.acontainers.com

Manufacturer and exporter of corrugated boxes
Owner: Leonard D Isban
misban@acontainers.com
CFO: Steve Tubes
Estimated Sales: $5 - 10 Million
Number Employees: 50-99

18743 American Conveyor Corporation
26-40 1st St.
Astoria, NY 11385-1002

718-386-0480
Fax: 718-456-1233

Supplier of belt and rollover conveyor, bagging & debagging, case packaging & unscrambling, case stackers, casers, checkweighers, corrugated case forming & top sealing, corrugated palletizing & banding, deunitizers, fillers, labeling &coding, metal detectors, palletizers, pushers, unitizers, unstackers, shrink wrap & stretch wrap, truck & dock leveling
Owner: Valdie Freidman
Estimated Sales: Below $5 Million
Number Employees: 20-49
Other Locations:
American Conveyor Corporation
Carlisle NY
American Conveyor Corporation
Overland Park KS
American Conveyor Corporation
Sarasota FL
American Conveyor Corporation
Uxbridge MA
American Conveyor Corporation
Murray KY
American Conveyor Corporation
St. Petersburg FL

18744 American Coolair Corp
3604 Mayflower St
Jacksonville, FL 32205-5378

904-389-3646
Fax: 904-387-3449 info@coolair.com
www.coolair.com

Manufacturer and exporter of ventilation fans and systems
President: Harry M Graves Jr
VP: Neal Taylor
Marketing/Sales Manager: Mark Fales
Estimated Sales: $20 - 50 Million
Number Employees: 100-249
Square Footage: 110000

18745 American Crane & Equip Corp
531 Old Swede Rd
Douglassville, PA 19518-1299

610-385-6061
Fax: 610-385-3191 info@americancrane.com
www.munckintl.com

Cranes and hoist trolleys
President: Oddvar Norheim
onorheim@americancrane.com
CFO: Dave Hope
Quality Control: Frank Yurich
VP of Sales: David Schaeffer
Purchasing Manager: Sandy Hoffman
Estimated Sales: $20 - 50 Million
Number Employees: 50-99
Square Footage: 60000

18746 American Creative Solutions
11145 Monroe Rd
Matthews, NC 28105

Fax: 731-925-3209 877-925-4406
info@amcreativesolutions.com
www.amcreativesolutions.com
Foodservice equipment manufacturer
President, Eagle Group: Larry McAllister
Parent Co: Eagle Group

18747 American Custom Dry Co
109 Elbow Ln
Burlington, NJ 08016-4123

609-387-3933
Fax: 609-387-7204
Spray drying and blending services
President: Richard Shipley
CFO: Michael Garger
Vice President: Svend Hansen
Quality Control: Fran Thornton
Public Relations: Jane Macey
Operations Manager: Larry Cutler
Estimated Sales: $10 - 20 Million
Number Employees: 50-99
Type of Packaging: Private Label, Bulk

18748 American Cut Edge Inc
480 Congress Park Dr
Dayton, OH 45459-4144

937-438-2390
Fax: 937-438-2398 888-252-3372
info@americancuttingedge.com
www.americancuttingedge.com
Industry standard blades and knives, high tolerant
blades and safety knives
President: Chuck Biehn
cbiehn@americancuttingedge.com
CFO: Don Cain
Estimated Sales: $5 - 10 Million
Number Employees: 20-49
Square Footage: 400000
Parent Co: CB Manufacturing & Sales Company

18749 American Cylinder Co
481 S Governors Hwy
Peotone, IL 60468-9116

708-258-3935
Fax: 708-258-3980 amcyl@americancylinder.com
www.americancylinder.com
President: Joseph White
amcyl@americancylinder.com
Estimated Sales: $20 - 50 Million
Number Employees: 20-49

18750 American Design & Machinery
430 Cummings Avenue NW
Grand Rapids, MI 49534-7984

616-791-4856
Fax: 616-791-4898
Food processing machinery
Marketing Director: Robert Cisleil
Contact: Joe Cisler
j_cisler@hotmail.com
Estimated Sales: $1-2.5 000,000
Number Employees: 19
Square Footage: 23000

18751 American Design Studios
6353 Corte Del Abeto Ste A106
Carlsbad, CA 92011

760-438-8880
Fax: 760-438-8488 800-899-7104
Manufacturer and importer of shirts with names and
logos
President: Robert Peritz
Marketing Director: Judy Morrill
Contact: Mike Srtingfellow
mike@mss.net
Estimated Sales: $10-20 Million
Number Employees: 10-19
Brands:
American Terrain

18752 American Dish Service
900 Blake St
Edwardsville, KS 66111-3820

913-422-3700
Fax: 913-422-2178 800-922-2178
www.americandish.com
Commercial dishwashers
President: James Andrews
jamie@americandish.com
Estimated Sales: $20-50 Million
Number Employees: 100-249

18753 American Dixie Group
250 Osborne Rd
Albany, NY 12205-1300

518-453-9000
Packaging machinery
Owner: Beth Wade
Estimated Sales: $5-10 Million
Number Employees: 5-9

18754 American Eagle Food Machinery
3557 S Halsted St
Chicago, IL 60609

773-376-0800
Fax: 773-376-2010 888-390-0800
Info@AmericanEagleMachine.com
www.americaneaglemachine.com
Manufacturer, importer and exporter of bakery ma-
chinery including mixers, bread slicers and grinders-
meat tenderizer, dough sheets, dough roller, dividers
of rounders and dough molders.
Owner: Spencer Yang
Contact: Didicher Grace
grace@ameagle.biz
Estimated Sales: $1-2,500,000
Number Employees: 10-19
Brands:
American Eagle

18755 American Electric Power
1 Riverside Plaza
Columbus, OH 43215-2372

614-716-1000
800-277-2177
www.aep.com
Electric utility systems.
Chairman/President/CEO: Nicholas Akins
EVP & Chief Financial Officer: Brian Tierney
EVP/General Counsel/Secretary: David Feinberg
EVP & Chief Administrative Officer: Lana
Hillebrand
SVP & Chief Customer Officer: Bruce Evans
SVP, Governmental Affairs: Tony Kavanagh
SVP & Chief Customer Officer: Thomas Kirkpatrick
Year Founded: 1906
Estimated Sales: $15 Billion
Number Employees: 18,000

18756 American Electronic Components
1101 Lafayette St
Elkhart, IN 46516-2615

574-295-6330
Fax: 574-293-8013 888-847-6552
Vice President: Patrick Conway
pconway@aecsensors.com
Vice President: Patrick Conway
pconway@aecsensors.com
Number Employees: 10-19

18757 American Engineering Corporation
PO Box 336
Collegedale, TN 37315-0336

423-396-3666
Fax: 423-396-3668
Food safety data collection
Estimated Sales: $5-10 Million
Number Employees: 3

18758 American Environmental International
1325 Remington Road
Schaumburg, IL 60173-4834

847-342-8600
Fax: 847-342-8500 800-343-8601
jstandon@aol.com www.aei-inc.com
Environmental control and resource recovery equip-
ment, emission control, solvent recovery systems, air
pollution control
Estimated Sales: $500,000-$1 Million
Number Employees: 5-9

18759 American Equipment Co
1080 Hardees Dr
Aberdeen, MD 21001-2637

410-272-2626
Fax: 410-272-2011 www.seamers.com
Refurbisher of can seamers; also, parts available
President: Charles Adams
cadams@americanequipment.us
General Manager: Mike Mangone
Estimated Sales: Below $5 Million
Number Employees: 5-9

18760 American Equipment Systems Inc
5458 Louie Ln
Reno, NV 89511-1832

775-852-1114
www.aes-sorma.com
President: Robert G Sapeta
bob@aes-sorma.com
Estimated Sales: $3 - 5 Million
Number Employees: 1-4
Parent Co: American European Systems

18761 American European Systems
5456 Louie Lane
Reno, NV 89510-7061

775-852-1114
Fax: 775-852-1163 info@aes-sorma.com
www.aes-sorma.com
Importer and wholesaler/distributor of cutting, peel-
ing, bagging and weighing equipment
President: Robert Sapeta
Sales/Marketing Executive: Don Bergin
Estimated Sales: $3 - 5 Million
Number Employees: 5-9
Square Footage: 32000

18762 American Excelsior Co
850 Avenue H E
Arlington, TX 76011-7720

817-385-3500
Fax: 817-649-7816 800-777-7645
www.americanexcelsior.com
Manufacturer, custom molder and exporter of foam
packaging products including inserts, contours, pro-
tectors, pads, liners and fillers
President, Chief Executive Officer: Terry A.
Sadowski
tsadowski@americanexcelsior.com
VP, CFO: Todd A. Eblen
Vice President of Sales and Marketing: Ken Starrett
Vice President of Operations: Kevin Stew
Estimated Sales: $5-10 Million
Number Employees: 50-99

18763 American Excelsior Co
850 Avenue H E
Arlington, TX 76011-7720

817-385-3500
Fax: 817-649-7816 800-777-7645
www.americanexcelsior.com
Plastic packaging products, erosion control prod-
ucts, evaporative cooling products and foam padding
General Manager: Rice Lake
Chairman: Robert Gregerson
CEO: Terry A Sadowski
Vice President of Sales and Marketing: Ken Starrett
Vice President of Operations: Kevin Stew
Estimated Sales: $20-50 Million
Number Employees: 50-99

18764 (HQ)American Extrusion Intl
498 Prairie Hill Rd
South Beloit, IL 61080-2563

815-624-6616
Fax: 815-624-6628
rickw@americanextrusion.com
www.americanextrusion.info
Supplier and exporter of direct expansion extruders
and auxiliary equipment including forced air ovens,
fryers, seasoning systems, wear parts, reel cutters,
mixers, tumblers and conveyors
President: Richard J Warner
rickw@americanextrusion.com
R&D: Dr. Samir El-Shatter
Director of Sales: Rick Warner
Sales Director: Rick Warner
General Manager: Daniel Thompson
Estimated Sales: $.5-$1 million
Number Employees: 50-99
Square Footage: 54000
Other Locations:
American Extrusion Internatio
South Beloit IL

Brands:
American Extrusion International

18765 American Fabric Filter Co Inc
29807 State Road 54
Wesley Chapel, FL 33543-4507
          813-991-9400
    Fax: 813-991-9700 800-367-3591
    info@americanfabricfilter.com
    www.americanfabricfilter.com
Manufacturers of custom made filter bags, dust bags
and transfer sleeves for the food, wood, processing
and baking industries. Our products are made specif-
ically to fit each application.
President: Derek Williams
CEO: Zoa Gomez
  zgomez@americanfabricfilter.com
CFO: Tim Robinson
Estimated Sales: Below $5 Million
Number Employees: 10-19

18766 American Felt & Filter Co
361 Walsh Ave
New Windsor, NY 12553-6727
          845-561-3560
    Fax: 845-561-0967 questions@affco.com
    www.affco.com
President/CEO: Wilson H. Pryne
  wpryne@affco.com
Vice President: Scott H. Pryne
Sales Manager: Mark A. Pryne
Estimated Sales: $10 - 20 Million
Number Employees: 50-99

**18767 American Fire SprinklerServices,
Inc**
16221 NW 57th Ave
Hialeah, FL 33014-6709
          305-628-0100
Fax: 305-628-3556 Sprinklerheads@bellsouth.net
    www.americanfiresprinklers.com
Manufacturer and exporter of sprinkler systems
Owner: Anisa Oweiss
Contact: Omar Oweiss
  sprinklerheads@bellsouth.net
Operations Director: Ken Oweis
Estimated Sales: $2.5-5 Million
Number Employees: 10-19
Type of Packaging: Consumer, Food Service

18768 American Flag & Banner Co Inc
28 S Main St
Clawson, MI 48017-2088
          248-288-3010
    Fax: 248-288-5630 800-892-5168
    flagsetc@aol.com
Manufacturer and exporter of flags, pennants and
banners
President: William S Miles
  flagsetc@aol.com
Sales Manager: Michelle Angle
Estimated Sales: Less Than $500,000
Number Employees: 1-4

18769 American Foam Corp
61 John St
Johnston, RI 02919-6210
          401-944-4990
    Fax: 401-944-0142 800-235-0010
    www.americanfoam.com
Flocked foam packaging materials
Vice President: Chad Martin
  chad@americanfoam.com
VP: Chad Martin
Estimated Sales: $20-50 Million
Number Employees: 50-99

18770 American Food Equipment
1301 N Miami Ave
Miami, FL 33136-2815
          305-377-8991
    Fax: 305-358-4328
  michael@americanfoodequipment.com
  www.americanfoodequipment.com
Manufacturer and supplier of restaurant equipment
such as coolers, freezers, and ice machines
Founder: Robert Green
President/Owner: Michael Clements
  americanfoodequipment@gmail.com
Estimated Sales: $460,000
Number Employees: 5-9
Square Footage: 28000
Parent Co: American Grinding And Equipment
Company.

Type of Packaging: Consumer, Private Label, Bulk

**18771 American Food Equipment
Company**
21040 Forbes Ave
Hayward, CA 94545-1116
          510-783-0255
    Fax: 510-783-0409 amfec@amfec.com
    www.amfec.com
Manufacturer and exporter of mixers, dumpers, belt
and screw conveyors, vacuum stuffers, tumblers and
massagers
President: Michael Botto
Quality Control: Melvin Hauss
Contact: Leticia Alexandre
  lalexandre@amfec.com
Controller: Simone Manos
Plant Manager: Ron Balthasar
Estimated Sales: $5 - 10 Million
Number Employees: 20-49
Square Footage: 80000
Brands:
  Amfec

18772 (HQ)American Forms & Labels
7448 W Mossy Cup St
Boise, ID 83709-2839
          208-562-0750
    Fax: 208-562-0151 800-388-3554
Pressure sensitive labels; also, bar code systems and
hardware
Owner: Kevin Curtin
Estimated Sales: $5-10 Million
Number Employees: 10-19
Square Footage: 60000

18773 American Formula
4720 Frederick Dr SW
Atlanta, GA 30336-1810
          404-691-7940
    Fax: 404-691-7943 800-282-1215
  pvcnet@aol.com www.americanformula.com
Industrial cleaning compounds
President: Don Hamilton
  dhamilton@americanformula.com
President: Phillip Consolino
General Manager: Michael Holtzman
Number Employees: 20-49
Parent Co: Holtco

18774 American Fruits & Flavors
10725 Sutter Ave
Pacoima, CA 91331
          818-899-9574
  SalesTeam@americanfruit.com
  www.americanfruits-flavors.com
Custom flavors, fruit juice blends, natural sweeten-
ers, juice concentrates and liquid powder blends.
Specializing in fruit, vegetable, sweet and savory
flavors, flavor bases, fruit concentrates, coconut
products, smoothies, andtropical blends.
President: Bill Haddad
CEO: Rodney Sacks
Corporate Controller: Michael Model
Senior Research & Development Chemist: Martin
Goldberg
Quality Control Chemist: Joanne Pallones
VP of Marketing: Richard Linn
Director of Human Resources: Regina Rodriguez
Year Founded: 1962
Estimated Sales: $168 Million
Number Employees: 200-500
Square Footage: 20000
Parent Co: Monster Beverage Corporation

18775 American Fuji Seal
1051 Bloomfield Rd
Bardstown, KY 40004-9794
          502-348-9211
    Fax: 502-348-9558 800-533-3854
    www.fujiseal.com
Shrink sleeves and application equipment
President: Takeo Sonoda
Senior VP: Bill Hayworth
  bhayworth@afseal.com
Estimated Sales: $20 - 50 Million
Number Employees: 250-499

**18776 American Gas & Chemical Co
LTD**
220 Pegasus Ave
Northvale, NJ 07647-1904
          201-767-7300
    Fax: 201-767-1741 800-288-3647
  contact@amgas.com www.amgas.com
Leak detection products and gas monitoring systems
President: Melanie Kershaw
  mkershaw@amgas.com
Quality Control and CFO: Jim Zanosky
Controller: Jim Zanosky
R&D: Scott Bruce
Marketing Director: Gerald Anderson
Sales Manager: John Hamilton
Estimated Sales: $10 - 20 Million
Number Employees: 20-49
Square Footage: 50000
Brands:
  Flaw Finder
  Leak-Tec
  Pin Point

18777 American Gas Association
400 North Capitol Street
Washington, DC 20001
          202-824-7000
    Fax: 703-841-8406 www.aga.org
Gas dispensing systems
President: Christopher Johns
President, Chief Executive Officer: Dave McCurdy
Senior Vice President: Chris Hermann
Sales Director: Axel Nordwall
Contact: Nadia Anderson
  nanderson@aga.org
President, Chief Operating Officer: Lawrence
Borgard
Estimated Sales: $1-5 Million
Number Employees: 5
Parent Co: Linde Technische

18778 American Gasket & Rubber Co
119 Commerce Dr
Schaumburg, IL 60173-5311
          847-882-9333
    Fax: 847-882-9333 www.tekni-plex.com
Number Employees: 100-249

18779 American Glass Research
349 Tomahawk Dr
Maumee, OH 43537-1611
          419-897-9000
    Fax: 419-897-9111
Laboratory providing analysis of packaging materi-
als, raw materials and problems such as foreign ma-
terials, package failure, etc
Manager: Diane Paskiet
Manager (Inorganic): James Hojuicki
Manager: Lindy Seagrave
  lindyseagrave@yahoo.com
Estimated Sales: $2.5-5 Million
Number Employees: 20-49
Square Footage: 24000

18780 American Glass Research
615 Whitestown Rd
Butler, PA 16001-8703
          724-482-2163
    Fax: 724-482-2767 agrsales@agrintl.com
    www.agrintl.com
Quality Assurance & Process Control Systems for
the Packaging Industry
CEO: Henry Dimmick Jr
Marketing: David Dineff
Operations: Robert Cowden
Estimated Sales: $20 - 50 Million
Number Employees: 100-249
Square Footage: 100000

18781 American Griddle Corp.
4416 New Haven Ave
Fort Wayne, IN 46803
          260-428-2685
    Fax: 260-428-2533 800-428-6550
  steamshell@americangriddle.com
  americangriddle.com
Steam griddle
Sales: Andy Garcia

18782 American Hawaiian Soy Company
274 Kalihi Street
Honolulu, HI 96819
          808-841-8435
          800-841-8435

Soybean
President: John Morita

18783 American Holt Corp
203 Carnegie Row
Norwood, MA 02062-5000
781-440-9993
Fax: 781-440-9994 sales@americanholt.com
www.americanholt.net
Replacement parts for industry
President: John Levy
jon@americanholt.com
Estimated Sales: $3 - 5 Million
Number Employees: 5-9

18784 American Housewares
755 E 134th St
Bronx, NY 10454-3419
718-665-9500
Fax: 718-292-0830
sales@americanhousewaresmfg.com
www.americanhousewaresmfg.com
Manufacturer and exporter of kitchen utensils and
equipment including strainers, colanders, basting
spoons, forks, pancake turners, mashers, fry baskets,
splatter screens, roast racks, kitchen tools and
gadgets
Owner: Paul Mayer
strainer4@juno.com
COO: Irving Spiegel
Estimated Sales: $5-10 Million
Number Employees: 50-99

18785 American Identification Industries
1319 Howard Drive
West Chicago, IL 60185-1625
630-231-4500
Fax: 630-231-4530 800-255-8890
Plastic cards
Sales Manager: Juan Sanjujo
Sales: Ginny Lacy
Sales Support: Sandy Brush
Estimated Sales: $5-10 Million
Number Employees: 5

18786 American Identity
1520 Albany Pl SE
Orange City, IA 51041
712-737-4925
Fax: 712-737-2408 800-369-2277
Manufacturer, importer and exporter of promotional
items including caps, jackets, uniforms, etc
Manager: Larry Sanson
Marketing Manager: Greg Ebel
Contact: Paul Awtry
paul.awtry@americanid.com
Estimated Sales: $50-100 Million
Number Employees: 250-499
Parent Co: American Marketing Industry
Brands:
   Glengate
   Identity
   K-Products
   Swingster

18787 American Industrial Supply Company
519 Potrero Ave
San Francisco, CA 94110-1431
415-826-1144
Fax: 415-552-3300
President: George Herbst
herbst@aiscmail.com
Estimated Sales: $50,000 - 1 Million
Number Employees: 1-4

18788 American Insulated Panel Co
75 John Hancock Rd
Taunton, MA 02780-1096
508-823-7003
Fax: 508-880-5476 800-924-2774
sales@aipanel.com
www.americaninsulatedpanel.com
Manufacturer and installer of walk in coolers and
freezers, cold storage doors, and glass display doors.
President: John Lynch
CFO: John Lynch
R&D: John Lynch
Quality Control: John Lynch
IT: Judith Lynch
judylynch@aipanel.com
Estimated Sales: $5 - 10 Million
Number Employees: 20-49
Square Footage: 35000

Type of Packaging: Bulk

18789 American International Electric
2835 Pellissier Pl
City of Industry, CA 90601-1512
562-908-5058
Fax: 562-908-5059 800-732-5377
www.aieco.com
CEO: Charles Chen
cchen@fastdry.com
Estimated Sales: $3 - 5 Million
Number Employees: 10-19

18790 American International Tooling
2516 Business Parkway
Suite A
Minden, NV 89423
775-267-6939
Fax: 775-267-697 866-248-8665
sales@seamertooling.com
Manufacturer seamer tooling for canning and bot-
tling industry
President: Lee Bertucci
Vice President Sales: John Konvicka
Contact: Cheryl Bertucci
cheryl@seamertooling.com
Production Manager: Anna Westmorland
Estimated Sales: $1 - 3 Million
Number Employees: 5-9

18791 American LEWA
132 Hopping Brook Road
Holliston, MA 01746
508-429-7403
Fax: 508-429-8615 888-539-2123
www.lewa.com
Manufacturer and exporter of precision metering and
mixing pumps and systems for blending and propor-
tioning all liquids; also, seal-less controlled volume
pumps for process services and moderate high
pressures
President/Owner: Mike Meraji
Contact: Larry Bell
houston@amlewa.com
Purchasing Director: Charlie Riordan
Number of Brands: 1
Number of Products: 4
Parent Co: OTT Holding Internationa GmbH
Brands:
   Lewa Ecodos
   Lewa Lab
   Lewa Modular
   Lewa Triplex

18792 (HQ)American Labelmark Co
5724 N Pulaski Rd
Chicago, IL 60646-6797
773-478-0900
Fax: 773-478-6054 800-621-5808
sales@labelmaster.com www.labelmaster.com
Manufacturer and exporter of signs including in-
door, outdoor, painted and silk screened for restau-
rants, food manufacturers, etc
President: Alan Schoen
CFO: Ed Kaplan
VP/Marketing: Marilyn Paprocki
Estimated Sales: $30-50 Million
Number Employees: 100-249
Type of Packaging: Food Service

18793 American Led-Gible
1776 Lone Eagle St
Columbus, OH 43228-3655
614-851-1100
Fax: 614-851-1121 www.ledgible.com
Light emitting electronic display signs
President: George Smith
ledgible@ledgible.com
Senior Management of Sales: Candy Chlam
Senior Production Management: Charles Morrison
Estimated Sales: $1-2.5 Million
Number Employees: 5-9
Square Footage: 40000
Brands:
   American Led-Gible, Inc.

18794 American Lifts
P.O. Box 1058
Guthrie, OK 73044
405-282-5200
Fax: 405-282-8105 877-360-6777
sales@autoquip.com www.americanlifts.com

Manufacturer, importer and exporter of lifts includ-
ing hydraulic scissor and stainless steel; also, hy-
draulic tilters, and pallet trucks
Manager: Clay Brinson
Estimated Sales: $10 - 20 Million
Number Employees: 50-99
Square Footage: 140000
Parent Co: Columbs McKinnon Corporation
Brands:
   Torklift

18795 American Liquid Pkgng Systs
440 N Wolfe Rd
Sunnyvale, CA 94085-3869
408-524-7474
Fax: 408-524-7470
Bottled water plants, accessories and plastic resin
Owner: Saeed Amidi
Estimated Sales: $20 - 50 Million
Number Employees: 1-4

18796 American Louver Co
7700 Austin Ave
Skokie, IL 60077-2603
847-470-3300
Fax: 847-470-0420 800-772-0355
Manufacturer and exporter of fluorescent lighting
louvers, acrylic mirror sheets, handheld shopping
baskets and convex security mirrors
President: Mark Comella
mcomella@plasticade.com
Chairman the Board: Walter Glass
VP: Barry Peterson
CFO: Lucy Polk
Marketing Manager: Butch Cavello
Estimated Sales: $20 - 50 Million
Number Employees: 50-99
Brands:
   Alumicube
   Paracube

18797 American Machinery Corporation
PO Box 3228
Orlando, FL 32802-3228
407-295-2581
Estimated Sales: $1 - 5 Million

18798 American Manufacturing-Engrng
4600 W 160th St
Cleveland, OH 44135-2630
440-899-9400
Fax: 440-899-9401 800-822-9402
info@ameco.com www.ameco-usa.com
Steel and stainless steel fabricated beverage and liq-
uid distribution/fillers, steam pressure vessels and
mixer components; exporter of stainless and regular
steel manufactured products
President and CEO: Michael Perkins
Sales/Marketing Manager: Fred Swanson
Sales Engineer: Tom Miller
Estimated Sales: $500,000-$1 Million
Number Employees: 20-49
Square Footage: 200000

18799 American Material Handling Inc
9013 Highway 165
PO Box 17878
N Little Rock, AR 72117-9728
501-375-6611
Fax: 501-375-8931 800-482-5801
sales@amermaterial.com www.amermaterial.com
Wholesaler/distributor and exporter of material han-
dling systems; also, design consultant
Owner: Jackie Lackie
General Manager: Jay Carman
VP of Marketing: Albert Redding
Sales Manager: Adam Dickens
Manager: Adam Dickens
adam.dickens@amermaterial.com
Estimated Sales: $5-10 Million
Number Employees: 10-19
Square Footage: 80000
Parent Co: Cetrum Industries

18800 American Menu Displays
4862 36th Street
Long Island City, NY 11101-1918
561-544-8047
Fax: 561-544-8048 877-544-8046
www.americandiscounttableware.com
Display signs and menu boards
President: Robet Subaj
Estimated Sales: $10 - 20 Million
Number Employees: 100-249

Brands:
Panel Lite

18801 American Metal Door Company
PO Box 2008
Richmond, IN 47375-2008
800-428-2737
Fax: 800-626-1490 800-428-2737
www.americanmetaldoor.com
Stainless steel and galvanized sliding doors; also,
high speed electric and pneumatic operators
Marketing Coordinator: Jennifer George
Sales Manager: Doug HolmesMidwest
Estimated Sales: $3 Million
Number Employees: 35
Square Footage: 108000
Brands:
Doors
Electric & Pneumatic Op.
Hardware

18802 American Metal Stamping
1 Nassau Ave
Brooklyn, NY 11222-3115
718-384-1500
Fax: 718-384-1523
Heavy duty bakers' pans and trays, food strainers,
institutional kitchen baking and roasting pans and
equipment smallwares
President: Stephanie Eisenberg
Estimated Sales: $5 - 10 Million
Number Employees: 20-49

18803 American Metalcraft Inc
3708 River Rd
Suite 800
Franklin Park, IL 60131-2158
708-345-1177
Fax: 708-345-5758 info@amnow.com
www.amnow.com
Manufacturer, importer, exporter and wholesaler/dis-
tributor of stainless steel restaurant/bar tabletop sup-
plies, funnels, pizza trays and food covers; serving
the food service market
President: David Kahn
davidk@amnow.com
Sales Manager: Richard Packer
Estimated Sales: $10-20 Million
Number Employees: 50-99
Square Footage: 240000
Type of Packaging: Food Service
Brands:
American Metalcraft

18804 American Municipal Chemical
1907 S 89th St
Milwaukee, WI 53227-1611
414-329-2920
Fax: 414-329-9043 800-598-3106
www.chemicalbargins.com
Cleaning compounds
President: Wayne Benz
wayne@wedor.com
VP: Eric Benz
Estimated Sales: $5-10 Million
Number Employees: 1-4
Square Footage: 60000

18805 American National Rubber
P.O. Box 878
Ceredo, WV 25507-6396
304-453-1311
Fax: 304-453-2347 www.anro.com
Manufacturer and exporter of sponge rubber includ-
ing gaskets and seals
Sales Manager: Ed Littlehales
Estimated Sales: $20-50 Million
Number Employees: 250-500

18806 American Olean Tile Company
1000 N Cannon Ave
Lansdale, PA 19446
215-855-1111
Contact: Nancy Wilson
nancy_wilson@americanolean.com
Estimated Sales: $1 - 5 Million
Parent Co: Armstrong World Industries

18807 American Packaging Corporation
P.O. Box 16223
Philadelphia, PA 19114-0223
215-676-8888
Fax: 215-698-7119 bkemp@ampkcorp.com
www.swalter.com

Flexible packages
CEO: Peter Schottland
CFO: Tom May
CEO: Andrew N Wilson
Quality Control: Jim Carlson
Estimated Sales: $81.3 Million
Number Employees: 100-249

18808 American Packaging Machinery
2550 S Eastwood Dr
Woodstock, IL 60098-9112
815-337-8580
Fax: 815-337-8583 888-755-2705
sales@apm-machinery.com
www.americanpackagingmachinery.com
High speed servo controlled shrink wrapping sys-
tems and high speed shrink bundling equipment
Owner: Tadiya Peric
apmmachinery@aol.com
Estimated Sales: $10 - 20 000,000
Number Employees: 10-19
Type of Packaging: Bulk

18809 American Packaging Machinery
2550 S Eastwood Dr
Woodstock, IL 60098-9112
815-337-8580
Fax: 815-337-8583 sales@apm-machinery.com
www.americanpackagingmachinery.com
Owner: Tadiya Peric
apmmachinery@aol.com
Estimated Sales: Below $5 Million
Number Employees: 10-19

18810 American Pallet Inc
1001 Knox Rd
Oakdale, CA 95361-9463
209-847-6122
Fax: 209-847-6154
Pallets, skids, bins and crates
President: Bill Montey
bill@americanpallet.com
VP: John Fauria
VP: John Fauria
Estimated Sales: $20 - 50 Million
Number Employees: 20-49

18811 American Pallets
2069 New Castle Rd.
Box 201
Portersville, PA 16051
724-658-5747

18812 American Pan Co
417 E Water St # 2
PO Box 678
Urbana, OH 43078-2178
937-652-3232
Fax: 937-652-1384 800-652-2151
sales@americanpan.com
www.americanpanuk.com
Commercial bakery pans
President: Gil T Bundy
gbundy@americanpan.com
Estimated Sales: $10-20 000,000
Number Employees: 50-99

18813 American Panel Corp
5800 SE 78th St
Ocala, FL 34472-3412
352-245-7055
Fax: 352-245-0726 800-327-3015
sales@americanpanel.com
www.americanpanel.com
Manufacturer and exporter of walk-in coolers and
freezers, blast chillers, refrigerated warehouses and
refrigeration systems
President: Danny E Duncan
danny@americanpanel.com
CEO: Marvin Duncan
VP: Harmon Lewis
Sales Manager: Kevin Graham
Sales Associate: Jenn Duncan
Estimated Sales: $20 - 50 Million
Number Employees: 100-249
Square Footage: 100000
Type of Packaging: Food Service
Brands:
American Panel

18814 American Pasien Co
109 Elbow Ln
Burlington, NJ 08016-4123
609-387-3130
Fax: 609-387-7204 info@109elbow.com
www.amcocustomdrying.biz
Functional protein ingredients and protein polymers
for edible applications
CEO: Jamil Ahmed
jamilahmed@americancasein.com
CEO: Dennis Bobker
CFO: Jack Pipala
Account Manager: Jane Macey
Sales Manager: Cliff Lang
Human Resources Manager/IT Manager: Ellen
Iuliucci
Facilities Manager: Chris Lockard
Estimated Sales: $5.8 Million
Number Employees: 20-49
Square Footage: 120000
Type of Packaging: Bulk

18815 American Pistachio Growers
9 E River Park Pl E # 410
Suite 410
Fresno, CA 93720-1530
559-353-2023
Fax: 559-475-0624 www.americanpistachios.org
Agricultural trade association representing members
who are pistachio growers, processors and industry
partners in California.
Executive Director: Richard Matoian
Director, Global Marketing: Judy Hirigoyen
Director, Member Services/Communications:
Catherine Byrnes
Number Employees: 10-19

18816 American Plant & Equipment
4200 S Church Street Ext
Roebuck, SC 29376-2912
864-574-4000
Fax: 864-576-7204
apesales@americanplantandequipment.com
www.forkliftsworld.com
Owner: Victor Le Bron
americanplant@americanplantandequipment.com
Quality Control: Cindy Forster
Estimated Sales: Less Than $500,000
Number Employees: 5-9

18817 American Plywood
7011 S 19th St
Tacoma, WA 98466-5333
253-565-6600
Fax: 253-565-7265 www.apawood.org
President: David L Rogoway
Director: Dennis Hardman
Estimated Sales: $10,000,000 - $19,999,999
Number Employees: 100-249

18818 American Printpak Inc
W225n6284 Village Dr
Sussex, WI 53089-3970
262-246-7300
Fax: 262-246-7388 800-441-8003
www.americanprintpak.com
Flexible packaging material including cohesive tape,
foil, rolls and sheets; also, heat seal coated lidding
and roll stock
President: Joseph Dollak
Director Sales/Marketing: Charles Holbrook
Customer Service: Anjanette Goetz
Estimated Sales: $5-10 Million
Number Employees: 20-49
Square Footage: 116000
Brands:
Touchseal

18819 American Production Co Inc
2734 Spring St
Redwood City, CA 94063-3524
650-368-5334
Fax: 650-368-4547 www.americanproduction.com
Manufacturer and exporter of commercial and indus-
trial stainless steel insulated food and beverage con-
tainers and thermal dispensers
Owner: Owen Conley
info@americanproduction.com
Estimated Sales: $2.5-5 Million
Number Employees: 5-9
Parent Co: Tilley Manufacturing Company
Brands:
Super Chef

18820 American Profol Inc.
4333 C St SW
Cedar Rapids, IA 52404-7461
319-365-0599
Fax: 319-365-1696 sales@profol.com
Plastic industrial film
CEO: Mark Thoeny
mthoeny@profol.com
CEO: Mark Thoeny
Estimated Sales: $20 - 50 Million
Number Employees: 100-249

18821 American Radionic Co Inc
32 Hargrove Grade
Industrial Park
Palm Coast, FL 32137-5106
386-445-6000
Fax: 386-445-6871 800-445-6033
www.americanradionic.com
HVAC capacitors
President: Robert Stockman
crezarad@aol.com
Sales Exec: Carl Rezendes
Estimated Sales: $10-20 Million
Number Employees: 50-99

18822 American Range
13592 Desmond St
Pacoima, CA 91331-2315
818-897-0808
Fax: 818-897-1670 888-753-9898
info@americanrange.com
www.americanrange.com
Manufacturer and exporter of commercial cooking
equipment including exhaust hoods, ranges, ovens,
hot plates, open burners, stock pot stoves, broilers,
griddles, woks, cheese melters, chicken rotisseries,
etc
President: Courtney Cochran
courtney.cochran@fetzer.com
Quality Control: Cristie Merriot
Estimated Sales: $10 - 20 Million
Number Employees: 100-249
Square Footage: 70000
Brands:
American Range

18823 American Renolit Corp LA
6900 Elm St
Commerce, CA 90040-2625
323-721-2720
Fax: 323-725-6466 www.renolit.com
Manufacturer and exporter of plastic materials in-
cluding PVC films, compounds and roll stock for
packaging and devices requiring food grade
applications
President: Rich Sterndahl
rich.sterndahl@renolit.com
Finance Executive: Laurie Dunbar
VP Sales: Mark Stern
Estimated Sales: $10-20 Million
Number Employees: 100-249
Square Footage: 170000

18824 American Resin Corp
6250 Southwest Pkwy
Wichita Falls, TX 76310-2897
940-692-8011
Fax: 940-692-8014
President: John Vitek
jwvitek@aol.com
Estimated Sales: Less Than $500,000
Number Employees: 1-4

18825 American Roland Food Corp
71 West 23rd Street
New York, NY 10010
800-221-4030
Fax: 516-694-9177
Development, manufacture and sale of antioxidants
including ethoxyquin, propyl gallate and tocopherols
for feed, food and industrial uses
Contact: Tyrus Brailey
tyrus.r.brailey@jpmorgan.com

18826 American Safety Technologies
565 Eagle Rock Ave
Roseland, NJ 07068-1501
973-403-2600
Fax: 973-403-1108 800-645-7546
www.insulcast.com
Contact: Bob Gasson
bob@compenv.com
Operations: Don Motta

Number Employees: 50-99

18827 American Services Group
850 Ridge Lake Blvd
Memphis, TN 38120
800-333-6678
Fax: 630-271-2710
alison.boyle@servicemaster.com
www.servicemaster.com
Consultant providing energy and waste manage-
ment, sanitation, maintenance and pest control
services
CEO: Robert J Gillette
Senior Vice President, General Counsel: Greer
McMullen
Senior Vice President of Corporate Commu: Peter
Tosches

18828 American Society of Brewing
3340 Pilot Knob Rd
Eagan, MN 55121-2055
651-454-7250
Fax: 651-454-0766 asbc@scisoc.org
www.asbcnet.org
Supplier of high quality malt based beverages and
ingredients
Executive Officer: Steve Nelson
snelson@scisoc.org
Member Public Relations Manager: Michelle
Bjerkness
VP Operations: Amy Hope
Number Employees: 50-99

18829 (HQ)American Solving Inc.
6519 Eastland Rd
Unit 5
Brook Park, OH 44142-1347
440-234-7373
Fax: 440-234-9112 800-822-2285
sales@solvinginc.com www.solvinginc.com
Manufacturer, importer and exporter of pneumatic
load-handling solutions
President: Andre Alho
andre.alho@solving.com
General Manager: Orley Aten
General Manager: Stanley Aten
Production Manager: Doug Eckert
Estimated Sales: $3 - 5 Million
Number Employees: 5-9
Square Footage: 12000
Brands:
American Solving
Numeri-Tech
Solving

18830 American Specialty Coffee & Culinary
204 14th Street NW
Atlanta, GA 30318-5304
404-607-1150
Fax: 404-876-1544
Espresso carts, espresso machines and accessories,
espresso pod machines

18831 American Specialty Machinery
456 Lake Hamilton Dr
Hot Springs, AR 71913-7424
713-828-2866
Fax: 713-926-2123
Owner: Jim West
Estimated Sales: $1 - 5 Million
Number Employees: 1-4

18832 American Star Cork Company
33-53 62nd Street
P.O. Box 770449
Woodside, NY 11377
718-335-3000
Fax: 718-335-3037 800-338-3581
www.amstarcork.com
Manufacturer, exporter and importer of cork and
cork products
President: Thomas Petrosino
amstarcork@gmail.com
Estimated Sales: $.5 - 1 million
Number Employees: 1-4

18833 American Store Fixtures
7700 Austin Avenue
Skokie, IL 60077-2603
Fax: 847-966-8074
Manufacturer and exporter of shopping baskets, se-
curity mirrors

CEO: Geoff Glass
CFO: Lucy Polk
Quality Control: Carol Salas
Marketing: Donna Kelner
Sales Manager: Debi Greenberg
Public Relations: Donna Kelner
Operations: Carol Salas
Plant Manager: Carol Salas
Estimated Sales: $1 - 5 Million
Number Employees: 100-250
Square Footage: 480000
Parent Co: American Louver

18834 American Style Foods
809 Riverside Drive
Old Hickory, TN 37138
615-847-0410
Consultant for food extrusion and product formula-
tion processes
President: Robert Garrison
Number Employees: 4

18835 American Sun Control Awnings
925 Mcfarland 400 Blvd
Alpharetta, GA 30004-3373
770-772-9900
Fax: 770-740-8668 800-245-6746
Commercial awnings
President: Glorio Patsy
Estimated Sales: $1-2,500,000
Number Employees: 10-19
Brands:
Fabri-Frame

18836 American Systems Associates
Leander Road
Hampton Bays, NY 11946
718-482-0408
800-584-3663
Gas powered cooking and refrigeration equipment;
also, food service design available
President: Johndavid Hensley
VP: Joyce Jones
Regional Director: Diane David
Number Employees: 1-4
Square Footage: 4000
Parent Co: FOOD

18837 American Technical Services Group
680 Oakbrook Parkway
Suite 165
Norcross, GA 30093
770-447-9444
Fax: 770-447-0319 800-893-1944
www.atsrmis.com
Service company providing instrumentation and
control system services including I/C installation,
ISO 9000 software, NIST calibration, integration,
maintenance and contract staffing
President: Robert Russo
Marketing Manager: Vicci Cogswell
VP Operations: Ray Green
Number Employees: 200
Parent Co: Strategic Distribution

18838 (HQ)American Textile Mills Inc
208 Bennington Ave
Kansas City, MO 64123-1914
816-842-2909
Fax: 816-842-8679
Disposable and reusable wiping towels
President: Dennis Wacknov
Estimated Sales: $5-10 Million
Number Employees: 10-19
Square Footage: 180000
Brands:
Nu-Wipes
Quik-Wipes

18839 American Time & Signal Co
140 3rd St
PO Box 707
Dassel, MN 55325-4511
320-275-2101
Fax: 320-275-2603 800-328-8996
theclockexperts@atsclock.com
www.american-time.com
Manufacturer and exporter of food preparation timers and clocks
President: Dieter Pape
dpape@atsclock.com

Estimated Sales: $10-20 Million
Number Employees: 50-99
Square Footage: 80000
Brands:
    American Time & Signal
    James Remind-O-Timer

18840 American Ultraviolet Co
212 S Mount Zion Rd
Lebanon, IN 46052-9479

765-483-9514
Fax: 765-483-9525 800-288-9288
www.americanultraviolet.com
Manufacturer and exporter of germicidal ultraviolet
air and water systems for air and water sterilization
President: Meredith C Stines
    mstines@auvco.com
Estimated Sales: $10 - 20 Million
Number Employees: 100-249
Number of Brands: 4
Square Footage: 70000
Type of Packaging: Food Service
Brands:
    Puritron
    Ultra-Cool
    Ultra-Gog
    Ultra-Spec

18841 American Variseal
510 Burbank St
Broomfield, CO 80020-1604

303-465-1727
Fax: 303-469-4874
Manager: Tom Potosky
Contact: Clae Jrwall
    claes.jorwall@trelleborg.com
Estimated Sales: $20 - 50 Million
Number Employees: 100-249

18842 American Ventilation Company
P.O. Box 227
Grafton, OH 44044-0227

440-365-4533
Fax: 440-365-5858 800-854-3267
Exhaust and make-up air fans for the food service
industry
Manager: Tammy Parron
General Manager: Michael Maynard
Estimated Sales: $1-2.5 Million
Number Employees: 5-9
Square Footage: 50000

18843 American Water Broom
3565 Mccall Pl
Doraville, GA 30340-2801

770-451-2000
Fax: 770-455-4478 800-241-6565
info@waterbrooms.com www.waterbrooms.com
Manufacturer and exporter of commercial and resi-
dential high pressure water brooms
Vice President: Archie Merlin
    amerlin@waterbrooms.com
VP: Beverly Roberts
Number Employees: 5-9
Brands:
    Jetaway
    Squirt

18844 American Wax Co Inc
3930 Review Ave
PO Box 1943
Long Island City, NY 11101-2020

718-361-4820
Fax: 718-482-9366
solutions@cleaning-solutions.com
www.heathsprings.net
Manufacturer and exporter of detergents, deodor-
ants, disinfectants, germicides, floor polish and soap
President: Michelle Devito
    michelled@cleaning-solutions.com
Vice President: Ronald Ingber
Sales Manager: Allen Winik
Purchasing Manager: Ron Ingber
Estimated Sales: $2.5 - 5 Million
Number Employees: 20-49
Square Footage: 124000

18845 American Whey Company
12 N State Route 17
Paramus, NJ 07652-2644

201-587-1444
Fax: 201-587-0310

18846 American Wholesale Equipment
4001 Hamilton Ave
Cleveland, OH 44114-3839

216-426-8882
Fax: 216-426-8883 877-220-8882
info@awrco.com www.awrco.com
Refrigerating equipment and machinery
President: John Paris
Manager: Larry Treb
    larry@awrco.com
Estimated Sales: Below $5 Million
Number Employees: 5-9

18847 American Wire Products
616 Industrial Park
Frankfort, KY 40601

502-695-0073
Manager: Carol Chamblain
Estimated Sales: $20 - 50 Million
Number Employees: 100-249

18848 American Wood Fibers
9841 Broken Land Pkwy # 302
Columbia, MD 21046-3073

410-290-8700
Fax: 410-290-6660 800-624-9663
www.awf.com
Sawdust, firelogs and wood floors
CEO: Ed Leland
    eleland@awf.com
CEO: Ed Leland
General Manager: Mark Fahner
Estimated Sales: $1 - 5 Million
Number Employees: 20-49

18849 American-Newlong Inc
5310 S Harding St
Indianapolis, IN 46217-9575

317-787-9421
Fax: 317-786-5225
newlong@american-newlong.com
www.american-newlong.com
Automated packaging equipment and bagging sys-
tems.
President/General Manager: Gary Wells
    gwells@american-newlong.com
CFO: Connie Parrin
North American Sales Manager: Garnet McMillian
Warehouse Manager: Mark Banholzer
Estimated Sales: $10-20 Million
Number Employees: 10-19

18850 (HQ)Americana Art China Company
PO Box 310
Sebring, OH 44672

330-938-6133
Fax: 330-938-9546 800-233-6133
amerimug@sbcglobal.net
Custom decorator of ceramic and glassware.
President/CEO: James Puckett
Research & Development: Lisa Cox
Manager of Quality Control: Wendy Davidson
Marketing Director: Jim Puckett
Operations: Jim Puckett
Estimated Sales: $1-3 Million
Number Employees: 32
Number of Products: 126
Square Footage: 80000
Type of Packaging: Private Label, Bulk
Other Locations:
    Americana Art China Co.
    Sebring OH

18851 Americana Marketing
840 Tourmaline Dr
Newbury Park, CA 91320

805-499-0451
Fax: 805-499-4668 800-742-7520
fdi@follmerdevelopment.com
www.follmerdevelopment.com
Aerosol nonstick cooking, baking and flavor sprays
President/CEO: Garrett Follmer
    fdi@follmerdevelopment.com
Sales/Marketing VP: David McKenzie
Number Employees: 50-99
Type of Packaging: Consumer, Food Service, Pri-
vate Label
Brands:
    Natural Lite
    Pure & Simple

18852 Americasia International
Hillsborough Business Center
1 Ilene Court, Building 8, Suite 12
Hillsborough, NJ 08844

609-608-6886
Fax: 908-262-2279 maria@americasia.net
americasia.net
Customized packaging and product displays
Other Locations:
    New Hampshire Office
    Dover NH

18853 Americo
601 E Barton Ave
West Memphis, AR 72301-2011

870-735-4848
Fax: 870-735-4129 800-626-2350
Laminated and vinyl table covers; also, upholstery
fabrics
President: Ed Straub
    ed@americo-inc.com
Chairman of the Board: Wallace Dunbar
Sales Director: Jerry Van Houten
Estimated Sales: $1-2.5 Million
Number Employees: 20-49

18854 Americode LLC
100 Redhaw Ct
Burleson, TX 76028-2540

817-447-9520
Fax: 817-447-3269 www.americodeusa.com
Printing systems
President: Jerry L Perry
Estimated Sales: $1 - 3 Million
Number Employees: 5-9

18855 Americraft Carton Inc
403 Fillmore Ave E
St Paul, MN 55107-1288

651-227-6655
Fax: 651-227-4713 www.americraft.com
Folding cartons
Manager: Jim Maher
    jim.maher@americraft.com
General Manager: Jim Maher
Plnt Mngr: Brian Lewindowski
Estimated Sales: $10 - 20 Million
Number Employees: 100-249
Parent Co: Americraft Carton

18856 Americraft Carton Inc
7400 State Line Rd # 206
Suite 206
Prairie Village, KS 66208-3445

913-387-3700
www.americraft.com
Folding cartons
Estimated Sales: $59 Million
Number Employees: 100-249
Square Footage: 135000
Parent Co: Americraft Carton Group

18857 Ameridia Innovative Solutions
20 Worlds Fair Dr
Suite F
Somerset, NJ 08873-1362

732-805-4003
Fax: 732-805-4008 dbar@ameridia.com
www.eurodia.com
Electrodialysis stacks and equipment; chromatogra-
phy and ion exchange systems; micro-, ultra-, and
non-afiltration systems
VP, Sales and Business Development: Daniel Bar
Estimated Sales: $5-10 Million
Number Employees: 5-9
Parent Co: Eurodia Industrie
Brands:
    Aqualyzer
    STARS

18858 Ameriglobe LLC
153 S Long St
Lafayette, LA 70506-3019

337-234-3211
Fax: 337-234-3213
marlener@ameriglobe-fibc.com
www.ameriglobe-fibc.com
Bulk bags and weigh/fill stations; also, bulk bag re-
furbishing services available
President: Daniel R Schnaars
    dans@ameriglobe-fibc.com
CFO: Randy Girourard
Marketing Director: Blaine Beck
Sales Director: Marlene Rodrigue

Estimated Sales: $50-100 Million
Number Employees: 50-99

18859 Amerikooler Inc
575 E 10th Ave
Hialeah, FL 33010-4639

305-888-5071
Fax: 305-884-8330 800-627-5665
marylo@amerikooler.net www.amerikooler.com
Walk-in coolers, freezers and refrigerated warehouses
President: Renate M Alonso
Vice President: Renato J. Alonso
Vice President of Sales: Gian Carlo Alonso
Purchasing: Macbeth Araque
Estimated Sales: $5 - 10 Million
Number Employees: 50-99

18860 Ameripak Packaging Equipment
2001 County Line Rd
Warrington, PA 18976-2486

215-343-1530
Fax: 215-343-5293 www.opschuman.com
Packaging equipment including horizontal wrappers, filled tray sealers, rigid box and thermoforming; rebuilt equipment available; importer of thermoforming equipment; exporter of rigid box machinery and horizontal wrappers
President: William T Schuman
schumanwt@opschuman.com
VP Marketing/Sales: Phil Kelly
Estimated Sales: $5-10 Million
Number Employees: 20-49
Number of Products: 5
Square Footage: 240000
Parent Co: SKS Equipment Company

18861 Ameripak Packaging Equipment
2001 County Line Rd
Warrington, PA 18976-2486

215-343-1530
Fax: 215-343-5293 www.opschuman.com
Horizontal form fill seals, flowpak wrapper, fill tray sealers for plastic or paperboard trays
President: William T Schuman
schumanwt@opschuman.com
Estimated Sales: $5-10 Million
Number Employees: 20-49

18862 Ameripec
6965 Aragon Cir
Buena Park, CA 90620

714-994-2990
Fax: 714-562-0849 www.ameripecinc.com
Contract packing of PET bottles and glass bottles of juices, juice drink, flavored drink and water at acidified pH
Contact: Mathew Bamberger
mathew@ameripec.com
Director of Operations: D Delacruz
Estimated Sales: $20-50 Million
Number Employees: 150
Square Footage: 130000
Type of Packaging: Private Label

18863 Ameristamp/Sign-A-Rama
1300 N Royal Ave
Evansville, IN 47715-7808

812-477-7763
Fax: 812-477-7898 800-543-6693
websales@SignsOverAmerica.com
www.signsoveramerica.com
Manufacturer and exporter of marking devices, including rubber stamps
Owner: Walter Valiant
walter@signsoveramerica.com
VP of Public Relations: Grant Valiant
Estimated Sales: $1-2.5 Million
Number Employees: 10-19
Square Footage: 6000
Type of Packaging: Consumer, Food Service, Bulk

18864 Ameritech Laboratories
12817 20th Ave
Flushing, NY 11356-2401

718-461-0475
Fax: 718-461-0187
Consultant providing a complete range of chemical, microbiological and nutritional tests and product development services
President: John Bonnes
Estimated Sales: Below $5 Million
Number Employees: 5-9
Square Footage: 20000

18865 Ameritech Signs & Banners
3015 Pico Blvd
Santa Monica, CA 90405-2003

310-829-9359
Fax: 310-998-1109 ameritechsigns@verizon.net
www.ameritechsigns.com
Pennants, signs and banners
Owner: Bill Gabriel
ameritechsigns@earthlink.net
Estimated Sales: Less Than $500,000
Number Employees: 1-4

18866 Amerivacs
1518 Lancaster Point Way
San Diego, CA 92154-7700

619-498-8227
Fax: 619-498-8222 www.amerivacs.com
Clean room compatible chamber and retractable nozzle vacuum sealers with gas purge for all heat sealable bags, including all ESD bags by using quiet, nonparticle generating, maintenance-free compressed air-driven vacuum pumps. Standardimpulse sealers also available. One week trial period. Custom designs upon request. One year limited warranty. Made in the USA
President: Peter Tadlock
petertadlock@amerivacs.com
Estimated Sales: $1 - 2.5 Million
Number Employees: 1-4
Number of Brands: 1
Number of Products: 8
Square Footage: 8000
Brands:
  Amerivacs

18867 Amerivap Systems Inc
31 Successful Way
Dawsonville, GA 30534-6841

706-531-1509
Fax: 404-350-9214 800-763-7687
Dry steam cleaning and sanitizing systems.
President: Werner Diercks
werner.diercks@amerivap.com
CFO: Paula Marshal
VP Marketing: Dolly Diercks
VP Sales: Gabriel Perez
Estimated Sales: $3 Million
Number Employees: 10-19
Square Footage: 20000

18868 Ameron International
P.O. Box 1629
Brea, CA 92822-1629

714-256-7755
Fax: 714-256-7750 www.ameron.com
General Manager: Edwin Steenis
Chairman of the Board, Chief Executive O: James Marlen
Vice President: Christine Stanley
Vice Division President of Operations: David Jones
Plant Manager: Ron Johnson
Estimated Sales: $1 - 5 Million
Number Employees: 1-4

18869 Ames Engineering Corporation
805 E 13th St
Wilmington, DE 19802

302-658-6945
Fax: 302-658-6946 800-628-7128
telesonics@aol.com www.telesoniconline.com
Horizontal form-fill, three and four side seal sachet, stand-up pouch and stick pack portion packaging machinery
Owner: Bernard Katz
Contact: Steve Ames
steveames@telesoniconline.com
Estimated Sales: $5 000,000
Number Employees: 1-4

18870 Ametco Manufacturing Corp
4326 Hamann Pkwy
Willoughby, OH 44094-5626

440-951-4300
Fax: 440-951-2542 800-321-7042
ametco@ametco.com www.ametco.com
Iron and steel security fencing; also, perforated plastics and expanded, perforated, heavy weld and bar metal gratings
President: Greg Mitrovich
ametco@ametco.com
Sales Manager: Ludwig Weber
Estimated Sales: $5-10,000,000
Number Employees: 20-49

18871 Ametek
900 E Clymer Ave
Sellersville, PA 18960-2628

215-257-6531
Fax: 215-257-4711 chatillon.fl-lar@ametek.com
www.usgauge.com
Test and calibration instruments
Manager: Joe Karpov
Estimated Sales: $30-50 Million
Number Employees: 10-19

18872 Ametek
900 E Clymer Ave
Sellersville, PA 18960-2628

215-257-6531
Fax: 215-257-4711 chatillon.fl-lar@ametek.com
www.usgauge.com
Manufacturer and exporter of pressure and temperature gauges
Manager: Joe Karpov
Sales Manager: Amil Demicco
Estimated Sales: $1 - 5 Million
Number Employees: 500-999
Parent Co: Ametek
Brands:
  U.S. Gauge

18873 Ametek Drexelbrook
205 Keith Valley Rd
Horsham, PA 19044-1408

215-674-1234
Fax: 215-674-2731 800-553-9092
drexelbrook.info@ametek.com
www.drexelbrook.com
Test and calibration instruments
General Manager: Jim Visnic
VP: Dave Hernance
Estimated Sales: $5,000,000 - $9,999,999
Number Employees: 50-99

18874 Ametek Technical & Industrial Products
627 Lake St
Kent, OH 44240

215-256-6601
Fax: 330-677-3306 www.ametektip.com
Air blowers and air knives for drying, dewatering and sterilization degassing applications; food grade products available, combustion blowers
Manager: Shannon Booth
Sales Director: Jay Jarboe
Contact: Chris Antwright
chris.antwright@ametek.com
Number Employees: 50-99
Parent Co: Ametek

18875 Ametek Us Gauge
205 Keith Valley Rd
Horsham, PA 19044-1408

215-674-1234
Fax: 215-323-9450 usg.sales@ametek.com
www.ametekusg.com
Test and calibration instruments
Manager: Joe Karpov
Number Employees: 20-49

18876 Amfec Inc
21040 Forbes Ave
Hayward, CA 94545-1116

510-780-0134
Fax: 510-783-0409
Food processing equipment.
Equipment Sales: Adam Quick
Contact: Melvin Huff
mhuff@amfec.com
Estimated Sales: Less Than $500,000
Number Employees: 1-4

18877 Amherst Milling Co
140 Union Hill Rd
Amherst, VA 24521-4053

434-946-7601
Grist mills
Manager: William H Wydner
General Manager/VP: Bill Wydner
Estimated Sales: $1 - 3 Million
Number Employees: 1-4
Square Footage: 6

18878 Amherst Stainless Fabrication
60 John Glenn Dr
Amherst, NY 14228

716-691-7012
Fax: 716-691-8202 www.amherstfab.com

Manufacturer of stainless steel equipment, parts and systems for the food and beverage industry
President/Owner: Gerald Bogdan
Square Footage: 45000

18879 Amiad Filtration Systems
120-J Talbert Road
Mooresville, NC 28117

704-662-3133
Fax: 704-662-3155 www.amiadusa.com
President: Tom Akehurst
Chief Executive Officer: Rami Molcho
Finance Executive: Inko Evrard
Sales Executive: Jim Lauria
Operations Executive: Jerry Weynand
Estimated Sales: $5 - 10 Million
Number Employees: 20-49

18880 Ammeraal Beltech
3720 3 Mile Rd NW
Grand Rapids, MI 49534-1270

616-791-0292
Fax: 616-791-1067 www.ammeraalbeltech.com
Process and conveyor belting equipment
President: Paul Hamilton
Manager: Jim Honeycutt
Sales Manager: Mike Wilde
Contact: Ron Jones
 rjones@ammeraalbeltechusa.com
Technical Services Manager: Jim Honeycutt
Estimated Sales: $20-50 Million
Number Employees: 20-49
Parent Co: Ammeraal International

18881 Ammeraal Beltech Inc
7501 Saint Louis Ave
Skokie, IL 60076-4033

847-673-6720
Fax: 847-673-6373 800-323-4170
info@ammeraalbeltechusa.com
www.ammeraal-beltech.com
Manufacturer, importer and exporter of belts for packaging machinery and the processing of cookies, crackers, confectionery items, bread, rolls, meat and poultry
President: Jeffrey W Nank
Vice President: Jim Ekedahl
Estimated Sales: $20-50 Million
Number Employees: 50-99
Square Footage: 55000
Parent Co: Verseidag
Brands:
 Beltech
 Burtek
 Polytek
 Rapplon
 Rapptex
 Volta

18882 Ammeraal Beltech Inc
7501 Saint Louis Ave
Skokie, IL 60076-4033

847-673-6720
Fax: 847-673-6373 800-323-4170
info@ammeraalbeltechusa.com
www.ammeraal-beltech.com
Manufacturer, importer and exporter of belts for packaging machinery and the processing of cookies, crackers, confectionery items, bread, rolls, meat and poultry
President: Jim Bateman
 jbateman@ammeraalbeltechusa.com
CFO: Jan Marion
Marketing Director: Mark Wierzbinski
Estimated Sales: $20 - 50 Million
Number Employees: 50-99
Square Footage: 55000
Brands:
 Beltech
 Burtex
 Polytek
 Rapplon
 Rapptex
 Volta

18883 Amodex Products
PO Box 3332
Bridgeport, CT 6605

203-335-1255
Fax: 203-330-9988 877-866-1255
www.amodexink.com
Stain removers and all-purpose industrial and house-hold cleaners for face and hands

President: Beverlee Fatse Dacey
Director, Finance & Technology: Nicolas Dacey
Director of Marketing: Alexander Dacey
Director of Operations: A. Peter Dacey
Estimated Sales: $.5 - 1 million
Number Employees: 1-4

18884 Amot Controls
401 1st Street
Richmond, CA 94801-2906

510-307-8300
info@amotusa.com
www.amot.com
President: James Mannebach
Contact: Lee Allen
 lee.allen@amotusa.com
Estimated Sales: $5 - 10 Million
Number Employees: 20-49

18885 Ampac Packaging, LLC
12025 Tricon Road
Cincinnati, OH 45246

513-671-1777
Fax: 513-671-2920 800-543-7030
www.ampaconline.com
Flexible packaging and bags
Contact: Ward Alexander
 ward.alexander@ourhouseinc.com
Brands:
 Ab Sealers
 All Packaging Machinery
 Chantland
 Fischbein Bag Closing
 Fujy
 Highlight Stretch Rappers
 Lift Products
 New London Eng
 Vaculet Usa

18886 Ampak
4580 E 71st St
Cleveland, OH 44125

216-341-2022
Fax: 216-341-2163 800-342-6329
www.heatsealco.com/about-ampak
Manufacturer and exporter of packaging machinery including bag/cup wrapping, skin and die cutting
Southeast Equipment Sales Manager: Dan Barnes
Customer Service: Troy Roberts
General Manager: Les Szakallas
Estimated Sales: $5-10 Million
Number Employees: 20-49
Square Footage: 80000
Parent Co: Heat Sealing Equipment Manufacturing Company
Brands:
 Master
 Maxima
 Rotocut

18887 Ampco Pumps Co Inc
2045 W Mill Rd
Milwaukee, WI 53209-3444

414-540-1597
Fax: 414-643-4452 800-737-8671
ampcocs@ampcopumps.com
www.ampcopumps.com
Manufacturer and exporter of pumps including centrifugal, sanitary, wastewater and water
Owner: Mike Nicholson
CFO: Loori Neisner
R&D: Loori Neisner
Quality Control: Oori Neisner
Midwestern Regional Manager: Matt Schultz
 mnicholson@ampcopumps.com
Estimated Sales: $1 - 2.5 Million
Number Employees: 10-19

18888 Ample Industries
4000 Commerce Center Dr
Franklin, OH 45005

937-746-9700
Fax: 937-746-2234 888-818-9700
Carry-out containers, food trays, french fry and pizza boxes and hot dog clam shells; exporter of pizza boxes
Vice President of Sales: David Ernst
Contact: Ty Gardner
 tgardner@huhtamaki.com
General Manager: Robert Fairchild, Jr.
Plant Manager: Bill Bausmith
Estimated Sales: $50 Million
Number Employees: 100-249
Square Footage: 110000

18889 Amplexus Corporation
9 Commercial Blvd #150
Novato, CA 94949

415-897-3700
Fax: 415-897-4897 800-423-8268
info@adssolutions.com
www.softwarefordistributors.com
Software for restaurant supply and food equipment distributors
President: Kenneth Levin
Marketing Manager: Rebecca Baker
Estimated Sales: $5 - 10 Million
Number Employees: 4
Brands:
 Amplexus Advantage
 Amplexus E3/Commerce

18890 Amri Inc
2045 Silber Rd # 100
Houston, TX 77055-2615

713-682-0000
Fax: 713-682-0080
President: William Leech
Manager: David Abbott
 dabbott@amrivalves.com
Estimated Sales: $5 - 10 Million
Number Employees: 20-49

18891 Amscor Inc
119 Lamar St
West Babylon, NY 11704-1301

718-383-4900
Fax: 718-383-7787 800-825-9800
sales@amscorinc.com www.amscorinc.com
Steel shelving
President: Michael Silberglied
 michael@amscorinc.com
Estimated Sales: $1-2.5 Million
Number Employees: 10-19
Square Footage: 20000
Parent Co: American Steel Corporation

18892 Amsler Equipment Inc
1245 Reid Street
Unit 1
Richmond Hill, ON, ON L4B 1G4
Canada

905-707-6704
Fax: 905-707-6707 877-738-2569
sales@amslerequipment.net
www.amslerequipment.net
Reheat stretch blow molding machines and related equipment.
President/CEO: Werner Amsler
Quality Control: Jason Amsler
Sales: Heidi Amsler
Estimated Sales: $3 Million
Number Employees: 15

18893 Amstat Industries
3012 N Lake Terrace
Glenview, IL 60026-1335

847-998-6210
Fax: 847-998-6218 800-783-9999
info@amstat.com www.amstat.com
Manufacturer and distributor of static electricity control products.
President: Larry Jacobson
Sales Director: Larry Jacobson
Estimated Sales: $3 - 5 Million
Number Employees: 10-19

18894 Amster-Kirtz Co
2830 Cleveland Ave NW
Canton, OH 44709-3204

330-535-6021
Fax: 330-437-2015 800-257-9338
www.amsterkirtz.com
Wholesaler/distributor of merchandise for convenience stores including; candy and grocery items
President: James Ulery
 jimu@amsterkirtzco.net
General Manager: Larry H
Sales Manager: Everett M
Number Employees: 50-99
Type of Packaging: Consumer, Bulk

18895 Amsterdam Printing & Litho Inc
166 Wallins Corners Rd
Amsterdam, NY 12010-1817

518-842-6000
Fax: 518-843-5204 800-203-9917
cs@amsterdamprinting.com
www.amsterdamprinting.com

Writing instruments including fine point, felt tip and ball point pens; also, advertising specialties including calendars, mugs, etc.; importer of roller ball pens
President: Robert Rosenthal
HR Executive: Donna Graham
dgraham@banyanincentives.com
Sales/Marketing: Jim Zuzzolo
Purchasing Manager: David Laemle
Estimated Sales: $10-20 Million
Number Employees: 500-999
Square Footage: 52000

18896 Amtab Manufacturing Corp
652 N Highland Ave
Aurora, IL 60506-2940
630-301-7600
Fax: 312-421-3448 800-878-2257
info@amtab.com www.amtab.com
Manufacturer and exporter of folding banquet tables
Owner: Greg Hanusiak
g_hanusiak@amtab.com
CEO: Chris Cornier
VP: Greg Hanusiak
Estimated Sales: $5-10 Million
Number Employees: 20-49
Square Footage: 70000
Type of Packaging: Food Service, Private Label

18897 Amtekco
1205 Refugee Rd
Columbus, OH 43207-2114
614-228-6590
Fax: 614-737-8017 800-336-4677
www.amtekco.com
Manufacturer and exporter of stainless steel tables, commercial sinks, wood cabinets, fixtures, table tops, bars and back bars.
President/Owner: Bruce Wasserstrom
brucewasserstrom@amtekco.com
CFO: Robert Hudgins
Research & Development: Roger Henry
Sales Manager: Nancy Green
Public Relations: Adena Bogdan
Plant Manager: Ron Fishking
Purchasing Manager: Hans Woschkolup
Estimated Sales: $18-20 Million
Number Employees: 100-249
Square Footage: 400000
Type of Packaging: Bulk

18898 Amwell
600 N Commons Dr # 116
Aurora, IL 60504-7928
630-898-6900
Fax: 630-898-1647 amwell@amwell-inc.com
www.amwell-inc.com
Owner: Art Benner
abenner@amwell-inc.com
Quality Control: Jim Martin
Estimated Sales: $3 - 5 Million
Number Employees: 10-19
Parent Co: McNish Corporation

18899 Amy Food Inc
3324 S Richey St
Houston, TX 77017-6259
713-910-5860
Fax: 713-910-4812 www.amyfood.com
Egg rolls, potstickers, empanadas and party platters, natural and organic foods.
Owner: Phyllis Hsu
amyfood@aol.com
Number Employees: 50-99
Square Footage: 40000
Type of Packaging: Consumer, Food Service, Private Label
Brands:
Jamy's Three Dragon

18900 Anaheim Manufacturing Company
P.O. Box 4146
Anaheim, CA 92803-4146
714-524-7770
Fax: 714-996-7073 800-767-6293
www.anaheimmfg.com
Manufacturer and exporter of garbage disposal units
President: Tom Dugan
Sales Supervisor: Alicia Oregel
Commercial Sales Manager: Grevor Wainwright
Estimated Sales: $20-50 Million
Number Employees: 100-249
Square Footage: 60000
Parent Co: Western Industries

Brands:
Sinkmaster
Waste King
Whirlaway

18901 Analite
24 Newtown Plz
Plainview, NY 11803-4506
516-752-1818
Fax: 516-752-0554 800-229-3357
Manufacturer and exporter of relative humidity and temperature probes, controllers and transmitters
President: Morris Wasser
Vice President: Julius Levin
Estimated Sales: $2.5-5 Million
Number Employees: 10-19
Square Footage: 15200
Brands:
A2000
Humitran
Humitran-C
Humitran-Dp
Humitran-T

18902 Analog Devices Inc
One Technology Way
P.O. Box 9106
Norwood, MA 02062
781-329-4700
800-262-5643
www.analog.com
Analog, mixed-signal and digital signal processing integrated circuits for electronic equipment.
President & CEO: Vincent Roche
SVP, Finance & CFO: Prashanth Mahendra-Rajah
Chief Technology Officer: Dan Leibholz
Year Founded: 1965
Estimated Sales: $6.2 Billion
Number Employees: 16,000

18903 Analog Technology Corporation
5220 4th St # 18
Baldwin Park, CA 91706-6600
626-856-5690
Fax: 626-472-6069
Manufacturers of industrial-graphic, bar code forms and label printers
President: James Lawrence
Estimated Sales: Below $5 Million
Number Employees: 1-4

18904 Analogic Corp.
8 Centennial Dr
Peabody, MA 01960
978-326-4000
Fax: 978-977-6809 www.analogic.com
Medical and security imaging products
CEO: Tom Ripp
CFO: Will Rousmaniere
CTO: Steve Urchuk
VPm Quality & Compliance: Brian Kinports
VP, Operations: Robert Lancaster
Year Founded: 1967
Estimated Sales: $486 Million
Number Employees: 1,500

18905 Analytical Development
65 Cavender Run
Dahlonega, GA 30533
770-237-2330
Fax: 770-237-2332
Manufacturer and exporter of hand-held portable luminometers
President: Ed Nemec
Estimated Sales: $500,000-$1 Million
Number Employees: 1-4
Brands:
Inspector

18906 Analytical Labs
1804 North 33rd Street Boise
Boise, ID 83703-5814
208-342-5515
Fax: 208-342-5591 800-574-5773
ali@analyticallaboratories.com
Laboratory specializing in microbiological and chemical analysis of food, water, waste water and fuel; also, nutritional labeling analysis and plant GMP inspections available
President: Mike Moore
Estimated Sales: Below $5 Million
Number Employees: 20-49
Square Footage: 24000

18907 Analytical Measurements
22 Mountain View Drive
Chester, NJ 07930
800-635-5580
phmeter@verizon.net
www.analyticalmeasurements.com
Manufacturer/supplier of pH and ORP instrumentation, probes, and other related materials
President: W Richard Adey
Contact: Frank G Paully
frank@analyticalmeasurements.com
Estimated Sales: 500,000
Number Employees: 3
Square Footage: 2000
Brands:
Universal Ph Doser

18908 Analytical Technologies Inc
11 Holt St
Westfield, NY 14787-1118
716-326-6444
Fax: 716-326-6468 800-345-1357
sales@testmilk.com www.testmilk.com
Dairy, electronic milk testing equipment
President: David Gross
ati@testmilk.com
Estimated Sales: $500,000-$1 000,000
Number Employees: 5-9

18909 Analyticon Discovery LLC
9700 Great Seneca Hwy
Rockville, MD 20850-3307
240-406-1256
Fax: 240-453-6208 info@ac-discovery.com
www.ac-discovery.com
Natural active ingredients and products.
CEO/Co-Founder: Lutz Muller-Kuhrt
CFO/Co-Founder: Jochen Gatter
VP Research & Development: Karsten Siems
North American/UK Sales Representative: Andrea Christes
Contact: Betsy Manikowski
b.manikowski@ac-discovery.com
VP Operations & Research: Martina Jaensch
Estimated Sales: $4.64 Million
Number Employees: 1-4

18910 Anbroco
7711 Old Plank Road
Stanley, NC 28164-7774
704-827-1255
Fax: 704-822-6266 800-228-4784
Agitators, aseptic processing equipment, blenders, batching and blending systems
Sales Manager: Ken Fincham
Number Employees: 22

18911 Anchor Conveyor Products
6830 Kingsley St
Dearborn, MI 48126-1941
313-846-6000
Fax: 313-846-6004 800-959-1347
sales@anchorconveyor.com
www.anchorconveyor.com
President: Bill Farmer
bfarmer@anchorconveyor.com
Estimated Sales: $1 - 3 Million
Number Employees: 10-19

18912 Anchor Crane & Hoist Service Company
455 Aldine Bender Road
Houston, TX 77060
281-405-9048
Fax: 281-448-7500 800-835-2223
anchor@anchorcrane.com
www.proservanchor.com
Manufacturer and exporter of overhead crane systems
Manager: Greg Salinas
Contact: Tommy Cochran
cochran@proservanchor.com
Purchasing Manager: Bob Steward
Number Employees: 100-249
Parent Co: RPC

18913 Anchor Glass Container Corporation
401 East Jackson St.
Suite 1100
Tampa, FL 33602

813-884-0000
Fax: 813-882-7859 Info@AnchorGlass.com
www.anchorglass.com
Premium glass containers for beverages, beer, liquor, and food products.
President/CEO: Nipesh Shah
Executive VP/CFO: Rachel Celiberti
VP/General Counsel: Sam Hijab
Chief Communications Officer: Robert Stewart
Executive VP, Operations: Arlo Sims
Year Founded: 1983
Estimated Sales: $297 Million
Number Employees: 2,840
Parent Co: BA Glass B.V.

18914 Anchor Hocking Operating Co
519 N Pierce Ave
Lancaster, OH 43130-2969

740-681-6275
Fax: 740-681-6040 800-562-7511
consumerar@anchorhocking.com
www.anchorhocking.com
Manufacturer and exporter of glass tabletop products including beverageware, stemware, dinnerware, ovenware and floral and table accessories
President: J David Reed
CEO: Mark Eichorn
Vice President Sales & Marketing: Jackie Sokol
Contact: Ben Baird
bb322801@ohiou.edu
Vice President of Operations: Margaret Homers
Estimated Sales: Less Than $500,000
Number Employees: 1-4
Parent Co: Newell Rubbermaid
Other Locations:
Anchor Hocking Glass Co.
Richmond Hill ON
Brands:
Clarisse
Excellency
Florentine
Optic Florentine
Stackables

18915 Anchor Industries
P.O. Box 3477
Evansville, IN 47733-3477

812-867-2421
Fax: 812-867-1429 custdiv@anchorinc.com
www.anchorinc.com
Commercial awnings
Founder: Louis Daus
CFO: Mike Elliott
Contact: Hubert Clark
hclark@anchorind.com
Estimated Sales: $30 - 50 Million
Number Employees: 500-999

18916 (HQ)Anchor Packaging
13515 Barrett Parkway Dr # 100
Ballwin, MO 63021-5870

314-822-7800
Fax: 314-822-2035 800-467-3900
info@anchorpackaging.com
www.anchorpackaging.com
Manufacturer and exporter of plastic microwaveable packaging and container supplies including films, containers, trays, food protective and cling wrap.
President: Jeff Wolff
jeff.wolff@anchorpack.com
CFO: Steve Riek
CEO: Brad Jensen
Marketing: Michael Thaler
Sales: Frank Baumann
Public Relations: Michael Thaler
Operations: Staya Garg
Estimated Sales: $20 - 50 Million
Number Employees: 20-49
Type of Packaging: Food Service, Private Label
Brands:
Aurity Wrap
Bonfaire
Culinary Classics
Fresh View
Micro Raves
Purity Wrap
Ultra Wrap

18917 Anco-Eaglin Inc
1420 Lorraine Ave
High Point, NC 27263-2040

336-855-7800
Fax: 336-855-7831 info@ancoeaglin.com
www.ancoeaglin.com
Batch rendering systems, continuous rendering systems, hydrolizing equipment, inedible rendering equipment and systems, prebreakers and presses
Owner: Clayton Eaglin
ancoeaglin@aol.com
US/European Sales: Brian Eaglin
Estimated Sales: Below $5 000,000
Number Employees: 20-49

18918 Andantex USA Inc
1705 Valley Rd
Ocean, NJ 07712-3949

732-493-2812
Fax: 732-493-2949 800-713-6170
info@andantex.com www.andantex.com
Power transmissions including robotic controls, speed reducers and right angle gear boxes
President: Mike Munn
mike@andantex.com
Vice President of Engineering: Dave Regiec
Systems Engineer: John Tashjian
VP of Marketing: Bruce Bradley
Sales Manager of Sales: Al Schwartz
Estimated Sales: $2.5-5 Million
Number Employees: 20-49

18919 Andco Environmental Processes
415 Commerce Dr
Amherst, NY 14228

716-691-2100
Fax: 716-691-2880 andco@localnet.com

www.localnet.com/~buffalo/customer/andco/andco
.htm
Manufacturer and exporter of waste and ground water pollution elimination systems
Sales Manager: Jack Reich
Chief Process Engineer: Michael Laschinger
Estimated Sales: less than $500,000
Number Employees: 5-9
Square Footage: 44000

18920 Andean Naturals LLC
393 Catamaran St
Foster City, CA 94404-2907

650-303-1780
Fax: 707-202-2838 info@andeannaturals.com
www.andeannaturals.com
Quinoa
Owner: Sergio Nunez De Arco
sergio_nunez@andeannaturals.com
Finance & Operations Manager: Marcos Guevara
Estimated Sales: $100 Thousand
Number Employees: 1-4
Type of Packaging: Bulk

18921 Andersen 2000
2011 Commerce Dr N
Peachtree City, GA 30269

770-486-2000
Fax: 770-487-5066 800-241-5424
Manufacturer and exporter of air pollution control systems for odor control, spray dryer dust and visible aerosol.
President/CEO: Jack Brady
CFO: Randall Morgan
CEO: Randall Morgan
Marketing/Sales: Tom Van Remmen
Contact: Randall Morgan
r.morgan@verantis.com
Purchasing Manager: Doug Topley
Number Employees: 50-99
Square Footage: 60000
Parent Co: Crown Andersen
Other Locations:
Andersen 2000
Sevenum

18922 Andersen Products Inc
3202 Caroline Dr
Haw River, NC 27258-9564

336-376-3000
Fax: 336-376-8153 www.anpro.com
President: H W Andersen
Quality Control: Lori Pfohl
HR Executive: Barbara England
bce@anpro.com
R&D: John Lindley

18923 Andersen Sign Company
1580 French Pond Road
Woodsville, NH 03785

603-787-6806
Advertising specialties including signs
Owner: Don Bowman
Estimated Sales: Less than $500,000
Number Employees: 1-4
Square Footage: 2500

18924 Anderson American Precision
2511 Friday Rd.
Cocoa, FL 32926

321-637-0728
www.feedscrewdesigns.com
Estimated Sales: $300,000-500,000
Number Employees: 1-4

18925 Anderson Chemical Co
325 S Davis Ave
Litchfield, MN 55355-3106

320-693-2477
Fax: 320-693-8238 www.accomn.com
Cleaning/sanitation and water treatment chemical compounds
President: Terry Anderson
terryanderson@andersonchemco.com
Number Employees: 20-49
Type of Packaging: Food Service

18926 Anderson Dahlen Inc
6850 Sunwood Dr NW
Ramsey, MN 55303-3601

763-852-4700
Fax: 763-852-4795 877-205-0239
sales@andersondahlen.com
www.andersondahlen.com
President: Thomas Knoll
thomasknoll@andersondahlen.com
Estimated Sales: $20 - 50 Million
Number Employees: 100-249

18927 Anderson Instrument Company
156 Auriesville Rd
Fultonville, NY 12072

518-922-5315
Fax: 518-922-8997 800-833-0081
marc.cognetti@danaher.com
www.anderson-negele.com
Sanitary temperature, pressure, liquid level monitoring and control instrumentation
Estimated Sales: $50 - 100 Million
Number Employees: 50-99
Parent Co: Danaher Corporation

18928 Anderson International Corp
4545 Boyce Pkwy
Stow, OH 44224-1770

216-641-1112
Fax: 216-641-0709 800-336-4730
www.expeller.info
Manufacturer and exporter of screw press machinery for the continuous extraction of vegetable oils and animal fats
President: Len Trocano
lenny.trocano@andersonintl.com
CFO: Kathleen O'Hearn
VP: Vincent Vavpot
Marketing: Vincent Vavpot
Sales: Bruce Brown
Plant Manager: Dave Botson
Estimated Sales: $10 - 20 Million
Number Employees: 50-99
Brands:
Dox Expander
Expeller
Hivex Expander
Solvex Expander

18929 Anderson Machine Sales
1066 Harvard Pl
P.O. Box 220
Fort Lee, NJ 07024-1630

Fax: 201-641-7952 amscapper@aol.com
Manufacturer and exporter of single spindle and rotary capping machines, pump placers and crimpers, conveyors and accumulating tables
Manager: Howard Cunningham

Estimated Sales: $2.5-5,000,000
Number Employees: 1-4
Parent Co: Anderson Machine Systems

18930 Anderson Products
1 Weiler Dr
Cresco, PA 18326-9804

    508-755-6100
Fax: 508-755-4694 800-729-4694
info@andersonproducts.com
www.andersonproducts.com
Power, paint and maintenance brushes including
wide face and strip, adapters, maintenance and hand,
rollers and accessories, etc
President: Richard Gommel
VP Sales/Marketing: Robert Levine
Contact: Ed Frymier
  efrymier@weilercorp.com
Estimated Sales: $20 - 50 Million
Number Employees: 100-249
Parent Co: Wilton Corporation

18931 Anderson Snow Corp
9225 Ivanhoe St
Schiller Park, IL 60176-2352

    847-678-3823
Fax: 847-678-0413 800-346-2645
www.anscorcoils.com
Heating and cooling coils
President: Ted Campbell
  tcamp5555@aol.com
Estimated Sales: $20-50 Million
Number Employees: 10-19

18932 Anderson Tool & Engineering Company
P.O. Box 1158
Anderson, IN 46015-1158

    765-643-6691
Fax: 765-643-5022
Manufacturer and exporter of packaging, automation
and material handling equipment; also, electrical de-
sign and assembly services available
President: Ted Fiock
Sales/Marketing Manager: David Keller
Operations Manager: Tom Tuterow
Purchasing Manager: Ron King
Estimated Sales: $10 - 20 Million
Number Employees: 100-249
Square Footage: 85000

18933 Anderson Wood Products
1381 Beech St
Louisville, KY 40211-3428

    502-778-5591
Fax: 502-778-5599 kenl@andersonwood.com
www.andersonwood.com
Wooden butchers' blocks and restaurant tabletops
Vice President: David Anderson
  davida@andersonwood.com
VP: David Anderson
Chairman of the Board: Sidney W Anderson Jr
Estimated Sales: $20 - 50 Million
Number Employees: 100-249
Square Footage: 140000

18934 Anderson-Crane Company
1213-19 Harmon Pl
Minneapolis, MN 55403

    612-332-0331
Fax: 612-332-0384 800-314-2747
www.anderson-crane.com
Manufacturers of stainless steel screw conveyors @
screw feeders to food grade specs.
President: Bob Crane
Director of Sales: Rob Crane
Contact: Steven Johnson
  steven.johnson@screw-conveyor.com
Estimated Sales: $10-20 Million
Number Employees: 20-49
Square Footage: 60000

18935 Anderson-Negele
156 Auriesville Rd
Fultonville, NY 12072

    518-922-5315
Fax: 518-922-8997 800-833-0081
info@anderson-negele.com
www.anderson-negele.com
sensors for food and life sciences.
General Manager: Parker Burke
Sr. Product and Marketing Manager: Paul Wagner
Director of Sales: Joe Gamradt

Estimated Sales: $50-60 Million
Number Employees: 100-249
Parent Co: Fortive Corporation

18936 Andex Corp
69 Deep Rock Rd
Rochester, NY 14624-3575

    585-328-3790
Fax: 585-328-3792
Manufacturer and exporter of paper coffee filters
President: Andrew Cherre
  andexcorp@aol.com
Estimated Sales: $1-2 Million
Number Employees: 20-49
Square Footage: 40000
Type of Packaging: Food Service, Private Label,
Bulk
Brands:
  Coffee's Choice
  Gourmay
  Tru Brew

18937 Andex Industries Inc
1911 4th Ave N
Escanaba, MI 49829-1435

    906-786-6070
Fax: 906-786-3133 800-338-9882
andex@andex.net www.andex.net
Printed blister cards and skin boards
President: John Anthony
CEO: John T Anthony
Estimated Sales: $10-20 000,000
Number Employees: 50-99

18938 Andfel Corporation
2350 W Fulton Street
Chicago, IL 60612-2256

    312-666-6375

18939 Andgar Corp
6920 Salashan Pkwy
Ferndale, WA 98248-8320

    360-366-9900
Fax: 360-366-5800 corporate@andgar.com
www.andgar.com
Conveyors, belts, vibrating feeders, custom stainless
steel design and fabrication, packaging equipment,
metal detectors, separators, scanning and sorting
equipment, complete processing lines, refrigeration
and freezing equipmenttemperature controls, stair-
ways, railings, catwalks, fabricated metal products
President: Gary Van Lou
  garyv@andgar.com
CFO: Gary Van Lou
CEO: Gary Van Loo
Quality Control: Gary Van Lou
R&D: Gary Van Lou
Estimated Sales: $10 - 20 Million
Number Employees: 100-249
Number of Brands: 4
Square Footage: 45000
Brands:
  Andgar
  Lakewood
  Langser Camp
  Sateline

18940 Andre Robin And Associates
8630 Farley Way
Fair Oaks, CA 95628-5353

    916-852-0177
Fax: 916-852-0192 800-998-6111
info@robin.com
President: Andre Robin
Estimated Sales: $5 - 10 Million
Number Employees: 10-19

18941 Andrea Basket
1401 Lakeland Ave
Bohemia, NY 11716-3317

    631-231-4888
Fax: 631-231-5635 888-272-8826
info@andreabaskets.com
Various styles of decorative baskets
President: Andrea Lieberman
Estimated Sales: $3.4 Million
Number Employees: 5-9

18942 Andrew H Lawson Co
2927 W Thompson St
Philadelphia, PA 19121-4547

    215-235-1119
Fax: 215-235-1727 800-411-6628
info@screengemsinc.com
www.screengemsinc.com
Tags, signs and labels
Owner: Edward Mitchell Sr
VP of Marketing: Regina Mitchell
Manager Operations: John Mitchell
Estimated Sales: $1 - 5 Million
Number Employees: 10-19
Square Footage: 40000

18943 Andrew W Nissly Inc
544 W Mill Ave
Lancaster, PA 17603-3426

    717-393-3841
Fax: 717-397-6239
Signs; also, industrial finishing and silk screen print-
ing available
President: Andrew Nissly
General Manager: Andrew Nissley
Estimated Sales: $500,000-$1 Million
Number Employees: 5-9

18944 Andrew's Fixture Co
1720 Puyallup Ave
Tacoma, WA 98421-2616

    253-627-8388
Fax: 253-627-8395
Store fixtures, custom cabinets and office furniture
President: Kenson Lee
  afco25@gmail.com
Secretary/Treasurer: Andrea Lee
Estimated Sales: $1 - 2.5 Million
Number Employees: 5-9
Square Footage: 20000

18945 Andritz Separation Inc
1010 Commercial Blvd S
Arlington, TX 76001-7130

    817-465-5611
Fax: 817-468-3961
Supplier of separation technologies in the municipal
and industrial sectors and of animal feed
technologies.
President: John Madden
  john.madden@andritz.com
Estimated Sales: $10-20 000,000
Number Employees: 500-999

18946 Andy J. Egan Co.
2001 Waldorf NW
Grand Rapids, MI 49544

    616-791-9952
Fax: 616-791-1037 800-594-9244
info@andyegan.com www.andritz.com
Manufacturer processing equipment for the baking,
confectionery and snack food industries.
Owner: Tom Jasper
Vice President/Treasurer: Casey Schellenboom
Engineer: Eric Schippers
Contact: Jack Alexander
  alexanderj@andyegan.com
Estimated Sales: 25 Million
Number Employees: 230
Square Footage: 70000

18947 Andy Printed Products
1258 Route 82
Lagrangeville, NY 12540-6015

    845-223-5101
Fax: 845-223-7426
Pressure sensitive and gummed labels
Owner: Thakur Nandlal
Estimated Sales: Less than $500,000
Number Employees: 1-4
Square Footage: 4000

18948 Anetsberger
P.O. Box 501
Concord, NH 06062

    603-225-6684
Fax: 603-225-8472
ANETS - Gas & Electric Fryers, Filter Systems,
Chrome Grills, Pasta Cookers
President: Paul Angrick
VP: Steve Spittle
VP Sales/Marketing: Bonnie Bolster
Contact: Tracy Doer
  tdoer@anets.com

Estimated Sales: $10-20 Million
Number Employees: 50-99
Parent Co: Middleby Corp
Brands:
  Anets'

18949 (HQ)Anguil Environmental Systems
8855 N 55th St
Milwaukee, WI 53223

414-365-6400
Fax: 414-365-6410 800-488-0230
sales@anguil.com www.anguil.com
Manufacturer and exporter of air pollution abatement and oxidation systems
President: Gene Anguil
CEO: Gene Anugil
Vice President: Chris Anguil
Marketing Director: Kevin Summ
Contact: Mathew Andrews
  mathew.andrews@anguil.com
Estimated Sales: $20-25 Million
Number Employees: 50-99
Square Footage: 25000

18950 Anhydro Inc
20000 Governors Dr Ste 301
Olympia Fields, IL 60461

708-747-7000
Fax: 708-755-8815 anhydroinc@anhydro.com
www.anhydro.com
Manufacturer and exporter of food drying equipment including spray, tower, flash, fluid bed and ring; also, consulting, design and engineering services available
President: Guy Lonergan
Contact: Dawn Braddy
  d.braddy@anhydro.com
Number Employees: 20-49
Square Footage: 80000
Parent Co: Drytec

18951 Anixter Inc
2301 Patriot Blvd
Glenview, IL 60026-8020

224-521-8000
Fax: 224-521-8100 www.anixter.com
President: Bob Eck
  bob.eck@anixter.com
CEO: Robert J Eck
CFO: Dennis Letham
Number Employees: 500-999

18952 Anko Food Machine USA Co LTD
390 Swift Ave # 2
South San Francisco, CA 94080-6221

650-624-8038
Fax: 650-624-8039 www.bakeryequsa.com
Owner: James Chung
  james@bakeryequsa.com
Estimated Sales: Less Than $500,000
Number Employees: 1-4

18953 Anko Products Inc
6012 33rd St E
Bradenton, FL 34203-5402

941-749-1960
Fax: 941-748-2307 800-446-2656
sales@ankoproducts.com www.ankoproducts.com
Manufacture of contamination-proof peristaltic pumps, and fractional horsepower gearmotors
Owner: Sharon Kottke
  sharon@ankoproducts.com
Estimated Sales: $20 - 50 Million
Number Employees: 20-49
Brands:
  Mitydrive
  Mityflex

18954 Ann Arbor Computer
34375 W 12 Mile Road
Farmington Hills, MI 48331-3375

248-553-1000
Fax: 248-553-1228 800-526-9322
info@jerviswebb.com
Manufacturer and exporter of computer software inventory control systems for warehouses and distribution centers; also, complete integrated control systems for material handling and factory automation

President & CEO: Brian Stewart
Sr. Vice President & CFO: John Doychich
Vice President Sales And Marketing: Bruce Buscher
Sales Manager: Art Fleischer
Vice President of Operations: Lon McAllister
Number Employees: 80
Square Footage: 148000
Parent Co: Jervis B. Webb Company
Brands:
  Basis
  Pc/Aim

18955 Ann Clark, LTD
112B Quality Lane
Rutland, VT 05701

802-773-7886
Fax: 802-775-6864 800-252-6798
info@annclark.com www.annclark.com
Shaped and holiday themed cookie cutters
President: Ann Clark
VP: John Clark Jr
Sales Manager: Elizabeth Clark
Contact: Pat Buchanan
  pat@annclark.com

18956 Annette's Donuts Ltd.
1965 Lawrence Ave W
Toronto, ON M9N 1H5
Canada

416-656-3444
Fax: 416-656-5400 888-839-7857
Bread, pastries and other bakery products
President: Nicolas Yannopoulos
Board Member: Ariadni Yannopoulos
Estimated Sales: $5.9 Million
Number Employees: 85
Square Footage: 124000
Type of Packaging: Consumer, Food Service, Bulk

18957 Annie's Frozen Yogurt
5200 W 74th St # A
Suite A
Minneapolis, MN 55439-2223

952-835-2110
800-969-9648
www.anniesyogurt.com
Soft serve equipment for frozen yogurt.
President: Lawrence Cerf
  ldcerf@aol.com
Number Employees: 10-19
Brands:
  Annie's

18958 Anova
211 N Lindbergh Blvd # 2
St Louis, MO 63141-7838

314-535-5005
Fax: 314-768-0835 800-231-1327
www.upbeat.com
Waste and recycling receptacles
President: William Gilbert
  eric@anovafurnishings.com
CFO: John Mueller
Estimated Sales: $5-10 Million
Number Employees: 50-99

18959 Anresco Laboratories
1375 Van Dyke Ave
San Francisco, CA 94124-3312

415-822-1100
Fax: 415-822-6615 800-359-0920
info@anresco.com www.microtracers.com
Laboratory providing consulting and analytical services including microbiology and food technology
Founder & President: David Eisenberg
Treasurer: Ngaly Frank
Lab Co-Direcotr: Mr. VuLam
Lab Co-Director: Ms. Cynthia Kushi
Quality Control Manager: Paleen Castenada
Marketing Director: Charleen Bizily
Purchasing Manager: Cynthia Kcohi
Estimated Sales: $3.85 Million
Number Employees: 50-99
Square Footage: 37600

18960 Anresco Laboratories
1375 Van Dyke Ave
San Francisco, CA 94124-3312

415-822-1100
Fax: 415-822-6615 info@anresco.com
www.microtracers.com

Analytical consultants for nutritional labeling, minerals, vitamins, sugars & sugar alcohols, fats & oils, protein, proximates, aflatoxins, trans fatty acids, preservatives, product stability and shelf life, extraneous mattermicroscopy, microbiological pathogens, dietary supplements and an extensive range of FDA automatic detention tests on imported foods.
Owner: David Eisenberg
CEO: Norlinda Cuesta
CFO: Mai Vo
Chemist: Aileen Borbon
Associate Lab Director: Vu Lam
Director of Marketing: Charleene Min
Manager: Bill Li
Estimated Sales: $2.6 Million
Number Employees: 50-99
Square Footage: 22000

18961 Anritsu Industrial Solutions
1001 Cambridge Dr
Elk Grove Vlg, IL 60007-2453

847-419-9729
Fax: 847-419-8266
Food inspection equipment.
President: Erik Brainard
  ebrainard@us.anritsu-industry.com
Number Employees: 20-49

18962 Ansell Healthcare Inc
111 Wood Ave S # 210
Iselin, NJ 08830-2700

732-345-5400
Fax: 732-219-5114 800-800-0444
info@ansell.com www.ansell.com
World's largest manufacturer of protective golves and clothing for the food service and processing industries.
Senior VP: James Albetta
  jamesalbetta@ansellpro.com
Manager: Willaim Gero
Number Employees: 100-249
Type of Packaging: Food Service

18963 Antek Industrial Instruments
PO Box 1130
Marble Falls, TX 78654-1130

830-693-5671
Fax: 830-798-8208 888-478-5387
www.antekhou.com
State-of-the-art testing and measurement of carbon dioxide and sulfur levels commonly found in the processing of soft drinks

18964 Anton Kimball Design
3777 SE Milwaukie Ave
Portland, OR 97202-3804

503-234-4777
Fax: 503-234-4687 www.bluestardecks.org
Specialty food packaging.
Owner: Anton C Kimball
  info@kimballdesign.com
Marketing: Anton Kimball
Estimated Sales: Less Than $500,000
Number Employees: 5-9

18965 Anton Paar USA Inc
10215 Timber Ridge Dr
Ashland, VA 23005-8135

804-550-1051
Fax: 804-550-1057 800-722-7556
info.us@anton-paar.com www.anton-paar.com
Laboratory density and brix meters, process brix and diet monitors, carbon dioxide monitors, laboratory and process beer analyzers
President: Bart Arts
  bart.arts@anton-paar.com
CEO: Niels Haggound
Product Manager: Thomas Luxbacher
Sales Manager: Erich Windischbacher
Estimated Sales: $2.5-5 Million
Number Employees: 50-99

18966 Antrim Manufacturing Inc
3530 N 127th St
Brookfield, WI 53005-2485

262-781-6860
Metal stampings and restaurant equipment including ovens and utility carts
Owner: Dan Antrim
  progrosup@aol.com
Office Manager: Patricia Antrim
Estimated Sales: $1 - 5 Million
Number Employees: 5-9

18967 Antunes Controls
180 Kehoe Blvd
Carol Stream, IL 60188-1814
630-784-1000
Fax: 630-784-1650 800-253-2991
www.ajantunes.com
Top Quality Counter Top Cooking Equipment, Advanced Membrane Filtration Equipment, Custom Electronics, and Air and Gas Pressure Switches
CEO: Glenn Bullock
National Sales Manager: Dan Huizinga
Estimated Sales: $5 - 10 Million
Number Employees: 250-499

18968 Anver Corporation
36 Parmenter Rd
Hudson, MA 01749
978-568-0221
Fax: 978-568-1570 800-654-3500
rfq13@anver.com www.anver.com
Full range of vacuum system components, from suction cups and vacuum cups, air and electric vacuum pumps and vacuum generations, and ergonomic vacuum lifters, to complete lifting systems
President: Anton Vernooy
CFO: Lynne Buttterworth
Marketing Director: Cully Murphy
Contact: Anver Anderson
anver@anver.com
Estimated Sales: $10 Million
Number Employees: 50-99
Square Footage: 60000

18969 Anzu Technology
3180 Imjin Rd # 155
Marina, CA 93933-5112
831-883-4400
Fax: 831-855-0220 twhite@anzutech.com
www.anzutech.com
Products and services include equipment for food processing, inspection and packaging.
President: Tom White
twhite@anzutech.com
Number Employees: 5-9

18970 Aoki Laboratory America
1240 Landmeier Rd
Elk Grove Village, IL 60007
847-981-6000
Fax: 847-981-6105 info@aokiusa.com
www.aokitech.co.jp
Container manufacturer
President/Owner: Shuichi Koshi
Number Employees: 5-9

18971 Apa
7011 S 19th St
Tacoma, WA 98466-5333
253-565-6600
Fax: 253-565-7265 www.apawood.org
President: David L Rogoway
Director: Dennis Hardman
Contact: Jeff Wagner
jwagner@engineeredwood.org
Estimated Sales: $10,000,000 - $19,999,999
Number Employees: 100-249

18972 Apache Inc
4805 Bowling St SW
Cedar Rapids, IA 52404-5021
319-365-0471
Fax: 319-365-2522 800-553-5455
info@apache-inc.com www.apache-inc.com
Wholesaler/distributor of hose and conveyor belting. Products for the food industry.
President/CEO: Tom Pientok
Chief Financial Officer: Randy Walter
Controller: Eric Hentges
Quality Engineer: Rick Coyle
Marketing & Communications Manager: Jill Miller
VP, Operations: Kyle Gingrich
VP, Business Development: John Shafer
VP, Product Management: Tom Weisenstine
Purchasing Manager: Randy James
Estimated Sales: $75-85 Million
Number Employees: 100-249
Square Footage: 125000

18973 (HQ)Apache Stainless Equipment
200 Industrial Dr
Beaver Dam, WI 53916-1136
920-356-9900
Fax: 920-887-0206 800-444-0398
www.apachestainless.com
Manufacturer and exporter of stainless steel food processing machinery including sanitary and ASME pressure vessels, tanks, blenders, mixers, conveyors, sanitary lifts, stuffers, dumpers and paced boning systems
President and R&D: D Foulkes
CAO: Fern Core
fcore@apachestainless.com
CFO: D Seifert
VP: W Lynn
Quality Control: Jerome Scharrer
Plant Manager: Duane Crouse
Estimated Sales: $5 - 10 Million
Number Employees: 100-249
Square Footage: 200000
Other Locations:
Apache Stainless Equipment Co
Beloit WI
Brands:
Vortron

18974 Apache Stainless Equipment
200 Industrial Dr
PO Box 538
Beaver Dam, WI 53916-1136
920-356-9900
Fax: 920-887-0206 800-444-0398
www.apachestainless.com
President: Duane Foulkes
CAO: Fern Core
fcore@apachestainless.com
V.P. of Sales & Marketing: Dennis Buehring
Estimated Sales: $5 - 10 Million
Number Employees: 100-249

18975 Apco/Valve & Primer Corporation
1420 Wright Blvd
Schaumburg, IL 60193
847-524-9000
Fax: 847-524-9007 factory@apcovalves.com
President: Robert Mauriello
r.mauriello@apcovalves.com
CEO: George Christofidis
CFO: Jack Mann
Engineering/Technical: Russell Voseurg
Estimated Sales: $10 - 20 Million
Number Employees: 50-99

18976 Apex Bakery Equipment
803 Main St
Belmar, NJ 07719-2783
888-571-3599
Fax: 954-364-6268 888-571-3599
sales@apex-equip.com www.apex-equip.com
President: Herbert Freedman
CFO: Barry McWatters
Quality Control: Mark Freedman
Contact: Jeffrey Liss
jeffreyliss@apex-equipment.com
Estimated Sales: $10 - 20 Million
Number Employees: 20-49

18977 Apex Fountain Sales Inc
1140 N American St
Philadelphia, PA 19123-1514
215-627-4526
Fax: 215-627-7877 800-523-4586
www.apexfountains.com
Manufacturer and exporter of champagne fountains, chafing dishes, punch bowls, candelabra and food stands
President: Abe Weinberg
info@apexfountains.com
Manager: Jody Clemente
Estimated Sales: $1-2.5 Million
Number Employees: 5-9

18978 Apex Machine Company
3000 NE 12th Ter
Oakland Park, FL 33334-4497
954-566-1572
Fax: 954-563-2844 email@apexmachine.com
www.apexmachine.com
Manufacturer and exporter, designs and engineers customized part handling and printing-packaging solutions for 3D products.
President: Todd Coningsby
CEO & Chairman: A. Robert Coningsby
toddc@apexmachine.com
Corp. Controller: Chris Bardelang
National Sales Manager: Russell Coningsby
Engineering Manager: Greg Coningsby
Director Production-Purchasing: Arthur Jordan

Estimated Sales: $5-10 Million
Number Employees: 50-99
Other Locations:
Capex Corporation
Fort Lauderdale FL
Desco Machine Company
Twinsburg OH

18979 Apex Packing & Rubber Co
1855 New Hwy # D
Farmingdale, NY 11735-1599
631-420-8150
Fax: 631-756-9639 800-645-9110
Manufacturer and exporter of sanitary replacement parts for the dairy, food, beverage and pharmaceutical industries
President: Ralph Oppenheim
ralph@apexgaskets.com
General Manager: Larry Hodes
Purchasing Agent: Leon Davidson
Estimated Sales: $2.5-5,000,000
Number Employees: 5-9
Brands:
Apex

18980 Apex Tool Works Inc
3200 Tollview Dr
Rolling Meadows, IL 60008
847-394-5810
Fax: 847-394-2739 apextool@apextool.com
www.apextool.com
Manufacturing equipment.
VP, Engineering: Edward Racutt
Estimated Sales: $5-10 Million
Number Employees: 20-49

18981 Apex Welding Inc
1 Industry Dr
Bedford, OH 44146-4413
440-232-6770
Fax: 440-232-6747 www.apex-bulkhandlers.com
Bins
President: D J Warner
Manager: Gary Warner
info@apex-bulkhandlers.com
Estimated Sales: Less Than $500,000
Number Employees: 10-19

18982 Apigent Solutions
5 N McCormick Street
Oklahoma City, OK 73127-6620
405-946-8228
Fax: 405-946-8242 800-664-8228
Specializes in software products taht enhance business performance and profitability by delivering reaL-time information from legacy business systems to site, field, and corporate personnel
CEO: Jim Melvin
Sales VP of the Americas: John Luidens
Public Relations: Ann Dickerson

18983 Aplen Sierra Coffee Company
2222 Park Place
Suite 1A
Minden, NV 89423
530-541-1053
Fax: 530-541-4412 800-531-1405
coffeentea@alpensierra.com
www.alpensierra.com
Supplier of specialty coffees.
Contact: Christian Waskiewicz
coffeentea@alpensierra.com
Estimated Sales: $1-2.5 Million
Number Employees: 5-9

18984 Apogee Translite Inc
593 Acorn St # B
Deer Park, NY 11729-3613
631-254-6975
Fax: 631-254-3860 www.apogeetranslite.com
Manufacturer and exporter of lighting fixtures for food processing range hoods, hose down and wet locations
President: Richard Nicolai
President: Mike Shada
Estimated Sales: $10 - 20,000,000
Number Employees: 20-49
Square Footage: 38000
Other Locations:
Apogee Lighting Group
Riverdale IL

18985 Apollo Acme Lighting Fixture
212 S 12th Ave
Mount Vernon, NY 10550
914-664-3600
Fax: 914-664-6091 800-833-9006
Fluorescent lighting fixtures
VP: Paul Verkleij
Estimated Sales: $1-2,500,000
Number Employees: 5-9
Square Footage: 33000

18986 Apollo Sheet Metal
1207 W Columbia Dr
Kennewick, WA 99336
509-586-1104
Fax: 509-586-3771 info@apollosm.com
www.apollosm.com
Food processing, handling and storage systems including conveyors, tanks, blanchers, ovens and fryers; also, installation services available.
President: Bruce Ratchford
CFO: Angie Haisch
VP: Keith Larson
Quality Control: Bill Meloy
Marketing Director: Connie Gillispie
Sales: Dan Briscoe
Contact: Emily Castle
ecastle@apollosm.com
Production: Cal Method
Estimated Sales: $20-50 Million
Number Employees: 250-499
Square Footage: 200000

18987 Apotheca Inc
201 Apple Boulevard
Woodbine, IA 51579
712-647-3133
Fax: 888-898-0401 800-736-3130
info@apothecacompany.com
www.apothecacompany.com
Homeopathics, botanical extracts, capsules, tablets and sports nutritionals
President: Kathryn Simon
Contact: Mike Evans
mike@apothecacompany.com
Estimated Sales: $10-20 Million
Number Employees: 100
Square Footage: 140000

18988 Appalachian Power
P.O. Box 1986
Charleston, WV 25327
800-956-4237
www.appalachianpower.com
Electric utility systems.
President & COO: Chris Beam
VP, Regulatory & Finance: Steven Ferguson
VP, External Affairs: Brad Hall
Estimated Sales: $1,000,000,000+
Parent Co: American Electric Power

18989 Apparel Manufacturing Co Inc
5405 Webb Pkwy NW
Lilburn, GA 30047-5470
770-638-1100
Fax: 770-638-8030 800-366-1608
www.apparelmanufacturing.com
Advertising specialties and uniforms; importer of caps
President: Michelle Dance
m.dance@ipcabc.org
Administrative Assistant to President: Chelley Young
Estimated Sales: $5 - 10,000,000
Number Employees: 50-99

18990 Apple-A-Day Nutritional Labeling Service
103 1/2 Avenida Del Mar
San Clemente, CA 92672-4017
949-855-8954
Fax: 949-855-8954
Provides computerized nutritional analysis based on submitted recipes. Nutritional facts labeling for food manufacturers following FDA guidelines and regulations

18991 Applegate Chemical Company
1325 N Old Rand Road
Wauconda, IL 60084-9764
847-487-2651
Fax: 847-487-2654
President: Donald F Colby

18992 Appleson Press
25 Tacoma Lane
Building 11
Syosset, NY 11791-6232
516-496-0004
Fax: 516-496-0006 800-888-2775
info@applesonpress.com www.applesonpress.com
Manufacturer of continuous business forms, envelopes and labels including printed cloth, linen, silk, pressure sensitive, promotional items; product labels
President: Kenneth Sands
CEO: Elyse Newman
Contact: Ken Sands
ksands@applesonpress.com
Plant Manager: John Samuels
Estimated Sales: $3-5 Million
Number Employees: 20-49
Square Footage: 40000
Type of Packaging: Food Service, Private Label, Bulk

18993 Applexion
9400 W Foster Avenue
Chicago, IL 60656-2860
773-243-0454
Fax: 773-243-0460 applexion@aol.com
Process engineering systems including ion exchange, chromatographic and membrane separation, fermentation, etc
President: Francois Rousset
Sales: Brian Burris
Production: Martha Turner
Estimated Sales: $1-2.5 Million
Number Employees: 1-4
Parent Co: Applexion S.A.
Brands:
Fast

18994 Application Software
211 Main St
New Paltz, NY 12561-1312
845-255-3226
Fax: 845-255-3295 800-888-9470
Bar code scanners, batching and blender systems
President: Greg Brandow
Estimated Sales: $1 - 3 Million
Number Employees: 1-4

18995 Applied Analytics
40 Kensington Cir
Chestnut Hill, MA 02467-2624
617-277-0906
Contact: Craig Miklencic
c.miklencic@a-a-inc.com

18996 Applied Chemical Technology
4350 Helton Dr
Florence, AL 35630
256-760-9600
Fax: 256-760-9638 800-228-3217
www.appliedchemical.com
Manufacturer and exporter of fluid beds, feeders and granulators. Development and engineering of processing plants available
President: A Ray Shirley
CFO: Ginger Lewey
VP: Curtis Lewey
Quality Control: Curtis Lewey
Marketing: Alan Nix
Contact: Craig Arnett
carnett@appliedchemical.com
Purchasing Manager: Roger Kilburn
Estimated Sales: Below $5 Million
Number Employees: 50
Square Footage: 70000

18997 Applied Fabric Technologies
P.O. Box 575
Orchard Park, NY 14127-0575
716-662-0632
Fax: 716-662-0636 www.afti.com
Conveyor belting including endless felts, endless belts, rotary moulder belts and bakery belts
President: Peter Lane
Sales Director: Matt Severied
Contact: Carole Lane
oilfence@aol.com
Estimated Sales: $20-50 Million
Number Employees: 10-19

Estimated Sales: $5 - 10 Million
Number Employees: 10

18998 Applied Handling NW
8531 South 222nd St
Kent, WA 98031
253-395-8500
Fax: 253-395-8585 888-395-3943
ahnwi@aol.com www.appliednw.com
Wholesaler/distributor of material handling equipment including package conveyors and pallet racks; rack jobber services available
President: Michael Tucker
Contact: Richard Chaffee
richc@appliednw.com
Estimated Sales: $5-10 Million
Number Employees: 10-19
Brands:
H.K. Systems
Prest Rack
Rapid Rack
Unarco
Western Pacific Storage Systems

18999 Applied Industrial TechInc
1 Applied Plz
Cleveland, OH 44115-2519
216-426-4000
Fax: 216-426-4845 877-279-2799
www.applied.com
CEO: Neil A Schrimsher
nschrimsher@ait-applied.com
CEO: David L Pugh
Estimated Sales: Over $1 Billion
Number Employees: 5000-9999

19000 Applied Membranes
2325 Cousteau Ct
Vista, CA 92081
760-727-3711
Fax: 760-727-4427 800-321-9321
sales@appliedmembranes.com
www.appliedmembranes.com
Reverse osmosis, ultrafiltration and nano filtration systems, RO membranes, filters, pressure vessels, residential and commercial components and resins
President: Gil Dhawan
Marketing: Jande Wysocki
Contact: Dorothy Adams
dadams@appliedmembranes.com
Estimated Sales: $5 - 10 000,000
Number Employees: 50-99

19001 Applied Product Sales
802 Angevine Court SW
Lilburn, GA 30047-4209
650-218-3104
Fax: 770-921-5814
info@appliedproductmarketing.com
Insulated shipping boxes and containers. Packaging and process machinery parts. Electro-mechanical power transmission components.
President: Tracey McHugh
CFO: Jim McHugh
Estimated Sales: $1.5 Million
Number Employees: 2
Number of Brands: 5
Type of Packaging: Food Service, Private Label, Bulk
Other Locations:
Applied Product Sales
Lilburn GA

19002 Applied Products Co
118 Sierra St
El Segundo, CA 90245-4117
310-322-5972
Fax: 310-640-2975 888-551-0447
appliedprods@att.net
Marking and numbering equipment
Owner: Richard Panacek
appliedprods@att.net
Estimated Sales: Less Than $500,000
Number Employees: 1-4

19003 Applied Robotics Inc
648 Saratoga Rd
Schenectady, NY 12302-5837
518-384-1000
Fax: 518-384-1200 800-309-3475
info@arobotics.com www.appliedrobotics.com
ARI is a leading provider of automation end-of-arm connectivity solutions designed to bring greater speed and flexibility to automation-based processes.

CEO: Michael F Quinn
mquinn@appliedrobotics.com
CEO: Tom Petronis
CFO: Paul Cullen
CEO: Thomas J Petronis
Research & Development: Clay Cooper
Quality Control: Mike Gallo
Marketing Director: Joanne Brown
Public Relations: Joanne Brown
Production Manager: Bob Butterfield
Plant Manager: John Sezfilippi
Estimated Sales: $10-20,000,000
Number Employees: 20-49
Square Footage: 18000
Brands:
   Quickstop
   Smartscan
   Xchange

19004 Applied Technologies
16815 W Wisconsin Ave
Brookfield, WI 53005-5714
262-784-7690
Fax: 262-784-6847 info@ati-ae.com
www.ati-ae.com
Consultant specializing in water and wastewater management
President: Dennis Totzke
Vice President: Dennis Totzke
Quality Control: Frank Tiefert
Marketing Director: Dennis Totzke
Number Employees: 20-49

19005 Applied Thermal Technologies
906 Boardwalk Ste B
San Marcos, CA 92069-4071
760-744-5083
Fax: 442-744-5031 800-736-5083
Manufacturer and exporter of water chilling systems for batch cooling, food, confectionery and dairy products.
President: Kimberly Howard
khoward@appliedthermaltech.com
Plant Manager: Dale Anderson
Estimated Sales: $500,000-$1 Million
Number Employees: 1-4
Square Footage: 10000
Brands:
   Hydro-Miser

19006 Apt-Li Specialty Brushes
231 Red Rose Rd
Kerrville, TX 78028-8957
830-995-5198
Fax: 830-995-4036
Brushes (for food and also for equipment) used in the food industry
Owner: Jerry O'Brien
Estimated Sales: $.5 - 1 million
Number Employees: 1-4

19007 Aptar Mukwonago
711 Fox St
Mukwonago, WI 53149-1419
262-363-7191
Fax: 262-363-3658 www.seaquistclosures.us
President: Eric Ruskoski
R & D: Jim Hammond
Data Processing: Michael Wedge
Manager: Asa Albritton
eem2rudy@aol.com
Number Employees: 250-499
Parent Co: Aptar Group

19008 Apv Crepaco Inc
395 Fillmore Ave
Tonawanda, NY 14150-2418
716-692-9967
Fax: 716-692-1715 800-828-7391
answers@invensys.com www.apv.com
Evaporators, dryers, membrane systems, distillation
Contact: Mamunur Rahman
mamunur.rahman@apv.com
Estimated Sales: $20-50 Million
Number Employees: 20-49

19009 Aqua Blast Corp Mfg
1025 W Commerce Dr
Decatur, IN 46733-7541
260-728-4433
Fax: 260-728-4517 800-338-7373
davidt@aquablast.com www.aquablast.com

High pressure cleaning systems. I order to meet certain food quality sterilization requirements, offers wash down motors, food grade oil and stainless steel.
President: Dave Tumbleson
abco@aquablast.com
Estimated Sales: $3 - 5 Million
Number Employees: 10-19

19010 Aqua Brew
3421 W Fordham Ave
Santa Ana, CA 92704
714-546-7117
Fax: 714-432-8802 800-888-BREW
www.aquabrew.com
Iced tea and coffee brewers, brewing devices and cleaners
Owner: Patrick Rolfes
Estimated Sales: $2.5 - 5 000,000
Number Employees: 20-49

19011 (HQ)Aqua Measure
9567 Arrow Rte # E
Suite E
Rancho Cucamonga, CA 91730-4550
909-941-7776
Fax: 909-941-6444 800-966-4788
sales@aquameasure.com www.finnagroup.com
Manufacturer and exporter of moisture meters and systems for measuring moisture content in solids for the food processing industry
Owner: John Lundrstrom
Sales: Gabriel Cote Jr
Contact: Steven Brunasso
sbrunasso@aquameasure.com
Estimated Sales: $2.5-5 Million
Number Employees: 5-9
Other Locations:
   Aqua Measure InstrumentCo.
   La Verne CA

19012 Aqua Tec Inc
1235 Shappert Dr
Machesney Park, IL 61115-1417
815-654-1500
Fax: 815-654-0038 rj.ryan@aquatecinc.com
www.aquatecinc.com
President: Richard Ryan
rj.ryan@aquatecinc.com
Estimated Sales: $3 - 5 Million
Number Employees: 20-49

19013 Aqua-Aerobic Systems Inc
6306 N Alpine Rd
Loves Park, IL 61111-4396
815-639-9803
Fax: 815-654-2508 800-940-5008
solutions@aqua-aerobic.com
www.aqua-aerobic.com
Manufacturer and exporter of water and wastewater treatment systems for both municipal and industrial market, including direct drive aerators, down draft mixers and sequencing batch reactors; also, shallow bed, gravity sand and clothmedia filtration equipment
President: Robert J Wimmer
rwimmer@aqua-aerobic.com
R&D: Lloyd Johnson
VP Marketing: Deb Lavelle
VP Sales: Steven Schupbach
VP International Sales: Sharon DeDoncker
Operations: Rick Reiland
Estimated Sales: $20-50 Million
Number Employees: 100-249
Square Footage: 100000
Brands:
   Aqua Br
   Aqua Cb12/24
   Aqua Dm
   Aqua Endura Disc
   Aqua Endura Tube
   Aqua Gf
   Aqua-Jet Aerator
   Aquadisk
   Thermo F10

19014 Aquafine Corp
29010 Avenue Paine
Valencia, CA 91355-4198
661-257-4770
Fax: 661-257-2489 800-423-3015
techsupport@aquafineuv.com
www.aquafineuv.com

Ultra-violet water treatment equipment for pure and ultrapure applications. Aquafine meets the most stringent specifications in a variety of industries ranging from semiconductor to bio-pharmaceutical, food and beverage to powergeneration. the systems adhere to rigid industry standards of performance and are available with UL, CE and TUV specifications to meet all standards
Manager: Rick Clark
CEO: Michael Murphy
CFO: Steven Smith
VP Operations: John Maskaluk
Research & Development: Tony Ng
Quality Control: Robert Rivard
Sales/Marketing: Greg Hoffman
Contact: Lobefaro Angelo
l.angelo@aquafineuv.com
Human Resource Director: Julie Weith
Engineering: Mike Quinn
Purchasing Manager: Paul Contreras
Estimated Sales: $10-20 Million
Number Employees: 50-99
Square Footage: 220000

19015 Aquair
PO Box 777
Glen Ellen, CA 95442-0777
800-834-4474
Fax: 707-996-9234 www.aquair.com

19016 Aquathin Corporation
950 South Andrews Avenue
Pompano Beach, FL 33069
954-781-7777
Fax: 954-781-7336 800-462-7634
info@aquathin.com www.aquathin.com
Manufacturer and exporter of water purification systems including reverse osmosis, softening and filtration
President: Alfred Lipshultz
Estimated Sales: $5 -14 Million
Number Employees: 20-49
Square Footage: 130000
Brands:
   Aqualite
   Aquathin
   Country Hutch
   Lead Out
   Megachar
   Platinum 90
   Sodia Lite
   Soft N Clean
   Yes

19017 Aquionics Inc
1455 Jamike Ave # 100
Suite 100
Erlanger, KY 41018-3147
859-341-0710
Fax: 859-341-0350 800-925-0440
sales@aquionics.com www.aquionics.com
Manufacturer and exporter of ultraviolet disinfection equipment
President: Oliver Lawal
oliver.law@aquionics.com
Manager: Rica Williams
Food/Beverage Sales Manager: Ralph Lopez
Number Employees: 20-49
Square Footage: 60000
Parent Co: Halma

19018 Aramark Uniform Svc
115 N First St # 203
Burbank, CA 91502-1857
818-973-3700
Fax: 818-973-3545 800-272-6275
www.aramarkuniform.com
Manufacturer and wholesaler/distributor of uniforms; serving the food service market
President, Uniform Services: Art Wake
COO: Brad Drummond
Estimated Sales: Over $1 Billion
Number Employees: 10000+
Parent Co: Aramark Services

19019 Aran USA
1704 Poplar Dr
Greer, SC 29651
864-479-0023
Fax: 864-479-0031 www.aran.co.il
Producer of bags for bag-in-box applications, including aseptic and non-aseptic liquid food.
Sales Manager North America: Mati Karni
Parent Co: Aran Group

19020 Arbee Transparent Inc
1450 Pratt Blvd
Elk Grove Vlg, IL 60007-5713
847-593-0400
Fax: 847-593-0291 800-642-2247
www.arbee.com
A supplier of Plastic Bags
President: Bob Harris
bagplastic@aol.com
Estimated Sales: $20-50 Million
Number Employees: 100-249
Square Footage: 25000

19021 (HQ)Arc Machines Inc
10500 Orbital Way
Pacoima, CA 91331-7129
818-896-9556
Fax: 818-890-3724 sales@arcmachines.com
www.arcmachines.com
Automatic orbital welding equipment
President: Mindegas E Gedgaudas
mindegas.gedgaudas@arcmachines.com
Estimated Sales: $30 - 50 Million
Number Employees: 100-249

19022 Arcar Graphics
450 Wegner Dr
West Chicago, IL 60185-2694
630-293-4453
Fax: 630-231-3716
President: Mark Denboer
Estimated Sales: Less Than $500,000
Number Employees: 1-4

19023 (HQ)Archer Daniels Midland Company
77 West Wacker Dr.
Suite 4600
Chicago, IL 60601
312-634-8100
www.adm.com
Food and feed ingredients, industrial chemicals and biofuels.
Chairman/CEO: Juan Luciano
Vice Chairman: Ray Young
Senior VP, General Counsel/Secretary: D. Cameron Findlay
Senior VP, Global Operations: Veronica Braker
Year Founded: 1902
Estimated Sales: $85.2 Billion
Number Employees: 38,000

19024 Archer Wire Intl Corp
7300 S Narragansett Ave
Chicago, IL 60638-6020
708-563-1700
Fax: 708-563-1740 www.archerwire.com
Stainless steel fry and wire baskets, barbecue grills, point of purchase displays, oven racks and stove grates; also, metal stamping services available
Owner: Lawrence Svabek
larrysv@archerwire.com
VP Sales: Rick Svabek
National Sales Manager: Dale Brines
VP Finance: Larry Svabek
Estimated Sales: $10-20 Million
Number Employees: 100-249
Square Footage: 376000

19025 Archibald Frozen Desserts
990 Progress Blvd
New Albany, IN 47150-2259
812-941-8267
Fax: 812-941-5374
Soft serve ice cream and frozen yogurt
CEO: Ed Meyer
Executive VP: Greg Gilbert
greg.gilbert@archibaldfrozendesserts.com
Sales & Marketing Coordinator: Lindsay Usher
National Sales Manager: Alex Mohler
Warehouse/Service Manager: Tim Coy
Estimated Sales: Less Than $500,000
Number Employees: 1-4

19026 Architectural Products
1 Lockhart Ln
Highland, NY 12528
845-691-8500
Fax: 845-691-2501
Lighting fixtures and emergency lighting; also, energy consultants
President: Stephen Lockhart
Contact: Mark Manning
mmanning@archprod.com

Estimated Sales: $500,000-$1,000,000
Number Employees: 1-4
Brands:
Api

19027 Architectural Sheet Metals LLC
1457 E 39th St
Cleveland, OH 44114-4198
216-361-9952
Fax: 216-431-6650 isminc@worldnet.att.net
www.architecturalsheetmetal.com
Sheet metal and stainless steel custom restaurant equipment including cooking, heating and food processing; also, store fixtures.
Owner: Art Petrauskis
Secretary/Treasurer: Donna Sens
Vice President: Jeff Dixon
Operations Manager: Guy DiSiena
Plant Manager: Guy DiSiena
Estimated Sales: $1-2.5 Million
Number Employees: 5-9
Square Footage: 24000

19028 Architectural Specialty Products
6312 W 74th St
Bedford Park, IL 60638
708-563-8510
Fax: 708-563-1860 800-388-0111
President: Rena Jahn
Owner: Lauren Jahn
Finance Executive: Tim Gibbons
Sales Executive: Warren Yoksas
Operations Executive: Pat Walsh
Estimated Sales: $1 - 5 Million
Number Employees: 20-49

19029 Architecture Plus Intl Inc
2709 N Rocky Point Dr # 201
Rocky Point, FL 33607-5562
813-281-9299
Fax: 813-281-9292 info@apiplus.com
www.apiplus.com
Manufacturer and exporter of aseptic packaging equipment and components, over and shrink wrappers and case packers, stackers and unstackers
President: Jean-Louis Limousin
CEO: Juan Romero
VP Sales: Keith Wennik
Number Employees: 50-99
Brands:
Api
Durajet
Duratech
Mastertech
Multitech
Versajet
Versatech

19030 Archon Industries
200 William Street
Rye Brook, NY 10573-4620
914-937-8030
Contact: Mario Faustini
sales@archonind.com
Estimated Sales: $1 - 5 Million
Number Employees: 20-50

19031 Archon Industries Inc
357 Spook Rock Rd
Suffern, NY 10901-5314
845-368-3600
Fax: 845-368-3040 800-554-1394
sales@archonind.com www.shoparchonind.com
Manufacturer, importer and exporter of washdown stations, sanitary fittings and ball, butterfly, gage and sanitary valves
CEO: Mario Faustini
Sales Manager: Linda Kyriakos
Engineering Manager: Konrad Mayer
Estimated Sales: $5 - 10 Million
Number Employees: 5-9

19032 Arco Coffee Co
2206 Winter St
Superior, WI 54880-1400
715-392-4771
Fax: 715-392-4776 800-283-2726
Pete@arcocoffee.com www.arcocoffee.com
Family owned coffee roasting company.
Owner: Don Andresen
donald@arcocoffee.com
Number Employees: 10-19
Type of Packaging: Consumer

Brands:
Arco Coffee

19033 Arcobaleno Pasta Machines
160 Greenfield Rd
Lancaster, PA 17601-5815
717-394-1402
800-875-7096
www.arcobalenollc.com
Pasta machinery and bakery processing lines, continuous and general purpose mixers, pasta preparation machinery, dough cutters and sheeters, pasteurizers, etc; exporter of calzone and pizza lines, ravioli machines and dough sheeters
President: Antonio Adiletta
info@arcobalenollc.com
VP, Marketing & Sales: Maja Adijetta
Number Employees: 10-19
Square Footage: 80000
Brands:
Arcobaleno

19034 Arcoplast Wall & Ceiling Systems
1873 Williamstown Drive
St Peters, MO 63376-8101
636-978-7781
Fax: 636-978-7782 888-736-2726
ghislain@arcoplast.com www.arcoplast.com
Integrated components necessary to design a contamination controlled environment. Product line includes ceilings, lights, air handling and microbial control systems, load-bearing and airtight walls and partitions, doors, windowspass-thru air locks, baseboards, structures, fasteners and other accessories.
President: Ghislain Beauregard
beauregard@arcoplast.com
Estimated Sales: $1-$5 Million
Type of Packaging: Food Service, Bulk

19035 Arctic Air
6440 City West Pkwy Ste 2
Eden Prairie, MN 55344
952-941-2270
Fax: 952-941-3066 800-853-3508
info@arcticairco.com www.arcticairco.com
Manufacturer and exporter of refrigerators including reach-in and NSF approved chest freezers.
Owner: Walter Broich Sr
wbroich@arcticairco.com
Estimated Sales: $10-20 Million
Number Employees: 4
Square Footage: 10000
Parent Co: Broich Enterprises
Brands:
Arctic Air

19036 Arctic Glacier Premium Ice
625 Henry Avenue
Winnepeg, MB R3A 0V1
Canada
204-772-2473
Fax: 204-783-9857 888-783-9857
info@arcticglacier.com www.arcticglacier.com
Bagged ice.
President & CEO: Richard Wyckoff
CFO: Marc Mongulla
Year Founded: 1996
Estimated Sales: $100-500 Million
Number Employees: 650
Parent Co: H.I.G. Capital

19037 Arctic Industries
9731 NW 114th Way
Medley, FL 33178
305-883-5581
Fax: 305-883-4651 800-325-0123
www.arcticwalk-ins.com
Manufacturer and exporter of walk-in coolers, freezers and cold storage facilities, as well as step-in freezers and coolers.
President: Donald Goodstein
Vice President: Barbara Bowman
Sales Director: Rio Giardinieri
Contact: Gary Albright
galbright@arcticwalkins.com
Office Manager: Barbara Bowman
Estimated Sales: $5 - 100 Million
Number Employees: 100-249
Square Footage: 50000
Brands:
Arctic
Penguin

19038 Arctic Seal & Gasket
2796 SW Bridgeway St
Palm City, FL 34990-1451
772-283-0080
Fax: 772-220-7437 800-881-4663
gaskets@bellsouth.net
Gaskets and seals for refrigeration units
Owner: Fred Froberd
VP: Fred Froberg
Sales: I Micheal Roth
Estimated Sales: $1-2.5,000,000
Number Employees: 1-4

19039 Arctic Star
3540 W Pioneer Pkwy
Pantego, TX 76013-4699
817-274-1396
Fax: 817-277-4828 800-229-6567
www.arcticstar.com
Refrigerated store displays
Owner: Jim Dunnagan
jdunnagan@arcticstar.com
Estimated Sales: $10-20 000,000
Number Employees: 10-19

19040 Arctica Showcase Company
88 Talbot St. E
P.O. Box 130
Cayuga, ON N0A 1E0
Canada
905-772-5214
Fax: 905-772-3179 800-839-5536
info@cayugadisplays.com cayugadisplays.com
Supplier of Hot Food, Deli, Meat, Seafood, Bakery, Candy Cafeteria showcases and more.
President: Rick Schotsman
Project Coordinator: Jennifer Zuidema
Vice President, Sales & Marketing: Chris Schotsman
Sales Director: Kirk Bessey
Number Employees: 85
Square Footage: 188000
Parent Co: Cayuga Displays Inc.
Brands:
Diamond 49 Series
Diamond 52 Series
M850 Series
Maxima Series
Omega 48 Series
Omega 52 Series
Omega Buffet Series

19041 Ardagh Group
8770 W Bryn Mawr Ave # 8
Chicago, IL 60631-3515
773-399-3000
Fax: 773-399-3354 www.ardaghgroup.com
Metal packaging manufacturer, aluminum can packaging
President: William Francois
CEO: Stephen Sefton
ssefton@rexambca.com
CEO: Harry Barto
Estimated Sales: $2.5-5 Million
Number Employees: 500-999

19042 Ardagh Group
1509 S Macedonia Ave
Muncie, IN 47302-3664
765-741-7000
Fax: 765-741-7012 www.ardaghgroup.com
Designs and manufactures glass containers for the food and beverage industries in North America.
CEO: Joseph R Grewe
joseph.grewe@saint-gobain.com
CEO: Joe Grewe
Marketing Director: Marilyn LaGrange
Sales Director: Jarrell Reeves
Estimated Sales: Over $1 Billion
Number Employees: 1000-4999
Parent Co: Ardagh Group S.A.

19043 Arde Inc
875 Washington Ave
Carlstadt, NJ 07072-3001
201-784-9880
Fax: 201-784-9710 800-909-6070
abmix@ardeinc.com www.ardeinc.com
Manufacturer and exporter of mixing equipment systems used to disperse gums and stabilizers to prepare emulsions

Manager: Sue Belaus
Sales/Engineering Manager: Roy Scott
Public Relations: Cindy Roehling
Purchasing: Tom Stephens
Estimated Sales: $5 Million
Number Employees: 50-99
Square Footage: 280000
Parent Co: Arde, Inc.

19044 Arde Inc
875 Washington Ave
Carlstadt, NJ 07072-3001
201-784-9880
Fax: 201-784-9710 800-909-6070
ABmix@Ardeinc.com www.ardeinc.com
Mixing equipment for beverage, sauces, preserves
Manager: Roy Scott
Manager: Kirk Sneddon
Estimated Sales: $2.5 - 5 000,000
Number Employees: 50-99
Square Footage: 20000

19045 Arden Companies
30400 Telegraph Road
Southfield, MI 48025
248-415-8500
Fax: 248-415-8520 www.ardencompanies.com
Manufacturer and exporter of aprons, chef coats, baker's mits, handle holders, cleaners, outdoor pads and cushions, grill covers, pot holders and oven mitts
President: Robert Sachs
CFO: John Connell
Sales/Marketing: William Sachs
Estimated Sales: $20-50 Million
Number Employees: 50-99
Square Footage: 675000
Type of Packaging: Consumer, Food Service

19046 Arena Products
2101 Mount Read Blvd
Rochester, NY 14615-3708
585-254-2180
Fax: 585-254-1046 844-762-0127
www.arenaproducts.com
Reusable, collapsible plastic containers for shipping liquid and cheese.
President: Anthony Arena
tarena@arenaproducts.com
Director of Marketing: Jim Roth
Plant Manager: Jeff Reeves
Estimated Sales: $5-10 Million
Number Employees: 5-9
Brands:
Arena 330 Shipper
Arena Shipper
Atlas 640 Shipper

19047 Argo & Company
182 Ezell Street
P.O. Box 2747
Spartanburg, SC 29304
864-583-9766
Fax: 864-585-5056 argosheen@bellsouth.net
Manufacturer and exporter of cleaning supplies including cotton pads, rug mops and carpet/upholstery chemicals and machines
President: Anne Sanders
Estimated Sales: $10-20 Million
Number Employees: 20-49
Square Footage: 200000
Brands:
Argomops
Argonaut
Argosheen

19048 Ari Industries Inc
381 S Ari Ct
Addison, IL 60101-4353
630-953-9100
Fax: 630-953-0590 800-237-6725
sales@ariindustries.com www.ariindustries.com
Manufacturer and exporter of temperature sensors and electric heaters
President: Dan Malcolm
brandi.crouch@lmco.com
VP Sales/Marketing: Dan Malcolm
Public Relations: Darlene Sosnowski
Operations: John Mulvey
Estimated Sales: $5-10 Million
Number Employees: 50-99
Square Footage: 56000

19049 Arizona Instrument LLC
3375 N Delaware St
Chandler, AZ 85225-1134
602-470-1414
Fax: 602-281-1745 800-528-7411
sales@azic.com www.azic.com
An ISO 9001:200 registered company that designs, manufactures, and markets Computrac precision moisture, solids, and ash analyzers and Jerome toxic gas analyzers.
President: George Hays
ghays@azic.com
Research & Development: Tom Hatfield
Quality Control: Blaine Nelson
Marketing: Shari Houtler
Operations Manager: Ben Brown
Estimated Sales: $10 Million
Number Employees: 50-99
Number of Brands: 4
Number of Products: 13
Brands:
Computrac Max
Computrac Vapor Pro
Jerome

19050 Arizona Store Equipment
2523 N 16th St
Phoenix, AZ 85006
602-252-4823
Fax: 602-258-3064 800-624-8395
Acrylic displays, showcases, slatwall, wall systems, shelving and store fixtures
Administrator: Bill James
Estimated Sales: $2.5-5,000,000
Number Employees: 1-4
Brands:
Cal Tuf
Diack
Discovery Plastics
Jahabow
Lozier
Marlite

19051 Arjo Wiggins
10901 Westlake Drive
Charlotte, NC 28273
704-587-3000
Fax: 704-587-1174 800-765-9278
www.polyart.com
Product and services are tag and label applications suitable for a variety of uses including that of: food labels; slaughterhouse meat tags; bar-coded labels, and self-adhesive labels.
Sales Representative: Chris Pelle
Contact: Bharath Chandra
bharath.chandra@arjobexamerica.com

19052 Arjobex
10901 Westlake Dr
Charlotte, NC 28273-3740
704-587-3000
Fax: 704-588-9506 800-POL-YART
www.polyart.com
Synthetic paper products
Vice President: David Brown
david.brown@arjobexamerica.com
VP: Vijay Yadav
Estimated Sales: $10-25 Million
Number Employees: 50-99

19053 Arkansas Glass Container Corp
516 W Johnson Ave
Jonesboro, AR 72401-1994
870-932-0168
Fax: 870-268-6217 800-527-4527
agcsalesdept@agcc.com www.agcc.com
Manufacturer and exporter of glass jars and bottles
CEO: Luann Sutton
lsutton@agcc.com
CEO: Anthony M Ramplex
VP Sales: Melton Harrison
VP Operations: Joel Sharp
Estimated Sales: $30 - 50 Million
Number Employees: 1-4
Square Footage: 450000

19054 Arkansas Poly
309 Phillips Rd
N Little Rock, AR 72117-4105
501-945-5763
Fax: 501-945-0276 800-342-7659
drew@arkpoly.com www.allampoly.com
Supplier of products for bottling, canning, food processing, and consumer packaging.

Manager: Jim Wilson
VP Sales/Marketing: Kip Johnson
Controller: Dave Robertson
Regional Sales Manager: Dave Schultz
Estimated Sales: $20 - 50 Million
Number Employees: 50-99
Brands:
   Arkansas Poly

19055 Arkansas Tomato Shippers
106 N John C Moss III St
Warren, AR 71671-2510
                      870-463-8258
            brooks@dakotacom.net
Distributor and processor of fresh produce
President: Charlie Sarcey
Estimated Sales: $1 - 5 Million
Number Employees: 6

19056 Arkfeld Mfg & Distributing Co
1230 W Monroe Ave
Norfolk, NE 68701-6664
                      402-371-9430
   Fax: 402-371-5137 800-533-0676
            arkfeldm@ncfcomm.com
Manufacturer, distributor and exporter of custom
metal fabricated poultry scales, livestock dial scales
and feed/grain hopper dial scales, custom automatic
watering systems and security and frozen product
storage cabinets.
President: Robert Arkfeld
CEO: Janet Arkfeld
CFO: Anthony Arkfeld
Sales Director: Janet Arkfeld
Sales: Robert Arkfeld
Number Employees: 10-19
Square Footage: 5000
Brands:
   Arkfeld Instant Way Dial Scales
   Arkfeld Security Cabinets
   Bunker Boxes

19057 Arla Foods Ingredients
106 Allen Rd
4th Floor, the Offices at Liberty Cor.
Basking Ridge, NJ 07920
                      908-604-8551
   Fax: 908-604-9310 ingredients@arlafoods.com
            www.arlafoodsingredients.com
Specialist provider of advanced innovative solutions
withing the milk-based ingredients industry such as
dairy, ice cream, meat, ready meals/fine foods, bak-
ery, infant nutrition and functional foods
applications.
CEO: Henrick Anderson
CFO: Klaus Kristiansen
Director R&D: Kristian Albertsen
Key Account Manager: Courtney Lopez
Sales Director: Carsten Valentin
Sales Director: Anders Steen Jergensen
Contact: Kay Breyer
   kbreyer@fultonbanknj.com
Account Manager: Nikolaj Beck
Product Manager: Adam Criscione
Estimated Sales: $5-10 Million
Number Employees: 5-9
Square Footage: 4000
Parent Co: Arla Foods Ingredients Group
Type of Packaging: Bulk
Brands:
   Capolac
   Lacprodan
   Miprodan
   Nutrilac

19058 Arlin Manufacturing Co
239 Industrial Ave E
Lowell, MA 01852-5113
                      978-454-9165
   Fax: 978-454-5265 sales@arlinmfg.com
            www.arlinmfg.com
Tear tapes, plastic film, plastic sheet
Owner: John Mitchell
   sales@arlinmfg.com
Estimated Sales: $5-10 Million
Number Employees: 20-49

19059 Arlington Display Industries
19303 W Davison St
Detroit, MI 48223
                      313-837-1212
                 Fax: 313-837-3425
Point-of-purchase displays
President: Carl Dumas

Number Employees: 50-99
Brands:
   Safe-Lode
   Traveler
   Versa-Panel

19060 Arlyn Johnson & Associates
1339 E Hanover St
Springfield, MO 65804-4232
                      417-886-3367
                 Fax: 417-886-4859
Poultry, poultry products, primarily fresh & frozen
turkey [roducts or further processing
President: Rex Johnson
Estimated Sales: Below $5,000,000
Number Employees: 1-4

19061 (HQ)Armaly Brands
1900 Easy St
Commerce Twp, MI 48390-3220
                      248-669-2100
   Fax: 248-669-3505 800-772-1222
   orderdesk207@armalybrands.com
            www.armalybrands.com
Manufacturer and exporter of sponges, scrubbers,
cotton cheesecloth and scouring pads
Owner: John Armaly
   jwarmaly@armalybrands.com
VP: Gilbert Armaly
Estimated Sales: $1 - 5 Million
Number Employees: 20-49
Square Footage: 400
Type of Packaging: Consumer, Food Service, Pri-
vate Label, Bulk
Brands:
   Auto Show
   Estracell
   Scourlite

19062 Armand Manufacturing Inc
2399 Silver Wolf Dr
Henderson, NV 89011-4431
                      702-565-7500
   Fax: 702-565-3838 sales@armandmfg.net
            www.armandmfg.com
President: Richard DE Heras
   rich@armandmfg.net
Estimated Sales: $10 - 20 Million
Number Employees: 20-49

19063 Armato & Associates
7825 Carlisle Dr
Hanover Park, IL 60133-2405
                      630-837-1886
                 Fax: 630-837-0813
Owner: Sam Armato
Estimated Sales: $1 - 5 Million
Number Employees: 1-4

19064 Armbrust Paper Tubes Inc
6255 S Harlem Ave # D
Chicago, IL 60638-3990
                      773-586-3232
   Fax: 773-586-8997 tubesrus@corecomm.net
            www.tubesrus.com
Manufacturer and exporter of packaging products
including paper tubes, cores, cans and push-ups for
frozen sherbet, gyros, etc.; also, containers for dry
goods
President: Bernard Armbrust
   bernard@tubesrus.com
VP: Chris Armbrust
Marketing: Bill Constable
Sales: Marc Armbrust
Secretary: Dorothee Johnstone
Plant Manager: Mike Johnstone
Estimated Sales: $5-10 Million
Number Employees: 20-49
Square Footage: 170000
Type of Packaging: Food Service, Private Label
Brands:
   Artpak
   Pinched Tube
   Push-Pops

19065 Armco
385 Todhunter Road
Monroe, OH 45050-1113
                      800-231-3748

19066 Armstrong Engineering Associates
PO Box 566
West Chester, PA 19381-0566
                      610-436-6080
                 Fax: 610-436-0374
            sales@armstrong-chemtec.com
                 www.rmarmstrong.com
President: Richard M Armstrong Jr
Sales: Gail Justi
Contact: Janine Stein
   janine@contentasia.tv
Estimated Sales: $1 - 5 Million
Number Employees: 50-99

19067 Armstrong Hot Water
221 Armstrong Blvd
Three Rivers, MI 49093-2374
                      269-279-3602
   Fax: 269-279-3150 www.armstrong-intl.com
Manufacturer and exporter of hose stations and ther-
mostatic mixing valves
President: David Armstrong
General Manager/Sales/Marketing Exec.: Paul
Knight
Purchasing Agent: Steven Shutes
Number Employees: 20-49
Parent Co: Armstrong International
Brands:
   Rada
   Steamix

19068 Armstrong International
900 Maple St
Three Rivers, MI 49093
                      269-273-1415
   Fax: 269-278-6555 marketing@armintl.com
                 www.armstronginternational.com
Steam traps, strainers, purgers, air vents, humidifiers
and liquid drainers, pressure reducing valves, instan-
taneous water heaters, radiator products, mixing
valves, hosestations, and heating and cooling coils
CEO: David Armstrong
Estimated Sales: $50-100 Million
Number Employees: 250-499

19069 Armstrong Manufacturing
2485 Haines Road
Mississauga, ON L4Y 1Y7
Canada
                      905-566-1395
   Fax: 905-566-8195 866-627-6588
Industrial cleaning products
CEO: David Armstrong
Estimated Sales: $1 - 5 Million
Number Employees: 100-250

19070 Armstrong-Hunt
816 Maple Street
Three Rivers, MI 49093
                      269-273-1415
   Fax: 269-278-6555 www.armstrong-hunt.com
President, Chief Executive Officer: Patrick
Armstrong
Contact: Zac Findlay
   zfindlay@armstronginternational.com

19071 Arneg LLC
750 Old Hargrave Rd
Lexington, NC 27295-7514
                      336-956-5300
   Fax: 610-746-9580 800-276-3487
            www.arnegusa.com
Display cases for meat, seafood, fish, cheese, deli
and frozen foods, etc
General Manager: Gianfrano Genovese
President: Rejean Lumiere
Sales Manager: Jim Christman
Manager: Louis Moschetta
   lmoschetta@arnegusa.com
Secretary: Sharon Sherman
Estimated Sales: $10-20 Million
Number Employees: 50-99
Square Footage: 140000
Parent Co: Arneg
Brands:
   Arneg

19072 Arnold Equipment Co
24400 Highpoint Rd # 5
Cleveland, OH 44122-6027
                      216-831-8485
   Fax: 216-831-8414 800-642-1824
            www.arnoldeqp.com

Wholesaler/distributor and exporter of blenders, ovens, agitators, filters, dryers, packaging plastic granulators, centrifuges, pumps, evaporators, condensers, kettles, homogenizers and material handling and laboratory testing equipment, etc
CEO: Jon Arnold
CFO: Seth Arnold
Estimated Sales: Less Than $500,000
Number Employees: 1-4
Square Footage: 120000

19073 Arol Closure Systems Spa
237 Graves Mill Road
Lynchburg, VA 24502-4203
800-423-5822
Fax: 434-832-8352 info@belvac.com
www.belvac.com

19074 Aroma Manufacturing Company
6469 Flanders Dr
San Diego, CA 92121
858-558-8866
Fax: 858-558-7300 800-276-6286
www.aroma-housewares.com
Rice and steam cookers; also, soup and rice warmers
Manager: David Kellerman
Marketing Director: Howard Ong
Contact: Peter Chang
pchang@aromaco.com
Estimated Sales: $3 - 5 Million
Number Employees: 5-9

19075 Aromascan PLC
14 Clinton Drive
Hollis, NH 03049-6595
603-598-2922
Fax: 603-595-9916
Instrumentation for the analysis of odors
Contact: Drwang Chong
drwang@aromascan.com
General Manager: Peter Debroczy
Estimated Sales: $1-2.5 Million
Number Employees: 24
Parent Co: Aromascan PLC
Brands:
The Aromo Scanner

19076 Aromatech USA
5770 Hoffner Avenue
Suite 103
Orlando, FL 32822
407-277-5727
Fax: 407-277-5725 americas@aromatech.com
www.aromatech.fr/en/f.usa.htm
Flavorings for beverages, candies, baking, snacks and pastries.

19077 (HQ)Arpac LP
9511 River St
Schiller Park, IL 60176-1019
847-678-9034
Fax: 847-671-7006 info@arpac.com
www.arpac.com
One stop shop packaging solutions. Manufacture shrink bundles, multipackers, horizontal shrink wrappers, corrugated tray and case erectors, box formers, corrugated board try and case packers, pallet stretch wrappers and pallet stretchhooders.
President: Michael Levy
Marketing Manager: Greg Levy
VP Sales: Gary Ehmka
Contact: Stephen Archer
sarcher@arpac.com
Estimated Sales: $10 - 50 Million
Number Employees: 5-9
Square Footage: 260000
Brands:
Brandpac
Tray Star

19078 Arpac LP
9511 River St
Schiller Park, IL 60176-1019
847-678-9034
Fax: 847-671-7006 info@arpac.com
www.arpac.com
Shrink wrappers, case packers and tray loaders
President: Michael Levy
Contact: James Barry
jbarry@arpac.com
Estimated Sales: $25-50 Million
Number Employees: 5-9

19079 Arpeco Engineering Ltd
7095 Ordan Drive
Mississauga, ON L5T 1K6
Canada
905-564-5150
Fax: 905-564-2943 sales@arpeco.com
Owner: Allan Prittie

19080 Arro Corp
7440 Santa Fe Dr # A
Hodgkins, IL 60525-5076
708-639-9063
Fax: 708-352-5293 877-929-2776
Sales@arro.com www.arro.com
Corn, peanut, salad, soybean and vegetable oils.
Owner: Pat Gaughn
arrosales@aol.com
Sales Exec: Timothy Mcnicholas
Estimated Sales: $500,000-1 Million
Number Employees: 50-99
Type of Packaging: Food Service, Private Label, Bulk
Other Locations:
Chicago IL
Hodgkins IL

19081 Arro Corp
7440 Santa Fe Dr # A
Hodgkins, IL 60525-5076
708-639-9063
Fax: 708-352-5293 877-929-2776
Sales@arro.com www.arro.com
Dry & liquid blending, dry & liquid processing, bulk handling & storage.
Sales Exec: Timothy Mcnicholas
Number Employees: 50-99
Square Footage: 600

19082 Arrow Plastic Mfg Co
701 E Devon Ave
Elk Grove Vlg, IL 60007-6700
847-595-9000
Fax: 847-595-9122 info@arrowplastic.com
www.arrowplastic.com
Manufacturer and exporter of plastic cutting boards
President: Robert Kleckauskas
rkleck@arrowplastic.com
Estimated Sales: $20-50 Million
Number Employees: 100-249
Type of Packaging: Food Service

19083 Arrow Sign & Awning Company
18607 Highway 65 NE
East Bethel, MN 55304-6784
763-755-8873
Fax: 763-755-1473 800-621-9231
john@arrowfenceco.com www.arrowsignmn.com
Design manufacturer of lit and unlit fabric and metal commercial awnings, neon signs and lighted channel letters, also pylon signs, LED lighting, parking lot lights, LED message centers.
President: Bruce Cardnial
CFO/VP: Connie Cardinal Ramberg
Research & Development: Kelli Keilty
Quality Control: Tony Ramberg
Marketing: Bruce Cardinal
Plant Manager: Tony Ramberg
Purchasing Manager: Ryan Thiede
Estimated Sales: $10 Million
Number Employees: 20-49
Square Footage: 72000

19084 Arrow Tank Co
16 Barnett Pl
Buffalo, NY 14215-3898
716-893-7200
Fax: 716-893-0693 sales@arrowtankco.com
www.arrowtankco.com
Manufacturer, exporter of wood tanks and tank hoops
President: William H Wehr
sales@arrowtankco.com
Operations: W H Wehr
Plant Manager: R Willis
Estimated Sales: $1-3,000,000
Number Employees: 5-9
Square Footage: 25000

19085 Arrow-Magnolia Intl Inc
2646 Rodney Ln
Dallas, TX 75229-3425
972-247-7111
Fax: 972-484-2896 800-527-2101
info@arrowmagnolia.com
www.arrowmagnolia.com
Industrial insecticides, grill cleaners, drain cleaners and deodorizers
President: Curtis Shaw
CEO: David Tippeconnic
Vice President of Sales: Jim Purcell
Operations Manager: Michael Campanaro
Number Employees: 50-99
Square Footage: 160000

19086 Art Craft Lighting
East Service Road
P.O. Box 1526
Champlain, NY 11919
718-387-8000
Fax: 516-593-9239 www.artcraftlighting.com
Electric lighting fixtures
President: Barry Spade
Estimated Sales: $1-2.5 Million
Number Employees: 5-9
Parent Co: Artcraft Lighting Company

19087 Art Poly Bag Co
70 Franklin Ave
Brooklyn, NY 11205-1504
718-243-9417
Fax: 718-422-8689 800-278-7659
Promotional poly tote bags
President: Erwin Katz
Estimated Sales: $500,000-$1 Million
Number Employees: 5-9

19088 Art Wire Works Co
6711 S Leclaire Ave
Chicago, IL 60638-6417
708-458-3993
Fax: 708-458-3008
dcollignon@artwireworks.com
www.artwireworks.com
Manufacturer and exporter of display racks, point of purchase displays, back room trays and hand carts
President: David Collignon
dcollignon@artwireworks.com
CFO: Ksenia Nalysnyk
R&D/Quality Control: Danny Tomasevich
Sales: Gayle Blakeslee
Plant Manager: Wally Kaim
Purchasing: Gayle Blakeslee
Estimated Sales: $5 Million
Number Employees: 20-49
Square Footage: 80000

19089 Art's Welding
3902 230th St
PO Box 909
Winsted, MN 55395
320-485-2471
Fax: 320-485-4466 888-272-2600
customerservice@awimfg.com www.awimfg.com
President: Gary Scherping
Sales Manager: Brent Johnson
Estimated Sales: $1 - 3 Million
Number Employees: 20-49
Square Footage: 90

19090 Art-Phyl Creations
16250 NW 8th Avenue
Hialeah, FL 33014-6415
305-624-2333
Fax: 305-621-4093 800-327-8318
info@art-phyl.com
Manufacturer and exporter of store display fixtures, peghooks, merchandising aids, point of purchase displays, etc.
President: Arthur Hochman
CEO: S Gwinn
CFO: C Pomerantz
Sales: William Rodriguez
Estimated Sales: $5 - 10 Million
Number Employees: 20-49
Number of Products: 400
Square Footage: 200000
Brands:
Kwik-Hook
Kwik-Hub
Poly-Pole
Scan-A-Plate

Short-Stop
Super Hook

19091 Art-Tech Restaurant Design
30 Woodland Avenue
Rockville Centre, NY 11570
516-593-9130
Fax: 516-593-9239
Consultant and designer of restaurant/food service interiors
President: Philip Starr
Consultant: Philip Starr
Estimated Sales: $1 - 2.5 Million
Number Employees: 5-9

19092 Artco Eq Co
40 Tillman St
Westwood, NJ 07675-2611
201-664-4455
Fax: 201-666-9243 800-664-5686
www.bagelbagel.com
Ovens, bagel machines, mixers, bagel kettles and smallwares
President: Howard Goldberg
Estimated Sales: $1-2.5 Million
Number Employees: 5-9

19093 Artcraft Badge & Sign Company
3512 John Carroll Drive
Olney, MD 20832
301-519-2939
800-739-0709
Plastic custom imprinted identification badges and interior signage. Produces personalized name badges, identification tags, signs, and deskplates
Owner: Janet Dinerman
Bookkeeper: Shirley Bowker
General Manager: Arthur Dinerman
Shipping Manager: Reina Roeder
Estimated Sales: $2.5-5 Million
Number Employees: 9
Square Footage: 3600
Type of Packaging: Bulk

19094 Artel Packaging SystemsLimited
PO Box 335
Gromley, ON L0H 1G0
Canada
905-888-9800
Fax: 905-888-9804
President: Fred McCatrney
Estimated Sales: Below $5 Million
Number Employees: 10

19095 Artex International
1405 Walnut St
Highland, IL 62249
618-654-2113
Fax: 618-654-0200
Manufacturer and exporter of table linens including covers, skirts, napkins and place mats, restaurant design, linen processing, trade show listing, linen presentations
Manager: Mike Kirchoff
Estimated Sales: $50-100 Million
Number Employees: 50-99

19096 Arthur Corporation
1305 Huron Avery Rd
Huron, OH 44839
419-433-7202
Fax: 419-433-7088 arthurcorp.com
Plastic cups, trays and containers
President: Charles Hensel
Contact: Russell Gibboney
russell.gibboney@arthurcorp.com
Estimated Sales: $10-20 Million
Number Employees: 100-249
Square Footage: 150000

19097 (HQ)Arthur D Little Inc.
68 Fargo Street
Suite 2810
Boston, MA 02110
617-532-9550
Fax: 617-261-6630 www.adlittle.com
Consultant specializing in technology, product and marketing services; also, management, environmental, health, safety, product formulation, sensory evaluation, research and development.
CEO/Pres.: C LaMantia
Sr. VP: P Ranganath Nayak
VP/Managing Director: C Gail Greenwald

Estimated Sales: $.5 - 1 million
Number Employees: 1,000-4,999
Square Footage: 800000

19098 Arthur G Russell Co Inc
750 Clark Ave
P.O. Box 237
Bristol, CT 06010-4065
860-583-4109
Fax: 860-583-0686 agr@arthurgrussell.com
www.arthurgrussell.com
Manufacturer and exporter of automated packaging, counting, inspecting and assembling equipment for food and disposable manufacturers; custom design services available
President: Robert J Ensminger
robert.ensminger@arthurgrussell.com
Applications Engr.: John Picoli
Vice President Sales & Marketing: William Mis
Human Resources Manager: Shelly Bove
robert.ensminger@arthurgrussell.com
Operations Manager: Craig Churchill
Estimated Sales: $10-20 Million
Number Employees: 100-249
Square Footage: 166000
Brands:
Uniplace
Vibro-Block

19099 Arthur Products Co
1140 Industrial Pkwy
Medina, OH 44256-2486
330-725-4905
Fax: 330-722-2698 800-322-0510
apc@apclsq.com www.arthurproducts.com
Vent tubes and nozzles
Owner: Richard Rauckhorst
rlr@apclsq.com
Sales Manager: Bob Peck
Estimated Sales: Below $5 Million
Number Employees: 5-9
Square Footage: 20000

19100 Artisan Controls Corp
111 Canfield Ave # B-18
Bldg B15-18
Randolph, NJ 07869-1127
973-598-9400
Fax: 973-598-9410 800-457-4950
sales@artisancontrols.com
www.artisancontrols.com
Controllers including time/temperature, dispensing, scheduling for pasta machines, fryers, ovens, etc.
President: Jack Murray
adonnelly@artisancontrols.com
Vice President: Larry Affelt
Sales Manager: Mary Ann Peterson
Plant Manager: Jack Cooper
Purchasing Manager: Angie Donnelly
Estimated Sales: $3 Million
Number Employees: 50-99
Square Footage: 24000
Type of Packaging: Private Label, Bulk
Brands:
Tyme Chef

19101 Artisan Industries
73 Pond St
Waltham, MA 02451-4594
781-893-6800
Fax: 781-647-0143 info@artisanind.com
www.artisanind.com
Equipment to purify, concentrate, deodorize or recover/remove solvents or fatty acids
President: Andrew Donevan
SVP/General Manager: Perry Alasti
Director Marketing/Sales: Richard Giberti
Contact: Louis Decker
lou@dectechassociates.com
Pilot Plant Services: Robert DiLoreto
Estimated Sales: $5-10 Million
Number Employees: 100
Brands:
Rototherm

19102 Artist Coffee
51 Harvey Road
Unit D
Londonderry, NH 03053-7414
603-434-9385
Fax: 603-216-8029 866-440-4511
Producer of gourmet coffee, tea and candy for promotional trade. Specializing in Custom Labeling with very special products.

President: Tom Rushton
Marketing Director: Dan Sewell
Estimated Sales: $3 - 5 Million
Number Employees: 1-4
Type of Packaging: Consumer, Private Label
Other Locations:
Lambent Technologies
Gurnee IL
Brands:
Cirashine
Erucical
Hodag
Lamchem
Lumisolve
Lumisorb
Lumulse
Oleocal
Polycal

19103 Artiste Flavor
35 Franklin Tpke
Waldwick, NJ 07463
201-447-1311
Ingredients, flavors, colors and additives
President: Joseph Raimondo
Contact: Tracy Hennig
thennig@artiste.us.com
Estimated Sales: $500,000- 1 Million
Number Employees: 5-9
Type of Packaging: Consumer

19104 Artistic Carton
1201 S Grandstaff Dr
Auburn, IN 46706-2660
260-925-6060
Fax: 260-925-1762 800-735-7225
customerserviceauburn@artisticcarton.com
www.artisticcarton.com
Folding cartons
President: Peter A Traeger
CFO: Mark Hopkinson
Manager: Brandy Aucunas
baucunas@artisticcarton.com
Estimated Sales: $10-20 Million
Number Employees: 50-99

19105 (HQ)Artistic Carton Co
1975 Big Timber Rd
Elgin, IL 60123-1139
847-741-0247
Fax: 847-741-8529 www.artisticcarton.com
Folding paper boxes and cartons
President: Peter A Traeger
CEO: Amanda Brown
brownamanda@artisticcarton.com
CFO: Mark Hopkinfon
Sales Manager: Patrick Driscoll
Estimated Sales: $20 - 50 Million
Number Employees: 20-49

19106 Artistic Packaging Concepts
PO Box 196
Massapequa Pk, NY 11762-0196
516-797-4020
Fax: 516-797-4020
Plain and printed plastic bags; also, blisters, blister cards, labels and paper printing foam envelopes
VP: S Falciana
Estimated Sales: $1 - 5 Million
Number Employees: 5

19107 Artkraft Strauss LLC
1776 Broadway # 1810
New York, NY 10019-2017
212-265-5156
Fax: 212-265-5262 info@artkraft.com
www.artkraft.com
Manufacturer and exporter of advertising signs
President: Tama Starr
CFO: Neil Vonknoblauch
Vice President Design & Engineering: Robert Jackowitz
VP Sales: Bob Neuberger
Manager: Amy Hu
alexandra.labrie@mercer.com
Estimated Sales: $10 - 20 Million
Number Employees: 5-9
Type of Packaging: Consumer, Food Service, Bulk

19108 Artx Limited
1770 W Lexington
Cincinnati, OH 45212-3508
513-631-0660
Fax: 513-631-3111 www.airtxinternational.com

President: Michael Rawlings
Estimated Sales: $5 - 10 Million
Number Employees: 1-4

19109 Asap Automation
503 S Westgate St # C
Suite C
Addison, IL 60101-4531

630-628-5830
Fax: 630-628-5831 800-409-0383
info@asapauto.com
Software and control systems
President: Steve Moore
sales@asap-automation.com
Board of Director: Bill Bastian
Marketing Manager: Lynsey Thomann
Sales Manager: Eric Cameron
Operations Manager: Hal Frary
Estimated Sales: Less Than $500,000
Number Employees: 1-4
Number of Products: 14
Type of Packaging: Private Label, Bulk

19110 Ascaso
524 North York Road
Bensenville, IL 60106

630-350-0066
Fax: 630-350-0005 info@expressoshoppe.com
www.expressoshoppe.com
Espresso equipment and espresso beans
Owner: David Dimbert
Estimated Sales: $300,000-500,000
Number Employees: 1-4
Parent Co: Ascaso Spa
Type of Packaging: Food Service
Brands:
   Ascaso

19111 Asepco
355 Pioneer Way # B
Mountain View, CA 94041-1542

650-691-4439
Fax: 650-691-9600 800-882-3886
www.asepco.com
President/CEO: Steve Joy
Executive Vice-President: Mark Embury
Quality Control Manager: Glenn Slusher
Contact: Arnold Brodskiy
arnoldbrodskiy@asepco.com
Purchasing: Ben Herbert
Estimated Sales: $3 - 5 Million
Number Employees: 10-19

19112 Aseptic Resources
10008 W 120th St
Overland Park, KS 66213-1647

913-897-4125
Fax: 913-327-5529
Consultant for aseptic systems
Estimated Sales: $1 - 5 Million

19113 (HQ)Asgco Manufacturing Inc
301 W Gordon St
Allentown, PA 18102-3136

610-821-0210
Fax: 610-778-8991 800-344-4000
info@asgco.com www.asgco.com
Conveyor and bulk material handling systems and
components including impact beds, belt cleaner,
conveyor components; also, lightweight belt for
food applications
President: Todd Gibbs
CFO: George Anthony
Executive VP: George Anthony
ganthony@asgco.com
Research & Development: George Mott
Marketing: Peggy Anthony
Inside Sales Manager: Steve Strella
Plant Manager: Steve Schubert
Estimated Sales: $10-20 Million
Number Employees: 50-99
Square Footage: 200000
Other Locations:
   ASGCO Manufacturing
   Newburgh NY

19114 Ash Enterprises
801 N 7th St
Salina, KS 67401-2903

785-825-5280
Fax: 785-825-5072 888-825-5280
dave@ashenterprisesonline.com
www.ashenterprisesonline.com

Specializing in awnings, livestock curtains, tarps
and sun shades.
CEO: Adrienne Ash
Estimated Sales: $5-9.9,000,000
Number Employees: 1-4
Brands:
   Chile Chews
   Hot Pops
   Jalea De Jalapeño
   Salsa Primo

19115 Ashcroft Inc
250 E Main St
Stratford, CT 06614-5145

203-212-5222
Fax: 203-385-0408 800-328-8258
info@ebro.com www.ashcroftinc.com
Ebro instruments can be used for applications in the
food and beverage industries. Ebro products are
high-precision measuring instruments for use in ap-
plications where reliability and performance are re-
quired. Ebro instruments canmeasure and store
temperature, pressure, humidity, pH, oil quality, cur-
rent/voltage, salt and RPM, as well as other physical
units.
CEO: Steven A Culmone
  steven.culmone@ashcroft.com
Managing Director: Wolfgang Klun
General Sales Manager: Iven Kruse
Quality Manager: Thomas Koch
Sales Manager USA: Frank Crisafulli
Marketing Manager: Norbert Niggl
Number Employees: 250-499
Number of Brands: 2
Square Footage: 325000
Brands:
   Ashcroft
   Ebro

19116 Ashland
8145 Blazer Dr
Wilmington, DE 19808

800-274-5263
www.ashland.com
Supplier of specialty resins, polymers, and adhe-
sives. Ashland's Water Technologies unit provides
papermaking chemicals and specialty chemicals to
markets such as pulp and paper, food and beverage,
municipal, and mining.
Chairman/Chief Executive Officer: Guillermo Novo
SVP/Chief Financial Officer: J. Kevin Willis
SVP/Chief Human Resources Officer: Anne
Schumann
SVP/CTO: Osama Musa
SVP, Global Operations: Keith Silverman
Year Founded: 1924
Estimated Sales: $4.9 Billion
Number Employees: 6,500
Brands:
   Aerowhip
   Aqualon
   Aquasorb
   Benecel
   Cellulose Gum
   HydraSperse
   Klucel
   Polyclar

19117 Ashland Nutritional Products
17751 Mitchell N
Irvine, CA 92614-6028

949-833-9500
Fax: 949-622-0954
Estimated Sales: $5 - 10 000,000
Number Employees: 5-9

19118 Ashlock Co
855 Montague St
P.O. Box 1676
San Leandro, CA 94577-4327

510-351-0560
Fax: 510-357-0329 info@ashlockco.com
www.ashlockco.com
Manufacturer and exporter of pitters for dates,
prunes, cherries and olives. Also olive slicers
President: Tom Rettagliata
   info@ashlockco.com
CFO: Sheryl Sullivan
R & D: Jeff Davis
Marketing Director: Alan Stender
Office Manager: S Sullivan
   info@ashlockco.com
Manager, Operations: Jeff Davis

Estimated Sales: $5-10 Million
Number Employees: 10-19
Square Footage: 24800
Parent Co: Vistan Corporation
Brands:
   Ashlock

19119 Ashworth Bros Inc
450 Armour Dl
Winchester, VA 22601-3459

540-662-3494
Fax: 540-662-3150 800-682-4594
ashworth@ashworth.com www.ashworth.com
Manufacturer and exporter of conveyor belts
President: Keith Almryde
keith.almryde@ashworth.com
VP: Joe Lackner
Quality Control: Jonathan Lasecki
Commercial Support Manager: Kenneth King
Sales: Marty Tabaka
Estimated Sales: $20 - 50 Million
Number Employees: 100-249
Brands:
   All Plastic Belting
   Balanceo Weave
   Cbs Baking Band
   Flat Wire
   Fusion Grid
   Hybri Flex
   Hybri Grio
   Omni Grid
   Omniflex
   Washer Holddown Mats
   Woven Wire

19120 Asi Food Safety Consultants
7625 Page Ave
St Louis, MO 63133-1009

314-333-6201
Fax: 314-727-2563 800-477-0778
asi@asifood.com
Consultant specializing in food safety audits and
training including manual and high pressure clean-
ing and sanitizing and foodborne illness prevention
and pest control; also, HACCP literature, videos and
training materials available
President: Tom Huge
CEO: Gary Huge
VP: Gary Huge
Quality Control: Michael Bushaw
Sales: Jeanette Huge
Number Employees: 50-99
Square Footage: 60000
Parent Co: Huge Company
Other Locations:
   ASI Food Safety Consultants
   Lakeland FL

19121 Asia and Middle East Food Traders
340 Pine Street
Suite 401
San Francisco, CA 94104

415-677-9700
Fax: 415-677-9711 info@arabellaadvisors.com
President: Lucy Bernholz
Number Employees: 10-19

19122 Aspect Engineering
7911 Linksview Cir.
Westerville, OH

614-638-7106
Fax: 614-416-6919
Consultant for product development and facility de-
sign; management advisory for food service compa-
nies and suppliers
Commun. Mgr.: Mark Wegner
Estimated Sales: $1 - 5 Million
Number Employees: 4
Square Footage: 4000

19123 Aspen Research Corp
8401 Jefferson Hwy
Maple Grove, MN 55369-4588

763-494-0273
Fax: 651-842-6199 answers@aspenresearch.com
www.aspenresearch.com
Vice President: John Biesboer
john.biesboer@aspenresearch.com
Vice President - Research & Development: Roger
Pearson, Ph.D.
Analytical Sales: Jan Fouks
VP of Manufacturing: Brian Woodman

Estimated Sales: $5 - 10 Million
Number Employees: 50-99

19124 Aspen Research Corporation
1800 Buerkle Rd
White Bear Lake, MN 55110

651-773-7961
Fax: 651-264-6270 answers@aspenresearch.com
www.aspenresearch.com
Contract applied research and development firm specializing in research on flavors, off-flavors, off odors and the interaction between food and food packaging
President: Andy Marine
VP Operations: Roger Worm
Estimated Sales: $20 - 50 Million
Number Employees: 50-99
Square Footage: 250000

19125 Aspen Systems
6930 E Chauncey Ln # 100
Suite 100
Phoenix, AZ 85054-5175

480-538-1970
Fax: 480-538-1971 800-767-1970
sales@aspen-systems.com
www.aspen-systems.com
Software developer for food industry
President: George Puype
CEO: Larry Andrews
landrews@aspen-systems.com
CFO: Jerry King
Quality Control: Stewart Ward
Estimated Sales: $10 - 20 000,000
Number Employees: 20-49

19126 Aspeon
16832 Red Hill Avenue
Irvine, CA 92606-4803

949-440-8000
Fax: 949-440-8087 800-574-1622
info@aspeon.com
Leading manufacturer and provider of point-of-sales systems, services and enterprise technology solutions for the retail and food markets

19127 Assembled Products Corp
112 E Linden St
Rogers, AR 72756-6035

479-636-5776
Fax: 479-636-5776 800-548-3373
techservice@assembledproducts.com
www.assembledproducts.com
Manufacturer and exporter of electric shopping carts for supermarkets and high pressure spray cleaning systems
President: Lori Barlar
lorib@martcart.com
Sr. VP Sales/Marketing: Steve Seroggine
Estimated Sales: $5-10 Million
Number Employees: 100-249
Square Footage: 256000
Parent Co: Assembled Products Corporation
Brands:
Mart Cart
Spray Master Technologies

19128 Assembly Technology & Test
12841 Stark Rd
Livonia, MI 48150-1525

734-522-1900
Fax: 734-522-9344
Designer and manufacturer of software for material handling implementation and electrified monorail systems for ingredient transport
Founder: Klaus Woerner
VP: James Diedrich
VP Sales/Marketing: Jim Anderson
Contact: Daniel Haubert
dhaubert@assembly-testww.com
Estimated Sales: $50-100 Million
Number Employees: 100-249
Square Footage: 200000
Parent Co: DT Industries

19129 Asset Design LLC
PO Box 3234
Mooresville, NC 28117

704-663-6170
Fax: 704-663-6177 888-293-1740

Consultant providing engineering solutions for process design and automation, plant design and operating procedures, feasibility studies, machine modifications and custom design. Also, project management, start-up assistance andefficiency training
Manager and R&D: Jeff Demback
Estimated Sales: $500,000 - $1,000,000
Number Employees: 1-4

19130 Assmann Corp of America
300 N Taylor Rd
Garrett, IN 46738-1844

260-357-3181
Fax: 260-357-3738 888-357-3181
info@assmann-usa.com www.assmann-usa.com
President: David Crager
dcrager@assmannusa.com
Quality Control: James Reynolds
Estimated Sales: $5 - 10 Million
Number Employees: 20-49

19131 Associated Bag Co
400 W Boden St
Milwaukee, WI 53207-6276

414-769-1000
Fax: 414-769-1820 800-926-6100
customerservice@associatedbag.com
www.associatedbag.com
Wholesaler/distributor of food grade stretch wrap and bags, gloves and shipping and packaging products
President: Herbert Rubenstein
hrubenstein@associatedbag.com
CFO: Sue Zelga
Quality Control: Mary Samanski
Marketing/Sales Director: Scott Pietila
Customer Service Manager: Philip Roedel
hrubenstein@associatedbag.com
Purchasing Manager: Sue Zylka
Estimated Sales: $20-50 Million
Number Employees: 100-249
Square Footage: 300000

19132 Associated Industrial Rubber
7550 West 2100 South
Magna, UT 84044

801-239-1670
Fax: 801-239-1675 800-526-6288
www.associated-rubber.com
Food handling hoses for beer, milk and juice
General Manager: Steve Williams
Controller: David George
Inside Sales: Steven Munz
Sales Agent: Wilson Dube
Branch Manager: Roger Morrison
Estimated Sales: $2.5-5 Million
Number Employees: 5-9
Square Footage: 120000
Parent Co: Associated Industrial Rubber

19133 Associated Packaging Enterprises
900 S Us Highway 1
Suite 207
Jupiter, FL 33477-6469

561-746-2414
Fax: 561-746-7192 info@aptechnologies.com

19134 Associated Packaging Equipment Corporation
70 Gibson Drive
Units 5 & 6
Markham, ON L3R 2Z3
Canada

905-475-6647
Fax: 905-479-9752
Manufacturer and exporter of roll fed labeling machinery
President: M Malthouse
Controller: Kenneth Bick
Sales Director: Klaus See
Plant Manager: John Malthouse
Purchasing Manager: R Manoharan
Estimated Sales: $1 Million
Number Employees: 15
Square Footage: 24000
Type of Packaging: Food Service, Private Label
Brands:
Polyclad

19135 Associated Products Inc
1901 William Flynn Hwy
P.O. Box 8
Glenshaw, PA 15116-1742

412-486-2255
Fax: 412-486-7710 800-243-5689
Manufacturer and exporter of air fresheners, deodorants and deodorizers; importer of essential oils and aromatic chemicals
President: Ralph Simons
mrsimon@sani-air.com
CFO: Harlan Simons
Estimated Sales: $2.5-5 Million
Number Employees: 20-49
Number of Products: 100
Square Footage: 360000
Type of Packaging: Consumer, Private Label, Bulk
Brands:
Ban Air
Mini Scents
Sani Air

19136 Association of Operative Millers
12351 w. 96th Terrace,
Suite 100
Lenexa, KS 66215

913-338-3377
Fax: 913-338-3553 aom@sky.net
www.iaom.info
Provider of educational resources and training for the milling industry.
Executive VP: Melinda Farris
Director (Association Services): Roger Gelsinger
Administration Assistant: Carole Smith
Number Employees: 1-4

19137 Association-Nutri
406 Surrey Woods Dr
St Charles, IL 60174-2386

630-587-6336
Fax: 630-587-6308 800-323-1908
info@anfponline.org www.anfponline.org
Dedicated to the practice of providing optimum nutritional care through foodservice management.
President: William S St John
nrubicz@anfponline.org
Quality Control: Pam Himrogh
Vice President of Development: Katherine Church
Marketing Manager: Kim Harden
Sales Exec: Nik Rubicz
Executive Vice President, Chief Operatin: Marla Isaacs
Estimated Sales: Below $5 Million
Number Employees: 20-49

19138 Astoria General Espresso
7912 Industrial Village Rd
Greensboro, NC 27409

336-393-0224
Fax: 336-393-0295 info@geec.com
www.usa.astoria.com
Manufacturer, importer and exporter of espresso and cappuccino machines, coffee grinders, espresso equipment accessories and sandwich grills
Owner: Roberto Daltio
CEO: Umberto Terreni
Accounting/Office Manager: Linda Sizemore
Sales & Marketing: Courtney Baber
Managing/Sales Director: Scott Gordon
Technical Support Specialist: Jimmy Wardell
Number Employees: 5-9
Number of Brands: 2
Number of Products: 36
Square Footage: 50000
Parent Co: CMA
Type of Packaging: Private Label
Brands:
Astoria
Grillmaster
Llsa

19139 Astoria Laminations
19803 E 9 Mile Rd
St Clair Shores, MI 48080-1774

586-944-2294
Fax: 586-775-0010 800-526-7325
www.lamseal.com
Point of sales systems and equipment including bar coders and pricers; also, laminators including thermal, pouch and roll
President: Dennis Oster
doster@lamseal.com
R & D: Anthony Sagese
VP: Anthony Sagese

Estimated Sales: $5-10 Million
Number Employees: 1-4
Square Footage: 2600

19140 (HQ)Astra Manufacturing Inc
21520 Blythe St # A
Canoga Park, CA 91304-6609
818-340-1800
Fax: 818-340-5830 877-340-1800
sales@astramfr.com www.astramfr.com
Manufacturer and exporter of espresso and cappuccino equipment including coffee grinders
President: Richard Hourizadeh
richard@astramfr.com
Estimated Sales: $3 Million
Number Employees: 5-9
Square Footage: 40000
Type of Packaging: Food Service
Brands:
Astra

19141 Astro Arc Polysoude
W133n5138 Campbell Dr
Menomonee Falls, WI 53051
262-783-2720
Fax: 262-783-2730 www.igmusa.com
President: Hans-Peter Mariner
Principal: Lynn Marek
Estimated Sales: $1 - 5 Million
Number Employees: 5-9

19142 Astro Machine Corp
630 Lively Blvd
Elk Grove Vlg, IL 60007-2016
847-364-6363
Fax: 847-364-9898 www.astromachine.com
President: George Selak
gselak@astromachine.com
Estimated Sales: $5 - 10 Million
Number Employees: 20-49

19143 Astro Physic Inc
21481 Ferrero
Walnut, CA 91789-5233
909-598-5488
Fax: 909-598-5546 800-251-9750
sales@astrophysicsinc.com
www.astrophysicsinc.com
Owner: Francois Zayek
fzayek@xaytek.com
Estimated Sales: $1 - 3 Million
Number Employees: 20-49

19144 Astro Plastics
PO Box 665
Oakland, NJ 07436-0665
201-337-8170
Manufacturer and extruder of plastic film bags
President: Steven Ringley
Contact: Lenore Clark
lenore.clark@astroplastics.com
Estimated Sales: $5 - 10 Million
Number Employees: 25

19145 Astro Pure Water
1441 SW 1st Way
Deerfield Beach, FL 33441-6753
954-422-8966
Fax: 954-422-8966
Manufacturer and exporter of water purifiers and filters
President and CFO: Roger Stefl
VP Sales: Mary Munn
Office Manager: Miki Kaye
Estimated Sales: Below $5 Million
Number Employees: 10-19
Number of Brands: 1
Number of Products: 39
Square Footage: 6000
Type of Packaging: Consumer, Food Service, Private Label, Bulk
Brands:
Astro-Pure

19146 Astro/Polymetron Zellweger
100 Park Avenue
League City, TX 77573-2446
281-332-2484
Fax: 970-669-2932 kcraig@hach.com
Water quality analyzers for silica, sodium, phosphate, chlorine, ozone, dissolved oxygen, hydrazine, pH/conductivity and on-line titrates

President: Tom Joyce
Marketing Manager: Karon Craig
Sales Mgr: Robert Blight
Number Employees: 500

19147 At-Your-Svc Software Inc
450 Bronxville Rd
Bronxville, NY 10708-1133
914-337-9030
Fax: 914-337-9031 888-325-6937
sales@costguard.com www.costguard.com
Develops Cost Guard restaurant and foodservice software
President: Matthew Starobin
CEO: Pamela Terr
Contact: Mathew Starobin
matt@costguard.com
Estimated Sales: $2.5-5 Million
Number Employees: 5-9
Brands:
Cost Guard
Smart Scaling
Vendor Transport

19148 Athea Laboratories
7855 N Faulkner Rd
Milwaukee, WI 53224
414-354-6417
Fax: 414-354-9219 800-743-6417
info@athea.com www.athea.com
Manufacturer and exporter of chemical specialties including ground and sewer maintenance chemicals, insecticides, aerosol, liquid and waterless hand cleaners and lotion; packager of aerosol and other products
President: Steve Hipp
VP Technical: Pete Martin
National Sales Manager: Ron Lloyd
Contact: Zech Ashba
zech.ashba@athea.com
Estimated Sales: $20-50 Million
Number Employees: 10
Parent Co: Share Company

19149 Athena Controls Inc
5145 Campus Dr # 1
Plymouth Meeting, PA 19462-1195
610-828-2490
Fax: 610-828-7084 800-782-6776
sales@athenacontrols.com
www.athenacontrols.com
Manufacturer and exporter of temperature, power and process controls
Manager: Bob Schlegel
Sales/Marketing: Jennifer Klinedinst
Manager: C Bill
bc@athenacontrols.com
Estimated Sales: $10-20 Million
Number Employees: 50-99
Parent Co: Inductotherm Industries
Other Locations:
Athena Controls
Plymouth Meeting PA

19150 Atkins Jemptec
6911 NW 22nd St
Gainesville, FL 32653-1249
352-378-5555
Fax: 352-335-6736 sdiuguid@cooper-atkins.com
Estimated Sales: $20 - 50 Million
Number Employees: 50-99

19151 Atkins Technical
6911 NW 22nd St
Gainesville, FL 32653-1249
352-378-5555
Fax: 352-335-6736 800-284-2842
Temperature recorders, digital thermocouple and thermistor thermometers
President: Carol Wallace
Sales/Marketing Executive: Stelli Dounson
Estimated Sales: $10-20 Million
Number Employees: 50-99
Parent Co: Cooper Instrumental Corporation

19152 Atkinson Dynamics
2645 Federal Signal Dr
University Park, IL 60484-3167
708-534-3400
Fax: 708-534-4852 888-751-1500
www.atkinsondynamics.com

President: Peter Guile
Quality Control: Dennis Stanberry
Contact: Sandy Belk
sbelk@fedsig.com
Number Employees: 500-999
Parent Co: Federal Signal Company

19153 Atlanta Burning Bush
3781 Happy Valley Cir
Newnan, GA 30263
770-253-4443
Fax: 770-253-9941 800-665-5611
Hot sauces, BBQ sauce. Supplier of food related products
Owner: Marilyn Witt
Estimated Sales: $500,000-$1,000,000
Number Employees: 1-4
Type of Packaging: Consumer, Bulk
Brands:
Atlanta Burning

19154 Atlanta SharpTech
403 Westpark Ct Ste 130
P.O. Box 11000
Peachtree City, GA 30269-3577
Fax: 404-752-9034 800-462-7297
Manufacturer and exporter of meat and bone cutting equipment including bandsaw blades, grinder plates, grinder knives, handsaw frames and handsaw blades
CEO: Tom Orelup
Estimated Sales: $20-50 Million
Number Employees: 100-249
Brands:
Atlanta Sharptech
Double Cut System
Kam-Lok
One Way Bands
Powermate System
Swift Tooth Bands

19155 Atlantic Coast CrushersInc
128 Market St
Kenilworth, NJ 07033-2026
908-259-9292
Fax: 908-259-9280 info@gocrushers.com
www.gocrushers.com
Owner: Jack Paddock
paddockj@gocrushers.com
Estimated Sales: $3 - 5 Million
Number Employees: 5-9

19156 Atlantic Foam & Packaging Company
2664 Jewett Ln
Sanford, FL 32771-1678
407-328-9444
Fax: 407-324-2299
Manufacturers and fabricators of polystyrene foam box liners for perishables and non perishables.
President: Peter Chorney
Estimated Sales: $2.5 - 5 Million
Number Employees: 10-19
Square Footage: 132000

19157 Atlantic Group Inc
16830 Barker Springs Rd # 405
Houston, TX 77084-5038
281-578-0366
info@agivalves.com
www.agivalves.com
CEO: Bobby Engelke
bengelke@agivalves.com
Estimated Sales: $1 - 5 Million
Number Employees: 5-9

19158 Atlantic Mills
1295 Towbin Ave
Lakewood, NJ 08701
732-363-9281
Fax: 732-363-4302 800-242-7374
Antimicrobial, sanitizing, disposable kitchen and industrial towels; also, aprons
President: Peter P Donnelly
Finance Executive: Warren Agate
Sales Director: Peter Donnelly
Contact: Cheryl Accoo
accoo@atlanticmills.com
Estimated Sales: $10 - 20,000,000
Number Employees: 20-49
Brands:
Katelin
Kerri Klean
Simple Solutions

19159 Atlantic Rubber Products

3065 Cranberry Hwy 13
East Wareham, MA 02538-1325

508-291-1211
Fax: 508-291-1123 800-695-0446
Manufacturer, importer and exporter of rubber safety flooring for kitchens, bars and entrance ways
Owner: John Donahue
Sales Director: Susan Boyens
Contact: Susan Donahue
donahue@atlanticrubber.com
General Manager: Jerry Donahue
Estimated Sales: $5-10 Million
Number Employees: 10-19
Number of Products: 85
Square Footage: 56000
Type of Packaging: Consumer, Food Service, Bulk
Brands:
  Comfort Zone
  Enter Clean
  Modular Tile
  Ultimate Comfort
  Work Right
  Work Right Interlock
  Work Station Airlock

19160 Atlantic Ultraviolet Corp

375 Marcus Blvd
Hauppauge, NY 11788-2026

631-273-0500
Fax: 631-273-0771 866-958-9085
sales@atlanticuv.com www.ultraviolet.com
Manufacturer and exporter of ultraviolet sterilization products for air, water and surfaces
CEO: Hilary Boehme
CFO: Arlene Metzroth
VP: Thomas Dituro Sr.
Director of Marketing: Ann Wysocki
Estimated Sales: $10 - 20 Million
Number Employees: 20-49
Square Footage: 50000
Brands:
  Hygeaire
  Magnum
  Megatron
  Mighty-Pure
  Minipure
  Nutripure
  Sanitaire
  Sanitron
  Tank Master

19161 Atlantis Industries Inc

1 Park St
Milton, DE 19968-1108

302-684-8542
Fax: 302-684-3367 contact@atlantisusa.com
www.atlantisusa.com
Manufacturer and exporter of injection molded plastic tumblers, dessert dishes, bowls, salad bowls and mugs
President: Kenneth Orr
kenneth@atlantisusa.com
VP: Ken Orr
Sales: Judie Brasure
Estimated Sales: $2.5-5 Million
Number Employees: 20-49
Square Footage: 56000
Brands:
  Sparkle-Lite

19162 Atlantis Pak USA Inc

75 Valencia Ave # 701
Coral Gables, FL 33134-6132

305-403-2603
Fax: 786-249-0454
customerservice@atlantis-pak.com
www.atlantis-pak.com
Meat Packing, manufacturer of acid free packing paper, and recycled paper for meat.
Principle: Vladimir Zhamgotsev
zhamgotsev@atlantis-pak.com
Number Employees: 1-4
Parent Co: Atlantis Pak

19163 Atlantis Plastics Linear Film

PO Box 9769
Tulsa, OK 74157-0769

918-446-1651
Fax: 918-227-2454 800-324-9727
paul.saari@atlantisplastics.com
Manufacturer and exporter of polyethylene stretch film

Manager: Randy Goodman
CFO: Paul G Saari
VP Sales: John Buchan
Estimated Sales: $10-20 Million
Number Employees: 100-249
Parent Co: Atlantis Films

19164 Atlas Bakery Machinery Company

4800 S.W. 51st Street
Suite 104
Davie, FL 33314-5511

954-316-6160
Fax: 954-316-1360 atlasbaker@aol.com
www.atlasshardwarecorp.com
Bread and roll make-up including dividers, rounders, proofers and mixers
President: Robert Atlass
Contact: Susan Baltus
sbaltus@atlasshardwarecorp.com
Estimated Sales: $2.5-5 Million
Number Employees: 5-9

19165 Atlas Body

PO Box 479
Amory, MS 38821-0479

601-256-5692
Fax: 601-256-2162 800-354-2192
Estimated Sales: $1 - 5 Million

19166 Atlas Case Inc

1380 S Cherokee St
Denver, CO 80223-3209

303-778-7058
Fax: 303-778-7102 888-325-2199
sales@atlascases.com www.atlascases.com
Trunks, cases and shipping containers
President: Randy Sabey
sales@atlascases.com
Estimated Sales: Below $5 Million
Number Employees: 5-9

19167 Atlas Copco Tools & Assembly

37735 Enterprise Court
Suite 300
Farmington Hills, MI 48331-3471

248-489-1260
Fax: 248-489-0130 800-359-3746
www.atlascopco.com
President: Frederik Moeller
Vice President of Corporate Communicatio: Annika Berglund

19168 Atlas Corporation

111 Ortona Court
Concord, ON L4K 3M3
Canada

905-669-6825
Fax: 905-669-8288 info@atlascorp.com
We are a construction company which offers the following services: General Contracting, Construction Management, Design Build, Project Management and LEED(Leadership in Engery and Environmental Design.
President: Andrew Famiglietti
VP Development: Adam Salehi
VP Operations: Eliseo Curto
Number Employees: 20-49

19169 Atlas Equipment Company

3111 Wyandotte St # 102
Kansas City, MO 64111-1369

816-842-9188
Fax: 816-842-9192 800-842-9188
2info@atlasequipment.com
www.atlasequipment.com
Wholesaler/distributor of storage and material handling systems, belt conveyors, steel shelving and pallet racks
President: Julie Duvall
Estimated Sales: $5-10 Million
Number Employees: 1-4
Square Footage: 600000

19170 Atlas Inspection

9001 Baltimore St NE
Minneapolis, MN 55449

763-783-7072
Fax: 763-783-7138
Xray inspection of food products
Founder: Ken Long
President: Jeffery Boisverg
Contact: Jeff Boisvert
atlas@atlasinspection.com

Estimated Sales: $2 Million
Number Employees: 5

19171 (HQ)Atlas Labels

11200 boul Pie 1X,
CP 280
Montreal, QC H1H 5L4
Canada

514-852-7000
Fax: 514-852-2000 info@cubart.com
Self-stick labels, silk screen, gold stampings, badges and folding boxes.
President: Rock Navy
Estimated Sales: $3 Million
Number Employees: 13
Number of Brands: 2
Number of Products: 114
Square Footage: 36000
Type of Packaging: Consumer, Food Service, Private Label, Bulk

19172 Atlas Match Company

45 Leadale Avenue
Toronto, ON M4G 3E9
Canada

416-929-8147
Fax: 416-961-3275 888-285-2783
nmackay11@rogers.com www.atlasmatch.com
Manufacturer, importer and exporter of custom designed wooden and book matches; also, reusable board coasters and cocktail and dinner napkins.
President: N Mackay
CFO: Sohan Kansal
Sales: W Teltz
Operations: Esther Tarahdmi
Number Employees: 5-9
Number of Brands: 2
Number of Products: 5
Square Footage: 8000
Type of Packaging: Food Service, Private Label, Bulk
Brands:
  Atlas
  Coasters Plus

19173 Atlas Match Corporation

1801 S Airport Cir
Euless, TX 76040

817-354-7474
Fax: 817-354-7478 800-628-2426
custserv@atlasmatch.com www.atlasmatch.com
Manufacturer, exporter and importer of matchbooks, box matches, scratchbooks and scratchpads
President: David Bradley
COO: Doug Lamb
Estimated Sales: $10-20 Million
Number Employees: 50-99
Square Footage: 130000

19174 Atlas Metal Industries

1135 NW 159th Dr
Miami, FL 33169

Fax: 305-623-0475 800-762-7565
atlasfoodserv.com
Cafeteria and restaurant counters, salad bars, food service tables and dispensers including cup, plate, self leveling, tray, bowl and napkin
President/Owner: David Meade
VP, Sales & Marketing: Jessica Meade DeMore
Year Founded: 1948
Estimated Sales: $10-20 Million
Number Employees: 100-249
Parent Co: Mercury Corporation
Brands:
  Levelmatic
  Precision
  Set-N-Serve

19175 (HQ)Atlas Minerals & Chemicals Inc

1227 Valley Rd
P.O. Box 38
Mertztown, PA 19539-8827

610-682-7171
Fax: 610-682-9200 800-523-8269
sales@atlasmin.com www.atlasmin.com
Manufacturer and exporter of construction materials including floor plates, drains and coatings and corrosion prevention; also, tanks for processing and storage

President: Francis X Hanson
fhanson@atlasmin.com
Marketing: Scott Gallagher
Sales: Steve Abernathy
Number Employees: 50-99
Type of Packaging: Food Service, Private Label

19176 Atlas Minerals & Chemicals Inc
1227 Valley Rd
Mertztown, PA 19539-8827
610-682-7171
Fax: 610-682-9200 800-532-8269
sales@atlasmin.com www.atlasmin.com
Flooring products include coating, sealers, polymer toppings and tile and brick floors
President: Francis X Hanson
fhanson@atlasmin.com
Estimated Sales: $10-20 Million
Number Employees: 50-99

19177 (HQ)Atlas Pacific Engineering
1 Atlas Ave
P.O. Box 500
Pueblo, CO 81001-4833
719-948-3040
Fax: 719-948-3058 sales@atlaspacific.com
Manufacturer and exporter of deciduous fruit and vegetable processing equipment including pitters, slicers, peelers, washers, cutters, sorters and scrubbers
President: Erik Teranchi
CFO: Don Freeman
VP Marketing: Robb Morris
Manager: Tom Ogrodny
tomo@atlaspacific.com
Estimated Sales: $20-50 Million
Number Employees: 100-249
Square Footage: 175000
Parent Co: Gulftech
Brands:
 Magnupeeler
 Magnuwasher
 N.F. Peeler
 Shufflo
 Super Carrot Cutter
 Super Cutter

19178 Atlas Packaging Inc
13165 NW 38th Ave
Opa Locka, FL 33054-4530
305-688-5096
Fax: 305-685-0843 800-662-0630
randy@atlaspackaginginc.com
www.atlaspackaginginc.com
Designer and manufacturer of all types of packaging, litho laminated boxes and displays. Also provides promotional items such as standers and casecards.
President: Penny Kroker
penny@flhosp.org
Sales Manager: Randy Macias
Estimated Sales: $5-10 Million
Number Employees: 50-99
Square Footage: 112000

19179 Atlas Restaurant Supply
3329 N Shadeland Ave
Indianapolis, IN 46226-6236
317-541-1111
Fax: 317-541-1404 877-528-5275
www.atlasrestaurantsupply.com
Manufacturers' representative for bar equipment, carts, concession supplies, dishwashers, display cases, ice machines, refrigerators, can openers, steam tables, etc.; serving supermarket chains and food service operators; kitchen andinterior design services
President: Thomas S Vavul
Manager: Jimmy Gravel
rickv@atlasrs.com
Estimated Sales: Below $5,000,000
Number Employees: 10-19

19180 Atlas Rubber Stamp & Printing
3755 E Market St # 3
York, PA 17402-2700
717-751-0459
Fax: 717-751-0459 sales@atlasrubberstamp.com
www.atlasrubberstamp.com
Stamps and markers
Owner: Paul Sipe
sales@atlasrubberstamp.com
Co-Owner: Hally Fontaine

Estimated Sales: Below $5 Million
Number Employees: 10-19

19181 Atlas Tag & Label Inc
2361 Industrial Dr
Neenah, WI 54956-4884
920-722-1557
Fax: 920-720-7900 800-558-6418
www.atlas-tag.com
Heat sealed bags, labels and tags
President: Mark Bissell
CFO: Dennis Novell
VP: Jerry Bultt
Head of Marketing: Kent Salomon
Manager: Dennis Prett
Account Manager: Mark White
Estimated Sales: $10-20 Million
Number Employees: 100-249
Parent Co: Atlas Tag & Label

19182 Atlas-Stord
7011-F Albert Pick Road
Greensboro, NC 27409
816-799-0808
Fax: 816-799-0812 info-usa@haarslev.com
www.haarslev.com/
Manager: Denise Gardner
CFO: Brad Rodgers
Estimated Sales: Below $5 Million
Number Employees: 20-49
Parent Co: Haarslev Industries A/S

19183 Atomizing Systems Inc
1 Hollywood Ave # 1
Suite 1
Ho Ho Kus, NJ 07423-1438
201-447-1222
Fax: 201-447-6932 www.coldfog.com
President: Michael Elkas
info@coldfog.com
Estimated Sales: $3 - 5 Million
Number Employees: 5-9

19184 (HQ)Attias Oven Corp
926 3rd Ave
Brooklyn, NY 11232-2002
347-619-0314
Fax: 212-979-1423 800-928-8427
info@attiasco.com www.attiasco.com
Manufacturer and exporter of pizza ovens, rotisseries, mixers, slicers, ice makers, refrigerators, freezers, dishwashers, toasters, blenders, sheeters, dividers and rounders
President: Simon Attias
Estimated Sales: $3 - 5 Million
Number Employees: 5-9

19185 Attracta Sign
14680 James Road
Rogers, MN 55374-9363
763-428-6377
Fax: 763-428-9097
Painted and electric signs
President: Greg Rendall
CFO: Greg Rendall
R&D/Quality Control: Greg Rendall
Estimated Sales: $1 - 2.5 Million
Number Employees: 10

19186 Attune Foods
535 Pacific Ave, 3rd Fl
San Francisco, CA 94133
415-486-2101
www.attunefoods.com
President: Rob Hurlbut
Director of Finance: Mike Centron
Director of Marketing: Daniel Wiser
Director of Sales: Steve Bernier
Contact: Idan Abada
iabada@piercecollege.edu
Production Manager: Marvin Malvar
Estimated Sales: $15 Million
Parent Co: Post Foods
Brands:
 ATTUNE
 EREWHON
 SKINNER'S
 UNCLE SAM

19187 AuNutra Industries Inc
5625 Daniels Street
Chino, CA 91710
909-628-2600
Fax: 909-628-8110 info@aunutra.com
www.aunutra.com
Manufacturer and supplier of botanicals and nutritional ingredients
VP Sales/Marketing: Ken Guest
Regional Sales Manager: Tara Trainor
Contact: Jing Ang
jang@aunutra.com

19188 Auburn Label & Tag Company
225 W 34th St
New York, NY 10122-9001
212-971-0338
Fax: 212-244-4397 www.ragnewyork.com
Labels including pressure sensitive and nonpressure sensitive
Owner: Max Greenstein
Vice President: Susan Alfender
Estimated Sales: $5-10 Million
Number Employees: 5-9

19189 Auburn Systems LLC
8 Electronics Ave # 1
Danvers, MA 01923-1045
978-777-8820
Fax: 978-777-8820 800-255-5008
sales@auburnsys.com
Auburn Systems, LLC designs, engineers, and manufactures dust monitoring equipment and systems. Auburn's product line ranges from simple broken bag detectors, flow switches and dust monitors to comprehensive bag leak detection systemsfor a wide variety of applications.
President: Ron Dechene
rond@auburnsys.com
Director/Business Development: Justin Dechene
VP/Sales: Earl Parker
Number Employees: 5-9

19190 Auburn Systems LLC
8 Electronics Ave # 1
Danvers, MA 01923-1045
978-777-8820
Fax: 978-777-8820 800-255-5008
sales@auburnsys.com
President: Ron Dechene
rond@auburnsys.com
Number Employees: 5-9

19191 (HQ)Audion Automation
1533 Crescent Dr # 102
Carrollton, TX 75006-3642
972-389-0777
Fax: 972-389-0790 info@clamcopackaging.com
www.audionltd.com
Manufacturer and exporter of flexible packaging machinery including bag opening, filling and heat sealing; also, shrink packaging
President: Mark Goldman
markg@paçaíds.com
CFO: David Johnson
Vice President Marketing & Sales: Dennis McGrath
Sales Manager: Bob Sorrentino
Operations Manager: David Bibb
Estimated Sales: $20 - 50 Million
Number Employees: 20-49
Square Footage: 56000
Brands:
 Sergeant
 Titan
 Vacumaster

19192 Audrey Signs
167 W 81st St
New York, NY 10024-7221
212-769-4992
Fax: 212-496-9649 audreysigns2@aol.com
www.audreysigns.com
Interior and exterior advertising signs including brass, aluminum, bronze, plastic, neon, cold cathode and cut-out letters; also, installation available
President and CEO: Harriet Black
audreysigns@aol.com
Estimated Sales: Below $5 Million
Number Employees: 10-19

19193 Audsam Printing
175 Park Blvd
Marion, OH 43302-3534
740-387-6252
Fax: 740-387-6251
Coupon books
President: J Saxby
VP: M Saxby
Secretary: S Saxby
Estimated Sales: $5-10 Million
Number Employees: 20-49

19194 Audubon Sales & Svc
850 Pennsylvania Blvd
Feastervl Trvs, PA 19053-7814
215-364-5377
Fax: 215-364-5538 800-523-0169
info@meshbelt.com www.meshbelt.com
President: Stephen I Weiss
accounting@meshbelt.com
Estimated Sales: $5 - 10 Million
Number Employees: 20-49

19195 Auger Fab
418 Creamery Way
Exton, PA 19341-2500
610-524-3350
Fax: 610-363-2821 800-334-1529
info@auger-fab.com www.augerfabrication.com
Manufacturer and exporter of stainless steel and
plastic liquid and powder filling equipment includ-
ing replacement augers and funnels
President: Erick Edginton
ericke@augerfab.com
CFO: Bill Egan
Regional Sales Manager: Allen Stewart
VP, Sales & Marketing: Kyle Edginton
Operations Manager: Rick Brennecke
Estimated Sales: $10-20 Million
Number Employees: 100-249
Square Footage: 100000

19196 Auger Fab
418 Creamery Way
Exton, PA 19341-2500
610-524-3350
Fax: 610-363-2821 800-334-1529
info@all-fill.com www.augerfabrication.com
Augers
President: Erick Edginton
ericke@augerfab.com
Estimated Sales: $10-20 000,000
Number Employees: 100-249

19197 Auger Manufacturing Spec
22 N Bacton Hill Rd # A
Malvern, PA 19355-1006
610-647-4677
Fax: 610-640-9085 800-544-1199
info@augermfgspec.com www.augermfgspec.com
Bag formers/fillers/sealers, cocoa packaging equipment, packaging machines, weighing machines and
augers
Owner: William E Day
info@augermfgspec.com
Estimated Sales: $5-10 000,000
Number Employees: 10-19

19198 August Thomsen Corp
36 Sea Cliff Ave
Glen Cove, NY 11542-3699
516-676-7100
Fax: 516-676-7108 800-645-7170
www.atecousa.com
Manufacturer, importer and exporter of pastry tubes,
pastry bags and other baking utensils
President: Jeffrey Schneider
jeff@atecousa.com
VP: Douglas Schneider
Estimated Sales: $10 - 20 Million
Number Employees: 20-49
Brands:
Ateco

19199 Aurora Air Products Inc
231c N Eola Rd
Aurora, IL 60502-9603
630-851-4515
Fax: 630-851-5165 ron@auroraair.com
www.auroraair.com
Owner: Rich Cibulskis
rich@auroraair.com
Quality Control: Don Cibulskis

Estimated Sales: $10 - 20 Million
Number Employees: 20-49

19200 Aurora Design Associates, Inc.
1308 South 1700 East
Suite 203
Salt Lake City, UT 84108
801-588-0111
Fax: 801-588-0333
Manufacturer and exporter of servers and ice buck-
ets for wine, water and champagne
President: Rob Norton
Contact: Robert Norton
robnorton1@att.net
Advertising Manager: Rick Daynes
Estimated Sales: Less than $500,000
Number Employees: 1-4
Number of Products: 6
Square Footage: 14000
Brands:
Chateau
Connoisseur
Evian Connoisseur

19201 Austin Brown Co
300 Reading Rd
Mason, OH 45040-1512
513-492-7933
Fax: 513-492-7932 800-421-9355
info@austinbrownco.com
www.austinbrownco.com
Manufacturers reps for insulated panels, cold storage
doors and high speed doors.
President: Doug Brown
doug@austinbrownco.com
Marketing: Douglas Brown
Inside Sales: Kevin Browning
Estimated Sales: $.5 - 1 million
Number Employees: 5-9
Number of Brands: 4

19202 Austin Co
6095 Parkland Blvd
Cleveland, OH 44124
440-544-2600
Fax: 440-544-2690 austin.info@theaustin.com
www.theaustin.com
Designing, engineering and construction architec-
tural firm that specializes in food and beverage pro-
cessing facilities including: production and bottling
plants; formulation and packaging plants for bulk in-
gredients; researchlaboratories; operations centers;
bulk storage warehouses; and automated distribution
centers.
President: Michael Pierce
VP, Finance: Jamie Hullman
VP Food & Beverage: Robert Graham
Director, Marketing & Communications: Tamara
Zupancic
SVP, Operations: Matt Eddleman
Year Founded: 1916
Estimated Sales: $100-500 Million
Number Employees: 1000-4999
Parent Co: Kajima USA

19203 Authentic Biocode Corp
4355 Excel Parkway
Suite 100
Addison, TX 75001
469-737-4400
Fax: 469-737-4409 866-434-1402
www.authentix.com
Invisible inks and food markers
Chief Financial/Operations Officer and P: Jeff Kupp
Chairman and CEO: Bernard C Bailey
CAO, General Counsel and Secretary: Mark L
Weintrub
Senior Vice President: Kevin McKenna
Chief Technology Officer: Jeff Conroy, Ph.D.
Chief Sales and Marketing Officer: Ryon Packer
Director Business Development: Jeffrey Slocum
CPO, GM and President: Dr. Mohamed Lazzouni
Estimated Sales: $3 - 5 Million
Number Employees: 8

19204 Autio Co
93750 Autio Loop
Astoria, OR 97103-8400
503-458-6191
Fax: 503-458-6409 800-483-8884
office@autioco.com www.autioco.com
Manufacturer and exporter of grinders and pumps

President: Marvin Autio
marvin.autio@autioco.com
Office Manager: Marilyn Anderson
Estimated Sales: $1 - 3 Million
Number Employees: 10-19

19205 Auto Chlor Systems
1000 Ridgeway Loop Rd Ste 100
Memphis, TN 38120
901-684-0600
Fax: 901-684-0620 800-477-3693
Glass cleaner, dishwasher detergents and dispensers
H.R. Dir.: Marie Brain
VP: Kirk Northcutt
Contact: Lisa Boswe
lisa@autochlor.net
Estimated Sales: $1 - 5 Million
Number Employees: 20-49
Parent Co: Unilever USA
Brands:
Glass Klean
Laundry Detergent Ii
Machine Detergent Ii

19206 Auto Labe
3101 Industrial Avenue
Suite 2
Fort Pierce, FL 34946
772-465-4441
Fax: 772-465-5177 800-634-5376
info@autolabe.com www.autolabe.com
Manufacturer and exporter of labeling equipment for
fruits and vegetables, bottles, cans, boxes, cartons,
bar coding, etc
President: Robert Smith
Marketing/Sales: Bob Peterson
Public Relations: Roy Shepherd
Production/Plant Manager: Dean Stauffer
Estimated Sales: $10-20 Million
Number Employees: 50-99
Square Footage: 50000
Parent Co: Booth Manufacturing Company

19207 Auto Pallets-Boxes
28000 Southfield Rd Fl 2
Lathrup Village, MI 48076-2864
248-559-7744
Fax: 248-559-6584 800-875-2699
www.apallets.com
Manufacturer and recycler of wooden pallets and
boxes
Owner: Mitchell B Foster
VP: Mitchell Foster
Estimated Sales: $1-2.5 Million
Number Employees: 10 to 19

19208 Auto Quotes
4425 Merrimac Ave
Jacksonville, FL 32210
904-384-2279
Fax: 904-384-1736 www.aqnet.com
Software for the food service market
President: Michael Greenwald
Chief Executive Officer: Kent Motes
CFO: Rene Butcher
Executive Vice President: Rob Morgan
VP, Program Development: Bill Kessler
Marketing Director: Kate Schmidt
EVP, Sales: Rosemary Connor
Contact: Rene Butcher
rbutcher@aqnet.com
CFO, Database Manager: Martin Smith
Estimated Sales: $3 - 5 Million
Number Employees: 1-4
Square Footage: 9600

19209 Auto-Mate Technologies
34 Hinda Blvd
Riverhead, NY 11901-4804
631-727-8886
Fax: 631-369-3903 info@automatetech.com
www.auto-matetech.com
Bottle labeling systems, induction cap systems, and
complete bottle inspection systems.
Owner: Kenneth Herzog
info@automatetech.com
Estimated Sales: $9-12 Million
Number Employees: 20-49

19210 AutoPak Engineering Corporation
PO Box 9024155
San Juan, PR 00902-4155
787-723-8036
Fax: 787-745-0030 mailbox@autopak.com
www.autopak.com
President: Ignacio Munoz
CFO: Astrid Robriguze
Quality Control: Amarilys Rivera
Estimated Sales: $30-40 Million
Number Employees: 10

19211 Autobar Systems
1800 Bloomsbury Ave
Asbury Park, NJ 07712-3975
732-922-3355
Fax: 732-922-2221 autobarcorp@aol.com
Manufacturer and exporter of alcoholic beverage
dispensers and control equipment for bars, conven-
tion centers and restaurants
CEO: Donald Ullery
Estimated Sales: Below $5 Million
Number Employees: 5-9
Square Footage: 8000
Brands:
Autobar
Autopor
Beermatic
Underbar
Winematic

19212 Autobox NA/Jit Box Machines
218 N Broadway Rd
Azle, TX 76020-3708
817-270-1019
Fax: 817-270-8430
President: Jerry Jenkins
Estimated Sales: $10 - 20 Million
Number Employees: 10-19

19213 Autocon Mixing Systems
2360 Vallejo St
St Helena, CA 94574-2432
707-963-3998
Fax: 707-963-3978 800-225-6192
tom@theosten.com www.autoconsystems.com
Manufacturer and exporter of continuous solid/liq-
uid feeders and dry blending processing systems
President: Thomas Haas
info@autoconsystems.com
Estimated Sales: $5 - 10 Million
Number Employees: 20-49
Square Footage: 10000

19214 Autofry
10 Forbes Rd
Northborough, MA 01532-2501
508-460-9800
Fax: 508-393-5750 800-348-2976
www.autofry.com
Deep fryers
Mktg. Manager: Heather Guerriero
Regional Sales Manager: Laird Hansberger
Sales Manager: Gary Santos
Estimated Sales: Less Than $500,000
Number Employees: 1-4
Brands:
Autofry

19215 Autoline
23243 Clayton Ave
Reedley, CA 93654-9547
559-638-5432
Fax: 559-638-6189
Fruit sorting equipent
President: Clarence Rasmussen
R&D: Jack Wis
Sales: Kelvin Farris
Quality Control: Brudy Hieberp
Contact: Alex Cordero
a.cordero@aweta.us
Estimated Sales: $5 - 10 Million
Number Employees: 20-49

19216 Automated Business Products
50 Clinton Pl # 1
Hackensack, NJ 07601-4562
201-489-1440
Fax: 201-489-9443 800-334-1440
Manufacturer, importer and exporter of money processing and handling systems, packagers, sorters,
counters and automatic wrappers; also, food stamp
counters, endorsers and microencoders

President: Robert J Mahalik
bmahalik@aol.com
Estimated Sales: $1-2,500,000
Number Employees: 10-19

19217 Automated Container Corp
2758 Centennial Rd
Toledo, OH 43617-1829
419-536-8393
Fax: 419-536-9686
ezosales@automatedcontainer.com
www.automatedcontainer.com
President: John Morrison
Number Employees: 5-9

19218 Automated Control Concepts
3535 State Route 66
Neptune, NJ 07753
732-922-6611
Fax: 732-922-9611
sysmail@automated-control.com
www.automated-control.com
Owner: Robert Tomasetta
Estimated Sales: $10 - 20 Million
Number Employees: 50-99

19219 Automated Feeding & Alignment
1921 W Wilson Street
Suite A171
Batavia, IL 60510-1680
630-761-3104
Fax: 630-761-3105
Controlled pick and place system and packaging au-
tomation special purpose machinery
Estimated Sales: $.5 - 1 000,000
Number Employees: 1-4

19220 Automated Flexible Conveyors
55 Walman Ave
Clifton, NJ 07011-3416
973-340-1414
Fax: 973-340-8216 800-694-7271
www.afcsolutions.com
Spiral and volumetric feeders, cartridge type bag
dump stations and bulk bag unloading equipment;
exporter of spiral feeders
President: Kevin Devaney
kfdevaney@aol.com
Vice President: Grace Faria
Estimated Sales: Below $5 Million
Number Employees: 5-9
Square Footage: 88000
Brands:
Dump Clean
Spiralfeeder
True Flow

19221 Automated Food Systems
1000 Lofland Dr
Waxahachie, TX 75165-6200
469-517-0470
Fax: 469-517-0476 sales@afstexas.com
www.afstexas.com
Manufacturer, exporter and importer of production
systems for corn dogs, kebabs, skewering, sausage
sticking and funnel cakes. Fryers, mixers, pumps;
special design
President: Robert Walser
robin@afstexas.com
CFO: Tina Walser
Marketing Director/Sales: Chris Consalus
Marketing Coordinator: Robin Seeton
Production Manager: Jerry Reidel
Plant Manager: Charles Stone
Purchasing Manager: Robert Walser
Estimated Sales: $2.5-5 Million
Number Employees: 10-19
Square Footage: 48000
Brands:
Cd-3 Vendor Cart
Fc-950
Kw-2001
Ptl-Condos Systems

19222 Automated Machine Technologies
10404 Chapel Hill Road
Suite 100
Morrisville, NC 27560-1186
919-361-0121
Fax: 919- 48- 212
Office@AMTLiquidFilling.com
www.amtliquidfilling.com
Packaging liquid filling equipment

Contact: David Kemnitz
dk@amtliquidfilling.com
Estimated Sales: $500,000-$1 Million
Number Employees: 2

19223 Automated Packaging Systems
10175 Philipp Pkwy
Streetsboro, OH 44241
330-342-2000
Fax: 330-342-2400 800-527-0733
info@autobag.com www.autobag.com
Manual, semi and fully automatic bagging equip-
ment; also, customer training and graphic design ser-
vices available.
VP, Sales, North America: Jay Patras
Year Founded: 1962
Estimated Sales: $100-500 Million
Number Employees: 100-249
Brands:
Autobag

**19224 Automated Production Systems
Corporation**
15556 Elm Dr
New Freedom, PA 17349
717-235-5220
Fax: 717-235-5274 888-345-5377
Conveyor systems, robotic palletizing and packing
machinery, cappers and in-line fillers
President: William Donohue
Contact: Jason Cambia
jasonc@atsinc.org
Estimated Sales: $5,000,000 - $9,999,999
Number Employees: 95

19225 Automated Retail Systems Inc
726 Boulevard # 18
Kenilworth, NJ 07033-1757
908-620-0008
Fax: 908-276-2214 800-355-0173
arsnj@aol.com www.arsnj.net
Distributor touch screen point of sale systems for
restaurants, software and peripherals
President: Robert Meyn
Vice President: Grace Ann Meyn
Estimated Sales: Less Than $500,000
Number Employees: 5-9
Square Footage: 2400

19226 Automatic Bar Controls Inc
790 Eubanks Dr
Vacaville, CA 95688-9470
707-448-5151
Fax: 707-448-1521 800-722-6738
sales@wunderbar.com
Portable bars and dispensers including soft drink, li-
quor, juice, wine, beer and condiment; importer of
beer dipensers; exporter of liquor, soft drink and
condiment dipensers
President: Rick Martindale
rick.martindale@wunderbar.com
Sales/Marketing: Brent Baker
Purchasing Agent: Tim Schroeder
Estimated Sales: $50 - 100 Million
Number Employees: 100-249
Square Footage: 70000
Brands:
Wunder-Bar

**19227 Automatic Electronic Machines
Company**
110 N 6th St
Brooklyn, NY 11211-3033
718-384-3211
Straw wrappers and automatic shears
Owner: Hannah Curtin
General Manager: George Casella
Estimated Sales: $1 - 5 Million
Number Employees: 1-4
Square Footage: 14000

19228 Automatic Feeder
921 Albion Ave
Schaumburg, IL 60193-4550
847-534-2300
Fax: 847-534-2354 888-534-2340
sales@automaticfeeder.com
www.automaticfeeder.com
Manufacturer, designer, and builder of specialty conveyor, feed (centrifugal linear and elevator) and assembly systems

President: Ken Eversole
VP: Kirk Verhasselt
VP: Jerry Kuntz
Marketing: Suzanne Eversole
Public Relations: Rochelle Verhasselt
Estimated Sales: $1-5 000,000
Number Employees: 10-19
Number of Brands: 4
Square Footage: 30000
Brands:
  Auto-Slide
  Flexlink
  Hoppmann

19229 Automatic Filters Inc
2672 S LA Cienega Blvd
Los Angeles, CA 90034-2604

310-839-2828
Fax: 310-839-6878 800-336-1942
info@tekleen.com www.tekleen.com
Fully automatic, self cleaning water filters
President: Gideon Brunn
info@tekleen.com
Estimated Sales: Less than $10,000,000
Number Employees: 5-9

19230 Automatic Handling Int
360 LA Voy Rd
Erie, MI 48133-9436

734-847-0633
Fax: 734-847-1823 info@automatichandling.com
www.automatichandling.com
Manufacturer and exporter of conveyors and conveyor systems, platforms, walkways and stairs; also, custom fabrication and custom stainless steel machinery available
President: Daniel Pienta
  dan.pienta@automatichandling.com
Operations Manager: Dennis Barutha
Estimated Sales: $1,5,000,000
Number Employees: 100-249
Square Footage: 66000
Parent Co: Automatic Handling

19231 Automatic Liquid Packaging Solutions
2445 E Oakton St
Arlington Heights, IL 60005

847-264-5349
Fax: 847-264-5348 www.alp-solutions.com
Manufacturer of sterile filling machines for sterile liquid packaging applications

19232 Automatic Products
PO Drawer 719
Williston, SC 29853

803-266-8891
Fax: 803-266-5150 800-523-8363
www.automaticproducts.com
Manufacturer and exporter of hot beverage vending machinery
President: Alan J Suitor
Sales Manager: Len McElhaney

19233 Automatic Products/Crane
165 Bridgepoint Dr
South St Paul, MN 55075-2500

651-288-2975
Fax: 651-224-5559 www.automaticproducts.com
Manufacturer and exporter of vending machinery including candy, pastry, snacks, coffee, hot drinks, ice cream and refrigerated/frozen foods
President & CEO: Max Mitchell
CFO: Richard Maue
SVP, General Counsel: Anthony D'lorio
CIO: Carey True
Estimated Sales: Less Than $500,000
Number Employees: 1-4

19234 Automatic Specialties Inc
422 Northboro Road Central # 2
Marlborough, MA 01752-1895

508-481-2370
Fax: 508-485-6276 800-445-2370
sales@auspin.com www.automaticspecialties.com
Manufacturer and exporter of wire racks and baskets, stainless steel fry baskets, trays and food machinery parts
President: Wilfred Moineau
Vice President: Bill Moineau
Marketing/Sales: Jay Graham
Public Relations: Jay Graham

Estimated Sales: $3 - 5 Million
Number Employees: 20-49
Square Footage: 60000

19235 Automatic Timing & Controls
8019 Ohio Riv
8019 Ohio River Blvd.
Newell, WV 26050

304-387-1200
Fax: 304-387-1212 800-727-5646
customerRFQ@marshbellofram.com
www.marshbellofram.com
Manufacturer and exporter of controls including temperature, counters, timers and photoelectric sensors
President: Arnold Siemer
Cmo: Dwight Nafziger
  dnafziger@marshbellofram.com
CFO: Roger Bailey
R&D: Tom Villano
Production Manager: J Tornetta
Production: E Allgyer
Estimated Sales: $10 - 20 Million
Number Employees: 50-99
Square Footage: 120000
Parent Co: Desco Corporation

19236 Automation Devices Inc
7050 W Ridge Rd
Fairview, PA 16415-2099
Canada

814-474-1818
Fax: 814-474-2131 sales@adlcan.com
www.autodev.com
Owner: Erdal Basaraner
  erdal_basaraner@kibele-pims.com
CFO: Garry Projanowski
Estimated Sales: Below $5 Million
Number Employees: 20-49

19237 Automation Equipment
E. Notherwest Highway
Dailas, TX 75228

469-212-9212
Fax: 419-663-1187
Custom designed machinery, material handling systems, metal fabricating, printing presses and special automatic machinery
Estimated Sales: $5-10 Million
Number Employees: 20-49

19238 Automation Group
6100 Hillcroft Street
Suite 300
Houston, TX 77081-1010

713-860-5200
Fax: 713-860-5298
Process control and automation and networking software
President: Steven E Paulson
Business Development Manager: Darryl Hazlett
Estimated Sales: $5 - 10 Million
Number Employees: 120

19239 Automation Ideas Inc
9945 Greenland Ave NE
Rockford, MI 49341-9338

616-874-4041
Fax: 616-874-3454 877-254-3327
jerry@automationideas.com
www.automationideas.com
Equipment for the water bottling, dairy and food processing industries.
President: Jerry Bott
  jerry@automationideas.com
Vice President: Mick Donahue
Sales, Midwest Region: Dave Westra
Operations Manager: Justin Bott
Parts orders / Purchasing / Logistics: Brandon Totten
Number Employees: 20-49

19240 Automation Intelligence
P.O. Box 704
Loganville, GA 30052-0704

404-241-1000
Fax: 770-497-8666 888-531-8213
Motion control
Owner: Jim Bowers
Estimated Sales: Below $5 Million
Number Employees: 5-9

19241 Automation Onspec Software
10923 Progress Ct # 743
Rancho Cordova, CA 95670-5667

916-362-5867
Fax: 916-362-5967 888-362-5867
sales@automationonspec.com
www.automationonspec.com
Provides SCADA/HMI software for process control and trending and reporting.
President: Mike McMann
CFO: Steve Schasser
Research & Development: Dedh Chisum
Quality Control: Mo Dhmed
Marketing Director: Ken Thompson
Sales Director: Ed Ireton
Estimated Sales: Below $5 Million
Number Employees: 5-9
Number of Brands: 1
Number of Products: 167

19242 Automation Packaging
6206 Benjamin Road
Suite 309
Tampa, FL 33634-5169

813-888-8488
Fax: 813-888-8113
Form, fill and seal wrappers, side-seal, lap-seal, shrink bundlers, automatic L-sealers and corrugated equipment
President: Jean Limousin
Estimated Sales: $5-10 000,000
Number Employees: 50-99

19243 Automation Products
8620 Richmond Ave # D
Houston, TX 77063-5649

713-785-3600
Fax: 713-869-7332 800-231-2062
www.packaging-online.com
Analyzers, tests, plant operations, total solids, batch control systems, chillers, filler monitoring systems, margarine processing equipment, meters, flow, milk, solids, process control
Owner: Vincent Gabory
National Sales Manager of Board: Brian Olesinski
Estimated Sales: $300,000-500,000
Number Employees: 1-4

19244 Automation Safety
24850 Drake Road
Farmington Hills, MI 48335-2506

248-473-1133
Fax: 248-473-3997 info@pilzusa.com
www.machinetoolsonline.com/doc/
Safety controls, industrial computers

19245 Automation Service
13871 Parks Steed Dr
Earth City, MO 63045-1406

314-785-6600
Fax: 314-785-6610 800-325-4808
info@automationservice.com
www.automationservice.com
Process control instrumentation
President: Rod Barnett
CEO: Wesley Rarick
  wesleyr@automationservice.com
Quality Control: Bob Bokel
R&D: Alex Muller
Marketing Director: Deanna Coppeans
Sales Director: Curt Sykes
Operations Manager: Mike Brunts
Production Manager: Michael Pruett
Purchasing Manager: Rich Kruse
Estimated Sales: $10 - 20 Million
Number Employees: 100-249

19246 Automotion Inc
11000 Lavergne Ave
Oak Lawn, IL 60453-5500

708-229-3700
Fax: 708-229-3799
info@automotionconveyors.com
www.automotionconveyors.com
Conveyors and sortation equipment
President: Merle Davis
  mdavis@autonotionconveyors.com
CFO: Dave Beesley
Vice President: John Hejmanowski
Marketing Director: Joe O'Connor
Estimated Sales: $20 - 50 Million
Number Employees: 100-249
Square Footage: 140000

19247 Autoprod
807 W Kimberly Rd
Davenport, IA 52806
563-391-1100
Fax: 563-391-0017
Manufacturer and exporter of packaging machinery
for filling and closing pre-formed metallic, paper
and plastic containers
President: Paul Desocio
CEO: Barry Shoulders
R & D: Hans Koule
Vice President Marketing & Sales: Tom Riggins
Sales: Barb Peeters
Trade Show Coordinator/Marketing: Mary Baltzell
Plant Manager: Larry Loftus
Purchasing Manager: Harvey Cassell
Number Employees: 50-99
Parent Co: IWKA Company
Type of Packaging: Consumer, Food Service, Private Label

19248 Autoquip Corp
1058 W Industrial Rd
Guthrie, OK 73044-6046
405-282-5200
Fax: 405-282-8105 877-360-6777
dcrabtree@autoquip.com www.autoquip.com
Manufacturer and exporter of material handling
equipment including scissor lifts, turntables and
tilters
President: Joe Robillard
jrobillard@autoquip.com
Plant Manager: Chris Curning
Manager, Marketing & Sales: Louis Coleman
Sales: Donnie Crabtree
Operations Director: Chris Kuehni
Engineering Director: Mike Adel
Supervisor, Parts & Services: Mike Calvert
Estimated Sales: $10 - 20 Million
Number Employees: 100-249
Parent Co: Autoquip Corporation

19249 Autosplice Inc
10121 Barnes Canyon Rd
San Diego, CA 92121-2725
858-678-3115
Fax: 858-535-0130 www.autosplice.com
President: Michael T Reagan
Contact: Jacques Belet
jbelet@psav.com
Estimated Sales: $50 Million
Number Employees: 50-99

19250 Autotron
195 W Ryan Rd
Oak Creek, WI 53154-4400
414-764-7500
Fax: 414-764-4298 800-527-7500
info@elwood.com www.elwood.com
Manufacturer and exporter of industrial photoelectric controls
President: Robert Larsen
Vice President/CFO: Terry Levin
Vice President: David Johnson
Quality Manager: John Hoeppner
Estimated Sales: $5 - 10 Million
Number Employees: 20-49
Square Footage: 60000

19251 Avalon Canvas & Upholstery Inc
4617 N Shepherd Dr
Houston, TX 77018-3315
713-607-9289
Fax: 713-697-9257 www.marygrove.com
Commercial awnings
Manager: Michael Falahee
Estimated Sales: Less Than $500,000
Number Employees: 1-4

19252 Avalon Foodservice
1 Avalon Drive
PO Box 536
Canal Fulton, OH 44614
330-854-4551
Fax: 330-854-7108 800-362-0622
marketing@avalonfoods.com
www.avalonfoods.com
Avalon is a member of UniPro Foodservice, Inc., a
cooperative of distributors with collective annual
sales of $58 billion. Avalon serves Ohio and parts of
Pennsylvania and West Virginia.
Contact: Adam Ables
adam.ables@avalonfoods.com
Square Footage: 114000

Brands:
Nestle
Stouffers
Tyson

19253 Avalon Manufacturer
509 Bateman Cir
Corona, CA 92880-2012
951-340-0280
Fax: 951-340-0283 800-676-3040
info@avalonmfg.com www.avalonmfg.com
Manufacturer and exporter of fryers, glazers and
stainless steel (aluminum) proof boxes
Owner: Troy Enger
troy@avalonmfg.com
VP: Troy Enger
Estimated Sales: $2.5-5 Million
Number Employees: 10-19
Square Footage: 80000

19254 Avantage Group Inc
250 N Harbor Dr # 311
Suite 311
Redondo Beach, CA 90277-2585
310-379-3933
Fax: 310-376-0591
Plastic bags
President: Mark E Daniels
Owner: Mark Daniels
mdaniels@avantage.nl
Estimated Sales: Below $5 Million
Number Employees: 5-9

19255 Avanti Polar Lipids
700 Industrial Park Dr
Alabaster, AL 35007-9105
205-663-0991
Fax: 205-663-0756 800-227-0651
info@avantilipids.com www.avantilipids.com
Analytical services, metal chellators, bulk products,
diagnostic kits, natural lipids, sterols, synthetic
lipids
President: Di Bush
dcl89@cornell.edu
VP: Rowena Shaw
Estimated Sales: $10-20 Million
Number Employees: 50-99

19256 Aveka Inc
2045 Wooddale Dr
St Paul, MN 55125-2904
651-730-1729
Fax: 651-730-1826 888-317-3700
aveka@aveka.com www.aveka.com
Contract manufacturer and research and development company that focuses on particle technology
including spray drying, particle coating or
microcapsule technologies.
Owner: John Anderson
aveka@avekamfg.com
CEO/Ownder: William Hendrickson
Environmental Manager: Shain Kroenecke
Process Engineer: Matthew Timmers
Number Employees: 50-99
Other Locations:
Aveka Manufacturing
Fredericksberg IA
Cresco Food Technologies
Cresco IA
Aveka Nutra Processing
Waukon IA
Aveka CCE Technologies
Cottage Grove MN

19257 Avena Foods Ltd.
316 1st Ave. E
Regina, SK S4N 5H2
Canada
306-757-3663
Fax: 306-757-1218 drichardson@avenafoods.com
www.avenafoods.com
Processor and supplier of gluten-free/wheat free oat
products for private label/ingredients market. Allergen free plant with GFCO and OU Kosher Certification. Products include rolled oats, quick flakes,
flour, steel cuts oats andbran.
Director: Kevin Meadows
Director: Maryellen Carlson
Quality Control: Nicole Gudmundsson
Sales: Dale Richardson
Operations: Rod Lechner
Plant Manager: Nathalie Paquin
Purchasing: Carryl Litzenberger
Estimated Sales: $746.93 Thousand
Number Employees: 26

Type of Packaging: Private Label, Bulk

19258 Aventics Corp
1953 Mercer Rd
Lexington, KY 40511-1021
859-254-8031
Fax: 859-281-3488 www.boschrexroth.com
Pneumatic and hydraulic cylinders and valves,
electropneumatic control systems and actuators, vacuum components
IT: Jerry Robinson
jerry.robinson@boschrexroth-us.com
Estimated Sales: $50-100 Million
Number Employees: 250-499

19259 Avery Dennison Corporation
8080 Norton Parkway
Mentor, OH 44060
440-534-6000
www.averydennison.com
Manufacturer and exporter of pressure sensitive labels.
Chairman/CEO: Mitch Butier
President/COO: Deon Stander
SVP/CFO: Greg Lovins
VP/Chief Legal Officer: Ignacio Walker
SVP/Chief Human Resources: Deena Baker-Nel
SVP, Global Operations/Supply Chain: Kamran
Kian
Year Founded: 1935
Estimated Sales: $8.4 Billion
Number Employees: 35,000
Other Locations:
Avery Research Center (AEM)
Irwindale CA
Business Media
Buffalo NY
Corporate
Framingham MA
Corporate Int'l Manufacturing
Covina CA
Corporate Office at Brea
Brea CA
Corporate Office at Framingham
Framingham MA
Corporate Shared EHS at Milford
Milford MA
Engineered Films Division
Greenfield IN
Engineered Films Division
Painesville OH

19260 Avery Filter Company
99 Kinderkamack Rd
Suite 209
Westwood, NJ 07675
201-666-9664
Fax: 201-666-3802 info@averyfilter.com
www.averyfilter.com
Supplier of used & reconditioned filter presses, pressure leaf, pressure plate and vacuum drum filtration
equipment & parts; paper & cloth filter media; and
technical consulting services.
Vice President Engineering & Sales: Ken Lindgren
Square Footage: 1000

19261 Avery Weigh-Tronix
1000 Armstrong Dr
Fairmont, MN 56031-1439
507-238-4461
Fax: 507-238-4195 877-368-2039
usinfo@awtxglobal.com
www.averyweigh-tronix.com
Manufacturer and exporter of industrial scales.
Estimated Sales: $533 Million
Number Employees: 5,500
Square Footage: 330000
Parent Co: Illinois Tool Works Inc.

19262 Avery Weigh-Tronix LLC
1000 Armstrong Dr
Fairmont, MN 56031-1439
507-238-4461
Fax: 507-238-4195 800-368-2039
usinfo@awtxglobal.com
www.averyweigh-tronix.com
Manufacturer, importer and exporter of point-of-sale
interface scales that link to cash registers and computers; also, portion control scales
Cmo: Peggy Trimble
peggi.trimble@weigh-tronix.com
VP: Peggy Trimble
Worldwide Marketing Director: P Trimble
Sales Director: D Cone

Number Employees: 250-499
Square Footage: 130000
Parent Co: Weigh-Tronix
Other Locations:
Weigh-Tronix
Tonbridge, Kent
Brands:
Nci

19263 Avestin
2450 Don Reid Drive
Ottawa, ON K1H 1E1
Canada
613-736-0019
Fax: 613-736-8086 888-283-7846
avestin@avestin.com
Manufacturer and exporter of high pressure homogenizers, filters, extruders and liposome extruders
President: Mark Ruzbie
Vice President: Hilde Linder
Marketing Manager: Sophie Sommerer
Number Employees: 10
Brands:
Emulsiflex
Liposofast

19264 Avins Fabricating Co
60 John Glenn Dr
Amherst, NY 14228-2118
716-691-7990
Fax: 716-691-8202 888-735-6907
info@goe-avins.com www.amherstfab.com
President: Gerald Bogdan
ccornwall@avinsfab.com
Estimated Sales: $3 - 5 Million
Number Employees: 20-49

19265 Avne Packaging Services
PO Box 863
Bronx, NY 10457-0863
718-716-7600

19266 Avon Tape
79 Florence St Apt 310s
Chestnut Hill, MA 2467
508-584-8273
Manufacturer and exporter of pressure-sensitive tapes
President: Howard Shuman
Estimated Sales: $5-10 Million
Number Employees: 50-99

19267 Avondale Mills
506 S Broad St
Monroe, GA 30655
770-267-2226
Fax: 803-663-5839
Manufacturers of fabrics for awnings
Manager: Doug Johnson
VP: Kevin Crean
Estimated Sales: $20-50 Million
Number Employees: 100-249
Parent Co: Avondale Mills

19268 Avtec Industries
9 Kane Industrial Dr
Hudson, MA 01749-2905
978-562-2300
Fax: 978-562-8900 www.avtecindustries.com
President: Anthony Camarota
inquiries@avtecindustries.com
Estimated Sales: $1 - 5 Million
Number Employees: 1-4
Parent Co: Dover Industries

19269 Avure Technologies Svc & Sales
3721 Corporate Dr
Columbus, OH 43231-4964
614-891-3498
Fax: 614-891-4568
Isostatic presses and thermocouples
Manager: Melanie Harter
Manager: Toddington Harper
todd.harper@fuelcellmarkets.com
Estimated Sales: $1 - 5 Million
Number Employees: 20-49

19270 Aw Sheepscot Holding CoInc
8809 Industrial Dr
Franksville, WI 53126-9337
262-884-9800
Fax: 262-884-9810 800-850-6110
sales@aw-lake.com www.awcompany.com

Manufacturer and distributor of flow control products including positive displacement flow meters, turbine flow meters, electronic sensors, flow computers, on-line optical sensors and signal conditioners.
President: Roger Tambling
Contact: Greg Baldwin
gbaldwin@aw-lake.com
Estimated Sales: $5 - 10 Million
Number Employees: 1-4
Square Footage: 60000
Brands:
Fluidpro
Proscan
Ta-3

19271 Award's of America's
the Cuisine Group 25 Kearny S
Suite 500
San Francisco, CA 94108
415-982-0701
Fax: 415-982-4580
Since 1985, has dedicated itself to the purveyance of taste and quality throughout the culinary industry and the search for the best of the best in food, beverage, and equipment. Expanded to include three division: American TestingInstitute, American Culinary Institute, and American Quality Institute

19272 Awb Engineers
1942 Northwood Dr
Salisbury, MD 21801-7824
410-742-7299
Fax: 410-742-0273 awbengs@aol.com
www.awbengineers.com
Consultant specializing in architecture, civil, constructural and mechanical engineering services for food processing facilities
President: Matt Smith
msmith@awbengineers.com
Director: John Shahan
Estimated Sales: $3 - 5 Million
Number Employees: 20-49
Square Footage: 23200

19273 Awmco Inc
11560 184th Pl
Orland Park, IL 60467-4904
708-478-6032
Fax: 708-478-6041 awmco@aol.com
www.awmcoinc.com
Manufacturer and exporter of baking decks and cooking stones for pizza, pretzel and bagel ovens
President: Mark O'Toole
Manager: Mark Otoole
Estimated Sales: $2 Million
Number Employees: 5-9
Number of Brands: 4
Number of Products: 12
Square Footage: 72000
Type of Packaging: Food Service
Brands:
Fibrament Baking Stone
Oven Stone

19274 Awning Co Inc
1668 Bhampton Sag Harbor Tpke
Sag Harbor, NY 11963-3706
631-725-3651
Fax: 631-725-7452 info@theawningcompany.com
www.theawningcompany.com
Commercial awnings
Owner: Michael Moody
michael.moody@awningcompany.com
Co-Ownr.: Susan Oi
Estimated Sales: $500,000-$1,000,000
Number Employees: 5-9

19275 Awning Enterprises
P.O. Box 1063
Frederick, MD 21702
301-631-0500
Fax: 301-695-7651 800-735-2453
awningenterprises@comcast.net
www.awningenterprises.com
Commercial awnings
Owner: Danny Baer
VP: Patrick O'Connell
Associate VP: Rita O'Connell
Estimated Sales: $.5 - 1,000,000
Number Employees: 1-4

19276 Awnings Plus
1405 W Bernard Dr # A
Suite A
Addison, IL 60101-4341
630-627-4700
Fax: 630-405-6105 888-627-4770
Commercial awnings
Owner: Kent Weber
CFO: Nancy Gomez
Marketing Director: Ken Miller
Sales Director: Erich Doering
kent@awningssigngroup.com
Purchasing Manager: Michael Moreth
Estimated Sales: Below $5,000,000
Number Employees: 20-49
Square Footage: 12000

19277 Awnings by Dee
24913 Northern Boulevard
Little Neck, NY 11362-1260
516-487-6688
Fax: 718-224-5614
Commercial awnings
Secretary: Laura Dee
Estimated Sales: $1-2,500,000
Number Employees: 10-19

19278 Axces Systems
265 Post Ave
Westbury, NY 11590-2233
516-333-8585
Fax: 516-333-4992 800-355-3534
www.access-systems.com
Consultant and marketing information specialist for companies with 3-tier distribution networks
Owner: Charlie Richgat
Estimated Sales: $1-2.5 Million
Number Employees: 5-9
Square Footage: 4000

19279 Axelrod, Norman N
445 E 86th St
New York, NY 10028-6433
212-369-2885
www.axelrodassociates.com
Manufacturer and exporter of optical sensing and vision systems for automated quality and process control systems for food processing and packaging. Consultant, market studies on optical sensing and control technologies
President: Norman N Axelrod, Phd
Manager of Systems Integration: C Chang
Manager Software Development: R Rolle
Estimated Sales: Less Than $500,000
Number Employees: 1-4

19280 Axia Distribution Corporation
247-2628 Granville Street
Vancouver, BC V6H 4B4
Canada
778-371-9885
Fax: 778-371-9000 info@axiadistribution.com
www.axiadistribution.com
Distributor & Manufacutuer of High Quality Rubber Mats. the Mats are molded with virgin rubber that offers durability, less odor, stability and anti-fatigue properties
Type of Packaging: Food Service

19281 Axiflow Technologies, Inc.
1955 Vaughn Road
Suite 103
Kennesaw, GA 30144
770-795-1195
Fax: 770-795-1342 www.axiflowtechnologies.com
Pumps, blenders and food processing machines for the food & beverage industries.

19282 Axiohm USA
2411 N Oak Street
Suite 203 C
Myrtle Beach, SC 29577
843-443-3155
Fax: 888-505-9555 namsales@Axiohm.com
www.axiohm.com
Manufacturer and exporter of magnetic strip card readers and thermal laser receipt printers
President and CEO: Lindsey Allen
Director Marketing/Communications: Mark Basla
Number Employees: 60
Brands:
Axiohm

19283 Axon Styrotech
3080 Business Park Dr # 103
Raleigh, NC 27610-3094
919-772-8383
Fax: 919-772-5575 800-598-8601
info@axoncorp.com www.axoncorp.com
Tamper evident sleeve labels
President: H Lane
Quality Control: Andy Perry
Manager: George Albrecht
gealb@axoncorp.com
General Manager: Victor Menayan
Estimated Sales: $10 - 20,000,000
Number Employees: 20-49
Brands:
E-Z Seal

19284 Axon Styrotech
3080 Business Park Dr # 103
Suite 103
Raleigh, NC 27610-3094
919-772-8383
Fax: 919-772-5575 800-598-8601
info@axoncorp.com www.axoncorp.com
Shrink and stretch sleeve labeling machines and systems
Sales Director: Ed Farley
Manager: George Albrecht
gealb@axoncorp.com
Estimated Sales: $1-2.5 Million
Number Employees: 20-49

19285 Axons Labeling
Gristmill Road
Wanaque, NJ 07465
973-616-7448
Fax: 973-616-7449
Labeling machines, labeling applicators/jar unscramblers

19286 Ay Machine Company
East King Street
PO Box 608
Ephrata, PA 17522-0608
717-733-0335
Fax: 717-733-2933 info@aymachine.com
www.aymachine.com
Custom built food processing machinery; also, spare parts and rebuilt equipment
President: Richard Ay
CEO: Rick Ay, Jr.
Estimated Sales: $2.5-5 Million
Number Employees: 10-19
Square Footage: 128000

19287 Ayer Sales Inc
2 Industrial Pkwy
Woburn, MA 01801-1997
781-933-1141
Fax: 781-933-3675 800-225-5736
customerservice@ayer.com www.ayer.com
Waste water treatment systems
Marketing Coordinator: Peter Quinn
Estimated Sales: $3 - 5 Million
Number Employees: 50-99
Parent Co: Ayer Sales

19288 Ayr King Corp
2013 Cobalt Dr
Louisville, KY 40299-2417
502-266-6270
Fax: 502-266-6274 866-266-6290
aurking@aol.com www.ayrking.com
Breading sifters, hoods and drive-thru windows
Owner: Don King
VP Engineering: Cha Harned
VP of Sales: James Bell
don@ayrking.com
Estimated Sales: $500,000-$1 Million
Number Employees: 5-9

19289 Azbar Plus
2755, av Dalton
Qu,bec, QC G1P 3T1
Canada
418-687-3672
Fax: 418-687-2987 azbar@total.net
azbarplus.com
Liquor and beverage control equipment and dispensers including electric and beverage
Estimated Sales: $1 - 5 Million

19290 Azco Corp
26 Just Rd
Fairfield, NJ 07004-3413
973-439-1428
Fax: 973-439-9411 cs@azcocorp.com
www.azcocorp.com
Dispensers, inserters, fan folders, cut-to-length assemblies
President: Andrew Zucaro
zucaro@azcocorp.com
Marketing: Tetie Milligan
Sales: John Perona
Estimated Sales: $1-2.5 Million
Number Employees: 20-49

19291 Azonix Corporation
101 Billerica Ave
Building 4
Billerica, MA 01862
978-670-6300
Fax: 978-670-8855 800-967-5558
www.azonix.com
President: Greg Balesta
Training/Sales Support: Craig Yelenick
Estimated Sales: $13 Million
Number Employees: 50-99

19292 Aztec Grill
PO Box 820037
Dallas, TX 75382
214-343-1897
Fax: 214-341-9996 800-346-8114
www.aztecgrill.com
Manufacturer and exporter of wood burning grills and rotisseries
Contact: Dennis Whiting
dennis@aztecgrill.com
Estimated Sales: $1 - 5 Million
Number Employees: 2
Square Footage: 16000
Type of Packaging: Food Service

19293 Azz/R-A-L
8500 Hansen Rd
Houston, TX 77075
713-943-0340
Fax: 713-943-8354 www.azz.com
Lighting fixtures for the food service industry.

19294 B & G Products
3631 44th St SE # E
Grand Rapids, MI 49512-3971
616-698-9050
Fax: 616-698-9271 sales@bgproducts.com
www.bgproducts.com
President: Kathleen Geddes
kgeddes@bgproducts.com
Vice President: Jacci Harding
Quality Control Manager: Mark Mastbergen
Sales: Paul Geddes
Estimated Sales: $5 - 10 Million
Number Employees: 10-19
Square Footage: 40000
Type of Packaging: Food Service

19295 (HQ)B & P Process Equipment
1000 Hess Ave
Saginaw, MI 48601-3729
989-757-1300
Fax: 989-757-1301 sales@bpprocess.com
www.bpprocess.com
Manufacturer and exporter of food processing machinery and equipment including automatic scales, sifters, etc
President: Alan Martin
alan@sandrofilm.com
R&D: Doug Hillman
Executive: Joe Flynn
CFO: Allen Martin
Estimated Sales: $20 - 50 Million
Number Employees: 50-99

19296 B & W Awning Co
219 Walton Ave
Lexington, KY 40502-1492
859-252-1619
Fax: 859-233-4354 lgille3607@aol.com
www.bwawning.com
Commercial awnings
President: Larry Gillespie
lgille3607@aol.com
Estimated Sales: $1 - 2,500,000
Number Employees: 5-9

19297 B C Holland Inc
45 Wilson Ave
Dousman, WI 53118-9369
262-965-2939
Fax: 262-965-3546 www.bcholland.net
Custom tanks and mixers
President: Brian Holland
CFO: Rom Able
VP: David Steward
Sales Manager: Jim Huth
VP Operations: Dave Stewart
Estimated Sales: $1-2.5 Million
Number Employees: 10-19
Square Footage: 20000

19298 B F Nelson Cartons Inc
12900 Eagle Creek Pkwy
Savage, MN 55378-1271
952-746-6300
Fax: 952-746-6399 800-328-2380
sales@bfnelson.com www.bfnelson.com
Folding cartons
President: Larry Ross
bfncartons@aol.com
Executive VP: Gary Sotebeer
VP Sales: Ron Anderson
Estimated Sales: $1 - 5 Million
Number Employees: 100-249

19299 B H Awning & Tent Co
2275 M 139
Benton Harbor, MI 49022-6190
269-925-2187
Fax: 269-925-2197 800-272-2187
sales@bhawning.com www.bhawning.com
Commercial awnings, banners, canopies and flags
President: Charles Dill
chuck@bhawning.com
Number Employees: 10-19

19300 B H Bunn Co
2730 Drane Field Rd
Lakeland, FL 33811-1325
863-647-1555
Fax: 863-686-2866 800-222-2866
info@bunntyco.com www.bunntyco.com
Bunn tying machines for poultry, pork and beef
Owner: John R Bunn
jbunn@bunntyco.com
Estimated Sales: $3 - 5 Million
Number Employees: 10-19
Square Footage: 68000
Brands:
Bunn

19301 B J Wood Products Inc
400 W 9th St S
Ladysmith, WI 54848-9514
715-532-6626
Fax: 715-532-7774 pauls@bjwood.com
www.bjwood.com
Custom wood and acrylic casework, cabinets, displays, counters and store fixtures
President: Paul Sieg
pauls@bjwood.com
VP: John Sieg
Estimated Sales: $5-10 Million
Number Employees: 10-19
Square Footage: 95000

19302 B M T USA LLC
14532 169th Dr SE # 142
#142
Monroe, WA 98272-2936
360-863-2252
Fax: 360-863-2366 sales@bmtus.com
www.bmtus.com
Offers a wide range of equipment for the food laboratory, including stability chambers, incubators, sterilization ovens, vacuum and dry-heat ovens, small, medium, and large steam sterilizers, and clean steam generators
President: Jim Atkinson
jatkinson@bmtus.com
Number Employees: 10-19

19303 B R Machinery
3312 E 2153rd Rd
Wedron, IL 60557
815-434-0427
Fax: 815-434-0428 800-310-7057
info@brmachine.us www.brmachine.us

Portable propane and custom portable grills, gas grill carts, personalized custom canopy and grill accessories
Owner: Robert Rogowski
VP: Nancy Rogowski
VP of Sales: Tony Rogowski
robertr@wedrongrills.com
Production Manager: Sam Brown
Estimated Sales: Less Than $500,000
Number Employees: 5-9
Square Footage: 40000
Brands:
Wedron Grills

19304 B S & B Safety Systems LLC
7455 E 46th St
Tulsa, OK 74145-6301
918-622-5950
Fax: 918-492-1559 800-272-3475
sales@bsbsystems.com www.bsbsystems.com
Manufactures overpressure protection safety products, pressure relief, both positive and vacuum with pressure relieving products including rupture disks.
VP: Dave Garrison
Number Employees: 5-9

19305 B S C Signs
7245 W 116th Pl
Broomfield, CO 80020-2955
303-464-0644
Fax: 303-464-0608 866-223-0101
sales@bscsigns.com www.bscsigns.com
Displays and signs including neon, lighted and nonilluminated; installation services available
President: Mike Nudd
VP: Jennifer Dent
Contact: John Dobie
john@bscsigns.com
Estimated Sales: Less Than $500,000
Number Employees: 1-4

19306 B T Engineering Inc
29 Bala Ave # 209
Bala Cynwyd, PA 19004-3269
610-664-9500
Fax: 610-664-0317 bte123123@aol.com
www.btengineering.com
Automated sanitary liquid food processing equipment and control systems including clean-in-place pipeline systems, pasteurizers and volumetric filling machines; exporter of skidded food systems; design services available
President/CEO: William Willard
CFO: Thomas Berger Sr
Secretary/Treasurer: Thomas Berger
Manager: W Willard
wilwillard@aol.com
Estimated Sales: $1-2.5 Million
Number Employees: 1-4
Square Footage: 5000
Type of Packaging: Food Service

19307 B W Cooney & Associates
28 Simpson Road
Bolton, Ontario, ON L7E 1G9
Canada
905-857-7880
Fax: 905-857-7883 info@bwcooney.ca
www.bwcooney.ca
Shrink wrapping and tray stretch machines, flow wrappers, verticle form fill & seal systems, packaging film and retail food trays.
President: Brian Cooney
Number Employees: 2

19308 B&B Neon Sign Company
2305 Donley Dr # 116
Austin, TX 78758-4535
512-765-4470
Fax: 512-719-4490 800-791-6366
customerservice@everythingneon.com
www.everythingneon.com
Point of purchase displays including neon and plexiglass signs; also, sign maintenance, refurbishing and repair services available
Owner: Tim O'Day
Estimated Sales: $300,000 -$500,000
Number Employees: 5-9

19309 B&G Machine Company
9124 S 53rd Ave
Oak Lawn, IL 60453-1665
708-499-1626
Fax: 631-589-9466 800-645-1191
www.bgmachine.com
Bins, hoppers, totes, ASME code vessels, storage tanks and mixing tanks
President: Barbara Ruehl
Vice President: Greg Ruehl
Estimated Sales: $5-10 Million
Number Employees: 5-9

19310 B&H Foods, Inc.
2122 Thrift Rd.
Charlotte, NC 28208
704-332-4106
Fax: 704-332-5980
Shellfish Shippers
President: Stan Bracey
Plant Manager: Dennis Frost
Year Founded: 1972
Estimated Sales: $20-50 Million
Number Employees: 40
Parent Co: B&H Foods

19311 B&H Labeling Systems
P.O. Box 247
Ceres, CA 95307
209-537-5785
Fax: 209-537-6854 marketing@bhlabeling.com
www.bhlabeling.com
Hot-melt roll-fed labeling machines capable of handling most container sizes, label substrates, and speeds for a diverse range of products and materials. Features and options include Computerized Registration System, Web TrackingOperator Alarms, Touch Screen Operation, Rapid Change Over Change Parts, ENDURA Shrink Labeling process, Precision Components
Owner: Carol Bright
CEO: Roman M Eckols
Contact: Lyn Bright
l.bright@bhlabeling.com
Plant Manager: Bruce Andrade
Number Employees: 100-249
Type of Packaging: Consumer, Food Service, Private Label

19312 B&J Machinery
11560 Rockfield Ct
Cincinnati, OH 45241-1919
513-771-7374
Fax: 513-771-3820 info@pe-us.com
www.pe-us.com
Packaging machinery and replacement parts
President: Bruno Negri
CFO: Bruno Negri
VP: Tom Kauffmann
Regional Sales Manager: Ryan Cooper
Estimated Sales: $10 - 20 Million
Number Employees: 20-49
Square Footage: 32000

19313 B&K Coffee
PO Box 1238
Oneonta, NY 13820-5238
607-432-1499
Fax: 607-432-1592 800-432-1499
www.bkcoffee.com
Manufacturer of coffee and tea.
Owner: Paul Karabinis
Owner: Gene Bettiol
Year Founded: 1991
Estimated Sales: $10-24.9 Million
Number Employees: 20-49
Number of Brands: 1
Type of Packaging: Private Label
Brands:
B&K Coffee

19314 B&R Industrial Automation Corp
1250 Northmeadow Parkway
Suite 100
Roswell, GA 30076
770-772-0400
office.us@br-automation.com
www.br-automation.com
Machine and factory control systems
President: Patrick McDermott
Number Employees: 1,000-4,999
Parent Co: ABB Group

19315 B.A.G. Corporation
11510 Data Dr
Suite 170
Richardson, TX 75081
800-331-9200
Fax: 214-340-4598 800-331-9200
www.bagcorp.com
Manufacturer and exporter of the Super Sack container, a woven polypropylene FIBC for shipping, handling, and storing dry-flowable and fluid products
President: Karl Reimers
Estimated Sales: $5-10 Million
Number Employees: 20-49
Type of Packaging: Food Service, Bulk
Brands:
Super Sack

19316 B.C.E. Technologies
616 S Ware Blvd
Tampa, FL 33619-4443
813-621-8128
Fax: 813-620-1206
President: Graham Lloyd
glloyd@bcetechnology.com
Number Employees: 20-49

19317 B.E. Industries
652 Glenbrook Rd # 4102
Stamford, CT 06906-1410
203-357-8055
Fax: 203-967-9537
Advertising specialties including key rings and magnets
President: Bruce Kahn
Estimated Sales: $2.5-5,000,000
Number Employees: 10-19

19318 B.E.S.T.
1071 Industrial Pkwy N
Brunswick, OH 44212
330-273-1277
Fax: 330-225-8740 sales@bestvibes.com
www.bestvibes.com
President: Ed Verbos
Estimated Sales: $5 - 10 Million
Number Employees: 20-49

19319 BAKERY Innovative Technology
139 N Ocean Ave
Patchogue, NY 11772-2018
631-758-3081
Fax: 631-758-3779
Software and automation: applying and installing computer and programmable controller automation for bakeries and food plants
Owner: Joe Vignati
joe.vignati@bit-corp.com
Estimated Sales: $2.5-5 Million
Number Employees: 10-19

19320 BAKERY Innovative Technology
139 N Ocean Ave
Patchogue, NY 11772-2018
631-758-3081
Fax: 631-758-3779
Owner: Mark Albert
mark.albert@bit-corp.com
Estimated Sales: $1 - 5 Million
Number Employees: 10-19

19321 BAW Plastics Inc
2148 Century Dr
Clairton, PA 15025-3654
412-384-2535
Fax: 412-384-2033 800-783-2229
www.allbrainscreatedreams.org
Coupon bags, transparent vinyl envelopes, vinyl checker aids, acrylic holders, lamination pouches, time and attendance badges and name tags, etc
Owner: Jim Slovonic
Sales Manager: Martin Slovonic
Sales Director: Francis Dusch
jslovonic@bawplastics.com
Estimated Sales: $10-20 Million
Number Employees: 100-249
Square Footage: 130000

19322 BBQ Pits by Klose
1355 Judiway Street #B
Houston, TX 77018-6005
713-686-8720
Fax: 713-686-8793 800-487-7487
www.bbqpits.com

Manufacturer, importer and exporter of barbecue equipment including grills and smokers; also, catering trailers; wood, charcoal and gas fired.
President: David Klose
Sales: Dana Harlow
Contact: Carla Hadley
 carla.hadley@bbqpits.com
Estimated Sales: $1-3 Million
Number Employees: 10-19
Number of Products: 500
Square Footage: 24000
Type of Packaging: Consumer, Food Service, Bulk
Brands:
 Klose

19323 BCN Research Laboratories
2491 Stock Creek Blvd
Rockford, TN 37853-3056
865-573-7511
Fax: 865-573-7513 800-236-0505
emilia.rico@bcnlabs.com www.bcnlabs.com
Consultant providing laboratory and research services including sanitation, testing and analysis; also, plant audits and training available
President: Emilia Rico
 emilia.rico@bcnlabs.com
VP: Shawn Johnson
Estimated Sales: $.5 - 1 million
Number Employees: 5-9
Square Footage: 12000

19324 BE&K Building Group
201 E McBee Ave
Suite 400
Greenville, SC 29601
864-250-5000
Fax: 864-250-5099 www.bekbg.com
Construction services
President & CEO: Frank Holley
EVP & Business Unit Leader: Mike Baumbach
Finance Controller: Kathy Harvey
VP, Preconstruction & Technology: Kevin Bredeson
SVP, Business Development: Jeff Thompson
VP, Human Resources: Candace Watson
Corporate Counsel: Leslie Sullivan
Marketing & Communications: Rick Helms
Year Founded: 1972
Estimated Sales: $2 Billion
Number Employees: 9,000
Other Locations:
 Atlanta GA
 Charlotte NC
 Greenville SC
 Brentwood TN
 Maitland FL
 Raleigh NC
 Vienna VA

19325 BEC International
2330 S Preston St
Louisville, KY 40217-2163
502-637-3852
Fax: 502-637-3803 877-232-4687
beci2001@hotmail.com
Consultant specializing in engineering and project management services
President: Richard Sorensen
Executive VP: James Winn
Number Employees: 1
Square Footage: 7200

19326 BEERCUP.COM
N22 W23685 Ridgeview Pkwy W
Waukesha, WI 53188
800-233-7287
Fax: 800-532-9287 beverage@boelter.com
BEERCUP.COM is an extension of the Boelter Companies' Beverage Group and provides the beverage industry with brand identified plastic cups, coasters, glassware, pitchers, buckets, and many other items used to serve beverage brands.
Director International Markets: Steve Dindorf

19327 BEI
1375 Kalamazoo St
South Haven, MI 49090
269-637-8541
Fax: 269-637-4233 800-364-7425
Manufacturer and exporter of berry harvesters and packing equipment
President: William De Witt Jr
Vice President: Butch Greiffendorf
Contact: Rodney Tolbert
 rtolbert@beiintl.com
Manager: J Greiffendorf

Estimated Sales: $5-10 Million
Number Employees: 20-49
Square Footage: 48000

19328 BEI
7230 Hollister Avenue
Goleta, GA 93117
805-968-0782
Fax: 805-968-3154 800-350-2727
www.beiresources.org
Insulated packaging
VP: Bob Belick
Marketing Manager: Bob Belick
Contact: Charles Crocker
 charles@beiied.com
Estimated Sales: Less than $500,000
Number Employees: 1-4
Brands:
 Thermal Cor

19329 BEMA
7101 College Boulevard
Suite 1505
Overland Park, KS 66210-2087
847-920-1230
Fax: 847-920-1253 info@bema.org
www.bema.org
President, Chief Executive Officer: Kerwin Brown
Operations Manager: Gay Poteet
Number Employees: 10

19330 BEUMER Corp
800 Apgar Dr
Somerset, NJ 8873
732-893-2800
Fax: 732-563-0905 usa@beumer.com
www.beumer.com
Manufacturer, importer and exporter of material handling equipment including automatic palletizing systems and automatic shrink and stretch hood unitizing systems
President: Matthias Erdsmannadoerf
 matthias.erdsmannadoerf@beumer.com
VP: Hanno Behm
Number Employees: 20-49
Square Footage: 10400
Parent Co: Beumer Maschinenfabrik GmbH & Company KG

19331 BEVCO
9354-194th Street Surrey
Canada, BC V4N 4E9
Canada
604-888-1455
Fax: 604-888-2887 800-663-0090
info@bevco.net www.bevco.net
Manufacturer and exporter of material handling and distribution equipment including accumulators, conveyors, conveyor systems, depalletizers and elevators; also, warmers and bottle rinsers
President: Brian Fortier
CEO: D Hargrove
CFO: Dianne Hargrove
Sales/Marketing Executive: Murray Kendrick
Estimated Sales: $5 - 10 Million
Number Employees: 45
Square Footage: 80000

19332 BEX Inc
836 Phoenix Dr
Ann Arbor, MI 48108-2221
734-464-8282
Fax: 734-389-0470 sales@bex.com
www.bex.com
Manufacture of spray nozzles and accessories for parts cleaning, rinsing and food processing.
Number Employees: 5-9

19333 BFB Consultants
5995 River Grove Avenue
Mississauga, ON L5M 4Z8
Canada
905-819-9856
Fax: 905-819-9857
Consultant specializing in food packaging, labeling and advertising in Canada and the U.S. in accordance with government regulations
Regional Affairs: Laurel Bellissimo
Sr. Technical Director: Gary Gnirss
Estimated Sales: $1 - 5 Million

19334 BFD Corp
15544 E Hinsdale Cir
Centennial, CO 80112-4225
303-363-6288
Fax: 303-363-6844 www.bfdcorp.com
Depackaging soft products/soft tissue separation; cutting-deboning-desinewing.
President: John Shook
 bfdcorp@aol.com
CFO: Mark Thomas
Sales Director: Harold Hodges
Number Employees: 10-19

19335 BFM Equipment Sales
209 Steel Road
P.O. Box 117
Fall River, WI 53932-0117
920-484-3341
Fax: 920-484-3077 info@bfmequip.com
www.bfmequip.com
Manufacturer, importer, exporter and wholesaler/distributor of food processing machinery, can end cleaners and dryers, replacement parts and supplies
Owner: Richard Bindley
Executive Manager: Russell Quandt
Contact: Leann Vick
 lvick@bfmequip.com
Estimated Sales: Below $5 Million
Number Employees: 1-4
Square Footage: 40000
Brands:
 Bfm

19336 BFT
3513 Transmitter Rd
Panama City, FL 32404
850-784-1231
Fax: 850-784-1343 800-871-1481
Gripper style air cleaner, bi-directional accumulation table, table top conveyors and a carry handle application machine for six-pack bottles and other containers and products
Estimated Sales: $2.5-5 000,000
Number Employees: 10

19337 BG Industries
305 Canal Street
Lemont, IL 60439-3603
630-257-1077
Fax: 630-257-0005 800-800-5761
www.bgindustry.com
Disposable plastic and metal catering products including chafing dishes, soup terrines and beverage urns
President: Paul Orednick
Estimated Sales: $1-2.5 Million
Number Employees: 9
Brands:
 Hot Buffet To Go
 Party Chafer

19338 BI Nutraceuticals
2550 El Presidio Street
Long Beach, CA 90810
310-669-2162
Fax: 310-637-3644
the largest supplier of botanical ingredients in the United States, for use in food & beverage, dietary supplements, personal care and pet care products. Products include botanical powders, teas, extracts, nutritional blends, vitaminsminerals, and more.
President/CEO: George Pontiakos
Chief Financial Officer: Christoph Kirchner
VP, North America: Bob Harvey
VP, Technical Services: Emilio Gutierrez
VP, Quality/Compliance: Rupa Das
Director, Marketing: Randy Kreienbrink
Contact: Patrisha Abergas
 patrishaabergas@tmmc.com
Director, Extract Operations: Dr. Bill Meer

19339 BINDER Inc.
545-3 Johnson Avenue
Bohemia, NY 11716
631-224-4340
usa@binder-world.com
www.binder-world.com
A simulation chamber specialist. Drying ovens
Contact: Jerry Jiang
 jerry.jiang@binder-world.com
Parent Co: BINDER GmbH

19340 BK Graphics
5270 Cub Cir Ste A
Morristown, TN 37814
423-581-4288
Fax: 423-581-9159 800-581-9159
www.bkgraphics.com
Advertising specialties; also, screen printing available
CEO: Brian Frankford
Quality Control: Kathy Frankford
Estimated Sales: $.5 - 1,000,000
Number Employees: 5-9

19341 BKI
1000 Broadway
Suite 410
Oakland, CA 94607
510-444-8707
Fax: 510-463-2690 www.bki.com
Technical management consultants
President: Robert Knight
Vice President: Brian Gitt
Contact: Julie Foster
jfoster@bki.com
Number Employees: 10

19342 BKI Worldwide
2812 Grandview Dr
Simpsonville, SC 29680-6217
864-963-3471
Fax: 864-963-5316 800-927-6887
customerservice@bkideas.com www.bkideas.com
Manufacturer and exporter of rotisseries, ovens, fryers, deli cases, ventless hood systems and food warmers
President: Randy A Karns
Controller: Reggy Skelton
COO: Dave Korcsmaros
Quality Control Manager: Wade Pitts
Operations Manager: Reed Walpole
Production Manager: Reed Walpole
Purchasing Manager: Wade Pitts
Number Employees: 100-249
Parent Co: Standex International Corporation
Brands:
   Bar-B-Que King
   Whisperflow

19343 BLH Electronics
75 Shawmut Rd
Canton, MA 02021
781-821-2000
Fax: 781-828-1451 sales@blh.com
www.blh.com
Manufacturer and exporter of process weighing and web tension systems, strain gauges and load systems/instruments
President: Robert E Murphy
Vice President: William Sheehan
Research & Development: David Scanlon
Sales Director: Art Koehler
Facilities Manager: Alan Sandman
Estimated Sales: $50-100 Million
Number Employees: 1-4
Square Footage: 55000
Parent Co: Spectra-Physics AB
Other Locations:
   BLH Electronics
   Toronto ON
Brands:
   Gate-Weigh

19344 BMH
19135 San Jose Avenue
City of Industry, CA 91748-1407
909-349-2530
Fax: 626-912-2477
Belt conveyors, automatic storage and handling systems and metal belting
Estimated Sales: $2.5-5,000,000
Number Employees: 20

19345 BMH Chronos Richardson
2 Stewart Place
Fairfield, NJ 07004-2202
973-227-3522
Fax: 973-227-8478 800-284-3644
info@premiertechchronos.com
www.bmhchronosrichardson.com
Contact: Bob Duran
info@chronosrichardson.com
Estimated Sales: $1 - 5 Million

19346 BNP Media
Beverage
Packaging Group
2401 W Big Beaver Rd, Su Troy
MI
480-4 -
248-362-3700
Henderson: Jim
*Estimated Sales:*www.bnpmedia.com
Type of Packaging: Food Service
Other Locations:
   Deerfield IL
   Marianna FL
   New York NY
   Paramus NJ
   Pittsburgh PA
   West Chester PA

19347 BNW Industries
7930 N 700 E
Tippecanoe, IN 46570-9613
574-353-7855
Fax: 574-353-8152 sales@norristhermal.com
Manufacturer and exporter of coolers and dehydrators; manufacturer of balance/single weave wire belts
Founder/President: Dan Norris
dnorris@bnwindustries.com
Vice President Sales: Aaron Norris
Purchasing Manager: Troy Eaton
Estimated Sales: $1-3 Million
Number Employees: 10-19
Square Footage: 52000
Parent Co: Lee Norris Construction & Grain Company
Brands:
   Belt-O-Matic
   Indiana Woven Wire

19348 BOC Gases
575 Mountain Ave
New Providence, NJ 07974
908-464-8100
Fax: 908-771-1701 800-742-4726
jobs@us.gases.boc.com www.boc.com
Full line of freezing and chilling equipment for beverage processing and carbonating needs
Marketing: Jon Lederman
Contact: Alexander Alvarado
   alex.alvarado@boc.com
Estimated Sales: $5 000,000
Number Employees: 1,000-4,999

19349 BOC Plastics Inc
90 Piedmont Industrial Drive
Suite 100
Winston Salem, NC 27107
336-767-0277
Fax: 336-767-2338 800-334-8687
Plastic cutlery kits
President: Robert Bach
CFO: Aren Petersen
Estimated Sales: $5 - 10 Million
Number Employees: 20-49

19350 BP
501 Westlake Park Blvd
Houston, TX 77079
281-366-2000
www.bp.com/en_us/united-states/home.html
Packaging materials including FDA approved resins and film.
CEO: Bernard Looney
Chair/President, BP America: Susan Dio
CFO: Brian Gilvary
EVP, Safety & Operational Risk: Bob Fryar
EVP/COO: Andy Hopwood
Year Founded: 1908
Estimated Sales: $3.4 Billion
Number Employees: 74,000
Parent Co: BP plc
Brands:
   Barex

19351 BPH Pump & Equipment
4126 W Orleans St
Mchenry, IL 60050-3972
815-578-0100
Fax: 815-578-0400 866-295-9161
www.sanitarypumpsandparts.com
Fluid handling equipment, system design, system fabrications, system engineering
Owner: Torres Beneth
   torres.beneth@accenture.com

Estimated Sales: $2.5 000,000
Number Employees: 5-9

19352 BPM Inc
200 W Front St
Peshtigo, WI 54157-1406
715-582-4551
Fax: 715-582-4853 800-826-0494
www.bpmpaper.com
Bond, mimeograph, duplicator, computer, copier rolls, MG and MF manifold, laminating stock, printed and plain waxed papers
President: Ronald Swanson
Vice President: Mitchell Mekaelian
   mm@bpmpaper.com
Plant Manager: Mark Bruemmer
Estimated Sales: $60 Million
Number Employees: 100-249

19353 BSI Instruments
101 Corporation Drive
Aliquippa, PA 15001-4859
724-378-1900
Fax: 724-378-1926 800-274-9851
bsischwa@sgi.net www.biospherical.com
On-line process control instrumentation including noninvasive level density systems
President: Bud Smith
VP of Marketing: Whit Little
Sales Manager: Aaron Tufts
Estimated Sales: $2.5-5 Million
Number Employees: 9
Square Footage: 60000

19354 BUCHI Corp
19 Lukens Dr # 400
Suite 400
New Castle, DE 19720-2787
302-652-8777
Fax: 302-225-2473 877-692-8844
us-sales@buchi.com www.buchi.com
Nutrition analysis systems
General Manager: Christopher Sopko
Finance Manager: Tony Casadei
Sales Director: John Pollard
Regional Sales Manager: Brad Miller
Regional Sales Manager: Charles Douglas
Estimated Sales: $5-10 Million
Number Employees: 20-49

19355 BUCHI Corp
19 Lukens Dr # 400
Suite 400
New Castle, DE 19720-2787
302-652-8777
Fax: 302-225-2473 877-692-8244
us-sales@buchi.com www.buchi.com
Lab instruments such as spray dryers, NIR spectroscopy instruments for quality control, solvent extraction equipment for food analysis, etc.
Finance Manager: Tony Casadei
Marketing Manager: Rudi Hartmann
Sales Director: John Pollard
Manager: Hodge Andy
   h.andy@genealogygoldmine.com
General Manager: Vahe Iplikci
Estimated Sales: $6.3 Million
Number Employees: 20-49

19356 BVL Controls
661, the Pit
Bois-Des-Filion, QC J6Z 4T2
Canada
450-965-0502
Fax: 450-965-8751 866-285-2668
info@bvlcontrols.com www.bvlcontrols.com
Manufacturer, importer and exporter of portion control and cooling equipment and supplies for beer, wine, soft drinks and liquors
President: Alvin Guerette
Controller: Josee Merchand
Vice President: Gilles Guerette
Estimated Sales: $1-3 Million
Number Employees: 10-19
Square Footage: 48000
Brands:
   Bvl
   Oberdorfer
   True Measure

19357 (HQ)BW Container Systems
1305 Lakeview Dr
Romeoville, IL 60446-3900
630-759-6800
Fax: 630-759-2299 sales@fleetinc.com
www.bwcontainersystems.com
Manufacturer and exporter of magnetic and specialized food handling and processing equipment including conveyors, capping, sealing, seaming, canning and food packing
Chairman of the Board: Robert H Chapman
CEO: Phil Ostapowicz
postapowicz@fgwa.com
CFO: David Brown
CEO: Phil Ostapowicz
VP Sales: Neil McConnellogue
Estimated Sales: $20 - 50 Million
Number Employees: 100-249
Square Footage: 200000
Parent Co: Barry-Wehmiller
Other Locations:
Fleetwood Systems
Orlando FL

19358 BW Controls
1080 North Crooks
Clawson, MI 48017
248-435-0700
Fax: 248-435-8120 800-635-0289
apt.orders@ametek.com www.ametekapt.com
Continuous and point level instruments, offering a line of 3-A approved magnetostictive level sensors
Manager: Bob Soeder
Bus Unit Manager: Robert Soeder
Business Development Director: Michael Geis
Estimated Sales: $5 Million
Number Employees: 100-249
Number of Brands: 4
Number of Products: 26
Square Footage: 520000

19359 BWI-PLC
1750 Corporate Drive
Suite 700
Norcross, GA 30093-2932
770-925-2004
800-605-6217
Packaging machinery, equipment and materials
Estimated Sales: $5-10 Million
Number Employees: 50

19360 BYK Gardner Inc
9104 Guilford Rd # 2
Columbia, MD 21046-2729
301-483-6500
Fax: 301-483-6555
Colors and color meters
VP: Mike Gogoel
Cio/Cto: Liza Wirkey
liza.wirkey@altana.com
General Manager: Mike Goegel
Estimated Sales: Over $1 Billion
Number Employees: 5000-9999

19361 Baader-Linco
2955 Fairfax Trfy
Kansas City, KS 66115-1317
913-621-3366
Fax: 913-621-1729 800-288-3434
www.baader.com
Designer, manufacturer and distributors of poultry and fish processing equipment.
President: Andy Miller
andy.miller@baaderna.com
Controller: Shaun Nicolas
Corporate Accounts/Sales Manager - US: Gehrig Chandler
Estimated Sales: $15.10 Million
Number Employees: 100-249
Square Footage: 13209
Parent Co: Baader Food Processing Machinery

19362 Babco International, Inc
911 S Tyndall
Tucson, AZ 85719
520-628-7596
Fax: 520-628-9622 contactus@babcotucson.com
www.babcotucson.com
Glassware, china, skirting, linen and silverware
Owner: Patrick Brodecky
patrick.brodecky@babcotucson.com
Marketing/Customer Service Director: Betsy Marco
Estimated Sales: $2.5-5 Million
Number Employees: 5-9

Brands:
Snap Drape
Syracuse

19363 Babcock & Wilcox MEGTEC
830 Prosper St
De Pere, WI 54115
920-336-5715
Manufacturer of environmental control technologies
Senior VP, B&W MEGTEC: Ken Zak
Parent Co: Babcock & Wilcox Enterprises

19364 Babcock & Wilcox Power Generation Group
20 S Van Buren Ave
Barberton, OH 44203-0351
330-753-4511
Fax: 330-860-1886 800-222-2625
slmccaulley@babcock.com www.babcock.com
Manufacturer and exporter of steam generation boilers and auxiliary equipment
President, COO: J. Randall Data
Senior Vice President, General Counsel,: James D. Canafax
SVP, CFO: Anthony S. Colatrella
SVP, Chief Administrative Officer: Kairus K. Tarapore
R&D Director: Stan Vecci
Manager Advertising: Phil Stillitano
Contact: Mel Albrecht
malbrecht@babcock.com
Director of Operation: Alan Nethery
Number Employees: 1,000-4,999
Parent Co: McDermott International

19365 Babcock Co
36 Delaware Ave
Bath, NY 14810-1607
607-776-3341
Fax: 607-776-7483 www.babcock.com
Manufacturer and exporter of small wooden crates
President: Marc Mc Connell
Sales/Marketing Executive: A Cranmer
Manager: Mike Bishop
Estimated Sales: $2.5-5 Million
Number Employees: 10-19
Square Footage: 154000

19366 Bacchus Wine Cellars
14027 Memorial Drive #228
Houston, TX 77079-9826
281-496-4495
Fax: 284-496-5855 800-487-8812
bacchuswinecellars.com
Manufacturer, importer and exporter of temperature and humidity controlled wine cellars, cabinets and storage equipment
President: Pierre Guinaudeau
Estimated Sales: Less than $500,000
Number Employees: 75
Square Footage: 40000
Brands:
Le Cellier

19367 Bacharach Inc
621 Hunt Valley Cir
New Kensington, PA 15068-7074
724-334-5000
Fax: 724-334-5001 800-736-4666
Help@MyBacharach.com www.mybacharach.com
Estimated Sales: $1 - 5 Million
Number Employees: 100-249

19368 Back Tech
388 2nd Avenue.
459
New York, NJ 10010
973-279-0838
Fax: 212-673-0386 backtech@liftsolutions.com
www.liftsolutions.com
Lightweight electrical lifting cart for up to 500 pounds, mobil, handling rolls and totes
Plant Manager: E Rydstedt
Estimated Sales: $1 000,000
Number Employees: 1-4

19369 Back to Basics
PO Box 2780
West Bend, WI 53095-0278
801-523-6500
800-688-1989
www.backtobasicsproducts.com
Confections, candy, equipment

Estimated Sales: $5 - 10 Million
Number Employees: 50-99
Brands:
Back To Basics
Hawaiice
Nutri Source
Peel Away

19370 Backus USA
602 W Dubois Ave
Suite 9
Du Bois, PA 15801
814-375-6999
Estimated Sales: $1 - 5 Million

19371 Backwoods Smoker Inc
8245 Dixie Shreveport Rd
Shreveport, LA 71107-8439
318-220-0380
Fax: 318-220-9022
backwoodssmoker@hughes.net
Meat smokers
Owner: Mike Mc Gowan
backwoodssmoker@hughes.net
VP: Charlene McGowan
Secy.: Larie McGowan
Estimated Sales: $1-2.5 Million
Number Employees: 1-4
Square Footage: 6000
Type of Packaging: Private Label
Brands:
Backwoods Smoker

19372 Bacon Products Corp
1605 Shepherd Rd
Chattanooga, TN 37421-2996
423-892-0414
Fax: 423-892-2065 800-251-6238
www.baconmail.com
Rodenticides and insecticides including pellets, glue traps, organic fly control products, ant, roach and spider spray, etc
Owner: Reed Bacon
jve@baconmail.com
R&D: Reed Bacon
Sales/Marketing: Karen Romito
VP of Production: James Edwards
Estimated Sales: $20 - 50 Million
Number Employees: 10-19
Brands:
Ant, Roach & Spider
Eagles-7
Final Bite!
Fly Eaters
Fly Ribbons
Last Step
Roach Destroyer
Septic Clean
Spray-Kill With Nylar
Wasp & Hornet Destroyer

19373 Baden Baden Food Equipment
3947 W Columbus Ave
Chicago, IL 60652
773-284-9009
Fax: 773-284-9109 877-368-8375
Sales of food and bakery equipment and wares
President: Vernon Condon
Contact: David Uhl
d.uhl@badenfoodequip.com
Estimated Sales: $1,500,000
Number Employees: 5-9
Square Footage: 12000

19374 Badger Meter Inc
4545 W Brown Deer Rd
P.O. Box 245036
Milwaukee, WI 53224
800-876-3837
www.badgermeter.com
Manufacturer and exporter of water meters and flowmeters.
President: Richard Meeusen
SVP & Chief Operating Officer: Kenneth Bockhorst
SVP, Finance/CFO/Treasurer: Richard Johnson
Vice President, Engineering: Fred Begale
VP/General Counsel/Secretary: Williams R.A. Bergum
VP, Business Development: Gregory Gomez
VP, Sales & Marketing: Kimberly Stoll
Vice President, Controller: Beverly L.P. Smiley
Vice President, Manufacturing: Raymond Serdynski
Vice President, Human Resources: Trina Jashinsky
Vice President, International Operations: Horst Gras

Year Founded: 1905
Estimated Sales: $100-500 Million
Number Employees: 1000-4999

19375 Badger Plug Co
N1045 Technical Dr
Greenville, WI 54942-8024

920-757-7300
Fax: 920-757-7339 sales@badgerplug.net
www.badgerplug.com
Plastic end plugs for cardboard tubes
President: Dan Voissem
dvoissem@badgerplug.net
Estimated Sales: $10 - 20 Million
Number Employees: 50-99

19376 Badger Wood Arts
PO Box 44698
Racine, WI 53404-7015

414-636-9902
Fax: 888-703-0383 800-331-9663
We design and produce food displays for retail point
of sale
Estimated Sales: $1 - 5 Million

19377 Bag Company
1650 Airport Rd NW
Suite 104
Kennesaw, GA 30144-7039

770-422-4187
Fax: 800-417-7273 800-533-1931
www.bagco.com
Manufacturer and exporter of polyethylene and
polypropylene bags; importer of plastic bags.
Director of Marketing: Katherine Remick
Estimated Sales: $13 Million
Number Employees: 10-19
Type of Packaging: Consumer

19378 Bag Masters
1540 19th St N
St Petersburg, FL 33713-5730

727-894-6797
Fax: 727-894-6734 800-330-2247
www.bagmastersusa.com
Converted and printed poly food and plastic bags
Owner: Eric Johannsen
eric@bagmastersusa.com
VP: Sandra Johannsen
General Manager: Eric Johannsen, Jr.
Estimated Sales: $1-2.5 Million
Number Employees: 10-19
Square Footage: 60000

19379 Bagcraft Papercon
3900 W 43rd St
Chicago, IL 60632-3490

773-254-8000
Fax: 773-254-8204 800-621-8468
www.bagcraft.com
Manufacturer and exporter of foil, film, paper, win-
dow and coffee bags and tin-tie
Vice President: Chuck Hathaway
chathaway@pkdy.com
Vice President, General Manager: Dan Vice
Director of Marketing: Barak Bright
Vice President of Sales: Chuck Hathaway
Customer Service Manager: Fredia Hess
chathaway@pkdy.com
Vice President - Operations: Grady Wetherington
Number Employees: 250-499
Square Footage: 1860000
Parent Co: Packaging Dynamics
Brands:
Cameo
Dubl-Fresh
Dubl-View
Dubl-Wax

19380 Bags Go Green
13 Ruths Place
Sequim, WA 98382

360-681-3876
Fax: 360-681-4877 info@bagsgogreen.com
www.bagsgogreen.com
Eco-friendly reusable bags
Marketing: Hena Marrero

19381 Bahnson Environmental Specs
4412 Tryon Rd
Raleigh, NC 27606-4246

919-829-9300
Fax: 919-833-9476 800-688-5859
jwalters@bahnson.com www.eschambers.com

Designs, manufactures, installs, and services a diverse line of controlled environmental chambers that
maintain precise conditions. We also offer a range of
enviornmental test and stability chambers designed
for high demand testing. Typical uses include stability, shelf life studies, freezing, refrigeration,
freeze-thaw and other product testing and/or
stability storage.
Business Development: John Walters
Number Employees: 50-99

19382 Bailey Moore Glazer Schaefer
16 Lunar Dr
Woodbridge, CT 06525-2397

203-397-7700
Fax: 203-397-7717 800-443-2362
www.baileymoore.com
Tea and coffee industry espresso machines and ac-
cessories, grinders
Partner: John Mooney
Manager: John J Mooney
Estimated Sales: Less than $500,000
Number Employees: 20-49

19383 Bailly Showcase & Fixture Company
2213 Paseo Ct
Las Vegas, NV 89117

702-947-6885
Fax: 323-232-6157
Store fixtures, cabinets and showcases
President: Gus Bailly
Estimated Sales: $1 - 2,500,000
Number Employees: 20

19384 (HQ)Baird & Bartlett Company
157 Green Street
Foxboro, MA 02035-2868

508-923-6400
Fax: 508-923-6060 800-752-4958
Cake collars and cardboard
President: Andrew Poce
CFO: George Whalen
Marketing Director: Andrew Londergan
Sales Director: Darck Ellwood
Plant Manager: Leo Sousa
Purchasing Manager: Lisa Omalley
Estimated Sales: $15 Million
Number Employees: 20
Square Footage: 60000
Type of Packaging: Consumer, Food Service, Pri-
vate Label, Bulk
Other Locations:
Baird & Bartlett Co.
Edison NJ

19385 Bake Star
1881 County Road C
Somerset, WI 54025-7508

763-427-7611
Fax: 763-323-9821 www.bakestar.com
Manufacturer and wholesaler/distributor of choco-
late spiral shavers, pre-depanners, semi-automatic
strawberry cappers, surplus topping removers and
UV surface sterilizers
CEO: Sherri Stumpl
President: Gary Hanson
R & D: Roger Hanson
Contact: Gary Hanson
grh230377@msn.com
General Manager: Laura Tuckner
Estimated Sales: Below $5 Million
Number Employees: 10
Square Footage: 36000

19386 Baker & Co
3541 Argonne Ave
Norfolk, VA 23509-2156

757-853-4325
Fax: 757-855-6252 800-909-4325
info@bakersheetmetal.com
www.bakersheetmetal.com
A fabrictor of custom and standard stainless steel
products including worktables, sinks, tables, workta-
bles and workstations, shelves and shelving,
countertops, furniture, range hoods, cabinets, galley
furniture, food service linespartitions
President: John Kronske
johnkronske@bakerco.com
Treasurer: Randy Bristow
CFO: R E Baker
Quality Control: C Winkler
Sales Director: John Kronske
Plant Manager: Paul Johnson

Estimated Sales: $10 - 20 Million
Number Employees: 50-99
Square Footage: 100000

19387 Baker Cabinet Co
2931 Grace Ln # C
Costa Mesa, CA 92626-4132

714-540-5515
Fax: 714-540-5515
Wood cabinets and store fixtures
Manager: Jim Thomas
bakercabinet@dslextreme.com
CEO: Tom Ouellette
Manager: Jim Thomas
bakercabinet@dslextreme.com
Estimated Sales: Less Than $500,000
Number Employees: 1-4

19388 Baker Concrete Construction
900 N Garver Rd
Monroe, OH 45050

513-539-4000
800-539-2224
www.bakerconcrete.com
Industrial concrete floor slab systems.
President: Brad Wucherpfennig
Exective Vice President: Tom Bell
President, Baker DC: Kenneth Fender
President, Northern Region: Todd Fox
Administration: Ben Goodin
President, Southwest Region: Jeff Miller
Human Resources: Mike Schneider
Year Founded: 1968
Estimated Sales: $856.94 Million
Number Employees: 1000-4999
Square Footage: 750000

19389 Baker Foodservice Design Inc
2220 East Paris Ave SE
Grand Rapids, MI 49546-6129

616-942-4011
Fax: 616-940-1415 800-968-4011
Marketing@BakerGroup.com
www.bakergroup.com
Award-winning foodservice consulting firm that has
provided expert support in evaluation, planning and
design for over two decades.
President/Principal: James Sukenik
consult@bakergroup.com
Estimated Sales: $1-2.5 Million
Number Employees: 5-9

19390 Baker Hughes
17021 Aldine Westfield
Houston, TX 77073

www.bakerhughes.com
Manufacturer and exporter of centrifuges and filters
for liquid/solid separations.
Chairman & CEO: Lorenzo Simonelli
CFO: Brian Worell
EVP, Turbomachinery & Process Solutions: Rod
Christie
Chief Marketing & Technology Officer: Derek
Mathieson
Year Founded: 1907
Estimated Sales: $22.8 Billion
Number Employees: 67,000

19391 Baker Perkins Inc
3223 Kraft Ave SE
Grand Rapids, MI 49512-2063

616-785-7500
Fax: 616-784-0973 800-458-2560
eriknadig@invensys.com www.bakerperkins.com
Manufacturer, importer and exporter of food pro-
cessing equipment including bakers and confection-
ers, mixing, forming, baking and product handling
equipment
Vice President: Paul Abbott
paul.abbott@bakerperkinsgroup.com
VP: John Lucas
R&D: Mark Glover
Marketing: Erik Nagig
VP Sales: Paul Abbott
Manager Process Optimization: Dan Smith
Number Employees: 50-99
Square Footage: 240000
Parent Co: APV plc

19392 Bakers Choice Products
4 Railroad Avenue Ext
Railroad Avenue Ext.
Beacon Falls, CT 6403
203-720-1000
Fax: 203-720-1004
Manufacturer, importer and exporter of sanitary food
containers and cups for candy, cookie and baking;
also, hot dog trays
Estimated Sales: $1 - 5 Million
Number Employees: 50-99
Square Footage: 120000
Parent Co: Reynolds Metals Company
Brands:
Baker's Choice
Chef's Choice

19393 Bakers Pride Oven Company
145 Huguenot St Ste Mz1
New Rochelle, NY 10801
914-576-0745
Fax: 914-576-0605 800-431-2745
sales@bakerspride.com www.bakerspride.com
Manufacturer and exporter of char-broilers and pizza
and counter top ovens
President: Hylton Jonas
VP: Tom Marston
Technical Writer: Daniel J Rivera
Quality Manager: Jim Ponnwitz
Estimated Sales: $20-50 Million
Number Employees: 100-249
Parent Co: APW/WYOTT Food Service Equipment
Brands:
Bakers Pride

19394 Bakery Associates
7 White Pine Ln
Setauket, NY 11733-3953
631-751-4156
Fax: 631-751-4156
Computerized bakery systems and commerical bak-
ery equipment including ovens, oven loaders and
unloaders
President: John Granger
wilcoven@aol.com
Estimated Sales: $1-2.5 Million
Number Employees: 10-19

19395 Bakery Crafts
P.O. Box 37
West Chester, OH 45071
513-942-0862
Fax: 513-942-3835 800-543-1673
Cake decorations: kits, edible decorations, candles,
and bakery supplies
President: San Guttman
Head of Marketing: Anne Rueho
Head of Sales: Keith Murcum
Contact: Shelley Adamson
s.adamson@bakerycrafts.com
Estimated Sales: $5 - 10 Million
Number Employees: 100-249

19396 Bakery Equipment Svc
118 Nevin Ave
Richmond, CA 94801-2900
800-842-4005
Fax: 510-236-7600 800-842-4005
www.bakery-equip.com
President: Kenneth Lind
Contact: Russell Cook
rcook@bakery-equip.com
Estimated Sales: $5 - 10 Million
Number Employees: 1-4

19397 Bakery Machinery & Fabrication
307 Bakery Ave
Peru, IL 61354
815-224-1306
Fax: 815-224-1396 www.bakerymachine.com
New and remanufactured bakery machinery for the
cookie, cracker, snack food and pet food industry
President: Cloyd Barnes
Estimated Sales: $1 - 2.5 000,000
Number Employees: 20-49

19398 Bakery Machinery Dealers
908 Colin Drive
Holbrook, NY 11741
631-567-6666
Fax: 631-567-6703
Bagel making and baking equipment
National Sales Manager: Rick Morrison

Number Employees: 12
Square Footage: 16000

19399 Bakery Refrigeration & Services
1125 Old Dixie Highway
Lake Park, FL 33403-2348
561-882-1655
Fax: 561-842-8106 waltman@flips.net
President: William Altman
Estimated Sales: Less than $500,000
Number Employees: 20-49

19400 Bakery Systems
7246 Beach Dr SW 1
Ocean Isle Beach, NC 28469
910-575-2253
Fax: 910-575-5057 800-526-2253
Importer, exporter and wholesaler/distributor of bak-
ery equipment nd supplies
President: Hayden O'Neil
patzcuaro@juno.com
Sales Manager: Lee Wagner
Estimated Sales: $2.5 Million
Number Employees: 5-9
Square Footage: 2000

19401 Bakeware Coatings
2915 Wilmarco Avenue
Baltimore, MD 21223-3223
410-664-2211
Fax: 410-664-1766
Coatings for baking pans and equipment

19402 Baking Machines
4577b Las Positas Road
Livermore, CA 94551-9615
925-449-3369
Fax: 925-449-2144 www.bakingmachines.com
Bagel, roll and variety systems, sheeter makeup
lines, tortilla equipment, troughs, elevators, baking
pans and carts, reciprocators, dustets, reservoirs,
etc.; also, custom design engineering services
available
President: James Long
VP of Sales: J William Long
Estimated Sales: $10-20 Million
Number Employees: 50-99
Square Footage: 30000

19403 Baking Technology Systems
5243 Royal Woods Pkwy # 120
Tucker, GA 30084-3081
770-270-5911
Fax: 770-270-5913
VP: Bob Miller
Sales Project Manager: Ben Marcum
Vice President, Director of Operations: Robert
Miller
Purchasing Manager: Glenda Arrington
Estimated Sales: $1 Million
Number Employees: 10-19

19404 Bakipan
9251 Van Horne Way
Richmond, BC V6X 1W2
Canada
604-278-1762
Fax: 604-278-3697
Estimated Sales: $1 - 5 Million

19405 Bakon Food Equipment
10117 Sepulveda Boulevard
Suite 205
Mission Hills, CA 91345-2600
818-895-7303
Fax: 818-892-1095 800-TRY-BAKO
Bakery equipment, glaze sprayers, chocolate ma-
chines, tartlet machine, whipping cream machine
Estimated Sales: 700000
Number Employees: 2

19406 Bal Seal Engineering Inc
19650 Pauling
Foothill Ranch, CA 92610-2610
949-460-2100
Fax: 949-460-2300 800-366-1006
sales@balseal.com www.balseal.com
Manufacturer and exporter of spring loaded PTFE
seals
President: Rob Sjostedt
CEO: Rick Dawson
rdawson@balseal.com
Sales Director: Michael Anderson

Estimated Sales: $20 - 50 Million
Number Employees: 250-499

19407 Bal/Foster Glass Container Company
1 Glass Pl
Port Allegany, PA 16743-1154
814-642-2521
Fax: 814-642-3204 www.sgcontainers.com
Manufacturer and exporter of glass bottles and jars
Plant Manager: Ed Stewart
Estimated Sales: $1 - 5 Million
Number Employees: 250-499

19408 Balchem Corp
52 Sunrise Park Rd
New Hampton, NY 10958
845-326-5600
www.balchem.com
Extensive line of encapsulated ingredients.
Chairman & CEO: Ted Harris
CFO: Martin Bengtsson
Year Founded: 1967
Estimated Sales: $100-500 Million

19409 Baldewein Company
9109 Belden Avenue
Lake Forrest, IL 60045
847-455-1686
Fax: 847-455-1706 800-424-5544
info@baldeweinco.com www.baldeweinco.com
Manufacturer and exporter of food processing
equipment including sanitary fittings, pumps,
valves, hose assemblies, brushes, steelware and
steam and water mixers
President: Valentin R Baldewein Jr
Sales: Tina Sanders
Treasurer: Val Baldwewin
Estimated Sales: Below $5 Million
Number Employees: 10
Square Footage: 40000
Brands:
Alpha Laval Flo
Lightnin
S.S.
S.S. Ware
Sani-Tech
Sparta
Strahman
Thermo-Tech
Tri-Clover
Vollrath

19410 Baldor Electric Co
5711 Rs Boreham Jr St
P.O. Box 2400
Fort Smith, AR 72901-8394
479-646-4711
Fax: 479-648-5792 www.baldor.com
Marketers, designers and manufacturers of industrial
electric motors, mechanical power transmission
products, drive and generators, specializing in prod-
ucts for the food and pharmaceutical industries. A
member of the ABB group since 2011.
CEO: Ronald Tucker
rtucker@baldor.com
VP, Finance and Corporate Secretary: Larry
Johnston
EVP: Edward Ralston
VP, Channel Management: Chris Keyser
VP Marketing: Tracy Long
Vice President, Sales: Randy Colip
COO, Baldor Operations: Wayne Thurman
Estimated Sales: Over $1 Billion
Number Employees: 5000-9999
Square Footage: 4000000

19411 Baldor Electric Co
5711 Rs Boreham Jr St
P.O. Box 2400
Fort Smith, AR 72901-8394
479-646-4711
Fax: 479-648-5792 800-241-2886
rjfleig@ra.rockwell.com www.baldor.com
Controls, energy management
CEO: Ronald E Tucker
rtucker@baldor.com
Chief Engineer: Alex McCutcheon
Estimated Sales: Over $1 Billion
Number Employees: 5000-9999

19412 Baldwin Richardson Foods

#2390, One Tower Lane
Oakbrook Terrace, IL 60181

866-644-2732
www.brfoods.com

Liquid ingredient manufacturer specializing in signature sauces, dessert toppings, beverage and pancake syrups, specialty fruit fillings and condiments. the company also offers processing options such as hot-fill, cold-fillhomogenization, and emulsion.
President & CEO: Eric Johnson
Chief Financial Officer: Evelyn White
Sr. Director of Sales: Cara Hughes
Year Founded: 1916
Estimated Sales: $5 - 10,000,000
Number Employees: 200 - 500
Square Footage: 900000
Type of Packaging: Consumer, Food Service, Private Label, Bulk
Other Locations:
Macedon Manufacturing Facility
Macedon NY
Williamson Manufacturing
East Williamson NY
Brands:
Mrs. Richardson Toppings
Nance's Mustards

19413 Baldwin Supply Co

2306 Washington Ave N
Minneapolis, MN 55411-2223

612-338-5070
Fax: 612-338-4877 800-897-1964
ghansen@baldwinsupply.com
www.baldwinsupply.com

President: Dave LA Rue
dave@baldwinsupply.com
Estimated Sales: $3 - 5 Million
Number Employees: 10-19

19414 Baldwin/Priesmeyer

1235 Hanley Industrial Ct
Saint Louis, MO 63144

314-535-2800
Fax: 314-535-2887 www.baldwinflags.com

Banners, flags, flagpoles and advertising specialties
Manager: Jim Schaper
CFO: Jannet Alexander
VP: Jim Schaper
Estimated Sales: $30-50 Million
Number Employees: 5-9
Parent Co: Baldwin Regalia

19415 Balemaster

980 Crown Ct
Crown Point, IN 46307-2732

219-663-4525
Fax: 219-663-4591 sales@balemaster.com

Automatic horizontal balers
President: Cornel Raab Jr
Cmo: Mike Connell
sales@balemaster.com
VP Sales/Marketing: Samuel Finlay
Estimated Sales: $300,000-500,000
Number Employees: 100-249

19416 Ball Corp

10 Longs Peak Dr
Broomfield, CO 80021

303-469-3131
info@ball.com
www.ball.com

Aluminum and steel beverage and food containers; also, lids, metal plastic food and beverage packaging, steel household packaging, plastic pails, ball aerospace.
Chairman/President/CEO: John Hayes
VP/General Counsel/Corporate Secretary: Charles Baker
VP/Controller: Nate Carey
SVP/Chief Financial Officer: Scott Morrison
SVP/Chief Operating Officer: Daniel Fisher
SVP: Robert Strain
SVP, Human Resources & Administration: Lisa Pauley
VP, Communications & Corp. Relations: Courtney Reynolds
Year Founded: 1880
Estimated Sales: $11 Billion
Number Employees: 18,300
Type of Packaging: Consumer, Food Service, Private Label

19417 Ball Design Group

1170 E Champlain Dr # 120
Suite 120
Fresno, CA 93720-5026

559-434-6100
Fax: 559-447-8596 john@balldesign.com
www.balldesign.com

Log and brand mark design, advertising website design, package and label design, and trade show displays for the produce and fruit industry
President: John Ball
john@balldesign.com
Estimated Sales: Less Than $500,000
Number Employees: 1-4

19418 Ball Foster Glass Container Company

1000 N Mission St
Sapulpa, OK 74066-3149

918-224-1440
Fax: 918-224-5280 us.verallia.com

Soft drink and tea glass bottles
Quality Control: Robert Beets
Plant Manager: Pat Hogan
Estimated Sales: $1 - 5 Million
Number Employees: 250-499
Square Footage: 4800000
Parent Co: American National Can Company

19419 Ball Glass Container Corporation

4000 Arden Drive
El Monte, CA 91731-1806

626-448-9831
Fax: 626-279-3225

Glass jars, bottles and containers
Plant Manager: Rich O'Neil
Estimated Sales: $50-100 Million
Number Employees: 250-499
Parent Co: St. Gobain

19420 (HQ)Ballantyne Food Service Equipment

4350 McKinley St
Omaha, NE 68112

402-453-4444
Fax: 402-453-7238 800-424-1215
www.ballantyne-omaha.com

Manufacturer and exporter of commercial restaurant equipment including electric pressure and gas pressure fryers, gourmet grills, cook and hold barbecue ovens, smokers and rotisseries
President/CEO: John Wilmers
Senior VP: Ray Boegner
VP: Michael Nulty
Estimated Sales: $1 - 5 Million
Number Employees: 100-249
Square Footage: 400000
Parent Co: Ballantyne of Omaha
Type of Packaging: Food Service, Private Label
Brands:
Ballatyne
Ballatyne Smokers
Bpe 2000

19421 Ballard & Wolfe Company

519 Interstate 30 #102
Rockwall, TX 75087-5408

214-704-8451
Fax: 817-652-1245 dbruner@ballardwolfe.com
www.ballardwolfe.com

Ice cream equipment
Estimated Sales: Below 1 Million
Number Employees: 2

19422 Balluff Inc

8125 Holton Dr
Florence, KY 41042-3009

859-727-2200
Fax: 859-727-4823 800-543-8390
balluff@balluff.com

Sensor, transducers and ID systems for automation
CEO: Chad Bramer
cbramer@bannerengineering.com
CEO: Kent Howard
Number Employees: 100-249

19423 (HQ)Bally Block Co

30 S 7th St
30 South Seventh Street
Bally, PA 19503-9665

610-845-7511
Fax: 610-845-7726 bbc@ballyblock.com
www.butcherblock.com

Manufacturer and exporter of cutting benches, blocks, tables and boards
President: James Reichart
Vice President of Sales and Marketing: Joe Barbercheck
Vice President Sales & Marketing: Pat Stanley
Vice President, Production: Emmet Wood
Estimated Sales: $5-10 Million
Number Employees: 50-99
Square Footage: 500000

19424 Bally Refrigerated Boxes Inc

135 Little Nine Rd
Morehead City, NC 28557-8483

252-240-2829
Fax: 252-240-0384 800-242-2559
ballysales@ballyrefboxes.com
www.ballyrefboxes.com

Walk-in cooler and freezers, refrigerated buildings, modular structures, blast chillers and refrigeration for the foodservice and scientific industries.
President: Michael Coyle
cm@ballyrefboxes.com
Sales Manager: William Strompf
Plant Manager: Alan Summers
Purchasing Manager: William Stomps
Estimated Sales: $20-50 Million
Number Employees: 250-499
Parent Co: United Refrigeration
Type of Packaging: Food Service
Other Locations:
Bally Refrigerated Boxes
King of Prussia PA
Brands:
Thermo-Plug

19425 Ballymore Company

220 Garfield Ave
West Chester, PA 19380-4512

610-696-3250
Fax: 610-593-8615 www.ballymore.com

Safety ladders, hydraulic lifts and special work platforms
Manager: Tom Richardson
Estimated Sales: $5 - 10 Million
Number Employees: 20-49

19426 Baltimore Aircoil Co

7600 Dorsey Run Rd
Jessup, MD 20794-9328

410-799-1300
Fax: 410-799-6416 info@baltimoreaircoil.com
www.baltimoreaircoil.com

Manufacturer and marketer of heat transfer and ice thermal storage products that conserve resources and respect the environment.
President: Steve Duerwachter
Contact: Glenn Babcock
amy@aafame.ccsend.com
Estimated Sales: $17 Million
Number Employees: 20-49
Parent Co: Amsted Industries
Brands:
Bacount
Bacross
Baltibond
Baltidrive
Easy Connect
Ejector
Energy Miser
High K
Ice Chiller
Ice Logic
Iobio
M Logic

19427 Baltimore Aircoil Co

7600 Dorsey Run Rd
Jessup, MD 20794-9328

410-799-1300
Fax: 410-799-6416 info@baltimoreaircoil.com
www.baltaircoil.com

President: Steve Duerwachter
Quality Control: John Hawkins
CFO: Robert Landstra
Contact: Glenn Babcock
amy@aafame.ccsend.com
Number Employees: 20-49

19428 Baltimore Sign Company

472 Cedar Haven Road
Arnold, MD 21012-1167

410-276-1500
Fax: 410-675-2420 www.baltimoresign.com

Signs, banners, displays, etc.; also, screen process and offset printing and collation
President: John Ferretti
Plant Manager: Hank Barret
Account Director: Kathie Schisler
Estimated Sales: $5 - 10 Million
Number Employees: 50-99

19429 Baltimore Spice Inc
9740 Reisterstown Rd
Owings Mills, MD 21117-4155
410-363-3209
Fax: 410-363-6619 800-376-0316
www.fuchsna.com
Spices
President: Jack M Irvin Jr
CEO: Del Almonia
padc@pworld.com
R&D: Elizabeth Morris
Quality Control: Joe Walters
Estimated Sales: $5 - 10 Million
Number Employees: 1-4

19430 Baltimore Tape ProductsInc
27 W Obrecht Rd
Sykesville, MD 21784-7702
410-795-0063
Printed and converted pressure sensitive labels and tape
Owner: Jeff Remmel
jeff.remmel@trw.com
Estimated Sales: Less Than $500,000
Number Employees: 1-4
Square Footage: 2000

19431 Bambeck Systems Inc
1921 Carnegie Ave # 3a
Santa Ana, CA 92705-5510
949-250-3100
Fax: 949-757-1610 800-334-3101
www.bambecksystems.com
President: Robert Bambeck
rjbambeck@bambecksystems.com
CFO: Anthony Fazzio
Quality Control: Anthony Fazzio
Estimated Sales: $5 - 10 Million
Number Employees: 20-49

19432 Bamco Belting
6 Andrews St
PO Box 8678
Greenville, SC 29601-3902
864-269-9750
Fax: 864-269-9754 800-258-2358
sales@bamcobelting.com www.bamcobelting.com
Distributor of flat transmission belting and textile, conveyor belting, and hose belt conveyors
President: Leonard Chace
Estimated Sales: $5 - 10 Million
Number Employees: 10-19
Type of Packaging: Bulk

19433 Bancroft Bag Inc
425 Bancroft Blvd
West Monroe, LA 71292-5703
318-387-2550
Fax: 318-324-2318 bbisales@bancroftbag.com
www.bancroftbag.com
Paper bags
President: Louis Rothschild
lrothschild@bancroftbag.com
Executive Assistant: Teresa Lucas
Estimated Sales: $50 - 100 Million
Number Employees: 250-499

19434 Banner Chemical Co
111 Hill St
Orange, NJ 07050-3901
973-676-0105
Fax: 973-676-4564 info@bannerchemical.com
www.bannerchemical.com
Cleaning products and sanitary maintenance chemicals including glass cleaners, floor cleaners, wates and strippers, kitchen and bathroom cleaners, disinfectants and many other chemicals for food service and industry.
President: Stanley Reichel
bannerchem@aol.com
VP: David Herman
Estimated Sales: $2.5 - 5 Million
Number Employees: 5-9

19435 Banner Day
1840 N Michigan Ave # 1
Saginaw, MI 48602-5562
989-755-0584
Fax: 989-775-1309 info@banner-day.com
www.banner-day.com
CEO: Joseph Day
joeday@banner-day.com
Project Engineer: Brian Lewis
Estimated Sales: $5 - 10 Million
Number Employees: 10-19

19436 Banner Engineering Corp
9714 10th Ave N
Minneapolis, MN 55441-5093
763-544-3164
Fax: 763-544-3123 888-373-6767
www.bannerengineering.com
Photoelectric sensor, safety light curtains, ultrasonics, measurement and inspection sensors, safety modules, safety switches, fiber optics and vision sensors
CEO: Ty Fayfield
CFO: Jason Pitts
Estimated Sales: $50-100 Million
Number Employees: 250-499
Square Footage: 100000
Brands:
   A Gage
   Beam-Array
   Beam-Tracker
   Duo-Touch
   Econo-Beam
   Ez-Beam
   Ez-Beam
   Ez-Screen
   L Gage
   Machine-Guard
   Maxi-Amo
   Maxi-Beam
   Micro-Amp
   Micro-Screen
   Mini-Array
   Mini-Beam
   Mini-Screen
   Multi-Beam
   Multi-Screen
   Omni-Beam
   Opto Touch
   Pico Guard
   Picodot
   Presence Plus
   Thin-Pak
   Ultra-Beam
   Ultra-Beam
   Vall-Beam
   Valu-Beam
   World-Beam

19437 Banner Equipment Co
1370 Bungalow Rd
Morris, IL 60450-8929
815-941-9600
Fax: 815-941-9700 800-621-4625
internetsales@bannerbeer.com
www.bannerbeer.com
Manufacturer and exporter of draft beer tapping and dispensing equipment
President: Jim Groh
jgroh@bannerbeer.com
VP: Michael Tannhauser
Estimated Sales: $10 - 20 Million
Number Employees: 20-49
Square Footage: 80000
Brands:
   Insta-Balance
   Perfecta Line
   Perfecta Pour

19438 Banner Idea
1400 Quail St
Newport Beach, CA 92660-2730
949-559-6600
Fax: 949-559-0861
Flags, pennants, banners and signs
Estimated Sales: less than $500,000
Number Employees: 5-9

19439 Bannerland
13360 Firestone Blvd Ste Ee
Santa Fe Springs, CA 90670-7040
Fax: 714-554-0579 800-654-0294
bannerland@aol.com

Banners, flags and poly pennants; also, silk screening available
Manager: Travis Townsend
Marketing/Sales: Terry Melanson
Plant Manager: Mike Slater
Estimated Sales: $26 Million
Number Employees: 10-19
Square Footage: 10000
Parent Co: AAA Flag & Banner

19440 Bar Equipment Corporation of America
7300 Flores Street
Downey, CA 90242
323-838-1770
Fax: 323-838-1778 888-870-2322
sales@lynxgrills.com www.lynxgrills.com
Bar equipment including undercounter refrigerators, bottle coolers, mug frosters and hand sinks
President: Michael Edwards
Director Sales: Dale Seiden
Estimated Sales: $3 - 5 Million
Number Employees: 5-9

19441 Bar Keepers Friend Cleanser
5240 Walt Pl
Indianapolis, IN 46254-5795
317-636-7760
Fax: 317-264-2192 800-433-5818
www.barkeepersfriend.com
Manufacturer and exporter of powdered and liquid cleansers for the removal of rust, lime, stains and mildew; also, polishes, bathroom and toilet bowl cleaners
President: Nick Childers
nchilders@barkeepersfriend.com
VP Sales: Tony Patterson
Estimated Sales: $20 - 50 Million
Number Employees: 20-49
Square Footage: 30000
Parent Co: SerVaas
Type of Packaging: Consumer, Private Label
Brands:
   Bar Keepers Friend
   Copper Glo
   Just 'n Time
   Shiny Sinks Plus

19442 Bar Maid Corp
2950 NW 22nd Ter
Pompano Beach, FL 33069-1045
954-960-1468
Fax: 954-960-1647 info@barmaidwashers.com
www.barmaidwashers.com
Manufacturer and exporter of portable, submersible and upright electric glass and muffin pan washers; also, low-sud detergents and sanitizers
President: George E Shepherd
CEO: Diane Michaud
diane@barmaidwashers.com
Marketing Director: Tammie Rice
Estimated Sales: Below $5 Million
Number Employees: 10-19
Number of Brands: 2
Square Footage: 16000
Brands:
   Bar Maid
   Losuds

19443 Bar NA, Inc.
PO Box 6599
Champaign, IL 61826-6599
217-687-4810
Fax: 217-687-4830 www.baraninc.com
Manufacturer, distribution and installation of small to medium capacity equipment for soy foods and vegetable oilseeds production and processing
President: Ramlakhan Boodram
Estimated Sales: $1-2.5 Million
Number Employees: 10-19

19444 Bar-B-Q Woods
800 E 14th Street
Newton, KS 67114-5700
316-284-0300
Fax: 316-283-8371 800-528-0819
www.flavorwood.com
Compressed wood in a can which is heated in a home Bar-B-Q grill to produce natural smoke blowing
President: Gary Hawkey
CEO: James Beery

Estimated Sales: $1-2.5,000,000
Number Employees: 4
Square Footage: 10000
Type of Packaging: Consumer, Food Service, Private Label, Bulk

19445 Bar-Maid Corp
362 Midland Ave # 1
Garfield, NJ 07026-1736

973-478-7070
Fax: 973-478-2106 800-227-6243
www.bar-maid.com
Refrigerators, minibars and freezers.
President: George Steele
CEO: James Steele
Vice President: John Steele
Marketing Director: Ken Lasini
Sales Director: K Zanda
Public Relations: Mike Castle
Estimated Sales: $50-100 Million
Number Employees: 50-99
Square Footage: 80000
Brands:
  Bar-Maids

19446 Bar-Ron Industries
58 Bryant Drive
Livingston, NJ 07039-1725

973-535-1406
Fax: 973-597-1996 www.grillit.com
Owner: Barry N Rein
Sales: Cindy Blanga
Sales: Rafi Blanga
Estimated Sales: $3 - 5 Million
Number Employees: 20-49
Brands:
  Grillit 1200
  Grillit 12x12

19447 Barbeque Wood Flavors Enterprises
141 Lyons Road
Ennis, TX 75119

972-875-8391
Fax: 972-875-8872
Manufacturer and exporter of wood firelogs
President and CEO: George C Wartsbaugh
Sales Manager: Charles Wartsbaugh
Estimated Sales: $5 - 10 Million
Number Employees: 10
Square Footage: 92000
Parent Co: Stephen Weber Production Company

19448 Barbour Threads
128 W 7th St
Anniston, AL 36201-5645

256-237-9461
Fax: 256-237-0646
Industrial nets and sports nets
President: Tony Foran
Plant Manager: Jim Landers
Estimated Sales: $5 - 10 Million
Number Employees: 50-99
Square Footage: 848000

19449 Barclay & Assoc PC
1525 Airport Rd # 101
Suite 101
Ames, IA 50010-8231

515-292-3023
Fax: 515-292-3053 tmbarclay@aol.com
Consultant providing automation solutions
President: T Michael Barclay
Contact: Dori Gass
  dori@drbarclay.com
Estimated Sales: Less Than $500,000
Number Employees: 1-4
Brands:
  Margin Minder Software
  Watch Dog

19450 Barco Inc
3059 Premiere Pkwy
Duluth, GA 30097-4905

678-475-8000
Fax: 678-475-8100 www.barco.com
Optical and X-ray sorting inspection equipment
President: Mohammad Abu-Dalou
  mohammad.abu-dalou@barco.com
Operations: Danny Claeys
VP Sales/Marketing: Richard McConeghy
Estimated Sales: $5-10 Million
Number Employees: 250-499
Parent Co: Barco

Brands:
  Elbicon
  Pulsarr

19451 Barco Inc
3078 Prospect Park Dr
Rancho Cordova, CA 95670-6000

888-414-7226
Fax: 916-376-0318 888-414-7226
www.ready2escape.com
President & Chief Executive Officer: Eric Van Zele
Chief Financial Officer: Carl Peeters
GM International Sales: Ney Corsino
Chief Human Resources Officer: Jan Van Acoleyen
Chief Operating Officer: Filip Pintelon
Estimated Sales: Less Than $500,000
Number Employees: 1-4
Parent Co: Barco

19452 Barcoding Inc
2220 Boston St # 2
Fl 2
Baltimore, MD 21231-3205

410-385-8532
Fax: 410-385-8559 888-412-7226
info@barcoding.com www.barcoding.com
Barcoding Inc works with companies within the Food and Beverage Industry to streamline their operations through the implementation of barcode and RFID systems.
CEO: Jay Steinmetz
  jay@barcoding.com
Media/Public Relations: Jon Stroz
Number Employees: 50-99
Type of Packaging: Consumer

19453 Bardes Plastics Inc
5225 W Clinton Ave
Milwaukee, WI 53223-4782

414-354-5300
Fax: 414-354-6331 800-558-5161
sales@bardesplastics.com
www.bardesplastics.com
Plastic and display boxes, lids, covers, food trays, sleeves, beaded rounds and cylindrical trays
President: Michael Heyer
CEO: Randolph Hamner
Sales: Steve Kopiske
Estimated Sales: $5-10 Million
Number Employees: 20-49
Square Footage: 160000
Type of Packaging: Consumer, Food Service, Private Label, Bulk

19454 Bardo Abrasives
1666 Summerfield St
Ridgewood, NY 11385

718-456-6400
Fax: 718-366-2104 www.bardoabrasives.com
Manufacturer and exporter of blending, finishing and buffing wheels for food processing equipment
President: Edwin F Doyle
VP: Ted Wood
Estimated Sales: $20 - 50 Million
Number Employees: 100-249
Square Footage: 90000
Parent Co: Barker Brothers
Brands:
  Bardo Flex
  Bardo Flex Deburring Wheels
  Barker Buffs

19455 Bargreen Ellingson
6626 Tacoma Mall Blvd # B
Tacoma, WA 98409-9002

253-722-2600
Fax: 253-896-3620 800-322-4441
www.bargreen.com
Restaurant equipment and supplies; interior and engineering design services available
Owner: Paul G Ellingson
  paul.ellingson@bargreen.com
President: Paul G Ellingson
Estimated Sales: $20 - 50 Million
Number Employees: 10-19

19456 Bargreen Ellingson
2925 70th Avenue East
Fife, WA 98424

425-740-2424
Fax: 425-740-2432 866-722-2665
Restaurant equipment, restaurant supplies, kitchen supplies, bar supplies, janitorial supplies, disposables, and restaurant design services.

President: Howard Bargreen
Sales Manager: Josh Pugh
Contact: Brie Adair
  b.adair@bargreen.com
Estimated Sales: $10-20 Million
Number Employees: 10-19
Parent Co: American Restaurant Supply
Brands:
  Bargreens
  Cafe Amore
  Golden Drip

19457 Barker Company
703 Franklin St
P.O. Box 478
Keosauqua, IA 52565

319-293-3777
Fax: 319-293-3776 www.barkercompany.com
Manufacturer and importer of refrigerated, hot and dry display cases
President: Pat Mahon
Contact: Amanda Brauns
  amanda.brauns@barkercompany.com
Estimated Sales: $10 - 20,000,000
Number Employees: 250-499
Square Footage: 84000

19458 Barker Wire
708 Water St
Keosauqua, IA 52565-7711

319-293-3176
Fax: 319-293-3182 www.barkerwire.com
Custom wire shelves, baskets and racks
Sales Manager: Roy Abriani
Plant Manager: Larry Begley
Estimated Sales: $10-20 Million
Number Employees: 50-99
Square Footage: 580000
Parent Co: Angola Wire Products
Other Locations:
  Barker Wire Products
  Angola IN

19459 Barkley Filing Supplies
PO Box 15789
Hattiesburg, MS 39404-5789

601-545-2200
Fax: 800-423-7589 800-647-3070
Stationery including envelopes and pressure sensitive labels
President: Joseph Compitello
Number Employees: 475

19460 Barksdale Inc
3211 Fruitland Ave
Vernon, CA 90058-3757

323-589-6181
Fax: 323-589-3463 mmueller@barksdale.com
www.barksdale.com
President: Ian Dodd
CFO: Dave Hefler
  dave.hefler@barksdale.com
Estimated Sales: $20,000,000 - $49,999,999
Number Employees: 100-249
Parent Co: Crane Company

19461 Barliant & Company
319 E Van Emmon St
Yorkville, IL 60560

630-553-6992
Fax: 630-553-6908 barliant@aol.com
www.barliant.com
Domestic and export broker of new and used food processing equipment including meat and poultry, as well as appraisals, liquidations, auctions and asset management programs.
Owner: Scott Swanson
Sales Manager: Kevin Chapman
Contact: Tom Baumgartner
  tom@centralice.com
Estimated Sales: $1.5 Million
Number Employees: 5
Square Footage: 152000

19462 Barlo Signs
158 Greeley St
Hudson, NH 03051-3422

603-880-8949
Fax: 603-882-7680 800-227-5674
www.barlosigns.com
Electric and interior point of purchase signs; also, screen printing available
President: Arthur Bartlett

Estimated Sales: $10-20 Million
Number Employees: 250-499
Parent Co: Barlo Group

19463 Barn Furniture Mart
6206 Sepulveda Blvd
Van Nuys, CA 91411-1110

818-785-4253
Fax: 818-785-4564 888-302-2276
www.barnfurnituremart.com
Manufacturer and exporter of chairs, barstools, bars, tables and booths; custom designing services available
Owner: Leon Tuberman
manya3@aol.com
VP: Leon Tuberman
Number Employees: 20-49
Square Footage: 840000

19464 Barnant Company
28092 W Commercial Ave
Lake Barrington, IL 60010

847-381-7050
Fax: 847-381-7053 800-637-3739
barnant@barnant.com www.barnant.com
Thermometers, tubing and vacuum pumps, controllers, data loggers, flow meters and mixers, and OEM pumps
President: Duncan Ross
Marketing: Greg Johnson
Marketing Director: Gregg Johnson
Contact: Jan Stadt
stadtj@barnant.com
Estimated Sales: $20-50 Million
Number Employees: 100-249

19465 Barnes Machine Company
2462 Emerson Avenue S
Saint Petersburg, FL 33712-1644

727-327-9452
Fax: 727-323-8791
Packaging machinery including carton erecting, closing, paper box, carton case, box sealing, etc
President: John Barnes
barnesmco@aol.com
CFO: Carla Barnes
Quality Control: John Barnes
Estimated Sales: Below $5 Million
Number Employees: 10 to 19
Square Footage: 30000
Brands:
Barnes Machine Company Bamco

19466 Barnstead/Thermolyne Corporation
P.O. Box 797
Dubuque, IA 52004-0797

563-556-2241
Fax: 563-589-0516 800-553-0039
www.barnstead.com
Laboratory equipment
President: Duncan Ross
CEO: Guy Broadband
Quality Control: Mike Reagan
Marketing Communication Officer: Kathy Regan
Estimated Sales: $50 - 100 Million
Number Employees: 250-499

19467 Baron Spices Inc
1440 Kentucky Ave
St Louis, MO 63110-3817

314-535-9020
Fax: 314-535-7227 sales@baronspices.com
www.baronspices.com
Wholesaler/distributor and contract packager of spices, seasonings, herbs, flavors and extracts
President: Tim Weigers
tewiegers@baronspices.com
Estimated Sales: $5-10 Million
Number Employees: 20-49
Number of Products: 300
Square Footage: 220000
Type of Packaging: Food Service, Private Label, Bulk
Brands:
Baron

19468 Barr Engineering Co
4700 W 77th St # 200
Minneapolis, MN 55435-4820

952-832-2600
Fax: 952-832-2601 800-632-2277
askbarr@barr.com www.barrengineering.com
Consulting engineering services

President: Doug Connell
R&D: Karin Clemon
CEO: Doug Conell
CFO: Terry Krohnverg
Contact: Lisa Andrews
eandrews@barr.com
Estimated Sales: $20 - 30 Million
Number Employees: 1-4

19469 Barr Refrigeration
1423 Planeview Dr
Oshkosh, WI 54904-9101

920-231-1711
Fax: 920-231-1701 888-661-0871
info@barrinc.com www.barrinc.com
Refrigeration equipment
VP, Sales: Erick Alatorre
Estimated Sales: $2,500,000 - $4,999,999
Number Employees: 20-49

19470 Barr Storage
1423 Planeview Dr
Oshkosh, WI 54904-9101

920-230-2600
Fax: 920-231-1701 888-661-0871
info@barrinc.com www.barrstorage.com
Refrigeration equipment
Owner: Thomas Barr
info@barrinc.com
Vice President: Jamie Barr
VP Marketing: Steve Morehead
Number Employees: 20-49

19471 Barr-Rosin
92 Boulevard Prevost
Boisbriand, QC J7G 2S2
Canada

450-437-5252
Fax: 450-437-6740 800-561-8305
sales.barr-rosin.ca@gea.com
President: Dell Lonvrgan
Quality Control: Haldgoudrvaulg Goudrvaulg
R & D: Paull Goudrvaulg
Number Employees: 10

19472 Barrette Outdoor Living
7830 Freeway Cir
Cleveland, OH 44130-6307

440-891-0790
Fax: 440-891-5267 800-336-2383
www.barretteoutdoorliving.com
Manufacturer and exporter of structural foam products, regular and tote trays, pallets, carts, plant displays, produce tables, lattice panels, plastic trellises, plastic arbors and plastic fencing
President: Karin Golan
karin.golan@us.ebarrette.com
CFO: Nick Kokotovich
Vice President: William Goslin
Marketing Director: Ron Smith
Sales Director: John Payne
Product Manager: Mark Sprague
Purchasing Manager: Steve Armstrong
Number Employees: 1000-4999
Square Footage: 1400000

19473 Barrington Nutritionals
500 Mamaroneck Avenue
Harrison, NY 10528

914-381-3500
Fax: 914-381-2232 800-684-2436
info@barringtonchem.com
www.barringtonchem.com
Offers custom granulation, blending and particle size reduction of products for the vitamin/nutrition industry
Owner: Stuart Gelbard
Vice President: Vice President
Controller: Cathy Annattone
cathyannattone@barringtonnutritionals.com *Year Founded:* 1991
Other Locations:
Utah Office
Bountiful UT

19474 Barrington Packaging Systems Group
500 Mamaroneck Ave # 201
Harrison, NY 10528-1636

914-381-3500
Fax: 914-381-2232 888-814-7999
sales@bpsgusa.com
Supplier of packaging equipment.

President: George Burny
Vice President - Marketing: Tom McClure
Sales Executive: Brian Fuller
Digital Data & eMarketing Director: Danny Lena
Chief Operating Officer: Larry Pence
Number Employees: 5-9

19475 Barrow-Agee Laboratories Inc
1555 Three Pl
Memphis, TN 38116-3507

901-332-1590
Fax: 901-398-1518 mhawkins@balabs.com
www.balabs.com
Analytical testing firm offering chemical and microbiological services
President: Lynn Hawkins
lhawkins@balabs.com
VP: Mike Hawkins
VP: John Peden
Estimated Sales: $2.5-5 Million
Number Employees: 20-49

19476 Barrow-Agee Laboratories Inc
1555 Three Pl
Memphis, TN 38116-3507

901-332-1590
Fax: 901-398-1518 customerservice@balabs.com
www.balabs.com
Private analytical laboratory
President and CEO: Lynn Hawkins
lhawkins@balabs.com
Estimated Sales: $5 - 10 Million
Number Employees: 20-49

19477 Barry Wehmiller DesignGroup
P.O. Box 245
New London, NH 3257

603-526-2585
Fax: 603-526-9468 866-526-2585
Full service engineering, architectural and construction management firm specializing in the food and beverage industry
President: Robert Stahlman
VP: Scott Pribula
Marketing: Scott Pribula
Estimated Sales: $5-10 Million
Number Employees: 50-99
Square Footage: 15000

19478 Barry Wehmiller Design
1006 Windward Ridge Pkwy
Alpharetta, GA 30005

770-667-6250
Fax: 770-667-6251 800-667-6250
info@cadencetech.com www.cadencetech.com
Consultant and design engineer specializing in systems integration and project management; installation services available
Owner: G H Brink
VP: David Bryant
Estimated Sales: $5-10 Million
Number Employees: 20-49
Square Footage: 26000

19479 Barry-Wehmiller Companies
8020 Forsyth Blvd
Clayton, MO 63105

314-862-8000
Fax: 314-862-8858 www.barrywehmiller.com
Leader in the packaging automation industry, world-wide provider of advanced technologies in filling, closing, converting, labeling, conveying, cartoning, case packing, and shrink-wrapping.
President: Kyle Chapman
Chairman & CEO: Robert Chapman
CFO: Mike Monarchi
Chief Information Officer: Frank Lanuto
Chief People Officer: Rhonda Spencer
Estimated Sales: $440 Million
Number Employees: 1000-4999

19480 Barry-Wehmiller Design Group
8020 Forsyth Blvd
St Louis, MO 63105-1707

314-862-8000
Fax: 314-862-2921 sales@barry-wehmiller.com
www.bwdesigngroup.com
Engineer consultant specializing in turnkey and line monitoring systems and project site management; also, feasibility studies, training programs, electrical control panels, validation, servo-motion control systems, equipmentprocurement and installation services available

Chairman/ CEO: Bob Chapman
VP/ CFO: Jim Lawson
Partner: Robyn Pikey
Director, Corporate Development: Jeff Giles
Chief Information Officer: Craig Hergenroether
Estimated Sales: $10,000,000 - $19,999,999
Number Employees: 100-249
Square Footage: 16000
Parent Co: Barry-Wehmiller Company
Other Locations:
Barry-Wehmiller Design Group
Cuyahoga Falls OH

19481 Baruch Box Company
85 South Bragg Street
Suite 503
Alexandria, VA 22312
703-642-0472
Fax: 703-941-7645 800-242-6948
ahe@baruchco.com www.baruchco.com
Boxes, crates, and baskets made out of wood. Wire, wicker and combination baskets, terra cotta, porcelain, silverplate
President: Andrew Eyck
ahe@baruchco.com
Estimated Sales: $2.5 - 5 000,000
Number Employees: 5-9

19482 Basic Adhesives
25 Knickerbocker Ave
Brooklyn, NY 11237
718-497-5200
Fax: 718-366-1425 info@basicadhesives.com
www.basicadhesives.com
President: Yale E Block Block
Contact: Michael Basch
mbasch@basicadhesives.com
Estimated Sales: $5 - 10 Million
Number Employees: 60

19483 Basic Concepts
6907 Mount Pleasant Dr
West Bend, WI 53090
262-247-2536
Fax: 262-673-2069 bio@execpc.com
www.execpc.com
SIS-Automatic saltine systems for cheese
President: James C Fischer
Estimated Sales: $1.6 000,000
Number Employees: 5-9

19484 (HQ)Basic Leasing Corporation
12a Port Kearny
Kearny, NJ 07032-4612
973-817-7373
Consultant specializing in the design of industrial kitchens; exporter of ice makers, dishwashers, etc.; importer of ice machines; wholesaler/distributor of equipment and fixtures and frozen drink machines and coffee machines
President: Harold Weber
VP: Johnathan Weber
Estimated Sales: $20-50 Million
Number Employees: 50-99
Square Footage: 28500

19485 Basic Polymers Industrial Flooring Systems
3628 W Holland Ave
Fresno, CA 93722-7808
559-230-1500
Fax: 559-266-6007 877-225-2549
www.basicpolymers.com/
Industrial flooring systems product line of which includes urethane, epoxy, MMA, flooring.
Owner: Jose Gonzalez
Sales Representative: Scott Hamilton

19486 Basiloid Products Corp
312 N East St
Elnora, IN 47529-3002
812-692-5511
Fax: 812-692-5512 866-692-5511
basiloid@dmrtc.net www.basiloid.net
Mechanical lift truck attachments
Owner: Rob French
rfrench@basiloid.com
Estimated Sales: $10-20 Million
Number Employees: 10-19

19487 Baskets Extraordinaires
1150 Shames Dr
Westbury, NY 11590
212-929-7259
Fax: 212-929-6124 800-666-1685
presentz@aol.com
Gift baskets
Owner: Michele Triester
Estimated Sales: less than $500,000
Number Employees: 5-9

19488 Batch
Boston, MA
617-416-1061
www.batchicecream.com
Manufacturer of natural ice cream.
Co-Owner: Susie Parish
Co-Owner: Veronica Janssens
Brands:
batch

19489 Batching Systems
50 Jibsail Dr
Prince Frederick, MD 20678-3467
410-414-8111
Fax: 410-414-8121 800-311-0851
info@BatchingSystems.com
www.batchingsystems.com
Manufacturer and exporter of optical part counting, scanning, filling and batching machines.
Owner: Don Wooldridge
Marketing: Raven Easton
Sales: David Wooldridge
sales@batchingsystems.com
Estimated Sales: $10-20 Million
Number Employees: 20-49
Brands:
Bagmaster
Batchmaster

19490 Batchmaster
PO Box 1303
Fayetteville, AR 72702-1303
479-521-9208
Fax: 479-442-5860 sales@bmaster.com
Owner: Paul Reagan
sales@bmaster.com
Estimated Sales: $1 - 3 Million
Number Employees: 5-9

19491 Batchmasters Software
23191 LA Cadena Dr # 101
Suite 101
Laguna Hills, CA 92653-1429
949-583-1646
Fax: 949-296-0912 info@batchmaster.com
www.batchmaster.com
PC-based software products designed specifically for controlling inventory, production, formulation, costing, etc
Owner: David Stanyo
President, Chief Executive Officer: Sahib Dudani
sdudani@batchmaster.com
Vice President, General Manager: Ingrid Leon
VP of Sales: Christy Hudson
Technical Specialist: Jeremy Wheaton
Number Employees: 100-249
Brands:
Batchmaster

19492 Baublys Control Laser
2419 Lake Orange Dr
Orlando, FL 32837
407-926-3500
Fax: 407-926-3590 866-612-8619
clcsales@controllaser.com www.controllaser.com
Fully integrated lasers and mechanical coding, marking, engraving, deep engraving, and 3D engraving systems and solution for the aerospace, automotive, coining and jewerly, consumer/commercial, electronic, medical, mold and diepackaging, tooling and trophy and awards industries. Our Laser Markink Systems are available: 10 Watt, 25 Watt, 50 Watt and CO2 with wigh power Nd:YAD and Nd:YLF lamp and diode pumped infrared, Green, UV and Deep UV systems.
President: Steve Graham
CEO: Antoine Dominic
Marketing Director: Monica Correal
Contact: Michele Fencik
mfencik@controllaser.com
Number Employees: 50-99
Number of Products: 20

Square Footage: 104000
Parent Co: Excel Technology
Brands:
Instamark Script
Instamark Signature
Instamark Stylus

19493 Bauermeister
601 Corporate Woods Pkwy
Vernon Hills, IL 60061-3111
847-415-5293
Fax: 847-793-8611 info@bauermeisterusa.com
www.bauermeisterusa.com
Food processing and chocolate machinery
President: Jeff Soldan
Estimated Sales: Below $5 Million
Number Employees: 10

19494 Baumer Limited
122 Spring St # C6
Suite C6
Southington, CT 06489-1534
860-621-2121
Fax: 860-628-6280 www.baumernet.com
President: Mike Labieniec
labieniec@baumer.com.br
Owner: Ken Talentino
Estimated Sales: $1 - 5 Million
Number Employees: 20-49

19495 Baumuller LNI
117 W Dudley Town Rd
Bloomfield, CT 06002
860-243-0232
Fax: 860-286-3080 www.baumuller.com
Contact: Chris Davis
c.davis@baumuller.com
Estimated Sales: $3 - 5 Million
Number Employees: 10-19

19496 Baur Tape & Label Co
130 Lombrano St
San Antonio, TX 78207-1832
210-738-3000
Fax: 210-738-0070 877-738-3222
baurlabel@swbell.net www.baurlabel.com
Manufacturer and exporter of shipping and metal labels
President: Leonard Humble
baurlabel@swbell.net
Sales Manager: Peter Humble
Estimated Sales: $1-2.5 Million
Number Employees: 5-9
Square Footage: 8000
Type of Packaging: Consumer, Food Service, Private Label, Bulk

19497 Baxter Manufacturing Inc
19220 State Route 162 E
Orting, WA 98360-9236
360-893-5554
Fax: 360-893-6836 800-777-2828
www.baxtermfg.com
Manufacturer and exporter of bakery and deli equipment including rack and revolving ovens, proof boxes, fryers, inventory supply items, ingredient bins, molders and dividers
Design/Marketing Manager: Laura Barrentine
Manager: Gabrielle Devault
gabrielle.devault@baxtermfg.com
Estimated Sales: $1 - 5 Million
Number Employees: 100-249
Square Footage: 228000
Parent Co: Hobart Corporation

19498 Bay Area Pallet Company/IFCO Systems
13100 Northwest Fwy # 625
Houston, TX 77040-6340
713-332-6145
Fax: 713-332-6146 877-430-4326
www.ifco-us.com
Re-manufacturer of wooden pallets and skids
President IFCO Systems North America: David Russell
Chairman: Bernd Malmstrom
Senior Vice President, Chief Financial O: Rich Hamlin
Senior VP: Mike Hachtman
Vice President of Sales: Dan Martin
Chief Operating Officer: Wolfgang Orgeldinger
Estimated Sales: $20-50 Million
Number Employees: 1,000-4,999
Parent Co: IFCO Systems

19499 Bayard Kurth Company
19321 Mount Elliott St
Detroit, MI 48234-2724
313-891-0800
Fax: 313-891-8966
Manufacturer and exporter of advertising displays, decalcomanias and packaging materials
President: Bayard Kurth Jr
VP: Bayard Kurth
Estimated Sales: $5-10 Million
Number Employees: 5-9
Type of Packaging: Consumer, Food Service, Bulk

19500 Bayer Environmental
95 Chestnut Ridge Road
Montvale, NJ 07645
201-307-9700
Fax: 201-307-3438
President: Helmut Schramm
Estimated Sales: Below $5 Million
Number Employees: 50-99

19501 Bayer/Wolff Walsrode
7330 S Madison St
Willowbrook, IL 60527-5588
630-789-8442
Fax: 630-789-8489 800-882-9987
Flexible packages, gas packaging materials, modified atmospheric packaging, vacuum packaging materials
CEO: Timothy McDivit
Estimated Sales: $5-10 000,000
Number Employees: 20-49

19502 Bayhead Products Corp.
173 Crosby Rd
Dover, NH 03820-4356
603-742-3000
Fax: 603-743-4701 800-229-4323
sales@bayheadproducts.com
www.bayheadproducts.com
Plastic and steel industrial items, tilt and box trucks, self-dumping hoppers, pallet containers, barrels, boxes, containment trays, totes, cases, tanks, steel racks and carts; exporter of tilt trucks and boxes
President: Elissa Moore
sales@bayheadproducts.com
Estimated Sales: $1.9 Million
Number Employees: 20-49
Square Footage: 50000
Type of Packaging: Bulk
Brands:
Haul-All

19503 Bayou Container & Supply Inc
14021 Hemley Rd
Coden, AL 36523-3146
251-824-2658
Fax: 251-824-2670 www.bayoucontainer.com
Owner/President: Mike Frederick
Estimated Sales: Less Than $500,000
Number Employees: 1-4

19504 Bayou Packing
9155 Little River Rd
Bayou La Batre, AL 36509
251-824-7710
Fax: 251-824-4061
Packages seafood
Owner: Richard Roush

19505 Bayside Motion Group
27 Seaview Boulevard
Port Washington, NY 11050-4610
516-484-5482
Fax: 516-484-5496 800-305-4555
www.baysideinfo.com
Manufacturer and exporter of environmentally sealed gear heads
Marketing Coordinator: Paul Gallagher
Estimated Sales: $5 - 10 Million
Number Employees: 150

19506 Bbc Industries
5 Capper Dr
Pacific, MO 63069-3603
636-343-5600
Fax: 636-343-3952 800-654-4205
info@bbcind.com www.hotyogaheaters.com
Industrial conveyor ovens and heaters
President and CFO: Ronald Vinyard
ron@bbcind.com
Head of R&D and Quality Control: Everett Graham

Estimated Sales: $5 - 10 Million
Number Employees: 10-19
Square Footage: 90400
Brands:
Baker's Best

19507 Bc Wood Products
11364 Air Park Rd
Ashland, VA 23005-3283
804-798-9154
Fax: 804-798-2672 info@bcwoodonline.com
www.bcwoodonline.com
Wooden pallets
Owner: Gordon Murdock
sales@bcwoodonline.com
Sales/Marketing: Reynolds Cowardin
Secretary/Treasurer: Carolyn Barrett
Purchasing Manager: Richard Barrett
Estimated Sales: $3-5 Million
Number Employees: 50-99
Square Footage: 100000

19508 Be & Sco
1623 N San Marcos
San Antonio, TX 78201-6436
210-734-5124
Fax: 210-737-3925 800-683-0928
sales@bescomfg.com www.minom.com
Manufacturer and exporter of flour tortilla and tamale equipment and grills
President: Robert Escamilla
robert@bescomfg.com
VP: Rosie Ecamilla
Estimated Sales: $2.5-5 Million
Number Employees: 20-49
Square Footage: 120000
Brands:
Beta Max
Beta-900
Mini-Wedge Press
Wedge Press

19509 Beach Filter Products
P.O. Box 505
555 Centennial Ave
Hanover, PA 17331
717-698-1403
Fax: 717-698-1610 800-232-2485
sales@beachfilters.com www.beachfilters.com
Manufacturer and exporter of compressed air filters, desiccant dehumidification bags, and breather filters.
President: Wesley Jones
abuckley@beachfilters.com
Sales Manager: Lori Prickitt
Production Manager: Leslie Doll
Plant Manager/Purchasing: Leslie Doll
Estimated Sales: $500 Thousand - $1 Million
Square Footage: 16000
Type of Packaging: Consumer, Bulk
Brands:
Polyclear II

19510 Beacon Engineering Co
162 Don Westbrook Ave S
Jasper, GA 30143-1161
706-692-6411
Fax: 706-692-3227 beacon6411@aol.com
www.beaconcan.com
Batch spinners, conveyors, cooling equipment, candy cutting machines, and automatic feeders
Owner: Susie Shields
susie@beaconcan.com
Estimated Sales: $1-2.5 000,000
Number Employees: 5-9

19511 Beacon Inc
12223 S Laramie Ave
Chicago, IL 60803-3129
708-544-9900
Fax: 708-544-9999 800-445-4203
www.beaconmetals.com
Stainless steel equipment for meat and poultry processing.
President: Jim Niemiec
sales@beaconmetals.com
Number Employees: 5-9

19512 Beacon Specialties
345 Bloome Street
New York, NY 10013
800-221-9405
Food service equipment parts and supplies including drains, casters, burners, grates, faucets, mixer parts, gaskets, refrigeration hardware, etc

VP: Steven Levine
Sales Manager: L Levine
Estimated Sales: $1 - 5 Million
Number Employees: 10
Square Footage: 10000

19513 Beam Industries
1700 W 2nd St
Webster City, IA 50595
515-832-4620
Fax: 515-832-6659 800-369-2326
lars.hybel@beamvac.com www.beamvac.com
Manufacturer and exporter of central vacuum cleaner systems and parts
President: Russell S Minick
CFO: Dave Thompson
Commercial Sales Manager: Bill Smith
Contact: Joel Fritz
joelfritz@beamsind.com
Estimated Sales: $20-50 Million
Number Employees: 100-249
Square Footage: 100000
Brands:
Beam

19514 Bean Machines
18619 Middlefield Rd
Sonoma, CA 95476-1998
707-996-0706
Fax: 707-996-0704
Manufacturer and exporter of soybean processing equipment used to produce soy milk, tofu, yogurt, etc.; importer of multiple filter centrifuges
President: W Rogers
CEO: S Fiering
Estimated Sales: $350,000
Number Employees: 6
Square Footage: 5600
Type of Packaging: Food Service

19515 Beaufurn
5269 US Highway 158
Advance, NC 27006-6905
336-941-3446
Fax: 336-941-3568 888-766-7706
info@beaufurn.com www.beaufurn.com
Manufacturer, importer and exporter of chairs and tables
President/CEO: Bill Bongaerts
bill@beaufurn.com
CFO: Monique De Proost
Sales: Lou Ann Bogulski
Public Relations: Janet Stanford
Estimated Sales: $3-4 Million
Number Employees: 20-49

19516 Beaumont Products
1560 Big Shanty Dr NW
Kennesaw, GA 30144-7040
770-514-7400
Fax: 770-514-7400 800-451-7096
cnatu31927@aol.com
www.beaumontproducts.com
Fruit and vegetable wash, citrus based and glycerine hand soaps, air fresheners and cleaners
Owner: Robert Rice
Vice President: Mark Woods
mwoods@beaumontproducts.com
Public Relations: Wat Bagley
Office Manager: Peggy Dunne
Estimated Sales: $10-20 Million
Number Employees: 20-49
Number of Brands: 5
Number of Products: 20
Square Footage: 52000
Parent Co: Beaumont Products, Inc.
Type of Packaging: Consumer, Private Label
Brands:
Clearly Natural

19517 Beaverite Corporation
9794 Bridge St
Croghan, NY 13327-2327
315-346-6011
Fax: 315-346-6221 800-424-6337
www.beaverite.com
Menu covers
Manager: Lucy Kniseley
Quality Control: Tom Becker
VP Manufacturing: Bob Burns
Estimated Sales: $20-50 Million
Number Employees: 20-49
Brands:
Beaverite

19518 Beayl Weiner/Pak

610 Palisades Drive
Pacific Palisades, CA 90272-2849

310-454-1354
Fax: 310-459-6545 weinerb@aol.com
Manufacturer and importer of flexible packaging
materials including printed and laminated roll stock,
bags and pouches
Owner: Jeanne Weiner
Number Employees: 95
Square Footage: 200000
Type of Packaging: Food Service, Private Label,
  Bulk

19519 Beckart Environmental Inc

6900 46th St
Kenosha, WI 53144-1779

262-656-7680
Fax: 262-656-7699 www.beckart.com
Wastewater treatment equipment
President: Arthur Fedrigon
CEO: Tom Fedrigon
  dfedrigon@beckart.com
CFO: Shawn Jensen
Estimated Sales: $5 - 10 000,000
Number Employees: 20-49

19520 Becker Brothers Graphite Co

39 Legion St
Maywood, IL 60153-2321

708-410-0700
Fax: 708-410-0701 sales@beckergraphite.com
  www.beckergraphite.com
Self-lubricating and heat resistant graphite bushings,
bearings, seals, rings and plates
President: Cheryl Ivanovich
  sales@beckergraphite.com
Sales: Linda Egelhart
Customer Service: Linda Egelhart
Director Operations: Pedro Espinoza
Plant Manager: Pedro Espinoza
Estimated Sales: $2.5-5,000,000
Number Employees: 5-9
Square Footage: 20000

19521 Becker Foods

15136 Goldenwest Cir
Westminster, CA 92683-5235

714-891-9474
www.beckerfoods.com
Custom processor and packager of; fresh and frozen
poultry, beef, pork, lamb, veal, cheese products, and
more
President: Stan Becker
  stan@beckerfoods.com
Vice President: Dian Vendel
Number Employees: 5-9
Type of Packaging: Food Service, Private Label

19522 Beckhoff Automation

12150 Nicollet Ave S
Burnsville, MN 55337

952-890-0000
Fax: 952-890-2888 www.beckhoffautomation.com
President: Gram Harris
R&D: Gram Harris
Quality Control: Gram Harris
Managing Director: Arnold Beckhoff
Contact: Dirk Bechtel
  d.bechtel@beckhoff.com
Estimated Sales: $5 - 10 Million
Number Employees: 20-49

19523 Beckman Coulter Inc.

250 S. Kraemer Blvd.
Brea, CA 92821-6232

714-993-5321
Fax: 800-232-3828 800-526-3821
  www.beckmancoulter.com
Diagnostic instruments for pharmaceutical compa-
nies.
President: Julie Sawyer Montgomery
Senior VP/Chief Financial Officer: Mark Kuhn
Year Founded: 1935
Estimated Sales: Over $1 Billion
Number Employees: 10000+

19524 Becton Dickinson & Co.

1 Becton Dr.
Franklin Lakes, NJ 07417-1880

201-847-6800
Fax: 201-847-6475 www.bd.com
Diagnostic tests and instruments for microbiology.

President/COO: Thomas Polen
Executive Chairman: Vincent Forlenza
  vincent_forlenza@bd.com
Executive VP/CFO/CAO: Christopher Reidy
Executive VP/General Counsel: Samrat Khichi
Executive VP/Chief Quality Officer: Davide Shan
Executive VP/Chief Marketing Officer: Tony Ezell
EVP/Chief Human Resources Officer: Betty Larson
Year Founded: 1897
Estimated Sales: $17.2 Billion
Number Employees: 70,000+

19525 Bedford Enterprises Inc

1940 W Betteravia Rd
Santa Maria, CA 93455-5926

805-922-4977
Fax: 805-928-7241 800-242-8884
bedfordscrap@gmail.com www.beibedford.com
Manufacturer and exporter of stainless platforms,
hand railing, stair treads, ladders and decking;
wholesaler/distributor of fiberglass gratings; instal-
lation services available
Vice President: Hugh Bedford
  bedford@tcsn.net
VP: David Thomas
Estimated Sales: $1-2.5 Million
Number Employees: 10-19
Brands:
  Bestdeck
  Bestread

19526 Bedford Industries

1659 Rowe Ave
P.O. Box 39
Worthington, MN 56187

507-376-4136
Fax: 507-376-6742 800-533-5314
  www.bedfordind.com
Manufacturer and exporter of identification ties and
tags, twist ties, recloseable twist ties, and ElasitTag
Products.
President: Kim Milbrandt
CEO: Bob Ludlow
Marketing Director: Deb Houseman
Sales Director: Martin Rickers
Estimated Sales: $20 - 50 Million
Number Employees: 100-249
Square Footage: 84000

19527 Bedrosian & Assoc

525 Veterans Blvd # 102
Suite 102
Redwood City, CA 94063-1140

650-367-0259
Fax: 650-367-0599 www.bedrosian-associates.com
Consultant for new product development
Owner: Ron Bedrosian
  rbedrosian@bedrosian-associates.com
Estimated Sales: less than $500,000
Number Employees: 10-19

19528 Bee's Wrap, LLC

PO Box 1016
Middlebury, VT 05753

802-643-2132
info@beeswrap.com
www.beeswrap.com
Sustainable, natural, and reusable alternatives to
plastic wrap for food storage, made of beeswax, or-
ganic GOTS-certified cotton, organic jojoba oil and
tree resin.
CEO: Tara Murphy
Director, Marketing: Carmen Reid
Director, Operations: Jason Miller
Year Founded: 2012
Estimated Sales: $3.1 Million
Number Employees: 22
Number of Brands: 1
Number of Products: 29
Square Footage: 6000
Brands:
  Bee's Wrap

19529 Beech Engineering

1134 Turnpike Road 73
Ashland, OH 44805

419-281-0894
Fax: 419-281-0894
Transfer carts, lift tables, mobile work stations,
stocking systems, etc
General Manager: Tracy McBride
Number Employees: 7

19530 Beehive- Provisur

9950 191st St
Mokena, IL 60448

801-561-4211
Fax: 801-562-5857 800-621-8438
  jim.varney@provisur.com
Food processing equipment, meat industry
President/CEO: Nick Lesar
Director: James Varney
Number Employees: 20-49

19531 Beehive/Provisur Technologies

9100 191st Street
Mokena, IL 60448

708-479-3500
Fax: 708-479-3598 www.provisur.com
Food processing equipment.

19532 Beemak-IDL Display

16711 Knott Ave
La Mirada, CA 90638-6013

714-367-5580
Fax: 310-764-0330 800-421-4393
info@beemak.com www.beemak-idl.com
Manufacturer and exporter of displays and holders
for recipe cards, brochures and pamphlets
President: Robert Gray
  robert@warden.com
CEO: Thomas Quinn
Finance Executive: Christy Harp
Manager Sales: Julia Alty
Estimated Sales: $10 - 20 Million
Number Employees: 50-99
Square Footage: 72000
Parent Co: Jordon Industries

19533 Beer Magic Devices

20 Railway Street
Hamilton, ON L8R 2R3
Canada

905-522-3081
Fax: 905-527-1957
Manufacturer, wholesaler/distributor and importer of
portion control dispensing machines for beer, wine
and liquor
President: Fred Palermo
Number Employees: 4

19534 Beford Technology

PO Box 609
Worthington, MN 56187-0609

507-372-5558
Fax: 507-372-5726 mail@bedfordtech.com
  www.bedfordtech.com
Contact: Larson Brian
  larson.brian@bedfordtech.com
Estimated Sales: $1 - 5 Million
Number Employees: 25-49

19535 Behlen Manufacturing Co.

4025 E. 23rd St.
Columbus, NE 68601

402-564-3111
Fax: 402-563-7441 behlen@behlenmfg.com
  www.behlenmfg.com
Grain storage bins, steel buildings, and grain dryers.
CEO: Phil Raimondo
Chairman: Tony Raimondo
Senior VP: Lyle Burbach
Year Founded: 1936
Estimated Sales: $98.6 Million
Number Employees: 1000-4999
Number of Products: 3
Square Footage: 850000
Brands:
  Behlen Big Bin
  Berico Dryers

19536 Behn & Bates/Haver Filling Systems

460 Gees Mill Business Ct NE
Conyers, GA 30013-1569

770-760-1130
Fax: 770-760-1181 sales@haverusa.com
  www.haverusa.com
High speed and in-line packaging systems
VP: Thomas Reckersdrees
Estimated Sales: $10 - 20 Million
Number Employees: 10-19

19537 Behnke Lubricants/JAX
W134 N 5373 Campbell Dr
Menomonee Falls, WI 53051
262-781-8850
Fax: 262-781-3906 800-782-8850
info@jax.com www.jax.com
Manufacturer and exporter of food grade and high
temperature synthetic lubricants
President: Eric Peter
Manager Central Region: Carter Anderson
Manager Western Region: Mitch Clark
Estimated Sales: $10-20 Million
Number Employees: 20-49
Parent Co: JAX
Brands:
  Jax

19538 Behrens Manufacturing LLC
1250 E Sanborn St
Winona, MN 55987
507-454-4664
Fax: 507-452-2106
customerservice@behrensmfg.com
www.behrensmfg.com
Steel and metal containers.
President: Keith Dau Schmidt
CEO: Steve Tuscic
Year Founded: 1911
Estimated Sales: $10-20 Million
Number Employees: 50-99
Number of Brands: 1
Type of Packaging: Bulk

19539 Beistle Co
1 Beistle Plz
Shippensburg, PA 17257-9684
717-532-2131
Fax: 717-532-7789 sales@beistle.com
www.beistle.com
New Year's Eve party goods
President: Tricia Lacy
VP Marketing: David Goode
Marketing Director: Michael Fague
Estimated Sales: $50 - 75 Million
Number Employees: 250-499
Number of Products: 4000
Type of Packaging: Private Label

19540 Beka Furniture
259 Bradwick Drive
Concord, ON L4K 1L5
Canada
905-669-4255
Fax: 905-669-3627 info@bekacasting.com
www.bekacasting.com
Tables, chairs and groupings
President: Maggie Dederian
National Sales Manager: Raffi Dayian
Parent Co: Beka Casting
Brands:
  Beka

19541 Bekum America Corp
1140 W Grand River Ave
Williamston, MI 48895-1394
517-655-4331
Fax: 517-655-4121 sales@bekumamerica.com
www.bekumamerica.com
Blow molding machinery
President: Martin Stark
  admin@bekumamerica.com
President: Martin Stark
CEO: Martin Stark
CFO: Owen Johnston
Estimated Sales: $30 - 50 Million
Number Employees: 100-249

19542 (HQ)Bel-Art Products
661 State Route 23
Wayne, NJ 07470-6814
973-694-0500
Fax: 973-694-7199 800-423-5278
www.belart.com
Manufacturer and exporter of plastic laboratory sup-
plies including sterile and nonsterile sampling de-
vices and magnetic stirring bars; also, laboratory
cleaning products
President: David Landsberger
CEO: William Downs
Estimated Sales: $10 - 20 Million
Number Employees: 100-249
Square Footage: 160000
Type of Packaging: Consumer, Private Label, Bulk

Other Locations:
  Bel-Art Products
  Pequannock NJ
Brands:
  Clavies
  Cleanware
  Spinbar
  Sterileware

19543 Bel-Ray Co LLC
1201 Bowman Ave
Wall Township, NJ 07727-3910
732-938-2421
Fax: 732-938-4232 www.belray.com
Formulated petroleum and synthetic oils and greases
CEO: Daryl Brosnan
Estimated Sales: $75 - 100 Million
Number Employees: 100-249
Square Footage: 150000
Brands:
  Molyube
  No-Tox

19544 Bel-Terr China
1001 Country Way SW
Warren, OH 44481-9699
Fax: 330-457-7524 800-900-2371
Pottery
President: Edward Massey
VP: Paul Ramponi
Estimated Sales: $10 - 20 Million
Number Employees: 20-49

19545 Belcan Corp
10200 Anderson Way
Blue Ash, OH 45242-4718
513-891-0972
Fax: 513-793-8618 888-263-3165
dlajoie@belcan.com www.belcan.com
President: Todd Cross
CEO: Mike McCaw
Chief Financial Officer: Michael J. Wirth
Sr. Vice President: Leigh Ann Pagnard
COO: Cleve Campbell
Number Employees: 5000-9999

19546 Belco Packaging Systems
910 S Mountain Ave
Monrovia, CA 91016-3641
626-930-0366
Fax: 626-359-3440 800-833-1833
info@belcopackaging.com
www.belcopackaging.com
Manufacturer and wholesaler/distributor of shrink
packaging equipment, carton sealers, shrink tunnels,
conveyors and accumulating tables
President: Michael A. Misik
CEO: Helen Misik
R&D: Tom Bolby
Quality Control: Dave Macneil
National Sales Manager: Thomas Misik
Distributor Sales Manager: Bruce Miles
Estimated Sales: $10 - 20 Million
Number Employees: 20-49
Square Footage: 70000
Brands:
  Belco

19547 Belgian Electronic Sorting Technology USA
65 Inverness Dr E
Suite 300
Englewood, CO 80112-5141
Fax: 720-870-2241
President: Eddy De Reyes
CEO: Bert Van Der Auwera
VP: Johan Peters
R & D: Mark Ruynen
Manager: Johan Peeters
Estimated Sales: $3 - 5 Million
Number Employees: 5-9

19548 (HQ)Bell & Howell Company
6802 N McCormick Boulevard
Lincolnwood, IL 60712-2709
847-675-7600
800-647-2290
www.bellhowell.com
Weighing systems, inserting systems, automated
guided mail delivery vehicles, remittance processing
equipment, labeling machinery and sorters

Principal: Mike Swift
Quality Control: Josecer David
CFO: Tom Werner
President: John Lomdard
Number Employees: 160

19549 Bell Container
615 Ferry St
Newark, NJ 07105-4404
973-344-6997
Fax: 973-344-0817 www.bellcontainer.com
Corrugated boxes
President: John Weining
  jweining@bellcontainers.com
Estimated Sales: $20-50 Million
Number Employees: 100-249

19550 Bell Flavors & Fragrances
500 Academy Dr
Northbrook, IL 60062-2497
847-291-8300
info@bellff.com
www.bellff.com
Manufacturer and exporter of natural and artificial
flavoring extracts for food and beverages; also, spice
compounds.
President/COO: Ron Stark
Director of Marketing: Kelli Heinz
Year Founded: 1912
Estimated Sales: $39 Million
Number Employees: 1,500+
Number of Brands: 1
Square Footage: 100000
Type of Packaging: Consumer, Food Service
Brands:
  Yuccafoam

19551 Bell Foods
134 Brookhollow Esplanade
New Orleans, LA 70123-5102
504-837-2355
Fax: 504-837-2365 www.bellfoods.net
Appetizers and prepared foods, USDA proteins,
Louisiana seafood, chemicals, dairy, paper products
Owner: John Bellina
  jb@bellfoods.net
Co-Owner/Dir., Sales: Shane Nicaud, Sr.
  jb@bellfoods.net
Co-Owner/Dir., Operations: John Bellini III
Number Employees: 20-49

19552 Bell Laboratories Inc
3699 Kinsman Blvd
Madison, WI 53704
608-241-0202
Fax: 608-241-9631 www.belllabs.com
Rodent control products including rodenticides, glue
traps and tamper resistant bait stations.
CEO: Steve Levy
Vice President, Sales - East: Sheila Haddad
Vice President, Sales - West: Patrick Lynch
Year Founded: 1974
Estimated Sales: $100-500 Million
Number Employees: 100-249
Square Footage: 5260000
Brands:
  Contrac
  Ditrac
  Final
  Protecta
  Trapper
  Zp

19553 Bell Packaging Corporation
3112 S Boots St
Marion, IN 46953
765-664-1261
Fax: 765-668-8127 800-382-0153
ryoung@prattindustries.com
www.prattindustries.com
Manufacturer corrugated shipping containers
President: Robert Young
Plant Manager: Terry Royal
Estimated Sales: $20 - 50 Million
Number Employees: 10
Square Footage: 250000
Parent Co: Pratt Industries

19554 (HQ)Bell-Mark Corporation
331 Changebridge Road
PO Box 2007
Pine Brook, NJ 7058
973-882-0202
Fax: 973-808-4616 info@bell-mark.com
www.bell-mark.com
Manufacturer and exporter of innovative coding and printing systems to the packaging and converting markets
President: John Marozzi
CFO: James Pontrella
VP: Tom Pugh
Marketing: Glenn Breslauer
Sales: Bob Batesko
Contact: Doug Buch
dbuch@bell-mark.com
Plant Manager: Dale Miller
Purchasing: Lou Ciccone
Estimated Sales: $16-20 Million
Number Employees: 50-99
Number of Brands: 5
Number of Products: 30
Square Footage: 90000
Brands:
Easyprint
Flexprint
Intelijet

19555 Bella Vita
PO Box 93204
Phoenix, AZ 85070
877-827-3638
Fax: 480-827-7630 sales@bellavitabags.com
www.bellavitabags.com
Wine bags and gourmet bags

19556 Belle Isle Awning
20220 Cornillie Dr
Roseville, MI 48066-1746
586-294-6050
Fax: 586-294-2487 www.belleisleawning.com
Commercial awnings
Owner: Blair Belloumo
info@belleisleawning.com
Estimated Sales: $2.5-5,000,000
Number Employees: 20-49

19557 Belleco Inc
414 Hill St
Biddeford, ME 04005-4334
207-283-8006
Fax: 207-283-8080 sales@bellecocooking.com
www.bellecocooking.com
Customized toasters, conveyor Pizza Ovens and Heat Lamps
President: Russ Bellerose
rbellerose@bellecocooking.com
CFO: Kevin Roche
Quality Control Manager: Gil Cole
Sales: Mike Clavet
Materials Manager: Ron Hevey
Number Employees: 10-19
Type of Packaging: Food Service

19558 Belleview
PO Box 122
Brookline, NH 3033
603-878-1583
Water and plastic milk cases
CEO: Alfred Stauble
Estimated Sales: $1 - 5 Million
Number Employees: 1-4

19559 Bellingham + Stanley
90 Horizon Dr
Suwanee, GA 30024
678-804-5730
Fax: 678-804-5729 800-678-8573
www.bellinghamandstanley.com
Manufactures refractometers and polarimeters
Administrator: Susan Davis
Parent Co: Bellingham + Stanley

19560 Belliss & Morcom
1800 Gardner expressway
Quincy, Il 62301
217-222-5400
Fax: 217-221-8728
belliss.red@gardnerdenver.com
www.belliss.com
High pressure oil-free air compressors for PET stretch blow molding
Marketing/Sales: Wendy Johnson

Estimated Sales: $1-2.5 Million
Number Employees: 5-9

19561 Bellsola-Pan Plus
7326 NW 46th Street
Miami, FL 33166-6425
305-406-9662
Fax: 305-406-9664 maquipanit@msn.com
Director of Product Development: Kirk Crowder

19562 Belltown Boxing Company
1717 Market St
Tacoma, WA 98402-3246
253-274-9000
Fax: 253-274-9009
Creative custom, packaging for the retail and food industries
President: Linda Ewing
VP: Andrew Levkass
Estimated Sales: $1-2.5 Million
Number Employees: 10-19
Type of Packaging: Private Label, Bulk

19563 Belly Treats, Inc.
210-200 Wellington St W
Toronto, ON M5V 3C7
Canada
416-418-3285
Fax: 905-479-4135 www.bellytreats.com
Candies and nuts
Owner/Sales & Marketing: George Tsioros
Estimated Sales: $1 Million
Number of Products: 500+
Type of Packaging: Bulk

19564 Belshaw Adamatic Bakery Group
814 44th St NW # 103
Suite 103
Auburn, WA 98001-1754
206-322-5474
Fax: 206-322-5425 800-578-2547
info@belshaw.com www.belshaw-adamatic.com
Machinery and production solutions for donut producers in every retail and wholesale category. Doughnut systems fryers, glazers, and icers; also pancake and batter depositers; and piston filler depostiters. One-hundred percentdedicated to the donut and to donut-makers worldwide.
President: Roger Faw
roger_faw@belshaw.com
CFO: William Yee
Marketing Coordinator: Mike Baxter
Sales: John DeMarre
Estimated Sales: $20 - 50 Million
Number Employees: 100-249
Square Footage: 120000
Parent Co: Welbilt Corporation
Type of Packaging: Food Service

19565 Belson Outdoors Inc
111 N River Rd
North Aurora, IL 60542-1324
630-264-2396
Fax: 630-897-0573 800-323-5664
sales@belson.com www.belson.com
Manufacturer and distributor of the finest outdoor cooking equipment available. Don't be misled, insist on certified (ul, csa, nsf) safe equipment. product line includes gas and charcoal grills, pig roasters, steam tables, trailerpits, smokers and more.
Manager: John Hauptman
hj@belson.com
Number Employees: 20-49
Brands:
Porta-Grills

19566 Belt Corporation of America
253 Castleberry Industrial Dr
Cumming, GA 30040
770-887-9725
Fax: 770-887-4138 800-235-0947
info@beltcorp.com www.beltcorp.com
Industrial belting, packing belts
Owner: Bill Levensalor
Estimated Sales: $5-10 000,000
Number Employees: 50-99
Type of Packaging: Consumer, Food Service, Private Label, Bulk

19567 (HQ)Belt Technologies Inc
11 Bowles Rd
Agawam, MA 01001-3812
413-786-9922
Fax: 413-789-2786 www.belttechnologies.com

Manufacturer and exporter of pulleys and metal belts used for conveyors, power transmissions, etc.; importer of backed belts
President: Alan Wosky
Quality Control: John Robertson
Sales Manager: Timothy Potrikus
Human Resources: Cindy Gadbois
Estimated Sales: Below $5 Million
Number Employees: 20-49
Square Footage: 46000
Other Locations:
Belt Technologies
Durham City
Brands:
Metrak
Transback

19568 Beltek Systems Design
30 Englehart Street
Suite C
Dieppe, NB E1A 6P8
Canada
506-857-4196
Fax: 506-857-0194
Chief Executive Officer: Michel Belzile
Chief Financial Officer: David Pugsley
Chief Technology Officer: Jason Janes
Estimated Sales: $15,000,000
Number Employees: 99
Parent Co: HighJump Software, LLC.

19569 Beltram Foodservice Group
6800 N Florida Ave
Tampa, FL 33604-5558
813-239-1136
Fax: 813-238-6673 800-940-1136
bfgtampa@beltram.com www.beltram.com
Wholesaler/distributor of food service supplies and equipment; serving the food service market
President: Dan Beltram
dan@beltram.com
CFO: Hal Herdman
VP: Allen Cope
VP: Kathy McCain
Purchasing Manager: John Zloch
Estimated Sales: $20 - 50 Million
Number Employees: 50-99
Parent Co: Beltram Foodservice Group

19570 Belvac Production Machinery
237 Graves Mill Rd
Lynchburg, VA 24502-4203
434-239-0358
Fax: 434-239-1964 800-423-5822
info@belvac.com www.belvac.com
Committed to provide our customers quality products, to be at the forefront of emerging technologies - to support our can makers and brands alike.
President: Richard S Steigerwald
CEO: Peggy Bell
peggy.bell@fema.gov
Director Marketing: Eric Hodge
Number Employees: 100-249

19571 Bematek Systems Inc
96 Swampscott Rd # 7
Salem, MA 01970-7004
978-744-5816
Fax: 978-922-7801 877-236-2835
bematek@bematek.com www.bematek.com
Manufacturer and exporter of food processing equipment including in-line mixers, colloid mills, homogenizers, grinders and dispersers; also, laboratory testing machinery for wet mixing and size reduction, continuous or batch
President: David Ekstrom
bematek@bematek.com
Technical Director: Stephen Masucci
Administration: Denise Raimo
Sales Manager: Lindsey Humphrey
Estimated Sales: $1 - 3 Million
Number Employees: 1-4
Square Footage: 8600
Brands:
Bematek
Colby
Speco

19572 Ben H. Anderson Manufacturers
7848 Morrison St
Morrisonville, WI 53571
608-846-5474
Fax: 608-846-8878 bklucey@merr.com
www.benhanderson.com

Dairy processing equipment
President: Dale Victor
Number Employees: 10

19573 Benchmark Thermal
13185 Nevada City Ave
PO Box 1799
Grass Valley, CA 95945-9568

530-477-5011
Fax: 530-477-6507 800-748-6189
thermal@benchmarkthermal.com
www.benchmarkthermal.com
Heating elements
President: Gil Mathew
CEO: Myles McKelo
Estimated Sales: $5-10 Million
Number Employees: 10-19
Square Footage: 24000

19574 Bendow
1120 Federal Road
Brookfield, CT 06804-1122

203-775-6341
Fax: 203-746-3728
Tea and coffee filters
Estimated Sales: $1 - 5 000,000
Number Employees: 3

19575 Benier
351 Thornton Rd # 123
Lithia Springs, GA 30122-1589

770-745-2200
Fax: 770-745-0050 www.benierusa.com
Provider of bakery equipment
President: Mike Hartnett
Estimated Sales: $5 - 10 Million
Number Employees: 20-49
Brands:
    Benier
    Daub
    Diosna
    Kaak
    Oddy
    Spiromatic

19576 Benier USA
351 Thornton Rd # 123
Lithia Springs, GA 30122-1589

770-745-2200
Fax: 770-745-0050 www.benierusa.com
Supplier of equipment for the automated production
of bread, rolls, pizza crust and tortillas
President: Mike Hartnett
CFO: Ron Tabor
Estimated Sales: $5 - 10 Million
Number Employees: 20-49
Square Footage: 148000
Brands:
    Benier
    Daub
    Diosna
    Koak Oddy

19577 Benko Products
5350 Evergreen Pkwy
Sheffield Vlg, OH 44054-2446

440-934-2180
Fax: 440-934-4052 info@benkoproducts.com
www.benkoproducts.com
Manufacturer or revolutionary ergonomic beverage
cart that eliminates the need to bend when loading
and unloading.
President: John Benko
    jbenko@benkoproducts.com
VP: Robert Benko
Sales/Marketing Manager: Laurie Benko
Estimated Sales: $10 Million
Number Employees: 50-99
Square Footage: 70000
Brands:
    G-Raff
    Sahara Hot Box

19578 Benner China & Glassware Inc
5329 Powers Ave
Jacksonville, FL 32207-8084

904-733-4620
Fax: 904-733-4622
Manufacturer, importer and exporter of glassware
and china
Vice President: Scott Miles
    smiles@odyseyfl.com
VP: Marie Wang
General Manager: Edward Mills

Estimated Sales: $5-10 Million
Number Employees: 20-49
Square Footage: 100000
Parent Co: Jacksonville Ginter Box Company
Brands:
    Odyssey

19579 Bennett Box & Pallet Company
200 River Street
Winston, NC 27968-9681

252-332-5026
Fax: 252-332-5799 800-334-8741
Skids and new and remanufactured pallets; also, pal-
let repair and removal services available
President: Barbara Perry
    barbara.perry@bennettpackaging.com
VP of Marketing: Shirley Walker
Estimated Sales: $10-20 Million
Number Employees: 50-99
Square Footage: 170000

19580 Bennett Manufacturing Company
13315 Railroad St
Alden, NY 14004-1390

716-937-9161
Fax: 716-937-3137 800-345-2142
info@bennettmfg.com www.bennettmfg.com
Custom built metal cabinets, waste receptacles, jani-
tor carts, racks, frames, etc.
President: Steven Yellen
Estimated Sales: $5-10 Million
Number Employees: 50-99
Square Footage: 300000

19581 Bennett's Auto Inc
W8136 Winnegamie Dr
Neenah, WI 54956-9401

920-836-3534
Fax: 920-836-3873 800-215-5464
bauto@bennettsauto.com www.bennettsauto.com
Disposable polyethylene products including bags,
aprons and gloves; also, latex gloves
Owner: Lowell Bennett
Product Manager (Film Sales): Larry Stelow
National Sales Manager (Healthcare): William
Rusch
Product Manager (Food Service): Ronald Green
Estimated Sales: $3 - 5 Million
Number Employees: 5-9
Square Footage: 992000

19582 Bennington Furniture Corporation
1371 Historic Route 7A
Bennington, PA 5201

802-447-3212
Fax: 802-447-0360
sales@benningtonfurniture.com
www.benningtonfurniture.com
Cushioned chairs and bar stools
President/CEO: Michael Fiacco
VP: Joseph Bennington
VP: Robert Bennington
Sales: Peg Caron
Customer Service/Accounts Payable M: Marcy
Rodd
Estimated Sales: $2.5-5 Million
Number Employees: 50-99
Brands:
    Bennington

19583 Bentley Instruments Inc
4004 Peavey Rd
Chaska, MN 55318-2344

952-448-7600
Fax: 952-368-3355 info@bentleyinstruments.com
www.bentleyus.com
Manufacturer and exporter of milk analyzers and
control systems
President: Bent Lyder
    blyder@bentleyinstruments.com
Estimated Sales: $2.5-$5 Million
Number Employees: 10-19
Square Footage: 38000
Type of Packaging: Food Service, Bulk
Brands:
    Bentley
    Somacount

19584 Bepex International LLC
333 Taft St NE
Minneapolis, MN 55413-2885

612-259-0699
Fax: 612-627-1444 800-607-2470
info@bepex.com www.bepex.net
Provider of thermal processing, polymer processing,
drying, agglomeration, size reduction, compaction,
briquetting, mixing and blending for the food, chem-
ical and polymer markets
President: Teri Butler
    t.butler@fairfieldinnandsuites.com
Estimated Sales: $20 Million
Number Employees: 50-99
Number of Brands: 4
Number of Products: 30+
Brands:
    Alpine
    Disintegrator
    Extructor
    Hosokawa
    Kg
    Mikropul
    Rietz
    Schugi
    Strong Scott

19585 Berco
1120 Montrose Ave
St Louis, MO 63104-1828

314-772-4700
Fax: 314-772-6241 888-772-4788
info@bercoinc.com www.bercodesigns.com
Tables and components for the food service industry
President: Maxine Berkowitz
Human Resources: Angie Balencie
Estimated Sales: $5-10 Million
Number Employees: 50-99
Square Footage: 340000

19586 Berenz Packaging Corp
N93w16214 Megal Dr
N93 W16214 Megal Drive
Menomonee Falls, WI 53051-1555

262-251-8787
Fax: 262-251-4710 www.berenzpackaging.com
Corrugated containers
President: Tom Berenz
    berenz@execpc.com
Sales Exec: Thomas Berenz
Estimated Sales: $10 - 20 Million
Number Employees: 20-49

19587 Berg Chilling Systems
51 Nantucket Blvd.
Toronto, ON, ON M1P 2N5
Canada

416-755-2221
Fax: 416-755-3874 bergsales@berg-group.com
www.berg-group.com
Manufacturer and exporter of industrial cooling
equipment, fluid recirculation, cold storage and
pumping systems, ice machines, chillers and cooling
towers
Chairman/CEO: Lorne Berggren
VP Sales: Stephanie Goudie
Estimated Sales: $20-50 Million
Number Employees: 100-249
Square Footage: 75000
Brands:
    Berg

19588 Berg Chilling Systems
51 Nantucket Blvd.
Toronto, ON M1P 2N5
Canada

416-755-2221
Fax: 416-755-3874 bergsales@berg-group.com
www.berg-group.com
Manufacturer and exporter of process cooling equip-
ment, large ice-making machines, freeze dryers,
turnkey food processing/refrigeration systems and
brine chillers for meat
VP: S Goudie
Estimated Sales: $1-2.5 Million
Number Employees: 1-4
Parent Co: Berg Chilling Systems

19589 Berg Co
2160 Industrial Dr
Monona, WI 53713-4805

608-221-4281
Fax: 608-221-1416 sales@berg-controls.com
www.bergliquorcontrols.com

Liquor dispensers, beer equipment and beverage dispensing systems
Estimated Sales: $2.5-5 Million
Number Employees: 10-19
Parent Co: DEC International
Brands:
   All-Bottle
   Berg
   Infinity
   Laser
   Tap 1

19590 Bergen Barrel & Drum Company
43 Obrien Rd
Kearny, NJ 07032-4212
   201-998-3500
   Fax: 201-998-0414
Tanks, pallets and plastic drums
Sales Coordinator: Lisa Goldstein
Estimated Sales: $1-2.5 Million
Number Employees: 5-9

19591 Berger Lahr Motion Technology
8001 Knightdale Blvd
Knightdale, NC 27545-9023
   734-459-8300
   Fax: 734-459-8622
Electric motors and drive controls
President: Steve Seabaugh
Sales Manager: Frank Eble
Contact: Alexander Filippenko
   alexander.filippenko@us.schneider-electric.com
Estimated Sales: $1-5 Million
Number Employees: 10

19592 Berghausen E Cheml Co
4524 Este Ave
Cincinnati, OH 45232-1763
   513-541-5631
   Fax: 530-683-4011 800-648-5887
   www.berghausen.com
Processor and finisher of quillaja and yucca extracts (powder and liquid forms) and food colors. Founded in 1863.
President: Beth Baker
   bbaker@berghausen.com
Quality Control Manager: Tom Davlin
Estimated Sales: $1-5 Million
Number Employees: 10-19

19593 Bergschrond
4458 51st Avenue SW
Seattle, WA 98116-4029
   206-763-3502
   Fax: 206-763-3767
Sereware
President: Karl Stephenson
VP of Marketing: Babette Easley
Estimated Sales: $1-2.5 Million
Number Employees: 20

19594 Bericap North America, Inc.
835 Syscon Court
CDN-Burlington, ON L7L 6C5
Canada
   905-634-2248
   Fax: 905-634-7780 info.na@bericap.com
   www.bericap.com
Manufacturer, importer and exporter of tamper-evident pourer closures, capsules for bottled liquids and flat top dispensing closures
President: Scott Ambrose
Number Employees: 10
Square Footage: 58000
Parent Co: Rical SA

19595 Berkshire PPM
PO Box 59
Litchfield, CT 06759-0059
   860-567-3118
   Fax: 860-567-3014
Reconditioner and exporter of used food and beverage packaging, processing machinery and tanks
President: James Rindos
Estimated Sales: $3 - 5 Million
Number Employees: 3
Square Footage: 30000

19596 Berlekamp Plastics Inc
2587 County Road 99
Fremont, OH 43420-9316
   419-334-4481
   Fax: 419-334-9094 sales@berlekamp.com
   www.berlekamp.com

Manufacturer and exporter of plastic signs and badges
President: Kenneth Berlekamp, Jr., CAS
Manager: Ken Berlekamp
   ken@berlekamp.com
Estimated Sales: $1-2.5 Million
Number Employees: 20-49

19597 Berlin Foundry & Mach Co
489 Goebel St
P.O. Box 127
Berlin, NH 03570-2338
   603-752-4550
   Fax: 603-752-2798 www.berlinfoundry.com
Manufacturer and exporter of wrapping and packaging machines for paper towels and toilet tissue.
Owner: Gary Hamel
Sales/Plant Manager: Gary Hamel
Manager: Helene Tardiff
   foundry2@verizon.net
Operations: Gary Hamel
Estimated Sales: $1.5 Million
Number Employees: 10-19
Square Footage: 60000

19598 Berlin Fruit Box Company
PO Box 47
Berlin Heights, OH 44814-0047
   419-588-2081
   Fax: 419-588-2800 800-877-7721
   contact@samuelpattersonbaskets.com
Wood veneer baskets for fruit and vegetables
President: Matthew Adelman
Contact: Anastasia Agee
   anastasia.agee@samuelpattersonbaskets.com
Estimated Sales: $1 - 2.5 Million
Number Employees: 10-19
Square Footage: 160000
Brands:
   Family Heritage

19599 Berloc Manufacturing & Sign Company
8010 Wheatland Ave
Ste G
Sun Valley, CA 91352-5317
   818-503-9823
   Fax: 818-503-0934
Signs including aluminum, engraved and vinyl; also, letters, directories and bulletin boards
Owner: Joan Adams
VP: Harry Adams
Sales Manager: Diana Gleason
Estimated Sales: $1 - 3 Million
Number Employees: 10
Square Footage: 10000

19600 Berlon Industries
434 Rubicon St
Hustisford, WI 53034
   920-349-3580
   Fax: 920-349-3081 800-899-3580
   www.berlon.com
Custom stainless steel products including boxes, casters and dairy equipment
President: Mike Ebben
CFO: Bill Olson
Contact: Cody Apfelbeck
   capfelbeck@berlon.com
Director Operations: Steve Griep
Estimated Sales: $1-2.5 Million
Number Employees: 20-49
Square Footage: 17200

19601 Bermar America
42 Lloyd Ave # A
Malvern, PA 19355-3000
   610-889-4900
   Fax: 610-889-0289 888-289-5838
   info@bermaramerica.com
   www.bermaramerica.com
Manufacturer and importer of vacuum and pressure seal wine preservation systems
Owner: Aline Bouilland
   alineb@bermaramerica.com
Estimated Sales: Less Than $500,000
Number Employees: 1-4

19602 Bernal Technology
2960 Technology Dr
Rochester Hills, MI 48309-3588
   248-299-3600
   Fax: 248-299-3601 800-237-6251
   sales@bernalinc.com www.bernalinc.info

Manufacturer and exporter of die cutting and packaging machines for cereal, coffee, snack foods, etc
President: Luigi Pessarelli
CFO: Kelly Lang
   lang@bernalinc.com
Director: Rey Hsu, Ph. D.
Vice President Sales & Marketing: Mark Voorhees
Sales Manager: Steven Leigh
Plant Manager: Frank Penksa
Estimated Sales: $20 Million
Number Employees: 20-49
Square Footage: 45000

19603 Bernard Wolnak & Associates
1721 Mission Hills Rd Apt 205
Northbrook, IL 60062-5715
   847-480-0427
   Fax: 847-480-0427
Consultant for the food processing industry providing consultation on food ingredients, processes, technology, planning, data acquisition and interpretation
President: Bernard Wolnak
Estimated Sales: $2.5-5 Million
Number Employees: 1 to 4
Square Footage: 9000

19604 Berndorf Belt Technology USA
59 Prairie Pkwy
Gilberts, IL 60136-4039
   847-931-5264
   Fax: 847-931-5299 800-393-8450
   danielw@berndorf-usa.com
   www.berndorf-usa.com
Manufacturer and service provider of solid steel belts, processing systems and complete turnkey plants for cooling, heat transfer, solidificationand casting applications.
VP: Larry Edwards
Marketing Director: Daniela Weishzar
Contact: Brian Brown
   brian.brown@berndorf-usa.com
Estimated Sales: Below $5 Million
Number Employees: 10-19
Square Footage: 23000
Parent Co: Berndorf Band Gesmb

19605 Berner International Corp
111 Progress Ave
New Castle, PA 16101-7601
   724-652-7106
   Fax: 724-652-0682 800-245-4455
   sales@berner.com www.berner.com
Berner International Corp. has established itself as the leading manufacturer of air doors for insect and climate control and cooler/freezer applications. Berner also has its own line of patio heaters, arctic seal doors, strip doorsand bakery rack covers.
Owner: Georgia Berner
   gberner@berner.com
Sales Manager: Michael Coscarelli
Estimated Sales: $10-20 Million
Number Employees: 50-99
Square Footage: 100000
Type of Packaging: Food Service
Brands:
   Aristocrat
   Berner
   Flystop
   Miniveil
   Posi-Flow
   Zephyr

19606 Berry Global
P.O. Box 959
Evansville, IN 47706-0959
   812-424-2904
   800-343-1295
   www.berryglobal.com
Manufacturer and exporter of injection molded plastic containers and lids; also, container fillers.
Chairman & CEO: Tom Salmon
Chief Financial Officer: Mark Miles
SVP & Strategic Corp. Development: Brett Bauer
EVP & Chief Information Officer: Debbie Garrison
EVP, Operations: Rodgers Greenawalt
EVP/Chief Legal Officer/Secretary: Jason Greene
EVP, Human Resources: Ed Stratton
Year Founded: 1967
Estimated Sales: $13 Billion
Number Employees: 48,000
Other Locations:
   Berry Plastics
   Henderson NV

19607 Berryhill Signs
597 Vandalia St
Memphis, TN 38112
901-324-1730
Fax: 901-389-3610 patberryhill@msn.com
www.berryhillsigns.com
Commercial plastic signs and designs
President: Kenneth M Berryhill
Contact: Patricia Berryhill
patricia.berryhill@berryhillsigns.com
Manager: Debbie Faber
Estimated Sales: Below $5 Million
Number Employees: dd.berryhill@ao

19608 Bert Manufacturing
1276 Pit Rd # 3
Unit 3
Gardnerville, NV 89460-8723
775-265-3900
Fax: 775-265-3939 bertmfg2@aol.com
www.bertmanufacturing.com
Manufacturer and exporter of chucks and rolls for
food processing machinery
Owner: Dennis Bertucci
bertmfg2@aol.com
Sales: Brian Bertucci
Technical Director: Paul Coleman
Engineering & Programming: Luis Martinez
Estimated Sales: Less Than $500,000
Number Employees: 1-4
Type of Packaging: Bulk

19609 (HQ)Bertek Systems Inc
133 Bryce Blvd
Fairfax, VT 05454-5491
802-752-3170
Fax: 802-868-3872 800-367-0210
www.berteksystems.com
Manufacturer and exporter of data processing and
pressure sensitive labels
Owner: Sam Peters
Sales and Marketing Director: Peter Kvam
0: Ken Whitcomb
MIS Systems Manager: Mike Saunders
Sales/Marketing Manager: Peter Kvam
Sales Representative: Danielle Ryea
HR/Ex Assistant: Amy Kimball
General Manager: Barney Kijeh
Account Executive: Debbie Chadwick
Estimated Sales: $10 - 20 Million
Number Employees: 100-249

19610 Bertels Can Company
1300 Brass Mill Road
Belcamp, MD 21017
410-272-0090
sales@independentcan.com
www.independentcan.com
Manufacturer of specialty metal cans and lithography
phy
President: Rick Huether
Director of Sales: Neil DeFrancisco
Plant Manager: Frank Sorokach
Estimated Sales: $20 - 50 Million
Number Employees: 20-49
Square Footage: 60000
Parent Co: Independent Can Company

19611 Berthold Technologies
99 Widway Lane
Oak Ridge, TN 37830
865-483-1488
Fax: 865-425-4309 Berthold-US@berthold.com
www.berthold-us.com
Measurement gauges and analyzers

19612 Bertie County Peanuts
217 U.S. 13 North
Windsor, NC 27983
252-794-2138
Fax: 252-794-9267 800-457-0005
jon@pnuts.net www.pnuts.net
Sugar-free, other chocolate, other candy, health, fit-
ness and energy bars, nuts, gift packs, private label.
Marketing: Jon Powell

19613 Beryl's Cake Decorating& Pastry Supplies
P.O. Box 1584
Springfield, VA 22151-0584
703-256-6951
Fax: 703-750-3779 800-488-2749
www.beryls.com

Specializes in mail order cake decorating and party
supplies.
Owner: Beryl Loveland
Sales: Linda Howe
Public Relations: Mara Lee
Estimated Sales: $.5 - 1 million
Number Employees: 1-4
Number of Products: 6000

19614 Besco Grain Ltd
PO Box 166
30 Railway Avenue
Brunkild, MB R0G 0E0
Canada
204-736-3570
Fax: 204-736-3575 www.bescograin.ca
Grains
President: Renee Caners
Quality Control: Carol Schulz
International Sales: Anthony Krijger
Sales Manager: Fred Nicholson
Office Manager: Sheri Hiebert
Plant Manager: Jamie Stelmachowich

19615 Bessamaire Sales Inc
10145 Philipp Pkwy # B
Unit B
Streetsboro, OH 44241-4706
330-650-5001
Fax: 440-439-1625 800-321-5992
bill@bessamaire.com www.bessamaire.com
Manufacturer and exporter of indirect heating equip-
ment for gas/oil, make-up air heating and summer
evaporative cooling units.
Owner: Bill Sullivan
Marketing Director: Joseph Marg
Product Manager: Mark McGinty
Contact: Joseph Marg
marg@bessamaire.com
Estimated Sales: Less Than $500,000
Number Employees: 1-4
Number of Brands: 1
Number of Products: 9
Square Footage: 100000
Type of Packaging: Food Service
Brands:
Bessam-Aire

19616 Bessco Tube Bending & Pipe Fabricating
18 Blackhawk Dr
Thornton, IL 60476-1127
708-339-3977
Fax: 708-339-9472 800-337-3977
Folding tables and trucks including hand, chair and
table
President: Ed Eggebrecht
CEO: Ruth Hartman
Marketing Director: Theresa Eggebrecht
Purchasing Manager: Henry De Vries
Estimated Sales: $1 - 3 Million
Number Employees: 5-9
Square Footage: 40000
Brands:
Handy-Cart
Hercules Tables

19617 Best
1071 Industrial Pkwy N
Brunswick, OH 44212
330-273-1277
Fax: 330-225-8740 800-827-9237
sales@bestvibes.com www.bestvibes.com
Manufacturer and exporter of pneumatic and electric
vibrators, bulk bag unloaders, bulk bag loaders, con-
veyors, tables, screeners and dry process systems.
President: Ed Verbos
VP of Engineering: Tim Conway
Marketing: S Fitzpatrick
Sales Manager: R Breudigam
Estimated Sales: $1-2,500,000
Number Employees: 10-19
Number of Products: 100+
Square Footage: 30000
Type of Packaging: Bulk

19618 Best & Donovan
5570 Creek Rd
Blue Ash, OH 45242-4004
513-791-9180
Fax: 513-791-0925 800-553-2378
info@bestanddonovan.com
www.bestanddonovan.com

Manufacturer and exporter of portable power meat
saws, skinners, hock cutters, dehiders and dehorners
Owner: Scott Andre
info@bestanddonovan.com
Finance Executive: Ken Park
VP: Scott Andre
Estimated Sales: $5 - 10 Million
Number Employees: 20-49
Square Footage: 110000
Brands:
B&D
Best & Donovan

19619 Best Brands Home Products
20 W 33rd St # 5
New York, NY 10001-3305
212-684-7456
Fax: 212-684-7630 www.bestbrands.com
Manufacturer and importer of towels, tablecloths,
place mats, pot holders, linen goods, display racks,
vinyl & fabric table cloths and place mats, oven and
barbecue mitts, barbecue aprons and vinyl coasters,
all bath towel products
President: Jack Albert
CEO: Jack Kassin
jacksr@bestbrands.com
Vice President: Rodnie Gindi
Marketing Director: Cari Bennett
Sales Director: Rodnie Gindi
Secretary: David Meyer
Estimated Sales: $25 Million+
Number Employees: 20-49
Type of Packaging: Consumer, Private Label
Brands:
American Greetings
Cannon
Norman Rockwell

19620 Best Buy Uniforms
500 E 8th Ave
Homestead, PA 15120-1904
412-461-4600
Fax: 412-461-4016 800-345-1924
customer-service@bestbuyuniforms.com
www.bestbuyuniforms.com
Manufacturer, wholesaler/distributor and importer of
image apparel uniforms; also, custom T-shirts, table
cloths, napkins and work uniforms; serving the food
service market
Owner: David Frischman
davidf@bestbuyuniforms.com
CEO: Lester Frischman
Estimated Sales: $1 - 5 Million
Number Employees: 5-9
Square Footage: 24000
Type of Packaging: Food Service

19621 Best Cooking Pulses, Inc.
110 10th St NE
Portage la Prairie, MB R1N 1B5
Canada
204-857-4451
margaret@bestcookingpulses.com
www.bestcookingpulses.com
Peas, chickpea, lentil and bean flours and pea fiber.
Certified Kosher, Halal, Conventional or Certi-
fied-Organic, free of all major allergens, and gluten
free.
President: Trudy Heal
Director, Sales & Marketing: Jennifer Evancio
General Manager: Mike Gallais
Estimated Sales: $11.25 Million
Number Employees: 23
Type of Packaging: Bulk

19622 Best Diversified Products
107 Flint Street
Jonesboro, AR 72401-6717
870-935-0970
Fax: 870-935-3661 800-327-9209
www.bestconveyors.com
Manufacturer and exporter of conveyors including
flexible, expandable, skatewheel and roller
President: James E Markley
Sales/Marketing Director: Charlie Appleby
Contact: Roger Haynes
rogerhaynes@bestconv.com
Estimated Sales: $20-50 Million
Number Employees: 100-249

19623 Best Label Co
13260 Moore St
Cerritos, CA 90703-2252
562-926-1432
Fax: 562-404-2076 800-404-2378
President: Donald Ingle
ingle@bestlabelinc.com
Estimated Sales: $10 - 20 Million
Number Employees: 100-249

19624 Best Manufacturers
6105 NE 92nd Dr
Portland, OR 97220-1321
503-253-1528
Fax: 503-253-0878 800-500-1528
sales@bestmfrs.com www.bestwhipsusa.com
Wire whips and mashers for beans and potatoes
Owner: Glennis Merrifield
VP Sales: Jeff Merrifield
glennis@bestmfrs.com
Estimated Sales: $2.5-5 Million
Number Employees: 1-4
Square Footage: 60000
Brands:
Best

19625 Best Manufacturing
10 Exchange Pl Unit 5
Jersey City, NJ 07302
201-356-3800
Fax: 201-356-3816 www.bestmfg.com
Manufacturers of aprons, bathrobes, bedspreads and
blankets, napkins, fabric, pillows, sheets and pillow
cases tablecloths and napkins, towels, cotton or
linen, uniforms, clothing
Manager: Eddie Chain
VP: Henry Garner
VP of Sales: Larry Miles
Number Employees: 100
Number of Products: 9

19626 Best Pack
10676 Fulton Ct
Rancho Cucamonga, CA 91730-4848
909-987-4258
Fax: 909-987-5189 sales@bestpack.com
www.bestpack.com
High speed carton erector without vacuum suction
cups and fully automatic L-sealer with shrink tunnel
President: David Lim
dlim@bestpackpackagingsystems.com
Estimated Sales: $1-2.5 000,000
Number Employees: 10-19

19627 Best Restaurant Equip &Design
4020 Business Park Dr
Columbus, OH 43204-5023
614-488-2378
Fax: 614-488-4732 800-837-2378
www.bestrestaurant.com
Wholesaler/distributor of furniture, cookware and
refrigeration, cooking and serving equipment; serving the food service market; installation and restaurant design services available
President: James Hanson
jhanson@betsrestaurant.com
CFO: Suzane Yosick
Estimated Sales: $10 - 20,000,000
Number Employees: 50-99

19628 Best Sanitizers Inc
17320 Penn Valley Dr
Penn Valley, CA 95946-9340
530-265-1800
Fax: 530-432-0752 888-225-3267
customerservice@bestsanitizers.com
www.gobrandstand.com
Hand sanitizing lotion, infrared no touch hand
sanitizer dispensers and sinks
President: Hillard Witt
htw@bestsanitizers.com
VP Sales/Marketing: Ryan Witt
Marketing Manager: Suzette Pool
Number Employees: 10-19
Square Footage: 40000

19629 Best Value Textiles
7240 Cross Park Drive
North Charleston, SC 29418
262-723-6133
Fax: 843-767-0494 800-858-8589
www.chefrevival.com

Manufacturer, importer and exporter of chef/crew
apparel and tools. Flame retardant items including
gloves, table linens, aprons, uniforms and oven mitts
Manager: Alex Onda
CFO: Tone Long
R&D: Elizabeth Weiler
Marketing: Rob Johnson
Sales: Claude Brewer
Production: Arturo Gomez
Purchasing Director: Elizabeth Weiler
Estimated Sales: $15 Million
Number Employees: 20-49
Square Footage: 85000
Parent Co: the Coleman Group
Type of Packaging: Food Service
Brands:
Gold Lion
Kut-Guard
Tri-Flex

19630 BestBins Corporation
1107 Hazeltine Blvd
Suite 470
Chaska, MN 55318
952-448-3114
Fax: 952-216-0155 866-448-3114
Provider of 'next generation' polycarbonate gravity
bins for bulk foods such as coffee, candy and natural
foods.
CEO: Robert Groenevelt
Vice President: Kyle McDonough
Estimated Sales: $1 - 3 Million
Number Employees: 1-4
Type of Packaging: Bulk

19631 Bestech Inc
442 S Dixie Hwy E
Pompano Beach, FL 33060-6910
954-785-4550
Fax: 954-785-4678 800-977-2378
bestek@aol.com
Manufacturer and exporter of water purification sys-
tems and vending machines
President: Gary Barr
bestek@aol.com
Director Sales: Gary Barr
Estimated Sales: $1-2.5 Million
Number Employees: 5-9
Square Footage: 20000

19632 Beta Screen Corp
707 Commercial Ave # A
Carlstadt, NJ 07072-2685
201-939-2400
Fax: 201-939-7656 800-272-7336
info@betascreen.com
Manufacturer and exporter of vinyl doors for auto-
matic kitchen dining room access
President: Arnold Serchuk
info@betascreen.com
Public Relations Director: Stu Serchuk
Estimated Sales: $3 - 5 Million
Number Employees: 5-9
Parent Co: Beta Industries
Type of Packaging: Food Service
Brands:
Betadoor

19633 Bete Fog Nozzle Inc
50 Greenfield St
Greenfield, MA 01301-1378
413-772-0846
Fax: 413-772-6729 800-235-0049
sales@bete.com www.bete.com
Manufacturer and exporter of nozzles for food and
dairy processing and spray drying nozzles for food
processing
President: Matthew Bete
mbete@bete.com
CEO: Lincoln Soule
Owner: David Bete
Research & Development: Dan Delesdernier
Quality Control: Tom Bassett
Sales Director: Susan Cole
Public Relations: Heidi Arnold
Estimated Sales: $15 Million
Number Employees: 100-249
Square Footage: 108000
Brands:
Bete Spiral
Mp Series
Sa Series
Xa Series

19634 Bethel Engineering & Equipment Inc
13830 McBeth Road
P.O. Box 67
New Hampshire, OH 45870
419-568-1100
Fax: 419-568-1807 800-889-6129
info@bethelengr.com www.bethelengr.com
Manufacturer and exporter of ovens, washers and
spray booths
Owner: David Whitaker
Director Sales/Marketing: Tom Shield
Estimated Sales: $5 - 10 Million
Number Employees: 20-49
Parent Co: Finishing Systems Holdings

19635 Bethel Grain Company
4220 Commercial Way
Glenview, IL 60025-3597
847-635-9960
Fax: 847-635-6801
President: Steve Grubb
Estimated Sales: $1 - 3 Million
Number Employees: 5-9

19636 Betsy Ross Manufacturing Company
251 Broadway
Paterson, NJ 07501-2033
973-278-7700
Fax: 973-278-5903 877-238-7976
brossmfg@aol.com
Flags and banners
Sales: Stacey Jung
Manager: Zahia Chehadeh
Estimated Sales: $1 - 5 Million
Number Employees: 5-9
Square Footage: 40000

19637 Bettag & Associates
116 N Central Dr
O Fallon, MO 63366-2337
636-272-4400
Fax: 636-272-1405 800-325-0959
customerservice@rdmproducts.net
www.rdmproducts.net
Cabinet enclosures for refrigeration units, theft de-
terrent cages, UL listed panel shop
President/CEO: Mike Bettag
Marketing: Carrie Ellis
Estimated Sales: Below $5 Million
Number Employees: 10-19
Square Footage: 30000
Brands:
Con-Pak
Ez-Lok
Pcu-2000

19638 Bettcher Industries Inc
6801 State Route 60
Wakeman, OH 44889-8509
440-965-4422
Fax: 440-965-4900 800-321-8763
sales@bettcher.com www.bettcher.com
Optimex breading machine and power knife
President: Don Esch
Chairman and Chief Executive Officer: Laurence A.
Bettcher
tclark@mobilityworks.com
Chief Financial Officer: Tim McNeil
Research/Development: Ed Steele
Quality Control: Mike Casteel
VP/Marketing: Paul Pirozzola
Public Relations: Wayne Daggett
Plant Manager: David Mears
Purchasing Director: Ed Gross
Number Employees: 100-249
Type of Packaging: Food Service

19639 Bettcher Industries Inc
6801 State Route 60
Wakeman, OH 44889-8509
440-965-4422
Fax: 440-965-4900 800-321-8763
vendas@bettcher.com.br www.bettcher.com
President: Laurence A Bettcher
Number Employees: 100-249

19640 Bettendorf Stanford Inc
1370 W Main St
Salem, IL 62881-3802
618-548-3555
Fax: 618-548-3557 800-548-2253
sales@bettendorfstanford.com
www.bettendorfstanford.com
Bread slicing and bagging equipment; also, cooling conveyors and slicing blades for bread, meat and fish
Manager: Matt Stanford
mstanford@bettendorfstanford.com
Sales: Chad Roberts
Shop Support: Merle Gwymon
Number Employees: 100-249

19641 Better Bilt Products
900 S Kay Avenue
Addison, IL 60101-4909
630-543-6767
Fax: 630-543-0524 800-544-4550
bbponline.com
Wire, metal and tubular products and point of purchase displays
President/Owner: Scott Camp
General Manager: Chris Wojcieszek
Year Founded: 1946
Estimated Sales: $50-100 Million
Number Employees: 51-100
Square Footage: 57000

19642 Better Life Foods, Inc.
17521 Railroad St
#J
City of Industry, CA 91748
626-810-5881
Fax: 626-810-9966 info@betterlifefoodsinc.com
www.betterlifefoodsinc.com
Prepared Asian dishes, including vegetable seafood chow mein, vegetable fried rice, pot stickers, spring rolls, special herbs and special vegetables.
CEO: Huaixiang Yang Yang *Year Founded:* 2021
Type of Packaging: Food Service
Other Locations:
 Plant
 Fresno CA

19643 Better Packages
4 Hershey Dr
Ansonia, CT 06401
203-926-3700
800-237-9151
info@betterpackages.com
www.betterpackages.com
Carton-sealing systems and packaging solutions
President & CEO: Philip White
Vice President Sales & Marketing: Jeffrey Deacon
Director Research & Development: Allen Crowe
Marketing Director: Lynn Padell
Director of Sales: Marc Schaible
Operations Director: Paul Kromberg
Number Employees: 100-249
Brands:
 Better Pack
 Big Inch
 Code Taper
 Counterboy
 Express
 Packer
 Penetron
 Simplex
 Tape Culator
 Tape Shooter
 Tape Squirt

19644 Betz Entec
200 Witmer Road
Horsham, PA 19044-2213
215-674-9200
800-877-1940
www.hazard.com
Water treatment products, boilers, process cooling systems, cookers and waste water treatment systems; also, engineering service available
President: Joseph Perugini
VP of Sales: A Moisey
VP Technical: D Henderson
Number Employees: 300
Square Footage: 240000
Parent Co: Betz Labs

19645 (HQ)Beverage Air
3779 Champion Blvd
Winston Salem, NC 27105-2667
336-245-6400
Fax: 336-245-6453 800-845-9800
sales@bevair.com www.beverage-air.com
Manufacturer and exporter of commercial beverage coolers and food service refrigeration equipment
President: Philippo Berti
CEO: Filippo Berti
fberti@bevair.com
National Sales Manager: Bill Stowik
VP Sales/Marketing: Jack McDonald
National Service Manager: Loran Tucker
Estimated Sales: $1 - 5 Million
Number Employees: 500-999
Square Footage: 2000000
Parent Co: Specialty Equipment Companies
Type of Packaging: Food Service
Other Locations:
 Beverage-Air
 Honea Path SC
Brands:
 Bever Marketeer
 Bree
 Maxi Marketeer

19646 Beverage Flavors Intl
3150 N Campbell Ave
Chicago, IL 60618-7921
773-248-3860
Fax: 773-248-3862 info@beverageflavorsintl.com
www.beverageflavorsinternational.com
Beverage flavor emulsions and concentrates to bottlers. Flavor selection includes citrus punch, tropical fruit punch, pineapple-banana, mango peach, apple, strawberry-kiwi, aloha punch and pineapple-guava.
Manager: Daniel Manoogian
Contact: Gregg Goga
ggoga@beverageflavorsintl.com
Office Manager: Barbara Martinez
Estimated Sales: Less Than $500,000
Number Employees: 1-4
Type of Packaging: Bulk

19647 Beverage World Inc.
590 South Service Rd.
Stoney Creek, ON L8E 2W1
Canada
905-643-7713
info@beverageworld.ca
www.beverageworld.ca
Non-alcoholic beverages.
Year Founded: 1999
Number of Brands: 9
Brands:
 Alo
 Arizona
 Calypso
 Faygo
 Milkadamia
 Mr Pure
 Sanavi
 The Popshoppe
 Vita Coco

19648 Bevistar
615 Vista Drive
Oswego, IL 60543-8129
847-758-1581
Fax: 847-758-1617 877-238-7827
Markets and distributes the newest technology in small-scale beverage dispensers and related consumable concentrate syrups. Specializes in systems comprised of patented technology ideal for the small volumeaccount/establishment/workplace
Marketing Director: Lynda Filicette
Sales Director: Saul Strankus
Plant Manager: Joe Rosado
Estimated Sales: $1 - 5 Million
Number of Brands: 1
Number of Products: 15
Square Footage: 18400
Parent Co: Isoworth Limited

19649 Bevles Company
729 3rd Ave
Dallas, TX 75230-2098
214-421-7366
Fax: 214-565-0976 800-441-1601
info@apwwyott.com www.apwwyott.com

Manufacturer and exporter of kitchen equipment including heated holding, transport and storage cabinets, low temperature roast and hold ovens, proofing cabinets and racks
President: Hylcon Jonas
CFO: Don Wall
Quality Control: Jim Austin
Marketing Assistant: Martha Patino
VP of Sales/Marketing: John Kossler
Estimated Sales: $20 - 50 Million
Number Employees: 100-249
Square Footage: 45000
Brands:
 Climate 2000
 Tendertouch
 Transitray

19650 Bevsource
219 Little Canada Road East
St. Paul, MN 55117
651-797-0113
Fax: 651-482-1337 866-956-4608
sales@bevsource.com www.bevsource.com
Ingredients and packaging for the beverage industry, specifically sweeteners, vitamin blends, juice concentrates, and alcohol.

19651 Bevstar
615 Vista Drive
Oswego, IL 60543-8129
847-758-1581
Fax: 847-758-1617 877-238-7827
www.bevstar.com
A beverage dispenser that dispenses hot, cold and sparkling bottled or filtered water, as well as soft drinks, juices, coffees and teas
General Manager/VP: Allan Wasserman
Estimated Sales: $1 - 5 Million

19652 Bi-O-Kleen Industries
820 SW 2nd Ave # 200
Portland, OR 97204-3087
503-224-6246
Fax: 503-557-7818
Nonhazardous cleaning products including spray and glass cleaners, dish and laundry powders, enzyme stain and odor eliminator, carpet cleaning, dish soaps and laundry liquid
Owner: Robert C Kline Jr
CFO: Brian Barnett
VP Sales/Marketing: Cindy Rimer
Estimated Sales: $1.5 Million
Number Employees: 1-4
Number of Brands: 15
Number of Products: 15
Square Footage: 26000
Brands:
 Bac Out
 Bi-O-Kleen

19653 Bi-Star Enterprise
P.O. Box 14016
Torrance, CA 90503
310-532-5829
Fax: 310-532-4216
Decorative tin boxes
President: Daniel Hsieh
Contact: Bi-Star Corp
shirleylh@yahoo.com
Estimated Sales: $1-2.5 000,000
Number Employees: 1-4

19654 Bia Diagnostics
480 Hercules Dr
Colchester, VT 05446
802-540-0148
Fax: 802-540-0147 sales@biadiagnostics.com
www.biadiagnostics.com
A food testing facility, specializing in food allergens.
CEO/Co-Owner: Thomas Grace
CFO/Co-Owner: Robin Grace
Contact: Robin Grace
robingrace@biadiagnostics.com

19655 Bib Pak
3205 Sheridan Road
Racine, WI 53403-3662
262-633-5803
Fax: 262-633-2606
Disposable food service and catering equipment
President: John Geshay
Quality Control and R&D: Jim Geshay
VP Sales: Jim Geshay

Estimated Sales: Below $5 Million
Number Employees: 6
Square Footage: 56000
Parent Co: Standalone
Brands:
  The Party Servers

19656 Bicknell & Fuller Paperbox Company
5600 Highway 169 N
Minneapolis, MN 55428-3027
617-361-8484
Fax: 617-361-3716
Quality Control: Manuel Santos
General Manager: George Preston
Estimated Sales: $5 - 10 Million
Number Employees: 130

19657 Big Apple Equipment Corporation
PO Box 408
Yonkers, NY 10705-0408
914-376-9300
Fax: 914-376-9375 800-225-2626
Commercial refrigeration
President: Sheldon J Bess
Estimated Sales: $5 - 10 000,000
Number Employees: 15

19658 Big Basket Company
5382 Forty One Court
Lavergne, TN 37086
615-793-7779
Fax: 615-793-7487 rsaulters@bigbasketco.com
Shopping baskets and carts
Marketing: Phil Goodell

19659 Big Beam Emergency Systems Inc
290 E Prairie St
Crystal Lake, IL 60014-4415
815-459-6100
Fax: 815-459-6126 info@bigbeam.com
www.bigbeam.com
Emergency lights and exit signs
President: Nick Shah
 nshah@bigbeam.com
Controller: Steve Loria
Quotations Manager: Pat Huber
Product Specialist: Frank Drew
Estimated Sales: $5-10 Million
Number Employees: 20-49
Brands:
  Big Beam

19660 Big Front Uniforms
4535 Huntington Dr S
Los Angeles, CA 90032-1940
323-227-4222
Fax: 323-227-4111 800-234-8383
Uniforms
President: Karen Katz
 info@bigfront.com
Marketing: Rou Pope
Estimated Sales: Less than $500,000
Number Employees: 20-49

19661 (HQ)Big John Corp
770 W College Ave
Pleasant Gap, PA 16823-7403
814-359-2755
Fax: 814-359-2621 800-326-9575
bjgrills@aol.com www.bigjohngrills.com
Barbecue grills including gas and charcoal
Owner: Jeff Derr
 bjgrills@aol.com
Sales & Marketing: Scott Gray
Marketing & Sales Director: Steve McLaughlin
Office Manager: Randy Czekaj
Estimated Sales: $2.5-5 Million
Number Employees: 5-9
Square Footage: 40000
Other Locations:
  Big John Grills & Rotisseries
  Frisco CO

19662 Big State Spring Companyy
2738 S Port Avenue
PO Box 5255
Corpus Christi, TX 78405-2035
361-884-6232
Fax: 361-884-1112 800-880-0244
billwilltx@aol.com
Refurbisher of food mixer whips

President: Bill Willette
 billwilltx@aol.com
Executive Officer: Armando Cantu
Craftsman: Manuel Ramos
 billwilltx@aol.com
Number Employees: 1-4
Square Footage: 12000

19663 Big-D Construction Corp
404 W 400 S
Salt Lake City, UT 84101
801-415-6000
Fax: 801-415-6900 skieffer@big-d.com
www.big-d.com
Designer and engineer providing construction management to food processors and distributors; turn key projects included.
Chairman: Jack Livingood
 jlivingood@big-d.com
Chief Executive Officer: Rob Moore
CFO: Blake Van Rosendaal
National President: Cory Moore
Executive Vice President & COO: Troy Thompson
President, Food & Beverage Group: Forrest McNab
Year Founded: 1967
Estimated Sales: $1 Billion
Number Employees: 1000
Square Footage: 15000000

19664 Bijur Lubricating Corporation
2250 Perimeter Park Dr.
Suite 120
Morrisville, NC 27560
919-465-4448
Fax: 919-465-0516 800-631-0168
info@bijurlube.com www.bijur.com
Manufacturer, exporter and importer of automatic lubricating equipment and fluid dispensers
CEO: Thomas Arndt
Marketing Communications Manager: Peter Sweeney
Sales: Kevin Ryan
Estimated Sales: $10 - 20 Million
Number Employees: 20-49
Square Footage: 160000
Parent Co: Vesper Corporation
Brands:
  Airmatic Lube
  Fluidflex
  Versa Iii Lub

19665 Bill Carr Signs
719 W 12th St
Flint, MI 48503-3851
810-232-1569
Fax: 810-232-6879 www.billcarrsigns.com
Vacuum formed, silk screened and advertising displays
President: Jeremy Elfstrom
CFO: Jergmy Elfstrom
Sales Executive: Mike Ellithorpe
Estimated Sales: $1 - 2.5 Million
Number Employees: 10-19

19666 Bill Davis Engineering
222 Hickman Drive
Suite 103
Sanford, FL 32771
407-328-1117
Fax: 407-330-5231 billdaviseng@bellsouth.net
www.davis-engineering.net
Packaging machinery
President: Rick Paulsen
Estimated Sales: $5 - 10 Million
Number Employees: 20-49
Parent Co: Davis Engineering

19667 Billboard Uniforms
101-1865 Dilworth Drive
Unit 395
Kelowna, BC V1Y 9T1
Canada
www.billboarduniforms.com
Manufacturer of apparel/uniforms for the food service industry. Products include chef coats/aprons, protective gear, and restaurant/waiter uniforms.
Year Founded: 2020
Number Employees: 11-50
Number of Brands: 1
Brands:
  BILLBOARD UNIFORMS

19668 Billie-Ann Plastics Packaging
360 Troutman St
Brooklyn, NY 11237-2614
718-497-3409
Fax: 718-497-6095 888-245-5432
info@billieannplastics.com
www.plasticcontainerswholesale-billieann.com
Cylinders and plastic boxes
Owner: Bill Rubenstein
 info@billieannplastics.com
Marketing: Bill Rubenstein
Estimated Sales: $3 Million
Number Employees: 1-4

19669 Billington Welding & Mfg Inc
1442 N Emerald Ave
PO Box 4460
Modesto, CA 95351-1115
209-526-9312
Fax: 209-521-4759 800-932-9312
info@billington-mfg.com
www.billington-mfg.com
Food processing equipment
President: Frances Billington
HR Executive: Lindy Broome
 lbroome@billington-mfg.com
Marketing Manager: Charles Billington
Estimated Sales: $5-10 Million
Number Employees: 20-49

19670 Bilt-Rite Conveyors
735 Industrial Loop Road
New London, WI 54961-3530
920-982-6600
Fax: 920-982-7750 www.bilt-rite.com
Manufacturer and exporter of stainless steel conveyors including belt, tabletop, chain and wire mesh
Owner: Jeffrey Bellig
R&D: Orlando Rojas
Contact: T Ramesh
 trramesh@bilt.ae
Estimated Sales: $5 - 10 Million
Number Employees: 20-49
Parent Co: Titan Industies, Inc.
Brands:
  Bilt-Rite
  Brico
  Speed-Flow

19671 Bimba Manufacturing Co
25150 S Governors Hwy
University Park, IL 60484-8895
708-534-8544
Fax: 708-235-2014 800-442-4622
support@bimba.com www.bimba.com
Rodless cylinders, double bore rectangular cross-section cylinders, rack and pinion rotary actuators, linear thrusters, hydraulic cylinders, import flow control valves and position sensing switches
President: Pat Ormsby
 ormsbyp@bimba.com
VP: Randy Dunlap
Head of Marketing Department: Dennis Kennedy
Head of Operations.: Randy Dunlap
Number Employees: 100-249

19672 Bimetalix
P.O. Box 8
Sullivan, WI 53178-0008
262-593-8066
Fax: 262-593-8067
A complete line of scraped surface heat exchanger cylinders for a variety of food processing
President: Forbes Hotchkiss

19673 Bindmax LLC
16595 W Stratton Dr
New Berlin, WI 53151-7301
262-796-2468
877-543-2463
tcolleton@bindmax.com
Protein products supplier utilized by meat, poultry and seafood companies to improve cook yield and flavor
Vice President: Tom Colleton
Contact: Rick Cassidy
 rcassidy@bindmax.com
Estimated Sales: $1 Million
Number Employees: 5-9

19674 Biner Ellison PackagingSysts
2685 S Melrose Dr
Vista, CA 92081-8783

760-598-6500
Fax: 760-598-7600 800-733-8162
sales@binerellison.com www.accutekcapping.com
Manufacturer and exporter of bottle labeling, conveying, liquid filling and capping machinery and integrated packaging systems
President: Tom Ellison Jr
Contact: Timothy Hussman
  timothy@newportmeat.com
Operations: Jeff Schwarz
Estimated Sales: $2.5-5 Million
Number Employees: 10-19

19675 Binks Industries Inc
1997a Aucutt Rd
Montgomery, IL 60538-1135

630-801-1100
Fax: 630-801-0819 info@binksindustries.com
www.binksindustries.com
Manufacturer and exporter of pin hole detection equipment
President: Carolyn Calkins
  binksinc@binksindustries.com
Estimated Sales: Less Than $500,000
Number Employees: 1-4
Square Footage: 12000
Brands:
  Binks Industries, Inc.

19676 Bintz Restaurant SupplyCompany
P.O. Box 1350
Salt Lake City, UT 84110-1350

801-463-1515
Fax: 801-463-1693 800-443-4746
sales@bintzsupply.com www.bintzsupply.com
Wholesaler/distributor and design consultant of hotel and restaurant equipment and supplies
President: Roger Brown
CFO: Troy Hanson
Vice President: Brad Garner
Sales Manager: Michael Bailey
Purchasing Manager: Christie Smith
Estimated Sales: $10-20 Million
Number Employees: 20-49
Square Footage: 40000

19677 Bio Cide Intl Inc
2845 Broce Dr # A
Norman, OK 73072-2448

405-329-5556
Fax: 405-329-2681 800-323-1398
www.bio-cide.com
Manufacturer and exporter of chlorine dioxide based products for sanitization, disinfection, deodorization and water treatment
CEO: B C Danner
Sales Director: Damon Dickinson
Contact: Mark Cochran
  mcochran@bio-cide.com
Chairman: B Danner
Estimated Sales: $1-2.5 Million
Number Employees: 20-49
Square Footage: 80000
Brands:
  Envirocon
  Odorid
  Oxine
  Purogene
  Sanogene

19678 Bio Huma Netics
1331 W Houston Ave
Gilbert, AZ 85233-1816

480-961-1220
Fax: 480-961-3501 800-961-1220
info@biohumanetics.com www.bhn.us
Odor control, sludge management, environmental compliance
President: Lyndon Smith
Contact: Rita Abi-Ghanem
  rita@bhn.us
Estimated Sales: $5-10 Million
Number Employees: 10-19

19679 Bio Industries
112 4th St
Luxemburg, WI 54217-8396

920-845-2355
Fax: 920-845-2439
Industrial and household cleaners including detergents, degreasers, etc

President: Irvin Vincent
Office Manager: Nancy Vincent
Estimated Sales: $1 - 5 Million
Number Employees: 3
Number of Brands: 2
Square Footage: 8000
Parent Co: NEW Plastics Corporation
Brands:
  Gp 101
  Hazel's

19680 Bio Pac Inc
584 Pinto Ct
PO Box 5288
Incline Village, NV 89451-8118

775-831-9493
Fax: 866-628-1662 800-225-2855
ceh@bio-pac.com www.bio-pac.com
Laundry and dish cleaners including citrus cleaner concentrates, liquid soap concentrate, laundry and bleach powder
President: Collin Harris
Estimated Sales: $1 Million
Number Employees: 1
Square Footage: 2000
Brands:
  Biopac
  Oasis

19681 Bio Zapp Laboratories
PO Box 20127
Sarasota, FL 34276

941-922-9199
Fax: 210-805-9196 biozapp@biozapp.com
www.biozapp.com
Manufacturer and exporter of odor elimination systems, degreasers, glass ans surface cleaners
Founder: Miky Gershenson
  miky@biozapp.com
Director Operations: Denise Novick
Estimated Sales: $5,000,000
Number of Products: 20
Type of Packaging: Consumer, Food Service, Private Label, Bulk
Brands:
  Grease Off

19682 Bio-Rad Laboratories Inc.
1000 Alfred Nobel Dr.
Hercules, CA 94547

510-724-7000
Fax: 510-741-5817 www.bio-rad.com
Supplier of laboratory equiptment and other supplies for the food industry.
Chairman/President/CEO: Norman Schwartz
  norman_schwartz@bio-rad.com
Executive VP/CFO: Ilan Daskal
Executive VP/Chief Strategy Officer: Giovannni Magni
Executive VP, Global Commercial Operat.: Mike Crowley
Executive VP/COO: Andrew Last
Year Founded: 1952
Estimated Sales: $2 Billion
Number Employees: 8,205+

19683 BioAmber
3850 Annapolis Ln N
Suite 180
Plymouth, MN 55447

763-253-4480
Succinic acid, BDO, plasticizers, polymers and C6 chemicals
President & CEO: Jean-Francois HUC
CTO: Jim Millis
CFO: Andrew Ashworth
Executive VP: Mike Hartmann
Chief Commercial Officer: Babette Pettersen
Contact: Marie Beaumont
  marie.beaumont@bio-amber.com
Chief Operations Officer: Fabrice Orecchioni
Estimated Sales: $560 Thousand
Number Employees: 74

19684 BioExx Specialty Proteins
33 Fraser Ave
Suite G11
Toronto, ON M6K 3J9
Canada

416-588-4442
Fax: 416-588-1999 www.bioexx.com
Oil and high-value proteins from Canola.

CEO & Director: Chris Schnarr
CFO: Greg Furyk
EVP: Samah Garringer
VP Operations: Clinton Smith

19685 BioSys
3810 Packard Street
Ann Arbor, MI 48108-2054

613-271-1144
Fax: 613-271-1148 800-458-5101
biosysinc@mail.com
E coliform
President: Brian Leek
Estimated Sales: $1-2.5 Million
Number Employees: 5-9

19686 BioTech Films, LLC
Ste 115
5370 College Blvd
Leawood, KS 66211-1884

813-628-0424
Fax: 813-628-0162 800-633-2611
Customized films made with food ingredients for packaging uses; edible, water-soluble films; edible plastic films; edible flakes for decoration
President: James Rossman
CEO: Graham Hind
Executive VP: Larry Shattles
Research & Development: Caroline Decker
Sales Director: Richard Fielder
VP Operations: George Tidy
Estimated Sales: $10 Million
Number Employees: 50-99
Number of Brands: 2
Number of Products: 20
Square Footage: 25000
Type of Packaging: Private Label, Bulk
Brands:
  Aquafilm
  Aquaflakes

19687 BioVittoria USA
357 N Milwaukee Rd
Libertyville, IL 60048

847-226-3467
Processor and supplier of monk fruit, a natural calorie-free sweetener that is a new alternative to sugar and artificial sweeteners.
President: Lan Fusheng
CEO: David Thorrold
CFO: Danny Wai Yen
VP: Garth Smith
VP Sales & Marketing: Paul Paslaski
Estimated Sales: $500 Thousand
Type of Packaging: Food Service, Private Label, Bulk

19688 Biobag Americas, Inc.
P.O. Box 369
Palm Harbor, FL 34682

727-789-1646
info@biobagusa.com
www.biobagusa.com
Compostable bags and films. Retail products: food scrap collection bin, food waste bags, sandwich bags, cling wrap, dog waste bags and garden bags. Commercial products: produce bags, shopping bags, can liners and films forpackaging.
Year Founded: 2001
Number of Brands: 1
Brands:
  BioBag

19689 Bioclimatic Air Systems LLC
600 Delran Pkwy # D
Delran, NJ 08075-1255

856-764-4300
Fax: 856-764-4301 800-962-5594
mail@bioclimatic.com www.bioclimatic.com
Manufacturer and exporter of air purification systems
President: Michele Bottino
  mbottino@bioclimatic.com
Estimated Sales: Below $5 Million
Number Employees: 20-49
Brands:
  Aeromat
  Aerotec

19690 (HQ)Biocontrol Systems Inc
12822 SE 32nd St
Bellevue, WA 98005-4340
425-603-1123
Fax: 425-603-0070 800-245-0113
bcs_us@biocontrolsys.com
www.biocontrolsys.com
Manufacturer and exporter of diagnostic microbiology test kits and equipment
President: Phillip Feldsine
CEO: Khyati Shah
shahkhyati123@gmail.com
R&D: David Kerr
Sr. Vice President: Carolyn Feldsine
Quality Control: Julia Terry
Director Marketing: Maritta Ko
Marketing Assistant: Jennifer Hawton
Estimated Sales: $3 - 5 Million
Number Employees: 50-99
Other Locations:
Biocontrol Systems
Westbrook ME

19691 Bioenergetics Inc
PO Box 259096
Madison, WI 53725-9096
608-255-4028
Fax: 608-251-0658
Research on flavor and nutrition, consutation and formulation
CEO: Roy Schenk
CFO: Roy Schenk
Estimated Sales: Less Than $500,000
Number Employees: 1-4

19692 Bioionix Inc
4603 Triangle St
Mc Farland, WI 53558-9445
608-838-0300
info@bioionix.com
www.bioionix.com
Disinfectants and oxidation systems for water treatment.
President/CEO: James Tretheway
Number Employees: 5-9

19693 Biolog Inc
21124 Cabot Blvd
Hayward, CA 94545-1130
510-785-2585
Fax: 415-782-4639 800-284-4949
csorders@biolog.com www.biolog.com
Manufacturer and exporter of microbiological identification products
President/CEO & CSO: Barry R Bochner
bbochner@biolog.com
Vice President of Finance/CFO: Edwin R Fineman
Vice President of Operations: Doug E Rife
Estimated Sales: $5,000,000 - $9,999,999
Number Employees: 20-49
Brands:
Microlog
Microplate
Rainbow Agar

19694 Biological Services
10835 NW Ambassador Drive
Kansas City, MO 64153-1241
913-236-6868
Fax: 913-236-6868
Consultant offering testing services for all bacteria; also, sanitation inspections and sampling
Estimated Sales: less than $500,000
Number Employees: 1-4

19695 Biomed Comm
2 Nickerson Street
Seattle, WA 98109-1652
206-284-3433
Fax: 206-284-6585 www.biomedcomm.com
Communications
CEO: Dr. Barbara Brewitt

19696 Biomedical Research & Longevity Society, Inc.
3600 West Commercial Boulevard
Fort Lauderdale, FL 33309
954-766-8433
Fax: 954-766-8433 info@brls.org
www.brlsociety.org
Health and nutritional supplements.

CEO: Paul Gilner
Co-Founder/Technical Director: Bill Faloon
Chief Medical Officer: Steven Joyal, M.D.
Chief Scientific Officer: Andrew Swick, M.S., Ph.D.
Chief Marketing Officer: Rey Searles
Vice President, Business Development: Carolyn Bouchard
Year Founded: 1980
Estimated Sales: $168 Million
Number Employees: 200-500
Number of Brands: 1
Type of Packaging: Consumer
Brands:
LIFE EXTENSION

19697 Biomerieux Inc
100 Rodolphe St
Durham, NC 27712-9402
919-620-2000
Fax: 800-968-9494 800-682-2666
www.biomerieux-usa.com
Manufacturer and exporter of food processing equipment including aseptic, bacterial detection and microbiological
Chairman: Jean Luc Belingard
CEO: Alexandre Merieux
CFO: Brian Armstrong
R&D: Brian Daniel
Quality Control: Katie Foushee
VP Sales: Harry Schrick
CVP, Human Resources & Communications: Michel Baugenault
Estimated Sales: $5 - 10,000,000
Number Employees: 500-999
Parent Co: Azko Nobel

19698 Biomerieux Inc
595 Anglum Rd
Hazelwood, MO 63042-2320
314-731-7787
Fax: 314-731-8800 www.biomerieux-usa.com
BioM,rieux features a full range of diagnostic products for use in the food industry, including rapid, automated testing solutions for pathogen detection, quality indicator enumeration, continuous bacterial monitoring, identificationstrain typing, environmental monitoring and sample preparation equipment.
Vice President: Scott Remes
scott.remes@biomed.com
Vice President: Scott Remes
scott.remes@biomed.com
Number Employees: 500-999

19699 Biomist Inc
573 N Wolf Rd
Wheeling, IL 60090-3027
847-850-5530
Fax: 847-803-0875 prmartin@biomistinc.com
Biomist Power Disinfecting System Spray.
Director of Sales & Operations: Robert Cook
rlcook@biomistinc.com
Director of Sales & Operations: Robert Cook
Vice President Customer Service: Eileen Bowery
Director of Sales and Operations: Peter Martin
Number Employees: 5-9

19700 Biopath
2611 Mercer Avenue
West Palm Beach, FL 33401-7415
800-645-2302
Fax: 888-645-2302 800-645-2302
rchiger@rxir.com www.biopathholdings.com
President: Peter Nielsen

19701 Bioscience International Inc
11333 Woodglen Dr
Rockville, MD 20852-3071
301-231-7400
Fax: 301-231-7277 bioinfo@biosci-intl.com
www.biosci-intl.com
Manufacturer and wholesaler/distributor of microbial air samplers for the food and beverage industry.
President: Don Queen
VP: Marsha Pratt
Customer Service: Don Queen
Number Employees: 1-4
Square Footage: 140000
Brands:
Sas Super 90

19702 Biotek Instruments Inc
100 Tigan St
Winooski, VT 05404-1356
802-655-4040
Fax: 802-655-7941 sales@biotek.com
www.biotek.com
Test kits for vitamins, mycotoxins, antibiotics, steroids/hormones, PSP, etc
President: Briar Alpert
CEO: Alpert Briar
briara@biotek.com
CFO: Klus Deutfcher
Quality Control: Mike Sevigny
R&D: Mike Kontorovich
Estimated Sales: $20 - 50 Million
Number Employees: 250-499

19703 Biotest Diagnostics Corporation
400 Commons Way
Rockaway, NJ 07866-2030
973-625-1300
Fax: 973-625-9454 800-522-0090
Manufacturer and exporter of environmental monitoring products
President: William Wiess
Quality Control: Lara Soltis
Marketing Director: Carol Julich
Contact: Angelene Atwal
angelene_atwal@bio-rad.com
Production Manager: Dan Behler
Estimated Sales: $10 - 20 Million
Number Employees: 20-49
Parent Co: Biotest AG
Type of Packaging: Bulk
Brands:
Apc Particle Counters
Hycom Contact Slides
Rcs Air Samplers

19704 Biothane Corporation
2500 Broadway
Camden, NJ 08104
856-541-3500
Fax: 856-541-3366 sales@biothane.com
www.biothane.com
Manufacturer and exporter of anaerobic biological waste water treatment systems
President: Robert Sax
VP: Jay Murphy
VP Marketing/Sales: Denise Johnston
Contact: William Donnell
b.odonnell@biothane.com
Estimated Sales: $3 - 5 Million
Number Employees: 30
Square Footage: 80000
Parent Co: Joseph Oat Corporation
Brands:
Biobed
Biopuric
Biothane

19705 Biovail Technologies
3701 Concorde Pkwy Ste 800
Chantilly, VA 20151
703-995-2400
Fax: 703-995-2490 biovail@btl.com
Consultant offering technology including controlled release and taste making applications, rapid dissolving tablets and long taste flavor systems
VP: Paul De Jardins
Contact: Myrna Gheen
myrna.gheen@biovail.com
Estimated Sales: $20 - 50 Million
Number Employees: 100-249
Square Footage: 32000

19706 Birko Corp
9152 Yosemite St
Henderson, CO 80640-8027
303-287-9604
Fax: 303-289-1190 800-525-0476
info@birkocorp.com
Inorganic industrial chemicals
President: Florence Powers
CEO: Josh Valdez
josh@seatosummit.com
CFO: Kelly Heffer
CEO: Mark Swanson
R&D and QC: Kerry McAninch
Estimated Sales: $20 - 50 Million
Number Employees: 50-99

19707 (HQ)Birko Corporation
19950 West 161st Street
Olathe, KS 66062
913-764-0321
Fax: 913-764-0779 800-444-8360
djohnson@birkocorp.com www.birkocorp.com
Manufactures 250 cleaning, sanitation and production chemicals, and specialized chemical delivery equipment for HACCP meat, poultry and food plants.
President: Mike Gangel
CEO: Mike Swanson
VP, Business Development: Kelly Green
Research/Development VP: Terry MacAninch
VP sales: Philip Snellen
Customer Service: Rosey Hohendorf
Estimated Sales: $9 Million
Number Employees: 20-49
Other Locations:
  Birko Distribution Center
  Atlanta GA
  Birko Distribution Center
  Boise ID
  Birko Distribution Center
  Louisville KY
  Birko Distribution Center
  Modesto CA
  Birko Distribution Center
  Philadelphia PA
  Birko Distribution Center
  Phoenix AZ

19708 Birmingham Controls
11144 Business Cir
Cerritos, CA 90703-5523
909-825-7311
Fax: 562-402-0485 800-527-8326
sales@bermingham.com www.bermingham.com
President: Ernest Chavez
  ernest.chavez@colostate.edu
Sales: Wes Selby
Number Employees: 50-99

19709 Birmingham Mop Manufacturing Company
115 Oxmoor Ln W
Birmingham, AL 35209-5901
205-942-6101
Fax: 205-942-6101
Mops, brooms, mopheads, etc
President: Glenn L Beacham Jr
  glenn.beacham@afflink.com
CEO: Mary Williams
Secretary: Frank Beacham
Estimated Sales: Below $5 Million
Number Employees: 11
Square Footage: 13000

19710 Biro Manufacturing Co
1114 W Main St
Lakeside Marblhd, OH 43440-2099
419-798-4451
Fax: 419-798-9106 sales@birosaw.com
www.birosaw.com
Manufacturer and exporter of meat cutting and processing equipment including grinders and mixer grinders, vacuum tumblers, tenderizers, horizontal slicing machines, cutters, meat mixers and industrial power saws; also, frozen foodflakers
President: Theresa Bahm
  tbahm@birosaw.com
VP of Sales & Marketing: D.L (Skip) Muir
Sales Manager: David Dursbacky
Estimated Sales: $5 - 10 Million
Number Employees: 50-99
Type of Packaging: Bulk
Brands:
  Biro

19711 Bishamon Industry Corp
5651 E Francis St
Ontario, CA 91761-3601
909-390-7093
Fax: 909-390-0060 800-358-8833
www.bishamon.com
Scissor and skid lifts, pallet trucks and manual levelers/positioners and mobile loading docks; exporter of pallet levelers/positioners; importer of pallet jacks
President: Wataru Sugiura
  wsugiura@bishamon.com
Quality Control: Margie Giordano
VP Sales/Marketing: Robert Clark
Sales Manager: Steve O'Connell

Estimated Sales: $10-20 Million
Number Employees: 20-49
Square Footage: 260000
Brands:
  Bishamon
  Ecoa
  Ez Loader
  Tad

19712 Bishop Machine Shop
2304 Hoge Ave
Zanesville, OH 43701-2166
740-453-8818
Fax: 740-453-6750 www.sprintermarking.com
Automatic contact ink marking machinery
Manager: Ron Barnhouse
Sales Manager: Bob Bishop
Estimated Sales: Less Than $500,000
Number Employees: 1-4
Brands:
  Ink-Koder

19713 Bismarck Caterers
1901 W Madison St
Chicago, IL 60612-2459
312-455-7500
Fax: 312-943-7898
Info@BismarckEnterprises.com
www.bismarckenterprises.com
Catering services, concessions
President: Peter Wirtz
Cmo: Erin Houlehen
  ehoulehen@bismarck-enterprises.com
Estimated Sales: $7,600,000
Number Employees: 250-499

19714 Bison Gear & Engineering Corp.
3850 Ohio Ave
St. Charles, IL 60174
630-377-4327
Fax: 630-377-6777 800-282-4766
info@bisongear.com www.bisongear.com
Power transmission equipment
Chairman: Ron Bullock
CEO: John Burch *Year Founded:* 1960

19715 Bivac Enterprise
357 Lake Shore Drive
Brick, NJ 08723-6013
732-920-0080
Fax: 609-693-8637
Thermoplastic sealing, vacuum and gas packing equipment

19716 Bivans Corporation
2431 Dallas St
Los Angeles, CA 90031
323-225-4248
Fax: 323-225-7316 sales@bivans.com
www.bivans.com
Packaging equipment for the food industry

19717 Bizerba USA
5200 Anthony Rd # F
Suite F
Sandston, VA 23150-1929
804-649-2064
Fax: 804-649-2064 us.info@bizerba.com
www.bizerba.com
Packaging equipment
Vice President: Rainer Dallairosa
  rainer.dallairosa@cporinc.com
CFO: Cheryll Ziemblicki
VP, Engineered Solutions: Rainer DallaRosa
Marketing Manager: Chuck Saje
Director Retail Systems: Robert Weisz
Operations Manager: Joanne Scuccimarri
Number Employees: 50-99

19718 Bizerba USA
31 Gordon Rd
Piscataway, NJ 08854
732-565-6000
Fax: 732-819-0429 www.bizerbausa.com
Retial scales, slicers, weigh price labeling equipment as well as checkweighers, industrial scales and software
President/CEO: Andreas Kraut
VP/Controller: Frank Thiry
Marketing Specialist: Gaudy Cruz
Contact: Manfred Beilharz
  manfred.beilharz@bizerba.com
Operations Manager: Keith Aumiller

Estimated Sales: $10-$20 000,000
Number Employees: 20-49
Type of Packaging: Food Service, Bulk

19719 Bjm Pumps
123 Spencer Plain Rd # 1
Old Saybrook, CT 06475-4051
860-399-5937
Fax: 860-399-7784 www.bjmpumps.com
Pumps and pump accesories for food industry
Owner: Steve Bjorkman
  sbjorkman@bjmcorp.com
Business Manager: Mike Bjorkman
Estimated Sales: $630,000
Number Employees: 10-19

19720 Black Bear Corp
2224 Buford Ave SW
Roanoke, VA 24015-5506
540-982-1061
Fax: 540-982-1066 800-223-1284
Specialty chemicals including municipal, institutional and industrial maintenance
President: Linda Jones
Estimated Sales: $2.5-5 Million
Number Employees: 1-4

19721 Black Bear Farm Winery
248 County Road 1
Chenango Forks, NY 13746-2208
607-656-9863
mamabear@blackbearwinery.com
www.blackbearwinery.com
Wines
President: Mark Stacey
Co-Owner: Sandy Stacey
Chief of Cider Production: Joe Stacey
Number Employees: 1-4

19722 (HQ)Black Brothers
501 9th Ave
PO Box 401
Mendota, IL 61342-1927
815-539-7451
Fax: 815-538-2451 800-252-2568
www.blackbros.com
Manufacturer and exporter of gluing, coating and laminating machines for packaging of food products
President: Matthew Carroll
CFO: Jeff Simonton
Director Sales/Service: Walter Weiland
Sales: Todd Phalen
IT: Jeffrey Simonton
  rburkhart@reimersinc.com
Estimated Sales: $10-20 Million
Number Employees: 50-99
Other Locations:
  Black Brothers Co.
  Warsaw IN
Brands:
  Black

19723 Black Horse Mfg Co
601 Cumberland St # B
Chattanooga, TN 37404-1922
423-624-0798
Fax: 423-624-7557 bhorse1178@aol.com
Advertising specialties
President: Larry Shope
  bhorse1178@aol.com
Estimated Sales: Below $5,000,000
Number Employees: 5-9

19724 Black River Caviar
0075 Sunset Dr
Breckenridge, CO 80424-7218
970-547-1542
Fax: 970-547-9707 888-315-0575
graham@blackrivercaviar.com
www.blackrivercaviar.com
Caviar
President: Graham Gaspard
Estimated Sales: $500 Thousand
Number Employees: 5
Type of Packaging: Consumer, Food Service

19725 Black River Pallet Co
410 E Roosevelt Ave
Zeeland, MI 49464-1342
616-772-6271
Fax: 616-772-6206 800-427-6515
bryan@blackriverpallet.com
www.blackriverpallet.com
Pallets and skids

President: Bryan Slagh
bryan@blackriverpallet.com
Estimated Sales: $1 - 2.5 Million
Number Employees: 20-49
Square Footage: 28000

19726 Black's Products of HighPoint
2800 Westchester Drive
High Point, NC 27262-8039

336-886-5011
Fax: 336-886-4734 www.blacksfurniture.com
Manufacturer and exporter of leather and restaurant
furniture polishes
Estimated Sales: $1 - 5 Million
Number Employees: 20-49
Square Footage: 40000
Brands:
Antique Blend
Apple Polisher
Blodis
Garde
Leather Care
Wood Care

19727 Blackhawk Molding Co Inc
120 W Interstate Rd
Addison, IL 60101

630-458-2100
Fax: 630-543-3904 www.blackhawkmolding.com
Manufacturer and exporter of Tamper-Evident clo-
sures for the dairy, juice, and bottled water
industries.
Automation Engineer: Andrew Dreasler
Year Founded: 1949
Estimated Sales: $100-500 Million
Number Employees: 100-249
Type of Packaging: Consumer, Food Service, Pri-
vate Label, Bulk

19728 Blackmer Co
1809 Century Ave SW
Grand Rapids, MI 49503-8017

616-241-1611
Fax: 616-241-3752 info@blackmer.com
www.psgdover.com/blackmer
Pumps and compressors
President: Carmine Bosco
CFO: Tom Madden
VP: John Pepper
Quality Control: Dick Sowa
Sales Manager: Peter Sturgeon
IT: Stephen Brown
kenneth.paine@alcoa.com
Number Employees: 100-249

19729 Blackwing Ostrich MeatsInc.
19588 Il Route 173
Antioch, IL 60002-7206

847-838-4888
Fax: 847-838-4899 800-326-7874
roger@blackwing.com www.blackwing.com
Organic beef, chicken, buffalo, ostrich and game
meats
President/Owner: Roger Gerber
VP: Beth Kaplan
bak@blackwing.com
Estimated Sales: $12 Million
Number Employees: 26
Number of Brands: 5
Number of Products: 140
Square Footage: 32000
Type of Packaging: Consumer, Food Service, Pri-
vate Label, Bulk
Brands:
Blackwing
Blackwing Organics
Solomon Glatt Kosher
Sport Stick

19730 Blade Runners
P.O. Box 49
New London, WI 54961-0049

920-982-9974
Fax: 920-982-0580
Computer systems and software, used and rebuilt
equipment, sausage linkers, smokehouses, accesso-
ries, stuffers and accessories, and vacuum pumps
Manager: John Mauthe
Estimated Sales: $1-2.5 000,000
Number Employees: 10-19

19731 Blake Corporation
W1902 Holy Hill Rd
Cecil, WI 54111

715-745-2700
Fax: 715-758-2080
Cheese equipment, cutters
Estimated Sales: $1 - 5 000,000
Number Employees: 1

19732 Blakeslee, Inc.
1228 Capital Drive
Addison, IL 60101

630-532-5021
Fax: 630-532-5020 blakeslee@blakesleeinc.com
www.blakesleeinc.com
Manufacturer and exporter of dishwashers, dish-
washer racks, mixers, grinders, peelers and slicers
President: Pirjo Stafseth
CFO: Gary Stafseth
Executive VP: Chirs Berg
Marketing/Sales: Pirjo Stafsethh
Contact: Blakeslee Glass
blakeslee@hfse.com
Plant Manager: Gary Berg
Purchasing Manager: Ron Pentis
Square Footage: 400000
Parent Co: Blako
Brands:
Blakeslee

19733 Blako Industries
P.O. Box 179
Dunbridge, OH 43414

419-833-4491
Fax: 419-833-5733
FDA and USDA approved low density polyethylene
films and bags. Polyethylene plastic film and bags
President: Ed Long
Quality Control: Brad Kickle
VP: Chuck Hansen
Director Quality: Ronald Rummel
Estimated Sales: $5 - 10 Million
Number Employees: 20-49
Square Footage: 50000

19734 Blanc Industries
88 King St # 1
Dover, NJ 07801-3655

973-537-0090
Fax: 973-537-0906 888-332-5262
email@blancind.com www.blancind.com
Manufacture, design and print point of sale promo-
tional signage, displays and fixtures for the food and
retail industry. Founded in 1997.
President: Didier Blanc
dblanc@blancind.com
Operations: Dorothy Vitiello
Number Employees: 20-49

19735 Blancett
8635 Washington Ave
Racine, WI 53406-3738

262-639-6770
Fax: 262-417-1155 800-235-1638
info@blancett.com www.blancett.com
Manufacturer and exporter of 3-A sanitary liquid
turbine flow meters
President: John Erskine
pascualespinoza@blancett.com
Sales: Pascual Espinoza
Purchasing Manager: Chuck Tucker
Estimated Sales: $3 - 5 Million
Number Employees: 100-249
Square Footage: 40000
Parent Co: Racine Federated
Type of Packaging: Bulk
Brands:
Floclean

19736 Blanche P. Field, LLC
1 Design Center Pl
Boston, MA 02210

617-423-0715
Fax: 617-330-6876 800-895-0714
www.blanchefield.com
Manufacturer and exporter of custom lamp shades
President: Stephen G W Walk
CEO: Mitchell Massey
Estimated Sales: $2.5-5 Million
Number Employees: 20-49
Brands:
Glanz French

19737 Blast It Clean
7800 E 12th St
Suite 7
Kansas City, MO 64126-2370

816-241-9199
Fax: 913-440-4725 877-379-4233
www.blastitclean.com
Industrial cleaning solutions
Owner: Rick Dillon
rdillon@blast-it-clean.com
Owner: Rick Salgado
Marketing Director: Erica Chen
Estimated Sales: $1.7 Million
Number Employees: 23
Square Footage: 160000

19738 Blaze Products Corp
1101 Isaac Shelby Dr
Shelbyville, KY 40065-8171

502-633-0650
Fax: 502-633-0685
blazesales@blazeproducts.com
www.blazeproducts.com
Manufacture chafing dish fuel
COO: Cindy Foster
Number Employees: 1-4

19739 Blendco Inc
8 J M Tatum Industrial Dr
Hattiesburg, MS 39401-8341

601-544-9800
Fax: 601-544-5634 888-253-6326
csr@blendcoinc.com www.blendcoinc.com
Dry food manufacturer. Provide custom blending
and packaging, as well as private labeling and con-
tract packaging services.
President: Charles McCaffrey
Chief Financial Officer: Ken Hrdlica
Estimated Sales: $8 Million
Number Employees: 20-49
Number of Brands: 2
Type of Packaging: Food Service, Private Label,
Bulk
Brands:
Chicken-To-Go
Ezy Time

19740 Blendex Co
11208 Electron Dr
Louisville, KY 40299

502-267-1003
Fax: 502-267-1024 800-626-6325
www.blendex.com
Dry ingredients blending company specializing in
batters, breadings, seasonings, seasonings and mari-
nades. 12 distribution warehouses located across the
US.
COO/President: Tony Jessee
CEO: Ronald Pottinger
rpottinger@blendex.com
Director: Olin Cook
Executive Vice President: Carla Hughes
Vice President Research/Development: Jordan
Stivers
Vice President Sales: Ron Carr
Year Founded: 1979
Estimated Sales: $28.5 Million
Number Employees: 50-99
Type of Packaging: Food Service, Private Label,
Bulk

19741 Blentech Corp
2899 Dowd Dr
Santa Rosa, CA 95407-7897

707-523-5949
Fax: 707-523-5939 info@blentech.com
Batch cookers, continuous batch cookers,
mixer-blenders, vacuum tumble mixers, tilt and
hi-lift dumpers, screw conveyors, pump feeders
President: Darrell Horn
CEO: Daniel Voit
Executive Vice President: Joe Yarnell
Estimated Sales: $5-10 Million
Number Employees: 50-99

19742 Blickman Supply Company
280 N Midland Avenue
Bldg M1
Saddle Brook, NJ 07663-5720

201-791-6680
Fax: 201-791-2288
Fry saver oil filtration machines for food service
Estimated Sales: $1-2.5 000,000
Number Employees: 19

19743 Blissfield Canning Company
PO Box 127
Blissfield, MI 49228-0127
517-486-3815
Fax: 517-486-4032
Canning
President: George Waigle
VP: Jerry Roessler
Estimated Sales: $2.5-5,000,000
Number Employees: 20-49

19744 Blodgett Co
10840 Seaboard Loop
Houston, TX 77099-3401
281-933-6195
Fax: 281-933-6196
info@theblodgettcompany.com
www.theblodgettcompany.com
Manufacturer and exporter of packaging equipment
including scales, controls and vertical form/fill/seal,
packaging machines
President: Amber Blodgett
ablodgett@theblodgettcompany.com
CFO and R&D: Bradley Blodgett
Purchasing Agent: Pete Duncan
Estimated Sales: $1 - 2.5 Million
Number Employees: 1-4
Square Footage: 11000

19745 Blodgett Corp
44 Lakeside Ave
Burlington, VT 05401-5242
802-658-6600
Fax: 802-864-0183 800-331-5842
literature@blodgett.com www.blodgett.com
Manufacturer and exporter of steamer ovens
President: Mark Pumphret
dreyn2@maytag.com
VP of Marketing: Des Hague
VP of Sales: Jeff Cook
Number Employees: 100-249
Parent Co: Maytag Corporation

19746 (HQ)Blodgett Oven Co
44 Lakeside Ave
Burlington, VT 05401-5274
802-860-3700
Fax: 802-864-0183 800-331-5842
literature@blodgett.com www.blodgett.com
Manufacturer and exporter of ovens including con-
vection, range, deck, pizza and conveyor; also,
steamers, fryers, kettles, grills, mobile food carts,
charbroilers, catering equipment and filtering
systems
President: Gary Mick
CFO: Gary Mick
IT Executive: Sarah Home
sarah@copelandfurniture.com
Director Corporate Communications: Ann Williams
IT Executive: Sarah Home
sarah@copelandfurniture.com
Number Employees: 100-249
Parent Co: Maytag Corporation
Brands:
  Blodgett
  Blodgett Combi
  Magikitch'n
  Pitco Frialator

19747 Bloemhof
1215 South Swaner Road
Salt Lake City, UT 84104
Canada
80- 42- 277
Fax: 801-973-6858 bert@bloemhof.com
www.bloemhof.com

19748 Blome International
1450 Hoff Industrial Ctr
O Fallon, MO 63366-1958
636-379-9119
Fax: 636-379-0388 support@blome.com
www.blome.com
Corrosion resistance coating materials.
President: Steven Blome
steven@blome.com
CEO: Steve Bloom
Number Employees: 5-9
Parent Co: Hempel

19749 (HQ)Blommer Chocolate Co
600 W Kinzie St
Chicago, IL 60610
800-621-1606
www.blommer.com
Processor and exporter of chocolate ingredients for
the bakery, dairy and confectionery industries in-
cluding milk and dark chocolate, confectioner and
pastel coatings, cookie drops, chocolate liquor, co-
coa butter, cocoa powder, icecream ingredients, etc.
President/COO: Peter Blommer
Founder/Chairman/CEO: Henry Blommer
Vice President/CFO: Neal Murphy
Year Founded: 1939
Estimated Sales: $38.4 Million
Number Employees: 500-1,000
Square Footage: 340000
Type of Packaging: Bulk
Other Locations:
  Union City CA
  East Greenville PA
  Campbellford ON

19750 Bloomfield Industries
10 Sunnen drive
St. Louis, MO 63143-3800
775-345-8200
Fax: 314-781-3445 888-356-5362
clientcare@wellsbloomfield.com
www.wellsbloomfield.com
Coffee and tea equipment including automatic and
satellite brewers, airpots and thermal servers, de-
canters and accessories, coffee warmers and grinders
and water filtration systems and filters
Vice President, Sales/Marketing, Wells-B: Paul
Angrick
Senior VP: Dave Ek
Estimated Sales: $500,000-$1 Million
Number Employees: 1-4
Parent Co: Carrier Commercial Refrigeration
Brands:
  Cafe Elite
  Integrity
  Koffe King

19751 Blower Application Co Inc
N114w19125 Clinton Dr
PO Box 279
Germantown, WI 53022-3013
262-255-5580
Fax: 262-255-3446 800-959-0880
sales@bloapco.com www.bloapco.com
Manufacturer and exporter of waste disposal sys-
tems and equipment shredders
President: John Stanislowski
bac@bloapco.com
Sales Director: Ric Johnson
Estimated Sales: $5 - 10 Million
Number Employees: 20-49
Square Footage: 80000
Brands:
  Blo Apco

19752 BluMetric EnvironmentalInc.
3108 Carp Road
P.O. Box 430
Ottawa, ON K0A 1L0
Canada
613-839-3053
Fax: 613-839-5376 info@blumetric.ca
www.blumetric.ca
Manufacturer and exporter of food processing
equipment including membrane and whey process-
ing and brine systems; also, filtration equipment and
water and waste water treatment systems.
President, Water: Dan L. Scroggins
CEO: Roger M. Woeller
Chief Financial Officer: Ian Malone, B.A. Hons.
Reaserch/Development: Sam Ali
Sales/Marketing: Gary Black
Director Process Development: Greg Choryhanna
Number Employees: 15
Square Footage: 34000
Type of Packaging: Bulk
Brands:
  Sepro Flow
  Sepro Kleen
  Sepro Pure

19753 Blue Bottle Coffee Co
300 Webster St
Oakland, CA 94607-4122
510-653-3394
support@bluebottlecoffee.com
www.bluebottlecoffee.com
Coffee, coffee grinders and brewers
Number Employees: 20-49

19754 Blue Cross Laboratories
20950 Centre Pointe Pkwy
Santa Clarita, CA 91350
bmahler@bc-labs.com
www.bc-labs.com
Cleaning products including air fresheners,
nonchlorine bleach, anti-bacterial liquid soap, health
and beauty care products.
President: Darrell Mahler
Formulation Development & Q.A.: Jagdish Koshti
Estimated Sales: $28 Million
Number Employees: 50-99
Number of Products: 150
Square Footage: 150000
Type of Packaging: Consumer, Private Label
Other Locations:
  Blue Cross Laboratories
  Phoenix AR
Brands:
  Admire
  Blue Too
  Capn Clean
  Carpet Scent
  Class
  Glass & More
  Glass Brite
  Mighty Pine
  Mr. John
  Now
  Pan Pal
  Royal Flush
  Scent Sation
  Sensation
  True Pine
  Ultra
  Wash & Clean

19755 Blue Diamond Growers
1802 C St.
Sacramento, CA 95811
800-987-2329
support@bdgrowers.com www.bluediamond.com
Processor, grower and exporter of almonds,
macadamians, pistachios and hazelnuts. Two thou-
sand almond products in many cuts, styles, sizes and
shapes for use in confectionery, bakery, dairy and
processed foods. in house R/D for customproducts.
President/Chief Executive Officer: Kai Bockmann
CFO: Dean LaVallee
Senior VP, General Counsel: Simone Denny
Senior Vice President, Procurement: David Hills
Year Founded: 1910
Estimated Sales: $709 Million
Number Employees: 1,100
Number of Brands: 9
Type of Packaging: Consumer, Food Service, Pri-
vate Label, Bulk
Brands:
  Almond Breeze
  Almond Toppers
  Blue Diamond
  Blue Diamond Almonds
  Blue Diamond Hazelnut
  Blue Diamond Macadamias
  California Nuts
  Nut Thins
  Smokehouse

19756 Blue Feather Products Inc
165 Reiten Dr
Ashland, OR 97520-9020
541-482-5268
Fax: 541-482-2338 800-472-2487
www.blue-feather.com
Manufacturer, importer and exporter of synthetic
chamois, magnetic picture frames and refrigerator
magnets
Vice President: John R King
johninashland@charter.net
VP: John King
Marketing Manager: Ashley Black
Office Manager: Lisa Gentle
Estimated Sales: Less Than $500,000
Number Employees: 1-4
Square Footage: 8000

Type of Packaging: Consumer
Brands:
 Clipwell
 Cougar Cloth
 Magnamight
 Vpeez

19757 Blue Giant Equipment Corporation
85 Heart Lake Road South
Brampton, ON L6W 3K2
Canada
905-457-3900
Fax: 905-457-2313 800-668-7078
sales@bluegiant.com www.bluegiant.com
Manufacturer and exporter of loading dock equipment, vehicle restraints, dock lifts, lift tables and industrial trucks and the Blue Genius Tech Control Panels
Chairman: Bill Kostenko
Director of Sales and Marketing: Steve Greco
VP of Sales/Marketing: Jeff Miller
Estimated Sales: $35 Million
Number Employees: 100-250
Square Footage: 85000

19758 Blue Lake Products
62 Greenmoor
Irvine, CA 92614-7476
949-786-0108
Fax: 949-786-3108 800-257-3477
Power transmission belting and specialty belting:
O-ring drive belts, flat woven endless belts, custom fabricated belts and foam covered belts
President: Dean Smeaton
 dean@bluelakeproducts.com
Estimated Sales: $3 - 5 Million
Number Employees: 1-4

19759 Blue Line Foodservice Distr
24120 Haggerty Rd
Farmington Hills, MI 48335-2645
248-478-6200
Fax: 248-442-4570 800-892-8272
Patricia.McGuire@bldcorp.com
www.bluelinedist.com
Restaurant equipment and supplies
Owner: Michael Ilitch
 militch@bluelinedist.com
Number Employees: 50-99

19760 Blue Print Automation
16037 Innovation Dr
S Chesterfield, VA 23834-5951
804-520-5400
Fax: 804-526-8164
sales@blueprintautomation.com
www.blueprintautomation.com
Fully integrated Turnkey Systems for applications that involve the loading of flexible and hard-to-handle packages into secondary containers such as cases, trays, cartons, crates and master bags
President: Peter Schneider
 peter.schneider@blueprintautomation.com
CEO: Martin Prakken
CFO: Tom O'Connell
Director Sales/Marketing: John French
Sales Manager: John Kertesz
Operations Manager: David Schoon
Purchasing: Louis Spartano
Estimated Sales: $10 - 25 Million
Number Employees: 100-249
Square Footage: 160000

19761 Blue Print Automation
16037 Innovation Dr
S Chesterfield, VA 23834-5951
804-520-5400
Fax: 804-526-8164
sales@blueprintautomation.com
www.blueprintautomation.com
Vision-guided robotics, case packing of flexible bags and rigid packages and complete turn-key packaging systems, taking control of the product in its naked state through packaging, utilizing and palletizing.
President: Mike Ganacoplos
Quality Control: Tom O'Connell
Marketing Director: Robbie Quinlin
Sales Manager: John Kertesz
Operations Manager: Jason Estes
Estimated Sales: $10 - 20 Million
Number Employees: 100-249
Square Footage: 40000

19762 Blue Ribbon Packaging Systems
4035 N 29th Ave
Hollywood, FL 33020-1011
954-922-9292
Fax: 954-922-9977 800-433-4974
sales@brpack.com www.blueribbonlabel.com
Owner: Robert Schwartz
Estimated Sales: $3 - 5 Million
Number Employees: 20-49

19763 Blue Ridge Converting
100 Fairview Road
Asheville, NC 28803
828-274-2100
Fax: 828-274-0000 800-438-3893
Manufacturer, importer and exporter of disposable and waterproof clothing and nonwoven wipers
CEO: Thomas Snell
Vice President: Daniel Neal
VP Sales: Daniel Neal
Purchasing: Jo Curtis
Estimated Sales: $2 Million
Number Employees: 24
Square Footage: 480000

19764 Blue Ridge Signs
1800 Barnett Dr
Weatherford, TX 76087-9440
817-594-0353
Fax: 817-598-0025 800-659-5645
blueridgesigns@aol.com
www.blueridgesigns.com
Indoor and outdoor painted signs including plywood, redwood and magnetic; also, display fixtures
Manager: Sherry Hamilton
Estimated Sales: Less Than $500,000
Number Employees: 1-4

19765 Blue Tech
PO Box 2674
Hickory, NC 28603
828-324-5900
Fax: 828-324-9712
Manufacturer and exporter of process control and air swept grinding systems, mixers, ribbon blenders, air filtration systems, etc
President: Dennis Harrow
VP: Charles Gero
Estimated Sales: $.5 - 1 million
Number Employees: 5-9
Square Footage: 16000

19766 BlueKey Inc
341 E Bay St
Charleston, SC 29401
843-628-6228
sales@bluekeyinc.com
www.bluekeyinc.com
Business consultants, areas of expertise include digital marketing, branding, web design and development, and content strategy.
Founder & Strategist: Ben Cash
Business Development: John Mulvey
Director of Client Services: Stacey Bailey
Digital Strategist: Matt McDonald
Digital Project Manager: Liz Wall
Digital Marketing Manager: Christy Jones
Year Founded: 2000
Number Employees: 11-50

19767 Bluebird Manufacturing
6670 St. Patrick
Montreal, QC H8N 1V2
Canada
514-762-2505
800-406-2505
admin@bluebird.ca www.bluebird.ca
Manufacturer, exporter and importer of metal cookware including pots, pans, fry baskets, etc; also, custom services available
President: Harvey Engelberg
Brands:
 Bluebird Products

19768 Bluegrass Packaging Industries
3651 Collins Ln
Louisville, KY 40245-1635
502-425-6442
Fax: 502-425-7201 800-489-3159
ellen@bluegrasspackaging.com
www.bluegrasspackaging.com
Co-packer of dried foods and snacks, beans, grain, gum balls, candy, coffee, etc

Owner: Terry Waddle
 twbpi@aol.com
CEO: Auggie Chick
Estimated Sales: $3 - 5 Million
Number Employees: 20-49
Square Footage: 100000

19769 Bluewater Environmental
704 Mara Street
Suite No. 201
Point Edward, ON N7V 1X4
Canada
519-337-0228
Fax: 519-337-9178 888-808-9782
eng@blueh2o.ca

19770 Bluff Manufacturing Inc
1400 Everman Pkwy # 156
Suite 156
Fort Worth, TX 76140-5034
817-293-3018
Fax: 817-293-7570 800-433-2212
jae@bluffmanufacturing.com
www.bluffmanufacturing.com
Manufacturers exporter of dockboards, dock plates and edge-of-dock levelers
President: Phillip Amrozowicz
 phillip@bluffmanufacturing.com
Director, Financing & Accounting: Bruce Parker
VP, Marketing: Amy Hamilton
Estimated Sales: $10-20 Million
Number Employees: 5-9

19771 Bluffton Motor Works
410 E Spring St
Bluffton, IN 46714-3737
260-827-2200
Fax: 260-827-2303 800-579-8527
www.blmworks.com
Electric motors for the dairy, beverage, meat and poultry industries.
CEO: Stacey Duncan
 sduncan@bcbsks.com
Number Employees: 250-499

19772 Bluffton Slaw Cutter Company
331 N Main St Ste 1
Bluffton, OH 45817
419-358-9840
Fax: 419-358-9840 www.blufftonslawcutter.com
Manufacturer and exporter of lid removers, cheese shredders, apple slicers and slaw cutters
President and CFO: Paul King
VP: T King
Quality Control: Louis Stier
Marketing Director: L King
Estimated Sales: Below $5 Million
Number Employees: 1-4
Square Footage: 2400
Brands:
 Top Loose

19773 Blumer
800A Prospect Hill Road
Windsor, CT 06095-1570
860-688-1589
Fax: 860-688-1539 marketing@blumerusa.com
www.blumerusa.com
Banding and labeling production machines
President: Kevin Coyle
VP: David Olbria
Estimated Sales: $2.5 - 5 Million
Number Employees: 5-9

19774 Bma Inc
100 Springdale Rd # 110
Suite 110
Cherry Hill, NJ 08003-3300
609-239-3638
Fax: 610-455-1491 information@maskell.com
www.maskell.com
Consulting firm, serving the needs of manufacturers and distributors
CFO: Nicholas S Katko
Contact: Bruce Baggaley
 bbaggaley@maskell.com
Estimated Sales: $1 - 5 Million

19775 Bmh Equipment Inc
1217 Blumenfeld Dr
P.O. Box 162109
Sacramento, CA 95815-3903

916-922-8828
Fax: 916-922-8820 800-350-8828
www.bmhe.com

Distributor/exporter of custom material handling equipment, hand trucks, casters, conveyor systems, dollies, pallet jacks and racks, aluminum ramps, dock boards, shelving and work tables; design and engineering for nonstandard materialhandling problems
President: Jack Alexander
jackalex@bmhequipment.com
VP: Jerry Berg
Conveyor Specialist: Richard Wales
Estimated Sales: $2.5-5 Million
Number Employees: 10-19
Square Footage: 20800

19776 Boardman Molded Products Inc
1110 Thalia Ave
Youngstown, OH 44512-1825

330-788-2401
Fax: 330-788-9665 800-233-4575
tbobonick@spacelinks1.com
www.boardmanmolded.com

Safety mats and flooring
Owner: Ron Kessler
Controller: Jim Bowser
QA Manager: Jeff Westlake
VP Marketing: Dan Kessler
VP of Sales: Tom Bobonick
rkessler@spacelinks1.com
Plant Manager: George Lolakis
Estimated Sales: $20 - 50 Million
Number Employees: 100-249
Brands:
Aisle Pro
Econo Pro
Entry Pro
Grip Top
Super Links
Water Pro

19777 Bodine Electric Co
201 Northfield Rd
Northfield, IL 60093-3311

773-478-3515
Fax: 773-478-3232 info@bodine-electric.com
www.bodine-electric.com

Components for food processing machinery including fractional hp and gear motors and controls
President: John Bodine
CEO: John R Bodine
john.bodine@bodine-electric.com
CFO: Jeff Stahl
Marketing Manager: Edmund Glueck
Estimated Sales: $20-50 Million
Number Employees: 50-99
Square Footage: 250000
Type of Packaging: Private Label, Bulk

19778 Bodolay Packaging
2401 Airport Rd
Plant City, FL 33563-1101

813-754-9321
Fax: 813-754-9321 www.bodolaypackaging.com

Horizontal form, fill and seal packaging machines
President: Mostafa Farid
mostafa@bodolaypackaging.com
Estimated Sales: Less Than $500,000
Number Employees: 1-4
Number of Products: 2
Type of Packaging: Consumer

19779 Bodycote Materials Testing
7530 Frontage Rd
Skokie, IL 60077-3213

847-676-2100
Fax: 847-676-3065 800-323-3657
www.bodycote.com

Materials testing, food and drug testing, packaging testing
Chief Executive Officer: Stephen Harris
CEO: Gordon Lawerance
Contact: Rebecca Alban
alban@bodycote.com
Estimated Sales: $2.5-5 Million
Number Employees: 50-99

19780 Boedeker Plastics Inc
904 W 6th St
Shiner, TX 77984-5608

361-594-2942
Fax: 361-594-2349 800-444-3485
info@boedeker.com www.boedeker.com

High performance engineering plastics such as vespel, torlon, ultem, peek, nylon, teflon, and delrin, in-house machine shop manufactures parts from prints or samples
President: Ray Anderson
randerson@boedeker.com
Marketing Director: Mike Randall
Sales: Jake Jalufka
Estimated Sales: $5-10 Million
Number Employees: 50-99

19781 Boehringer Mfg. Co. Inc.
6500 Highway 9
Unit F
Felton, CA 95018

831-704-7732
Fax: 831-704-7731 800-630-8665

Manufacturer and exporter of burlap sack needles, block scrapers, dough cutters, boning, meat hooks, and specialty blades; custom plastic injection moldings; also bbq tools and accessories
Secretary: Mark Fowles
Estimated Sales: $300-500,000
Number Employees: 5-9
Number of Products: 50
Square Footage: 2500
Parent Co: Boehringer Manufacturing Company
Type of Packaging: Consumer, Private Label

19782 Boekels
P.O. Box 7004
Oakland, NJ 07436-7004

201-651-0500
Fax: 201-651-0505
President: Mark Schultz

19783 Boelter Industries
202 Galewski Dr
Winona, MN 55987

507-452-2315
Fax: 507-452-2649
dboelter@boelterindustries.com

Folding cartons and special paper products
President: Dennis Boelter
CEO: Lester Boelter
VP: Dixie Breitenfeldt
R&D: Dean Boelter
Contact: Terrie Klug
tklug@boelterindustries.com
Estimated Sales: $20 - 50 Million
Number Employees: 130
Square Footage: 325000
Type of Packaging: Consumer, Food Service, Private Label, Bulk

19784 Bogner Industries
199 Trade Zone Drive
Ronkonkoma, NY 11779-7362

631-981-5123
Fax: 631-981-3792

Manufacturer, engineer and designer of hi-tech and high quality production of stainless steel processing and packaging equipment for the food and beverage industries.
Owner: Erwin Bogner
Owner: Ruediger Albrecht
Sales Director: Tina Hadizadeh
Type of Packaging: Food Service

19785 Bohler Bleche
11525 Brittmoore Park Drive
Houston, TX 77041-6916

800-852-8556
Fax: 281-856-5458 www.iadd.org/LISTAD.HTM - 101k

Specialty steel sheet and plate products used in producing knives for food processing
Head of Marketing Dept.: John Leonard
Operations Manager: John Leonard

19786 Bohn & Dawson
3500 Tree Court Industrial Blv
St Louis, MO 63122-6685

636-225-5011
Fax: 636-825-6111 800-225-5011

Manufacturer and exporter of metal fabricators, tubular parts and assemblies; also, tool and die services available

President: Steven L Hurster
Engineer: J Koopman
VP: R Wiele
CFO: Steve Leibach
Quality Control: Mike Schneider
Estimated Sales: $20 - 50 Million
Number Employees: 10-19

19787 Bohnert Construction Company
PO Box 34320
Kansas City, MO 64120-4320

816-231-2281
Fax: 816-241-5236 800-701-2281
Manager: Eric Limoges
Quality Control: Emmie Cobins
Estimated Sales: $5 - 10 Million
Number Employees: 10

19788 Boise Cascade Co
1111 W Jefferson St # 300
Suite 300
Boise, ID 83702-5389

208-384-6161
Fax: 208-384-7189 www.bc.com

Corrugated containers
President: Stanley Bell
Chief Executive Officer: Thomas Carlile
Chief Financial Officer: Wayne Rancourt
Senior Vice President: Thomas Corrick
Manager: Bill Bialkowsky
Vice President of Sales & Marketing: Dennis Huston
Vice President of Operations: Dan Hutchinson
Estimated Sales: Over $1 Billion
Number Employees: 5000-9999

19789 Boise Cascade Corporation
1544 W 27th St
Burley, ID 83318

208-678-3531
Fax: 208-677-7719 www.bc.com

Containers and boxes
CEO: Thomas Corrick
Estimated Sales: $50 - 100 Million
Number Employees: 100-249
Parent Co: Boise Cascade Corporation

19790 Boise Cold Storage Co
495 S 15th St
Boise, ID 83702-6846

208-344-8477
Fax: 208-344-8598 www.boisecoldstorage.com

Ice; warehouse providing cold, dry and freezer storage; also, distribution available
Owner: Tim Johnson
tfj@boisecold.com
Office Manager: B Grover
General Manager: M Tallent
Estimated Sales: $1-2,500,000
Number Employees: 20-49
Square Footage: 100000

19791 Boldt Co
2525 N Roemer Rd
Appleton, WI 54911-8623

920-739-6321
Fax: 920-739-4409 info@boldt.com
www.theboldtcompany.com

Offering consulting, construction and maintenance solutions throughout the United States
President/COO: Robert DeKoch
CEO: Thomas Boldt
thomas.boldt@boldt.com
CFO: Dale Von Behren
CEO: Thomas J Boldt
Chairman: Oscar Boldt
Marketing Director: Paula Wydeven
President, Chief Operating Officer: Bob DeKoch
Estimated Sales: $1-$3 Million
Number Employees: 1000-4999

19792 Boldt Technologies Corporation
812 10th Street
West Des Moines, IA 50265-3507

515-277-4848
Fax: 515-277-2775

Pouch machines, bag formers/fillers/sealers, cocoa packaging equipment, teabag machinery
President: Donald Vanoort
Estimated Sales: Less than $500,000
Number Employees: 25

19793 Bolling Oven & Machine Company

1101 Jaycox Road
Avon, OH 44011-1394

440-937-6112
Fax: 440-937-6875

Compact revolving tray baking ovens
VP: Lynn Bolling
Sales: Dennis Szalai
Estimated Sales: less than $500,000
Number Employees: 6
Square Footage: 22000

19794 Bollore Inc

60 Louisa Viens Dr
Dayville, CT 06241-1106

860-774-2930
Fax: 860-774-8895 sales@bolloreinc.com
www.bolphane.com

Tea, coffee filters (paper) and shrinkfilms
President: Stephen Brunetti
Estimated Sales: $20-50 Million
Number Employees: 50-99

19795 Bollore Inc

60 Louisa Viens Dr
Dayville, CT 06241-1106

860-774-2930
Fax: 860-774-8895 sales@bolloreinc.com
www.bolphane.com

Specialty plastic films; high performance multipur-
pose, specialty and cross-linked shrink packaging
films. ISO 9001:2000 certified.
President: Stephen Brunetti
  sbrunetti@seniorsnorth.com
CEO: Stephen Brunetti
Estimated Sales: $20 - 50 Million
Number Employees: 50-99

19796 Bolzoni Auramo

17635 Hoffman Way
Homewood, IL 60430-2186

708-957-8809
Fax: 708-957-8832 800-358-5438
sales.us@bolzoni-auramo.com
www.bolzoni-auramo.it

Manufacturer, importer and exporter of lift truck at-
tachments
Vice President: Ad Artuso
  eartuso@bolzoni-auramo.com
VP: Ad Artuso
VP Sales: Ronnie Keene
VP Operations: Ed Artuso
Plant Manager: Jose Cardonas
Purchasing Manager: Brian Cummings
Estimated Sales: $20 Million
Number Employees: 20-49
Square Footage: 14700
Parent Co: Bolzoni SPA

19797 Bolzoni Auramo

17635 Hoffman Way
Homewood, IL 60430-2186

708-957-8809
Fax: 708-957-8832 800-358-5438
sales.us@bolzoni-auramo.com
www.bolzoni-auramo.it

Manufacturer and exporter of lift truck attachments
President: Roberto Scotti
Vice President: Ad Artuso
  eartuso@bolzoni-auramo.com
General Manager: Dick Fennessey
Estimated Sales: $5-10 Million
Number Employees: 20-49
Parent Co: Auramo O.Y.

19798 Bon Chef

205 State Route 94
Lafayette, NJ 07848-4617

973-383-8848
Fax: 973-383-1827 800-331-0177
info@bonchef.com www.bonchef.com

Food presentation items. Products include chafing
dishes, coffee urns, sandstone servingware, buffet
bars, custom counter-tops and more.
President: Salvatore Torre
Vice President: Anthony Lo Grippo
Director of Sales Administration: Amy Passafaro
Estimated Sales: $2.5-5 Million
Number Employees: 20-49

19799 Bonar Engineering & Constr Co

565 Edgewood Ave S
Jacksonville, FL 32205-5332

904-389-6700
Fax: 904-389-6003 henry3rd@bonareng.com
www.bonareng.com

Owner: Henry Bonar
  hank@bonarengineering.com
Estimated Sales: $3 - 5 Million
Number Employees: 5-9

19800 Bonar Plastics

1005 Atlantic Dr
West Chicago, IL 60185

402-465-6497
Fax: 402-465-1220 800-295-3725
www.bonarplastics.com

Custom plastic rotational molded bulk bins, tanks,
hoppers, drums, combo bins, etc
President: John Bielby
CFO: Don Layng
Quality Control: Gustavo Cuevas
Sales Director: Jerry Ankiewicz
  jankiewicz@bonarplastics.com
Plant Manager: Gustavo Cuevas
Estimated Sales: Below $5 Million
Number Employees: 50-99
Square Footage: 200000

19801 Bonar Plastics

6111 S 6th Way
Ridgefield, WA 98642

360-887-2230
Fax: 360-887-3553 800-972-5252
www.bonarplastics.com

Bulk food handling bins
President: John Bielby
CFO: Lee Robinson
Sales/Marketing: Larry Hughes
Contact: Joel Carter
  jcarter@bonarplastics.com
Plant Manager: Jeff Harms
Estimated Sales: $20-50 Million
Number Employees: 100-249
Square Footage: 100000
Parent Co: Low & Bonar
Brands:
    Bonar
    Payloader
    Polar
    Two-Can

19802 (HQ)Bonneau Company

3334 South Tech Boulevard
Miamisburg, OH 45342

937-886-9100
Fax: 937-886-9300 800-394-0678
www.bonneaucompany.com

Manufacturer, importer and exporter of commercial
and industrial dyes including paraffin,
microcrystalline waxes and blends
President: Timothy Muldoon
VP/Technical Director: Paul Guinn
Estimated Sales: $5 - 10 Million
Number Employees: 1-4
Square Footage: 60000
Brands:
    Bonn Dye
    Bonn Trace

19803 Bonnot Co

1301 Home Ave
Akron, OH 44310-2654

330-896-6544
Fax: 330-896-0822 info@thebonnotco.com
www.thebonnotco.com

Manufacturer and exporter of extruders for food,
chemicals, ceramics, catalysts, etc
President: George Bain
CFO: Becky Goulden
VP: John Negrelli
Engineering Manager: Kurt Houk
General Manager: George W. Bain
Contact: Vince Damicone
  damicone@thebonnotco.com
Controller: Becky Bouldon
Estimated Sales: $2.5 - 5 Million
Number Employees: 10-19
Square Footage: 160000

19804 Bonsai World

PO Box 2634
Union City, CA 94587-7634

510-784-8880
Fax: 510-784-8882 888-744-5444

Decorative water fountains
General Manager: Yoshi Nozawa
Marketing Manager: Francis Marsal
Number Employees: 7
Brands:
    Fountainside

19805 Booth

2007 Royal Ln
Dallas, TX 75229-3263

972-243-0014
Fax: 912-243-8075 800-497-2958

Beverage dispensers
President: J Raulerson
Vice President: Robert Weeks
Marketing Director: JoAnn Leach
Sales Director: Jon Noble
Estimated Sales: $10-20 Million
Number Employees: 1-4
Parent Co: Welbilt Corporation

19806 Borgwaldt KC

7741 Whitepine Rd
N Chesterfield, VA 23237-2212

804-271-6471
Fax: 804-275-9070 www.borgwaldt.hauni.com

Wine industry pH valves and manufactures of ma-
chinery for tobacco industry
President: Michael Connor
  michaelc@borgwaldt-kc.com
Managing Director: Shawn Maxwell
Estimated Sales: $2.5-5 Million
Number Employees: 20-49

19807 Bormioli Rocco Glass Company

41 Madison Ave
New York, NY 10010-2202

212-719-3605
Fax: 212-719-3605
lmonastero@bormiolirocco.com
www.bormiolirocco.com

Storage containers: jars, hermetic closures with wire
bail mechanism, terrines with wire bail closures,
bottles, decanters, vacuum jars
President: Greg Simone
Contact: Paolo Abbreviato
  paolo_abbreviato@bormiolirocco.com
Estimated Sales: $10-20 Million
Number Employees: 5-9

19808 Born Printing Company

1125c Destro Rd #C
Baltimore, MD 21223-3222

410-646-7768
Fax: 410-644-6638

Can and bottle labels
President: Michael Born
VP: Timothy Born
VP: Richard Born
VP: Timothy Born
Estimated Sales: $1 - 2.5 Million
Number Employees: 10-19
Square Footage: 9600

19809 Borroughs Corp

3002 N Burdick St
Kalamazoo, MI 49004-3483

269-342-0161
Fax: 269-342-4161 800-748-0227
www.borroughs.com

Manufacturer and exporter of industrial and com-
mercial steel shelving, checkout counters and office
filing units
President: Timothy Tyler
  ttyler@borroughs.com
Sales: Rick Stear
Estimated Sales: $20-50 Million
Number Employees: 250-499
Square Footage: 450000

19810 Bosch Packaging Svc

2440 Sumner Blvd
Raleigh, NC 27616-3275

919-877-0886
Fax: 919-877-0887 888-546-5744
www.siggroup.com

Bag and pouch sealers, bag filling and sealing machines, brush wrapping, foiling, carton machines: closing, filling, forming, horizontal form and fill, sear machines, robotics, pharmaceutical packaging
Vice President: Tod Torey
VP: Tod Torey
Estimated Sales: $5 - 10 Million
Number Employees: 50-99

19811 Bosch Packaging Technology
869 S Knowles Ave
New Richmond, WI 54017-1745
715-246-6511
Fax: 715-246-6539 www.boschpackaging.com
Manufacturer and exporter of carton and tray forming and sealing machines, horizontal wrappers and bag closing machines
President: William Heilhecker
CFO: Julie Foss
Sales: Mike Wilcox
Director Sales: John Bowerman
Director Operations: Mark Hanson
Estimated Sales: $30 - 50 Million
Number Employees: 100-249
Parent Co: SIG
Brands:
At
Bd-Iii
Cbs-B
Cbs-Ch
Hd-900
J-Series
Microtronic
Mustang
Mustang Iv
Pc-1200
S-Ch
Scotty Ii
Servotronic
Super H
Super Mustang

19812 Bosch Packaging Technology Inc
8700 Wyoming Ave N
Minneapolis, MN 55445-1836
763-424-4700
Fax: 763-493-6776 www.boschpackaging.com
Phamaceutical and nutraceutical packaging
President: Don Demorett
CEO: Tom Mcdaniel
tom.mcdaniel@bosch.com
CFO: Jack Tsahalis
CEO: Tom McDaniel
R & D: Al Peterson
Quality Control: L S Gagnerls
Number Employees: 100-249

19813 Bosch Packaging Technology Inc
8700 Wyoming Ave N
Minneapolis, MN 55445-1836
763-424-4700
Fax: 763-493-6776
pharm-na@boschpackaging.com
www.boschpackaging.com
Supplier of filling, processing, and packaging technology for piece goods and bulk items in the food, pharmaceutical, and confectionery sectors as well as for health and hygiene products.
CEO: Tom Mcdaniel
tom.mcdaniel@bosch.com
Chief Executive Officer: Tom McDaniel
Number Employees: 100-249

19814 Bosch Packaging Technology
869 S Knowles Ave
New Richmond, WI 54017-1745
715-246-6511
Fax: 715-246-6539 www.boschpackaging.com
Packaging machinery inclusing bag sealers, horizontal flow wrappers, vertical form-fill-seal machines, carton formers, carton closers, and delta robotics.
Sales: Mike Wilcox
Number Employees: 100-249
Parent Co: Robert Bosch GmbH

19815 Bosch Packaging Technology
9890 Red Arrow Hwy
Bridgman, MI 49106-9001
269-466-4000
Fax: 269-466-4040 vtnf@boschpackaging.com
www.boschpackaging.com
VP: John Staruch
Number Employees: 50-99

19816 Bosch Rexroth Corp
14001 S Lakes Dr
Charlotte, NC 28273-6791
800-739-7684
info@boschrexroth-us.com
www.boschrexroth-us.com
Linear actuators, linear guides, subassemblies, machine bases and frames.
President & CEO: Paul Cooke
EVP & CFO: Christoph Kleu
SEVP, Technical & Engineering: Matthias Aberle
EVP, Hydraulics: Erwin Wieckowski
Year Founded: 2001
Estimated Sales: $5.9 Billion
Number Employees: 33,100
Parent Co: Bosch Rexroth AG
Brands:
Star

19817 Boska Holland
40-4 Radio Circle Drive
Mt Kisco, NY 10549
914-241-3600
Fax: 914-663-5158 usa@boskaholland.com
www.boska.com
Cheese, accessories/supplies i.e. picninc baskets, cooking implements/housewares, display fixtures.
Marketing: Esther Booth

19818 Boss Linerless Label Company
15990 N Greenway Hayden Loop
Suite 900
Scottsdale, AZ 85260-1655
480-348-6362
Fax: 480-348-6399 randkir@hotmail.com
Linerless label applicators for pressure sensitive labels
Estimated Sales: $1 - 5 000,000

19819 Boss Manufacturing Co
1221 Page St
Kewanee, IL 61443-2159
309-852-2131
Fax: 309-852-0848 800-447-4581
custserv@bossgloves.com
Manufacturer, importer and exporter of gloves, boots, protective clothing and aprons
CEO: Louis Graziado
lgraziado@bossgloves.com
VP Sales/Marketing: Brian Wise
Sales Manager: Gerry Stockelman
Purchasing Manager: Summer Cohen
Estimated Sales: $40 Million
Number Employees: 50-99
Parent Co: Boss Holdings
Type of Packaging: Consumer, Food Service, Private Label, Bulk
Other Locations:
Boss Manufacturing Co.
Concord ON
Brands:
Boss (Boots and Gloves)
Tuff Grip (Gloves)

19820 Bossar
650 Hurricane Shoals Rd NW
Lawrenceville, GA 30046-4460
941-351-3023
Fax: 770-817-5031 ckoellner@bossar.com
Horizontal form, fill and seal pouch machines for three or four side sachets, gusset and stand-up pouches with recloseable zipper, spouts, valves, handles or a straw inside for fruit juices
Commercial Manager: Roger Stainton
CFO: Geanne Kaight
Contact: Ken Anderson
kanderson@bossar.com
Estimated Sales: $5 - 10 Million
Number Employees: 10-19
Parent Co: Bossar

19821 Bostik Inc
211 Boston St
Middleton, MA 01949-2128
978-777-0834
Fax: 978-750-7802 888-571-8558
info@booth.com
Adhesives in film, hot melt, liquid, web and Vitol resins
Key Person: Pat Lamb
CEO: Michael Klonne
michael.klonne@bostik-us.com
CEO: Mike Klonne
Number Employees: 100-249

19822 Boston Gear
229 Berkeley St
Suite 410
Boston, MA 02116
617-859-8439
Fax: 617-479-6238 888-999-9860
info@bostongear.com
www.bostongroundwater.org
the Colfax Power Transmission Group is a leading supplier of mechanical and electrical power transmission products to the food processing and packaging machinery industries. With hundreds of years of industry experience Colfax PT hasdeveloped some of the premier products, delivery programs and services available today.
Executive Director: Elliott Laffer
Marketing VP: Craig Schuele
Sales VP: Gerald Ferris
Estimated Sales: $5 - 10 Million
Number Employees: 20-49
Type of Packaging: Bulk
Brands:
Bost-Kleen
Boston Gear
Centrie Clutch

19823 Boston Rack
300 Main Street
223
North Easton, MA 02356
508-230-5755
Fax: 508-880-5449 800-640-5723
info@1stopmth.com www.bostonrack.com
Boston Rack is a nationwide storage and material handling systems integrator. the sales and engineering teams specialize in specific industries including Archive, Food and Beverage, Retail, 3rd Party Logistics, Petroleum, andGovernment.
President/Chief Executive Officer: Peter Murphy
Chief Financial Officer: Sean Medeiros
National Sales Engineer: Alex Hultron
Systems Enginer: Stephen Nolan
GSA Development Manager: Woody Farrow
Operations Manager: Jennifer Aguiar

19824 (HQ)Boston Retail
400 Riverside Ave
Medford, MA 02155-4949
781-395-2656
Fax: 781-395-0155 800-225-1633
info@bostonretail.com www.bostonretail.com
Manufacturer and exporter of space frame systems, damage control products, bumper guards, fixtures and display products
President & CEO: Russell Rubin
rrubin@bostonretail.com
CFO & Vice President: Victor Martin
Estimated Sales: $20 - 50 Million
Number Employees: 50-99
Other Locations:
Boston Retail Products
Youngstown OH
Brands:
Boston Beam
Boston Bumper
Boston Colorguard
Boston Tuffguard
Carts

19825 Boston Shearpump
234 Abby Rd
Manchester, NH 03103-3332
603-627-2340
Fax: 603-627-2019 mixing@admix.com
www.admix.com
President: Lou Beaudette
Estimated Sales: $5 - 10 Million
Number Employees: 20-49

19826 Boston's Best Coffee Roasters
43 Norfolk Ave
South Easton, MA 02375-1190
508-238-8393
Fax: 508-238-6835 800-898-8393
sales@bostonsbestcoffee.com
www.bostonsbestcoffee.com
Coffee, mixers and filters
President: Jacqueline Dovner
CEO: Stephen Fortune
Director of Fundraising Sales: Erin Woodard
Contact: Mary Burke
marymb@bostonsbestcoffee.com
Production Manager: Rocky Raposa

Estimated Sales: Less Than $500,000
Number Employees: 5-9
Square Footage: 5692
Type of Packaging: Consumer, Food Service, Private Label, Bulk
Brands:
David's Gourmet Coffee
Gold Star Coffee
Premier Coffee
Tropical Coffee

19827 Bottom Line Processing Technologies, Inc.
901 Blue Sky Ridge
Snellville
Largo, GA 30078

678-344-7353
Fax: 678-623-9950 888-834-4552

Small scale candy making equipment, batch cookers, continuous cookers, chocolate makers and beverage processing equipment.

19828 Boulder Bar
2635 Ariane Drive
San Diego, CA 92117-3422

858-274-1049
Fax: 858-274-1207

Marketing & Advertising: Lorie Zapf

19829 Bouras Mop Manufacturing Company
1330 Dolman Street
Saint Louis, MO 63104-2908

314-241-5800
Fax: 314-241-9759 800-634-9153

Manufacturer and exporter of corn brooms and brushes, mop heads, deck mops, dust mops and applicators
President: Virgil Bouras
R & D: James Bouras
Estimated Sales: Below $5 Million
Number Employees: 10
Square Footage: 200000

19830 Bower's Awning & Shade
366 N 9th St
Lebanon, PA 17046-3465

717-273-2351
Fax: 717-273-2351

Commercial awnings
Owner: Fred Bowers
Estimated Sales: Less Than $500,000
Number Employees: 1-4

19831 Bowers Process Equipment
487 Lorne Avenue E
Stratford, ON N5A 6T3
Canada

519-271-4757
Fax: 519-271-1092 800-567-3223

mail1@clemmersteelcraft.com www.steelcraft.ca
Manufacturer and exporter of agitators, blenders, bins, kettles, tube fillers, portable air-driven mixers and dairy equipment; also, tanks including mixing
President: Keith Zehr
Chief Executive Officer: Paul Summers
Quality Control: Roy Langford
Marketing: Chris Wyatt
Division Manager, Engineered Products Di: Darcy Vanneste
Operations Manager: Jayson Barlow
Number Employees: 150
Square Footage: 640000
Parent Co: Clemmer Steelcraft Technologies Inc.

19832 Bowlswitch
6580 Valley Center Dr # 6
Fairlawn, VA 24141-5691

540-633-6733
Fax: 540-633-6735 800-338-6733

19833 Bowman Hollis Mfg Corp
2925 Old Steele Creek Rd
Charlotte, NC 28208-6726

704-374-1500
Fax: 704-333-5520 888-269-2358
www.bowmanhollis.com

A full service industrial distributor specializing in industrial belting of all types.
President: Tom Bowman
tbowman@bowmanhollis.com
Marketing/Sales: Steve Broadwell
Sales: Rick Siler
Production Manager: Tom Bowman

Estimated Sales: $5-10 Million
Number Employees: 20-49

19834 Bowtemp
5700 Cote De Liesse Road
Mont-Royal, QC H4T 1B1
Canada

514-735-5551
Fax: 514-735-0751

Thermometers
President: Sam Bern
Manager of Sales: Wayne Pregent
Purchasing Manager: David Parker
Number Employees: 100-249
Brands:
Bowtemp

19835 Boxco
2326 Grissom Dr
St Louis, MO 63146-3311

314-569-9984
Fax: 314-567-4991 800-654-2932
sales@boxcoindustries.com
www.boxcoindustries.com

Specialty food packaging i.e. gift wrap/labels/boxes/containers.
Vice President: David Wolf
Vice President: David Wolf
Marketing: David Wolf
Number Employees: 1-4

19836 (HQ)Boxes.com
184 S Livingston Avenue
Suite 9
Livingston, NJ 07039

201-646-9050
Fax: 201-646-0990 www.boxes.com

Manufacturer and exporter of paper folding boxes, point of purchase displays and cardboard inserts
Estimated Sales: $1 - 5 Million
Number Employees: 19
Square Footage: 100000
Type of Packaging: Consumer, Food Service, Private Label
Brands:
Quick 'n Easy
Quik Lok
Qwik Pak
Swifty

19837 Boyd Lighting Company
30 Liberty Ship Way
Suite 3150
Sausalito, CA 94965

415-778-4300
Fax: 415-778-4319 info@boydlighting.com
www.boydlighting.com

Manufacturer, exporter and importer of decorative and architectural interior lighting; designing services available
President: John Sweet Jr
CEO: Jay Sweet
Design Director: Doyle Crosby
Director of Marketing: Erin Geiszler
Sales Manager: Jane Culligan
Estimated Sales: $10 - 20 Million
Number Employees: 50-99
Square Footage: 80000
Parent Co: Boyd Lighting Company
Other Locations:
Boyd Lighting Co.
Colorado Springs CO

19838 Boyd's Coffee Co
9120 NE Alderwood Road
Portland, OR 97220

800-735-2878
customerservicena@farmerbros.com
www.boydscoffeestore.com

Coffees, teas, cocoa, hot and frozen beverages.
CEO: Jeffrey Newman
Treasurer & Chief Financial Officer: Steve Weeks
Year Founded: 1912
Estimated Sales: $41.6 Million
Number Employees: 100
Number of Brands: 1
Parent Co: Farmer Bros Co
Type of Packaging: Food Service
Other Locations:
Boyd's Coffee Company
Coeur D Alene ID
Brands:
Boyd's Coffee

19839 Boyer Corporation
PO Box 10
La Grange, IL 60525

708-352-2553
Fax: 708-352-2573 800-323-3040
www.boyercorporation.com

Liquid and dry drain openers, metal polishes, lubricants, etc
President: Harold Hurwitz
VP: James Burgener
Contact: Harold Herwitz
h.herwitz@boyercorporation.com
Estimated Sales: Less than $500,000
Number Employees: 1-4
Square Footage: 4000
Brands:
Boyer

19840 Boyle's Famous Corned Beef, LLC
1638 Saint Louis Ave
Kansas City, MO 64101-1130

816-221-6283
Fax: 816-221-3888 800-821-3626

Steaks, corn beef, pastrami and pot roast.
President: Gregg Ouverson
Vice President: Christy Chester
Year Founded: 1955
Estimated Sales: $20-50 Million
Number Employees: 35
Square Footage: 10000
Type of Packaging: Food Service, Private Label, Bulk

19841 Brad's Raw Foods
PO Box 210
Pipersville, PA 18947-0210

215-766-3739
info@bradsrawfoods.com

Raw chips, crackers, kale and onion rings. Organic, gluten free, vegan, non gmo, and kosher.
Owner: Brad Gruno
Contact: Nancy Berger
execoffice@bradsrawchips.com
Number Employees: 5-9
Type of Packaging: Consumer

19842 Bradford A Ducon Company
N25 W23040 Paul Road
Pewaukee, WI 53072-2537

Fax: 800-789-4046 800-789-1718
info@bradfordfittings.com
www.bradfordfittings.com

Manufacturer and importer of stainless steel sanitary fittings, clamps, valves, machined castings and forgings
Quality Control: Bruce Anderson
Marketing: William Duyser
Sales: Jeff Casillo
Operations: Sally Besgrove
Number Employees: 5-9
Square Footage: 40000
Parent Co: Dixon Valve & Coupling

19843 Bradford Co
13500 Quincy St
Holland, MI 49424-9460

616-399-6538
Fax: 616-399-8989 info@bradfordco.com
www.bradfordco.com

Manufacturer of packaging products and material handling systems.
President: Hulda Grin
hgrin@championhealthandfitness.com
Estimated Sales: $2.5-5 Million
Number Employees: 100-249

19844 Bradford Derustit Corp
21660 Waterford Dr
Yorba Linda, CA 92887-2650

714-695-0899
Fax: 714-965-0840 877-899-5315
www.derustit.com

Chemical metal cleaners
President: Ann Denney
VP: Anne Denney
Number Employees: 1-4

19845 (HQ)Bradford Soap Works Inc
200 Providence St
West Warwick, RI 02893-2511

401-821-2141
Fax: 401-821-1660 info@bradfordsoap.com
www.bradfordsoap.com
Manufacturer and exporter of cake soap and industrial detergents
CEO: John H Howland
jhowland@bradfordsoap.com
CEO: John H Howland
VP Sales: Ed Windsor
Estimated Sales: $20-50 Million
Number Employees: 250-499
Type of Packaging: Private Label

19846 Bradley Industries
1 Westbrook Corp Ctr Ste 300
Westchester, IL 60154

815-469-2314
Fax: 815-469-7089
Matchbooks
President: Jon Bradley
Vice President: John Bradley
Estimated Sales: $5-10 Million
Number Employees: 50-99
Square Footage: 120000

19847 Bradley Lifting
1030 Elm St
York, PA 17403-2597

717-848-3121
Fax: 717-843-7102 www.bradleylifting.com
Manufacturer and exporter of material handling
equipment including slab and ingot tongs, plate and
sheet lifters and coil and paper roll grabs
President: Tom Thole
info@bradleylifting.com
CFO: Winfred Bradley
Estimated Sales: $5 - 10 Million
Number Employees: 20-49
Parent Co: Xtek, Inc.

19848 Bradley Ward Systems
635 Montauk Way
Alpharetta, GA 30022-4704

770-754-5899
Fax: 770-754-5876 www.bwsys.com
Manufacturing execution systems for packaging
President: Garry Diver

19849 Bradman Lake Inc
3050 Southcross Blvd
Rock Hill, SC 29730-9055

803-366-3688
Fax: 704-588-3302 usa@bradman-lake.com
www.bradman-lake.com
Specializes in the design and manufacture of packaging machinery
Manager: Steve Irwin
Marketing Director: Mervat El RaFei
Sales Director: Nick Bishop
Plant Manager: Sam Hunnicutt
Estimated Sales: Less Than $500,000
Number Employees: 1-4
Parent Co: Bradman Lake Ltd
Type of Packaging: Bulk
Other Locations:
Bradman Lake Group
Charlotte NC

19850 Brady Enterprises Inc
167 Moore Rd
East Weymouth, MA 02189-2332

781-337-5000
Fax: 781-337-9338 www.bradyenterprises.com
Manufacturer and exporter of cocktail, powdered
drink, stuffing and meatloaf mixes and seasonings;
importer of seasoning; also, spray drying and dish
detergent
President: Kevin Maguire
Chairman/CEO: John Brady
CFO: Mary Gudalawicz
Director QC/R&D: Mike Waytowich
Director Sales/Marketing: Desi Gould
Human Resources: Jack Brady Jr.
Estimated Sales: $11.60 Million
Number Employees: 100-249
Number of Brands: 3
Number of Products: 16
Type of Packaging: Consumer, Food Service
Brands:
Bar-Tenders

Bells
Dishwasher Glisten

19851 Brady Worldwide
P.O. Box 2131
Milwaukee, WI 53201

414-358-6600
Fax: 414-228-5979 www.whbrady.com
Safety signage and regulatory training products:
pipe markers, floor marking materials, numbering
and coding markers, aluminum, fiberglass and vinyl
siding
President: Katherine Hudson
CEO: Frank Jaehnert
Estimated Sales: $50 - 100 Million
Number Employees: 100-249

19852 Bragard Professional Uniforms
201 E 42nd St # 1805
New York, NY 10017-5710

212-759-0202
Fax: 212-353-0318 800-488-2433
customersupport@bragardusa.com
www.bragardusa.com
Manufacturer, importer and exporter of uniforms
and special clothing including aprons, linens, chef's
hats and coats, footwear, cloth towels, etc.; complete
embroidery services available
CEO: Lu Aranzamendez
lua@bragardusa.com
Vice President: Peter Isom
Chief Operating Officer: Benjamin Bragard
Estimated Sales: $1-2.5 Million
Number Employees: 1-4
Parent Co: Bragard SA
Brands:
Bragard
Cooking Star By Bargard

19853 Bran & Luebbe
1234 Remington Rd
Schaumburg, IL 60173-4812

847-882-8116
Fax: 847-882-2319 www.pumpsandprocess.com
Manufacturer and exporter of metering pumps, food
blending systems and analyzers for determination of
protein, fat, moisture and other parameters in food
products
President: Robert Arcaro
Marketing Coordinator: Kelly Breitlando
Director Sales: Jim Hunson
Estimated Sales: $20-50 Million
Number Employees: 50-99
Square Footage: 36000
Parent Co: Bran & Luebbe GmbH

19854 Brand Castle
5111 Richmond Rd
Bedford, OH 44146-1354

216-292-7700
Fax: 216-292-7701 jimmyz@brandcastle.com
www.brandcastle.com
Cookie making kits and decorations
President/Founder: Jimmy Zeilinger
Marketing: Jimmy Zellinger
VP Sales/Marketing: Jim Shlonsky
Contact: Abby Barton
abby_barton@rand.org
Operations Manager: Jeff Berger
Estimated Sales: Less Than $500,000
Number Employees: 5-9

19855 Brand Specialists
PO Box 381146
Duncanville, TX 75138-1146

972-283-8491
Fax: 972-572-9292 888-323-3708
Consultant specializing in product development in-
cluding frozen, fresh and dry items for the retail and
food service markets
President: Dalton Lott
Member of the Board: Daniel F Pickering
VP of Operations: Jon Davies
Estimated Sales: $5-10 Million
Number Employees: 10

19856 Brandstedt Controls Corporation
3600 NW 115th Ave
Doral, FL 33178

305-477-0034
Fax: 305-477-0035 800-426-5488

19857 Branford Vibrator Company
3600 Cougar Drive
Peru, IL 61354-9336

815-224-1200
Fax: 815-224-1241 800-262-2106
www.cougarindustries.com
Manufacturer and exporter of pneumatic and electric
vibrators
President: D Pedritti
Manager: T Zagorski
Estimated Sales: $20-50 Million
Number Employees: 50
Parent Co: Cougar Industries
Brands:
Branford

19858 Branson Ultrasonics Corp
41 Eagle Rd # 1
P.O. Box 1961
Danbury, CT 06810-4179

203-796-0400
Fax: 203-796-0450 www.emersonindustrial.com
the industry leader in the design, development, man-
ufacture, and marketing of plastics joining, precision
cleaning, ultrasonic processing, and ultrasonic metal
welding equipment.
President: Ed M Boone
eboone@bransonultrasonics.com
VP Finance: Robert Tibbets
VP/General Manager-North America: Richard
Gehrin
VP Sales: Rodger Martin
VP Operations: Anthony Prioreschi
Number Employees: 1000-4999

19859 Brass Smith
5125 Race Court
Denver, CO 80216

303-331-8777
Fax: 303-331-8444 800-662-9595
www.zguard.com
Manufacturer and exporter of sneeze guards, hot
merchandising display cases, railing systems, crowd
control posts, menu stands, etc
Human Resources: Dave Carr
Marketing: Wayne Sirmons
Regional Sales Manager: Benny Martinez
Contact: Michael Ackerman
mackerman@bsidesigns.com
Estimated Sales: $5-10 Million
Number Employees: 50-99
Square Footage: 400000
Parent Co: BSI
Brands:
Beltway
Brass Master
Lustre Rail
Z Guard

19860 Braun Brush Co
43 Albertson Ave
Albertson, NY 11507-2198

516-741-6000
Fax: 516-741-6299 800-645-4111
sales@brush.com
Manufacturer, importer and exporter of sanitary
cleaning brushes used for baking, confectionery pro-
cessing, etc
President: Lance Cheney
lance@brush.com
Business Development Director: Peter Lassen
Customer Service: Jerilyn Leis
Accounting: Joan Egidio
Estimated Sales: $2 Million
Number Employees: 20-49
Square Footage: 28000
Parent Co: Braun Industries
Type of Packaging: Consumer, Food Service, Pri-
vate Label, Bulk
Brands:
Saniset

19861 Braun Brush Co
43 Albertson Ave
Albertson, NY 11507-2198

516-741-6000
Fax: 516-741-6299 800-645-4111
sales@brush.com
Manufacturer, importer and exporter of USDA standard and custom designed brushes

President: Lance Cheney
 lance@brush.com
President: Max Cheney
Director of Business Development: Peter Lassen
Customer Service: Jerilyn Leis
Accounting: Joan Egidio
Estimated Sales: $2.5-5 Million
Number Employees: 20-49
Square Footage: 28000

19862 Brazilian Consulate
2601 S Bayshore Dr # 5
Miami, FL 33133-5417
 305-446-3900
 Fax: 305-461-4466

Owner: Raul Arlacon

19863 Brechbuhler Scales
1414 Scales St SW
Canton, OH 44706
 330-453-2424
 Fax: 330-453-5322 www.brechbuhler.com
Manufacturer and exporter of scales including dormant, flour, warehouse, portable, etc
Contact: Mike Ambs
 mambs@bscales.com
Manager: Roger Doerr
Branch Manager: Rick Spradling
Estimated Sales: $1-2.5 Million
Number Employees: 160
Parent Co: Brechbuhler Scales
Type of Packaging: Bulk

19864 Brechteen
30060 23 Mile Rd
Chesterfield, MI 48047-5718
 586-949-2240
Manufacturer and importer of packaging materials
including plastic, cellulose, collagen and fibrous;
manufacturer of stuffing equipment
VP of Sales: Roger Allen
Number Employees: 100-249

19865 Brecoflex Co LLC
222 Industrial Way W
Eatontown, NJ 07724-2206
 732-460-9500
 Fax: 732-542-6725 888-463-1400
 www.brecoflex.com
Manufacturer, and exporter of polyurethane, USDA
and FDA approved timing belts, pulleys, and accessories
President: Bernie Fulleman
VP: Rudolf Schoendienst
Research & Development: Johnathan Weir
Quality Control: Dararith Son
Marketing Director: Joy Guigo
Estimated Sales: $2.5 - 5,000,000
Number Employees: 1-4
Brands:
 Breco
 Brecoflex
 Esband

19866 Breddo Likwifier
1230 Taney N.
Kansas City, MO 64116
 816-561-9050
 Fax: 816-561-7778 800-669-4092
 don.wolfe@corbion.com www.breddo.com
Manufacturer and exporter of high shear blender
with scraped surface heat transfer
President: Ron Ashton
Sales: Don Wolfe
 dwolfe@caravaningredients.com
Estimated Sales: $5 Million
Number Employees: 10-19
Parent Co: American Ingredients Company

19867 Bremer Manufacturing CoInc
W2002 County Road Q
Elkhart Lake, WI 53020-1109
 920-894-2944
 Fax: 920-894-2881 sales@bremermfg.com
 www.bremermfg.com
Aluminum hand scoops
President: Tom Dolack
 tdolack@bremermfg.com
Sales: Tim St Clair
Purchasing: Glen Leahn
Shipping Manager: J Thome
Estimated Sales: $10 - 20 Million
Number Employees: 100-249
Square Footage: 60000

19868 Bren Instruments
308 Century Court
Franklin, TN 37064-3918
 615-794-6825
 Fax: 615-794-7478 info@breninc.com
 www.breninc.com
Automated decal and stencil systems
President: Murray O Wilhoite
 bren308@msn.com
CFO: Brenda Wilhoite
Quality Control Manager: Phill Thomas
Director Marketing/VP: Murray Wilhoite
Estimated Sales: $500,000 - $1 Million
Number Employees: 8

19869 (HQ)Brenner Tank LLC
450 Arlington Ave
Fond Du Lac, WI 54935-5571
 920-922-5020
 Fax: 920-922-3303 800-558-9750
 sales@brennertank.com www.brennertank.com
Manufacturer, importer and exporter of stainless
steel tank transports and intermodal tank containers
President: Bruce D Yakley
 byakley@brennertank.com
Sales Manager: Thomas Ballon
Estimated Sales: $20-50 Million
Number Employees: 100-249
Square Footage: 300000
Parent Co: Wabash National Corp.

19870 Brenton Engineering Co
4750 County Road 13 NE
Alexandria, MN 56308-8022
 320-852-7705
 Fax: 320-852-7621 800-535-2730
 bec@becmail.com
 www.roboticpackagingsystems.com
Manufacturer and exporter of case packers, handling, robotics, and shrink wrappers
President: Jeff Bigger
Sales: Scott Leuschke
Marketing Director: Karen Kielmeyer
Vice President Sales: Troy Snader
Estimated Sales: $20-50 Million
Number Employees: 100-249
Parent Co: ProMach
Brands:
 Brenton

19871 Brentwood Plastics In
8734 Suburban Trak
PO Box 440160
St Louis, MO 63144-2734
 314-968-1135
 Fax: 314-968-4276
Polyethylene films
President: Sam Longstreth
Estimated Sales: $5-10 Million
Number Employees: 20-49
Square Footage: 80000

19872 Bresco
2428 6th Ave S
Birmingham, AL 35233-3322
 205-252-0076
 Fax: 205-323-8630 sales@brescoinc.com
 www.brescoinc.com
Wholesaler/distributor of restaurant equipment and
supplies; design services available
President: George Tobia
 gtobia@brescoinc.com
Estimated Sales: $10-20 Million
Number Employees: 50-99

19873 Brevard Restaurant Equipment
565 Gus Hipp Blvd.
Rockledge, FL 32955 - 48
 321-631-0318
 Fax: 321-631-6040
Wholesaler/distributor of new and used equipment;
serving the food service market; also, design and
layout plans
President: John Schneider
VP: Diana Schneider
General Manager: Glenn Pierson
Estimated Sales: $1-2.5 Million
Number Employees: 1-4
Square Footage: 30000

19874 Brewer-Cantelmo Inc
55 W 39th St # 205
New York, NY 10018-0573
 212-244-4600
 Fax: 212-244-1640 bc@brewer-cantelmo.com
 www.brewer-cantelmo.com
Custom handed crafted menus, room directories, reservation books, check presenters, wine lists, presentation tools.
President: Niyazi Bozkurt
 bozkurt@computeq.com
Vice President: David Kirschenbaum
Estimated Sales: $2 Million
Number Employees: 20-49
Square Footage: 37500

19875 Brewers Outlet-Chestnut Hill
7401 Germantown Ave
Philadelphia, PA 19119-1605
 215-247-1265
 Fax: 215-247-1855 www.mybrewersoutlet.com
Craft and specialty beers
Owner: Paul Egonopoulos
Estimated Sales: $2.5-5 Million
Number Employees: 5-9
Square Footage: 15000
Parent Co: Brewers Outlet

19876 Brewmatic Company
P.O. Box 2959
Torrance, CA 90509
 310-787-5444
 Fax: 310-787-5412 800-421-6860
Manufacturer and exporter of thermal coffee servers,
commercial and domestic drip brewing equipment
and accessories; importer of espresso machines
Manager: Ed Esteban
Research & Development: Traian Zaionciuc
Quality Control: Ron Mann
Marketing Director: Eddison Esteban
Sales Director: Cindi Watson Kramer
Plant Manager: John Galvin
Purchasing Manager: Frank Cherry
Number Employees: 50-99
Square Footage: 300000
Parent Co: Farmer Brothers Company
Type of Packaging: Food Service, Private Label
Other Locations:
 Brewmatic Company
 St. Louis MO
Brands:
 Brewmatic

19877 Bridge Machine Company
614 Kennedy Street
Palmyra, NJ 8065
 856-829-1800
 Fax: 856-786-8147 877-754-1800
 sales@bridgeonline.com www.bridgeonline.com
Designs and manufactures a complete line of food
processing equipment such as patty formers, tenderizers, dumpers/meat tubs, hand tenderizers, cutlet
flatteners, meatball formers, macerators, spreading
conveyors, dicers and stripcutters
President: Terry Bridge
Contact: David Hicks
 david.hicks@bridgeonline.com
Estimated Sales: $10 - 20 Million
Number Employees: 50-99
Square Footage: 28000

19878 Bridgewell Resources LLC
124020 SE Carpenter Dr
Clackamas, OR 97015
 800-481-3557
 webinfo@bridgewellres.com
Edible oils, flours, grains and pulses.
President: Pat McCauley
CEO: Pat McCauley
Chief Financial Officer: Jay Wilson
Vice President of Human Resources: Donna Lesch
Food & Agriculture General Manager: Craig Mullen
Parent Co: Bridgewell Resources
Type of Packaging: Consumer, Food Service, Private Label, Bulk

19879 Briel America
3888 Bluffview Pt
Marietta, GA 30062
 770-509-3006
 Fax: 770-518-6624
Espresso machines, accessories, grinders
President: Wesley Smith
 wesley@smithagy.net

Estimated Sales: $.5 - 1 000,000
Number Employees: 1-4

19880 Bright Technologies
127 N. Water Street
PO Box 296
Hopkins, MI 49328

269-793-7183
Fax: 269-793-8793 800-253-0532
www.brightbeltpress.com
De-packaging compactors, hydraulic cart dumpers, factory direct installation, service, patented Xtractors, patented HighDensity Extruders, patented Belt Filter Presses, mobile, trailer mounted and stationary equipment.
President: Brent Sebright
R&D/Sales: Dennis Sprick
Marketing Director: Jeannie Jansma
Contact: Doug Sebright
 doug@brightbeltpress.com
Operations: T Stuart Sebright
VP Purchasing: Lee Murray
Estimated Sales: $5-10 Million
Number Employees: 50-99
Number of Brands: 2
Number of Products: 80

19881 Bright of America
200 Greenbrier Rd
PO Box 460
Summersville, WV 26651

304-872-3000
Fax: 304-872-3040 www.brightwv.com
Place and counter mats
President: Steve Pridemore
Contact: John Whelan
 jwhelan@brightwv.com
Estimated Sales: $10 - 20 Million
Number Employees: 20-49
Square Footage: 400000
Parent Co: Russ Berrie & Company

19882 Bril-Tech
1506 Baltimore Street
Defiance, OH 43512-1908

419-782-2430
Fax: 419-784-9717
Air pollution control, drying rooms, ovens, smokehouses, refrigeration systems and tempering systems

19883 Brill Manufacturing Co
715 S James St
Ludington, MI 49431-2368

231-843-2430
Fax: 231-845-9966 866-896-6420
www.brillcompany.com
Pine and oak tables, chairs and booths
President: David Field
 dfield@brillcompany.com
Estimated Sales: $2.5-5 Million
Number Employees: 50-99
Square Footage: 192000

19884 Brimrose Corporation ofAmerica
19 Loveton Cir
Hunt Valley Loveton Center
Sparks Glencoe, MD 21152-9201

410-472-7070
Fax: 410-472-7960 office@brimrose.com
www.brimrose.com
Manufacturer of AOTF-NIR spectrometers for process control with accelerated speeds of up to 16,000 wavelengths per second.
Vice President of Sales & Marketing: Benjamin Fried

19885 (HQ)Brinkmann Corporation
4215 McEwen Rd
Dallas, TX 75244

972-387-4939
800-468-5252
Manufacturer and exporter of smokers and cookers; also, lighting including portable emergency, flashlights, lanterns, electronic flashers and electronic assemblies
President: Jon Brinkmann
VP: Erma Eddins
Contact: Brad Adams
 badams@thebrinkmanncorp.com
Estimated Sales: $20-50 Million
Number Employees: 100-249

19886 Brinkmann Instruments, Inc.
6555 Pelican Creek Circle
Riverview, FL 33578-8653

813-316-4700
Fax: 516-334-7506 800-645-3050
www.brinkmann.com
Seward blenders, grinding mills and sievers, binders and ovens, fat determination systems, universal solvent extraction systems and lab equipment
President & Chief Executive Officer: Michael Melingo
Contact: Felicia Nelson
 f.nelson@metrohmusa.com
Estimated Sales: $20.40 Million
Number Employees: 143

19887 Brisker Dry Food Crisper
PO Box 7000
Oldsmar, FL 34677

813-854-5231
Fax: 800-854-3069 800-356-9080
Manufacturer and exporter of electric kitchen countertop storage appliances designed to keep crackers, chips, cereals, etc. free of humidity
CEO: Anita Rybicki
Estimated Sales: $1 - 5 Million
Number Employees: 7
Number of Brands: 1
Number of Products: 1
Square Footage: 48000
Type of Packaging: Consumer, Food Service
Brands:
 Brisker

19888 Bristol Associates Inc
5777 W Century Blvd # 855
Suite 865
Los Angeles, CA 90045-5671

310-670-0525
Fax: 310-670-4075 www.bristolassoc.com
Executive recruitment firm serving the food industry
President: Ben Farber
Executive VP: Roberta Borer
 rborer@bristolassoc.com
Director Marketing: Laurie Stern
Number Employees: 5-9

19889 Britt Food Equipment
684733 HWY 2
RR 3
Woodstock, ON N4S 7V7
Canada

519-533-0365
Fax: 519-533-6315
Equipment and machinery to the red meat, poultry, fish and pet food industries
President: Brad Britton
Vice President: Greg Britton
Estimated Sales: $750,000
Number Employees: 3

19890 Britt's Barbecue
1678 Montgomery Highway
Suite 104
Birmingham, AL 35216

205-612-6538
Stationery and trailer commercial smokers
Owner: James Britt

19891 Bro-Tex Inc
800 Hampden Ave
St Paul, MN 55114-1299

651-645-5721
Fax: 651-646-1876 800-328-2282
www.brotex.com
Polishing cloths, industrial paper and cloth wipers and Turkish bar mops
President: Arlys Freeman
CEO: Roger Greenberg
Estimated Sales: $21 Million
Number Employees: 100-249
Square Footage: 200000
Brands:
 Bx-100
 Dual-Tex

19892 Broadcom Inc.
1320 Ridder Park
San Jose, CA 95131

learn@broadcom.com
www.broadcom.com
Software for systems, financial and warehouse management, etc.

President & CEO: Hock Tan
CFO: Tom Krause
Chief Legal Officer: Mark Brazeal
VP/Corporate Controller: Kristen Spears
Senior VP/Chief Sales Officer: Charlie Kawwas
Year Founded: 1961
Estimated Sales: $20.8 Billion
Number Employees: 15,000

19893 Broadmoor Baker
1301 5th Ave
Seattle, WA 98101-2603

206-624-3660
Fax: 206-464-1389
Consultant specializing in the development and marketing of specialty bread recipes
Owner: Paul Suzman
Estimated Sales: less than $500,000
Number Employees: 1-4

19894 Broadway Companies
6161 Ventnor Ave
Dayton, OH 45414

937-890-1888
Fax: 937-890-5678 billbirch@aol.com
Innovations for custom molds, preforms and bottle designs, prototyping and production, injection preform models, blow molds, family molds that combine multiple sizes and finishes
Owner: Bill Gaiser
Contact: Ken Enneking
 kenneking@broadwayco.com
Estimated Sales: $10-20 000,000
Number Employees: 100-249

19895 Broaster Co LLC
2855 Cranston Rd
Beloit, WI 53511-3991

608-365-0193
Fax: 608-363-7957 800-365-8278
broaster@broaster.com
www.genuinebroasterchicken.com
Manufacturer and exporter of gas and electric pressure fryers, ventless fryers, warmers, broilers and rotisseries
President: Richard Schrank
 rschrank@broaster.com
Vice President: Tracy Choppi
Marketing Director: Mark Markwardt
Sales Director: Randy McKinney
Plant Manager: Gene Halley
Purchasing Manager: Lee Blehinger
Number Employees: 50-99
Brands:
 Aristo-Ray
 Bro-Tisserie
 Broaster
 Broaster Chicken
 Broaster Foods
 Broaster Recipe
 Perfect Hold Deli Case
 Snack-Mate

19896 Brock Awnings LTD
211 E Montauk Hwy # 1
Hampton Bays, NY 11946-2035

631-728-3367
Fax: 631-728-0134 sales@brockawnings.com
www.brockawnings.com
Commercial awnings
President: Earl Brock
Estimated Sales: $500,000-$1,000,000
Number Employees: 5-9

19897 Brogdex Company
1441 W 2nd St
Pomona, CA 91766

909-622-1021
Fax: 909-629-4564
Manufacturer and exporter of cleaners and chemicals for use in film/wax coatings for fresh fruits and vegetables; exporter of fruit and vegetable processing and handling equipment
President: Kirk Bannerman
Vice President: Greg Appel
Contact: Linda Smith
 lindas@paceint.com
Number Employees: 50-99
Brands:
 Britex

19898 Brooklace
P.O. Box 2038
Oshkosh, WI 54903-2038

Fax: 203-937-4583 800-572-4552
www.brooklace.com
Manufacturer and exporter of paper, foil, glassine
and grease-proof doilies, place mats, tray covers,
baking cups, cake decorating triangles and hot dog
trays
President: Charles Foster
VP of Sales: Brian Schofield
VP of Manufacturing: James Stryker
Estimated Sales: $30 - 50 Million
Number Employees: 50-99
Square Footage: 50000
Parent Co: Hoffmaster
Brands:
   Brooklace

19899 Brooklyn Boys Pizza & Pasta
9967 Glades Rd
Boca Raton, FL 33434-3920

561-477-3663
Manufacturer and wholesaler of knives, cutlery,
china, dinnerware and related table-setting products
Owner: Carlos Sierra
Estimated Sales: $1 - 5 Million
Number Employees: 10-19

19900 Brooks Barrel Company
8 W Hamilton St
Baltimore, MD 21201-5008

410-228-0790
Fax: 410-221-1693 800-398-2766
brooksbarrel@shorenet.net
www.brooksbarrel.com
Wooden barrels, kegs, planters and buckets; whole-
saler/distributor of bushel baskets and crates for
shipping and display
President: Kenneth Knox
Office Manager: Tammy Doege
Estimated Sales: $500,000 - $1 Million
Number Employees: 15
Square Footage: 40000

19901 Brooks Instrument LLC
407 W Vine St
Hatfield, PA 19440-3000

215-362-3500
Fax: 215-362-3745 888-554-3569
brooksam@brooksinstrument.com
www.brooksinstrument.com
Manufacturer and exporter of measurement instru-
mentation for gas and liquid flow
President: Jim Dale
Cmo: Jim Hollis
   jim.hollis@emersonprocess.com
CFO: Joe Doeters
Quality Control: Kevin Gallagher
R & D: Steve Glaudel
Marketing: T Hannigan
Sales: R Fravel
Number Employees: 100-249
Parent Co: Emerson Electric Company
Brands:
   Brooks

19902 Brookshire Grocery Company
P.O. Box 1411
Tyler, TX 75710-1411

903-534-3000
888-937-3776
www.brookshires.com
Regional supermarket chain in Texas, Louisiana and
Arkansas.
Chairman/CEO: Brad Brookshire
Year Founded: 1928
Estimated Sales: $3.4 Billion
Number Employees: 14,000+
Number of Brands: 8
Brands:
   Brookshire's
   Full Circle
   Goldenbrook Farms
   PAWS Premium
   Tasty Bakery
   Top Care
   Valu Time
   World Classics

19903 Brose Chemical Company
702 Bridge St
Twin Falls, ID 83301

208-733-1045
Fax: 208-733-1320
Manufactures chemicals for food processing and
mining industries
President: David Brose
Vice President: Susan Brose
Research & Development: Jim Brose
Sales Director: Ken Stewart
Production Manager: Dick Clarkson
Estimated Sales: 1-5 000,000
Number Employees: 10-19
Number of Brands: 1
Type of Packaging: Private Label, Bulk

19904 Brothers Manufacturing
PO Box 220
Hermansville, MI 49847-0220

906-498-7771
Fax: 906-498-2150 888-277-6117
Storage tanks and liquid handling systems
Operations Manager: Bob Triest
Estimated Sales: $10-20,000,000
Number Employees: 50-99
Square Footage: 33000

19905 Brothers Metal Products
1780 E McFadden Ave #117
Santa Ana, CA 92705-4648

714-972-3008
Fax: 714-632-5032
Manufacturer and exporter of vegetable slicers and
dryers; also, wash tank conveyors and packaging
and receiving tables
President: Gregory Siegmann
Estimated Sales: $600,000
Number Employees: 4
Square Footage: 22000
Type of Packaging: Food Service
Brands:
   Legrow

19906 Broughton Foods LLC
1701 Greene St
Marietta, OH 45750

740-373-4121
Fax: 740-373-2861 800-395-7004
www.dairypure.com
Milks, premium and homestyle ice cream, novelty
ice cream, juices and fruit drinks, cottage cheese,
sour cream, and chip dip.
Principal: Michael McCullum
General Manager: David Broughton
Executive Vice President: George Broughton
Estimated Sales: $46.6 Million
Number Employees: 100-249
Square Footage: 8000
Parent Co: Dean Foods
Type of Packaging: Consumer, Food Service, Bulk

19907 Brower
609 Main Street
P.O. Box 2000
Houghton, IA 52631

319-469-4141
Fax: 319-469-4402 800-553-1791
sales@hawkeyesteel.com www.hawkeyesteel.com
Manufacturer and exporter of poultry processing
equipment including scalders, pickers, evicerating
equipment and related accessories. Specialize in
small and medium plants.
President: Tom Wenstrand
VP Sales: Cindy Wellman
Estimated Sales: $10 - 20 Million
Number Employees: 50-99
Square Footage: 400000
Parent Co: Hawkeye Steel Products
Type of Packaging: Consumer
Brands:
   Batch Pik
   Brower
   Super Pik
   Super Scald

19908 Brower Equipment Co
3750 Getwell Cv
Memphis, TN 38118-5909

901-365-7991
Fax: 901-367-2925 info@browerequipment.net
www.browerequipment.net
Process tank, controls, installation pumps, fittings
and valve designs

President: Chandler Brower
   cbrower@browerequipment.net
Estimated Sales: $5-10 000,000
Number Employees: 5-9

19909 Brown & Caldwell
201 N Civic Dr # 115
Suite 115
Walnut Creek, CA 94596-3865

925-937-9010
Fax: 925-932-9026 800-727-2224
info@brwncald.com
Environmental engineer and consultant offering san-
itation, waste water, testing and analytical services
President: Craig Goehring
Finance Administration Manager: Angela Ferrif
Director Marketing: Diana Levin
Contact: Norman Abrams
   nabrams@conet.ucla.edu
Director Operations: Jim Meehan
Estimated Sales: $3 - 5 Million
Number Employees: 1-4

19910 Brown Chemical Co
302 W Oakland Ave
Oakland, NJ 07436-1381

201-337-0900
Fax: 201-337-9026 800-888-9822
sales@brownchem.com www.brownchem.com
Liquid packaging, contract warehousing, vendor
managed inventory programs, custom blending, reg-
ulatory compliance assistance, USP, food grade and
kosher packaging
Owner: Doug Blum
   dougblum@subway.com
VP: Patrick Brown
VP Finance and Operations: Dave Lyle
Executive Secretary: Eileen Lyness
Office Manager: Doug Blum
Manager Information Systems: Rob Eckert
Operations Manager: Mark Donatiello
Estimated Sales: $20-50 Million
Number Employees: 10-19

19911 (HQ)Brown Fired Heater
300 Huron St
Elyria, OH 44035-4829

440-323-3291
Fax: 440-323-5734 www.enerconsystems.com
Manufacturer and exporter of process temperature
control systems, fluid heat systems and incinerators
President: David Hoecke
   dhoecke@enerconsystemsinc.com
Vice President: John Somodi
Estimated Sales: $3 Million
Number Employees: 10-19
Square Footage: 100000
Brands:
   Consertherm
   Super-Trol
   Ventomatic

19912 Brown International Corp LLC
333 Avenue M NW
Winter Haven, FL 33881-2405

863-299-2111
Fax: 863-294-2688 info@brown-intl.com
www.brown-intl.com
Manufacturer and exporter of fruit and vegetable
processing equipment including extractors, pulpers,
finishers, dewaterers, sizers and processing lines
President: Scott Alexander
COO: Pete Devito
   pete.d@brown-intl.com
VP: Ann Williams
Sales: Jim Sheppard
Operations: Bryce Adolph
Purchasing: Bruce Strong
Estimated Sales: $20-50 Million
Number Employees: 50-99
Number of Brands: 1
Number of Products: 85
Square Footage: 70000
Brands:
   Brown

19913 Brown International Corp LLC
333 Avenue M NW
Winter Haven, FL 33881-2405
Canada

863-299-2111
Fax: 863-294-2688 contact@brown-intl.com
www.brown-intl.com
Plastic bottles, closures and sprayers

President: Howard Bassel
COO: Pete Devito
pete.d@brown-intl.com
Number Employees: 50-99

19914 Brown Machine LLC
330 N Ross St
Beaverton, MI 48612

989-435-7741
Fax: 989-435-2821 877-702-4142
brownmachinegroup.com
Thermoforming machinery
Vice President, Operations & COO: Brian Keeley
Estimated Sales: $42 Million
Number Employees: 100-249
Number of Brands: 1
Square Footage: 140000

19915 Brown Manufacturing Company
125 New St Ste A
Decatur, GA 30030

404-378-8311
Fax: 404-378-8311 www.bottleopener.com
Manufacturer and exporter of stationary bottle openers; custom imprinting available.
President: David Brim
Number Employees: 1-4
Square Footage: 5000
Brands:
Starr

19916 Brown Paper Goods Co
3530 Birchwood Dr
Waukegan, IL 60085-8334

847-688-1450
Fax: 847-688-1458
jlabuda@brownpapergoods.com
www.brownpapergoods.com
Cake pan liners and bags including food, garbage, greaseproof, paper, plastic and sandwich
President: Alan Mones
CEO: Allen Mons
amons@brownpapergoods.com
Estimated Sales: $20-50 Million
Number Employees: 100-249

19917 Brown Plastics & Equipment
683 Main Street # 1
Falmouth, MA 02540-3221

508-540-3990
Fax: 508-540-3963 www.falmouthlawyer.com
Partner: Paula M Barbosa
Estimated Sales: $300,000-500,000
Number Employees: 1-4

19918 Brown's Sign & Screen Printing
8299 Hazelbrand Road NE
Covington, GA 30014-3406

770-786-2257
Fax: 770-784-1324 800-540-3107
Manufacturer and exporter of flags, pennants, banners, signs and advertising specialties; screen printing and lettering services available
President: Mike Brown
Estimated Sales: Less than $500,000
Number Employees: 4

19919 Brown/Millunzi & Associates
3305 Tampa St
Houston, TX 77021-1143

713-747-2870
Fax: 713-237-0761 800-460-3387
Consultant specializing in the design of food and beverage facilities; also, project management services available
Prin.: Daniel Brown
Prin.: Robert Millunzi
Prin.: Robert Pursell
Estimated Sales: $300,000-500,000
Number Employees: 1-4

19920 Browne & Company
100 Esna Park Drive
Markham, ON L3R 1E3
Canada

905-475-6104
Fax: 866-849-4719 sales@browneco.com
www.browneco.com
A leading supplier of glassware, dinnerware and smallwares to the food service industry in Canada

President: Michael Browne
CFO: Alen Budish
Vice President: Brian Wood
Marketing Director: Katherine Dilk
Sales Director: Brian Wood
Number Employees: 10
Type of Packaging: Food Service

19921 Bruce Industrial Co Inc
4049 New Castle Ave
New Castle, DE 19720-1496

302-655-9616
Fax: 302-656-4327 866-866-4331
service@bruceindustrial.com
www.bruceindustrial.com
Wholesaler/distributor of material handling equipment including overhead and modular lifts, enclosures, rigging, etc
President: Clem Bason
sales@bruceindustrial.com
CEO: Doug Johnston
Estimated Sales: $10 Million
Number Employees: 50-99
Square Footage: 40000
Brands:
Akro-Mils
Aleco
Alm
Ballymore
Bishamon
Bluegiant
Cm
Cotterman
Eagle
Faultless
Fred Silver
Gorbel
Hamilton
Hytrol
Keymaster
Langley
Lift-Rite
Magline
Omni Spaceguard
Palamatic
Presto
Republic

19922 Bruins Instruments
P.O. Box 1023
Salem, NH 03079

603-898-6527
Fax: 978-485-0055 info@bruinsinstruments.com
www.bruinsinstruments.com
NIR analyzers for the agricultural and food industries.
President: Hans Joachim Bruins
Contact: Hans Bruins
hans.bruins@bruinsinstruments.com

19923 Brulin & Company
2920 Dr Andrew J Brown Ave
Indianapolis, IN 46205

317-923-3211
Fax: 317-925-4596 800-776-7149
www.brulin.com
Manufacturer and exporter of sanitation products including disinfectants, hand care, food sanitation and floor care chemicals. ISO 9002 certified
President: Charles Pollnow
VP Sales/Marketing: Michael Falkowski
Marketing Coordinator: Janet Cleary Salisbury
Marketing Manager (Commerical Products): Garry Thornley
Estimated Sales: $10-20 Million
Number Employees: 100-249
Brands:
815 Mx
Quat Clean Sanitizer
Spotlight

19924 Bruni Glass
2750 Maxwell Way
Fairfield, CA 94534-9708

707-421-2946
Fax: 707-752-6201 877-278-6445
info@bruniglass.com
Glass packaging, specialty and custom glass jars and bottles
Contact: Samantha Bieganowski
samantha.bieganowski@bruniglass.com
Number Employees: 1-4

19925 Bruni Glass Packaging
1449 46TH Ave
Lachine Montreal, QC H8T 3C5
Canada

514-633-9247
Fax: 514-633-9878 877-771-7856
info@bruniglass.com www.bruniglass.com
Glass containers for food, pharmaceutical and related products; bottles for distillates, wine, oil and vinegar
President: Roberto Delbon
CEO: Gino Delbon
Marketing: Mark Bassel
Number Employees: 26

19926 Brush Research Mfg Co Inc
4642 Floral Dr
Los Angeles, CA 90022-1288

323-261-6162
Fax: 323-268-6587 info@brushresearch.com
Manufacturer and exporter of conveyor brushes.
President: Tara Rands
sales@brushresearch.com
VP: Robert Fowlie
General Manager: Don Didier
Estimated Sales: $5-10 Million
Number Employees: 50-99
Square Footage: 300000
Brands:
2-Flap
Flex-Hone
Nam Power

19927 Bruske Products
7447 Duvan Dr
Tinley Park, IL 60477-3714

708-532-3800
Fax: 708-532-3977
customersupport@bruskeproducts.com
www.bruskeproducts.com
Brushes and brooms
President: Steve Schafer
steve.schafer@bruskeproducts.com
Executive Administrator: Susan Bruske
Sales/Marketing Executive: David Cohea
Retail Sales Manager & VP: Steve Schafer
Estimated Sales: $10-20 Million
Number Employees: 50-99
Square Footage: 60000

19928 Brute Fabricators
PO Box 1621
Castroville, TX 78009-1621

210-648-2370
Fax: 210-648-5811 800-777-2788
www.bruterack.com
Manufacturer and exporter of heavy structural steel pallet racks including drive-in, drive-thru and cantilever drive-in
President: Fred Siebrecht
CEO: Brandie Siebrecht
CFO: Ben Cogdell
Number Employees: 20
Square Footage: 81000
Parent Co: Brute Fabricators
Brands:
Brute Rack

19929 Bry-Air Inc
10793 E State Route 37
Sunbury, OH 43074-9311

740-965-2974
Fax: 740-965-5470 877-379-2479
info@bry-air.com www.bry-air.com
Manufacturers of industrial dehumidifiers.
President/CEO: Mel Meyers
bryair1@bry-air.com
Executive VP: Doug Howery
Quality Control: Rick Frenier
Plant Manager: Ron Busch
Purchasing Director: Debra Kemmer
Estimated Sales: $5-10 Million
Number Employees: 20-49

19930 Bryan Boilers
783 Chili Ave
Peru, IN 46970

765-473-6651
Fax: 765-473-3074 inquires@bryansteam.com
www.bryanboilers.com
Manufacturer and exporter of boilers, blow down separators, boiler feed systems and de-aerators

President: Tom May
CEO: Dale Bowman
Sales/Marketing Manager: Dick Holmquist
Estimated Sales: $20,000,000 - $49,999,999
Number Employees: 250-499
Parent Co: Bryan Steam LLC

19931 Bryant Glass
619 Main St
Wilmington, MA 01887-3215
978-988-9300
Fax: 978-988-9111 800-369-2782
bryantglass@verizon.net www.bryantglassco.com
High pressure pumps and homogenizers
Owner: Bob Bryant
Estimated Sales: Less Than $500,000
Number Employees: 1-4

19932 Bryant Products Inc
W1388 Elmwood Ave
Ixonia, WI 53036-9437
920-206-6920
Fax: 920-206-6929 800-825-3874
www.bryantpro.com
Manufacturer and exporter of tensioning devices for
conveyors, straight and tapered rollers, machine
grade conveyor pulleys
President: Fred Thimmel
Vice President: Dave Roessler
dave@bryantpro.com
Purchasing: Jody Mack
Estimated Sales: $20-50 Million
Number Employees: 20-49
Square Footage: 50000
Brands:
Airform
Telescoper
Tieltrack

19933 Bryce Corp
4505 Old Lamar Ave
P.O. Box 18338
Memphis, TN 38118-7063
901-369-4400
Fax: 901-367-5670 800-238-7277
www.brycecorp.com
Convertable flexible packaging including candy
wrappers and potato chip bags
President: John Bryce
CEO: Tom Bryce
VP Sales: Paul Rickman
R & D: Mark Montsinger
Number Employees: 1000-4999

19934 Bubbla Inc
7931 Deering Ave
Canoga Park, CA 91304-5008
818-884-2000
Fax: 818-884-2164 www.bubbla.com
President: Andrew Cooper
Marketing: Cindy Daley
Estimated Sales: $3 - 5 Million
Number Employees: 1-4

19935 Buck Ice & Coal Co
2400 12th Ave
Columbus, GA 31901-1354
706-322-5451
Fax: 706-322-5453
Manufacturer and packager of ice. Private label
packaging available
Owner: William C Buck
mailbucki@aol.com
CEO: W Buck, Jr.
Estimated Sales: $1 - 3 Million
Number Employees: 5-9
Number of Products: 1
Square Footage: 120000
Type of Packaging: Consumer, Food Service, Pri-
vate Label
Brands:
Buck Ice

19936 Buck Knives
660 S Lochsa St
Post Falls, ID 83854-5200
208-262-0500
Fax: 208-262-0738 800-326-2825
www.buckknives.com
Manufacturer and exporter of fish fillet knives and
cutlery.

Chairman: Charles Buck
CEO: Cj Buck
chuckbuck@buckknives.com
VP Sales/Marketing: Rob Morgan
Estimated Sales: $20-50 Million
Number Employees: 100-249
Square Footage: 200000
Brands:
Buck

19937 (HQ)Buckeye Group
4700 Wilmington Pike
South Charleston, OH 45368
937-462-8361
Fax: 937-462-7071
Wooden packaging including boxes
President: Sam McAdow
Estimated Sales: $10-20 Million
Number Employees: 50-99
Other Locations:
Buckeye Group
South Charleston OH

19938 Buckeye International
2700 Wagner Pl
Maryland Heights, MO 63043-3400
314-291-1900
Fax: 314-298-2850
www.buckeyeinternational.com
Manufacturer and exporter of cleaning chemicals in-
cluding hand soap and floor polish for restaurants
President: Kristopher Kosup
Cio/Cto: Noel Haden
nhaden@buckeyeinternational.com
Estimated Sales: $20-50 Million
Number Employees: 100-249
Type of Packaging: Food Service, Bulk

19939 Buckhorn Canada
8028 Torbram Road
Brampton, ON L6T 3T2
Canada
905-791-6500
Fax: 905-791-9942 800-461-7579
www.buckhorninc.com/
Manufacturer, importer and exporter of reusable
plastic pallets and boxes for storage, processing,
dipping and freezing
Sales Manager: Tim Walsh
Number Employees: 20
Square Footage: 180000
Parent Co: Myers Industries
Brands:
Akro-Bins
Ameri-Kart
Maxi-Bins
Nestier

19940 (HQ)Buckhorn Inc
55 W Techne Center Dr # A
Milford, OH 45150-9779
513-831-4402
Fax: 513-831-5474 800-543-4454
sales@buckhorninc.com www.buckhorninc.com
Manufacturer and exporter of reusable plastic pack-
aging systems, including plastic totes, bulk boxes,
containers, trays & pallets for shipping & in-process
use.
President: R. David Banyard
CEO: R. David Banyard
Dir. Engineering & Product Development: Jack
Fillmore
Director of Sales: Lane Pence
Director of Human Resources: Lorraine Gibbs
Parent Co: Meyers Industries Inc.
Brands:
Akro-Mils
Buckhoen

19941 Budget Blinds Inc
1927 N Glassell St
Orange, CA 92865-4313
714-637-2100
Fax: 714-637-1400 800-800-9250
corporateoffice@budgetblinds.com
Manufacturer and exporter of decorative items including centerpieces, candleabras, vases, candlesticks, etc
CEO: John Akins
centralbirmingham@budgetblinds.com
Executive VP: Mark Frankel
Office Manager: Cindy Mason

Number Employees: 1-4
Square Footage: 60000
Brands:
Band-It
Finesse
Franklinware
Garden Romance

19942 Buffalo China
658 Bailey Avenue
Buffalo, NY 14206-3003
716-824-8515
Fax: 716-825-5783 lester.rickard@oneida.com
www.oneida.com
Tabletop products and supplies including china
Sales Manager: Frank Fan
Manager: Charles Goehrig
VP Engineering: Paul Graeber
Estimated Sales: $1 - 5 Million
Number Employees: 500-999
Parent Co: Oneida Foodservice

**19943 (HQ)Buffalo Technologies
Corporation**
750 E Ferry Street
Buffalo, NY 14211-1106
716-895-2100
Fax: 716-895-8263 800-332-2419
sales@buflovak.com www.btcorp.com
Manufacturer and exporter of food dryers, flaking
drums, material handling and lifting equipment,
coolers, evaporators, heat exchangers, conveyors,
mills, etc
CEO/Chairman: Theodore Dann
Product Manager: Todd Murray
Production Manager: Patrick Scanlon
Estimated Sales: $10-20 Million
Number Employees: 2
Square Footage: 500000
Brands:
Bar Nun
Bke
Buflovak
Gump

19944 Buffalo Wire Works Co Inc
1165 Clinton St
Buffalo, NY 14206-2825
716-821-7866
Fax: 716-826-8271 800-828-7028
info@buffalowire.com www.buffalowire.com
Buffalo Wire Works offers screening media for in-
dustrial and food processing, including circular
screens, taped edge, hooked panel and rolled goods
for all major OEM's
CEO: Joseph Abramo
jabramo@buffalowire.com
CFO: George Ulrich
VP of Technalogy: Erich Steadman
R&D: Zach Hall
Quality Control: Rick Zimmer
Marketing: Melissa Kenneweg
Executive VP of Sales: Dominic Nasso
Customer Service: Beth Dajka
Operations: Kevin Shoemaker
Production: Terrie Battaglia
Plant Manager: Kevin Shoemaker
Purchasing Director: Tom Duriak
Estimated Sales: $10 - 20 Million
Number Employees: 100-249
Type of Packaging: Food Service

19945 Buffet Enhancements Intl
PO Box 1000
Point Clear, AL 36564
251-990-6119
Fax: 251-990-9373 www.buffetenhancements.com
Display products for banquets and catering includ-
ing decorative fountains, illuminated ice displays,
food display trays, beverage housings and center-
piece trays; also, seafood display containers
Owner: Mike Anderson
Quality Control: Paul Lepiane
Marketing Director: Mike Anderson
Contact: Kevin Caldwell
kevinc@buffetenhancements.com
Estimated Sales: $10 - 20 Million
Number Employees: 50-99
Square Footage: 10000
Brands:
Banquet Boats
Chef Stone
Marquis Fountains

19946 (HQ)Buffet Partners
2701 E Plano Pkwy # 200
Plano, TX 75074
214-291-2900
Fax: 214-291-2467 888-626-6636
www.furrs.net
Food gift certificates
Manager: Jill Laird
CFO: Monty Standifer
Number Employees: 20-49

19947 Buhler Aeroglide Corp
100 Aeroglide Dr
Cary, NC 27511-6900
919-851-2000
Fax: 919-851-6029 www.buhlergroup.com
Design and manufacture of custom industrial dryers,
roasters, and coolers for food processing.
President: Fred Kelly
Senior VP: Mark Paulson
mpaulson@aeroglide.com
Sales Director: Tom Barber
Number Employees: 100-249

19948 Buhler Inc.
13105 12th Ave N
Plymouth, MN 55441-4509
763-847-9900
buhler.minneapolis@buhlergroup.com
www.buhlergroup.com
Supplies technologies and methods for processing
grain into flour and feed; the production of pasta &
chocolate; die casting, wet grinding & surface
coating.
President: Rene Steiner Jr
rene.steiner@buhlergroup.com
Number Employees: 100-249
Other Locations:
Buhler Inc
Minneapolis MN
Buhler Inc (Grinding & Dispersion)
Mahwah NJ
Buhler Aeroglide (Drying)
Cary NC
BuhlerPrince, Inc (Die Casting)
Holland MI
Buhler Inc (Optical Sorting)
Stockton CA
Buhler (Canada) Inc
Markham, Ontario
Buhler Mexico
Metepec, Mexico
Brands:
C.G. Sargent's Sons
Fec
National Drying Wachinery

19949 Bulk Lift International, LLC
1013 Tamarac Dr
Carpentersville, IL 60110-1967
847-428-6059
Fax: 847-428-7180 800-879-2247
www.bulklift.com
industrial bulk packaging, food packaging and bulk
shipping bag products.
President/CEO: Brian Kelly
VP of Sales & Product Development: Gary Nattrass
Marketing Manager: Elizabeth Prosser
Vice President of Sales & Marketing: Ron Lanier
Human Resources Manager: Brenda Kardys
Vice President of Operations: Mike Sanchez
Purchasing: James Morrow
Square Footage: 200000
Brands:
Bulklift
Ohmega
Sea Bag

19950 Bulk Pack
1025 N 9th St
Monroe, LA 71201
318-387-3260
Fax: 318-387-6362 800-498-4215
sales@bulk-pack.com www.bulk-pack.com
Manufacturer and exporter of bulk containers in-
cluding flexible and intermediate
President: Peter Anderson
Quality Control: Jane Burden
VP Marketing/Sales: Peter Anderson
Sales: Ron Shemwell
Estimated Sales: $1 - 3 Million
Number Employees: 5-9
Square Footage: 90000
Type of Packaging: Bulk

19951 (HQ)Bulk Sak Intl Inc
103 Industrial Dr
Malvern, AR 72104-2009
501-332-8745
Fax: 501-332-8438 bags@bulksak.com
www.bulksak.com
Bulk shipping containers; importer and exporter of
bulk bags
President: Grant Patterson
gpatterson@bulksak.com
VP: Grant Patterson
Vice President/Sales: David Whitt
Plant Manager: Mike Nissen
Estimated Sales: $8,000,000
Number Employees: 50-99
Square Footage: 48500
Type of Packaging: Bulk
Other Locations:
Bulk Sak
Memphis TN

19952 Bulldog Factory Svc LLC
25880 Commerce Dr
Madison Heights, MI 48071-4151
248-541-3500
Fax: 248-541-5095 bmullins@santannatool.com
www.bulldogfactory.com
Conveyors and mixing machinery
President: Joseph Newton
CEO: Jamilce Newton
jsnewton@santannatool.com
Sales: Brad Mullins
Estimated Sales: $5-10 Million
Number Employees: 20-49

19953 Bullet Guard Corporation
3963 Commerce Dr W
West Sacramento, CA 95691
916-373-0402
Fax: 916-373-0208 800-233-5632
Sheila@bulletguardmail.com
www.bulletguard.com
Manufacturer and exporter of drive-through and
walk-up windows including bullet resistant; also, in-
terior counter enclosures; installation and custom
fabrication available
President: Karlin Lynch
CFO: Marcia Lynch
Vice President: Ken Lynch
Production Manager: Kevin Lynch
Marketing Director: Jeannine Ricci
Sales Manager: Sheila Lynch
Estimated Sales: $3 - 5 Million
Number Employees: 25
Square Footage: 30000
Brands:
Bullet Guard
Food Chute

19954 Bulman Products Inc
1650 Mcreynolds Ave NW
Grand Rapids, MI 49504-2091
616-363-4416
Fax: 616-363-0380 bulman@bulmanproducts.com
www.bulmandirect.com
Manufacturer and exporter of metal dispensers for
rolled butcher paper, films, aluminum foil, bag seal-
ing tape, etc.; importer of bag sealers
Owner: Ann Hall
akirkwoodhall@bulmanproducts.com
R&D: Marc Wierenga
Operations: Ann Kirkwood
Plant Manager/Purchasing: Nils Reichert
Estimated Sales: $3-4 Million
Number Employees: 20-49
Square Footage: 52000

19955 (HQ)Bunn-O-Matic Corp
1400 Adlai Stevenson Dr
Springfield, IL 62703-4291
217-529-6601
Fax: 217-585-7699 800-352-2866
www.bunnautomatic.com
Manufacturer and exporter of coffee brewers, decanters, grinders and warmers as well as coffee and
iced tea filters, hot water systems, iced tea brewers,
water filtration systems, and hot powdered and
frozen drink systems

President/CEO: Arthur Bunn
CFO: Gene Wilken
R&D: Robert Kobylarz
Quality Control: Kurt Powell
Sales: John Kielb
Public Relations: Melinda McDonald
Production: John Vanderveldt
Plant Manager: Doug Schwartz
Purchasing Director: John Essig
Estimated Sales: $10 - 20 Million
Number Employees: 500-999
Other Locations:
Bunn-O-Matic Corporation
Cerritos CA
Brands:
Bunn
Bunn-O-Matic
Easy Pour
Pour-O-Matic

19956 Bunn-O-Matic Corporation
280 Industrial Parkway S
Aurora, ON L4G 3T9
Canada
905-841-2866
Fax: 905-841-2775 800-263-2256
order.cdn@bunn.com www.bunn.com/canada
Coffee brewing equipment
VP of Sales: Ken Cox
General Manager: Ross Anderson
Estimated Sales: $1 - 5,000,000
Number Employees: 100
Parent Co: Bunn-O-Matic Corporation

19957 Bunting Magnetics Co
500 S Spencer Rd
Newton, KS 67114-4109
316-284-2020
Fax: 316-283-4975 800-835-2526
bmc@buntingmagnetics.com
www.buntingmagnetics.com
Magnetic and nonmagnetic conveyors in steel and
aluminum extruded frames, magnetic separators and
all metal detection equipment for both dry and wet
lines
President: Robert J. Bunting
CEO: Matt Anderson
manderson@buntingeurope.com
CFO: Jana L. Davis
Vice President: Richard Meister
Marketing Director: Michael Wilks
Sales Director: Rod Henricks
General Manager: Barry Voorhees
Estimated Sales: $21.7 Million
Number Employees: 100-249
Square Footage: 122000
Other Locations:
Bunting Magnetics Company
Elk Grove Village IL
Brands:
Mag Slide
Powertrac

19958 Bunzl Distribution USA
One CityPlace Dr
Suite 200
St. Louis, MO 63141
314-997-5959
Fax: 314-997-1405 888-997-5959
www.bunzldistribution.com
Outsourced food packaging, disposable supplies,
and cleaning and safety products to food processors,
supermarkets, retailers, convenience stores and other
users.
President & CEO: Patrick Larmon
Executive Vice President: Jeff Earnhart
Year Founded: 1981
Estimated Sales: Over $1 Billion
Number Employees: 5,000
Parent Co: Bunzl PLC
Type of Packaging: Food Service, Private Label,
Bulk
Other Locations:
Bunzl Distribution
West Valley City UT

19959 Bunzl Processor Distribution LLC
5710 NW 41st St
Riverside, MO 64150
816-448-4300
Fax: 816-561-3286 www.bunzlpd.com

Leading supplier to the meat and food processing industry, providing everything from packaging materials to work and safety apparel. Also available is a private label product line called Prime Source, featuring various products for thefoodservice, janitorial, industrial and healthcare industries
Director, Marketing: Reese Naftel
International Sales Representative: Patricia Vargas
Number Employees: 500-999
Type of Packaging: Food Service, Private Label
Brands:
 Prime Source

19960 Burd & Fletcher
5151 E Geospace Dr
Independence, MO 64056-3321
816-257-0291
Fax: 816-257-9928 800-821-2776
www.burdfletcher.com
Carton containers for food products
Number Employees: 250-499
Type of Packaging: Food Service, Bulk

19961 Burdock Group
859 Outer Rd # 710
Orlando, FL 32814-6652
407-802-1400
Fax: 407-802-1405 info@burdockgroup.com
www.burdockgroup.com
Consulting team that provides clients with solutions to scientific and regulatory issues affecting FDA and USDA regulated products.
President: George Burdock, Ph.D
 gburdock@burdockgroup.com
Director of Business Development: John Geisler
Marketing Coordinator: Alexandra Smith
Controller: Gina Radcliff
Estimated Sales: $300,000-500,000
Number Employees: 10

19962 Burford Corp
11284 Highway 74
Maysville, OK 73057-9669
405-867-4467
Fax: 405-867-4219 877-287-3673
cburford@burford.com
www.burford.publishpath.com
Bag and pouch sealers, bag labeling equipment, closing equipment, coders, daters, imprinters, computer systems, cooling equipment, cooling tunnels and computer programs
Executive VP: Fred Springer
 fspringer@burford.com
CFO: Fred Speringr
Vice President: Don Ivey
R & D: Scott Clemons
Sales Manager: Teresa Ruder
Estimated Sales: $10-20 000,000
Number Employees: 50-99
Type of Packaging: Private Label, Bulk

19963 Burger Maker Inc
666 16th St
Carlstadt, NJ 07072-1922
201-939-0444
Fax: 201-939-1965 www.schweidandsons.com
Hamburger patties
Owner: David Schweid
 davidschweid@burgermaker.com
EVP Operations: Brad Schweld
EVP Sales: Jamie Schweld
Regional Manager: Chip Crenshaw
Regional Manager: Bill Breslin
Regional Manager: John Jernagan
 davidschweid@burgermaker.com
Number Employees: 100-249

19964 Burgess Enterprises, Inc
1000 SW 34th St
Bldg W2 Suite A
Renton, WA 98057
206-763-0255
Fax: 206-763-8039 800-927-3286
www.burgessenterprises.net
Carts and kiosks; importer and exporter of espresso machines
President/CEO: Robert S Burgess
CFO: Don Paschal
Sales: Robert Connor
Contact: Bob Connor
 bconnor@burgessenterprises.net
Estimated Sales: Below $2.5 Million
Number Employees: 5-9

Number of Brands: 4
Number of Products: 12
Brands:
 Burgess
 Faema

19965 Burgess Mfg. - Oklahoma
1250 Roundhouse Rd
P.O. Box 237
Guthrie, OK 73044-4700
405-282-1913
Fax: 405-282-7132 800-804-1913
bmfg@sbcglobal.net www.burgesspallets.com
Manufacturer and exporter of pallets, boxes, crating and lumber; wholesaler/distributor of lumber, plywood, stretch film, plastic pallets, chipboard and plastic components
Plant Manager: Lee Williams
Estimated Sales: $3 Million
Number Employees: 20-49
Square Footage: 42000

19966 Burghof Engineering & Mfg Co
16051 W Deerfield Pkwy # 1
Prairie View, IL 60069-9629
847-634-0737
Fax: 847-634-0870
Automatic fillers and packers
President: Kaspar Kammerer
Manager: Jeff Mell
Estimated Sales: $2.5-5 Million
Number Employees: 10-19

19967 Burke Industrial Coatings
6200 NE Campus Drive
Suite B
Vancouver, WA 98661-6800
360-944-8465
Fax: 360-759-4989 800-348-3245
USDA accepted water base industrial coatings
President: James P Harris
Quality Control: Barreal Badertscher
Vice President: Darrell Badertscher
Estimated Sales: Below $5 Million
Number Employees: 10

19968 Burkert Fluid Control
2572 White Rd
Irvine, CA 92614-6236
949-251-1224
Fax: 949-223-3198 800-325-1405
marketing-usa@burkert.com www.burkert.com
Water treatment systems.
President: Harm Stratman
 harm.stratman@burkert.com
Inside Sales: Ebert Bautista
Number Employees: 20-49

19969 Burling Instrument Inc
16 River Rd
P.O. Box 298
Chatham, NJ 07928-1988
973-635-9481
Fax: 973-635-9530 800-635-2526
www.burlinginstruments.com
Manufacturer and exporter of temperature controls, limits and sensors; importer of thermostats
President: Bruce Freed
 bfreed@burlinginstruments.com
Sr. VP: Roger Nation
VP of Sales: Michael Wetterer
Estimated Sales: $2.5-5 Million
Number Employees: 10-19
Square Footage: 44000

19970 Burnett Bros Engineering
20 Magnolia Via
Anaheim, CA 92801-1034
714-526-2448
Fax: 714-526-4961 info@burnettbros.com
www.burnettbros.com
Manufacturers and importers of machinery including bunch and shrink wrappers, carton overwrappers, colloid, roll-fed labelers for water, soft drink and milk bottles. Also produce wrapper for cauliflower, cabbage, iceberg lettuceetc
President: Malcolm Burnett
 mfburnett@aol.com
Sales VP: Malcolm Burnett
Estimated Sales: Less Than $500,000
Number Employees: 1-4

19971 Burnishine Products
755 Tri State Pkwy
Gurnee, IL 60031
847-356-0222
Fax: 253-856-1003 800-818-8275
www.burnishine.com
Sanitizers, disinfectants, sterilants, cleaners and polishers
President: Carl Demasi
Human Resources: Laura Welch
Purchasing Manager: Michelle Hogan
Number Employees: 20-49
Number of Brands: 4
Number of Products: 250
Square Footage: 200000
Parent Co: Herbert Stanley Company
Type of Packaging: Consumer, Private Label, Bulk

19972 (HQ)Burns & Mcdonnell Inc
9400 Ward Pkwy
Kansas City, MO 64114-3319
816-333-9400
Fax: 816-333-3690 rdick@burnsmcd.com
www.burnsmcd.com
Consulting engineers and construction for various industries including the food
General Manager: Ronald Colas
CEO: Ray Kowalik
 rkowalik@burnsmcd.com
CEO: Greg Graves
Estimated Sales: $5 Million
Number Employees: 5000-9999

19973 Burns Chemical Systems
3100 Hamilton Ave
Cleveland, OH 44114-3701
724-327-7600
Fax: 724-327-8049
Dish washers
President: John Burns
Contact: Melissa Mitchell
 mmitchell1@statechemical.com
Controller: Robert Rummel
Estimated Sales: $10-20,000,000
Number Employees: 100-249

19974 Burns Engineering Inc
10201 Bren Rd E
Hopkins, MN 55343-9066
952-935-4400
Fax: 952-935-8782 800-328-3871
info@burnsengineering.com
www.burnsengineering.com
Resistant thermometer devices (RTD) and thermocouple sanitary temperature sensors, transmitters and thermowells; calibration services available
Owner: David Ciervo
Sales Director: Stefan Tudor
 dciervo@burns-group.com
Purchasing Manager: Wendi Fetter
Estimated Sales: $10 - 20 Million
Number Employees: 50-99

19975 Burns Industries
1150 Bethlehem Pike
Line Lexington, PA 18932
215-822-8778
Fax: 215-822-1006 800-223-6430
Vacuum lifting systems
Manager: Tim Burns
Number Employees: 50
Square Footage: 60000
Brands:
 Vacuhoist

19976 Burrell Cutlery Company
100 Rockwell Ave.
Ellicottville, NY 14731
716-699-2343
Fax: 716-699-2683
Carving, culinary, fruit, slicing, steak, household, specialty and kitchen knives
President: John Burrell
Estimated Sales: $2.5-5 Million
Number Employees: 10

19977 Burrows Paper Corp
501 W Main St # 1
Little Falls, NY 13365-1899
315-823-2300
Fax: 315-823-0867 800-272-7122
papersales@burline.com www.burrowspaper.com
Integrated paper manufacturer with operations in the US and Europe.

President/CEO: R W Burrows
Corporate Secretary: Margaret Goldman
Corporate VP: Michael Lengvarsky
VP/General Manager: Hai Ninh
Vice President, Sales: Duane Judd
Estimated Sales: $20-50 Million
Number Employees: 1000-4999
Square Footage: 120000
Type of Packaging: Food Service
Brands:
    Plastawrap

19978 Burrows Paper Corp
501 W Main St # 1
Little Falls, NY 13365-1899

    315-823-2300
Fax: 315-823-0867 800-272-7122
papersales@burrowspaper.com
www.burrowspaper.com
Pizza boxes, carry-out food containers, sandwich wrap, and micro-flute packaging
President/CEO: R W Burrows
Cmo: Joe Healey
    jhealey@burline.com
CFO: Philip Paras
Vice President: Hai Ninh
Research & Development: Terry McMillen
Quality Control: Melinda Bird
VP OF Sales: Duane Judd
Sales Director: Ed Amodei
Operations Manager: Jeffrey Hall
Production Manager: Jeffrey Hall
Plant Manager: Chris Kitchel
Purchasing Manager: Ralph Renzulli
Number Employees: 1000-4999
Type of Packaging: Consumer, Food Service, Private Label

19979 Burry Foods
1750 E Main Street
Suite 160
Saint Charles, IL 60174

    630-584-9976
www.burryfoodservice.com
Frozen food service supplier of Thomas', Boboli and Entenmann's
CEO/Founder: Tony Hyler
CFO/VP Information Technology: Dave Phillips
Contact: Christopher Orlando
    christopher.orlando@burryfoods.com
Operations Manager/VP Supply Chain: Gerard Mitchell
Estimated Sales: $28.15 Million
Number Employees: 17
Square Footage: 7853
Type of Packaging: Food Service

19980 Busch LLC
516 Viking Dr
Virginia Beach, VA 23452-7316

    757-463-7800
Fax: 757-463-7407 800-872-7867
www.buschusa.com
Vacuum packaging equipment, vacuum systems, rendering pumps, vacuum pumps
President: Charles Kane
    ckane@bushusa.com
CFO: Doug Clark
Quality Control: Kelly Wood
Marketing Director: Terry McMahan
VP of Engineering: Wayne Benson
Estimated Sales: $10 - 25 000,000
Number Employees: 100-249

19981 Bush Refrigeration Inc
1700 Admiral Wilson Blvd # A
Pennsauken, NJ 08109-3990

    856-963-1801
Fax: 856-361-2772 800-220-2874
info@bushrefrigeration.com
www.bushrefrigeration.com
Manufacturer and exporter of walk in, display and storage coolers and freezers. Refrigerated deli and bakery display cases. Prep tables and under the counter prep tables.
Owner: Alex Bush
    abush@bushrefrigeration.com
Estimated Sales: $2.5-5 Million
Number Employees: 20-49

19982 Bush Tank Fabricators Inc
222 Thomas St
Newark, NJ 07114-2614

    973-596-1121
Fax: 973-596-1662
Ribbon blenders, custom fabricated tanks, mixers, agitators and hoppers
President: Thomas Horenburg
    bushtank@aol.com
Vice President: Martin Koppel
Estimated Sales: $10-20,000,000
Number Employees: 5-9

19983 Bushman Equipment Inc
W133n4960 Campbell Dr
Menomonee Falls, WI 53051-7056

    262-790-4200
Fax: 262-790-4202 800-338-7810
www.bushman.com
Manufacturer and exporter of material handling equipment including cranes, hooks, coil, sheet and pallet lifters, beams, spreaders, blocks and tongs
President: Ralph Deger
    custinfo@bushman.com
Sales Manager: Chuck Nettesheim
Estimated Sales: $20-50 Million
Number Employees: 20-49

19984 Business Control Systems
1173 Green St
Iselin, NJ 08830-2011

    732-283-1301
Fax: 732-283-1192 800-233-5876
www.businesscontrol.com
Point of sale systems and software
Owner: Alexander Want
    alexw@businesscontrol.com
Number Employees: 10-19

19985 Business Facilities
44 Apple St # 3
Tinton Falls, NJ 07724-2672

    732-842-7433
Fax: 732-458-6634 800-524-0337
dgoldstein@busfac.com
www.businessfacilities.com
Manager: Ted Coene
Manager: B Barbara
    bbaldwin@americanrunning.org
Number Employees: 20-49

19986 Buss America
455 Kehoe Blvd
Carol Stream, IL 60188-5203

    630-933-9100
Fax: 630-933-0400 www.busscompounding.com
Kneading extruders
Contact: Ryan Buss
    r.buss@summitradiology.com
Product Manager: Edmund Meier
Estimated Sales: $20-50 Million
Number Employees: 5-9
Square Footage: 66000
Parent Co: George Fisher

19987 Busse/SJI Corp
124 N Columbus St
Randolph, WI 53956-1204

    920-326-3131
Fax: 920-326-3134 800-882-4995
inquiry@arrowheadsystems.com
www.arrowheadsystems.com
Manufacturer and exporter of palletizers and depalletizers for glass, can and plastic beverage containers; also, retort crate loading and unloading
President: Thomas Young
    tyoung@arrowheadsystems.com
Marketing Director: Nick Osterholt
Sales Manager: Dan Erdman
General Manager: George Vroom
Number Employees: 50-99
Parent Co: Arrowhead Systems
Other Locations:
    Busse
    Shelton CT
Brands:
    Advantage
    Eclipse
    Turbo
    Viper

19988 Busse/SJI Corp
124 N Columbus St
Randolph, WI 53956-1204

    920-326-3131
Fax: 920-326-3134 www.arrowheadsystems.com
Conveyors
President: Thomas J Young
    tyoung@arrowheadsystems.com
Estimated Sales: $10-25 Million
Number Employees: 50-99

19989 Butler Winery
6200 E Robinson Rtd
Bloomington, IN 47408

    812-332-6660
vineyard@butlerwinery.com
www.butlerwinery.com
Wine and wine making supplies
President/CEO: James Butler
Secretary/Treasurer: Susan Butler
Manager: Amy Butler
Estimated Sales: $540,000
Number Employees: 5
Brands:
    Butler

19990 Butterworth Inc
16737 W Hardy Rd
Houston, TX 77060-6241

    281-821-7300
Fax: 281-821-5550 info@butterworth.com
www.butterworth.com
Tank cleaning machines
Owner: Daniel Elko
CFO: Craig Cooper
R & D: Dan Elko
Director Sales: James Slaughter
    dabbuhl@repeatbusinesssystems.com
Estimated Sales: $1-2.5 Million
Number Employees: 20-49

19991 Buyers Laboratory Inc
108 John St
Hackensack, NJ 07601-4130

    201-489-6439
Fax: 201-488-0461 info@buyerslab.com
www.buyerslab.com
Owner: Burt Meerow
Chief Executive Officer: Michael Danziger
Vice President of Sales: Patti Clyne
Chief Operating Officer: Mark Lerch
Estimated Sales: $.5 - 1 million
Number Employees: 5-9

19992 Buypass Corporation
360 Interstate North Pkwy SE
Atlanta, GA 30339-2204

    770-953-2664
Fax: 770-916-3391 www.firstdata.com
Electronic payment systems for debit, credit, EBT and check authorization purposes
Co- Founder: George Roberts
Chief Executive Officer, Chairman: Michael Capellas
Vice President of Community Relations: Ellen Sandberg
Client Executive: Rich Toland
Number Employees: 250-499
Parent Co: Electronic Payment Services

19993 Bynoe Printers
167 W 126th Street
New York, NY 10027-4412

    212-662-5041
Manufacturer and wholesaler/distributor of advertising specialties including labels, raffle tickets and paper cups
President: Mark Bynoe
Estimated Sales: $1-2,500,000
Number Employees: 1-4

19994 Byrton Dairy Products
28354 N Ballard Dr
Lake Forest, IL 60045

    847-367-8300
Fax: 847-367-8332
President: Richard Tondi
Estimated Sales: $2.5-5 000,000
Number Employees: 5-9

19995 C & D Robotics
4780 S 23rd St
Beaumont, TX 77705-2632
409-840-5252
Fax: 409-840-4660 800-967-6268
www.cdrobot.com
Material handling for finished goods, industrial
contry robots, specialty machinery, conveyers and
material handling systems
President: Charles Davis
Estimated Sales: $10-20 000,000
Number Employees: 20-49

19996 C & D Valve Mfg Co
201 NW 67th St
Oklahoma City, OK 73116-8247
405-843-5621
Fax: 405-840-0443 800-654-9233
www.cdvalve.com
Manufacturer and exporter of valves for refrigera-
tion equipment
President: Brad Denning
bdenning@cdvalve.com
Estimated Sales: $5 - 10 Million
Number Employees: 20-49

19997 C & K Machine Co
56 Jackson St # 1
Holyoke, MA 01040-5582
413-536-8122
Fax: 413-532-9819 email:ckmachine.com
www.ckmachine.com
Manufacturer and exporter of nonshrink, conform-
ing wrapping machines for cookies, candies and
sandwiches; also, bakery slicing machines and gum
and candy cartoners
President: James Tallon
jjtallon@hge.net
Sales/Marketing: James Tallon
Estimated Sales: $1-3 Million
Number Employees: 1-4
Square Footage: 24000
Brands:
   Redington
   Wrap King

19998 C & L Wood Products Inc
62 Walnut Rd
Hartselle, AL 35640-5348
256-502-9650
Fax: 256-773-3238 800-483-2035
hbowman@clwoodproducts.com
www.clwoodproducts.com
Pallets and crates including hardwood and pine
Manager: Henry Bowman
hbowman@clwoodproducts.com
Plant Manager: Rodger Glaz
Estimated Sales: $2.5-5 Million
Number Employees: 50-99
Square Footage: 30000

19999 C & R Inc
5600 Clyde Moore Dr
Groveport, OH 43125-1081
614-497-1130
Fax: 614-497-1585 888-497-1130
www.crproducts.com
Fabrication and installation of stainless process
equipment and process piping; distributors of G and
H products and AMPCO centrifugal pumps, heat
exchangers, tubular, ice equipment, ice builders,
flow diversion stations, pipingfittings and tubing
President: R Murphy
Estimated Sales: $5-10 000,000
Number Employees: 20-49

20000 C E Rogers Co
1895 Frontage Rd
PO Box 118
Mora, MN 55051-7133
320-679-2172
Fax: 320-679-2180 800-279-8081
www.cerogers.com
Manufacturer, exporter and importer of free-stand-
ing multi-effect and waste water evaporators, hori-
zontal and vertical spray dryers and related heating
and cooling equipment; installation service available
President/Sales: Howard Rogers
hrogers@cerogers.com
Chief Engineer: Steven Degeest
Parts: Carol Dutton
Estimated Sales: $5-10 Million
Number Employees: 20-49

Square Footage: 8000
Parent Co: CFR Group

20001 C F Napa Brand Design
2787 Napa Valley Corporate Dr
Napa, CA 94558-6216
707-265-1891
Fax: 707-265-1899 dschuemann@cfnapa.com
www.cfnapa.com
Designer of labels, containers, boxes, etc
Owner: David Schuemann
Principal: John Farrell
Marketing Director: Susan Rouzie
Estimated Sales: Below $5 Million
Number Employees: 10-19
Square Footage: 18000

20002 C H Babb Co Inc
445 Paramount Dr
Raynham, MA 02767-5178
508-977-0600
Fax: 508-977-1985 sales@chbabb.com
www.tunnelovens.com
Manufacturer and exporter of automated final
proofers, tunnel ovens, cooling conveyors and com-
plete systems for pizza, bagels, breads and rolls,
pastries, pies, etc
President: Charles Foran
cforan@babbco.com
Sales Representative: William Foran
Number Employees: 20-49
Square Footage: 150000
Brands:
   Babbco

20003 C M Becker Inc
1604 Falcon Dr
PO Box 1022
Desoto, TX 75115-2418
972-228-1690
Fax: 972-224-2191 Info@CMBecker.com
www.cmbecker.com
Precision parts for the beverage industry
Owner: Michael Korkisch
Estimated Sales: Below $5 000,000
Number Employees: 1-4

20004 C M Processing Solutions
235 Benjamin Dr # 102
Suite 102
Corona, CA 92879-8098
951-808-4376
Fax: 951-808-8657 sales@cmpsolutions.net
www.cmpsolutions.net
Supplier of stainless steel hygiene equipment and
food processing equipment for the beef, pork, poul-
try, seafood and produce industry
CEO: Mark Corser
Number Employees: 1-4

20005 C Nelson Mfg Co
265 N Lake Winds Pkwy
Oak Harbor, OH 43449-9012
419-898-3305
Fax: 419-898-4098 800-922-7339
nelsonoh@aol.com
Manufacturer and exporter of refrigerated pushcarts
and ice cream storage cabinets
Owner: Kelley Smith
Sr. Engineer: Paul Cox
Sales Manager: Tammy Almendinger
nelsonoh@aol.com
Account Manager: Tammy Almendinger
Purchasing: Paul Zylka
Estimated Sales: $10-20 Million
Number Employees: 20-49
Square Footage: 40000

20006 C Nelson Mfg Co
265 N Lake Winds Pkwy
Oak Harbor, OH 43449-9012
419-898-3305
Fax: 419-898-4098
Manufacturer of ice cream cabinets, ice cream carts
and related equipment.
Owner: Kelley Smith
nelsonoh@aol.com
Marketing/Sales: George Dunlap
Purchasing: Paul Zylka
Estimated Sales: $10-20 000,000
Number Employees: 20-49

20007 C P Industries
560 N 500 W
Salt Lake City, UT 84116-3429
801-521-0313
Fax: 801-539-0510 800-453-4931
info@cpindustries.net
Manufacturer and exporter of industrial and house-
hold cleaners, ice melters and detergents
Owner: Ann Lieber
ann@cpindustries.net
National Detergent Manager: Ted Olsen
Estimated Sales: $10 - 20 Million
Number Employees: 20-49
Square Footage: 500000
Type of Packaging: Consumer, Food Service, Pri-
vate Label, Bulk
Brands:
   Generic Liquid Dish
   Generic Liquid Laundry
   Mountain White
   Power Clean
   Sparkle

20008 C Palmer Mfg Co Inc
5 Palmers Rd
West Newton, PA 15089-2014
724-872-8200
Fax: 724-872-8302 www.cpalmermfg.com
Pizelle irons
President: John Palmieri
CEO: John Palmeri
President: John Palmeri
VP: Kathryn Palmeri
CFO: Philpe Palmieri
Sales Manager: Parcy Smose
Estimated Sales: $1 - 2.5 Million
Number Employees: 5-9

20009 C R Daniels Inc
3451 Ellicott Center Dr
Ellicott City, MD 21043-4191
410-461-2100
Fax: 410-461-2987 800-933-2638
info@crdaniels.com www.crdaniels.com
Manufacturer and exporter of conveyor belting,
trucks and plastic totes, carts, hampers and tubs; im-
porter of cotton duck
President: Gary Abel
CEO: Gary V Abel
Vice President: Vic Keeler
Quality Control: J Singh
Estimated Sales: $20 - 50 Million
Number Employees: 100-249
Square Footage: 250000
Brands:
   Dandux

20010 C R Mfg
10240 Deer Park Rd
Waverly, NE 68462-1416
402-786-2000
Fax: 402-786-2096 877-789-5844
lisag@pmc-group.com
Manufacturer and exporter of plastic pour spouts,
scoops, spreaders, spatulas, funnels, knives, spoons,
bowls, pitchers, corkscrews, tongs, etc
General Manager: Daryl Chapelle
Quality Control: Ace Dettinger
Vice President: Mary Gaber
mary.gaber@pmc-group.com
Estimated Sales: $5 - 10 Million
Number Employees: 100-249
Brands:
   Betterway
   Dispos-A-Way
   Exacto-Pour
   Ezy-Way
   Jigg-All
   Lidd Off
   Magic-Flo
   Magic-Mesh
   Margarita Made Easy
   Pop-N-Pull
   Posi-Pour
   Posi-Pour 2000
   Pour Mor
   Pour-Eaz
   Save-A-Nail
   Shooters Made Easy
   Table Lev'lr
   Whiskygate

20011 C R Mfg
10240 Deer Park Rd
Waverly, NE 68462-1416

402-786-2000
Fax: 402-786-2096 877-789-5844
Plastic supplies and smallwares to the food service, food prep, bakery, restaurant, scoop and scoop accessories, specialty items, pourers and pourer accessories, bar supply and bar accessories markets
Vice President: Mary Gaber
  mary.gaber@pmc-group.com
Vice President: Mary Gaber
  mary.gaber@pmc-group.com
Customer Service: Gary Knaub
Marketing/Sales: Sheila Camprecht
National Sales: Scott Donalds
Plant Manager: Bob Cooper
Estimated Sales: $20 Million
Number Employees: 100-249
Number of Brands: 27
Number of Products: 29
Square Footage: 120000
Parent Co: PMC Group Companies
Type of Packaging: Food Service, Private Label, Bulk
Brands:
  3-Cup Measurer
  Betterway Pourers
  Cake Comb
  Cr Food Baskets
  Cr Scoops
  Crystal Shooter Tubes
  Drip Catchers
  Econo Pourer
  Exacto-Pour Tester
  Ezy-Way Pourer
  Jigg-All
  Jumbo Straws
  Kover All Dust Cap
  Lid-Off Pail Opener
  Magic-Mesh
  Marga-Ezy
  Pizza Slicer
  Polar Pitcher
  Posi-Pour 2000 Pourer
  Posi-Pour Pourer
  Pour Mor
  Pro-Flo Pourer
  Roxi Rimming Supplies
  Roxi Sugar and Salt Spices/Flavors
  Shakers Prepackaged Accessories
  Shotskies Gelatin Mixes
  Steakmarkers
  Super Slicer
  Whisky Gate Pourer

20012 C S Bell Co
170 W Davis St
PO Box 291
Tiffin, OH 44883-1337

419-448-0791
Fax: 419-448-1203 888-958-6381
info@csbellco.com www.csbellco.com
Manufacturer and exporter of grist and hammer mills, conveyors and recycling and size reduction equipment; also, custom fabrication available.
President: Daniel White
Estimated Sales: Less Than $500,000
Number Employees: 5-9
Square Footage: 20000
Brands:
  Bell

20013 C W Cole & Co
2560 Rosemead Blvd
South El Monte, CA 91733-1593

626-443-2473
Fax: 626-443-9253 info@colelighting.com
www.colelighting.com
Custom lighting fixtures for cooking hoods, walk-in coolers and salad bar/pie cases; also, refrigerator door light switches
President: Stephen W Cole
  scole@colelighting.com
Co-Owner: Donald Cole
Sales Manager: Sam Serrano
Sales Engineer: Kevin Brummett
Engineering & Design: Dan Wilkins
Plant Manager: Gustavo Castillo
Purchasing Manager: Jim Cotney
Estimated Sales: $5 Million
Number Employees: 20-49
Square Footage: 50000

20014 C&H Chemical
222 Starkey St
St Paul, MN 55107-1813

651-227-4343
Fax: 651-227-2485 www.secole.com
Cleaning compounds
President: Greg Elliott
Food Industry Specialist: John Jesmok
Estimated Sales: $5-10 Million
Number Employees: 20-49

20015 C&H Packaging Company
1401 W Taylor St
Merrill, WI 54452

715-536-5400
Fax: 715-536-4678 www.chpack.com
Flexographic printing, lamination, pouching
VP: Gene Wagner
Marketing: Bob Madderom
Sales: Bob Madderom
Operations: Larry Offerman
Plant Manager: Dave Welch
Estimated Sales: $3.5 000,000
Number Employees: 100-249
Type of Packaging: Consumer, Food Service, Private Label

20016 C&H Store Equipment Company
2530 S Broadway
Los Angeles, CA 90007

213-748-7165
Fax: 213-749-6135 800-648-4979
Manufacturer, wholesaler/distributor and exporter of store fixtures, office furniture, showcases, and metal shelving
CEO: Cheon Kim
Estimated Sales: $2.5-5,000,000
Number Employees: 10-19
Brands:
  Lozier Reeve

20017 (HQ)C&R Refrigation Inc
PO Box 93
Center, TX 75935

936-598-2761
Fax: 936-598-7858 800-438-6182
www.crrefrig.com
Custom Metal Fabrication-3A tanks, process piping installation, platforms, flow panels, valve clusters, hoppers, skid systems, dryers, orbital welding. Distributor for Alfalaval, Ampco Pumps, Definix Valves.
President: Ronald Murphy
VP: Phillip McKitrick
Sales Manager: Jim McAnaul
Estimated Sales: $5-10 Million
Number Employees: 11
Square Footage: 160000
Other Locations:
  C&R
  Largo FL

20018 C&R Refrigeration
405 Center St
P.O. BOX 93
Center, TX 75935

936-598-2761
Fax: 409-598-7858 800-438-6182
www.crrefrig.com
Rebuilt ammonia compressors, ice machines and other industrial refrigeration equipment
President: Robert Reeves
Founder: Willard Reeves
Estimated Sales: $10-20 Million
Number Employees: 50-99

20019 C-P Flexible Packaging
122 Penns Trl
Newtown, PA 18940-1815

215-860-7676
Fax: 215-860-6170 800-448-8183
Polyethylene sleeve labels, specialty bags and roll stock; also, polypropylene roll feed labels
COO: Gney Lane
Marketing VP/Sales: Art Bucci
Manager: Bill Owen
  bowen@aa.com
Estimated Sales: $30 Million
Number Employees: 5-9

20020 C-P Flexible Packaging
15 Grumbacher Rd
York, PA 17406-8417

717-764-1193
Fax: 717-764-2039 www.cpflexpack.com
Snack food bags, cellophane lamination, polypropylene and polyethylene, slitting, resource recovery, quality assurance
President: Tony Vaudo
  tvaudo@cpconverters.com
Information Technologist: Brad Gates
Estimated Sales: $20-50 Million
Number Employees: 100-249
Number of Products: 6
Square Footage: 120000

20021 C-P Flexible Packaging
122 Penns Trl
Newtown, PA 18940-1815

215-860-7676
Fax: 215-860-6170 800-448-8183
Polyethylene stretch sleeve labels, oriented polypropylene roll-fed labels, shrink sleeves, and shrink roll-fed labels.
Sales: Jennifer Hirsch
Manager: Bill Owen
  bowen@aa.com
Estimated Sales: $15 Million
Number Employees: 5-9
Type of Packaging: Private Label

20022 C-Through Covers
4955 Curry Drive
San Diego, CA 92115-2631

619-286-0671
Fax: 619-286-7991
Reinforced vinyl and canvas covers for bakery rack, freezers, etc
Sales Manager: Marta Stulberger
Estimated Sales: $1 - 5 Million

20023 C. Cretors & Company
3243 N California Ave
Chicago, IL 60618

773-588-1690
Fax: 773-588-2171 800-228-1885
info@cretors.com www.cretors.com
Manufacturer and exporter of popcorn machines and cotton candy equipment and supplies
President: Andrew Cretors
CFO: Dan Williams
Quality Control: Walter Karzak
Marketing Manager: Beth Cretors
Product Manager: John Concannon
Estimated Sales: $10 - 20 Million
Number Employees: 100-249
Square Footage: 106000
Brands:
  Caramelizer
  Cretors
  Flo-Thru
  Ringmaster I
  Ringmaster Ii

20024 C.B. Dombach & Son
252 N Prince St
Lancaster, PA 17603

717-392-0578
Fax: 717-392-1210 info@cbdombach.com
www.cbdombach.com
Commercial awnings
President: Scott Underwood
Contact: Scott Pino
  scott@cbdombach.com
Estimated Sales: $1 - 2.5 Million
Number Employees: 10-19

20025 C.F.F. Stainless Steels
1840 Burlington Street East
Hamilton, ON L8H 3L4
Canada

905-549-2603
Fax: 905-549-2994 800-263-4511
sales@cffstainless.com www.cffstainless.com
Supplier of stainless steel products to the pharmaceutical, chemical, beverage, mining, water purification, food and dairy industries
President: Brian McComb
Vice President Sales: John Burns

20026 C.H. Robinson Co.
14701 Charlson Rd
Eden Prairie, MN 55347-5076
952-683-2800
Fax: 952-933-4747 855-229-6128
solutions@chrobinson.com www.chrobinson.com
Provides: freight transportation (TL, intermodal, ocean, and air freight), cross docking, LTL, customs brokerage, freight forwarding and trucking services, fresh produce sourcing, and information services.
CEO: Bob Biesterfeld
President, NA Surface Transportation: Mac Pinkerton
CFO: Mike Zechmeister
President, Global Freight Forwarding: Michael Short
Year Founded: 1905
Estimated Sales: $14.87 Billion
Number Employees: 15,074
Type of Packaging: Consumer, Food Service, Bulk

20027 C.J. Machine
1183-73 1/2 Avenue NW
Fridley, MN 55432
763-767-4630
Fax: 763-767-4633
Conveyors, casers, stackers, dolly cart loaders and elevators
President: Chuck Voller
VP: Jeff Anderson
Number Employees: 10
Brands:
Built Rite

20028 C.J. Machine
11551 Eagle Street NW
Suite 1
Coon Rapids, MN 55448-3051
763-506-0968
Fax: 763-767-4633
Estimated Sales: $300,000-500,000
Number Employees: 1-4

20029 C.J. Zone ManufacturingCompany
1615 N 25th St
St Louis, MO 63106-2545
314-771-7107
Fax: 314-771-1292
Owner: Bud Zone
Estimated Sales: $10 - 20 Million
Number Employees: 20-49

20030 C.M. Lingle Company
100 Millard Drive
Henderson, TX 75652-5034
903-657-5557
Fax: 903-657-9749 800-256-6963
Walk-in coolers and freezers and cold storage doors
President: Fred Lingle
VP: James Lingle
Estimated Sales: $10-20 Million
Number Employees: 50-99
Square Footage: 140000

20031 C.W. Brabender Instruments
50 E Wesley St
P.O. Box 2127
South Hackensack, NJ 07606-1495
201-343-8425
Fax: 201-343-0608 foodsales@cwbrabender.com
www.cwbrabender.com
Instrumentation for testing physical properties and quality of various materials utilized in the food industry. Product line includes the world renowned Farinograph, Extensograph, as well as viscometers, mills andextruders.
President: Richard Thoma
VP of Sales & Marketing - Food Division: Sal Iaquez
Vice President of Customer Services: Kai Kunicke
Purchasing: Tony Grambone
Estimated Sales: $5 - 10 Million
Number Employees: 20-49
Brands:
Extensograph
Farinograph
Plasti-Corder

20032 C.W. Shasky & Associates Ltd.
2880 Portland Drive
Oakville, ON L4K 5P2
Canada
905-829-9414
Fax: 905-760-7715 www.shasky.com
Manufacturers' representative for foodservice, club and HMR segments
President: Michael Shasky
VP: James Shasky
Estimated Sales: $7.3 Million
Number Employees: 25
Brands:
Angostura Bitters
Au Pain Dore
Catania-Spagna
Dole Food Products
Eli's Cheesecake Company
Farmland Foods
Haagen-Dazs
Japan Food Canada/Kikkoman
McIlhenny Company Tabasco
Mimi Foods
Mission Foods
National Importers/Twinnings
Nestle Ice Cream
Norpac
Otis Spunkmeyer
Patak's
Rosina Food Products
Sea Watch International
Stanislaus Food Products
Tate & Lyle

20033 CA Griffith International
PO Box 1785
Huntington, NY 11743-0460
631-385-7521
Fax: 631-424-3639
Meat packaging
Estimated Sales: $5-10 000,000

20034 CAE Alpheus
9370 7th Street
Unit E
Rancho Cucamonga, CA 91730-5509
Fax: 513-831-3672 800-777-9101
info@coldjet.com www.dryiceblasting.com
Dry Ice blasting machines
Estimated Sales: $1-2.5 Million
Number Employees: 1-4

20035 CAL Controls
1675 Delany Road
Gurnee, IL 60031
800-866-6659
Fax: 847-782-5223 800-447-6690
NA@West-CS.com www.cal-controls.com
Temperature and process controllers for OEM and Plant MRO
President: Alan Bates
Estimated Sales: $1-2.5 Million
Number Employees: 5-9

20036 CAM Campak/Technician
119 Naylon Ave
Livingston, NJ 07039-1005
973-597-1414
Fax: 973-992-4713 info@campak.com
www.campak.com
Thermoformers, intermittent motion horizontal cartoners, automatic wrappers, automatic bundlers and shrink tunnels
President: Thomas Miller
Estimated Sales: $5-10 Million
Number Employees: 10-19

20037 CANBERRA Industries Inc
800 Research Pkwy
Meriden, CT 06450-7169
203-238-2351
Fax: 203-235-1347 800-656-1114
www.canberra.com
Temperature recorders and monitors
Cmo: Bud Sielaff
bsielaff@canberra.com
Number Employees: 1000-4999

20038 (HQ)CB Mfg. & Sales Co.
4475 Infirmary Rd
Miamisburg, OH 45342
937-866-5986
Fax: 937-528-2006 800-543-6860
sales@cbmfg.com www.cbmfg.com
Manufacturer and distributor of industrial knives and blades
Chief Executive Officer: Chuck Biehn
CFO: Don Cain
VP Manufacturing: Roger Adams
Contact: Jess Ahern
jahern@cbmfg.com
Purchasing Manager: Angie Matheney
Estimated Sales: $10-20 Million
Number Employees: 10
Square Footage: 200000
Type of Packaging: Private Label, Bulk
Other Locations:
CB Manufacturing & Sales Company
Centerville OH

20039 CBI Freezing Equipment
6202 214th St SW
Mountlake Terrace, WA 98043
425-775-7424
Fax: 425-775-1715
President: Ed Cloudy
Estimated Sales: $3 - 5 Million
Number Employees: 5-9

20040 (HQ)CBORD Group Inc
61 Brown Rd
Ithaca, NY 14850-1247
607-257-2410
Fax: 607-257-1902 sales@cbord.com
www.cbord.com
Looking for major food cost savings? Net-based foodservice programs? Cashless cafeteria system to increase revenue? the CBORD provides everything from enterprise-wide food production management to single-facility inventory tracking.Catering and event modules are also available. NetNutrition provides nutrition information with just the click of a mouse. the Nutrition Service Suite delivers support tools to clinical services. Award winning 24/7 telephone support. CBORD offerssuccess w/out risk
President: Max Steinhardt
mxs@cbord.com
CEO: Tim Tighe
Director of Sales: Mohammad Ramzy
Estimated Sales: $10 - 20 Million
Number Employees: 250-499
Other Locations:
CBORD Group
Indianapolis IN
Brands:
Catermate
Foodservice Suite
Gerimenu
Nutrition Service Suite

20041 CBORD Group Inc
61 Brown Rd
Ithaca, NY 14850-1247
607-257-2410
Fax: 607-257-1902 800-982-4643
sales@cbord.com www.cbord.com
Manufacturer and exporter of computer software that generates LTC food service, tickets, nourishment labels, production tallies, recipes, inventory, nutritional analysis, etc
President: Max Steinhardt
mxs@cbord.com
Vice President of Client Support and Edu: Nancy Sullivan
Vice President of Human Resources: Lisa Patz
Executive Vice President: Bruce Lane
Director of Development, Odyssey Systems: Shane Boyer
VP, Marketing: Cindy McCall
VP, Sales: Read Winkelman
Director of Contract Administration: Chris Curkendall
Senior Director, Service Operations: Jodi Denman
Estimated Sales: Below $5 Million
Number Employees: 250-499
Parent Co: GeriMenu
Brands:
Gerimenu

20042 CBS International
P.O. Box 70
Currituck, NC 27929-0070
252-232-3378
Fax: 252-232-3470
Manager: Spence Castello
Estimated Sales: $1-2.5 000,000
Number Employees: 1-4

20043 CBi Freezing Equipment
6202 214th St SW
Mountlake Terrace, WA 98043-2097
425-775-7424
Fax: 425-775-1715
President: Ed Cloudy
Estimated Sales: $3 - 5 Million
Number Employees: 20

20044 CC Custom Technology Corporation
18201 S Miles Road
Cleveland, OH 44128-4231
216-662-5500
Fax: 216-662-2623
Waxes and cleaners
President: April Esner
Quality Control: Don Pierce
VP Manufacturing: Charles Silk
Estimated Sales: $2.5-5 Million
Number Employees: 10

20045 CCL Container
1 Llodio Dr
Hermitage, PA 16148-9015
724-981-4420
Fax: 724-342-1116 www.cclcontainer.com
Collapsible metal tubes and plastic closures
Vice President: Karen Krebs
kkrebs@cclind.com
Vice President: Karen Krebs
kkrebs@cclind.com
Estimated Sales: $10-20 000,000
Number Employees: 100-249

20046 CCL Container
105 Gordon Baker Rd
Suite 500
Toronto, ON M2H 3P8
Canada
416-756-8500
ccl@cclind.com
www.cclind.com
Manufacturer and exporter of aluminum aerosol
cans and tubes
President & CEO: Geoffrey Martin
Executive Chairman: Donald Lang
Vice President, General Manager: Andy Iseli
Sales Manager: Joe Meldrew
Senior Vice President of Corporate Commu: Janis
Wade
Estimated Sales: $1 - 5 Million

20047 CCL Label Inc
1187 Industrial Rd
Cold Spring, KY 41076-8799
859-781-6161
Fax: 859-781-6339 800-422-6633
www.ccllabel.com
Pressure sensitive and promotional labels
President: Eric Schaffer
Cio/Cto: Marty Butherus
mbutherus@cclind.com
Quality Control: Liary Guys
Director Operations: Tom McDonald
Estimated Sales: $10-20 Million
Number Employees: 50-99
Brands:
    On-Pak

20048 CCL Label Inc
208 Spring Dr
St Charles, MO 63303-3118
636-946-2439
Fax: 314-724-4670 888-ETL-ABEL
www.cclind.com
Computerized numbering and bar coding devices;
pressure sensitive labels
President: Brian Madden
CEO: Chuck Jongeward
R & D: John Dultz
Quality Control: Steve Harding
Human Resources: Sheila Eicheo
Office Manager: Jeanne Hodges

20049 CCL Labeling Equipment
1616 S California Avenue
Monrovia, CA 91016-4622
626-305-8056
Fax: 626-301-0405 800-423-6569
www.ccllabel.com
Stepper motor labeling heads with integrated electronics, in-line and rotary labeling systems, synchronous and transfer label applicators; prime and
promotional label designs including rotating labels
and multipanel labels

20050 CCP Industries, Inc.
26301 Curtiss-Wright Parkway
Cleveland, OH 44143
440-449-6550
Fax: 800-445-8366 800-321-2840
ccporders@ccpind.com www.ccpind.com
Industrial wiping materials, hand, glass and all pur-
pose cleaners, disposable clothing, uniforms and
safety products
President: Allen Menard
Quality Control: James Fulls
V.P.: Norman Sull
Marketing Manager: Dave Williams
Contact: Michael Alberico
    michaelalberico@ccpind.com
Number Employees: 1,000-4,999
Square Footage: 500000
Parent Co: Tranzonic Companies

20051 CCR Data Systems
128 Airport Rd
Concord, NH 03301-5296
603-224-7757
Fax: 603-224-7709 800-633-6500
www.ccrdata.com
Supplier of software packages for retail applications
President: David Woetzel
Contact: Gerri Cote
    gerri-cote@ncr.com
Estimated Sales: $20 - 50 Million
Number Employees: 50-99

20052 CCR USA LLC
5810 Wison Road
Suite 200
Houston, TX 77396
281-436-1121
Fax: 281-436-1108 www.ccrcontainers.com
A global provider of stainless steel, portable containers to the food processing, cosmetics, pharmaceutical and chemical industries.

20053 CCS Creative, Inc.
3889 Chesswood Dr
Toronto, ON M3J 2R8
Canada
416-633-9733
Fax: 416-633-0677 888-633-2079
info@ccscreative.com ccscreative.com
Assisting with digital marketing, branding, menu
and recipe development for restaurants.
President: Cynthia Hollidge
Vice President: Lesley Greenberg
Operations Manager: Steve Mauro
Number Employees: 7

20054 CCS Stone, Inc.
9-11 Caeser Place
Moonachie, NJ 07074-1702
201-933-1515
Fax: 201-933-5744 800-227-7785
info@ccsstone.com www.ccsstone.com
Manufacturer and importer of restaurant and bar fur-
niture including chairs, barstools, marble and granite
tabletops and bases
President: Donald Mitnick
Controller: Corey Mitnick
VP: John Mitnick
Purchasing Manager: Michael Rivkin
Estimated Sales: $5-10 Million
Number Employees: 20-49
Square Footage: 200000

20055 CCi Scale Company
PO Box 1767
Clovis, CA 93613
559-325-7900
Fax: 888-693-2792 800-900-0224
sales@cciscale.com www.cciscale.com

Estimated Sales: $5-10 Million
Number Employees: 50-99

Manufacturer and importer of mechanical, electronic
digital, portable, portion control, receiving, counting
and battery operated scales
CEO: Tom Bouton
Sales Manager: Terri McGinn
Estimated Sales: Below $5 Million
Number Employees: 1-4
Brands:
    Cci

20056 CDF Corp
77 Industrial Park Rd
Plymouth, MA 02360-4868
508-747-5858
Fax: 508-747-6333 800-443-1920
www.cdf1.com
Liners and other value added products used in industrial shipping and storage containers.CDF offers the
following products: cheer pack; cheertainer bag in
box; IBC aseptic; form-fit; pillow & high-barrier foil
liners & accessories;DrumSaver liners for steel,plas-
tic and fiber drums; PailSaver liners for steel & plastic pails & dust caps, cover sheets, lids and strainers
for drums and pails.
President: Joe Sullivan
    jsullivan@cdf1.com
Marketing: Amanda Verash-Morris
Operations: Buddy Morgan
Number Employees: 100-249
Type of Packaging: Food Service, Bulk

20057 CDI Service & Mfg Inc
2181 34th Way
Largo, FL 33771-3952
727-536-2207
Fax: 727-536-2208 www.cdimfg.com
Manufacturer and exporter of booths, tables and
bars; also, custom design services available.
President: David Goudy
VP: Deborah Goudy
Sales Director: David Goudy
Estimated Sales: Less than $900,000
Number Employees: 5-9
Square Footage: 15200
Type of Packaging: Food Service, Private Label

20058 CE International Trading Corporation
13450 SW 134th Ave
Suite B-5
Miami, FL 33186-4530
305-254-3448
Fax: 305-254-3182 800-827-1169
edwin@ceinternationaltrading.com
http://ceinternational.marcorojas.com/index.htm
Vibratory and separation systems. Food and beverage usage includes batch operations to screen and
scalp powders, granules, or liquids in different
locations.
Sales Representative: Edwin Rojas
Contact: Vanessa Perez
    vanessa@ceinternationaltrading.com

20059 CEA Instrument Inc
160 Tillman St # 2
Suite 1
Westwood, NJ 07675-2624
201-967-5660
Fax: 201-967-8450 888-893-9640
ceainstr@aol.com www.ceainstr.com
Manufacturer, importer and exporter of monitors for
toxic and combustible gas and oxygen levels
Manager: Steven Adelman
    ceainstr@aol.com
Vice President: Steve Adelman
General Manager: Martin Adelman
Estimated Sales: $2-3 Million
Number Employees: 5-9
Number of Brands: 4
Number of Products: 18
Square Footage: 8000
Brands:
    Cea 266
    Gas Baron
    Gas Baron 2
    Md-16
    Series U

20060 CEM Corporation
3100 Smith Farm Rd
Matthews, NC 28104-5044
704-821-7015
Fax: 704-821-7894 800-726-3331
info@cem.com www.cem.com

Manufacturer and exporter of microwave instruments for moisture/solids, protein and fat analysis; also, digestion and solvent extraction systems and muffle furnaces.
Owner: Michael Collins
Senior Research & Development Scientist: Alicia Stell
Marketing Manager: Keller Barnhardt
Director of North American Sales: Bobbie McManus
Director of Manufacturing: Cathy McDonald
Estimated Sales: $20 - 30 Million
Number Employees: 100-249
Square Footage: 60000
Brands:
  Fas-9001
  Mars 5
  Mars-X
  Mas-7000
  Profat 2
  Smart System 5
  Star Systems

20061 CERT ID LC
500 N 3rd St
Suite 204
Fairfield, IA 52556
641-209-1899
www.cert-id.com
Certifies food processing and packaging operations in which food is handled, processed, packed, stored or distributed.
Vice President of Business Development: Joan Moeller
General Manager: Lisa Eberman

20062 CF Chef
4030 Black Gold Dr
Dallas, TX 75247-6304
214-905-1518
Fax: 214-905-9817 800-332-8812
cfmails@cfchefs.com
Sell roux as an ingredient to chef and other food companies throughout the world
Owner: W R Seeds
R & D: Eugene Wisakowsky
Vice President, Controller: Campbell Tagg
Contact: Ann Geddes
  ageddes@cfchefs.com
Director Operations: Donald Capone
  ageddes@cfchefs.com
Vice President of Production: James Michel
Estimated Sales: $10 - 20 Million
Number Employees: 20-49
Brands:
  Cf Chefs
  Country Flavor Kitchens
  Flavor Roux
  Skillet Style

20063 CFC International, Inc.
500 State St
Chicago Heights, IL 60411-1293
708-891-3456
Fax: 708-758-5989 cfcinfo@cfcintl.com
www.cfcintl.com
Holographic patterns, images in laminating films, hot and cold stamp foils and other label materials.
Chairman: Roger Huby
President: Richard Grathwaite
Sales: Mark Mitravich
Estimated Sales: $10-25 000,000
Number Employees: 250-499
Parent Co: ITW

20064 CFS North America
3179 99th Street
Urbandale, IA 50322
515-278-1559
844-808-2063
www.camlinfs.com
Shelf life extension solutions
General Manager: Jennifer Igou

20065 CGI Processing Equipment
275 Innovation Drive
Romeoville, IL 60446
888-746-0275
Fax:.815-221-5301 info@cgimfg.com
www.cgimfg.com
Brine systems, bacon processing equipment and accesories, continuous sausage processing systems, cookers, smokehouses, accessories, trucks and cages
Sales Manager: Mike Willis

Estimated Sales: $5-10 Million
Number Employees: 60

20066 CH Imports
3410 Deep Green Dr
Greensboro, NC 27410
336-282-9734
Fax: 336-288-3375
Essential oils and aromatherapy supplies
Owner: Jack Bollini
Estimated Sales: Below $5 000,000
Number Employees: 1-4

20067 CHEP Pallecon Solutions
37564 Amrhein Rd
#100
Livonia, MI 48150
734-542-9150
Fax: 734-542-9628 888-873-2277
info.containers@chep.com
Provide food and beverage container rentals for dry or liquid products.
Business Development Manager: Katelyn Byrom
Marketing Specialist: Katie Hanka
Director of Technology Solutions: Keith Schall

20068 CHL Systems
476 Meetinghouse Rd
Souderton, PA 18964-2314
215-723-7284
Fax: 215-723-9115 sales@chlsystems.com
www.chlsystems.com
Food handling and conveyor systems, and material handling equipment; custom designed systems available
President: Dan Landis
  dan.landis@chlsystems.com
CFO: Kevin Albvefer
Sales Manager: Leon Kartz
Estimated Sales: $20 - 50 Million
Number Employees: 100-249
Square Footage: 80000
Parent Co: Clayton H. Landis Company

20069 CHS Inc.
5500 Cenex Dr.
Inver Grove Hts., MN 55077
651-355-6000
800-328-6539
www.chsinc.com
Agriculture, energy, transportation and business services company, with food products through subsidiary Ventura Foods.
President/CEO: Jay Debertin
Executive VP/CFO/Chief Strategy Officer: Olivia Nelligan
Executive VP/General Counsel: Brandon Smith
Year Founded: 1929
Estimated Sales: $38.4 Billion
Number Employees: 10,000
Type of Packaging: Consumer, Food Service, Private Label, Bulk

20070 CIDA
15895 SW 72nd Ave
Suite 200
Portland, OR 97224
503-226-1285
Fax: 503-226-1670 888-226-1285
www.cidainc.com
President: David G Welsh
Architect: Jennifer Beattie
Contact: Sam Corbin
  samc@cidainc.com
Estimated Sales: $3 - 5 Million
Number Employees: 20-49

20071 CII Food Svc Design
545 N Saginaw St # A
Lapeer, MI 48446-2337
810-667-3100
Fax: 810-667-3101 JimP@CiiFSD.com
Consultant specializing in food service design
President: Jim Peterson
Estimated Sales: Less Than $500,000
Number Employees: 1-4

20072 CIM Bakery Equipment ofUSA
836 E Rand Road
Pmb 198
Arlington Heights, IL 60004-4008
847-818-8121
Fax: 847-818-8894 www.cimbakery.com
Estimated Sales: $1 - 5 Million

20073 CK Products
310 Racquet Dr
Fort Wayne, IN 46825-4229
260-484-2517
Fax: 800-837-2686 800-424-6839
mail@ckproducts.com www.ckproducts.com
Cake decorating and candy making products
President: Orlie Brand
Contact: Steve Burdick
  steve.burdick@ckproducts.com
Estimated Sales: $2.5-5 Million
Number Employees: 50-99

20074 CKS Packaging
350 Great SW Pkwy
Atlanta, GA 30336
404-691-8900
Fax: 404-691-0086 800-800-4257
www.ckspackaging.com
Clear plastic containers
Chairman: Charles K Sewell
President/CEO: John R Sewell
CFO: Dan Fischer
EVP: Dewayne Phillips
COO, Operations: Scott K Sewell
Estimated Sales: $10-20,000,000
Number Employees: 100-249
Parent Co: CKS Packaging

20075 CL&D Graphics
1101 Wests 2nd Street
Oconomowoc, WI 53066-0644
Fax: 262-569-4075 800-777-1114
marketing@cldgraphics.com
www.cldgraphics.com
Manufacturer and exporter of pressure sensitive labels and unsupported opp film
President: Mike Dowling
CFO: Scott Demski
Quality Control: Patrick Dillon
R&D: Greg McLain
Sales Manager: Ned Price
Estimated Sales: $20 - 50 Million
Number Employees: 100-249
Type of Packaging: Bulk

20076 CLARCOR Air Filtration Prods
100 River Ridge Cir
Jeffersonville, IN 47130-8974
502-969-2304
Fax: 502-961-0930 866-247-4827
mailbag@airguard.com www.clcair.com
Air filtration products including extended surface pleated, pocket and cartridges filter media, bag filters, fiberglass filter media, panel filters, streamline polyester filter medias, and synthetic automatic roll filter media, HEPAfilters
President: Rich Larson
  rlarson@clcair.com
CFO: Jim Snoedy
R&D: Monroe Britt
Marketing Director: Gary Heilmann
Sales Director: Joe Hevekamp
Operations Manager: Tom Justire
Number Employees: 1000-4999
Brands:
  Clean-Pak
  Dp
  Mieloguard
  Powerguard
  Vari-Pak

20077 CLECO Systems
1395 S Marietta Pkwy SE
Bldg 750
Marietta, GA 30067-4440
770-392-0330
Fax: 770-795-8093 www.clecosys.com
Pallet and case handling systems and equipment
President: Kenneth Matson
Quality Control: Ban Santonato
Sales Manager: Paul Sartore
Estimated Sales: Below $5 Million
Number Employees: 10
Brands:
  Condor
  Maestro
  Raven
  Titan
  Viking

20078 CM Ambrose Company
PO Box 3037
Arlington, WA 98223-3037
360-435-1411
Fax: 360-435-8200 ambroseinc@aol.com
Liquid packaging equipment
Contact: John Bowman
john.bowman@ambroseco.com
Estimated Sales: $2.5-5 000,000
Number Employees: 19

20079 CM Packaging
800 Ela Rd
Lake Zurich, IL 60047
847-438-2171
Fax: 847-438-0369 800-323-0422
info@cmpackaging.com
President: Mark Faber
Contact: Jenny Bryan
j.bryan@packagingdirect.com

20080 CMA Group
61 Broadway
10th Floor
New York, NY 10006
212-382-1822
Fax: 212-382-2126 800-913-2531
www.cma.net
Corporate Financial Consultants
Contact: Ted Conwell
tconwell@lighthousefinance.no

20081 CMC America Corporation
208 South Center Street
Joliet, IL 60436
815-726-4337
Fax: 815-726-7138 Info@cmc-america.com
www.cmc-america.com
Bakery machinery including mixers, water handling
equipment and cookie depositing systems
President: Edward Fay
Executive Consultant: James Fay
Plant Manager: Michael Baron
Estimated Sales: $3 Million
Number Employees: 10-19
Number of Brands: 1
Number of Products: 4
Square Footage: 80000
Brands:
Champion

20082 CMD Corp
2901 E Pershing St
Appleton, WI 54911-8670
920-730-6888
Fax: 920-730-6880 info@cmd-corp.com
www.cmd-corp.com
High speed plastic film converting equipment for the
production of trash can liners and bag rolls. Also
vertical form fill and seal packaging equipment and
modular pouch making systems.
President: Steve Sakai
steve.sakai@cmd-corp.com
Research & Development: Ron Buchinger
Quality Control: Curt Frievalt
Marketing/Public Relations: Lisa Kain
Sales: Margaret Valinski
Sales: Rich Camp
Operations Manager: Don Wiedenheft
Production Manager: Curt Frievalt
Plant Manager: Don Wiedenheft
Purchasing Manager: Colleen Frederick
Estimated Sales: $20-50 Million
Number Employees: 100-249
Number of Brands: 2
Number of Products: 40
Square Footage: 50000
Parent Co: CMD Corporation
Type of Packaging: Consumer, Food Service, Private Label, Bulk
Brands:
Cmd Converting Solutions
Cmd Packaging Systems
Modular Pouch Machine
Vffs Packaging System

20083 CMD Corp
2901 E Pershing St
Appleton, WI 54911-8670
920-730-6888
Fax: 920-730-6880 info@cmd-corp.com
www.cmd-corp.com
Vertical form, fill and seal packaging equipment,
washdown equipment

President: Steve Sakai
steve.sakai@cmd-corp.com
CFO: Tim Lamerf
Quality Control: Mark Heindel
Regional Sales Manager: David Andrews
Director of Operations: Ron Buchinger
Number Employees: 100-249

20084 CMD Corporation
2901-3005 East Pershing Street
PO Box 1279
Appleton, WI 54912-1279
920-730-6888
Fax: 920-730-6880 info@cmd-corp.com
www.cmd-corp.com
Plastic bottles
President: John Smith
R & D: Larry Mikeosjy
Corporate Market Manager, Research and C: Lisa
Karin
VP Marketing and Sales: Timothy B. Lewis
Regional Sales Manager: David Andrews
Contact: Christie Sweeney
christie.sweeney@cmd-corp.com
Director of Operations: Ron Buchinger
Product Line Manager: Scott Fuller
Number Employees: 10

20085 CMF Corp
1524 W 15th St
Long Beach, CA 90813-1207
562-437-2166
Fax: 562-495-1857 800-350-8979
info@jack-frost.com www.jack-frost.com
President: Larry Sackrison
Estimated Sales: $3 - 5 Million
Number Employees: 5-9

20086 CMS Fine Foods
4791 Dry Creek Rd
Healdsburg, CA 95448
707-473-9561
Fax: 707-473-9765 www.cmsfinefoods.com
sauces, dressings, mustards, marinades and other
condiments; offers co-packing and private label services.
Type of Packaging: Consumer, Food Service, Private Label, Bulk

20087 CMT
P.O. Box 297
Hamilton, MA 01936
978-768-2555
Fax: 978-768-2525 cmtinc@tiac.net
Manufacturer and exporter of temperature and humidity monitors, alarms and controls sustems for climate sensitive goods such as wine and cigars.
President: David C De Sieye
Estimated Sales: $500,000-$1 Million
Number Employees: 1-4
Number of Products: 50
Square Footage: 8000

20088 CNL Beverage Property Group
450 South Orange Avenue
Orlando, FL 32801-3383
407-650-1000
Fax: 407-316-0457 800-522-3863
www.cnl.com
President: Robert Bourne
CFO: Lynn Rose
CEO: James Seneff
R & D: Courtney Powell
Contact: Christian Abreu
christian@cnl.com
Number Employees: 10-19

20089 COMPRESSOR Engrg. Corp.
5440 Alder Dr
Houston, TX 77081-1798
713-664-7333
Fax: 713-664-6444 800-879-2326
sales@ceconet.com www.tryceco.com
President: Richard Hotze
CEO: Bruce R Hotze
bruceh@ceconet.com
CFO: Mark Hotze
Estimated Sales: $20 - 50 Million
Number Employees: 100-249

20090 COTT Technologies
14923 Proctor Ave
La Puente, CA 91746-3206
626-961-0370
Fax: 626-333-9307 800-373-1968
Sanitary Piston Pumps, Liquid Fillers, Custom Process Piping and machinery
Owner: Gilbert De Cardenas
Marketing: Dennis Gonzalez
Production: Westly Brown
Plant Manager: Westly Brown
Estimated Sales: $10 - 20 Million
Number Employees: 20-49
Number of Brands: 1
Brands:
Cott

20091 COVERIS
501 Williams St
Tomah, WI 54660-1454
608-372-2153
Fax: 608-372-5702 www.coveris.com
Manufacturer and exporter of polyethylene film and
bags
Quality Control: Don Bergum
President: Stan Bikulege
Sales Manager: Bruce Baker
Plant Manager: Terry Smith
Estimated Sales: $20 - 50 Million
Number Employees: 250-499
Parent Co: Union Camp Corporation
Type of Packaging: Consumer, Bulk

20092 COW Industries Inc
1875 Progress Ave
Columbus, OH 43207-1781
614-443-6537
Fax: 614-443-9600 800-542-9353
www.cowind.com
Bakers' equipment, flour hoppers, pans, racks, tanks,
trays, etc
President: George Combs
gcombs@invacare.com
CFO: John Burns
Executive VP Sales: David Burns
VP Production: Rock Kauser
Estimated Sales: $20 - 50 Million
Number Employees: 20-49
Square Footage: 100000

20093 COX Technologies
69 McAdenville Rd
Belmont, NC 28012
704-825-8146
Fax: 704-825-4498 800-848-9865
www.coxtec.com
President: James L Cox
james.cox@coxtec.com
CFO: Jack Mason
Vice President: Dave Caskey
Quality Control: Bob Hiatt
Marketing/Sales: Maryy Norris
Operations/Production/Plant Manager: Margaret
Hiatt
Purchasing Manager: Pamela Jackson
Estimated Sales: $10 000,000
Number Employees: 100
Parent Co: COX Technologies

20094 CPI Packaging
50 Jiffy Rd
Somerset, NJ 08873
732-431-3500
Fax: 732-568-0440 www.cpipkg.com
Foam and plastic packaging products
COO: Joseph Lomando
COO: Joseph Mormondo
Contact: Anthony Distefano
apiantieri@amrindustries.com
Estimated Sales: $20 - 50 Million
Number Employees: 10,000

20095 CPM Century Extrusion
2412 W Aero Park Ct
Traverse City, MI 49686-9102
231-947-6400
Fax: 231-947-8400 sales@centuryextrusion.com
www.centuryextrusion.com
Manufacturer & supplier of extruders and extrusion
parts.
President: Bob Urtel
urtelb@centuryextrusion.com
General Manager: Charlie Spearing

Number Employees: 50-99
Parent Co: CPM Extrusion Group

20096 CPM Roskamp Champion
2975 Airline Cir
Waterloo, IA 50703-9631
319-232-8444
Fax: 319-236-0481 800-366-2563
www.cpm.net
Manufacturer and exporter of particle sizing equipment including roller and hammer mills, flakers, crushers, pallet mills, coolers and crumblers for food processing; also, testing/lab facility available
President: Ted Waitman
CEO: Heath Hartwig
CFO: Doug Ostrich
Research & Development: Ron Fuller
Marketing Director: Scott Anderson
Sales Director: Linda Kruckenberg
Manager: J Manning
 julie.manning@cpm.net
Operations Manager: Jim Hughes
Plant Manager: Terry Tackenberg
Purchasing Manager: Stuart Downs
Estimated Sales: $20 Million
Number Employees: 50-99
Square Footage: 50000
Parent Co: California Pellet Mill
Brands:
 Champion
 Roskamp

20097 (HQ)CPM Wolverine Proctor LLC
121 Proctor Ln
Lexington, NC 27292-7630
336-248-5181
Fax: 336-248-5118 www.wolverineproctor.com
Manufacturer and exporter of energy efficient equipment including conveyor dryers, roasters, toasters, coolers, ovens and the JETZONE fluidized dryers, puffers and toasters for the processing of fruits, vegetables, nuts, bakery, snackfoods, meat, poultry, pet foods, etc. Also offers batch drying equipment including tray, truck and laboratory dryers. Fully equipped Tech Centers available for demonstration purposes and development of new products and processes.
CEO: Steven Chilenski
CFO: Mark Brown
VP: Paul E Smith
Sales: Terry Midden
Estimated Sales: $15-25 Million
Number Employees: 50-99
Square Footage: 60000
Brands:
 Jetzone
 Proctor

20098 CPM Wolverine Proctor LLC
251 Gibraltar Rd
Horsham, PA 19044-2305
215-443-5200
Fax: 215-443-5206
sales@cpmwolverineproctor.com
www.wolverineproctor.com
Manufacturer and designer of processing equipment including energy efficient continuous dryers, roasters, toasters, coolers, impingement ovens, and jetzone fluid bed dryers for the processing of fruits, vegetables, nuts/seeds, bakerysnack foods, meat, poultry, pet foods, etc. Also batch drying equipment including tray, truck and laboratory dryers; ultra sanitary design conveyor dryer and new pizza infrared fuser/melter.
Lab Manager: Lisa Geck
Director of Sales & Marketing: Kevin Van Allen
Vice President, Sales & Marketing: Paul Smith
Vice President of Operations: Rick Diefes
General Manager: Paul Finnerty
Estimated Sales: $13.1 Million
Number Employees: 20-49
Square Footage: 180000
Parent Co: CPM Extrusion Group
Type of Packaging: Food Service
Other Locations:
 USA Operations Office
 Lexington NC
 European Office
 Glasgow, UK
 South American Office
 Sao Paulo, Brazil

20099 CPT
415 E Fulton St
Edgerton, WI 53534-1923
608-884-2244
Fax: 608-884-2288 info@cptplastics.com
www.cptplastics.com
Manufacturers of foamed polypropylene rollstock and trays for case-ready and other applications requiring extended shelf life; pre-formed trays and barrier shrink lidstock, foamed barrier PP is microwaveable, lightweight andeasy-to-form, specializes in
President: Linda Bracha
Estimated Sales: $10 - 20 Million
Number Employees: 20-49

20100 CRC Inc
3218 Nebraska Ave
Council Bluffs, IA 51501-7035
712-323-9477
Fax: 712-323-3573 www.bradley-refrigeration.com
Stainless steel variable speed blenders and mixers
Vice President: Jim Crossley
 jimc@crcinconline.com
Secretary: Joan Collins
VP: Jim Crossley
Estimated Sales: $2.5-5,000,000
Number Employees: 5-9

20101 CRF Technologies
PO Box 32414
Charlotte, NC 28232-2414
704-554-2253
Fax: 704-554-3900 800-875-0275
Cut resistant gloves, apparel and uniforms
Estimated Sales: $1 - 5 000,000

20102 CRS Marking Systems
3315 NW 26th Ave #1
Portland, OR 97210-1856
503-228-7624
Fax: 503-228-2464 800-547-7158
info@crsdatasolutions.com
Manufacturer and wholesaler/distributor of marking, coding, printing, labeling and bar code equipment
CEO: Julia Farrenkopf
Customer Service: Dwaine Brandson
COO: David Snmodgrass
Estimated Sales: $1 - 3 Million
Number Employees: 10 to 19

20103 CRT Custom Products Inc
7532 Hickory Hills Ct
Whites Creek, TN 37189-9289
615-876-5490
Fax: 615-876-0096 www.crtcustomproducts.com
Printing, packing, supplies
Sales: Ken Gereen
Estimated Sales: Less Than $500,000
Number Employees: 1-4

20104 CSAT America
7007 Johnson Cir
Longmont, CO 80503-7667
303-652-0370
Fax: 303-652-8736 888-904-2728
www.csat.de

20105 CSC Scientific Co Inc
2799 Merrilee Dr # B
Fairfax, VA 22031-4419
703-564-4306
Fax: 703-280-5142 800-621-4778
www.cscscientific.com
Manufacturer and exporter of sieves and laboratory analyzers to measure water, moisture, filtration equipment, solids, surface tension, particle size and consistency; also, calibration services available
President: Al Gatenby
 agatenby@cscscientific.com
Vice President: Tim Comwell
Marketing Director: Wendy Liu
Operations Manager: Theresa Andreoni
Estimated Sales: $2.5 - 5 Million
Number Employees: 20-49
Brands:
 Aquapal
 Cfc Dunouy Tensiometer
 Cfc Us Standard
 Digital Moisture Balance

20106 (HQ)CSC Worldwide
4401 Equity Dr
Columbus, OH 43228-3856
614-850-1460
Fax: 614-850-0741 800-848-3573
Manufacturer, designer and exporter of refrigerated and heated display cases; also store fixtures
CEO: Carl J Aschinger Jr
Marketing: Jennier Bobbitt
Contact: Carl Aschinger
 c.aschingerjr@cscworldwide.com
Estimated Sales: $20-50 Million
Number Employees: 100-249

20107 CSI Tools
2700 N Partnership Blvd
Springfield, MO 65803-8208
417-831-1411
Fax: 417-831-5314 800-258-0133
Leading provider of tube and pipe facing and cutting equipment for the sanitary process piping industry; also supply users of this equipment with top quality consumables for these tools such as blades, bits
President: Mark Cook
CFO: Joe Reynolds
Vice President of Systems: Beth Ipock
Manager: Mark Wilson
Marketing Director: Ryan Tiller
Sales Manager: Liz Braden
Contact: Charlie Jockers
 charlie@csitools.com
Vice President of Operations: Bryan Billmyer
Estimated Sales: $10-20 Million
Number Employees: 50-99
Type of Packaging: Food Service

20108 CSM Bakery Solutions
c/o Brill Inc
1912 Monteal Rd
Tucker, GA 30084
770-724-8200
www.csmbakerysolutions.com
Develops, produces and sells a wide selection of bakery ingredients and products to professional bakeries, top consumer food companies, grocers and retailers. Products include brownies, cakes, cookies croissants, fillings, glazesicing & toppings, mixes, muffins, puff pastry, sweet rolls, filled pastries, and turnovers.
President & CEO: Marianne Kirkegaard
SVP & Chief Administrative Officer: Michael Delaney
SVP & Chief Financial Officer: Maarten Bok
SVP, Sales & Chief Commercial Officer: John Lindsay
SVP & Chief Supply Chain Officer: Steve Jones
VP, Marketing: Val Burnett
SVP, Sales: Troy Hendricks
VP, Customer Solutions: James Mayer
VP, Manufacturing: John Doyle
Year Founded: 1919
Estimated Sales: $2.1 Billion
Number Employees: 7,000+
Other Locations:
 CSM Bakery Products
 Atlanta GA
 Caravan Ingredients
 Kansas City MO
 BakeMark USA
 Pico Rivera CA
Brands:
 Brill
 Henry & Henry
 Multifoods
 Scoop-N-Bake
 Sensibly Indulgent Cupcakes
 Thaw-N-Sell
 Transmart

20109 CSM Worldwide
1100 Globe Ave
Mountainside, NJ 07092
908-233-2882
Fax: 908-233-1064 www.csmworldwide.com
Tea and coffee industry pollution control equipment
President: Mike Torstup
Contact: Michael Sohnen
 msohnen@csmworldwide.com
Estimated Sales: $2.5-5 000,000
Number Employees: 20-49

20110 CSPI
43 Manning Rd
Billerica, MA 01821-3925
978-663-7598
Fax: 978-663-0150 info@cspi.com
www.cspi.com
Scanning equipment
CEO: Alexander R Lupinetti
Marketing Coordinator: Bernard Pelon
Contact: Jim Duffy
jdufffy@cspi.com
Estimated Sales: $30 - 35 Million
Number Employees: 100-249

20111 CSS Inc
122 Rogers St
Hartsville, TN 37074
615-374-0601
Fax: 615-374-0610 choicecutsurplus@comcast.net
www.choicecut.net
Meat packing and food handling equipment
President: Randy Beach
Chief Executive Officer: Robert Paxton

20112 CSS International Corp
2061 E Glenwood Ave
PO Box 19560
Philadelphia, PA 19124-5674
215-533-6110
Fax: 215-288-8030 800-278-8107
sales@cssintl.com
Manufacturer and exporter of container handling
equipment and packaging machinery
Vice President: Eugene Fijalkowski
gene@cssintl.com
Vice President: Albert Andrew
VP Productions: Gene Fijalkowski
Number Employees: 20-49
Parent Co: CSS International Corporation
Type of Packaging: Consumer, Food Service, Private Label

20113 CSV Sales
44450 Pinetree Dr
Plymouth, MI 48170-3869
734-453-4544
Fax: 248-669-3000 800-886-6866
info@nationalfoodgroup.com www.csvsales.com
Supplier of closeouts, surplus, salvage and liquidator
items including baked goods, poultry, meats and
off-grade, frozen and value added foods
President: Bud Zecman
Owner: Sean Zecman
Finance Executive: Scott Kaman
Sales Executive: Justin Sarrach
Contact: Tracey Daraban
tracey.daraban@nationalfoodgroup.com
Operations Manager: Justin Sarrach
Purchasing/Sales Support: Roger Cary
Estimated Sales: $5-10 Million
Number Employees: 5-9
Brands:
Awrey's
Bakery Chef
House of Raeford
Pierre
Pilgrim's Pride
Tyson

20114 CTC
11 York Ave
West Caldwell, NJ 07006-6486
973-228-2300
Fax: 973-228-7076 info@ctcint.com
www.ctcint.com
Supplier of automatic splicers for packaging lines.
President: Erwin L Herbert

20115 CTI Celtek Electronics
3609 Robertson St
Metairie, LA 70001-5844
504-832-0049
Fax: 504-832-8117
Level controls, inventory management
Owner: Jack Graves
Estimated Sales: $1 - 5 Million
Number Employees: 1-4

20116 CTK Plastics
1815 Stadacona Street W.
Moose Jaw, SK S6H 7K8
Canada
306-693-7075
Fax: 306-693-9944 800-667-8847

Plastic bottles and sheeting; importer of resin and
bottling equipment; exporter of plastic bottles and
rigid sheeting
President: Dennis Wastle
Sales/Marketing: Dennis Wastle
General Manager: Brian McGuigan
Supervisor: Bernice Larose
Number Employees: 10
Square Footage: 120000
Parent Co: CTK Developments

20117 CTS Bulk Sales
P.O. Box 8318
Northfield, IL 60093
847-267-0837
Fax: 847-267-0838
President: Charles L Brooks
R&D: Ginger Brooks
Estimated Sales: Below $5 000,000
Number Employees: 5-9

20118 CUTCO Corp
1116 E State St
Olean, NY 14760-3814
716-372-3111
Fax: 716-790-7160 www.cutco.com
Manufacturer and exporter of knives, forks and
spoons
President: Brent Driscoll
CEO: James E Stitt
jstitt@alcas.com
President: James Stitt
Executive Vice President of Eastern Regi: Amar
Dave
President, Chief Operating Officer: John Whelpley
Estimated Sales: $50,000,000 - $99,999,999
Number Employees: 1000-4999
Parent Co: Alcas-Cutco Corporation
Type of Packaging: Consumer

20119 CVC Technologies Inc
10861 Business Dr
Fontana, CA 92337-8235
909-355-0311
Fax: 909-355-0411 sales@cvcusa.com
www.cvcusa.com
Labelers with automatic job set up, memory for 50
jobs and self-diagnostics. Also counters, cappers, indexing cappers, cartoners and blister packers
Manager: Yulie Luo
Vice President: Andy Span
Quality Control: Oscar Esparza
Marketing Director: Brit Sten
Sales Director: Andy Span
Manager: Joseph Levy
jlevy@osgoodcapital.com
Plant Manager: Oscar Esparza
Estimated Sales: $7-12 000,000
Number Employees: 20-49
Number of Brands: 1
Number of Products: 9
Brands:
302 Hawk Labelers
Cvc 300

20120 CVP Systems Inc
2518 Wisconsin Ave
Downers Grove, IL 60515-4230
630-852-1190
Fax: 630-852-1386 800-422-4720
sales@cvpsystems.com www.cvpsystems.com
Manufacturer and exporter of cost effective, bags
and packaging machinery including microbial reduction units, wrap around label systems and vacuum
and modified atmosphere systems
President: Wesley Bork
VP: L Mykleby
Estimated Sales: $10 - 20 Million
Number Employees: 20-49
Type of Packaging: Consumer, Food Service, Private Label, Bulk
Brands:
Cvp Fresh Vac
Dynarap

20121 CXR Co
2599 N Fox Farm Rd
PO Box 1114
Warsaw, IN 46580-6536
574-269-6020
Fax: 574-269-7140 800-817-5763
info@cxrcompany.com www.cxrcompany.com
Industrial x-ray machines; also, x-ray inspection services available

President: Cassandra Stewart
cstewart@cxrcompany.com
Vice President: Paula Zeigler
Research & Development: Tim Murphy
Sales Manager: Scott Stewart
Plant Manager: John Sherman
Estimated Sales: $5-10 Million
Number Employees: 10-19
Square Footage: 32000
Brands:
Accuvue

20122 CXR Co
2599 N Fox Farm Rd
Warsaw, IN 46580-6536
574-269-6020
Fax: 574-269-7140 800-817-5763
info@cxrcompany.com www.cxrcompany.com
Safety X-ray inspection for contaminants
President: Cassandra Stewart
cstewart@cxrcompany.com
CEO: Barb Colbes
Vice President: Paula Zeigler
Research/Development: Tim Murphy
Sales: Scott Stewart
Plant Manager: John Sherman
Estimated Sales: $5-10 Million
Number Employees: 10-19

20123 CYBER BEARINGS, INC
4821 S. Eastern Ave
Bell, CA 90201
562-272-8032
Fax: 562-272-8588 888-288-9889
info@cyberbearings.com www.cyberbearings.com
Solid stainless steel bearing inserts with
thermoplastic housing, bearing units (pillow block,
flange), bearing inserts with nickel plated cast iron
housing, mast guide bearings, agricultural bearings
and ISO-9002 certified
President: Kevin Lee
Contact: Robyn Chung
robyn@cyberbearings.com

20124 Ca Polytechnic State/Alumni
1 Grand Ave
San Luis Obispo, CA 93407-0707
805-756-2586
Fax: 805-756-5052 lgay@calpoly.edu
www.calpolylink.com
President: Warren Baker
Manager: Dennis Elliot
delliot@calpoly.edu
Number Employees: 5-9

20125 Cab Technology Inc
87 Progress Ave # 1
Tyngsboro, MA 01879-1441
978-649-0293
Fax: 978-649-0294 info.us@cab.de
www.cab.de
President: Joachim Komus
Operations Executive: Mark Cavanaugh
Estimated Sales: Below $5 Million
Number Employees: 10-19

20126 Caboo Paper Products, Inc.
112-2323 Boundary Road
Vancouver, BC V5M 4V8
604-299-1193
info@cabooproducts.com
cabooproducts.com
Tree-free, bamboo-based paper products, including
toilet paper, paper towels, and flushable wipes.
Eco-friendly, sustainable alternative.
CEO & Founder: Albert Addante
Year Founded: 2012
Estimated Sales: $6.3 Million
Number Employees: 11-50
Number of Brands: 1
Brands:
caboo

20127 Cabot Corp
2 Seaport Ln # 1300
Boston, MA 02210-2019
617-345-0100
Fax: 617-342-6312 www.cabot-corp.com
Manufacturer and exporter of treated and untreated
fumed silica

President/CEO: Patrick Prevost
CEO: Sean D Keohane
  sean_keohane@cabot-corp.com
Executive Vice President/CFO: Eduardo Cordeiro
Vice President: James Belmont
Vice President, Research & Development: Yakov Kutsovsky
National Sales Manager: James Litrun
Vice President, Operations: James Turner
Estimated Sales: Over $1 Billion
Number Employees: 1000-4999
Parent Co: Cabot Corporation
Brands:
  Cab-O-Sil

20128 Cabot/Norit Americas Inc
3200 University Ave
Marshall, TX 75670-4842
                            903-923-1000
        Fax: 903-938-9701 800-641-9245
                            www.norit.com
Activated carbon
Vice President: Nikki Gurule
  ngurule@norit-americas.com
Vice President: Nikki Gurule
  ngurule@norit-americas.com
Number Employees: 250-499

20129 Cabot/Norit Americas Inc
3200 University Ave
Marshall, TX 75670-4842
                            903-923-1000
        Fax: 903-938-9701 800-641-9245
                            www.norit.com
Manufaturer activated carbon, a filter media
Vice President: Doug Dallmer
  ddailmer@norit-americas.com
Vice President: Doug Dallmer
  ddailmer@norit-americas.com
Number Employees: 250-499
Parent Co: Cabot Corp

20130 Cacao Prieto
218 Conover Street
Brooklyn, NY 11231
                            347-225-0130
                            www.cacaoprieto.com
Fine chocolates
President/CEO: Dan Preston
VP & Art Director: Michele Clark
Sales Director: Mike Dirksen
Contact: Michele Clark
  michele@cacaoholdings.com
Chief Operating Officer: Dennis Walsh
Number Employees: 20

20131 Cache Box
2009 14th Street N
Suite 415
Arlington, VA 22201-2514
                            703-276-2500
        Fax: 703-276-2504 800-603-4834
Manufacturer and exporter of touchscreen turn-key
point of sale systems
CEO: Lorenzo Salhi
VP Engineering: Murali Nagaraj
CTO: Dilip Ranade
VP, Technical Marketing: Shaloo Shalini
Contact: John Groff
  john@cachebox.com
COO: John Groff
Estimated Sales: $5-10 Million
Number Employees: 20-49
Brands:
  Chromium

20132 Cache Creek Foods LLC
411 N Pioneer Ave
Woodland, CA 95776-6122
                            530-662-1764
        Fax: 530-662-2529 www.cachecreekfoods.com
Custom flavoring and wholesale manufacturing of
almond, cashew, pistachio, nut products and nut
butters
President: Nicholas Celek
  ncelek@thelabb.com
CEO: Matthew Morehart
Sales and Marketing Executive: Mike Leonard
Office Manager: Connie Stephens
Production: Ana Contreras
Estimated Sales: $10 Million
Number Employees: 20-49
Number of Products: 75
Square Footage: 60000

Type of Packaging: Consumer, Food Service, Private Label, Bulk
Brands:
  Private Label

20133 Cache Cuisine, Inc.
1565 Brittania Road East
Suites #18-20
Mississauga, ON L4W 2V6
Canada
                            905-564-5083
        info@cachecuisine.com
        www.cachecuisine.com
Manufacturer and distributor of specialty dry food
blends and mixes.
President: Constantine Kentros
Type of Packaging: Food Service

20134 Cactus Mat ManufacturingCompany
4131 Arden Dr
El Monte, CA 91731-1999
                            626-579-6287
        Fax: 626-401-2003 cactuskid@cactusmat.com
                            www.cactusmat.com
Floor mats including rigid wood, interlocking rub-
ber, entrance and rubber for food preparation areas
President: C W Hartranft Jr
CEO: Debra De Ring
CFO: Les De Ring
Contact: Debbie Dering
  debbie@cactusmat.com
Estimated Sales: $5 - 10 Million
Number Employees: 20-49
Square Footage: 120000
Brands:
  Cactus Kid
  Contempo
  Cushion Walk
  Kaktus
  Monterey
  Softread
  Vip
  Vip Lite

20135 Caddy Corporation of America
509 Sharptown Road
Bridgeport, NJ 08014-0345
                            856-467-4222
        Fax: 856-467-5511 mbodine@caddycorp.com
                            www.caddycorp.com
Manufacturer and exporter of food service equip-
ment including conveyors, transport/delivery carts,
kitchen ventilation hoods and utility distribution
systems
President: Harry Schmidt
CEO: Craig Cohen
CFO: John McNamee
VP of Corporate Services: Al Scuderi
Vice President, Sales: Phil Bailis
National Sales Manager: Donald Morrison
Engineering Manager: Brad Wallace
Purchasing: Robin Corma
Estimated Sales: $5-10 Million
Number Employees: 50-99
Square Footage: 288000
Brands:
  21c
  Caddy
  Caddy Cold
  Caddy Connections
  Caddy-Flex
  Caddy-Veyor
  Caddymagic
  Circle-Air
  Ds Special
  Dura-San Belt
  Fogg-It
  Mega-Temp
  Pacemaker
  Servi-Shelf
  Simplex
  Speed-Lift
  Temp-Lock
  Temp-Lock Ii
  Thermo-Lock
  Xl-1

20136 Cadie Products Corp
151 E 11th St
Paterson, NJ 07524-1228
                            973-278-8300
        Fax: 973-278-0303 www.cadieproducts.com

Manufacturer and exporter of cloths including dust-
ing, polishing, cheese, pastry and sponge; also,
cooking parchment, microwave cooking bags, seat
covers, salad bags, ice cube bags, hamburger (patty)
bags, and non-stick oven liner
President: Edwin Meyers
CFO: Bob Appelbaum
Vice President: Kenny Meyers
Estimated Sales: $20 - 50 Million
Number Employees: 20-49
Square Footage: 35000
Type of Packaging: Consumer, Private Label, Bulk
Brands:
  Cadie
  Chef's Favorite
  Krazy Kloth
  Super Power

20137 Cadillac Pallets
7000 15 Mile Rd
Sterling Heights, MI 48312-4520
                            586-264-2525
                       Fax: 248-879-7420

20138 Cadillac Plastics
2855 Coolidge Highway
Suite 300
Troy, MI 48084-3217
                            248-205-3100
        Fax: 248-205-3173 800-488-1200
                            www.cadillacplastic.com
Engraved plastics: rods, sheets, tubes and film; ad-
hesive and graphic arts products
Estimated Sales: $2,500,000 - $4,999,999
Number Employees: 19

20139 Cadillac Products Inc
5800 Crooks Rd # 200
Troy, MI 48098-2830
                            248-879-5000
        Fax: 248-879-7420 www.cadprod.com
Tea and coffee industry flexible packaging, bags and
packaging film supplies materials
Chairman of the Board: Robert Williams Sr
CEO: Robert J Williams Jr
Estimated Sales: $50-100 Million
Number Employees: 250-499

20140 Cady Bag Co
41 Project Cir
Pearson, GA 31642-7428
                            912-422-3298
        Fax: 912-422-3155 www.cadybag.com
Polypropylene, woven bags
President: William Cady
Vice President: John Moore
Estimated Sales: $20 - 50 Million
Number Employees: 100-249

20141 Cafe Del Mundo
229 E 51st Ave
Anchorage, AK 99503
                            907-562-2326
        Fax: 907-562-3278 800-770-2326
                            www.cafedelmundo.com
Coffee, espresso equipment
Owner: Perry Merkel
Manager: Monique Johnston
Purchasing: Perry Merkel
Estimated Sales: $800,000
Number Employees: 12
Type of Packaging: Private Label, Bulk
Brands:
  Cafe Del Mundo

20142 Cain Awning Co Inc
1301 3rd Ave S
Birmingham, AL 35233-1406
                            205-323-8379
        Fax: 877-640-6739 info@cainawning.com
                            www.cainawning.com
Commercial awnings
Owner: Hank Lawson
  info@cainawning.com
Estimated Sales: $1-2,500,000
Number Employees: 10-19

20143 Cal Ben Soap Co
9828 Pearmain St
Oakland, CA 94603-2312
                            510-638-7092
        Fax: 510-638-7827 800-340-7091
        calbenco@yahoo.com www.calbenpuresoap.com
Soaps including laundry, dish, etc

President: Martin Schachter
calbenco@yahoo.com
Estimated Sales: Below $5 Million
Number Employees: 10-19

20144 Cal Controls
1675 Delany Road
Gurnee, IL 60031

Fax: 847-782-5223 800-866-6659
NA@West-CS.com www.cal-controls.com
Manufacturer and exporter of temperature and machine controllers for packaging and processing equipment
Sales Manager: Dave Chylstek
Estimated Sales: $15 Million
Number Employees: 21
Brands:
Cal
Calcomms
Calgrafix
Calogix

20145 Cal Western Pest Control
5417 Peck Road
Arcadia, CA 91006-5847

661-808-7378
Fax: 323-721-0377 800-326-2847
Consultant for pest and sanitation control programs for food processors and distributors
Owner: John Lemm
Manager: Dave Conner
General Manager: Marc Canipe
Estimated Sales: $2.5-5 Million
Number Employees: 50-99

20146 Cal-Coast Manufacturing
P.O. Box 1864
Turlock, CA 95381-1864

209-668-9378
Fax: 209-668-9382
Dairy equipment, storage tanks and auger systems. Also dairy construction and public scale
President: L Baptista
Controller: D Baptista
Estimated Sales: $1 - 3,000,000
Number Employees: 5-9

20147 Cal-Mil Plastic Products Inc
4079 Calle Platino
Oceanside, CA 92056-5805

760-630-5100
Fax: 760-630-5010 800-321-9069
www.calmil.com
Manufacturer, exporter and importer of acrylic counter top cabinets, mirrored displays, crocks, platters, risers, bowls, pedestals, tables, domes, etc. for the catering and banquet industries.
President: Barney Callahan
bcallahan@calmil.com
Marketing Director: Mike Juneman
Sales Director: Mike Juneman
Estimated Sales: $10-20 Million
Number Employees: 20-49
Number of Products: 1460
Type of Packaging: Bulk

20148 Calcium Chloride Sales Inc
713 W Main St
Grove City, PA 16127-1198

724-458-5778
Fax: 724-458-4250 800-228-3879
cacl2@zoominternet.net
www.calciumchloridesales.com
Food grade calcium chloride including liquid and flake
President: Jim Mc Lean
cacl2@zoominternet.net
Secretary: Larry Bowie
Estimated Sales: $2.5 Million
Number Employees: 5-9
Number of Products: 1
Square Footage: 16000
Type of Packaging: Private Label, Bulk

20149 Caldwell Group
5055 26th Avenue
Rockford, IL 61109

815-229-5667
Fax: 815-229-5686 800-628-4263
contact@caldwellinc.com www.caldwellinc.com
Manufacturer and exporter of crane lifting attachments

Owner: Howard Will
VP: William McLeod
Estimated Sales: $5-10 Million
Number Employees: 50-99

20150 Calgene
1920 5th St
Davis, CA 95616

530-753-6313
Fax: 530-753-1510 800-992-4363
rhonda.ryan@monsanto.com www.calgene.com
Research in genetics, and biotechnology of food
Contact: Julie Alvarez
julie.alvarez@monsanto.com
Estimated Sales: $10 - 15 000,000
Number Employees: 100-249

20151 Calgon Carbon
300 GSK Drive
Moon Township, PA 15108

412-787-6700
www.calgoncarbon.com
Activated carbon products
President & CEO: Randy Dearth
Estimated Sales: $555 Million
Number Employees: 1,100
Parent Co: Kuraray Co., Ltd.

20152 Calhoun Bend Mill
PO BOX 520
Libuse, LA 71348

318-640-0060
Fax: 318-339-9099 800-519-6455
sales@calhounbendmill.com
www.calhounbendmill.com
Fruit cobbler mixes, cornmeal and seafood coating.
President/CEO: Patrick Calhoun
Treasurer: Monica Calhoun
Vice President: Nathan Martin
Sales Manager: Emma Cash
Corporate Secretary: Martie Hoover
Estimated Sales: $400,000
Number Employees: 5
Number of Brands: 2
Number of Products: 25
Square Footage: 34000
Type of Packaging: Consumer, Food Service, Private Label, Bulk
Brands:
Calhoun Bend Mill
Orchard Mills

20153 Calia Technical
420 Jefferson Boulevard
Staten Island, NY 10312-2334

718-967-9757
Fax: 718-967-0275
Inspection, control systems, bar code verification systems, bottle and cap inspection and machine vision solutions; web bar code verification systems to verify multiple bar codes on thermoformer lidstock
President: Anthony Calia
VP: Robert Santagata
Engineer: Elias Hawileh
Estimated Sales: $.5 - 1 million
Number Employees: 1-4
Number of Products: 2

20154 Calico Cottage
210 New Hwy
Amityville, NY 11701-1116

631-841-2100
Fax: 631-841-2401 800-645-5345
www.calicocottage.com
Fudge mixes, flavors and colorings.
President & CEO: Mark Wurzel
m.wurzel@calicocottage.com
Chief Financial Officer: Michael Lobaccaro
Vice President: Larry Wurzel
Executive VP, Sales & Marketing: David Sank
Director, Human Resources & Admin: Barbara Stone-Carroll
Sr. VP, Operations & Technology: Thomas Montoya
Estimated Sales: $5 Million
Number Employees: 50-99
Square Footage: 45000
Type of Packaging: Consumer
Brands:
Calico Cottage Fudge Mix
Mister Fudge

20155 Calif Canning Peach Assn
2300 River Plaza Dr # 110
Sacramento, CA 95833-4241

916-925-9131
Fax: 916-925-9030 ccpa@calpeach.com
www.calpeach.com
Cooperative for cling peach processors providing marketing, price negotiation, etc
President: Rich Hudgins
rhudgins@calpeach.com
VP/COO: Rich Hudgins
Number Employees: 1-4

20156 California Blending Co
2603 Seaman Ave
El Monte, CA 91733-1929

626-448-1918
Fax: 626-448-1998
Pizza spices, dough mixes, dressing mixes, steak salts, and garlic blends. Also provided; custom blending
President: Bill Morehart
calblending@aol.com
Vice President: Roger Morehart
Estimated Sales: Less Than $500,000
Number Employees: 1-4
Square Footage: 14600
Type of Packaging: Private Label, Bulk

20157 California Caster & Handtruck
1400 17th St
San Francisco, CA 94107-2412

415-552-6750
Fax: 415-552-0463 800-950-8750
customerservice@californiacaster.com
Stainless steel hand trucks and carts, dollies, casters, leveling pads and oven and bun pan racks; wholesaler/distributor of casters
Owner: Alan Mc Clure
alanm@californiacaster.com
VP: Terry Cavannaugh
Estimated Sales: $5-10 Million
Number Employees: 10-19
Square Footage: 33000
Brands:
Dareon
Darnell
Dutro
Faultless
Magline
Meese
Morton Kaciff
Rack & Roll
Vlier
Werner

20158 California Hi-Lites
12500 Slauson Ave Ste C3
Santa Fe Springs, CA 90670-2631

562-696-1777
Fax: 562-696-8917 www.hilites.com
Co-packing, labeling, over wrapping, display construction, handwork, light assembly, bundling, gluing, collating, QC projects, order fulfillment, FDA approved cleanroom, alcoholic beverage license, organic food license and more
Owner: Hans Blom
Owner: Robert Landinl
Owner: Jim Yoder
Estimated Sales: $3-5 Million
Number Employees: 23
Square Footage: 80000
Type of Packaging: Consumer, Food Service, Private Label, Bulk
Brands:
Feast of Eden
Hi-Lites
Nature's Candy
Val Linda

20159 California League of Food Processors
1755 Creekside Oaks Drive
Suite 250
Sacramento, CA 95833

916-640-8150
Fax: 916-640-8156 www.clfp.com
Represents the business interest for California's food industry.
President/CEO: Rob Neenan
COO/Treasurer: Janet Planck
Marketing Manager: Amy Alcorn
Meetings & Events Manager: Alissa Dillon

Estimated Sales: $1 - 5 Million
Number Employees: 7

20160 California Milk Advisory
400 Oyster Point Blvd # 211
Suite 211
South San Francisco, CA 94080-1998
650-871-6455
Fax: 650-583-7328 jgiambroni@cmab.net
www.realcaliforniamilk.com
Other cold non-carbonated beverages, butter, cheese, other dairy and eggs, yogurt, ice cream/sorbet, foodservice, private label.
Manager: Jim Jones
CEO: Adri Boudewyn
Marketing: Jennifer Giambroni
Estimated Sales: $1-2.5 Million
Number Employees: 5-9

20161 California Saw & Knife Works
721 Brannan St
San Francisco, CA 94103-4927
415-861-0644
Fax: 415-861-0406 888-729-6533
calsaw@calsaw.com www.calsaw.com
Manufacturer and exporter of machine knives and circular saws for food processing equipment
President: Warren Bird
wbird@calsaw.com
CFO: Mike Weber
Vice President: Benson Joseph
VP Production: S Bird
Estimated Sales: $5-10 Million
Number Employees: 10-19
Square Footage: 36000
Brands:
Calsaw

20162 California Toytime Balloons
554 West Seventh Street
PO Box 1876
San Pedro, CA 90733
310-548-1234
Fax: 310-548-1237
Printed advertising specialties including buttons, balloons, golf tees, bumper stickers and emery boards
Chairman: Bob Bershad
Sales: Richard Petrosino
Estimated Sales: $5-10 Million
Number Employees: 10-19
Parent Co: Bershad Advertising Products Company

20163 California Vibratory Feeders
1725 N Orangethorpe Park
Anaheim, CA 92801-1139
714-526-3359
Fax: 714-526-3515 800-354-0972
Custom design and build automation equipment
President: Donn Robinson
Marketing: Sandy Chester
Sales: Peter Speers
Operations: Kelly Reece
Estimated Sales: $5 - 10 Million
Number Employees: 20-49

20164 Caljan America
3600 E 45th Ave
Denver, CO 80216-6510
303-321-3600
Fax: 303-321-6767 www.caljan.com
Telescopic conveyors for trailer loading and unloading
President: Lonnie Watkins
Contact: Henrick Olsen
olsen@caljan.com
Estimated Sales: $5-10 Million
Number Employees: 20-49

20165 Callanan Company Alloy Company
1844 Brummel Avenue
Elk Grove Village, IL 60007-2121
847-364-4242
Fax: 847-364-4373 800-732-5123
alloyd@alloyd.com www.alloyd.com
Radio frequency heat sealing and packaging equipment
Estimated Sales: $5-10 Million
Number Employees: 40

20166 Caloritech
1420 West Main Street
P.O. Box 146
Greensburg, IN 47240
812-663-4141
Fax: 812-663-4202 800-473-2403
info@ccithermal.com www.caloritech.com
Manufacturer and exporter of components for electrical cooking equipment, air heating immersion and clamp-on radiant equipment
President: Harold Roozen
VP Sales/Marketing: Bob Pender
Number Employees: 200
Square Footage: 440000
Parent Co: CCI Thermal Technologies
Brands:
X-Max

20167 (HQ)Calzone Case Co
225 Black Rock Ave
Bridgeport, CT 06605-1204
203-367-5766
Fax: 203-336-4406 800-243-5152
www.calzonecase.com
Custom transporting cases including shipping and storage containers
President: Joe Calzone
joe.calzone-@calzonecase.com
CFO: Stephen Bajda
Executive VP: Vin Calzone
Marketing: Kim Bullard
Estimated Sales: $5 - 10,000,000
Number Employees: 50-99
Other Locations:
Calzone Case Co.
City of Industry CA

20168 Cam Spray
520 Brooks Rd
Iowa Falls, IA 50126-8005
641-648-5011
Fax: 641-648-5013 800-648-5011
sales@camspray.com www.camspray.com
Manufacturer and exporter of high pressure washers; importer of pumps
Manager: Jim Gillestie
CFO: Jim Gillispie
Estimated Sales: $5-10 Million
Number Employees: 20-49
Square Footage: 150000
Parent Co: Campbell Supplies
Brands:
Cam Spray

20169 Cam Tron Systems
444 W Interstate Rd
Addison, IL 60101-4518
630-543-2884
Fax: 630-543-8153
Pressure sensitive labeling equipment
President: Micheal Ahern
Contact: Mike Ahern
ahern_mike@hotmail.com
General Manager: Frank Ross
Estimated Sales: Below $5 Million
Number Employees: 20-49
Parent Co: Cameron Group
Brands:
Cam Tron

20170 Cambelt International Corporation
2820 W 1100 S
Salt Lake City, UT 84104-4594
801-972-5511
Fax: 801-972-5522 www.cambelt.com
Conveyor belt and automatic reclaiming systems
President: Colin Campbell
VP Marketing: Rex Wood
Estimated Sales: $20 - 50 Million
Number Employees: 50-99

20171 (HQ)Cambridge Intl. Inc.
105 Goodwill Rd
PO Box 399
Cambridge, MD 21613-2980
410-228-3000
Fax: 410-221-1100 800-638-9560
www.cambridge-intl.com
Manufacturer and Exporter of conveyor belting, filters, vibration screens and filter leaves

Manager: Jody Padelko
CEO: Tracy Tyler
ttyler@cambridge-intl.com
International Sales Manager: Bart Shellabarger
Belt Sales Manager: Larry Windsor
Director of Sales: Larry Windsor
Customer Service Manager: Breanne Hemphill
Estimated Sales: $300,000-500,000
Number Employees: 250-499
Brands:
Cam-Grid
Cambri-Link
Continu-Weld

20172 (HQ)Cambridge Viscosity, Inc.
101 Station Lndg
Medford, MA 02155-5134
781-393-6500
Fax: 781-393-6515 800-554-4639
info@cambridgeviscosity.com
www.cambridgeapplied.com
Manufacturer and exporter of viscometers
President: Robert Kasameyer
Marketing Manager: Art MacNeill
Contact: Victoria Benea
beneavictoria@paclp.com
Director Engineering: Dan Airey
Estimated Sales: $1 - 2.5 Million
Number Employees: 20-49
Brands:
Cambridge
Visco Lab 400
Visco Pro 1000
Visco Pro 2000

20173 Cambro Manufacturing Co
5801 Skylab Rd
Huntington Beach, CA 92647-2056
714-848-1555
800-833-3003
webmaster@cambro.com www.cambro.com
Food service equipment and supplies including bus boxes, insulated food carriers, carts and beverage containers, plastic insert pans, fiberglass trays and polyethylene boxes.
President: Argyle Campbell
acampbell@cambro.com
Chief Financial Officer: David Capestro
Year Founded: 1951
Estimated Sales: $74 Million
Number Employees: 250-499
Type of Packaging: Food Service
Other Locations:
Warehouse
Brampton, Canada
Customer Service Center
Stuttgart, Germany
Manufacturing Facility
Mebane NC
Brands:
Cambro

20174 Camco Chemicals
8150 Holton Dr
Florence, KY 41042-3010
859-727-3200
Fax: 859-727-1508 800-554-1001
www.camco-chem.com
Contract packager of janitorial supplies, laundry detergents, lubricants, soaps and cleaners
President: Thomas Cropper
CEO: Richard Rolfes
CFO: Richard Rolfes
CEO: Richard Rolfes
Estimated Sales: $20 - 50 Million
Number Employees: 100-249

20175 Camcorp Inc
8224 Nieman Rd
Overland Park, KS 66214-1507
913-831-0740
Fax: 913-831-9271 info@camcorpinc.com
www.camcorpinc.com
Owner: Frank Hanwork
VP Sales/Marketing: Ted Remmers
Contact: Leydy Galindez
lgalindez@cam.com.co
Estimated Sales: $5 - 10 Million
Number Employees: 5-9

20176 Camel Canvas Shop

8910 Valgro Rd
Knoxville, TN 37920-9137

865-573-2804
Fax: 865-573-9677 800-524-2704
www.camelcanvas.com
Commercial awnings, and custom canvas products
Owner: Christian Cain
Sales: Brad Young
ccain@camelcanvas.com
Plant Manager: Brenda Young
Purchasing: Rayma Stasen
Estimated Sales: $5 - 10 Million
Number Employees: 5-9
Square Footage: 6400

20177 Cameo Metal Products Inc

127 12th St
Brooklyn, NY 11215-3891

718-788-1106
Fax: 718-788-3761 sales@cameometal.com
www.cameometal.com
Cameo Metal Products Manufactures metal closures
for the food and beverage industry.
President: Vito Di Maio
cameosales@cameometals.com
Finance Manager: Adolsopoll Cruz
Director of Sales/Plant Manager: Robert Geddis
Director of Operations: Anthony Di Maio
Estimated Sales: $5.8 Million
Number Employees: 20-49
Square Footage: 100000

20178 Cameron Intl. Corp.

Park Towers South
Houston, TX

281-285-4376
www.slb.com/companies/cameron
Manufacturer and exporter of oil-free centrifugal
compressors.
CEO, Schlumberger: Olivier Le Peuch
VP, Finance: Jeff Altamari
Year Founded: 1920
Estimated Sales: $9.8 Billion
Number Employees: 23,412
Parent Co: Schlumberger Limited
Brands:
    Joy

20179 Camerons Brewing Co.

1165 invicta Drive
Oakville, ON L6H 4M1
Canada

905-849-8282
Fax: 905-849-5578 info@cameronsbrewing.com
www.caemronsbrewing.com
Manufacturer and exporter of micro brewing equipment
President: Gary Deathe
Number Employees: 17

20180 Camie Campbell

9225 Watson Industrial Park
Saint Louis, MO 63126

314-968-3222
Fax: 314-968-0741 800-325-9572
camie@camie.com www.camie.com
Lubricants, pressure sensitive adhesives, rust corrosion silicones, spray adhesive and silicone sealants
President: Vince Doder
CEO: Tom Shelby
CFO: Vincent Doder
Natl. Sales Rep.: Steve Hartley
Credit Manager: Claudia Grissin
Estimated Sales: $10-20 000,000
Number Employees: 20-49
Type of Packaging: Bulk

20181 Campak Inc

119 Naylon Ave
Livingston, NJ 07039-1005

973-597-1414
Fax: 973-992-4713 info@campak.com
www.campak.com
Thermoformer, intermittent motion horizontal cartons, automatic wrapper, automatic bundler and
shrink tunnel
CEO: Rugel Franz
rugel@campak.com
CEO: Thomas Miller
Estimated Sales: $5-10 Million
Number Employees: 10-19

20182 Campbell Wrapper Corporation

1415 Fortune Ave
De Pere, WI 54115-8104

920-983-7100
Fax: 920-983-7300 www.campbellwrapper.com
Manufactures Horizontal Fin Seal Wrappers for food
and nonfood applications. On-Edge Wrappers for
cookies and crackers; In-line Feed Systems for confectionery and bakery; Bar Distribution Systems for
health bars, confectionery, bakeryetc.
President: John Dykema
dykemaj@campbellwrapper.com
Chief Financial Officer: Todd Goodwin
Engineering Manager: Jeffrey Ginzl
Vice President Sales & Marketing: Don Stelzer
Regional Sales Manager: Steve Joosten
Service Manager: Marv Calaway
Materials Manager/Wrapper Assembly Mgr: Jeff
Jende
Estimated Sales: $10 - 20 Million
Number Employees: 50-99
Type of Packaging: Consumer

20183 Campbell-Hardage

305 Old Commerce Rd
Athens, GA 30607

706-548-4615
Fax: 706-543-2139
Machinery for distribution systems and automatic
product loading
President: Tim Wayne Hardage
CFO: Ark Campbell
Estimated Sales: $2.5 - 5 000,000
Number Employees: 30

20184 Campus Collection, Inc.

PO Box 2904
Tuscaloosa, AL 35403

205-758-0678
Fax: 205-758-4848 800-289-8744
www.campuscollection.net
Manufacturer and exporter of printed and embroidered T-shirts, hats
President: Chet Goldstein
Contact: Chris Ballard
chris@campuscollection.net

20185 Camstar Systems

100 Century Center Ct # 500
San Jose, CA 95112-4536

408-559-5700
Fax: 408-558-9350 800-237-2841
partners@camstar.com www.camstar.com
Production line software systems
President: James David Cone
President, Chief Executive Officer: Scott Toney
Vice President of Marketing: Karim Lokas
Chief Technical Officer: Scott Jones
Vice President of Sales: Jay Antonellis
Contact: Sean Henry
shenry@camstar.com
Estimated Sales: $20 - 50 Million
Number Employees: 100-249

20186 Camtech-AMF

2115 West Laburnum Avenue
Richmond, VA 23227-4315

804-355-7961
Fax: 804-355-1074 sales@amfbakery.com
www.amfbakery.com
Industrial baking equipment
President: Ken Newsome
Number Employees: 100-249

20187 Camtron Systems

444 W Interstate Rd
Addison, IL 60101-4518

630-543-2884
Fax: 630-543-8153
Labels and label applicators
Owner: Mike Ahern
ahern_mike@hotmail.com
Estimated Sales: $1 - 2.5 000,000
Number Employees: 20-49

20188 Can & Bottle Systems, Inc.

2525 SE Stubb St
Milwaukie, OR 97222-7323

503-236-9010
Fax: 503-232-8453 866-302-2636
www.canandbottle.com
Manufacturer, sales and service and exporter of reverse vending machines and systems for beverage
container redemption and recycling. Can, plastic and
glass beverage container crushers/recyclers
President: Bill Janner
Number Employees: 20-49
Number of Products: 15
Square Footage: 40000
Brands:
    Cando

20189 Can Corp of America Inc

326 June Ave
Blandon, PA 19510-9566

610-926-3044
Fax: 610-926-5041 www.cancorpam.com
Steel food cans.
President & CEO: Ronald Moreau
Vice President, Sales & Marketing: Phil Butler
Year Founded: 1975
Estimated Sales: $100-500 Million
Number Employees: 100-249
Square Footage: 150000
Other Locations:
    Can Corp. of America
    Reading PA

20190 Can Creations

PO Box 848576
Pembroke Pines, FL 33084

954-581-3312
Fax: 954-581-2523 800-272-0235
www.cancreations.com
Bags, baskets and containers, boxes, cellophane, gift
wrap, pull bows, shrink wrap.

20191 Can Creations

PO Box 8576
Pembroke Pines, FL 33084

954-581-3312
Fax: 954-581-2523 orders@cancreations.com
www.cancreations.com
Decorative boxes, shrink wrap, ribbons, bows and
bags
Estimated Sales: $1 - 5 Million
Number Employees: 12
Brands:
    Crystal Wrap

20192 Can Lines Engineering Inc

9839 Downey Norwalk Rd
P.O. Box 7039
Downey, CA 90241-7039

562-861-2996
www.canlines.com
Can and bottle handling conveyors.
President: Keenan Koplien
Director, Mechanical Engineering: Steve Lusa
Director, Operations: Darwin Smock
Year Founded: 1960
Estimated Sales: $20 Million
Number Employees: 10-19
Square Footage: 40000

20193 Can-Am Instruments

2851 Brighton Road
Oakville, ON L6H 6C9
Canada

905-829-0030
Fax: 905-829-4701 800-215-4469
psmyth@can-am.net www.can-am.net
Food machinery and equipment
President: Mark Reeves
Director: Richard Reeves
Director: Greg Reeves
Estimated Sales: $3 Million
Number Employees: 12

20194 CanPacific Engineering

7331 Vantage Way
Delta, BC V4G 1C9
Canada

604-946-1680
Fax: 604-946-1620 www.canpacific.com
Industrial can openers and can seam inspection
equipment
President: Wun Chong
Number Employees: 5-9
Brands:
    Canguard

20195 Canada Coaster
44 Head St.
Dundas, ON L9H 3H3
Canada

905-627-6910
Fax: 905-627-7608 866-233-7628
sales@canadacoaster.com
www.canadacoaster.com
Manufacturers of beer and drink coasters
Type of Packaging: Food Service, Private Label,
Bulk

20196 Canada Goose Wood Produc
2489 Del Zotto Avenue
Gloucester, ON K1T 3V6
Canada

613-822-2575
Fax: 613-822-2232 888-890-6506
www.canada-goose.com
Wooden cutting boards, butcherblocks, trays and
fajita griddle underliners

20197 Canada Pure Water Company Ltd
7 Kodiak Crescent
Toronto, ON M3J 3E5
Canada

416-631-5800
Fax: 416-635-1711 800-361-2369
info@canadapure.com www.canadapure.com
Wholesaler/distributor of flavored spring water and
teas
President: David Tavares
Marketing Assistant: Sophia Ahmed
Director Purchasing: Tracy Tavares
Number Employees: 10-19

20198 Canadian Display Systems
60 Corstate Ave
Concord, ON L4K 4X2
Canada

905-265-7888
Fax: 905-265-7692 800-895-5862
cds1@on.aibn.com
www.canadiandisplaysystems.com
Display coolers
President: Gary Sohi
Number Employees: 15

20199 Canarm, Ltd.
2157 Parkedale Avenue
PO Box 367
Brockville, ON K6V 5V6
Canada

613-342-5424
Fax: 800-263-4598 info@canarm.ca
www.canarm.com
Manufacturer and importer of ceiling fans
President: James A. Cooper
Vice President - HVAC & Agri Products: Doug
Matthews
Marketing Manager: John McBride
Sales Manager: Tim Sutton
Director Operations: Steven Read
Number Employees: 30
Type of Packaging: Consumer, Food Service, Pri-
vate Label
Brands:
Four Seasons
Pleasantaire

20200 Candle Lamp Company
1880 Compton Avenue
Ste. 101
Corona, CA 92881

951-682-9600
Fax: 951-784-5801 877-526-7748
www.candlelamp.com
Chafing dish and lamp fuel; also, table lamps for the
restaurant/hotel industry
President: Daniel Stoner
VP: L Murlin
Marketing Services: J Van Osdel
Contact: Karina Garcia
kgarcia@sternocandlelamp.com
Estimated Sales: $10 - 20 Million
Number Employees: 100-249
Brands:
Safe Heat
Soft Light

**20201 Candy & Company/Peck's
Products Company**
4100 West 76th Street
Chicago, IL 60652

800-837-9189
daleyinternational.com/
Manufacturer and exporter of industrial disinfectant
cleaners, janitorial supplies, sanitizers, laundry sup-
plies and specialty cleaning chemicals
President: Joh Daley
Sales Manager: Joann Stoskoph
Estimated Sales: $1 - 5 Million
Number Employees: 1-4
Square Footage: 160000
Parent Co: J.F. Daley International
Brands:
Camagsolv
Pepcocide

20202 Candy Manufacturing Co
5633 W Howard St
Niles, IL 60714-4011

847-588-2639
Fax: 847-588-0055 info@candycontrols.com
www.candycontrols.com
Manufacturer and exporter of industrial timing con-
trols including differentials, positioners, cam
switches, timing hubs, and web handling systems
President: Robert Hendershot
Quality Control: Al Rosenow
Sales Director: Jacob Ninan
Estimated Sales: Below $5 Million
Number Employees: 5-9
Square Footage: 60000

20203 CandyMachines.com
27721 N Twin Oaks Valley Rd
San Marcos, CA 92069-9742

760-734-1414
Fax: 866-863-5867 800-853-3941
info@candymachines.com
www.candymachines.com
Distributor of gumball and candy vending machines,
sticker, capsule machines, and bulk products, and re-
fill supplies
Manager: Tonya Bryhie
CFO: Irving Korn
Vice President: Harris Harris
Marketing Director: Jerry Korn
Estimated Sales: Less Than $500,000
Number Employees: 1-4
Number of Brands: 500+
Number of Products: 5000
Parent Co: RM Electronics
Type of Packaging: Consumer, Bulk

20204 Canning & Filling
PO Box 7501
Burlingame, CA 94011

650-401-6654
Fax: 650-401-6535

20205 Cannon Equipment Company
324 W Washington St
Cannon Falls, MN 55009

507-263-6400
800-825-8501
info@cannonequipment.com
www.cannonequipment.com
Point-of-purchase displays, front-end merchandisers,
distribution and display carts, and material handling
equipment and system.
President: Robyn Walker
VP, Finance: Stephanie Zabel
VP, Business Development: John Serpiello
VP, Operations: Rob Schettle
Year Founded: 1981
Estimated Sales: $100-250 Million
Number Employees: 250-499
Number of Brands: 15
Number of Products: 100
Parent Co: IMI,PLC
Type of Packaging: Consumer, Food Service, Pri-
vate Label, Bulk
Other Locations:
Cannon Equipment Company
Passaic NJ
Cannon Equipment Company
College Point NY
Cannon Equipment Company
Chattanooga TN
Cannon Equipment Company
Garden Grove CA
Cannon Equipment Company
Cannon Falls MN
Brands:
Connect-A-Bench
Ez-Lock
Ez-Reach
Magna-Bar
Ship 'n Shop
Slip

20206 Canon Potato Company
P.O. Box 880
Center, CO 81125

719-754-3445
Fax: 719-754-2227 sales@canonpotato.com
www.canonpotato.com
Potatoes including Centennials, McClures,
Norkotahs, Nuggets, Reds, Russets, Sangres and Yu-
kon Gold.
Manager: Jim Tonso
Sales Representative: Matt Glowczewski
Sales Manager: David Tonso
d.tonso@canonpotato.com
General Manager: Jim Tonso
Office Manager: Sandy Tonso
Estimated Sales: $10-20 Million
Number Employees: 50-99
Square Footage: 865020
Type of Packaging: Consumer, Food Service, Bulk

20207 Canongate Technology
2045 S Arl Hts Rd Ste 109
Arlington Hts, IL 60005

847-593-1832
Fax: 847-593-1629 800-221-4051
sales@canongatetechnology.co.uk
www.canongatetechnology.com
Inline instruments and analyzers sensing dissolved
CO2, O2, % alcohol, O.G. and Brix
Group Managing Director: Robin Cuthbertson
VP: Ron Mc Rae
Estimated Sales: $500,000-$1 000,000
Number Employees: 1-4

20208 Cantech Industries Inc
2222 Eddie Williams Rd
Johnson City, TN 37601-2871

423-926-9748
Fax: 423-928-0311 800-654-3947
www.cantechtn.com
Manufacturer and exporter of pressure sensitive
tapes including duct, masking, box sealing, filament,
double-coated, and electrical for industrial, automo-
tive and retail markets
CEO: Darryl Bezaire
Estimated Sales: $50 Million
Number Employees: 50-99
Number of Brands: 2
Number of Products: 70
Square Footage: 100000
Parent Co: Canadian Technical Tape
Type of Packaging: Consumer, Food Service, Pri-
vate Label, Bulk
Brands:
Cantech
Clipper

**20209 Cantley-Ellis Manufacturing
Company**
1200 South Eastman Road
Kingsport, TN 37660-5408

423-246-4671

Wooden pallets
General Manager: Jim Cantley
Estimated Sales: $2.5-5 Million
Number Employees: 20-49

20210 Cantol
199 Steelcase Road West
Markham, ON L3R 2M4
Canada

905-475-6141
800-387-9773
info@cantol.com www.cantol.com
Liquid detergents, soaps, herbicides, insecticides, lu-
bricants, solvents and degreasers and floor care
products, drain treatment chemicals, turf products,
odor control, food processing and dietary chemicals
President & CEO: Ja Brightman
VP: Richard Petscha
Plant Manager: Ellwood Barth
Estimated Sales: $10-20 Million
Number Employees: 20-49

Number of Products: 13
Parent Co: Cantol
Type of Packaging: Private Label, Bulk

20211 (HQ)Canton Sign Co
222 5th St NE
Canton, OH 44702-1262
330-456-7151
Fax: 330-456-7152 cantonsign@aol.com
www.cantonsignco.com
Metal, electric, plastic and wood signs and displays
President: Timothy Franta
cantonsign@aol.com
VP: Mark Franta
VP: Timothy Franta
Estimated Sales: $500,000-$1 Million
Number Employees: 1-4

20212 (HQ)Canton Sterilized Wiping Cloth
1401 Waynesburg Dr SE
Canton, OH 44707-2115
330-455-8157
Fax: 330-455-2003
Cheesecloth wiping rags
President: Robert Shapiro
Estimated Sales: $5 - 10 Million
Number Employees: 10-19

20213 (HQ)Cantwell-Cleary Co Inc
7575 Washington Blvd
Elkridge, MD 21075
301-773-9800
Fax: 301-773-9257 support@cantwellcleary.com
www.cantwellcleary.com
Distributors of corrugated boxes and containers.
Chairman/CEO: Vincent Cleary
Year Founded: 1914
Estimated Sales: $14 Million
Number Employees: 20-49
Square Footage: 45000

20214 Cantwell-Cleary Co Inc
4263-I Carolina Ave
Richmond, VA 23222
804-329-9800
Fax: 804-329-5780 support@cantwellcleary.com
www.cantwellcleary.com
Distributors of corrugated boxes and containers.
Chairman & CEO: Vincent Cleary
Year Founded: 1914
Estimated Sales: $14 Million
Number Employees: 20-49

20215 Canvas Products
580 25 Rd
Grand Junction, CO 81505-1230
970-242-1453
Fax: 970-241-4801 www.canvas-products.com
Commercial awnings
Owner: Greg L Coren
Estimated Sales: $1-2,500,000
Number Employees: 5-9

20216 CapSnap Equipment
2080 Brooklyn Road
Jackson, MI 49203
517-787-3481
Fax: 517-787-2349 sales@capsnapequipment.com
www.capsnapequipment.com
HOD water bottling equipment and service.

20217 Capaco Plastics
9231 Billy the Kid St
El Paso, TX 79907-4738
915-772-1395
Fax: 915-772-1396 www.capcoplastics.com
Thermoform company specializing in blister, clamshell and trifold packages.
President: Robert Arno
Vice President, General Manager: Bob Arno
Estimated Sales: Less Than $500,000
Number Employees: 1-4

20218 Cape Systems
100 Allentown Parkway
Suite 218
Allen, TX 75002
800-229-3434
Fax: 908-756-2332 www.capesystems.com
Pallets, load planning, optimization, transportation-software; warehouse management software order fulfillment and inventory system

Executive Chairman: Hugo Biermann
Director/CEO/CFO: Nicholas Toms
CEO: Nicholas R Toms
International Marketing: Peter Ayling
Vice President Group Sales: Brad Leonard
Contact: Kennedy Allen
akennedy@capesystems.com
Chief Operating Officer/CTO: David Sasson
Vice President Software Sales: Heidi Larsen
Estimated Sales: Below $5 Million
Number Employees: 20-49
Number of Brands: 8

20219 Capital City Container Corporation
150 Precision Drive
Buda, TX 78610
512-312-1222
Fax: 512-312-1349
Corrugated shipping containers
Manager: Mike McDonald
VP of Marketing: Doug King
Contact: Mike Mcdonald
m.mcdonald@boiseinc.com
Estimated Sales: $10 - 20 Million
Number Employees: 148

20220 Capital City Signs
2714 Industrial Dr
Monona, WI 53713-2250
608-222-1881
Fax: 608-222-1889
Luminous tube and plastic signs
President: Rosemary Zimmerman
info@capitalcitysigns.net
VP/Secretary: Rosemary Zimmerman
Estimated Sales: Below $5 Million
Number Employees: 5-9
Square Footage: 16000

20221 Capital Industries
PO Box 1693
Mattituck, NY 11952-0929
631-298-6300
Fax: 631-298-2077 info@kwikbond.com
www.kwikbond.com
Kwik-Bond, floor repair
Estimated Sales: $5 - 10 Million
Number Employees: 20-49

20222 Capital Packaging
PO Box 873
Panacea, FL 32346
229-228-0006
Fax: 912-228-6405
Packaging
C.E.O: Polybus B. Joseph
Secretary: Polybus T. Frances
Sales Manager: Randy Eason

20223 (HQ)Capital Plastics
15060 Madison Rd
Middlefield, OH 44062-9450
440-632-5800
Fax: 440-632-0012 collector@capitalplastics.com
www.capitalplastics.com
Manufacturer and exporter of custom plastic displays for acrylic cutting boards, clip boards, plaques and trophies
President: Lyle Schwartz
Estimated Sales: $2.5 - 5 Million
Number Employees: 10-19

20224 Capitol Awning Co Inc
10515 180th St
Jamaica, NY 11433-1818
718-454-6444
Fax: 718-657-8374 800-241-3539
www.capitolawning.com
Commercial awnings, banners, sign faces and graphics
President: Fred Catalano
Estimated Sales: $2.5-5,000,000
Number Employees: 20-49

20225 Capitol Carton Company
8333 24th Avenue
Sacramento, CA 95826
916-388-7848
Fax: 916-388-7840
Corrugated boxes
President: Neal Gurevitz
VP: Thomas Milligan
Plant Supervisor: James Wodarczyk

Estimated Sales: $1 - 5 Million
Number Employees: 5-9
Square Footage: 100000

20226 Capitol City Container Corp
8240 Zionsville Rd
Indianapolis, IN 46268-1627
317-875-0290
Fax: 317-876-6694 800-233-5145
Custom corrugated boxes and stock packaging supplies
President: Rich Purcell
rich@capcitycontainer.com
VP: Mike Purcell
Plant Manager: Jim Plank
Estimated Sales: $10 - 20 Million
Number Employees: 20-49
Square Footage: 130000

20227 Capitol Hardware, Inc.
402 N Main Street
P.O. Box 70
Middlebury, IN 46540-2573
800-327-6083
Fax: 800-544-4054
Manufacturer and exporter of retail store fixtures, peripheral display hardware and electric lighting fixtures
President: Joe Shelby
capitolhardware@leggett.com
Senior Vice President: David DeSonier
Executive Vice President of Sales: Joel Katterhagen
Executive Vice President of Operations: Ron McComas
Estimated Sales: $2.5-5 Million
Number Employees: 20-49
Square Footage: 1000000
Parent Co: Leggett & Platt Store Fixtures Group
Brands:
Capitol Hardware

20228 Capitol Recruiting Group
712 Gum Rock Ct
Newport News, VA 23606-2524
757-812-8677
Executive search firm specializing in selection and placement of consumer packaged goods industry personnel including sales, marketing, category, broker and senior level management positions
Contact: Robyn Tragesser
robyn.tragesser@capitolrecruitinggroup.com
General Manager: Buford Sims
Number Employees: 10-19
Other Locations:
Washington DC
Boston MA
New York NY

20229 Capitol Vial
151 Riverside Drive
Fultonville, NY 12072-1824
518-853-3377
Fax: 518-853-3409 sales@capitolvial.com
www.capitolvial.com
Contact: Jeff Steiger
jsteiger@capitolvial.com
Estimated Sales: $5-10 Million
Number Employees: 20-49

20230 Capmatic, Ltd.
12180 Boul. Albert-Hudon
Monreal North, QC H1G 3K7
Canada
514-332-0062
Fax: 514-322-0063 info@capmatic.com
www.capmatic.com
Manufacturer and exporter of packaging machinery and bottling equipment
President: Charles Lacasse
CFO: Nicole Murray
President: Alioscia Bassani
Sales Director: Christian Normandin
Number Employees: 20

20231 Capone Foods
14 Bow St. Union Square
Somerville, MA 02143
617-629-2296
Fax: 617-776-0318 albert@caponefoods.com
www.caponefoods.com

Producer of pasta and sauces. Some of their products include fresh pasta, ravioli, tortellini, gnocchi, pizza, entr,es, meatballs, sausage, empanadas and many more items. Their products can be found in several store locationsthroughout Massachusetts, such as Bedford, Boston, Brighton, Brookline, Cambridge, Concord, and other locations.
Owner: Albert Capone
Manager: Jennifer Capone
Estimated Sales: $320,000
Number Employees: 7
Brands:
    Capone Foods

20232 Capresso
81 Ruckman Rd
PO Box 775
Closter, NJ 07624-2102
201-564-7273
Fax: 201-767-9684 800-767-3554
contact@capresso.com www.capresso.com
Espresso machines and accessories, coffee makers, coffee grinders, coffee/espresso centers and toasters.
President: Michael Kramm
Manager: Barbara Leung
    barbara@jura.com
Estimated Sales: $10 - 20 000,000
Number Employees: 10-19
Type of Packaging: Bulk

20233 Capricorn Coffees Inc
353 10th St
San Francisco, CA 94103-3804
415-621-8500
Fax: 415-621-9875 800-541-0758
www.capricorncoffees.com
Coffee, Tea, Accessories
Manager: Annie Ngo
Manager: Rachel Akins
    rachel.akins@capricorncoffees.com
Estimated Sales: $1-2.5 Million
Number Employees: 10-19
Type of Packaging: Private Label

20234 Capricorn Coffees Inc
353 10th St
San Francisco, CA 94103-3804
415-621-8500
Fax: 415-621-9875 www.capricorncoffees.com
Espresso machines and accessories
Manager: Megan Patterson
CFO: Craig Edwards
Quality Control: Craig Edwards
Manager: Rachel Akins
    rachel.akins@capricorncoffees.com
Estimated Sales: $1 - 2.5 000,000
Number Employees: 10-19

20235 Capway Conveyor Systems Inc
725 Vogelsong Rd
York, PA 17404-1765
717-843-0003
Fax: 717-843-1654 877-222-7929
sales@capwayusa.com www.capwayusa.com
Manufacturer and exporter of bakery and food processing equipment including depanners, proofers, coolers, pan storage systems, conveyors, etc
President: Frank Achterberg
    fachterberg@capwayusa.com
General Manager: Frank Achterberg
Estimated Sales: $5-10 Million
Number Employees: 20-49
Square Footage: 72000
Parent Co: Capway Systems
Brands:
    Capway

20236 Cara Products Company
9192 Tara Boulevard
Jonesboro, GA 30236-4913
770-478-9802
Fax: 770-471-3715
Manufacturer and exporter of stainless steel, fiberglass and wood free standing and hot food counters. Custom stainless steel kitchen equipment, serving lines, buffets and salad bard, portable hot and cold carts and custom millwork
President: W Casey
VP: David Pearson
Marketing: Bill Steadman
Sales Manager: Bill Steadman
Purchasing: Dan Casey
Estimated Sales: $20-25 Million
Number Employees: 200

20237 Carando Technologies Inc
345 N Harrison St
Stockton, CA 95203-2801
209-948-6500
Fax: 209-948-6757 sales@carando.net
www.carando.net
Manufacturer and exporter of container production machinery
President: Sid Schuetz
CFO: Laura Keir
    lkeir@carando.net
Sales Coordinator: Laura Keir
Estimated Sales: $5-10 Million
Number Employees: 10-19

20238 (HQ)Caraustar
5000 Austell Powder Springs Rd
Suite 300
Austell, GA 30106
770-948-3101
www.caraustar.com
Contract packager.
President & CEO: Mike Patton
Year Founded: 1938
Estimated Sales: $20-50 Million
Number Employees: 5000-9999
Other Locations:
    Consumer Packaging
    Pineville NC
    Chicago IL
    Grand Rapids MI
    Kingston Springs TN
    Cleveland OH
    Randleman NC
    Burlington NC
    Los Angeles CA
    Industrial Products
    Arlington TX
    Atlanta GA
    Augusta GA
    Austell GA
    Bay Minette AL

20239 Caraustar
115 Quail Road
Franklin, KY 42134
270-586-9565
info@caraustar.com
www.caraustar.com
Advertising novelties and specialties including plastic lids, tips and spouts
Division Manager: Mark Bamberger
Estimated Sales: $5-10 Million
Number Employees: 20-49

20240 Caraustar Industries, Inc.
3900 Comanche Drive
Archdale, NC 27263-3158
770-948-3101
800-223-1373
info@caraustar.com www.caraustar.com
Manufacturer and exporter of composite cans, tubes, metal ends and injection molded plastic products used for packaging wet and dry, hot fill and frozen products
Marketing Director: Andrew McGowan
Type of Packaging: Consumer, Food Service

20241 Caravan Company
237 Chandler St
Worcester, MA 01609
508-752-3777
Fax: 508-753-4717
Coffee
President/Treasurer: George Drapos
Vice President: Arthur Drapos
Clerk: Alex Drapos
Estimated Sales: $2.1 Million
Number Employees: 17

20242 Caravan Packaging Inc
6427 Eastland Rd
Brookpark, OH 44142-1305
440-243-4100
Fax: 440-243-4383 info@caravanpackaging.com
www.caravanpackaging.com
Manufacturer and exporter of wooden boxes and custom packaging
President: Fred Hitti
    fred@caravanpackaging.com
Estimated Sales: $500,000-$1 Million
Number Employees: 1-4
Type of Packaging: Food Service, Bulk

20243 Carbis Inc
1430 W Darlington St
Florence, SC 29501-2124
843-669-6668
Fax: 843-662-1536 800-948-7750
sales@carbissolutions.com
Stainless steel products, including loading racks, arms, stairs, platforms and handrails
President: Sam Cramer
    sam.cramer@carbissolutions.com
Marketing Director: Rob Cooksey
General Manager: Ron Bennett
Number Employees: 250-499
Square Footage: 1200000

20244 Carboline Co
2150 Schuetz Rd
St Louis, MO 63146-3517
314-644-1000
Fax: 314-644-4617 800-848-4645
www.carboline.com
High-performance, anti-corrosive coatings
President: Richard Wilson
    richard_wilson@carboline.com
Estimated Sales: $87 Million
Number Employees: 10-19

20245 Carbon Clean Industries Inc
216 Courtdale Ave
Kingston, PA 18704-1123
570-288-1155
Fax: 570-288-1227 carbonclean@aol.com
Chemical cleaners for the removal of burnt and carbonized food products; also, dispensers
President: Ernest J Clamar
    carbonclean@aol.com
CFO: Ernest J Clamar Sr
Estimated Sales: $5 - 10,000,000
Number Employees: 10-19

20246 Carbone Fine Food LLC
4100 NE 1st Ave
Miami, FL 33137
845-344-7806
carbonefinefood.com
Pasta sauces.
CEO: Eric Skae
Year Founded: 2020
Estimated Sales: $3.8 Million
Number Employees: 11
Number of Brands: 1
Number of Products: 10
Brands:
    CARBONE

20247 Carbonic Machines Inc
2900 5th Ave S
Minneapolis, MN 55408-2497
612-824-0745
Fax: 612-824-1974 info@shamrockgroup.net
www.shamrockgroup.net
Ice machines and beer, wine and soda dispensing systems for restaurants
Owner: Nabil Gadros
    nabil.gadros@bavaria.com
VP Marketing: Steven Kelly
Estimated Sales: $20 - 50 Million
Number Employees: 20-49

20248 Carbonic Reserves
4754 Shavano Oak # 102
San Antonio, TX 78249-4027
210-479-0100
Fax: 210-479-0070 800-880-1911
www.airgas.com
Freezers and cooling tunnels and spirals; processor of dry ice
President: Bob Bradshaw
Vice President of HR: Ann Rice
Sales Manager: Jay Loo
Vice President of Operations: Don Goldschmidt
Estimated Sales: $1 - 5 Million
Number Employees: 100-249
Brands:
    Penguin Brand

20249 Card Pak Inc
29601 Solon Rd
Cleveland, OH 44139-3451
440-542-3100
Fax: 440-542-3399 800-824-3342
sgraham@cardpak.com
Owner: Shelby David
dshelby@cardpak.com

Estimated Sales: $20 - 50 Million
Number Employees: 100-249

20250 Cardan Design
227 Rutgers St
Maplewood, NJ 07040-3229
973-762-2186
Fax: 973-762-2753
Owner: Bert Ghavami
Contact: Cristi Mosco
cristimosco@techniedge.com
Estimated Sales: $1 - 5 000,000
Number Employees: 50-99

20251 Cardinal Container Corp
750 S Post Rd
Indianapolis, IN 46239-9745
317-898-2715
Fax: 317-899-6747 800-899-2715
www.cardinalcontainercorp.com
Corrugated cartons
President: Fred Beers
fbeers@cardinalcontainercorp.com
Controller: Mark Prosser
Estimated Sales: $10-20 Million
Number Employees: 20-49

20252 Cardinal Kitchens
165 Exeter Road
London, ON N6L 1A4
Canada
519-652-3295
Fax: 519-652-9853 800-928-0832
Laboratory providing food testing services
President: David M. Lucy
Parent Co: Cardinal Biologicals
Brands:
Snack Rite

20253 Cardinal Packaging
PO Box 959
Evansville, IN 47706-0959
812-424-2904
Fax: 330-562-4875 800-343-1295
www.berryplastics.com
Plastic round and rectangular containers
President: Ira Booth
CFO: Mike Cutnam
VP: Bill Regan
Quality Control: Warren Blazy
VP Sales: Bill Regan
Regional Manager: Norma Seevers
Plant Manager: Kurt Hamlin
Number Employees: 100-249
Square Footage: 760000
Parent Co: Cardinal Packaging

20254 Cardinal Packaging Prod LLC
300 Exchange Dr # A
Suite A
Crystal Lake, IL 60014-6290
815-444-6000
Fax: 815-444-6379 866-216-4942
info@cardinalpack.com www.cardinalpack.com
Manufacturer and exporter of set-up paper boxes, specialty folding cartons, incorporating domicut platforms, etc. Also hot leaf (foil) stamping
President: Bob Colletti
b.colletti@cardinalpkgproducts.com
Sales: Steve Overlee
Estimated Sales: Less Than $500,000
Number Employees: 1-4

20255 Cardinal Professional Products
57 Matmor Rd
Woodland, CA 95776-6008
530-666-1020
Fax: 530-666-3170 800-548-2223
info@cardinalproproducts.com
www.cardinalproproducts.com
Insecticides
President: John Sansone
Vice President: Ed Hosoda
ehosoda@cardinalproproducts.com
Estimated Sales: $.5 - 1 million
Number Employees: 10-19
Parent Co: Cal-Ag Industrial Supply

20256 Cardinal Rubber & Seal Inc
1545 Brownlee Ave SE
Roanoke, VA 24014-2609
540-982-0091
Fax: 540-982-6750 800-542-5737
sales@cardinalrubber.com
www.cardinalrubber.com
Manufacturer and exporter of rubber seals, gaskets, O-rings, hoses, etc.
CEO: Loren Bruffey, Sr.
Vice President: Pat Lawhorn
Inside Sales: Pat Worley
Purchasing: Connie Dowdy
Estimated Sales: $10-20 Million
Number Employees: 20-49

20257 Cardinal Scale Mfg Co
203 E Daugherty St
P.O. Box 151
Webb City, MO 64870-1929
417-673-4631
Fax: 417-673-5001 800-441-4237
cardinal@cardet.com www.cardinalscale.com
Manufacturer and exporter of scales
Owner: Brock Dawson
bdawson@detecto.com
CEO: W Perry
CFO: Charles Nasters
Vice President: Herbert Harwood
Estimated Sales: $50 - 100 Million
Number Employees: 500-999
Square Footage: 400000

20258 (HQ)Care Controls, Inc.
PO Box 12014
Mill Creek, WA 98082
425-745-1252
Fax: 425-745-8934 800-593-6050
info@carecontrols.com www.carecontrols.com
Manufacturer and exporter of on-line inspection systems including check weighers, vacuum and pressure detectors, etc
President: Ray Pynsky
Marketing: Rob Laroche
Contact: Brenda Ballard
brenda@carecontrols.com
Brands:
Canalyzer
Ivis
Quantum

20259 (HQ)Cargill Inc.
15407 McGinty Rd W
Wayzata, MN 55391
800-227-4455
www.cargill.com
Stores, trades, processes and distributes grains, oilseeds, vegetable oils and meals; raises livestock and produces animal feed; produces food ingredients such as starches, glucose syrups, oils and fats.
President/CEO: Brian Sikes
Chief Compliance Officer/General Counsel: Anna Richo
Chief Human Resources Officer: Stephanie Lundquist
Year Founded: 1865
Estimated Sales: $165 Billion
Number Employees: 166,000
Type of Packaging: Bulk

20260 Cargill Kitchen Solutions Inc.
15407 McGinty Rd. W.
Wayzata, MN 55391
833-535-5205
CustomerService_Protein@Cargill.com
www.sunnyfresh.com
Eggs and breakfast products for foodservice operatos, convenience stores, chain restaurants, healthcare foodservice facilities, and schools.
Parent Co: Cargill Inc.
Type of Packaging: Bulk
Brands:
Sunny Fresh

20261 Carhartt
P.O. Box 600
Dearborn, MI 48121-0600
313-271-8460
Fax: 313-271-3455 800-358-3825
www.carhartt.com
CFO: Linda Hubbard
CEO: Mark Valade
Number Employees: 1,000-4,999

20262 Carhoff Company
13404 Saint Clair Ave
Cleveland, OH 44110
216-541-4835
Fax: 216-541-4022
Manufacturer and exporter of silicone and chemically treated cleansing tissues
V.P.: Jim Lauer
Estimated Sales: $5-10 Million
Number Employees: 10-19

20263 Carico Systems
4211 Clubview Dr
Fort Wayne, IN 46804
260-432-6738
Fax: 260-432-2461 800-466-6738
Material handling, wire carts, containers
President: Jon Marler
Estimated Sales: $500,000 - $1 000,000
Number Employees: 1-4

20264 Caristrap International
1760 Fortin Boulevard
Laval, QC H7S 1N8
Canada
450-667-4700
Fax: 450-663-1520 800-361-9466
info@caristrap.com www.caristrap.com
Manufacturer and exporter of polyester cord strapping
President: Audrey Karass
Operations: Gerry Elis
Plant Manager: Norm Stevenson
Number Employees: 150
Brands:
Strapping

20265 Carl Strutz & Company
440 Mars-Valencia Road
PO Box 509
Mars, PA 16046
724-625-1501
Fax: 724-625-3570 info@strutz.com
www.strutz.com
Direct screen printing equipment for glass and plastic containers
Director: Frank Strutz Jr
Director: James Strutz
President: Carl Strutz Jr
Contact: Larry Collingwood
lcollingwood@lovemystrutz.com
General Manager: Edward Zwigert
Estimated Sales: $5 - 10 Million
Number Employees: 10-19
Square Footage: 52000

20266 Carleton Helical Technologies
30 S Sand Rd
Doylestown, PA 18901-5123
215-230-8900
Fax: 215-230-8033 sales@feedscrew.com
www.carletonhelical.com
Container handling products and systems including timing screws, invertors, inline air rinsers, carton twisters, etc
President: Nick Carleton
ncarleton@feedscrew.com
Operations Manager: Connie McDermott
Production Manager: Mike Anrein
Production: Mark McDermott
Purchasing Manager: Edward Amrein
Estimated Sales: $2 - 3 Million
Number Employees: 10-19
Number of Brands: 5
Number of Products: 1
Square Footage: 52000

20267 Carleton Helical Technologies
30 S Sand Rd
Doylestown, PA 18901-5123
215-230-8900
Fax: 215-230-8033 sales@feedscrew.com
www.carletonhelical.com
Packaging and container handling
President: Nick Carleton
ncarleton@feedscrew.com
Engineering Dept./ Manager: Connie McDermott
Estimated Sales: Below $5 Million
Number Employees: 10-19

20268 Carleton Technologies Inc
10 Cobham Dr
Orchard Park, NY 14127-4195
716-662-0006
Fax: 716-662-0747 www.cobham.com
Manufacturer and exporter of testing equipment for
flexible package seal integrity and strength
President/CEO: Paddy Cawdery
Cmo: Stuart Buckley
stuart.buckley@cobham.com
Estimated Sales: $20-50 Million
Number Employees: 100-249
Square Footage: 93000
Parent Co: FR Group PLC
Brands:
Test-A-Pack

20269 Carlin Manufacturing
466 West Fallbrook Avenue
Suite 106
Fresno, CA 93711
559-276-0123
Fax: 559-222-1538 888-212-0801
info@carlinmfg.com www.carlinmfg.com
Manufacturer and exporter of custom mobile kitch-
ens, military field kitchens and specialty vehicles.
Owner: Kevin Carlin
Sales/FMP/CEO: Bob Farrar
Contact: Robin Goldbeck
goldbeck@carlinmfg.com
Estimated Sales: $5-10 Million
Number Employees: 10-19
Number of Brands: 1
Square Footage: 74000

20270 Carlisle Food Svc Products Inc
4711 E Hefner Rd
Oklahoma City, OK 73131
405-475-5600
Fax: 800-872-4701 800-654-8210
customerservice@carlislefsp.com
www.carlislefsp.com
Dishware, tabletop accessories, coffee and tea sup-
plies, buffet service, food bars and accessories, food
service trays, bar supplies, catering equipment,
kitchen accessories, storage and handling and
cleaning tools.
President: Trent Freiberg
trentfreiberg@carlislefsp.com
Chief Financial Officer: Carolyn Ford
Vice President: Todd Manor
Vice President of Sales: Jim Calamito
Year Founded: 1946
Estimated Sales: $238.8 Million
Number Employees: 250-499
Number of Brands: 100
Number of Products: 1600
Square Footage: 150000
Type of Packaging: Food Service
Other Locations:
Central Distribution Center
Oklahoma City OK
Western Distribution Center
Reno NV
Eastern Distribution Center
Charlotte NC
Brands:
Aria
Bistro
Bravo
Catarcooler
Celebration
Che Series
Classic
Clutter Busters
Coldmaster
Crescendo
Crystalite
Delivers
Designer Displpayer
Elan
Elegant
Elegant Impressions
Excelibur
Expressions
Fall'n Go
Festival Traus
Flex - All
Galaxy
Glasted
Griptite
Hi - Lo
Ice Sculptures
Lexington
Meteor

Miracryl
Mosar Design Displayware
Munchie
Napkin Deli
Omni
Orchid
Perma - Sam
Perma - Sil
Petal Mist
Poly - Tuf
Poura - Clam
Queen Anne
Sani - Pail
Save - All
Signature Select
Six Star
Sleep'n Bag
Sparta
Spectrum
Ssal 2000
Stackable
Star Plus
Steclite
Sted Stock Ii
Steeluminum
Store'n Pour
Suds - Pail
Supreme
Symphony
Textile Design Collection
The Gotham Collection
The Lions Head Collection
The Mediterranean Collection
The New World Collection
The Oceana Collection
The Resort Collection
Thermoinsulator
Top Notch
Trimlina
Thermoinsulator
Top Notch
Trimlina
Tulip Deli
Universal
Weavewear

20271 Carlisle Plastics
1401 W 94th St
Minneapolis, MN 55431
952-884-1309
Fax: 952-884-6438
Polyethylene bags, film and sheeting; also, garbage
bags
Number Employees: 250-499
Parent Co: Tyco International
Brands:
Color Scents
Film-Gard
Ruffies
Sure Sak

20272 Carlisle Sanitary Mntnc Prods
4711 E Hefner Rd
PO Box 53006
Oklahoma City, OK 73131-6114
405-475-5600
Fax: 405-475-5607 800-654-8210
www.carlislefsp.com
Manufacturer and exporter of custom-designed
brushes including floor scrub, clean-up, fryers, ny-
lon paddle scraper, grill, grease, glass and washing
CEO: Ruth Marciniec
ruthmarciniec@carlislefsp.com
Director Sales/Marketing: Christopher Meaney
General Manager: Robert Daley, Jr.
Estimated Sales: $200,000
Number Employees: 6
Square Footage: 16652
Type of Packaging: Food Service, Bulk
Brands:
Broiler Master
Galaxy
Hercules
Hi-Lo
Long Reach
Meteor
Venus

20273 Carlo Gavazzi Inc
750 Hastings Dr
Buffalo Grove, IL 60089-6904
847-465-6100
Fax: 847-465-7373 sales@carlogavazzi.com
www.gavazzionline.com
Importer of solid-state relays, electronic plug-in control modules and sensors, digital electronic counters
and meters
President: Fred Shirzadi
fshirzadi@carlogavazzi.com
Estimated Sales: $10 - 20 Million
Number Employees: 20-49

20274 Carlson Engineering Inc
505 NE 37th St
Fort Worth, TX 76106-3713
817-877-3815
Fax: 817-335-4712
office@carlsonengineeringinc.com
www.carlsonengineeringinc.com
Software development and systems integration
President: John Carlson
Estimated Sales: Below $5 000,000
Number Employees: 20-49

20275 Carlson Products
4601 N Tyler Rd
P.O. Box 429
Maize, KS 67101-8734
316-722-0265
Fax: 316-721-0158 800-234-1069
sales@carlsonproducts.com
www.carlsonproducts.com
Manufacturer and exporter of lightweight dou-
ble-acting aluminum impact and sliding aluminum
cooler and freezer doors; also pizza pans
President: Austin Peterson
austin@carlsonproducts.com
Sales Manager: Rich Dreiling
Estimated Sales: $5-10 Million
Number Employees: 50-99
Square Footage: 100000
Parent Co: Jay Ca

20276 Carlton Industries
PO Box 280
La Grange, TX 78945-0280
979-242-5055
Fax: 979-242-5058 800-231-5988
sales@carltonusa.com www.carltonusa.com
Product identification labels, decals, tags, tapes,
signs, placards, etc
President: Kay Carlton
Vice President: Richard Carlton
Marketing Director: Colette Merchant
Estimated Sales: Less Than $500,000
Number Employees: 1-4
Square Footage: 80000

20277 Carlyle Compressor
Carrier Parkway, TR-4
PO Box 4808
Syracuse, NY 13221
315-432-6000
Fax: 315-432-3274 800-462-2759
www.carlylecompressor.com
President: Richard Laubstein

20278 Carman And Company
12 Wilmington Rd
Burlington, MA 1803
781-221-3500
Fax: 781-221-3508
Counter display cabinets
Owner: Dan Carman
Contact: Seth Farmer
sfarmer@carmansite.com
Estimated Sales: $500,000-$1 Million
Number Employees: 5-9

20279 Carman Industries Inc
1005 W Riverside Dr
Jeffersonville, IN 47130-3143
812-288-4710
Fax: 812-288-4707 800-456-7560
info@carmanindustries.com
www.carmanindustries.com
Vibratory material handling and fluid-bed drying
equipment including conveyors, feeders, bin dischargers and spiral elevators
President: Jim Hyslop
VP: Carl Porter
VP: Carl Porter

Estimated Sales: $2.5-5 Million
Number Employees: 50-99
Square Footage: 80000

20280 Carman Industries Inc
1005 W Riverside Dr
Jeffersonville, IN 47130-3143
812-288-4710
Fax: 812-288-4707 800-456-7560
info@carmanindustries.com
www.carmanindustries.com
Bulk material handling and processing equipment including vibrating feeders, vibrating conveyors, vibrating spiral elevators, vibrating bin dischargers and fluid bed dryers, heaters and coolers
President: Jim Hyslop
CFO: Jack Ising
Quality Control: Bill Whearthon
Estimated Sales: $2.5 - 5 000,000
Number Employees: 50-99

20281 Carmel Engineering
PO Box 67
Kirklin, IN 46050
317-896-9367
Fax: 765-896-5713 888-427-0497
sales@carmeleng.com
www.carmelengineering.com
Supplier of food processing equipment that include heat exchangers, product tubes, heat exchanger parts, resting tubes, dump tanks and accumulator tanks and convection systems
Owner: Randy Weaver
VP: Randy Weaver
Contact: Allan Roden
aroden@carmeleng.com
Estimated Sales: $1.5 Million
Number Employees: 10-19

20282 Carmel Engineering
PO Box 67
Kirklin, IN 46050
317-896-9367
Fax: 765-896-5713 888-427-0497
sales@carmeleng.com
www.carmelengineering.com
Supplier of food processing equipment that include heat exchangers, product tubes, heat exchanger parts, resting tubes, dump tanks and accumulator tanks and convection systems
Owner: Randy Weaver
VP: Randy Weaver
Contact: Allan Roden
aroden@carmeleng.com
Estimated Sales: $1.5 Million
Number Employees: 10-19

20283 (HQ)Carmi Flavor & Fragrance Company
6030 Scott Way
Commerce, CA 90040-3516
323-888-9240
Fax: 323-888-9339 800-421-9647
sales@carmiflavors.com www.carmiflavors.com
High quality natural and artificial flavors in liquid or powder form; supplier of packaging products.
President: Eliot Carmi
CEO: Eliot Carmi
Chief Operating Officer: Dan Carmi
Estimated Sales: $12 Million
Number Employees: 40
Number of Brands: 1
Number of Products: 500
Square Footage: 60000
Type of Packaging: Private Label, Bulk
Other Locations:
Carmi Flavor & Fragrance
Port Coquitlam, Canada
Midwest Office & Manufacturing
Waverly IA
Southern Office & Warehouse
Lawrenceville GA
Brands:
Carmi Flavors
Flavor Depot

20284 Carmona Designs
737 3rd Ave
Chula Vista, CA 91910-5827
619-425-2800
Fax: 619-425-0225 carmonadgs@aol.com
Design consultant specializing in restaurants
President: Armando Carmona
General Manager: Armando Carmona

Estimated Sales: $1 - 2.5 Million
Number Employees: 10-19

20285 Carmun International
702 San Fernando Street
San Antonio, TX 78207-5041
210-224-1781
Fax: 210-227-5332 800-531-7907
Stainless steel fittings, aluminum cold plates, CO2 regulators and bar guns
Contact: Luther Cowden
luther.cowden@cornelius.com
General Manager: Luther Cowden
Estimated Sales: $20-50 Million
Number Employees: 250-499
Parent Co: IMI Cornelius

20286 Carnegie Manufacturing Company
20 Montesano Road
Fairfield, NJ 07004-3310
973-575-3449
Fax: 973-575-2575
Aluminum molds
President: Barbara Carnegie
Estimated Sales: $1-2.5 Million
Number Employees: 5-9

20287 Carnegie Textile Co
31100 Solon Rd # A
Cleveland, OH 44139-3463
440-542-1180
Fax: 440-542-1188 800-633-4136
kerry@carnegietextile.com
www.carnegietextile.com
Terry cloth wipes, bar mops, tablecloths, napkins and uniforms
Owner: Carren Kay
General Manager: Carren Kay
Estimated Sales: $10-20 Million
Number Employees: 10-19
Square Footage: 68000
Parent Co: Surgical Manufacturing Company
Type of Packaging: Bulk

20288 Carnes Company
PO Box 930040
Verona, WI 53593
608-845-6411
Fax: 608-845-6470 carnes@carnes.com
www.carnes.com
Carnes Company is a manufacturer of commercial HVAC equipment. Its product line offering includes registers, grilles, diffusers. terminal units, ventilation equipment, louvers, penthouses, fire and smoke dampers, steam humidifiers andenergy recovering ventilators. Carnes has been a supplier of HVAC equipment since 1939.
VP, Sales & Marketing: David Stankevich
dstankevich@carnes.com
Estimated Sales: $50-100 Million
Number Employees: 11-50
Square Footage: 93000

20289 Carolina Container
909 Prospect St
High Point, NC 27260-8273
336-883-7146
Fax: 336-883-7576 800-627-0825
www.carolinacontainer.com
Corrugated containers
President: Ronald Sessions
rsessions@carolinacontainer.com
CEO: Ron Sessions
General Sales Manager: David Mitchell
Estimated Sales: $20 - 50 Million
Number Employees: 100-249

20290 Carolina Cracker
P.O. Box 374
Garner, NC 27529-0374
919-779-6899
Fax: 919-779-6899 www.carolinacracker.net
Nut crackers for soft shell nuts, shelled pecans in bulk
President: Dot Woodruff
CEO: Harold Woodruff
Estimated Sales: $1-2.5 Million
Number Employees: 10-19
Number of Brands: 3
Square Footage: 4
Type of Packaging: Bulk
Brands:
The Carolina Cracker

20291 Carolina Glove Co
116 S Mclin Creek Rd
PO Box 999
Conover, NC 28613-9024
828-464-1132
Fax: 828-464-1710 800-335-1918
sales@carolinaglovecompany.com
www.carolinaglove.com
Gloves including plastic, rubber, leather, cotton and knit
President: Robert Abernethy
rabernethy@carolinaglovecompany.com
National Sales Director: Marshall Fisher
Manager: Fred Abernethy
Estimated Sales: $5 - 10 Million
Number Employees: 20-49
Brands:
Eagle
Golden Hawk
Master Rigger
Patriot
Tiger Tuff
Tuff-Dot
Warm Grip

20292 Carolina Knife
224 Mulvaney St
Asheville, NC 28803-1499
828-253-6796
Fax: 828-258-0693 800-520-5030
info@cknife.com
Manufacturer and exporter of machine knives
President: Walter Ashbrook
wally@cknife.com
Sales Manager: Paul Turner
Technical Rep.: Bart Loudermilk
Estimated Sales: $2.5-5 Million
Number Employees: 20-49
Square Footage: 12000
Parent Co: Hamilton Industrial Knife & Machine

20293 Carolina Mop
819 Whitehall Road
Anderson, SC 29625-2119
864-225-8351
Fax: 864-225-1917 800-845-9725
www.carolinamop.com
Manufacturer, importer and exporter of dust mops, wet mops, brooms and broom handles
President: Pam Ritter
Estimated Sales: $5 - 10 Million
Number Employees: 20-49
Square Footage: 100000
Brands:
Camoco
Cotton Queen

20294 Carolina Summit Mountain Spring Water
6557 Garden Road
Unit 9
Riviera Beach, FL 33404-6307
561-841-8841
Fax: 828-743-5483 water123@bellsouth.net
bottledwater123.com
Bottled water
President: Tom Mitchell
Estimated Sales: $1-2.5 Million
Number Employees: 10-19
Parent Co: Mountain Valley Spring Company

20295 Carometec Inc
8548 Kapp Dr
Peosta, IA 52068-9759
563-582-4230
Fax: 563-582-4130 js@carometec.com
www.carometec.com
Food equipment for carcass grading and quality control
President: Henrrick Anderson
Sales: Jeb Supple
Manager: Jeb Supple
js@carometec.com
Estimated Sales: Under $500,000
Number Employees: 1-4
Parent Co: Carometec

20296 Caron Products & Svc Inc
27640 State Route 7
P.O. Box 715
Marietta, OH 45750-5146
740-373-6809
Fax: 740-374-3760 800-648-3042
sales@caronproducts.com
www.caronproducts.com
Test chambers, temperature/humidity,photostability
chambers,and reach in CO_
Manager: Terry St Peter
CEO: Steve Keiser
Vice President: Joyce Abicht
j.abicht@caronproducts.com
R&D: David Figel
Estimated Sales: Below $5 Million
Number Employees: 10-19
Square Footage: 20000

20297 Carotek Inc
700 Sam Newell Rd
Matthews, NC 28105-4515
704-847-4406
Fax: 704-847-5101 terri.smedley@carotek.com
www.carotek.com
Positive displacement pumps including internal and
external rotary gear, magnetic drive and rotary lobe.
air-operated double diaphragm pumps and abrasives,
solids, corrosives and aggressive materials
President: Rebecca Adler
rebecca.adler@carotek.com
Sales Engineer: Mike Mercredy
Sales and Marketing Assistance: Terri Smedley
Quality Control: Mack A Stewart
Manager: Stephen Bell
Estimated Sales: $20 - 50 Million
Number Employees: 1-4

20298 Carpenter Advanced Ceramics
13395 New Airport Rd
Auburn, CA 95602
530-823-3401
Fax: 530-888-1087 800-288-8730
cacsales@cartech.com www.cartech.com
President: James West
Quality Control: Marc Fichou
Financial Controller: Sonia Souron
Contact: Janet Brown
jbrown@cartech.com
Estimated Sales: $20 - 30 Million
Number Employees: 100-249

20299 Carpenter Emergency Lighting
2 Marlen Drive
Hamilton, NJ 08691
609-689-3090
Fax: 609-689-3091 888-884-2270
sales@carpenterlighting.com
www.carpenterlighting.com
Manufacturer and exporter of emergency lighting
equipment, emergency exit, portable and rechargeable lights
President: Avinash Diwan
National Sales Manager: Philip Salvatore
Contact: Evi Nash
info@carpenterlighting.com

20300 Carpenter-Hayes Paper Box Company
8 Walnut Avenue
East Hampton, CT 06424-1222
203-267-4436
Fax: 203-425-1769
Folding paper cartons
President: Bill Salinsky
CFO: Bill Salinsky
R&D: Bill Salinsky
Quality Control: Bill Salinsky
Estimated Sales: $5 - 10 Million
Number Employees: 15

20301 Carpet City Paper Box Company
36 Finlay Street
Amsterdam, NY 12010
518-842-5430
Paper set-up boxes for ravioli and nonperishable
food products
Owner: John Bogdan
Estimated Sales: Less than $500,000
Number Employees: 4
Square Footage: 8400

20302 Carpigiani Corporation of America
3760 Industrial Drive
Winston Salem, NC 27105
336-661-9893
Fax: 336-661-9895 800-648-4389
info@carpigiani-usa.com
www.carpigiani-usa.com
Manufacturer, importer and exporter of self serve
frozen dessert and drink machines, whip cream dis-
pensers and batch ice cream freezers
VP: Randy Karns
General Manager: Jim Hall
Sales Manager: Jim Marmion
Operations Manager: Bill Van Hine
National Sales Manager: Jerry Hoefer
Estimated Sales: $5-10 Million
Number Employees: 10-19
Square Footage: 80000
Parent Co: Carpigiani Viaemilia
Type of Packaging: Food Service
Other Locations:
Coldelite Corp. of America
Bologna
Brands:
Coldelite
Colore
Kwik Whipper

20303 Carrageenan Company
200 E 61st St Apt 27a
New York, NY 10065-8580
Fax: 714-850-9865
Processor, importer and exporter of gum and
hydrocolloide blends; also, custom blending of
carrageenan products for dairy, meat and poultry
President: Vincent Zaragoza
Executive Director: Javier Zaragoza
Marketing Director: Yolanda Zaragoza
Sales Director: Carla Gonzales
Public Relations: Cristina Gonzales
Managing Director: Vincente Zaragoza
Estimated Sales: Below $5 Million
Number Employees: 5-9
Type of Packaging: Private Label
Brands:
Carrabind
Carrafat
Carralite
Carralizer
Carraloc
Carravis

20304 Carrier Corp
1 Carrier Pl
Farmington, CT 06032-2562
800-227-7437
www.carrier.com
Manufacturer and exporter of refrigerating units for
delivery trucks, marine containers and commercial
refrigeration equipment.
President & CEO: Dave Gitlin
Executive VP & CFO: Tim McLevish
VP & Chief Legal Officer: Kevin O'Connor
VP, Communications & Marketing: Mary Milmoe
VP, Operations: Rishi Grover
Year Founded: 1902
Estimated Sales: $12.5 Billion
Number Employees: 55,000
Brands:
Automated Logic
Autronica
Carrier
Chubb
Delta Security Solutions
Det-tronics
Edwards
Fireye
GST
Interlogix
Kidde
Lenel-S2
Marioff
Noresco
Onity
Sensitech
Sicli
Supra
UTEC

20305 Carrier Rental Systems
9655 Industrial Dr
Bridgeview, IL 60455-2323
847-847-2220
Fax: 847-847-7330 800-586-8336
www.nutemp.com
Refrigeration, chiller sales, rentals and investment
recovery
Manager: Laurie Werner
Marketing Manager: David Brockemeyer
Contact: Thomas Benedict
thomas.benedict@carrier.com
Estimated Sales: $5 - 10 Million
Number Employees: 50-99

20306 Carrier Transicold
1 Carrier Pl
Farmington, CT 06032-2562
www.carrier.com
Manufactures refridgerated units for trucks and trail-
ers.
President: David Appel
Chief Financial Officer: Martha Ingram
Parent Co: Carrier Corporation

20307 (HQ)Carrier Vibrating EquipInc
3400 Fern Valley Rd
Louisville, KY 40213-3554
502-969-3171
Fax: 502-969-3172 cve@carriervibrating.com
www.carriervibrating.com
Manufacturer and exporter of custom designed
screening conveyor systems and feeders, bin dis-
chargers, stainless steel dairy dryers, coolers and
bulk handling vibrating equipment
CEO: Brian M Trudel
CEO: Brian M Trudel
Sales Manager: Steve Baker
Estimated Sales: $30 Million
Number Employees: 100-249
Square Footage: 185000
Other Locations:
Carrier Europe
Nivelles, Belgium

20308 Carroll Chair Company
411 Mason Street
Onalaska, WI 54650
608-779-7505
Fax: 608-779-7508 800-331-4704
info@carrollchair.com www.carrollchair.com
Bar, restaurant and lounge seating
Member of the Board: Anthony Wilson
Contact: Bill Dykema
bill.dykema@carrollchair.com
General Manager: Keith Martin
Estimated Sales: $10 - 20 Million
Number Employees: 100-249
Parent Co: Hospitality International
Brands:
Carroll Chair

20309 Carroll Co
2900 W Kingsley Rd
Garland, TX 75041-2378
972-278-1304
Fax: 972-840-0678 800-527-5722
info@carrollco.com www.carrollconverting.com
Manufacturer and exporter of soap, cleaners, disin-
fectants and germicides
President: Kyle Ogden
CEO: Frank Antonacci
fantonacci@carrollco.com
VP Technical: Ron Cramer
VP Sales: Craig Neely
Estimated Sales: $20-50 Million
Number Employees: 500-999
Square Footage: 220000

20310 Carroll Co
2900 W Kingsley Rd
Garland, TX 75041-2378
972-278-1304
Fax: 972-840-0678 800-527-5722
www.carrollconverting.com
Plastic bags and rollstock; also, printing services
available
President: Gene Stys
CEO: Frank Antonacci
fantonacci@carrollco.com
Sales Manager: Gary Denenak
Estimated Sales: $2.5-5 Million
Number Employees: 500-999

20311 Carroll Manufacturing International
23 Vreeland Rd
Florham Park, NJ 07932-1510
973-966-6000
Fax: 973-966-0315 800-444-9696
info@carrollmi.com www.carrollmi.com
Manufacturer and exporter of exhaust systems, fire protection equipment, heat reclaim units and utility distribution systems
Chairman of the Board: Barry J Carroll
VP Sales: Richard Moon
Contact: Bill Burrus
 info@carrollmi.com
General Manager: Byron Read
Estimated Sales: $10 - 15 Million
Number Employees: 10-19
Square Footage: 150000
Parent Co: Carroll International Corporation
Brands:
 Aquafire
 Carroll
 Environair
 Hmr Merchandiser
 Transporter
 Udisco

20312 Carroll Packaging
PO Box 780
Dearborn, MI 48121-0780
313-584-0400
Fax: 313-584-2022
Plastic packaging equipment
President: Hazen Carroll
Estimated Sales: $10 - 20 Million
Number Employees: 50-99

20313 Carron Net Co Inc
1623 17th St
PO Box 177
Two Rivers, WI 54241-2995
920-793-2217
Fax: 920-793-2122 800-558-7768
sales@carronnet.com www.carronnet.com
Manufacturer and exporter of hardware and netting for racks and conveyors
President/CEO: Bill Kiel Jr
 bkieljr@carronnet.com
EVP/ CFO: Troy Christiansen
VP: Donald Schweiger
Estimated Sales: $5-10 Million
Number Employees: 20-49
Type of Packaging: Bulk

20314 Carry-All Canvas Bag Co.
1983 Coney Island Ave
Brooklyn, NY 11223-2328
718-375-4230
Fax: 718-375-4230 888-425-5224
sales@carryallbag.com www.carryallbag.com
Advertising specialties, bags and aprons; importer of tote bags; logo imprinting services available
Owner: Mitchel Kraut
Estimated Sales: $400,000

20315 Carson Industries
801 Corporate Center Dr
Pomona, CA 91768
909-592-6272
Fax: 909-592-7971 800-735-5566
info@carsonind.com www.carsonind.com
Plastic bulk containers and pallets
President: Richard Gardner
CEO: Richard Gordinier
Sales Coordinator: Roscoe Bes
Estimated Sales: $20-50 Million
Number Employees: 20-49
Brands:
 Titan I
 Titan Ii

20316 Carson Manufacturing Company
PO Box 750338
Petaluma, CA 94975-0338
707-778-3141
Fax: 707-778-8691 800-423-2380
sales@carsonmanufacturing.com
www.carsonmfg.com
Manufacturer and exporter of vinyl aprons
President: Curtis Lang
Number Employees: 10-19
Type of Packaging: Private Label, Bulk

20317 Cart Mart
PO Box 686
Itasca, IL 60143-0686
630-628-6655
Fax: 630-628-6855 800-628-3183
Material handling products including pallet rack, carts and used equipment
Estimated Sales: $1-2.5 000,000
Number Employees: 1-4

20318 Carter & Burgess Food and Beverage Division
777 Main Street
Fort Worth, TX 76102-5304
817-735-600
Fax: 817-735-6148
Carter & Burgess' Food & Beverage professionals specialize in the design, construction, and management of facilities for meat, poultry, RTE prepared foods, beverage, dairy, produce, bakery and seafood.
Senior Consultant Food Processing: Jim Short
Contact: Deepak Agarwal
 deepak.agarwal@c-b.com

20319 Carter Products
2871 Northridge Dr NW
Grand Rapids, MI 49544-9109
616-647-3380
Fax: 616-647-3387 888-622-7837
sales@carterproducts.com
www.carterproducts.com
Manufacturer and exporter of guide line and inspection lights; also, bandsaw guides, wheels and tires
President: Peter Perez
 perez@carterproducts.com
VP: Terry Camp
Marketing Director: Kip Walworth
Operations Manager: Jeff Folkert
Purchasing Manager: Char Mooney
Estimated Sales: $3 - 5 Million
Number Employees: 20-49
Square Footage: 30000
Brands:
 Carter
 Flip-Pod
 Guidall
 Inspecto-Light
 Laser
 Laser Diode
 Micro-Precision

20320 Carter-Day International Inc
500 73rd Ave NE # 100
Minneapolis, MN 55432-3271
763-571-1000
Fax: 763-571-3012 bulldog@carterday.com
www.carterday.com
Manufacturer and exporter of grain cleaning and sizing equipment
President: Paul Ernst
HR Executive: Tim Ryan
 bulldog@carterday.com
Director International Agribusiness: Matthew Ernst
Estimated Sales: $10 - 20 Million
Number Employees: 100-249

20321 Carter-Hoffmann LLC
1551 Mccormick Blvd
Mundelein, IL 60060-4491
847-362-5500
Fax: 847-367-8981 800-323-9793
sales@carter-hoffmann.com
www.carter-hoffmann.com
Manufacturer and exporter of stainless steel food carts including refrigerator, banquet and heated holding/transport
President: Bob Fortmann
 jfagan@carter-hoffman.com
CFO: Jim Fagan
CEO: Robert Fortman
Research & Development: Jim Minard
Marketing Director: Kim Aaron
Sales Director: Mark Anderson
IT Executive: Jim Fagan
Production Manager: John Bartoski
Purchasing Manager: Vince Unger
Estimated Sales: $20-25 Million
Number Employees: 100-249
Number of Products: 300+
Brands:
 Carter-Hoffmann

20322 Carteret Coding Inc
1431 Raritan Rd
Clark, NJ 07066-1230
732-574-0900
Fax: 732-574-9212 ccisales@carteretcoding.com
www.carteretcoding.com
Date and lot coding systems
Owner: Charles Vill
Number Employees: 1-4

20323 Carthage Cup Company
115 Kodak Blvd
Longview, TX 75602
903-238-9833
Plastic cups, plates, bowls, deli containers and portion cups; also, hotel/motel wrapped cups with printing capability available
President: C Mark Abernathy
VP Consumer Sales: William Tostlebe
VP Institutional Sales: Brent Abernathy
Number Employees: 1 to 4
Parent Co: John Waddington
Brands:
 Carthage
 Cool Cups
 Holiday

20324 Carton Closing Company
P.O. Box 629
Butler, PA 16003-0629
724-287-7759
Fax: 724-287-2811
Industrial staples and staplers for corrugated carton closing
Marketing Manager: Mary Lawler
Sales Manager: Robert McHugh
Purchasing Manager: Paul Lucas
Estimated Sales: $1 - 5 Million
Number Employees: 100-249

20325 Carton Service Co
2 Franklin Ave
Shelby, OH 44875-1661
419-342-5010
Fax: 419-342-4804 800-533-7744
www.cartonservice.com
Boxes and cartons; contract packaging services available
Vice President: Scott Garverick
 scott.ferguson@rauantiques.com
VP: Mike Robinette
Marketing/Sales: Scott Garverick
Estimated Sales: $20-50 Million
Number Employees: 250-499

20326 Cartonplast
609 Burton Blvd
De Forest, WI 53532-1289
608-846-2516
Fax: 608-849-4496 info@cartonplast.com
www.cartonplast.com
Plastic tier sheets, plastic layer pads, layer pad pool system
Estimated Sales: less than $500,000
Number Employees: 1-4

20327 Cartpac Inc
245 E North Ave
Carol Stream, IL 60188-2021
630-510-1100
Fax: 630-629-6575 www.fraingroup.com
Rebuilt cartoner and case filling equipment; repair services available
President: Richard Frain
 rfrain@fraingroup.com
CEO: Rich Frain
CFO: Chris Hostert
Senior Engineer: Thomas Suchan
Sales Manager: Steve Norman
HR Director: Olga Sivek
General Manager: Kenneth Campbell
Manager Engineer: Len Thomsen
Estimated Sales: Below $5 Million
Number Employees: 50-99
Square Footage: 126000
Parent Co: Frain Industries

20328 Carts Food Equipment
113 8th St
Brooklyn, NY 11215-3115
718-788-5540
Fax: 718-788-4962 www.cartsfoodeqp.com

Sinks, reach-in and underbar refrigerators and marble top pizza and stainless steel work tables; exporter of mobile food vending carts
Owner: David Nadler
  dave@cartsfoodeqp.com
CFO: Florence Rosenberg
VP: Dave Nadler
Estimated Sales: $2.5-5 Million
Number Employees: 10-19
Square Footage: 120000

20329 Carts of Colorado Inc
5420 S Quebec St # 204
Suite 204
Greenwood Vlg, CO 80111-1902
  303-329-0101
  Fax: 303-329-6577 800-227-8634
  carts@cartsofcolorado.com
  www.cartsofcolorado.com
Manufacturer and exporter of mobile food carts, kiosks, and modular systems
President: Dan Gallery
  dgallery@cartsofcolorado.com
Accountant: Bill Sheakin
Research & Development: Craig Green
Quality Control Manager: Jeff Clonk
Sales Director: John Gallery
Operations Manager: Jim Covey
Purchasing Manager: Deborah Gallery
Estimated Sales: $500,000 - $1 Million
Number Employees: 10-19
Number of Brands: 4
Number of Products: 10
Square Footage: 240000
Brands:
  Carts of Colorado
  Mobile Merchandising Systems
  Peckam Carts
  Power Carts

20330 Casa Herrera
2655 Pine St
Pomona, CA 91767-2115
  909-392-3930
  Fax: 909-392-0231 800-624-3916
  rudyh@casaherrera.com www.casaherrera.com
Manufacturer and exporter of tortilla and corn chip machinery including cookers, millers, sheeters, bakers, coolers, dividers, pressers, seasoners, etc
President: Michael Herrera
  michaelh@casaherrera.com
CEO: Ron Meade
VP Sales: Christopher Herrera
Manager: Susana Herrera
Estimated Sales: $20-50 Million
Number Employees: 100-249
Square Footage: 100000

20331 Casa Herrera
2655 Pine St
Pomona, CA 91767-2115
  909-392-3930
  Fax: 909-392-0231 800-624-3916
  alfredoj@casaherrera.com www.casaherrera.com
Food processing machines for commercial and industrial food makers
President: Michael Herrera
  michaelh@casaherrera.com
Manager: Christopher Herrera
Mngr.: Susana Herrera
Estimated Sales: $20-50 Million
Number Employees: 100-249

20332 Casabar
42 Court St
Morristown, NJ 07960-5199
  973-605-8995
  Fax: 973-401-1519 877-745-8700
Instant Dip silver cleaner and polishing cloths
President: Mel Appelbaum
  m3@casabar.com
Administrative Assistant: Irene Carpio
General Manager: Mel Sales
Estimated Sales: Less than $500,000
Number Employees: 1-4
Brands:
  Instant Dip

20333 Cascade Earth Sciences
3511 Pacific Blvd SW
Albany, OR 97321-7727
  541-926-7737
  Fax: 503-967-7619 albany@cascade-earth.com
  www.cascade-earth.com
President: Perry Rahe
CAO: Dayla Rabe
  dayla@cascade-earth.com
CEO: Steel Maloney
Estimated Sales: $20,000,000 - $49,999,999
Number Employees: 5000-9999

20334 Cascade Signs & Neon
2166 Wayside Ter NE
Salem, OR 97301-0323
  503-378-0012
  Fax: 503-362-8154 info@cascade-signs.com
  www.cascade-signs.com
Electric neon signs
Owner: Jay Kinnee
  jay@cascade-signs.com
Estimated Sales: $500,000-$1 Million
Number Employees: 5-9

20335 Cascade Wood Components
15 Herman Creek Road
Cascade Locks, OR 97014
  541-374-8413
  Fax: 541-374-9054
Wooden pallets
President: Gary Hegewald
Manager: Gene Shultz
  gschultz@cascadewood.com
Sales Manager: Tim Todd
Office Manager: Gene Hill
Estimated Sales: $10-20 Million
Number Employees: 10 to 19

20336 Case Lowe & Hart Architects
2484 Washington Blvd # 510
Suite 510
Ogden, UT 84401-2346
  801-399-5821
  Fax: 801-399-0728 kevinl@clhae.com
  www.clhae.com
President: Kevin Lewis
  kevinl@clhae.com
Estimated Sales: $1 - 3 Million
Number Employees: 10-19

20337 Case Manufacturing Company
14304 29th Rd
Flushing, NY 11354-2312
  914-965-5100
  Fax: 914-965-2362 casestaty@aol.com
Tea and coffee industry coffee canisters
President: Jerome Sudnow
Estimated Sales: $1 - 5 000,000
Number Employees: 10

20338 Caselites
PO Box 161000
Hialeah, FL 33016-0017
  305-819-7766
  Fax: 305-819-8198 www.caselites.com
Lighting for steam tables, and refrigerated/nonrefrigerated cases. Also special lighting for food equipment
President: Barry Spade
R & D: Fred Morgan
Estimated Sales: $50-100 Million
Number Employees: 10
Square Footage: 10000

20339 Casella Lighting
10183 Croydon Way # C
Suite C
Sacramento, CA 95827-2103
  916-363-2888
  Fax: 888-489-9543 Info@CasellaLighting.com
  www.casellalighting.com
Manufacturer and exporter of portable floor and table lamps, wall scones, chandeliers and solid brass fixtures
Owner: Chuck Bird
  chuck@casellalighting.com
Buyer: Margig Yaka
Office Manager: Ronda Simi
Estimated Sales: $5-10 Million
Number Employees: 5-9
Square Footage: 120000
Type of Packaging: Food Service
Brands:
  Casella
  Grag Studios

20340 Cash Caddy
PO Box 13770
Palm Desert, CA 92255-3770
  760-772-8884
  Fax: 760-772-8885 888-522-2221
  cashcaddy@aol.com
Change, dinner check and tip trays
Sales Manager: Eddie Robinson
General Manager: Judy Wilkins
Number Employees: 30
Square Footage: 12000
Parent Co: Plastic By Design
Brands:
  Cash Caddy
  Dinner Check

20341 Cashco Inc
607 W 15th St
Ellsworth, KS 67439-1624
  785-472-4461
  Fax: 785-472-3539 sales@cashco.com
  www.cashco.com
Regulators, control valves and sanitary biotechnological products for the food and pharmaceutical industry
President: Philip Rogers
  philipr@cashco.com
National Sales Manager: Robert Schroeder
Estimated Sales: $10-20 Million
Number Employees: 100-249

20342 Cass Saw & Tool Sharpening
3916 N Cass Ave
Westmont, IL 60559-1103
  630-968-1617
  Fax: 630-968-7767
Saw and knife sharpeners, carbide retipping and chain and circular saws
Owner: Sam Robertson
Manager: Joseph Robertson
Estimated Sales: Less than $500,000
Number Employees: 1 to 4

20343 Cassel Box & Lumber Co Inc
1100 Falls Rd
Grafton, WI 53024-9728
  262-377-9503
  Fax: 262-377-4421 www.casselboxlumber.com
Wooden boxes, crates, skids and pallets
President: John Cassel
Vice President: Craig Cassel
  craigcassel@casselboxlumber.com
Manager: John Cassel
Estimated Sales: $500,000-$1 Million
Number Employees: 10-19

20344 Casso-Solar Corporation
506 Airport Executive Park
P.O. Box 163
Nanuet, NY 10954
  845-354-2010
  Fax: 845-547-0328 800-988-4455
  sales@cassosolartechnologies.com
  www.cassosolar.com
Manufacturer and exporter of dryers, ovens, and electric and gas conveyor systems
President: Doug Canfield
VP Finance: Harry Lyons
Quality Control Manager: Alex Mankiewicz
VP Sales/Marketing: Frank Lu
Plant Manager: Jan Michalski
Purchasing Manager: John Moles
Estimated Sales: $10 Million
Number Employees: 20-49
Number of Products: 100
Square Footage: 50000
Brands:
  Solar Infrared Heater

20345 Cast Film Technology
7455 E Adamo Drive
Tampa, FL 33619-3433
  847-487-8899
  Fax: 847-487-7288
Edible plastic films, customized films made with food ingredients for packaging and barrier uses
President: James Rossman
Vice President: Scott Schaneville
Research & Development: Caroline Decker
Estimated Sales: $8 Million
Number Employees: 50
Number of Products: 15
Square Footage: 80000

20346 Cast Nylons LTD
4300 Hamann Pkwy
Willoughby, OH 44094-5626
440-269-2300
Fax: 440-269-2323 800-543-3619
cnlmail@castnylon.com
Manufacuturer of cast nylon materials
President: Jack Thorp
jackthorp@castnylon.com
CFO: Dan Welsh
VP: Steve Tischler
Quality Control: Tom Schaffer
Marketing Head: Shelly Pike
Sales: Traci Deiner
Estimated Sales: $10-20 000,000
Number Employees: 50-99
Type of Packaging: Bulk

20347 Castell Interlocks Inc
150 N Michigan Ave # 800
Sutie 800
Chicago, IL 60601-7585
312-360-1516
Fax: 312-268-5174 ussales@castell.com
www.castell.com
Dock locks
President: Bryan Gregory
bgregory@castell.com
Number Employees: 10-19

20348 Castella Imports Inc
60 Davids Dr
Hauppauge, NY 11788
631-231-5500
Cheeses, spices, olives and olive oils.
Estimated Sales: $100+ Million
Number Employees: 51-200
Square Footage: 66000

20349 Castino Restaurant Equipment
50 Utility Ct
Rohnert Park, CA 94928-1659
800-238-0404
Fax: 707-585-7306 800-238-0404
solutions@castinosolutions.com
www.castinosolutions.com
Wholesaler/distributor of restaurant equipment,
kitchen equipment, furniture, refrigeration hood sys-
tems, chinaware, glassware, pots, pans, etc
President/CEO: David Castino
david_castino@castinosolutions.com
Purchasing Manager: Ron Nasuti
Estimated Sales: $8 Million
Number Employees: 5-9
Square Footage: 60000
Parent Co: Castino Refrigeration Company

20350 Castle Bag Co.
115 Valley Rd.
Wilmington, DE 19804
302-656-1001
Fax: 302-656-2830
sales@castlebagcompany.comcastbiz.net
www.castlebag.com
Polyethylene bags.
Owner: Harry Russell
Year Founded: 1969
Estimated Sales: $750 Million
Number Employees: 1-4
Number of Brands: 1
Square Footage: 6000
Type of Packaging: Consumer, Food Service, Pri-
vate Label, Bulk
Brands:
Castle Bag

20351 Castrol Industrial
201 N Webster St
White Cloud, MI 49349-9678
231-689-0002
Fax: 231-689-0372 800-582-3266
lubeconcc@castrol.com www.lubecon.com
Lubrication equipment, conveyor cleaners, lubri-
cants, machinery lubrication
BDM: Frank Langley
BDM: Ted Edwards
BDM: Jerry Robinson
Site Manager: Michael Bailey
michael.bailey@castrol.com
Production Manager: Kathy Crickmore
Purchasing Manager: Chris Warren
Estimated Sales: $10-20 Million
Number Employees: 10-19
Square Footage: 10000

20352 Cat Inc
201 S Erie Ave
Russellville, AR 72801-5265
479-890-3433
Fax: 479-967-2651 888-890-3433
www.gocatgo.biz
Supplier of chilling systems, whole muscle pumps,
plant monitoring and weighing systems
CEO: Mike Miller
mike.miller@catsquared.com
CEO: Michael Miller
Principal: Dion Henson
Estimated Sales: $26 Million
Number Employees: 50-99

20353 Cat Pumps
1681 94th Ln NE
Minneapolis, MN 55449-4372
763-780-5440
Fax: 763-780-2958 techsupport@catpumps.com
www.catpumps.com
Manufacturer and exporter of pumps including
high-pressure, positive displacement, piston and
plunger, stainless steel, hightemp, custom designed
power units, submersible and end-suction
centrifugal
CEO: William Bruggeman
CEO: William Bruggeman
Marketing Director: Darla Jean Thompson
Sales: Scott Stelzner
Estimated Sales: $50-100 Million
Number Employees: 100-249
Square Footage: 130000
Brands:
Cat Pumps

20354 (HQ)Catalent Pharma Solutions Inc
1100 Enterprise Dr
Winchester, KY 40391-9668
859-745-8679
Fax: 859-745-6636 www.catalent.com
Consultant offering agglomeration, instantizing, en-
capsulation and solids drying services
President: David Heyens
President, Chief Executive Officer: John Chiminski
Vice President of Audit: Charles Silvey
Senior Vice President of Quality: Sharon Johnson
Senior Vice President of Sales and Marke: Will
Downie
Manager: Steve Havel
shavel@cardinalhealth.com
VP Business Development: Michael Valazza
Estimated Sales: $19.7 Million
Number Employees: 250-499
Square Footage: 200000
Other Locations:
International Processing Corp
Ramsey NJ

20355 Catalina Cylinders
7300 Anaconda Ave
Garden Grove, CA 92841-2930
714-890-0999
Fax: 714-890-1744 sales@catalinacylinders.com
www.catalinacylinders.com
Empty aluminum high pressure CO2 cylinders alu-
minum cylinders to the compressed gas industry
President: Tom Newell
Quality Control: Ward Dekker
Sales Director: Michael Krupsky
Manager: Doug Burtt
d.burtt@catalinacylinders.com
Estimated Sales: $10-20 000,000
Number Employees: 100-249

20356 Catalyst International
1285 101st Street
Lemont, IL 60439
630-972-9800
Fax: 630-972-9876 800-236-4600
info@cdcsupply.com www.cdcsupply.com
Manufacturer and exporter of computer software for
warehouse management
President: J Scott Pearson
CEO: Mitchell Radar
CFO: Tim Ward
Office Manager: Laurie Goodwin
VP, Business Development: Thomas Geza Varga
Controller: Mike Grecco
Marketing Coordinator: Wendy Erwin
Director of Sales: Bryan Gaines
VP Operations: James H Martin
Number Employees: 70

Type of Packaging: Bulk

20357 Catalytic Products IntlInc
980 Ensell Rd
Lake Zurich, IL 60047-1557
847-438-0334
Fax: 847-438-0944 info@cpilink.com
www.cpilink.com
Air pollution control equipment, baking oven emis-
sion control, catalytic and thermal oxidizers
President: Dennis Lincoln
Vice President: Scott Christopher
scott.christopher@cpilink.com
Marketing Manager: Jan Carlson
Estimated Sales: $1 - 2.5 000,000
Number Employees: 20-49

20358 CaterMate
61 Brown Road
Ithaca, NY 14850-1247
800-486-2283
Fax: 607-257-1902 www.catermate.com
Software for catering and event management
President: John Alexander
VP: Tim Tighe
Marketing: Susie Stephnson
Sales Manager: Ron Prorus
Contact: Peter Martini
petermartini@cbord.com
Number Employees: 10-19
Parent Co: the CBORD Group, Inc.
Type of Packaging: Food Service
Brands:
Eventmaster

20359 Catering Co
24833 Commercial Ave
Orange Beach, AL 36561-3845
251-974-5000
Fax: 251-974-5640 www.catering.com
Owner: J Schenck
hazels@gulftel.com
Vice President: J Hall Schenck
Estimated Sales: Below 1 Million
Number Employees: 10-19

20360 Cates Mechanical Corp
3901 Corporation Cir
Charlotte, NC 28216-3420
704-392-8932
Fax: 704-392-8932
ernest.cates@catesmechanical.com
www.catesmechanical.com
Packaging machinery
President: John Cates
tom.cates@catesmechanical.com
Estimated Sales: Below $5 000,000
Number Employees: 5-9

20361 Catskill Craftsmen Inc
15 W End Ave
Stamford, NY 12167-1296
607-652-7321
Fax: 607-652-7293 info@catskillcraftsmen.com
www.catskillcraftsmen.com
Manufacturer and exporter of butcher block tables,
cutting boards, solid maple housewares and kitchen
furniture and work counters
President: Duncan Axtel
catskill@telenet.net
Vice President: Kenneth Smith
Quality Control: John Locastro
VP Sales: Dick Carpenter
Purchasing Manager: Hank Cioccari
Estimated Sales: $5 - 10 Million
Number Employees: 50-99
Number of Products: 17
Square Footage: 208000
Type of Packaging: Consumer, Food Service, Pri-
vate Label

20362 Cattron Group International
25 W Shenango St
Sharpsville, PA 16150-1123
724-962-1629
Fax: 724-962-4310
Cattron Group International, including the Cattron,
Remtron, Theimeg and Vectran brands, provides industrial radio remote control systems for overhead
cranes, hoists, conveyors, yard locomotives, overhead doors, boom trucks, concretepumps or anywhere the operator of equipment can be moved to a
safer, more efficient location.

President/CEO: John Paul
CFO: Mike Pearson
Marketing/Public Relations: Amanda Bailey
Sales: Jeremy Pearson
Contact: Alan Anglemyer
  aanglemyer@cattron-theimeg.com
Production: Rich Patterson
Estimated Sales: $10-20 Million
Number Employees: 100-249
Number of Brands: 6
Parent Co: Laird Technologies
Other Locations:
  Cattron Group-Remtron
  Escondido CA
Brands:
  Cattron
  Remtron
  Theimeg
  Vectran

20363 Catty Inc
6111 White Oaks Rd
Harvard, IL 60033-8307

815-943-2288
Fax: 815-943-4473 plawther@cattycorp.com
www.cattycorp.com
Manufacturer and exporter of flexible packaging including foil, foil/paper, poly structures, margarine and candy wraps and lidding
President: Vincent Jefferson
  vince.jefferson@comcast.net
CFO: Bill Schmiederer
Marketing and Sales Coordinator: Kristen Dahm
Sales Manager: Sheri Morelli
Operations Manager: Chuck DiPietro
Vice President, Engineering: Ron Klint
Number Employees: 50-99
Square Footage: 270000

20364 Cavalla Inc
111 Union St
Hackensack, NJ 07601-4083

201-343-3338
Fax: 201-487-1096 www.cavalla.com
Equipment
President: Arthur Pisani
  apisani@cavalla.net
Estimated Sales: $5 - 10 Million
Number Employees: 20-49

20365 Cavanna Packaging USA Inc
2150 Northmont Pkwy # A
Suite A
Duluth, GA 30096-5835

770-688-1501
Fax: 973-383-0741 www.cavanna.com
Wholesaler/distributor of horizontal flow wrapping machinery
President: William Stoebling
Contact: Adam Caplan
  a.caplan@cavannagroup.com
Estimated Sales: Below $5 Million
Number Employees: 10-19

20366 (HQ)Cavert Wire Co
620 Forum Pkwy
Rural Hall, NC 27045-8934

336-969-2601
Fax: 336-969-2621 800-245-4042
cspittler@cavertwire.com www.cavertwire.com
Single loop wire bale ties used in supermarkets for waste corrugated boxes
Owner: Chuck Spittler
CFO: Harry Sages
VP Sales: Ben Shifler
  cspittler@cavertwire.com
Estimated Sales: $20 - 50 Million
Number Employees: 20-49
Square Footage: 200000
Other Locations:
  Cavert Wire Co.
  Atlanta GA

20367 Cawley Co
1544 N 8th St
PO Box 2110
Manitowoc, WI 54220-1902

920-686-7000
Fax: 920-686-7080 800-822-9539
info@cawleyco.com www.thecawleyco.com
Manufacturer and exporter of engravable badges, plates, plaques and awards; also, electronic personalization systems for do-it-yourself engraving

President/CEO: Jim Peterson
CFO: Jerry Harris
HR Executive: Jean Slaby
  jeans@thecawleyco.com
R & D: Jim Peterson
Quality Control: Paul Mueller
Marketing Director: Molly Peterson
Public Relations: Molly Peterson
Operations/Productions Manager: Paul Mueller
Plant Manager: Diane Fogltanz
Estimated Sales: Below $5 Million
Number Employees: 100-249
Square Footage: 112000
Parent Co: Contemporary
Brands:
  Champ Awards
  Chrom-A-Grav
  Engravable Gifts

20368 Cayne Industrial Sales Corp
429 Bruckner Blvd
Bronx, NY 10455-5007

718-993-5800
Fax: 718-402-9465
Manufacturer and exporter of industrial racks, handling equipment and food lockers including custom plastic.
President: Steven Cayne
Manager: Hank Cayne
  hankcayne@aol.com
Estimated Sales: Less Than $500,000
Number Employees: 1-4
Square Footage: 20000
Brands:
  Uni-Steel Lockers

20369 Cci Industries-Cool Curtain
350 Fischer Ave # A
Costa Mesa, CA 92626-4508

714-662-3879
Fax: 714-662-0943 800-854-5719
www.coolcurtain.com
Freezer curtains, fly traps and broiler griddles
President: Michael Robinson
Sales Manager: Randy Wall
VP Production: Marion Mills
Estimated Sales: $5-10 Million
Number Employees: 1-4
Square Footage: 16000
Brands:
  Clear Vu

20370 Ccw Products
5861 Tennyson St
Arvada, CO 80003-6902

303-427-9663
Fax: 303-427-1608 vickie.h@ccwproducts.com
www.ccwproducts.com
Manufacturer and exporter of clear wide-mouth plastic containers used for food packaging and point-of-purchase displays
President: David Teneyck
CEO: Mort Saffer
Sales Manager: Donald Johnston
Contact: Mirza Beg
  beg@ccwproducts.com
Operations Manager: Roger Lamb
Estimated Sales: Less Than $500,000
Number Employees: 1-4
Number of Products: 300+
Square Footage: 160000
Type of Packaging: Consumer, Food Service, Private Label, Bulk

20371 Cecor
102 Lincoln St
Verona, WI 53593-1599

608-845-6771
Fax: 608-845-6792 800-356-9042
cecor@cecor.net www.chipcarts.com
Waste handling equipment including dumping containers, sump cleaners and filter units for separation of solids from liquids
President: Dennis Johnson
  djohnson@cecor.net
Production Manager: Paul Elmer
Estimated Sales: $2.5-5 Million
Number Employees: 5-9
Brands:
  Cecor

20372 Cedar Box Co
2012 Cedar Ave S
Minneapolis, MN 55404-3199

612-332-4287
Fax: 612-332-8619 sales@cedarboxco.com
www.cedarboxcompany.com
Corrugated and wooden boxes, wooden pallets skids, specialty wood bases, and specialty wood blocking
President: Michael Mintz
  mike@cedarboxco.com
Owner: Jefferey Migershone
CFO: Michael Mintz
Purchasing Agent: C Skjeveland
Estimated Sales: $5-10 Million
Number Employees: 20-49
Square Footage: 30000

20373 Ceilcote Air Pollution Control
7251 Engle Rd
Suite 300
Middleburg Hts, OH 44130

440-243-0700
Fax: 440-243-9854 800-554-8673
1us@verantis.com www.verantis.com
Manufacturer and exporter of air pollution control equipment including fans, tower packing, blowers, mist eliminators, resin systems and ionizing wet scrubbers, turn key systems, emergency vapor spill equipment
President: Larry Hein
CEO: Lars Buttkus
Sales: John Tonkewicz
Engineering Director: Nat Dickinson
Number Employees: 20-49
Square Footage: 100000
Brands:
  Duracor
  Iws
  Tellerette

20374 Celebrity Promotions
P.O. Box 200
Remsen, IA 51050

712-786-1100
Fax: 712-786-2900 800-332-6847
sewncm@midlands.net
Aprons and re-usable cloth shopping bags including washable and poly-cotton; screen printing and embroidery available
CFO: Connie Mueller
QC and R&D: Paul Mueller
VP Marketing: Mark Mueller
Estimated Sales: Below $5 Million
Number Employees: 20-49
Square Footage: 36000
Brands:
  Celebrity Stars

20375 Celite Corporation
2500 San Miguelito Rd
Lompoc, CA 93436

805-736-1221
Fax: 805-736-1222 info@worldminerals.com
www.worldminerals.com
Manufacturer and exporter of diatomite filter aids and functional fillers; also, absorbents, synthetic calcium silicate and mineral fillers
CEO: John Oskam
Contact: George Christoferson
  christofersong@worldminerals.com
Estimated Sales: $5 - 10 Million
Number Employees: 250-499

20376 Cell-O-Core Company
6935 Ridge Road
PO Box 342
Sharon Center, OH 44274-0342

330-239-4370
Fax: 330-239-4403 800-239-4370
cellocore@cellocore.com www.cellocore.com
Cocktail stirrers, straws and wooden and plastic toothpicks
President: Craig Cook
Quality Control: Damm Damwillan
R&D: Mathew Willam
CFO: Creak Cook
Director: Hugh Alpeter
Director: Jill Hoffman
Contact: Thomas Allen
  allenthomas@cellocore.com
(Distributor Service): Dede Beynon

Estimated Sales: $5 - 10 Million
Number Employees: 20-49
Square Footage: 60000
Brands:
Cell-O-Core

20377 Cellier Corporation
135 Robert Treat Paine Drive
Taunton, MA 02780-7266
508-655-5906
Fax: 508-653-2508
Paper coatings and kitchen lube oil
Acting General Manager: Stephen Noworski
Number Employees: 10

20378 Cello Bag Company
123 Willamette Lane
Bowling Green, KY 42101-9170
800-347-0338
Fax: 270-782-7478
Packaging materials including plastic bags and film
Number Employees: 25

20379 Cellofoam North America
1917 Rockdale Industrial Blvd
PO Box 406
Conyers, GA 30012
770-483-4491
Fax: 770-929-3608 800-241-3634
info@cellofoam.com www.cellofoam.com
Manufacturer and exporter of expanded polystyrene
foam insulation
President: Steve Gardner
VP Sales/Marketing: Cliff Hanson
Estimated Sales: $10-20 Million
Number Employees: 100-249
Brands:
Cello Foam
Permafloat
Permaspan
Poly Shield
Super Sheath

20380 Cellotape, Inc.
39611 Eureka Dr
Newark, CA 94560
510-651-5551
Fax: 510-651-8091 sales@cellotape.com
cellotape.com
Adhesive panels and pressure sensitive labels
President & CEO: Peter Offerman
VP, Sales: Steve Suppa
Estimated Sales: $50-100 Million
Number Employees: 100-249
Square Footage: 35000

20381 Cellox Corp
1200 Industrial St
Reedsburg, WI 53959-2154
608-524-2316
Fax: 608-524-2362 sales@cellox.com
www.cellox.com
Manufacturer and exporter of packaging supplies
and plastic molding for advertising displays
President: Craig Hutchison
Estimated Sales: $10 - 20 Million
Number Employees: 50-99

20382 (HQ)Cellucap Manufacturing Co
4626 N 15th St
Philadelphia, PA 19140-1197
215-324-1541
Fax: 215-324-1290 800-523-3814
sales@cellucap.com www.cellucap.com
Personal protective apparel with a full range of
headwear, disposable apparel, aprons and gloves
President: Jane Harris
cellucap@aol.com
Executive VP: Mark Davis
VP Sales: John Twamley
VP Sales: Nancy Lozoff
Operations Manager: David Richman
Estimated Sales: $2.5-5 Million
Number Employees: 20-49
Type of Packaging: Food Service

20383 Celplast Metallized Products Limited
67 Commander Boulevard
Unit 4
Toronto, ON M1S-3M7
Canada
416-293-4330
Fax: 416-293-9198 800-866-0059
jim@celplast.com http://cmp.celplast.com
Producer and manufacturer of metallized films for
the food industry.
President/Founder: Chuck Larsen
CEO: Dante Ferrari
Vice President: Bill Hellings
Technical Representative: Dante Ferrari
Technical Sales: Jim Lush
Account Manager: Naomi Panagrapka

20384 Celsis
400 W Erie St Ste 300
Chicago, IL 60654
312-476-1200
Fax: 312-476-1201 800-222-8260
ATP bioluminescence end product screening systems
CEO: Jay Le Coque
Contact: Lori Daane
ldaane@celsis.com
Estimated Sales: $5-10 000,000
Number Employees: 5-9

20385 Celsis Laboratory Group
600 W. Chicago Avenue
Suite 625
Chicago, IL 60654-2822
312-476-1282
Fax: 312-476-1201 800-222-8260
RDinfo@celsis.com www.celsis.com
Consultant and independent testing laboratory spe-
cializing in microbiology, analytical chemistry and
toxicology testing services
Chief Executive Officer: Jay Lecoque
Manager Marketing Development: Martin Gilman,
Ph.D.
Contact: Bhavna Solanki
bsolanki@celsis.com
Associate Director: William Gilman
Estimated Sales: $5-10 Million
Number Employees: 50-99
Square Footage: 140000
Parent Co: Celsis Laboratory Group

20386 Centennial Moldings
1830 Centennial Ave
1900 Summit Ave
Hastings, NE 68901-6712
402-462-2173
Fax: 402-461-3219 888-883-2189
www.centennialplastics.com
Manufacturer and exporter of plastic tanks and
drums
CEO: G Peter Konen
Sales Manager: Jeff Armstrong
Product Manager: Val Kopke
Plant Manager: Bob Shockey
Estimated Sales: $1 Million
Number Employees: 5-9
Number of Brands: 1
Number of Products: 3
Square Footage: 600000
Type of Packaging: Food Service, Private Label,
Bulk
Brands:
Pure-Life

20387 Centennial Transportation Industries
P.O. Box 708
Columbus, GA 31902-0708
706-323-6446
Fax: 706-327-9921
Manager: Bob Hudak
Estimated Sales: $10 - 20 Million
Number Employees: 50-99

20388 Centent Co
3879 S Main St
Santa Ana, CA 92707-5787
714-979-6491
Fax: 714-979-4241 info@centent.com
www.centent.com
Manufacturer and exporter of industrial controls for
factory automation including computer guided multiple axis positioning systems

President: August Freimanis
august.freimanis@centent.com
Estimated Sales: $2.5-5 Million
Number Employees: 10-19

20389 Center for Packaging Education
358 Route 202
Somers, NY 10589-3234
914-276-0425
Fax: 914-276-0428
Consultant and educators in packaging, provide ex-
pert testimony in legal conflicts
President: Dr. Robert Goldberg
Vice President: Mark Goldsberg
Estimated Sales: Less than $500,000
Number Employees: 1-4
Square Footage: 4000

20390 Centi Mark Corp
401 Technology Dr # 2
Canonsburg, PA 15317-7538
724-514-8700
Fax: 724-743-7770 jason.meyers@centimark.com
www.centimark.com
Cleaners, flooring, floor grating, floor and wall coat-
ing materials, paints and enamels
President: Timothy Dunlap
Contact: Robert Detweiler
robert.detweiler@centimark.com
Estimated Sales: $50,000,000 - $99,999,999
Number Employees: 20-49

20391 Central Bag Co
4901 S 4th St
Leavenworth, KS 66048-5003
913-250-0325
Fax: 913-727-1760 www.centralbagcompany.com
Bags including burlap, cotton and polypropylene
multi-wall; also, shrink wrap
President: Walter Cordova
waltercordova@centralbagcompany.com
Sales: Dog Cross
Estimated Sales: $5-10 Million
Number Employees: 50-99

20392 Central Coated ProductsInc
2025 Mccrea St
Alliance, OH 44601-2794
330-821-9830
Fax: 330-821-3114
www.centralcoatedproducts.com
Coated paper packaging materials
President: Thomas Tormey
sporter@centralcoatedproducts.com
VP: Steve Porter
Sales Exec: Steve Porter
Estimated Sales: $10 - 20 Million
Number Employees: 50-99

20393 Central Decal
6901 High Grove Blvd
Burr Ridge, IL 60527-7583
630-325-9892
Fax: 630-325-9878 800-869-7654
info@centraldecal.com www.centraldecal.com
Manufacturer and exporter of flexible nameplates,
pressure sensitive labels and decals
President: Bob Keflin
bkeflin@centraldecal.com
CFO: Jennifer Loconte
VP: Robert Kaplan
Sales Manager: George Labine
Estimated Sales: $10 - 20 Million
Number Employees: 50-99
Square Footage: 60000

20394 Central Electropolishing Company
124 N Lawrence Ave
Anthony, KS 67003
620-842-3701
Fax: 620-842-3208 877-200-5488
steve@celcoinc.com www.celcoinc.com
Electropolishing, passivation and oxygen cleaning
of stainless steel and other alloys
President: Kenneth Bellesine
CFO: Kim Bell
Quality Control: Jerry Smith
Estimated Sales: $2.5-5 000,000
Number Employees: 20-49

20395 Central Fabricators Inc
408 Poplar St
Cincinnati, OH 45214-2481
   513-621-1240
  Fax: 513-621-1243 800-909-8265
  esales@centralfabricators.com
   www.centralfabricators.com
Manufacturer and exporter of stainless and carbon
steel pressure vessels, heat exchangers, storage
tanks, condensers, cookers, evaporators and kettles;
also, other alloys available
President: Mike Lewis
 mlewis@centralfabricators.com
CEO: Dave Angner
CFO: Dan Meade
Vice President: Tim Maly
Operations Manager: Troy Black
Estimated Sales: $3 - 5 Million
Number Employees: 10-19
Square Footage: 40000

20396 Central Fine Pack Inc
7707 Vicksburg Pike
Fort Wayne, IN 46804-5549
   260-432-3027
  Fax: 260-432-9275 www.dwfinepack.com
Plastic disposable food packaging and trays
Director Sales/Marketing: David Brown
Plant Manager: Russ Stephens
Estimated Sales: $20-50 Million
Number Employees: 20-49

20397 Central Ice Machine Co
6279 S 118th St
Omaha, NE 68137-3574
   402-731-4690
  Fax: 402-731-0823 800-228-7213
  customerservice@centralice.com
   www.refrigerationsupplies.net
Compressors, control valves, hand valves, relief
valves, condensers and evaporators, gauges, refrigeration controls, refrigeration pumps, purgers,
X-pando pipe joint compound, MSA gas masks, sulphur sticks, litmus paper and neverseez
President: Don Erftmier
 customerservice@centralice.com
Number Employees: 1-4

20398 Central Missouri Sheltered Enterprises
PO Box 10147
Columbia, MO 65205-4002
   573-442-6935
  Fax: 573-499-0586 www.cmse.org
Promotional items and packaging for barbecue sauce
and rice cakes
Executive Director: Bruce Young
Executive Director: Bruce Young
Estimated Sales: $20-50 Million
Number Employees: 100-249

20399 Central Ohio Bag & Burlap
1000 E, Fifth Ave
Columbus, OH 43203
   614-294-4495
  Fax: 614-294-4362 800-798-9405
  info@centralohiobagandburlap.com
   www.centralohiobagandburlap.com
Bags and packaging materials
President: James Stout
Estimated Sales: $1 - 3,000,000
Number Employees: 5-9

20400 Central Package & Display
3901 85th Ave N
Minneapolis, MN 55443-1907
   763-425-7444
  Fax: 763-425-7917
 customerservice@centralcontainer.com
   www.centralpackage.com
Manufacturer and wholesaler/distributor of corru-
gated boxes, cushion packaging, flexible films, litho
labels and static control products
President: James E Haglund
CEO: Mike Haglund
 mhaglund@centralpackage.com
Sales: Steve Braun
VP Sales/Marketing: Steve Braun
General Manager: Jerry Condon
Estimated Sales: $10-20 Million
Number Employees: 100-249
Square Footage: 300000

20401 Central Pallet Mills Inc
5745 Paradise Rd
Central City, KY 42330
   270-754-2900
  Fax: 270-754-2902
Lift truck pallets
President: Jack Brewer
 jackbrewer28@aol.com
Estimated Sales: $20-50 Million
Number Employees: 20-49

20402 Central Paper Box
2911 Belleview Avenue
Kansas City, MO 64108-3538
   816-753-3126
  Fax: 816-753-6923
Paper boxes including candy, paper and set-up; also,
folding cartons
General Manager: Lon Wilkerson
Estimated Sales: $20-50 Million
Number Employees: 50-100
Square Footage: 125000

20403 Central Solutions Inc
401 Funston Rd
Kansas City, KS 66115-1213
   913-621-6542
  Fax: 913-621-7031 800-255-0262
  markn@centralsolutions.com
Disinfectants and cleaners; also, custom formulating
available
President: Mark Nobrega
CEO: Mike Noberga
HR Executive: Mike Nobrega
 miken@centralsolutions.com
Estimated Sales: $10-20 Million
Number Employees: 50-99

20404 Central States Indl Eqpt & Svc
2700 N Partnership Blvd
Springfield, MO 65803-8208
   417-831-1411
  Fax: 417-831-5314 800-654-5635
  sales@csidesigns.com
Fluid handling systems for food process and CIP
Owner: Bryan Billmyer
 billmyerb@csitools.com
Estimated Sales: $10-20 000,000
Number Employees: 100-249

20405 Centrifuge Solutions
2232 S Main Street
Suite 357
Ann Arbor, MI 48103-6938
   734-424-0713
  Fax: 734-426-9016
 sales@centrifugesolutions.com
   www.centrifugesolutions.com
Custom blended seasonings.
President: Tom Czartoski
Sales: Ron Mederski

20406 Centrisys
9586 58th Pl
Kenosha, WI 53144-7805
   262-654-6006
  Fax: 262-654-6063 info@centrisys.us
   www.centrisys.us
Centrifuges and separators; also, centrifuge services
available
President: Michael Copper
 michael.copper@centrisys.us
Marketing Manager: Michael Kopper
Estimated Sales: $2.5-5 Million
Number Employees: 20-49
Brands:
 Centrisys

20407 Century 21 Manufacturing
8008 Harney Street
Omaha, NE 68114-4451
   402-391-2104
High quality vending machines
President: R Lebron

20408 Century Box Company
2412 W Cermak Road
Chicago, IL 60608-3704
   773-847-7070
  Fax: 773-847-7868 info@centurybox.com
   www.centurybox.com
Wooden boxes
President: Daniel Leon

Estimated Sales: Less than $500,000
Number Employees: 1-4
Square Footage: 25000

20409 Century Chemical Corp
28790 County Road 20
Elkhart, IN 46517-1125
   574-293-9521
  Fax: 574-522-5723 800-348-3505
  sales@centurychemical.com
Manufacturer and exporter of industrial and house-
hold deodorants and sanitizers; also, nontoxic
anti-freeze
President: Edward A Fetters
 edfetters@centurychemical.com
Office Manager: Bobbi Holdeman
Plant Manager: David Eller
Estimated Sales: $1-2.5 Million
Number Employees: 5-9
Brands:
 Travel-Jon

20410 Century Crane & Hoist
210 Washington Ave
Dravosburg, PA 15034
   412-466-6987
  Fax: 412-469-0813 888-601-8801
  info@centurysteel.com www.centurysteel.com
Energy absorbing bumpers, overhead electric cranes
and hoists; also, repair services and OSHA inspections
President: Don Taylor
Sales Representative: Frank Marchese

20411 Century Foods Intl LLC
400 Century Ct
Sparta, WI 54656-2468
   608-269-1900
  Fax: 608-269-1910 800-269-1901
   www.centuryfoods.com
Century Foods International is a manufacturer of nutritional powders and ready-to-drink beverages un-
der private label and contract manufacturing
agreements for food, sports, health and nutritional
supplement industries. Other servicesprovided in-
clude agglomeration, blending and instantizing, re-
search and development, analytical testing, and
packaging from bulk to consumer size.
President: Tom Miskowski
VP R&D: Julie Wagner
VP Sales/Marketing: Gene Quast
VP Operations: Wade Nolte
Number Employees: 250-499
Square Footage: 1680000
Parent Co: Hormel Foods Corporation
Type of Packaging: Private Label, Bulk
Brands:
 Cenprem
 Lacey Delite
 Pizazz
 Ready Cheese

20412 Century Glove Corp
145 John Bankston Dr
Summerville, GA 30747-5124
   706-857-6444
  Fax: 706-857-6446 www.centuryglove.com
Manufacturer and importer of cotton work and uni-
form gloves
Manager: Mary Seiler
Sales: Mary Seiler
Estimated Sales: less than $500,000
Number Employees: 20-49

20413 Century Industries Inc
299 Prather Ln
Sellersburg, IN 47172-1739
   812-246-3371
  Fax: 812-246-5446 800-248-3371
   www.centuryindustries.com
Manufacturer and exporter of mobile concession
trailers and kitchens
President: Robert Uhl
 robertuhl@centuryindustries.com
VP: John Uhl
Sales Manager: Matt Gilland
Estimated Sales: $5-10 Million
Number Employees: 20-49
Type of Packaging: Food Service
Brands:
 Goldrush

20414 Century Products
1 Doulton Place
Peabody, MA 01960-3817
978-535-9001
Fax: 978-535-9002 800-225-3472
info@poolcover.com www.poolcover.com
Air bubble cushioning materials and shipping bags
Estimated Sales: $10-20 Million
Number Employees: 100-249

20415 Century Refrigeration
P.O. Box 1206
Pryor, OK 74362-1206
918-825-6363
Fax: 918-825-0723 century@rae-corp.com
Commercial and industrial refrigeration equipment
including condensing units, unit coolers, product
coolers and chillers
President/CEO: Eric Swank
VP/CTO: Vickie Stephens
VP/Engineering: Jay Kindle
Manager of Quality: John Martin
Manager Marketing: Lisa Schrader
VP/Sales: Kevin Trowhill
Contact: Rawls Bill
  robm@rae-corp.com
Vp/Operations: Jerry Salcher
Purchasing Manager: Jerry Douglas
Estimated Sales: $50-100 Million
Number Employees: 275
Square Footage: 125000
Parent Co: RAE Corporation

20416 Century Rubber Stamp Company
121 Fulton St Fl 2
New York, NY 10038
212-962-6165
Numbering machinery, stamps, stencils, etc
Manager: Harry Gold
Estimated Sales: $500,000-$1 Million
Number Employees: 5-9

20417 Century Sign Company
1622 Main Ave # E
Fargo, ND 58103-1553
701-235-5323
Fax: 701-235-5325
Neon and plastic signs
President: Matt Brasel
CFO: Steven Fliflet
Estimated Sales: $5 - 10 Million
Number Employees: 20-49

20418 Cenveo Inc
3001 N Rockwell St
Chicago, IL 60618-7917
773-267-3600
Fax: 773-267-2440 800-388-8406
www.cenveo.com
Envelopes including advertising clasp, string, win-
dow, postage saver, pressure sensitive, billing, etc
Chairman, CEO: Robert G. Burton Sr.
CFO: Scott Goodwin
VP: Ian Scheinmann
Estimated Sales: $1-2.5 Million
Number Employees: 100-249
Square Footage: 1080000

20419 Cepco
2400 Turner Avenue NW
Suite A
Grand Rapids, MI 49544-2004
616-364-8454
Fax: 616-364-8442
Management

20420 Ceramic Color & Chemical Mfg
13th St & 11th Ave
New Brighton, PA 15066
724-846-4000
Fax: 724-846-4123 www.ceramiccolor.com
Inorganic pigments
Owner: Bill Wenning
  cccmfg@verizon.net
Sales Manager: Tom Knox
Sales/Shipping Coordinator: Sally Antonini
Estimated Sales: $20-50 Million
Number Employees: 10-19

20421 Ceramic Decorating Co Inc
4651 Sheila St
Commerce, CA 90040-1003
323-268-5135
Fax: 323-268-5108
sales@ceramicdecoratingco.com
www.ceramicdecoratingco.com
Supplier of custom made packaging labels.
President: Caitlyn Anaya
  caitlyn@ceramicdecoratingco.com
CEO: Chad Johnson
Number Employees: 10-19

20422 Ceramica De Espana
7700 NW 54th St
Doral, FL 33166-4106
305-597-9161
Fax: 305-597-9161
Manufacturer and importer of ceramic tableware,
vases and candlesticks, bathroom, table top, cook-
ware, table accessories, pottery, garden pottery
President: Monica Ruiz
Estimated Sales: $5-10 Million
Number Employees: 5-9
Type of Packaging: Consumer, Food Service

20423 Cermex
5600 Sun Court
Norcross, GE 30092
678-221-3570
Fax: 678-221-3571
Side loading case packer specifically developed for
pharmaceutical industry, pick and place robot for
plastic bottles, top loading machines, compact machine integrating case erection and high speed
shrinkwrapping machine of cans andbottles
Manager: Marc Daniel
Contact: Guy Ayel
  guy.ayel@gebocermex.com

20424 Certified Grocers Midwest
1 Certified Dr
Hodgkins, IL 60525
708-579-2100
Fax: 708-354-7502 www.certisaver.com
Grocery supplier
President: James Bradley
CEO: Jim Denges
Number Employees: 100-249

20425 Certified Labs
200 Express St
Plainview, NY 11803-2423
516-576-1400
Fax: 516-576-1410 800-237-8522
corp@800certlab.com
www.certified-laboratories.com
Full service laboratory
General Manager: Martin Mitchell
  mmitchell@certified-laboratories.com
Estimated Sales: $10 - 20 Million
Number Employees: 50-99

20426 Certified Labs of California
6460 Dale St
Buena Park, CA 90621-3115
714-562-8622
Fax: 714-562-8799 888-366-3522
cflabs@certified-laboratories.com
www.certified-laboratories.com
Providing laboratory testing services for the food in-
dustry.
President: Martin Mitchell
  mmitchell@800certlab.com
Vice President: Steven Mitchell
Estimated Sales: $5-10 Million
Number Employees: 20-49

20427 Certified Machinery Inc
3175 Princeton Pike # A
Lawrenceville, NJ 08648-2331
609-912-0300
Fax: 609-912-0144 www.certifiedmachinery.com
Inkjet and labeling product handling equipment in-
cluding off line coding and labeling, base coding di-
verter, l-sealers and heat tunnels
President: Randy Camacho
  randy.camacho@certifiedmachinery.com
Estimated Sales: Below $5 Million
Number Employees: 5-9
Square Footage: 50000

20428 Certified Piedmontese Beef
100 West Harvest Drive
PO Box 82545
Lincoln, NE 68521
402-458-4442
Fax: 402-458-4531 800-414-3487
info@piedmontese.com www.piedmontese.com
Prime cuts of beef
President: Billy Swain

20429 Cesco Magnetics
93 Utility Ct
Rohnert Park, CA 94928-1614
707-585-2402
Fax: 707-585-3886 877-624-8727
www.cescomagnetics.com
Manufacture magnetic separation equipment and
sanitary valves
President: Alfred Truslow
Estimated Sales: $1 - 3 Million
Number Employees: 20-49
Brands:
  Cesco

20430 Cha's Organics
3700 Saint-Patrick St.
Suite 234
Montreal, QC H4E 1A2
Canada
514-369-8175
info@chasorganics.com
chasorganics.com
Organic plant-based foods, including: coconut milk
and cream, coconut oil, heirloom rice, thai curries,
jackfruit and tropical fruit, spices, snacks like water-
melon chips and coconut rolls.
Co-Founder & VP, Marketing: Marise May
Co-Founder: Chanaka Kurera
Year Founded: 2006
Number of Brands: 1
Type of Packaging: Food Service
Brands:
  Cha's Organics

20431 Chad Co Inc
19950 W 161st St # A
Olathe, KS 66062-2717
913-764-0321
Fax: 913-764-0779 800-444-8360
Manufacturer and exporter of automated washing
and pasteurizing equipment for meat slaughtering
operations
President: Mike Gangel
  mike@chadcompany.com
Estimated Sales: Below $5 Million
Number Employees: 10-19
Square Footage: 10400

20432 Chaffee Co
4111 Citrus Ave # 10
#10
Rocklin, CA 95677-4009
916-630-3980
Fax: 916-630-3987 chaffee@chaffeeco.com
Barrier laminate, cellophane and polyethylene seal-
ers, and sealer systems.
President: Charlie Harper
Estimated Sales: $2.5-5 Million
Number Employees: 5-9
Brands:
  Chaffee

20433 Chain Restaurant Resolutions
Suite 5
Toronto, ON M5S 1T8
Canada
416-934-4334
Fax: 416-934-4333
Consultant providing physical and financial restruc-
turing to the restaurant and fast food industries
Estimated Sales: $1 - 5,000,000
Number Employees: 2

20434 (HQ)Chain Store Graphics
2220 E Logan Street
Decatur, IL 62526-5133
217-428-4695
Fax: 217-423-4010 800-443-7446
Advertising materials including paper and plastic
signs, sign kits and decals; also, OEM decals and
fleet markings
VP: Scott Bowers

Estimated Sales: $500,000-$1 Million
Number Employees: 4
Square Footage: 50000

20435 (HQ)Chaircraft
P.O. Box 608
Hickory, NC 28603-0608

828-326-8458
Fax: 828-326-8447 www.centuryfurniture.com
Chairs and bar stools
President: Cick Finch
Plant Manager: Kevin Boyle
Estimated Sales: $20 - 50 Million
Number Employees: 100-249
Parent Co: Century Furniture

20436 (HQ)Challenger Pallet & Supply Inc
24 N 3210 E
Idaho Falls, ID 83401-5174

208-523-1969
Fax: 208-523-1972 800-733-0205
www.challengerpallet.com
Pallets, stakes, wedges and saw dust
President: Tad Hegsted
just_hegs@yahoo.com
R&D: Justin Hegsted
VP Operations: Kelly Bennion
Estimated Sales: $5 - 10 Million
Number Employees: 20-49
Square Footage: 60000
Other Locations:
  Challenger Pallet & Supply
  Midvale UT

20437 Chalmur Bag Company, LLC
1426 Frankford Avenue
Philadelphia, PA 19125

215-425-0400
Fax: 215-425-4749 800-349-2247
chalmurbag@msn.com
chalmurbag.homestead.com/
Printed bags including polyethylene, cellophane,
mini-lock and pre-opened on rolls, extruded narrow
width tubing and cellophane sheets; also, carton and
drum lining
Manager: Bob Livingston
blivingston@chalmurbag.com
Sales Manager: John Yarris
Plant Manager: Jon Ashley
Estimated Sales: $5 - 10 Million
Number Employees: 10-19
Square Footage: 64000

20438 (HQ)Chamberland Engineering
PO Box 817
West Warwick, RI 02893

800-687-1136
Fax: 401-615-7758 vibrate020@aol.com
www.chamberlandengineering.com
Vibrating screens, vibrating separators, vibrating
sieves, bin and hopper vibrators, point and strip
samplers, rotary tray dryers, ball valves, dust collec-
tors,cyclones, scrubbers, electromechanical feeders,
dosing feeders, air sweeprssystems, weigh belt feed-
ers, bulk bag unloaders, BIC bins, blenders and mix-
ers, ingredient dispensing systems
President: David Chamberland
VP: Steven Chamberland
R & D: Albert Bleau
Estimated Sales: $3.5 Million
Number Employees: 4
Number of Brands: 5
Number of Products: 27
Square Footage: 40000
Type of Packaging: Food Service

20439 Chambers Container Company
145 Bluedevil Dr
Gastonia, NC 28056-8610

704-377-6317
Fax: 704-864-4022
Corrugated boxes
Manager: Roger Powers
Controller: Beth Hudson
VP: Scott Chambers
Estimated Sales: $20-50 Million
Number Employees: 50-99
Square Footage: 54000

20440 Champaign Plastics Company
PO Box 6413
Champaign, IL 61822

217-359-3664
Fax: 217-359-0091 800-575-0170
products@champaignplastics.com
www.champaignplastics.com
Manufacturer and wholesaler/distributor of disposable aprons, gloves, boots, shoe covers, hats, beard
restraints, sleeves, children's and adult bibs and banquet rolls
President: Donna Williams
Contact: Joseph Bateman
  joseph.bateman@champaignplastics.com
Estimated Sales: Below $5,000,000
Number Employees: 1-4

20441 Champion Chemical Co
8319 Greenleaf Ave
Whittier, CA 90602-2998

562-945-1456
800-621-7868
service@championchemical.com
www.cleanthatpot.com
Manufacturer and exporter of carbon and grease re-
movers
Owner: Andrew Ellis
  service@championchemical.com
Estimated Sales: $1 - 5 Million
Number Employees: 10-19
Square Footage: 72000
Brands:
  Sokoff

20442 Champion Industries Inc
3765 Champion Blvd
Winston Salem, NC 27105-2667

336-661-1556
Fax: 336-661-1979 800-532-8591
info@championindustries.com
www.championindustries.com
Manufacturer and exporter of commercial dishwash-
ers, pot and pan washers and waste disposal systems
Owner: Luciano Berti
Chairman of the Board: Luciano Berti
CEO: Hank Holt
CFO: Christa Miller
R & D: Perry Money
Director Sales: Pete Michailo
Advertising Manager: Patrick Elworth
  lberti@championindustries.com
Purchasing Manager: Donna Mealka
Estimated Sales: $20-50 Million
Number Employees: 100-249
Square Footage: 130000
Parent Co: Comenda-Alispa
Type of Packaging: Food Service
Brands:
  Champion
  Moyer Diebel

20443 Champion Plastics
220 Clifton Blvd
Clifton, NJ 07011

Fax: 800-526-1238 800-526-1230
sales@championplastics.com
www.championplastics.com
Manufacturer and exporter of polyethylene bags and
films.
Founding Partner: John Callaghan
Year Founded: 1972
Estimated Sales: $20-30 Million
Number Employees: 100-249
Square Footage: 96000
Parent Co: X-L Plastics
Brands:
  Champtuf Polyethylene

20444 (HQ)Champion Trading Corporation
P.O. Box 227
Marlboro, NJ 07746

732-780-4200
Fax: 732-780-9839 info@champtrading.com
www.champtrading.com
Manufacturer and exporter of used and rebuilt pro-
cessing and packaging machinery
Principal: David Matthews
Co-Owner: James Matthew
Co-Owner: Michael Matthews
Contact: Adrienne Schere
  schere@champtrading.com
Plant Manager: S Bassett

Estimated Sales: $1-2,500,000
Number Employees: 5-9
Square Footage: 50000

20445 Champlin Co
236 Hamilton St
Hartford, CT 06106-2910

860-951-9217
Fax: 860-951-3464 800-458-5261
info@champlincompany.com
www.champlincompany.com
Wooden and corrugated boxes
President: Rory Poole
  champlinco@snet.net
VP: W James Schumaker
Estimated Sales: $3 - 5 Million
Number Employees: 20-49

20446 Chandre Corporation
14 Catharine Street
Poughkeepsie, NY 12601-3104

845-473-8003
Fax: 845-473-8004 800-324-6252
www.chandre.com
Chocolate tempering machines
Estimated Sales: 700000
Number Employees: 10

20447 (HQ)Chaney Instrument Co
965 S Wells St
P.O. Box 70
Lake Geneva, WI 53147-2468

262-248-4449
Fax: 262-248-8707 800-777-0565
info@chaney-inst.com www.acurite.com
Manufacturer and exporter of digital and analog
kitchen thermometers, timers and clocks
President: Valerie Wilson
  v.wilson@laonastatebank.com
National Sales Manager Food Service: Allan Ahrens
Number Employees: 100-249
Square Footage: 95000
Type of Packaging: Consumer, Food Service, Pri-
vate Label, Bulk
Other Locations:
  Chaney Instruments
  Lake Geneva WI
Brands:
  Acu-Rite
  Chaney Instrument

20448 Change Parts Inc
185 S Jebavy Dr
Ludington, MI 49431-2460

231-845-5107
Fax: 231-843-4907 www.changeparts.com
Custom designed changeover parts including fillers,
cleaners, cappers, timing screws, stars and guides,
nozzles, drive wheels and belts; also,
remanufactured and used packaging equipment
President: Jeff Pelc
  j.pelc@apcoe.com
CFO: Greg Simsa
VP: Greg Simsa
Marketing: Dori Bray
National Sales Manager: Jon Goad
Operations Manager: Andy Kmetz
Production: Andy Kmetz
Estimated Sales: $2.5-5 Million
Number Employees: 20-49
Square Footage: 90000

20449 Chantland Company, The
PO Box 69
Humboldt, IA 50548

515-332-4040
Fax: 515-332-4923 www.chantlandpulley.com
Manufacturer and exporter of belt conveyors, bag
filling equipment and bag palletizers
CEO: Donald Sosnoski
Year Founded: 1943
Estimated Sales: $33 Million
Number Employees: 200
Square Footage: 140000

20450 Chapman Corp
3366 Tree Court Industrial Blv
St Louis, MO 63122-6688

636-225-5313
Fax: 636-825-2610 800-843-1404
sales@chapmanstl.com www.chapmanstl.com
Replacement knives, blades, slitters and perforators
for processing and packaging equipment.

Executive VP: Mark Zumbehl
mzumbehl@chapmanstl.com
Estimated Sales: $2.5-5,000,000
Number Employees: 10-19

20451 Chapman Manufacturing Co Inc
481 W Main St
Avon, MA 02322-1695
508-587-7592
Fax: 508-587-7592 info@chapmanco.com
www.chapmanco.com
Manufacturer and exporter of lamps and lighting fixtures, encompasses table and floor lamps, chandeliers, sconces, accent furniture and decorative accessories. Authentic reproductions, traditional adaptations and transitional andoriginal contemporary designs
President: Richard Amaral
ramaral@chapmanco.com
Estimated Sales: $10-20 Million
Number Employees: 50-99

20452 Chapman Sign
23253 Hoover Rd
Warren, MI 48089-1934
586-758-1600
Fax: 586-758-1610
Electric signs
Manager: Harold Chapman
*Estimated Sales:*less than $500,000
Number Employees: 5

20453 Charles Beck Machine Corporation
400 W Church Road
King of Prussia, PA 19406-3185
610-265-0500
Fax: 610-265-5627 beckmachine@verizon.net
www.beckmachine.com
Manufacturer and exporter of set-up box lidders and rotary shear sheet cutters
President: Arthur Beck
Manager Parts/Service: Robert Pickell
Estimated Sales: Below $5 Million
Number Employees: 10

20454 Charles Beseler Company
2018 W Main St
P.O. Box 431
Stroudsburg, PA 18360
570-517-0400
Fax: 800-966-4515 800-237-3537
www.beselershrinkpackaging.com
Manufacturer and exporter of shrink wrap machinery.
Estimated Sales: $100-500 Million

20455 Charles Craft Inc
21381 Charles Craft Ln
Laurinburg, NC 28352
910-844-3521
Fax: 910-844-9846 www.charlescraftinc.com
Towels including dish, pot holders and aprons
President: Charles G Buie Jr
Cmo: Marybeth Zadel
mzadel@charlescraft.com
President: Clifton Buie
Estimated Sales: $50-100 Million
Number Employees: 100-249
Brands:
Charles Craft

20456 Charles E. Roberts Company
539 Fairmont Rd
Wyckoff, NJ 07481-1318
973-345-3035
Fax: 973-345-8516 800-237-2684
Manufacturer and exporter of embossed ribbon for awards, badges, prizes, contests, emblems, fairs and conventions
Owner/President: Bernard Gallant
Estimated Sales: $5-10 Million
Number Employees: 10-19
Square Footage: 28000

20457 Charles Engineering & Service
1 Tye Green Paddoc
Belcamp, MD 21017-0428
410-272-1090
Temperature sensitive containers; custom design available
Sr. VP: Charles Furlong

Estimated Sales: $300,000-500,000
Number Employees: 7
Square Footage: 32000

20458 Charles Gratz Fire Protection
241 W Oxford St
Philadelphia, PA 19122-3798
215-235-5800
Fax: 215-236-2510
Manfacturer of fire alarm systems and fire extinguishers
Owner: Harry Gratz
Office Manager: Deborah DeSimone
Estimated Sales: Below $5 Million
Number Employees: 5 to 9

20459 Charles H Baldwin & Sons
1 Center St
P.O. Box 372
West Stockbridge, MA 01266-9502
413-232-7785
Fax: 413-232-0114 www.baldwinextracts.com
Flavoring extracts and flavors, maple table syrup and supplier of baking supplies.
Owner: Jackie Moffatt
jackie@baldwinextracts.com
Estimated Sales: $500,000-$1 Million
Number Employees: 1-4
Brands:
Baldwin

20460 Charles Lapierre
56 Etna Road
Lebanon, NH 03766-1403
Canada
603-448-0300
Fax: 603-448-4810 800-432-2990
info@njmpackaging.com
President: Charles Lapierre
Vice President of Operations: Andre Caumartin
R&D: Louis Lasluer
Director of International Sales: Marc Lapierre
Number Employees: 25

20461 Charles Mayer Studios
105 E Market St
Suite 114
Akron, OH 44308-2037
330-535-6121
Fax: 330-434-2016
Manufacturer, exporter and importer of hotel and restaurant menu boards, white liquid chalk boards, bulletin boards, easels, trade show displays and to-day's specials boards, custom tables
Owner: Jeffrey Mayer
Executive VP: M Barton
Estimated Sales: $1-3 Million
Number Employees: 20-49
Square Footage: 210000
Type of Packaging: Food Service
Brands:
Mayer Hook N' Loop
Mayer Magna

20462 (HQ)Charles Ross & Son Co
710 Old Willets Path
Hauppauge, NY 11788-4193
631-234-0500
Fax: 631-234-0691 800-243-7677
mail@mixers.com www.mixers.com
Manufacturer, importer and exporter of mixing, blending and dispersion equipment
President: Richard Ross
rross@mixers.com
Executive VP: Bogard Lagman
Estimated Sales: $20-50 Million
Number Employees: 100-249
Square Footage: 150000
Other Locations:
Ross, Charles, & Son Co.
Savannah GA
Brands:
Double Planetary
Powermix
Ross
X-Series

20463 Charles Ross & Son Co
710 Old Willets Path
Hauppauge, NY 11788-4193
631-234-0500
Fax: 631-234-0691 800-243-7677
sales@mixers.com www.mixers.com
Emulsifying equipment

President: Richard Ross
rross@mixers.com
Executive Vice President: Bogard Lagman
Product Manager: Shannon Wolf
Regional Sales Manager: Chip Nipps
Estimated Sales: $20-50 Million
Number Employees: 100-249

20464 Charles Tirschman Pallet Co
1936 Graves Ct
Dundalk, MD 21222-5508
410-282-6199
Pallets and skids
Owner: Charles Tirschman
Estimated Sales: $500,000-$1 Million
Number Employees: 5-9

20465 Charles Walker North America
2901 Stanley Ave
Fort Worth, TX 76110
817-922-9834
Fax: 817-922-9854 cissy@charlesalaninc.com
www.charlesalanfurniture.com
Furniture manufacturer
Owner: Margaret Sevadjian
Vice President: Jim Boston
Operations Manager: Steve McDonald
Square Footage: 120
Brands:
Waiker Conveyor Belt & Equipment

20466 Charlotte Tent & Awning
5901 N Hill Cir
Charlotte, NC 28213-6237
704-921-8743
Fax: 704-921-3034
www.charlottetentandawning.com
Commercial awnings
President: Dale Michael
dale@charlottetentandawning.com
Estimated Sales: $1-2,500,000
Number Employees: 20-49

20467 Charlton & Hill
655 30th Street N
Lethbridge, AB T1H 5G5
Canada
403-328-3388
Fax: 403-328-3533 www.charltonandhill.com
Conveyors; wholesaler/distributor of ranges, coolers and hot plates; serving the food service market; also, metal fabrication available
Sales Manager: Dwayne Huber
Estimated Sales: $1 - 5 Million
Number Employees: 100-250

20468 Charm Sciences Inc
659 Andover St
Lawrence, MA 01843-1032
978-687-9200
Fax: 978-687-9216 info@charm.com
www.charm.com
Manufacturer and exporter of food safety diagnostic instruments for antibiotic, aflatoxin and pesticide residues, ATP sanitation/hygiene, pasteurization efficiency and doneness in meat products
President: Dr Stanley Charm
VP Sales: Gerard Ruth
Contact: Rami Abraham
r.abraham@charm.com
Estimated Sales: Less Than $500,000
Number Employees: 1-4
Brands:
Chef Test
Cidelite
Paslite
Pathogel
Pocketswab
Sl Test

20469 Chart Applied Technologies
3505 County Road 42 W
Burnsville, MN 55306-3803
952-882-5000
Fax: 952-882-5172 888-877-3093
www.mve-inc.com
VP: Eric M Rottier
Estimated Sales: $1 - 5 Million
Number Employees: 250-499

20470 (HQ)Chart Inc
407 7th St NW
New Prague, MN 56071-1010
952-758-4484
Fax: 952-758-8293 800-428-3777
www.chartindustries.com
Turnkey liquid nitrogen systems for food freezing,
turnkey liquid nitrogen injection systems for still
product manufacturing and bulk carbon dioxide sys-
tems for beverage carbonation
VP Industrial Gases Marketing: Ron' Stark
Manager: Bruce Lyman
bruce.lyman@chart-ind.com
VP Technical Engineering: Jon Wikstrom
VP Restaurant Products: Paul Plooster
Number Employees: 500-999
Square Footage: 844000
Other Locations:
Minnesota Valley Engineering
Canton GA

20471 (HQ)Chart Industries Inc
1 Infinity Corporate Ctr # 300
Cleveland, OH 44125-5370
440-753-1490
Fax: 440-753-1491 800-247-4446
www.chartindustries.com
Manufacturer and exporter of CO2 storage tanks
used for carbonation in soda dispensing machines
President: John Wikstrom
CEO: William C Johnson
william.johnson@chart-ind.com
VP: Eric M Rottier
Marketing Director: Mary Nelson
Sales Director: Dick Mich
Estimated Sales: $20-50 Million
Number Employees: 1000-4999
Type of Packaging: Food Service

20472 Charter House
200 N Franklin St # B
Zeeland, MI 49464-1075
616-741-4301
Fax: 616-796-1199 800-314-7659
www.sperrysmoviehouse.com
Food service dining room furniture
President: Chuck Reid
Cmo: Scott Simpson
scott.simpson@charter-house.com
Finance Executive: Jacob Burroughs
Director/Managing Engineer: Bill Regan
Plant Manager: Harriet Trethewey
Purchasing Manager: Bill Forslund
Estimated Sales: $10 - 20 Million
Number Employees: 50-99
Square Footage: 80000
Parent Co: Franke

20473 Chase Doors
10021 Commerce Park Dr.
Cincinnati, OH 45246
513-860-5565
Fax: 800-245-7045 800-543-4455
Manual, electric sliding cold storage room, swing
and vertical lift doors for walk-in coolers and freez-
ers. Full line of parts. Commercial refrigeration
sales, service, and installation
Owner: Jeff Staples
Contact: Vicki Byrd
vbyrd@chasedoors.com
General Manager: David Canady
Estimated Sales: $2.5-5 Million
Number Employees: 1-4
Square Footage: 64000

20474 Chase Doors
10021 Commerce Park Dr
Cincinnati, OH 45246
513-860-5565
Fax: 800-245-7045 800-543-4455
info@chasedoors.com www.chasedoors.com
Impact traffic doors, service doors, flexible doors,
security doors, corrosion resistant doors, fire and
service doors, pharmaceutical doors, door opera-
tions, cold storage doors and dock seals and shelters
President: Jim Lindsay
CEO: Robert W Muir
Contact: Vicki Byrd
vbyrd@chasedoors.com
Estimated Sales: $10-25 000,000
Number Employees: 100-249

20475 Chase Industries Inc
10021 Commerce Park Dr
West Chester, OH 45246-1333
513-860-5565
Fax: 513-860-0933 800-543-4455
www.chasedoors.com
Chase Industries, Inc. manufactures a full line of
manual and semi-automatic L-Sealers, Shrink Tun-
nels, and Bar Sealers as well as fully automatic
Sleeve Wrappers, Bundlers, Blister Sealers, Clam
Shell Sealers, Curing Systems and Formfill equip-
ment. Our goal as a manufacturer, is to provide top
performance and top quality to the customer in as
many combinations of size and options as possible.
We like to work closely with our distributors and
their customers for the bestpossible standards
CEO: Robert W Muir
bmuir@chaseind.com
CEO: Elizabeth Braslow
CEO: Jim Braslow
R&D: James Braslow
Purchasing: Jose Garcia
Estimated Sales: $5 - 10 Million
Number Employees: 250-499
Number of Brands: 10
Square Footage: 30000
Brands:
Chase
Cii
Ultrablister
Ultrasealer

20476 (HQ)Chase-Doors
10021 Commerce Park Dr
Cincinnati, OH 45246
513-860-5565
Fax: 513-245-7045 800-543-4455
www.chasedoors.com
Manufacturer and exporter of vinyl and roll up
doors, fire and insulated doors, door operators and
air curtains
CEO: Dan O'Connor
CFO: Drew Bachman
CEO: Robert W Muir
R&D: Rory Falato
Marketing: Rory Falato
General Manager: Carl Johnson
Plant Manager: Rick Schweitzer
Purchasing Director: Diane Wells
Estimated Sales: $20 - 50 Million
Number Employees: 100-249
Number of Brands: 10
Number of Products: 35
Other Locations:
Chase-Durus
Memphis TN

20477 Chase-Logeman Corp
303 Friendship Dr
Greensboro, NC 27409-9332
336-665-0754
Fax: 336-665-0723 info@chaselogeman.com
Manufacturer and exporter of liquid filling, plugging
and screw capping machinery, tray loaders and
unloaders, conveyors, unscramblers, rotary tables,
accumulators and monoblocks; also, custom
designing available
President: Alan Gillespie
alang@chaselogeman.com
Vice President: Joel Slazyk
Quality Control: Louis Stier
Plant Manager: Lew Stier
Estimated Sales: $1 Million
Number Employees: 10-19
Square Footage: 36000
Brands:
Chaselock

20478 (HQ)Chaska Chocolate
821 Oriole Lane
Chaska, MN 55318-1131
952-448-5699
Fax: 952-448-6719
Consultant for the oilseed extraction, fats and oils,
chocolate and coffee industries; also, food technol-
ogy research available
Contact: Phillip Arendt
parendt@aol.com
Estimated Sales: $1 - 5 Million
Number Employees: 2
Square Footage: 2200
Other Locations:
Chaska Chocolate
Chicago IL

20479 Chatelain Plastics
413 N Main St
PO Box 1464
Findlay, OH 45840-3541
419-422-4323
Fax: 419-422-1122 866-421-4323
sales@chatelainplastics.com
www.chatelainplastics.com
Advertising signs
Owner: Tom Klein
tom@chatelainplastics.com
President: Jim Chatelain
Estimated Sales: Below $5 Million
Number Employees: 1-4

**20480 (HQ)Chatfield & Woods Sack
Company**
651 Enterprise Dr
Harrison, OH 45030-1691
513-202-9700
Fax: 513-202-0900
Paper sacks
President: Alan Bicknayer
General Manager: Mark Mitter
Number Employees: 5
Square Footage: 60000
Other Locations:
Chatfield & Woods Sack Co.
Harrison OH

20481 Chatillon
8600 Somerset Dr
Largo, FL 33773-2700
727-536-7831
Fax: 727-538-2400 chatillon.fl-lar@ametek.com
www.ametek.com
Mechanical and electronic calibration equipment for
hydraulic, pneumatic, materials testers
Quality Control: Mike Guglicelli
Manager: Nick Hoiles
Estimated Sales: $10 - 20 Million
Number Employees: 50-99
Parent Co: Amatek

20482 Chattanooga Labeling Systems
P.O. Box 2492
Chattanooga, TN 37409-0492
423-825-2125
Fax: 423-825-2173 www.clsdeco.com
Pressure sensitive, heat transfer and shrink sleeve la-
bels; glassware and plastic screen printing
President: Marvin Smith
CFO: Dave Houseman
Head of Customer Service Dept.: Chris Gonzalez
Office Manager: Jenny Hughes
Production Manager: Don Gilbert
Estimated Sales: $20 - 30 Million
Number Employees: 20-49

**20483 Chattanooga Rubber Stamp &
Stencil Works**
P.O. Box 443
Sale Creek, TN 37373-0443
423-894-1163
Fax: 423-894-1164 800-894-1164
crs4018@aol.com
Rubber stamps
President: John L McNair Jr
Estimated Sales: Less than $500,000
Number Employees: 3

20484 Chattin Awning Company
85 Newfield Ave
Edison, NJ 08837
732-225-8800
Fax: 732-225-2110 800-394-3500
mainattractions3500@gmail.com
www.mainattractions.com
Commercial awnings
President: Rocky Sconda
CEO: Kevin Bova
Contact: Theresa Ascolese
tascolese@mainattractions.com
Operations Manager: Dean Dialfonso
Estimated Sales: $5 - 10 Million
Number Employees: 20-49

20485 Chaucer Foods, Inc.
2238 Yew Street
Forest Grove, OR 97116
503-359-2050
chaucerfoods.com

Supplier of freeze-dried fruit, vegetables and baked ingredients. *Year Founded:* 1980

20486 Chaucer Press Inc
535 Stewart Rd
Hanover Twp, PA 18706-1454
570-825-2005
Fax: 570-825-0535 www.chaucerpress.com
Communnicone and Xtenda-cone collars for on-pack promotion, folding cartons, pressure-sensitive and cut labels, and other printed materials
CEO: Patricia A. Frances
COO: Frank A. Franzo
Plant Manager: Al Saldy
Estimated Sales: $2.5-5 000,000
Number Employees: 20-49

20487 Check Savers Inc
529 Shepherd Dr
Garland, TX 75042-6830
972-272-7533
Fax: 972-276-8315 800-276-8315
Checks
President: R P Mc Nabb
CEO: Bret Woods
National Sales Rep.: Mike Voight
Number Employees: 20-49

20488 Checker Bag Co
10655 Midwest Industrial Blvd
St Louis, MO 63132-1281
314-423-3131
Fax: 314-423-1329 800-489-3130
www.checkerbag.com
Manufacturer, importer and exporter of polyethylene, polypropylene and cellophane bags including bakery, confection and gourmet
President: Robert Freund
VP: Al Stix
Number Employees: 20-49

20489 Checker Machine
2701 Nevada Ave N
Minneapolis, MN 55427-2879
763-544-5000
Fax: 763-544-1272 888-800-5001
cm@checkermachine.com
Spiral conveyors, ovens and freezers
President: Steve Lipinski
CFO: John Ackerman
Vice President: Steve Lipinski
Sales/Marketing Manager: Don Hockman
Production Manager: Brad Schmitt
Plant Manager: Steve Lipinski
Estimated Sales: $5 - 10 Million
Number Employees: 50-99
Square Footage: 400000
Parent Co: Checker Machine
Brands:
  Checker
  Stein/Checker

20490 Cheese Merchants of America
248 Tubeway Dr
Carol Stream, IL 60188
630-768-0317
Fax: 630-221-0584 www.cheesemerchants.com
Processors of custom blends of Italian cheeses, converters of hard Italian cheeses to grated, shredded, and shaved.
EVP/Managing Partner: Robert Greco
Director Purchasing/Quality Assurance: Paul DelleGrazie
Central Regional Sales Manager: Mark Lewis
EVP Sales: Jim Smart
Contact: Brian Barrett
  brianb@cheesemerchants.com
Estimated Sales: $19.3 Million
Number Employees: 90
Square Footage: 105000
Type of Packaging: Consumer, Food Service, Bulk

20491 Cheese Outlet Fresh Market
400 Pine St
Burlington, VT 5401
802-863-3968
Fax: 802-865-1705 800-447-1205
www.freshmarketgourmetvt.com
Retail gourmet bakery of cheeses, produce and gourmet items, prepared foods, wine and Vermont products
President: Simon Pozirekides
Manager: Sherie Cyr

Estimated Sales: $5 - 10 Million
Number Employees: 20-49
Square Footage: 10000

20492 Cheesemakers Inc
2266 S Walker Rd
Cleveland, TX 77328-6336
281-593-1319
Fax: 281-593-2898 www.cheesemakers.com
General Manager: James Keliehor
  jck@cheesemakers.com
Estimated Sales: $2.5-5 Million
Number Employees: 10-19

20493 Chef Revival
7240 Cross Park Drive
North Charleston, SC 29418
800-858-8589
Fax: 843-767-0494 800-248-9826
www.chefrevival.com
Manufacturer, importer and exporter of traditional and contemporary chef uniforms including jackets,aprons,pants, hats,clogs,as well as a full line of ladies and chilrens clothing.
President: Jerry Rosenblum
VP: Kim dela Villefromoy
Marketing Director: Kelly Gloor
Sales: Jack Kramer
Contact: Rob Johnson
  rob@chefrevival.com
Production: Louis Nardella
Plant Manager: Paul Brady
Number Employees: 20
Square Footage: 16000
Type of Packaging: Consumer, Food Service
Brands:
  Chef Revival
  Chefcare
  Chefcutlery
  Knife & Steel

20494 Chef Specialties
411 W Water St
Smethport, PA 16749-1199
814-887-5652
Fax: 814-887-2021 800-440-2433
info@chefspecialties.com
www.chefspecialties.com
Manufacturer, exporter and importer of metal and wood kitchen specialties including peppermills, spice mills, salad bowls and cutting boards
Owner: Jack Pierotti
Sales: Mike Wagner
  info@chefspecialties.com
Estimated Sales: $500,000-$1 Million
Number Employees: 5-9
Square Footage: 50000
Type of Packaging: Consumer, Food Service, Private Label, Bulk
Brands:
  Chef

20495 Chef's Choice Mesquite Charcoal
1729 Ocean Oaks Rd
PO Box 707
Carpinteria, CA 93014-0707
805-684-8284
Fax: 805-684-8284
Manufacturer and importer of mesquite charcoal
Owner: Bill Lord
Number of Products: 2
Type of Packaging: Food Service
Brands:
  Chef's Choice

20496 Chefwear
2300 W Windsor Ct # C
Addison, IL 60101-1491
312-427-6700
Fax: 630-396-8337 800-568-2433
info@chefwear.com www.chefwear.com
Manufacturer and exporter of culinary apparel and accessories
President: Rochelle Huppin Fleck
CEO: Gary Fleck
Vice President: Carol Mueller
  carol.mueller@chefwear.com
VP Sales/Marketing: Carol Mueller
Sales Director: Glenn Woerz
General Manager: Rob James
Estimated Sales: Less than $500,000
Number Employees: 50-99
Square Footage: 24000

Brands:
  Chef-R-Alls
  Chefwear
  Pint Size Duds

20497 Cheil Jedang Corporation
105 Challenger Rd
Ridgefield Park, NJ 07660-2101
201-229-6050
Fax: 201-229-6058 annie@cheiljedang.com
Flavor enhancers
President: Ben Heo
Estimated Sales: $10 - 20 Million
Number Employees: 50-99

20498 Chem Mark International
635 E Chapman Ave
Orange, CA 92866-1604
714-633-8560
Fax: 310-557-1976
Broker of commercial dishwashing machines, chemicals, air purification equipment, bar glass washer and flying insect control products. Also exporter of commercial dishwashing machines
President: Darol Carlson
VP: Betty Carlson
Marketing Director: Jay Jaeger
Estimated Sales: $1-2.5 Million
Number Employees: 1 to4

20499 Chem Pack Inc
2261 Spring Grove Ave
Cincinnati, OH 45214-1797
513-241-6616
Fax: 513-241-6664 800-421-2700
info@chem-pack.com www.chem-pack.com
Contract packager of multi-packaged food products, health and beauty aids, skin and blister packaging, shrink wrap, liquids, powders, etc.; also display assembly.
President: John Pierce
Contact: Sanya Mishevski
  sanya@chem-pack.com
Estimated Sales: $1-2.5 Million
Number Employees: 20-49
Square Footage: 100000

20500 Chem Pruf Door Co LTD
5224 Ruben Torres Sr Blvd
5224 FM 802
Brownsville, TX 78526-5217
956-544-1000
Fax: 956-544-7943 800-444-6924
info@chem-pruf.com www.chem-pruf.com
Noncorrosive fiberglass doors and wall windows, louver systems and fiberglass frames; also, stainless steel hardware available
Owner: Tony Mc Dermid
CFO: Bill Stirling
HR Executive: Mary Chapa
  mary@chem-pruf.com
Estimated Sales: $10 - 20 Million
Number Employees: 50-99
Square Footage: 80000
Type of Packaging: Food Service, Private Label
Brands:
  Chem-Pruf

20501 Chem-Tainer Industries Inc
361 Neptune Ave
West Babylon, NY 11704-5800
631-661-8300
Fax: 631-661-8209 800-275-2436
sales@chemtainer.com
Manufacturer and exporter of plastic tanks and containers
President: James Glen
VP Marketing: Tony Lamb
Contact: Joan Flaxman
  joanflaxman@chem-tainer.com
Estimated Sales: $5-10 Million
Number Employees: 1-4
Square Footage: 1000000
Brands:
  Haz Mat

20502 Chem-Tainer Industries Inc
361 Neptune Ave
West Babylon, NY 11704-5800
631-661-8300
Fax: 631-661-8209 800-938-8896
sales@chemtainer.com www.chemtainer.com
Manufacturer and exporter of plastic tanks, containers and material handling equipment

President: James Glen
Executive VP: A Lamb
Contact: Joan Flaxman
  joanflaxman@chem-tainer.com
Estimated Sales: $5-10,000,000
Number Employees: 1-4
Square Footage: 40000
Parent Co: Chem-Trainer Industries

20503 ChemTreat, Inc.
4461 Cox Rd
Glen Allen, VA 23060-3331
                              804-935-2000
    Fax: 804-965-0154 800-648-4579
  cs_orders@chemtreat.com www.chemtreat.com
Manufacturer and exporter of water treatment chemicals for boilers and cooler, cooker and waste water treatment and clarification systems
Contact: Roy Arnett
  arnett@chemtreat.com
Manager,Food Industry Marketing: David Anthony
Dierctor Food Industry Division: Dennis Martin
Purchasing Manager: Steve Hemmis
Estimated Sales: $300,000-500,000
Number Employees: 1-4

20504 Chemclean Corp
13045 180th St
Jamaica, NY 11434-4194
                              718-525-4500
    Fax: 718-481-6470 800-538-2436
  info@chemclean.com www.chemclean.com
Manufacturer and exporter of industrial cleaners, degreasers, disinfectants, and deodorizers
President: Alberto Bodhert
  alberto@chemclean.com
CEO: Frank Bass
Manager: S Emil Johnsen
Estimated Sales: $20-50 Million
Number Employees: 20-49
Square Footage: 20000
Brands:
  D-Carb 297
  D-Scale
  Multichlor
  Neutraclean
  Sparkleen 310

20505 Chemco Products Inc
1349 Grand Oaks Dr
Howell, MI 48843-8579
                              517-546-7800
  Fax: 517-546-5163 www.chemcoproducts.net
USDA sanitation chemicals, boiler, cooling tower and wastewater treatment; provides and installs related dispensing equipment, controllers, tanks, CIP systems, lube systems, pressure washers
President: Janis Utz
CFO: Elaine Cooper
CEO: Joe Mickunas
Quality Control: Elaine Cooper
VP Sales: Dave McCalo
Manager: Julie Blank
  julieblankpt@aol.com
Estimated Sales: $10 - 20 000,000
Number Employees: 10-19

20506 Chemdet Inc
730 Commerce Center Dr # D
Sebastian, FL 32958-3128
                              772-388-2755
    Fax: 772-388-8813 800-645-1510
  info@chemdet.com www.chemdet.com
Manufacturer and exporter of stainless steel tank washers
President: Phillip Joachim
Estimated Sales: $2.5-5 Million
Number Employees: 10-19
Brands:
  Chem Disc
  Clip Disc
  Fury
  Rotaball
  Spray Ball
  Turbodisc

20507 Chemetall
675 Central Ave
New Providence, NJ 07974-1560
                              908-464-6900
    Fax: 908-464-4658 800-526-4473
          www.chemetallna.com
President: Joris Merckx
  joris.merckx@chemetall.com

Number Employees: 500-999

20508 Chemetrics Inc
4295 Catlett Rd
Midland, VA 22728-2003
                              540-788-9026
    Fax: 540-788-9302 800-356-3072
          www.chemetrics.com
Water analysis test kits
President: Bruce Rampy
Cmo: Henry B Castaneda
  henryc@chemetrics.com
International Business Manager: Shirley Ward
Estimated Sales: $20 - 50 Million
Number Employees: 50-99

20509 Chemex Division/International Housewares Corporation
11 Veterans Drive
Chicopee, MA 1022
                              413-499-2370
    Fax: 413-443-3546 800-243-6399
          www.chemexcoffeemaker.com
Manufacturer, importer and exporter of drip coffee makers and filters
President: Eliza Grassy
Estimated Sales: $1 - 3 Million
Number Employees: 5-9
Type of Packaging: Consumer
Brands:
  Chemex

20510 Chemglass Life Sciences
3800 N Mill Rd
Vineland, NJ 08360-1528
                              856-696-0014
    Fax: 856-696-9102 800-843-1794
  customer-service@cglifesciences.com
          www.cglifesciences.com
Manufacturer of high quality laboratory glassware and equipment. Products include glassware and plastics, hotplates, overhead stirrers, stirrer bars, chromatography and reaction vials, beakers, cylinders, volumetric flasks, shakersvortexers, rotators, mini centrifuges, UV lamps, melting point apparatus, clamps, supports and bossheads.
Sales Exec: Craig Beesecker
Export Manager: Linnea Warren
Number Employees: 100-249

20511 Chemi-Graphic Inc
340 State St
PO Box 410
Ludlow, MA 01056-3439
                              413-589-0151
              Fax: 413-589-7448
  customer.service@chemi-graphic.com
          www.chemi-graphic.com
Etched, lithographed and silk screened name plates, dials and scales
President: Paul R Pohl
  sales@chemi-graphic.com
Executive VP: Donald Devine
Estimated Sales: Below $5 Million
Number Employees: 50-99

20512 Chemicolloid Laboratories, Inc.
P.O. Box 251
New Hyde Park, NY 11040-0251
                              516-747-2666
              Fax: 516-747-4888
  customersupport@colloidmill.com
          www.colloidmill.com
Manufacturer and exporter of colloid mills used in applications to process materials being dispersed, suspended, emulsified, homogenized or comminuted, and process equipment.
VP: Robert Best
Marketing: Susan Okeefe
Sales Director: George Ryder
Purchasing: Steve Best
Estimated Sales: $3 - 5 Million
Number Employees: 20-49
Square Footage: 144000
Brands:
  Charlotte
  Colloid Mills

20513 Chemifax
11641 Pike St
Santa Fe Springs, CA 90670
                              562-908-0405
    Fax: 562-908-0077 800-527-5722
  info@carrollco.com www.carrollco.com

Manufacturer and exporter of cleaning products including floor waxes, finishes, detergents, soaps and chemical specialties
Manager: Mohammed Nilchian
Sales Manager: Mike Greene
Contact: Eddie Ayala
  eayala@carrollco.com
Sales Manager: Mike Meller
Estimated Sales: $20 - 50 Million
Number Employees: 50-99
Square Footage: 80000
Parent Co: Carroll Company
Brands:
  Airx
  Nature's Orange
  Show Patrol
  Shower Patrol Plus
  Solar System
  Trewax Hardware
  Trewax Industrial
  Trewax Janitorial

20514 (HQ)Chemindustrial Systems Inc
W 53 N 560 Highl & Dr
Cedarburg, WI 53012
                              262-375-8570
    Fax: 262-375-8559 info@chemindustrial.com
          www.chemindustrial.com
Manufacturers of pH control, neutralizing process systems and hydrocyclones.
CEO: Michael Lloyd
  mlloyd@chemindustrial.com
Sales Manager: Michael Lloyd
Estimated Sales: $5-10 Million
Number Employees: 10-19
Square Footage: 6000
Brands:
  Chemindustrial

20515 Chemineer
P.O. Box 1123
Dayton, OH 45401-1123
                              937-454-3200
    Fax: 937-454-3379 chemineer@nov.com
          www.chemineer.com
Agitators and mixers
Manager: Patty Breig
Contact: Cherie Buhler
  c.buhler@chemineer.com
Estimated Sales: $10 - 50 Million
Number Employees: 250-499

20516 Chemir Analytical Svc
2672 Metro Blvd
Maryland Heights, MO 63043-2412
                              314-291-6620
    Fax: 314-291-6630 800-659-7659
              www.chemir.net
Provides investigative analytical services for the food & beverage industry. Services include contaminant identification, material/foreign object identification, off-colors/off-odors/off-flavors analysis, extractables/leachablestoxicological evaluations, packaging failure analysis and litigation support.
Chairman: Shri Thanedar
  sthanedar@chemir.com
Number Employees: 50-99

20517 ChemtranUSA.com
5634 Shirley Ln
Houston, TX 77032-2640
                              281-590-9400
    Fax: 763-476-8155 800-523-9033
  info@ChemTranUSA.com www.chemtranusa.com
Specialize in packaging for shipment of infectious substances; suppliers of UN Performance-Oriented Packaging
Owner: Randy Hill
  randy@chemtranusa.com
Number Employees: 10-19

20518 Chemtreat
4461 Cox Rd # 106
Glen Allen, VA 23060-3331
                              804-935-2000
    Fax: 804-965-6974 800-442-8292
  michaelk@chemtreat.com www.chemtreat.com
Contact: Jackie Allen
  allen@chemtreat.com
Estimated Sales: $1 - 5 Million
Number Employees: 1-4

20519 Chemtura Corp
199 Benson Rd
Middlebury, CT 06762-3218

203-573-2000
Fax: 203-573-3711 800-295-2392
www.chemtura.com
CEO: Ron Abbott
ron.abbott@chemtura.com
Estimated Sales: Over $1 Billion
Number Employees: 500-999

20520 Chep
8517 Southpark Cir # 100
Orlando, FL 32819-9062

407-370-2437
Fax: 407-355-6211 800-243-7872
President: Michael Lamb
Contact: Amanda Abbott
amanda.abbott@chep.com
Estimated Sales: Less Than $500,000
Number Employees: 1-4

20521 Cherry's Industrial Eqpt Corp
600 Morse Ave
Elk Grove Vlg, IL 60007-5102

847-364-0200
Fax: 800-350-8454 800-350-0011
sales@cherrysind.com www.cherrysind.com
Manufacturer and exporter of aluminum shipping
containers and pallet transfer machines, inverters
and retrievers; importer of pallet inverters
President: David Novak
david@cherrysind.com
National Accounts Manager: James Woods
Estimated Sales: $500,000-$750,000
Number Employees: 10-19
Square Footage: 60000

20522 Cheshire Signs
201 Old Homestead Highway
Keene, NH 03431-4441

603-352-5985
Neon and plastic signs
President: Anthony A Magaletta
Estimated Sales: $500,000-$1 Million
Number Employees: 1 to4

20523 Chesmont Engineering CoInc
619 Jeffers Cir
Exton, PA 19341-2540

610-594-9200
Fax: 610-594-1909 heatpro@aol.com
www.chesmont-engineering.com
Fume incinerators for volatile organic compounds
and odors; also, process heating systems, fuel and
propane standby systems and baking ovens
Owner: Christopher Mohler
heatpro@aol.com
Office Administrator: Lois Lanza
VP: Christopher Mohler
Office Manager: Kathy Tiffany
Estimated Sales: Below $1Million
Number Employees: 1-4
Square Footage: 8000

20524 Chester Hoist
PO Box 449
Lisbon, OH 44432

330-424-7248
Fax: 330-424-3126 800-424-7248
www.chesterhoist.com
Manufacturer and importer of hoists including man-
ual chain, worm-drive and electrical low headroom;
exporter of manual and electric chain hoists
Manager: Bob Burkey
Quality Control: Bob Eusanio
Sales Rep.: Chris Reynolds
Application Engineer: Vince Anderson
Product Manager: Joe Runyon
Estimated Sales: $10-20 Million
Number Employees: 50-99
Parent Co: Columbus McKinnon Corporation
Brands:
Chester
Model Am
Zephyr

20525 Chester Plastics
Highway 3
P.O. Box 460
Chester, NS B0J 1J0
Canada

902-275-3522
Fax: 902-275-5002

Manufacturer and exporter of rigid plastic packaging
and thermoformed plastic bottles; importer of plastic
sheeting
President: George Nemskeri
General Manger: John Babiak
Marketing Manager: Ed Baker
General Manager: Michael Johnston
Number Employees: 90
Square Footage: 108000

20526 (HQ)Chester-Jensen Co., Inc.
345 Tilghman St
Chester, PA 19013-3432

610-876-6276
Fax: 610-876-0485 800-685-3750
htxchng@chester-jensen.com
www.chester-jensen.com
stainless steel food processing equipment, including
sanitary chillers, ice builders (thermal storage),
batch mixing processors, plate heat exchangers &
cook-chill equipment.
President: Richard Miller
CEO: Steven Miller
Sales Director: Robert Skoog
Estimated Sales: $10-20 Million
Square Footage: 76000
Type of Packaging: Consumer, Food Service, Pri-
vate Label, Bulk
Other Locations:
Chester-Jensen Company
Cattaraugus NY

20527 Chesterfield Awning Co
9301 S Western Ave
Chicago, IL 60643-6736

773-239-1513
Fax: 708-848-4309 800-339-6522
www.chesterfieldawning.com
Commercial awnings
Owner: David Ausema
Vice President: Dave Ausema
dave@chesterfieldawnings.com
Estimated Sales: $1 - 3,000,000
Number Employees: 20-49

20528 Chesterfield Awning Co
16999 Van Dam Rd
South Holland, IL 60473-2660

708-596-4434
Fax: 708-596-9469 800-339-6522
david@chesterfieldawning.com
www.chesterfieldawning.com
Commercial awnings
President: David Ausema
dave@chesterfieldawning.com
Estimated Sales: Less Than $500,000
Number Employees: 1-4

20529 Chestnut Labs
3233 E. Chestnut Expressway
Springfield, MO 65802

417-829-3788
Fax: 417-829-3787
information@chestnutlabs.com
www.chestnutlabs.com
Laboratory testing for food microbiology pathogens
such as Salmonella and Listeria testing, and water
analysis testing.
Contact: Kristen Acker
kristenacker@chestnutlabs.com

20530 Chevron Global Lubricants
555 Market Street
San Francisco, CA 94105-2800

415-894-4646
Fax: 415-894-1297
Number Employees: 10,000 +

20531 Chicago Automated Labeling Inc
44 N 450 E
Valparaiso, IN 46383-9310

219-531-0646
Fax: 219-462-8315 www.chicagoautolabel.com
Manufactuerers of labeling equipment
Owner: Mark Walker
sales@chicagoautolabel.com
CEO: Ken Walker
Estimated Sales: $2 000,000
Number Employees: 10-19

20532 Chicago Conveyor Corporation
330 S La Londe Avenue
Addison, IL 60101-3309

630-543-6300
Fax: 630-543-2308
Pneumatic conveying systems for powder or granu-
lar materials, storage spaces and related equipment,
weighing bathcing and controls
VP Sales: Tom Hodanovac
Contact: Mike Stogdill
mstogdill@chicagoconveyor.com
Purchasing Manager: Keith Stark
Estimated Sales: $5-10 Million
Number Employees: 20
Square Footage: 60000

20533 Chicago Dowel Co Inc
4700 W Grand Ave
Chicago, IL 60639-4695

773-622-2000
Fax: 773-622-2047 800-333-6935
sales@chicagodowel.com
www.chicagodowel.com
Skewers for candy, apples, corn dogs and meat
President: Paul Iacono
piacono@chicagodowel.com
Sales Director: Jay Goodwin
Manager: George Iacono
Estimated Sales: $5 - 10 Million
Number Employees: 20-49
Square Footage: 100000

20534 Chicago Ink & Research Co
97 Ida Ave
Antioch, IL 60002-1887

847-395-1078
Fax: 847-395-3568
Industrial marking and rubber stamp inks
President: Charles Doty
sales@chicagoink.com
General Manager: F Arthur Doty
Estimated Sales: $1-2.5 Million
Number Employees: 5-9
Square Footage: 16000

20535 Chicago Scale & Slicer Company
2359 Rose St
Franklin Park, IL 60131-3504

847-455-3400
Fax: 847-455-3450
Manufacturer, importer and exporter of hand oper-
ated and electric slicers; also, grinders and knives
Owner: Eugene Dee
Estimated Sales: $1 - 5 Million
Number Employees: 10 to 19
Square Footage: 28000
Parent Co: Lawndale Corporation
Brands:
Digi
Globe

20536 Chicago Show Inc
851 Asbury Dr
Buffalo Grove, IL 60089-4525

847-955-0200
Fax: 847-955-9996 www.chicagoshow.com
Point of purchase advertising displays and signs;
also, fixtures
CEO: Andrew Prantner
prantner@mail.med.upenn.edu
CEO: James M. Snediker
CFO: B Fier
Estimated Sales: $5 - 10 Million
Number Employees: 50-99
Square Footage: 200000

20537 Chicago Stainless Eqpt Inc
1280 SW 34th St
Palm City, FL 34990-3308

772-781-1441
Fax: 772-781-1488 800-927-8575
www.chicagostainless.com
Since 1937, manufacturer of high quality sanitary
pressure gauges, homogenizer gauges and digital
thermometers
Manager: Jerry Williamson
VP of Marketing: Mark Mistarz
Sales Director: Jerry Williamson
Manager: John Kalousek
john@chicagostainless.com
Estimated Sales: $2.5-5 Million
Number Employees: 10-19

Brands:
  Pharma-Flow
  Sani-Flow

20538 Chicago Trashpacker Corporation
290 N Prospect St
Marengo, IL 60152-3235
815-568-5116
800-635-5745
Trash compactors, can and glass crushers
President/CEO: Fredrick Gohl
VP/R&D/Quality Control: Bill Phillips
Estimated Sales: Below $5 Million
Number Employees: 10
Number of Products: 12
Square Footage: 2000
Brands:
  Trashpacker

20539 Chickadee Products
1208 N Swift Road
Addison, IL 60101-6104
773-523-7972
Fax: 773-523-9066 800-621-5046
donaldmk@aol.com
Custom blending
Estimated Sales: $5-10 Million
Number Employees: 10-19

20540 Chickasaw Broom Mfg Co Inc
7710 Jamison Rd
Little Rock, AR 72209-5541
501-562-0311
www.thehatchergroup.com
Brooms and mops
CEO: Everette Hatcher
ehatcher@thehatchergroup.com
Number Employees: 10-19

20541 Chief Industries
PO Box 848
Kearney, NE 68848-0848
308-237-3186
Fax: 308-237-2650 800-359-8833
agri@chiefind.com www.chiefind.com
Manufacturer and exporter of grain drying and han-
dling equipment; also, bins
President: Roger Townsend
Research & Development: Jim Moffit
Sales Director: Ed Benson
Plant Manager: Duene McCann
Purchasing Manager: Rob Morris
Estimated Sales: $20-50 Million
Number Employees: 100-249
Number of Brands: 3
Number of Products: 12
Square Footage: 90000
Parent Co: Chief Industries
Type of Packaging: Bulk
Brands:
  Caldwell Manufacturing
  Chief
  York

20542 Chil-Con Products
PO Box 1385
Brantford, ON N3T 5T6
Canada
519-759-3010
Fax: 519-759-1611 800-263-0086
www.henrytech.com
Manufacturer and exporter of pressure vessels, oil
separators, condensers, process cooling heat
exchangers, direct expansion and flooded chillers
General Manager: Scott Rahmel
President, Chief Executive Officer: Michael
Giordano
Business Manager: Harry Stewart
Plant Manager: Myron Harasym
Number Employees: 95
Square Footage: 400000
Parent Co: Valve, Henry, Company

20543 Childres Custom Canvas Prods
711 E Highway 67
Duncanville, TX 75137-3407
972-298-4943
Fax: 972-709-7453 info@childresproducts.com
www.childresproducts.com
Awnings
Owner: Gary Childres
info@childresproducts.com
CFO: Linda Childres

Estimated Sales: $2,500,000
Number Employees: 20-49
Square Footage: 20000

20544 Chili Plastics
4 Pixley Industrial Pkwy
Rochester, NY 14624-2399
585-889-4680
Fax: 585-889-6199
Molded plastics including containers
Manager: Mike Curley
Estimated Sales: $.5 - 1 million
Number Employees: 5-9

20545 Chill Rite Mfg
2371 Gause Blvd W
Slidell, LA 70460-6501
985-641-4865
Fax: 985-641-0183 800-256-2190
www.chillrite32.com
Beverage dispensing and delivery systems
Owner: Buddy Abraham
info@chillrite32.com
Estimated Sales: $1 - 5 Million
Number Employees: 20-49
Brands:
  Chill Rite
  Desco

20546 Chillers Solutions
101 Alexander Ave # 3
Pompton Plains, NJ 07444-1854
973-835-2800
Fax: 973-835-3222 800-526-5201
www.edwards-eng.com
Manufacturer and exporter of heating/cooling equip-
ment and products, control components, hydronic
heating/cooling systems and vapor recovery units for
pollution and process control; also, packaged
industrial chillers
President: R Waldrop
VP Engineering: G Passaro
Manager: Aaron Herl
aherl@frhsd.com
Plant Manager: Jose Mercedes
Estimated Sales: $40 Million
Number Employees: 50-99
Brands:
  Box'fin
  Quiet' Slide

20547 Chilson's Shops Inc
8 Industrial Pkwy
Easthampton, MA 01027-1164
413-529-8062
Fax: 413-529-2022 chilsons@chilsons.com
www.chilsons.com
Commercial awnings
President and R&D and QC: Edward Ghareeb
chilsons@chilsons.com
Estimated Sales: $1 - 2,500,000
Number Employees: 10-19

20548 Chilton Consulting Group
PO Box 129
Rocky Face, GA 30740-0129
706-694-8325
Fax: 706-694-8316 info@chiltonconsulting.com
www.chiltonconsulting.com
Consulting firm providing HACCP development,
validation and training, food safety and quality au-
dits, crisis management, environmental sanitation
audits, employee safety training, etc
President: Jeff Chilton
General Manager: Brent Heldt
Contact: Jorge Acosta
jacosta@chiltonconsulting.com

20549 China D Food Service
2535 S Kessler Street
Wichita, KS 67217-1044
316-945-2323
Fax: 316-945-5557
Food service and management
Purchasing: Lisa Diez
Estimated Sales: $300,000-500,000
Number Employees: 1-4
Type of Packaging: Food Service

**20550 China Food Merchant
Corporation**
1601 N Hale Avenue
Fullerton, CA 92831-1218
714-773-0803
Fax: 714-773-1082

20551 China Lenox Incorporated
1414 Radcliffe Street
Bristol, PA 19007-5413
267-525-7800
www.lenox.com
Manufacturer and exporter of fine china dinnerware
and giftware
CEO: Bob Burbank
Estimated Sales: $91 Million
Number Employees: 1,500
Square Footage: 9774
Parent Co: Brown-Foreman
Type of Packaging: Food Service

20552 Chinet Company
722 Barrington Circle
Winter Springs, FL 32708-6117
407-365-5372
Fax: 407-359-8381 800-539-3726
www.mychinet.com
Biodegradable disposable tableware; serving the
food service industry
District Sales Manager: Marvin Tolley

20553 Chinet Company
27601 Forbes Rd # 59
Laguna Niguel, CA 92677-1242
949-348-1711
Fax: 949-489-2043
Disposable plastic and paper tableware
Owner: Xiao Qiu
Regional Sales Manager: Ronald Shillings
Estimated Sales: Less than $500,000
Number Employees: 10-19
Brands:
  Chinet

20554 Chino Works America Inc
22301 S Western Ave # 105
Sutie 105
Torrance, CA 90501-4155
310-787-8899
Fax: 310-787-8899 888-321-9118
info@chinoamerica.com www.chinoamerica.com
Recorders, controllers, infared technology (pyrome-
ters) and noncontact moisture reading on line
President: Toshikazu Inden
Sales, OEM and Tech Support: Toshi Toshi
Vice President: Akemi Adachi
akemi@chinoamerica.com
Sales Engineer: Mike Matsuno
Estimated Sales: $500,000-$1 Million
Number Employees: 5-9
Number of Products: 100

20555 Chipmaker Tooling Supply
7352 Whittier Ave
Whittier, CA 90602-1131
562-698-5840
Fax: 562-698-5646 800-659-5840
chipmakerca@yahoo.com www.chip-makers.com
A major supplier of machines and parts to the food
industry.
Manager: Patty Rivera
Contact: Stephen Smith
chipmakerca@yahoo.com
Office Manager/Purchasing Agent: Laura Kurbel
Estimated Sales: $3 - 5 Million
Number Employees: 1-4
Square Footage: 48000

20556 Chiquita Brands LLC.
2051 SE 35th St
Fort Lauderdale, FL 33316
954-924-5700
www.chiquita.com
Fruit and vegetable grower and producer of fresh
and prepared food products.
President/CEO: Carlos Lopez Flores
Year Founded: 1899
Estimated Sales: $3 Billion
Number Employees: 20,000
Number of Brands: 3
Parent Co: Cutrale-Safra
Type of Packaging: Consumer, Food Service, Pri-
vate Label, Bulk

Brands:
Bites
Chiquita
Fresh Express

20557 Chlorinators Inc
1044 SE Dixie Cutoff Rd
Stuart, FL 34994-3436
772-288-4854
Fax: 772-287-3238 800-327-9761
regal@regalchlorinators.com
www.regalchlorinators.com
Manufacturer and exporter of gas chlorinators, waste water treatment systems, sulphonators, dual cylinder scales, chlorine gas detectors, flow pacing control valves and vacuum monitors
President: Diane Haskett
Vice President: Chris Myers
Marketing Manager: Jill Majka
Operations Manager: John Hentz
Estimated Sales: $3 - 5 Million
Number Employees: 20-49
Square Footage: 20000
Brands:
Regal

20558 Chocolate Concepts
114 S Prospect Ave
Hartville, OH 44632-8906
330-877-3322
Fax: 330-877-1100 cc@dmpweb.net
Manufacturer, importer and exporter of chocolate equipment including tempering tanks, measuring pumps, vibrating tables, cooling conveying tunnels, coin machines and kettles; manufacturer and exporter of plastic standard and custom molds
Owner: Scott Huckestein
shuckestein@dmpweb.net
Estimated Sales: $1 - 2.5 Million
Number Employees: 5-9
Number of Products: 55
Square Footage: 120000
Parent Co: LCF
Brands:
Chocolate Concepts

20559 (HQ)Choctaw-Kaul Distribution Company
540 Vinewood Avenue
Detroit, MI 48208
313-894-9494
Fax: 313-894-7977 jgreer@choctawkaul.com
www.choctawkaul.com
Gloves, personal protective equipment and safety related products
CEO: Kenny Tubby
Estimated Sales: $21 Million
Number Employees: 125
Square Footage: 110000

20560 Choklit Molds LTD
23 Carrington St
Lincoln, RI 02865-1702
401-725-7377
Fax: 401-724-7776 800-777-6653
www.choklitmolds.com
Manufacturer and exporter of reusable plastic chocolate molds. Wholesaler of packaging supplies for the candy retail.
President: Lea Goyette
CEO: Richard Goyette
VP/Treasurer: Lea Goyette
Contact: Richard Oyette
choklitmolds@cox.net
Plant Manager: Chris Mottram
Purchasing: Kelly Mottram
Number Employees: 1-4
Square Footage: 20000
Type of Packaging: Bulk

20561 Chop-Rite Two Inc
531 Old Skippack Rd
Harleysville, PA 19438-2203
215-256-4620
Fax: 215-256-4363 800-683-5858
info@chop-rite.com www.chop-rite.com
Meat grinders, cherry stoners and juice extractors
Owner: Nancy Saeger
info@chop-rite.com
Estimated Sales: $5 - 10 Million
Number Employees: 10-19

20562 Chord Engineering
P.O. Box 518
Niwot, CO 80544
303-449-5812
Fax: 303-546-6405 www.chord.org
On-line inspection equipment for cans
Estimated Sales: Below $500,000
Number Employees: 2

20563 Chore-Boy Corporation
411 E Water Street
Centerville, IN 47330
765-855-5434
Fax: 765-855-1311
Sanitary pumps
President: Ronald Napier
Estimated Sales: $500,000-$1 Million
Number Employees: 5-9
Square Footage: 14000
Brands:
Chore-Boy
Kleen-Flo

20564 Chori America
154 Veterans Drive
Northvale, NJ 07647-2302
201-750-7050
Fax: 201-750-7055 866-420-7050
Flexible pouch filling and sealing equipment
Estimated Sales: $1 - 3 Million
Number Employees: 1-4
Brands:
Hisaka Works Ltd
Toyo Jidoki

20565 (HQ)Christianson Systems Inc
20421 15th St SE
PO Box 138
Blomkest, MN 56216-9706
320-995-6141
Fax: 320-995-6145 800-328-8896
info@christianson.com www.onyxrp.com
Manufacturer and exporter of pneumatic conveyors and ship and barge unloaders
President: Jim Gerhardt
jger@christianson.com
Marketing Manager: Barbara Gilberts
Sales: Tim Flaan
Estimated Sales: $5-10 Million
Number Employees: 50-99
Square Footage: 170000
Brands:
Chem-Vac
Handlair
Push-Pac
Superportable
Supertower
Vac-U-Vator

20566 Christman Screenprint Inc
2822 Wilbur St
Springfield, MI 49037-7954
269-962-6274
Fax: 269-962-9411 800-962-9330
dtc@christmanscreenprint.com
www.christmanscreenprint.com
Decals, labels, signs, aprons, shirts, jackets and hats
President: David Christman
dtc@christmanscreenprint.com
Secretary: Dana Christman
VP: Michael Christman
Estimated Sales: Less than $500,000
Number Employees: 1-4

20567 Christy Industries Inc
1812 Bath Ave # 1
Brooklyn, NY 11214-4690
718-236-0211
Fax: 718-259-3294 800-472-2078
www.christy-ind.com
Manufacturer and exporter of fire and burglar alarms; wholesaler/distributor of intercoms and television equipment including security and closed circuit
President: Statz Cheryl
s.cheryl@alarmdistributor.com
Estimated Sales: $1 - 3 Million
Number Employees: 5-9
Square Footage: 6000

20568 Christy Machine Co
118 Birchard Ave
P.O. Box 32
Fremont, OH 43420-3008
419-332-6451
Fax: 419-332-8800 888-332-6451
www.christymachine.com
Manufacturer and exporter of conveyers; also, filling, icing and glazing machinery
President: Randy L Fielding
cmc1@cros.net
Estimated Sales: $1 - 2.5 Million
Number Employees: 10-19

20569 Chroma Color Corp
3900 W Dayton St
McHenry, IL 60050-8378
877-385-8777
www.chromacolors.com
Color concentrates for thermoplastic, pre-colored, natural and clear materials.
CEO: Michael Clementi
Year Founded: 1964
Estimated Sales: $100-500 Million
Number Employees: 100
Square Footage: 250000

20570 Chroma Tone
P.O. Box 4
Saint Clair, PA 17970
214-321-8601
Fax: 214-320-3791 800-878-1552
Metal and plastic signs, decals, point of purchase displays and candy rail strips
President: Matthew Parulis
Marketing Director: Nan Merchant
Plant Manager: Jerry Watts
Estimated Sales: $2.5-5 Million
Number Employees: 20-49
Square Footage: 60000

20571 Chromalox Inc
103 Gamma Dr # 2
Pittsburgh, PA 15238-2981
412-967-3800
Fax: 412-967-3938 800-443-2640
www.chromalox.com
Manufacturer and exporter of electric heating elements for commercial cooking equipment
CEO: Scott Dysert
Estimated Sales: $161 Million
Number Employees: 100-249
Square Footage: 20259
Parent Co: Emerson Electric Company
Brands:
Chromalox

20572 Chronos Richardson
2 Stewart Place
Fairfield, NJ 07004-2202
973-227-3522
Fax: 973-227-8478 800-284-3644
www.bmhchronosrichardson.com
Bags, batching systems, form, fill and seal, palletizing
Mktg. Manager: Mike Hudak
Contact: Bob Duran
info@chronosrichardson.com
Number Employees: 415

20573 Chroust Associates International
22311 Ventura Boulevard
Suite 115
Woodland Hills, CA 91364-1555
818-348-1438
Fax: 818-348-1094 chroust@aol.com
www.members.aol.com/chroust/associates.html
Consultant specializing in engineering and design for restaurants, schools, hotels, casinos, schools and universities
Principal: Thomas Chroust
Product Manager: Ivan Benes
Number Employees: 3
Square Footage: 6000

20574 Chrysler & Koppin Co
7000 Intervale St
Detroit, MI 48238-2498
313-491-7100
Fax: 313-491-8769 800-441-0038
dkoppin@aol.com www.chryslerkoppin.com
Pre-fabricated walk-in refrigerators and freezers

President: Douglas G Koppin
CEO: Dean Koppin
CFO: Karen Oakley
  kare@chryslerkoppin.com
Estimated Sales: $5-10 Million
Number Employees: 5-9

20575 Chu's Packaging Supplies
10011 Santa Fe Springs Rd
Santa Fe Springs, CA 90670-2921
                    562-944-6411
    Fax: 562-944-7113 800-377-4754
              www.chuspkg.com
Owner: Pao Chu
  pao@movingpad.com
Estimated Sales: $10 - 20 Million
Number Employees: 10-19

20576 Chuppa Knife Manufacturing
133 N Conalco Drive
Jackson, TN 38301
                    731-424-1212
    Fax: 731-424-8937 chuppak@aol.com
Manufacturer and exporter of stainless steel and aluminum handle cutlery
President: Elmer Rausch
Estimated Sales: $1 - 2.5 Million
Number Employees: 8
Number of Products: 350
Type of Packaging: Consumer, Food Service, Private Label

20577 Church & Dwight Co., Inc.
Princeton South Corporate Center
500 Charles Ewing Boulevard
Ewing, NJ 08628
                    609-806-1200
                    800-833-9532
              www.churchdwight.com
Personal care, household cleaning, fabric care, and health and well-being products for the consumer market. Manufacturer of Arm & Hammer brand sodium bicarbonate (baking soda), and other leavening products for the baking industry.
Chairman/President/CEO: Matthew Farrell
Executive VP/CFO/Head, Business Ops.: Rick Dierker
Executive VP/General Counsel/Secretary: Patrick de Maynadier
Executive VP/Chief Technology Officer: Carlos Linares
Executive VP/Chief Marketing Officer: Barry Bruno
Executive VP/Chief Commercial Officer: Paul Wood
Executive VP/Chief Supply Chain Officer: Rick Spann
Year Founded: 1846
Estimated Sales: $4.15 Billion
Number Employees: 5,100
Number of Brands: 31
Type of Packaging: Consumer, Food Service, Bulk
Brands:
    AIM
    ARM & HAMMER
    Answer
    Arrid
    Batiste Dry Shampoo
    Close-Up
    Clump & Seal
    FIRST RESPONSE
    FelinePine
    Flawless
    KABOOM
    L'il Critters
    Legatin
    Nair
    Orajel
    Orange GLO
    OxiClean
    PB8
    Pepsodent
    Pre-Seed
    RepHresh
    Replens
    Simply Saline
    Spinbrush
    Toppik
    Trojan Brands
    Vitafusion
    Viviscal
    Water Pik
    Wellgate
    XTRA

20578 Church Offset Printing Inc
1731 Margaretha Ave
P.O. Box 988
Albert Lea, MN 56007-3270
                    507-373-6485
    Fax: 507-373-2716 800-345-2116
    sales@churchoffsetprinting.com
    www.churchoffsetprinting.com
Labels for automatic or hand application; also, specializing in flexographic printing
Owner: Michael Kruse
  mikek@churchoffsetprinting.com
Financial Manager: Dan Bodensteiner
Plant and Project Manager: Todd Hoenisch
Estimated Sales: Below $1 Million
Number Employees: 20-49

20579 (HQ)CiMa-Pak Corp.
50 Lindsay Ave
Dorval, QC H9P 2T8
Canada
                    514-631-6222
    Fax: 514-631-7361 877-631-2462
    info@cima-pak.com www.cima-pak.com
Trays and tray-sealing equipment
President: Tim Dawson
Sales Manager: Todd Trudel
Other Locations:
    Mississauga, ON
    Mooers NY

20580 Cielo Foods
9238 Bally Ct
Rancho Cucamonga, CA 91730-5313
                    909-945-2323
    Fax: 909-945-9090 877-652-4356
              www.cielousa.com
Frozen yogurt
Owner: Dan Kim
  info@cielousa.com
Number Employees: 5-9

20581 Cimino Box & Pallet Co
8500 Clinton Rd # J
Cleveland, OH 44144-1000
                    216-961-7377
              Fax: 216-961-4054
Pallets
Owner: Frank Ritson
  ciminobox@aol.com
VP: Frank Ritson
Estimated Sales: Less Than $500,000
Number Employees: 5-9

20582 Cin-Made Packaging Group
3150 Clinton Ct
Norcross, GA 30071
                    770-476-9088
    Fax: 513-541-5945 800-264-7494
              info@cin-made.com
Manufacturer and exporter of paper composite cans and tubes for specialty markets including wine and spirits, fancy foods and teas.
Manager: Hartmut Geisselbrecht
CFO: John Ewalt
Quality Control: Erik Frey
Marketing Director: Hartmut Geisselbrecht
Sales Manager: Janet Pickerell
Plant Manager: Eric Frey
Purchasing Manager: Phyllis Dietrich
Estimated Sales: $10-20 Million
Number Employees: 20-49
Type of Packaging: Consumer, Private Label

20583 Cincinnati Convertors Inc
1730 Cleneay Ave
Cincinnati, OH 45212-3506
                    513-731-6600
              Fax: 513-731-6605
    info@cincinnaticonvertors.com
    www.cincinnaticonvertors.com
Up to 6 color printed and plain flexible packaging for food, pharmaceutical and chemical applications: cellophane bags, confectioners' bags, heat sealed bags, food bags, plastic packaging, thermoformed cups, pouch lidding materials andtea bag tags
President: Donald Ellsworth Jr
VP: Donald Ellsworth, Jr.
Office Manager: Kristin Goltra
  kristin@cincinnaticonvertors.com
COO: Kristin Goltra
Estimated Sales: $2.5 - 5 Million
Number Employees: 10-19

20584 Cincinnati Foam Products
3244 McGill Rd
Cincinnati, OH 45251
                    513-741-7722
              Fax: 513-741-7723
Manufacture high quality foam shipping containers, protective packaging, molded EPS and fabricated foam.
Founder: Carl Welage
Plant Manager: John Shearer
Estimated Sales: Below $5 Million
Number Employees: 5-9
Square Footage: 20000
Type of Packaging: Consumer, Food Service, Private Label, Bulk

20585 Cincinnati Industrial Machry
4600 N Mason Montgomery Rd
Mason, OH 45040-9176
                    513-923-5600
    Fax: 513-769-0697 800-677-0076
    sales@cinind.com www.thearmorgroup.com
Warewashing equipment for bakeries, supermarkets, food processing, and institutions
Owner: Frank Ahaus
  fahaus@cinind.com
Global Sales Director: George Shillcock
  fahaus@cinind.com
Estimated Sales: $5 - 10 Million
Number Employees: 250-499
Number of Brands: 2
Square Footage: 320000
Parent Co: the Armor Group, Inc
Type of Packaging: Food Service

20586 Cincinnati Industrial Machry
4600 N Mason Montgomery Rd
Mason, OH 45040-9176
                    513-923-5600
    Fax: 513-769-0697 800-677-0076
    sales@cinind.com www.thearmorgroup.com
Manufacturer and exporter of baking ovens and can washing equipment; also turnkey finishing systems and cleaning/drying/curing systems
Owner: Frank Ahaus
  fahaus@cinind.com
Marketing Director: Liz Chamberlain
Public Relations: Liz Chamberlain
Operations Manager: Joe Bohlen
Estimated Sales: $20 - 25 Million
Number Employees: 250-499
Square Footage: 317000

20587 Cinelli Esperia
380 Chrislea Road
Woodbridge, ON L4L 8A8
Canada
                    905-856-1820
              albert@cinelli.com
    www.gcinelli-esperia.com
Manufacturer and exporter of spiral mixers, bagel and roll machinery, steam proofers, baguette and bread molders, automatic bun dividers, rounders, sheeters, etc.; importer of coffee machines and revolving rack and convection ovens
President: Guido Cinelli
Sales/Marketing Manager: Albert Cinelli
Number Employees: 50
Square Footage: 160000
Brands:
    G. Cinelli-Esperia Corp.

20588 Cintas Corp
6800 Cintas Blvd
Cincinnati, OH 45262
    Fax: 800-864-3888 800-864-3676
              www.cintas.com
Business uniforms; also, rental uniform service available.
EVP/Chief Administrative Officer: Mike Thompson
Chairman & Chief Executive Officer: Scott Farmer
  farmers@cintas.com
EVP/Chief Financial Officer: J. Michael Hansen
SVP/General Counsel/Secretary: Thomas Frooman
Vice President & Treasurer: Paul Adler
EVP/Chief Operating Officer: Todd Schneider
Year Founded: 1929
Estimated Sales: $4.9 Billion
Number Employees: 45,000

20589 Cintex of America

283 E Lies Rd
Carol Stream, IL 60188

630-588-0900
Fax: 425-962-4600 800-424-6839
www.centex.com
Manufacturer and exporter of metal detection check weighing equipment, x-ray inspection systems and vision systems
President: Anthony Divito
CEO: Simon Armstrong
CFO: Richard Harwood Smith
Marketing: Dan Izzard
Sales: Dan Izzaro
Production: Jeff Hoffman
Plant Manager: Jeff Hoffman
Purchasing: Sandy Sell
Estimated Sales: $10-20 Million
Number Employees: 50-99
Number of Brands: 10
Number of Products: 4
Square Footage: 60000
Brands:
  Autosearch
  Eclipse
  Insight

20590 Cipriani

30271 Tomas
Rancho Sta Marg, CA 92688-2123

949-589-3978
Fax: 949-589-3979 www.ciprianicorp.com
Manufacturer, distributor and importer of hygienic stainless steel valves
President: Maria Carlo
  mg@ciprianicorp.com
CEO: Robert Moreno
Vice President: Maria Grazia Cipriani
Marketing/Sales VP: Carlo Cipriani
Sales Manager: Chris P Winsek
Estimated Sales: $1,000,000
Number Employees: 5-9
Square Footage: 6000

20591 Ciranda Inc.

221 Vine St
Hudson, WI 54016

715-386-1737
Fax: 715-386-3277 www.ciranda.com
Global supplier of organic, non-GMO and fair trade ingredients, specializing in tapioca syrups; starches and derivatives; honey and agave; cocoa and chocolates; coconut; soy and sunflower lecithin; and various oils and fats.
Contact: Patty Gfrerer
  pgfrerer@gmail.com
Chief Financial Officer: Mark Cross
Marketing Manager: Tonya Lofgren
Human Resources Manager: Karen Brabec
Director of Commerical Operations: Joe Rouleau

20592 Circle Packaging Machinery Inc

2020 American Blvd
De Pere, WI 54115-9139

920-983-3420
Fax: 920-983-3421 www.circlepackaging.com
Vertical and horizontal form/fill/seal machines. F/F/S machines can be used to package a wide verity of liquids, tablet, capsules and other food and beverage products.
President: John Dykema
  john@circlepackaging.com
VP Marketing & Sales: Don Stelzer
Product Manager: Craig Stelzer
Production Manager: Steve Joosten
Parts & Service Manager: Ralph Ruggiero
Estimated Sales: Less than $500,000
Number Employees: 20-49
Type of Packaging: Consumer

20593 Circuits & Systems Inc

59 2nd St
East Rockaway, NY 11518-1236

516-593-4607
Fax: 516-593-4607 800-645-4301
sales@arlynscales.com www.arlynscales.com
Manufacturer and exporter of electronic scales
President: Arnold Gordon
  a.gordon@chaverware.com
Estimated Sales: Below $5 Million
Number Employees: 20-49
Square Footage: 20000

20594 Cisco Eagle

2120 Valley View Ln
Dallas, TX 75234-8911

972-331-3000
Fax: 972-406-9577 www.cisco-eagle.com
Carton erecting and sealing equipment; conveyors, conveyor systems, storage systems
President: Steve Strifler
  steve.strifler@cisco-eagle.com
Chairman the Board: Warren W Gandall
CEO: Warren W Gandall
Office Manager: Marc Dewall
Estimated Sales: $20 - 50 Million
Number Employees: 50-99
Type of Packaging: Bulk

20595 Citadel Computer Corporation

60A State Route 101A
Amherst, NH 03031-2213

603-672-5500
Fax: 603-672-5590 www.citadelcomputer.com
Industrial computer systems for advanced information management and data collection applications in industrial warehousing, transportation and logistics-product configurations include integrated touchscreens and multilple displaysizes
President: Gregory Walker
CFO: Lesley Sillion
Manager: Andy Nacard
VP Sales: Brandy Herring
Estimated Sales: $10 - 25 Million
Number Employees: 2

20596 Citect Inc

30000 Mill Creek Ave Ste 300
Alpharetta, GA 30022

770-521-7511
Fax: 770-521-7512 sales-americas@citect.com
www.citect.com
Services include integrated solution systems that facilitate productivity, product quality and traceability. CitectSCADA Reports system includes advanced data management tools for tracking production and serving as a reporting tool anddata transfer engine. Ampla Suite system facilitates the streamlining of the production process thereby increasing throughput and eliminating downtime, reducing wastage, improving quality levels, tracking resource genealogy and achieving industrycompliance.
Manager: Scott Mack
Chief Technology Officer: Paul Francis
Chief Human Resources Officer: Andrea Bidwell
Global Director SCADA Systems: Stephen Flannigan
Global Director Ampla Systems: Colette Munro
Global Director Meta Systems: Kurt Lovell
Global Director S-Business Systems: James Cowie
Director Global Partner Programs: Brooke Mauro
Contact: Danie Badenhorst
  daniebadenhorst@citect.com
Estimated Sales: $61.5 Million

20597 Citra-Tech

2 Prespas Street
Lefkosia, CY 33811

info@citra-tech.com
www.citra-tech.com
Manufacturer and exporter of fruit handling and processing machinery; consultant specializing in the design and construction of fresh and citrus fruit processing facilities
President: P M Irby
VP: P Irby, Jr.
Number Employees: 25
Square Footage: 8000

20598 Citrus and Allied Essences

3000 Marcus Ave, Ste 3e11
New Hyde Park, NY 11042

516-354-1200
Fax: 516-354-1502 www.citrusandallied.com
Supplier of essential oils, oleoresins, aromatic chemicals and specialty flavor ingredients.
President/CEO/Owner: Richard Pisano Jr.
Executive Vice President: Stephen Pisano
Sales Manager: Ann Heller
Contact: Jodi Adams
  jadams@citrusandallied.com
Director Purchasing: Rob Haedrich
Number Employees: 100+
Type of Packaging: Food Service, Bulk

20599 City Box Company

4390 Liberty Street
Aurora, IL 60504-9502

773-277-5500
Fax: 773-277-9541
Corrugated cartons; also, inner packaging
Marketing/Sales: Mark Rosenhlatt
Estimated Sales: less than $500,000
Number Employees: 20
Square Footage: 178000

20600 City Canvas

750 W San Carlos St
San Jose, CA 95126-3532

408-287-2688
Fax: 408-287-1727 info@citycanvas.com
www.citycanvas.com
Commercial awnings, canopies, backyard products, custom projects and yards. Also custom fabrication and installation of the finest commercial and residential retractable styles
President: Johnny Cerrito
  cccanvas@aol.com
Estimated Sales: $1-2,500,000
Number Employees: 10-19
Number of Brands: 25

20601 City Grafx

243 Grimes Street
Suite D
Eugene, OR 97402

541-345-1101
Fax: 541-345-1942 800-258-2489
www.citygrafx.com
Manufacturer and exporter of tabletop signs, table numbers, specialty merchandising boards, custom signs, menu boards and dimensional graphics
President: Jeff Phoenix
  j.phoenix@citygrafx.com
VP: Mary Phoenix
Estimated Sales: Below $5 Million
Number Employees: 1-4
Square Footage: 16000

20602 City Neon Sign Company

3117 E Glass Ave Ste C
Spokane, WA 99217

509-483-5171
Advertising, neon, electric and plastic signs
Owner: Thomas Quigley
Estimated Sales: less than $500,000
Number Employees: 1-4

20603 City Sign Svc Inc

3914 Elm St
Dallas, TX 75226-1218

214-826-4475
Fax: 214-826-4722 css1956@aol.com
citysignservices.com
Signs including advertising, neon, painted, indoor and outdoor
President: Kenneth Waits
  css1956@aol.com
CFO: Shelly Peters
Quality Control: Kenneth Waits
Estimated Sales: $2.5 - 5 Million
Number Employees: 20-49

20604 City Signs LLC

65 Bonwood Dr
Jackson, TN 38301-7785

731-424-5551
Fax: 731-427-9096 877-248-9744
Electric, plastic and neon signs, billboards and electronic message centers
Owner: John Mc Caskill
Marketing Director: Paul Anderson
National Sales Manager: Scott Rogers
Estimated Sales: $2.5-5 Million
Number Employees: 10-19

20605 City Stamp & Seal Co

1308 W Anderson Ln # A
Austin, TX 78757-1496

512-452-2578
Fax: 512-452-2979 800-950-6074
Rubber stamps, badges, wall signs and embossing seals
Owner: Spencer Daniel
Office Manager: Sharon Smith
  orders@city-stamp.com
General Manager: Stacy Daniel

Estimated Sales: Less Than $500,000
Number Employees: 5-9
Square Footage: 8400

20606 City-Long Beach Pubc Library
101 Pacific Ave
Long Beach, CA 90822-1003

562-570-7500
Fax: 562-628-2312 sara@lbplfoundation.org
www.lbpl.org
Information
Executive Director: Sara Myers
Contact: Mario Adame
madame@lbpl.org
Number Employees: 10-19

20607 Claire Manufacturing Company
500 S Vista Ave
Addison, IL 60101

630-543-7600
Fax: 630-543-4310 800-252-4731
www.clairemfg.com
Cleaning compounds, glass cleaners, aerosols, disinfectants, polishers and insecticides
President: Tony Schwab
CFO: Roger Hayes
VP Sales/Marketing: Bob Potvin
Contact: Mark Kubiak
mkubiak@clairemfg.com
Estimated Sales: $20,000,000 - $49,999,999
Number Employees: 250-499
Square Footage: 85000
Parent Co: Oakite Products
Brands:
    Dust Up
    Fast Kill
    Fly Jinx
    Gleme
    Mister Jinx

20608 Clamco Corporation
775 Berea Industrial Parkway
Berea, OH 44017

216-267-1911
Fax: 216-267-8713 www.clamcocorp.com
Manufacturer and exporter of shrink packaging machinery and bag sealers
Owner: Serge Bergun
CEO: Mark Goldman
VP: Dennis McGrath
R&D: Rob Patton
Marketing: Dennis McGrath
Sales Director: Bruce Howell
Contact: Sandy Waite
swaite@clamcocorp.com
General Manager: Larry Boyles
Purchasing: Bob Snyder
Estimated Sales: $5-10 Million
Number Employees: 40
Square Footage: 48000
Parent Co: PAC Machinery Group
Type of Packaging: Consumer, Food Service, Private Label, Bulk

20609 Clamp Swing Pricing Co Inc
8386 Capwell Dr
Oakland, CA 94621-2114

510-567-1600
Fax: 510-567-1830 800-227-7615
cspinfo@clampswing.com www.clampswing.com
Manufacturer and exporter of pricing tags, sign holders, display hooks, hand trucks, handheld plastic shopping baskets, etc
President: Trageser Ed
ed@clampswing.com
Sales/Marketing Executive: Kamran Faizi
Purchasing Manager: Ron Coffman
Estimated Sales: $3 - 5 Million
Number Employees: 20-49
Brands:
    Celographics
    Deligraphics
    Doubletalk
    Frameworks
    Fresh Facts
    Kick-Off
    Monorail
    Spacesaver
    Vari-Extenders
    View-Lok

20610 Clanton & Company
2204 E Vista Canyon Rd
Orange, CA 92867

714-282-7980
Fax: 714-978-7103 fssearch@aol.com
Executive recruitment firm specializing in the placement of sales and management personnel within the food and disposable manufacturing industry
Owner: Diane Clanton
Estimated Sales: Less than $500,000
Number Employees: 1-4

20611 (HQ)Claridge Products & Equipment
601 US 32
Harrison, AR 72602

Fax: 870-743-1908 orders@claridgeproducts.com
www.claridgeproducts.com
Manufacturer and exporter of menu signs and boards, display cases and cabinets, easels, chalkboards, markerboards, etc.; importer of raw materials
President: Helen Clavey
CFO: Leslie Eddings
VP: Paul Clavey
Purchasing Director: John Wilson
Number Employees: 250-499
Square Footage: 300000
Other Locations:
    Claridge Products & Equipment
    Mamaroneck NY
    Claridge Products & Equipment
    Palatine IL
    South Central Claridge
    Farmers Branch TX
    Claridge Products & Equipment
    San Leandro CA
Brands:
    Claridge Cork
    Fabricork
    Lcs
    Vitracite

20612 Clark Caster Company
RR 1 Box 210A
Cave in Rock, IL 62919

708-366-1913
Fax: 708-366-5103 800-538-0765
sales@clarkcaster.com www.clarkcaster.com
Casters, wheels
President: James Clark
Estimated Sales: $2.5 - 5 Million
Number Employees: 5-9
Square Footage: 12000

20613 Clark Richardson-Biskup
1251 NW Briarcliff Pkwy # 500
Suite 500
Kansas City, MO 64116-1795

816-880-9800
Fax: 816-880-9898 www.crbusa.com
A full-service network of engineers, architects, constructors and consultants assisting food, nutrition and consumer product organizations in the planning, design, construction and operations support of facilities across the globe.
President: Doyle Clark
VP, Facility Integration: Mark Von Stwolinski
Associate/Core Team Leader: Aaron Saggars
Process Specialist: Marc Pelletier
Senior Associate: J. Lee Emel
General Manager, Midwest Region: Larry Klein
Process Engineer/Senior Associate: Bill Jarvis
Number Employees: 50-99

20614 Clark-Cooper Division Magnatrol Valve Corporation
855 Industrial Highway
Unit 4
Cinnaminson, NJ 08077

856-829-4580
Fax: 856-829-7303 techsupport@clarkcooper.com
www.clarkcooper.com
Metering pumps and valves; exporter of pumps and skid systems
Manager: Brian White
CEO: Brian Hagan
CFO: Kevin Hagan
Contact: John Bush
    johnb@clarkcooper.com
Plant Manager: John Chando

Estimated Sales: $3 - 5 Million
Number Employees: 10-19
Square Footage: 32000
Brands:
    Chemtrol

20615 Clarke American Sanders
14600 21st Ave N
Minneapolis, MN 55447-4617

336-372-8080
800-253-0367
info@clarkeus.com www.americansanders.com
Floor maintenance equipment such as floor polishers, floor sanders, carpet extractors and vacuum cleaners
CEO: Mark Hefty
CFO: Niels Olsen
R&D: Tom Benton
Marketing: Rob Godlewski
Sales: John Castaldo
Estimated Sales: $10-20 Million
Number Employees: 300
Number of Products: 150
Square Footage: 500000
Parent Co: Incentive Group
Brands:
    A.L. Cook Technology
    American Sanders Technology
    American-Lincoln Technology
    Clarke Technology
    Delco Technology
    Kew Technology
    Simpson Technology

20616 Clarkson Supply
213 Main St
Williamsport, PA 17702-7312

570-323-3631
Fax: 570-323-1899 800-326-9457
clarksonmurphy@gmail.com
www.clarksonsupply.com
Warewashing and laundry washing products; also, chemicals for hydro-therapy equipment
President: Michael I Stuempfle
mikes@clarksonchemical.com
Estimated Sales: $1-2.5 Million
Number Employees: 5-9

20617 Classic Signs Inc
13 Columbia Dr # 15
Amherst, NH 03031-2331

603-883-0384
Fax: 603-882-2962 800-734-7446
ptripp@classicsignsnh.com
www.classicsignsnh.com
Electric signs including interior, vehicle and changeable letter
President: Paul Tripp
ptripp@classicsignsnh.com
Estimated Sales: Below $5 Million
Number Employees: 5-9

20618 Classico Seating
801 N Clay St
Peru, IN 46970-1068

765-473-6691
Fax: 800-242-9787 800-968-6655
Manufacturer and exporter of metal chairs, barstools, dinettes, tables and table bases
President: Kim Regan
CFO: Hank Richardson
Estimated Sales: $20 - 50 Million
Number Employees: 100-249
Square Footage: 125000
Type of Packaging: Consumer, Food Service
Brands:
    Classico Seating

20619 Classy Basket
9275 Trade Place
San Diego, CA 92126-6318

858-274-4901
Fax: 858-274-0795 888-449-4901
info@patent.org www.classybasket.com
Novelty food gift baskets
Estimated Sales: $1 - 5 Million
Number Employees: 2

20620 Claude Neon Signs
1808 Cherry Hill Rd
Baltimore, MD 21230-3522

410-685-7575
Fax: 410-837-3154

Electric, neon and fluorescent signs, floodlights and bullet resistant protection equipment
President: Alan Nethen
Estimated Sales: $1 - 2.5 Million
Number Employees: 20-49
Square Footage: 16000

20621 Clauss Tools
60 Round Hill Road
Fairfield, CT 6824
877-412-7467
Fax: 419-332-8077 800-835-2263
orders@shopatron.com www.clausco.com
Hand tools: ergonomic food processing shears
President: Scott Sprause
Marketing Director: William Miller
Sales Director: E Ted Miller
Estimated Sales: $5-10 Million
Number Employees: 10
Type of Packaging: Bulk

20622 Clawson Container Company
4545 Clawson Tank Dr
Clarkston, MI 48346
248-625-3921
Fax: 248-625-3066 800-325-8700
Complete line of steel, composite, and rotationally and blow molded polyethylene intermediate bulk containers. Container management services include daily rental program and ReturnNet System for the Passport IBC, which picks upreconditions and recycles the container for the customer; ISO 9001:200 certified.
President: Dick Harding
VP: Robert Harding
Quality Control: Peter Ricketts
Marketing: Carol Abid
Sales: Dave McKenna
Contact: Larry Bricco
lbricco@ibcna.com
Estimated Sales: $20 - 50 Million
Number Employees: 20-49
Type of Packaging: Bulk
Brands:
Enviroclean Gold
Jumbo Bin

20623 Clawson Machine Co Inc
12 Cork Hill Rd
Franklin, NJ 07416-1304
973-827-8209
Fax: 973-827-4613 800-828-4088
eclipse@nac.net www.clawsonmachine.com
Cole slaw cutters and ice crushers and shavers for sno-cones; exporter of ice crushers, ice shavers and slaw cutters
Owner: Charles Fletcher
Customer Service: Diane Olsen
eclipse@nac.net
Estimated Sales: $10 - 20 Million
Number Employees: 20-49
Square Footage: 20000
Parent Co: Technology General Corporation
Type of Packaging: Food Service
Brands:
Hail Queen
Plus Crusher
Princess Chipper
Snow Ball Ice Shavers

20624 Clayton & Lambert Manufacturing
3813 West Highway 146
Buckner, KY 40010
502-222-1411
Fax: 502-222-1415 800-626-5819
info@claytonlambert.com
www.claytonlambert.com
Manufacturer and exporter of galvanized and stainless steel tanks for storage
President: John Lambert
Estimated Sales: $2.5-5 Million
Number Employees: 10-19
Square Footage: 700000
Brands:
Herd King
Silver Shield

20625 Clayton Corp.
866 Horan Dr
Fenton, MO 63026-2416
636-349-5333
Fax: 636-349-5335 800-729-8220
rberger@claytoncorp.com www.claytoncorp.com

Aerosol Valves, Actuators, Dispensing Systems, Covers, Barrier Packaging and assorted plastic moulded parts
President & CEO: Barry Baker
bakerb@claycorp.com
Director of Sales: Ric Berger
Number Employees: 100-249
Type of Packaging: Bulk

20626 Clayton Industries
17477 Hurley St
City of Industry, CA 91744-5106
626-435-1200
Fax: 626-435-0180 800-423-4585
sales@claytonindustries.com
www.claytonindustries.com
Manufacturer and exporter of steam generators
President: Boyd Calvin
boyd.calvin@claytonind.com
Chairman: William N
CFO: Boyd Calvin
Quality Control: Jess Alvear
Sales: Marsha Ashley
Plant Manager: Robin Pope
Purchasing Director: Maria Serna
Estimated Sales: $20-50 Million
Number Employees: 500-999

20627 Clayton L. Hagy & Son
5000 Paschall Ave
Philadelphia, PA 19143-5136
215-844-6470
Fax: 215-724-9983
Wiping cloths and cheesecloth
Owner: Andriea Bookbinder
Estimated Sales: $1 - 3 Million
Number Employees: 10 to 19
Parent Co: American By Products

20628 Clayton Manufacturing Company
7873 Catherine Street
Derby, NY 14047-9597
716-549-0392
Fax: 716-549-0392 claytonmfg@aol.com
www.claytonindustries.com
Pie crimpers and cake slicers
President: John Clayton
Vice President: Jim Oetinger
Square Footage: 70000
Type of Packaging: Food Service

20629 Clean Room Products
1800 Ocean Ave
Ronkonkoma, NY 11779-6532
631-588-7000
Fax: 631-588-7863 800-777-2532
pjcarcara@knfcorporation.com
www.knfcorporation.com
Clean rooms and equipment, controls, energy controls, piping, fittings and tubing, sanitary, processing and packaging
President: Phil Cacara
Sales Manager: Lee Gordon
General Manager: John Stuerzel
Estimated Sales: $10-20 Million
Number Employees: 50-99

20630 Clean That Pot
PO Box 5429
Whittier, CA 90607
909-674-8332
Fax: 909-674-8395 800-621-7868
service@championchemical.com
www.cleanthatpot.com
Provides effective solutions for the coffee industry's toughest cleaning challenges.
President: Andrew Ellis
VP: Dennis Hall
Estimated Sales: $1.4 Million
Number Employees: 8
Square Footage: 32000

20631 Clean Water Systems
2322 Marina Dr
PO Box 146
Klamath Falls, OR 97601-9110
541-882-9993
Fax: 541-882-9994 866-273-9993
www.cleanwatersysintl.com
Manufacturer and exporter of solid state ballasts, UV sensing, monitor and control system, ultraviolet water, and waste water treatment systems and air ozone units
President/CEO: Charles Romary

Estimated Sales: Less Than $500,000
Number Employees: 1-4
Square Footage: 6000
Parent Co: C G Romary & Son
Type of Packaging: Private Label
Brands:
Cws

20632 Clean Water Technology
151 W 135th St
Los Angeles, CA 90061-1645
310-380-4658
Fax: 310-380-4658 www.cleanwatertech.com
Wastewater treatment systems
VP: Linda Englander Mills
Manager: Joanna Parra
jparra@cleanwatertech.com
Number Employees: 10-19
Parent Co: the Marvin Group
Brands:
GEM System

20633 Clean-All Pool Svc
838 Erie Blvd W
Syracuse, NY 13204-2228
315-472-7665
Fax: 315-472-3904
Owner/President: Severino Gonnella
CEO/Finance Executive: August Gonnella
Sales Executive: August Gonnella
Manager: Severino Gonnella
Estimated Sales: Below $5 Million
Number Employees: 5-9

20634 Cleanfreak
3900 N Providence Ave
Appleton, WI 54913-8017
920-380-0777
Fax: 920-380-0878 888-722-5508
info@cleanfreak.com www.cleanfreak.com
Maufacturer and supplier of cleaning equipment and supplies
Vice President: Steve Menzner
smenzner@pti-1.com
Number Employees: 10-19
Parent Co: Packaging Tape Inc.

20635 Clear Bags
4949 Windplay Dr # 100
Suite 100
El Dorado Hills, CA 95762-9318
916-933-4700
Fax: 916-933-4717 800-233-2630
sales@clearbags.com www.clearbags.com
Accessories/supplies i.e picnic baskets, specialty food packaging i.e .gift wrap/labels/boxes/containers.
Marketing: Danielle Badeaux
Number Employees: 20-49

20636 Clear Lam Packaging
1950 Pratt Blvd
Elk Grove Village, IL 60007
847-439-8570
Fax: 847-439-8589 www.clearlam.com
Flexible and rigid packaging materials printed and laminated films for form/fill/seal and lidding.
President & CEO: R. Howard Coker
VP & CFO: Julie Albrecht
EVP: Rodger Fuller
VP & Chief Information Officer: Rick Johnson
Estimated Sales: $100-500 Million
Number Employees: 250-499

20637 Clear Products Inc.
6156 Mission Gorge Rd
Suite C
San Diego, CA 92120
619-521-0327
Fax: 619-283-3913 888-257-2532
mail@clearproductsinc.com
www.clearproductsinc.com
Manufacturing
Owner: Del Neville
Estimated Sales: $300,000-500,000
Number Employees: 1-4

20638 (HQ)Clear View Bag Co Inc of Nc
5 Burdick Dr
Albany, NY 12205-6407
518-458-7153
Fax: 518-458-1401 800-458-7153
sales_info@clearviewbag.com
www.clearviewbag.com

Plastic bags
President: William Romer
CFO: Virginia Trimarchi
Quality Control: Todd Romer
Sales Manager: Trent Romer
General Manager: William Todd Romer
Estimated Sales: $10 Million
Number Employees: 50-99
Square Footage: 128000
Type of Packaging: Consumer, Food Service, Private Label, Bulk
Other Locations:
  Clear View Bag Co.
  Thomasville NC

20639 Clear View Bag Company
7137 Prospect Church RD
Thomasville, NC 27360-8839

336-885-8131
Fax: 336-885-1044

Plastic bags
VP: Joe Romer
Manager: Daniel A Jones
Estimated Sales: $5-10 Million
Number Employees: 50-99
Parent Co: Clear View Bag Company

20640 ClearWater Tech LLC
P.O. Box 15330
San Luis Obispo, CA 93406

805-549-9724
Fax: 805-549-0306 800-262-0203
sales@cwtozone.com www.cwtozone.com

ClearWater Tech's water purification systems produce ozone-enriched water that uses few to no chemicals in order to eliminate pathogens and many other organic and inorganic contaminants, leaving no residue in the water or on theproduct.
President: Cameron Tapp
Factory Representative: Ed Knueve
Factory Representative: John Dittbemer
Contact: Richard Camp
  rcamp@cwtozone.com

20641 Clearr Corporation
6325 Sandburg Rd
Minneapolis, MN 55427-3629

763-398-5400
Fax: 763-398-0134 800-548-3269
www.clearrcorp.com

Pop displays, signage, light boxes, poster frames
President/Owner: Andy Steinfeldt
VP: Pete Nelson
Marketing: Ryan Lester
Sales: Darryl Helleman
Estimated Sales: $10 Million
Number Employees: 50-99
Number of Products: 15
Square Footage: 40000
Parent Co: Stylmark
Brands:
  Alcon Plus
  Edge Lite
  Luminate Ultra
  Moving Pix
  Pointframe
  Stretch Frame
  Tension
  Triad
  Triola

20642 Cleartec Packaging
409 Parkway Dr
Park Hills, MO 63601-4435

314-543-4150
Fax: 314-543-4054 800-817-8967
sales@cleartecpackaging.com
www.cleartecpackaging.com

Sales Manager: Michael Wester
Contact: Amanda Merritt
  amerritt@mocap.com
Estimated Sales: $1 - 5 Million

20643 Clearwater Packaging Inc
615 Grand Central St # B
Clearwater, FL 33756-3438

727-442-2596
Fax: 727-447-3587 800-299-2596
www.clearwaterpackaging.com

Manufacturer and exporter of packaging machinery
President: Jon Hoover
  sales@clearwaterpackaging.com
Estimated Sales: $5 - 10 Million
Number Employees: 20-49

20644 Clearwater Paper Corporation
Suite 1100
Spokane, WA 99201

509-344-5900
877-847-7831
www.clearwaterpaper.com

Manufacturer and exporter of paper packaging products
President/CEO: Arsen Kitch
SVP, CFO: Michael Murphy
SVP/General Counsel/Corporate Secretary: Michael Gadd
Estimated Sales: $1.87 Billion
Number Employees: 3,860
Parent Co: Bell Fibre Company
Type of Packaging: Consumer, Bulk
Brands:
  Rap-In-Wax
  Wax Tex

20645 Cleasby Manufacturing Co
1414 Bancroft Ave
PO Box 24132
San Francisco, CA 94124-3603

415-822-6565
Fax: 415-822-1843 800-253-2729
info@cleasby.com www.cleasby.com

Tar buckets, kettles, dump trailers and hoisting equipment
President: John Cleasby
  john@cleasby.com
Estimated Sales: $10-20 Million
Number Employees: 10-19

20646 Cleaver-Brooks Inc
221 Law St
Thomasville, GA 31792

229-226-3024
800-250-5583
info@cleaverbrooks.com cleaverbrooks.com

Manufacturer and exporter of packaged steam and hot water boilers; applications include food processing, packaging, sterilization, heating/ventilation/air conditioning, etc.
President & CEO: Bart Aitken
President, Boiler Systems: Earle Pfefferkorn
Chief Financial Officer: Darren Allen
Year Founded: 1929
Estimated Sales: $100-500 Million
Number Employees: 1,400

20647 Cleco Systems
1395 S Marietta Pkwy SE
Bldg 750
Marietta, GA 30067-4440

770-392-0330
Fax: 770-795-8093

President: Kenneth Matson
R&D: Percy Nay
Quality Control: Ban Sandlnato
Estimated Sales: $5 - 10 Million
Number Employees: 15

20648 Cleland Manufacturing Company
2125 Argonne Dr NE
Columbia Heights, MN 55421-1317

763-571-4606
Fax: 763-571-4606
clealandmanufacturing@tcq.net

Manufacturer and exporter of grain/seed cleaners and spiral separators
President: Robert Maxton
Quality Control: George Maxton
VP: Mary Maxton
Contact: Bob Maxton
  glen@agmercury.com
Estimated Sales: Less than $500,000
Number Employees: 2
Square Footage: 6000
Brands:
  Expert Line

20649 (HQ)Cleland Sales Corp
11051 Via El Mercado
Los Alamitos, CA 90720-2878

562-598-6616
Fax: 562-598-3858
sales@blizzardbeersystems.com
www.blizzardbeersystems.com

Manufacturer, importer and exporter of automatic refill devices, beer chillers and beverage and dry powder dispensers.

President: Arlene Cleland
Vice President: Jimmy Cleland
Sales Director: Mike Pollock
Manager: Kevin Wesley
  kevin@clelandsales.com
Estimated Sales: $1 - 3 Million
Number Employees: 5-9
Square Footage: 40000
Type of Packaging: Food Service
Other Locations:
  Cleland Sales Corp.
  Los Alamitos CA
Brands:
  Automate
  Automix
  Blizzard Beer Systems
  Choc-O-Lot
  Dove
  Starline

20650 Clements Industries Inc
50 Ruta Ct
South Hackensack, NJ 07606-1709

201-440-5500
Fax: 201-440-1455 800-222-5540
steven@tach-it.com www.tach-it.com

Tape and label dispensers, twist tie equipment and supplies
President: Alan Clements
  alan@tach-it.com
CEO: Steven Clements
CFO: Steven Clements
Vice President: Steven Clements
Research & Development: Steven Clements
VP Marketing: Steven Clements
VP Sales: Steven Clements
Operations Manager: Steven Clements
Production Manager: Alan Clements
Plant Manager: Steven Clements
Purchasing: Marilyn Ring
Number Employees: 10-19
Parent Co: Tech-It

20651 Clerestory
1740 Ridge Avenue
Suite 117
Evanston, IL 60201

312-640-5777
Fax: 312-915-5933 www.clstory.com

Tea and coffee industry cans
Founding principal and managing partner: Linda Toops
Founding principal and partner: Michelle Kerr
Contact: Asad Ali
  aali@clstory.com
Estimated Sales: Below $5 Million
Number Employees: 5-9

20652 Cleveland Canvas Goods Mfg Co
1960 E 57th St
Cleveland, OH 44103-3804

216-361-4567
Fax: 216-361-1728 sales@clevelandcanvas.com
www.clevelandcanvas.com

Insulated carrying cases and filter bags
President: Mark Howard
  m.howard@clevelandcanvas.com
Treasurer: W Morton
  m.howard@clevelandcanvas.com
VP Sales: M Howard
Estimated Sales: $2.5-5 Million
Number Employees: 20-49
Square Footage: 64000
Brands:
  The Coldholder

20653 Cleveland Menu Printing
1441 E 17th St
Cleveland, OH 44114-2012

216-241-5256
Fax: 216-241-5696 800-356-6368
web_sales@clevelandmenu.com
www.clevelandmenu.com

Manfacturer and exporter of menus and menu boards, covers, holders and displays
Owner: Thomas Ramella
  tramella@clevelandmenuprinting.com
Estimated Sales: $2.5-5 Million
Number Employees: 20-49

20654 Cleveland Metal Stamping Company
1231 W Bagley Rd #1
Berea, OH 44017-2942
440-234-0010
Fax: 440-234-8050
Manufacturer and exporter of bottle openers, burner bowls for gas ranges and metal shelf extenders; also, barbecue utensils including spatulas and forks.
Manager: Frank Ghinga
CFO: Dorina Ghinga
VP: Pascu Ghinga
Estimated Sales: $1 - 3 Million
Number Employees: 50 to 99
Number of Products: 200
Square Footage: 86000
Type of Packaging: Private Label, Bulk

20655 Cleveland Mop Manufacturing Company
5261 W 161st St
Cleveland, OH 44142-1606
216-898-5866
Fax: 216-898-5867 800-767-9934
clevelandmop@hotmail.com
Wet mop heads, mop head handles, dust and bowl mops, floor machine pads, push brooms and broom handles
Owner: David Rhodes
Estimated Sales: $5-10 Million
Number Employees: 1-4
Square Footage: 40000
Brands:
  Dumor
  Eagle
  Kleen Mor

20656 Cleveland Motion Controls
7550 Hub Pkwy
Cleveland, OH 44125
216-524-8800
Fax: 216-642-2199 800-321-8072
www.cmccontrols.com
Electronic industrial controls and systems
Managing Director: Chris Williams
Estimated Sales: $50 - 100 Million
Number Employees: 100-249
Parent Co: IMC

20657 Cleveland Plastic Films
41740 Schadden Road
Elyria, OH 44035-2294
440-324-2222
Fax: 440-324-2790 800-832-6799
Polyethylene films and printed and plain polyethylene bags for poultry, meat and pastries
CFO: Thomas Tyler
Vice President: James Hendershot
Sales Director: Frank Szabo
Plant Manager: Dan McDonald
Purchasing Manager: Paul Mirka
Estimated Sales: $5 - 10 Million
Number Employees: 100
Square Footage: 240000
Parent Co: Global Film & Packaging Corporation
Type of Packaging: Food Service, Bulk

20658 Cleveland Range
8251 Keele St
Concord, ON L4K 1Z1
CAN
www.clevelandrange.com
Manufacturer and exporter of steam cooking equipment including convection steamers, kettles, skillets, combi-ovens and cook-chill systems
Estimated Sales: $48 Million
Number Employees: 100-249
Square Footage: 150000
Parent Co: the Manitowac Company, Inc.
Type of Packaging: Food Service
Brands:
  Cleveland
  Combicraft
  Spectrum
  Steamcraft

20659 (HQ)Cleveland Specialties Co
6612 Miami Trails Dr
Loveland, OH 45140-8044
513-677-9787
Fax: 513-683-4132

Plastic closures, plastic shrink film, milk carton handles and polycoated paperboard products including folding boxes and cartons; importer of packaging products
President: Nancy Hartmann
Vice President: James Downing
Estimated Sales: Less Than $500,000
Number Employees: 1-4
Type of Packaging: Consumer, Food Service, Private Label, Bulk

20660 Cleveland Vibrator Co
2828 Clinton Ave
Cleveland, OH 44113-2998
216-241-7157
Fax: 216-241-3480 800-221-3298
cvc@clevelandvibrator.com
www.clevelandvibrator.com
Industrial vibrators including air piston, air ball, electromagnetic and rotary electric; also, air and electric brute force feeders and screeners and vibratory tables and conveyors
President: William Lee Gardner
CEO: Julia Hoverson
  julia.hoverson@gmail.com
CFO: Mike Valore
VP: Glen Roberts
CEO: Jeff Chokel
Marketing: Susan Koblyski
Sales: Jack Steinbuch
Public Relations: Suasan Kobylski
Plant Manager: Mike Weisinger
Estimated Sales: Below $5 Million
Number Employees: 20-49
Square Footage: 56000
Type of Packaging: Bulk
Brands:
  Hybrute
  Vibra-Ball
  Vibra-Might

20661 Cleveland Wire Cloth & Mfg Co
3573 E 78th St
Cleveland, OH 44105-1596
216-341-1832
Fax: 216-341-1876 800-321-3234
cleveland@wirecloth.com www.wirecloth.com
Manufacturer, importer and exporter of woven wire cloth and wire cloth products.
President: C Crone
CFO: Joe Sarasa
VP Marketing: Larry Schrader
Estimated Sales: $5 - 10 Million
Number Employees: 20-49
Square Footage: 200000

20662 Cleveland-Eastern Mixers
4 Heritage Park Rd
Clinton, CT 06413-1836
860-669-1199
Fax: 860-669-7461 800-243-1188
Manufacturer and exporter of industrial fluid mixers
President: James Donkin
Sales Director: Sean Donkin
Estimated Sales: $10 Million
Number Employees: 20-49
Number of Brands: 30
Number of Products: 2
Square Footage: 50000
Parent Co: EMI Inc Technology Group
Brands:
  Cleveland
  Eastern

20663 Clevenger Frable Lavallee
39 Westmoreland Ave # 114
White Plains, NY 10606-1970
914-997-9660
Fax: 914-997-9671 marketing@cfldesign.com
www.cfldesign.com
Consultant specializing in the design of commercial food facilities
President: Foster Frable Jr
CFO: James Lavalle
VP: James LaVallee
Contact: David Bell
  dbell@excelsior.edu
Estimated Sales: Less Than $500,000
Number Employees: 1-4
Square Footage: 8000

20664 Clextral USA
14450 Carlson Cir
Tampa, FL 33626
813-854-4434
Fax: 813-855-2269 www.clextral.com
Manufacturer and exporter of food processing machinery including twin screw extruders.
President: Jose Coelho
Sales Manager, North America: Justin Montgomery
Contact: Alice Albaret
  aalbaret@clextral.com
Pilot Plant Manager: Julie Probst
Estimated Sales: Below $5 Million
Number Employees: 10-19
Parent Co: Clextral

20665 Climate Master Inc
7300 SW 44th St
Oklahoma City, OK 73179-4307
405-745-6000
Fax: 405-745-6058 877-436-0263
cyperry@climatemaster.com
www.climatemaster.com
Manufacturer and exporter of heat pumps, air conditioners, filters and controls
President: Daniel Ellis
CEO: Dan Ellis
  dellis@climatemaster.com
Estimated Sales: $50,000,000 - $99,999,999
Number Employees: 250-499
Parent Co: LSB Corporation
Brands:
  Climate Master

20666 Climax Industries
11836 Judd Ct
Suite 320
Dallas, TX 75243
972-881-8860
Fax: 972-424-0293 800-854-5063
Estimated Sales: $1 - 3 Million
Number Employees: 5-9

20667 Climax Packaging Machinery
25 Standen Dr
Hamilton, OH 45015-2209
513-874-1664
Fax: 513-874-3375 info@climaxpackaging.com
www.climaxpackaging.com
Manufacturer and exporter of uncasing and case packing equipment, bottle conveyors, lane dividers, tray stackers and carton and flap openers
President: William George
Marketing/Sales: Jack Bunce
Manager: Nick Jody
  njody@climaxpackaging.com
Purchasing: Barb Ruthwell
Estimated Sales: $5 - 10 Million
Number Employees: 20-49
Square Footage: 40000
Parent Co: GL Industries
Brands:
  Air Cush'n
  Sof-Pac

20668 Clipco
5841 Melshire Drive
Dallas, TX 75230-2117
972-239-8028
Fax: 972-980-7552
Plastic containers

20669 Clippard Instrument LabInc
7390 Colerain Ave
Cincinnati, OH 45239-5396
513-521-4261
Fax: 513-521-4464 sales@clippard.com
www.clippard.com
President: Amy Dryer
clippardinstrumentlaboratoryinc@exhibitorinvites.com
R&D: Sid Hendry
Chairman of the Board: William L Clippard III
Estimated Sales: $20 - 50 Million
Number Employees: 100-249

20670 Clipper Belt Lacer Company
1995 Oak Industrial Dr NE
Grand Rapids, MI 49505
616-459-3196
Fax: 616-459-4976 info@flexco.com
www.flexco.com

Manufacturer and exporter of mechanical belt fastening systems for conveyors
Manager: Nancy Ayres
CFO: Lee Merys
Marketing Specialist: Beth Miller
Estimated Sales: $10-20 Million
Number Employees: 50-99
Square Footage: 304000
Parent Co: Flexco - Grand Rapids
Brands:
　Baler Belt Lacer
　Clipmark
　Clipper
　Microlacer
　Roller Lacer
　Unibar
　Valulacer

20671 Clock Associates
1629 SE 11th Ave
Portland, OR 97214-4795

503-234-0202
Fax: 503-238-0420 www.clockassociates.com
Manufactures food product machinery
Owner: Pat Clock
　pclock@clockassociates.com
Estimated Sales: Less Than $500,000
Number Employees: 1-4

20672 Clofine Dairy Products Inc
1407 New Rd
P.O. Box 335
Linwood, NJ 08221

609-653-1000
Fax: 609-653-1027 800-441-1001
info@clofinedairy.com www.clofinedairy.com
Fluid and dried dairy products; proteins, cheeses, milk replacement blends, tofu and soymilk powders, vital wheat gluten, etc.
Chairman: Larry Clofine
　lclofine@clofinedairy.com
President/CEO: Frederick Smith
CFO: Butch Harmon
Warehouse Coordinator: Pamela Gerety
Estimated Sales: $20-50 Million
Number Employees: 10-19
Number of Brands: 5
Number of Products: 100
Type of Packaging: Food Service, Private Label, Bulk
Other Locations:
　Midwest Officer
　Chicago IL
Brands:
　Fine-Mix Dairy
　Food Blends
　Soy Products
　Soyfine
　Soymilk

20673 Clorox Company
1221 Broadway
Oakland, CA 94612

510-271-7000
800-227-1860
corporate.communications@clorox.com
www.thecloroxcompany.com
Dips, dip mixes, bbq sauces, marinades, and dressings; plastic bags and wrap; disinfectants.
CEO: Linda Rendle
EVP/CFO: Kevin Jacobsen
SVP/Chief Marketing Officer: Eric Schwartz
EVP/COO: Eric Reynolds
Year Founded: 1913
Estimated Sales: $7.1 Billion
Number Employees: 9,000
Number of Brands: 49
Brands:
　Agua Jane
　Ayudin
　Blessed Herbs
　Brita
　Burt's Bees
　Champion Performance
　Chux
　Clorinda
　Clorox
　Clorox 2
　Clorox Healthcare
　Clorox Total 360
　CloroxPro
　Dispatch
　Ever Clean
　Formula 409

　Fresh Step
　Glad
　Green Works
　Handi Wipes
　Hidden Valley
　KC Masterpiece
　Kingsford
　Kitchen Bouquet
　Lestoil
　Limpido
　Liquid-Plumr
　Match Light
　Mistolin
　Mortimer
　Natural Vitality
　Neocell
　OSO
　Objective
　Pine-Sol
　PinoLuz
　Poett
　Rainbow Light
　Ready Mop
　RenewLife
　S.O.S
　Scoop Away
　Selton
　Soy Vay
　Stop Aging Now
　Tilex
　Trenet
　True Health
　Wash N Dri

20674 Closure Systems Intl Inc
7702 Woodland Dr # 200
Suite 200
Indianapolis, IN 46278-2709

317-390-5000
Fax: 317-390-5079 800-311-2740
www.csiclosures.com
Suppliers of closures for carbonated soft drinks, bottled water, juice & isotonic, milk and dairy products, alcoholic beverages, packaged foods and wine.
President: Rafael Pantigoso
　rafael.pantigoso@csiclosures.com
President: Ruth Mack
VP Finance: Robert Smith
EVP: Lawrence Purtell
Quality Manager: Praveen Mathur
VP Human Resources: Arrigo Bodda
Number Employees: 1000-4999
Square Footage: 64000
Parent Co: Rank Group Limited

20675 Cloud Inc
4855 Morabito Pl
San Luis Obispo, CA 93401-8748

805-549-8093
Fax: 805-549-0131 800-234-5650
mkemp@cloudinc.com www.cloudinc.com
Manufacturer and exporter of rotary tank cleaning machines
Owner: Brian Buell
Product and Marketing Manager: Mike Kemp
Regional Sales Manager: Lee LaFond
　brian@cloudinc.com
Division Manager: Greg Boege
Job Shop Division Mgr.: Richard Riggs
Manufacturing Mngr.: Brad Erickson
Estimated Sales: Less Than $500,000
Number Employees: 1-4
Brands:
　Cloud

20676 Cloudy & Britton
6202 214th St SW
Mountlake Ter, WA 98043-2097

425-775-7424
Fax: 425-775-1715
Refrigeration systems including industrial refrigerators, freezing tunnels and spiral and plate freezers
President: Edward Cloudy
Purchasing Agent: Gordon Derksema
Estimated Sales: $5-10 Million
Number Employees: 5-9
Brands:
　Cloudy & Britton

20677 Club Coffee
55 Carrier Drive
Toronto, ON M9W 5V9
Canada

416-675-1300
contactus@clubcoffee.ca
www.clubcoffee.com
Coffee blends.
CEO: John Morrison Pigott
President: Steve Malinowski
CFO: Sandeep Aggarwal, CPA-CGA CPA
Year Founded: 1906
Estimated Sales: $27 Million
Number Employees: 300+
Number of Brands: 4
Square Footage: 300000
Parent Co: Olam International
Type of Packaging: Consumer, Food Service, Private Label
Brands:
　Beaniac Craft Roasted Coffee
　ClubCoffee Craft Roasters
　Good Host
　Simply Sensational 100% Coffee

20678 Cluster Goods Inc
6 Martel Way
Georgetown, MA 01833-2223

978-965-3434
Fax: 978-965-3438 info@clustergoods.com
www.clustergoods.com
Offers Private Label Services and export operations for manufacturers in the US. Other services include consolidation, procurement, shipping, and logistics.
Director/Partner: Sam Haddad
Type of Packaging: Private Label
Brands:
　CEDAR'S PREMIUM BEVERAGES
　DIPPY DONUTS
　FROSTY MOUNTAIN JUICE DRINKS
　PATISSERIE CROISSANTS
　VIDA POP
　ZAGHI'S TIRAMISU

20679 Clyde Bergemann Eec
3700 Koppers St
Halethorpe, MD 21227-1019

410-712-4280
Fax: 410-368-6721
www.clydebergemannpowergroup.com
Air cleaning systems and air filters
President, Chief Executive Officer: Franz Bartels
Vice President & CFO: Graham Lees
Contact: Matt Rodgers
　mrodgers@clydebergemanneec.com
VP Finance & Chief Operating Officer: Patrick von Hagen
Estimated Sales: Less Than $500,000
Number Employees: 1-4

20680 Cma Dishmachines
12700 Knott St
Garden Grove, CA 92841-3904

714-898-8781
Fax: 71- 89- 214 800-854-6417
sales@cmadishmachines.com
Manufacturer, importer and exporter of commercial dishmachines, glasswashers and dishtables
President: David Crane
Vice President: Mike Belleville
　mike.belleville@cmadishmachines.com
Marketing Director: Matt Swift
Sales Assistant: Kimberly Feldstein
Plant Manager: Mike Belleville
Number Employees: 50-99
Square Footage: 135000
Parent Co: S.C. Johnson & Son
Brands:
　Energy Mizer

20681 Co-Rect Products Inc
7105 Medicine Lake Rd
Golden Valley, MN 55427-3675

763-542-9200
Fax: 763-542-9205 800-328-5702
customerservice@co-rectproducts.com
www.co-rectproducts.com
Bar and restaurant supplies; serving the food service market
President & CEO: Michael Pierce
Vice President: Steve Ess
Sales Manager: Bryan Mattson
Accounts Representative: Brian Mattson
Purchasing: Rose Bruhn

Estimated Sales: $10-20 Million
Number Employees: 20-49
Number of Brands: 20
Square Footage: 60000
Type of Packaging: Food Service, Private Label, Bulk

20682 Coast Controls Inc
7500 Commerce Ct
Sarasota, FL 34243-3217

941-355-7555
Fax: 941-359-2321 800-513-2345
sales@coastcontrols.com www.coastcontrols.com
Industrial process controls
President: Thomas Marks
tmarks@coastcontrols.com
Vice President: Kyle Koontz
Contact-Marketing/Sales: Rodney Shrock
Estimated Sales: Below $5 000,000
Number Employees: 10-19

20683 Coast Label Co
17406 Mount Cliffwood Cir
Fountain Valley, CA 92708-4101

714-426-1410
Fax: 714-426-1440 800-995-0483
sales@coastlabel.com www.coastlabel.com
Offset, letterpress, flexography and seal press printed labels
President: Craig Moreland
cmoreland@coastlabel.com
Chief Executive Officer: Craig Moreland
Quality Control: Dave Fox
VP Sales: Tom Miller
Estimated Sales: $1 - 2.5 Million
Number Employees: 20-49

20684 Coast Packing Co
3275 E Vernon Avenue
Vernon, CA 90058

323-277-7700
www.coastpacking.com
Quality shortening products for the restaurant, baking, and food industries. A supplier of animal fat and vegetable oil shortenings.
President: Ronald Gustafson
ronald.gustafson@coastpacking.com
CEO: Eric Gustafson
HR Manager: Washington Paredes
Director of Operations: Chavis Ferguson
Number Employees: 50-99
Type of Packaging: Consumer, Food Service
Brands:
 Bake Lite All Soy
 Bake Lite Soy/Cotton
 Coast Refined Lard
 Flavor King Blue
 Flavor King Red
 Gold Coast
 Golden Bake
 Supreme
 VIVA Manteca Mixta
 Viva Lard
 Viva Retail Lard

20685 Coast Paper Box Company
205 S Frank Bland Drive
San Bernardino, CA 92408

909-382-3475
Fax: 909-382-3481
Folding paper boxes
Number Employees: 50-99

20686 Coast Scientific
P.O. Box 185
Rancho Santa Fe, CA 92067

Fax: 800-791-8999 800-445-1544
www.medcosupplies.com
Manufacturer and exporter of adhesive mats, aprons, polyethylene bags, bouffant caps, carts, shelving, latex and vinyl gloves, convection ovens and disposable wipers
Manager: Alex Sardarian
Director Operations: Stacy Camp
Estimated Sales: $2.5-5 Million
Number Employees: 10-19

20687 Coast Signs & Graphics
520 Cypress Ave
Hermosa Beach, CA 90254

310-379-9921
Fax: 310-372-2160

Banners and signs of all types; also, screen printing, graphi design, digital, large and small format available
President: Bill Febbo
Owner: William Febbo
Marketing Director: Linda Hopkins
Art Director: Wayne Morris
Estimated Sales: Less than $500,000
Number Employees: 1-4
Square Footage: 6

20688 Coastal Canvas Products
73 Ross Rd
P.O. Box 22834
Savannah, GA 31405-1660

912-236-2416
Fax: 912-232-7884 800-476-5174
sales@coastalcanvas.net
Commercial canvas awnings, roll curtains, storon protection machinery covers, sunscreens, and strip curtians
Owner: Ellen Barber
ebarber@coastalcanvas.net
CFO: Marlene Wood
Vice President: Duane Wood
Estimated Sales: $2.5-5,000,000
Number Employees: 20-49

20689 Coastal Mechanical Svc Inc
33 Parker Ave
Stamford, CT 06906-1713

203-359-3070
Fax: 203-995-9129 www.coastalmechanical.com
Consultant specializing in design of HVAC and refrigeration systems; also, engineering and installation services available
President: David Besterfield
Estimated Sales: $1-2,500,000
Number Employees: 5-9

20690 Coastal Pallet Corp
135 E Washington Ave
Bridgeport, CT 06604-3607

203-333-6222
Fax: 203-333-1892 www.coastalpallet.com
Wooden pallets and boxes
President: Peter G. Standish
coastalpallet@msn.com
Estimated Sales: $1-2.5 Million
Number Employees: 20-49

20691 Coastal Products Company
PO Box 208
Westbrook, ME 04098-0208

207-854-5616
Fax: 207-854-2118
Chemicals
President: Herb Pressman

20692 Coastline Equipment Inc
2235 E Bakerview Rd
Bellingham, WA 98226-7153

360-734-8509
Fax: 360-734-9321 www.coastline-equipment.com
Designer and manufacturer of processing and handling equipment. A complete package from design to fabrication and start-up. Family owned for 30 years
President: Kurt Lunde
admin@coasteq.com
Sales Manager: Brian Claudon
Estimated Sales: $5 - 10 Million
Number Employees: 20-49
Square Footage: 128000

20693 Coating Technologies International
805 Birch Street
Algonquin, IL 60102-2213

847-854-9620
Fax: 847-854-9621 mrgintl@aol.com
Lolipop processing equipment, pans and pan lids

20694 Coats American Industrial
745 Gotham Pkwy
Carlstadt, NJ 07072-2413

201-935-0200
Fax: 201-804-9392
Tea and coffee industry packaging
Estimated Sales: $3 - 5 000,000
Number Employees: 5-9

20695 Coats North America
3430 Toringdon Way # 301
Charlotte, NC 28277-2576

704-329-5800
Fax: 704-329-5820 800-631-0965
www.coats.com
Thread
CFO: Donna Armstrong
CEO: Max Perks
 max.perks@coats.com
CEO: Max Perks
CEO: Max Perks
Estimated Sales: $5 - 10 Million
Number Employees: 5000-9999

20696 Cobatco
1327 NE Adams St
Peoria, IL 61603

309-676-2663
Fax: 309-676-2667 800-426-2282
info@cobatco.com www.cobatco.com
Manufacturer and exporter of specialty baking equipment for waffles, waffle cones, doughnuts, edible shells, etc.; also, mixes including vanilla and chocolate waffle cone, regular and multigrain waffle and vanilla and chocolatedoughnut
President: Donald Stephens
Contact: Brett Crosthwaite
 bcrosthwaite@cobatco.com
Estimated Sales: $2.5-5 Million
Number Employees: 10-19
Square Footage: 240000
Type of Packaging: Food Service
Brands:
 Cobatco
 Cobatco Olde Time

20697 Cobb & Zimmer
7900 Mack Avenue
Detroit, MI 48214-1766

313-923-0350
Fax: 313-923-1916
Bar fixtures, laminated counter and table tops and tables including wood and steel
Estimated Sales: $1 - 5 Million
Number Employees: 1
Square Footage: 30000

20698 Cobb Sign Co Inc
528 Elmira St
Burlington, NC 27217-1328

336-227-0181
Fax: 336-227-0206
Neon and plastic signs
President: Jody Speagle
 jodys@cobbsignco.com
President: Kenneth Speagle
Manager: Jody Speagle
Estimated Sales: $1-2.5 Million
Number Employees: 5-9

20699 Cober Electronics, Inc.
151 Woodward Ave
Norwalk, CT 06854-4721

203-855-8755
Fax: 203-855-7511 800-709-5948
sales@cober.com www.cober.com
Manufacturer and exporter of batch and continuous conveyorized microwave ovens for the food scientist and production floor; also, laboratory and pilot plant services, process development and engineering design
CEO: Bernard Krieger
 bern@cober.com
President: Martin Yonnone
VP Engineering: Martin Yonnone
Estimated Sales: $30-50 Million
Number Employees: 20-49
Square Footage: 39000

20700 Cobitco Inc
5301 Bannock St
Denver, CO 80216-1623

303-296-8575
Fax: 303-297-3029 info@cobitco.com
www.cobitco.com
Cobitco is a private label and branded chemical solutions provider with 20+ years experience and over 10,000 product formulations. Markets include jan-san, automotive, industrial, bulk, health care and marine.

President: Lee E Morgan
 lee.morgan@cobitco.com
Marketing Director: Ray Harter
Sales Director: Greg Dauer
Number Employees: 10-19
Number of Brands: 10
Number of Products: 1200
Square Footage: 200000
Type of Packaging: Food Service, Private Label,
 Bulk
Brands:
 Car Chem
 Cobit+Care
 Enviro~Chem
 Enviro~Chem Gold
 Norseman
 Pressure Patch
 Pro-Magic
 Tidal Marine

20701 Coblentz Brothers Inc
7101 S Kohler Rd
Apple Creek, OH 44606-9613

330-857-7211
 Fax: 330-857-4966 www.coblentzbros.com
Wooden pallets
President: Wayne Liechty
 wayne@coblentzbros.com
Business Manager: Don Yoder
Vice President: Jonas Coblentz
Estimated Sales: $2.5-5 Million
Number Employees: 20-49
Square Footage: 40000

20702 (HQ)Coburn Company
P.O. Box 147
Whitewater, WI 53190-0147

262-473-2822
 Fax: 262-473-3522 800-776-7042
 www.coburn.com
Manufacturer and exporter of dairy equipment in-
cluding milking and sanitation
President: Jim Coburn
Finance: Jason Alexander
Marketing: Ginny Coburn
Sales: Joe Coburn
Operations: Thayer Coburn
Export Manager: Jack Kolo
Purchasing: Jim Coburn
Estimated Sales: $5-10 Million
Number Employees: 20-49
Type of Packaging: Bulk

20703 (HQ)Coca-Cola Europacific Partners
Pemberton House
Bakers Road
Uxbridge, Middx, UB8 1EZ
UK

800-418-4223
 Connect@ccep.com www.cocacolaep.com
Coca-Cola brand products.
CEO: Damian Gammell
CFO: Nik Jhangiani
General Counsel/Company Secretary: Clare Wardle
Estimated Sales: $10.9 Billion
Number Employees: 33,200
Number of Brands: 41
Type of Packaging: Consumer, Food Service, Bulk
Brands:
 Adez
 Apollinaris
 Appletiser
 Aquarius
 BonAqua
 Burn Energy Drink
 Capri-Sun
 Chaqwa
 Chaudfontaine
 Coca-Cola
 Coca-Cola Energy
 Coca-Cola Signature Mixers
 Coca-Cola Zero Sugar
 Costa Coffee
 Diet Coke
 Fanta
 Finley
 Fuze Tea
 Glacéau Smartwater
 Honest
 Krystal
 Kuli
 Lift Apfel Schorle
 Mer

Mezzo Mix
Minute Maid
Monster Energy
Nalu Fruity Energizer
Nestea
Nordic Mist
Oasis
Powerade
Reign Total Body Fuel
Relentless Energy
Royal Bliss
Schuss
Schweppes
Schwepps
Seagram's
Sprite
Sprite
TAB X-tra
Toscal
Tropico
Urge
Urge
ViO
ViO BiO LiMO
Vilas del Turbon
Vio Schorle
Viva

20704 Coconut Code
4490 N Federal Hwy
Lighthouse Point, FL 33064

954-786-0252
 Fax: 954-481-9360
Software for financial reporting, inventory control,
product/menu analysis, time and attendance for food
service operations
Chairman of Board: Jack Abdo
CEO/President: Mark Wotell
President: Mark Woterl
VP/R&D: E Wotell
Estimated Sales: $5 - 10 Million
Number Employees: 50-99
Square Footage: 14000
Brands:
 Coconut Code
 Food Service Management Systems
 Remotecontroller
 Timeware

20705 Coddington Lumber Co
19501 Shaft Rd SW
Frostburg, MD 21532-3723

301-689-8816
 Fax: 301-689-1629

Pallets
President: Carl Mazer
 pallets@allcolink.com
Estimated Sales: $2.5 - 5 Million
Number Employees: 5-9

20706 Codeck Manufacturing
PO Box 2940
Sausalito, CA 94966-2940

415-331-9509
 Fax: 415-331-9469 800-878-5663
Manufactures coding equipment for various indus-
tries
Estimated Sales: $500,000-$1 000,000
Number Employees: 4

20707 Codema
11790 Troy Ln N
Maple Grove, MN 55369

763-428-2266
 Fax: 763-428-4411 info@codemallc.com
Manufacturer, importer and exporter of processing
equipment; packaging systems. Also have recondi-
tioned and used equipment.
President: Heinz Baecker
 h.baecker@codemallc.com
VP: Steve Parker
VP sales: Larry Yarger
VP Engineering: Rick Gilles
Estimated Sales: $1-2.5 Million
Number Employees: 5-9
Square Footage: 70000

20708 Coding Products
111 W Park Dr
Kalkaska, MI 49646-8794

231-258-5521
 Fax: 231-258-6120 800-748-0525
 www.codingproducts.com

Hot stamp ribbons, thermal transfer ribbons, inks
and hot ink rollers for packaging applications
Sales Executive: Rob Fickling
Plant Manager: Ron Maxey
Estimated Sales: $50-100 Million
Number Employees: 50-99
Parent Co: Illinois Tool Works

20709 Cody Consulting Services
509 Whitney
Cedar Hill, TX 75104

972-291-7268
Customized quality and food safety program devel-
opment. Food safety audits, audit preparation.
President: Deborah Cody
Number of Products: 4

20710 Coe & Dru Inc
589 W Terrace Dr
San Dimas, CA 91773-2915

909-599-5500
 Fax: 909-599-2005 800-722-7538
 inquiry@coedru.com www.coedru.com
Supplies baskets to those who make gift baskets.
President: Frank Chu
 fchu@coedru.com
Sales Manager: Steve Wemane
Human Resources Manager: Lena Chu
Production Manager: Kwok Lai
Purchasing Manager: Kwonk Wong
Estimated Sales: $1.6 Million
Number Employees: 10-19

20711 Coextruded Packaging Technologies
3706 Enterprise Drive
Janesville, WI 53546

608-314-2020
 Fax: 608-314-2021 info@cptplastics.com
 www.cptplastics.com
Barrier foamed polypropylene trays
President: Linda Bracha
Contact: Katrina Bennett
 katrina@cptgroup.com
Estimated Sales: $5-10 Million
Number Employees: 20-49

20712 Coffee Brothers Inc
1204 Via Roma
Colton, CA 92324-3909

909-370-1100
 Fax: 909-370-1101 888-443-5282
 info@coffeebrothers.com
 www.coffeebrothers.com
Coffee and espresso; importer and wholesaler/dis-
tributor of espresso machines
Owner: Cal Amodemo
 cal@coffeebrothers.com
General Manager: Max Amodeo
Estimated Sales: $2.5-5 Million
Number Employees: 1-4
Square Footage: 44000
Type of Packaging: Private Label, Bulk
Brands:
 Coffee Brothers
 Il Caffe
 Sigma

20713 Coffee Enterprises
32 Lakeside Ave
Burlington, VT 05401-5242

802-865-4480
 Fax: 802-865-3364 800-375-3398
 www.coffeeenterprises.com
Coffee extracts and chilled coffee-based beverage
concentrates; laboratory specializing in the testing
and analyzing services for coffee; consultant special-
izing in the marketing and promotion of coffee
Owner/President: Daniel C Cox
 dancox@coffee-ent.com
Administrative Assistant: Christine Hibma
Office Manager: Judy Mammorella
Estimated Sales: $1 - 3 Million
Number Employees: 10-19
Square Footage: 14000
Type of Packaging: Bulk

20714 Coffee Express RoastingCo
47722 Clipper St
Plymouth, MI 48170-2437

734-459-4900
 Fax: 734-459-5511 800-466-9000
 info@coffeeexpressco.com
 www.coffeeexpressco.com

Wholesaler roaster of specialty coffees; distributors
of associated products.
President: Tom Isaia
Office Manager: Joyce Novak
Contact: Genevieve Boss
 g.boss@coffeeexpressco.com
Production: Scott Novak
Estimated Sales: Less Than $500,000
Number Employees: 1-4
Number of Brands: 8
Number of Products: 20
Square Footage: 32000
Type of Packaging: Consumer, Food Service, Pri-
vate Label, Bulk
Brands:
 Coffee Express
 Mountain Country

20715 Coffee PER
111 Freeport Circle
Fallon, NV 89406-2823
775-423-8857
Fax: 775-423-8859 866-957-9233
coffee@phonewave.net www.coffeeper.com
Roasting machines
President: Sherman Dodd
CFO: Phyliss Dodd
Estimated Sales: $1-5 Million
Number Employees: 5-9

20716 Coffee Processing Systems
3666 Swenson Ave
St. Charles, IL 60174-3442
630-443-0034
Fax: 630-443-0049
Automatic controls, bin silo systems and storage,
conveying equipment, elevators, machiners and
buckets
Estimated Sales: Less than $500,000
Number Employees: 4

20717 Coffee Sock Company
PO Box 10023
Eugene, OR 97440-2023
541-344-7698
Fax: 541-344-7672
jason@coffeesockcompany.com
www.coffeesockcompany.com
Reusable cloth coffee filters and household storage
products
Director Sales/Marketing: Robert Thomas
Estimated Sales: $5-10 Million
Number Employees: 5-9

20718 Coffee-Inns of America
3617 E La Salle St
Phoenix, AZ 85040
602-438-8286
Fax: 602-437-2270 800-528-0552
www.coffeeinns.com
Brewers
Owner: John Bergmann
 john.bergmann@2mfg.com
Estimated Sales: $10-20 000,000
Number Employees: 100-249

20719 Cog-Veyor Systems, Inc.
371 Hanlan Road
Woodbridge, Ontario, ON L4L 3T1
Canada
416-798-7333
Fax: 416-743-7196 888-337-2358
frubino@ontariobelting.com www.cog-veyor.com
Conveyor's designed for use in the food processing,
canning and bottling industries.
Production Manager: Brian Kilbride

20720 Cognitive
4403 Table Mountain Dr Ste A
Golden, CO 80403
303-273-1400
Fax: 303-273-1414 800-765-6600
sales@cognitive.com www.cogsol.com
Labelers, label printing equipment and printing sys-
tems
VP: Arthu Kennedy
Marketing Manager: Vic Barezyk
Estimated Sales: $20-50 Million
Number Employees: 100-249
Parent Co: Axiohm Transaction Solutions

20721 Colbert Packaging Corp
28355 N Bradley Rd
Lake Forest, IL 60045-1173
847-367-5990
Fax: 847-367-4403 847-367-5990
www.colbertpkg.com
Rigid paper heart-shaped candy boxes.
President: Jim Hamilton
 jhamilton@colbertpkg.com
Chairman: Nancy Colbert MacDougall
Sales Manager: Dave Sult
Sales Representative: Michael Baker
General Manager: Tim Price
Estimated Sales: $10 - 20 Million
Number Employees: 100-249
Square Footage: 230000
Type of Packaging: Consumer

20722 Colbert Packaging Corp
28355 N Bradley Rd
Lake Forest, IL 60045-1173
847-367-5990
Fax: 847-367-4403 jhamilton@colbertpkg.com
www.colbertpkg.com
Rigid paper heart-shaped candy boxes
President: Jim Hamilton
 jhamilton@colbertpkg.com
Sales Manager: Dave Sult
General Manager: Tim Price
Estimated Sales: $32 Million
Number Employees: 100-249
Square Footage: 115000
Parent Co: Colbert Packaging Corporation

20723 Colbert Packaging Corp
28355 N Bradley Rd
Lake Forest, IL 60045-1173
847-367-5990
Fax: 847-367-4403 www.colbertpkg.com
Rigid paper heart-shaped candy boxes
President: Jim Hamilton
 jhamilton@colbertpkg.com
Sales Manager: Dave Sult
General Manager: Tim Price
Estimated Sales: $20 - 50 Million
Number Employees: 100-249
Square Footage: 115000
Parent Co: Colbert Packaging Corporation

20724 Colborne Foodbotics
28495 N Ballard Dr
Lake Forest, IL 60045-4510
847-724-5070
Fax: 847-724-5081 jenny@questequipment.co.uk
www.colbornefoodbotics.com
Cutting systems ideal for cutting sticky, fragile and
difficult to cut products and bakery industry turn-
over systems
President: Richard Hoskins
Quality Control: Don Guther
Manager: Brenda Anderson
 brendaa@colbornefoodbotics.com
Estimated Sales: $5 - 10 Million
Number Employees: 100-249

20725 Cold Chain Technologies
29 Everett St
Holliston, MA 1746
508-429-1395
Fax: 508-429-9056 800-370-8566
info@coldchaintech.com www.coldchaintech.com
Manufacturer and exporter of insulated shipping
containers and refrigerant packs for perishable food
shipments
President: Larry Gordon
VP, General Manager: Bob Bohne
R&D Manager: Richard Formato
VP Sales/Marketing: TJ Rizzo
Contact: Paul Anderson
 panderson@coldchaintech.com
Number Employees: 100-249
Square Footage: 80000
Type of Packaging: Food Service, Private Label,
Bulk
Brands:
 Fdc
 Koolit

20726 Cold Jet, LLC
455 Wards Corner
Loveland, OH 45140
513-831-3211
Fax: 513-831-1209 800-337-9423
service@coldjet.com www.coldjet.com

Manufacturer and exporter of dry ice cleaning solu-
tions and dry ice production equipment.
President & CEO: Gene Cooke III
Vice President of Global Marketing: Christian
Rogiers
Sr. Vice President of Sales: Brian Allen
Human Resources Manager: Jennifer Ellspermann
Chief Operating Officer: Scott Gatje
Estimated Sales: $1-2.5 Million
Number Employees: 1-4

20727 Cold Storage Building Products
510 Turtle Cove Boulevard
Suite 100
Rockwall, TX 75087-5374
972-771-7824
Fax: 972-771-7822 888-544-4225
Estimated Sales: $3 - 5 Million
Number Employees: 1-4

20728 ColdZone
8101 E Kaiser Blvd Ste 110
Anaheim, CA 92808-2661
Fax: 714-529-8503
Manufacturer and exporter of refrigeration equip-
ment including remote racks and fluid coolers
President: Jim Grob
VP: Ken Falk
National Sales Manager: R Echols
Contact: Sherry Rister
 sherry.rister@htpgusa.com
Product Manager: R Dotson
Estimated Sales: $20 - 50 Million
Number Employees: 100-249
Square Footage: 260000
Parent Co: Ardco
Type of Packaging: Food Service
Brands:
 C/Z
 Cold Saver
 Enviro-Cool
 Enviro-Therm
 Fc-Pack
 Mini-Pak
 Parallel-Pak
 Uni-Pak

20729 Colder Products Co
1001 Westgate Dr
St Paul, MN 55114-1092
651-645-0091
Fax: 651-645-6938 800-444-2474
brad.ferstan@colder.com www.cpcworldwide.com
Industrial connectors
President: Gary Rychley
 gary.rychley@colder.com
Number Employees: 250-499

20730 Coldmatic Building Systems
8500 Keele Street
Concord, ON L4K 2A6
Canada
905-326-7600
Fax: 905-326-7600 800-668-4165
markgalea@rogers.com www.coldmatic.com
President: MARK GALEA
Sales Manager: DEREK FRANCIS
Estimated Sales: $1 - 5 Million

20731 Coldmatic Refrigeration
8500 Keel Street
Concord, ON L4K 2A6
Canada
905-326-7600
Fax: 905-326-7601 mark@summitproducts.com
www.coldmatic.com
Manufacturer and exporter of automatic and manual
doors including cold storage, double acting, plastic
and refrigerator
President: Mark Galea
CFO: Stafford Mass
VP: Rex Palmatier
Marketing Director: Dan Gregero
Sales Manager- Ontario & Eastern Canada: Mike
Robbie
Plant Manager: Derrick Lee
Estimated Sales: $1 - 3 Million
Number Employees: 5-9
Parent Co: Coldmatic Refrigeration

20732 Coldstream Products Corporation
10 McCool Crescent
P.O. Box 878
Crossfield, AB T0M 0S0
Canada
403-946-4097
Fax: 403-946-0148 888-946-4097
Manufacturer and exporter of coolers, freezers and display cases
President: George Zafir
VP: Trevor Rees
VP Marketing: Trevor Rees
Director of Sales: Ken Savard
Operations: Rick Lewis
Purchasing: Les Lewis
Number Employees: 100-249
Number of Brands: s
Number of Products: 75
Square Footage: 1000000
Parent Co: Coldmatic Group of Companies
Brands:
   Cold Tech
   Coldstream

20733 Cole-Parmer Instrument Co LLC
625 Bunker Ct
Vernon Hills, IL 60061-1844
847-549-7600
Fax: 847-247-2929 800-323-4340
info@coleparmer.com www.coleparmer.com
Centrifuges, meters, flow, piping, fittings and tubing, nonsanitary, sanitary
President: Andy Greenawalt
CEO: Bernd Brust
   bbrust@coleparmer.com
Quality Control: Robert Czapla
Estimated Sales: $20 - 50 Million
Number Employees: 250-499

20734 Colecraft Commercial Furnishings
1021 Allen Street
Jamestown, NY 14701
716-488-2810
Fax: 716-488-2824 800-622-2777
www.colecraftcf.com
Plastic laminated food service tables
Manager: Dave Messinger
CEO: Robert Benzel
Vice President: Peter Cardinale
Contact: Martin Buescher
   mbuescher@colecraftcf.com
Plant Manager: Neil Hergott
Purchasing Manager: Pat Cleary
Estimated Sales: $8 Million
Number Employees: 50-99
Square Footage: 400000
Parent Co: TR Manufacturing

20735 Coleman Manufacturing Co Inc
48 Waters Ave
Everett, MA 02149-2099
617-389-0380
Fax: 617-389-0769 www.coleman.com/home
Manufacturer and exporter of hand cleaners
President: Richard Coleman
   dickcoleman@coleman.com
Estimated Sales: $1 - 2.5 Million
Number Employees: 5-9
Square Footage: 40000

20736 Coleman Resources
PO Box 8129
Greensboro, NC 27419-0129
336-852-4006
Fax: 336-854-8469
Business printed materials
Manager: Tom Byerly
Estimated Sales: Below $5 Million
Number Employees: 20-49

20737 Coleman Rubber Stamps
171 Madison Ave
Daytona Beach, FL 32114-2177
386-252-8597
Fax: 386-257-5301
Rubber stamps, signs, seals, etc
President: Carole C Ford
VP: Carole Ford
Estimated Sales: $5 - 10 Million
Number Employees: 5-9

20738 Coley Industries
11885 Granger Road
Wayland, NY 14572-9745
716-728-2390
Woodenware, wooden and gourmet salad bowls, pepper grinders, salt and pepper shakers and mounted/unmounted time and hour glasses
President: John Coley

20739 Colgate-Palmolive Professional Products Group
895 Don Mills Rd
North York, ON M3C 1W3
Canada
800-468-6502
Manufacturer and exporter of cleaning supplies
CEO: Noel Wallace
Estimated Sales: $100-500 Million
Number Employees: 1,000-4,999
Type of Packaging: Food Service
Brands:
   Ajax
   Colgate
   Fabuloso
   Irish Spring
   Murphy Oil Soap
   Palmolive
   Softsoap

20740 Collectors Gallery
2601 E Main St
St Charles, IL 60174-4289
630-584-5235
Fax: 630-584-1224 800-346-3063
www.studiostyle.com
Extensive line of decorative boxes, bags and wraps
Executive Director: Kevin Hughes
   kevinh@studiostyle.com
Project Manager: Sandy Peterman
Number Employees: 100-249

20741 Collegeville Flag & Manufacturing Company
24 W 4th Avenue
Collegeville, PA 19426-2601
610-489-4131
Fax: 610-489-4164 800-523-5630
in store displays, flags and banners including U.S., custom logo, advertising, etc.; also, poles and accessories
Chairman: Richard Doyle
Account Executive: Jennifer Engle
Estimated Sales: $10-20 Million
Number Employees: 50-99
Parent Co: Collegeville Flag & Banner

20742 Colliers International
3439 Brookside Rd # 108
Suite 108
Stockton, CA 95219-1754
209-475-5100
Fax: 209-475-5102 www.colliers.com
Partner: Michael Goldstein
Senior Vice President: Lisa Hodgson
   lhodgson@colliersparrish.com
Vice President: Adam Lucatello
Operations Manager: Maria Marquez
Estimated Sales: Below $500,000
Number Employees: 10-19

20743 Collins & Aikman
1212 7th St SW
Canton, OH 44707
330-253-3826
Fax: 330-456-0849 800-321-0244
Manufacturer and exporter of rubber and vinyl matting
Quality Control: Chris Carpenter
CEO: Mike Geaghan
Contact: Michelle Petruska
   michellepetruska@devry.edu
VP Merchandising: Scot Landeis
Production Manager: Gary Taylor
Plant Manager: Todd Weber
Estimated Sales: $.5 - 1 million
Number Employees: 20-49
Type of Packaging: Food Service
Brands:
   Aqua Trap
   Cushion Ease

20744 Collins Manufacturing Company Ltd
9835 199 A Street
Langley, BC V1M 2X7
Canada
604-888-2812
Fax: 604-888-7689 800-663-6761
www.collinsmfg.com
Refrigerated and dry freight van-bodies and flat-decks ditributor of Maxon liftgates, Parco-Hesse beverage bodies and Utilimaster walk-in bodies
President: Michael Sondergaard
Finance: Bobbie Hiscock
Director, Sales & Marketing: Guy Perrault
Account Manager: Brent Wilson
Plant Manager: Jerry Brownlee
Number Employees: 50-99
Brands:
   Collins
   Maxon
   Parco-Hesse
   Utilimaster

20745 Collins Technical
8330 Route a i a S
St Augustine, FL 32086
904-461-4546
Fax: 904-461-4539
Moulding equipment
Sales Manager: Jack Collins
Estimated Sales: $1 - 5 000,000
Number Employees: 6

20746 Colmac Coil Mfg Inc
370 N Lincoln St
Colville, WA 99114-2342
509-684-2595
Fax: 509-684-8331 800-845-6778
mail@colmaccoil.com www.colmaccoil.com
Owner: Scott Mc Millan
   scott.mcmillan@colmac.ind.com
Sales Manager: Jeremy Olberding
   scott.mcmillan@colmac.ind.com
Estimated Sales: $20 - 50 Million
Number Employees: 100-249
Square Footage: 225000

20747 Colmar Storage Co Warehouse
6695 NW 36th Ave
Miami, FL 33147-7519
305-696-1614
Fax: 305-836-5800
Storage of coffee (green coffee), samplers and weighers
manager: Robert Olmedo
   rolmedo@colmarstoragellc.com
Manager: Robert Olmedo
Estimated Sales: $2.5-5 000,000
Number Employees: 10-19
Type of Packaging: Private Label

20748 Colonial Marketing Assoc
400 Broadway
Freehold, NJ 07728-1494
732-462-2100
Fax: 732-431-3419
Marketing consultant for the egg industry
Owner: Abe Opatut
Partner: Henry Opatut
   henry.opatut@nextfinancial.com
Number Employees: 5-9

20749 Colonial Paper Company
P.O. Box 310
Silver Springs, FL 34489-0310
352-622-4171
Fax: 352-422-7247 cpcweb@aol.com
Paper goods, disposable tabletop items and janitorial, dishwashing and warewashing equipment and supplies
President: William H Tuck Sr
Estimated Sales: $10-20 Million
Number Employees: 20-49

20750 Colonial Transparent Products Company
870 S Oyster Bay Road
mail.com
Hicksville, NY 11801-3576
516-822-4430
Fax: 516-822-4292
Plastic films, sleeve labels and polyethylene bags; also, design, printing and converting available

President: L Goldstein
VP: E Goldstein
Office Manager: C Bland
Estimated Sales: $5-10 Million
Number Employees: 20-49
Square Footage: 50000

20751 Colony Brands Inc
1112 7th Ave
Monroe, WI 53566-1364

608-328-8400
Fax: 608-328-8457 800-544-9036
www.colonybrands.com
Cakes, tortes & pies; cookies & bars; pastries; petits fours; candy & chocolate; boxed assortments of all kinds; cheeses; sausage, ham and other meats; nuts & pre-mixed snacks; home furniture; home d,cor; electronics; jewelry; fitnessequipment; unisex apparel; small appliances
CEO: John Baumann
Chairman: Pat Kubly
VP/CIO: Steve Cretney
Content Marketing Manager: Matt Stetler
Director of Strategic Planning: Ryan Kubly
Number Employees: 1000-4999
Square Footage: 13236
Parent Co: Colony Brands, Inc.
Brands:
   Swiss Colony Foods

20752 Color Ad Tech Signs
6500 S Washington St
Amarillo, TX 79118-7817

806-374-8117
Advertising signs
Owner: Truet Cargill
Estimated Sales: $1 - 3 Million
Number Employees: 5-9
Square Footage: 15000

20753 Color Box
623 S G St
Richmond, IN 47374

765-966-7588
Fax: 765-962-5584 www.gp.com
Manufacturer and exporter of paper boxes and cartons
Manager: Jeff Pobanz
VP Sales: Frank Mazzei
Contact: Michael Adams
   madams@cskcorp.com
VP Manufacturing: Mike Roark
Estimated Sales: $20-50 Million
Number Employees: 250-499
Parent Co: Georgia Pacific
Type of Packaging: Consumer, Bulk

20754 Color Carton Corp
341 Canal Pl
Bronx, NY 10451-6091

718-665-0840
Fax: 718-993-1776
customerservice@colorcarton.com
www.colorcarton.com
Folding paper boxes
President: Debbie Loprinzi
   dloprinzi@colorcarton.com
VP: Nicholas LoPrinzi
Treasurer: Vincent LoPrinzi
Estimated Sales: $5-10 Million
Number Employees: 20-49

20755 Color Communications Inc
4000 W Fillmore St
Chicago, IL 60624-3916

773-638-1400
Fax: 773-638-0887 www.ccicolor.com
Creates visual quality colors control standards and color tolerance to communicate your product
President: Steve Winter
   hpham@ccicolor.com
VP: Steven Winter
General Manager: Harry Lerner
Marketing Director: Jill Goldstein
Estimated Sales: $50 - 100 Million
Number Employees: 250-499
Type of Packaging: Bulk

20756 Color-Box Inc
1275 S Granada Dr
Madera, CA 93637-4803

559-674-1049
Fax: 559-674-1050
Wine industry bag, box and carton packaging

Manager: Tim McCoy
VP: Barbara Fox
Manager: Brad Alling
   bpalling@gapac.com
Number Employees: 50-99

20757 Colorado Mills
P.O. Box 1155
Lamar, CO 81052

719-335-8452
www.comills.com
Sunflower oil.
CEO: Richard Robbins
Year Founded: 1999
Estimated Sales: $14.8 Million

20758 Colorado Nut Co
2 Kalamath St
Denver, CO 80223-1550

303-733-7311
800-876-1625
sales@coloradonutco.com
www.coloradonutco.com
Manufactures and Imports candies, chocolates, unique trail mixes, snack mixes, dried fruits and gift baskets for any occasion. Also roast nuts on site. Also offer products with private labeling and customized logos for a variety ofspecialized events.
Owner: Mark Goodman
   mgoodman@coloradonutco.com
Owner: Roger Renaud
Estimated Sales: Less Than $500,000
Number Employees: 5-9
Type of Packaging: Consumer, Private Label

20759 Colorcon Inc
275 Ruth Rd
Harleysville, PA 19438-1952

215-256-7700
Fax: 215-661-2626 www.colorcon.com
Custom dispersed colorant systems, natural colorants, pearlescent color systems, barrier coatings, glazes, FD&C certified pigments, color blends and monogramming and nontoxic printing inks for food packaging applications; exporter offood colorants, coatings, inks, etc.
CEO: William Motzer
   wmotzer@colorcon.com
Senior Business Manager - Naturals/Food: Lou Palermo
Business Manager - Food/Confectionary: John Jaworski
Estimated Sales: $50-100 Million
Number Employees: 250-499
Parent Co: Berwind Pharmaceutical Services
Type of Packaging: Bulk
Other Locations:
   NA Headquarters
   Westpoint PA
   Colorcon No-Tox Products
   Chalfont PA
   Colorcon, Inc.
   Irvine CA
   Colorcon, Inc.
   Indianapolis IN
   Colorcon, Inc.
   Stoughton WI
   Colorcon P.R., Inc.
   Humacao PR
   Colorcon, Inc.
   St. Laurent, Canada

20760 Colortec Associates Inc
28 Center St # 1
Clinton, NJ 08809-2632

908-735-2248
Fax: 908-236-7865 www.formulatorus.com
Develops and markets technologically advanced PC software and color instruments for industrial applications and point-of-sale merchandising; delivering color measuring instruments and nutritional labeling software to the food andagriculture industry.
President: James Degroff
   jdegroff@color-tec.com
Vice President: C Womer
Estimated Sales: $1 - 3 Million
Number Employees: 5-9
Number of Brands: 3
Number of Products: 3

20761 Colson Caster Corp
3700 Airport Rd
Jonesboro, AR 72401-4463

870-932-4501
Fax: 870-932-1446 800-643-5515
info1@colsoncaster.com www.colsoncaster.com
Manufacturer and exporter of casters, wheels and bumpers
CEO: Tom Blashill
Estimated Sales: $50 - 100 Million
Number Employees: 100-249

20762 Colter & Peterson
414 East 16th Street
Paterson, NJ 07514

973-684-0901
Fax: 973-684-0260 contact@colterpeterson.com
www.colter-peterson.com
New and rebuilt machinery for set-up, folding and corrugated boxes
Manager: Lawrence Harris
VP: Lawrence Harris
Contact: Bob Allan
   ballan@colter-peterson.com
Assistant Manager: Jo Taylor
Estimated Sales: $1-2.5 Million
Number Employees: 5-9

20763 Columbia Equipment & Finance
586 Silver Lake Dr
Danville, CA 94526-6226

925-314-1242
Fax: 925-314-1240 800-733-3939
information@columbialeasing.com
www.columbialeasingusa.com
Equipment lease financing and small business loans
President: Stan Nathanson
Estimated Sales: $.5 - 1 million
Number Employees: 1-4

20764 (HQ)Columbia Jet/JPL
750 Almeda Genoa Road
Houston, TX 77047-4106

713-433-4511
Fax: 713-434-1397 800-876-4511
Lighting fixtures
Director Sales: Mack Pyle
Marketing Manager: Tom Scott
Sales Manager: Les Simpson
Estimated Sales: $1 - 5 Million

20765 Columbia Labeling Machinery
1580 Dale Ave
PO Box 5290
Benton City, WA 99320

Fax: 509-588-5080 888-791-9590
sales@rippedsheets.com www.columbialabel.com
Manufacturer and exporter of automatic and semi-automatic labeling machines and supplies; also, bar code printing and labeling equipment
President: Raymond MacNeill
Sales: Catherine Bryson
Estimated Sales: $1-2.5 Million
Number Employees: 4
Square Footage: 100000

20766 Columbia Lighting
701 Millennium Blvd.
Greenville, SC 29607

864-678-1000
Fax: 864-678-1740
www.hubbell.com/columbialighting/en
Lighting fixtures including electric and fluorescent.
Year Founded: 1897
Estimated Sales: $100-500 Million
Number Employees: 500-999
Number of Brands: 1
Square Footage: 680000
Parent Co: Hubbell Lighting
Brands:
   Columbia

20767 Columbia Machine Inc
107 Grand Blvd
Vancouver, WA 98661-7795

360-694-1501
Fax: 360-695-7517 800-628-4065
pallsales@colmac.com
www.columbiamachine.com
Floor, high level and robotic palletizers for cases, bags, pails, bales and trays

President: Jerry Finolay
CEO: Rick Goode
 ricgoo@colmac.com
CFO: Winston Asai
CEO: Rick Goode
Sales Director: Richard Armstrong
Estimated Sales: $50 - 100 Million
Number Employees: 100-249
Square Footage: 186530

20768 Columbia Okura LLC
301 Grove St
Vancouver, WA 98661
360-735-1952
Fax: 360-905-1707 taygoo@colmac.com
www.columbiamachine.com
Robotic palletizing experts.
President: Rick Goode
Contact: Robert Alley
 robert.alley@columbiaokura.com
Estimated Sales: $20 - 50 Million
Number Employees: 10-19

20769 Columbian TecTank
2101 S 21st St
Parsons, KS 67357
620-421-0200
Fax: 620-421-9122 800-421-2788
www.columbiantectank.com
Manufacturer and exporter of bolted and welded carbon steel, stainless steel and aluminum storage tanks and silos
Contact: Robert Baker
 rwbaker@columbiantectank.com
Plant Manager: Steve Allen
Estimated Sales: $20 - 50 Million
Number Employees: 100-249
Brands:
 Aquastore
 Harvestove
 Peabody Tectank
 Seal Weld

20770 Columbus Instruments
950 N Hague Ave
Columbus, OH 43204-2121
614-279-9607
Fax: 614-276-0529 800-669-5011
sales@colinst.com www.colinst.com
Manufacturer and exporter of respirometers for measuring the sterility, bacterial and fungal growth, biodegradation and oxidation of fats; also, calorimeters, precision gas mixers and air dryers
President: Jan A Czekajewski
Manager: Frank Pence
 frank.pence@service.colinst.com
Estimated Sales: $2.5 - 5 Million
Number Employees: 20-49
Square Footage: 40000
Brands:
 Micro-Oxymax
 Oxymax

20771 Columbus McKinnon Corporation
205 Crosspoint Pkwy.
Getzville, NY 14068
716-689-5400
800-888-0985
www.cmworks.com
Chains, hoists, forgings, lift tables, jib arms, manipulators and conveyors.
Chairman: Richard Fleming
President/CEO: Mark Morelli
Vice President, Finance/CFO: Gregory Rustowicz
Vice President, Information Services: Mark Paradowski
Year Founded: 1875
Estimated Sales: $597 Million
Number Employees: 3,328
Brands:
 Abell-Howe
 Alltec
 Budgit
 CES
 CM
 CMCO
 Cady
 Chester Hoist
 Coffing
 Duff Norton
 Little Mule
 Magnetek
 Pfaff Silberblau
 STAHL CraneSystems

STB Stahlhammer Bommern
Shaw-Box
Unified Industries
Yale

20772 Columbus Paperbox Company
595 Van Buren Dr
Columbus, OH 43223
419-628-2381
Fax: 419-628-3105 800-968-0797
info@globusprinting.com
www.globusprinting.com/
Folding cartons and rigid set-up boxes
President: William Reiber
VP: Robert Reiber
VP Sales: Thomas Kasle
Estimated Sales: $5-10 Million
Number Employees: 20-49
Square Footage: 240000
Parent Co: Globus Printing & Packaging, Inc.
Brands:
 Conoco Lubricants
 Conoco/Andero
 Hydroclear

20773 Com-Pac International Inc
800 W Industrial Park Rd
Carbondale, IL 62901-5514
618-529-2421
Fax: 618-529-2234 888-297-2824
compac@com-pac.com www.com-pac.com
In-line reclosable zipper system with air-tight seal
President: Greg Sprehe
 greg.sprehe@com-pac.com
CEO: Don Wright
R&D: Chris Pemberton
Quality Control: Kendall Henkins
Marketing: Durrell McDannel
Sales: Darrell McDannel
Estimated Sales: Below $5 Million
Number Employees: 100-249
Number of Brands: 4
Number of Products: 20
Type of Packaging: Consumer, Food Service, Private Label
Brands:
 Integra
 Integra Cm
 Integra T
 Rtr 1000
 Z Patch

20774 Com-Pak International
11615 Cardinal Circle
Garden Grove, CA 92843-3814
714-537-5772
Fax: 714-537-4326
Wholesaler/distributor of food and chemical processing and packaging equipment
President: Billy Fielder
VP: David West
Estimated Sales: $1 - 3 Million
Number Employees: 7
Square Footage: 72000
Parent Co: Garden Grove
Other Locations:
 Com-Pak International
 Hemet CA

20775 Comalex
419-B Gordon Avenue
Van Buren, AR 72956
866-343-2594
renewberry@comalex.com www.comalex.com
Manufacturers computer software designed to automate Point-of-Sale (POS) food service operations in K-12 public and private schools and colleges
President: Richard Newberry
Number Employees: 16
Square Footage: 12400

20776 Comark Instruments
P.O. Box 9029
Everett, WA 98206-9029
360-435-5571
Fax: 360-403-4243 800-555-6658
sales@comarkusa.com global.bayliner.com
Supplier of electronic measurement instruments inculding food and industrial thermometers, thermocouples, temperature probes, data loggers, data management systems and timers plus humidity and pressure instruments.

President: Jeff Behan
Marketing Manager: Alan Mellinger
National Sales Manager: Bob Bader
Estimated Sales: $5-10 Million
Number Employees: 1,000-4,999
Number of Brands: 1
Number of Products: 200
Parent Co: Brunsik Corporation
Type of Packaging: Food Service
Brands:
 Comark
 Kane-May/Km

20777 Comasec Safety, Inc.
8 Niblick Road
Enfield, CT 06082
860-749-0506
Fax: 860-741-0881 800-333-0219
Manufacturer and importer of gloves including PVC/nitrile, knit lined latex, plastic, cotton/mesh lined, heavy unlined rubber; exporter of knit lined latex gloves
General Manager: P Gelinas
Tecnical Manager: Joe Krocheski
Estimated Sales: $5-10 Million
Number Employees: 10-19
Brands:
 Astroflex

20778 Comax Flavors
130 Baylis Rd
Melville, NY 11747
Fax: 631-249-9255 800-992-0629
info@comaxflavors.com www.comaxflavors.com
Supplier of flavors.
President: Weisz Agneta

CEO: Peter Calabretta
CFO: Virginia Wyan
Vice President: Paul Calabretta
Sr. Flavor Chemist: Mike Crain
Quality Control: Frank Vollaro
EVP Sales/Marketing: Bill Graham
PR/Communications Manager: Laura Ferrante

VP Operations: Joe Piazza
Production Manager: Jorge Quintanilla
Plant Manager: Marion Cunningham
Purchasing Manager: Michael Keppel
Estimated Sales: $15 Million
Number Employees: 250-499

20779 Combake International
3050 Royal Boulevard S
Suite 150
Alpharetta, GA 30022-4454
770-667-4944
Fax: 770-677-3440 wpib@aol.com

20780 Combi Packaging Systems LLC
5365 E Center Dr NE
PO Box 9326
Canton, OH 44721-3734
330-456-9333
Fax: 330-456-4644 866-472-5236
sales@combi.com www.combi.com
30 year manufacturer of case erectors, case packers and case sealers, robotic pick and place pakcers with integrated case erectors; ergonomic hand packaging stations and drop packers with integrated case erectors.
President/CEO: John Fisher
 jfisher@combi.com
CFO: Barb Karch
Research & Development: Bill Mitchell
Marketing Director: Sue Lewis
Sales Director: Mark Freidly
Plant Manager: Brian Miller
Estimated Sales: $10-20 Million
Number Employees: 100-249
Square Footage: 270000
Brands:
 Combi America
 Laser 2000
 Z-Ez

20781 Combined Computer Resource
2777 N Stemmons Fwy Ste 1046
Dallas, TX 75207
214-267-1010
Fax: 214-267-1019 800-956-1866
www.winocular.com

Suppliers of management software solutions that solve problems with paper and electronic document movement,retrieval,storage and archival or retention
Owner: Nick Sanders
Quality Control: Kim Roberts
VP: Rocky Chesnutt
VP: Kim Roberts
Estimated Sales: $4 000,000
Number Employees: 10-19

20782 Combustion Systems Sales
12946 SE Kent Kangley Road
300
Kent, WA 98030-7940
206-623-1141
Fax: 501-556-4104
Roasters (machines), conveying equipment (elevators, machiners and buckets), repair services

20783 Comco Signs
1624 Toal St
Charlotte, NC 28206-1522
704-375-2338
Fax: 704-333-3335
Signs
President: John W Ulery
Estimated Sales: Below $5 Million
Number Employees: 20 to 49

20784 Comet Signs
235 W Turbo Dr
San Antonio, TX 78216-3313
210-341-7244
Fax: 210-341-7279 info@cometsigns.com
www.cometsigns.com
Indoor and outdoor signs including advertising and electric
President: Arthur Sitterle
CEO: Tim Edmonds
tim@cometneon.com
VP: Pete Sitterle
Estimated Sales: $5-10 Million
Number Employees: 50-99

20785 Comm-Pak
2406 Frederick Rd
Opelika, AL 36801-7222
334-749-6201
Fax: 334-749-1948
Point of purchase displays and pressure sensitive decals and labels; also, custom printing of plastic drinkware available
President: Trey Gafford
Estimated Sales: $1-2.5 Million
Number Employees: 10 To 19
Square Footage: 36000

20786 Command Belt Cleaning Systems
700 Hoffman Street
Hammond, IN 46327-1894
219-931-1450
Fax: 219-931-0209 800-433-7627
www.screwconveyor.com
Automated conveyor belt cleaning systems
Operations Manager: Frank Pennino
General Manager: John Rice
Number Employees: 20-49
Square Footage: 20000
Parent Co: Pari Industries

20787 Command Communications
14510 E Fremont Ave
Centennial, CO 80112-4233
304-839-4051
Fax: 303-792-0899 800-288-3491
Manufacturer and exporter of wireless, staff, guest, hostess and waitress paging systems. Also communication products designed to reduce the number of phone lines— saving monthly phone line expenses
President/CEO: Craig Hibbard
chibbard@commandcom.com
VP Operations: Mary Larson
Director of Communications/Online Mkting:
Michael Rose
National Accounts Sales Manager: Charla Martin
Estimated Sales: $3 - 5 Million
Number Employees: 10-19
Number of Products: 10
Type of Packaging: Consumer, Food Service, Private Label, Bulk

20788 Command Electronics Inc
15670 Morris Industrial Dr
Schoolcraft, MI 49087-9628
269-679-4011
Fax: 269-679-5410
info@commandelectronics.com
www.commandelectronics.com
Manufacturer and exporter of fluorescent and incandescent lighting
President: Cary Campagna
Vice President: Dan Campagna
Estimated Sales: $1 - 5 Million
Number Employees: 10-19
Square Footage: 52000
Brands:
Porta-Lamp

20789 Command Line Corporation
1090 Kng Geo Pst Rd Ste 802
Edison, NJ 8837
732-738-6500
Fax: 732-738-6504 www.commandlinecorp.com
Customized purchasing, distribution and manufacturing management software systems for multi-site inventory control, requisitions, receiving, bar coding, A/P interfaces, warehouse locator systems, etc
President: Donald Staffin
Estimated Sales: $1-2.5 Million
Number Employees: 10-19

20790 Command Packaging
3840 E 26th St
Vernon, CA 90058-4107
323-980-0918
Fax: 323-260-7047 800-996-2247
info@commandpackaging.com
www.commandpackaging.com
Elegant, upscale, and value added bags for retail stores including, bakeries and delies, restaurants, and grocery stores. We specialize in bags for restaurant carry out
President: Albert Halimi
CEO: Pete Grande
Vice President: Scott Ellingson
scottellingson@cox.net
Marketing Director: Vicki Stiling
Operations Manager: Carol Bullock
Estimated Sales: $10 - 20 Million
Number Employees: 100-249
Square Footage: 100000
Type of Packaging: Food Service

20791 (HQ)Commencement Bay Corrugated
13414 142nd Ave E
Orting, WA 98360-9560
253-845-3100
Fax: 253-445-0772 www.cbcbox.com
Manufacturer and exporter of corrugated paper boxes
Manager: Paul Winber
Sales Coordinator: James Kressler
Manager: Steve Mc Donald
mcdonald@cbcbox.com
General Manager: Joe McQuade
Plant Manager: Randy Snow
Estimated Sales: $20 - 50 Million
Number Employees: 100-249
Square Footage: 130000

20792 Commercial Corrugated Co Inc
4101 Ashland Ave
Baltimore, MD 21205-2924
410-522-0900
Fax: 410-522-6184 800-242-8861
jpauly@commercialcorrugated.com
www.commercialwagner.com
Corrugated boxes and containers; also, point of purchase displays
President: John Pauley Sr
Contact: Wanda Battaglia
wbattaglia@commercialwagner.com
Estimated Sales: $10 - 20 Million
Number Employees: 10-19
Type of Packaging: Private Label, Bulk

20793 Commercial Creamery Co
159 S Cedar St
Spokane, WA 99201
509-747-4131
sales@cheesepowder.com
www.cheesepowder.com
Dried cheese and yogurt powders; processor and exporter of snack seasoning and spray dried dairy flavors
Owner/VP Sales & Marketing: Megan Boell
mboell@cheesepowder.com
Year Founded: 1908
Estimated Sales: $28 Million
Number Employees: 5-9

20794 (HQ)Commercial Dehydrator Systems
256 Bethel Dr
Eugene, OR 97402-2504
541-688-5282
Fax: 541-688-5989 800-369-4283
darryl@dryer.com www.dehydrator.com
Berry crate washers, insect sterilization chambers, roasters, cookers and dryers including continuous belt, bin and tray; exporter of dryers/roasters and sorting/grading belting.
President: David Stone
marketing@dryer.com
Vice President: David Stone
National Sales Manager: Darryl Hastings
Field Representative: Darryl Hastings
Estimated Sales: $1-2.5 Million
Number Employees: 50-99
Square Footage: 54000

20795 Commercial Envelope Manufacturing Company
350 Wireless Blvd Ste 102
Hauppauge, NY 11788-3947
Fax: 631-242-6935
Envelopes
President: Alan Kristel
Estimated Sales: $20-50 Million
Number Employees: 100-249

20796 (HQ)Commercial Furniture Group Inc
810 W Highway 25 70
Newport, TN 37821-8044
423-623-0031
Fax: 423-587-8872 800-873-3252
www.commercialfurnituregroup.com
Manufacturer and exporter of chairs, benches, booths and tables
Manager: Bob Branstetter
CFO: Neal Restivo
Marketing Specialist: Teri Winters
IT: Stefanie Thompson
sthompson@commercialfurniture.com
Number Employees: 1000-4999
Type of Packaging: Food Service
Brands:
Epic
Falcon
Howe
Shelby Williams
Thonet

20797 Commercial Kitchen Co
3219 W Washington Blvd
Los Angeles, CA 90018-1249
323-732-2291
Fax: 323-732-2729 www.commercialkitchen.com
Stainless steel hoods, tables and shelving
President: Armando Carmona
commercialkitchen18@yahoo.com
Estimated Sales: $500,000-$1,000,000
Number Employees: 1-4

20798 Commercial Lighting Design
43 S Dudley St
Memphis, TN 38104
901-774-5771
Fax: 901-946-2478 800-774-5799
www.lumalier.com
Manufacturer and exporter of lighting fixtures
President: Charles Dunn
CEO: Charles Dunn, Sr.
VP: Charles Dunn, Jr.
Estimated Sales: $1-2,500,000
Number Employees: 10-19
Brands:
Lumalier

20799 Commercial Manufacturing
2432 S Railroad Ave
Fresno, CA 93706-5187

559-237-1855
Fax: 559-266-5149 info@commercialmfg.com
www.commercialmfg.com
Manufacturer and exporter of bin handling systems, conveyors, bucket elevators, air dryers, coolers and cleaners, washers, centrifuges, food pumps, graders and mix and blend systems
President: Larry Hagopian
 info@commercialmfg.com
Sales Manager: Jack Kraemer
Sales Engineer: Jim MacKenzie
Sales Engineer: Bob Peschel
Estimated Sales: $10-20 Million
Number Employees: 50-99

20800 Commercial Packaging
8425 Fairway Pl
Middleton, WI 53562-2501

608-836-7181
Fax: 608-831-9632 800-500-9519
info@commercialpackaging.com
Packaging material
Manager: Bonnie Dahlk
 bdahlk@commercialpackaging.com
VP: Aaron Egbers
Estimated Sales: $5 - 10 Million
Number Employees: 1-4
Parent Co: Commercial Packaging

20801 Commercial Printing Company
P.O. Box 10302
Birmingham, AL 35202-0302

205-251-9203
Fax: 205-251-6133 800-989-9203
Manufacturers of printers and printing related services like scanning, digital and conventional stripping, multicolor printing, bindery, on demand printing and elkote finishing
President: Thomas Arledge
Executive Vice President: Mike Leathers
Account Executive: Alex Berger
Contact: Don Thompson
 dthompson@cprintingco.com
Estimated Sales: $10-20 Million
Number Employees: 50-99

20802 Commercial Refrigeration Service, Inc.
2501 West Behrend Drive
Suite 39
Phoenix, AZ 85027-4148

623-869-8881
Fax: 623-869-8882 www.comrefsvc.com
Manufacturer and exporter of beverage dispensers
Contact: Sandra Forsythe
 s.forsythe@crhinc.com
Estimated Sales: $1 - 5 Million
Number Employees: 100-250
Square Footage: 240000
Type of Packaging: Food Service
Brands:
 Jet Spray

20803 Commercial Seating Specailists
481 Laurelwood Rd
Santa Clara, CA 95054-2416

408-453-8983
Fax: 408-453-8986 www.comseat.com
Booths and table tops.
Owner: Jim Day
CEO: Patricia Day
Marketing Director: Rich Buchner
Sales Director: Mike Alexander
 jday@comseat.com
Purchasing Manager: Scott Wallace
Estimated Sales: $1-2.5 Million
Number Employees: 10-19

20804 Commercial Testing Lab Inc
514 Main St
Colfax, WI 54730-9001

715-962-3121
Fax: 715-962-4030 800-962-5227
ctlfoods@ctlcolfax.com
An analytical microbiology Testing Lab testing water, food, calibrations, and feed and forage.
President: Peter Klug
 peterk@ctlcolfax.com
R&D: Cheryl Bean
Estimated Sales: $2.5 - 5 000,000
Number Employees: 20-49

20805 Commodity Traders International
101 E. Main Street
P.O. Box 6
Trilla, IL 62469-0006

217-235-4322
Fax: 217-235-3246 sales@commoditytraders.biz
www.commoditytraders.biz
Manufacturer and exporter of new and used milling, grain handling and seed processing machinery
Executive Trustee: Charles Stodden

20806 Common Sense Natural Soap & Bodycare Products
109 Lincoln Avenue
Rutland, VT 05701-3226

802-773-0582
Fax: 561-753-8207
Natural soap products
General Manager: Michael Delaney
Estimated Sales: $5-10 Million
Number Employees: 10-19

20807 Compacker Systems LLC
9104 N Zenith Ave
P.O. Box 2026
Davenport, IA 52806-6432

563-391-2751
Fax: 563-391-8598
Manufacturer and exporter of case packing and sealing equipment including case erectors, wrap-around and top and bottom sealers, traymakers, etc
President: Keith Tucker
CEO: John Curtis
 compacker@compacker.com
Quality Control: Jane Bower
Marketing Manager: Michael Bower
General Manager: Keith Tucker
Estimated Sales: $5-10 Million
Number Employees: 10-19
Square Footage: 80000
Brands:
 Bottom Line
 Compacker Ii
 Compacker Ii Abf-3
 Compacker Iii
 Endpacker
 Rap-Up 90
 Tm1000

20808 Compact Industries Inc
3945 Ohio Ave
St Charles, IL 60174-5467

630-513-9600
Fax: 630-513-9655 800-513-4262
www.compactind.com
Private label and contract packager: dry product packaging, in-house blending, formulating
President/CEO: Michael Brown
CFO: Steve Zaruba
VP Sales: Gary Johnson
Estimated Sales: $9 Million
Number Employees: 100-249
Square Footage: 300000
Type of Packaging: Consumer, Food Service, Private Label, Bulk
Brands:
 Casa Verde
 Cool Off
 Geneva Freeze
 John Foster Green

20809 Compact Mold
3436 Turfway Road
Erlanger, KY 41018-3169

859-371-3250
Fax: 859-371-2290
Blow molds
Estimated Sales: $1-5 000,000
Number Employees: 12

20810 Compactors Inc
71 Lighthouse Rd # 221
Hilton Head Isle, SC 29928-7297

843-363-5077
Fax: 843-686-3290 800-423-4003
info@compactorsinc.com
www.compactorsinc.com
Manufacturer and exporter of can and bottle crushers, trash compactors and densifiers
President: Mike Pierson
 mike@compactorsinc.com
VP: Bill Phillips
Estimated Sales: Below $5 Million
Number Employees: 1-4

Square Footage: 8000
Parent Co: Hilton Head SC
Brands:
 Pac Crusher I

20811 Compass Group Canada
1 Prologis Blvd
Suite 400
Mississauga, ON L5W 0G2
Canada

800-465-2203
www.compass-canada.com
Foodservices and support services for sports and leisure venues, executive dining rooms and cafes, schools, universities, seniors' residences, hospitals, remote camps and off-shore oil rigs.
CEO: Saajid Khan
CFO: Brent Mooney
SVP/General Counsel: Ian Baskerville
Chief Growth Officer, Canada: Peter Kourtis
Chief People & Culture Officer: Lauren Davey
Estimated Sales: $28 Billion
Number Employees: 25,000
Parent Co: Compass Group PLC
Type of Packaging: Food Service

20812 Compatible Components Corporation
1213 West Loop North
Suite 180
Houston, TX 77055

713-688-2008
Fax: 713-688-2993 sales@cccmix.com
www.compatible-components.com
Mixing/blending products and separating/dewatering products
President: Gerald Lott
Contact: Anthony Lerma
 alerma@cccmix.com

20813 Complete Automation
1776 W Clarkston Rd
Lake Orion, MI 48362-2267

248-814-4967
Fax: 248-693-0503 marketing@completeco.com
www.completeco.com
Coolant filtration systems and filtration products.
President: Kenneth Matheis
IT: Ryan Rausch
 rmrausch@completeco.com
Number Employees: 50-99
Square Footage: 45000

20814 (HQ)Complete Packaging & Shipping
83 Bennington Ave
Freeport, NY 11520-3913

516-546-2100
Fax: 516-546-0717 877-269-3236
johnc@completepackage.com
www.completesupplyusa.com
Corrugated boxes; exporter and importer of tapes, cartons, stretch film, impulse sealers and plastic strapping materials. 3000 box sizes in stock
Owner: Jeffery Berkowitz
Director of Sales: Tom DiGiacomo
Estimated Sales: $10-20 Million
Number Employees: 10-19

20815 Complete Packaging Solutions
325 Curie Dr
Alpharetta, GA 30005-2264

770-751-7400
Fax: 770-751-0706 800-417-3178
info@kallfass.com www.kallfass.com
Fully automatic l-sealer, side sealers and sleeve wrapper, shrink tunnels and semiautomatic l-sealer
Owner: Bodo Goepfert
 bodo@kallfass-us.com
Vice President: Bodo Goepfert
Marketing/Sales Manager: Cece Loft
Estimated Sales: $1-2.5 000,000
Number Employees: 5-9

20816 Complete Packaging Systems
2411 Loma Avenue
South El Monte, CA 91733-1415

626-579-4670
Fax: 626-579-2015
Prints blister cards and thermoforms blisters
President: Bruce Romfo
Estimated Sales: $10-20 000,000
Number Employees: 100-249

20817 Complex Steel & Wire Corp
36254 Annapolis St
Wayne, MI 48184-2094
734-326-1600
Fax: 734-326-7421 www.complexsteel.com
Wire rack decking and partitions.
President: Vincent Fedell
complexsteel@aol.com
Sales Manager: Gary Snarkas
Estimated Sales: $2.5 - 5 Million
Number Employees: 20-49

20818 Compliance Control Inc
1595 Cabin Branch Dr
Hyattsville, MD 20785-3816
301-773-6485
Fax: 301-773-4044 800-810-4000
info@hygenius.com www.tempgenius.com
Manufacturer and exporter of handwashing verification systems
President: Neil Segal
nsegal@compliancecontrolinc.com
Executive VP: Bill Karlin
Estimated Sales: $2.5-5 Million
Number Employees: 20-49
Type of Packaging: Food Service, Private Label
Brands:
Hygenius

20819 (HQ)Component Hardware Group Inc
1890 Swarthmore Ave
Lakewood, NJ 08701-4530
323-888-9395
Fax: 732-363-9864 800-526-3694
Manufacturer, importer and exporter of food service equipment including beverage preparation and serving products, dispensers, faucets, spray washers, water stations, tables including legs and bases, drains, grease filters, castersetc
President: Alfred Klein
VP Marketing: William Matthaei
VP Sales: Pat Campbell
Contact: Steve Bruno
sbruno@chgusa.com
Estimated Sales: Less Than $500,000
Number Employees: 1-4
Square Footage: 96000
Brands:
Encore
Standard-Keil

20820 Composite Can & Tube Institute
50 S Pickett St # 110
Alexandria, VA 22304-7206
703-823-7234
Fax: 703-823-7237
Representing the interests of manufacturers of composite paperboard cans, containers, canisters, tubes, cores, cones, fibre drums, spools, ribbon blocks, bobbins and related or similar composite products.
VP: Kristine Garland
ccti@cctiwdc.org
Estimated Sales: $2.5 - 5,000,000
Number Employees: 1-4

20821 Composition Materials Co Inc
249 Pepes Farm Rd
Milford, CT 06460-3671
203-874-6500
Fax: 203-874-6505 800-262-7763
info@compomat.com www.compomat.com
Plastic Blasting Media, a distributor of a multitude of filers and extenders, supplier of Walnut Shell grits and flours, and importer of birch wood flour from Sweden.
President: Alan Nudelman
nudelman@compomat.com
Chairman: Theodore Diamond
Sales Representative: Steven D. Essex
Product Operations Manager: David M. Elster
Estimated Sales: $2.5-5 Million
Number Employees: 10-19
Square Footage: 30000
Brands:
Clear-Cut
Cob Dry
Plasti-Grit
Resistat

20822 Compris Technologies
2651 Satellite Blvd
Duluth, GA 30096-5810
770-418-4616
Fax: 770-795-3333 800-615-3301
www.compristech.com
Manufacturer and exporter of computer software including point of sale, labor, inventory, scheduling, executive information and cash management
President: Alaa Pasha
Vice President, Development: Eric Kobres
Area VP Sales: Ron Small
Contact: Mills Bronson
brown.james@ncr.com
Estimated Sales: $5 - 10 Million
Number Employees: 100-249

20823 Compusense Inc.
P.O. Box 1116
Guelph, ON N1H 6n3
Canada
519-836-9993
Fax: 519-836-9898 800-367-6666
info@compusense.com www.compusense.com
A leader in sensory and consumer research, Compusense's software and services guide leading food and beverage companis in making informed business decisions.

20824 Computer Aid Inc
1390 Ridgeview Dr # 300
Allentown, PA 18104-9065
610-530-5000
Fax: 610-530-5298 800-327-4243
blake@computeraid-llc.com www.compaid.com
In-house payroll, automated time and attendance software
President: Joe Angronaco
CEO: Anthony J Salvaggio
tony_salvaggio@compaid.com
Program System Analyst: Kyle Bonney
Estimated Sales: $3 - 5 Million
Number Employees: 1000-4999
Square Footage: 3000
Brands:
Pay Master
Pay Master Plus

20825 Computer Aided Marketing
PO Box 4990
Chapel Hill, NC 27515-4990
919-401-0996
Fax: 919-489-4980
Restaurant back office software for frequent diners
VP Sales/Marketing: Bill Ryan
Number Employees: 6
Brands:
Cam Frequent Diners

20826 Computer Assocs. Intl.
2950 Express Dr S Ste 106
Central Islip, NY 11749
631-342-2984
Fax: 631-342-5329 800-225-5224
www.ca.com
Prepackaged software publishing
C.E.O: Sanjay Kumar
Quality Control: Douglas Robinson
C.T.O: Yogesh Gupta
G.M. Global Mkting.: Kenneth Fitzpatrick
Executive VP/GM: Stephen Richards
Exec. V.P. Administrative Services: Gary Quinn
Estimated Sales: $1 - 5 000,000
Number Employees: 1,000-4,999

20827 Computer Communications Specialists
2960 Shallowford Rd # 102
Marietta, GA 30066-3093
770-509-5321
888-231-4227
Designer and manufacturer of integrated information response systems
Manager: Andy Pereira
Marketing Specialist: David Gay
Estimated Sales: $10 - 20 Million
Number Employees: 1-4
Brands:
Acca
First Line

20828 Computer Controlled Machines
1 Magnuson Ave
Pueblo, CO 81001-4889
719-948-9500
Fax: 719-948-9540 sales@magnusoncorp.com
www.magnusoncorp.com
Manufacturer and exporter of vegetable processing equipment for sweet corn, green beans and peas
Owner: Bob Smith
VP/General Manager: Craig Furlo
Estimated Sales: $5 - 10 Million
Number Employees: 20-49
Parent Co: Atlas-Pacific Engineering

20829 Computer Group
4212 N Arlington Heights Rd
Arlington Hts, IL 60004-1372
847-818-9200
Fax: 847-818-9300 dsj@computer-group.com
Service computers and internet services
Owner: Dave Besser
Estimated Sales: $5-10 000,000
Number Employees: 10-19
Square Footage: 4500

20830 (HQ)Computerized Machinery Systs
11733 95th Ave N
Maple Grove, MN 55369-5551
763-493-0099
Fax: 763-493-0093 sales@cmsitechnologies.com
www.labelmart.com
Manufacturer and exporter of pressure sensitive labels; wholesaler/distributor and exporter of barcode printers, label scanners and applicators
Owner: Kate Jackson
Sales: Eric Sorensen
kate@labelmart.com
Estimated Sales: Below $5 Million
Number Employees: 20-49
Brands:
Dura-Kote

20831 Computerway Food Systems
635 Southwest Street
High Point, NC 27260
336-841-7289
Fax: 336-841-2594 sales@mycfs.com
www.mycfs.com
Our systems include overhead sizing, grading and weighing lines as well as fully integrated computerized production and inventory systems for food processing plants.
President: William Altenpohl
Contact: Elhanan Bone
ebone@mycfs.com
Estimated Sales: $2.5-5 000,000
Number Employees: 20-49

20832 Computrition
19808 Nordhoff Pl
Chatsworth, CA 91311
818-701-5544
Fax: 818-701-1702 800-222-4488
info@computrition.com www.computrition.com
Offers completely integrated food service and nutrition care management software systems for operations of all size. Software features include diet order, recipe, menu and inventory management, online order entry and nutrientanalysis
President: Luros Luros-Elson RD
CEO: Scott Saklad
R&D: Joseph Bibbo
Manager, Marketing: Marty Yadrick, RD
Sales: Scott Saklad
Contact: Bindu Amin
bamin@computrition.com
Operations: Kim Goldberg
Estimated Sales: $20-50 Million
Number Employees: 50-99
Square Footage: 17000
Type of Packaging: Food Service
Brands:
Hospitality Suite

20833 (HQ)Computype Inc
2285 County Road C W
St Paul, MN 55113-2567
651-633-0633
Fax: 651-633-5580 800-328-0852
www.computype.com
Manufacturer and exporter of bar code labels, printers and applicators

President: R Huntsinger
CEO: Sonia Artola
 soniaartola@hotmail.com
VP: J Ammann
CEO: William Roche
Estimated Sales: $20-50 Million
Number Employees: 100-249
Other Locations:
 Computype
 Concord NH

20834 Comstar Printing Solutions
10175 Philipp Pkwy
Streetsboro, OH 44241-4706

330-528-2800
Fax: 330-528-2828 info@printpro.com
www.printpro.com
In-line and thermal transfer imprinters for in-line
packaging and table top labeling systems
Executive Assistant: Sharon Spaeth
Production Manager: Jeff Burke

20835 Comstock Castle Stove Co
119 W Washington St
Quincy, IL 62301-3860

410-829-4199
Fax: 217-223-0007 800-637-9188
sales@castlestove.com www.castlestove.com
Manufacturer, importer and exporter of cooking
equipment including gas broilers, deep fat fryers,
ovens, griddles, ranges, hot plates, etc
Vice President: Tim Spake
 tspake@comstockcastlestoveco.com
Vice President: Timothy Spake
Marketing/Sales: Curtis Spake
Purchasing Manager: Bob Speckhart
Estimated Sales: $5-10 Million
Number Employees: 20-49
Square Footage: 170000
Type of Packaging: Food Service, Private Label
Brands:
 Castle
 Economy

20836 Comtec Industries
10210 Werch Dr
Suite 204
Woodridge, IL 60517

630-759-9000
Fax: 630-759-9009
feedback@comtecindustriesltd.com
www.comtecindustriesltd.com
Baking equipment and supplies including dough
formers for pot pies, hors d'oeuvres and top/bottom
crusts; also, dies and tooling for pies, tarts, cheese-
cakes, etc.; exporter of dough presses
President: James Reilly
Contact: Dolores Reilly
 dreilly@comtecindustriesltd.com
Estimated Sales: $1 - 3 Million
Number Employees: 10
Square Footage: 8000
Brands:
 Comtec

20837 Comtek Systems
309 Breesport Street
San Antonio, TX 78216-2699

210-340-8253
Fax: 210-340-8255
Point of sale systems
President: Thomas Hayes
Plant Manager: M Hayes
Number Employees: 5-9
Square Footage: 5000
Brands:
 Comtek Supercharger

20838 Comus Restaurant Systems
9667 Fleetwood Court
Frederick, MD 21701

301-698-6208
Manufacturer and exporter of point of sale and full
back office software
Marketing: Fred Ihrer
Estimated Sales: $2.5-5 Million
Number Employees: 10
Square Footage: 4000
Parent Co: Comus Software
Brands:
 Comus Restaurant Systems

20839 Con-tech/Conservation Technology
2783 Shermer Rd
Northbrook, IL 60062-7708

847-559-5505
Fax: 847-559-5505 800-728-0312
www.con-techlighting.com
Manufacturer, importer and exporter of lighting
products and industrial fans
President: John Ranshaw
Secretary: Sandy Grossman
VP: John Ranshow
Sales/Marketing Executive: Olga Draqunsky
Contact: Sally Baybutt
 sbaybutt@con-techlighting.com
Purchasing Agent: Larry Sabatino
Estimated Sales: $20-50 Million
Number Employees: 20-49
Square Footage: 36000
Brands:
 Con-Tech

20840 Conagra Brands Inc
222 W. Merchandise Mart Plaza
Chicago, IL 60654

312-549-5000
877-266-2472
www.conagrafoods.com
Consumer brands.
President/CEO: Sean Connolly
Executive VP/CFO: David Marberger
EVP/General Counsel/Corporate Secretary: Carey
Bartell
Year Founded: 1919
Estimated Sales: $11.7 Billion
Number Employees: 17,000
Number of Brands: 70
Type of Packaging: Consumer, Food Service, Bulk
Brands:
 ACT II
 Alexia
 Andy Capp's
 Angie's BOOMCHICKAPOP
 Armour Star
 BIGS
 Banquet
 Bernstein's
 Bertoli
 Birds Eye
 Birds Eye C&W
 Birds Eye Voila
 Blake's
 Blue Bonnet
 Brooks
 Celeste Pizza for One
 Chef Boyardee
 Crunch 'n Munch
 DAVID Seeds
 Dennison's
 Duke's
 Duncan Hies Wilderness
 Duncan Hines
 Duncan Hines Comstock
 EVOL
 Earth Balance
 Egg Beaters
 Erin's
 Fiddle Faddle
 Fleischmann's
 Frontera
 Gardein
 Glutino
 Gulden's
 H.K. Anderson
 Hawaiian Snacks
 Healthy Choice
 Hebrew National
 Hungry-Man
 Hunt's
 Husman's
 Jiffy Pop
 Kangaroo
 Kid Cuisine
 La Choy
 Lender's
 Libby's
 Log Cabin
 Manwich
 Marie Callender's
 Mrs.Butterworth's
 Mrs.Paul's
 Nalley
 Odom's Tennessee Pride
 Open Pit

 Orville Redencacher's
 P.F. Chang's Home Menu
 PAM
 Parkay
 Pearl Milling Company
 Penrose
 Peter Pan
 Poppycock
 RO*TEL
 Ranch Style Beans
 Reddi-wip
 Rosarita
 Ranch Style Beans
 Reddi-wip
 Rosarita
 Sandwhich Bros. of Wisconsin
 Slim Jim
 Smart Balance

20841 Conagra Foodservice
222 W. Merchandise Mart Plaza
Suite 1300
Chicago, IL 60654

312-549-5000
877-266-2472
www.conagrabrands.com
Supplies restaurants, retailers, commercial custom-
ers and other foodservice suppliers.
President/CEO: Sean Connolly
EVP/CFO: David Marberger
EVP/General Counsel/Corporate Secretary: Carey
Bartell
EVP/Co-COO: Tom McGough
Estimated Sales: $1,000,000+
Number Employees: 10,000+
Number of Brands: 70
Square Footage: 11042
Parent Co: Conagra Brands
Type of Packaging: Consumer, Food Service, Bulk
Other Locations:
 ConAgra Headquarters
 Kennewick WA
 ConAgra Headquarters
 Naperville IL
 Sales Office
 Anaheim CA
 Sales Office
 Mesa AR
 Sales Office
 San Antonio TX
 Sales Office
 Plano TX
 Sales Office
 Tampa FL
 Sales Office
 Baltimore MD
 Sales Office
 Mason OH
 Sales Office
 Troy OH
Brands:
 ACT II
 Alexia
 Andy Capp's
 Angie's BOOMCHICKAPOP
 Armour Star
 BIGS
 Banquet
 Bernstein's
 Bertoli
 Birds Eye C&W
 Birds Eye Voila
 Birds Eye
 Blake's
 Blue Bonnet
 Brooks
 Celeste Pizza for One
 Chef Boyardee
 Crunch 'n Munch
 DAVID Seeds
 Dennison's
 Duke's
 Duncan Hies Wilderness
 Duncan Hines Comstock
 Duncan Hines
 EVOL
 Earth Balance
 Egg Beaters
 Erin's
 Fiddle Faddle
 Fleischmann's
 Frontera
 Gardein
 Glutino
 Gulden's

H.K. Anderson
Hawaiian Snacks
Healthy Choice
Hebrew National
Hungry-Man
Hunt's
Husman's
Jiffy Pop
Kangaroo
Kid Cuisine
La Choy
Lender's
Libby's
Log Cabin
Manwich
Marie Callender's
Mrs.Butterworth's
Mrs.Paul's
Nalley
Odom's Tennessee Pride
Open Pit
Orville Redenbacher'S
P.F. Chang's Home Menu
PAM
Parkay
Pearl Milling Company
Penrose
Peter Pan
Poppycock
RO*TEL
Ranch Style Beans
Reddi-wip
Rosarita
Ranch Style Beans
Reddi-wip
Rosarita
Sandwhich Bros. of Wisconsin
Slim Jim
Smart Balance

20842 Conam Inspection
192 Internationale Blvd
Glendale Heights, IL 60139-2094

630-681-0008
Fax: 630-681-0009
www.mistrasgroup.com/services/
Consultant providing nondestructive testing laboratory services, lubricant and fuel analysis and chemical and environmental testing
President: Laurie Todd
Contact: Stephen Bertolet
stephen.bertolet@conaminsp.com
Estimated Sales: $10-20 Million
Number Employees: 50-99

20843 Conatech Consulting Group, Inc
501 N Lindbergh Blvd Ste 105
Saint Louis, MO 63141

314-995-9767
Fax: 314-995-9766 rjbockserman@conatech.com
www.conatech.com
Consulting engineering firm, processing-packaging-distribution of food products. Product and package development, line integration, federal regulations, expert testimony trial, research and discovery; product liability, patentinfringement research and discovery, depositions, trial testimony
President: Robert Bockserman
Estimated Sales: $500,000-$1 Million
Number Employees: 42
Number of Products: 42

20844 Conax Buffalo Technologies
2300 Walden Ave
Buffalo, NY 14225-4779

716-684-4500
Fax: 716-684-7433 800-223-2389
conax@conaxtechnologies.com
www.conaxbuffalo.com
Manufacturer and exporter of measurement systems including temperature sensors, sealing devices and fiber optic systems
President: Robert Fox
Marketing Director: Richard Paluch
Director of Sales and Marketing: Michael Valachos
Purchasing: Joe Kelly
Estimated Sales: $10-20 Million
Number Employees: 50-99
Square Footage: 186000

20845 Conbraco Industries Inc
701 Matthews Mint Hill Rd
Matthews, NC 28105-1706

704-841-6000
Fax: 704-841-6020 www.apollovalves.com
Water gauge valves
President: Glenn Mosack
CFO: Eric Miller
Estimated Sales: Below $5 Million
Number Employees: 50-99

20846 Concept Foods Inc
141 Covington Dr
Bloomingdale, IL 60108-3107

630-539-3107
Fax: 630-539-3109 800-762-1734
www.cafortune.com
President: Dorothy Rzeszutko
Estimated Sales: $20 - 50 Million
Number Employees: 1-4

20847 Concept Hospitality Group
325 Cutwater
Foster City, CA 94404

650-357-1224
Fax: 760-323-0170
Consultant specializing in image enhancement, product marketing and promotion for the hospitality and service markets
Managing Partner: Tom Kelley
Number Employees: 5

20848 Concepts & Design International, Ltd
203 Foxwood Road
West Nyack, NY 10994-2507

845-358-1558
Fax: 845-358-1558
Design and engineering consultant for food facilities including restaurants, schools and hotels.
President: Philip Amato
CFO: Adrienne Amato
Estimated Sales: $300,000-$500,000
Number Employees: 1
Square Footage: 156
Type of Packaging: Food Service

20849 Concord Chemical Co Inc
1700 Federal St
Camden, NJ 08105-1716

856-966-1526
Fax: 856-963-0246 800-282-2436
www.concordchemical.com
Producer of eco-friendly cleaners, soaps, lubricants, release agents, dust control products and more.
President/CEO: Miguel Castillo
VP Product Development: Jack Cram
VP Sales: Carol Griffiths
VP Purchasing: Lauren DeSilvio
Number Employees: 1-4
Square Footage: 120000
Parent Co: Seacord Corporation
Brands:
22 K Gold Finish
3-D Degreaser
Creamedic
Harley Activated Pine
Lemonee-8

20850 Conductive Containers Inc
4500 Quebec Ave N
Minneapolis, MN 55428-4915

763-537-2090
Fax: 763-537-1738 800-327-2329
info@corstat.com www.corstat.com
Manufacturer and exporter of containers including conductive fiberboard, corrugated, chipboard and plastic
President: Brad Ahlm
VP: Paul Granning
VP Operations/R&D: Robert Marlovits
Estimated Sales: $1-2.5 Million
Number Employees: 50-99
Square Footage: 100000
Brands:
Corstat

20851 ConeTech
1450 Airport Blvd Ste 180
Santa Rosa, CA 95403

707-577-7500
Fax: 707-577-7511 info@conetech.com
www.conetech.com

President: Anthony Dann
CFO: Robert E Williams
Estimated Sales: $1-2.5 000,000
Number Employees: 5-9

20852 Conesco Conveyor Corporation
953 Paulison Avenue
Clifton, NJ 07011-3641

973-365-1440
Fax: 973-365-1923 conesco@aol.com
Belt and chain conveyors
President: John Garratt
VP: Jim Garratt
Estimated Sales: Below $5 Million
Number Employees: 4
Square Footage: 40000

20853 Confection Art Inc
3636 North Williams Avenue
Portland, OR 97227

503-505-0481
info@chocolatecraftkits.com
www.chocolatecraftkits.com
Molded chocolates
President: Nancy Baggett
Master Pastry Chef: Pierre Herme
Number Employees: 8

20854 Conflex Incorporated
6637 N Sidney Pl
Germantown, WI 53022

262-512-2665
Fax: 262-512-1665 800-225-4296
jmorrissey@conflex.com www.conflex.com
President: Kevin Laird

20855 Conflex, Inc.
W130 N10751 Washington Drive
Germantown, WI 53022

262-512-2665
Fax: 262-512-1665 800-225-4296
info@conflex.com www.conflex.com
Manufacturer and exporter of shrink wrapping equipment
President: Bill Morrissey
CEO: Joe Morrissey
CFO: Jim Benton
Research & Development: Mark Kubisiak
Tech Services: Kevin Thomas
Product Manager: Joe Morrissey
Purchasing Manager: Bill Morrissey, Jr.
Number Employees: 20-49
Square Footage: 320000
Type of Packaging: Consumer, Food Service, Bulk

20856 Conflow Technologies, Inc.
18 Regan Road
Units 28 & 29
Brampton, ON L7A 1C2
Canada

905-840-6800
Fax: 905-840-6799 800-275-9887
sales@conflow.ca www.conflow.ca
Manufacturer and importer of food processing machinery including certified milk reception and loadout systems, in-plant sanitary flow meters and calibration services and batch and blend control systems; also, transport custodydispensing systems
President: Gary Collins
CFO: Anna Lynn Wiebe
Vice President: Gerry Camirand
Research & Development: Anna Lynn
Quality Control: Gerry Camirand
Number Employees: 7
Square Footage: 5400
Brands:
Contrec
Flowdata, Inc.
Hoffer Flow Controls Inc.
Proces-Data

20857 Congent Technologies
11140 Luschek Drive
Cincinnati, OH 45241-2434

513-469-6800
Fax: 513-469-6811
Bioluminescence lighting system
President: Jim Leroy
Estimated Sales: $2.5-5 000,000
Number Employees: 5-9
Square Footage: 2000

20858 Conifer Paper Products
4911 Central Avenue
Richmond, CA 94804-5842

510-527-8222
Fax: 510-526-3376
Tea and coffee industry bags and packaging film
supplies
Number Employees: 104

20859 Conimar Corp
1724 NE 22nd Ave
Ocala, FL 34470-4702

352-732-3262
Fax: 352-732-6888 800-874-9735
corp@conimar.com www.conimar.com
Beverage coaster, flexible cutting mats and bamboo
cutting boards
Owner: Terry Crawford
CFO: Eric Robinson
VP: Ron Dampier
Marketing: Terry Putty
Estimated Sales: $10-15 Million
Number Employees: 50-99
Square Footage: 140000
Type of Packaging: Private Label

20860 (HQ)Conn Container Corp
455 Sackett Point Rd
North Haven, CT 06473-3199

203-248-0241
Fax: 203-248-0241 www.unicorr.com
Corrugated boxes, containers, displays, foam and
plastic packaging
President: Harry Perkins
hperkins@unicorr.com
President: Lawrence Perkins
Sales Manager: B Etra
Estimated Sales: $20 - 50 Million
Number Employees: 250-499

20861 Connecticut Culinary Institute
230 Farmington Avenue
Suite 5
Farmington, CT 06032-1973

860-677-7869
Fax: 860-676-0679 ct.culinary.inst@snet.net
Consulting firm providing assistance for food ser-
vice operators
President: David Tine
Contact: Tad Handley
admissions@ctculinary.com
Number Employees: 20-49
Square Footage: 20000
Parent Co: Hartine Corporation

20862 Connecticut Laminating Co Inc
162 James St
New Haven, CT 06513-3845

203-787-2184
Fax: 203-787-4073 800-753-9119
info@ctlaminating.com www.ctlaminating.com
Manufacturer and exporter of plastic laminated ad-
vertising signs, place mats, tags, menus and cards
President: Henry Snow
henry@ctlaminating.com
VP: Steve Snow
Estimated Sales: $10 Million+
Number Employees: 100-249
Square Footage: 110000

20863 Connerton Co
1131 E Wakeham Ave
Santa Ana, CA 92705-4145

714-547-9218
Fax: 714-547-1969
sales@connertoncompany.com
www.connertoncompany.com
Commercial gas cooking equipment including broil-
ers, hot plates, griddles, stock pot stoves and
over/under broilers
Vice President: Craig Reynolds
sales@connertoncompany.com
VP: Craig Reynolds
Number Employees: 10-19
Brands:
Connerton

20864 Conpac
131 Industrial Dr
Warminster, PA 18974

215-322-2755
Contract packaging
President: Sam Gerbino

Estimated Sales: Less than $500,000
Number Employees: 1-4

20865 Conquest International LLC
1108 SW 8th St
Plainville, KS 67663-3106

785-434-2483
Fax: 785-434-2736 conquest@ruraltel.net
www.envirolyteconquestusa.com
Water treatment and purification systems. Turn-key
bottled water plants and water stores.
President: Ned Colburn
CFO: Jeffrey Van Dyke
Estimated Sales: Under $500,000
Number Employees: 1-4
Square Footage: 40000
Brands:
Natural Pure

**20866 Consolidated Baling Machine
Company**
P.O. Box 6922
Jacksonville, FL 32236-6922

904-358-3812
Fax: 904-358-7013 800-231-9286
sales@intl-baler.com www.intl-baler.com
Manufacturer and exporter of balers, compactors
and drum crushers/packers
President: William Nielsen
CEO: Roger Griffin
Sales Manager: Jerry Wise
Estimated Sales: $10,000,000 - $19,999,999
Number Employees: 50-99
Square Footage: 8000
Parent Co: Waste Technology Corporation
Brands:
Cmbc
Consolidated Baling Machine Co.
Ibc
International Baler Corp.
International Press & Shear
Ips
Wpc

20867 Consolidated Can Co
15725 Illinois Ave
Paramount, CA 90723-4112

562-634-5245
Fax: 562-634-8689 888-793-2199
www.consolidatedcan.com
Manufacturer and exporter of tin cans; also, tops,
bottoms, plugs and caps for containers
Owner: Doug Lampson
consilidatedcan@aol.com
CFO: Doug Lampson
Estimated Sales: $1 - 2.5 Million
Number Employees: 1-4
Square Footage: 6000
Type of Packaging: Bulk

**20868 Consolidated Commercial
Controls**
200 International Way
Winsted, CT 6098

860-738-7112
Fax: 860-738-7140 800-227-1511
CustServ@AllPointsFPS.com
www.allpointsfps.com
Manufacturer and exporter of commercial cooking
and refrigeration equipment parts; importer of cast
iron parts and supplies.
CEO: John Hanby
CFO: Dan Cox
Vice President: Azie Kahn
Research & Development: Azie Kahn
Marketing Director: John McDermott
Sales Director: Phil Wisehart
Contact: Rick Hernandez
rhernandez@allpointsfps.com
Purchasing Manager: Linda Feichtl
Estimated Sales: $15-20 Million
Number Employees: 20-49
Square Footage: 90000
Type of Packaging: Food Service

20869 Consolidated Container Co
221 Grove St
New Castle, PA 16101-4022

724-658-0549
Fax: 724-658-7427 www.cccllc.com
Plastic containers for liquids including orange juice
and syrup

Sales Manager: John Wolfgang
General Manager: Joe Smarrelli
Plant Manager: Nick Shuler
Purchasing Manager: Bill Bullano
Estimated Sales: $20-50 Million
Number Employees: 50-99
Parent Co: Rostan Corporation

**20870 (HQ)Consolidated Container Co
LLC**
3101 Towercreek Pkwy SE # 300
Suite 300
Atlanta, GA 30339-3256

678-742-4600
Fax: 678-742-4750 888-831-2184
www.cccllc.com
Manufacturer and exporter of blow molded plastic
bottles
Estimated Sales: $237 Million
Number Employees: 1000-4999
Square Footage: 16000
Parent Co: Altium Packaging

20871 Consolidated Container Co
8 Harbor View Rd
South Burlington, VT 05403-7850

802-658-6588
Fax: 802-658-6596
Plastic bottles
President: Eugene Torvend
etorvend@shelburneplastics.com
Vice President of Sales: John Wolfgang
Estimated Sales: $10-20 Million
Number Employees: 50-99

20872 Consolidated Container Co LLC
3101 Towercreek Pkwy SE # 300
Suite 300
Atlanta, GA 30339-3256

678-742-4600
Fax: 678-742-4750 888-831-2184
www.cccllc.com
Blow molded plastic packaging for the dairy, water,
beverage and food industries.
President/CEO/Director: Jeffrey Greene
jeffrey.greene@cccllc.com
CFO: Richard Sehring
EVP Sales/Market Development: Kenneth Branham
VP Human Resources: Bradley Newman
COO: Robert Walton
Number Employees: 1000-4999
Square Footage: 16000
Type of Packaging: Consumer, Food Service

20873 Consolidated Display CoInc
1210 US Highway 34
Oswego, IL 60543-8939

630-851-8666
Fax: 630-851-8756 888-851-7669
buzzp@aol.com www.letitsnow.com
Food props for displays
President: Sebastian Puccio
VP: Anthony Puccio
Estimated Sales: Below $5 Million
Number Employees: 10-19
Square Footage: 60000

20874 Consolidated Label Company
925 Florida Central Pkwy
Longwood, FL 32750

407-339-2626
Fax: 407-331-1711 800-475-2235
liz@consolidatedlabel.com
www.consolidatedlabel.com
Manufacturer and exporter of pressure sensitive la-
bels and tags
President: Joel Carmany
National Sales Manager: Beau Bowman
Plant Manager: Dick St Hilaire
Estimated Sales: $20-50 Million
Number Employees: 50-99
Square Footage: 35000
Type of Packaging: Private Label, Bulk

20875 Consolidated Plastics Co Inc
4700 Prosper Rd
Stow, OH 44224-1068

330-689-3000
Fax: 800-858-5001 800-858-5001
www.consolidatedplastics.net
Blow molded plastic bottles
Number Employees: 50-99

20876 Consolidated Thread Mills, Inc.
P.O. Box 1107
Fall River, MA 02722
508-672-0032
Fax: 508-674-3773
www.consolidatedthreadmills.com
Manufacturer and exporter of bounded and waxed industrial twine including nylon, polyester, rayon and cotton
Owner: Colleen Pacheco
Estimated Sales: $1 - 5 Million
Number Employees: 5-9

20877 Consorcio, MG SA DE CV
4812 N 10th Street
Apt 503
McAllen, TX 78504-2880
956-664-9793
Fax: 956-664-9793

20878 Constantia Colmar
92 County Line Rd
Colmar, PA 18915-9606
215-997-6222
Fax: 215-997-3976
Manufacturer and exporter of foil, juice and yogurt lids, butter wrappers, etc
CEO: Jerry Decker
jerryd@hnpack.com
CEO: Jerry Decker
Estimated Sales: $50-100 Million
Number Employees: 50-99
Parent Co: H&N Packaging
Type of Packaging: Bulk

20879 Constantia Colmar
92 County Line Rd
Colmar, PA 18915-9606
215-997-6222
Fax: 215-997-3976
CEO: Jerry Decker
jerryd@hnpack.com
CEO: Jerry Decker
Estimated Sales: $20 - 50 Million
Number Employees: 50-99

20880 Constar International
41605 Ann Arbor Road
Plymouth, MI 48170
734-455-3600
info@plastipak.com
Plastic containers and bottles for soft drinks, mustard, edible oils, wine and liquors
President: Mike Hoffman
CFO: Bill Rymer
R&D: Don Deual
Production: Craig Renton
Estimated Sales: $2.5 - 5 Million
Number Employees: 20
Parent Co: Crown Cork & Seal

20881 Consulting Nutritional Services
26500 Agoura Road
Suite 210
Calabasas, CA 91302-3550
818-880-6774
Fax: 818-880-6797 cns@foodsafe.com
www.foodsafe.com

20882 Consumer Cap Corporation
PO Box 7259
New Castle, PA 16107-7259
724-657-9440
Fax: 724-654-8573 800-545-5504
Plastic closures
Number Employees: 100

20883 Consumers Packing Company
Plum & Liberty Street
Lancaster, PA 17603
717-397-6141
Fax: 717-397-0322
Packaging supplies
Estimated Sales: $1 - 3 Million
Number Employees: 5-9

20884 Contact Industries
9200 SE Sunnybrook Blvd # 200
Suite 200
Clackamas, OR 97015-5767
503-228-7361
Fax: 503-221-1340 800-345-2232
sales@contactind.com www.contactind.com

Contract packager of aerosols, adhesives, cements, insecticides, room deodorants and oven cleaners
President: Frank Pearson
Quality Control: Leo Hu
Estimated Sales: $10 - 20 Million
Number Employees: 1-4
Parent Co: Safeguard Chemical Corporation
Type of Packaging: Food Service, Private Label

20885 Containair Packaging Corporation
37 E 6th St
Paterson, NJ 7524
973-523-1800
Fax: 973-523-1818 888-276-6500
Manufacturer and exporter of semi-bulk containers for food ingredients; also, slotted cartons and graphic displays available
CEO/President: Lawrence Taylor
VP: Paul Davis
Plant Manager: Ken Kutner
Estimated Sales: $2.5-5 Million
Number Employees: 20-49
Square Footage: 94000
Brands:
  K Box
  Kl Box

20886 Container Handling Systs Corp
621 E Plainfield Rd
Countryside, IL 60525-6913
708-482-9900
Fax: 708-482-8960 sales@chsc1.com
www.containerhandlingsystems.com
Conveyors and conveyor systems
President: Matt Nalbach
neco@nalbach.com
R&D: David Haskell
Estimated Sales: $5 - 10 000,000
Number Employees: 20-49

20887 Container Machinery Corporation
1060 Broadway
Albany, NY 12204
518-694-3310
Fax: 608-719-8380 www.cmc-kuhnke.com
High speed notching presses; exporter of seam quality inspection and measuring systems; importer of can making machinery
Managing Director: Thomas Duve
VP: Alex Grossjohann
Technical Service Manager: Markus Kellner
Marketing Manager: Aura Marcks
Sales Manager Southeast Asia: Ning Qian
Customer Service Manager: Jose Rodriguez
Vice President, Managing Director: Alex Grossjohann
Estimated Sales: $1 - 3 Million
Number Employees: 5-9
Square Footage: 60000
Brands:
  Bertil-Ohlsson
  Imeta
  Krupp (Sig Cantech)
  Lanico
  Mbt (Lubeca)
  Mh Press Systems
  Sanyu
  Wegro Metal Crown

20888 Container ManufacturingInc
50 Baekeland Ave
Middlesex, NJ 08846-2601
732-563-0100
Fax: 732-563-0704 www.containermfg.com
Plastic containers
President: David Jennings
Estimated Sales: $5-10 000,000
Number Employees: 20-49

20889 Container Services Company
PO Box 1115
Warrenton, OR 97146-1115
503-861-3338
Fax: 503-861-0287 cscastoria@aol.com
Estimated Sales: $1 - 5 Million

20890 Container Specialties
1950 N Mannheim Rd
Melrose Park, IL 60160
708-615-1400
Fax: 708-615-0381 800-548-7513
www.midwestcan.com
Plastic bottles and sanitary cans

Owner: John Trippi Sr
CFO: Janet Johnson
Quality Control: John Trippi Jr
Sales/Marketing: Alan Trippi
Estimated Sales: $10 - 20 Million
Number Employees: 20-49
Square Footage: 160000
Parent Co: Midwest Can Company

20891 Container Supply Co
12571 Western Ave
Garden Grove, CA 92841-4012
562-594-0937
Fax: 714-892-3824
tbertoglio@containersupplycompany.com
www.containersupplycompany.com
Manufacturer and exporter of tin cans and plastic pails and containers
Owner: Robert Hurtt
cscmaster@aol.com
Quality Control: C Bonnet
Regional Sales Manager: T Carlson
Director Sales: Tony Bertoglio
Export Sales: F Ceja
Estimated Sales: $20 - 50 Million
Number Employees: 100-249
Square Footage: 160000

20892 Container Testing Lab
607 Fayette Ave
Mamaroneck, NY 10543
914-381-2600
Fax: 914-381-0143 800-221-5170
Laboratory and consulting service specializing in container materials and systems including package engineering, related material handling and package testing certification
President: Vasilis Morfoupolous
Contact: Anton Cotaj
sales@packagelab.com
Lab Manager: S Brooks
Technical Director: C Coleman, Ph.D.
Estimated Sales: Less than $500,000
Number Employees: 5 to 9
Square Footage: 43500

20893 Container-Quinn TestingLab
170 Shepard Ave # A
Wheeling, IL 60090-6061
847-537-9470
Fax: 847-537-9098 spowell@container-quinn.com
Consultant offering package testing, design development, engineering and systems services
President: Todd R Nelson
Manager: Steven Powell
spowell@containerquinn.com
Lab Director: Stephen Powell
Estimated Sales: less than $500,000
Number Employees: 1-4

20894 (HQ)Containment Technology
1105 Highway 30
St Gabriel, LA 70776-5011
225-642-3963
Fax: 225-642-9629 800-388-2467
contectun.bin@aol.com
FDA approved steel containers for liquid and dry hazardous and nonhazardous materials
President: Robert Allen
Vice President: Sylvia Allen
Marketing: Roderick Franklin
VP Sales: Gerald Scruggs
Estimated Sales: $1-2.5 Million
Number Employees: 10-19
Square Footage: 40000
Type of Packaging: Bulk
Other Locations:
  Material Containment
  City of Commerce CA
Brands:
  Blend Tanks
  Fda Steel Container
  Greane Bins

20895 Contec, Inc.
2680 New Cut Rd
Spartenburg, SC 29303
864-503-8333
Fax: 864-503-8444 800-289-5762
www.contecinc.com
Designer and manufacturer of science based cleaning products for food manufacturing facilities.
Estimated Sales: $2.5-5 Million
Number Employees: 5-9

Other Locations:
Contec, Inc. - Automotive Division
Toledo OH
Contec Cleanroom Technology Co, Ltd
Suzhou, China
Contec
France

20896 Contech Enterprises Inc
314 Straight Ave SW
Grand Rapids, MI 49504-6439
616-818-1520
Fax: 616-459-4140 800-767-8658
Manufacturer and exporter of pesticide-free insect trapping adhesives
President and CEO: Mark Grambart
VP of Sales and Marketing: Allen Spigelman
VP of Sales and Marketing: Allen Spigelman
Contact: John Borden
john.borden@contech-inc.com
VP of Operations: Bill Jones
Estimated Sales: $2.5 - 5 Million
Number Employees: 5-9
Square Footage: 80000
Type of Packaging: Private Label
Brands:
Tangle-Trap
Tanglefoot

20897 Contemporary Product Inc
273 Hein Dr
Garner, NC 27529-7221
919-779-4228
Fax: 919-779-9734
Manufacturer and importer of award plaques and shields, trophies and cup bases
VP: David Hamilton
Manager: Joan Squillini
Manager: Joan Squillini
Estimated Sales: $1 - 5 Million
Number Employees: 1-4

20898 (HQ)Contico Container
15510 Blackburn Ave
Norwalk, CA 90650
562-921-9967
Fax: 562-926-4979 www.contico.com
Manufacturer and exporter of polyethylene containers
Engineering-R&D: Michael Angelo
Contact: Nick Man
nickm@conticospraychem.com
Estimated Sales: $20 - 50 Million
Number Employees: 100-249
Parent Co: Contico International

20899 Continental Carbonic Products
2985 East Harrison Avenue
Decatur, IL 62526
217-428-2068
Fax: 217-424-2325 800-379-4232
www.continentalcarbonic.com
Specializes in the manufacture and distribution of dry ice and liquid carbon dioxide, along with sales and rental of dry ice blasting equipment.
President: John Funk
Vice President/Chief Financial Officer: Randy Spitz
General Manager, Manufacturing: Phil Wood
Vice President, Business Development: David Butts
Vice President, Distribution: Jason Taulbee
VP, Manufacturing & Distribution: Mark Hatton

20900 Continental Cart by Kullman Industries
1 Kullman Corporate Campus Dr
Lebanon, NJ 08833-2163
908-236-0220
Fax: 908-236-0848 888-882-2278
Manufacturer and exporter of carts and kiosks; also, modular construction for diners, schools and correctional facilities
President: Amy Marks
CEO: Avi Telyas
Vice President of Operations: Michael Hathaway
Vice President of Production: Bobby Pohlman
Estimated Sales: $50 - 60 Million
Number Employees: 250-499

20901 Continental Commercial Products
305 Rock Industrial Park Dr.
Bridgeton, MO 63044
314-656-4301
Fax: 800-327-5492 800-325-1051
janics@contico.com
www.continentalcommercialproducts.com
Wastebaskets, recycle collection and trash receptacles, utility carts, liners, mopping equipment, squeegees, trigger sprayers, caution signs, plastic shelves, food service products and mobile equipment
President: Mike Boland
VP: Jim Dunn
Contact: Gary Anton
ganton@continentalcommercialproducts.com
Number Employees: 250-499
Square Footage: 11999999
Parent Co: Katy Industries
Brands:
Guardsboy
Guardsmen
Huskee
King Kan
Kleen Aire
Kleen Mist
Roun' Top
Snapoff
Steeline
Structolene
Swing Top
Tip Top
Wall Hugger

20902 Continental Disc Corp
3160 W Heartland Dr
Liberty, MO 64068-3385
816-792-1500
Fax: 816-792-2277 pressure@contdisc.com
www.contdisc.com
Food processing machinery parts including rupture discs for overpressure protection
President: Kenneth R Shaw
CEO: David Brown
dbrown@contdisc.com
Estimated Sales: $20 - 50 Million
Number Employees: 100-249

20903 Continental Envelope
1700 Averill Rd
Geneva, IL 60134-1668
630-578-3300
Fax: 630-262-1450 800-621-8155
sales@continentalenvelope.com
www.continentalenvelope.com
Custom made printed flexo and lithographed envelopes
President: Fred Margulies
fred@convelope.com
Estimated Sales: $20 - 50 Million
Number Employees: 100-249
Square Footage: 120000

20904 Continental Equipment Corporation
P.O. Box 18662
6103 N. 76th Street
Milwaukee, WI 53218
414-463-0500
Fax: 414-463-3199 www.ceceq.com
Manufacturer and exporter of custom washing machinery
President: Will Leistikow
Manager: Mark Kelso
VP Sales: Doug Piszczek
Engineer: Brennen Cullen
Estimated Sales: $3-5 Million
Number Employees: 20-49
Square Footage: 60000
Brands:
Aqucous Washing Systems

20905 Continental Extrusion Corporation
11 Cliffside Drive
Cedar Grove, NJ 07009-1234
973-239-4030
Fax: 973-239-9289 800-822-4748
Bags including specialty squared bottom HDPE and SOS style
VP Sales/Marketing: Ronald Basso
Estimated Sales: $10-20 Million
Number Employees: 100
Square Footage: 266

Brands:
Superbag
Superbag Jr.

20906 Continental Girbau Inc
2500 State Road 44
Oshkosh, WI 54904-8914
920-231-8222
Fax: 920-231-4666 800-256-1073
www.cgilaundry.com
Manufacturer and exporter of commercial and industrial laundry equipment
President: Mike Floyd
mike.floyd@continentalgirbau.org
VP Sales & Customer Service: Joel T Jorgensen
Director Human Resources: Kelly Zabel
Number Employees: 20-49
Parent Co: Girbau S.A.
Brands:
Continental

20907 Continental Identification
140 E Averill
Sparta, MI 49345
616-887-7341
Fax: 616-887-0154 800-247-2499
cipinfo@continentalid.com
www.continentalid.com
Manufacturer and exporter of counter mats, screen printed decals and cooler doors danglers
President: James Clay
Contact: John Begerow
jbegerow@continentalid.com
Operations Manager: Dave Clay
Estimated Sales: $10 - 20 Million
Number Employees: 100-249
Parent Co: Celia Corporation

20908 Continental Industrial Supply
6935 Grande Vista Way S
South Pasadena, FL 33707-4702
727-341-1100
Fax: 727-343-3606
Flooring, trenchdrains, gratings and water conditioners and steamers (dry steamers)
Owner: Mike Marshall
Brands:
Kitchen Best
Never Scale
Polycast

20909 Continental Packaging Corporation
1327-29 Gateway Drive
Elgin, IL 60124
847-289-6400
Fax: 847-289-9048 info@continentalpkg.com
www.continentalpkg.com
Custom flexible packaging materials including bags and printed and plain overwrap
President: Rory Lent
CEO: Christian Krupsha
Contact: Joseph Barsano
joseph@continentalpkg.com
Estimated Sales: $5 Million
Number Employees: 20-50
Square Footage: 60000

20910 Continental Plastic Container
2515 McKinney Avenue
Suite 850
Dallas, TX 75201-7617
972-303-1825
Fax: 972-303-1829
Blow molded plastic bottles
Director Marketing: John Murphy
VP Sales/Marketing: John Roesch

20911 Continental Products
2000 W Boulevard St
Mexico, MO 65265-1209
573-581-5568
Fax: 573-581-8711 800-325-0216
mail@adbags.com www.continentalproducts.com
Plastic and cloth shopping bags
Owner: Pat Mcguire
National Sales Manager: Thad Fisher
Estimated Sales: $1-2.5 Million
Number Employees: 100-249

20912 Continental Refrigeration
539 Dunksferry Rd
Bensalem, PA 19020

215-244-1400
Fax: 215-244-9579 800-523-7138
www.continentalrefrigerator.com
Commercial foodservice refrigeration equipment.
Year Founded: 1989
Estimated Sales: $50-100 Million
Number Employees: 100-249

20913 (HQ)Continental Refrigerator
539 Dunksferry Rd
Bensalem, PA 19020-5908

215-244-1400
Fax: 215-244-9579 800-523-7138
www.nrproducts.com
Refrigeration and air conditioning equipment
Cmo: Tara Migatz
tmigatz@nrac.com
CEO: Brian Kelly
Marketing Director: Tara Montvydas
Sales Manager: Mike Coyle
Operations Manager: Ed Carruthers
Purchasing Manager: Amy Ahern
Estimated Sales: $50-100 Million
Number Employees: 100-249
Square Footage: 87000
Brands:
  Continental Refrigerator
  Hvac

20914 Continental Refrigerator
539 Dunksferry Rd
Bensalem, PA 19020-5908

215-244-1400
Fax: 215-244-9579 800-523-7138
www.nrproducts.com
President: Brian Kelly
Cmo: Tara Migatz
tmigatz@nrac.com
Estimated Sales: $50 - 100 Million
Number Employees: 100-249

20915 Continental Terminals
112 Port Jersey Blvd
Jersey, NJ 07305

973-578-2702
Fax: 973-578-2795
infonj@continentalterminals.com
www.continentalterminals.com
Tea and coffee industry reconditioners, samplers and
weighers
Owner: Vito Difalco
Estimated Sales: Less than $500,000
Number Employees: 10-19

20916 Continental-Fremont
Airport Industrial Park 1685 S. County
PO Box 489
Tiffin, OH 44883

419-448-4045
Fax: 419-448-4048
Manufacturer and exporter of carbon and stainless
steel storage tanks, plating, bins, hoppers, and silos;
sanitary and metal fabrication services available
President: C William Harple
CFO: Melissa Hoover
Quality Control: Ron Ranson
Marketing/Sales: Don Harple
Operations Manager: Ron Ransom
Estimated Sales: Below $5 Million
Number Employees: 20-49
Square Footage: 100000

20917 Contour Packaging
637 W Rockland St
Philadelphia, PA 19120

215-457-1600
Fax: 215-457-5040
Manufacturer and exporter of stand-up pouches and
blow molded plastic bottles and containers; also,
screen printing and hot foil stamping services
available
President: Stephen D Mannino
Sales Engineer: Mark Rysak
Estimated Sales: $10-20 Million
Number Employees: 50-99

20918 Contour Products
4001 Kaw Dr
Kansas City, KS 66102

913-321-4114
Fax: 913-321-8063 800-638-3626

Molded foam
President: Richard Nickloy
Sales Manager: E Brandt
Contact: Mark Deal
  mdeal@contourliving.com
Estimated Sales: $2.5-5 Million
Number Employees: 1-4

20919 Contract Chemicals
201 Concourse Boulevard
Suite 102
Glen Allen, VA 23059-5640

804-967-9761
Fax: 804-967-9764
Specialty chemicals
Estimated Sales: $1-2.5 Million
Number Employees: 4

20920 Contract Comestibles
2004 Beulah Ave
East Troy, WI 53120-1202

262-642-9400
Fax: 262-642-9404 www.execpc.com
Packagers
Owner: Matt Nitz
  mnitz@contractcomestibles.com
Purchasing: Matthew Nitz
Estimated Sales: $1-2,500,000
Number Employees: 5-9

20921 Contrex Inc
8900 Zachary Ln N
Maple Grove, MN 55369-4018

763-424-7800
Fax: 763-424-8734 info@contrexinc.com
www.contrexinc.com
Manufacturer and exporter of electronic controls in-
cluding universal motor speed, universal motor syn-
chronizing, rotary die/knife synchronizing,
cut-to-length/indexing and digital DC motor
President: Gary C Hansen
VP: Glen Gauvin
Estimated Sales: $5-10 Million
Number Employees: 10-19
Brands:
  M-Cut
  M-Drive
  M-Rotary
  M-Shuttle
  M-Track
  M-Traverse
  M-Trim

20922 Control & Metering
6500 Kestrel Road
Mississauga, ON L5T 1Z6
Canada

905-795-9696
Fax: 905-795-9654 800-736-5739
sales@candm.ca
Manufacturer and exporter of dry material handling
equipment including bulk bag dischargers, fillers
and controls
President: Chris Gadula
COO: Don Mackrill
Marketing Manager: Don Mackrill
Operationa Manager: Carmine Cacciarro
Number Employees: 15

20923 Control Beverage
PO Box 578
Adelanto, CA 92301-0578

330-549-5376
Fax: 330-549-9851
Manufacturer and exporter of drink dispensers in-
cluding liquor and soft drink; also, portable bars
President: P Beeghly
VP/Division Manager: Glenn Lewis
Sales Director: Kenneth Wogberg
Manager Technical Services: Dan Pershing
Purchasing Manager: Glenn Lewis
Estimated Sales: $1-3 Million
Number Employees: 6
Square Footage: 10000
Parent Co: International Carbonic
Brands:
  Bevcon

20924 Control Chief Holdings Inc
200 Williams St
Bradford, PA 16701-1411

814-362-6811
Fax: 814-368-4133 sales@controlchief.com
www.controlchief.com

Wireless industrial remote control manufacturer
President: Doug Bell
CEO: Greg Caggiano
  gcaggiano@controlchief.com
CFO: David Dedionisio
R&D: David Higgs
Quality Control: Christine Foster
Marketing Director: Allison Ambrose
Sales: Brian Landries
Operations: Paul McCord
Production: Jack Zelina
Purchasing Director: Dan Johnston
Estimated Sales: $10 - 20 Million
Number Employees: 20-49

20925 Control Concepts Inc.
18760 Lake Dr E
Chanhassen, MN 55317-9384

952-474-6200
Fax: 952-474-6070 800-765-2799
www.ccipower.com
Manufacturer and exporter of electric temperature
process controls. Not to be confused with Control
Concepts, Inc. located in Putnam, CT.
President: Gary Gretenhuis
CEO: Stan Kintigh
CEO: Stanley S Kintigh
Director Sales Support: William Rovick
Contact: Lynn Abraham
  lynn@controlconcepts.net
Operations Manager: Don Christomer
Production Manager: Linh Nguyen
Number Employees: 20
Square Footage: 28000

20926 Control Concepts, Inc.
100 Park St
Putnam, CT 06260

860-928-6551
Fax: 860-928-9450
sales@controlconceptsusa.com
controlconceptsusa.com
Productivity equipment, including Airsweep Sys-
tems, SpeedSwitch Devices and AcoustiClean Sonic
Horns. Not to be confused with Control Concepts
Inc. located in Chanhassen, MN.
President: Henry Tiffany III

20927 Control Instrument Service
3607 Ventura Drive E
Lakeland, FL 33811-1229

863-644-9838
Fax: 863-644-8608 800-644-9839
Instrumentation, valves, weighing equipment includ-
ing temperature, pressure, level, flow and weight
Chairman: John Benedict
Estimated Sales: $1-2.5 Million
Number Employees: 9
Type of Packaging: Bulk

20928 Control Instruments Corp
25 Law Dr # 1
Fairfield, NJ 07004-3295

973-575-9114
Fax: 973-575-0013 info@controlinstruments.com
www.controlinstruments.com
Manufacturer and exporter of hazardous gas detec-
tion systems
CEO: Chris Schaeffer
  cschaeffer@controlinstruments.com
CEO: Chris Schaeffer
Marketing Manager: Patty Gardner
Sales Director: Debra Woods
Estimated Sales: $5-10 Million
Number Employees: 50-99
Type of Packaging: Private Label

20929 Control Module
89 Phoenix Ave
Enfield, CT 6082

860-745-2433
Fax: 860-741-6064 800-722-6654
info@controlmod.com www.controlmod.com
Manufacturer and exporter of bar code data collec-
tion equipment including label printers, laser scan-
ners, data collection terminals and cluster buffers
President: James Bianco
VP: John Fahy
VP Marketing/Sales: James Bianco
Contact: Denise Batalha
  dbatalha@controlmod.com
Estimated Sales: $10-20 Million
Number Employees: 50-99
Square Footage: 80000

Brands:
Bioscan Ii
Linc
Savetime
Securcode Ii

20930 Control Pak Intl
11494 Delmar Dr # 100
Suite #100
Fenton, MI 48430-9018
810-735-2800
Fax: 734-761-2880 info@controlpak.com
www.controlpak.com
Manufacturer and exporter of energy management control systems for temperature, humidity and HVAC applications
Owner: Tim Glinke
Office Manager: Julie Bodziak
Engineer: Len Poma
Estimated Sales: Less Than $500,000
Number Employees: 5-9

20931 Control Products Inc
1724 Lake Dr W
Chanhassen, MN 55317-8580
952-448-2217
Fax: 952-448-1606 800-947-9098
www.protectedhome.com
Digital electronic temperature, humidity and pressure controls including timers, alarms, indicators and controllers; also, custom design available
President: Chris Berghoff
VP Operations: Paul Carlson
IT Executive: John Abbott
jabbott@controlproduictsinc.com
Director Foodservice Industry: Jerry Brown
Marketing Manager: Mark Bjornstad
National Sales Manager: Greg Colvin
IT Executive: John Abbott
jabbott@controlproductsinc.com
Estimated Sales: $20 - 50 Million
Number Employees: 100-249

20932 Control Systems Design
PO Box 647
Forest Hill, MD 21050-0647
410-296-0466
Fax: 410-337-8360
www.controlsystemsdesign.com
Industrial control and data acquisition systems
President: Eldon Hiebert
Part Owner: Jay King
Estimated Sales: $1-2.5 Million
Number Employees: 9
Square Footage: 6000

20933 Control Techniques
7078 Shady Oak Rd
Eden Prairie, MN 55344
952-995-8000
Fax: 952-995-8020 800-893-2321
info.cta@mail.nidec.com acim.nidec.com
Supplier of intelligent drives for commercial and industrial motor control applications. Products help increase productivity, save energy and reduce operating costs.
Parent Co: Nidec Motor Corp.
Other Locations:
Grand Island NY
York PA
Fort Meyers FL
Portland OR
Salt Lake City UT
Cleveland OH
Toronto, ON
Calagary AB Canada

20934 Control Technology Corp
25 South St # E
Hopkinton, MA 01748-2231
508-435-9596
Fax: 508-435-2373 800-282-5008
sales@ctc-control.com
www.controltechnologycorp.com
Designs, manufactures and markets products that enable electronic automation device to be controlled, configured, or reprogrammed over the internet and/or internets.

President: Kenneth Crater
crater@powermotionsales.com
Controller: Lisa St George
Director of Research & Development: Kevin Halloran
Quality Control: Tim Leavitt
Sales Director: Karl Chambers
Operations Manager: Tim Leavitt
Estimated Sales: $4 - 5 Million
Number Employees: 20-49
Other Locations:
Control Technology Corporation
Mequon WI

20935 Convay Systems
9800 Bren Road East
Suite 300
Minnetonka, MN 55343
Canada
905-279-9970
Fax: 888-329-1099 800-334-1099
Manufacturer and exporter of washing and drying systems, pasteurizers, coolers, warmers and dry trash removal systems for the food, beverage and dairy industries
President: Roger Potts
Controller: Carol Ruggiero
Engineering Manager: Michael Voss
Number Employees: 18
Square Footage: 28000

20936 Convectronics
111 Neck Rd
Ward Hill Industrial Park
Haverhill, MA 01835-8027
978-374-7714
Fax: 978-374-7794 800-633-0166
info@convectronics.com www.convectronics.com
Manufacturer and exporter of electric air heaters and thermocouples
President: Philip G Aberizk Jr
VP/Quality Control: Steve Becker
sbecker@connectronics.com
R&D: Bryce Budrow
Sales: Leslie Woodfall
Estimated Sales: Below $5 Million
Number Employees: 10-19
Square Footage: 40000

20937 Convergent Label Technology
620 S Ware Blvd
Tampa, FL 33619
813-621-8128
Fax: 813-620-1206 800-252-6111
Manufacturer and exporter of weigh price labeling equipment and labels
President: Graham Lloyd
Marketing Director: Paula Nelson
Sales/Marketing: Chris Walker
Contact: Nancy Solman
n_solman@discovery-academy.org
Purchasing Manager: Steve Halbrook
Estimated Sales: $60 Million
Number Employees: 100-249
Square Footage: 166000
Type of Packaging: Food Service

20938 Conveyance Technologies LLC
24803 Detroit Rd
Cleveland, OH 44145
440-899-7440
Fax: 440-835-3107 800-701-2278
billwalzer@conveyancecart.com
www.conveyancecart.com
Manufacturer, importer and exporter of material handling products including mobile loading docks, stocking systems, hydraulic lifts, nestable warehouse carts, stocking carts, conveyors, pallet carriers and platform trucks
President: William Walzer
Sales Manager: Sam Aquino
Estimated Sales: $1 - 2 Million
Number Employees: 20-49
Square Footage: 220000
Brands:
Roll-A-Bench
Thru-Put
Uni-Cart
Uni-Lift

20939 Conveying Industries
3795 Paris St # B
Denver, CO 80239-3369
303-373-2035
Fax: 303-373-5149 877-600-4874
info@conveyind.com www.palletizing.us
Conveyors and palletizers
Manager: Don Simmonds
Sales Manager: Bob Carr
Manager: Bill Priday
billpriday@conveyind.com
Estimated Sales: $5-10 Million
Number Employees: 10-19

20940 Conveyor Accessories
7013 High Grove Blvd
Burr Ridge, IL 60527-7593
630-655-4205
Fax: 630-655-4209 800-323-7093
cai@conveyoraccessories.com
www.conveyoraccessories.com
Manufacturer and exporter of conveyor belt fasteners, tools and accessories
President: Thomas Richardson
sales@conveyoraccessories.com
Estimated Sales: $10-20 Million
Number Employees: 20-49
Square Footage: 60000

20941 Conveyor Components Co
130 Seltzer Road
Croswell, MI 48422-9180
810-679-4211
Fax: 810-679-4510 800-233-3233
info@conveyorcomponents.com
www.conveyorcomponents.com
Quality engineered conveyor accessories including emergency stop switches & pull cords, compact stop controls, belt mi-alignment switches, tripper position switches, bucket elevator alignment switches, damaged belt detectors, bulkmaterial flow switches, motion controls and zero speed switches, aeration pads, level controls including rotating paddles and tilt switches, skirtboard clamps, a rotary brush style belt cleaner as well as a wide variety of other conveyor beltcleaners.
President/CEO: Clint Stimpson
General Manager: Barb Stimpson
Sales Manager: Rich Washkevich
Purchasing Coordinator: Sandy VanBrande
Estimated Sales: $5-10 Million
Number Employees: 50-99
Square Footage: 80000
Brands:
Insul-Air
Insul-Glare

20942 Conveyor Components Co
130 Seltzer Rd
Croswell, MI 48422-9180
810-679-4211
Fax: 810-679-4510 800-552-3337
info@cotterman.com
www.conveyorcomponents.com
Manufacturer and exporter of rolling safety and fixed ladders including powder-coated and aluminum; also, portable elevating work platforms
President/CEO: C Stimpson
CFO: B Stimpson
Research & Development: J Kerr
Sales Manager: David Taylor
Manufacturing Manager: Robert Stimpson
Production Manager: L Higgins
Purchasing Manager: G Smith
Estimated Sales: $20-50 Million
Number Employees: 50-99
Square Footage: 60000
Parent Co: Material Control
Brands:
Maxi-Lift
Stockmaster
Tiltnroll
Workmaster

20943 Conveyor Dynamics Corp
7000 W Geneva Dr
St Peters, MO 63376-5712
636-279-1111
Fax: 636-279-1121
info@conveyordynamicscorp.com
www.conveyordynamicscorp.com
Manufacturer and exporter of vibratory processing machinery for bulk and material handling applications

President: Michael Didion
  info@conveyordynamicscorp.com
Engineer: Scott Milsark
Estimated Sales: $500,000 - $1,000,000
Number Employees: 1-4
Square Footage: 72000

20944 Conveyor Equipment Manufacturers Association
6724 Lone Oak Blvd
Naples, FL 34109-6834
                              239-514-3441
        Fax: 239-514-3470 bob@cemanet.org
                        www.cemanet.org
Serves the manufacturers and designers of conveyor
equipment worldwide.
President: George Huber III
Executive VP: Robert Reinfried
Marketing/Membership Manager: Kim MacLaren
Contact: Phil Hannigan
  phil@cemanet.org
Executive Secretary: Philip Hannigan
Estimated Sales: $500,000-$800,000
Number Employees: 1-4

20945 Conveyor Mart
3972 S Us Highway 45
Oshkosh, WI 54902-7351
                              920-233-2724
                         Fax: 920-233-3159
On-line conveyors and conveyor parts
President: James L Nerenhausen
Quality Control: Kurt Frank
Estimated Sales: Below $5 Million
Number Employees: 50-99

20946 Conveyor Supply Inc
1334 Dartmouth Ln
Deerfield, IL 60015-4066
                              847-945-5670
      Fax: 847-945-5676 conveyorsupply2@att.net
Conductors and conveyor systems
Owner: Walter Weiss
CEO: Keith Weiss
Number Employees: 1-4
Square Footage: 8000

20947 Conveyor Systems & Components
21 Norman Ave
Riverside, NJ 08075-1009
                              856-461-8084
    Fax: 856-764-9367 info@conveyorsystems.com
                     www.conveyorsystems.com
Conveyors and conveyor systems
Owner: Thomas Mc Larney
Estimated Sales: $5-10 Million
Number Employees: 1-4

20948 Conveyor Technologies Intergraded
1001 W Waukau Ave
Oshkosh, WI 54902
                              920-233-2756
                         Fax: 920-233-3159
Material handling equipment, packaging machinery,
material handling and conveyor equipment
Number Employees: 5-9

20949 Conviron
572 S 5th St
Suite 2
Pembina, ND 58271-4309
                              701-280-9635
        Fax: 204-786-7736 800-363-6451
                     sales@conviron.com
Refrigerated structures, walk-in coolers and freezer
building and construction consultants, meat distrib-
uting center
President: Steve J Kroft
  steve@conviron.com
Estimated Sales: $1-2.5 Million
Number Employees: 100-249

20950 Convoy
PO Box 8589
Canton, OH 44711
                              330-453-8163
        Fax: 330-453-8181 800-899-1583
Manufacturer and exporter of plastic collapsible
containers and plastic tote boxes
President: Phillip Dannemiller
National Sales Manager: Daren Newman
Estimated Sales: $2.5 - 5 Million
Number Employees: 10-19

Type of Packaging: Bulk

20951 Conwed Global Netting Sltns
530 Gregory Ave NE
Roanoke, VA 24016-2129
                              540-981-0879
        Fax: 540-345-8421 800-368-3610
                     www.conwedplastics.com
Manufacturer and exporter of bags including vented
plastic netting and netting header, onion netting,
mesh linings and netting pallet wrap for fruits, vege-
tables and meats; also, fruit and vegetable juice filter
support cartridges
President: Lawrance Ptaschek
Sales Manager: Michael Woldanski
Controller: Del Ramsey
Plant Manager: Charlie Boxler
Estimated Sales: $10 - 20 Million
Number Employees: 50-99
Parent Co: Siemens Corporation
Brands:
  Polynet

20952 Conwed Plastics LLC
2810 Weeks Ave SE
Minneapolis, MN 55414-2835
                              612-623-1700
        Fax: 612-623-2500 800-426-0149
                     contact@conwedplastics.com
                     www.conwedplastics.com
Netting
Manager: John Burke
CEO: Chris Hatzenbuhler
  chris.hatzenbuhler@conwedplastics.com
Quality Control: Tim Downes
Estimated Sales: $5 - 10 Million
Number Employees: 50-99

20953 Conxall Corporation
601 E Wildwood Ave
Villa Park, IL 60181
                              630-834-7504
        Fax: 630-834-8540 sales@conxall.com
                     www.conxall.com
Custom nonmetallic product connectors and cable
assemblies for processing and controls
President: Keith Bandolik
CFO: Dave Bandolik
Quality Control: Jim Collado
Plant Manager: Rob Smith
Estimated Sales: $20 - 50 Million
Number Employees: 100-249
Square Footage: 45000
Brands:
  Maxi-Con
  Mega-Con
  Micro-Con
  Mil-E-Qual
  Mini-Con
  Multi-Con

20954 Cook & Beals Inc
221 S 7th St
Loup City, NE 68853-8041
                              308-745-0154
        Fax: 308-745-0154 www.cooknbeals.com
Manufacturer and exporter of honey processing
equipment including rotary knife uncappers, spin
float honey-wax separators, heat exchange units,
honey pumps, wax melters, etc
President: Patrick Kuehl
  info@cooknbeals.com
Secretary: Carol Kuehl
VP: Lawrence Kuehl
Estimated Sales: $1-2.5 Million
Number Employees: 5-9

20955 Cook Associates
212 W Kinzie St
Second Floor
Chicago, IL 60654
                              312-329-0900
                         Fax: 312-329-1528
Executive search firm for the food and beverage in-
dustry
President: Arnie Kins
CEO: Mary Kier
VP: Jessica Gentile
Contact: Joe Bilanzic
  jbilanzic@cookma.com
Division Manager: Walter Rach
Estimated Sales: $2.5-5 Million
Number Employees: 50-99

20956 Cook Neon Signs
5382 New Manchester Hwy
Tullahoma, TN 37388-6783
                              931-455-0944
        Fax: 931-455-4536 800-488-0944
        rhonda@cookneon.com www.cookneon.com
Internally illuminated signs
Owner: Charles Callaway
  charles@cookneon.com
Estimated Sales: Below $5 Million
Number Employees: 10-19

20957 CookTek
156 N. Jefferson Street
Suite 300
Chicago, IL 60661-1436
                              312-563-9600
        Fax: 312-432-6220 888-266-5835
                     www.cooktek.com
Manufacturer and exporter of induction cooking sys-
tems
President: Robert Wolters
Quality Control: Robbe Gibb
Marketing Director: Tricia Cleary
Contact: Steven Lopez
  slopez@cooktek.com
Estimated Sales: $.5 - 1 million
Number Employees: 1-4
Number of Brands: 1
Number of Products: 5
Square Footage: 100000
Parent Co: Wolters Group International
Brands:
  Cooktek

20958 Cookie Kingdom
1201 E Walnut St
Oglesby, IL 61348-1344
                              815-883-3331
        Fax: 815-883-3332 ckingdomoffice@gmail.com
                     www.cookiekingdom.com
Manufacturer of cookies, ice cream wafers and dairy
inclusions; co-packer for private label companies;
and builder and upgrader of dairy equipment for
lease or purchase.
President: Cliff Sheppard
  ckingdom@ivnet.com
Director: Patty Smith
Estimated Sales: $13 Million
Number Employees: 100-249
Type of Packaging: Consumer, Private Label, Bulk

20959 Cooking Systems International
76 Pelican Ln
Redwood City, CA 94065
                              650-556-6222
        Fax: 203-377-8187 info@mysck.com
                     www.sck.com
Manufacturer and exporter of rethermalizing units
for cook chill, sous vide, precooked and frozen food
Chairman: B Koether
Executive VP: Scott Wakeman
VP Sales/Marketing: George Koether
Part Time Controller: Scott C Kennedy
Estimated Sales: $10 - 20 Million
Number Employees: 25
Square Footage: 80000
Type of Packaging: Food Service
Brands:
  Csi

20960 Cookshack
2304 N Ash St
Ponca City, OK 74601-1109
                              580-765-3669
        Fax: 580-765-2223 800-423-0698
        info@cookshack.com www.cookshack.com
Sauces & spices, smoking wood accessories for
better barbeque, Cookshack smoked foods cook-
books, electric smoker ovens, pellet fired smokes,
charbroilers, pellet grills
President: Brent Matthews
CEO: Sara Birch
  j.kenney@varde.com
VP: Edward Aguiar Jr
Marketing Coordinator: Cayley Armstrong
Finance/Marketing/Sales Manager: John Shiflet
General Manager: Stuart Powell
Production Manager: Jim Linnebur
Estimated Sales: $4 Million
Number Employees: 20-49
Number of Brands: 2
Number of Products: 1
Square Footage: 44000

Type of Packaging: Consumer, Food Service, Private Label, Bulk
Brands:
  Fast Eddy's

20961 Cookson Plastic Molding
787 Watervliet Shaker Road
Latham, NY 12110-2285

518-951-1000
Fax: 518-783-0004 888-738-8800
www.pacificpools.com

President: Bruce Quay
Technical Services Manager: Peter Morgan

20962 Cool Care
4020 Thor Drive
Boynton Beach, FL 33426-8407

561-364-5711
Fax: 561-364-5766 www.coolcarehvac.com
Manufacturer, importer and exporter of ripening rooms for produce with cold storage and controlled atmosphere; also, vacuum coolers, ice injectors, etc.; installation services available
President: Mike Bianco
Director Sales: Ron Roberts
Engineering Manager: Bob Windecker
Number Employees: 20-49
Square Footage: 100000
Parent Co: Dole Food Company

20963 Cool Cargo
5324 Georgia Highway 85
Forest Park, GA 30297-2475

770-994-0338
Temperature control systems.
President: Burt Pedowitz

20964 Cool-Pitch Co
5948 Rocky Mount Dr
Jacksonville, FL 32258-5415

904-260-1876
800-938-0128
www.cool-pitch.com
Pitcher coolers
President: William Coker
Estimated Sales: $1 - 3,000,000
Number Employees: 5-9
Brands:
  Cool-Pitch

20965 CoolBrands International
4175 Veterans Memorial Highway
3rd Floor
Ronkonkoma, NY 11779-7639

631-737-9700
Fax: 631-737-9792 www.eskimopie.com
Distributor of frozen desserts including ice cream, also flexible packaging
CFO: Gary Stevens
Estimated Sales: $35 Million
Number Employees: 35
Type of Packaging: Food Service, Bulk
Brands:
  Breyers
  Care Bears
  Chipwich
  Crayola
  Disney
  Dogsters
  Eskimo Pie
  Fruit a Freeze
  Godiva Ice Cream
  No Pudge
  Snapple
  The Sopranos
  Trix
  Tropicana
  Wholefruit
  Yoplait

20966 Cooling Products Inc
500 N Pecan Ave
Broken Arrow, OK 74012-2333

918-251-8588
Fax: 918-251-8837
Manufacturer and exporter of heat exchangers, radiators, finned tubes and condensers
Manager: Steve Chalmers
  schalmers@coolprod.com
Production: Harold Gordon
Sales Manager: Stephen Chalmers
Estimated Sales: $20 - 50 Million
Number Employees: 50-99

20967 Cooling Technology Inc
1800 Orr Industrial Ct
Charlotte, NC 28213-6342

704-596-4109
Fax: 704-597-8697 800-872-1448
info@coolingtechnology.com
www.coolingtechnology.com
Manufacturer and exporter of temperature controllers, chillers and evaporative cooling and pumping systems.
Owner: Chrystel Baker
Marketing Director: Chris Fore
Director of Sales and Marketing: Laura Walker
  cbaker@coolingtech.gd
Operations Manager: Sheetal Desai
Estimated Sales: $3-5 Million
Number Employees: 20-49
Number of Products: 20
Square Footage: 40000

20968 Cooper Decoration Company
PO Box 81
Weston, MA 02493-0005

315-475-1661
Fax: 315-475-1664 tsmallcoop@aol.com
Christmas lights and decorations; also, food show decorator
President: Jon Cooper
VP: Lou Galtieri
Operations Manager: Jim Cooper
Estimated Sales: $1-2.5 Million
Number Employees: 10
Parent Co: Cooper Drapery Company

20969 Cooper Instrument Corporation
P.O. Box 450
Middlefield, CT 06455-0450

860-349-3473
Fax: 860-349-8994 800-835-5011
sbennett@cooperinstrument.com
www.cooper-atkins.com
CEO: Carol P Wallace
Director of Marketing: Cherylann Hunt
Estimated Sales: $1 - 5 Million
Number Employees: 100-249

20970 Cooperheat/MQS
P.O. Box 123
Alvin, TX 77512-0123

281-331-6154
Fax: 281-331-4107 800-526-4233
Manufacturer and exporter of heat treating equipment, accesories and services, heat tracing equipment and services; also, induction equipment and nondestructive testing
President: Kenneth Tholan
VP Sales: Charels Silver
VP International Sales: Jim Campbell
Number Employees: 20-49
Square Footage: 160000
Parent Co: International Industrial Services
Brands:
  Eagle
  Versatrace

20971 Copack International
1270 Belle Ave # 115
Winter Springs, FL 32708-1905

407-699-7507
Fax: 407-699-7543 padamission@copack.com
www.copack.com
Food packaging materials
President: Paul J Adamission
Contact: Paul Adamission
  p.adamission@copack.com
Estimated Sales: $4 Million
Number Employees: 50-99
Square Footage: 400000
Type of Packaging: Consumer, Food Service, Private Label, Bulk

20972 Cope Plastics Inc
4441 Industrial Dr
Alton, IL 62002-5939

618-466-0221
Fax: 618-466-7975 800-851-5510
mi@copeplastics.com www.copeplastics.com
FDA, 3A and USDA compliant plastic components

President & CEO: Jane Saale
CEO: Grant Benner
  grant@thegoalieclub.com
VP of Finance: John Theen
Quality Manager: Mike Chism
Director of Marketing: Cindy Smalley
VP of Sales: John Lee
VP of Operations: Josh Kuhnash
Manufacturing Manager: Jerry Dunnagan
Estimated Sales: $1-2.5 Million
Number Employees: 100-249
Parent Co: Cope Plastics

20973 Coperion Corp
590 Woodbury Glassboro Rd
Sewell, NJ 08080-4558

854-253-3265
info@coperionktron.com
www.coperion.com
Provide process automation, equipment, systems and solutions for bulk material handling.
Vice President: Thomas Hummel
Vice President: Thomas Hummel
Business Development Manager - Food: Sharon Nowark
Number Employees: 100-249

20974 Copesan
W175n5711 Technology Dr
Menomonee Falls, WI 53051-5673

262-783-6261
Fax: 262-783-6267 800-267-3726
info@copesan.com www.copesan.com
Provides effective pest management services for all your pest management needs, including insect, rodent stored product pest, bird and weed control, and fumigations
President: Deni Naumann
Vice President of Finance: Kevin Fixel
Vice President: Mike Campbell
Quality Control: Jim Snkiele
Technical Advisor: Jim Snkiele
Marketing Director: Elizabeth Johnson
VP, Sales: Aric Schroeder
Director, HR: Jessica Janiszewski
Operations Manager: Carl Griswold
Estimated Sales: $2.5 - 5 Million
Number Employees: 20-49

20975 Copper Brite
PO Box 50610
Santa Barbara, CA 93150-0610

805-565-1566
Fax: 805-565-1394
Manufacturer and exporter of insecticides and wood rot fungicides; also, cleaner and polish for copper, brass and stainless steel
President/ CEO: Alan D. Brite
CFO: Alan Brite
Executive VP: Terry Brite
R&D: Alan Brite
Quality Control: Terry Brite
Estimated Sales: $2.5 - 5 Million
Number Employees: 1-4
Brands:
  Copper Brite
  Roach Prufe
  Termite Prufe

20976 Copper Clad
600 S 9th St
Reading, PA 19602-2506

610-375-4596
Fax: 610-375-3557
Metal polish cleaners including silver, brass, copper and stainless steel
President: Thomas Ziemer
Estimated Sales: $10 - 20 Million
Number Employees: 10-19
Square Footage: 144000
Brands:
  Farberware
  Revere

20977 Copper Hills Fruit Sales
4337 N Golden State Boulevard
Suite 102
Fresno, CA 93722-3801

559-432-5400
Fax: 559-432-5620
Packers of peaches, plums, nectarines, apricots, pomegranates, and persimmons
Managing Member: Wilma J. Deniz

20978 Copperwood InternationalInc
9249 S Broadway
Unit 200-238
Highland Ranch, CO 80129-5692
303-683-1234
Fax: 303-683-0933 800-411-7887
copperwoodfoods@aol.com
Broker of a wide variety of closeout, excess and dis-
counted food items
Sales Director: Michael Casey
Estimated Sales: $5,000,000
Number Employees: 4
Number of Brands: 76
Number of Products: 127
Square Footage: 50000

20979 Coral LLC
5576 Bighorn Dr # B
Carson City, NV 89701-1474
775-883-9853
Fax: 775-883-9858 800-882-9577
sales@coralcalcium.com www.coralcalcium.com
Natural minerals
Sales Director: Alberto Galdamez
Contact: Matt Cuhadar
matt@coralcalcium.com
Number Employees: 5-9

20980 Corben Packaging & Display
976 Grand Street
Brooklyn, NY 11211-2707
718-388-7666
Fax: 718-388-6592 packitgood@aol.com
Full service contract packaging includes shrink
wrapping, poly bagging, blister packaging, custom
packaging, clam shells and folding boxes
Estimated Sales: $1-2.5 000,000
Number Employees: 12

20981 Corbett Timber Co
1200 Castle Hayne Rd
Wilmington, NC 28401-8885
910-763-9991
Fax: 910-763-3426 800-334-0684
Wooden wirebound crates
President: Scott Corbett
Partner: William Corbett
Sales Manager (Containers): Donald Williamson
Estimated Sales: $10-20 Million
Number Employees: 50-99
Square Footage: 300000

20982 Corbox-Meyers Inc
6701 Hubbard Ave
Cleveland, OH 44127-1475
216-441-0150
Fax: 216-441-4213 800-321-7286
www.corbox.com
Shipping containers, bins and storage boxes
Owner: Kathy Zenisek
VP: Clyde Zenisek
Estimated Sales: $1-2.5 Million
Number Employees: 20-49
Square Footage: 96000
Parent Co: Corbox

20983 Corby Hall
3 Emery Ave
Randolph, NJ 07869-1308
973-366-8300
Fax: 973-366-9833 info@corbyhall.com
www.corbyhall.com
Manufacturer and exporter of stainless steel and sil-
ver plated flatware and hollowware; importer of
flatware
Vice President: Bill Adams
bill.adams@hollowick.com
CFO: Alan Millward
Vice President: Adrian Millward
Quality Control: Andrew Millward
VP Marketing: Andrew Millward
Estimated Sales: $500,000 - $1 Million
Number Employees: 5-9
Square Footage: 30000
Type of Packaging: Food Service
Brands:
Algarve
Corby Hall
Riviera
St. Moritz

20984 Cord Tex
136 Industrial Ave
New Orleans, LA 70121-2902
504-834-2862
Fax: 504-837-7645
Distributor, importer and exporter of manila, sisal
and synthetic rope and twine
President: Carl Ruch
VP: Gerard Ruch
Estimated Sales: $1 - 3 Million
Number Employees: 5-9

20985 Core Products Co
401 Industrial Park
PO Box 669
Canton, TX 75103-2817
903-567-1341
Fax: 903-567-1346 800-825-2673
www.coreproductsco.com
Manufacturer and exporter of odor control agents,
carpet and upholstery cleaning products, stain and
rust removers, degreasers and cleaners for tub, tile,
glass, chrome and stainless steel
President: Brent Crawford
core@coreproductsco.com
CFO: Debbie Crawford
VP: Debbie Crawford
Sales Manager: Brian Hawkins
Estimated Sales: $500,000-$1 Million
Number Employees: 10-19
Square Footage: 80000
Brands:
Believe It
Beta-Kleen
Bonnet Buff
De-Foamer
Hot Water Extract
Incredible Blue
Juice Out
Leather Magic
Mal-X
Perfect Image
Plus Ii
Preconditioner Traffic Lane
Rust Bust'r
Tann-X
Unbelievable Green
Unbelievable!

20986 Corenco
3275 Dutton Ave
Santa Rosa, CA 95407-7891
707-824-9868
Fax: 707-528-3197 888-267-3626
ngorsuch@corenco.biz www.corenco.biz
Manufactures size reduction equipment for the food
processing industry.
President/CEO: Chris Cory
ccory@corenco.biz
Corporate Secretary/Accounting: Saraj Cory
VP/COO: Jeff Boheim
Inside Machinery Sales: Neil Gorsuch
Production Manager: Matt Young
Estimated Sales: $1-2.5 Million
Number Employees: 5-9
Number of Brands: 1
Number of Products: 14
Square Footage: 14000
Brands:
Corenco

20987 Corfab
6700 S Sayre Avenue
Chicago, IL 60638
708-458-8750
Corrugated paperboard partitions, boxes, file folders
and displays
President: R Izenstark
VP: Sy Ginsberg
Plant Manager: Frank Fandl
Estimated Sales: $20-50 Million
Number Employees: 50-99

20988 Corinth Products
74 Hob Rd
Corinth, ME 4427
207-285-3387
Fax: 207-285-7738
Wooden pallets and boxes
President/CEO: Peter Higgins
Estimated Sales: Below $5 Million
Number Employees: 10

20989 Cork Specialties
1454 NW 78th Ave #305
Miami, FL 33126
305-477-1506
Fax: 305-591-0593 corkspec@aol.com
Manufacturer, importer and exporter of corks and
plastic top stoppers
President: Rafael Figueroa
VP: Orlando Barranco
Estimated Sales: Below $5 Million
Number Employees: 5-9

20990 Corman & Assoc Inc
881 Floyd Dr
Lexington, KY 40505-3694
859-233-0544
Fax: 859-253-0119 ted@cormans.com
www.cormans.com
Point of purchase displays and store fixtures
President: Ted Corman
ted@cormans.com
Estimated Sales: $5-10 Million
Number Employees: 50-99
Square Footage: 220000

20991 Corn States Metal Fabricators
1323 Maple St
PO Box 65635
West Des Moines, IA 50265-4397
515-225-7961
Fax: 515-225-9382 www.cornstates.com
Conveyors and elevators
President and CEO: Randall Golay
Vice President: Mitch Golay
mitchg@cornstates.com
Estimated Sales: $5-10 Million
Number Employees: 20-49
Square Footage: 60000

20992 Cornelia Broom Company
756 Hoyt St
Cornelia, GA 30531
706-778-4434
Fax: 706-778-9814 800-228-2551
Brushes, brooms, mops and handles
President: Joby Scroggs
Secretary: Fran Chastain
VP: Marcia Scroggs
Estimated Sales: $5 - 10 Million
Number Employees: 24
Square Footage: 40000

20993 Cornelius
2421 15th SW
Mason City, IA 50401
641-424-3601
800-238-3600
www.cornelius.com
Manufacturer and exporter of ice makers and dis-
pensers.
Year Founded: 1931
Estimated Sales: $100-$500 Million
Number Employees: 4,500
Type of Packaging: Food Service

20994 Cornelius Inc.
101 Broadway St. W
Osseo, MN 55369
763-488-8200
Fax: 763-488-4298 800-238-3600
publications@cornelius.com
www.cornelius-usa.com
Beverage dispensing and ice making equipment.
Year Founded: 1931
Estimated Sales: $241.8 Million
Number Employees: 4,500+
Number of Brands: 4
Number of Products: 6
Parent Co: Marmon Beverage Technologies Inc.
Type of Packaging: Food Service
Other Locations:
IMI Cornelius
Norwood MA
Brands:
Cornelius
Jet Spray
Rencor
Wilshire

20995 Cornelius Wilshire Corporation
2401 N Palmer Dr
Schaumburg, IL 60196-0001
847-397-4600
Fax: 847-539-6960 www.cornelius-usa.com

Ice makers and juice dispensers
President: Tim Hubbard
Sales/Marketing: Michael Orlando
Brands:
    Wilshire

20996 Cornell Machine Co
45 Brown Ave
Springfield, NJ 07081-2992
973-379-6860
Fax: 973-379-6854 info@cornellmachine.com
www.cornellversator.com
Manufacturer and exporter of food processing
equipment including homogenizers, emulsifiers,
mixers, oxygen removers, deaerators and defoaming
equipment
President: Martin Huska
Contact: Alan Huska
    ajhuska@cornellmachine.com
Estimated Sales: $1-2.5 Million
Number Employees: 5-9
Brands:
    Cornell Versator

20997 Cornell Pump Company
P.O. Box 6334
Portland, OR 97228-6334
503-653-0330
Fax: 503-653-0338 info@cornellpump.com
www.cornellpump.com
Manufacturer, importer and exporter of pumps for
food product handling, hot oil circulation, refrigera-
tion and waste handling
President: Jeff Markham
Marketing: Brenda Case
Number Employees: 100-249
Parent Co: Roper Industries
Brands:
    Cycloseal
    Redi-Prime

20998 Cornerstone
750 Patrick Pl
Brownsburg, IN 46112-2211
317-852-6522
Fax: 317-852-6433 800-659-7699
info@cornerstoneflooring.com
www.cornerstoneflooring.com/industries/industrie
s.shtml
Manufacturer and installer of high performance
polymer flooring, lining and coating materials for a
variety of industries including that of food and
beverage.
President: Dann Hess
Sales Manager: Tracy Figley
Contact: Charles Joslin
    cjoslin@cornerstoneflooring.com
Estimated Sales: $1 - 5 000,000
Number Employees: 20-49

20999 Corniani
501 Southlake Blvd
Richmond, VA 23236-3042
804-794-6688
Fax: 804-794-6187
President: Giuseppe Venturi
    gventuri@middleburgbank.com
Number Employees: 100-249

21000 Corning Life Sciences
836 North Street
Tewksbury, MA 01876
978-442-2200
800-492-1110
inquiries@corning.com
www.corning.com/worldwide/en/products/life-scie
nces.html
Pyrex Laboratory glassware, Corning brand instru-
ments and equipment, and Cornin and Costar brand
plasticware.
Chairman & CEO: Wendell Weeks
Vice Chairman/Corporate Development: Lawrence
McRae
Senior VP & GM, Life Sciences: Ronald Verkleeren
Executive VP & CFO: Tony Tripeny
Estimated Sales: $10.5 Billion
Number Employees: 45,000
Parent Co: Corning Inc
Brands:
    Checkmate
    Checkmite
    Corex Ii
    Corning
    Costar

Pyrex
Pyrex Plus
Scholar
Vycor

21001 Cornish Containers
205 W Sophia Street
Maumee, OH 43537-2166
419-893-7911
Fax: 419-893-5146
Chest and door type insulated and refrigerated con-
tainers
CEO: Jody Holbrook
Sales Director: Tim McNulty
Estimated Sales: $1-2.5 Million
Number Employees: 6
Square Footage: 50000
Brands:
    Frigi-Top
    Transafe

21002 Coronet Chandelier Originals
12 Grand Blvd # 16
Brentwood, NY 11717-5195
631-273-1177
Fax: 631-273-1247
Manufacturer and exporter of custom chandeliers;
importer of chandelier crystals, wrought iron tables,
wall solders, pendents
President: Irwin Goldberg
Estimated Sales: $1 - 3 Million
Number Employees: 10-19
Square Footage: 60000

21003 Corp Somat
165 Independence Ct
Lancaster, PA 17601-5838
717-392-6714
Fax: 717-291-0877 800-237-6628
www.somatcompany.com
Manufacturer and exporter of waste pulping and
dewatering systems for processing and reduction of
food service wastes
Manager: Scott Witmer
R&D: Steve Eno
Marketing: Lin Sensenig
Food Service Equipment Sales: Herman Williams
Contact: Dolores Alexander
    dalexander@somat.com
Production: Barry Alexander
Plant Manager: Rich Zimmerman
Number Employees: 5-9
Square Footage: 78000
Brands:
    Somat Classic
    Somat Evergreen

21004 Corpak
PO Box 364747
San Juan, PR 00936-4747
787-787-9085
Fax: 787-740-5230
Paperboard boxes
VP Sales: Minerva Medina
Estimated Sales: $1 - 5 Million
Number Employees: 50-99

21005 Corporate Safe Specialists
14800 S Mckinley Ave
Posen, IL 60469-1547
708-371-4200
Fax: 708-371-3326 800-342-3033
curreyj@corporatesafe.com
CSS is an industry leader providing innovative secu-
rity solutions to the restaurant and retail industries
globally. CSS safes, smart safes and kiosks can be
configured to provide closed-loop cash management
to deter armed robberyburglary and internal theft.
President: Edward McGunn
CEO: Ed McGunn
CFO: Lisa Marsh
Vice President: Rosemary Leonard
Marketing Director: Peter Muiznieks
Sales Director: James Currey
Operations Manager: Adam Saggese
Estimated Sales: $35 Million
Number Employees: 5-9
Square Footage: 60000
Brands:
    Power Lever
    Quik Lock Ii

21006 Corpus Christi Stamp Works
502 S Staples St
Corpus Christi, TX 78401-3333
361-884-4801
Fax: 361-884-1038 800-322-4515
sales@ccstampworks.com
www.ccswsignsystems.com
Marking devices, rubber and pre-inked stamps and
engraved signs and name badges
President: Harry Lee Chester
    hches92383@aol.com
VP: Catherine Ray
Office Manager: Mildred Ashmore
Estimated Sales: $2.5-5 Million
Number Employees: 20-49
Square Footage: 10000

21007 Corr Pak Corp
8000 Joliet Rd # 100
Mc Cook, IL 60525-3256
708-442-7806
Fax: 708-442-0467 haltaylor@corr-pak.com
Corrugated boxes, containers and point of purchase
displays; silk screen printing available
President: Jim Hagenseker
    hagensekerjim@corr-pak.com
VP, Display Division: Jim Hagenseker
Sales: Barry Smith
Estimated Sales: Below $5 Million
Number Employees: 20-49

21008 Corrections Dept
1920 Technology Pkwy
Mechanicsburg, PA 17050-8507
717-728-2573
Fax: 717-975-2242 ra-contactdoc@pa.gov
www.cor.state.pa.us
Industrial school
Manager: Franklin Tennis
Quality Control: Carroll Healey
Manager: John E Wetzel
    jowetzel@state.pa.us
Number Employees: 10000+

21009 Corrigan Corporation of America
104 Ambrogio Dr
Gurnee, IL 60031-3373
847-263-5955
Fax: 847-263-5944 800-462-6478
sales@corriganmist.com www.corriganmist.com
Produce misting, meat humidification and water fil-
tration systems
Owner: J Michael Corrigan
Account Manager: Charles Noland
Estimated Sales: $3 - 5 Million
Number Employees: 10-19
Parent Co: Corrigan Corporation of America
Brands:
    Hypersoft
    Optimist
    Ultramist
    Vaporplus

21010 Corro-Shield International Inc
7059 Barry St
Rosemont, IL 60018-3401
847-298-7770
Fax: 847-298-7784 800-298-7637
www.corroshield.com
Industrial floors and wall coatings.
Manager: Bret Snider
    bsnider@corroshield.com
Number Employees: 5-9

21011 Corrobilt Container Company
7888 Marathon Dr
Livermore, CA 94550-9325
925-373-0880
Fax: 209-249-3130
Corrugated containers
President: Edward Childe
Number Employees: 5 to 9
Type of Packaging: Bulk

21012 Corrugated Inner-Pak Corporation
51 Washington Street
Conshohocken, PA 19428
610-825-0200
Fax: 610-828-0907
Corrugated paper and foam plastic packaging specialties and wooden boxes and crates; contract packaging available for the government and commercial
industries

President: Robert E Doyoe
Treasurer: Ben Watson
VP: John McCarthy
Estimated Sales: Below $5 Million
Number Employees: 9
Parent Co: Inter-Pack Corporation

21013 Corrugated Packaging
1683 Cattlemen Rd
Sarasota, FL 34232
941-371-0000
Fax: 941-378-5637
Packaging materials including corrugated boxes,
pads, folders and die cuts
Owner: Nancy James
President: Arthur James Jr
Marketing Director: Herbert Markham
Purchasing Manager: Robert Mecall
Estimated Sales: $2.5-5 Million
Number Employees: 10
Square Footage: 53000

21014 Corrugated Specialties
352 12th St # 2
Plainwell, MI 49080-1154
269-685-9821
Corrugated paper and boxes
Owner: Jim Skrobot
President: James Skrobot
Estimated Sales: $1-2.5 Million
Number Employees: 1 to4

21015 Corrugated Supplies Co.
5043 W 67th St
Bedford, IL 60638
708-458-5525
Fax: 708-458-0013 888-826-2738
www.corrugatedsuppliescompany.com
Manufacturer of corrugated cardboard sheets
CEO: John Potocsnak
Estimated Sales: $21 Million
Number Employees: 50-99
Square Footage: 100000
Type of Packaging: Consumer, Food Service, Bulk

21016 Corrupad Protective Packaging
89 Oleary Dr
Bensenville, IL 60106-2270
630-238-8090
Fax: 630-238-8096
Recycled paper packaging materials
President: Norman Lynn
Estimated Sales: $10-25 Million
Number Employees: 20-49

21017 Corsair Display Systems
5560 Airport Rd
Canandaigua, NY 14424
585-396-3480
Fax: 585-396-5953 800-347-5245
sales@corsairdisplay.com
www.corsairdisplay.com
Merchandising stations, pastry cases, carts, kiosks,
menu systems and bulkhead signs
President: David Mansfield
Vice President: Alison Leet
Marketing/Sales: Bruce Meckling
Operations Manager: Cindy DeRycke
Purchasing Manager: Eric Rands
Estimated Sales: $3-5 Million
Number Employees: 20-49
Square Footage: 80000

21018 Corson Manufacturing Company
20 Michigan Street
24
Lockport, NY 14094-2628
716-434-8871
Fax: 716-434-8801
Paper boxes for cereal, snacks, cookies, etc
CEO: Anthony Gioia
Estimated Sales: $3 - 5 Million
Number Employees: 230

21019 Corson Rubber Products Inc
105 Smith St
Clover, SC 29710-1333
803-222-7779
Fax: 803-222-9022 info@corsonrubber.com
www.corsonrubber.com
Color coded sanitation was FDA compliant knobby
mats.
President: Denis Garvey
Plant Manager: Terry Wallace

Estimated Sales: $9-15 Million
Number Employees: 10-19
Type of Packaging: Consumer, Food Service, Private Label, Bulk
Brands:
Corson

21020 Cortec Aero
4119 White Bear Pkwy
St Paul, MN 55110-7634
651-429-1100
Fax: 651-429-1122 800-426-7832
info@cortecvci.com www.cortecvci.com
Polyethylene film and bags including plain and
printed
General Manager: Usama Jacir
CEO: Boris Miksic
bmiksic@cortecvci.com
Vice President of Sales: Cliff Cracauer
Regional Sales Manager: Ashlee Meints
Plant Manager: Tim Bliss
Estimated Sales: $1 - 3 Million
Number Employees: 100-249
Square Footage: 106400

21021 Cortec Aero
4119 White Bear Pkwy
St Paul, MN 55110-7634
651-429-1100
Fax: 651-429-1122 800-426-7832
info@cortecvci.com www.cortecvci.com
Cortec Corporation is a pioneer of environmentally
friendly, corrosion protection Vapor Phase Corrosion
Inhibitors(VpCIin), a Migratory corrosion Inhibitors(MCI) Technologies for the packaging industry.
ISO 9001:2000 & 14001Registered
President: Boris Miksic
bmiksic@cortecvci.com
Estimated Sales: $10 - 20 000,000
Number Employees: 100-249
Number of Brands: 5
Number of Products: 400+
Type of Packaging: Consumer, Food Service, Private Label, Bulk

21022 Cosco Home & Office Products
2525 State St
Columbus, IN 47201
Fax: 636-745-1005 800-628-8321
customer.service@coscoproducts.com
www.coscoproducts.com
Manufacturer and exporter of home and office furniture.
President & CEO: Troy Franks
Year Founded: 1939
Estimated Sales: $100-500 Million
Number Employees: 1000-4999
Parent Co: Dorel Home Furnishings
Type of Packaging: Food Service
Brands:
Cosco

21023 Cosense Inc
155 Ricefield Ln
Hauppauge, NY 11788-2031
631-231-0735
Fax: 631-231-0838 sales@cosense.com
Designs and manufactures lliquid level sensors utilizing patented ultrasonic technology.
Owner: Naim Dam
Sales Director: Kevin Conlin
Contact: Bill Allhusen
ballhusen@cosense.com
Estimated Sales: $5-10 Million
Number Employees: 20-49
Square Footage: 20000
Brands:
Millennuim
Pointsense
Sentio
Sonic Eye

21024 Cosgrove Enterprises Inc
14300 NW 77th Ct
Miami Lakes, FL 33016-1534
305-820-5600
Fax: 305-623-6935 800-888-3396
orders@e-cosgrove.com
www.cosgroveenterprises.com
Manufacturer, exporter and importer of cleaning
equipment and janitorial supplies including brooms,
brushes and paper products

President: Robert Cosgrove
robert@cosgroveenterprises.com
Quality Control: Louides Cohen
VP: Randy Shelton
Estimated Sales: $500,000 - $1 Million
Number Employees: 20-49
Square Footage: 220000

21025 Cosmic Co
151 Haskins Way # A
South San Francisco, CA 94080-6200
650-742-0888
Fax: 650-742-6777 cosmic@cosmicco.us
www.cosmicco.us
Boxes, thermal-formed trays, compartments,
semi-rigid clear containers
VP: Agnes Cheung
Estimated Sales: $2.5-5 000,000
Number Employees: 10-19

21026 Cosmo/Kabar
140 Schmitt Blvd
Farmingdale, NY 11735-1461
631-694-6857
Fax: 631-694-6846 info@cosmos-kabar.com
www.cosmos-kabar.com
President: Bruce McKee
R&D: Bryan Matty
CFO: Bruce McKee
Contact: Paolo Bruschi
pbruschi@cosmos-kabar.com
Estimated Sales: $2 Million
Number Employees: 20-49

21027 Cosmos International
PO Box 7740
Burbank, CA 91510-7740
626-330-8499
Fax: 626-333-4210
Canned fruit
Office Manager: Janet Muna

21028 Coss Engineering Sales Company
3943 S Creek Drive
Ts
Rochester Hills, MI 48306-4729
248-370-0707
Fax: 248-370-9211 800-446-1365
Manufacturer and exporter of pneumatic conveying
systems, surge hoppers and storage silos
CEO and President: Carter Coss
Estimated Sales: Less than $500,000
Number Employees: 4

21029 Costa Broom Works
3606 E 4th Ave
Tampa, FL 33605-5835
813-385-1722
Fax: 813-247-6060
Brooms, mops, mop heads and brushes; importer of
related products for cleaning
Owner: Frank J Costa
Estimated Sales: $1-2.5 Million
Number Employees: 20-30
Type of Packaging: Food Service, Bulk

21030 Cott Technologies
14923 Proctor Ave
La Puente, CA 91746-3206
626-961-0370
Fax: 626-333-9307
Automated vacuum packaging machines and refrigerator display cases
Owner: Gilbert De Cardenas
Estimated Sales: $10 - 20 Million
Number Employees: 20-49
Brands:
Vari-Pack

21031 Cotter Brothers Corp
8 Southside Rd
Danvers, MA 01923-1409
978-777-5001
Fax: 978-750-6219 info@cotterbrothers.com
www.cotterbrothers.com
High purity process piping and skid mounted systems; also, installation available
President: Randolph Cotter
randy@cotterbrothers.com
VP: David Cotter
Director Business Development: Frank Armstrong
Estimated Sales: $10-20 Million
Number Employees: 20-49

21032 (HQ)Cotton Goods Mfg Co
259 N California Ave
Chicago, IL 60612-1903
773-265-0088
Fax: 773-265-0096 cotton2@earthlink.net
www.cottongoodsmfg.com
Manufacturer and exporter of table skirts and linens
President/CEO: Edward Lewis
cotton2@earthlink.net
Sales Manager: Kevin Higgins
Estimated Sales: $3 - 5 Million
Number Employees: 10-19
Square Footage: 20000
Brands:
Grip Clips

21033 Couch & Philippi
10680 Fern Ave
PO Box A
Stanton, CA 90680-2600
714-527-2261
Fax: 714-827-2077 800-854-3360
sales@couchandphilippi.com
Designing and producing innovative products for
restaurants and beverage copmanies nationwide.
President: Steve Ellsworth
sellsworth@primus-group.com
Estimated Sales: $5 - 10 Million
Number Employees: 50-99

21034 Cougar Packaging Concepts, Inc.
612 Stetson Ave
St. Charles, IL 60174
630-689-4050
www.cougarpackaging.com
Developer of packaging systems to help food safety
and shelf life extension. Creator of a Modified Atmosphere Packaging (AMP) process combined with
Pulsed Ultra Violet (PUV) light technology that creates a sanitization method to cleanproduct lines,
packaging and even food products, without ad-
versely affecting the taste of the products.
President: Mark Cottone
CEO: Tiffany DeSalvo
Marketing & Admin/Sales Support: Brooke
Shipbaugh
Vice President of Tech Sales: Steve Kligis

21035 Cougar Packaging Solutions
12301 New Ave
Unit E
Lemont, IL 60439
630-231-7800
Fax: 630-231-1286 sales@cougargroup.com
www.cougargroup.com
Provides packaging services, including Modified At-
mosphere Packaging equipment, thermoformed trays
and lidded films.
President: John Senese
Senior Account Executive: Pam Anderson
Vice President of Sales: Dan Ferguson

21036 Country Save Products Corp
19704 60th Ave NE
Arlington, WA 98223-4736
360-435-9868
Fax: 360-435-0896 info@countrysave.com
www.countrysave.com
Manufacturer and exporter of phosphate-free laun-
dry detergent and dishwashing powder; also, chlo-
rine-free powdered bleach
President: Kris Anderson
krisa@countrysave.com
Estimated Sales: $2.5-5 Million
Number Employees: 5-9
Brands:
Country Save

21037 County Neon Sign Corporation
PO Box 504
Plainview, NY 11803-0504
516-349-9550
Fax: 516-349-0090
Lighting fixtures and electric and neon signs
President: George Schneider
VP: Joe Miller
Estimated Sales: $2.5-5,000,000
Number Employees: 20-49

21038 Couprie Fenton
4282 Belair Frontage Rd
Suite 5
Augusta, GA 30909
706-650-7017
Fax: 706-868-1534
Crab, conch, crabmeat, dogfish, full line seafood,
halibut, lobster, lobster meat
Manager: Yves Latremouille
Estimated Sales: $.5 - 1 million
Number Employees: 1-4

21039 Courtesy Signs
3101 S Fillmore St
Amarillo, TX 79110-1025
806-373-6609
Fax: 806-373-2953 courtesy@arn.net
www.bestsigns.com
Window signs, over-the-wire banners, point of pur-
chase markers, aisle product signs, pennant banners,
flags, etc
Manager: Bruce Milton
CFO: Wesley Ninemire
Sales: Dixie Flaherty
Manager: Victor Newton
Estimated Sales: Below $5 Million
Number Employees: 5-9
Square Footage: 148000

21040 Courtright Companies
26749 S. Governors Hwy.
Monee, IL 60449-8095
708-534-8400
Fax: 708-534-9140 sales@right-tape.com
www.right-tape.com
Manufacturer & exporter of reusable shipping con-
tainers, Teflon tapes, shellac adhesives, tensilized
polypropylene and stretch film
Owner: Patricia Schoenbeck
Sales Director: Ted Bachand
Purchasing Manager: Ted Bachand
Estimated Sales: $3-5 Million
Number Employees: 6
Square Footage: 40000
Type of Packaging: Food Service, Private Label

21041 Cousins Packaging
105 Claireport Crescent
Etobicoke, ON M9V 6P7
Canada
416-743-1341
Fax: 416-743-1831 888-209-4344
info@cousinspackaging.com
www.cousinspackaging.com
Number Employees: 50

21042 Covance Inc.
210 Carnegie Center
Princeton, NJ 08540-6233
609-452-4440
Fax: 609-452-9375 888-268-2623
www.covance.com
Analytical testing services to the food, dietary sup-
plement and biotechnology industries.
Executive Chairman: David King
CEO: Adam Schechter
Executive VP/CFO: Glenn Eisenberg
Senior VP/Global General Counsel: Sandra van der
Vaart
Chief Human Resources Officer: Judi Seltz
Year Founded: 1996
Estimated Sales: Over $1 Billion
Number Employees: 50,000
Parent Co: LabCorp

21043 Cove Four
195 E Merrick Rd
Freeport, NY 11520-4012
516-379-4232
Fax: 516-379-4563 www.covefour.com
Wire products including corkscrews and custom;
also, forming available
President: Barry Jaffe
erikcovefour@aol.com
VP Marketing: Bill Freedman
Sales Exec: Erik Christopher
Estimated Sales: $10 - 20 Million
Number Employees: 50-99

21044 Cove Woodworking
20 Kettle Cove Lane
Gloucester, MA 01930
978-526-4755
Fax: 978-526-4188 800-273-0037
whit33@msn.com
Restaurant tables, bars, bar stools, booths, chairs,
bases, built-ins and custom work.
President: Andrew Marques
CFO: Patty Kenaedy
Production Manager: Paul Hargreaves
Estimated Sales: $1 Million
Number Employees: 10-19
Square Footage: 17000
Type of Packaging: Food Service

21045 Covergent Label Technology
620 S Ware Boulevard
Tampa, FL 33619-4443
800-252-6111
Fax: 813-620-1206
Weighing and labeling systems
Contact: Nancy Solman
n_solman@discovery-academy.org
Estimated Sales: $20 - 25 Million
Number Employees: 100-250

21046 Coveris
1701 Johnson Industrial Dr
Excelsior Springs, MO 64024
contact.rigidna@coveris.com
Rigid packaging solutions
CEO: Jakob Mosser
Brands:
Aqua Crystal
Instabowl
Repellence
Safe-T-Strip
Serve-N-Seal
Slide-Rite

21047 Covestro LLC
119 Salisbury Rd
Sheffield, MA 01257-9706
413-229-8711
Fax: 413-229-8717 800-628-5084
www.covestro.com
Extruded plastic sheets for window glazing, signs,
displays, architectural products and industrial appli-
cations
President: Dennis Duff
Cmo: Kurt Glaser
curt.glaser@bayerbms.com
CFO: David Martin
Quality Control: Sherley Alarie
Estimated Sales: $20 - 50 Million
Number Employees: 100-249
Square Footage: 160000
Parent Co: Bayer Corporation

21048 Coy Laboratory ProductsInc
14500 Coy Dr
Grass Lake, MI 49240-9207
734-433-9296
Fax: 734-475-1846 sales@coylab.com
www.coylab.com
Glove boxes, anaerobic chambers, controlled envi-
ronment
President: Richard Coy
Cmo: Brian Coy
brian@coylab.com
Estimated Sales: $2.5 - 5 000,000
Number Employees: 20-49

21049 Cozzini Inc
2400 Highway 18 E
Algona, IA 50511-7204
515-295-7234
Fax: 515-295-9568 888-295-1116
sales@afeco.com www.cozzini.com
Vat and barrel dumpers, belt and screw conveyors,
curing and blending systems, pallet lifts, platforms,
tables, tanks, and smokehouse racks
President: Jeffrey Christensen
Director Sales/Marketing: Mike Rooney
Manager: Mike Broughton
mike.broughton@afeco.com
Manager Production/Engineering: Jeffery Philips
Number Employees: 50-99
Square Footage: 200000

21050 (HQ)Cozzini LLC
4300 W Bryn Mawr Ave
Chicago, IL 60646-5943

773-478-9700
Fax: 773-478-8689 sales@cozzini.com
www.rapidpaktec.com
Manufacturer and exporter of meat processing
equipment and blades
President: Peter J Samson
psamson@cozzini.com
VP: Oscar Cozzini
R&D: Greg Grady
Quality Control: Mario Lucchesi
Catalog Sales Technical Assistance: Pete Pierazzi
Estimated Sales: $20 Million
Number Employees: 100-249
Square Footage: 65000
Other Locations:
  Cozzini
  Soucy
Brands:
  Cozzini
  Ergo
  Primedge
  Suspentec

21051 Cozzini LLC
4300 W Bryn Mawr Ave
Chicago, IL 60646-5943

773-478-9700
Fax: 773-478-8689 888-295-1116
cozzini@cozzini.com
Meat processing and packaging equipment: chutes,
boning systems, canning systems, custom machinery
President: Peter J Samson
psamson@cozzini.com
Estimated Sales: $5-10 Million
Number Employees: 100-249

21052 Cozzoli Machine Co
50 Schoolhouse Rd
Somerset, NJ 08873-1289

732-564-0400
Fax: 732-564-0444 www.cozzoli.com
Designs and manufactures integrated precision pack-
aging systems solutions.
President: Frank Cozzoli
General Manager: Fred Hart
Controller: Michael Shanker
Marketing Director: Crystal Basiluk
Sales: Bruce Teeling
Purchasing Manager: Steve Turkus
Estimated Sales: $10-20 Million
Number Employees: 5-9
Number of Brands: 2
Number of Products: 200
Square Footage: 180000
Parent Co: Cozzoli Machine Company
Type of Packaging: Food Service
Brands:
  Inline Fill-To-Level Filler
  Inline Piston Filler
  Rotary Fill-To-Level Filler
  Rotary Piston Filler
  Versa-Cap
  Versa-Fil

21053 Craft Corrugated Box Inc
4674 Acushnet Ave
New Bedford, MA 02745-4736

508-998-2115
Fax: 508-998-8112
Corrugated boxes and other corrugated products
President: Ronald Mardula
Estimated Sales: Below $5 Million
Number Employees: 5-9

21054 Craft Industries
26-35 47th Avenue
Long Island City, NY 11101

252-753-3152
Fax: 252-753-3154
Portable LP gas cookers and trailers for caterers;
also, custom made cookers and trailers available
President and CFO: Jim Craft Jr
VP Financing: Sylvia Craft
Estimated Sales: Below $5 Million
Number Employees: 1-4
Square Footage: 80000
Brands:
  Craftmaster
  Steelcraft

21055 Craig Manufacturing
30 Loretto St
Irvington, NJ 7111

973-923-3211
Fax: 973-923-1767 800-631-7936
buycraig@aol.com
Deli cases, steam tables, back bars, refrigerators and
sandwich units
President: Craig Dubov
Estimated Sales: $5 - 10 Million
Number Employees: 50-99
Square Footage: 150000
Type of Packaging: Food Service

21056 Crain Walnut Shelling, Inc.
10695 Decker Ave
Los Molinos, CA 96055-9628

530-529-1585
Fax: 530-529-1458 crainwalnut@crainwalnut.com
www.crainwalnut.com
Shelled walnuts supplying industrial ingredient
needs.
President: Grant Skognes
gskognes@ridefox.com
Owner: Harold Crain
Vice President of Sales & Logistics: Vicki Lapera
Quality Assurance: Devan Wilson
Sales Administrator: Kimberly Gonsalves
Number Employees: 100-249
Type of Packaging: Bulk

21057 Cramer Company
105 Nutmeg Rd S
South Windsor, CT 6074

877-684-6464
Fax: 860-610-0897
customer-service@mhrhodes.com
Manufacturer and exporter of motors and timers for
process control systems
President: Kenneth Mac Cormac
VP: Wayne Taylor
Director Operations: Frank Darmig
Estimated Sales: $3 - 5 Million
Number Employees: 5-9
Square Footage: 220000
Parent Co: Owosso Corporation
Type of Packaging: Bulk

21058 Cramer Inc
1523 Grand Blvd
Kansas City, MO 64108-1403

816-471-4433
Fax: 816-471-7188 800-366-6700
nick@cramerinc.com www.cramerinc.com
Industrial steel seating, step stools and ladders
President: Nick Christianson
nick@cramerinc.com
CEO: Jason Rann
Director Marketing: J Sanders
VP Sales/Marketing: Jeff Meyer
Director Product Development: Lee Denny
Estimated Sales: $10-20 Million
Number Employees: 10-19
Parent Co: Rotherwood Corporation

21059 Cramer Products
381 Park Ave S
New York, NY 10016-8806

212-645-2368
Fax: 212-242-6799 www.abpaonline.org
Manufacturer and exporter of temperature controlled
storage units, humidors, wire and wood storage
racks and cooling panels for wine and cheese
President: Richard Rothschild
Treasurer: Valerie Tomaselli
Vice President: Nancy Hall
Estimated Sales: Less than $500,000
Number Employees: 1-4
Brands:
  Cmc
  Cool-Kit
  Cool-Safe
  Cramarc
  Well Tempered

21060 Crandall Filling Machinery
80 Gruner Rd
Buffalo, NY 14227-1007

716-897-3486
Fax: 716-897-3488 800-280-8551
cai@conveyoraccessories.com www.crandall.com
Manufacturer and exporter of filling, packaging and
closing machinery

Owner: Scott Reed
Technician: Scott Reed
VP sales: Charles Wood
dave@crandall.com
Estimated Sales: $1 - 3 Million
Number Employees: 1-4
Square Footage: 16000

21061 Crane Carton Corporation
555 N Tripp Avenue
Chicago, IL 60624-1079

773-722-0555
Fax: 773-722-3510
Folding paper boxes
Estimated Sales: $20 - 50 Million
Number Employees: 100-249

21062 Crane Composites Inc
23525 W Eames St
Channahon, IL 60410-3220

815-467-8600
Fax: 815-467-8666 800-435-0080
sales@cranecomposites.com
www.cranecomposites.com
Fiber-reinforced composite materials.
President: Thomas Jeff Craney
Cmo: Cleve Madlock
cmadlock@cranecomposites.com
VP of Building Products: Kelly Erdmann
Eastern Regional Sales Manager: Kevin Bellinger
Western Regional Sales Manager: Chris Schamer
Number Employees: 100-249

21063 Crane Environmental
2650 Eisenhower Ave Ste 100a
Norristown, PA 19403

610-631-7700
Fax: 610-631-6800 800-633-7435
www.cranenv.com
Manufacturer and exporter of water treatment equip-
ment including reverse osmosis, demineralizers,
softeners, filters, CB pumps, deaerators and steam
specialty items
Manager: Russ Burke
Marketing Manager: Russell Burke
Purchasing Agent: Sandra Bisci
Estimated Sales: $20-30 Million
Number Employees: 1-4
Square Footage: 100000
Parent Co: Crane Company
Brands:
  Accu-Spray
  Delta
  Epro
  Spiraflow
  Uni-Mod
  Uni-Pac

21064 Crane National Vendors
12955 Enterprise Way
Bridgeton, MO 63044

314-298-0055
Fax: 314-298-3534 www.cranems.com
Tea and coffee industry dispensers
President: Brad Ellis
Contact: Anne Barks
abarks@cranems.com
Estimated Sales: $50 - 100 Million
Number Employees: 100-249

21065 Crane Pumps & Systems
420 Third St
Piqua, OH 45356

937-778-8947
Fax: 937-773-7157
cranepumps@cranepumps.com
www.cranepumps.com
Manufacturer and exporter of pumps for the agricul-
tural and food processing industries.
President: Brian Sweeney
Year Founded: 1946
Estimated Sales: $100-$500 Million
Number Employees: 250-499
Square Footage: 400000
Parent Co: Crane Pumps & Systems
Brands:
  Midland
  Weinman

21066 (HQ)Crane Research & Engineering
617 Regional Dr
Hampton, VA 23661-1800
757-826-1707
Fax: 757-838-3728
Crab processing, picking and cleaning machinery
Owner: John Biggs
john.biggs@craftbearing.com
Plant Manager: Dan Schrum, Jr.
Estimated Sales: $5-10 Million
Number Employees: 20-49
Square Footage: 33000
Brands:
Quik-Pik

21067 Crate Ideas by Wilderness House
P.O. Box 675
Cave Junction, OR 97523-0675
541-592-2106
Fax: 541-592-6670 800-592-2206
Custom wooden and decorative gift crates
President: Eugene Schreiber
Sales Director: Sarah Peiffer
Estimated Sales: $1 - 3 Million
Number Employees: 10-19

21068 Crawford Packaging
1609 N Capitol Avenue
Indianapolis, IN 46202-1202
317-924-2494
Fax: 317-283-1817
Estimated Sales: $1 - 5 000,000
Number Employees: 20-49

21069 Crayex Corp
1747 Commerce Dr
Piqua, OH 45356-2601
937-773-7000
Fax: 937-773-4823 800-837-1747
crayex@crayex.com www.crayex.com
Low density polyethylene film and bags for shrink
packaging and wrapping
President: Mimi Crawford
mimi.crawford@crayex.com
Founder & CEO: Clifford R. Alexander
CFO: Lori Webster
Quality Control: Jeff Gower
Manager: Keith Killingsworth
Estimated Sales: $10 - 20 Million
Number Employees: 50-99
Square Footage: 180000

21070 Crc Industries Inc
885 Louis Dr
Warminster, PA 18974-2869
301-843-5226
Fax: 215-674-2196 800-556-5074
kcantwell@crcindustries.com
www.crc-industries.com
Manufacturer and exporter of cleaners, degreasers,
lubricants, corrosion inhibitors, hand cleaners, adhe-
sives and sealants; also, cleaning compound
dispensers
Global CEO: Perry Cozzone
Estimated Sales: $91 Million
Number Employees: 10-19
Brands:
3-36
Hydroforce
Mechanix Orange
Power Lube
Screwloose
Super

21071 Cream of the Valley Plastics
5750 Lamar Street
Arvada, CO 80002
303-425-5499
Fax: 303-425-0734
Milk and juice containers
Plant Supervisor: Bart Hurley
Estimated Sales: $2.5-5 Million
Number Employees: 10-19
Parent Co: Southern Foods

21072 Creamery Plastics Products, Ltd
8989 Charles Street
Chilliwack, BC V2P 2V8
Canada
604-792-0232
Fax: 604-792-1890 www.icechiller.net

Cream and condiment dispensers; also, buffet dis-
plays and ice chillers to keep foods & beverages
chilled for many hours.
President: Lucy Vales
CEO: Tony Rapaz
Purchasing Agent: Tony Rapaz
Number Employees: 4

21073 Creative Automation
5404 Jedmed Court
Saint Louis, MO 63129-2221
800-745-9539
Fax: 314-845-7779
Contact: Paul Habinstript
ph@creative-automation.com

21074 Creative Automation
61 Willet St Ste 3b
Passaic, NJ 7055
973-778-0061
Fax: 973-614-8336
Manufacturer and exporter of automatic feeders, bar
code verification equipment, turnkey systems, leaflet
inserters and outserters, vertical, form, fill and seal
equipment
President: John Calabrese
jcalabrese@creative-auto.com
CEO: John Bartlo
VP: John Calabrese
Estimated Sales: $1-2.5 Million
Number Employees: 1-4

21075 Creative Canopy Design
4272 Columbus Dr
Hernando Beach, FL 34607
866-970-5200
Fax: 303-424-0172 866-970-5200
Portable canopies/shade structures, commercial
tents, banner flags, screen printing and dyesub printing.
Owner: Laura Uribe

21076 Creative Coatings Corporation
28 Charron Avenue
1165
Nashua, NH 03063-1783
603-889-8040
Fax: 603-889-3780 800-229-1957
flocking@aol.com
Packaging materials including laminated vinyls,
metallized barrier and pressure sensitive films, etc.;
importer of bakery and confectionery mixers and
homogenizers
CEO: Robert Borowski
Customer Service Manager: Barbara Landry
Number Employees: 5
Square Footage: 20000

21077 Creative Converting Inc
255 Spring St
Clintonville, WI 54929-1159
715-823-3104
Fax: 715-823-5232 800-826-0418
www.creativeconverting.com
Paper table cloths, napkins, plates and cups
Estimated Sales: $50-100 Million
Number Employees: 100-249
Square Footage: 105000
Parent Co: Hoffmaster Group, Inc.
Brands:
Every Occasion

21078 Creative Cookie
8673 Commerce Dr
Suite 7
Easton, MD 21601
410-819-0091
Fax: 410-819-0255 800-451-4005
www.creativecookieetc.com
Manufacturer and exporter of themed fortune cook-
ies and candy boxes
Owner: Marty Schwartz
Vice President: Joan Schwartz
General Manager: Martin Schwartz
Estimated Sales: Less than $500,000
Number Employees: 1-4
Number of Products: 80
Type of Packaging: Consumer, Food Service, Pri-
vate Label, Bulk
Brands:
A World of Good Fortune
Anniversary
Baseball Trivia
Bible Verse

Birthday
Calling Card
Christmas
Congratulations!
Doctor's
Easter
Executive
For Kid's Only
Get Well
Golfer's
Halloween
Holiday Greetings
Housewarming
Irish
It's a Baby!
Italian
Jewish
Millenium Message
Mother's Day
Movie Trivia
Naughty But Nice!
Over the Hill
Romantic
Sports Trivia
Teachers
Thank You
Trivia
Valentine
Wedding
Year 2000
You're the Greatest!

21079 Creative Enterprises
12 Rochelle Drive
Kendall Park, NJ 08824-1405
732-422-0300
Fax: 732-422-0008
Platforms, point of purchase and store displays,
dump tables and cabinets
President: S Y Goldberg
Estimated Sales: Below $5 Million
Number Employees: 2

21080 Creative Essentials
2155 5th Ave
Ronkonkoma, NY 11779-6908
631-467-8370
Fax: 631-467-4255 800-355-5891
sales@menudesigns.com
Manufacturer and exporter of menu covers, acrylic
stands, placemats, recipe holders, menus and check
presenters
President: Allen Fischer
Sales Manager: Jonathan Sunshine
Sales: Karen Chalson
Number Employees: 20-49
Square Footage: 64000

21081 Creative Foam Corp
300 N Alloy Dr
Fenton, MI 48430-2649
810-629-4149
Fax: 810-629-7368 www.creativefoam.com
Manufacturer and exporter of packaging and mate-
rial handling systems
President: David Swallow
daswallow@creativefoam.com
Sales Manager: David Rosser
Estimated Sales: $20 - 50 Million
Number Employees: 100-249
Type of Packaging: Bulk

21082 Creative Forming
PO Box 128
Ripon, WI 54971-0128
920-748-7285
Fax: 920-748-9466 www.creativeforming.com
Manufacturer and exporter of thermoformed plastic
trays
President: Glen Yurjevich
General Manager: John Beard
Estimated Sales: $20 - 50 Million
Number Employees: 100-249
Parent Co: Wellman
Type of Packaging: Consumer, Food Service, Bulk

21083 Creative Impressions
7697 9th St
Buena Park, CA 90621-2898
714-521-4441
Fax: 714-522-2733 800-524-5278
email@emenucovers.com
Clear and soft plastic menu covers in 30 colors and
textures; also, inserts available

President: Marc Abbott
email@emenucovers.com
Estimated Sales: $5-10 Million
Number Employees: 20-49

21084 Creative Industries Inc
1024 Western Dr
Indianapolis, IN 46241-1437

317-248-2068
Fax: 317-247-4953 800-776-2068
mike.clark@creativeind.com
www.creativeind.com
Pass- and talk-thru, plastic laminated and bulletproof
windows
President: Mark Clark
Estimated Sales: Below $5 Million
Number Employees: 5-9
Type of Packaging: Private Label

21085 Creative Label Designers
3890 SW Harbor Drive
Lees Summit, MO 64082-4679

816-537-8757
Fax: 816-537-8757
Pressure sensitive printed and thermal bar code labels
President: Dale G Wheat
Number Employees: 4
Square Footage: 8000

21086 Creative Mobile SystemsInc
189 Adams St
Manchester, CT 06042-1919

860-649-6272
Fax: 860-643-2830 800-646-8364
cms189@ntplx.net www.hotdog325.com
Catering trucks, hot dog carts and concession trailers
President: Brian Smith
rlumpkin@cmsc.com
CFO: Mary Davis
VP: Richard Lumpkin
VP: Richard Lumpkin
Purchasing Manager: John Izzo
Estimated Sales: Below $5 Million
Number Employees: 1-4
Square Footage: 24000
Brands:
Cms, Inc.

21087 Creative Packaging
2249 Davis Ct
Hayward, CA 94545-1113

510-785-6500
Fax: 510-785-6349
www.cpccreativepackaging.com
Wooden crates and containers including corrugated,
foam, urethane and styrofoam
Owner: Jim Oliver
jim@ivccreativepackaging.com
General Manager: J Hunter
Estimated Sales: $5-10 Million
Number Employees: 10-19
Square Footage: 190000

21088 Creative Packaging Corporation
700 Corporate Grove Dr
Buffalo Grove, IL 60089

847-459-1001
Fax: 847-325-3919
Manufacturer and exporter of dispensing closures
President: John Weeks
CFO: Mike Farreoo
Quality Control: Samantha Gibson
VP Sales/Marketing: Jeff Teth
Corporate Manager: Robert Giles
Estimated Sales: $50-75 Million
Number Employees: 10
Square Footage: 1100000
Parent Co: Courtesy Corporation
Brands:
Shear Pak
Sports Cap

21089 Creative Printing Co
200 Lakewood Cir
Burr Ridge, IL 60527-6340

630-734-3244
www.creativeprinting.net
Menus
Owner: Rick Styfer
Estimated Sales: $500,000-$1 Million
Number Employees: 10-19

21090 Creative Signage System
9101 51st Place
College Park, MD 20740

301-345-3700
Fax: 301-220-0289 800-220-7446
creative@creativesignage.com
www.creativesignage.com
Plastic signs
President: John Mayer
Sales: Peter Van Allen
Estimated Sales: $2.5 - 5 Million
Number Employees: 20-49

21091 Creative Storage Systems
2700 Barr Lks Blvd NW Ste 500
Kennesaw, GA 30144

770-514-0711
Fax: 770-514-0622 888-370-8810
marketing@creativestorage.com
www.creativestorage.com
High density dynamic warehouse storage systems,
conveyors/gravity, flow-through pallet systems, pal-
lets/racks, racks/storage, storage
President: Robert Lawless
Estimated Sales: $10-20 000,000
Number Employees: 20-49

21092 Creative Techniques
2441 N Opdyke Rd
Auburn Hills, MI 48326

248-373-3050
Fax: 248-373-3458 800-473-0284
www.creativetechniques.com
Manufacturer and exporter of packaging and mate-
rial handling products
President: Richard Yeakey
Sales Manager: Stanley Shore
Contact: Joe Banfield
banfieldj@creativetechniques.com
Estimated Sales: $20-50 Million
Number Employees: 100-249

21093 Creegan Animation Company
508 Washington St
Steubenville, OH 43952-2140

740-283-3708
Fax: 740-283-4117
Manufacturer and exporter of animations, costume
characters and audio-animatronics
Owner: George Creegan
Contact: Sandy Baumgard
sandy.baumgard@creegans.com
Estimated Sales: $1 - 5 Million
Number Employees: 20-49

21094 Creekstone Farms Premium Beef
604 Goff Industrial Park Rd
PO Box 869
Arkansas City, KS 67005-8880

620-741-3100
Fax: 620-741-3353 www.creekstonefarms.com
Their own line of Creekstone Farms Natural and
Premium Black Angus Beef marketed under the
USDA Process-Verified Tender Beef label.
President: John Stewart
Genetics Division: Joe Bill Meng
Bull and Semen Sales: Danny Rankin
Feeder Calf Program: Ryan Meyer
Natural Beef Program: Matt Bode
Number Employees: 500-999
Type of Packaging: Food Service

21095 Crepas & Associates
15w725 Virginia Lane
Elmhurst, IL 60126-1259

630-833-4880
Fax: 630-833-0580
Consultant providing structural engineering services
for facility renovations new contruction renovation
specialize in floors concrete and epoxy
President: Robert Crepas
Estimated Sales: Less than $500,000
Number Employees: 4

21096 Cres Cor
5925 Heisley Rd
Mentor, OH 44060-1833

440-350-1100
Fax: 440-350-7267 877-273-7267
www.crescor.com
A complete line of quality mobile food service
equipment including hot cabinets, utility cabinets
and racks, banquet cabinets, dish dollies, ovens and
more. Since 1936...There is no equal.

President: Clifford D Baggott
cbaggott@crescor.com
VP: Rio DeGennaro
Director of Engineering: Heather Stewart
Sales/Marketing Director: Michael Capretta
Number Employees: 100-249
Brands:
Cres Cor

21097 Cresco Food Technologies
717 2nd Ave SE
Cresco, IA 52136-1703

563-547-4241
Fax: 563-547-4504 cft@iowatelecom.net
www.aveka.com
Nutraceutical and food processing facility.
Manager: John Anderson
john_@iowatelecom.net
Number Employees: 50-99
Parent Co: Aveka, Inc.

21098 Crespac Incorporated
5032 N Royal Atlanta Drive
Tucker, GA 30084

770-938-1900
Fax: 770-939-4900 800-438-1900
info@crespac.com
Disposable thermoformed food trays and containers;
exporter of produce and food containers
CEO: Jeff Moon
Estimated Sales: $5-10 Million
Number Employees: 50-99
Square Footage: 400000
Brands:
Big Green

21099 Cresset Chemical Company
One Cresset Center
PO Box 367
Weston, OH 43569

419-669-2041
Fax: 419-669-2200 800-367-2020
cresset@cresset.com www.cresset.com
Manufacturer and exporter of hand cleaners, release
agents and admixtures
President: Mike Baty
CFO: Roger Davis
Vice President: Mike Baty
Quality Control: Rick Reynolds
Inside Sales Representative: Shanelle Scott
Estimated Sales: Below $5 Million
Number Employees: 10
Brands:
Crete-Lease
Crete-Trete
Han-D
Sol-Zol
Spatter-Cote
Super Strip
Super-Trete

21100 Crest Foods Inc
502 Brown Ave
Ashton, IL 61006

815-453-7411
800-435-6972
www.crestfoods.com
Processor of food ingredients including emulsifying
agents, proteins, caseinates, whey, stabilizers and
flavors for dips, bases and seasonings. Contract
packaging available.
President: Jeff Meiners
Sales/Research Manager: Gaven Meiners
VP Manufacturing: Mike Meiners
Supply Manager: Jamie Cooper
Year Founded: 1946
Estimated Sales: $20-50 Million
Number Employees: 250-499
Type of Packaging: Consumer, Food Service, Pri-
vate Label

21101 Cresthill Industries
196 Ashburton Ave
Yonkers, NY 10701-4001

914-965-9510
Fax: 914-965-9534 www.whereorg.com
Manufacturer and exporter of bag closures
President: Christopher Rie
Treasurer: J Rie
Contact: Rhoda Needelman
rhoda@cresthillindustries.com
Estimated Sales: $10-20 Million
Number Employees: 50-99
Parent Co: Cresthill Industries

Brands:
  Kisco Bip

21102 Crestware
520 N Redwood Rd
PO Box 540210
North Salt Lake, UT 84054-2747

      801-292-0656
Fax: 801-295-5732 800-345-0513
sales@crestware.com www.crestware.com
Manufacturer and importer of china, flatware, steamtable pans, chafers, pots, pans, smallwares, thermometers and scales
President: Hal Harrison
Vice President: Julie Jackson
  jjackson@crestware.com
VP Marketing: Stephen Jordan
VP Operations: Greg Harrison
Estimated Sales: $10 - 20 Million
Number Employees: 10-19
Square Footage: 160000
Brands:
  Crestware

21103 Cretel Food Equipment
303 Little Station Road
Holland, MI 49424-2618

      616-786-3980
Fax: 616-786-0299
Bags for beef, ham, bacon and sausage; films, laminates, flexible packages, vacuum packaging materials and equipment, processing equipment, skinning machines, fish processing equipment, plant layout and product flow
Owner: James Smith
Estimated Sales: $1 - 3 Million
Number Employees: 5
Number of Brands: 4
Number of Products: 10
Type of Packaging: Consumer, Food Service

21104 Cretorr
3243 N California Ave
Chicago, IL 60618-5890

      773-588-1690
Fax: 773-588-2171 800-228-1885
marketing@cretors.com www.cretors.com
Popcorn machines
President: Charles D Cretors
Quality Control: Wally Krzak
Vice President of Sales and Marketing: Shelly Olesen
Estimated Sales: $10 - 20 Million
Number Employees: 100-249

21105 Crippen Manufacturing Co
400 Woodside Dr
St Louis, MI 48880-1057

      989-681-4323
Fax: 989-681-3818 800-872-2474
www.crippenmfg.com
Grain separators, polishers and conveyors
President: Darren Losey
  darrenl@crippenmfg.com
System Technician: Daniel Kelley
CFO: Shane Gascho
V P/Sales: Douglas Clark
V P and Mktg: Kevin Kennedy
Conveying and Systems Product Mgr: Jerry Valch
Density Specialist: William Donnell
New Equipment Sales: Kevin Vogt
Customer Service: Kevin Vogt
Design Eng'r /Air Screen Equipment: James Strawder
Design Eng'r/Density Equipment: Robert Gilbert
Materials Mgr: Darren Losey
Product Specialist: Steve Galgoczi
Estimated Sales: $1-2.5 Million
Number Employees: 20-49
Square Footage: 260000

21106 Crisci Food Equipment Company
P.O. Box 8327
New Castle, PA 16107-8327

      724-654-6609
Fax: 724-654-9266
Stainless steel food services equipment, ladders, step stools and conveyors
President: Sally Firmi
Estimated Sales: $2.5-5 000,000
Number Employees: 10-19

21107 Crispy Lite
10 Sunnen Drive
St. Louis, MO 63143-3800

      775-689-5700
Fax: 314-781-5445 888-356-5362
clientcare@wellsbloomfield.com
www.wellsbloomfield.com
Manufacturer and exporter of display cases, filters, pressure fryers, fans, hoods and food warmers
Vice President, Sales/Marketing, Wells-B: Paul Angrick
VP Sales/Marketing: David Moore
Mngr.: D Joseph Lambert
Number Employees: 250-499
Square Footage: 248000
Parent Co: Wells Bloomfield Company
Type of Packaging: Food Service

21108 Critzas Industries Inc
4041 Park Ave Frnt
St Louis, MO 63110-2391

      314-773-8510
Fax: 314-773-4837 800-537-1418
goop@earthlink.net www.goophandcleaner.com
Manufacturer and exporter of premium waterless hand cleaner.
President/Treasurer: John Critzas
Contact: Gerald Pogue
  critzas@aol.com
Estimated Sales: $10-20 Million
Number Employees: 10-19
Square Footage: 120000
Brands:
  Goop

21109 Criveller East
6935 Oakwood Drive
Niagara Falls, ON L2E 6S5
Canada

      905-357-2930
Fax: 905-374-2930 888-894-2266
info@criveller.com www.criveller.com
President: Mario Criiveller
CFO: Jim Farlane
Number Employees: 10

21110 Croll Reynolds Inc
6 Campus Dr # 5
Suite 1
Parsippany, NJ 07054-4406

      908-232-4200
Fax: 908-232-2146
Manufacturer and exporter of food processing machinery including combined evactor/condenser/liquid ring vaccum, vapor recovery and vacuum cooling systems and ejectors
Vice President: Philip Reynolds
  preynolds@croll.com
CEO: Samuel W. Croll
CEO: Samuel W Croll Iii
Division Manager: Henry Hage
Plant Manager: Ellis Production/Shipping
Estimated Sales: $5 - 10 Million
Number Employees: 20-49
Brands:
  Chill-Vactor
  Core-Chill
  Evactor
  Rotajector
  Scrub-Vactor

21111 Croll-Reynolds Engineering Company
2400 Reservoir Ave
Trumbull, CT 06611-4793

      203-371-1983
Fax: 203-371-0615 creco@att.net
Design and manufacture backwashable, liquid pressure, tubular element polishing type filters and strainers.
President/CEO: John Quinlan
Sales Manager: Louis Ancillai
Estimated Sales: $200,000
Number Employees: 3
Number of Brands: 3
Number of Products: 3
Square Footage: 10000
Brands:
  Clarite
  Flexodisc
  Flexoleed

21112 Crompton Corporation
One American Lane
Greenwich, CT 06831-2560

      203-573-2000
Fax: 203-552-2010 800-295-2392
Chemical ingredients and food additives
Chairman/ President/ CEO: Craig A. Rogerson
CFO/ SVP: Stephen C. Forsyth
VP/ Corporate Controller/ Principal Acco: Laurence Orton
Global Market Manager: Bob Ruckle
Sales Director: Rick Beitel
Contact: Paul Ellis
  paul.ellis@chemtura.com
Number Employees: 20-49

21113 Crosfield Company
111 Ingalls Ave
Joliet, IL 60435-4373

      815-727-3651
Fax: 815-774-2804 www.ineossilicas.com
Manufacturer and exporter of silicon dioxide gels and precipitates; also, silica hydrogel
Plant Manager: Pat Murphy
Estimated Sales: $1 - 5 Million
Number Employees: 100-249
Brands:
  Gasil
  Neosyl

21114 Crossroads Espresso
P.O. Box 23610
Eugene, OR 97402

      541-344-4600
Fax: 541-344-8992
Espresso parts and espresso machines
President: James Glang
Contact: Susan Schultheis
  sue@crossroads-espresso.com
Estimated Sales: $1-5 000,000
Number Employees: 10-19

21115 Crosswind Foods
P.O. Box 29
Sabetha, KS 66534

      785-284-3462
Fax: 785-284-3940 www.crosswindindustries.com
Contract food manufacturing
President: Ken Matson
Vice President: Bob Niehues
Quality Control: Gary Lierz
Plant Manager: Chris Shelly
Estimated Sales: $5 - 10 000,000
Number Employees: 20-49
Type of Packaging: Consumer, Private Label, Bulk
Other Locations:
  Crosswind Industries
  Kansas City MO

21116 Crouch Dairy Supply
305 S Main St
Fort Worth, TX 76104-1226

      817-332-2118
Fax: 817-332-6511 800-825-1110
k.kertis@crouchinc.com www.crouchinc.com
Distribution of process and refrigeration equipment, supplies and services
Vice President: Mike Davis
Vice President: Mike Davis
Sales: Karyn Kertis
Number Employees: 10-19

21117 Crouse-Hinds
1201 Wolf St
Syracuse, NY 13208

      Fax: 315-477-5179 866-764-5454
crousecustomerctr@eaton.com www.eaton.com
Manufacturer and exporter of outdoor and emergency lighting
President/Owner: Scott Hearn
Estimated Sales: $135 Million
Number Employees: 1,300
Parent Co: Eaton

21118 Crouzet Corporation
3237 Commander Drive
Carrollton, TX 75006-2506

      972-620-7713
Fax: 972-250-3865 800-677-5311
www.crouzet.com

Manufacturer and exporter of OEM products for packaging and processing equipment: timers, proximity sensors, counters, control relays, solid state relays and temperature controllers
President: Gerald Vincent
VP Marketing: Phillipe Dubois
Contact: Rosemary Martinez
  martinezr@us.crouzet.com
Estimated Sales: $20-50 Million
Number Employees: 100-249
Parent Co: Crouzet
Brands:
  Crouzet
  Gordos
  Syrelec

21119 Crown Battery Mfg
1445 Majestic Dr
Fremont, OH 43420-9190
419-334-7181
Fax: 419-334-7416 800-487-2879
www.crownbattery.com
Manufacturer and exporter of industrial batteries used in lift trucks and food service equipment
President: Hal Hawk
Senior VP: Bill Bessire
  bbessire@crownbattery.com
Director Marketing: Mark Kelley
Estimated Sales: $20 - 50 Million
Number Employees: 250-499
Square Footage: 200000

21120 Crown Chemical Products
6125 Netherhart Road
Mississauga, ON L5T 1G5
Canada
905-564-0904
Fax: 905-564-0906 crownchemical@bellnet.ca
Sanitation and janitorial chemicals including hand cleaners, degreasers, disinfectants, deodorants, plumbing and carpet chemicals, etc.; custom blending available
President: Keith Chan
Quality Control: Annie Chan
Number Employees: 10
Square Footage: 30000
Type of Packaging: Food Service, Private Label

21121 Crown Closures Machinery
1765 W Fair Ave
Lancaster, OH 43130-2325
740-681-6593
Fax: 740-681-6527 sheila.heath@crowncork.com
www.crowncork.com
Capping/sealing equipment since 1913. Formerly known as Anchor Hocking Packaging. Member of Crown Cork and Seal family of corporations. Precision CNC machining capabilities. Machine building and rebuilding
CAO: Amanda Marutz
  amanda.marutz@crowncork.com
Operations Manager: Sheila Heath
Plant Manager: Ed Schott
Purchasing Manager: Greg Henwood
Estimated Sales: Below $5 Million
Number Employees: 20-49
Square Footage: 192000
Parent Co: Crown Cork & Seal

21122 Crown Controls Inc.
2316 Crown Point Executive Drive
Charlotte, NC 28227
704-841-1622
Fax: 704-841-1655 800-541-7874
crowncontrols@windstream.net
www.crowncontrols.com
Manufacturer and exporter of level controls and open channel flow meters; also, food processing equipment
President: Charles Stevens
Number Employees: 20-49
Brands:
  Capaciagage
  Sonargage
  Sonarswitch

21123 Crown Cork & Seal Co Inc
1 Crown Way
Philadelphia, PA 19154-4599
215-698-5100
Fax: 215-698-5201 www.crowncork.com
Metal cans

CEO: John W Conway
  john.conway@crowncork.com
Sales Department: Bill Keith
Number Employees: 100-249

21124 Crown Custom Metal Spinning
1-176 Creditstone Road
Concord, ON L4K 4H7
Canada
416-243-0112
Fax: 416-243-0112 800-750-1924
sales@crowncookware.ca
www.crowncookware.ca
Manufacturer and exporter of bakery racks and aluminum cookware including stockpots and cake and pizza pans; importer of stainless steel mixing bowls
President: David P Vella
CFO: Franco Mazzuca
Customer Service: Carmen D'Cruze
Administrator: Gilda Leib
Number Employees: 10
Square Footage: 80000
Type of Packaging: Consumer, Food Service, Bulk

21125 Crown Equipment Corp.
44 S. Washington St.
New Bremen, OH 45869
419-629-2311
Fax: 419-629-2900 www.crown.com
Lift trucks.
Chairman/Chief Executive Officer: James Dicke

President: James Dicke

VP: Keith Sinram
Senior Vice President: James Mozer
Senior Vice President: Timothy Quellhorst
Senior Vice President: John Tate
Vice President, Sales: Christopher Rahe
Vice President, Engineering: Steven Dues
Vice President, Design: Michael Gallagher
Vice President, Manufacturing Operations: David Beddow
Year Founded: 1945
Estimated Sales: $3.48 Billion
Number Employees: 16,100

21126 Crown Holdings, Inc.
770 Township Line Rd.
Yardley, PA 19067
215-698-5100
ir@crowncork.com
www.crowncork.com
Bottle caps, can tops, crowns and cans including tin, beer and ale; also, bottling machinery.
President/CEO/Chairman: Timothy Donahue
Senior VP/CFO: Kevin Clothier
VP/Treasurer: David Beaver
Executive VP/COO: Gerard Gifford
Year Founded: 1892
Estimated Sales: $11.6 Billion
Number Employees: 33,000
Type of Packaging: Consumer, Food Service, Private Label, Bulk
Other Locations:
  Crown Cork & Seal Co.
  Apopka FL

21127 Crown Industries
155 N Park St
East Orange, NJ 7017
973-672-2277
Fax: 973-672-7536 877-747-2457
www.4rails.com
Furniture including railings and fittings: brass; also, crowd control stanchion and ropes; tables, easels and dance floors
President: Gene Loebner
VP: Mario Camerota
Contact: Mario Camerota
  mario.camerota@crowncork.com
VP: Carmen Ware
Estimated Sales: $500,000-$1 Million
Number Employees: 5-9
Square Footage: 56000

21128 (HQ)Crown Iron Works Company
2500 County Road C W # A
Roseville, MN 55113-2523
651-639-8900
Fax: 651-639-8051 888-703-7500
sales@crowniron.com www.crowniron.com
Manufacturer and exporter of oil extractors, oil/fat processing systems and dryer/cooler systems.

Product Sales Manager: Richard Ozer
General Manager: Bill Antilla
Estimated Sales: $1 - 5 Million
Number Employees: 50-99
Brands:
  Crown
  Wurster & Sanger

21129 Crown Jewels Marketing
423 W Fallbrook Ave # 203
Suite 204
Fresno, CA 93711-6138
559-438-2335
Fax: 559-438-2341
mail@crownjewelsproduce.com
www.crownjewelsproduce.com
President: Rob Mathias
  robm@crownjewelsmarketing.com
Sales: Rob Mathias
Administration: Danell Wright
Estimated Sales: $5 - 10 Million
Number Employees: 20-49

21130 Crown Label Company
663 Young Street
Santa Ana, CA 92750
714-557-3830
Fax: 714-557-0401 800-422-3590
sales@crownlabel.com www.crownlabel.com
Labels, decals and tags; also, silk screening available
Owner: Gary Siposs
Estimated Sales: $1 - 2,500,000
Number Employees: 10-19

21131 Crown Manufacturing Corporation
147 Cross Rd
Waterford, CT 06385-1216
860-442-4325
Fax: 860-442-9658
Cabinets and boxes
President: David Parker
  crownmanufacturing@snet.net
Estimated Sales: $1-2.5 Million
Number Employees: 5 to 9
Type of Packaging: Bulk

21132 Crown Marking
1000 Boone Ave. N.
Suite 680
Minneapolis, MN 55427
763-543-8243
Fax: 800-488-4034 800-305-5249
sales@crownmarking.com
www.crownmarking.com
Stamps, stamp pads and name plates, signs and ID badges
CEO: Gregg Prest
VP: Thomas Knauer
Contact: Karen Prest
  kprest@crownmarking.com
Estimated Sales: $1-2.5 Million
Number Employees: 5-9
Square Footage: 9200
Brands:
  Bates
  Cosco
  X-Stamper

21133 Crown Metal Manufacturing Company
765 South State
Route 83
Elmhurst, IL 60126-4228
630-279-9800
Fax: 630-279-9807 ca-sales@crownmetal.com
www.crownmetal.com
Manufacturer and exporter of store fixtures including wall standards, brackets, showcase hardware and sign holders
Manager: Mike Volosin
Operations Manager: Mike Volosin
Estimated Sales: Less than $500,000
Number Employees: 1-4
Parent Co: Crown Metal

21134 (HQ)Crown Metal Mfg Co
8768 Hellman Ave
Rancho Cucamonga, CA 91730-4418
909-291-8585
Fax: 909-291-8587 ca-sales@crownmetal.com
www.crownmetal.com

Manufacturer and exporter of metal store fixtures, pegboard equipment and sign holders
Manager: Mike Volosin
Vice President: Glenn Dalglerish
Research & Development: Steve Varon
Sales Director: Scott Durham
Manager: Chris Montoya
  cmontoya@crownmetal.com
Production Manager: Wayne Baker
Estimated Sales: Less Than $500,000
Number Employees: 1-4
Number of Brands: 8
Number of Products: 500
Square Footage: 340000
Type of Packaging: Bulk
Other Locations:
  Crown Metal Manufacturing Co.
  Rancho Cucamonga CA

21135 Crown Packaging
17854 Chesterfield Airport Road
Chesterfield, MO 63005
636-681-8000
Fax: 636-681-9600 800-883-9400
www.crownpack.com
Wholesaler/distributor of packaging machinery and materials
Estimated Sales: $70 Million
Number Employees: 95
Square Footage: 18800
Other Locations:
  Atlanta GA
  Baltimore MD
  Baton Rouge LA
  Boston MA
  Charlotte NC
  Cincinnatti OH
  Cleveland OH
  Dallas/Ft. Worth TX
  Des Moines IA
  Evansville IN
  Indianapolis IN
  Knoxville TN
  Lenexa KS

21136 Crown Plastics Inc
12615 16th Ave N
Minneapolis, MN 55441-4609
763-557-6000
Fax: 763-557-6638 800-423-2769
www.crystalpalacecupcaketree.com
Tea and coffee industry dispensers; whisper blend sound enclosures.
CEO: Tom Van Beusekon
Estimated Sales: $2.5-5 000,000
Number Employees: 20-49
Number of Brands: 1
Number of Products: 1
Square Footage: 30000
Type of Packaging: Food Service, Bulk

21137 Crown Steel Mfg
177 Newport Dr # A
San Marcos, CA 92069-1470
760-471-1188
Fax: 760-471-1189 info@crownsteelmfg.net
www.crownsteelmfg.net
Kitchen and restaurant equipment including tables and sinks
President: Dave Carr
  carrdj@pacbell.net
VP: David Carr
Estimated Sales: $3 - 5 Million
Number Employees: 20-49
Square Footage: 80000

21138 Crown Tonka Walk-Ins
15600 37th Ave N # 100
Minneapolis, MN 55446-3204
763-541-1410
Fax: 763-541-1563 800-523-7337
sales@crowntonka.com www.crowntonka.com
Manufacturer and exporter of walk-in coolers and freezers
President: Mike Kahler
  mikek@crowntonka.com
Senior Vice President Sales & Marketing: Greg Sullens
Estimated Sales: $5-10 Million
Number Employees: 50-99
Type of Packaging: Consumer, Food Service

21139 Crown Uniform & Linen Service
309 Battles St
Brockton, MA 02301
800-221-2725
CustomerSupport@CrownUniform.com
crownuniform.com
Supplier of uniform programs, healthcare apparel programs, and linen services throughout New England.
Co-President: George Spilios
Co-President: Plato Spilios
Year Founded: 1914
Estimated Sales: $17.5 Million
Number Employees: 201-500

21140 Crown Verity
37 Adams Boulevard
Brantford, ON N3S 7V8
Canada
519-751-1800
Fax: 519-751-1802 888-505-7240
info@crownverity.com www.crownverity.com
Manufacturer and exporter of stainless steel barbecues
President: William Verity
Founder: Bill Verity
CFO: Tracy McIngrrey
Quality Control: Allan Frennett
R & D: William Verity
Sales Manager: John Foulger
Number Employees: 10
Square Footage: 48000
Brands:
  Chef's Choice

21141 Crown-Simplimatic
1200 S Newkirk Street
Baltimore, MD 21224-5308
410-563-6700
Fax: 410-563-6782

21142 Crownlite Manufacturing Corporation
1546 Ocean Ave
Bohemia, NY 11716-1916
631-589-9100
Fax: 631-589-4584
Manufacturer and exporter of fluorescent and HID lighting fixtures and supplies; specializing in super-market lighting
President: William Siegel
Sales Executive: Lois Carbonaro
Sales Manager: C Longo
Estimated Sales: $5 - 10 Million
Number Employees: 50 to 99

21143 Crucible Chemical Co
10 Crucible Ct
Greenville, SC 29605-5411
864-277-1284
Fax: 864-299-1192 800-845-8873
www.cruciblechemical.com
Food grade defoamers
President: Mark Chandler
  markchandler.ccc@gmail.com
Assistant to the President: Kathryn Stroud
Lab Manager: Danny Hawkins
Estimated Sales: $10-20 Million
Number Employees: 20-49
Brands:
  Foamkill

21144 Crunch Time Information Systems
129 Portland Street
Boston, MA 02114
857-202-3000
www.crunchtime.com
Purchasing and inventory control information systems
President: Bill Bellissimo
Chief Operating Officer: David Daugherty
Vice President of Client Services: Jean Fogarty
VP, Prodcut Development: James Krawcynski
Director of Marketing: Chris Bauer
Sales Manager: Michelle Bullock
Contact: Elizabeth Russo
  erusso@crunchtime.com
Chief Operating Officer: David Daugherty
Estimated Sales: $500,000-$1 Million
Number Employees: 1-4

21145 Cruvinet Winebar Co LLC
610 S Rock Blvd # 115
Sparks, NV 89431-8118
775-827-4044
Fax: 800-873-7894 800-278-8463
info@cruvinetsys.com www.cruvinetsys.com
Manufacturer, importer and exporter of wine dispensing/preserving systems, nitrogen-based preserving systems and wine storage cases; also, service, repair and preventative maintenance for all makes and models of wine dispensing andcellaring systems
President/CEO: Matt Kuchnis
Vice President: Jennifer Kuchnis
Director of Sales: Matt Kuehnis
Production: Matt Kuehnis
Estimated Sales: Less Than $500,000
Number Employees: 1-4
Square Footage: 19960
Brands:
  Cruvinet Collector
  Cruvinet Estate
  Le Cavernet
  Le Grand Cruvinet
  Le Grand Cruvinet Mobile
  Le Grand Cruvinet Premier
  Le Sommelier
  Petite Sommelier
  Petite Sommelier Cruvinet
  The Cruvinet
  Ultra Cruvinet

21146 Cryochem
PO Box 20268
St Simons Island, GA 31522-8268
912-262-0033
Fax: 912-262-9990 800-237-4001
sales@cryochem.com www.cryochem.com
Manufacturer and exporter of cryogenic freezing and chilling equipment including single and tri-deck freezers, immersion and batch cabinets; also, custom-designed systems
Marketing Manager: Bryan Smith
General Manager: Frank Grillo
Estimated Sales: $1 - 5 Million
Number Employees: 18
Square Footage: 120000
Parent Co: Cryogenic Industries
Brands:
  Kryospray

21147 Cryogenic Systems Equipment
2363 136th St
Blue Island, IL 60406-3233
708-385-4216
Fax: 708-385-4390 dsink@cryobrain.com
www.cryobrain.com
Cryogenic food processing equipment, exhaust, parts
President: Brian Sink
  bsink@cryobrain.com
CFO: Devin Sink
Marketing Director: Todd Czernik
Sales Director: Brian Sink
Operations Manager: Peter Kruse
Purchasing Manager: Gary Magdziarz
Estimated Sales: $3.2 Million
Number Employees: 10-19
Number of Products: 15
Square Footage: 30

21148 Cryopak
6818 Jarry Street E
St. Leonard, QC H1P 1W3
Canada
514-324-4720
Fax: 514-324-9623 888-423-7251
bstapleton@cryopak.com www.cryopak.com
A wide range of gel packs and insulated containers for shipping perishables
President: Maurice Barakat
VP: Raj Gill
Marketing/Sales: Bruce Stapleton
Estimated Sales: $1 - 5 Million

21149 Cryovac
2415 Cascade Pointe Blvd
Charlotte, NC 28208
980-430-7000
800-391-5645
www.sealedair.com
Micro-layered shrink films.

President & CEO: Ted Doheny
SVP & Chief Commercial Officer: Karl Deily
VP & Chief Human Resources Officer: Susan Edwards
VP & Chief Human Resources Officer: Angel Willis
SVP & Chief Strategy Officer: Sergio Pupkin
SVP & Chief Financial Officer: Jim Sullivan
SVP & Chief Supply Chain Officer: Emile Chammas
Estimated Sales: $1,000,000,000+
Number Employees: 10-19
Parent Co: Sealed Air Corp

21150 Crystal Chem Inc.
1536 Brook Dr
Suite A
Downers Grove, IL 60515
630-889-9003
Fax: 630-889-9021 sales@crystalchem.com
www.crystalchem.com
Food allergen and vitamin kits for easy to use detection of allergens in both raw and processed food.
President: Priyavadan Shah
VP: Hema Shah
Safety Manager: Robert Kyle
Sales Manager: Sachin Shah
Contact: Dawn Conklin
dawn@crystalchem.com
Estimated Sales: $3 Million

21151 Crystal Creative Products
PO Box 450
Middletown, OH 45042
513-423-0731
Fax: 513-423-0516 800-776-6762
Manufacturer, importer and exporter of tissue including wrapping and industrial
President: James Akers
Vice President: John Crider
Sales Director: Ed Miller
Purchasing Manager: Randy Clark
Estimated Sales: $20-50 Million
Number Employees: 100-249
Brands:
Crystal
Crystalized
Fantasy Wrap
Radiant Wrap
Tiara

21152 Crystal Lake Mfg Inc
2225 Highway 14 W
Autaugaville, AL 36003-2541
334-365-3342
Fax: 334-365-3332 800-633-8720
www.homeworkclean.com
Manufacturer and exporter of brooms, mops and handles
President: James Pearson
james.pearson@crystallakemfg.com
Chairman: Theresa Dunn
Chairman the Board: Theresa Dunn
Sales Director: Ron Poole
Estimated Sales: $10 - 20 Million
Number Employees: 100-249
Square Footage: 406000
Type of Packaging: Consumer, Food Service, Private Label, Bulk
Brands:
Crystal Lake

21153 Crystal-Flex Packaging Corporation
10 Oxford Road
Rockville Centre, NY 11570-2122
770-218-3556
Fax: 732-967-9839 888-246-7325
sales@crystalflex.com www.crystalflex.com
Manufacturer and exporter of polyethylene bags, plastic and barrier film, food packaging, pouches and laminations
President: Lesley Craig Litt
Number Employees: 6
Brands:
Flexbarrier
Oven Pak

21154 Crystal-Vision Packaging Systems
23870 Hawthorne Blvd
Torrance, CA 90505-5908
310-373-6057
Fax: 310-373-6157 800-331-3240
don@crystalvisionpkg.com
www.crystalvisionpkg.com

Shrink film; printed shrink labels; dry food weigh/fill machines; packaging machines and bag sealers; food bags; & printed stand-up food bags.
President/CEO/CFO: Donald Hilmer
Quality Control: Emilio Diaz
Sales: Karl Behrens
Contact: Mark Bayless
mbayless@drbayless.com
General Manager: Jeff Hilmer
Purchasing: Bernie Johnson
Estimated Sales: $5 Million
Number Employees: 11
Square Footage: 60000
Parent Co: AID Corporation
Brands:
Aie
Cal Vac
Crystal Vision
Curwood
Good Year
Multivac

21155 Cube Plastics
190 Maplecrete Road
Concord, Ontario, ON L4K 2B6
Canada
905-669-8669
Fax: 905-669-8646 877-260-2823
Microwavable food containers in a variety of sizes.

21156 Cucamonga Sign Shop LLC
9223 Archibald Ave # A
Rancho Cucamonga, CA 91730-5237
909-945-5888
Fax: 909-941-7395 www.signshopofrc.com
Custom vinyl banners, wood and metal signs, name plates, labels, etc.; also, screen printing and lettering services available
Owner: Andy Megaw
sales@signshopofrc.com
Estimated Sales: Less Than $500,000
Number Employees: 1-4
Brands:
The Bob-O-Bear

21157 Cuerden Sign Co
PO Box 187
Conway, AR 72033-0187
501-375-7705
Fax: 501-327-3438 cuerden@swbell.net
Signs including interior, outdoor and electric
Owner: Jasper Burton
cuerden@nwbell.net
VP Sales: Jap Burton
Estimated Sales: $1-2.5 Million
Number Employees: 10-19
Square Footage: 20000

21158 Cugar Machine Co
3579 Mccart Ave
Fort Worth, TX 76110-4694
817-927-0411
Fax: 817-927-0473 www.cugarmachine.com
Food processing machinery including bin dumpers, trimlines, pivot conveyors, catwalks, washing systems, onion peelers, etc
President: Gary Greene
Estimated Sales: $1-2.5 Million
Number Employees: 5-9

21159 Culicover & Shapiro
220 S Fehrway
Bay Shore, NY 11706-1208
631-918-4560
Fax: 631-918-4561
Floor brooms and brushes
President: Richard Shapiro
Marketing: David Shaw
Estimated Sales: $500,000-$1 Million
Number Employees: 5 to 9
Square Footage: 16000

21160 Culinar
4945 Ontario Rue E
Montreal, QC H1V 1M2
Canada
514-255-2811
Fax: 514-251-2184
Consultant providing research and development for cookies
Director Sales: Daniel Merci
Estimated Sales: $1 - 5 Million
Parent Co: Culinar Canada

21161 Culinart Inc
7609 Production Dr
Cincinnati, OH 45237-3208
513-244-2999
Fax: 513-244-2555 800-333-5678
Tallow sculptures and specialty candles; also, bulk tallow in white, butter, cheddar and chocolate available
President/ Culinary Artist: Dominic Palazzolo
culinart@yahoo.com
Estimated Sales: $500,000 - $1 Million
Number Employees: 1-4
Type of Packaging: Bulk

21162 Culinary Collective
12407-B Mukilteo Speedway
Suite 245
Lynnwood, WA 98087
425-398-9761
Fax: 425-398-9765 info@culinarycollective.com
www.culinarycollective.com
Spanish and Peru foods
Co-Founder: Betsy Power
Co-Founder: Pere Selles
Sales Manager: Marion Sproul
Estimated Sales: $3 - 5 Million
Number Employees: 5-9

21163 (HQ)Culinary Depot
2 Melnick Dr.
Monsey, NY 10952
Fax: 845-352-2700 888-845-8200
customerservice@culinarydepot.biz
www.culinarydepotinc.com
Kitchen and restaurant equipment, janitorial supplies, restaurant furniture and food storage and transport materials
Founder/President: Sholem Potash
CEO: Michael Lichter

21164 Culinary Papers
10 Maybrook Dr
Toronto, ON M1V 4B6
Canada
416-757-6768
Fax: 416-757-5183
Accessories/supplies i.e. picnic baskets, cooking implements/housewares.
Marketing: Bill Benson

21165 Culligan Company
1 Culligan Parkway
Northbrook, IL 60062-6287
877-530-2676
feedback@culligan.com www.culligan.com
Manufacturer and exporter of commercial/industrial water softeners, filters, deionizers, dealkalizers and reverse osmosis units
President: Tim Tousignant
Sales Director: Doug Dickinson
Contact: Nisha Aggarwal
naggarwal@culligan.com
Estimated Sales: $35 - 40 Million
Number Employees: 250-500
Number of Brands: 4
Square Footage: 120000
Brands:
Bruner
Bruner-Matic
Iqs/3
Salt-Master

21166 Culligan International Co
9399 W Higgins Rd # 1100
Suite 1100
Rosemont, IL 60018-4940
847-430-2800
Fax: 732-512-0166 800-231-9283
www.culligan.com
Water Systems, Water
Manager: Bob Prigen
President: Scoot Levy
Chairman: Peter Dixon
Estimated Sales: Under $500,000
Number Employees: 5000-9999
Parent Co: Culligan Water Technologies

21167 Culmac
720 Hanford St # 2
Geneseo, IL 61254
309-944-6494
Fax: 309-944-6495
Flexographic printing presses

President: Archie Cullen
Estimated Sales: $1-2.5 000,000
Number Employees: 10-19

21168 Cumberland Box & Mill Co
215 W Elder St
Cumberland, MD 21502-4606
301-724-1010
Fax: 301-777-0700
Wooden skids and lids
President: James L Ketterman
Estimated Sales: $1 - 2.5 Million
Number Employees: 5-9

21169 Cumberland Container Corp
1027 N Chestnut St
Monterey, TN 38574-1062
931-839-2227
Fax: 931-839-3971
service@cumberlandcontainer.com
www.cumberlandcontainer.com
Corrugated containers
President: Eugene Jared
CFO: Tim Dunn
Quality Control: Patti Davis
Sales Manager: Randy Swallows
Computer: Randall Hardison
Plant Manager: Chris Landers
Estimated Sales: Less than $500,000
Number Employees: 100-249

21170 Cumberland Farms
100 Crossing Blvd
Framingham, MA 01702
781-828-4900
Fax: 781-828-9012 www.cumberlandfarms.com
Milk and ice cream
Chairman: Lily Bentas
VP: George Haseotes, Sr.
Senior VP: Don Holt
Sales Director: Barbara Paidy
Contact: Ahmed Ali
aali@cumberlandfarms.com
VP Manufacturing: Emanuel Cavaco
Number Employees: 250-499
Parent Co: Suiza Foods

21171 Cummings
PO Box 23194
Nashville, TN 37202-3194
615-673-8999
Fax: 615-782-6699
stacey.hawke@cummingssigns.com
Manufacturer and exporter of electric signs and marquees
President: Stephen R Kerr
Sr VP: Bruce Cornett
Contact: T Cummings
t.cummings@thesign.com
Executive VP National Accounts: Jerry Morrison
Estimated Sales: $20-50 Million
Number Employees: 50-99
Square Footage: 175000

21172 Cummins Label Co
2230 Glendenning Rd
Kalamazoo, MI 49001-4189
269-345-3386
Fax: 269-345-6657 800-280-7589
customerservice@cumminslabel.com
www.cumminslabel.com
Pressure sensitive labels and seals
President: Phil Nagel
pnagel@cumminslabel.com
Vice President: Kevin Nagel
Chairman: Gordon Nagle
Marketing/Sales Executive: Len Boekhoven
Estimated Sales: $5 - 10 Million
Number Employees: 20-49
Type of Packaging: Private Label, Bulk

21173 Cummins Power Generation Inc.
500 Jackson St.
Columbus, IN 47201
812-377-5000
www.cummins.com
Electric generators and engines.
Chairman/CEO: Tom Linebarger
Vice President/CFO: Mark Smith
Vice President/General Counsel: Sharon Barner
President/COO: Tony Satterthwaite
Year Founded: 1919
Estimated Sales: $23.77 Billion
Number Employees: 58,600

21174 Cunningham LP Gas
400 Carswell Ave
Daytona Beach, FL 32117-4418
386-672-2507
Fax: 386-254-5007
paul@cunninghamresearch.com
Sensory research for the food industry
President: Stacy Cunningham
General Manager: Tom Brett
VP Corporate Operations: Frankie Tonelli
Number Employees: 50-99

21175 Cup Pac Packaging Inc
777 Progressive Ln
South Beloit, IL 61080-2618
815-624-7060
Fax: 815-624-8170 877-347-9725
info@cuppac.com www.cuppac.com
Manufacturer and exporter of machinery for filling,
tamper-evident sealing, lidding and code dating
plastic cups; contract packaging available
President: Dennis James
Vice President: Jim Philipp
VP Sales: Russell James
Estimated Sales: $4 Million
Number Employees: 20-49
Square Footage: 68000
Type of Packaging: Consumer, Food Service, Private Label, Bulk

21176 Cup Pac Packaging Inc
777 Progressive Ln
South Beloit, IL 61080-2618
815-624-7060
Fax: 815-624-8170 info@cuppac.com
www.cuppac.com
President: Dennis James
Vice President: Jim Philipp
Estimated Sales: $20 - 50 Million
Number Employees: 20-49

21177 Currie Machinery Co
1150 Walsh Ave
Santa Clara, CA 95050-2647
408-727-0422
Fax: 408-727-8892 currieco@aol.com
www.curriepalletizers.com
Manufacturer and exporter of material handling
equipment including automatic palletizers, case elevators, beverage pallet stackers and powered discharge conveyors; also, dispensers including pallet,
slip and tier sheet
President: Bradley Patrick
b.patrick@curriepalletizers.com
Marketing Director: Gerry Haase
Estimated Sales: $5-10 Million
Number Employees: 1-4
Square Footage: 160000

21178 Curry Enterprises
1248 Zonolite Road NE
Atlanta, GA 30306-2006
404-873-1163
800-241-7308
Screen printed point of purchase displays and merchandising systems
Sales Manager: Steve Cornett
Estimated Sales: $1 - 5 Million
Number Employees: 17

21179 (HQ)Curtainaire
6000-T S. Gramercy Place
Los Angeles, CA 90047
323-753-4266
Fax: 323-753-6460
Air curtains
President: Ken Burns
VP Sales: Gary Burns
Estimated Sales: $5-10 Million
Number Employees: 19
Square Footage: 64000
Brands:
Curtainaire

21180 Curtis 1000
1725 Breckinridge Pkwy
Suite 500
Duluth, GA 30096-8994
770-925-4500
877-287-8715
www.curtis1000.com
Labels; digital and commercial printing

President/Owner: Steve Geiger
Contact: Kelli Hayes
kmhayes@curtis1000.com
Estimated Sales: $50-75 Million
Number Employees: 20-49

21181 Curtis Packaging
44 Berkshire Rd
Sandy Hook, CT 06482-1499
203-426-5861
Fax: 203-426-2684 www.curtispackaging.com
Manufacturer and exporter of folding paper boxes;
also, hot stamping and UV coating available
Chairman, President & CEO: Donald Droppo
Estimated Sales: $35 Million
Number Employees: 100-249
Square Footage: 150000

21182 Curtis Restaurant Equipment
P.O. Box 7307
Springfield, OR 97401
541-746-7480
Fax: 541-746-7384 sales@curtisresteq.com
www.curtisresteq.com
Consultant specializing in design for the food service market; wholesaler/distributor of equipment
and supplies; serving the food service market
CEO: Daniel Curtis
Chief Financial Officer: Bill Kettas
Estimated Sales: $20-30 Million
Number Employees: 50-99
Square Footage: 38000

21183 Curwood Specialty Films
2200 Badger Ave
PO Box 2968
Oshkosh, WI 54904-9118
920-303-7300
Fax: 920-303-7309 800-544-4672
www.curwood.com
Supplier of films, trays, lids and other packaging
materials for the food and beverage industries.
Founder: Howard Curler
Founder: Bob Woods
Contact: Tom Bordona
tsbordona@bemis.com
Estimated Sales: Less Than $500,000
Number Employees: 5-9

21184 Curzon Promotional Graphics
1013 S 75th St
Omaha, NE 68114-4658
402-393-2020
Fax: 402-393-1502 800-769-7446
Banners, posters, decals and screen printed point of
purchase displays
President: Kirby Smith
CFO: E J Stanek
Sales Manager: Bob Drake
Product Manager: Ray Serfass
Estimated Sales: $2.5 - 5 Million
Number Employees: 10-19
Square Footage: 80000

21185 Cush-Pak Container Corporation
904 State Highway 64 W
Henderson, TX 75652-5516
903-657-0555
Corrugated and wooden boxes and containers
Estimated Sales: $20-50 Million
Number Employees: 20-49

21186 Cusham Enterprises
441 Commonwealth Avenue
Erlanger, KY 41018-1425
859-727-9727
Fax: 859-727-9796
Buys and sells food equipment and companies and
then resells their machinery and parts
Estimated Sales: $1 - 5 Million

21187 Custom Baking Products
111 Erick Street
Suite 129
Crystal Lake, IL 60014-1314
877-455-4938
Fax: 815-455-2735
info@custombakingproducts.com
www.custombakingproducts.com

21188 Custom Bottle of Connecticut
P.O. Box 979
Naugatuck, CT 06770-0979
　　　　　　　　203-723-6661
Fax: 203-723-6687 www.custombottle.com
Plastic blow molded bottles and extruded containers
Vice President of Engineering: William Padgett
Vice President of Sales: Ed Jacquette
Contact: William Padgett
　padgett@custombottle.com
Executive Vice President, Chief Operatin: Richard Allen
Estimated Sales: $30 - 50 Million
Number Employees: 100-249
Square Footage: 75000

21189 Custom Brands Unlimited
PO Box 500
Solebury, PA 18963-0500
　　　　　　　　215-297-9842
Fax: 215-297-0161
Private-label gourmet mixes, candy, tea, snack items and fruit
Owner: David Vissor

21190 (HQ)Custom Business Interiors
1701 Athol Avenue
Henderson, NV 89011-4072
　　　　　　　　702-564-6661
Fax: 702-564-6767 cbilv@aol.com
Store fixtures
General Manager: John Filar
Estimated Sales: $1 - 5 Million
Number Employees: 20
Other Locations:
　Custom Business Interiors
　Ventura CA

21191 Custom Business Solutions
12 Morgan
Irvine, CA 92618
　　　　　　　　949-380-7674
Fax: 949-380-7644 800-551-7674
info@cbsnorthstar.com www.cbsnorthstar.com
Point of sale hardware and software
Founder & CEO: Art Julian
Chief Financial Officer: Michael Block
VP, Software Development: Joseph Castillo
VP, Sales & Marketing: Gary Stotko
Inside Sales: Jason Perovich
Contact: Cyndy Allen
　cyndy.allen@custombusinesssolutions.com
Square Footage: 16528
Other Locations:
　San Diego CA
　Dallas TX

21192 Custom Card & Label Corporation
P.O. Box 433
Lincoln Park, NJ 07035-0433
　　　　　　　　973-492-0022
Fax: 973-492-0022
Pressure sensitive labels
Owner: John Miller
Sales Manager: John Miller
Estimated Sales: $1-2.5 Million
Number Employees: 1-4

21193 Custom Color Corp
14320 W 101st Ter
Lenexa, KS 66215-1123
　　　　　　　　816-595-6800
Fax: 913-730-9301 888-605-4050
info@customcolor.com www.customcolor.com
Menu boards
CEO: Matthew Keith
Director Strategic Marketing: Jan Ray
Corporate Sales Rep.: Joe Goodwin
Estimated Sales: $5-10 Million
Number Employees: 50-99

21194 Custom Control Products
1300 N Memorial Dr
Racine, WI 53404
　　　　　　　　262-637-9225
Fax: 262-637-5728 800-279-9225
Batch control systems, cleaning equipment, distributed control systems, expert systems, flow diverson stations, instruments/sensors, process control, process software, heat exchangers, plate, scraped surface, tubular
Estimated Sales: $1-5 000,000
Number Employees: 15

21195 Custom Conveyor & Supply Corp.
PO Box 668
Racine, WI 53401-0668
　　　　　　　　262-634-4920
Fax: 262-634-1787
Manufacturer and designer of belt and chain conveyors and lifts
President: George Seater, Jr.
VP: Thomas Fountas
Estimated Sales: $1-2.5 Million
Number Employees: 9

21196 Custom Craft Laminates
4705 N Manhattan Ave
Tampa, FL 33614-6981
　　　　　　　　813-877-7100
Fax: 813-877-5285 800-486-4367
mblanton@Humidorstore.com
www.mycabinetcompany.com
Store fixtures
Owner: James E Blanton
　james@mycabinetcompany.com
Estimated Sales: $5 - 10 Million
Number Employees: 10-19

21197 Custom Diamond International
895 Munck Avenue
Laval, QC H7S 1A9
Canada
　　　　　　　　450-668-0330
Fax: 450-662-1326 800-363-5926
info@diamond-group.com
www.diamond-group.com
Refrigerators, work tables, buffets, ovens, dispensers, glass washers, etc
President: Ron Diamond
CFO: Craig Aronoff
Quality Control: Hilly Diamond
Number Employees: 50
Parent Co: the Diamond Group

21198 Custom Diamond Intl.
895 Munck Avenue
Laval, QC H7S 1A9
Canada
　　　　　　　　450-668-0330
Fax: 450-662-1326 800-326-5926
Smokers, ovens, combi-oven systems, food transport systems, heated and refrigerated stainless steel tables, counters, carts, dollies, feeding systems, etc.; exporter of food service equipment including ovens, prison food carts, andrethermalization food systems
President/CEO: Ron Diamond
CFO: D Bucci
Vice President: Allan Weber
R&D: Jason B
Marketing: Alex Malikian
Sales/Public Relations: Nick V
Production/Plant Manager: Paul Nesi
Plant Manager: H Diamond
Purchasing: George D
Square Footage: 204000
Type of Packaging: Bulk
Brands:
　Brute
　Custom
　Diamond

21199 Custom Extrusion Technologies
1650 Corporate Rd W
Lakewood, NJ 08701-5920
　　　　　　　　732-367-5511
Fax: 732-367-2908 coburn@aol.com
www.cetfilms.com
President: Roger Jacobs
Cmo: Guy Leigh
　gleigh@cetfilms.com
Vice President: James Putvinski
Number Employees: 20-49

21200 (HQ)Custom Fabricating & Repair
1932 E 26th St
Marshfield, WI 54449-5500
　　　　　　　　715-387-6598
Fax: 715-384-3768 800-236-8773
dawn.isenberg@gotocfr.com www.gotocfr.com
Stainless steel filtration and cheese processing equipment; wholesaler/distributor of fittings, valves and pumps
President: Kyle Balcom
　kyle.balcom@gotocfr.com
VP: Dawn Isenberg
Sales Director: Jay Moore
Estimated Sales: $7 Million
Number Employees: 50-99
Square Footage: 130000
Other Locations:
　Custom Fabricating & Repair
　Fridley MN
Brands:
　Custom Fab

21201 Custom Foam Molders
122 Mulberry St
Foristell, MO 63348-0100
　　　　　　　　636-441-2307
Packaging including expandable polystyrene, food protective and thermal insulation
VP: Mike Loyet
Estimated Sales: $500,000-$1 Million
Number Employees: 1-4
Square Footage: 32000

21202 (HQ)Custom Food Machinery
1881 E Market Street
Stockton, CA 95205-5673
　　　　　　　　209-463-4343
Fax: 209-463-3831
Rebuilder, importer and exporter of machinery including canning, beverage and beer bottling, fruit and vegetable, processing, filling, sterilization, can closing, packaging, cartoning, etc
President: Ron McNiel Sr
VP Sales/Advertising (Inventory): Richard Gomez-Stockton
VP Operations: Ron McNiel, Jr.
Estimated Sales: $10 - 20 Million
Number Employees: 50-99
Other Locations:
　Custom Food Machinery
　Sampron Nakornpathom

21203 Custom ID Systems
3506 E Venice Ave
Venice, FL 34292-2535
　　　　　　　　941-488-8430
Fax: 941-485-1969 800-242-8430
Signs, displays and name badges
Quality Control: Jerry Barnes
　j.barns@custom-id.com
Estimated Sales: Less Than $500,000
Number Employees: 1-4

21204 Custom Lights & Iron
3101 Hoover Ave
National City, CA 91950-7221
　　　　　　　　858-274-7070
Fax: 619-474-8596 www.customlightsandiron.com
Lighting fixtures
Owner: Paul Bell
　paul@customlightsandiron.com
Sales Manager: Joe Campbell
Estimated Sales: Less Than $500,000
Number Employees: 1-4
Square Footage: 24000

21205 Custom Machining Inc
1204 Hale Rd
P.O. Box 192
Shelbyville, IN 46176-2371
　　　　　　　　317-392-2328
Fax: 317-398-8856 www.custommachininginc.com
Pumpkin processing equipment, including washers, cutters, deseeders and dryers; tapered auger dryer, pork cutter depositor
Owner: Darrell Mollenkotpf
　mike@custommachininginc.com
Sales Exec: Mike Walker
Estimated Sales: Less than $500,000
Number Employees: 20-49

21206 Custom Metal Crafts
2332 E Division St
Springfield, MO 65803-5197
　　　　　　　　417-862-9324
Fax: 417-864-7575
cmcsales@custom-metalcraft.com
www.custom-metalcraft.com
Process vessels and food processing equipment including material handling systems.
President: Dwayne Holden
　dwayneh@custom-metalcrafts.com
CEO: Jerry Cowan
CFO: Sharon Saunders
Marketing Director: Nikki Holden
Sales Director: Drew Holden
Production Manager: Scott Higgins
Purchasing Manager: Tom Georges

Estimated Sales: $30 Million
Number Employees: 10-19
Number of Brands: 35
Square Footage: 125000
Brands:
    Cm-L Lifters
    Flex Bag
    Invert-A-Bin
    Transchem
    Transitainer
    Transtore
    Voyager

21207 Custom Metal Design Inc
921 W Oakland Ave
Oakland, FL 34760-8855

    407-656-7771
Fax: 407-656-6230 800-334-1777
sales@custommetaldesigns.com
www.custommetaldesigns.com
Manufacturer and exporter of material handling equipment including conveyors and systems, depalletizers, elevators, accumulators and bagging equipment and supplies
President: Dennis Bankowitz
  dennis@custommetaldesigns.com
Estimated Sales: $10-20 Million
Number Employees: 20-49
Type of Packaging: Bulk

21208 Custom Metalcraft, Architectural Lighting
65 Sprague Street
Boston, MA 02136

    617-242-0868
Fax: 617-242-0743 info@custommetalcraft.com
www.custommetalcraft.com
Electric lighting fixtures
Owner: Mike Elson
Sales/ Quotations: Mike Elson
Contact: Guil Dasilva
  gds@custommetalcraft.com
Estimated Sales: $1-2.5 Million
Number Employees: 5-9

21209 Custom Millers Supply Co
511 S 3rd St
Monmouth, IL 61462-2235

    309-734-6312
Fax: 309-734-7466
Grain processing equipment including corn cutters, hammer mills and trailers
President: L Howard White
Secretary: Wanda White
VP: Loran White
Estimated Sales: $1-2.5 Million
Number Employees: 1-4
Square Footage: 20000
Brands:
    Big Chief
    White

21210 Custom Mobile Food Equipment
275 South 2nd Road
Hammonton, NJ 08037-0635

    609-561-6900
Fax: 609-567-9318 800-257-7855
info@foodcart.com
www.customsalesandservice.com
President: William Sikora
Estimated Sales: $5 - 10 Million
Number Employees: 100-249

21211 (HQ)Custom Molders
PO Box 7100
Rocky Mount, NC 27804-0100

    919-688-8061
Fax: 919-688-8439
Injection custom-molded plastics including trays
President/CEO: Hwa-Yong Jo
Contact: George Perfon
  gperfon@custommolders.com
VP Manufacturing: Chung-Yong Jo
Estimated Sales: $20 - 30 Million
Number Employees: 100-250
Other Locations:
    Custom Molders
    Morrisville NC

21212 Custom Pack Inc
662 Exton Cmns
Exton, PA 19341-2446

    610-363-1900
Fax: 610-321-2526 800-722-7005
sales@custompackinc.com
www.custompackinc.com
Converter of plastic films, bags, and lidding stick
President: Frank Menichini
  sales@cpispecimen.com
Estimated Sales: $6 Million
Number Employees: 20-49
Square Footage: 54000
Brands:
    Poleguards

21213 Custom Packaging Inc
1003 Commerce Rd
Richmond, VA 23224-7007

    804-232-3299
Fax: 804-232-6230 www.custompack.com
Manufacturer and exporter of corrugated boxes and point of purchase displays
President: Ed Beadels
  custompackaging@verizon.net
VP: Jackie Cowden
VP Sales: Gary West
Estimated Sales: $20-50 Million
Number Employees: 10-19

21214 Custom Packaging Systems
200 W North Avenue
Northlake, IL 60164-2402

    231-723-5211
Fax: 231-723-6301 800-968-5211
scholle@scholle.com www.scholle.com
Rhino spouted form-fit dry liners; multiply liquid liners; liquid squeeze bags for fill and discharge of highly viscous products; bulk bags; Rhino protecto tank and the Rhino mussle pack bag-in-box
President: Lee Lefleur
Estimated Sales: $10 - 20 Million
Number Employees: 150

21215 Custom Plastics Inc
250 Laredo Dr
Decatur, GA 30030-2294

    404-373-1691
Fax: 404-373-8605 www.custom-plasticsinc.com
Acrylic sneeze guards for salad bars, indoor plastic signs and skylights; also, custom acrylic fabrication available
President: Scarlett Luke
  scarlett@custom-plasticsinc.com
Estimated Sales: $1-2.5 Million
Number Employees: 5-9
Square Footage: 24000

21216 Custom Poly Packaging
3216 Congressional Pkwy
Fort Wayne, IN 46808-4417

    260-483-4008
Fax: 260-484-5166 800-548-6603
info@custompoly.com www.custompoly.com
Polyethylene, polypropylene, trash, shopping and laboratory bags; importer of sample bags
Owner: Michael Carpenter
  info@custompoly.com
Estimated Sales: $2.5-5,000,000
Number Employees: 10-19
Square Footage: 13000

21217 Custom Pools Inc
373 Shattuck Way
Portsmouth, NH 03801-2828

    603-431-7800
Fax: 603-431-5109 800-323-9509
info@custompools.com www.custompools.com
Manufacturer and wholesaler/distributor of ultraviolet disinfection equipment for opaque fluids, juices, etc
President: Kelsey Hemming
  kelsey.hemming@gmail.com
Vice President: Darrel Short
VP: David Short
Estimated Sales: $3 - 5 Million
Number Employees: 20-49

21218 Custom Quality Products
1645 Blue Rock St
Cincinnati, OH 45223

    513-541-1191
Fax: 513-541-1192 800-477-4720
www.cqpinc.com

Temperature controls, cold storage doors and hardware
President: George White
Contact: Chuck Lovinski
  chuckl@cqpinc.com
Estimated Sales: $2.5-5 000,000
Number Employees: 20-49

21219 Custom Rubber Stamp Co
326 5th St NE
Crosby, MN 56441-1513

    218-545-4977
Fax: 866-485-9205 888-606-4579
orders@crstamp.com www.crstamp.com
Manufacturer, exporter and importer of custom rubber stamps, self-inking and pre-inked stamps, embossers, engraved plastic signs, name tags and inks
President: James Grimes
Co-Owner: Jean Grimes
Employee: Paula Steigauf
Estimated Sales: Less Than $500,000
Number Employees: 1-4
Square Footage: 4000
Brands:
    2000 Plus
    Aero
    Albany
    Base Lock
    Brailltac
    Brooklyn
    Comet
    Cooke
    Cosco
    Dapon
    Eagle Zephyr
    Imprintz
    Quik
    Rowmark
    Triumph
    X-Stamper

21220 Custom Sales & Svc Inc
275 S 2nd Rd
Hammonton, NJ 08037-8445

    609-561-6900
Fax: 609-567-9318 800-257-7855
info@foodcart.com
Manufacturer and exporter of mobile food equipment including trucks, trailers, vans and cart systems
CEO: William Sikora
VP Sales/Marketing: Lynda Sikora
IT: Jay Celona
  jay.celona@foodcart.com
Estimated Sales: $5-10 Million
Number Employees: 100-249
Square Footage: 140000

21221 (HQ)Custom Stamp Company
37449 Regal Blue Trail
Anza, CA 92539-8806

    323-292-0753
Fax: 323-292-0754
Manufacturer and exporter of pressure sensitive labels, rubber stamps, name plates, stencils, daters, marking products, metal tags and serial numbering on metal
President: Jack Coleman
Sales Manager: Steve Glass
Number Employees: 8
Square Footage: 7200
Type of Packaging: Food Service
Brands:
    Cosco
    Custom
    Dymo
    Garvey
    Jrs
    Melind
    Roovers

21222 (HQ)Custom Stamping & Manufacturing
1340 SE 9th Ave
PO Box 14340
Portland, OR 97293-0340

    503-238-3700
Fax: 503-238-3742
Custom metal stampers and foil food containers
Owner: Dave Stoudt
General Manager: D Stoudt
Engineer: D Marcotte
Estimated Sales: $10-20 Million
Number Employees: 50-99
Square Footage: 240000

21223 Custom Systems Integration Co
PO Box 130414
Carlsbad, CA 92013-0414
760-635-1099
Fax: 760-766-3307 bill@csicinc.com
Machinery and services for the packaging and automation industries serving the food and beverage markets. Including feeders, conveyors and custom automation
Owner: Bill Davis
feeders@att.net
Estimated Sales: $500,000-$1 Million
Number Employees: 1-4
Square Footage: 20000
Type of Packaging: Food Service, Private Label
Brands:
Archimedes

21224 Custom Table Pads
455 Hayward Ave N
St Paul, MN 55128-5374
651-714-5720
Fax: 651-501-9246 800-325-4643
Table pads and cloths; also, place mats
Owner: Steve Mc Kay
Estimated Sales: $10 - 20 Million
Number Employees: 20-49

21225 Custom Tarpaulin Products Inc
8095 Southern Blvd
Youngstown, OH 44512-6336
330-758-1801
Fax: 330-758-9872 888-394-5054
info@customtarpaulin.com
www.customtarpaulin.com
Commercial awnings
President: Gerald Robinson
Estimated Sales: $10-20 Million
Number Employees: 10-19

21226 Customized Equipment SE
4186 Railroad Ave
Tucker, GA 30084-4484
770-934-9300
Fax: 770-934-0610
Manufacturer and exporter of packaging machinery including automatic and semi-automatic baggers and sealers; also, random and fixed size carton taping machinery
President: Kermit Cooper
Sales Director: Bruce Cooper
Estimated Sales: $1 - 5 Million
Number Employees: 10 to 19
Square Footage: 40000

21227 (HQ)Cutler Brothers Box & Lumber
711 W Prospect Ave
PO Box 217
Fairview, NJ 07022-1523
201-943-2535
Fax: 201-943-8532 cutler711@aol.com
www.cutlerpallets.com
Wooden and reconditioned pallets; also, scrap wood removal and pallet repair services available
Owner: Greg Cutler
cutler711@aol.com
VP: Greg Cutler
VP: Jed Cutler
Estimated Sales: $12 Million
Number Employees: 50-99
Square Footage: 60000
Other Locations:
Cutler Brothers Box & Lumber
Woodland PA

21228 Cutler Industries
8300 Austin Avenue
Morton Grove, IL 60053-3209
847-965-3700
Fax: 847-965-8585 800-458-5593
Manufacturer and exporter of revolving tray, rack and utility ovens and under counter proofers
Director Marketing Support: Kathleen Casey
Estimated Sales: $1 - 5 Million
Number Employees: 50-99
Square Footage: 340000

21229 Cutler-Hammer
811 Green Crest Drive
Westerville, OH 43081-2838
614-882-3282
Fax: 614-895-7111 www.ch.cutler-hammer.com

Open control and automation solutions including software, logic products, operator interface, sensors, acuators, and industrial PC's
Estimated Sales: $30 - 50 Million
Number Employees: 250-500

21230 Cutrite Company
PO Box 851
Fremont, OH 43420-0851
419-332-1380
Fax: 419-334-2383 800-928-8748
sales@arius-eickert.com
Manufacturer and exporter of cooking knives, poultry shears and meat processing specialty tools and utensils
Sales Manager: Ramon Eickert
General Manager: Becky Smith
Estimated Sales: $3-5 Million
Number Employees: 20-50
Square Footage: 100000
Parent Co: A. Eickert Company
Brands:
Arius-Eickert
Cutrite
Proline

21231 Cutter Lumber Products
10 Rickenbacker Cir
Livermore, CA 94551-7211
925-443-5959
Fax: 925-443-0648 sales@cutterlumber.com
www.cutterlumber.com
Pallets and skids
President: Tony Palma
tony@cutterlumber.com
Sales Manager: Todd Samuels
Estimated Sales: $1-2.5 Million
Number Employees: 1-4
Other Locations:
Cutter Lumber Products
Willits CA

21232 Cyborg Equipment Corporation
8 Graham St
Wareham, MA 02571
508-291-0999
Fax: 781-297-0097
Packaging, vacuum, tumblers, crede machine, form, fill and seal machines, temp monitoring device
Manager: Jennifer Lawrence
Estimated Sales: $1 - 2.5 000,000
Number Employees: 1-4

21233 Cyclamen Collection
2140 Livingston St
Oakland, CA 94606
510-434-7620
Fax: 510-434-7624 CYCLAMENCOLL@aol.com
www.cyclamencollection.com
Manufacturer and exporter of dinnerware, serveware, bakeware and vitrified stoneware, pitchers, vases, and lamps
Owner: Julie Sanders
julie.sanders@cyclamencollection.com
Sales: Julie Sanders
julie.sanders@cyclamencollection.com
Estimated Sales: $500,000-$1,000,000
Number Employees: 5-9
Number of Products: 200+
Type of Packaging: Bulk
Brands:
Calla
Cyclamen
Ergo
Fallingwater
Fiamma
Forma
Mosaica
Nelson
Nova
Patchwork
Stella

21234 Cycle Computer Consultants
95 Jerusalem Ave
Hicksville, NY 11801
516-733-1892
Fax: 516-935-0697
Consultant offering computer services for food distributors
Owner: Anthony Manzillilo
Marketing Manager: Frank Berelson
Number Employees: 10-19
Parent Co: Tomark-Cyber Associates

21235 Cyclonaire Corp
2922 N Division Ave
P.O. Box 366
York, NE 68467-9775
402-362-2000
Fax: 402-362-2001 800-445-0730
sales@cyclonaire.com www.cyclonaire.com
Manufacturer and exporter of pneumatic conveying equipment and accessories
President: Dan Reckner
dreckner@ddreckner.com
CEO: Don Baker
VP: Scott Schmidt
Sales: Joe Morris
Plant Manager: Deryl Kliewer
Purchasing: Sheila Miller
Estimated Sales: $10 - 20 Million
Number Employees: 20-49
Square Footage: 80000
Brands:
Cyclojet
Cyclolift
Cyclolok
Cyclonaire
Vibra Pad

21236 Cynter Con Technology Adviser
656 Quince Orchard Road
7th Floor
Gaithersburg, MD 20878-1409
301-208-3958
Fax: 301-990-3434 800-287-1811
Consultant specializing in technology for the food service and retail industries
Business Development Manager: Francis Carmello
Number Employees: 12
Square Footage: 40000

21237 (HQ)Cyntergy Corporation
400 E Gude Dr
Rockville, MD 20850-1365
301-315-8610
Fax: 301-315-8611 800-825-5787
info@cyntergy.com www.cyntergy.com
Consultant specializing in project management, training, implementation/training and documentation for the food service and retail industries
President: Mitchell Rambler
Chairman/CEO: Rob Grimes
VP Sales/Marketing: Cort Grey
Estimated Sales: $5-10 Million
Number Employees: 50-99
Type of Packaging: Bulk

21238 Cyplex
6311 Primrose Ave Apt 18
Los Angeles, CA 90068-4413
Fax: 323-436-0190 www.cyplex.net
Developer of point of sale hardware and software
Estimated Sales: $1-2,500,000
Number Employees: 10-19
Brands:
Alliance

21239 Cypress Systems
40365 Brickyard Dr # 101
Suite 101
Madera, CA 93636-9520
559-229-7850
Fax: 559-225-9007 800-235-2436
www.cypsystems.com
Electrochemical instrumentation
President: Paul Willis
paul.willis@cypsystems.com
Business Manager: Huei Chi Alice Sutherland
Estimated Sales: Less Than $500,000
Number Employees: 1-4

21240 Cyprus Embassy Trade Ctr
13 E 40th St
New York, NY 10016-0110
212-213-9100
Fax: 212-213-2918 ctcny@cyprustradeny.org
www.cyprustradeny.com
Agency/Trade Organization.
Marketing: Aristos Constantine
Manager: Aristos Constantine
ctcny@aol.com
Number Employees: 1-4

21241 Cyrk
14224 167th Avenue
Monroe, WA 98272
Fax: 800-545-8840 800-426-3125
Manufacturer and exporter of advertising novelties
including screen printed promotional materials
Sales Manager: Steve Paradiso
Contact: Kathy Heineman
kheineman@cyrk.com
Estimated Sales: $40 Million
Number Employees: 250-500
Type of Packaging: Food Service

21242 Cyro Industries/Degussa
P.O. Box 677
Parsippany, NJ 07054-0677
973-541-8000
Fax: 973-541-8445 800-631-5384
cyro@degussa.com www.cyro.com
Manufacturer and exporter of molding and extrusion
compounds for food bins and displays
President: Thomas Bates
Marketing Director: Cynthia Zey
Public Relations: Gail Wood
Number Employees: 500-999
Parent Co: Cytec Industries/Rohm GmbH
Brands:
Cyrolite G-20
Xt

21243 Cyvex Nutrition
1851 Kaiser Ave
Irvine, CA 92614
949-622-9030
Fax: 949-622-9033 888-992-9839
sales@cyvex.com www.cyvex.com
High quality, reliable and accurate refractometers
and polarimeters for liquid concentration control
Director, Operations: Quang La
R&D: Denise Lam
Marketing: Charlene Lee
Contact: Michelle Adelman
michelle.adelman@reachlocal.com
Number Employees: 5-9
Number of Brands: 1
Number of Products: 3
Square Footage: 15000
Brands:
Atago Brand

21244 D & F Equipment
8641 Highway 227 North
PO Box 275
Crossville, AL 35962
256-528-7842
Fax: 256-528-7171 800-282-7842
terrycleghorn@dfequip.com www.dfequip.com
Equipment and machinery for meat processing
Owner: Larry Fortenberry
Owner: Lynn Fortenberry
Owner: Dawn Knox
SVP: Greg Cagle
Director of Engineering: Gary Cambron
Corporate Purchasing/Marketing: Gene Pledger
Sales Manager: Terry Cleghorn
Contact: Joey Knott
projects@dfequip.com
VP of Operations & Service: Joey Knott
Accounts Receivable: Cathy Sims
Accounts Payable: Towania Williams
Number Employees: 20

21245 D & L Manufacturing
1818 S 71st St
Milwaukee, WI 53214
414-256-8160
Fax: 414-476-0564 sales@kempsmith-dl.com
www.kempsmith-dl.com
Manufacturer and exporter of machinery including
file folder, paper converting, cutting, creasing, fold-
ing carton, folding and glueing, laminating, printing,
embossing and rotary die cutting
President: Brett Burris
CEO: Robert Burris
Sales Director: Judy Lewis
Estimated Sales: $10-20 Million
Number Employees: 20-49
Square Footage: 116000

21246 D & S Mfg
14 Sword St # 4
Auburn, MA 01501-2170
508-799-7812
Fax: 508-753-3468
Knives; also, screens for granulators and choppers
President: Graham Scarsbrook
Contact: Robert Johnson
dsmanufacturing@aol.com
Estimated Sales: $1 - 2.5 Million
Number Employees: 10-19
Parent Co: L. Hardy

21247 D & W Fine Pack
800 Ela Rd
Lake Zurich, IL 60047-2340
847-438-2171
Fax: 847-438-0369 800-323-0422
www.dwfinepack.com
Manufacturer and exporter of metal baking pans for
muffins, cupcakes, breads, baguettes, pizza, cakes,
pies, buns and rolls; also, aluminum foil containers,
plastic domes, plastic containers, and plastic
clamshells
President & CEO: Dave Randall
Cio/Cto: Mike Jenkins
CFO, VP Finance: Tom Nickele
VP, CIO: Michael Casula
VP Sales Grocery & Processor: Rick Barton
SVP Operations: Jay DuBois
Number Employees: 100-249
Square Footage: 1200000
Type of Packaging: Consumer, Food Service, Pri-
vate Label, Bulk
Brands:
Bakalon
Bake King
Chicago Metallic
Cm Packaging
Sure-Bake
Sure-Bake & Glaze
Ultraslik
Village Bakers

21248 D & W Fine Pack
4162 Georgia Blvd
San Bernardino, CA 92407-1852
909-880-1781
Fax: 909-474-4384 800-232-5959
www.dwfinepack.com
Disposable food containers
President: Andrew Falcon
Controller: Rick Blanton
rickb@cmfinepack.com
Estimated Sales: $20,000,000 - $49,999,999
Number Employees: 100-249
Brands:
Fine Pak

21249 D A Berther Inc
9000 W Becher St
Milwaukee, WI 53227-1510
414-328-1995
Fax: 414-328-1818 877-357-9622
info@daberther.com www.daberther.com
Stainless steel food equipment, supplies, tables and
sinks
President/CEO: David A. Berther
jeff@daberther.com
CFO: David Berther
Vice President/Sales Consultant: Jeff Berther
Inside Sales/Rental Manager: Jim Lidwin
Estimated Sales: $1 - 2.5 Million
Number Employees: 10-19
Square Footage: 42000

21250 D A C Labels & Graphic
10491 Brockwood Rd
Dallas, TX 75238-1641
214-340-2055
Fax: 214-340-2272 800-483-1700
daclbl@aol.com www.daclabels.com
Printed labels and tags; wholesaler/distributor of
thermal transfer printers and ribbons
Vice President: Judy Benson
daclbl@aol.com
CEO: Jay Fair
R & D: Greg Swindle
VP: Judy Vinson
Marketing Manager: Greg Towers
Customer Support: Michelle Ywhite
Estimated Sales: $5 - 10 Million
Number Employees: 10-19

21251 D D Bean & Sons Co
207 Peterborough St
Jaffrey, NH 03452-5868
603-532-8311
Fax: 603-532-6001 800-326-8311
info@ddbean.com www.ddbean.com
Manufacturer and exporter of matchbooks
President: D Bean
CEO: Delcie D Bean
dbean@ddbean.com
VP: Peter Leach
Manager: Terry Fecto
Estimated Sales: $20-50 Million
Number Employees: 50-99
Square Footage: 100000
Type of Packaging: Food Service, Private Label

21252 D D Williamson & Co Inc
1901 Payne St
Louisville, KY 40206-1902
502-895-2438
Fax: 502-895-7381
Global manufacturer of natural colour for the food
and beverage industries with facilities in Africa,
Asia, Europe and North and South America.
Chairman & CEO: Ted Nixon
Type of Packaging: Bulk

21253 D F Ingredients Inc
127 Elm St # 200
Suite 200
Washington, MO 63090-2140
636-583-0802
Fax: 630-583-4877 888-583-0802
michael@dfingredients.com
www.dfingredients.com
Ingredients and dairy products
President: Michael Husmann
Vice President: Larry Rice
Sales Rep: Richard Kuddes
Sales Rep: Kenneth Johnson
Sales Rep: Jim Wesselschmidt
Manager: Megan Bade
megan@dfingredients.com
Number Employees: 1-4

21254 D I Mfg LLC
13335 C St
Omaha, NE 68144-3601
402-330-5650
www.dimanufacturing.com
Specialty food products including gluten free foods,
garlic bread, wrapped breads, pizza, cookie dough
Contact: Zack Best
zbest@dimanufacturing.com
Number Employees: 10-19
Type of Packaging: Food Service, Bulk

21255 D M Sales & EngineeringCo
1325 Sunday Dr
Indianapolis, IN 46217-9334
317-783-5493
Fax: 317-787-5642 www.dmsales-eng.com
Decorative and thermoforming plastic molding and
plastic packaging products
President: Dave Mickel
davemickel@dmsaleseng.com
Estimated Sales: $2.5-5 Million
Number Employees: 20-49

21256 D R Technology Inc
73 South St
Freehold, NJ 07728-2317
732-780-4664
Fax: 732-780-1545 sales@DRTechnologyInc.com
www.drtechnologyinc.com
Manufacturer and exporter of wet scrubbers used to
control atmospheric emissions in food manufactur-
ing plants
President: Richard Schwartz
CEO: Doris Schwartz
drtinfo@aol.com
Marketing Director: Debra Kruggen
Estimated Sales: $.5 - 1 million
Number Employees: 5-9
Square Footage: 5000

21257 D W Davies & Co
3200 Phillips Ave
Racine, WI 53403-4309
262-637-6133
Fax: 262-637-3933 800-888-6133
dwdavies@dwdavies.com www.dwdavies.com

Chemicals, cleaners, floor finishes, boiler compounds and dishwashing detergents.
Owner: D J Davies
  dwdavies@dwdavies.com
President: Daniel Davies
CFO: David Rubenstein
Estimated Sales: $10-20 Million
Number Employees: 20-49
Square Footage: 40000
Type of Packaging: Consumer, Private Label
Brands:
  D.W. Concentrate

21258 D&D Sign Company
6232 Southwest Pkwy
Wichita Falls, TX 76308-0803
940-692-4643
Fax: 940-692-1344
Metal, electric, neon, plexiglass and wooden signs; also, installation and services available
Co-Owner: Mark Patterson
Estimated Sales: $1-2.5 Million
Number Employees: 5-9

21259 D&L Manufacturing
1818 S 71st St
Milwaukee, WI 53214
414-256-8160
Fax: 414-476-0564 sales@kempsmith-dl.com
www.kempsmith-dl.com
Bottle washers and fillers
President: Les Johnson
CEO: Robert E Burris
Estimated Sales: $10 - 20 Million
Number Employees: 20-49

21260 D&M Pallet Company
118 Morris St
Neshkoro, WI 54960-9599
920-293-4616
Fax: 920-293-4660
Pallets, skids, crates and boxes
President: David Heinzelman
Estimated Sales: $500,000 - $1 Million
Number Employees: 1 to4

21261 D&M Products
2310 Michigan Avenue
Santa Monica, CA 90404
310-453-0485
Fax: 310-828-9670 800-245-0485
sales@dm-products.com www.dm-products.com
Hydro-air pressure guns for cold stream cleaning
President and CFO: Karl Hirzel
Contact: Dennis Markle
  dennis@dmproducts.net
Estimated Sales: Below $5 Million
Number Employees: 1-4
Brands:
  D&M

21262 D'Ac Lighting
420 Railroad Way
PO BOX 262
Mamaroneck, NY 10543-2257
914-698-5959
Fax: 914-698-6061 www.daclighting.com
Manufacturer and importer of lighting fixtures including electric and flourescent
President: Robert N Haidinger
Customer Service: Peggy Guglielmo
General Manager: Moshe Toledo
Estimated Sales: $1-2.5 Million
Number Employees: 50-99
Square Footage: 100000

21263 D'Addario Design Associates
123 W 44th Street
New York, NY 10036-4000
212-302-0059
Fax: 212-764-7262
Design consultant specializing in labels, cartons, logos, wooden boxes and POS and merchandising aids
President: Thomas D'Addario
VP: Adam D'Addario
Estimated Sales: Less than $500,000
Number Employees: 1-4
Square Footage: 4000

21264 D'Lights
533 West Windsor Road
Glendale, CA 91204
818-956-5656
Fax: 818-956-2157 www.dlights.com

Manufacturer and exporter of lighting fixtures and food warmers
President: Kent Erle Sokolow
General Manager: Steve Sink
Estimated Sales: Below $5 Million
Number Employees: 10

21265 D. Picking & Company
119 S Walnut St
Bucyrus, OH 44820
419-562-6891
Fax: 419-562-0078
Copper kettles for use in the processing of apple butter and decorative items
Owner: Helen Picking-Neff
Office Manager: Steve Schifer
Director: Sylvia Cooper
Estimated Sales: $5-10 Million
Number Employees: 5-9

21266 D.A. Colongeli & Sons
16 Pomeroy Street
Cortland, NY 13045-2241
607-753-0888
Fax: 607-756-2997 800-322-7687
Established in 1970; purveyors of fine foods.
President: Donald Colongeli
Number Employees: 1
Square Footage: 4000
Type of Packaging: Food Service
Brands:
  Fancy
  Fine
  Gourmet
  Haco Foods
  Knorr

21267 D.D.& D. Machinery
7620 Seneca St
East Aurora, NY 14052-9457
716-652-4410
Fax: 716-652-0677
President: Norbert Gerhard
Estimated Sales: $3 - 5 Million
Number Employees: 1-4

21268 D.R. McClain & Son
7039 E Slauson Ave
Commerce, CA 90040-3620
323-722-7900
Fax: 323-726-4700 800-428-2263
Bakery equipment including dough rollers, sheeters and molders
Owner: Jeff Branstein
National Sales Manager: Norm Gwinn
Estimated Sales: $1 - 5 Million
Number Employees: 50-99
Square Footage: 76000

21269 D2 Ingredients, LP.
1244 Enterprise Dr
De Pere, WI 54115
920-425-8870
Fax: 920-964-0116 info@d2ingredients.com
d2ingredients.com
Functional ingredients and products, including smoke flavorings, alginate products, extrudable yeast-less doughs and savory fillings; spice blends, caramelized sugars and commodities; injection and tumbling products for poulty andmeat. Also provide
Vice President of Sales & Marketing: Dan Rose
Type of Packaging: Private Label, Bulk

21270 (HQ)DBE Inc
310 Rayette Road
Concord, ON L4K 2G5
Canada
905-738-0353
Fax: 905-738-7585 800-461-5313
www.dbe-vsi.com
Manufacturer, importer and exporter of seafood equipment including commercial fish/lobster tanks, electrical fish sealers, customized seafood tanks
President: Fima Dreff
Marketing Director: Lesya Sklyarenko
Sales Director: Joe Albis
Public Relations: Lesya Sklyarenko
Plant Manager: Jean-Pierre Paquette
Estimated Sales: $10 - 20 Million
Number Employees: 15
Number of Brands: 6
Square Footage: 100000

Other Locations:
  DBE Food Equipment
  Kyiv
Brands:
  Dde

21271 (HQ)DCI, Inc.
600 54th Ave N
St Cloud, MN 56303-2043
320-252-8200
Fax: 320-252-0866 sales@dciinc.com
www.dciinc.com
Manufacturer and exporter of stainless steel processing and storage tanks as well as OEM components (tank heads, manways, mixers/agitators,parts). Also offering DCI Site-Fab (field fabrication of any size tank up to 500,00 gallons).
Chief Financial Officer: Chad Leither
Executive Vice President: Chad Leither
Estimated Sales: $20 - 50 Million
Number Employees: 100-249
Square Footage: 88000
Other Locations:
  Manufacturing/Site-Fab Facility
  Sparta MO
  Manufacturing/Site-Fab Facility
  Fresno CA

21272 (HQ)DCL Solutions LLC
4201 Torresdale Ave
Philadelphia, PA 19124-4701
215-743-4201
Fax: 215-288-0847 800-426-1127
sales@dclsolutions.com www.big3packaging.com
Manufacturer and exporter of floor finishes, strippers, oven/grill cleaners, hand soaps, degreasers and portion control water soluble packets
Owner: Steve Seneca
  sseneca@pakit.com
CFO: Bill Harry
VP: Bill Paris
Estimated Sales: $5 - 10 Million
Number Employees: 50-99
Square Footage: 120000
Brands:
  Chemical Service
  Pak It
  Vapguard

21273 DCM Tech Corp
4455 Theurer Blvd
PO Box 1304
Winona, MN 55987-1593
507-452-4043
Fax: 507-452-7970 800-533-5339
interest@dcm-tech.com www.dcm-tech.com
Supplier of metal cutting tools and machines
President: Chris Arnold
  chris@luminet.net
Financial Controller: Jennifer Fruth
Technical Specialist: Mike Anderson
Engineering Manager: Jerry Lawson
Purchasing Manager: Denise Aitken
Estimated Sales: $4 Million
Number Employees: 50-99

21274 DCS IPAL Consultants
1043 Autoroute Chomedey
Laval, QC J7W 4V3
Canada
450-973-3338
Fax: 450-973-3339 www.sidel.com
Consultant specializing in packaging and process engineering
Engineering & Material Handling: Marc Aury
Controls and Automation Dir.: Franck Klotz
Director Operations: Alex Gieysztor
Number Employees: 250
Square Footage: 56000
Parent Co: Gebo Industries

21275 DCS Sanitation Management
7864 Camargo Rd
Cincinnati, OH 45243
513-271-9300
Fax: 513-271-5710 800-837-8737
www.pssi.co
Consultants and sanitation programs for the meat industry; sanitation supplies and equipment, including cleaning compounds and solutions, cleaning and washing equipment and accessories, and sanitizers
President: Tom Murray
Estimated Sales: $1 - 5 Million
Number Employees: 1-4

21276 DCV BioNutritionals
3521 Silverside Road
Wilmington, DE 19810-4900
800-641-2001
Fax: 302-695-5188 800-641-2001
Microencapsulation of nutrition, baking and specialty food ingredients: choline and betaine salts
Contact: Becky Price
 becky.price@airepel.com
Estimated Sales: $50 - 100 Million
Number Employees: 50-99

21277 DECI Corporation
One Todd Drive
Burgettstown, PA 15021
724-947-3300
Fax: 724-947-3621
Consultant specializing in food processing plant engineering and design
Vice President: Bruce Mahoney
Contact: Michael Gialames
 michael.gialames@deccorp.com
Estimated Sales: $2.5-5 Million
Number Employees: 20-50
Square Footage: 29824

21278 DEFCO
165 Sawmill Road
Landenberg, PA 19350-9302
215-274-8245
Fax: 610-274-0342
Fiberglass reinforced thermoset plastic process equipment; also, installation and maintenance available
VP: John Field
Estimated Sales: $1-2.5 Million
Number Employees: 10-19
Square Footage: 32000

21279 DEL-Tec Packaging Inc
4020 Pelham Ct
Greer, SC 29650-4804
864-288-7390
Fax: 864-288-7237 800-747-8683
sales@del-tec.com www.del-tec.com
Totes, bins, trays and vacuum and thermoformed plastic containers
Owner: Robert Kocis
VP Finance: Jere Davis
VP Sales: Bob Kocis
 rkocis@mainstay.net
Customer Service: Joy McCullough
Plant Manager: Tim Shea
Estimated Sales: $1-2.5 Million
Number Employees: 20-49
Square Footage: 260000

21280 DEMACO
411 S Ebenezer Road
Florence, SC 29501-7916
407-952-6600
Fax: 407-952-6683

21281 DFL Laboratories
111 E. Wacker Dr.
Suite 2300
Chicago, IL 60601
312-938-5151
Fax: 209-521-1005
Consultant specializing in chemical and microbiological testing services
Manager: Stephanie Campbell
Estimated Sales: $10-20,000,000
Number Employees: 100-249

21282 DH/Sureflow
402 SE 31st Avenue
Portland, OR 97214-1929
503-236-9263
Fax: 503-236-9264 800-654-2548
sureflow@dhsales.com
Manufacturer and exporter of drain cleaning machinery and power snakes
Owner and President: Doug Hemenway
VP: Geoff Hemenway
Number Employees: 3
Square Footage: 10000
Brands:
 Sureflow

21283 DHM Adhesives Inc
509 S Wall St # A
Calhoun, GA 30701-2536
706-629-7960
Fax: 706-625-2819 800-745-1346
www.dhmadhesives.com
Pressure sensitive and hot melt adhesives
President: Matt Devine
 mdevine@dhmadhesives.com
CFO: Bill Matthews
Vice President of Procurement: Bob Goodman
Vice President of Sales and Marketing: Bob Shumaker
Plant Manager: David Chase
Purchasing Manager: Milton Bryson
Estimated Sales: $5 - 10 Million
Number Employees: 20-49

21284 DHP
1911 Rustic Pl
Farmington, NM 87401
Fax: 505-327-2934 877-711-4347
info@dhptraining.com www.dhptraining.com
Water treatment, training, products and service
President & CEO: Charles Bedford
VP, Marketing & Software: Darrell Cunningham
VP, On-Site Sales: Dick Youmans
Year Founded: 1988
Estimated Sales: $100-200 Million
Number Employees: 20-49

21285 DIC International
35 Waterview Blvd Ste 100
Parsippany, NJ 07054-1270
Fax: 201-836-4962
www.dic.co.jp/eng/products/pps/global.html
Manufacturer, importer and exporter of a natural nontoxic chlorophyll colorant
President: Shintaro Asada
CFO: Yuzi Koike
Marketing Manager: Y Akiyama
Contact: Christine Medordi
 christine@dica.com
Number Employees: 20-49
Parent Co: Dainippou Ink & Chemicals
Brands:
 Co-Enzyme Q-10
 Linablue A
 Pantethine
 Sqvalene

21286 DIPIX Technologies
1051 Baxter Road
Ottawa, ON K2C 3P2
Canada
613-596-4942
Fax: 613-596-4914 info@dipix.com
www.dipix.com
President: Anton Kitai
Director of Sales: Geoff Evans
Chief Operating Officer: Peter Wakeman
Estimated Sales: $1 - 5 Million
Number Employees: 20-50

21287 DL Enterprises
399 Cameron St
Etters, PA 17319-9775
717-938-1292
Fax: 717-938-5110
www.panetwork.com/aisle-a-gator
Battery powered wet/dry vacuum cleaners for grocery warehouses, distribution centers, food processors, warehouses and retail stores
President: Dick Lewis
Estimated Sales: $300,000-500,000
Number Employees: 1-4
Square Footage: 10000
Brands:
 The Aisle-A-Gator

21288 DLX Industries
1609 Roote 202
Pomona, NY 10970-2902
845-517-2200
www.dlxonline.com
Manufacturer and exporter of vinyl-imprinted advertising specialties and promotional items
Estimated Sales: $78,000
Number Employees: 2
Number of Products: 120
Square Footage: 12804
Parent Co: DLX

21289 DMC-David ManufacturingCompany
1600 12th Street NE
Mason City, IA 50401-2543
641-424-7010
Fax: 641-424-7017
Manufacturer and exporter of grain-handling equipment including cleaners and dryers; also, moisture sensing devices for flowing or moving material
CEO and President: Wes Cagle
Sales/Marketing Manager: Jim Balk
Estimated Sales: $20-50 Million
Number Employees: 100-249
Square Footage: 157000
Brands:
 Cal-Cu-Dri
 Calc-U-Dryer
 Hi-Cap
 Stirator

21290 DMG Financial Inc
950 S Cherry St # 424
Suite 424
Denver, CO 80246-2612
303-756-1794
Fax: 303-756-9484 888-331-3882
info@dmgfinancial.com www.dmgfinancial.com
Management consultants specializing in management consulting, mergers and acquisitions, financial services
President: Douglas Bilenski
 dbilenski@dmgfinancial.com
Estimated Sales: Less Than $500,000
Number Employees: 1-4

21291 DMN Inc
220 S Woods St
West Memphis, AR 72301-4304
870-733-9100
Fax: 870-733-9101 www.dmnwestinghouse.com
Rotary valves, diverter valves
Owner: Rob Kabel
 rkabel@dmn-inc.com
Estimated Sales: Below $5 Million
Number Employees: 5-9

21292 DOWL LLC
4041 B St
Anchorage, AK 99503-5906
907-562-2000
Fax: 907-563-3953 800-478-3695
Glycine, chelating agents, surfactants, dispersing agents and emulsion polymers
President: Stewart G Osgood
 sosgood@dowlhkm.com
CEO: Andrew Liveris
Executive VP: Geoffery Merszel
Marketing Manager: Art Paulidis
Commercial Manager: Mark DeGeorge
Estimated Sales: $2.5-5 Million
Number Employees: 250-499

21293 DPC
21 W Fornance St # 150
Norristown, PA 19401-3300
610-277-3000
Fax: 610-277-1264 800-220-9473
Disposable and nonwoven counter and table wipers in folded, roll and portion control dispenser box form
President: Jim Drucker
CFO: Daniel Chojnacki
VP: Jeff Berk
Director Marketing: D Bancroft
Estimated Sales: $1-2.5 Million
Number Employees: 50-99
Square Footage: 600000
Parent Co: RTR Industries
Other Locations:
 D.P.C.
 Greenville SC

21294 DPI Specialty Foods Inc.
601 Rockefeller Ave.
Ontario, CA 91761
909-975-1019
Fax: 909-975-7238 www.dpispecialtyfoods.com
Gourmet, natural, organic, gluten free, local and ethnic foods.
CEO: Russ Blake
Chief Financial Officer: Marc Barth
Chief Information Officer: Nadia Rosseels
Chief Operating Officer: Christopher Erklenz

Year Founded: 1963
Estimated Sales: Over $1 Billion
Number Employees: 1000-4999

21295 DR McClain & Son
PO Box 95
Pico Rivera, CA 90660-0095

562-699-4542
Fax: 562-692-0026 800-428-2263
Dough rollers and sheeters

21296 DSA Software
34 School St # 201
Foxboro, MA 02035-2318

508-543-0400
Fax: 508-543-0856 sales@dsasoft.com
www.dsasoft.com
Warehouse management software
President: David Petri
lpetri@dsasoft.com
Estimated Sales: Below $5 Million
Number Employees: 5-9
Brands:
Foxware Dc Label
Foxware Dc Manager
Foxware Edi Manager
Foxware Rf Manager

21297 DSI
15304 NE 95th St
Redmond, WA 98052

425-885-5223
Fax: 425-882-2025
Cutting, boning devices and processing equipment,
defatting machines, trimming devices, dicers, and
slicers
President: Jim Heber
Estimated Sales: $5-10 000,000
Number Employees: 20-49

21298 DSI Process Systems
4630 W Florissant Ave
St Louis, MO 63115-2233

314-382-1525
Fax: 314-382-5234 800-342-5374
jack@dsiprocess.com www.statco-dsi.com
Conveyor systems, stainless steel food processing
equipment, tanks, and sanitary piping
President: Robert Goetz
rgoetz@statco-dsi.com
Marketing Contact: Jack Luechtefeld
Estimated Sales: $10 - 20 Million
Number Employees: 50-99

21299 DSM Nutritional Products LLC
45 Waterview Blvd
Parsippany, NJ 07054

973-257-8500
info.dnp@dsm.com

www.dsm.com/corporate/about/businesses/dsm-nut
ritional-products.html
Supplier of vitamins, carotenoids and other fine
chemicals to the feed, food, pharmaceutical and per-
sonal care industries.
President: Chris Goppelsroeder
Parent Co: Koninklijke DSM N.V.
Type of Packaging: Bulk

21300 DSO Fluid Handling Company
300 McGaw Drive,
Raritan Center Edison
Irvington, NJ 08837

732-225-9100
Fax: 732-225-9101 1 8-0 5-7 68
Owner: Darrin Oppenheim
Estimated Sales: $10-20 000,000
Number Employees: 10-19

21301 DSW Converting Knives
1504 8th Avenue N
Birmingham, AL 35203

205-322-2021
Fax: 205-322-2576
Manufacturer and exporter of machine knives
President: Chris Mc Ilvaine
Estimated Sales: Below $5 Million
Number Employees: 10-19
Type of Packaging: Bulk

21302 DT Converting Technologies - Stokes
207 Mill St
Bristol, PA 19007-4808

215-788-3500
Fax: 215-781-1122 800-635-0036
stokes-info@dtindustries.com
www.dtindustries.com
Manufacturer tablet presses, granulators, tablet
deduster, tornado mills
President: Ken Peterson
Vice President: George Graff
Research & Development: Dave Breen
Marketing Director: Barb McDevitt
Sales Director: George Graff
Number Employees: 20-49
Parent Co: DT Industries
Brands:
Genesis Removable Head Press
Tablet Press 328
Valitah 3000

21303 (HQ)DT Industrials
949 S McCord Rd
Holland, OH 43528

567-703-8550
Fax: 419-866-4656 sales@dtindustrials.com
dtindustrials-lubricants.com
Food grade oils and greases
Sales & Marketing: Erica Jaspers

21304 DT Packaging Systems
18105 Trans Canada
Kirkland, QC H9J 3Z4
Canada

514-694-2390
Fax: 514-694-6552 888-384-3343
lvilleneuve@kalishdti.com www.dtindustries.com

21305 DT Packaging Systems
7 New Lancaster Road
Leominster, MA 01453-5224

978-537-8534
Fax: 978-840-0730 800-851-1518
Line integration conveyors, online quality assurance,
filling by count, bulk handling
President: Jim Ririe
Contact: Burckhart Cory
stewart.harvey@imanova.com
Plant Manager: Stewart Harvey
Estimated Sales: $5-10 Million
Number Employees: 100-249

21306 DWL Industries Company
65 Industrial Road
Lodi, NJ 07644

973-916-9958
Fax: 973-916-9959 888-946-2682
cs@wincous.com www.wincodwl.com
Wholesaler/distributor, importer and exporter of
knives, utensils and tableware; serving the food ser-
vice market
President: David Li
Officer: Jieyui Ding
VP Sales: Steve Chang
Contact: Steven Chu
1and1admin@wincous.com
Number Employees: 15
Square Footage: 40000

21307 Dabrico Inc
1555 Commerce Dr
Bourbonnais, IL 60914-4600

815-939-7798
Fax: 815-939-7798 888-439-0580
sales@dabrico.com www.dabrico.com
President: Efrain A Davila
efrain@dabrico.com
Marketing Manager: Maria Carter
Director of Sales and Marketing: Chuck Goranson
Purchasing Manager: Mario Trevino
Estimated Sales: $3 - 5 Million
Number Employees: 10-19

21308 Dacam Corporation
PO Box 310
Madison Heights, VA 24572-0310

434-929-4001
Fax: 434-847-4487 www.dacammachinery.com
Manufacturer and exporter of packaging machinery
President: Ed Tolle
Sales And Marketing: Dean Hargis
Director Engineering: David Vaughan

Estimated Sales: $2.5-5 Million
Number Employees: 20-49
Square Footage: 80000
Brands:
Dacam

21309 Dacam Machinery
113 N Amherst Highway
Madison Heights, VA 24572

434-369-1259
Fax: 434-369-1949
Produces high quality packaging and material han-
dling equipment for the food and beverage indus-
tries.
Estimated Sales: $2.5-5 Million
Number Employees: 20-49

21310 Dadant & Sons Inc
51 S 2nd St # 2
Hamilton, IL 62341-1397

217-847-3324
Fax: 217-847-3660 888-922-1293
dadant@dadant.com www.dadant.com
Injection molded hardware and honey handling and
processing equipment; also, chocolate melters
President: Tim Dadant
Cio/Cto: Terry Avis
dadant@dadant.com
CFO: Tom Ross
VP: T Ross
Quality Control: Gary Stanspery
Estimated Sales: $1-2.5 Million
Number Employees: 100-249

21311 Dade Canvas Products Company
12067 Tech Road
Silver Spring, MD 20904

301-680-2500
Fax: 301-680-0851 thomasawning@prodigy.net
www.thomasawning.com
Commercial awnings
Owner: Michael Riley
Estimated Sales: $1-2.5 Million
Number Employees: 1-4

21312 Dade Engineering
15150 Nighthawk Drive
Tampa, FL 33625

813-264-2273
Fax: 813-343-8117 800-321-2112
richard@starsouth.us www.daeco.net
Manufacturer and exporter of walk-in coolers and
freezers and cold storage doors
President: Joanne Goodstein
Estimated Sales: $5 - 10 Million
Number Employees: 10-19
Square Footage: 80000
Brands:
Daeco

21313 Daesang America Inc
1 University Plz # 505
Hackensack, NJ 07601-6203

201-488-4010
Fax: 201-488-4625 www.daesangamerica.com
President: David Park
Contact: Han Chang
chan@daesangamerica.com
Estimated Sales: $20 - 50 Million
Number Employees: 5-9

21314 Daga Restaurant Ware
500 Alakawa St Rm 220c
Honolulu, HI 96817

808-847-3100
Fax: 808-843-2977
Restaurant supplies
Owner: Noreen Quirk
Vice President: Alfred Coscina
Estimated Sales: $2.5-5 000,000
Number Employees: 1-4

21315 Dagher Printing
11775 Marco Beach Dr
Jacksonville, FL 32224-7616

904-998-0921
Fax: 904-998-0921 www.dagher.com
Commercial printer of business stationery; color
printing available
Owner: Anthony Fredrickson
afredrickson@dagherprintingonline.com
Treasurer: Mouma Khourly
VP: Sam Dagher

Estimated Sales: $1-2.5 Million
Number Employees: 10-19
Square Footage: 16000

21316 Dahl-Tech Inc
5805 Saint Croix Trl N
Stillwater, MN 55082-6593

651-439-2946
Fax: 651-439-2976   800-626-5812
daltechinc@qwestoffice.net
www.dahltechplastics.com
Custom blew molding company and manufacturer of plastic containers, devices, and hollow structures for the food packaging, chemical, automotive, agricultural, healthcare, recreational, and household products industries.
President: Bob Dahlke
  bob.dahlke@dahltechplastics.com
Sales: Nichole Blekum
Plant Manager: Brian Hell
Estimated Sales: $5 Million
Number Employees: 50-99
Square Footage: 128000
Type of Packaging: Consumer, Food Service, Private Label, Bulk

21317 Dahmes Stainless
6300 County Road 40
New London, MN 56273

320-354-5711
Fax: 320-354-5712   info@dahmes.com
www.dahmes.com
President: Forrest Dahmes
CFO: Dan DeGeest
Sales Director: Steve Frank
Production Manager: Jeff Kampsen
Purchasing Manager: Brad Doyle
Estimated Sales: $5-10 000,000
Number Employees: 20-49
Type of Packaging: Consumer, Bulk

21318 Daido Corp
1031 Fred White Blvd
Portland, TN 37148-8369

615-323-4020
Fax: 615-323-4015   866-219-9972
www.daidocorp.com
President: Mike Kato
  carrierl@daidocorp.com
CEO: Steve Pudles
Sales Exec: Lee Carrier
Estimated Sales: $10 - 20 Million
Number Employees: 20-49

21319 Daily Printing Inc
2333 Niagara Ln N
Plymouth, MN 55447-4712

763-475-2333
Fax: 763-449-6320   800-622-6596
info@dailyprinting.com   www.dailyprinting.com
Manufacturer and exporter of size reduction equipment for grinding, deagglomerating and pulverizing feeds, foods, spices, etc
President: Pete Jacobson
  pjacobson@dailyprinting.com
CFO: Ken Rein
EVP: Don Bergeron
VP of Sales and Marketing: Tom Moe
Estimated Sales: $10 - 20 Million
Number Employees: 50-99
Square Footage: 200000

21320 DairiConcepts
3253 E Chestnut Expy
Springfield, MO 65802-2540

417-829-3400
Fax: 417-829-3401   877-596-4374
mwilliams@dairiconcepts.com
www.dairiconcepts.com
CEO: Jeff Miyake
  jeffmiyake@dairiconcepts.com
Number Employees: 1-4

21321 Dairiconcepts
3253 E Chestnut Expy
Springfield, MO 65802-2540

417-829-3400
Fax: 417-829-3401   877-596-4374
www.dairiconcepts.com
CEO: Jeff Miyake
  jeffmiyake@dairiconcepts.com
Number Employees: 1-4

21322 (HQ)Dairy Conveyor Corp
38 Mount Ebo Rd S
Brewster, NY 10509-4005

845-278-7878
Fax: 845-278-7305   info@dairyconveyor.com
www.dairyconveyor.com
Manufacturer and exporter of material handling equipment for dairies and ice cream plants
President: Karl Kleinschrod
CEO: Karl Kleinsahrod
Southeast Regional Sales Manager: Greg Reid
Eastern Regional Sales Manager: Tony Gomez
Estimated Sales: $12 Million
Number Employees: 100-249
Square Footage: 24000

21323 Dairy Foods
1050 IL Route 83
Suite 200
Bensenville, IL 60106

630-694-4341
Fax: 630-227-0527   www.bnp.com
Publications
Market Analyst: Jerry Dryer
Contact: M Sarah
  kennedys@dairyfoods.com
Estimated Sales: Below $5 Million
Number Employees: 10

21324 Dairy Service & Mfg
1818 Linn St
Kansas City, MO 64116-3627

816-472-0011
Fax: 816-472-7935   800-825-0011
dsikc@dsiprocess.com
Custom fabrication, processing and packaging
Owner: Jack W Luechtefeld
Controller: Charlie Siebert
Accounts Manager: Gordon Gosejohan
Vice President: Gary Rinck
Technical Sevices/Refrigeration Manager: Dave Smith
Customer service: Brandon Barr
Marketing Manager: Lori Collier
Inside Sales: Nicole Wohletz
Customer Service: Dawn Jinson
Operations Manager: Georgia Pilla
Project Engineer: Paul Wallace
Estimated Sales: $2.5 - 5 000,000
Number Employees: 1-4

21325 Dairy Services Inc
450 W Meadow St
Stratford, WI 54484-9498

715-687-8091
800-221-3947
Owner: Barb Nikolai
  barb.nikolai@gmail.com
Number Employees: 10-19
Square Footage: 32000

21326 Dairy Specialties
8536 Cartney Ct
Dublin, OH 43017

614-764-1216
Fax: 614-855-3114   dsibrown@aol.com
Exporter, importer and wholesaler/distributor of milk proteins, flavor producing enzymes and dried dairy ingredients
President: David Brown
  d.brown@dsm.com
CEO: V Brown
Estimated Sales: $2 Million
Number Employees: 1-4
Square Footage: 6000
Type of Packaging: Bulk

21327 Dairyland Plastics Company
N 8986 County Rd
Colfax, WI 54730-4500

715-962-3425
Plastic bags
Owner: David Haugle

21328 Dakota Blenders
1350 South Kingshighway
St. Louis, MO 63110

314-898-9926
Fax: 314-531-3789   800-383-0958
www.dakotablenders.net
A leading supplier of quality blends for top wholesale bakeries, as well as numerous other divisions of the industry.

21329 Dakota Corrugated Box
4501 N 2nd Ave
Sioux Falls, SD 57104-0676

605-332-3501
Fax: 605-332-3496
Corrugated containers
President: Robert Bittner
CFO: Bob Bittner
Sales Manager: Mike Bartlett
General Manager: Mike Bartlett
Estimated Sales: $2.5 - 5 Million
Number Employees: 20 to 49

21330 Dakota Valley Products,Inc.
419 3rd St.
Willow Lake, SD 57278

605-625-2526
Fax: 605-352-0558
Agricultural products marketing company
Estimated Sales: $1 - 5 Million
Number Employees: 4

21331 Dalare Associates Inc
217 S 24th St
Philadelphia, PA 19103-5593

215-567-1953
Fax: 215-567-1168   info@dalarelab.com
www.dalarelab.com
Analytical and Environmental analysis through a full range of laboratory services.
President: Joseph J Strug Jr
Estimated Sales: $500,000-$1 Million
Number Employees: 5-9

21332 Dalebrook Supplies Ltd.
27-01 Queens Plaza N
13th Floor
Long Island City, NY 11101

sales@dalebrook.com
www.dalebrook.com
Supplier of melamine catering supplies to the food industry sector.
Number of Brands: 1
Brands:
  Dalebrook

21333 Daleco
1000 Wilmont Mews
5th Floor
West Chester, PA 19382

610-429-0181
Fax: 610-429-0818   www.dalecoresources.com
Steamed cheeseburger making machines
President: Robert Gattilia
Estimated Sales: $.5 - 1 million
Number Employees: 1-4
Brands:
  Burg'r Tend'r

21334 Dalemark Industries
575 Prospect St
Bldg. 211
Lakewood, NJ 08701-5040

732-367-3100
Fax: 732-367-7031   sales@dalemark.com
www.dalemark.com
Manufacturer and exporter of coding, imprinting and labeling equipment
President: Michael Delli Gatti
CFO: Kathy Scalzo
Research & Development: Thurman Becker
Marketing: Maria Rau
Sales: Maria Rau
Purchasing: Maria Rau
Estimated Sales: $1 Million
Number Employees: 10-19
Number of Brands: 15
Number of Products: 25
Square Footage: 24000
Type of Packaging: Food Service
Brands:
  Codaire
  Dotmark

21335 (HQ)Dallas Container Corp
8330 Endicott Ln
Dallas, TX 75227-2305

214-381-7148
Fax: 214-381-8279   800-381-7148
www.dallascontainer.com
Corrugated containers
President & Owner: Rod Turnipseed
  rturnipseed@dallascontainer.net
Plant Manager: James Cullen

Estimated Sales: $10-20 Million
Number Employees: 50-99
Other Locations:
Dallas Container Corp.
Albuquerque NM

21336 Dallas Group of America Inc
374 US Highway 22
Whitehouse, NJ 08888-9800
908-534-7800
Fax: 908-534-0084 800-367-4188
info@dallasgrp.com
Magnesium silicate, frying oil purifiers, filter aids
and absorbents; exporter of magnesium silicate
Owner: Bob Dallas Sr
Estimated Sales: $10-20,000,000
Number Employees: 20-49
Type of Packaging: Food Service, Bulk
Brands:
Dalsorb
Haze-Out
Magnesol
Xl

21337 Dallas Roth Young
100 N Cottonwood Drive
Suite 108
Richardson, TX 75080-4772
972-233-5000
Fax: 972-235-5210
Executive search firm specializing in selection and
placement of food industry personnel
President: Ben Dickerson
Sales/Marketing Manager: Chad Dickerson
Number Employees: 3
Square Footage: 1600
Parent Co: Winston Franchise Corporation

21338 Dalloz Safety
10 Thurber Blvd
Smithfield, RI 02917-1858
401-233-0333
Fax: 401-232-1830 800-977-9177
jwomer@dallozsafety.com
Ear muffs, laser eyewear, safety spectacles, goggles
and disposable and reusable respirators and ear
plugs
Estimated Sales: $50-100 Million
Number Employees: 10-19
Brands:
Bilsom
Glendale
Gpt

21339 Dalls Semiconductor
160 Rio Robles
San Jose, CA 95134
972-702-9250
Fax: 972-371-3748 888-629-4642
sales-us@maximintegrated.com
www.maxim-ic.com
President and Chief Executive Officer:

Tun‡ Doluca
SVP and Chief Financial Officer: Bruce E. Kiddoo
President; Chief Executive Officer; Dire: Tunc
Doluca
Vice President, Test Engineering: Rob Georges
Vice President, Quality: Bryan Preeshl
Vice President of Sales and Marketing: Walter
Sangalli
Vice President of Human Resources: Steve
Yamasaki
SVPof Manufacturing Operations: Vivek Jain

Estimated Sales: $1 - 5 Million
Parent Co: Maxim Integrated

21340 Dalmec North America
469 Fox Ct
Bloomingdale, IL 60108-3110
630-307-8426
Fax: 630-307-8436 800-935-8686
sales@dalmecusa.com www.dalmec-na.com
Industrial manipulators for handling rolls, barrels,
boxes, pails or custom product manufacture highly
ergonomic manipulators, combined with bispoke
tooling heads, custom-built to handle a specific
product
Manager: Al Izzo
Sales Manager: Al Killian
Branch Manager: Allan Izzo

Estimated Sales: $2.5-5 000,000
Number Employees: 10-19

21341 Dalton Electric HeatingCo
28 Hayward St
Ipswich, MA 01938-2096
978-356-9844
Fax: 978-356-9846 dalton@daltonelectric.com
www.daltonelectric.com
Industrial heating products-Wall-Flex Cartridge
Heaters.
Owner: Thomas A Shields
tshields@daltonelectricheatingco.com
Sales: E W Whitney III
tshields@daltonelectricheatingco.com
Plant Manager: Steve Lounes
Estimated Sales: $5-10 000,000
Number Employees: 20-49
Square Footage: 17000

21342 Damas Corporation
1977 N Olden Avenue Ext
Suite 289
Trenton, NJ 08618-2112
609-695-9121
Fax: 609-695-9225
Manufacturer and exporter of washing and drying
equipment for laboratory glassware, trays, tote bins,
tubs, pallets and carts
President: David M Smith
Engineer: Dave Smith
Estimated Sales: $1-2,500,000
Number Employees: 5-9
Brands:
Aquasan
Thermajet

21343 Damascus/Bishop Tube Company
795 Reynolds Industrial Park Road
Greenville, PA 16125-4203
724-646-1500
Fax: 724-646-1514
FDA approved steel stainless pipe and tubing for
dairy processors
President: Brent Ward
Estimated Sales: $1 - 5 Million
Number Employees: 100-249

21344 Damon Industries
12435 Rockhill Ave NE
Alliance, OH 44601
Fax: 330-821-6355 800-362-9850
info@damonq.com damonq.com
Manufacturer cleaning chemicals and disinfectants;
consultant specializing in food safety and HACCP
President/Owner: Amy Damon
Executive Vice President: Scott Butterfield
Estimated Sales: $50-100 Million
Number Employees: 100-249
Square Footage: 45000

21345 Damons Graoo
11 Green Pond Road
Rockaway, NJ 07866-2001
973-664-1000
Fax: 973-664-1305
Manufacture high pressure enjection molded prod-
ucts for food and agriculture
Estimated Sales: $300,000-500,000
Number Employees: 10

21346 Damp Rid
W.M. Barr
P.O. Box 1879
Memphis, TN 38101-6948
407-851-6230
Fax: 407-851-6246 888-326-7743
www.damprid.com
Manufacturer and exporter of mildew preventatives,
moisture absorbers and odor eliminators
President: Darien Jalka
CFO: Ken Lasseter
Quality Control: Oliver Cunanan
Sales Director: Darin Galka
Purchasing Manager: Roy Rosado
Estimated Sales: $5-10 Million
Number Employees: 10
Square Footage: 288000
Parent Co: Tetra Technologies Incorporated
Type of Packaging: Consumer
Brands:
Damp Rid

Fresh-All
Magic Disk

21347 Damrow Company
894 S Military Rd
Fond Du Lac, WI 54935
920-922-1500
Fax: 920-922-1502 800-236-1501
Dairy and food processing equipment including
cheese making, automated control systems, process
and storage tanks, evaporators, CIP systems and pro-
cess piping; exporter of cheese making equipment
Manager: Gary Ring
Sales Director: Mark Steffens
Operations: Todd Martin
Estimated Sales: $10 - 20 Million
Number Employees: 5-9
Square Footage: 300000
Parent Co: Carlisle Process Systems

21348 Dan Mar Co
2131 N Collins St
B433-738
Arlington, TX 76011
817-822-5767
Fax: 218-338-5909 danmarco1@msn.com
www.danmarco.net
Supplier of products in antimicrobial control for
beef, pork and poultry industries
President: Paul Edwards
Estimated Sales: Under $500,000
Number Employees: 1-4

21349 Dan-D Foods Ltd
11760 Machrina Way
Richmond, BC V7A 4V1
Canada
604-274-3263
Fax: 604-274-3268 800-633-4788
www.dan-d-pak.com
Fine food importer, manufacturer and distributor of
cashews, dried fruits, rice crackers, snack foods,
spices etc. from around the world.
Chairman/President/CEO/Founder: Dan On
Number Employees: 500
Type of Packaging: Food Service, Bulk

21350 (HQ)Dana Labels
7778 SW Nimbus Ave
Beaverton, OR 97008-6423
503-646-7933
Fax: 503-641-4728 800-255-1492
Labels and labeling machines
Owner: Wilfredo Rabanal
Sales Manager: Dave Pancoast
Estimated Sales: $20 - 50 Million
Number Employees: 20-49
Brands:
Axcess

21351 Dana S. Oliver & Associates
21 Island Drive
Savannah, GA 31406-5238
912-354-1455
Fax: 912-354-2455
Consultants for executive searches and placement in
the food and beverage industry
President: Dana Oliver

21352 (HQ)Danafilms Inc
5 Otis St
Westborough, MA 01581-3311
508-366-8884
Fax: 508-898-0106 www.danafilms.com
Manufacturer and exporter of polyethylene films for
packaging.
President: Sherman Olson
solson@danafilms.com
VP Sales: Bob Simoncini
Marketing Director: Steve Crimmin
Sales Manager: Steve Crimmin
General Manager: Alan Simoncini
Purchasing Manager: Alan Simoncini
Estimated Sales: $20-30 Million
Number Employees: 50-99
Square Footage: 40000
Type of Packaging: Consumer, Food Service, Pri-
vate Label, Bulk
Other Locations:
Danafilms
Hopedale MA

21353 Danbury Plastics
239 Castleberry Industrial Dr
Cumming, GA 30040-9051
678-455-7391
Fax: 203-790-6801 www.danburyplastics.com
Manufacturer, importer and exporter of compression and injection molded bottle caps as well as linings and gaskets
President: Michael Da Cruz
Quality Control: Diana Cepada
Sales: Donna Dyke
Plant Manager: Rocco Grosse
Estimated Sales: $2.5-5 Million
Number Employees: 10-19
Square Footage: 18000
Type of Packaging: Consumer, Private Label

21354 Dandelion Chocolate
740 Valencia St
San Francisco, CA 94110-1735
415-349-0942
800-785-2301
www.dandelionchocolate.com
Chocolates
Owner: Maggi Mcconnell
maggi.m@gmail.com
CEO: Todd Masonis
Number Employees: 5-9

21355 Danfoss Drives
2995 Eastrock Drive
Rockford, IL 61109-1737
815-398-2770
Fax: 815-398-2869
CEO: Jergen Clausen
Executive VP & CFO: Frederik Lotz
Estimated Sales: $1 - 5 Million

21356 Danfoss Drives
4401 N Bell School Rd
Loves Park, IL 61111
888-326-3677
www.danfossdrives.com
Electronic AC motor controls.
President & CEO: Kim Fausing
EVP & Chief Financial Officer: Jesper Christensen
President, Power Solutions: Eric Alstrom
President, Cooling: Jurgen Fischer
President, Drives: Vesa Laisi
President, Heating: Lars Tveen
Year Founded: 1933
Estimated Sales: Over $1 Billion
Number Employees: 26,000
Parent Co: Danfoss

21357 Danger Men Cooking
3 Lumen Ln
Highland, NY 12528-1903
845-691-7029
Fax: 845-691-2852
BBQ accesories and gear for men
President: Peter Rooney
Estimated Sales: $10 - 20 Million
Number Employees: 10-19
Brands:
  Bbq Sauce
  Danger Men Cooking
  Hot Sauce
  Ketchupepper
  Steak Sauce
  Tough Guy's
  Wussy Hot Sauce

21358 Daniel Boone Lumber Industries
1375 Clearfork N
Morehead, KY 40351
606-784-7586
Fax: 606-783-1858
New and reconditioned wooden pallets and skids
President: Gail Lincoln
Regional Sales Manager: Mike Coburn
Sales Manager: Mike Coburn
Plant Supervisor: Elvis Middleton
Estimated Sales: Below $5 Million
Number Employees: 10-19
Square Footage: 50000

21359 Daniel J. Bloch & Company
PO Box 263
Essex, CT 06426-0263
860-767-8204
Fax: 860-767-8205
Roasters and roasting machines
Owner: Daniel Bloch

21360 Daniel Woodhead Company
3411 Woodhead Drive
Northbrook, IL 60062-1892
847-272-7990
Fax: 847-272-8133
General packing house electrical and safety equipment and devices; AC Waterlite plugs and connectors, quick disconnect molded control connectors, temporary lighting, portable outlet boxes, electric reels, wire mesh grips, DC batteryconnectors and push b
Contact: Debbie Dickinson
ddickinson@danielwoodhead.com
Estimated Sales: $2.5-5 000,000
Number Employees: 10-19

21361 Danieli Awnings
2530 Oak St
Napa, CA 94559-2227
707-257-6100
Fax: 707-257-0318
Commercial awnings
President: Charles Gibson
charles@danielis.com
Estimated Sales: $500,000-$1,000,000
Number Employees: 5-9

21362 Daniels Food Equipment
310 N Clayborn Ave
PO Box 341
Parkers Prairie, MN 56361-4748
218-338-5000
Fax: 218-338-5909 danielsfood@midwestinfo.net
www.danielsfood.com
Supplier of stainless steel products for meat industry; including grinders, stuffers, grinders, mixers, etc
President: Gary Haavig
garyhaavig@midwestinfo.net
President: Marty Weibye
Estimated Sales: $2 Million
Number Employees: 1-4

21363 Danish Food Equipment
1633 E Madison St
Petaluma, CA 94954-2320
707-763-0110
Fax: 707-763-1303
Owner: Flemming Maersk
Vice President: Flemming Maersk
Estimated Sales: $1 - 5 Million

21364 Daniso USA
PO Box 653
Pine Brook, NJ 07058-0653
201-784-9300
Fax: 201-784-0604
Estimated Sales: $1 - 5 Million

21365 Danlac Inc
1917 Twilight Ln
Hudson, WI 54016-9271
715-381-5575
Fax: 715-381-5576
Butter processing and dairy equipment
Owner: Liane Hoier
liane@danlacinc.com
Estimated Sales: less than $500,000
Number Employees: 1-4

21366 Danmark Packaging Systems
PO Box 560901
Lewisville, TX 75056-6901
972-625-8311
Fax: 972-370-9113
Shrink packaging machinery including semi and fully automatic L-sealers and shrink tunnel combinations, horizontal form, fill, seal machines and semi and fully automatic sleeve wrap and bundling systems with in-line and multi-packcollating capabilities

21367 Dansk International Designs
P.O. Box 2006
Suite 301
Bristol, PA 19007-0806
914-697-6400
Fax: 914-697-6464 www.dansk.com
China, crystal, housewares, tabletop items, giftware, etc
President: David Herman
VP Merchandising: Jeanne Allen
Estimated Sales: $1 - 5 Million
Number Employees: 250-500
Parent Co: Lenox

21368 Danville Economic Development
427 Patton St # 203
Danville, VA 24541-1215
434-793-1753
Fax: 434-797-9606
Manager: Jeremy Stratton
Number Employees: 5-9

21369 Dap Technologies Corporation
8945 South Harl Avenue
Suite 112
Tempe, AR 85284
813-969-3271
Fax: 813-969-3334 800-229-2822
www.daptech.com
Packaging equipment specializing in bar code scanner technology
President: Yzes Oaroctue
CEO: Michel Oatointe
Contact: Jim Higgins
jimhiggins@daptech.com
Estimated Sales: $2.5-5 Million
Number Employees: 9

21370 Dapec
1000 Evenflo Dr
Ball Ground, GA 30107
770-345-2841
Fax: 770-345-5926
Processing equipment
President: Scott Russell
Chairman of the Board: Jack Hazenbroek
Estimated Sales: $20 - 50 Million
Number Employees: 20-49

21371 Dapec/Numafa
1000 Evenflo Dr
Ball Ground, GA 30107-4544
770-345-2841
Fax: 770-345-5926 www.dapec.com
Conveyor systems and accessories, sanitation supplies, temperature control equipment
President: Scott Russell
Estimated Sales: $10-20 Million
Number Employees: 20-49

21372 Dar-B-Ques Barbecue Equipment
2300 Minnehaha Ave S
Minneapolis, MN 55404
612-724-7425
www.coastalseafoods.com
Barbecue grills and pig roasters
President: Freddrew Freddrew
Estimated Sales: Below $5 Million
Number Employees: 1-4
Square Footage: 150000
Brands:
  Dar-B-Ques

21373 Darcor Casters
7 Staffordshire Place
Toronto, ON M8W 1T1
Canada
416-255-8563
Fax: 416-251-6117 800-387-7206
casters@darcor.com www.darcor.com
Manufacturer and exporter of casters and wheels
President: Rob Hilborn
Controller: Dan Watson
Engineering Manager: Adrian Steenson
Director of Marketing: Kirk Tobias
Number Employees: 75
Square Footage: 320000
Parent Co: Darcor Casters
Brands:
  Carpet Master
  Cartwashable
  Solid Elastomer

21374 Darcy Group
1350 Home Ave Ste L
Akron, OH 44310
330-633-4700
Fax: 330-633-8779
Manager: Jodi Westphal
Quality Control: Bob Tredd
Estimated Sales: $2.5 - 5 000,000
Number Employees: 50-99

21375 Darfill
750 Green Crest Dr
Westerville, OH 43081-2837
614-890-3274
Fax: 614-890-4230 info@darifill.com
www.darifill.com
Equipment that offers a variety of filling, packaging styles and sealing methods for the dairy and ice cream industries.
President: Lisa Aspery
lisa@darifill.com
Number Employees: 10-19

21376 Dari Farms Ice Cream Inc
1501 State St
Bridgeport, CT 06605-2010
203-384-0820
Fax: 203-336-3235
www.dairyfarms.com/error.html
Manager: Richard Corraro
rcorraro@dairyfarms.com
General Manager: Michael Carraro
Estimated Sales: $3 - 5 Million
Number Employees: 20-49

21377 Darlington Dairy Supply Co Inc
17332 State Road 81
Darlington, WI 53530-9257
608-776-4064
Fax: 608-776-4092 800-877-4064
daveg@ddsco.com www.ddsco.com
Heat exchangers, plate, tubular, process control
President: Mae Thuli
dds@mhtc.net
Marketing: Torry Thuli
Estimated Sales: $5-10 000,000
Number Employees: 10-19

21378 Darlington Sign Awning & Neon
221 Jefferson Blvd
Warwick, RI 02888-3818
401-734-5800
Fax: 401-231-1481 custserv@aathriftysign.com
www.aathriftysign.com
Neon signs and awnings; installation services available
Owner: David Solomon
Operations Manager: Tom Grenga
Estimated Sales: $5 - 10 Million
Number Employees: 20-49
Square Footage: 20000

21379 Darmex Corporation
71 Jane Street
Roslyn Heights, NY 11577-1359
516-621-3000
Fax: 516-621-3627 800-645-6368
info@fuchs.com
Sanitary lubricants
Estimated Sales: $50-100 Million
Number Employees: 140

21380 Darnell-Rose Inc
17915 Railroad St
City of Industry, CA 91748-1113
626-912-1688
Fax: 626-912-3765 800-327-6355
www.casters.com
Manufacturer and exporter of casters and wheels, including stainless steel models and other mobility products
President: Brent Bargar
bbargar@casters.com
Research & Development: Bob Siegried
Quality Control: Phil Mazzolini
Marketing Director: Brent Bargar
Sales Director: Bob Siegried
Operations Manager: Richard Martinez
Purchasing Manager: Robbie McCullah
Estimated Sales: $10-20 Million
Number Employees: 50-99
Square Footage: 170000
Type of Packaging: Food Service, Bulk

21381 Darson Corp
7650 Chrysler Dr # 150
Suite 150
Detroit, MI 48211-1734
313-875-7781
Fax: 313-875-1666 800-783-7781
www.thedarsoncorp.com
Screen printed decals, labels and name plates

President: Mary Ellen Darge
Controller: Shirley Lyle
Production Manager: David Breuhan
Estimated Sales: $1-2.5 Million
Number Employees: 10-19

21382 Dart Canada Inc.
2121 Markham Rd.
Toronto, ON M1B 2W3
Canada
416-293-2877
800-465-9696
canadainfo@dartcanada.ca
www.dartcanada.com/ca
Paper, plastic and foam cups and plates; also, plastic knives, forks and spoons.
Estimated Sales: $1,000,000,000+
Number Employees: 5,000-9,999
Parent Co: Dart Container Corp.
Brands:
Lily

21383 Dart Container Corp.
500 Hogsback Rd.
Mason, MI 48854
Fax: 517-676-3883 800-248-5960
sales@dart.biz www.dartcontainer.com
Disposable tabletop supplies including foam cups, containers and lids, plastic cups and lids, fusion cups, foam plastic dinnerware, foam hinged lid containers, clear containers, portion containers and lids, and plastic cutlery.
President: Jim Lammers
Executive VP/CFO: Christine Waltz
Executive VP, Sales: Robert Novak
Year Founded: 1960
Estimated Sales: Over $1 Billion
Number Employees: 15,000
Number of Brands: 37
Brands:
Anthora
Bare by Solo
ClearPac
Concord
Conex ClearPro
Conex Complements
Conex ProMotions
Creative Carryouts
Duo Shield
Eco Expressions
Expressions
Flexstyle
Fusion
Galaxy
Guildware
Impress
Impulse
J Cup
LX
M-Line
MicroGourmet
MicroGreen
PresentaBowls
Prima
Quiet Classic
Ready Roll
Regal
Reliance
SafeSeal
Silent Service
Solo
SoloServe
StayLock
ThermoGlaze
ThermoGuard
Traveler
Trophy

21384 Dashco
17 Westpark Drive
Gloucester, ON K1B 3G6
Canada
613-834-6825
Fax: 613-834-6826
Manufacturer and exporter of degradable plastic carry-out/check-out bags
President: Dave Paul
Number Employees: 2
Brands:
Biosolo
Dashco

21385 Data 2
1099 Essex Ave
Richmond, CA 94801-2112
510-232-6200
Fax: 510-235-2176 800-227-2121
www.data2.com
Wine industry UPC bar code labels
Manager: Alan Gaber
alan@data2.com
Estimated Sales: $1 - 5 Million
Number Employees: 20-49

21386 Data Consultants
P.O. Box 180
Pleasant Hill, MO 64080
805-748-3427
Fax: 703-330-2436 www.dataconsultantsinc.com
PCs and management of and access to critical business information
Owner: Mike Mc Neall
Accountant and Public Relations: Shelly Haines
Marketing: Mark Frund
Contact: Aaron Donatello
aaron.donatello@dciasp.com

21387 Data Consulting Associates
18000 Coleman Valley Rd
Occidental, CA 95465-9236
707-874-3067
Fax: 707-874-3848
Wine industry computer software
Owner: Carey Dubbert
Estimated Sales: $1 - 3 Million
Number Employees: 1-4

21388 Data Management
1 Time Clock Drive
San Angelo, TX 76904
325-223-9500
Fax: 325-223-9104 800-749-8463
www.timeclockplus.com
Software for restaurants including programs for recording and calculating payroll hours, taking orders, customer service, P.O.S., delivery systems, time, attendance and scheduling packages
President: Jorge Ellis
Director Marketing: Scott Turner
Sales/Technical Manager: Mark Moorman
Estimated Sales: $1-2.5 Million
Number Employees: 10-19
Square Footage: 3400
Brands:
Timeclock Plus

21389 Data Scale
42430 Blacow Rd
Fremont, CA 94539-5621
510-651-7350
Fax: 510-651-6343 800-651-7350
sales@datascale.com www.datascale.com
Liquid drum and pail filling systems
Owner: Terry B Lowe
tlowe@datascale.com
Sales Director: Tim DuClos
Estimated Sales: $1-2,500,000
Number Employees: 10-19
Type of Packaging: Consumer, Food Service
Brands:
Data Scale

21390 Data Specialists
1021 Proctor Dr # 1
Elkhorn, WI 53121-2027
262-723-5726
Fax: 262-723-5767 800-211-1545
info@dataspecialist.com www.dataspecialists.com
Manufacutrer of computers and software designed for the dairy industry including production, costing, inventory, distribution, payroll, etc.; installation and start-up services available
President: Sherrie Mertes
Estimated Sales: $2.5-5 Million
Number Employees: 20-49

21391 Data Specialists
1021 Proctor Dr # 1
Elkhorn, WI 53121-2027
262-723-5726
Fax: 262-723-5767 www.dataspecialists.com
Process accountablity and reconciliatoin business software for food and dairy industry
President: Sherrie Mertes
Estimated Sales: $2.5-5 Million
Number Employees: 20-49

21392 Data Visible Corporation
PO Box 7767
Charlottesville, VA 22906-7767
434-296-5608
Fax: 434-977-1076 800-368-3494
www.datavisible.com
Quick reference cash register units, flip cards,
job-aids for bulk pricing and instructions, color
coded folders, labels, filing cabinets, etc
President: A Patton Janssen Jr
Executive VP: Gary Sloan
Number Employees: 10
Brands:
  Data Visible
  Dataflex

21393 Datalogic ADC
959 Terry St
Eugene, OR 97402-9150
541-683-5700
Fax: 541-687-7998 800-929-3221
info.adc.us@datalogic.com www.datalogic.com
Sensors, capacitive sensors, photoelectrics, linear
transducers and identification for packaging and
electronic sensors for automation manufacturer of
both CCD and LASER bar code reading
technologies
President: Darrell Owens
CFO: Mack Ruacker
Estimated Sales: $5 - 10 000,000
Number Employees: 20-49

21394 (HQ)Datapaq
187 Ballardvale St
Wilmington, MA 01887-1082
978-988-9000
Fax: 978-988-0666 800-326-5270
websales@datapaq.com www.datapaq.com
Monitors the temperature profiles of a food product
as it passes through continuous cook, bake, chill,
freeze, and fry processes. A Datapaq system is comprised of four major components: a data logger, a
protective thermal barrier toprotect the logger, ther-
mocouple probes, and easy-to-use software to ana-
lyze and store temperature data collected during a
process. Detailed graphical information gives a com-
plete picture of the continuous process
President: Michael E White
Marketing Director: Kathleen Higgins
Sales Director: Bill Adaschik
Contact: D Abbrat
  abbrat@datapaq.com
Estimated Sales: $5-10 Million
Number Employees: 10-19
Square Footage: 19200
Other Locations:
  Datapaq
  Cambridge
Brands:
  Datapaq Multi-Tracker System

21395 Datapax
11225 North 28th Drive
Suite D-102
Phoenix, AZ 85029
602-212-9202
Fax: 602-274-1476 877-328-2729
Computer programming, management systems and
services for bakeries and food processing in modular
and integrated system format
Owner: Tyson Philippi
Estimated Sales: $2.5-5 000,000
Number Employees: 5-9

21396 Datu Inc
159 Maxwell Ave
Geneva, NY 14456-1538
315-787-2240
Fax: 315-787-2284
GCO systems for analysis of odors
President: Terry Accree
CEO: Stephen Wyckoff
Manager: Steve Wyckoff
Number Employees: 1-4

21397 Daubert Cromwell LLC
12701 S Ridgeway Ave
Alsip, IL 60803-1526
708-293-7750
Fax: 708-293-7765 info@daubertcromwell.com
Rust inhibiting paper, film and paper converting

President: Francis Houlihan
CEO: Oscar Abello
  oabello@daubert.com
CEO: Martin J Simpson
Estimated Sales: $5-10 000,000
Number Employees: 50-99

21398 Daubert VCI
1333 Burr Ridge Pkwy Ste 200
Burr Ridge, IL 60527
630-203-6800
Fax: 630-203-6900 800-535-3535
www.daubert.com
Corrosion-preventive packaging products paper,
film, emitters
President: M Lawrence Garman
CFO: Peter Miehl
Estimated Sales: $50,000,000 - $99,999,999
Number Employees: 100-249

21399 Dave's Imports
6824 N Main Street
Jacksonville, FL 32208-4726
904-764-6886
Fax: 904-764-7131 800-553-2837
Advertising specialties
Graphic Artist/Admin.: Kimberly Pratt
Estimated Sales: less than $500,000
Number Employees: 1

21400 Davenport Machine
301 Second St
PO Box 6635
Rock Island, IL 61201
309-786-1500
Fax: 309-786-0771
Manufacturer and exporter of rotary dryers and cool-
ers, foundry equipment and continuous dewatering
presses
President: R Nixon Jr
General Sales Manager: Lauren Reimer
Chief Engineer: R Bateman
Estimated Sales: $5-10 Million
Number Employees: 20-50
Square Footage: 172000
Parent Co: Middle States Corporation

21401 David A Lingle & Son Mfg
104 S Knoxville Ave
Russellville, AR 72801-5315
479-968-2500
Fax: 479-968-1998
Walk-in coolers and freezers, cold storage doors and
insulated specialties
Owner: David L Lingle
Partner: Larry Lingle
CFO: Jean Harbison
Estimated Sales: $1 - 3 Million
Number Employees: 20-49
Square Footage: 40000

21402 (HQ)David Dobbs EnterpriseInc.
4600 US 1 N
St Augustine, FL 32095
904-824-6171
Fax: 904-824-9989 800-889-6368
sales@menudesigns.com www.menudesigns.com
Vinyl and leather menu covers, wine lists and guest
service directories; also, promotional items includ-
ing hats, T-shirts, tote bags, aprons and pizza bags
President: David Dobbs
CFO: Peggy Dobs
Executive VP: Jay Maguire
Quality Control: Terry Sechen
Sales Manager: J Michael Davis
Estimated Sales: $10-20 Million
Number Employees: 50-99

21403 David E. Moley & Associates
PO Box 920
Wrightsville Beach, NC 28480
910-256-3826
Fax: 910-256-8639 moleyusa@aol.com
Executive search consultant for food service manu-
facturers seeking sales and marketing executives
VP: Gloria Moley
Estimated Sales: less than $500,000
Number Employees: 5

21404 David Roberts Food Corp.
2351 Upper Middle Rd. E
Oakville, ON L6H 6P7
Canada
905-502-7700
Fax: 905-502-7701 800-361-4028
www.davidrobertsfood.com
Supplier of nuts, dried fruits, candies, and baking in-
gredients.
Controller: Bill Simeon
Vice President: Ron Melocco
Vice President, Sales: David Abrams
Plant Manager: Sean Whitfield
Year Founded: 1987
Estimated Sales: $5.5 Million
Number Employees: 20+
Number of Brands: 1
Square Footage: 125000
Type of Packaging: Consumer, Food Service, Pri-
vate Label, Bulk
Brands:
  David Roberts

21405 David's Goodbatter
PO Box 102
Bausman, PA 17504-0102
717-872-0652
Fax: 717-872-8152
Processor, packager and exporter of organic pan-
cakes and baking mixes, pasta, couscous, Irish oat-
meal, dried beans, bean blends and gluten-free and
wheat-free foods; importer of maple candies and
syrup; also, custom packaging andprivate labeling
available
Owner: Jane David
Estimated Sales: $1-2.5 Million appx.
Number Employees: 1-4
Square Footage: 52000
Type of Packaging: Consumer, Food Service, Pri-
vate Label, Bulk
Brands:
  David's Goodbatter
  Gabriel & Rose

21406 Davidson's Safest Choice Eggs
2963 Bernice Road
Lansing, IL 60438
708-418-8500
Fax: 708-418-1235 800-410-7619
www.safeeggs.com
Pasteurized eggs
President: Greg West
CFO: Michael Smith

21407 Davis & Small Decor
1888 Clements Ferry Rd
Charleston, SC 29492
843-881-8990
Fax: 800-227-7398 800-849-5082
orders@dsdecor.com
Manufacturer and exporter of decorative wall items
for restaurants
President: Thomas M Davis
Estimated Sales: $3 - 5 Million
Number Employees: 20-49

21408 Davis Brothers Produce Boxes
8264 Haynes Lennon Highway
Evergreen, NC 28438-0069
910-654-4913
Packaging material including wooden containers and
boxes
President: Bedford S David Jr
Estimated Sales: $1 - 5 Million
Number Employees: 20

21409 Davis Core & Pa
1140 Davis Rd SW
Cave Spring, GA 30124-2422
706-777-3675
Fax: 706-777-8690 800-235-7483
sales@daviscore.com www.daviscore.com
Custom molded expanded polystyrene packaging
materials, cold storage shipping containers and dis-
posable shipping pallets; industrial sizes available
President: Joel Davis
  joel@daviscore.com
Estimated Sales: $5 Million
Number Employees: 20-49
Square Footage: 60000
Brands:
  Kol-Boy Products

21410 Davlynne International
3383 E Layton Ave Stop 3
Cudahy, WI 53110
414-481-1011
Fax: 414-481-3155 800-558-5208
Manufacturer and exporter of strip curtains and
doors, custom cart covers and enclosures
President: Kristin Larson
CEO: Randall Larson
Marketing Director: Krista Larson
Estimated Sales: $2.5-5 Million
Number Employees: 7
Square Footage: 13000
Brands:
    Glare-Eze
    Inhibidor

21411 Davron Technologies Inc
4563 Pinnacle Ln
Chattanooga, TN 37415-3811
423-870-1888
Fax: 423-870-1108 sales@davrontech.com
www.davrontech.com
Manufacturer and exporter of all types of custom
process equipment including, but not limited to, ov-
ens, conveying systems, washing systems and frying
systems
President: Ronald Speicher
Director Sales/Marketing: Jimmy Evans
Contact: Bobby Bishop
    bbishop@davrontech.com
Equipment Design Manager: David Craft
Estimated Sales: $10 - 20 Million
Number Employees: 50-99

21412 Day & Zimmermann Group Inc
1500 Spring Garden St # 500
Philadelphia, PA 19130-4070
215-299-8000
Fax: 215-299-8208 800-523-0786
media.relations@dayzim.com www.dayzim.com
Electrical, electronic and construction engineering
equipment and services for food and beverage
industry
President: Steve Selfridge
    sselfridge@davita.com
Vice President: Anthony Bosco Jr.
Marketing Manager: Tamara Dean
Chief Operating Officer: Michael McAreavy
Estimated Sales: Over $1 Billion
Number Employees: 10000+

21413 Day & Zimmermann International
610 Minuet Lane
Charlotte, NC 28217-2723
704-943-5007
Fax: 704-943-5112 www.dayzim.com
CEO: Harold Yoh III
Vice President And CIO: Anthony Bosco Jr.
Marketing Manager: Tamara Dean
Chief Operating Officer: Michael McAreavy

21414 Day Basket Factory
PO Box 724
North East, MD 21901
410-398-5150
Fax: 410-287-8835
daybasketcompany@gmail.com
www.daybasketfactory.com
Hand-made white oak baskets including grocery and
shopping
Owner: Robert Fredrick
Estimated Sales: $500,000-$1 Million
Number Employees: 1-4
Type of Packaging: Private Label

21415 Day Lumber Company
34 South Broad Street
Westfield, MA 01085
413-568-3511
Fax: 413-568-6668 allen@daylumber.com
www.daylumber.com
Wooden skids and pallets; also, plywood containers
President: Arthur Grodd
VP Sales / General Manager: Allen Nadler
Operations Manager: Lee Krieg
Estimated Sales: $2.5-5 Million
Number Employees: 10-19

21416 Day Manufacturing Company
419 E Lamar St
Sherman, TX 75090
903-893-1138
Fax: 903-892-0218
Folding cartons
President: Herald W Totten
VP: Curry Vogelsang
Operations Manager: Rick Smith
Estimated Sales: $10-20 Million
Number Employees: 20-49
Square Footage: 107000
Parent Co: Washington Iron Works

21417 Day Nite Neon Signs
PO Box 2716
Dartmouth, NS B3B 1E3
Canada
902-469-7095
Fax: 902-469-2124
Illuminated and architectural signs and interior
graphics
President: Chris Boone Jr
CFO: Allen Fraser
Sales Director: Wayne Stewart
Number Employees: 10

21418 Day-O-Lite
126 Chestnut St
Warwick, RI 02888-2104
401-467-8232
Fax: 401-941-2960 sales@dayolite.com
www.dayoliteled.com
Fluorescent lighting fixtures
President: Steven Weisman
    steve@dayolight.com
Estimated Sales: $20-50 Million
Number Employees: 50-99
Square Footage: 4000

21419 Dayco
4681 107th Circle N
Clearwater, FL 33762-5006
727-573-9330
Fax: 727-573-2879 www.daycoindia.com
Stainless steel custom chef lines and tables
President: James Ashbaugh
Sales Director: Ron Rogers
Estimated Sales: $2.5-5 Million
Number Employees: 10
Square Footage: 60000

21420 Daydots
1801 Riverbend West Dr
Fort Worth, TX 76118
817-590-4500
Fax: 817-590-4501 800-321-3687
sales@daydots.com www.daydots.com
A goal of making the world a safer place to eat.
Daydots offers more than 4,000 products and ser-
vices including original day of the week food safety
labels. Produce and distribute products for food rota-
tion, temperture control;cross-contamination preven-
tion; personal hygiene and sanitation and cleaning,
employee safety and food safety education.
President/Owner: Mark Smith
Marketing: Paul McGinnis
Sales: Laura Manatis
Contact: Shawn Blazuir
    shawnb@daydots.com
Operations: Chad Logan
Number Employees: 50-99
Number of Products: 4000
Square Footage: 200000
Type of Packaging: Food Service, Private Label
Brands:
    Coders
    Daydots

21421 Daymark Safety Systems
12830 S Dixie Hwy
Bowling Green, OH 43402-9697
419-353-2458
Fax: 419-354-0514 corgan@daymarklabel.com
www.daymarksafety.com
Manufacturer, importer and exporter of dissolve-a-way food labels, coding, dating and marking
equipment, label applicators and food rotation
systems
VP/General Manager: Jeff Palmer
    jpalmer@daymarsafety.com
Estimated Sales: $1 - 3 Million
Number Employees: 5-9

Square Footage: 172000
Parent Co: CMC Group
Brands:
    Daymark
    Dissolve-A-Way

21422 Daymark Safety Systems
12830 S Dixie Hwy
Bowling Green, OH 43402-9697
419-353-2458
Fax: 419-354-0514 866-517-0490
international@daymarklabel.com
www.daymarksafety.com
President: Jeff Palmer
    jpalmer@daymarsafety.com
Vice President: Tammy Corral
Director, Inside Sales: Heidi Chambers
Estimated Sales: $1 - 3 Million
Number Employees: 5-9

21423 Daystar
12530 Manor Road
Glen Arm, MD 21057-9503
410-592-3106
Fax: 410-592-3362 800-494-6537
sales@lenoxlaser.com www.lenoxlaser.com
Micro leaks for can and bag testing valves for gas
handling, laser systems, rapid prototyping and small
hole drilling services
Quality Control: John Whelan
General Manager: Gary Thornton
Number Employees: 10
Square Footage: 18000
Parent Co: Lenox Laser
Brands:
    Microleak

21424 Daytech Limited
70 Disco Road
Toronto, ON M9W 1L9
Canada
416-675-1195
Fax: 416-675-7183 877-329-1907
info@daytechlimited.com
www.daytechlimited.com
Illuminated and nonilluminated signage shelters,
parking lot kiosks, shopping cart corrals, smoking
shelters and covered walkways
President, COO: Dion McGuire
VP Operations: Dave Bradley
Sales & Marketing Manager: John Duthie
Purchasing Manager: Rick Rankin
Estimated Sales: $5 - 10 Million
Number Employees: 25

21425 Dayton Bag & Burlap Co
322 Davis Ave
Dayton, OH 45403-2900
937-258-8000
Fax: 937-258-0029 800-543-3400
info1@daybag.com www.daybag.com
Manufacturer and exporter of bags including burlap,
feed, grain, greaseproof, paper, paper lined, plastic
and polypropylene for shipping commodities
President: Samuel Lumby
    slumby@daybag.com
VP Marketing: Sue Spiegel
Industrial Sales Manager: Sue Spiegel
Customer Service: Delilah Oda
Estimated Sales: $1 - 3 Million
Number Employees: 100-249
Square Footage: 150000
Type of Packaging: Bulk

21426 Dayton Marking Devices Company
1681 Ladera Trl
Dayton, OH 45459-1401
937-432-0285
Fax: 937-254-9638
Rubber stamps, printing dies, steel stamps and dies,
engraved/etched nameplates, time equipment and
signaling devices
Owner: Michael Dunham
Estimated Sales: Below $5 Million
Number Employees: 10

21427 Dayton Reliable Tool
618 Greenmount Blvd
Dayton, OH 45419
937-298-7391
Fax: 937-298-7190 postoffice@drtusa.com
www.drtusa.com

Specializes in the design of conversion systems for all types of easy-open end applications including SOT, ringpull and full aperture, spare parts tooling for all types of cans including conversion systems, shell systems and cuppers
President: Gary Van Gundy
CFO: James Sass
CEO: Gary L Vangundy
Quality Control: George Kloos
R & D: Paul Klips
Contact: David Geis
  david.geis@drtusa.com
Estimated Sales: $20-50 Million
Number Employees: 100-249

21428 Dayton Wire Products
7 Dayton Wire Pkwy
Dayton, OH 45404-1282

937-236-8000
Fax: 937-236-8300 888-265-1711
www.daytonwireproducts.com
Wire store display racks
Owner: Brian Schissler
Estimated Sales: $10 - 20 Million
Number Employees: 50-99

21429 Dc Tech
619 E 19th St
Kansas City, MO 64108-1743

816-842-9090
Fax: 816-842-4121 877-742-9090
sales@dctech-inc.com www.dctech-inc.com
Meat packing and food processing equipment including carts, tables, smokehouse trucks and vats. Manufacturer of grocery store and restaurant equipment, and custom stainless steel fabrication. Polished aluminum performance car partsbattery covers and turbo shields
President: Buddy Mitchum
  buddy@dctech-inc.com
Sales/Marketing Executive: Buddy Mitchum
Purchasing Manager: Robert Mitchum
Estimated Sales: $3 - 5 Million
Number Employees: 10-19
Square Footage: 148000

21430 De Felsko Corp
802 Proctor Ave
Ogdensburg, NY 13669-2205

315-393-4450
Fax: 315-393-8471 800-448-3835
techsale@defelsko.com www.defelsko.com
Automatic liquor pourers
President: David Bamish
  davidbamish@defelsko.com
Estimated Sales: $5-10 Million
Number Employees: 20-49
Brands:
  Accupour

21431 De Iorio's Foods Inc
2200 Bleecker St
Utica, NY 13501-1739

315-732-7612
Fax: 315-732-7621 800-649-7612
www.deiorios.com
Manufacturer of dough products. Products include dough balls, flats, shells, self rise, breads and sub rolls, breadsticks, and more.
Chairman & CEO: Robert Ragusa
VP, Business Development: Robert Horth
Manager: Fabio Faro
  ffaro@deiorios.com
Manager: Donald King
Estimated Sales: $5-10,000,000
Number Employees: 100-249
Number of Brands: 1
Number of Products: 87
Type of Packaging: Consumer, Food Service, Private Label
Other Locations:
  De-Iorio's Frozen Dough
  Utica NY
Brands:
  DeIorio's

21432 De Laval
11100 N Congress Ave
Kansas City, MO 64153-1222

816-891-7700
Fax: 816-891-1606
www.delavalcleaningsolutions.com

Manufacturer and suppliers of cleaning and sanitizing products for the dairy, food, and beverage processing industies.
Number Employees: 100-249

21433 De Leone Corp
1258 SW Lake Rd
Redmond, OR 97756-8611

541-504-8311
Fax: 541-504-8411 sam@deleone.com
www.cascadelabel.com
Manufacturer and exporter of pressure sensitive and custom labels; wholesaler/distributor of label dispensers
President: Samuel A DE Leone
  steve@deleone.com
General Manager: David Hawes
Sales Director: Diana Jibiden
Estimated Sales: $5-10 Million
Number Employees: 20-49

21434 De Leone Corp
1258 SW Lake Rd
Redmond, OR 97756-8611

541-504-8311
Fax: 541-504-8411 www.cascadelabel.com
Labels and labeling material
President: Samuel A DE Leone
  steve@deleone.com
Quality Control: David Hawes
Sales Representative: Diana Jibiden
Estimated Sales: $5-10 000,000
Number Employees: 20-49

21435 De Leone Corp
1258 SW Lake Rd
Redmond, OR 97756-8611

541-504-8311
Fax: 541-504-8411 www.cascadelabel.com
President: Samuel A DE Leone
  steve@deleone.com
Estimated Sales: $5 - 10 Million
Number Employees: 20-49

21436 De Paul Industries
4950 NE M L King Blvd
Portland, OR 97211-3354

503-281-1289
Fax: 503-284-0548 800-518-6637
www.depaulindustries.com
DePaul Industries provides food and consumer goods packaging services.
CEO: Dave Shaffer
  dshaffer@depaulindustries.com
CEO: Bennett Johnson
Foods & Consumer Goods Packaging Manager: Chris Cusack
Business Development Manager: Lori Fletcher
Number Employees: 10-19
Type of Packaging: Consumer

21437 De Royal Textiles
100 E York St
Camden, SC 29020

803-432-1103
Fax: 803-425-4566 800-845-1062
textiles@deroyal.com www.deroyaltextiles.com
Wipers and cheesecloth
President: Steve Ward
Quality Control: John Getting
VP: E Steven Ward
Sales Manager: Jay Green
Plant Manager: John Gettys
Estimated Sales: Below $5 Million
Number Employees: 1-4
Square Footage: 550000
Brands:
  Hermitex
  Idealfold
  Jiffy Roll

21438 De Ster Corporation
225 Peachtree Street
Suite 400
Atlanta, GA 30303-1727

404-659-9100
Fax: 404-659-5116 800-237-8270
info@dester.com www.dester.com
Manufacturer, importer and exporter of disposable and reusable trays, plates, flatware, containers, cups and cutlery
Executive VP: Gerrit de Kiewit
Director Marketing/Development: John Squire
Senior VP Sales: Dan Whitehead

Estimated Sales: $5-10 Million
Number Employees: 150-200
Square Footage: 640000
Parent Co: De Ster Holding BV
Type of Packaging: Consumer, Food Service, Private Label, Bulk
Brands:
  Isobox
  Microstar
  Octaview

21439 De Vere Co Inc
1923 Beloit Ave
Janesville, WI 53546-3028

608-752-0576
Fax: 608-752-6625 800-833-8373
www.deverechemical.com
Cleaning and sanitizing chemicals including dishwashing detergents
President: Cynthia Shackelford
  cshackelford@deverechemical.com
VP: Frank Drew
Estimated Sales: Below $5 Million
Number Employees: 10-19
Square Footage: 52000

21440 Deacom
950 W Valley Rd
Wayne, PA 19087-1824

610-971-2278
Fax: 610-971-2279
Technology software
President: Jay Dookins
Marketing Manager: Susan Shaw
Sales Manager: Jim Reilly
Contact: Dave Beyel
  dbeyel@deacom.com
Estimated Sales: $300,000-500,000
Number Employees: 1-4

21441 Deadline Press
1652 N Roberts Road NW
Suite C-2
Kennesaw, GA 30144-3634

770-419-2232
Fax: 770-419-2933
Advertising specialties, flags, pennants, banners and labels
Owner: Susan Lester
Other Locations:
  Deadline Press
  Atlanta GA

21442 Dean Custom Awning
529 Route 303
Orangeburg, NY 10962-1303

845-425-6678
Fax: 845-425-6678
mail@deancustomawnings.com
www.deancustomawnings.com
Commercial awnings
President: Charles Collishaw
  deancustomawning@aol.com
Estimated Sales: Less Than $500,000
Number Employees: 1-4

21443 (HQ)Dean Foods Co.
P.O. Box 961447
El Paso, TX 79996

800-395-7004
deanfoods@casupport.com www.deanfoods.com
Milk, ice cream, cultured dairy products, juices, teas and bottled water.
President/CEO: Eric Beringause
Chief Financial Officer: Thomas Sancho
Year Founded: 1925
Estimated Sales: $7.3 Billion
Number Employees: 14,500
Number of Brands: 33
Type of Packaging: Food Service, Private Label
Brands:
  Alta Dena Dairy
  Borden Cheese
  Breakstone's Butter
  Cache Valley
  Cass Clay
  Country Fresh
  Creamland Dairy
  Dairy Maid Dairy
  Deans Dairy
  Falfurria Butter
  Gandy's Dairy
  Garelick Farms
  Guida's Dairy

Hotel Bar Butter
Hygeia Dairy
Jilbert Dairy
Keller's Creamery Butter
Kemps
La Vaquita
Lehigh Valley Dairy Farms
Live Real Farms
Meadow Gold Dairy
Oak Farms Dairy
Oakhurst Dairy
PET
Plugra Butter
Price's Dairy
Purity Dairy
Reiter Dairy
Sport Shake
Swiss Premium Dairy
T.G. Lee Dairy
Tuscan Dairy Farms

21444 Dean Industries
14501 S Broadway
Gardena, CA 90248
310-353-5000
Fax: 310-327-3343 800-995-1210
salesmkt@frymaster.com
Manufacturer and exporter of fryer baskets and deep
fat fryers
Owner: Jimmy Dean
General Manager: Al Cote
Estimated Sales: $300,000-500,000
Number Employees: 1-4
Parent Co: ENODIS

21445 Dearborn Mid-West Conveyor Co
8245 Nieman Rd # 123
Overland Park, KS 66214-1509
913-384-9950
Fax: 913-261-2470
Manufacturer and exporter of material handling sys-
tems including conveyors, palletizers and palletizing
systems
President, CEO: Tony Rosati
Executive VP: Sudy Ohra
sudyv@dmwcc.com
Manager of Sales: Gerry Cohen
Number Employees: 20-49

21446 Dearborn Mid-West Conveyor Co
20334 Superior Rd
Taylor, MI 48180-6301
734-288-4400
Fax: 734-288-1914 jwp@dmwcc.com
www.dmwcc.com
Automated material handling systems
President: Jeff Homenik
jeffh@dmwcc.com
CEO: Tony Rosati
Controller: Sherry Gavito
VP: Jeff Homenik
Quality Control: Mark Duxter
Director, Marketing & Sales: John Confer
Human Resources: Kelly Schafer
Plant Manager: Bruce Mazarowski
Purchasing: Katarina Katsavrias
Estimated Sales: $500,000 - $1 Million
Number Employees: 50-99
Number of Products: 5

21447 Deb Canada
42 Thompson Rd W
Waterford, ON N0E 1Y0
Canada
519-443-8697
Fax: 519-443-5160 888-332-7627
www.debgroup.com/us/contact-us/global-contact
Hand and body cleansers, protective creams,
anti-bacterial, gel, heavy duty and waterless soaps
and soap dispensers
Controller: Dan Balan
General Manager: Didier Bauton
Asst. to General Manager: Theresa Sulisz
Number Employees: 50-99
Square Footage: 80000
Parent Co: Deb Group
Type of Packaging: Private Label
Brands:
Debba
Ensuite
Florafree
Great White
Hands
Heiress

Hypor
Inhibit
Lanimol
Maxipor
Mitzi
Quick Shift
Sceptre
Suprega
Tiv Plus
Tuf'n Ega

21448 Debbie Wright Sales
5852 E Berry St
PO Box 15554
Fort Worth, TX 76119-1803
817-429-8282
Fax: 817-429-8882 800-935-7883
www.debbiewrightsales.net
Manufacturer and wholesaler/distributor of stud
welding equipment and supplies
Owner: Debbie Wright
Sls. Rep.: Allan Yarber
Estimated Sales: $1-2.5 Million
Number Employees: 5-9

21449 Debelak Technical Systems
W6390 Quality Drive
Greenville, WI 54942-8015
920-757-9980
Fax: 920-757-9987 800-888-4207
Control systems including clean-in-place, instrument
monitoring, pasteurization and temperature for the
food and dairy industries
President: William Debelak
Production Manager: Lee Fintelmann
Estimated Sales: $5-10 Million
Number Employees: 10

21450 Debelis Corp
5000 70th Ave
Kenosha, WI 53144-1762
262-657-5000
Fax: 262-656-8326 800-472-7462
www.puratos.com
R&D: Gloria Brandes
Quality Control: Eillen Walo
Contact: Brian Hogan
bhogan@puratos.com
Manager: Benoit Keppenne
Estimated Sales: $10 - 20 Million
Number Employees: 20-49

21451 Deborah Sales LLC
109 Meeker Ave
Newark, NJ 07114-1300
973-344-8466
Fax: 973-344-3981 crei@deborahsales.us
Advertising specialties and premiums
President: Carlos Rei
crei@deborahsales.us
Estimated Sales: $1-2.5 Million
Number Employees: 1-4

21452 Decade Products
3910 Plainfield Ave NE
Grand Rapids, MI 49525-1602
616-365-2887
Fax: 616-956-9492 www.decadeproducts.com
Owner: Cindy Douthett

21453 Decagon Devices Inc
2635 NE Hopkins Court
Pullman, WA 99163
509-332-2756
Fax: 509-332-5158 800-755-2751
sales@aqualab.com www.aqualab.com
Scientific instruments.
Research/Development: Brady Carter
Product Design: Ken Byers
Marketing Assistant: Tyler Zollinger
Sales Support: John Russell

21454 Decal Techniques Inc
25 Mahan St # A
West Babylon, NY 11704-1306
631-491-1800
Fax: 631-491-1816 800-735-3322
decalinfo@earthlink.net www.decaltech.com
Silk screened labels, posters, banners and displays
President: Gene Snyder
Contact: Eugene Snyder
e.snyder@decaltech.com

Estimated Sales: $1 - 2.5 Million
Number Employees: 10-19
Square Footage: 10000

21455 Decartes Systems Group
120 Randall Drive
Waterloo, ON N2V 1C6
Canada
519-746-8110
Fax: 519-747-0082 info@descartes.com
www.descartes.com
Computer accounting systems for the dairy, bever-
age and food industries
Executive Vice President of Information: Raimond
Diederik
Regional Manager: Rick Spencer
Estimated Sales: $1 - 5 Million
Type of Packaging: Bulk

21456 Deccofelt Corp
555 S Vermont Ave
Glendora, CA 91741-6206
626-963-8511
Fax: 626-914-2734 800-543-3226
sales@deccofelt.com
www.greenmoisturebarrier.com
Industrial tapes including adhesive coated, heat acti-
vated and laminated
President: Jerry Heinrich
jheinrich@deccofelt.com
Director Sales: Kathy Smith
Estimated Sales: $5-10 Million
Number Employees: 20-49
Square Footage: 120000

21457 Decernis
1250 Connecticut Avenue NW
Suite 200
Washington, DC 20036
240-428-1800
Fax: 301-990-1086 www.decernis.com
Provides regulatory compliance, supply chain track-
ing and information management systems for food
additives, food contact materials and consumer
product manufacturers.
Chief Executive Officer: Andrew Waldow
Director, International Business Dev.: Jacques
Desarnauts
Director, Data Services: Clive Raven
Director, System Development: Yong Zou
Chief Operating Officer: Kevin Kenny
VP, Business Development Americas: Craig Henry

21458 (HQ)Decision Analyst Inc
604 Avenue H E
Arlington, TX 76011-3119
817-649-5241
Fax: 817-640-6567 800-262-5974
jthomas@decisionanalyst.com
Consultant performing consumer testing and adver-
tising pre-testing; market researcher including new
product development and strategy
President: Jerry W. Thomas
CEO: Vivian Allan
vallan@secondarydata.com
EVP: Bonnie Kenoly
Marketing Director: Cristi Johnson
Number Employees: 100-249
Square Footage: 100000
Brands:
Copytest
Optima

21459 Decker Plastics
1104 2nd Ave
Council Bluffs, IA 51501-4012
712-323-9995
Fax: 712-328-8617 866-869-6293
www.deckerplastics.com
Polyethylene bags, tubes and sheeting
President: Robert A Decker
CFO: Sherry Deckar
sherrydeckar@deckerplastics.com
Estimated Sales: $1-2.5 Million
Number Employees: 20-49
Square Footage: 50000

21460 Decker Tape Products Inc
6 Stewart Pl
Fairfield, NJ 07004-2202
973-227-5350
Fax: 973-808-9418 800-227-5252
www.deckertape.com

Pressure sensitive tapes and stock labels and in-house converting services include custom imprinting 2-color, die cutting, spooling, laminating, sheeting, narrow width and long length rolls
Owner: Jack Decker
jdecker@deckertape.com
Estimated Sales: $20-50 Million
Number Employees: 50-99

21461 Decko Products Inc
2105 Superior St
Sandusky, OH 44870-1891

419-626-5757
Fax: 419-626-3135 800-537-6143
shumphrey@decko.com www.decko.com
Edible cake and candy decorations and packaged rings, gels
President: F William Niggemeyer
Marketing Director: Sara Humphrey
Estimated Sales: $10 Million
Number Employees: 50-99
Square Footage: 105000
Type of Packaging: Private Label
Brands:
Royal Icing Decoration

21462 Deco Labels & Tags
28 Greensboro Drive
Toronto, ON M9W 1E1
Canada

416-247-7878
Fax: 416-247-9030 888-496-9029
www.decolabels.com
Pressure sensitive labels, shipping tags, stickers, decals and seals; also, silk screening, data processing and hot stamping available
President: Doug Ford
Quality Control: Brian Burke
General Manager: Douglas Ford
Assistant Manager: Robbie Ford
Number Employees: 10
Square Footage: 72000
Brands:
Data-Tabs
Hard-Tac
Sof-Tac

21463 Deco Pac Inc
3500 Thurston Ave # 100
Anoka, MN 55303-1061

763-574-0091
Fax: 763-574-1060 tana.krona@decopac.com
President: Christine McKenna
CEO: Mike Mcglynn
mike.mcglynn@decopac.com
CFO: Mike McGlynn
Quality Control: Kim Roy
Estimated Sales: $10 - 20 Million
Number Employees: 100-249

21464 Decolin
9150 Parc Avenue
Montreal, QC H2N 1Z2
Canada

514-384-2910
Fax: 514-382-1305 www.decolin.com
Table cloths and runners; also, place mats
President: Leonard Mendel
CFO: Alissa Ratpatort
Number Employees: 50

21465 Decorated Products Company
PO Box 580
Westfield, MA 01086-0580

413-568-0944
Fax: 413-568-1875
Labels including food product, carton and computer pin feed
President: Mike Goepfert
Sales Manager: Joe Menh
Contact: William Chevalier
wchevalier@decorated.com
Operations Manager: Stafford Springs
Number Employees: 10
Square Footage: 180000

21466 Decoren Equipment
133 Chaucer Court
Willowbrook, IL 60527-8418

708-789-3367
Fax: 708-789-3367
Carts including specialty, china and plate
Marketing Manager (West): Howard Charles
Administrative Manager: Jule Arvans

Estimated Sales: $1 - 5 Million

21467 Dedert Corporation
20000 Governors Dr # 3
Olympia Fields, IL 60461-1034

708-747-7000
Fax: 708-755-8815 info@dedert.com
www.anhydro.com
Manufacturer and exporter of evaporators, filters, centrifuges and liquid/solid separation equipment; importer of filters, liquid/solid separation equipment and centrifuges
President: Guy Lonergan
Marketing Director: John Ruhl
Contact: Pat Baumgartner
p.baumgartner@dedert.com
Estimated Sales: $20-50 Million
Number Employees: 20-49
Brands:
Dedert
Lfc
Reineveld

21468 Defontaine of America
16720 W Victor Rd
New Berlin, WI 53151

262-754-4665
Fax: 262-797-5735 sternw2@earthlink.net
Sanitary butterfly, check valves, air-operated valves, pigging systems, mixproof valves
President: William Stern
Marketing: Wayne Johnson
Estimated Sales: $1-2.5 000,000
Number Employees: 1-4

21469 (HQ)Defranco Co
1000 Lawrence St
Los Angeles, CA 90021-1620

213-627-8575
Fax: 213-627-9837 800-992-3992
Defrancomp@aol.com www.defrancoandsons.com
We are a family owned business that offers fresh produce and nuts.
Manager: Paul De Franco
CEO: Paul DeFranco
CFO: Jerry De Franco
VP: Gerald DeFranco
R&D: Salvatore DeFranco
Estimated Sales: $15 Million
Number Employees: 20-49
Square Footage: 150000
Type of Packaging: Consumer, Food Service, Private Label, Bulk
Brands:
Sunripe

21470 Defreeze Corporation
PO Box 330
Southborough, MA 1772

508-485-8512
Fax: 508-481-1491 albezanson@defreeze.com
www.defreeze.com
Industrial microwave processing and frozen fish slicing equipment
President: Allan Bezanson
Estimated Sales: $1 - 3 Million
Number Employees: 1-4

21471 Degussa BioActives
P.O. Box 1609
Waukesha, WI 53187-1609

262-547-5531
Fax: 262-547-0587 800-342-5724
Estimated Sales: $1 - 5 Million
Number Employees: 50-99

21472 Degussa Flavors
1000 Redna Ter
Cincinnati, OH 45215-1187

513-771-4682
Fax: 513-771-8748 888-771-2448
flavors.us@degussa.com
Number Employees: 20-49

21473 Dehyco Company
1000 Kansas Street
Memphis, TN 38106-1925

901-774-3322
Fax: 901-774-2076
Manufacturer and exporter of hammer mills, custom grinders, pulverizers, separators and packaging machinery
President: Mike Broussard
VP: Albert Harris, Jr.

Estimated Sales: $10-20 Million
Number Employees: 20-49

21474 Dehydration & Environmental System
864 Saint Francis Way
Rio Vista, CA 94571-1250

707-374-7500
Fax: 707-374-7505 800-992-9113
sales@desllc.biz www.desllc.biz
Dewatering and drying equipment; by-product used to process both food and waste
President: Dan Simpson
Estimated Sales: $2.5-5 Million
Number Employees: 5-9

21475 Deibel Laboratories
407 Cabot Rd
South San Francisco, CA 94080

650-952-4209
Fax: 650-952-4518 Sales@DeibelLabs.com
www.deibellabs.com
Analytical laboratory specializing in chemical and microbiological food testing including nutrition labeling, dietary fiber, cholesterol, sulfites, vitamins, trace minerals, sugar profiles, etc
President and CEO: Dr. Robert Deibel
Research & Development: Dr. Lawrence Rosner
Manager: Dean Reed
Contact: Judy Tran
southsanfrancisco@deibellabs.com
Plant Manager: Dan Coules
Number Employees: 10
Square Footage: 14000

21476 Deibel Laboratories
3530 NW 97th Blvd
Gainesville, FL 32606

352-331-3313
Fax: 352-332-2050 www.deibellabs.com
Analytical laboratory specializing in chemical and microbiological food testing including nutrition labeling, dietary fiber, cholesterol, sulfites, vitamins, trace minerals, sugar profiles, etc
Research & Development: Dr Lawrence Rosner
Manager: Kirsten Hunt
Manager: Dean Reed
Plant Manager: Dan Coules
Estimated Sales: $.5 - 1 million
Number Employees: 1-4
Square Footage: 7000

21477 Deibel Laboratories Inc
103 S 2nd St
Madison, WI 53704-5216

608-241-1177
Fax: 608-241-2252 madison@deibellabs.com
www.deibellabs.com
Analytical laboratory specializing in chemical and microbiological food testing including nutrition labeling, dietary fiber, cholesterol, sulfites, vitamins, trace minerals, sugar profiles, etc
President: Robert H Deibel
Contact: Richard Boehme
deibelmad@ameritech.net
Director of Operations: Kristen A. Hunt
Plant Manager: Dan Coules
Estimated Sales: $3 - 5 Million
Number Employees: 20-49
Square Footage: 14000

21478 Deibel Laboratories Inc
7165 Curtiss Ave
Sarasota, FL 34231-8012

941-925-1579
Fax: 941-925-2130 SarasotaLab@DeibelLabs.com
www.deibellabs.com
Analytical laboratory specializing in chemical and microbiological food testing including nutrition labeling, dietary fiber, cholesterol, sulfites, vitamins, trace minerals, sugar profiles, etc
President: Robert H Deibel
Research & Development: Dr. Lawrence Rosner
Manager: Dean Reed
Plant Manager: Dan Coules
Estimated Sales: $300,000-500,000
Number Employees: 1-4
Square Footage: 7000

21479 Deibel Laboratories of Il
7120 N Ridgeway Ave
Lincolnwood, IL 60712-2622
847-329-9900
Fax: 847-329-9903
LincolnwoodLab@DeibelLabs.com
www.deibellabs.com
Analytical laboratory specializing in chemical and microbiological food testing including nutrition labeling, dietary fiber, cholesterol, sulfites, vitamins, trace minerals, sugar profiles, etc
President: Charles Deibel
charlesdeibel@deibellabs.com
Research & Development: Dr. Lawrence Rosner
Manager: Dean Reed
Plant Manager: Dan Coules
Estimated Sales: $1 - 3 Million
Number Employees: 10-19
Square Footage: 7000

21480 Deibel Laboratories of Il
7120 N Ridgeway Ave
Lincolnwood, IL 60712-2622
847-329-9900
Fax: 847-329-9903
LincolnwoodLab@DeibelLabs.com
www.deibellabs.com
Analytical laboratory specializing in chemical and microbiological food testing including nutrition labeling, dietary fiber, cholesterol, sulfites, vitamins, trace minerals, sugar profiles, etc
President: Charles Deibel
charlesdeibel@deibellabs.com
Research & Development: Dr. Lawrence Rosner
Manager: Dean Reed
Plant Manager: Dan Coules
Number Employees: 10-19
Square Footage: 14000

21481 Deitz Company
1750 Route 34
PO Box 1108
Wall, NJ 07719
732-681-0200
Fax: 732-681-8468 800-394-2709
www.deitzco.com
Machinery
President: James L Deitz
VP Engineering: John Deitz
Estimated Sales: $2.5 - 5 000,000
Number Employees: 10-19

21482 (HQ)Del Monte Fresh Produce Inc.
241 Sevilla Ave
Coral Gables, FL 33114
305-520-8400
Fax: 305-567-0320 800-950-3683
salesinquiry@freshdelmonte.com
www.freshdelmonte.com
Fresh and fresh-cut fruit and vegetables.
EVP/COO: Mohammed Abbas
Chairman/CEO: Mohammad Abu-Ghazaleh
mabughazaleh@freshdelmonte.com
Senior VP/CFO: Monica Vicente
Senior VP/General Counsel/Secretary: Effie D. Silva
Senior VP, Corporate R&D: Hans Sauter
Year Founded: 1886
Estimated Sales: $3.9 Billion
Number Employees: 40,000+
Number of Brands: 11
Type of Packaging: Consumer, Food Service
Other Locations:
Del Monte Fresh Plant
Forest Park GA
Del Monte Fresh Plant
Kankakee IL
Del Monte Fresh Plant
Jessup MD
Del Monte Fresh Plant
Kansas City MO
Del Monte Fresh Plant
Bloomfield NJ
Del Monte Fresh Plant
Mappsville VA
Del Monte Fresh Plant
Canton MA
Del Monte Fresh Plant
Mulberry FL
Del Monte Fresh Plant
Richmond CA
Del Monte Fresh Plant
Eddystone PA
Del Monte Fresh Plant
Chicago IL
Del Monte Fresh Plant
Plant City FL
Del Monte Fresh Plant
Columbus OH
Brands:
De L'Ora
Del Monte Fresh
Fruitini
Golden Ripe
Just Juice
MAG Melon
Mann's
Mission
National Poultry Company
Rosy
UTC

21483 Del Monte Fresh Produce Inc.
9880 S Dorchester Ave
Chicago, IL 60628
773-221-9480
Fax: 773-221-9388 www.freshdelmonte.com
Distribution center providing a variety of services including ripening, sorting, re-packing, fresh cut processing, and delivery of fruits and vegetables
Type of Packaging: Consumer, Food Service

21484 Del Monte Fresh Produce Inc.
2200 Westbelt Dr
Columbus, OH 43228
614-527-7398
Fax: 614-527-8575 800-348-8878
www.freshdelmonte.com
Distribution center providing a variety of services including ripening, sorting, re-packing, fresh cut processing, and delivery of fruits and vegetables
Type of Packaging: Consumer, Food Service

21485 Del Monte Fresh Produce Inc.
1400-1500 Parker St
Dallas, TX 75215
214-428-3600
Fax: 214-428-8836 800-428-3600
www.freshdelmonte.com
Distribution center providing a variety of services including ripening, sorting, re-packing, fresh cut processing, and delivery of fruits and vegetables
Type of Packaging: Consumer, Food Service

21486 Del Monte Fresh Produce Inc.
3101 SW 42nd St
Ft. Lauderdale, FL 33312
954-791-4828
Fax: 954-583-8648 www.freshdelmonte.com
Distribution center providing a variety of services including ripening, sorting, re-packing, fresh cut processing, and delivery of fruits and vegetables
Type of Packaging: Consumer, Food Service

21487 Del Monte Fresh Produce Inc.
7780 Westside Industrial Dr
Unit 5
Jacksonville, FL 32219
904-378-0051
Fax: 904-378-0260 www.freshdelmonte.com
Distribution center providing a variety of services including ripening, sorting, re-packing, fresh cut processing, and delivery of fruits and vegetables
Type of Packaging: Consumer, Food Service

21488 Del Monte Fresh Produce Inc.
6311 Deramus Ave
Kansas City, MO 64120
816-241-6242
Fax: 816-483-4050 www.freshdelmonte.com
Distribution center providing a variety of services including ripening, sorting, re-packing, fresh cut processing, and delivery of fruits and vegetables
Type of Packaging: Consumer, Food Service

21489 Del Monte Fresh Produce Inc.
1001 Industrial Hwy
Building D
Eddystone, PA 19022
610-499-9049
www.freshdelmonte.com
Distribution center providing a variety of services including ripening, sorting, re-packing, fresh cut processing, and delivery of fruits and vegetables
Type of Packaging: Consumer, Food Service

21490 Del Monte Fresh Produce Inc.
3602 W Washington St
Suite 200
Phoenix, AZ 85009
602-252-3290
www.freshdelmonte.com
Distribution center providing a variety of services including ripening, sorting, re-packing, fresh cut processing, and delivery of fruits and vegetables
Type of Packaging: Consumer, Food Service

21491 Del Monte Fresh Produce Inc.
14550 W La Estrella
Goodyear, AZ 85338
623-925-0900
www.freshdelmonte.com
Distribution center providing a variety of services including ripening, sorting, re-packing, fresh cut processing, and delivery of fruits and vegetables
Type of Packaging: Consumer, Food Service

21492 Del Monte Fresh Produce Inc.
3306 Sydney Rd
Plant City, FL 33566
813-752-5145
Fax: 813-759-8625 www.freshdelmonte.com
Distribution center providing a variety of services including ripening, sorting, re-packing, fresh cut processing, and delivery of fruits and vegetables
Type of Packaging: Consumer, Food Service

21493 Del Monte Fresh Produce Inc.
10730 Patterson Pl
Santa Fe Springs, CA 90670
562-777-1127
Fax: 562-777-9498 www.freshdelmonte.com
Distribution center providing a variety of services including ripening, sorting, re-packing, fresh cut processing, and delivery of fruits and vegetables
Type of Packaging: Consumer, Food Service

21494 Del Monte Fresh Produce Inc.
504 42nd St NE
Suite 101
Auburn, WA 98002
253-850-3190
Fax: 253-850-3182 www.freshdelmonte.com
Distribution center providing a variety of services including ripening, sorting, re-packing, fresh cut processing, and delivery of fruits and vegetables
Type of Packaging: Consumer, Food Service

21495 Del Monte Fresh Produce Inc.
7970 Tar Bay Dr
Jessup, MD 20794
410-799-4440
Fax: 410-799-3828 www.freshdelmonte.com
Distribution center providing a variety of services including ripening, sorting, re-packing, fresh cut processing, and delivery of fruits and vegetables
Type of Packaging: Consumer, Food Service

21496 Del Monte Fresh Produce Inc.
105 Shawmut Rd
Shamut Industrial Park
Canton, MA 02021-1438
781-830-2600
Fax: 781-830-2699 www.freshdelmonte.com
Distribution center providing a variety of services including ripening, sorting, re-packing, fresh cut processing, and delivery of fruits and vegetables
Type of Packaging: Consumer, Food Service

21497 Del Monte Fresh Produce Inc.
15845 E 32nd Ave
Suite D
Aurora, CO 80011
720-857-9678
Fax: 720-857-9956 www.freshdelmonte.com
Distribution center providing a variety of services including ripening, sorting, re-packing, fresh cut processing, and delivery of fruits and vegetables
Type of Packaging: Consumer, Food Service

21498 Del Monte Fresh Produce Inc.
6532 Judge Adams Rd
Suite 170
Whitsett, NC 27377
336-446-7408
www.freshdelmonte.com
Distribution center providing a variety of services including ripening, sorting, re-packing, fresh cut processing, and delivery of fruits and vegetables
Type of Packaging: Consumer, Food Service

21499 Del Monte Fresh Produce Inc.
C/O Holt Marine Terminal
701 North Broadway
Gloucester City, NJ 08030
856-742-9202
Fax: 856-742-9209 www.freshdelmonte.com
Distribution center providing a variety of services
including ripening, sorting, re-packing, fresh cut
processing, and delivery of fruits and vegetables
Type of Packaging: Consumer, Food Service

21500 Del Monte Fresh Produce Inc.
9243 N Rivergate Blvd
Portland, OR 97203-6615
503-285-0992
Fax: 503-285-1040 www.freshdelmonte.com
Distribution center providing a variety of services
including ripening, sorting, re-packing, fresh cut
processing, and delivery of fruits and vegetables
Type of Packaging: Consumer, Food Service

21501 Del Monte Fresh Produce Inc.
1810 Academy Ave
Sanger, CA 93657
559-875-5000
Fax: 559-875-1301 www.freshdelmonte.com
Distribution center providing a variety of services
including ripening, sorting, re-packing, fresh cut
processing, and delivery of fruits and vegetables
Type of Packaging: Consumer, Food Service

21502 Del Monte Fresh Produce Inc.
P.O. Box 755
Galveston, TX 77553
409-762-4638
Fax: 409-762-5358 www.freshdelmonte.com
Distribution center providing a variety of services
including ripening, sorting, re-packing, fresh cut
processing, and delivery of fruits and vegetables
Type of Packaging: Consumer, Food Service

21503 Del Monte Fresh Produce Inc.
300 Broadacres Drive
Suite 205
Bloomfield, NJ 07003
973-338-8591
Fax: 973-338-1523 www.freshdelmonte.com
Distribution center providing a variety of services
including ripening, sorting, re-packing, fresh cut
processing, and delivery of fruits and vegetables
Type of Packaging: Consumer, Food Service

21504 Del Monte Fresh Produce Inc.
P.O. Box 520
Port Hueneme, CA 93044
805-488-0881
Fax: 805-488-2428 www.freshdelmonte.com
Distribution center providing a variety of services
including ripening, sorting, re-packing, fresh cut
processing, and delivery of fruits and vegetables
Type of Packaging: Consumer, Food Service

21505 Del Monte Fresh Produce Inc.
200 Del Monte Way
Palmetto, FL 34221-6609
941-722-3060
Fax: 941-722-7075 www.freshdelmonte.com
Distribution center providing a variety of services
including ripening, sorting, re-packing, fresh cut
processing, and delivery of fruits and vegetables
Type of Packaging: Consumer, Food Service

21506 Del Monte Fresh Produce Inc.
118-A Forest Pkwy
Forest Park, GA 30297
404-366-3699
Fax: 404-366-6945 www.freshdelmonte.com
Distribution center providing a variety of services
including ripening, sorting, re-packing, fresh cut
processing, and delivery of fruits and vegetables
Type of Packaging: Consumer, Food Service

21507 Del Monte Fresh Produce Inc.
14 Stuart Dr
Kankakee, IL 60901
815-936-7400
Fax: 815-936-7409 www.freshdelmonte.com
Distribution center providing a variety of services
including ripening, sorting, re-packing, fresh cut
processing, and delivery of fruits and vegetables
Type of Packaging: Consumer, Food Service

21508 Del Monte Fresh Produce Inc.
15141 Finney Mason Lane
Mappsville, VA 23407
757-824-4703
www.freshdelmonte.com
Distribution center providing a variety of services
including ripening, sorting, re-packing, fresh cut
processing, and delivery of fruits and vegetables
Type of Packaging: Consumer, Food Service

21509 Del Monte Fresh Produce Inc.
5050 State Route 60 W
Mulberry, FL 33860
863-844-5836
www.freshdelmonte.com
Distribution center providing a variety of services
including ripening, sorting, re-packing, fresh cut
processing, and delivery of fruits and vegetables
Type of Packaging: Consumer, Food Service

21510 Del Monte Fresh Produce Inc.
14516 Heathrow Forest Pkwy
Houston, TX 77032
281-912-6900
Fax: 281-912-6931 www.freshdelmonte.com
Distribution center providing a variety of services
including ripening, sorting, re-packing, fresh cut
processing, and delivery of fruits and vegetables
Type of Packaging: Consumer, Food Service

21511 Del Monte Fresh Produce Inc.
3151 Regatta Blvd
Suite E
Richmond, CA 94804
510-236-2719
Fax: 510-236-2029 www.freshdelmonte.com
Distribution center providing a variety of services
including ripening, sorting, re-packing, fresh cut
processing, and delivery of fruits and vegetables
Type of Packaging: Consumer, Food Service

21512 Del Monte Fresh Produce Inc.
936 Bankhead Hwy
Winder, GA 30680
770-307-4013
Fax: 770-307-2960 www.freshdelmonte.com
Distribution center providing a variety of services
including ripening, sorting, re-packing, fresh cut
processing, and delivery of fruits and vegetables
Type of Packaging: Consumer, Food Service

21513 Del Monte Fresh Produce Inc.
940 Thornton Rd S
Oshawa, ON L1J 7E2
Canada
905-743-5900
Fax: 905-743-5935 www.freshdelmonte.com
Distribution center providing a variety of services
including ripening, sorting, re-packing, fresh cut
processing, and delivery of fruits and vegetables
Type of Packaging: Consumer, Food Service

21514 Del Monte Fresh Produce Inc.
1570 rue Ampere
Suite 501
Boucherville, QC J4B 7L4
Canada
450-641-7373
Fax: 450-641-2269 www.freshdelmonte.com
Distribution center providing a variety of services
including ripening, sorting, re-packing, fresh cut
processing, and delivery of fruits and vegetables
Type of Packaging: Consumer, Food Service

21515 Del Packaging Inc
18113 Telge Rd
Cypress, TX 77429-1301
281-653-0099
Fax: 281-653-0077 sales@delpackaging.com
www.delpackaging.com
Packaging equipment
President: Dwayne Harthorn
dharthorn@delpackaging.com
Quality Control: Paro Patrick
CFO: Patrick Paro
Estimated Sales: Below $5 000,000
Number Employees: 50-99

21516 Delavan Spray Technologies
PO Box 969
Bamberg, SC 29003-0969
803-245-4347
Fax: 803-245-4146 800-982-6943
delavansales@goodrich.com
www.delavaninc.com
Manufacturer, importer and exporter of spray noz-
zles and accessories including flat spray, straight
stream, hollow and solid cone, etc
EVP: Terrence G Linnert
Senior VP: Stephen R Huggins
VP: Joseph F Andolino
Contact: Allen Priester
allen.priester@goodrich.com
Plant Manager: Roger Young
Estimated Sales: $1 - 5 Million
Number Employees: 100-249

21517 Delavan Spray Technologies
2730 W Tyvola Rd # 600
Charlotte, NC 28217-4578
704-423-7000
Fax: 704-423-4098 www.goodrich.com
Manufacturer, importer and exporter of spray noz-
zles and accessories including flat spray, straight
stream, hollow and solid cone, etc
President: Ray Davis
Division Controller: Carolin Kirsch
CEO: Marshall O Larsen
Contact: Tom Barrow
tom.barrow@utas.utc.com
Executive Vice President of Operation: Jerry
Witowski
Estimated Sales: $5-10 Million
Number Employees: 10,000
Parent Co: Coltec Industries
Brands:
Mini Sdx
Sdx
Sdx Iii

21518 Delavan-Delta
11 Rado Drive
Naugatuck, CT 06770-2220
203-720-5610
Fax: 203-720-5616
Manufacturer and exporter of level controls
Sales/Marketing Manager: Dean Cheramie
Number Employees: 65
Parent Co: Coltec Industries

21519 (HQ)Delco Tableware
19 Harbor Park Dr
Port Washington, NY 11050-4657
516-484-7965
Fax: 516-625-0859 800-221-9557
Flatware, holloware, steak knives and chinaware
Executive VP: Robert Delman
VP Distributor Sales: Holly Newme
Other Locations:
Delco Tableware
Port Washington NY
Brands:
Atlantic
Ceramicor
Delco
Hotel America
Table De France

21520 Delfield Co
980 S Isabella Rd
Mt Pleasant, MI 48858
989-773-7981
Fax: 800-669-0619 800-733-8821
www.delfield.com
Manufacturer and exporter of freezers and cabinets,
display cases, cafeteria/restaurant serving counters,
dispensers, ventilation systems, commercial refriger-
ators, mobile cafeteria systems, salad bars, pizza ta-
bles and stationary andmobile hot tables.
Year Founded: 1949
Estimated Sales: $100-500 Million
Number Employees: 500-999
Parent Co: the Manitowoc Company
Brands:
Air Tech
Mark V
Shelleyglass
Shelleymatic

21521 Delfin Design & Mfg
23301 Antonio Pkwy
Rancho Sta Marg, CA 92688-2664
949-888-4644
Fax: 949-888-4626 800-354-7919
john@delfinfs.com www.delfinfs.com
Manufacturer and exporter of plastic displayware including crocks, bowls, platters, trays, domes and covers
President: John Rief
john@delfinff.com
VP Sales: Gary Mazzone
Estimated Sales: $2.5-5,000,000
Number Employees: 20-49
Square Footage: 25000

21522 Deli-Boy Inc
100 Matthews Ave
Syracuse, NY 13209-1500
315-488-4411
Fax: 315-488-4155 www.deli-boy.com
Owner: Lon Frocione
lon.frocione@deli-boy.com
Estimated Sales: $20 - 50 Million
Number Employees: 50-99
Brands:
Grande
Premier/Nugget

21523 Delice Global Inc
150 Roosevelt Pl
Palisades Park, NJ 07650-1153
201-438-0300
Fax: 201-947-0320 info@deliceusa.com
www.deliceglobal.com
Baking equipment
Number Employees: 10-19

21524 Deline Box Co
3700 Lima St
Denver, CO 80239-3309
303-376-1283
Fax: 303-373-2325 webmaster@delinebox.com
Corrugated boxes
President: Dade Deline
Sales Manager: Jim Davis
Contact: Ricardo Alvarez
alvarez.ricardo@delinebox.com
Estimated Sales: $10 - 20 Million
Number Employees: 20-49

21525 Delkor Systems, Inc
8700 Rendova St NE
Minneapolis, MN 55014
763-783-0855
Fax: 763-783-0875 800-328-5558
sales@delkorsystems.com
www.delkorsystems.com
Provides end-of-line packaging systems that deliver robust, innovative solutions for carton forming, loading, and closing, top load case and tray packing, flat pad shrink wrapping, and robotic palletizing. Delkor's packaging solutionsare engineered for maximum versatility and flexibility to help customers meet ever-changing market requirements while preserving their capital investments.
Owner: Dale Andersen
CFO: Terry Cook
Contact: Dave Ackley
dackley@delkorsystems.com
Estimated Sales: $10 - 20 Million
Number Employees: 50-99

21526 Dell Marking Systems
721 Wanda St
Ferndale, MI 48220
248-547-7750
Fax: 248-544-9115 info@dellid.com
www.dellid.com
Marking and identification systems
President: Michael Grattan
sales@dellid.com
Estimated Sales: $1-2.5 000,000
Number Employees: 10-19

21527 Delmonte Fresh
3151 Regatta Ave
Suite E
Richmond, CA 94804
510-236-8968
Fax: 510-236-2029
contact-us-executive-office@freshdelmonte.com
www.freshdelmonte.com
Distribution center providing a variety of services including ripening, sorting, re-packing, fresh cut processing, and delivery of fruits and vegetables.
President/Chief Operating Officer: Hani El-Naffy
Chief Executive Officer/Chairman: Mohammad Abu-Ghazaleh
SVP/Chief Financial Officer: Richard Contreras
SVP/General Counsel & Secretary: Bruce Jordan
VP/Research-Development Agricultural Svs: Thomas Young
efiroozabady@freshdelmonte.com
SVP/North American Sales & Product Mgmt: Emanuel Lazopoulos
VP/Human Resources: Marissa Tenazas
SVP/North American Operations: Paul Rice
Number Employees: 10-19
Parent Co: Del Monte Fresh Produce Company
Type of Packaging: Consumer, Food Service

21528 Delmonte Fresh Produce Co
118 Forest Pkwy
Forest Park, GA 30297
404-366-3996
contact-us-executive-office@freshdelmonte.com
www.freshdelmonte.com
Distribution center providing a variety of services including ripening, sorting, re-packing, fresh cut processing, and delivery of fruits and vegetables.
President: Mike Ford
mford@freshdelmonte.com
Chief Executive Officer/Chairman: Mohammad Abu-Ghazaleh
mford@freshdelmonte.com
SVP/Chief Financial Officer: Richard Contreras
SVP/General Counsel & Secretary: Bruce Jordan
VP/Research-Development Agricultural Svs: Thomas Young
mford@freshdelmonte.com
SVP/North American Sales & Product Mgmt: Emanuel Lazopoulos
VP/Human Resources: Marissa Tenazas
SVP/North American Operations: Paul Rice
Site Manager: Mike Ford
Parent Co: Del Monte Fresh Produce Company
Type of Packaging: Consumer, Food Service

21529 Delphi Food Machinery
625 S Smith Rd # 21
Suite 21
Tempe, AZ 85281-2967
480-483-8361
Fax: 480-483-8396
foodmachinery@delphifm.com
www.delphifm.com
Dealers of used processing equipment
Owner: Peter Yioulos
Estimated Sales: $.5 - 1 million
Number Employees: 1-4

21530 Delran Label Corporation
1829 Underwood Boulevard
Suite 10
Delran, NJ 08075-1241
856-764-1336
Fax: 856-764-3470
Wine industry labels

21531 Delta Carbona
376 Hollywood Ave # 208
Fairfield, NJ 07004-1807
973-808-6260
Fax: 973-808-5661 888-746-5599
www.carbona.com
Stain removers
President: Tim Wells
dbudhan@carbona.com
Marketing Director: Sherry Polevoy
Purchasing Manager: Eileen Hirschfield
Estimated Sales: $1-2.5 Million
Number Employees: 5-9
Square Footage: 80000
Brands:
Carbona Cleanit! Oven Cleaner
Carpet Wizard
Color Run Remover
Pet Stain & Odor Remover
Stain Devils
Stain Stop
Stain Wizard
Stain Wizard Wipes

21532 Delta Chemical Corporation
P.O. Box 73054
Baltimore, MD 21273-3054
410-354-3253
Fax: 410-354-1021 800-282-5322
jack@deltachemical.com www.deltachemical.com
Chlorine liquid bleaches
President: John Besson
CEO: Rebecca Besson
Director of Technology: Jim Dulko
Natl Sls Mgr: Jack Colgan
Director of Technology: Jim Dulko
Sales Manager (South): Joe Shemanski
Northern Regional Sales: Dan Moyer
Western/Caribbean Regional Sales Manager: Ed Penick
Vice President, Marketing & Sales: Terry Badwak
Estimated Sales: $20 - 50 Million
Number Employees: 100-249

21533 Delta Container Corporation
220 Plantation Rd
New Orleans, LA 70123
504-733-7292
Fax: 504-734-8920 800-752-7292
www.prattindustries.com
Corrugated containers
President: Gary Byrd
CEO: Brian McPheely
CFO: Gary Byrd
Quality Control: Mark May
COO: David Dennis
Estimated Sales: $10 - 20 Million
Number Employees: 50-99
Square Footage: 170000
Parent Co: Pratt Industries

21534 Delta Cooling Towers Inc
41 Pine St # 103
Suite 103
Rockaway, NJ 07866-3139
973-586-2201
Fax: 973-586-2243 800-289-3358
sales@deltacooling.com www.deltacooling.com
Polyethylene non-corroding cooling towers and air strippers
President: John Flaherty
Sales: David Jurgensen
Contact: Frank Przyhocki
fprzyhocki@deltacooling.com
Estimated Sales: Above $10MM
Number Employees: 5-9
Brands:
Paragon
Pioneer
Premier
Vanguard

21535 Delta Cyklop Orga Pac
2601 Westinghouse Blvd
Charlotte, NC 28273-6517
704-588-2510
Fax: 704-588-6838 800-446-4347
www.itwpbna.com
Polyester, steel, cord and polypropylene strapping; also, tape dispensers, strapping machines and elastic string tying equipment
VP Sales/Marketing: James Prieb
Estimated Sales: $10 - 20 Million
Number Employees: 20-49
Parent Co: Illinois Tool Works

21536 Delta Engineering Corporation
3 Freedom Way
Walpole, MA 02081
781-729-8650
Fax: 781-729-6149
info@deltaengineeringcorp.com
www.deltaengineeringcorp.com
Electronic counting and weighing systems, boxing and bagging equipment
Manager: Peter Knobel
R&D: Herb Mac Rae
Sales: Steve Hill
Production: Richard Pooler
Plant Manager: Pete Knobel
Estimated Sales: $2.5-5 000,000
Number Employees: 1-4
Number of Products: 25
Type of Packaging: Consumer, Food Service, Bulk

21537 Delta F Corporation
4 Constitution Way Ste I
Woburn, MA 01801
781-935-4600
Fax: 781-938-0531
Oxygen analyzers
VP: John Swyers
Sales Manager: Margaret Lanoue
Contact: John Swyers
 j.swyers@delta-f.com
Estimated Sales: $50-100 Million
Number Employees: 50-99
Parent Co: TGE Group

21538 Delta Industrial Services
11501 Eagle St NW
Coon Rapids, MN 55448
800-279-3358
Fax: 763-755-7799 800-279-3358
www.deltaind.com
Narrow web converting, packaging
Contact: Greg Sorensen
 gsorensen@deltaind.com
Estimated Sales: $1-5 000,000
Number Employees: 50-99

21539 Delta Machine & Maufacturing
137 Teal St
St Rose, LA 70087-4022
504-949-8304
Fax: 504-467-0071 debra@deltamachinemfg.com
Manufacturer and exporter of bakery equipment including trough elevators
President/Owner: Dale Kessler
CEO: Andrew Kessler, Jr.
CFO: Debra Kessler
Estimated Sales: Below $1 Million
Number Employees: 1-4

21540 Delta Plastics
106 Delta Pl
Hot Springs, AR 71913
501-760-3000
Fax: 501-760-3005 sales@deltaplastics.com
www.deltaplastics.com
Packaging supplies for the food industry. Rexam PLC has now acquired the company as of September 2005
CEO: Lothar Schweigert
VP: Kurt Nyberg
VP Sales: Kurt Nyberg
Contact: Leanne Mitchell
 lmitchell@deltapl.com
Estimated Sales: $50 Million
Number Employees: 250-499
Parent Co: Rexam PLC
Type of Packaging: Food Service

21541 Delta Pure Filtration Corp
11011 Richardson Rd
Ashland, VA 23005-3418
804-798-2888
Fax: 804-798-3923 800-785-9450
tfurbee@deltapure.com www.deltapure.net
Manufacturer and exporter of active carbon cartridge filters for water, juice, vegetable oil, etc
President: Todd Furbee
 tfurbee@deltapure.com
Operations Manager: Frank Williams
Number Employees: 20-49
Square Footage: 36000
Type of Packaging: Bulk
Brands:
 Aquatrust
 Delta Pure

21542 Delta Signs
1802 Hickory Dr
Haltom City, TX 76117
817-838-0213
Fax: 817-665-0167 866-643-3582
Electric signs and awnings; also, installation available with crane service
Owner: Steve Jessup
CEO: Sergio Contreras
CFO: Steve Jessup
Quality Control: N Cao
Estimated Sales: Below $5 Million
Number Employees: 5-9
Square Footage: 20800

21543 Delta Systems Inc
535 W Dyke Rd
Rogers, AR 72758-6443
479-631-2210
Fax: 479-631-2217 800-631-2214
www.delta-systems-inc.com
Horizontal flow wrapping machinery, turnkey packaging systems, automatic feeding equipment, distribution equipment
President: Jake Bushey
CEO: Charles Bruce
 c.bruce@delta-systems-inc.com
Director of Sales: Liam Buckley
Estimated Sales: $5-10 Million
Number Employees: 20-49

21544 Delta T Construction
10838 Old Mill Rd # A
Omaha, NE 68154-2649
402-333-0830
Fax: 402-333-6635 info@deltatconstruction.com
www.deltatconstruction.com
Cold storage doors and hardware, insulated building panels, insulation-floors, ceilings, and refrigerated structures
Manager: Ty Kestel
 tyk@deltatconstuction.com
Estimated Sales: Less Than $500,000
Number Employees: 1-4

21545 Delta Technology Corp
1602 Townhurst Dr
Houston, TX 77043-3283
713-464-7407
Fax: 713-461-6753 info@deltatechnology.com
www.deltatechnology.com
Electronic color sorting equipment
VP/Sales: Eduardo Libin
Estimated Sales: $5-10 Million
Number Employees: 10-19

21546 Delta Trak
PO Box 398
Pleasanton, CA 94566-0039
925-249-2250
Fax: 925-249-2251 800-962-6776
salesinfo@deltatrak.com www.deltatrak.com
Innovator of cold chain managament and food safety solutions. Product line includes a wide range of temperature, humidity, and pH monitoring and recodring devices such as data loggers, wireless systems, and a variety of professionalthermometers.
President/Founder: Fredrick Wu
R&D Director: George Krasten
Marketing/Business Development Director: Ray Caron
Operations Director: Steve Hibbs
Production Manager: Satwant Chand
Estimated Sales: $10-15 000,000
Number Employees: 70+
Number of Brands: 4
Number of Products: 220+
Square Footage: 6000
Brands:
 Air Repair
 Coldtrak
 Flash Link
 Temp Dot
 Thermotrace

21547 Delta Wire And Mfg.
29 Delta Drive
Harrow, ON N0R 1G0
Canada
519-738-3514
Fax: 519-738-3468 800-221-3794
contact@deltawire.com www.deltawire.com
Manufacturer and exporter of welded wire mesh products including pallet racks and containers
President: Geoffrey Scully
CFO: Geoffrey Scully
National Sales Manager: Larry Cunningham
Estimated Sales: $10 - 20 Million
Number Employees: 10-19

21548 Delta/Ducon
Three Tun Center
33 Sproul Road
Malvern, PA 19355
610-695-9700
Fax: 610-695-9724 800-238-2974
sales@deltaducon.com www.deltaducon.com
Pneumatic conveying equipment for flour, unloading rail cars, in-plant transfer and dust capture systems.

Manager: Gini Krisciunas
Sales Director: Ron Tempesta
Engineering: Dave Lizzi
Purchasing Manager: Cathy Heinser
Estimated Sales: $5 Million
Number Employees: 10-19
Brands:
 Perma/Flo
 Perma/Lok
 Spira/Flo
 Xl Airlock

21549 DeltaTrak
P.O. Box 398
Pleasanton, CA 94566
925-249-2250
Fax: 925-249-2251 800-962-6776
salesinfo@deltatrak.com www.deltatrak.com
DeltaTrak, Inc. is a leading innovator of cold chain management and temperature monitoring solutions. DeltaTrak offers a wide range of temperature and humidity data loggers and wireless systems. DeltaTrak develops and manufactures highquality portable test instruments that monitor/record temperature and humidity. DeltaTrak's comprehensive cold chain management systems also include professional digital probe and infrared thermometers.
Quality Assurance Manager: Tony Trapolino
VP Marketing & Business Development: Ray Carson
Director, Operations: Rick Delgado
Estimated Sales: $8,000,000
Number Employees: 250
Number of Brands: 20
Number of Products: 80+
Type of Packaging: Food Service, Private Label, Bulk
Brands:
 Flash Link
 Thermotrace

21550 Delux Manufacturing Co
4650 Airport Rd
PO Box 1027
Kearney, NE 68847-3761
308-237-2274
Fax: 308-234-3765 800-658-3240
info@deluxmfg.com www.deluxmfg.com
Manufacturer and exporter of grain dryers
President: Eric D Michel
 eric.dm@deluxmfg.com
VP/Sales Manager: Bob Schultz
Estimated Sales: $2.5-5 Million
Number Employees: 20-49
Square Footage: 144000

21551 Deluxe Equipment Company
P.O. Box 11390
4414 28th St. West
Bradenton, FL 34207
941-753-3184
Fax: 941-753-4529 800-367-8931
deluxe@gte.net www.deluxeovens.com
Manufacturer and exporter of ovens, proofers, warmers.
President: Gib Smith
CFO: Sandra Smith
VP/Sales: Russ D'Aiuto
Estimated Sales: $2.5-5 Million
Number Employees: 10-19
Square Footage: 50000
Brands:
 Convect a Ray
 Deluxe

21552 (HQ)Dema Engineering Co
10020 Big Bend Rd
St Louis, MO 63122-6457
314-966-3533
Fax: 314-965-8319 800-325-3362
sales@demaeng.com
Manufacturer and exporter of warewash, laundry and liquid soap dispensers including injectors, proportioning detergent feeders, rinse pumps and foamers
President: Jonathan Deutsch
 jonathand@demaeng.com
VP, Marketing: Dan Gillespie
SVP, Global Sales: Ron Dickerson
Purchasing Manager: David Deutsch
Estimated Sales: $10-20 Million
Number Employees: 20-49
Square Footage: 56000

Other Locations:
Dema Engineering Co.
Gerald MO

21553 Demaco
4645 Metropolitan Ave
Ridgewood, NY 11385

Fax: 718-417-9264 www.demaco.nl/en/
Manufacturer and exporter of pasta equipment
President: Leonard Defrancisci
VP: John Deluca
Mngr: Amy Casaburri
Estimated Sales: $10-20 Million
Number Employees: 20-49
Parent Co: Howden Food Equipment

21554 Demag Cranes & Components Corp
29201 Aurora Rd
Cleveland, OH 44139-1895

440-248-2400
Fax: 440-248-3086 www.demagcranes.us
Manufacturer and exporter of cranes and hoists
President: John Paxton
Corp Comms: Dan Konstantinovsk
Administrative Assistant: Maureen Tilly
Estimated Sales: $50,000,000 - $99,999,999
Number Employees: 250-499
Parent Co: Demag Material Handling

21555 Demarle Inc
8 Corporate Dr # 1
Cranbury, NJ 08512-3630

609-395-0219
Fax: 609-395-1027 888-353-9726
info@demarleusa.com www.sasademarle.com
Silicone applied mold and trays for baking and
freezing
President: Hatsuo Takeuchi
Vice President: Pierre Bonnet
pierre@sasademarle.com
Sales Manager: Eliane Feiner
Estimated Sales: $5 - 10 000,000
Number Employees: 10-19
Brands:
Flexipan
Silform
Silpat

21556 Dematic Corp
8012 Tower Point Dr
Charlotte, NC 28227-7726

704-845-1110
Fax: 704-845-1111
President: Mats Herrstromer
CEO: Terry Dunn
CFO: Bob Consoli
Quality Control: Janet Hill
Estimated Sales: $10 - 20 Million
Number Employees: 20-49

21557 Dematic Corp
2855 S James Dr
New Berlin, WI 53151-3662

262-860-7000
Fax: 262-860-7010 800-424-7365
www.dematic.com
Chairman of the Board: John Splude
Cmo: Mike Kotecki
mike.kotecki@dematic.com
Vice President and CFO: James P Purko
Vice President, Corporate Marketing: Cheryl Falk
Estimated Sales: $20 - 30 Million
Number Employees: 250-499

21558 Dematic USA
507 Plymouth Ave NE
Grand Rapids, MI 49505-6029

616-451-6200
Fax: 616-913-7701 877-725-7500
logisticsresults@dematic.com www.dematic.com
Material handling, systems and management.
President/ CEO: Ulf Henricksson
CEO: David Abbey
david.abbey@dematic.com
CFO: Richard Paradise
EVP/ General Counsel: Ben Clark
EVP R&D: Jim Strollberg
EVP Human Resources: Dutch Burfield
EVP Global Operations: Robert Arguelles
Number Employees: 20-49
Parent Co: Siemens Dematic AG

Brands:
Dematic
Direct It
Pick Director
Q-Can
Rapid Sort
Rapistan
Siplace
Sort Director
Staging Director

21559 Dembling & Dembling Architects
307 Washington Ave
Albany, NY 12206-3074

518-463-8066
Fax: 518-463-8610 daved@ddarch.com
www.ddarch.com
Consultant specializing in the design of food service
and hospitality establishments
President: Daniel Dembling
dand@ddarch.com
Partner: David Dembling
Estimated Sales: Below $5 Million
Number Employees: 5-9

21560 Demeyere Na, Llc
3 Dorchester Dr
Westport, CT 06880-4037

203-255-2402
Fax: 203-255-2406 800-338-7304
dem.breeden@prodigy.net
Commercial stainless steel cookware with seven ply
construction, industry rated for all energy sources
especially efficient induction
President: John Walters
Contact: John Breeden
info@demeyere.be
Estimated Sales: $50 Million+
Number Employees: 1-4
Number of Brands: 11
Number of Products: 1700
Square Footage: 120000

21561 Dempster Systems
PO Box 1388
Toccoa, GA 30577-1424

706-886-2327
Fax: 706-886-0088
Manufacturer and exporter of refuse handling systems
President: John Boonstra
Estimated Sales: $20-50 Million
Number Employees: 100-249
Parent Co: Technology
Type of Packaging: Consumer, Food Service, Bulk

21562 Demptos Glass Corporation
2300 Cordelia Rd
Fairfield, CA 94534

707-422-9999
Fax: 707-422-1242 david@demptos.com
Manufacturers of wine bottles, champagne bottles,
spirits bottles, beer bottles etc
Manager: John Symank
COO: Rob Belke
rob@demptos.com
General Manager: John Symank
Estimated Sales: $20-50 Million
Number Employees: 50-99

21563 (HQ)Den Mar Corp
1005 Reed Rd
North Dartmouth, MA 02747-1567

508-999-3295
Fax: 508-999-6108 henrydenmar@corp.com
www.denmar-corp.com
Stainless steel and wood tables including dish, work
and steam; also, shelving and sinks
President: George Henriques
Partner: Henry Martin
henry@denmar-corp.com
Production Manager: Aaron Magrath
Estimated Sales: $1 - 2.5 Million
Number Employees: 10-19
Square Footage: 56000
Other Locations:
Denmar Corp.
North Dartmouth MA
Brands:
Aqua-Vent
Denmar
Simplex

21564 Den Ray Sign Company
1057 Whitehall St
Jackson, TN 38301

731-427-5466
Fax: 731-427-5473 800-530-7291
sales@denraysign.com www.denraysign.com
Plastic and neon signs; custom designs, service and
maintenance available
President: Rhea Deming
Estimated Sales: $500,000-$1 Million
Number Employees: 10-19

21565 Denair Trailer Company
P.O. Box 1389enue
Yuma, AZ 85366

928-627-4716
Fax: 928-627-4717 denairtrailer.com
Wine industry agricultural trailers.
Estimated Sales: $100-500 Million
Number Employees: 10-19

21566 Denice & Filice LLC
10001 Fairview Rd
Hollister, CA 95023-9209

831-637-7492
Fax: 831-637-4174
Contact: Vince Brigantino
vince.brigantino@denicefilice.com
Estimated Sales: $20 - 50 Million
Number Employees: 20-49

21567 Denman Equipment
2020 Satinwood Dr
Memphis, TN 38119-5631

901-755-7135
Fax: 901-754-0105 www.denserv.com
Dealer of used and rebuilt food processing equipment for the meat and poultry industry
Owner: Pierce Denman
Estimated Sales: $.5 - 1 million
Number Employees: 1-4

21568 Dennis Engineering Group
1537 Main St # 2
Springfield, MA 01103-1463

413-787-1785
Fax: 413-787-1786 info@dennisgrp.com
www.dennisgrp.com
Offers complete planning, design, architectural, engineering and construction management services.
President: Calen Burr
burr@dennisgrp.com
Principal: Tan McCreary
VP: John Lapinksi
Finance Executive/HR Director: Alissa Boudreau
Number Employees: 10-19
Square Footage: 32000

21569 (HQ)Dennsi Group
1537 Main St
Springfield, MA 01103-1458

413-737-1353
Fax: 413-787-1786 info@dennisgrp.com
www.dennisgroup.com
Full-Service architectural, engineering, process design and construction management firm providing total project solutions, from conception through start-up, exclusively to the food and beverags industries.
President: Thomas Dennis
Sales: Dan McCreary
Estimated Sales: Less Than $500,000
Number Employees: 1-4
Other Locations:
Salt Lake City UT
San Diego CA
Wheaton IL
Toronto, Canada

21570 Denstor Mobile Storage Systems
2966 Wilson Drive NW
Walker, MI 49534

616-735-9100
Fax: 616-988-4045 800-234-7477
sales@pippmobile.com www.denstor.com
High density mobile storage systems
President, CEO: Craig J. Umans
Chief Financial Officer: Keith Carpentier
Director of Retail Sales: Len Kowalski
lkowalski@denstor.com
Operations Manager: Tom French
Estimated Sales: $5 - 10 Million
Number Employees: 20
Parent Co: Pipp Mobile Storage Systems, Inc

21571 DentalOne Partners
17300 Dallas Parkway
Suite 1070
Dallas, TX 75248-7725

972-755-0800
Fax: 972-387-9774
Printing materials, film coextruded, film laminated,
film LLDPE, film LDPE, stand-up pouch, film
stretch, film shrink, film oriented polxprotylene, film
coated
CEO: R Kirk Huntsman
Contact: Robert Anders
robert.anders@dental-one.com
Estimated Sales: $3 - 5 Million
Number Employees: 20-49

21572 Denver Instrument Company
5 Orville Dr.
Bohemia, NY 11716

303-431-7255
Fax: 303-423-4831 800-321-1135
www.denverinstrumentusa.com
Balances, multiple weighing units
Manager: Karen Ware
Contact: Denice Pracht
denice@denverinstrument.com
Estimated Sales: Below $5 Million
Number Employees: 10-19
Brands:
Apex

21573 Denver Mixer Company
6565 Vine Ct
Denver, CO 80229

303-287-0025
Fax: 303-287-0924
President: Chris Barnhill
Estimated Sales: $2.5-5 000,000
Number Employees: 5-9

21574 Denver Reel & Pallet Company
4600 Monaco Parkaway
Denver, CO 80216

303-321-1920
Fax: 303-321-1949 denverreel@aol.com
www.denverreelandpallet.com
Pallets, reels, skids, boxes and crates
President: Kurt Heimbrock
CFO: Kurt Heimbrock
VP: Darold Herrera
R&D: Kurt Heimbrock
Quality Control: Kurt Heimbrock
VP of Sales: Dareld Herrera
Estimated Sales: $2.5 - 5 Million
Number Employees: 20-49
Square Footage: 32000
Brands:
Dratco

21575 Dependable Machine, Inc.
308 S. 14th St. - Coeur
d'Alene, ID 83814

973-239-7800
Fax: 973-239-7855 866-967-0146
dmi-cnc.com
Manufacturer, importer and exporter of screen and
pad printing equipment, printing inks and accesso-
ries
President: Thomas Skeels
VP: Brett Skeels
Estimated Sales: $2.5 - 5 Million
Number Employees: 10-19
Square Footage: 40000

21576 (HQ)Derse Inc
3800 W Canal St
Milwaukee, WI 53208-4150

414-977-0002
Fax: 414-257-3798 800-562-2300
www.derse.com
Custom exhibits and highway business signs
CEO: William Haney
CEO: Aaron Bartelt
abartelt@derse.com
President: Adam Beckett
VP Sales/Marketing: Kent Jones
Estimated Sales: $10-20 Million
Number Employees: 100-249
Other Locations:
Derse
Carrollton TX

21577 Des Moines Stamp Mfg Co
851 6th Ave
Des Moines, IA 50309-1229

515-288-7245
Fax: 515-288-0418 888-236-7739
info@dmstamp.com www.dmstamp.com
Rubber stamps, notary seals and stencils
Owner: Tom Child
tchild@dmstamp.com
Estimated Sales: $2.5-5 Million
Number Employees: 20-49
Square Footage: 80000

21578 Desco Equipment Corporation
1903 Case Pkwy
Twinsburg, OH 44087-2343

330-405-1581
Fax: 330-405-1584 www.descoequipment.com
Innovators of high quality, cost-efficient printing
systems for the container and closure industry.
President: Leo Henry
Contact: Phyllis Faiken
pfaiken@descoequipment.com
Purchasing Manager: Dennis Sweeney
Estimated Sales: $3.7 Million
Number Employees: 26
Square Footage: 200000
Brands:
Desco

21579 Descon EDM
54 W Main St
PO Box 189
Brocton, NY 14716

716-792-9300
Fax: 716-792-9363 us.kompass.com/
Manufacturer and exporter of material handling
equipment including vibrating and belt conveyors,
graders, etc
CEO: David Beehler
R&D: Christopher Beehler
General Manager: C Beehler
Estimated Sales: Below $5 Million
Number Employees: 1-4
Square Footage: 20000

21580 Desert Box & Supply Corporation
P.O. Box 281
Thermal, CA 92274-281

760-399-5161
Wooden boxes, packaging materials and corrugated
boxes
President: Michael Wills
Co-Owner: Ann Wills
Estimated Sales: Less than $500,000
Number Employees: 10

21581 Deshazo Crane Company
P.O. Box 1450
Alabaster, AL 35007-2062

205-664-2006
Fax: 205-664-3668 www.deshazo.com
Manufacturer and exporter of cranes including over-
head bridge, gantry and semi-gantry
CEO: Guy K Mitchell Jr
Estimated Sales: $20-50 Million
Number Employees: 100-249
Type of Packaging: Bulk

21582 Desiccare
10600 Shoemaker Avenue
Suite C
Santa Fe Springs, CA 90670-4073

888-932-0405
Fax: 562-903-2272 800-446-6650
desiccant@desicare.com www.desicare.com
Silica gel, clay, molecular sieve and activated carbon
desiccants ranging in size from 0.25 grams to 2,500
grams
President: Ken Blankenhorn
Contact: Wayne Pelletier
wpelletier@desicare.com
Estimated Sales: $10-20 Million
Number Employees: 50-99

21583 Design Group
1002 S Prospect Ave
Clearwater, FL 33756-4042

727-441-2825
Fax: 727-446-0388
thedesigngroup@tampabay.rr.com
www.thedesigngroupincusa.com

Interior design services for hospitality - hotels and
restaurants. Licensed in the state of Florida (ID -
0001657, IBC - 000317)
President: Jeanette Brewer
thedesigngroupinc@verizon.net
Vice President: Delayna Cowley Nestell
Marketing: Jeanetter Brewer
Sales: Delayna Nestell
Production: Irene Bishop
Purchasing Manager: Delayna Cowley Nestell
Estimated Sales: Less than $500,000
Number Employees: 1-4
Square Footage: 12000
Brands:
Daniel Paul
Flexsteel Contract
Lexmark Carpet
McI Group
Mtj Seating
Shelly Williams Seating

21584 Design Ideas
2521 Stockyard Rd
P.O. Box 2967
Springfield, IL 62702-1437

217-753-3081
Fax: 217-753-3080 800-426-6394
designideas@designid.com
Containers, gift packaging, and candle holders
Owner: Court Hager
chager@designideas.net
Director Sales/Marketing: Christine Netznik
Number Employees: 50-99
Number of Products: 1500

21585 Design Label Manufacturing
7 Capitol Dr
East Lyme, CT 6333

860-739-6266
Fax: 860-739-7659 800-666-1575
www.designlabel.com
Pressure sensitive and promotional labels, clam shell
and polystyrene inserts and coupons
President: Jeff P Dunphy
Controller: Kim Dunphy
Contact: David Arroyo
darroyo@designlabel.com
Estimated Sales: $10-20 Million
Number Employees: 20-49

21586 Design Packaging Company
100 Hazel Ave
Glencoe, IL 60022-1731

773-486-8100
Fax: 773-486-2160 800-321-7659
Polypropylene and polyethylene bags and sheets;
importer of polyethylene and polyproplyne bags; ex-
porter of polyethylene sleeves and bags
President: Myron Horvitz
CFO: Greg Horvitz
VP: Randy Block
Sales Representative: Greg Horvitz
Contact: Conrad Capulong
conrad.capulong@designpackaging.net
Purchasing Agent: Randy Block
Estimated Sales: $5 - 10 Million
Number Employees: 20-49
Square Footage: 80000
Brands:
Designbags
Foiltex
Kristalene

21587 Design Plastics Inc
3550 Keystone Dr
Omaha, NE 68134-4800

402-572-7177
Fax: 402-572-0500 800-491-0786
www.designplastics.com
Plastic packaging and containers for dry and frozen
foods
President: Rick Breden
HR Executive: Nancy Janne
njanne@designplastics.com
Director Marketing: Sylvio Rebolloso
Estimated Sales: $10-20 Million
Number Employees: 50-99

21588 Design Specialties Inc
1890 Dixwell Ave # 200
Hamden, CT 06514-3171

203-288-3587
Fax: 203-288-3594 800-999-1584
design@duralux4you.com www.duralux4you.com

Reusable plastic tableware including flatware, trays, dishes, tumblers, mugs and bowls; also, insulated trays and high temperature dishes available for cooking and chilling
Owner: Patricia Whitlock
  design@duralux4you.com
VP: Patricia Whitlock
Estimated Sales: $5 - 10 Million
Number Employees: 5-9
Number of Brands: 1
Number of Products: 40
Brands:
  Duralux

21589 Design Systems Inc
38799 W 12 Mile Rd # 100
Farmington Hills, MI 48331-2903
  248-489-4300
  Fax: 248-489-4321 800-660-4374
  pmunzenberger@dsidsc.com www.dsidsc.com
Process engineering company specializing in lean manufacturing and controls integration, through put simulation
Manager: Steve Puranen
Sales Director: Paul Munzenberger
Manager: David Goings
  dgoing@ofisolutions.com
Estimated Sales: $35 Million
Number Employees: 100-249

21590 Design Technology Corporation
5 Suburban Park Drive
Billerica, MA 01821-3904
  978-663-7000
  Fax: 978-663-6841
Custom designed and built food processing, material handling, packaging, inspection and assembly equipment
President: Marvin Menzin
Estimated Sales: $5-10 Million
Number Employees: 20-49
Square Footage: 120000

21591 Design Technology Corporation
26 Mason Street
Lexington, MA 02421
  781-862-5107
  Fax: 303-440-5127 800-597-7063
Manufacturer and exporter of material handling equipment, food processing machinery and process control systems
President: Marvin Menzin
Estimated Sales: $1-2,500,000
Number Employees: 4

21592 Design-Mark Industries
3 Kendrick Rd
Wareham, MA 02571-1093
  508-295-9591
  Fax: 508-295-6752 800-451-3275
  sales@design-mark.com www.design-mark.com
Manufacturer and exporter of labels, nameplates and membrane switch panels
President: Carl Burquist
Cmo: Denise Shurtleff
  denise@design-mark.com
Quality Control: Jim Brawders
Operations: Jon Winzler
Marketing Director: Denise Shurtley
Estimated Sales: $14 Million
Number Employees: 50-99
Square Footage: 40000
Type of Packaging: Bulk

21593 Designers Folding Box Corp
84 Tennessee St
Buffalo, NY 14204-2797
  716-853-5141
  Fax: 716-853-5149
  sales@designersfoldingbox.com
  www.designersfoldingbox.com
Folding paper boxes and carry-out trays and boxes; also, die cut inserts
President: Jeffrey Winney
CSR: Teri McAndrews
Manager: Eugene Zilka
  ezilka@designers.com
PA: Donald Rounds
Estimated Sales: $5-10 Million
Number Employees: 20-49
Type of Packaging: Consumer, Food Service, Private Label, Bulk

21594 Designers Plastics
12880 Automobile Blvd # G
Suite G-I
Clearwater, FL 33762-4711
  727-573-1643
  Fax: 727-572-7078 sales@designersplastics.com
  www.designersplastics.com
Acrylic displays
President: Bruce Ely
  desplastic@aol.com
CFO and Quality Controller: Penny Carrigan
Estimated Sales: $1 - 2.5 Million
Number Employees: 5-9

21595 Designpro Engineering
20092 Edison Circle East
Clearwater, MN 55320
  320-558-6000
  Fax: 320-558-6110 800-221-4144
  www.franklinoutdoor.com
Poultry cutting machinery
Owner: Keith Franklin
Director: John Boughner
Head Technical Department: Jon Boughner
Estimated Sales: $500,000-$1 Million
Number Employees: 1-4
Square Footage: 28000

21596 Despro Manufacturing
PO Box 2503
Cedar Grove, NJ 07009-2503
  973-239-0202
  Fax: 973-239-1595 800-292-9906
  mailbox@emcoplastics.com
  www.emcoplastics.com
Acrylic bulk food containers and bins, steel shelving, display racks, point of purchase displays, awnings and pastry cases
President: James Mc Namara
VP: Mark Mercadante
Estimated Sales: $20 - 50 Million
Number Employees: 100-249
Square Footage: 40000
Parent Co: Emco Industrial Plastics

21597 Detectamet Inc
5111 Glen Alden Dr
Richmond, VA 23231
  804-303-1983
  844-820-7244
  sales@us.detectamet.com www.detectamet.com
Designer and manufacturer of tools and equipment used to detect plastic contamination in food products.
Group Managing Director: Angela Musson-Smith
CEO: Sean Smith
Managing Director: James Chrismas
Parent Co: Detectamet

21598 Detecto Scale Co
203 E Daugherty St
Webb City, MO 64870-1929
  417-673-4631
  Fax: 417-673-5001 800-641-2008
  detecto@cardet.com www.detecto.com
Manufacturer and exporter of scales including portion control, top loading, price computing, bench, platform, counter, pre-packaging, hanging and receiving
Estimated Sales: $50 - 60 Million
Number Employees: 10-19
Square Footage: 400000
Parent Co: Cardinal Scale Manufacturing Company
Type of Packaging: Food Service
Brands:
  Cardinal
  Detecto

21599 Detecto Scale Co
203 E Daugherty St
Webb City, MO 64870-1929
  417-673-4631
  Fax: 417-673-5001 800-641-2008
  detecto@cardet.com www.detecto.com
Weighing scales
President: David H Perry
  brockdawson@detecto.com
Chief Financial Officer: Elise Crume
Vice President: Larry Hicks
Research/Development: Tony Herrin
Quality Control: Ginger Harper
Marketing: Jonathan Sabo
Sales Exec: Brock Dawson
Operations/Production: Matt Stovern

Estimated Sales: $45 Million
Number Employees: 10-19
Square Footage: 350000
Parent Co: Cardinal Scale Manufacturing Company

21600 Detex Corp
302 Detex Dr
New Braunfels, TX 78130-3099
  830-629-2900
  Fax: 830-620-6711 www.detex.com
Security locks, alarms, panels, switches and electric and manual guard tour clocks
President: John Blodgett
  dta@detex.com
Chairman of the Board: Philip Haselton
R & D: George Val
Director Sales/Marketing: Gary Hackney
National Accounts Sales Manager: Ken Khueler
IT: David Alexander
Production Manager (Hardware): Greg Drake
Estimated Sales: $5-10 Million
Number Employees: 100-249

21601 Detroit Forming
19100 W 8 Mile Rd
Southfield, MI 48075-5792
  248-440-1317
  Fax: 248-352-0445 sales@detroitforming.net
  www.detroitforming.net
Manufacturer and exporter of plastic food trays for meat, produce, ice cream and cookies
President: Leigh Rodney
  leigh.rodney@detroitforming.net
National Sales Manager: Ken Sherry
Estimated Sales: $10 - 20 Million
Number Employees: 100-249
Type of Packaging: Food Service

21602 Detroit Marking Products
15100 Castleton St
Detroit, MI 48227
  313-838-9760
  Fax: 800-831-4243 800-833-8222
  www.dmpco.com
Rubber stamps
President: William Foerg
Contact: Joe Foerg
  jfoerg@dmpco.com
Estimated Sales: $1-2.5 Million
Number Employees: 10-19

21603 Detroit Quality Brush Mfg Co
32165 Schoolcraft Rd
Livonia, MI 48150-1833
  734-525-5660
  Fax: 734-525-0437 800-722-3037
  sales@dqb.com www.dqb.com
Manufacturer and exporter of brooms and brushes
Owner: Donald Weinbaum
  don@gqb.com
Manufacturing Manager: Mike Lindemoth
Estimated Sales: $2.5-5 Million
Number Employees: 50-99
Square Footage: 200000
Parent Co: Erco Housewares
Type of Packaging: Consumer, Food Service, Private Label, Bulk

21604 Devar Inc
706 Bostwick Ave
Bridgeport, CT 06605-2396
  203-368-6751
  Fax: 203-368-3747 800-566-6822
  sales@devarinc.com www.devarinc.com
Process control instruments including indicators, data acquisition recorders and temperature transmitters, alarms and panel meters; also, pH analyzers and instrument calibrators
President: A J Ruscito
  jhead@devarinc.com
VP Engineering: A Gura
VP Sales: Terry Tomasko
Estimated Sales: $2.5 - 5 Million
Number Employees: 20-49
Square Footage: 40000
Brands:
  Smart Chart

21605 Developak Corporation
2525 Pioneer Ave
Vista, CA 92081-8419
  760-598-7404
  Fax: 760-598-7402
Custom packaging machinery

President: Brian Pike
Executive VP: Annette Watson
Estimated Sales: Less than $500,000
Number Employees: 1-4
Square Footage: 4000

21606 Development Workshop Inc
555 W 25th St
Idaho Falls, ID 83402-4527

208-524-1550
Fax: 208-523-3148 800-657-5597
www.dwinc.org
Plastic trash liners and specialty and grain bags;
also, hand cleaners and wooden pallets
President: Dwight Whittaker
VP: Gerald Hodges
CFO: Bruce Cook
CEO: Michael O'Bleness
Mktg Mgr and Sales Mgr and Pub Relns Mgr: Gregg
Katainen
Operations Mgr: Mike O'Bleness
Prodn Mgr: Joe Hodge
VP Operations: Gerry Hodges
VP Upper Valley Industries: Rose Murphy
Estimated Sales: $2.5-5 Million
Number Employees: 250-499

21607 Deville Technologies
8515 Bourassa West
St Laurent, QC 4Y5 1P7
Canada

514-366-4545
Fax: 514-366-9606 866-404-4545
info@devilletechnologies.com
www.devilletechnologies.com
Manufacturers of high capacity food reduction
equipment such as shredders, graters, dicers, strip
cutters
President: Angelo Penta
Marketing: Lou Penta
Sales: Terry Baggott
Number Employees: 15

21608 Dewatering Equipment Company
6002 SW Texas Court
Portland, OR 97219-1175

503-246-8899
Fax: 503-248-7016 800-426-1723
Number Employees: 4

21609 Dewey & Wilson Displays
5635 Bancroft Avenue
Lincoln, NE 68506-4517

402-489-0868
Advertising signs, posters and emblems
President: Lynn Wilson
Estimated Sales: $500,000-$1 Million
Number Employees: 1-4

21610 (HQ)Dewied International Inc
5010 Interstate 10 E
San Antonio, TX 78219-3352

210-661-6161
Fax: 210-662-6112 800-992-5600
www.dewied.com
Natural and synthetic sausage casings specializing in
hog, sheep and beef casings
President: Phil Bohlender
philb@dewiedint.com
VP Sales: George Burt
Estimated Sales: $10-20 Million
Number Employees: 50-99
Brands:
Dewied

21611 Dex-O-Tex Crossfield Products Corporation
3000 E Harcourt St
Compton, CA 90221-5589

310-886-9100
Fax: 310-886-9119 jodih@cpcmail.net
www.crossfieldproducts.com
Seamless sanitary flooring
President/CEO: Bradford Watt
CFO: David Johnson
Marketing Director: Jodi Hood
Estimated Sales: $30 Million
Number Employees: 100-249
Number of Brands: 3
Number of Products: 25

21612 Dexter Laundry Inc
2211 W Grimes Ave
Fairfield, IA 52556

641-472-5131
800-524-2954
www.dexter.com
Laundry machines.
President: Craig Kirchner
Year Founded: 1894
Estimated Sales: $100-500 Million
Number Employees: 100-249

21613 Dexter Russell Inc
44 River St
Southbridge, MA 01550-1834

508-765-0201
Fax: 508-764-2897 800-343-6042
sales@dexter1818.com www.dexter1818.com
Manufacturer and exporter of knives, turners and
spatulas
President: Alan Peppel
apeppel@dexter1818.com
Sales: Kevin Clark
Estimated Sales: $10 - 20 Million
Number Employees: 250-499
Brands:
Connoisseur
Dexter Russell
Russell Green River
Russell International
Sani-Safe
Sofgrip

21614 Di Engineering
1658 Cole Blvd # 290
Lakewood, CO 80401-3304

303-235-0050
Fax: 303-231-0050 www.diec-group.com
Export and import of cans and end making machin-
ery, fill line equipment, spare parts, and associated
technologies, equipment sales and service
VP: Patty Locke
Estimated Sales: $2.5-5 Million
Number Employees: 1-4

21615 Diablo Chemical
216 Court Dale Ave
Kingston, PA 18704

Fax: 570-288-1227 800-548-1384
diablochemicalco@aol.com
Manufacturer and exporter of soaps, detergent and
oven cleaners
President: Ernest Clamar

VP, Sales & Marketing: E.J. Clamar

Estimated Sales: $2.8 Million
Number Employees: 1-4
Brands:
Diablo

21616 Diablo Valley Packaging
2373 N Watney Way
Fairfield, CA 94533-6746

707-422-4300
Fax: 707-422-4545
Wine industry bottles and packaging
Owner: Jeffrey Jones
jeffj@dvpackaging.com
VP: William Bronson
Estimated Sales: $25 Million
Number Employees: 20-49

21617 Dial Corporation
19001 N Scottsdale Rd
Scottsdale, AZ 85255

480-754-3425
Fax: 480-754-1098 www.henkelna.com
Cleaning products including bath and liquid soaps,
floor polish and detergents
President: Jeffery C, Piccolomini
Corporate SVP: Alan Syzdek
Senior VP Research & Development: Richard
Theiler
Senior VP Sales: Tracy VanBibber
Number Employees: 775
Parent Co: Henkel KGaA
Brands:
Armour Star Canned Foods

21618 Diamond & Lappin
20-21 Wagaraw Road
Bldg 30a
Fair Lawn, NJ 07410-1322

973-636-9550
Fax: 973-636-9590 877-527-7461
Consultant specializing in private label designing in-
cluding photography, pre-press and print, digital and
conventional production. Package design and manu-
facture, labeling
Estimated Sales: $1 - 5 Million
Number Employees: 5
Square Footage: 16000
Parent Co: Lappin Marketing Group

21619 Diamond Automation
23550 Haggerty Rd
Farmington Hills, MI 48335

248-426-9394
Fax: 248-476-0849 www.diamondsystems.com
Manufacturer and exporter of automated packaging
equipment; also, egg production and processing
equipment
President: Michel Defenbau
Estimated Sales: $20 - 50 Million
Number Employees: 1-4

21620 Diamond Chain
402 Kentucky Ave
Indianapolis, IN 46225-1174

317-635-8422
Fax: 317-633-2243 800-872-4246
custsvc@diamondchain.com
www.diamondchain.com
Manufacturer and exporter of transmission chains
and chain drives
President: Mike Fwiderski
VP Operations: Jerry Randich
CFO: Sheeley Faback
Quality Control: Joe Fossard
VP Sales/Marketing: Douglas Bademoch
Contact: Kristen Abbott
kabbott@diamondchain.com
VP Operations: Pat Taylor
Purchasing Manager: Barbara Heacock
Number Employees: 1-4
Parent Co: Amsted Industries

21621 Diamond Chemical & Supply Co
524 S Walnut St # B
Wilmington, DE 19801-5243

302-656-7786
Fax: 302-656-3039 800-355-7786
sales@diamondchemical.com
www.diamondchemical.com
Wholesaler/distributor of paper products, commer-
cial dishwashing and laundry chemicals, floor main-
tenance and janitorial equipment and insecticides
President: Susan Hartzel
susan@diamondchemical.com
CFO: Saeed Malik
VP: Richard Ventresca
Sales Manager: Gene Mirolli
Warehouse: Ryan Rynar
Estimated Sales: $5 Million
Number Employees: 20-49
Square Footage: 52000

21622 Diamond Chemical Co Inc
Union Ave & Dubois St
East Rutherford, NJ 7073

201-935-4300
Fax: 201-935-6997 800-654-7627
sales@diamondchem.com
www.diamondchem.com
Manufacturer and exporter of detergents and clean-
ers for meat and poultry plants; also, laundry deter-
gent and bleach
President: Harold Diamond
hdiamond@diamondchem.com
CFO: R Diamond
Estimated Sales: $20 - 50 Million
Number Employees: 100-249
Square Footage: 137000
Brands:
Diamond

21623 Diamond Electronics
2530 E Main St
Lancaster, OH 43130-8490

800-700-2791
Fax: 740-687-4201 800-443-6680
www.diamondpower.com

Closed circuit camera and discreet dome surveillance systems
Director Marketing: Pat Kula
Customer Service Manager: Lee Montgomery
Estimated Sales: $1 - 5 Million
Number Employees: 10-19

21624 Diamond Machining Technology
85 Hayes Memorial Dr # 1
Marlborough, MA 01752-1892
508-481-5944
Fax: 508-485-3924 800-666-4368
www.dmtsharp.com
Manufacturer and exporter of knife sharpeners
President: Christine Miller
Chairman: Elizabeth Powell
R&D: Stan Watson
Sales Manager: George Pettee
Manager: Kris Byron
dmtcustomercare@dmtsharp.com
Estimated Sales: $1 - 2.5 Million
Number Employees: 1-4
Square Footage: 40000
Brands:
Diamond

21625 (HQ)Diamond Packaging
111 Commerce Dr
Rochester, NY 14623-3503
585-334-8030
Fax: 585-334-9141 800-333-4079
sales@diamondpkg.com
www.diamondpackaging.com
Folding carton manufacturing and contract packaging services
President/Owner: Kirsten Werner
CEO/Owner: Karla Fichter
kfichter@diamondpkg.com
CFO: Keith Robinson
CEO: Karla Fichter
Research & Development: Dave Ziemba
Quality Control: Heidi Ingersol
Director of Marketing: Dennis Bacchetta
Director of Business Development: Sue Julien
Director of Business Development: Dave Semrau
Plant Manager: Dan Gurbacki
Estimated Sales: $20 - 50 Million
Number Employees: 100-249
Square Footage: 90000
Type of Packaging: Consumer, Private Label
Other Locations:
Diamond Packaging Company
Rochester NY

21626 Diamond Pheonix Corporation
P.O. Box 1608
Lewiston, ME 04241-1608
207-784-1381
Fax: 207-786-0271
President: E Strayhorn
CFO: Peter Pacetti
President, Chief Executive Officer: Tom Coyne
Director of Sales: Dennis Duell
Estimated Sales: $20 - 50 Million
Number Employees: 50-99

21627 Diamond Roll-Up Door
295 Commerce Way
Upper Sandusky, OH 43351-9079
419-294-3373
Fax: 419-294-3329
diamondinfo@australmonsoon.com
www.diamondrollupdoor.com
Tractor trailer and cargo van roll-up doors; industrial roll-up doors
President: Ray Vangunten
rvangunten@diamonddoor.com
Admin Manager: Sheri Gatchell
Estimated Sales: $10 - 20 000,000
Number Employees: 20-49

21628 Diamond Sign Co
2950 Airway Ave # D9
Costa Mesa, CA 92626-6002
714-545-1440
Fax: 714-545-1449 diamondsignco@aol.com
Flags, pennants, banners, signs, displays and exhibits; screen printing service available
Owner: John Kasell
diamondsignco@aol.com
Partner: Nancy Gill
Estimated Sales: Less Than $500,000
Number Employees: 1-4
Square Footage: 3000

21629 Diamond Water Conditioning
PO Box 39
Hortonville, WI 54944-0039
920-779-9940
Fax: 920-779-9950 800-236-8931
info@diamondh2o.com www.diamondh2o.com
Water treatment and purification systems including filters, softeners, etc
President: Tom Griesbach
Sales Commercial/Industrial: Bill Calabria
Estimated Sales: Below $5 Million
Number Employees: 10
Square Footage: 20000

21630 Diamond Wipes Intl Inc
4651 Schaefer Ave
Chino, CA 91710-5542
909-230-9888
Fax: 909-230-9885 800-454-1077
info@diamondwipes.com
www.diamondwipes.com
Manufacturer and exporter of pre-moistened paper towels
Founder, Owner & President: Eve Yen
eyen@diamondwipes.com
R&D: Map Taing
Quality Control: Anthony Castro
Marketing: Anthony Reyes
Estimated Sales: $5 - 10 Million
Number Employees: 50-99
Square Footage: 15000
Brands:
Diamond Wipes
La Fresh
With Our Compliment

21631 Diazteca Inc
993 E Frontage Rd
Rio Rico, AZ 85648-6234
520-761-4621
Fax: 520-281-1024 www.diazteca.com
Processor and distributor of Mexican fresh mangos, fresh hot peppers, granulated cane sugar, refrigerated and frozen lean beef, frozen shrimp, frozen IQF fruits and vegetables, aseptic fruit purees and other food products.
Owner/President: Ismael Diaz
Vice President: Roderigo Diaz
Estimated Sales: Less Than $500,000
Number Employees: 5-9
Type of Packaging: Consumer, Private Label, Bulk

21632 Dibpack USA
196 Coolidge Avenue
Englewood, NJ 07631-4522
201-871-8787
Fax: 201-871-8908 800-990-3424
Packaging, graphic and printing services
President: Ira Dermanski
CEO: Peter Quercia
CFO: Ira Dermanski
Number Employees: 20

21633 Dickey Manufacturing Company
3632 Stem Avenue
St Charles, IL 60174
630-584-2918
Fax: 630-584-0261 info@securityseals.com
www.securityseals.com
Manufacturer and exporter of security and tamper proof seals for containers, rail cars, trucks, etc.; also, locking devices
Manager: Terry Mauger
Sales: Dan Bemis
General Manager: Terry Mauger
Estimated Sales: Below $5,000,000
Number Employees: 20-49
Square Footage: 80000

21634 Dicks Packing Plant
7745 State Route 37 E
New Lexington, OH 43764-9512
740-342-4150
Fresh meats
Owner: Dick Knipe
regina_knipe@yahoo.com
Partner: Blanche Knipe
Partner: Rex Knipe
Estimated Sales: $320,000
Number Employees: 5-9
Square Footage: 11865
Type of Packaging: Consumer, Food Service, Bulk

21635 Dickson
930 S Westwood Ave
Addison, IL 60101-4917
630-543-3747
Fax: 630-543-0498 800-757-3747
dicksoncsr@dicksondata.com
www.dicksondata.com
High temperature stainless steel data loggers for tracking, sterilization, pasteurization, autoclave and oven temperatures
President: Michael Unger
CFO: Mike Kohlmeier
Quality Control: Dan Gawel
Contact: Eugene Deleplanque
edeleplanque@dickson-constant.com
Estimated Sales: Below $5 Million
Number Employees: 50-99

21636 Dickson Company
930 S Westwood Ave
Addison, IL 60101-4917
630-543-3747
Fax: 630-543-0498 800-757-3747
dicksoncsr@dicksondata.com
www.dicksondata.com
Data loggers, chart recorders and indicators.
President: Michael Unger
Marketing: Kathy Donovan
Contact: Eugene Deleplanque
edeleplanque@dickson-constant.com
Estimated Sales: $5 - 10 Million
Number Employees: 50-99

21637 Die Cut Specialties Inc
12543 Rhode Island Ave
Savage, MN 55378-1136
952-890-7590
Fax: 952-890-7590
Manufacturer and exporter of packaging materials and bulk boxes for sugar, cocoa etc
President: Robert Jones
Plant Manager: Mike Jones
Estimated Sales: $500,000-$1 Million
Number Employees: 10-19
Square Footage: 20000
Type of Packaging: Bulk

21638 Diebel Manufacturing Company
6505 Oakton Street
Morton Grove, IL 60053-2736
847-967-5678
Fax: 847-967-0655 jeffs@diebel.com
www.diebel.com
President and CEO: Richard H Schaefer Sr
Chief Executive Officer: Mike Chester
Quality Control: Victor Rivera
Contact: Jeffrey Schaefer
jschaefer@diebel.com
Estimated Sales: $10 - 20 Million
Number Employees: 40

21639 Diebolt & Co
100 Halls Rd
Old Lyme, CT 06371-1456
860-434-2222
Fax: 860-434-0370 800-343-2658
sales@dieboltco.com www.heatedhose.com
Steam transfer and Teflon hoses for filtering cooking oil
President: Mark Diebolt
mdiebolt@diebold.com
Sales Manager: Terrence Murphy
Estimated Sales: Below $5,000,000
Number Employees: 5-9
Brands:
Electroflo
Kleenflo
Steamflo

21640 Diehl Food Ingredients
136 Fox Run Dr
Defiance, OH 43512
419-782-5010
Fax: 419-783-4319 800-251-3033
Lactose free beverages, powdered fat, coffee creamers and whip topping bases.
President: Charles Nicolais
CFO: Darren Lane
CEO: Peter Diehl
Research & Development: Joan Hasselman
Quality Control: Kelly Roach
Marketing Director: Dennis Reid
Sales Director: Jim Holdrieth

Number Employees: 100-249
Parent Co: Diehl
Type of Packaging: Consumer, Food Service, Bulk
Brands:
Chocomite
Vitamite

21641 Diequa Inc
180 Covington Dr
Bloomingdale, IL 60108-3105

630-980-1133
Fax: 630-980-1232 info@diequa.com
www.diequa.com
Power transmission and drive components
President: Michael Quaas
mquaas@diequa.com
Estimated Sales: $10-20 000,000
Number Employees: 20-49

21642 Diequa Inc
180 Covington Dr
Bloomingdale, IL 60108-3105

630-980-1133
Fax: 630-980-1232 800-480-1095
info@diequa.com www.diequa.com
President: Michael Quaas
mquaas@diequa.com
CFO: Norman Quaas
Marketing Coordinator: Jeff Gibbons
Inside Sales Manager: Jeff White
Motion Products Manager: Tom Kahn
Number Employees: 20-49

21643 Dietzco
6 Bigelow St
Hudson, MA 01749-2697

508-481-4000
Fax: 508-481-4004 www.entwistleco.com
Spiral winding equipment for production of composite, paper and fiber cans; exporter of paper converting equipment
President: H Corkin
CEO: V Robinson
VP: R J Heidel
Estimated Sales: $20,000,000 - $49,999,999
Number Employees: 100-249
Square Footage: 200000
Parent Co: Entwistle Company

21644 Digatex
4301 Westbank Drive
Suite B
Austin, TX 78746-4400

512-346-8090
Fax: 512-328-3556 800-285-1636
sales@digatex.com www.digatex.com
Complete route accounting software solutions for Direct Store Distribution companies. Includes accounting routing, production, sales, inventory and more!
Estimated Sales: $2.5-5 Million
Number Employees: 10-19

21645 Digital Design
67 Sand Park Rd
Cedar Grove, NJ 07009-1281

973-857-0900
Fax: 973-857-9375 800-469-2205
edg@ddiworldwide.com
Marking devices
Manager: Richard Coventryu
Manager: Michael Liddawi
mike@ddiworldwide.com
Estimated Sales: $5-10 000,000
Number Employees: 20-49

21646 Digital Dining
7370 Steel Mill Dr
Springfield, VA 22150-3600

703-912-3000
Fax: 703-912-4305
Point of sale software
Owner: Carol Boden
carol.boden@menusoft.com
Estimated Sales: $5-10 Million
Number Employees: 5-9
Brands:
Digital Dining

21647 Digital Dynamics Inc
5 Victor Sq
Scotts Valley, CA 95066-3531

831-438-4444
Fax: 831-438-6825 800-765-1288
sales@digitaldynamics.com
www.digitaldynamics.com
Wash down safe industrial computers, and computer work stations
President: James B Jerde
jjerde@digitaldynamics.com
Vice President Engineering: Craig Nelson
Sales Manager: Steve Wait
Estimated Sales: $5 - 10 Million
Number Employees: 20-49
Number of Brands: 4
Square Footage: 200000

21648 Digital Image & Sound Corporation
11 Denonville Rdge
Rochester, NY 14625

585-381-0410
Fax: 585-381-0428 jfroom@aol.com
Computer hardware, software and systems for dairy and food processors; also, package design consultant
President: James Froom
Treasurer: Kathryn Froom
Sales Manager: Chris Ince
Contact: Jim Froom
jfroom@aol.com
Estimated Sales: Less than $500,000

21649 Dilley Manufacturing Co
215 E 3rd St
Des Moines, IA 50309-2095

515-288-7289
Fax: 515-288-4210 800-247-5087
www.dilleymfg.com
Menu covers
President: David Dilley
CEO: Robert Dilley
kflagg@dilleymfg.com
Estimated Sales: $5-10 Million
Number Employees: 10-19

21650 Dillin Automation Systems Corp
8030 Broadstone Rd
Perrysburg, OH 43551-4856

419-666-6789
Fax: 419-666-4020 www.dillinautomation.com
Accumulators and conveyor systems; merge, divert, elevate and orientation equipment; caselifts; gripper lifts; air conveyor and accumulation
President: David Smith
david.smith@dillinautomation.com
Estimated Sales: $10-20,000,000
Number Employees: 50-99
Square Footage: 80000
Brands:
Air Deck
Over-The-Top
Roe-Lift

21651 Dillin Automation Systems Corp
8030 Broadstone Rd
Perrysburg, OH 43551-4856

419-666-6789
Fax: 419-666-4020 www.dillinautomation.com
Engineered conveyor systems, vertical accumulators, case lifts and compression belts
President: David Smith
david.smith@dillinautomation.com
Estimated Sales: $10-20 Million
Number Employees: 50-99

21652 Dillons Food Stores
2700 E 4th Ave
Hutchinson, KS 67501-1903

620-665-5511
Fax: 620-669-3167 www.dillons.com
Supermarket chain
President: Colleen Juergensen
colleen.juergensen@kroger.com
Plant Manager: Albert Garcia
Number Employees: 100-249
Parent Co: Kroger

21653 Dimension Graphics Inc
800 Burton St SE
Grand Rapids, MI 49507-3320

616-245-1447
Fax: 616-245-2899 855-476-1281
dime@dimensiongraphics.com
www.dimensiongraphics.com
Advertising signs including banners, point of purchase and silk-screened
President: Ken Blessing
dime@dimensiongraphics.com
Estimated Sales: $500,000 - $1 Million
Number Employees: 5-9

21654 Dimensional Insight
111 S Bedford St
Burlington, MA 01803-6807

781-229-9111
Fax: 781-229-9113 info@dimins.com
Integrated data visualization, analysis and reporting solution that delivers information with unparalleled speed and simplicity
President: Frederick A Powers
CEO: Nancy Berkowitz
nberkowitz@dimins.com
CFO: Cathy Sweet
R&D: Stan Zanarotti
Estimated Sales: $10 - 20 000,000
Number Employees: 20-49

21655 Dimplex Thermal Solutions
2625 Emerald Dr
Kalamazoo, MI 49001-4542

269-349-6800
Fax: 269-349-8951 bbutch@dimplexthermal.com
www.dimplexthermal.com
Supplier of cooling solutions
President: Steve Cummings
scummings@dimplexthermal.com
National Sales Manager: William Butch
Director of Operations: Mark Siegfried
Estimated Sales: $34 Million
Number Employees: 100-249

21656 Dinex International
4711 E. Hefner Rd
Oklahoma City, OK 73131

800-872-4701
Fax: 405-475-5600 800-654-8210
customerservice@carlislefsp.com www.dinex.com
CEO: Kick Dzuvin
Chairman of the Board: Barry Taintor
VP: Jacqueline Gustafson
Quality Control: Marc Ginnett
Estimated Sales: $3 - 5 Million
Number Employees: 50-99

21657 Dings Co Magnetic Group
4740 W Electric Ave
Milwaukee, WI 53219-1626

414-672-7830
Fax: 414-672-5354 magnets@dingsco.com
www.dingsmagnets.com
Manufacturer and exporter of magnetic separators for the removal of ferrous metal contaminants from free-flowing powders and granular materials
President: Harold Bolstad
CEO: Brian Nahey
Manager: Gene Poker
Estimated Sales: $10-20 Million
Number Employees: 50-99

21658 Dinosaur Plastics
2815 Gulf Fwy
Houston, TX 77003

713-923-2278
Fax: 713-923-4454
Plastic signs, name badges and buttons, T-shirts, multi-color counter cards, window posters, pennants, banners, promotional products and give-aways; also, letters including plastic, metal and zip change
Owner: Jinny Stephens
Marketing: Chris Conrad
Estimated Sales: Less than $500,000
Number Employees: 5-9
Square Footage: 6000
Brands:
Gemini
Wagner

21659 Dinovo Produce Company
135 Wilson Street
Newark, OH 43055-4921
740-345-4025
Fax: 740-349-7276
Fruit and vegetables
President: Mark Dinovo
Estimated Sales: $2.5 - 5 000,000
Number Employees: 4
Type of Packaging: Private Label, Bulk

21660 Dipix Technologies
1051 Baxter Road
Ottawa, ON K2C 3P2
Canada
613-596-4942
Fax: 613-249-7341 info@dipix.com
www.dipix.com
Manufacturer and exporter of two dimensional and
three dimensional vision inspection systems for the
detection of defects in the color, size and shape of
baked goods
President: Anton Kitai
Chairman And Acting CEO: Don Gibbs
VP Engineering: Andy Peters
VP Marketing/Sales: John Lawrence
Director of Sales: Geoff Evans
Chief Operating Officer: Peter Wakeman
Square Footage: 60000
Brands:
Dipix Vision Inspection Systems

21661 Dipwell Co
106 Industrial Dr
Northampton, MA 01060-2327
413-587-4673
Fax: 413-587-4609 rinse@dipwell.com
www.dipwell.com
Manufacturer and exporter of food processing
equipment including creamery, ice cream, mashed
potatoes, butter, sour cream, cole slaw and peas;
also, stainless steel running water wells to keep
scoops sanitary
Owner: Tom Baird
rinse@dipwell.com
President: Lynn Perry-Alstadt
VP: Fred Perry, Jr.
Estimated Sales: Less Than $500,000
Number Employees: 1-4
Square Footage: 5000
Type of Packaging: Food Service
Brands:
Collar-Dip
Dipwell

21662 Direct Fire Technical
45 Bounty Road W
Benbrook, TX 76132-1043
817-568-8778
Fax: 817-568-8784 888-920-2468
Manufacturer and exporter of industrial hot water
heaters and steam generators
President: J Baker
VP: Jack Nichols
Estimated Sales: $1-2,500,000
Number Employees: 20-49
Brands:
Dft Series
Direct Fire Technical, Inc.

21663 Direct South
P.O. Box 2445
Macon, GA 31203-2445
478-746-3518
Fax: 478-745-5668
Food service equipment
Chairman of the Board: Danny Truelove
danny.truelove@directsouth.com
Estimated Sales: $5-10 Million
Number Employees: 20-49

21664 Dirt Killer Pressure Washer
1708 Whitehead Rd # 103
Gwynn Oak, MD 21207-4021
410-944-9966
Fax: 410-944-8866 800-544-1188
info@dirtkiller.com www.dirtkiller.com
Manufacturer and wholesaler/distributor of pressure
washers, accessories and cleaning soaps
President: Jeffrey Paulding
jpaulding@dirtkiller.com
Sales Director: Ken Rankin

Estimated Sales: $3 - 5 Million
Number Employees: 5-9
Square Footage: 60000
Brands:
China-Brite
Dirt Killer
Kranzle

21665 Discovery Chemical
2141 Carlyle Drive
Marietta, GA 30062-5836
770-973-5661
800-973-9881
Wastewater treatment chemicals, sanitizers, insecticides, degreasers, etc
Estimated Sales: $2.5-5,000,000
Number Employees: 2

21666 Discovery Products Corporation
13619 Mukilteo Speedway # 1180
Lynnwood, WA 98087-1626
425-267-9577
Fax: 425-267-9156
President: Dennis A Clark
Vice President of Sales and Marketing: David Muir
Estimated Sales: $300,000-500,000
Number Employees: 1-4

21667 Diskey Architectural Signs
450 E Brackenridge St
Fort Wayne, IN 46802-3521
260-424-0233
Fax: 260-424-0668 Orders@DiskeySign.com
www.diskeysign.com
Interior and exterior signs
Owner: Stacie Breen
sbreen@diskeysign.com
Estimated Sales: $1 - 3 Million
Number Employees: 10-19

21668 Dispensa-Matic Label Dispense
28220 Playmor Beach Road
Rocky Mount, MO 65072
573-392-7684
Fax: 573-392-1757 800-325-7303
info@dispensamatic.com www.dispensamatic.com
Pressure sensitive label dispensers for roll labels and
computer printouts
President: David Pocost
Marketing: Richard Shannon II
Sales Manager: Rich Laycob
Contact: Richard Shannon
richard@dispensamatic.com
Estimated Sales: $5 - 10 Million
Number Employees: 1-4
Parent Co: Commercial Mailing Accessories

21669 Dispense Rite
2205 Carlson Dr
Northbrook, IL 60062
847-753-9595
Fax: 847-753-9648 800-772-2877
sales@dispense-rite.com www.dispense-rite.com
Dispensing equipment for the foodservice industry
President: Robert Gapp
R&D: Robert Riley
Quality Control: Don Hitchcock
VP Marketing/Sales: Ronald Klein
Contact: Donald Hitchcock
dhitchcock@dispense-rite.com
Plant Manager: Don Hitchcock
Purchasing Agent: Robert Gapp
Estimated Sales: $3 - 5,000,000
Number Employees: 20-49
Number of Brands: 1
Number of Products: 250
Parent Co: Diversified Metal Products
Brands:
Dispense Rite

21670 Display Concepts
Rr 3
Trenton, ME 04605
207-667-3386
Fax: 207-667-4103 800-446-0033
Store decor letters and signs including neon; also,
aisle markers, trim and graphics
President: S Shelton
CEO: K Shelton
Number Employees: 20-49
Square Footage: 120000
Brands:
Iridescents
Neoneon

21671 Display Craft Mfg Co
3939 Washington Blvd
Halethorpe, MD 21227-4185
410-242-0400
Fax: 410-242-0475 sales@displaycraft.com
www.displaycraftmfg.com
Store fixtures
CEO: Ronald Weitzmann
ron@storesbydc.com
CEO: Ronald Weitzman
Estimated Sales: $5-10 Million
Number Employees: 50-99

21672 Display Creations
PO Box 70449
Brooklyn, NY 11207-0449
718-257-2300
Fax: 718-257-2558 ron@displaycreations.com
Manfacturer of lucite displays, store fixtures and
point of purchase displays
President: Ronald Newman
Sales Director: Michael Mathless
Purchasing Manager: Jeffry Baum
Estimated Sales: $5-10 Million
Number Employees: 50-99
Square Footage: 320000

21673 Display One
621 N Wacker Dr
Hartford, WI 53027-1001
262-673-5880
Fax: 262-670-2008 info@menasha.com
www.menasha.com
Corrugated boxes and containers including shipping
and display
CFO: Arthur Huge
President, Chief Executive Officer: James Kotek
Vice President of Corporate Development: Evan
Pritz
Sales Manager: Mike Waite
Estimated Sales: $20 - 50 Million
Number Employees: 100-249
Parent Co: Menasha Corporation

21674 Display Pack Inc
1340 Monroe Ave NW # 1
Grand Rapids, MI 49505-4604
616-451-3061
Fax: 616-451-8907 info@displaypack.com
Contract packaging and materials, vacuum and
thermoformed plastics,printed packaging and
phone-card packaging
President: Roger Hansen
CEO: Victor Hansen
vhansen@displaypack.com
Estimated Sales: $20-50 Million
Number Employees: 250-499
Square Footage: 400000
Type of Packaging: Private Label, Bulk

21675 Display Studios Inc
5420 Kansas Ave
Kansas City, KS 66106-1143
913-754-8900
Fax: 913-754-8901 800-648-8479
www.displaystudios.com
Manufacturer and exporter of displays and exhibits
President: John Mc Coy
jmccoy@displaystudios.com
Estimated Sales: $2.5 - 5 Million
Number Employees: 20-49

21676 Display Technologies
11101 14th Ave
College Point, NY 11356-1405
914-699-2666
Fax: 718-939-4034
info@display-technologies.com
www.display-technologies.com
Computer display, monitors and systems
President: Glenn Affonso
gaffonso@display-technologies.com
CFO: Leslie Tannenbaum
Estimated Sales: $30 - 50 Million
Number Employees: 50-99

21677 Display Tray
5475 Royalmount Avenue
Mont-Royal, QC H4P 1J3
Canada
514-735-2988
Fax: 514-735-8933 800-782-8861
displaytray@hotmail.com

Manufacturer and exporter of high impact styrene food display and market trays; also, plastic proof and bagel boards
President: Gail Cantor
CEO: Simy Oliel
Sales: Yoel Acoca
Number Employees: 4
Square Footage: 8000

21678 Dispoz-O Plastics
3736 Abercrombie Rd
Fountain Inn, SC 29644

864-862-4004
Fax: 864-862-4511 pgehrels@dispozo.com
www.dispozo.com
Plastic cutlery
President: Joseph D Lancia
CFO: Todd Linecerger
Estimated Sales: $75 - 100 Million
Number Employees: 500-999

21679 Distaview Corp
121 W Wooster St # 201
Bowling Green, OH 43402-2920

419-353-6080
Fax: 419-353-6080 800-795-9970
sales@distaview.com
Manufacturer and exporter of liquid and material process controllers
President: Rick Kramer
rkramer@distaview.com
Estimated Sales: Less Than $500,000
Number Employees: 5-9
Square Footage: 27200
Brands:
2point
Levelair
Liquavision
Twoview
Vacview

21680 Distillata
1608 E 24th Street
Cleveland, OH 44114

800-999-2906
www.distillata.com
Bottler of spring and distilled water, as well as water filtration systems, water coolers, water fountains, and pool filling services.
Owner: Kevin Schroeder
Head of Sales: Adam Schroeder
Operations Manager: Heather Schroeder
Estimated Sales: $10-20 Million
Number Employees: 100-249
Type of Packaging: Consumer, Food Service, Private Label, Bulk
Brands:
Distillata

21681 Distinctive Embedments
110 Kenyon Ave
Pawtucket, RI 2861

401-729-0770
Fax: 401-729-0772
Advertising novelites including key tags and paper weights
President: Mario Carosi
General Manager: Mario Carosi
Estimated Sales: $10 - 20 Million
Number Employees: 20 to 49

21682 Distributed Robotics
172 Lockrow Rd
Troy, NY 12180-9622

518-279-3419
Fax: 518-279-3611
derbys@distributedrobotics.com
www.distributedrobotics.com
President: Steven Derby
Contact: Stephen Derby
sderby1@gmail.com
Estimated Sales: Below $5 Million
Number Employees: 5-9

21683 Distribution Results
900 Moe Dr
Akron, OH 44310-2519

330-633-0727
Fax: 330-633-0728 800-737-9671
sales@icsponge.com www.icsponge.com
Manufacturer, importer and exporter of cellulose sponges for the bakery, dairy and candy industries

Owner: Larry Rowlands
VP: Larry Rowlands
Research & Development: Jeff Shaffer
Quality Control: Carol Schaffer
Sales: Sherwood Shoemaker
Contact: Dotty Barrett
dotty@icsponge.com
Operations: Dotty Barrott
Estimated Sales: $1 Million
Number Employees: 10-19
Square Footage: 60000
Parent Co: Distribution Results

21684 Dito Dean Food Prep
10200 David Taylor Drive
Charlotte, NC 28262

916-652-5824
Fax: 704-547-7401 866-449-4200
dito-foodservice@electrolux.com
professional.electroluxusa.com
Manufacturer and exporter of blenders, cheese shredding and cubing equipment, cutters, slicers, food and vegetable processors, salad dryers and verticle cutters and mixers
President: Gary Probert
Estimated Sales: $1-2.5 Million
Number Employees: 5-9
Parent Co: WCI
Type of Packaging: Food Service

21685 Ditting USA
1000 Air Way
Glendale, CA 91201-3030

818-247-9479
Fax: 818-247-9722 800-835-5992
info@ditting.com www.ditting.com
Manufacturer, importer and exporter of commercial coffee grinders
President: Albert Bezjian
nancy@ditting.com
CEO: Nancy Wideman
CFO: Mike Hatun
Estimated Sales: Below $5 Million
Number Employees: 5-9
Number of Brands: 1
Square Footage: 16000
Brands:
Ditting

21686 Divercon Inc
9684 N 109th Ave
Omaha, NE 68142-1124

402-571-5115
Fax: 402-571-1742 www.scottent.com
Consultant specializing in the design and engineering of food manufacturing, warehouse and distribution facilities
President: Scott Seaton
Executive VP: S Shain Humphrey
Vice President: Tim Wood
Estimated Sales: $5-10 Million
Number Employees: 5-9
Square Footage: 40000

21687 Diversified Capping Equipment
8030 Broadstone Road
Perrysburg, OH 43551-4856

419-666-2566
Fax: 419-666-0275
Manufacturer and exporter of closure application machines, cap sorters and cap conveying equipment
VP: Jack Weber
Engineering Manager: John Louy
Estimated Sales: $2.5-5 Million
Number Employees: 10-19
Square Footage: 128000
Brands:
Diversified (Dce)

21688 Diversified Label Images
136 Industrial Dr
Birmingham, AL 35211-4466

205-942-4791
Fax: 205-942-4896 800-777-4791
www.diversifiedlabel.com
Point of sale for beer, beverage and snack industry; also labels
President: Greg Boggis
gboggis@diversifiedlabel.com
Marketing Director: Jennifer Davis
Sales Director: Chad Johnson
Number Employees: 20-49

21689 Diversified Lighting Diffusers Inc
175-B Liberty St
Copiague, NY 11726

631-842-0099
Fax: 631-980-7668 800-234-5464
info@receilit.com www.1800ceiling.com
Manufacturer and distributor of fluorescent safety sleeves and vapor-tight lenses; also, custom fabrication of acrylic and lexan diffusers
CEO: Joe Broser
COO: Colleen Baum
Estimated Sales: $1 - 3 Million
Number Employees: 5-9
Square Footage: 100000

21690 Diversified Metal Engineering
54 Hilstrom Ave.
PO Box 553
Charlottetown, PE C1E 2C6
Canada

902-628-6900
Fax: 902-628-1313
Manufacturer and exporter of washers, cookers, conveyors, graders and coolers for fish; also, brewery and dairy tanks, potato and vegetable shapers, turnkey microbrewery systems, portion packing equipment and piping systems andconveyors for dairy products, pressure vessels, complete skid systems and tanks.
President: Peter Toombs
VP Marketing/Sales: Barry MacLeod
Marketing Director: Kelly Lantz
Director of Sales and Marketing: David Campbell
Production Manager: Blair MacKinnon
Purchasing Manager: Ralph MacDonald
Estimated Sales: $7 Million
Number Employees: 50-99
Square Footage: 80000
Brands:
Dme

21691 Diversified Metal Manufacturing
2661 Alvarado St
San Leandro, CA 94577-4304

510-667-9900
Fax: 510-667-9700
Tea and coffee industry carts
Owner: Shawn O'Leary
Estimated Sales: Less than $500,000
Number Employees: 1-4

21692 Diversified Metal Products Inc
2205 Carlson Dr
Northbrook, IL 60062-6705

847-753-9595
Fax: 847-753-9648 800-772-2877
sales@dispense-rite.com www.dispense-rite.com
Dispensing equipment for the foodservice industry
President: Robert Gapp
rgapp@dispense-rite.com
CFO: Paul Gapp
R&D: Robert Riley
Quality Control: Don Hitchcock
Marketing Director: Ronald Klein
Sales Administration Manager: Ronald Klein
Plant Manager: Don Hitchcock
Purchasing Manager: Robert Gapp
Estimated Sales: $3 - 5 Million
Number Employees: 20-49
Number of Brands: 3
Number of Products: 350
Square Footage: 60000
Brands:
Dispense-Rite

21693 Diversified Panel Systems
2345 Statham Blvd
Oxnard, CA 93033-3911

805-487-9241
Fax: 805-988-4630
President: Richard C Bell
rich@dpspanels.com
Estimated Sales: $1 - 3 Million
Number Employees: 10-19

21694 Diversified Plastics Corp
120 W Mount Vernon St
Nixa, MO 65714-7827

417-725-2622
Fax: 417-725-5925 sales@dpcap.com
www.dpcap.com
Custom molded polystyrene packaging materials, plastic molding and foam fabricating

President: Justin Carter
jcarter@divplast.com
Quality Control: Shane Boston
Estimated Sales: $20-50 Million
Number Employees: 250-499

21695 Diversified Products

1460 Kings Wood Lane
Eagan, MN 55122

651-269-9091
Fax: 651-454-8079 800-942-2282
www.divprod.com
Wine industry packaging
President: James Crea
Contact: Jeff Knight
jeff@select-a-vision.com
Estimated Sales: $500,000-$1 Million
Number Employees: 1-4

21696 Diversiplast Products

7425 Laurel Ave
Minneapolis, MN 55426-1501

763-540-9700
Fax: 763-540-9709 800-828-6114
www.diversiplast.com
Corrugated plastic sheets and containers
Manager: Lanny Jass
Estimated Sales: $2.5-5 000,000
Number Employees: 20-49

21697 Dividella

14501 58th Street North
Clearwater, FL 33760

727-532-6509
Fax: 727-532-6537 info@kmedipak.com
www.dividella.com
Carton packaging for vials, ampoules, cartridges, syringes, tablet blisters, blistercards, sachets and similar products and automatic tray and carton loading systems for vials
Contact: Christoph Hammer
c.hammer@dividella.ch
Estimated Sales: $1 - 5 Million

21698 Divine Menu Covers Ltd.

219 Norseman St
Etobicoke, ON M8Z 2R5
Canada

416-253-5849
866-706-6368
divinemenucovers.com
Manufacturer of custom menu covers.
Year Founded: 1953
Estimated Sales: $7 Million
Number Employees: 1-4

21699 Divis Laboratories

325 Columbia Tpk
3rd Fl Suite 305
Florham Park, NJ 07932

973-993-1060
Fax: 973-993-1070 www.divisnutraceuticals.com
Carotenoids and specialty vitamins
CEO: Murali Krishna Prasad Divi
Director of Research & Development: Gundu Rao Padakandla
Contact: Punna Aml
punnarao@divislaboratories.com
Head of Manufacturing: Madhusudana Rao Divi
Number Employees: 5000

21700 Dixie Canner Machine Shop

326 Commerce Blvd
Athens, GA 30606-0824

706-549-0592
Fax: 706-549-0137 sales@dixiecanner.com
www.dixiecanner.net
Manufacturer and exporter of low-volume canning equipment including seamers, retorts, exhausters and vacuum closers; also, blanchers, pulpers/finishers and lye peelers
President: B Gentry
Chairman: W Stapleton Sr
VP Manufacturing: J Campbell
VP Sales: Parrish Stapleton
Contact: Bill Gentry
bill@dixiecanner.com
Estimated Sales: $1-2.5 Million
Number Employees: 5-9
Square Footage: 24000
Brands:
  Dixie

21701 Dixie Flag Mfg Co

1930 N Interstate 35
San Antonio, TX 78208-1925

210-227-5039
Fax: 210-227-5920 800-356-4085
dixieflg@dixieflag.com www.dixieflag.com
Manufacturer and exporter of flags, street net banners and pennants
President: Henry P Van Deputte Jr
pete@dixieflag.com
VP: Sally Van de Putte
VP: Glenda Krueger
Estimated Sales: $5 - 10 Million
Number Employees: 20-49

21702 Dixie Graphics

636 Grassmere Park
Nashville, TN 37211-3697

615-832-7000
Fax: 615-832-7621 info@dixiegraphics.com
www.dixiegraphics.com
Rubber printing plates, photo engraving and color separations
President: J R Meadows
jmeadows@dixiegraphic.com
Estimated Sales: $10-20 000,000
Number Employees: 50-99

21703 Dixie Maid Ice Cream Company

206 E 2nd St
Deridder, LA 70634-5004

337-463-8835
Ice cream novelties
Owner: L C Kern
Estimated Sales: $5-10 Million
Number Employees: 7
Type of Packaging: Consumer

21704 Dixie Neon Company

3001 W Granada St
Tampa, FL 33629

813-248-2531
Fax: 813-247-6230
Signs including advertising, electric and plastic
Owner: Freddie Hevia Iii
Estimated Sales: $1-2.5 Million
Number Employees: 5-9

21705 Dixie Poly Packaging

916 Tanner Road
Greenville, SC 29607-6036

864-268-3751
Fax: 864-268-0511
Polyethylene poultry bags
Owner: Whit Jordan
Estimated Sales: $5-10 Million
Number Employees: 20-49

21706 Dixie Printing & Packaging

7354-58 Baltimore-Annapolis Blvd
Glen Burnie, MD 21061

410-766-1944
Fax: 410-761-4032 800-433-4943
www.primepkg.com
Folding paper boxes
Owner: A Newth Morris Iii
VP Sales: Bill Linchan
General Manager: Raymond Bedell
Estimated Sales: $15 - 20 Million
Number Employees: 100-249
Square Footage: 135000
Type of Packaging: Consumer, Food Service, Private Label

21707 Dixie Rubber Stamp & Seal Company

PO Box 54616
Atlanta, GA 30308-0616

404-875-8883
Fax: 404-872-3504 plates@dixieseal.com
Rubber stamps and ink products
President: Jack Anders
Plant Manager: Brad Grice
Estimated Sales: $10 - 20 Million
Number Employees: 80

21708 Dixie Search Associates

316 Audubon Place
Dauphin Island, AL 36528

770-675-7300
Fax: 770-850-9295 www.dixiesearch.com
Executive search agency specializing in supermarket, food sales/marketing, manufacturing and hospitality industries

President: Clifford G Fill
clifford.fill@dixiesearch.com
Senior VP: Ellyn Fill
Estimated Sales: $300,000-500,000
Number Employees: 10-19
Square Footage: 6000
Parent Co: Fill Corporation

21709 Dixie Signs Inc

2930 Drane Field Rd
Lakeland, FL 33811-1329

863-644-3521
Fax: 863-644-3524 www.dixiesignsinc.com
Interior and exterior signs and graphics
President: Roger Snyder
Estimated Sales: $2.5-5 Million
Number Employees: 20-49

21710 Dixon Lubricants & Specialty Pro Group

P.O. Box 144
Asbury, NJ 08802-0144

908-537-2155
Fax: 908-537-2908 sendinfo@asbury.com
www.asbury.com
Chief Executive Officer: Stephen Riddle
Vice President of Manufacturing: Gary Ziegler
Quality Manager: Ken Newton
Sales Manager: Debra Nowacki
Plant Manager: Michael Mares
Estimated Sales: $1 - 5 Million
Number Employees: 500-999

21711 Dize Co

1512 S Main St
Winston Salem, NC 27127-2707

336-722-5181
Fax: 336-761-1334 800-583-8243
Commercial awnings, tarps, window coverings, and food cart covers
President: Cr Skidmore
CFO: Mike Durr
Marketing/Sales: Carl Livengood
Operations Manager: Jim Shaver
Estimated Sales: Less Than $500,000
Number Employees: 1-4
Square Footage: 160000
Type of Packaging: Bulk

21712 Do-It Corp

1201 Blue Star Hwy
PO Box 592
South Haven, MI 49090-9784

269-639-2600
Fax: 269-637-7223 800-426-4822
sales@do-it.com www.do-it.com
Manufacturer, importer and exporter of self-adhesive plastic hangers and hang tabs; also, contract packaging available
President: Mark Mc Clendon
sales@do-it.com
Director Marketing: John Deschaine
VP Sales: Chuck Miller
Estimated Sales: $5-10 Million
Number Employees: 50-99
Square Footage: 80000
Brands:
  Do-It

21713 Dober Chemical Corporation

14461 S Waverly Ave
Midlothian, IL 60445

630-410-7300
Fax: 630-410-7444 800-323-4983
doberinfo@dober-group.com
Liquid and powdered soap; also, cleaning chemicals for metal finishing
President: John G Dobrez
CFO: Jim Harper
SVP: Scott Smith
VP Sales: Tom Blakmore
Contact: Scott Dobrez
sdobrez@dobergroup.com
Estimated Sales: $10-20 Million
Number Employees: 50-99

21714 Doering Co

6343 River Rd SE
Clear Lake, MN 55319-9611

320-743-2276
Fax: 320-743-3723 info@doering.com
www.doering.com

Stainless steel valves for high pressure directional control, manually operated stainless steel pumps for high pressure hydraulic service and manually activated hand wash water valves UHMW and stainless construction
President: Jon Boughner
 jonb@doering.com
Sales Director: Kris King
Estimated Sales: $3 - 5 Million
Number Employees: 10-19
Square Footage: 20000
Brands:
  Doering
  Water Miser

21715 Doering Machines Inc
2121 Newcomb Ave
San Francisco, CA 94124-1300
415-526-2131
 Fax: 415-526-2136 sales@doeringmachines.com
 www.doeringmachines.com
Manufacturer and exporter of pumping, extruding, portioning, metering, cartoning and wrapping systems for high viscosity products including dough, butter, cheese and polymers
President: Richard Doering
 richard.doering@doeringmachines.com
CEO: Tim Doering
Estimated Sales: $2.5-5 Million
Number Employees: 5-9
Square Footage: 60000

21716 Dolcera
155 Bovet Rd # 302
Real #305
San Mateo, CA 94402-3111
650-269-7952
 Fax: 866-690-7517 info@dolcera.com
Provides clients with the technical, intellectual property and business information they need to develop new products and ideas, and to understand the competitive landscape and market environment.
Chief Executive Officer: Samir Raiyani
 info@dolcera.com
Founder: Lakshmikant Goenka
Founder: Ed Rozenberg
Number Employees: 1-4

21717 Dolco Packaging Co
2110 Patterson St
Decatur, IN 46733-1892
260-728-2161
 Fax: 260-728-9958 www.tekni-plex.com
Manufacturer and exporter of polystyrene foam packaging
CEO: Steve Harvey
 steve.harvey@tekni-plex.com
Vice President: Norm Patterson
Quality Control: Doug Keller
Marketing Director: Phil Laughlin
Public Relations: Amy Geradoj
Production Manager: Jeff Brown
Plant Manager: Roger Lichtle
Purchasing Manager: Terry Alberson
Estimated Sales: $20-50 Million
Number Employees: 100-249
Parent Co: Tekni Plex
Type of Packaging: Food Service

21718 (HQ)Dole Refrigerating Co
1420 Higgs Rd
Lewisburg, TN 37091-4402
931-359-6211
 Fax: 931-359-8664 800-251-8990
 sales@doleref.com www.kencoplastics.com
Manufacturer and exporter of truck refrigeration units including eutectic plate and blower; also, quick freeze plates for food processing, double contact quick freezing freezers and fiberglass coolers
President: John Cook
 johnjr@doleref.com
CFO: Joe Mulliniks
Sales Manager: Bobby Dunnivant
Chief Engineer: Rod Hardy
Estimated Sales: $20 - 50 Million
Number Employees: 50-99
Square Footage: 55000
Brands:
  Cold-Cel
  Freze-Cel

21719 DomainMarket
9812 Falls Road Ste.
Suite 290
Potomac, MD 20854
973-366-7500
 Fax: 973-366-7453 888-694-6735
 contact@DomainMarket.com
Manufacturer and exporter of converting equipment for food packaging
CEO: John Wilkes
Estimated Sales: $10-20 Million
Number Employees: 50-99

21720 Dometic Mini Bar
P.O. Box 490
Elkhart, IN 46515-0490
574-294-2511
 Fax: 574-293-9686 800-301-8118
In-room refreshment products including honor bars, automated systems, carts, safes, etc
CEO: John Waters
National Sales Manager: Tyler Ellendorff
Contact: Bryan Bergin
 bryan.bergin@dometicusa.com
General Manager: Hans Disch
Estimated Sales: $10,000,000 - $19,999,999
Number Employees: 20-49
Parent Co: A.B. Electrolux

21721 Dominion Pallet Inc
9644 Cross County Rd
Mineral, VA 23117-2915
540-894-5401
 Fax: 540-894-0108 800-227-5321
 info@dominionpallet.com
 www.dominionpallet.com
Lift truck pallets
Owner: Dan Yancey
 dompal@aol.com
CFO: Bernon Aenos
Buyer (Lumber): Scott Walton
General Manager: Vernon Jones
Estimated Sales: $10 - 20 Million
Number Employees: 20-49

21722 Dominion Regala
4 Overlea Blvd
Toronto, ON M4H 1A4
Canada
416-752-9987
 Fax: 416-752-9986 866-423-4086
 info@dominionregalia.com
 www.dominionregalia.com
Patio umbrellas, flags, banners and continously printed ribbons
President: Ross Chafe
Quality Control: Summer Zurawski
Director Marketing: Connie Murphy
Number Employees: 10

21723 Domino Amjet Inc
1290 Lakeside Dr
Gurnee, IL 60031-2499
847-244-2501
 Fax: 847-244-1421 800-444-4512
 service@domino-na.com
 www.dominodigitalprinting.com
Digital printing solutions used for date coding, product markings, serialization and variable printing.
Estimated Sales: $39 Million
Number Employees: 1000-4999
Square Footage: 72000
Parent Co: Domino Printing Sciences PLC

21724 Don Lee
1114 W. Berks St.
Philadelphia, PA 19122-6090
760-745-0707
 Fax: 760-746-2856 connieberry@aol.com
 www.don-lee.com
Dough cutters and dividers.
President: Lee Berry
CFO: Kim Key
Vice President: Connie Berry
Number Employees: 20-49
Number of Products: 2
Square Footage: 20000
Type of Packaging: Private Label
Brands:
  Cloverleaf
  Roll Former/Divider

21725 Don Walters Company
11630 Western Ave
Stanton, CA 90680
714-892-0275
 Fax: 714-901-1852 donwaltersco@aol.com
 www.donwaltersinc.com
Wholesaler/distributor of restaurant equipment; also, design consulting available
President/CEO: Roger Criswell
CFO/VP: Mindy Criswell
Estimated Sales: $1-2,500,000
Number Employees: 5-9
Type of Packaging: Food Service

21726 Don's Prepared Foods
4461 Township Line Rd
Schwenksville, PA 19473
888-321-3667
 donspreparedfoods.com
Salads, gourmet cream cheese spreads, soups, dips, entrees and desserts.
President & CEO: Victor Skloff
Head of Marketing: Melanie Skloff
Region Sales Manager: Lisa Brauckmann
Year Founded: 1970
Estimated Sales: $5-25 Million
Number Employees: 51-200
Number of Brands: 3
Brands:
  Artisan Deli
  Don's Salads
  Melanie's Medleys

21727 (HQ)Donahower & Company
15615 S Keeler Ter
Olathe, KS 66062-3509
913-829-2650
 Fax: 913-829-5494
Manufacturer and exporter of conveyors including package handling, flat top chain and material handling; also, lidding and capping machinery and bottle rotators
President: Carol Brooks
Vice President: Ken Koelzer
Estimated Sales: $1-2.5 Million
Number Employees: 5-9
Square Footage: 10000

21728 Donalds & Associates
3900 Kilroy Airport Way # 190
Long Beach, CA 90806-6815
562-290-8440
 Fax: 562-438-2668
Consultant specializing in restaurant conceptualization
President: Steve Donalds

21729 Donaldson Co Inc
1400 W 94th St
Bloomington, MN 55431
952-887-3131
 www.donaldson.com
Manufacturer, importer and exporter of dust control and filtration equipment.
Chairman, President & CEO: Tod Carpenter
 tod.carpenter@donaldson.com
Senior VP & CFO: Scott Robinson
Year Founded: 1915
Estimated Sales: $2.85 Billion
Number Employees: 11,700
Brands:
  Dce Dalamatic
  Dce Siloair
  Dce Sintamatic
  Dce Unicell
  Dce Unimaster

21730 Dong Us I
2590 Main St
Irvine, CA 92614-6227
949-251-1768
 Fax: 949-251-8865 888-580-0088
 info@dongyu.us www.dongyu.us
Manufacturer and distributor of L-Carnitine products, amino acids, vitamins, sweeteners, sports nutrition ingredients, food and beverage ingredients
Manager: Weili Zhang
Number Employees: 10-19
Square Footage: 40000

21731 Donnelly Industries, Inc
557 Route 23 South
Wayne, NJ 07470
973-672-1800
Fax: 973-323-8699
www.donnellyconstruction.com
Wooden boxes
President: Gerard J Donnelly Jr
CEO: Rod Donnelly
VP: Christopher Powers
Estimated Sales: $1 - 2.5 Million
Number Employees: 5-9

21732 Donnick Label Systems
1450 Lane Ave N
Jacksonville, FL 32254
Fax: 904-786-7301 800-334-7849
Direct thermal scale and product labels, thermal
printers and ribbons
President: Jerry Smith
Owner: Anne Smith
ms@donnick.com
CFO: Anne Smith
Sales/Marketing: David Frederick
Estimated Sales: $.5 - 1 million
Number Employees: 5-9
Square Footage: 14000

21733 Donoco Industries
P.O. Box 3208
Huntington Beach, CA 92605
714-893-7889
Fax: 714-897-7968 888-822-8763
info@encoreplastics.com
www.encoreplastics.com
Manufacturer and exporter of plastic mugs and tum-
blers
President: Richard Harvey
Estimated Sales: $5 - 10 Million
Number Employees: 25
Brands:
Encore

21734 Dontech Industries Inc
76 Center Dr
Gilberts, IL 60136-9712
847-428-8222
Fax: 847-428-6855 rap@micropure.com
www.dontechindustriesinc.com
Ultraviolet disinfection systems for food processing,
sanitation, water and wastewater treatment
Owner: Bill Cataldo
w.cataldo@hotmail.com
Estimated Sales: $1-2.5 Million
Number Employees: 5-9

21735 Doosan Industrial Vehicle America Corp
2475 Mill Center Parkway
Suite 400
Buford, GA 30518
678-745-2200
Fax: 678-745-2250 www.doosanlift.com
Manufacturer, importer and exporter of industrial
trucks.
VP & CEO: Tony Jones
National Sales Director: Jeff Powell
Year Founded: 1962
Estimated Sales: $7 Billion
Number Employees: 7,728
Square Footage: 150000
Parent Co: Doosan Group

21736 Dorado Carton Company
Carr 693
Dorado, PR 00646-0546
787-796-1670
Fax: 787-796-2988
Paper, pizza and food service boxes, doilies, place
mats and shelf and wrapping paper; also, coated
stock available
President: Keneth Schulman
VP F.C. Meyer Division: Paul Robinson
Business Manager: Nazira Wightman
Number Employees: 16
Square Footage: 44000
Parent Co: Frank C. Meyer Company/Mafcote In-
dustries

21737 Doran Scales Inc
1315 Paramount Pkwy
Batavia, IL 60510-1460
630-879-1200
Fax: 630-879-0073 800-365-0084
sales@doranscales.com www.doranscales.com
Stainless steel washdown safe scales.
President: Mark Podl
markp@doranscales.com
Chairman/CEO: William Podl
CEO: William Podl
Marketing Coordinator: Mark Anderson
Applications Engineer: Mark Podl
Estimated Sales: $5 - 10 Million
Number Employees: 20-49
Square Footage: 80000
Brands:
Digibar

21738 Dordan Manufacturing Co
2025 Castle Rd
Woodstock, IL 60098-9271
815-334-0087
Fax: 815-334-0089 800-663-5460
sales@dordan.com www.dordan.com
Heat sealing and plastic vacuum formed packaging
products
President: Oney Pineda
opineda@coppersmith.com
Estimated Sales: $2.5-5 Million
Number Employees: 20-49

21739 Dorden & Co
7446 Central St
Detroit, MI 48210-1037
313-834-7910
Fax: 313-834-1178 www.dordensqueegee.com
All types of rubber floor and window squeegees
CEO: Bruce M Gale
bgale@dordensqueegee.com
Public Relations: Bruce Gale
Purchasing: Bruce Gale
Estimated Sales: $.5 - 1 million
Number Employees: 1-4
Square Footage: 30000
Type of Packaging: Food Service, Private Label,
Bulk

21740 (HQ)Dorell Equipment Inc
80 Veronica Ave # 60
Somerset, NJ 08873-3498
732-247-5400
Fax: 732-247-5700
Food and beverage packaging equipment including
tray and case erectors, and loaders, shrink wrapping
systems, collation and stacking systems.
Manager: Lu Mado
Vice President: Joseph Minond
Marketing/Sales: Jon Levin
Sales Representative: Eli Schloss
Plant Manager: Ray Jenito
Purchasing Manager: Tami Minond
Estimated Sales: $2.5-5 Million
Number Employees: 20-49
Type of Packaging: Bulk
Other Locations:
Dorell Equipment Company
Cincinati OH
Dorell Equipment Company
Atlanta GA
Brands:
Dorell

21741 Dormont Manufacturing Co
6015 Enterprise Dr
Export, PA 15632-8969
724-733-4800
Fax: 724-733-4808 800-367-6668
info@dormont.com www.dormont.com
Safety system flexible stainless steel gas appliance
connectors and gas connection accessories; also,
pre-rinse assemblies and faucets
Vice President: Joey Kelly
joey@rynopro.com
CEO: Evan Segal
VP: Mark Humenansky
Marketing Manager: Judi D'Amico
VP Sales: David Berstein
Purchasing Manager: Norman Czarnecki
Estimated Sales: $50,000,000 - $99,999,999
Number Employees: 100-249
Square Footage: 70000
Parent Co: Watts Water Technologies

Type of Packaging: Food Service, Private Label,
Bulk
Brands:
Cimfast
Hi-Psi-Flex(Water)
Power Force
Supr Swivel
Supr-Safe (Gas)

21742 Dorner Manufacturing Corp
975 Cottonwood Ave
975 Cottonwood Ave
Hartland, WI 53029-2461
262-367-7600
Fax: 262-367-5827 800-397-8664
www.dornerconveyors.com
Belt conveyors
President: Werner Dorner
President: Scott Lucas
CFO: Dale Visgar
Engineering Manager: Michael Hosch
Marketing Director: Gary Wemmert
Sales Director: Mark Wedell
Operations Manager: Randy Meis
Purchasing Manager: Greg Sipek
Estimated Sales: $10 - 20 Million
Number Employees: 100-249

21743 Dorpak
1780 Dreman Avenue
Cincinnati, OH 45223-2456
513-681-2323
Fax: 513-541-5945 info@cin-made.com
High graphic, re-closable, rectangular paperboard
drums
President: Robert Fry
CFO: John Ewalt
Quality Control: Brian Kilpatrick
Estimated Sales: Below $5 Million
Number Employees: 10

21744 Dorton Incorporated
3436 N Kennicott Ave
Arlington Hts, IL 60004-7814
847-577-8600
Fax: 847-392-6212 800-299-8600
www.dortongroup.com
President: Ed Collins
CFO: Al Nowak
VP: Marie Collins
R&D: Milt Lynn
Marketing: Micki Bagnuolo
Sales: Micki Bagnuolo
Public Relations: Ed Collins
Operations Manager: Michelle Gilbert
Production: M Levinberg
Purchasing: Cindy Byrne
Number Employees: 10-19
Number of Brands: 2
Number of Products: 12
Square Footage: 15200
Type of Packaging: Food Service
Brands:
Dor-Blend
Dor-Mixer
Dor-Opener
Dorton

21745 Dosatron International Inc
2090 Sunnydale Blvd
Clearwater, FL 33765-1201
727-443-5404
Fax: 727-447-0591 800-523-8499
mailbox@dosatronusa.com
www.swinemedicator.com
Distributor of Dosatron water powered chemical injectors used int he food processind sanitation process. They are easy to adjust and automatically
compensate for changes in water pressure or flow,
allowing for a fine tuned chemical mixthat provides
improved results and reduced waste.
President: Edward Kelly
Contact: Courtney Boettcher
c.boettcher@dosatronusa.com
Number Employees: 20-49

21746 Dot-It Food Safety Products
2011 E Randol Mill Rd
Arlington, TX 76011
817-275-7714
Fax: 817-275-0122 800-642-3687
Labels and tags

Manager: Ben Nicholson
Director Sales: Robert Galan
General Manager: Sonya Peterson
Estimated Sales: $1 - 3 Million
Number Employees: 5-9
Square Footage: 72000
Parent Co: Craftmark Label Graphics

21747 Double E Co LLC
319 Manley St # 301
West Bridgewater, MA 02379-1034
508-588-8099
Fax: 508-580-2915 doublee@doubleeusa.com
www.ee-co.com
Core chucks anad core shafts for packaging and paper, film and foil converting
President: Mark Fortin
mfortin@doubleeusa.com
CEO: Redward Flagg
Estimated Sales: $10 - 20 000,000
Number Employees: 100-249

21748 Double E Co LLC
319 Manley St # 301
West Bridgewater, MA 02379-1034
508-588-8099
Fax: 508-580-2915 www.ee-co.com
Engineering
President: Mark Fortin
mfortin@doubleeusa.com
Estimated Sales: $10 - 20 Million
Number Employees: 100-249

21749 (HQ)Double Envelope Corp
7702 Plantation Rd
Roanoke, VA 24019-3225
540-362-3311
Fax: 540-366-8401 www.double-envelope.com
Pressure sensitive labels, bind-in order forms and envelopes
Sales Manager: Jim Long
Manager: Bill Howell
bhowell@double-envelope.com
Estimated Sales: $20-50 Million
Number Employees: 100-249

21750 Double H Plastics
50 W Street Rd
Warminster, PA 18974-3203
215-674-4100
Fax: 215-674-4109 800-523-3932
phaney@doublehplastics.com
www.doublehplastics.com
President: Harry J Harp Iii
phaney@doublehplastics.com
Sales Exec: Peter Haney
Estimated Sales: $20-50 Million
Number Employees: 100-249

21751 Double Wrap Cup & Container
728 W Jackson Blvd
Ste 1002
Chicago, IL 60661
312-337-0072
Fax: 847-777-0586
High quality,low cost insulated wrap for paper coffee cups.
CEO: Ted Alpert
VP: Ted Alpert
Marketing Director: Ted Alpert
Sales Director: Ted Alpert
Public Relations: Ted Alpert
Operations Manager: Ted Alpert
Estimated Sales: $3 - 5 Million
Number Employees: 10-19
Type of Packaging: Food Service

21752 Doucette Industries
20 Leigh Dr
York, PA 17406-8474
717-718-8944
Fax: 717-845-2864 800-445-7511
info@doucetteindustries.com
www.doucetteindustries.com
Manufacturer and exporter of suction line and vented double wall heat exchangers, CO2 Vaporizers, coaxial coils, counterflow condensers and vibration absorbers for air conditioning, refrigeration and hydronic applications
President: John Lebo
johnl@doucetteindustries.com
Number Employees: 20-49

21753 DoughXpress
1201 E 27th Terrace
Pittsburg, KS 66762
620-231-8568
Fax: 620-231-1598 800-835-0606
sales@hixcorp.com www.doughxpress.com
Bakery equipment including bread slicers, dough dividers, rounders, air compressors, release agents, storage carts, dough dockers, dual heated, presses, air automatic pizza presses, flat grills, and meat presses
President: Doug Condra
Chairman: Jack Deboer
Treasurer: Kay Stroud
Marketing & Product Manager: Tim McNally
Sales & Marketing Manager: Lorin Rigby
National Sales Manager: Willie Anderson
Contact: Isabel Ianieri
isabel.ianieri@doughxpress.com
Plant Manager: Jim Mattson
Purchasing Manager: Dave Gromer
Estimated Sales: $8.2 Million
Number Employees: 60
Square Footage: 222000
Parent Co: Hix Corporation
Type of Packaging: Food Service, Bulk

21754 Doughmakers, LLC
PO Box 10034
Terre Haute, IN 47801
812-299-8750
Fax: 812-299-7788 888-386-8517
www.doughmakers.com
Manufacturer and distributor of bakeware pans, sheets, and tins
Quality Control: Tony Buck
Manager: Robert Bossar
Estimated Sales: $5 - 10 Million
Number Employees: 20-49

21755 Doughpro
20281 Harvill Ave
Perris, CA 92570
800-624-6717
Fax: 562-869-7715 800-594-5528
Pizza presses and wood fired ovens
President: Eugene Raio
Contact: Michael Cole
mcole@doughpro.com
Number Employees: 10

21756 Douglas Battery Manufacturing Company
1255 Creekshire Way
Suite 221
Winston Salem, NC 27103
800-368-4527
info@douglasbattery.com
Industrial batteries & generators.
Year Founded: 1921
Estimated Sales: $100-500 Million

21757 (HQ)Douglas Machine Inc
3404 Iowa St
Alexandria, MN 56308-3399
320-763-6587
Fax: 320-763-5754 info@douglas-machine.com
www.douglas-machine.com
Manufacturer and exporter of packaging machinery including high speed continuous and multi-range intermittent motion case packers, case openers, bottom sealers, integrated conveyor systems, shrink wrappers, tray formers, palletizerssleevers, cartoners, multipackers and provide rebuild/conversion services
President: Jon Ballou
CEO: Vern Anderson
Estimated Sales: $94 Million
Number Employees: 500-999
Square Footage: 218000
Parent Co: Douglas
Type of Packaging: Consumer, Food Service, Private Label, Bulk

21758 Douglas Machine Inc
3404 Iowa St
Alexandria, MN 56308-3399
320-763-6587
Fax: 320-763-5754 info@douglas-machine.com
www.douglas-machine.com
Standard, custom continuous and intermittent-motion cartoners, automatic placers, robotic palletizers, etc

President: Vernon Anderson
CEO: John Ballou
Marketing Director: Jon Ballone
Sales Director: Mike Huss
Operations Manager: Bill Lawrence
Estimated Sales: $20-50 Million
Number Employees: 500-999
Square Footage: 85000
Parent Co: Douglas Machine

21759 Douglas Machines Corp
2101 Calumet St
Clearwater, FL 33765-1310
727-461-3477
Fax: 727-449-0029 800-331-6870
info@dougmac.com www.dougmac.com
Douglas Machines Corporation specializes in the design and manufacture of automated industrial and commercial washers and sanitizing equipment for all containers commonly found in the Bakery, Food Processing, Food Service andDistribution industries.
President: Gerri Boyce
boyce@jea.com
Executive Vice President: Kevin Lemen
Vice President Finance & Accounting: Susan Mader
Engineering Manager: Josef Weinberger
Service Manager: Dale Breedlove
Sales & Marketing Coordinator: Rosie Rachel
Operations Manager: Jim Beadling
Technical Support Specialist: John Jurski
Purchasing Manager: Karen McCrae
Number Employees: 50-99

21760 Douglas Machines Corp.
4500 110th Ave North
Clearwater, FL 33762
727-461-3477
Fax: 727-449-0029 800-331-6870
info@dougmac.com www.dougmac.com
Automated industrial and commercial washing and sanitizing equipment
President/Owner: Dave Ward
VP, Finance: Susan Mader
Marketing Manager: Darcel Schouler
Sales Manager: Kevin Quinn
Operations Manager: Dale Breedlove
Estimated Sales: $5-10 Million
Number Employees: 50-99
Number of Brands: 3
Number of Products: 40
Square Footage: 50000
Brands:
Douglas

21761 (HQ)Douglas Products
1550 E Old State Route 210
Liberty, MO 64068-9459
816-781-4250
Fax: 816-781-1043 800-223-3684
info@douglasproducts.com
Custom packager of liquid products
President: Jerry McCaslin
CEO: Bill R Fuller
bill.fuller@douglasproducts.com
CEO: Bill R Fuller
General Manager: Jim Osment
Estimated Sales: $10-20 Million
Number Employees: 20-49
Square Footage: 110000
Type of Packaging: Private Label, Bulk

21762 Douglas Stephen Plastics Inc
22 Green St # 36
Paterson, NJ 07501-2825
973-523-3030
Fax: 973-523-0643
bmccullough@douglasstephen.com
www.douglasstephen.com
Plastic containers and trays
President and CFO: Stewart Graff
Cmo: Ellen Sciancalepore
esciancalepore@douglasstephen.com
National Sales Manager: Brian McCullough
VP Operations: Doug Graff
Estimated Sales: $10 - 20 Million
Number Employees: 100-249

21763 Dove Screen Printing Co
18 Salem Rd
Royston, GA 30662-7406
706-245-4975
Fax: 706-245-7500 www.dovescreenprinting.com

Manufacturer and exporter of advertising specialties, signs and restaurant aprons; importer of caps and coffee mugs
Owner: Ronny Dove
  ronnydove@aol.com
Estimated Sales: Less Than $500,000
Number Employees: 1-4

21764 Dover Chemical Corp
3676 Davis Rd NW
Dover, OH 44622-9771

330-343-7711
Fax: 330-364-1579 800-321-8805
www.doverchem.com
Manufacturer and exporter of bleaches, muratic acids and antioxidants
President: Kevin Burke
  burke@cranechempharma.com
CFO: Mike Caffrey
Quality Control: Dave Schlarb
Quality Issues: Carol Churilla
Marketing Coordinator: Wendy Finch
US Sales Manager: Chad McGlothlin
Purchasing Agent: Robert Ren
Number Employees: 100-249
Parent Co: ICC Industries
Brands:
  Dover Phos Foods

21765 Dover Hospitality Consulting
6 Tallforest Crescent
Etobicoke, ON M9C 2X2
Canada

416-622-9294
Fax: 416-622-5944
Consultant specializing in chain restaurant marketing and operations
President: Bill Dover
Number Employees: 1

21766 Dover Industries
3005 Highland Parkway
Downers Grove, IL 60515

630-541-1540
Fax: 630-743-2671 www.doverind.com
President: Michael Zhang
President, Chief Executive Officer: Robert Livingston
CFO: Robert Scheuer
Vice President, Treasurer: Brian Moore
Operations Manager of Sales: Greg Smith
Contact: Marcel Berkhout
  mberkhout@dovergrp.com
Estimated Sales: $1.2 Million
Number Employees: 1,000-4,999

21767 Dover Metals
4768 Hwy M-63
Coloma, MI 49038

269-849-1411
Fax: 269-849-2903
Accessories and supplies for the food service and hospitality industry
President/Owner: Deborah Bedwell
VP: Nick Anders
Estimated Sales: $2.8 Million
Number Employees: 8

21768 Dover Parkersburg
PO Box 610
Follansbee, WV 26037-610

Fax: 304-485-3214
Manufacturer and importer of tinware including baking pans, garbage cans, buckets, tubs, wringers and mopping equipment
Sales: Donna Burns
Director Operations: William Cusack, Jr.
Estimated Sales: $10-20 Million
Number Employees: 50-99
Parent Co: Louis Berkman
Type of Packaging: Bulk

21769 Dover Products Company
607 W Jefferson St # 1
Bloomington, IL 61701-8208

309-821-1271
Fax: 502-633-3798 800-351-5582
Grease, oil and tallow
President: Egerton M Dover
Plant Manager: Robert Kepfer
Estimated Sales: $500,000-$1 Million
Number Employees: 5 to 9

21770 Dow Agro Sciences LLC
9330 Zionsville Rd
Indianapolis, IN 46268-1053

317-337-3000
Fax: 317-337-4140 800-258-3033
www.dowagro.com
Wine industry vineyard chemicals
Director: Rogelio Lara
CEO: Jerry Britt
  jlbritt@dow.com
Estimated Sales: Over $1 Billion
Number Employees: 5000-9999

21771 Dow Cover Co Inc
373 Lexington Ave
New Haven, CT 06513-4061

203-469-5394
Fax: 203-469-0742 800-735-8877
mark@dowcover.com www.dowcover.com
Canvas covers and aprons including custom logo, screenprint and embroidery
President: Mark Steinhardt
  mark@dowcover.com
Estimated Sales: $5-10 Million
Number Employees: 50-99
Square Footage: 68000
Brands:
  Dowsport America

21772 Dow Industries
271 Ballardvale St
Wilmington, MA 01887-1081

978-658-8200
Fax: 978-658-2307 800-776-1201
sales@dowindustries.com www.smythco.com
Manufacturer and exporter of pressure sensitive labels and automatic labeling equipment
President: Walter Dow
CEO: Andy Farquharson
CFO: John Morrison
Quality Control: Scott Boucher
Senior VP: Bill Donovan
Operations Manager: D Apgar
Estimated Sales: $20 Million
Number Employees: 50-99
Square Footage: 64000
Type of Packaging: Consumer, Private Label

21773 Dow Packaging
2211 H.H. Dow Way
Midland, MI 48674

989-636-1000
Fax: 989-382-1456 800-331-6451
www.dow.com
Processor and exporter of ethylene oxide/ethylene glycol, coating materials, industrial performance chemicals, polyolefin resins and compounds, solvents intermediates and monomers, UCAR emulsion systems, specialty polymers andproducts.
Chairman & CEO: Andrew Liveris
President & COO: James Fitterling
Vice Chairman & CFO: Howard Underleider
EVP & General Counsel: Charles Kalil
Controller/VP of Controllers & Tax: Ron Edmonds
Year Founded: 1917
Number Employees: 2,300
Parent Co: the Dow Chemical Company
Type of Packaging: Bulk

21774 Dow Water and Process Solutions
7600 Metro Boulevard
Edina, MN 55439

800-447-4369
www.dowwaterandprocess.com
Product line includes food grade ion exchange resins, adsorbents and membranes used to recover, isolate and purify nutritional ingredients such as polyphenols, taste mask unwanted flavors, stabilize victims, immobilize enzymesdecolorize juice streams, produce clean water, efficiently reduce waste and more.

Director, Finance: Ken Swanson
Director, Business Unit Ion Exchange: Rajat Mehta
Director, Communications: Kimberly Kupiecki
Director, Business Unit Reverse Osmosis: Lance Johnson
Director, Research & Development: Dr. George Barclay
Director, Business Manufacturing/Tech: Vicky Biedenstein
Legal Counsel: Janaki Catanzarite
Global Business Director: Snehal Desai
Contact: Randy Blom
  rblom@dow.com
Director, Human Resources: Kim Fisher
Global Supply Chain Director: Christophe Gay-Bellile

21775 Dowling Signs Inc
1801 Princess Anne St
Fredericksburg, VA 22401-3544

540-373-6675
Fax: 540-371-7543 800-572-2100
www.dowlingsignsinc.com
Signs specializing in ADA (American Disabilities Act) approved including illuminated and nonilluminated identification
President: Allen Malocha
  signsdsi@aol.com
Secretary and Treasurer: Susanne Bradley
General Manager: Allen Malocha
Production Manager: Charles Ward
Estimated Sales: $2.5-5 Million
Number Employees: 20-49
Square Footage: 60000

21776 Downeast Chemical
88 Scott Dr
Westbrook, ME 04092-1927

207-773-9668
Fax: 207-773-0832 800-287-2225
Detergents, degreasers and boiler treatment compounds; also, custom blending
President: Joseph Brita
VP: John Bowns
Customer Service: Heather Bowns
Estimated Sales: $1 - 3 Million
Number Employees: 9
Square Footage: 16800

21777 Downs Crane & Hoist Co Inc
8827 Juniper St
Los Angeles, CA 90002-1899

323-589-6061
Fax: 323-589-6066 800-748-5994
sales@downscrane.com www.downscrane.com
Manufacturer and exporter of lifting devices including grabs, tongs, spreaders, manipulators, hooks, cranes and crane wheels and assemblies
President: John W Downs Jr
Number Employees: 5-9
Type of Packaging: Bulk
Brands:
  Grabmaster

21778 Doyen Medipharm
4030 S Pipkin Rd Ste 102
Lakeland, FL 33811

863-683-6335
Fax: 863-683-6857
Packaging machinery for food industry
President: Ray Johnson
VP: Martin Beriswill
Estimated Sales: $2.5-5 000,000
Number Employees: 20-49

21779 Doyle Signs Inc
232 W Interstate Rd
Addison, IL 60101-4563

630-543-9490
Fax: 630-543-9493 info@doylesigns.com
www.doylesigns.com
Interior and exterior electric identification signs; also, design, installation and maintenance services available
President: Terrence J Doyle
  terrence@doylesigns.com
VP: P Doyle
Sales Director: J Doyle
Estimated Sales: $10 Million
Number Employees: 50-99
Square Footage: 74000

21780 Doyon Equipment
1255 Rue Principale
Liniere, QC G0M 1J0
Canada
418-685-3431
Fax: 418-685-3948 800-463-4273
sales@nu-vu.com www.doyon.qc.ca
Baking equipment
President: Karl Doyon
Research & Development: Pierre Poirier
Marketing Director: Jennifer Letourneau
Regional Sales Director: John Herbert
Regional Sales Director: Jim Markee
Estimated Sales: $10-20 Million
Number Employees: 20
Brands:
Doyon
Jet Air

21781 Drackett Professional
8600 Governors Hill Drive
Cincinnati, OH 45249-1360
513-583-3900
Fax: 513-583-3968
Cleaners and mops
National Sales Director: Steve Moser
Director Advertising/PR: Diego Esquibel
General Manager: Terry Conlon
Number Employees: 20-49
Parent Co: S.C. Johnson Wax
Brands:
Beer Clean
Draino
Easy Paks
Glade
Ice-Foe
Raid
Windex

21782 Draeger Safety Inc
101 Technology Dr
Pittsburgh, PA 15275-1005
412-787-8383
Fax: 412-787-2207 800-922-5518
www.draeger.com
Develops safety technology for manufacturing industry.
President: Ralf Drews
CFO: Graeme Roberts
Contact: Elaine Adie
elaine.adie@draeger.com
Estimated Sales: $50 - 100 Million
Number Employees: 100-249

21783 Draiswerke Inc
40 Whitney Rd
Mahwah, NJ 07430-3130
201-847-0600
Fax: 201-847-0606 800-494-3151
www.buhlergroup.com
Tea and coffee industry mills for micro wet grinding and dispersing, mixers, dryers, reactors, and compounding systems
President: Gilbert Schall
gschall@draiswerke-inc.com
Estimated Sales: $10 - 20 000,000
Number Employees: 20-49

21784 Drake Co
1401 Greengrass Dr
Houston, TX 77008-5005
713-869-9121
Fax: 713-869-3512 800-299-5644
Manufacturer and exporter of corrugated boxes and lithographic displays
CEO: John Carrico
CFO: Shelley Golden
sgolden@drakecompany.com
Sales/Service Manager: Kevin Fiedler
Estimated Sales: $1 - 5 Million
Number Employees: 100-249

21785 Drapes 4 Show
12811 Foothill Blvd
Sylmar, CA 91342-5316
818-838-0852
Fax: 818-222-7469 800-525-7469
staff@drapes.com www.drapes.com
Tabletop accessories including napkins, table skirting and table linens
CEO: Karen Honigberg
Customer Service: Kathryn Pereyra

Estimated Sales: Below $5 Million
Number Employees: 20-49
Square Footage: 12800

21786 Dreaco Products
172 Reaser Court
Elyria, OH 44035-6285
440-366-7600
Fax: 440-365-5858 800-368-3267
Manufacturer and exporter of exhaust hoods and fans; also, make-up air fans
Owner and President: Robert Gargasz
Sales/Marketing Executive: Karen Kauk
Purchasing Agent: Michael Gargasz
Estimated Sales: $2.5-5 Million
Number Employees: 20-49
Square Footage: 100000
Brands:
Dreaco

21787 DreamPak LLC
4717 Eisenhower Avenue
Alexandria, VA 22304
703-751-3511
877-687-4662
info@dreampak.com www.dreampak.com
On-the-go beverages
President/CEO: Dr. Aly Gamay
Executive Vice President: Terry Schneider
Contact: Taufeeque Ali
tali@dreampak.com
Vice President, Operations: Randy Cook
Brands:
Chocolate Slim
Dogflex
Enhance To Go
Fruitslim
Joker's Wild Energy
Soluflex
Trimma
Zeniht

21788 Drehmann Paving & Flooring Company
847 Bethel Ave
Pennsauken, NJ 08110-2605
856-486-0202
Fax: 856-486-0808 800-523-3800
Manufacturer and exporter of brick floor coatings, plates and drains; installation services available
President: William Varra
VP: J Kline, Jr.
Executive VP: Horace Furman
Research & Development: M Bojesuk
Quality Control: S Furman
Contact: J Kline
kklinejr@drehmann.com
Estimated Sales: $5,000,000
Number Employees: 75-100
Number of Brands: 1
Number of Products: 10
Square Footage: 36000
Type of Packaging: Private Label

21789 Drehmann Paving & Flooring Company
2101 Byberry Road
Philadelphia, PA 19116-3017
215-464-7700
Fax: 215-673-9755 800-523-3800
www.drehmann.com
Industrial brick flooring, epoxy, joint materials, expansion joints,cast iron floor drains and stainless steel floor drains

21790 Drescher Paper Box Inc
459 Broadway St
Buffalo, NY 14204-1697
716-854-0288
Fax: 716-854-1920
Rigid set-up paper boxes, jigsaw puzzles, board games
President: Jb Langworthy
CEO: Joyce MacLeod
Estimated Sales: $10-20 Million
Number Employees: 10-19
Square Footage: 96000

21791 Dresco Belting Co Inc
122 East St
PO Box 890026
East Weymouth, MA 02189-2198
781-335-1350
Fax: 781-340-0500 sales@drescobelt.com
www.drescobelt.com
Manufacturer and exporter of conveyor and transmission belting
Owner: James Dresser
jim.dresser@drescobelt.com
VP, Manufacturing & Technology: James G. Dresser
VP, Sales: Norman K. Dresser
Estimated Sales: $1-2.5 Million
Number Employees: 1-4
Square Footage: 40000

21792 Dreumex USA
3445 Board Rd
York, PA 17406-8409
717-767-6881
Fax: 717-767-6888 800-233-9382
dreumex@dreumex.com www.dreumex.com
Manufacturer and exporter of waterless gel and lotion hand cleaners and liquid soap; also, hand and multi-purpose wipes, dispensing systems, and car/truck wash
President/CEO: Jim Strickler
Research & Development: Gail Shermeyer
Quality Control: Gail Shermeyer
Marketing Director: Karen Hansen
Sales Director: Jim Strickler
Contact: Craig Bennett
c.bennett@dreumex.com
Operations Manager: Jeff Strickler
Production Manager: Jim Mitzel
Plant Manager: Jim Mitzel
Purchasing Manager: Bob Keyser
Estimated Sales: $5 - 10 Million
Number Employees: 20-49
Number of Brands: 13
Number of Products: 13
Square Footage: 160000
Type of Packaging: Private Label
Brands:
Citrus
Gent-L-Kleen
Grime Grabber
Power Wipes Formula Z
Premium Blue
Pumicizied Advantage Plus
Skin Armor
Zapper

21793 Dri Mark Products
15 Harbor Park Dr
Port Washington, NY 11050
516-484-6200
Fax: 516-484-6279 800-645-9118
www.drimark.com
Manufacturer and exporter of pens including nylon, felt and plastic tip, ball point, roller ball and counterfeit detector; also, watercolor and permanent markers, highlighters and drawing sets
President: Charles Reichmann
CFO: Cathy Owens
VP Sales: Mark Dobbs
Purchasing Manager: Mickey Cirrani
Estimated Sales: $20 - 50 Million
Number Employees: 100-249
Square Footage: 70000
Brands:
Buffalo
Color Graphic
Communication
Mr. Doodler
Perma Graphic

21794 Driall Inc
1144 E 800 N
Attica, IN 47918-8027
765-295-2255
Fax: 317-272-1097
Manufacturer and exporter of grain dryers and air curtain destructors for controlled open residue burning
Manager: Dave Scott
Estimated Sales: Less Than $500,000
Number Employees: 1-4
Type of Packaging: Food Service, Bulk

21795 Driam USA Inc
181 Access Rd
Spartanburg, SC 29303-1775
864-579-7850
Fax: 864-579-7852 info@driamusa.com
Confectionary and candy sorting and inspection machinery. Coating equipment for the pharmeceutical and confectionary industry
Owner: Marilyn Drumm
Sales Manager: Hans Peter Schwendeler
Manager: Rose Michael
rosemichael@driamusa.com
Estimated Sales: Less Than $500,000
Number Employees: 1-4
Parent Co: Driam

21796 Dried Ingredients, LLC.
9010 NW 105th Way
Miami, FL 33178
786-999-8499
Fax: 888-893-6595 info@driedingredients.com
www.driedingredients.com
Maufacturer of organic, precooked pulses (beans, lentils, peas); also teas, tea ingredients, herbs, spices, essential oils & dried vegetables. Provide product development & logistics services.
President: Armin Dilles
armin.dilles@driedingredients.com
Sales Manager: Maria Rosello
Parent Co: Dried Ingredients GmbH
Type of Packaging: Food Service, Bulk

21797 Driscoll Label Company
19 West Street
East Hanover, NJ 07936
973-585-7291
Fax: 973-585-7295 www.driscolllabel.com
Wine industry pressure sensitive labels
President: John Riguso
Vice President: Patricia Biava
Sales Director: Patricia Vargas
Contact: Gail Chill
gailchill@driscolllabel.com
Estimated Sales: $10-20 000,000
Number Employees: 20-49

21798 Drives Incorporated
901 19th Ave
Fulton, IL 61252
815-589-2211
Fax: 815-589-4420 custserv@drivesinc.com
Power transmission products, conveyor chain, screw conveyors
President: David J Vogel
CFO: Michael Landers
Contact: Steven Eggemeyer
eggemeyers@drivesinc.com
Estimated Sales: $50-100 Million
Number Employees: 250-499

21799 DropperBottles.com
2801 Technology Dr.
#127
Plano, TX 75074
844-526-8853
sales@dropperbottles.com dropperbottles.com
Wholesale glass and plastic dropper bottles supplier.
President: Ben Ganter

21800 Drs Designs
217 Greenwood Ave
Bethel, CT 06801-2113
203-744-2858
Fax: 203-743-4389 888-792-3740
www.drsdesigns.com
Rubber stamps, engraved signs and pressure sensitive labels; also, general printing, laminating and hot stamping services available
Manager: Samantha Conrad
Manager: Dave Spence
dspence@drsdesigns.com
Estimated Sales: $500,000-$1 Million
Number Employees: 1-4
Square Footage: 2400

21801 Drum-Mates Inc.
PO Box 636
Lumberton, NJ 08048-0636
609-261-1033
Fax: 609-261-1034 800-621-3786
info@drummates.com www.drummates.com
Manufacturer and supplier of sanitary duty drum and IBC heaters, mixers, pumps, hand dispensing nozzles, bung equipment, fittings, global ThreadConverters and adapters.
Technical Sales: David Marcmann
Estimated Sales: $1 - 5 Million
Number Employees: 20
Square Footage: 100000
Brands:
  Drum-Mate
  Quikmix
  Threadconverter
  Threadguard

21802 Drying Technology Inc
500 Highway 327 E
Silsbee, TX 77656-5018
409-385-6422
Fax: 409-385-6537 drying@moisturecontrols.com
www.moisturecontrols.com
Moisture controls
President: John Robinson
Estimated Sales: Below $5 000,000
Number Employees: 1-4

21803 Dryomatic
7924 Reco Avenue
Frederick, MD 70814
301-668-8200
Fax: 225-612-7407 sales@dryomatic.com
www.dryomatic.com
Parent Co: Airflow Company

21804 Dsl
6504 Mayfair St
Houston, TX 77087-3422
713-645-9177
Fax: 713-645-9131 800-460-3164
sales@dslformers.com www.dslformers.com
Forming collars to fit draw bar, pull belt, vacuum pull belt and continuous motion baggers and packaging machinery
President: Louis Posada
R & D: Simon Gonales
Marketing Manager: Simon Gondales
Contact: Simon Gonzales
sg@dslformers.com
Estimated Sales: Below $5 000,000
Number Employees: 5-9

21805 Dsr Enterprises
38404 Hidden Creek Way
Mechanicsville, MD 20659-7203
301-472-4990
Fax: 610-942-4273 800-238-0310
dsr@dsrenterprises.com www.dsrenterprises.com
Electrical panel management schedules and estimates loads
Partner: Randy Junkins
President: David Groh
Estimated Sales: Less Than $500,000
Number Employees: 1-4
Square Footage: 1500
Type of Packaging: Private Label

21806 Du Bois Chemicals
3630 E Kemper Rd
Cincinnati, OH 45241-2046
513-326-8800
Fax: 513-326-8309
charlie.weber@diverseylever.com
www.duboischemicals.com
CEO: Mike Gallico
mikeg@johnson-company.com
Estimated Sales: $1 - 5 Million
Number Employees: 100-249

21807 Du-Good Chemical Laboratory & Manufacturing Company
1215 S Jefferson Ave
Saint Louis, MO 63104-1992
314-773-5007
Fax: 314-773-5007
Dishwashing detergent and waterless hand cleaning products
President: Lincoln I Diuguid
VP: Lewis Diuguid
Manager: V Diuguid
Estimated Sales: $.5 - 1 million
Number Employees: 5 to 9
Square Footage: 13150
Brands:
  Du-Good
  Rainbow Delight

21808 DuBois Chemicals
3630 E Kemper Rd
Sharonville, OH 45241-2011
800-438-2647
www.duboischemicals.com
Supplier of cleaning and hygiene systems for dairy, beverage, brewing and food industries.
President & CEO: Jeff Walsh
Technical Advisor: Michael Askren
VP, Operations: James Walker
Year Founded: 1920
Estimated Sales: $2 Billion
Number Employees: 150
Square Footage: 105000

21809 (HQ)DuPont
939 Centre Rd.
Wilmington, DE 19807
302-774-1000
800-441-7515
www.dupont.com
Collaborates with equipment manufactureres, converters, brand owners and retailers to develop application-specific packaging solutions; tecnhologies include packging resins and sealants, anti-counterfeit solutions, non-wovensubstrates, grease-resistant coatings and liquid packaging solutions.
Executive Chairman/CEO: Edward Breen
CFO: Lori Koch
Senior VP/General Counsel: Erik Hoover
President, Nutrition & Biosciences: Matthias Heinzel
Senior VP/Chief Operations & Engineering: Daryl Roberts
Year Founded: 1802
Estimated Sales: $25 Biliion
Number Employees: 34,000
Number of Brands: 169

21810 DuPont Nutrition & Biosciences
4 New Century Pkwy
New Century, KS 66031
913-764-8100
www.food.dupont.com
Ingredients for baking, bars, beverages, confectionery, culinary, diary, frozen desserts, fruit applications, meat alternatives, meat/poultry/seafood, oils and fats, and pet food.
Estimated Sales: $4.4 Billion
Number Employees: 10,000
Number of Brands: 6
Parent Co: DuPont
Type of Packaging: Consumer, Bulk
Other Locations:
  Central Soya Company - Processing Decatur IN
  Central Soya Company - Processing Gibson City IL
  Central Soya Company - Processing Marion OH
  Central Soya Company - Grain Plant Indianapolis IN
  Central Soya Company - Processing Bellevue OH
  Central Soya Company - Grain Plant Cincinnati OH
  Central Soya Company - Processing Delphos OH
  Central Soya Company - Mfg Remington IN
  Central Soya Company - Processing Morristown IN
  Central Soya Company - Grain Jeffersonville OH
  Central Soya Company - Grain Waterloo IN
  Central Soya Company - Bulk Oil Pawtucket RI
  Central Soya Company - Mfg New Bremen OH
Brands:
  FIBRIM
  Gardenburger
  Medifast
  Mori-Nu
  Solae
  V8 Splash
  Yves Veggie Cuisine

21811 Dual Temp
4301 S Packers Ave
Chicago, IL 60609-3311
773-254-9800
Fax: 773-254-9840 800-255-9801
sales@dualtempcompanies.com
www.dualtempcompanies.com

President: Mary Akers
 marya@dualtempcompanies.com
Estimated Sales: $1 - 5 Million
Number Employees: 20-49

21812 Dualite Sales & Svc Inc
1 Dualite Ln
Williamsburg, OH 45176-1121

    513-724-7100
Fax: 513-724-9029 dualite@dualite.com
www.dualite.com

National account sign manufacturer
President: Frank W Schube
 fschube@dualite.com
Executive VP Administration: E Lynn Webb
R&D: Pat Seggerson
National Sales Manager: Robert Stephany
Plant Manager: Jerry Hinnenkamp
Purchasing: Greg Hoffer
Estimated Sales: $35-50 Million
Number Employees: 250-499
Square Footage: 600000
Parent Co: Dualite

21813 Dub Harris Corporation
2875 Metropolitan Place
Pomona, CA 91767

    909-596-6300
Fax: 909-596-6336 dubharris@dubharris.com
www.dubharris.com

Plastic bags; wholesaler/distributor of corrugated
boxes and packaging materials
President: Maurice Harris
Contact: Ming Yu
 dubharris@dubharris.com
Estimated Sales: $2.5-5 Million
Number Employees: 5-9

21814 Dubor GmbH
4801 Harbor Pointe Dr.
Suite 1305
North Myrtle Beach, SC 29016-9458

    803-691-8941
Fax: 803-754-7755
benmuller@mullerinternational.com
www.mullerinternational.com

21815 Dubuit of America Inc
70 Monaco Dr
Roselle, IL 60172-1955

    630-894-9500
Fax: 847-647-1796 www.dubuit.com

Printers and screen printing equipment
President: Pierre Crozet
 pcrozet@dubuitamerica.com
Estimated Sales: $3 000,000
Number Employees: 5-9

21816 Dubuque Steel Products Co
1500 Radford Rd
Dubuque, IA 52002-2115

    563-556-6288
Fax: 563-583-7365
www.dubuquesteelproducts.com

Stainless steel tubs, trucks, dollies, racks, drums and
vats
President: Thomas A Geisler
 sales@dubuquesteelproducts.com
CEO: Dave Geisler
Vice President: Todd Geisler
Estimated Sales: $2.5-5 Million
Number Employees: 5-9
Parent Co: Geisler Brothers Company

21817 Duck Waok
44535 Main Road
PO Box 962
Water Mill, NY 11976-0962

    631-765-3500
Fax: 631-765-3509 www.duckwalk.com

Wines
Owner: Alexander Damianos
VP and General Manager: Alex Zamianos
Estimated Sales: Below $5 Million
Number Employees: 10-19

21818 Duct Sox Corp
9866 Kapp Ct
Peosta, IA 52068-9451

    563-588-5300
Fax: 563-588-5330 866-563-7729
cpinkalla@ductsox.com www.ductsox.com
Fabric air dispersion systems

President: Cary Pinkalla
 cpinkalla@ductsox.com
Key Person: Lou Wiegand
Number Employees: 250-499

21819 Dudson USA Inc
5604 Departure Dr
Raleigh, NC 27616-1841

    919-877-0200
Fax: 919-877-0300 800-438-3766
usasales@dudson.com

Importer and wholesaler/distributor of dinnerware
including china; serving the food service market
President: Elmer Carr
VP: Lorraine Delois
VP Marketing/Sales: Joel DeNoble
VP Corporate Accounts: Maire-Anne Bassil
Manager: Steve Abourisk
Estimated Sales: $1-2.5 Million
Number Employees: 10-19
Square Footage: 180000
Parent Co: Dudson Company
Type of Packaging: Food Service

21820 Duerr Packaging Co Inc
892 Steubenville Pike
Burgettstown, PA 15021-9510

    724-947-1234
Fax: 724-947-4321 www.duerrpack.com

Rigid paper boxes, transformed plastics
CEO: Samuel Duerr Jr
 sam@duerrpack.com
CFO: Wayne Albroght
VP: David Duerr
Sales Exec: Sam Duerr
Estimated Sales: $2.5 - 5 Million
Number Employees: 20-49

21821 Dufeck Manufacturing Co
210 Maple St
Denmark, WI 54208

    920-863-2354
Fax: 920-863-2054 888-603-9663
info@dufeckwood.com www.dufeckwood.com

Wooden cheese and wine boxes, custom display
units, containers, gift boxes and baskets and wooden
pallets
President: Paul Dufeck
 paul@duffeckwood.com
Finance: Jeanette Dufeck
R&D: Junette Dufeck
Plant Manager: Al Bouressa
Estimated Sales: $10 - 20 Million
Number Employees: 50-99
Square Footage: 40000

21822 Dugussa Texturant Systems
3582 McCall Pl
Atlanta, GA 30340-2802

    770-455-3603
Fax: 770-986-6216 800-241-9485
texturants@degussa.com

President: Ed Baranski
Number Employees: 50-99

21823 Dukane Corp
2900 Dukane Dr
St Charles, IL 60174-3395

    630-797-4900
Fax: 630-797-4949 usservice@dukcorp.com
www.dukane.com

Ultrasonic food cutting
President: Jean Stone
CEO: Michael W Ritschdorff
 mritschdorff@dukcorp.com
CEO: Michael W Ritschdorff
Marketing Communications: Kathy Jensen
Sales Director: Joe Re
Estimated Sales: $20,000,000 - $49,999,999
Number Employees: 250-499
Brands:
 Ultrasonic Equipment

21824 Dukane Corp
2900 Dukane Dr
St Charles, IL 60174-3395

    630-797-4900
Fax: 630-797-4949 usuntl@dukane.com
www.dukane.com

CEO: Michael W Ritschdorff
 mritschdorff@dukcorp.com
CEO: Michael W Ritschdorff
Estimated Sales: $1 - 5 Million
Number Employees: 250-499

21825 Duke Manufacturing Co
2305 N Broadway
St Louis, MO 63102-1420

    314-231-1130
Fax: 314-231-5074 800-735-3853
www.dukemfg.com

Manufacturer and exporter of ingredient bins, cabi-
nets, sneeze guards, conveyors, counters, filters,
freezers, ovens, steam tables, pans, racks, coolers,
kiosks, fire extinguishing systems, sinks, carts, etc
President: Jack Hake
 jhake@dukemfg.com
CFO: Larry Reader
Quality Control: Art Lamley
Estimated Sales: $20-50 Million
Number Employees: 100-249
Square Footage: 300000

21826 Duluth Sheet Metal
P.O. Box 16582
Duluth, MN 55816-0582

    218-722-2613
Fax: 218-727-8870

Stainless steel tables, stands, shelves, counter tops,
cabinets, sinks and vapor hoods; custom fabricator
of conveyors, platforms, tanks, etc
President: Mark Jam
Contact: Barney Revier
 revier@duluthsheetmetal.com
Estimated Sales: $1-2.5 Million
Number Employees: 10-19
Square Footage: 24000

21827 Dunbar Co
1186 Walter St
Lemont, IL 60439-3993

    630-257-2900
Fax: 630-257-3434 dunbar@dunbarsystems.com
www.dunbarsystems.com

Producer of serpentine baking systems for cookies,
cakes, biscuits, bread, pies, pastries, muffins and
puddings.
President/Owner: Mark Dunbar
CEO/Owner: Mike Dunbar
Senior Sales Engineer: Chuck Kazen
Manager: George Dunbar
 george@dunbarsystems.com
Vice President of Operations: Doug Hale
Estimated Sales: $9.7 Million
Number Employees: 10-19
Type of Packaging: Food Service

21828 Dunbar Manufacturing Co
390 N Gilbert St
South Elgin, IL 60177-1398

    847-741-6394
Fax: 847-741-6394
www.dunbarmanufacturing.com

Manufacturer and exporter of caramel and regular
popcorn equipment including mixers, tumblers,
poppers and sprayers
President: Ray Goode Jr
 rgoode4@gmail.com
Estimated Sales: Less than $500,000
Number Employees: 1-4
Number of Products: 40
Square Footage: 12000
Brands:
 Popt-Rite

21829 Dunhill Food Equipment Corporation
PO Box 496
Armonk, NY 10504

    718-625-4006
Fax: 718-625-0155 800-847-4206

Manufacturer and exporter of cafeteria and kitchen
equipment including cashier stands, serving coun-
ters, sinks, refrigerated display cases and tables
President: Geoffrey Thaw
VP: Larry Dubow
Estimated Sales: $5-10 Million
Number Employees: 10-19
Square Footage: 100000
Parent Co: Esquire Mechanical Group
Type of Packaging: Food Service
Brands:
 Dunhill

21830 Dunkin' Brands, Inc.
130 Royall St.
Canton, MA 02021
S

781-737-3000
800-859-5339
www.dunkindonuts.com
Coffee, baked goods and premium ice cream.
CEO: David Hoffmann
Executive Chairman: Nigel Travis
CFO: Kate Jaspon
Chief Marketing Officer: Jill McVicar
Chief Operating Officer: Rick Colon
Year Founded: 1950
Estimated Sales: $860.5 Million
Number Employees: 270,000
Number of Brands: 2
Parent Co: Inspire Brands
Type of Packaging: Food Service
Brands:
  Baskin-Robbins
  Dunkin' Donuts

21831 Dunkley International Inc
1910 Lake St
Kalamazoo, MI 49001-3274

269-343-5583
Fax: 269-343-5614 800-666-1264
Manufacturer and exporter of pitters, de-stemmers and electronic sorters, inspection systems and conveyors
President: Richard L Bogard
Manager: Nick Hatzinikolis
  nhatzinikolis@dunkleyinyl.com
General Manager: Ernest Kenneway
Plant Manager: Rob Prange
Estimated Sales: $1 - 3 Million
Number Employees: 10-19
Square Footage: 120000
Parent Co: Cherry Central

21832 Dunn Woodworks
536 S Main Street
Shrewsbury, PA 17361-1739

717-235-1144
Fax: 717-227-2828 877-835-8592
woodpilot@aol.com
Manufacturer, broker and wholesaler/distributor of custom designed displays, kiosks, racks, P.O.P. P.O.S. and merchandisers. Custom designed wine racks and display headers. Over ten thousand displays made annually
Owner: Henry Dunn
Estimated Sales: $1 - 3,000,000
Number Employees: 5
Square Footage: 10000

21833 Dunrite Inc
3405 N Yager Rd
Fremont, NE 68025-7880

402-721-3061
Fax: 402-721-3040 800-782-3061
www.dunrite.com
Pneumatic grain conveyors, grain elevator vacuums and accessories including respirators, dust masks and duct tape
Manager: Leroy Klinzing
VP: Leroy Klinzing
Estimated Sales: $2.5-5 Million
Number Employees: 5-9
Brands:
  Buckskin Bill
  Harvestvac

21834 Duo-Aire
39 Third Street SW
Suite 606
Winter Haven, FL 33880

863-294-2272
Fax: 863-294-2704 info@duoaire.com
www.duoaire.com
Commercial kitchen ventilation systems
President: Gary Smith
Accounting: Jan Smith
Sales & Parts: Jody Reynolds
Estimated Sales: $470,000
Number Employees: 4
Square Footage: 14836
Parent Co: Ventilation Marketing Services

21835 Duplex Mill & Mfg Co
415 Sigler St
Springfield, OH 45506-1144

937-325-5555
Fax: 937-325-0859 www.dmmc.com
Diverter valves and mixing, blending, conveying, elevating, size reduction and slide gate machinery; exporter of mixers, conveyors and hammer mills
CEO: Eric Wise
  eww@dmmc.com
Sales Manager: Eric Wise
Production Manager: Eric Brickson
Plant Manager: Eric Brickson
Estimated Sales: $2-3 Million
Number Employees: 10-19
Square Footage: 320000
Brands:
  Kelly Duplex

21836 Dupps Co
548 N Cherry St
Germantown, OH 45327-1185

937-855-0623
Fax: 937-855-6554 info@dupps.com
www.dupps.com
Manufacturer and exporter of process equipment and protein waste recovery systems including cookers and dryers; also, computerized control and information systems, screw presses, conveyor systems, high viscosity material pumps and sizereduction equipment
President: John A Dupps Jr
VP: Frank Dupps
  frank.dupps@dupps.com
Quality Control: Tim Seebach
Marketing Manager: Rich Hollmeyer
Estimated Sales: $20-50 Million
Number Employees: 100-249
Square Footage: 120000
Brands:
  Equacookor
  Precrushor
  Pressor
  Ring Dryer

21837 Dupuy Storage & Forwarding LLC
4300 Jourdan Rd
New Orleans, LA 70126-3731

504-245-7600
Fax: 504-245-7643 www.dupuygroup.com
Tea and coffee industry bulk silo services, reconditioners, samplers and weighers
President: Allan B Colley
  abcolley@dupuystorage.com
Estimated Sales: $50-100 Million
Number Employees: 50-99

21838 Dur-Able Aluminum Corporation
1555 Barrington Rd
Hoffman Estates, IL 60169-1019

847-843-1100
Fax: 847-843-0764
Manufacturer and exporter of aluminum foil bakeware including pans, plates, trays and cooking and baking utensils
Estimated Sales: $20-50 Million
Number Employees: 1-4
Type of Packaging: Food Service, Bulk

21839 Dura Electric Lamp Company
64 E Bigelow Street
Newark, NJ 07114-1699

973-624-0014
Fax: 973-624-3945
Manufacturer and exporter of incandescent and fluorescent lamps and starters
President: Lawrence Portnow
General Manager: A Gross
Estimated Sales: $2.5-5 Million
Number Employees: 5-9
Square Footage: 80000
Brands:
  Dura
  Durelco

21840 Dura-Flex
95 Goodwin St
East Hartford, CT 06108-1146

860-528-9838
Fax: 860-528-2802 877-251-5418
contact_us@dur-a-flex.com www.dur-a-flex.com
Commercial and seemless industrial flooring systems and wall coatings and polymer components - epoxies, urethanes and methyl methacrylates (MMA) plus premium colored quartz aggregates.
CEO: Robert Smith
  roberts@dur-a-flex.com
Marketing: Mark Paggioli
Number Employees: 50-99
Square Footage: 260000
Brands:
  Cryl-A-Chip
  Cryl-A-Flex
  Cryl-A-Floor
  Cryl-A-Quartz
  Poly-Crete

21841 Dura-Pack Inc.
7641 Holland Rd
Taylor, MI 48180

313-299-9600
Fax: 313-299-9988 sales@dura-pack.com
dura-pack.com
Custom bags and packaging; machinery for bagging
President: Tim Harrison
Year Founded: 1971
Estimated Sales: $550,000
Number Employees: 20

21842 (HQ)Dura-Ware Company of America
PO Box 53006
Oklahoma City, OK 73152-3006

405-475-5600
Fax: 405-475-5607 800-664-3872
customerservice@carlislefsp.com
www.carlislefsp.com
Manufacturer, importer and exporter of commercial cookware and servingware including stock pots, frying pans, sauce pans, pasta cookers, chafers, etc
President: David Shannon
VP Sales: David Wasserman
Estimated Sales: $20 - 50 Million
Number Employees: 50-99
Square Footage: 70000
Brands:
  Celebration
  Dura-Ware
  Signature
  Ssal
  Symphony

21843 Durable Corp
75 N Pleasant St
Norwalk, OH 44857-1218

419-668-8138
Fax: 419-668-8068 800-537-1603
sales@durablecorp.com www.durablecorp.com
Dock bumpers, wheel chocks and floor mats and matting
President: Thomas Secor
CEO: Hilary Alexander
  alexander@durablecorp.com
Sales Director: Phil Lorcher
Estimated Sales: $20-50 Million
Number Employees: 50-99
Type of Packaging: Private Label

21844 Durable Engravers
521 S County Line Rd
Franklin Park, IL 60131

630-766-6420
Fax: 630-766-0219 800-869-9565
www.durable-tech.com
Manufacturer and exporter of steel and brass codes, logo blocks and holders for the food and pharmaceutical industries
CEO: Gary Berenger
  g.berenger@durable-tech.com
VP: Jim Maybach
Estimated Sales: $1-2.5 Million
Number Employees: 20-49
Square Footage: 20000
Type of Packaging: Food Service, Bulk

21845 Durable Packaging Corporation
5117 Dansher Rd
Countryside, IL 60525-6905

708-387-2253
Fax: 708-387-2211 800-700-5677
www.okcorp.com
Case erectors and sealers
Manager: Adam Kwiek
Sales/Marketing Manager: Carol Crouse
General Information: Leslie Hickey

Estimated Sales: $5 - 10 Million
Number Employees: 10-19

21846 Duralite Inc
15 School St
Riverton, CT 06065-1013

860-379-3113
Fax: 860-379-5879 888-432-8797
sales@duralite.com www.duralite.com
Manufacturer and exporter of quartz tubes for heating/cooking equipment with element enclosed is tube or wrapped around tube, also heating elements (electric) heating and cooking, coiled or not
Owner: Mark Jessen
markj@duralite.com
CEO: Elliott Jessen
Chairman: Elliot Jessen
Sales Director: Barbara Asselin
markj@duralite.com
Estimated Sales: $1 Million+
Number Employees: 10-19
Square Footage: 15000

21847 (HQ)Durand-Wayland Inc
101 Durand Rd
Lagrange, GA 30241-2501

706-882-8161
Fax: 706-882-0052 800-241-2308
sales@durand-wayland.com
www.durand-wayland.com
Manufacturer and exporter of fruit processing and packing machinery including conveyors, cleaners, sizers, sorters, blemish graders and sprayers
President: Brooks Lee
brooksl@durand-wayland.com
VP Sales: Ray Perry
Marketing Director: Ashley Scott
Sales Manager: Suzanne Bryan
Purchasing Manager: Savral Patel
Number Employees: 100-249
Other Locations:
Durand-Wayland
Reedley CA

21848 (HQ)Durango-Georgia Paper
4301 Anchor Plaza Parkway
Suite 360
Tampa, FL 33634

813-286-2718
Fax: 912-576-0713
Manufacturer and exporter of bleached boards for folding cartons; also, grease resistant decorative paper plates and lightweight cups, bleached and natural kraft paper
VP Marketing: Joseph Meighan
Estimated Sales: $1 - 5 Million
Parent Co: Corporation Durango.

21849 Durant Box Factory
916 Crooked Oak Dr
Durant, OK 74701-2218

580-924-4035
Fax: 580-924-7276
Hardwood pallets and skids
Estimated Sales: $1-2.5 Million
Number Employees: 20
Square Footage: 50000

21850 Durashield USA
601 W Cherry St
Sunbury, OH 43074-9803

740-965-3008
Fax: 740-965-4485 www.americanpan.com
Non-stick coatings
Operations Manager: Brad Moore
bradmoore@richardsapex.com
Estimated Sales: $1 - 2.5 000,000
Number Employees: 10-19

21851 (HQ)Durasol Awnings
225 Tower Dr
Middletown, NY 10941

845-692-1100
Fax: 845-692-1101 800-444-6131
Custom-made awnings and awning products
President: Rich Lemond
Contact: Lauri Blake
lblake@durasol.com
Estimated Sales: $50 - 100 Million
Number Employees: 50-99
Square Footage: 50000
Other Locations:
Durasol
Tolleson AZ

21852 Durastill Export Inc
86 Reservoir Park Dr
Rockland, MA 02370-1062

781-878-5577
Fax: 781-878-2224 800-449-5260
sales@durastill.com www.durastill.com
Manufacturer and exporter of water distillation systems
Owner: M Anthony
Director Sales: Horace Mansfield
Sales: Jeff Thompson
Estimated Sales: Less Than $500,000
Number Employees: 1-4
Parent Co: Master Pitching Machine Company

21853 Durham Manufacturing Co
201 Main St
Durham, CT 06422-2108

860-349-3427
Fax: 860-349-8572 800-243-3744
info@durhammfg.com www.durhammfg.com
Manufacturer and exporter of pallet rack and industrial duty steel shelving
President: Paul H Frick Jr
Sales/Marketing Administrative Manager: David Massie
Estimated Sales: $2.5-5 Million
Number Employees: 100-249

21854 Duske Drying Systems
6901 Industrial Loop
Greendale, WI 53129-2445

414-529-0240
Fax: 414-529-0362 www.uzelacind.com
Drying systems
President: Mike Uzelac
Estimated Sales: $2.5 000,000
Number Employees: 10-19

21855 Dusobox Company
233 Neck Rd
Haverhill, MA 01835-8029

978-372-7192
Fax: 978-372-7198
Corrugated boxes
Manager: Peter Grogan
General Manager: Peter Grogan
Estimated Sales: $2.5-5 Million
Number Employees: 10 to 19
Parent Co: Dusobox Company

21856 Dutchess Bakers' Machinery Co
302 Grand Ave
Superior, WI 54880-1243

715-394-2387
Fax: 715-394-6199 800-777-4498
www.dutchessbakers.com
Dutchess Bakers' Machinery Company has been manufacturing high quality dough dividers and dough divider rounders for the foodservice industry since 1886! We are the originator and most respected & recognized name in the world for thiskind of equipment; also offers the bun & bagel slicer.
President: Kent Phillips
Marketing Director: Tony Marino
Plant Manager: John Skandel
Estimated Sales: $3 - 5 Million
Number Employees: 20-49
Square Footage: 120000
Parent Co: Superior-Lidgerwood-Mundy Corporation
Brands:
Dutchess

21857 Dutro Co
675 N 600 W # 2
Logan, UT 84321-3197

435-752-3921
Fax: 435-752-6360 866-388-7660
contact@dutro.com www.dutro.com
Manufacturer and exporter of carts, dollies and trucks
President: Josh Adams
j.adams@dutro.com
CEO: William Dutro
Estimated Sales: $17,483,702
Number Employees: 50-99
Number of Products: 16

21858 Dutter's Food
2700 Lord Baltimore Drive
Baltimore, MD 21244-2648

410-298-3663
Fax: 410-298-1625

Food Plans & Programs and Grocery stores
President: Vernon Mules
Estimated Sales: $10 - 20 Million
Number Employees: 10-19

21859 Duval Container Co
91 S Myrtle Ave
Jacksonville, FL 32204-2117

904-355-0711
Fax: 904-350-9709 800-342-8194
www.duvalcontainer.com
Corrugated boxes; wholesaler/distributor of containers and packaging materials
President: Richard L Gills
CFO: Mary Geller
Contact: William Erwin
william@duvalcontainer.com
Estimated Sales: $10 - 20 Million
Number Employees: 20-49

21860 Dwinell's Central Neon
101 Butterfield Rd
Yakima, WA 98901-2008

509-248-3772
Fax: 509-457-8026 800-932-8832
Indoor and outdoor signs including advertising, electric, neon and painted
President: Chuck Colmenero
President: Glenn Terrell
Estimated Sales: $5 - 10 Million
Number Employees: 50-99

21861 Dwyer Instruments Inc
102 Indiana Highway 212
Michigan City, IN 46360-1956

219-879-8000
Fax: 219-872-9057 800-872-3141
info@dwyer-inst.com www.dwyer-inst.com
Manufacturer and exporter of HVAC instruments including air filter gauges, thermostats, air velocity transmitters, temperature and process controllers and mercury switches
President: Steve Clark
CFO: Tom Dhaeze
Quality Control: Don Goad
Manager: Dave Lange
dlange@love-controls.com
Purchasing Manager: Dave Pilarski
Estimated Sales: $50 - 100 Million
Number Employees: 250-499

21862 Dycem Limited
83 Gilbane St
Warwick, RI 02886-6901

401-738-4420
Fax: 401-739-9634 800-458-0060
Contamination control systems including contamination mats for entranceways dealing with heavy pedestrian flow and wheeled machinery. Also, detergents and cleaners, cleaning equipment (vacuums, mops, buckets), and also stabilizing matsfor laboratory use.
President: Mark Dalziel
VP: Leo Lake
Research Microbiologist: Caroline Clibbon
Quality Officer: Cherie Jackson
Marketing Coordinator: Emma Truby
Sales Manager: Thomas Mulligan
Contact: Katlyn Babb
katlynn.babb@dycemusa.com
Purchasing: Lee Hamilton
Number Employees: 5-9

21863 Dyco
50 Naus Way
Bloomsburg, PA 17815-8784

570-752-2757
Fax: 570-752-7366 800-545-3926
sales@dyco-inc.com www.dyco-inc.com
Manufacturer and exporter of material handling equipment including case conveyors, car conveyors, diverter gates, fittings, and can rinsers
President: David M Rauscher
VP Sales/Marketing: David Rauscher, Jr.
Manager: Lewis Abram
labram@dyco-inc.com
Office Manager: Lea Ann O'Quinn
Estimated Sales: $2.5-5 Million
Number Employees: 50-99
Square Footage: 10000

21864 Dyco
50 Naus Way
Bloomsburg, PA 17815-8784
570-752-2757
Fax: 570-752-7366 800-545-3926
sales@dyco-inc.com www.dyco-inc.com
Conveyers, bagger and debagger machines
Finance Executive: Dan Bierdziewski
Manager: Lewis Abram
labram@dyco-inc.com
Estimated Sales: $1 - 5 Million
Number Employees: 50-99

21865 Dyco
6951 Naus Way
Bloomsburg, PA 17815
570-752-2757
Fax: 570-752-7366 800-545-3926
sales@dyco-inc.com www.dyco-inc.com
Provides custom engineered container handling solutions
President: Peter Yohe
Finance Executive: Dan Bierdziewski
Sales Manager: Kevin John
Contact: John Petty
jpetty@dyco-inc.com
Operations Manager: John Wittman
Number Employees: 50-99

21866 Dylog USA Vanens
7213 Sandscove Court
Suite 5
Winter Park, FL 32792-6901
407-265-9385
Fax: 407-265-9003

21867 Dyna-Veyor Inc
10 Hudson St
Newark, NJ 07103-2804
973-484-1119
Fax: 973-484-7790 800-326-5009
dynaveyor@aol.com www.dyna-veyor.com
Manufacturer and exporter of plastic conveyor chain belting, sprockets, idlers and corner tracks for the food processing, beverage, canning, pharmaceutical, packaging and container industries
Owner: Tony Ayre
dynaveyor@aol.com
Estimated Sales: $5-10 Million
Number Employees: 10-19

21868 Dynabilt Products
31 Industrial Drive
Readville, MA 02136-2355
617-364-1200
Fax: 617-364-7643 800-443-1008
http://dynabilt.com
Pallet racking and mezzanine systems, floor trucks and refuse and recycling containers
President: Charles Burtman
VP: Mark Goodman
National Sales Manager: Paul Venini
Estimated Sales: $10-20 Million
Number Employees: 50-99
Square Footage: 240000
Parent Co: Burtman Iron Works

21869 Dynablast Manufacturing
94 Riverside Drive
Mississauga, ON V5N 7K5
Canada
905-567-4126
Fax: 905-567-4330 888-242-8597
sales@dynablast.com www.dynablast.com
Gas fired pressure washers for kitchen degreasing and hot water and steam drain cleaning
President: Max Minkhorst
CFO: Don Kent
General Manager: William Duff
Purchasing Manager: Harry Bowker
Number Employees: 10
Square Footage: 340000
Brands:
Dynablast

21870 Dynaclear Packaging
500 W Main St
Suite 12
Wyckoff, NJ 07481-1439
201-337-1001
Fax: 201-337-5001 gerard@shrinkfilm.com
www.shrinkfilm.com
Manufacturer and supplier of packaging equipment and supplies.

Chairman/CEO: Peter Quercia
peterquercia@gmail.com
Manager: Jim Quercia
CFO: Barbara Kaywork
Manager of Sales: Michael Kintzley
Estimated Sales: $3.4 Million
Number Employees: 5-9
Other Locations:
Warehouse & Shipping
Wyckoff NJ

21871 Dynaco USA
935 Campus Dr
Mundelein, IL 60060-3830
847-562-4910
Fax: 847-562-4917 800-459-1930
dynaco@dynacodoor.us
High performance roll-up doors.
President: Bryan Gregory
CEO: Dirk Wouters
d.wouters@dynacodoor.us
Estimated Sales: Below $5 Million
Number Employees: 20-49

21872 Dynalab Corp
175 Humboldt St # 300
Suite 300
Rochester, NY 14610-1058
585-334-2060
Fax: 585-334-0241 800-828-6595
labinfo@dyna-labware.com www.dynalon.com
Distributor of a full line of plastic lab supplies including world renowned brands such as Azlon, Cowie, Kartell, and Sterilin.
President: Martin Davies
martin@dyna-labware.com
Number Employees: 20-49

21873 Dynalon Labware
175 Humboldt St
Suite 300
Rochester, NY 14610
585-334-2064
Fax: 585-334-0241 800-334-7585
dynaloninfo@dyna-labware.com
www.dynalabcorp.com
Wholesaler and distributor of plastic lab supplies
President & CEO: Martin Davies
Data Processing: Brian Genter
Product Manager: Steve Yudicky
Human Resources Director: Patti Zimmer
Engineering Manager: William Potter
Manager: Christine Leskovar
Plant Manager: Robert Pfeil
Estimated Sales: $6.7 Million
Number Employees: 35
Square Footage: 100000
Brands:
Ads Laminaire
Azlon
Baritainer Jerry Cans
Bio-Bin Waste Disposal
Burkle
Delrin
Kartell
Kydex
Kynar
Noryl
Sintra
Sterilin
Stuart
Ultem

21874 Dynamet
7687 N 6th St
Kalamazoo, MI 49009-8865
269-385-0006
Fax: 269-385-4750 dynamet@net-link.net
Specialty bulk material handling conveyors including flexible screw, tubular drag and oscillating; also, hydraulic dumpers
President: Robert Sutton
Estimated Sales: $1 - 3 Million
Number Employees: 10 to 19
Square Footage: 10000

21875 Dynamic Air Inc
1125 Willow Lake Blvd
St Paul, MN 55110-5193
651-484-2900
Fax: 651-484-7015 info@dynamicair.com
www.dynamicair.com
Pneumatic conveying of bulk solids for the processing industries.

President: James Steele
james.steele@dynamicair.com
National Sales Manager: Tom Acheson
Estimated Sales: $20-50 Million
Number Employees: 100-249

21876 Dynamic Automation LTD
4525 Runway St
Simi Valley, CA 93063-3479
805-584-8476
Fax: 805-584-8479 info@dynamicautomation.com
www.dynamicautomation.com
Bottling, bag closing, food and dairy processing, packaging, material handling and conveyor systems and equipment
Owner: Marc Freedman
mark@dynamicautomation.com
Sales Executive: Randy Gray
Estimated Sales: $2.5-5,000,000
Number Employees: 10-19

21877 Dynamic Coatings Inc
3315 W Sussex Way
Fresno, CA 93727-1320
559-225-4605
Fax: 559-225-4606 info@dynamiccoatingsinc.net
Product and service line is concrete restoration and protective coating products for floors and walls applications of which include that of food processing plants, kitchens, wineries, dairies, bakeries and breweries.
Owner: Jose A Gonzales
President: Scott Hamilton
Sales Representative: Jose Gonzalez
Estimated Sales: $857,000
Number Employees: 12

21878 Dynamic Cooking Systems
5900 Skylab Rd
Huntington Beach, CA 92647-2061
714-372-7000
Fax: 714-372-7096 800-433-8466
info@dcsappliances.com www.dcsappliances.com
Manufacturer and exporter of ranges, broilers, counter equipment, drop-in-cook tops, wall and convection ovens, ventilation hoods, outdoor barbecues and patio heaters
President: Mike Goadby
President: Michael Markowich
VP: Randy Rummel
CFO: Jeff Elder
Quality Control: Chillie Waiemas
Marketing Manager: Scott Davies
Contact: Vince Barott
vince.barott@fisherpaykel.com
Estimated Sales: $5 - 10 Million
Number Employees: 500-999
Square Footage: 66000
Brands:
Professional

21879 Dynamic International
PO Box 3322
Champlain, NY 12919-3322
514-956-0127
Fax: 877-668-6623 800-267-7794
www.dynamicmixers.com
Contact: Tony Tsirigoris
tony@dynamicmixers.com

21880 Dynamic Packaging
5725 International Pkwy
Minneapolis, MN 55428-3079
763-535-8669
Fax: 763-535-8768 800-878-9380
www.dynamicpkg.com
Printed and laminated flexible packaging films, roll stock and bags including simplex style and wicketed side-weld polyethylene; importer of polypropylene and polyester packaging films
Owner: George Butgusaim
VP Sales: James Pater, Jr.
Contact: Cindy Carr
ccarr@packaging-specialties.com
VP Production: Thoams Guerity
Estimated Sales: $1-2.5 Million
Number Employees: 10-19
Square Footage: 80000

21881 Dynamic Pak LLC
102 W Division St # 100
Suite 100
Syracuse, NY 13204-1428
315-474-8593
Fax: 315-474-8795 www.dynamicpak.us
Thermoforming and contract packaging including labeling andpackaging.
President: Tm Coyne
tcoyne@dynamicpak.us
Sales Executive: Herman Garcia
Estimated Sales: $1 - 3 Million
Number Employees: 5-9

21882 Dynamic Storage SystemsInc.
15315 Flight Path Dr.
Brooksville, FL 34604
Fax: 254-221-4106 800-974-8211
info@dynamicstorage.com www.hi-linerack.com
Sales storage and pallet racks, belt conveyors, canti-levers and guided rail entries
VP Sales: Robert Egner
Estimated Sales: $2.5-5 Million
Number Employees: 20-49
Brands:
Flexi-Guide
Gold Shield
Hi-Line
Hipir Kart

21883 Dynapar Corp
1675 N Delany Rd
Gurnee, IL 60031-1237
847-662-2666
Fax: 847-662-6633 800-873-8731
dancon@dancon.com www.dynapar.com
Industrial controls, counters, encoders, tachometers, temperative controllers
Vice President: Susan Ottmann
sottmann@dancon.com
VP: Susan Ottmann
Estimated Sales: $20 - 50 Million
Number Employees: 1000-4999
Number of Products: 8

21884 Dynaric Inc
5740 Bayside Rd
Virginia Beach, VA 23455-3004
757-460-3725
Fax: 757-363-8016 800-526-0827
gd@d-y-c.com www.dynaric.com
Manufacturer and exporter of strapping machinery and nonmetallic strapping
President: Joseph Martinez
CEO: Mike Moses
CFO: John Guzdus
Plant Manager: Vernon Wilson
Assistant Marketing Manager: Brian Cosgrove
Manager: Dennis Fuller
dennisf@dynaric.com
Plant Manager: Dennis Fuller
Number Employees: 100-249
Square Footage: 200000
Type of Packaging: Consumer, Food Service, Private Label, Bulk
Brands:
Durastrap
Dynaric
Dynastrap

21885 Dynasty Transportation
4021 Ambassador Caffery Prkwy
Suite 200 Bldg A
Lafayette, LA 70503
337-291-6700
Fax: 811-764-9229 866-626-3845
uvlwebsitesupport@uvlogistics.com
www.uvlogistics.com
Refrigerated and dry less than truckload and truckload service
Sales Director: Garland Hutson
Estimated Sales: $1 - 3 Million
Number Employees: 10-19
Parent Co: UV Logistics Holding Corp.

21886 Dynasys Technologies
2106 Drew Street
Suite 104
Clearwater, FL 34698-7880
727-443-6600
Fax: 727-443-4390 800-867-5968
dynasys@dyna-sys.com www.dyna-sys.com

Products for automatic identification datacapture, temperature indicators, and other products
President: Robert Scher
CEO/owner: Bobby Burkett
Director of R&D/COO: Tomas Grajales
Contact: Darrick Olson
darrickolson@dyna-sys.com
Estimated Sales: $5 - 10 Million
Number Employees: 20-49

21887 Dynatek Laboratory Inc
105 E 4th St
Galena, MO 65656-9649
417-357-6155
Fax: 417-357-6327 800-325-8252
www.dynateklabs.com
Texture analysis and adhesive testing
President: Elaine R Strope
Estimated Sales: $1-5 000,000
Number Employees: 10-19

21888 (HQ)Dynic USA Corp
4750 NE Dawson Creek Dr
Hillsboro, OR 97124-5799
503-693-1070
Fax: 503-648-1185 800-326-1249
enrique@dynic.com www.dynic.com
Labeling and printing products
President: Gwen Robinson
leej@smccd.edu
CEO/President: Shigeru Tamura
Director of Marketing: Mindy Nybert
Sales Engineer: Cesar Santa
Customer Service Rep: James Brandow
Estimated Sales: $25 Million
Number Employees: 50-99
Parent Co: Dynic Corporation
Other Locations:
Dynic UK Ltd
Cardiff, South Wales UK
Dynic Corporation
Minatoku, Tokyo, Japan HK
Brands:
Cabin Air Filters
Cetus Textile Fabrics
Oled Desiccant
Sirius Ttr

21889 (HQ)Dynynstyl
855 NW 17th Avenue
Suite A
Delray Beach, FL 33445-2520
561-547-5585
Fax: 561-547-0993 800-774-7895
Manufacturer and exporter of china, flatware, hollowware, chafing dishes, trays, buffetware, etc.; also, polishers, burnishers, silver cleaners and canned fuel for chafing dishes, etc.; silver and stainless steel repair servicesavailable
CEO: Dennis Paul
Vice President: Debra Cosner
Estimated Sales: $1 - 5 Million
Number Employees: 10
Brands:
Dynynstyl
Eco Lamp
Eco Pure Aqua Straw
Ecofuel
Emperor
Empress
Fold Flat

21890 Dzignpak LLC Englander
701 Texas Central Pkwy
Waco, TX 76712-6507
254-776-2360
Fax: 254-776-1213 888-314-5259
info@englanderdzp.com www.englanderdzp.com
Corrugated boxes
CEO: Marty Englander
CFO: Hal Whitaker
Estimated Sales: $23 Million
Number Employees: 50-99
Square Footage: 100000

21891 E & E Process Instrumentation
4-40 North Rivermede Road
Concord, Ontario, ON L4K 2H3318
Canada
905-669-4857
Fax: 905-669-2158 info@eeprocess.com
www.eeprocess.com

Manufacturer, importer and exporter of thermometers, hygrometers and hydrometers. Instruments for quality control and research and development. Nist certification of test instruments for FDA & USDA compliance
President: Todd Teichert
Estimated Sales: $1-2.5 Million
Number Employees: 5-9
Square Footage: 16000
Parent Co: E & E Process Instrumentation
Brands:
Brooklyn

21892 E & M Electric & Machinery Inc
126 Mill St
Healdsburg, CA 95448-4438
415-392-4834
Fax: 707-431-2558 www.eandm.com
Wine industry machinery
President: Judith Deas
steve.deas@enm.com
Sales Exec: Steven Deas
Estimated Sales: $20 - 50 Million
Number Employees: 50-99

21893 E A Bonelli & Assoc
8450 Edes Ave
Oakland, CA 94621-1306
510-740-0155
Fax: 510-740-0160 marco@eabonelli.com
President: Marco Di Gino
marco@eabenelli.com
Estimated Sales: $3 - 5 Million
Number Employees: 20-49

21894 E C Shaw Co
1242 Mehring Way
Cincinnati, OH 45203-1836
513-721-6334
Fax: 513-721-6350 866-532-7429
johnpinkley@ecshaw.com www.ecshaw.com
Flexographic plates, marking devices, nameplates, brass dies and steel stamps
President: Joseph C Grome
ajgrome@ecshaw.com
Rubber Stamp Sales: Marilyn Schalk
Customer Service Manager: Diana Randolph
Plant Manager: Joe Moffitt
Estimated Sales: $3 - 5 Million
Number Employees: 20-49

21895 E F Bavis & Assoc Inc
201 Grandin Rd
Maineville, OH 45039-9762
513-677-0500
Fax: 513-677-0552 info@bavis.com
www.bavis.com
Manufacturer and exporter of drive-thru and vertical conveyor systems including transaction cash drawers
President: William Sieber
wps@bavis.com
R&D: Mike Brown
Director Marketing/Sales: Terry Roberts
Estimated Sales: $5 - 10 Million
Number Employees: 20-49
Number of Products: 2
Type of Packaging: Food Service
Brands:
Transaction Drawer
Vittleveyor

21896 E F Engineering
9710 Humboldt Ave S
Minneapolis, MN 55431-2623
952-888-6596
Fax: 952-888-3619 sales@efengineering.com
www.efengineering.com
Owner: Eyal Fine
eyalf@chemserv.com
Number Employees: 10-19

21897 E H Wachs Co
600 Knightsbridge Pkwy
Lincolnshire, IL 60069-3617
847-537-8800
Fax: 847-520-1147 800-323-8185
sales@ehwachs.com www.ehwachs.com

President: Ken Morency
VP Finance: Nate Drucker
Quality Control: Peter Mullally
Marketing: John Geis
Sales: Chris Bauer
Public Relations: John Geis
Plant Manager: Craig Lewandowski
Purchasing: Ken Jarasz
Estimated Sales: $10-20 000,000
Number Employees: 100-249

21898 E J Mckernan Co
800 S Rock Blvd
Reno, NV 89502-4122

          775-356-6111
Fax: 775-356-2181 800-787-7587
surplus@mckernan.com www.mckernan.com
President: Timothy Mckernan
timm@mckernan.com
Chief Operating Officer: Frank Maggio
Estimated Sales: $20 - 50 Million
Number Employees: 20-49

21899 E K Lay Co
3469 Belgrade St
Philadelphia, PA 19134-5419

          215-739-1141
Fax: 215-739-7470 800-523-3220
www.eklay.com
Cutlery, utensils, foam plates and hinge take-out
containers and cups
President: Jim O'Brien
job@eklay.com
VP: James O'Brien
Sales: William Gallen
Estimated Sales: $10-20 Million
Number Employees: 10-19

21900 E-Control Systems
5170 Sepulveda Blvd
Suite 240
Sherman Oaks, CA 91403

          818-783-5229
Fax: 818-783-5219 888-384-3274
sales@econtrolsystems.com
www.econtrolsystems.com
CEO: Abraham Bernstein
Estimated Sales: $10 - 20 Million
Number Employees: 50-99

21901 E-Cooler
4320 S. Knox Avenue
Chicago, IL 80632

          773-284-9975
Fax: 773-284-9973 866-955-3266
www.e-cooler.com
Supplier of corrugated boxes and custom designed
boxes for the meat, seafood and produce industries.

21902 E-J Industries Inc
1275 S Campbell Ave
Chicago, IL 60608-1013

          312-226-5023
Fax: 312-226-5976 www.e-jindustries.com
Manufacturers of contract commercial seating and
cabinetry for the hospitality industry.
Vice President: Bill Colles
bcolles@ejindus.com
CEO/CFO: Keith Weitzman
VP: Keith Weitzman
Quality Control: W Nowak
Estimated Sales: $7 Million
Number Employees: 50-99
Square Footage: 240000

21903 E-Lite Technologies
2285 Reservoir Ave
Trumbull, CT 06611

          203-371-2070
Fax: 203-371-2078 877-520-3951
Manufacturer and exporter of electroluminescent
lamps
President: Mark Appelberg
President: Mark Appleberg
VP/COO: Mark Appelberg
Contact: Paul Burge
pburge@elitetechnologies.uk.com
Office Manager: Judith Sepelak
Estimated Sales: Below $5,000,000
Number Employees: 10-19
Brands:
   Flatlite

21904 E-Pak Machinery
1555 S State Road 39
La Porte, IN 46350

          219-393-5541
Fax: 219-324-2884 800-328-0466
sales@epakmachinery.com
www.epakmachinery.com
President: Lyle Lucas
CEO: Ron Sarto
Vice-President: Chris Ake
Contact: Brandon Pudlo
brandonpudlo@epakmachinery.com
Purchasing Director: Susie Nehal
Estimated Sales: $10 - 20 Million
Number Employees: 50-99

21905 E-Quip Manufacturing
230 Industry Ave
Frankfort, IL 60423-1641

          815-464-0053
Fax: 815-464-0059 www.e-quipmfg.com
OEM stainless steel equipment for food applications
President: Milt Minyard
sales@e-quipmfg.com
CFO: Marge Minyard
Estimated Sales: $2.5-5 000,000
Number Employees: 20-49

21906 E-Saeng Company
17316 Edwards Rd # 240
Cerritos, CA 90703-2450

          562-404-1844
Fax: 562-404-1774
Plastic bottle, container and tray, multi-layer plastic
sheet, flexible package, co-extruded
VP: K J Chang
Estimated Sales: $1 - 3 000,000
Number Employees: 1-4

21907 E-Z Dip
2048 S State Road 39
Frankfort, IN 46041-7655

          317-575-1088
Fax: 765-659-9687 866-347-3279
Electric ice cream scoop dips hard ice cream quickly
and easily. Ideal for caterers, convention centers, ho-
tels, cruise ships. Commercial grade, cast aluminum
President: Tom Shoup
Vice President: Amy Mennem
Marketing Director: Katherine Russell
Estimated Sales: $150,000
Number Employees: 5
Number of Brands: 1
Number of Products: 1
Square Footage: 9600
Brands:
   E-Z Dip

21908 E-Z Edge Inc
6119 Adams St
West New York, NJ 07093-1505

          201-295-1171
Fax: 201-295-1115 800-232-4470
order@e-zedge.com www.e-zedge.com
Manufacturer, exporter and importer of food pro-
cessing equipment including shears, knives and
grinders for meat, fish and poultry; importer of
stainless steel fish shears, bowl cutter knives and
cutlery
Owner: Michael Maffei
ezedgeusa@aol.com
VP: Michael Maffei
Manager: Paul Povinelli
Estimated Sales: Less Than $500,000
Number Employees: 1-4
Square Footage: 15000
Brands:
   Finney
   Giesser
   Speco
   Steffens
   Triumph
   Victorianox
   Zico

21909 E-Z Edge Inc
6119 Adams St
West New York, NJ 07093-1505

          201-295-1171
Fax: 201-295-1115 800-232-4470
order@e-zedge.com www.e-zedge.com
Supplier of custom made blades and saws, injector
needles, packing blades, bowl choppers, etc

Owner: Michael Maffei
ezedgeusa@aol.com
Manager: April Carazani
Estimated Sales: Less Than $500,000
Number Employees: 1-4

21910 E-Z Lift Conveyors
2000 S Cherokee St
Denver, CO 80223-3917

          303-733-5642
Fax: 303-733-5642 800-821-9966
ez@ezliftconveyors.com
www.ezliftconveyors.com
Manufacturer and exporter of lightweight conveyors
for beans, fruits, nuts and vegetables including
troughing belt, belt bucket, bottom dump car un-
loader and floor-to-floor
President: Kenneth B Drost
Estimated Sales: $1-2.5 Million
Number Employees: 10-19
Square Footage: 20000
Brands:
   E-Z Lift

21911 E-Z Shelving Systems Inc
5538 Merriam Dr
Shawnee, KS 66203-2548

          913-384-1331
Fax: 913-384-3399 800-353-1331
info@e-zshelving.com
www.walkincooler-shelving.com
Heavy duty cantilever shelving systems for walk-in
coolers, back room storage and sales areas
President: Ralph Larkin
ralph.larkin@e-zshelving.com
Estimated Sales: $1-2.5 Million
Number Employees: 10-19
Square Footage: 16000
Type of Packaging: Consumer, Food Service, Pri-
vate Label, Bulk

21912 E.G. Staats & Company
608 N Iris Rd
Mount Pleasant, IA 52641

          319-385-2116
Fax: 319-385-2429 800-553-1853
info@staatsawards.com www.staatsawards.com
Custom award ribbons
Contact: Rick Garbers
rick@staatsbikes.com
General Manager: Robert Mendenhall
Manager: Andy Zinkle
Estimated Sales: $5 - 10 Million
Number Employees: 20-49
Parent Co: Midwest Publishing Company

21913 (HQ)E.L. Nickell Company
385 Centreville St
Constantine, MI 49042

          269-435-2475
Fax: 616-435-8216
Manufacturer and exporter of pressure vessels and
heat exchangers
President: Brian Hicks
Sales Manager: Roger Bainbridge
Estimated Sales: $5-10 Million
Number Employees: 20-49
Square Footage: 60000

21914 E2M
3300 Breckinridge Blvd
Duluth, GA 30096-8983

          770-449-7383
Fax: 770-328-2880 800-622-4326
fskwira@e2m.com
Specializing in the integration of people, machines,
controls, procedures, materials and laytout into
seamless highly efficient packaging systems
President: Waye Young
Vice President of Development: Don Baldwin
General Manager: Fran Skwira
Estimated Sales: $20-50 Million
Number Employees: 50-99

21915 EAS Consulting Group LLC
1700 Diagonal Rd # 750
Suite 750
Alexandria, VA 22314-2841

          703-548-3270
Fax: 703-684-4428 877-327-9808
esteele@easconsultinggroup.com
www.easconsultinggroup.com

A leading provider of regulatory services to the food, dietary supplement, cosmetic, pharmaceutical, medical device, and tobacco industries.
President/Chief Operating Officer: Dean Cirotta
Chairman/Chief Executive Officer: Edward Steele
 esteele@easconsultinggroup.com
Chief Financial Officer: Brett Steele
Director, Regulator Info & Submissions: Charles Celeste
Number Employees: 1-4

21916 EB Box Company

20 Pollard Street
Unit #3
Richmond Hill, ON L4B 1C3
Canada

905-889-5600
Fax: 905-889-5602 800-513-2269
sales@ebbox.com www.ebbox.com
Paper boxes for fish and chips, Chinese food, doughnuts andpatties, auto parts, computer parts, health products, cosmetics, garments, innerboxes, trays and custom boxes
Number Employees: 5-9

21917 EB Eddy Paper

P.O. Box 5003
Port Huron, MI 48061-5003

810-982-0191
Fax: 810-982-4057 www.domtar.com
Manufacturer and exporter of packaging and specialty coated papers
Vice President: Mark Ushpol
Marketing Manager: Rob Belanger
Contact: John Beecroft
 johnbeecroft@domtar.com
Production Manager: David Rushton
Estimated Sales: $30 - 50 Million
Number Employees: 20-49
Parent Co: Domtar

21918 EB Metal Industries

Poultney St
Whitehall, NY 12887-0149

518-499-1222
Fax: 518-499-2220
Vending equipment, zinc die castings and sheet metal fabrication
Sales Director: Stu Tesser
Purchasing Director: Patti Abbott

21919 EBM Technology

641 Keeaumoku Street
Suite 5
Honolulu, HI 96814

330-929-8929
Fax: 808-945-3105 866-212-6127
info@ebmtech.com www.ebmtech.com
Fully automated, highspeed collating and packing system which will top load or side load with gantry robots, two axis robots or pushers
President: Martin Dannenberg
Contact: Bell Hsu
 bell@ebmtech.com
Number Employees: 5200

21920 EBS

14657 Pebble Bend Drive
Houston, TX 77068

713-939-1000
Fax: 281-444-7900 www.ebs-next.com
Software for material handling systems
President/ COO: Ron Rogers
VP, Development & Software Support: Jay Spencer
Director, Business Development: Kim Prevost
Contact: Steve Benedict
 steve@ebsoftware.com
Estimated Sales: $1 - 3,000,000
Number Employees: 30

21921 ECHO Inc

400 Oakwood Rd
Lake Zurich, IL 60047-1564

Fax: 847-540-9670 800-432-3246
www.echo-usa.com
Wine industry hoses and sprayers.
President & CEO: David Erickson
Year Founded: 1950
Estimated Sales: $220 Million
Number Employees: 500-999

21922 ECOM Agroindustrial Corporation Ltd

13760 Noel Rd
Ste 500
Dallas, TX 75240

214-520-1717
Fax: 214-520-1859 www.ecomtrading.com
Cotton, cocoa, coffee and sugar.
CEO: Andrew Halle
Year Founded: 1849
Estimated Sales: $5.1 Billion
Number Employees: 6,000
Type of Packaging: Consumer, Food Service, Private Label, Bulk
Other Locations:
 New York NY
 Hayward CA

21923 EDT Corp

1006 NE 146th St # J
Vancouver, WA 98685-1411

360-574-7294
Fax: 360-574-3834 www.edtcorp.com
Sanitary bearings and bearings for extreme environments
President: Carl Klinge
Manager: Carl G Klinge
 carl@edtcorp.com
Estimated Sales: $1 - 5 000,000
Number Employees: 10-19

21924 EFA Processing EquipmentCompany

13308 C St
Omaha, NE 68144-3602

402-592-9360
Fax: 402-592-9366
Cutters, boning devices and slaughtering equipment, skinning machines and stunning apparatus
Manager: Donald Novonty
Estimated Sales: $500,000-$1 000,000
Number Employees: 1-4

21925 EFCO Products Inc

130 Smith St
Poughkeepsie, NY 12601

800-284-3326
info@efcoproducts.com www.efcoproducts.com
Leading supplier of mixes, fruit and creme style fillings, jellies, jams and concentrated icing fruits to the baking industry.
CEO: David Miller
Vice President: Andy Herzing
Senior Director of Sales & Marketing: Mark Lowman
Director of Manufacturing Operations: Veronica Miller
Year Founded: 1903
Estimated Sales: $2.5-5 Million
Number Employees: 50-99

21926 EFP Corp

223 Middleton Run Rd
Elkhart, IN 46516-5488

574-295-4690
Fax: 574-295-6512 www.efpcorp.com
Molders and fabricators of expanded polystyrene for packing, insulation, flotation and foundry patterns
President: Bill B Flint
Cmo: Joann Phillips
 jphillips@efpcorp.com
Estimated Sales: $20,000,000 - $49,999,999
Number Employees: 50-99

21927 EG&G Instruments

100 Midland Rd
Oak Ridge, TN 37830

Fax: 865-483-0396 800-251-9750
info@signalrecovery.com www.ortec-online.com
Modular research instrumentation; gamma and alpha semiconductor detectors
VP: Jon P Kidder
Estimated Sales: $25-50 Million
Number Employees: 250-499

21928 EGA Products Inc

4275 N 127th St
Brookfield, WI 53005-1890

262-781-7899
Fax: 262-781-3586 800-937-3427
www.egaproducts.com
Material handling equipment; also, cabinets, racks and containers

President: David Young
Marketing/Sales: John Kuhnz
Estimated Sales: $10 - 20 Million
Number Employees: 50-99

21929 EGS Electrical Group

7770 Frontage Rd
Skokie, IL 60077

847-679-7800
Fax: 847-268-6011
Manufacturer and exporter of electrical products including controls, switches and lighting fixtures
President: Eric Meyer
CFO: Michael Bryant
Quality Control: L Engler
Marketing Communication Manager: Michelle Miller
Contact: Peter Strong
 pstrong@egseg.com
Estimated Sales: $20 - 50 Million
Number Employees: 100-249
Parent Co: EGS Electrical Group

21930 EGW Bradbury Enterprises

479 US Highway 1
PO Box 129
Bridgewater, ME 04735-0129

207-429-8141
Fax: 207-429-8188 800-332-6021
info@bradburybarrel.com
www.bradburybarrel.com
Manufacturer and exporter of tongue and groove white cedar barrels, tubs and barrelcraft and wooden display fixtures; also, custom wooden displays, fixtures and accessories
President/CEO: Adelle Bradbury
Sales/Marketing Manager: Wayne Bradbury
Office Manager: Jennifer Griffin
Estimated Sales: $5-10 Million
Number Employees: 20-49

21931 EIT

532 W Lake St
Elmhurst, IL 60126-1408

630-279-3400
Fax: 630-279-3420 eitpromo@aol.com
Manufacturer and exporter of flags and promotional products
Owner: Mark Tober
CFO: Lucille Tobor
VP: Mark Tobor
Quality Control: Beth Pirc
Chairman of the Board: Earl Tobor
Estimated Sales: Below $5 Million
Number Employees: 5 to 9
Square Footage: 32000

21932 EJ Brooks Company

2727 Paces Ferry Road
Atlanta, GE 30339

973-597-2900
Fax: 973-597-2919 800-458-7325
info@tydenbrooks.com www.tydenbrooks.com
Security seals and locking devices.
President/CEO: John Roessner
Sales Director: Paul Dietlin
Director Purchasing: George Weber
Estimated Sales: $5-10 Million
Number Employees: 250-499

21933 EKATO Corporation

700 C Lake St
St Ramsey, NJ 07436

201-825-4684
Fax: 201-825-9776 jerry.baresich@ekato.com
Manufacturer and exporter of industrial mixers and agitators for fluids and solids
President: Paul Dwelle
Sales Director: Michael Starer
Estimated Sales: $5-10,000,000
Number Employees: 10-19
Parent Co: EKATO Ruhr Und Mischtechnik-GmbH
Brands:
 Ekato
 Esd
 Fluid
 Unimix

21934 ELAU-Elektronik Automatiions

4201 W Wrightwood Avenue
Chicago, IL 60639-2095

773-342-8400
Fax: 773-342-8404 sales@elau.com
www.elau.com

Motion control systems
CEO: Thomas Cord
Business Manager: Ronda Dade
Estimated Sales: $2.5-5 Million
Number Employees: 1-4
Parent Co: Elau Germany

21935 ELBA
4717 Sweden Road
Charlotte, NC 28273-5935

704-643-5777
Fax: 704-643-2010
Complete bag making systems, ice cube bags, systems for producing extruded netting and systems to produce mesh bags from extruded material
President: Carlo Louni
CFO: Angle Louni
Contact: Paolo Azimonti
paolo@elba-spa.it
Warehouse Manager: Bill Lebact
Estimated Sales: $3 - 5 000,000
Number Employees: 10

21936 ELF Machinery
1555 S State Road 39
La Porte, IN 46350-6301

219-325-3060
Fax: 219-324-2884 800-328-0466
www.elfmachines.com
Manufacturer and exporter of liquid packaging equipment including fillers, cappers, labelers, induction sealers, coders, bottle cleaners, unscramblers, conveyors, turntables, etc
President: Thomas Ake Reed
CEO: Ron Sarto
International Sales Manager: Eric Thorgren
Number Employees: 100-249
Square Footage: 320000
Type of Packaging: Food Service
Brands:
  Elf

21937 ELISA Technologies, Inc.
2501 NW 66th Ct
Gainesville, FL 32653-1693

352-337-3929
Fax: 352-337-3928 info@elisa-tek.com
www.elisa-tek.com
Developed of enzyme immunoassay technology for use in the food industry.
Scientific Director: Justin Bickford
justin.bickford@elisa-tek.com
Sales & Marketing: Nick Lafferman
Administrative Director: Natalie Rosskopf
Estimated Sales: $500,000 - $1 Million
Number Employees: 10-19

21938 ELP Inc
366 Grant St
Elizabeth, CO 80107

303-688-2240
Fax: 303-688-2240
Packer of meat including beef, lamb, goat and pork
President: Mike Hundley
VP: Robert Hundley
Estimated Sales: $1-2.5 Million
Number Employees: 10-19
Type of Packaging: Consumer

21939 EM Industries
480 S Democrat Rd
Gibbstown, NJ 08027-1239

914-592-4660
Fax: 914-592-9469
Specialty chemicals
Contact: Kalyan Nuguru
knuguru@emindustries.com
Estimated Sales: $10 - 15 Million
Number Employees: 50-99

21940 EMCO
170 Monarch Ln
Miamisburg, OH 45342

661-294-9966
Fax: 937-865-6605 800-722-3626
www.emcolabels.com
Manufacturer and exporter of code labelers and printers for price marking and UPC/EAN code printing
President: Robert H Hay
Sales Manager: Morris Bargorch
Estimated Sales: $5-10 Million
Number Employees: 10

Brands:
  Coronet
  Mark Ii
  Medalist
  Regal
  Signet

21941 EMCO Packaging
2100 Commonwealth Ave
North Chicago, IL 60064

847-689-2200
Fax: 847-689-8470 www.emcochem.com
Contract packager of detergents
President & CEO: Edward Polen
Estimated Sales: $31 Million
Number Employees: 385
Parent Co: Emco Chemical Distributors, Inc.

21942 EMD Performance Materials
One International Plaza
#300
Philadelphia, PA 19113

908-591-7496
Fax: 484-652-5749 888-367-3275
Specialty testing products for the Food and Beverage industry including Microbiology Culture Media featuring granulated media for safety and convenience; the MAS-100 Eco, a lightweight, portable air sampling instrument; the HYLiTE 2system, a portable system for determining the cleanliness of surfaces and work spaces; and Test Strip Kits for rapid testing of Ions and pH measurement. Manufactures a mineral based line of colors for use in foods, dietary supplements and drugs.
President/CEO: Meiken Krebs
Contact: Matthew Girard
mgirard@emdchemicals.com
CFO: Klaus Brandt
Vice President: Octavio Diaz
Research & Development: Jim Morgera
Quality Control: Stephen Bates
Marketing Director: Rebecca Vaiarelli
Key Account Manager: Taina Franke
Public Relations: Rina Spatafore
Operations Manager: Thorsten Hartis
Production Manager: John Alestra
Plant Manager: Bob Jones
Purchasing Manager: Ron Wisda
Estimated Sales: $10-25 Million
Number Employees: 500-999
Parent Co: Merck KgaA Darmstadt

21943 EMD Products
33 Zarpa Way
Hot Springs Village, AR 71909-7108

847-549-8308
Fax: 501-922-4873 800-910-4000
emdproduct@aol.com www.emdproducts.com
Servo motion control products, single axis positioning brushless servo systems, multi-axis controllers and analog and digital brushless servo systems and software
Member: Ray Eimerman
emdproduct@aol.com

21944 EMI
4 Heritage Park Rd
Clinton, CT 06413

860-669-1199
Fax: 860-669-7461 800-243-1188
info@clevelandmixer.com
Fluid mixing and blending, wine industry tank mixers
President: Emmett Barker
Contact: Jullian Anderson
janderson@emi1.com
Estimated Sales: $10-20 000,000
Number Employees: 20-49

21945 ENJAY Converters Limited
495 Ball Street
Cobourg, ON K9A 3J6
Canada

905-372-7373
Fax: 905-377-8066 800-427-5517
sales@enjay.com www.enjay.com
Manufactures complete line of laminated and grapped cake circles and sheets

21946 ENM Co
5617 N Northwest Hwy
Chicago, IL 60646-6177

773-775-8400
Fax: 773-775-5968 enmco@aol.com
www.enmco.com
Manufacturer and exporter of counting and number devices and hour meters; also, mechanical, electro-mechanical and electronic digital counters
Owner: Nicholas Polydoris
npolydoris@enmco.com
Sales Manager: Dale Hall
Sales Manager: Lee Bryant
Sales Engineer: Megan Fitzgerald
Estimated Sales: $20 - 50 Million
Number Employees: 50-99

21947 ENSCO Inc
5400 Port Royal Rd
Springfield, VA 22151-2312

703-321-9000
Fax: 703-321-4529 williams.susan@ensco.com
www.ensco.com
Vision based food product color verification inspection systems; instantaneous feedback process control for food processing applications
President: Gregory B Young
gregory.young@ensco.com
CEO: Paul W Broome Iii
Director Marketing: Tom Cirillo
Estimated Sales: $80 Million
Number Employees: 100-249

21948 EP Minerals LLC
9785 Gateway Dr # 1000
Reno, NV 89521-2991

775-824-7600
Fax: 775-824-7601 www.epminerals.com
Wine industry filter aids
President: Randy Moore
CEO: David Treadwell
Vice President of Technology: Greg Miller
Director of Quality Assurance: Forrest Reed
Estimated Sales: $50,000,000 - $99,999,999
Number Employees: 20-49

21949 EPCO
P.O. Box 20428
Murfreesboro, TN 37129-0428

615-893-8432
Fax: 615-890-3196 800-251-3398
www.useco.com
Manufacturer and exporter of food service equipment including bun racks, heater/proofer cabinets, banquet carts, can racks and air curtain refrigerators
Controller: Philip Keller
VP/General Manager: Thomas Taylor
VP Sales/Marketing: James Jean
Number Employees: 10-19
Square Footage: 400000
Parent Co: Standex International Corporation
Type of Packaging: Food Service

21950 EPD Technology Corporation
14 Hayes St
Elmsford, NY 10523-2502

914-592-1233
Fax: 914-347-2181 800-892-8926
Steam management products, software and services; also, infrared thermometers and ultrasonic test instruments.
President: Gary Mohr
CEO: Helen Clint
VP Marketing: Alan Bardes
Estimated Sales: $5-10 Million
Number Employees: 20-49
Square Footage: 40000
Parent Co: UE Systems

21951 EPI Labelers
1145 E Wellspring Rd
New Freedom, PA 17349-8426

717-235-8344
Fax: 717-235-0608 800-755-8344
sales@epilabelers.com www.epilabelers.com
Pressure sensitive label applicators and premium inserting equipment
President: Randy Cottalier
sales@epilabelers.com
Co-Owner: Lynn Vonderhorst
R&D: Linda Fulginiti
General Manager: Linda Fulginiti
Estimated Sales: $5 - 10 Million
Number Employees: 10-19

21952 EPI World Graphics
3824 147th St Ste F
Midlothian, IL 60445-3460

708-389-7500
Fax: 708-389-7522
Nameplates and labels; also, imprinting services
available
President: Nancy Kolar
VP: Karen R Steffey
Purchasing: Chuck Tanner
Estimated Sales: $5-10 Million
Number Employees: 5 to 9
Square Footage: 50000

21953 EPL Technologies
237 Lancaster Avenue
Suite 2002
Devon, PA 19333

610-254-8600
Fax: 610-521-5985 800-637-3743
www.bloomberg.com
Consultant providing technology, products and ser-
vices to maintain the quality of fresh cut produce
President: Paul L. Devine
CEO: Antony E. Kendall
VP Technology: William R. Romig
Commercial Manager: Lisa Herickhoff
Number Employees: 221

21954 ERC Parts Inc
4001 Cobb International Blvd N
Kennesaw, GA 30152-4374

770-984-0276
Fax: 770-951-1875 800-241-6880
marketing@erconline.com www.erconline.com
Drive-thru displays, recording devices and timers
and battery chargers; importer of cash register parts;
exporter of point of sale systems, parts and software;
wholesaler/distributor of VAR products; serving the
food service market
Owner: Chuck Rollins
cerollins@erconline.com
CFO: Stuart Dobson
Vice President: Charles Barnes
Research & Development: Timothy Adams
Marketing Director: Bryon Finkel
Parts/Manufacturing Division: Eric Hart
Purchasing Manager: Rob Haight
Estimated Sales: $1 - 2.5 Million
Number Employees: 50-99
Square Footage: 180000
Other Locations:
ERC Parts
Louisville KY
ERC Parts
Lexington KY
ERC Parts
Cleveland OH
ERC Parts
Las Vegas NV
ERC Parts
Baltimore MD
ERC Parts
Greensboro NC
ERC Parts
Raleigh NC

21955 ERO/Goodrich Forest Products
19255 SW 65th Ave # 110
Tualatin, OR 97062-9717

503-885-9414
Fax: 503-625-5825 800-458-5545
Manufacturer and exporter of plywood shipping
containers and pallets
Manager: Elizabeth Brashear
Sales Manager: Harry Nelson
Estimated Sales: $1 - 5 Million
Number Employees: 16
Type of Packaging: Bulk

21956 ERS International
488 Main Avenue
Norwalk, CT 06851-1008

203-849-2500
Fax: 203-849-2501 800-377-4685
Electronic displays and shelf labels
CEO and President: Bruce Failing
Number Employees: 50-99
Square Footage: 20000
Brands:
Shelfnet

21957 ES Robbins Corp
2802 Avalon Ave
Muscle Shoals, AL 35661-3748

256-248-2400
Fax: 256-248-2410 800-633-3325
info@esrchairmats.com www.esrobbins.com
Expandable and collapsible reusable beverage and
food storage containers, plastic measuring caps and
canisters
Owner: Amanda Berryman
CFO: Ron Mansel
CEO: Edward S Robbins Iii
VP Sales/Marketing: Steve Doerr
berryman@esrchairmats.com
Purchasing Manager: Nancy Hamilton
Estimated Sales: $10 - 20 Million
Number Employees: 100-249
Parent Co: E.S. Robbins Corporation
Brands:
Flex-Flo
Kleer-Measure
Poptite

21958 ESD Energy Saving Devices
1751 Highway 36 E
St Paul, MN 55109-2108

651-222-0849
Fax: 651-222-4626
Commercial and industrial fluorescent and vapor
tight lighting fixtures
President: Kerry Petersen
VP: Mike Holder
Estimated Sales: Below $5 Million
Number Employees: 5-9

21959 ESD Waste2water Inc
495 Oak Rd
Ocala, FL 34472-3005

352-680-9134
Fax: 352-867-1320 800-277-3279
info@waste2water.com www.waste2water.com
Manufacturer and exporter of water treatment equip-
ment
Manager: Kevin Hawkins
Estimated Sales: $2.5-5 Million
Number Employees: 20-49
Square Footage: 100000
Parent Co: Zentox
Brands:
Cascade

21960 ESE Inc
3600 Downwind Dr
Marshfield, WI 54449-8656

715-387-4778
Fax: 715-387-0125 800-236-4778
sudat@ese1.com www.eseautomation.com
Owner: Mark Weber
CEO: Michael Richart
richartm@ese1.com
Director of Sales: Brandon Teachman
Director of Operations: Justin Hobson
Estimated Sales: $2.5 - 5 Million
Number Employees: 20-49

21961 ESE, Inc
PO Box 1107
Marshfield, WI 54449-7107

715-387-4778
Fax: 715-387-0125 800-236-4778
sudat@ese1.com www.ese1.com
Process control systems; also, specialty applications
and integration services available for PC based
systems
President: Mark Weber
Director of Sales: Brandon Teachman
Contact: Gwen Irvan
irvang@ese1.com
Director of Operations: Justin Hobson
Estimated Sales: $5-10 Million
Number Employees: 5-9
Square Footage: 68000

21962 ESI Group
950 Walnut Ridge Dr
Hartland, WI 53029-9388

262-369-3535
Fax: 262-369-3536 866-369-3535
sales@esigroupusa.com www.esigroupusa.com

ESI is an industry leading design-build firm focused
on the new construction, expansion and renovation
of foodservice facilities. Our single source approach
streamlines the building process allowing the team
at ESI to remain focusedon the needs of the customer, the success of their project and their financial
bottom line.
President: Brad Barke
bbarke@esigroupusa.com
Number Employees: 50-99

21963 ESI Qual Intl
968 Washington St # 2
Stoughton, MA 02072-2973

781-344-6344
Fax: 781-341-3978 800-443-0511
info@esiqual.com www.esiqual.com
Enviromental services and equipment, laboratory
testing equipment, sanitation supplies and equip-
ment, environmental, occupational, and food safety
consultants.
President/CEO: Phil Ventresca
info@esiqual.com
Vice President: Vince Vantresca
Estimated Sales: Below 1 Million
Number Employees: 5-9

21964 ESKAY Corporation
5202 D Corrigan Way Ste 100
Salt Lake City, UT 84116

801-363-6100
Fax: 801-359-9911 800-253-1003
Designs, sells, installs, and supports a complete line
of world-class logistics systems for automated material handling in factory, distribution, and cleanroom
environments. Full range of advanced-technology
products forrefrigerated/frozen food distribution includes conveyors, sortation systems, transport vehicles, order-picking systems, automated storage
buffers, and real-time warehouse management
software (WMS)
President: Itsud Oyamatsu

21965 ESS Technologies
3160 State St
Blacksburg, VA 24060-6603

540-961-5716
Fax: 540-961-5721 info@esstechnologies.com
www.esstechnologies.com
Supplier of packaging equipment including
overwrapping and bundling; shrinkwrapping, stretch
banding, automatic cartoning and case packing;
candy wrapping equipment; filling and packaging
equipment; turnkey lines and integrationservices.
President: Kevin Browne
Vice President: Linda Browne
Director, Global Business Development: Walter
Langosch
Estimated Sales: $1-2.5 Million

21966 ESummits
PO BOX 27946
Scottsdale, AZ 90831-0002

562-983-8050
Fax: 562-983-8051 800-643-0797
www.esummits.com
Marketing company, promote food products globally
Chief Executive Officer, Director: Paul Ortman
Estimated Sales: Below $500,000
Number Employees: 1-4

21967 ET International Technologies
3705 Kipling Street
Suite 103
Wheat Ridge, CO 80033

303-854-9087
Fax: 303-722-7379 855-412-5726
Manufacturer and exporter of hot tapping machines
for the HVAC/R and piping industries
President: Greg Apple

21968 ETS Laboratories
899 Adams St # A
St Helena, CA 94574-1160

707-963-4806
Fax: 707-963-1054 info@etslabs.com
www.etslabs.com
Wine, beer, and spirits testing, ISO Guide 25 accred-
ited
President: Gordon Burns
gburns@etslabs.com
Estimated Sales: $1-2.5 000,000
Number Employees: 20-49

21969 EVAPCO Inc
5151 Allendale Ln
Taneytown, MD 21787-2155
410-876-3782
Fax: 410-756-6450 marketing@evapco.com
www.evapco.com
Manufacturer and exporter of industrial refrigeration equipment including evaporative condensers, cooling towers, evaporators, vessels, valves, recirculator packages, rooftop hygienic air systems, and closed circuit coolers
President: Bill Bartley
bbartley@evapco.com
CFO: Harold Walsh
VP: Joseph Mondato
VP Marketing/Sales: Dave Rule
Number Employees: 5-9
Square Footage: 360000

21970 EXE Technologies
8787 N Stemmons Fwy
Dallas, TX 75247
214-775-6000
Fax: 214-775-0900 800-393-8324
Warehouse management systems, supply chain distribution
CEO: Raymond Hood
Senior VP Professional Services/CFO: Michael Burstein
Contact: Miroslav Buran
miroslav.buran@exe.sk
Director: Adam Belsky
Estimated Sales: $35 - 40 Million
Number Employees: 100

21971 EZ-Tek Industries
7041 Boone Avenue
Brooklyn Park, MN 55428
800-835-9344
Fax: 763-795-8867 800-796-3279
www.eztek.com
Manufacturer and exporter of case sealers, tapers, material handling and packaging equipment; importer of case sealers, tapers and strappers
President: Bob Kops
CFO: Bob Kops
Estimated Sales: $1 Million
Number Employees: 4
Brands:
Easy Gluer
Easy Strapper
Easy Taper

21972 EZE-Lap Diamond Products
3572 Arrowhead Dr
Carson City, NV 89706-2006
775-888-9500
Fax: 775-888-9555 800-843-4815
sales@eze-lap.com www.eze-lap.com
Sharpeners and sharpening stones for knives, slicing wheels, saw chains and pizza cutters; also, grinding equipment
President: Jack Fletcher
sales@eze-lap.com
Sales Coordinator: Donna Long
Office Manager: Lisa Fletcher
sales@eze-lap.com
General Manager: Ralph Johnson
Estimated Sales: $1 - 20,000,000
Number Employees: 10-19
Brands:
Diamond

21973 Eagle Bakery Equipment
9989 Lickinghole Road
Ashland, VA 23005
804-798-8920
Fax: 804-752-6828
support@eaglebakeryequipment.com
www.eaglebakeryequipment.com
Bun, bread make-up lines and equipment, dough pumps, tortillia and speciality equipment
Manager: Paul Peebles
CFO: Wd David Abbott
R&D: Howard Brandon
Quality Control: Howard Brandon
Sales: Mac Broddus
Estimated Sales: Below $5 000,000
Number Employees: 1-4

21974 Eagle Box Company
1 Adams Blvd Ste 1
Farmingdale, NY 11735
212-255-3860
Fax: 212-249-4517 info@eaglebox.com
www.eaglebox.com
Printed folding paperboard cartons
Owner: Jay Hoffman
Sales Director: Jim Fahlgren
Plant Manager: Steve Williamson
Estimated Sales: $10 Million
Number Employees: 20-49
Square Footage: 160000

21975 Eagle Flexible Packaging
1100 Kingsland Dr.
Batavia, IL 60510
630-406-1760
info@eagleflexible.com
www.eagleflexible.com
Biodegradable packaging and reusable bags
President: Frank Vacca
CEO: Ed Walenga
VP, Operations: Scott Deringer
Year Founded: 1994
Estimated Sales: $20.7 Million
Square Footage: 52000

21976 Eagle Foodservice Equipment
100 Industrial Blvd
Clayton, DE 19938
302-653-3000
Fax: 302-653-2065 800-441-8440
answers@eaglegrp.com www.eaglegrp.com
Manufacturer and exporter of wire, solid and polymer shelving, work tables, sinks, handsinks, countertop equipment, underbar equipment, bun pans, as well as custom fabricated items
Owner: Larry N McAllister
Sales Director: Linda Donavon
Number Employees: 250-499
Type of Packaging: Food Service

21977 Eagle Group
100 Industrial Blvd
Clayton, DE 19938-8903
302-653-3000
Fax: 302-653-2065 800-441-8440
customerservice@eaglegrp.com
Manufacturer and exporter of stainless steel food service equipment including shelving, sinks, tables, cookers, warmers and bar equipment
Owner: Larry Mccallister
Sales: Linda Donavon
lmccallister@eaglegroup.com
Estimated Sales: $50 - 75 Million
Number Employees: 250-499
Parent Co: Eagle Group
Brands:
Lifestore
Panco

21978 Eagle Home Products
1 Arnold Dr # 1
Huntington, NY 11743-3981
631-673-3500
Fax: 631-673-6700 www.eaglehomeproducts.com
Manufacturer, importer and exporter of cleaning aids and rubber gloves
Owner: Robert Chemtob
rchemtob@eaglehomeproducts.com
Vice President: Andre Chemtob
Estimated Sales: $5-10 Million
Number Employees: 20-49
Square Footage: 200000
Brands:
Denta Brite
Diamond Brite
Diamond Grip
Eagle
Eagle Absolute
Soft Touch

21979 Eagle Labeling
1741 Industrial Dr
Sterling, IL 61081-9290
815-625-1858
Fax: 815-625-8554 800-527-7549
Custom label applicators, labeling in-line, label dispensors, automation
Estimated Sales: Below $500,000
Number Employees: 5-9

21980 Eagle Packaging Corp
2100 Dennison St
Oakland, CA 94606-5236
510-533-3000
Fax: 510-534-3000 800-824-EAGL
pesales@parsons-eagle.com www.eaglepack.net
Vice President: Russ Davis
r.davis@eaglepack.net
Vice President: Russ Davis
r.davis@eaglepack.net
Estimated Sales: $20-50 Million
Number Employees: 10-19

21981 Eagle Packaging Corp
2100 Dennison St
Oakland, CA 94606-5236
510-533-3000
Fax: 510-534-3000 800-824-3245
President: Peter Hatchell
Vice President: Pierce Butler
Product Manager: Jeff Reed
Vice President of Sales: Pete Butler
Estimated Sales: $10 Million
Number Employees: 10-19

21982 Eagle Products Company
P.O. Box 431601
Houston, TX 77243-1601
713-690-1161
Fax: 713-690-7661 info@eaglechair.com
www.eaglechair.com
Quality manufacturer and exporter of booths, chairs, bar stools, tabletops and bases
Executive Director: Maximillian Yurgulich
CEO: Natalia Jurcic-Koc
CFO: Nathalai Kac
Contact: Max Yuglich
max@eaglechair.com
Director of Operations: Max Yuglich
Estimated Sales: $5 - 10 Million
Number Employees: 10-19
Square Footage: 80000
Parent Co: Eagle Chair
Type of Packaging: Food Service
Brands:
Eagle Chair

21983 Eagle Protect PBC.
3079 Harrison Ave #21
South Lake Tahoe, CA 96150
800-384-3905
eagleprotect.com
Protective clothing supplier, including disposable gloves and clothing. Eagle Protect is the world's only disposable glove and clothing specialist to be B Corp certified.
CEO & Founder: Steve Ardagh
Co-Founder & VP, Marketing: Lynda Ronaldson
Chief Operating Officer: Aaron French *Year Founded:* 2006

21984 Eagle Research Inc
2375 Bush St
San Francisco, CA 94115-3123
415-495-3131
Fax: 415-441-6709 info@xeaglex.com
www.xeaglex.com
Custom software for any indsutry
President: Allen Gleazer
allen@xeaglex.com
Vice President: Nina Rosa carino
Vice President: Nina Carino
Estimated Sales: $1-5 000,000
Number Employees: 1-4

21985 Eagle Wire Works
3173 E 66th St
Cleveland, OH 44127
216-341-8550
Fax: 216-341-6460
Refrigerator racks and stands and racks to hold plastic bags
President: James J Malik
Contact: Jim Bartolotta
jimb@eaglewireworks.com
Estimated Sales: $1-2.5 Million
Number Employees: 5-9

21986 Eagle-Concordia Paper Corporation
1 Adams Blvd
Farmingdale, NY 11735-6611
212-255-3860
Fax: 212-249-4530 info@eaglebox.com
www.eaglebox.com
Wholesaler/distributor of boxes, cartons, packaging tape, bubble wrap, etc.; also, package design services available
Owner: Michael Hoffman
Estimated Sales: $10-20 Million
Number Employees: 20-49

21987 Eagles Printing & Label
1206 International Dr
Eau Claire, WI 54701-7052
715-835-6631
Fax: 715-835-1601 eagles@eaglesprinting.com
www.eaglesprinting.com
Commercial printing and labels
President: Barb Sands
eagles@eaglesprinting.com
Estimated Sales: $1-2.5 Million
Number Employees: 20-49

21988 Eagleware Manufacturing
12683 Corral Pl
Santa Fe Springs, CA 90670
562-20 -100
Fax: 314-527-4314
Contact: J Gross
j.gross@alegacy.com
Parent Co: Harold Leonard & Company

21989 Eagleware Manufacturing
2835 E Ana Street
Compton, CA 90221-5601
310-604-0404
Fax: 310-604-1748
Manufacturer and exporter of cookware
President: Jesse Gross
Vice President: Brett Gross
Estimated Sales: Below $5,000,000
Number Employees: 10
Square Footage: 140000
Parent Co: Harold Leonard & Company
Brands:
Eagleware

21990 Eam
19 Pomerleau St
Biddeford, ME 04005-9457
207-283-3001
Fax: 207-283-3023 info@eaminc.com
www.eaminc.com
Owner: John Grondin
Outside Sales: Kevin Call
jgrondin@prescottmetal.com
Estimated Sales: $3 - 5 Million
Number Employees: 20-49

21991 Eam-Mosca Corporation
675 Jaycee Dr
Hazle Township, PA 18202
570-459-3426
Fax: 570-455-2442 info@eammosca.com
www.eammosca.com
Plastic strapping systems for pallets, off-line and in-line strappers, side-seal pallet strappers, drive-thru pallet strappers and horizontal pallet strapper
President: Daniel Dreher
Regional Sales Manager: Jim Gum
Contact: Sal Carsia
america2@americanpigeonracing.com
Sales Coordinator: Denise Casanova
Estimated Sales: $30 - 50 Million
Number Employees: 50-99

21992 Earl Soesbe Company
1347 Enterprise Drive
Romeoville, IL 60446-1015
219-866-4191
Fax: 219-866-7979
Bulk material handling equipment including self-dumping hoppers
President: Jerry Schlottmann
Sales Manager: Claas Schlottmann
Estimated Sales: $2.5-5 Million
Number Employees: 10-19
Square Footage: 106000

21993 Earthstone Wood-Fire Ovens
6717 San Fernando Rd
Glendale, CA 91201-1704
818-553-1134
Fax: 818-553-1133 800-840-4915
info@earthstoneovens.com
www.earthstoneovens.com
Manufacturer/exporter of wood and gas fire ovens including pre-assembled, commercial kit and residential; also, wood fire training available
Principal: Maurice Yotnegparian
Principal: Jean-Paul Yotnegparian
Estimated Sales: $3 - 5 Million
Number Employees: 15
Square Footage: 60000
Brands:
Earthstone

21994 Earthy Delights
1161 E Clark Road
Suite 260
Dewitt, MI 48820
517-668-2402
Fax: 517-668-1213 800-367-4709
info@earthy.com www.earthy.com
Specialty foods
President: Ed Baker
eb@earthy.com
Marketing: Angie Padgett
Estimated Sales: $2.5 Million
Number Employees: 12

21995 Eash Industries
120 Rush Ct
Elkhart, IN 46516
574-295-4450
Fax: 574-389-1190
High gloss bar tops and tables; also, custom logos and inlaid graphics available
President: Todd Eash
Contact: Lisa Eash
eashindustries@hotmail.com
Estimated Sales: $2.5-5,000,000
Number Employees: 5-9
Brands:
Diamond Clear

21996 East Bay Fixture Co
941 Aileen St
Emeryville, CA 94608-2805
510-652-4421
Fax: 510-652-5915 800-995-4521
rick@ebfc.com www.eastbayfixture.com
Store fixtures
Owner: Richard Laible
rick@ebfc.com
Estimated Sales: $5-10 Million
Number Employees: 20-49

21997 East Coast Group New York
23209 Merrick Boulevard
Springfield Gardens, NY 11413-2116
718-527-8464
Fax: 718-527-8498
Garbage, insulated, multi-wall and plastic bags and packaging materials
Sr Partner: Trevor Ford
Estimated Sales: $500,000-$1,000,000
Number Employees: 9
Brands:
East Coast

21998 East Coast Mold Manufacturing
30 Eastern Ave # 1
Deer Park, NY 11729-3100
631-253-2397
Fax: 631-254-6682 800-933-9533
Candy and confectionery equipment
President: Sebastian Piccione
Number Employees: 5-9

21999 East Memphis Rubber Stamp Company
6246 Acorn Dr
Bartlett, TN 38134-4608
901-384-0887
Fax: 901-384-3507
Rubber stamps
President: Buddy Good
VP Marketing: Buddy Good
Estimated Sales: Below $5 Million
Number Employees: 1 to4

22000 Easterday Belting Company
1400 E Touhy Ave # 409
Des Plaines, IL 60018-3341
847-297-8200
Fax: 847-803-9290
Thermal and solid color jet inks, for small character jet printers
Owner: Azam Nizamudiz
Estimated Sales: $5-10 000,000
Number Employees: 10-19

22001 Easterday Fluid Technologies
4343 S Kansas Ave
Saint Francis, WI 53235
414-482-4488
Fax: 414-482-3720
Supplies the food processing industry thermal sensitive coding links. Manufactures thermal sensitive, solid color, and UV jet inks for noncontact jet printers for tough, reliable product codes on retorted food containers andpasteurization processes of the beer and beverage industry
President: Max Baum
Director Operations: Lee Robbins
National/International Services Manager: Paul Oetlinger
Estimated Sales: $1-3 Million
Number Employees: 5-9
Square Footage: 12000
Brands:
Easterday

22002 Eastern Bakery Co
475 Stevens Rd
York Haven, PA 17370-9236
717-938-8278
Fax: 717-938-3060
Manufacturers of bakery equipment
President and R&D: Ken Johson
CFO: Cindy Ng
Quality Control: Jeff Love
Manager: Jeff Love
jlove@eb-sys.com
Plant Manager: Jeff Love
Estimated Sales: Below $5 000,000
Number Employees: 10-19
Parent Co: Gemini Bakery Equipment Company

22003 Eastern Cap & Closure Company
726 N Kresson Street
Baltimore, MD 21205-2907
410-327-5640
Fax: 410-522-6068
Caps and closures for bottles and jars
Manager: John Lepus
Number Employees: 30
Square Footage: 98000
Parent Co: Penn Bottle & Supply Company

22004 Eastern Container Corporation
60 Maple St
Mansfield, MA 02048-1505
508-337-0400
Fax: 508-339-8493 www.smurfitstone.com
Corrugated shipping containers and displays
General Manager: Randy Thrasher
Estimated Sales: $5 - 10 Million
Number Employees: 250-499
Parent Co: Eastern Container
Brands:
Radio Pack

22005 Eastern Design & Development Corporation
PO Box 440
Hershey, PA 17033-0440
717-533-2452
Fax: 717-533-2036
Confectionary and baking equipment
Estimated Sales: $1-2.5 000,000
Number Employees: 20-49

22006 Eastern Envelope
5 Laurel Dr
Flanders, NJ 07836-4701
973-584-3311
Fax: 973-584-4125
Envelopes
President: Jerome Kessler
Estimated Sales: $1-2.5 Million
Number Employees: 5-9

22007 Eastern Machine
80 Turnpike Dr # 2
Middlebury, CT 06762-1830
203-598-0066
Fax: 203-598-0068
Manufacturer and exporter of capping machinery for metal and plastic screw and snap caps; also, cap tighteners, fitment applicators and trigger sprayers
President: David Baker
Number Employees: 5-9
Square Footage: 20000

22008 Eastern Plastics
PO Box 1266
Pawtucket, RI 02862-1266
401-724-8050
Fax: 401-728-3770 800-442-8585
Clear acrylic products including bulk food bins, step up racks, product displays, bag holders, description holders, literature dispensers, recipe card holders, etc
President: Jim Rosenthal
Sales Representative: Irene Champagne
Number Employees: 20
Square Footage: 20000

22009 Eastern Poly Packaging Company
53 Prospect Park W
Brooklyn, NY 11215-2629
718-788-4700
Fax: 718-788-5463 800-421-6006
www.easternpoly.com
Printed and plain bags including polypropylene and polyethylene
Owner: Stephen Somers
General Manager: Tran Van Lam
Director: Tran Minh Tam
Estimated Sales: $2.5-5 Million
Number Employees: 20-49
Parent Co: X

22010 Eastern Tabletop Mfg
1943 Pitkin Ave
Brooklyn, NY 11207-3312
718-240-9595
Fax: 718-240-9797 888-422-4142
sales@easterntabletop.com
www.easterntabletop.com
High quality silver plated and stainless steel food service equipment including chafing dishes, coffee urns, trays, serving and tabletop accessories, punchbowls and candelabras
President: Sol Basch
sol@easterntabletop.com
Estimated Sales: $10 - 20 Million
Number Employees: 10-19
Brands:
Eastern

22011 Eastey Enterprises
7041 Boone Avenue
Brooklyn Park, MN 55428
800-835-9344
Fax: 763-795-8867 800-835-9344
parts_eastey@dgi.net www.eastey.com
Electric or air operated L-sealers, shrink tunnels, high speed tunnels, banding tunnels, bundling tunnels and manual or automatic sleeve wrapping systems
President: Jeff Eastey
Contact: John Belden
john@eastey.com
Estimated Sales: $4 Million
Number Employees: 20-49

22012 Easy Lift Equipment Co Inc
2 Mill Park Ct
Newark, DE 19713-1986
302-737-8784
Fax: 302-737-7333 800-233-1800
sales@easylifteqpt.com www.easylifteqpt.com
Manufacturers of Drum & Roll handling Equipment
President: Lorea Eastbrun
eastbrun@easylifteqpt.com
Estimated Sales: $5-10 Million
Number Employees: 5-9

22013 Easy-Care Environs
7002 Maplewood Court SW
Olympia, WA 98512-2031
360-754-1013
Fax: 360-754-1013
Specialty walls and ceilings (glass, FRP)

22014 Easybar Corp
19799 SW 95th Ave # A
Suite A
Tualatin, OR 97062-7584
503-624-6744
Fax: 503-624-6741 888-294-7405
info@easybar.com www.easybar.com
Manufacturer and exporter of liquor, beer, wine and soda dispensers.
President: Gorham Nicol
gnicol@easybar.com
CEO: James Nicol
Marketing: Sarah Puglia
Sales: Margo Winquist
Estimated Sales: $5 - 10 Million
Number Employees: 20-49
Brands:
Easybar

22015 (HQ)Easyup Storage Systems
18271 Andover Park W
Tukwila, WA 98188-4706
206-394-3330
Fax: 206-575-6829 800-426-9234
www.easyupusa.com
Boltless steel storage and shelving systems
President: Dave Saman
VP: Kyle Jones
VP/C-Store Manager: Ken Davis
Estimated Sales: Less Than $500,000
Number Employees: 1-4
Square Footage: 56000
Brands:
Easy Up

22016 Eatec Corporation
1900 Powell St
Suite 230
Emeryville, CA 94608
510-594-9011
Fax: 510-549-1959 877-374-4783
www.agilysys.com
A provider of enterprise back-office software and services for the foodservice and hospitality industries. EatecNetX, Eatec's proven software solution, is recognized as a state-of-the-art foodservice management system that iscentralizzed, scalable, web-centric and user-friendly for food and beverage operators of every variety.
Contact: Scot Benbow
s.benbow@eatec.com
Manager: Jeff Gebhardt
Estimated Sales: $5 - 10 Million
Number Employees: 20-49
Brands:
Catertec
Clubtec
Eatec Netx
Eatec System

22017 Eatem Foods Co
1829 Gallagher Dr
Vineland, NJ 08360-1548
856-692-1663
Fax: 856-692-0847 800-683-2836
sales@eatemfoods.com www.eatemfoods.com
Food base manufacturing; supplier of savory flavor systems, flavor concentrates, broth concentrates and seasoning bases.
Vice President: Gerrie Bouchard
gerriebouchard@gmail.com
Chief Technical Officer: John Randazzi
Chief Financial Officer: Danine Freeman
Vice President, Treasurer: Mario Riviello
Director, R&D: Bill Cawley
Marketing Manager: Gerrie Bouchard
Vice President, Sales: Don Witherspoon
Director of Operations: Jerry Santo
Estimated Sales: $14 Million
Number Employees: 50-99
Square Footage: 12916
Type of Packaging: Consumer, Food Service, Bulk
Brands:
Eatem

22018 (HQ)Eaton Corporation
1000 Eaton Blvd
Beachwood, OH 44122
800-386-1911
www.eaton.com
Manufacturer and exporter of emergency, indoor and outdoor lighting

Chairman & CEO: Craig Arnold
Vice Chairman & CFO: Richard Fearon
Executive VP & General Counsel: April Miller Boise
Executive VP, Supply Chain Management: Rogerico Branco
Estimated Sales: $21.4 Billion
Number Employees: 97,000

22019 Eaton Electrical Sector
1000 Cherrington Pkwy
Moon Township, PA 15108
877-386-2273
www.eaton.com/Eaton/ProductsServices/Electrical
Controls and control systems, electrical distribution, electronics components, lighting, metering, monitoring and protection.
President & COO, Electrical Sector: Uday Yadav
President, Americas: Brian Brickhouse
Parent Co: Eaton Corporation

22020 Eaton Equipment
5210 State Road 133
PO Box 55
Boscobel, WI 53805-9134
608-375-2256
Fax: 608-375-2256 www.mwt.net
Homoginizers, cheese equipment, custom fabrication, heat exchangers, plate, agitators, cookers, ford, hoop washers, hoops, knives, molds, automatic presses, manual presses, piping, fittings and sanitary tubing
President: Don Eaton
eatoneq@mwt.net
Estimated Sales: $500,000-$1 Million
Number Employees: 1-4

22021 Eaton Filtration, LLC
44 Apple Street
Tinton Falls, NJ 07724
732-212-4700
Fax: 952-906-3706 800-859-9212
www.filtration.eaton.com
Manufacturer and exporter of fluid filters and strainers
Chairman & CEO: Craig Arnold
President & COO, Industrial Sector: Heath Monesmith
Vice Chairman & CFO: Richard H. Fearon
Number Employees: 50-99
Parent Co: Eaton Corporation
Brands:
Ronningen-Petter

22022 Eaton Manufacturing Co
1201 Holly St
Houston, TX 77007-6241
713-223-2331
Fax: 713-223-2342 800-328-6610
www.eatonmfg.com
Manufacturer and exporter of labels, laminated films, cash control envelopes and bags including polyethylene, polypropylene and ice
President: Tom B Eaton Jr
General Manager: Joe Williams
Estimated Sales: $5-10 Million
Number Employees: 20-49
Square Footage: 100000

22023 Eaton Quade Plastics & Sign Co
1116 W Main St
Oklahoma City, OK 73106-7854
405-236-4475
Fax: 405-236-4520 doug@eatonquade.com
www.eatonquade.com
Custom formed plastics including sneeze protectors, displays, food display covers, etc
President: Doug Swindell
doug@eatonquade.com
Estimated Sales: $1-2.5 Million
Number Employees: 5-9
Square Footage: 30000

22024 (HQ)Eaton Sales & Service
PO Box 16405
Denver, CO 80216
303-296-4800
Fax: 303-296-5749 800-208-2657
sales@eatonmetal.com www.eatonmetalsales.com
Atmospheric and pressure tanks; also, installation services available

President: Timothy J Travis
CFO: Dorothy Martin
General Manager Administration: Kirby Boutelle
Estimated Sales: $20 - 50 Million
Number Employees: 50-99

22025 Ebel Tape & Label
1832 Westwood Ave
Cincinnati, OH 45214-1347

513-471-1067
Fax: 513-471-5657
Tapes including gummed and pressure sensitive;
also, pressure sensitive labels
President: Greg Dulle
CFO: James Dulle
Contact: Larry Heidemann
  ebellabel@fuse.net
Estimated Sales: Below $5 Million
Number Employees: 5 to 9

22026 Ebenezer Flag Company
64 Spring St
Newport, RI 02840-6803

401-846-1891
Fax: 401-849-1640
Flags and banners
President: Tina Croce
*Estimated Sales:*less than $500,000
Number Employees: 1 to4

22027 Eberbach Corp
505 S Maple Rd
Ann Arbor, MI 48103-3836

734-665-8877
Fax: 734-665-9099 800-422-2558
info@eberbachlabtools.com
www.eberbachlabtools.com
Laboratory and pilot-plant equipment, instruments,
apparatus, shakers, mixers, homogenizers and
blenders
President: Ralph O Boehnke Jr
CFO: Ralph O Boehnke Jr
R&D: Chris Boehnke Jr
Quality Control: Ralph O Boehnke Jr
Estimated Sales: Below $5 000,000
Number Employees: 10-19

22028 EcFood.Com
4655 Old Ironsides Dr
Santa Clara, CA 95054-1808

408-496-2900
Fax: 408-566-6148 877-532-7253
Estimated Sales: $1 - 5 Million
Number Employees: 1-4

22029 EcFood.com
410 Jessie St
San Francisco, CA 94103-1834

415-869-6100
Fax: 415-869-6148 877-532-7253
President: Dave Laukat
Estimated Sales: $10 - 20 Million
Number Employees: 20-49

22030 Eckels Bilt
7700 Harwell St
Fort Worth, TX 76108-1806

817-246-4555
Fax: 817-246-7139 800-343-9020
info@eckelsbilt.com www.eckelsbilt.com
Manufacturer and exporter of conveyor belt auto-
matic tracking systems
President: John Mic Kunas
  johnm@eckelsbilt.com
Sales Manager: Tony Keeton
Estimated Sales: $5-10 Million
Number Employees: 10-19
Square Footage: 15000
Brands:
  True Tracker

22031 Ecklund-Harrison Technologies
11000 Metro Pkwy # 40
Fort Myers, FL 33966-1245

239-936-6032
Fax: 239-936-6327 www.ecklund-harrison.com
Manufacturer and exporter of heat penetration
equipment and pasteurization monitor computers
President: Daneil Highbaugh
  kathy@ecklund-harrison.com
Estimated Sales: $500,000
Number Employees: 1-4

22032 Eclipse Electric Manufacturing
6512 Walker St
St Louis Park, MN 55426

952-929-2500
Fax: 952-929-0024 emailchico@aol.com
Electric custom lighting fixtures
President: David Jenkins
  emailchico@aol.com
VP Marketing: Dave Jenkins
Estimated Sales: $1-2.5 Million
Number Employees: 5-9
Square Footage: 40000

22033 Eclipse Espresso Systems
1733 Westlake Avenue N
Seattle, WA 98109-3014

206-587-3767
Fax: 206-587-0339
members.aol.com/eclsystm/parts.htm
Tea and coffee industry blending and mixing equip-
ment, dryers and feeders, evaporators
Estimated Sales: $500,000-$1 Million
Number Employees: 5

22034 Eclipse Innovative Thermal Solutions
5040 Enterprise Blvd
Toledo, OH 43612

419-729-9726
Fax: 419-729-9705 800-662-3966
sales@exothermics.com
Industrial air-to-air heat exchangers and heat recov-
ery equipment; exporter of industrial heat
exchangers
Manager: Paul Wilde
R&D: Bob Shaffer
Contact: Sheryl Holbrook
  sholbrook@eclipsenet.com
Number Employees: 20-49
Square Footage: 70000
Parent Co: Eclipse

22035 Eclipse Systems Inc
943 Hanson Ct
Milpitas, CA 95035-3166

408-263-2201
Fax: 408-559-2252
Manufacturer and exporter of mixers including elec-
tric and pneumatic drive
Owner: Jerry Grose
CFO: Helen Fletcher
Sales Director: Diane Olsen
  jerrygrose@eclipsesystems.com
Estimated Sales: $20-50 Million
Number Employees: 1-4
Square Footage: 30000
Parent Co: Technology General Corporation
Brands:
  Pneumix

22036 Eco Fish Inc
340 Central Ave # 303
Suite 305
Dover, NH 03820-3770

603-834-6034
Fax: 603-430-9929 comments@ecofish.com
www.ecofish.com
Distributor and promoter of ecologically sound sea-
food
President: Henry Lovejoy
  henry@ecofish.com
Manager: Hector Gudino
Estimated Sales: $1 - 3 Million
Number Employees: 5-9

22037 Eco-Air Products
7466 Carroll Rd # 101
San Diego, CA 92121-2356

858-271-8111
Fax: 858-578-3816 800-284-8111
pcurrie@shoreline.com
Manufacturer and exporter of air, rangehood and
grease filters
President: Wesley Measamer
CFO: John Hodson
Vice President of Division: Charlie Kwiatkowski
Manager: Robert Jaquay
Quality Control: Bill Stevens
VP Marketing: Bill O'Brien
Director of Sales: Bill Cawley
Senior Vice President of Operations: Kirk Dominick
Estimated Sales: $30-50 Million
Number Employees: 20-49
Square Footage: 110000

22038 Eco-Bag Products
23-25 Spring St, #302
Ossining, NY 10562

914-944-4556
Fax: 914-271-4867 800-720-2247
sales@ecobags.com www.eco-bags.com
Manufacturer, importer and exporter of natural and
organic cotton bags including shopping and promo-
tional tote, lunch and produce; printing services
available
President: Sharon Rowe
Marketing: Ellen Ornato
PR & Communications: Rob Bradey
Estimated Sales: Below $5 Million
Number Employees: 1-4
Type of Packaging: Consumer, Food Service, Bulk
Brands:
  Eco-Bags

22039 Eco-Pak Products Engineering
P.O. Box 179
Fenton, MO 63026-0179

636-305-9800
Fax: 636-305-9800
Multi-packaging for beverage and food products,
customizing packaging with or without full color
graphics
President: Helly Miller
Estimated Sales: Less than $500,000
Number Employees: 1-4

22040 Ecodyne Water Treatment, LLC
1270 Frontenac Rd
Naperville, IL 60563

630-961-5043
Fax: 630-671-8846 800-228-9326
Manufacturer and exporter of water treatment equip-
ment including softeners, filters and reverse osmosis
systems
President: Patrick O'Neill
Finance Executive: Todd Mc Gee
Research & Development: Wayne Simpson
Quality Control: Mark Thenhaus
Sales Director: Patrick O'Neill
Public Relations: Patrick O'Neill
Operations Manager: Mark Thenhaus
Production Manager: Mark Thenhaus
Plant Manager: Mark Thenhaus
Purchasing Manager: Mark Thenhaus
Estimated Sales: $5 - 10,000,000
Number Employees: 20-49
Square Footage: 50000
Brands:
  Red Line

22041 Ecolab Inc
1 Ecolab Place
St. Paul, MN 55102-2233

Fax: 651-225-3098 800-352-5326
institutionalorders@ecolab.com www.ecolab.com
Cleaning and sanitizing products, equipment, sys-
tems and services for the agribusiness, beverage,
brewery, pharmaceutical, dairy, meat, poultry and
food processing industries.
Chairman & Chief Executive Officer: Douglas
Baker, Jr.
President & Chief Operating Officer: Christophe
Beck
Chief Financial Officer: Daniel Schmechel
EVP & President, Global Institutional: Timothy
Mulhere
EVP & GM, Global Food & Beverage: Nicholas
Alfano
EVP & President, Global Nalco Water: Christophe
Beck
EVP & Chief Information Officer: Anil Arcalgud
EVP & Chief Technical Officer: Dr. Larry Berger
EVP & Chief Supply Chain Officer: Mike Duijser
EVP, Corporate Strategy: Angela Busch
SVP & Corporate Controller: Scott Kirkland
Year Founded: 1923
Estimated Sales: $13.84 Billion
Number Employees: 48,400
Square Footage: 24135
Type of Packaging: Food Service

22042 Ecolo Odor Control Systems Worldwide
59 Penn Drive
North York, ON M9L 2A6
Canada

416-740-3900
Fax: 416-740-3800 800-667-6355
info@ecolo.com www.ecolo.com
Manufacturer and exporter of odor control systems and air solutions to deodorize washrooms, garbage rooms, transfer stations, waste water treatment plants, etc
President: Calvin Sager
Vice President: Ian Howard
Marketing Director: Cindy Pickard
Director Manufacturing: John Linthwaite
Number Employees: 20
Square Footage: 60000
Parent Co: Sager Industries
Brands:
  Air Solution
  Ecolo

22043 Ecological Labs Inc
13 Hendrickson Ave
Lynbrook, NY 11563-1201

516-823-3441
Fax: 516-379-3632 800-645-2976
info@propump.com www.microbelift.com
Live bacterial cultures
President: Barry Richter
  barryrichter@microbelist.com
Estimated Sales: $5-10 Million
Number Employees: 10-19
Type of Packaging: Bulk

22044 Econo Equipment
PO Box 250
Westfield, WI 53964-0250

608-296-3646
Fax: 608-296-4029
Packaging equipment
President: Michael Johnson
Estimated Sales: $1-2.5 000,000
Number Employees: 19

22045 Econo Frost Night Covers
PO Box 40
Shawnigan Lake, BC V0R 2W0
Canada

250-743-1222
Fax: 250-743-1221 800-519-1222
info@econofrost.com www.mgvinc.com
Manufacturer, importer and exporter of color corrected lighting and night covers for refrigerated display cases
President: Mark Granfar
Marketing: Samantha Criddle
International Sales Director: Carlos Paniagua
Product Development: Trevor Brien
Number Employees: 20-49
Number of Products: 1
Square Footage: 6000
Parent Co: MGV Inc
Type of Packaging: Food Service
Brands:
  Econofrost
  Instamark
  Mgv
  Mr16
  Multichrome
  Promolux
  Samark

22046 Econocorp Inc
72 Pacella Park Dr
Randolph, MA 02368-1791

781-986-7500
Fax: 781-986-1553 www.econocorp.com
Manufacturer and exporter of carton sealing machinery
President: Wayne Goldberg
  wayne@econocorp.com
Quality Control: Richard Norton
VP: Mark Jacobson
Estimated Sales: $10 - 20 Million
Number Employees: 50-99
Square Footage: 42000
Brands:
  Econoseal

22047 Econofrost Night Covers
Box 40
Shawnigan Lake, BC V0R 2W0
Canada

250-743-1222
Fax: 250-743-1221 800-519-1222
info@econofrost.com www.econofrost.com
Night covers for the refrigerated display cases in supermarkets.
President: Mark Granfar
Marketing: Lyn Rose
Sales: Trevor Brian
Sales: Scott Werhun
Sales: Jamie Farr
International Sales: Carlos Paniagua
Number Employees: 15
Number of Brands: 2
Square Footage: 3000
Type of Packaging: Private Label
Brands:
  Econofrost

22048 Economic Sciences Corp
1516 Le Roy Ave
Berkeley, CA 94708-1914

510-841-6869
Fax: 510-644-1943
Computer software
President: Bill F Roberts
  bill@econsci.com
VP: Helen Chin
Estimated Sales: Less Than $500,000
Number Employees: 1-4

22049 Economy Folding Box Corporation
2601 S La Salle St
Chicago, IL 60616

312-225-2000
Fax: 312-225-3082 800-771-1053
Manufacturer and exporter of paper boxes
President: Michael M Mitchel
CEO: Clifford Moos
  guizhou@yahoo.com
VP/Treasurer: Michael Mitchel
Purchasing Officer: Marie Hernandez
Sales Manager: Joseph Moos
Estimated Sales: $10 - 20 Million
Number Employees: 50-99
Square Footage: 330000
Type of Packaging: Consumer, Food Service, Private Label

22050 Economy Label Sales Company
515 Carswell Ave
Daytona Beach, FL 32117-4411

386-253-4741
Fax: 386-238-0775
Manufacturer and exporter of flexible plastic and vinyl labels including pressure sensitive, plain, hot-stamped and printed
Estimated Sales: $5-10 Million
Number Employees: 50-99
Parent Co: Meadow USA

22051 Economy Novelty & Printing Co
407 Park Ave S # 26a
Suite 26A
New York, NY 10016-8420

212-481-3022
Fax: 212-481-4514 info@thinkideas.com
www.thinkideas.com
Manufacturer and importer of advertising specialties including badges, medals, decals and ribbons
President: Robert Becker
  einfo@thinkideas.com
VP: Warren Becker
Estimated Sales: Less Than $500,000
Number Employees: 1-4
Square Footage: 2000
Parent Co: Economy Novelty
Brands:
  Thinkideas

22052 Economy Paper & Restaurant Co
180 Broad St
Clifton, NJ 07013-1299

973-279-5500
Fax: 973-279-4140 sales@economysupply.com
www.economysupply.com
Soaps, degreasers and custom fabricated equipment; wholesaler/distributor and exporter of food service equipment, disposables, janitorial supplies, smallwares, glassware, flatware and china; installation and consulting available
President: L J Konzelman
CFO: Susan Majors
VP: Micheal Konzelman
R&D: Alex Nasarone
Public Relations: Susan Majors
Purchasing: Kevin Konzelman
Estimated Sales: $3 - 5 Million
Number Employees: 10-19
Square Footage: 50000
Type of Packaging: Food Service
Brands:
  Econo-Flash
  Econo-Suds

22053 Economy Tent Intl
2995 NW 75th St
Miami, FL 33147-5943

305-694-1234
Fax: 305-835-7098 800-438-3226
sales@economytent.com www.mmicreateweb.com
Supplier and exporter of party tents for the food service industry
Owner: Hal Lapping
  hlapping@economytent.com
VP Marketing: Hal Lapping
Estimated Sales: $1 - 2.5 Million
Number Employees: 20-49
Type of Packaging: Food Service

22054 Ecover
PO Box 911058
Los Angeles, CA 90091-1058

323-720-5730
Fax: 323-720-5732 www.ecover.com
Natural bases, environmentally safe cleaning products.
CEO: Philip Malmberg
Sales Manager: Maureen Davis
Estimated Sales: $3 - 5 Million
Number Employees: 5-9

22055 Ecs Warehouse
2381 Fillmore Ave
Buffalo, NY 14214-2129

716-833-7380
Fax: 716-833-7386 permerling@emerfood.com
www.ecswarehouse.com
A warehouse that understands your needs. Frozen, dry, refrigerated warehouse on Canadian border, within 500 miles of 70% of the entire Canadian population and 55% of the entire USA population. Services include: pick & pack, crossdocking, express service, repacking, distribution, TL & LTL, rail, consolidation, salvage, quick access to NYC, Boston, D.C., Cleveland, Buffalo, Toronto, Rockland, Syracuse, Detroit and Cincinnati. If you have special product needs, call us.
CEO: Peter Emerling
  pemerling@emerfood.com
Number Employees: 10-19
Square Footage: 500000
Type of Packaging: Bulk
Brands:
  Chocolate Moose
  Flathead Lake Monster Gourmet Soda
  Havana Cappuccino
  Hill-Tween Farms
  Ocean Spray

22056 Ed Smith's Stencil Works LTD
4315 Bienville St
P O Box 791837
New Orleans, LA 70119-4621

504-525-2128
Fax: 504-525-2157 sales@edsmiths.net
www.edsmiths.net
Marking devices, rubber stamps, checks, name badges, price markers, stencils and plastic signs
Owner: Mike Rowan
VP: Ronald Schaefer
Assistant Sales Manager: Michael Rowan
  mike@edsmiths.net
Estimated Sales: $1-2.5 Million
Number Employees: 10-19
Square Footage: 27168

22057 Edco Industries
203-249 Dekalb Ave
Bridgeport, CT 6607
203-333-8982
Fax: 203-333-7950 www.edcoindustries.com
Molded plastic products including housewares, ice buckets, tumblers, trays, coasters, etc.; also, hot stamping available
President: John Thomas Szalan
VP: Anna Marie Szalan
Plant Manager: Hector Mendez
Estimated Sales: $1 Million
Number Employees: 10-19
Square Footage: 26800

22058 Edco Supply Corp
323 36th St
Brooklyn, NY 11232-2599
718-499-7005
Fax: 718-788-7481 800-221-0918
info@edcosupply.com www.edcosupply.com
Antistatic packaging including antistatic bags, commercial translucent static shielding materials, desiccant, indicator cards, caution labels and VCI papers
Owner: Sylvia Freyer
sylvia@edcosupply.com
Estimated Sales: $5 - 10 000,000
Number Employees: 20-49

22059 Ederback Corporation
505 South Maple Road
Ann Arbor, MI 48103
734-665-8877
Fax: 734-665-9099 800-422-2558
info@eberbachlabtools.com
www.eberbachlabtools.com
Manufacturer and exporter of laboratory equipment including shakers, mixers, homogenizers and blenders
President: Ralph Boehnke Jr
Estimated Sales: $3 - 5 Million
Number Employees: 10-19

22060 (HQ)Edge Food Equipment
110 Arrow Rd
North York, ON M9M 2M1
Canada
416-744-9995
edgefoodequipment.com
Supplier of restaurant equipment.
Owner: John Paul Cesario
Year Founded: 1949
Number Employees: 5-9

22061 Edge Food Equipment
234 William St
London, ON N6B 3B9
Canada
519-438-2991
edgefoodequipment.com
Supplier of restaurant equipment.

22062 Edge Food Equipment
50 Clarke St S
Woodstock, ON N4S 8Y7
Canada
416-744-9995
edgefoodequipment.com
Supplier of restaurant equipment.
Square Footage: 50000

22063 Edge Resources
1 Menfi Way
Unit 20
Hopedale, MA 01747-1542
508-634-8214
Fax: 508-634-9888 888-849-0998
info@edgeresources.com
www.edgeresources.com
Manufacturer and importer of food service equipment and supplies; consultant specializing in marketing and sales services
President/CEO: Frank Curty
Estimated Sales: $500,000-$1 Million
Number Employees: 5-9
Square Footage: 16000

22064 Edgecraft Corp
825 Southwood Rd
Avondale, PA 19311-9765
610-268-0500
Fax: 610-268-3545 800-342-3255
www.chefschoice.com
Manufacturer and exporter of manual and power driven sharpeners slicer and cutlery
President: Samuel Weiner
samuel.weiner@edgecraft.com
CEO: Daniel Friel Sr
Estimated Sales: $20,000,000 - $49,999,999
Number Employees: 100-249
Brands:
Chef's Choice

22065 Edgemold Products
37031 E Wisconsin Ave
PO Box 88
Oconomowoc, WI 53066
262-567-9313
Fax: 262-567-9339 800-450-0051
info@fiberesin.com www.edgemold.com
Urethane-edged tables and tabletops
President & CEO: Mike MacDougal
National Sales Manager: Lonie Wise
Director of Manufacturing: Jeff Bahr
Estimated Sales: $1 - 5 Million
Number Employees: 10-19
Parent Co: Fibersin Industries
Brands:
Edgemold

22066 Edgerton Corporation
22560 Lunn Rd
Strongsville, OH 44149
440-268-0000
Fax: 440-268-0300 www.edgerton.com
Computer systems for material handling
President: Bob Walters
CFO: Susan Sponsler
Executive VP: Barry Zimmerman
COO: Jed Cavadas
Estimated Sales: $10 - 20,000,000
Number Employees: 20-49

22067 Edhard Corp
279 Blau Rd
Hackettstown, NJ 07840-5221
908-850-8444
Fax: 908-850-8445 888-334-2731
meter@edhard.com www.edhard.com
Bakers' equipment and supplies including plastic injection molds and dies
President: Ed Bars
ed@edhard.com
CFO: Joe Englert
Sales Manager: Nancy Neri
Estimated Sales: $2.5 - 5 Million
Number Employees: 20-49
Brands:
Edhard Injectors & Depositors

22068 Edible Software
3603 Westcenter Dr # 100
Suite 100
Houston, TX 77042-5222
713-592-8200
Fax: 832-200-8001 sales@ediblesoftware.com
www.ediblesoftware.com
Accessories/supplies i.e. picnic baskets
CEO: Trevor Morris
info@ediblesoftware.com
President, Chief Executive Officer: Henri Morris
Senior Vice President: Trevor Morris
Number Employees: 20-49

22069 Edison Price Lighting
4150 22nd St
Long Island City, NY 11101-4815
718-685-0700
Fax: 718-786-8530 jlattanzio@epl.com
Manufacturer and exporter of architectural, energy efficient, recessed and surface mounted lighting fixtures
President: Emma Price
eprice@epl.com
Finance: MaryAnna Romano
R&D: Richard J. Shaver
Sales/Marketing: Joel Seigel
Sales Service: Joanie Lattanzio
Customer Service: Stephanie Smith
Administration: James D. Vizzini
purchasing/operations: George H. Closs
Number Employees: 100-249
Brands:
Anglux
Artima
Autotrak
Bablux
Duplux
Multipurpose
Sight Line
Simplux
Spredlite
Triples

22070 Edl Packaging Engineers
1260 Parkview Rd
Green Bay, WI 54304-5619
920-336-7744
Fax: 920-336-8585 sales@edlpackaging.com
www.edlpackaging.com
Manufacturer and exporter of shrink and stretch bundling machinery
President: Ken Carter
sales@edlpackaging.com
Director of Sales: Larry D Cozine
Product Manager/Bagged Product: Jariath Harkin
Estimated Sales: $5 - 10,000,000
Number Employees: 50-99
Number of Products: 4
Square Footage: 50000
Parent Co: EDL UK
Type of Packaging: Consumer, Food Service, Private Label, Bulk

22071 Edlund Co
159 Industrial Pkwy
Burlington, VT 05401-5494
802-862-9661
Fax: 802-862-4822 800-772-2126
scrane@edlundco.com www.edlundco.com
Develops and manufactures operator-oriented stainless steel equipment for the food service industry product line of which includes can crushers; manual, electric and air-powered can openers; high speed industrial systems; mechanical and digital portion control scales; mechanical and digital receiving scales; knife sharpeners; knife racks; and tongs.
President: Willett S Foster Iv
Cmo: Peter Nordell
pnordell@edlundco.com
Vice President: Peter Nordell
Vice President of Sales and Marketing: David Sebastianelli
Estimated Sales: $10-25 Million
Number Employees: 100-249
Brands:
Edlund

22072 Edmeyer
315 27th Ave NE
Minneapolis, MN 55418-2715
651-450-1210
Fax: 651-450-0003 www.edmeyerinc.com
Manufacturer and exporter of casers, conveyors, case packers and palletizers
President: Larry Smith
VP: Jerry Kisch
Sales Manager: Greg Reid
Estimated Sales: $20-50 Million
Number Employees: 20-49
Square Footage: 12000

22073 Edson Packaging Machinery
215 Hempstead Drive
Hamilton, ON L8W 2E6
Canada
905-385-3201
Fax: 905-385-8775 800-493-3766
value@edson.com www.edson.com
Manufacturer and exporter of robotic top load packers, packaging machinery including case openers, robotic palletizers, stretch bundlers, sealers and automatic packers
CEO: Robert Hattin
Vice President, General Manager: Gary Evans
Engineering Manager: Bob Krouse
Quality Control: Bob Krause
Account Manager: Scott Killins
Estimated Sales: $10 Million
Number Employees: 70
Number of Brands: 5
Square Footage: 96600
Type of Packaging: Consumer, Food Service
Brands:
Edson

22074 (HQ)Educational Products Company
P.O. Box 295
Hope, NJ 07844
908-459-4220
Fax: 908-459-4770 800-272-3822
cookiecutters1947@hotmail.com
www.cookiecutters.com
3-D cookie cutters
President: Christopher Maier
Manager: Lucy Kise
Estimated Sales: $500,000 - $1 Million
Number Employees: 1-4
Brands:
Cookie Craft

22075 Edward & Sons Trading Co
4420 Via Real # C
Carpinteria, CA 93013-1635
805-684-8500
Fax: 805-684-8220 www.edwardandsons.com
Innovative natural and organic vegetarian foods
President: Joel Dee
edwardsons@aol.com
Number Employees: 10-19

22076 Edwards Fiberglass
P.O. Box 1252
Sedalia, MO 65302-1252
660-826-3915
Fax: 660-827-2793 www.edwardsfiberglass.com
Above and below ground fiberglass storage tanks
President: Robert L Edwards
VP: Shane Edwards
Sales: Donna Schoolman
Estimated Sales: $20 - 50 Million
Number Employees: 20-49
Square Footage: 31000

22077 Edwards Products
1223 Budd St
Cincinnati, OH 45203
513-851-3000
Fax: 513-851-9300 800-543-1835
Stock trucks and storage racks
President: Thomas Reilly
Quality Control: Kevin Reilly
General Manager: John Sloniker
Estimated Sales: $20 - 50 Million
Number Employees: 20-49
Square Footage: 30000

22078 Efficient Frontiers
2021 W.Las Positas Ct.Ste 127
Livermore, CA 94551
925-456-6700
Fax: 925-456-6701 888-433-4725
Automated software for event sales, dining reservations and club membership
Director Sales/Marketing: Beth Goodell
Contact: Ron Goodell
ron.goodell@reserveinteractive.com
Brands:
Efficient Frontiers
Reserve

22079 Eggboxes Inc
PO Box 8651
Deerfield Beach, FL 33443
954-410-5565
Fax: 954-783-3456 800-326-6667
www.eggboxes.com
Egg cartons, baskets, egg washing supplies, hatchery supplies, bird care, incubating trays, feeders, scales, and nest accessories
President: James Tongle

22080 Ehmke Manufacturing
4200 Macalester St
Philadelphia, PA 19124-6014
215-324-4200
Fax: 215-324-4210
www.ehmkemanufacturing.com
Commercial awnings
President: Louis Verna
CEO: Bob Rosania
Manager, Quality Assurance: Richard Ludwig
Director, Sales & Marketing: Brad Milnes
Sales Manager: Brad Daniels
COO: Cliff Stokes
Number Employees: 100-249

22081 Ehrgott Rubber Stamp Company
4615 E 10th St
Indianapolis, IN 46201-2823
317-353-2222
Fax: 317-357-7750 www.ehrgott.com
Rubber stamps, engraved signs and name tags
President and CFO: Mary Clevenger
Estimated Sales: $500,000 - $1 Million
Number Employees: 1-4

22082 Eichler Wood Products
5477 Mauser Street
Laurys Station, PA 18059-1317
610-262-6749
Fax: 610-262-4454
Wooden pallets, boxes, crates and skids
Owner: Henry Taylor
Business Manager: Thomas R Nemeth
Estimated Sales: $1 - 3 Million
Number Employees: 30
Square Footage: 40000

22083 Eide Industries Inc
16215 Piuma Ave
Cerritos, CA 90703-1528
562-402-8335
Fax: 562-924-2233 800-422-6827
info@eideindustries.com www.eideindustries.com
Manufacturer and exporter of commercial awnings, canopies, tension structures and custom fabric covers
President: Luis Barragan
barraganl@gmail.com
VP Manufacturing/ Chairman: Jesse Borrego
Secretary/VP Marketing: Joe Belli
VP Sales & Marketing: Dan Neill
Human Resources: Lourdes Jordan
Production Coordinator: Ignacio Pellegrin
Chairman/VP Manufacturing: Jesse Borrego
Estimated Sales: $8 Million
Number Employees: 50-99
Square Footage: 82000

22084 Einson Freeman
200 Robin Road
Paramus, NJ 7652
201-221-2800
Fax: 201-226-9262 info@cafsnj.org
www.cafsnj.org
Manufacturer and exporter of point of purchase displays, exhibits and sales promotion items
President & CEO: Jerrold B. Binney
Treasurer & CFO: Joanne Mandry
EVP & Chief Development Officer: Elizabeth Mason
Senior Project Manager: Jeff Shapiro
Estimated Sales: $10 - 20 Million
Number Employees: 50-99
Parent Co: WPP Group PLC

22085 Eirich Machines
4033 Ryan Rd
Gurnee, IL 60031-1255
847-336-2444
Fax: 847-336-0914 eirich@eirichusa.com
www.eirich.com/en/eirich-machines
Manufacturer and exporter of high speed, ribbon, paddle, plow and fluidized zone mixers, finishers, bag dump work stations, viscous pumps, blenders and hoppers
Co-President: Paul Eirich
VP Sales: Richard Zak
Estimated Sales: $10-20 Million
Number Employees: 100-249
Square Footage: 150000
Parent Co: Maschinenfabrik G. Eirich GmbH

22086 Eirich Machines
4033 Ryan Rd
Gurnee, IL 60031-1255
847-336-2444
Fax: 847-336-0914 eirich@eirichusa.com
www.eirichusa.com
High quality mixers, dryers, reactors and ancillary equipment
Sales: Richard Zak
VP Sales: Richard Zak
Estimated Sales: $20-50 Million
Number Employees: 100-249
Parent Co: Elrich Machines

22087 Eisai
3 University Plz
Hackensack, NJ 07601-6208
201-692-0999
Fax: 201-692-1972 www.eisaiusa.com
Fully automated inspection machines for parenternal products
President: Micheal De La Montaign
Contact: Stephen Breckenridge
emu@eisai.com
Estimated Sales: $10 - 15 Million
Number Employees: 10-19

22088 Eischen Enterprises
10111 S Cedar Ave
Fresno, CA 93725-9107
559-834-0013
Fax: 559-834-9183 veischen@aol.com
www.eischenenterprisesinc.com
Sell food processing equipment, used and reconditioned.
President: Virgil Eischen
Marketing: Janice Jepsen
Sales: Virgil Eischen
Estimated Sales: Less Than $500,000
Number Employees: 1-4

22089 Eisenmann Corp USA
150 E Dartmoor Dr
Crystal Lake, IL 60014-8710
815-455-4100
Fax: 815-455-1018 www.eisenmann.com
Manufacturer and exporter of turnkey material handling systems including electrified monorail systems and belt, power, chain, overhead chain and free conveyors; system design services available
VP: Craig Benner
Manager: Jeff Wehner
info@eisenmann.com
General Manager (General Industry): R Trenn
Estimated Sales: $50-100 Million
Number Employees: 20-49
Square Footage: 300
Parent Co: Eisenmann Corporation
Type of Packaging: Bulk

22090 El Cerrito Steel
1424 Kearney St
El Cerrito, CA 94530-2397
510-230-4709
Fax: 510-233-0116
Steel canning and preserving kettles
President: John Kim
Estimated Sales: $1-2.5 Million
Number Employees: 1-4

22091 El Dorado Packaging Inc
204 Prescolite Dr
El Dorado, AR 71730-6677
870-862-4977
Fax: 870-862-8520 www.eldoradobag.com
Manufacturer and exporter of paper bags
President: Louis Hall
CEO: Louis T Hall Iii
Estimated Sales: $20 - 50 Million
Number Employees: 100-249
Type of Packaging: Consumer

22092 Elan Vanilla Co
268 Doremus Ave
Newark, NJ 07105
973-344-8014
Fax: 973-344-5880 sales@elanvanilla.com
www.elanvanilla.com
Organic kosher certified vanilla extract, flavoring and synthetic and natural aromatic chemicals.
President: Jocelyn Manship
jmanship@elan-chemical.com
Quality Control Manager: Phil Kapp
VP Sales: David Pimentel
Director of Customer Service: Marilyn Santiago
Year Founded: 1922
Estimated Sales: $20-50 Million
Number Employees: 50-99
Type of Packaging: Bulk

22093 Elanco Food Solutions
2500 Innovation Way
PO Box 708
Greenfield, IN 46140
317-276-9846
800-428-4441
www.elanco.com
Food safety products and services

President: Jeff Simmons
Contact: Summer Amado
summeramado@hotmail.com
Number Employees: 2,500

22094 Elba Pallets Company
PO Box 276
Elba, AL 36323-0276

334-897-6034
Fax: 334-897-6421

Wooden pallets
President: L Little
Estimated Sales: $5-10 Million
Number Employees: 19

22095 Elberta Crate & Box Company
231 W Main Street
Suite 207
Carpentersville, IL 60110-1769

847-426-3491
Fax: 847-426-3520 888-672-9260

Manufacturer and exporter of wirebound boxes,
crates and expendable pallets
CEO: Ramsay Simmons
Sales Director: Walter Eschenbach
Public Relations: Todd Mills
Estimated Sales: $1 - 5 Million
Number Employees: 1-4
Parent Co: Elberta Crate & Box Company
Type of Packaging: Food Service, Bulk
Brands:
  Elberta
  Skee
  Woodkor

22096 Eldetco
20 Anson Road
Burlingame, CA 94010-7226

650-579-7655
Fax: 650-579-7650

Conveyors and conveying equipment
President: Don Lunghi
Estimated Sales: $1 000,000
Number Employees: 9

22097 Eldorado Miranda Manufacturing Company
1744 12th St SE Ofc
Largo, FL 33771

727-586-0707
Fax: 727-585-4797 800-330-0708
www.eldoradomfg.com

UL listed ventmatic hoods; also, stainless steel work
tables, square corner sinks, shelving and commercial
dishwasher tables
President: Andrew Miranda Jr
Quality Control: Cora Miranda
VP: Andrew Miranda
Estimated Sales: Below $5 Million
Number Employees: 5-9
Square Footage: 90000
Brands:
  Eldorado Miranda

22098 Elecro-Craft/Rockwell Automation
6950 Washington Ave S
Eden Prairie, MN 55344-3407

952-942-3600
Fax: 612-942-3636 800-752-6946
eesemea@ra.rockwell.com www.electro-craft.com

Programmable limit switches and electornic rotary
cam switches used to control food processing and
packaging machinery
General Manager: Philip Martin
President, Chief Executive Officer: James Elsner
Senior VP: William Calisse
Vice President of Business Development: Rob
Kerber
VP: David Dorgan
Vice President of Sales: Tom Ouellette
Plant Manager: Rick Roberts
Estimated Sales: $50 - 100 Million
Number Employees: 100-249
Number of Products: 4
Square Footage: 279000
Type of Packaging: Bulk

22099 Electra-Gear
1110 N Anaheim Boulevard
Anaheim, CA 92801-2502

714-535-6061
Fax: 714-535-2489

Manager: Katherine Garrison
Human Resoures and Administration: Anna Alvarez
Estimated Sales: $3 - 5 Million
Number Employees: 1
Parent Co: Regal-Beloit Company

22100 Electric City Signs & Neon Inc.
701 US Hwy 28 By Pass
PO Box 656
Anderson, SC 29622

864-225-5351
Fax: 864-225-9050 800-270-5851
www.electriccitysigns.com

Plastic and neon signs
Owner: Darrell Ridgeway
Secretary and Treasurer: Patricia Ridgeway
Contact: Chad Ridgeway
cridgeway@electriccitysigns.com
Production Manager: Chris Bowser
Estimated Sales: $2 Million
Number Employees: 20-49
Square Footage: 60000

22101 Electric Contract Furniture
450 Fashion Ave # 2710
Suite 2701
New York, NY 10123-2710

212-967-5504
Fax: 212-760-8823 888-311-6272
eclecticinc@aol.com www.eclecticcontract.com

Tables, chairs, booths and barstools
Owner: Junior Ferma
junior@eclecticcontract.com
Estimated Sales: Less than $500,000
Number Employees: 1-4

22102 Electrical Engineering & Equip
953 73rd St
Windsor Heights, IA 50324-1031

515-273-0100
Fax: 515-273-0101 800-955-3633
www.3e-co.com

Conveyors, elevators, bins and other material han-
dling systems
President/ CEO: Jeff Stroud
CFO: Dave Moench
EVP: John Pilmer
Corporate Marketing Director: Tim Pruch
SVP, Sales & Operations: Steve VanBrocklin
Sr. Director of Operations: Barry Tegels
Estimated Sales: $10-20 Million
Number Employees: 250-499

22103 Electro Alarms
24 S Washington St
Tiffin, OH 44883

419-447-3062
800-261-9174

Broker of burglar and fire alarm systems. Repair and
installation services available
Owner: Howard Beisner
Sales Director: Howard Beisner
Estimated Sales: $1-2.5 Million
Number Employees: 1-4

22104 Electro Cam Corp
13647 Metric Rd
Roscoe, IL 61073-9717

815-389-2620
Fax: 815-389-3304 800-228-5487
info@electrocam.com www.electrocam.com

Manufacturer and exporter of packaging and food
processing controls and software including program-
mable and electric switches
President: Donald Davis
application@electrocam.com
Quality Control: Mike Engevretson
Marketing Manager: Barbara Scheeberger
Sales Manager: John Straw
Estimated Sales: $5 - 10 Million
Number Employees: 20-49
Brands:
  Plus
  Plusnet
  Slimline

22105 Electro Freeze
2116 8th Ave
East Moline, IL 61244

309-755-4553
Fax: 309-755-9858 sales@electrofreeze.com
www.hcduke.com

Manufacturer, importer and exporter of soft serve ice
cream, slush, shake and frozen yogurt equipment

Marketing: Joe Clark
Contact: Shane Allen
sallen@electrofreeze.com
Estimated Sales: $20 - 50 Million
Number Employees: 100-249
Square Footage: 115000
Parent Co: H.C. Duke & Son

22106 Electro Freeze of New England
340 Commerce Way
Unit 3
Pembroke, NH 03275

800-922-2629
acananortheast.com

Manufacturer of industrial ice cream equipment. *Year
Founded:* 1953
Type of Packaging: Food Service

22107 Electro Lift Inc
204 Sargeant Ave
Clifton, NJ 07013-1932

973-471-0204
Fax: 973-471-2814 info2@electrolift.com
www.electrolift.com

Manufacturer and exporter of hoists for monorail,
dual rail, hatchway or base-mounted applications
Owner: Deborah Rechtschaffer
debbie@electrolift.com
Estimated Sales: $5 - 10 Million
Number Employees: 20-49
Type of Packaging: Bulk

22108 Electro-Lite Signs
9155 Archibald Ave # 303
Rancho Cucamonga, CA 91730-5258

909-945-3555
Fax: 909-945-9805 www.els4signs.com

Electric signs
Owner: Ken Brown
els4signs@aol.com
Estimated Sales: $500,000-$1,000,000
Number Employees: 5-9

22109 Electro-Sensors Inc
6111 Blue Circle Dr
Minnetonka, MN 55343-9108

952-930-0100
Fax: 952-930-0130 1 8-0 3-8 61
sales@electro-sensors.com
www.electro-sensors.com

Electro-Sensors, Inc. manufactures a complete line
of motion monitoring and speed control systems for
industrial machinery including: Speed Sensors,
Speed Sensitive Switches, Tachometers, Counters,
Speed to Analog Converters, DigitalPulse Genera-
tors, Closed Loop Motor Speed Control Systems,
and Material Level Controls
President/CEO': Brad Slyle
CEO: David L Klenk
dklenk@electro-sensors.com
CFO: Gloria Grundhoefer
Marketing/Sales: Philip Rae
Estimated Sales: $5-10 000,000
Number Employees: 20-49

22110 Electro-Sensors Inc
6111 Blue Circle Dr
Minnetonka, MN 55343-9108

952-930-0100
Fax: 952-930-0130 800-323-6170
sales@electro-sensors.com
www.electro-sensors.com

Speed monitoring systems, speed switches, tachome-
ters, counters, speed to analog converters, ratemeters
CEO: David L Klenk
dklenk@electro-sensors.com
CEO: Brad Flye
CEO: Bradley D Slye
Manager: Mike Kroening
Estimated Sales: $5,000,000 - $9,999,999
Number Employees: 20-49
Number of Products: 14

22111 Electro-Steam GeneratorCorp
50 Indel Ave
PO Box 438
Rancocas, NJ 8073

609-288-9071
Fax: 609-288-9078 866-617-0764
sales@electrosteam.com www.electrosteam.com

Manufacturer all-electric steam generators that are
used in industry for ovens, proofers, kettles, and for
cleaning, sanitizing, and heating

President: Robert Murnane
Cio/Cto: Sal Negro
 sal@electrosteam.com
Quality Control: Barbara Aikens
Marketing/National Sales Manager: Jack Harlin
Operations: Jack Harlin
Manufacturing Executive: Sal Negro
Plant Manager: Barbara Aikens
Purchase Executive: Gary Lango
Estimated Sales: $1-3 Million
Number Employees: 10-19
Number of Brands: 4
Square Footage: 52000
Type of Packaging: Private Label
Brands:
 Baby Giant
 Little Giant
 Low Boy
 Space Savers

22112 (HQ)Electrodex
4554 19th St Ct E
Bradenton, FL 34203
                    941-753-5663
 Fax: 941-753-7049 800-362-1972
Manufacturer and exporter of lighting fixtures
President: Mike Guritz
Sales Manager: Warren Dalton
Estimated Sales: $2.5-5 Million
Number Employees: 10-19
Type of Packaging: Food Service

22113 Electrol Specialties Co
441 Clark St
South Beloit, IL 61080-1363
                    815-389-2291
 Fax: 815-389-2294 www.esc4cip.com
Clean-in-place, computer and control systems, sanitation equipment, transfer panels and tanks; custom fabrication services available
President: Nicholas Amsbaugh
 nick@amsbaugh.net
Quality Control: Roger Schwartz
VP/General Manager: John Franks
Senior Sales Engineer: Dick Gleed
Estimated Sales: $5 - 10,000,000
Number Employees: 50-99
Square Footage: 100000
Type of Packaging: Bulk

22114 Electron Machine Corp
15824 County Road 450
P.O. Box 2349
Umatilla, FL 32784-8176
                    352-669-3101
 Fax: 352-669-1373 sales@electronmachine.com
                    www.electronmachine.com
Microprocessor refractometers
President: C A Vosburg
 ca@electronmachine.com
Estimated Sales: $2.5-5 000,000
Number Employees: 20-49

22115 Electronic Development Labs
244 Oakland Drive
Danville, VA 24540
                    434-799-0807
 Fax: 434-799-0847 800-342-5335
 sales@edl-inc.com www.edl-inc.com
Provides products and service, the most reliable precision temperature meassuring sensors, equipment, accessories, and calibrators; customized to customer specifications as needed. EDL offers an extensive line of calibratorsthermocouples, RTD's, thermistors, wire, high temperature bore thru compression fittings, bimetals, lab thermometers, recorders, infrared, high temperature insulations, over 10,000 sensors, and a full range of precision handheld pyrometers.
President and CFO: Donald Polsky
Quality Control: Steve Winnes
Marketing: Kristen Gusler
Sales: Jean Moore
Contact: John Lollar
 jlollar@emory.edu
Purchasing: Stephanie King
Number Employees: 35

22116 Electronic Filling Systems
574 Barrow Park Drive
Winder, GA 30680-3416
                    770-621-9200
 Fax: 770-934-0959

In-line liquid filling systems including volumetric piston liquid fillers, stainless steel tabletop chain conveyors, rotary unscramblers and accumulators and ink jet imagers
Estimated Sales: $5-10 000,000
Number Employees: 10-19

22117 Electronic Liquid Fillers
P.O. Box 387
Kingsbury, IN 46345-0387
                    219-393-5571
 Fax: 219-393-5283 800-328-0466
Owner: Mitch Juszkiewicz
CEO and CFO: Ronald Sarto
Number Employees: 50-99

22118 Electronic Machine Parts
400 Oser Ave # 2000
Hauppauge, NY 11788-3658
                    631-434-3700
 Fax: 631-434-3718 www.empregister.com
Registration controls, rebuilding labeling machines
President: Maureen Mc Adam
 loubier_gabriel@jpmorgan.com
Estimated Sales: $10-20 Million
Number Employees: 10-19

22119 Electronic Weighing Systems
664 Fisherman Street
Opa Locka, FL 33054
                    305-685-8067
 Fax: 305-685-2440
Manufacturer and exporter of electronic scales for receiving, counter, heavy duty, warehouse and crane scale
VP: Victor Perez, Jr.
Estimated Sales: $2.5-5 Million
Number Employees: 7
Square Footage: 84000
Brands:
 Ews

22120 Electrostatics Inc
352 Godshall Dr
Harleysville, PA 19438-2017
                    215-513-0850
 Fax: 215-513-0855 888-782-8427
sales@electrostatics.com www.electrostatics.com
Static neutralizing-generating and related contamination control equipment including static measuring locator and meter, high and low pressure guns, nozzles and blowers, static neutralizing bars, power units, static inducingequipment
President: Peter Mariani
 ken@electrostatics.com
Marketing: Maryjane Vielhauer
Sales: Maryjane Vielhauer
Director Engineering: Bob Meyers
Production: Keri Farrington
Purchasing: Janet Benfield
Estimated Sales: $2.5-5 000,000
Number Employees: 20-49

22121 Electrotechnology Applications Center
3835 Green Pond Rd
Bethlehem, PA 18020
                    610-861-4552
 Fax: 610-861-5060 877-862-3696
                    www.etctr.com
Infrared, ultraviolet, microwave, and radiofrequency energy to improve heating, drying, curing, and coating processes

Number Employees: 9

22122 Elegant Awnings
13831 Oaks Avenue
Chino, CA 91710-7009
                    626-575-3556
 Fax: 626-575-3567 800-541-9011
Commercial awnings
President: Mike Chiovare
CFO: Tony Chiovare
sales manager: Mike Chiovare
Estimated Sales: Below $5 Million
Number Employees: 10-19

22123 Elegant Packaging
5253 W Roosevelt Rd
Cicero, IL 60804-1222
                    708-652-3400
 Fax: 708-652-6444 800-367-5493
                    www.elegantpackaging.com

Manufacturer and designers of customized rigid specialty boxes, presentation binders, soft sewn packaging and compression thermal forming.
Estimated Sales: $11 Million
Number Employees: 50-99
Square Footage: 96000
Type of Packaging: Consumer, Food Service, Private Label, Bulk

22124 Elemental Containers
860 Springfield Rd
Union, NJ 07083-8614
                    908-687-7720
 Fax: 908-687-5157 800-577-7624
                    www.aluminumbottles.com
Industrial aluminum bottles used for liquids, viscous and solid products, keeping out light, moisture and oxidation.
President: Luc Tournaire
Account Manager: Patricia Cataldo
Sales & Marketing Manager: Benoit Ramet
Director of Operations: Madeline Cicalese
Estimated Sales: $6 Million
Number Employees: 5-9
Square Footage: 44000

22125 Elementar Americas Inc
520 Fellowship Rd # D408
Suite D-408
Mt Laurel, NJ 08054-3409
                    856-787-0022
 Fax: 856-787-0055 www.elementaramericas.com
Represents the worldwide leading German manufacturer of analytical instrumentation for non-metallic elements like carbon, nitrogen, hydrogen, oxygen and chlorine in all organic materials. Also offers isotope ratio massspectrometers.
President: Georg Schick
 sandy_hughes@elementar-inc.com
Number Employees: 10-19

22126 Elettric 80 Inc
8100 Monticello Ave
Skokie, IL 60076-3326
                    847-329-7717
 Fax: 847-329-9923 www.elettric80.com
Robotic palletizers, laser-guided vehicle systems
President: Johan Castegren
Vice President: Marco Ferrarini
 ferrarini.m@electric80.it
Estimated Sales: Below $5 Million
Number Employees: 50-99

22127 Elgene
299 Welton St
Hamden, CT 06517-3938
                    203-562-9948
 Fax: 203-562-2053 800-922-4623
 answers@elgene.com www.chargar.com
Industrial cleaning compounds
President: Tim Reason
VP: Giulio Fraenza
Estimated Sales: $1 - 3 Million
Number Employees: 1-4
Number of Brands: 22
Number of Products: 22
Square Footage: 60000
Parent Co: Chargar Corporation
Brands:
 Fabulene

22128 (HQ)Eliason Corp
9229 Shaver Rd
Portage, MI 49024-6799
                    269-327-7003
 Fax: 269-327-7006 800-828-3655
                    doors@eliasoncorp.com
Manufacturer and exporter of swing doors and night covers for open refrigerated cases and freezers.
Owner: Edwanda Eliason
CEO: Doug Morrison
 dmking851027@gmail.com
Marketing Director: Michael Woolsey
Estimated Sales: $5 - 10 Million
Number Employees: 50-99
Square Footage: 350000
Other Locations:
 Eliason Corporation
 Woodland CA
Brands:
 Easy Swing
 Econo-Cover
 Eliason

22129 Elite Forming Design Solutions
15 Commerce Ct SE
Rome, GA 30161-6848
706-232-3021
Fax: 706-232-3121 www.eliteforming.com
Manufacturer and supplier of OEM plates and parts.
Owner: Jim Mauer
Number Employees: 10-19

22130 Elite Spice Inc
7151 Montevideo Rd
Jessup, MD 20794-9308
410-796-1900
Fax: 410-379-6933 800-232-3531
jbrandt@elitespice.com www.elitespice.com
Spice, seasoning, capsicum, oil & oleoresin, and de-hydrated vegetable producer.
Co-Founder/President: Isaac Samuel
EVP/Treasurer: Anton Samuel
Quality Control Manager: Justin Ai
VP, Sales: Paul Kurpe
Year Founded: 1988
Estimated Sales: $105 Million
Number Employees: 500
Square Footage: 800000
Type of Packaging: Private Label

22131 Elite Storage SolutionsInc
1118 W Spring St
Monroe, GA 30655-1755
770-207-0002
Fax: 770-207-0101 800-367-0572
www.basemfg.com
Pallet rack systems; also, design and installation available
President: Steve South
ssouth@elitena.com
Chairman of the Board: Dan South
VP Sales: Lee Bissell
Estimated Sales: $10-20 Million
Number Employees: 250-499
Square Footage: 360000

22132 Elkay Plastics Co Inc
6000 Sheila St
Commerce, CA 90040-2405
323-722-7073
Fax: 323-869-3911 800-809-8393
www.sirane.biz
Manufacturer and distributor of flexible polyethyl-ene packaging
President: Louis Chertkow
CFO: Stuart Hortwiz
Quality Control: Christina Lucas
IT: Raul Cruz
r.cruz@elkayplastics.com
Estimated Sales: $20 - 50 Million
Number Employees: 10-19

22133 Ellab
1299 Del Mar Ave
San Jose, CA 95128-3548
408-938-0506
Fax: 408-280-0979 888-533-5588
www.phfspec.com
Estimated Sales: $300,000-500,000
Number Employees: 1-4

22134 Ellab
Trollesmindealle 25
Hilleroed, DK 3400
454-452-0500
Fax: 454-453-0505 info@ellab.com
www.ellab.com
Temperature, pressure and relative humidity moni-toring
Estimated Sales: $1-2.5 Million
Number Employees: 1-4

22135 Ellehammer Industries
20146 100 A Avenue
Langley, BC V1M 3G2
Canada
604-882-9326
Fax: 604-882-9703
Manufacturer and exporter of plastic bags and film
Quality Control: Jack Tucker
Plant Manager: Ralph Schnitzer
Number Employees: 50

22136 Ellenco
4419 41st Street
Brentwood, MD 20722-1515
301-927-4370
Fax: 301-927-4376
Manufacturer and exporter of fire alarm systems
VP: Bob Harding
Estimated Sales: $1 - 5 Million
Number Employees: 20-50

22137 Ellett Industries
1575 Kingsway Avenue
Port Coquitlam, BC V3C 4E5
Canada
604-941-8211
Fax: 604-941-6854
Manufacturer and exporter of fabricated alloy metal, tanks, stills, heat exchangers, vessels, stainless steel and titanium pipes and fittings
President/CEO: J Ellett
Vice President: Bob Gill
Sales Director: L Osberg
Production Manager: David Clift
Purchasing Manager: Don Young
Estimated Sales: $20 Million
Number Employees: 100-250
Square Footage: 120000

22138 Ellingers Agatized WoodInc
923 S 21st St
Sheboygan, WI 53081-4702
920-457-7746
Fax: 920-457-2972 888-287-8906
jenny@ellingerswoodproducts.com
www.agatized.com
Manufacturer and exporter of wood bowls, bar trays, cutting boards and wood bowl gift sets.
President: Joyce Neese
jennye@bytehead.com
Sales Director: Jennifer Stafford
Estimated Sales: $800,000
Number Employees: 10-19
Number of Products: 35
Square Footage: 25000
Type of Packaging: Consumer, Food Service

22139 Elliot Horowitz & Co
675 3rd Ave
New York, NY 10017-5704
212-972-7500
Fax: 212-972-7050
ehorowitz@elliothorowitz.com
www.elliothorowitz.com
Manufacturers' representative for food service equipment and supplies including smallwares and heavy cooking and freezing equipment
Owner: Elliot Horowitz
Estimated Sales: $.5 - 1 million
Number Employees: 5-9
Type of Packaging: Food Service
Brands:
Brewmatic
Doyen
Piper Industries

22140 Elliot Lee
445 Central Ave Unit 100
Cedarhurst, NY 11516
516-569-9595
Fax: 516-569-8088 sales@misterpromotion.com
www.misterpromotion.com
Manufacturer, importer and wholesaler/distributor of advertising specialties including sign holders, awards, badges, bags, cups, pens and plaques
President/CFO: Victor Deutsch
CFO: Elliot Deutsch
Marketing Director: Elliot Deutsch
Estimated Sales: Below $5 Million
Number Employees: 5-9

22141 Elliott Bay Espresso
950 NW Elford Drive
Seattle, WA 98177-4125
206-467-6838
Fax: 206-467-6819
Espresso machines and accessories

22142 Elliott Manufacturing Co Inc
2664 S Cherry Ave
Fresno, CA 93706-5494
559-233-6235
Fax: 559-233-9833 elliottmfg@elliott-mfg.com
www.elliott-mfg.com
Manufacturer and exporter of date and raisin pro-cessing machinery and olive, date and prune pitters; also, packaging machinery including erectors, seal-ers, cartoners and case packers
President, Chief Executive Officer: Terry Aluisi
National Sales Manager: John Rea
Estimated Sales: $1-5 Million
Number Employees: 20-49
Square Footage: 120000

22143 Elliott-Williams Company
3500 E 20th St
Indianapolis, IN 46218
317-635-1660
Fax: 317-453-1977 800-428-9303
Manufacturer and exporter of blast chillers, walk-in coolers, freezers and refrigerators; also, pre-fabri-cated refrigerated warehouses
Owner: Stuart Mc Keehan
CFO: R Scott
Contact: Michael Elliott
mark.m.elliott@williams.com
Purchasing Manager: K McCoy
Estimated Sales: $20-50 Million
Number Employees: 100-249
Square Footage: 100000
Brands:
Correctchill
Faster Freezer

22144 Ellis Corp
1400 W Bryn Mawr Ave
Itasca, IL 60143-1384
630-250-9222
Fax: 630-250-9241 800-611-6806
ksiriano@elliscorp.com www.elliscorp.com
President: Robert H Fesmire
rfesmire@elliscorp.com
Chief Executive Officer: Bob Fesmire
CEO: Robert H Fesmire
Estimated Sales: $10-20 Million
Number Employees: 50-99

22145 Elm Packaging Company
5837 Distribution Dr
Memphis, TN 38141-8204
901-795-2711
Fax: 901-795-8035 www.tekni-plex.com
Foam carry out containers
President: Kenneth Baker
CFO: Glean Davis
Plant Manager: Rick Nelson
Estimated Sales: $20 - 30 Million
Number Employees: 100-249

22146 Elmar Industries
200 Gould Ave
Depew, NY 14043-3138
716-681-5650
Fax: 716-681-4660 800-433-3562
www.elmarworldwide.com
Filling machines: rotary piston (both rotary and ver-tical valve), bottom fill, gravity, true monoblock vol-umetric pocket, and vacuum syruper product fillers
President: Mark Dahlquist
Cio/Cto: Unggit Tjitradjaja
unggitt@elmarworldwide.com
Estimated Sales: $10-20 000,000
Number Employees: 100-249

22147 Elmar Worldwide
200 Gould Avenue
P.O. Box 245
Depew, NY 14043-0245
716-681-5650
Fax: 716-681-4660 800-433-3562
elmar@elmarworldwide.com
www.elmarworldwide.com
Manufacturer, exporter and designer of rotary valve piston fillers, multi-flex particulate fillers, vacuum syrupers and monoblock systems; also, re-manufac-turing, R&D, computer/electronic line control sys-tems, product testing andflush-in place systems
President: Mark Dahlquist
CEO: Martin Jolden, Jr.
CFO: Linda Gregorio
Sales: Tom Depczynski
Estimated Sales: $10 - 20 Million
Number Employees: 50-99
Brands:
Elmar

22148 Elmark Packaging Inc
901 S Bolmar St # 1j
West Chester, PA 19382-4550
610-692-2455
Fax: 610-692-8793 800-670-9688
sales@elmarkpkg.com www.elmarkpkg.com
Provider of equipment, products and knowledge to
enable customers to add information to their prod-
ucts and packages in plant, on-line with self-adhe-
sive labels and/or all forms of printing
President: Heather Skerlak
apar@elmarkpkg.com
Estimated Sales: Below $5 Million
Number Employees: 5-9
Square Footage: 16400
Brands:
    Mini-Pro

22149 Elmeco SRL
5700 Ferguson Road
Suite 8
Bartlett, TN 38134-4557
901-385-0490
Fax: 901-373-7091
Slush machines
President: David Roberts
Number Employees: 4

**22150 Elmo Rietschle - A Gardner
Denver Product**
1800 Gardner Expressway
Quincy, IL 62305
217-222-5400
Fax: 217-228-8243
Compressors and pumps for the beverage and food
production industries.
President & CEO: Barry Pennypacker
Chairman Board of Directors: Frank Hansen
frank.hansen@garnerdenver.com

22151 Elmwood Sensors
500 Narragansett Park Dr
Pawtucket, RI 00861
401-727-1300
Fax: 401-728-5390 800-356-9663
linda.lundgren@invensys.com
www.elmwoodsensors.com
Manufacturer and exporter of thermostats and con-
trols
VP/General Manager: Steven Fof
Estimated Sales: $50-100 Million
Number Employees: 100-250
Square Footage: 160000
Parent Co: Fasco

22152 Elo Touch Systems
301 Constitution Dr
Menlo Park, CA 94025-1110
650-361-4800
Fax: 650-361-4721 800-557-1458
eloinfo@elotouch.com www.elotouch.com
Manufacturer and exporter of operator interfaces
and point of sale systems
General Manager: Mark Mendenhall
Chief Executive Officer: Craig Witsoe
CFO: Roxi Wen
Vice President, Chief Technical Officer: Bruno
Thuillier
VP, Corporate Development: Sharon Segev
VP, Global Quality: Anita Chang
Manager of Marketing: Fumiko Sasaki
Vice President of Global Sales: Sean Miller
Contact: Thuillier Bruno
bruno.thuillier@elotouch.com
Vice President of Operations: Mike Moran
Number Employees: 500-999
Parent Co: Amp
Type of Packaging: Food Service
Brands:
    Ad-Touch
    Info Board
    Smart Frame
    Total Touch
    Touch in a Box

22153 Elopak Americas
46962 Liberty Dr
Wixom, MI 48393
248-486-4600
www.elopak.com
Cartons, aseptic and plastic pouches, form/fill/seal
systems and packaging equipment for paper and
plastic; importer of filling machinery.
Director, National Accounts, Americas: Julia Viter

Year Founded: 1906
Estimated Sales: $13 Billion
Number Employees: 2,800
Square Footage: 175000
Parent Co: Ferd Groups
Brands:
    Elopouch
    Pure-Pak
    Unifill

22154 Elreha Controls Corporation
2510 Terminal Drive South
St Petersburg, FL 33712
727-327-6236
Fax: 727-323-7336 sales@elreha.com
www.elreha.com
Electronic timers, cooking computers and thermom-
eters
President: Abdul Hamadeh
Contact: Junis Hamadeh
jhamadeh@elreha.com
General Manager: Bonnie DelGrosso
Estimated Sales: $5 - 10 Million
Number Employees: 100-249
Square Footage: 260000

22155 Elrene Home Fashions
261 5th Ave
New York, NY 10016-7794
212-213-0425
Fax: 212-481-1738
Place mats and tablecloths including plastic and fab-
ric
CEO: Mark Siegel
CFO and QC: Ron Selber
Estimated Sales: $2.5 - 5 Million
Number Employees: 100-249
Parent Co: Elrene Manufacturing Company

22156 (HQ)Elro Signs
400 W Walnut St
Gardena, CA 90248-3137
310-380-7444
Fax: 310-380-7452 800-927-4555
sales@elrosigns.com www.elrosigns.com
Electric, plastic, neon and metal signs; installation
service available nationwide
President: Max Rhodes
VP: Frank Rhodes
Manager: Dan Materman
sales@elrosigns.com
Estimated Sales: $4 Million
Number Employees: 20-49
Square Footage: 72000
Other Locations:
    Elro Sign Co.
    Marietta GA

22157 Elwell Parker
4200 Casteel Drive
Coraopolis, PA 15108
216-432-0638
Fax: 216-881-7555 800-272-9953
nick@elwellparker.com www.elwellparker.com
Manufacturer and exporter of material handling
equipment including rider style, electric fork and
platform trucks
Sales and Marketing: Nick Marshall
VP Sales/Marketing: Jeff Leggett
Manager Sales/Parts/Service/Support: Curt Roupe
Estimated Sales: $3 - 5 Million
Number Employees: 5-9

22158 Elwood Safety Company
2180 Elmwood Ave
Buffalo, NY 14216
716-308-0573
Fax: 716-874-2110 866-326-6060
www.elwoodsafety.com
Manufacturer and exporter of protective clothing in-
cluding aprons, coveralls, sweatbands, lab coats and
flame retardant clothing; also, voltage testers, food
and beverage coolers and filtration systems
VP/ Sr. Sales Representative: Leslie Meyers
Estimated Sales: $1 - 5 Million
Number Employees: 10-19
Square Footage: 30000

22159 Embee Sunshade Co
722 Metropolitan Ave # 1
Brooklyn, NY 11211-3722
718-387-8566
Fax: 718-782-2642 info@embeesunshade.com
www.embeesunshade.com

Umbrellas for carts and tables
Owner: Barnett S Brickner
info@embeesunshade.com
Estimated Sales: $2.5-5 Million
Number Employees: 10-19
Square Footage: 48000

22160 Emblem & Badge
123 Dyer Street
Suite 2
Providence, RI 02903-3907
401-365-1265
Fax: 401-365-1263 800-875-5444
sales@recognition.com www.recognition.com
Manufacturer, importer and exporter of plaques, tro-
phies, advertising novelties, name badges, desk sets,
glassware, custom awards, etc
President: David Resnik
Vice President: Mike Hersherits
Sales: RI Johnston
Contact: Dinna Finnegan
dinna@recognition.com
Number Employees: 50-99
Square Footage: 100000
Type of Packaging: Bulk
Brands:
    Awards America
    Emblem & Badge

22161 Embro Manufacturing Company
400 Nassau Street E
East Canton, OH 44730-1330
330-489-3500
Fax: 330-488-3131
O.E.M. wire forms, point of purchase and displays
Customer Service: Joni Nelson
Production Manager: Gary Wilson
Estimated Sales: $2.5-5 Million
Number Employees: 20-49
Square Footage: 136000

22162 Emc Solutions
302 S Ash St
Celina, OH 45822-2210
419-586-2388
Fax: 419-586-3311 sales@emcconveyor.com
www.emcconveyor.com
Stainless steel and painted overhead trolley convey-
ors.
Owner: Jeffrey Hazel
econo-mfg@bright.net
Estimated Sales: Less Than $500,000
Number Employees: 1-4
Square Footage: 20000
Type of Packaging: Food Service

22163 Emco Industrial Plastics
99 Commerce Rd
Cedar Grove, NJ 07009
973-239-0202
Fax: 973-239-1595 800-292-9906
mailbox@emcoplastics.com
www.emcoplastics.com
Supplier of plastic sheet, rod, tubing and films in-
cluding plexiglass, cutting boards, and vinyl door
strip. Manufacturer of plastic point of purchase dis-
plays including bulk food containers, bagel bins,
pastry cases, candy binsframes, sign holders, and
sneeze guards.
President: James Mc Namara
Vice President: Mark Mercadante
Sales Manager: Jim McNamara
Estimated Sales: $20-50 Million
Number Employees: 50-99
Square Footage: 50000
Type of Packaging: Food Service

22164 Emedco
2491 Wehrle Dr
Williamsville, NY 14221-7141
716-626-1616
Fax: 716-626-1630 877-765-8386
customerservice@emedco.com www.emedco.com
Signs and marking and safety devices including
warning flags, tags, convex mirrors and laminated
metal and pressure sensitive labels
President: David Ewert
Quality Control: Bill Meehen
Marketing Director: Kathleen Brunner
Sales Manager: Joseph Reinhart
Manager: Pascal Deman
Estimated Sales: $10 - 20 Million
Number Employees: 100-249
Square Footage: 140000

Brands:
  Economarks
  Kwik-Koils

22165 Emerald City Closets Inc
301 - 30th St. NE, #106
Auburn, WA 98002
425-497-8808
Fax: 425-497-8311 800-925-1521
www.emeraldcc.com
Manufacturer, importer and exporter of induction
ranges and ovens
Owner: John Pearson
  johnp@emeraldcc.com
Purchasing Manager: Winston Chiu
Estimated Sales: $2.5-5 Million
Number Employees: 1-4
Square Footage: 30000
Type of Packaging: Food Service, Private Label
Brands:
  Fuji Electric

22166 Emerald Packaging Inc
33050 Western Ave
Union City, CA 94587-2157
510-429-5700
Fax: 510-429-5715 www.empack.com
Polyethylene bags
President: Kevin Kelly
CEO: Esmeralda Barriga
  ebarriga@cisco.com
Estimated Sales: $20-50 Million
Number Employees: 100-249

22167 Emerling International Foods
2381 Fillmore Ave
Suite 1
Buffalo, NY 14214-2197
716-833-7381
Fax: 716-833-7386 pemerling@emerfood.com
www.emerlinginternational.com
Bulk ingredients including: Fruits & Vegetables;
Juice Concentrates; Herbs & Spices; Oils & Vinegars; Flavors & Colors; Honey & Molasses. Also
produces pure maple syrup.
President: J Emerling
  jemerling@emerfood.com
Sales: Peter Emerling
Public Relations: Jenn Burke
Year Founded: 1988
Estimated Sales: $10-20 Million
Number Employees: 20-49
Square Footage: 500000

22168 Emerson Industrial Automation
7078 Shady Oak Rd
Eden Prairie, MN 55344
952-995-8000
800-893-2321
info.us@mail.nidec.com
Automation solutions.
Contact: Steve Burts
  steve.burts@emersonct.com
Number Employees: 100-249
Parent Co: Emerson Electric Co.

22169 Emerson Process Management
7070 Winchester Cir
Boulder, CO 80301-3506
303-527-5200
Fax: 303-530-8459 800-522-6277
flowcustomercare.americas@emerson.com
www2.emersonprocess.com
Measurement and process controls for the food and
beverage industry, as well as solutions for water and
wastewater treatments.
Business Leader: Steven Sonnenberg
Number Employees: 500-999

**22170 Emery Thompson Machine
&Supply Company**
15350 Flight Path Drive
Brooksville, FL 34604-6861
718-588-7300
Fax: 352-796-0720
STEVE@EMERYTHOMPSON.COM
www.emerythompson.com
Manufacturer, importer and exporter of ice cream,
Italian ice, frozen lemonade and frozen custard making machinery
President: Steve Thompson
CEO: Ted Thompson

Estimated Sales: $2.5-5 Million
Number Employees: 20-49
Square Footage: 180000

22171 Emery Winslow Scale Co
73 Cogwheel Ln # A
Seymour, CT 06483-3930
203-881-9333
Fax: 203-881-9477 www.emerywinslow.com
Industrial scale manufacturer
Owner/CEO: Walter Young
CEO: Rudi Baisch
  emeryscale@aol.com
CFO/President: Bill Fischer
VP/Marketing: Rudi Baisch
Research & Development: Sam Sagarsee
Sales: David Young
Operations Manager: Bill Rosser
Plant Manager: Jim Evinger
Purchasing Manager: Jonathan Young
Estimated Sales: $20 Million+
Number Employees: 20-49
Number of Brands: 3
Square Footage: 120000
Other Locations:
  Pennsylvania Scale Company
  Lancaster PA
Brands:
  Emery
  Flattop
  Genesis
  Hydrostatics
  Hytronics
  Lifemount
  Totalizer
  Weighsquare
  Winslow

22172 Emico
13570 Larwin Circle
Santa Fe Springs, CA 90670
562-926-9600
Fax: 562-926-9611 info@emicoinc.com
www.emicoinc.com
Magnetic pan indexer, dough maker, zig-zag board
rotary and boards, bread moulder, up-down pan indexer, wet onion applicator, bread and bun cooler,
and screw pan; parts and service
Contact: Ron Fender
  rfender@emicoinc.com
Estimated Sales: $1 - 5 Million

22173 Emiliomiti
219 9th St
San Francisco, CA 94103-3806
415-621-1909
Fax: 415-621-4613 866-867-2782
info@pastabiz.com www.pastabiz.com
Wholesaler/distributor of espresso coffee machines,
pasta machines and wood burning brick pizza ovens;
serving the food service market
CEO: Emilio Mitidieri
Estimated Sales: 900000
Number Employees: 10-19
Number of Brands: 5
Number of Products: 16
Square Footage: 12000
Brands:
  Capitani
  Emiollomiti
  Libitalia
  Pastabiz
  Technomachine

22174 Emjac
1075 Hialeah Dr
Hialeah, FL 33010-5551
305-883-2194
Fax: 305-883-2197 www.emjacindustries.com
Walk-in coolers and freezers
President: David Dorta
  davidd@emjacindustries.com
Estimated Sales: $20 - 50 Million
Number Employees: 100-249

22175 Emmeti
101 Sherwood Drive
Boalsburg, PA 16827-1612
816-466-2781
Fax: 816-466-2782 emmeti@nauticom.net
Fully automatic, floor level, bulk palletizers, intelligent bottle stacker, automatic layer pad, top frame
and empty pallet inserters

President: Kevin Zarnick
Marketing Manager/Owner: Fausto Savazzi
Sales Manager and PET Industry: Paolo Biondi
V P: Beth Zarnick-duffy
Sales Manager: Fabrizio Boschi
Technical Manager: Luis Garcia

22176 Emmeti USA
7320 East Fletcher Avenue
Tampa, FL 33637
813-490-6252
Fax: 813-490-6253 www.emmetiusa.com
President: Kevin Zarnick
Vice President: Fausto Savazzi
USA Sales Manager: Beth Zarnick-Duffy

22177 Emoshun
10022 6th Street
Rancho Cucamonga, CA 91730-5746
909-484-9559
Fax: 909-484-9560
Insulated bags and bottles
Estimated Sales: $1 - 5 Million

22178 Empire Bakery Equipment
1 Enterprise Pl # C
Hicksville, NY 11801-5347
516-681-1500
Fax: 516-681-1510 800-878-4070
info@empirebake.com
Distributor of mixers, dough dividers, rounders,
moulders, stampers, bagel machines, retarders,
freezers, refrigerators, ovens, display cases, tables,
slicers, etc
Owner: S Wechsler
  info@empirebake.com
VP: C Zarate
Estimated Sales: Below $8 Million
Number Employees: 10-19
Square Footage: 64000

22179 Empire Candle Mfg LLC
2925 Fairfax Trfy
Kansas City, KS 66115-1317
913-621-4555
Fax: 913-621-3444 800-231-9398
Candles including scented and seasonal citronella
Owner: Rick Langley
  rlangley@langleyempirecandle.com
CEO: Drummond Crews
CFO: Mick Buttress
Marketing: Brenda Cherpitel
Operations Manager: Eric Coulter
Purchasing: Larry Palmer
Estimated Sales: $10 - 20 Million
Number Employees: 50-99

22180 Empire Safe Company
6 E 39th St
New York, NY 10016-0112
212-226-2255
Fax: 212-684-5550 info@empiresafe.com
www.empiresafe.com
Safes including burglar resistant and cash depositing
President: Richard Krasilovsky
CFO: Andy Genett
Contact: Tom Iacobellis
  tom@empiresafe.com
Director of Operations: Mark Rubin
Estimated Sales: $5-10 Million
Number Employees: 5-9
Square Footage: 80000

22181 Empire Screen Printing Inc
N5206 Marco Rd
Onalaska, WI 54650-8818
608-783-3301
Fax: 608-783-3306 www.empirescreen.com
Empire is a leader in the latest printing processes including flexographic, screen & digital printing, as
well as doming. Empire is a supplier to the appliance, retail, food, and beverage industries. Products
include retail signagepackage labels, and marketing
support items.

President: Johns Freismuth
CEO: James Brush
 jamesbr@empirescreen.com
Vice President: James Schwinefus
Research & Development: Keith Cole
Quality Control: Steve Johnson
Marketing Director: Douglas Billings
Sales Director: Kathleen Cuellar
Public Relations: Douglas Billings
Operations Manager: John Johnsonth
Plant Manager: Lee Vieth
Purchasing Manager: Lori Taube
Estimated Sales: $25 Million
Number Employees: 250-499
Number of Brands: 2
Square Footage: 150000
Type of Packaging: Food Service, Private Label

22182 Emtrol
425 E Berlin Rd
York, PA 17408-8810

717-846-4000
Fax: 717-846-3624 800-634-4927
cgales@emtrol.com
www.weldonmachinetool.com
Manufacturer, importer and exporter of material handling equipment and controls, plant automation equipment and custom warehouse/inventory software
President: George Sipe
Executive VP: Matthew Anater
VP Sales/Marketing: Nicholas Selch
Estimated Sales: $20-50 Million
Number Employees: 50-99
Square Footage: 52000

22183 Emulso
2750 Kenmore Ave
Tonawanda, NY 14150-7707

716-854-2889
Fax: 716-854-2809 info@emulso.com
www.emulso.com
General and specialty cleaning compounds
President/Owner: Chris Miller
Estimated Sales: $10 Million
Number Employees: 25
Square Footage: 34000
Type of Packaging: Private Label, Bulk
Brands:
 Emulso

22184 En-Hanced Products Inc
229 E Broadway Ave
Westerville, OH 43081-1656

614-882-7400
Fax: 614-882-7549 800-783-7400
www.en-hancedproducts.com
Food grade elevators and conveyors; also, hand and power seed cleaners.
President: James Hance
 jhance@en-hancedproductsinc.com
Sales Director: Dennis James
Production Manager: Tim Woodruff
Purchasing Manager: Dennis James
Estimated Sales: $750,000
Number Employees: 5-9
Square Footage: 28000

22185 EnWave Corporation
744 W Hastings St
Suite 425
Vancouver, BC V6C 1A5
Canada

604-806-6110
info@enwave.net
www.enwave.net
Dehydration of food, live or active bulk liquids, and sensitive pharmaceuticals.
President & CEO: Tim Durance
Executive Chairman: John P.A. Budreski
Chief Financial Officer: Dan Henriques
SVP, Research & Development: Dr. John Zhang
SVP, Technical Services & Director: Dr. Gary Sandberg
Director, R&D, Biomaterials: Dr. Rehaineh Noorbakhsh
SVP, Sales & Business Development: Brent Charleton
SVP, Manufacting & Chief Engineer: Leon Fu
Year Founded: 1996
Estimated Sales: $14.9 Million
Number Employees: 35

22186 Encapsulation Systems
1489 Baltimore Pike
Suite 109
Springfield, PA 19064-3958

610-543-0800
Fax: 610-543-0688
Manufacturers of specially controlled release products for use in the pharmaceutical and medical-device field
President and CEO: Bruce Retting
Executive Vice President, Licensing: Cyril Burke
Number Employees: 10

22187 Encompass Supply
3505 Autumn Ct
Kalispell, MT 59901

406-756-5900
Fax: 406-756-1203 888-852-7590
info@encompass-supply.com
encompass-supply.com
Commercial janitorial supply company

22188 Encore Glass
4345 Industrial Way
Benicia, CA 94510

707-745-4444
Fax: 707-748-4444 sales@Encoreglass.com
www.encoreglass.com
Wine industry recycled equipment
Sales Director: Dave Hammond
Contact: Rannie Dada
 rannie.dada@encoreglass.com
Estimated Sales: $5-10 000,000
Number Employees: 40

22189 Encore Image Inc
303 W Main St
Ontario, CA 91762-3843

909-986-4632
Fax: 909-988-6376 800-791-1187
info@encoreimage.com www.encoreimage.com
Exterior and interior electric and neon signs; also, menus and awnings
Chairman of the Board: Terry Wilkins
HR Executive: Sarah Quevada
 s.quevada@encoreimage.com
VP Sales: Corey Northncott
Estimated Sales: $3-4,000,000
Number Employees: 20-49
Square Footage: 30000

22190 Encore Plastics
P.O. Box 3208
Huntington Beach, CA 92605

714-893-7889
Fax: 714-897-7968 888-822-8763
info@encoreplastics.com
www.encoreplastics.com
Manufacturer and exporter of beverageware and plastic stemware
President: Richard Harvey
Quality Control: David Martin
VP: Donald Okada
Contact: Donald Okada
 dokada@encoreplastics.com
Estimated Sales: $500,000-$1 Million
Number Employees: 10
Parent Co: Donoco Industries

22191 Endress & Hauser
P.O. Box 246
Greenwood, IN 46142-0246

317-535-7138
Fax: 317-535-1489 800-428-4344
info@us.endress.com www.us.endress.com
Electronic process control instruments
Manager: Todd Lucey
VP Controller: Nancy Winter
Executive VP: Joseph Schaffer
Contact: David Jackson
 david.jackson@us.endress.com
VP Manufacturing: Phil Tumey
Estimated Sales: $20-50 Million
Number Employees: 250-499
Square Footage: 78000
Parent Co: Endress & Hauser Consult

22192 Endurart Inc
20 W 22nd St
New York, NY 10010-5804

212-779-8522
Fax: 212-691-4751
Advertising novelties and specialties including awards, trophies, embedments and coins

Manager: William Kalsman
Estimated Sales: $5-10 Million
Number Employees: 1-4

22193 Enercon
PO Box 773
Menomonee Falls, WI 53052-0773

262-255-6070
Fax: 262-255-7784 www.enerconind.com
Corona treaters and power supplies
Owner: Don Nimmer
CEO: Donald Nimmer
Contact: Sarah Bauer
 sbauer@enerconmail.com
Estimated Sales: $10-20 000,000
Number Employees: 100-249

22194 Enerfab Inc.
4430 Chickering Ave.
Cincinnati, OH 45232

513-641-0500
enerfab.com
Stainless and carbon steel tanks, bulk aseptic storage systems, epoxy tank linings, sanitary manways and gasket materials.
CEO: Aaron Landolt
CFO: Trisha Cole
COO: Jacob Snyder
Year Founded: 1901
Estimated Sales: $251 Million
Number Employees: 1000-4999
Square Footage: 250000

22195 Energy Sciences Inc
42 Industrial Way # 1
Wilmington, MA 01887-3471

978-658-3731
Fax: 978-694-9046 www.ebeam.com
Manufacturer and exporter of electron beam processing machinery used for drying and curing packaging materials, printed foil, etc
Estimated Sales: $7 Million
Number Employees: 50-99
Square Footage: 52000
Parent Co: Iwasaki Electric

22196 Energymaster
105 Liberty St
Walled Lake, MI 48390

248-624-6900
Fax: 248-624-6975 www.energymasterusa.com
Manufacturer and exporter of energy conservation equipment for heating and cooling, summer/winter ventilation and make-up air
President: Erik Hall
Estimated Sales: $2.5 - 5 Million
Number Employees: 10-19
Square Footage: 3600
Type of Packaging: Consumer, Food Service
Brands:
 Energymaster
 Seasonmaster
 Ventilation

22197 Enerquip Inc
611 North Rd
611 North Road
Medford, WI 54451-1154

715-748-5888
Fax: 715-748-6484 ronherman@enerquip.com
www.enerquip.com
Designer and fabricator of stainless steel shell and tube heat exchangers and custom components.
President & CEO: Jeannie Deml
Parts and Service: Sue Rhyner
Quality Control: John Barna
Director of Sales & Marketing: Ron Herman
Thermal Design and Inside Sales: Ron Herman
Manager: Ryan Ballinger
 ryanballinger@enerquip.com
Number Employees: 20-49

22198 Engineered Automation
19 Pomerleau St.
Suite 101
Biddeford, MI 4005

207-200-8301
Fax: 207-283-3023 www.eaminc.com
Packaging machinery including rotary lidders, puck inserters and removers and rotary overcappers
National Sales Manager: Suzanne Farrell
Number Employees: 20

22199 Engineered Food Systems
PO Box 821
Aurora, OR 97002-0821

503-699-6682
Fax: 503-699-6658

Equipment for Tortilla, Snack, Bakery and Packaging industries

22200 Engineered Plastics Inc
211 Chase St
PO Box 227
Gibsonville, NC 27249-2877

336-449-4121
Fax: 336-449-6352 800-711-1740
www.engplas.com

Illuminated buffet and ice sculpture display equipment, acrylic serving bowls and trays and specialty display items
President: Dwight M Davidson
 engplas@triad.rr.com
Sales Manager: Robert Ratliff
Food Service Manager: W Mottinger
Estimated Sales: $2.5-5 Million
Number Employees: 20-49
Square Footage: 150000
Brands:
 Glo-Ice

22201 Engineered Products
12202 Missouri Bottom Rd
Hazelwood, MO 63042-2318

314-731-5744
Fax: 314-731-5744 800-474-1474
tdaugherty@enprod.com

President: Dave Wendel
Estimated Sales: $10 - 20 Million
Number Employees: 50-99

22202 (HQ)Engineered Products
12202 Missouri Bottom Rd
Hazelwood, MO 63042-2318

314-731-5744
Fax: 314-731-5744 www.epico.com

Custom plastic injection molding including containers
President: Dave Wendel
VP/General Manager: Ron McGee
Estimated Sales: $10-20 Million
Number Employees: 50-99
Square Footage: 96000
Other Locations:
 Engineered Products
 Dequeen AR

22203 Engineered Products Corp
355 Woodruff Rd # 204
Greenville, SC 29607-3494

864-234-4888
Fax: 864-234-4860 800-868-0145
sales@engprod.com www.engprod.com

Manufacturer and exporter of pallet storage racks, gravity flow storage systems and conveyors; also, turnkey warehouse engineering services available
Manager: David Shupe
Sales/Marketing Executive: Charles Rouse
Manager: Andre Butler
 asbutler@epco.com
Purchasing Agent: Allen Griffith
Estimated Sales: $5-10 Million
Number Employees: 100-249
Square Footage: 400000
Parent Co: Gower
Brands:
 Deepflo
 Durabit
 Pushbak Cart
 Selectrak
 Traytrak

22204 Engineered Products Group
P.O. Box 8050
Madison, WI 53708

608-222-3484
Fax: 608-222-9314 800-626-3111
www.boumatic.com

Manufacturer and exporter of heat transfer equipment, jacketed shells, troughs, baffles and tanks, plates for fluid bed coolers and heaters, process vessels and storage and mixing tanks; also, carbon steel, stainless stell, titaniumand other alloys available
Owner: John Kotts
Sales: R Albrecht

Estimated Sales: $1-2.5 Million
Number Employees: 250-499
Parent Co: DEC International

22205 Engineered Security System Inc
1 Indian Ln
Towaco, NJ 07082-1015

973-257-0555
Fax: 973-257-0550 800-742-1263
info@engineeredsecurity.com
www.engineeredsecurity.com

Manufacturer and exporter of computer based security systems; closed circuit TV monitoring available
Owner: David George
 dgeorge@engineeredsecurity.com
Estimated Sales: $20-50 Million
Number Employees: 50-99
Square Footage: 8500

22206 Engineered Systems & Designs
119 Sandy Dr # A
Newark, DE 19713-1148

302-456-0446
Fax: 302-456-0441 esd@esdinc.com
www.esdinc.com

Wine industry laboratory equipment
President: Robert Spring
Estimated Sales: Below $5 Million
Number Employees: 1-4

22207 Engineered Textile Products
715 Loeffler St
Mobile, AL 36607-1317

251-476-8001
Fax: 251-476-0956 800-222-8277
ken@etpinfo.com www.etpinfo.com

Commercial awnings
President: Kenneth Robinson
 ken@etpinfo.com
Estimated Sales: $1-2.5 Million
Number Employees: 20-49
Brands:
 Artcraft

22208 Engineering & Mgmt Consultants
742 Butternut Dr
Franklin Lakes, NJ 07417-2243

201-847-0748
Fax: 201-847-0748 rhmeeremc@aol.com

Consultant specializing in plant operations, production and inventory control, laboratory and technical activities, marketing, regulatory and financial affairs, processing functions, certification, etc
President: Richard H Meer
 rhmeeremc@aol.com
Estimated Sales: Less Than $500,000
Number Employees: 1-4

22209 England Logistics
4701 West 2100 South
Salt Lake City, UT 84120

801-972-2712
Fax: 801-977-5795 800-887-0764
info@englandlogistics.com
www.englandlogistics.com

Transportation firm providing local, short and long haul trucking; also, contract warehousing available
President: Dan England
CEO: Dean England
Senior Vice President Chief Financial Of: Keith Wallace
Vice President: Brandon Harrison
Executive Vice President of Corporate Sa: David Kramer
Contact: Rolina Camello
 rolina.camello@crengland.com

22210 English Manufacturing Inc
11292 Sunrise Park Dr
Rancho Cordova, CA 95742-6599

916-638-9902
Fax: 916-638-9961 800-651-2711
www.englishmfg.com

Stainless steel sneeze gaurds and food guards, glass racks and partition posts.

President: Doug English
CFO: Diana English
Vice President: Jennifer Kogler
Research & Development: Shawn Rice
Quality Control: A J Wells
Marketing Director: Andrew Nelson
Sales Director: Cindy Lucas
Contact: Mark Dallara
 markdallara@freudenbergmedical.com
Operations Manager: Mike Richardson
Production Manager: Sara Stefanik
Estimated Sales: Less Than $500,000
Number Employees: 1-4
Number of Brands: 2
Number of Products: 12
Square Footage: 10000
Type of Packaging: Food Service, Private Label
Brands:
 Matrix Sneezegaurd

22211 Engraph Label Group
1187 Industrial Rd
Cold Spring, KY 41076-8799

859-781-6161
Fax: 859-781-6339 800-422-6633

Wine industry label printers
President: Eric Schaffer
Estimated Sales: $3 - 5 Million
Number Employees: 10-19

22212 Engraving Services Co.
818 Port Road
Woodville South, SA 05011
www.engravingservices.com.au

Manufacturer and exporter of labels, nameplates, decals and engraved plastic and electric signs
Sales/Marketing Director: Peter Vasic
Production Manager: Jamie Smale
Estimated Sales: $5-10 Million
Number Employees: 50-99
Type of Packaging: Bulk

22213 Engraving Specialists
503 N Washington Ave
Royal Oak, MI 48067-1756

248-542-2244
Fax: 248-542-1847

Engraved promotional items, award plaques and name badges; also, signage including ADA, directional, label, vinyl letter and logo available
Owner: Marc Milosevich
VP/Secretary/Treasurer: Dick Lang
Estimated Sales: $500,000-$1 Million
Number Employees: 1-4
Square Footage: 5600

22214 Enhance Packaging Technologies
201 S Blair Street
Whitby, ON L1N 5S6
Canada

905-668-5811
Fax: 905-666-7005 www.packagingdigest.com

Liquid pouch form/fill/seal equipment including pasteurized and aseptic fillers; also, films matched to application and equipment
Marketing Development Manager (US Dairy): Harry Akamphuber
Marketing Development: Wayne Naumowich
Marketing Development: Joe Shields
Parent Co: DuPont Canada
Brands:
 Mini-Sip

22215 Enjay Converters Ltd.
495 Ball Street
Cobourg, ON K9A
Canada

905-372-7373
Fax: 905-377-8066 800-427-5517
sales@enjay.com www.enjay.com

Manufactures a complete line of laminated and wrapped cake circles and shieets
President: Jay Cassidy
Number Employees: 10

22216 Ennio International
1005 N. Commons Drive
Aurora, IL 60504-4100

630-851-5808
Fax: 630-851-7744 www.enniousa.com

Manufacturer and supplier of high quality netting and casings for the meat and poultry industries.

Director of Sales: Ralph Schuster
Contact: Ennio Hand
ennio.hand@enniousa.com

22217 Ennis Inc.
2241 Presidential Pkwy.
Midlothian, TX 76065

972-775-9801
Fax: 800-645-8339 800-972-1069
HOTLine@ennis.com www.ennis.com
Restaurant supplies including menus, place mats and paper items.
Chairman/CEO/President: Keith Walters
Interim CFO: Vera Burnett
Executive Vice President/Secretary: Michael Magill
Year Founded: 1909
Estimated Sales: $370 Million
Number Employees: 2,300+
Number of Brands: 33
Brands:
Adams McClure
Admore
Allen-Bailey
Atlas Tag & Label
B&D Litho of Arizona
Block Graphics
Calibrated
ColorWorx
Ennis
Falcon Business Forms
Folder Express
Forms Manufacturers
GenForms
General Financial Supply
Hayes Graphics
Hoosier Data Forms
Independant Folders
Kay Toledo Tag
Major Business Systems
Mutual Graphics
National Imprint Corporation
Northstar
Print Graphics
PrintXcel
Printegra
Royal
Special Service Partners
Specialized Printed Forms
Star Award Ribbon Co.
Trade Envelopes
Tri-C Business Forms
Wisco Envelope
Witt Printing

22218 Enotech Corporation
PO Box 576
Palo Alto, CA 94302-0576

650-851-2040
Fax: 650-851-2034
Wine industry equipment

22219 Enpoco
4263 Carolina Avenue
Suite J
Richmond, VA 23222-1400

804-228-9934
Fax: 703-668-1400 800-338-2581
Grease interceptors
CEO: Patrick Okeefe
Interceptor Production Manager: Roy Hetzler
Estimated Sales: $2.5-5 Million
Number Employees: 10-19
Parent Co: Watts Industries

22220 Enrick Co
150 E 1st St
PO Box 37
Zumbrota, MN 55992-1552

507-732-5215
Fax: 507-625-6570 rollorkari@yahoo.com
www.enrickco.com
Manufacturer and exporter of hand trucks, dollies and carts
Owner: Vince Small
Estimated Sales: $1-2.5 Million
Number Employees: 5-9

22221 Ensign Ribbon Burners LLC
101 Secor Ln
Pelham, NY 10803-2791

914-813-0815
Fax: 914-738-0928 info@erbensign.com
Industrial gas burners

President: John F Cavallo
Vice President: Mario Anelich
mario@erbensign.com
Estimated Sales: $2.5-5 Million
Number Employees: 10-19

22222 Ensign Ribbon Burners LLC
101 Secor Ln
PO Box 8369
Pelham, NY 10803-2791

914-813-0815
Fax: 914-738-0928 info@erbensign.com
Vice President: Mario Anelich
mario@erbensign.com
Vice President: James Pezzuto
Director of Sales: Mario Anelich
Estimated Sales: $3 - 5 Million
Number Employees: 10-19

22223 Ensinger Inc
365 Meadowlands Blvd
Washington, PA 15301-8900

724-746-6050
Fax: 724-746-9078 800-243-3221
sales@ensinger-ind.com www.ensinger-inc.com
Manufacturer and exporter of plastic packaging materials
President: Frank Bavaro
fbavaro@ensinger-inc.com
Director Sales/Marketing: Bruce Dickinson
Technical Director: Ken Schwartz
Estimated Sales: $10 - 20 Million
Number Employees: 20-49
Parent Co: Dana Her Corporation
Type of Packaging: Bulk

22224 Entech Instruments Inc.
2207 Agate Court
Simi Valley, CA 93065

805-527-5939
www.entechinst.com
Developer and manufacturer of analytical instruments.
Founder & Presdient: Dan Cardin
Director, Marketing & Information System: John Quintana
Customer Care & Service Manager: Tom Wilber
National Service Manager: Tim Raub

22225 Entech Systems Corp
607 Maria St
Kenner, LA 70062-7400

504-469-6541
Fax: 504-465-9192 800-783-6561
entech@msn.com www.entech.com
Manufacturer and exporter of automatic ULV insect fogging systems for killing crawling and flying insects; also, semi-automatic and portable systems, sanitation audits and insecticides
President: Robert Drude
robert.drudge@entech.cc
Corporate Secretary: Gail Stumpf
Purchasing Manager: Marcus Curtis
Estimated Sales: Below $5 Million
Number Employees: 5-9
Square Footage: 16000
Brands:
Auto Fog
Entech Fog

22226 Entergy's Teamwork Louisiana
4809 Jefferson Highway
Jefferson, LA 70121-3126

504-840-2562
Fax: 504-840-2512 800-968-8243
laed@entergy.com www.entergy.com
Chairman of the Board; Chief Executive O: Wayne Leonard
Senior Vice President: Donna Jacobs
Contact: Cain Merite
cmerite@entergy.com
Estimated Sales: $1 - 5 Million

22227 Enterprise
7800 Sovereign Row
Dallas, TX 75247-4887

214-688-5223
Fax: 214-638-2016 800-527-9431
Contact: Frederick Goes
fred@goesent.com
Estimated Sales: $10-20 000,000
Number Employees: 5-9

22228 Enterprise Box Company
10 Burnside Street
Montclair, NJ 07043-1325

973-509-2200
Fax: 973-509-1910
Paper boxes and envelopes
VP: Lenore Klein
Estimated Sales: Less than $500,000
Number Employees: 1-4

22229 Enterprise Company
616 S Santa Fe
Santa Ana, CA 92705

714-835-0541
Fax: 714-543-2856
Manufacturer and exporter of baling presses
President: Orval Gould
VP: Albert Gould
Marketing Director: John Gould
Contact: Dan Scott
dan@enterpriseco.com
Estimated Sales: $2.5-5 Million
Number Employees: 50-99
Type of Packaging: Bulk

22230 Enterprise Dynamics Corporation
1577 N Technology Way # A
Orem, UT 84097-2395

801-224-6914
Fax: 801-224-6984
Software
Owner: Bill Nordgren
Estimated Sales: $1 - 3 Million
Number Employees: 10-19

22231 Enterprise Envelope Inc
920 Ken O Sha Ind Park Dr SE
Grand Rapids, MI 49508-8215

616-247-1301
Fax: 616-247-1343 800-422-4255
orders@enterpriseenvelope.com
www.enterpriseenvelope.com
Envelopes including lithographed, commercial catalog, special size and window; up to four color process
President: Gary Helmholdt
gary@enterpriseenvelope.com
Estimated Sales: $1-3 Million
Number Employees: 10-19
Square Footage: 42000

22232 Enterprise Products
6875 Suva St
Bell Gardens, CA 90201-1998

562-928-1918
Fax: 562-927-8413
Wire display racks and shelving; also, tubing goods and stampings
CEO: Ron Spicer
Contact: Stephanie Happel
stephanie.happel@georgfischer.com
Estimated Sales: $20-50 Million
Number Employees: 100-249

22233 Enting Water Conditioning Inc
3211 Dryden Rd Frnt
Moraine, OH 45439-1400

937-456-5151
Fax: 937-294-5485 800-735-5100
sales@enting.com www.enting.com
Manufacturer and exporter of water treatment systems including softeners, reverse osmosis, cartridge filters and ultra-violet purifiers
President: Mel Entingh
President/COO: Dan Entingh
info@enting.com
Estimated Sales: $5-10 Million
Number Employees: 10-19
Square Footage: 86800
Brands:
Aquamate
Enting
Kane
Watermate

22234 Entoleter LLC
251 Welton St
Hamden, CT 06517-3944

203-787-3575
Fax: 203-787-1492 800-729-3575
info@entoleter.com www.entoleter.com
Manufacturer, exporter of centrifugal impact mills, wet scrubbers and wet electrostatic precipitators

President: Ernie Carr
  ecarr@entoleter.com
Sales Manager: Todd Gardner
Sales Manager: Dick Steinsuaag
  ecarr@entoleter.com
Estimated Sales: $5-10 000,000
Number Employees: 20-49
Square Footage: 62000
Parent Co: Spinnaker Industries
Brands:
  Centrified
  Centrimil
  Eid
  Esa

22235 Enviro Doors By ASI Technologies
5848 N. 95th Court
Milwaukee, WI 53225-2613
                                414-464-6200
        Fax: 414-464-9863 800-558-7068
        sales@asidoors.com www.asidoors.com
President: George C Balbach
Estimated Sales: $6 Million
Number Employees: 100-249

22236 Enviro-Clear Co
152 Cregar Rd
High Bridge, NJ 08829-1003
                                908-638-5507
        Fax: 908-638-4636 info@enviro-clear.com
                        www.enviro-clear.com
Manufacturer and exporter of clarifiers and belt and
pressure filters and separators
President: Joe Muldowney
  sales@enviro-clear.com
VP Marketing: Cindy Meyer
Sales: James Grau
Estimated Sales: $3 - 5 Million
Number Employees: 5-9
Square Footage: 40000
Brands:
  Enviro-Clear
  Pronto

22237 Enviro-Pak
15450 SE For Mor Ct
PO Box 1569
Clackamas, OR 97015
                                503-655-7044
        Fax: 503-655-6368 800-223-6836
        sales@enviro-pak.com www.enviro-pak.com
Manufactures food processing ovens, smokers, dryers, steam cabinets and chillers for further processing of meat, fish and poultry. Products are also now
being used in different industries such as pet foods,
fruits, vegetables, tofubakery products, mushrooms,
and more.
Owner: Gil Martini
Contact: Kim Bryant
  kim.bryant@enviropak.com
Estimated Sales: $10 - 20 Million
Number Employees: 20-49

22238 Enviro-Safety Products
8248 West Doe Ave
Visalia, CA 93291-9263
                                559-625-5592
        Fax: 559-651-1320 800-637-6606
        info@envirosafetyproducts.com
                www.envirosafetyproducts.com
Wine industry powdered spray and sulfur helmets,
protective clothing, respirators of all types
Manager: Scott Newton
R & D: Peggy Dahlvang
Contact: Bob Brussel
  b.brussel@envirosafetyproducts.com
Estimated Sales: $500,000
Number Employees: 20-49
Brands:
  3m
  Aearo/Peltor
  Paulson
  Sas

22239 Enviro-Test/Perry Laboratories
8102 Lemont Rd Ste 1500
Woodridge, IL 60517-7776
                                630-324-6685
        Fax: 630-734-9534 www.envirotest-perry.com
Laboratory testing and analysis firm
President: Maria Lenos
VP Sales: Detrie Zacharias
Lab Director: George Lenos

Estimated Sales: Less than $500,000
Number Employees: 10 to 19
Square Footage: 9000

22240 Enviro-Ware
100 Sandusky Street
2nd Floor
Pittsburgh, PA 15212-5822
                                412-642-2222
        Fax: 412-642-2223 888-233-7857
                        www.enviro-ware.com
Manufacturers of biodegradable dinnerware and
packing
Estimated Sales: $1 - 5 Million
Brands:
  Enviro-Ware

22241 Envirolights Manufacturing
50 Viceroy Road
Concord, ON L4K 2L8
Canada
                                905-738-0357
        Fax: 905-738-0647
Pest and insect control systems and devices includ-
ing industrial electrocution and glue board type in-
sect light traps
President: Ken Nayler
VP: Douglas Nayler
Number Employees: 5-9
Parent Co: Envirolights Manufacturing
Brands:
  Electri-Fly
  Flintrol
  The Flylight

22242 Enviromental Structures
950 Walnut Ridge Dr
Hartland, WI 53029-9388
                                262-369-3535
        Fax: 262-369-3536
President: Brad Barke
Contact: Kathryn Macdonald
  kathryn.macdonald@aurora.org
Estimated Sales: $10 - 20 Million
Number Employees: 20-49

22243 Environmental Consultants
391 Newman Ave
Clarksville, IN 47129-3247
                                812-282-8481
        Fax: 812-282-8554
Environmental consultants specializing in pollution
control, testing and analysis
President: Robert Fuchs
Office Manager: Patti Kinchlow
Estimated Sales: $1-2.5 Million
Number Employees: 5 to 9

22244 Environmental Express
2345 Charleston Regional Pkwy
Charleston, SC 29492-8405
                                843-881-6560
        Fax: 843-881-3964 800-343-5319
        suggestions@envexp.com www.envexp.com
Supplier of environmentally safer laboratory equip-
ment for the food and beverage research &
develepent industry.
CEO: Dennis Pope
CFO: Nikki Truman
  nikkit@envexp.com
Vice President: Paul Strickler
Technical Sales Representative: Allison Ditullio
Manager: Paula Borgstedt
Estimated Sales: $5.2 Million
Number Employees: 50-99

22245 Environmental Products
730 Commerce Dr
Venice, FL 34292
                                941-486-1325
        Fax: 941-480-9201 800-828-2447
                www.cranenv.com/index1
Reverse osmosis based water purification equip-
ment, including pre-treatment and post-treatment
systems
Estimated Sales: $10-20 000,000
Number Employees: 50-99

22246 (HQ)Environmental Products Corp
99 Great Hill Rd
Naugatuck, CT 06770-2227
                                203-720-4059
        Fax: 203-720-9302 800-275-3861

Reverse-vending machinery; also, container ac-
counting and collection services available
President: Bhajun G Santchurn
CFO: Pilraj Chuwla
Sales: Bill Donnelly
Contact: David Baltimore
  davidb@envipco.com
Operations Manager: Charles Ricey
Plant Manager: Harry Yerrick
Estimated Sales: $.5 - 1 million
Number Employees: 5-9
Square Footage: 160000
Other Locations:
  Environmental Products Corp.
  Fairfax VA

22247 Environmental Products Company
197 Poplar Place #3
North Aurora, IL 60542-8191
                                630-892-2414
        Fax: 630-892-2467 800-677-8479
Manufacturer and exporter of polyvinyl chloride
strip doors, heat recycling fans and welding screens
Manager: Kurt Pfoutz
  kpfoutz@hotmail.com
Office Manager: Kurt Pfoutz
Estimated Sales: $5 - 10 Million
Number Employees: 10 to 19
Square Footage: 30000
Parent Co: Material Control

22248 Environmental Systems
218 N Main St
Culpeper, VA 22701-2620
                                540-825-6660
        Fax: 540-825-4961 800-541-2116
        info@ess-services.com www.ess-services.com
Consultant specializing in dairy and sanitation test-
ing, quality control and analysis including water,
wastewater, microbiological and shelf-life
President: Robert Jebson
  robertj@ess-services.com
VP: Donald Hearl
Estimated Sales: $5 - 10 Million
Number Employees: 20-49
Square Footage: 20000

22249 Environmizer Systems Corporation
25 W Highland Avenue
Atlantic Highlands, NJ 07716-2804
                                732-291-4700
        Fax: 732-291-4720
Magnetic scale removal in evaporators, separators,
pasteurizers
Estimated Sales: Less than $500,000
Number Employees: 4

22250 Enviropak Corp
4203 Shoreline Dr
Earth City, MO 63045-1209
                                314-739-1202
        Fax: 314-739-2422 info@enviropak.com
                        www.enviropak.com
Molded pulp packaging
President: John Wichlenski
CEO: Chris Miget
  chris@enviropak.com
Estimated Sales: $5-10 000,000
Number Employees: 50-99

22251 Enviropak Corp
4203 Shoreline Dr
Earth City, MO 63045-1209
                                314-739-1202
        Fax: 314-739-2422 sales@enviropak.com
                        www.enviropak.com
Pulp packaging for numerous industries including
that of food and beverage.
President: John Wichlenski
CEO: Chris Miget
  chris@enviropak.com
Treasurer: Joseph Walsh
VP: Jon Smith
Vice President Sales & Marketing: Bill Noble
Sales Coordinator: Kay Walsh
Vice President Manufacturing: Rodney Heenan
Estimated Sales: $4 Million
Number Employees: 50-99
Square Footage: 40000

22252 Epcon Industrial Systems
17777 I-45 South
Conroe, TX 77385
936-273-3300
Fax: 936-273-4600 800-447-7872
sales@epconlp.com www.epconlp.com
Manufacturer and exporter of air pollution control systems for enclosures, odor control systems and oxidizers; also, general bake ovens
President and R&D: Aziz Jamaluddin
CFO: Sunny Naidu
Quality Control: Mike Paddie
Sales Engineer: Brad Morello
Engineer Designer: Nedzad Hadzajlic
Estimated Sales: $5 - 10 Million
Number Employees: 50-99
Square Footage: 400000

22253 Epic Industries
1007 Jersey Ave
New Brunswick, NJ 08901
732-249-6867
Fax: 732-249-7683 800-221-3742
www.epicindustries.com
Institutional and industrial cleaning
President and CFO: Ted Bustany
Quality Control: John Nelson
Director: Sam Levine
Estimated Sales: $1 - 2.5 000,000
Number Employees: 50-99
Square Footage: 55000

22254 Epic Products
2801 S Yale St
Santa Ana, CA 92704
714-641-8194
Fax: 714-641-8217 800-548-9791
info@epicproductsinc.com
www.epicproductsinc.com
Bar supplies including plastic wine glasses, acrylic glassware, servingware, wine racks, cork pullers and drink stirrers
Owner: Ardeen Dubow
VP: Matt DuBow
Contact: Rocio Brooks
brooks@epicproductsinc.com
Estimated Sales: $5 - 10 Million
Number Employees: 20-49

22255 Epsen Hillmer Graphics Co
13748 F St
Omaha, NE 68137-1166
402-342-7000
Fax: 402-342-9284 800-228-9940
www.ehg.net
Manufacturer and exporter of labels including pressure sensitive, glue applied litho, in-mold and PET beverage
President: Tom Hillmer
thillmer@ehg.net
VP Opers.: Thomas Hillmer
VP Sales/Marketing: R Craig Cunran
VP Operations: Thomas Hillmer
Estimated Sales: $.5 - 1 million
Number Employees: 50-99

22256 Epsilon Industrial
2215 Grand Avenue Pkwy
Austin, TX 78728
512-251-1500
Fax: 512-251-1593
Provides food technologists with instrumentation to perform multicomponent analysis on clear or cloudy liquids, slurries, powders, solids
Estimated Sales: $1-2.5 000,000
Number Employees: 5-9

22257 Epsilon-Opti Films Corporation
132 Case Dr
South Plainfield, NJ 07080-5109
908-791-1732
Fax: 908-791-1030 800-235-8383
Polyolefin shrink films
Number Employees: 20-49

22258 Epstein
600 W Fulton St # 9
Chicago, IL 60661-1253
312-454-9100
Fax: 312-559-1217 information@epstein-isi.com
www.epsteinglobal.com
Design and construction of food manufacturing and distribution facilities

President: John Patelski
CFO: Jim Jirsa
jimjirsa@epstein-isi.com
Executive VP: Allen L Pomerance
Quality Control: Darrin McCormies
R&D: Andrea Velasquez
Estimated Sales: $20 - 50 Million
Number Employees: 250-499

22259 Epstein
600 W Fulton St # 9
Chicago, IL 60661-1253
312-454-9100
Fax: 312-559-1217 information@epstein-isi.com
www.epsteinglobal.com
CFO: Jim Jirsa
jimjirsa@epstein-isi.com
Executive VP: Allen L Pomerance
Estimated Sales: $20-50 Million
Number Employees: 250-499

22260 Equichem International Inc
510 Tower Blvd
Carol Stream, IL 60188-9426
630-784-0432
Fax: 630-784-0436 mail@equichem.com
www.equichem.com
Custom vitamin and mineral premixes and enzyme blends.
President: Luis C Lovis
llovis@equichem.com
Research/Development Director: Luis J Lovis
Sales Director: Anna Lovis
Number Employees: 5-9
Type of Packaging: Bulk

22261 Equilon Lubricants
1111 Bagby Street
Houston, TX 77002-2551
713-752-6695
Fax: 713-752-4678 800-645-8237
www.shell-lubricants.com
Synthetic and mineral based fluids and greases for food or beverage processing plants
Chief Executive Officer: Peter Voser
Research & Development: Kris Kaushik
Marketing Director: David Rowe
Sales Director: Larry Cekella
Parent Co: Shell International Petroleum Company
Brands:
Cassida Fluids and Greasers
Cyenus Fluids and Greasers
Shell Fm Fluids and Greasers

22262 Equipex Limited
765 Westminster St
Providence, RI 02903-4018
401-273-3300
Fax: 401-273-3328 800-649-7885
sales@equipex.com www.equipex.com
Manufacturer and exporter of ovens and restaurant equipment
President: Loretta Clark
lorettac@equipex.com
VP: Val Ginzburg
Sales/Marketing Division: Irina Mirsky-Zayas
Operations: Loretta Fortier
Estimated Sales: $2.5-5,000,000
Number Employees: 1-4

22263 Equipment Design & Fabrication
722 N Smith St
Charlotte, NC 28202-1454
704-372-4513
Fax: 704-372-4514 800-949-0165
Materials handling, railroad maintenance, textile & furniture manufacturing equipment
President: Terry D Miller
edfterry@bellsouth.net
Purchasing Manager: Tony Walkins
Number Employees: 5-9

22264 Equipment Distributing of America
1776 Country Road M
PO Box 213
Wahoo, NE 68066
402-592-9360
Fax: 402-443-1384 efa.efa-usa@windstream.net
www.efa-germany.de
Supplier of meat processing machines and industrial tools
Manager: David Weinert

Estimated Sales: Under $500,000
Number Employees: 1-4
Parent Co: EFA Germany

22265 Equipment Enterprises
6670 E Harris Blvd
Charlotte, NC 28215-5101
704-568-3001
Fax: 704-536-3259 800-221-3681
sales@wardtank.com www.wardtank.com
Water treatment systems
President: Donald Ward
President, Chief Executive Officer: Jon Ward
President, Chief Executive Officer: Jon Ward
Operations Sales Manager: Rick Shepherd
Vice President of Operations: Bob Besh
Estimated Sales: $5 - 10 Million
Number Employees: 20-49
Square Footage: 64000
Parent Co: Ward Tank & Heat Exchanger

22266 Equipment Enterprises
1875 Graves Road
Norcross, GA 30093-1022
770-368-9789
Fax: 770-368-0587 800-221-3681
Water treatment systems including lime coagulation, direct filtraton, membranes, carbon purifiers, filters, ozanators, and ultraviolet units
Estimated Sales: $1-5 000,000
Number Employees: 9

22267 Equipment Equities Corporation
866 United Nations Plaza
Suite 440
New York, NY 10017-1838
212-688-8800
Fax: 212-688-0061
Estimated Sales: $3 - 5 Million
Number Employees: 1-4

22268 Equipment Exchange Co
10042 Keystone Dr
Lake City, PA 16423-1060
814-774-0888
Fax: 814-774-0880 info@eeclink.com
www.eeclink.com
Buyers and sellers of used food process machinery. Choppers, grinders, patty, meat forming and portion, smokehouses and accessories, seasonings, ingredients, batters and breading
President: Robert J Breakstone
info@eeclink.com
Estimated Sales: $2.5 - 5 Million
Number Employees: 10-19
Square Footage: 120000

22269 Equipment Express
60 Wanless Court
Ayr, ON N0B 1E0
Canada
519-740-8008
Fax: 519-740-6297 800-387-9791
carrief@equipmentexpress.com
equipmentexpress.com
Unscramblers, air and wet bottle cleaners, conveyors, fillers, cappers, induction sealers, labelers, coders, tapers, case erectors, case packers, palletizer, bundlers, pallet warppers, turnkey bottled water plants, including watertreatment systems, specialty machines
President: Jeff Ake
VP Marketing: Liliana Ake
Production Manager: Kurt Organ
Plant Manager: John Naughton
Purchasing Manager: Teresa Mago
Estimated Sales: $1-4 Million
Number Employees: 20

22270 Equipment Innovators
800 Industrial Park Dr
Marietta, GA 30062-2498
770-427-9467
Fax: 678-391-9120 800-733-3434
sales@equipmentinnovators.com
www.equipmentinnovators.com
President: Richard C McCamey
CEO: Joe Rubin
Vice President: Doug Edwards
dedwards@equipmentinnovators.com
Estimated Sales: $10 - 20 Million
Number Employees: 20-49

22271 Equipment Outlet
199 N Linder Road
Meridian, ID 83642-2440
208-887-1472
Fax: 208-887-4874
Supplier of packaging equipment materials
Salesman: Brian Maglecic
Estimated Sales: $1-2.5 Million
Number Employees: 10

22272 Equipment Specialists Inc
9489 Hawkins Dr
Manassas, VA 20109-3907
703-361-2227
Fax: 703-361-4965
www.equipmentspecialistsinc.com
Manufacturer and exporter of new and used food
processing and packaging equipment
Owner: Allan Tousha
CEO: Beverly Gordon
Vice President: Jeremy Gordon
Sales Director: Mariano Montealegre
  allan@esitrucks.com
Operations Manager: Jose Macy
Plant Manager: Reinaldo Mendoza
Purchasing Manager: Eric Ball
Estimated Sales: $10-20 Million
Number Employees: 10-19
Square Footage: 300000
Type of Packaging: Food Service

22273 Equipment for Coffee
71 Lost Lake Ln
Campbell, CA 95008-6642
650-259-7801
Fax: 650-259-7603
Tea and coffee industry colorimeters, pollution con-
trol equipment, vacuum packaging machinery
Contact: Robert Hensley
  rh@specialtycoffee.com
Plant Manager: Gordon McNeil
Estimated Sales: Less than $500,000
Number Employees: 1-4
Square Footage: 3000

22274 Erb International
290 Hamilton Road
New Hamburg, ON N3A 1A2
Canada
519-662-2710
Fax: 519-662-3316 800-665-2653
werb@erbgroup.com www.erbgroup.com
President: Vernon D Erb
CFO: Kevin Copper
Number Employees: 10

22275 Erca-Formseal
1210 Campus Dr
Morganville, NJ 07751-1262
732-536-8770
Fax: 732-536-8850 www.oystarusa.com
President: Charles Ravalli
Estimated Sales: $3 - 5 Million
Number Employees: 10-19

22276 Erell Manufacturing Co
2678 Coyle Ave
Elk Grove Vlg, IL 60007-6404
847-427-3000
Fax: 847-663-9970 800-622-6334
Plastic aprons; exporter and manufacturer of vinyl
industrial and promotional products
President: Randy Silton
  randy@erell.com
Estimated Sales: $1-2.5 Million
Number Employees: 10-19
Square Footage: 34000
Brands:
  Plasti-Guard

22277 Ergonomic Handling Systems
PO Box 338
Line Lexington, PA 18932-0338
215-822-8778
Fax: 215-822-8088 800-223-6430
General and CNC machining, drilling, boring, cut-
ting and honing, general welding, fabricating and
material handling
Sales Director: Tim Burns
Estimated Sales: $1-2.5 Million
Number Employees: 20-50

22278 Erickson Industries
717 Saint Croix St
River Falls, WI 54022
715-426-9700
Fax: 715-426-9701 800-729-9941
Manufacturer and exporter of refrigerators, freezers,
walk-in coolers and pre-fabricated cooling and
freezing warehouses; also, manufacturer of tubular
towers and planter grids
Owner: Paul Erickson
Sales: Debbie Huppert
Sales Engineering: Joel Johnson
Advertising Manager: H Walsh
Estimated Sales: $1-2.5 Million
Number Employees: 1-4
Square Footage: 80000
Brands:
  Chill-Air
  Erickson
  Kool-Rite

22279 Erie Container
4700 Lorain Ave
Cleveland, OH 44102-3443
216-631-1650
Fax: 216-631-1249
Paper tubes and containers
President: Frank Lipinski
  flipinski@containers-cases.com
VP: Joseph Lipinski
Estimated Sales: $5 - 10 Million
Number Employees: 5-9

22280 Erie Cotton Products
1112 Bacon St
Erie, PA 16511-1732
814-459-6644
Fax: 814-453-7816 800-289-4737
sales@eriecotton.com www.eriecotton.com
Towels including burlap, cheesecloth, nonwovens,
dish, glass, bar and disposable; also, janitorial sup-
plies, gloves, disposable aprons and hair caps
President: Gregory Rubin
  rags@eriecotton.com
CFO: Louise Clemens
General Manager: Rick Gore
Estimated Sales: $5 - 10 Million
Number Employees: 20-49

22281 (HQ)Erie Foods Intl Inc
401 7th Ave
PO Box 648
Erie, IL 61250
309-659-2233
Fax: 309-659-2822 glindsey@eriefoods.com
www.eriefoods.com
Co-dried and concentrated milk proteins; also so-
dium, calcium, combination and acid-stable
caseinates and dairy blends; importer of milk
proteins
President/CEO: David Reisenbigler
  dreisenbigler@eriefoods.com
CFO: Mark Delaney
COO: Jim Klein
Technical Services Manager: Craig Air
Quality Manager: Rene Perla
Purchasing Manager: Jake VanDeWostine
Process Development Manager: Jim Jacoby
Purchasing Manager: Shawn Larson
Estimated Sales: $1-2.5 Million
Number Employees: 10-19
Square Footage: 120000
Parent Co: Erie Foods International Inc
Type of Packaging: Bulk
Other Locations:
  Erie Foods International
  Beenleigh QLD
Brands:
  Ecco
  Erie

22282 Eriez Magnetics
4700 W 23rd St
Erie, PA 16506
Fax: 814-838-4960 800-346-4946
eriez@eriez.com www.eriez.com
Manufacturer and exporter of vibratory feeders and
conveyors, magnetic separators, metal detectors, vibratory and material-sizing screeners, lifting magnets and magnetic conveyors.

Chairman: Richard Merwin
President/CEO: Lukas Guenthardt
CFO: Andrew Olsen
Global Director, Marketing & Brand: John Blicha
Estimated Sales: $50 - 100 Million
Number Employees: 250-499
Square Footage: 110000
Brands:
  E-Z Tec
  Hi-Vi
  Metalarm
  Safehold

22283 Erika Record LLC
37 Atlantic Way
Clifton, NJ 07012-1141
973-614-8500
Fax: 973-614-8503 800-682-8203
max@erikarecord.com www.bake-easier.com
Bun divider and rounder, bakery equipment
President: Max Oehler
Manager: Austin Archdeacon
  austin@erikarecord.com
Estimated Sales: Below $5 000,000
Number Employees: 10-19
Type of Packaging: Bulk

22284 Ermanco
6870 Grand Haven Rd
Norton Shores, MI 49456
231-798-4547
Fax: 231-798-8322 www.ermanco.com
Manufacturer and exporter of conveyors including
belt/live roller, lineshaft driven, belt driven and
sortation; also, turnkey systems
President: Leon Kirschner
Quality Control: Bob Dorgan
VP of Marketing: Lee Schomberg
VP of Sales: Gordon Hellberg
Contact: Tom Bergy
  tombergy@ermanco.com
Estimated Sales: $30 - 50 Million
Number Employees: 100-249
Square Footage: 100000
Parent Co: Paragon Technologies
Brands:
  Accurol
  Ers Sorter
  Intellorol
  Nbs Sorter
  Swing Arm Diverter
  Xenopressure Xenorol

22285 Ernest F Mariani Co
573 W 2890 S
Salt Lake City, UT 84115-3456
801-359-3744
Fax: 801-531-9615 800-453-2927
sales@efmco.com www.efmco.com
Accumulating of bottling supplies and equipment
President: Wil Fiedler
  wil@efmco.com
Finance Manager: Clay Dalton
Estimated Sales: $5 - 10 Million
Number Employees: 10-19

22286 Ernst Timing Screw Co
1534 Bridgewater Rd
Bensalem, PA 19020-4508
215-639-1438
Fax: 215-639-2873 ernstime@comcat.com
www.ernsttiming.com
Feed screws, change parts, star wheels, center guides
President: Suzanne Cannon
  t.cannon@ernsttiming.com
CEO: Lee Cannon
Estimated Sales: $1 - 2,500,000
Number Employees: 10-19

22287 Ertelalsop
132 Flatbush Ave
Kingston, NY 12401-2202
845-331-4552
Fax: 845-339-1063 800-553-7835
sales@ertelalsop.com www.ertelalsop.com
Manufacturer and exporter of filtration equipment,
filter media and mixers for liquids; also, glass crush-
ing equipment
President: George Quigley
VP: George Quigley
Marketing Manager Food & Beverage: Mike Kelly
VP Sales/Marketing: William Kearney
Estimated Sales: $5 - 10 Million
Number Employees: 50-99

Brands:
Alpha-Media
Bottle-Buster
Micro-Deck
Micro-Media
Vapor-Master

22288 Erving Industries
97 East Main Street
Erving, MA 01344
413-422-2700
Fax: 413-422-2710 www.ervingpaper.com
Custom printed and plain paper products including napkins, placemats, traycovers and table covers
President & CEO: Morris Housen
Estimated Sales: $50-100 Million
Number Employees: 1-4
Square Footage: 130000
Brands:
Savlin

22289 Erwin Food Service Equipment
2915 Horton Rd
Fort Worth, TX 76119-5635
817-535-0021
Fax: 817-535-2999
Stainless steel cooking and heating equipment, tables, sinks, counters and hoods
President: Al Erwin
Office Manager: Barbara Vandever
Estimated Sales: $500,000-$1 Million
Number Employees: 1 to4
Square Footage: 20000

22290 Erwyn Products Inc
200 Campus Dr # C
Morganville, NJ 07751-2101
732-972-1440
Fax: 732-972-1263 800-331-9208
steve@erwyn.com www.erwyn.com
Manufacturer, importer and exporter of waste paper baskets and ice buckets
President: Randy Grant
randy.grant@erwyn.com
Estimated Sales: $10 - 20 Million
Number Employees: 20-49

22291 Esbelt of North America: Divison of ASGCO
301 W Gordon Street
Allentown, PA 18102-3136
610-821-0216
Fax: 610-778-8991 rlehman@asgco.com
www.asgco.com
Heavyweight conveyor belts
Estimated Sales: $1 - 5 Million

22292 Escher Mixers, USA
2770 W Commerce Street
Suite 100
Dallas, TX 75212-4913
214-572-7777
Fax: 214-572-8888

22293 Esco Manufacturing Inc
2020 4th Ave SW
Watertown, SD 57201-3413
605-886-9668
Fax: 605-882-1205 800-843-3726
wholesale@escomfg.com
www.escomanufacturing.com
Signs and displays
President: Mark Stein
mstein@escomfg.com
Senior Account Manager of Sales: Rob Fjerstad
Manufacturing Manager: Kevin Morris
Resources Manager of Purchasing: Laurie Gates
Estimated Sales: $10-20 Million
Number Employees: 100-249

22294 Esco Manufacturing Inc
2020 4th Ave SW
PO Box 1237
Watertown, SD 57201-3413
605-886-9668
Fax: 605-882-1205 800-843-3726
www.escomanufacturing.com
Indoor and outdoor signs including neon, electric and painted

Owner: Mark Stein
mstein@escomfg.com
Engineering Manager/Account Representati: Dave Bartels
Paint Supervisor: Jeremy Raap
Manufacturing Manager: Kevin Morris
Resources Manager: Laurie Gates
Senior Account Manager: Rob Fjerstad
Estimated Sales: less than $500,000
Number Employees: 100-249
Parent Co: Esco

22295 Esco Products Inc
5325 Glenmont Dr # D
Suite D
Houston, TX 77081-2050
832-649-5684
Fax: 713-666-5877 800-966-5514
www.escopro.com
Rebuilt and reconditioned food processing equipment, dashers, freezer barrels, thermometers, homo blockes, piston plungers, pumps, etc.; also, OEM, machining and grinding services available
President: Chris Haught
chaught@escopro.com
Number Employees: 10-19

22296 Esha Research
4747 Skyline Rd S # 100
Suite 100
Salem, OR 97306-5700
503-540-7518
Fax: 503-585-5543 800-659-3742
info@esha.com www.esha.com
Software for formulation development and nutrition labeling; exporter of nutritional labeling software
CEO: Craig Bennett
c@esha.com
CEO: Robert Geltz
Vice President: David Hands
Sales Director: Scott Hadsall
Estimated Sales: $2 Million
Number Employees: 20-49
Number of Brands: 6
Number of Products: 6
Square Footage: 1000
Brands:
Genesis R&D

22297 Eskay Metal Fabricating
83 Doat St
Buffalo, NY 14211-2048
716-893-3100
Fax: 716-893-0443 800-836-8015
www.specialtystainless.com
Food preparation equipment including sinks, chef's tables, restaurant, cafeteria, serving and specialty counters, etc.; also, cabinets, coolers and self contained mobile hot dog and display carts.
President: Jeff Subra
Public Relations: Kathy Bristol
Engineering Manager: Ken White
Estimated Sales: $1 Million
Number Employees: 5-9
Square Footage: 32000
Parent Co: Schuler-Subra
Brands:
Buffalo Grill

22298 Espresso Carts and Supplies
429 United States Avenue
Lindenwold, NJ 08021-2658
856-782-1775
Fax: 856-782-1775 74274.60@compuserve.com
Carts, espresso carts, espresso machines and accessories, bars, kiosks displays
Vie President of Sales/Marketing: Anthony Santangelo
Estimated Sales: 250000
Number Employees: 3
Type of Packaging: Bulk

22299 Espresso Roma
1310 65th St
Emeryville, CA 94608-1119
510-420-8898
Fax: 510-420-8980 800-437-1668
sandydboyd@aol.com
www.sweetonyouberkeley.com
Processor and wholesaler/distributor of roast coffee; manufacturer and wholesaler/distributor of espresso machines and restaurant equipment

President: Sandy Boyd
VP: Pat Weigt
Sales Manager: Sandy Boyd
Estimated Sales: $1-2.5 Million
Number Employees: 10-19

22300 Esquire Mechanical Corp.
PO Box 496
Armonk, NY 10504
718-625-4006
Fax: 718-625-0155 800-847-4206
sales@dunhill-esquire.net
www.dunhill-esquire.com
Manufacturer and exporter of cafeteria and kitchen equipment including cashier stands,serving counters,sinks,refrigerated display cases,tables and bbq and rotisserie machines.
President: Geoffrey Thaw
Estimated Sales: $1 - 5 Million
Number Employees: 10-19
Square Footage: 240000
Parent Co: Dunhill Food Equipment
Type of Packaging: Food Service

22301 Esselte Meto
1200t American Road
Morris Plains, NJ 07950-2453
973-359-0947
Fax: 201-455-7492 800-645-3290
Manufacturer and exporter of handheld labeling and merchandising systems, thermal and laser bar code printers and supplies, tags and labels
President: Travis Howe
VP Marketing: Bob Cantono
VP Sales: Bob Evans
Estimated Sales: $300,000-500,000
Number Employees: 50-99
Square Footage: 270000
Parent Co: Esselte AB
Type of Packaging: Consumer, Private Label
Brands:
Essette Meto
Laser-Link
Meto
Meto/Primark
Price Marquee
Take a Number
Turn-O-Matic

22302 Essential Industries Inc
28391 Essential Rd
Merton, WI 53056
262-538-1122
Fax: 262-538-1354 800-551-9679
sales@essind.com www.essind.com
Manufacturer and exporter of household and industrial hand, glass and window cleaners, liquid and powder dishwashing compounds and soap, detergents and floor polish
President & CEO: Michael Wheeler
Director, Purchasing: Kathleen Leemon
Estimated Sales: $15 Million
Number Employees: 50-99
Square Footage: 110000
Type of Packaging: Private Label, Bulk
Brands:
Durabrite
Silhouette
Sport Kote
Superbase
Trust

22303 Essentra Packaging Inc.
1625 Ashton Park Drive
Suite D
Colonial Heights, VA 23834-5908
804-518-1803
Fax: 804-518-1809 800-849-0633
info@essentrapackaging.com
Pressure sensitive tear tape
President: Bob Donnahoo
Contact: Jame Belton
jamesbelton@payne-worldwide.com
Estimated Sales: $5 - 10 Million
Number Employees: 30

22304 Esstech
13911 NW 3rd Court
Vancouver, WA 98685-5703
360-546-5662
Fax: 360-546-5664

Boxes, multi-wall and plastic bags designed to eliminate or reduce the use of banding and stretch wrapping without damaging package graphics or appearance
President: Paul Mazi
Estimated Sales: $500,000-$1 000,000
Number of Employees: 1-4
Type of Packaging: Bulk

22305 Ester International
29 Junction Pond Lane
Monmouth Junction, NJ 08852-2924
732-967-0561
Fax: 732-967-0563
Plain, corona treated, chemically treated film, polyester film, milky white film, colored film and different types of polyester resins
General Manager: S Shridhar
Number of Employees: 4
Number of Brands: 1

22306 Esterle Mold & Machine Co Inc
1539 Commerce Dr
Stow, OH 44224-1783
330-686-1685
Fax: 330-686-9434 800-411-4086
info@esterle.com www.esterle.com
Peel boards made from 100% long-lasting high impact, virgin and prime rigid plastic; standard 18 in. x 26 in. and custom sizes. Hygienic and FDA approved; 100% recyclable
President: Richard Esterle
resterle@esterle.com
VP: Kathleen Sawyer
Vice President: Kathleen Sawyer
Chairman: Adam Esterle
Sales Director: Patrick Miller
Operations Manager: Mark Starnes
Purchasing Manager: Steve Staszak
Estimated Sales: Below $5 Million
Number of Employees: 50-99
Square Footage: 120000

22307 Et Oakes Corp
686 Old Willets Path
Hauppauge, NY 11788-4102
631-232-0002
Fax: 631-232-0170 info@oakes.com
Food processing equipment including mixers, depositors, blenders, controllers, creme injectors, agitators, emulsifiers, extruders, homogenizers, fillers and lidders, and cake depositors
President: W Peter Oakes
Vice President: Bob Peck
Marketing Director: Karen Oakes
Sales Director: Chris Oakes
Estimated Sales: Below $5 Million
Number of Employees: 20-49

22308 Etched Images
1758 Industrial Way # 101
Napa, CA 94558-3302
707-252-5450
Fax: 707-252-2666 www.etchedimages.com
Wine industry applications; bottle design
Owner: Stu Mc Farland
stu@etchedimages.com
Estimated Sales: $20-50 Million
Number of Employees: 20-49

22309 Etna Sales
1112 W Barkley Avenue
Orange, CA 92868-1213
714-520-5204
Fax: 714-563-0339
Brewing devices, coffee urn cleaners

22310 Ettore
2100 N Loop Rd
Alameda, CA 94502-8010
510-748-4130
Fax: 510-638-0928 info@ettore.com
Manufacturer and exporter of window and floor squeegees and window washing equipment
Chairman of the Board: Michael Smahlik
michael.smahlik@ettore.com
VP Sales/Marketing: Patrick Murphy
National Sales Manager: Herman Miron
Estimated Sales: $1 - 2.5 Million
Number of Employees: 50-99
Type of Packaging: Consumer, Food Service, Bulk
Brands:
Ehore

22311 Etube & Wire
50 W Clearview Dr
Shrewsbury, PA 17361-1103
717-227-0280
Fax: 717-428-2974 800-618-4720
sales@etubeandwire.com www.etubeandwire.com
Wire fryer baskets, displays, hooks, hangers, rings, screens, grills, filters, guards, fan guards, and shelving
Owner: Glenn Eyster
General Manager: Larry Krumrine
Contact: Jed Beckman
jbeckman@eysters.com
Manager: Larry Krumrwe
Estimated Sales: $2.5 Million
Number of Employees: 20-49
Square Footage: 120000

22312 Euchner-USA
6723 Lyons St
East Syracuse, NY 13057-9332
315-701-0315
Fax: 315-701-0319 info@euchner-usa.com
www.euchner-usa.com
Suppliers of sensors for automation, safety and man-machine interface products including safety interlocking swithces, enabling switches, trip dogs and rails, encoders, read & write coding systems, read only identification systemsjoysticks and operator panels.
President & CEO: Mike Ladd
Customer Service Supervisor: Margie Krayenhof
Operations Manager: Doug Hatch
Number of Employees: 500 - 1000

22313 Eugene Welding Company
2420 Wills St
Marysville, MI 48040
810-364-7421
Fax: 810-364-4347
Manufacturer and exporter of racks including pallet storage, drive-in, push back and cantilever
President: Charles Vamella
CEO: Jim Bradshaw
Sales: Scott Samples
Public Relations: Dawne Kimberley
Plant Maanger: Wes Boyne
Purchasing: Dave Campa
Estimated Sales: $20-50 Million
Number of Employees: 250-499
Square Footage: 120000
Parent Co: Eugene Welding Company
Brands:
Spacerak

22314 Eunice Locker Plant
1232 Main Street
Eunice, NM 88231
505-394-2060
Slaughterer and packer of beef and pork
Owner: Louie Miller
Estimated Sales: $1-2.5 Million
Number of Employees: 1-4
Type of Packaging: Consumer

22315 Eureka Company
807 N Main St
Bloomington, IL 61701
309-828-2367
Fax: 309-823-5335 800-282-2886
kathy.luedke@eureka.com www.eureka.com
Manufacturer and exporter of commercial vacuums including canisters, uprights, home cleaning, built-ins and rechargeable
President: John Case
CEO: Jan Wolansky
VP Advertising: Don Johnson
Quality Control: Steve Knuth
Contact: Bruce Gold
bruce.gold@electrolux.com
Number of Employees: 250-499
Parent Co: White Consolidated Industries
Type of Packaging: Consumer
Brands:
Eureka

22316 Eureka Door
PO Box 276
Ballwin, MO 63022-0276
314-256-1949
800-673-8735

22317 Eureka Ice & Cold Storage Company
12 Waterfront Dr
Eureka, CA 95501-0368
707-443-5663
Fax: 707-443-6481
http://eurekaice.com/index.html
Warehouse providing freezer and cooler storage and a manufacturer of ice. Eureka Ice also offers Blast Freezing, a quick freezing of up to 80 tons of product in a short time.
Manager: Tom Devere
Manager: Tom Devero
Estimated Sales: $2.5-5 Million
Number of Employees: 5-9
Square Footage: 140000

22318 (HQ)Eureka Paper Box Company
PO Box 1476
Williamsport, PA 17703-1476
570-326-9147
Fax: 570-326-7239
Custom paper folding cartons
Co-Owner: Jim Waters
Co-Owner: John McInerney
CFO: Bob Bernaski
Production Manager: Joseph Cioffi
Estimated Sales: $5 - 10 Million
Number of Employees: 80
Square Footage: 212000
Other Locations:
Eureka Paper Box Co.
Syracuse NY

22319 Euro-Pol Bakery Equipment
2770 W Commerce St
Dallas, TX 75212-4913
214-637-2253
Fax: 214-637-2257
President: Mariusz B. Bandurski

22320 Eurobar Sales Corporation
12b W Main Street
Elmsford, NY 10523-2401
914-592-5770
Fax: 914-592-6004
Espresso machines and accessories

22321 Eurodib
PO Box 1798
1320 State Route 9
Champlain, NY 12919
450-641-8700
Fax: 451-641-8705 888-956-6866
shaun@eurodib.com www.eurodib.com
Importer of citrus and centrifugal juicers, dispensers, coffee grinders, blenders, vegetable cutters, grills, mandolines, cookware, and dishwashers
President: Jean Yves Dumaine
VP: Shaun McDonald
Marketing: Shaun McDonald
Contact: Shaun Mcdonald
jydumaine@eurodib.com
Purchasing Manager: Robert Perrier
Number of Employees: 14
Number of Brands: 15
Number of Products: 500
Square Footage: 176000

22322 Eurodispenser
6480 Majors Lane
Decatur, IL 62521-9697
217-864-4061
Fax: 217-864-6722
Quality dispensing equipment including condiments, sauces, toppings, syrups, soap and cleaning compounds
Estimated Sales: $1-2.5 Million
Number of Employees: 1-4

22323 Eurofins DQCI
5205 Quincy St
St Paul, MN 55112-1438
763-785-0484
Fax: 763-785-0584 dqciinfo@eurofinsus.com
www.dqci.com
Laboratory providing chemical analysis and testing services to the dairy industry; also, calibration standards
Owner: Tom Janas
tom@dqci.com
Estimated Sales: $5 - 10,000,000
Number of Employees: 20-49

22324 Eurofins S-F AnalyticalLabs
2345 S 170th St
New Berlin, WI 53151-2701
262-754-5300
Fax: 262-754-5310 800-300-6700
www.eurofinsus.com
Laboratory performing chemical analysis and micro-biological testing of food and food related products. Nutritional labeling anf USDA Fat Claims are specialties.
President/CEO: David Kliber
Manager: Bryan Dieckelman
bdieckelman@sflabs.com
Number Employees: 20-49
Type of Packaging: Food Service

22325 (HQ)Eurofins Scientific Inc
2200 Rittenhouse St # 150
Suite 175
Des Moines, IA 50321-3157
515-265-1461
Fax: 515-266-5453 800-841-1110
ENACclientservices@eurofinsus.com
www.eurofins.com/food
Laboratory offering nutrition labeling, food analysis, microbiology, nutritional bioassays, toxicology and independent testing
President: Brandi Augustine
augustine@eurofinsus.com
Quality Assurance Director: Rhonda Krick
VP Sales/Marketing: Michael Meyers
Client Services Representative: Sophies Holbrook
Account Manager: Charles Hecht
Estimated Sales: $5 - 10 Million
Number Employees: 100-249
Parent Co: Eurofins Group
Other Locations:
Eurofins Scientific
Teltow/Berlin

22326 Eurofins Scientific Inc.
4500 Wadsworth
Suite 110
Dayton, OH 45414
937-276-7800
Fax: 937-276-7805 800-880-1038
info@eurofinsus.com www.eurofinsus.com/food
Laboratory specializing in nutrition analysis for amino acids, dietary fibers, microbiological, proxi-mate and vitamins; also, pesticide and residue test-ing, mycotoxin screening, authenticity, and GMO/ONA testing
President: Gary Wnorowski
CFO: Jean-Denis Giraudet
Quality Assurance Director: Rhonda Krick
Marketing Director: Lori Overstreet
Sales Director: Jay Kurmaski
Contact: Jennifer Durando
jenniferdurando@eurofinsus.com
Estimated Sales: $1-2.5 Million
Number Employees: 5-9

22327 Europa Company
11289 Slater Ave
Fountain Valley, CA 92708-5421
714-432-0112
Fax: 714-432-7246 www.europa-co.com
Espresso machines and accessories, grinders
Estimated Sales: Less than $500,000
Number Employees: 1-4

22328 European Gift & Houseware
514 S 5th Ave
Mt Vernon, NY 10550-4408
914-664-3448
Fax: 914-664-3257 800-927-0277
sales@europeangift.com www.europeangift.com
Espresso machines and accessories.
Owner: Angelo Forzano
afsales@europeangift.com
Estimated Sales: $5 - 10 Million
Number Employees: 5-9

22329 European Packaging Machinery
PO Box 40
Tennent, NJ 07763-0040
732-845-3557
Fax: 732-845-3844 www.epmincorporated.com
Packaging form-fill-seal, fill-seal, filling, inspection equipment, special engineering and customized han-dling and assembling equipment
President: Klans Huenecke
Brands:
Alfa-Kortogleu

Asg
Deltamat
Siebler

22330 Eurosicma
36 Lake St
Wilmington, MA 01887-3708
978-657-8841
Fax: 978-657-8847 www.eurosicma.it
Pillow pack wrapping machine for hard boiled candy, chewing-gum balls, deposited candies and milk tablets
Estimated Sales: $1 - 5 Million
Number Employees: 1-4

22331 Eurotherm
44621 Guilford Dr # 100
Ashburn, VA 20147-6070
703-726-0138
Fax: 703-724-7301 info@eurotherm.com
www.eurotherm.com
Supplier of precision process and temperature con-trol instrumentation including single and multiloop digital controllers, alarms and indicators.
President: John Searle
Executive: Dan Dudici
Marketing Director: Al Betz
Sales Director: Al Betz
IT: Terry Ackerman
terry.wolfe@invensys.com
Estimated Sales: $50 Million
Number Employees: 50-99
Number of Brands: 5
Number of Products: 1000
Parent Co: Invensys Intelligent Automation

22332 Eutek Systems
2925 NW Aloclek Dr
Hillsboro, OR 97124-7523
503-601-0843
Fax: 503-615-2906
Manufacturer and exporter of wastewater reclama-tion and reuse equipment; also, grit removers
Operations: Steve Tansley
Contact: Mohamed Abu
mabu@hydro-int.com
Estimated Sales: Less Than $500,000
Number Employees: 1-4

22333 Eval Company of America
1001 Warrenville Rd # 110
Lisle, IL 60532-1392
312-347-0126
Fax: 312-893-8510 800-423-9726
Plastic containers for food applications like ketchup or juice, coextruded films for flexible packaging of food, coextruded plastic tubing, coated paperboard and films in both standard and biaxially oriented forms
Owner: Rodger Bloch
Vice President of Sales: George Avdey
Director of Sales: Jim Claggett
Estimated Sales: $20-50 Million
Number Employees: 10-19

22334 Evans Adhesive Corp LTD
925 Old Henderson Rd
Columbus, OH 43220-3779
614-451-9778
Fax: 614-451-1373 800-868-0925
orders@evansadhesive.com
www.evansadhesive.com
Packaging adhesives for all applications
President: Rusty Thompson
Estimated Sales: $10 Million
Number Employees: 20-49

22335 Evanston Awning Co
2801 Central St
Evanston, IL 60201-1200
847-864-4520
Fax: 847-864-5886 www.evanstonawnings.com
Commercial awnings
President: Edward Hunzinger Jr
Estimated Sales: $1-2,500,000
Number Employees: 10-19

22336 Evant
2300 Windy Ridge Parkway
10th Floor
Atlanta, GA 30339
770-955-7070
Fax: 770-955-0302 877-596-9208

Management software for manufacturers and whole-salers in the food industry used to optimize purchas-ing. Manhattan Associates has now acquired this company who is a provider of supply chain planning and replenishment solutions
President/CEO: Eddie Capel
EVP and CFO: Dennis Story
Chief Marketing Officer: Jonathan Colehower
Senior Vice President, Americas Sales: Bob Howell
SVP and Chief Human Resources Officer: Terry Geraghty
SVP, International Operations: Steve Smith
Parent Co: Manhattan Associates, Inc

22337 Evaporator Dryer Technologies
1805 Ridgeway St
Hammond, WI 54015-5044
715-796-2313
Fax: 715-796-2378 info@evapdryertech.com
www.evapdryertech.com
Engineering and supply of custom evaporators and spray drying systems, heat recovery, dust collection, and exclusive sanitary designed components: liq-uid-activated, retractable CIP spray nozzles and sys-tems, fire suppression systemssanitary, heavy-duty manways and inspection ports
Owner: Peter Jensen
info@evapdryertech.com
Purchasing: Jeff Derrick
Estimated Sales: $3-10 Million
Number Employees: 10-19
Square Footage: 13000
Other Locations:
Stainless Steel Machining Division
Fond du Lac WI

22338 Ever Extruder Co
7 Goodwin Dr
Festus, MO 63028-4122
636-937-8830
Fax: 636-937-6111
Custom designer & manufacturer of new extruder bases, power transmissions, barrel assemblies and dischargers to fit existing aftermarket extruder systems.
President: Tommy Davis
tommydavis@everextruder.com
Chief Engineer: Steve Stewart
Number Employees: 100-249

22339 (HQ)Everbrite LLC
4949 S. 110th St.
Greenfield, WI 53228
414-529-3500
800-558-3888
sales@everbrite.com www.everbrite.com
Signs and displays including indoor, outdoor, neon, electric and menu boards.
Vice President, Sales/Marketing: Jay Jensen
Year Founded: 1927
Estimated Sales: $74.8 Million
Number Employees: 500-999
Square Footage: 1000000
Type of Packaging: Food Service

22340 Everedy Automation
345 Renninger Rd
Frederick, PA 19435
610-754-1775
Fax: 610-754-1108
Manufacturer and exporter of bakery machinery for batter, scaling, cake cutting, icing, splitting, slicing, cake sandwich, pie, custard and fruit filling and me-ringue/cream topping; also, raisin cleaning and stemming equipmentavailable.
President: Irv Fisher
Sales Director: Irv Fisher
Number Employees: 2
Square Footage: 31200

22341 Everest Interscience
2102 N.Forbes Blvd.
Suite 107
Tucson, AZ 85705-6429
Fax: 520-792-4545 www.everestinterscience.com
Wine industry infrared thermometers
President: Charles Everest
sales@everestinterscience.com
CFO: Marilin Everest
Estimated Sales: $1 - 5 000,000
Number Employees: 5-9

22342 Everett Rubber Stamp
2933 Wetmore Ave
Everett, WA 98201-4016

425-258-6747
Fax: 425-252-8858
Rubber stamps and plastic signs
Owner: Jeff Hathaway
  everettstamp@frontier.com
Owner: Jeffrey Hathaway
Estimated Sales: Less Than $500,000
Number Employees: 1-4

22343 Everfilt Corp
3167 Progress Cir
Mira Loma, CA 91752-1112

951-360-8380
Fax: 951-360-8384 800-360-8380
everfilt@everfilt.com www.everfilt.com
Water and waste water filtration and separation
equipment for food processing plants, packing
houses, etc
Contact: Barbara Andrew
  b.andrew@everfilt.com
Operations Manager: Brian Tolson
Estimated Sales: $2.5-5 Million
Number Employees: 5-9
Square Footage: 21200
Brands:
  Everfilt

22344 Evergreen Packaging
5350 Poplar Ave
Suite 600
Memphis, TN 38119

901-821-5350
evergreenpackaging.com
Gable top packaging equipment and gable top cartons.
President & CEO: John Rooney
Estimated Sales: $5.5 Billion
Number Employees: 3,800
Square Footage: 40000
Type of Packaging: Consumer, Food Service

22345 Everidge
15600 37th Ave N
Suite 100
Plymouth, MN 55446

888-227-1629
www.everidge.com
ThermalRite division manufactures commercial re-
frigeration systems
President & CEO: Chris Kahler
CFO: Mike Polis
SVP, Foodservice Sales & Marketing: Steve Gill
President & COO: Mike Kahler
Brands:
  CROWNTONKA
  ICS
  THERMALRITE

22346 Everpure, LLC
1040 Muirfield Drive
Hanover Park, IL 60133

630-307-3000
Fax: 630-307-3030 info@everpure.com
www.everpure.com
Manufacturer and exporter of water filters
Contact: Peter Gorr
  gorr@everpure.com
Estimated Sales: $35 - 40 Million
Number Employees: 1-4
Parent Co: Culligan International Company

22347 Everson Spice Co
2667 Gundry Ave
Signal Hill, CA 90755-1808

562-595-4785
Fax: 562-988-0219 800-421-3753
customerservice@eversonspice.com
www.eversonspice.com
Seasonings, dry rubs, stuffing mixes and marinades
Owner: Tom Everson
  tomeverson@eversonspice.com
President: Ken Hopkins
CEO: Kim Everson
Estimated Sales: $2.5-5 Million
Number Employees: 50-99
Type of Packaging: Food Service

**22348 Evonik Corporation North
America**
299 Jefferson Rd
Parsippany, NJ 07054

973-929-8000
corporate.evonik.us
Precipitated and fumed silica used to improve the
flow properties of food products, prevent caking,
transfer liquids into free-flowing powders, improve
dispersability, and function as processing aids in
spray drying and millingapplications.
President, North America Region: John Rolando
Estimated Sales: $3.5 Billion
Number Employees: 4,800
Parent Co: Evonik Industries AG
Other Locations:
  Production/Health & Nutrition
  Blair NE
  Production/Inorganic Materials
  Clavert City KY
  Production/R&D
  Chester PA
  Production/Coatings & Additives
  Deer Park TX
  Production/Performance Polymers
  Fortier LA
  Production/Advanced Intermediates
  Galena KS
  Production/Consumer Specialties
  Garyville LA
  Production/R&D
  Greensboro NC
  Production/Coatings & Additives
  Hopewell VA
  Production/Coatings & Additives
  Horsham PA
  Production/Consumer Specialties
  Janesville WI
  Customer Services/Health/Nutrition
  Kennesaw GA
  Tippecanoe Laboratories
  Lafayette IN

22349 Evoqua Water Technologies
1828 Metcalf Ave
Thomasville, GA 31792-6845

229-226-5733
Fax: 229-226-4793 800-841-1550
www.evoqua.com
Water and wastewater treatment equipment.
President: Roger Radke
  radker@kusfilter.com
CEO: Roger Radke
Marketing Manager: Doug Davis
Estimated Sales: $50 - 100 Million
Number Employees: 100-249
Square Footage: 40000

22350 Ex-Cell KAISER LLC
11240 Melrose Ave
Franklin Park, IL 60131-1332

847-451-0451
Fax: 847-451-0458 service@ex-cell.com
www.ex-cell.com
Manufacturer and exporter of metal check order
rails, long handle dust pans, handheld dust pans,
waste receptacles, bus tub and water carts, bar speed
rails, bottlecap catchers, mobile coat racks, condi-
ment trays, luggage racks, andluggage carriers
President: Jeffrey Speizman
Human Resources/Purchasing: Elaine Abba
Estimated Sales: $8 Million
Number Employees: 100-249
Square Footage: 70000
Brands:
  Banquet Series
  Ex-Cell
  Landscape Series
  Note Minder
  Quicksilver
  Safeguard
  Service Solutions Series

22351 Ex-Tech Plastics
11413 Burlington Road
PO Box 576
Richmond, IL 60071

847-829-8100
Fax: 847-829-8190 sales@extechplastics.com
www.extechplastics.com
Extruded, plastic film and sheet PVC, PET, COPP,
HOPP, and PLA
President: Jeff Fidler
Marketing: Laura Pichon
Contact: Lettitia Kokan
  lkokan@extechplastics.com

Estimated Sales: $10 - 20 000,000
Number Employees: 50-99

22352 Exact Equipment Corporation
20 N Pennsylvania Ave
Morrisville, PA 19067-1110

215-295-2000
Fax: 215-295-2080 www.exactequipment.com
Automatic and manual wrapping equipment, indexer
labelers, scales and printers
Manager: Rich Lee
National Sales Manager: F Basil
VP Operations: S Smith
Estimated Sales: $5 - 10 Million
Number Employees: 50-99
Brands:
  Exact Weight
  Power Pack
  Pre-Pac
  Speedmaster
  Work Horse

22353 Exact Mixing Systems Inc
4739 S Mendenhall Rd
Memphis, TN 38141-8202

901-362-8501
Fax: 901-362-5479 jwarren@exactmixing.com
www.readingbakery.com
Continuous dough mixers and ingredient metering
systems
President: Jim Warren
CFO and Corporate Secretary: Cheryl Followell
Chairman/VP: Robert Followell
Estimated Sales: $2.5-5 Million
Number Employees: 5-9
Square Footage: 40000

22354 Exact Mixing Systems Inc
4739 S Mendenhall Rd
Memphis, TN 38141-8202

901-362-8501
Fax: 901-362-5479 exactmix@aol.com
Mixing equipment
President: Jim Warren
Estimated Sales: $5 - 10 Million
Number Employees: 5-9

22355 Exact Packaging
1145 E Wellspring Rd
New Freedom, PA 17349-8426

717-235-8345
Fax: 717-235-0608 800-755-8344
President: Randy Cotteleer
Contact: Bill Berg
  bberg@epilabelers.com

22356 Exaxol Chemical Corp
14325 60th St N
Clearwater, FL 33760-2708

727-524-7732
Fax: 727-532-8221 800-739-2965
info@exaxol.com www.exaxol.com
Manufacturer and exporter of food quality control
laboratory chemicals
Owner: Joe Papa
Estimated Sales: $1 - 2,500,000
Number Employees: 1-4

22357 Excalibur Bagel & Bakery Eqpt
4-01 Banta Pl
Fair Lawn, NJ 07410-3026

201-797-2788
Fax: 201-797-2711 excaliburequip@aol.com
www.excaliburequip.com
Manufacturing ovens, mixers (spiral), two-arm mix-
ers, bagel machines
Owner: Richard Zinn
  excaliburequip@aol.com
Estimated Sales: $1-2.5 000,000
Number Employees: 10-19

22358 Excalibur Miretti Group LLC
285 Eldridge Rd
Fairfield, NJ 07004-2508

973-808-8399
Fax: 973-808-8398 sales@exequipment.com
www.exequipment.com
Explosion-proof forklifts, electric and forklift
trucks, exporter of forklifts
President: Angelo Miretti
Number Employees: 20-49
Square Footage: 88000

Brands:
Go Getters
Gregory

22359 Excalibur Seasoning
1800 Riverway Dr
Pekin, IL 61554-9307

309-347-1221
Fax: 309-347-9086 800-444-2169
sales@excaliburseasoning.com
www.excaliburseasoning.com
Seasoning
President: Jay Hall
CEO: Blake Taylor
btaylor@lumc.edu
Estimated Sales: $5 - 10 Million
Number Employees: 50-99

22360 Excel Chemical Company
2385 Corbett St
Jacksonville, FL 32204-1705

904-356-0446
Fax: 904-356-1906
Cleaning compounds
President: William D Gladney
Contact: Joan Gladney
joan.gladney@americanchemical.net
Number Employees: 5 to 9

22361 Excel Engineering
100 Camelot Dr
Fond Du Lac, WI 54935-8333

920-926-9800
Fax: 920-926-9801 info@excelengineer.com
www.excelengineer.com
Architectural design, surveyor and engineering resources
President: Jeff Quast
CEO: Steve Soodsma
Business Development Director: Tony LeShay
Estimated Sales: Less Than $500,000
Number Employees: 1-4

22362 Excel-A-Tec Inc
3695 N 126th St # N
Brookfield, WI 53005-2424

262-252-3600
Fax: 262-252-3664 www.excelatec.com
Heat recovery systems, homogenizers, aseptic processing equipment, cheese equipment, blenders, deactators, heat exchangers, piping, fittings and tubing, sanitary, process control, process software
President: Herve Bronnert
Vice President: Joan Bronnert
Estimated Sales: $5 - 10 Million
Number Employees: 10-19

22363 Excell Products Inc
2500 Enterprise Blvd
Choctaw, OK 73020-8400

405-390-4491
Fax: 405-390-4493 800-633-7670
sales@excellproducts.com
Screen painting, offset painting, signing systems, aisle markers, plastic extruding, spiral painting systems
President and CFO: Merle Medcalf
merle@excellproducts.com
Estimated Sales: $500,000 - $1 Million
Number Employees: 20-49

22364 Excellence Commercial Products
1750 N University Dr
Pompano Beach, FL 33071-8903

954-752-0010
Fax: 954-752-0080 800-441-4014
howard@stajac.com www.stajac.com
Wholesaler/distributor, importer and exporter of coolers, freezers and ice cream cabinets
President: Howard Noskowicz
Quality Control: Catherina Derr
Number Employees: 1-4
Parent Co: Stajac Industries

22365 Excellent Bakery Equipment Co
315 Fairfield Rd
Fairfield, NJ 07004-1930

973-244-1664
Fax: 973-244-1696 staff@excellent-bagels.com
www.excellent-bagels.com

Bakery machinery, graters and shredders, triple action mixers, spiral mixers, rack ovens, formers and dividers, removable owl and self tipping mixers, bagel ovens and kettles, deck ovens, and volumetric dough dividers
President: Karin Seruga
Estimated Sales: $5 - 10 000,000
Number Employees: 10-19

22366 Excelsior Transparent Bag Manufacturing
159 Alexander St
Yonkers, NY 10701-2520

914-968-1300
Fax: 914-968-6567
Printed flexible packaging and laminated materials, bags and envelopes
President: Arleen Neustein
CFO: Ron Shenesh
VP: Cynthia Gaines
Contact: Jeff Marger
info@yonkerschamber.com
Estimated Sales: $10 - 20 Million
Number Employees: 50 to 99

22367 ExecuChef Software
862 Sir Francis Drake Boulevard
Suite 282
San Anselmo, CA 94960-1914

415-488-9600
Fax: 415-488-9690
Computer software including back-of-the-house management, inventory, cost, etc
Brands:
Chef Apprentice
Chef Explosion
Execuchef Pro

22368 Executive Line
30 Church St
Chatham, NY 12037-0352

518-392-5761
Fax: 518-392-5156 800-333-5761
Advertising specialties including tags, badges, pins, magnets, name plates, calendars, rulers, etc
President: Danny Crellin
VP Finance: Bernie Rizzo
Sales Manager: Jane Ryan
Estimated Sales: $2.5-5 Million
Number Employees: 1 to49
Square Footage: 5000

22369 Executive Match Inc
PO Box 693
Salem, OH 44460-0693

330-332-2674
Fax: 330-332-2673 800-860-2674
President: William Penfold
exmatch@neo.rr.com
Estimated Sales: Less Than $500,000
Number Employees: 1-4

22370 Executive Referral Services
5440 N Cumberland Ave
Chicago, IL 60656-1490

773-693-6622
Fax: 773-693-8466 866-466-3339
info@facilitec-sw.com www.facilitec-sw.com
International consultant specializing in operations and sales management positions for grocery, convenience store, retail, food service and manufacturing organizations
Owner: Bruce Freier
Vice President: Mark Gray
Accounting Executive: Garry Chesla
Estimated Sales: $1-2.5 Million
Number Employees: 5-9

22371 Exel
509 Lee Ave
Lincolnton, NC 28092-2522

704-735-6535
Fax: 704-735-4899 www.excelhandling.com
Manufacturer and exporter of industrial hand, flat deck, order picking and specially fabricated trucks. Also, material handling carts, dollies, pin trucks, and yarn and beam transports
President/CEO: Charles Eurey
ceurey@excelcontainer.com
VP Administration/Sales: Jim Eurey
Estimated Sales: $20-50 Million
Number Employees: 10-19
Square Footage: 65000

22372 Exhausto
PO Box 720651
Atlanta, GA 30358-2651

770-587-3238
Fax: 770-587-4731 800-255-2923
steenh@exhausto.com www.exhausto.com
Manufacturer, importer and exporter of kitchen exhaust/grease fans
President: Steen Hagensen
Marketing Director: Kelly Johnson
Sales Director: Mark Sylvia
Purchasing Manager: Joan Chenier
Estimated Sales: $40 Million
Number Employees: 100
Number of Brands: 1
Square Footage: 18000
Parent Co: Exhausto A/S
Type of Packaging: Bulk
Brands:
Exhausto

22373 Exhibitron Co
505 SE H St
Grants Pass, OR 97526-3262

541-471-7400
Fax: 541-471-7200 800-437-4571
info@exhibitroncorp.com
www.exhibitroncorp.com
Screen printing commercial signage, and decor products and garments, aisle markers for grocery and retail stores; also, general fabrication and screen printing available
Owner: Ken Northrup
exhibitron@uci.net
CEO: Kenneth Northup
Vice President: Marlene King
Estimated Sales: Less Than $500,000
Number Employees: 1-4
Square Footage: 13000

22374 Exhibits & More Shopworks
7843 Goguen Dr
Liverpool, NY 13090-2514

315-652-0383
Fax: 315-652-8020 888-326-9100
bobd@exhibitsandmore.com
Store fixtures
Owner: Bob Davidson
bobd@exhibtsandmore.com
CEO: Frank Carnovale
VP of Sales: Valerie Low
bobd@exhibtsandmore.com
COO: Jeff Vandeyacht
Estimated Sales: $500,000-$1 Million
Number Employees: 10-19
Other Locations:
Victor NY

22375 (HQ)Eximco Manufacturing Company
5311 N Kedzie Ave
Chicago, IL 60625-4711

773-463-1470
Fax: 773-583-5131
Fluorescent lighting fixtures, light bulbs, energy-saving lighting, alkaline batteries and fluorescent ballasts; importer and exporter of lamps
President: R Ramsden
General Manager: John Perell
Estimated Sales: $2.5-5 Million
Number Employees: 20-49
Square Footage: 40000
Other Locations:
Eximco Manufacturing Co.
Chicago IL

22376 Expanko Cork Co
180 Gordon Dr # 113
Suite 113
Exton, PA 19341-1340

610-363-0735
Fax: 610-363-0735 800-345-6202
sales@expanko.com www.expanko.com
Wine industry corks and closures
President: Rob Mc Kee
Estimated Sales: $2.5-5 000,000
Number Employees: 5-9

22377 Expert Industries Inc
848 E 43rd St
Brooklyn, NY 11210-3502

718-434-6060
Fax: 718-434-6174 www.rubiconhx.com

545

Custom fabricated ribbon blenders, tanks, hoppers, mixers, dispersers, agitators, batch containers, cooling towers, half pipe coils, reactors, polishing pans, liquid and powder transporting bins, etc
Manager: Matt Rubinberg
Sales: E Senatore
General Manager: M Sterling
Estimated Sales: $10-20,000,000
Number Employees: 20-49

22378 Expo Displays
3401 Mary Taylor Rd
Birmingham, AL 35235-3234

205-439-8284
Fax: 205-439-8201 800-367-3976
www.expodisplays.com
Manufacturer and exporter of portable and modular displays and exhibits for tradeshow exhibition and marketplace display
Owner: Jeff Colton
jeff@expodisplays.com
CEO: Jeff Culton
VP: Jay Burkette
Marketing: Sara Mathews
Public Relations: Jay Burkette
Estimated Sales: $10 - 20 Million
Number Employees: 50-99
Square Footage: 60000
Brands:
2001
Airlite
Eclipse
Expoaire
Expoframe
Odyssey
Quantum
Visions

22379 Expo Instruments
1122 Aster Ave Ste E
Sunnyvale, CA 94086

408-554-8822
Fax: 408-554-8822 800-775-EXPO
info@expoinstruments.com
www.expoinstruments.com
Custom liquid level sensors, moniters, controls
President: George Rauchwerger
Estimated Sales: Below $5 000,000
Number Employees: 1-4

22380 Express Card & Label CoInc
2012 NE Meriden Rd
Topeka, KS 66608-1737

785-233-0369
Fax: 785-233-2763 absales@expresscl.com
Labeling equipment
President: John George
CEO: Stephen Atha
CFO: Mark Tillings
HR Executive: Pam Whitfield
express@expresscl.com
Estimated Sales: $5 - 10 Million
Number Employees: 50-99

22381 Express Packaging
Highway 67
PO Box 1333
Pembroke, GA 31321

912-653-2800
Fax: 912-653-2801 www.expresspkg.com
President: John Reardon
Vice President/Sales Manager: Mike Reardon
Estimated Sales: $10 - 20 Million
Number Employees: 20-49

22382 Expresso Shoppe Inc
524 N York Rd
Bensenville, IL 60106-1607

630-350-0066
Fax: 336-393-0295 info@expressoshoppe.com
www.expressoshoppe.com
Owner: David Dimbert
david@expressoshoppe.com
Estimated Sales: Below $5 Million
Number Employees: 1-4

22383 Expro Manufacturing
2800 Ayers Avenue
Vernon, CA 90058

323-415-8544
Fax: 323-268-4060
Manufacturer and packager of food ingredients, including custom dry powder blends

President: Peter Ernster
CEO: Douglas Kantner
R&D: Greg Rowland
VP Sales: Michele Mullen
Contact: Daniel Diaz
ddiaz@expromfg.com
Purchasing: James Ernster
Number Employees: 20

22384 Exquis Confections
17629 Wheat Fall Drive
Derwood, MD 20855-1151

301-926-7043
Fax: 301-926-6432

22385 Extech Instruments
285 Bear Hill Rd
Waltham, MA 02451

781-890-7440
Fax: 781-890-7864 extech@extech.com
www.extech.com
Test and measurement instruments
Marketing Coordinator: Tracy Milhomme
Number Employees: 50-99

22386 Extrutech Plastics Inc
5902 W Custer St
Manitowoc, WI 54220-9790

920-684-2065
Fax: 920-684-4344 888-818-0118
info@epiplastics.com www.epiplastics.com
Plastic panels that are lightweight and easy to install. Panels can be used both indoors and out for dairy barns, foodplants, car washes and will not rust, peel, rot or corrode and are very easy to clean.
President/CEO/CFO: Greg Sheehy
Research/Development: Mike Sheehy
Quality Control: Ashley Shulz
Marketing: Greg Sheehy
Sales Representative: Scott Charles
Senior Project Engineer: Chuck Grozis
Estimated Sales: $10 Million
Number Employees: 5-9

22387 Exxon Mobil
5959 Las Colinas Blvd
Irving, TX 75039-2298

972-940-6000
www.exxonmobil.com
Industrial fuels and lubricants, among other business divisions.
Chairman & CEO: Darren Woods
SVP: Jack Williams
SVP & Principal Financial Officer: Andrew Swiger
SVP: Neil Chapman
Estimated Sales: $279.3 Billion
Number Employees: 71,000

22388 Exxon Mobil Chemical Company
22777 Springwoods Village Prkw
Spring, TX 77389-1425

www.exxonmobilchemical.com
Pressure sensitive oriented polypropylene labels, roll stock cut and stack.
Chairman & Chief Executive Officer: Darren Woods
President, ExxonMobil Chemical: Karen McKee
Year Founded: 1999
Estimated Sales: $279.3 Billion
Number Employees: 71,000
Parent Co: Exxon Mobil Corporation
Brands:
Label-Lyte

22389 Ez Box Machinery Company
6126 Brookshire Blvd Ste E
Charlotte, NC 28216

704-399-0727
Fax: 704-393-3629 sales08@ezbox.com
www.ezbox.com
Box machines, slitters, corrugated boxes
President: Andrew Dunn
Sales Director: Johnnie Quinn
Contact: Jim Rasmussen
jimrasmussen@ezbox.com
Number Employees: 1-4

22390 F & A Fabricating Inc
104 Arbor St
Battle Creek, MI 49015-3068

269-965-8371
Fax: 269-965-8371 www.fa-fabricating.com
Manufacturer and exporter of stainless steel fabricated products including belt conveyors
President: Hiep Nguyen

Estimated Sales: $2.5-5 Million
Number Employees: 20-49
Type of Packaging: Food Service, Bulk

22391 F & F and A. Jacobs & Sons, Inc.
1100 Wicomico St
Baltimore, MD 21230

410-727-6397
Fax: 800-426-4595 www.rjuniform.com
Military, commercial and institutional uniforms
President: Robert Friedlander
Estimated Sales: $1 - 5 Million
Number Employees: 20-49

22392 F & S Awning & Sign Co
13 Coral St
Edison, NJ 08837-3242

732-738-4110
Fax: 732-738-7255 www.fsawning.com
Commercial awnings
Owner: Bob Trotte
Estimated Sales: $1-2,500,000
Number Employees: 10-19

22393 F & S Engraving Inc
1620 W Central Rd
Mt Prospect, IL 60056-2269

847-870-8400
Fax: 847-870-8414 fsengrav@aol.com
www.fandsengraving.com
Bronze rotary cookie and cracker molds, and steel dye engraving
President: Jim Fromm
fsengrav@aol.com
Estimated Sales: $5 - 10 000,000
Number Employees: 50-99

22394 F C MEYER Packaging LLC
2531 Thomas St
Jeannette, PA 15644-1876

724-523-5565
Fax: 724-527-3575 www.mafcote.com
Paper boxes for pasta, frozen poultry, pizza, etc
Manager: Tracey Moranduzzo
Manager: Paul Parisi
pparisi@spc.cc
Estimated Sales: $20-50 Million
Number Employees: 10-19

22395 F G Products Inc
3000 Pioneer Ave
Rice Lake, WI 54868-2433

715-234-2334
Fax: 715-234-6259 800-247-3854
info@fgproducts.com www.fgproducts.com
Insulated and return air bulkheads and center partition systems for the refrigerated transportation industry
Owner: Chad Nelson
Marketing Director: Matthew Nelson
Sales Manager: Ron Hagen
info@fgproducts.com
Estimated Sales: $10 - 20 Million
Number Employees: 50-99
Square Footage: 50000

22396 F N Sheppard & Co
1261 Jamike Ave
P. O. Box 18520
Erlanger, KY 41018-3115

859-525-2358
Fax: 859-525-8467 800-733-5773
beltinfo@fnsheppard.com www.fnsheppard.com
Manufacturer and exporter of industrial belting for packaging including custom, flat, surreys and power transmission; also, design assistance, custom fabrication, field service, splicing tools and equipment available
CEO: James E. Reilly
Vice President: Frank Klaene
R&D: Tim Reilly
Quality Control: Bob Black
Marketing Director: Flint Coltharp
Sales Director: Wayne Siemer
Manufacturing Executive: Dan Martin
Plant Manager: Jim Reilly, Jr.
Purchasing Manager: Jack Fassel
Estimated Sales: $10 - 20 Million
Number Employees: 50-99
Square Footage: 40000

22397 F N Smith Corp
1200 S 2nd St
P.O. Box 179
Oregon, IL 61061-2330
815-732-2171
Fax: 815-732-6173 fnsmith@fnsmithcorp.com
www.fnsmithcorp.com
Bins, conveyors, packaging and extrusion equipment, knives, cartoning equipment and forming rolls for flaking/forming food; exporter of oat hullers and grain steamers
President: Ed Smith
CEO: Fred Smith
fnsmith@fnsmithcorp.com
CFO: Fred Smith
VP: Edward Smith
Estimated Sales: $2.5-5 Million
Number Employees: 20-49
Square Footage: 70000

22398 F P Intl
1090 Mills Way
Redwood City, CA 94063-3120
650-261-5300
Fax: 650-361-1713 800-866-9946
www.fpintl.com
Manufactures cushioning material for protective packaging
President: Joe Nezwek
joenezwek@fpintl.com
CFO: Dennis Fernandes
Marketing: Larry Lenhart
Estimated Sales: $30 - 50 Million
Number Employees: 5-9

22399 F R Drake Co
1410 Genicom Dr
Waynesboro, VA 22980-1956
540-949-6215
Fax: 540-949-8363 sales@drakeloader.com
www.drakeloader.com
Designs and manufactures automatic loading systems for cylindrical products and frozen patties. Frankfurters and other cylindrical products are loaded into packages at speeds up to 1,800 pieces per minute
President: Russ Martin
Vice President of Engineering: George Reed
Sales Manager of North America: Tyrone Beatty
Number Employees: 50-99
Type of Packaging: Food Service, Bulk

22400 F&G Packaging
US Highway 17
Yulee, FL 32097
904-225-5121
Fax: 904-225-9500
Paper bags
General Manager: Allan Young
Number Employees: 177
Parent Co: Stone Container

22401 F-D-S Mfg Co
2200 S Reservoir St
Pomona, CA 91766-6408
909-591-1733
Fax: 909-591-1571 custserv@fdsmfg.com
www.fdsmfg.com
Fruit and vegetable packaging
Chairman: Sameul Stevenson
Cmo: Dan Stevenson
dstevenson@fdsmfg.com
Estimated Sales: $20 - 50 Million
Number Employees: 100-249

22402 F.B. Leopold
227 S Division St
Zelienople, PA 16063
724-452-6300
Fax: 724-452-1377 sales@fbleopold.com
Wine industry filtration equipment
VP: Robert M Clements
Contact: Francis Daugherty
pdaugherty@fbleopold.com
Estimated Sales: $1 - 5 Million
Number Employees: 50-99

22403 F.B. Pease Company
1450 E Henrietta Road
Rochester, NY 14623-3184
585-475-1870
Fax: 716-475-9621
Paring, coring, slicing and conveying machinery for apples, kiwifruit, potatoes, squash and eggplant; exporter of apple parers, corers and slicers
Chairman: Warren Pease
President: Dudley Pease
Export Manager: Vivian Bubel
Estimated Sales: $2.5-5 Million
Number Employees: 19
Square Footage: 88000
Parent Co: Pease Development Company

22404 F.E. Wood & Sons
5 Brown Road
West Baldwin, ME 4091
207-286-5003
Fax: 207-787-2575 www.fewoodenergy.com
Wooden pallets, bins and skids
CEO: Tony Wood
VP: Anthony Wood
Contact: Dean Wood
dean@fewoodenergy.com
Head, Procurement & Logistics: Dean Wood
Estimated Sales: $1-2.5 Million
Number Employees: 20-49

22405 F.M. Corporation
1360 SW 32nd Way
Deerfield Beach, FL 33442-8110
954-570-9860
Fax: 954-570-9865
Manufacturer and exporter of kitchen ventilation equipment including oven hoods
Plant Manager: Twayn Katz
Estimated Sales: $1 - 5,000,000
Number Employees: 20-50
Parent Co: Hood Depot
Type of Packaging: Food Service

22406 F.P. Smith Wire Cloth Company
11700 W Grand Avenue
Northlake, IL 60164-1373
708-562-3344
Fax: 800-310-8999 800-323-6842
Manufacturer and exporter of woven and welded wire cloth
VP of Manufacturing: John Crupper
VP Sales: Ted Kapp
VP Manufacturing: Dr. John Crupper
Estimated Sales: $2.5-5 Million
Number Employees: 500
Square Footage: 114000
Brands:
Metaloom

22407 FAN Separator
466 Randy Road
Carol Stream, IL 60188-2120
922-793-8400
Fax: 922-793-8444 800-451-8001
info@fan-separator.de www.fan-separator.de
Liquids, solid separation
President: Friedrich Wiegand
Estimated Sales: $1 - 2.5 Million
Number Employees: 2

22408 FASTCORP LLC
22 Shelter Rock Lane
Danbury, CT 06810
973-455-0400
Fax: 973-455-7401 888-457-0716
fastcorp1@aol.com www.fastcorpvending.com
Contact: Jay Bender
jay.bender@fastcorpvending.com
Estimated Sales: $3 - 5 Million
Number Employees: 20-49

22409 FBM/Baking Machines Inc
1 Corporate Drive
Cranbury, NJ 08512
800-449-0433
Fax: 609-860-0576 800-449-0433
info@fbmbakingmachines.com
www.fbmbakingmachines.com
Ovens and machines, VMI mixers, Panimatic retarders/proofers and ovens
President: Oliver Frot
CFO: Beatrice Harmett
Contact: Frank Signorile
fsignorile@fbmbakingmachines.com
Number Employees: 5-9

22410 FCD Tabletops
812 Snediker Ave
Brooklyn, NY 11207
718-649-1002
Fax: 800-938-0818 800-822-5399
Manufacturer and exporter of table, bar and counter tops
Sales Manager: Eric Grossman
VP Sales: Peter Stagg
Estimated Sales: $5-10,000,000
Number Employees: 20-49
Square Footage: 35000

22411 FCF Ginseng, LLC
3225 Halder Dr
Mosinee, WI 54455
715-693-3166
Fax: 715-693-5541
President: Lawrence Murray
CFO: Yvonne Murray
Estimated Sales: Below $5 Million
Number Employees: 1-4

22412 FCI Inc
4661 Giles Rd
Cleveland, OH 44135-3794
216-251-5200
Fax: 216-251-5206 800-321-1032
www.fci-usa.com
Change parts for bottle fillers and cappers, replacement parts fore beverage equipment, vent tubes
President: Kenneth J Edgar
Operations Manager: Mike Peronek
Estimated Sales: $10-20 Million
Number Employees: 20-49

22413 FCN Publishing
1725 K St NW # 506
Washington, DC 20006-1401
202-887-6320
Fax: 202-887-6339
Publish food chemical news, food tracebility report newsletter, lawyers, regulators, food industry execs. in bulk commodities
Manager: David Acord
Estimated Sales: $3 - 5 Million
Number Employees: 5-9

22414 FDL/Flair Designs
P.O. Box 606
Kokomo, IN 46903-0606
765-452-6000
Fax: 765-452-5882 www.fdlinc.com
Chairs, cushions, pads and bar/counter stools
Contact: Stephen Striebel
stephen.striebel@eyeweardesigns.com
Estimated Sales: $1-2.5 Million
Number Employees: 20-49

22415 FECO/MOCO
1745 Overland Avenue
Warren, OH 44483
330-372-8511
Fax: 330-372-8608 800-547-1527
www.ajaxtocco.com
Custom designing and manufacturing industrial ovens and thermal processing equipment Engineering and design capabilities include the unique ability to combine heat-processing and curing technologies with material handling andconveying methods
President: Dave Ekers
Project Manager Conveyors: Jim Hercik
Project Manager Ovens: Alan Semetana
Purchasing Manager: Jack Specker
Estimated Sales: $10-20 Million
Number Employees: 10
Square Footage: 240000
Parent Co: Park Ohio Company

22416 FEI Co
1125 Berryhill St # 2
Harrisburg, PA 17104-1704
717-232-2310
Fax: 888-381-6910
Warehouse providing cooler, freezer, humidity-controlled and dry storage
Manager: Greg Shipe
Estimated Sales: Less Than $500,000
Number Employees: 5-9
Square Footage: 160000
Type of Packaging: Consumer, Food Service

22417 FEI Inc
934 S 5th Ave
Mansfield, TX 76063-2794
817-473-3344
Fax: 817-473-3124 800-346-5908
sales@feiconveyors.com www.feiconveyors.com
Manufacturer and exporter of sanitary and anti-corrosive conveyors including gravity, powered and stainless steel skate wheels; also, conveyor components
President: Duane Murray
duane@feiconveyors.com
VP: David Murray
Estimated Sales: $5-10 Million
Number Employees: 20-49
Square Footage: 68000

22418 FES West
2617 Willowbrook Ln
Aptos, CA 95003-6022
831-462-6603
Fax: 831-462-9781 800-251-6603
Wine industry refrigeration systems
Owner: Harold Paul
Estimated Sales: $1-2.5 Million
Number Employees: 1-4

22419 (HQ)FFE Transportation Services
P.O. Box 655888
Dallas, TX 75265-5888
Fax: 214-819-5625 800-569-9200
ir@ffex.net www.ffex.net
To get to any information for the other FFE sites please visit the web address in this listing, transportation firm providing refrigerated local, long and short haul trucking and van service, LTL, and TL
CEO: Stoney M Stubbs Jr
Contact: Leonard Bartholomew
lbartholmew@ffex.net
Estimated Sales: $2,500,000 - $4,999,999
Number Employees: 250-499
Other Locations:
FFE Transportation Services
Oakland CA

22420 FFI Corporation
2330 Sweet Meadow Rd
Baltimore, MD 21209
908-810-7100
ffi-corp.com
Manufacturer and exporter of continuous flow commercial and industrial grain dryers
Estimated Sales: $50-100 Million
Number Employees: 250-499

22421 FFR Merchandising Inc
8181 Darrow Rd
Twinsburg, OH 44087-2303
440-505-6919
Fax: 440-505-6900 800-422-2547
info@ffr.com www.ffr.com
Since 1962, has been developing innovative merchandising systems and accesories to effectively position brands at retail. Offers custom design services and fullfillment
President/CEO: Donald Kimmel
CEO: Stanley Burson
stanley.burson@ffr.com
CFO: Nathaniel Smith
CEO: Stanley Burson
Research & Development: Daniel Kump
Marketing Director: Paul Bloom
Sales Director: Michael DeJohn
Operations Manager: Drew Phillips
Estimated Sales: $50 - 100 Million
Number Employees: 100-249
Number of Brands: 40
Number of Products: 1700
Square Footage: 100000

22422 FIB-R-DOR
10021 Commerce Park Dr.
P.O. Box 13268
Cincinnati, OH 45246
501-758-9494
Fax: 501-758-9496 800-342-7367
www.fibrdor.com
Manufacturer and exporter of fiberglass doors, etc.
President: Jason Dileo
Marketing Director: Wes Lacewell
Sales Director: Mike Ferrell
Estimated Sales: $2.5 Million
Number Employees: 10-19

Number of Products: 3
Square Footage: 50000
Parent Co: Advance Fiberglass
Type of Packaging: Bulk
Brands:
Fib-R-Dor

22423 (HQ)FILTEC-Inspection Systems
3100 Fujita St
Torrance, CA 90505-4007
310-325-5633
Fax: 310-530-1000 888-434-5832
www.filtec.com
Manufacturer and exporter of automatic inspection systems for empty bottles, cases, missing caps, labels, filler/seamer monitors and packaging line detectors
President/CEO: James Kearbey
Purchasing Agent: Bill Herich
Estimated Sales: $44 Million
Number Employees: 250-499
Square Footage: 155000
Type of Packaging: Food Service
Other Locations:
Industrial Dynamics Co.Ltd.
Hamburg 30, West
Brands:
Dairyvision
Ebi-Ultraline
Ft-50
Omnivision 1200
Omnivision 900

22424 FJC International
2418 Hilton Way
Gainesville, GA 30501-6192
770-718-0100
Fax: 770-718-0909 info@fjcinternational.com
www.fjcinternational.com
Provides equipment and turnkey operations for poultry processing plants
President: Juan Chiarella
info@fjcinternational.com
Estimated Sales: $1.3 Million
Number Employees: 5-9

22425 (HQ)FLEXcon Company
1 FLEXcon Industrial Park
Spencer, MA 01562-2642
508-885-8200
Fax: 508-885-8400 www.flexcon.com
Pressure sensitive film and adhesive products
President & CEO: Neil McDonough
CEO: Neil McDonough
Number Employees: 1,000-4,999

22426 FMB Company
RR 1
Box 564
Broken Bow, OK 74728-9780
580-513-5309
Fax: 580-584-2971 fmbco@octm.com
Consultant providing design and building services for food and industrial plants
President: Fred Bray
Director Marketing: Tonya Laffey
Estimated Sales: Below $5 Million
Number Employees: 1
Square Footage: 6400

22427 FMC Corporation
2929 Walnut St
Philadelphia, PA 19104
215-299-6000
Fax: 215-299-5998 www.fmc.com
Natural soda ash for sodium bicarbonate, sodium cyanide, sodium sesquicarbonate and caustic soda, hydrogen peroxide, active oxidants, phosphorus chemicals and phosphoric acid.
Chairman/CEO: Pierre Brondeau
EVP & CFO: Andrew Sandifer
EVP/General Counsel/Secretary: Michael Reilly
President & CEO-Elect: Mark Douglas
Year Founded: 1883
Estimated Sales: Over $1 Billion
Number Employees: 7,000

22428 FMC Fluid Control
103 E Maple Street
Hoopeston, IL 60942-1699
217-283-8300
Fax: 217-283-8424
Wine industry vineyard sprayers

Co- Owner: Thomas Hamilton
Chairman, President, Chief Executive Off: John Gremp
Vice President of Infrastructure: Barry Glickman
Regional Sales Manager: Ellen Hao
Contact: Lavonda Sherrill
lavonda_sherrill@fmc.com
Estimated Sales: $10-20 Million
Number Employees: 50-99

22429 FMI Display
360 Glen Way
Elkins Park, PA 19027-1740
215-663-1998
Fax: 215-763-7099
Wire display racks and point of purchase displays including paper and plastic; also, screen printing services available
President: Kenneth Hoffman
Number Employees: 10
Square Footage: 10000

22430 FMI Fluid Metering
5 Aerial Way
Suite 500
Syosset, NY 11791-5593
516-922-6050
Fax: 516-624-8261 800-223-3388
pumps@fmipump.com www.fmipump.com
Dispensers, ingredients, lubricant, ingredient feeders
President: Harry Pinkerton
Contact: Hank Pinkerton
pumps@fmipump.com
Number Employees: 50-99

22431 FMS
328 Commerce Blvd # 8
Bogart, GA 30622-2200
706-549-2207
Fax: 706-548-1724 fmssales@fmsathens.com
www.fmsathens.com
Manager: Eric Gunderson
Estimated Sales: $10 - 20 Million
Number Employees: 20-49

22432 FMS Company
338 Alana Drive
New Lenox, IL 60451-1784
815-485-4955
Fax: 815-485-4011 800-992-2814
Wine industry financial software
Estimated Sales: $2.5-5 000,000
Number Employees: 1-4

22433 FOODesign from tna
29103 SW Kinsman Rd
Wilsonville, OR 97070-8701
503-685-5030
Fax: 503-685-5034 info@foodesign.com
www.foodesign.com
Supplier of commercial and industrial cooking & baking equipment, fryers, Cryo-Jet, cooling units, coating & seasoning equipment, food grade bulk packaging handling conveyers and specialty cooking equipment.
Vice President: Daniel Luna
Project Manager: Jason Heisler
Estimated Sales: $5 - 10 million
Number Employees: 20
Parent Co: tna

22434 FORT Hill Sign ProductsInc
13 Airport Rd
Hopedale, MA 01747-1547
781-321-4320
Fax: 781-397-0452 fh@forthillsigns.com
www.forthillsigns.com
Plastic cut letters and logos, name plates and signs
Owner: Amy Clark
amy.clark@forthillsigns.com
Estimated Sales: $3 - 5 Million
Number Employees: 5-9

22435 FP Packaging Company
193 Camino Dorado
Napa, CA 94558-6213
707-258-3940
Fax: 707-258-3949 www.collopack.com
Wine industry packaging and wine corks
CEO: Gregory Fulford
Founder, Executive Vice President Sales: Phil Giacalone
Founder, Vice President of Sales: Joe Mironicki

Estimated Sales: $10 - 20 Million
Number Employees: 10-19
Type of Packaging: Bulk

22436 FPC Corp
355 Hollow Hill Rd
Wauconda, IL 60084-9794
847-487-4583
Fax: 847-487-0174 www.surebonderindustrial.com
Glue sticks, staples and staple guns
President: Michael Kamins
glueguns@aol.com
CFO: Patrick Kamins
Quality Control: M Bernard Kamins
Estimated Sales: $10-20 000,000
Number Employees: 20-49

22437 FPEC Corp
2216 Ford Ave
Springdale, AR 72764-4722
479-751-9392
Fax: 479-751-9399 salesark@fpec.com
www.fpec.com
Processing equipment for beef, chicken, sausage,
fish and ham
President: Alan Davison
Estimated Sales: $5-10 Million
Number Employees: 20-49

22438 FPEC Corporation
13623 Pumice St
Santa Fe Springs, CA 90670-5105
562-802-3727
Fax: 562-802-8621 salescal@fpec.com
www.fpec.com
Manufacturer and exporter of food processing
equipment including blenders, conveyors and vac-
uum tumblers
President: Alan Davison
Contact: Laura Flynn
flynnl@fpec.com
Plant Manager: Dwayne Lee
Estimated Sales: $5 - 10 Million
Number Employees: 20-49
Square Footage: 212000
Brands:
Fpec

22439 FRC Environmental
1635 Oakbrook Dr
Gainesville, GA 30507
770-534-3681
Fax: 770-535-1887
Manufacturer and exporter of stainless steel waste
water treatment equipment and systems
President: Lonnie Finley
Estimated Sales: $2,600,000
Number Employees: 25
Square Footage: 72000
Type of Packaging: Bulk

22440 FRC Systems International
1770 Ridgefield Drive
Roswell, GA 30075
770-534-3681
Fax: 770-992-2289 info@FRCsystems.com
www.frcsystems.com
Water and wastewater treatment systems for the
dairy, poultry, meat & seafood processing industries.

22441 FRICK by Johnson Controls
5757 N Green Bay Ave
P.O. Box 591
Milwaukee, WI 53201
414-524-1200
855-270-5546
www.jci.com/frick
Industrial refrigeration, food and beverage, petro-
chemical, oil and gas extraction.
Chairman & CEO: George Oliver
Estimated Sales: $100-500 Million
Number Employees: 500
Parent Co: Johnson Controls

22442 FRS Industries
1021 Center Ave.
Moorhead, MN 56560
701-365-1000
Fax: 218-287-2907 800-747-4795
www.frsind.com
Advertising novelties and specialites including
award ribbons, rosettes, trophies, promotional buttons, imprinted T-shirts, jackets, caps, etc

Owner: Sheri Larson
Controller: Timothy Dockter
Sales Manager: Sheri Larson
Contact: Eric Bacon
ebacon@heatsoftware.com
Estimated Sales: $5-10 Million
Number Employees: 20-49

22443 FSFG Capital
814 Fontana Avenue
Richardson, TX 75080-3002
972-783-0611
Fax: 972-235-5310
Investment firm for food companies
Vice President: Richard Harju

22444 FTC International Consulting
19021 Mitchell Road
Pitt Meadows, BC V3Y 1Y1
Canada
604-288-2719
Fax: 604-288-8565 contact@ftcinternational.com
www.ftcinternational.com
Consulting: product development, nutrition analysis,
regulatory consulting, quality programs
President: Walter Dullemond
Operations Manager: Eva Savova

22445 FTI International Automation Systems
10914 N 2nd Street
Machesney Park, IL 61115-1400
815-877-4080
Fax: 815-877-0073
www.ftiautomationsystems.com

22446 FTL/Happold Tensil Structure Design & Engineering
44 East 32nd Street
3rd Floor
New York, NY 10016
212-732-4691
Fax: 212-385-1025 ngoldsmith@ftlstudio.com
www.ftlstudio.com
Commercial tents, fabric structures
Owner: Todd Dalland
Genetics Department: Andre Chaszar
Engineer: Wayne Rendeley
Estimated Sales: $1 - 5 Million
Number Employees: 20-49
Parent Co: Buro Happold

22447 FTR Processing Equipment
2101 Troy Ave
South El Monte, CA 91733-2535
626-452-1870
Fax: 626-452-1857 ftrequipment@yahoo.com
ftrequipment.com
Packaging, processing and slaughtering equipment
Owner: Francisco Prejo
ftrprocessingequipment@yahoo.com
Vice President: Gloria Trejo
Sales Director: Jair Trejo
Estimated Sales: Below $5 000,000
Number Employees: 10-19
Number of Brands: 55

22448 FX Technology & Products
900 Factory Rd
PO Box 547
Fremont, NE 68026
402-727-5222
Fax: 402-721-5154 866-938-8388
Proteins
Regional Sales Manager: Rick Young
Office Manager: Debbie Vacha
Estimated Sales: Under $500,000
Number Employees: 10-19

22449 FX-Lab Company
725 Lehigh Avenue
Union, NJ 07083-7642
908-810-1212
Fax: 908-810-1630
Manufacturer and exporter of beneficial bacterial
cleaning compounds and liquefiers for septic tanks
and cesspools
President: George Weinik
Number Employees: 5
Square Footage: 4800

22450 Fab-X/Metals
PO Box 1903
Washington, NC 27889-1903
252-977-3229
Fax: 252-977-6605 800-677-3229
Manufacturer and wholesaler/distributor of chairs,
ovens, sinks, spoons, tables, etc.; also, supermarket
equipment including store fixtures and racks; serv-
ing the food service market
President: Jonathan Turner
COO: Cyrus Watson
Quality Control: Carol Causeway
Estimated Sales: $10-20 Million
Number Employees: 10
Square Footage: 200000

22451 Fabco
PO Box 754
Albertville, AL 35950-0012
256-878-5010
Fax: 256-878-7879 www.fabcoinc.com
CEO: Rocky Frazier
Director of Sales: Stephen Frazier
Manufacturing Manager: Phillip Murphree
Estimated Sales: $20-50 Million
Number Employees: 20-49

22452 Fabick CAT
11200 W Silver Spring Rd
Milwaukee, WI 53225-3118
414-461-9100
Fax: 414-461-8899 sal@fabco.com
Disinfection of pumpable foods and drinking water
CEO: Jere Fabick
j.fabick@fabco.com
Estimated Sales: $500,000-$1 Million
Number Employees: 50-99

22453 Fabohio Inc
521 E 7th St
Uhrichsville, OH 44683-1613
740-922-4233
Fax: 740-922-4785 www.fabohio.com
Manufacturer and exporter of protective clothing
and products including drum liners, meat cutters'
aprons and smocks and shoe covers. Also custom
fabrication available.
President: Don Coy
dcoy@fabohio.com
CEO: Kurt Shelley
CFO: Kurt Shelley
Purchasing Manager: Dennis Sautters
Estimated Sales: $1-3 Million
Number Employees: 20-49
Square Footage: 50000

22454 Fabreeka International
315 Ruthar Dr
Newark, DE 19711
302-452-2500
Fax: 302-452-2505 www.derco.com
Equipment
Manager: Paul O'Connor
Estimated Sales: $3 - 5 Million
Number Employees: 10-19

22455 Fabreeka International
696 W Amity Rd
Boise, ID 83705-5401
208-342-4681
Fax: 208-343-8043 800-423-4469
www.beltservice.com
Manufacturer and exporter of lightweight custom
conveyor belting including food grade, food grade
incline, special profile, harvester, PVC and
polyurethane
Branch Manager: Bob Holda
General manager: Toby Grindstaff
Division Manager: Toby Grindstaff
Assistant Division Manager: Mitz Pellicciotta
Estimated Sales: Below $5 Million
Number Employees: 10-19
Square Footage: 400000
Parent Co: Fabreeka International
Other Locations:
Fabreeka International
Oakville ON
Brands:
Fablene
Fablon
Fabreeka
Fabsyn

22456 Fabreeka International Inc
1023 Turnpike St
Stoughton, MA 02072-1156
781-341-3655
Fax: 781-341-3983 800-322-7352
info@fabreeka.com www.fabreeka.com
Integrally molded cleated and special profile rubber
belting and European style thermoplastics belting
President: Pat Norton
pnorton@fabreeka.com
Estimated Sales: $25 - 30 Million
Number Employees: 1-4

22457 Fabri-Kal Corp
600 Plastics Pl
Kalamazoo, MI 49001-4882
269-385-5050
Fax: 269-385-0197 800-888-5054
info@fabri-kal.com www.fabri-kal.com
Thermoformed plastic containers and cups including
custom designed, prototype, production, stock food
service line, clear or colored and FDA certified
CEO: Scott Abel
sabel@f-k.com
CEO: Robert P Kittredge
Marketing Manager: Scott Tindall
Estimated Sales: $10-20 Million
Number Employees: 50-99
Brands:
Kal-Tainer

22458 Fabricated Components Inc
2018 W Main St
PO Box 431
Stroudsburg, PA 18360
570-421-4110
Fax: 570-421-2553 800-233-8163
info@fabricatedcomponents.com
www.fabricatedcomponents.com
Manufacturer and exporter of pallets, dollies, carts,
cabinetry and containers
President: Bob Deinarowicz
Estimated Sales: $2.5-5 Million
Number Employees: 20-49
Square Footage: 200000
Type of Packaging: Private Label

22459 Fabricating & Welding Corp
12246 S Halsted St
Chicago, IL 60628-6400
773-928-2050
Fax: 773-928-4950
www.fabricatingandwelding.com
Steel skids, base plates and motor bases
President: Greg Delcotto
gregdelcotto@fabricatingandwelding.com
CFO: Elizabeth Pecora
Research & Development: Steven Samecak
Production Manager: Jim Foley
Purchasing Manager: Robert Del Cotto
Estimated Sales: $5 - 10 Million
Number Employees: 10-19
Square Footage: 60000

22460 Fabrication Specialties
2898 Crestridge Dr
Centerville, TN 37033-5941
931-729-2283
Fax: 931-729-2585
www.fabricationspecialties.com
Wood pallets and shipping skids
Owner: Mike Goodpasture
fabspec@hughes.net
VP: William Goodpasture
Estimated Sales: $2.5-5 Million
Number Employees: 20-49
Square Footage: 40000

22461 Fabrichem Inc
2226 Black Rock Tpke # 206
Fairfield, CT 06825-3240
203-366-1820
Fax: 203-366-1850 sales@fabricheminc.com
www.fabricheminc.com
Aspartame, amino acids, L-Tyrosine, botanical ex-
tracts, L-theanine, Lutein, D-Glucuronolactone
Owner: Jacob Tallathra
Estimated Sales: $5-10 000,000
Number Employees: 10
Number of Brands: 4
Number of Products: 50

22462 Fabricon Products Inc
1721 W Pleasant St
River Rouge, MI 48218-1099
313-841-8200
Fax: 313-841-4819 bdinda@fabriconproducts.com
www.fabriconproducts.com
Manufacturer, importer and exporter of flexible
packaging materials including printed waxed and
coated paper, films, frozen/novelty food packaging
and wrapping, preformed paper bags and film lami-
nated pouches; also, package designservices
available
President: Bruce Dinda
bdinda@fabriconproducts.com
CFO: Roland David
Sales Director: Bruce L Dinda
Customer Service: Becky Smith
Production Manager: Mike Aslanian
Plant Manager: John Kuzawinski
Purchasing Manager: Colleen Loweifer
Estimated Sales: $9 Million
Number Employees: 50-99
Square Footage: 302000
Type of Packaging: Consumer, Food Service, Pri-
vate Label, Bulk

22463 Fabriko
P.O. Box 67
Altavista, VA 24517-0067
434-369-1170
Fax: 434-369-1169 888-203-8098
afbriko@voyager.net www.fabriko.com
Manufacturer and importer of barbecue and waist
aprons, coolers and bags including lunch, grocery
and shopping
Owner: Ranata Allbeck
Sales Manager: Jerry Fischer
Estimated Sales: $3 - 5 Million
Number Employees: 10-19

22464 Fabwright Inc
13912 Enterprise Dr
Garden Grove, CA 92843-4021
714-554-5544
Fax: 714-554-5545 800-854-6464
Manufacturer and exporter of custom stainless steel
kitchen equipment fabrication; complete line of
commercial food waste disposers
Owner: Della Williams
della@fabwrightinc.com
Vice President: J Wright
Purchasing Manager: D Yeardley
Number Employees: 10-19
Type of Packaging: Food Service

22465 Facilitec
73 S Riverside Dr
Elgin, IL 60120-6425
847-931-9500
Fax: 847-931-9629
Estimated Sales: $1 - 5 Million
Parent Co: Ecolab

22466 Facilities Design Inc
100 Brubaker Rd
Lititz, PA 17543-8662
717-626-1880
Fax: 717-285-3102 www.facilitiesdesign.net
Full-service design capabilities including construc-
tion services with special expertise in cold storage
warehousing and food processing facilities, com-
plete architectural engineering and materials
handling design
President: Joe Shaffer
Marketing Director: Jack Stone
Estimated Sales: Less Than $500,000
Number Employees: 1-4

22467 Facility Group
2233 Lake Park Dr SE Ste 100
Smyrna, GA 30080
770-437-2700
Fax: 770-437-3900 www.facilitygroup.com
Fully integrated planning, engineering and construction management firm specializing in turn-key services for the food processing and distribution
industries. Refrigeration engineering and insulation
technology, materials handlingequipment selection
CEO: Ennis Parker
Estimated Sales: $50
Number Employees: 250-499

22468 Faciltec Corporation
73 S Riverside Dr
Elgin, IL 60120-6425
847-931-9500
Fax: 847-931-9629 800-284-8273
Manufacturer and exporter of a rooftop grease con-
tainment system for food service and industrial mar-
kets; also, cleaning services available
Executive VP: Christopher Barry
National Sales/Service Manager: Patrick Molloy
Estimated Sales: $1 - 5 Million
Number Employees: 50-99
Square Footage: 104000
Type of Packaging: Food Service
Brands:
Afc
G2 Grease Guard
Grease Guard

22469 Factory Cat
1509 Rapids Drive
Racine, WI 53404-2383
262-681-3583
Fax: 262-632-3335 800-634-4060
www.factorycat.com
Industrial, walk-behind and rider sweepers and
scrubbers

22470 FactoryTalk
1201 S 2nd St
Milwaukee, WI 53204
414-382-2000

www.rockwellautomation.com/en_NA/products/fa
ctorytalk
Software to support advanced industrial applications, including system design, operations, plant
maintenance, and analytics.
VP, Architecture & Software: Fran Wlodarczyk
Parent Co: Rockwell Automation Inc

22471 Fair Publishing House
15 Schauss Ave
PO Box 350
Norwalk, OH 44857-1851
419-668-3746
Fax: 419-663-3247 orders@fairsupplies.com
www.fairpublishing.com
Manufacturer and exporter of award ribbons, tickets
and signs including advertising
President: Kevin Doyle
kevin@fairsupplies.com
Sales Director: Charles Doyle
Production Manager: Kenneth Kosie
Estimated Sales: $3 - 5 Million
Number Employees: 20-49
Square Footage: 50000
Parent Co: Rotary Printing Company
Other Locations:
Fair Publishing House
Norwalk OH

22472 Fairbanks Scales
6800 W 64th St
Overland Park, KS 66202
816-471-0231
Fax: 816-471-0241 800-451-4107
www.fairbanks.com
Manufacturer and exporter of stainless steel hostile
environment scales including bench, unirail,
omnicells, digital indicators, bench and portable
scales, and bar code dataprinter
CEO: F.A. Norden
Estimated Sales: $81 Million
Number Employees: 20-49
Square Footage: 12000
Parent Co: Fancor, Inc.

22473 Fairborn USA Inc
205 Broadview St
Upper Sandusky, OH 43351-9628
419-294-4987
Fax: 419-294-4980 800-262-1188
info@fairbornusa.com www.fairbornusa.com
Manufacturer and exporter of truck and rail loading
dock enclosures
President: Mark Dillon
dillonm@fairbornusa.com
General Manager: Mark Dillon
Number Employees: 100-249

22474 Fairchester Snacks Corp
100 Lafayette Ave
White Plains, NY 10603-1612
914-761-2824
www.nysnacks.com
Salty biscuits
Owner: John Barisano
Estimated Sales: $300,000-500,000
Number Employees: 5-9

22475 Fairchild Industrial Products
3920 Westpoint Blvd
Winston Salem, NC 27103-6727
336-659-3400
Fax: 336-659-9323 800-334-8422
sales@fairchildproducts.com www.soldousa.com
Manufacturer and exporter of industrial controls including electro-pneumatic transducers and pneumatic pressure regulators; also, mechanical power transmission equipment including differential and draw transmissions
President: Mark Cuthbert
CEO: Bryan Buono
bryan.buono@rotork.com
Director, Finance: David C. Velten
VP Industrial Controls: Thomas McNichol
Quality Control: Greg Argrabright
R&D: Andy Askew
Director of Sales: Claudio Borges
VP Power Transportation Equipment: Jack Dunivant
Estimated Sales: $10 - 20 Million
Number Employees: 100-249
Square Footage: 176000
Brands:
　Cubic
　Fairchild
　Harmonic
　Specon
　Vari-Chain

22476 Fairfield Line Inc
605 W Stone Ave
PO Box 500
Fairfield, IA 52556-2223
641-472-3191
Fax: 641-472-3194 800-247-3383
www.fairfieldlineinc.com
Manufacturer, importer and exporter of work gloves including cotton, leather, leather-palm, coated and string knits
President: Nicole Vivacqua
nvivacqua@fairfieldline.com
VP: Larry Sheffler
Sales Manager: Larry Ray Sheffler
Estimated Sales: $5 - 10 Million
Number Employees: 20-49
Parent Co: Fairfield Line

22477 Falco Technologies
1245 Rue Industrielle
La Prairie, QC J5R 2E4
Canada
450-444-0566
Fax: 450-444-2227 www.falcotechnologies.com
Manufacturer and exporter of stainless steel food processing equipment including silos, tanks, hoppers, mixing kettles, wine storage units, brewery machinery, dairy processing equipment and custom fabrication turn key solutions tosimple and complex problems - from tank installation to complete process
Co-President: Bertrand Blanchette
Co-President: Marc Regnaud
Quality Control: Andre Pichette
Marketing/Sales: Nicolas Courchesne
Vice President of Sales and Marketing: Stephane Audy
Production/Plant Manager: Jonathan Gingras
Purchasing: Susan Hynes
Estimated Sales: $10 Million
Number Employees: 75
Square Footage: 130000
Parent Co: Falco
Brands:
　Falco

22478 Falcon Belting
8338 SW 15th Street
Oklahoma City, OK 73128-9594
405-495-7563
Fax: 405-495-7911 800-922-0878
Plastic belts
Estimated Sales: $5-10 000,000
Number Employees: 60

22479 Falcon Fabricators Inc
422 Allied Dr
Nashville, TN 37211-3304
615-832-0027
Fax: 615-832-0048 www.falconnashville.com
Stainless steel work tables, hot fat filters, chicken marinators, etc.; also, replacement parts available
President: Gary Heckle
gheckle@falconnashville.com
President: Gary Heckle
Account Manager: Jan Wilson
Estimated Sales: $20-50 Million
Number Employees: 10-19
Square Footage: 50000
Parent Co: Trendco

22480 Fallas Automation Inc.
7000 Imperial Dr
Waco, TX 76712-6816
254-772-9524
Fax: 254-751-1242 sales@fallasautomation.com
www.fallasautomation.com
Automatic packaging machinery
President: Dave Fallas
dfallas@fallasautomation.com
Vice President: Mark McAninch
Sales Manager: Chris Calebrese
Spare Parts Manager: Curtis Gross
Estimated Sales: $10 - 20 Million
Number Employees: 50+
Square Footage: 130000
Type of Packaging: Consumer, Food Service, Private Label, Bulk

22481 Falls Chemical Products
123 Caldwell Ave
Oconto Falls, WI 54154
920-846-3561
Fax: 920-846-4830 fallschemical@ez-net.com
Cleaners, sanitizers, soaps and dish washing detergent for restaurant, bar and janitorial services; also, dairy chemicals
Owner/President: Sam Scimemi
Number Employees: 2

22482 Falls Filtration Technologies
115 E Steels Corners Rd
Stow, OH 44224-4919
330-928-4100
Fax: 330-928-0122 info@fallsfti.com
Air and oil filters
President: David Casper
dcasper@fallsfti.com
CFO: Bradley Lane
Quality Manager: Jeff Patrick
Director of Commercial Marketing: Andy Blair
Director of Sales: Andy Blair
Customer Service Rep.: Simone Edwards
Senior Buyer: Jean Balcer
Estimated Sales: $10 - 20 Million
Number Employees: 20-49

22483 Fallshaw Wheels & Casters
6848 Moorhen Place
Oceanside, CA 92009
760-476-9713
Fax: 760-476-9714 jdavitt@fallshaw.com.au
Estimated Sales: $1 Million
Number Employees: 1

22484 Fallwood Corp
75 S Broadway
Suite 494
White Plains, NY 10601-4413
914-304-4065
Fax: 914-304-4063 ana@fallwoodcorp.com
www.fallwoodcorp.com
Manufacturer and supplier of all natural nutraceutical ingredients and raw materials. All glanulars - Bovine and Porcine Enzymes
President/CEO: Jorge Millan
Vice President: Graciela Rocchia
Sales: Wayne Battenfield
Manager: Anne-Marie Rodriguez
anna@fallwoodcorp.com
Adminstration: Anne Marie Rodriguez
Estimated Sales: Under $500,000
Number Employees: 1-4
Parent Co: Loboratorio Opoterapico Argentino

22485 Famco Automatic SausageLinkers
P. O. Box 8647
Pittsburgh, PA 15221
412-241-6410
Fax: 412-242-8877 info@famcousa.com
www.famcousa.com
Linking machines for sausage and frankfurter production
President: Charles Allen
Vice President: R. Robert Allen
Sales: Dick Carson

22486 Famco Sausage Linking Machines
421 N Braddock Ave
Pittsburgh, PA 15208-2514
412-241-6410
Fax: 412-242-8877 info@famcousa.com
www.famcousa.com
Sausage linkers
Owner: Bob Allen
VP: R Robert Allen
Estimated Sales: $1 - 5 Million
Number Employees: 20-49

22487 Family Farms Group
31832 Dehli Rd.
Brighton, IL 62012
618-372-7400
877-221-3276
www.familyfarmsgroup.com
Services including coaching and management consulting, networking, human resources, cost savings, crop financing, and crop marketing.
CEO: Jeff Haferkamp
EVP: Harold Birch
Director, Sales & Marketing: Dave Bryden
Year Founded: 2006
Number Employees: 50-200

22488 Family Tree Farms
41646 Road 62
Reedley, CA 93654
559-591-6280
www.familytreefarms.com
Plumcots, white peaches and nectarines, donut peaches and nectarines, yellow peaches and nectarines, apricots, apriums, plums, blueberries, cherries, satsumas.
Owner/Farmer: David Jackson
Owner/Farmer: Rick Jackson
Owner/Farmer: Daniel Jackson
Owner/Farmer: Andy Muxlow
Estimated Sales: $20-50 Million
Number Employees: 250-499
Number of Brands: 6
Brands:
　Eat Smart
　Farmers Market
　Flavor Safari
　Great Whites
　River Run
　Summerripe

22489 Famous Software LLC
8080 N Palm Ave # 210
Suite 210
Fresno, CA 93711-5797
559-431-8100
Fax: 559-447-6339
support@FamousSoftware.com
www.famoussoftware.com
Wine industry computer systems
President: Kirk Parrish
kirkp@famoussoftware.com
CFO: Rick Desehr
Estimated Sales: $5 - 10 Million
Number Employees: 50-99

22490 Fan Bag Company
4307 W Division St
Chicago, IL 60651-1714
773-342-2752
Fax: 773-342-4413
Plastic bags
CEO: Florian Nocek
VP Marketing: Carl Nocek
Estimated Sales: $5 - 10 Million
Number Employees: 25

22491 Fantapak
12150 Merriman Rd
Livonia, MI 48150-1914
734-838-1300
Fax: 248-743-2970 800-856-3803
sales@fantapak.com www.fantapak.com
President: Chia Chang
j.chang@fantapakinternational.com
Estimated Sales: $5 - 10 Million
Number Employees: 20-49

22492 Faraday
805 S Maumee St
Tecumseh, MI 49286-2053
517-423-2111
Fax: 517-423-2320 www.faraday.com
Manufacturer and exporter of fire alarm systems
Manager: Tim Wertz
Contact: Hugo Hortiz
hugo@faradaybikes.com
Estimated Sales: $20 - 50 Million
Number Employees: 100-249
Parent Co: Cerberus Pryotronics
Brands:
Faraday

22493 Fargo Automation
969 34th St N
Fargo, ND 58102-3071
701-239-1656
Fax: 701-232-1929 888-616-0188
sales@fargoautomation.com
www.fargoautomation.com
Owner: Kevin Biffert
kevin.biffert@fargoautomation.com
Estimated Sales: $20 - 50 Million
Number Employees: 20-49

22494 Faribault Foods, Inc.
3401 Park Ave. NW
Fairbault, MN 55021
507-331-1400
ConsumeResponse@faribaultfoods.com
www.faribaultfoods.com
Canned vegetables, sauced beans, refried beans,
baked beans, pasta, soup, chili, and organic and
Mexican specialties.
President/CEO: Albert Hoflack
CFO: Mike Weber
Executive VP, Sales/Marketing: Frank Lynch
Year Founded: 1895
Estimated Sales: $164 Million
Number Employees: 5
Number of Brands: 10
Parent Co: Arizona Canning Company, LLC
Type of Packaging: Consumer, Private Label, Bulk
Other Locations:
Faribault Foods Distribution
Faribault MN
Faribault Foods Plant
Cokato MN
Brands:
Butter Kernel Vegetables
Chilli Man
Kuner's
Luck's
Mrs. Grimes
Otoe's Finest
PASTA SELECT
PRIDE
SW
SunVista

22495 Faribault ManufacturingCo
820 20th St NW
Faribault, MN 55021-2396
507-334-0464
Fax: 507-334-0674 800-447-6043
tcook.sales@faribomfg.com www.faribomfg.com
Plastic light globes, food containers, dunnage racks
and ingredient bins; also, custom roto molded com-
ponents available.
President: Timothy M. Hoschette
National Sales/Marketing Manager: Tom Cook
National Sales/Marketing Manager: Kristy
Hoffstatter
kristy.orders@faribomfg.com
Purchasing Manager: Tim Hoschette
Estimated Sales: $2.5-5 Million
Number Employees: 10-19
Number of Brands: 2
Number of Products: 150+
Square Footage: 108000
Parent Co: Hoschette Enterprises

22496 Farmer Direct Foods, Inc
PO Box 326
511 Commercial
Atchison, KA 66002
913-367-4422
Fax: 913-367-4443 800-372-4422
www.farmerdirectfoods.com
Provides white and whole wheat baking products,
bread recipes, and tips for using bread machines.
Chief Executive Officer: Kent Symns
sales@farmerdirectfoods.com
Director: Dave Pfefer
Operations Director: Marcia Walters
Estimated Sales: $2.5 - 5 Million
Number Employees: 20-49

22497 Farmer's Co-Op ElevatorCo
3302 Prospect St
P.O. Box 219
Hudsonville, MI 49426-1420
616-669-9596
Fax: 616-669-0490 800-439-9859
info@fcelevator.com www.fcelevator.com
Corrugated cartons and wooden shipping crates,
boxes and baskets
President: Jim Roskam
jroskam@fcelevator.com
General Manager: Jim Roskam
Estimated Sales: $1 - 5 Million
Number Employees: 20-49
Parent Co: Farmer's Cooperative Elevator Co., Inc.

22498 Farnell Packaging
30 Ilsley Avenue
Dartmouth, NS B3B 1L3
Canada
902-468-9378
Fax: 902-468-3192 800-565-9378
sales@farnell.ns.ca www.farnell.ns.ca
Flexible packaging, plastic films and pressure sensi-
tive labels
President: Donald Farnell
CFO: Bill Morash
Quality Control: Danny Christianson
Sales/Marketing Manager: D Stanfield
General Manager: H Christianson
Number Employees: 160
Square Footage: 75000

22499 Fas-Co Coders
422 Thornton Rd # 103
Lithia Springs, GA 30122-1581
770-739-7798
Fax: 480-545-1998 800-478-0685
Manufacturer and exporter of coding and marking
equipment
Owner: Victor Er
CFO: Roger Van Steenkiste
VP: Dan Piercy
Quality Control: Ty Martin
Estimated Sales: $6,000,000
Number Employees: 20-49
Square Footage: 30000

22500 Fasson Employee FCU
250 Chester St
Painesville, OH 44077-4118
440-358-2100
Fax: 440-358-2102 www.fasson.com
Wine industry labeling equipment
Manager: Laurie Hall
lhall@fasson.com
Estimated Sales: Less Than $500,000
Number Employees: 1-4

22501 Fast Bags
2501 Ludelle Street
Fort Worth, TX 76105-1036
817-534-9950
Fax: 817-534-1771 800-321-3687
Paper and plastic bags and labels
Estimated Sales: $1 - 5,000,000
Parent Co: Daydots International

22502 Fast Industries
1850 NW 49th St
Fort Lauderdale, FL 33309-3304
954-776-0066
Fax: 954-776-5387 800-775-5345
Manufacturer and exporter of label placement systems, sign holders and merchandising aids; also,
cleaning supplies including stain, laundry, rust and
odor removers

President: Jacob Fast
Market Manager: Mike Brinkman
Estimated Sales: $10 - 15 Million
Number Employees: 100 to 249
Square Footage: 190000
Brands:
Carpet Gun
Ez View
Frontrunner
One Drop
One Spray
Rust Gun
Sell Strip
Smoking Gun
Stain Gun

22503 Fast Stuff Packaging
2 Village Road
Suite 10
Horsham, PA 19044-3816
877-388-3278
Fax: 215-830-9332
Void fill packaging system

22504 Fastcorp
1 Cory Road
Morristown, NJ 07960-3103
973-455-0400
Fax: 201-939-0255
Estimated Sales: $500,000-$1 000,000
Number Employees: 5-9

22505 Fata Automation
6050 19 Mile Rd
Sterling Heights, MI 48314
586-323-9400
Fax: 248-553-6013 www.fatainc.com
Conveyors, integrated systems and controls
President: Piero Bugnone
Sales Manager: Ron Benish
Contact: Anthony Calabrese
acalabrese@fatainc.com
Estimated Sales: $75 Million
Number Employees: 100
Square Footage: 65000
Parent Co: Fata Automation Group

22506 Fato Industries
462 S 5000w Rd
Kankakee, IL 60901-7905
815-932-3015
Fax: 815-932-9839 fatoindustries@gmail.com
Fiberglass and polyethylene tanks, covers, trays and
totes
President: Thomas Fato
otaf226@yahoo.com
CFO: Chris Fato
Quality Control: Tom Fato
R&D: Tom Fato
Estimated Sales: Below $5,000,000
Number Employees: 1-4
Square Footage: 20000

22507 Faubion Central States Tank Company
P.O. Box 26085
Shawnee Mission, KS 66225-6085
913-681-0069
Fax: 913-681-0150 800-450-8265
dfaubion@faubiontank.com
www.faubiontank.com
Food grade and heated stainless steel storage tanks
Owner: Dan Faubion
VP: Tom Thompson
Plant Manager: Dave Hill
Estimated Sales: $1-2.5 Million
Number Employees: 5-9
Square Footage: 160000

22508 Faulkenberg Inc
3660 2nd St
Hubbard, OR 97032-9560
503-981-3200
Fax: 503-981-9143 www.falkenberginc.net
High pressure pumps, nozzles and accessories
Owner: Gary Faulkenberg
Estimated Sales: $2.5-5 000,000
Number Employees: 5-9

22509 Faultless Caster
1421 N Garvin Street
Evansville, IN 47711-4687
866-316-2163
Fax: 800-322-9329 800-322-7359
www.faultlesscaster.com
Casters and wheels
Sales Manager: Matt Olson
Contact: Mary Heskett
mheskett@iupui.edu
Manager (Industrial Distribution): Brian Robb
Sales/Production Manager: Denny Garness
Number Employees: 250-499
Parent Co: FKI Industries
Brands:
  Dynatred
  Heavy Metal
  K-Wheel
  Rt

22510 Favorite Foods Inc
29 Interstate Dr
Somersworth, NH 03878-1227
603-692-4990
Fax: 603-692-4993 800-NUT-S4YO
favorite99@aol.com
www.midtownfavoritebeef.com
Vertical mixers, moulding and nut processing equipment
Owner: Fred Lewin
CEO: Chris Barstow
VP: Tom Myers
Estimated Sales: $2.5-5 Million
Number Employees: 20-49

22511 Fawema Packaging Machinery
1701 Desoto Road
Palmetto, FL 34221-3066
941-351-9597
Fax: 941-351-4673 www.fawema.com
Manufacturer, importer and exporter of bag packaging systems including formers, fillers and closers; also, control modules, checkweighers and hot melt glue applicators
Customer Service Manager: Frank Potvin
Estimated Sales: $1-2.5 Million
Number Employees: 1-4
Square Footage: 20000
Parent Co: Fawema Maschinenfabrik GmbH
Brands:
  Allen Bradley
  Electro Cam
  Emerson
  Hi-Speed
  Nordson

22512 Fax Foods
1205 Activity Dr
Vista, CA 92081-8510
760-599-6030
Fax: 760-599-6040
Manufacturer and exporter of plastic food replica.
Owner: Judy Preston
Square Footage: 60000
Parent Co: Fax Plastics
Type of Packaging: Food Service
Brands:
  Foodart By Francesco
  Replikale

22513 Fay Paper Products
124 Washington St # 101
Foxboro, MA 02035-1368
781-769-4620
Fax: 781-769-8522 800-765-4620
Manufacturer and exporter of cash register rolls and stationery items
President: Gregory Steele
VP: Peter Steele
Estimated Sales: $5-10 Million
Number Employees: 20-49
Brands:
  Fay-Vo-Rite

22514 Feather Duster Corporation
10 Park St
Amsterdam, NY 12010-4214
518-842-3690
Fax: 518-842-3754 800-967-8659
Manufacturer, importer and exporter of dusters including ostrich feather and wool; also, applicator pads

President and CFO: Neil Stravitz
Quality Control: Susan Spagnola
Plant Manager: Susan Spagnola
Estimated Sales: Below $5 Million
Number Employees: 5-9
Square Footage: 20000

22515 Fedco Systems
500 S Vandemark Road
Sidney, OH 45365-8991
813-920-6641
Fax: 813-920-3564 800-922-6641
Rollerbar mixer

22516 Federal Engineered Systems
141 Ben Burton Cir
Bogart, GA 30622-1791
706-543-8101
Fax: 706-543-7934
Owner: Micheal Van Drunen
mvandurnen@federalengineeredsystems.com
Estimated Sales: Less Than $500,000
Number Employees: 1-4

22517 Federal Heath Sign Co LLC
3609 Ocean Ranch Blvd # 204
Suite #204
Oceanside, CA 92056-8601
760-901-7447
Fax: 760-727-2279 800-527-9495
marketing@federalheath.com
www.federalheath.com
Manufacturer and exporter of custom interior and exterior signs including plastic and metal; also, installation and maintenance available
CEO: Kevin Stotmeister
kstotmeister@fedsign.com
Account Executive: Randy Cearlock
Estimated Sales: $1-2.5 Million
Number Employees: 100-249
Square Footage: 300000
Parent Co: Federal Signal Corporation

22518 Federal Industries
215 Federal Ave
Belleville, WI 53508-9201
608-424-3331
Fax: 608-424-3234 800-356-4206
geninfo@federalind.com www.federalind.com
Refrigerated and nonrefrigerated display cases for bakery and deli products
National Sales Manager (Food Service): Bill Rice
Plant Manager: Gary Hamburg
Estimated Sales: $20-50 Million
Number Employees: 50-99
Parent Co: Standex International Corporation

22519 Federal Industries Inc
2550 Niagara Ln N
Minneapolis, MN 55447-8761
763-476-1500
Fax: 763-476-8155 800-523-9033
chemtran@aol.com www.chem-tran.com
Shipping systems for hazardous materials
President: Chuck Goldman
chemtran@aol.com
Estimated Sales: $1-2.5 000,000
Number Employees: 1-4

22520 Federal Label Systems
7920 Barnwell Avenue
Elmhurst, NY 11373-3727
718-899-2233
Fax: 718-397-1921 800-238-0015
Product merchandising tags, pressure sensitive labels, on-product coupons, display and card packaging
President: Alan Rothchild
Co-Chairman: Herbert Rothchild
Executive VP: Paul Rothchild
Estimated Sales: $10-20 Million
Number Employees: 100-249
Square Footage: 90000
Parent Co: Rothchild Printing Group

22521 Federal Machine Corp
8040 University Blvd
Clive, IA 50325-1118
515-274-1555
Fax: 515-274-9256 800-247-2446
www.vending.com

Manufacturer and exporter of vending machines for snacks, candy, pastries, milk, canned drinks, gum, mints, hot beverages, frozen foods and ice cream; also machine parts (full line vending equipment manufacturing company).
President: Todd Wiggins
twiggins@wittern.com
CFO: Ray Lantz
CEO: F A Wittern Jr
Sales: Gary Bahr
Director Operations: Gary Bahr
Estimated Sales: $5-10 Million
Number Employees: 5-9
Number of Brands: 10
Number of Products: 20
Square Footage: 1400000
Type of Packaging: Food Service, Private Label
Brands:
  Fs1
  Us1

22522 Federal Mfg Co
201 West Walker Street
Milwaukee, WI 53204
414-384-3200
Fax: 414-384-8704 www.federalmfg.com
Designers and Manufacturers of bottle filling and capping systems and specialty products for the Dairy, Juice, Water, Food, and Pharmaceutical Industries.
President: Otis Cobb
CEO: Marjorie Fee
Contact: Gilbert Alba
galba@federalmfg.com
Estimated Sales: $5-10 Million
Number Employees: 50-99
Square Footage: 240000

22523 Federal Sign
135 Dean St
PO Box 1
Providence, RI 02903-1603
401-421-9643
Fax: 401-351-2233 federalsigns@cox.net
www.federalsigns.net
Advertising signs including electric, luminous and billboards.
Manager: Frank Benell
federalsigns@cox.net
VP: William Benell
Estimated Sales: Less Than $500,000
Number Employees: 5-9
Square Footage: 60000
Parent Co: Hub Sign Company

22524 Federal Sign
135 Dean St
Providence, RI 02903-1603
401-421-9643
Fax: 401-351-2233 www.federalsigns.net
Manufacturer, designer and installer of electrical signs
President: Frank Benell Jr
federalsigns@cox.net
VP: William Benell
Estimated Sales: Less Than $500,000
Number Employees: 5-9
Square Footage: 34000
Parent Co: Federal Sign Company

22525 Federal Stamp & Seal Manufacturing Company
2210 Marietta Blvd NW
Atlanta, GA 30318-2020
404-525-6103
Fax: 404-525-3320 800-333-7726
www.fessco.net
Pre-inked and self-inking rubber stamps; also, engraved signs, seals, numbering machines, ink and ink pads
President: Don Bradshaw
fesco@fescogroup.net
Plant Manager: Gary D'Andrea
Purchasing Manager: Mick Mortensen
Number Employees: 20-49

22526 Federated Mills
3620 Tamiami Trl N
Naples, FL 34103-3705
239-659-5450
Fax: 518-734-5805 888-692-6226

Mold inhibitors for mycoban calcium propionate, mycoban sodium propionate, supreme brand dykon (sodium diacetate), potassium sorbate, sorbic acid, sodium citrate, sodium benzoate, xantham gum, citric acid
VP: Douglas Sweet
VP: Doug Sweet
Estimated Sales: Below $5 Million
Number Employees: 1-4

22527 Feed the Party
2055 Nelson Miller Pkwy
Louisville, KY 40223
partyon@feedtheparty.com
feedtheparty.com
Supplier of the finest butcher shop quality meats, including steak, pork, chicken, and lamb.
President & Founder: Matt Kenney
Estimated Sales: $100+ Million
Number Employees: 2-10
Number of Brands: 7
Square Footage: 89000
Type of Packaging: Food Service, Bulk
Brands:
  A. Thomas Meats
  Berkwood Farms
  Big Fork
  Border Springs Farm Lamb
  Joyce Farms
  Shire Gate
  Shuckman's Fish Co. & Smokery, Inc.

22528 Feedback Plus
2222 W Spring Creek Pkwy
#114
Plano, TX 75023
972-661-8989
Fax: 972-661-5414 800-882-7467
www.feedbackplusinc.com
Consulant offering market research
CEO: Vickie Henry
VP Marketing: Bill Waston
Food Service Sales Representative: Kelly Heatly
Contact: Sharon Karlebach
  sharon.karlebach@gofeedback.com
VP of Store Operations: Monica Rattay
Estimated Sales: $2.5-5,000,000
Number Employees: 10-19

22529 Fehlig Brothers Box & Lbr Co
1909 Cole St
St Louis, MO 63106-3506
314-241-6900
Fax: 314-436-0315 fehligbrothers@sbcglobal.net
www.fehligbrotherslumber.com
Custom made wooden crates, boxes and pallets
President: John Oleary
  markf10355@aol.com
Treasurer: Tim O'Leary
Estimated Sales: Below $5 Million
Number Employees: 20-49
Square Footage: 152000

22530 Felco Packaging Specialist
4001 E Baltimore St
Baltimore, MD 21224-1544
410-675-2664
Fax: 410-276-2367 800-673-8488
Manufacturer, importer and exporter of corrugated boxes, tapes, burlap, canvas, pallets, paper products and bags
President: Jeffrey Feldman
  jeff@felcoinc.com
Controller: Sherry Feldman
Estimated Sales: $5 - 10 Million
Number Employees: 10-19
Square Footage: 150000

22531 (HQ)Feldmeier Equipment Inc
6800 Townline Rd
Syracuse, NY 13211-1325
315-454-8608
Fax: 315-454-3701 sstanks@feldmeier.com
www.feldmeier.com
Manufacturer and exporter of heat exchangers, pasteurizers, stainless steel tanks, processing vessels, strainers, and stainless steel ice builders
President: John Feldmeier
CEO: Robert Feldmeier
CFO: Margaret Feldmeier
VP: Robert Feldmeier
Estimated Sales: $40 Million
Number Employees: 100-249

Other Locations:
  Feldmeier Equipment
  Little Falls NY
  Feldmeier Equipment
  Reno NV
  Feldmeier Equipment
  Cedar Falls IA
Brands:
  Across-The-Line
  Feldmeier
  Torpedo

22532 Felins USA Inc
8306 W Parkland Ct
Milwaukee, WI 53223-3832
414-355-7747
Fax: 414-355-7559 800-343-5667
sales@felins.com www.felins.com
Manufacturer, importer and exporter of manual and automatic bundling, tying, wrapping, strapping and banding equipment; also, automated banding systems for multi-packing food products
Manager: Bruce Bartelt
Owner: James Chisholm
CFO: Ron Kuzia
Marketing: Peter Chapman
Sales: Mark Meyer
Public Relations: Neal Donding
Production: Bruce Lanham
Estimated Sales: $8.5 Million
Number Employees: 20-49
Square Footage: 50000
Brands:
  Flexstrap
  Loop Plus
  Pak Tyer 2000

22533 Felix Storch Inc
770 Garrison Ave
Bronx, NY 10474-5603
718-328-8101
Fax: 718-842-3093 800-932-4267
sales@summitappliance.com
www.summitappliance.com
Manufacturer, importer and exporter of beer taps, wine coolers, ice cream freezers and beverage merchandisers, minibars and coolers
President: Floria Lee
  lee.floria@gmail.com
Vice President of Marketing: Steve Ross
R&D: Phil Yacht
Quality Control: Jeff Musnikow
Sales Director: Stephen Ross
Vice President: Paul Storch
Estimated Sales: $25 Million
Number Employees: 100-249
Square Footage: 140000
Parent Co: Felix Storch
Brands:
  Summit

22534 Fell & Co Intl Inc
3266 Winbrook Dr
Memphis, TN 38116-3644
901-332-6669
Fax: 901-332-6433 800-356-8588
info@fellcoinc.com www.fellcoinc.com
Cocoa and chocolate preparation equipment including batch kneaders, block shavers, conches, enrobing, refiners, cooling equipment and cooling tunnels, cream machines, depositors and nut processing equipment, bean cleaners, roasterswinnowers, liquor grinders, cocoa powder systems, mixer/kneaders, pre-refiners, continuous conches, storage and pumps/piping, moulding machine
President/CEO/CFO: Marc Fell
  fellandcompany@aol.com
Sales Manager: Mike Dunn
Sales/ Operations Manager: Marc Fell
Estimated Sales: $1-2.5 Million
Number Employees: 1-4
Square Footage: 48000

22535 Femc
22201 Aurora Rd
Cleveland, OH 44146-1273
216-663-1208
Fax: 216-663-9337 info@femc.com
www.femc.com
President: Dan Auvil
  dauvil@femc.com
Estimated Sales: $5 - 10 Million
Number Employees: 20-49

22536 Fenco
2210 County A
Three Lakes, WI 54562
715-546-8077
Fax: 715-546-3561
Conveyor components, plastic conveyor belt, and wearstrips
Estimated Sales: Less Than $500,000
Number Employees: 1-4

22537 Fenner Drives
311 W Stiegel St
Manheim, PA 17545-1747
717-665-2421
Fax: 717-665-2649 800-243-3374
info@fennerdrives.com
Industrial transmission conveyor belts
President: Debbie Adler
  d.adler@phillyjcc.com
CEO: Nick Hobson
Marketing Director: Robin Palmer
Sales Director: Craig Harris
Estimated Sales: $50+ Million
Number Employees: 100-249
Type of Packaging: Private Label, Bulk
Brands:
  Orange Belt

22538 Fenner Drives
311 W Stiegel St
Manheim, PA 17545-1747
717-665-2421
Fax: 717-665-2649 800-327-2288
info@fennerdrives.com
Industrial belting, power transmission and motion control components, maintains extensive engineering, development, and testing facilities
President: Debbie Adler
  d.adler@phillyjcc.com
CEO: Nick Hobson
Marketing Director: Robin Palmer
Sales Director: Craig Harris
Estimated Sales: $30 - 50 Million
Number Employees: 100-249
Number of Products: +0
Type of Packaging: Bulk
Brands:
  Clear - Go
  Minikeeper
  Orange - Go
  Powertwist
  Quik - Go
  Red - Go
  Torquekeeper
  Trantorque
  Veelos

22539 Fenner Dunlop Americas Inc
1000 Omega Dr # 1400
Pittsburgh, PA 15205-5001
412-249-0700
Fax: 412-249-0701
www.fennerdunlopamericas.com
Conveyors and elevator belting
President: Cassandra Pan
CEO: David Jones
  david.jones@fennerdunlop.com
Chief Financial Officer: William Mooney
Chief Operating Officer: Mark Hardwick
Estimated Sales: $1 - 5 Million
Number Employees: 250-499
Brands:
  Duratrax

22540 Fenster Consulting Inc
29 Davis Rd
Port Washington, NY 11050-3935
516-944-7108
Fax: 516-944-7953 fred@fensterconsulting.com
www.fensterconsulting.com
Consultant specializing in factory, warehouse and material handling, packaging and storage system design
President: Fred Fenster
  fensterf@fensterconsulting.com
Vice President: Linda Necroto
Sales Director: Jordan Fenster
Purchasing Manager: Sandra Lee
Number Employees: 5-9
Square Footage: 20000

22541 Fenton Art Glass Company
700 Elizabeth St
Williamstown, WV 26187

304-375-6122
Fax: 304-375-7833 800-933-6766
askfenton@fentonartglass.com
www.fentonartglass.com
Manufacturer and exporter of decorative glassware
and lamps
President: George Fenton
CFO: Stan Van Lanqingham
VP: Tom Fenton
R&D: Nancy Fenton
Quality Control: Tom Bobbitt
Sales VP: Scott Fenton
Public Relations: Terry Nutter
Purchasing Director: Mike Fenton
Estimated Sales: $25-30 Million
Number Employees: 250-499
Type of Packaging: Consumer, Bulk
Brands:
　Fenton Art Glass

22542 Ferguson Containers
20 Industrial Rd
Phillipsburg, NJ 08865-4081

908-454-9755
Fax: 908-454-7144 mail@fergusoncontainers.com
www.fergusoncontainers.com
Corrugated boxes and containers
Owner: Stuart Ferguson
　ferguson@silo.com
General Manager: Ed Reichard
Estimated Sales: $5 Million
Number Employees: 20-49
Square Footage: 42000

22543 Ferm-Rite Equipment
PO Box 1233
Woodbridge, CA 95258-1233

209-794-2700
Fax: 209-794-8164
Wine industry bungs
President: Martyn Nastasian
Bookkeeper: Jil Nastasian
Number Employees: 2

22544 Fernholtz Engineering
15471 Victory Boulevard
Van Nuys, CA 91406-6241

818-785-5800
Fax: 818-785-8406
Manufacturer and exporter of mills, sifting and
screening machinery, wet and dry magnetic separa-
tors, mixers, blenders and agitators
President: Vivian Fernholtz
VP: Frank Fernholtz
Estimated Sales: $500,000-$1 Million
Number Employees: 1-4

22545 Fernqvist Labeling Solutions
2544 Leghorn St
Suite C
Mountain View, CA 94043-1614

650-967-3766
Fax: 650-428-1615 800-426-8215
customercare@fernqvist.com www.fernqvist.com
Label and bar code printing systems, labels, thermal
transfer ribbons, dispensers, bar code verifiers, scan-
ners, etc
President: Per Fernqvist
VP: Bill Goodman
Manufacturing Manager: Richard Hernandez
Estimated Sales: Below $5 Million
Number Employees: 1-4
Square Footage: 7000
Brands:
　Fernqvist Prodigy Max

22546 Fernqvist Labeling Solutions
2544 Leghorn St
Mountain View, CA 94043-1614

650-967-3766
Fax: 650-428-1615 800-426-8215
sales@fernqvist.com www.fernqvist.com
Digital and flexo labels provided nationally, thermal
transfer printers, labling software, TT ribbons, and
other labling supplies.
President: Per Fernqvist
Operations/Production Officer: Richard Hernandez
Estimated Sales: $3 - 5 Million
Number Employees: 1-4

22547 Ferrell-Ross
PO Box 50669
Amarillo, TX 79159

806-359-9051
Fax: 806-359-9064 800-299-9051
info@ferrellross.com www.ferrellross.com
Manufacturer and exporter of grinding and flaking
mills for breakfast cereals, spices and snack foods;
also, grain and cereal blenders, grain and seed clean-
ing machinery
President: David Ibach
Vice President: Philip Petrakos
Sales Director: Clay Gerber
Estimated Sales: $10 - 20 Million
Number Employees: 10
Square Footage: 50000
Parent Co: Bluffton Agri Industrial Corporation
Other Locations:
　Ferrell-Ross
　Bluffton IN
Brands:
　Clipper Precision
　Ferrell-Ross

22548 Ferrer Corporation
415 Calle San Claudio
San Juan, PR 00926-4206

787-761-5151
Fax: 787-755-0450
Manufacturer and exporter of interior and exterior
signs including electric, metal, neon and plastic
President: Juan Ferrer Davila
Controller: Jose Vazquez
Sales Manager: Enid Cintron
Number Employees: 50
Square Footage: 80000
Brands:
　Rotulos Ferrer

22549 Ferrite Components Inc
165 Ledge St
Nashua, NH 03060-3061

603-881-5234
Fax: 603-881-5406 info@ferriteinc.com
www.ferriteinc.com
President: Richard Wolfe
CEO: Ron Clark
　ascholder@digcommunications.com
Quality Control: Bill Tabonnu
Estimated Sales: $50 - 100 Million
Number Employees: 5-9

22550 Ferro Corporation
6060 Parkland Blvd
Suite 250
Mayfield Heights, OH 44124

216-875-5600
Fax: 216-875-5627 www.ferro.com
Manufacturer and exporter of printing inks, labels
and label supplies.
Chairman/President/CEO: Peter Thomas
VP/Chief Financial Officer: Ben Schlater
VP/General Counsel/Secretary: Mark Duesenberg
Year Founded: 1919
Estimated Sales: $1,075 Million
Number Employees: 4,846
Parent Co: Ferro Corporation

22551 Festo Corp
395 Moreland Rd
Hauppauge, NY 11788-3900

631-435-0800
Fax: 631-435-8026 800-99F-ESTO
www.festo.com
Offers one of the largest selections of pneumatic
components and controls available from a single
source. Select from over 90 product families, including pneumatic valves, cylinders and controls. Festo
has the engineering expertiseto design and build
President: Hans Zobel
CFO: Sven Doerge
　sven.doerge@us.festo.com
Estimated Sales: $20 - 50 Million
Number Employees: 250-499

22552 Fetco
600 Rose Rd
Lake Zurich, IL 60047-1560

847-719-3000
Fax: 847-719-3001 800-338-2699
info@fetco.com www.fetco.com
Manufacturer, importer and exporter of food service
equipment including coffee carts, tea brewing equip-
ment servers, commissary systems and coffee and
tea equipment
President: Zbigniew Lassota
　zlassota@fetco.com
CFO: Zeel Lasoda
VP: Christopher Nowak
VP of Marketing and Sales: Richard Baggett
Estimated Sales: $10 - 20 Million
Number Employees: 100-249

22553 Fettig Laboratories
900 Godfrey Ave SW
Grand Rapids, MI 49503

616-245-3000
Fax: 616-245-3299 radonman01@aol.com
Laboratory providing nutritional analysis and label-
ing, bacteriological testing, QC/QA program design
and management, shelf life testing, contamina-
tion/adulteration identification and witness service
President: Patricia Fettig
Marketing Director: Gregory Painter
Estimated Sales: $500,000-$1 Million
Number Employees: 5-9

22554 Fetzer Vineyards
12901 Old River Rd
Hopland, CA 95449

707-744-1250
Fax: 707-744-7605 800-846-8637
Fernando.Avalos@fetzer.com www.fetzer.com
Manufacturer and exporter of table wines, barrels
and cork.
Head Operations: Pat Voss
Manager: Tim Nall
Director Winemaking: Dennis Martin
Estimated Sales: $45 Million
Number Employees: 250-499
Number of Brands: 3
Parent Co: Brown-Forman Corporation
Type of Packaging: Consumer, Food Service, Pri-
vate Label, Bulk
Brands:
　Bel Arbors
　Bon Terra
　Fetzer

22555 Fever-Tree Drinks & Mixers
37 West 26th Street
New York, NY 10010

800-263-7054
info@fever-tree.com fever-tree.com
Tonic waters and mixers, including club soda, pre-
mium tonic water, ginger beer, and ginger ale.
CEO: Charles Gibb
VP of Marketing: Amanda Stein
Head of Supply Chain: Sebastian Tondo
Year Founded: 2007
Number Employees: 51-200
Number of Brands: 1
Type of Packaging: Food Service
Brands:
　FEVER-TREE

22556 Fiber Does
1470 N 4th Street
San Jose, CA 95112-4715

408-453-5533
Fax: 408-453-9303
Manufacturer and exporter of fiber optic lighted
signs including indoor, outdoor and window display
CEO: Song Lee
Sales/Customer Service Manager: Rick Perez
Estimated Sales: $3,000,000
Number Employees: 20-50
Brands:
　Fiberpro
　Optickles

22557 Fibercell Packaging LLC
46 Brooklyn St
Portville, NY 14770-9529

716-933-8703
Fax: 716-933-6948 800-545-8546
www.fibercel.com
Bulk packaging
General Manager: Mitch Gray
Sales Administrator: Geoff Buckner
Manager: Bruce Olson
　bolson@fibercel.net
Estimated Sales: $20 - 50 Million
Number Employees: 50-99

22558 Fibergrate Composite Strctrs
5151 Belt Line Rd # 1212
Dallas, TX 75254-6740
972-250-1633
Fax: 972-250-1530 800-527-4043
info@fibergrate.com www.fibergrate.com
Manufacture fiberglass, reinforced plastic, gratings
and products for the food and beverage industry
President: Eric Breiner
ebreiner@fibergrate.com
CFO: Sean Lovison
Operations Manager: Wendell Hollingsworth
Estimated Sales: $10-25 Million
Number Employees: 20-49
Brands:
Chemgrate
Fibergrate
Rigirtex0

22559 Fibergrate Composite Strctrs
5151 Belt Line Rd # 1212
Suite 1212
Dallas, TX 75254-6740
972-250-1633
Fax: 972-250-1530 800-527-4043
www.fibergrate.com
President: Eric Breiner
ebreiner@fibergrate.com
CFO: Travis Kirsch
Quality Control: Ray Blackshear
Number Employees: 20-49

22560 Fiberich Technologies
3280 Gorham Ave Ste 202
St Louis Park, MN 55426
952-920-8054
Fax: 952-920-8056
Pea fiber, vegetable fiber, bean and lentil precooked
whole and powders
President: Edward Schmidt
edward.schmidt@popp.net
Estimated Sales: $1-2.5 000,000
Number Employees: 1-4
Type of Packaging: Bulk

22561 Fiberich Technologies
3280 Gorham Ave
Suite 202
St Louis Park, MN 55426
952-920-8054
Fax: 952-920-8056 fiberichtech@popp.net
Processes and markets peas, beans and lentil based
ingredients
President: Ed Schmidt
Contact: Edward Schmidt
edward.schmidt@popp.net
Type of Packaging: Consumer, Bulk

22562 Fibertech Inc
11744 Blue Bell Rd
Elberfeld, IN 47613-9455
812-983-2642
Fax: 812-983-4953 800-304-4600
www.fibertechinc.net
President: William Scott
Contact: Tabitha Devasier
tdevasier@fibertechinc.net
Estimated Sales: Less Than $500,000
Number Employees: 1-4

22563 Fibertech Inc
11744 Blue Bell Rd
Elberfeld, IN 47613-9455
812-983-2642
Fax: 812-983-4953 800-304-6400
www.fibertechinc.net
Supplies fiber materials used in food industry manu-
facturing
Contact: Tabitha Devasier
tdevasier@fibertechinc.net
Estimated Sales: Less Than $500,000
Number Employees: 1-4

22564 Fibre Containers Inc
15250 Don Julian Rd
City of Industry, CA 91745-1001
626-968-5897
Fax: 626-330-0870 www.fleetwood-fibre.com
Corrugated shipping containers
President: Tony Pietrangelo
Vice President: Mark White
white@fibrecontainers.com
Director Sales: Lloyd Kennedy

Estimated Sales: $20-50 Million
Number Employees: 5-9

22565 Fibre Converters Inc
1 Industrial Park Dr
PO Box 130
Constantine, MI 49042-8735
269-279-1700
jamey.southland@fibreconverters.com
www.fibreconverters.com
Manufacturer and exporter of die cut slip sheets for
replacement of pallets as well as special laminated
or solid fibre paperboard
Owner: Jim Stuck
st@net-link.net
Chairman: David T Stuck
Operations Manager: Stephen Reed
Estimated Sales: $25 Million
Number Employees: 50-99
Square Footage: 160000
Brands:
Fiber-Pul
Fico
Valdor

22566 Fibre Leather Manufacturing Company
686 Belleville Avenue
New Bedford, MA 02745-6093
508-997-4557
Fax: 508-997-7268 800-358-6012
Manufacturer and exporter of latex-impregnated and
coated paper for box coverings; also, base stock for
pressure sensitive tapes and jean label stock.
President: Daniel Finger
fibreleather@earthlink.net
VP: Louis Finger
Production Manager: Ellen Hull
Shipping Manager: Charles Hull
Estimated Sales: $10-20 Million
Number Employees: 50-99
Square Footage: 400000

22567 Fibreform Containers Inc
N115w19255 Edison Dr
Germantown, WI 53022-3092
262-251-1901
Fax: 262-251-1941
customersupport@fibreforminc.com
www.fibreforminc.com
Model pulp protective packaging
President: Edward Gratz
jeffgratz@fibreforminc.com
Sales Exec: Jeff Gratz
Estimated Sales: $20 - 50 Million
Number Employees: 20-49

22568 (HQ)Fiebing Co
421 S 2nd St
Milwaukee, WI 53204-1612
414-271-5011
Fax: 414-271-3769 800-558-1033
custserv@fiebing.com www.fiebing.com
Manufacturer and exporter of soap and
waterproofers
President: Richard Chase
jchase@fiebing.com
R&D: Mansur Abul
VP: Dennis Kendall
Estimated Sales: $10 - 20 Million
Number Employees: 5-9
Square Footage: 140000
Brands:
Fiebing
Kelly
Snow Proof

22569 Fiedler Technology
84 Malmo Court
Units 13-15
Maple, ON L6A 1R4
Canada
905-832-0493
Primary and secondary packaging machinery for
nonstandard packages
President: Edgar Fiedler
Number Employees: 5-9
Square Footage: 12000

22570 Field Manufacturing Corporation
2535 Maricopa St.
Torrance, CA 90503
310-781-9292
Fax: 310-781-9386 www.fieldmfg.com

Plastic molded store fixtures
President: Steven Fields
Vice President: Mary McWilliams
Research & Development: Omar Balley
Contact: Katarina Field
katarina.field@norcomfg.com
Estimated Sales: $5 - 10 Million
Number Employees: 100

22571 Fife Corp
222 W Memorial Rd
Oklahoma City, OK 73114-2317
405-755-1600
Fax: 405-755-8425 800-639-3433
fife@fife.com www.maxcessintl.com
Automatic process controls
President: Terry Brookes
CFO: Merlyn Devries
mdevries@fife.com
CEO: Bruce Ryan
CEO: Bruce E Ryan
Estimated Sales: $20 - 50 Million
Number Employees: 100-249

22572 Filet Menu
P.O. Box 352161
Los Angeles, CA 90035
310-202-8000
Fax: 310-559-0917
Manufacturer and designer of menus, point of pur-
chase displays, table cards, dinner napkins, place
mats, etc
Owner: Michael Le Vine
Marketing: Marcia Petersen
Estimated Sales: $2.5-5,000,000
Number Employees: 20-49
Type of Packaging: Food Service

22573 Filler Specialties
440 100th Ave
Zeeland, MI 49464-2061
616-772-9235
Fax: 616-772-4544 filler@filler-specialties.com
www.filler-specialties.com
Manufacturer and exporter of capping and closing
equipment, conveyor systems and fillers and filling
equipment
President: Ron Slagh
rslagh@filler-specialties.com
Sales Manager: Jim Grant
Estimated Sales: $5-10,000,000
Number Employees: 10-19

22574 Filling Equipment Co Inc
1539 130th St
Flushing, NY 11356-2481
718-445-2111
Fax: 718-463-6034 800-247-7127
filling@fillingequipment.com
www.fillingequipment.com
Manufacturer and exporter of packaging equipment,
tables, conveyors, automatic cap tighteners, etc
President: Robert Hampton
Sales: G Hite
Sales: J Popper
Estimated Sales: $1-2.5 Million
Number Employees: 10-19

22575 Fillit
18105 Trans Canada Highway
Kirkland, QC H9J 3Z4
Canada
514-694-2390
Fax: 514-694-6552 rzajko@kalishdti.com
Manufacturer and exporter of conveying, filling,
capping and counting equipment
President/Owner: ý
Production Manager: Richard Zajko
Number Employees: 100-249
Brands:
Fillit
Fillkit
Kapit
Power Fillit
Torquit

22576 Film X
20 Louisa Viens Dr
Dayville, CT 6241
860-779-3403
Fax: 860-779-3406 800-628-6128
Packaging materials including film; also, extrusion
coating and slitting services available

Manager: Michael Quarry
Sr. Account Manager: Peter Hendrickson
Contact: Steve English
  senglish@webindustries.com
General Manager: Jon Pluff
Estimated Sales: $5 - 10 Million
Number Employees: 1-4
Parent Co: Web Industries

22577 Film-Pak Inc
201 S Magnolia St
Crowley, TX 76036-3110
　　　　　　　　817-297-4341
　　Fax: 817-572-7568 800-526-1838
　　　　　www.film-pak.com
Film and plain and printed bags
President: Rossi Callender
Sales Manager: Chris Walters
Manager: Melissa Blyleo
Estimated Sales: $5-10 Million
Number Employees: 20-49
Square Footage: 32000

22578 Filmco Inc
1450 S Chillicothe Rd
Aurora, OH 44202-9264
　　　　　　　　330-562-6111
　　Fax: 330-562-2740 800-545-8457
　　　　　www.linpac.com
Manufacturer and exporter of PVC film
President: Rolland Castellanos
Customer Service: Marianne Martone
General Manager: Richard Pohland
Purchasing Manager: Susan Burkholder
Estimated Sales: $20-50 Million
Number Employees: 50-99
Parent Co: Linpac Plastics Inc.
Brands:
  Britepak
  Crustpak

22579 (HQ)Filmpack Plastic Corporation
266 Ridge Rd
Dayton, NJ 8810
　　　　　　　　732-329-6523
　　　　Fax: 732-329-8543
Plastic translucent polystyrene cold drinking cups
President: Morris Herman
VP: Moric O'Streicher
Estimated Sales: $5-10 Million
Number Employees: 20-49

22580 Filter Equipment Co
1440 State Route 34
Wall Township, NJ 07753-6807
　　　　　　　　732-938-3312
　　Fax: 732-938-3312 800-445-9775
　　　sales@filter-equipment.com
　　　www.filter-equipment.com
Filtration equipment
Owner: Herman Groh
  herman@filter-equipment.com
VP: Scott Groh
Estimated Sales: $5 - 10 000,000
Number Employees: 10-19

22581 Filter Products
8314 Tiogawoods Dr
Sacramento, CA 95828
　　　　　　　　916-689-2328
　　　　Fax: 916-689-1035
Wine industry filtration equipment
President: Paris Rivera
Estimated Sales: $5 - 10 000,000
Number Employees: 20-49

22582 Filtercarb LLC/ Filtercorp
9805 NE 116th St
Suite A-200
Kirkland, WA 98034-4245
　　　　　　　　425-820-4850
　　Fax: 425-820-2816 800-473-4526
　　rbernard@filtercorp.com www.filtercorp.com
President: Robin Bernard
Estimated Sales: $5-10 Million
Number Employees: 10-19

22583 Filtercold Corporation
1840 E University Drive
Suite 2
Tempe, AZ 85281-7760
　　　　　　　　800-442-2941
Tea and coffee industry filtration equipment

22584 (HQ)Filtercorp
2585 S Sarah Street
Fresno, CA 93706-5034
　　　　　　　　559-495-3140
　　Fax: 559-495-3145 800-473-4526
　　　　　www.filtercorp.com
Manufacturer, importer and exporter of nonwoven cellulose fiber filter pads used for cooking fats and oils
President: Don Eskes
  sales@filtercorp.com
Estimated Sales: $500,000-$1 Million
Number Employees: 4
Square Footage: 24000
Brands:
  Supersorb
  Unifit

22585 Filtration Solutions
4361 Charlotte Hwy # 301
Suite 301
Lake Wylie, SC 29710-7063
　　　　　　　　803-831-8379
　　Fax: 803-931-8476 800-598-1897
　　sales@filtrationsolutions.com
　　www.filtrationsolutions.com
Filtration products and systems.
President: Billie Wells
  billie@filtrtionsolutions.com
Office Manager: Tamara Hartman
Engineerig Consultant: Larry Seitz
Sales Representative: April Sadler
Sales Representative: Pete Dawes
Customer Service Representative: Robbie Putnam
Number Employees: 5-9

22586 Filtration Systems
10304 NW 50th St
Sunrise, FL 33351-8007
　　　　　　　　954-572-2700
　　Fax: 954-572-3401 service@filtsys.com
　　　　www.filtrationsystems.com
Liquid filters, pressure vessels and filter media
President: Sidney Goldman
VP: Michael Goldman
Contact: Michael Goldman
  mgoldman@filtsys.com
Estimated Sales: $2.5-5 Million
Number Employees: 10-19
Parent Co: Mechanical Manufacturing Corporation

22587 Filtration Systems Prods Inc
8506 Herrington Ct
Pevely, MO 63070-1601
　　　　　　　　314-721-2888
　　Fax: 314-721-4519 800-444-4720
　　info@fsptbm.com www.fsptbm.com
OEM filter products including cartridges, bags, paper rolls, pressure plates, HVAC and frame sheets.
Vice President: David Harrell
  dharrell@fsptbm.com
VP: David Harrell
Research & Development: Andy Burns
Sales Director: Dave Kassabaum
Production: Russell Brown
Estimated Sales: $5 - 10 Million
Number Employees: 20-49
Square Footage: 100000

22588 Filtrine Manufacturing
15 Kit St
Keene, NH 03431-5911
　　　　　　　　603-352-5500
　　Fax: 603-352-0330 800-930-3367
　　　　　www.filtrine.com
Water filtration systems and ingredient water coolers for baked goods, confections, brewing, etc
Chairman: John Hansel
President: Peter Hansel
Sales: Philip Tussing
IT: David Hansel
  dhansel@filtrine.com
Estimated Sales: $10 - 20 Million
Number Employees: 50-99
Square Footage: 500000
Brands:
  Filtrine
  Larco
  Steri-Flo
  Taste Master

22589 Final Filtration
139 Columbia Dr.
Williamsville, NY 14221
　　　　　　　　716-568-8080
　　Fax: 716-568-8079 800-454-2357
　　info@cleanerpools.net www.cleanerpools.net
Filtration for wine and beverages
President: David Privitera
Estimated Sales: $500,000 - $1 Million
Number Employees: 5-9

22590 Fine Cocoa Products
224 48th St
Brooklyn, NY 11220-1012
　　　　　　　　201-244-9210
　　Fax: 201-244-8555 info@cocoasupply.com
　　　　　www.cocoasupply.com
Importers and distributors of conventional, organic, and kosher cocoa and other ingredients. Some of their products include Cocoa Powders, Cacao Nibs & Beans, Cocoa Butter, Cocoa Liquor/Mass, Chocolate Couvertures and more.
Estimated Sales: Less Than $500,000
Number Employees: 2 - 10
Type of Packaging: Consumer, Food Service, Private Label, Bulk
Brands:
  Bergenfield Cocoa
  Cafiesa
  Doncella Chocolates
  Eve's Organic Cocoa

22591 Fine Foods Intl
9907 Baptist Church Rd
St Louis, MO 63123-4903
　　　　　　　　314-842-4473
　　Fax: 314-843-8846 ffinylp@aol.com
　　　　　www.dek.de
Tea and coffee industry bags (brick packs), coffee and cappuccino mixes
Manager: Carole Garnett
  cagarnett1@aol.com
VP: Keith Sheller
Operations: Carole Garnett
Estimated Sales: Less Than $500,000
Number Employees: 1-4
Type of Packaging: Bulk

22592 Fine Woods Manufacturing
2413 East Jones
Phoenix, AZ 85040
　　　　　　　　602-258-3868
　　Fax: 602-258-3868 800-279-2871
　　info@finewoodsmfg.com
　　　www.finewoodsmfg.com
Store fixtures including steel, wood and laminate cabinet displays
President: Dennis Thomas
Estimated Sales: $5 - 10,000,000
Number Employees: 20-49

22593 Fingerlakes Construction Co
10269 Old Route 31
Clyde, NY 14433-9742
　　　　　　　　315-923-7777
　　Fax: 315-923-9158 800-328-3522
　　　www.fingerlakesconstruction.com
Winery construction
President: Rex Brigham
  rbrigham@fingerlakesconstruction.com
Estimated Sales: $50-100 Million
Number Employees: 50-99

22594 (HQ)Finlays
10 Blackstone Valley Place
Lincoln, RI 02865
　　　　　　　　401-333-3300
　　　　　　　　800-288-6272
　　americas@finlays.net www.finlays.net
Roaster and extractor of gourmet coffee and tea; also, coffee extracts, syrups, concentrates, iced cappuccino, iced coffee, espresso and smoothies available; services include retail, distributor, OCS, food service and foodingredients
Managing Director: Guy Chambers
Finance Director: Julian Rutherford
Technical Director: Wolfgang Tosch
Year Founded: 1895
Number Employees: 100-249
Square Footage: 180000
Parent Co: Swire
Type of Packaging: Consumer, Food Service, Private Label

Brands:
Autocrat
Eclipse
Newport Coffee Traders

22595 Finn & Son's Metal Spinning Specialists
PO Box 72
South Lebanon, OH 45065-0072

513-494-2898
Fax: 513-494-2885

Metal spun professional bowls and pans
Estimated Sales: $500,000-$1,000,000
Number Employees: 3
Square Footage: 5000

22596 Finn Industries
1921 S Business Pkwy
Ontario, CA 91761

909-930-1500
Fax: 909-930-1510

PVC containers, folding cartons and rigid boxes
President: William Finn
Contact: Wes Biel
wbiel@finnindustriesinc.com
Estimated Sales: $5-10,000,000
Number Employees: 20-49

22597 Fiore Di Pasta
4776 E Jensen Ave
Fresno, CA 93725-1704

559-457-0431
Fax: 559-457-0164 info@fioredipasta.com
www.fioredipasta.com

Fresh and frozen organic pastas, sauces, and entrees
Owner: Shanaz Ahmed
ahmed.sarah81@gmail.com
Chief Operating Officer: Benedetta Primavera
Vice President: Anthony Primavera
Purchasing Director: John Day
Number Employees: 20-49
Square Footage: 120000

22598 Fioriware
333 Market Street
Zanesville, OH 43701-3429

740-454-7400
Fax: 740-454-7790

Flatware
President: Howard Peller
Estimated Sales: $.5 - 1 million
Number Employees: 10
Brands:
Fioriware

22599 Fire & Flavor
375 Commerce Blvd
Athens, GA 30606-0825

706-369-9466
Fax: 706-369-9468 866-728-8332
info@fireandflavor.com www.fireandflavor.com

Grilling planks, grilling papers, brine mixes, rubs & sals, skewers & spice
CEO: Genevieve Knox
CFO: Davis Knox
Contact: George Carlton
george@fireandflavor.com
Estimated Sales: Less Than $500,000
Number Employees: 1-4

22600 Fire Protection Industries
1765 Woodhaven Dr
Bensalem, PA 19020-7107

215-245-1830
Fax: 215-245-8819 ausmfpi@cswebmail.com

Fire sprinkler systems; installation available
President: Aus Marburger
Sales Manager: Galen Young
Contact: David Herron
david_herron@thebluebook.com
Estimated Sales: $5-10 Million
Number Employees: 100-249
Parent Co: Williard Company

22601 Firebird Artisan Mills
500 North St W
Harvey, ND 58341-1012

701-324-4330
Fax: 701-324-4334 www.firebirdmills.com

Manufactuer of gluten free flour and mixes; custom blending available.
President Sales & Procurement: Chris Cairo
Plant Manager: Don Franke

Number Employees: 20-49
Parent Co: Agspring LLC
Type of Packaging: Consumer, Food Service, Private Label, Bulk

22602 (HQ)Firematic Sprinkler Devices
900 Boston Turnpike
Shrewsbury, MA 1545

508-845-2121
Fax: 508-842-3523 800-225-7288

Manufacturer and exporter of fire protection devices and control valves
Sales Manager: Greta Heath
Estimated Sales: $10-20 Million
Number Employees: 20-49

22603 Firl Industries Inc
321 W Scott St
Fond Du Lac, WI 54937-2121

920-921-6942
Fax: 920-921-7329 800-558-4890
info@firlindustries.com www.firlindustries.com

Manufacturer and exporter of doors and accessories including vinyl strip-traffic.
President: John M Buser
Estimated Sales: Less Than $500,000
Number Employees: 10-19
Brands:
Roll-Up

22604 Firmenich Inc.
250 Plainsboro Rd.
Plainsboro, NJ 08536

609-452-1000
Fax: 609-520-9780 800-257-9591
www.firmenich.com

Flavors and fragrances.
Chairman: Patrick Firmenich
CEO: Gilbert Ghostine
CFO: Benoit Fouilland
General Counsel/Secretary: Jane Sinclair
Chief Research Officer: Dr. Sarah Reisinger
COO: Eric Nicolas
Chief Supply Chain Officer: Boet Brinkgreve
Year Founded: 1895
Estimated Sales: $4 Billion
Number Employees: 10,000
Other Locations:
Firmenich Chemical Plant
Newark NJ
Fermenich Citrus Center
Safety Harbor FL
Corporate Office
Princeton NJ
Corporate Office
New York NY
Corporate Office
Golden Valley MN
Corporate Office
New Ulm MN
Corporate Office
Anaheim CA
Corporate Office
Newark NJ
Corporate Office
Lakeland FL
Corporate Office
St. Louis MO
Corporate Office
Los Angeles CA
Corporate Office
Calhoun MI
Corporate Office
Cherokee GA

22605 First Bank of Highland P
633 Skokie Blvd
3rd Floor
Northbrook, IL 60062-2871

847-272-1300
Fax: 847-562-2000 www.firstbankhp.com

Consultant specializing in market research, strategic planning, direct marketing and point of sale merchandising; manufacturer of food display magnetic base counter signs
Chief Executive Officer: Randy L. Green
Estimated Sales: $.5 - 1 million
Number Employees: 1-4
Square Footage: 3200

22606 First Choice Sign & Lighting
610 Rock Springs Rd
Escondido, CA 92025-1623

760-746-5069
Fax: 760-746-5393 800-659-0629

Neon lighting, channel letters and architectural and electrical monument signs
Owner: Noel Johnson
Manager: Robby Seeds
Estimated Sales: Less than $500,000
Number Employees: 1-4

22607 First DataBank
1111 Bayhill Dr # 350
San Bruno, CA 94066-3056

650-827-4555
Fax: 650-588-6867 800-633-3453
cs@firstdatabank.com www.firstdatabank.com

Software programs for analyzing diets, menus, formulations and individual food items for nutrient content
President: Joe Hirshman
VP Sales/Marketing: Jim Wilson
Sales Representative: Michele O'Reilly-Kim
Contact: Ron Ross
rross@fdbhealth.com
Production Manager: Judy Lichtman
Estimated Sales: $20 - 50 Million
Number Employees: 100-249
Parent Co: Hearst Corporation/First Data Bank
Brands:
Nutritionist Iv

22608 First Midwest of Iowa Corporation
616 10th Street
Des Moines, IA 50309-2621

515-243-0768
Fax: 515-243-8103 800-247-8411

Multi-wall paper bags
Estimated Sales: $2.5-5 Million
Number Employees: 50-99
Square Footage: 110000

22609 First Plastics Co Inc
22 Jytek Rd
Leominster, MA 01453-5966

978-840-6908
Fax: 978-840-6908 ed@firstplastics.com

Plastic restaurant supplies including cake keepers, round platters and salad tongs
Owner: Ed Mazzaferro
CEO: Mary Anne Taylor
Office Manager: Lisa Butler
Estimated Sales: Below $5 Million
Number Employees: 50-99
Square Footage: 120000
Parent Co: Art Plastics Manufacturing Corporation
Type of Packaging: Consumer
Brands:
Handy-Home Helpers

22610 First Source LLC
3612 LA Grange Pkwy
Toano, VA 23168-9347

757-566-5360
Fax: 757-566-5379 800-296-0273
www.wythewill.com

Distributor of specialty foods and fine confections across the US
President: Keith McDaniel
Owner: John McCurry
CFO & VP Finance: Rod Hogan
VP: Belton Joyner
Director of Sales & Marketing: David Mastricola
Director of Human Resources: Lisa Weakland
Operations Manager: Bill Hall
Purchasing Manager: Nanette Ross
Estimated Sales: $8.9 Million
Number Employees: 50-99
Square Footage: 200000
Type of Packaging: Consumer, Bulk

22611 Fischbein LLC
151 Walker Rd
Statesville, NC 28625-2535

704-838-4600
Fax: 704-872-3303 sales@fischbein.com
www.fischbein.com

Manufacturer and exporter of bag closing equipment including bag closing, sealing and flexible material handling

President: Craig Blaske
cblaske@fischbein.com
VP of Sales/Marketing: Lee Thompson
Manager: Mike Hersey
VP Sales/Marketing: Sean O'Flynn
Sales Development Manager: Tom Conroy
Operations Manager: Lynn McDonald
Purchasing Manager: Curt Poppe
Estimated Sales: $5,000,000
Number Employees: 100-249
Number of Brands: 3
Number of Products: 21
Square Footage: 56000
Parent Co: AXIA
Brands:
   Fischbein
   Inglett
   Saxon

22612 Fischer Paper Products Inc
179 Ida Ave
Antioch, IL 60002-1838
847-395-6060
Fax: 847-395-8619 800-323-9093
bags@fischerpaperproducts.com
www.fischerpaperproducts.com
Specialty paper bags for foodservice, prescription, merchandise and industrial applications.
President: Josh Fischer
jfischer@fischerpaperproducts.com
Vice President: William Fischer
VP Sales: William Fischer
Estimated Sales: $10-15 Million
Number Employees: 50-99
Square Footage: 140000
Type of Packaging: Food Service

22613 Fish Oven & Equipment Co
120 Kent Ave
PO Box 875
Wauconda, IL 60084-2441
847-526-8686
Fax: 847-526-7447 877-526-8720
info@fishoven.com www.fishoven.com
Manufacturer and exporter of mechanical revolving tray, rotating rack, and woodburning ovens for baking, roasting, supermarket, food service and institutions.
President: James M Campbell III
j.campbell@browardschools.com
Sales Manager: Sandra Bradley
Estimated Sales: $2.5-5 Million
Number Employees: 20-49
Square Footage: 160000
Parent Co: Campbell International

22614 Fisher Manufacturing Company
1900 South O Street
PO Box 60
Tulare, CA 93274
559-685-5200
Fax: 800-832-8238 800-421-6162
info1@fisher-mfg.com www.fisher-mfg.com
Manufacturer and exporter of stainless steel faucets, spray washers and water stations
President: Ray Fisher Jr
Quality Control: Delbert Poole
CFO: Rudy Fernandes
Contact: Michael Emoff
michael.emoff@outtathebox.com
Estimated Sales: $10 - 20 Million
Number Employees: 50-99
Type of Packaging: Food Service

22615 Fisher Scientific Company
2000 Park Lane Dr
Pittsburgh, PA 15275-1104
412-490-8300
Fax: 412-490-8759 www.fishersci.com
Manufacturer and exporter of food grade laboratory chemicals
Contact: Lawrence Crooks
larry.cook@fishersci.com
Estimated Sales: $50-100 Million
Number Employees: 500-999
Parent Co: Fisher Scientific International

22616 Fisher Scientific Company
2844 Soquel Ave
Santa Cruz, CA 95062-1411
831-425-7240
Fax: 800-926-1166 800-766-7000
www.fisherscientific.com
Wine industry laboratory equipment

Owner: William Fisher
Estimated Sales: $.5 - 1 million
Number Employees: 1-4

22617 Fishers Investment
8950 Rossash Road
Cincinnati, OH 45236-1210
513-731-3400
Fax: 513-731-8113 800-833-5916
Manufacturer and exporter of cleaning equipment and supplies including glass cleaners, hand soap, dishwashing and washing compounds
Number Employees: 10
Type of Packaging: Food Service, Private Label

22618 Fishmore
1231 East New Haven Avenue
PO Box 24018
Melbourne, FL 32901
321-723-4751
Fax: 321-726-0939
Manufacturer, exporter and importer of custom fish processing equipment including automatic scaling, heading and gutting machines, glazers, conveyors, cutting tables etc
President: Al Sebastian
VP: Tim Cojocari
Estimated Sales: $300,000-500,000
Number Employees: 4
Square Footage: 12000
Brands:
   Simor

22619 Fiskars Brands Inc.
PO Box 320
Baldwinsville, NY 13027-0320
315-635-9911
Fax: 315-635-1089 consumeraffairs@fiskars.com
www.fiskars.com
Manufacturer and exporter of casual resin and aluminum furniture for restaurants and cafes; also, clocks, plaques and wall mirrors
President: Ray Carrock
R&D: Melisa Rader
CFO: Michael Read
Quality Control: Tom Norgrack
Number Employees: 250-499

22620 Fiske Brothers RefiningCo
129 Lockwood St
Newark, NJ 07105-4782
973-589-9150
Fax: 973-589-4432 800-733-4755
www.lubriplate.com
USDA H-1/H-2/FDA lubricants for use in food and beverage processing, petroleum-based and synthetic lubricants
President: Richard McCouskey
CEO: Richard T Mccluskey
richardm@lubriplate.com
CEO: Richard T Mc Cluskey
Sales/Marketing: James Girarg
Estimated Sales: $20,000,000 - $49,999,999
Number Employees: 50-99
Brands:
   Lubriplate

22621 Fitec International Inc
3525 Ridge Meadow Pkwy # 200
Suite 200
Memphis, TN 38115-4081
901-366-9144
Fax: 901-366-9446 800-332-6387
www.castnets.com
Manufacturer, importer and exporter of cotton and nylon mesh bags; also, netting, twine and rope
President: Mark Hall
hall@castnets.com
Sales: Mark Hall
Estimated Sales: $5 - 10 Million
Number Employees: 5-9
Type of Packaging: Bulk

22622 Fittings Inc
3300 Fisher Ave
Fort Worth, TX 76111-4506
817-332-3300
Fax: 817-332-5102 800-473-3301
sales@fitandcp.com
Stainless steel fittings and cold plates for premix and postmix dispensing equipment

Owner: Mark Gannon
mark@fitandcp.com
Partner: Mark Gannon
mark@fitandcp.com
Estimated Sales: $5-10 000,000
Number Employees: 50-99

22623 Fitzpatrick Brothers
10700 88th Ave
Pleasant Prairie, WI 53158
773-722-3100
Fax: 773-722-5133 800-233-8064
boconnor@oldsfitz.com
Manufacturer and exporter of scouring powders, cleansers and detergents
General Manager/VP: Odie Ramien
VP: William O'Connor
VP: Tim McAvoy
Plant Manager: Vic Luburich
Estimated Sales: $.5 - 1 million
Number Employees: 1-4
Parent Co: Olds Products Company
Brands:
   Babo
   Kitchen Klenzer
   Old Dutch
   Tip Top

22624 Fitzpatrick Co
832 N Industrial Dr
Elmhurst, IL 60126-1179
630-592-4425
Fax: 630-530-0832 info@fitzmill.com
www.fitzmill.com
Manufacturer and exporter of grinder and hammer mills, fluid bed dryers, roll compactors and continuous mixers
President: Scott Patterson
Quality Control: Jose Molimar
CFO: Gary Minta
R&D: Scott Waemmnerstrun
Director Development/Marketing: Scott Wennerstrum
Manager, Sales: Tom Kendrick
Plant Manager: Al Cedno
Estimated Sales: $20 - 50 Million
Number Employees: 100-249
Square Footage: 150000
Brands:
   Chilsonator
   Fitzmill
   Guiloriver
   Malaxator

22625 Fitzpatrick Container Company
6923 Schantz Rd.
North Wales, PA 19454
215-699-3515
Fax: 215-699-7603 www.fitzbox.com
Corrugated containers and point of purchase displays
President: Thomas J Shallow Jr
VP: Thomas Shallow
Estimated Sales: $2.5-5 Million
Number Employees: 50-99

22626 Five Continents
P.O. Box 2134
Darien, IL 60561-7134
773-927-0100
Fax: 773-927-5113
Marketing Manager: Marilyn Mara
Estimated Sales: $30 - 35 Million
Number Employees: 100-250

22627 Five-M Plastics Company
178 N State Street
Allentown, PA 18106
610-628-4291
Fax: 610-395-7336
Manufacturer and installation, indoor/outdoor signs and displays
Owner: John Chapman
Sales Manager: Phil George
Estimated Sales: $500,000-$1 Million
Number Employees: 9

22628 Fixtur World
1555 Interstate Dr
Cookeville, TN 38501-4124
931-528-7259
Fax: 931-528-9214 800-634-9887
www.fixturworld.com

Manufacturer and exporter of wooden and stainless steel furniture including stands, benches, booths, chairs, cushions, pads, counters/tabletops and hot food tables; custom fabrications available
President: Randy Dyer
rdyer@fixturworld.com
Sales Director: Bobby Hull
General Manager: Al Paker
Estimated Sales: $10-20 Million
Number Employees: 100-249
Square Footage: 240000

22629 Fixtures Furniture
4121 Rushton Street
Florence, AL 35630
855-321-4999
Fax: 800-831-9821 www.izzyplus.com
Tables, stools and benches
Founder/CEO: Chuck Saylor
Estimated Sales: $2.5 - 5 Million
Number Employees: 50
Parent Co: JSJ Corp.
Brands:
Albi
Astro
Baby Bola
Bola
D Chair
Encore
Jazz
Ole
Romo

22630 Flair Electronics
212 Mercury Cir
Pomona, CA 91768-3212
626-963-6077
Fax: 626-335-2080 800-532-3492
www.flairsecurity.com
Glass break detectors, water sensors and door annunciators and contacts
Estimated Sales: $1 - 2.5 Million
Number Employees: 10-19
Type of Packaging: Bulk

22631 Flair Flexible Packaging Corp
2605 S Lakeland Dr
Appleton, WI 54915-4193
920-574-3121
Fax: 920-574-3122 www.flairpackaging.com
Flair Flexible Packaging is a fully integrated packaging solutions company providing complete in-house services within the United States and Canada since 1992. Product line includes printing and manufacturing of rolls and bags:multilayer lamination; dry lamination; extrusion lamination and tandem extrusion lamination.
Director/Operations: Cheryl Miller Balster
cheryl@flairpackaging.com
Number Employees: 50-99
Type of Packaging: Consumer

22632 Flakice Corporation
6920 Seaway Blvd
Everett, WA 98203
425-347-6100
Fax: 425-446-5116 800-654-4630
www.fluke.com
Manufacturer and exporter of fluid chillers and industrial ice machines
President: Antoine Hajjar
Vice President: Robert Butler
Chairman: William Adelman
Number Employees: 25
Square Footage: 50000
Brands:
Flakice
Instant-Ice
Liquid Freeze

22633 Flambeau Inc
100 Grace Dr
Weldon, NC 27890-1200
252-536-2171
Fax: 252-536-2201 800-344-5716
info@flambeau.com www.flambeau.com
Plastic blow molded and injection molded packaging
Plant Manager: David Burke
Estimated Sales: $1 - 5 Million
Number Employees: 100-249
Square Footage: 5600000

22634 Flame Gard
1890 Swarthmore Avenue
PO Box 2020
Lakewood, NJ 08701
800-526-3694
Fax: 732-364-8110 sales@flamegard.com
www.flamegard.com
Manufacturer and exporter of UL classified and commercial grease extracting filters, baffles for kitchen exhaust hoods and grease containment products
President: Lawrence Capalbo
CFO: Gary Barros
VP: Gary Barros
Estimated Sales: Below $5 Million
Number Employees: 20-49
Square Footage: 48000
Parent Co: Component Hardware Group, Inc.
Brands:
Flame Gard
Flame Gard Iii

22635 Flamingo Food Service Products
3095 E 11th Ave
Hialeah, FL 33013
305-691-4641
Fax: 305-696-7342 800-432-8269
info@flamingopaper.com
www.flamingopaper.com
Manufacturer and exporter of paper napkins
President: Tonny Arias
Operations Manager: Evelyn Hernandez
Estimated Sales: $1 - 5 Million
Number Employees: 10-19
Type of Packaging: Consumer, Food Service

22636 Flanders Corp
531 Flanders Filter Rd
Washington, NC 27889-7805
252-946-8081
Fax: 252-946-3425 800-637-2803
customerservice@flanderscorp.com
www.flanderscorp.com
Air filters for heating, air conditioning and ventilation systems
President: John Oakley
joakley@flanderscorp.com
Chief Executive Officer: Harry L. Smith, Jr.
SVP: Charlie Kwiatkowski
Senior Vice President of Sales: Travis Stephenson
Number Employees: 1000-4999

22637 FlashBake Ovens Food Service
47817 Fremont Boulevard
Fremont, CA 94538-6506
510-498-4200
Fax: 510-498-4224 800-843-6836
Cooking and heating equipment including visible light wave ovens
Director Sales/Marketing: Nora Romo
VP Sales: Rick Schoenberg
Estimated Sales: $300,000-500,000
Number Employees: 1-4
Parent Co: Quadlux

22638 Flashfold Carton Inc
1140 Hayden St
Fort Wayne, IN 46803-2040
260-423-9431
Fax: 260-423-4351
Folding cartons
Contact: Ralph Clanton
rclanton@gppkg.com
Estimated Sales: $20-50 Million
Number Employees: 100-249

22639 Flat Plate Inc
2161 Pennsylvania Ave
York, PA 17404-1793
717-767-9060
Fax: 717-767-9160 888-854-2500
www.flatplate.com
Manufacturer and exporter of brazed plate heat exchangers
President: Steven Wand
CEO: Charles Schmidt
CFO: Mike Losties
Quality Control: Brian Emery
R&D: Brian Emery
Marketing Head: Steve Wand
Estimated Sales: Less Than $500,000
Number Employees: 1-4

22640 Flatten-O-Matic: Universal Concepts
1147 SW 1st Way
Deerfield Beach, FL 33441-6640
954-327-0194
Fax: 954-792-4502 flattenomatic@aol.com

22641 Flavor Burst
499 Commerce Dr
Danville, IN 46122-7848
317-745-2952
Fax: 317-745-2377 800-264-3528
support@flavorburst.com www.flavorburst.com
Owner: Ernie Gerber
erniegerber@flavorburst.com
Estimated Sales: $5 - 10 Million
Number Employees: 10-19

22642 Flavor Wear
28425 Cole Grade Road
Valley Center, CA 92082-6572
760-749-1332
Fax: 760-749-6164 800-647-8372
www.flavorwear.com
Manufacturer and exporter of uniform accessories including ties, vests, hair accessories, hats, suspenders, bows, shirts and aprons
President: Lawrence Schleif
Owner/CEO: Martin Anthony
Vice President: Annie Smith
Estimated Sales: $2 Million
Number Employees: 23
Number of Brands: 2
Number of Products: 50
Square Footage: 40000
Parent Co: Anthony Enterprises
Type of Packaging: Food Service, Private Label
Brands:
Designs By Anthony
Flavor Classics
Flavor Touch
Flavor Trim
Flavor Wear
Flavor Weave

22643 Flavorseal
35179 Avon Commerce Pkwy
Avon, OH 44011
440-937-3900
Fax: 440-937-3901 877-827-5962
www.flavorseal.com
Supplies shring bags, cooking bags, netting, casings and other accessories
Principal: Ron Mitchell
Contact: Eric Aites
aites.eric@flavorseal.com
Estimated Sales: $1-2.5 Million
Number Employees: 50-99
Square Footage: 133
Parent Co: Carroll Manufacturing and Sales

22644 Flavourtech Americas
9505 N. Congress Ave
Kansas City, MO 64153-1811
816-880-9321
Fax: 707-829-6211 www.flavourtech.com
President: Anthony Dann
Number Employees: 19

22645 Fleet Wood Goldco Wyard
10615 Beaver Dam Rd
Cockeysville, MD 21030-2204
410-785-1934
Fax: 410-785-2909 service@fgwa.com
www.barrywehmiller.com
Manufacturer and exporter of mechanical conveyors and low pressure accumulating conveying and blending systems; also, package line engineering and integration of systems
President: Tom Spangenberg
VP: John Molite
R&D: Tom Spangenberg
Marketing: Dee Yakel
Sales: Michael Tymowezak
Contact: Don Powell
dpowell@bwcontainersystems.com
Operations: Bob Jones
Estimated Sales: $30 Million
Number Employees: 20-49
Square Footage: 50000
Type of Packaging: Consumer, Food Service, Private Label, Bulk

Brands:
Air Flow
Ambec 10
Ambec 10r
Can Jet
Double Density Miniroller
Isometric
Lite Touch
Ring Jet

22646 Fleetwood InternationalPaper
2721 E 45th Street
Vernon, CA 90058-2301
    323-588-7121
Fax: 323-588-9219
Corrugated cartons and displays
Marketing Manager: Clive Costa
Contact: Mike Hinton
hinton@fleetwoodcontainer.com
Estimated Sales: $20-50 Million
Number Employees: 100-249

22647 Fleetwood Systems
1264 La Quinta Dr
Orlando, FL 32809-7724
    407-855-2282
Fax: 407-857-4453 800-432-5433
www.hardwareimagination-tech.com
Material handling systems and components including conveyor belts, chains, vacuums, elevators and lowerators
Sales Applications: Norman Nissen
General Manager: Gerald Janesek
Number Employees: 50-99
Square Footage: 120000
Parent Co: Fleetwood Systems
Type of Packaging: Private Label, Bulk

22648 FleetwoodGoldcoWyard
1305 Lakeview Dr
Romeoville, IL 60446
    630-759-6800
Fax: 630-759-2299 www.fgwa.com
Manufacturer and exporter of depalletizers, brewery pasteurizers, warmers, coolers, complete turnkeys, conveyors and rinsers; also, engineering and installation services available
President: David Brown
CEO: Phil Ostapowicz
R&D: Neil McConnellogue
Chairman of the Board: Robert Chapman
General Sales Manager: Richard Witte
Contact: Ronald Burns
rburns@bwcontainersystems.com
Number Employees: 100-249
Square Footage: 200000
Parent Co: Barry-Wehmiller Co.
Brands:
Ez-Just

22649 Fleming Packaging Corporation
411 Hamilton Blvd # 1518
Peoria, IL 61602-1185
    309-676-7657
Fax: 309-676-8776
Partner: John Fleming
CEO: Ken Lyons
CFO: Paul Wayvon
General Manager: J Willard Briggs
Estimated Sales: $1 - 3 Million
Square Footage: 164000

22650 Flex Pack USA
6321 Emperor Dr
Orlando, FL 32809-5513
    407-857-2883
Fax: 407-857-6970
Packaging/bags
Owner: Mark Dorey
Estimated Sales: $5 - 10 Million
Number Employees: 50-99

22651 Flex Products
640 Dell Rd # 1
Carlstadt, NJ 07072-2202
    201-933-3030
Fax: 201-933-2396 800-526-6273
www.flex-products.com
Manufacturer and exporter of plastic extruded tube containers, closures and caps
President: Ed Friedhoff
Vice President: Bill Rooney
Sales Director: Darby Rosa
Plant Manager: Chris Smolar

Estimated Sales: $5-10 Million
Number Employees: 10-19
Square Footage: 130000
Brands:
Flexshape

22652 Flex Sol Packaging Corp
1531 NW 12th Ave
Pompano Beach, FL 33069-1730
    954-941-6333
Fax: 954-956-4200 877-353-9765
www.flexsolpackaging.com
Custom industrial extruder of flexible packaging film and bag
President: Brian Stevenson
bstevenson@flexsolpackaging.com
Estimated Sales: $43 Million
Number Employees: 250-499
Type of Packaging: Food Service, Bulk
Other Locations:
Flex Sol Packaging
Chicago IL
Flex Sol Packaging
Newark NJ
Flex Sol Packaging
Nashville TN
Flex Sol Packaging
Marshville NC

22653 Flex Sol Packaging Corp
1531 NW 12th Ave
Pompano Beach, FL 33069-1730
    954-941-6333
Fax: 954-956-4200 800-231-4191
www.flexsolpackaging.com
Plastic film and bags
President: Brian Stevenson
bstevenson@flexsolpackaging.com
Number Employees: 250-499

22654 Flex-Hose Co Inc
6801 Crossbow Dr
East Syracuse, NY 13057-1026
    315-437-1611
Fax: 315-437-1903 sales@flexhose.com
www.flexhose.com
Manufacturer and exporter of hoses including Teflon, stainless steel and rubber flexible; also, couplings and expansion joints
President: Philip Argersinger
pbargersinger@flexhose.com
VP: Philip Argersinger
Quality Assurance: Chuck Phillips
Sales Management: Philip Argersinger
Operations Coordinator: Charles Phillips
Purchasing: Bill Wells
Estimated Sales: Below $5 Million
Number Employees: 10-19
Square Footage: 20000
Brands:
Flexzorber
Guideline
Pumpsaver
Te-Flex
Tri-Flex Loop

22655 Flex-O-Glass
1100 N Cicero Ave # 1
Chicago, IL 60651-3213
    773-379-7878
Fax: 773-261-5204 www.flexoglass.com
Ionomer skin packaging film
Owner: Harold Warp
Manager: Jeff Whittington
Estimated Sales: $10-20 000,000
Number Employees: 5-9

22656 FlexBarrier Products
5350 Campbells Run Road
Pittsburgh, PA 15205
    412-787-9750
Fax: 412-787-3665 800-888-9750
Manager: Rick M Rochelle
Estimated Sales: $1 - 3 Million
Number Employees: 5-9
Parent Co: TMI, LLC

22657 Flexco
2525 Wisconsin Ave
Downers Grove, IL 60515-4241
    630-971-0150
Fax: 630-971-1180 800-323-3444
info@flexco.com www.flexco.com
Single source for light-duty endless and mechanical belt splicing solutions.

President/CEO: Richard White
CFO: Glen Paradise
EVP/COO: Tom Wujek
Marketing: Mike Stein
Sales: Dick Reynolds
Public Relations: Kelly Clancy
Estimated Sales: $20-50 Million
Number Employees: 250-499
Square Footage: 175000
Other Locations:
Australia
Chile
China
England
Germany
Mexico
India
Singapore
South Africa
Brands:
Alligator
Clipper
Flexco
Novitool

22658 Flexco
2525 Wisconsin Ave
Downers Grove, IL 60515-4241
    630-971-0150
Fax: 630-971-1180 800-541-8028
info@flexco.com www.flexco.com
Fasteners for conveyor belts, endless splicing products and other products that improve conveyor productivity.
President: Richard White
EVP: Tom Wujek
VP Marketing: Michael Stein
Sales Manager: Richard Reynolds
PR Specialist: Kelly Clancy
Estimated Sales: $20-50 Million
Number Employees: 250-499
Other Locations:
Grand Rapids MI

22659 Flexco
2525 Wisconsin Ave
Downers Grove, IL 60515-4241
    630-971-0150
Fax: 630-971-1180 800-323-3444
info@flexco.com www.flexco.com
Supplier of belt conveyor products
President: Richard White
Number Employees: 250-499

22660 (HQ)Flexible Foam Products
1900 W Lusher Ave
Elkhart, IN 46517
    574-294-7694
Fax: 574-522-4823 800-678-3626
Foamed polyurethane plastic products including containers; also, custom cutting to specific shapes available
General Manager: Jerry Egan
Contact: Beckie Smith
bsmith@flexiblefoam.com
Chemist: Karl Baier
Plant Manager: John Noble
Estimated Sales: $20-50 Million
Number Employees: 100-249

22661 Flexible Material Handling
410 Horizon Dr Ste 200
Suwanee, GA 30024
    216-587-1575
Fax: 216-587-2833 800-669-1501
www.flexmh.com
Conveyors including portable, flexible gravity and powered; also, portable storage racks
Sales Administration: Nancy Stohlman
Sales/Marketing Manager: Karl Dearnley
Contact: Teresa Blanton
tblanton@flexmh.com
Estimated Sales: $20-50 Million
Number Employees: 50-99
Parent Co: Axia

22662 Flexible Tape & Label Co
243 Jefferson Ave
Memphis, TN 38103-2376
    901-522-1410
Fax: 901-523-0073 art@flexiblelabel.com
www.flexiblelabelgroup.com
Printed pressure sensitive labels

Owner: Alan Magnus
orderlabel@aol.com
VP: Melanie Magnus
Estimated Sales: $1-2.5 Million
Number Employees: 5-9

22663 Flexicell Inc
10463 Wilden Dr
Ashland, VA 23005-8134

804-550-7300
Fax: 804-550-4898 www.flexicell.com
Manufacturer and exporter of robotic packaging machinery for case packing, collating, palletizing and conveying
President: Hans Dekoning
hdekoning@flexcon.com
R & D: Jack Morris
VP of Sales: Stuart Cooper
Operations Manager: Allen Bancroft
Manufacturing Specialist: Jack Mouris
Plant Manager: John Architzel
Purchasing Manager: Jim Golob
Estimated Sales: Below $5 Million
Number Employees: 20-49
Square Footage: 48000
Brands:
Flexi-1850
Flexi-Cell
Flexilinear
Flexiloader

22664 (HQ)Flexicon
2400 Emrick Blvd
Bethlehem, PA 18020-8006

610-814-2400
Fax: 610-814-0600 888-353-9426
sales@flexicon.com www.flexicon.com
Manufacturer and exporter of flexible screw conveyor systems, bulk bag dischargers, weigh batching systems and bulk handling systems with automated controls
CEO: William S Gill
Number Employees: 50-99
Other Locations:
Flexicon Corporation
Kent
Brands:
Batch-Con
Bev-Con
Flow-Flexer
Pop-Top

22665 Flexicon
165 Chicago St
Cary, IL 60013

847-639-3530
Fax: 847-639-6828
Flexible packaging materials for the food and pharmaceuticalical industries, supplied in rollstock for thermoforming, lidding, and form fill and seal applications. Preformed pouches are also supplied. Specializing in rollstock orpouches for boil and freeze applications.
President: Robert Biddle
CEO: Greg Baron
Estimated Sales: $20 Million
Number Employees: 50-99
Type of Packaging: Consumer, Food Service, Private Label

22666 Flexlink Systems Inc
6580 Snowdrift Rd # 200
Allentown, PA 18106-9331

610-954-7000
Fax: 610-973-8345 800-782-1399
us1.marketing@flexlink.com www.flexlink.com
Plastic chain conveyor systems and automation components
President: Dave Clark
CFO: Nino Dipietrroo
IT: Jeff Russo
jeff.roth@flexlink.com
Estimated Sales: $20-50 Million
Number Employees: 50-99

22667 Flexlume Sign Corp
1464 Main St
Buffalo, NY 14209-1780

716-884-2020
Fax: 716-881-0361 info@flexlume.com
www.flexlume.com
Indoor and outdoor signs
Owner: Curtis Martin
cmartin@signweb.com

Estimated Sales: Below $5 Million
Number Employees: 5-9

22668 Flexo Graphics
900 S Georgia St
Amarillo, TX 79102-1204

806-374-5363
Fax: 806-371-7104 866-533-5396
Labels including die-cut and pressure sensitive
Owner: Kevin Ahrens
flexo@arn.net
Sales: Ray Clark
Office Manager: Dylan Clark
Estimated Sales: $500,000-$1 Million
Number Employees: 1-4
Square Footage: 7000

22669 Flexo Printing Equipment Corp
416 Hayward Ave N
St Paul, MN 55128-5379

651-731-9499
Fax: 651-731-0525 www.flexo-siat.com
Die cutting and slitting capability for tape and labels
President: Wynn Lidell
wynn@flexo-siat.com
Estimated Sales: Below $5 000,000
Number Employees: 1-4

22670 Flexo Transparent Inc
28 Wasson St
Buffalo, NY 14210-1544

716-825-7710
Fax: 716-825-0139 877-993-5396
Flexographic printer, manufacturer and exporter of custom designed and printed plastic films up to ten colors including process print. Flexible packaging materials including: bags, rollstock, bottle sleeves, sheeting, reclosablezipper, resealable tape, pallet covers, specialty prepared foods totes, custom shaped packaging, etc. EDI and VMI capable; Just in Time Deliveries; Fast turnaround shipments.
President: Ronald Mabry
HR Executive: Debbi Gauthier
dgauthier@flexotransparent.com
Sales: Mark Barrile
Estimated Sales: $20-50 Million
Number Employees: 50-99
Number of Brands: 4
Square Footage: 84000
Type of Packaging: Consumer, Food Service, Private Label, Bulk
Brands:
Chicken Keeper
Crispy Keeper
Rotisserie Keeper
Safti Keeper

22671 (HQ)Flint Boxmakers Inc
2490 E Bristol Rd
Flint, MI 48529-1325

810-743-0400
Fax: 810-743-9577 www.michiganmall.com
Corrugated boxes
President: Steve Landaal
Number Employees: 5-9

22672 Flint Rubber Stamp Works
3518 Fenton Rd
Flint, MI 48507

810-235-2341
Fax: 810-235-3919 rodzinaind@aol.com
Marking and coding devices including rubber stamps
President: Robert Cross Jr
Estimated Sales: $500,000-$1 Million
Number Employees: 5-9
Parent Co: Rodzina Industries

22673 Flo-Cold
29290 Wall St,
PO Box 930317
Wixom, MI 48393

248-348-6666
Fax: 248-348-6667
Coolers, freezers and racked modular refrigeration systems
President: Dean M Koppin
Engineer: Albert Durand
Estimated Sales: $2.5 - 5 Million
Number Employees: 60
Parent Co: Chrysler & Koppin Company
Brands:
Flo-Cold

22674 Flo-Matic Corporation
1982t Belford North Drive
Belvidere, IL 61008-8565

815-547-5650
Fax: 815-544-2287 800-959-1179
Manufacturer and exporter of washers and washing systems
Chief Engineer: Edward Herman
Estimated Sales: $1 - 5,000,000

22675 Floaire
1730 Walton Rd # 203
Suite # 203
Blue Bell, PA 19422-2301

484-530-2601
Fax: 610-239-8941 800-726-5623
sales@floaire.com www.floaire.com
Ventilation equipment and commercial cookware
President: Clark S Fuller
Marketing Administration: Dawn Kearny
VP Sales Food Service: Richard Kinzler
Manager: Cory Scott
sales@floaire.com
Estimated Sales: Less Than $500,000
Number Employees: 1-4
Parent Co: Ralph Kearney & Sons

22676 Flodin
PO Box 1578
Moses Lake, WA 98837-0245

509-766-2996
Fax: 509-766-0157
Manufacturer and exporter of potato processing equipment including conveyors, dumpers, friers, dryers and frozen concertrate, thawing and breaker systems, etc
Sales Executive: Bill Flodin
Purchasing Agent: Rod Wright
Estimated Sales: $2.5-5 Million
Number Employees: 10-19
Square Footage: 92000
Brands:
Flodin

22677 Flojet
20 Icon
Foothill Ranch, CA 92610-3000

949-859-4945
Fax: 949-859-1153 800-235-6538
www.flojet.com
Manufacturer, importer and exporter of bag-in-box packaging pumps, motor pump units and power sprayers for soda, beer, cider, wine, condiments and water
President: Russ Davis
Marketing Director: Brud LeTourneav
Sales Director: Jon Byrd
Estimated Sales: $50 - 100 Million
Number Employees: 250

22678 Flomatic International
2100 Future Drive
Sellersburg, IN 47172

503-775-2550
Fax: 812-246-7020 800-367-4233
www.manitowocbeverage.com
Manufacturer and exporter of post-mix soft drink dispensing valves
VP: John Cochran
Estimated Sales: $10-20 Million
Number Employees: 20-49
Square Footage: 43200
Parent Co: Manitowoc Foodservice Group
Brands:
Flomatic

22679 Floor Master Inc
1157 Hooker Rd
Chattanooga, TN 37407-3248

423-867-4525
Fax: 423-867-4563 www.floormasterinc.net
Floor sweeping compounds
President: Johnny Bailey
floormaster@bellsouth.net
Estimated Sales: $2.5-5 Million
Number Employees: 10-19
Square Footage: 20000

22680 Florart Flock Process
13870 W Dixie Hwy
North Miami, FL 33161-3343

305-643-3900
Fax: 305-981-9929 800-292-3524
www.flagusa.com

Manufacturer and exporter of flags, flagpoles, pennants, indoor flag sets and banners
Owner: Barbara Dabney
CEO: Stephanie Ledlow
Number Employees: 5-9
Square Footage: 20800
Brands:
  Annin
  Cf
  Eder
  Valley Forge

22681 Florida Knife Co
1735 Apex Rd
Sarasota, FL 34240-9386
    941-371-2104
Fax: 941-378-9427 800-966-5643
sales@florida-knife.com www.florida-knife.com
Manufacturer and exporter of knives for ice, candy and packaging; also, food processing machine knife blades
President: Tom Johanning
  tjohanning@florida-knife.com
Sales: Tom Johanning Jr
Personnel: Debbie Dean
Estimated Sales: $2.5-5 Million
Number Employees: 10-19
Square Footage: 48000

22682 Florida Plastics Intl
10200 S Kedzie Ave
Evergreen Park, IL 60805-3735
    708-499-0400
Fax: 708-499-4620 800-499-0400
Manufacturer and exporter of point of purchase displays, signs and menu boards
Owner: Bill Kaiser
  bkaiser@keyser-group.com
CEO: Donald Keyser
Quality Control: Tom Page
Estimated Sales: $10 - 20 Million
Number Employees: 1-4
Square Footage: 120000
Type of Packaging: Food Service

22683 Florida Seating
6100 Mears Ct
Clearwater, FL 33760-2337
    727-540-9802
Fax: 727-540-9403 www.floridaseating.com
Manager: Jeremy Williams
Manager: Joe Bonnetti
  joe@floridaseating.com
Estimated Sales: $1 - 5 Million
Number Employees: 20-49

22684 Florin Box & Lumber Company
PO Box 292338
Sacramento, CA 95829-2338
    916-383-2675
Fax: 916-383-1397 800-767-2675
Wine industry gift boxes, packaging, wood crates
Estimated Sales: $5-10 000,000
Number Employees: 20-49

22685 Flour City Press-Pack Company
P.O. Box 398198
Minneapolis, MN 55439-8198
    952-831-1265
    Fax: 612-378-9441
Paper boxes including set-up and folding
Owner: Gene N Fuller
Quality Control: Richard Hall
Estimated Sales: $300,000-500,000
Number Employees: 1-4

22686 Flow Aerospace
1635 Production Rd
Jeffersonville, IN 47130-9624
    812-283-7888
Fax: 812-284-3281 www.flowwaterjet.com
Manufacturer and exporter of positioning systems for waterjet cutting pick and place robots
Manager: Anthony Neeley
Vice President of Global Sales: Dick LeBlanc
Manager: Kent Eubank
  keubank@flowcorp.com
General Manager: Gerald Malmrose
Chief Engineer: Mark Saberton
Estimated Sales: $1 - 5 Million
Number Employees: 100-249
Square Footage: 108000
Parent Co: Flow International

22687 (HQ)Flow International Corp.
23500 64th Ave. S
Kent, WA 98032
    253-850-3500
Fax: 253-813-9377 800-446-3569
info@flowcorp.com www.flowwaterjet.com
Food processing and high-pressure waterjet cutting and cleaning equipment.
President/CEO: Marc Michael
Year Founded: 1974
Estimated Sales: $200 Million
Number Employees: 680
Square Footage: 150000
Brands:
  Fresher Under Pressure

22688 Flow Technology
P.O. Box 52103
Phoenix, AZ 85072-2103
    480-240-3400
Fax: 480-240-3401 800-528-4225
ftimarket@ftimeters.com www.ftimeters.com
Instrumetation and controls, flow meters
President: Alan Eschbach
Quality Control: Randy Larrison
Estimated Sales: $10 - 20 Million
Number Employees: 50-99

22689 Flow Technology Inc
8930 S Beck Ave # 107
Suite #107
Tempe, AZ 85284-2864
    480-240-3400
Fax: 480-240-3401 800-833-2448
ftimarket@ftimeters.com www.ftimeters.com
Positive displacement and turbine flow meters
President: C Foran, Jr.
Vice President: Ralph Duffill
Number Employees: 50-99
Square Footage: 60000
Brands:
  Decathlon Series
  Exact Series

22690 Flow of Solids
1 Technology Park Drive
Westford, MA 01886-3139
    978-392-0300
Fax: 978-392-9980 www.jenike.com
Portable and stationery containers including silos, bins, hoppers, feeders, tumble blenders, chutes, solid pumps and slide gates
Director Sales/Marketing: Roderick Hossfeld
National Sales Manager: Brian Pittenger
Estimated Sales: $3 - 5 Million
Number Employees: 20-49
Parent Co: Jenike & Johanson

22691 Fluid Air Inc
2580 Diehl Rd # E
Aurora, IL 60502-5309
    630-665-5001
Fax: 630-851-1244 fluidairinfo@spray.com
    www.fluidairinc.com
Manufacturer and exporter of milling equipment for fine grinding and dryers/agglomerators for drying, agglomerating, coating and encapsulating foods and flavors
President: Martin Bender
CEO: Thomas Tappen
Director Process Development: Donald Verbarg
Estimated Sales: $5 - 10 Million
Number Employees: 20-49
Square Footage: 64000
Parent Co: Spraying Systems Company

22692 Fluid Energy Processing& Eqpt
2629 Penn St
Hatfield, PA 19440-2344
    215-368-2510
Fax: 215-368-6235 sales@fluidenergype.com
    www.fluidenergype.com
Manufacturer and exporter of jet/micronizing grinding mills, pulverizers and flash drying equipment
President: Jerry Leimkuhler
Estimated Sales: $5 - 10 Million
Number Employees: 50-99
Brands:
  Jet-O-Mizer
  Micro-Jet
  Roto-Jet
  Roto-Sizer
  Thermajet

22693 Fluid Imaging Technologies Inc
200 Enterprise Dr
Scarborough, ME 04074-7636
    207-846-6100
Fax: 207-846-6110 info@fluidimaging.com
    www.fluidimaging.com
Continuous-imaging particle analysis instruments for food and beverage research and development and inspection.
President: Chris Sieracki
CEO: Kent Peterson
  kent@fluidimaging.com
Marketing Assistant: Faith Baker
Estimated Sales: $2.5 Million
Number Employees: 20-49

22694 Fluid Metering Inc
5 Aerial Way # 500
Syosset, NY 11791-5593
    516-922-6050
Fax: 516-624-8261 800-223-3388
pumps@fmipump.com www.fmipump.com
Manufacturer and exporter of metering pumps, dispensers and accessories including valveless and variable positive displacement piston pumps
President: Hank Pinkerton
  hank.pinkerton@fmipump.com
Marketing Manager: Herb Werner
VP Sales: David Peled
Purchasing Director: Anthony Mennella
Estimated Sales: $10-20 Million
Number Employees: 10-19
Square Footage: 24000
Brands:
  Fmi
  Micro-Petter
  Ratiomatic

22695 Fluid Systems
10054 Old Grove Rd
San Diego, CA 92131
    858-695-3840
Fax: 858-695-2176 800-525-4369
Crossflow membrane filtration processes and systems for the industrial, good, water, chemical, and biotechnology markets
CFO: William Colins
Contact: William Liht
  fluid.systems@ksb.com

22696 Fluted Partition Inc
850 Union Ave
Bridgeport, CT 06607-1137
    203-368-2548
Fax: 203-367-5266 www.valleycontainer.com
Fluted partitions, corrugated and solid fiber boxes
Owner: Arthur W Vietze Jr
VP: Richard Jackson
Vice President: Rudolph Niedermeier
  cellpak@aol.com
Estimated Sales: $5-10 000,000
Number Employees: 10-19
Number of Products: 1
Type of Packaging: Private Label, Bulk

22697 Flux Pumps Corporation
4330 Commerce Cir SW
Atlanta, GA 30336
    404-691-6010
Fax: 404-691-6314 800-367-3589
  contact-flux-usa@flux-pumpen.de
Manufacturer and exporter of pumps including centrifugal, pneumatic, positive displacement, progressive cavity and sanitary
President: L G Eastman
Vice President: Mike O'Toole
Contact: Fred Bryant
  fbryant@flux-pumps.com
Estimated Sales: $1-2,5,000,000
Number Employees: 5-9
Parent Co: Flux Pumps Corporation
Type of Packaging: Bulk

22698 Flynn Burner Corporation
425 5th Ave
New Rochelle, NY 10801
    914-636-1320
Fax: 914-636-3751 800-643-8910
    www.flynnburner.com
Industrial gas burners for baking and surface treating (3D and flat web), paper, plastic
CEO: Edward S Flynn
Number Employees: 50-99
Type of Packaging: Food Service, Private Label

22699 Foam Concepts Inc
44 Rivulet St
PO Box 410
Uxbridge, MA 01569-3134
508-278-7255
Fax: 508-278-3623 sales@foamconcepts.com
www.foamconcepts.com
Manufacturer and exporter of custom molded insulated foam shipping containers and custom packaging for perishables
Owner: Mark Villamaino
mvillamaino@filmconcepts.com
VP Sales: Philip Michaelson
mvillamaino@filmconcepts.com
Estimated Sales: $5 - 10 Million
Number Employees: 20-49
Square Footage: 160000

22700 Foam Fabricator-Corp
8722 E San Alberto Dr # 200
Scottsdale, AZ 85258-4353
480-607-7330
Fax: 480-607-7333
scottsdale@foamfabricatorsinc.com
www.foamfabricatorsinc.com
Custom molded polystyrene packaging materials, expanded polystyrene, expanded polypropylene, expanded polyethylene
President: Jeffrey Askins
jaskins@foamfabricatorsinc.com
CFO: James Hughes
Estimated Sales: $5 - 10 Million
Number Employees: 10-19

22701 Foam Pack Industries
72 Fadem Rd
Springfield, NJ 07081-3116
973-376-3700
Fax: 973-467-9850 foampack@verizon.net
www.foampackindustries.com
Polystyrene packaging materials and containers; also, ice packs
President: Harvey Goodstein
CFO: David Goodstein
Sales Manager: Lacy Seabrook
Estimated Sales: $5 - 10 Million
Number Employees: 5-9

22702 Foam Packaging Inc
35 Stennis Rd
Vicksburg, MS 39180-9175
601-638-4871
Fax: 601-636-2655 800-962-2655
info@foampackaging.com
www.foam-packaging.com
Manufacturer and exporter of food service trays and insulated food containers for eggs, poultry and produce
President: Ray B English
renglish@vicksburg.com
Estimated Sales: $1-2.5 Million
Number Employees: 1-4

22703 Foamex
18801 Old Statesville Rd
Cornelius, NC 28031-9306
704-892-8081
Fax: 704-892-0409 www.foamex.com
Polyurethane foam
General Manager: Fran Conard
Finance Executive: Jennifer Hughes
Contact: Richard Centeno
rcenteno@fxi.com
Manager of Laminated Products: L Peterson
Estimated Sales: $20-50 Million
Number Employees: 10-19

22704 Foamold Corporation
34 Birchwood Dr
PO Box 95
Oneida, NY 13421-0095
315-363-5350
Fax: 315-363-4518
Foam packaging materials
Plant Manager: Jay Rheinhardt

22705 Focke & Co Inc
5730 Millstream Rd
Whitsett, NC 27377-9789
336-449-7200
Fax: 336-449-5444 sales@fockegso.com
www.focke.com
Packaging machinery

Vice President: Johann Betschart
jbetschart@fockegso.com
Financial Controller: Alec Pratto
VP: Johann Betschart
Estimated Sales: $10 - 20 000,000
Number Employees: 50-99

22706 Focus
2852 Anthony Ln S
Minneapolis, MN 55418-3233
612-706-4444
Fax: 612-706-0544
food@focusexecutivesearch.com
www.focusexecutivesearch.com
Executive search firm specializing in personnel for general management, sales, research and development, operations, production and administration positions
President: Tim Mc Lafferty
CFO: Gayle Hope
Vice President: Tim Schultz
R & D: Nicholas Kallenbach
Sales Director: Tony Misum
Contact: Gayle Holt
gh@focusexecutivesearch.com
Estimated Sales: Below $5 Million
Number Employees: 5-9
Square Footage: 400000

22707 (HQ)Fogel Jordon CommercialRefrigeration Company
2501 Grant Avenue
Philadelphia, PA 19114-2307
215-535-8300
Fax: 215-289-1597 800-523-0171
Manufacturer and exporter of refrigerators, walk-in cabinets, refrigerated display cases, beverage coolers, cooling rooms, etc
Secretary/Treasurer: Gene Sterner
Sales Manager: Howard Smith
Estimated Sales: $20-50 Million
Number Employees: 50-99
Square Footage: 200000
Type of Packaging: Consumer, Bulk
Brands:
Fogel
Jordon
Jordon Scientific

22708 Fogel Rubin & Fogel
44 W Flagler St # 350
Miami, FL 33130-6813
305-577-4905
Fax: 305-372-0936
Commercial refrigerators specifically designed for beverage and beer industries
Partner: Joel D Fogel
Estimated Sales: $300,000-500,000
Number Employees: 5-9

22709 Fogg Filler Co
3455 John F Donnelly Dr
Holland, MI 49424-9207
616-786-3644
Fax: 616-786-0350 info@foggfiller.com
Manufacturer and exporter of packaging machinery including bottle fillers and cappers, and rinsers for flowable liquid, and noncarbonated products
President: Mike Fogg
Vice President: Al Nienhuis
Marketing Director: Susan Lamar
Sales Director: Ben Fogg
Plant Manager: Randy Dewaard
Estimated Sales: $10-20 Million
Number Employees: 100-249
Square Footage: 80000
Type of Packaging: Consumer, Food Service, Private Label, Bulk
Brands:
Clip Go Valve
Easi-63
Filt Pro 5000
Ventraflow

22710 Foilmark Inc
5 Malcolm Hoyt Dr
Newburyport, MA 01950-4082
978-462-7300
Fax: 978-462-0831 sales@itwfoilmark.com
Wine industry fillers
President: David Bales
dbales@itwfoils.com

Estimated Sales: $50-100 Million
Number Employees: 100-249

22711 (HQ)Fold-Pak Corporation
Van Buren Street
Newark, NY 14513
315-331-3159
Fax: 315-331-0093
Manufacturer and exporter of folding ice cream and carry out food cartons
President/CEO: Karl De May
Senior VP Sales/Marketing: Robert Mullally
VP Sales: Max Richter
Estimated Sales: $50-100 Million
Number Employees: 100-249
Type of Packaging: Consumer, Private Label
Other Locations:
Fold-Pak Corp.
Hazleton PA

22712 Fold-Pak South
3961 Cusseta Rd
Columbus, GA 31903-2045
706-689-2924
Fax: 706-689-2308
Manufacturer and exporter of food trays, soup containers and wire-handled food pails including Oriental and microwaveable; available with or without pagoda design
Quality Control: Coral Vessel
Contact: April Butler
aprilb@fold-pak.com
Plant Manager: Carl Vessell
Estimated Sales: $10 - 20 Million
Number Employees: 20-49
Type of Packaging: Food Service
Brands:
Bio-Pak

22713 Folding Carton/FlexiblePackaging
12323 Sherman Way
North Hollywood, CA 91605-5517
818-896-3449
Fax: 818-982-9039
Paper boxes, cartons, blister cards and skin sheets
General Manager: Tom Hiraishi
Number Employees: 60
Parent Co: Marfred Industries

22714 Folding Guard Co
5858 W 73rd St
Chicago, IL 60638-6216
708-924-1359
Fax: 312-829-3278 800-622-2214
Manufacturer and exporter of partitions, gates and lockers
Manager: J Lipa
jlipa@foldingguard.com
Operations Manager: Keith Stadwick
Estimated Sales: $10-20 Million
Number Employees: 50-99
Type of Packaging: Bulk
Brands:
Quik-Fence

22715 Foley Sign Co
572 Mercer St
Seattle, WA 98109-4618
206-324-3040
Fax: 206-328-4953 www.foleysign.com
Manufacturer and exporter of signs
Owner: Mark Metcalf
mark@foleysign.com
Estimated Sales: $1-2.5 Million
Number Employees: 10-19

22716 Foley's Famous Aprons
3441 Filbert St
Wayne, MI 48184-1974
734-641-9507
Fax: 734-721-8426 800-634-3245
Work cloths, caps and aprons
Owner: Terrence Foley
Secretary: Kevin Foley
VP: Tom Foley
Estimated Sales: $300,000-500,000
Number Employees: 1-4
Square Footage: 10000

22717 Follett Corp
801 Church Ln
Easton, PA 18040-6637
610-252-7301
Fax: 610-250-0696 800-523-9361
www.follettice.com
Manufacturer and exporter of high quality, innovative ice storage bins, ice storage and transport systems, ice and water dispensers, ice and beverage dispensers, and Chewblet ice nugget ice machines
President/CEO: Steven Follett
fsteven@follettice.com
CFO: Thomas Rohrbach
Executive VP: Robert Bryson
Marketing Director: Lois Schneck
VP Sales: Ed Barr
Manager, Marketing Services: Robin Porter
VP Operations: David Tumbusch
Manager, Materials: Jeff Craig
Number Employees: 100-249
Type of Packaging: Food Service

22718 Fona International
1900 Averill Rd
Geneva, IL 60134
630-578-8600
Fax: 630-578-8601 www.fona.com
Flavoring extracts and syrups.
President & COO: Jeremy Thompson
Chairman/CEO, McCormick: Larence Kurzius
EVP: Manon Daoust
Estimated Sales: $100-500 Million
Number Employees: 200-500
Parent Co: McCormick

22719 Fonda Group
PO Box 519
Goshen, IN 46527-0519
574-534-2515
Fax: 574-533-6330
Paper plates
President: William Lester
Principal: Meg Amadeo
Number Employees: 50

22720 Food & Agrosystems
1289 Mandarin Drive
Sunnyvale, CA 94087-2028
408-245-8450
Fax: 408-748-1826 www.foodagrosys.com
Consultant specializing in process engineering, product/process development, plant/process layout, equipment design, feasibility analysis, production problem-solving, management assistance, etc
President: Thomas Parks
VP Marketing: Robert Marquardt
Estimated Sales: $1-2.5 Million
Number Employees: 10

22721 Food & Beverage Consultants
1260 Oaklawn Ave
Cranston, RI 02920-2628
401-463-5784
Fax: 401-463-7931
Consultant specializing in food and beverage development, flavor modification, food service and institutional consulting, recipe and menu development, quality control, food labeling, sensory evaluation and training programs
President: Demetri Kazantzis
Contact: Abel Martinez
amartinez@hpaconsultants.co.uk
Estimated Sales: $.5 - 1 million
Number Employees: 1-4

22722 Food Allergy & Anaphylaxis Network
7925 Jones Branch Dr.
Suite 1100
McLean, VA 22102
703-691-3179
Fax: 703-691-2713 800-929-4040
www.foodallergy.org
To improve the quality of life and the health of individuals with food allergies.
Founder/CEO: Anne Munoz-Furlong
Contact: Alyssa Ackerman
aackerman@foodallergy.org
Number Employees: 10-19

22723 (HQ)Food Business Associates
PO Box J
Temple, ME 04984-0539
207-778-2251
Fax: 207-778-5097
Consultant and market development specialist providing growth strategy planning and consumer and trade acceptance research; also, supermarket supervisor training services available
President: Robert Bull
VP: Stephen Bull
Estimated Sales: Less than $500,000
Number Employees: 4

22724 Food Consulting Company
13724 Recuerdo Drive
Del Mar, CA 92014-3430
858-793-4658
Fax: 800-522-3545 800-793-2844
info@foodlabels.com www.foodlabels.com
Consultant specializing in nutrition analysis and food labeling
Contact: Susan Drew
jim.wurbel.b7hq@statefarm.com
Estimated Sales: Below $500,000
Number Employees: 1

22725 Food Development Centre
PO Box 1240
Portage La Prairie, NB R1N 3J9
Canada
306-933-7555
Fax: 306-933-7208 800-870-1044
info@foodcentre.sk.ca www.foodcentre.sk.ca
Consultant specializing in product development, packaging, equipment, food analyses, nutritional profiles, QC programs, food research and development, food processing, process engineering, etc.; full service food science and technologylibrary in house; also, seminars available
CEO: Dave Donaghy
Research & Development: AlPhonSus Utioh
Marketing Director: Markus Schmulgen
Number Employees: 25
Square Footage: 80000
Parent Co: Manitoba Agriculture & Food

22726 Food Engineering Network
1050 Il Route 83
Bensenville, IL 60106-1049
630-616-0200
Fax: 630-227-0204 www.bnpmedia.com
CEO: Jim Henderson
Contact: Joyce Fassi
fasslj@bnpmedia.com
Estimated Sales: $1 - 5 000,000

22727 Food Engineering Unlimited
1501 N Harbor Blvd Ste 103
Fullerton, CA 92835-4128
714-879-8762
Fax: 714-773-0911 feu@earthlink.net
Conveyors,material handling systems, bakery ovens, mixers and spiral freezers; also, installation services available
President: Russ Juergens
Contact: Rosalie Hofmaenner
rosalie.hofmaenner@food-eng.com
Estimated Sales: $1-2,500,000
Number Employees: 1-4

22728 Food Equipment BrokerageInc
PO Box 6541
Key West, FL 33041
800-968-8881
febinc@mo.net
We do turn key c-stores across the United States and Canada. We also export to Asia
CEO: Michael Hesse
Marketing: J R Kim
Sales: Dave Schuller
Number Employees: 110
Number of Brands: 400
Type of Packaging: Food Service, Private Label

22729 Food Equipment Manufacturing Company
22201 Aurora Rd
Bedford Heights, OH 44146
216-672-5859
Fax: 216-663-9337 info@femc.com
www.femc.com
Manufacturer and exporter of packaging machinery including fillers, de-stackers, sealers and slicers

President: Robert Sauer
rls@femc.com
CFO: Obert Sauer
VP: Joseph Lukes
Sales Manager: Daniel Auvil
Estimated Sales: $5-10 Million
Number Employees: 20-49
Square Footage: 120000

22730 Food Executives Network
10415 West Michigan Street
Milwaukee, WI 53226
414-962-7684
Fax: 414-962-6261
careers@foodexecsnetwork.com
Search firm speacializing in the selection and placement of executive, managerial and technical professionals.
President and CEO: Thomas Brenneman
VP: Kay Boxer
Business Manager: Christine Brennemen
Director of BD, SE Office: Kay Boxer
Contact: Tom Brenneman
chris.brenneman@gmail.com
Business Manager, Milwaukee Office: Christine Brenneman
Estimated Sales: $300,000-500,000
Number Employees: 1-4
Square Footage: 6000
Parent Co: Winston Franchise Corporation

22731 Food Handling Systems
8948 SW Barbur Boulevard
Suite 720
Portland, OR 97219-4047
877-266-6972
Fax: 503-691-0917
Gentle food handling, horizontal motion conveyors and vibratory equipment
Chairman: Richard Frank
President/CEO: Trevor Fagerskog
CFO: Steven Reiss
VP Sales/Marketing: Karen Orton Katz
Type of Packaging: Bulk

22732 (HQ)Food Industry ConsultingGroup
21050 SW 93rd Lane Road
Dunnellon, FL 34431-5802
352-489-8919
Fax: 352-489-8919 800-443-5820
Consultant specializing food service systems especially food procurement productivity in food preparation and service
CEO: J Hill
Operations: James Mixon
Estimated Sales: $1 - 5 Million
Number Employees: 6
Square Footage: 5000
Other Locations:
Food Industry Consulting Group
Silver Spring MD

22733 Food Industry Equipment
1121 W 14th Street
Lorain, OH 44052-3800
440-246-3150
Fax: 440-246-1739
Defattting machines, skinnning machines and accessories and trimming devices, deboning equipment/meat, knives/powered, sharpening systems, boning machines, meat and poultry, cutters/knives, cutters/trimmers, consultants/processingequipment and consultants/processing equipment
Manager Customer Support: Pam Agocki

22734 Food Insights
1100 Connecticut Avenue NW
Suite 430
Washington, DC 20036
202-296-6540
Fax: 901-755-1006 info@foodinsight.org
www.foodinsight.org
Consultant specializing in marketing research, operating systems and management strategy services, customer relationship management
CEO: Judy Patton
Marketing: Carolyn Thomas
Operations: Sandy Brickley
Purchasing: Larry Ruggles
Estimated Sales: $300,000-500,000
Number Employees: 1-4

22735 Food Institute
10 Mountainview Rd # S125
Suite S125
Upper Saddle Rvr, NJ 07458-1942
      201-791-5570
Fax: 201-791-5222 www.foodinstitute.com
A non-profit organization founded in 1928. Provides
information covering the entire food industry issues
and food industry news.
President: Brian Todd
HR Executive: Cathy Sloan
  csloan@foodinstitute.com
Order Status/Billing: April Brendel
Estimated Sales: $2.5-5 Million
Number Employees: 10-19

22736 Food Instrument Corp
115 Academy Ave
Federalsburg, MD 21632-1202
      410-754-8606
Fax: 410-754-8796 800-542-5688
  kickout@verizon.net
www.foodinstrumentcorporation.com
Manufacturer, wholesaler/distributor and exporter of
microprocessor based quality control instrumenta-
tion including closure seal testers, rejectors, data an-
alyzers, can orienters and diverters
President: Richard V Kudlich
Sales Director: James Boehm
Estimated Sales: $1-5 Million
Number Employees: 1-4
Number of Brands: 1
Number of Products: 6
Square Footage: 40000
Brands:
  Adr
  Das Ii
  Div-10
  Vrr

22737 Food Machinery Sales
328 Commerce Blvd # 8
Bogart, GA 30622-2200
      706-549-2207
Fax: 706-548-1724 fmssales@fmsathens.com
www.fmsathens.com
Manufacturer and exporter of product handling and
packaging machinery for the biscuit and cracker in-
dustries
Manager: Eric Gunderson
Estimated Sales: $10-20 Million
Number Employees: 20-49

22738 Food Machinery of America
3115 Pepper Mill Court
Mississauga,, ON L5L 4X5
Canada
      905-823-5522
Fax: 905-607-0234 800-465-0234
  sales@omcan.com www.omcan.com
Estimated Sales: $1 - 5 Million

22739 Food Makers Equipment
16019 Adelante St
Irwindale, CA 91702-3255
      626-358-1343
Fax: 626-358-1613 www.bakeryequipment.net
Owner: Tom Fowler
  tom@fmbe.com
Estimated Sales: $10 - 20 Million
Number Employees: 20-49

22740 Food Management Search
235 State St # 326
Suite 326
Springfield, MA 01103-1749
      413-732-2666
Fax: 413-732-6466
recruiters@foodmanagementsearch.com
www.foodmanagementsearch.com
Contingency firm specializing in recruiting food industry career professionals in the areas of food production, supermarket and distribution, food service,
restaurant, culinary, hotel food and beverage and
sales and marketingnationwide. Position salaries
range between $40K and $150K
Contact: Allison Wellman
  allisonw@chap-con.com
Estimated Sales: Less Than $500,000
Number Employees: 1-4

22741 Food Marketing Servives
419 Friday Rd
Pittsburgh, PA 15209
      412-821-8960
www.leepercompanies.com
Provides sales and marketing services to manufac-
turers of Consumer Packaged Goods, sold generally
through grocery, drug and mass merchant stores.
President: James Leeper
Year Founded: 1987
Estimated Sales: $20-50 Million
Number Employees: 100-249
Parent Co: Louis F Leeper

22742 (HQ)Food Pak Corp
2300 Palm Ave
San Mateo, CA 94403-1817
      650-341-6559
Fax: 650-341-2110
Chili seasonings, board and food coatings; manufac-
turer and exporter of custom packaging products in-
cluding flexible X-ray film, insulated and sandwich
bags, containers, folding cartons, shopping bags,
flexible packaging bags, paper &foil bags
CEO: Steve Kanaga
Estimated Sales: Less Than $500,000
Number Employees: 1-4
Square Footage: 14000
Type of Packaging: Food Service, Private Label,
Bulk
Brands:
  A.B. Curry's
  Hyfroydol
  Safety Pak
  Scoop It
  Sta-Hot
  Zest

22743 Food Plant Companies
15945 N 76th Street
Scottsdale, AZ 85260-1781
      480-991-6534
Fax: 480-991-1243

22744 Food Plant Engineering
PO Box 9906
Yakima, WA 98909-0906
      509-248-5530
Fax: 509-453-3008
Meat industry services: architects and engineers,
building and construction consultants, temperature
controls, refrigerated structures and refrigeration
systems

22745 Food Plant Engineering
10816 Millington Ct # 110
Cincinnati, OH 45242-4025
      513-488-8888
Fax: 513-641-0057
mail@foodplantengineering.com
www.foodplantengineering.com
We specialize in facility design, engineering, architectural and construction management services for
expansions, renovations and new construction. We
provide master planning, production capacity studies, plant flow investigationprocess and equipment
layouts, process design, lean manufacturing principle implementation and process simulation analysis.
We offer a variety of project formats including competitive bidding, construction management and
design build
President: Mark Redmond
Marketing Director: Jennifer Redmond
Project Manager: Michael Cowgill
Estimated Sales: $2,500,000 - $4,999,999
Number Employees: 10-19

22746 Food Processing Concepts
4212 Happy Valley Cir
Newnan, GA 30263
      628-478-4700
www.foodprocessingconcepts.com
Equipment for food industry used in the production
process
Sales: David McKinney

22747 Food Processing Equipment Co
13623 Pumice St
Santa Fe Springs, CA 90670-5105
      562-802-3727
Fax: 562-802-8621 salesark@fpec.com
www.fpec.com

Manufacturer and exporter of food processing and
material handling equipment including vacuum tumblers, blenders and mixers, chilled massage blenders, conveyors, dumpers, screw conveyors, cart lifts,
screw loaders, vacuum hoppers, openblenders and
mixers, etc
Owner: Alan Davison
Sales Manager: Larry Butler
Estimated Sales: $5 - 10 Million
Number Employees: 1-4
Square Footage: 72000

22748 Food Processors Institute
1350 I St NW # 300
Washington, DC 20005-3377
      202-393-0890
Fax: 202-639-5932 800-355-0983
Non-profit association that provides education for
food processors and affiliated industries
CEO: Cal Dooley
Contact: Carla Mitchell
  cmitchell@fpa-food.org
Executive Director: Lisa Weddnig
Number Employees: 1-4

22749 Food Products Lab
12003 NE Ainsworth Cir # 105
Portland, OR 97220-9034
      503-253-9136
Fax: 503-253-9019 800-375-9555
www.fplabs.com
Manager: Nidel Kahl
Quality Control: Nadil Kahl
Estimated Sales: $3 - 5 Million
Number Employees: 20-49

22750 Food Resources International
250 Rayette Rd.
Units 13 & 14
Concord, ON L4K 2G6
Canada
      905-482-8967
Fax: 905-482-8968 ifr@rogers.com
Manufacturer and exporter of food processing
equipment including dairy machinery, membrane
systems and spray dryers; also, reconditioned equip-
ment available; importer of casein and whey and
milk protein concentrates
President: Jon Chesnut
VP: Karen Chesnut
Number Employees: 10-19

22751 Food Safety Net Services Ltd
199 W Rhapsody Dr
San Antonio, TX 78216-3105
      210-308-0675
Fax: 210-525-1702 888-525-9788
tcornett@food-safetynet.com www.fsns.com
Laboratory specializing in microbiological, nutri-
tional, and chemical analysis, consulting and audit-
ing, education and training
President: Gina R. Bellinger
CEO: John W. Bellinger
CFO/COO: Alan W. Uecker
VP of Operations: Dr. Randal Garrett
Quality Control: Micheal Devine
Marketing Director: Tesa Cornett
Business Development Manager: Tim Deary
Business Development Manager: Tony Nguyen
Lead Special Scientist: Amit Morey PhD
Estimated Sales: Below $5 Million
Number Employees: 50-99
Square Footage: 24000
Type of Packaging: Food Service
Other Locations:
  Food Safety Net Services
  Richardson TX

22752 Food Sanitation Svc Inc
64 Fulton St # 702
New York, NY 10038-2752
      212-732-9540
Fax: 212-608-7862
Consultant specializing in food sanitation and safety
President: Barbara Kleiner
  bkleiner@food-san.com
CEO: Martin Muchanic
CFO: Barbara Kleiner
Estimated Sales: $1-2.5 Million
Number Employees: 10-19

22753 Food Scene
P.O. Box 459
Colts Neck, NJ 07722
732-431-1132
Fax: 732-577-8445
Owner: Barry Kahn
Contact: John Pauciullo
jpauciullo@foodscene.com
Estimated Sales: $20-50 Million
Number Employees: 10-19

22754 Food Science Associates
PO Box 525
Crugers, NY 10521-0525
914-739-7541
Fax: 914-739-7541
Consultant providing product development, nutritional labeling, culinary assistance, regulatory compliance, etc
VP: Frank del Valle
Estimated Sales: $1 - 5 Million
Number Employees: 14

22755 Food Science Consulting
PO Box 30992
Walnut Creek, CA 94598-7992
925-947-6785
Fax: 925-947-2811 www.foodonline.com
Consultant for product formulation and development, process development, plant implementation, recipe development, food styling and commercialization of recipes
President: Dorothy Keefer
Number Employees: 1

22756 Food Service Equipment Corporation
727 Del Prado Boulevard N
Cape Coral, FL 33909-2254
941-574-7767
New and used hotel restaurant, deli, cafeteria equipment and heavy duty equipment and small wares
President: J Furdell
Estimated Sales: $500,000-$1 Million
Number Employees: 4

22757 Food Tech Structures LLC
10 Crescent Rd
Riverside, CT 06878
203-637-2471
Fax: 203-637-2527 800-880-0118

22758 Food Technologies
10001 Wayzata Boulevard
Golden Valley, MN 55405
763-544-8586
Fax: 763-544-0999
Consultant specializing in food product development, program design and marketing for food processors
President: William Drier, Ph.D.
Marketer: C Carroll Hicks
Production Developer: Gene Monroe
Number Employees: 3
Square Footage: 4000

22759 Food Technology Corporation
45921 Maries Rd
Suite 120
Sterling, VA 20166-9278
703-444-1870
Fax: 703-444-9860 info@foodtechcorp.com
www.foodtechcorp.com
Manufacturer and exporter of food texture testing systems and measurement equipment including texture profile analysis, pea tenderometers, peak force measurement systems, and kramer shear press
President: Shirl Lakeway
srkim@mcik.co.kr
Estimated Sales: $3 Million
Number Employees: 5
Square Footage: 6000
Brands:
  Kramer Shear Press
  Tenderometers
  Tenore Measurement Equipment

22760 Food Tools
315 Laguna St
Santa Barbara, CA 93101-1716
805-962-8383
Fax: 805-966-3614 877-836-6386
www.foodtools.com

Manufacturer and exporter of de-panners, cake slabbers, crumb spreaders and ultrasonic slicers and mechanical slicers
Owner: Marty Grano
martyg@foodtools.com
Vice President: Mike Christenson
Vice President: Doug Petrovich
VP of Engineering: Matt Browne
VP of Production: Gary Grand
Estimated Sales: $5 - 10 Million
Number Employees: 20-49
Square Footage: 78000

22761 Food Tools
315 Laguna St
Santa Barbara, CA 93101-1716
805-962-8383
Fax: 805-966-3614 877-836-6386
www.foodtools.com
Owner: Marty Grano
martyg@foodtools.com
Chairman of the Board: Martin Grano
Estimated Sales: $5-10 Million
Number Employees: 20-49

22762 Food Warming Equipment Co
338 Memorial Dr # 300
Crystal Lake, IL 60014-6262
815-444-6394
Fax: 815-459-7989 800-222-4393
www.fwe.com
Manufacturer and exporter of stainless steel heated and refrigerated utility carts and mobile cabinets
President: Chuck Deck
c-deck@fweco.net
CEO: Deron Lichte
CFO: Chris Huffman
VP Marketing/Sales: Curt Benson
Estimated Sales: $5 - 10 Million
Number Employees: 50-99
Square Footage: 280000
Brands:
  Prm-Ii (Prime Rib Master)
  Weather-All Bars

22763 Food and Dairy ResearchAssociates
107 Homer St
Commerce, GA 30529-1859
706-335-9703
Fax: 706-335-9704
Owner: Steve Green
Estimated Sales: $.5 - 1 000,000
Number Employees: 5-9

22764 Food-Tek
9 Whippany Rd Bldg C-2
Whippany, NJ 7981
973-257-4000
Fax: 973-257-5555 800-648-8114
info@foodtek.com www.foodtek.com
Consultant specializing in product development services for food manufacturers
President: Gilbert Finkel
CFO: Gilbert Finkel
Vice President: Victor Davila
R&D: Gilbert Finkel
Quality Control: Gilbert Finkel
Estimated Sales: $5 - 10 Million
Number Employees: 5-9
Square Footage: 10000

22765 FoodHandler
2301 Lunt Avenue
Elk Grove Village, IL 60007
516-338-4433
Fax: 516-338-4405 800-338-4433
www.foodhandler.com
Disposable gloves, aprons, hair restraints, bibs, worker protection and food safety training
Contact: Don Allegretti
dallegretti@foodhandler.com
Number Employees: 20-49

22766 FoodLogiQ
2655 Meridian Pkwy.
Durham, NC 27713
866-492-4468
info@foodlogiq.com www.foodlogiq.com
Solutions for all sectors of the food industry, including compliance and regulations, supplier management, recall management, safety and quality control, and blockchain management.

CEO: Sean O'Leary
CFO: Faith Kosobucki
Chief Marketing & Strategy Officer: Katy Jones
VP, Sales: Julie Hepner
Chief Product Officer: Todd Dolinsky
Year Founded: 2006
Number Employees: 80-200

22767 Foodchek Systems
1414 8 St SW
Suite 450
Calgary, AB T2R 1J6
Canada
403-269-9424
Fax: 403-263-6357 877-298-0208
info@foodcheksystems.com
www.foodcheksystems.com
Supplier of food safety pathogen tests
President: William Hogan
Estimated Sales: $500,000- 1 Million
Number Employees: 8

22768 Fooddesign Machinery & Systems
29103 SW Kinsman Rd
Wilsonville, OR 97070-8701
503-685-5030
Fax: 503-685-5034 sales@foodesign.com
President: Joseph Mistretta
joe.mistretta@foodesign.com
Estimated Sales: $5 - 10 Million
Number Employees: 1-4

22769 Fooddesign Machinery & Systems
29103 SW Kinsman Rd
PO Box 2449
Wilsonville, OR 97070-8701
503-685-5030
Fax: 503-685-5034 sales@foodesign.com
Supplier of heavy-duty precision built cooking and processing machines
President: Joseph Mistretta
joe.mistretta@foodesign.com
Sales Executive: Daniel Luna
Number Employees: 1-4

22770 Foodmark, Inc.
180 Linden Street
Wellesley, MA 02482
781-237-7088
Fax: 781-237-7455 800-535-3447
ggavris@foodmark.com
Offers prospective clients a variety of brand development and sales management possibilties, as well as capital investment opportunities when necessary.
Partner: George Gavris
Partner: Rob Simmons
Partner: Lee Gavris
Contact: George Banis
gbanis@foodmark.com
Estimated Sales: $950 Thousand
Number Employees: 10

22771 (HQ)Foodpro International
P.O. Box 1119
Stockton, CA 95202
209-943-8400
Fax: 408-227-4908 888-687-5797
bwashburn@foodpro.net www.foodpro.net
Consultant provides engineering services including studies, plans and specifications development, construction and equipment installation management; exporter of fruit fly extermination systems
President: M W Washburn
CEO: M Wm Washburn
CFO: Lou Kong
Research & Development: Olga Osipova
Marketing Director: Richard Jennings
Branch Manager: Alex Tarasov
Estimated Sales: $1 - 3 Million
Number Employees: 12

22772 Foods Research Laboratories
130 Newmarket Sq # 3
Boston, MA 02118-2675
617-442-3322
Fax: 617-442-2013
Laboratory providing microbiological and chemical analysis of food and nutrition labeling; also, consultant services include plant sanitation, quality control and HACCP audits and verifications
Owner: Andrea Fontaine
Lab Director: Andrea Fontaine
Chemist: Regina Pierce

Estimated Sales: Less than $500,000
Number Employees: 1-4

22773 Foodservice ConsultantsSociety International
P.O. Box 4961
Louisville, KY 40204

502-379-4122
Info@fcsi.org
www.fcsi.org
Promotion professionalism in foodservice and hospitality consulting.
President: Mr. Jonathan Doughty
Secretary, Treasurer: James Petersen
Estimated Sales: $5-10 Million
Number Employees: 50-99

22774 Foodservice Design Associates
10207 General Dr
Orlando, FL 32824-8529

407-896-4115
Fax: 407-895-7022
p.bean@foodservice-design.com
www.foodservice-design.com
Consultant specializing in architectural design and specification services for the food service industry
Principal: Philip Bean
Estimated Sales: $150,000
Number Employees: 1-4

22775 Foodservice East
197 8th St # 728
Charlestown, MA 02129-4234

617-242-2217
Fax: 617-742-5938 800-852-5212
www.foodserviceeast.com
Estimated Sales: Less Than $500,000
Number Employees: 1-4

22776 Foodservice Equipment &pplie
110 Schiller
Suite 312
Elmhurst, IL 60126

847-390-2010
Fax: 800-630-4169 800-630-4168
maureen@zoombagroup.com www.fesmag.com
Contact: Cindy Cardinal
cindy@zoombagroup.com

22777 Foodservice Equipment Distributors Association
2250 Point Boulevard
Suite 200
Elgin, IL 60123

224-293-6500
Fax: 224-293-6505 feda@feda.com
www.feda.com
Trade association for foodservice and supplies dealers.
President: Brad Pierce
Executive Vice President: Raymond W. Herrick
Secretary: Jay Ringelheim
Number Employees: 5-9

22778 Foodservice Innovation Network
335 North River Street
Batavia, IL 60510

630-879-3006
Fax: 630-879-3014

22779 Foodworks
400 N 4th Street
La Grange, KY 40031-1512

502-222-0135
Fax: 502-222-0135 easyhaccp@aol.com
Consultant providing HACCP training, food safety seminars, food plant sanitation and food safety auditing
President: Dotty Heady
Executive VP: Kazmer Wolkensperg
Number Employees: 4

22780 Foote & Jenks
1420 Crestmont Ave
Camden, NJ 08103-3182

856-966-0700
Fax: 856-966-6137

President: Castro Alexander
castro@footeandjenks.com
Estimated Sales: $20-50 Million
Number Employees: 10-19

22781 For Life
1811 W Mahalo Pl
Compton, CA 90220-5429

310-638-6386
Fax: 310-638-6305 info@forlifedesign.com
www.forlifedesign.com
Accessories/suplies i.e. picnic baskets, cooking implements,/housewares.
President: Masa Fujii
masa@forlifedesign.com
Number Employees: 5-9

22782 Foran Spice Inc
7616 S 6th St
P.O. Box 109
Oak Creek, WI 53154-2049

414-764-1220
Fax: 414-764-8803 800-558-6030
email@asenzya.com www.asenzya.com
Re-cleaned and sterilized spices, custom engineered seasonings, and value-added food products
President: Patty Goto
patty.goto@foranspice.com
CFO: Andy Gitter
Vice President: Joy Hauser
VP of Business Development & Marketing: Chris Anderson
VP Sales: Paul Duddleston
Engineer: Alan Goto
Estimated Sales: $19 Million
Number Employees: 100-249
Square Footage: 213000
Type of Packaging: Food Service, Private Label, Bulk

22783 Forbes Industries
1933 E Locust St
Ontario, CA 91761-7608

909-923-4549
Fax: 909-923-1969 sales@forbesindustries.com
www.forbesindustries.com
Manufacturer and exporter of banquet cabinets and carts, tables, sign stands, boards, easels, bins, carts, menus, etc.; also, bars including salad, soup and portable.
President: Tim Sweetland
tsweetland@forbesindustries.com
Estimated Sales: $50-100 Million
Number Employees: 100-249

22784 Forbes Products Corp
45 High Tech Dr
Rush, NY 14543-9746

585-334-4800
Fax: 585-334-6180 800-316-5235
www.forbesproducts.com
Customized vinyl office products and promotional items including pocket planners, binders, desk and carrying portfolios, proposal covers, clear envelopes and business card holders
President: Jim Mcdermott
jmcdermott@forbesproducts.com
VP Sales: Rick Blowers
Estimated Sales: $2.5-5 Million
Number Employees: 10-19
Square Footage: 300000

22785 (HQ)Forbo Siegling LLC
12201 Vanstory Dr
Huntersville, NC 28078-8395

704-948-0800
Fax: 704-948-0995 800-255-5581
siegling.us@forbo.com www.forbo.com
Transilon conveyor belts, extremultus flat transmission belts, transfer conveyor belting, prolink plastic modular belts, proposition high-efficiency timing belts and other related products specifically designed for the food andbeverage industry.
President: Wayne Hoffman
VP Sales/Marketing: John Casal
Research & Development: Jay Leighton
Quality Control: Natalie Deal
Marketing Director: Kitty Spence
National Sales Manager: Dany Bearden
Contact: Stacy Bennett
stacy.bennett@forbo.com
VP Production: Chris Flannigan
Number Employees: 500-999
Square Footage: 200000
Other Locations:
Siegling America
Wood Dale IL
Siegling America
Englewood NJ

Siegling America
Fullerton CA
Siegling America
Manteca CA
Siegling America
Kansas City MO
Siegling America
Mobile AL
Siegling America
Stone Mountain GA
Siegling America
Mansfield TX
Brands:
Extremultus
Transilon
Transtex

22786 Foreign Candy Company
1 Foreign Candy Dr
Hull, IA 51239-7499

712-439-1496
Fax: 712-439-3207 800-831-8541
www.foreigncandy.com
Developer and distributor of candy.
CEO, President & Owner: Peter De Yager
VP, Marketing & Sales: Bill Lange
HR Manager: Bethany Bosma
Estimated Sales: $5-10 Million
Number Employees: 11 - 50
Type of Packaging: Private Label
Brands:
Mega Warheads
Rips Toll

22787 Foreman Group
P.O. Box 189
Zelienople, PA 16063

724-452-9690
Fax: 724-452-0136 www.foremangroup.com
Owner: Phil Foreman
Contact: Mark Follen
m.follen@foremangroup.com
Estimated Sales: $10 - 20 Million
Number Employees: 50-99

22788 Foremost Machine Builders Inc
23 Spielman Rd
Fairfield, NJ 07004-3488

973-227-0700
Fax: 973-227-7307 sales@foremostmachine.com
Manufacturer and exporter of plastic scrap recovery and bulk material handling systems
President: Marlene Heydenreich
mheydenreich@foremostmachine.com
VP/General Manager: Clifford Weinpel
Assistant Sales Manager: Drew Schmid
Estimated Sales: $10 - 20 Million
Number Employees: 50-99
Square Footage: 110000

22789 Forest Manufacturing Co
1665 Enterprise Pkwy
Twinsburg, OH 44087-2284

330-425-3805
Fax: 330-425-9604
Manufacturer/exporter of flags, pennants, banners, pressure-sensitive product markings and decals
President: Forest Bookman
CFO: Bob Briggs
Sales Manager: Dick Dragonnette
General Manager: John Hammons
Estimated Sales: $20 - 30 Million
Number Employees: 50-99
Square Footage: 135000

22790 Formaticum
165 Court Street
Apt 104
Brooklyn, NY 11201

503-922-3866
Fax: 503-389-7675 800-830-0317
mark@formaticum.com www.formaticum.com
Accessories/supplies i.e. picninc baskets, cooking implements/housewares, dispaly fixtures, specialty food packaging i.e. gift wrap/labels/boxes/containers.
Marketing: Mark Goldman
Contact: Mark Goldman
mark@formaticum.com

22791 Formation Systems
144 Turnpike Rd Ste 310
Southborough, MA 01772
508-303-6200
Fax: 508-303-6250 info@formationsystems.com
www.formationsystems.com
A provider of product lifecycle management solutions for process manufacturing companies. Info, a large software provider has acquired this company
President: Trent Landreth
CFO: Leo Casey
Contact: G Casey
g.casey@formationsystems.com
Estimated Sales: $10 - 20 Million
Number Employees: 60
Parent Co: Infor

22792 Formel Industries
2355 N. 25th Ave
Franklin Park, IL 60131
847-455-3300
Fax: 847-928-9655 800-373-3300
www.formelinc.com
Cellophane bags
President: Don O' Malley
Sales/ Marketing: Sam O'Malley
Plant Manager: Mike Cinquepalmi
Estimated Sales: $5 - 10 Million
Number Employees: 20-49

22793 Former Tech
9367 Winkler Drive
Houston, TX 77017-5915
713-944-5336
Fax: 713-944-2194 800-843-8914
President and CEO: Ron Hokanson
Estimated Sales: $5 - 10 Million
Number Employees: 25

22794 Formers By Ernie
7905 Almeda Genoa Rd # B
Suite B
Houston, TX 77075-2007
713-991-3455
Fax: 713-991-0048 866-991-3455
www.formersbyernie.net
Metal and aluminum bag formers and packaging machinery equipment
President: Ernie Sanchez
sales@formersbyernie.com
CFO: Terry Sanchez
Quality Control: Ernie Jr Sanchez
R&D: Dennis Kokkins
Estimated Sales: $2 000,000
Number Employees: 10-19

22795 Formers of Houston
3533 Preston Ave
Pasadena, TX 77505
281-998-9570
Fax: 281-998-9692 800-468-5224
info@formers.com www.formers.com
Packaging machinery parts
President: John Dominguez Jr
Vice President: John Dominguez
Quality Control: Chico Marquez
Sales Director: Patty O'Neal
Contact: Cynthia Alaniz
cynthia@formers.com
Production Manager: Ben Dominguez
Estimated Sales: $5 - 10 000,000
Number Employees: 20-49
Square Footage: 9500
Type of Packaging: Consumer

22796 Formflex
70 N Main St
Bloomingdale, IN 47832
765-498-8900
Fax: 765-498-5200 800-255-7659
de@formflexsales.com
www.formflexproducts.com
Manufacturer and exporter of polyolefin sheets, signs, and packaging
CEO: Martha Alexander
kwformflex@bloomingdaletel.com
CEO: Brent Thompson
Marketing Director: David Elliott
Sales Director: Brent Thompson
Public Relations: Janice Stewart
Estimated Sales: $10-20 Million
Number Employees: 250-499
Square Footage: 60000
Parent Co: Futurex Industries

Type of Packaging: Bulk
Brands:
Formflex

22797 Formic Technologies Inc.
445 W Erie St
Suite 101
Chicago, IL 60654
844-436-7642
formic.co
Automation machinery manufacturing for food products.
CEO: Saman Farid
Treasurer & VP, Finance: Jack Wagler
Year Founded: 2020
Estimated Sales: $26.5 Million

22798 Formost Packaging Machines
19211 144th Ave NE
Woodinville, WA 98072
425-483-9090
Fax: 425-486-5656 sales@formostfuji.com
Manufacturer and exporter of high-speed automated horizontal and vertical bagging and wrapping machines including formers/fillers/sealers
President: Norm Formo
normf@formostpkg.com
CFO: Dan Semanskee
Executive VP: Norm Formo
VP Sales: Dennis Gunnell
Plant Manager: Al Shelton
Purchasing Manager: Michelle Richards
Number Employees: 50-99
Type of Packaging: Consumer, Food Service, Private Label, Bulk

22799 Formula Espresso
65 Commerce Street
Brooklyn, NY 11231-1642
718-834-8724
Fax: 718-834-9022 www.espressosystems.com
Manufacturer and exporter of commercial stainless steel espresso equipment
Owner: George Ilardo
Estimated Sales: $1-2.5 Million
Number Employees: 5-9
Type of Packaging: Food Service
Brands:
Formula

22800 Formulator Software, LLC
28 Center St
Clinton, NJ 08809-2635
908-735-2248
Fax: 908-236-7865 jdegroff@formulatorus.com
www.formulatorus.com
Offering barcode solutions and products including route accounting softwareand implementation, warehouse management software and wireless integration.
Managing Partner: James Degroff
Technical Manager: C Womer
Research & Development: C Longfield
Estimated Sales: $1 - 3 Million
Number Employees: 12
Number of Brands: 20
Number of Products: 8000
Brands:
Eltron
Hhp
Symbol
Zebra

22801 Forpack
16905 Neill Path
Hastings, MN 55033-8743
651-438-2115
Fax: 651-437-8755
President: Loyd Lowweden
CFO: Loyd Lowweden
Quality Control: Dave Lege
Estimated Sales: $3 - 5 Million
Number Employees: 10

22802 Forpak
16901 Neill Path
Hastings, MN 55033-8743
651-438-2115
Fax: 651-437-8755
President: Lloyd Lodewegen
CFO: Suzanne Lloyd
Estimated Sales: $1 - 2.5 000,000
Number Employees: 7

22803 Forrest Engraving Company
92 1st St
New Rochelle, NY 10801-6121
914-632-9892
Fax: 914-632-7416
Manufacturer and exporter of plastic and metal nameplates and signs
President: Thomas Giordano
tom@forrestpermasigns.com
Manager: Tom Giordano
Estimated Sales: $500,000-$1 Million
Number Employees: 5 to 9

22804 Forster & Son
1900 B St
Ada, OK 74820-2831
580-332-6021
Fax: 580-332-6021
Flour and feed mill machinery; also, custom steel fabrication, steel perforation and mining equipment
Owner: John Forster
jforster40@hotmail.com
Estimated Sales: Less Than $500,000
Number Employees: 1-4

22805 Fort Dearborn Company
1530 Morse Ave
Elk Grove, IL 60007
847-357-9500
Fax: 847-357-8726 info@fortdearborn.com
www.fortdearborn.com
Label supplier
CEO: Kevin Kwilinski
CFO: Timothy Trahey
COO: Bill Johnstone
Year Founded: 1925
Estimated Sales: $526 Million
Number Employees: 1,675

22806 Fort James Canada
137 Bentworth Avenue
Toronto, ON M6A 1P6
Canada
416-784-1621
Fax: 416-789-0170
Disposable cups including paper, plastic and foam
National Sales Manager: Phil Wahl
Number Employees: 500-999
Parent Co: James River Corporation

22807 Fort Lock Corporation
3000 River Road
River Grove, IL 60171-1097
708-456-1100
Fax: 708-456-9476
Manufacturing, electronic and mechanical locks for the vending industry
President: Jay Fine
VP: Gary Myers
Estimated Sales: $10 - 20 000,000
Number Employees: 3

22808 Fort Wayne Awning
7105 Ardmore Ave
Fort Wayne, IN 46809-9541
260-478-1636
Fax: 260-747-0466 800-404-1636
mccawning@aol.com www.fortwayneawning.com
Commercial awnings
Owner: Mel Mc Clain
mccawning@aol.com
Estimated Sales: Below $5,000,000
Number Employees: 5-9

22809 Forte Technology
58 Norfolk Ave.
Suite 4
South Easton, MA 02375-1055
508-297-2363
Fax: 508-297-2314 info@forte-tec.com
www.forte-tec.com
Manufacturer and exporter of electronic moisture measurement systems
President: Patricia White
Contact: Tom Gorman
t.gorman@forte-tec.com
Plant Manager: Mark Donohowski
Estimated Sales: $2.5-5 Million
Number Employees: 5-9
Square Footage: 28000
Brands:
Forte

22810 Fortenberry Mini-Storage
3128 Fortenberry Rd
Kodak, TN 37764-2020
865-933-2568
Fax: 865-933-2568
Ice
President: Arvil Fortenberry
arvil@fortenberrymm.com
Estimated Sales: Less Than $500,000
Number Employees: 1-4

22811 Fortifiber Building Systs Grp
300 Industrial Dr
Fernley, NV 89408-8905
775-575-5557
Fax: 775-333-6411 800-773-4777
buildingproducts@fortifiber.com
www.fortifiber.com
Paper bags, building papers and linings
Manager: Bill Rieger
CEO: Stuart Yount
syount@fortifiber.com
Plant Manager: Greg Hobbs
Estimated Sales: $5-10 Million
Number Employees: 10-19
Brands:
  Fibreen Economy
  Super Bar

22812 Fortress Technology
51 Grand Marshall Drive
Scarborough, ON M1B 5N6
Canada
416-754-2898
Fax: 416-754-2976 888-220-8737
sales@fortresstechnology.com
www.fortresstechnology.com
Fortress Technology is a world leader in the design
and manufacture of the highest quality metal detec-
tor systems for the food processing, material han-
dling and packaging operations.
President: Steve Gidman
Marketing Director: Adam Lang
Sales Director: Steve Mason
Number Employees: 60
Number of Brands: 4
Number of Products: 20

22813 Fortress Technology
51 Grand Marshall Dr
Toronto, ON M1B 5N6
Canada
416-754-2898
Fax: 416-754-2976 888-220-8737
info@fortresstechnology.com
www.fortresstechnology.com
Food safety detector equipment

22814 Fortune Plastics, Inc
P.O Box 637
Williams Ln.
Old Saybrook, CT 06475
Fax: 860-388-9930 800-243-0306
Manufacturer and exporter of plastic bags
Contact: Jay Adamski
jadamski@fortuneplastics.com
Estimated Sales: $5 - 10 Million
Number Employees: 20-49
Parent Co: Hilex Poly Co. LLC

22815 Fortune Products Inc
2010 Windy Ter # A
Cedar Park, TX 78613-4559
512-249-0334
Fax: 830-693-6394 contact@accusharp.com
www.accusharp.com
Manufacturer and exporter of manually operated
knife and scissor sharpeners
President: Jay Cavanaugh
info@accusharp.com
VP: Dale Fortenberry Jr
Operations: Randy Fortenberry
Estimated Sales: Less Than $500,000
Number Employees: 5-9
Square Footage: 13000
Type of Packaging: Consumer, Food Service, Pri-
vate Label, Bulk
Brands:
  Accusharp
  Sharp 'n' Easy
  Shear Sharp

22816 Fort, Products
4801 Main St
Suite 205
Kansas City, MO 64112
816-741-3000
www.forteproducts.com
Retail fixtures for the food service industry
CFO: Scott Morris

22817 Forum Lighting
900 Old Freeport Rd
Pittsburgh, PA 15238-3130
412-781-5970
Fax: 412-244-9032 www.forumlighting.com
Manufacturer and exporter of fluorescent and HID
linear lighting; custom designs available
Special Projects: Paula Garret
Controller: Julie McElhattan
Senior VP: Jonathan Garret
Special Projects: Paula Garret
Vice President of Sales: Steve Seligman
Plant Manager: Bill Dapper
Estimated Sales: $20-50 Million
Number Employees: 20-49
Square Footage: 70000

22818 Foss Nirsystems
12101 Tech Rd
Silver Spring, MD 20904-1915
301-755-5200
Fax: 301-236-0134
Manufacturer and exporter of rapid quality control
analysis equipment including moisture, fat, protein
and sugar for laboratory and in-plant application using near infrared technology
IT Executive: Dan Cipriaso
dcipriaso@foss.dk
IT Executive: Dan Cipriaso
dcipriaso@foss.dk
Estimated Sales: $20 Million
Number Employees: 1-4

22819 Foster Farms Inc.
1000 Davis St.
PO Box 306
Livingston, CA 95334
800-255-7227
www.fosterfarms.com
Poultry producer.
CEO: Dan Huber
Year Founded: 1939
Estimated Sales: Over $1 Billion
Number Employees: 10,000+
Number of Brands: 6
Type of Packaging: Consumer, Food Service, Pri-
vate Label, Bulk
Brands:
  Foster Farms Always Natural
  Foster Farms Fresh & Natural
  Foster Farms Naturally Seasoned
  Foster Farms Organic
  Foster Farms Saut, Ready
  Foster Farms Simply Raised

22820 Foster Forbes Glass
E Charles St
Marion, IN 46952
765-668-1200
Fax: 765-668-1389
Glass containers
Sr. VP Sales/Marketing: R Deneau
VP Operations/Service: J Fordham
Manager of Purchasing: T Moreland
Estimated Sales: $1-2.5 Million
Number Employees: 5-9
Parent Co: American National Can Company

22821 Foster Miller Inc
350 2nd Ave
Waltham, MA 02451-1196
781-684-4000
Fax: 781-290-0693 www.qinetiq-na.com
Custom food processing and vending equipment; de-
sign services available engineering and R&D ser-
vices from 200+ engineers and scienctists
President: Michael G. Stolarik
CEO: Duane P. Andrews
Executive VP: David Shrum
david.shrum@qinetiq-na.com
Marketing: Peter Debakker
Number Employees: 20-49
Square Footage: 380000

22822 Foster Refrigerator Corporation
PO Box 718
Kinderhook, NY 12106
518-828-3311
Fax: 518-828-3315 888-828-3311
fosterusa@yahoo.com www.Foster-us.com
Manufacturer and exporter of commercial refrigera-
tors, freezers, coolers and ovens
Owner: James Dinardi
Estimated Sales: $1 - 5 Million
Number Employees: 1-4
Square Footage: 200000
Type of Packaging: Food Service
Brands:
  Fosters

22823 Foster-Forbes Glass Company
4855 E 52nd Pl
Vernon, CA 90058
323-562-5100
Fax: 323-560-4165 800-767-4527
www.sgcontainers.com
Glass bottles
Plant Manager: Art Jones
Estimated Sales: $1 - 5 Million
Number Employees: 250-499
Parent Co: Sant' Gobian

22824 Fotel
1125 E St Charles Rd Ste 100
Lombard, IL 60148-2085
630-932-7520
Fax: 630-932-7610 800-834-4920
Bar code film masters, pre-printed bar code labels
and equipment, RFID systems for manufacturing bar
code verifiers.
President: John Nachtries
CEO: John Nachtrieb
Marketing Director: Beverly Nachtries
Operations Manager: Kevin Sousa
Plant Manager: Cathy Letza
Estimated Sales: $2.5-5 Million
Number Employees: 20-49
Square Footage: 40000

22825 Foth & Van Dyke
P.O. Box 19012
Green Bay, WI 54307-9012
920-497-2500
Fax: 920-497-8516 foth@foth.com
www.foth.com
Consultant for custom machine development and de-
sign, packaging line layout and design and modifica-
tions and upgrades to lines and equipment
CEO: Tim Weyenberg
CEO: Tim Weyenberg
Contact: Dorothi Cummings
dcummings@foth.com
Estimated Sales: $50 Million
Number Employees: 250-499

22826 Fountainhead
1726 Woodhaven Drive
Bensalem, PA 19020-7108
215-245-7300
Fax: 215-245-7390 800-326-8998
info@towelettes.com www.towelettes.com
Manufacturer and exporter of stainless steel bever-
age dispensers, fountains, hoods and fans
General Manager: Ralph Kearney
Number Employees: 50-99
Parent Co: Floaire

22827 Four Corners Ice
801 W Arrington St
Farmington, NM 87401-5530
505-325-3813
Ice
Owner: Shirley Whipple
Estimated Sales: $500,000-$1 Million
Number Employees: 5-9

22828 Four M Manufacturing Group
210 San Jose Avenue
San Jose, CA 95125-1033
408-998-1141
www. four m manufacturing.com
Paper products including plates, cups, partitions and
corrugated cardboard boxes
President: Dennis Mechiel
Owner: Frank Martinez
Executive VP: Peter Mechiel
Estimated Sales: Less than $500,000
Number Employees: 4

22829 Four Seasons Produce Inc
400 Wabash Rd
PO Box 788
Ephrata, PA 17522-9100
717-721-2800
Fax: 717-721-2597 800-422-8384
www.sunrisetransportinc.com
Fruits and vegetables
Owner: David Hollinger
VP Finance: Loretta Radanovic
Quality Manager: Daniel Oloro
National Sales Manager: Stan Paluszewski
davidh@fsproduce.com
VP/General Manager: Rob Kurtz
Number Employees: 500-999
Square Footage: 261000

22830 Four Star Beef
Omaha, NE
www.fourstarbeef.com
Beef
Parent Co: JBS USA, LLC.
Other Locations:
Tolleson AZ
Green Bay WI
Plainwell MI
Souderton PA

22831 Fourinox Inc
1015 Centennial St
Green Bay, WI 54304-5562
920-336-0621
Fax: 920-336-0089 www.fourcorp.com
Manufacturer and exporter of ASME certified process vessels
President: Ben Meeuwsen
ben.meeuwsen@fourinox.com
Marketing/Sales: John Ruppel
Estimated Sales: $10-20 Million
Number Employees: 20-49
Square Footage: 110000

22832 Fowler Products Co LLC
150 Collins Industrial Blvd
Athens, GA 30601-1516
706-549-3300
Fax: 706-548-1278 877-549-3301
sales@fowlerproducts.com
www.fowlerproducts.com
Manufacturer and exporter of bottling, capping and packaging machinery
President: Don Cotney
Vice President: Randy Uebler
ruebler@fowlerproducts.com
VP Sales: Andy Monroe
Estimated Sales: Less Than $500,000
Number Employees: 1-4
Square Footage: 150000

22833 Fox Brush Company
29 Tiger Hill Road
Oxford, ME 4270
207-539-2208
Fax: 207-539-2208
Wholesaler/distributor of corn, road, push and street sweeper brooms and brushes; manufacturer of specialty brushes
Owner: Linda Cushman
Manager: Thomas Cushman
Estimated Sales: Below $5 Million
Number Employees: 1

22834 Fox Iv Technologies
6011 Enterprise Dr
Export, PA 15632-8969
724-387-3500
Fax: 724-387-3516 877-436-2434
www.foxiv.com
Labels and packing supplies
President/CEO: Rick Fox
Estimated Sales: $10 - 20 Million
Number Employees: 20-49

22835 Fox Stamp Sign & Specialty
618 W Airport Rd
Menasha, WI 54952-1407
920-725-2683
Fax: 920-725-2037 office@foxstamp.com
www.foxstamp.com
Rubber and pre-inked stamps, daters, stamp pads, inks, engraved signs and badges, notary and other embossers; also, advertising and political buttons
Owner: Jon Ceninger
jon@foxstamp.com
Sales Director: Steve Kryscio
Production Manager: Jason Burmeister
Purchasing Manager: Deb Zuck
Estimated Sales: Below $5 Million
Number Employees: 5-9
Square Footage: 4400
Parent Co: Fox Stamp, Sign & Specialty

22836 Fox Valley Wood Products Inc
W811 State Highway 96
Kaukauna, WI 54130-9653
920-766-4069
Fax: 920-766-1220
jeff@foxvalleywoodproducts.com
www.foxvalleywoodproducts.com
Pallets, crates and boxes
President: Dale Van Zeeland
jeff@foxvalleywoodproducts.com
VP: Dale Van Zeeland
Sales Manager/ Design/ Customer Service: Jeff Van Zeeland
Plant Manager: Travis Van Zeeland
Purchasing Manager/ Controller: Dale Van Zeeland
Estimated Sales: $1-2.5 Million
Number Employees: 20-49

22837 Fox-Morris Associates
9140 Arrow Point Boulevard
Suite 380
Charlotte, NC 28273-8140
704-522-8244
Fax: 704-529-1465 800-777-6503
Executive search firm specializing in the bakery and food industry
VP Executive Search: Toni Marie
Estimated Sales: $500,000-$1,000,000
Number Employees: 5-9

22838 FoxJet
P.O. Box 83
South Canaan, PA 18459-0083
570-937-4921
Fax: 570-937-3229 800-572-3434
info@loveshaw.com www.loveshaw.com
Marking and coding equipment and barcodes/labeling equipment
Marketing Director: Mark Gilvey
Plant Manager: Mark Gilvy
Estimated Sales: $10-20 Million
Number Employees: 100-249
Parent Co: Illinois Tool Works
Brands:
Foxjet
Lablex
System Master
Waxjet

22839 Foxboro Company
10900 Equity Drive
Houston, TX 77041
713-329-1600
Fax: 508-543-8764 888-369-2676
ips.csc@invensys.com www.foxboro.com
Manufacturer and exporter of microprocessor based enterprise network systems, instruments and controls
President: Mike Caliel
Industry Consultant: John Blanchard
VP: Ken Brown
Contact: Alexander Johnson
ajohnson@foxboro.com
Manager: Joe Fillion
Number Employees: 6000
Parent Co: Siebe

22840 Foxcroft Equipment & Svc Co
2101 Creek Rd
Glenmoore, PA 19343-1421
610-942-2888
Fax: 610-942-2769 800-874-0590
sales@foxcroft.com www.foxcroft.com
Chlorine control equipment, on-line analyzers, gas pacing valves, loop (set point) controllers and toxic gas detectors
Owner: Roger W Irey Jr
General Manager: Sandra Moriarity
postoffice@foxcroft.com
Estimated Sales: $2.5-5 000,000
Number Employees: 10-19

22841 Foxfire Marketing Solutions
750 Dawson Drive
Newark, DE 19713
302-533-2240
Fax: 302-533-2241 800-497-0512
Point of purchase displays and sales aids including tissue decor kits, special event cards, contest boxes and parking lot pennants.
President: Gerry Senker
Marketing Director: Jeanne Nooney
Sales Director: Bob Wegbreit
Estimated Sales: $5-10 Million
Number Employees: 50-99

22842 Foxjet
2016 E Randol Mill Road
Suite 409
Arlington, TX 76011-8223
817-795-6056
Fax: 817-795-7101 800-369-5384
www.foxjet.com
Marketing Manager: Dina Garland
Sales Director: Steve Shoup
Contact: Debbie Arling
ddarling@foxjet.com

22843 Foxon Co
235 W Park St
Providence, RI 02908-4881
401-421-2386
Fax: 401-421-8996 800-556-6943
www.quicktest.com
Manufacturer and exporter of pressure sensitive, flexible and embossed/debossed foil and paper labels
President: William Ewing
wewing@foxonlabels.com
Estimated Sales: $10-20 Million
Number Employees: 20-49

22844 Fp Development
402 S Main St
Williamstown, NJ 08094-1729
856-875-7100
Fax: 856-875-6717 sales@fpdevelopments.com
www.fpdevelopments.com
Specialized packaging equipment
President: Fred Pfleger
fpfleger@fpdevelopments.com
Estimated Sales: $5-10 Million
Number Employees: 20-49

22845 Frain Industries
245 E North Ave
Carol Stream, IL 60188-2021
630-629-9900
Fax: 630-629-6575 847-629-6575
sales@fraingroup.com www.frainindustries.com
Wholesaler/distributor of used packaging and processing equipment; rental/leasing services
Owner: Richard Frain
rfrain@fraingroup.com
CEO: David Eggleston
Marketing Director: Suzanne Eaton
Estimated Sales: $14 Million
Number Employees: 50-99
Square Footage: 350000

22846 Framarx Corp
3224 Butler St
S Chicago Hts, IL 60411-5505
708-755-3530
Fax: 708-755-3617 800-336-3936
saus@framarx.com www.framarx.com
Manufacturer and exporter of waxed and coated papers
Vice President: Cindy Cofran
ccofran@framarx.com
Vice President: Cindy Cofran
Marketing Coordinator: Julia Saeid
Sales: Deborah M
Operations Manager: Christopher Czaszwicz
Production Manager: Jim Merrell
Estimated Sales: $20 - 50 Million
Number Employees: 20-49
Type of Packaging: Food Service, Private Label, Bulk

22847 FranRica Systems
PO Box 30127
Stockton, CA 95213-0127
209-948-2811
Fax: 209-948-5198

Food processing and filling equipment, including heat exchangers (tubular, scraped surface, aseptic flash cooling, steam injection), hot break systems, evaporators, control panels, pre-made aseptic bag fillers, aseptic bulk storage systems, complete syst
President: Eric Kurtz
CFO: Marty Menz
R&D: Bill Kreaner
Contact: Jerry Hougland
  jerry.hougland@fmc.com
Estimated Sales: $20 - 30 Million
Number Employees: 125

22848 France Personalized Signs
1559 E 17th St
Cleveland, OH 44114-2921
216-241-2198
Fax: 216-771-5111
Signs, banners, decals, interior graphics and displays
President: Stephen Treitinick Jr
Estimated Sales: less than $500,000
Number Employees: 1-4

22849 (HQ)Francis & Lusky Company
1437 Donelson Pike
Nashville, TN 37217-2957
615-242-0501
Fax: 615-256-0862 800-251-3711
Manufacturer, importer and exporter of advertising calendars; distributor of promotional products
President: Richard Francis
VP Marketing: Eric Wittel
VP Sales: Jeff Brown
Estimated Sales: $20 - 50 Million
Number Employees: 20-49

22850 Francis Restaurant Industry Equipment Services (F.R.I.E.S.)
14 Automatic Road
Unit 33
Brampton, ON L6S 5N5
Canada
905-838-2060
Fax: 905-838-2050 customerservice@friesinc.com
www.friesinc.com
Food equipment service supplier.
Year Founded: 1998
Number of Brands: 1
Brands:
  F.R.I.E.S.

22851 (HQ)Francorp
20200 Governors Dr
Olympia Fields, IL 60461
708-481-2900
Fax: 708-481-5885 800-327-6244
info@francorp.com www.francorp.com
Management consulting firm specializing in franchise development providing legal, financial, operational and marketing services
CEO: Donald Boroian
President: L Patrick Callaway
Executive VP/COO: Mary Kennedy
Contact: Ahmed Alrefai
  ahmad.alrefai@reedsunaidiexpo.com
COO: Mary Kennedy
Estimated Sales: $10-15 Million
Number Employees: 20-49
Square Footage: 26000
Other Locations:
  Francorp
  Seville

22852 Frank B Ross Co Inc
970 New Brunswick Ave # H
Rahway, NJ 07065-3814
732-669-0810
Fax: 732-669-0814 www.frankbross.com
Natural waxes and wax blends
President: Larry Powell
VP: Donald Ayerlee
Estimated Sales: $1 - 5 Million
Number Employees: 5-9
Square Footage: 160000

22853 Frank Haile & Assoc
2650 Freewood Dr
Dallas, TX 75220-2596
214-357-6659
Fax: 214-357-9321 800-544-2511
n4fh@aol.com www.fha-usa.net
Bulk and minor ingredients handling systems

President/CEO: Frank Haile
  n4fh@aol.com
CFO: Dale Fehlman
Vice President: Elaine Cook
Estimated Sales: $2.5 000,000
Number Employees: 5-9
Square Footage: 6400

22854 Frank O Carlson & Co
3622 S Morgan St # 2r
Chicago, IL 60609-1576
773-847-6900
Fax: 773-847-6924 dcarlson@focarlson.com
www.focarlson.com
Indoor advertising signs and graphics
President: Rose Carlson
  rcarlson@focarlson.com
Quality Control: Earl Raas
VP: Douglas Carlson
Number Employees: 5-9

22855 Frank Torrone & Sons
400 Broadway
Staten Island, NY 10310-2096
718-273-7600
Fax: 718-447-5103 atorrone@aol.com
Electric signs
Owner: Arthur Torrone
Estimated Sales: $1-2.5 Million
Number Employees: 10-19

22856 Franke Americas
3050 Campus Dr
Suite 500
Hatfield, PA 19440
215-822-6590
Fax: 800-789-6201 www.franke.com/us
Manufacturer of foodservice and coffee systems
President, Franke Coffee Systems NA: Corrie Byron
Parent Co: Franke Group

22857 Franklin Automation Inc
1981 Bucktail Ln
Sugar Grove, IL 60554-9609
630-466-1900
Fax: 630-466-1902 info@franklinautomation.com
www.franklinautomation.com
Form, fill and seal machine for packaging small consumer products
President: Frank Kigyos
  frank@franklinautomation.com
Estimated Sales: $3 - 5 Million
Number Employees: 10-19

22858 Franklin Crates
P.O. Box 279
Micanopy, FL 32667
352-466-3141
Fax: 352-466-0708 fcrates@bellsouth.net
Fruit and vegetable wirebound crates
President: Ben O Franklin Iii
Secretary: W Davis
Estimated Sales: $5-10 Million
Number Employees: 50-99

22859 Franklin Equipment
P.O. Box 8246
Greenville, TX 75404-8246
903-883-2002
Fax: 903-883-3210 800-356-7591
www.thehenrygroup.com
Food plant construction services, stainless fabrication services, matching of replacement part for food equipment
President, Chief Executive Officer, Owne: Troy Henry
Estimated Sales: $10-25 Million
Number Employees: 100-249

22860 Franklin Machine Products
PO Box 992
Marlton, NJ 08053-0992
856-983-2500
Fax: 800-255-9866 800-257-7737
sales@fmponline.com www.fmponline.com
Wholesaler/distributor of parts and accessories: serving the food service market
CEO: Carol Adams
Vice President: Michael Conte, Sr.
Estimated Sales: $20-50 Million
Number Employees: 100-249
Square Footage: 50000

22861 Franklin Rubber Stamp Co
301 W 8th St
Wilmington, DE 19801-1553
302-654-8841
Fax: 302-654-8860 orders@franklinstamps.com
www.franklinstamps.com
Rubber stamps and magnetic and engraved plastic signs
President: Tom Tanzilli
Manager: Russell Protas
Estimated Sales: $1-2.5 Million
Number Employees: 10-19

22862 Franklin Uniform Corporation
3946 Cloverhill Rd
Baltimore, MD 21218-1707
410-235-8151
Fax: 410-347-7607
Uniforms and special clothing
Owner: Paula A Franklin
Estimated Sales: $1-2.5 Million
Number Employees: 1-4

22863 Frankston Paper Box Company of Texas
699 N Frankston Hwy
Frankston, TX 75763
903-876-2550
Fax: 903-876-4458
admin@frankstonpackaging.com
www.frankstonpackaging.com
Rigid set-up, paper, plastic and folding boxes
Owner: Norm Bollock
  nbollock@frankstonpackaging.com
CFO: Norm Bullock
Quality Control: Edwin Adcock
Sales: D'Wayne Odom
Production Manager: Charles Montrose
Plant Manager: Bill McHam
Estimated Sales: $20 - 50 Million
Number Employees: 50-99
Square Footage: 45000

22864 Franmara
560 Work St
Salinas, CA 93901-4350
831-422-4000
Fax: 831-422-7000 800-423-5855
franksr@franmara.com www.modularackusa.com
Wine industry tasting room supplies
President: John Chiorazzi
  johnc@franmara.com
Estimated Sales: $10 - 20 Million
Number Employees: 20-49
Number of Products: 19

22865 Franrica Systems
PO Box 30127
Stockton, CA 95213-0127
209-948-2811
Fax: 209-948-5198
Manufacturer, importer and exporter of aseptic fillers, heat exchangers, tanks, pumps, evaporators, flash coolers, tomato paste processing plants, etc
Director: Eric Curtz
Controller: Marty Menz
Contact: Jerry Hougland
  jerry.hougland@fmc.com
Estimated Sales: $20 - 30 Million
Number Employees: 125
Square Footage: 70000
Parent Co: FMC Technologies
Brands:
  Franrica

22866 Frantz Co Inc
12314 W Silver Spring Dr
Milwaukee, WI 53225-2918
414-462-8700
Fax: 414-462-6655 inform@frantzcompany.com
www.frantzcompany.com
Smokehouse sawdust
President: Steve Frantz
  steve@frantzcompany.com
CFO: John Tesensky
Estimated Sales: $5-10 Million
Number Employees: 10-19

22867 Franz Haas Machinery-America
6207 Settler Rd
Henrico, VA 23231-6044
804-222-6022
Fax: 804-222-0217 www.haasusa.com
Bakery machinery including ovens

Manager: Michael Fleetwood
Director Sales/Marketing: M Fleetwood
General Manager: Michael Fleetwood
Application Engineer: Bill Redden
Estimated Sales: $10-20 Million
Number Employees: 20-49
Parent Co: Franz Haas Machinery of America

22868 Fraser Stamp & Seal
215 N Desplaines St # 2n
Chicago, IL 60661-1073
312-922-4970
Fax: 312-922-2692 800-540-8565
fraserstamp@aol.com www.aerubberstamp.com
Sealing stamps, stamp pad inks and marking stencils
President: Phil DE Francisco
aerbrstamp@aol.com
Estimated Sales: Less Than $500,000
Number Employees: 1-4

22869 Frazier & Son
101 Longview St
Conroe, TX 77301-4075
936-494-4040
Fax: 936-494-4045 800-365-5438
info@frazierandson.com www.frazierandson.com
Manufacturer and exporter of power operated packaging machinery including fillers for frozen food; also, bucket elevators
Owner: Mark Frazier
Sales/Engineer: Robert Gennario
Manager: Nicole Baird
nicole.baird@lrsus.com
Estimated Sales: $2.5 - 5 Million
Number Employees: 10-19
Square Footage: 20000
Brands:
Whiz-Lifter

22870 Frazier Industrial Co
91 Fairview Ave
Long Valley, NJ 07853-3381
908-876-3001
Fax: 908-876-3615 800-859-1342
frazier@frazier.com www.frazier.com
Structural steel pallet rack systems
CEO: William L Mascharka
wmascharka@frazier.com
Estimated Sales: $50 - 100 Million
Number Employees: 100-249

22871 Frazier Precision InstrCo
925 Sweeney Dr
Hagerstown, MD 21740-7128
301-790-2585
Fax: 301-790-2589 info@frazierinstrument.com
www.frazierinstrument.com
Manufacturer and exporter of test instruments and measuring equipment
President: Thomas F Scrivener
Estimated Sales: $1 - 2.5 Million
Number Employees: 5-9

22872 Frazier Signs
1304 N 20th St
Decatur, IL 62521
217-429-2349
Fax: 217-429-2340
Signs including neon, plastic, metal, magnetic, vinyl and pressure sensitive; also, maintainenance, installation and repair services available
Manager (Vinyl Graphics): Robert Frazier
Estimated Sales: less than $500,000
Number Employees: 1-4
Square Footage: 12000

22873 Fred Beesley's Booth & Upholstery
264 Brookfield Ln
Centerville, UT 84014-1474
801-364-8189
Restaurant booths, counters and tables
President: Fred Beesley
Marketing Director: Fred Beesley
Estimated Sales: Below $5 Million
Number Employees: 10

22874 (HQ)Fred D Pfening Co
1075 W 5th Ave
Columbus, OH 43212-2691
614-294-5361
Fax: 614-294-1633 sales@pfening.com
www.pfening.com

Manufacturer and exporter of bakers' machinery including proof boxes, sifters and water metering devices; also, material handling equipment
President: Fred Pfening
ebrackman@pfening.com
VP of Sales/Marketing: Norm Meulenberg
Sales Exec: Edward Brackman
Purchasing Agent: Patrick Inskeep
Estimated Sales: $10 - 20 Million
Number Employees: 50-99
Square Footage: 150000
Brands:
Wat-A-Mat

22875 Fredman Bag Co
5801 W Bender Ct
Milwaukee, WI 53218-1609
414-462-9400
Fax: 414-462-9409 800-945-5686
www.fredmanbag.com
Printed packaging materials including recloseable polyethylene bags and breathable films
President: Charles Akins
charlesakins29@yahoo.com
Executive VP: Tim Fredman, Jr.
Number Employees: 50-99
Square Footage: 50000

22876 Fredrick Ramond Company
33000 Pin Oak Parkway
Avon Lake, OH 44012
440-653-5550
Fax: 440-653-5555 800-446-5539
service@hinkleylighting.com
www.fredrickramond.com
Manufacturer, importer and exporter of decorative light fixtures
President: Fredrick Glassman
National Sales Manager: Alan Dubrow
Inside Sales: David Brusius
Support Manager: Carol Romero
Estimated Sales: $10-20 Million
Number Employees: 100-249
Brands:
F. Ramond
Palm Springs

22877 Free Flow Packaging Corporation
1090 Mills Way
Redwood City, CA 94063
650-261-5300
Fax: 650-361-1713 800-888-3725
Interior cushioning material for protective packaging; also, dispersing systems for loose-fill cushioning materials
President: Arthur Graham
Marketing Manager: Jim Jensen
National Sales Manager: Harry Reynolds
Contact: Jim Birkle
james.binkle@fpintl.com
Number Employees: 350
Brands:
Flo-Pak
Flo-Pak Bio 8

22878 Freedom Packaging
195 Aviation Way # 201
Watsonville, CA 95076-2059
831-722-3565
Fax: 831-724-0995 laura@freedompackaging.com
www.freedompackaging.com
Packaging supplies for frozen foods
Owner: Tom Prague
Owner/CEO: Thomas Sprague
CEO: Thomas Sprague
Contact: Paul Hurlburt
phurlburt@choc.org
Estimated Sales: Less Than $500,000
Number Employees: 1-4

22879 Freely Display
12401 Euclid Ave
Cleveland, OH 44106-4314
216-721-6056
Fax: 216-721-6081
Manufacturer and exporter of wood store fixtures and displays
Controller: Bernadette Gello
Operations Manager: Thomas Olechiw
Estimated Sales: $2.5-5 Million
Number Employees: 5-9

22880 Freeman Co
911 Graham Dr
Fremont, OH 43420-4086
419-334-9709
Fax: 419-334-3426 800-223-7788
info@freemancompany.com
www.freemancompany.com
Cutting equipment, presses, dies, tooling
President: Greg Defisher
COO: Mike Mullholand
mmullholand@freemancompany.com
CEO: Louis G Freeman III
CFO: Scott Clifford
Estimated Sales: $2.5-5 Million
Number Employees: 50-99

22881 Freeman Electric Co Inc
534 Oak Ave
Panama City, FL 32401-2648
850-785-7448
Fax: 850-747-1162
Plastic and neon signs
President: Tommy Duncan
freemanelectricc@bellsouth.net
Estimated Sales: $1-2.5 Million
Number Employees: 10-19

22882 FreesTech
PO Box 2156
Sinking Spring, PA 19608
717-560-7560
Fax: 717-560-7587 info@freestech.com
www.freestech.com
Palletizers, freezing and cooling systems, conveyors and storage and retrieval machines for warehouse applications.
Contact: Richard Greener
dgreener@freestech.com
Year Founded: 1967
Estimated Sales: $500 Million-$1 Billion
Number Employees: 10
Brands:
Auto-Pal
Fusion Cell
Milk-Stor
Tri-Flow
Tri-Stacker
Tri-Tray

22883 Frelco
PO Box 316
Stephenville, NL A2N 2Z5
Canada
709-643-5668
Fax: 709-643-3046
Manufacturer, importer and exporter of conveyors, hoppers, tables and cabinets

22884 Frem Corporation
60 Webster Place
Worcester, MA 01603-1920
508-791-3152
Fax: 508-791-7969
Manufacturer and exporter of injection molded plastic housewares including food storage bins, crates and waste baskets
CEO: M.L. Sherman
CFO: D.A. Denovellis
Vice President: J.J. Althoff
Manager: Tim Eunice
Parent Co: Ekco Group

22885 Fremont Die Cut Products
3177 E State St
Fremont, OH 43420
419-334-2626
Fax: 419-334-3327 800-223-3177
Corrugated plastic products including bulk and sleeve packs, sheets and containers
President: Les Mintz
Estimated Sales: $1 - 5 Million
Number Employees: 20-49
Square Footage: 320000

22886 French Awning & Screen Co Inc
4514 S Mcraven Rd
Jackson, MS 39204-2031
601-922-1132
Fax: 601-922-9671 800-898-1132
kerry@frenchcanvasawnings.com
www.frenchcanvasawnings.com
Commercial awnings
President: Kerry French
kerry@frenchcanvasawnings.com

Estimated Sales: Less Than $500,000
Number Employees: 1-4

22887 French Oil Mill Machinery Co

1035 W Greene St
P.O. Box 920
Piqua, OH 45356-1855

937-773-3420
Fax: 937-773-3424 sales@frenchoil.com
www.frenchoil.com
Manufacturer and exporter of vegetable oilseed processing equipment including cracking and flaking mills, conditioners, full, extruder and pre-presses, dewatering and drying presses, liquid-solid separation equipment and hydraulicpresses
President: Daniel French
CEO: Jason P Mcdaniel
jmcdaniel@frenchoil.com
CFO: Dennis Bratton
CEO: Jason P McDaniel
Quality Control: Jason McDaniel
Sales Director: James King
Public Relations: Eric Brockman
Estimated Sales: $10 - 20 Million
Number Employees: 50-99
Square Footage: 450000

22888 Fres-Co SYSTEM USA Inc

3005 State Rd
Telford, PA 18969-1021

215-256-4172
Fax: 215-721-0747 contact@fresco.com
www.fresco.com
Tea and coffee industry bag formers/fillers/sealers, bagging machines, bags and packaging film supplies, espresso pod machines, foil laminates, machinery for coffee roasters, packaging (flexible), vacuum packaging machinery, scalesteabag machinery, pac
President: Tullio Vigano
tvigano@fresco.com
Estimated Sales: $20-50 Million
Number Employees: 250-499

22889 Fresca Foods Inc.

195 CTC Blvd.
Louisville, CO 80027

303-996-8881
Fax: 303-645-4884 hello@frescafoodsinc.com
frescafoodsinc.com
Supply chain management services.
CEO: Todd Dutkin
CFO: Zan Powell
Chief Commercial Officer: Brandon Viar
CMO: Liz Myslik
COO: Mark Bible
Year Founded: 1993
Number Employees: 150-500

22890 Fresh Express, Inc.

P.O. Box 80599
Salinas, CA 93912

800-242-5472
www.freshexpress.com
Certified organic salads and lettuce, cole slaw & shreds, delicious kits, flavorful spinach, gourmet cafe salads, harvest originals, refreshing mixes, tasty greens mixes, and tender leaf mixes.
President: John Olivo
Year Founded: 1926
Estimated Sales: $368.3 Million
Number Employees: 5,000+
Number of Brands: 1
Square Footage: 20000
Parent Co: Chiquita Brands International, Inc
Type of Packaging: Bulk
Brands:
  Fresh Express

22891 Fresh Mark Inc.

1888 Southway St. SW
Massillon, OH 44646

330-832-7491
Fax: 330-830-3174 www.freshmark.com
Bacon, ham, weiners, deli and luncheon meats, dry sausage and other specialty meat items.
CEO: Neil Genshaft
President/COO: Brent Patmos
Year Founded: 1920
Estimated Sales: $219 Million
Number Employees: 500-999
Number of Brands: 2
Square Footage: 80000

Type of Packaging: Consumer, Food Service, Private Label
Other Locations:
  Canton OH
  Salem OH
Brands:
  Sugardale
  Superior's Brand

22892 Freshloc Technologies

15443 Knoll Trail Dr
Suite 100
Dallas, TX 75248

972-759-0111
Fax: 972-759-0090 888-225-9458
sales@freshloc.com
President/CEO: Alan C Heller
Founder: Richard G. Fettig
Vice President of Sales & Operations: JD Donnelly
Sales Director: Donna Fettig
Contact: Larah Cooley
larah@freshloc.com
Estimated Sales: $2.5 - 5 Million
Number Employees: 10-19

22893 Freshway Distributors

50 Ludy St
Hicksville, NY 11801-5115

516-870-3333
www.freshway.com
Refrigerating company and also offers transportation services

22894 Fresno Neon Sign Co Inc

5901 E Clinton Ave
Fresno, CA 93727-8641

559-292-2944
Fax: 559-292-2980 www.fresnoneon.com
Signs including point of purchase, neon luminous tube and plastic
President: Ken Block
block@fresnoneon.com
Manager: Bill Kratt
Estimated Sales: $1-2.5 Million
Number Employees: 10-19

22895 Fresno Pallet, Inc.

PO Box 268
Sultana, CA 93666

559-591-4111
Fax: 559-591-6116
Fencing, skids, plywood bins and wooden and plastic pallets; also, rail and truck unloading services available
Owner: Steven Johnson
Sales Manager: Steve Johnson
Operations Manager: Michael Johnson
Estimated Sales: $2.5-5 Million
Number Employees: 10-19

22896 Fresno Tent & Awning

100 M St
Fresno, CA 93721-3117

559-264-4771
Fax: 559-485-5629 www.yahoo.com
Commercial awnings
President: Pat Haun
fresnotent@yahoo.com
Estimated Sales: $2.5 - 5,000,000
Number Employees: 1-4

22897 Freudenberg Nonwovens

2975 Pembroke Road
Hopkinsville, KY 42240

270-887-5115
Fax: 270-886-5069
HVAC@freudenberg-filter.com
www.freudenberg-filter.com
Manufacturer and importer of air and liquid filters; also, filtration media
Estimated Sales: $50-100 Million
Number Employees: 100-249
Brands:
  Micronair
  Viledon

22898 (HQ)Friedman Bag Company

865 Manhattan Beach Boulevard
Suite 204
Manhattan Beach, CA 90266-4955

213-628-2341
Fax: 213-687-9772

Manufacturer and exporter of burlap, cotton, polyethylene, open mesh bags; wholesaler/distributor of paper bags, cartons and packaging supplies
President: Al Lanfeld
VP/Operations Manager: David Friedman
Sales/Service: Diane Dal Porto
Estimated Sales: $20-50 Million
Number Employees: 250-499
Square Footage: 400000

22899 Friedr Dick Corp

33 Allen Blvd
Farmingdale, NY 11735-5611

631-454-6955
Fax: 631-454-6184 800-554-3425
www.fdick.us
Manufacturer and distributor of cutlery
Sales: Morgan
Manager: Steve Kurek
s.kurek@feiedrdick.us
Operations: Scott Belovin
Number Employees: 5-9
Number of Brands: 7
Number of Products: 600
Square Footage: 10000
Type of Packaging: Consumer, Food Service, Bulk
Brands:
  Friedr. Dick

22900 Friedrich Metal Products

6204 Technology Dr
Browns Summit, NC 27214-9702

336-375-3067
Fax: 336-621-7901 800-772-0326
info@friedrichproducts.com
www.friedrichproducts.com
Manufacturer and exporter of smokehouses, bakery ovens, smokers, deli equipment, etc
President: Jennifer Prago
jprago@friedrichproducts.com
CFO: Bob Friedrich
Vice President: Laura Friedrich-Bargebuhr
Quality Control: Axel Dender
Estimated Sales: $1 - 3 Million
Number Employees: 20-49
Square Footage: 60000

22901 Friend Box Co

90 High St
Danvers, MA 01923-3196

978-774-0240
Fax: 978-777-7921 www.friendbox.com
Boxes including rigid paper and loose wrap candy
President: Debbie Bertolino
debbie@friendbox.com
Quality Control: Rich Lombardo
CEO: Charlie Walker
VP Sales: Fran Dollard
VP Operations: Larry Comeau
Estimated Sales: $5 - 10 Million
Number Employees: 50-99

22902 Friendly City Box Co Inc

520 Oakridge Dr
Johnstown, PA 15904-6915

814-266-6287
Fax: 814-266-9757
Folding paper cartons
Owner: Lance Blackburn
fcboxco@floodcity.net
Estimated Sales: $1-2.5 Million
Number Employees: 5-9

22903 Frigid Coil

13711 Freeway Drive
Santa Fe Springs, CA 90670-5688

562-921-4310
Fax: 562-921-6412
Manufactures refrigeration and air conditioning equipment for commercial use
President: David Myers
Quality Control: Thomas Serry
R & D: Gary Price
Estimated Sales: $1-2.5 Million
Number Employees: 10

22904 Frigidaire Co.

10200 David Taylor Dr.
Charlotte, NC 28262

866-449-4200
Fax: 704-547-7401 www.frigidaire.com
Freezers and fridges.

Estimated Sales: $100-500 Million
Number Employees: 1000-4999
Parent Co: Electrolux
Brands:
  Gibson
  Kelvinator
  White Westinghouse

22905 Frigoscandia
9577 153rd Ave NE
Redmond, WA 98052-2513
425-883-2244
Fax: 425-882-0948 800-423-1743
Freezing/refrigeration equipment including in-line quick freezing and spiral freezers, freezer control systems and pre-packaged refrigeration systems; also, steam pasteurization systems for carcasses
Vice President: Charlie Cannon
Director Sales: Mike Kish
Contact: Jared Larson
  vijay_lamba@fmc.com
Number Employees: 20-49
Parent Co: FMC Corporation
Brands:
  Flofreeze
  Frigopak
  Gyrocompact
  Gyrostack
  Lewis Iqf
  Sps

22906 Frigoscandia Equipment
1700 Cannon Road
Northfield, MN 55057-1680
507-645-9546
Fax: 507-645-6148 800-426-1283
www.fmctechnologies.com
Manufacturers inline spiral freezer for food processing industry
President: Simoau Jeff
Quality Control: Chucks Moder
Regional Sales Manager: Ellen Hao
Estimated Sales: $20 - 50 Million
Number Employees: 100

22907 Frigoscandia Equipment
1700 Cannon Road
Northfield, MN 55057-1680
507-645-9546
Fax: 507-645-6148 800-426-1283
www.frigoscandia-equipment.com
Freezing systems, specializing in in-process line freezers, chillers, coolers, bakery proofers, dehydrators, bottle elevators, conveyors, fluidized belt freezers, trolley freezers
President: Joseph Nertherland
Marketing Manager: Larry DeBoer
Estimated Sales: $20 - 50 Million
Number Employees: 75

22908 Frisk Design
PO Box 504
Saint Helena, CA 94574-5004
707-944-1655
Fax: 707-944-1655
Wine industry bottle etching and design

22909 (HQ)Friskem Infinetics
PO Box 2330
Wilmington, DE 19899
302-658-2471
Fax: 302-658-2475
Manufacturer and exporter of detectors including metal, pilferage, passive magnetometer and active field
CEO: M Schwartz
Brands:
  Friskem
  Friskem-Af
  Tellem

22910 Fristam Pumps USA LLP
2410 Parview Rd
Middleton, WI 53562-2521
608-831-5001
Fax: 608-831-8467 800-841-5001
fristam@fristampumps.com www.fristam.com
Manufacturer and exporter of stainless steel, centrifugal and positive displacement pumps, blenders and mixers.

President: Pete Herb
CEO: Wolfgang Stamp
VP: Pete Skora
Quality Control/Operations: Duane Ehlke
Marketing Supervisor: Dan Funk
Sales Director: Larry Cook
Public Relations: Wendy Andrew
Number Employees: 100-249
Number of Products: 80
Brands:
  Fristam

22911 Fristam Pumps USA LLP
2410 Parview Rd
Middleton, WI 53562-2521
608-831-5001
Fax: 608-831-8467 sales@fristampumps.com
www.fristam.com
Centrifugal pumps, shear pumps, powder mixers and positive displacement pumps
President: Scott Haman
  shaman@fristam.com
Number Employees: 100-249

22912 Fritsch
921 Proton Rd
San Antonio, TX 78258-4203
210-227-2726
Fax: 210-227-5550
Industrial bakery equipment (sheeting equipment) roll-fix USA (retail reversible sheeters)
President: Claus Fritsch
General Manager: Danny Kelly
Off. Mngr.: Joseph Mouyer
Estimated Sales: $300,000-500,000
Number Employees: 1-4

22913 Fritsch USA
2706 Treble Crk Ste 200
San Antonio, TX 78258
210-491-9309
Fax: 210-227-5550
Sheeting and laminating equipment
President/General Manager: Danny Kelly
Estimated Sales: $300,000-500,000
Number Employees: 1-4

22914 Frobisher Industries
6260 Rte 105
Waterborough, NB E4C 2Y4
Canada
506-362-2198
Fax: 506-362-9090
Manufacturer and exporter of hamper baskets, veneer and wooden boxes for fruits and vegetables
President: George Staples
CFO: George Lorriaine
Number Employees: 10
Square Footage: 48000

22915 (HQ)Frohling Sign Co
419 E Route 59
Nanuet, NY 10954-2908
845-623-2258
Fax: 845-623-2799 bocfrohlingsign@aol.com
Plastic, wood, interior, exterior, neon and metal signs; also, plaques
President: Brian O'Connor
  brian@frohlingsign.com
Estimated Sales: $1-2.5 Million
Number Employees: 5-9

22916 Frommelt Safety Products& Ductsox Corporation
4343 Chavenelle Rd
Dubuque, IA 52002-2653
563-556-2020
Fax: 563-589-2776 800-553-5560
Fabric air dispersion products for open ceiling architecture
President: Cary Pinkalla
Sr. Sales Promotion Specialist: Mary Jo Kluesner
Contact: Lou Wiegand
  l.wiegand@ritehite.com
Plant Manager: Lou Wiegand
Estimated Sales: $2 million
Number Employees: 5-9

22917 Frontage Enterprises
14111 Freeway Dr
Santa Fe Springs, CA 90670-5822
562-407-9345
Fax: 562-404-3602

22918 Frontier Bag
5720 E State Route 150
Kansas City, MO 64147-1003
816-765-4811
Fax: 816-765-6603 www.yellowbagpeople.com
Plastic, shrink and meat bags, polyethylene bag liners, pallet covers and sheeting; exporter of plastic bags; importer of polyethylene raw materials bager plain and printed
President: Mark Gurley
  m.gurley@yellowbagpeople.com
Owner: Ron Gurley
VP Sales: Tom Hauser
VP Production: Ron Avery
Estimated Sales: $20-50 Million
Number Employees: 50-99
Square Footage: 90000

22919 Frontier Bag Co Inc
2420 Grant St
Omaha, NE 68111-3825
402-342-0992
Fax: 402-342-2107 800-278-2247
customerservice@frontierbagco.com
www.frontierbagco.com
Burlap and cotton bags; wholesaler/distributor of paper and plastic bags; serving the food service market
President: Judy Pearl-Lee
  jplee@frontierbagco.com
Sales Manager: Judy Pearl-Lee
Estimated Sales: $1-2.5 Million
Number Employees: 10-19

22920 Frontier Packaging Company
1938 Occidental Avenue S
Seattle, WA 98134-1413
206-682-7800
Fax: 206-682-1669 800-737-7333
Wine industry packaging
Estimated Sales: $1-2.5 000,000
Number Employees: 19

22921 Frost ET Inc
2020 Bristol Ave NW
Grand Rapids, MI 49504-1402
616-301-2660
Fax: 616-453-2161 800-253-9382
frost.sales@frostinc.com www.frostinc.com
Overhead, inverted and conveyor trolleys, guide rollers, conveyor roll bearings, and food processing components.
President: Chad Frost
  cfrost@frostinc.com
Number Employees: 10-19

22922 Frost Food Handling Products
2020 Bristol Ave NW
Grand Rapids, MI 49504
616-453-7781
Fax: 616-453-2161 800-253-9382
frost@frostinc.com www.frostinc.com
Conveying components for food handling applications
CEO: Chad Frost
CFO: Fred Sytsma
Sales Director: Joe Jakeway
Estimated Sales: $10-20 Million
Number Employees: 50-99
Square Footage: 120000
Parent Co: Frost Industries
Brands:
  Attachments
  Blue Poly Trolleys
  Sani-Link Chain
  Sani-Trolley
  Sani-Wheel
  Stainless Steel Bearings
  Stainless Steel Trolleys
  Stainless Steel X-Chain
  X-Chain

22923 Frost Manufacturing Corp
173 Grove St # 1
Worcester, MA 01605-1715
508-756-4685
Fax: 508-757-5604 800-462-0216
info@frostmanufacturing.com
www.frostmanufacturing.com
Rubber stamps, signs, name plates, stencils, menu boards, inks, labels, banners and name badges
President: Douglas Frost
  dfrost@frostmanufacturing.com
VP Marketing: Julieane Frost

Estimated Sales: $1 - 2.5 Million
Number Employees: 5-9

22924 Frosty Factory of America Inc
2301 S Farmerville St
Ruston, LA 71270-9042

    318-255-1162
    Fax: 318-255-1170 800-544-4071
dolph@frostyfactory.com www.frostyfactory.com
Manufacturer and exporter of frozen beverage, soft
serve ice cream and shake machines
President: Heath Williams
  ruston186@aol.com
Finance Executive: Penny Taylor
Sales/Marketing: Craig Moss
Sales Executive: Christopher Williams
Engineer: Ralph Pettijohn
Purchasing Manager: Ralph Pettijohn
Estimated Sales: $5 Million
Number Employees: 20-49
Square Footage: 80000
Brands:
  Petite Sorbeteer
  Soft-Serve Ice Cream
  Sorbeteer

22925 Frozen Specialties, Inc.
1718 Indian Wood Circle
Maumee, OH 43537

    419-867-2005
    www.frozenspecialties.com
Private label pizza and pizza bites.
President/CEO: Ric Alvarez
  rich.alvarez@frc.com
Controller: Paul Nungester
  rich.alvarez@frc.com
Director, Marketing: Lori Hamilton
Vice President, Sales: Dan Burdick
Year Founded: 1969
Estimated Sales: $49.99 Million
Number Employees: 10-19
Number of Brands: 2
Number of Products: 6
Square Footage: 13395
Type of Packaging: Consumer, Private Label, Bulk
Brands:
  Fox Deluxe
  Mr. P's

22926 Fruehauf Trailer Services
12813 Flushing Meadows Dr
St Louis, MO 63131-1835

    314-822-1113
Refrigerated trailers; service available
CEO: Derek Nagle
Director Marketing/Advertising: Steve Havens
Number Employees: 10-19
Parent Co: Wabash National Company
Brands:
  Fruehauf

22927 Fruit Growers Package Company
4693 Wilson Avenue SW
Suite H
Grandville, MI 49418-8762

    616-724-1400
Manufacturer and exporter of wood veneer products,
craft baskets and wooden shipping crates for berries
President: Diane Taylor
VP: Dennis Palasek
Contact: Dennis Palasek
  dennis.palasek@fruitgrowers.com
Estimated Sales: $600,000
Number Employees: 10
Square Footage: 80000
Type of Packaging: Consumer, Bulk

22928 Fruitcrown Products Corp
250 Adams Blvd
Farmingdale, NY 11735-6615

    631-694-5800
    Fax: 631-694-6467 800-441-3210
info@fruitcrown.com www.fruitcrown.com
Aseptic fruit flavors and bases for beverage, dairy
and baking industries
President: Robert Jagenburg
  orjagenburg@fruitcrown.com
Number Employees: 50-99
Type of Packaging: Bulk
Brands:
  Asp
  Exquizita
  Fruitcrown
  Huntingcastle

22929 Fruition Northwest LLC
29345 NW W Union Rd
PO Box 130
North Plains, OR 97133

    503-880-5193
High-quality infused-dehydrated berry fruits to the
wholesale market.
Owner: Alan Krassowski
Estimated Sales: $210 Thousand
Type of Packaging: Bulk

22930 Fruvemex
233 Paulin Ave
Calexico, CA 92231

    760-203-1896
    Fax: 760-203-2389 fcaballero@fruvemex.com
    www.fruvemex.com
Refrigerated and frozen fruit and vegetable products
President: Gustavo Caballero
VP Sales/Marketing: Yvonne Brewer
Year Founded: 1986
Number Employees: 85
Square Footage: 180000
Type of Packaging: Bulk

22931 Fry Tech Corporation
4430 Dodge Street
Dubuque, IA 52003-2600

    319-583-1559
    Fax: 319-557-8602 frytech@mwci.net
Fryers including ventless counter-top and auto-lift
fryers with built-in air filtration and fire suppression
systems
Owner: Rod Christ
VP: Donna Christ
Number Employees: 2
Square Footage: 7000
Brands:
  Alpaire
  Fan-C-Fry
  U-Fry-It

22932 Frye's Measure Mill
12 Frye Mill Rd
Wilton, NH 03086-5010

    603-654-6581
    Fax: 603-654-6103 www.fryesmeasuremill.com
Manufacturer and exporter of wooden dry measures,
specialty packaging, veneer containers, colonial pan-
try and shaker boxes
President: Harley Savage
  harleysavage@tds.net
Quality Control: Harley Savage
Estimated Sales: Below $5 Million
Number Employees: 5-9
Brands:
  Frye's Measure Mill
  Old Tyme

22933 Frymaster
8700 Line Ave
Shreveport, LA 71106-6800

    318-865-1711
    Fax: 318-868-5987 800-221-4583
webmaster@frymaster.com www.frymaster.com
Supplier of commercial fryers, frying systems, wa-
ter-bath rethermalizers, pasta cookers, and of the
equipment related to these technologies.
Chief Executive: David Mosteller
Estimated Sales: $60 Million
Number Employees: 500-999
Square Footage: 180000
Parent Co: Welbilt
Type of Packaging: Food Service
Brands:
  Frymaster
  Master Jet

22934 Fsi Technologies
668 E Western Ave
Lombard, IL 60148-2005

    630-932-9380
    Fax: 630-932-0016 800-468-6009
info@fsinet.com www.fsinet.com
Machine vision and systems, automatic inspection
systems, rotary shaft encoders, electronic counters
and displays for motion variables, specialized photo-
electric sensors.
President: Scott Tobey
  scott@fsinet.com
VP: Fred Turek
Sales: Kim Jackson
Estimated Sales: $2.5-5 Million
Number Employees: 20-49

Brands:
  Checker Vision System
  Cirrus
  Defender
  Ese
  Hde
  Indicoder
  Pulsar
  Rse
  Tuff-Coder

22935 Fuji Health Science/Inc
3 Terri Ln # 12
Unit 12
Burlington, NJ 08016-4903

    609-386-3030
    Fax: 609-386-3033 www.fujichemicalusa.com
Markets and manufacturers natural specialty food in-
gredient, AstaReal astaxanthin, a powerful anti-oxi-
dant
National Sales Manager: Joe Kuncewitch
  kuncewitch@fujihealthscience.com
Estimated Sales: Under $500,000
Number Employees: 10-19

22936 Fuji Labeling Systems
2025 S Arl Hts Rd Ste 100
Arlington Heights, IL 60005

    847-690-1725
    Fax: 847-690-1734 fujiusa@aol.com
Standard series labels
Estimated Sales: $300,000-500,000
Number Employees: 1-4

22937 Fujitso Transaction Solutions
11085 N Torrey Pines Road
La Jolla, CA 92037-1015

    858-457-9900
    Fax: 858-457-2701 800-340-4425
Lightweight and rugged pen-based hand-held com-
puters, route accounting, distributing
President: Hiroaki Kurokawa
Marketing Manager: Sandy Watts
Estimated Sales: $20 - 50 Million
Number Employees: 50

22938 Ful-Flav-R Foods
P.O. Box 82
Alamo, CA 94507

    925-838-0300
    Fax: 925-838-0310 www.fulflavr.com
Premium Ground Garlic, Minced Garlic (in oil &
water), Ground and Minced Ginger, Ground Roasted
Garlic, Ground Onion, diced Sweet Bell Peppers,
Ground and Diced Jalepeno's, Fire Roasted Ana-
heim chili's, Ground Chili-Garlic Blends andother
unique custom formulated blends. All of our prod-
ucts are pasteurized and pH controlled.
President: Joseph Farrell
Chief Operations Officer: Glen Farrell
Director Sales/Marketing: Steve Linzmeyer
Plant Manager: John Small
Estimated Sales: $1-2.5 Million
Number Employees: 5-9
Type of Packaging: Food Service, Bulk
Brands:
  Ful-Flav-R

22939 Full-View Display Case
PO Box 79200
Fort Worth, TX 76179-0200

    817-847-0775
    Fax: 817-232-0214 800-252-1667
Refrigerated and nonrefrigerated display cases for
the gourmet candy and bakery industries
Estimated Sales: $1-2.5 Million
Number Employees: 10-19

22940 Fuller Box Co
150 Chestnut St
North Attleboro, MA 02760-3205

    508-695-2525
    Fax: 508-695-2187 www.fullerbox.com
Cardboard and steel packaging and packaging ma-
chinery; also, metal stamping machinery
President: Peter C Fuller
CFO: John Backner
Vice President: A Fuller
Sales/Marketing Executive: Thomas Mercer
Estimated Sales: $10 - 20 Million
Number Employees: 100-249
Square Footage: 194000
Parent Co: Fuller Companies

22941 Fuller Flag Company

1092 Main Street
Holden, MA 01520-1247

508-829-6016
Fax: 508-829-7767 800-348-6723
tjaitken@earthling.net

Flags and pennants, retail and wholesale flags
Sales Manager: Samantha McDonald
Office Manager: Samatha McDonald
Estimated Sales: $300,000-500,000
Number Employees: 1-4

22942 Fuller Industries LLC

1 Fuller Way
Great Bend, KS 67530-2466

620-792-1711
Fax: 620-792-1906 800-522-0499
customer@fuller.com www.fullerindustriesllc.com

Manufacturer and exporter of detergents, mops,
floor polish, brooms and plastic bottles
President: G Robert Gey
CEO: David Sabin
dsabin@fuller.com
VP: Lewis L Gray
VP Sales: Dolores McConnaughy
VP Sales: Bill McCoy
Number Employees: 250-499
Square Footage: 1000000

22943 Fuller Packaging Inc

1152 High St
PO Box 198
Central Falls, RI 02863-1506

401-725-4300
Fax: 401-726-8050
customerservice@fullerbox.com
www.fullerbox.com

Manufacturer, importer and exporter of boxes in-
cluding paper and counter display
President: Peter Fuller
Product Development Manager: Alvin Fuller
Estimated Sales: $10-20 Million
Number Employees: 50-99
Square Footage: 154000

22944 Fuller Ultra Violet Corp

9416 Gulfstream Rd
Frankfort, IL 60423-2524

815-469-3301
Fax: 815-469-1438 www.fulleruv.com

Liquid sweetener tank storage, water purification
President: William Eckstrom
fulleruvcorp@mindspriomng.com
Number Employees: 10-19
Number of Brands: 1
Number of Products: 12
Square Footage: 16000

22945 Fuller Weighing Systems

1600 Georgesville Road
Columbus, OH 43228-3616

614-882-8121
Fax: 614-882-9594 www.fullerweighing.com

Manufacturer and exporter of bulk weighing sys-
tems, feeders and automatic net-weigh container fill-
ing systems for liquids and dry materials
VP Sales: Tim Schultz
General Manager: Karl Hedderich
Production: David Patterson
Number Employees: 50
Square Footage: 60000
Parent Co: Cardinal Scale Manufacturing Company

22946 Fulton Boiler Works Inc

3981 Port St
Pulaski, NY 13142-4604

315-298-5121
Fax: 315-298-6390 service@fulton.com
www.fulton.com

Process, heat, steam for baking, cooking, frying
President: Nathan Fulton
nathan@nathanfulton.com
Chairman: Ronald B Palm
Estimated Sales: $20 Million
Number Employees: 250-499

22947 (HQ)Fulton-Denver Co

3500 Wynkoop St
Denver, CO 80216-3650

303-294-9292
Fax: 303-292-9470 800-521-1414
www.fultondenver.com

Bags including burlap, mesh, poly, paper, bulk, cot-
ton, vexar and wool; also, cartons, wrap, sheets,
twine and thread
Manager: Steve Potter
spotter@fultondenver.com
President: Rhett Schuller
Estimated Sales: $5 - 10 Million
Number Employees: 1-4

22948 Fun City Popcorn

3211 Sunrise Ave
Las Vegas, NV 89101

702-367-2676
Fax: 702-876-1099 800-423-1710
www.funcitypopcorn.com

Caramel, cheese and butter popcorn; manufacturer
of popcorn processing machinery
President/CEO: Richard Falk
CFO: Maryann Talavera
Estimated Sales: $1-3 Million
Number Employees: 5-9
Square Footage: 40000
Type of Packaging: Consumer, Food Service, Pri-
vate Label, Bulk

22949 Fun-Time International

433 W Girard Ave.
Philadelphia, PA 19123

215-925-1450
Fax: 215-925-1884 800-776-4386
orders@krazystraws.com www.krazystraws.com

Manufacturer and exporter of novelty drinking
straws, eating utensils and drinking containers; also,
novelty candy items
Owner: Erik Lipson
Estimated Sales: $3 - 5 Million
Number Employees: 10-19
Square Footage: 2000
Brands:
Candy Bracelets
Connecter
Crazy Glasses
Funstraws
Krazy Koolers
Krazy Strawston
Krazy Utensils
Spookyware

22950 Funke Filters

P.O. Box 30097
Cincinnati, OH 45230-0097

513-528-5535
Fax: 513-528-5575 800-543-7070

Filters and filtration equipment
President: William F Funke
Estimated Sales: Below $5 000,000
Number Employees: 1-4

22951 Funny Apron Co

PO Box 1780
Lake Dallas, TX 75065-1780

940-498-3308
Fax: 800-515-8076 800-835-5802
info@funnyaprons.com www.funnyaprons.com

Imprinted aprons with humorous food themed de-
signs
President: Ellice Lovelady
CFO: Charles Lovelady
Sales Director: Terri Whiting
Estimated Sales: Under $1 Million
Number Employees: 1-4
Number of Products: 90+
Parent Co: the Imagination Association LLC
Type of Packaging: Consumer

22952 Furgale Industries Ltd.

324 Lizzie Street
Winnipeg, NB R3A 0Y7
Canada

204-949-4200
Fax: 204-943-3191 800-665-0506

Provider of cleaning tools to the north american
market - tools include: brooms, mops & brushes
President: Jim Furgale
VP: Terry Gibb
Customer Service: Kate Furgale
Number Employees: 70
Number of Brands: 10
Number of Products: 250
Square Footage: 280000
Type of Packaging: Consumer, Private Label
Brands:
Furgale
Home Commercial
No Name
Northwest Co
Pro Seris
Shop Master
Western Family

22953 Furnace Belt Company

2316 Delaware Avenue
Suite 217
Buffalo, NY 14216
Canada

Fax: 800-354-7215 800-354-7213
fbc@furnacebeltco.com www.furnacebeltco.com

Manufacturer and exporter of wire processing belts
for heat treating, brazing, annealing, sintering,
quenching, freezing and baking
President: J Tatone
Number Employees: 40
Square Footage: 90000

22954 Furniturelab

106 S Greensboro St # E
Carrboro, NC 27510-2266

919-913-0270
Fax: 919-913-0271 800-449-8677
sales@furniturelab.com www.furniturelab.com

Manufacturer and exporter of wood and laminated
tables, tabletops, chairs and bases
President: Greg Rapp
sales@furniturelab.com
Marketing: Courtney Smith
Sales Director: Nathan Bearman
Estimated Sales: $1 - 3 Million
Number Employees: 10-19
Square Footage: 14000

22955 Futura 2000 Corporation

8861 SW 132nd Street
31
Miami, FL 33176-5926

305-256-5877
Fax: 718-349-2485

Menu boards and systems and point of purchase
signage; also, retrofitting services available
VP: Diana Amengual
Sales Manager: Rocco Colafrancesco
Estimated Sales: $300,000-500,000
Number Employees: 1-4

22956 Futura Coatings

6614 Grant Road
Houston, TX 77066

281-397-0033
Fax: 281-397-6512

Wine industry tank linings and coating
CFO: David Wicks
Contact: Dannie Vickers
dvickers@futuracoatings.com
Estimated Sales: $5-10 000,000
Number Employees: 50-99

22957 Futura Equipment Corporation

460 McLaughlin Rd
Yakima, WA 98908-9659

509-972-3300
Fax: 509-972-3377 888-886-2233

President: Andy Briesmeister
Estimated Sales: $1 - 3 Million
Number Employees: 5-9

22958 Future Care Packaging Inc.

1410 Bayly St
Unit 11-13
Pickering, ON L1W 3R3
Canada

905-508-9881
Info@futurecarepackaging.com
www.futurecarepackaging.com

Manufacturer of eco-friendly & biodegradable paper
straws.
General Manager: Giancarlo Lombardi
Manager, Product Development: Robert Zeidenberg

22959 Future Commodities IntlInc

10676 Fulton Ct
Rancho Cucamonga, CA 91730-4848

909-987-4258
Fax: 909-987-5189 888-588-2378
sales@bestpack.com www.bestpack.com

Manufacturer and exporter of carton sealers, erectors
and end line packaging machinery

President: David Lim
VP: Chery Lim
Sales Manager: Patrick Brennan
Contact: Mike Byrne
  mbyrne@bestpack.com
Estimated Sales: $5 - 10 Million
Number Employees: 1-4
Square Footage: 108000
Parent Co: Future Commodities International
Brands:
  Bestpack

22960 Future Foods
945 W. Fulton Marke
Chicago, IL 60607
312-987-9342
Fax: 773-561-0307
Consultant providing marketing services to the food service industry; also, product development available
President: Andrew Patterson
VP Sales: Ron Gulyas
Estimated Sales: $.5 - 1,000,000
Number Employees: 1-4

22961 Futures
P.O. Box 60
Barrington, NH 03825-0060
603-664-5811
Fax: 603-664-5864 info@futuressearch.com
www.cri-mms.com
Executive search firm specializing in food service sales and marketing
Manager: Peter Dutton
VP: Richard Mazzola
Estimated Sales: $500,000-$1 Million
Number Employees: 5-9
Square Footage: 8000

22962 Fygir Logistic Information Systems
25 Mall Road
Suite 300
Burlington, MA 01803-4144
781-270-0683
Fax: 781-238-6725
Production planning for developing and monitoring production resources
Estimated Sales: Under $500,000

22963 Fyh Bearing Units USA Inc
285 Industrial Dr
Wauconda, IL 60084-1078
847-487-9111
Fax: 847-882-5360 www.fyhusa.com
Mounted bearing units and insert bearings; inch and metric shaft sizes, heavy duty, medium duty, standard duty, and light duty units; specialty series include solid stainless steel, bright white thermoplstic, clean series, taper borelocking UK-series
Manager: J Frasor
CFO: Rodney Jones
Executive VP: Tohru Yamashita
Contact: Jay Frasor
  jfrasor@fyhusa.com
General Manager: Charles Horwitz
Estimated Sales: $10 - 20 000,000
Number Employees: 5-9
Type of Packaging: Private Label

22964 (HQ)G & C Packing Co
240 S 21st St
Colorado Springs, CO 80904-3304
719-634-1587
Fax: 719-636-1038
Supplier of slaughtering services only
President: Frank Grindinger
  gcpack@qwestoffice.net
Estimated Sales: $7.6 Million
Number Employees: 20-49
Square Footage: 23850
Type of Packaging: Consumer, Food Service, Bulk

22965 G & D Chillers Inc
3498 W 1st Ave # 1
Eugene, OR 97402-5453
541-345-3903
Fax: 541-345-8835 800-555-0973
www.gdchillers.com
Wine industry, glycol and process chiller
Owner: Justin Thomas
  justin@gdchillers.com
VP: Ray Tatum

Estimated Sales: Below $5 000,000
Number Employees: 5-9

22966 G & F Mfg
5555 W 109th St
Oak Lawn, IL 60453-5070
708-424-4170
Fax: 708-424-4922 800-282-1574
gandf@gandf.com www.gandf.com
Designing and manufacturing high quality chemical resistant, durable and rugged Stainless steel products such as steel tanks, filling machines, piston filters, cappers, and labeling.
President: Rob Bais
  rbais@gfmfg.com
Purchasing Manager: Ron Bais
Number Employees: 10-19
Square Footage: 15000
Type of Packaging: Food Service

22967 G & J Awning & Canvas Inc
1260 10th St N
Sauk Rapids, MN 56379-2500
320-255-1733
Fax: 320-255-0130 800-467-1744
info@gjawning.com www.gjawning.com
Commercial awnings including interior and exterior
Owner: Gary Buermann
CEO: Janice Buermann
CFO: Janice Beurmann
Vice President: Janice Buermann
Manager: Beth Brenny
  beth@gjawning.com
Estimated Sales: Below $5,000,000
Number Employees: 10-19
Square Footage: 19800

22968 (HQ)G & S Metal Products CoInc
3330 E 79th St
Cleveland, OH 44127-1878
216-441-0700
Fax: 216-441-0736 www.gsmetal.com
Aluminum and steel bakeware and housewares including pans
President & CEO: Mark Schwartz
Estimated Sales: $50-100 Million
Number Employees: 250-499
Brands:
  Baker-Eze
  Black Beauty
  Ez Baker
  Silverstone

22969 G A Systems Inc
17872 Gothard St
Huntington Beach, CA 92647-6217
714-848-7529
Fax: 714-841-2356 sales@gasystemsmfg.com
www.gasystemsmfg.com
Stainless steel food service equipment and display cabinets
President: Steve Anderson
Founder: Gordon Anderson
Chief Financial Officer: Pat Devalle
Vice President: Steven Anderson
Sales: Virginia Anderson
Estimated Sales: $2.5-5 Million
Number Employees: 10-19
Square Footage: 64000

22970 G C Evans Sales & Mfg Co
3300 S Woodrow St
Little Rock, AR 72204-6550
501-664-5095
Fax: 501-663-8690 800-382-6720
sales@gcevans.com www.gcevans.com
Cooling tunnels, warmers and pasteurizers
President: Gerald Mc Namer
  jenniferb@gcevans.com
Sales/Marketing: Mark McNamer
Operations/Production: David McNamer
Estimated Sales: $5-10 000,000
Number Employees: 20-49
Square Footage: 50000

22971 G C Evans Sales & Mfg Co
3300 S Woodrow St
Little Rock, AR 72204-6550
501-664-5095
Fax: 501-663-8690 800-382-6720
sales@gcevans.com www.gcevans.com
Accumulating conveyors
President: Gerald Mc Namer
  jenniferb@gcevans.com

Estimated Sales: $5-10 000,000
Number Employees: 20-49

22972 G K & L Inc
20910 Peach Tree Rd
Dickerson, MD 20842-9159
301-948-5538
Fax: 301-972-7641 GKandL@aol.com
www.gkandl.com
Grease interceptors, floor sinks and solid strainers for restaurants
Owner: Gene Wilkes
  gkandl@aol.com
Estimated Sales: $1-2.5 Million
Number Employees: 1-4
Brands:
  Renn

22973 G L Packaging Products Inc
1135 Carolina Dr
West Chicago, IL 60185-1713
630-231-5440
Fax: 630-231-5447 866-935-8755
info@glpackaging.com www.glpackaging.com
Corrugated and wooden pallets
President: Todd Tomala
  toddt@glpackaging.com
Sales Director: Len Kats
Operations Manager: Dale Komarek
Estimated Sales: $5 - 10 Million
Number Employees: 20-49
Square Footage: 160000

22974 G Lighting
9777 Reavis Park Dr
St Louis, MO 63123-5315
314-631-6000
Fax: 314-631-7800 800-331-2425
sales@glighting.com www.glighting.com
Designer and manufacturer of decorative commercial lighting fixtures
President: Nick Gross
  nick@glighting.com
CEO: Robert Gross
Executive Vice President: Linton Gross
Marketing/R&D: Brent Paiva
Marketing/R&D: Brent Paiva
President, Sales Manager: Nick Gross
Customer Service: Kara Gross
Office Manager, Purchasing Manager: Jenny Cole
Production Manager: Dan Dickinson
Office Manager, Purchasing Manager: Jenny Cole
Estimated Sales: $5 - 10 Million
Number Employees: 20-49
Square Footage: 16000

22975 G P 50 New York LTD
2770 Long Rd
Grand Island, NY 14072-1223
716-773-9300
Fax: 716-773-5019 meltsales@gp50.com
www.gp50.com
Controls: transducers and transmitters
President: Donald Less
  don@gp50.com
Vice President: Ken Brodie
Director: Bob Atwood
Director: Bob Atwood
Estimated Sales: $10-20 000,000
Number Employees: 50-99
Square Footage: 30000

22976 G W Berkheimer Co
1011 E Wallace St
Fort Wayne, IN 46803-2591
260-744-4156
Fax: 260-456-2177 800-535-6696
webmaster@gwberkheimer.com
www.gwberkheimer.com
Heating equipment
Manager: Chris Wamsley
  chriswamsley@gwberkheimer.com
Branch Manager: Curt Rees
Estimated Sales: $10-20,000,000
Number Employees: 20-49
Parent Co: G.W. Berkheimer Company

22977 G&H Enterprises
344 McLaws Cir
Williamsburg, VA 23185-5648
757-258-1230
Fax: 757-258-1231

Case packaging machinery, case packing, box erection, top sealing custom automated machinery and components
Estimated Sales: $1-2.5 000,000
Number Employees: 10-19

22978 G&K Vijuk Intern. Corp
715 Church Rd
Elmhurst, IL 60126
630-530-2203
Fax: 630-530-2245 info@guk-vijuk.com
Bindery finishing equipment, miniature folders
President: Joseph Vijuk
Contact: Steve Kozak
skozak@vijukequip.com
Estimated Sales: $10-20 Million
Number Employees: 35

22979 G&R Graphics
PO Box 7095
West Orange, NJ 7052
973-380-8317
Fax: 973-731-7438 813-503-8592
gnrstamp@aol.com
Manufacturer and exporter of rubber printing plates, corporate seals, rubber stamps, inks and pads
President: David Gonzalez
Contact: Anibal Gonzalez
agonzalez@grgraphicsinc.com
Estimated Sales: $1 - 5 Million
Number Employees: 5-9
Square Footage: 8000

22980 G-3 Enterprises
500 S Santa Rosa Ave
Modesto, CA 95354-3717
209-341-4100
Fax: 209-341-3034 888-264-3225
www.g3enterprises.com
Wine, Champagne, Beer, Soda, Water and Sake industries. Aluminum screw caps, corks, capsules
President, Chief Executive Officer: Robert Lubeck
Director Marketing/Sales: Lee McDonald
Customer Care Specialist: Jack Leguria
Estimated Sales: $20-50 Million
Number Employees: 100-249

22981 G.F. Frank & Sons
9075 LeSaint Dr Fairfield
Fairfield, OH 45014
513-870-9075
Fax: 513-870-0579 john@GFFrankAndSons.com
www.gffrankandsons.com
Manufacturer and exporter of meat hooks, skewers, trolleys and smokehouse shelving
President: George Frank
Vice President: John Frank
Estimated Sales: $10-20 Million
Number Employees: 10-19

22982 G.G. Greene Enterprises
2790 Pennsylvania Avenue
West Warren, PA 16365
814-723-5700
Fax: 814-723-3037
awillingham@greenegroup.com
www.greenegroup.com
Manufactures guns, howitzers, mortars & related equipment; manufactures small arms ammunition; manufactures stamped or pressed metal machine parts; plate metal fabricator
Manager: Brent Long
Estimated Sales: $4,500,000
Number Employees: 20-49
Square Footage: 850000
Type of Packaging: Consumer, Food Service

22983 G.V. Aikman Company
6312 Southeastern Avenue
Indianapolis, IN 46203-5828
317-353-8181
Fax: 317-352-7695 800-886-4029
Designer of commercial kitchens for schools, institutions, etc
Estimated Sales: $2.5-5,000,000
Number Employees: 20-49

22984 G.W. Dahl Company
8439 Triad Dr
Greensboro, NC 27409-9018
336-668-4444
Fax: 336-668-4452 800-852-4449
info@purolator-facet.com
www.purolator-facet.com

Filters including water, oil and air; also, I/P transducers, P/I transmitters and pneumatic relays
President: Bruss Stellfox
Quality Control: Stlee Bigary
Marketing Manager: John Mello
Sales Administration: Debbie Froelich
Number Employees: 100-249
Square Footage: 340000
Parent Co: Purolator Products Company

22985 GA Design Menu Company
28710 Wall Street
Wixom, MI 48393-3516
313-561-2530
Fax: 313-561-1049
Laminated menus including inserts and covers
Owner: Gary Anoshka
Number Employees: 3
Square Footage: 6000

22986 GAF Seelig Inc
5905 52nd Ave
Flushing, NY 11377-7480
718-899-5000
Fax: 718-803-1198
Wholesaler and distributor of juice, milk, cheese, yogurt, sour cream, purees, raviolis and pastas, oils and vinegars, chocolate and many more food service items.
President: Rodney Seelig
rseelig@gafseelig.com
Executive Vice President: Gary Lavery Sr.
Director of Sales: John Arena
Estimated Sales: $5-10 Million
Number Employees: 100-249

22987 GBS Foodservice Equipment, Inc.
951 Matheson Boulevard E
Mississauga, ON L4W 2R7
Canada
905-897-2333
Fax: 905-897-2334 888-402-1242
pdouglas@gbscooks.com www.gbscooks.com
Distributor of foodservice equipment including; combi-ovens, open well fryers, rotisseries, blast chillers, for hot & cold merchandisers
General Manager: S Jaffer
Estimated Sales: $1 - 5 Million
Number Employees: 10-20

22988 GCA
5122 Bolsa Ave # 104
Huntington Beach, CA 92649-1050
714-379-4911
Fax: 714-379-4913 julie@gcalabels.com
www.gcalabels.com
Bar code equipment and supplies, labels, packaging, printers, software and marking devices; laser marking service available
Owner: Karen Schade
kschade@schoollane.org
Office Manager: Kim Benudict
Estimated Sales: Less Than $500,000
Number Employees: 1-4
Brands:
Loftware
Monarch

22989 GCJ Mattei Company
927 E Madison St
Louisville, KY 40204
502-583-4774
Fax: 502-583-4776
Displays
Owner: Louis Mattei
Estimated Sales: $500,000-$1 Million
Number Employees: 1-4
Square Footage: 24000

22990 GD Packaging Machinery
501 Southlake Blvd
Richmond, VA 23236-3078
804-794-9777
Fax: 804-794-6187
CFO: Lich Polchinski
Marketing: Glen Coater
Number Employees: 250-499

22991 GDM Concepts
15330 Texaco Ave
Paramount, CA 90723-3920
562-633-0195
Fax: 562-633-1561
Store fixtures

President: George Myers
info@gdmconcepts.com
Estimated Sales: $10-20,000,000
Number Employees: 20-49

22992 GE Appliances
Appliance Park
Louisville, KY 40225-0001
877-959-8688
www.geappliances.com
Appliances for home and businesses.
President & CEO: Kevin Nolan
VP & CFO: Marc Charnas
VP, Legal: Jason Brown
VP, Human Resources: Tom Quick
Chief Commercial Officer: Rick Hasselbeck
COO: Melanie Cook
Number Employees: 12,000
Parent Co: Haier Group Corporation
Brands:
Cafe
GE
GE Profile
Haier
Hotpoint
Monogram

22993 GE Interlogix Industrial
12345 SW Leveton Dr
Tualatin, OR 97062-6001
503-692-4052
Fax: 503-691-7377 800-247-9447
www.interlogix.com
Manufacturer and exporter of noncontract safety switches, position sensors and safety relays
Estimated Sales: $50-100 Million
Number Employees: 500-999
Square Footage: 140000
Parent Co: Interlogix
Brands:
Failsafe Guardswitch
Guardswitch

22994 GE Lighting
1975 Noble Rd
Cleveland, OH 44112-6300
800-435-4448
www.gelighting.com
Lighting and lighting fixtures including incandescent, flourescent, HID, outdoor and mercury
CEO: Bill Lacey
bill.lacey@ge.com
Estimated Sales: $3 Billion
Number Employees: 17,000
Parent Co: General Electric Company
Other Locations:
GE Lighting
Elmwood Park NJ

22995 GEA Evaporation Technologies LLC
9165 Rumsey Rd
Columbia, MD 21045-1929
410-997-8700
Fax: 410-997-5021
President: Eric Bryars
Contact: Ramash Quasba
ramash.quasba@geagroup.com
Estimated Sales: $20 Million
Number Employees: 100-249

22996 GEA FES, Inc.
44840 Les SoriniŠres
York, PA 17406
025-119-1051
Fax: 024-005-7381 geneglace@gea.com
Industrial refrigeration components.
President: John Ansbro
Service Manager: Randy Keefer

22997 GEA Filtration
1600 Okeefe Rd
Hudson, WI 54016-2290
715-386-9371
Fax: 715-386-9376
President: Steve Kathleen
VP: Eric Bryars
Manufacturing Manager: Gerry Nelson
Sales: Bob Keefe
Contact: Jamie Atwell
jamie.atwell@gea.com
Estimated Sales: $20 - 50 Million
Number Employees: 100-249

22998 GEA Niro Soavi North America
10 Commerce Park North
Building 7
Bedford, NH 03110
603-606-4060
Fax: 603-606-4065
Manufacturer and supplier of high pressure pumps
and homogenizers for the food industry.

22999 (HQ)GEA North America
1880 Country Farm Dr
Naperville, IL 60563-1089
630-369-8100
Fax: 630-369-9875
Manufacturer and exporter of dairy farm equipment
including cleaners
President: John Ansbro
 john.ansbro@geagroup.com
CEO: Dirk Hejnal
CFO: Dr. Ulrich Hullman
Sales: Vern Foster
Business Unit, Milking & Cooling: Dr. Armin
Tietjen
Estimated Sales: Below $5 Million
Number Employees: 100-249
Other Locations:
 Babson Brothers Co.
 Galesville WI
Brands:
 Surge

23000 GEA PHE Systems North America, Inc.
100 Gea Drive
York, PA 17406-8469
717-268-6200
Fax: 717-268-6162 800-774-0474
info.phe-systems.usa@gea.com
www.geaphena.com
Heat exchangers, industrial evaporating equipment,
spray dryers
Manager: Steve Lovell
VP Sales: Clemens Starzinski
Contact: Dave Berry
 dave.berry@geagroup.com
Estimated Sales: $7 Million
Number Employees: 5-9

23001 GEA Refrigeration NorthAmerica
3475 Board Rd
York, PA 17406-8414
717-767-6411
Fax: 717-764-3627 800-888-4337
sales.gearna@gea.com www.gea.com
Industrial refrigeration equipment
President: John Ansbro
 john.ansbro@geagroup.com
CFO: John Lutz
Quality Control: Jim Mesbitt
VP: Dennis Halsey
Marketing Manager: Teresa Sauble
Sales: John Miranda
Estimated Sales: $500,000 - $1 Million
Number Employees: 250-499

23002 GEBO Corporation
6015 31st Street E
Bradenton, FL 34203-5382
941-727-1400
Fax: 941-727-1200
Packaging machinery
Marketing Director: George Rouli
Estimated Sales: $20-50 Million
Number Employees: 100-250

23003 GED, LLC
28107 Beaver Dam Branch Rd
Box 140
Laurel, DE 19956-9801
302-856-1756
Fax: 302-856-9888 gedllc@yahoo.com
Importers and exporters of cans, plus dealers of food
processing machines and parts
Estimated Sales: $1 - 5 Million
Number Employees: 3

23004 GEE Manufacturing
2200 S Golden State Blvd
P.O. Box 397
Fowler, CA 93625
559-834-2929
Fax: 559-834-1715 800-433-1620
info@geemanufacturing.com
www.geemanufacturing.com

Wine industry stainless steel tanks
President and Owner: Glen Gee
Estimated Sales: $5-10 000,000
Number Employees: 20-49

23005 GEI Autowrappers
700 Pennsylvania Drive
Exton, PA 19341-1129
610-321-1115
Fax: 610-321-1199
Manufacturer and exporter of electronic flow wrap-
pers
Sales Manager: Richard Landers
Number Employees: 120
Square Footage: 160000
Parent Co: GEI International

23006 GEI PPM
569 W Uwchlan Ave
Exton, PA 19341-1563
610-524-7178
Fax: 610-321-1199 800-345-1308
Manufacturer and exporter of pressure sensitive and
multi-head/in-line rotary labelers
Owner: Jin Guo
Estimated Sales: $1 - 5 Million
Number Employees: 1-4
Square Footage: 320000
Parent Co: GEI International

23007 GEI Turbo
700 Pennsylvania Drive
Exton, PA 19341-1129
610-321-1100
Fax: 610-321-1199 800-345-1308
Manufacturer and exporter of hand-held and auto-
matic high and low temperature filling equipment
Estimated Sales: $1 - 5 Million
Parent Co: GEI International

23008 GEM Equipment of OregonInc
2150 Progress Way
Woodburn, OR 97071-9765
503-982-9902
Fax: 503-981-6316 gem@gemequipment.com
www.gemequipment.com
Manufacturer and exporter of blanchers, conveyor
systems and components, fryers, dumpers, mixers,
preheaters and batter mix systems
President: Edward McKenney
CEO: Steve Ross
 sross@gemequipment.com
COO: Steve Ross
Vice President of Sales: Jerry Bell
Plant Manager: Ray Rowe
Purchasing Manager: Ray Rowe
Estimated Sales: $20-50 Million
Number Employees: 50-99
Square Footage: 100000

23009 GEM Equipment of OregonInc
2150 Progress Way
P.O. Box 2449
Woodburn, OR 97071-9765
503-982-9902
Fax: 503-981-6316 gem@gemequipment.com
www.gemequipment.com
President: Edward T McKenney
CEO: Steve Ross
 sross@gemequipment.com
Vice President, Sales: Jerry Bell
R&D: Dill Larson
Quality Control: Tony Meehl
Technical Sales: Jim Caughlin
Estimated Sales: $10 - 20 Million
Number Employees: 50-99

23010 GENESTA
1850 E Interstate 30
Rockwall, TX 75087-6201
Canada
972-771-1653
Fax: 972-722-1179 info@genesta.com
www.genesta.com
Extruded formed fluorescent lighting fixtures and
vacuum formed display components
Partner: Kelson Elam
 kelam@genesta.com
VP: Merv Schwantz
Number Employees: 10-19

23011 GEO Graphics-Spegram
PO Box 305
Mystic, CT 06355-0305
860-572-8507
Fax: 860-536-3961 gspmystic@gsptoday.com
www.gsptoday.com
Wine industry labelers
CEO: Erik H Ljungberg
Contact: Erik Ljungberg
 eljungberg@gsptoday.com
Estimated Sales: $10-20 Million
Number Employees: 10-19

23012 GERM-O-RAY
1641 Lewis Way
Stone Mountain, GA 30083-1107
770-939-2835
Fax: 770-621-0100 800-966-8480
sales@insect-o-cutor.com
www.insect-o-cutor.com
Manufacturer and exporter of air disinfection fix-
tures and germicidal fluorescent, UV and UVC
lamps; available in in-room, in-duct and custom
styles
CEO: Bill Harris
Marketing Director: J Harris
Advertising: D Johnson
Systems Engineer: J Baum
Estimated Sales: $1 - 3 Million
Number Employees: 10-19
Brands:
 Germ-O-Ray

23013 GET Enterprises LLC
1515 W Sam Houston Pkwy N
Houston, TX 77043-3112
713-467-9394
Fax: 713-467-9396 800-727-4500
info@get-melamine.com www.get-melamine.com
Importer and wholesaler/distributor of dinnerware,
high chairs, tray stands, tumblers, platters and soup
and coffee mugs; serving the food service market
President: Glen Hou
HR Executive: Joyce Liu
 joyceliu@get-melamine.com
VP Sales/Marketing: Eve Hou
Estimated Sales: $5-10 Million
Number Employees: 50-99
Square Footage: 40000

23014 GFI Stainless
2084 Lapham Dr # A
Building A
Modesto, CA 95354-3909
209-571-1684
Fax: 209-571-2445 800-221-2652
sales@gfistainless.com www.gfistainless.com
Wine industry fluid handling products
President: Gordon Fluker
 g_fluker@gfistainless.com
Vice President: Fred Elwood
Estimated Sales: $1-2.5 Million
Number Employees: 10-19

23015 (HQ)GHM Industries Inc
100 Sturbridge Rd # A
Charlton, MA 01507-5323
508-248-3941
Fax: 508-248-0639 800-793-7013
sales@millerproducts.net www.millerproducts.net
Manufacturer and exporter of textile machinery in-
cluding automatic roll wrappers and polywraps
President: Paul Jankovic
 pjankovic@millerproducts.net
Estimated Sales: $2.5-5 Million
Number Employees: 5-9

23016 GJ Glass Company
1019 Lincoln Street
Cedar Falls, IA 50613-3248
319-266-4444
Fax: 319-266-2041 800-422-8807

23017 GKI Foods
7926 Lochlin Road
Brighton, MI 48116
248-486-0055
Fax: 248-486-9135 www.gkifoods.com
Milk chocolate, sugar free chocolate, yogurt and
cards products, panned and enrobed, bulk or packaged. Also produces custom granola (all natural,
highly nutritional, low in fat and fat free), trail
mixes, etc. Custom formulation. Aidcertified, GMP
and HACCP accreditation.

President: Sue Wilts
Contact: Nancy Fletcher
nancy.fletcher@gkifoods.com
General Manager: Jim Frazier
Number Employees: 20-49
Square Footage: 60000
Type of Packaging: Consumer, Private Label, Bulk

23018 (HQ)GM Nameplate
2040 15th Ave W
Seattle, WA 98119-2783

206-284-2200
Fax: 206-284-3705 800-366-7668
webnet@gmnameplate.com
www.gmnameplate.com
Manufacturer and exporter of nameplates, labels,
membrane switches, injection and compression
molding.
President: Brad Root
brad@gmnameplate.com
Chairman & CEO: Donald Root
New Product Manager: Dennis Cook
Research & Development: Debbie Anderson
Marketing Manager: Shannon Kirk
VP Sales & Marketing: Gerry Gallagher
Operations Executive: Mark Samuel
Plant/Production Manager: Marc Doan
Purchasing Agent: Jim Davis
Number Employees: 1000-4999
Square Footage: 560000
Other Locations:
Elite Plastics Division
Beaverton OR
Canada Division
Surrey BC
California Division
San Jose CA
North Carolina Division
Monroe NC
SuperGraphics Division
Seattle WA
Brands:
Color Cal
Mark Cal
Poly Cal

23019 GMF
9201 NW 78th
St Weatherby Lake, MO 64152

816-505-9900
Fax: 816-505-9995 www.andritzgouda.com
GMF-Gouda supplies specialized machinery to the
chemical and food industries.
President: Mark Mc Kee
Estimated Sales: $.5 - 1 million
Number Employees: 170
Parent Co: ANDRITZ Separation

23020 GN Thermoforming Equipment
345 Old Trunk 3
PO Box 710
Chester, NS B0J 1J0
Canada

902-275-3571
Fax: 902-275-3100 gn@gncanada.com
www.gnplastics.com
President: Georg Nemeskeri
Quality Manager: Curtis Dowe
Marketing Manager: Jerome Romkey
Sales Representative: Colin MacDonald
Number Employees: 100+

23021 GNTUSA Inc
660 White Plains Rd # 6
Tarrytown, NY 10591-5139

914-332-6663
Fax: 914-524-0681 877-468-8727
info@gntusa.com www.gnt-group.com
GNT manufactures Exberry natural colors and
Nutrifood fuit and vegetable extracts.
President and CEO: Stefan Hake
gnt-orders@gntusa.com
Marketing: Jeannette O'Brien
Number Employees: 10-19
Parent Co: GNT International B.V.
Type of Packaging: Food Service, Private Label,
Bulk

23022 GOBI Library Solutions
999 Maple St
Hopkinton, NH 03229-3374

603-746-3102
Fax: 603-746-5628 800-258-3774
service@ybp.com
Information resource

Director, Finance & Accounting: Andy Fries
Senior VP: Amy Alcorn
a_alcorn@salemstate.edu
Senior Vice President, Sales and Operati: Mark
Kendall
Vice President, Operations: Nathaniel Bruning
Estimated Sales: $5,000,000 - $9,999,999
Number Employees: 250-499

23023 GOJO Industries Inc
1 Gojo Plz # 500
Akron, OH 44311-1085

330-255-6000
Fax: 330-255-6119 800-321-9647
www.gojo.com
Manufacturer and exporter of hand cleaners and
soap dispensers
President/CEO: Carey Jaros
Executive Chair: Marcella Kanfer Rolnick
CEO: Joseph Kanfer
Lab Manager: Dan Willis
Purchasing: Debbie Topliff
Estimated Sales: $75 Million
Number Employees: 250-499
Square Footage: 500000
Brands:
Derma-Pro
Go-Jo

23024 GP Plastics Corporation
8900 NW 77th Court
Medley, FL 33166-2102

305-888-3555
Fax: 305-885-4204
Extruded polyethylene products including trash and
produce bags
Division Manager: Pam Hauserman
Manager (Southeast): Elaine Kurau
Plant Manager: Bob Riber
Estimated Sales: $20-50 Million
Number Employees: 100-249

23025 GPI USA LLC.
10062 190th Place
Suite 107
Mokena, IL 60448

706-850-7826
Fax: 708-785-0608 800-929-4248
karen.haley@foodgums.com
Specialize in carageenan used for stabilization and
as an additive for both dairy products and in the red
meat and poultry industries.

23026 GSC Blending
3600 Atl Ind Pkwy NW
Atlanta, GA 30331

404-696-6200
Fax: 404-696-4546 800-453-9997
SShapiro@gaspiceco.com www.gaspiceco.com
President/Owner: Selma Shapiro
President: Robert S Shapiro
Estimated Sales: $10 - 20 Million
Number Employees: 16

23027 GSC Packaging
3715 Atlanta Industrial Pkwy
Atlanta, GA 30331-1049

404-505-9925
Fax: 404-696-2667 800-453-9997
www.gscpackaging.com
President and CEO: Robert Shapiro
Estimated Sales: $10 - 20 Million
Number Employees: 20-49

23028 GSMA Division of SWF Co
1949 E. Manning Avenue
Suite 5
Reedley, CA 93654

559-638-8484
Fax: 559-38 -478 800-344-8951
info@swfcompanies.com
www.swfcompanies.com
Automated robotics, barcode scanners, proofreaders
President: Roland Parker
Vice President / General Manager: Ed Suarez
Product Manager - Robotics: Matt Garcia
AMP Manager: Mark Freitas
Product Manager: Craig Friesen
General Manager: Mark Senti
Estimated Sales: $1-5 Million
Number Employees: 10

23029 GSW Jackes-Evans Manufacturing Company
4427 Geraldine Avenue
Saint Louis, MO 63115-1217

314-385-4132
Fax: 314-385-0802 800-325-6173
Manufacturer, importer and exporter of barbecue
equipment and accessories
President: Rob Harris
BBQ Products: Joe Fernandez
Director Sales (Heating Products): Ron Bailey
Number Employees: 200
Square Footage: 500000
Parent Co: GSW
Type of Packaging: Consumer, Private Label, Bulk
Brands:
Chef Shop
E-Z Fit Barbecue
Party Chef
Super Chef

23030 GT International
1400 Post Oak Boulevard
Suite 270
Houston, TX 77056-3008

713-494-8779
Fax: 713-629-8908
Plasic pallets, plastic crates, bottled water
Estimated Sales: $500,000-$1 000,000
Number Employees: 1-4

23031 GTCO CalComp
14557 N. 82nd Street
Scottsdale, AZ 85260

410-381-3450
Fax: 480-948-5508 800-856-0732
calcomp.sales@gtcocalcomp.com
Manufacturer and exporter of wide-format graphic
printers and tablets
Sales Director: Kim Plasterer
VP Sales: Don Lightfoot
Contact: Debra Melcher
dmelcher@gtcocalcomp.com
Number Employees: 1,000-4,999
Parent Co: eInstruction
Type of Packaging: Food Service

23032 GTI
12650 W 64th Ave # F
Arvada, CO 80004-3887

303-420-6699
Fax: 303-420-6699 www.greatclips.com
Manufacturer and exporter of seamers
President: Charlie Simpson
Chairman of the Board: Ray Barton
Vice President: Michelle Sack
Senior Vice President of Operations: Steve Hockett
Estimated Sales: $1 - 5 Million
Brands:
Ease Out

23033 GW&E Global Water & Energy
2404 Rutland Drive
Austin, TX 78758

512-697-1930
Fax: 512-697-1931
Supplier of wastewater treatment and
bio-waste-to-energy solutions with sludge management, scrubbing & utilizations sytems, reuse/reclaim
water systems, and biological treatments.
Contact: Jeff Faldyn
jfaldyn@globalwaterengineering.com

23034 Gabriel Container Co
8844 Millergrove Dr
Santa Fe Springs, CA 90670-2013

323-685-8844
Fax: 562-699-3284
Corrugated containers
President: Ron Gabriel
r.gabriel@gabrielcontainer.com
Estimated Sales: $20-50 Million
Number Employees: 100-249

23035 Gabriella Imports
5100 Prospect Ave
Cleveland, OH 44103

216-432-3651
Fax: 216-432-3654 800-544-8117
Manufacturer, importer and exporter of automatic
espresso equipment and granita machines and
products
Estimated Sales: $500,000-$1 Million
Number Employees: 35

Brands:
  Gabriella

23036 Gadren Machine Company
PO Box 117
Mount Ephraim, NJ 08059-0117
856-456-4329
Fax: 856-456-2238 800-822-4233
gadreninfo@comcast.net
Wine industry valves and fittings
Estimated Sales: $3 Million
Number Employees: 20

23037 Gaetano America
9460 Telstar Ave
El Monte, CA 91731-2904
626-442-2858
Fax: 626-401-1988 gaetanorf@aol.com
Manufacturer and exporter of ceramic bowls, platters, serving pieces and dinnerware
Owner: Irving Chait
VP Sales/Marketing: Rick Frovich

23038 Gafco-Worldwide
6302 Harrison Avenue
Suite 5
Cincinnati, OH 45247-6413
513-574-2257
Fax: 513-574-2362 gafcoww@aol.com
Accumulating conveyors and bar code scanners, spare parts, export management brewery and soft drink applications
President: Frank May
Estimated Sales: $5-10 000,000
Number Employees: 9

23039 Gage Industries
P.O. Box 1318
Lake Oswego, OR 97035
503-639-2177
Fax: 503-624-1070 800-443-4243
Manufacturer and exporter of plastic thermoformed packaging products including freezable and dual-ovenable food trays, cutting trays, totes, plastic containers, etc
President: Jeff Gage
Executive VP: Lizbeth Gage
Sales: Scott Tullis
Estimated Sales: $50 - 100 Million
Number Employees: 250-499
Number of Brands: 3
Number of Products: 70
Square Footage: 200000
Type of Packaging: Consumer, Food Service, Private Label, Bulk
Brands:
  Gage

23040 Gainco Inc
1635 Oakbrook Dr
Gainesville, GA 30507-8492
770-534-0703
Fax: 770-534-1865 800-467-2828
Sales@gainco.com www.gainco.com
Automated weighing and sorting systems for the meat and poultry industry
Manager: Gene Parets
Manager: Joe Cowman
jcowman@gainco.com
Number Employees: 20-49
Parent Co: Bettcher Industries

23041 Gainco Inc
1635 Oakbrook Dr
Gainesville, GA 30507-8492
770-534-0703
Fax: 770-534-1865 800-467-2828
Sales@gainco.com www.gainco.com
Portion sizing and distribution equipment, sorting, counting, weighing, and bagging systems, as well as bench and floor scales for the poultry, meat and food processing industries.
Manager: Joe Cowman
jcowman@gainco.com
Number Employees: 20-49

23042 Gainesville Neon & Signs
1405 NW 53rd Ave
Gainesville, FL 32609-6104
352-376-2750
Fax: 352-373-5734 800-852-1407
sales@gainesvilleneon.com
www.gainesvilleneon.com

Lighted signs including neon, wooden, vinyl, luminous tube and billboard
Owner: Daryl Tomlinson
accounting@gainesvilleneon.com
General Manager: Robert Jammer
Estimated Sales: Below $5 Million
Number Employees: 10-19
Square Footage: 40000

23043 Gainesville Welding & Mntnc
37 Henry Grady Hwy
Dawsonville, GA 30534-5717
706-216-2666
Fax: 706-216-4282 www.gwrendering.com
Cookers, dryers, prebakers, presses, tanks and storage units
Owner: Terry Stephens
Estimated Sales: $500,000-$1 000,000
Number Employees: 10-19
Type of Packaging: Bulk

23044 Galaxy Chemical Corp
2041 Whitfield Park Ave
Sarasota, FL 34243-4085
941-755-8545
Fax: 941-751-9412 gccgps@aol.com
Manufacturer and exporter of hand cleaners
Owner: Allan M Sanger
gccgps@aol.com
Manager: Tim San
Estimated Sales: $5 - 10 Million
Number Employees: 10-19

23045 Galbraith Laboratories Inc
2323 Sycamore Dr
Knoxville, TN 37921-1700
865-546-1335
Fax: 865-546-7209 877-449-8797
labinfo@galbraith.com www.galbraith.com
Consultant specializing in chemical microanalyses and analyses for all elements including trace analyses, TOX, ION chromatography, ICP metal scans and molecular weights
President: Brenda S Thornburgh
brendathornburgh@galbraith.com
CFO: Jim Cunnings
Senior VP: Lee Bates
Quality Control: Robert Logan
Estimated Sales: $10 - 20 Million
Number Employees: 50-99
Square Footage: 51000

23046 (HQ)Galbreath LLC
410 East 150 South
Winamac, IN 46996
574-946-6631
www.galbreathproducts.com
Manufacturer and exporter of detachable container systems, roll-off hoists and recycling containers, lugger boxes, self-dumping hoppers, dock carts, material-handling equipment, compactors, utility, trailers and balers
Director, Sales: Peyton Cox
Estimated Sales: $10 Million
Number Employees: 75
Square Footage: 250000
Parent Co: Wastequip, Inc.
Other Locations:
  Galbreath
  Ider AL
Brands:
  Combo-Pack
  Pack-Man
  Super Pack-Man

23047 Gallard-Schlesinger Industries
245 Newtown Road
Plainview, NY 11803-4316
516-683-6900
Fax: 516-683-6990 800-645-3044
Chemicals for food products
President: Karl Dorn
CFO: Jelle Westra
Quality Control: Henry Medello
Contact: Sandra Riquelme
sriquelme@gallard.com
Estimated Sales: $20 - 50 Million
Number Employees: 40

23048 Galley
50 South US Highway One
Jupiter, FL 33477-5107
561-748-5200
Fax: 561-748-5250 800-537-2772
galley@galleyline.com www.galleyline.com
Manufacturer and exporter of modular and mobile cafeteria and buffet equipment, salad bars, hot food tables and portable freezers
President: Alice Spritzer
CEO: Larry Spritzer
Estimated Sales: $500,000-$1 Million
Number Employees: 1-4
Square Footage: 11000
Brands:
  Galley
  Galley Line
  Mate-Lock

23049 Gallimore Industries
PO Box 158
Lake Villa, IL 60046
847-356-3331
Fax: 847-356-6224 800-927-8020
mark@gallimoreinc.com
Manufacturer and exporter of in-pack coupons and coupon inserters
President: Claris Gallimore
CEO: C Clay Gallimore
Quality Control: Mark Gallimore
Equip. VP/Production Manager: Kent Gallimore
Print VP/Production Manager: Mark Gallimore
Estimated Sales: Below $5 Million
Number Employees: 10-19
Square Footage: 42000

23050 Gallo
3600 S Memorial Dr
Racine, WI 53403-3822
262-752-9950
Fax: 262-752-9951
Manufacturer and exporter of resealable plastic bag sealers
President: Mary Sollman
VP: Thomas Sollman
Estimated Sales: $1 - 2.5 Million
Number Employees: 10-19
Square Footage: 32000
Brands:
  Easy-Lock

23051 Galvinell Meat Co Inc
461 Ragan Rd
Conowingo, MD 21918-1224
410-378-3032
galvinell@zoominternet.net
www.galvinell.com
Custom meat processor, also cooker services and products and private label, custom slaughtering, and party platters, salads, charcoal and ice also available. Beef, pork, goat, and lamb.
President: Dennis Welsh
dennis@galvinell.com
Estimated Sales: $730 Thousand
Number Employees: 5-9
Type of Packaging: Consumer, Food Service, Private Label, Bulk

23052 Gamajet Cleaning Systems
604 Jeffers Circle
Exton, PA 19341-2524
610-408-9940
Fax: 610-408-9945 800-289-5387
sales@gamajet.com www.gamajet.com
Manufacturer and exporter of tank cleaning equipment and CIP systems for fermenters, reactors, tank trucks, storage tanks and industrial process vessels
Chairman: Robert Delaney
Sales/Customer Service: Linda Chappell
Estimated Sales: $1-2.5 Million
Number Employees: 10-19
Square Footage: 19200
Parent Co: Alfa Laval Group
Brands:
  Gamajet

23053 Gamecock Chemical Co Inc
23 Plowden Mill Rd
Sumter, SC 29153-8909
803-773-7391
Fax: 803-775-8362
Sweeping compounds
Owner: George Self Jr
General Manager: Tommy Self

Estimated Sales: $1-2.5 Million
Number Employees: 5-9
Square Footage: 19000

23054 Gamewell Corporation
251 Crawford Street
Northborough, MA 01532-1234
508-231-1400
Fax: 508-231-0900 888-347-3269
www.gamewell.com
Manufacturer and exporter of fire alarm systems
President: Bill Abraham
Estimated Sales: $20-50 Million
Number Employees: 50-99

23055 Gamse Lithographing Co Inc
7413 Pulaski Hwy
Rosedale, MD 21237-2580
410-866-4700
Fax: 410-866-5672 gamse@gamse.com
www.gamse.com
Wine industry label design
President: Daniel Canzoniero
m.holland@bishophouse.com
CFO: Shelly Welling
Vice President: Ivan Sigris
Marketing Director: Joan Ziegler
Production Manager: Bob Markel
Estimated Sales: $20 - 50 Million
Number Employees: 100-249

23056 Ganau America Inc
21900 Carneros Oak Ln
Sonoma, CA 95476-2824
707-939-1774
Fax: 707-939-0671 800-694-CORK
www.ganau.com
Wine industry corks and cork stoppers
President: Mariella Ganau
mariella@ganauamerica.com
Sales Consultant: Kerry Smith
Accounting Manager: Gina Isi
Estimated Sales: $1-2.5 Million
Number Employees: 10-19

23057 Gann Manufacturing
1607 Wicomico St
Baltimore, MD 21230-1705
410-752-5040
Fax: 410-727-3521 800-922-9832
Safety products including gloves, liners, rainwear,
boots and disposable clothing
CEO: Stuart Levin
Exec. Sales: Grace Gracey
Estimated Sales: $2.5-5 Million
Number Employees: 1-4

23058 Gannett Outdoor of New Jersey
185 Us Highway 46
Fairfield, NJ 07004-2321
973-575-6900
Fax: 973-808-8316 www.viacomoutdoor.com
Outdoor advertising items including bulletins, post-
ers and backlights
VP: George Gross
Local Sales Manager: Gerald Allen
VP/General Sales Manager: Seth Bosin
Estimated Sales: $1 - 5 Million
Number Employees: 100-249
Parent Co: Gannett Company

23059 Ganz Brothers
12 Mulberry Ct
Paramus, NJ 7652
201-845-6010
Fax: 201-384-1329
Manufacturer and exporter of wrapping machinery
including high speed, paperboard, multipack and
shrink film for cans, bottles, cups and tubs
President: Christopher Ganz
cganz@ganz.com
VP: Jay Ganz
VP: Jay Ganz
Manager: Lisa Noch
Estimated Sales: $2.5-5 Million
Number Employees: 19
Square Footage: 24000

23060 Gar Products
170 Lehigh Ave
Lakewood, NJ 08701-4526
732-364-2100
Fax: 732-370-5021 800-424-2477
elliotb@garproducts.com www.garproducts.com

Manufacturer and exporter of indoor and outdoor
barstools, chairs, tables and bases; importer of chair
frames and table base castings
President: Jay Garfunkel
jaygar@garproducts.com
Vice President: Ellen Garfunkle
Quality Control: Sam Garfunkle
Sales Director: Elliot Bass
Operations Manager: Sam Garfunkle
Plant Manager: Jose Lopez
Purchasing Manager: Daniel Hyams
Number Employees: 20-49
Square Footage: 300000

23061 Garb-El Products Co
240 Michigan St # 1
Lockport, NY 14094-1797
716-434-6010
Fax: 716-434-9148 jcarbonejr@garb-el.com
www.garb-el.com
Manufacturer and exporter of food waste disposal
equipment and prep stations
President/ CEO: James M. Carbone, Jr.
VP: Deborah Carbone
Contact: Deborah Carbone
jcarbonejr@garb-el.com
Estimated Sales: $1-2.5 Million
Number Employees: 10-19
Square Footage: 30000
Brands:
Garb-El

23062 Garden City Community College
801 N Campus Dr
Garden City, KS 67846-6398
620-276-7611
Fax: 620-276-9573 www.gcccks.edu
President: Carol Ballantyne
Executive Vice President: Dee Wigner
Administrative Assistant: Ruth Drees
Number Employees: 250-499

23063 Gardenville Signs
4622 Hazelwood Ave
Baltimore, MD 21206-2812
410-485-4800
Fax: 410-485-4805
Electric signs
Owner: Conley D Reems
Marketing: Conley Reams
Estimated Sales: $500,000-$1 Million
Number Employees: 5 to 9

23064 Gardiner Paperboard
721 Water Street
Gardiner, ME 04345-2013
207-582-3230
Fax: 207-582-8207
Paper board
CEO: Jeffrey Hinderliter
Estimated Sales: $20-50 Million
Number Employees: 50-99
Parent Co: Newark Group

23065 Gardner Denver Inc.
222 E Erie St
Suite 500
Milwaukee, WI 53202
www.gardnerdenver.com
Compressed air, blower and vacuum applications.
President & CEO, Industrials Group: Vicente
Reynal
Parent Co: Ingersoll Rand Inc
Brands:
CompAir
Elmo Rietschle
Gardner Denver
Hydrovane
Robusch

23066 Gardner Manufacturing Inc
1201 W Lake St
Horicon, WI 53032-1819
920-485-4303
Fax: 920-485-4370 800-242-5513
www.gardnermfg.com
Manufacturer and exporter of insect electrocuting
systems, traps and lamps
Owner: John S Jones
johnjones@gardnermfg.com
Quality Control: Mark Sullivan
Sales Division: Robert Marschke

Estimated Sales: $10 - 20 Million
Number Employees: 100-249
Square Footage: 190000
Brands:
Zap

23067 Garland Commercial Ranges Ltd.
1177 Kamato Road
Mississauga, ON L4W 1X4
Canada
905-624-0260
www.garland-group.com
Manufacturer and exporter of commercial cooking
equipment including ranges, ovens, gas and electric
broilers and griddles; custom cooking equipment
available
CFO: Angelo Ascidne
CEO: Dale Kostick
Senior VP: Dale Kostick
Regional Manager: Jeff McGowan
Number Employees: 250-499
Number of Brands: 2
Number of Products: 1005
Square Footage: 904000
Parent Co: ENODIS

23068 Garland Commercial Ranges
1177 Kamato Road
Mississauga, ON L4W 1X4
Canada
905-624-0260
Fax: 905-624-5669 www.garland-group.com
Commercial holding, warming and cooking equip-
ment including ranges, ovens, gas and electric broil-
ers, griddles, steam cookers and fryers; also,
warming and ventilation equipment
President: Jack Seguin
CFO: Angelo Ascione
Quality Control: Keith Milmine
Group VP Sales/Marketing: Ian Osborne
Regional Manager: Jeff McGowan
Number Employees: 300
Parent Co: Welbilt Corporation

23069 Garland Floor Company
4500 Willow Pkwy
Cleveland, OH 44125-1042
216-883-4100
Fax: 216-883-9076 800-321-2395
Industrial flooring, thermal-shock/chemical resistant
flooring systems
CEO: Byron Smith
Estimated Sales: $10-20 Million
Number Employees: 20-49

23070 Garland Truffles, Inc.
3020 Ode Turner Rd
Hillsborough, NC 27278
919-732-3041
Fax: 919-732-6037 sheila@garlandtruffles.com
www.garlandtruffles.com
Mushrooms including rare truffle mushrooms, also,
truffle tree nursery
Estimated Sales: $1.6 Million
Number Employees: 11
Type of Packaging: Food Service

23071 Garland Writing Instruments
1 S Main St
Coventry, RI 2816
401-828-9582
Fax: 401-823-7460
customerservice@garlandpen.com
www.garlandpen.com
Quality writing instruments and accessories.
USA-made writing collections offer a full color logo
top. All writing instruments and accessories can be
customized
President: Louise Lanoie
VP: Kevin Bittle
Estimated Sales: $10 - 20 Million
Number Employees: 20-49
Number of Brands: 1
Square Footage: 130000

23072 Garman Co Inc
401 Marshall Rd
Valley Park, MO 63088-1817
636-923-2121
Fax: 636-923-2144 800-466-5150
nancyl@vapcoproducts.com
www.vapcoproducts.com
Ice machine cleaners.

President: Scott Garner
  scottg@vapcoproducts.com
Research & Development: Dr Joseph Raible
Marketing Director: Nancy Leppo
Sales Director: Bill Taylor
Estimated Sales: $2.5-5 Million
Number Employees: 10-19
Type of Packaging: Private Label
Brands:
  Blow Out
  Foaming Coil

23073 Garman Routing Systems Inc
1612 Barthel Road
PO Box 1126
Taylor, TX 76574

410-561-8085
Fax: 410-561-8086 512-535-0178
www.garmanrouting.com

Route accounting and distribution software for all route distribution applications including that of sales order entry; sales analysis; inventory control; full service vending; truck dispatch. Food industry uses include soft drinkbottlers, bottled water delivery, snack food distributors, dairy delivery, and coffee delivery services.
Sales Manager: Chip Sturm

23074 Garrity Equipment Company
31 Georgia Trl
Medford, NJ 08055-8938

609-953-0007
Fax: 609-953-0022 markg8@yahoo.com

Dryers, drum, fluid bed, roller, spray, tunner, fillers, filtration equipment, heat exchangers, homogenizers, ice cream equipment, margarine processing equipment, custom fabrication, distributed control systems, processing andpackaging, pilot plants
Estimated Sales: $500,000-$1 000,000
Number Employees: 1

23075 Garroutte
830 NE Loop 410 # 203
San Antonio, TX 78209-1207

210-826-2321
Fax: 210-824-5253 888-457-4997

Manufacturer and exporter of custom designed food processing equipment
President: Bob Garrett
Sales Support Manager: Richard Knappen
International Rep.: John Wurster
Operations Manager: Dan Southwood
Estimated Sales: $5-10 Million
Number Employees: 5-9
Square Footage: 120000
Brands:
  Waterfall Hydrochiller

23076 Garver Manufacturing Inc
224 N Columbia St
PO Box 306
Union City, IN 47390-1432

765-964-5828
Fax: 765-964-5828 www.garvermfg.com

Manufacture a wide variety of industrial centrifuges, bottle shakers, and bottle washers as well as custom equipment.
President: Michael Read
  garvermfg@woh.rr.com
Estimated Sales: Less Than $500,000
Number Employees: 1-4
Number of Brands: 2
Number of Products: 5
Square Footage: 16000

23077 Garvey Corp
208 S Route 73
Hammonton, NJ 08037-9565

609-561-2450
Fax: 609-561-2328 800-257-8581
garvey@garvey.com www.garvey.com

Conveyors and accumulators; exporter of conveyor systems and components; also, installation and start-up services available
President: Mark Garvey
Cmo: Ruth Caldwell
  rcaldwell@garvey.com
VP: William Garvey
Sales: Michael Earling
Estimated Sales: $20 - 50 Million
Number Employees: 50-99
Type of Packaging: Bulk

23078 Garvey Products
5428 Duff Dr
West Chester, OH 45246-1323

513-771-8710
Fax: 888-218-5551 800-543-1908
garveycares@garveyproducts.com
www.garveyproducts.com

A comprehensive supplier of handheld labeling equipment, custom labels, safety box cutters, handheld tagging equipment, handheld shopping baskets and carts, stampers and ink refills, and a variety of other retail supplies, for foodservice, deli or retail.
President: Chad Heminover
Marketing Manager: Benita Dorn
Customer Service Manager: Douglas Kelly
Director of Operations: Richard Williams
Estimated Sales: $5 Million+
Parent Co: Cosco Industries
Type of Packaging: Consumer, Food Service, Private Label, Bulk
Brands:
  Garvey

23079 Garvey Products
871 Redna Terrace
Cincinnati, OH 45215-1174

513-771-8710
Fax: 513-771-5108 www.garveyproducts.com

Price marking equipment, pressure sensitive labels, ink cutters, blades and express baskets
President: Rick Gmoch
Quality Control: Dave Ramey
VP: Dennis Feltner
R&D: Dave Ramey
Marketing Director: Dan Cork
Estimated Sales: $5 - 10 Million
Number Employees: 60
Parent Co: Cosco Industries

23080 Garvin Industries
3700 Sandra St
Franklin Park, IL 60131-1114

847-455-0188
Fax: 773-276-5580 847-451-6500

Manufacturer and designer of fluorescent lighting fixtures, backlighted menu display systems and transparency illuminators
Owner: Raheel Baig
  jim@ntisterling.com
Estimated Sales: $1 - 5 Million
Number Employees: 10-19

23081 Garvis Manufacturing Company
212 E 3rd Street
Des Moines, IA 50309-2006

515-243-8054
Fax: 515-243-1488

Steam cookers
President/Co-Owner: Robert Williams
VP/Co-Owner: Phillip Williams
Estimated Sales: Less than $500,000
Number Employees: 1-4
Parent Co: Fabricon

23082 Gary Manufacturing Company
2626 Southpoint Wat
Suite E
National City, CA 91950

619-429-4479
Fax: 619-429-4810 800-775-0804
www.garymanufacturing.com

Manufacturer and exporter of plastic and fabric table covers, aprons and napkins
Co-Owner: Helen Smith
Estimated Sales: $2.5-5 Million
Number Employees: 5-9
Square Footage: 20000

23083 Gary Plastic Packaging Corporation
3539 Tiemann Ave
Bronx, NY 10469-1636

718-231-4285
Fax: 203-629-1160 800-221-8151
sales@plasticboxes.com www.plasticboxes.com

Manufacturer and exporter of plastic boxes, containers and packaging materials; also, package design service available
Owner: Valerie A Gray
Sales: Rich Satone
Estimated Sales: 25-50 Million
Number Employees: 1-4

23084 Gary Plastic Packaging Corporation
3539 Tiemann Ave
Bronx, NY 10469-1636

718-231-4285
Fax: 203-629-1160 800-227-4279
sales@plasticboxes.com www.plasticboxes.com

Advertising specialties, plastic packaging and candy boxes; exporter of packaging products
Owner: Valerie A Gray
VP: Marilyn Hellinger
Sales: Rich Satone
Estimated Sales: $24 Million
Number Employees: 1-4
Square Footage: 4000
Brands:
  Garyline

23085 Gary Sign Co
3289 E 83rd Pl
Merrillville, IN 46410-6542

219-942-3191
Fax: 219-942-3077

Signs and advertising displays
Owner: Paul Grochowski
  garysignco@verizon.net
Estimated Sales: $1-2.5 Million
Number Employees: 5-9

23086 Gary W. Pritchard Engineer
5082 Bolsa Ave Ste 112
Huntington Beach, CA 92649

714-893-5441
Fax: 714-893-8405

Food processing machinery and sanitary fittings
President: Gary Pritchard
Sales Manager: Lisa Carlson
Estimated Sales: $1-2,500,000
Number Employees: 19

23087 Gasser Chair Co Inc
4136 Logan Way
Youngstown, OH 44505-1797

330-759-2234
Fax: 330-759-9844 800-323-2234
sales@gasserchair.com www.gasserchair.com

Wood and metal chairs, barstools and tables
President: Gary Gasser
  gary.gasser@gasserchair.com
CEO: George L Gasser
President: Mark Gasser
VP Sales/Marketing: Cindy Gasser
Estimated Sales: $10-20 Million
Number Employees: 50-99
Square Footage: 300000

23088 (HQ)Gaston County Dyeing Mach Co
1310 Charles Raper Jonas Hwy
Mt Holly, NC 28120-1234

704-822-5000
Fax: 704-822-0753 info@gaston-county.com
www.gaston-county.com

Heat exchangers, pressure vessels, tanks, dryers and electronic assemblies
President: Hubert Craig
Cmo: Ted J Hiley
  thiley@gaston-county.com
CEO: Joseph Mahoney
Advertising Manager: Sally Davis
Operations: Scott Davis
Purchasing: Scott Jonas
Estimated Sales: $20-50 Million
Number Employees: 500-999
Square Footage: 370000

23089 Gastro-Gnomes
22 Brightview Drive
West Hartford, CT 06117-2001

860-236-0225
Fax: 860-236-7967 800-747-4666

Manufacturer and exporter of plastic and thematic menu stands, menus and pop-out menu inserts
President: Allan Grody
Vice President: Marjorie Grody
Number Employees: 4

23090 Gates
PO Box 90
West Peterborough, NH 03468-0090

603-924-3394
Fax: 603-924-9677 888-543-6316

Wooden boxes

President: Mike Herz
Marketing Manager: John Naylor
Estimated Sales: $1-2.5 Million
Number Employees: 10-19

23091 Gates Corp
1144 15th St
Denver, CO 80202

303-744-5800
www.gates.com
Application-specific fluid power and power transmission solutions.
Chief Executive Officer: Ivo Jurek
Chief Financial Officer: Brooks Mallard
Chief Operating Officer: Walt Lifsey
EVP, Human Resources: Roger Gaston
Chief Information Officer: Michael Rhymes
SVP/Chief Marketing Officer: Tom Pitstick
Year Founded: 1911
Estimated Sales: Over $1 Billion
Number Employees: 14,000
Square Footage: 234264

23092 Gates Manufacturing Company
6924 Smiley Avenue
Saint Louis, MO 63139

314-647-5662
Fax: 314-645-7003 800-237-9226
www.gatesmfg.com
Custom commercial kitchen equipment including bins, conveyors, dish tables, refrigerators and tray make-up systems
President: Earl Gates Jr
Marketing/Sales: Robert Martin
Estimated Sales: $5-10 Million
Number Employees: 50

23093 Gates Mectrol Inc
9 Northwestern Dr
Salem, NH 03079-4809

603-890-1515
Fax: 603-890-1616 800-394-4844
www.gatesmectrol.com
Urethane timing belts, speed reducers and motion controle components
President: Bret Morrison
Estimated Sales: $20-50 Million
Number Employees: 100-249
Square Footage: 45000

23094 Gates Mectrol Inc
9 Northwestern Dr
Salem, NH 03079-4809

603-890-1515
Fax: 603-890-1616 800-394-4844
contact@gatesmectrol.com
www.gatesmectrol.com
Timing pulleys and polymer based automation components and synchronous timing belts.
President: Mark Appleton
appleton@gatesmectrol.com
Number Employees: 100-249

23095 Gateway Packaging Co
5910 Winner Rd
Kansas City, MO 64125-1626

816-483-9800
Fax: 618-876-4856
marketing@gatewaypackaging.com
Multiwall, small and specialty paper bags
Owner: Roger Miller
VP/CFO: Judy Samayda
Estimated Sales: $1 - 5 Million
Number Employees: 100-249
Square Footage: 300000

23096 Gateway Packaging Corp
2240 Boyd Rd
Export, PA 15632-8974

724-327-7400
Fax: 724-325-7447 888-289-2693
sales@gatepack.com www.gatepack.com
Corrugated boxes
President: Benjamin Getty
VP: Thomas Gill
Contact: Thomas Gill
gill@gatepack.com
General Manager: Scott Getty
Estimated Sales: $10-20 Million
Number Employees: 50-99
Square Footage: 196000

23097 Gateway Plastics Inc
5650 W County Line Rd
Mequon, WI 53092-4751

262-242-2020
Fax: 262-242-7262 www.gatewayplastics.com
Plastic caps and closures, custom plastic packaging
President: Carl Vogel
carl.vogel@gatewayplastics.com
Marketing/Sales: Bob Proudfoot
Estimated Sales: $20+ Million
Number Employees: 100-249
Number of Brands: 2
Square Footage: 200000
Type of Packaging: Consumer, Food Service, Private Label, Bulk
Brands:
  Gateway Closures
  Gateway Plastics

23098 Gateway Printing Company
3425 N Ridge Avenue
Arlington Heights, IL 60004-1496

847-394-0625
Fax: 847-727-1200 www.gateway-printing.com
Printing on skin and blister packaging board
General Manager: Bill Waters
CEO: John Rohrer
Estimated Sales: $10-20 Million
Number Employees: 50-99

23099 (HQ)Gatewood Products LLC
814 Jeanette St
3001 Gateman Drive
Parkersburg, WV 26101

304-422-5461
Fax: 304-485-2714 800-827-5461
Wood and wood-and-metal containers, pallets, skid shocks and wire-bounds; also, dry warehousing and transportation service available
President/CEO/Vice Chairman: Perry Smith
Estimated Sales: $20-50 Million
Number Employees: 20-49
Square Footage: 1150000

23100 Gavco Plastics Inc
9840 S 219th East Ave
Broken Arrow, OK 74014-5911

918-455-7888
Fax: 918-455-3695 www.gavcoplastics.com
President: Randall Gavlik
randygavlik@gavcoplastics.com
Estimated Sales: $1 - 5 Million
Number Employees: 50-99

23101 Gaychrome Division of CSL
220 D Exchange Drive
Crystal Lake, IL 60014

815-459-6000
Fax: 815-459-6105 800-873-4370
sales@csltd.com www.csltd.com
Tray stands, high chairs, etc., for the hospitality and food service industries.
President: Jay Maher
Director Sales: Rus Budde
Plant Manager: Joe Mancuso
Purchasing Manager: Sharri Kapaldo
Estimated Sales: $10-20 Million
Number Employees: 20-49
Type of Packaging: Consumer, Food Service, Private Label

23102 Gaylord Container Corporation
8700 Adamo Dr
Tampa, FL 33619-3524

813-621-3591
Fax: 813-621-3318 www.templeinland.com
Manufacturer and exporter of corrugated shipping containers, boxes and cartons
Manager: Wayne Parker
Controller: P Wilkins
General Manager: John Thrift
Production Supervisor: R Piepenbring
Estimated Sales: $20-50 Million
Number Employees: 100-249

23103 Gaylord Container Corporation
2301 Wilbur Ave
Antioch, CA 94509

925-779-3200
Fax: 925-779-4960 800-727-2699
Wine industry packaging

President: Michael Keough
CEO: Marvin Pomerantz
CFO: Daniel Casey
Senior VP: Lawrence Rogna

23104 Gaylord Industries
10900 SW Avery St
Tualatin, OR 97062-8578

503-691-2010
Fax: 503-692-6048 800-547-9696
www.gaylordventilation.com
or more than 75 years, Gaylord's ventilation systems have been known for durability, dependability, and meticulous attention to detail. They continue to revolutionize the industry with groundbreaking new designs as well as an innovative approach to solving the two main priorities facing foodservice operators: enrg savings and labor optimization.
President: Dan Shoop
CFO: Jeana Randall
R&D: Biucazx Lukins
Sales Manager: Keven Hass
Estimated Sales: $10 - 20 Million
Number Employees: 100-249
Square Footage: 150000
Brands:
  Gaylord

23105 Gaynes Labs Inc
9708 Industrial Dr
Bridgeview, IL 60455-2305

708-233-6655
Fax: 708-233-6985 gayneslabs@aol.com
www.gaynestesting.com
Consultant and testing laboratory for packaging materials
President: Yury Beyderman
gayneslabs@aol.com
Estimated Sales: $1-2.5 Million
Number Employees: 10-19
Square Footage: 33000

23106 Gbn Machine & Engineering
17073 Bull Church Rd
Woodford, VA 22580-2412

804-448-2033
Fax: 804-448-2684 800-446-9871
gbnmach@verizon.net www.nailerman.com
Manufacturer and exporter of pallet assembly systems, lumber stackers and conveyors
Vice President: Paul Bailey
paul@nailerman.com
Estimated Sales: Below $5 Million
Number Employees: 5-9

23107 Gbs
7233 Freedom Ave NW
North Canton, OH 44720-7123

330-494-5330
800-552-2427
marketing@gbscorp.com www.gbscorp.com
Manufacturer and exporter of plastic film, pressure sensitive labels and tags
VP: Jim Lee
VP/General Manager: James Lee
Marketing Director: Jackie Davidson
Plant Manager: Bruce Budney
Estimated Sales: $4 Million
Number Employees: 1-4
Square Footage: 120000

23108 (HQ)Gch Internatonal
330 Boxley Ave
Louisville, KY 40209-1845

502-636-1374
Fax: 502-636-0125 www.gchintl.com
Manufacturer and exporter of surge bins, vibrating sizing conveyors, enrobers and separators; also, freezers including spiral, tunnel and trolley
Chief Operating Officer: Haldun Turgay
CEO: John Thornton
jthornton@gchintl.com
VP Business Development: Edward Ward
Sales Manager Food: Thomas Fahed
Estimated Sales: $1-2.5 Million
Number Employees: 50-99
Square Footage: 360000
Parent Co: GCH International
Other Locations:
  Cardwell Machine Co.
  Farnborough NH
Brands:
  Spiro-Freeze
  Trolly-Freeze

Uni-Freeze
Vibe-O-Bin
Vibe-O-Vey

23109 Ge-No's Nursery
12285 Road 25
Madera, CA 93637-9013
559-674-4752
Fax: 559-674-3724
Grapevines for wine industry
Manager: Martin Nonin
Estimated Sales: Below $5 000,000
Number Employees: 10-19

23110 Gea Intec, Llc
4319 S Alston Ave
Suite 105
Durham, NC 27713
919-433-0131
Fax: 919-433-0140
Single and variable retention time freezers/chillers
for the food and beverage industries.
Contact: Jennifer Shambley
jshambley@gearefrigeration.com
Parent Co: Intec USA

23111 Gea Process EngineeringInc
9165 Rumsey Rd
Columbia, MD 21045-1929
410-997-8700
Fax: 410-997-5021 gea-pe.us@gea.com
www.geapharmasystems.com
Liquid and powder processing equipment for the
dairy and food and beverage industries.
President: Steve Kaplan
steve.kaplan@geagroup.com
Number Employees: 100-249

23112 Gea Processing
1600 Okeefe Rd
Hudson, WI 54016-7206
715-386-9371
Fax: 715-386-9376 800-376-6476
Powder and liquid processing equipment for the
dairy and food & beverage industries.
Vice President: Ron Matzek
ron.matzek@geagroup.com
Vice President: Ron Matzek
ron.matzek@geagroup.com
Number Employees: 100-249

23113 Gea Us
20903 W Gale Ave
Galesville, WI 54630-7276
608-582-3081
Fax: 608-582-2581
Manufacturer, importer and exporter of dairy farm
equipment and machinery including milk meters,
processors and coolers
Manager: Ralph Rottier
Cio/Cto: Kathy Snyder
kathy.snyder@westfaliasurge.com
VP: Ralph Rottier
Estimated Sales: $20-50 Million
Number Employees: 100-249
Square Footage: 140000
Parent Co: Babson Brothers Company
Brands:
Surge
Tru-Test

**23114 Gebo Conveyors, Consultants &
Systems**
1045 Autoroute Chomedey
Laval, QC H7W 4V3
Canada
450-973-3337
Fax: 450-973-3336 www.sidel.com
Manufacturer and exporter of stainless steel tabletop
conveying systems and equipment including pack-
age line controls, pressure-free combiners, packer
infeed systems and line audits
President: Mark Aury
Sales Manager: Jean Dion
Project Director: Mike De Cotiis
Number Employees: 250
Square Footage: 260000
Parent Co: Gebo Industries
Brands:
Gebo

23115 Gebo Corporation
6015 31st Street E
Bradenton, FL 34203-5382
941-727-1400
Fax: 941-727-1200
Manufacturer, importer and exporter of conveyors
including air trans and cap feeder
President: Mark Aury
Marketing Director: George Louli
General Manager: Christian Fitsch-Mouras
Estimated Sales: $20-50 Million
Number Employees: 100-249
Square Footage: 40000
Parent Co: Sidel Corporation
Brands:
Flat Top
Garro
Magneroll
Uf Feeder

23116 Gecko Electronics
Riedtlistrasse 72
CH-8006
Zurich, SW G2E 5W6
Canada
418-872-4411
Fax: 418-872-0920 contact@gecko-research.com
www.gecko-research.com
President: Michel Authier
R&D: Bemoit Laslamme
Number Employees: 350

23117 Geerpres Inc
1780 Harvey St
Muskegon, MI 49442-5396
231-773-3211
Fax: 231-773-8263 sales@geerpres.com
www.geerpres.com
Manufactures cleaning tools for the maintenance
supply industry in a business-to-business environ-
ment: steel, stainless steel, plastic, microfiber and
metal components.
President: Scott Ribbe
scott@geerpres.com
CFO: Bryan Depree
R&D: Joe Fodrocy
Quality Control: Jeff Kulbe
Marketing Director: Megan Schihl
Sales Director: Ted Moon
Purchasing Manager: Barb McAttnen
Estimated Sales: Below $5 Million
Number Employees: 20-49
Square Footage: 340000

23118 Gehnrich Oven Sales Company
2675 Main Street
East Troy, WI 53120
262-642-3938
Fax: 262-363-4018 sales@wisoven.com
www.wisoven.com/gehnrich-oven
Manufacturer and exporter of convection baking and
cooking ovens
President: Richard Gehnrich
Treasurer: Leon Pedigo, Jr.
VP: Wayne Pedigo
Estimated Sales: $1-2.5 Million
Number Employees: 20-49
Square Footage: 45000
Parent Co: Nevo Corporation

23119 Gei International Inc
100 Ball St
East Syracuse, NY 13057-2359
315-463-9261
Fax: 315-463-9034 800-345-1308
info@geionline.com www.geionline.com
Complete food processing and packaging systems
Estimated Sales: $1 - 5 Million
Number Employees: 10-19

23120 Geiger Bros
70 Mount Hope Ave
Lewiston, ME 04240-1021
207-755-2000
Fax: 207-755-2422 geigerorders@geiger.com
www.geiger.com
Manufacturer and exporter of advertising specialties
Regional VP East: Fred Snyder
Owner, CEO: Gene Geiger
CFO: Bob Blaisdell
Owner, Executive Vice President: Peter Geiger
V.P. Marketing: Gary Biron
V.P. Sales & Marketing: Jim Habzda
Vice President of Operations: Sheila Olson

Estimated Sales: $500,000 - $1 Million
Number Employees: 500-999
Square Footage: 40000
Brands:
Farmer's Almanac
Time By Design

23121 Gelberg Signs
6511 Chillum Pl NW
Washington, DC 20012-2192
202-882-7733
Fax: 202-882-1580 800-443-5237
sales@gelbergsigns.com www.gelbergsigns.com
Menu boards, signs and point of purchase displays
President: Neil Brami
nbrami@gelbergsigns.com
CFO: Bruce Gersh
Executive VP: Christopher Smith
Human Resource: Sarah Armour
Production Manager: Mark McCluney
Estimated Sales: Below $5 Million
Number Employees: 50-99
Square Footage: 50000

**23122 Gem Electric Manufacturing
Company**
20 Commerce Dr
Hauppauge, NY 11788-3910
631-273-2230
Fax: 631-273-9876 800-275-4361
Electrical wiring devices and electrical lighting ac-
cessories
President: Harvey Cooper
Vice President: Peter Massa
Marketing Director: Neal Massa
Contact: Andy Aqkr
andy@btn.net
Plant Manager: Andy Aqkr
Estimated Sales: Over $10 Million
Number Employees: 30
Number of Brands: 1
Number of Products: 8000
Square Footage: 140000
Parent Co: Gem Electric Manufacturing Company
Type of Packaging: Consumer, Private Label

23123 Gem Refrigerator Company
7340 Milnor St
Philadelphia, PA 19136-4211
215-426-8700
Fax: 215-426-8731
Refrigerators and freezers including walk-in and
reach-in, also custom boxes
President: Bruce Gruhler
Sales: John Greenwood
Plant Manager/Sales: Tony Iacono
Estimated Sales: $5 - 10 Million
Number Employees: 20 to 49
Square Footage: 80000

23124 Gemini Bakery Equipment
9991 Global Rd
Philadelphia, PA 19115-1005
215-676-9508
Fax: 215-673-3944 800-468-9046
sales@geminibe.com www.geminibe.com
Manufacturer and importer of bakery equipment
CEO/ Founder: Mark Rosenberg
Marketing Coordinator: Laura Albright
Sales Exec: Lou Giliberti
Estimated Sales: $10-20 Million
Number Employees: 20-49

23125 Gemini Data Loggers Inc
3685 Lakeside Dr
Suite A
Reno, NV 89509-5280
406-721-1958
Fax: 877-799-5198 sales@geminidataloggers.com
www.geminidataloggers.com
Contact: Neil Vass
nvass@geminidataloggers.com
Number Employees: 5-9

23126 Gemini Plastic Films Corporation
535 Midland Ave
Garfield, NJ 7026
973-340-0700
Fax: 973-340-1045 800-789-4732
customerservice@geminiplasticfilms.com
www.geminiplasticfilms.com
FDA/USDA approved plastic bags, sheeting, tubing,
pallet covers and film

President: Richard Hulbert Jr
Marketing/Sales: Frank Fusaro
Maintenance Manager: Pasquale Pavillo
Contact: Gemini Corp
  r.hulbert@geminiplasticfilms.com
Production Manager: Jack Pezdic
Purchasing Manager: Richard Primo
Estimated Sales: $5-10 Million
Number Employees: 20-49
Square Footage: 100000
Type of Packaging: Consumer, Food Service, Private Label, Bulk

23127 Gems Sensors & Controls
1 Cowles Rd
Plainville, CT 06062-1107
860-747-3000
Fax: 860-793-4531 www.gemssensors.com
Manufacturer and exporter of conductance actuated liquid level controls including sanitary probes and fittings; also, underground leak detection services available
President: Blue Lane
  twanbentlage@yahoo.com
Marketing Specialist: Tony Mancin
Estimated Sales: $50,000,000 - $99,999,999
Number Employees: 100-249
Square Footage: 29000
Parent Co: Danaher Corporation

23128 Gems Sensors & Controls
1 Cowles Rd
Plainville, CT 06062-1107
860-747-3000
Fax: 860-793-4531 800-378-1600
info@gemsensors.com www.gemssensors.com
Designs and manufacturers a broad portfolio of liquid level, flow and pressure sensors, miniature solenoid valves, and pre-assembled fluidic systems to exact customer application and manufacturing requirements.
President: Douglas Banks
  douglas.banks@danaher.com
Estimated Sales: $50,000,000 - $99,999,999
Number Employees: 100-249

23129 Gemtek Products LLC
3808 N 28th Ave
Phoenix, AZ 85017-4733
602-265-8586
Fax: 602-265-7241 800-331-7022
info@gemtek.com www.gemtek.com
Manufacturer and supplier of safe solvents, cleaners, and lubrications
President: Sarah Kristoff
  sarah.hunt@cdctn.org
Number Employees: 5-9
Other Locations:
  Manufacturing Plant
  Hayward CA
  Manufacturing Plant
  Mecedonia OH

23130 Genarom International
41 Mountain Blvd
Warren, NJ 07059-2630
908-753-8484
Fax: 908-753-9635 800-352-8672
Owner: Kenny Woo

23131 Genecor International
925 Page Mill Road
Palo Alto, CA 94304
650-846-7500
Fax: 585-256-6952 800-847-5311
www.genencor.com
Enzymes, such as amylases, cellulases, xylanases, glucose-oxidase, catalase and proteases
Contact: Lilia Babe
  lbabe@genencor.com
Number Employees: 73

23132 Genemco Inc
4455 Carter Creek Pkwy
Bryan, TX 77802-4416
979-268-7447
Fax: 979-268-7447 877-268-5865
sales@genemco.com
Agitation systems, milk and tank, cheese equipment, vacuum chambers, centrifuges, chillers, dryers, drum, fluid bed, roller, spray, tunnel, homogenizers, ice equipment, ingredient feeders, fillers, air gravity, milk, steam, filtrationequipment, flow div
Owner: Diane Lafving
  blafving@gmail.com

Estimated Sales: $500,000-$1 Million
Number Employees: 10-19

23133 General Analysis Corporation
PO Box 528
Norwalk, CT 06856-0528
203-852-8999
Fax: 203-838-1551
Diet and carbonation monitors for soft drink, beer, tea, and juice lines; lab testers for measuring CO2 in packaged beverage products
Estimated Sales: $1 - 5 000,000
Number Employees: 20-50

23134 General Bag Corporation
3368 W 137th St
Cleveland, OH 44111
216-941-1190
Fax: 216-476-3401 800-837-9396
generalbag@aol.com
Manufacturer and distributor of all packaging materials paper bags, poly, mesh. Boxes all sizes, bulk and waxed produce cartons; also packaging machinery
President: Rob Sprosty
Sales Manager: Dan Juba
Sales Representative: Larry Sprosty
Contact: Robert Sprosty
  generalbag@aol.com
Estimated Sales: $5 - 10 Million
Number Employees: 20-49
Square Footage: 160000

23135 General Cage
238 N 29th St
Elwood, IN 46036-1702
765-552-5039
Fax: 765-552-6962 800-428-6403
Manufacturer and exporter of wire products including forms, specialties, cages, display racks, partitions, grills, etc
Member: Bruce D Cook
Estimated Sales: $10-20 Million
Number Employees: 100-249
Square Footage: 216000

23136 General Chemical Corporation
90 E Halsey Rd Ste 301
Parsippany, NJ 07054
973-515-0900
Fax: 973-515-3232 info@genchemcorp.com
Industrial specialty and fine chemicals
CEO: William E Redmond Jr
Contact: Anny Ally
  a.ally@gentek-global.com
Estimated Sales: $20,000,000 - $49,999,999
Number Employees: 1,000-4,999

23137 General Conveyor Company
245 Industrial Parkway South
Auroua, ON L4G 4J9
Canada
905-727-7922
Fax: 905-841-1056 gcc@gccl.com
www.gccl.com
Design and manufacture a wide range of standard and customized conveyors, accumulators, end-of-line automation and custom machinery. Our primary focus is in the food, personal care, pharamceutical, beverage, irrafiation and plasticsmarkets.

23138 General Corrugated Machinery Company
269 Commercial Avenue
Palisades Park, NJ 07650-1154
201-944-0644
Fax: 201-944-7858 70451.2363@compuserve.com
Manufacturer and exporter of corrugated box formers; also, case formers, sealers, case packers and palletizers
Sales Manager: John Lavin
Estimated Sales: $1 - 5 Million
Brands:
  Galaxy
  Model Cf
  Nova

23139 General Cutlery Co
1918 N County Road 232
Fremont, OH 43420-9595
419-332-2316
Fax: 419-334-7119
Cutlery including knives

President: David Reitz
  dreitz@generalcutlery.com
VP: David Reitz
Estimated Sales: Below $5 Million
Number Employees: 10-19
Square Footage: 40000
Brands:
  Hard-Edge

23140 General Data Co Inc
4354 Ferguson Dr
Cincinnati, OH 45245-1667
513-752-7978
Fax: 513-752-6947 www.general-data.com
President: Peter Wenzel
Quality Control: Marsha Doon
Estimated Sales: $20-30 Million
Number Employees: 100-249

23141 General Electric Company
3135 Easton Turnpike
Fairfield, CT 06828
203-373-2211
www.geconsumerandindustrial.com
Household appliances including freezers and garbage disposal units
President & Chief Executive Officer: Ferdinando Beccalli-Falco
CEO: Jeff Immelt
CEO: James P Campbell
VP Marketing: Bruce Albertsons
Estimated Sales: $500,000-$1 Million
Number Employees: 10,000

23142 General Electric Company
5 Necco St
Boston, MA 02210
617-443-3078
800-417-0575
directors@corporate.ge.com www.ge.com
Electricity provider, as well as other segments such as additive manufacturing.
Chairman & CEO: H. Lawrence Culp, Jr
VP & CEO, GE Additive: Jason Oliver
SVP & CFO: Carolina Dybeck Happe
SVP & General Counsel: Mike Holston
SVP & President & CEO, GE Power: Russell Stokes
Year Founded: 1892
Estimated Sales: $95.2 Billion
Number Employees: 205,000

23143 General Equipment & Machinery Company
1617 NW 79th Avenue
Doral, FL 33126-1105
305-471-0802
Fax: 305-471-6196
Machinery for PET stretch blow molding, form-fill seal, injection molding and film shrink wrap packing
Estimated Sales: $2.5-5 Million
Number Employees: 8

23144 General Espresso Equipment
7912 Industrial Village Rd
Greensboro, NC 27409-9691
336-393-0224
Fax: 336-393-0295 info@geec.com
www.astoriausaparts.com
Espresso machine cleaners, espresso machines/accessories, espresso pod machines
Owner: Roberto Daltio
Manager: Randy Brewer
Estimated Sales: $500,000-$1 000,000
Number Employees: 10-19

23145 General Films Inc
645 S High St
Covington, OH 45318-1182
937-473-3033
Fax: 937-473-2403 888-436-3456
www.generalfilms.com
Manufacturer and exporter of plastic bags, packaging coextruded films and bag-in-box bulk liquid packaging
President: Tim Weikert
Quality Control: Norman Slade
Sales (Food Pkg.): Linda Lyons
Sales Manager (Industrial Pkg.): Howard Stutzman
Sales (Bag-in-Box): Cindy Grogean
Estimated Sales: $20 - 50 Million
Number Employees: 50-99
Square Footage: 60000
Brands:
  Duratuf

23146 General Floor Craft
4 Heights Ter
Little Silver, NJ 07739-1323
973-742-7400
Fax: 973-742-0004
Manufacturer and exporter of vacuums and carpet
cleaning machinery
Owner: Barry Gore
VP: Jeff Gore
Estimated Sales: $2.5-5 Million
Number Employees: 20-49
Square Footage: 54000

23147 General Formulations
309 S Union St
Sparta, MI 49345-1529
616-887-7387
Fax: 616-887-0537 800-253-3664
mclay@generalformulations.com
www.generalformulations.com
Manufacturer and exporter of self-adhesive and
floor advertising films
CEO: James Clay
CEO: James Clay
Marketing Manager: Mike Clay
Regional Sales Manager: Jeff Balasko
Estimated Sales: $20-50 Million
Number Employees: 50-99
Square Footage: 100000
Brands:
 Permalar
 Traffic Graffic

23148 (HQ)General Grinding Inc
801 51st Ave
Oakland, CA 94601-5694
510-261-5557
Fax: 510-261-5567 800-806-6037
ggrind@aol.com www.generalgrindinginc.com
Knife sharpeners; also, replacement parts for ma-
chinery including curling and beading rings; repair
services available
President: Michael Bardon
ggrind@aol.com
Sales Manager: Daniel Bardon
Estimated Sales: $5-10 Million
Number Employees: 20-49
Square Footage: 42000

23149 General Industries Inc
3048 Thoroughfare Rd
PO Box 1279
Goldsboro, NC 27534-7728
919-751-1791
Fax: 919-751-8186 888-735-2882
tanks@gitank.com www.gitank.com
Vaulted tire rated, mix/process, above ground and
underground steel storage tanks and oil/water sepa-
rators also carbon steel and stainless steel
President: John T Wiggins
tommyw@gitank.com
Sales Marketing: Nancy Lilly
Purchasing Manager: Jody Vernon
Estimated Sales: $6 Million
Number Employees: 20-49
Square Footage: 160000
Brands:
 Fireguard
 Permatank

23150 General Machinery Corp
1831 N 18th St
PO Box 717
Sheboygan, WI 53081-2312
920-458-2189
Fax: 920-458-8316 888-243-6622
sales@genmac.com www.genmac.com
Manufacturer and exporter of meat and cheese pro-
cessing equipment including meat flakers, slicers,
dicers, mechanical tenderizers, grinders, pork rind
chippers and cheese cutters; also, cake and bun
slabbers, pan washers and beltconveyors.
President: Michael Horwitz
CFO: Marsha Binversie
VP Operations: Robert Jeske
Production Manager: Gary Mueller
Estimated Sales: $2.5-5 Million
Number Employees: 10-19
Brands:
 Cannon
 Hydraucuber Super Slicer
 Hydrauflakers
 M-8 Slitter
 Multislicer

Rotary Dicer
S/M Flaker
Sp-250 Flattener
Tenderit
Tu-Way

23151 General Magnaplate Corp
1331 W Edgar Rd
Linden, NJ 07036-6496
908-862-6200
Fax: 908-862-6110 800-852-3301
info@magnaplate.com www.magnaplate.com
Metal finishing, surface enhancement coatings for
food and drug processing and packaging equipment,
wear and corrosion resistant coatings for metal parts.
CEO: Candida Aversenti
caversenti@magnaplate.com
Estimated Sales: $12 Million
Number Employees: 100-249

23152 General Methods Corporation
3012 SW Adams Street
Peoria, IL 61602
309-497-3344
Fax: 309-497-3345
Manufacturer and exporter of coupon and premium
dispensers; also, contract thermoform packaging and
seal integrity verification equipment
President: Dale Kuykendall
Chief Tech.: Ken Brackett
Estimated Sales: Less than $500,000
Number Employees: 3
Square Footage: 26000

23153 General Neon Sign Co
900 Buena Vista St
San Antonio, TX 78207-4308
210-227-1203
Fax: 210-227-0067 www.generalsignsinc.com
Signs including neon, plastic, vinyl, advertising,
electric, etc.; also, installation and repair services
available
Owner: Jason Kaupert
Quality Control: Jason Kaupert
Estimated Sales: Below $5 Million
Number Employees: 10-19

23154 General Packaging Equipment Co
6048 Westview Dr
Houston, TX 77055-5420
713-686-4331
Fax: 713-683-3967 sales@generalpackaging.com
www.generalpackaging.com
Manufacturer and exporter of packaging machinery
including bag forming and net weighers
President: Robert C Kelly
rkelly@generalpackaging.com
Director of Sales: Tom Wilson
Estimated Sales: $5-10 Million
Number Employees: 20-49
Square Footage: 66000
Type of Packaging: Consumer, Food Service, Pri-
vate Label
Brands:
 General Packager
 Hydrafeed

23155 General Packaging Products Inc
1700 S Canal St
Chicago, IL 60616-1189
312-226-8380
Fax: 312-226-4027 800-621-1921
info@generalpk.com www.generalpk.com
Wrappers and protective packages for food industry
President: William K Kellogg III
william@generalpk.com
CFO: Tom Woods
CEO: William Kellogg
Quality Control: Eric Courtney
Sales (Central Region): Tim Schoolman
VPO: Volney Bunch
Plant Manager: Joe Bunch
Estimated Sales: $10-25 Million
Number Employees: 100-249
Type of Packaging: Private Label

23156 General Press Corp
110 Allegheny Dr
PO Box 316
Natrona Heights, PA 15065-1902
724-224-3500
Fax: 724-224-3934 www.generalpress.com

Manufacturer and exporter of die cut paper labels
for food and beverage containers; also, heat seal foil
lids for single serve jelly cups, injection mold labels
and lightweight plastic labels.
President: Scott Poorbaugh
spoorbaugh@generalpress.com
Sales Manager: David Wolff
VP Operations: T Conroy
Estimated Sales: $5-10 Million
Number Employees: 50-99
Square Footage: 120000

23157 General Processing Systems
12838 Stainless Drive
Holland, MI 49424
616-399-2220
Fax: 616-399-7365 800-547-9370
jswiatlo@nbe-inc.com www.productsaver.com
Manufacturer and exporter of bag opening equip-
ment and custom designed product recovery
systems.
President: Ed Swiatlo
Sales Manager: Jeff Swiatlo
Contact: Joe Reed
todd@nbe-inc.com
Estimated Sales: $3 - 5 Million
Number Employees: 10-19
Square Footage: 40000
Parent Co: General Processing Systems

23158 General Resource Corporation
P.O. Box 470
Dassel, MN 55325-0470
952-933-7474
Fax: 952-933-9777
Airlock, gates, air slides
President: Joseph Pausch
VP: Jim Masterman
Estimated Sales: $1 - 3 Million
Number Employees: 1-4

23159 General Shelters of Texas LTD
1639 State Highway 87 N
P.O. Box 2108
Center, TX 75935
936-598-3389
Fax: 936-598-1432 www.generalshelters.com
Manufacturer of portable buildings.
President: Rick Campbell
Year Founded: 1973
Estimated Sales: $50-100 Million
Number Employees: 100-249
Square Footage: 300000

23160 General Sign Co
2723 N Jackson Hwy
Sheffield, AL 35660-3430
256-383-3176
Fax: 256-383-3170
Identification and deco electrical signage
General Manager: Ted Martin
CEO/President: Lenn Scheibal
Controller: Kris Sneed
Engineer: Dean Precival
Sales Director: Kim Underwood
Estimated Sales: Less Than $500,000
Number Employees: 5-9
Square Footage: 280000
Type of Packaging: Bulk

23161 General Steel Fabricators
927 S Schifferdecker Ave
Joplin, MO 64801-3528
417-623-2224
Fax: 417-623-2204 800-820-8644
Tanks, bucket elevators and dust and cyclone collec-
tors
Manager: Stan Rife
General Manager: Stan Rife
Assistant General Manager: Paul Howey
Purchasing Manager: Jim Cruzan
Estimated Sales: $10 - 20 Million
Number Employees: 50-99
Square Footage: 80400
Parent Co: Doane Pet Care

23162 General Tank
328 West Front Street
P O Box 488
Berwick, PA 18603-2138
570-752-4528
Fax: 570-752-6121 800-435-8265
Conveyors, fittings, pumps, valves, tanks, washers
and control systems

President: Dan Bower
Contact: Gebby Bankoski
 gbankoski@generaltank.com
Estimated Sales: Below 1 Million
Number Employees: 1-4

23163 General Tape & Supply
28505 Automation Blvd
Wixom, MI 48393-3154
248-357-2744
Fax: 248-357-2749 800-490-3633
Manufacturer and exporter of pressure sensitive labels
President: Mary Raden
COO: Jack Hooker
Research & Development: Debbie Wojcik
Sales Director: Julie Stallings
Estimated Sales: $2.5 - 5 Million
Number Employees: 30

23164 General Trade Mark Labelcraft
55 Lasalle St
Staten Island, NY 10303
718-448-9800
Fax: 718-448-9808
Embossed and printed labels, price tag seals and stickers; exporter of printed labels
Owner: Richard Capuozzo
CEO: V Kruse
Estimated Sales: $10 - 20 Million
Number Employees: 20-49
Square Footage: 40000
Brands:
 Sure-Stik

23165 General Truck Body Mfg
7110 Jensen Dr
Houston, TX 77093-8703
713-692-5177
Fax: 713-692-0700 800-395-8585
www.generalbody.com
Truck bodies including van, slide-ins, cold plates and refrigerated
President: Barbara Paull
 barbara.paull@generalbody.com
CEO: Barbara Paull
Sales: Clayton Price
Plant Manager: Tollan Maxwell
Estimated Sales: $10 - 20 Million
Number Employees: 50-99

23166 General Wax & Candle Co
6863 Beck Ave
North Hollywood, CA 91605-6206
818-765-5800
Fax: 818-764-3878 800-929-7867
www.generalwax.com
Manufacturer and exporter of candles
Owner: Jerry Baker
 jbaker@generalwax.com
VP: Mike Tapp
Estimated Sales: $10 - 15 Million
Number Employees: 50-99
Type of Packaging: Food Service

23167 General, Inc
3355 Enterprise Ave.
Suite 160
Weston, FL 33331
954-202-7419
Fax: 954-202-7337 info@generalfoodservice.com
www.generalfoodservice.com
Manufacturer, importer and exporter of slicers, grinders and mixers; manufacturer of food and organic waste disposers
President: John Westbrook
VP Sales/Marketing: Harry Ristan
Purchasing Manager: Dean Council
Estimated Sales: $5-10 Million
Number Employees: 100-249
Square Footage: 80000
Parent Co: Standex International Corporation
Type of Packaging: Food Service
Brands:
 General Slicing

23168 Genesee Corrugated
2022 North St
Flint, MI 48505
810-228-3702
Fax: 810-235-0350 www.genpackaging.com
Manufacturer and exporter of corrugated shipping containers and interior packing materials

President: Luella Kautman
 lkautman@co.genesee.mi.us
Material Control: Bobbi Jackson
Estimated Sales: $23.1 Million
Number Employees: 20-49
Type of Packaging: Bulk

23169 Genesis Machinery Products
400 Eagleview Blvd Ste 100
Exton, PA 19341
610-458-4900
Fax: 610-458-4939 800-552-9980
President: Bruce Smith
CFO: Bill Seiler
Contact: Bill Bogle
 bbogle@gen-techno.com
Estimated Sales: $5 - 10 000,000
Number Employees: 20-49

23170 Genesis Nutritional Labs
391 S Orange St
Salt Lake City, UT 84104-3524
801-973-8824
Fax: 801-973-8807 www.gnlabs.net
Testing services offered for chemical and microbiological nutraceutical and food needs.
Managing Partner: Jeff Reynolds
Technical Account Manager: Melissa Robbins
Business Development: Rachelle Maass
On-Staff Physician: Joe Giacalone
 edgar@genysislabs.com
Sr Laboratory Manager: Edgar Grigorian
Manager: Edgar Grigorian
 edgar@genysislabs.com
Microbiology Manager: Scott Larsen
Number Employees: 1-4

23171 Genesis Total SolutionsInc
3524 Decatur Hwy # 104
Suite 104
Fultondale, AL 35068-1366
205-631-5334
Fax: 205-877-3224 gts@gts-genesis.com
www.gts-genesis.com
rovides quality software solutions to the Food & Beverage Industry for over 35 years. We have users located throughout the United States, in Canada and overseas. Our applications include Accounting, Distribution, Production, and OrderFulfillment. All of our applications were developed by, and are supported through our staff of responsive professionals. Our solutions were designed to address the specific requirements of the F/B industry and an be used by both large and smallbusinesses.
President and Owner: Bill Miller
 bmiller@gts-genesis.com
Vice President: Chris Miller
Technical Director: Camille Bourque
Estimated Sales: Below $5 Million
Number Employees: 1-4
Square Footage: 6000

23172 Geneva Awning & Tent Works Inc
96 Lewis St
Geneva, NY 14456
315-789-3151
Fax: 315-789-2695 800-789-3151
www.genevatent.com
Commercial awnings and tents,also rental and sales
Owner: Sam Heakel
VP: Dan Warder
Estimated Sales: $1 - 2.5 Million
Number Employees: 5-9

23173 Geneva Lakes Cold Storage
PO Box 39
Darien, WI 53114-0039
262-724-3295
Fax: 262-724-4200
Warehouse offering cooler, freezer and dry storage for frozen, refrigerated and nonperishable food items; transportation firm providing refrigerated truck and van services including local, short and long haul
Number Employees: 1-4

23174 Genflex Roofing Systems
250 West
96th Street
Indianapolis, IN 46260
972-233-4100
Fax: 817-588-3099 800-443-4272
info@fbpe.be www.genflex.com

Partner: Rick L Cohen
Sales Manager: Bob Marini
QBS Regional Manager: Brian Stevenson
Sales Manager: Tim Creagan
Sales Manager: Mike Melito
Customer Service Representative: Linda Monroe
Estimated Sales: $1 - 3 000,000
Number Employees: 5-9

23175 Genpak
25 Aylmer Street
P O Box 209
Peterborough, ON K9J 6Y8
Canada
705-743-4733
Fax: 705-743-4798 800-461-1995
info@genpak.com www.genpakca.com
Manufacturer and exporter of plastic containers, cups and lids; also, single-serve packaging machinery for butter, margarine, creamers, etc
Quality Control: Jennifer Seeley
R&D: Jennifer Seeley
National Sales Manager: Kevin Callahan
Production Manager: Bernie Logan
Plant Manager: Brian May
Number Employees: 60
Type of Packaging: Bulk
Brands:
 Purity Pat
 Sealcup

23176 Genpak LLC
8235 220th St W
Lakeville, MN 55044-8059
952-881-8673
Fax: 952-881-9617 800-328-4556
www.genpak.com
Plain and printed new and recycled polyethylene bags and film, flexible packaging, laminations and pouches for various food and snack food applications.
President: Kim Lenhardt
Sales: Kevin Callahan
Plant Manager: Russ Snyder
Estimated Sales: $20 - 50 Million
Number Employees: 100-249
Number of Products: 100+
Square Footage: 140000
Parent Co: Jim Pattison Group
Other Locations:
 Strout Plastics
 Lakeville MN
Brands:
 Bags Again
 Flip & Grip
 Mr. Neat
 Value Tough

23177 Genpak LLC
10601 Westlake Dr
Charlotte, NC 28273
800-626-6695
info@genpak.com www.genpak.com
Manufacturer and exporter of plastic and styrofoam take out containers including plates, bowls and take-out containers. Dual oven meal solutions and bakery trays in opet plastic for retail packs. Packaging for processor, food serviceand retail applications.
President: Kevin Kelly
Estimated Sales: $100-500 Million
Number Employees: 1000-4999

23178 Gensaco Marketing
1751 2nd Ave
New York, NY 10128-5388
212-876-1020
Fax: 212-876-1003 800-506-1935
espmachine@aol.com
Coffee bars, espresso and cappuccino machines; importer of grinders; exporter of espresso machines, ice cream machines - restaurant equipment
Partner: Edward V Giannasca
CEO: Al Elvino
VP Sales: Lawrence Coal
VP Purchasing: Carbone Lorenzo
Estimated Sales: $1 Million
Number Employees: 5-9
Square Footage: 34000
Parent Co: Gensaco
Brands:
 Gensaco

23179 Gentile Packaging Machinery
8300 Boettner Rd
Saline, MI 48176-9642

734-429-1177
Fax: 734-429-4714 info@gentilemachinery.com
www.gentilemachinery.com
Packaging machinery
President: Aliseo Gentile
al@xelapack.com
Vice President: Anthony Gentile
Plant Manager: Rob Wilkerson
Estimated Sales: $1 - 2.5 000,000
Number Employees: 50-99

23180 Geo. Olcott Company
PO Box 267
Scottsboro, AL 35768-0267

256-259-4937
Fax: 256-259-4942 800-634-2769
Manufacturer and exporter of glass bead blast-clean-
ing cabinets, degreasing tanks, magnetic detectors
and jet spray washers
President: Richard Olcott
Vice President: Marilyn Olcott
Estimated Sales: $1-2.5 Million
Number Employees: 9
Square Footage: 16800
Brands:
Olcott

23181 Georg Fischer Central Plastics
39605 Independence St
Shawnee, OK 74804-9203

405-273-6302
Fax: 405-273-5993 800-654-3872
www.centralplastics.com
Molded plastic boxes
Contact: Cameron Laplante
cameronlaplante@yahoo.com
Estimated Sales: $1 - 5 Million
Number Employees: 50-99

23182 Georg Fischer Disa PipeTools
PO Box 40
Holly, MI 48442-0040

248-634-8251
Fax: 248-634-2507
Pipe cutting and beveling equipment
CEO: Kurt Stirnemann
Estimated Sales: $20-50 Million
Number Employees: 100-249

23183 George Basch Company
PO Box 188
Freeport, NY 11520

516-378-8100
Fax: 516-378-8140 info@nevrdull.com
www.nevrdull.com
Metal cleaners and polishes
President: Laurie Basch-Levy
Vice President: Mark Ax
Estimated Sales: $5-10 Million
Number Employees: 10-19
Number of Brands: 1
Number of Products: 1
Brands:
Nevr-Dull Polish

23184 George G. Giddings
61 Beech Road
Randolph, NJ 07869-4548

973-361-4687
Fax: 973-887-1476
Consultant for food processing preservation
Consultant: George Giddings, Ph.D.
Number Employees: 1

23185 George Glove Company, Inc
301 Greenwood Ave
Midland Park, NJ 07432

201-251-1200
Fax: 201-251-8431 800-631-4292
steve@georgeglove.com www.georgeglove.com
Importer of white gloves
President/CEO: Andrew Wilson
CFO: Andrew Wilson
Marketing Director: Roy Miller
Sales: Roy Miller
Contact: Sharon Jubelt
sjubelt@newconceptoffice.com
Operations Manager: Juan Mino
Estimated Sales: $2 Million
Number Employees: 7
Square Footage: 48000

Brands:
Beauty
Dermal
While-U-Color

23186 George Gordon Assoc
12 Continental Blvd
Merrimack, NH 03054-4302

603-424-5204
Fax: 603-424-9031 sales@ggapack.com
www.ggamfg.com
Packaging machinery, kits packaging, pouching sys-
tems, case/carton/gaylord loaders
President: Don Blanger
VP Sales/Marketing: Ron Downing
Purchasing Manager: Maurice Demarais
Estimated Sales: $10-20 000,000
Number Employees: 5-9

23187 George Lapgley Enterprises
4988 E Rolling Glen Drive
Pipersville, PA 18947

267-221-2426
Fax: 215-766-1687
Specialist in food safety & security consulting.
Liason with regulatory agencies. Production, retail,
food service, HACCP Plans, food safety training, ex-
pert testimony, food safety audits

23188 George Lauterer Corp
310 S Racine Ave # 6
6th Floor North
Chicago, IL 60607-2841

312-913-1881
Fax: 312-913-1811 sales@lauterer.com
www.lauterer.com
Advertising novelties and specialties including
flags, banners, badges and buttons
Owner: Earl Joyce
johnj@lauterer.com
VP Marketing: John Joyce
Sales Exec: John Joyce
Estimated Sales: $2.5-5 Million
Number Employees: 20-49

23189 George Risk Industries Inc
802 S Elm St
Kimball, NE 69145-1599

308-235-4645
Fax: 308-235-3561 800-445-5218
www.grisk.com
Reed-type panel mount pushbutton switches, burglar
alarms, door, window and keyboard switches, alpha-
numeric keyboards and proximity systems
CEO: Stephanie Risk-McElroy
gricfo@embarqmail.com
CFO: Stephanie Risk
VP Sales: Mary Ann Brothers
Quality Control: Bonnie Heaton
Sales Administration: Sharon Westby
Estimated Sales: $10,000,000 - $19,999,999
Number Employees: 100-249

23190 George's Bakery Svc
1525 Macarthur Blvd # 4
Suite 4
Costa Mesa, CA 92626-1413

714-437-7143
Fax: 714-437-1016 www.georgesbakery.com
Owner: George Grezaud
george@georgesbakery.com
Estimated Sales: Less Than $500,000
Number Employees: 1-4

23191 Georgia Cold Storage
503 Ship St
Tifton, GA 31794-9617

229-382-5800
Fax: 912-382-5803
Cold Storage
Estimated Sales: $300,000-500,000
Number Employees: 1-4

23192 (HQ)Georgia Duck & Cordage Mill
21 Laredo Drive
Scottdale, GA 30079

404-297-3170
Fax: 404-296-5165
Manufacturer and exporter of conveyor and elevator
belting including vinyl, rubber and urethane

President: Raymond Willoch
VP Sales/Marketing: Ken Dangelo
Sales Manager/National Accounts: Jim Hinson
Sales Manager: Jim Panter
Number Employees: 490

23193 Georgia Pacific
P.O. Box 19130
Green Bay, WI 54307

920-435-8821
Fax: 920-496-9445 www.gp.com
Facial tissue, hand towels, napkins, wipers, dispens-
ing systems and printed specialty products
VP: Russ Mc Collister
Sr. VP Sales: George Hartmann
VP Sales: Paul Farren
Contact: Dean Baumgartner
dean.baumgartner@gapac.com
Estimated Sales: $1 - 5 Million
Number Employees: 1,000-4,999
Brands:
Adnaps
Belnap
Bevnaps
Bi-Tex
Billow
Commander Ii
Dari-Dri
Dine-A-Wipe
Dine-A-Wipe Plus
Drize
Dust 'n Clean
Elfin
Essence
Fornap
Fort Howard
Generation Ii
Handifold
Hy-Tex
Hynap
Miltex
Mini-Mornap
Mornap
Mynap
Nornap Jr.
Nu-Nap
Palmer
Paperlux
Perfection
Plyfold
Pom
Pom-Etts
Prim
Pul-A-Nap
Ritenap
Selford
Shur-Wipe
Sirnap
So-Dri
Sof-Knit
Soft 'n Fresh
Soft 'n Gentle
Spread
Staynap
Studio Colors
Stylene
Texnap
Tidynap Jr.
Twin-Tex
Ultra Wipe
Wipe Away

23194 Georgia Tent & Awning
1356 English St NW
Atlanta, GA 30318

404-523-7551
Fax: 404-525-0601 800-252-2391
info@georgiatent.com www.georgiatent.com
Commercial awnings
President: Ken Spooner
Quality Control: Mike Hill
VP: Bob Spooner
CFO: Gary Meacher
Chairman of the Board: Robert Spooner
Contact: Leonard Buccellato
leonard.buccellato@georgiatent.com
Estimated Sales: $5 - 10,000,000
Number Employees: 50-99

23195 Georgia Watermelon Association
4109 Country Way
PO Box 1109
LaGrange, GA 30241
706-845-8575
Fax: 706-883-8215
Our purpose is watermelon promotion from production to consumption.
President: Ricky Tucker
Executive Secretary/Treasurer: Nancy Childers
Estimated Sales: $1-2.5 Million
Number Employees: 1-4

23196 Georgia-Pacific LLC
133 Peachtree St. NE
Atlanta, GA 30303
404-652-4000
800-283-5547
www.gp.com
Manufacturer and exporter of corrugated shipping cases.
President/Chief Executive Officer: Christian Fischer
SVP, Operations: Jeff Koeppel
SVP/Chief Financial Officer: Tyler Woolson
SVP/Communications, Gov't & Pub. Affairs: Sheila Weidman
Year Founded: 1927
Estimated Sales: Over $5 Billion
Number Employees: 30,000+
Parent Co: Koch Industries
Type of Packaging: Consumer

23197 Gerber Innovations
24 Industrial Park Rd W
Tolland, CT 6084
Fax: 978-694-0055 800-331-5797
www.gerberinnovations.com
Manufacturer and exporter of computer plotters and sample makers for packaging design
Director of Sales & Marketing: Don Skenderian
Vice President, Business Development: Mark Bibo
Technical Manager: Ken Hooks
VP Sales: Steven Gore
General Manager: W Staniewicz
Estimated Sales: $10 - 20 Million
Number Employees: 50-99
Parent Co: Data Technology

23198 Gerber Legendary Blades
14200 SW 72nd Ave.
Portland, OR 97224-8010
503-639-6161
Fax: 503-403-1102 800-950-6161
www.gerbergear.com
Culinary knives including steak, carving, slicing, etc.
Year Founded: 1939
Estimated Sales: $100 Million
Number Employees: 250-499
Parent Co: Fiskars

23199 Germantown Milling Company
6098 Brooksville Germantown Rd
Germantown, KY 41044-9060
606-728-5857
Fax: 606-883-3172
Feed
President: Jack Myrick
Estimated Sales: Below $5 Million
Number Employees: 2
Square Footage: 900000

23200 Gerrity Industries
PO Box 121
Monmouth, ME 04259
207-933-2804
Fax: 207-933-1081 877-933-2804
info@gerrityindustries.com
www.gerrityindustries.com
Pallets and skids
President: Peter Gerrity
Sales: Leo Moody
Contact: Wally Fish
fish@gerrityindustries.com
Estimated Sales: Below $5 Million
Number Employees: 20-49
Square Footage: 120000

23201 Gerstel Inc
701 Digital Dr # J
Suite J
Linthicum Hts, MD 21090-2236
410-609-0856
Fax: 410-247-5887 800-413-8160
info@gerstelus.com www.gerstelus.com
Gas chromatographic systems for analysis of complex samples in the flavoring and food additive business including thermal desorption, static headspace, fraction collectors and multi-column switching systems
President: Bob Collins
CFO: Robert Collins
Vice President: Robert Collins
R&D: Ed Pfannkoch
IT: Robert Collins
sales@gerstelus.com
Estimated Sales: Below $5 Million
Number Employees: 10-19
Parent Co: Gerstel GmbH
Brands:
Gerstel

23202 Gervasi Wood Products
2611 W Beltline Highway
Madison, WI 53713-2349
608-274-6752
Counters
Estimated Sales: $500,000-$1 Million
Number Employees: 5-9

23203 Gessner Products
241 N Main St
PO Box 389
Ambler, PA 19002-4224
215-646-7667
Fax: 215-646-6222 800-874-7808
sales@gessnerproducts.com
www.gessnerproducts.com
Manufacturer and exporter of plastic ashtrays, credit card trays, coasters, signs, condiment jars, sugar caddies and restaurant smallwares
President: Edward H Gessner
Controller: Neo Brown
Executive VP: Geoffrey Ries
Quality Control: Steve Fuhrmeister
National Sales Manager: Michael Salemi
Production Manager: Chuck Denoncour
Estimated Sales: $5 - 10 Million
Number Employees: 100-249

23204 Geyersville Printing Company
21001 Geyersville Avenue
Geyserville, CA 95441
707-857-1704
Fax: 707-857-1705
Wine industry labels
Estimated Sales: less than $500,000
Number Employees: 6

23205 Ghibli North American
14 Germay Drive
Wilmington, DE 19804
302-654-5908
Fax: 302-652-7159 ghibli@frontiernet.net
Manufacturer and exporter of high pressure and hot water cleaning equipment
General Manager: Gordon Thomas
Estimated Sales: $1 - 5 Million
Number Employees: 5 to 9
Brands:
Ghibli

23206 (HQ)Giant Gumball Machine Company
200 Macarthur Blvd
Grand Prairie, TX 75050-4739
972-262-2234
Fax: 972-262-3167
Manufacturer and exporter of vending machines
President: Dan Clemson
d.clemson@productsales.com
National Sales Manager: Bob Rogers
National Sales Manager: Dan Wright
Estimated Sales: $300,000-500,000
Number Employees: 1-4

23207 Giant Packaging Corporation
545 W Lambert Road
Suite F
Brea, CA 92821-3916
714-256-8498
Fax: 714-256-8499 giant@gus.net

Strapping and wrapping machines, carton sealers, impulse sealers, and strapping hand tools
Estimated Sales: $2.5-5 000,000
Number Employees: 1-4

23208 Gibbs Brothers Cooperage
113 Overton St
Hot Springs, AR 71901-6312
501-623-8881
Fax: 501-623-9610 gibbsbro@swbell.net
White oak wooden kegs and barrels
President: James Gibbs Sr
Manager: Jay Gibbs
Estimated Sales: $1-2.5 Million
Number Employees: 5-9
Square Footage: 48000

23209 (HQ)Gibraltar Packaging Group Inc
2000 Summit Ave
Hastings, NE 68901-6703
402-463-1366
Fax: 402-463-2467
Folding cartons, litho-laminated cartons, regular and corrugated cartons and flexible packaging including converted bags and rollstock
President and COO: Richard Hinrichs
rhinrichs@rosmarpackaging.com
CEO: Walter E Rose
Chairman of the Board: Walter E Rose
VP Sales: Mark Lessor
Corporate Marketing/Investor Rel. Mgr: Leslie Schroeder
Estimated Sales: Below $5,000,000
Number Employees: 100-249
Other Locations:
Gibraltar Packaging Group
Mount Gilead NC

23210 Giddings & Lewis
P.O. Box 1960
Fond Du Lac, WI 54936-1960
920-921-7100
Fax: 920-906-7669 800-558-4808
mwl@giddings.com
Automotion controls, measurement, sensing
Manager: Pete Winkelmann
President, Chief Executive Officer: Lawrence Culp
Estimated Sales: $50 - 100 Million
Number Employees: 100-249

23211 Giesecke & Devrient America
45925 Horseshoe Dr # 100
Dulles, VA 20166-6588
703-480-2000
Fax: 703-480-2060 800-856-7712
www.gi-de.com
Manufacturer and exporter of high speed currency counters, dispensers and endorsers
President: Scott Marquardt
scott.marquardt@gdai.com
Director Distribution: Bill Chamberlain
Estimated Sales: $50-100 Million
Number Employees: 250-499
Parent Co: G&D America

23212 Giffin International
1900 Brown Rd
Auburn Hills, MI 48326-1701
248-478-5115
Fax: 248-478-1321 info@giffinusa.com
Cooking and chilling systems; smoke houses, air chillers, batch and continuous systems
Owner: Shawn Drury
shawn.drury@giffinusa.com
Estimated Sales: Less Than $500,000
Number Employees: 1-4

23213 Gilbert Industries, Inc
5611 Krueger Drive
Jonesboro, AR 72401-6818
870-932-6070
Fax: 870-932-5609 800-643-0400
mailbox@gilbertinc.com www.gilbertinc.com
Electronic wall-mounted flytraps
President: David Gilbert
Sales: Stephen Goad
Sales: Libby Mackey
Estimated Sales: $1 - 5 Million

23214 Gilbert Insect Light Traps
5611 Krueger Dr
Jonesboro, AR 72401-6818
870-932-6070
Fax: 870-932-5609 800-643-0400
mailbox@gilbertinc.com www.gilbertinc.com
Manufacturer and exporter of professional flytraps,
emergency lighting and LED exit signs; also, con-
sultant on flying insect control
President/ILT Research/Customer Service: David
Gilbert
ILT Sales/Customer Service: Stephen Goad
Executive Administrator/Customer Service: Libby
Mackey
Estimated Sales: $1 - 3 Million
Number Employees: 20-49
Number of Brands: 2
Number of Products: 15
Square Footage: 152000
Parent Co: Gilbert Industries
Brands:
   Gilbert

23215 Gilchrist Bag Co Inc
907 Sharp Ave
Camden, AR 71701-2603
870-836-6416
Fax: 870-836-8379 800-643-1513
sales@gilchristbag.com www.gilchristbag.com
Manufacturer and exporters of a wide variety of
quality paper bags, sacks and specialty supplies used
by a variety of markets.
Owner: Tom Gilchrist
tgilchrist@gilchristbag.com
Director Operations Marketing: Randy Robertson
Plant/Production Manager: Larry Starnes
Plant Manager: Louis Hammond
Estimated Sales: $5-10,000,000
Number Employees: 20-49
Square Footage: 350000
Type of Packaging: Consumer, Food Service, Pri-
vate Label

23216 (HQ)Giles Enterprises Inc
2750 Gunter Park Dr W
P.O. Box 210247
Montgomery, AL 36109-1098
334-272-1457
Fax: 334-239-4117 800-288-1555
intsales@gilesent.com www.gfse.com
Manufacturer and exporter of kitchen and deli
equipment including ventless hood fryers
President: David Byrd
dbyrd@gfsequipment.com
Financial Director: Ken Robinson
Quality Control: Sheila Munday
VP Sales: David Byrd
Estimated Sales: $10 - 20 Million
Number Employees: 100-249
Square Footage: 160000
Brands:
   Chester Fried
   Giles

23217 Gillis Associated Industries
750 Pinecrest Dr
Prospect Heights, IL 60070-1806
847-541-6500
Fax: 847-541-0858 www.gillisindustries.com
Wire systems for shelving, carts, palletainer stacking
wire containers, rack decking, high-density mobile
storage and rivet rack with wire decking
President: Harvey Baker
President, Chief Executive Officer: Steven DarnelL
Vice President of Business Development: Dave
Mack
VP Sales: Mark Jones
Vice President of Operations: Bob Buehler
Estimated Sales: $5-10 Million
Number Employees: 20-49

23218 Gilson Co Inc
7975 N Central Dr
Lewis Center, OH 43035-9409
740-548-5314
Fax: 740-548-5314 800-444-1508
www.globalgilson.com
Liquid handling
President: Trent R Smith
tsmith@gilsonco.com
CEO: Robert H Smith
Marketing Director: Carl Kramer
Technical Development Manager: Jim Bibler

Estimated Sales: $12-20 Million
Number Employees: 50-99
Brands:
   Fristch Mills
   Gilsonic Autosiever
   Ultra Siever

23219 Giltron Inc
61 Endicott St
PO Box 427
Norwood, MA 02062-3046
781-762-4310
Fax: 508-359-4317 sales@giltron.com
www.giltron.com
Induction heat cap foil sealers for bottles and jars
President: Fred Giltron
CFO: A Stanley Pittman
Quality Control: Bruce Green
R & D: Mike Sievert
Service Manager: William Koivu
VP Operations: Fred Pittman
Estimated Sales: Below $5 Million
Number Employees: 1-4
Square Footage: 14000
Brands:
   Giltron Foilsealer

23220 Ginnie Nichols Graphic Design
780 W Napa St
Sonoma, CA 95476-6452
707-996-0164
Fax: 707-938-3855 800-399-7890
Package design
President: Jenny Nichols
Estimated Sales: $300,000-500,000
Number Employees: 1-4

23221 Ginseng Up Corp
16 Plum St
Worcester, MA 01604-3600
508-799-6178
Fax: 508-799-0686 800-446-7364
info@ginsengup.com www.ginsengup.com
Natural soft drinks; contract packaging available
President: Sang Han
Manufacturing Executive: Courtney Craite
courtney@ginsengup.com
Estimated Sales: $3 - 5 Million
Number Employees: 10-19
Parent Co: One Up
Type of Packaging: Consumer
Brands:
   Cold/Hot Pack Tunnel Pasterized
   Flavor
   Ginseng Up

23222 Gintzler Graphics Inc
100 Lawrence Bell Dr
Buffalo, NY 14221-7089
716-631-9700
Fax: 716-631-0075 sales@gintzler.com
Pressure sensitive labels
President: Jeff Amato
amato.jeff@gintzler.com
Sales Manager: James Calamita
Estimated Sales: $20-50 Million
Number Employees: 50-99

23223 Girard Spring Water
1100 Mineral Spring Ave
North Providence, RI 02904-4104
401-725-7298
Fax: 401-725-7913 800-477-9287
Spring water and water coolers
President: John Ponton
Estimated Sales: $500,000-$1 Million
Number Employees: 1 to 4
Square Footage: 7500
Type of Packaging: Consumer, Private Label, Bulk

23224 Girard Wood Products Inc
802 E Main St
Puyallup, WA 98372-3364
253-845-0505
Fax: 253-845-5463 800-532-0505
greg@girardwoodproducts.com
Wooden pallets and skids; also, pallet recycling services including retrieval, repair and disposal available

President: Anthony Hubbs
anthony@girardwoodproducts.com
VP of Sales: Greg Vipond
Sales Manager: Dave Loden
Operations Manager: Scott Vipond
Plant Manager: Virgil Vwngwirth
Purchasing Manager: Stan Henry
Estimated Sales: $10 - 20 Million
Number Employees: 20-49

23225 Girton Manufacturing Co
160 W Main St
Millville, PA 17846-5004
570-458-5521
Fax: 570-458-5589 info@girton.com
www.girton.com
Manufactures stainless steel washing equipment for
the Food & Dairy Processing Industries, including
COP tanks, bin and tub washing systems for pallets,
drums, cases, etc. Girton MFG co Inc also manufac-
tures King Zeero Ice Builders.
President: Dean Girton
info@girton.com
Sales: Wm Bruce Michael
Plant Manager: Jim Eves
Purchasing Director: Donna Bender
Estimated Sales: $10 - 20 Million
Number Employees: 50-99
Square Footage: 45000
Brands:
   Girton King Zeero

23226 Giunta Brothers
2612 S 17th St
Philadelphia, PA 19145-4502
215-389-9670
Culinary strainers and graters
Owner: Anthony P Giunta
Estimated Sales: less than $500,000
Number Employees: 1 to 4

23227 Gl Mezzetta Inc
105 Mezzetta Ct
American Canyon, CA 94503-9604
707-648-1050
Fax: 707-648-1060 800-941-7044
www.mezzetta.com
Glass-packed peppers and olives
President: Jeff Mezzetta
Founder: Giuseppe Luigi Mezzetta
HR Executive: Maritza Monge
mmonge@mezzetta.com
General Manager: Ronald Mezzetta
Estimated Sales: $12.3 Million
Number Employees: 100-249

23228 Glamorgan Bakery
3919 Richmond Rd SW
Building 19
Calgary, AB T3E 4P2
Canada
403-232-2800
glamorganbakery@gmail.com
www.glamorganbakery.com
Freshly baked goods
President/Owner: Douwe Nauta
General Manager: Don Nauta
Sales/Customer Service: Jeremy Nauta
Number Employees: 8

23229 Glaro Inc
735 Calebs Path # 1
Hauppauge, NY 11788-4201
631-234-1717
Fax: 631-234-9510 info@glaro.com
www.glaro.com
Manufacturer and exporter of waste containers, en-
graved signs, aluminum tray stand equipment, crowd
control stanchions, planters, coat racks, etc
Vice President: Robert Betensky
robert@glaro.com
CEO: Michael Glass
VP: Robert Betensky
Estimated Sales: $20-50 Million
Number Employees: 10-19
Square Footage: 50000

23230 Glasko Plastics
3123 W Alpine St
Santa Ana, CA 92704
714-751-7830
Fax: 714-751-4039
Plastic containers

Estimated Sales: $2.5-5 Million
Number Employees: 20-49

23231 Glass Industries America LLC
340 Quinnipiac St # 3
Wallingford, CT 06492-4050
203-269-6700
Fax: 203-269-8782 www.wallingfordglass.com
Manufacturer and exporter of lighting fixtures including bent and decorated glassware
Owner: George Sutherland
glass.industries@snet.net
Manager: Jack Jackson
Estimated Sales: $2.5-5 Million
Number Employees: 5-9
Parent Co: L.D. Kichler

23232 Glass Pro
2300 W Windsor Ct
Addison, IL 60101-1491
630-268-9494
Fax: 800-875-6243 888-641-8919
Manufacturer and exporter of glass washing machinery, sanitizers and accessories
President: Robert Joesel
CEO: Evelyn Joesel
R&D: Robert Joesel
Quality Control: Robert Joesel
Estimated Sales: Below $5 Million
Number Employees: 5-9
Number of Brands: 4
Number of Products: 3
Square Footage: 12000
Type of Packaging: Food Service, Private Label
Brands:
Brush-Rite
Glass Maid
Glass Pro

23233 Glass Tech
23780 NW Huffman St # 101
Hillsboro, OR 97124-5976
503-646-3989
Fax: 503-626-2890 www.glasstechweb.com
Wine industry tasting room supplies
Contact: Patricia Patton
patricia@glasscellar.com
Estimated Sales: $1-2.5 000,000
Number Employees: 10-19

23234 Glassline Corp
28905 Glenwood Rd
Perrysburg, OH 43551-3020
419-666-0857
Fax: 419-666-1549 www.glasslinecompanies.com
Hot and cold seal packaging machinery
Owner: Tom Ziems
sales@glassline.com
Estimated Sales: $10-20 Million
Number Employees: 100-249

23235 Glastender
5400 N Michigan Rd
Saginaw, MI 48604-9700
989-752-4275
Fax: 989-752-4444 800-748-0423
info@glastender.com www.glastender.com
Manufacturer and exporter of bar and restaurant equipment including glass washers, cocktail stations, underbar and refrigerated backbar equipment, mug frosters, beer and soda line chillers, ice cream freezers and coolers
President: Todd Hall
thall@glastender.com
CFO: Jamie Rievert
VP Admin: Kim Norris
Quality Control: David Burk
VP Operations: Mark Norris
Plant Manager: Mark Norris
Purchasing Manager: Zoa May
Estimated Sales: $10 - 20 Million
Number Employees: 100-249
Square Footage: 200000

23236 Glatech Productions LLC
325 2nd St
Lakewood, NJ 08701-3329
732-364-8700
Fax: 732-370-0877 info@kosherGELATIN.com
www.koshergelatin.com
Producer of Kolatin Kosher gelatin and Elyon kosher confectionery products.

CEO: Moshe Eider
glatech@gmail.com
Marketing: Chez Eider
Estimated Sales: $1 - 5 Million
Number Employees: 1-4
Number of Brands: 2
Type of Packaging: Bulk
Brands:
Elyon
Kolatin

23237 Glatfelter P H Co
96 S George St # 520
Suite 500
York, PA 17401-1434
717-225-4711
Fax: 717-846-7208 866-744-7680
info@glatfelter.com www.glatfelter.com
Teabag paper, bags and packaging film supplies, coffeebag paper, coffeebag paper (metallized)
CEO: Dante C Parrini
dante.parrini@glatfelter.com
CEO: George Glatfelter
CFO: John Jacunski
Number Employees: 1000-4999

23238 Glatt Air Techniques Inc
20 Spear Rd
Ramsey, NJ 07446-1288
201-825-8700
Fax: 201-825-0389 info@glattair.com
Process controls, material handling equipment, coaters, fluid bed dryers, granulators, etc
EVP: Stephen Sirabian
General Manager Sales: John Carey
Vice President: Steve Sirabian
ssirabian@glattair.com
Director Business Development: Ted Wisniewski
VP Sales/Technical Operations: Stephen Sirabian
Estimated Sales: $30 - 50 Million
Number Employees: 100-249
Square Footage: 60000
Parent Co: Glatt GmbH
Other Locations:
Glatt Air Techniques
San Leandro CA

23239 Glawe Manufacturing Company
851 Zapata Dr
Fairborn, OH 45324-5165
937-754-0064
Fax: 937-754-1780 800-434-8368
bhughes@glaweawning.com
www.glaweawning.com
Commercial awnings
CEO: L Vernon Schaefer
Contact: L Schaefer
l.schaefer@glaweawnings.com
Estimated Sales: $2.5-5 Million
Number Employees: 20-49

23240 Gleason Industries
3013 Douglas Boulevard
Suite 230
Roseville, CA 95661-3847
916-784-1302
Fax: 310-679-5581
Converting box boards and layerboards for the candy and bakery industries
President: Michael Richards
CEO: Mike Richards
VP Finance: John Mahar
Sales Director: Carlene Milligan
Plant Manager: Tony Concad
Estimated Sales: $1 - 3 Million
Number Employees: 85
Other Locations:
Gleason Industries
Sacramento CA
Gleason Industries
Summer WA
Gleason Industries
Millwaukie OR
Gleason Industries
West Valley City UT
Gleason Industries
Rancho Cocamonca CA

23241 Gleeson Construct & Engineers
2015 7th St
P.O. Box 625
Sioux City, IA 51101-2003
712-258-9300
Fax: 712-277-5300 www.gleesonllc.com

Specializes in the construction of food processing facilities, freezers, cold storage facilities and distribution centers.
President: Harlan Vandezandschul
h.vandezandschul@gleesonllc.com
Number Employees: 1-4

23242 Glen Mills Inc.
220 Delawanna Ave
Clifton, NJ 07014-1550
973-777-0777
Fax: 973-777-0070 sales@glenmills.com
Laboratory and small-scale production equipment
Director: Stanley Goldberg
Marketing: Lisa McCormack
Sales Engineer: Ross Kaplan
Estimated Sales: $2.5-5 Million
Number Employees: 6
Square Footage: 48000
Brands:
Kakuhunter
Retsch
SEPR
Turbula

23243 Glen Raven Custom Fabrics LLC
1831 N Park Ave
Burlington, NC 27217-1137
336-227-6211
Fax: 336-226-8133 oford@glenraven.com
www.glenraven.com
Solutions dyed acrylic fabrics for awnings and umbrellas
Chairman/ CEO: Allen E Gant Jr
President/ COO: Leib Oehmig
SVP, CFO & Treasurer: Gary Smith
SVP, Secretary & General Counsel: Derek Steed
R&D: John Coates
Sales/Marketing Administration: Harry Gobble
National Sales Manager: Ocie Ford
Contact: Emily Eby
eeby@glenraven.com
Number Employees: 20-49
Parent Co: Glen Raven Custom Fabrics LLC
Type of Packaging: Food Service

23244 Glenmarc Manufacturing
2001 S.Blue Island Ave.
Chicago, IL 60608
312-243-0800
Fax: 312-243-4670 800-323-5350
glenmarc@aol.com
Manufacturer and exporter of adhesive dispensing equipment. Also 304/316 stainless steel pressure tanks
President: John Sims
Chairman, Chief Executive Officer: John Chen
CEO: Don Deloach
Senior Vice President of Operations: Billy Ho
Purchasing Manager: Steve Eichele
Estimated Sales: Below $500,000
Number Employees: 5-9
Square Footage: 26000

23245 (HQ)Glenro Inc
39 Mcbride Ave
Paterson, NJ 07501-1799
973-279-5900
Fax: 973-279-9103 888-453-6761
info@glenro.com www.glenro.com
Hot air and infrared ovens for food packaging
President: Bill Bacher
bbacher@glenro.com
Vice President: Jim Karrett
Sales Director: Jim Karrett
Estimated Sales: $10-15 Million
Number Employees: 10-19

23246 Glenroy Inc
1437 Wells Dr
Bensalem, PA 19020-4469
215-245-3575
Fax: 215-245-3589 800-441-2230
www.glenroylabels.com
Labeling technologies, bar code scanners
Owner: Patrick Larkin Jr
Vice President: Terry la Ruffa
CFO: Vince Laruffa
Estimated Sales: $5-10 000,000
Number Employees: 20-49

23247 Glit Microtron
305 Rock Industrial Park Dr
Bridgetown, MO 63044
877-947-7117
Fax: 800-327-5492 800-325-1051
CustomerService@contico.com
www.continentalcommercialproducts.com
Abrasive coated synthetic sponge, scour pads and
scrub sponges
President: Gordan Kirsch
Research Manager: Alan Christopher
Number Employees: 250-499
Parent Co: Katy Industries

23248 Glit/Disco
13330 Lakefront Drive
Earth City, MO 63045-1513
314-770-9919
Fax: 800-327-5492 contmfg@contico.com
www.continental-mfg.com
Estimated Sales: $1 - 5 Million
Parent Co: Katy Company

23249 Glo Germ Company
P.O. Box 189
Moab, UT 84532
435-259-6034
Fax: 435-259-5930 800-842-6622
info@glogerm.com www.glogerm.com
Handwashing training
President: Joe D Kingsley
Estimated Sales: $1 000,000
Number Employees: 5-9
Type of Packaging: Consumer, Bulk
Brands:
Superior Systems

23250 Glo-Quartz Electric Heater
7084 Maple St
Mentor, OH 44060-4932
440-255-9701
Fax: 440-255-7852 800-321-3574
tstrokes@gloquartz.com www.gloquartz.com
Electric immersion heaters and tubular metal and
quartz heating elements for food processing and
packaging; also, temperature controls; exporter of
electric heaters
President: George Strokes
VP: Thomas Strokes
Sales: John Paglia
Contact: Jeffrey Payne
jpayne@gloquartz.com
Plant Manager: Jeff Payne
Estimated Sales: $3 - 5 Million
Number Employees: 20-49
Square Footage: 88000
Brands:
Glo-Quartz

23251 Global Canvas Products
5000 Paschall Ave
Philadelphia, PA 19143-5136
267-634-6207
Fax: 610-284-4323 kanvasking@globecanvas.com
www.globecanvas.com
Wholesale manufacturer and distributor, with a diverse product mix comprised of 60% awning, 25%
athletic pads for track and field, 10% industrial covers and 5% bags.
President: Kevin Kelly
kevin@globecanvas.com
Estimated Sales: $1-2.5 Million
Number Employees: 1-4
Square Footage: 72000

23252 Global Carts and Equipment
640 Herman Road
Suite 2
Jackson, NJ 08527-3068
732-899-9555
Fax: 732-899-1719 800-653-0881
foodman40@aol.com
Supplier of hot dog carts, soup carts and food.
Estimated Sales: $2.5-5 Million
Number Employees: 5-9
Square Footage: 104000

23253 Global Environmental Packaging
221 3rd Street
Newport, RI 02840-1087
401-847-4603
Fax: 401-847-4654 800-729-4210

23254 Global Equipment Co Inc
11 Harbor Park Dr
Port Washington, NY 11050-4646
516-608-7000
Fax: 516-625-8415 888-628-3466
www.globalindustrial.com
Manufacturer, exporter and importer of steel bins,
benches, wire shelving and material handling equip-
ment
Purchasing Manager: Eric Bertel
Estimated Sales: $28 Million
Number Employees: 100-249
Square Footage: 85000
Parent Co: Systemax

23255 Global Manufacturing
1801 E 22nd St
Little Rock, AR 72206-2501
501-374-7416
Fax: 501-376-7147 800-551-3569
www.globalmanufacturing.com
Manufacturer and exporter of vibrators including
hydraulic, pneumatic, electric, air blasters and
turbine
President: Catherine Janosky
cjanosky@globalmanufacturing.com
Quality Control: Wilfred Coney
Marketing: April Crocker
Sales: Perry Schnebelen
Operations: Tom Janosky
Production: Stan Kligman
Plant Manager: Rod Treat
Purchasing Director: Howard Stewart
Estimated Sales: $3 - 5,000,000
Number Employees: 10-19
Brands:
Quiet Thunder
Silver Sonic
Yellow Jacket

23256 Global Marketing Enterprises
1801 S Canal St # C
Chicago, IL 60616-1522
312-733-0000
Fax: 312-733-8010
President: Eduardo Chua
echua@globalmsi.com
Estimated Sales: $5 - 10 Million
Number Employees: 10-19

23257 Global New Products DataBase
333 West Wacker Drive
Suite 1100
Chicago, IL 60606
312-932-0400
Fax: 312-932-0469 helpdesk@mintel.com
www.gnpd.com
Comprehensive database that monitors worldwide
product innovation in consumer packaged goods
markets
Manager: Jon Butcher
CFO: John Weeks
Estimated Sales: $5 - 10 Million
Number Employees: 20-49

**23258 Global Nutrition Research
Corporation**
3120 S Potter Dr
Tempe, AZ 85282
602-454-2248
Fax: 602-454-2249
Provide a comprehensive database of herbal supple-
ments, health products, and herbal companies avail-
able on the internet. We are not only an information
provider, but also an herbal and alternative medicine
community site.
President: Ken Ardisson
Sales Contact: Shannon Purcell
Estimated Sales: $20 - 50 Million
Number Employees: 20-49

23259 Global Organics
68 Moulton St
Cambridge, MA 02138-1119
781-648-8844
Fax: 781-648-0774 info@global-organics.com
www.global-organics.com
Organic ingredients
President: Dave Alexander
Vice President: Roland Hoch
Account Manager: Dino Scarsella
Sales and Marketing Coordinator: Ravi Arori
Estimated Sales: Under $500,000
Number Employees: 25

23260 Global Package
PO Box 634
Napa, CA 94559
707-224-5670
Fax: 707-224-8170 info@globalpackage.net
www.globalpackage.net
International packaging solutions for wine, spirits
and food
CEO: Erica Harrop
Sales: Kathy Feder
Estimated Sales: $5 Million
Number Employees: 3
Type of Packaging: Food Service

**23261 Global Packaging Machinery
Company**
1500 Cardinal Drive
Little Falls, NJ 07424
973-450-4601
Fax: 973-450-4603
global@globalpackmachinery.com
www.globalpackmachinery.com
President: Daniel Waldron
R & D: Mike Kurgyla
Vice President/Mechanical Engineer: Herman
Andrade
Contact: Michael Kurdyla
global@globalpackmachinery.com
Estimated Sales: Below $5 Million
Number Employees: 10

23262 Global Payment Tech Inc
170 Wilbur Pl # 4
Bohemia, NY 11716-2416
631-563-2500
Fax: 631-563-2630 www.gptx.com
Paper currency validators, lockable stackers for use
in the gaming, beverage and vending industries
President: Thomas Oliveri
CFO: William L Mcmahon
wmcmahon@gptx.com
Quality Control: Dede Lisa
Sales Director: Mary Russell
Number Employees: 20-49

**23263 Global Product Development
Group**
3501 Woodhead Drive
Suite 10
Northbrook, IL 60062
847-504-0464
Fax: 608-224-0455 info@globalpdg.com
www.globalpdg.com
Laboratory providing research and development,
consulting and contract research services
President: Michael Maloney
Estimated Sales: $1 - 3 Million
Number Employees: 5-9
Square Footage: 15000

23264 Global Sticks, Inc.
13555-23A Avenue
Surrey, BC V4A 9V1
Canada
604-535-7748
Fax: 604-535-7749 866-433-5770
Wooden ice cream spoons & sticks, corn dog sticks
& coffee stirrers.
President: Reggie Nukovic
General Manager: Earl Metcalf

23265 Global USA Inc
1990 M St NW # 200
Washington, DC 20036-3468
202-296-2400
Fax: 202-296-2409 info@globalusainc.com
www.globalusainc.com
CEO: H Lottie
lottie@globalusainc.com
Chairman and Chief Executive Officer: Dr. Bo
Denysyk
Senior Vice President: David C. Fine
Director - Research and Analysis: Viktor Sulzynsky
Number Employees: 10-19

23266 Global Water & Energy
2404 Rutland Dr
Suite 200
Austin, TX 78758
512-697-1930
Fax: 512-697-1931 mail.usa@globalwe.com
www.globalwaterengineering.com

Industrial wastewater treatment and bio-waste-to-energy solution provider for food industries
Chairman/CEO: Jean-Pierre Ombregt
Contact: Erin Booth
  ebooth@globalwaterengineering.com
Controller: Mike Herbert
Estimated Sales: $1 Million
Number Employees: 5
Parent Co: GLV

23267 Global Water Group Inc
8601 Sovereign Row
Dallas, TX 75247-4613

214-678-9866
Fax: 214-678-9811 info@globalwater.com
www.globalwater.com
Mobile, self-contained and fixed based water purification systems, wastewater processing equipment, and gray water recycling equipment
President: Alan Weiss
  amweiss@globalwater.com
COO: Rick Stafford
CFO: Rd Stafford
Vice President: N Kanmer
Research & Development: Jacob Kupersztoch
Quality Control: Thomas Boutwell
Public Relations: Cherie Weiss
Estimated Sales: $10 Million
Number Employees: 20-49
Number of Brands: 6
Number of Products: 50
Square Footage: 40000

23268 (HQ)Globe Fire Sprinkler Corp
4077 Airpark Dr
Standish, MI 48658-9533

989-846-4583
Fax: 989-846-9231 800-248-0278
Bob733@aol.com www.globesprinkler.com
Manufacturer, importer and exporter of commercial, industrial and residential fire sprinklers, deluge/preaction, alarm, dry pipe and check valves, water motor alarms and accessories for sprinkler systems
President: Steven R. Worthington, I.M.B..A
Chairman/ CEO: Robert C. Worthington, P.E.
  bob733@aol.com
EVP: Buck Buchanan
Dir. of Marketing & Information System: John D. Corcoran
VP, Sales: Randy Lane
VP, Operations: Terry Bovee
Estimated Sales: $10-20 Million
Number Employees: 100-249
Square Footage: 80000
Brands:
  Globe
  Kennedy
  System Sensor

23269 Globe Food Equipment Co
2153 Dryden Rd
Moraine, OH 45439-1739

937-299-5493
Fax: 937-299-4147 800-347-5423
www.globefoodequip.com
Manufactures slicers, vegetable cutters, mixers, choppers and scales
President: Hilton Gardner
  hgardner@globeslicers.com
Marketing: Alicia Sanders
Sales: Bob Adams
Number Employees: 20-49
Brands:
  Chefmate
  Globe
  Protech

23270 Globe Machine
902 E E St
Tacoma, WA 98421-1839

253-572-9637
Fax: 253-572-9672 800-523-6575
sales@globemachine.com
www.globemachine.com
Manufacturer and exporter of material handling equipment including hydraulic lift tables, conveyors, personnel carriers, tilters, dumpers and transfer cars
Special Projects Manager: Mark Allen
Operations Manager: Michael Natucci
Estimated Sales: $20 - 50 Million
Number Employees: 1-4
Square Footage: 225000
Parent Co: Globe Machine Manufacturing Company

23271 Globe Packaging Co
368 Paterson Plank Rd
Carlstadt, NJ 07072-2306

201-939-3335
Fax: 201-939-3325 888-221-0989
sales@globecasing.com www.globecasing.com
Natural casing for meat industries
Owner: Isreal Bank
  issy@globecasing.com
VP: David Knoebel
Estimated Sales: $2 Million
Number Employees: 10-19

23272 (HQ)Globe Ticket & Label Company
300 Constance Dr
Warminster, PA 18974

215-443-7960
Fax: 215-956-2493 800-523-5968
www.globeticket.com
Tickets, coupons and labels including heat seal, pressure sensitive and EDP
COO: Randy Hicks
  sales@globeticket.com
CFO: Don Schilling
Treasurer: Maddalena Krause
Estimated Sales: $20-50 Million
Number Employees: 100-249
Brands:
  Tak-A-Number

23273 Globex America
2324 Shorecrest Dr
Dallas, TX 75235-1804

214-353-0328
Fax: 214-353-0074 jerry@globexamerica.net
Brewing devices
President: Bonnie Itzig
  info@globexamerica.net
CFO: Jerry Itziq
R & D: Donnie Itziq
Estimated Sales: $1 - 3 Million
Number Employees: 5-9

23274 Glopak
4755 Boulevard De Grandes Prairies
St Leonard, QC H1R 1A6
Canada

514-323-4510
Fax: 514-323-5999 800-361-6994
www.glopak.com
Manufacturer and exporter of packaging equipment and supplies including bags, fillers, filling equipment, films, flexible packaging, pouches and wrapping material
President: Ritchie Baird
CEO: Harold Martin
CFO: John Mireault
Quality Control: Hens Pohl
R&D: Eves Quiten
Number Employees: 130
Type of Packaging: Bulk

23275 Gloucester Engineering
11 Dory Rd
Gloucester, MA 01931

978-281-1800
Fax: 978-282-9111
Film extrusion products
Year Founded: 1961
Estimated Sales: $100+ Million
Number Employees: 250-499
Parent Co: Davis-Standard

23276 Glover Latex
PO Box 167
Anaheim, CA 92815

714-535-8920
Fax: 714-535-3635 800-243-5110
Plastic, rubber and protective gloves
President: Paul Babcock
CEO: Sandra Robles
Sales Director: R Fisher
Estimated Sales: $2.5-5 Million
Number Employees: 20-49
Square Footage: 34000
Type of Packaging: Consumer, Food Service, Private Label, Bulk

23277 Glover Rubber Stamp & Crafts
1015 Goodnight Blvd
Wills Point, TX 75169-3134

214-824-6900
Fax: 214-824-6906 anna@gloverstamp.com
www.gloverstamp.com
Rubber stamps and signs
Manager: Anna Prile
  anna@gloversstamps.com
Estimated Sales: $500,000 - $1 Million
Number Employees: 1-4

23278 Glowmaster Corporation
312 Lexington Ave
Clifton, NJ 07011-2366

973-772-1112
Fax: 973-772-4040 800-272-7008

www.e-hospitality.com/storefronts/glowmaster.html
Manufacturer and importer of cooking and heating equipment including portable tabletop butane stoves and fuel, chafers, griddles, service carts and induction cooking systems; exporter of portable butane stoves
Owner: Juan Travezano
CFO: Linda Smith
Director Sales: Frank Palatiello
Number Employees: 10-19
Square Footage: 28000
Brands:
  Chafermate
  Glowmaster

23279 Glue Dots International
5515 S Westridge Dr
New Berlin, WI 53151

262-814-8500
Fax: 262-814-8505 888-688-7131
info@gluedots.com www.gluedots.com
Providing adhesive solutions to people, businesses and industries worldwide. Packaging/product assembly, printing and bindery, direct mail/sales promotion, gift baskets, balloon decorating, candlemaking, greeting cards, customproducts, kids and school, scrapbooking and rubber stamping and many more.
Manager: Paul Ellsworth
Marketing/Communications Manager: Jennie Staghano
Contact: Dave Angus
  dangus@gluedots.com
Estimated Sales: $10 - 20 Million
Number Employees: 10-19
Type of Packaging: Consumer, Bulk

23280 Glue Fast
3535 State Route 66 # 1
Neptune, NJ 07753-2623

732-918-4600
Fax: 732-918-4646 800-242-7318
info@gluefast.com www.gluefast.com
Pressure sensitive adhesives, packaging adhesive, adhesive applicators, faux finish texture coating/texturizing products, hot melt glue systems, coating and laminating equipment, palletizing glue, mountin and laminating products andmuch more.
President: Lester Mallet
  lmallet@gluefast.com
General Manager: Joe Benenati
Vice President: Amy Altman
Estimated Sales: $5 - 10 Million
Number Employees: 5-9

23281 Glue Fast
3535 State Route 66 # 1
Neptune, NJ 07753-2623

732-918-4600
Fax: 732-918-4646 800-242-7318
info@gluefast.com www.gluefast.com
Adhesives and applicators used for packaging, labeling, palletizing, gluing and hot melts
President: Lester Mallet
  lmallet@gluefast.com
Vice President: Amy Altman
Estimated Sales: $2.8 Million
Number Employees: 5-9
Square Footage: 68000

23282 Gluemaster
12620 Wilmot Rd
Kenosha, WI 53142-7360

262-857-7212
Fax: 262-857-7430

595

Labeling and packaging machinery
President: Darlene Sanew
Contact: Sherri Longshore
  slongshore@kamind.com
Estimated Sales: $1 - 2.5 Million
Number Employees: 5-9

23283 Godshall Paper Box Company
146 Algoma Boulevard
Oshkosh, WI 54901
920-235-4040
Fax: 920-235-2326
Candy boxes for chocolate candy manufacturers and
cheese manufacturers
President: Patrick Kogutkiewiez
CEO: Terry Tormoen
Estimated Sales: $2.5 - 5 Million
Number Employees: 15
Square Footage: 42000

23284 Goebel Fixture Co
528 Dale St SW
Hutchinson, MN 55350-2397
320-587-2112
Fax: 320-587-2378 888-339-0509
www.gf.com
Wooden and plastic cutting boards and knife storage
blocks
President: Matt Field
  mfield@environmentsinc.com
VP: Richard Goebel
General Manager: Bob Croatt
Department Manager: Brian Koehler
Estimated Sales: $10 - 20 Million
Number Employees: 100-249
Square Footage: 200000

23285 (HQ)Goeman's Wood Products
PO Box 270240
5840 Highway 60 East
Hartford, WI 53027-0240
262-673-6090
Fax: 262-673-6459
Shipping crates, pallets and skids
President: Danny Guzman
Chairman/ CEO: Danny Goeman
Controller: Rich Blair
CEO: Danny Goeman
Regional Sales Manager: Dale Cordy
General Manager: Don Woods
Purchasing: Gary Hyber
Estimated Sales: $10-20 Million
Number Employees: 50-99
Square Footage: 80000
Other Locations:
  Goeman's Wood Products
  Hartford WI

23286 Goergen-Mackwirth Co Inc
765 Hertel Ave
Buffalo, NY 14207-1992
716-874-4800
Fax: 716-874-4715 800-728-4446
sales@gomac.com www.goergenmackwirth.com
Stainless steel and aluminum custom metal bins;
also, conveyors
President: Drew Fossum
  djfossum@albanyhousing.org
Project Manager: Paul Kruger
Estimated Sales: $5 - 10 Million
Number Employees: 20-49
Square Footage: 48000

23287 Goex Corporation
2532 Foster Ave
Janesville, WI 53545
608-754-3303
Fax: 608-754-8976 goex@goex.com
www.goex.com
Manufacturer and exporter of packaging materials
including rigid plastic sheet products
President: Joshua D Gray
Sales Manager: Richard Hamlin
Contact: Vicky Bladl
  vbladl@goex.com
Estimated Sales: $50-100 Million
Number Employees: 50-99

23288 Gold Bond Inc
5485 Hixson Pike
Hixson, TN 37343-3235
423-842-5844
Fax: 423-842-7934 www.goldbondinc.com

Advertising novelties including pencils, pens, rulers
and wooden nickels; also, custom plastic injection
molding available
CEO: Donald W Godsey
  donaldg@goldbondinc.com
CEO: Donald W Godsey
Estimated Sales: $20-50 Million
Number Employees: 250-499

23289 Gold Medal Products Co
10700 Medallion Dr
Cincinnati, OH 45241-4807
513-769-7676
Fax: 513-769-8500 800-543-0862
info@gmpopcorn.com www.gmpopcorn.com
Manufacturer and exporter of food products and
concession equipment including popcorn machines,
supplies and staging cabinets, butter dispensers, caramel, kettle and cheese corn, cotton candy machines
and supplies, shave ice & sno-conemachines, drinks
and frozen beverages, fried foods & bakers, nachos
& cheese dispensers, hot dog grills & cookers,
candy & caramel apples, whiz bang carnival games
and more.
President: Dan Kroeger
  dkroeger@gmpopcorn.com
Senior VP: John Evans
National Sales: Chris Petroff
International Sales: David Garretson
Estimated Sales: $20 - 50 Million
Number Employees: 250-499
Square Footage: 325000
Type of Packaging: Consumer, Food Service, Pri-
  vate Label, Bulk
Brands:
  Love My Popper

23290 Gold Star Products
21680 Coolidge Hwy
Oak Park, MI 48237-3109
248-548-9840
Fax: 248-548-9844 800-800-0205
info@goldstarmail.com
Restaurant equipment including refrigerators,
stoves, freezers, etc.; also, trays, forks, napkins, etc
Owner: Frouke Bruinsma
  frouke-bruinsma@g-star.com
Estimated Sales: $5-10,000,000
Number Employees: 20-49

23291 (HQ)Goldco Industries
5605 Goldco Dr
Loveland, CO 80538
970-663-4770
Fax: 970-663-7212 www.goldcointernational.com
Manufacturer and exporter of container and material
handling equipment including depalletizers,
palletizers and container, case and pallet handling
systems
President: Richard Vander Meer
Marketing: Jim Parker
Sales: Jim Parker
Contact: Sharon Hogan
  sharon.hogan@fgwa.com
Estimated Sales: $1 - 3 Million
Number Employees: 5-9
Square Footage: 200000
Other Locations:
  Goldco Industries
  Appleton WI

23292 Golden Eagle ExtrusionsInc
1762 State Route 131
Milford, OH 45150-2649
513-248-8292
Fax: 513-248-8300 800-634-3355
info@goldeneagleextrusions.com
www.goldeneagleextrusions.com
Owner: Paul Eagle
  info@goldeneagleextrusions.com
CEO: Jenny Eagle
CFO: Jenney Dunkin
Product Development: Pat Delany
Plant Supervisor: Joe Herzog
Estimated Sales: $3 - 5 Million
Number Employees: 5-9

23293 Golden Needles Knitting& Glove Company
1300 Walnut Street
Coshocton, OH 43812-2262
919-667-5102
Fax: 919-838-2753 www.ansell.com
Manufacturer and exporter of protective gloves

Managing Director, Chief Executive Offic: Magnus
Nicolin
Senior Vice President, Director of Asia: Denis
Gallant
Communications Director: Wouter Piepers
Senior Vice President of Operations: Steve Genzer
Estimated Sales: $1 - 5 Million
Number Employees: 1000
Type of Packaging: Consumer, Food Service, Pri-
  vate Label, Bulk
Brands:
  Hotpan'zers
  Polar Bear

23294 (HQ)Golden Star
PO Box 12539
N Kansas City, MO 64116
816-842-0233
Fax: 816-842-1129 800-821-2792
goldenstar@goldenstar.com www.goldenstar.com
Manufacturer and exporter of floor and furniture
polish, mops, dry carpet cleaner solvent, mats and
mattings
President: Gary Gradinger
Executive VP: Bill Gradinger
National Sales Manager: Steve Lewis
Contact: Heather Moll
  moll@goldenstar.com
Estimated Sales: $20-50 Million
Number Employees: 20-49
Square Footage: 350000
Type of Packaging: Consumer, Food Service, Pri-
  vate Label
Brands:
  Admiral
  Barricade
  Clencher
  Comet Blend
  Disposo-Treet
  Dus-Trol
  Golden Star
  Healthcare
  Infinity Twist
  King
  Performer
  Quality
  Quik-Change
  Set-O-Swiv
  Sno-White
  Soil Sorb
  Sta-Flat
  Starborne
  Wearever

23295 Golden West Packaging Concept
24342 Muirlands Blvd
Lake Forest, CA 92630-3679
949-855-9646
Fax: 949-645-7043
Custom and stock plastic packaging
General Manager: Connie Nash
Number Employees: 5-9
Square Footage: 10000

23296 Goldenwest Sales
16730 Gridley Rd
Cerritos, CA 90703-1730
562-924-7909
Fax: 562-924-7930 800-827-6175
info@gwsales.com www.gwsales.com
Manufacturer and exporter of tote boxes, magnetic
flatware retriever systems and cutlery bins, covers,
and rapid cooling flash chill bottles
Owner: Jitu Patel
  jitu@sftech.com
Treasurer: Estee Edwards
Estimated Sales: $.5 - 1 million
Number Employees: 10-19
Square Footage: 60000
Brands:
  The Chute
  Tough Guy Totes

23297 Goldman Manufacturing Company
13697 Elmira St
Detroit, MI 48227-3015
313-834-5535
Fax: 313-834-0496
Cardboard boxes, box partitions and separator pads;
also, die cutting services available
Owner: Cherrie L Goldman
Office Manager: Elaine Patterson

Estimated Sales: $2.5-5 Million
Number Employees: 10 to 19

23298 Goldmax Industries
17747 Railroad St
City of Industry, CA 91748-1111
626-964-8820
Fax: 626-964-6629 sales@goldmax.com
Manufacturer and importer of wooden and bamboo toothpicks, chopsticks, stirrers, plastic bags, glove dispensers, skewers, disposable gloves and aprons; also, cocktail and party straws and picks
President: Helen Chen
helenchen@goldmax-polyking.com
COO: Marcelo Mancilla
Sales Director: David Wang
Production: Manuel De La Roja
Purchasing Manager: William Hsing
Estimated Sales: $1 - 2.5 Million
Number Employees: 10-19
Type of Packaging: Food Service

23299 (HQ)Gonterman & Associates
5411 S Grand Blvd
Saint Louis, MO 63111
314-771-0600
Fax: 314-771-0610
Manufacturer and exporter of custom calendars and other advertising specialties
Estimated Sales: $1 - 5 Million
Number Employees: 5
Square Footage: 6000000
Brands:
S-Line

23300 Good Idea
351 Pleasant St
PMB 224
Northampton, MA 01060
413-586-4000
Fax: 413-585-0101 800-462-9237
info@larien.com www.larien.com
Manufacturer and exporter of bagel slicers and replacement blades.
President: Rick Ricard
Sales/Marketing Executive: Jim Dodge
Contact: Elizabeth Devito
bdevito@larien.com
Estimated Sales: $1 - 3 Million
Number Employees: 1-4
Brands:
Bagel Biter
Smartblade

23301 Good Pack
500 E Plume Street
Suite 509
Norfolk, VA 23510-2312
757-627-8889
Fax: 757-627-8989
Steel cargo carrier shipping baskets
Estimated Sales: $1-5 000,000
Number Employees: 10

23302 Goodall Rubber Company
Quakerbridge Executive Drive
Lawrenceville, NJ 08648
609-799-2000
Fax: 609-799-4582 800-524-2650
Wine industry transfer and washing hoses
Estimated Sales: $1 - 5 000,000

23303 Goodell Tools
9440 Science Center Dr
New Hope, MN 55428-3624
763-531-0053
Fax: 763-531-0252 800-542-3906
Manufacturer and exporter of grill scrapers and ice picks
Owner: Rick Garon
Marketing/Sales: Linda Alexander
Estimated Sales: $5 - 10 Million
Number Employees: 20-49
Square Footage: 88000
Type of Packaging: Private Label, Bulk
Brands:
Goodell

23304 Goodman & Company
401 Cooper Street
Camden, NJ 8102
856-225-6070
Fax: 856-225-6559 www.cgoodman.com
Filter cloths for filter presses, centrifuges, others

President: Arnold H Goodman
Estimated Sales: $5 - 10 Million
Number Employees: 50

23305 Goodman Wiper & Paper Co
120 Mill St
Auburn, ME 04210-5647
207-784-5779
Fax: 207-777-1717 ken@goodmanwiper.com
www.goodmanwiper.com
New and recycled wiping cloths; distributor of paper towels, towel systems, trash liners, linen and terry towels, cleaners, gloves, oil absorbent pads and compounds.
Owner: Ken Goodman
CFO: Ken Goodman
VP/Plant Manager: Steve Goodman
Sales/Purchasing Director: Ken Goodman
kengoodman@goodmanwiper.com
Plant Manager: Steven Goodman
Estimated Sales: $10 - 20 Million
Number Employees: 10-19
Square Footage: 12000
Type of Packaging: Consumer, Food Service, Private Label

23306 Goodnature Products
3860 California Rd
Orchard Park, NY 14127
716-855-3325
Fax: 716-855-3328 800-875-3381
sales@goodnature.com www.goodnature.com
Manufacturer and exporter of food and juice processing equipment
President/Treasurer: Dale Wettlaufer
President: Diane Massett
Marketing: Angela Dedlin
Estimated Sales: $3.5 Million
Number Employees: 20-49
Number of Brands: 1
Number of Products: 21
Brands:
Cmp Pasteurizer
Juice-It
Maximizer
Squeezebox
X-1

23307 Goodway Industries Inc
175 Orville Dr
Bohemia, NY 11716-2503
631-567-2929
Fax: 631-567-2423 800-943-4501
Manufacturer, importer and exporter of batch mixers, emulsifiers, dispersers, homogenizers, foamers, injectors, fillers, toppers and depositors
Director Sales/Marketing: Phillip Branning
Estimated Sales: $1 - 3,000,000
Number Employees: 5-9

23308 Goodway Technologies Corp
420 West Ave
Stamford, CT 06902-6329
203-359-4709
Fax: 203-359-9601 800-333-7467
goodway@goodway.com www.goodway.com
Manufacturer and exporter of tube cleaning equipment, vacuums and pressure washers
President: Per Reichdlin
CEO: Amanda Williams
awilliams@11id.com
CFO: David Lobelson
CEO: Per K Reichborn
Director Marketing: Chris Van Name
Estimated Sales: $10 - 20,000,000
Number Employees: 50-99
Square Footage: 70000
Brands:
Awt-100
Jet Cleaner
Rea-A-Matic
Soot-A-Matic
Soot-Vac

23309 (HQ)Goodwin Co
12102 Industry St
Garden Grove, CA 92841-2814
714-894-0531
Fax: 714-897-7673 www.goodwinnc.com
Manufacturer and exporter of detergents
President: Tom Goodwin
tom.goodwin@goodwinlnc.com
General Manager: Rusty Peters

Estimated Sales: $20 - 50 Million
Number Employees: 50-99

23310 Goodwin-Cole Co Inc
8320 Belvedere Ave
Sacramento, CA 95826-5902
916-381-8888
Fax: 916-383-3499 800-752-4477
info@goodwincole.com www.goodwincole.com
Commercial awnings, party tents and flags
President: Roger Gilleland
roger@goodwincole.com
Estimated Sales: $1-2,500,000
Number Employees: 10-19

23311 Goodwrappers Inc
1920 Halethorpe Farms Rd
Halethorpe, MD 21227-4501
410-536-0400
Fax: 410-536-0484 800-638-1127
www.goodwrappers.com
Manufacturer and exporter of pallet stretch wrapping systems, printed stretch and black, red, orange, green, blue and white opaque and color tinted films and stretch netting
President: Bea Parry
CEO: John Parry
VP Marketing: David Parry
Estimated Sales: $10-20 Million
Number Employees: 20-49
Brands:
Goodwrappers Handwrappers
Goodwrappers Identi-Wrap

23312 Goodyear Tire & Rubber Company
200 Innovation Way
Akron, OH 44316-0001
330-796-2121
Fax: 330-796-2222 800-321-2136
www.goodyear.com
Tires for most applications.
Chairman, President & CEO: Richard Kramer
President, Americas: Steve McClellan
EVP & Chief Financial Officer: Darren Wells
SVP, Global Operations & Technology: John Bellissimo
SVP & Chief Technology Officer: Chris Helsel
SVP & Chief Human Resources Officer: Gary Vanderlind
SVP & Chief Communications Officer: Laura Duda
SVP & General Counsel: David Phillips
Year Founded: 1898
Estimated Sales: $15.3 Billion
Number Employees: 64,000

23313 Gorbel Inc
600 Fishers Run
Victor, NY 14564-9732
585-924-6262
Fax: 585-924-6273 www.gorbel.com
Manufacturer and exporter of aluminum and steel track cranes
President: David Reh
VP: David Butwid
Manager: Deb Rader
debrad@gorbel.com
Estimated Sales: $20.9 Million
Number Employees: 100-249
Parent Co: Raytek Group

23314 Gordon Graphics
15 Digital Drive
Suite A
Novato, CA 94949-5792
415-883-0455
Fax: 415-883-5124
Wine industry labels
President: Gordon Lindstron
Estimated Sales: $5-10 Millon
Number Employees: 10

23315 Gorilla Label
7466 E Monte Cristo Avenue
Scottsdale, AZ 85260-1208
480-443-0303
Fax: 480-368-7923 800-615-7277

23316 Goring Kerr
642 Blackhawk Dr
Westmont, IL 60559-1116
847-842-2397
Fax: 630-734-1497 866-269-0070
www.goring-kerr.com

Manager: Aaron Soto
Estimated Sales: $1 - 5 Million
Number Employees: 1-4
Parent Co: Thermo Fisher Scientific Inc

23317 Goshen Dairy Company
1026 Cookson Ave SE
New Philadelphia, OH 44663-9500
330-339-1959
Fax: 330-339-2252
Distributer of ice cream.
President: Jerry Bichsel
Estimated Sales: $5-9.9,000,000
Number Employees: 20-49
Parent Co: Smith Dairy

23318 Gotham Pen Co Inc
1827 Washington Ave
Bronx, NY 10457-6203
212-675-7904
Fax: 718-294-9044 800-334-7970
gothampen@aol.com
Pens and pencils; also, custom imprinting services
available
Owner: Marshall Sutterman
Estimated Sales: Less Than $500,000
Number Employees: 5-9

23319 Gough-Econ Inc
9400 N Lakebrook Rd
Charlotte, NC 28214-9008
704-399-4501
Fax: 704-392-8706 800-204-6844
sales@goughecon.com www.goughecon.com
Bucket elevator and conveyor systems; exporter of
bucket elevator systems; also, multiple discharges
available. Also manufacturer of complete line of vi-
bratory conveyors, feeders, screens and belt
conveyors
CEO: David Risley
drisley@goughecon.com
VP: Don Calvert
Marketing: Angela Gallagher
Sales: Andrew Leitch
Estimated Sales: $5-10 Million
Number Employees: 20-49
Square Footage: 160000

23320 Gourmet COFFEE Roasters
46956 Liberty Dr
Wixom, MI 48393-3693
248-669-1060
Fax: 248-669-1111 800-933-6300
www.javamasters.com
In-store coffee roasters
President: Richard C Sewell
javausa@aol.com
VP Retail Development: Terry Immel
Estimated Sales: $10-20,000,000
Number Employees: 5-9
Square Footage: 34000

23321 Gourmet Display
6040 S 194th St # 102
Suite 102
Kent, WA 98032-1191
206-767-4711
Fax: 206-764-6094 800-767-4711
info@gourmetdisplay.com
www.gourmetdisplay.com
Mirrored and marble serving equipment for buffets
and banquets
Owner: Precious Chuop
Vice President: Mark Vollmar
Marketing Manager: T Ecker
Sales Manager: Julien Chomette
pchuop@gourmetdisplay.com
General Manager: T Schueler
Estimated Sales: $2.5-5 Million
Number Employees: 5-9
Parent Co: Plastic Dynamics
Brands:
  Riser Rims
  Serving Stone
  Texture Tone

23322 Gourmet Foods Intl
255 Ted Turner Dr SW
Atlanta, GA 30303-3705
404-954-7600
Fax: 404-954-7672 800-966-6172
Full-line oils, full-line chocolate, cheese, frozen desserts, hors d'oeuvres/appetizers, full-line
meat/game/pate, full-line spices, olives.

Owner: Russell Mc Call
rmccall@gfifoods.com
Marketing: Doug Jay
Number Employees: 250-499

23323 Gourmet Gear
1413 Westwood Blvd
Los Angeles, CA 90024-4911
310-268-2222
Fax: 310-301-4115 800-682-4635
Culinary apparel
Owner: Farhad Besharati
CEO: Newton Katz
Director Marketing: Marcee Katz
Estimated Sales: $500,000-$1 Million
Number Employees: 1-4

23324 Gourmet Table Skirts
9415 W Bellfort St
Houston, TX 77031-2308
713-666-0602
Fax: 713-666-0627 800-527-0440
gkammerman@gourmet-table-skirts.com
www.tableskirts.com
Manufacturer and exporter of table cloths, skirts and
runners, napkins, place mats and aprons
Owner: Glenn Kammerman
glenn@tableskirts.com
Estimated Sales: $2.5-5 Million
Number Employees: 50-99
Square Footage: 64000
Type of Packaging: Consumer, Food Service
Brands:
  Permalux
  Permanent Press
  Polytwill
  Visa

23325 Governair Corp
4841 N Sewell Ave
Oklahoma City, OK 73118-7820
405-525-6546
Fax: 405-528-4724 info@governair.com
Manufacturer and exporter of air handling units,
evaporative condensing package water chillers, etc
General Manager: Jim Durr
Quality Control: Bill Taylor
R & D: Mark Sly
Marketing: Mark Fly
Sales: Buddy Cross
Plant Manager: Brad Campbell
Purchasing: Vickey Hopper
Estimated Sales: $20-30 Million
Number Employees: 100-249
Square Footage: 150000
Parent Co: Nortek
Brands:
  Governair

23326 Government Food Service
P.O. Box 1500
Westbury, NY 11590-0812
516-334-3030
Fax: 516-334-3059 ebm-mail@ebmpubs.com
www.ebmpubs.com
President: Murry Greenwald
R & D: Fred Shaen
Estimated Sales: $10 - 20 Million
Number Employees: 20-49

23327 Grace Instrument Co
9434 Katy Fwy # 300
Houston, TX 77055-6309
713-783-1560
Fax: 713-974-7144 800-304-5859
info@graceinstrument.com
www.graceinstrument.com
Manufacturer and importer of thermometers includ-
ing bi-metal, digital, pocket test, vapor tension dial,
refrigeration, oven, barbecue grill and deep fry
Owner: Hongfeng Bi
Marketing Manager: Michelle Dahm
Estimated Sales: $1 - 5 Million
Number Employees: 20-49

23328 Grace Tea Co
14 Craig Rd
Acton, MA 01720-5405
978-635-9500
Fax: 978-635-9701
customerservice@gracetea.com
www.gracetea.com
Teas

Owner: Hartley Johnson
hejohnson1@gracetea.com
VP: Richard Verdery
Operations Director: Richard Sanders
Estimated Sales: $48,000
Number Employees: 5-9
Number of Brands: 1
Number of Products: 20
Square Footage: 4000
Brands:
  China Yunnan Silver Tip Choice
  Connoisseur Master Blend
  Darjceling Superb 6000
  Demitasse After Dinner Tea
  Earl Grey Superior Mixture
  Flowery Jasmine-Before the Rain
  Formosa Oolong Champagne of Tea
  Gun Powder Pearl Pinhead Green Tea
  Lapsang Souchong Smoky #1 Blend
  Mountain-Grown Fancy Ceylon
  Owner's Blend Premium Congou
  Pure Assam Irish Breakfast
  Russian Caravan Original China
  Winey Keemun English Breakfast

23329 Grace-Lee Products
2450 2nd Street NE
Minneapolis, MN 55418
612-379-2711
Fax: 763-789-6263
Detergents and institutional cleaning products
President: Barry Graceman
Executive VP: Sherman Gleekel
Institutional Sales Manager: Tom Pross
Number Employees: 75
Square Footage: 110000

23330 (HQ)Graco Inc
88 11th Ave NE
Minneapolis, MN 55413-1829
612-623-6000
Fax: 612-378-3505 877-844-7226
info@graco.com www.graco.com
Manufacturer and exporter of industrial and portable
cleaners, sanitary pumps and dispensers.
Chairman/President/CEO: David Roberts
Chief Administrative Officer: Mark Sheahan
Chief Financial Officer/Treasurer: James Graner
CEO: Patrick J McHale
Sales & Marketing Director: Rick Berkbigler
Vice President Operations: Charles Rescoria
Estimated Sales: Over $1 Billion
Number Employees: 1000-4999
Brands:
  Graco, Inc.

23331 Graco Inc
88 11th Ave NE
Minneapolis, MN 55413-1829
612-623-6000
Fax: 612-378-3505 www.graco.com
Manufacturer and exporter of conveyor lubrication
equipment and specialty lubricants
HR Manager: Kathy Buechel
CEO: Patrick J Mc Hale
pmchale@graco.com
Vice President, General Counsel, Secreta: Karen
Gallivan
Service Manager: Gary Knutson
Plant Manager: Ryan Eidenschink
Estimated Sales: Over $1 Billion
Number Employees: 1000-4999
Parent Co: IDEX

23332 Graff Tank Erection
RR 1
Box 246
Harrisville, PA 16038-9511
814-385-6671
Fax: 814-385-6657
Above-ground steel storage tanks, bins and hoppers;
field based erection and repair services available
Owner: William Graff
Controller: Rose Graff
Quality Control: Rose Graff
President: William Graff
Engineer Manager: Raymond Graff
Estimated Sales: $500,000 - $1 Million
Number Employees: 10
Square Footage: 32000

23333 Grafoplast Wiremarkers Inc
6875 E 48th Ave
Denver, CO 80216-5310
303-321-5995
Fax: 303-399-5054 800-864-3874
sales@grafoplast.com www.grafoplast.com
Markers for terminal blocks, relays, wire, and cable
Manager: Maureen Wilkins
Manager: Priscilla Hobdell
priscilla@grafoplast.com
Estimated Sales: $1-2.5 Million
Number Employees: 1-4

23334 Grafoplast Wiremarkers Inc
6875 E 48th Ave
Denver, CO 80216-5310
303-321-5995
Fax: 303-399-5054 800-864-3874
www.grafoplast.com
Manager: Priscilla Hobdell
priscilla@grafoplast.com
Estimated Sales: $3 - 5 Million
Number Employees: 1-4

23335 (HQ)Graham Engineering Corp
1203 Eden Rd
York, PA 17402-1965
717-848-3755
Fax: 717-846-1931 www.grahamengineering.com
Manufacturer and exporter of blow-molded plastic
bottles and containers
President: Steven F Wood
CEO: Wendy Brown
wendy_brown@uscourts.gov
VP: Joe Spohr
CEO: Wolfgang Liebertz
CFO: Rich Rutkowski
VP Sales/Marketing: F White
Estimated Sales: $20 - 50 Million
Number Employees: 50-99

23336 Graham Ice & Locker Plant
328 Elm Street
Graham, TX 76450-2514
940-549-1975
Ice; slaughterer, processor and wholesaler/distributor of deer
Owner: James Black
Estimated Sales: Less than $500,000
Number Employees: 1 to 4
Type of Packaging: Consumer

23337 Graham Pallet Co Inc
3234 Celina Rd
Tompkinsville, KY 42167-8207
270-487-6609
Fax: 270-487-9420 888-525-0694
www.millwoodinc.com
Wooden pallets and skids
President: Rick Miller
Sales Exec: Mike Scoby
mscoby@grahampallet.com
Customer Service: Carolyn Turner
mscoby@grahampallet.com
General Manager: Terry Marr
Production Manager: Carolyn Grove
Plant Manager: Keith Ainsley
Estimated Sales: $5 - 10 Million
Number Employees: 50-99
Square Footage: 100000

23338 Grain Machinery Mfg Corp
1130 NW 163rd Dr
Miami, FL 33169-5816
305-620-2525
Fax: 305-620-2551 grainman@bellsouth.net
www.grainman.com
Manufacturer and exporter of grain elevators, dryers,
graders, cleaners, pea and bean hullers, casting and
rice machinery, bagging scales and conveyor belts;
importer of casting and rice machinery
Owner: Manny Diaz
grainman@bellsouth.net
Treasurer: Librada Dieguez
Vice President: Cary Dieguez
Sales Director: Jose Martinez
Purchasing Manager: Brissa Pichardo
Estimated Sales: $3 - 5 Million
Number Employees: 10-19
Square Footage: 86000
Brands:
Cell-O-Matic
Grainman
Rimac

23339 (HQ)Gralab Instruments
900 Dimco Way
Centerville, OH 45458-2710
937-433-7600
Fax: 937-433-0520 800-876-8353
www.gralab.com
Electromechanical and electronic timing devices for
commercial cooking and baking applications, food
testing laboratories, process control systems and
sanitation; also, thermoset and thermoplastic compression and injection moldedproducts.
President & CEO: Michael Sieron
msieron@dimcogray.com
Treasurer: Terry Tate
Quality Control: Lyle Crum
Sales & Marketing Manager: Linda Raisch
Production: James Daulton
Number Employees: 50-99
Number of Brands: 1
Number of Products: 20
Parent Co: Dimco-Gray Corporation

23340 (HQ)Gram Equipment of America
1212 N 39th St # 438
Tampa, FL 33605-5890
813-248-1978
Fax: 813-248-2314 www.gram-equipment.com
Box/carton formers, ice cream makers, feeders,
freezers and heat exchangers
President: Morten Borup
mgs@gram-equipment.com
Number Employees: 10-19
Type of Packaging: Food Service, Bulk

23341 GranPac
4709 39th Avenue
Wetaskiwin, AB T9A 2J4
Canada
780-352-3324
Fax: 780-352-3387 www.granpac.com.br
Polyethylene plastic food containers
Sales Manager: G Jacobson
Managing Director: J Patel
Estimated Sales: $1 - 5 Million
Number Employees: 20-50
Square Footage: 80000

23342 Granco Manufacturing Inc
2010 Crow Canyon Pl # 100
Suite 100
San Ramon, CA 94583-1344
510-652-8847
Fax: 510-652-1565 info@grancopump.com
www.grancopump.com
Manufacturer and exporter of hydraulically driven
and low shear pumping systems; also, rotary positive
pumps for displacement of viscous liquids.
President: Ivan Dimcheff
CEO: Michael Alessandro
Operations: Ivan Dimcheff
Production Manager: David Kenzler
Estimated Sales: $.5 - 1 million
Number Employees: 5-9
Square Footage: 64000
Parent Co: Challenge Manufacturing Company
Type of Packaging: Private Label
Brands:
Grandco
Hy-Drive Systems

23343 Grand Cypress
6087 NW 90th Avenue
Parkland, FL 33067-3722
954-255-5686
Fax: 954-255-5926 grandcypressintl@comcast.net
President: Bart Ostroff

23344 Grand Rapids Chair Company
625 Chestnut St SW
Grand Rapids, MI 49503
616-774-0561
Fax: 616-774-0563 tom@grandrapidschair.com
www.grandrapidschair.com
Chairs
Owner: Jill Miller
Contact: Aladin Brakic
abrakic@grandrapidschair.com
Estimated Sales: $5 - 10 Million
Number Employees: 20-49

23345 Grand Rapids Label
2351 Oak Industrial Dr NE
Grand Rapids, MI 49505-6017
616-776-2778
Fax: 616-459-4543 www.grlabel.com
Manufacturer and exporter of pressure sensitive and
heat seal labels including advertising and
supermarket
President: William Muir
CFO: John Laninga
R&D: Tony Maravalo
Quality Control: Christine Howlett
VP Sales: Tom Topel
Estimated Sales: $10 - 20 Million
Number Employees: 50-99
Type of Packaging: Bulk

23346 Grand Silver Company
289 Morris Avenue
Bronx, NY 10451-6198
718-585-1930
Fax: 718-402-4724 grandsilve@aol.com
Silver plated holloware, coffee pots, sugar bowls
and creamers; also, repairing and replating services
available
CEO: Barry Kostrinsky
Estimated Sales: $2.5-5 Million
Number Employees: 20-49

23347 Grand Valley Labels
4417 Broadmoor Ave SE
Grand Rapids, MI 49512-5367
Fax: 616-784-2915
Pressure sensitive labels, tags, envelopes, bar codes,
label printing systems, packaging, etc.
Estimated Sales: $5-10 Million
Number Employees: 1-4
Square Footage: 10000

23348 Grande Chef Company
21 Stewart Court
Orangeville, ON L9W 3Z9
Canada
519-942-4470
Fax: 519-942-4440
Manufacturer, importer and exporter of stainless
steel cooking equipment including cookers, kettles,
ovens and broilers
President: Frank Edmonstone
Sales/Marketing Executive: Lisa Ashton
Sales/Marketing Executive: Alex Mackay
Operations Manager: Lisa Ashton
Purchasing Manager: Frank Edmonstone
Number Employees: 5-9
Brands:
Grande Chef

23349 Grande Ronde Sign Company
2302 Cove Avenue
La Grande, OR 97850-3907
541-963-5841
Fax: 541-963-4337 www.whereorg.com
Signs including neon, wood, plastic and vinyl
President: Mat Barber
Contact: Earl Barber
gabebarber@gmail.com
Office Manager: Jenne O'Daol
Estimated Sales: Below $5 Million
Number Employees: 1 to 4

23350 Granite State Stamps Inc
8025 S Willow St # 102
Manchester, NH 03103-2311
603-669-9322
Fax: 603-669-5182 800-937-3736
sales@granitestatestamps.com
www.granitestatestamps.com
Engraved name pins and rubber stamps
President: Lynn A Hale
lynn@granitestatestamps.com
VP Sales: Lynn Hale
Estimated Sales: $1-2.5 Million
Number Employees: 5-9
Square Footage: 20000

23351 Grant Chemicals
PO Box 13
New Hope, PA 18938-0013
215-331-3350
Fax: 215-331-2394
Wine industry chemicals

23352 Grant Laboratories
14688 Washington Ave
San Leandro, CA 94578-4218

510-483-6070
Fax: 510-483-9846
grant-laboratories-inc.san-leandro.ca.amfibi.company

Insecticides including ant and insect granular
CEO: William E Brown
COO: Louis Antonali
Sales Director: Samantha Sturdivant
COO: Quazui Iqbal
Estimated Sales: $5-10 Million
Number Employees: 5 to 9
Square Footage: 52000
Parent Co: Central Garden & Pet
Type of Packaging: Consumer
Brands:
   Grants Kill Ants

23353 Grant-Letchworth
110 Mullen Street
Tonawanda, NY 14150-5424

716-692-1000
Fax: 716-692-3638 response@letchworth.com
www.letchworth.com
Grinders, mixers and stuffers
President: W Keith Jackson
Sales Manager: James Smith
Estimated Sales: $1-2.5 Million
Number Employees: 4

23354 Granville ManufacturingCo
45 Mill Rd
Granville, VT 05747-9669

802-767-4747
Fax: 802-767-3107 800-828-1005
bowlmill@madriver.com www.woodsiding.com
One piece wooden bowls made from premium hardwoods in Vermont
President: Robert Fuller
Vice President: Jeff Fuller
   woodsiding@woodsiding.com
Marketing Director: Cindy Fuller
Purchasing Manager: Cindy Fuller
Estimated Sales: $1,000,000
Number Employees: 1-4
Square Footage: 10000

23355 Graphic Apparel
2365 Industrial Park Road
Inniasfil, ON L9S 3W1
Canada

705-436-6137
Fax: 705-436-6139 800-757-4867
Distributor of career apparel and promotions
President: Werner Syndikus
Sales Manager: Mitch Dawkins
Number Employees: 10
Square Footage: 32000
Type of Packaging: Food Service

23356 Graphic Arts Center
709 Silver Palm Ave
Suite H
Melbourne, FL 32901

321-725-0710
Fax: 321-984-3783 888-345-7436
gac@yourlink.net
Graphic designer of packages, labels, advertising materials, cartons, displays, literature and trade show displays
Owner: D D Rhem
Estimated Sales: $500,000-$1 Million
Number Employees: 1-4
Square Footage: 9600
Parent Co: Rhem Group
Type of Packaging: Consumer, Food Service, Private Label, Bulk

23357 Graphic Calculator Company
234 James Street
Barrington, IL 60010-3388

847-381-4480
Fax: 847-381-5370
Manufacturer and exporter of advertising novelties including slide rules, printed calculators and feature demonstrators
President: Capron Gulbronsen
VP: Lorraine Gorski
Estimated Sales: $5 - 10 Million
Number Employees: 10

23358 Graphic Impressions of Illinois
8538 Grand Ave
River Grove, IL 60171

708-453-1100
Fax: 708-453-1169
Quality flexographic labels and printing plates. Custom labels priced by specification. Complete design for flexible packaging. ValueStar certified. A family owned business since 1956
Estimated Sales: $1-2,500,000
Number Employees: 5-9

23359 Graphic Packaging Corporation
4455 Table Mountain Drive
Golden, CO 80403

720-497-4724
Fax: 303-273-2935 800-677-2886
www.graphicpkg.com
Labels, bottle carriers and beverage and carrier cartons
Chairman/ President/ CEO: David W. Scheible
CFO/ SVP: Daniel J. Blount
SVP, Flexible Division: R. Allen Ennis
Plant Manager: Jeffrey Coors
Estimated Sales: $1 - 5 Million
Number Employees: 100-249
Parent Co: Graphic Packaging Corporation

23360 Graphic Packaging International
1500 Riveredge Parkway NW
Atlanta, GA 30328

770-240-7200
www.graphicpkg.com
Paperboard containers
President & CEO: Michael Doss
EVP/Chief Financial Officer: Stephen Scherger
EVP, Human Resources: Stacey Panayiotou
EVP/General Counsel: Lauren Tashma
President, Americas: Joseph Yost
Estimated Sales: Over $1 Billion
Number Employees: 13,000
Parent Co: Graphic Pakaging Holding Company

23361 Graphic Packaging Intl
1500 Nicholas Blvd
Elk Grove Vlg, IL 60007-5516

847-437-1700
Fax: 847-956-9291 www.graphicpkg.com
Manufacturer and exporter of folding cartons
President: Larry Field
Cmo: Larry Janis
   larry.janis@fieldcontainer.com
Number Employees: 250-499

23362 (HQ)Graphic Promotions
7418 SW 23rd Court
Topeka, KS 66614-6079

785-234-6684
Fax: 785-354-1519 gpromotion@aol.com
Consultant specializing in promotional services and support including point of purchase signage, labels, specialty items, fulfillment, creative art/graphics, design, inventory manangement and printing
VP: Kurt Oswald
Number Employees: 100-249
Square Footage: 144000
Other Locations:
   Graphic Promotions
   Topeka KS

23363 Graphic Technology
301 Gardner Dr
New Century, KS 66031

913-764-5550
Fax: 913-764-0320 800-767-9920
Manufacturer, exporter and importer of bar coded and nonbar coded shelf labels for product unit pricing; bar code printers and software; also, picking labels
VP Sales/Marketing: Tom Pooton
Contact: Robert Mccurdy
   rob@graphictech.com
Estimated Sales: $1 - 5 Million
Number Employees: 500-999
Square Footage: 500000
Parent Co: Nitto Denko Corporation

23364 Graphics Unlimited
10477 Roselle St # B
San Diego, CA 92121-1593

858-453-4031
Fax: 858-453-5337
www.graphicsunlimitedusa.com

Decals, name plates and banners; also, screen printing available
Owner: Les Burge
   les@unlimitedgraphics.com
Estimated Sales: $1-2,500,000
Number Employees: 5-9

23365 Graphite Metalizing Corp
1050 Nepperhan Ave
Yonkers, NY 10703-1421

914-968-8400
Fax: 914-968-8468 sales@graphalloy.com
www.graphalloy.com
Manufacturer and exporter of graphalloy high-temperature self-lubricating bearings for ovens
President: Eben Walker
Quality Control: Mohmed Youssef
Director Marketing: Eric Ford
Estimated Sales: $10 - 20 Million
Number Employees: 50-99
Square Footage: 50000
Brands:
   Graphalloy
   Graphilm

23366 Grasselli SSI
410 Charles St
Throop, PA 18512

570-489-8001
Fax: 570-485-8005 800-789-4353
info@grasselli-ssi.com www.grasselli-ssi.com
Processing equipment for meat and fish industries; slicing and skinning
President: David Atcherley
Vice President: Helga Harrington
Contact: Benjamin Conner
   benc@grasselli-ssi.com
Estimated Sales: $8 Million
Number Employees: 12

23367 Grasso
1101 N Governor Street
Evansville, IN 47711-5069

812-465-6600
Fax: 812-465-6610 800-821-3486
grasso@fessystems.com
Industrial reciprocating and screw refrigeration compressors, custom-built refrigeration packages for any refrigerant including ammonia; self-limiting automatic purgers for refrigeration systems
President: Jake Grifford
Manager of Quality: Harald Wilke
Marketing Manager: Martina Chao
Manager of International Sales: Siegfried Pitsch
Estimated Sales: $20-50 Million
Number Employees: 10

23368 Grating Pacific Inc
3651 Sausalito St
Los Alamitos, CA 90720-2436

562-598-4314
Fax: 562-598-2740 800-321-4314
sales@gratingpacific.com
www.gratingpacific.com
Distributor of industrial flooring.
President: Ron Robertson
   ronrobertson@gratingpacific.com
Year Founded: 1971
Estimated Sales: $20 - 30 Million
Number Employees: 50-99

23369 Graver Technologies LLC
200 Lake Dr
Newark, DE 19702-3327

302-731-1700
Fax: 302-731-1707 800-249-1990
info@gravertech.com www.gravertech.com
Microfiltration membranes
President: John Almeida
   jalmeida@gravertech.com
VP Finance and Administration: Sharon Gatta
VP and General Manager Liquid Filters: Bill Cummings
Product Manager: Scott Wittwer
Number Employees: 50-99

23370 Gray Woodproducts
297 Swetts Pond Rd
P.O. Box 7126
Tacoma, WA 98417

253-752-7000
Fax: 207-825-3200
www.graylumber.com/products.php
Pallets and skids

President/Sales Manager: Mac Gray
Treasurer/Secretary: Steve Gray
Vice President: W Douglas Gray, Jr.
Asst. Sales Manager: Jack deLeon
Operations Manager: Paul VanDyken
Estimated Sales: $500,000-$1 Million
Number Employees: 1-4

23371 Graybill Machines Inc
221 W Lexington Rd # 1
Lititz, PA 17543-9400

717-626-5221
Fax: 717-626-1886 info@graybillmachines.com
www.graybillmachines.com
Designs and builds custom food machinery, specializing in finishing systems, product registration/handling, process machinery and specialized packaging
President: David Fyock
dfyock@graybillmachines.com
Marketing Director: Matthew Randolph
Sales Director: John Stough
Estimated Sales: $2.5-$5 Million
Number Employees: 10-19
Square Footage: 44000

23372 Grayco Products Sales
100 Tec Street
Hicksville, NY 11801-3650

516-997-9200
Fax: 516-870-0510
Wholesaler/distributor and exporter of paper and disposable products including tabletop and industrial equipment, packaging and printing supplies
Owner: Helen Kushner
CEO: Adrienne Kushner
Vice President: Alan Kushner
Operations Manager: D Pascale
Estimated Sales: $1 - 5 Million
Number Employees: 2
Square Footage: 10000
Parent Co: ASK Sales

23373 Graydon Lettercraft
81 Cuttermill Rd
Great Neck, NY 11021-3153

516-482-0531
Fax: 516-482-5632
Advertising specialties and custom printed brochures and stationery
Owner: Pasquale Riccardi
VP: Ruth Theobald
Estimated Sales: $300,000-500,000
Number Employees: 1-4

23374 Grayline Housewares Inc
2711 International St
Suite 105
Columbus, OH 43228-4604

614-850-7000
Fax: 614-850-7111 800-222-7388
www.graylinehousewares.com
Coated-wire space savers and organizers including bag and pot holders, bars, wall grids and racks including can, kitchen and wire
President: Fred Rosen
Director: Paul Nearpass
Estimated Sales: $500,000-$1 Million
Number Employees: 10-19

23375 Grayling Industries
1008 Branch Dr
Alpharetta, GA 30004-3391

770-751-9095
Fax: 770-751-3710 800-635-1551
raymond.joyner@graylingmail.com
www.graylingindustries.com
Director of Sales: Raymond Joyner
Contact: Salvador Abreu
sabreu@graylingindustries.com
Estimated Sales: Less Than $500,000
Number Employees: 1-4
Parent Co: ILC Dover
Type of Packaging: Food Service, Bulk

23376 Grays Harbor Stamp Works
110 N G St
Aberdeen, WA 98520-5226

360-533-3830
Fax: 360-533-3210 800-894-3830
graysharborstamp@olynet.com
www.graysharborstamp.com
Promotional buttons, engraved signage and rubber stamps

Partner: Ronald Windell
Partner: Ron Windell
Partner: Kenneth Windell
Estimated Sales: $2.5-5 Million
Number Employees: 5-9

23377 Graytech Carbonic
9460 230th Street E
Lakeville, MN 55044-8137

952-461-8020
Fax: 952-461-8022
Estimated Sales: $1-2.5 000,000
Number Employees: 1-4

23378 Grease Master
608 Matthews Mint Hill # 105
Suite 105
Matthews, NC 28105-1763

704-844-6907
Fax: 704-844-8013 info@greasemaster.com
www.greasemaster.com
Kitchen ventilation systems including wall mounted and exhaust only canopies
Division Manager: David Breidt
david.breidt@greasemaster.com
Sales Quotations Design: Harvey Worrell
Division Manager: David Breidt
Plant Manager: Nick Nakos
Estimated Sales: Less Than $500,000
Number Employees: 1-4
Square Footage: 92000
Parent Co: Custom Industries
Brands:
Grease Master

23379 Great Dane LP
222 N LaSalle St
Suite 920
Chicago, IL 60601

773-254-5533
www.greatdane.com
Refrigerated tractor trailers.
President: Dean Engelage
Year Founded: 1900
Estimated Sales: $257.6 Million
Number Employees: 1000-4999
Brands:
Great Dane

23380 Great Lakes Brush
6859 Audrain Road #9139
Centralia, MO 65240

573-682-2128
Fax: 573-682-2121
Manufacturer and importer of brushes and wire drawn products
President: Matthew Kallas
Estimated Sales: $500,000-$1 Million
Number Employees: 1-4
Square Footage: 8000

23381 Great Lakes Cold Storage
6531 Cochran Rd
Cleveland, OH 44139-3959

440-248-3950
Fax: 440-248-4315 888-248-9600
info@glcsinc.com www.glcsinc.com
Terminal
President: Pat Gorbett
pgorbett@glcsinc.com
Accounts Payable and Receivable: Daphne Bengough
Chief Engineer: Phil Watson
VP National Sales and Marketing: Ken Mossgrove
IT/HR Manager: Regina Twining
pgorbett@glcsinc.com
Director of Operations: Tom Johnson
Estimated Sales: $3 - 5 Million
Number Employees: 50-99

23382 Great Lakes Foods
1230 48th Ave
Menominee, MI 49858-1002

906-863-5503
Fax: 906-863-2102 800-800-7492
jvan@greatlakesfoods.com
Canned mushrooms; fruit and vegetable canning, pickling and drying
President: Tom Ireland
Owner: Jerry Vandelaarschot
CFO: Don Kressin
dkressin@greatlakefood.com
Vice President: Johanne Ubbels

Estimated Sales: $1-2.5 Million
Number Employees: 50-99
Parent Co: Ubbelea Farms
Type of Packaging: Consumer, Food Service, Private Label
Brands:
Chateau
Riviera

23383 Great Lakes Scientific
2847 Lawrence St
Stevensville, MI 49127-1257

269-429-1000
www.glslab.com
An independent laboratory offering confidential testing services for food, water and environmental samples. A USDA recognized (microbiology) and accredited (chemistry) laboratory.
President: Wayne Gleiber
gls@glslab.com
Estimated Sales: $1-2.5 Million
Number Employees: 20-49
Square Footage: 10000

23384 Great Lakes Software ofMichigan
P.O. Box 2222
Howell, MI 48844

517-548-4333
Fax: 517-548-4433 www.greatlakessoftware.com
C.I.M.S.(computerized inventory and logistic management system) designed for beverage industry manufacturing, distribution, warehousing and sales
Owner: Gene Chandler
Estimated Sales: $1 - 2.5 000,000
Number Employees: 1-4

23385 Great Lakes-Triad Package Corporation
3939 36th Street
Grand Rapids, MI 49512

616-241-6441
Fax: 616-241-4145 www.glpkg.com
Corrugated boxes and containers
Estimated Sales: $50-100 Million
Number Employees: 50-99

23386 Great Northern Corp
421 Palmer St
Chippewa Falls, WI 54729-1449

715-723-1801
Fax: 715-723-7744 800-472-1800
www.greatnortherncorp.com
Corrugated shipping containers, inner packaging partitions and point of purchase displays
CEO: John Kell
CEO: John Kell
Plant Production Manager: Rick Gates
Estimated Sales: $30 - 50 Million
Number Employees: 100-249
Square Footage: 250000

23387 Great Northern Corp
1800 South St
Racine, WI 53404-1518

262-639-4700
Fax: 262-639-8103 800-558-4711
www.greatnortherncorp.com
Corrugated boxes
CEO: John Davis
Estimated Sales: $50-100 Million
Number Employees: 100-249
Square Footage: 70058
Parent Co: Great Northern Corporation
Type of Packaging: Bulk

23388 Great Northern Corp.
395 Stroebe Rd.
Appleton, WI 54914

800-236-3671
www.greatnortherncorp.com
Expandable polystyrene plastic packaging products including boxes and containers.
President/CEO: John Davis
Year Founded: 1962
Estimated Sales: $100-500 Million
Number Employees: 500-999
Type of Packaging: Bulk
Brands:
Instore
Laminations
Packaging
Rollguard
StrataGraph

23389 Great Plains Software
1 Lone Tree Road S
Fargo, ND 58104-3911
701-281-0550
Fax: 701-282-9243 800-456-0025
Backoffice accounting software
Sr. VP (Marketing Communications): Michael Olsen
Franchise Marketing Manager: Judy Felch

23390 Great Southern Corp
3595 Regal Blvd
Memphis, TN 38118-6117
901-365-1611
Fax: 901-365-4498 800-421-7802
sales@greatsoutherncorp.com
www.gsmemphis.com
Manufacturer, importer and exporter of licensed
gloves consisting of leather, cotton, plastic and rub-
ber gloves; also, rubber bands
President: Scott Vaught
Chairman: C Vaught
Manager: Jeff Harrell
j.harrell@greatsoutherncorp.com
Estimated Sales: $20 - 50 Million
Number Employees: 5-9
Square Footage: 48000
Parent Co: Great Southern Corporation
Brands:
Sirco

23391 Great Southern Industries
PO Box 22488
Jackson, MS 39225
601-969-1434
Fax: 601-969-3838 877-638-3667
sales@netdoor.com netdoor.com
Corrugated shipping containers
President: Charles Ellis
President, Chief Executive Officer: Tom Tiernan
CFO: Nancy Hocutt
Executive Vice President, General Manage: Michael
Elia
Production Manager: Bill Dahlman
Estimated Sales: $10-20 Million
Number Employees: 100-249

**23392 Great Western Chemical
Company**
5200 SW Macadam Ave # 200
Portland, OR 97239-3800
503-228-2600
Fax: 503-228-8471 800-547-1400
Manufacturer and wholesaler/distributor of cleaning
and sanitation chemicals and food ingredients in-
cluding acidulants, preservatives, etc
Manager: Jason Keyes
Bus. Mgr.: Tom Cervenka
Bus. Mgr.: Andy Pollard
VP Marketing: Tami Mainero
Estimated Sales: $50-100 Million
Number Employees: 5-9

23393 Great Western Co LLC
30290 US Highway 72
Hollywood, AL 35752-6134
256-259-3578
Fax: 256-259-7087 www.gwproducts.com
Processor and exporter of popcorn, popping corn oil,
cotton candy, sno-cone syrup, candy apple coatings,
funnel cakes, waffle cones, corn dog mix, and other
consession items
Contact: Tim Ferguson
timf@gwproducts.com
Estimated Sales: Less Than $500,000
Number Employees: 1-4
Number of Brands: 6
Type of Packaging: Consumer, Food Service, Pri-
vate Label, Bulk
Brands:
Chillee Snow Cones
Frostee Snow Cones
Great Western Products Company
Peter's Movie Time Products
Premium America
Sunglo

**23394 Great Western Manufacturing
Company**
2017 So. 4th Floor
PO Box 149
Leavenworth, KS 66048
913-682-2291
Fax: 913-682-1431 800-682-3121
sifter@gwmfg.com www.gwmfg.com
Screening machines, shakers, sifters, screens and
sieves.
CFO: Michael Bell
General Manager: Robert Ricklefs
Sales, Services & Applications Engineeri: Bob
Recklifs
Production Manager: Steve Wood
Purchasing Manager: Michael Glassford
Estimated Sales: $5-10 Million
Number Employees: 10
Type of Packaging: Food Service
Brands:
Hs
Tru Balance

23395 Grecon
15875 SW 74th Ave # 100
Suite 100
Tigard, OR 97224-7934
503-641-7731
Fax: 503-641-7508 sales@grecon-us.com
www.grecon-us.com
Spark detection and extinguishing systems, as well
as quality assurance measuring systems.
Contact: Walter Crosson
wcrosson@grecon.us
Number Employees: 10-19

23396 Greeley Tent & Awning Co
2209 9th St # C
Greeley, CO 80631-3088
970-352-0253
Fax: 970-352-2013
Commercial awnings
Owner: Julie Heyer
greeleytentawning@gmail.com
CFO: Barbara Hendricks
Estimated Sales: Less than $500,000
Number Employees: 5-9

23397 Green Bag America Inc.
15430 Cabrito Road
Unit 1
Van Nuys, CA 91406
818-787-6223
Fax: 818-453-0316 877-224-2299
sales@greenbagamerica.com
www.greenbagamerica.com
Accesories/supplies i.e. picninc baskets, display fixtures, specialty food packaging i.e. gift wrap/la-
bels/boxes/containers.
Marketing: Tom Maor
Contact: Richelle Kim
richellekim@greenbagamerica.com

23398 Green Bay Machinery
P.O. Box 19010
Green Bay, WI 54307
920-455-6749
Fax: 920-455-2203 www.gbm-co.com
Estimated Sales: $2.5-5 000,000
Number Employees: 250-499

23399 (HQ)Green Bay Packaging Inc.
1700 North Webster Court
Green Bay, WI 54302
920-433-5111
Fax: 920-433-5471 www.gbp.com
Corrugated shipping containers and labels including
coated and stock.
President/CEO: William Kress
bkress@gbp.com
Senior VP/General Counsel: Scott Wochos
Year Founded: 1933
Estimated Sales: $850 Million
Number Employees: 3,200
Type of Packaging: Consumer, Food Service, Pri-
vate Label, Bulk

23400 Green Bay Packaging Inc.
5350 East Kilgore Ave.
Kalamazoo, MI 49048
269-552-1000
www.gbp.com
Printed and plain corrugated shipping containers
President: Will Kress

Year Founded: 1933
Estimated Sales: $20 - 30 Million
Number Employees: 50-99
Square Footage: 312000
Parent Co: Green Bay Packaging

23401 Green Bay Packaging Inc.
5901 W 55th St.
Tulsa, OK 74107
918-446-3341
www.gbp.com
Corrugated boxes.
President: William Kress
Year Founded: 1933
Estimated Sales: $20-50 Million
Number Employees: 100-249
Parent Co: Green Bay Packaging

23402 Green Belt Industries Inc
45 Comet Ave
Buffalo, NY 14216-1710
716-873-6923
Fax: 716-873-1728 800-668-1114
www.greenbelting.com
Manufacturer and exporter of Teflon-coated con-
veyor belting for baking pans and trays
Manager: Gail Lipka
Marketing Director: Joe Smith
Manager: Sue King
sking@greenbelting.com
Operations Manager: Scott O Hearn
Purchasing Manager: Jennifer White
Estimated Sales: $5-10 Million
Number Employees: 20-49
Square Footage: 200000

23403 Green Brothers
43 Massasoit Avenue
Barrington, RI 2806
401-245-9043
Steel rule dies and paper boxes
President: James McClelland
Estimated Sales: $1-2.5 Million
Number Employees: 19

23404 Green Earth Bags
815C Tecumseh
Point-Claire, QC H9R 4B1
Canada
514-694-9440
Fax: 514-694-6311
keberwein@fiberlinktextiles.com
www.fiberlinktextiles.com
Accessories/supplies i.e. picninc baskets, specialty
food packaging i.e. gift wrsp/labels/boxes/contain-
ers.
Marketing: Kassandra Eberwein

23405 Green Metal Fabricating
536 Houston St # A
West Sacramento, CA 95691-2253
916-371-2951
Fax: 916-371-7541
Sheet metal and stainless steel fabrications for use in
restaurants
Owner: Harry Green Jr
hgreen32@yahoo.com
Estimated Sales: Below $5 Million
Number Employees: 5-9

23406 Green Mountain Awning Inc
36 Marble St
West Rutland, VT 5777
802-438-2951
Fax: 802-438-2774 800-479-2951
Flags, pennants and banners
President: Robert Pearo Sr
Vice President: Robert Pearo, Jr.
Marketing Director: Robert Pearo, Jr.
Estimated Sales: Less Than $500,000
Number Employees: 1-4

23407 Green Mountain Graphics
P.O. Box 1417
Long Island City, NY 11101
718-472-3377
Fax: 718-472-4040 www.gm-graphics.com
Manufacturer and wholesaler/distributor of signs,
awards and promotional products
President: Eric Greenberg
VP Sales: Steve Goldman
Estimated Sales: $1 - 2,500,000
Number Employees: 10-19

Square Footage: 6000
Parent Co: Eastern Concepts

23408 Green Pond Development
92 Greenport Road
Rockaway, NJ 07866
973-983-1023
Land developers

23409 Green Seams
11605 100th Avenue N
Maple Grove, MN 55369-3203
612-929-3213
Fax: 612-929-3027
Totes, bags, uniforms and promotional garments
Owner: Francis Green

23410 Green Spot Packaging
100 S Cambridge Ave
Claremont, CA 91711-4842
909-625-8771
Fax: 909-621-4634 800-456-3210
info@greenspotusa.com www.lagunaliquid.com
Beverages, flavors and fragrances; aseptic packaging services available
CEO: John Tsu
Finance Executive: Don Koury
Sales Executive: Greg Faust
Chief Operating Officer: Dana Staal
Plant Manager: Roy Cooley
Estimated Sales: $6.5 Million
Number Employees: 20-49
Square Footage: 200000
Type of Packaging: Consumer, Food Service, Private Label, Bulk
Brands:
  Action Ade
  Apple Delight
  Apple Royal
  Awesome Orange
  Black Cherry Royal
  Citrus Royal
  Galactic Grape
  Good Buddies
  Green Spot
  Peach Royal
  Superstar Strawberry
  Tropical Royal

23411 Green Sustainable Solutions
1624 Staunton Ave # 101
Parkersburg, WV 26101-5073
304-422-5461
Fax: 304-428-7530 800-827-5461
custserv@gssllc.us.com www.gssllcus.com
CEO: Perry D. Smith
Marketing: Eric Watkins
Manager: Kristen Deem
  kdeem@greenpak.com
Estimated Sales: $1 - 5 Million
Number Employees: 100-249

23412 Green Tek
3708 Enterprise Dr
Janesville, WI 53546-8737
608-754-7336
Fax: 608-754-7334 800-747-6440
greentek@green-tek.com www.green-tek.com
Plastic pallets and trays for oven use and manual heat sealers to package meals for ovens and microwaves. Manufacturer of disposable, dual-ovenable and microwavable food trays and lids
President: Linda Bracha
  lbrach@green-tek.com
CFO: Sandy Boyer
Sales Representative: Steve Guertin
General Manager: Paul Jacobson
Estimated Sales: $20 - 50 Million
Number Employees: 20-49
Square Footage: 10000
Brands:
  Green-Tek
  Polyziv
  Seal N' Serve

23413 Greenbridge
6277 Heisley Rd
Mentor, OH 44060
440-357-1500
Fax: 440-352-9553 www.polychem.com
Polyester strapping/polypropylene strapping.

President & CEO: Omar Abuaita
CFO: Joe Italiano
VP, Sales & Marketing: Vito Cafagna
COO: Norm Christoffersen
Year Founded: 1974
Estimated Sales: $100 Million
Number Employees: 100-249

23414 Greenbush Tape & Label Inc
40 Broadway # 3
PO Box 1488
Albany, NY 12202-1020
518-465-2389
Fax: 518-465-5781 www.greenbushlabel.com
Manufacturer and exporter of pressure sensitive tapes and labels
President: James Chenot
Estimated Sales: Below $5 Million
Number Employees: 20-49
Type of Packaging: Consumer, Food Service, Private Label, Bulk

23415 Greene Brothers
134 Broadway
Brooklyn, NY 11211-6031
718-388-6800
Fax: 718-782-4123
Manufacturer and exporter of lighting fixtures
Fmn.: Matthew Santoro
Number Employees: 5-9
Parent Co: Greene's Lighting Fixtures

23416 Greene Industries
65 Rocky Hollow Rd
East Greenwich, RI 02818-3513
401-884-7530
Fax: 401-885-9370 rallengreene@aol.com
Plywood and fiberboard cases and wooden shipping crates
President: Allison Greene
  agreene@greeneinc.org
Estimated Sales: Below $5 Million
Number Employees: 5-9

23417 Greener Corp
4 Helmly St
Bayville, NJ 08721-2188
732-269-0107
Fax: 732-286-7842 800-634-9933
custserve@greencorp.com www.greenercorp.com
Bag and pouch sealers, closing equipment; bag closure, heat seal
President: Ted Wojtech
IT Executive: Donna Pilla
  donnap@greenercorp.com
R&D: Matt Wojtech
IT Executive: Donna Pilla
  donnap@greenercorp.com
Estimated Sales: Below $5 000,000
Number Employees: 20-49

23418 Greenfield Disston
7345 W Friendly Ave # G
Greensboro, NC 27410-6252
336-855-4200
Fax: 336-299-0616
Industrial cutting tools including machine knives
CEO: Henry Libby
Marketing Manager: Holly Oakley
Estimated Sales: $3 - 5 Million
Number Employees: 10-19
Square Footage: 16000
Parent Co: Rule Industries

23419 Greenfield Packaging
39 Westmoreland Avenue
White Plains, NY 10606-1937
914-993-0233
Fax: 203-934-7172 gpind@aol.com
We sell stock and custom plastic, glass and aluminum bottles, jars and caps; also, print logos, hex-packs and drums available
President: Debra Greenfield
Executive VP: Barbara Greenfield
Estimated Sales: $1 - 5,000,000

23420 Greenfield Paper Box Co
55 Pierce St
Greenfield, MA 01301-1740
413-773-9414
Fax: 413-774-5134 gpbox123@verizon.net
Manufacturer and designer of set-up and folding boxes for candy, cookies, cereal, etc

President: Brian T Lowell
Vice President: Robert Fischlein
  rfischlein@greenfieldpaperboxcoin.com
VP Marketing: Brian Lowell
VP Manufacturing: Robert Fischlein
Production Manager: Roger Phillips
Estimated Sales: $2.5 - 5 Million
Number Employees: 20-49
Square Footage: 40000
Type of Packaging: Private Label

23421 Greenheck Fan Corp
P.O. Box 410
Schofield, WI 54476
715-359-6171
info@greenheck.com
www.greenheck.com
Manufacturer and exporter of kitchen ventilation equipment including exhaust and supply fans, air units and exhaust hoods; also, pre-piped fire suppression systems including wet chemical and water spray.
Chairman & CEO: James McIntyre
President, Operations: Dave Kallstrom
CFO/Treasurer: Rich Totzke
Plant Manager: Mark Haase
Year Founded: 1947
Estimated Sales: $203.7 Million
Number Employees: 250-499
Square Footage: 1000000
Brands:
  Greenheck

23422 Greensburg Manufacturing Company
513 N Depot Street
Greensburg, KY 42743-1300
270-932-5511
Fax: 270-932-7866
Cutting boards and butcher blocks with lacquer finishes
General Manager: Daryl Parnell
Estimated Sales: $1 - 3 Million
Number Employees: 160
Parent Co: Kimball International

23423 Greenville Awning Company
325 New Neely Ferry Rd
Mauldin, SC 29662
864-288-0063
Fax: 864-288-3683 www.greenvilleawning.com
Commercial awnings
President: Gerhard Kuhn
  info@greenvilleawning.com
Estimated Sales: $10-20,000,000
Number Employees: 20-49

23424 Greenwood Mop & Broom Inc
312 Palmer St
Greenwood, SC 29646
864-227-8411
Fax: 864-227-3200 800-635-6849
gmb@emeraldis.com
www.greenwoodmopandbroom.com
Brooms, dry and wet mops, handles and brushes
CEO: Henry Bonds
Vice President of Finance: Craig Glanton
VP: Freida Bonds
VP Sales/Marketing: Sid Johnston
Chief Operating Officer: Sid G. Johnston
Estimated Sales: $10-20 Million
Number Employees: 20-49
Square Footage: 314000

23425 (HQ)Greer's Ferry Glass Work
PO Box 797
Dubuque, IA 52004-0797
501-589-2947
Fax: 800-310-0525 gfgw@hotmail.com
Manufacturer and exporter of thermometers, refractometers and hydrometers for testing salt, alcohol, sugar, etc
Sales: Brenda Marler
Operations: Bob Mallis
Estimated Sales: $1-2.5 Million
Number Employees: 5-9
Other Locations:
  Greer's Ferry Glass Works
  West Paterson NJ
Brands:
  Brix
  Salometers

23426 Greerco High Shear Mixers
125 Flagship Dr
North Andover, MA 01845-6119
978-687-0101
Fax: 978-687-8500 800-643-0641
inquiry@kenics.com www.chemineer.com
Homogenizers, colloid mills, laboratory homogenizers, self contained systems and high shear mixers
Manager: Mark Raymond
Estimated Sales: $20 - 50 Million
Number Employees: 20-49

23427 Grefco
23705 Crenshaw Blvd
Torrance, CA 90505-5236
310-660-8840
Fax: 213-517-0794
Wine industry filter acids
Estimated Sales: $2.5-5 Million
Number Employees: 10-19

23428 Gregg Industries Inc
5048 Vienna Dr
Waunakee, WI 53597-9746
608-846-5143
Fax: 608-846-5143 gregginD@gregginc.com
www.smokehouseparts.com
Smokers, parts, and equipments
President: Wes Gillespie
greggind@gregginc.com
Estimated Sales: $300,000-500,000
Number Employees: 1-4

23429 Gregg Industries Inc
5048 Vienna Dr
Waunakee, WI 53597-9746
608-846-5143
Fax: 608-846-5143 gregginD@gregginc.com
www.smokehouseparts.com
Industrial equipment for meat industries; smokehouse door air seals, wet bulb socks and silicone gasket
President: Wes Gillespie
greggind@gregginc.com
Vice President: Kathleen Triggs
Estimated Sales: Under $500,000
Number Employees: 1-4

23430 Gregor Jonsson Inc
13822 W Laurel Dr
Lake Forest, IL 60045-4529
847-247-4200
Fax: 847-247-4272 sales@jonsson.com
www.jonsson.com
Manufacturer and exporter of shrimp peeling systems
President: Frank Heurich
Vice President: Beth Dancy
Computer Support/Database Design: Ann Curry
Operations Manager: Scott Heurich
Operations Manager: Scott Heurich
Estimated Sales: $10 - 20 Million
Number Employees: 10-19
Square Footage: 80000

23431 Greif Brothers Corporation
3113 W 110th Street
Cleveland, OH 44111-2753
216-941-2021
Fax: 216-476-8209 800-424-0342
www.greif.com
Corrugated cartons
Product Manager: Rick Volker
Sales Manager: Michael Blatt
Plant Manager: Bob Dozer
Estimated Sales: $20-50 Million
Number Employees: 100-249

23432 Greif Inc
425 Winter Rd
Delaware, OH 43015-8903
740-549-6000
Fax: 740-549-6100 800-476-1635
www.greif.com
Specialty packaging, signage and displays including point of purchase
President, Chief Executive Officer: David B. Fischer
CEO: Peter G Watson
watson@greif.com
EVP: Gary R. Martz
COO: Peter G. Watson
Estimated Sales: Over $1 Billion
Number Employees: 10000+
Square Footage: 260000

23433 Greif Inc
425 Winter Rd
Delaware, OH 43015-8903
740-549-6000
Fax: 740-549-6100 www.greif.com
Bulk boxes, die cuts and curtain contained corrugated shipping containers
Manager: George Petzelt
CEO: Peter G Watson
watson@greif.com
VP Sales/Marketing: Dan Lautermilch
Sales Representative: David Mackson
Estimated Sales: Over $1 Billion
Number Employees: 10000+

23434 Greif Inc
425 Winter Rd
Delaware, OH 43015-8903
740-549-6000
Fax: 740-549-6100 www.greif.com
Fiber and plastic packaging, steel drums, corrugated containers, etc
CFO: Donald S Huml
CEO: Peter G Watson
watson@greif.com
CEO: Michael J Gasser
Product Manager: Rick Volker
Estimated Sales: Over $1 Billion
Number Employees: 10000+

23435 Greif Inc
4300 W 130th St
Alsip, IL 60803-2003
708-371-4777
Fax: 708-371-2047 800-233-0004
www.greif.com
Steel and plastic shipping containers and drums, specialty containers, stainless steel batch containers and process drums
President: Tony Riley
Estimated Sales: $49.5 Million
Number Employees: 100-249

23436 Greig Filters Inc
412 High Meadows Blvd
P.O. Box 91675
Lafayette, LA 70507-3417
337-237-3355
Fax: 337-233-9263 800-456-0177
gfi@greigfilters.com www.greigfilters.com
Manufacturer and exporter of filtration systems for cooking oil and beverages
Owner: Alan Greig
gfi@greigfilters.com
Office Manager: Tammy Roy
Engineer: Shane Hulin
Estimated Sales: $1-2.5 Million
Number Employees: 5-9
Square Footage: 40000
Brands:
Greig Filters
Pressure Leaf Filter
Purifry

23437 Greitzer
P.O. Box 2008
Elizabeth City, NC 27906
252-338-4000
Fax: 252-338-5445 kevin@greitzer.com
Conveyors and ventilators
Owner: Kevin Gilroy
Estimated Sales: $300,000-500,000
Number Employees: 1-4

23438 Greydon Inc
391 Greendale Rd # 2
York, PA 17403-4638
717-848-3875
Fax: 717-843-6435 info@greydon.com
www.greydon.com
Inline printing for packaging
President: Gregory Rochon
Vice President: John Rochon
Sales Director: Leo Zitella
Plant Manager: Jim Buchmver
Purchasing Manager: Brian Newman
Estimated Sales: $2.5-5 000,000
Number Employees: 20-49

23439 Gribble Stamp & StencilCo
121 St Emanuel St
Houston, TX 77002-2355
713-228-5358
Fax: 713-228-2127

Rubber and steel stamps, stencils, engraved signs, security seals and plaques
President: C W Gribble
sales@gribblestamp.com
President: C Gribble
Number Employees: 1-4

23440 Gridpath, Inc.
328 Glover Road
Stony Creek, ON L8E 5M3
Canada
905-643-0955
Fax: 905-643-6718
High pressure processing equipment for non-thermal pasteurization and packaging for the food processing industry.
President: Rick Marshall

23441 Griffin Automation
240 Westminster Rd
Buffalo, NY 14224-1930
716-674-2300
Fax: 716-674-2309 www.griffinautomation.com
Design adn build automation machinery
CEO: Gerald Bidlack
VP Finance: John Shepherd
VP Engineering: Robert Kern
Sales: Richard Hacker
Manager: Randy Reed
rreed@griffinautomation.com
Plant Manager: Mike Baines
Purchasing Manager: Chuck Peskir
Estimated Sales: $5-10 000,000
Number Employees: 20-49
Number of Products: 20
Square Footage: 40000
Type of Packaging: Private Label

23442 (HQ)Griffin Bros Inc
3033 Industrial Way NE
Salem, OR 97301-0042
503-540-7886
Fax: 503-540-7929 800-456-4743
griffinbros1@yahoo.com
Manufacturer and exporter of disinfectants, polymer floor finish, etc
President: Rod Bennett
rod@griffinbrothers.com
Account Sales Manager: Rod Bennett
Production Manager: Mike Allison
Estimated Sales: $1 - 3 Million
Number Employees: 5-9
Type of Packaging: Consumer, Food Service

23443 Griffin Food Co
111 S Cherokee St
Muskogee, OK 74403-5420
918-687-6311
Fax: 918-687-3579 800-866-6311
www.griffinfoods.com
Contract packager and wholesaler/distributor of sauces, vegetables and condiments including jams and syrups
Owner: John Griffin
johngriffin@griffinfoods.com
Vice President: David Needham
VP Sales/Marketing: Sam Ramos
Director Midwest Sales: D.C. Smith
Director Southeast Region Sales: Wayne Fuller
Estimated Sales: $16,000,000
Number Employees: 50-99
Square Footage: 648297
Type of Packaging: Consumer, Food Service, Private Label, Bulk
Brands:
Cherokee Maid
Delta
Griffin
Lucky Dutch
Old Santa Fe
Olde Farm
Prize Taker

23444 Griffin Products
P.O. Box 90
Wills Point, TX 75169
903-873-6388
Fax: 903-873-6389 800-379-9709
sales@griffinproducts.com
www.griffinproducts.com
Stainless steel sinks and tables including work and dish

President: Shane Griffin
CFO: Kenneth Fratcher
Sales: Janet Griffen
Sales: Mike Whitus
Estimated Sales: $2.5 - 5,000,000
Number Employees: 20-49

23445 Griffin Rutgers Co Inc
1170 Lincoln Ave # 12
Holbrook, NY 11741-2286

631-981-4141
Fax: 631-981-4171 800-237-6713
custserv@griffinrutgers.com
www.griffinrutgers.com
Supplying printing
Owner: Jim Umbdenstock
jim@griffin-rutgers.com
Estimated Sales: $1-2.5 Million
Number Employees: 5-9

23446 Griffith Foods Inc.
1 Griffith Center
Alsip, IL 60803

708-371-0900
Fax: 708-371-4783 www.griffithfoods.com
Protein, side-dish and snack seasonings; sauces, gravies, and soups mixes; salsa and condiments; and bakery and dough blends.
Owner/Executive Chairman: Brian Griffith
CEO: TC Chatterjee
Executive VP/CFO: Matt West
Group President, North America: Wim van Roekel
Global VP, Marketing: Rob Pellicano
Year Founded: 1919
Estimated Sales: $286.8 Million
Number Employees: 1,000-4,999
Square Footage: 250000
Type of Packaging: Food Service, Private Label, Bulk
Other Locations:
Lithonia GA
Toronto, Ontario, Canada
Hidalgo, Mexico
Nuevo Leon, Mexico

23447 Grigg Box Company
18900 Fitzpatrick Street
Detroit, MI 48228-1428

313-273-9000
Fax: 313-273-9356 rocco@griggbox.com
www.griggbox.com
Packaging equipment
President: Rocco Franco
General Manager: R Gary Turnbull
Packaging Sales: Leon Cote
Contact: Alan Gentinne
alan@griggbox.com
Plant Manager: Ed Schlacht
Estimated Sales: $10-20 Million
Number Employees: 1-4

23448 Grigsby Brothers Paper Box Manufacturers
817 NE Madrona Street
PO Box 11189
Portland, OR 97211

503-285-8341
Fax: 503-285-3334 866-233-4690
And folding cartons; package design and full service printing available
President: Terry Grigsby
CFO: Jane Hewitt
VP: Terry Grigsby
R&D: Todd Grigsby
Estimated Sales: $2.5 - 5 Million
Number Employees: 10-19

23449 Gril-Del
400 Southbrook Circle
Mankato, MN 56001-4782

507-776-8275
Fax: 507-776-8276 800-782-7320
Manufacturer and exporter of outdoor cooking utensils for the barbecue grill including spatulas, tongs and knives; also, aprons, salt and pepper shakers, handmade baskets, mitts and meat platters
President: Steven Saggau
VP: Connie Saggau
Number Employees: 10
Square Footage: 12000
Type of Packaging: Consumer, Food Service, Private Label, Bulk

Brands:
Gril-Classics
Gril-Del

23450 Grill Greats
PO Box 568
Saxonburg, PA 16056-0568

724-352-1511
Fax: 724-352-1266 sales@du-co.com
www.du-co.com
Manufacturer and exporter of ceramic briquettes for barbecue grills
President: Tom Arbanas
Quality Control: Paul Sekeras
Sales: Mike Carson
Estimated Sales: $50 - 100 Million
Number Employees: 100-249
Square Footage: 150000
Type of Packaging: Private Label, Bulk
Brands:
Grill Greats

23451 Grillco Inc
1775 Mallette Rd
Aurora, IL 60505-1319

630-906-0290
Fax: 630-906-0289 800-644-0067
Portable grills including charcoal, gas and pit barbecue; also, rotisseries, hoods, shelves and racks
Sales Director: Brian Ruseitti
Manager: Brian Ruscitti
sales@grillcoinc.com
Estimated Sales: Less Than $500,000
Number Employees: 1-4
Brands:
Grillco, Inc.

23452 Grills to Go
5659 W San Madele Avenue
Fresno, CA 93722-5066

559-645-8089
Fax: 559-645-8088 877-869-2253
Manufacturer, Distributor and Exporter of commerical barbecue equipment, smoker ovens, Southern Pride brand ovens and Rotisseries and supplies
President: Michael Hall
CEO: Nora Hall
Estimated Sales: $1-2.5 Million
Number Employees: 1-4
Square Footage: 12000
Brands:
Grills To Go

23453 Grimes Co
600 Ellis Rd N
Jacksonville, FL 32254-2801

904-786-5711
Fax: 904-786-7805 800-474-6378
www.grimescompanies.com
Heat sealers, tong welders, impulse sealers, impulse bar sealers, and rotary hospital sealers
Owner: Nicole Adler
nadler@grimescompanies.com
Estimated Sales: Less than $500,000
Number Employees: 20-49

23454 (HQ)Grindmaster-Cecilware Corp
4003 Collins Ln
Louisville, KY 40245-1602

502-425-4776
Fax: 502-425-4664 800-695-4500
info@gmcw.com www.gmcw.com
Manufacturers of a complete line of hot, cold and frozen beverage dispensing equipment.
CEO: Michael G Tinsley
mtinsley@grindmaster.com
CEO: Tom McDonald
Plant Manager: Jim Howell
Estimated Sales: $5 - 10 Million
Number Employees: 100-249
Brands:
American Metal Ware
Crathco
Espressimo
Grindmaster
Wilch

23455 Grinnell Fire ProtectionSystems Company
4985 Quail Rd NE
Sauk Rapids, MN 56379

320-253-8665
Fax: 320-253-4540

Fire protection and sprinkling systems
Branch Manager: Harry Ramler
Estimated Sales: $10 - 20 Million
Number Employees: 100
Parent Co: TYCO International Company

23456 Grinnell Fire ProtectionSystems Company
50 Technology Drive
Westminster, MA 1441

320-253-8665
Fax: 320-253-4540 800-746-7539
www.tycosimplexgrinnell.com
Fire extinguishers and kitchen hood systems
Regional Manager: Don Molloy
VP Human Resource: Dana Smith
Estimated Sales: $10 - 20,000,000
Number Employees: 250
Parent Co: TYCO International Company

23457 Grocery Manufacturers Assn
1350 I St NW # 300
Washington, DC 20005-3377

202-639-5900
Fax: 202-639-5932 www.gmaonline.org
Representing the food products industry.
President: John Cady
CEO: Pamela G Bailey
pbailey@nfpa-food.org
CEO: Cal Dooley
Estimated Sales: $5 - 10 Million
Number Employees: 50-99

23458 Grocery Products Distribution
14 Ridgedale Ave # 106
Cedar Knolls, NJ 07927-1106

973-538-1035
Fax: 973-538-0944 richgpds@aol.com
Consultant specializing in distribution marketing services for public grocery distribution centers
President: Rich Richards
richgpds@aol.com
VP: Florence Richards
Staff Assistant: Barbara Brown
Estimated Sales: $.5 - 1 million
Number Employees: 5-9

23459 Groeb Farms
10464 Bryan Hwy
Onsted, MI 49265-0269

517-467-2065
Fax: 517-467-2840 800-530-9969
Honey; UPC labeling, tamper-evident packaging, re-closable cap, easy pour handle and shatterproof containers
President & CEO: Ernest Groeb
VP & CFO: Jack Irvin Jr
VP/COO: Troy Groeb
Director Retail Sales: Jim McCoy
Chief Procurement Officer: Alison Tringale
Type of Packaging: Consumer, Food Service, Private Label, Bulk
Other Locations:
Belleview FL
Miller's American Honey
Colton CA
Brands:
Gourmet Jose
Groeb Farms

23460 Groen Process Equipment
271 Country Commons Rd # F
Trout Valley, IL 60013-2545

847-462-1865
Fax: 847-462-1950
Manager: Frank Lobes
flobes@gpeequipment.com
Estimated Sales: Below $5 Million
Number Employees: 250-499

23461 Groen-A Dover Industries Co
1055 Mendell Davis Dr
Byram, MS 39272-9788

601-371-4417
Fax: 601-373-9587 800-676-9040
info@groen.com www.unifiedbrands.net
Manufacturers of steam jacketed kettles, braising pans, convection steamers, combi ovens, cook-chill and continuous processing systems for food service operators and industrial processors worldwide

President: Bill Strenglis
CFO: Scott Stevenson
R&D: Pam Holmes
Quality Control: Mike Blackwell
Sales/Marketing: Clay Thames
Estimated Sales: $10 - 20 Million
Number Employees: 50-99
Parent Co: Dover Industries

23462 Groen-A Dover Industries Co
1055 Mendell Davis Dr
Byram, MS 39272-9788

601-371-4417
Fax: 888-864-7636 webmaster@unifiedbrands.net
www.unifiedbrands.net
President: Bill Strenglis
CFO: Scott Stevenson
R&D: Pam Holmes
Quality Control: Mike Blackwell
V.P. of Sales and Marketing: Blair Alfdord
Estimated Sales: $10 - 20 Million
Number Employees: 50-99

23463 Grosfillex Inc
230 Old West Penn Ave
Robesonia, PA 19551-8904

610-693-6213
Fax: 610-693-5414 800-233-3186
info@grosfillexfurniture.com
www.grosfillexfurniture.com
Supplier, importer and exporter of commercial out-
door resin furniture
CEO: Frans Govers
Estimated Sales: $50-100 Million
Number Employees: 100-249
Parent Co: Grosfillex SARL
Other Locations:
  Grosfillex Contract Furniture
  Chino CA
Brands:
  Grosfillex

23464 Gross & Co Licensed BusPro
1208 Sunset St
Middletown, OH 45042-2890

513-424-6035
Fax: 513-420-9260 www.grossinc.com
Chill rolls, hearto rolls and process water systems
Owner: M Dtannreuther
dtannreuther@grossinc.com
Estimated Sales: Less Than $500,000
Number Employees: 5-9

23465 Grote Co
1160 Gahanna Pkwy
Columbus, OH 43230-6615

614-868-8414
Fax: 614-863-1647 888-534-7683
www.grotecompany.com
Manufacturer and exporter of food processing
equipment including high yield slicer applicators,
multi-purpose slicers, cheese shredders, pizza top-
ping lines and paper sheeter systems
President: Jelff Rawef
aschneider@grotecompany.com
CEO: Bruce Hohl
Chairman: James Grote
Quality Control: Jon Feifeit
Marketing Communication/Sales Coord.: Terri
Hoover
Sales Exec: Andy Schneider
Estimated Sales: $10 - 20 Million
Number Employees: 100-249
Square Footage: 140000
Brands:
  Grote

23466 Groth Corp
13650 N Promenade Blvd
Stafford, TX 77477-3972

281-295-6800
Fax: 713-295-6999 800-354-7684
sales@grothcorp.com www.grothcorp.com
Consultant specializing in sales and marketing for
U.S. companies overseas through exclusive
distributorships and joint venture arrangements
President: David Brown
dbrown@grothcorp.com
Managing Director: Helen Groth
Estimated Sales: $1 - 5 Million
Number Employees: 50-99
Square Footage: 600

23467 Group One Partners
21 W 3rd St
Boston, MA 02127-1133

617-268-7000
Fax: 617-268-0209 info@grouponeinc.com
www.grouponeinc.com
Consultant specializing in food service design for
facilities including kitchens and restaurants; also,
food service programming and interior design
President: Mary Fraria
m_fraria@lysibishop.com
Principal: Kevin Mullin
Principal: Harry Wheeler
Director Food Service Design: William Stenstrom
Estimated Sales: $1 - 2.5 Million
Number Employees: 20-49

23468 Gruenewald ManufacturingCompany
100 Ferncroft Rd Ste 204
Danvers, MA 1923

978-777-0200
Fax: 978-777-9432 800-229-9447
info@whipcream.com www.whipcream.com
Manufacturer, importer and exporter of dispensers
for food products, including ice cream and whipped
cream
Owner: Fredrick Gruenewald
fredrick@whipcream.com
Sales/Marketing: Kevin Muldoon
VP Sales: Thomas Muldoon
Sales: Joseph Ransom
Estimated Sales: $10-20 Million
Number Employees: 10-19
Square Footage: 30000
Type of Packaging: Food Service
Brands:
  Refillo
  River of Cream
  Rocket

23469 Grueny's Rubber Stamps
210 S Gaines St
Little Rock, AR 72201-2218

501-376-0393
Fax: 501-376-6327
Price markers and rubber stanps
President and CFO: John Ward Jr
Quality Control: Bob Pinkerton
Sales Manager: Brit Wood
Estimated Sales: Less than $500,000
Number Employees: 1 to 4

23470 Guardsman
4999 36th St SE
Grand Rapids, MI 49512-2005

616-940-2900
Fax: 616-285-7870 www.guardsman.com
Carpet and fabric cleaners, degreasers and adhesive
removers
Manager: Kate Bass
New Business Development Manager: Sandi
Brogger
Estimated Sales: $10 - 20 Million
Number Employees: 100-249
Parent Co: Lilly Industries
Brands:
  Afta
  Carpet Guard
  Goof Off
  One-Wipe

23471 Guest Supply
P.O. Box 902
Monmouth Jct, NJ 08852

609-514-9696
Fax: 609-514-2692 800-448-3787
eservice@guestsupply.com www.guestsupply.com
Cleaning equipment and chemicals
President: Clifford Stanley
Number Employees: 100

23472 Gulf Arizona Packaging
7720 FM 1960 East
Humble, TX 77346

281-582-6700
Fax: 281-852-1590 800-364-3887
Manufacturer and wholesaler/distributor of packag-
ing equipment and materials including bags, con-
tainers, closures, conveyors, labels, linings, tapes,
ties, etc
Manager: Paul Corley
General Manager: Paul Corley
General Manager: Jay Crabb

Estimated Sales: $5 - 10 Million
Number Employees: 5-9
Parent Co: Gulf Systems

23473 Gulf Coast Plastics
9314 Princess Palm Ave
Tampa, FL 33619-1364

813-621-8098
Fax: 813-623-1408 800-277-7491
sales@gulfcoastplastics.com
www.gulfcoastplastics.com
Manufacturer and exporter of anti-static plastic bags
Owner: Karen Santiago
karens@gulfcoastplastics.com
CFO: Tom Coryn
Quality Control: Tom Coryn
Manager: Thomas Coryn
Estimated Sales: Below $5 Million
Number Employees: 20-49
Square Footage: 24000
Parent Co: Dairy Mix
Type of Packaging: Consumer, Food Service, Bulk

23474 Gulf Coast Sign Company
380 Clematis Street
Pensacola, FL 32503-2839

850-438-2131
Fax: 850-432-6367 800-768-3549
gulfcoastsign@hotmail.com
U.L. approved neon, plastic, electric and sandblasted
signs; also, maintenance, repair and erection ser-
vices
CEO: William Terry
Estimated Sales: $1-2.5 Million
Number Employees: 19
Square Footage: 40000

23475 Gulf Packaging Company
323 9th Avenue N
Safety Harbor, FL 34695

727-725-4424
Fax: 727-725-2885 800-749-3466
Folding, paper, set-up and transparent boxes; also,
blister and skin cards
President: Jeffrey A Herran
Chairman: F Edward Herran
Plant Manager: Patrick Herran
Estimated Sales: $2.5 - 5 Million
Number Employees: 20
Square Footage: 32000

23476 Gulf Systems
801 E Fronton St
Brownsville, TX 78520

800-217-4853
Fax: 956-504-9800 www.gulfpackaging.com
Wholesaler/distributor of packaging equipment and
materials
Manager: Blanca Puga
bpuga@gulfsys.com
CFO: Debby Malone
Customer Service Representative: Cathy Wyatt
Estimated Sales: Below $5,000,000
Number Employees: 5-9
Parent Co: Gulf Systems

23477 Gulf Systems
2109 Exchange Dr
Arlington, TX 76011

817-261-1915
Fax: 817-861-0092
Wholesaler/distributor of packaging equipment and
materials
Manager: Denise Stiger
Contact: Todd Williams
todd_esala@lselectric.com
Estimated Sales: $20 - 50 Million
Number Employees: 20-49
Parent Co: Gulf Systems

23478 Gulf Systems
7720 fm 960 e
Humble, TX 77346

405-528-2293
Fax: 281-852-1590 800-364-3887
customerservicehumble@gulfpackaging.com
www.gulfpackaging.com
Wholesaler/distributor of packaging equipment and
materials
Customer Service Representative: Cathy Wyatt
Estimated Sales: $2.5-5,000,000
Number Employees: 5-9
Parent Co: Gulf Systems

23479 Gulf Systems
7720 fm 960 e
Humble, TX 77346
405-528-2293
Fax: 281-852-1590 800-364-3887
www.gulfpackaging.com
Wholesaler/distributor of packaging equipment and materials
Customer Service Representative: Cathy Wyatt
Estimated Sales: $1 - 5,000,000
Number Employees: 5-9
Parent Co: Gulf Systems

23480 Gulf Systems
3815 N Santa Fe Ave
Oklahoma City, OK 73108
800-364-3887
Fax: 405-557-0903
Wholesaler/distributor of packaging equipment and materials
Customer Service Representative: Cathy Wyatt
Estimated Sales: $5-10,000,000
Number Employees: 5-9
Parent Co: Gulf Systems

23481 Gunter Wilhelm Cutlery
20-10 Maple Ave # 35g
Fair Lawn, NJ 07410-1591
201-569-6866
Fax: 201-369-4679 sales@gunterwilhelm.com
www.gunterwilhelm.com
Cookware, cooking implements
Founder: Paul Hellman
CEO: David Malek
Contact: Cherry Dan
sales@gunterwilhelm.com
Number Employees: 1-4

23482 Gusmer Enterprises Inc
81 M St
Fresno, CA 93721-3215
559-485-2692
Fax: 559-485-4254 866-213-1131
www.gusmerenterprises.com
Manufacturer and exporter of filter and fiber media for food and beverages
CEO: Marla Jeffrey
mjeffrey@gusmerenterprises.com
CEO: Marla Jeffrey
VP/Technical Sales: Phil Crantz
Estimated Sales: $5 - 10 Million
Number Employees: 50-99
Square Footage: 240000
Parent Co: Gusmer Enterprises
Other Locations:
Cellulo Co.
Crawford NJ
Brands:
Cellu Flo
Cellu Pore
Cellu Stacks
Kolor Fine
Oak Mor

23483 Gustave A Larson Co
W233n2869 Roundy Cir W
Pewaukee, WI 53072-6285
262-542-0200
Fax: 262-542-1400 www.galarson.com
Heating equipment
President: Devon Becker
devon.becker@jpmorgan.com
Branch Manager: John Hirsch
Estimated Sales: $2.5-5,000,000
Number Employees: 250-499
Parent Co: Indiana Supply Company

23484 Guth Lighting
PO Box 7079
Saint Louis, MO 63177
314-533-3200
Fax: 314-533-9127
Manufacturer and exporter of sealed and gasketed fluorescent and high-intensity discharge lighting equipment for use in water wash down and corrosive environments
Manager: Robert Catone
VP and Controller: Sue Pries
VP/General Manager: Robert Catone
Research & Development: Mike Kurtz
Estimated Sales: $20 - 50 Million
Number Employees: 50-99
Square Footage: 100000
Parent Co: JJI

Brands:
Duraclamp
Enviroguard
Kleenseal
Plascolume
Railtite
Steeltite

23485 H & H Metal FabricationInc
3066 Faulkner Rd
PO Box 1505
Belden, MS 38826-9649
662-489-4626
Fax: 662-489-4626 hhmetalfab@earthlink.net
www.hhmetalfab.com
Manufactures electrical enclosures & panels; residential & commercial fluorescent light fixtures; steel sheet metal fabricating; punch press work & welding
President: Michael Huey
hhmetalfab@earthlink.net
Number Employees: 10-19

23486 H & M Bay Inc
1600 Industrial Park Rd
Federalsburg, MD 21632
410-754-5167
Fax: 410-754-3495 800-932-7521
information@hmbayinc.net www.hmbayinc.net
Warehouse offering cooler and freezer storage of seafood; transportation firm providing refrigerated trucking services including local, short and long haul
Co-Owner: Walter Messick
CFO: Al Nulph
Marketing And Sales Manager: Scott Steinhardt
Manager: Randy Hind
rhind@hmbayinc.com
COO: Michael Ryan
Number Employees: 100-249

23487 H A Phillips & Co
770 Enterprise Ave
Dekalb, IL 60115-7904
630-377-0050
Fax: 630-377-2706 info@haphillips.com
www.haphillips.com
Manufacturer and exporter of float controls, valves and pressure vessels for ammonia refrigeration systems; wholesaler/distributor and importer of pressure regulating and solenoid valves
President/Chief Executive Officer: Michael R. Ryan
Executive Director: John Schroeder
Vice-President of Finance: Janet L. Jones
Vice-President of Engineering: Steve L. . Yagla, P.E
R&D/Quality Control: Mike Ryan
Sales/Marketing: Ed Murziuski
Corporate Sales Manager: Thomas W. Herman
Secretary/Vice President of Human Resour: Mary Wright
Operations Manager: Andrew McCullough
Vice President of Manufacturing: Brian J. Youssi
Plant Manager: David Williams
Purchasing Manager: Rou Coleman
Estimated Sales: $4.2 Million
Number Employees: 20-49
Square Footage: 60000
Brands:
Dump Trap
Live Brine
Phillips
Phillips Level-Edge

23488 H A Sparke Co
1032 Texas Ave
PO Box 674
Shreveport, LA 71101-3341
318-222-0927
Fax: 318-222-2731 info@hasparke.com
www.hasparke.com
Manufacturer and exporter of restaurant fixtures including pot, pan and utensil racks; also, guest check handling equipment
President: Richard W Sparke
Estimated Sales: $1-2.5 Million
Number Employees: 5-9
Square Footage: 14000

23489 H A Stiles
386 Bridgton Rd # A1
Westbrook, ME 04092-3606
207-854-8458
Fax: 207-854-3863 800-447-8537
askhastiles@hastiles.com www.hastiles.com

Manufacturer and exporter of wooden kitchen utensils and bread and cake boards; also, toothpicks
President: Ambrose Berry
Estimated Sales: Less Than $500,000
Number Employees: 10-19

23490 H B Fuller Co
1200 Willow Lake Blvd
P.O. Box 64683
St. Paul, MN 55164-0683
651-236-5900
www.hbfuller.com
Adhesives including hot melt, palletizing and low temperature application.
President & Chief Executive Officer: Jim Owens
EVP & Chief Operating Officer: Ted Clark
EVP & Chief Financial Officer: John Corkrean
Year Founded: 1887
Estimated Sales: $2.8 Billion
Number Employees: 3,700
Brands:
Adventra
H.B. Fuller
Palletite
Potimelt

23491 H C Bainbridge Inc
718 N Salina St
Syracuse, NY 13208-2511
315-475-5313
Fax: 315-475-5469
bainbridgeflags@twcny.rr.com
Flags, flag poles and banners.
President: Marilyn Swetland
bainbridgeflags@twcny.rr.com
Estimated Sales: Less than $500,000
Square Footage: 8000

23492 H C Duke & Son Inc
2116 8th Ave
East Moline, IL 61244-1800
309-755-4553
Fax: 309-755-9858 sales@electrofreeze.com
www.electrofreeze.com
Manufacturer and exporter of soft serve ice cream machines
Marketing: Joe Clark
VP Sales: Jim Duke
Estimated Sales: $20-50 Million
Number Employees: 100-249
Square Footage: 115000
Type of Packaging: Food Service
Brands:
Electro Freeze
H.C. Duke & Son

23493 H F Staples & Co Inc
9 Webb Dr # 5
PO Box 956
Merrimack, NH 03054-4876
603-889-8600
Fax: 603-883-9409 800-682-0034
info@hfstaples.com
www.naturalfurniturecare.com
Manufacturer and exporter of wood filler, wax and ladder accessories. Contract private label tube filling of viscous products
President: John Murphy
john.murphy@staples.com
Vice President: Thomas Stratton
Estimated Sales: $5 - 10 Million
Number Employees: 5-9
Square Footage: 52000
Type of Packaging: Private Label

23494 H G Weber & Co
725 Fremont St
Kiel, WI 53042-1352
920-894-2221
Fax: 920-894-3786 info@hgweber.com
www.holwegweber.com
Manufacturer and exporter of paper and film bag machinery, flexographic printers and vertical case conveyors
President: Mike Odom
modom@hgweber.com
CFO: John Smith
Senior VP: Donald Ludwig
Marketing Director: Jeff Vogel
Sales Director: Brian Niemuth
Estimated Sales: $20 - 50 Million
Number Employees: 50-99
Square Footage: 130

Brands:
  Presto Flex
  Upender
  Weber-Univers

23495 H G Weber & Co
725 Fremont St
Kiel, WI 53042-1352
                        920-894-2221
        Fax: 920-894-3786 info@hgweber.com
                        www.holwegweber.com
Bag making machines
President: Mike Odom
  modom@hgweber.com
Estimated Sales: $20-50 Million
Number Employees: 50-99

23496 H H Franz Co
3201 Fallscliff Rd
Baltimore, MD 21211-2792
                        410-889-2975
        Fax: 410-889-2160 www.hhfranzfillers.com
Packaging, bottle fillers
President: Bob Mintiens Jr
  bmintiens@hhfranzco.com
Estimated Sales: $1-2.5 000,000
Number Employees: 1-4

23497 H H Franz Co
3201 Fallscliff Rd
Baltimore, MD 21211-2792
                        410-889-2975
        Fax: 410-889-2160 800-731-3309
        franz@qis.net www.hhfranzfillers.com
Food processing equipment
President: Bob Mintiens Jr
  bmintiens@hhfranzco.com
Estimated Sales: $1 - 2.5 000,000
Number Employees: 1-4

23498 H P Mfg Co
3705 Carnegie Ave
Cleveland, OH 44115-2750
                        216-361-6500
        Fax: 216-361-6508 info@hpmanufacturing.com
Plastic items including sheets, rods and tubes
President: John Melchiorre
CFO: Ken Lutke
Quality Control: Paul Glozer
Chairman of the Board: Terry Poltorek
VP Sales/Marketing: Bob Roman
Contact: Denise Arcangelini
  darcangelini@hpmanufacturing.com
Estimated Sales: $5 - 10 Million
Number Employees: 10-19

23499 H S Crocker Co Inc
12100 Smith Dr
Huntley, IL 60142-9618
                        847-669-3600
        Fax: 847-669-1170 www.hscrocker.com
Specialty, gravure, flexographic and letterpress
printing; paper and pressure sensitive labels; tickets;
pharmaceutical, portion pack, foil, juice and yogurt
lids
CFO: John Dai
CEO: Endilch Andy
  endilch.andy@hscrocker.com
CFO: John Dai
CEO: Ron Giordano
Marketing Manager: Ron Giordano
Estimated Sales: $20 - 30 Million
Number Employees: 50-99

23500 H S Inc
1301 W Sheridan Ave
Oklahoma City, OK 73106-5233
                        405-239-6864
        Fax: 405-239-2242 800-238-1240
        sales@hsfoodservers.com
Thermal food containers for tabletop service
President: Esther Feiler
Owner: Ester Stephenson
  estherstephenson@coxinet.net
Sales Manager: Sue Garcia
Estimated Sales: $2.5-5 Million
Number Employees: 10-19
Parent Co: ACO

23501 H T I Filtration
30241 Tomas
Rancho Sta Marg, CA 92688-2123
                        949-546-0745
        Fax: 949-269-6438 877-404-9372
                        info@htifiltration.com
Manufacturer and exporter of filtration equipment
including oil, and hydraulic, specializing in water re-
moval from oils
CEO: Steven Parker
Technical Service: Ron Hart
  r.hart@htifiltration.com
Estimated Sales: $1 - 5 Million
Number Employees: 10-19
Square Footage: 40000
Parent Co: Temcor
Type of Packaging: Private Label
Brands:
  H-F 201
  H-F 211
  H-S 410
  Hydra-Supreme
  Hydro-Fil

23502 H&H Lumber Company
11100 SE 3rd Ave
Amarillo, TX 79118
                        806-335-1813
        Fax: 806-335-3734
Wooden pallets
Owner: Doyle Herring
Estimated Sales: Less than $500,000
Number Employees: 1-4
Square Footage: 12000

23503 (HQ)H&H Wood Products
5600 Camp Rd
Hamburg, NY 14075
                        716-648-5600
        Fax: 716-648-3246 hhwood1@aol.com
Wooden pallets; heat treating service
President: William Heussler
  williamheussler@voestalpine.com
Production Coordinator: Richard Perez
Estimated Sales: $3 Million
Number Employees: 20-49
Square Footage: 52000
Type of Packaging: Bulk
Other Locations:
  H&H Wood Products
  Hamburg NY

23504 H&H of the Americas
225 W 34th Street
Suite 1310
New York, NY 10122-1310
                        212-695-4980
        Fax: 212-695-7153 johntripas@msn.com
Processing equipment for the meat industry
President: Barbara Negron
CFO: Barbara Negron
Estimated Sales: Below $5 000,000
Number Employees: 6

23505 H. Arnold Wood Turning
220 White Plains Road
Suite 245
Tarrytown, NY 10591
                        914-381-0801
        Fax: 914-381-0804 888-314-0088
        staff@arnoldwood.com www.arnoldwood.com
Wooden items including mini crates and boxes,
broom and mop handles, turned handles, rolling
pins, flag poles, skewers and dowels; importer of
broom and mop handles and dowels
VP: Johnathan Arnold
VP Sales: Jonathan Arnold
Contact: Ann Arnold
  ann@arnoldwood.com
Estimated Sales: $500,000-$1 Million
Number Employees: 5-9

23506 H. Gartenberg & Company
260 Blackthorn Drive
Buffalo Grove, IL 60089-6341
                        847-821-7590
        Fax: 773-268-6402
Commercial drying, pulverizing and blending equip-
ment for dried egg processing; also, dehydration ser-
vices available
President: Melvin Gartenberg
Estimated Sales: $2.5-5 Million
Number Employees: 10
Square Footage: 60000

Type of Packaging: Bulk

23507 H. Reisman Corporation
377 Crane St
Orange, NJ 07050
                        973-677-9200
        Fax: 973-675-2766 800-631-3424
President: David Holmes
Sales/Marketing Manager: Dillon McLellan
Estimated Sales: $5 - 10 000,000
Number Employees: 20-49

23508 H. Yamamoto
8 Hickory Road
Port Washington, NY 11050-1504
                        718-821-7700
        Fax: 718-366-1619
Zinc and aluminum die castings

23509 H.B. Wall & Sons
1560 W Skyline Ave
Ozark, MO 65721
                        417-581-1902
        Fax: 417-581-2010 800-373-1616
        scott@welhenerawning.com www.hbwall.com
Commercial awnings
Owner: Greg Casey
Estimated Sales: Below $5,000,000
Number Employees: 10-19

23510 H.C. Foods Co. Ltd.
6414 Gayhart St
Commerce, CA 90040
                        323-722-8648
                        sales@hcfoods.net
                        www.hcfoods.net
Asian foodstuffs, including rice and tea
President/Owner: Ken Hsiao
Co-Owner: Anthony Sher
Number of Products: 3000
Square Footage: 70000

23511 H.F. Coors China Company
PO Box 59
New Albany, MS 38652-0059
                        310-338-8921
        Fax: 310-641-9429 800-782-6677
Manufacturer and exporter of cookware and table-
ware including high strength china, health care ser-
vice dishes, cups and mugs; also, custom decorated,
colored, decal and banding available
Controller: George Holzheimer
General VP: Robert Gasbarro
Ceramics Engineer: Leo Suzuki
Number Employees: 50-99
Square Footage: 400000
Parent Co: Standex International Corporation
Type of Packaging: Food Service, Private Label,
  Bulk
Brands:
  Alox
  Chefsware
  Roca Beige

23512 H.J. Jones & Sons
1155 Dundas Street
London, ON N5W 3A9
Canada
                        519-451-5250
        Fax: 519-451-0545 800-667-0476
                        jonesy@farmline.com
Packaging materials including stretch pak and blister
cards and folding cartons
President: Michael Jones
Controller: Scott Switzer
Vice President: Doug Jones
Marketing Director: Les Meeneil
Purchasing Manager: Glen Davies
Number Employees: 50

23513 (HQ)H.L. Diehl Company
9 Babcock Hill Rd
South Windham, CT 6266
                        860-423-7741
        Fax: 860-423-2654 info@giant-vac.com
                        www.giant-vac.com
Manufacturer and exporter of power cleaning equip-
ment including industrial vacuum cleaners
President: Anton Janiak
  anton.janiak@giant-vac.com
VP: Gail Marie Diehl
Estimated Sales: $10 - 20 Million
Number Employees: 50-99

23514 H.P. Neun
75 N Main St
Fairport, NY 14450
585-388-1360
Fax: 585-388-0184
Manufacturer and exporter of foam products and paper boxes including corrugated, folding, candy, set-up and fancy.
President: Mike Hanna
Estimated Sales: $20-50 Million
Number Employees: 100-249

23515 HAABTEC Inc
116 Bohannon Park
Shacklefords, VA 23156
804-785-4408
Fax: 804-785-3208
Packaging equipment
Owner: Robert Haab
eric@haabtec.com
Estimated Sales: $5-10 000,000
Number Employees: 5-9

23516 HABCO Beverage Systems
501 Gordon Baker Road
Toronto, ON M2H 2S6
Canada
416-491-6008
Fax: 416-491-6982 800-448-0244
Manufacturer and exporter of reach-in refrigerators, freezers, and merchandisers.
Vice President/Marketing: Scott Brown
EVP/Sales: Jim Maynard
Number Employees: 100
Number of Brands: 2
Number of Products: 27
Brands:
Cold Space
Habco
Signature Series

23517 HAMBA USA, Inc
2050 Trade Center Dr E
Saint Peters, MO 63376
Fax: 636-281-1503
Filler for still beverages and almost any liquid or pasty product
President: Gary Pyles
VP: Ken Hicks
Number Employees: 10-19

23518 (HQ)HBD Industries
PO Box 948
Salisbury, NC 28145
704-636-0121
Fax: 704-633-3880 800-438-2312
info@hbdthermoid.com www.hbdthermoid.com
Industrial hoses for nondairy or alcoholic applications
President: Robert Lyons
Manager: David Dockins
Customer Service Manager: Pat Stubbs
Contact: John Backscheider
j.backscheider@hbdthermoid.com
General Manager: Lou Smith
Plant Manager: Dave Dockins
Estimated Sales: $20-50 Million
Number Employees: 100-249
Square Footage: 300000

23519 HBD Thermoid, Inc.
1301 W Sandusky Ave
Suite 110
Bellefontaine, OH 43311-1082
614-526-7000
Fax: 614-526-7027 800-543-8070
info@hbdthermoid.com www.hbdthermoid.com
industrial rubber products since 1883.
President & CEO: Tom Pozda
President, Rubber Products Group: Chris Denick
Vice President & CFO: Eric Houser
Finance Director, Rubber Products Group: Kent Carleton
Director, Sales & Marketing: David Schempp
Dir. of Marketing, Rubber Products Group: Subin Sethuram
Vice President, Human Resources: Emily Ritchey
Estimated Sales: $1 - 5 Million
Number Employees: 250-499
Type of Packaging: Consumer, Private Label, Bulk

23520 HCI Corp
28 S 5th St
Geneva, IL 60134-2111
630-208-3100
Fax: 630-208-3111 www.hci-search.com
Executive search and placement firm
President: Frank Cianchetti
frankc@hci-search.com
Estimated Sales: Less Than $500,000
Number Employees: 5-9

23521 HCR
Highway 87 West
Lewistown, MT 59457
406-538-7781
Fax: 406-538-5506 800-326-7700
www.hcr-inc.com
President: Peter Smith
Estimated Sales: $10 - 20 Million
Number Employees: 20-49
Parent Co: the Jamison Door Company

23522 HD Barcode
334 4th Ave
Indialantic, FL 32903-4214
321-952-2490
Fax: 321-952-2475 sales@hdbarcode.com
www.hdbarcode.com
Barcoding technologies
President: Gary Parish
mbrandon@completeinspectionsystems.com
Marketing: Angela Kirshon
Sales Exec: Michael Brandon
Estimated Sales: $1 - 3 Million
Number Employees: 10+
Brands:
HD Barcode
HD SecureID
HD SmartCode

23523 HD Electric Co
1475 S Lakeside Dr
Park City, IL 60085-8314
847-473-4882
Fax: 847-473-4981 www.hdeinnovations.com
Manufacturer and exporter of electrical test equipment and portable/emergency lighting products
CEO: M Hoffman
mhoffman@hdelectriccompany.com
CEO: M Hoffman
Marketing Manager: Kimberly Higgins
Sales: Berstrom
Estimated Sales: $2.5-5 Million
Number Employees: 20-49
Brands:
Digivolt
Halo
Mark
Quickcheck
Versa-Lite

23524 HDT Manufacturing
RR 9
Salem, OH 44460
330-337-8565
Fax: 330-337-8576 800-968-7438
Manufacturer and exporter of industrial trailers and trucks
President: Dave Lawless
VP: Shawn Lawless
Purchasing Manager: Don Souce

23525 HH Controls Company
6 Frost Street
Arilington, MA 02474-1012
781-646-2626
Heat storage/exchange devices for full size convection ovens
Estimated Sales: Less than $500,000
Number Employees: 1-4

23526 (HQ)HHP Inc
14 Buxton Industrial Dr
PO Box 489
Henniker, NH 3242
603-428-3298
Fax: 603-428-3448 hhp@conknet.com
www.hhp-inc.com
Manufacturer and exporter of wooden pallets; also, saw mill
President: Ross D Elia
hhp@conknet.com
Sales: Nancy Kocsis

Estimated Sales: $5-10 Million
Number Employees: 50-99

23527 HI-TECH Filter
80 Myrtle Street
North Quincy, MA 02171-1728
617-328-7756
Fax: 617-773-4192 800-448-3249
Air filters

23528 HID Global
6533 Flying Cloud Dr # 1000
Eden Prairie, MN 55344-3334
952-942-5258
Fax: 952-941-7836 sales@fargo.com
www.fargo.com
ID CARD printers
President: Gary Holland
Cmo: Alan Fontanella
afontanella@hidglobal.com
Quality Control: Jeff Sasse
VP: Thomas C Platner
CFO: Paul Stephenson
Sales Manager: Mark Anderson
Number Employees: 100-249

23529 HMC Corp
284 Maple St
Hopkinton, NH 03229-3339
603-746-4691
Fax: 603-746-4819 petertaylor@hmccorp.com
www.hmccorp.com
Manufacturer and exporter of saw mill conveyors
President: Peter Taylor
petertaylor@hmccorp.com
Estimated Sales: $20-50 Million
Number Employees: 50-99

23530 HMG Worldwide
8710 Ferris Avenue
Morton Grove, IL 60053-2841
847-965-7100
Fax: 947-965-7141
Custom and stock in-store marketing programs and displays
President: Stephen Dopp
Number Employees: 50
Parent Co: Howard Marlboro Group

23531 (HQ)HMG Worldwide In-Store Marketing
371 7th Ave
New York, NY 10001-3984
212-736-2300
Fax: 212-564-3395
Manufacturer and exporter of point-of-sale displays, integrated merchandising systems and interactive electronics; also, in-store related research, market planning, package design and space management services available
CEO Director: Andrew Wahl
CEO: Michael Lipman
Estimated Sales: $1 - 5 Million
Number Employees: 5-9
Square Footage: 1200000
Other Locations:
HMG Worldwide In-Store Market
Chicago IL

23532 HPI North America/Plastics
900 Apollo Rd
Eagan, MN 55121-2477
651-454-2520
Fax: 651-229-5470 800-752-7462
Disposable plastic dinnerware including plates, tumblers, trays, coffee cups, barware, etc
Estimated Sales: $1 - 5 Million
Number Employees: 250-499
Parent Co: Newell Companies

23533 HPI North America/Plastics
4501 W 47th St
PO Box 2830
Chicago, IL 60632
773-890-0523
800-327-3534
homzinfo@homzproducts.com
www.homzproducts.com
Disposable plastic tableware and drinkware
President: Frank Biller
VP Merchandising: Jim Schmidt
Contact: George Haminton
ghamilton@homz.biz

Number Employees: 500-999
Parent Co: Newell Companies
Brands:
    Beverageware
    Dinnerware
    Flip-N-Fresh
    Gourmet To Go
    Hi-Heat
    Legacy
    Microproof
    Microware
    Pop-Tops
    Prestige
    Scrollware
    Stow Away
    Swirl

23534 HSI
9977 North 90th Street
Suite 300
Scottsdale, AZ 85258
480-596-5456
Fax: 480-707-6223 info@hsi-solutions.com
Hospitality application software
Controller: Ron McNamee
General Manager And VP: Cyndi Shepley
Contact: Hany Ahmed
    hany.ahmed@oracle.com
Director of Operations: Norbert Holzmann
Purchasing Director: Jim Nicholas
Number Employees: 100-249

23535 HSI Company
3002 Hempland Rd
Lancaster, PA 17601-1992
717-392-2987
Fax: 717-392-0723
Ice cream hardening machinery and warehouse storage systems
Estimated Sales: $10-25 000,000
Number Employees: 10-19

23536 HW Theller Engineering
1540 Crown Rd
Petaluma, CA 94954-1487
707-762-3820
Fax: 707-769-0874
Hot tack heatsealer tester, mini tensile tester, precision heatsealer tester
Contact: Theller Hutton
    mcaprara@bottinifuel.com
Estimated Sales: $1-2.5 Million
Number Employees: 5-9

23537 Haake
33 N Century Rd
Paramus, NJ 07652-2810
201-262-3628
Fax: 201-265-1977 800-631-1369
Rheological instrumentation including viscometers, rheometers, thermal analyzers and circulators/water baths
Sales Director: Stephen Dieter
Estimated Sales: $1 - 5 Million
Number Employees: 1-4
Brands:
    Minilab Micro Compouuder
    Polylab
    Rheostress Rs1
    Rheostress Rs150
    Rheostress Rs300
    Rheostress Rv1
    Vt-550

23538 Haarslev Inc
9700 NW Conant Ave
Kansas City, MO 64153-1832
816-799-0808
Fax: 816-799-0812 info-usa@haarslev.com
www.haarslev.com
Supplier of processing equipment to meat and fish industries
President: Matthew Aguilera
    maguilera@haarslev.com
CEO: Hans Nissen
VP Sales: Bob McKay
Number Employees: 20-49

23539 Haas Tailoring Company
3425 Sinclair Ln
Baltimore, MD 21213-2030
410-732-3804
Fax: 410-732-9310
Clothes and service uniforms

Comptroller: Mark McLean
President of Sales: Matthew Haas
Estimated Sales: $5-10 Million
Number Employees: 100-249

23540 Haban Saw Company
9301 Watson Industrial Park
St.Louis, MO 63126
314-968-3991
Fax: 314-968-1240 info@habansaw.com
www.habansaw.com
Manufacturer and exporter of butcher handsaws and blades
Estimated Sales: $1-2.5 Million
Number Employees: 4

23541 Habasit America
805 Satellite Blvd NW
Suwanee, GA 30024-2879
678-288-3600
Fax: 800-422-2748 800-458-6431
info.america@us.habasit.com www.habasit.com
Manufacturer, importer and exporter of belting
Chairman: Thomas Habegger
CEO: Andrea Volpi
CFO: Beat Stebler
Vice Chairman: Alice Habegger
R&D: Bill Humsby
Marketing: Allison Cox
National Sales Manager: Bert Fliegi
Segment Manager: Mike Creo
Head of Product Division Fabrics: Maarten Aarts
Estimated Sales: $5 - 10 Million
Number Employees: 100-249
Parent Co: Habasit-AG
Type of Packaging: Bulk

23542 Habasit America PlasticDiv
825 Morgantown Rd
Reading, PA 19607-9533
610-373-1400
Fax: 610-373-7448 800-445-7898
Manufacturers of modualar plastic conveyor belts, chains and flat top chains
President: Christopher Nigon
VP Marketing/Sales: Joe Gianfalla
Marketing: Galina Rodzirosky
Estimated Sales: $10,000,000 - $19,999,999
Number Employees: 100-249
Type of Packaging: Bulk

23543 Habasit Belting
3453 Pierce Drive NE
Chamblee, GA 30341-2496
770-458-6431
Fax: 770-454-6164 800-458-6431
hbi.habasit@us.habasit.com www.habasitusa.com
Industrial flat belting
President: Harry Cardillo
Estimated Sales: $10-25 Million
Number Employees: 115

23544 Habasit Canada Limited
2275 Bristol Circle
Oakville, ON L6H 6P8
Canada
905-827-4131
Fax: 905-825-2612
Canada.CustomerCare@habasit.com
www.habasit.ca
Food handling conveyor belts, modular belts and flat power transmission belts.
President: John Visser
Plant Manager: Marty Ahearn
Number Employees: 30
Square Footage: 100000
Parent Co: Habasit AG

23545 Habco
1262 Windermere Way
Concord, CA 94521-3344
925-682-6203
Fax: 925-686-2036
Custom kitchen and galley equipment including steam tables, cabinets, counters and foodstands
Owner: Heidi Linder
CEO: Sarah Trissel
Estimated Sales: 500000
Number Employees: 1-4
Number of Brands: 50
Number of Products: 100
Square Footage: 2400

23546 Hach Co
5600 Lindbergh Dr
Loveland, CO 80538-8842
970-669-3050
Fax: 970-669-2932 800-227-4224
httc@hach.com www.hach.com
Supplier of water and wastewater analysis equipment, including products for laboratory and microbiology testing, on-line analysis, and flow and sampling measurement equipment
President: Kevin Klau
    kklau@hach.com
CFO: Jary Dreher
Number Employees: 1000-4999

23547 Hach Co
5600 Lindbergh Dr
Loveland, CO 80538-8842
970-669-3050
Fax: 970-669-2932 800-227-4224
info@gliint.com www.hach.com
Wine industry flow and level gauges
President: Kevin Klau
    kklau@hach.com
Number Employees: 1000-4999

23548 Hach Co.
PO Box 389
Loveland, CO 80539-0389
970-669-3050
Fax: 970-669-2932 800-227-4224
techhelp@hach.com
Manufacturer of oxygen sensors and water analysis products for the beverage and water bottling industries. Also manufactures, designs, and distributes test kits for testing the quality of water in food industry applications.
Contact: Leon Moore
    lmoore@hach.com

23549 Hackney Brothers
911 West 5th Street
Box 880
Washington, NC 27889
252-946-6521
Fax: 252-975-8340 800-763-0700
kgodley@vthackney.com
www.hackneybeverage.com
Manufacturer and exporter of refrigerated truck bodies and trailers; also, refrigeration systems and ice cream vending carts
Estimated Sales: $50-100 Million
Number Employees: 100-249
Square Footage: 220000
Type of Packaging: Food Service
Brands:
    Hackney
    Hackney Champion
    Hackney Classic
    Short Stop
    Sno Van
    Starlite
    Vari-Temp

23550 Haden Signs of Texas
1102 30th St
Lubbock, TX 79411
806-744-4404
Fax: 806-744-1327 hadensigns@nts-online.net
Illuminated and nonilluminated signs including neon, plexiglass, metal and vinyl; also, electronic message centers; service and installation available
President: Curt Jones
CFO: Delwin Jones
Estimated Sales: Below $5 Million
Number Employees: 5-9

23551 Hager Containers Inc
1015 Hayden Dr
Carrollton, TX 75006-5741
972-416-7660
Fax: 972-417-8875 www.englanderdzp.com
Corrugated boxes, partitions, point of purchase displays and value added packaging
President: Carl Renner
VP/General Manager: Carl Renner
Sales/Marketing Manager: Steve Main
Estimated Sales: $10-20 Million
Number Employees: 50-99

23552 Hagerty Foods
987 N Enterprise St
Suite J
Orange, CA 92867
714-628-1230
Condiments
President: Francisco Esquivel
Estimated Sales: $220,000
Number Employees: 3
Square Footage: 20000
Type of Packaging: Consumer, Food Service, Private Label
Brands:
Hagerty Foods
La Napa
Winemaker's Choice

23553 Hahn Laboratories
1111 Flora St
Columbia, SC 29201-4569
803-799-1614
Fax: 803-256-1417
Consultant and chemical analyst providing agricultural and food service testing
Owner: Frank Hahn
hahnlab@bellsouth.net
Lab Manager: Frank Hahn
Estimated Sales: $500,000-$1 Million
Number Employees: 1-4

23554 Haier American Trading
1356 Broadway
New York, NY 10018-7300
212-594-3330
Fax: 212-594-3434 www.haieramerica.com
Owner: Michael Jamal
Contact: Sal Alberta
salberta@haieramerica.com
Estimated Sales: $1 - 5 Million
Number Employees: 5-9

23555 Haifa Chemicals
6800 Jericho Tpke
Suite 216w
Syosset, NY 11791-4488
516-921-0044
Fax: 516-921-0228 800-404-2368
Sales Manager: JoAnn Sprung
Estimated Sales: $2.5-5 Million
Number Employees: 9

23556 Haines Packing Company
5 Mile Mud Bay Rd.
PO Box 290
Haines, AK 99827
907-766-2883
gennyrietze@gmail.com
www.hainespacking.com
Salmon, crab, halibut, and shrimp.
President/CEO: William Weisfield
Year Founded: 1917
Estimated Sales: 100 Million
Number Employees: 40
Number of Brands: 2
Square Footage: 5963
Type of Packaging: Consumer, Food Service, Bulk
Other Locations:
Whitehorse YT
Brands:
Northern Pride
Pirate

23557 Hairnet Corporation of America
151 W 26th St # 2
New York, NY 10001-6810
212-675-5840
Fax: 212-685-6225
Manufacturer and exporter of hairnets
President: E Gard
Secretary: M Moron
VP: T Persad
Estimated Sales: $2.5-5 Million
Number Employees: 1-4
Square Footage: 3500
Brands:
Jac-O-Net
Lady Swiss
Mirage

23558 Hal Mather & Sons
11803 Il Route 120
Woodstock, IL 60098-1900
815-338-4000
Fax: 815-338-3003 800-338-4007
Tags, labels and tickets
President: Douglas Mather
CFO: Paul Weathersby
VP: Jim Mather
General Manager: David Diverde
Estimated Sales: $5 - 10 Million
Number Employees: 1-4

23559 Hal-One Plastics
801 E Highway 56
Olathe, KS 66061-4999
913-782-3535
Fax: 913-764-7369 800-626-5784
Manufacturer and wholesaler/distributor of reusable plastic tableware and trays
CEO: Joyce Stawarz
1st Executive VP Sales: Galen Soule
Estimated Sales: $10 - 20 Million
Number Employees: 50-99
Square Footage: 60000

23560 Hall China Co
1 Anna St
East Liverpool, OH 43920-3675
330-385-2900
Fax: 330-385-6185 800-445-4255
custserv@hallchina.com www.hlcdinnerware.com
Chinaware
President: Chuck Henderson
chenderson@hallchina.com
National Sales Manager: Jim Clunk
National Distributor Account Manager: Joe Owen
National Chain Account Manager: Joe Brice
Estimated Sales: $20 - 50 Million
Number Employees: 100-249

23561 Hall Manufacturing Co
297 Margaret King Ave
Ringwood, NJ 07456-1423
973-962-6022
Fax: 973-962-7652 kerry@hallmanufacturing.com
Manufacturer and exporter of extruded plastic tracks for refrigeration industry; also, co-extrusions and tubing
President: Mike Goceljak
kerry@hallmanufacturing.com
Sales Manager: Kerry Goceljak
Estimated Sales: $2.5-5 Million
Number Employees: 10-19
Square Footage: 42000

23562 Hall Manufacturing Company
1321 Industrial Drive
Henderson, TX 75652-5019
903-657-4501
Fax: 903-657-4502
Tote bags
Contact: Steve Strain
steve@hallmfgco.com
Estimated Sales: $1-2.5 Million
Number Employees: 5-9

23563 Hall Safety Apparel
1020 W 1st St
Uhrichsville, OH 44683-2210
740-922-3671
Fax: 740-922-4880 800-232-3671
www.hallssafety.com
Protective Clothin Manufacturing; Supplier, Importer and Exporter
President: Delores Schneider
delores.schneider@pro-am.com
VP: Delores Schneider
Public Relations: Arnold Ziffel
Estimated Sales: $1-3 Million
Number Employees: 5-9
Square Footage: 42000
Parent Co: Schneider Enterprises USA
Type of Packaging: Food Service, Private Label, Bulk
Brands:
Polytex
Solvaseal

23564 Hall-Woolford Wood TankCo Inc
5500 N Water St
Philadelphia, PA 19120-3093
215-329-9022
Fax: 215-329-1177 jackhillman@woodtank.com
www.woodtank.com
Manufacturer and exporter of noncorrosive wood tanks, vats and tubs; wholesaler/distributor of flexible tank liners; industrial wood products; all products FDA approved. Also industrial wood products

President: Scott Hochhauser
woodtanks@aol.com
Sales Manager: Jack Hillman
Operations Manager: Robert Riepen
Estimated Sales: $1 - 3 Million
Number Employees: 5-9
Square Footage: 38000

23565 Hallams
5204 N 10th Ave
Ozark, MO 65721
417-581-3786
Fax: 417-581-3786 rzkozark@yahoo.com
Owner: Robert Zoppelt
Vice President: Katherine Zoppelt
Marketing Director: Robert Zoppelt
Estimated Sales: 300000
Number Employees: 1-4
Number of Brands: 1
Square Footage: 1800
Type of Packaging: Private Label

23566 Hallberg Manufacturing Corporation
PO Box 23985
Tampa, FL 33623-3985
800-633-7627
Fax: 800-253-7323
Manufacturer and exporter of industrial hand soap
President: Charles Hallberg
VP: Linda Werlein
Estimated Sales: $300,000-500,000
Square Footage: 20000
Brands:
Aloe Jell Water Less
Citra Jell
Pumice Jell
Surety Pwd Hand Soap

23567 Hallmark Equipment Inc
11040 Monterey Rd
Morgan Hill, CA 95037-9362
408-782-2600
Fax: 408-782-2605 hallmark@heiusa.com
www.heiusa.com
Supplier of used packaging and food processing equipment
Owner: Ron Wilson
hallmark@heiusa.com
Estimated Sales: $1 - 3 Million
Number Employees: 5-9

23568 Hallock Fabricating Corp
324 Doctors Path
Riverhead, NY 11901-1509
631-727-2441
Fax: 631-369-6021
Stainless steel and carbon steel exhaust hoods and countertops; also, custom metal fabrication
Owner: Cory Hallock
hallockfabricating@gmail.com
Estimated Sales: $1 - 5 Million
Number Employees: 1-4
Square Footage: 18400

23569 Halmark Systems Inc
354 Page St
Stoughton, MA 02072-1104
781-344-8616
Fax: 781-341-4505 800-225-5823
sales@halmarksystems.net
www.halmarksystems.net
Price marking equipment, custom-printed labels, and date marking equipment
President: Mark Crean
mark@halmarksystems.net
Operations: Lisa Allen
Estimated Sales: $5-10 Million
Number Employees: 10-19

23570 Halpak Plastics
10 Burt Dr
Deer Park, NY 11729-5702
631-242-1100
Fax: 631-242-6150 800-442-5725
Shrink bands and labels
Marketing Director: Sande Kaplan
Estimated Sales: $5-10 Million
Number Employees: 20-49

23571 Halton Company
101 Industrial Dr
Scottsville, KY 42164

270-237-5600
Fax: 270-237-5700 800-442-5866
Manufacturer and exporter of stainless steel hoods, filters and fans; also, fire suppression and ventilation systems
President: Rick Bagwell
R&D: Andre Livchak
Controller: Chris Gentry
National Sales Manager: Rich Catan
Contact: Ben Barshaw
  b.barshaw@petersoncat.com
Plant Manager: Phil Meredith
Purchasing Manager: Eric Key
Estimated Sales: $10 - 20 Million
Number Employees: 1250
Square Footage: 100000
Parent Co: Halton O.Y.
Brands:
  Capture Jet
  Capture Rey

23572 Halton Packaging Systems
1045 S Service Road W
Oakville, ON L6L 6K3
Canada

905-847-9141
Fax: 905-847-9145
Manufacturer and exporter of pallet packaging machinery including stretch wrapping, conveyors, and pallet handling machinery
President: Peter Hughes
Estimated Sales: $2 Million
Number Employees: 10-19
Square Footage: 120000
Brands:
  Halton

23573 Hamer Inc
14650 28th Ave N
Plymouth, MN 55447-4821

763-231-0100
Fax: 763-231-0101 800-927-4674
packaging@hamerinc.com www.hamerinc.com
Form-fill-seal systems, bag closers, bag fillers, balers
President: Dan Brown
  dan@hamerinc.com
Sales Manager: Jerome Eller
Estimated Sales: $5-10 Million
Number Employees: 20-49

23574 Hamersmith, Inc.
3200 NW 125 Street
Miami, FL 33167

305-685-7451
Fax: 305-681-6093 office@hamersmith.com
www.hamersmith.com
Shortenings, margarines, oils, puff paste, pan releases and spices; packagaing services
President: Calvin Theobald
Sales Director: Gerald Delmonico
Estimated Sales: $2.5-5 Million
Number Employees: 10
Number of Brands: 20
Number of Products: 9
Square Footage: 60000
Type of Packaging: Food Service, Private Label, Bulk

23575 Hamilton Awning Co
469 Market St
Beaver, PA 15009-2130

724-774-7644
Fax: 724-775-4221
Commercial awnings
Owner: Dave Mulcahy
Estimated Sales: $1-2,500,000
Number Employees: 5-9

23576 Hamilton Beach Brands
261 Yadkin Rd
Southern Pines, NC 28387-3415

910-692-7676
Fax: 910-692-7959 800-851-8900
www.hamiltonbeach.com
Foodservice equipment for restaurant, bars, nursing homes, healthcare facilities, hotels, and more
CEO: Michael J Morecroft
Sales Director: Steve Sarfaty
Public Relations: Kirby Kriz

Estimated Sales: $1 - 5 Million
Number Employees: 100-249
Parent Co: Nacco Industries
Type of Packaging: Food Service
Brands:
  Hamilton Beach
  Proctor Silex

23577 Hamilton Caster
1637 Dixie Hwy
Hamilton, OH 45011-4087

513-896-3541
Fax: 513-863-5508 888-699-7164
info@hamiltoncaster.com
www.hamiltoncaster.com
Manufacturer and exporter of nonpowered material handling carts, hand trucks, trailers, industrial casters and wheels
Vice President: Steve Lippert
  steve.lippert@hamiltoncaster.com
Executive VP: Steven Lippert
Quality Control: Mary Latimer
Marketing Director: Mark Lippert
Sales Director: James Lippert
Estimated Sales: $10 - 20 Million
Number Employees: 50-99
Brands:
  Ace-Tuf
  Aqualite
  Bondalast
  Cush-N-Aire
  Cush-N-Flex
  Cush-N-Tuf
  Duralast
  Ebonite
  Eleva-Truck
  Flexonite
  Freightainer
  Hi-Lo
  Instoematic
  Job-Built
  Leader
  Lite-N-Tuff
  Lube-Gard
  Maxi-Duty
  Nu-Flex
  Nu-Last
  Plastex
  Poly-Tech
  Roll Models
  Roll-N-Stor
  Stack-N-Roll
  Steeltest
  Super-Flex
  Superlast
  Ultra-Lite
  Unilast
  Versa-Tech
  Vulcalite

23578 Hamilton Kettles
2898 Birch Drive
Weirton, WV 26062-5142

304-794-9400
Fax: 304-794-9430 800-535-1882
Manufacturer and exporter of sanitary stainless steel and steam jacketed kettles, mix-cookers, pressure cookers, agitators, vacuum kettles and custom designed processing kettles and mixers
President: Charles Friend
Quality Control: Ed Henderson
VP/General Manager: George Gruner
R&D: Ed Henderson
Sales Director: Peggy Miller
Production Manager: Kenneth Henderson
Estimated Sales: $5 - 10 Million
Number Employees: 25
Square Footage: 128000
Parent Co: Allegheny Hancock Corporation

23579 Hamilton Manufacturing Corp
1026 Hamilton Dr
Holland, OH 43528-8210

419-867-4858
Fax: 419-867-4850 888-723-4858
www.hamiltonmfg.com
Currency validators and changemakers
President: Pam Anderson
  panderson@horstengineering.com
Sales: Tim Morgan
Estimated Sales: $10-20 Million
Number Employees: 50-99

23580 Hamilton Soap & Oil Products
51 Bleeker Street
Paterson, NJ 7524

973-225-1031
Fax: 973-225-0268
Soap and detergent; also, private label and contract packaging services available
Estimated Sales: $1 - 5 Million

23581 Hammar & Sons
71 Bridge St
PO Box 184
Pelham, NH 03076-3479

603-635-2292
Fax: 603-635-7904 800-527-7446
www.signsnownh.com
Signs including neon, wood, sandblasted window, in-store and aisle markers; also, banners and posters; installation and repair services available
Owner: Al Hammar
VP: Mike Hammar
Estimated Sales: Less Than $500,000
Number Employees: 5-9
Square Footage: 24000
Brands:
  Hammar

23582 Hammer Packaging Inc
200 Lucius Gordon Dr
West Henrietta, NY 14586

585-424-3880
Fax: 585-424-3886 www.hammerpackaging.com
Labels for the food and beverage industry; holticulture, wine and spirits and household products.
President & CEO: Jim Hammer
CFO: Mike Guche
SVP: Lou Iovoli
VP, Research & Innovation: Hart Swisher
VP, Manufacturing: Jason Hammer
VP, Sales: Matthew Kellman
Estimated Sales: $100-500 Million
Number Employees: 100-249
Square Footage: 92000
Type of Packaging: Consumer, Food Service, Private Label

23583 Hammerstahl Cutlery
3232 Woodsmill Drive
Melbourne, FL 32934

561-373-1925
Fax: 321-253-0737 felipe.florida@netzero.com
www.hammerstahl.com
Contact: Zuleik Urquiola
zuleik.urquiola@hammerstahl.com

23584 Hampden Papers Inc
100 Water St
Holyoke, MA 01040-6298

413-536-1000
Fax: 413-532-9161 www.hampdenpapers.com
Embossed and plain foil and glazed, laminated and gift wrapping paper, packaging components, FDA compliant
President/COO: Richard Wells
CEO: Robert Fowler
HR Executive: Marylou Mccormick
  mmccormick@hampdenpapers.com
Vice President of Sales and Marketing: Bob Adams
VP Operations: Michael Archambeault
Estimated Sales: $33 Million
Number Employees: 100-249
Square Footage: 400000

23585 Hampton Roads Box Company
619 E Pinner St
Suffolk, VA 23434

757-934-2355
Fax: 757-539-4918
Manufacturer and exporter of pallets, wooden boxes and shipping crates
President: Mark Sullivan
Estimated Sales: $1.2 Million
Number Employees: 5-9

23586 Hampton-Tilley Associates
740 Goddard Ave
Chesterfield, MO 63005

636-537-3353
Fax: 636-536-4114 813-418-3340
info@dcreng.com www.dcreng.com

Consultant specializing in automation and engineering services; designer of software for recipes, cooking, processing, packaging and quality control/validation
Manager: Pat Finefield
VP: C Tilley
Estimated Sales: $5 - 10 Million
Number Employees: 10-19
Square Footage: 42000

23587 Hamrick Manufacturing &Svc
1436 Martin Rd
PO Box 5
Mogadore, OH 44260-1591

330-628-4877
Fax: 330-628-2180 800-321-9590
marketing@hamrickmfg.com
www.hamrickmfg.com
Manufacturer and exporter of packaging machinery including case packers, case sealers, bottled water case packers, lock tab pullers/breakers, liter tray packers, four flap openers, uncasers, etc.; custom built machinery available
President: Phil Hamrick
phamrick@hamrickmfg.com
CEO: Luther Hamrick
VP Sales: Tom Hamrick
VP of Production: Phil Hamrick
Purchasing Director: Kurt Kothmayer
Estimated Sales: $5-10 Million
Number Employees: 20-49
Number of Products: 18
Square Footage: 56000
Brands:
    Hms

23588 Hanco Manufacturing Company
1301 Heistan Place
Memphis, TN 38104

901-725-7364
Fax: 901-726-5899 800-530-7364
Disinfectants, insecticides, cleaners and degreasers
VP: Scott Hanover
Estimated Sales: $1-2.5 Million
Number Employees: 19
Square Footage: 60000
Brands:
    Hanco

23589 Hand Made Lollies
465 S Orlando Avenue
Suite 205
Maitland, FL 32751

877-784-2724
Fax: 877-249-6419 info@handmadelollies.com
www.handmadelollies.com
Handmade and personalized lollipops
President: Timothy Lang

23590 Handgards Inc
901 Hawkins Blvd
El Paso, TX 79915-1202

915-779-6606
Fax: 915-779-1312 800-351-8161
sales@handgards.com www.handgards.com
Manufacturer and exporter of disposable plastic gloves, aprons and bags; importer of latex and PVC gloves
CEO: Bob Mclellan
bmclellan@handgards.com
CEO: Bob McLellan
Estimated Sales: $500,000-$1,000,000
Number Employees: 250-499
Square Footage: 280000
Type of Packaging: Food Service, Private Label
Brands:
    Handgards
    Neatgards
    Tuffgards
    Valugards
    Zipgards

23591 Handi-Foil Corp
135 E Hintz Rd
Wheeling, IL 60090-6059

847-520-8347
Fax: 847-229-8000 www.handi-foil.com
Foil wrap
CEO: Norton Sarnoff
nsarnoff@handi-foil.com
CEO: Norton Sarnoff
Estimated Sales: $1 - 3 Million
Number Employees: 20-49

23592 Handicap Sign Inc
1142 Wealthy St SE
Grand Rapids, MI 49506-1599

616-454-9416
Fax: 616-454-4999 800-690-4888
handicapsign@gmail.com www.hsisign.com
Custom screen printing, vinyl graphics and hand lettering for decals, signs, posters, banners and P.O.P displays
President: Charles Tasma
handicapsign@gmail.com
VP: Kim Tasma
Estimated Sales: $500,000-$1 Million
Number Employees: 5-9
Square Footage: 15000

23593 Handling Specialty
PO Box 279
Niagara Falls, NY 14304-0279

716-694-6333
Fax: 716-694-6903 800-559-8366
info@handling.com www.handling.com
Manufacturer and exporter of material handling equipment including lifting systems for very hot or cold environments, tilters, rotators, fork truck service lifts and robotic indexing tables
President: Thomas Beach
Marketing Director: Lydia Macugajlo
Direct Sales: Mike Roper
Contact: Linda Videto
lvideto@handling.com
Estimated Sales: $1,000,000 - $2,499,999
Number Employees: 10-19
Parent Co: Handling Specialty
Brands:
    Forklevator

23594 Handtmann
28690 N.
Ballard Drive
Lake Forest, IL 60045

847-808-1100
Fax: 847-808-1106 800-477-3585
www.handtmann.com
Vacuum fillers with in-line grinders, and high speed clipping machines
President: Steve Tennis
Sales Director: Robert Kors
Estimated Sales: $5 - 10 000,000
Number Employees: 20-49

23595 Handtmann Inc
28690 N Ballard Dr
Lake Forest, IL 60045-4500

847-808-1100
Fax: 847-808-1106 800-477-3585
www.handtmann.us
Filling, portioning and linking machines for the sausage and meat industries. Also manufacture deli product systems and grinding machines.
President: Tom Kittle
tom.kittle@handtmann.us
Number Employees: 20-49

23596 Handy Manufacturing Co Inc
337 Sherman Ave
Newark, NJ 07114-1507

973-242-1600
Fax: 973-733-2185 800-631-4280
www.handystorefixtures.com
Manufacturer and exporter of store and wall fixtures, show cases, gondolas and shelving units
President: Paul Kurland
richardkurland@handystorefixtures.com
CFO: Scott McClymont
Executive VP: Richard Kurland
VP Sales: Walter Pincus
Number Employees: 50-99
Square Footage: 1200000
Type of Packaging: Food Service

23597 Handy Roll Company
1236 Anna Lane
San Marcos, CA 92069-2160

760-471-6214
Carton cutters
Co-Owner: Glenn Spear
Co-Owner: Margaret Spear
Number Employees: 1
Brands:
    Handy Blade

23598 Handy Wacks Corp
100 E Averill St
P.O. Box 129
Sparta, MI 49345

800-445-4434
customerserv@handywacks.com
www.handywacks.com
Waxed packaging products including sandwich and interfolded high density polyethylene wrap, baking cups, hot dog trays, and steak, freezer, locker, delicatessen and bakery tissue and paper.
CIS Director: Bruce Stevens
Sales Director: George Siwik
Purchasing Manager: Mike Moberly
Year Founded: 1929
Estimated Sales: $20-25 Million
Number Employees: 50+
Number of Brands: 12
Number of Products: 225
Square Footage: 90000
Type of Packaging: Food Service
Brands:
    Handy Wacks

23599 Hanel Storage Systems
121 Industry Dr
Pittsburgh, PA 15275-1015

412-787-3444
Fax: 412-787-3744 info@hanel.us
www.hanel.us
Manufacturer, importer and exporter of vertical storage systems
President: Joachim Hanel
CEO: Brian Cohen
bcohen@hanel.us
Vice President: Brian Cohen
VP: Brian Cohen
Sales Director: Michael Fanning
Estimated Sales: $5-10 Million
Number Employees: 20-49
Parent Co: Hanel GmbH
Brands:
    Hanel Lean-Lift
    Hanel Vertical Carousels

23600 Haney, Inc.
5657 Wooster Pike
Cincinnati, OH 45227

513-561-1441
haneypkg.com
Manufacturer of packaging and containers.
Co-Founder & President: Dan Haney
CEO: Matt Haney
Year Founded: 1990
Estimated Sales: $13.8 Million

23601 Hangzhou Sanhe USA Inc.
20536 Carrey Rd
Walnut, CA 91789

909-869-6016
Fax: 909-869-6015 www.sanheinc.com
Food ingredients and additives.
President: Aili Chen
Contact: Yun Qian
yunqian@sanheinc.com
Estimated Sales: $1 Million
Type of Packaging: Bulk

23602 Hank Rivera Associates
13600 W Warren Ave
Dearborn, MI 48126-1421

313-581-8300
Manufacturer and exporter of uniforms, aprons and pizza delivery equipment including heat retention/insulated food bags, nylon pan pullers, beverage carriers and pizza lid supports
President: Dante Rivera
Secretary/Treasurer: Hank Rivera
Number Employees: 10-19
Square Footage: 25000
Brands:
    Hank's

23603 Hankin Specialty Elevators Inc
3237 Fitzgerald Rd
Rancho Cordova, CA 95742-6813

916-381-2400
Fax: 916-381-2481 800-831-8395
info@hankinspecialty.com
www.hankinspecialty.com
Wine industry pallet postitioners
President and QC: Neil Hankin
neilh@hankinspecialty.com
CFO: Mike Seebode

Estimated Sales: $5 - 10 Million
Number Employees: 10-19

23604 Hankison International
1000 Philadelphia St
Canonsburg, PA 15317-1700

724-746-1100
Fax: 724-745-6040 www.spx-hankison.de
Manufacturer and exporter of compressed air dryers, filters, condensate drains and air purifiers
Manager: Neal Horrigan
Marketing: Bill Kennedy
Sales: Rod Smith
Manager: Ken Gorman
Estimated Sales: $5-10 Million
Number Employees: 20-49
Square Footage: 808000
Parent Co: Hansen

23605 Hanley Sign Company
26 Sicker Rd
Latham, NY 12110

518-783-6183
Fax: 518-783-0128 ltymchyn@hanleysign.com
Signs and advertising displays
President: Lisa Tymchyn
Quality Control: Lisa Tymchyn
Contact: Kerry Blinn
 kblinn@hanleysign.com
Estimated Sales: Below $5 Million
Number Employees: 20-49
Square Footage: 16000

23606 Hanna Instruments
584 Park E Dr
Woonsocket, RI 02895

401-765-7500
Fax: 401-765-7575 800-426-6287
info@hannainst.com
Manufacturer and exporter of electro-analytical instruments including sodium chloride and chlorine analyzers, conductivity, pH and relative humidity meters, temperature recorders and thermo hygrometers.
President: Martino Nardo
Vice President: Pamela Nardo
General Manager: Harry Lau
Year Founded: 1978
Estimated Sales: $100 Million
Number Employees: 20-49
Number of Products: 3000
Square Footage: 26000
Type of Packaging: Consumer, Food Service, Bulk
Brands:
 Agricare
 Bravo
 Champ
 Checker
 Checktemp
 Conmet
 Elth
 Food Care
 Hydrocheck
 Key
 Micro Phep
 Phandy
 Phep
 Piccolo
 Temp Care
 Temp Check

23607 Hannan Products
220 N Smith Ave
Corona, CA 92880-1740

951-735-1587
Fax: 951-735-0827 800-954-4266
sales@hannanpak.com
Manufacturer and exporter of machinery and materials for skin and blister packaging; also, for die cutting
President: Damon Lewis
 damon@hannanpak.com
CFO and QC and R&D: Alfred Ramos
Sales Manager: Lawrence Jenkins
Estimated Sales: $5 - 10 Million
Number Employees: 20-49

23608 Hannay Reels
553 State Route 143
Westerlo, NY 12193-2691

518-797-3791
Fax: 518-797-3259 877-467-3357
reels@hannay.com www.hannay.com

Metal reels for hose & cable, water, washdown, fluid handling
President: Eric Hannay
COO: Elaine Gruener
Quality Control: Ken Fritz
Marketing Manager: Jennifer Wing
Sales Manager: Mark Saker
Public Relations: Maureen Bagshaw
President/CEO: Eric Hannay
Production: Mike Ferguson
Facilities Manager: Walt Scram
Materials Manager: Dick Storm
Estimated Sales: $25-50 Million
Number Employees: 100-249
Square Footage: 118612

23609 Hannic Freight Forwarders Inc
16214 S Lincoln Hwy
PO Box 445
Plainfield, IL 60586-5146

815-436-4521
Fax: 815-436-1734 800-786-4521
www.hannic.net
Owner: Hans Maass
 hans@hffi.net
Vice President: Hans Maass
Estimated Sales: $.5 - 1 million
Number Employees: 5-9

23610 Hano Business Forms
PO Box 275
Wilbraham, MA 01095-0275

413-781-7800
Fax: 413-781-7808 www.hano.com
Printed documents
CEO and President: John Sindstorm
VP: Jim Michill
Number Employees: 50

23611 Hansaloy Corp
820 W 35th St
Davenport, IA 52806-5800

563-386-1131
Fax: 563-386-7707 800-553-4992
sales@hansaloy.com www.hansaloy.com
Manufacturer and exporter of blades including slicing/dicing, band and reciprocating with scalloped and straight edges for slicing bread and boneless meat
Owner: Diane Artioli
CEO: Howard H Cherry Iii
Quality Control: Stephen Wright
VP Sales/Marketing: K Brenner
VP Sales: Allen Wright
 d.artioli@hansaloy.com
Estimated Sales: $5 - 10 Million
Number Employees: 50-99
Square Footage: 80000

23612 Hansen Technologies Corporation
400 Quadrangle Dr Ste F
Bolingbrook, IL 60440

630-325-1565
Fax: 630-325-1572 800-426-7368
info@hantech.com www.hantech.com
Hansen Technologies Corporation offers an extensive line of components for industrial refrigeration systems including sealed motor valves, control valves, shut-off valves, pressure-relief valves, refrigerant pumps, air purgers, defrostcontrols, and liquid level controls
President: Jeffrey Nank
CEO: Jeff Markham
CFO: Mark Sebben
R&D: John Yencho
Marketing Manager: Denise Ernst
Sales: Harold Streicher
Contact: Phillip Beste
 pbeste@hantech.com
Operations: Jim Flurry
Purchasing Director: Joe Reicher
Estimated Sales: $20 - 50 Million
Number Employees: 100-249
Number of Brands: 3
Number of Products: 300

23613 Hansen's Laboratory
N67w33880 Loghouse Ct
Oconomowoc, WI 53066-1936

262-966-4952
Fax: 414-607-5959
Culture research
Owner: Marsha Hanson

Estimated Sales: $1 - 3 000,000
Number Employees: 5-9

23614 Hanset Stainless Inc
1729 NE Argyle St
Portland, OR 97211-1801

503-283-8822
Fax: 503-283-8875 800-360-7030
info@hansetstainless.com
www.hansetstainless.com
Custom stainless steel food service equipment
President: Jim Hanset
 jim@hansetstainless.com
Estimated Sales: $20-50 Million
Number Employees: 50-99
Square Footage: 25000

23615 Hanson Box & Lumber Company
12 New Salem Street
Wakefield, MA 01880-1979

617-245-0358
Fax: 781-245-8043
Plywood and pine boxes, shipping containers, pallets and skids
President: Kirk Hanson

23616 Hanson Brass Rewd Co
7530 San Fernando Rd
Sun Valley, CA 91352-4344

818-767-3501
Fax: 818-767-7891 888-841-3773
info@hansonbrass.com www.hansonhl.com
Sneeze guards, copper carts and brass, chrome and copper lamps; exporter of carving units, food displays; wholesaler/distributor of restaurant equipment and supplies; serving the food service market, alto shaam test kitchen
President: Tom Hanson
VP: Jim Hanson
CFO: Tom Hanson
 info@hansonbrass.com
Vice President: Robert Hanson
Plant Manager: Mark Denny
Estimated Sales: $6-7 Million
Number Employees: 10-19
Number of Brands: 2
Square Footage: 32000
Brands:
 Hanson Brass

23617 Hanson Brass Rewd Co
7530 San Fernando Rd
Sun Valley, CA 91352-4344

818-767-3501
Fax: 818-767-7891 888-841-3773
info@hansonbrass.com www.hansonhl.com
President: Tom Hanson Jr
CEO: Jim Hanson
CFO: Tom Hanson Sr
VP: Robert Hanson
Plant Manager: Mark Denny
Number Employees: 10-19

23618 Hanson Lab Furniture Inc
814 Mitchell Rd
Newbury Park, CA 91320-2215

805-498-3121
Fax: 805-498-1855 info@hansonlab.com
www.hansonlab.com
Manufacturer and exporter of laboratory furniture, fume hoods and accessories; also, installation and lab planning services available
Owner: Joe Matta
 joe@hansonlab.com
VP: Mike Hanson
Estimated Sales: $5 - 10 Million
Number Employees: 5-9
Parent Co: Norlab

23619 (HQ)Hantover Inc
10301 Hickman Mills Dr # 200
Kansas City, MO 64137-1600

816-761-7800
Fax: 816-761-0044 800-821-7849
contactus@hantover.com
Manufacturer and exporter of vacuum packaging machinery and stainless steel cutlery and utensils
Chairman: Bernard Huff
General Manager: David Philgreen
Estimated Sales: $20 - 50 Million
Number Employees: 100-249
Type of Packaging: Food Service

Other Locations:
Hantover
Kansas City MO

23620 Hapco Inc
390 Portage Blvd
Kent, OH 44240-7283
330-678-9353
Fax: 330-677-8282 800-345-9353
www.hapcoinc.com
Hot air tools, sealing equipment
Owner: Charles George
mike@hapcoinc.com
VP: Mike Harrison
Estimated Sales: $10-20 Million
Number Employees: 20-49

23621 Hapco Inc
390 Portage Blvd
Kent, OH 44240-7283
330-678-9353
Fax: 330-677-8282 800-345-9553
www.hapcoinc.com
Owner: Charles George
mike@hapcoinc.com
Estimated Sales: $10 - 20 Million
Number Employees: 20-49

23622 Hapman Conveyors
6002 E N Ave
Kalamazoo, MI 49048-9775
269-343-1675
Fax: 269-349-2477 800-968-7722
info@hapman.com
Manufacturer and exporter of flexible screw, pneumatic and tubular drag conveyors, bulk bag unloaders, manual bag dump stations, batch weigh equipment and silo dischargers
President: Edward Thompson
info@hapman.com
Quality Control: Randy McBroom
Marketing: Greg Nowak
Estimated Sales: $20 - 50 Million
Number Employees: 50-99
Square Footage: 100000
Parent Co: Prab
Brands:
Helix
Mini-Vac

23623 Happy Chef Inc
22 Park Pl # 2
Suite 2
Butler, NJ 07405-1377
973-492-2525
Fax: 973-492-0303 800-347-0288
info@happychefuniforms.com
www.happychefuniforms.com
Manufacturer and wholesaler/distributor of uniforms and table linens for kitchen and waiter/waitress personnel. Serving the food service market
Vice President: Howard Curtin
info@happychefuniforms.com
VP: Howard Curtin
VP, Sales/Marketing: Howard Curtin
Estimated Sales: $10 Million
Number Employees: 20-49
Square Footage: 30000
Type of Packaging: Private Label

23624 Harbor Group Inc
1520 N Main Ave
Sioux Center, IA 51250-2111
712-722-1662
Fax: 712-722-1667 bdev@interstates.com
www.interstates.com
Electrical engineering, electrical construction and automation
Chairman of the Board: Larry Den Herder
CEO: Scott Peterson
scott.peterson@harborcg.com
CFO: Scott Peterson
Estimated Sales: $40 - 60 Million
Number Employees: 100-249
Number of Brands: 4

23625 Harbor Pallet Company
301 W Imperial Hwy
Anaheim, CA 90631
714-871-0932
Fax: 714-871-3483 pomonabox@att.net
www.harborpallet.com
Wooden and plastic pallets and skids and wooden boxes and containers

President: Ross Gilroy
Estimated Sales: $2.5-5 Million
Number Employees: 5-9

23626 Harborlite Corporation
PO Box 519
Lompoc, CA 93438-0519
800-342-8667
Fax: 805-735-5699 info@worldminerals.com
www.worldminerals.com
Manufacturer and exporter of perlite filter aids and functional fillers
Contact: Mike Mcdonald
mike.mcdonald@worldminerals.com
Type of Packaging: Food Service, Bulk

23627 Harborlite Corporation
P.O. Box 462908
Escondido, CA 92046-2908
760-745-5900
Fax: 760-745-6349 www.worldminerals.com
Wine industry filtration and wastewater systems
Manager: Darin Jackman
d.jackman@imerys.com
Estimated Sales: $2.5-5 Million
Number Employees: 10-19

23628 Harbour House Bar Crafting
737 Canal Street
Bldg 16
Stamford, CT 06902-5930
203-348-6906
Fax: 203-348-6190 800-755-1227
bigbars@snet.net www.harbourhouse.com
Manufacturer solid wooden bars, tables, booths and carts
President: Steven Kline
VP: Jeff Watkins
Estimated Sales: $1-2.5 Million
Number Employees: 10
Type of Packaging: Food Service

23629 Harbour House Furniture
37 Canal Street
Bldg 16
Stamford, CT 06902-5930
203-348-6906
Fax: 203-348-6190 bigbars@snet.net
www.harbourhouse.com
President: Steven Kline

23630 Harbro Packaging Co
2635 N Kildare Ave
Chicago, IL 60639-2051
773-489-6520
Fax: 773-489-6584 877-428-5812
www.purepoolcleaning.com
Distributor of tabletop and stand - alone vacuum machines
President: Hershcel Brohman
rand_thomas@harbro.net
CFO: Susan Thomas
Quality Control: Rand Thomas
Estimated Sales: $5 - 10 Million
Number Employees: 10-19

23631 Harco Enterprises
675 the Parkway
Peterborough, ON K9J 7K2
Canada
705-743-5361
Fax: 705-743-4312 800-361-5361
sales@harco.on.ca www.harco.on.ca
Manufacturer, wholesaler/distributor and exporter of promotional items including hot stamping, pad printing, multi-color imprints, glow-in-the-dark custom products, coasters, swizzle sticks, toys, flyers, key tags, spoons, etc; servingthe food service market. Supplier of spare parts to the dairy and food industries
President: Ray Harris
VP Finance: Kathy Perry
VP: Terry Harris
VP Marketing: Kathy Perry
VP Administration: Joan Harris
Number Employees: 10
Square Footage: 64000
Type of Packaging: Food Service

23632 Harcros Chemicals Inc
5200 Speaker Rd
Kansas City, KS 66106-1048
913-321-3131
Fax: 913-621-7718 KansasCityCS@harcros.com
www.harcroschem.com
Surface active agents and medicinal chemicals
President, Chief Executive Officer: Kevin Mirner
kmirner@harcros.com
Vice President: Dan Larsen
Director of Operations: Dan Johnson
Number Employees: 250-499

23633 Hardi-Tainer
P.O. Box 201
South Deerfield, MA 01373-0201
413-665-2163
Fax: 413-665-4801 800-882-9878
hardiggacct@hardigg.com www.hardigg.com
Returnable and reusable intermediate bulk containers with wide mouth openings
President, Chief Executive Officer: Lyndon Faulkner
CEO: James S Hardigg
Vice President of Research: Kevin Deighton
Vice President of Sales: Mark Rolfes
Estimated Sales: $20 - 50 Million
Number Employees: 250-499
Square Footage: 100000
Parent Co: Hardigg Industries
Brands:
Hardi-Tainer

23634 Hardin Signs Inc
3663 N Meadowbrook Rd
Peoria, IL 61604-1214
309-688-4111
Fax: 309-688-3217
Signs including neon plastic; also, lettering, installation and maintenance services available
President: William Hardin
sales@hardinsigns.com
CFO: Marian Hardin
VP: James Hardin
Estimated Sales: $2.2 Million
Number Employees: 10-19
Square Footage: 48000
Type of Packaging: Bulk

23635 Hardt Equipment Manufacturing
1756 50th Avenue
Lachine, QC H8T 2V5
Canada
888-848-4408
www.hardt.ca
Designer and manufacturer of food service equipment including commercial rotisseries, heated merchandisers, counter-top heated display cases and a cleaning apparatus for cookin utensils and accessories.
Purchasing Manager: Tony Morrone
Number Employees: 75
Square Footage: 112000
Brands:
Inferno
Snack Zone
The Cleaning Solution
Zone

23636 Hardware Components Inc
1021 Park Ave
New Matamoras, OH 45767
740-865-2424
Fax: 740-865-2534
hci@hardwarecomponents.com
www.hardwarecomponents.com
Manufacturer and importer of ferrous and nonferrous castings, stampings, forgings, furniture and cabinets
Vice President: Dan Gautschi
hci@hardwarecomponents.com
VP/General Manager: Danny Gautschi
VP Sales: Chris Dickinson
Estimated Sales: $5 - 10,000,000
Number Employees: 1-4

23637 Hardwood Products Co LP
31 School St
Guilford, ME 04443-6388
207-876-3311
Fax: 207-876-3130 800-289-3340
www.hwppuritan.com

Manufacturer and exporter of wooden ice cream sticks and spoons, stir sticks and skewers; also, industrial cleaning swabs, cocktail forks, cocktail spears, corn dog sticks, flag sticks, fan paddles, dawels
Chief Finacial Officer: Scott Welman
Quality Control: William Young
Sales Manager: Ann Erickson
Sales Exec: Timothy Templet
CSR Rep: Jessica Brown
ttemplet@hwppuritan.com
VP of Operations: James Cartwright
Plant Manager: Bruce Jones
Purchasing Agent: Joseph Cartwright
Estimated Sales: $20-50 Million
Number Employees: 250-499
Square Footage: 600000
Type of Packaging: Consumer, Food Service, Private Label, Bulk
Brands:
 Gold Bond
 Puritan
 Purswab
 Trophy

23638 Hardy Diagnostics
1430 W Mccoy Ln
Santa Maria, CA 93455-1005
805-346-2766
Fax: 805-346-2760 800-266-2222
techservice@hardydiagnostics.com
www.hardydiagnostics.com
Owner: Jay Hardy
burksr@hardydiagnostics.com
CFO: Nathaniel Gragssle
Estimated Sales: $10-20 000,000
Number Employees: 100-249

23639 Hardy Process SolutionsInc
9440 Carroll Park Dr # 150
San Diego, CA 92121-5201
858-278-2900
Fax: 858-278-6700 800-821-5831
hardyinfo@hardyinst.com
www.hardysolutions.com
Designer and manufacturer of process weighin, tension control and vibration monitoring equipment serving the food, chemical, petrochemical, pharamautical, feed and grain, mining and metal, pulp and paper, oil and gas, and generalautomation industries.
Manager: Jim Ephraim
Sales: Jerry Samaniego
Manager: Steven Barron
sbarron@hardyinst.com
Number Employees: 50-99

23640 Hardy Systems Corporation
610 Anthony Trl
Northbrook, IL 60062
847-272-4400
Fax: 847-272-4471 800-927-3956
Manufacturer and exporter of bins, batching scales, conveying systems and flow control panels
President: Richard Walter
Sales Manager: J Soling
Head Engineer: D Acker
Estimated Sales: Below $5,000,000
Number Employees: 5-9

23641 Hardy-Graham
P.O. Box 487
Ambler, PA 19002
215-699-6111
Fax: 215-699-6106 800-445-4271
www.hardy-builtfastener.com
Knock-down, returnable, reusable crates and containers made of wood, metal, plastic
President: A Stuart Graham
CFO: A Stuart Graham
Contact: Diane Alexander
adiane@hardy-builtfastener.com
Estimated Sales: Below $5 Million
Number Employees: 5-9

23642 Harford Duracool LLC
P.O. Box 1026
Aberdeen, MD 21001-6026
410-272-9999
Fax: 410-272-8508
Walk-in coolers
President: Arley Mead
Operations: Charles Mike
Sales Manager: Scott Smith

Number Employees: 50-99
Parent Co: IPC Industries
Brands:
 Harford Duracool

23643 Harford Systems Inc
2225 Pulaski Hwy
Havre De Grace, MD 21078-2145
410-272-3400
Fax: 410-273-7892 800-638-7620
pwatson@harfordsystems.com
www.harfordsystems.com
Manufacturer and exporter of alarm systems and refrigeration equipment and machinery
President: Ralph Ahrens
VP: George Gabriel
HR Manager: Kate Pelonquin
Estimated Sales: $20-50 Million
Number Employees: 100-249
Parent Co: Bio Medic Corporation
Brands:
 Duracool

23644 Harlan Laws Corp
304 Muldee St
Durham, NC 27703-2332
919-596-2124
Fax: 919-596-0421 800-596-7602
sales@harlanlaws.com www.harlanlaws.com
Signs including electric and neon
Owner: Kenny Lester
klester@harlanlaws.com
VP: Gary Hester
Estimated Sales: $10-20 Million
Number Employees: 100-249
Square Footage: 100000

23645 Harland America
1803 Underwood Blvd
Delran, NJ 08075
856-764-9622
Fax: 856-764-9615
us.enquiries@harland-hms.com
Manager: John Lyall
Contact: Mike Habeck
mikehabeck@harland-hms.com
Estimated Sales: $2.5 - 5 Million
Number Employees: 10-19

23646 Harland Simon Control Systems USA
Windsor Office Plaza
210 West 22nd Street, Suite 138
Oakbrook, IL 60523
630-572-7650
Fax: 630-572-7653 sales@harlandsimon.com
Manufacturer and exporter of control systems including drive systems
Systems Sales Manager: Robert Picknell
National Sales Support Manager: Scott Mincher
Number Employees: 70
Square Footage: 164000
Parent Co: Monotype Systems
Brands:
 Micropower
 Micropower Ac
 Symtec

23647 Harmar
2075 47th St
Sarasota, FL 34234-3109
941-351-2776
Fax: 941-351-5801 800-833-0478
garys@harmar.com www.harmar.com
Custom wire displays and wire forms; also, bending spot welding and coated parts available
President: Robert Williams
Founder, President, Chief Executive Offi: Chad Williams
Vice President of Sales: Paul Johnson
Vice President of Operations: Todd Walters
Estimated Sales: $10-20 Million
Number Employees: 5-9
Square Footage: 90000

23648 Harmony Enterprises
704 Main Ave N
Harmony, MN 55939-8839
507-886-6666
Fax: 507-886-6706 800-658-2320
info@harmony1.com www.harmony1.com

Manufacturer and exporter of waste handling and recycling equipment including indoor and outdoor compactors, vertical balers, beverage extraction equipment and full product destruction equipment. Some of their brands include HarmonyPower Packer, Harmony Insite Wireless Monitoring, Harmony SunPak Solar Options, Harmony Equipment Rental, Harmony ExtractPack and more.
President: Steve Cremer
Office Manager & Finance: Lana Soppa
New Business Development Manager: Lane Powell
Vice President, Sales & Marketing: Brent Christiansen
National Sales Manager: Nick Roberts
Vice President, Operations: Ramon Hernandez
Purchasing: Sid Polley
Estimated Sales: $24 Million
Number Employees: 75
Other Locations:
 Harmony MN
Brands:
 Gpi

23649 Harold F Haines Manufacturing Inc
243 Main St
Presque Isle, ME 04769-2899
207-762-1411
Fax: 207-762-1412
Potato handling equipment, sizers and washers
Owner: Fred Haines
VP: Harold Haines
Estimated Sales: $2.5-5 Million
Number Employees: 10-19

23650 Harold Import Co Inc
747 Vassar Ave
Lakewood, NJ 08701-6908
732-367-2800
Fax: 732-364-3253 800-526-2163
www.hickitchen.com
Paper, brewers (tea), filters (cloth, cotton), grinders.
President: Mildred Laub Polansky
mpolansky@haroldimport.com
Estimated Sales: $50 - 100 Million
Number Employees: 100-249

23651 Harold Leonard Southwest Corporation
1812 Brittmoore Road
Suite 230
Houston, TX 77043-2216
713-467-8105
Fax: 713-467-0072 800-245-8105
Manufacturer and wholesaler/distrbutor of smallwares
President: Carl Marcus
CEO: Herb Kelleher
Marketing Director: Roger Randall
Sales Representative: Jerry Williams
Estimated Sales: $1-2.5 Million
Number Employees: 6
Square Footage: 100000
Parent Co: Harold Leonard & Company
Brands:
 Eagleware

23652 Harold M. Lincoln Company
2130 Madison Ave
Suite 101
Toledo, OH 43604-5135
419-255-1200
Broker of confectionery and dairy/deli products, frozen foods, general merchandise, groceries, etc. Marketing, sales planning and promotional tracking services available
President: David Lincoln
Chairman: Harold Lincoln
VP/Account Manager: John Lincoln
Estimated Sales: $20-50 Million
Number Employees: 7
Square Footage: 7000

23653 Harold Wainess & Assoc
2045 N Dunhill Ct N
Arlington Hts, IL 60004-3179
847-259-6400
Fax: 847-259-6460 847-722-8744
kenderson@aol.com www.haroldwainess.com
Food safety consultant providing audits, food equipment evaluations and testing
V.P.: Kenneth Anderson
kenderson@aol.com
R&D: Erickson

Estimated Sales: Below $5 Million
Number Employees: 1-4

23654 Harpak-ULMA Packaging LLC
175 John Quincy Adams Rd
Taunton, MA 02780-1035

508-238-8884
Fax: 508-238-8885 www.harpak-ulma.com
Flexible packaging machinery
President: Linda Harlfinger
lindaharlfinger@harpak.com
VP: Harvey Fine
Number Employees: 20-49
Type of Packaging: Consumer, Food Service, Private Label, Bulk
Brands:
Ulma

23655 Harpak-ULMA Packaging LLC
3035 Torrington Dr
Ball Ground, GA 30107-4543

770-345-5300
Fax: 770-345-5322 www.harpak-ulma.com
Packaging machines and packaging solutions such as traysealers, vertical and side seal packaging, blister packaging and film.
Manager: Ron Hartwig
ronhartwig@harpak-ulma.com
Number Employees: 10-19

23656 Harpak-Ulma
175 John Quincy Adams Rd
Taunton, MA 02780-1035

508-884-2500
Fax: 508-884-2501 800-813-6644
info@harpak-ULMA.com www.harpak-ulma.com
Supplier of engineered packaging equipment and complete automated systems.
Field Sales Manager: Jerry Rundle
Estimated Sales: $60 Million
Number Employees: 88
Type of Packaging: Food Service, Private Label, Bulk
Brands:
Rama

23657 Harper Associates
31000 Northwestern Hwy # 240
Farmington Hills, MI 48334-2564

248-932-1170
Fax: 248-932-1214 Info@HarperJobs.com
www.harperjobs.com
Personnel placement specialist for the hospitality industry
President: Ben Schwartz
ben@harperjobs.com
Vice President: Cindy Kramer
CEO: Ben Schwartz
Estimated Sales: $500,000 - $1 Million
Number Employees: 5-9

23658 Harper Brush Works Inc
400 N 2nd St
Fairfield, IA 52556-2416

641-472-5186
Fax: 641-472-3187 800-223-7894
www.harperbrush.com
Manufacturer and exporter of brooms, brushes, mops and squeegees
CEO: Barry Harper
barry.harper@harperbrush.com
Marketing: Pat Adam
Sales: Jerry Armstrong
Public Relations: Pat Adam
Operations: Don Sander
Purchasing Director: Randy Rhoads
Estimated Sales: $20 - 50 Million
Number Employees: 100-249
Type of Packaging: Consumer, Food Service, Bulk

23659 Harper Trucks Inc
1522 S Florence St
Wichita, KS 67209-2634

316-942-1381
Fax: 316-942-8508 800-835-4099
www.harpertrucks.com
Manufacturer and exporter of industrial trucks

President: Phil G Ruffin
pruffin@harpertrucks.com
CFO: Phillip Ruffin
Vice President: Gary Leiker
Marketing Director: David Rife
Sales Director: Judy Darnell
Plant Manager: Hugh Sales
Purchasing Manager: Sonya Kellogg
Estimated Sales: $20 Million
Number Employees: 100-249
Number of Brands: 1
Square Footage: 350000

23660 Harrington Hoists Inc
401 W End Ave
Manheim, PA 17545-1703

717-665-2000
Fax: 717-665-2861 800-233-3010
www.harringtonhoists.com
Material handling equipment including hoists, lever pullers and cranes
President: Ned Hunter
Manager of Quality & Engineering: Drew Schoenberger
National Sales Manager: W David Merkel, Jr.
Customer Service Manager: Hope Arment
COO: Carlo Lonardi
Plant Manager: Guy Haney
Estimated Sales: $10-20 Million
Number Employees: 100-249
Parent Co: Kito Corporation

23661 Harrington's Equipment Co
475 Orchard Rd
Fairfield, PA 17320-9399

410-756-2506
Fax: 302-422-7149 800-468-8467
RSH5@live.com www.harringtonsequipment.com
Dealer of rebuilt can seamers, replacement parts and change parts
President: Thomas H Harrington Jr
Number Employees: 5-9

23662 Harris & Company
980 Salem Pkwy
Salem, OH 44460

330-332-4127
Fax: 330-332-9627 info@harrisandcompany.com
CIS labels, self adhesive labels in sheets, coated paper and printed boards
President: Charles M Day
Owner: Charles W. Harris
VP (Pre-Press): George Ritchie
VP Sales: Norm Ritchie
Contact: David Harris
davidh@hjpchartered.com
Estimated Sales: $1 Million
Number Employees: 5-9
Square Footage: 22000

23663 Harris Equipment Corp
2040 N Hawthorne Ave
Melrose Park, IL 60160-1106

708-343-0866
Fax: 708-343-0995 800-365-0315
customer_service@harrisequipment.com
www.harrisequipment.com
Heat exchangers; wholesaler/distributor of oil free air compressors and compressed air filtration equipment, oil flooded compresser air dryers, stainless steel vavles, filter regulated lubricators
President: Gary Pollack
gpollack@harrisequipment.com
VP: John Pearson
Marketing: Tony Beaman
Purchasing Manager: Humer Lovett
Estimated Sales: $10-20 Million
Number Employees: 20-49
Square Footage: 56000

23664 Harris Specialty Chemicals
P.O. Box 2789
Jacksonville, FL 32203-2789

904-598-9808
Fax: 904-598-9833 800-537-4722
Polymer floor systems
CEO: Ellen Harris
Estimated Sales: $1 - 5 Million
Number Employees: 5-9

23665 Harrison Electropolishing
13002 Brittmoore Park Dr
Houston, TX 77041-7231

832-467-3100
Fax: 832-467-3111 info@harrisonep.com
www.m.harrisonep.com
Specializes in mechanical, electropolishing and passivation for brew kettles, fermenters and lagering tanks.
President: Tom Harrison
Manager: Ginger Happacher
ginger@harrisonep.com
Number Employees: 50-99

23666 Harrison of Texas
7142 Siena Vista Dr
Houston, TX 77083-2938

281-498-8206
Fax: 713-981-9589 800-245-5707
Electropolishing and mechanical polishing service for stainless steel food processing equipment; also, oxygen cleaning and mil-spec passivation services available
President: Tom Harrison
Office Manager: Patricia Bays
Operations Manager: Matt Buck
Estimated Sales: $300,000-500,000
Number Employees: 1-4
Square Footage: 60000

23667 Harro Hofliger Packaging Systems
4 W Oakland Ave # 2
Doylestown, PA 18901-4243

215-345-4256
Fax: 215-345-4994
Supplier of Packaging Equipment
President: Allen Shane
Contact: Seth Blau
sblau@hofliger.com
Estimated Sales: $1 - 3 Million
Number Employees: 5-9

23668 Harry Davis & Co
1725 Blvd of the Allies
Pittsburgh, PA 15219-5991

412-765-1170
Fax: 412-765-0910 800-775-2289
sales@harrydavis.com www.harrydavis.com
CEO: Stanford Davis
sdavis@harrydavis.com
CEO: Martin Davis
Estimated Sales: $20 - 50 Million
Number Employees: 10-19

23669 Harsco Industrial IKG
1801 Forrest Park Dr
Garrett, IN 46738

260-357-6900
Fax: 260-357-0027 800-467-2345
salesikg@harsco.com www.harscoikg.com
Manufacturer and exporter of fiberglass grating used for flooring in food processing plants
Marketing Manager: Tom Toler
VP Sales/Marketing: Ray Palombi
Contact: Heidi Malcolm
h.malcolm@ikgindustries.com
Estimated Sales: $1 - 5 Million

23670 (HQ)Hart Design & Mfg
1940 Radisson St
Green Bay, WI 54302-2092

920-468-5927
Fax: 920-468-5888 www.hartdesign.com
Designs and constructs specialty, standard and proprietary equipment for use in the Food and Dairy industry. Our packaging machinery includes process cheese wrappers, automatic puching, filling and sealing lines for process and creamcheese, a ribbon cheese casting, slitting, slice stacking equipment, automatic product feeders, and portion cutting equipment for block and barrel cheese.
President: Timm Schaetz
CEO: John Adams
Founder/CEO: Gerald Schaetz
Marketing Manager: Dennis Adelmeyer
Sales Manager: Dennis Adelmeyer
Estimated Sales: $4 Million
Number Employees: 20-49
Square Footage: 80000
Brands:
Hart

23671 (HQ)Hart Designs LLC
PO Box 1387
Ruston, LA 71273-1387
318-278-0473
Fax: 318-255-8328 800-592-3500
www.hart-designs.com
Electric lighting fixtures
CEO: Charles Hart
Quality Control: Sandra Hart
Sales: Amy Foster
Estimated Sales: Less Than $500,000
Number Employees: 1-4

23672 Hartford Containers
PO Box 399
Terryville, CT 06786-0399
860-584-1194
Fax: 860-582-5051
Corrugated containers
President: Bob Braverman
Estimated Sales: $20 - 50 Million
Number Employees: 50-99

23673 Hartford Plastics
10861 Mill Valley Rd
Omaha, NE 68154
Fax: 860-683-8484
Manufacturer and exporter of plastic bottles and
containers; also, custom blow molding, labeling, hot
stamping and silk screening available
VP Marketing: Anthony Roncaioli
Estimated Sales: $10-20 Million
Number Employees: 50-99
Parent Co: Comtrol

23674 Hartford Stamp Works
201 Locust Street
Hartford, CT 6114
860-249-6205
Fax: 860-409-4110
Rubber stamps, name plates, seals, name pins,
self-inking stamps, etc.; also, inks
CEO: Ramani Ayer
Contact: Kyle Shorty
hartfordstamp@aol.com
Office Manager: Sandy Williams
Estimated Sales: $1-2.5 Million
Number Employees: 10-19
Square Footage: 15000

23675 Harting Graphics
111 N Cleveland Ave
Wilmington, DE 19805-1714
302-622-8911
Fax: 302-622-8909 800-848-1373
Advertising signs and point of purchase posters and
banners
President: Theodore Harting
Sales/Marketing Executive: Susan Cuttance
Purchasing Agent: Kim Livermore
Estimated Sales: Below $5 Million
Number Employees: 5-9
Square Footage: 40000

23676 Hartness International
1200 Garlington Road
P.O. Box 26509
Greenville, SC 26509
864-297-1200
Fax: 864-297-4486 800-845-8791
www.hartness.com
Manufacturer and exporter of packaging equipment
and machinery including case packers, decasers, sin-
gle filers/laners and conveyor and mass product flow
systems
CEO: Sean Hartness
VP & General Manager: Tim Hudson
Director, Procurement: Dianne Hall
Estimated Sales: $50-75 Million
Number Employees: 250-499
Brands:
  Dynac

23677 Hartstone Pottery Inc
1719 Dearborn St
Zanesville, OH 43701-5299
740-452-9999
Fax: 800-506-9627
Manufacturer, importer and exporter of stoneware,
dinnerware, cookware, bakeware, tabletop accessories, oven dishwashers and microwave safe cookie
molds

Manager: Wess Foltz
wess@hartstonepottery.com
VP/General Manager: Patrick Hart
Sales Manager: Mike Flynn
Operations Manager: Shawn McGee
Estimated Sales: $7 Million
Number Employees: 20-49
Square Footage: 400000
Parent Co: Carlisle Companies
Type of Packaging: Consumer, Food Service
Brands:
  Hartstone
  The Original Cookie & Shortbread
  The Wine Tote

23678 Hartzell Fan Inc
910 S Downing St
Piqua, OH 45356
937-773-7411
Fax: 937-773-8994 800-336-3267
info@hartzellfan.com www.hartzell.com
Manufacturer and exporter of general and process
ventilation fans and centrifugal fans and blowers
President: George D Atkinson
CEO: Sean Steimle
customerservice@hartzell.com
Sales: George Atkins
Operations Manager: R Wallace
Estimated Sales: $20-50 Million
Number Employees: 100-249
Brands:
  Duct Axial

23679 Harvard Folding Box Company
71 Linden St
Lynn, MA 1905
781-598-1600
Fax: 781-598-2950 www.idealboxmakers.com
Manufacturer and exporter of folding paper boxes
President: Leon Simkins
VP: David Simkins
Logistics Manager: Tony Geraneo
Contact: Mike Hios
mhios@idealboxmakers.com
Operational Manager: Chris Robertson
Plant Manager: Jimmy Mc Gee
Estimated Sales: $10 - 20 Million
Number Employees: 100-249
Parent Co: Simkins Industries

23680 Harvey W Hottel Inc
18900 Woodfield Rd # A
Gaithersburg, MD 20879-6704
301-921-9599
Fax: 301-948-1892 jhottel@harveyhottel.com
www.harveyhottel.com
Air conditioning, heating and refrigeration items, fi-
nancing, food service, HVAC, plumbing, de-
sign/build case study
President: Richard Hottel
CEO: Dick Hottel
VP: Jeff Hottel
VP Sales: Bernard Mejean
Estimated Sales: $10 - 20 Million
Number Employees: 100-249
Square Footage: 20000

23681 Harvey's Indian River Groves
3700 US Highway 1
Rockledge, FL 32955-4925
321-636-6072
Fax: 321-633-4132 800-327-9312
www.harveysgroves.com
Fruit gift baskets
President: Jim Harvey
Manager: Ann Manerino
Estimated Sales: $2.5-5 Million
Number Employees: 100-249

23682 Harwil Corp
541 Kinetic Dr
Oxnard, CA 93030-7923
805-988-6800
Fax: 805-988-6804 800-562-2447
www.harwil.com
Manufacturer and exporter of bag closing machinery, heat sealers and flow and liquid level switches.
Also manufature fluid liquid level switches, liquid
level pumpup/plumpdown controlles, pump emergency shutdown controllers andachemical feed
pump interface module
VP: Bruce Bowman
Sales Exec: Ellis Anderson
Number Employees: 20-49

23683 Hasco Electric Corporation
84 S Water St Ste 1
Greenwich, CT 06830
203-531-9400
Fax: 203-531-9408
Lighting fixtures
Owner: Donna Sagona
VP: Brad Sagona
Estimated Sales: $5-10,000,000
Number Employees: 20-49
Square Footage: 58000

23684 Hassia USA
1210 Campus Dr
Morganville, NJ 07751-1262
732-536-8770
Fax: 732-536-8850
President: Charles Ravalli
Estimated Sales: $3 - 5 Million
Number Employees: 10-19

23685 Hastings Lighting Company
1206 Long Beach Ave
Los Angeles, CA 90021
213-622-2009
Fax: 213-622-9157
Fluorescent showcase lighting fixtures for use in
show cases
President: Jim Culbertson
VP: Jeffrey Colby
Office Manager: Joan Culbertson
Estimated Sales: $1-2.5 Million
Number Employees: 1-4
Square Footage: 9600

23686 Hasty Bake Charcoal Grills
1313 S Lewis Ave
Tulsa, OK 74104-4215
918-665-8220
Fax: 918-665-8225 800-426-6836
info@hastybake.com www.hastybake.com
Charcoal ovens and barbecue accessories
Owner: Richard Alexander
ralexander@hastybake.com
Estimated Sales: $2.5-5 Million
Number Employees: 10-19

23687 Hatco Corp
635 S 28th St
Milwaukee, WI 53215-1298
414-671-6350
Fax: 414-615-1226 800-558-0607
www.hatcocorp.com
Manufacturer and exporter of heating, warming,
toasting, cooking and equipment including display
warmers, holding cabinets, low temperature and
slow cookers and booster and sink heaters for hot
water, toasters, etc
President: Dave Rolston
drolston@hatcocorp.com
Co-Founder: Lareine Hatch
Vice President - Sales: Michael Whiteley
National Sales Manager: Mark Pumphret
Number Employees: 50-99
Type of Packaging: Food Service
Brands:
  Chef System
  Flav-R-Fresh
  Flav-R-Savor
  Glo-Ray
  Hatco
  Toast King
  Toast Rite
  Toast-Qwik

23688 Hathaway Stamps
635 Main St # 1
Cincinnati, OH 45202-2524
513-621-1052
Fax: 513-621-7339 contact@hathawaystamps.com
www.hathawaystamps.com
Rubber stamps
Manager: Larry Schultz
VP: Robert Ruwe
Estimated Sales: $1 - 2.5 Million
Number Employees: 10-19
Square Footage: 8000
Parent Co: Volk Corporation

23689 Hatteras Packaging Systems
8753 S Highway A1a
Melbourne Beach, FL 32951-4008
321-728-0908
Fax: 321-984-7252 hatteraspk@aol.com

Number Employees: 10

23690 Haug Quality Equipment
18443 Technology Dr
Morgan Hill, CA 95037-2822
                 408-465-8160
    Fax: 408-842-1265 sales@haugquality.com
                 www.haugquality.com
Leak detecting equipment for food packaging
President: Brian Haug
  bhaug@haugmfg.com
Secretary: Gale Craft
Sales Manager: Thomas Hoffman
Estimated Sales: $1 - 3 Million
Number Employees: 10-19
Brands:
  Haug

23691 Haumiller Engineering Co
445 Renner Dr
Elgin, IL 60123-6991
                 847-695-9111
    Fax: 847-695-2092 sales@haumiller.com
                 www.haumiller.com
Manufacturer and exporter of high-speed automatic
custom assembly machines, flip top closure closing
machines, cappers, spray tip and fitment applicators,
reducer plug inserters and collar placers
President: Russ Holmer
  rholmer@haumiller.com
VP Sales: John Giacopelli
Estimated Sales: $5-10 Million
Number Employees: 50-99
Square Footage: 90000

23692 Hauser Packaging
44 Exchange Street
Suite 202
Portland, ME 04101-5018
                 207-899-3306
    Fax: 207-899-3970 888-600-2671
info@hauserpack.com www.hauserpack.com
Wine industry bottles
Contact: Thomas Houser
  thouser@hauserpack.com

23693 Hautly Cheese Co
251 Axminister Dr
Fenton, MO 63026-2938
                 636-533-4400
    Fax: 653-533-4401 info@hautly.com
                 www.hautly.com
Cheese, cheese products
Owner: Alan Hautly
  a_hautly@hautly.com
Estimated Sales: Less than $500,000
Number Employees: 20-49

23694 Have Our Plastic Inc
6990 Creditview Road
Unit 4
Mississauga, ON L5N 8R9
Canada
                 905-821-7550
    Fax: 905-821-7553 800-263-5995
                 sales@hop.ca
Manufacture and distribute synthetic paper, plastic
and wire binding products, laminating equipment
and supplies, other equipment and supplies, restau-
rant menu covers, display and merchandising
products and PVC.
Estimated Sales: $5,000,000
Number Employees: 16
Number of Brands: 1
Square Footage: 96000
Type of Packaging: Private Label, Bulk
Brands:
  E-Binder
  H.O.P.
  Hop-Syn
  Print Protector
  The Menu Roll

23695 Haven's Candies
87 County Rd
Westbrook, ME 04092-3807
                 207-772-1557
    Fax: 207-775-0086 800-639-6309
        info@havenscandies.com
        www.havenscandies.com
Chocolates and other confectionary; custom chocolate molding available

---

Owner: Andy Charles
Marketing Director: Krista Viola
Production Manager: Arthur Dillon
Estimated Sales: $1-2.5 Million
Number Employees: 20-49
Square Footage: 24000
Type of Packaging: Consumer, Private Label, Bulk

23696 Haviland Enterprises Inc
421 Ann St NW
Grand Rapids, MI 49504-2019
                 616-734-0250
    Fax: 616-361-9772 800-456-1134
Industrial, food grade and U.S.P. specialty cleaners
and wastewater treatment chemicals; wholesaler/dis-
tributor of various food grade and U.S.P. process
chemicals
President: E Bernard Haviland
Cmo: Graham Torr
  grahamt@havilandusa.com
CFO: Tom Simmons
Quality Control: Terry Schoew
Sales/Marketing Manager: Eric Earl
Estimated Sales: $20 - 50 Million
Number Employees: 100-249
Square Footage: 185000

23697 Haward Corporation
29 Porete Ave
North Arlington, NJ 7031
                 201-991-8777
    Fax: 201-991-1903 800-342-9041
Metal finisher whose services include teflon and
plastic coating and electropolishing of stainless steel
President: Dean Ward
Vice President: Keith Schumacher
Sales Director: Gary Horman
Estimated Sales: $5-10 Million
Number Employees: 20-49
Square Footage: 60000

23698 Hawkeye Corrugated Box
725 Ida St
Cedar Falls, IA 50613-2112
                 319-268-0407
    Fax: 319-268-0057 www.buckeyecorrugated.com
Corrugated boxes
President: Matt Highland
  highland@hawkeyebox.com
Estimated Sales: $20-50 Million
Number Employees: 20-49

23699 Hawkeye Pallet Co
6055 NW Beaver Dr
Johnston, IA 50131-1349
                 515-276-0409
Wooden pallets
Owner: Bill Haller
Estimated Sales: Less Than $500,000
Number Employees: 1-4

23700 Hayes & Stolz Indl Mfg LTD
3521 Hemphill St
PO Box 11217
Fort Worth, TX 76110-5212
                 817-926-3391
    Fax: 817-926-4133 800-725-7272
  sales@hayes-stolz.com www.hayes-stolz.com
Manufacturer and exporter of batch mixers, continu-
ous blenders, liquid coaters, bucket elevators, valves
and rotary screeners
President: B J Masters
  marhay@hayes-stolz.com
VP: Mark Hayes
Chairman of the Board: Vernon Hayes
Sales Exec: Mark Hayes
Sales Engineer: Kris Helsley
Estimated Sales: $10 - 20 Million
Number Employees: 100-249

23701 Hayes Machine Co Inc
3434 106th Cir
Des Moines, IA 50322-3700
                 515-252-1216
    Fax: 515-252-1316 800-860-6224
         www.hayesmachine.com
Packaging and cartoning machines
President: Luca Berrone
CFO: John Stone
R & D: Allan Anderson
Inside Sales Manager: Julie Reincke
Manager: Allan Andersen
  aandersen@sacmiusa.com
Plant Manager: Allan Anderson

Estimated Sales: Below $5 Million
Number Employees: 20-49
Square Footage: 32000
Parent Co: Gram Equipment of America

23702 Haynes Manufacturing Co
24142 Detroit Rd
Westlake, OH 44145-1528
                 440-871-2188
    Fax: 440-871-0855 800-992-2166
info@haynesmfg.com www.haynesmfg.com
Manufacturer and exporter of food grade lubricants
Owner: Tammy Doctor
Sales and Marketing Coordinator: Tammy Doctor
  tdoctor@haynesmfg.com
Estimated Sales: Less Than $500,000
Number Employees: 1-4
Type of Packaging: Food Service, Private Label,
  Bulk
Brands:
  Haynes

23703 (HQ)Hayon Manufacturing
9682 Borgata Bay Blvd
Las Vegas, NV 89147-8080
                 702-562-3377
    Fax: 702-562-3351 hayonmfg@aol.com
         www.eggwashsprayer.com
Manufacturer and exporter of bakery machinery in-
cluding automatic pan greasers and coaters, egg
washers and icing/glaze applicators
Owner: Z Hayon
  hayonmfg@aol.com
VP: Ziona Hayon
Estimated Sales: Below $500,000
Number Employees: 1-4
Brands:
  Hayon Select-A-Spray

23704 Hayssen Flexible Systems
225 Spartangreen Blvd
Duncan, SC 29334-9400
                 864-486-4000
    Fax: 864-486-4412 sales@hayssen.com
                 www.hayssen.com
Manufacturer and exporter of horizontal flow wrap-
ping and horizontal and vertical form/fill/seal
machinery
President: Daniel L Jones
Vice President: Dan Minor
  dan.minor@hayssensandiacre.com
Vice President of Sales and Marketing: Dan Minor
Estimated Sales: $50 Million
Number Employees: 250-499
Parent Co: Barry Wehmiller Companies
Brands:
  Edge
  Rt
  Servo Ii
  Turbo
  Ultima
  Ultra

23705 Hayssen Flexible Systems
225 Spartangreen Blvd
Duncan, SC 29334-9400
                 864-486-4000
    Fax: 864-486-4412 www.hayssen.com
Packaging machinery and machinery parts, vertical
form fill and seal bagmakers and horzaontal flow
wrappers
Founder: Herman Hayssen
General Manager: Troy Snader
Vice President: Dan Minor
  dan.minor@hayssensandiacre.com
Vice President of Sales and Marketing: Dan Minor
Estimated Sales: $8-10 Million
Number Employees: 250-499
Parent Co: Molins Richmond

23706 Hayward Gordon
6660 Campobello Road
Mississauga, ON L5N 2L9
Canada
                 905-567-6116
    Fax: 905-567-1706 info@haywardgordon.com
             www.haywardgordon.com
President: John Hayward
CFO: Jeanne Gray
Number Employees: 10

23707 Hayward Industries Inc
1 Hayward Industrial Dr
Clemmons, NC 27012-9737
        336-712-9900
    Fax: 336-712-9523 www.haywardindustries.com
Manufacturer and exporter of cartridge filters, pipe-line strainers, gas/liquid separators, plastic valves and flow meters
President: Robert Davis
HR Executive: Mathieu Bienvenue
  mbienvenue@haywardnet.com
Marketing Communication Manager: D Treslan
Number Employees: 500-999
Brands:
  Flosite
  Loeffler
  Qic
  Strainomatic
  Wright-Austin

23708 Hazen Paper Co
240 S Water St
Holyoke, MA 01040-5979
        413-538-8204
    Fax: 413-533-1420 customerservice@hazen.com
    www.hazen.com
Paper including foil and metallized film laminations, heat sealing, fancy, printed and embossed paper
President: Royal Casino
  sdximuhb@amazinhazen.org
Quality Control: Alfred Zuffoletti
R&D: Kyle Parent
VP Sales: Steve Smith
Purchasing Manager: Larry Hoague
Estimated Sales: $20 - 50 Million
Number Employees: 50-99

23709 Hazmat Business Ideas
1620 i St NW Ste 925
Washington, DC 20006
        202-293-5800
    Fax: 202-463-8998
Provides a forum for the gathering and exchange of information for the shipment and distribution of hazardous materials.
Number Employees: 20-49

23710 Hcs Enterprises
Plot No. 333, Rai Industrial Estate
Sonipat
Haryana, 131029
India
    www.hcsbakerymachines.com
Manufacturer, supplier and exporter of a comprehensive range of bakery plants, machines and equipment including steel flour sifters, bread slicing machines, baking proofer ovens, planetary mixers, infrared ovens, rack ovens
Managing Director: Bhupinder Singh
Estimated Sales: $1 Million
Number Employees: 26-50

23711 Healdsburg Machine Company
2584 Rim Rock Way
Santa Rosa, CA 95404-1819
        707-433-3348
    Fax: 707-433-3340
Manufacturer and exporter of grape crushing and stemming machinery; also, special pumps for the canning industry
President: Arthur Rafanelli
  yvette.moseman@mosemanlaw.com
VP: Ron Rafanelli
Marketing: Ron Rafanelli
Estimated Sales: $1-2.5 Million
Number Employees: 10
Square Footage: 180000
Parent Co: Healdsburg Machine Company

23712 Health Products Corp
1060 Nepperhan Ave
Yonkers, NY 10703-1432
        914-423-2900
    Fax: 914-963-6001 www.hpc7.com
Psyllium and nutritional herbs, tablets and capsules; contract packager of blending and filling powders
President: Joseph Lewin
  zurion2@aol.com
Number Employees: 50-99
Brands:
  Aspi-Cor
  Khg-7
  Lactalins

  Malpotane
  Tick Stop

23713 Health Star
80 Pacella Dr
Randolph, MA 02368
        781-961-5400
    Fax: 781-961-5456 800-545-3639
    info@HealthStaronline.com
    www.healthstaronline.com
New, and rebuilt processing and packaging machinery including liquid fillers
Marketing Manager: Bonnie Cote
Sales: Patl Lais
Estimated Sales: $2.5-5 Million
Number Employees: 50-99
Brands:
  Level Star Ls Level Sensing Fillers
  Purecop
  Purefil

23714 HealthFocus
1140 Hightower Trail
Suite 201
Atlanta, GA 30350-2988
        770-645-1999
    Fax: 770-518-0630 www.healthfocus.net
Market research firm specializing in consumer health and nutrition trends
Marketing Director: Julie Johnson
Estimated Sales: $500,000-$1 Million
Number Employees: 1
Square Footage: 8000

23715 Healthline Products
100 N Santa Fe Avenue
Los Angeles, CA 90012-4021
        213-620-8600
    Fax: 213-620-8636 800-473-4003
Pot holders, gloves, towels, uniforms, etc
President: Courtney Sapin
National Sales Manager: Trina Brown
Customer Service: Rita Recio
Estimated Sales: $5-10,000,000
Number Employees: 19
Square Footage: 15000

23716 Healthstar Inc
1 Randolph Rd
Randolph, MA 02368-4321
        781-961-5400
    Fax: 781-961-5456 800-LIK-ENEW
    info@healthstaronline.com
    www.healthstaronline.com
Pre-owned, rebuilt, and new processing and packaging equipment
President: William Grabowski
CFO: Scott Johnson
Contact: Robert Bean
  rbean@healthstaronline.com
Estimated Sales: $10 - 20 Million
Number Employees: 20-49

23717 Healthy Dining
4849 Ronson Ct Ste 115
San Diego, CA 92111
        858-541-2049
    Fax: 858-541-0508 800-266-2049
    erica@healthy-dining.com
    www.healthydiningfinder.com
Consultant specializing in marketing and promoting healthy restaurant menu items; also, computerized nutrition analysis of menu items available
President/ Founder: Anita Jones Mueller
VP/ Director Strategic Partnerships: Erica Bohm, M.S.
Research & Communications Coordinator: Nancy Snyder, M.S.
Director Nutrition, Quality Assurance: Lauren Rezende, M.P.H., R.D.
Contact: Rick Bayless
  rick@healthydiningfinder.com
Director Operations: Andrew Packer, M.A.
Estimated Sales: Below $5,000,000
Number Employees: 5-9

23718 Healthy Grain Foods LLC
4125 Yorkshire Ln
Northbrook, IL 60062-2915
        847-272-5576
    Fax: 847-272-5576
Cereals; research and development
President: Harold Zukerman
  haroldzukerman@gmail.com

Estimated Sales: $1-2,500,000
Number Employees: 5-9

23719 Healthy Truth, LLC
87 West Street
Walpole, MA 02081
        774-202-9986
    info@healthytruth.com
    www.healthytruth.com
Organic plant-based, keto, gluten-free, and dairy-free nuts, powder blends, and protein bars.
CEO: Andrew Weiss
Year Founded: 2014
Estimated Sales: $4.1 Million
Number Employees: 20

23720 Heart Smart International
6702 E Clinton St
Scottsdale, AZ 85254-5254
        480-948-7631
    Fax: 480-948-9834 800-762-7819
    www.heartsmartinternational.net
Consultant specializing in the computer analysis of menu items, product marketing and nutritional training assistance
Owner: Jay Philips
Director Customer Relations: Judy Peters
Production Manager: Joe Cox
Estimated Sales: less than $500,000
Number Employees: 1-4
Square Footage: 2000
Parent Co: Best of Taste

23721 Heart of Virginia
PO Box 937
Lynchburg, VA 24505-0937
        804-847-1732
    Fax: 804-847-2067 kbutler@region2000.org

23722 Hearthside Food Solutions
3500 Lacey Rd
Suite 300
Downers Grove, IL 60515
        630-967-3600
    info@hearthsidefoods.com
    www.hearthsidefoods.com
Nutrition and energy bars, cookies, crackers, snack foods, cereal and granola, and food packaging.
Chairman/CEO & Co-Founder: Rich Scalise
Senior VP/CFO: Fred Jasser
Senior VP Human Resources: Steve England
Year Founded: 2009
Number Employees: 5000-9999
Type of Packaging: Consumer, Private Label

23723 Heartland Farms Dairy & Food Products, LLC
3668 South Geyer Road
Suite 205
St. Louis, MO 63127
        314-965-1110
    Fax: 314-965-1118 888-633-6455
    info@heartlandfarmsdairy.com
    www.heartlandfarmsdairy.com
Dairy products
President: Tom Jacoby
Marketing Assistant: Pat Hittmeier
Sales of Dry Products: Tim Fann
Contact: Christine Anderson
  canderson@heartlandfarmsdairy.com
Weights and Tests: Jenn Jacoby
Type of Packaging: Consumer, Bulk

23724 Heartland Ingredients LLC
802 West College Street
Troy, MO 63379
        Fax: 877-841-2067 800-557-2621
    contactus@heartlandingredients.net
    www.heartlandingredients.net
Ingredients, food and technical grade chemicals and colors, dairy products, meat products, sugar, artifical sweeteners, close dated finished products.

23725 Heartwood
5063 Arrow Hwy
Montclair, CA 91763-1304
        909-626-8104
    Fax: 909-626-7636
    www.heartwoodcountertops.com
Solid surfacing materials and store fixtures
Estimated Sales: Less than $500,000
Number Employees: 1-4

23726 Heat Seal
4580 E 71st St
Cleveland, OH 44125-1048
216-341-2022
Fax: 216-341-2163 800-342-6329
custserv@heatsealco.com www.heatsealco.com
Horizontal form/fill/seal machines, shrink packaging systems, rotary blister packaging machinery, high speed shrink tunnels and vertical L-sealer bagger
Owner: Ron Skalsky
Contact: Brent Ferns
 brferns@heatsealequipment.com
Estimated Sales: $20-50 Million
Number Employees: 100-249

23727 Heat-It Manufacturing
12050 Crownpoint Dr
San Antonio, TX 78233-5362
210-650-9112
Fax: 210-967-8345 800-323-9336
Manufacturer and exporter of canned heating fuels for buffets, catering, camping and emergencies
Manager: Lisa Garza
General Manager: Georgina Yoast
Estimated Sales: $.5 - 1 million
Number Employees: 1-4
Square Footage: 60000
Brands:
 Heat-It

23728 Heatcraft Refrigeration Prods
2175 W Park Place Blvd
Stone Mountain, GA 30087-3535
770-465-5600
Fax: 770-465-5990
hrrdp.feedback@heatcraftrpd.com
www.heatcraftrpd.com
Manufacturer and exporter of commercial refrigeration equipment
Cmo: Grady Mcadams
VP: Ken Rothgeb
Director Marketing: Jeff Almond
Director Sales: Mark Westphal
General Manager: J Jones
Estimated Sales: $10-20,000,000
Number Employees: 100-249
Square Footage: 140000
Parent Co: Lennox International
Brands:
 Bohn
 Chandler
 Climate Control
 Larkin

23729 Heatcraft Worldwide Refrig
5201 Transport Blvd
Columbus, GA 31907-1961
706-568-1514
Fax: 706-568-8990 800-866-5596
marietta.oneill@heatcraftrpd.com
www.kysorwarren.com
Manufacturer and exporter of refrigerated display fixtures, walk-in coolers/freezers and refrigeration systems
President: Ralph Schmitt
Director of Sales-Eastern U.S. & Canada: Larry Norton
Director of Sales-Western U.S.: Robert Greene
Executive VP: Cliff Hill
Sales Manager: Brian Eddins
Dealer Development Manager: Oscar Stuart
Estimated Sales: $1 - 5 Million
Number Employees: 500-999
Square Footage: 980000
Parent Co: Heatcraft Worldwide Refrigeration
Brands:
 Dual Jet
 Kysor/Warren

23730 Heatec
P.O. Box 72760
Chattanooga, TN 37407
423-821-5200
Fax: 423-821-7673 800-235-5200
heatec@heatec.com www.heatec.com
Heaters, storage tanks and related products
President: Richard Dorris
VP/Marketing: Tom Wilkey
Sales: Jerry Vautrease
Parent Co: Astec Industries

23731 Heath & Company
3411 Johnson Ferry Road
Roswell, GA 30075-5205
770-650-2724
Fax: 678-623-3475 info@heathandco.com
www.heathandco.com
Signs including advertising, changeable letter, electric, luminous tube, etc
Founder & Managing Partner: David W. Health
Contact: Pooja Mehta
 pooja@jkworld.net
Manager: Ken Plass
Number Employees: 150
Parent Co: Jim Patterson Group

23732 Heath & Company
3411 Johnson Ferry Road
Roswell, GA 30075-5205
770-650-2724
Fax: 678-623-3475 info@heathandco.com
www.heathandco.com
Signs including electric advertising, plastic and luminous tube
Founder & Managing Partner: David W. Health
Contact: Pooja Mehta
 pooja@jkworld.net
Manager: Ken Plass
Estimated Sales: $1,000,000 - $2,499,999
Number Employees: 150
Parent Co: Jim Patterson Group

23733 Heath Signs
278 Hillcrest Dr
Reno, NV 89509-3705
775-359-9007
Fax: 775-359-2527
Neon signs
President: Steve Scharfe
Secretary: Cathleen Wallman
Estimated Sales: Less than $500,000
Number Employees: 10

23734 Heatrex
P.O. Box 515
231 Chestnut St., Suite 410
Meadville, PA 16335-0515
814-724-1800
Fax: 814-333-6580 800-394-6589
sales@heatrex.com www.heatrex.com
Manufacturer and exporter of heaters including tubular/finned tubular, flanged/screw plug immersion, circulation, defrost, high temperature duct, infrared and radiant process; also, heater controls
Owner: Fred O'Polka
CFO: Fred O Polka
R&D: Larry Clever
Quality Control: Kim Lenhart
Marketing: Earl Pifer
Sales: Earl Pifer
Contact: Cindy Andrews
 andrews@heatrex.com
Operations Manager: Earl Pifer
Plant Manager: Kim Lenhart
Estimated Sales: $10 - 20 Million
Number Employees: 50-99
Brands:
 Heatzone
 Quartzone

23735 Heatron Inc
3000 Wilson Ave
Leavenworth, KS 66048-4637
913-651-4420
Fax: 913-651-5352 chrisk@heatron.com
www.heatron.com
Custom designers and manufacturers of patented non-stick cartridge heaters, Max2000 mica band and strip heater, Ceramix ceramic bands, Extruheat tubular channel bands, aluminum and bronze cast in heaters, flexible silicone rubberetched-foil
CEO: Mike Keenan
 mikek@heatron.com
CEO: Michael W Keenan
Estimated Sales: $5-10 000,000
Number Employees: 100-249

23736 (HQ)Hebeler Corp
2000 Military Rd
Tonawanda, NY 14150-6704
716-873-9300
Fax: 716-873-7538 800-486-4709
info@hebeler.com www.hebeler.com
Stainless steel food processing machinery including bakers' mixers, candy, syrup and beverage coolers, food dryers, deaerators, distillation units, evaporative condensers, separators, heat exchangers and preheaters
President: Ken Snyder
Purchasing: Lori Neidlinger
Estimated Sales: $25 Million
Number Employees: 100-249
Square Footage: 100000
Other Locations:
 Hebeler Corp.
 Vicksburg MS

23737 Hebenstreit GmbH
2465 Byron Station Dr. SW,
Suite B
Byron Center, MI 49315
616-583-1458
Fax: 616-583-1646 bryan@bainbridge-assoc.com
www.hebenstreit.de
Representative: Ross Brainbridge

23738 Hector Delorme & Sons
1631 Route 235
Farnham, QC J2N 2R2
Canada
450-293-5310
Fax: 450-293-5319
High pressure washers
President: Yves Cloutier
Number Employees: 5
Brands:
 Cyclone

23739 Hectronic
4300 Highline Blvd # 300
Oklahoma City, OK 73108-1843
405-946-3574
Fax: 405-946-3564 info@hetronic.com
www.hetronic.com
Manufacturer and exporter of material handling equipment including remote control systems
President: Dave Krueger
Executive VP: Torsten Rempe
VP: Torsten Rempe
Marketing: Laurel Benjamin
Sales: Bob Peddycoart
Contact: Stefan De
 deboor@hectronic.com
Estimated Sales: $5 - 10 Million
Number Employees: 20-49
Parent Co: Hectronic

23740 Hedges Neon Sales
616 Reynolds St
Salina, KS 67401-1932
785-827-9341
Fax: 785-827-1411
Signs including luminous tube, painted, wooden, etc
President: Nancy Hedges
 nhedges@hedgesonline.com
Estimated Sales: Less Than $500,000
Number Employees: 1-4

23741 Hedgetree Chemical Manufacturing
119 Prosperity Drive
Savannah, GA 31408-9551
912-691-0408
Fax: 912-692-0440
Organic and biodegradable household and industrial cleaning compounds; also, freezer, food and meat processing equipment cleaners
President: Larry Skinner Sr
Sales/Marketing: James Wallace
Estimated Sales: $1 - 2.5 Million
Number Employees: 7
Square Footage: 27200
Brands:
 U.N.L.O.C.C.

23742 Hedland Flow Meters
PO Box 081580
Racine, WI 53408
262-639-6770
Fax: 262-639-2267 800-433-5263
hedlandsales@racinefed.com www.hedland.com
President: John Erksine
Sales Manager: Mark Leveille
Estimated Sales: $10 - 20 Million
Number Employees: 100-249

23743 Hedstrom Corporation
1401 Jacobson Ave
Ashland, OH 44805
419-289-9310
Fax: 419-281-3371 700-765-9665
www.hedstrom.com
Rotationally molded polyethylene and vinyl bins,
material handling containers, hoppers, etc
President: Jim Braeunit
VP: James Braeunig
VP (Industrial Sales): Marty Fickenscher
Sales Manager (Technical): Jim Cotter
Contact: Tommy Bauer
  t.bauer@hedstrom.com
VP Operations: James Braeunig
Estimated Sales: $20 - 50 Million
Number Employees: 100-249
Square Footage: 300000
Parent Co: GAI Partners

23744 Hedwin Division
1600 Roland Heights Ave
Baltimore, MD 21211-1299
410-467-8209
Fax: 410-889-5189 800-638-1012
www.hedwin.com
Manufacturer and exporter of plastic products in-
cluding containers, film bags, shipping trays and
drum protector lids; also, dispensing systems, drum
and film liners, pails and flexible packaging
President: David E Rubley
CEO: Randy Wolfinger
  rwolfinger@hedwin.com
Sales Service Manager: Wayne Deal
Number Employees: 500-999
Parent Co: A. Solvay America Company
Brands:
  Cubitainer
  Ecoset
  Hedliner
  Hedpak
  Payliner
  Topliner
  Winliner
  Winpak

23745 Heely-Brown Co Inc
1280 Chattahoochee Ave NW
Atlanta, GA 30318-3683
404-352-0022
Fax: 404-350-2693 800-241-4628
info@heely-brown.com www.heelybrown.com
President: Bill Brown
CEO: William H Brown
  williamb@heelybrown.com
CFO: Mike Spencer
Estimated Sales: $20 - 50 Million
Number Employees: 50-99

23746 Hefferman Interactive
1196 Easton Road
Horsham, PA 19044-1405
610-517-2877
Fax: 215-441-5292
Estimated Sales: $500,000-$1 000,000
Number Employees: 1-4

23747 Heico Chemicals Inc
Route 611
Delaware Wtr Gap, PA 18327
570-420-3900
Fax: 570-421-9012 800-344-3426
www.vertellus.com
Organic and inorganic fine chemicals and organic
performance chemicals
Vice President of Business Development: Dan
Giambattisto
Manager of Corporate Sales: Joshua Kley
Estimated Sales: $10-25 Million
Number Employees: 20-49

23748 Heimann Systems Corporation
3203 Regal Dr
Alcoa, TN 37701
865-379-1670
Fax: 865-379-1677
President: Brad Mueller
Estimated Sales: $20 - 50 Million
Number Employees: 50-99

23749 Heinlin Packaging Svc
3121 South Ave
Toledo, OH 43609-1331
419-385-2681

Industrial and food packaging machinery
Manager: John Heinlin
VP: John Heinlin
Estimated Sales: $1-2.5 000,000
Number Employees: 5-9
Square Footage: 25000

23750 Heinrich Envelope Corp
925 Zane Ave N
Minneapolis, MN 55422-4692
763-544-3571
Fax: 763-544-6287 800-346-7957
information@heinrichenvelope.com
www.heinrichenvelope.com
Envelopes
President: Bill Berkner
Sales Manager: Don Schindle
Manager: Wesley Clerc
  wfclerc@heinrichenvelope.com
Estimated Sales: $10 - 20 Million
Number Employees: 50-99
Parent Co: Taylor Corporation

23751 Heinzen Sales
405 Mayock Rd
Gilroy, CA 95020-7040
408-842-6678
Fax: 408-842-6678 hmisales@heinzen.com
www.heinzen.com
Manufacturer and exporter of food processing
equipment including fruit peelers, dryers, dumpers,
trim lines and conveyors with complete engineering
service for new plant layout and equipment
President: Allan Heinzen
Sales: Gary M Hertzog
Estimated Sales: $10-20 Million
Number Employees: 1-4
Square Footage: 44000

23752 Heisler Machine & Tool Co
224 Passaic Ave
Fairfield, NJ 07004-3581
973-227-6300
Fax: 973-227-7627 heislersales@heislerind.com
www.heislerind.com
Packaging equipment amd 5 gallon pail handling
equipment; denesters, lid placers, lid closers, label-
ers, palletizers, case packers, gray packers,
lipstackers, line integration, pail orientation,
bail-o-matic,spcialty equipment.
President: Richard Heisler
  rheisler@heislerind.com
VP Sales: James Lamb
Sales Administrator: Judy Vinson
Estimated Sales: $3 - 5 Million
Number Employees: 50-99
Number of Products: 12
Square Footage: 100000
Type of Packaging: Food Service, Bulk
Brands:
  Casettraypackers
  Denester
  Lid Placers
  Lid Press

23753 Helken Equipment Co
171 Erick St # Q1
Crystal Lake, IL 60014-4539
847-697-3690
Fax: 847-697-3692 info@helkenequipment.com
Used and rebuilt food processing equipment
Owner: Kent Redmond
  kent@helkenequipment.com
Estimated Sales: $1-2.5 Million
Number Employees: 1-4
Square Footage: 29600

23754 Heller Truck Body Corp
138 US Highway 22
Hillside, NJ 07205-1888
973-923-9200
Fax: 973-923-9269 800-229-4148
dnovak2491@hotmail.com
Truck bodies, trailers, cargo containers, service and
repair all major brands of liftgates.
President: D Novak
  contactus@hellertruck.com
Estimated Sales: $1-2.5 Million
Number Employees: 1-4

23755 Helm Software
4722 N 24th Street
Suite 225
Phoenix, AZ 85016-9140
602-522-2999
Fax: 602-522-8046
Provide trade spending and equipment program soft-
ware to food service manufacturing
President: Daniel Buckstaff
Executive VP: Doug McFetters
Quality Control: Douglas McFetters
Estimated Sales: Below $5 Million
Number Employees: 15

23756 Helman International
4196 Suffolk Way
Pleasanton, CA 94588-4119
925-484-5000
Fax: 925-484-5007 pahelman@attb.com
www.aimblending.com
Ribbon blenders
President: Phil Helman
Contact: Jessica Hanscom
  jessicahanscom@aimblending.com
Estimated Sales: $2.5-5 Million
Number Employees: 20-49

23757 Helmer
14395 Bergen Blvd.
Noblesville, IN 46060
317-773-9073
Fax: 800-743-5637 317-773-9082
sales@helmerinc.com www.helmerinc.com
Refrigerators and freezers.
President: David Helmer
Market Integration Manager: Ann Marie Rohe
Contact: Steve Cloyd
  scloyd@helmerinc.com

23758 Hemco Corp
711 S Powell Rd
Independence, MO 64056-2602
816-796-2900
Fax: 816-796-3333 800-779-4362
info@hemcocorp.com www.hemcocorp.com
Complete line of laboratory fume hoods, lab furni-
ture, countertops, sinks, and fixture plumbing op-
tions. Large floor mount hoods, ventilation
equipment, emergency shower decontamination
booths, and Modular Clearn Labs
class1,000-100,000.
President: David Campbell
Owner: Ron Hill
Marketing: Jerry Schwarz
Contact: Sue Chandler
  suechandler@hemcocorp.com
Estimated Sales: 3 Million
Number Employees: 20-49
Square Footage: 60000
Brands:
  CE AireStream Hoods
  EnviroMax Enclosures
  HazMax Enclosures
  UniFlow Fume Hoods
  UniFlow SE
  UniLine Casework
  UniMax Large Floor Mount Hoods

23759 Hench Control, Inc.
3701 Collins Avenue
Suite 8C
Richmond, CA 94806
510-741-8100
Fax: 510-307-9804 sales@henchcontrol.com
www.henchcontrol.com
Efficiently controlling compressors , condensers,
evaporaters, vessels, heat exchangers, pumps and total alarms.
Chief Executive Officer: Alex Daneman
Contact: Patrick Cardon
  pcardon@lightpointe.com

23760 Hendee Enterprises Inc
9350 S Point Dr
Houston, TX 77054-3724
713-796-2322
Fax: 713-796-0494 800-231-7275
sales@hendee.com www.hendee.com
Commercial awnings
President: Robert Veasey
  robertv@hendee.com
Quality Control: Buddy Teairfon
CEO: John Macfarlane
Sales: Kathy Davis

Estimated Sales: $10 - 20 Million
Number Employees: 50-99

23761 Henkel Consumer Adhesive
32150 Just Imagine Dr
Avon, OH 44011

440-937-7000
Fax: 440-937-7077 800-321-0253
ask.a.duck@us.henkel.com
Manufacturer and exporter of pressure sensitive
tapes including masking, strapping, packaging, iden-
tification, cloth, foil, electrical and specialty
President: Jack Kahle
CEO: John Kahle
Contact: Melanie Amato
melanie.amato@manco.com
Number Employees: 250-499
Type of Packaging: Consumer, Food Service

23762 Henkel Corp.
200 Elm St
Stamford, CT 06902-3800

475-210-0230
www.henkel-northamerica.com
Adhesive technologies
President/Owner: Jerry Perkins
Director, Operations: Drew Thaler
drew.thaler@henkel.com
Estimated Sales: $4.4 Billion
Number Employees: 8,200
Brands:
AQUENCE
BONDERITE
LOCTITE
TECHNOMELT
TEROSON

23763 (HQ)Henley Paper Company
4229 Beechwood Dr
Greensboro, NC 27410-8108

336-668-0081
Fax: 336-605-9366 Atlanta@AtlanticPkg.com
www.atlanticpkg.com
Manufacturer and wholesaler/distributor of die cut-
ting, hosiery inserts, slitting, rewinding, sheeting,
transfer tissue, electrical insulator paper
VP Sales/Marketing: Bill Parks
Estimated Sales: $10 - 20 Million
Number Employees: 50-99

23764 Henningsen Foods Inc
9350 Excelsior Blvd
Suite 300
Hopkins, MN 55343

952-258-4000
info@michaelfoods.com
michaelfoods.com/brands/henningsen-foods/
Dried meats ingredients.
President, Michael Foods: Mark Westphal
Estimated Sales: $10-49.9 Million
Number Employees: 100-249
Square Footage: 12000
Parent Co: Michael Foods
Type of Packaging: Food Service, Private Label,
Bulk

23765 Henny Penny, Inc.
1219 US 35 W.
PO Box 60
Eaton, OH 45320

937-456-8400
Fax: 937-456-8402 800-417-8417
www.hennypenny.com
Pressure and open fryers, heated holding equipment,
combination convection and steamer ovens, rotisser-
ies, filters, etc.
CEO: Rob Connelly
Executive VP: Steve Maggard
Executive VP: Carolyn Wall
Year Founded: 1957
Estimated Sales: $200 Million
Number Employees: 600
Square Footage: 400000
Brands:
Climaplus
Hot N' Tender
Sure Chef
Sure Chef Climaplus Combi

23766 Henry & Sons Inc
58480 Frudden Rd
Bradley, CA 93426-9674

805-472-2600
Fax: 805-472-2626 800-752-7507
mark@dhenryandsons.com
www.dhenryandsons.com
Weight control systems, casing stuffer, extruders,
ham stuffing equipment, sausage linkers, stuffers
and accessories
Vice President: Mark Henry
mark@dhenryandsons.com
Vice President: Mark Henry
Estimated Sales: $1.5 Million
Number Employees: 1-4

23767 Henry Group
3734 State Highway 34 S
Greenville, TX 75402-5133

903-883-2002
Fax: 903-883-3210 www.thehenrygroup.com
Custom food processing equipment and food plant
reconstruction services
Owner: Troy Henry
troy@thg1.com
VP Business Development: Darren Jackson
Estimated Sales: $5 - 10 Million
Number Employees: 100-249

23768 Henry Hanger & Fixture Corporation of America
450 Seventh Ave 23rd Floor
New York City, NY 10123

212-279-0852
Fax: 212-594-7302 877-279-0852
www.henryhanger.com
Manufacturer and exporter of store fixtures and gar-
ment hangers
President: Henry Spitz
VP: Nancy Spitz Bittan
VP: Astrid Spitz Metsos
Estimated Sales: $5-10 Million
Number Employees: 50-99

23769 Henry Ira L Co
802 Elm St
Watertown, WI 53098-2538

920-261-0648
Fax: 920-261-3525 info@irabox.com
Custom set-up paper boxes and gameboards
Owner: Gregory Farado
Sales Director: Keith Thomas
Customer Service Manager: Joanne Duckworth
jduckworth@iralhenry.com
Design & Production Manager: Clark Farago
Plant Manager: Bob Wolfram
Estimated Sales: $1-3 Million
Number Employees: 20-49

23770 Henry Molded Products Inc
71 N 16th St
Lebanon, PA 17042-4502

717-273-3714
Fax: 717-274-3743 henry@henry-molded.com
Pressed and molded pulp goods, fiber containers and
custom packaging service, including pharmaceutical
and wine bottles, etc
President: J Brian
bj@henrymolded.com
CEO: Sue Wymann
CFO: Susan Weiman
Estimated Sales: $20-50 Million
Number Employees: 50-99
Brands:
Stakker

23771 Henry Troemner LLC
201 Wolf Dr
West Deptford, NJ 08086-2245

856-686-1600
Fax: 856-686-1601 856-686-1600
www.troemner.com
Manufacturer and exporter of laboratory stirrers and
mixers for research and development and quality as-
surance applications
COO: Steve Butler
sbutler@troemner.com
Sales/Marketing: Linda Sears
Estimated Sales: $1-2.5 Million
Number Employees: 100-249
Brands:
T-Line

23772 Henschel Coating & Laminating
15805 W Overland Dr
New Berlin, WI 53151-2814

262-786-1750
Fax: 262-786-3852 800-866-5683
warren@henschelcoating.com
www.henschelcoating.com
Coated and laminated paper
President: Warren Henschel
warren@henschelcoating.com
R & D: Brian Lemke
VP: Warren Henschel
Estimated Sales: Below $5 Million
Number Employees: 20-49

23773 Herbert Miller
1548 Old Skokie Rd
Highland Park, IL 60035-2704

847-831-2083
Fax: 847-831-2193
Aseptic processing systems, including packaging
and all forms of processing equipment
Owner: Herb Miller
Estimated Sales: Less than $500,000
Number Employees: 1-4

23774 Herche Warehouse
4735 Leyden Street
Denver, CO 80216-3301

303-371-8186
Manufacturer and wholesaler/distributor of packag-
ing equipment and materials including bags, con-
tainers, closures, conveyors, labels, linings, tapes,
ties, etc
Customer Service Representative: Cathy Wyatt
Estimated Sales: $1 - 5,000,000
Parent Co: Gulf Systems

23775 Herculean Equipment
4917 Encinita Ave
Temple City, CA 91780

626-286-7057
Fax: 626-286-7922 800-441-3455
Owner: Steven Law
Estimated Sales: $300,000-500,000
Number Employees: 1-4

23776 Hercules Food Equipment
145 Millwick Drive
Weston, ON M9L 1Y7
Canada

416-742-9673
Fax: 416-742-6486 hercules@interlog.com
Custom stainless steel sinks, counters and exhaust
canopies; also, refrigerated and heated display units,
barbecue ovens and Chinese cooking equipment;
wholesaler/distributor of food service equipment;
serving the food servicemarket
President: R Barron
CEO: M Lepage
Number Employees: 20-49
Square Footage: 34000

23777 Herdell Printing Inc
340 Mccormick St
St Helena, CA 94574-1457

707-963-3634
Fax: 707-963-5002 866-963-3634
www.herdellprinting.com
Wine industry labels
President: Mike Herdell
info@herdellprinting.com
VP: Michael Herdell
Quality Control: Steve Herdell
Estimated Sales: $2.5-5 000,000
Number Employees: 20-49

23778 Heritage Bag Co
501 Gateway Pkwy
Roanoke, TX 76262-3481

214-432-3644
Fax: 972-247-3843 800-527-2247
infot@heritage-bag.com www.hunt2recovery.com
Plastic trash bags
CEO: Carl Allen Jr
Contact: Adina Aghinitei
aaghinitei@heritage-bag.com
Estimated Sales: $10-20 Million
Number Employees: 500-999

23779 Heritage Corrugated BoxCorporation
454 Livonia Ave
Brooklyn, NY 11207
718-495-1500
Fax: 718-922-9553
Manufactures corrugated & solid fiber boxes
President: Jeff Schatz
 jeff@heritagecontainer.com
Estimated Sales: $5.2 Million
Number Employees: 50-99
Type of Packaging: Bulk

23780 Heritage Equipment Co
9000 Heritage Dr
Plain City, OH 43064-8744
614-873-3941
Fax: 614-873-3549 800-282-7961
eric@heritage-equipment.com
www.heritage-equipment.com
Owner: Louis Castelli
VP: Lisa Zwirner
Ops Mgr: Lou Costillo
Estimated Sales: $5 - 10 Million
Number Employees: 20-49

23781 Heritage Packaging
625 Fishers Run
Victor, NY 14564-8905
585-742-3310
Fax: 585-742-3311 sales@heritagepackaging.com
www.heritagepackaging.com
Manufacturer and exporter of shipping containers
and packaging for equipment
President: William S Smith
 sales@heritagepackaging.com
Estimated Sales: $1-2.5 Million
Number Employees: 50-99

23782 Herkimer Pallet & Wood Products Company
Arthur Street Extension
Herkimer, NY 13350-1440
315-866-4591
Fax: 315-866-4591
Wooden crates, boxes, pallets, etc
President: Michael Lennon
CFO: Karen Dass
VP Marketing: Dave Bass
Manager: Karen Bass
Estimated Sales: Below $5 Million
Number Employees: 1 to 4

23783 Hermann Laue Spice Company
119 Franklin Street
Uxbridge, ON L9P 1J5
Canada
905-852-5100
Fax: 905-852-1113 www.helacanada.ca
Custom blended spices; technical assistance available
President: Walter Knecht
Director of Sales and Marketing: Eric Nummelin
Number Employees: 35
Square Footage: 228000
Parent Co: Laue, Herman, GmbH
Type of Packaging: Food Service
Brands:
 Hela

23784 Herrmann Ultrasonics
1261 Hardt Cir
Bartlett, IL 60103-1690
630-626-1626
Fax: 630-626-1627 www.herrmannultrasonics.com
Ultrasonic packaging sealing equipment
President: Thomas Herrmann
Marketing Director: Emily Rutkoske
Number Employees: 20-49

23785 Hersey Measurement Company
PO Box 4585
Spartanburg, SC 29305-4585
864-574-8964
Fax: 864-578-7308 800-845-2102
hersey@worldnet.att.net
Batch control systems
Estimated Sales: $20-50 Million
Number Employees: 100-249

23786 Hershey Co.
100 Crystal A Drive
Hershey, PA 17033
800-468-1714
www.thehersheycompany.com
Chocolate, confectionery, snack, refreshment and
grocery products.
Chairman/President/CEO: Michele Buck
Senior VP/CFO: Steve Voskuil
VP/General Counsel/Secretary: James Turoff
Year Founded: 1894
Estimated Sales: $8 Billion
Number Employees: 10,000+
Number of Brands: 33
Type of Packaging: Consumer, Food Service, Private Label
Other Locations:
 Lancaster PA
 Hazleton PA
 Hershey PA
 Memphis TN
 Stuarts Draft VA
 Robinson IL
 Mississauga, Canada
 Sao Paulo, Brazil
 Mandideep, India
 Tokyo, Japan
 Korea, Seoul
 Johor/Malaysia, Singapore
 Guadalajara, Mexico
Brands:
 5th Avenue
 Allan
 Almond Joy
 Brookside
 Bubble Yum
 Cadbury
 Good & Plenty
 Heath
 Hershey's
 Hershey's Bliss
 Hershey's Kisses
 Ice Breakers
 Jolly Rancher
 KitKat
 Krackel
 Lancaster
 Milk Duds
 Mounds
 Mr.Goodbar
 Payday
 Reese's
 Reese's Pieces
 Rolo
 Skor
 Symphony
 Take 5
 Twizzlers
 Whatchamacallit
 Whoppers
 York
 Zagnut
 Zero
 breathsavers

23787 Hess Machine Intl
1040 S State St
Ephrata, PA 17522-2355
717-733-0005
Fax: 717-733-2255 800-735-4377
www.hessmachine.com
Manufacturer and exporter of water treatment equipment including ozone analyzers, ozone generators
and filteration equipment.
President: Richard Hess
Marketing Director: Lynn Martin
Manager: Terry Good
 terry@ozonesolutions.com
Plant Manager: Calburn McEllheauey
Estimated Sales: Less Than $500,000
Number Employees: 1-4

23788 Heuft USA Inc
2820 Thatcher Rd
Downers Grove, IL 60515-4051
630-968-9011
Fax: 630-968-8767 edi.e.gilich@heuft.com
www.heuft.com
Container inspection equipment including online
empty and full container inspectors, valve monitors
and bottle sorting equipment
General Manager: Carl Bonnan
Marketing Manager: Bob Klien
Sales Manager: Carl Bonnan
Administrative Manager: Edi Gilch

Estimated Sales: $10-20 Million
Number Employees: 20-49
Parent Co: Heuft SystemTechnik GmbH

23789 Hevi-Haul InternationalLTD
N90w14555 Commerce Dr
Menomonee Falls, WI 53051-2338
262-502-0333
Fax: 262-502-0260 800-558-0577
www.langelift.com
Manufacturer and exporter of rollers and material
handling equipment
President: Daniel Knaebe
 sales@hevihaul.com
VP: S Knaebe
Sales/Marketing Executive: M Knaebe
Purchasing Agent: M Knaebe
Estimated Sales: $1-2.5 Million
Number Employees: 5-9

23790 Hewitt Manufacturing Co
5365 S 600 E
Waldron, IN 46182-9559
765-525-9829
Fax: 765-525-7185 hewittmfg@tds.net
www.hewittmfg.com
Wire goods including display and refrigerator racks
President: Donald Hewitt
hewittmfg@tds.net
Estimated Sales: $1-2.5 Million
Number Employees: 5-9

23791 Hewitt Soap Company
654 Residenz Pkwy # H
Dayton, OH 45429-6290
937-293-2697
Fax: 937-258-3123 800-543-2245
www.hewittsoap.com
Manufacturer and exporter of bar soap
Vice President of Marketing: Deb McDonough
Estimated Sales: $33.9 Million
Number Employees: 1-4
Square Footage: 400000
Parent Co: ASR

23792 Hewlett-Packard
1000 NE Circle Blvd
Corvallis, OR 97330-4291
541-757-2000
Fax: 541-715-6925 www.hp.com
Printers, computers, desktops, laptops, printer ink
Estimated Sales: $20-50 Million
Number Employees: 5000-9999

23793 Hexion Inc
180 E Broad St
Columbus, OH 43215
614-986-2497
888-443-9466
www.hexion.com
Chemical manufacturer.
Chairman/President/CEO: Craig Rogerson
EVP & Chief Financial Officer: George Knight
EVP/General Counsel/Secretary: Douglas Johns
EVP, Human Resources: John Auletto
EVP, Environmental Health & Safety: Stephanie
Couhig
EVP & Chief Procurement Officer: Nathan Fisher
EVP & Chief Administrative Officer: Matt Sokol
Year Founded: 2005
Estimated Sales: $3.8 Billion
Number Employees: 4,300
Brands:
 Prince

23794 Hi Roller Enclosed BeltConveyors
5100 W 12th St
Sioux Falls, SD 57107-0551
605-332-3200
Fax: 605-332-1107 800-328-1785
sales@hiroller.com www.hiroller.com
Manufacturer and exporter of enclosed belt conveyors and related accessories
Owner: Philip Clark
Controller: Sally Dieltz
Sales Manager: Mike Spillum
General Manager: John Nelson
General Manager: Steve Tweet
Estimated Sales: $10 - 20 Million
Number Employees: 20-49
Square Footage: 120000
Parent Co: Hansen Manufacturing Corporation
Brands:
 Hi Roller

23795 Hi-Tech Packaging Inc
1 Bruce Ave
Stratford, CT 06615-6102
203-378-2700
Fax: 203-378-1344 sales@hitechpackaging.net
www.hitechpackaging.com
Packaging machinery
Manager: Al Thibault
athibault@hitechpackaging.net
Estimated Sales: $1-5 000,000
Number Employees: 20-49

23796 Hi-Temp Inc
820 Mississippi St
PO Box 478
Tuscumbia, AL 35674-4741
256-383-5066
Fax: 256-383-5175 800-239-5066
hitemp@hitemp.net www.hitemp.biz
Check and plug valves, pump impellers, valve
stems, plastic mallets, rubber pipe grommets, gas-
kets, dies and floor drains
CEO: Billy Rumbley
Plant Manager: Randy Inman
Estimated Sales: $5-10 Million
Number Employees: 20-49
Square Footage: 76200

23797 Hibco Plastics
1820 US 601 Hwy
PO Box 157
Yadkinville, NC 27055-6347
336-463-2391
Fax: 336-463-5591 800-849-8683
www.hibco.com
Plastic foam
President: Mark Pavlansky
Chairman Board/CEO: Dan Pavlansky
Quality Control: Landon Hardy
Sales: Chris Pavlansky
Accounts Receivable: Sharon Renegar
Purchasing Manager: Mike Russell
Estimated Sales: $10 - 20 Million
Number Employees: 50-99
Square Footage: 240000

23798 Hibrett Puratex
7001 Westfield Avenue
Pennsauken, NJ 8110
856-662-1717
Fax: 856-662-0550 800-260-5124
www.hibrettpuratex.com
Manufacturer and wholesaler/distributor of com-
pound cleaning chemicals and water treatment
products
CEO: Jerome Ellerbee
Sales: Nelissa Abreu
Contact: Stefanie Geoghegan
sgeoghegan@hibrettpuratex.com
Number Employees: 20
Number of Products: 1000
Square Footage: 42000
Parent Co: Hibrett Puratex
Type of Packaging: Private Label

23799 Hickory Industries
4900 W Side Ave
North Bergen, NJ 00047
201-223-4382
Fax: 201-223-0950 800-732-9153
www.hickorybbq.com
Manufacturer and exporter of cooking equipment in-
cluding grills, warmers, ovens and rotisseries; also,
barbecue machinery and accessories
President: Steven Maroti
VP Sales/Marketing: Joe Slusz
Contact: Beth Beyer
beth.beyer@hickorybbq.com
Estimated Sales: $20 - 50 Million
Number Employees: 100-249
Square Footage: 50000
Brands:
Hickory
Old Hickory

23800 Hickory Zesti Smoked Specialties
783 Old Hickory Boulevard
Suite 300
Brentwood, TN 37027-4508
615-373-8838
Fax: 615-371-1780 800-251-2076
www.hickoryspecialties.com
Liquid smoke products
President: Pat Moeller

Estimated Sales: $5 - 10 Million
Number Employees: 110

23801 Hiclay Studios
3015 Locust Street
St Louis, MO 63103-1328
314-533-8393
Fax: 314-533-8397
Displays and signs
President: Harold A Lutz Jr
Estimated Sales: $1-2.5 Million
Number Employees: 1-4

23802 High Ground of Texas
401 N. 3rd Street
PO Box 716
Stratford, TX 79084-0716
806-366-7510
Fax: 806-366-7511 www.highground.org
Estimated Sales: Below $500,000
Number Employees: 1-4

23803 High-Purity Standards
7221 Investment Drive
North Charleston, SC 29418
843-767-7900
Fax: 843-767-7906 866-767-4771
www.highpuritystandards.com
Manufactures single and multielement standards of
extremely high purity for the calibration of analyti-
cal instruments such as the AAS, ICP, ICP-MS and
IC.
President: Theodore Rains
CEO: Connie Hayes
Contact: Stephanie Audette
stephanie@hps.net
Estimated Sales: $1,904,757
Number Employees: 20-49
Square Footage: 40000

23804 Highland Plastics Inc
3650 Dulles Dr
Mira Loma, CA 91752-3260
951-360-9587
Fax: 951-360-9465 800-368-0491
mmurphy@hiplas.com www.hiplas.com
Lid capping equipment and containers, cups and clo-
sures; also, custom printing and labeling available
CEO: James Nelson
jnelson@hiplas.com
CEO: James Nelson
Marketing Director: Mark Murphy
Estimated Sales: $10-20 Million
Number Employees: 250-499
Square Footage: 162000

23805 Highland Sugarworks
49 Parker Rd
Wilson Industrial Park, P.O. Box 58
Websterville, VT 5678
802-479-1747
Fax: 802-479-1737 800-452-4012
www.highlandsugarworks.com
Pure maple syrup and pancake mixes
President: Jim Mac Isaac
jim@highlandsugarworks.com
Sales/Marketing: Jim Close
Operations: Deb Frimodig
Estimated Sales: $500,000-$1 Million
Number Employees: 10-19
Square Footage: 60000
Type of Packaging: Consumer, Food Service, Pri-
vate Label, Bulk
Brands:
Highland Sugarworks

23806 Highland Supply Corp
1111 6th St
Highland, IL 62249-1408
618-654-2161
Fax: 618-654-3911 800-472-3645
orderdesk@highlandsupply.com
www.billkreitzer.com
Converted printed, tinted and clear film; also, shred-
ded material and pre-cut covers
President: Donald Weder
dweder@highlandsupply.com
Sales Service Manager: Scott Greathouse
Estimated Sales: $20 - 50 Million
Number Employees: 250-499
Brands:
Speed Cover

23807 Highlight Industries
2694 Prairie St SW
Wyoming, MI 49519-2461
616-531-2464
Fax: 616-531-0506 800-531-2465
info@highlightindustries.com
www.highlightindustries.com
Manufacturer and exporter of stretch wrapping ma-
chinery, case sealing, case strapping, and shrink
wrap machinery
Owner: Kurt Riemenschneide
Estimated Sales: $10-20 Million
Number Employees: 50-99
Square Footage: 120000
Brands:
Freedom
Poly Packer
Revolver
Synergy

23808 Hilden Halifax
1044 Commerce Lane
P.O. Box 1098
South Boston, VA 24592-1098
434-572-3965
Fax: 434-572-4781 800-431-2514
www.hildenamerica.com
Manufacturer, importer and exporter of table linens
and kitchen textiles
President: Russell Basch
Vice President of Sales: Tom Hall
Sales: Sharlene Gulley
Estimated Sales: $2.5-5 Million
Number Employees: 20-49
Square Footage: 160000
Parent Co: Hilden Manufacturing Company
Brands:
Village Square

23809 Hildreth Wood Products Inc
825 Mount Vernon Rd
Wadesboro, NC 28170-7108
704-826-8326
Fax: 704-826-8097
www.hildrethwoodproducts.com
Wooden pallets and skids
Owner: Blake E Hildreth Jr
bhildreth@hildrethwoodproducts.com
General Manager: Leon Hildreth
Estimated Sales: $3 - 5 Million
Number Employees: 20-49

23810 Hilex Company
990 Apollo Rd # A
Eagan, MN 55121-2390
651-454-1160
Fax: 651-454-2507
Bleaches, sanitizers and disinfectants
President: Tom Gates
COO: Ray Lee
Estimated Sales: $5-10 Million
Number Employees: 20 to 49
Square Footage: 120000
Brands:
Hilex 6-40

23811 Hill Brush, Inc.
811 Rolyn Ave
Baltimore, MD 21237
410-325-7000
Fax: 410-325-6477 800-998-1515
www.hillbrushinc.com/index.htm
Cleaning systems for hygienically sensitive areas
within food and beverage production facilities, res-
taurants & kitchens, catering, dairies and hospitals.
Color coded manual cleaning tools.
President: Philip Coward
Manager: Ernest Atkinson
VP: Peter Coward
National Sales Director: James Sokaitis
Contact: Lori Cain
lori@hillbrush.com
Manager: Margie Gessinger
Estimated Sales: $600 Thousand
Type of Packaging: Food Service, Bulk

23812 Hill Manufacturing Co Inc
1500 Jonesboro Rd SE
Atlanta, GA 30315-4085
404-522-8364
Fax: 404-522-9694 www.hillmfg.com

Manufacturer, importer and exporter of USDA cleaning products including hand cleaners, liquid washing and industrial cleaning compounds, germicide disinfectants and floor polish
President: Stewart Hillman
VP: Jack Hillman
Estimated Sales: $20-50 Million
Number Employees: 100-249
Square Footage: 110000
Type of Packaging: Bulk
Brands:
  Hilco

23813 Hill Parts
211 Hogan Pond Ln
Ball Ground, GA 30107-4380
    770-735-4181
Fax: 770-735-4494 800-241-4003
sales@hillparts.com www.hillparts.com
Equipment and parts for poultry processing
Owner: Donald Hill
Chief Executive: Billy Hill
Account Manager: Marty Lee
Number Employees: 5-9
Parent Co: Cooperatieve Meyn

23814 Hillards Chocolate System
275 E Center St
West Bridgewater, MA 02379-1813
    508-587-3666
Fax: 508-587-3735 800-258-1530
sales@hilliardschocolate.com
www.hilliardschocolate.com
Candymaking utensils and manufacturers of chocolate machinery
President: James S Bourne
Contact: Daniel Andersen
  dandersen@hilliardschocolate.com
Estimated Sales: $1 Million
Number Employees: 5-9
Type of Packaging: Bulk
Brands:
  Hilliard

23815 Hilliard Corp
100 W 4th St
Elmira, NY 14901-2190
    607-733-7121
Fax: 607-737-1108 hilliard@hilliardcorp.com
www.hilliardcorp.com
Motion control products, oil filtration and reclaiming equipment, starters for industrial gas, diesel engines and gas turbines, and plate and frame filter presses used in the food and beverage industry.
President: Paul Webb
CEO: Nelson Mooers Van Den
  n.vandenblink@hilliardcorp.com
CEO: Nelson Mooers Van Den
CEO: Nelson Mooers Van Den Blink
Regional Sales Manager: Gerry Lachut
Estimated Sales: $50 - 75 Million
Number Employees: 500-999

23816 Hillside Metal Ware Company
1060 Commerce Ave
Union, NJ 07083-5026
    908-964-3080
Fax: 908-964-3082
Manufacturer and exporter of aluminum cookware and bakeware including molds, black steel pizza, springform and cake pans
Estimated Sales: $2 Million
Number Employees: 20-49
Square Footage: 120000
Brands:
  Hillware

23817 Hilltop Services LLC
6616 Fribay Road
Byron, IL 61010
    815-234-8600
Fax: 815-234-3028 mmhilltop@verizon.net
Supplies prep equipment/machinery
President: Michael Lingel
CFO: Mary Lingel
Sales/PR: Mike Lingel

23818 Hillyard Inc
302 N 4th St
P.O. Box 909
St Joseph, MO 64501-1720
    816-233-1321
Fax: 816-383-8414 800-365-1555
www.hillyard.com

Manufacturer and exporter of floor seals, finishes, waxes, polishes and cleaners
President: Jim Corolus
CFO: Jana Hessemyer
Purchasing Manager: Tom Armstrong
Estimated Sales: $66 Million
Number Employees: 500-999
Square Footage: 325600

23819 Hilter Stainless
614 Eau Placine Street
Stratford, WI 54484
    715-387-8260
Fax: 715-387-0148
Estimated Sales: $1-2.5 Million
Number Employees: 15

23820 Himolene
1648 Diplomat Drive
Carrollton, TX 75006-6847
    203-731-3600
Fax: 203-731-3620 800-777-4411
High density industrial can liners
VP/General Manager: Paul Hart
Marketing Manager: Dave Shewmaker
Estimated Sales: $1-2.5 Million
Number Employees: 5-9
Parent Co: First Brands Corporation
Brands:
  Stick 'n Stay
  Tie-Tie

23821 (HQ)Hinchcliff Products Company
13477 Prospect Road
Strongsville, OH 44149
    440-238-5200
Fax: 440-238-5202 sales@hinchcliffproducts.com
www.hinchcliffproducts.com
Manufacturer and exporter of wooden pallets, skids, boxes, crates and containers
President: Jay D Phillips
VP of Sales: Don Phillips
Contact: Donald Phillips
  sales@hinchcliffproducts.com
Purchasing Manager: Scott Phillips
Estimated Sales: $500,000-$1 Million
Number Employees: 1-4
Number of Products: 3
Square Footage: 200000

23822 Hinds-Bock Corp
2122 222nd St SE
Bothell, WA 98021-4430
    425-885-1183
Fax: 425-885-1492 www.hinds-bock.com
Manufacturer and exporter of standard and custom piston filling machines, depositors and transfer pumps for liquids and viscous products with delicate particulates
President: Gary Hinds
CFO: John Davis
VP Sales/Marketing: Lance Aasness
Estimated Sales: $5 - 10 Million
Number Employees: 20-49
Square Footage: 96000

23823 Hines III
1650 Art Museum Dr
Suite 18
Jacksonville, FL 32207-2188
    904-398-5110
Fax: 904-396-1867
Fiberglass, steel and wood benches/seats; also, planters, ash and trash receptacles, tables, table tops and planter/bench combinations
CEO: Samuel Hines
Estimated Sales: Below $5 Million
Number Employees: 1-4
Square Footage: 64000

23824 Hinkle Manufacturing
5th & D Streets Ampoint Industrial Park
Perrysburg, OH 43551
    419-666-5550
Fax: 419-666-5367 419-666-5367
www.hinklemfg.com
Corrugated boxes and recyclable plastic and foam packaging
Manger: Taber Hinkle
VP Marketing: Malcolm Eddy
General Manager: John Mayland
Estimated Sales: $10-20 Million
Number Employees: 50-99

23825 Hino Diesel Trucks
41180 Bridge Street
Novi, MI 48375
    248-699-9300
Fax: 248-699-9310 daniels@hino.com
www.hino.com
VP: Francis Merz
IT Manager: Brad Czischke
VP Marketing and Dealer Operations: Glenn Ellis
SM, Human Resources and Administration: Joseph Whalen
VP of Service Operations: George M. Daniels

23826 Hishi Plastics
600 Ryerson Road
Lincoln Park, NJ 07035-2057
    973-633-1230
Fax: 973-872-8381
customerservice@hishiplastics.com
www.hishiplastics.com
Food and HBA packaging materials
President: Shawn Kawazato
Contact: Kathy Ammirata
  kammirata@hishiplastics.com
Estimated Sales: $5-10 Million
Number Employees: 50-99

23827 Hiss Stamp Company
100 N Grant Ave
Columbus, OH 43215-5119
    614-224-5119
Fax: 614-224-0464
Manufacturer and wholesaler/distributor of stamps and FDA approved inks
Manager: Michael Gaborcik
Estimated Sales: Less than $500,000
Number Employees: 4
Square Footage: 7000
Parent Co: Cosco Industries

23828 Hitachi Maxco LTD
1630 Cobb International Blvd
Kennesaw, GA 30152-4353
    770-424-9350
Fax: 770-424-9145 800-241-8209
twalker@hitmax.com www.hitmax.com
President: Martin Bando
  mbando@hitmax.com
CFO: Douglas Roberts
Number Employees: 20-49

23829 Hitec Food Equipment
818 Lively Blvd
Wood Dale, IL 60191-1202
    630-521-9460
Fax: 630-521-9466 information@hitec-usa.com
www.hitec-usa.com
Owner: Charles Chacon
  cchacon@hitec-usa.com
CFO: Takeshi Kojima
Estimated Sales: Below $5 000,000
Number Employees: 5-9

23830 Hitec Food Equipment
818 Lively Blvd
Wood Dale, IL 60191-1202
    630-521-9460
Fax: 630-521-9466 information@hitec-usa.com
www.hitec-usa.com
Food processing machines for the ham and sausage industry.
Owner: Charles Chacon
  cchacon@hitec-usa.com
Number Employees: 5-9

23831 Hiwin Technologies Corporation
520 E Business Center Drive
Mt Prospect, IL 60056-2186
    847-827-2270
Fax: 847-827-2291 info@hiwin.com
www.hiwin.com.tw
High quality linear motion products
President: Joe Jou
Sales Engineer: Fred Chevalau
Sales Engineer: Joe Long
Sales Engineer: Chuck Haas
Accounting Dept.: Geneva Wang
Inventory Control: Andrew Choi
Estimated Sales: $5 - 10 Million
Number Employees: 30

23832 Hixson Architecture Engrng
659 Van Meter St
Cincinnati, OH 45202-1568

513-241-1230
Fax: 513-241-1287 info@hixson-inc.com
www.hixson-inc.com
Hixson provides engineering and design solutions
that enable food and beverage processors to increase
production speed and thoughput, improve product
quality and consistency, reduce costs, and deliver
capital projects more effectively.Design capabilities
include process, packaging, material handling, automation, electrical, HVAC, plumbing, refrigeration,
civil and structural engineering, architecture, environmental, health and safety compliance, project
management, constructionadministration.
President: Michael Follmer
m.follmer@hixson-inc.com
Sales: Jim Rivard
Sales: Mike Steur
Estimated Sales: $20 - 30 Million
Number Employees: 100-249

23833 Hixson Architecture Engrng
659 Van Meter St
Cincinnati, OH 45202-1568

513-241-1230
Fax: 513-241-1287 info@hixson-inc.com
www.hixson-inc.com
Engineering and design solutions that enable food
and beverage processors to increase production
speed and through-put, improve product quality and
consistency, reduce costs, and deliver capital projects more effectively. Designcapabilities include
process, packaging, material handling, automation,
electrical, HVAC, plumbing, refridgeration, civil and
structural. Hixson assists companies with renovations, expansion, site selection, master planning,
utility improvements andmore.
President: Bryan Suutherly
bsuutherly@hixson-inc.com
Chief Financial Officer: Thomas Banker
Vice President: William Sander NCARB
Marketing/Sales: Mike Steur
Sales: Jim Rivard
Public Relations: Patricia Helmbrook
Estimated Sales: $20-30 Million
Number Employees: 100-249

23834 Hoarel Sign Co
819 NE 7th Ave
Amarillo, TX 79107-5417

806-373-2175
Fax: 806-373-2329 www.hoarelsign.com
Point of purchase displays and signs including ad-
vertising, changeable letter, electric, interchange-
able, luminous tube and plastic
President: Gary Cox
Treasurer: Linda Cox
VP: Ray Cox
Estimated Sales: $1-2.5 Million
Number Employees: 10-19
Square Footage: 32000

23835 Hobart
701 S Ridge Ave
Troy, OH 45374-0001

888-378-1338
www.hobartcorp.com
Bakery machinery and equipment.
Year Founded: 1897
Estimated Sales: Above $5 Billion
Number Employees: 1,000-4,999
Parent Co: ITW Food Equipment Group LLC

23836 Hodge Design Assoc PC
22 Chestnut St
Evansville, IN 47713-1022

812-422-2558
Fax: 812-422-3337 info@hodgestructural.com
Wine industry label design
Owner: Gray Hodge
ghodge@hodgedesign.com
Estimated Sales: $1 - 5 000,000
Number Employees: 5-9

23837 Hodge Manufacturing Company
55 Fisk Ave
Springfield, MA 01107

413-781-6800
Fax: 413-349-8235 800-262-4634
www.durhammfg.com

Steel work benches, carts, platforms, shelf and hand
trucks, recycle receptacles, waste material contain-
ers, shelving racks, hook-on bins, storage cabinets,
safety equipment, wire carts, etc
Manager: Bob Hall
Contact: Edwin Kossoy
e.kossoy@hodgemfg.com
Estimated Sales: $10-20,000,000
Number Employees: 50-99
Square Footage: 50000

23838 Hodges
PO Box 187
Vienna, IL 62995-0187

618-658-9070
Fax: 773-379-8102 800-444-0011
Racks, shelving, casters, dolly trucks, utilty carts
and mobile storage equipment
National Sales Manager: Chris Geurden
Estimated Sales: $1 - 5,000,000
Number Employees: 100-249
Square Footage: 240000
Parent Co: Leggett & Platt Storage Products Group
Brands:
Postmaster

23839 Hoegger Alpina
PO Box 175918
Covington, KY 41017-5918

865-344-8642
Fax: 865-344-8743
Commerical meat processing machines, choppers,
stuffers, and chip machines

23840 Hoegger Food Technology
3555 Holly Ln N # 10
Suite 10
Minneapolis, MN 55447-1285

763-233-6930
Fax: 802-223-5499 877-789-5400
info.usa@hoegger.com www.hoegger.com
Meat presses for bacon, pork and strip steaks, as
well as post packaging pasteurization products for
hams, sausage and other meat products as well as
pasta and vegetables.
Manager: Mike Collins
Number Employees: 5-9

23841 Hoffer Flow Controls Inc
107 Kitty Hawk Ln
P.O. Box 2145
Elizabeth City, NC 27909-6756

252-331-1997
Fax: 252-331-2886 800-628-4584
info@hofferflow.com www.hofferflow.com
Manufacturer and exporter of sanitary turbine
flowmeters for batch controlling, flow rate indica-
tion and totalization.
President: Bob Carrell
bcarrell@hofferflow.com
CEO: Ken Hoffer
CEO: Sandra Kelly
Quality Control: Wendy Brabble
Marketing Manager: Janna Critcher
Sales: Linda Markham
Production Manager: Deborah Blakeney
Purchasing: Melissa Stallings
Estimated Sales: $5-10 Million
Number Employees: 50-99
Square Footage: 80000
Brands:
Hoffer

23842 Hoffman & Levy Inc Tasseldepot
3251 SW 13th Dr # 3
Deerfield Beach, FL 33442-8166

954-698-0001
Fax: 954-698-0009 info@tasseldepot.com
www.tasseldepot.com
Manufacturer and exporter of napkin rings and deco-
rative items including tassles and chair tie-backs
President: Roger Leavy
info@tasseldepot.com
Marketing/Design: April Leavy
Estimated Sales: $1-2.5 Million
Number Employees: 50-99
Square Footage: 46000

23843 Hoffman Co
1306 Laredo St
Corpus Christi, TX 78401-3249

361-882-9281
Fax: 361-883-1677 sales@hoffman-co.com
www.hoffmanandcompany.com

Doors, cabinets and store fixtures
President: Bryan Hoffman
bhoff@hoffmancompany.com
Marketing Manager: Brian Hoffman
Estimated Sales: $5-10 Million
Number Employees: 20-49

23844 Hoffmann LA Roche
340 Kingsland St
Nutley, NJ 07110-1199

973-235-4761
Fax: 973-235-3775 800-526-6367
President: George B Abercrombie
Chief Financial Officer: Ivor MacLeod
Contact: Sophie Actis
sophie.actis@roche.com
Number Employees: 1-4
Parent Co: Roche Group

23845 Hoffmaster Group Inc
2920 N Main St
Oshkosh, WI 54901-1221

920-235-9330
Fax: 920-235-1642 800-367-2877
info@solocup.com www.hoffmaster.com
Institutional and consumer food service items: bak-
ing, eclair, portion, burger cups; hot dog trays; pan
liners; bath mats/car mats; doilies; lace and linen
placemats, printed and custom designed placemats;
plain and printed napkins;tray sovers and table
covers
President: Robert Korzenski
CEO: Dennis Mehiel
CFO: Haris Heinsen
VP Operations: Bryan Hollenbach
Marketing Director: Beth Dahlke
Sales Director: John Lewchenko
Public Relations: Jenny Leichtfuss
Plant Manager: Tom Glaeser
Purchasing Manager: Mike Marquardt
Number Employees: 500-999
Number of Brands: 9
Square Footage: 970000
Parent Co: SF Holdings Group
Other Locations:
Fonda Group
Lakeland FL
Fonda Group
Goshen IA
Fonda Group
Glens Falls NY
Fonda Group
Williamsberg PA
Fonda Group
St. Albans VT
Fonda Group
Appleton WI
Fonda Group
Augusta GA
Fonda Group
Indianapolis IA
Brands:
American
Budgetware
Dollarwise
Firmware
Fonda
Hoffmaster
Linen-Like
Sensations
Smartware

23846 Hoffmaster Group Inc
2920 N Main St
Oshkosh, WI 54901-1221

Fax: 920-235-1642 800-327-9774
marketing@hoffmaster.com www.hoffmaster.com
Manufacturer and exporter of strip lace, place mats,
baking cups, tray covers and doilies including paper
lace, linen, glassine, grease-proof and foil
CEO: Rory Leyden
rory.leyden@creativeconverting.com
Customer Service Manager: Lori Hart-Noyes
General Manager: Wayne Grant
Number Employees: 500-999
Square Footage: 50000
Type of Packaging: Consumer, Private Label, Bulk
Brands:
Gay 90's

23847 Hoffmaster Group Inc.
2920 N. Main St.
Oshkosh, WI 54901

800-558-9300
www.hoffmaster.com
Disposable tableware including plates, napkins, table covers, cups, bowls, trays, take-out containers, etc.
President/CEO: Rory Leyden
Year Founded: 1947
Estimated Sales: $100-500 Million
Number Employees: 500-999
Number of Brands: 17
Brands:
  Bello Lino
  CaterWrap
  Classy Kid
  Combo Packs
  Earth Wise Tree Free
  Earth Wise
  FashnPoint
  Linen-Like Natural
  Linen-Like Supreme
  Linen-Like
  Linen-Like Select
  Multipack
  Party in a Box
  Quickset
  S!mply Baked
  Spunbond
  SturdyStyle

23848 Hoffmeyer Corp
1600 Factor Ave
San Leandro, CA 94577-5618

510-895-9014
Fax: 510-895-9014 888-744-1826
sales@hoffmeyerco.com
Manufacturer and fabricator of conveyor belting, gaskets, seals, hoses, fittings and assemblies
Owner: Frederick O Shay
Chairman Board/CEO: Frederick Oshay
Chairman: Frederick Oshay
Contact: Mike Alberts
  malberts@hoffmeyerco.com
Estimated Sales: $5 - 10 Million
Number Employees: 1-4
Square Footage: 34000

23849 Hoge Brush Company
701 S Main Street
State Route 29
New Knoxville, OH 45871

419-753-2351
Fax: 419-753-2893 800-494-4643
www.hoge.com
Counter dusters, dairy, floor, sweeping, garage and window brushes, street brooms, etc
President: John Hoge
Sales/Marketing Executive: David Zwiep
Production Manager: Ray Slone
Plant Manager: Dave Zwiep
Purchasing Manager: David Zwiep
Estimated Sales: $1 - 3 Million
Number Employees: 5-9
Square Footage: 71484
Parent Co: Hoge Lumber Company
Brands:
  Hoge

23850 Hogshire Industries
2401 Hampton Blvd
Norfolk, VA 23517

757-877-2297
Fax: 757-624-2328 www.bigleycanvas.com
Commercial awnings
Estimated Sales: $1-2,500,000
Number Employees: 20-49

23851 Hogtown Brewing Company
2351 Royal Windsor Drive
Unit 6
Mississauga, ON L5J 4S7
Canada

905-855-9065
Fax: 905-822-0990 www.hogtownbrewers.org
Beers; bottling services
President: Maria Lopez
General Manager: Peter Lazaro
Number Employees: 5-9
Type of Packaging: Consumer, Food Service

23852 Hohn Manufacturing Company
200 Sun Valley Cir
Fenton, MO 63026

636-349-1400
Fax: 636-349-1440 800-878-1440
hohnmfginc@toast.net
Manufacturer and exporter of furniture polishes, cleaning compounds, soaps, detergents, tablets, etc
President: Larry Harrington
Estimated Sales: $1-4 Million
Number Employees: 5-9
Square Footage: 72000
Type of Packaging: Private Label
Brands:
  Vita Lustre

23853 Hohner Corporation
PO Box 3004
Beamsville, ON L0R 1B3
Canada

905-563-4924
Fax: 905-563-7209 800-295-5693
hohner@hohner.com www.hohner.com
President: Walter Bloechle
Number Employees: 10

23854 (HQ)Holcor
13603 S Halsted Street
Riverdale, IL 60827-1163

708-841-3800
Fax: 708-841-3941
Fluorescent, incandescent and mercury lighting
President: S Larson
Estimated Sales: $20-50 Million
Number Employees: 50-99
Square Footage: 5000

23855 (HQ)Holden Graphic Services
607 Washington Ave N
Minneapolis, MN 55401-1220

612-339-0241
Fax: 612-349-0433 holden@usinternet.com
Printed cash register tapes, coupons and business forms
President: George T Holden
CFO: Gary Plager
Sales Manager: Dave Brow
Contact: Craig Fixell
  cfixell@holdenonline.com
Estimated Sales: $5-10 Million
Number Employees: 20-49
Other Locations:
  Holden Graphic Services
  Minneapolis MN

23856 Holland Applied Technologies
7050 High Grove Blvd
Burr Ridge, IL 60527-7595

630-325-5130
Fax: 630-654-2518 information@hollandapt.com
www.hollandapt.com
Packaging equipment and materials, clean-in-place systems, filters, gauges, heat exchangers and valves
President: Dave Cheney
VP: Fred Kramer
Estimated Sales: $25 Million
Number Employees: 50-99

23857 Holland Chemicals Company
4590 Rhodes Drive
Windsor, ON N8W 5C2
Canada

519-948-4373
Fax: 519-945-2256 info@hollandcleaning.com
www.hollandcleaning.com
Floor finishes and detergents
Manager: Mike Shalub

23858 Holland Co Inc
153 Howland Ave
Adams, MA 01220-1199

413-743-1292
Fax: 413-743-1298 800-639-9602
info@hollandcompany.com
www.hollandcompany.com
Manufacturer and exporter of food grade additives including ammonium, potassium and iron-free aluminum sulfates
President: Daniel J Holland
Estimated Sales: $10-20,000,000
Number Employees: 20-49

23859 Holland Manufacturing Co Inc
15 Main St
Succasunna, NJ 07876-1747

973-584-8141
Fax: 973-584-6845 www.hollandmfg.com
Converted paper products and packaging tapes
President: Jack Holland
CEO: Edelina Zajac
  edelina@hollandmfg.com
CFO: Mitch Cantor
R&D: Donald Thoren
Estimated Sales: $20 - 50 Million
Number Employees: 50-99

23860 Hollander Horizon International
16 Wall St
Princeton, NJ 08540-1513

609-924-7577
Fax: 609-924-8626 www.hhisearch.com
Hollander Horizon International is the premier executive search firm specializing in the technical sector of the food and consumer products industry. the areas we serve are: research and development, manufacturing and engineeringquality control, and quality assurance.
East Coast Senior Partner: Michael Hollander
West Coast Senior Partner: Arnold Zimmerman
Contact: Sheri Baker
  sbaker@hhisearch.com
Estimated Sales: $300,000-500,000
Number Employees: 5-9
Parent Co: Hollander Horizon International

23861 Hollandia Bakeries Limited
PO Box 100
Mt Brydges, ON N0L 1W0
Canada

519-264-1020
800-265-3480
www.hollandiacookies.com
Cookies
President: Joop De Voest Jr
Controller: Rick Bannister
Quality Control: Mike Hobley
VP Sales: Doug Smith
Brands:
  Gourmet Specialty Cookies
  Hard Cookies
  Kerleens
  Mini Tubs
  Red Label
  Soft Cookies
  Sugar Free Cookies

23862 Hollingsworth Custom Wood Products
284 N Street
Sault Ste. Marie, ON P6A 7B8
Canada

705-759-1756
Fax: 705-759-0275
Manufacturer and exporter of butchers' blocks, cutting boards and wooden bakers' tops
Marketing Director: Paul Hollingsworth
Customer Service: Ruth Bradley
General Manager: Jim Webb
Estimated Sales: $1 - 5 Million
Number Employees: 15
Parent Co: Soo Mill Lumber
Brands:
  Woodwelded

23863 Hollowell Products Corporation
570 Central St
Wyandotte, MI 48192-7123

734-282-8200
Fax: 734-282-0678
Industrial vacuum cleaners including mobile, gas and electric powered
President: John F Hollowell
Contact: John Hollowell
  jhollowell@elephant-vac.com
Estimated Sales: Below $5 Million
Number Employees: 5-9

23864 Hollowick Inc
100 Fairgrounds Dr
Manlius, NY 13104-1699

315-682-2163
Fax: 315-682-6948 800-367-3015
info@hollowick.com
Manufacturer and exporter of liquid candle lamps, lamp fuel, wax candles, chafing fuel and silk flowers ceramic vases

President: Alan Menter
info@hollowick.com
CFO: Eugene Duffy
Marketing: Mike Cleveland
Sales: Mike Cleveland
Plant Manager: Tom Palmeter
Estimated Sales: $5-10 Million
Number Employees: 20-49
Brands:
　Easy Florals
　Easy Heat
　Select Wax

23865 Holly International
PO Box 265
Lake Elsinore, CA 92531-0265
909-678-8386
Fax: 909-678-7856

Equipment

23866 Hollymatic Corp
600 E Plainfield Rd
Countryside, IL 60525-6900
708-579-3700
Fax: 708-579-1057 hollyinfo@hollymatic.com
www.hollymatic.com
Manufacturer, exporter and importer of food processing equipment and supplies including tenderizers, grinders, mixers/grinders/ patty machines, meat saws, etc.
President: James Azzar
R&D: Hardev Somal
Marketing Manager: Rob Kovack
Manager: Jim Trejo
jtrejo@hollymatic.com
Estimated Sales: $5 - 10 Million
Number Employees: 20-49
Type of Packaging: Food Service
Brands:
　Hollymatic

23867 Hollywood Banners
539 Oak St
Copiague, NY 11726-3261
631-842-3000
Fax: 631-842-3148 800-691-5652
info@hollywoodbanners.com
www.hollywoodbanners.com
Manufacturer and exporter of indoor and outdoor banners including plastic and cloth
President: Daniel F Mahoney
dmaoney@hollywoodbanners.com
Sales Exec: Daniel F Mahoney
Production Manager: Hugo Canedo
Estimated Sales: $1-3 Million
Number Employees: 20-49
Square Footage: 100000

23868 Holman Boiler Works
1956 Singleton Blvd
Dallas, TX 75212
214-637-0020
Fax: 214-637-2539 800-331-1956
Manufacturer and exporter of watertube and firetube boilers; also, burners
President: John Campollo
sales@holmanboiler.com
CEO: Richard Maxson
Quality Control: Greg Martinez
Manager Business Development: Gary Perskhini
Estimated Sales: $50 - 100 Million
Number Employees: 50-99
Parent Co: Copes-Vulcan
Brands:
　E.D.G.E.

23869 Holman Cooking Equipment
10 Sunnen Dr
Saint Louis, MO 63143-3800
888-356-5362
Fax: 800-264-6666
Food service equipment including conveyor toasters, conveyor ovens and specialty/finishing ovens
CFO: Mike Barber
CEO: Frank Ricchio
VP Engineering: Doug Vogt
Marketing Manager: Candi Benz
Number Employees: 100-249
Square Footage: 80000
Parent Co: Star Manufacturing International

23870 Holmco Container Manufacturing, LTD
1501 TR 183
Baltic, OH 43804-9677
330-897-4503
Fax: 330-698-3200
Manufacturer and exporter of stainless steel milk containers.
Owner: Eli Troyer
Number Employees: 2
Square Footage: 38400
Type of Packaging: Food Service

23871 Holo-Source Corporation
12280 Hubbard St
Livonia, MI 48150
734-427-1530
Fax: 734-525-8520 888-995-7799
sales@holo-source.com www.holo-source.com
Holographic materials for packaging and label applications
CEO: Rob Levy
Year Founded: 1986
Estimated Sales: $100,000,000 - $499,999,999
Number Employees: 51-200

23872 Holophane
P.O. Box 3004
Newark, OH 43058-3004
740-587-7218
Fax: 740-349-4451 sbacklund@holophane.com
www.holophane.com
Lighting and control equipment, glass reflectors and HID lighting fixtures, emergency lighting systems, and back-up power supplies
President: Crawford Lipsey
CFO: Daren Cox
Vice President: Bob Petro
Quality Control: Lowry Pierce
Manufacturing Director: Kim Lombardi
Contact: William Gordon
bgordon@holophane.com
Estimated Sales: $50 - 100 Million
Number Employees: 10-19

23873 Holsman Sign Svc
15002 Woodworth Rd
Cleveland, OH 44110-3310
216-761-4433
Fax: 216-761-4439
Signs including neon, electric, plastic, wood, vinyl, metal, etc.; also, service and installation available
Branch Manager: J Burge
Estimated Sales: $1 - 5 Million
Number Employees: 10-19
Square Footage: 120000
Parent Co: Identitek

23874 Holstein Manufacturing
5368 110th St
Holstein, IA 51025-8131
712-368-4342
Fax: 712-368-2351 800-368-4342
hmi@pionet.net www.holsteinmfg.com
Barbecue equipment, portable grills and flatbed, livestock and concession trailers
Vice President: Darrin Schmidt
dlshmidt@ruralwaves.us
VP: Darrin Schmidt
Estimated Sales: $1-2.5 Million
Number Employees: 5-9

23875 Home City Ice Co
6045 Bridgetown Rd # 1
Cincinnati, OH 45248-3047
513-598-3000
Fax: 513-574-5409 800-759-4411
www.homecityice.com
Packaged and block ice
Manager: Robert Everly
Estimated Sales: $1-2.5 Million
Number Employees: 20-49

23876 Home Plastics Inc
5250 NE 17th St
Des Moines, IA 50313-2192
515-265-2562
Fax: 515-265-8872 info@homeplastics.com
www.homeplastics.com
Manufacturer and exporter of polyethylene heat sealed bags, tubes and liners; also, plastic film and plain and printed slip-on sleeve labels, political signs

President and QC: Samuel Siegel
Manager: Bob Rees
brees@homeplastics.com
Estimated Sales: $20 - 50 Million
Number Employees: 100-249
Type of Packaging: Consumer, Food Service, Private Label, Bulk

23877 Home Rubber Co
31 Wolverton St
Trenton, NJ 08611-2429
609-394-1176
Fax: 609-396-1985 800-257-9441
info@homerubber.com www.homerubber.com
Manufacturer and exporter of industrial rubber food and milk unloading hoses, belting, molded goods and sheet rubber
President: Rich Balka
VP: Stephen Kelley
Estimated Sales: $10-20 Million
Number Employees: 20-49
Brands:
　Sterling

23878 (HQ)Homer Laughlin China Co
672 Fiesta Dr
Newell, WV 26050-1299
304-387-1300
Fax: 304-387-0593 800-452-4462
hlc@hlchina.com
Manufacturer and exporter of dinnerware china
President: Elizabeth Mc Ilvain
emcilvain@hlchina.com
CEO: Joseph Wells
Marketing Director: Kimberly Faloon
Production Manager: Wilbur Waigoneer
Plant Manager: John Bennley
Purchasing Manager: Otto Jirianni
Estimated Sales: Less Than $500,000
Number Employees: 5-9
Square Footage: 1700000
Brands:
　Ameriwhite
　Best China
　Fiesta
　Gothic
　Lyrica
　Milford
　Pristine
　Seville

23879 (HQ)Honeywell International
World Headquarters
Charlotte, NC 07950
877-841-2840
www.honeywell.com
Fire alarm systems and controls, among other safety and productivity products.
Chairman/CEO: Darius Adamczyk
President, Safety & Productivity: John Waldron
Senior VP/Chief Financial Officer: Greg Lewis
Senior VP/General Counsel: Anne Madden
Senior VP, HR/Security & Communications: Mark James
Year Founded: 1906
Estimated Sales: $41.8 Billion
Number Employees: 114,000
Square Footage: 15803

23880 Honeywell Sensing & Internet of Things
302-613-4491
800-537-6945
info.sc@honeywell.com sensing.honeywell.com
Switches and sensors for packaging lines (smart distributed systems): photoelectric, proximity, pressure, cuttent and ultrasonic.
Chairman/CEO: Darius Admczyk
Estimated Sales: $500 Million-$1 Billion
Number Employees: 1000-4999
Parent Co: Honeywell International

23881 Honeywell UOP
25 E. Algonquin Road
P.O. Box 5017
Des Plaines, IL 60017-5017
847-391-2000
800-877-6184
www.uop.com
Treatment of food production-related wastewater.
President: John Gugel

23882 Honiron Corp
400 Canal St
Jeanerette, LA 70544-4504
337-276-6314
Fax: 337-276-3614 sales@honiron.com
www.honiron.com
Manufacturer and exporter of sugar machinery
Owner: John Deere
COO: Dennis Banta
dbanta@honiron.com
Estimated Sales: $1 - 5 Million
Number Employees: 50-99
Type of Packaging: Bulk

23883 (HQ)Hood Packaging
25 Woodgreen Pl
Madison, MS 39110
601-853-7260
Fax: 601-853-7299 800-321-8115
www.hoodpkg.com
Paper and plastic packaging supplies.
President: Robert Morris
Year Founded: 1978
Estimated Sales: $250-500 Million
Number Employees: 250

23884 Hood Packaging
2380 McDowell Road
Burlington, ON L7R 4A1
Canada
905-637-5611
Fax: 905-637-9954 877-462-6627
www.hoodpkg.com
Paper and plastic packaging supplies.
President: Robert Morris
Year Founded: 1978
Estimated Sales: $250-500 Million
Number Employees: 250

23885 Hoover Company
7005 Cochran Rd.
Glenwillow, OH 44139
330-499-9499
Fax: 330-497-5065 www.hoover.com
Extractors, vacuum cleaners and supplies including
bags, belts, air freshener tablets and steamvac clean-
ing solutions.
Year Founded: 1908
Estimated Sales: $350-400 Million
Number Employees: 1000-4999
Square Footage: 527000
Parent Co: Techtronic Industries

23886 Hoover Materials Handling Group
2135 Highway 6 S
Houston, TX 77077-4319
800-844-8683
Manufacturer and exporter of containers and tanks.
Year Founded: 1911
Estimated Sales: $103.2 Million
Parent Co: Hoover Group
Brands:
Apr
Bdi
Bdii
Bdiii
Liquitote
Mamor
Suredrain

23887 Hop Growers of Washington
301 W Prospect Rd
Moxee, WA 98936-9811
509-453-4749
Fax: 509-457-8561 info@usahops.org
Represents and promotes the interests of U.S. growers both domestically and internationally. As the national organization, HGA provides support,
coordination and communication to growers, brewers and the world hop industry in areas of common
interest, including; marketing statistics, promotion,
education and research.
Administrator: Ann George
info@usahops.org
Public Relations: Michelle Palacios
Number Employees: 1-4

23888 Hope Chemical Corporation
PO Box 908
Pawtucket, RI 2862
401-724-8000
Fax: 401-724-8076
Industrial cleaning compounds

President: R Bernstein
Contact: Robert Bernstein
robert.bernstein@mannsvillechemical.com
Number Employees: 50

23889 Hope Industrial Systems
1325 Northmeadow Pkwy # 100
Suite 100
Roswell, GA 30076-3896
678-762-9790
Fax: 678-762-9789 877-762-9790
sales@hopeindustrial.com
Flat panel touchscreens and monitors for the food
processing and dairy industries.
Contact: Bo Bowling
bo.bowling@hopeindustrial.com
Number Employees: 5-9

23890 Hope Paper Box Company
33 India Street
Pawtucket, RI 02860-5510
401-724-5700
Corrugated paper boxes and partitions
President: Timothy H Hayes
VP: Gregory Yates
Estimated Sales: $2.5-5 Million
Number Employees: 20-49

23891 Hopp Co Inc
815 2nd Ave
New Hyde Park, NY 11040-4869
516-358-4170
Fax: 516-358-4178 800-889-8425
Sales@HoppCompanies.com
www.HoppCompanies.com
Plastic chips, strips, restocking tags, label backers
and covers used as label holders, overlays and deco-
rative coverings for shelf moldings
Owner: Robert Hopp
bob@hoppcompanies.com
CEO: Cani Hopp
CEO: Bob Hopp
Estimated Sales: $2.5-5 Million
Number Employees: 10-19
Number of Brands: 1

23892 Hoppmann Corporation
13129 Airpark Dr # 120
Elkwood, VA 22718-1761
540-825-2899
Fax: 540-829-1724 800-368-3582
sales@ShibuyaHoppmann.com
www.shibuyahoppmann.com
Manufacturer and exporter of assembly packaging
systems including feeders, pre-feeders, conveyors,
turnkey systems, etc.; also, integration services
available
President: Mark Flanagan
flanagan@hoppmann.com
CEO: Peter Hoppmann
Executive Vice President: Kazuhiro Miyamae
VP Finance: Maryanne Flusher
Product Manager: Chad Roberts
Sales Director: Dave Martin
Number Employees: 100-249

23893 Horix Manufacturing Co
1384 Island Ave
Mc Kees Rocks, PA 15136-2593
412-771-1111
Fax: 412-331-8599 info@horix.net
www.horix.info
Manufacturer, importer and exporter of liquid fill-
ing, capping, labeling and rinsing machinery for
cans and bottles
President: Linda Fzramowski
Plant Manager: Felgon Robert
Research & Development: Russell Myers
CEO: Linda M Szramowski
Sales Director: David Becki
Plant Manager: Robert Feltop
Purchasing Manager: Brad Barber
Estimated Sales: $5 - 10 Million
Number Employees: 20-49
Square Footage: 120000
Brands:
Dura-Base
Flo-Fil
Hytamatic
Posi-Sync
Screen-Flo
Ultra-Fil
Var-I-Vol

Volufil
Weigh-Master

23894 Horizon Plastics
Northam Industrial Park, Bldg 3
PO Box 474
Cobourg, ON K9A5V7
Canada
905-372-2291
Fax: 905-372-9397 855-467-4066
info@horizonplastics.com
www.horizonplastics.com

23895 Horizon Software International
2915 Premiere Parkway
Suite 300
Duluth, GA 30097
770-554-6353
Fax: 770-554-6331 800-741-7100
Point of sale and back office solutions for all your
food service management needs
President: Randy Eckels
VP/Finance: Jason Hayes
Senior VP/R&D: Robbie Payne
VP/Sales: Sharon McGuire
Contact: Nikki Bridwell
nbridwell@horizonsoftware.com
Estimated Sales: $10 - 20 Million
Number Employees: 50-99
Brands:
Fast Lane 2000
Visual Boss

23896 Hormann Flexan Llc
20a Avenue C
Leetsdale, PA 15056-1305
412-749-0400
Fax: 412-749-0410 800-365-3667
Manufacturer and exporter of industrial/commercial
doors and loading dock equipment including deliv-
ery truck ramps.
President: Christoph Hormann
CEO: Charles A De La Porte
VP: Patrick Boyle
Marketing: Alic Permigiani
Contact: Peter Burnham
p.burnham@hormann-flexon.com
Plant Manager: Mark Permigiani
Purchasing: David Palmosina
Estimated Sales: $10 - 20 Million
Number Employees: 20-49
Square Footage: 180000
Parent Co: Hexon
Brands:
Easy Hinge
Flexidoor
Weathershield

23897 Hormel Foods Corp.
1 Hormel Pl.
Austin, MN 55912
507-437-5611
www.hormelfoods.com
Meat and grocery products.
Chairman/President/CEO: Jim Snee
Executive VP/CFO: Jacinth Smiley
Senior VP/General Counsel: Lori Marco
Senior VP, R&D/Quality Control: Kevin Myers
Vice President, Quality Management: Richard
Carlson
Year Founded: 1891
Estimated Sales: $11.4 Billion
Number Employees: 20,000
Number of Brands: 52
Type of Packaging: Consumer, Food Service, Pri-
vate Label
Other Locations:
Manufacturing Facility
Austin MN
Manufacturing Facility
Algona IA
Manufacturing Facility
Alma KS
Manufacturing Facility
Atlanta GA
Manufacturing Facility
Aurora IL
Manufacturing Facility
Barron WI
Manufacturing Facility
Beloit WI
Manufacturing Facility
Bondurant IA
Manufacturing Facility
Bremin GA
Manufacturing Facility

Browerville MN
Manufacturing Facility
Dayton OH
Manufacturing Facility
Dubuque IA
Manufacturing Facility
Eldridge IA
Brands:
Applegate
Austin Blues BBQ
Bacon 1
Black Label Bacon
Bufalo
Burke
Cafe H
Chi-Chi's
Columbus
Compleats
Cure 81
Dan's Prize
Del Fuerte
Deli Meats
DiLusso Deli Company
Dinty Moore
Don Miguel
Doña María
Embasa
Evolve
Fire Braised Meats
Fontanini
Fuse Burger
Gatherings
Herbox
Herdez
Hormel
Hormel Chili
Hormel Health Labs
Hormel Pepperoni
Hormel Side Dishes
Hormel Taco Meats
House of Tsang
Jennie-O Turkey
Justin's
La Victoria
Little Sizzlers
Lloyds Barbeque Co
Mary Kitchen
Muscle Milk
Natural Choice
Not So Sloppy Joe
Old Smokehouse
Premium Chicken Breast
Real Bacon Toppings
Refrigerated Entre,s
SPAM
Skippy
Stagg Chili
Valley Fresh
Vital Cuisine
Wholly Guacamole

23898 Horn & Todak
10505 Judicial Dr # 101
Fairfax, VA 22030-5157

703-352-7330
Fax: 703-352-6940
Partner: Bob Horan
Estimated Sales: Below $5 Million
Number Employees: 5-9

23899 Horner International
5304 Emerson Drive
Raleigh, NC 27609

919-787-3112
Fax: 919-787-4272 sales@hornerintl.com
www.hornerinternational.com
Natural extracts and flavors
Contact: Ladiner Blaylock
ladiner.blaylock@hornerintl.com
Parent Co: Horner International

23900 Horton Fruit Co Inc
4701 Jennings Ln
Louisville, KY 40218-2967

502-969-1375
Fax: 502-964-1515 800-626-2245
Tomatoes, onions, spinach, kale, coleslaw, bananas,
avocados, pineapples and caramel apples
Chairman/CEO: Albert Horton
ahorton@hortonfruit.com
President/COO: Jackson Woodward
Treasurer: Steve Edelen
Vice President: Bill Benoit
Sales/Procurement: Tom Smith
Transportation Manager: Bobby Harlow

Number Employees: 100-249
Square Footage: 400000
Type of Packaging: Consumer, Food Service, Private Label
Other Locations:
Louisville Produce Terminal
Louisville KY

23901 Hosch Properties
1002 International Dr
Oakdale, PA 15071-9226

724-695-3002
Fax: 724-695-3603 800-695-3310
hosch@hoschusa.com www.hoschusa.com
Scrapers for conveyor belt cleaning.
Owner: Kevin Carpol
kevinc@hoschusa.com
Operations: Grace Barkhurst
Estimated Sales: $5-10 Million
Number Employees: 20-49

23902 Hose Master Inc
1233 E 222nd St
Euclid, OH 44117-1121

216-481-2020
Fax: 216-481-7557 info@hosemaster.com
www.hosemaster.com
Manufacturer and exporter of gas, steam and water
connectors
CEO: Sam Foti
Quality Control: Mike Thompson
CEO: Sam J Foti
Estimated Sales: $20 - 50 Million
Number Employees: 250-499
Square Footage: 130000
Brands:
Live Link
Smart

23903 Hoshizaki
530 Lakeview Plaza Blvd # F
Worthington, OH 43085-4710

614-848-7702
Fax: 614-848-7706 800-642-1140
www.hoshizaki.com
VP: Gary Peffly
Estimated Sales: $1 - 5 Million
Number Employees: 5-9

23904 Hoshizaki America Inc
618 Highway 74 S
Peachtree City, GA 30269-3016

770-487-2331
Fax: 770-487-1325 800-438-6087
marketing@hoshizaki.com
www.hoshizakiamerica.com
Commercial ice machines and refrigeration equipment.
CEO: Youki Suzuki
Executive VP: Mark McClanahan
Quality Control: Carter Davis
Marketing Director: Carter Davis
Operations Manager: Jim Procuro
Production Manager: Jim Procuro
Plant Manager: Jim Procuro
Number Employees: 500-999
Parent Co: Hoshizaki Electric Company
Brands:
Cleancycle 12
Cyclesaver
Evercheck
Hoshizaki America
Temp Guard

23905 Hosokawa Confectionery &Bakery Technology and Systems
10 Chatham Rd
Summit, NJ 07901-1310

908-273-6360
Fax: 908-273-7432 www.hosokawa.com
Agglomeration, size reduction, compaction/briquetting, mixing/blending, thermal reactors,
disintegrators and drying and cooling machinery;
consultant for process designs, engineering, research, testing, istallation, etc. available.Small scale
food grade production agreements, AIG certified
Manager: Rob Vorhees
CEO: Masuo Hosokawa
Estimated Sales: $5 - 10 Million
Number Employees: 1,000-4,999
Parent Co: Hosokawa Micron Corporation

23906 Hosokawa Micron Powder Systems
10 Chatham Rd
Summit, NJ 07901-1310

908-273-6360
Fax: 908-273-7432 800-526-4491
info@hmps.hosokawa.com
www.hmicronpowder.com
Weighing machines and augers, blending and mixing
equipment (coffee), brewing devices (urns, cleaners,
coffeemakers), bulk silo services (green coffee), dryers, feeders, grinders, agglomeration, size reduction,
compaction, thermalreactors and packaging
Manager: Rob Vorhees
Contact: Greg Boyer
gboyer@hmps.hosokawa.com
Estimated Sales: $10-25 Million
Number Employees: 1-4

23907 Hosokawa/Bepex Corporation
PO Box 880
Santa Rosa, CA 95402-0880

707-586-6000
Fax: 707-585-2325 info@hmfg.hosokawa.com
www.hosokawamicron.com
Food processing equipment including size reduction,
liquid/solid separation, mixing/blending and thermal
processing
CEO: Masuo Hosokawa
Vice President And COO: Kiyomi Miyata
Estimated Sales: $1 - 5 Million
Number Employees: 100-249
Brands:
Rietz
Strong-Scott

23908 Hospitality International
W6636 L B White Rd
Onalaska, WI 54650

608-783-2800
Fax: 608-783-6115 info@carrollchair.com
www.hospitalityinternational.com
President: Anthony Wilson
Vice President of Development: Ron Provus
Contact: Al Hebers
ahebers@hospitalityinternational.com
Estimated Sales: $10 - 20 Million
Number Employees: 100-249

23909 Hoss-S
12985 Dunnings Hwy
PO Box 219
Claysburg, PA 16625-8202

814-693-3453
Fax: 814-239-5922 800-438-7439
www.hosswares.com
Prepared foods
Owner: Bill Campbell
VP: Mark Spinazzola
Plant Manager: Rocky Rhodes
Estimated Sales: Less Than $500,000
Number Employees: 5-9

23910 Hot Food Boxes
451 East County Line Road
Mooresville, IN 46158

317-831-7030
Fax: 317-831-7036 800-733-8073
schirico@theramp.net www.secoselect.com
Manufacturer and exporter of insulated stainless
steel and aluminum equipment for hot and cold
foods; also, steam tables and heated bulk food carts
for banquet service.
President: John Schirico
Vice President: Pat Darre
Estimated Sales: $2.5-5 Million
Number Employees: 20-49
Square Footage: 100000
Brands:
Piper
Road Warrior

23911 Hot Mama's Foods
134 Avocado St
Springfield, MA 01104

413-737-6572
Fax: 413-737-6793
Gourmet foods, including salsa, hummus, pesto, prepared salads, dips and ready-to-cook products; custom packaging and consulting

President: Matt Morse
Finance & Business Development: Herb Heller
Executive Chef: Josh Cooper
Director of Human Resources: Lisa Dufour
Director of Operations: Jim Boyle
Estimated Sales: $14.9 Million
Number Employees: 90
Square Footage: 13500

23912 Hotshot Delivery System
155 Covington Dr
Bloomingdale, IL 60108-3107
630-924-8817
Fax: 630-924-8819 sales@deliveryconcepts.com
www.hotshotdeliverysystems.com
Mobile vending trucks for hot, cold and refrigerated foods
Owner: Bernard Pfeiffer
hdsbernie@aol.com
General Sales Manager: Nick Prestia
Estimated Sales: $10 - 20 Million
Number Employees: 5-9

23913 Hotsy Corporation
10099 Ridgegate Pkwy # 280
Lone Tree, CO 80124-5534
303-792-5200
Fax: 303-792-0547 800-525-1976
info@hotsy.com www.hotsy.com
Pressure washers
Vice President of Sales: Frank Rotondi
Estimated Sales: $1 - 5 Million
Number Employees: 50-99

23914 Houdini Inc
4225 N Palm St
Fullerton, CA 92835-1045
714-525-0325
Fax: 714-996-9605
www.winecountrygiftbaskets.com
Gourmet food, wine and gift baskets
Owner: Tim Dean
tdean@houdiniinc.com
Estimated Sales: $500,000 - $1 Million
Number Employees: 10-19
Brands:
California Pantry
Wine Country

23915 House Stamp Works
20650 South Cicero
Chicago, IL 60443
312-939-7177
Fax: 312-939-8520 info@housestampworks.com
www.housestampworks.com
Stamps, dies, seals, etc
President: Edward Leppert
Estimated Sales: Less than $500,000
Number Employees: 1-4

23916 Houser Neon Sign Company
6411 Airline Dr
Houston, TX 77076-3507
713-691-5765
Lighted signs
Owner: Kimberly Mallett
Division Manager: Robert Betz
Estimated Sales: Less than $500,000
Number Employees: 1-4
Parent Co: Southwest Neon Signs

23917 Houston Atlas
1201 N Velasco Street
Angleton, TX 77515-3009
409-849-2344
Fax: 409-849-2166
Analytical instrumentation
President: Hammond Rood
Estimated Sales: $5-10 000,000
Number Employees: 50

23918 Houston Label
909 Shaver St
Pasadena, TX 77506-4411
713-477-6995
Fax: 713-477-0023 800-477-6995
sales@houstonlabel.com www.houstonlabel.com
Manufacturer and exporter of labels including pressure sensitive, printed, unprinted, color processed, UPC and inventory automatic labeling equipment
Owner: Richard Ryholt
Executive VP: Hans Ryholt
Outside Sales Manager: Willie Hager
rryholt@houstonlabel.com

Estimated Sales: $5-10 Million
Number Employees: 50-99
Square Footage: 92000
Type of Packaging: Consumer, Food Service, Private Label, Bulk
Other Locations:
Houston Tape & Label Co.
Pasadena TX
Brands:
3m
Fasson
Mactac
Technicote

23919 Houston Stamp & Stencil Company
601 Jackson Hill St
Houston, TX 77007
713-869-4337
Fax: 713-869-4339 sales@houstonstamp.com
www.houstonstamp.com
Plastic signs, rubber stamps, nameplates and marking dies
President: Bruce La Roche
Contact: Bruce Laroche
roche@houstonstamp.com
Estimated Sales: $1 - 5 Million
Number Employees: 5-9

23920 Houston Wire Works, Inc.
1007 Kentucky
South Houston, TX 77587
713-946-2920
Fax: 713-946-3579 800-468-9477
info@houstonwire.com www.houstonwire.com
Manufacturer and exporter of water bottle display, refrigerator, wine and wire racks; also, steel platform ladders and hand carts; exporter of storage racks
President: Ken Legler
CEO: Barbara Leagler
VP Sales/Marketing: Steve Foster
Sales Director: Melanie Houser
Contact: Barbara Legler
barbaralegler@att.net
Sales Manager: Bill Watkins
Purchasing Manager: Raquel Garza
Estimated Sales: $3 - 5 Million
Number Employees: 45
Square Footage: 280000
Type of Packaging: Food Service
Brands:
Hww
Space-Saver

23921 Hovair Systems Inc
6912 S 220th St
Kent, WA 98032-1906
253-872-0405
Fax: 253-872-0406 800-237-4518
info@hovair.com www.hovair.com
Manufacturer and exporter of air film material handling equipment. Manufactures air bearing systems and air film products for a wide variety of applications, with particular emphasis on the movement of heavy loads and equipment withintoday's industry.
Manager: Betty Roberts
robertsb@hovair.com
Marketing: Betty Roberts
Operations: Betty Roberts
Plant Manager: Jeff Grow
Estimated Sales: $3 - 5 Million
Number Employees: 10-19

23922 Hovus Inc
272 Brodhead Rd # 200
Bethlehem, PA 18017-8956
610-997-8800
Fax: 610-997-0485 sales@hovus.com
www.hovus.com
HOVUS Incorporated is a flexible packaging consultation and sales organization that is focused on the needs of wholesale food manufacturer's in the private, public and not-for-profit sectors.
Owner: Alfred Haus
ahaus@hovus.com
Number Employees: 10-19

23923 Howard Fabrication
PO Box 90550
City of Industry, CA 91715-0550
626-961-0114
Fax: 626-961-8533
Custom stainless steel mixing and storage tanks for food, pharmaceutical and dairy products

President: John Gill
Sales Manager: Ron Reed
Estimated Sales: Below $5 Million
Number Employees: 10
Square Footage: 160000

23924 Howard Imprinting Machine Company
4519 Terrace Manor Drive
PO Box 15027
Houston, TX 77041
713-869-4337
Fax: 813-881-1554 800-334-6943
howard.imprinting@gte.net
www.howardimprinting.com
Manufacturer and exporter of hot stamp imprinting machinery
President: James Wrobbel
Estimated Sales: $3 - 5 Million
Number Employees: 5-9

23925 Howard Overman & Sons
517 N Bradford Street
Baltimore, MD 21205-2403
410-276-8445
Fax: 410-254-6358
Household and commercial brooms
Estimated Sales: Less than $500,000
Number Employees: 4

23926 (HQ)Howard-Mccray
831 E Cayuga St
Philadelphia, PA 19124-3815
215-464-6800
Fax: 215-969-4890 800-344-8222
www.howardmccray.com
Manufacturer and exporter of commercial refrigerators and freezers, open merchandisers; deli, fish, poultry and red meat service cases; produce cases; bakery display, proofers, retarders; glass door; step in and reach in units. Alsodistribute beer frosters, bottle coolers, beer dispensers, under counter coolers, and prep tables.
President: Annette Ramsey
aramsey@howardmccray.com
CFO: Marie Ginon
Marketing Director: Diane Scott
Plant Manager: Brian Tyndall
Estimated Sales: $1 - 10 Million
Number Employees: 100-249
Number of Products: 60
Square Footage: 460000
Parent Co: HMC Enterprises,LLC

23927 Howard-Mccray
831 E Cayuga St
Philadelphia, PA 19124-3815
215-464-6800
Fax: 215-969-4890 hmccray850@aol.com
www.howardmccray.com
President: Will Bell
wbell@howardmccray.com
Estimated Sales: $10 - 20 Million
Number Employees: 100-249

23928 Howden Group
900 W Mount St
Connersville, IN 47331
765-827-9200
www.howden.com
Rotary and centrifugal air and gas blowers, compressors, high vacuum and industrial compressor equipment.
Chief Executive Officer: Ross Shuster
Estimated Sales: Over $1 Billion

23929 Howe Corp
1650 N Elston Ave
Chicago, IL 60642-1585
773-235-0200
Fax: 773-235-1530 webinfo@howecorp.com
www.howecorp.com
Specialty refrigeration equipment including flake ice machines, bin transport systems, packaged refrigeration systems, compressors and pressure vessels

President: Mary C Howe
craig@cmvsharperfinish.com
CFO: M Aguilar
Senior VP: Kevin McCool
Research & Development: A Ahuja
Marketing Director: K McCool
VP Sales: A Ortman
Director Sales/Marketing: Chuck Janovsky
IT: Andrew Ortman
Production Manager: Steve Bokor
Plant Manager: John Myrda
Purchasing Manager: Bob Dondzik
Estimated Sales: $20-50 Million
Number Employees: 20-49
Square Footage: 65000
Brands:
Conditionaire
Rapid Freeze

23930 Howell Brothers Chemical Laboratories
5007 Overbrook Ave
Philadelphia, PA 19131-1402
215-477-0260
Manufacturer and exporter of glass cleaners and hair products
President: Douglas C Howell
Manager: David Hart
Production Manager: Charles Thomson
Estimated Sales: $2.5-5 Million
Number Employees: 7
Square Footage: 24000
Type of Packaging: Consumer, Private Label

23931 Howell Consulting
1611-A South Melrose Dr
211
Vista, CA 92081
760-536-3456
Fax: 760-536-3457
www.howellconsultinggroup.com
Control systems, design assembly, installation and service. Consultant and systems integrator for process control systems
Owner: Rodney A Howell
Estimated Sales: Below $5 000,000
Number Employees: 10

23932 Howes S Co Inc
25 Howard St
Silver Creek, NY 14136-1097
716-934-2611
Fax: 716-934-2081 888-255-2611
sales@showes.com www.pressureleaffilter.com
Manufacturer and exporter of job engineered processing and materials handling equipment including classifiers, conveyors, crushers, rotary cutters, horizontal/vertical mixers, continuous liquid mixers and feeders, sifters, elevatorsauger packers and scales
President: Wayne Mertz
bryantd@showes.com
Vice President: Frederick Mertz
Sales: Diana Bryant
Estimated Sales: $10-20,000,000
Number Employees: 10-19

23933 Howes S Co Inc
25 Howard St
Silver Creek, NY 14136-1097
716-934-2611
Fax: 716-934-2081 888-255-2611
sales@showes.com www.pressureleaffilter.com
Bins for bulk storage; hoppers, conveyors, bucket elevators
President: Wayne Mertz
bryantd@showes.com
VP: Fred Mertz
Sales: Diana Bryant
Estimated Sales: $10 - 20 Million
Number Employees: 10-19
Parent Co: MetalWorks

23934 Howlett Farms
1112 East River Rd.
Avon, NY 14414
585-226-8340
www.howlettfarms.com
Offers marketing and risk management services.
President: Bruce Howlett
Operations Manager: David Walthew *Year Founded:* 1880

23935 Hoyer
753 Geneva Pkwy N
Lake Geneva, WI 53147-4579
262-249-7400
Fax: 262-249-7500
Ice cream processing equipment
President: Gustav Korsholm
Estimated Sales: $5-10 Million
Number Employees: 20-49

23936 (HQ)Hoyt Corporation
251 Forge Rd
Westport, MA 2790
508-636-8811
Fax: 508-636-2088 hoytinc@hoytinc.com
www.hoyt-corp.com
Manufacturer and exporter of vapor recovery systems and dry cleaning equipment including commercial washer extracts, laundry dryers and extractors
Chairman: Jean H Olinger
VP Marketing: Pat King
Contact: Gil Abernathy
gil.abernathy@hoyavc.com
Estimated Sales: $10-20 Million
Number Employees: 10-19
Brands:
Petro-Miser
Sniff-O-Miser
Solvo-Miser

23937 Huard Packaging
685 Discovery Bay Boulevard
Discovery Bay, CA 94514-9443
650-857-1501
Fax: 650-852-8138 800-752-0900

23938 Hub City Brush Co
106 Mc Aulay Dr
Petal, MS 39465-4008
601-584-7314
Fax: 601-544-2600 800-278-7452
www.hubcityindustries.net
Commercial brooms, mops and brushes
Owner: Tyler Cedotal
tcedotal@hubcitybrush.com
VP: Cecil Cedotal
Quality Control: Russel Herrin
Estimated Sales: Less Than $500,000
Number Employees: 10-19
Square Footage: 36720

23939 Hub Electric Company
6207 Commercial Rd
Crystal Lake, IL 60014
815-455-4400
Fax: 815-455-1499 richardvaralightinc@juno.com
Manufacturer and exporter of dimming systems and special lighting equipment
President and CFO: Richard Latronica
VP: Kenneth Hansen
Estimated Sales: Below $1 Million
Number Employees: 5-9

23940 Hub Folding Box Co
774 Norfolk St
Mansfield, MA 02048-1826
508-339-0102
Fax: 508-339-0102 www.hubfoldingbox.com
Paper folding boxes
Owner: Fred Di Rico
fdirico@hubfoldingbox.com
Sales Manager: Lucy Gilligan
Estimated Sales: $20-50 Million
Number Employees: 100-249

23941 Hub Labels Inc
18223 Shawley Dr
Hagerstown, MD 21740-2462
301-790-1660
Fax: 301-745-3646 800-433-4532
jdoyle@hublabels.com www.hublabels.com
Adhesive and pressure sensitive labels
President: Mary Dahbura
thomson_natascha@emc.com
CEO: Abbud S Dahbura
Quality Assurance Manager: Mark Stahle
Sales/Marketing: Belinda Smith
Manager: Pam Kunkle
Production Manager: John Potterfield
General Manager: Mary Dahbura
Purchasing Manager: Nick Myers
Estimated Sales: $10 Million
Number Employees: 100-249
Square Footage: 32000

23942 Hub Pen Company
230 Quincy Avenue
Quincy, MA 02169-6741
617-471-9900
Fax: 617-471-2990 www.hubpen.com
Manufacturer and exporter of felt tip markers, pens, pencils, etc
President: Helen Fleming
Quality Control: Howard Ernest
Sales Manager: Robert McGaughey
Contact: Cheryl Brugliera
cbrugliera@hubpen.com
Estimated Sales: $10 - 20 Million
Number Employees: 65
Square Footage: 20000
Brands:
Hub Pen

23943 Hubbell Electric HeaterCo
45 Seymour St
PO Box 288
Stratford, CT 06615-6170
203-380-3306
Fax: 203-378-3593 800-647-3165
info@hubbellheaters.com
www.hubbellheaters.com
Manufacturer and exporter of electric hot water booster heaters for sanitizing water
President: William E Newbauler
Head of Quality Control: Clifford Dineson
Sales Director: Sean Clarker
IT: Jessica Delvalle
jessicad@hubbellheaters.com
Estimated Sales: $5 - 10 Million
Number Employees: 50-99
Brands:
Hubbell

23944 Hubbell Lenoir City Inc
2911 Industrial Park Dr
Lenoir City, TN 37771-3209
865-986-9726
Fax: 865-986-4186 800-346-3061
www.hubbell.com
Polymer concrete drain systems
General Manager: John Downey
Cio/Cto: Danny Bowden
dbowden@hubbell.com
Finance Executive: David Redman
Estimated Sales: $20 - 50 Million
Number Employees: 100-249

23945 Hubbell Lighting Inc
701 Millennium Blvd
Greenville, SC 29607-5251
864-678-1000
Fax: 864-678-1065 www.hubbelllighting.com
Manufacturer and exporter of industrial, commercial, emergency, exit, recessed and track lighting
Vice President: Scott H Muse
smuse@prescolite.com
VP: Scott Veil
VP Sales/Marketing: Richard Barrett
VP Sales: James O'Hargan
Number Employees: 500-999
Parent Co: Hubbell

23946 (HQ)Hubber Technology Inc
9735 Northcross Center Ct # A
Huntersville, NC 28078-7331
704-949-1010
Fax: 704-949-1020 huber@hhusa.net
Huber Technology offers different treatment systems to provide clean and healthy drinking water in order to meet the requirements of different surface water qualities and customer preferences. the systems process includes: coarsematerial separation; oxygenation; fine material separation: flocculation and sedimentation; filtration; oxidation and disinfection; absorption; network protection and water storage.
President: Forstner Gerhard
CEO: Mr. Dana Hicks
Marketing: T.R. Gregg
Number Employees: 10-19
Square Footage: 96000
Parent Co: Hans Huber AG

23947 Hubco Inc
215 S Poplar St
PO Box 1286
Hutchinson, KS 67501-7456
620-663-8301
Fax: 620-663-5053 800-563-1867
www.hubcoinc.com

Manufacturer, importer and exporter of bags including drawstring, cotton, flannel, polypropylene and burlap for flour, rice, popcorn, nuts, etc.; also, specialty food packaging available
President: Merlin Prehein
VP: Trey McPherson
VP: Jim Schmidt
Plant Manager: Fred Moore
Estimated Sales: $5 - 10 Million
Number Employees: 50-99
Square Footage: 284000
Brands:
    Protexo
    Sentry
    Sentry Ii

23948 Huck Store Fixture Company
1100 N 28th St
Quincy, IL 62301-3447
    217-222-0713
Fax: 217-222-0751 800-680-4823
Store fixtures
VP: Mark Flegel
Purchase: Cory Phipps Phipps
Sales and Marketing: Romhamann Hamann
Marketing Director: Christopher Peters
VP Production: Ron Hamann
Number Employees: 250-499
Square Footage: 1208000

23949 Hudson Belting & Svc CoInc
85 E Worcester St
Worcester, MA 01604-3649
    508-756-0090
Fax: 508-753-6844 www.hudsonbelting.com
Manufacturer and wholesaler/distributor of food grade belting including leather, rubber, conveyor and timing; installation services available
President: Tom Jennette
  hudsonbelting@charter.net
Plant Manager: John Whitney
Estimated Sales: Less Than $500,000
Number Employees: 5-9
Square Footage: 15000
Type of Packaging: Consumer, Food Service

23950 Hudson Control Group Inc
10 Stern Ave
Springfield, NJ 07081-2905
    973-376-8265
Fax: 973-376-8265 info@hudsoncontrol.com
    www.hudsoncontrol.com
Manufacturer and exporter of custom designed and integrated robotic automation systems including case packers/unpackers; also, software
President: Phil Farrelly
CSO: Cliff Olson, Ph.D.
VP Sales/Marketing: Tom Gilman
Contact: John Celecki
  jcelecki@hudsoncontrol.com
Estimated Sales: $1 - 2.5 Million
Number Employees: 5-9
Square Footage: 12000
Brands:
    Hudson's Total Control For Windows
    Packit

23951 Hudson Poly Bag Inc
578 Main St
Hudson, MA 01749-3099
    978-562-7566
Fax: 978-568-0797 800-229-7566
sales@hudsonpoly.com www.hudsonpoly.com
Plain and printed polyethylene and poly propylene bags and sheets, film and narrow width tubing.
President: Marilyn Kinder
  marilynkinder@staples.com
CEO: Richard Renwick
Marketing/General Manager: Jim Chapman
Estimated Sales: $5 - 10 Million
Number Employees: 10-19
Square Footage: 35000
Type of Packaging: Consumer, Food Service, Private Label, Bulk

23952 Hudson Valley Hops
PO Box 292
Beacon, NY 12508
    845-202-2398
    admin@hvhops.com
    www.hvhops.com
Harvester, processor and distributor of hops to brewers in the Hudson Valley

Co-Founder: Justin Riccobono
Co-Founder: Shawn McLearen *Year Founded:* 2013
Type of Packaging: Bulk

23953 Hudson-Sharp Machine Co
975 Lombardi Ave
Green Bay, WI 54304-3735
    920-494-4571
Fax: 920-496-1322 800-950-4362
Manufacturer and exporter of packaging machinery including bag makers and pouch makers and fillers
President: Don Pansier
VP: Gilas Blaser
Sales Director: Dennis Jimmel
Plant Manager: Jack Hendrickson
Estimated Sales: $20-50 Million
Number Employees: 50-99
Square Footage: 60000
Brands:
    Amplas Converting Equipment
    Totani Pouch M/C

23954 Hudson-Sharp Machine Company
P.O. Box 13397
Green Bay, WI 54307-3397
    920-494-4571
Fax: 920-496-1322 sales@hudsonsharp.com
    www.hudsonsharp.com
Manufacturer and exporter of converting and pouch and plastic bag making equipment
President: Peter Hatchell
CFO: Gary Reinert
CEO: Rod Drummond
Research & Development: Danford Anderson
Marketing Director: Mark Smith
Sales Director: Paul Staab
Contact: Michele Allamprese
  michele.allamprese@hudsonsharp.com
Operations Manager: Scott Romenesko
Estimated Sales: $50-100 Million
Number Employees: 50-99

23955 Hueck Foils LLC
1955 State Route 34
Suite 2
Wall, NJ 07719-9703
    732-974-4100
Fax: 732-974-4111 www.hueckfoils.com
Hueck ia a foil converter supplying flexible packaging materials for the food and pharmecutical industries
Quality Control: Rosalyn White
Marketing: Angela Boggenhofer
Sales: Kevin Judd
Plant Manager: Manfred Rauer
Estimated Sales: $3 - 5 Million
Number Employees: 5-9
Parent Co: Hueck Folien

23956 Huettinger Electronic Inc
4000 Burton Dr
Santa Clara, CA 95054-1509
    408-454-1180
Fax: 408-454-1181 800-910-0035
info-us@huettinger.com www.huettinger.com
Induction cap sealing equipment and power supplies
President: Juergen Mertens
VP Sales: Paul Oranges
Contact: David Fostervold
  david.fostervold@us.trumpf.com
Estimated Sales: $3 - 5 000,000
Number Employees: 5-9

23957 Hughes Co
1200 W James St
Columbus, WI 53925-1028
    920-623-2000
Fax: 920-623-4098 866-535-9303
    hughes@hughesequipment.com
    www.hughesequipment.com
Food processing equipment
President/CEO: Ross Lund
  rosslund@hughescompany.biz
Sales Manager: Tracey Lange
Sales Manager: Ryan Metzdorf
Director of Engineering: Todd Belz
Plant Manager: Bill Wandersee
Estimated Sales: $10 - 20 Million
Number Employees: 20-49
Brands:
    Digisort
    Hughes

23958 Hughes Co
1200 W James St
Columbus, WI 53925-1028
    920-623-2000
Fax: 920-623-4098
    hughes@hughesequipment.com
    www.hughesequipment.com
Machinery for the food processing industry including air cleaners; bins; rotary blanchers and cookers; rotary coolers; bulk unloading feeders; fillers; graders; inspection tables, etc.
President: Ross Lund
  rosslund@hughescompany.biz
Sales Manager: Doug Zadra
Manufacturing Manager: Bill Wandersee
  rosslund@hughescompany.biz
Director of Engineering: Todd Belz
Sales Coordinator: Lisa Adam
Number Employees: 20-49

23959 Hughes Manufacturing Company
2301 W Highway 290
Giddings, TX 78942
    979-542-0333
Fax: 979-542-0335 800-414-0765
    www.hughesmanufacturing.com
Manufacturer and exporter of nylon and plastic flags, pennants and banners
Manager: Lisa Marek
Operations Manager: Larry Conlee
Operations Manager: Larry Conlee
Estimated Sales: Below $5 Million
Number Employees: 10-19
Square Footage: 40000

23960 Huhtamaki Food Service Plastics
100 N Field Drive
Suite 300
Lake Forest, IL 60045-2520
    847-295-6100
Fax: 847-295-9862 800-244-6382

23961 Huhtamaki Inc
9201 Packaging Dr
De Soto, KS 66018-8600
    913-583-3025
Fax: 913-583-8756 800-255-4243
President: Clay Dunn
  clay.dunn@us.huhtamaki.com
Chief Executive Officer: Jukka Moisio
Estimated Sales: $50 - 100 Million
Number Employees: 500-999

23962 Huls America
220 Davidson Avenue
Somerset, NJ 08873-4149
    732-980-6800
Fax: 732-980-6970
Wine industry enzymes
CEO: Joseph Fuhrman
Marketing Manager: Tom Wickett
Number Employees: 1000

23963 Hungerford & Terry
226 Atlantic Ave
PO Box 650
Clayton, NJ 8312
    856-881-3200
Fax: 856-881-6859 sales@hungerfordterry.com
    www.hungerfordterry.com
Manufacturer and exporter of water treatment systems including filters, softeners, demineralizers and reverse osmosis
President: Allen Davis
Executive VP: Vernon Dawson
VP Sales: Kenneth Sayell
Contact: Douglas Bateman
  dbateman@hungerfordterry.com
Estimated Sales: $10-20 Million
Number Employees: 50-99
Square Footage: 40000
Brands:
    Ferrofilt
    Ferrosand
    H&T
    Hungerford & Terry
    Invercab

23964 Hunt Midwest
8300 NE Underground Drive
Kansas City, MO 64161
816-455-2500
Fax: 816-455-2890
mediacontact@huntmidwest.com
www.huntmidwest.com
President: Ora Reynolds
Chairman of the Board: Jim Holland
Vice President and CFO: Don Hagan
Assistant General Manager of Sales: Dick Ringer
Number Employees: 50-99

23965 Hunter Fan Co
7130 Goodlett Farms Pkwy # 400
Cordova, TN 38016-4991
901-743-1360
Fax: 901-248-2258 techsupport@hunterfan.com
www.hunterfan.com
Ceiling fans, programmable thermostats, air purifiers
and humidifiers
President: Robert Beasley
CEO: John Alexander
jalexander@hunterfan.com
Director Sales/Special Markets: Rick Neuman
VP Sales: Brennon Byrney
Estimated Sales: $50-100 Million
Number Employees: 500-999

23966 Hunter Graphics
140 N Orlando Avenue
Suite 140
Umatilla, FL 32784
407-644-2060
Fax: 407-644-0957 www.huntergraphics.com
Consultant specializing in the design of packaging
and labels; support services available
President: Brian Hunter
Estimated Sales: Below $500,000
Number Employees: 1
Square Footage: 14000
Parent Co: Optimal Graphics

23967 Hunter Lab
11491 Sunset Hills Rd # 1
Reston, VA 20190-5280
703-471-6870
Fax: 703-471-4237 sales@hunterlab.com
www.hunterlab.com
Manufacturer and exporter of color measurement
systems
Owner: Phil S Hunter
CFO: Teresa Demangos
R & D: Jim Freal
Quality Control: Ambur Daley
Sales Manager: Paul Barnes
hunter@hunterlab.com
Estimated Sales: $10-20 Million
Number Employees: 50-99
Square Footage: 140000
Brands:
Colortrend Ht

23968 Hunter Packaging Corporation
865 Commerce Drive
South Elgin, IL 60177-2633
847-741-4747
Fax: 847-741-1100 800-428-4747
Corrugated boxes and displays
Vice President: Tom Pabelick
Office Manager: Susan Brown
Estimated Sales: $3-5 Million
Number Employees: 31
Square Footage: 140000

23969 Hunter Woodworks
21038 S Wilmington Ave
Carson, CA 90810
310-835-5671
Fax: 323-775-2540 800-966-4751
info@hunterpallets.com www.hunterpallets.com
Wooden pallets, boxes and crates
General Manager: Bruce Benton
CEO: Bill Hunter
Sales Manager: Frank Gower
Contact: Jeremy Benz
jeremy@hunterpallets.com
General Manager: Bruce Benton
Number Employees: 100-249
Square Footage: 1000000

23970 Huntington Foam Corp
101 N 4th St
Jeannette, PA 15644-3331
724-522-5144
Fax: 814-265-8627 www.huntingtonfoam.com
Construction and packaging foam
President: Gary B. McLaughlin
CFO: Tom Kuehl
Director of Sales & Enginnering: Ed Flynn
Manager: Jeff Jones
Director of Operations: Benjamin Raygoza
Estimated Sales: $5-10 000,000
Number Employees: 5-9

23971 Huntington Park Rbr Stamp Co
2761 E Slauson Ave
PO Box 519
Huntington Park, CA 90255-3048
323-582-6461
Fax: 323-582-8046 800-882-0029
hprubberstamp@pacbell.net
www.hprubberstamp.com
Marking devices including rubber stamps
President: Mary Barlam
hprubberstamp@pacbell.net
Sales Manager: Robert Barlam
Estimated Sales: $1 - 2.5 Million
Number Employees: 10-19
Square Footage: 12500

23972 Huntsman Packaging Corporation
PO Box 11085
Birmingham, Bi 35202-1085
205-328-4720
Fax: 205-322-2505
Plastic film
President/CEO: John Huntsman
Controller: John Clark
Production Manager: Pete Lenzer
Plant Manager: Larry Bearden

23973 Hurlingham Company
1158 W 11th Street
Apt F
San Pedro, CA 90731-3479
310-538-0236
Fax: 310-538-4436
Store fixtures
President: Eusebio Espejo
VP Sales: Michele Duston
Estimated Sales: Below $5,000,000
Number Employees: 30
Square Footage: 25000

23974 Hurri-Kleen Corporation
6000 Southern Industrial Dr
Birmingham, AL 35235
205-655-8808
Fax: 205-655-5392 800-455-8265
Manufacturer and dirtributor of intermediate bulk
containers and related parts and accessories
Estimated Sales: $1-5,000,000
Number Employees: 1-4
Square Footage: 100000
Brands:
Hurri-Kleen

23975 Hurst Corp
175 Strafford Ave # 1
Wayne, PA 19087-3340
610-687-2404
Fax: 610-687-7860 sales@hurstcorp.com
www.hurstcorp.com
De-labeling machinery
Owner: Richard Hurst
sales@hurstcorp.com
Estimated Sales: $5-10 Million
Number Employees: 10-19

23976 Hurst Labeling Systems
20747 Dearborn St
PO Box 5169
Chatsworth, CA 91311-5914
818-701-0710
Fax: 818-701-8747 800-969-1705
info@hurstinternational.net
www.hurstinternational.net
Manufacturer and exporter of pressure sensitive labels and label application equipment

Owner: Ari Lichtenberg
CFO: Rita Rebera
Quality Control: Rick Aranbul
Sales Representative: Melody Nichols
Sales Representative: Chaylon Holland
ari@hurstinternational.net
Estimated Sales: $3 - 5 Million
Number Employees: 10-19
Square Footage: 26000

**23977 Hurt Conveyor
EquipmentCompany**
6615 8th Ave
Los Angeles, CA 90043-4353
323-541-0433
Fax: 323-541-0442
Belt and chain conveyors
President: Ramesh Soni
VP: Saroj Soni
Number Employees: 7
Type of Packaging: Private Label

23978 (HQ)Huskey Specialty Lubricants
1580 Industrial Ave
Norco, CA 92860-2946
951-340-4000
Fax: 951-340-4011 888-448-7539
sales@huskey.com www.huskey.com
Manufacturer and exporter of food grade grease and
lubricating oils for food processing machinery
President: Sheldy Huskey
R&D: Jim Landry
Vice President: Mike Montgomery
Research & Development: Hugh Woodworth
Foreign Sales Manager: Denis Alonso
Contact: Michael Montgomery
mmontgomery@huskey.com
Plant Manager: Chris Kimball
Purchasing Manager: Cathy Merlo
Estimated Sales: $10 - 20 Million
Number Employees: 5-9
Square Footage: 120000
Type of Packaging: Private Label, Bulk
Other Locations:
Huskey Specialty Lubricants
Twinsburg OH
Brands:
Huskey

23979 Hussmann Corp
12999 Saint Charles Rock Rd.
Bridgeton, MO 63044-2483
314-291-2000
www.hussmann.com
Commercial and display refrigerators and coolers.
President/CEO: Tim Figge
CFO: Cathy Haigh
Senior VP, Retail Services: Jay Welu
Year Founded: 1906
Estimated Sales: Over $1 Billion
Number Employees: 5000-9999
Parent Co: Panasonic Corporation of North America
Brands:
Impact
Protochill
Protocol

23980 Hutchison-Hayes International
P.O. Box 2965
Houston, TX 77252-2965
713-455-9600
Fax: 713-455-7753 800-984-3397
sales@hutch-hayes.com www.hutchhayes.com
Centrifuges
Owner: Richard Parks
Quality Control and R&D: Lee Hilpert
Chairman: John Joplin
Estimated Sales: $10 - 20 Million
Number Employees: 50-99

23981 Huther Brothers
1290 University Avenue
Rochester, NY 14607-1674
585-473-9462
Fax: 585-473-9476 800-334-1115
Manufacturer and exporter of industrial food pro-
cessing cutting blades and circular, straight and spe-
cialty knives
President: George W Huther Iii
CFO: James Aldridge
Bookkeeper: Margie Campaigne
Foreman: Eric Nash

Estimated Sales: $3 - 5 Million
Number Employees: 10-19
Square Footage: 38000

23982 Hutz Sign & Awning
2415 Hubbard Rd
Youngstown, OH 44505

330-743-5168
Fax: 330-743-2319 hutzsigns@worldnet.att.net
Advertising signs
President: Tom Kling
VP: David Hutz
Estimated Sales: $3 - 5 Million
Number Employees: 10-19

23983 Hy-Ko Enviro-MaintenanceProducts
PO Box 26116
Salt Lake City, UT 84126-0116

801-973-6099
Fax: 801-973-9746 sales@hyko.com
www.hyko.com
Cleaners including hand, dairy, glass, household and
industrial, pipe, toilet bowl and window; also, wash-
ing compounds, disinfectants and floor polishes
President: Ron Starr
CFO: Ron C Starr Sr
Sales Manager: John Hille
Estimated Sales: $10 - 20 Million
Number Employees: 20-49

23984 Hy-Ten Plastics Inc
38 Powers St
Milford, NH 03055-4982

603-673-1611
Fax: 603-673-0970 sales@hy-ten.com
www.hy-ten.com
Designer of custom injection molded products
President: Rich Staples
rich.staples@hy-ten.com
Sales/Engineer: Peter Fritsch
VP Operations: Mike McGown
Estimated Sales: $10-20 Million
Number Employees: 50-99
Square Footage: 60000

23985 Hy-Trous/Flash Sales
3R-T Green Street
Woburn, MA 1801

781-933-5772
Hand soaps and cleaning compounds
Estimated Sales: $1 - 5 Million
Number Employees: 5
Square Footage: 30000
Parent Co: Hy-Trous Corporation
Brands:
Flash
Hy-Trous Plant Foods
Skat

23986 Hyatt Industries Limited
1572 West 4th Avenue
Vancouver, BC V6J 1L7
Canada

604-736-7301
Fax: 604-736-7305 800-482-7446
sales@hyatt-ind.com
President: Lindsay Lawrence
Number Employees: 10

23987 Hybrinetics Inc
225 Sutton Pl
Santa Rosa, CA 95407-8199

707-585-0333
Fax: 707-585-7313 800-247-6900
www.voltagevalet.com
Manufacturer and exporter of dimmer controls for
incandescent and fluorescent lighting
President: Rick Rosa
hybrinet@voltagevalet.com
Estimated Sales: $20 - 50 Million
Number Employees: 20-49
Brands:
Aladdin Products
Star Controls

23988 Hycor Corporation
562 E Bunker Court
Vernon Hills, IL 60061-1831

847-473-3700
Fax: 847-473-0477 technology@parkson.com
www.parkson.com
Wine industry wastewater treatment
CEO: Zain Mahmood

Estimated Sales: $10-25 Million
Number Employees: 250-499

23989 Hyde & Hyde Inc
300 El Sobrante Rd
Corona, CA 92879-5757

951-279-5239
Fax: 951-270-3526 www.hydeandhyde.com
Condiments for the fresh-cut produce industry; cus-
tom packaging and co-packaging
President: Tim Hyde
Number Employees: 250-499
Type of Packaging: Consumer, Private Label

23990 Hyder North America
270 Granite Run Dr
Lancaster, PA 17601-6804

717-569-7021
Fax: 717-560-0577 info@thearrogroup.com
www.thearrogroup.com
Water and wastewater treatment, total outsourcing
solutions
President: G Matthew Brown
CFO: Susan L Long
Estimated Sales: $10 - 20 Million
Number Employees: 50-99

23991 Hydra-Flex Inc
32975 Industrial Rd
Livonia, MI 48150-1617

734-522-9090
Fax: 734-522-9579 800-234-0832
customerservice@hydra-flex.com
www.hydra-flex.com
Manufacturer and wholesaler/distributor of hoses,
valves, fittings, tubing, etc
President: Charley Blank
cblank@hydra-flex.com
R&D: Jim Poole
VP: Bill Berlin
Sales Manager: Bill Berlin
Warehouse Manager: Jason Pinard
Estimated Sales: $10 - 20 Million
Number Employees: 10-19

23992 Hydranautics (A Nitto Denko Company)
9119 Princeton Rd
Woodbury, MN 55125

651-739-0443
www.hydranautics.com
Reverse osmosis, nanofiltration, ultrafiltration and
microfiltration crossflow membranes and elements
for food, dairy, and beverage production as well as
water and wastewater applications. Concentration of
proteins, amino acids, fishmeat and vegetable extracts, enzymes, sugars, vitamins, flavors, vinegar,
coffee, tea, maple sap and colorants. Also remove
color from juices, syrups, flavorings and beverages
and can adjust alcohol content.
President: Yukio Nagira
Estimated Sales: $33.34 Million
Number Employees: 60

23993 Hydrel Corporation
12881 Bradley Ave
Sylmar, CA 91342-3828

818-362-9465
Fax: 818-362-6548 www.hydrel.com
Manufacturer and exporter of outdoor lighting fix-
tures including flood, ingrade and underwater; also,
custom environment fixtures
President: Craig Jennings
VP: Dwight Hochstein
VP: Mark Blackford
CFO: John Gay
VP Marketing: Hal Madsen
Sales Manager: Dan Roth
Contact: Trilby Jasinski
tjasinski@hrblock.com
Estimated Sales: $20 - 50 Million
Number Employees: 100-249
Parent Co: GTY Industries
Brands:
9000 Series
Hypak
Sunlite

23994 Hydrite Chemical Co
300 N Patrick Blvd # 2
Brookfield, WI 53045-5816

262-792-1450
Fax: 262-792-8721 sales@hydrite.com
www.hydrite.com

Manufacturer and wholesaler/distributor of indus-
trial cleaning, sanitaring ingredients and water treat-
ment chemicals
CEO: John Honkamp
john.honkamp@hydrite.com
Sales Director: Rob Adams
Sales Director (Special Chemicals): Rich
Carmichael
Purchasing Manager: Chuck Krior
Number Employees: 1000-4999

23995 Hydro Life
503 Maple St
Bristol, IN 46507

574-848-1661
Fax: 574-848-1400 800-626-7130
www.hydrolife.com
President: La Von Troyer
Sales: Roger Egli
Estimated Sales: $1 - 3 Million
Number Employees: 5-9

23996 Hydro Seal Coatings Company
12151 Madera Way
Riverside, CA 92503-4849

760-723-8992
Fax: 760-723-7206
Wine industry coatings
Vice President of Technology: Sergio Franyutti

23997 Hydro-Miser
906 Boardwalk # B
San Marcos, CA 92069-4071

442-744-5083
Fax: 442-744-5031 800-736-5083
Manufacturer and exporter of portable and thermal
storage chillers and cooling towers and systems;
also, food processing equipment and supplies
President/CEO: Kimberly Howard
Estimated Sales: $1-2.5 Million
Number Employees: 1-4
Parent Co: Applied Thermal Technologies
Brands:
Copeland
Gould

23998 Hydro-Tech EnvironmentalSystems
410 Petaluma Blvd S # A
Petaluma, CA 94952-4278

707-769-9247
Fax: 707-769-9140 800-559-3102
info@htes.com www.htes.com
Wastewater treatment, bad reduction, product recov-
ery, product concentration
Manager: Susan Stone
CFO and CTO: Aron Lavner
Estimated Sales: $.5 - 1 million
Number Employees: 5-9
Square Footage: 6800

23999 Hydro-Thermal Corp
400 Pilot Ct
Waukesha, WI 53188-2439

262-548-8900
Fax: 262-548-8908 262-902-0121
info@hydro-thermal.com
www.hydro-thermal.com
Direct contact steam injection heaters and heat
exchangers for liquids and slurries for both indus-
trial and 3A applications
President: Jim Zaiser
jzaiser@hydro-thermal.com
VP: John Warne
Marketing: Kristie Anderson
Estimated Sales: $5-10 Million
Number Employees: 50-99
Brands:
Hydroheater
Hydrohelix

24000 HydroCal
22732 Granite Way Ste A
Laguna Hills, CA 92653

949-455-0765
Fax: 949-455-0764 800-877-0765
don@hydrocal.com www.hydrocal.com
Wastewater treatment equipment
President: Donald Meylor
VP: Oilie Breen
Director Marketing/Operationss: Jorge Funez
Sales: Ollie Breen
Contact: Oliver Breen
breen@hydrocal.com

Estimated Sales: $500,000-$1 000,000
Number Employees: 5-9
Number of Products: 8

24001 Hydrocal Inc
23011 Moulton Pkwy # G5
Suite G5
Laguna Hills, CA 92653-1228
949-455-0765
Fax: 949-455-0764 800-877-0765
ollieb@hydrocal.com www.hydrocal.com
President: Don Meylor
info@hydrocal.com
Estimated Sales: $1,000,000 - $3,000,000
Number Employees: 5-9

24002 Hydromax Inc
4 Creamery Way
Emmitsburg, MD 21727-8803
301-447-3800
Fax: 301-668-3700 800-326-0602
info@hydromax.net www.hydromax.net
Manufacturer and exporter of water filtration and
purification equipment including reverse osmosis,
ultraviolet, ozone and filtration technologies
President: Frederick N Reidenbach
Estimated Sales: $1-2.5 Million
Number Employees: 5-9

24003 Hydron
14550 E Easter Avenue
Centennial, CO 80112-4263
303-792-9988
Fax: 303-792-5772
Water and waste water clean uo in processing plants

24004 Hydropure Water Treatment Co
5727 NW 46th Dr
Coral Springs, FL 33067-4005
954-340-3331
Fax: 954-971-0801 800-753-1547
Exporter of rotary vane pumps and water filtration,
purification and reverse osmosis systems.
President: Vittorio Sordi
VP: Susan Shasser
Estimated Sales: $1.6 Million
Number Employees: 5-9
Number of Brands: 4
Number of Products: 78
Type of Packaging: Consumer, Food Service
Brands:
  Carbonetor Pumps
  Hydropure Pumps

24005 Hyer Industries
91 Schoosett St
Pembroke, MA 02359-1839
781-826-8101
Fax: 781-826-7944 mail@thayerscale.com
www.thayerscale.com
Manufacturer and exporter of continuous scale
weighing systems, flow aid devices, volumetric
feeders and pre-blending and continuous compound
feeder networks for extrusion processes
Owner: Frank Hyer
  sales@thayerscales.com
CFO: Bruce Edward
R & D: Rick Tolles
VP Sales/Marketing: Charles Wesley
Purchasing Agent: Lou Sawyer
Estimated Sales: $10-20 Million
Number Employees: 50-99
Square Footage: 164000
Parent Co: Hyer Industries

24006 Hygiena LLC
941 Avenida Acaso
Camarillo, CA 93012-8755
805-388-8007
Fax: 805-388-5531 www.hygiena.com
All-in-one bacterial testing products for the food and
beverage industries
Director of Sales/Business Development: Steve
Nason
Contact: Edgar Abarca
  eabarca@hygiena.com
Manager: Fred Nason
Estimated Sales: $400 Thousand
Number Employees: 1-4
Brands:
  Aller-Snap Protein Residue Test
  Aquasnap Water Atp Sample Testing
  Ensure Quality Check System
  Pro-Clean Hygiene Surface Test

Q-Swab Environmental Collection
Qd-Loop Rapid Dilution Devices
Snapshot Universal Atp Sample Test
Spotcheck Hygiene Surface Test
Spotcheck Plus Hygiene Surface Test
Supersnap High Sensitivity Atp Test
Systemsure Plus Atp Hygiene
Ultrasnap Atp Test Devices

24007 Hygiene-Technik
4743 Christie Drive
Beamsville, ON L0R 1B4
Canada
905-563-4987
Fax: 905-563-6266 info@gotoHTI.com
www.gotoHTI.com
Specializing in the design, development and manu-
facturing of proprietary dispensing systems.
President: Heiner Ophardt
VP/General Manager: Tony Kortleve-Snider
Business Development Manager: Marina Nava
Number Employees: 50
Square Footage: 180000
Brands:
  Ingo-Man
  Ingo-Top

24008 Hygienic Fabrics Inc
118 S Broad St
P.O. Box 34
Lanark, IL 61046-1204
815-493-2502
Fax: 815-493-1098 sales@hyfab.com
www.hyfab.com
Cheese equipment, firesavers, bandages, fillers, milk
Manager: Shirley Gothard
Vice President: Thomas Laiken
Manager: Rachel Moll
  rmoll@hyfab.com
Production Supervisor: Kelly Leicht
Plant Manager: Shirley Gothard
Estimated Sales: Less Than $500,000
Number Employees: 1-4

24009 Hygrade Gloves
30 Warsoff Pl
Brooklyn, NY 11205
718-488-9000
Fax: 718-694-9500 800-233-8100
Manufacturer, importer and exporter of protective
and disposable clothing including gloves, aprons,
goggles, hair nets, uniforms, boots and dust masks
President: Lazar Follman
Contact: Ryan Bowling
  r.bowling@hygradesafety.com
Estimated Sales: $1 - 5 Million
Number Employees: 20-49
Square Footage: 440000
Parent Co: LDF Industries
Brands:
  American Optical
  Comfiwear

24010 Hypro
375 5th Ave NW
St Paul, MN 55112-3288
651-766-6300
Fax: 651-766-6600 800-424-9776
mattc@hypropumps.com
Wine industry pumps, fluid handling products for
the agricultural, pressure cleaning, fire services, in-
dustrial, semiconductor equipment and marine
markets
President: Donald Jorgensen
CFO: Steve Dickhaus
CEO: Paul Meschke
R&D: Bruce Maki
Contact: Tony Engebretson
  imtech@pentair.com
Executive Assistant: Myrna Press
Estimated Sales: $75 - 100 Million
Number Employees: 5-9

24011 Hyster Company
7227 Carroll Rd
San Diego, CA 92121
858-566-4181
Fax: 858-578-6165 800-437-8371
www.hyster.com
CFO: Kevin Kelley
Vice President/GM: David Ohm
General Sales Manager: Bob Pilon
Manager: Scott Stearne
General manager: Steve Smith

Number Employees: 10-19
Parent Co: Hyster-Yale Materials Handling

24012 Hyster Company
7227 Carroll Rd
San Diego, CA 92121
855-804-2118
Fax: 858-578-6165 www.johnson-lift.com
Manufacturer and exporter of automatic storage and
handling systems and industrial trucks; also, service
and rental available
Manager: Scott Stearne
Service Manager: Steve Lacroix
Estimated Sales: $5-10 Million
Number Employees: 10-19
Parent Co: Johnson Machinery
Brands:
  Hyster

24013 Hytrol Conveyor Co Inc
2020 Hytrol St
Jonesboro, AR 72401-6712
870-935-3700
Fax: 800-852-3233 info@hytrol.com
www.hytrol.com
President: Gregg Goodner
  ggoodner@hytrol.com
VP of Business Operations: Bob West
VP of Manufactoring Operations: Don Wilson
Estimated Sales: $80 Million
Number Employees: 500-999

24014 I C Technologies
613 W Manlius St # 1
East Syracuse, NY 13057-2168
315-423-5051
Fax: 315-423-0086 800-554-2832
sra@blistertech.com www.pinholedetector.com
President: Steve Antonacci
  sra@blistertech.com
Estimated Sales: $1,000,000 - $5,000,000
Number Employees: 5-9

24015 I J White Corp
20 Executive Blvd
Farmingdale, NY 11735-4710
631-293-2211
Fax: 631-293-3788 info@ijwhite.com
www.ijwhite.com
Spiral systems for both the food processing and bakery industries: blast freezing, refrigerated cooling,
proofing, elevating, accumulating, drying, and
pasteurizing
President: Peter J. White
  pwhite@ijwhite.com
Estimated Sales: $5-10 Million
Number Employees: 50-99

24016 I M A North America
7 New Lancaster Rd
Leominster, MA 01453-5224
978-537-8534
Fax: 215-826-0400 toddima@aol.com
Bag formers/fillers/sealers, carton machines (fold-
ing, lining, filling, closing), pouch machines, shrink
wrap machine, teabag machinery, wrapping ma-
chines, blister machines
President: Warren Roman
CEO: Krouchiek
CFO: Jerry Krouchick
Estimated Sales: $20 - 50 Million
Number Employees: 20-49
Parent Co: IMA North America

24017 I. Fm Usa Inc.
9490 Franklin Ave
Franklin Park, IL 60131
847-288-9500
Fax: 847-288-9501 866-643-6872
info@ifmusa.com www.sirman.com
Slicers, panini grills, meat & food processors and
bar equipment.

24018 I.W. Tremont Company
79 4th Ave
Hawthorne, NJ 07506
973-427-3800
Fax: 973-427-3778 www.iwtremont.com
Manufacturer and exporter of filter media including
inspection, analysis, sampling and testing systems

President: Sal Averso
CFO: Andrew Averso
Contact: Salvatore Averso
 jimaverso@iwtremont.com
Production Manager: Andrew Averso
Production Manager: James Averso
Estimated Sales: $20 - 50 Million
Number Employees: 10-19
Square Footage: 10000

24019 IAFIS Dairy Products Evaluation Contest
1451 Dolley Madison Boulevard Suite 10
Mc Lean, VA 22101-3847
703-761-2600
Fax: 703-761-4334 www.fpsa.org
President, Chief Executive Officer: David Seckman
Vice President of Development: Andy Drennan
Director of Sales: Grace Yee
Number Employees: 20-49

24020 IASE Co Inc
161 Industrial Pkwy # 6
Branchburg, NJ 08876-6023
908-218-1104
Fax: 908-218-1337 www.iase.net
Robotic packaging equipment
President: Michael Degidio
 miked@iase.net
Estimated Sales: $2.5-5 Million
Number Employees: 20-49

24021 IB Concepts
657 Dowd Avenue
Elizabeth, NJ 07201-2116
215-739-9960
Fax: 215-739-9963 888-671-0800
www.celwa.com
Manufacturer and exporter of printed, embossed and molded crepe wadding inserts and liners; also, absorbent cellulose doilies, pulpboard coasters, die cut polyester discs, and die cut foam
General Manager: Robert Pettus
Operations Manager: Michael Hersh
Number Employees: 25
Square Footage: 80000

24022 IBA
P.O. Box 37
Florham Park, NJ 07932-0037
973-660-9334
Fax: 908-647-6560 pastoretec@aol.com
Estimated Sales: $1 - 5 Million
Number Employees: 1-4

24023 IBA Food Safety
6000 Poplar Avenue
Suite 426
Memphis, TN 38119-3981
901-681-9006
Fax: 901-681-9007 800-777-9012
Sterilization, gamma irradiation, electron beam radiation and microorganism reduction systems; materials processing services and installation available
President: Rick Doscher
VP Perishable Foods: Chip Colonna
Number Employees: 1300
Parent Co: IBA Chemin Du Cyclotron
Brands:
 Sterigenics

24024 IBC Shell Packaging
1981 Marcus Ave
New Hyde Park, NY 11042
516-352-5138
rsamaroo@ibcshell.com
ibcshell.com
Custom packaging, display boxes and point of purchase displays for specialty foods.
Chief Executive Officer: Norman Kay
Managing Director & Partner: Phillip Schoonmaker
Logistics Manager: Mike Walker
 mikew@ibcshell.com
Estimated Sales: $20-50 Million
Number Employees: 250-499

24025 ICB Greenline
5808 Long Creek Park Dr # Q
Suite Q
Charlotte, NC 28269-3748
704-333-3377
Fax: 704-334-6146 800-331-5312
info@icb-usa.com

Manufacturer and exporter of overhead conveyors for poultry and meat processing
President: Heinz Dremel
Manager: Iris Chasteen
Estimated Sales: $5.6 Million
Number Employees: 10-19
Square Footage: 200000
Brands:
 Dura-Plate
 Greenline

24026 ICI Surfactants
Strawinskylaan 2555
Amsterdam, ZZ 1077
302-762-0555
Fax: 302-762-4750 800-424-3696
www.ici.com
Food surfactants for bakery, edible oil, dairy, confectionery, and miscellaneous food processors
Manager: Amber Prichett
CFO: Alan Brown
Technical Manager: Wei Shi
Estimated Sales: $.5 - 1 million
Number Employees: 1-4

24027 ICM Controls
7313 William Barry Blvd
North Syracuse, NY 13212
315-233-5266
800-365-5525
www.icmcontrols.com
HVAC controls.
President: Ronald Kadah
Chair & CEO: Joseph Bonacci
VP: Zach Kadah
Director, Operations: Bruce Hahn
Estimated Sales: $100-500 Million
Number Employees: 200-500

24028 ICOA Inc
111 Airport Rd # 1
Warwick, RI 02889-1049
401-648-0690
Fax: 401-648-0699 888-408-0600
Wireless internet services (design, deployment management)
Chairman/CEO: George Strouthopoulos
 gstrouthop@icoacorp.com
Director/CFO: Erwin Vahlsing
Sales Director: Joe Farrugla
Operations Manager: Chris Browne
Estimated Sales: $4 Million
Number Employees: 20-49
Number of Brands: 7
Brands:
 Airport Network Solutions
 Authdirect
 Cafe.Com
 Idockusa
 Linkspot
 Toll Booth
 Webcenter
 Wisezone

24029 ID Images
2991 Interstate Pkwy
Brunswick, OH 44212
330-220-7300
Fax: 330-220-3838 866-516-7300
customerservice@idimages.com
www.idimages.com
Baggers and printers
Marketing Director: Lisa Stang
Contact: Megan Bailey
 mbailey@idimages.com
Estimated Sales: $500,000-$1,000,000
Number Employees: 5
Brands:
 Pack Star
 Park Star Plus
 Versa Color

24030 IDC Food Division
1879 Capital Cir NE
Tallahassee, FL 32308-4598
850-656-5600
Fax: 850-656-3032 800-831-6340
Estimated Sales: $1 - 5 Million

24031 IDEX Corp
1925 W Field Ct # 200
Suite 200
Lake Forest, IL 60045-4862
847-498-7070
Fax: 847-498-3940 800-843-8210
www.idexcorp.com
Chairman and Chief Executive Officer: Andrew Silvernail
 asilvernail@idexcorp.com
Senior Vice President-Chief Financial Of: Heath Mitts
Vice President, Tax and International Fi: Gerald Carter
Senior Vice President, Fluid & Metering: Brett Finley
Senior Vice President-Health, Science &: Eric Ashleman
Senior Vice President-Chief Human Resour: Jeffrey Bucklew
COO: James W Patterson
Estimated Sales: Over $1 Billion
Number Employees: 5000-9999

24032 IDL
4250 Old William Penn Hwy
Monroeville, PA 15146-1626
724-733-2234
Fax: 724-327-6420
Advertising decals including pressure sensitive and reflective
Sales Manager: Jim Krentz
Estimated Sales: $20-50 Million
Number Employees: 100-249

24033 IEW
49 W Federal Street
Niles, OH 44446
330-652-0113
Manufacturer and exporter of industrial electronic weighing devices and scales for mobile material handling equipment
Estimated Sales: $1 - 5 Million
Brands:
 Criterion
 Sos

24034 IFC Disposables Inc
250 Kleer Vu Dr
Brownsville, TN 38012-2199
731-779-0959
Fax: 731-772-2282 800-432-9473
info@cascades.com www.cascades.com
Nonwoven wiping towels and tissue products
President and CFO: Robert E Briggs
Cmo: Laura Brooks
 lbrooks@ifcdisposables.com
Marketing: Laura Brooks
Purchasing Agent: Sherry Elliot
Estimated Sales: $10 - 20 Million
Number Employees: 50-99
Parent Co: Wyant Corporation
Brands:
 Busboy
 Dusterz

24035 IFS North America
5451 E Williams Blvd Ste 181
Tucson, AZ 85711
520-512-2000
Fax: 520-512-2001 info@ifsna.com
www.ifsna.com
President: Theresa Sheridan
CFO: Mitch Dwight
R&D: William Grant
Contact: Mike Collins
 mike.collins@ifsworld.com
Estimated Sales: $20 - 50 Million
Number Employees: 100-249

24036 IFoodDecisionSciences
P.O. Box 82475
Kenmore, WA 98028-2475
206-219-3703
info@idsfoodsafety.com
www.idsfoodsafety.com
Offers software solutions for the agriculture industry, including growing, harvesting, packing and processing, distribution, and pricing.
CEO: Diane Wetherington
Year Founded: 2013
Number Employees: 25-50

24037 IGEN
16020 Industrial Dr
Gaithersburg, MD 20877
301-208-3784
Fax: 301-947-6990
Laboratory testing equipment and kits; safety equipment

24038 IGEN International
16020 Industrial Dr
Gaithersburg, MD 20877-1414
301-208-3784
Fax: 301-947-6990 800-336-4436
m-series@igen.com
Provides biotechnical services to the food and beverage industry
President: Samuel Wohlstadter
Number Employees: 100-249

24039 IGS Store Fixtures
58 Pulaski St
Peabody, MA 01961-3767
978-532-0010
Fax: 617-569-0201
Store fixtures and counters
CFO: Harvey Gordon
Estimated Sales: $10-20 Million
Number Employees: 100-249
Square Footage: 96000
Brands:
Jahbo Showcases
Lozier

24040 IHS Heath Information
15 Inverness Way E
Englewood, CO 80112-5710
800-716-3447
Fax: 800-716-6447 800-525-5539
info@ihs.com
Meat industry services (computer systems and software, importing-exporting, publications and information, nutrition labeling, quality control instruments, sanitation programs); seasonings and ingredients; meat products
Contact: Clark Pollard
clark.pollard@ihs.com

24041 IMAS Corporation
2905 Brittany Court
St. Charles, IL 60175
630-584-7011
847-274-9383
sphelps@IMASLtd.com www.xspec.com
Software for specification management; also, information management consulting available
Vice President: Steven Meier
Estimated Sales: $2.5-5 Million
Number Employees: 20-49
Brands:
Winspex
Xspec

24042 IMC Instruments
N60w 14434 Kaul Avenue
Menomonee Falls, WI 53051
262-252-4620
Fax: 262-252-4623 sales@imcinstruments.com
www.imcinstruments.com
Instrumentation for temperature, pressure, humidity, vacuum and air flow measurement
President: Louis Frias
VP: Ronald Frias
Estimated Sales: $2.5-5 Million
Number Employees: 10
Square Footage: 32000

24043 IMC Teddy Food Service Equipment
50 Ranick Drive East
PO Box 338
Amityville, NY 11701
631-842-2200
Fax: 631-842-2203 800-221-5644
www.imcteddy.com
Stainless steel shelving, floor troughs and gratings, sinks, can washers, counter tops, floor drains, tables and cabinets
Partner and President: Asit Majundar
Marketing Manager: Suzane Girrsoli
General Sales Manager: Joe Campbell
Contact: Madelin Fernandez
madelin@imcteddy.com
Purchasing Manager: Madelin Fernandez

24044 IMECO Inc
3820 S IL Route 26
Polo, IL 61064-9006
815-946-2351
Fax: 815-946-3409 www.imeco.com
Manufacturer and exporter of refrigeration equipment including prime surface evaporative condensers and sub-zero blast freezers
President: Mark Stencel
Managing Director: Elias Salloum
Estimated Sales: $50-100 Million
Number Employees: 100-249
Square Footage: 135000
Parent Co: York International

24045 IMI Cornelius
2401 N Palmer Dr
Schaumburg, IL 60196-0001
847-397-4600
Fax: 847-539-6960 800-323-4789
www.cornelius.com
Manufacturer and exporter of ice making and dispensing equipment including beverage, ice, juice and beer
President: Tim Hubbard
t.hubbard@imi-cornelius.com
Executive VP Sales/Marketing: Joseph Asfoud
President (Wilshire Canada): David Noble
Estimated Sales: $1 - 5 Million
Number Employees: 250-499
Parent Co: IMI Cornelius

24046 IMI Precision Engineering
325 Carr Dr
Brookville, OH 45309-1921
937-833-4033
Fax: 937-833-4205 www.imi-precision.com
Pneumatic components for the packaging industry including aluminum and steel NFPA interchangeable cylinders, rodless cylinders, small bore cylinders and directional control valves
President: Peter Wallace
Quality Control: John Campbell
Senior VP: Patty Lynch
plynch@usa.norgren.com
Technical Marketing Manager (Actuators): Douglas Kelly
Estimated Sales: $20 - 50 Million
Number Employees: 100-249
Square Footage: 47000
Parent Co: IMI Norgren
Brands:
Airserv
Airswitch
Decel-Air
Fast/Bak
Pak-Lap
Tiny Tim

24047 IMI Precision Engineering
72 Spring Ln
Farmington, CT 06032-3140
860-677-0272
Fax: 860-677-4999 800-722-5547
www.imi-precision.com
Solenoid valves, liquid level controls, pressure switches
Executive Director: Gary Fett
Cmo: Joshua Denison
jdenison@norgren.com
Quality Control: Ned Lanfranco
Marketing: Karen Markie
Operations: Gary Fett
Purchasing: Dave Simons
Estimated Sales: $10-20 Million
Number Employees: 100-249
Parent Co: IMI Norgren

24048 IMO Foods
P.O. Box 236
Yarmouth, NS B5A 4B2
Canada
902-742-3519
Fax: 902-742-0908 imofoods@ns.sympatico.ca
www.imofoods.com
Canned fish
President: Sidney Hughes
Executive VP/General Manager: Phillip Le Blanc
Director Marketing: David Jollimore

Number Employees: 100-249
Parent Co: IMO Foods
Type of Packaging: Consumer, Food Service, Private Label
Other Locations:
Brands:
Golden Treasure
Kersen
West Island

24049 IMS Food Service
1-2 Corporate Dr #136
Shelton, CT 06484-6208
203-929-2254
Fax: 203-926-0916 800-235-7072
Web based foodservice management software
President/Owner: Arnold D'Angelo
VP: Thomas O'Hara
Sales Executive: Scott Ricci
Estimated Sales: $5 - 10 Million
Number Employees: 33
Parent Co: International Marketing Systems
Type of Packaging: Consumer, Food Service

24050 INA Co
837 Industrial Rd # G
San Carlos, CA 94070-3333
650-631-7066
Fax: 650-873-4729 www.sovaleather.com
Importer of china and plastic bags and garbage bags
Owner: Philip Wong
Estimated Sales: Less than $500,000
Number Employees: 1-4
Brands:
Ina

24051 (HQ)INDEECO
425 Hanley Industrial Ct
St Louis, MO 63144-1511
314-644-4300
Fax: 314-644-5332 800-243-8162
sales@indeeco.com www.indeeco.com
Electric heating elements and systems including heat transfer systems, circulation and pipeline impedance; exporter of electric heaters and controls
President: Fred Epstein
CEO: John Eulich
Research & Development: Steve Links
Quality Control: Jana Jensen
Marketing Director: Kevin Healy
Operations Manager: Ron Kohlman
Production Manager: Cathy Luster
Purchasing Manager: John ie Harrington
Estimated Sales: $50 - 100 Million
Number Employees: 100-249
Square Footage: 200000
Other Locations:
INDEECO
Saint Louis MO
Brands:
Hynes

24052 IPEC
185 Northgate Circle
New Castle, PA 16105
800-377-4732
Fax: 724-658-3054
Plastic closures and capping equipment
President: Charles Long
CEO: Joseph Giordano
CFO/Secretary/Treasurer: Shawn Fabry
VP Operations: Jay Martin
Number Employees: 75
Square Footage: 12922

24053 IPG International Packaging Group
5611 Foxwood Drive
Apt B
Agoura Hills, CA 91377-3982
818-865-1428
Fax: 818-889-9691
Consultant specializing in product marketing and packaging design including structural and graphic for the consumer market; importer of finished printed packages
Design: Debbiz Zakrzeudski
Design: Tyson Marquardt
Estimated Sales: Less than $500,000
Number Employees: 4
Type of Packaging: Consumer

24054 (HQ)IPL Inc
140 Commerciale
Saint-Damien, QC GOR-2Y0
Canada

418-789-2880
Fax: 418-789-3153 800-463-4755
info-ipl@ipl-plastics.com www.ipl-plastics.com
Producer of molded plastic products through injection and extrusion for various industrial sectors, specially food
President: Julien M, Tivier
CEO: Serge Bragdon
Estimated Sales: $10-$20 Million
Number Employees: 10-19
Type of Packaging: Consumer, Food Service, Private Label

24055 IPL Plastics
20 Boyd St
Edmundston, NB E3V 4H4
Canada

506-739-9559
Fax: 506-739-1028 800-739-9595
Manufacturer and exporter of thin wall plastic food containers; also, molding and printing services available
Sales Manager: Pierre Boilard
Administrative Services: Claude Nadeau
Operations Manager: Mario Gaudieault
Number Employees: 100
Square Footage: 180000
Parent Co: IPL

24056 IPM Coffee Innovations LLC
1130 Springtown Road
Suite A
Alpha, NJ 08865

610-865-1900
Fax: 888-762-2173 ipmcoffee@gmail.com
www.ipmcoffee.com
Cappuccino machines
Owner & President: George Strysky
Owner & Office Manager: Lela Evans Strysky

24057 IPS International
20124 Broadway Ave
Snohomish, WA 98296

360-668-5050
Fax: 360-415-9056 info@ipsintl.com
www.independentpetsupply.com
Manufacturer and exporter of thermal and insulated handling and shipping containers
Estimated Sales: less than $500,000
Number Employees: 1
Brands:
Pal Pac
Sof-Pak
Speedwall

24058 IQ Scientific Instruments
PO Box 389
Loveland, CO 80539-0289

Fax: 970-669-2972 800-227-4224
www.phmeters.com
Manufacturer and exporter of pH meters
President: Malcolm Mitchell
Marketing Director: Kate Roberts
Sales Director: Rod Stark
Estimated Sales: $10 - 20 Million
Number Employees: 10-19
Brands:
Iq120 Minilab
Iq125 Minilab
Iq150
Iq240
Minilab

24059 IR Systems
725 N Highway A1a
Jupiter, FL 33477-4571

561-743-7171
Fax: 561-743-2121 800-893-7540
info@infrared-systems.com
www.infrared-systems.com
Infrared and conveyorized oven systems
Owner: J J Cunningham
Estimated Sales: less than $500,000
Number Employees: 1-4
Square Footage: 8800

24060 ISM Carton
PO Box 629
Butler, PA 16003-0629

800-378-3430
Fax: 800-827-4762 800-378-3430
Quality products for construction, industrial and packaging applications
CEO: Mark Kania
CEO: Steve Macefe
Director Operations: Luciano Aldeghi
Estimated Sales: $50-100 Million
Number Employees: 100-249
Type of Packaging: Private Label, Bulk

24061 ISS/GEBA/AFOS
23 Water St
PO Box 480
Ashburnham, MA 01430-1258

978-827-3160
Fax: 978-827-3162 800-269-2367
sales@intlsmokingsystems.com
www.intlsmokingsystems.com
Vacuum packaging equipment, slicers, smokehouses
President: Mark Carlisle
Estimated Sales: $5-10 Million
Number Employees: 1-4

24062 ISi North America
175 Route 46 West
Fairfield, NJ 07004-7316

973-227-2426
Fax: 973-227-4520 800-447-2426
customerservice@isinorthamerica.com
Hand held whippers and soda siphons.
President: Richard W Agresta
Estimated Sales: $5 - 10 Million
Number Employees: 10-19
Brands:
Espuma

24063 (HQ)ITC Systems
49 Railside Road
Unit 63
Toronto, ON M1H 2X1
Canada

416-289-2344
Fax: 416-289-4790 877-482-8326
sales@itcsystems.com www.itcsystems.com
Manufacturer, importer and exporter of cash card systems hardware and software for prepaid services at vending machines and manual food operations; manufacturer of photo identification cards with on-line debit/credit balances
Chief Executive Officer, President: Cam Richardson
Vice President of Business Development: Dan Bodolai
Director Sales: David Hulbert
Purchasing Manager: Janet Exconde
Number Employees: 10
Square Footage: 44000
Other Locations:
ITC Systems
Longwood FL

24064 ITC Systems
49 Railside Road
Toronto, ON M3A 1B3
Canada

416-289-2344
Fax: 416-289-4790 877-482-8326
service@itcsystems.com www.itcsystems.com
Manufacturer, importer and exporter of cash card systems hardware and software for prepaid services at vending machines and manual food operations; manufacturer of photo identification cards with on-line debit/credit balances
Chief Executive Officer, President: Cam Richardson
R&D: Igor Irlin
Director of Sales: Dave Hulbert
Director Sales: David Hulbert
Plant Manager: Bryan Bull
Purchasing Manager: Janet Exconde
Number Employees: 25
Square Footage: 22000
Parent Co: ITC Systems

24065 ITS/ETL Testing Laboratories
27611 La Paz Rd # C
Laguna Niguel, CA 92677-3938

949-448-4100
Fax: 949-448-4111
Laboratory specializing in microbiological and chemical testing; also, sanitation and electrical inspection

Manager: Bill Bocchini
Estimated Sales: $5-10 Million
Number Employees: 1-4

24066 ITT Inc
33 Centerville Rd
Lancaster, PA 17603-4068

717-509-6496
Fax: 717-509-2336 800-366-1111
engvalvescustserve@fluids.ittind.com
www.engvalves.com
Valves: Cam-Line, Cam-Tite, Dia-Flo, Pure-Flo, Fabri-Valve, Skotch, Richter products
Cmo: Heather Sandoe
heather.sandoe@itt.com
Estimated Sales: $2.5-5 Million
Number Employees: 10-19

24067 ITT Jabsco
1485 Dale Way
Foothill Ranch, CA 92610

949-609-5106
Fax: 949-853-1254 www.jabsco.com
Manufactures food and dairy products pumps
President: Russ David
VP: Oliver Dupre
R&D: Scott Shimer
Quality Control: John Ebeling
Sales Manager: David Farrer
Estimated Sales: $20 - 50 Million
Number Employees: 250

24068 ITW Angleboard
113 Censors Road
Villa Rica, GA 30180-2120

770-459-5747
Fax: 770-459-1305 www.itw.com
Manufacturer and exporter of protective packaging profiles for shipping, unitizing and palletizing
CEO: David Speer
CFO: James Wooten Jr.
Investor Relations: John Brooklier
Estimated Sales: $1 - 5 Million
Brands:
Edgeboard

24069 ITW Auto-Sleeve
2003 Case Pkwy S
Suite 3
Twinsburg, OH 44087

330-487-2200
Fax: 330-487-3700 800-852-4571
CFO: Roy Marschke
Estimated Sales: Below $5 Million
Number Employees: 10-19

24070 ITW Diagraph
1 Research Park Dr
St Charles, MO 63304-5685

636-300-2000
Fax: 636-300-2003 800-722-1125
www.diagraph.com
Automated coding and labeling systems for product identification, case marking, shipment addressing and barcoding
Manager: Cathie Windle
Marketing Director: Quentin Griesenauer
VP Slaes: John Campbell
Estimated Sales: $50-100 Million
Number Employees: 100-249

24071 ITW Dymon
805 E Old 56 Highway
Olathe, KS 66061

913-829-6296
Fax: 913-397-8707 800-443-9536
cservice@dymon.com
Cleaning supplies including disinfectants, hand sanitizer wipes and polishing clothes
R&D: Jason McCauley
Quality Control: David Madsen
General Manager: Paul Taylor
Marketing Manager: Andrew Bolin
National Sales Manager: Alan Smith
Contact: Charles Manz
manzcharlesj@itwprobrands.com
General Manager: Paull Taylor
Estimated Sales: Below $5,000,000
Number Employees: 50-99
Parent Co: Illinois Tool Works
Brands:
Antimicrobial Sanitizer Scrubs
Lemon Glo

Metal Polish Scrubs
Scrubs In-A-Bucket

24072 ITW Dynatec
31 Volunteer Dr
Hendersonville, TN 37075-3156
615-824-3634
Fax: 615-264-5248 info@itwdynatec.com
www.itwdynatec.com
Hot melt glue systems
President: Zent Myer
CFO: Doug Betew
CFO: Doug Detew
R & D: Marie McLain
Number Employees: 100-249

24073 ITW Engineered Polymers
2425 N Lapeer Rd
Oxford, MI 48371-2425
248-628-2587
Fax: 248-628-7136 info@ironout.com
Manufacturer and exporter of polyurea elastomeric
coatings, urethane foam systems, application equip-
ment and set-up processing stations. ITW Foamseal
is currently supplying a wide range of urethane
products for many uses in the automotive, manufac-
tured housing, fenestration, furniture, sports equip-
ment, recreational vehicle, medical, tolling and
infrastructure markets
Manager: Gary Maxson
General Manager: Ted Stolz
Business Manager: Tim Walsh
Estimated Sales: $20-50 Million
Number Employees: 5-9
Square Footage: 50000
Parent Co: Illinois Tool Works
Type of Packaging: Private Label
Brands:
Infraseal

24074 ITW Food Equipment Group
702 S Ridge Ave
Troy, OH 45374
888-978-8381
www.itwfoodequipment.com
Cooking and baking, refrigeration, food preparation,
clean up, holding, weighing and wrapping, ventila-
tion and service.
Chairman/CEO: E. Scott Santi
Vice Chairman: Christopher O'Herlihy
SVP/CFO: Michael Larsen
SVP/General Counsel: Norman Finch

SVP/Chief Human Resources Officer: Mary Lawler
Estimated Sales: $14.1 Billion
Number Employees: 45,000
Parent Co: Illinois Tool Works Inc
Brands:
Avery Berkel
Baxter
Berkel
Bonnet
Elro
Foster
Gamko
Gaylord
Hobart
Kairak
Master
Peerless Food Equipment
Perfecta
Red Goat
Somat
Stero
Traulsen
Vesta
Vulcan
Wittco Foodservice Equipment
Wolf

24075 ITW Hi-Cone
1140 W Bryn Mawr Ave
Itasca, IL 60143-1599
630-438-5300
Fax: 630-438-5315 www.hicone.com
Multi-pack plastic ring carriers for cans and bottles
of beverages, vegetables, fruits, pasta and soup.
President: Tim Gardner
Cmo: Jeff Meitzel
jmeitzel@hi-cone.com
VP Sales: Steve Henn
Estimated Sales: $5-10 Million
Number Employees: 100-249
Parent Co: Illinois Tool Works

Brands:
Hi-Cone

24076 ITW Plastic Packaging
4950 Colorado Blvd
Denver, CO 80216
303-316-6816
Plastic transport packaging products: slip sheets, tier
sheets, EZ Grab LoadLoc, pallets, top frams,
DuraSheets and Replastec Separators, pallets
Contact: Roberta Andersen
roberta.andersen@chilis.com

24077 ITW United Silicone
4471 Walden Ave
Lancaster, NY 14086-9778
716-681-8222
Fax: 716-681-8789 info@unitedsilicone.com
www.unitedsilicone.com
Designer and manufacturer of product decorating
and packaging equipment, supplies, tooling and heat
seal solutions.
President: Kim Jackson
kjackson@unitedsilicone.com
Marketing Manager: Laura Baumann
Sales Director: Eric Steinwachs
Estimated Sales: $20-50 Million
Number Employees: 100-249
Square Footage: 18000
Parent Co: Illinois Toolworks
Type of Packaging: Consumer, Food Service

24078 IVEK Corp
10 Fairbanks Rd
N Springfield, VT 05150-9743
802-886-2238
Fax: 802-886-8274 800-356-4746
ivek@ivek.com www.ivek.com
Precision liquid metering and dispensing systems.
President, CEO & R&D: Mark Tanny
mtanny@ivek.com
CFO: Dennis Crowley
VP, Sales: Frank Dimaggio
Quality Control: Ed Lawrence
Marketing: Tracey Tanny
Public Relations: Pauline Asselin
Operations: Gary Blake
Production: Brad Doody
Plant Manager: Gary Blake
Purchasing: Wade McAllister
Estimated Sales: $3 - 5 Million
Number Employees: 50-99
Square Footage: 68000
Brands:
Digispense 2000
Digispense 700
Digispense 800
Microspense Ap
Multiplex
Multispense
Ox/Digifeeder
Sanitary Split Case Pump
Syncrospense

24079 IVEK Corp
10 Fairbanks Rd
N Springfield, VT 05150-9743
802-886-2238
Fax: 802-886-8274 800-356-4746
ivek@ivek.com www.ivek.com
Precision small volume liquid dispensing and meter-
ing systems
President: Mark Tanny
mtanny@ivek.com
CFO: Dennis Crowley
Vice President: Frank DiMaggio
Research & Development: Mark Tanny
Quality Control: Ken Neal
Marketing Director: Tracey Tanny
Sales Director: Frank DiMaggio
Public Relations: Pauline Asselin
Operations Manager: Gary Blake
Production Manager: Tara Curtis
Plant Manager: Brad Deedy
Purchasing Manager: Wade McAllister
Estimated Sales: Below $5 Million
Number Employees: 50-99

24080 IVEX Packaging Corporation
610 Beriault Rd.
Longueuil, QC J4G 1D8
Canada
450-651-8887
Fax: 450-651-0093 www.ivexpackaging.com

Manufacturer and exporter of packaging materials
including corrugated paper and trays.
President: Paul Gaulin
Year Founded: 2008
Estimated Sales: $710 Million
Parent Co: Induspac Inc.
Brands:
Grand Stands
Ivex
M&R
Prime Time
Reflections
Selectware
Sho-Bowls
Ultra Pac

24081 IWS Scales
9885 Mesa Rim Road
Suite 128
San Diego, CA 92191
Fax: 858-784-0542 800-881-9755
iwsscales.com
Manufacturer, importer and exporter of mechanical
and electronic scales including platform, receiving,
portion, racking, computing, etc
Estimated Sales: $1 - 3 Million
Number Employees: 50
Square Footage: 40000
Parent Co: Western Scale
Brands:
Airway
West Weigh

24082 Ice-Cap
P.O. Box 292
Piermont, NY 10968-292
718-729-7000
Fax: 718-392-4193 888-423-2270
Manufacturer and exporter of air conditioners
CEO: Mo Siegel
CFO: Mo Siegel
Estimated Sales: $20 - 50 Million
Number Employees: 10

24083 Icee-USA Corporation
4701 E Airport Dr
Ontario, CA 91761-7817
909-390-4233
Fax: 909-390-4260 800-426-4233
www.icee.com
Manufacturer and exporter of frozen carbonated
beverage dispensers; also, point of sale signs and
displays available
President: Dan Fachner
CFO: Kent Galloway
VP: Rod Sexton
Contact: Michael Acosta
macosta@icee.com
Estimated Sales: $5 - 10 Million
Number Employees: 100-249
Square Footage: 88000
Parent Co: J&J Snack Foods Company

24084 Iceomatic
11100 E 45th Ave
Denver, CO 80239-3006
303-371-3737
Fax: 303-371-6296 800-423-3367
customer.service@iceomatic.com
www.iceomatic.com
Ice making equipment since 1952 including cubers,
flakers, dispensers, bins and accessories. Provides
equipment for restaurants, bars, hotels/motels, hos-
pitals, etc
President: Kevin Fink
kevin.fink@iceomatic.com
CFO: Dave Weller
Quality Control: David Spiciarich
Marketing Director: Keith Kelly
Public Relations: Linda Gleeson
Plant Manager: Randy Karas
Number Employees: 250-499
Brands:
Ice-O-Matic Ice Machines

24085 Ickler Co Inc
2832 1st St S
St Cloud, MN 56301-3894
320-251-8282
Fax: 320-251-8389 800-243-8382
ickler@ickler.com www.ickler.com
Machine shop services, custom fabrication, and retail bearing sales

Owner: Todd Mc Gonagle
ickler@ickler.com
Estimated Sales: $600,000-$700,000
Number Employees: 10-19

24086 Iconics Inc
100 Foxboro Blvd # 130
Foxboro, MA 02035-2883

508-543-8600
Fax: 508-543-1503 800-946-9679
us@iconics.com www.iconics.com
ICONICS is the lead supplier of HMI SCADA, Energy Management, and Productivity Analytics software solutions to the Food and Beverage Industry. ICONICS GENISIS64 HMI/SCADA and Analytix software improves operational performance andproductivity by providing 360 degrees of visibility and real time control for business and production systems.
CEO: Russell Agrusa
russ@iconics.com
VP Finance/Administration, CFO: Paula Agrusa
VP Worldwide Sales: Chris Volpe
Business Development Manager for Buildin: Oliver Gruner
VP Product Marketing: Gary F. Kohrt
VP, Worldwide Sales: Mark Hepburn
Estimated Sales: $5,000,000 - $9,999,999
Number Employees: 20-49
Square Footage: 96000
Brands:
  Alarmwork Multimedia
  Genesis For Windows
  Genesis32 Enterprise Edition
  Pocket Genesis
  Winworx
  Winworx Open Series

24087 Id Technology
2051 Franklin Dr
Fort Worth, TX 76106-2204

817-626-7779
Fax: 817-626-0553 888-438-3242
marketing@idtechnology.com
www.idtechnologytx.net
Labels, label printer/applicators, label applicators, laser marketing, inkjet coding, thermal transfer overprinting
President: Robert Zuilhof
robert.zuilhof@idtechnology.com
CFO: Tina Millwood
VP: Alan Shipman
Marketing: Hilary Taylor
Estimated Sales: $75 Million
Number Employees: 100-249
Other Locations:
  Pewaukee WI
  Fresno CA

24088 Id Technology
2051 Franklin Dr
Fort Worth, TX 76106-2204

817-626-7779
Fax: 817-626-0553 888-438-3242
marketing@idtechnology.com
www.idtechnologytx.net
Labeling, coding and marking equipment
President: Robert Zuilhof
robert.zuilhof@idtechnology.com
CEO/CFO: Tina Millwood
VP: Alan Shipman
R&D: Mark Snedecor
Marketing: Hillary Taylor
Sales: Alan Shipman
Public Relations: Hillary Taylor
Plant Manager: Kim Pulliam
Purchasing: Kim Pulliam
Estimated Sales: $50 Million
Number Employees: 100-249
Parent Co: Pro Mach Inc

24089 Idaho Beverages Inc
2108 1st Ave N
Lewiston, ID 83501-1604

208-743-6535
Fax: 208-746-2273 dprasil@lewistonpepsi.com
www.lewistonpepsi.com
Distributer of beverages to the food service industry. Brands distributed include Pepsi, Mountain Dew, 7 Up, Cheerwine Soft Drink, Gatorade, Aquafina, Starbucks Coffee and more.
Owner: Dan Prasil
Estimated Sales: $5-10 000,000
Number Employees: 51 - 200

Type of Packaging: Food Service

24090 Idaho Steel Products Inc
255 E Anderson St
Idaho Falls, ID 83401-2016

208-522-1275
Fax: 208-522-6041 sales@idahosteel.com
www.idahosteel.com
Manufacturer and exporter of food processing equipment including blanchers, cookers, coolers, drum dryers and complete processing lines
President: Delynn Bradshaw
delynn@idahosteel.com
CFO: Craig Parker
Engineering Manager: Alan Bradshaw
Marketing/Public Relations: Davis Christiansen
Sales Director: Bruce Ball
Operations Manager: D Bradshaw
Purchasing Manager: Adam French
Estimated Sales: $10 - 20 Million
Number Employees: 100-249
Square Footage: 100000

24091 Ideal Office Supply & Rubber Stamp Company
222 E Center Street
Kingsport, TN 37662-0935

423-246-7371
Fax: 423-246-3535
Office supplies including rubber stamps and plastic signs
President: Cynthia Culberton
Number Employees: 12

24092 Ideal Packaging Systems
1662 Broughton Court
Atlanta, GA 30338-4633

770-352-0210
Fax: 770-352-0106 ioealvr@yahoo.com
Pallet stretch wrapping and bundle shrink wrapping equipment
Estimated Sales: $10-20 Million
Number Employees: 5

24093 Ideal Pak Inc
4607 Dovetail Dr
Madison, WI 53704-6302

608-241-1118
Fax: 608-241-4448 800-383-1128
sales@ideal-pak.com www.idealstorage.biz
Industrial liquid filling and closing equipment
Owner: Steve Bethke
steve@ideal-pak.com
Sales & Marketing Director: Russell Schlager
Vice President: Bruce Bierman
Marketing Manager: Steven Meyer
National Sales Manager: Robert D. Whetstone
steve@ideal-pak.com
Operations Manager: Bruce Bierman
Purchasing Manager: Aric Riley
Estimated Sales: $1 Million +
Number Employees: 20-49
Number of Brands: 3
Square Footage: 30000
Type of Packaging: Food Service, Private Label, Bulk

24094 Ideal Sleeves
182 Courtright St
Wilkes Barre, PA 18702-1802

570-823-8456
Fax: 570-823-8458
Tamper evident shrink seals, multipak, sleeves, shrink labels, preforms, seamed and seamless materials including PVC and Pet-G
Manager: Dave Frable
Chief Executive Officer, President: James Dwyer
G.M.: Arlene Warnuck
Manager: Henry Shuffler
henrys@idealsleeves.com
Estimated Sales: $5 - 10 Million
Number Employees: 20-49

24095 Ideal Stencil Machine &Tape Company
5307 Meadowland Parkway
Marion, IL 62959-5893

618-233-0162
Fax: 618-233-5091 800-388-0162
Manufacturer and exporter of ink including meat branding, hog tattoo, coding and jet printer; also, fountain brushes, conveyor line coders, ink applicators, metal markers and electronic stencil and embossing machines

Sales Manager: Jim Boyd
Executive VP Operations: Marco Ziniti
Estimated Sales: $2.5-5 Million
Number Employees: 20-49
Square Footage: 240000
Brands:
  Handy A&C
  Ht80
  Ideal Mark
  Ideco
  M074
  Meat Marking
  Roll-Eze
  Speedry

24096 Ideal Wire Works
820 S Date Ave
Alhambra, CA 91803-1414

626-282-0886
Fax: 626-282-2674
Manufacturer and exporter of custom wire display racks, rings and parts in steel or stainless steel
Vice President: Liz Maro
lizmaro@idealwireworks.com
VP: Jim Freitag
Estimated Sales: $2.5 - 5 Million
Number Employees: 20-49
Square Footage: 40000

24097 Ideal Wrapping Machine Company
81 Sprague Avenue
Middletown, NY 10940-5223

845-343-7700
Fax: 845-344-4248
Manufacturer and exporter of forming, cutting and wrapping machinery for caramel, nougat and toffee candies
President: Lee Quality Tire
General Manager: Jim Horton
Number Employees: 5-9

24098 Ideal of America
205 Regency Executive Park Drive
Suite 309
Charlotte, NC 28217-3989

704-523-1604
Fax: 704-523-1635
Packaging equipment including bundlers, shrink wrappers and automatic baggers
VP: David Katz
Sales Manager: Lana Taylor
Estimated Sales: $1 - 5 Million
Number Employees: 100-250
Square Footage: 80000

24099 Ideal of America/ValleyRio Enterprise
1662 Broughton Court
Atlanta, GA 30338-4633

770-352-0210
Fax: 770-352-0106 idealvr@yahoo.com
Manufacturer and exporter of stainless steel packaging equipment including fully automated shrink and stretch wrappers
Vice President: Alan Pullock
Estimated Sales: $10 Million
Number Employees: 100-250
Square Footage: 210000
Parent Co: Ideal of America
Brands:
  Ideal

24100 Ideas Etc Inc
8305 Dawson Hill Rd
Louisville, KY 40299-5317

502-231-4303
Fax: 502-239-0555 800-733-0337
ideasetc@msn.com www.ideas-etc.com
Manufacturer and exporter of shot and martini glasses, beverage containers and 4-necker T-shirts; importer of martini glasses. Designers and printers of food service calendars and planners
President: Tiffany Gaskin
tiffanygaskin@hotmail.com
Estimated Sales: $500,000+
Number Employees: 1-4
Brands:
  Palm Tree Cooler
  Splitshot
  Yardski

24101 Ideas Well Done LLC

276 E Allen St # 5
Winooski, VT 05404-1570

802-654-8603
Fax: 802-654-8618 877-877-1224
www.ideaswelldone.com

Manufacturer, boilerless atmospheric steamers in 4 and 6 pan sizes, stackable up to 12 pan configuration. convection fan and automatic waterfill makes steam convection and simple
President: Michael G Colburn
  mcolburn@ideaswelldone.com
CFO: Bob McLaughlin
VP: Mary Treat
Quality Control: Stephen Bogner
Marketing: Mary Treat
Sales/Public Relations: Mary Esthertrout
Purchasing: Steve Bogner
Estimated Sales: Below $5 Million
Number Employees: 5-9
Number of Brands: 1
Number of Products: 3
Square Footage: 20000
Brands:
  Steller Steam

24102 Ideas in Motion

P.O. Box 8504
New Castle, PA 16107-8504

724-924-9680
Fax: 724-924-9665 800-367-3535

Owner: Brian Crisci
Estimated Sales: $1-2.5 Million
Number Employees: 20-49

24103 Idec Corp

1175 Elko Dr
Sunnyvale, CA 94089-2209

408-747-0550
Fax: 408-744-9055 800-262-IDEC

Control components, switches, pushbuttons, sensors and relays
Chairman of the Board: Toshiyuki Funaki
VP: Sada O'Hara
Manager: Jc Aguirre
  aguirre.jc@idec.com
Estimated Sales: $50 - 100 Million
Number Employees: 100-249
Number of Products: 5500

24104 IdentaBadge

3219 Johnston St
Lafayette, LA 70503

337-984-8888
Fax: 337-984-1666 800-325-8247

Name badges, directional signs and advertising specialties and awards
Owner: D A Savoie
CEO: Dale Savoie
VP: Sidney Savoie
Sales: Dottie Blanchard
Public Relations: Dottie Blanchard
Estimated Sales: $5 - 10 Million
Number Employees: 5-9
Number of Brands: 1
Number of Products: 25
Square Footage: 11000
Parent Co: Trophyland
Type of Packaging: Bulk

24105 Idesco Corp

37 W 26th St # 10
New York, NY 10010-1097

212-784-1800
Fax: 212-889-7033 800-336-1383
info@idesco.com www.idesco.com

Manufacturer and exporter of integrated security systems
President: Andrew Schonzeit
  andrew@idesco.com
CFO: Ray O' Connor
VP of Sales: Michael Perlow
VP Sales: Andy Goldstone
Operations Manager: Brian Simpson
Estimated Sales: $10-20 Million
Number Employees: 20-49
Square Footage: 20000
Brands:
  Vita

24106 Idexx Laboratories Inc

1 Idexx Dr
Westbrook, ME 04092-2041

207-556-0300
Fax: 207-556-4346 800-548-6733
www.idexx.com

Manufacturer and exporter of cleaning and validation systems including testing kits for salmonella, coliforms/E coli in water, residues in milk and microbiological; also, dehydrated culture media.
President/CEO: Jay Mazelsky
EVP/Chief Financial Officer/Treasurer: Brian McKeon
Corp VP/Software & Engineering Officer: Jeff Dixon
Corp VP/General Counsel/Secretary: Sharon Underberg
Corp VP/Worldwide Operations: John Hart
Corp VP/Chief Information Officer: Ken Grady
Corp VP/Chief Technology Officer: Jeffrey Thomas
Year Founded: 1983
Estimated Sales: $2.4 Billion
Number Employees: 7,000
Brands:
  Acumedia
  Bind
  Colilert
  Lightning
  Simplate
  Snap

24107 Ifm Efector

782 Springdale Dr
Exton, PA 19341-2850

610-524-2000
Fax: 610-524-2020 800-441-8246
customer_service@ifmefector.com
www.ifmefector.com

Industrial sensors including capacitive, inductive and plug-connector type proximity switches, photoelectric controls, flow monitor switches, pressure switches, and temperature sensors
Contact: Deven Ott
  deveno@fedex.com
Estimated Sales: $70 Million
Number Employees: 100-249

24108 Igloo Products Corp

777 Igloo Rd
Katy, TX 77494

866-509-3503
www.igloocoolers.com

Ice chest coolers, insulated catering chests, softside catering carriers and beverage and cup dispensers.
President & CEO: Dave Allen
Year Founded: 1947
Estimated Sales: $108.90 Million
Number Employees: 1,200
Number of Products: 500+
Square Footage: 10000000
Parent Co: ACON
Type of Packaging: Food Service
Brands:
  Igloo
  Igloo 2go
  Igloo Stralth

24109 Igus Inc

50 N Broadway # 1
Rumford, RI 02916-2600

401-438-2200
Fax: 401-438-7270 800-521-2747
sales@igus.com www.igus.com

Packaging machinery components, cable carriers, high flex cables, bearings and linear guides
Vice President: Carsten Blase
  cblase@igus.com
VP: Carsten Blase
Number Employees: 100-249
Square Footage: 352000
Parent Co: Igus GmbH

24110 Ika-Works Inc

2635 Northchase Pkwy SE
Wilmington, NC 28405-7419

910-452-7059
Fax: 910-452-7693 800-733-3037
process@ikausa.com www.ikausa.com

Laboratory, pilot plant and processing equipment including particle size reducers, dispersers and homogenizers; also, continuous and vertical kneaders, overhead stirring motors and magnetic stirrers; sanitary design servicesavailable

Owner: Rene Steigelman
Vice President: Robert Hardin
Marketing/Sales: Linn Wilson
Sales Director: Michael Janssen
Number Employees: 100-249
Square Footage: 60000
Parent Co: IKA Werke
Brands:
  Conterna
  Dispax Reactor
  Eurostar
  Ikamag
  Planetron
  Ultra-Turrax

24111 Il Valley Container Inc

2 Terminal Rd
Peru, IL 61354-3700

815-223-7200
www.ivcontainer.com

Corrugated containers
President: Timothy Alter
  timothyalter@ivcontainer.com
General Manager: Jim Ewert
Estimated Sales: $5-10 Million
Number Employees: 20-49

24112 Ilapak Inc

105 Pheasant Run
Newtown, PA 18940-1820

215-579-2900
Fax: 215-579-9959 marketing@ilapak.com
www.ilapak.com

Flexible horizontal and vertical packaging machinery including fin seal and shrink wrappers, vertical form/fill/seal, four-side seal pouch, horizontal modified atmosphere, etc
President: Andrew G Axberg
CEO: Edward Young
  eyoung@ilapak.com
CFO: Frank Zellucci
VP Sales: Randy Rice
Estimated Sales: $10 - 20 Million
Number Employees: 20-49
Square Footage: 36000
Parent Co: Ilapak Holding
Brands:
  Alfa
  Carrera 1000 M
  Carrera 1000 Pc
  Carrera 2000 Pc
  Carrera 500 M
  Cougar
  Delta
  Delta 3000 D-Cam
  Delta 3000 Ld
  Delta 3000 Sb
  Indy
  Rose Forgrove
  Sandiacre
  Vegatronic 1000
  Vegatronic 2000
  Vegatronic 3000
  Vegatronic 3000

24113 Ilapak Inc

105 Pheasant Run
Newtown, PA 18940-1820

215-579-2900
Fax: 215-579-9959 www.ilapak.com

Supplier of industrial wrapping machinery for food industry
CEO: Edward Young
  eyoung@ilapak.com
CEO: Andrew Axberg
Office Manager: Claire Paczkowski
Number Employees: 20-49

24114 Ilc Dover

1 Moonwalker Rd
Frederica, DE 19946-2080

302-335-3911
Fax: 302-335-0762 800-631-9567
customer_service@ilcdover.com
www.ilcdover.com

Pharmaceutical packaging material.
President: Fran DiNuzzo
Year Founded: 1947
Estimated Sales: $100-500 Million
Square Footage: 225000
Brands:
  Keg Wrap

24115 Illinois Lock Co
301 W Hintz Rd
Wheeling, IL 60090-5700
                              847-537-1800
          Fax: 847-537-1881 800-733-3907
    sales@illinoislock.com www.illinoislock.com
Producers of custom engineered key locks, keyless
locks, electric switch locks, high - security locks,
and wire harness lock assemblies
Sales Exec: Paul Sletzer
Manager: Len Samela
Estimated Sales: $10-20 Million
Number Employees: 50-99
Parent Co: Eastern Company

24116 Illinois Range Company
9555 Ainslie St
Schiller Park, IL 60176-1115
                              847-928-2490
          Fax: 847-928-2782 800-535-7041
Custom stainless steel kitchen equipment including
counters, hoods, ranges, ovens, smallwares, etc
President: John Domdek
Estimated Sales: Below $5 Million
Number Employees: 1-4
Square Footage: 504000

24117 Illinois Restaurant Association
33 W. Monroe
Suite 250
Chicago, IL 60603
                              312-787-4000
          Fax: 312-787-4792 800-572-1086
          info@illinoisrestaurants.org
          www.illinoisrestaurants.org
To serve the needs of the foodservice industry and
support its future.
President: Sam Toia
Project Manager: Ashley Brandon
Assistant Director of Finance & Administ: Maria
Bello
Contact: Rick Brands
    rbrands@mcmaster.com
VP, Operations: Mary Kay Bonoma
Number Employees: 20-49

24118 Illinois Tool Works
155 Harlem Ave
Glenview, IL 60025
                              224-661-8870
          www.itw.com
Dishwashing, cooking, refrigeration and food pro-
cessing equipment
Chairman/CEO: E. Scott Santi
Vice Chairman: Christopher O'Herlihy
Senior VP/General Counsel/Secretary: Norman
Finch

Senior VP/CFO: Michael Larsen
Estimated Sales: $13.6 Billion
Number Employees: 50,000

24119 Illinois Wholesale CashRgstr
2790 Pinnacle Dr
Elgin, IL 60124-7943
                              847-310-4200
          Fax: 847-310-8490 800-544-5493
          www.illinoiswholesale.com
Refurbished point of sale equipment
President: Al Moorhouse
    amoorhouse@illinoiswholesale.com
Vice President of Accounting: Bob Tracy
Chief Operating Officer, Vice President: Darin
Moorhouse
Operations Manager: Jeff Burton
Estimated Sales: $10 - 20 Million
Number Employees: 100-249

24120 Illuma Display
P.O. Box 1531
Brookfield, WI 53008-1531
                              262-446-9220
          Fax: 262-446-9260 800-501-0128
Manufacturer and exporter of curved light boxes,
graphic stands and backlit displays
President: Joe Galati
VP: Tony Galati
Estimated Sales: Less than $500,000
Number Employees: 1-4

24121 Illumination Products Inc
175 Calle Federico Costa
Tres Monjitas Park
San Juan, PR 00918-1307
                              787-754-7193
                    Fax: 787-250-7813
Fluorescent light fixtures and lamps
President: Robert Santiago
Quality Control: Raul Millan
Estimated Sales: Below $5 Million
Number Employees: 5-9

24122 Ilsemann Corp
398 Circle of Progress Dr # 10
Suite 102
Pottstown, PA 19464-3814
                              610-323-4143
          Fax: 610-323-4709 sales@ilsemannusa.com
          www.ilsemann.com/index.php?id=company&L=1
Estimated Sales: $1,000,000 - $3,000,000
Number Employees: 5-9
Parent Co: Heino Ilsemann GmbH

24123 Image Development
PO Box 218
Plymouth, CA 95669-0218
                              209-267-1850
          Fax: 209-267-1850 id@bauerengraving.com
Chocolate coin imprinting, dies, candy
President: William Bratt
Number Employees: 2

24124 Image Experts Uniforms
1623 Eastern Pkwy
Schenectady, NY 12309-6011
                              518-377-4523
          Fax: 518-374-1236 800-789-2433
          www.imageexpertsuniforms.com
Manufacturer and exporter of uniforms
Owner: Tom Salamone
    tom@imageexperts.com
CEO: Thomas J Salamone
Estimated Sales: $1-2.5 Million
Number Employees: 10-19
Square Footage: 8000
Parent Co: Image Experts Uniforms
Brands:
    Chef Direct
    Really Cookin' Chef Gear

24125 Image Fillers
735 Fox Chase # 111
Suite 111
Coatesville, PA 19320-1897
                              610-466-1440
          Fax: 610-466-0116 www.imagefillers.com
Owner: Mike Kelly Sr
Number Employees: 5-9

24126 Image National Inc
16265 Star Rd
Nampa, ID 83687-8415
                              208-345-4020
          Fax: 208-336-9886 jcarico@imagenational.com
Manufacturer and exporter of electric signs, store
fronts and interior graphics
President: Doug Bender
    doug.bender@imagenational.com
CEO/CFO: Chuck White
Service Install Manager: Jeff Carico
Sales Manager: Tony Adams
General Manager: Doug Bender
Estimated Sales: $5 - 10 Million
Number Employees: 100-249
Parent Co: Futura Corporation

24127 Image Plastics
5919 Jessamine Street
Houston, TX 77081-6506
                              713-772-2811
          Fax: 713-772-6445 800-289-2811
Insulated and noninsulated plastic drinkware
VP: Jim Houseal
Director Marketing: Gary Opperman
Director Sales: Mike Barrow
Estimated Sales: $20-50 Million
Number Employees: 100-249
Brands:
    Automug
    Sportsmate

24128 Imaging Technologies
445 Universal Drive
Cookeville, TN 38506-4603
                              931-432-4191
          Fax: 931-432-4199 800-488-2804
          www.icglink.com
Manufacturer and exporter of high resolution ink jet
printing systems for printing bar codes, alphanumer-
ics and graphics on porous surfaces
President: Loyd Tarver
Controller: Ted Bonnay
Vice President of Marketing: Chris Jones
Marketing Manager: Steve Shoup
Contact: Mark Doyle
    sales@itiworldwide.com
Number Employees: 30
Square Footage: 24000
Brands:
    Iti
    Kd Jet Streamer
    Marksman
    Porelon

24129 Imaje
1650 Airport Rd NW # 101
Kennesaw, GA 30144-7017
                              678-594-7153
          Fax: 770-421-7702 www.markem-imaje.us
Coding, dating and marking equipment, barcoding
systems and inks for food packaging; importer of ink
jet coders; exporter of ink jet coders, inks and
additives
Manager: Linda Kaimesher
CFO: Steve Wakeford
Marketing Director: Alisha Curd
Sales Director: Tim Sines
Contact: Luis Davila
    ldavila@markem-imaje.com
Purchasing Manager: Norm Coon
Estimated Sales: $20,000,000 - $49,999,999
Number Employees: 1-4
Parent Co: Dover Technologies
Brands:
    Crayon
    Crayon Z-Tra
    Imaje 7s
    Lightjet
    Lightjet Vector
    McP
    McP Barcode
    McP Series
    Prima
    Pulsar
    S8 1p65
    S8 Classic
    S8 Contrast
    S8 Master

24130 Iman Pack
5762 E Executive Dr
Westland, MI 48185-9125
                              734-467-9016
          Fax: 734-467-8642 800-810-4626
          www.imanpack.com
Manufacturer and importer of automatic packaging
equipment including horizontal and vertical
form/fill/seal machinery, shrink wrappers, counting
and weighing scales, case packers, palletizers, etc
President: Antonio Bonotto
Sales/Marketing: Lori Scheinman
National Sales Director: Fred Barbarotto
Contact: Mauro Ferrari
    m.ferrari@imanpack.it
Estimated Sales: $1 - 3 Million
Number Employees: 5-9
Parent Co: Iman Pack SRL
Brands:
    Gianopac
    Ultravert

24131 Iman Pack
5762 E Executive Dr
Westland, MI 48185-9125
                              734-467-9016
          Fax: 734-467-8642 www.imanpack.it
Packaging equipment including vertical form, fill
and seal baggers
President: Antonio Bonotto
VP: Giovanni Bonotto
Contact: Mauro Ferrari
    m.ferrari@imanpack.it
Estimated Sales: $1 - 3 Million
Number Employees: 5-9
Parent Co: Imanpak

24132 Iman Pack Sigma System
5762 E Executive Dr
Westland, MI 48185
734-467-9016
Fax: 734-467-8642 www.imanpack.com
President: Antonio Bonotto
VP Sales: Massimo Denipoti
Contact: Mauro Ferrari
m.ferrari@imanpack.it
Estimated Sales: $1 - 5 Million
Number Employees: 5-9

24133 Imar
2301 Collins Avenue
Miami Beach, FL 33139-1639
305-531-5757
Fax: 305-538-2957
Manufacturer, importer and exporter of packaging
machinery for pouches
CEO: Thomas Tennant
Parent Co: Imar
Brands:
Imar

24134 Imdec
2061 Freeway Dr
Suite E
Woodland, CA 95776
530-661-9091
Fax: 530-661-9206
Tomato and fruit processing equipment
President: Glen Langstaff
Contact: David Matthews
trgshop@yahoo.com
Estimated Sales: $1 - 2.5 Million
Number Employees: 9

24135 Imex Vinyl Packaging
2559 Plantation Center Drive
Matthews, NC 28105
704-815-4600
Fax: 704-815-4601 800-938-4639
sales@imexvp.com www.imexpackaging.com
Clear vinyl bags and packaging.
President & Owner: Steve Jefferey
Operations Manager: Danny Love
Number Employees: 10
Type of Packaging: Consumer, Private Label, Bulk

24136 Impact Awards & Promotions
748 Us Highway 27 N
Avon Park, FL 33825-2639
561-394-8002
Fax: 561-394-9002 888-203-4225
www.impactpromotions.com
Signs, trophies, awards, nameplates and name tags
Owner: Doug Singletary
Marketing: Doug Singletary
Contact: San Woodlee
swoodlee@impactpromotions.com
Estimated Sales: Less than $500,000
Number Employees: 1-4
Square Footage: 6000

24137 Impact Nutrition
1155 S Havana Street
Suite 11-392
Aurora, CO 80012-4019
720-374-7111
www.impactnutrition.net.au
Contract packager of vitamins, minerals, herbal and
nutritional supplements, sports nutrition products,
capsules, tablets and powders
President: Patrick Frazier
General Manager: Julene Frazier
Estimated Sales: $10-20 Million
Number Employees: 20-49
Square Footage: 30000

24138 Impact Products LLC
2840 Centennial Rd
Toledo, OH 43617-1898
419-841-2891
Fax: 419-841-7861 800-333-1541
custserv@impact-products.com
www.impact-products.com
Wholesaler/distributor of toilet bowl mops, soap dis-
pensers, dust pans, plastic pumps, disposable plastic
gloves and washroom accessories
President/CEO: Steve Shultz
VP, Marketing: Robb Borgen
VP, Sales: Chris Tricozzi
Director, Operations: Randy Allison
Procurement Manager: James Knechtges

Estimated Sales: $29 Million
Number Employees: 100-249
Square Footage: 155000

24139 Impaxx Machines
550 Burning Tree Rd
Fullerton, CA 92833-1400
714-449-5155
Fax: 714-526-0300 info@label-aire.com
www.label-aire.com
Provides advanced and reliable pressure-sensitive
labeling machinery to blue-chips firms world over
V P: Stuart Moss
CEO: Ken Phillips
Contact: Isaac Zukerman
izukerman@label-aire.com
Estimated Sales: $20 - 50 Million
Number Employees: 100-249

24140 Imperial
303 Paterson Plank Rd
Carlstadt, NJ 07072-2307
201-288-9199
Fax: 201-288-8990 800-526-6261
imperial@imperialusa.com www.imperialusa.com
Bar stools
Contact: Zachary Dimotta
zdimotta@imperialusa.com
Estimated Sales: $1 - 5 Million
Number Employees: 15

24141 Imperial
6300 W Howard St
Niles, IL 60714
847-581-3300
Fax: 847-647-3105 800-967-4442
Wholesale bakery
President: Betty Dworkin
Estimated Sales: $2.5-5 000,000
Number Employees: 20-49

24142 Imperial Broom Company
PO Box 8018
Richmond, VA 23223-0018
804-648-7840
Fax: 804-648-0113 888-353-7840
Brooms
Owner: Matthew J Robinson Jr
General Manager: Carlton Robinson
Estimated Sales: less than $500,000
Number Employees: 1-4
Square Footage: 20800

24143 Imperial Containers
13400 Nelson Ave
City of Industry, CA 91746
626-333-6363
Fax: 714-630-2737
Corrugated containers and inner packing
Estimated Sales: $10-20 Million
Number Employees: 20-49
Parent Co: Orange County Container

24144 Imperial Industries Inc
505 W Industrial Park Ave
Rothschild, WI 54474-7917
715-359-0200
Fax: 715-355-5349 800-558-2945
indsales@imperialind.com www.imperialind.com
Bulk storage silos and tanks, liquid waste tanks both
self-contained and truck mounted, portable toilets,
wash sinks and barricades. Also Asme certified
tanks and DOT 407/412 truck mounted tanks.
President: Russ Putnam
HR Executive: Doug Hagen
doug@iimperialind.com
Reaserch/Development: Rial Potter
Quality Control: Doug Hagen
Marketing/Sales Manager: T Aerts
Plant Manager: K Mannel
Purchasing Director: Lisa Schultz
Number Employees: 100-249
Square Footage: 75000
Parent Co: Wausau Tile
Type of Packaging: Bulk

24145 Imperial Manufacturing Co
1128 Sherborn St
Corona, CA 92879-2089
951-281-1830
Fax: 951-281-1879 800-343-7790
imperialsales@imperialrange.com
www.imperialrange.com

Ranges, convection ovens, fryers and filter systems,
char-broilers, hot plates, griddles, roasters,
cheesemelters and griddles/broilers
Sales Manager (Eastern): Daniel Monfort
Manager: Matt Wise
mwise@imperialrange.com
Number Employees: 100-249
Brands:
Elite

24146 Imperial Packaging Corporation
1 Campbell Street
PO Box 2383
Pawtucket, RI 2861
401-753-7778
Fax: 401-765-5537 info@imperialpkg.com
www.imperialpkg.com
Paper folding boxes
VP: Steven Felici
Owner: Ronald Felici
VP Sales/Marketing: Stevem Felici
Contact: Patrick Gilmartin
pgilmartin@imperialpkg.com
General Manager: Robert Gilmore
Estimated Sales: $10 - 20 Million
Number Employees: 20-49

24147 Imperial Plastics Inc
21320 Hamburg Ave
PO Box 907
Lakeville, MN 55044-9032
952-469-4951
Fax: 952-469-4724 www.imperialplastics.com
Plastic signs, trays and boxes
President: Dennis Erler
erler.dennis@yahoo.com
Number Employees: 100-249

24148 Imperial Plastics Inc
21320 Hamburg Ave
PO Box 907
Lakeville, MN 55044-9032
952-469-4951
Fax: 952-469-4724 www.imperialplastics.com
Manufacturer and exporter of plastic stoppers and
advertising novelties
President: Dennis Erler
erler.dennis@yahoo.com
Number Employees: 100-249
Type of Packaging: Private Label

24149 Imperial Schrade Corporation
7 Schrade Ct
Ellenville, NY 12428
212-210-8600
Fax: 845-210-8671 www.schradeknives.com
Knive sharpeners, forks, spoons, fish splitting and
stainless knives, shears, etc
Estimated Sales: $75 Million
Number Employees: 500

24150 Imperial Signs & Manufacturing
924 Eglin St
Rapid City, SD 57701-9525
605-348-2511
Fax: 605-399-2705
Signs including neon, plastic and painted
Estimated Sales: $1-2.5 Million
Number Employees: 10-19

24151 Importers Service Corp
65 Brunswick Ave
Edison, NJ 08817-2512
732-248-1946
Fax: 201-332-4152
Manufacturers of gum arabic, gum acacia, gum
karaya, gum tragacanth and gum ghatti
President: Eric Berliner
Plant Engineer: Chris Berliner
cberliner@importersservice.com
Quality Control: David Hulmes
Product Manager: David Hulmes
Director Sales: Robert Vilim
Office Manager: Nancy Meurer
Plant Manager: Henry Schleckser
Estimated Sales: $20-50 Million
Number Employees: 50-99
Square Footage: 70000
Type of Packaging: Private Label, Bulk

24152 Impress Industries
PO Box 477
Emmaus, PA 18049-0477
610-967-6027
Fax: 610-844-9521
Corrugated boxes for cakes, candy, etc
President: Thomas Galiardo
Controller: Debbie White
Sales Manager: Peter Tisi
Estimated Sales: $20-50 Million
Number Employees: 100-249
Square Footage: 81000

24153 Impress USA Inc
936 Barracuda St
San Pedro, CA 90731
310-519-2400
Fax: 310-519-2281 www.ardaghgroup.com
Manufacturer of metal packaging for the food industry
Quality Control: Rudy Shufeldt
Sales: Linda Zottola
Number Employees: 1-10
Parent Co: Ardagh Group

24154 Imprinting Systems Specialty
803 Pressley Rd # 104
Charlotte, NC 28217-0971
704-527-4545
Fax: 704-527-4546 800-497-1403
www.imprintinginc.com
Pressure-sensitive labels
President: Glenn E Randolph
issilbl@bellsouth.net
Marketing Manager: Mark Kessler
Estimated Sales: $500,000-$1 Million
Number Employees: 5-9

24155 Improved Blow Molding
27 Hillside Dr
Hollis, NH 03049-6158
603-465-6190
Fax: 603-465-6190 800-256-1766
Manufacturer and exporter of plastic blow molding machinery for food packaging
Owner: Ron Beaulieu
VP Marketing: H Lance Goldberg
VP Engineering: Ronald Beaulieu
Estimated Sales: $500,000-$1 Million
Number Employees: 1-4
Square Footage: 140000
Parent Co: Goodman Equipment Company
Brands:
Automa
Impco

24156 Impulse Signs
25 Advance Road
Toronto, ON M8Z 2S6
Canada
416-231-3391
Fax: 416-236-2116 866-636-8273
mgisborne@impulsesigns.com
Manufacturer and exporter of menu boards and table signs
President/General Manager: Alex Cachia
Director, Marketing: Ron Wynne
VP, Sales: Carole Lynch
Estimated Sales: $1 - 5 Million
Number Employees: 20-50
Square Footage: 96000
Brands:
Impulse

24157 Imsco Technology
40 Bayfield Drive
North Andover, MA 01845-6016
978-689-2080
Fax: 978-689-2585
Filtration equipment
Chairman/CEO: Timothy Keating
Estimated Sales: $500,000-$1 Million
Number Employees: 5-9

24158 Imtec Acculine Inc
49036 Milmont Dr
Fremont, CA 94538-7301
510-770-1800
Fax: 802-463-4334 800-854-6832
www.imtecacculine.com
High preformance automated identification systems
President: Paul Mendes
pmendes@imtecacculine.com
CEO: Tim Thompson

Number Employees: 20-49

24159 in Sink Erator
4700 21st St
Racine, WI 53406-5093
262-554-5432
Fax: 262-554-3639 800-558-5700
www.insinkerator.com
Garbage disposal units and hot water dispensers
President: Tim Ferry
tim.ferry@insinkerator.com
CFO: William Ivy
Secretary and Marketing: Cathy Davis
Number Employees: 1000-4999
Parent Co: Emerson Electric Company
Brands:
In-Sink-Erator

24160 In-Line Corporation
11121 Excelsior Blvd
Hopkins, MN 55343-3434
952-938-0046
Fax: 952-938-0046
Wrappers and skin packaging and premium and promotional packaging
Sales Manager: Chris Thornby
Operations Manager: Don Steen
Estimated Sales: $5-10 Million
Number Employees: 50-99
Square Footage: 340000
Type of Packaging: Bulk

24161 In-Line Labeling Equipment
7282 Spa Road
North Charleston, SC 29418-8437
843-569-2530
Fax: 843-569-2531 800-465-4630
info@labeling.net www.labeling.net
Pressure sensitive labellers and cold glue labellers
President: Greg L Brandon
CFO: Greg L Brandon
Contact: Mark Cowart
mcowart@labeling.net
Estimated Sales: $2.5 - 5 Million
Number Employees: 10-19
Square Footage: 80000

24162 In-Touch Products
555 W 1100 N
North Salt Lake, UT 84054
801-298-4466
Fax: 801-298-1955 www.intouchhealth.com
Custom thermoformed trays, blisters, clam shells and other packaging supplies
President: Tim Keniewfki
CEO: Yulun Wang, Ph.D.
CFO: Stephen L. Wilson
EVP, Research & Development: Steve Jordan
EVP, Marketing: Michael Chan
Sales Representative: Douglas Johnson
Operations: Curtis Reeves
Estimated Sales: $5-10 Million
Number Employees: 10

24163 InFood Corporation
1575 Oak Avenue
Evanston, IL 60201-4274
773-338-8485
Software for food processors including inventory, nutritional analysis/labeling, formulations/BOM, costing, lot tracking, production planning/scheduling, work orders, yield analysis, QC/statistical sampling, etc
Estimated Sales: $1 - 5 Million
Number Employees: 4

24164 InHarvest
1012 Paul Bunyan Dr SE
Bemidji, MN 56601
Fax: 218-751-8519 800-346-7032
www.inharvest.com
Wild rice and specialty grain importer and distributor
CFO: Jeffrey Buelow
VP, Foodservice Sales: Pete Linder
Type of Packaging: Food Service, Bulk

24165 InHarvest Inc.
1277 Santa Anita Ct
Bemidji, MN 56601
218-751-8500
Fax: 218-751-8519 800-346-7032
sales@inharvest.com www.inharvest.com

Beans, grains, pastas and specialty rice blends.
CFO: Jeffrey Buelow
Director, Culinary Development: Michael Holleman
Year Founded: 1978
Estimated Sales: $20-50 Million
Number Employees: 201-500
Number of Brands: 1
Type of Packaging: Consumer, Food Service, Private Label, Bulk
Brands:
InHarvest

24166 Incinerator International Inc
2702 N Main St
Houston, TX 77009-6838
713-227-1466
Fax: 713-227-0884 sales@incinerators.com
www.incinerators.com
Manufacturer and importer of material handling equipment including incinerators, balers, compactors, containers, crushers, trucks, hoppers and environmental; exporter of incinerators
Owner: Tom Leervig
sales@incinerators.com
Estimated Sales: $2.5-5 Million
Number Employees: 5-9
Square Footage: 10000
Parent Co: International Environmental Equipment Company
Brands:
Iii

24167 Incinerator Specialty Company
6018 Golden Forest Dr
Houston, TX 77092-2360
713-681-4207
Manufacturer and exporter of destructors, afterburners and incinerators including pathological, garbage, waste, burners and parts
President: Mick Kromer
Estimated Sales: $1-2.5 Million
Number Employees: 4

24168 Incomec-Cerex Industries
1515 Black Rope Type
Fairfield, CT 06432
203-335-1050
Fax: 203-366-7305 cerexpro@aol.com
Manufacturer and exporter of grain processing equipment, flavoring spray booths, puffing guns, drying and infrared toasting ovens and continuous popcorn popping and caramelizing coating systems
President: Stephan Vandenberghe
Executive Vice Presient: Dennis Norberg
Market Development: Jeff Norberg
Estimated Sales: $25 Million
Number Employees: 60
Number of Brands: 5
Number of Products: 34
Square Footage: 300000

24169 Incredible Logistics Sol
112 W Boca Raton Road
Phoenix, AZ 85023-6249
602-548-1295
Fax: 602-548-0322

24170 Indco
PO Box 589
New Albany, IN 47151-0589
812-945-4383
Fax: 812-944-9742 800-942-4383
info@indco.com www.indco.com
Industrial mixers
President: Mark Hennis
CFO: J T Sims
Vice President: Kris Wilberding
Contact: Linda Potts
linda@indco.com
Estimated Sales: $5 - 10 Million
Number Employees: 30

24171 Indeco Products Inc
140 Ridge Dr
San Marcos, TX 78666-2052
512-396-5814
Fax: 512-396-5890 888-246-3326
info@indecoproducts.com
www.indecoproducts.com
Plastic strapping and packaging systems and polyester meat slings
President: Daniel R Springs
R & D: Jesse Hinojosa
General Manager: David Behal

Estimated Sales: $2-5 Million
Number Employees: 10-19
Square Footage: 34000
Brands:
  Linear
  Net-Rap
  Polychem

24172 Indemax Inc
1 Industrial Dr
Vernon, NJ 07462-3466

973-209-2424
Fax: 973-209-2644 800-345-7185
sales@indemax.com www.indemax.com
Manufacturer and exporter of parts for hot melt equipment
President: A Infurna
Vice President: P Infurna
Quality Control: P Infurna
Sales Director: R Infurna
Plant Manager: C Peterson
Purchasing Manager: J Tapscnyi
Estimated Sales: $5-10 Million
Number Employees: 5-9

24173 (HQ)Independent Can Co
1300 Brass Mill Rd
Po Box 370
Belcamp, MD 21017-1236

410-272-0090
Fax: 410-272-7500
salesdept@independentcan.com
www.independentcan.com
Manufacturer, importer and exporter of decorative tin containers for coffee, peanuts, cookies, cakes, popcorn, candies, ice cream, etc
Manager: Cathy Mc Clelland
CEO: Richard D Huether
Marketing: Neil Defrancisco
Sales: Frank Shriver
Public Relations: George R McClelland
Opertaions: G William Goodwin
Plant Manager: Frank Currens
Purchasing: Page Edwards
Estimated Sales: $20-50 Million
Number Employees: 100-249
Square Footage: 360000
Type of Packaging: Consumer, Private Label
Other Locations:
  Independent Can Co.
  Ontario CA

24174 Independent Can Company: Western Specialty Division
2040 S Lynx Ave
Ontario, CA 91761-8010

909-923-6150
Fax: 909-923-6052 johnt@westernspecialty.com
www.independentcan.com
Owner: John Thompson
VP: John Thompson
Contact: Omar Becerra
  omar@independentcan.com
Estimated Sales: $3 - 5 Million
Number Employees: 5-9

24175 Independent Dealers Advantage
780 Buford Highway Bldg
C-100
Suwanee, GA 30024

678-720-0555
Fax: 678-720-0650 www.idallc.com
Packaging inspection, robotic positioning, 2D datamatrix code reading
President: Larry Pierson
CEO: Dr. Robert Shillman
CFO: Richard Morin
Senior Vice President: Richard Morin
Estimated Sales: $5-10 000,000
Number Employees: 50-99

24176 Independent Energy
42 Ladd Street
Suite 6
E Greenwich, RI 02818-4358

401-884-6990
Fax: 401-885-1500 800-343-0826
info@IndependentEnergyLLC.com
www.independentenergyllc.com
Wine industry temperature controls
Estimated Sales: $2.5-5 Million
Number Employees: 20-49

24177 Independent Ink
13700 Gramercy Pl
Gardena, CA 90249-2455

310-523-4657
Fax: 310-329-0943 800-446-5538
www.independentink.com
Marking machines and coding and ink jet inks; exporter of inks and solutions
Owner: Barry Brucker
  bbrucker@independentink.com
Executive VP/COO: Randa Nathan
International Sales: Nora Valdez
Estimated Sales: $5-10 Million
Number Employees: 20-49
Square Footage: 50000
Type of Packaging: Consumer, Private Label

24178 Independent Packers Corporation
2001 W Garfield St
C102
Seattle, WA 98119

206-285-6000
Fax: 206-285-9236
Fresh and frozen seafood including crab, cod, halibut, salmon and tuna
President: Jeffery Buske
Contact: Tammy Findlay
  tammy@bbaybrewery.com
Estimated Sales: $3-5 Million
Number Employees: 100-249
Square Footage: 60000
Type of Packaging: Food Service, Private Label

24179 Independent Stave Co
1078 S Jefferson Ave
PO Box 104
Lebanon, MO 65536-3601

417-588-4151
Fax: 417-588-3344
info@independentstavecompany.com
www.independentstavecompany.com
Barrels for wine and whisky producers
Founder: T W Boswell
President: Brad Boswell
Number Employees: 500-999

24180 Index Instruments Us Inc
3305 Commerce Blvd
Kissimmee, FL 34741-4655

407-932-0232
Fax: 407-932-3686 IndexUS@aol.com
www.indexinstrumentsus.com
Refractometers used to measure jams, jellies, candies, crude oil, sugars, edible oils, plastics, beers, adhesives, fruit juices, and many more.
President: Linnell Oakes
Vice President: Jennifer Horn
Estimated Sales: $400 Thousand
Number Employees: 1-4

24181 Indian Valley Industries
PO Box 810
Johnson City, NY 13790-0810

607-729-5111
Fax: 607-729-5158 800-659-5111
www.iviindustries.com
Manufacturer and exporter of burlap and textile bags; also manufacturers and supplies products relating to environmental protection, erosion control, and the containment of both air and waterborn pollutants.
President: Wayne Rozen
CEO: Nilton Rozen
VP Marketing: Phil March
Contact: John Brauer
  brauer@iviindustries.com
Estimated Sales: $10 - 20 Million
Number Employees: 10-19

24182 Indiana Bottle Co
300 W Lovers Ln
Scottsburg, IN 47170-6729

812-752-8700
Fax: 812-752-8702 800-752-8702
mccarty@indianabottle.com
www.indianabottle.com
Custom blow molded, high and low density polyethylene and polypropylene bottles; also, screen printing services available
President: David Keener
  mccarty@hsonline.net
Sales Exec: Mike Mc Carty
General Manager: David Baker
  mccarty@hsonline.net

Estimated Sales: $3.9 Million
Number Employees: 20-49
Square Footage: 50000

24183 Indiana Carton Co Inc
1721 W Bike St
PO Box 68
Bremen, IN 46506-2123

574-546-3848
Fax: 574-546-5953 800-348-2390
salesservice@indianacarton.com
www.indianacarton.com
Manufacturer and exporter of boxes and cartons
President: David Petty
  davidpetty@indianacarton.com
Chairman of the Board: Kenneth Petty
Estimated Sales: $10-20 Million
Number Employees: 50-99

24184 Indiana Glass Company
37 West Broad Street
Columbus, OH 43215

614-224-7141
Fax: 513-563-9639 800-543-0357
www.lancastercolony.com
Manufacturer and exporter of housewares including candleholders, glasses and other beverage containers
Human Resources: Cathy Durham
VP/Marketing: Jerry Vanden Eynden
National Sales Manager: Mark Cunningham
International Sales Manager: Alex Morroni
Estimated Sales: $1 - 5 Million
Number Employees: 500-999
Parent Co: Lancaster Colony Corporation
Type of Packaging: Bulk

24185 Indiana Michigan Power
110 Wayne St
Fort Wayne, IN 46802

800-311-4634
www.indianamichiganpower.com
Electric utility systems.
President & COO: Toby Thomas
VP, Finance & Customer Experience: David Lucas
VP, Regulatory & External Affairs: Marc Lewis
Estimated Sales: $1,000,000,000+
Number Employees: 2,400
Parent Co: American Electric Power

24186 Indiana Vac Form Inc
2030 N Boeing Rd
Warsaw, IN 46582-7860

574-269-1725
Fax: 574-269-2723 bret@invacform.com
www.invacform.com
Manufacturer and exporter of custom plastic vacuum and thermoformed products including containers and refrigerator liners
Owner: Donald Robinson
  ins@invacform.com
Operations Manager: Roy Szymanski
Production Manager: Bob Stevents
Estimated Sales: $2.5-5 Million
Number Employees: 20-49
Square Footage: 90000
Type of Packaging: Food Service

24187 Indiana Wiping Cloth
2340 Schumacher Dr
Mishawaka, IN 46545

574-255-9666
Fax: 574-255-9676 800-446-9645
Wiping cloths and absorbent products
Manager: Darren Sauer
Estimated Sales: $5-10 Million
Number Employees: 10-19

24188 Indiana Wire Company
803 S Reed Rd
PO Box 947
Fremont, IN 46737

260-495-1231
Fax: 260-495-0087 877-786-6883
www.indianawireco.com
Wire mesh decking, shelving, baking equipment and wire products
Sales Manager: Jackie Masternik
Sales Manager: Greg Bosk
Plant Manager: Jeremy Breen
Estimated Sales: $5-10,000,000
Number Employees: 50-99
Parent Co: Indiana Wire Company
Brands:
  Indiana Wire

24189 Indianapolis Container Company
PO Box 40006
Indianapolis, IN 46240
317-580-5000
Fax: 800-760-3319 800-760-3318
sales@containerworks.com
www.containerworks.com
Plastic and glass bottles and jars; also, pails
Manager: Stephen Roco
sroco@containerworks.com
CFO: Nancy Heidt
VP: Nancy Lilly
Owner: Tom Asher
Estimated Sales: Below $5 Million
Number Employees: 10-19
Square Footage: 112000

24190 Industrial Air Conditioning Systems
1883 W Fullerton Avenue
Chicago, IL 60614-1923
773-486-4236
Fax: 773-486-4238
Proof boxes, dough rooms, bread and cake coolers
and stainless steel sanitary pan trucks
VP: Albert Wentzel
Estimated Sales: $2.5-5 Million
Number Employees: 5-9
Square Footage: 30000

24191 Industrial Automation Specs
17 Research Dr
Hampton, VA 23666-1324
757-766-7520
Fax: 757-766-7505 800-916-4272
sales@iascorp.net www.iascorp.net
Manufacturer and exporter of analog chart recorder
CEO: Kathy Burton
preston@iascorp.net
Owner: Kathy Burton
Marketing Supervisor: Don Crawford
Estimated Sales: $1-2.5 Million
Number Employees: 10-19
Brands:
Pricorder

24192 Industrial Automation Systems
28440 Redwood Canyon Place
Santa Clarita, CA 91390-5724
661-257-3482
Fax: 661-257-7627 888-484-4427
Bag making and closing, food processing, labeling
and packaging machinery; also, material handling
equipment and conveyor systems
Manager: Peter Adams
Manager: Guido Pydde
Estimated Sales: Less than $500,000
Number Employees: 1-4

24193 Industrial Brush Corporation
P.O. Box 2608
Pomona, CA 91769-2608
909-591-9341
Fax: 909-627-8916 800-228-6146
ibcsales@industrial-brush.com
www.industrialbrush.com
Brushes for industry and food processing
President: John Cottam
Vice Presient: Greg Tripp
Estimated Sales: $10 - 25 Million
Number Employees: 50-99
Square Footage: 360000

24194 Industrial Ceramic Products
14401 Suntra Way
Marysville, OH 43040
937-642-3897
Fax: 937-644-2646 800-427-2278
sales@industrialceramic.com
www.industrialceramic.com
Manufacturer and exporter of ceramic pizza stones
President: R C Oberst
Contact: Clay Foreman
cforeman@industrialceramic.com
Estimated Sales: $5 - 10 Million
Number Employees: 20-49
Square Footage: 100000

24195 Industrial Chemical
136 Long Ridge Rd
Bedford, NY 10506
914-234-9303
Fax: 914-234-9305 800-431-1075
sales@industrialchemicaldiv.com

Natural fast deodorization and organic waste diges-
tion
Director of Sales: Andy Sinclair
Estimated Sales: $1-2.5 Million
Number Employees: 10-19

24196 Industrial Chemicals Inc
2042 Montreat Dr # A
Vestavia, AL 35216-4040
205-823-7330
Fax: 205-978-0485 800-476-2042
www.industrialchem.com
Ingredients to water and wastewater treatment chem-
istry
President: Bill Welsch
CEO: Bill Welch
wlwelsch@industrialchem.com
Sales Manager: L Pickens
Estimated Sales: $20-50 Million
Number Employees: 100-249

24197 Industrial Consortium
110 Gilmer St
Sulphur Springs, TX 75482-2703
903-885-6610
Fax: 903-885-6701 www.icthruput.com
Consultant providing engineering services for pack-
aging companies
President: Dale Stephens
Estimated Sales: $10 Million
Number Employees: 5-9

24198 Industrial ConstructionSvc
215 15th St S
St James, MN 56081-2438
507-375-4633
Fax: 507-375-7513 800-795-8315
cbrown@icsmn.com www.icsmn.com
Design and construction of contamination controlled
environments, services of which include
biocontainment laboratories, clean rooms,
antimicrobial atmospheres for pharmaceutical, bio-
medical, and nutraceutical development, and
sanitaryenvironments for food and beverage
processing and manufacturing.
President: Clint Brown
cbrown@icsmn.com
Sales Representative: Josh Brown
Number Employees: 20-49

24199 Industrial Container Corp
107 Motsinger St
High Point, NC 27260-8836
336-886-7031
Fax: 336-886-2044 www.iccpackage.com
Plain, printed and wax corrugated boxes
President: Bernard Rosinsky
CEO: Randy Chambers
randy@iccpkg.com
General Manager: Ron Horney
Number Employees: 10-19

24200 Industrial Contracting & Rggng
41 Ramapo Valley Rd
Mahwah, NJ 07430-1118
201-444-7504
Fax: 201-529-3754 888-427-7444
info@icrnj.com www.industrialcontracting.com
Trucking, rigging, crating & storage machinery
Owner: Joseph Sensale
icrnj@aol.com
Engineer: James Certaro
VP Marketing: Joseph Sensale
Estimated Sales: $1-2.5 Million
Number Employees: 10-19

24201 (HQ)Industrial Crating & Packing
15450 Nelson Pl
Tukwila, WA 98188-5504
425-226-9205
Fax: 425-226-9205 800-942-0499
Corrugated boxes and wooden shipping crates
President: Tom Kalil
sales@indcrate.com
Estimated Sales: $1-2.5 Million
Number Employees: 10-19

24202 Industrial Custom Products
2801 37th Ave NE
Minneapolis, MN 55421-4217
612-782-9048
Fax: 612-781-1144 877-784-2415
icp@industrialcustom.com
www.industrialcustom.com

Specialists in forming heavy-gauge plastics for
OEM and material-handling applications. the com-
pany specializes in custom applications and is expe-
rienced in die-cutting and fabricating a broad range
of
President: Herb Houndt
Estimated Sales: $10-20 Million
Number Employees: 20-49

24203 Industrial Design Corporation
2020 SW 4th Ave
Portland, OR 97201-4953
503-224-6040
Fax: 503-223-1494 800-224-0707
Facility services including planning, site selection,
environmental/permitting, facility design and engi-
neering, industrial engineering, system integration,
waste treatment, construction management, commis-
sioning/startup andoperations/maintenance
President: George Lemmon
Corporate Management: Sue King
Vice President: Jim Hall
Marketing Director: Jeff Cross
Contact: Patti Glaze
3635@idc-ibg.com
Purchasing Manager: Mark Varon
Number Employees: 250-499

24204 Industrial Design Fab
2501 Murray St # A
Suite A
Sioux City, IA 51111-1141
712-224-5600
Fax: 712-873-5859 877-873-5858
info@idfi.com www.idfi.com
Designer and manufacturer of conveyor systems for
the food industry.
President: Todd Jager
tjager@idfi.com
Number Employees: 20-49

24205 Industrial Devices Corporation
3925 Cypress Drive
Petaluma, CA 94954-5695
707-789-1000
Fax: 707-789-0175 sales@idcmotion.com
Electric linear actuators, servo controls and position-
ing systems for packaging equipment
VP Sales/Marketing: Al Statz
Customer Service Manager: Joe Ording
Estimated Sales: $10-20 Million
Number Employees: 50-99

24206 Industrial EnvironmentalPollution Control
127 Bruckner Boulevard
Bronx, NY 10454-4698
718-585-2410
Fax: 718-292-8353
Air pollution control, bacteria control equipment,
cleaning and washing equipment and accessories,
detergent dipensing systems, drain and sewer clean-
ing compounds, floor scrubbers and sweepers, odor
control equipment, pan, vat and moldwashing,
pressure
Manager: James Albanese
Vice President: Mike Mouracade
Food Safety Specialist: Alex Mouracade
Estimated Sales: $1-5 Million
Number Employees: 10-19
Brands:
Foamatic

24207 Industrial Equipment Company
35 Maple St
Suite 2
Derry, NH 3038
603-432-2037
Fax: 603-437-7539
Hand and electric power trucks and fork-lifts
President/CFO: Robert Shaver
Manager: Bob Shaver
Estimated Sales: $2 - 3 Million
Number Employees: 1-4

24208 Industrial Grinding Inc
2306 Ontario Ave
Dayton, OH 45414-5692
937-277-6579
Fax: 937-277-4536 888-322-6579
sales@industrialgrinding.com
www.industrialgrinding.com

President: Marcus Wendling
mwendling@industrialgrinding.com
CFO: Sabrina Welch
Estimated Sales: $1 - 2.5 Million
Number Employees: 10-19

24209 (HQ)Industrial Hardwood
521 F St
Perrysburg, OH 43551

419-666-2503

Wooden boxes, pallets and skids
Owner: Ashvin Shah
ashvins@hardwoodind.com
General Manager: William Eckel
Estimated Sales: $2.5-5 Million
Number Employees: 1-4
Square Footage: 15000
Other Locations:
Industrial Hardwood
Oak Harbor OH

24210 Industrial Hoist Service
21525 N Highway 288b
Angleton, TX 77515-4888

979-798-7077
Fax: 979-798-1963 800-766-7077
www.industrialhoist.com

Air chain hoists
Manager: James Kowalk
Chief Executive Officer: Kevin Rodgers
Senior Vice President, General Manager o: James Kowalik
Vice President of Sales, Division I: Anthony Piwonka
Vice President of Sales: Kurt Charpentier
President, Chief Operating Officer: Mitch Hausman
Vice President of Purchasing: Tony DAmico
Estimated Sales: $20-50 Million
Number Employees: 50-99
Number of Brands: 3
Square Footage: 130000

24211 Industrial Information Systems
393 Cumberland St
Memphis, TN 38112-2712

901-324-5535
Fax: 901-324-0104 800-494-7916

Developer of training software for ammonia refrigeration operating engineers
President: Hanns Wittjen
Estimated Sales: $500,000 - $1 Million
Number Employees: 5-9

24212 (HQ)Industrial Kinetics
2535 Curtiss St
Downers Grove, IL 60515

630-655-0300
Fax: 630-655-1720 800-655-0306
ikiinfo@iki.com www.iki.com

Manufacturer and exporter of material handling and conveyor systems
Owner: George Huber
Marketing/Sales: Dwight Pentzien
Operations Manager: Dennis Harsnbarger
Production Manager: John Zienda
Plant Manager: John Zienda
Estimated Sales: $10-20 Million
Number Employees: 50-99
Square Footage: 180000
Other Locations:
Industrial Kinetics
Atlanta GA
Brands:
Olson Conveyors
Pallet-Pro

24213 Industrial LaboratoriesCo
4046 Youngfield St
Wheat Ridge, CO 80033-3862

303-287-9691
Fax: 303-287-0964 800-456-5288
www.industriallabs.net

Full service analytical support to the food industry, dietary and sports supplements, veterinary regulatory and therapeutic monitoring. Analytical support includes food chemistry, food safety monitoring, nutritional analyses, andtesting for other potential contaminants. Provides BAX analyses fo E. coli 0157:H7, Salmonella and Listeria, food safety monitoring

President: Seth Wong
swong@industriallabs.net
Controller: Lisle Goeldner
Supervisor: Geoff Henderson
Manager: Joanne Compton
Business Development Manager: Larisa Moore
Customer Services: Kathie Inman
Lab Manager: Mike Gross
Estimated Sales: $2.5-5 Million
Number Employees: 20-49
Square Footage: 24000

24214 Industrial Laboratory Eqpt Co
3210 Piper Ln
PO Box 220245
Charlotte, NC 28208-6442

704-357-3930
Fax: 704-357-3940 ile@ile-textiles.com
www.ile-textiles.com

Manufacturer and exporter of industrial testing equipment including custom, food and portion scales for analytical, counting and inventory use
President: Harry Simmons
ile@ile-textiles.com
VP: Harry Simmons
Estimated Sales: $1-2.5 Million
Number Employees: 5-9
Square Footage: 20000
Brands:
Ile
Multi-Scale
Ohaus

24215 Industrial Labsales
PO Box 30628
Portland, OR 97294-3628

800-524-8224
Fax: 503-255-8367

24216 Industrial Lumber & Packaging
925 W Savidge St
Spring Lake, MI 49409

616-842-1457
Fax: 616-842-9352

Pallets, skids and wooden boxes and shipping crates
Owner: Jim Walsh
Number Employees: 7
Square Footage: 29600

24217 Industrial Machine Manufacturing
8140 Virginia Pine Ct
Richmond, VA 23237

804-271-6979
Fax: 804-275-0813 www.uniflow1.com

Customized hot melt dispensing machinery
President: Marvin Garrett
R & D: Leo Moore
VP Marketing: Leo Moore
Estimated Sales: $1-2.5 Million
Number Employees: 10-19

24218 Industrial Magnetics
1385 S M 75
Boyne City, MI 49712-9689

231-582-3100
Fax: 231-582-0622 800-662-4638
imi@magnetics.com www.magnetics.com

Manufacturer and exporter of magnetic separation devices for the removal of ferrous and metals.
CEO: Walter Shear
doleary@magnetics.com
Chief Financial Officer: Robin Wottowa
Engineering Manager: Dan Allore
Business Development, Marketing Manager: Dennis O'Leary
Plant Manager, Purchasing: Casey House
Estimated Sales: $25-30 Million
Number Employees: 51 - 200
Number of Products: 2000
Square Footage: 76000
Brands:
Bullet

24219 Industrial Marking Equipment
4152 Lazy Hammock Road
Palm Beach Gardens, FL 33410-6114

561-845-2828
Fax: 561-848-8930

Custom printing systems, printing attatchments for converting and packaging applications
Estimated Sales: $1-2.5 Million
Number Employees: 5-9

24220 Industrial Nameplate Inc
29 Indian Dr
Warminster, PA 18974-1487

215-322-1111
Fax: 215-953-1161 800-878-6263
www.industrialnameplate.com

Labels, tapes, tags, folding paper boxes, point of purchase displays, shelf talkers, styrene cards, etc
President: Chuck Mascaro
info@industrialnameplate.com
Manager Marketing: Fred Knup
Estimated Sales: $2.5 - 5 Million
Number Employees: 20-49
Square Footage: 28000

24221 Industrial Neon Sign Corp
6223 Saint Augustine St
Houston, TX 77021-2612

713-748-6600
Fax: 713-748-6621

Architectural, electrical, magnetic, metal, neon, painted, plastic, silk screen, vinyl lettering & wooden signs
Owner: Sarah Jones
Estimated Sales: $470,000
Number Employees: 10-19

24222 Industrial Netting Inc
7681 Setzler Pkwy N
Minneapolis, MN 55445-1883

763-496-6355
Fax: 763-971-0872 800-328-8456
info@industrialnetting.net
www.industrialnetting.com

Plastic netting for meat racks, separators, bird netting and fencing
Owner: Greg Frandsen
gfrandsen@industrialnetting.com
Vice President: David Brentz
Sales: Karen Slater
Estimated Sales: $72,000
Number Employees: 20-49

24223 (HQ)Industrial Piping Inc
800 Culp Rd
PO Box 518
Pineville, NC 28134-9469

704-588-1100
Fax: 704-588-5614 800-951-0988

Manufacturers and exporter of custom fabricated process equipment including coils, columns, condensers, exchangers, mix tanks, piping systems, pressure vessels, reactors and towers
President: Robert Jones
CEO: Mike Jones
mjones@goipi.com
VP: Michael Roberts
Quality Control: Ron Miller
Business Development: Earl Dowdy
Estimated Sales: $10-20 Million
Number Employees: 20-49
Square Footage: 136000

24224 Industrial Plastics Company
8307 Ball Rd
Fort Smith, AR 72908-8435

479-646-8293
Fax: 479-646-6020 800-850-0916

VP: Jim Rahn
Manager: Kyle Dejaeger
Estimated Sales: $20 - 50 Million
Number Employees: 100-249
Parent Co: Jarden Corporation

24225 Industrial Product Corp
1 Hollywood Ave # 30
Suite 30
Ho Ho Kus, NJ 07423-1438

201-652-5913
Fax: 201-652-2494 800-472-5913

Manufacturer and exporter of standard and custom industrial blades for food processing machinery for pasta, pretzel and baked goods
Owner: Ken Dohner
kendohner@ipdco.com
Estimated Sales: Less Than $500,000
Number Employees: 1-4
Square Footage: 16200

24226 Industrial Pump Sales &Svc
37 William S Canning Blvd
Tiverton, RI 02878-3003
401-624-2977
Fax: 401-624-3373 sales@ipspump.com
www.ipspump.com
Pumps and mixers
President: Bruce Levesque
Estimated Sales: $3-5 Million
Number Employees: 20-49

24227 Industrial Razorblade
575 Nassau St
Orange, NJ 07050-1262
973-673-4286
Fax: 973-673-7165 sales@industrialrazor.com
www.industrialrazor.com
Knives and blades specializing in strip ground
blades; custom manufacturing available
Owner: Frank Florey
frank@industrialrazor.com
VP: Francis Florey
Estimated Sales: Less Than $500,000
Number Employees: 1-4
Square Footage: 10000

24228 Industrial Refrigeration Services
403 Dividend Drive
Hampton, GA 30228
770-946-9235
Fax: 770-946-3115 800-334-0273
C.E.O: Terry Childers

24229 Industrial Screw Conveyors Inc
4133 Conveyor Dr
Burleson, TX 76028-1819
817-641-0691
Fax: 817-556-0224 800-426-4669
sales@screwconveyors.com
www.screwconveyors.com
Dedicated to the design, engineering, and fabrication
of helical flighting, helical screw assemblies, and
helical screw conveyors using helical flighting.
President: Ralph Jones
indscrew@aol.com
Estimated Sales: $5,000,000
Number Employees: 50-99
Square Footage: 480000

24230 Industrial Sign Company
9635 Klingerman Street
South El Monte, CA 91733-1726
562-602-2420
Fax: 562-602-2599 800-596-3720
Point of purchase displays, flags, pennants, banners
and electric signs
Owner: Maria Saavetra
Estimated Sales: $1-2,500,000
Number Employees: 20-49

24231 Industrial Signs
1109 N. AL Davis Rd.
Suite B
Elmwood, LA 70123
504-736-0600
Fax: 504-736-9285 www.industrialsigns.net
Signs including electrical, neon, industrial, etc
President: William F Hunter
Estimated Sales: $2.5 - 5 Million
Number Employees: 20-49

24232 Industrial Systems Group
5140 Moundview Drive
Red Wing, MN 55066-1100
651-388-2267
Fax: 651-385-2279 800-ROB-OTIC
Estimated Sales: $1 - 5 Million

24233 Industrial Test SystemsInc
1875 Langston St
Rock Hill, SC 29730-7314
803-329-2999
Fax: 803-329-9743 800-861-9712
its@sensafe.com www.sensafe.com
Tests for water quality parameters.
Owner: Ivars Jaunakais
ivars@sensafe.com
VP: Lea Jaunakais
Marketing: Mike McBride
Sales: George Bailey
Plant Manager: Angelo Perry
Estimated Sales: $5-10 Million
Number Employees: 20-49

24234 Industrial Washing Machine Corporation
PO Box 1509
Jackson, NJ 08527-0266
732-304-9203
Fax: 732-286-0862 inwamacorp@yahoo.com
Pot and pan washers.
President: Joseph Gangi
Number Employees: 10-19
Square Footage: 40000
Brands:
Industrial

24235 Industrial Washing Machine Corporation
PO Box 506
Matawan, NJ 07747-0506
732-566-4660
Fax: 732-566-2201
Pot and pan washers
President: Joseph Gangi
Estimated Sales: $1-3 Million
Number Employees: 19
Square Footage: 20000
Brands:
Industrial

24236 Industrial Woodfab & Packaging
18620 Fort St
Riverview, MI 48193-7443
734-284-4808
Fax: 734-284-5308 www.industrialwoodfab.com
Wooden crates, boxes and pallets
President: Richard E Ott
rott@industrialwoodfab.com
Engineer: Tom DeFeyten
Manager: Frank Nicnski
Estimated Sales: $1-2.5 Million
Number Employees: 10-19
Square Footage: 130000

24237 Industries For the Blind
445 S Curtis Rd
Milwaukee, WI 53214-1016
414-778-3040
Fax: 414-933-4316 800-642-8778
info@ibmilw.com www.ibmilwaukee.com
Manufacturer and exporter of household cleaning
supplies including plastic window brushes and
brooms
President: Charles Lange
VP, Manufacturing: Helen Ritter
National Federal Sales Director: Dan Bailey
IT: Cindy Pinkley
cindy.pinkley@ibmilw.com
Estimated Sales: $10-20 Million
Number Employees: 50-99
Parent Co: Industries For the Blind
Type of Packaging: Consumer, Food Service, Bulk

24238 Industries Inc Kiefer
400 Industrial Dr
Random Lake, WI 53075-1653
920-994-2332
Fax: 920-994-4005
Food service equipment including stainless steel ta-
bles
Owner: James Eischen
kieferindustries@yahoo.com
Estimated Sales: $1-2.5 Million
Number Employees: 10-19

24239 Industries of the Blind
920 West Lee Street
Greensboro, NC 27403
336-274-1591
Fax: 336-544-3739 info@iob-gso.com
www.industriesoftheblind.com
Mops including cotton, rayon, wet and dry; also,
brooms, wooden mop handles, clipboards and pens
Executive Director: Mike Burge
Contact: Donald Bassett
dbassett@iob-gso.com
General Manager: Derek Davis
Plant Manager: Jack Permer
Purchasing Manager: Bob Gwyn
Estimated Sales: $10 - 20 Million
Number Employees: 100-249
Square Footage: 260000
Type of Packaging: Consumer

24240 Industrious Software Solutions
500 W Florence Ave
Inglewood, CA 90301-1011
310-672-8700
Fax: 310-419-6000 800-351-4225
www.1st-accounting.com
Developer of operations management software for
wholesalers/distributors, manufacturers, exporters
and importers
President: David Goguen
david.goguen@iss.com
Quality Control: Gary Zenun
Estimated Sales: $10-20 Million
Number Employees: 20-49

24241 Industronics Service Co
489 Sullivan Ave
PO Box 649
South Windsor, CT 06074-1942
860-289-1551
Fax: 860-289-3526 800-878-1551
service@industronics.com www.industronics.com
Incinerators and commercial furnaces and ovens
President: James Wyse
jwyse@industronics.com
VP: Dean Hills
Estimated Sales: Below $5 Million
Number Employees: 20-49
Brands:
Consertherm

24242 Indy Lighting
12001 Exit 5 Pkwy
Fishers, IN 46037
317-849-1233
Fax: 317-576-8006
Incandescent, compact fluorescent, recessed, surface
and track lighting fixtures
VP Sales: Steve Fetter
VP Marketing: Barry Hindman
Contact: Roger Michel
rmichel@indyltg.com
Manager: Kevin Fagan
Estimated Sales: $10 - 20 Million
Number Employees: 50-99
Square Footage: 250000
Parent Co: Juno Lighting

24243 Infanti International
3075 Richmond Terrace
Staten Island, NY 10303-1300
718-447-5632
Fax: 718-447-5667 800-874-8590
www.infanti.com
Manufacturer and exporter of serving carts and
chairs
Estimated Sales: $3 - 5 Million
Number Employees: 20-49
Type of Packaging: Food Service

24244 Inficon
2 Technology Pl
East Syracuse, NY 13057
315-434-1100
Fax: 315-437-3803 reachus@inficon.com
www.inficon.com
Instruments for gas leak detection
CEO: Lukas Winkler
Estimated Sales: $373 Million
Number Employees: 1,000

24245 Infinity Tapes LLC
300 Canal St # 7
Lawrence, MA 01840-1420
978-686-0632
Fax: 978-683-5202
Adhesives
Owner: Craig Allard
callard@shepcompany.com
Quality Control: Craig Aalard
Estimated Sales: $20-50 Million
Number Employees: 50-99

24246 Infitec Inc
6500 Badgley Rd
East Syracuse, NY 13057-9667
315-433-1150
Fax: 315-433-1521 800-334-0837
sales@infitec.com www.infitec.com
Timing controls (industrial/time delay), speed controls, flashers, and custom controls.

CEO/CFO/President: George Ehegartner, Sr
HR Executive: Kim Bremerman
kb@infitec.com
Quality Control/Marketing: George Ehegartner, Jr
kb@infitec.com
VP Sales: David Lawrie
Estimated Sales: $10-20 Million
Number Employees: 50-99
Square Footage: 50000
Type of Packaging: Bulk
Brands:
Inc
Infitec

24247 Inflatable Packaging
75 Glen Rd # 103
Sandy Hook, CT 06482-1176
203-426-2900
Fax: 203-426-6976 800-520-3383
sales@inflatablepackaging.com
www.inflatablepackaging.com
Air bag dunnage system for internal packaging designed to replace peanuts, compressed paper, expansion foam and air bubble materials. Manufacture Void-Fill Bags, En-Cap Sleeves, and Waffle-Paks in various sizes to meet your shippingrequirements
President: Michell Tschantz
mich@inflatablepackaging.com
Estimated Sales: $1 - 3 Million
Number Employees: 5-9

24248 Infometrix
11807 N Creek Pkwy S # 111
Suite B-111
Bothell, WA 98011-8804
425-402-1450
Fax: 425-402-1040 info@infometrix.com
www.infometrix.com
Analyses for quality control, online monitoring of processes, sensory evaluation and research in the food and beverage industries
President: Brian Rohrback
CEO: Marlana Blackburn
marlana_blackburn@infometrix.com
Sales/Marketing Manager: Paul Bailey
Estimated Sales: Below $5 Million
Number Employees: 10-19
Brands:
Biocount
Ein Sight
Pirouette

24249 Infopro Inc
2920 Norwalk Ct
Aurora, IL 60502-1310
630-978-9231
Fax: 734-638-6139 info@sysmaker.com
www.corrflow.com
Menuing and application development systems
CEO: Sue Graham
Vice President And CFO: Eileen Anderson
Executive Vice President And COO: Greg Capella
Administrative Manager: Susan Boarden
Estimated Sales: $500,000-$1 Million
Number Employees: 5-9
Brands:
Guidemaker
Systemaker

24250 Infor
641 Avenue of the Americas
New York, NY 10011
646-336-1700
866-244-5479
www.infor.com
Software for process industries: ERP and EAM software for meat, poultry and beverage processing; software for safety, cost containment, inventory
General Manager, Americas: Rod Johnson
CEO: Kevin Samuelson
CFO: Jay Hopkins
CTO/President, Products: Soma Somasundaram
EVP/Global Chief Customer Officer: Nancy Mattenberger
Estimated Sales: $2.8 Billion
Number Employees: 17,000

24251 Information Access
8801 E Pleasant Valley Rd
Cleveland, OH 44131-5599
216-328-0100
Fax: 216-328-0913 info@infoaccess.net
www.infoaccess.net
Software for food brokers

24252 Information Resources
150 N Clinton St
Chicago, IL 60661
312-726-0005
888-262-5973
Supplier of market content, analytic services, and business performance management solutions.
Chairman: Romesh Wadwani
CEO: John Freeland
CFO: Michael Duffy
CEO: John Freeland
Contact: Christine Aceron
christine.aceron@infores.com
Grp President/International Operations: Mark Tims
CTO/CIO: Marshall Gibbs
Estimated Sales: $554 Million
Number Employees: 1,000-4,999
Other Locations:
Information Resources
LK, Bel
Information Resources - UK
Berkshire, GBR
IRI Hellas
New Ionia, Athens
IRI France
Chambourcy, France
IRI USA
Waltham MA

24253 Informed Beverage Management
420 Minuet Ln
Charlotte, NC 28217
704-527-1709
Fax: 704-527-8509 800-438-5058
www.highjump.com
Computer software and hardware
Manager: Pel Dael
Manager: Jerry Morrow
Manager: Ed Browning
Estimated Sales: $5-10 Million
Number Employees: 10-19

24254 Infra Corp
5454 Dixie Hwy
P.O. Box 300997
Waterford, MI 48329-1615
248-623-0400
Fax: 248-623-1766 888-434-6372
sales@infracorporation.com
www.infracorporation.com
Bar and restaurant equipment, stainless and brass small wares
President: Bryan A Mc Graw
bryan@infracorporation.com
Estimated Sales: $1 - 3 Million
Number Employees: 5-9
Square Footage: 48000

24255 InfraTech Corporation
939 N Vernon Avenue
Azusa, CA 91702-2202
626-331-9400
Fax: 626-858-1951 800-955-2476
joe@infratech-usa.com
Comfort heat for patios
President/CEO: Sam Longo
Research & Development: Joe Petro
Marketing Director: Joe Petro
Sales Manager: Joseph Petro
Estimated Sales: $.5 - 1 million
Number Employees: 90
Square Footage: 150000

24256 Ingersoll Rand Inc
N58 W14686 Shawn Cir
Menomonee Falls, WI 53051
262-232-7275
www.ingersollrand.com
Rotary screw, reciprocating and sliding vane compressors, multistage and positive displacement, centrifugal and side-channel blowers, vacuum technology and mobile transport products.
CEO: Vicente Reynal
SVP, Industrial Technologies: Todd Wyman
SVP & Chief Financial Officer: Emily Weaver
SVP, General Counsel & CCO: Andrew Schisel
VP, Global Sourcing & Logistics: Chris Neubauer
Year Founded: 1859
Estimated Sales: $2.3 Billion
Parent Co: Kohlberg Kravis Roberts

Brands:
ARO
Club Car
Ingersoll Rand

24257 Ingles Markets, Inc.
2913 US Highway 70 W
Black Mountain, NC 28711-9103
828-669-2941
Fax: 828-669-3678
customerservice@ingles-markets.com
www.ingles-markets.com
Cakes, cookies, and deli products
President/CEO: James Lanning
Year Founded: 1963
Estimated Sales: $4.987 Billion
Number Employees: 26,000
Number of Brands: 2
Other Locations:
Dairy Manufacturing
Asheville NC
Brands:
Milko
Sealtest

24258 Inglett & Company
151 Walker Road
Statesville, NC 28625-2535
706-738-1488
Fax: 706-736-5416 tFspitzer@hotmail.com
Automatic packaging machinery
Estimated Sales: $5-10 Million
Number Employees: 20-50

24259 Ingman Laboratories
2945 34th Avenue S
Minneapolis, MN 55406-1707
612-724-0121
Fax: 612-724-0603 http://inglabs.pconline.com
Consultant specializing in product development, food labeling and laboratory services including chemical and microbiological analysis for the food and agricultural industries
President: Pete Meland
Public Relations: Kipp Barksdale
Office Manager: Dick Davidson
Chief Chemist: Glenn Kyle
Number Employees: 24
Square Footage: 40000

24260 Ingredient Masters
1080 Nimitzview Dr
Suite 302
Cincinnati, OH 45230
513-231-7432
Fax: 513-231-3104 sales@ingredientmasters.com
www.ingredientmasters.com
Custom-designing bulk dry ingredient and dispensing systems
President: Scott Culshaw
Contact: Ben Culshaw
culshaw@ingredientmasters.com
Estimated Sales: Below $5 Million
Number Employees: 1-4

24261 (HQ)Ingredients Solutions Inc
631 Moosehead Trl
Waldo, ME 04915-3402
207-722-4172
Fax: 207-722-4271 800-628-3166
info@ingredientssolutions.com www.isi.us.com
Independent supplier of Carrageenan. Offers a full range of Natural and Organic allowed products including Xanthan Gums, Sodium Alginates and Carrageenans for use in dairy, meat & poultry, sauces & dressings, bakery, confections, petfood, pharmaceuticals and personal-care applications.
Owner: Donna Ravin
info@ingredientssolutions.com
CEO: Scott Rangus
CFO: Janine Mehuren
Lab Manager: Kevin Johndro
Purchasing: Kristin Grover
Number Employees: 10-19
Type of Packaging: Bulk

24262 Ingredion Incorporated
5 Westbrook Corporate Ctr.
Westchester, IL 60154
708-551-2600
Fax: 708-551-2700 800-713-0208
www.ingredion.com
Sweeteners, starches, corn syrups, glucose, and oils used in food and beverage products.

President/CEO/Director: James Zallie
Executive VP/CFO: James Gray
Senior VP/Chief Innovation Officer: Jeremy Xu
Year Founded: 1906
Estimated Sales: $6 Billion
Number Employees: 11,000
Number of Brands: 16
Type of Packaging: Bulk
Other Locations:
    Bedford Park IL
    Belcamp MD
    Berwick PA
    Cardinal, Canada
    Cedar Rapids IA
    Englewood CO
    Fort Fairfield ME
    Grand Forks ND
    Idaho Falls ID
    Indianapolis IN
    London, Canada
    Mapleton IL
    Mississauga, Canada
Brands:
    Abc Carrier
    Brewer's Crystals
    Buffalo
    Cerelose
    Enzose
    Fiberbond
    Globe
    Globe Plus
    Invertose Hfcs
    Proferm
    Royal
    Royal-T
    Stablebond
    Surebond
    Ultrabond
    Unidex

24263 Inject Star of the America's
355 Industrial Dr
Mountain View, AR 72560-8872
870-269-7778
Fax: 203-740-8331 800-253-6475
www.injectstar.com
Meat processing equipment and food packaging
equipment
Owner: John Engle
Estimated Sales: Below $5 Million
Number Employees: 5-9

24264 Inksolv 30, LLC.
2495 N Ave
PO Box 66
Emerson, NE 68733
515-537-5344
info@inksolv30.com
www.inksolv30.com
Manufacturer and exporter of powdered hand soap
President: Kevin Wilson
Contact: Allison Franklin
allison.franklin@inksolv30.com
Estimated Sales: $2.5-5 Million
Number Employees: 1-4

24265 Inland Consumer Packaging
17507 S Dupont Hwy
Harrington, DE 19952-2370
302-398-4211
Fax: 302-398-1422 www.gp.com
Folding paper boxes
President: Brent Paugh
Executive Vice President: Christian Fischer
Executive Vice President of Operations: Wesley
Jones
Estimated Sales: $20 - 50 Million
Number Employees: 100-249

24266 Inland Label & Marketing Svc
2009 West Ave S
La Crosse, WI 54601-6207
608-783-4700
Fax: 608-787-5870 800-657-4413
info@inlandlabel.com www.inlandlabel.net
Labels
Owner: Steve Winterfield
CEO: Mark Glenndenning
mglenndenning@inlandlabel.com
Director of Sales: Don Iverson
Number Employees: 100-249
Square Footage: 41138

24267 Inland Paper Company
1826 S Taylor Pl
Ontario, CA 91761
909-923-4505
Fax: 909-923-9808 www.inlandpaper.com
Stock boxes, poly bags, anti-static bags, packaging
material such as bubble wrap and foam, shipping
supplies such as carton sealing tapes, stretch film,
strammping, and wrapping papers. Janitorial and
safety supples also available.
Vice President: Al Fertal
Year Founded: 1980
Estimated Sales: Less Than $500,000
Number Employees: 11-50

24268 Inland Paperboard & Packaging
210 Mount Phillips Street
Rock Hill, SC 29730-3340
803-366-4103
Fax: 803-366-1648
Corrugated containers, boxes and sheets
CEO: Dale Stahl
Sales Manager: Mannonum Heller
General Manager: George Hare
Estimated Sales: $20-50 Million
Number Employees: 100-249
Parent Co: Temple Inland Company

24269 Inland Showcase & Fixture Company
1473 N Thesta St
Fresno, CA 93703-3791
559-237-4158
Fax: 559-237-7238
Restaurant and store fixtures including plastic counters
Purchasing Manager: Richard Bertad
Estimated Sales: $10-20 Million
Number Employees: 50-99
Square Footage: 60000

24270 Inline Automation
14758 Bluebird St NW
Anoka, MN 55304
763-434-2828
Fax: 763-755-5757
President: Gerald Jilts
Number Employees: 10

24271 Inline Filling Systems
216 Seaboard Ave
Venice, FL 34285-4618
941-486-8800
Fax: 941-486-0077 sales101@fillers.com
www.fillers.com
Manufacturer and exporter of liquid filling equipment, capping machinery, conveyors and unscramblers
President: Sam Lubus
slubus@inlinefillingsysteminc.com
R&D: Jay Carlson
VP Sales: Joe Schemenauer
Estimated Sales: $10,000,000
Number Employees: 20-49
Square Footage: 20000
Brands:
    Levelhead 2

24272 Inline Plastic Corp
100 Constitution Dr
McDonough, GA 30253
678-466-3467
Fax: 770-957-4492 www.inlineplastics.com
Clear plastic containers for cakes and desserts, fresh
baked goods, salads, and cut veggies and fruit.
President: Thomas Orkisz

24273 (HQ)Inline Plastic Corp
42 Canal St
Shelton, CT 06484
Fax: 203-924-0370 800-826-5567
www.inlineplastics.com
Clear plastic containers for cakes and desserts, fresh
baked goods, salads, and cut veggies and fruit.
President: Thomas Orkisz
Year Founded: 1968
Estimated Sales: $100-500 Million
Number Employees: 200-499

24274 Inline Services
27731 Commercial Park Rd
Tomball, TX 77375-6532
713-973-0079
Fax: 713-973-6614 888-973-0079
www.inlineservices.com
Pigging systems for product displacement and
batching pipe cleaning
President: Gary Smith
glsmith@inlineplc.com
Financial Director: Deanne Schillaci
Vice President: Harvey Diehl
Sales: Jessica Nichols
General Manager: Rick Meade
Warehouse: Russell Williams
Accounts Payable: Susan Thomas
Estimated Sales: $1.5 Million
Number Employees: 20-49

24275 Inman Foodservices Group LLC
3807 Charlotte Ave
Nashville, TN 37209-3736
615-321-5591
Fax: 615-321-5689
foodservicedesign@inman-inc.com
www.inman-inc.com
Consultant specializing in food service facility planning and design
Owner: John Feilmeier
john.feilmeier@inman-inc.com
Vice President: Brandi Hale
Estimated Sales: $5-10 Million
Number Employees: 5-9

24276 Inmark, Inc
675 Hartman Road
Suite 100
Austell, GA 30168
770-373-3300
Fax: 770-373-3301 800-646-6275
service@inmarkinc.com www.inmarkinc.com
Packaging supplies, plastic food containers
President: Brian Murphy
Vice President: James Curlee
Contact: Chuck Albert
chucka@inmarkpackaging.com
Estimated Sales: $20 - 50 Million
Number Employees: 50-99

24277 Inmotion Technologies
211 Overlook Dr
Sewickley, PA 15143-2459
412-749-0710
Fax: 412-749-0705
Multi-axis motion control systems for advanced
packaging and printing featuring accurate coordination and synchronization functions
President, Chief Executive Officer: Lawrence Culp
Contact: David Birarda
david.birarda@inmotiontechnology.com
Estimated Sales: $1 - 5 Million
Number Employees: 5-9

24278 Innavision Global Marketing Consultants
1615 Count Turf Ln.
Racine, WI 53402
262-633-1000
Equipment manufacturers, distributors and representatives.
Estimated Sales: $190,000
Number Employees: 2

24279 Innerspace Design Concepts
16015 Van Aken Boulevard
Apt 104
Shaker Heights, OH 44120-5345
216-295-1589
Fax: 216-295-1593 innerspace@stratos.net
Complete design services for restaurants and stores
CEO: Steven Goldschel
Number Employees: 12
Square Footage: 3500

24280 Innio
1101 W St Paul Ave
Waukesha, WI 53188
contact.en@innio.com
www.innio.com
Jenbacher and Waukesha gas engines.
CEO: Carlos Lange
President, INNIO Waukesha: Bud Hittie
Parent Co: INNIO Jenbacher GmbH & Co OG

24281 Innophos Holdings Inc.
259 Prospect Plains Rd.
Building A
Cranbury, NJ 08512

609-495-2495
Fax: 609-860-0138 www.innophos.com
Specialty ingredient solutions for food, health, and
industrial markets, including phosphates, minerals,
botanicals, protiens and other nutrition ingredients.
CEO: Richard Hooper
CFO: Dennis Loughran
Year Founded: 2004
Estimated Sales: $785 Million
Number Employees: 1,400
Number of Brands: 9
Other Locations:
    Manufacturing Site
    Chicago IL
    Manufacturing Site
    East Hanover NJ
    Manufacturing Site
    Geismar LA
    Manufacturing Site
    Nashville TN
    Manfuacturing Site
    North Salt Lake UT
    Manufacturing Site
    Taicang City, Jiangsu
    Manfacturing Site
    Lowbanks, Ontario, Canada
    Manufacturing Site
    Coatzacoalcos, Mexico
    Manufacturing Site
    Guanajuato, Mexico
    Administrative Site
    Miguel Hidalgo, Mexico
    Administrative Site
    SÆo Paulo, Brazil
    Administrative Site
    Taicang City, China
    Administrative Site
    Miguel Higalgo
Brands:
    Advantra Z
    Aminogen Advanced
    Bergavit 40
    Cera-Q
    Chelamax
    CranSmart
    MaitakeGold
    Oxyjun
    QU995

24282 Innoseal Systems Inc
10900 S Commerce Blvd # B
Charlotte, NC 28273-7133

704-521-6068
Fax: 704-521-6038 sales@innoseal.com
President: Jeff Rebh
jeff.rebh@innovativetape.com
Number Employees: 5-9
Parent Co: Twinseal Systems B.V.

24283 Innova Envelopes
7213 Rue Cordner
La Salle, QC H8N 2J7
Canada

514-595-0555
Fax: 514-595-1112 www.supremex.com
Manufacturer and exporter of envelopes
President: Gilles Cyrcs
CFO: Stephan Lavigne
VP/General Manager: Gilles Cyr
R&D: Alain Tremblay
Estimated Sales: $30 - 50 Million
Number Employees: 200
Parent Co: Supremex

24284 Innova-Tech
1500 E Lancaster Ave # 100
Paoli, PA 19301-1500

610-640-9350
Fax: 610-640-2670 800-523-7299
www.innovatechnologies.in
Wastewater treatment equipment and dissolved air
flotation units
President: John Murphy
Chief Engineer: Greg Laurent
Number Employees: 1-4
Square Footage: 109200

24285 Innovation Moving Systems
310 S 10th St
P.O. Box 700169
Oostburg, WI 53070-1301

920-564-6272
Fax: 920-564-2322 800-619-0625
president@lectrotruck.com www.lectrotruck.com
USA manufacturer of the ORIGINAL battery oper-
ated stail climbing hand truck for over 40 years.
Safely move heavy loads from 600lbs/272kg to
1500lbs/680kg in less time. All models include free
battery, battery charger, strap bar(s), 2year motor
warranty and a 1year entire unit warranty.
President: Kevin Peters
president@lectrotruck.com
Sales/Marketing Executive: Jason Tagel
Estimated Sales: Below $5 Million
Number Employees: 1-4
Square Footage: 34000
Brands:
    Lectro Truck

24286 Innovations Expressed LLC
Po Box 1823
Sparta, NJ 07871-3850

201-452-0557
Specialty food packaging i.e. gift wrap/la-
bels/boxes/containers.
Marketing: Jody Shampton-Moore

24287 Innovations by Design
19 Foothill Path
Chadds Ford, PA 19317-9146

610-558-0160
Fax: 610-558-1960
Consultant specializing in food service design, cad
layouts and project administration for cafeterias,
prisons, schools, hospitals, sports arenas, etc
President & CEO: Jon Shaw
VP of Operations: John Fogleman
Director of Marketing: Scott Huggins
Director of Sales: Allen Wells

24288 Innovative Ceramic Corp
432 Walnut St
East Liverpool, OH 43920-3130

330-385-6515
Fax: 330-385-6510 info@innovativeceramic.com
www.innovativeceramic.com
Rubber stamps and high temperature inks
President: Orville Steininger
Estimated Sales: Below $5 Million
Number Employees: 1-4
Square Footage: 20000

24289 Innovative Components
P.O. Box 294
Southington, CT 06489-0294

860-621-7220
Fax: 860-620-0288 800-789-2851
info@liquidlevel.com www.liquidlevel.com
Manufacturer and exporter of sanitary liquid level
instrumentation for level indication, alarms and
controls
Owner: Pete Meade
Sales: Pete Meade
Production: Joe Kubisek
Estimated Sales: $1-2.5 Million
Number Employees: 5-9
Square Footage: 10000

24290 Innovative Controls Corp
1354 E Broadway St
Toledo, OH 43605

419-691-6684
Fax: 419-691-0170
www.innovativecontrolscorp.com
Provides the following services to the food & beverage industry: packaging integration; packaging machine rebuilds and retrofits; automated process
control panels; conveyor systems; bar coding;
verticle form fill seal bagging machines;cup feeders
- auger and filling; rebuilds and retrofits of processing equipment; transfer feeds; materials handling
distribution; mills - sugar, flour & meal; process
controls for weighing, blending, & batching; PLC
controlled robotics. Individualconsulting.
President & CEO: Louis Soltis
Marketing Director: Angela Hitchens
Sales Director: Michael Hitchens
Contact: Mark Benton
mbenton@innovativecontrolscorp.com
Director of Operations: Robert Simon

Estimated Sales: $5-7 Million
Number Employees: 20-49
Square Footage: 70000

24291 Innovative Energy
10653 W 181st Ave
Lowell, IN 46356-9451

219-696-3639
Fax: 219-696-5220 info@insul.net
www.insul.net
Specialty food packaging i.e. gift wrap/la-
bels/boxes/containers.
President: Robert Wadsworth
info@insul.net
Marketing: Tammy Snyder
Number Employees: 20-49

**24292 Innovative Folding Carton
Company**
901 Durham Ave
South Plainfield, NJ 07080

908-757-0205
Fax: 908-757-6464
Folding cartons and pressure sensitive labels
President: Shawn Smith
CFO: Bob Sgaitierri
CFO: Robert S Pierre
Quality Control: Will Suton
VP Sales: Shawn Smith
VP Operations: Ray Karst
Estimated Sales: $20-50 Million
Number Employees: 100-249
Square Footage: 100000
Parent Co: Impaxx

24293 Innovative Food Processors Inc
2125 Airport Dr
Faribault, MN 55021-7798

507-334-2730
Fax: 507-334-7969 800-997-4437
www.ifpinc.biz
Custom manufacturing services including agglomer-
ation, encapsulation, and packaging for food and
beverage powders
CEO: Ephi Eyal
eeyal@ifpinc.biz
Marketing Director: Anna Batsakes
Sales Director: Scott Sijan
Estimated Sales: $23.4 Million
Number Employees: 250-499

24294 Innovative Food Solutions LLC
4516 Kenny Road
Suite 320
Columbus, OH 43220-3711

614-326-1421
Fax: 614-326-1443 800-884-3314
Consulting firm ready to assist you to quickly launch
new food products and manufacturing processes,
new food industry ingredients, perform technical
troubleshooting and produce prototype samples for
trade shows and market researchstudies. Areas of
experience include organic, natural and
nutraceutical/functional food products, including
aseptic and retort liquids, and spray dried powders.
President: Jeff Liebrecht
R&D: Jeff Liebrecht

24295 Innovative Foods, Inc.
338 N Canal
Suite 20
South San Francisco, CA 94080

650-871-8912
Fax: 650-871-0837
Infused foods, including using product forming, fla-
voring, coloring and value added to underutilized
raw materials.
Owner: Gilbert Lee
VP/Secretary & Treasurer: Fay Hirschberg
Research & Development: Edward Hirschberg
Contact: David Terry
dterry@innovfoods.com
Estimated Sales: $190 Thousand
Square Footage: 74000

24296 Innovative Marketing
11801 Pierce St.
2nd Floor
Riverside, CA 92505

951-710-3135
Fax: 952-949-8865 800-438-4627
innovativemarketingca.com
Manufacturer and exporter of lid openers for plastic
containers

653

President: Brad Pappas
Operations Manager: Amy Vinar
Estimated Sales: 150000
Number Employees: 1-4
Square Footage: 40000
Brands:
  Pco
  The Lid Cutter

24297 Innovative Molding
6775 McKinley Ave
Sebastopol, CA 95472

707-829-2666
Fax: 707-829-5212
whunt@innovativemolding.com
www.innovativemolding.com
Manufacturer and exporter of threaded plastic caps
and lids for jars and bottles.
Administrator: Alan Williams
  awilliams@innovativemold.com
Vice President: Ron Cook
Operations Manager: Warren Hunt
Estimated Sales: $5-10 Million
Number Employees: 50-99
Square Footage: 56000

24298 Innovative Packaging Solution
1692 12th Street
Martin, MI 49070-8745

616-656-2100
Fax: 616-656-2101
Litho cut and stack labels, seals, stickers, label ap-
plication equipment and computerized artwork
CEO: James Rand
Sr VP: Jim English
Communications Director: Kate Hunter
Estimated Sales: $20-50 Million
Number Employees: 100-249
Square Footage: 30000
Parent Co: Excellence Group

24299 Innovative Plastech
1260 Kingsland Dr
Batavia, IL 60510

630-232-1808
Fax: 630-232-1978 ghernandez@inplas.com
www.inplas.com
Custom thermoforming, tool and package designing,
plastic trays
President: Jim Gustafson
CFO: Jake Clever
VP: Edward Gustafson
R&D: Denny Bahl
Quality Control: Girish Raval
Sales: Dave Lyons
Contact: Dennis Bahl
  d.bahl@inplas.com
Production: Martine Del Toro
Plant Manager: John Martinez
Purchasing: Larry Rosales
Estimated Sales: $15 Million
Number Employees: 64
Square Footage: 90000
Type of Packaging: Consumer, Private Label

24300 Innovative Plastics Corp
400 Route 303
Orangeburg, NY 10962-1340

845-359-7500
Fax: 845-359-0237
service@innovative-plastics.com
www.innovative-plastics.com
Thermoformed plastics packaging and contract
packaging services
President: Don D'Antonio
  don@inoplas.com
VP: Bud Macfarlane
Estimated Sales: $35 - 40 Million
Number Employees: 100-249
Square Footage: 60000
Type of Packaging: Consumer
Other Locations:
  Innovative Plastics Corporation
  Nashville TN

24301 Innovative Rotational Molding
2300 W Pecan Ave
Madera, CA 93637-5056

559-673-4764
Fax: 559-673-4716 CustServe@IRM-CORP.Com
www.irm-corp.com
Sales and marketing information systems to food
and beverage manufacturers, distributors and
brokers.

President: Shelly Humphries
  shumphries@irm-corp.com
CEO: Art Harding
Sales: Tim Shine
Number Employees: 10-19
Other Locations:
  IRM Corporation
  Dallas TX
Brands:
  Compass Forecast System
  Discovery System
  Promo Assist

24302 Innovative Space Management
2645 Brooklyn Queens Expressway
Woodside, NY 11377-7826

718-278-4300
Fax: 718-274-0973 contact@ny.diam-int.com
Manufacturer, exporter and designer of shelf man-
agement systems and point of purchase displays
VP/General Manager (ISM Division): Bryan
Yablans
VP Sales: Winn Esterline
VP Operations: Valerie Vignola
Number Employees: 850
Square Footage: 300000
Parent Co: POP Displays

24303 Inovar Packaging Group
611 Magic Mile St # 205
Arlington, TX 76011-5109

817-277-6666
Fax: 817-275-2770 800-285-2235
info@inovarpkg.com www.inovarpkg.com
Custom printed labels, tags and decals. Also, distrib-
ute label applicators and packaging equipment.
President: Gary Cooper
CEO: Dave Young
  dyoung@inovarpkg.com
CFO: Kyle Dailey
Research & Development: Alton Berry
Quality Control: Sonya Ayers
Marketing/Sales: Steve Nevil
Operations Manager: Darryl Parham
Purchasing Manager: Mark Ingus
Estimated Sales: $15,000,000
Number Employees: 20-49
Square Footage: 106000
Parent Co: Conti Industries
Type of Packaging: Consumer, Food Service, Pri-
vate Label, Bulk
Brands:
  Kraftmark

24304 Inovatech
3911 Mount Lehman Road
Abbotsford, BC V4X 2N1
Canada

604-857-9080
Fax: 604-857-0843 www.inovatech.com
Number Employees: 10

24305 Inovpack Vector
40 Vreeland Avenue
Suite 107
Providence, RI

888-227-4647
Fax: 203-852-0136
Casings

24306 Inpaco Corporation
PO Box 286
Nazareth, PA 18064-0286

610-759-8544
Fax: 610-759-9021
Wine industry bags

24307 Inpak Systems Inc
540 Tasman St
Madison, WI 53714-3162

608-221-8180
Fax: 608-221-4473 sales@inpaksystems.com
www.inpaksystems.com
Distributor of industrial packaging equipment
President: Gerald Hoague
  info@inpaksystems.com
VP: Ronn Ferrell
Marketing: Tom McDonnell
Sales: Dennis Murphy
Operations: Mike Kennedy
Estimated Sales: $3-4 Million
Number Employees: 1-4
Square Footage: 8000
Type of Packaging: Bulk

24308 Inscale
1607 Maple Ave
Terre Haute, IN 47804-3234

812-232-0893
Fax: 812-232-6876 855-839-9147
incell@inscale-incell.com
Checkweighing devices, weight control systems,
scales
Owner: Fred Herrmann
General Manager: Paul Herrmann
Estimated Sales: $5-10 Million
Number Employees: 20-49
Square Footage: 140000
Type of Packaging: Bulk

24309 Insect-O-Cutor Inc
1641 Lewis Way
Stone Mountain, GA 30083-1107

770-939-2835
Fax: 770-621-0100 800-966-8480
sales@insect-o-cutor.com
www.insect-o-cutor.com
Industrial commercial grade insect light traps; 110
volt, 220 volt, stainless steel, scatterproof, en-
ergy-efficient
President: W A Harris
Number Employees: 10-19
Type of Packaging: Private Label
Brands:
  Germ-O-Ray
  Guardian
  Insect-O-Cutor

24310 Insects Limited Inc
16950 Westfield Park Rd
Westfield, IN 46074-9374

317-896-9300
Fax: 317-867-5757 800-992-1991
insectsltd@aol.com www.fumigationzone.com
Manufacturer, exporter and wholesaler/distributor of
pest control systems including traps, lures, insect
monitoring and detection devices, fumigation prod-
ucts, etc.; importer of cigarette beetle pheromone
traps; also, pest controlaudits and seminars available
President: David Mueller
  d.mueller@insectslimited.com
CFO: Barbara Bass
VP: John Mueller
General Manager: Patrick Kelley
Estimated Sales: $1 Million
Number Employees: 10-19
Square Footage: 6000
Brands:
  Bullet Lure
  Lasio
  No Survivor
  Serrico
  Storgard

24311 Insight Distribution Systems
222 Schilling Cir
Suite 275
Hunt Valley, MD 21031-8638

410-403-1100
Fax: 410-329-1114 800-310-3548
Beverage distribution software, specilizing in mo-
bile computers, route accounting, inventory,
financials, account management software
President: Bob Jenkin
Estimated Sales: $10-20 Million
Number Employees: 10

24312 Insight Packaging
1000 Muirfield Drive
Hanover Park, IL 60133-5468

630-980-4314
Fax: 630-980-4316 info@insightpack.com
www.insightpack.com
Package food items for other companies
President: Gregory Batton
Estimated Sales: $10 - 20 Million
Number Employees: 10

24313 Insignia Systems Inc
8799 Brooklyn Blvd
Minneapolis, MN 55445-2398

763-392-6200
Fax: 763-392-6222 800-874-4648
info@insigniasystems.com
www.insigniasystems.com
Manufacturer and exporter of promotional items including signage and software for bar coding and
large format printing

President/CEO: Glen P. Dall
VP, Finance: John C. Gonsior
CFO: John C. Gonsior
Quality Control: Bob Norman
VP Marketing: Scott Simcox
Number Employees: 50-99
Brands:
Insignia Pops
Stylus

24314 (HQ)Insinger Co
6245 State Rd
Philadelphia, PA 19135-2996
215-624-4800
Fax: 215-624-6966 800-344-4802
sales@insingermachine.com
www.insingermachine.com
Manufacturer and exporter of commercial dishwashers potato peelers, garbage disposal units, french fry cutters, tray washers and driers and dish, glass, pot and pan washers
President: John Stern
CEO: Robert Cantor
acantor@insingermachine.com
VP Sales/Marketing: Ari Cantor
Chief Engineer: Jim Bittner
Quality Control: Kris Hogan
Marketing Director: Annemarie Fisher
Regional Sales Manager: Don Gazzillo
Vice President of Operations: Kristine Hogan
Purchasing Manager: Kristine Hogan
Estimated Sales: $10 - 20 Million
Number Employees: 50-99
Square Footage: 130000

24315 Inspired Automation Inc
5321 Derry Ave # D
Agoura Hills, CA 91301-5064
818-991-4598
Fax: 818-597-4820 www.inspiredautomation.com
Automatic net weighing, counting, in-line batching and filling machinery; exporter of automatic net weighing, in-line batching and counting machinery
President: Robert Homes
bob@inspiredautomation.com
Sales: Buzz Holmes
Plant Manager: Joesph Gonzales
Estimated Sales: $3 - 5 Million
Number Employees: 5-9
Number of Brands: 1
Number of Products: 22
Square Footage: 4000
Type of Packaging: Consumer, Food Service, Private Label, Bulk

24316 Insta-Pro International
10104 Douglas Ave
Urbandale, IA 50322-2007
515-254-1260
Fax: 515-276-5749 800-383-4524
www.insta-pro.com
Manufacturer and exporter of processing equipment for textured soy products
Vice President: Ray Goodwin
rgoodwin@insta-pro.com
President, Chief Executive Officer: Kevin Kacere
R&D: Wilmot Wijeratne
VP: Karl Arnold
Chairman: Wayne Fox
VP International Marketing: Tom Welby
Vice President of Operations: Hennie Pieterse
Estimated Sales: $5 - 10 Million
Number Employees: 10-19
Parent Co: Triple F
Brands:
Express
Insta-Pro

24317 Instabox
1139 40th Avenue North East
Calgary, AB T2E 6M9
Canada
403-250-9217
Fax: 403-250-8075 800-482-6173
www.instabox.com
Corrugated cardboard boxes and shipping supplies
President: Jim Mace
CFO: Greg Mace
CEO: Greg Mace
Office Manager: Linda Burgher
Manager: Richard Bain
Order Desk: Dale Beck
Number Employees: 40

24318 (HQ)Instacomm Canada
Unit 1, Suite 376
Oakville, ON L6M 2Y1
Canada
905-465-1266
Fax: 905-465-0644 877-426-2783
info@instacomm.com www.instacomm.com
Distributor of guest and server oaging systems
Estimated Sales: $1 - 5 Million
Number Employees: 1-4
Other Locations:
Instacomm Canada
Creedmoor NC

24319 Institute of Packaging Professionals
1833 Centre Point Circle
Suite 123
Naperville, IL 60563
630-544-5050
Fax: 630-544-5055 info@iopp.org
www.iopp.org
Association for packaging professionals
Religious Leader: Paul Kim
Contact: Eric Berkley
eberkley@iopp.org
Number Employees: 10-19

24320 Institutional & Supermarket
7362 NW 5th St
PO Box 17440
Plantation, FL 33317-1605
954-584-3100
Fax: 954-584-5591 info@iseinc.org
www.iseinc.org
Industrial food serving equipment
Executive Director: Philip Polunsky
phil@iseinc.org
Estimated Sales: $1-2.5 Million
Number Employees: 10-19

24321 Institutional EquipmentInc
704 Veterans Pkwy # B
Bolingbrook, IL 60440-5094
630-771-0990
Fax: 630-771-0994 www.ieiusa.net
Stainless steel counters, shelving and tables including steam
President: Frank Fiene
ffiene@ieiusa.net
VP Manufacturing: Don Wasielweski
Estimated Sales: $5-10 Million
Number Employees: 50-99
Square Footage: 160000

24322 Instrumented Sensor Technology
4704 Moore St
Okemos, MI 48864-1722
517-349-8487
Fax: 517-349-8469 info@isthq.com
www.isthq.com
Owner: Greg Hoshal
hoshal@isthq.com
Estimated Sales: $1 - 3 Million
Number Employees: 5-9

24323 Insulair
35275 S Welty Rd
Vernalis, CA 95385-9733
209-839-0911
Fax: 209-839-1353 800-343-3402
Manufacturer and exporter of insulated triple-wall paper cups and plastic lids
President: Claus Sadlier
CFO: Larry Nally
Quality Control: Dale Houglant
Sales Director: Frank Gavin
Estimated Sales: $5 - 10 Million
Number Employees: 5-9
Brands:
Insulair

24324 Intec Video Systems
23301 Vista Grande Dr
Laguna Hills, CA 92653-1497
949-859-3800
Fax: 949-859-3178 800-468-3254
info@intecvideo.com www.intecvideo.com
Rear vision cameras systems
President: Don Nama
Marketing Director: Manuel Mendez
Sales Director: Roy Barbatti
Manager: John Hoover
jhoover@avanquest.com

Estimated Sales: $12 000,000
Number Employees: 20-49

24325 Intech
3825 Grant St
Washougal, WA 98671-2810
360-835-8785
Fax: 360-835-5144 www.intechenterprises.com
President: Tom Cunning
tomc@intechenterprises.com
Estimated Sales: Below $5 Million
Number Employees: 10-19

24326 Intedge Manufacturing
1875 Chumley Rd
Woodruff, SC 29388-8561
864-969-9601
Fax: 864-969-9604 866-969-9605
customer.service@intedge.com www.intedge.com
Food service equipment including textiles, smallware, baking supplies, timers, thermometers, utensils, and much more.
Plant Manager: Debi Collier
Number Employees: 20-49
Type of Packaging: Food Service, Private Label
Brands:
Intedge
Metalwash

24327 Integrated Barcode Solutions
856 3rd St NW
Valley City, ND 58072
Fax: 530-273-4725
Portable terminal or fixed station data capture applications that employ bar code technology
Estimated Sales: less than $500,000
Number Employees: 1

24328 Integrated Distribution
2110 S 169th Plz # 200
Omaha, NE 68130-4650
937-445-1936
Fax: 402-397-8451
Computer software for food distribution
President/ CEO/ Chairman: Wiliam Nuti
SVP/ CFO/ Chief Accounting Officer: Bob Fishman
Vice President of Information Technology: Bob Mawyer
EVP, Services, Hardware Solutions & EQ: Rick Marquardt
Head of Marketing: Oren Betzaleli
Executive Vice President of Retail Sales: Mike Todd
SVP/ Corp. Services/ Chief HR Officer: Andrea Ledford
Estimated Sales: $10 - 20 Million
Number Employees: 50-99

24329 Integrated Packaging Systems
3 Luger Rd # 5
Suite 5
Denville, NJ 07834-2638
973-664-0020
Fax: 973-263-2992 www.ipsnj.com
Tablet counting and liquid filling
President: Michael Fuzia
mfuzia@ipsnj.com
Vice President: Michael McNeila
Technical Manager: Michael Frusteri
Sales Director: Marianne Mooney
General Manager: Phil DePalma
Estimated Sales: $4-5 Million
Number Employees: 5-9
Brands:
Procount Salt Counter
Versaflow Liquid Filler

24330 Integrated Restaurant Software/RMS Touch
9 West Ridgely Road
Timonium, MD 21093
201-461-9096
Fax: 410-902-5468
Manufacturer and exporter of P.O.S. touch screen software for restaurants, bars, cafeterias, etc
President: Richard Adler
VP Sales: Peter Polizanno
Estimated Sales: $2.5 - 5 Million
Number Employees: 10-19
Square Footage: 12000

655

24331 Integrated Systems
1904 SE Ochoco Street
Portland, OR 97222-7315

503-654-7886
Fax: 503-654-7868 800-705-6401
Palletizers and depalletizers available in high or low
level infeed with rates up to five layers a minute, options include depalletizing, pallet dispensers, tie
sheets and fully automated multi-palletizer cells
Estimated Sales: $1 - 5 Million

24332 Intelligent Controls
PO Box 638
Saco, ME 4072

207-283-0156
Fax: 207-283-0158 800-872-3455
webadmin@incon.com www.incon.com
Manufacturer and exporter of microprocessor and
programmable controls including liquid level measurement and process multiplexing systems, supervisory control and data acquisition systems
CEO: Scott Tremble
Director Marketing: John Eastman
VP: Dean Richards
Contact: Vitaliy Demin
vdemin@franklinfueling.com
Estimated Sales: $10,000,000 - $19,999,999
Number Employees: 1,000-4,999
Square Footage: 28000
Parent Co: Franklin Fueling Systems

24333 Intelplex Designers
9607 Dielman Rock Island Indus
St Louis, MO 63132-2149

314-983-9996
Fax: 314-983-9989 intouch@intelplex.com
Consultant specializing in the design of restaurant
equipment
Owner: Alan Sherman
intouch@intelplex.com
Estimated Sales: $1-2.5 Million
Number Employees: 1-4

24334 Intentia Americas
1700 E Golf Rd # 9
Schaumburg, IL 60173-5816

847-762-0900
Fax: 847-762-0901 800-796-6839
www.lawson.com
Managing Director, Intentia Australia/Ne: Linus
Parker
Chief Executive Officer, President: Harry Debes
Vice President of Sales: Mikael Anden
Contact: Christine Roe
christine.roe@lawson.com
Estimated Sales: $10 - 20 Million
Number Employees: 20-49

24335 (HQ)Inteplast Bags & Films Corporation
7503 Vantage Pl.
Delta, BC V4G 1A5
Canada

604-946-5431
Fax: 604-946-5343 www.inteplast.com
Polyethylene produce bags, film, trash can liners and
corrugated sheets
President: John Young
Estimated Sales: $12.4 Million
Number Employees: 90

24336 Inteplast Group LTD
9 Peach Tree Hill Rd
Livingston, NJ 07039-5702

973-994-8000
Fax: 973-994-8028 info@inteplast.com
www.inteplast.com
BOPP films, stretch wrap, and plastic concentrates
and compounds.
President: John D Young
jyoung@inteplast.com
Number Employees: 1000-4999

24337 Inter-Access
100 Carrier Drive
Etobicoke, ON M9W 5R1
Canada

514-744-6262
Fax: 514-744-3176
Executive search firm; also, consultant providing
company re-engineering, manufacturing automation,
ISO quality implementation, business planning and
market surveys

President: Mohamed Geledi-Nami
VP: Edith Chandonnet
Senior Consultant: Tom Schopflocher
Number Employees: 5-9
Square Footage: 2000
Parent Co: Le Groupe Consortium Canada

24338 Inter-City Welding & Manufacturing
10058 E Wilson Rd
Independence, MO 64053-1541

816-252-1770
Fax: 816-252-8321
Industrial belt conveyors
Manager: Mary Robinett
Estimated Sales: $500,000-$1 Million
Number Employees: 1-4

24339 (HQ)Inter-Pack Corporation
PO Box 691
Monroe, MI 48161-0691

734-242-7755
Fax: 734-242-7756
Manufacturer and exporter of corrugated paper and
foam plastic; contract packaging services available
Manager: Frank Calandra
Estimated Sales: $20 - 50 Million
Number Employees: 20-49

24340 InterCrate, Inc.
657 Marine Dr
West Vancouver, BC V7T 1A4

855-922-4446
sales@intercratecontainer.com intercrate.com
North American manufacturer of plastic hand-held
containers for food service, food processing and restaurant operations.
President: Justin Elvin-Jensen
U.S. Sales: Bradley Fry
Number Employees: 2-10

24341 InterMetro Industries
Wilkes-Barre, PA 18705

570-825-2741
Manufacturer of space and productivity solutions
Year Founded: 1929
Number Employees: 400
Number of Products: 30K
Brands:
Metromax
Super Adjustable
Super Erecta

24342 InterSect Business Systems Inc
1921 Kent Road
Kelowna, BC V1Y 7S6
Canada

250-860-0829
Fax: 250-860-0876 sales@distrib-u-tec.com
www.distrib-u-tec.com
Distrib-u-tec Software is a fully integrated operations and cost accounting information management
system designed specifically for food distributors,
processors and packers.
Sales/Marketing: Corrina Cross

24343 InterXchange Market Network
32 Laurens Street
Charleston, SC 29401-1565

803-577-4794
Fax: 803-577-4794 800-577-4794
rrabago@halcyon.com
Brokers and commondity exchanges, computer systems and software
Number Employees: 45

24344 Interactive Sales Solutions
616 Shadowcrest Ln
Coppell, TX 75019-3401

214-352-9575
Fax: 214-352-5729 800-352-9575
www.issi-ivr.info
Sales force automation software utilizing touch-tone
phones for consumer sales, food service and retail
food broker operations
President: William Godbey
bgodbey@issi-ivr.com
VP: Dean Schenkel
Operations Manager: John Williamson
bgodbey@issi-ivr.com
Estimated Sales: $500,000-$1 Million
Number Employees: 5-9
Square Footage: 8000
Type of Packaging: Bulk

Brands:
Interactive Sales Manager

24345 Interactive Services Group
600 Delran Pkwy # C
Delran, NJ 08075-1268

856-824-9401
Fax: 856-824-9415 800-566-3310
jbdickinson@isg-service.com
Hand-held computer system maintenance and support. Specialize in supporting Intermec and Symbols
systems. Company also has priority software applications for route accounting industry
Owner: Igor Lukov
i.lukov@isg-service.com
CEO: J Dickinson
Director Human Resources: Michele Galan
Estimated Sales: $4 Million
Number Employees: 20-49
Square Footage: 36000

24346 Interamerican Coffee
19500 State Hwy 249 # 255
Houston, TX 77070

713-462-2671
Fax: 713-912-7072 800-346-2810
Green coffee importer and distributer
President: Guy Burdett
Controller: Samantha Marino
Vice President of Operations: John Mason
Estimated Sales: $5-10 Million
Number Employees: 20-49

24347 Interbrand Corporation
555 Market Street
Suite 900
San Francisco, CA 94105

347-334-3502
Fax: 415-593-2250 877-692-7263
inquiries@interbrand.com www.interbrand.com
Consultant for brand logos, packaging, identification
and naming
Global CEO: Jez Frampton
Global Chief Creative Officer: Andy Payne
Global CFO & COO: Kelly Gall
Global Chief Strategy Officer: Leslie Butterfield
Contact: Paulette Fox
fox.paulette@interbrand.com
Director of Operations: Michael Levtchenko
Estimated Sales: $5 - 10 Million
Number Employees: 20-49
Parent Co: Omnicom
Other Locations:
Interbrand Corp.
Chicago IL

24348 Intercard Inc
1884 Lackland Hill Pkwy # 1
St Louis, MO 63146-3569

314-275-8066
Fax: 314-275-4998 info@intercardinc.com
Manufacturer and exporter of credit and debit card
systems
CEO: Ray Sherrod
CFO: Gerry Schmidt
Quality Control: Lynn Soreden
Estimated Sales: $10 - 20 Million
Number Employees: 20-49

24349 Intercomp
3839 County Road 116
Hamel, MN 55340-9342

763-476-2531
Fax: 763-476-2613 800-328-3336
info@intercompcompany.com
www.intercompco.com
Manufacturer and exporter of electronic scales including crane, platform, pallet and portable truck,
floor, bench and hanging
Owner: Robert Kroll
Quality Control: Mark Browne
Plant Manager: Jeff Weyandt
Estimated Sales: $20 Million
Number Employees: 50-99
Square Footage: 90000
Brands:
Cs 750
Cw 250
Cw 500
Pw 800
Pw 850

24350 Interfood Ingredients
777 Brickell Ave
Suite 210
Miami, FL 33131
786-953-8320
info@interfood.com
www.interfood.com
Dairy ingredients and products
CEO: Frank van Stipdonk
CFO: Constantijn Stan Sweep
Chief Commercial Officer: Edwin van Stipdonk
Chief Information Officer: Ran Panday
Chief Human Resources Officer: Mirjam van der Horst
Year Founded: 1970
Estimated Sales: $235 Million
Number Employees: 200
Parent Co: Interfood Holding

24351 Intergraph Corp
7840 N Sam Houston Pkwy W # 20
Suite 100
Houston, TX 77064-3503
281-671-1013
Fax: 281-890-3301 800-899-8787
sales@coade.com www.intergraph.com
Provides software for multiple plant design and engineering disciplines.
Senior VP: Rick Allen
rick.allen@intergraph.com
Estimated Sales: $5-10 000,000
Number Employees: 50-99

24352 Interior Systems Inc
241 N Broadway # 600
Suite 600
Milwaukee, WI 53202-5860
414-224-0957
Fax: 414-224-0972 800-837-8373
info@isiamerica.com www.isiamerica.com
Food service fixtures, furniture, play equipment, artwork and signage
President/CEO: Tony Lutz
tlutz@isiamerica.com
Chairman: Lindsey Bovinet
CFO: Bill Stoll
Vice President - Fulfillment: Mark Huck
IT Manager: Robert Graf
Director of Sales: Jason Fredrickson
Director - Human Resources: Jim Carlson
Director of Operations: Darin Grobe
Creative Director: Tony Pagliuca
Controller: Zach Schaefer
Estimated Sales: $5 - 10 Million
Number Employees: 50-99

24353 Interlab
4200 Research Forest Dr # 150
The Woodlands, TX 77381-3237
281-298-9410
Fax: 281-298-9411 888-876-2844
www.polyseed.org
Manufacturer and exporter of microbial products for drain maintenance, odor control, septic systems, etc.; also, in-house and field technical support available
President: Peter Perez
Estimated Sales: $3 - 5 Million
Number Employees: 5-9
Square Footage: 28400
Brands:
Bio Free Trap Clear
Biofree Septic Clear

24354 Interlake Mecalux
1600 N. 25th Ave.
Melrose Park
Chicago, IL 60160
708-344-9999
Fax: 708-343-9788 www.interlakemecalux.com
Steel racking, warehouse automation, warehouse management software and other storage solutions.
Founder/President: Jose Luis Carrillo Rodriguez
Year Founded: 2000
Estimated Sales: $100-$500 Million
Number Employees: 500-999
Brands:
Esmena
Interlake

24355 Interliance
200 E Sandpointe Ave 510
Santa Ana, CA 92707
714-540-8889
Fax: 714-540-6113 800-540-7917
info@interliance.com www.interliance.com
Consultant providing performance improvement, process improvement, quality strategies, policies and procedures, regulatory compliance programs, site specific training, etc
President: Brad Kemp
CFO: Brad Kamth
Quality Control: Brad Kamth
Contact: Linda Apple
lapple@interliance.com
Estimated Sales: $5 - 10,000,000
Number Employees: 1-4

24356 Intermec Technologies Corporation
6001 36th Ave W
Everett, WA 98203-1264
425-348-2600
Fax: 425-267-2983 info@intermec.com
Labels and tags
Estimated Sales: $50-100 Million
Number Employees: 1,000-4,999
Parent Co: Intermec

24357 Intermec/Norand Mobile Systems
6001 36th Avenue West
Everett, WA 98203 - 12
425-348-2600
Fax: 425-355-9551 800-755-5505
info@intermec.com www.intermec.com
President: Tom Miller
Interim President, Chief Executive Offic: Allen Lauer
Senior Vice President of Solutions: Earl Thompson
Chief Technical Officer: Arvin Danielson
Senior Vice President of Sales and Marke: James McDonnell
Contact: Aaron Fu
afu@radiax.com
Senior Vice President of Operations: Dennis Faerber
Estimated Sales: $1 - 5 Million
Number Employees: 250-499

24358 Intermex Products USA
1375 Ave S.
Suite 300
Grand Prairie, TX 75050
972-988-1333
Fax: 972-660-5941 800-508-8475
ravera@cydsa.com www.intermexproducts.com
Cydsa, cellophane, bi-oriented polypropylene, coextrusions, printed and laminated plastic films
Contact: Juan Carlos
jcarlos@intermexproducts.com
Estimated Sales: $5-10 Million
Number Employees: 5-9
Parent Co: La Torre

24359 Intermold Corporation
30 Old Mill Rd
Greenville, SC 29607
864-627-0300
Fax: 864-627-0005 sales@intermoldcorp.com
www.intermoldcorp.com
Manufacturer and exporter of plastic injection molding products including bakery proofer cups; custom molding for the baking industry available
President: Alan Butcher
sales@intermoldcorp.com
VP: Jane Butcher
Estimated Sales: $1-2.5 Million
Number Employees: 10-19
Square Footage: 32000

24360 International Adhesive Coating
6 Industrial Dr
PO Box 240
Windham, NH 03087-2020
603-893-1894
Fax: 603-898-9025 800-253-4450
Manifactures a complete line of double coated, single-coated, transfer tapes, bag sealing, foam and high tack/low tack products along with a wide range of coating and converting capabilities.
Manager: Dennis Salois
dsalois@itctapes.com
Estimated Sales: $5 - 10 Million
Number Employees: 20-49

24361 International Approval Services
8501 East Pleasant Valley Road
Cleveland, OH 44131-5516
216-524-4990
Fax: 216-642-3463 877-235-9791
Testing service for gas powered cooking equipment
President & CEO: Ash Sahi
EVP, Finance & Administration: Esteban De Bernardis
Regional Vice President, U.S. & Mexico: Rich Weiser
EVP, Science & Engineering: Helene Vaillancourt
Chief Operating Officer: Magali Depras
Estimated Sales: $1 - 5 Million
Number Employees: 100-249
Parent Co: CSA

24362 International Automation
332 Ramapo Valley Road
Oakland, NJ 7004
201-651-0500
Fax: 201-760-9960 www.iaiusa.com
Checkweighers
President: Mark Schultz
Estimated Sales: $.5 - 1 million
Number Employees: 5-9

24363 International Carbonic
P.O. Box 578
Adelanto, CA 92301
760-246-3900
Fax: 760-246-4044 www.ici.us
Carbonated beverage dispensing equipment, including carbonators, valves, fittings and systems; complete sheet metal facility
President: Joe Suarez
Estimated Sales: $20-50 Million
Number Employees: 20-49

24364 International Coatings
2925 Lucy Ln
Franklin Park, IL 60131
847-451-0279
Fax: 847-451-0379 800-624-8919
Flooring, coatings
President: Mike Kramer
Marketing Director: Raymond Hurley
Contact: Eileen Henquinet
ehenq@icocoat.com
Estimated Sales: $10 - 20 Million
Number Employees: 10-19

24365 International Cold Storage
215 E 13th St
Andover, KS 67002-9329
316-218-4100
Fax: 316-733-2434 800-835-0001
www.icsco.com
Walk-in coolers and freezers; exporter of walk-in coolers
President: Matt Madeksza
CFO: Carlos Tlusty
carlos.tlusty@carrier.utc.com
VP, Sales, West: Jim Cook
VP, Sales, Midwest: Mark Norvold
Plant Manager: Jay Risley
Estimated Sales: $10 - 20 Million
Number Employees: 100-249
Square Footage: 160000
Parent Co: Tyler Refrigeration Company

24366 International ContainerSystems
5401 W Kennedy Boulevard
Suite 711
Tampa, FL 33609-2447
813-287-8940
Fax: 813-286-2070 800-444-4274
Carton and container systems
Estimated Sales: $1-2.5 Million
Number Employees: 5-9

24367 International Cooling Systems
300 Granton Drive
Richmond Hill, ON L4B 1H7
Canada
416-213-5566
Fax: 416-213-9666 888-213-5566
Manufacturer, importer and exporter of turnkey process cooling systems, cooling towers, chillers, flake and pumpable flow ice machines and water/fluid recirculation stations
President: Victor Gardiman
VP: Otto Novak
Plant Manager: Steve Novak

Number Employees: 10-19
Square Footage: 96000

24368 International Envelope Company

2 Tabas Ln
Exton, PA 19341

610-363-0900
Fax: 610-363-2999

Specialty mailing envelopes and filing products
CEO: Sandy Moyer
VP Marketing: Sandy Moyer
Contact: Jennifer Dyer
   jdyer@goiec.com
Estimated Sales: $1 - 5 Million
Number Employees: 250-499
Square Footage: 300000
Parent Co: American Business Products

24369 International Environmental Solutions

6860 Gulfport Blvd S.
Suite 131
South Pasadena, FL 33707-2108

727-573-1676
Fax: 727-573-0747   800-972-8348
davidleeti@aol.com   www.drycamping.com

Automatic faucet controls
President: Steve Gordon
Estimated Sales: Less than $500,000
Number Employees: 20-49
Square Footage: 16000
Brands:
   Ez Flo
   Med Flo
   Quik Flo
   Sani-Flow

24370 International EquipmentTrading

960 Woodlands Parkway
Vernon Hills, IL 60061-3103

847-913-0777
Fax: 847-913-0785   800-438-4522
info@ietltd.com   www.ietltd.com

Buy, lease, rent, trade, sell refurbished analytical
isntruments
President: Turgay Kaya
Contact: Ceylan Bilgin
   ck@ietltd.com
Estimated Sales: $3 - 5 Million
Number Employees: 5-9

24371 International Flavors &Fragrances Inc.

521 W. 57th St.
New York, NY 10019

212-765-5500
Fax: 212-708-7132   www.iff.com

Scents and flavors.
CEO: Frank Clyburn
Executive VP/CFO: Glenn Richter
Year Founded: 1889
Estimated Sales: $5.1 Billion
Number Employees: 13,700
Number of Products: 38K
Type of Packaging: Bulk

24372 International Food Information Service

the Granary, Bridge Farm
Reading Road, Arborfield
Reading, Berkshire, RG2 9HT
UK

Organization provides high quality food science in-
formation products and services to food industry
professionals worldwide which includes FSTA/Food
Science and Technolcogy Abstracts and Food Sci-
ence Central. Telephone number is +44118 988
3895 and Fax is +44 118 988 5056.
Marketing Director: Danielle Woolley
Other Locations:
   International Food Information Srvc
   Shinfield/Reading UK

24373 International Food Products

150 Larkin Williams Industrial Ct
Fenton, MO 63026

800-227-8427
info@ifpc.com   www.ifpc.com

Food ingredients and additives.

Chairman: Fred Brown

CEO: Clayton Brown
VP, Finance: Kathy Langan
General Manager: Jamie Moritz
VP, Supply Chain: Jennifer Hoerchler
VP, Manufacturing: Mark Warren
Director, Research & Development: An Ho
Human Resources Director: Carrie Harmon
VP, Supply Chain: Jennifer Hoerchler
Year Founded: 1974
Estimated Sales: $150 Million
Number Employees: 50-200
Square Footage: 230000
Type of Packaging: Consumer, Food Service
Other Locations:
   St. Louis MO
   Joplin MO
   Kansas City MO
   Houston TX
   Dallas TX
   Laredo TX
   San Antonio TX
   Indianapolis IN
   Cleveland OH
   Denver CO
   Atlanta GA
   Spokane WA
   Plant City FL
Brands:
   Dairy House Chocolate Dairy Powder
   Dairy House Milk Flavors
   Dairy House Stabalizers
   Dairy House Vitamins
   Ingredion

24374 International Foodservice Manufacturers' Association

180 N Stetson Ave
Suite 850
Chicago, IL 60601-6766

312-540-4400
Fax: 312-540-4401   ifma@ifmaworld.com
www.ifmaworld.com

President/CEO: Phil Kafarakis
Chief Financial Officer: Jennifer Tarulis
SVP, Member Value: Mike Schwartz
Senior Director, Marketing: Alvaro Rojas
VP, Sales/Member Services: Anthony DePaolo
Estimated Sales: $20-50 Million
Number Employees: 10-19

24375 International Fresh-CutProduce Association

1600 Duke Street
Suite 440
Alexandria, VA 22314-3400

703-299-6282
Fax: 703-299-6288
www.creativew.com/sites/ifpa/index_main.html

Represents leaders in the fresh-cut produce industry
who specialize in today's growing fresh food cate-
gory.
President: Edith Garrett
VP, Technical and Regulatory Affairs: James
Roman Gorny, PhD.
Director, Communications: Ken Hodge
Director, Marketing: Loren Queen
Director Membership: Reta Jones
Administrator: Seneta Burns
Number Employees: 5-9

24376 International Fruit Marketing

1201 S Orlando Ave # 340
Winter Park, FL 32789-7107

407-628-1121
Fax: 407-628-1829   intlfruit@aol.com

Fruit drinks, pure concentrates and citrus purees
President/CEO: Gene Hays
CFO: Robert Keyes
Vice President: Leland Anderson
Estimated Sales: $13 Million+
Number Employees: 1-4
Parent Co: SECO & Golden 100

24377 International Group Inc

2875 N Main St
Oshkosh, WI 54901-1517

920-233-5500
Fax: 920-233-4345

Petroleum wax and wax blends, hot melt coatings
and cheese wax

Manager: Gary Fraaza
   gfraaza@igtwax.com
General Manager: Gary Fraaza
Production Manager: Tom Brunner
Number Employees: 20-49
Square Footage: 120000

24378 International Inflight Food Service Association

455 S 4th St # 650
Louisville, KY 40202-2554

502-583-3783
Fax: 502-589-3602   ifsa@hqtrs.com

End to end direct marketing provider.
President: David Cawood
Director Administration: Aimee Spigner
Executive of Administration: Phillip Cooke
Estimated Sales: $5-10 Million
Number Employees: 50-99

24379 International Ingredients Corporation

4240 Utah Street
Saint Louis, MO 63116-1820

314-776-2700
Fax: 314-776-3395   iicag@iicag.com
www.iicag.com

Processing of food plant waste
President: Bill Holtgrieve
Chairman: Fred E Brown Jr
Contact: Lisa Filkins
   lfilkins@ifpc.com
Estimated Sales: $30 - 50 Million
Number Employees: 130

24380 International Knife & Saw

1435 N Cashua Dr
Florence, SC 29501-6950

843-662-6345
Fax: 843-664-1103   800-354-9872
www.iksinc.com

Manufacturer and exporter of fruit and vegetable
slicing machinery; also, machine knives
President: Don Weeks
Vice President of Division: Terry Isaacs
Vice President, Metal & Printing Divisio: Jim
Ranson
Sales: Warren Balderson
Manager: Robb Kirkpatrick
   rkirkpatrick@iksinc.com
Vice President, Finance & Manufacturing: Mike
Gray
Purchasing Manager of Materials: Sarah Strother
Estimated Sales: $60 Million
Number Employees: 50-99

24381 International Kosher Supervision

351 Keller E Price Street
Suite 200
Keller, TX 76248

817-337-4700
Fax: 817-337-4901   www.ikckosher.com

Kosher food certification agency with rabbinical
staff
Rabbinical Administration: Rabbi Dovid Jenkins
General Manager: Jerry Dillig
Parent Co: Texas K International

24382 International MachineryXchnge

214 N Main St
Deerfield, WI 53531-9644

608-764-5481
Fax: 608-764-8240   800-279-0191
sales@imexchange.com   www.imexchange.com

Manufacturer and exporter of re-manufactured ma-
chinery including refrigeration, cheese making, cen-
trifuges, compressors and heat exchangers; also,
tanks and custom control systems
President: Greg Mergen
   sales@imexchange.com
Sales Director: George Bamman
Estimated Sales: $5-10 Million
Number Employees: 10-19
Square Footage: 80000

24383 International Meat Inspection Consultants

P.O. Box 264
Germantown, MD 20875-0264

301-570-1058
Fax: 240-821-5939   imic@thefoodtrainer.com
www.thefoodtrainer.com

Consultants, importing/exporting, label expediting

President: Barbara Bennett
CFO: John Cucl
Estimated Sales: $.5 - 1 million
Number Employees: 1-4

24384 International Media & Cultures
1250 South Parker Road Ste. 203
Denver, CO 80231
303-337-4028
Fax: 303-337-5140 mantha@earthnet.net
www.askimac.com
Cheese anti-caking agent and starter media
President: Malireddy Reddy
Plant Manager: Ed Price
Estimated Sales: $5 - 10 Million
Number Employees: 10-19

24385 International Molded Packaging Corporation
206 Central Main Street
Central City, SD 57754-2070
605-578-2500
Fax: 605-578-3933 800-307-2194
www.impakcorp.com
President and CEO: Rod Galland
Estimated Sales: Below $5,000,000
Number Employees: 10

24386 International Omni-Pac Corporation
2079 Wright Ave
La Verne, CA 91750-5822
909-593-2833
Fax: 909-593-2829 bobdavis@omni-pac.com
www.omni-pac.com
Manufacturer and exporter of packaging systems
and juice and soft drink bottle carriers
President: Richard Erickson
Sales Manager: Bob Davis
Contact: Bill Johnston
 bjohnston@omni-pac.com
Estimated Sales: Below $5 Million
Number Employees: 5-9
Square Footage: 40000

24387 International PackagingMachinery
PO Box 8597
Naples, FL 34101-8597
941-643-2020
Fax: 941-643-2708 800-237-6496
Manufacturer and exporter of stretch wrapping ma-
chinery including film tensioners and stretch film
delivery systems
Estimated Sales: $5-10 Million
Number Employees: 20-49
Square Footage: 42000
Brands:
 Ipm
 Roller-Brake
 Uni-Tension

24388 International PackagingNetwork
409 N Jefferson Street
Kearney, MO 64060-8379
816-628-3002
Fax: 800-247-4904 800-932-3597
High performance and flexibility polyolefin film
Estimated Sales: $500,000-$1 Million
Number Employees: 1-4

24389 (HQ)International Paper BoxMachine Company
PO Box 787
Nashua, NH 03061-0787
603-889-6651
Fax: 603-882-2865
Manufacturer, exporter and importer of carton fold-
ing and gluing machinery; also, corrugated convert-
ers including liquid-tight packaging
President: Hugh McAdam
Marketing Manager: Larry Macko
Marketing Communications Manager: Michael
Sutcliffe
Estimated Sales: $20-50 Million
Number Employees: 100-249
Square Footage: 165000

24390 International Paper Co.
6400 Poplar Avenue
Memphis, TN 38197
www.internationalpaper.com

Fiber-based packaging, pulp and paper. Products in-
clude coated paperboard, containerboard, corrugated
packaging, and other foodservice packaging
material.
Chairman/Chief Executive Officer: Mark Sutton
SVP, Paper the Americas: W. Michael Amick, Jr.
SVP, Corporate Development: John Sims
SVP/Chief Financial Officer: Tim Nicholls
SVP, Industrial Packaging the Americas:
Jean-Michel Ribieras
SVP/Human Resources/Global Citizenship: Thomas
Plath
SVP/General Counsel/Corporate Secretary: Sharon
Ryan
SVP/Global Cellulose Fibers: Catherine Slater
SVP/North American Container: Gegory Wanta
Year Founded: 1898
Estimated Sales: $21.7 Billion
Number Employees: 56,000

24391 International Patterns,Inc.
50 Inez Dr
Bay Shore, NY 11706-2238
631-952-2000
Fax: 516-938-1215
Manufacturer and exporter of illuminated and
nonilluminated menu, changeable letter and write-on
boards, nonneon signs, banners, point of purchase
displays, tray stands, ice-free wine coolers and youth
chairs
President: Shelley Beckwith
 shelleyb@u.washington.edu
CFO: Shelly Beckwi
Vice President: Shellay Beckwith
R & D: Paul Kaplan
VP Marketing: Murray Gottieb
VP Sales: Andrew Replan
Production Manager: Ran Alvaeri
Purchasing Manager: Nancy St. Nicholas
Estimated Sales: $5-10 Million
Number Employees: 50-99
Number of Brands: 1
Number of Products: 50
Square Footage: 140000
Type of Packaging: Food Service
Brands:
 City Lites
 Comet
 Grandstand
 Lite Writer
 Magnetic Menumaster
 Menu Master
 Menu Master

24392 International Polymers Corp
426 S Aubrey St
Allentown, PA 18109-2769
610-437-5463
Fax: 610-437-1799 800-526-0953
ipc@fast.net www.ipc.org.nz
Reprocessed polyethylene, polypropylene and poly-
styrene
President: David Bates
CEO: Brian Taschler
 btaschler@ipc.org
CFO: Frank Pope
Marketing: Bob Barette
VP Production: Blair Manning
Estimated Sales: $20 - 50 Million
Number Employees: 50-99

24393 International Process Plants-IPP
17 Marlen Drive
Hamilton, NJ 08691-1634
609-586-8004
Fax: 609-586-0002 michaelj@ippe.com
www.ippe.com
Buyers and sellers of new, rebuilt and used process
equipment and plants worldwide. Has an inventory
of over 20,000 items that allow them to offer
on-time and on-budget process solutions
President: Ronald Gale
Executive VP: Jan Gale
VP Sales: Michael Joachim
Number Employees: 500-999

24394 International Reserve Equipment Corporation
46 Chestnut Avenue
Clarendon Hills, IL 60514-1238
708-531-0680
Fax: 630-325-7045

Manufacturer, importer and exporter of food pro-
cessing equipment including centrifuges, separators,
dryers, screeners, mills, filters, mixers and blenders;
also, pollution control; wastewater treatment and
sludge de-wateringequipment
Owner: Robert Mertz
Marketing Manager: Thomas Mertz
Estimated Sales: $1 - 5 Million
Number Employees: 2
Brands:
 Centrifuges
 Dewater Equipment
 Filtration Equipment
 Screeners
 Separators

24395 International Roasting Systems
3450 N State St
Ukiah, CA 95482-3055
707-462-6164
Fax: 707-462-5258
Cleaners, blending and mixing equipment (coffee),
afterburners, automatic controls, grinders, bin silo
systems and storage, bin vibrators, bulk silo services, roasters, smoke control equipment and afterburners, quality controlinstruments and conveying
equipment
Owner: Steve Pardini
Management Consultant: Jane Pfeiffer
Estimated Sales: Less Than $500,000
Number Employees: 5-9

24396 International Smoking Systems
23 Water St
PO Box 480
Ashburnham, MA 01430
978-827-3160
Fax: 978-827-3162 800-269-2367
www.intlsmokingsystems.com
Provides smoking and defrosting kilns for salmon
and fish processing needs
President: Mark Carlisle
Estimated Sales: Under $500,000
Number Employees: 2

24397 International Tank & Pipe Co
PO Box 590
Clackamas, OR 97015-0590
503-288-0011
Fax: 503-493-0372 888-988-0011
Info@WoodTankandPipe.com
woodtankandpipe.com
Manufacture wood stove tanks and pipe. Install new
wood stove tanks and pipe and repair existing tanks
and pipe.
President/CEO: Michael Bye
CFO: Jacqueline Bye
R&D/Purchasing Director: Kent Huschka
Quality Control: Matthew Bye
Marketing/Sales/Production: Michael Bye
Estimated Sales: $2-4 Million
Number Employees: 12
Number of Brands: 2
Square Footage: 40000
Type of Packaging: Consumer
Other Locations:
 Portland OR
Brands:
 International Tank & Pipe
 National Tank & Pipe

24398 International Thermal Dispensers
67 Batterymarch St # 600
Boston, MA 02110-3211
617-239-3600
Fax: 617-239-3650 www.atlanticretail.com
Espresso, hot and cold food vending carts and con-
cession equipment
Managing Partner: Bryan W. Anderson
Partner: Brian Mc Donald
Partner: Ben Starr
Broker: James C. Bagley
 Broker: Adam Cirel
 Broker: Tom Sibley
 Broker: Brian Roache
Sales Manager: Anne McCormick
Estimated Sales: $300,000-500,000
Number Employees: 5-9

24399 International Tray Pads
3299 NC Highway 5
P.O. Box 307
Aberdeen, NC 28315-8619

910-944-1800
Fax: 910-944-7356 www.pactiv.com
Manufacturer and supplier of tray pads for meats and case liners for produce and dairy products.
Contact: Larry Norpoth
lrnorpoth@traypads.com
Number Employees: 20-49

24400 International Wax Refining Company
3 Mountain Blvd
Warren, NJ 07059-5613

908-561-2500
Fax: 908-561-7411 www.villagetravel.com
Bee's wax
President: J D Panella
Executive VP: L Powell
Number Employees: 10-19

24401 International Wood Industries
12027 Three Lakes Rd
Snohomish, WA 98290

360-568-3185
Fax: 509-965-6141 800-922-6141
www.nepapallet.com
Manufacturer and exporter of skids, wooden pallets and bins, couch boxes, baggage boxes, household goods
President: Denton Sherry
General Manager: Joe Carlos
Estimated Sales: $10-20 Million
Number Employees: 100-249
Parent Co: International Wood Industries

24402 (HQ)Interplast
1400 Lytle Road
Troy, OH 45373-9401

937-332-1110
Fax: 937-332-0672
Manufacturer and exporter of plastic custom-injection moldings
Sales Manager: Bob Garton
Contact: Jared Langman
jlangman@interplastinc.com
Estimated Sales: $5-10 Million
Number Employees: 50-99

24403 Interroll Corp
3000 Corporate Dr
Wilmington, NC 28405-7422

910-799-1100
Fax: 910-392-3822 800-830-9680
www.interroll.us
Manufacturer and exporter of conveyor components and flow storage systems
President: Tim Mcgill
t.mcgill@interroll.com
VP: Richard Keely
VP Sales/Marketing: Steve Vineis
Estimated Sales: $20-50 Million
Number Employees: 100-249
Square Footage: 250
Parent Co: Interroll Holding AG
Brands:
    Driveroll
    Joki
    Logix
    Taperhex Gold

24404 Interroll Corp
3000 Corporate Dr
Wilmington, NC 28405-7422

910-799-1100
Fax: 910-392-3822 800-830-9680
www.interroll.us
President: Tim Mcgill
t.mcgill@interroll.com
VP: Richard Keely
Estimated Sales: $20 Million
Number Employees: 100-249

24405 Interstate Monroe Machinery
2230 1st Avenue S
Seattle, WA 98134-1408

206-682-4870
Fax: 313-891-5449
Manufacturer and exporter of controls and instrumentation equipment
General Manager: Larry Gruendike

Estimated Sales: $1-2.5 Million
Number Employees: 9
Square Footage: 30000
Parent Co: Statco Engineering & Fabrication

24406 Interstate Packaging
2285 Highway 47 N
White Bluff, TN 37187-4126

615-797-9000
Fax: 615-797-9411 800-251-1072
ldoochin@interstatepkg.com
www.interstatepkg.com
Manufacturer and exporter of pressure sensitive labels and poly bags; manufacturer of printed flexible films
President: Michael Doochin
mdoochin@interstatepkg.com
Sales Manager: Lawrence Doochin
Customer Service Representative: Robert Garlock
Purchasing Manager: Liz Gilliam
Estimated Sales: $20-50 Million
Number Employees: 250-499
Square Footage: 100000
Type of Packaging: Consumer

24407 Interstate Showcase & Fixture Company
PO Box 402
West Orange, NJ 07052-0402

973-483-5555
Fax: 973-669-0200
Store fixtures, showcases, wallcases and refrigerated candy cases
CEO: L Miller
Estimated Sales: Less than $500,000
Number Employees: 1-4
Square Footage: 50000

24408 Intertape Polymer Group
741 4th St
Menasha, WI 54952-2801

920-725-4335
Fax: 920-729-4217 800-558-5006
www.itape.com
Manufacturer and exporter of printed and plain pressure sensitive and gummed tapes: kraft paper and reinforced carton sealing; pressure sensitive carton sealing machine systems
President: Dale McSween
Manager: Bob Mc Donald
rmcdonal@itape.com
Product Manager: Steve Pistro
Product Manager: Tom Zettler
Plant Manager: John Cullen
Estimated Sales: $2.5-5 Million
Number Employees: 100-249
Parent Co: Intertape Polymer Group

24409 Intertape Polymer Group
100 Paramount Dr
Suite 300
Sarasota, FL 34232

888-898-7834
www.itape.com
Manufacturer of paper- and film-based, pressure-sensitive and water-activated tapes
President & CEO: Gregory Yull
CFO: Jeffrey Crystal
SVP, Sales: Shawn Nelson
SVP, Operations: Douglas Nalette
Year Founded: 1981
Number Employees: 2,200

24410 (HQ)Intertech Corp
3240 N Ohenry Blvd
Greensboro, NC 27405-3808

336-621-1891
Fax: 336-621-1893 800-364-2255
www.ezgowalker-ball.com
Plastic bottles
President: Jack Worsham
VP: Leon Worsham
VP: Jim Sitton
Estimated Sales: $5-10 Million
Number Employees: 50-99
Square Footage: 232000

24411 (HQ)Intertek USA
70 Codman Hill Rd
Boxborough, MA 01719-1737

978-263-7086
Fax: 978-264-9403 800-967-5352
icenter@intertek.com www.intertek.com

Laboratory specializing in the testing of food service equipment
President: Greegg Tiemann
Chief Executive Officer: Wolfhart Hauser
Division Executive Vice President: Andrew Swift
Marketing Director: Erik Holladay
Business Development Manager: Carlos Velasco
Estimated Sales: $30 - 50 Million
Number Employees: 50-99
Square Footage: 150000
Other Locations:
    Intertak Testing Services
    Cortland NY

24412 Intralox LLC
301 Plantation Rd
Harahan, LA 70123-5326

504-733-0463
Fax: 504-734-0063 800-535-8848
www.intralox.com
Manufacturer and exporter of USDA accepted and FDA compliant modular plastic screw conveyors and conveyor belting
President: James Lapeyre Jr
Marketing Manager: Michelle Waite
National Sales Manager: Da Waters
Number Employees: 500-999
Parent Co: Laitram Corporation
Brands:
    Intralox, Inc.

24413 Intralox LLC
301 Plantation Rd
Harahan, LA 70123-5326

504-733-0463
Fax: 504-734-0063 www.intralox.com
Designers and manufacturers of conveyor belt systems for the meat, poultry, seafood and beverage industries.
President: James M Lapeyre Jr
Number Employees: 500-999

24414 Intralytix
701 E Pratt St # 400
Rm 4036
Baltimore, MD 21202-3190

410-625-1224
Fax: 410-625-2506 877-489-7424
info@intralytix.com www.intralytix.com
Produces bacteriophage-based products to control bacterial pathogens in food processing
Number Employees: 10-19

24415 Intrex
149 Grassy Plain St
Bethel, CT 06801-2851

203-792-7400
Fax: 203-778-3991
Waste receptacles, smoking urns and planters; custom design available
President: Steven Decker
CEO: Mary Edgerton
Quality Control: Jim Patnaude
Chairman: Philip Feinman
Estimated Sales: Below $5 Million
Number Employees: 20-49

24416 Introdel Products
1339 Industrial Drive
PO Box 723
Itasca, IL 60143-1847

630-773-4250
Fax: 907-562-8517 800-323-4772
Water conditioning and filtration products including nonchemical cartridges for use in steamers, combi ovens, warewashing equipment, ice machines, water wash hoods, coffee and tea equipment, post mix applications, etc
Estimated Sales: $500,000-$1,000,000
Number Employees: 19

24417 Invensys APV Products
10900 Equity Drive
Houston, TX 77041

713-329-1600
Fax: 920-648-1441 apvproducts.us@apv.com
Supplier of a wide range of pumps, valves, heat exchangers and homogenisers designed for use in the food, dairy and brewing industries
Executive Director: Jim Keene
Marketing Communications Manager: Antonella Crimi
Contact: Frank Alphonsoo
frank.alphonsoo@invensys.com

Parent Co: Invensys Limited
Type of Packaging: Food Service, Bulk

24418 Invensys Process Systems
5100 River Road
3rd Floor
Schiller Park, IL 60176-1058

847-678-4300
Fax: 847-678-4300 888-278-9087
answers@apv.com www.apv.com
Project Sales Manager: Enrique Hinojosa
Contact: Anna Butorac
anna.butorac@invensys.com

24419 Invictus Systems Corporation
5505 Seminary Rd Apt 2210n
Suite 202
Falls Church, VA 22041-3544

Fax: 703-503-8064
www.govcon.com/storefronts/invictus
Manufacturer and exporter of custom computer software for the food industry including facts panel creation, nutrition calculators, formula costing, time to market analysis and operations planning. Our services include custom websoftware for both internal and external use
President: Anthony Latta
CFO: Kim Witney
Chief Scientist: Kenneth Latta
Quality Control: Benson Wetta
Business Developer: Scott Weaver
Estimated Sales: Below $5 Million
Number Employees: 20-49
Number of Products: 3
Square Footage: 30000
Type of Packaging: Bulk

24420 Iowa Rotocast Plastics Inc
1712 Moellers Dr
Decorah, IA 52101-7304

563-382-9636
Fax: 563-382-3016 800-553-0050
irp@irpinc.com
Portable bars, special event carts and super coolers
President: Floyd Mount
VP Sales: Steve Rolfs
Estimated Sales: $10 Million
Number Employees: 100-249

24421 (HQ)Ipec
185 Northgate Circle
New Castle, PA 16105

800-377-4732
Fax: 724-658-3054 www.ipec.biz
Supplier of plastic closures and capping equipment
President: Joseph Giordano Jr
Sales Manager: Robert Harding
Estimated Sales: $22 Million
Number Employees: 75

24422 Irby
2913 S Church St
Rocky Mount, NC 27803

252-442-0154
Fax: 252-442-4909 www.irby.com
Custom fabricated metal food service equipment including conveyors, racks, stampers, welders, parts, etc
President: Mike Wigton
Chief Financial Officer: John Honigfort
Vice President of Supply Chain: Dave Armstrong
Vice President of Sales: Chad Cravens
Chief Operating Officer: Andy Waring
Plant Manager: Tony Whitley
Estimated Sales: $.5 - 1 million
Number Employees: 1-4
Square Footage: 112000

24423 Iron Out
7201 Engle Rd
Fort Wayne, IN 46804-2228

260-483-2519
Fax: 260-483-2277 888-476-6688
info@summitbrands.com
Cleaning products
Owner: Joel Harter
Executive VP: Stan Stuart
Contact: Mike Brown
mbrown@summitbrands.com
Estimated Sales: $5-10 Million
Number Employees: 5-9
Brands:
All Out

Drain Out
Super Iron Out
Super Iron Out Dignio
Yellow Out

24424 Ironwood Displays
PO Box 632
Niles, MI 49120-0632

231-683-8500
Fax: 231-683-6803
Store fixtures and wooden and plexiglass display racks
Director Marketing: Judy Truesdell
Number Employees: 25

24425 Irresistible Cookie Jar
PO Box 3230
Hayden Lake, ID 83835-3230

208-664-1261
Fax: 208-667-1347
service@irresistiblecookiejar.com
Cookie and muffin mixes, cookie cutters and decorations
President: Wanda Hall
Estimated Sales: $300,000-500,000
Number Employees: 10
Brands:
Boyds' Kissa Bearhugs
Mimi's Muffins
Susan Winget

24426 Irvine Analytical Labs
10 Vanderbilt
Irvine, CA 92618

949-951-4425
Fax: 949-951-4909 877-445-6554
info@ialab.com www.irvinepharma.com
Laboratory offering chemical and microbiological analysis for food and food supplements
President: Iassad Kazeminy
CEO: Assad J. Kazeminy
Lab Director: Assad Kazeminy
Regional Sales Representative: JoAnne Nordel
Contact: Tandis Kazeminy
tandis.kazeminy@irvinepharma.com
Business Development Manager: Rambod Omid
Estimated Sales: Less than $500,000
Number Employees: 50-99
Square Footage: 50000
Parent Co: Irvine Analytical Labs

24427 Irvine Pharmaceutical Services
10 Vanderbilt
Irvine, CA 92618

949-951-4425
Fax: 949-951-4909 877-445-6554
www.irvinepharma.com
Contract laboratory, chemical and microbiological testing services
President: Iassad Kazeminy
Laboratory Director: Abbass Kamalizad
Contact: Ayla Acosta
ayla.acosta@irvinepharma.com
Business Development Manager: Gregory McLaughlin
Estimated Sales: $10 - 20 Million
Number Employees: 50-99

24428 Irwin Research & Development
2601 W J St
Yakima, WA 98902-5291

509-248-0494
Fax: 509-248-3503 www.irwinresearch.com
Thermoforming equipment, tooling and granulators.
President: Jere Irwin
Sales and Marketing Representative: Craig Richardson
Estimated Sales: $10-20 Million
Number Employees: 100-249

24429 Isbre Holding Corporation
225 Glen Rd
Woodcliff Lake, NJ 07677

201-802-0005
Fax: 201-802-0006
Bottled spring drinking water.
President: Stevan A Sandberg
Regional Director of Sales: Rene Skanning

24430 Island Delights, Inc.
5104 Greenwich Road
Seville, OH 44273

330-769-2800
Fax: 330-769-3935 866-877-4100
acrall@islanddelights.com
www.islanddelights.com
Coconut candies
Sales: Ann Crall
Sales: Greg Miller
Estimated Sales: $5-10 Million
Number Employees: 15

24431 Island Oasis Frozen Cocktail
3400 Millington Rd.
Beloit, WI 53511

508-660-1177
Fax: 508-660-1435 800-777-4752
www.kerryfoodservice.com/pages/island-originals
Non-alcoholic beverage mixes, ice shavers and blenders.
Estimated Sales: $20-50 Million
Number Employees: 100-249
Number of Products: 16
Square Footage: 25000
Parent Co: Kerry Food Services

24432 Island Poly
514 Grand Blvd
Westbury, NY 11590-4712

516-338-4433
Fax: 516-338-4405 800-338-4433
Gloves including vinyl, natural latex, poly and cut resistant; also, natural rubber nitrile, neoprene and poly aprons, bouffant head caps and beard covers
President: Dan Grinberg
Controller: Denise Ramo
Director Marketing: Jane Donnelly
Estimated Sales: $2.5 - 5 Million
Number Employees: 20-49
Brands:
Foodhandler
Jobhandler

24433 Island Scallops
5552 Island Highway W
Qualicum Beach, BC V9K 2C8
Canada

250-757-9811
Fax: 250-757-8370 www.islandscallops.com
Fresh and frozen scallops; marine research hatchery
President/CEO: Robert Saunders
R&D: Barb Bunting
Processing Manager: Lorraine Hopps
Estimated Sales: $1 Million
Number Employees: 10
Type of Packaging: Consumer, Food Service

24434 Isotherm Inc
7401 Commercial Blvd E
Arlington, TX 76001-7142

817-472-9922
Fax: 817-472-5878 info@iso-therm.com
www.iso-therm.com
President: Zahid Ayub
info@iso-therm.com
Engineering Manager: Adnan Ayub
Production Manager: Al Faisal
Estimated Sales: $5 - 10 Million
Number Employees: 10-19

24435 It's A Corker
P.O. Box 11549
Chattanooga, TN 37401-2549

423-756-1200
Fax: 423-266-5913
Wine industry closures
President: Robert P Corker
Executive Assistant, Chief Executive Off: Carolyn Stringer
Controller: Beth Robertson
CEO: Kim Hudson White
Estimated Sales: $.5 - 1 million
Number Employees: 5-9

24436 Itac Label & Tag Corp
179 Lexington Ave
Brooklyn, NY 11216-1114

718-625-2148
Fax: 718-625-3806
Manufacturer and exporter of labels including pressure sensitive, magnetic, shipping, bar code and file folder; also, tags and decals

President: Sidney Alder
CEO: James H C Tao
Estimated Sales: $5-10 Million
Number Employees: 10-19
Square Footage: 28000
Brands:
  Ul

24437 Italgi USA
2 Titan Drive
Chestnut Ridge, NY 10977-6727
800-706-9338
Fax: 845-371-6145
Manufacturer of professional pasta machines

24438 Italtech
3425 NW 112 STREET
Miami, FL 33167
305-256-9651
Fax: 305-685-0990 800-547-5075
Pasta and noodle equipment, extruders, dryers, mixers, dies, pasteurizers, noodle cutters, sheeters, Italian equipment for confectionery industry
Engineering Director: Romolo Battistini
Estimated Sales: $2.5-5 Million
Number Employees: 1-4

24439 Item Products
16111 Park Entry Drive
Suite 100
Houston, TX 77041-4077
281-893-0100
Fax: 281-893-4836 800-333-4932
Manufacturer and exporter of carts and storage racks; also, consultant specializing in the design of custom machinery
Marketing Coordinator: Claudia Sears
National Marketing Manager: Jim Boyd
Estimated Sales: $10-20,000,000
Number Employees: 20-49
Square Footage: 60000

24440 Ito Packing Company
707 W South Ave
Reedley, CA 93654
559-638-2531
Fax: 559-638-2282 craigi@itopack.com
Packs and ships fruit
President: Craig Ito
Contact: James Ito
  stephi93654@yahoo.com
Estimated Sales: $45 Million
Number Employees: 1,000-4,999
Brands:
  Red Jim
  Ufo

24441 Iug Business Solutions
132 Nassau Street
Room 1402
New York, NY 10038-2424
212-404-6168
Fax: 212-404-6180 dphelps@iug.net
Accessories/supplies i.e. picnic baskets, display fixtures.
Marketing: Edward Ip
Contact: Edward Ip
  sales@iug.net
Chief Operating Officer: Michael Lazarus

24442 Ivarson Inc
3100 W Green Tree Rd
Milwaukee, WI 53209-2535
414-351-0700
Fax: 414-351-4551 sales@ivarsoninc.com
www.ivarsoninc.com
Manufacturer and exporter of process and packaging equipment and parts for butter, cheese and margarine industries; also, set-up boxes
President: Glenn Ivarson
  givarson@ivarsoninc.com
Engineering Manager: Chuck Ellingson
Manager Technical Services: Jim Wycklendt
Sales Director: Mark Mullinix
Estimated Sales: $10 - 20 Million
Number Employees: 50-99
Square Footage: 100200

24443 Ivarson Inc
3100 W Green Tree Rd
Milwaukee, WI 53209-2535
414-351-0700
Fax: 414-351-4551 cellingson@ivarsoninc.com
www.ivarsoninc.com

Brining systems, butter processing equipment, cheese equipment, custom fabrication, cutting equipment, heat exchangers, scraped surface, margarine processing equipment, piping, fittings and tubing
President and R&D: Glenn Ivarson
  givarson@ivarsoninc.com
CFO: Lennie Ivarson
Estimated Sales: $20 - 50 Million
Number Employees: 50-99

24444 Ives-Way Products
2030 N Nicole Ln
Round Lake Beach, IL 60073-2288
847-740-0658
Manufacturer and exporter of automatic can sealers for food, giftware or other sealed shipping containers
VP: Laura Ours
Estimated Sales: Less Than $500,000
Number Employees: 1-4
Square Footage: 4000

24445 Iwatani International Corporation of America
2200 Post oak Blvd.
Suite 1150
Houston, TX 77056
713-965-9970
Fax: 713-963-8497 800-775-5506
www.iwatani.com
Manufacturer and importer of portable butane stoves and induction cookers.
Regional Sales Manager: Karen Buquicchio
National Sales Manager: Gary Rodgers
Estimated Sales: $5-10 Million
Number Employees: 5-9
Parent Co: Iwatani International
Brands:
  Cassette Feu

24446 Izabel Lam International
204 Van Dyke Street
Brooklyn, NY 11231-1038
718-797-3983
Fax: 718-797-0030 info@izabellam.com
www.izabellam.com
Manufacturer and exporter of tabletop products including cutlery, dinnerware and drinkware
Estimated Sales: $500,000-$1 Million
Number Employees: 1-4
Square Footage: 112000
Type of Packaging: Consumer, Food Service
Brands:
  Glacier
  Golden Wind
  Morning Tide
  Mt. Rainbow Series
  Pale Wind
  Rushing Tide
  Sphere
  Splash
  Wind Over Water

24447 J & J Industries Inc
107 Gateway Rd
Bensenville, IL 60106-1950
630-595-8878
Fax: 630-595-9010
Nonmetallic die cut parts including gaskets and noise control materials
Owner: Jerry Haug
  jgasket@hotmail.com
General Manager: Grant Cramer
Estimated Sales: $1-2.5 Million
Number Employees: 1-4

24448 J & J Window Sales Inc
600 Cepi Dr
Chesterfield, MO 63005-1244
636-532-3320
Fax: 636-532-3864
www.jandjsidingandwindows.com
Commercial awnings
President: Sue Gittemeier
  sue@jandjwindows.com
Estimated Sales: $500,000-$1 Million
Number Employees: 10-19

24449 J & L Honing
4150 S Nevada St
St Francis, WI 53235-4515
414-744-9500
Fax: 414-744-9515 800-747-9501
contact@jlhoning.com www.jlhoning.com

Sanitary finishing for stainless steel tubing; also, ID polishing and honing of tubing and piping available
President: David Putney
VP: David Putney
Operations Manager: Dana Felske
Estimated Sales: Below $5 Million
Number Employees: 5-9
Square Footage: 60000

24450 J & M Industries Inc
300 Ponchatoula Pkwy
Ponchatoula, LA 70454-8311
985-386-6000
Fax: 985-386-9066 800-989-1002
www.jm-ind.com
Packaging supplies
President & CFO: Maurice Gaudet IV
  marnold@jm-ind.com
Quality Control: Tim Sanders
Marketing Director: Ricky Brossard
Sales Exec: Mark Arnold
Plant Manager: Lance Powers
Plant Manager: Lance Powers
Purchasing: Ruth Sweeney
Estimated Sales: $20 - 50 Million
Number Employees: 100-249

24451 J & R Mfg Inc
820 W Kearney St # B
Mesquite, TX 75149-8804
972-289-0801
Fax: 972-288-9488 800-527-4831
sales@jrmanufacturing.com
www.jrmanufacturing.com
Manufacturer and exporter of barbecue pits, broilers, grills, rotisseries and combo broiler/rotisseries
Vice President: Trent Hamrick
  trent.hamrick@jrmanufacturing.net
VP: Larry Bellows
Estimated Sales: $5 - 10 Million
Number Employees: 20-49
Square Footage: 60000
Brands:
  Combo
  Fabuloso
  Little Red Smokehouse
  Oyler
  Smoke-Master
  Spinnin' Spits
  Wood Show

24452 J A Emilius Sons
537 Woodland Ave
Cheltenham, PA 19012-2195
215-379-6162
Fax: 215-663-8985 800-224-6162
sales@emilius.com www.emilius.com
Machine shop, conveyors, conveyor belt, confectionery equipment confectionery, bakery, food process equipment
Owner: Carl A Emilius Iii
CFO: Beth Emilius
Sales: Vince McCabe
Estimated Sales: $1 - 2.5 Million
Number Employees: 10-19
Number of Brands: 4

24453 J A Heilferty & Co
133 Cedar Ln # 104
Teaneck, NJ 07666-4416
201-836-5060
Fax: 201-836-3275 info@primepak.com
www.primepakcompany.com
Manufacturer, importer and exporter of HDPE and LLDPE poly bags, sheeting, box and trash can liners, T-sacks and plain and printed bags
Owner: William Poppe
Chief Financial Officer: Mike Heilferty
VP Sales: William Heilferty
VP Operations: Chris Poppe
Estimated Sales: $20 - 50 Million
Number Employees: 20-49
Square Footage: 120000
Brands:
  Prime Liner
  Primeliner Sacks
  Primeliners

24454 J C Ford Co
901 S Leslie St
La Habra, CA 90631-6841
714-871-7361
Fax: 714-773-5827 www.jcford.com

Manufacturer and exporter of cooling conveyors, corn masa feeders, tamale steamers and extruders, tortilla and chip ovens, tortilla sheeter and corn cookers and grinders
Sales: Robert Meyer
Customer Service: Desi Sanchez
Engineer: Thomas Dosch
Estimated Sales: $5-10 Million
Number Employees: 5-9
Square Footage: 40000
Brands:
  J.C. Ford Co.

24455 J C Industries Inc
89 Eads St
West Babylon, NY 11704-1186
631-420-1920
Fax: 631-420-0467 800-322-1189
Refuse handling equipment
President: Joseph Celano
  jcelano@jcindustriesinc.com
Sales Exec: James Celano
Estimated Sales: $3 - 5 Million
Number Employees: 20-49

24456 (HQ)J C Whitlam Mfg Co
200 W Walnut St
Wadsworth, OH 44281-1379
330-334-2524
Fax: 330-334-3005 800-321-8358
www.whitlampaint.com
Manufacturer and exporter of refrigeration chemicals, waterless hand cleaners and other cleaning chemicals
President: Jack Whitlam
  sales@jcwhitlam.com
CFO: Doug Whitlam
Senior VP: Doug Whitlam
VP Operations: Steve Carey
Estimated Sales: $5-10 Million
Number Employees: 20-49
Square Footage: 280000

24457 J E M Mfg LLC
1901 Parrish Dr SE
Rome, GA 30161-9576
706-232-1709
Fax: 706-802-1175 www.jemmfg.com
Water pollution treatment and monitoring, analytical laboratory services
Owner: Chris Mauer
  cmauer@jemsalesinc.com
Estimated Sales: $2.5-5 Million
Number Employees: 10-19

24458 J L Becker Co
41150 Joy Rd
Plymouth, MI 48170-4634
734-656-2000
Fax: 734-656-2009 800-837-4328
www.jlbecker.com
Manufacturer and exporter of heat treating furnaces and conveyor belts including wire mesh and flat wire
President: John Becker
CEO: Wayne Webbe
CFO: Ellen Beckor
Vice President: John Beckor
Sales Manager: David Peterson
Estimated Sales: $10-20 Million
Number Employees: 20-49
Type of Packaging: Bulk

24459 J L Clark Corp
923 23rd Ave
Rockford, IL 61104-7173
815-962-8861
Fax: 815-966-5862 www.jlclark.com
Manufacturer and exporter of decorative tin cans and injection molded plastic dispensing closures
President: Bob Morris
CFO: Christine Albert
Estimated Sales: $50,000,000 - $99,999,999
Number Employees: 250-499
Parent Co: Clarcor Consumer Products
Type of Packaging: Consumer, Food Service, Private Label

24460 J Leek Assoc Inc
145 Peanut Dr
Edenton, NC 27932-9604
252-482-4456
Fax: 252-482-5370

Laboratory providing aflatoxin, microbiological, pesticide residue and chemical/physical analyses of food and feed products; services also include product development, packaging, shelf life and sensory studies, etc
Manager Analytical Services: Mike Jackson
Manager: Mike Jackson
Estimated Sales: $1-2.5 Million
Number Employees: 10-19
Square Footage: 21600
Parent Co: Seabrook Enterprises

24461 (HQ)J M Canty Inc E1200 Engineers
6100 Donner Rd
Lockport, NY 14094-9227
716-625-4227
Fax: 716-625-4228 sales@jmcanty.com
www.cantylight.com
Manufacturer and exporter of fiber optic lighting, image processing and inspection and color analysis
President: Thomas Canty
Quality Control: Dan Raby
VP: Tod Canty
Manager: Chris Miller
  chrism@jmcanty.com
Estimated Sales: $5 - 10 Million
Number Employees: 20-49
Square Footage: 152000
Other Locations:
  Canty
  Dublin, Ireland
Brands:
  Canty

24462 J M Packaging Co
26300 Bunert Rd
Warren, MI 48089-3639
586-771-7800
Fax: 586-771-5440 www.jmindustries.com
Manufacturer and exporter of printed tapes and labels; contract packaging available
Owner: Corey Bunch
  cbunch@jmindustries.com
VP: Michael Jones
Estimated Sales: $5-10 Million
Number Employees: 50-99
Type of Packaging: Bulk

24463 J M Swank Co
395 Herky St
North Liberty, IA 52317-8523
319-626-3683
Fax: 319-626-3662 800-593-6375
www.jmswank.com
Food ingredients for the dairy, beverage, meat, bakery, snack, confection, ethnic and prepared foods industries
CEO: Shawn Meaney
Chief Financial Officer: Philip Garton
Senior Vice President: Paul Hillen
Vice President, Sales & Customer Service: Linda Loucks
Vice President, Operations: Reggie Hastings
Estimated Sales: $6 Million
Number Employees: 100-249
Parent Co: Conagra Brands
Other Locations:
  Swank Great Lakes
  Carol Stream IL
  Swank South
  Dallas TX
  Swank West
  Denver CO
  Tolleson AZ
  Buena Park CA
  Modesto CA
  Atlanta CA
  Cedar Rapids IA
  Iowa IA
  Kansas KS
  Wichita KS
  Louisville KY
  Mansfield MA

24464 J R Short Milling Co
1580 Grinnell Rd
Kankakee, IL 60901-8246
815-523-9987
Fax: 815-937-3981 800-544-8734
www.shortmill.com
A bakery ingredient supplier company that transforms natural grains into functional foods.

Founder: J.R. Short
COO: Sonny Beckman
  sbeckman@shortmill.com
Year Founded: 1910
Estimated Sales: $10-20 Million
Number Employees: 100-249

24465 J Rettenmaier USA LP
16369 US Highway 131 S
Schoolcraft, MI 49087-9150
269-679-2340
Fax: 269-679-2364 877-895-4099
info@jrsusa.com www.jrs.de
Researcher, developer and processor of organic fibers derived from vegetable raw materials that are used as functional additives and pulps.
Director of Administration & Controlling: Gerhard Goss
CEO: Thorsten Willmann
Director of Business Development: Curtis Rath
Director of Sales, Food Division: Dia Panzer-Biddle
Manager: Katie Bush
  eyeluvme1991@yahoo.com
Estimated Sales: $12 Million
Number Employees: 50-99
Parent Co: J. Rettenmaier & Sohne GmbH & Co KG

24466 J W Hulme Co
678 7th St W
St Paul, MN 55102-3198
651-222-7359
Fax: 651-228-1181 800-442-8212
sales@jwhulmeco.com
Sport bags, gun cases, duffles, breifcases and luggage.
Owner: Chuck Bidwell
  cbidwell@jwhulmeco.com
Estimated Sales: $500,000-1,000,000
Number Employees: 20-49

24467 J&J Corrugated Box Corporation
210 Grove St
Franklin, MA 02038-3119
508-528-6200
Fax: 508-528-2316
Corrugated boxes
Manager: Dan McKinney
General Manager: Richard Koestner
Estimated Sales: $20-50 Million
Number Employees: 100-249
Parent Co: Georgia-Pacific

24468 J&J Mid-South ContainerCorporation
1745 Doug Barnard Pkwy
Augusta, GA 30906-9277
706-798-7420
Fax: 706-793-6947 800-395-1025
www.georgiapacific.com
Corrugated shipping containers
President: Brent Paugh
Chief Executive Officer, President: James Hannan
Executive Vice President: Christian Fischer
Executive Vice President of Operations: Wesley Jones
Estimated Sales: $20-50 Million
Number Employees: 100-249
Parent Co: Georgia-Pacific Corporation

24469 J&M Laboratories
12 Nordson Dr
Dawsonville, GA 30534
706-216-1520
Fax: 706-216-1517 www.nordson.com
Tea and coffee industry filters
VP: George Porter
Contact: Justin Clark
  jclark@nordson.com
Estimated Sales: $30 - 50 Million
Number Employees: 100-249

24470 J. James
723 Lorimer Street
Brooklyn, NY 11211-1311
718-384-6144
Fax: 718-384-6112 www.jjames.com
Place mats and tray covers
Estimated Sales: less than $500,000
Number Employees: 1-4

24471 J. R. Simplot Co.
PO Box 27
Boise, ID 83707-0027

208-336-2110
jrs_info@simplot.com
www.simplot.com
Food manufacturing, seed production, farming, fertilizer manufacturing and frozen-food processing.
Chairman: Scott Simplot
President/CEO: Garrett Lofto
Year Founded: 1929
Estimated Sales: $6 Billion
Number Employees: 11,000
Number of Products: 1000
Type of Packaging: Consumer, Food Service, Private Label
Other Locations:
J.R. Simplot Potato Processing
Aberdeen ID
J.R. Simplot Potato Processing
Caldwell ID
J.R. Simplot Potato Processing
Grand Forks ND
J.R. Simplot Potato Processing
Moses Lake WA
J.R. Simplot Potato Processing
Nampa ID
J.R. Simplot Potato Processing
Othello WA
J.R. Simplot Vegetable Processing
West Memphis AR
Brands:
Batter Bites
Bent Arm Ale
Conquest
Farmhouse Originals
Freezefridge
Infinity
JR Buffalos
Kitchen Craft
Krunchie Wedges
Megacrunch
NaturalCrisp
Old Fashioned Way
RoastWorks
SIDEWINDERS
SeasonedCrisp
Select Recipe
Simplot Classic
Simplot Daily Pick
Simplot Good Grains
Simplot Harvest Fresh Avocados
Simplot Simple Goodness
Simplot Sweets
Simplot Thunder Crunch
Simply Gold
Skincredibles
Spudsters
Tater Pals
Traditional
True Recipe

24472 J. Scott Company
175 Barneveld Ave
San Francisco, CA 94124

415-824-1743
Fax: 415-824-5849   888-OIL-LUBE
jscottco@aol.com
Oils and lubricants
Contact: John Scott
jscottco@msn.com
Manager: John Scott
Estimated Sales: Below $5 Million
Number Employees: 5-9

24473 J.A. Thurston Company
Route 2
Rumford, ME 04276

207-364-7921
Fax: 207-369-9903
Manufacturer and exporter of chairs and stools
VP: John Thurston
Sales: Cindy Giroux
Estimated Sales: $5 - 10 Million
Number Employees: 5-9

24474 J.C. Products Inc.
66 Ranger Rd
Haddam, CT 6438

860-267-5516
Fax: 860-267-5519
Wire products including displays, racks and bread, roll and rotisserie baskets
Owner: Charles Helenek

Estimated Sales: $2.5-5 Million
Number Employees: 10-19

24475 J.E. Roy
60 Boulevard Begin
St Claire, QC G0R 2V0
Canada

418-883-2711
Fax: 418-838-8008
Manufacturer, importer and exporter of plastic bottles and bottle nasal plugs
President: Ronald Leclair
Quality Control: Nicoles Mertileau
VP Sales: Sylvie Lefevbre
Number Employees: 55
Square Footage: 18000
Type of Packaging: Consumer, Food Service, Private Label
Brands:
Ropak
Roy

24476 J.G. Machine Works
2182 Route 35 South
Holmdel, NJ 07733

732-203-2077
Fax: 732-203-2078 sales@jgmachine.com
www.jgmachine.com
Rotary fillers
Manager: Don Nelson
dnelson@jgmachine.com
National Sales Manager: John McArdle
Number Employees: 20-49

24477 J.H. Carr & Sons
37 S Hudson Street
Seattle, WA 98134-2416

206-763-1937
Fax: 206-763-7033 800-523-8842
jerryacarr@msn.com www.jhcarr.com
Bars, tables and bases, chairs, booths, barstools and service cabinets
VP Marketing/General Manager: Jerry Carr
Sales Manager: Wayne Muliner
Contact: James Carr
jim.carr@jhcarr.com
Estimated Sales: $5 Million
Number Employees: 25-49
Square Footage: 200000

24478 J.H. Thornton Company
879 N Jan Mar Ct
Olathe, KS 66061

913-764-6550
Fax: 913-764-1314
Manufacturer, exporter and wholesaler/distributor of conveyor systems; installation services available
President: Douglas Metcalf
Estimated Sales: $3 - 5 Million
Number Employees: 10

24479 J.I. Holcomb Manufacturing
6400 Rockside Road
Independence, OH 44131-2309

800-458-3222
Fax: 216-524-4381
Cleaners including hand, toilet and bowl, dishwashing and washing compounds, mops, brooms, floor polish, soap, insecticides, etc
Estimated Sales: $52 Million
Number Employees: 500
Number of Products: 1600
Parent Co: Premier Industrial Corporation

24480 J.K. Harman, Inc.
1139 Dixwell Ave
Hamden, CT 06514

203-777-9726
Fax: 203-782-6575 800-248-1627
Custom store fixtures
President: D Harman
Estimated Sales: $5-10 Million
Number Employees: 10-19

24481 J.M. Rogers & Sons
PO Box 8725
Moss Point, MS 39562-0011

228-475-7584
Pallets, drag line mats, skids, lumber, etc.; exporter of pallets
Owner: Louis Rogers
Number Employees: 50

24482 J.M. Swank Company
520 W Penn St
North Liberty, IA 52317-9775

319-626-3683
Fax: 319-626-3662 800-567-9265
www.jmswank.com
Ingredient blending, label and special palletizing, inventory management, quality control and freight consolidation
President: Taylor Strubell
VP: Ron Pardekooper
Contact: George Nulty
george.nulty@conagrafoods.com
Estimated Sales: $29.5 Million
Number Employees: 175
Parent Co: Conagra Brands

24483 J.R. Ralph Marketing Company
4317 E Genesee Street
Suite 210
Syracuse, NY 13214-2114

315-445-0255
Fax: 315-445-0245
Consultant specializing in the introduction and expansion of products to the food industry
Partner: Chris Ralph
Estimated Sales: $1-2.5 Million
Number Employees: 1-4

24484 J.S. Ferraro
130 Adelaide St. W
Ste. 810
Toronto, ON M5H 3P5
Canada

416-306-0018
Fax: 416-583-2456 800-278-0018
info@jsferraro.com jsferraro.com
Offers market intelligence, risk management, and supply chain solutions.
CEO: Alexander Cave
Executive Chairman: John Ferraro
CFO: Eric Nie
EVP, Research & Analysis: Dr. Rob Murphy
SVP, Sales & Merchandising: Roger Despres *Year Founded:* 1988

24485 J.V. Reed & Company
1939 Goldsmith Ln
Suite 121
Louisville, KY 40218-3175

502-454-4455
Fax: 502-587-6025 877-258-7333
Manufacturer and exporter of dust pans, metal waste baskets, signs, tabs, labels, burner covers, hot pads, stove and counter mats, canister sets, etc
Owner: Jean Reid
Chairman Board: Marc Ray
Estimated Sales: $10-20 Million
Number Employees: 1-4
Square Footage: 160000

24486 J/W Design Associates
401 Terry Francois St
Suite 212
San Francisco, CA 94158

415-546-7707
Fax: 415-546-4004 info@webbdesign.com
www.webbdesign.com
Design consultant for restaurants, hotels and resorts
Owner: Kim Webb
Designer: Jack Donald Webb
Estimated Sales: $1 - 3 Million
Number Employees: 10-19

24487 JAS Manufacturing Company
3228 Skylane Dr
PO Box 702041
Carrollton, TX 75370-2041

972-380-1150
Fax: 972-931-6218
Dust and mist collectors and bakery equipment
Director Production: Jim Singleton
Estimated Sales: $2.5-5 Million
Number Employees: 20-49

24488 JBA International
3701 Algonquin Road
Rolling Meadows, IL 60008-3127

847-590-0299
Fax: 847-590-0394 800-522-4685
Wine industry computer software

24489 JBC Plastics
2239 Gravois Ave
St Louis, MO 63104-2852

314-771-2279
Fax: 314-771-0910 877-834-5526
mail@jbcplastic.com www.jbcplastic.com
Displays, napkin holders and signs
Owner: Cheryl Mc Grath
Customer Service: Jennifer Ward
Estimated Sales: $.5 - 1 million
Number Employees: 1-4

24490 (HQ)JBT Food Tech
400 Fairway Ave
Lakeland, FL 33801

863-683-5411
Fax: 863-680-3677 hello@jbtc.com
www.jbtc.com
Food processing machinery including fruit and vegetable juice extractors, blanchers, freezers, can closers, corers, pitters, choppers, etc
President & CEO: Brian Deck
EVP/CFO: Matthew Meister
EVP/President, JBT Aerotech: David Burdakin
EVP/President, Protein: Paul Sternlieb
Year Founded: 1884
Estimated Sales: $1,350 Million
Number Employees: 5,000
Parent Co: FMC Corporation

24491 JBT Wolf-Tec Inc
20 Kieffer Ln
Kingston, NY 12401-2209

845-340-9727
Fax: 845-340-9732 www.wolf-tec.com
Massagers and tumblers, pickle injectors, sausage linkers
CEO: Ralf Ludwig
ralf@wolf-tec.com
Estimated Sales: $20-50 Million
Number Employees: 50-99

24492 JC Food
PO Box 5121
Ridgewood, NJ 07451

201-444-4172
Fax: 201-444-3622 info@jc-food.com
www.jc-food.com
School foodservice services from menu planning to providing fresh foods
Owner/President: Joseph Civita
jcivita@jc-food.com
Estimated Sales: $700,000
Number Employees: 5

24493 JCH International
978 E Hermitage Rd NE
Rome, GA 30161-9641

706-295-4111
Fax: 706-295-4114 800-328-9203
info@jchinternational.com
Manufacturer and exporter of industrial and commercial mats and matting for entrance, meat cutting and produce areas; also, specialty flooring available; importer of heavy duty carpets
President: John Hoglund
jchoglund@yahoo.com
Number Employees: 5-9
Type of Packaging: Food Service
Brands:
Champions Sports Tile
Drainthru
Floorsaver
Locktile

24494 JCS Controls, Inc.
460 Buffalo Road
Suite 200
Rochester, NY 14611-2020

585-227-5910
Fax: 585-723-3213 sales@jcs.com
www.jcs.com
JCS has strong core competence in product development (R&D), Aseptic Processing, Mass Balanced Digital In-Line Blending Application, S88 Compliant Batching Systems, and many advanced technology processing systems such as EvaporationSpray Drying, Cheese VAT control, Membrane Processes, and more.
Founder: Philip Frechette
VP: Don Frechette
Operations: Rob Frechette
Estimated Sales: $3.7 Million
Number Employees: 20

Other Locations:

24495 JDG Consulting
2-8 Brookhollow Avenue
Suite 407
Baulkham Hills, NS 2153

312-621-8900
Fax: 312-621-0162 800-243-7037
info@jdgconsulting.com.au
www.greenfuture.com.au
Consultant providing market research and communications
VP: Alan Levitt
Administrative Assistant: Ann Marie Alanes
Number Employees: 3

24496 JDO/LNR Lighting
7980 Pat Booker Road
Suite A1
Live Oak, TX 78233-2603

210-637-6244
Fax: 210-637-6910 800-597-1570
Electric lighting fixtures
VP Marketing: Bob Windro
Manager: Leonard Almendarez
Number Employees: 30

24497 JEM Wire Products
2303 South Main Street
PO Box 2606
Middletown, CT 6457

860-347-0447
Fax: 860-347-9743
Wire products for baskets, displays, racks and shelves; also, custom wire forming and spot welding services available
President: Edward Muzik
Vice President: Tom Muzik
Marketing/Sales: Yale Gordon
Estimated Sales: $2.5-5 Million
Number Employees: 10-19

24498 JGB Enterprises Inc
115 Metropolitan Park Dr
Liverpool, NY 13088-5389

315-451-2770
Fax: 315-451-8503 www.jgbhose.com
Hose assemblies
President: Bob Zywicki
bzywicki@jgbhose.com
Quality Control: Glenn Beede
CFO: Bod Zywicki
Estimated Sales: $50 - 100 Million
Number Employees: 250-499

24499 JH Display & Fixture
P.O. Box 432
Greenwood, IN 46142

317-888-0631
Fax: 317-888-0671
Manufacturer, importer and exporter of wood, acrylic, metal and glass fixtures. Also custom shelving and tables available. Antique and vintage decorative props for all types of settings
Owner: John Holbrook
VP/Owner: Trudy Holbrook
Estimated Sales: $1-2.5 Million
Number Employees: 5-9

24500 JIT Manufacturing & Technology
4101 Stuart Andrew Boulevard
Suite D
Charlotte, NC 28217-1580

800-804-3910
Fax: 704-522-1603
Art patented print and apply equipment, bar coding systems, distribution programming, labeling and inventory control

24501 JJI Lighting Group, Inc.
11500 Melrose Ave.
Franklin Park, IL 60131-1334

847-451-0700
Manufacturer, importer and exporter of lighting fixtures and systems
CEO: Robert Haidinger
Contact: Claude Sarti
claude.sarti@philips.com
Estimated Sales: $55 Million
Number Employees: 650
Number of Products: 15
Type of Packaging: Private Label, Bulk

24502 JL Industries Inc
4450 W 78th Street Cir
Bloomington, MN 55435-5416

952-835-6850
Fax: 952-835-2218 800-554-6077
www.activarcpg.com
Manufacturer, exporter and importer of fire extinguishers and cabinets, other fire and emergency AED cabinets, metal access panels and roof hatches, dirt control floor mats and gratings, and detention specialties.
President: Carl Coleman
cecoleman@jlindustries.com
Marketing: Nona Peterson
Estimated Sales: $10 - 20 Million
Number Employees: 50-99
Square Footage: 116000
Parent Co: Activar

24503 JM Huber Chemical Corporation
907 Revolution St
Havre De Grace, MD 21078-3723

410-939-3500
Fax: 410-939-7302 hubermaterials@huber.com
www.huber.com
Industrial inorganic chemicals
President: Tom Lamb
President, Chief Executive Officer: Michael Marberry
R&D: John Clrnelius
Vice President of Environmental: Andrew Miles
Quality Control: Matt Hall
Contact: Chris Bible
etceb@huber.com
Plant Manager: Pat Jackson
Estimated Sales: $20 - 30 Million
Number Employees: 100-249

24504 JMA
658 Blue Point Road
Holtsville, NY 11742-1848

631-475-0023
Fax: 631-475-0549 800-428-8377
info@crazyhatter.com www.crazyhatter.com
Wine industry bottles
Owner: Jeffery Leibowitz
Estimated Sales: $1 - 3 Million
Number Employees: 10-19

24505 JMC Packaging Equipment
3470 Mainway Drive
Burlington, ON L7M 1A8
Canada

905-335-4196
Fax: 905-335-4201 800-263-5252
davidk@jmcpackaging.com
www.jmcpackaging.com
Manufacturer and exporter of bagging and bag sealing machinery
Sales Manager: David Kay
Office Manager: Linda Campbell
Number Employees: 10-19
Type of Packaging: Consumer, Food Service, Private Label, Bulk

24506 JP Plastics, Inc.
67 Green Street
Foxboro, MA 02035

508-203-2420
Fax: 508-203-2401 sales@jp-plastics.com
www.jp-plastics.com
Custom vacuum formed packaging products
President: John P Cheever
Contact: Mike Graves
mgraves@clarkeus.com
Estimated Sales: Below 1 Million
Number Employees: 7
Square Footage: 64000

24507 JPS Packaging Company
1972 Akron Peninsula Rd
Akron, OH 44313-4810

330-923-5281
Fax: 330-923-9637
Manufacturer and converter of flexible packaging and label products for use by customers in the food and beverage industry and other niche markets
Plant Manager: Anthony Oakes
Estimated Sales: $1 - 5 Million
Number Employees: 100-249

24508 JS Giles Inc
8810 Emmott Street
Suite 400
Houston, TX 77040-3592
713-690-3333
Fax: 713-690-3353 800-254-0709
sales@jfgilesinc.com www.jfgilesinc.com
Medium intensity horizontal and vertical mixers
President: John Giles
R & D: Peter Foxon
Estimated Sales: Below $5 Million
Number Employees: 5-9

24509 JUMO Process Control Inc
6733 Myers Rd
East Syracuse, NY 13057-9787
315-437-5866
Fax: 315-697-5860 800-554-5866
www.jumo.net
Meat thermometers, temperature control probes and
refrigeration controllers.
President: Carsten Juchheim
CEO: Bernhard Juchheim
Manager: Katherine Blume
katherine.blume@jumo.net
Number Employees: 20-49

24510 JVC Rubber Stamp Company
PO Box 2338
Elkhart, IN 46515
574-293-0113
Fax: 574-293-0113
Rubber stamps
Owner: Ron Cataldo
Estimated Sales: Less than $500,000
Number Employees: 1-4

24511 JVM Sales Corp.
3401 A Tremley Point Rd
Linden, NJ 07036
908-862-4866
Fax: 908-862-4867 anthony@jvmsalescorp.com
jvmsales.com
Italian grated cheeses; custom blends
President & CEO: Mary Beth Tomasino
VP of Sales & Marketing: Anthony Caliendo
Estimated Sales: $2-4 Million
Square Footage: 150000
Type of Packaging: Consumer, Food Service, Private Label, Bulk
Other Locations:
JVM Sales South
Delray Beach FL

24512 JVNW
390 S Redwood St
Canby, OR 97013
503-263-2858
Fax: 503-263-2868 800-331-5869
www.jvnw.com
Brewing vessels
President: Donald Jones
CFO: Donald Jones
Contact: Nicole Souter
nicole.s@jvnw.com
Estimated Sales: $5 - 10 Million
Number Employees: 100-249

24513 JVR/Sipromac
100 W Drullard Ave
Lancaster, NY 14086-1670
716-206-2500
Fax: 716-897-4731 www.jvrinc.com
Vacuum packaging, processing equipment
President: John Radziwon
Parts & Service Manager: Kevin Monk
Contact: Marta Guerra
guerram@hss.edu
Estimated Sales: $2.5 Million
Number Employees: 5-9

24514 JW Aluminum
435 Old Mt Holly Rd
Mt Holly, SC 29445
843-572-1100
Fax: 843-572-1049 800-568-1100
www.jwaluminum.com
Aluminum foil
Chief Executive Officer: Lee McCarter
Chief Financial Officer: Philip Cavatoni
Chief Commercial Officer: Ryan Roush
Chief Operating Officer: Stan Brant
Estimated Sales: $1 - 5 Million
Number Employees: 10-19

Type of Packaging: Food Service

24515 JW Aluminum Co
2475 Trenton Ave # 5
Williamsport, PA 17701-7904
570-323-4430
Fax: 570-323-6866 www.jwaluminum.com
Aluminum
CEO: Craig Eddy
Estimated Sales: $50 - 100 Million
Number Employees: 100-249

24516 JW Leser Company
4408 W Jefferson Blvd
Los Angeles, CA 90016-4090
323-731-4173
Fax: 323-731-4175
Sell and manufacture fillers, pumps, homogenizers,
tanks, mixers, and filters
President: Ray Leser
Number Employees: 1-4
Brands:
Alesco
In-Shear

24517 Jack Langston Manufacturing Company
3700 Elm Street
Dallas, TX 75226-1214
214-821-9844
Fax: 214-824-5777
Commercial refrigerators and walk-in coolers and
freezers
President: Olden Phil Paul
Chairman Board: J Langston, Jr.
Plant Manager: David Cormican
Number Employees: 25
Parent Co: Camp Langston

24518 Jack Stack
221 Sheridan Blvd
Inwood, NY 11096-1226
516-371-5214
Fax: 516-371-6880 800-999-9840
info@jackstack.com www.interfreight.net
Manufacturer and importer of mobile plate racks
Manager: Tom Staub
tom@interfreight.net
Managing Director: Tom Staub
Sales Manager: John Falzarano
Sales Manager: Pascale Steingueldoir
Estimated Sales: Less than $500,000
Number Employees: 5-9
Parent Co: Jackstack International

24519 Jack Stone Lighting & Electrical
3131 Pennsy Dr
Landover, MD 20785
301-322-3323
Fax: 301-322-8407 service@jackstone.net
www.jackstone.net
Electrical signs
President: Trevor Stone
Contact: Spencer Stone
sstone@jackstone.net
Operations Manager: Spencer Stone
Estimated Sales: $5-10 Million
Number Employees: 50-99

24520 Jack the Ripper Table Skirting
4003 Greenbriar Drive
Suite A
Stafford, TX 77477
281-240-1024
Fax: 281-240-0343 800-331-7831
www.tableskirting.com
Manufacturer and exporter of table skirting, table
cloths, napkins, place mats and tray stand covers
Director Sales: Erik Dean
Customer Service: Jessie Carpenter
Estimated Sales: $1 Million
Number Employees: 20-50

24521 Jacks Manufacturing Company
PO Box 50695
Mendota, MN 55150-0695
651-452-1474
Fax: 651-452-1477 800-821-2089
Manufacturer and exporter of boiler compounds and
carpet and upholstery cleaners
Chairman Board: C Nimis
Director: S Nimis
Office Manager: Sharon Bruesile

Estimated Sales: $2.5-5 Million
Number Employees: 1-4

24522 Jackson Corrugated Container
225 River Rd
Middletown, CT 6457
860-346-9671
Fax: 860-346-9320
Supplier of corrugated packaging.
President: William P Herlihy
info@jacksonbox.com
Estimated Sales: $5.2 Million
Number Employees: 20-49

24523 Jackson Msc LLC
6209 N US Highway 25e
Gray, KY 40734-6583
606-523-1438
Fax: 606-523-9196 888-800-5672
www.jacksonwws.com
Commercial dishwashers and ovens
President: David Crane
david.crane@jacksonmsc.com
VP Sales/Marketing: Mark Whalen
Production/Inventory Control Manager: Teresa
Doan
Purchasing Manager: Sheila Reeder
Estimated Sales: $5-10 Million
Number Employees: 100-249
Square Footage: 436000
Parent Co: ENODIS

24524 Jackson Restaurant Supply
1119 Highway 45 Byp
Jackson, TN 38301-3277
731-664-5100
Fax: 731-664-0978 800-424-8943
usamfg@usamanufacturing.com
Automatic barbecue cookers
President: James Griffith
Estimated Sales: $5-10 Million
Number Employees: 1-4
Square Footage: 64000
Brands:
Hickory Creek Bar-B-Q Cooker

24525 Jacksonville Box & Woodwork Co
5011 Buffalo Ave
Jacksonville, FL 32206-1573
904-354-1441
Fax: 904-354-6088 800-683-2699
info@jaxbox.com www.jaxbox.com
Packaging products including wooden bins for juice,
fruit, egg and vegetable boxes, collapsible pallet
mats for melons and wooden shipping crates
President: Jennings B King
Vice President: J King, Jr.
Sales: Tom More
Manager: Steve Farford
Estimated Sales: $5-10 Million
Number Employees: 10-19

24526 Jaco Equipment Corporation
3166 Main Street
Buffalo, NY 14214-1311
716-836-3755
Fax: 716-836-3756
Forming case packing, cleaning air bottling, cleaning washing bottling
President: Maurice Osterman
Number Employees: 5-9

24527 Jacob Holtz Co.
10 Industrial HWY MS-6 Airport Business
Lester, PA 19029
215-423-2800
Fax: 215-634-7454 800-445-4337
info@jacobholtz.com
Supplier and exporter of self-adjusting table glides
Estimated Sales: Below $5 Million
Number Employees: 3
Square Footage: 9600
Brands:
Superlevel

24528 Jacob Tubing LP
3948 Willow Lake Blvd
Memphis, TN 38118-7040
901-566-1110
Fax: 901-566-1910 info@jacob-tubing.com
www.jacob-tubing.com
Primary supplier of modular tubing systems with
pull ring connections to major industries worldwide.

CEO: Birte Mathis
Manager: Volker Eynck
Number Employees: 20-49
Parent Co: Jacob Soehne

24529 Jacob White Packaging
12720 Pennridge Drive
Bridgeton, MO 63044-1235

314-791-6448
Fax: 314-291-6913 800-248-6448
www.jacobwhite.com
Fully automatic horizontal end load cartoner
Estimated Sales: $1 - 3 Million
Number Employees: 10

24530 Jacobi Lewis Co
622 S Front St
PO Box 1289
Wilmington, NC 28401-5034

910-763-6201
Fax: 910-763-5610 800-763-2433
jl@jacobi-lewis.com www.jacobi-lewis.com
Wholesaler/distributor of equipment, supplies, furniture, etc.; serving the food service market
President: Greg Lewis
Chairman: French Lewis
Vice President: Gloria Ludewic
Marketing/Sales: Chris Gannon
Purchasing Manager: Wilson Horton
Estimated Sales: $7 Million
Number Employees: 10-19
Number of Brands: 700
Square Footage: 45000

24531 Jacobs Engineering Group
1999 Bryan St
Suite 1200
Dallas, TX 75201

214-638-0145
Fax: 214-638-0447 www.jacobs.com
Global, full-service engineering, procurement, construction management and operations firm
Chairman & CEO: Steve Demetriou
President & CFO: Kevin Berryman
Year Founded: 1947
Estimated Sales: $14.98 Billion
Number Employees: 52,000
Other Locations:
Lockwood Greene
Atlanta GA
Lockwood Greene-Enterprise Mill
Augusta GA
Lockwood Greene
Cincinnati OH
Lockwood Greene
Dallas TX
Lockwood Greene
Hampton VA
Lockwood Greene
Knoxville TN
Lockwood Greene
Long Beach CA
Lockwood Greene
Nashville TN
Lockwood Greene
New York NY
Lockwood Greene
Moon Township PA
Lockwood Greene
Saint Louis MO
Lockwood Greene
Pooler GA
Lockwood Greene
Somerset NJ

24532 Jade Products Co
2650 Orbiter St
Brea, CA 92821-6265

714-528-4486
800-884-5233
dpack@maytag.com www.jaderange.com
OEM equipment including commercial cooking ranges and refrigerators
President: Ray Williams
VP Sales: Lex Poulos
Customer Service Manager: Susan Hopkins
Production Engineering Manager: Peng Wang
Estimated Sales: $2.5-5 Million
Number Employees: 100-249
Parent Co: Maytag Corporation
Brands:
Dynasty
Jade Range
Jade Refrigeration
Utility Refrigeration

24533 Jagenberg
PO Box 1229
Enfield, CT 06083-1229

860-741-2501
Fax: 860-741-2508 www.jagenberg.com
Automatic folding carton gluers and packers
VP: C Himmelsbach
VP Converting Gruop: A Groat
Estimated Sales: $20-50 Million
Number Employees: 100-249
Parent Co: Jagenberg-Werke AG
Brands:
Jagenberg Diana

24534 Jagla Machinery Company
26 Woodland Ave
San Rafael, CA 94901

415-457-7672
Fax: 415-457-1143
Wine industry equipment fabricators
President: Lee Jagla
Estimated Sales: Below $5 Million
Number Employees: 5-9
Square Footage: 5000

24535 Jagulana Herbal Products
PO Box 45
Badger, CA 93603

559-337-2200
Fax: 559-337-2354 888-465-3686
www.immortalityherb.com
Dedicated to researching, developing and marketing jiaogulan and jiaogulan-based herbal products of the highest quality
President: Chris Gleen
Research: Michael Blumert
Estimated Sales: $1 - 3 Million
Number Employees: 1-4

24536 James Austin Co
115 Downieville Rd
P.O. Box 827
Mars, PA 16046

724-625-1535
Fax: 724-625-3288 www.jamesaustin.com
Household chlorine bleaches, laundry and dishwashing detergents, disinfectants, ammonia, pines oil cleaners, windshield washer fluid, fabric softeners and glass cleaners.
President: Harry Austin III
hgaustin@jamesaustin.com
Board Member: John Austin
Board Member: Doug Austin
Board Member: Jack Rea
Year Founded: 1889
Estimated Sales: $52 Million
Number Employees: 100-249
Number of Brands: 10
Number of Products: 30
Square Footage: 180000
Type of Packaging: Consumer, Food Service, Private Label
Other Locations:
Ludlow MA
Statesville CA
DeLand FL
Brands:
101
A-1
Austin
Snoee
Wipe Away

24537 James River Canada
137 Bentworth Avenue
North York, ON M6A 1T6
Canada

416-789-5151
Fax: 416-789-3590
Disposable cups, plates and cutlery
Estimated Sales: $1 - 5,000,000
Number Employees: 250
Parent Co: James River Corporation

24538 (HQ)James Thompson
381 Park Ave S
Rm 718
New York, NY 10016-8806

212-686-5306
Fax: 212-686-9528 inquiry@jamesthompson.com
www.jamesthompson.com
Manufacturer and exporter of buckrams, netting, cotton goods, burlap, cheesecloth, etc

President: Robert B Judell
Treasurer: Barry Garr
Vice President, Sales/Marketing: Marc Bieler
Site Manager: Steve Luchansky
Vice President, Manufacturing: Steve Luchansky
Merchandise Manager: Gail Boyle
Estimated Sales: $300,000-500,000
Number Employees: 5-9

24539 James V. Hurson Associates
200 N. Glebe Road
Suite 321
Arlington, VA 22203-3755

703-524-8200
Fax: 703-525-8451 800-642-6564
info@hurson.com www.hurson.com
Consultant specializing in food labeling, trademarks and patents
President: James Hurson
Manager: J Hurson
Estimated Sales: $2.5 - 5 Million
Number Employees: 20-49

24540 James Varley & Sons
1200 Switzer Ave
Saint Louis, MO 63147

314-383-4372
Fax: 314-383-4379 800-325-8891
General purpose and meat room cleaners, degreasers, sanitizers, housekeeping chemicals, floor polish and hand soap
President: John Daley
CEO: Jack Daley
Estimated Sales: $5-10 Million
Number Employees: 20-49
Parent Co: Daley International, Ltd
Brands:
Everwear
Med-I-San

24541 Jamestown Awning
289 Steele St
Jamestown, NY 14701

716-483-1435
Fax: 716-483-3995
service@jamestownawning.com
www.jamestownawning.com
Commercial awnings
President: Mark Saxton
mark@jamestownawning.com
Estimated Sales: $1 - 2,500,000
Number Employees: 10-19

24542 Jamestown Container Corporation
2775 Broadway St
Suite 250
Buffalo, NY 14227

216-831-3700
Fax: 216-831-3709 855-234-4054
www.jamestowncontainer.com
Corrugated cartons
President: Larry Hudson
Sales Manager: Jeffrey Davidson
Estimated Sales: $10-20 Million
Number Employees: 50-99
Parent Co: Willamette Industries

24543 Jamieson Wellness Inc.
1 Adelaide St E
Suite 2200
Toronto, ON M5C 2V9
Canada

800-265-5088
consumeraffairs@jamiesonlabs.com
www.jamiesonvitamins.com
Kefir, yogurt, cod liver oil, vitamins, mineral supplements; water purifying systems and filters.
President/CEO: Mike Pilato
Year Founded: 1922
Estimated Sales: $42 Million
Number Employees: 501-1000
Number of Brands: 22
Square Footage: 40000
Parent Co: CCMP Capital Advisors LLC
Type of Packaging: Consumer
Other Locations:
Toronto ON
Brands:
Arthrimin GS
Baby-D
BodyGUARD
Digestive Care
Effervescent

Exxtra-C
FluShield
Healthy SLEEP
Mega Cal
NEM
Neurosome
Nutrisentials
Omega Complete
Omega-3 Brain
Omega-3 Calm
Omega-3 Select
ProVitamina
Prostease
Red Dragon
Relax & Sleep
Slimdown
Stressease

24544 Jamison Door Co
55 Jv Jamison Dr
Hagerstown, MD 21740
301-733-3100
Fax: 240-329-5155 800-532-3667
www.jamisondoor.com
Cold storage refrigerator and freezer doors.
CEO: John T Williams
jw@jamisondoor.com
Purchasing: Don Wilson
Number Employees: 100-249
Number of Brands: 3

24545 Jamison Plastic Corporation
5001 Crackersport Rd
Allentown, PA 18104
610-391-1400
Fax: 610-391-1414
Manufacturer and designer of custom and plastic injection molded products
President: Marc Solda
Contact: Dan Gawer
dan.gawer@npiplastic.com
Estimated Sales: $10-20 Million
Number Employees: 50-99
Square Footage: 210000

24546 Janedy Sign Company
27 Carter St
Everett, MA 2149
617-776-5700
Fax: 617-387-5822
Signs
Owner: William Penney
Estimated Sales: $500,000-$1 Million
Number Employees: 5-9

24547 Janows Design Associates
5323 W Pratt Avenue
Lincolnwood, IL 60712-3121
847-763-0620
Fax: 847-763-0621
Consultant specializing in engineering and design of commercial food service equipment
President: Quintilla Janows
Principal: Sherwin Janows
Estimated Sales: $500,000-$1 Million
Number Employees: 5-9

24548 Jantec
1777 Northern Star Dr
Traverse City, MI 49696-9244
231-941-4339
Fax: 231-941-1460 800-992-3303
accounting@jantec.com www.jantec.com
Manufacturer and exporter of belt, angle-edge and spiral conveyors; also, power turns and specialty stainless steel conveying equipment for food and washdown applications
Owner: Ronald Sommerfield
ronalds@jantec.com
Number Employees: 20-49

24549 January & Wood Company
PO Box 308
Maysville, KY 41056-0308
606-564-3301
Fax: 606-564-8425
Cotton and cotton/polyester twine
Estimated Sales: $5-10 Million
Number Employees: 50-99

24550 Japan External Trade Organization (JETRO) New York
1221 Avenue of the Americas
42nd Floor
New York, NY 10020-1079
212-997-0400
Fax: 212-944-8808
Tea
Marketing: Yumika Tanaka

24551 Jarboe Equipment
411 N Bedford St
Georgetown, DE 19947-2197
302-856-7988
Fax: 302-856-7408 800-699-7988
Dealer of new and used food processing equipment
Owner: Ronald Snyder
Estimated Sales: $1 - 5 Million
Number Employees: 1-4

24552 Jarchem Industries
414 Wilson Ave
Newark, NJ 07105
973-578-4560
Fax: 973-344-5743 info@jarchem.com
www.jarchem.com
Acetates and chlorides
VP: Arthur Hein
CEO: Arnold Stern
Sales Manager: Steve Yonder
Contact: Hein Arthur
hein.arthur@jarchem.com
Estimated Sales: $20-50 Million
Number Employees: 1-4

24553 Jarden Home Brands
1800 Cloquet Ave
Cloquet, MN 55720-2141
218-879-6700
Fax: 218-879-6369 www.jardenhomebrands.com
Matches, toothpicks, plastic cutlery, ice cream sticks, candles, etc
Estimated Sales: $20-50 Million
Number Employees: 250-499

24554 Jarden Home Brands
14611 W. Commerce Road
P.O Box 529
Daleville, IN 47334
800-392-2575
Fax: 765-557-3250 info@jardenhomebrands.com
www.diamondbrands.com
Cocktail forks, toothpicks, corn-on-the-cob holders, skewers, candy sticks, spoons, etc; exporter of woodware and cutlery; importer of toothpicks and candy apple sticks
Sales Manager: Phil Dvorak
Contact: Jared Anderson
janderson@jardencs.com
Brands:
Diamond
Forster
Permaware
Universal

24555 Jarisch Paper Box Company
1560 Curran Highway
North Adams, MA 01247-3900
413-663-5396
Fax: 413-664-4889
Boxes including set-up paper and plastic; also, partitions
General Manager: Gary Mallows
Number Employees: 45

24556 Jarke Corporation
750 Pinecrest Dr
Prospect Hts, IL 60070
847-520-4774
Fax: 847-541-0858 800-722-5255
www.gillisindustries.com
Steel pallets and skids; also, racks including portable stacking, pallet storage and cantilever; nonpowered trucks and carts for warehouse coolers and freezers available
President: Harvey Baker
Marketing Director: Liz Cheevers
Sales: George Luft
Estimated Sales: $10-20 Million
Number Employees: 20-49
Square Footage: 240000
Brands:
Airector
Button-On

Cupl-Up
Hi-Drum
Mini-Module
Minitree
Quiktree
Steeltree
Tri-Drum
Utilitier

24557 Jarlan Manufacturing
8701 Avalon Blvd
Los Angeles, CA 90003-3512
323-752-1211
Fax: 323-752-2037
Bar tops and ice bins
President: Craig Malburg
jarlan55@yahoo.com
Estimated Sales: $500,000-$1 Million
Number Employees: 5-9

24558 Jarvis Caster Company
881 Lower Brownsville Rd
Jackson, TN 38301-9667
731-554-2138
800-995-9876
inof@jarviscaster.com www.jarviscaster.com
Manufacturer and exporter of industrial casters and wheels
President: Rodney Brooks
CFO: Ronnie Fondrun
Vice President: Scott Lackey
Research & Development: Harry Green
Marketing Director: Cary Gillespie
Sales Director: Scott Lackey
Contact: Zachary Minner
zminner@emdeon.com
Operations Manager: Harold Clark
Purchasing Manager: Tracy Hall
Number Employees: 100-249
Square Footage: 800000
Parent Co: Standex International Corporation
Type of Packaging: Bulk
Other Locations:
Jarvis East
Mississauga ON

24559 (HQ)Jarvis Products Corp
33 Anderson Rd
Middletown, CT 06457-4926
860-347-7271
Fax: 860-347-9905 sales@jarvisproducts.com
Meat and poultry processing equipment.
President: Peter Brown
peterdouglas@hotmail.com
Estimated Sales: $14.8 Million
Number Employees: 100-249
Square Footage: 24000
Brands:
Jarvis

24560 Jarvis-Cutter Company
184 Bremen Street
Boston, MA 02128-1738
617-567-7532
Fax: 617-567-5644
General, infectious and pathological waste incinerators and heat recovery boilers
Estimated Sales: $.5 - 1 million
Number Employees: 6
Parent Co: Jarvis-Cutter

24561 Jasper Seating Company
P.O. Box 231
Jasper, IN 47547-0231
812-481-9259
Fax: 812-482-1548 www.jasperseating.com
Technical Services Manager: Amilcar Ubiera
Sales Territory Manager: Jimi Barreiro
Estimated Sales: $10 - 20 Million
Number Employees: 100-249

24562 Java Jacket
910 NE 57th Ave # 300
Portland, OR 97213-3615
503-281-6240
Fax: 503-281-6462 800-208-4128
info@javajacket.com www.javajacket.com
Manufacturer and exporter of hot and cold paper cup coffee sleeves, joe to go boxes and custom sized sleeves.
President: Jay Sorensen
jay@javajacket.com
CEO: Colleen Sorensen

Estimated Sales: $500,000-$1 Million
Number Employees: 5-9
Brands:
Java Jacket

24563 Jax Inc
W134n5373 Campbell Dr
Menomonee Falls, WI 53051-7023
262-781-3906
Fax: 262-781-3906 800-782-8850
info@jax.com
Jax INC is a manufacturer of high technology, indus-
trial, synthetic and food grade lubricants. Founded in
1955, JAX produces conventional and extreme per-
formance synthetic lubricants for food processing
and numerous other industrysegments. JAX lubrica-
tion products are distributed worldwide.
President/CEO: Eric Peter
CFO: Steve Matiacci
Vice President: Carter Anderson
Marketing Director: Tracey Huebner
Manager: Keely Marlowe
keely@jax.com
Estimated Sales: $10-20 Million
Number Employees: 50-99
Parent Co: Pressure-Lube
Type of Packaging: Private Label, Bulk
Other Locations:
Benhkle Lubricants/Western Regional
Sacramento CA
Brands:
Jax Lubricants

24564 Jax Inc
W134n5373 Campbell Dr
Menomonee Falls, WI 53051-7023
262-781-3906
Fax: 262-781-3906 800-782-8850
Food grade lubricants including antiwear food grade
greases, hydraulic oils and gear oils, food grade air-
line oils, chain and conveyor lubricants and extreme
temperature lubricants
President: Eric J Peter
Manager: Keely Marlowe
keely@jax.com
Estimated Sales: $10 - 20 Million
Number Employees: 50-99

24565 Jay Packaging Group Inc
100 Warwick Industrial Dr
Warwick, RI 02886-2486
401-244-1300
Fax: 401-738-0137 www.jaypack.com
Manufacturer and exporter of displays, blister cards,
skin sheets and thermoformed trays and blisters
President: Richard E Kelly
CFO: Fernando Lemos
flemos@jaypack.com
VP Sales: Jim Nattiucci
Estimated Sales: $20 - 50 Million
Number Employees: 100-249

24566 Jay R Smith Mfg Co
2781 Gunter Park Dr E
Montgomery, AL 36109-1405
334-277-8520
Fax: 334-272-7396 sales@jrsmith.com
www.jrsmith.com
Grease remediation systems and grease intercepters
CFO: Dale Evans
CEO: Jay Smith
Marketing: Charles White
Vice President of Domestic Sales: John Roberts
Plant Manager: Jeff Cannon
Purchasing Director: Bruce Tomlinson
Estimated Sales: $40 Million
Number Employees: 250-499
Number of Products: 200
Square Footage: 250000
Parent Co: Smith Industries

24567 Jay-Bee Manufacturing Inc
522 N Beverly Ave
Tyler, TX 75702-5932
903-597-9343
Fax: 903-593-8725 800-445-0610
jaybeemfg@suddenlinkmail.com
www.jaybeehammermills.com
Manufacturer and exporter of stainless steel hammer
mills for particle reduction of fruits, rice cakes and
spices
President: Edwina Granberry

Estimated Sales: $1-2.5 Million
Number Employees: 10-19
Square Footage: 280000
Brands:
Jay Bee

24568 Jayhawk Boxes
1150 S Union St
Fremont, NE 68025-6137
402-721-6101
Fax: 402-721-7958 800-642-8363
jaystevr@lpco.net www.lpco.co
Corrugated shipping boxes
Estimated Sales: $20 Million
Number Employees: 50-99
Parent Co: Lawrence Paper Company

24569 Jayhawk Manufacturing Co Inc
1426 N Grand Street
Hutchinson, KS 67501-2135
620-669-8269
Fax: 620-669-9815 866-886-8269
www.jayhawkmills.com
Manufacturer and exporter of wet process, stone
grinding and colloid mills used primarily in the pro-
duction of condiments
President: Merle Starr
Estimated Sales: $500,000-$1 Million
Number Employees: 1-4
Brands:
Jayhawk Mills

24570 Jayone Foods, Inc.
7212 Alondra Blvd
Paramount, CA 90723-3902
562-633-7400
Fax: 562-633-7401 info@jayone.com
www.jayonefoods.com
Gluten-free, vegan, non-GMO, sugar-free specialty
items; tea, juices, cider; condiments, yogurt, sauces;
and other snacks.
President: Seung Hoon Lee
info@jayone.com
Marketing Manager: Janis Kim
Year Founded: 1999
Estimated Sales: $30 Million
Number Employees: 50
Number of Brands: 2
Type of Packaging: Private Label
Brands:
Jayone
Sea's Gift

24571 Jeb Plastics
3519 Silverside Rd Ste 106
Wilmington, DE 19810
302-479-9223
Fax: 302-479-9227 800-556-2247
www.jebplastics.com
Wholesaler/distributor/broker of poly bags, vinyl
bags, heat sealers and packaging supplies
Owner: Sherri Lindner
Estimated Sales: Below $500,000
Number Employees: 1-4
Square Footage: 4000

24572 Jeco Plastic Products LLC
885 Andico Rd
Plainfield, IN 46168-9659
317-839-4943
Fax: 317-839-1209 800-593-5326
www.jecoplastics.com
FDA approved plastic pallet and containers
President/CEO: Craig Carson
craigc@jecoplastics.com
CFO: Sherry Arndt
R & D: Roger Streling
Sales: Paul Koehl
Sales/Customer support: Ann Carson
Plant Manager: Don Andrews
Estimated Sales: Below $5 Million
Number Employees: 20-49
Square Footage: 74000
Type of Packaging: Bulk
Brands:
Perfect Pallet

24573 Jedwards International Inc
141 Campanelli Dr
Braintree, MA 02184-5206
781-848-1473
Fax: 617-472-9359 sales@bulknaturaloils.com
www.bulknaturaloils.com

Organic specialty oils, essential oils, butters, waxes
and botanicals
Contact: Jeremy Bamsch
jeremy@bulknaturaloils.com

24574 Jeffcoat Signs
1611 S Main St
Gainesville, FL 32601-8608
352-377-2322
Fax: 352-377-4249 877-377-4248
info@jeffcoatsigns.com www.jeffcoatsigns.com
Signs including plastic, neon and painted; installa-
tion services available
President: Kevin Jeffers
kevin@jeffcoatsigns.com
Estimated Sales: Less Than $500,000
Number Employees: 5-9
Square Footage: 90000

24575 Jefferson Packing Company
765 Marlene Drive
Gretna, LA 70056-7639
504-366-4451
Fax: 504-366-9382
Packaging solutions
President: William Marciante

24576 Jefferson Smurfit Corporation
1228 Tower Rd
Schaumburg, IL 60173-4308
847-884-1200
Fax: 847-884-7206
Flexible packaging
President: Gary Mc Daniel
VP: Mark A Polivka
Estimated Sales: $20 - 50 Million
Number Employees: 100-249

24577 Jemolo Enterprises
100 S Westwood Street
Spc 126
Porterville, CA 93257-7708
559-784-5566
Fax: 209-823-2506 jemoloente@aol.com
www.jemolo.en.ec21.com
Manufacturer and exporter of environmental technological building systems including water purification
and waste water and sanitation treatment; also, reverse osmosis water treatment systems
President: Fred Niswonger

24578 Jen-Coat, Inc.
132 North Elm Street
PO Box 274
Westfield, MA 01086
877-536-2628
Fax: 413-562-8771 info@jencoat.com
Manufacturer and exporter of plastic coated paper
President: James Kauffman
Contact: Michelle Cotham
michellec@workplacestaff.com
Estimated Sales: $1 - 5 Million
Number Employees: 250-499
Parent Co: Ana Business Products

24579 Jenco Fan
6393 Powers Ave
Jacksonville, FL 32217-2217
904-731-4711
Fax: 904-737-8322 www.breidert.com
Owner: Patrick M Williams Sr
Contact: Josh Cosgrove
jcosgrove@solerpalau-usa.com
Estimated Sales: $20 - 50 Million
Number Employees: 100-249
Parent Co: Breidert Air Products

24580 (HQ)Jenike & Johanson Inc
400 Business Park Dr
Tyngsboro, MA 01879-1077
978-649-3300
Fax: 978-392-9980 www.bulk-solids-flow.com
Manufacturer, design engineer and consultant for
bulk solid handling equipment including portable
and stationary containers, hoppers, bins and silos
President: Orlando Andrs
aorlando@jenike.com
V.P. of Technology: T Anthony Royal
Marketing Director: Rod Hossefeld
Sales Director: Brian Pittenger
Estimated Sales: $2.5-5 Million
Number Employees: 20-49
Type of Packaging: Bulk

Other Locations:
Jenike & Johanson
Westford MA
Brands:
Binsert

24581 Jenkins Sign Co
1400 Mahoning Ave
Youngstown, OH 44509-2503

330-799-3205
Fax: 330-799-3024 jenkinsadmin@neo.rr.com
www.jenkinsign.com
Plastic, metal and neon signs
President: J Jenkins
jenkinssales@neo.rr.com
Administrative Assistant: Sue Kaden
Estimated Sales: $3 - 5 Million
Number Employees: 20-49

24582 Jensen Fittings Corporation
107 Goundry Street
111
North Tonawanda, NY 14120-5998

800-255-4111
Fax: 800-523-4165 800-255-4111
Sanitary stainless steel valves, pumps, and fittings
Estimated Sales: $10-20 Million
Number Employees: 19

24583 Jentek
PO Box 809
North Branford, CT 06471-0809

203-488-5334
Fax: 203-481-9006
Dry coating equipment for ice cream sticks
President: Susanna Jensen
Plant Manager: Christian Jensen
Estimated Sales: $500,000-$1 Million
Number Employees: 1-4

24584 Jergens Inc
15700 S Waterloo Rd
Cleveland, OH 44110-3898

216-486-2100
Fax: 216-481-6193 800-537-4367
info@jergensinc.com www.jergensinc.com
Knobs and handles, cranks, threaded inserts, quick
change devices and hardware, automated tape dis-
pensing equipment, toggle clamps, grippers, slides,
vacuum generators, rotary actuators, pick-n-place,
and remote IO transmissiondevices
President: Jack Schrøn
jschron@jergensinc.com
CFO: W Howard
Quality Control: J Klindenerg
Estimated Sales: $20 - 50 Million
Number Employees: 100-249

24585 Jersey Shore Steel Co
70 Maryland Ave
Jersey Shore, PA 17740-7113

570-753-3000
Fax: 570-753-3782 800-833-0277
sales@jssteel.com www.jssteel.com
Wine industry metal grape stakes
Owner: Lorraine Barone
lbarone@jssteel.com
Estimated Sales: $63.40 Million
Number Employees: 250-499

24586 Jervis B WEBB Co
30100 Cabot Dr
Novi, MI 48377

248-553-1000
www.daifuku.com/us
Manufacturer and exporter of conveyor and inte-
grated material handling systems.
President: Tim Hund
Year Founded: 1919
Estimated Sales: $100-250 Million
Number Employees: 1,000
Parent Co: Daifuku Co.
Other Locations:
Webb, Jervis B., Co.
Chardon OH

24587 Jesco Industries
950 Anderson Rd
Litchfield, MI 49252

517-542-2353
Fax: 517-542-2501 800-455-0019
www.jescoonline.com
Manufacturer, importer and exporter of hoppers,
dumpers, security trucks, carts, dollies, baskets, wire
mesh partitions, security cages, window guards and
enclosures, etc
Vice President: Tom Sebastian
toms@jescolion.com
VP: B Desjardin
Marketing Director: Bonny DesJardin
Sales Engineer: Phil Risedorph
Estimated Sales: $8 Million
Number Employees: 100-249
Square Footage: 360000
Brands:
Jesco
Wipco

24588 (HQ)Jescorp
300 E Touhy Avenue
Suite C
Des Plaines, IL 60018-2669

847-299-7800
Fax: 847-299-7822
Manufacturer and exporter of thermoformed and
laminated containers and films, integrated gas flush-
ing systems, gas flush tray sealers and vacuum
seamers
VP Direct Sales: Jim Sanfilippo
Number Employees: 64
Square Footage: 280000
Brands:
Belt-Vac
Map-Fresh
Map-Seal
Ms-1400
Ms-25
Ms-55
Ms-700
Nitro-Flush
Vbt-1100
Vbt-250
Vbt-550

24589 Jess Jones Vineyard
6496 Jones Ln
Dixon, CA 95620-9601

707-678-3839
Fax: 707-678-3898 www.jessjonesvineyard.com
Wines
President: Jess Jones
CEO: Mary Ellen Jones
Estimated Sales: $700,000
Number Employees: 1-4
Square Footage: 20000
Type of Packaging: Consumer, Bulk
Brands:
California Golden Pop
Customer's Bags
Jess Jones Farms

24590 Jesse Jones Box Corporation
499 E Erie Avenue
Philadelphia, PA 19134-1104

215-425-6600
Fax: 215-425-4705
Set-up and folding boxes, specialty containers and
point of purchase displays
Director Sales: Harvey Brenner
Contact: William Fenkel
jjibill@aol.com
Production Manager: Joseph Pomray
Estimated Sales: $3-5 Million
Number Employees: 50-75
Square Footage: 90000
Parent Co: Jesse Jones Industries
Type of Packaging: Bulk

24591 Jessup Paper Box
211 S Railroad St
Brookston, IN 47923

765-490-9043
Fax: 765-563-3424 www.jessuppaperbox.com
Paper boxes and novelties
President: Butch Huber
CFO: Butch Huber
General Manager: Donald Winship
Plant Manager: Donald Cross
Purchasing Manager: Peggy Ruckdeschel
Estimated Sales: Below $5 Million
Number Employees: 20-49

24592 Jet Box Co
1822 Thunderbird
Troy, MI 48084-5479

248-362-1260
Fax: 248-362-2736
Corrugated boxes
Chairman of the Board: Lynda K Zardus
Estimated Sales: Below $5 Million
Number Employees: 20-49

24593 Jet Lite Products
PO Box 279
Highland, IL 62249

618-654-2217
Fax: 618-654-2217
Lighting fixtures and neon signs
President: John D Kutz Jr
Vice President: Roger Huber
Plant Manager: Joe Kutz
Estimated Sales: Below $5 Million
Number Employees: 10-19
Square Footage: 24000

24594 Jet Plastica Industries
1100 Schwab Rd
Hatfield, PA 19440

www.dwfinepack.com
Manufacturer and exporter of molded plastics in-
cluding packaging kits, tumblers, cutlery and straws
Estimated Sales: $43 Million
Number Employees: 600
Square Footage: 300000
Parent Co: D&W Fine Pack

24595 Jetnet Corp
505 North Dr
79 North Industrial Park
Sewickley, PA 15143-2339

412-741-0100
Fax: 412-741-0140 800-245-1036
info@jetnetcorp.com www.jetnetcorp.com
Cutting and boning devices, general packinghouse
equipment, uniforms, aprons and clothing; process-
ing equipment, netting and tying machines
President: Donald Sartore
CEO: Bill Attiya
billa@jetnetcorp.com
Estimated Sales: $5-10 Million
Number Employees: 50-99

24596 Jetstream Systems
400 South Emporia St.
Wichita, KN 67202

316-462-9784
Fax: 303-371-9012 855-861-6916
jetstreamsys.com
Manufacturer and exporter of mechanical and air
conveyors, palletizers and depalletizers, bottle and
can fillers and rinsers
Director Sales: Neal McConnellogue
Director Applications: Vince Jones
Number Employees: 153
Square Footage: 264000
Parent Co: Barry-Wehmiller Company

24597 Jewel Case Corp
110 Dupont Dr
Cranston, RI 02907-3181

401-943-1400
Fax: 401-943-1426 800-441-4447
contact@jewelcase.com www.jewelcase.com
Manufacturer and exporter of gift and promotional
packaging for candy, confections, gourmet foods and
cutlery/tableware
President: Terri Eisen
teisen@jewelcase.com
Controller: Terry Eisen
Marketing Manager: Lynn Johnson
Sales: Richard Dobuski
Estimated Sales: $10 - 20 Million
Number Employees: 100-249
Square Footage: 200000
Type of Packaging: Consumer, Private Label, Bulk

24598 Jewell Bag Company
228 Yorktown St
Suite B
Dallas, TX 75208-2045

214-749-1223
Fax: 214-749-1226
FDA approved polyethylene bags
President: Michael Smith
Estimated Sales: $1-2.5 Million
Number Employees: 1-4

24599 Jhrg LLC
303 S Pine St
Spring Hope, NC 27882-9551
    252-478-4997
Fax: 252-478-4998 800-849-4997
info@hsarmor.com www.hsarmor.com
Owner: John Holland
  jholland@hsarmor.com
Partner: John Holland
  jholland@hsarmor.com
Estimated Sales: $1 - 5 Million
Number Employees: 50-99

24600 (HQ)Jif-Pak Manufacturing
1451 Engineer St # A
Vista, CA 92081-8841
    760-597-2665
Fax: 760-597-2667 800-777-6613
info@jifpak.com www.jifpak.com
Manufacturer and exporter of elastic and nonelastic nettings, stockinettes, stuffing horns, semi and automatic netting machines and elastic trussing loops
President: Gary Cleppe
  garycleppe@kalleusa.com
Marketing Executive: John Connelly
Operations Ex: Lee Jared
Estimated Sales: $1 - 5 Million
Number Employees: 5-9
Brands:
  Casing-Net
  Jif-Pak

24601 Jiffy Mixer Co Inc
1691 California Ave
Corona, CA 92881-3375
    951-272-0838
Fax: 951-279-7651 800-560-2903
www.jiffymixer.com
Nonelectric mixers including portable and heavy duty
President: Jeff Johnson
  jeff@jiffymixer.com
Production Manager: Douglas Kaus
Office Manager: Al Measham
Estimated Sales: Below $5 Million
Number Employees: 5-9
Square Footage: 12000

24602 Jilson Group
20 Industrial Rd
Lodi, NJ 7644
    973-471-2400
Fax: 973-471-3993 800-969-5400
heretohelp@jilson.com www.jilson.com
Manufacturer and importer of casters, wheels, noncorrosive bearings and bearing housings as well as plastic packaging ties.
Chief Financial Officer: Pete Rennard
VP: David Baughn
Products Manager: Steven Becher
Vice President Sales: David Baughn
Contact: Tony Alfano
  talfano@jilson.com
Purchasing Manager: Tony Alfano
Estimated Sales: $2.5-5 Million
Number Employees: 10-19
Square Footage: 40000
Brands:
  Steinco Casters

24603 Jim Did It Sign Company
PO Box 17
Allston, MA 2134
    617-782-2410
Fax: 781-782-5433
Manufacturer and exporter of commercial signs for supermarkets and other businesses
Owner: Robert Thompson
Estimated Sales: $500,000-$1 Million
Number Employees: 5-9

24604 Jim Lake Companies
1350 Manufacturing St # 101
Dallas, TX 75207
    214-741-5018
Fax: 214-741-5020 info@jimlakeco.com
www.jimlakeco.com
Rubber stamps and seals
Founder: Jim Lake
Marketing Coordinator: Monica Diodati
Estimated Sales: $500,000-$1 Million
Number Employees: 10-19

24605 Jim Scharf Holdings
PO Box 305 Ave K & 9th St
Perdue, SK S0K 3C0
Canada
    306-237-4365
Fax: 306-237-4362 800-667-9727
sales@ezeewrap.com www.ezeewrap.com
Manufacturer and exporter of plastic wrap dispensers, process refrigerator/freezer odor absorbers, shopping bag handles, bagel cutters and lettuce knives; processor of instant lentils
President: Bruna Scharf
Marketing: Leanna Carr
Plant Manager: Mary Ann Cotterill
Estimated Sales: Below $5,000,000
Number Employees: 10
Square Footage: 24000
Brands:
  Bagel Buddy
  Bakeware Buddy
  E-Zee Wrap
  Grocery Grip
  Heavenly Fresh
  Kitchen Buddy
  The Lettuce Knife

24606 Jimbo's Jumbos Inc
185 Peanut Dr
Edenton, NC 27932-9604
    252-482-2193
Fax: 252-482-7857 800-334-4771
Snacks and peanuts; custom formulation
Manager: Hal Burns
Manager: Debbie Miller
  dmiller@jimbosjumbos.com
Number Employees: 100-249
Type of Packaging: Private Label

24607 Jl Analytical Svc Inc
217 Primo Way
Modesto, CA 95358-5749
    209-538-8111
Fax: 209-538-3966
Laboratory specializing in food analysis and water testing
President: Mary Jacobs
CEO: Richard Jacobs, Ph.D.
VP: Mark Jacobs
Estimated Sales: $5 - 10 Million
Number Employees: 50-99

24608 Jms Packaging Consultants Inc
10 Lenbar Cir
New City, NY 10956-4908
    845-708-0701
Fax: 845-708-0702
jstrassman@jmspackaging.com
www.jmspackaging.com
Custom gift packaging, plastic set-up and folding boxes
Owner: Joel Strassman
  jmspkg@aol.com
CEO: Joel Strassnan
Estimated Sales: Less Than $500,000
Number Employees: 1-4

24609 Jo Mar Laboratories
583 Division St # B
Campbell, CA 95008-6915
    408-374-5920
Fax: 408-374-5922 800-538-4545
info@jomarlabs.com www.jomarlabs.com
Health products; contract packaging
President: Joanne Brown
  joanne@jomarlabs.com
Estimated Sales: $1 - 3 Million
Number Employees: 10-19
Square Footage: 14000
Parent Co: Jo Mar Labs
Type of Packaging: Consumer, Private Label

24610 Jogue
14731 Helm Court
Plymouth, MI 48170
    734-207-0100
Fax: 734-207-0200 800-521-3888
www.jogue.com
Flavor development
President: Dattu Sastry
Estimated Sales: $5 Million
Number Employees: 20-49
Type of Packaging: Food Service, Private Label

24611 Johanson TransportationSvc
5583 E Olive Ave
Fresno, CA 93727-2559
    559-458-2200
Fax: 559-458-2234 800-742-2053
LJohanson@johansontrans.com
www.johansontrans.com
Transporters of dry and temperature controlled freight.
President: Larry Johanson
  ljohanson@johansontrans.com
CFO: Janice Spicer
Vice President: Craig Johanson
Chief Operations Officer: Jerry Beckstead
Corporate Accounting & Administration Ma: Becky Martin
Number Employees: 20-49

24612 John Bean Technologies Corp
400 Highpoint Dr
Chalfont, PA 18914-3924
    215-822-4600
Fax: 215-822-4553 888-362-3622
www.jbtc-agv.com
Automated guided vehicles
Manager: Barry Douglas
  barry.douglas@jbtc.com
Advertising Manager: Amy Porter
Estimated Sales: $50 - 100 Million
Number Employees: 100-249

24613 (HQ)John Boos & Co
3601 S Banker St
PO Box 609
Effingham, IL 62401-2899
    217-347-7701
Fax: 217-347-7705 888-431-2667
www.johnboos.com
Manufacturer and exporter of cutting boards, butchers' blocks, dining room tables and chairs and stainless steel work tables and sinks
President: Edward Surowiec
  gerencia@cibersam.es
Executive Chef: Dustin Muroski
VP Sales: Eric Johnson
Estimated Sales: $10-20 Million
Number Employees: 20-49
Square Footage: 260000
Other Locations:
  John Boos & Co.
  Philipsburg PA
Brands:
  Cucina Americana
  Pro Bowl
  Pro Chef
  Stallion
  The Table Tailors

24614 John Burton Machine Corporation
3251 John Muir Pkwy
Rodeo, CA 94572
    510-799-5000
Fax: 510-799-5003 800-664-4178
Packaging machines and case conveyor, case conveyors for cardboard boxes and tote boxes
President: Burton Rice
Sales Director: Burton Rice
Estimated Sales: Below $5 Million
Number Employees: 1-4
Brands:
  Chain-In-Channel

24615 John Crane Mechanical Sealing Devices
227 W Monroe St
Suite 1800
Chicago, IL 60606
www.johncrane.com
Manufacturer and exporter of mechanical seals, bearing isolators, couplings, lubrication systems, heat exchangers and pressure reservoirs.
President & CEO: Jean Vernet
CFO: Celine Boland
Chief Technology Officer: Cyrille Levesque
Vice President, Global Quality: Terri Willis
Year Founded: 1910
Estimated Sales: $900 Million
Number Employees: 6,550
Square Footage: 9000
Parent Co: TI Group

24616 John E. Ruggles & Company
PO Box 8179
New Bedford, MA 02742-8179
508-992-9766
Fax: 508-992-9734
Manufacturer, importer and exporter of varietal fiber regular and dyed rope, twine and braid
President: John Ruggles
Estimated Sales: $5-10 Million
Number Employees: 50-99
Square Footage: 100000

24617 John Henry Packaging
10005 Main St
Penngrove, CA 94951
707-664-8018
Fax: 707-762-1253 800-327-5997
Producer of digital, flexo, embossed, screened labels and cartons
Owner: John Herpeck
Digital Print Manager/Marketing Director: Dan Welty
Number Employees: 5-9
Number of Brands: 30
Square Footage: 8000
Parent Co: John Henry Company
Type of Packaging: Consumer, Food Service, Private Label, Bulk

24618 John J. Adams Die Corporation
10 Nebraska St
Worcester, MA 01604-3628
508-757-3894
Fax: 508-753-8016 jadamsdie@aol.com
Knives; exporter of cutting dies
President and CFO: Richard Adams
General Manager: John J Adams II
Marketing: John Adams
Estimated Sales: $2.5 - 5 Million
Number Employees: 1-4
Square Footage: 40000

24619 John L. Denning & Company
330 N Washington St
Wichita, KS 67202
316-264-2357
Fax: 316-264-3521
Brooms
President: Ed Collins
Number Employees: 4

24620 John Larkin & Co Inc
96 Ford Rd # 15
Denville, NJ 07834-1359
973-627-7779
Fax: 973-627-7809 john.larkin@verizon.net
www.johnlarkinandcompany.com
Tea and coffee industry repair service
President: John Larkin
john.larkin@verizon.net
Estimated Sales: $1 - 2.5 Million
Number Employees: 1-4

24621 John Morrell Food Group
PO Box 405020
Cincinnati, OH 45240
800-722-1127
www.johnmorrell.com
Meat products including; ham and turkey, bacon, hot dogs, smoked sausage, lunchmeat, and special reserve hams.
President/CEO, Smithfield Foods: Kenneth Sullivan
Year Founded: 1827
Estimated Sales: Over $1 Billion
Number Employees: 5000-9999
Parent Co: Smithfield Foods
Type of Packaging: Consumer, Food Service, Private Label, Bulk
Brands:
  John Morrell

24622 John Plant Co
112 Greenhill Rd
Ramseur, NC 27316-8749
336-824-2366
Fax: 336-824-3177 800-334-2711
gloves@johnplant.com www.johnplant.com
Manufacturer and importer of gloves and safety supplies
Owner: Robert Jarman
jarman@johnplant.com
CEO: Ron Tesh
Estimated Sales: $2.5 - 5 Million
Number Employees: 10-19

24623 John R Nalbach Engineering Co
621 E Plainfield Rd
Countryside, IL 60525-6913
708-579-9100
Fax: 708-579-0122 neco@nalbach.com
www.nalbach.com
Manufacturer and exporter of high speed powder fillers for instant coffee, ground coffee and drink mixes; also, plastic bottle unscrambles, container orientors and aerosol filling lines.
Owner: Matt Nalbach
CEO: John Nalbach
VP Engineering: David Nowaczyk
VP Marketing: Edward Atwell
VP Sales: Gary Lange
mnalbach@nalbach.com
VP Manufacturing: Phil Testa
Estimated Sales: $5 - 10 Million
Number Employees: 20-49
Square Footage: 280000

24624 John Rock Inc
500 Independence Way
Coatesville, PA 19320-1689
610-857-4809
Fax: 610-857-4809 www.johnrock.com
Recycled wooden pallets
President: Bill Mac Cauley
bill@johnrock.com
Finance: Steve Hedrick
Lumber: Penn Cooper
Sales: Mike Veneziale
Customer Service: Jeanne Ryan
Operations: Ed Healy
Administration: Robyn Stoltzfus
Facilities/Fleet: Steve Marrs
Estimated Sales: $5 - 10 Million
Number Employees: 50-99
Square Footage: 200000

24625 John Rohrer ContractingCo
2820 Roe Ln # S
Kansas City, KS 66103-1560
913-236-5005
Fax: 913-236-7291
www.johnrohrercontracting.com
Manufacturer and exporter of concrete floors
Owner: Kirt Courkamp
kirtcourkamp@jrcccolorado.net
EVP: Brandon McMullen
Estimated Sales: $1-2.5 Million
Number Employees: 10-19

24626 John W Keplinger & Sons
2789 Egypt Rd
Norristown, PA 19403-2254
610-666-6191
Fax: 610-666-6215
Flags, banners and flagpoles
Owner: John W Keplinger
Estimated Sales: Less Than $500,000
Number Employees: 1-4

24627 John W. Spaulding Brokerage
2035 W McDowell Rd
Phoenix, AZ 85009-3012
602-254-4777
Fax: 602-258-5623
Wholesaler/distributor of salt products including food grade, water softener, agricultural, etc.; serving the food service market
Owner: John W Spalding Iii
CEO: John Spaulding
Estimated Sales: $500,000-$1 Million
Number Employees: 7
Type of Packaging: Food Service, Private Label, Bulk

24628 Johnson & Sons Manufacturing
534-D West 2nd St.
Elgin, TX 78261
512-285-2462
Fax: 512-285-2464
info@johnsonbaggingequipment.com
www.johnsonbaggingequipment.com
Contact: Brent Johnson
brent@johnsonbaggingequipment.com
Estimated Sales: $300,000 - $500,000
Number Employees: 1-4

24629 Johnson & Wales University
8 Abbott Park Pl
Providence, RI 02903-3775
401-598-1000
Fax: 401-598-2880 800-342-5598
President: John J Bowen
Executive VP: Richard J Kosh
rkosh@jwu.edu
Number Employees: 1000-4999

24630 Johnson Associates
600 W Roosevelt Rd
Unit B-2
Wheaton, IL 60187
630-690-9200
Fax: 630-690-9910 sjohnson@jasearch.com
www.jasearch.com
Executive search firm specializing in the food, non-food and beverage industries
President: Scott Johnson
VP: Mary Johnson
Contact: Don Huston
dhuston@jasearch.com
Estimated Sales: Below $5 Million
Number Employees: 1-4

24631 Johnson Brothers Manufacturing Company
412 W 3rd Street
Elgin, TX 78621-2117
512-285-2462
Fax: 512-285-2464
Bagging scales
Estimated Sales: $1 - 5 Million
Number Employees: 1-4

24632 Johnson Brothers Sign Co Inc
307 S State St
PO Box 345
South Whitley, IN 46787-1409
260-723-5161
Fax: 260-723-6778 800-477-7516
info@johnsonbros-sign.com
www.johnsonbros-sign.com
Electric, neon and plastic signs
President: Les Cripe
les@johnsonbros-sign.com
Estimated Sales: $1-2.5 Million
Number Employees: 10-19
Square Footage: 37600

24633 Johnson Controls Inc
5757 N Green Bay Ave
P.O. Box 591
Milwaukee, WI 53209-4408
414-524-1200
Fax: 414-524-2077 www.johnsoncontrols.com
Gas and electronic and electromechanical refrigeration controls, HVAC/refrigeration/lighting store management systems
Chairman & CEO: George Oliver
EVP & CFO: Olivier Leonetti
Estimated Sales: Over $1 Billion
Number Employees: 10000+

24634 Johnson Corrugated Products Corporation
PO Box 246
Thompson, CT 06277
860-923-9563
Fax: 860-923-2531
Corrugated packaging materials inlcuding corrugated and paper boxes; also, cake and pizza circles
Manager: Andrew Baumont
General Manager: Dick Clark
Estimated Sales: $20-50 Million
Number Employees: 10-19

24635 Johnson Diversified Products
1408 Northland Dr
Suite 406
Mendota Heights, MN 55120-1013
651-688-0014
Fax: 952-686-7670 800-676-8488
info@jdpinc.com www.jdpinc.com
Wholesaler/distributor of food service equipment, and HACCP related instruments, tools and systems; serving the food service market
CEO: Thomas Johnson
Vice President: Paul Johnson
Estimated Sales: $5 - 10 Million
Number Employees: 5-9

24636 (HQ)Johnson Food Equipment Inc
2955 Fairfax Trfy
Kansas City, KS 66115-1317
913-621-3366
Fax: 913-621-1729 800-288-3434
www.baader-johnson.com
Poultry processing equipment
President: Andy Miller
CEO: Oliver Hahn
oliver.hahn@baaderna.com
CFO: Shawn Nicholas
Sr VP: David Crawford
General Sales Manager: Steve Abram
Sales Manager (Food Systems): Bruce Sterling
Estimated Sales: $20 - 50 Million
Number Employees: 10-19
Square Footage: 70000
Other Locations:
Johnson Food Equipment
Kitchener ON

24637 Johnson Industries Intl
6391 Lake Rd
Windsor, WI 53598-9708
608-846-4499
Fax: 608-846-7195 info@johnsonindint.com
www.johnsonindint.com
Manufacturer and exporter of mozzarella cheese
making machinery
President: Gary Nesheim
gnesheim@johnsonindint.com
Estimated Sales: $5 - 10 Million
Number Employees: 50-99
Square Footage: 77408
Brands:
Supreme

24638 Johnson Industries Intl
6391 Lake Rd
Windsor, WI 53598-9708
608-846-4499
Fax: 608-846-7195 info@johnsonindint.com
www.johnsonindint.com
Manufacturer cheese processing equipment
President: Gary Nesheim
gnesheim@johnsonindint.com
Owner and Cheese Industry Expert: Peter Nelles
Sales Director: Todd Martin
Plant Manager: Eric Severson
Director Purchasing: Scott Peterson
Number Employees: 50-99
Number of Brands: 4
Square Footage: 200000

24639 Johnson International Materials
2908 Boca Chica Blvd
Brownsville, TX 78521-3506
956-541-6364
Fax: 956-541-1446
Manufacturer and exporter of wiping rags
President: Jim Johnson
VP Marketing: Bob Ewing
Estimated Sales: $20-50 Million
Number Employees: 100-249

24640 Johnson Pump of America
1625 Hunter Rd
Hanover Park, IL 60133-6767
847-671-7867
Fax: 847-671-7909 www.johnson-pump.com
Positive displacement rotary lobe pumps
CEO: Jerry Assessor
VP Sales: Mitch Pixley
Contact: Gregg Pardus
johnson-pump.americas.marine@spx.com
Production Manager: Tony Wuethrich
Estimated Sales: $20 - 50 Million
Number Employees: 50-99
Parent Co: Johnson Pumps of America
Brands:
Albin

24641 (HQ)Johnson Refrigerated Truck
215 E Allen St
Rice Lake, WI 54868-2203
715-234-7071
Fax: 715-234-4628 800-922-8360
jtbsales@johnsontruckbodies.com
Manufacturer and exporter of fiberglass composite
plastic refrigerated truck bodies and trailers, and
all-electric truck refrigeration systems.

President: Ron Ricci
rricci@johnsontruckbodies.com
VP Sales/Marketing: Mayo Rude
Public Relations: Nicole King
VP Operations: Chris Olson
Number Employees: 250-499
Square Footage: 268000
Type of Packaging: Food Service

24642 Johnson Starch Molding
13549 W Greenview Drive
Wadsworth, IL 60083-9309
847-872-1989
Fax: 847-872-1988
Boards, starch, conveyors, cooling equipment, cool-
ing tunnels, elevators, bucket, feeder belts
Estimated Sales: $1 - 5 Million
Number Employees: 4

24643 Johnson-Rose Corporation
5303 Crown Dr
Lockport, NY 14094
716-434-2711
Fax: 716-434-2762 800-456-2055
info@johnsonrose.com www.johnsonrose.com
Aluminum cookware and bakeware; importer and
exporter of commercial kitchen utensils including
ladles, spoons, tongs, mixing bowls, collanders,
steam pans, etc
President: Ernie Berman
ernieberman@johnsonrose.net
CFO: Viola Wilson
Director of Marketing: Mark Kuligowski
Operations Manager: D Kuligowski
Inventory Control: Darrell Szyprygada
Estimated Sales: $2.5-5 Million
Number Employees: 20-49
Square Footage: 82000
Parent Co: Johnson-Rose

24644 Johnston Boiler Co Inc
300 Pine St
Ferrysburg, MI 49409-5131
616-842-5050
Fax: 616-842-1854 info@johnstonboiler.com
www.johnstonboiler.com
Boilers, generators, heat recovery systems, burners,
energy savings, JBC engineering, emission data,
JBC specifications, driving directions
President: R Kim Black
COO: Rick Ewing
rewing@johnstonboiler.com
Director: Pat Baker
Estimated Sales: $5 - 10 Million
Number Employees: 1-4

24645 Johnston Equipment
#105-581 Chester Road
Annacis Island
Delta, BC V3M 6G7
Canada
604-524-0361
Fax: 604-524-8961 800-237-5159
couttsd@johnstonequipment.com
www.johnstonequipment.com
Manufacturer, wholesaler/distributor and exporter of
material handling equipment including electric fork-
lifts and pallet racking/shelving systems
President & CEO: Michael Marcotte
Regional Sales Manager: John Binns
Sales Manager: Curt Snigol
Estimated Sales: $1 - 5 Million
Number Employees: 50-99
Square Footage: 66000
Brands:
Pacific Westeel
Serco

24646 Johnstown Manufacturing
1055 S Hamilton Rd
Columbus, OH 43227-1309
614-236-8853
Fax: 614-876-6797
Plastic straws and stirrers
Manager: John Scott
Number Employees: 50-99

24647 Jokamsco Group
22 Lea Ave
Waterford,, NY 12118-1927
518-237-6416
Fax: 518-233-7203 Jokamsco@aol.com
www.hudsonrivergrinding.com

Gears and machine replacement parts for the food
and beverage industry; also, industrial knife grind-
ing available
President: Colleen Swedish
Estimated Sales: $300,000-500,000
Number Employees: 1-4
Square Footage: 10000

24648 Jomac Products
7525 N Oak Park Avenue
Niles, IL 60714-3819
215-343-0800
Fax: 215-343-0912 800-566-2289
Manufacturer and exporter of terrycloth, cut-resis-
tant and nomex gloves, mitts, aprons, pads and
sleeves
Marketing Manager: Charlie Lake
Sales Manager: Jim Podall
Number Employees: 499
Type of Packaging: Food Service, Bulk
Brands:
Cool Blues
Pott Holdr
The Shield

24649 Jomar Corp
115 E Parkway Dr
Egg Harbor Twp, NJ 08234-5112
609-646-8000
Fax: 609-645-9166 www.jomarcorp.com
Manufacturer and exporter of plastic injection blow
molding machinery and plastic molds and dies
President: William Petrino
Founder: Joseph Johnson
Senior VP: Walter Priest
Contact: Ed Burns
eburns@jomarcorp.com
Estimated Sales: $10-20 Million
Number Employees: 20-49
Square Footage: 90000
Parent Co: Inductotherm Industries
Brands:
Aquatral
Jomar

24650 Jomar Plastics Industry
1304 Shoemaker St
Nanty Glo, PA 15943-1255
814-749-9131
Fax: 814-749-8079 800-681-4039
info@floodcity.net
Plastic bags for bakery, meat and poultry
President: Pam Harkcom
VP: Susan Ott
Estimated Sales: $500,000-$1 Million
Number Employees: 1-4
Square Footage: 10000

24651 Joneca Corp
4332 E LA Palma Ave
Anaheim, CA 92807-1806
714-993-5997
Fax: 714-993-2126 info@joneca.com
www.joneca.com
Manufacturer and exporter of dehydrators and waste
reduction and water purification systems
President: Edward E Chavez
contactus@joneca.com
Estimated Sales: Below $5 Million
Number Employees: 10-19
Parent Co: Anaheim Marketing International
Brands:
Aquacare
Commodore
Compacta
Mr. Scrapy

24652 Jones Automation Company
11838 W Carroll Rd
Beloit, WI 53511
608-879-9307
Fax: 608-879-2266
Forming, filling and sealing equipment, stacking and
interleaving equipment, vacuum packaging equipment, wrapping and overwrap machines, slicers and
weigh-convey systems
Estimated Sales: $1-5 Million
Number Employees: 10

24653 Jones Environmental
2404 Rutland Dr Ste 200
P.O. Box 5387
Fullerton, CA 92838
714-449-9937
Fax: 714-449-9685 www.jonesenv.com
Waste treatment plants capable of anaerobic and aerobic processes for the food and beverage industries; custom design services available
President: Jim Porteous
CEO: Dick Johnson
CFO: Nelda Tallman
Chairman: Richard Johnson
Marketing Assistant: Ann Perry
Production: Arthur Shaffer
Estimated Sales: Less than $500,000
Number Employees: 20-49

24654 Jones Packaging Machinery
8005 Wolftever Dr
Ooltewah, TN 37363
423-238-4558
Fax: 423-238-6018
Packaging machinery
President: Charles Abernathy
CFO: Charles Abernathy
Quality Control: Jeff Smith
Plant Manager: James Dillard
Estimated Sales: Below $5 Million
Number Employees: 10
Square Footage: 24000

24655 Jones-Hamilton Co
30354 Tracy Rd
Walbridge, OH 43465-9792
419-666-9838
Fax: 419-666-1817 888-858-4425
info@jones-hamilton.com
www.jones-hamilton.com
Producer of natural acidulants and pHase.
CFO: Brian Brooks
EVP: Bernard Murphy
Director Research & Development: Carl Knueven
IT: Daniel Dias
dad@jones-hamilton.com
Plant Manager: Chuck Almroth
Estimated Sales: $64 Million
Number Employees: 50-99

24656 Jones-Zylon Co
305 N Center St
West Lafayette, OH 43845-1001
740-545-6341
Fax: 740-545-6671 800-848-8160
miker@joneszylon.com www.joneszylon.com
Institutional tableware, compartments and serving trays, tumblers, cups, bowls, plates and reusable plastic flatware; exporter of dinnerware and flatware
President: Todd Kohl
toddk@joneszylon.net
CEO: Tracey Jackrich
Quality Control: Chuck Laney
Sales (Mid Atlantic): Mike Robertson
Sales (West): Myron Vile
Chairperson: Marion Mulligan-Sutton
Estimated Sales: $5 - 10 Million
Number Employees: 10-19
Square Footage: 81600
Parent Co: Jones Metal Products Company
Brands:
Jones Zylon

24657 Jonessco Enterprises
2801 Regal Road
Suite 103
Plano, TX 75075-6315
972-985-7961
Fax: 972-612-1741 www.whereorg.com
Consultant specializing in food technology, marketing and promotion for the supermarket and food service industries
President: Buck Jones
CFO: Buck Jones
R&D: Bill Jacob
Estimated Sales: Below $5 Million
Number Employees: 5
Type of Packaging: Bulk

24658 Jordan Box Co
140 Dickerson St
PO Box 1054
Syracuse, NY 13202-2309
315-422-3419
Fax: 315-422-0318 sales@JordanBoxCo.com
www.jordanboxco.com
Paper boxes
President: Richard M Casper
rick@jordanboxco.com
Estimated Sales: $1-2.5 Million
Number Employees: 10-19

24659 Jordan Paper Box Co
5045 W Lake St
Chicago, IL 60644-2596
773-287-5362
Fax: 773-287-5362
Manufacturer, importer and exporter of paper boxes
President: John M Jordan
jordanpaperbox@att.net
President: Jam Jordan
Estimated Sales: $1 - 2.5 Million
Number Employees: 5-9
Square Footage: 60000
Type of Packaging: Bulk

24660 Jordan Specialty Company
1245 Route 1 South
Brooklyn, NY 11215-4603
Fax: 718-238-3221 877-567-3265
Transparent card cases, covers, holders and menu covers
Manager: Joshua Handler
Manager: Soul Handler
Estimated Sales: $1-2.5 Million
Number Employees: 20-49
Square Footage: 50000
Brands:
Bondstar

24661 Jordon Commercial Refrigerator
2200 Kennedy Street
Philadelphia, PA 19137-1820
215-535-8300
Fax: 215-289-1597 800-523-0171
Manufacturer, importer and exporter of refrigerators and freezers
President: Gene Sterner
VP, Sales: Jim Duff
Purchasing Manager: Jerry Joyce
Number Employees: 100-249
Square Footage: 296000
Parent Co: Jordon/Fleetwood/Fogel, LLC
Other Locations:
Jordon Commercial Refrigerato
Fleetwood PA
Brands:
Fleetwood
Fogel
Jordon

24662 Jordon-Fleetwood Commercial Refrigerator Company
2200 Kennedy Street
Philadelphia, PA 19137-1820
215-535-8300
Fax: 215-289-1597 www.keepitcool.com

24663 (HQ)Josam Co
525 W US Highway 20
Michigan City, IN 46360-6835
219-872-5531
Fax: 219-874-9539 800-365-6726
www.josam.com
Drains, interceptors, backwater valves, carriers, hydrants and water hammer arrestors
President: Barry Hodgkins
President, Chief Executive Officer: Scott Holloway
CFO: David Szerencse
Vice President of Sales and Marketing: Paula Bowe
Chief Operating Officer: Barry Hodgekins
Estimated Sales: $20 - 50 Million
Number Employees: 100-249

24664 Josef Kihlberg of America
2400 Galvin Dr
Elgin, IL 60124
Fax: 315-452-9597 800-437-9818
Stapling and strapping tools and fasteners
Estimated Sales: $1 - 3 Million
Number Employees: 10-19

24665 Joseph Manufacturing Company
5011 Antioch Road
Overland Park, KS 66203-1314
913-677-1660
Fax: 913-677-1658 800-373-6671
Automated and manual label dispensing and applying equipment
V.P.: Shawn Hornung
Estimated Sales: $5-10 Million
Number Employees: 19

24666 Joseph Struhl Co Inc
195 Atlantic Ave
PO Box N
New Hyde Park, NY 11040-5027
516-741-3660
Fax: 516-742-3617 800-552-0023
info@magicmaster.com www.magicmaster.com
Manufacturer and exporter of signs including open/closed self-adhesive reusable and removable static vinyl and stock and custom using static cling vinyl
Managing Director: Cliff Stevens
cliff@magicmaster.com
Sales Manager: H Green
Manager: Cliff Stevens
Estimated Sales: $1 - 2.5 Million
Number Employees: 10-19
Brands:
Design Master
Magic Master
Ready Made
Super Moderna

24667 Joseph Titone & Sons
1006 Jacksonville Rd
Burlington, NJ 08016-3802
Fax: 609-386-8978 800-220-4102
www.metrolace.com
Nets and hair nets for food handlers
President: Alfred Titone
CFO/Attorney: John Titone
V.P.: Edward Dormand
Number Employees: 20-49
Square Footage: 110000

24668 Joul, Engineering StaffiSolutions
1245 Route 1 South
Raritan Plaza 1
Edison, NJ 8837
732-548-1069
Fax: 732-632-9795 800-341-0341
Consultant of custom design plant modernization and automation equipment
Senior VP: Howard Moseman
Estimated Sales: $1 - 5 Million
Number Employees: 50-99
Parent Co: Joule

24669 Jowat Corp.
PO Box 1368
High Point, NC 27261
336-434-9000
Fax: 336-434-9019 800-322-4583
info@jowat.com www.jowat.com
Packaging hot melts, anti-slip hot melts, casein glues, pressure sensitives, dextrins, water-based dispersions
President/Owner: Rainhard Kramme
Estimated Sales: $10,000,000 - $19,999,999
Number Employees: 1,100

24670 Joyce Dayton Corp
3300 S Dixie Dr # 101
Moraine, OH 45439-2318
937-294-6261
Fax: 937-297-7173 800-523-5204
sales@joycedayton.com www.joycedayton.com
Lifts including hydraulic and mechanical powered
President: Patty Deppen
jgoodman@mcdonald-partners.com
CFO: Kim Gockal
Director Sales: Warren Webster
Estimated Sales: $10 - 20,000,000
Number Employees: 50-99

24671 Joyce Engraving Co Inc
1262 Round Table Dr
Dallas, TX 75247-3504
214-638-1262
Fax: 214-638-5432 sales@joyceengraving.com
www.joyce-engraving.com

Steel stamps, stencils and branding equipment including burning, meat and tire
VP: Rick Joyce
  ricky@joyceengraving.com
VP: R Joyce
Estimated Sales: Less Than $500,000
Number Employees: 1-4
Square Footage: 40000

24672 Joylin Food Equipment Corporation
51 Chestnut Ln
Woodbury, NY 11797-1918

Fax: 516-742-2123 800-456-9546
joylin1961@aol.com
Manufacturers' representative for food service equipment
President: Rich Kirsner
Marketing Director: Tom Pitts
Sales Director: M Kohn
Operations Manager: Tom DiRusso
Purchasing Manager: Yvette Western
Estimated Sales: $20-50 Million
Number Employees: 21
Number of Brands: 16
Square Footage: 12000

24673 Jr Mats
1519 Mcdaniel Dr
West Chester, PA 19380-7037

610-344-7225
Fax: 610-696-6760 800-526-7763
justrightmats@aol.com
Manufacturer and distributor of quality entry matting, kitchen matting and antifatigue matting. Custom logo mats
Owner: Jay Mc Grath
Sales/Marketing: Jay McGrath
  jrmats@comcast.net
General Manager: Jeri Delahanty
Estimated Sales: $1 Million
Number Employees: 1-4
Number of Brands: 10
Number of Products: 25
Square Footage: 116000
Type of Packaging: Consumer, Food Service, Private Label, Bulk
Brands:
  Silver Streak

24674 Judel Products
45 Knollwood Road
Suite 24
Elmsford, NY 10523-2822

914-592-6200
Fax: 914-592-1216 800-583-3526
Manufacturer, importer and exporter of glassware
President: Mel Schulweis
VP: John Rufus
Sales Director: Stven Fox
Office Manager: Dorothy See
Estimated Sales: $500,000 - $1 Million
Number Employees: 1-4
Parent Co: Tiffany & Company
Type of Packaging: Food Service
Brands:
  Durobor
  Judel
  Opticrystal
  Vintner's Ii
  Vintner's Selection

24675 Judge
300 Conshohocken State Rd #300
W Conshohocken, PA 19428-3820

610-667-7700
Fax: 610-667-1058 888-228-7162
wgladstone@judge.com www.judgeinc.com
Executive search agency specializing in operations and distribution management
President: Michael F Ferreri
CEO: Martin Judge, Jr.
Estimated Sales: $1 - 5 Million
Number Employees: 20-49
Parent Co: Judge Group

24676 Juice Merchandising Corp
9237 Ward Pkwy # 104
Suite 104
Kansas City, MO 64114-3382

816-361-5343
Fax: 816-361-2033 800-950-1998

Plastic juice bottles as well as wholesaler/distributor of juice processing equipment
Owner: Bob Bushman
  juice@micro.ct
CEO: Helen Bushman
Manager, Operations: Bill Young
Estimated Sales: Below $5 Million
Number Employees: 1-4
Square Footage: 4000
Type of Packaging: Private Label

24677 Juice Tree
10861 Mill Valley Road
Omaha, NE 68154-3975

714-891-4425
Fax: 714-892-3699
Manufacturer and exporter of citrus juice extractors, pineapple peelers, mobile ice display tables for fresh fruit products and capped plastic containers for juice
President: James Beck
Plant Administrator: B Copeland
Estimated Sales: $1-2.5 Million
Number Employees: 19
Brands:
  Juice Tree

24678 Juicy Whip Inc
1668 Curtiss Ct
La Verne, CA 91750-5848

909-392-7500
Fax: 626-814-8016 www.juicywhip.com
Hispanic beverage concentrates
President/CEO: Gus Stratton
Purchasing: Craig Allen
Estimated Sales: $4 Million
Number Employees: 5-9
Square Footage: 88000
Brands:
  Juicy Whip

24679 Junction Solutions
9785 Maroon Cir
Suite 410
Englewood, CO 80112

877-502-6355
Fax: 303-327-8804
webinfo@junctionsolutions.com
www.junctionsolutions.com
Advanced enterprise software that allows food and beverage processors to improve control over operations, quality, and compliance
CEO/President: Jeff Grell
CFO: Jeff Allen
Product Marketing: George Casey
VP Sales: Michael Frauenhoffer
Contact: Hillary Mccrea
  hillary.mccrea@airtalk.com
COO: Jeff Grell
VP Product Development: Greg Penn

24680 Jupiter Mills Corporation
20 Walnut Dr
Roslyn, NY 11576

516-484-1166
Fax: 516-484-1242 800-853-5121
info@jupitermillscorp.com
Manufacturer and exporter of bags, barrels, drums, bottles, boxes, cans, cartons, cases, containers, foam, packaging materials, paper, partitions, tapes and tubes
President: Fred Fisher
Customer Service: Harvey Chestman
Office Manager: Pat Fisher
Estimated Sales: $5,000,000
Number Employees: 20-49
Square Footage: 2000

24681 Jus-Made
9761 Clifford Dr Ste 100
Dallas, TX 75220

972-241-5544
Fax: 972-241-3399 800-969-3746
Beverages and beverage mixes; beverage equipment
President: Gene Barfield
VP Sales: Jim Tanner
Contact: Matt Cook
  mcook@jus-made.com
Operations Manager: Mike Sayre
Estimated Sales: $1 - 3 Million
Number Employees: 50-99
Square Footage: 14000
Type of Packaging: Consumer, Food Service, Private Label, Bulk

Other Locations:
Jus-Made
Houston TX
Brands:
  Floria Julep
  Orogold

24682 Just Plastics Inc
250 Dyckman St
New York, NY 10034-5354

212-569-8500
Fax: 212-569-6970 info@justplastics.com
www.justplastics.us
Manufacturer and exporter of custom acrylic point of purchase displays, signs, sneeze guards, menu holders, tent card holders and containers
President: Robert Vermann
  info@justplastics.com
VP: Lois Vermann
Sales Associate: Tommy de Los Angeles
VP: Robert Vermann
Estimated Sales: $20 - 50 Million
Number Employees: 10-19
Square Footage: 15000

24683 Justman Brush Co
828 Crown Point Ave
Omaha, NE 68110-2828

402-451-4420
Fax: 402-451-1473 800-800-6940
www.justmanbrush.com
Manufacturer and exporter of twisted-in-wire brushes including bottle, toilet bowl, hospital and laboratory
Owner: Justman Company
  justmanbrush@aol.com
Estimated Sales: $1-2.5 Million
Number Employees: 20-49
Square Footage: 24000

24684 Justrite Rubber Stamp &Seal
1701 Locust St
Kansas City, MO 64108-1401

816-421-5010
Fax: 816-421-1939 800-229-5010
sales@justriterubberstamp.com
www.justriterubberstamp.com
Rubber stamps, daters, self-inking and pre-inked, custom logos and kits.
Owner: Paul Thomas
  justrite01@aol.com
CFO/R&D: Paul Thomas
Estimated Sales: $1 - 2.5 Million
Number Employees: 1-4
Square Footage: 20000

24685 Jutras Signs & Flags
711 Mast Rd
Manchester, NH 03102-1425

603-622-2344
Fax: 603-623-3562 800-924-3524
graphics@jutrassigns.com
Signs including interior and exterior illuminated, billboards and neon and electronic message centers; also, flagpoles and accessories available
President: Cathy Champagne
Contact: Susan Gelinas
  sgelinas@jutrassigns.com
General Manager: Joe Champagne
Estimated Sales: Less Than $500,000
Number Employees: 1-4
Square Footage: 40000

24686 Juvenal Direct
PO Box 5449
Napa, CA 94581-0449

707-254-2000
Fax: 707-642-2288 888-254-2060
Grape presses, membrane presses and wine corks
CEO: Manuel Santiago
Number Employees: 8

24687 Jwc Environmental
290 Paularino Ave
Costa Mesa, CA 92626-3314

949-833-3888
Fax: 949-833-8858 800-331-2277
jwce@jwce.com www.jwce.com
Heavy duty solids reduction grinders, screening, and dewatering equipment

President: Ron Duecker
CFO: John Harrison
Marketing Director: Fritz Egger
Sales Director: Pete Garcia
Contact: Scot Anderson
    scota@jwce.com
Estimated Sales: $20 - 30 Million
Number Employees: 1-4
Square Footage: 55000
Parent Co: JWC International
Brands:
    Auger Monster
    Channel Monster
    Muffin Monster

24688 K & H Corrugated Corp
330 Lake Osiris Rd
Walden, NY 12586-2605
                            845-778-3555
        Fax: 845-778-7417 www.unicorr.com
Corrugated boxes
Manager: Mark Andrews
    m.andrews@unicorr.com
Estimated Sales: $20-50 Million
Number Employees: 20-49
Parent Co: K&H Corrugated Case Corporation

24689 K & I Creative Plastics& Wood
582 Nixon St
Jacksonville, FL 32204-3010
                            904-387-0438
    Fax: 904-387-0430 www.kicreativeplastics.net
Displays, sneeze guards, engraved signs, food bins
and condiment trays; also, metal engraved signs,
custom plastic fabricating available, and point of
purchase displays
Owner: Bonnie Osterman
Manager: Bob Korda
    sales@kicreativeplastics.net
Estimated Sales: $1 - 3 Million
Number Employees: 5-9
Square Footage: 24000

24690 K & L Intl
1929 S Campus Ave
Ontario, CA 91761-5410
                            909-923-9258
    Fax: 909-923-9228 888-598-5588
        info@knl-international.com
        www.knl-international.com
Manufacturer, Importer and Exporter of chopsticks,
toothpicks, guest checks, napkins, plastic T-Shirt
bags, bamboo skewers, matches, sushi containers,
wood sushi plates, wood sushi boats (bridge), swirl
bowls, dried seaweed, eel(unagi), wasabi powder
and soybean (edamame).
President: David Kao
VP: Susan Lin
Marketing Director: Richard Yeang
Manager: May Lin
Estimated Sales: $5 - 10 Million
Number Employees: 10-19
Number of Products: 20
Square Footage: 100000
Type of Packaging: Food Service, Private Label

24691 K & M Intl Inc
1955 Midway Dr # A
Twinsburg, OH 44087-1961
                            330-425-2550
    Fax: 330-425-3777 www.wildrepublicretail.com
LED signs for display
Owner: G B Pillai
CFO: G Pillai
Sales Manager: Marianne Zmyslinski
    gpillai@kmtoys.com
Estimated Sales: $20 - 50 Million
Number Employees: 20-49

24692 K B Systems Inc
90 Jacktown Rd
Bangor, PA 18013-9504
                            610-588-7788
        Fax: 610-588-7785 www.geminibe.com
Material hadling systems flour/sugar; roll, pita bread
and tortilla equipment
President: Karl Brunner
    kbrunner@kbsystemsinc.com
Estimated Sales: $5-10 Million
Number Employees: 20-49

24693 K C Booth Co
1760 Burlington St
N Kansas City, MO 64116-3892
                            816-471-1921
        Fax: 816-471-2461 800-866-5226
        info@kcbooth.com www.kcbooth.com
Manufacturer and exporter of benches, front-end
booths, tables and chairs
President: Scott Neuman
    scott@kcbooth.com
VP: Scott Neuman
Operations Manager: Jack Buddemeyer
Estimated Sales: $5-10 Million
Number Employees: 20-49
Type of Packaging: Food Service

24694 (HQ)K Katen & Company
65 E Cherry Street
Rahway, NJ 07065-4011
                            732-381-0220
Manufacturer and importer of linen goods including
tablecloths, napkins, pillowcases and kitchen towels
VP: Pauline Katen
Manager: Benny Yabut
Manager: Steven Richards
Number Employees: 3
Square Footage: 4000
Type of Packaging: Consumer
Brands:
    Keepsake Table Fashions

24695 K Trader Inc.
1452 W. 9th Street
Suite D
Upland, CA 91786
                            909-949-0327
    Fax: 909-992-3471 sales@ktraderinc.com
                        www.ktraderinc.com
Exporter of fresh fruits, vegetables and meats to
overseas markets.
President: Robert Amakasu
Manager: Kay Shimivu
Estimated Sales: $1 Million
Number Employees: 10

24696 K&H Container
126 S Turnpike Road
Wallingford, CT 06492-4371
                            203-265-1547
                        Fax: 203-269-6837
Corrugated shipping containers
VP/General Manager: Steve Wasko
Customer Service Manager: Lou Carigliano
Plant Manager: Mark Andres
Estimated Sales: $5-10 Million
Number Employees: 20-49
Square Footage: 70000
Parent Co: K&H Corrugated Case Company

24697 K&R Equipment
2033 Gateway Place
Suite 500
San Jose, CA 95110
                            408-573-6427
                        Fax: 408-573-6471
Case forming, poly bag insertion, decuffing, case
sealing
President: Owen Kellep
CFO: Adam Kwiek
VP: Richard Lee
Marketing/Sales: Dennis Alexander
Plant Manager: Fred Kruger
Estimated Sales: Below $5 Million
Number Employees: 20-49
Number of Products: 15
Square Footage: 30000

24698 K-C Products Company
16780 Stagg Street
Van Nuys, CA 91406-1635
                            818-267-1600
                        Fax: 323-261-5882
Plastic bags and covers; also, vinyl and fabric table
cloths, chair pads, place mats, appliance covers, etc
VP: Ingrid Albrechtson
Operations Manager: George Chamberlain
Estimated Sales: $1 - 5 Million
Number Employees: 1-4

24699 K-Coe Isom
6125 Sky Pond Dr.
Ste. 200
Loveland, CO 80538
                            970-685-3500
                            800-461-4702
                            www.kcoe.com
Accounting and financial advisement for the agricul-
tural industry.
Year Founded: 1932
Number Employees: 300-500

24700 K-Patents
1804 Centre Point Cir # 106
Naperville, IL 60563-4849
                            630-955-1545
    Fax: 630-955-1585 info@kpatents-usa.com
                        www.kpatents.com
Process refractometer for in-line liquid concentra-
tion measurement
Vice President: Eric Gronowski
    eric.gronowski@kpatents-usa.com
Estimated Sales: $1 - 3 Million
Number Employees: 1-4
Parent Co: K-Patents OY

24701 K-Tron
PO Box
Salina, KS 67402-0017
                            785-825-1611
        Fax: 785-825-8759 info@ktron.com
Manufacturer and exporter of pneumatic conveying
and feeding systems
General Manager: Todd Smith
Estimated Sales: $20-50 Million
Number Employees: 100-249
Square Footage: 115000
Parent Co: K-Tron America

24702 K-Tron International
Routes 55 and 553
P.O. Box 888
Pitman, NJ 08071-0888
                            856-589-0500
    Fax: 856-256-3281 800-203-4130
Maqnufacture feeders for low to high feed rate ap-
plications, precision feeding and material control
with complete PLC-DCS system integration, vac-
uum loaders and receivers. Offer volumetric screw
feeders, weighbelt feeders, vibratingfeeders, etc
President: Kevin Bowen
Estimated Sales: $77.50 Million
Number Employees: 727
Square Footage: 92000
Parent Co: K-Tron International
Brands:
    Digi-Drive
    K-Commander
    K-Link
    K-Modular
    K-Tron Soder
    K10s
    K2-Modular
    Smart Flow Meter
    Smart Force Transducer

24703 K-Way Products
759 W Commercial St
Mount Carroll, IL 61053-9762
                            815-244-2800
        Fax: 815-244-2799 800-622-9163
Manufacturer and exporter of soda, juice, beer and
coffee dispensing equipment including pre and
post-mix ice chests, carbonator/chiller dry refriger-
ated systems and soda and liquor guns
VP Marketing: Gene Deleeuw
VP Sales: John Hiney
Estimated Sales: $5-10 Million
Number Employees: 20-49
Square Footage: 76000
Type of Packaging: Food Service
Brands:
    Bar-O-Matic
    K-Way

24704 K. Sidrane, Inc.
24 Baiting Place Road
Farmingdale, NY 11735
                            631-393-6974
                        www.ksidrane.com
Packaging and containers manufacturer, specializing
in beverage labels and shrink sleeves.

President: Neil Sidrane
Vice President: Adam Sidrane
Vice President: Zachary Sidrane
Director, Marketing: Arielle Sidrane
Chief Operations Officer: Michael Liff
Year Founded: 1948
Estimated Sales: $8.8 Million

24705 K.F. Logistics
10045 International Boulevard
Cincinnati, OH 45246-4845

513-874-0788
Fax: 513-881-5383 800-347-9100
www.buschman.com
Manufacturer and exporter of case conveyors and
sortation products
CFO and Sr VP Finance: Robert Duplain
Sr VP Sales/Marketing: Lawrence Frey
Number Employees: 10
Square Footage: 1200000

24706 KANE Bag Supply Co
1200 S East Ave
Baltimore, MD 21224-5099

410-732-5800
Fax: 410-675-0079
Plastic bags
Owner: Karen Kane
kaneandtarp@aol.com
VP: Karen Kane
Estimated Sales: $1-2.5 Million
Number Employees: 10-19
Square Footage: 40000

24707 KAPCO
1000 Cherry Street
PO Box 626
Kent, OH 44240

330-678-1626
Fax: 330-678-3922 800-843-5368
converting@kapco.com www.kapco.com
Manufacturer and exporter of coated and converted
pressure sensitive flexible materials, labels, tapes
and paper
President: Edward Small
Contact: Dan Barlett
dbarlett@kapco.com
Operations Manager: Phil Zavracky
Estimated Sales: $10 - 20 Million
Number Employees: 50-99
Square Footage: 180000

24708 KAPS All Packaging
200 Mill Rd.
Riverhead, NY 11901-3125

631-727-0300
Fax: 631-369-5939 www.kapsall.com
Packaging machinery including fluid filling, bottle
capping, bottle orienting and bottle cleaning; also,
unscramblers, torque meters cap sealers and con-
veyor systems.
President: Kenneth Herzog
Packaging Solutions: Michael Herzog
mherzog@kapsall.com
Year Founded: 1941
Estimated Sales: Less Than $500,000
Number Employees: 1-4
Square Footage: 65000
Brands:
Filz-All
Kaps-All
Orientainer
Torq-All

24709 KASCO Sharp Tech Corp
1569 Tower Grove Ave
St Louis, MO 63110-2287

314-771-1550
Fax: 314-771-5162 800-325-8940
service@kascocorp.com www.kascocorp.com
Seasonings and ingredients, knives, chopper plates,
grinder plates and other meat processing equipment
President: Brian Turner
bturner@kascocorp.com
CEO: Tom Orelup
Manufacturing Director: Bill McGuire
R & D: Jerry Peterson
Sales: Mark Dobson
Public Relations: David Neu
Production: Larry Jones
Plant Manager: Bill McGuire
Purchasing: Jerry Brooks
Estimated Sales: $10-25 Million
Number Employees: 50-99

24710 KASE Equipment
7400 Hub Pkwy
Cleveland, OH 44125-5735

216-642-9040
Fax: 216-986-0678 info@plastechnic.com
www.kaseequip.com
Manufacturer and exporter of printers for cups,
pails, lids and closures
President: Patrick Hawkins
patrick.hawkins@kaseequip.com
CEO: Edward Thomas
Estimated Sales: $50 - 100 Million
Number Employees: 50-99
Type of Packaging: Consumer, Food Service, Pri-
vate Label

24711 KATZ Marketing Solutions
295 S Dawson Ave
Columbus, OH 43209-1736

614-252-7824
Fax: 614-252-6113
info@katzmarketingsolutions.com
www.katzmarketingsolutions.com
A marketing and brand management consulting firm
specializing in consumer products and food bever-
age marketing
CEO: Carl Riis
carl.riis@katz-solutions.com
CEO: Tammy Katz
Estimated Sales: Less Than $500,000
Number Employees: 1-4
Type of Packaging: Consumer
Brands:
Boost
Borden
Dearfoams
Enfamil
Frito Lay
Miller Lite
Mount Vernon Mantel Company
Pathlire
Rice Select
Scotts
Sopakco
Titebond

24712 KBR Building Group
5605 Carnegie Boulevard
Suite 200
Charlotte, NC 28209

704-551-2700
Fax: 919-859-9011 www.bekbuildinggroup.com
Products and services for the food and beverage in-
dustry includes: processing facilities; pilot
plants/test kitchens; distribution and storage facili-
ties (low temperature/food service); research and de-
velopment facilities;laboratories; offices; and
commissaries.
President: Philip Southerland
Chairman/Chief Executive Officer: Luther Cochrane
CFO and CAO: Trilby Carriker
VP: Frank Holley
Vice President Business Development: John
McLauglin
Contact: Chris Gentry
cgentry@humana.com
Senior Vice President, Texas Operations: Matt
Daniel
Number Employees: 43
Square Footage: 24194

24713 KCL Corporation
PO Box 629
Shelbyville, IN 46176-0629

317-392-2521
Fax: 317-392-4772
Reclosable poly zipper packaging
Estimated Sales: $20-50 Million
Number Employees: 100-249

24714 KD Kanopy
3755 W 69th Pl
Westminster, CO 80030

303-650-1310
Fax: 303-650-5093 800-432-4435
askme@kdkanopy.com www.kdkanopy.com
Manufacturer and exporter of instant set-up canopies, tents and banners; also, customized graphics
available

President: John T Matthews
CFO: John T Matthews
Director Marketing: Helene Schmid
Sales: Scott Rudin
Contact: Shelly Bangs
shelly@kdkanopy.com
Sales: Matt Lehman
Estimated Sales: $1 - 2.5 Million
Number Employees: 20-49
Square Footage: 40000
Brands:
Kd Bannerpole
Kd Majestic
Kd Party Shade
Kd Starshade
Kd Starstage

24715 (HQ)KEMCO
8 Thatcher Lane
Wareham, MA 02571-1076

508-295-5959
Fax: 508-291-2364 800-231-5955
www.kemco.or.kr/eng
New and used stainless steel fabrications including
sinks, tables, push and tow along carts, exhaust
hoods, walk-in coolers and freezers and food service
equipment
President & CEO: Byun Jong-Rip
Purchasing/AR/AP: Beverly Limpus
Number Employees: 17
Square Footage: 80000

24716 KES Science & Technology Inc
3625 Kennesaw N Industrial Pkw
Kennesaw, GA 30144-1234

678-290-8619
Fax: 770-425-0837 800-627-4913
info@kesair.com
Food safety air sanitation system for maximum
shelf/storage life, optimum product integrity and re-
duced food spoilage
President: John Hayman
Marketing Manager: Kristi George
National Sales Manager: Jimmy Lee
Billing Contact: Scott Hayman
Estimated Sales: $8 Million
Number Employees: 20-49

24717 KETCH
1006 E Waterman St
Wichita, KS 67211-1525

316-383-8700
Fax: 316-383-8715 800-766-3777
rpasmore@ketch.org www.ketch.org
Electrical extension cords, wooden pallets, shipping
boxes and air filters; contract packaging services
available
President/CEO: Ron Pasmore
rpasmore@ketch.org
Chairman: Fred Badders
CFO: Coral Houdyshell
Vice President of Finance: Sheila Brown
R&D: Pattie Knauff
Vice President of Quality Assurance: Sallie Jensen
Vice President of Human Resources: Pattie Knauff
Estimated Sales: Less Than $500,000
Number Employees: 250-499
Square Footage: 120000

24718 KHL Engineered Packaging
1640 S Greenwood Ave
Montebello, CA 90640

323-721-5300
Fax: 323-725-0312
Manufacturer and wholesaler/distributor of flexible
packaging equipment and materials including shrink
and stretch film, tape, poly and corrugated boxes,
chipboard, skin film and poly bags
VP: Jed Wockensuss
General Sales Manager: Bill Browne
Contact: Peter Szymanski
peter.szymanski@khlengpkg.com
Estimated Sales: $5-10 Million
Number Employees: 1,000-4,999
Square Footage: 100000

24719 KHM Plastics Inc
4090 Ryan Rd # B
Gurnee, IL 60031-1201

847-249-4910
Fax: 847-249-4976 dankay@khmplastics.com
www.khmplastics.com
Custom bulk acrylic food bins; importer of acrylic
sign holders. Custom displays for food service

President: Daniel Kay
  dankay@khmplastics.com
Marketing Director: Dan Kay
Sales Director: Glenn Murphy
Operations Manager: Dan Bunting
Estimated Sales: $2.5-5 Million
Number Employees: 20-49
Square Footage: 200000
Brands:
  Photo-Mates

24720 (HQ)KHS Co
25 Fox Den Road
West Simsbury, CT 06092

860-658-9454

Prints tags and labels.
Director: Pete Payne
CEO: Kevin Keane
Vice President: Russell Jackson
Marketing Executive: Kesha Briley
Sales Executive: Kerwin Spangler
Estimated Sales: 500,000
Number Employees: 20-49

24721 KIK Custom Products
3900 Joliet St
Denver, CO 80239

303-728-0871
Fax: 303-728-0880 kikcorp.com
Contract packager of aerosols, liquids and sticks.
Year Founded: 1993
Estimated Sales: $50-100 Million
Number Employees: 500-999
Type of Packaging: Bulk

24722 KIK Custom Products
24 Mill Ln
P.O. Box 660
Salem, VA 24153

540-389-5401
Fax: 540-904-0113 kikcorp.com
Contract packager of aerosols, liquids and sticks.
Number Employees: 50-99
Brands:
  Blue Ridge

24723 (HQ)KIK Custom Products
101 MacIntosh Blvd
Concord, ON L4K 4R5
Canada

905-660-0444
Fax: 905-660-9310 800-276-8260
www.kikcorp.com
Contract packager of aerosols, liquids and sticks.
President & CEO: Jeffrey Nodland
EVP & Chief Administrative Officer: Ben Kaak
EVP, Finance & CFO: Alay Shah
Year Founded: 1993
Estimated Sales: $50-100 Million
Number Employees: 500-999

24724 KION North America
2450 W 5th North St
Summerville, SC 29483-9621

843-875-8000
Fax: 843-875-8329 trucksales.na@kiongroup.com
www.kion-na.com
Dealer of forklifts and similar vehicles made by
Linde and Baoli.
President, CEO & CFO: Max Heller
VP, Operations: Daniel Schlegel
VP, Sales: Michael Gore
VP, Product Development: Christian Loew
Estimated Sales: $50,000,000 - $99,999,999
Number Employees: 100-249
Parent Co: Linde Material Handing

24725 KISS Packaging Systems
1399 Specialty Drive
Vista, CA 92081-8521

760-714-4177
Fax: 760-714-4188 888-522-3538
sales@kisspkg.com www.kisspkg.com
Manufacturer and exporter of liquid fillers, cappers,
conveyors, turntables, feeders/orienters, labelers and
integrated packaging systems
Estimated Sales: $2.5-5 Million
Number Employees: 19
Square Footage: 34000

24726 KISS Packaging Systems
1399 Specialty Drive
Vista, CA 92081-8521

760-714-4177
Fax: 760-714-4188 sales@kisspkg.com
Packaging machinery
Estimated Sales: $2.5-5 Million
Number Employees: 19

24727 KL Products, Ltd.
234 Exeter Road
London, ON N6L 1A3
Canada

519-652-1070
Fax: 519-652-1071 800-388-5744
kadmin@klproducts.com www.klproducts.com
Automated food processing equipment. Poultry and
hatchery equipment and washing systems.
President: Patrick Poulin
Vice President, Sales & Marketing: Rick Bennett

24728 KLEEN Line Corp
7 Opportunity Way
Newburyport, MA 01950-4044

978-463-0827
Fax: 978-463-0847 800-259-5973
info@kleenline.com www.kleenline.com
Stainless steel conveyors, wash-down duty, custom
conveyors, single units, complete systems. Manufacturer and system integrator of custom stainless steel
sanitary conveyors and equipment, including controls and automation. Engineering and consulting
services available for material handling
requirements.
President: James Laverdiere
Vice President: Dave Larcenaire
  dave@kleenline.co.za
Sales: Stuart Olsen
Plant Manager: Scott Fallovollita
Estimated Sales: $1-5 Million
Number Employees: 20-49

24729 KLLM Transport Svc LLC
135 Riverview Dr
Richland, MS 39218-4401

601-939-2545
Fax: 601-936-7151 800-925-1000
lpurvis@kllm.com www.kllm.com
President/CEO: James M. Richards, Jr.
Chairman of the Board: William J. Liles III
CFO: Terry Thornton
Vice President - Strategic Partnerships: Milton
Tallant, Jr
V.P. of Sales and Marketing: Moe Shroter
Vice President of Human Resources: Steve SzaboVP
of Operations: Greg Carpenter
Estimated Sales: $1 - 5 Million
Number Employees: 1000-4999

24730 KM International Corp
320 N Main St
Kenton, TN 38233-1130

731-749-8700
Fax: 256-539-9799 www.kminternational.com
Manufacturer, importer and exporter of plastic bags
and film
President: Kourosh Vakili
CEO: Kevin Vakili
  kevinb@kmigroup.com
Estimated Sales: $20 - 50 Million
Number Employees: 10-19

24731 KMT Aqua-Dyne Inc
635 W 12th St
Baxter Springs, KS 66713-1940

620-856-6222
Fax: 713-864-0313 800-826-9274
sales@aqua-dyne.com www.aqua-dyne.com
Manufacturer and exporter of water blasting and
tank cleaning equipment; also pumps
Manager: Deiter Tischler
VP: Jennifer Rankin
Regional Sales Manager: Jorge Elarba
Marketing: Dennis Williams
Sales/Marketing: Paul Bako
Public Relations: Dennis Williams
Purchasing: Jennifer Rankin
Estimated Sales: $5-10,000,000
Number Employees: 20-49
Square Footage: 170000
Brands:
  Aqua-Dyne

24732 KNF Flexpak Corporation
Rr 3 Box 6b
Tamaqua, PA 18252

570-386-3550
Fax: 570-386-3703 800-823-7786
pfloro@knfcorporation.com
www.knfcorporation.com
Nylon, polyethylene, pan liners, co-extrusion, oven
bags, cook chill, cashings and vacuum bags
Sales Director: David Dunphy
Estimated Sales: $12 Million
Number Employees: 50-99
Number of Brands: 4
Number of Products: 250
Square Footage: 28000
Type of Packaging: Consumer, Food Service, Pri-
vate Label, Bulk

24733 KNOX Stove Works Inc
PO Box 751
Knoxville, TN 37901-0751

865-524-4113
Fax: 865-637-2461 knoxstove@gmail.com
www.knoxstove.com
Coal and wood cooking ranges
President: Joe Anderson
Acct.: David Oglesby
Estimated Sales: $10-20 Million
Number Employees: 5-9
Square Footage: 42000

24734 KOF-K Kosher Supervision
201 the Plaza
Teaneck, NJ 7666

201-837-0500
Fax: 201-837-0126 ceo@kof-k.org
www.kof-k.org
Consultant specializing in kosher certification
CEO: Rabbi Dr. H. Zecharia Senter
Contact: Francine Adler
  fadler@kof-k.org
Number Employees: 100-249
Square Footage: 15000

24735 KOFLO Corp
309 Cary Point Dr # A
Cary, IL 60013-2901

847-516-3700
Fax: 847-516-3724 800-782-8427
info@koflo.com www.koflo.com
Static mixers, calibration columns and injection
quills.
President: James Federighi
  jf@koflo.com
VP: Anthony Federighi
Estimated Sales: $5-10 Million
Number Employees: 10-19
Brands:
  Calibration Columns
  Injection Quills
  Static Mixers

24736 KP Aerofill
P.O. Box 3848
Davenport, IA 52808-3848

563-391-1100
Fax: 563-391-4951 800-257-5622
CEO: Barry Shoulders

24737 KROHNE Inc
4100 N Sam Houston Pky W # 220
Building C - Suite 220
Houston, TX 77086-1466

281-598-0050
Fax: 281-598-0051 866-689-1250
oilandgas@krohne.com us.krohne.com
Flow meters
Marketing: Joe Incontri
Manager: Ron Garcia
Number Employees: 5-9

24738 KSW Corp
1731 Guthrie Ave
PO Box 3224
Des Moines, IA 50316-2197

515-265-5269
Fax: 515-265-9072 kswborp@aol.com
www.kswcorporation.com
Manufacturer and exporter of mechanical blades and
knives
President: Paul Naylor
  kswcorpdsm@aol.com
National Sales Manager: Michelle Struble

Estimated Sales: $3 - 5 Million
Number Employees: 10-19
Type of Packaging: Consumer, Food Service

24739 KTG
11353 Reed Hartman Hwy
Cincinnati, OH 45241-2443
513-793-5366
Fax: 866-533-6950 888-533-6900
Wireless temperature tracking computer software
CEO: Jim Flood
VP: Jack Kennamer
VP Sales: Jeff Carletti
VP Operations: Susan Payne
Estimated Sales: $10-20 Million
Number Employees: 5-9
Square Footage: 200000
Brands:
　Bladerunner
　Board-Mate
　Code Red Kit
　Cook-Eze
　Disposer Saver
　Fridgekare
　K-Mars
　Katchall
　Kleen-Cup
　Kleen-Pail
　Kolor Cut
　Kool-Tek
　Kwik-Flo
　Linen-Saver
　Magnetic Scrap Board
　N'Ice Ties
　Poly-Roll
　Poly-Slice
　Polyliner
　Rapi-Kool
　Safetywrap
　Sat-T-Ice
　Sat-T-Mop
　Side Swipe Spatula
　Tableware Retrievers
　Traysaver
　Tuff-Cut
　Whizard Gloves

24740 KTR Corp
122 Anchor Rd
Michigan City, IN 46360-2802
219-879-2792
Fax: 219-872-9150 ktr-us@ktr.com
www.ktrcorp.com
Shaft couplings
President: Bill Ketchum
　w.ketcham@ktr.com
CFO: Tedd Slesinsky
Marketing Director: Marshall Marcos
Estimated Sales: $5-10 Million
Number Employees: 20-49

24741 KTech by Muckler
1190 Meramac Road
Suite 207
Manchester, MO 63021
314-631-7616
Fax: 314-631-7409 800-952-0241
ktechinfo@mucklerktech.com
www.mucklertech.com

24742 KUKA Robotics Corp
51870 Shelby Parkway
Shelby Township, MI 48315-1787
800-459-6691
www.kuka.com
Manufacturer and importer of automated robotic material handling and palletizing systems and system integrators
President, KUKA Robotics Corp US: Joseph Gemma

Estimated Sales: Over $1 Billion
Number Employees: 14,256
Parent Co: KUKA Robotics Corporation

24743 KWIK Lok Corp
2712 S 16th Ave
Yakima, WA 98903-9530
509-248-4770
Fax: 509-457-6531 800-688-5945
sales@kwiklok.com www.kwiklok.com
Manufacturer and exporter of bag closures and bag closing machinery using plastic clips and labels

Vice President: Hal Miller
　halm@kwiklok.com
VP: Hal Miller
Quality Control: Jim Paxton
Sales: Rich Zaremba
Public Relations: Bill Klancke
Purchasing Director: Kohen Kelly
Estimated Sales: $10-20 Million
Number Employees: 50-99
Brands:
　Kwik Lok
　Striplok

24744 KWIK Lok Corp
2712 S 16th Ave
Yakima, WA 98903-9530
509-248-4770
Fax: 509-457-6531 800-688-5945
www.kwiklok.com
Vice President: Hal Miller
　halm@kwiklok.com
VP: Hal Miller
VP Sales: James Forsthe
Estimated Sales: $20 - 50 Million
Number Employees: 50-99

24745 KWS Manufacturing Co LTD
3041 Conveyor Dr
Burleson, TX 76028-1857
817-295-2247
Fax: 817-447-8528 800-543-6558
sales@kwsmfg.com www.kwsmfg.com
Manufacturer and exporter of bulk elevators and conveyors including belt and screw; also, spare parts and repair services available. Installation and field service available
Owner: Claressa Moore
　cmoore@drivetime.com
CEO: Tim Harris
CFO: Olin Miller
Marketing Director: Bill Porterfield
Plant Manager: Joe Radloff
Purchasing Manager: Eddie Maxwell
Estimated Sales: $10 - 20 Million
Number Employees: 100-249
Square Footage: 250000
Parent Co: J.B. Poindexter & Co., Inc.
Type of Packaging: Bulk

24746 Kadon Corporation
55 W Techne Center Drive
Milford, OH 45150-8901
937-299-0088
Fax: 513-831-5474
Manufacturer and exporter of plastic pallets, tote boxes, storage containers and wash baskets; OEM services available
Sales Manager: Chuck Acton
Administrative Assistant: Linda Brandeburg
Type of Packaging: Bulk

24747 Kady International
30 Parkway Dr
Scarborough, ME 04074-7155
207-883-4141
Fax: 207-883-8241 800-367-5239
kady@kadyinternational.com
www.kadyinternational.com
Manufacturer and exporter of high speed dispersion mills for mixing, blending, dispersing, emulsifying and cooking
President: Robert Kritzer
VP: Todd Kritzer
Sales: Todd Kritler
Estimated Sales: $5-10 Million
Number Employees: 10-19
Square Footage: 200000
Brands:
　Kady
　Kadyzolvers

24748 Kaeser Compressors Inc
511 Sigma Dr
Fredericksburg, VA 22408-7330
540-898-2207
Fax: 540-898-5520 info.usa@kaeser.com
www.oilfreeair.com
Rotary screw compressors, SmartPipe, Rotary screw vacuum packages, Rotary lobe blowers, portable compressors.
President: Reiner Mueller
　reiner.mueller@kaeser.com
Number Employees: 100-249

24749 Kafko International LTD
3555 Howard St
Skokie, IL 60076-4052
847-763-0333
Fax: 847-763-0334 800-528-0334
sales@oileater.com www.kafkointl.com
Manufacturer and supplier of cleaning products
President: Ena Dora
　edora@kafkointl.com
Number Employees: 100-249

24750 Kagetec
309 Elm Avenue SW
Montgomery, MN 56069
612-435-7640
Fax: 612-435-7641 kagetecusa@gmail.com
www.kagetec.com
Industrial flooring for the dairy, food and brewery industries.

24751 KaiRak
1158 N. Gilbert St
Anaheim, CA 92801
714-870-8661
Fax: 866-210-7542 literature@kairak.com
www.kairak.com
Manufacturer and exporter of remote refrigeration systems, pan chillers and sandwich and pizza prep tables
President/General Manager: Mark Curran
VP Sales & Marketing: Steve Asay
National Sales Manager: Steve Asay
Contact: Brian Casserilla
　bcasserilla@kairak.com
Administrative Assistant: Susie Parodi
Estimated Sales: $15 Million
Number Employees: 20-49
Square Footage: 160000
Parent Co: Hobart Corporation
Type of Packaging: Consumer, Food Service
Other Locations:
　KaiRak
　Gardena CA
Brands:
　Advantage Rak
　Pan Chillers

24752 Kaines West Michigan Co
211 E Dowland St
Ludington, MI 49431-2308
231-845-1281
Fax: 231-843-2259 kwmco@aol.com
www.kwmco.com
Custom welded wire products including racks, trays, refrigerator/freezer shelving, etc
President: John Kaines
　mikefelty@kwmco.com
CEO: Les Kaines
Engineering: Mike Felty
Human Resources: Jody Stewart
Materials Management: Jim Negele
Shipping Manager: Kevin Marcoux
Ordering Department: Nancy Van Liere
Estimated Sales: $5 - 10 Million
Number Employees: 50-99
Square Footage: 96000

24753 Kal Pac Corp
10 Factory St
Montgomery, NY 12549-1202
845-457-7013
Fax: 845-457-7009 800-852-5722
info@kalpac.com www.kalpac.com
Manufacturer, importer and exporter of plastic take out bags
CEO: Mike Nozawa
Sales Representative: Henry Meola
Estimated Sales: $10-20 Million
Number Employees: 10-19
Square Footage: 60000
Type of Packaging: Food Service

24754 Kalco Enterprises
443 Park Avenue South
New York, NY 10016-7322
212-627-5311
Fax: 212-627-3323 800-396-6600
kalconet@aol.com
Handmade food packaging products.
President: Ariel Kalaty
Sales Manager: Silverio Baranda
Type of Packaging: Consumer, Private Label, Bulk

24755 Kalix DT Industries
36 4th Street
Somerville, NJ 08876-3206
514-694-2390
Fax: 514-694-6552
Filling machines, conveyors, cappers

24756 Kalle USA Inc
5750 Centerpoint Ct
Suite B
Gurnee, IL 60031-5279
847-775-0781
Fax: 847-775-0782 www.kalle.de
Sausage casings and other meat processing supplies.
Sales Manager: John Lample
Number Employees: 10-19
Brands:
Pullulan
Sunmalt
Trehalose

24757 Kalman Floor Co Inc
1202 Bergen Pkwy # 110
Suite 110
Evergreen, CO 80439-9559
303-674-2290
Fax: 303-674-1238 866-266-7146
Karl.Johnson@kalmanfloor.com
www.kalmanfloor.com
Seamless industrial concrete floors suitable for the
food and beverage industries.
President: Donald Ytterberg
CEO: Robin Balliet
robin.balliet@kalmanfloor.com
Sales Engineer: Karl Johnson
Sales Engineer: Jeffrey Brown
Number Employees: 5-9

24758 (HQ)Kalsec
3713 W Main St
Kalamazoo, MI 49006
269-349-9711
800-323-9320
www.kalsec.com
Natural flavors, colors, extracts; spice oleoresins and
essential oils.
Executive Chairman: George Todd
Research & Development: Don Berdahl
Plant Manager: Harry Todd
Estimated Sales: $3-5 Million
Number Employees: 100-249
Parent Co: Kalamazoo Holdings
Type of Packaging: Food Service, Bulk
Brands:
Kalsec

24759 Kamflex Corp
1321 W 119th St
Chicago, IL 60643-5109
630-682-1555
Fax: 630-682-9312 800-323-2440
kamflex@kamflex.com
Manufacturer and exporter of FDA and USDA ap-
proved stainless steel conveyors and systems with
fabric, plastic or steel belts, rotary turntables, air op-
erations, etc
President: Kirit Kamdar
Vice President: Jose Ceja
jceja@kamflex.com
Marketing Director: John Tomaka
Operations Manager: Dave Matan
Estimated Sales: $5 - 10 Million
Number Employees: 5-9
Square Footage: 70000
Brands:
Elevair

24760 Kammann Machine
235 Heritage Ave
Portsmouth, NH 03801
978-463-0050
Fax: 630-377-7759
Printing machinery for packaging.
Vice President of Sales and Marketing: Steve
Gilbertson
Sales Manager: Barney Hanrahan
bhanrahan@kammann.com
Estimated Sales: $2.5-5 Million
Number Employees: 5-9
Square Footage: 400000
Brands:
K-14

24761 Kamran & Co
411 E Montecito St
Santa Barbara, CA 93101-1718
805-957-1551
Fax: 805-962-5915 800-480-9418
www.kamranco.com
Preparation tables
President: Firouzeh Amiri
firouzeh@kamranco.com
Estimated Sales: $5 - 10 Million
Number Employees: 20-49
Square Footage: 55200
Type of Packaging: Private Label, Bulk

24762 Kapak Corporation
5305 Parkdale Dr
Minneapolis, MN 55416
952-541-0730
Fax: 952-541-0735 info@kapak.com
Flexible high barrier packaging and sealing equip-
ment; also, rollstock retort films, preformed
pouches, die cuts, handles and closures
CEO: Gary Bell
Sales: Craig Rutman
National Sales Manager: Brian Bell
Director Manufacturing: Kathy Cyracks
Estimated Sales: $20-50 Million
Number Employees: 50-99
Brands:
Coffee-Pak
Kap-Pak
Stan-Pak

24763 Karl Schnell
903 North St
New London, WI 54961-1000
920-982-9974
Fax: 920-982-0580 sales@karlschnell.com
www.karlschnell.com
Food pumps, emulsifiers, mixers/blenders, cookers,
etc
Manager: John Mauthe
john@karlschnell.com
Estimated Sales: $2.5-5,000,000
Number Employees: 1-4
Square Footage: 10000
Parent Co: Karl Schnell Gmbh
Brands:
Karl Schnell

24764 Karma
500 Milford Street
Watertown, WI 53094
920-262-8688
Fax: 920-261-3302 800-558-9565
Manufacturer and exporter of hot and cold beverage
and mashed potato dispensers; also, warmers includ-
ing hot fudge
President: Chris Gorski
Vice President: Jerry Scheiber
Marketing VP: Elizabeth Brennecke
VP Sales: Jeremy Scheiber
Contact: Brittany Brantley
brantleyb@karma-inc.com
Estimated Sales: $10-20 Million
Number Employees: 20-49
Square Footage: 120000
Brands:
Cafe-Matic
Choco-Matic
Drink-Master
Insti-Mash
Juice-Master
Tea-Master
Whip-Master

24765 Karolina Polymers
1508 S Center Street
Hickory, NC 28602-5220
828-328-2247
Fax: 828-322-3674
Plastic film
President: Paul Kolis
VP: Jim Koshinski
Contact: Beth Lail
markf@agri-fab.com
Estimated Sales: $5-10 Million
Number Employees: 20-49
Type of Packaging: Bulk

24766 Karyall Telday Inc
8221 Clinton Rd
Cleveland, OH 44144-1095
216-281-4063
Fax: 216-281-5428 karyall@core.com
www.karyalltelday.com
Shop pans and tote boxes including aluminum, steel
and stainless steel
President: James Mindek
karyall@core.com
Estimated Sales: $10-20,000,000
Number Employees: 20-49

24767 Kasel Engineering
5911 Wolf Creek Pike
Dayton, OH 45426-2439
937-854-8875
Fax: 937-854-8875 www.kaselengineering.com
Bacon equipment, slicing machines and scales.
Owner: Don Kasel
dkasel@kaselengineering.com
Estimated Sales: Under $500,000
Number Employees: 5-9

24768 Kasel Industries Inc
3315 Walnut St
Denver, CO 80205-2429
303-296-4417
Fax: 303-293-9825 800-218-4417
www.kasel.net
Manufacturer and exporter of meat slicers, convey-
ors and automatic loaders
Owner: Ray Kasel
ray@kasel.net
Sls./Mktg. Mgr.: Jon Toby
Quality Control: Galana Kasel
Estimated Sales: $32 Million
Number Employees: 10-19

24769 Kasel Industries Inc
3315 Walnut St
Denver, CO 80205-2429
303-296-4417
Fax: 303-293-9825 800-218-4417
sales@kasel.net www.kasel.net
Slicers
Owner: Ray Kasel
ray@kasel.net
CFO: Oigita Jrausau
Quality Control: Galinajasto Kasel
Estimated Sales: $2.5 - 5 Million
Number Employees: 10-19

24770 Kashrus Technical Consultants
PO Box 172
Lakewood, NJ 08701-0172
732-364-8046
Fax: 732-363-5451 kashrusy@aol.com
www.kosherconsumer.org
Consultant specializing in the kosher food industry
Owner: Yehuda Shan
Number Employees: 10
Type of Packaging: Consumer, Food Service

24771 Kason
8889 Whitney Dr
Lewis Center, OH 43035-7106
740-549-2100
Fax: 740-549-0701 Central@kasonind.com
www.kasonind.com
Food bins, bumper systems for walls and strip doors;
wholesaler/distributor of commercial refrigeration
hardware and bulk food merchandisers
Manager: Rich Kaiser
central@kasonind.com
Estimated Sales: $1 - 5 Million
Number Employees: 5-9

24772 Kason Central
7099 Huntley Road
Columbus, OH 43229-1073
614-885-1992
Fax: 614-888-1771
Manufacturer, exporter and wholesaler/distributor of
refrigerator latches and hinges, strip curtains, hood
lights, grease filters, gaskets, stainless steel food ser-
vice hardware, thermometers for ovens and refriger-
ators and plumbingfixtures
Manager: David Katz
Sales Representative: Rich Kaiser
Office Manager: Greg Murray
General Manager: David Katz
Estimated Sales: $1-2.5 Million
Number Employees: 5-9

Square Footage: 8000
Parent Co: Kason Industries
Type of Packaging: Consumer, Food Service, Private Label

24773 Kason Industries
140 Herring Road
Newnan, GA 30265

770-254-0553
Fax: 770-253-3370 vinyl@kasonind.com
www.kasonind.com
Commercial food service equipment hardware and accessories including hinges, latches, feet, legs, door closers, panel fasteners, sliding door ware, vinyl strip doors, heated vents, grease extracting filters, etc
Estimated Sales: $50-100 Million
Number Employees: 8
Number of Products: 400
Square Footage: 6572
Parent Co: Kason Industries
Other Locations:
  Kason Industries
  Forest Hills NY
Brands:
  Doorware
  Easimount
  Panelock
  Safeguard
  Thermal Flex
  Trapper

24774 Kason Vinyl Products
57 Amlajack Blvd
Newnan, GA 30265-1093

770-254-0553
Fax: 770-253-3370 800-472-7450
www.kasonind.com
Vinyl strip curtains and swing doors for refrigeration and storage
President: Peter Katz
National Sales Manager: Larry Crabtree
Estimated Sales: $50-100 Million
Number Employees: 100-249
Parent Co: Kason Industries
Brands:
  Easimount
  Maximount
  Thermal Flex

24775 Kastalon, Inc.
4100 West 124th Place
Alsip, IL 60803-1876

708-389-2210
Fax: 708-389-0432 800-527-8566
sales@kastalon.com www.kastalon.com
Polyurethane parts and products
President & CEO: Bruce DeMent
Year Founded: 1963
Estimated Sales: $100+ Million
Number Employees: 68

24776 Kathabardehum Idification
1 Executive Dr
Suite 410
Somerset, NJ 08873-4002

732-560-0565
Fax: 732-356-0643 888-952-8422
sales@kathabar.com www.kathabar.com
Dehumidification for all food processing, baking candy, enrobing, freeze drying, coating, drying, spraying, dehydration, packaging, etc.
President: Pedro Correa
Global Sales Director: Nick Honko
Vice President: Bill Szabo
Sales Director: Stephen Constant
Contact: Skip Koski
  skoski@kathabar.com
Product Manager: Michael Harvey
Estimated Sales: $5-10 Million
Number Employees: 30
Number of Brands: 1
Number of Products: 24

24777 Kaufman Engineered Systems
1260 Waterville Monclova Rd
Waterville, OH 43566-1016

419-878-9727
Fax: 419-878-9726 info@kaufmanengsys.com
www.kaufmanengsys.com
Industrial stretch wrappers, conveyor systems, pick and place machinery, palletizers and stackers

President: Charlie Kaufman
  charlie.kaufman@kaufmanengsys.com
VP: Bob Kaufman
Estimated Sales: $20-50 Million
Number Employees: 50-99

24778 Kaufman Paper Box Company
187 N Main St
Providence, RI 02903-1220

401-272-7508
Fax: 401-272-9738
Set-up boxes for candy and other related products
Owner: Arnold Kaufman
Estimated Sales: $1-2.5 Million
Number Employees: 5-9
Square Footage: 24000
Type of Packaging: Private Label, Bulk

24779 Kauling Wood Products Company
15735 Old Us Hwy 50
Beckemeyer, IL 62219

618-594-2901
Fax: 618-594-4218
www.woodfibre.com/trade/aa009934.html
Material handling equipment including hardwood pallets and skids; also, pallet mattes/tops
General Manager: Jim Kauling
Estimated Sales: $1 - 5 Million
Number Employees: 1-4

24780 Kawneer Co Inc
555 Guthridge Ct
Norcross, GA 30092

770-449-5555
Fax: 770-734-1560 www.kawneer.com
Engineering products and solutions.
Chief Executive Officer: Charles "Chip" Blankenship
Chief E&C Officer: Cynthia Durkin
EVP, Chief Financial Officer: Ken Giacobbe
VP, Treasurer: Peter Hong
EVP, Technology: Raymond Kilmer
EVP, Strategy & Development: Mark Krakowiak
VP, General Counsel: Max Laun
VP, Controller: Paul Myron
EVP, Legal: Kate Ramundo
Year Founded: 1906
Estimated Sales: $50-100 Million
Number Employees: 500-999

24781 Kay Home Products Inc
90 Mcmillen Rd
Antioch, IL 60002-1845

847-395-4940
Fax: 847-395-3305 800-600-7009
www.kayhomeproducts.com
Manufacturer and exporter of patio and tray tables, lap trays, barbecue grills, etc
Chairman: Edward Crawford
CEO: Jack Murray
Estimated Sales: $1 - 5 Million
Number Employees: 50-99
Square Footage: 600000
Parent Co: Park-Ohio Industries
Brands:
  Marshallan
  Quaker

24782 Kaye Instruments
101 Billerica Avenue
Suite 7
N Billerica, MA 01862-1256

978-262-0273
Fax: 978-439-8181 800-343-4624
kaye@ge.com www.kayeinstruments.com
Manufacturer and exporter of data acquisition systems for process monitoring, controlling, archiving and reporting
President: Kenneth B Hurley
CEO: Ken Hurley
CFO: Al Parenteau
VP Sales/Marketing: Karen Huffman
Number Employees: 120
Square Footage: 240000
Brands:
  Autograph
  Dialog
  Digi-Link
  Digistrip
  Fix Dmacs
  Netpac

24783 Keating of Chicago Inc
8901 W 50th St
Mc Cook, IL 60525-6001

708-246-3000
Fax: 708-246-3100 800-532-8464
keating@keatingofchicago.com
www.keatingofchicago.com
Manufacturer and exporter of fryers, frying baskets, serving equipment, griddles, griddle brushes, pasta cookers, food warmers, hot plates, salting/bagging stations and grease/oil filtration systems.
President: Eliza Keating
IT: Eliza Moravec
  elizaann@keatingofchicago.com
Estimated Sales: $2.5-5 Million
Number Employees: 5-9
Brands:
  Instant Recovery Fryer
  Keating's Incredible Frying Machine
  Miraclean Griddle
  Pasta Plus System

24784 Kedco Wine Storage Systems
564 Smith St
Farmingdale, NY 11735-1111

631-454-7800
Fax: 631-454-4876 800-654-9988
www.kedcowinestoragesystems.com
Manufacturer and importer of store fixtures, glass doors, temperature-controlled wine storage equipment, display cabinets and refrigeration and wine racks
VP: David Windt
VP: Ken Windt
Contact: Helene Windt
  helene.windt@kedco.com
Estimated Sales: Less Than $500,000
Number Employees: 5-9
Square Footage: 50000

24785 Keen Kutter
20608 Earl St
Torrance, CA 90503

310-370-6941
Fax: 310-370-3851 rshaver814@aol.com
www.keenkutter.shaverspecialty.com
Manufacturer and exporter of vegetable cutters
President: George W Shaver
Manager: Scott Shaver
Estimated Sales: $2.5-5 Million
Number Employees: 20-49
Brands:
  Keen' Kutter

24786 Keena Corporation
25 Lenglen Road
Suite 4
Newton, MA 02458-1420

617-244-9800
Fax: 617-527-0056
Reinforced gummed paper, fiberglass, gummed tape
President: Harvey Epstein
Business Manager: Leslie Kent
Estimated Sales: $5 Million
Number Employees: 1-4
Square Footage: 80000

24787 Keene Technology Inc
14357 Commercial Pkwy
South Beloit, IL 61080-2621

815-624-8989
Fax: 815-624-4223 info@keenetech.com
www.ktiusa.com
Automatic zero speed splicers, rewinders, web tension controls, infeeds, unwind/rewind stands and related web handling equipment.
President: Danny Pearse
  dpearse@keenetech.com
Sales Manager: Darrel Spors
Plant Manager: Bill Carpenter
Estimated Sales: $5-10 Million
Number Employees: 50-99
Square Footage: 260000

24788 Keenline Conveyor Systems
1936 Chase Dr
Omro, WI 54963-1788

920-685-0365
Fax: 920-235-0825 www.keenline.com
Manufacturer and exporter of conveying equipment including tabletop chain, belt and case conveyors, accumulators, indexers, pushers, counters, clamps, mergers, dividers, combiners and gripper elevators/de-elevators

President: David Kersztyn
davidk@keenline.com
Vice President: Ed Gamoke
Estimated Sales: $5 - 10 Million
Number Employees: 20-49
Square Footage: 30000
Brands:
Keenline

24789 Keeper Thermal Bag Co
1006 Poplar Ln
Bartlett, IL 60103-5649

630-213-0125
Fax: 630-213-0134 800-765-9244
keepertb@sbcglobal.net
www.keeperthermalbags.com
Manufacturer and exporter of insulated bags including food, pizza and catering; also, beverage carriers
Owner: Mike Leel
Manager: Mike Leel
Estimated Sales: $1 - 3 Million
Number Employees: 5-9
Brands:
Kee-Per

24790 (HQ)Kehr-Buffalo Wire FrameCo Inc
127 Kehr St
Buffalo, NY 14211-1522

716-893-4276
Fax: 716-897-2389 800-875-4212
sales@kbwf.net www.kbwf.net
Manufacturer and exporter of custom fabricated store fixtures and point of purchase displays for baked goods, produce and beverage products
Owner: James A Rogers Jr
jrogers@rogersindustrialspgs.com
CFO: James Rogers
Research & Development: James Rogers
Quality Control: James Rogers
Sales Director: George Rogers
Estimated Sales: $3 - 5 Million
Number Employees: 10-19
Square Footage: 50000
Type of Packaging: Bulk

24791 Keith Machinery Corp
34 Gear Ave
Lindenhurst, NY 11757-1078

631-957-1200
Fax: 631-957-9264 sales@keithmachinery.com
www.keithmachinery.com
Agitators, attritors, autoclaves, bag filling and sealing machines, bag labeling equipment, blenders, bundling machines, carton machines: closing, filling, sealing, checkweighers
VP: John Hatz
Estimated Sales: $10-20 Million
Number Employees: 50-99

24792 Keller-Charles of Philadelphia
2413 Federal St
Philadelphia, PA 19146-2431

215-732-2614
Fax: 215-732-4327

Tea and coffee industry cans
Owner: Peggy Fields
kcpfields@aol.com
Estimated Sales: $20-50 Million
Number Employees: 20-49

24793 Kelley Advisory Services
PO Box 2193
Northbrook, IL 60065-2193

847-412-9234
Fax: 847-412-9235
Consultant specializing in industrial ingredients, finished products, marketing, sales and distribution
President: H Kelley
VP: M Kelley
Customer Service: Karen Bass
Number Employees: 5
Square Footage: 30000

24794 Kelley Company
1612 Hutton Dr
Suite 140
Carrollton, TX 75006

972-466-0707
800-558-6960
kelley@entrematic.com kelleyentrematic.com
Hydraulic, mechanical and air-powered dock levelers, restraints, controls and seals for loading dock shelters.

Year Founded: 1953
Estimated Sales: $100-500 Million

24795 Kelley Supply Inc
704 Industrial Dr
Colby, WI 54421-9778

715-223-3614
Fax: 715-223-6383 800-782-8573
info@kelleysupply.com www.kelleysupply.com
Cheese equipment, defoamers, dispensers, lubricant
Owner: Bernie Alberts
balberts@kelleysupply.com
Estimated Sales: $5 - 10 Million
Number Employees: 20-49

24796 Kelley Wood Products
85 River St
Fitchburg, MA 01420-3093

978-345-7531
Fax: 978-343-3070 kwpmainoffice@cc.com
www.kelleywoodpro.com
Wooden skids, boxes, shooks and pallets
Owner: Stephen Kelley
info@kelleywoodpro.com
VP: John Kelley
Estimated Sales: $1 - 2.5 Million
Number Employees: 10-19

24797 Kelly Box & Packaging Corp
2801 Covington Rd
Fort Wayne, IN 46802-6969

260-432-4570
Fax: 260-432-2042 dcope@kellybox.com
www.kellybox.com
Corrugated cartons and corrugated and wooden boxes
CEO: Thomas J Kelly Jr
Sales Manager: Doug Cope
Customer Service Manager / Estimator: Chris Dowty
Estimated Sales: $5-10 Million
Number Employees: 100-249

24798 Kelly Dock Systems
6720 N Teutonia Avenue
Milwaukee, WI 53209-3119

414-352-1000
Fax: 414-352-2093
Manufacturer and exporter of dock equipment including levers and restraints
Sales/Marketing Manager: Steve Sprunger
Estimated Sales: $20-50 Million
Number Employees: 100-249

24799 Kelmin Products
P. O. Box 1108
Plymouth, FL 32768

407-886-6079
Fax: 407-886-6579 kelminwik@aol.com
www.kelminproductsinc.com
Chafing fuel, chafing heaters, wick, chafin dish fuel, diethylenol glycol
President: Robert Jankun
CEO: Betty J Jankun
Estimated Sales: $1 - 3 Million
Number Employees: 10-19
Number of Brands: 1
Number of Products: 3
Square Footage: 28000
Type of Packaging: Food Service, Private Label, Bulk
Brands:
Ultra Pumps
Witte Pumps

24800 Kem A Trix Inc
PO Box 580
Champlain, NY 12919-0580

206-764-4668
Fax: 206-764-7213 888-215-8237
mpenton@kematrix.com www.kematrix.com
Specialty lubricants manufacturer as well as sealants for pumps and valves
President: Norman Katz
Marketing: Jeffrey Katz
Contact: Mable Benton
info@kematrix.com
Estimated Sales: Less Than $500,000
Number Employees: 1-4
Number of Products: 34
Type of Packaging: Consumer, Food Service, Private Label, Bulk

24801 Kemco Systems Inc
11500 47th St N
Clearwater, FL 33762-4955

727-573-2323
Fax: 727-573-2346 800-633-7055
sales@kemcosystems.com
www.kemcosystems.com
System equipment for meat and poultry industry, heaters-water, heat reclaiming systems, water pollution treatment and monitoring, total plant sanitation and waste water treatment systems
President: Carol Gorrel
carolgorrel@kemcosystems.com
CEO: Lee Kesbering
VP: Gerald Van Gils
R & D: Gerald Van Gils
Marketing: Bernie Weintraub
VP Sales: Al Jenneman
Plant Manager: David Gregg
Purchasing: Rod Kummer
Estimated Sales: $10-25 Million
Number Employees: 50-99
Number of Brands: 18
Square Footage: 60000

24802 Kemex Meat Brands
2400 T Street NE
Washington, DC 20002-1919

301-277-2444
Fax: 301-277-0235
Manufacturer and exporter of USDA inspection legend insert labels
Owner: Mary Ellen Campbell
Estimated Sales: Less than $500,000
Number Employees: 4

24803 Kemin Industries Inc
2100 Maury St
P.O. Box 70
Des Moines, IA 50317-1100

515-559-5100
Fax: 515-559-5232 800-777-8307
kftcs.am@kemin.com www.kemin.com
Liquid products which help to enhance the shelf life of food items.
Co- Founder: Mary Nelson
CEO: Jennifer Brown
jennifer-l-brown@uiowa.edu
Number Employees: 100-249

24804 Kemper Bakery Systems
300 Forge Way
Rockaway, NJ 07866-2032

973-625-1566
Fax: 973-586-2091

24805 Kemutec Group Inc
130 Wharton Rd # A
Keystone Industrial Park
Bristol, PA 19007-1685

215-788-8013
Fax: 215-788-5113 sales@kemutecusa.com
www.kemutecusa.com
Manufacturer, importer and exporter of blenders, mixers, centrifugal sifters, grinding mills and valves
President: Karin Galloway
klg@kemutecusa.com
Director of Marketing: Kathy Moncur
Estimated Sales: $5-10 Million
Number Employees: 5-9
Square Footage: 40000
Brands:
Kek
Mucon

24806 Kemwall Distributors LTD
250 Avenue W
Brooklyn, NY 11223-4610

718-372-0486
Fax: 718-372-3421 fldwr@msn.com
Manager: Charles Feldman
c.feldman@feldware.com
Estimated Sales: $1 - 3 Million
Number Employees: 5-9

24807 Ken Coat
P.O. Box 575
Bardstown, KY 40004-575

Fax: 270-259-9858 888-536-2628
Manufacturer and exporter of plastisol-coated, metal outdoor furniture including tables, benches, chairs, etc.; also, trash receptacles

President: J R Davis
Sls.: Philip Clemens
Estimated Sales: $5-10 Million
Number Employees: 10-19
Square Footage: 75000

24808 Ken's Beverage Inc
10015 S Mandel St
Plainfield, IL 60585

800-285-2292
orders@kbiparts.com www.kbiparts.com
Beverage dispensing services and equipment for the
food service market.
Owner/President/CEO: Ken Reimer
Year Founded: 1985
Estimated Sales: $50-100 Million
Number Employees: 100-249

24809 Kendall Frozen Fruits, Inc.
9777 Wilshire Blvd
Suite 818
Beverly Hills, CA 90212-1908

310-288-9920
Fax: 310-288-9913 susan@kendallfruit.com
www.kendallfruit.com
Frozen fruits including dried, juice concentrates, pu-
rees, freeze dried fruit, fruit powders, vegetable
products, chocolate covered dried fruit, and yogurt
covered dried fruit
President: Susan Kendall
Manager/Berkeley: Deborah Kendall
Manager/Littleton: Larry Kendall
VP Finance: Debra Olk
VP: Mike Daems
VP: Frank Abarca
VP: Kelly Marks
Estimated Sales: $3.6 Million
Number Employees: 14

24810 Kendall Packaging Corporation
633 W Wisconsin Ave
Milwaukee, WI 53203-1918

414-276-4770
Fax: 414-276-5668 800-237-0951
www.kendallpkg.com
Flexible, food, and industrial packaging
President and COO: Eric Erickson
VP Marketing/Sales: Stuart Zeisse
Manager: Randy Mjelde
Contact: Rebecca Kuehl
rebecca@kendallpkg.com
Estimated Sales: $10-20 Million
Number Employees: 20-49

24811 Kendel
5320 Dansher Rd
Countryside, IL 60525-3124

708-813-1520
Fax: 708-813-1539 800-323-1100
www.welchpkg.com
Folding paper boxes; flexo printing and structural
and graphic designing services available
Manager: Ian Mercer
VP: Gary Davidson
Manager Account Services: Rick Berg
Estimated Sales: $10-20 Million
Number Employees: 50-99
Square Footage: 280000

24812 Kendon Candies Inc
460 Perrymont Avenue
San Jose, CA 95125

408-297-6133
Fax: 408-297-4008 800-332-2639
Lollipops
President: Kate Glass
Contact: Holly Anderson
h.anderson@kendoncandies.com

24813 Kendrick Johnson & Assoc Inc
9609 Girard Ave S
Minneapolis, MN 55431-2619

952-888-2847
Fax: 952-888-8336 800-826-1271
www.kendrick-johnson.com
Plastic dish covers, trays, plates, tumblers, cups and
soup and cereal bowls
President: Byron C Hamilton
bhamilton@kendrick-johnson.com
Vice President: Nancy Hamilton
Sales Director: Lori Green
Estimated Sales: Less than $500,000
Number Employees: 1-4

24814 Kennedy Enterprises
4910 Rent Worth Dr
Lincoln, NE 68516-2507

402-423-3210
Fax: 402-423-5129 800-228-0072
www.kennedyenterprisesinc.com
Greases and oils, accessory equipment, forming, fill-
ing and sealing equipment, vacuum packaging
equipment
President: Rick Kennedy
rickkei@windstream.net
Chairman: Maxine Kennedy
Estimated Sales: $1 - 2.5 Million
Number Employees: 5-9

24815 Kennedy Group
38601 Kennedy Pkwy
Willoughby, OH 44094-7395

440-951-7660
Fax: 440-951-3253
kennedygroup1@kennedygrp.com
www.kennedygrp.com
Developer and manufacturer of labeling, packaging,
promotional labels, and identification systems. Man-
ufactures prime labels, clear labels, booklets, cou-
pons, blister cards, instant digital labels, case pack
labels, versa-cards, tab-onads, shrink labels, etc
Owner: Patrick Kennedy
kennedypatrick@kennedygrp.com
Marketing/Sales: Patrick Kennedy
Operations Manager: Todd Kennedy
Estimated Sales: $10 - 20 Million
Number Employees: 50-99
Square Footage: 160000
Type of Packaging: Consumer, Food Service, Pri-
vate Label, Bulk

24816 Kennedy's Specialty Sewing
Box 250
Erin, ON N0B 1T0
Canada

519-833-9306
Fax: 519-833-2357
Flags, canvas goods, coffee filters and aprons
President: Brenda Broughton
Number Employees: 10-19

24817 Kenray Associates
11576 Highway 150
Greenville, IN 47124-9213

812-923-9884
Fax: 812-923-2820 sales@kenray.com
www.kenray.com
Data processing systems for brokers, distributors
and manufacturers including multi-office capability,
hardware/software training, integrated e-commerce,
EDI and support
President: Kenneth Mcgee Sr
Contact: Sandy Yoshida
syoshida@kenray.biz
Estimated Sales: $1-2.5 Million
Number Employees: 5-9

24818 Kenro
200 Industrial Dr
Fredonia, WI 53021

262-692-2411
Fax: 262-692-9141
Plasticware including trays, dishes and dinnerware
Contact: Sharon Fay
sharon.fay@kenro.com
Estimated Sales: $20-50 Million
Number Employees: 100-249
Parent Co: Carlisle Company

24819 Kensington Lighting Corp
593 Rugh St
Greensburg, PA 15601-5637

724-850-2433
Fax: 724-837-8087 800-434-5005
info@kensingtonUS.com www.kensingtonus.com
Manufacturer and exporter of energy efficient light-
ing fixtures and flourescent lighting
Owner: Gary Whiteknight
gary@kensingtonus.com
Estimated Sales: $500,000-$1 Million
Number Employees: 5-9
Parent Co: Adience Equities
Type of Packaging: Consumer, Food Service

24820 Kent Co
13301 Biscayne Blvd
North Miami, FL 33181-2039

305-944-4041
Fax: 305-944-1106 800-521-4886
kentcomp@aol.com www.kent-company.com
Rubber de-feathering fingers for use in chicken or
turkey processing machines.
Sales: Dolly Tomlinson
Manager: Dolly Tomlinson
kentcomp@aol.com
Technical: Edd Woike
Number Employees: 1-4

24821 Kent Corp
4446 Pinson Valley Pkwy
Birmingham, AL 35215-2940

205-856-3621
Fax: 205-856-3622 800-252-5368
sales@kentcorp.com www.kentcorp.com
Manufacturer and exporter of store fixtures includ-
ing modular steel display shelving
President: Mera Craws
crawsm@asme.org
CEO: V Albano
CFO: Sharron Harbison
Sales Director: Allan Solomon
Estimated Sales: $20 - 50 Million
Number Employees: 100-249
Square Footage: 250000

24822 Kent District Library System
814 W River Center Dr NE
Comstock Park, MI 49321-8955

616-784-2007
Fax: 616-647-3828 lwerner@kdl.org
www.kdl.org
Material handling equipment including skids and
factory trucks
Chairman: Charles R. Myers
Treasurer: Scott Petersen
Technology Director: Mike Carpenter
IT: Shane Hinds
shinds@kdl.org
Plant Supervisor: John McKay
Number Employees: 20-49
Square Footage: 40000
Brands:
Globe
Wheel-Ezy

24823 Kent Precision Foods Group Inc
2905 US-61
Muscatine, IA 52761

800-442-5252
www.precisionfoods.com
Pickle and tomato mixes, pectins, jams, jellies, fruit
preservatives, blended spices and seasonings, des-
sert mixes; exporter of dry soft serve and dessert
mixes.
President, Kent Corp.: David Tsai
Year Founded: 1992
Estimated Sales: $69.4 Million
Number Employees: 20-49
Number of Brands: 6
Square Footage: 200000
Parent Co: Kent Corporation
Type of Packaging: Consumer, Food Service, Pri-
vate Label, Bulk
Other Locations:
Manufacturing Location
Bolingbrook IL
Brands:
DOLE SOFT SERVE
Foothill Farms
Frostline Frozen Treats
LAKND O'LAKES
PFLfreeze
Sqwincher

24824 Kent R Hedman & Assoc
3312 Woodford Dr # 200
Arlington, TX 76013-1139

817-277-0888
Executive search firm
President: Kent Hedman
Principal: K Dunbar
Estimated Sales: Less Than $500,000
Number Employees: 1-4

24825 Kentfield's
180 Nadina Way
Greenbrae, CA 94904
415-461-7454
Fax: 415-461-5553 888-461-7454
21tchen towels, canvas aprons, canvas totes, cocktails napkins
Owner: Donna Vanmalder
CFO: Donna Vanmalder
Estimated Sales: Below $5 Million
Number Employees: 4

24826 Kentmaster Manufacturing Co
1801 S Mountain Ave
Monrovia, CA 91016-4270
626-359-8888
Fax: 626-303-5151 800-421-1477
sales@kentmaster.com
Manufacturer and exporter of portable power beef and hog slaughtering equipment
Owner: Ralph Karubian
rk@kentmaster.com
Sls./Svce. Mgr.: Joe Leamen
Estimated Sales: $5-10 Million
Number Employees: 20-49

24827 Kentucky Grocers Assn Inc
512 Capital Ave
Frankfort, KY 40601-2839
502-696-9153
Fax: 502-875-1595 info@kgaonline.org
www.kgaonline.org
Committed to being a positive change in the grocery and convenience store industries.
Executive Director: Ted Mason
ted@kgaonline.org
Estimated Sales: $300,000-500,000
Number Employees: 1-4

24828 Kentucky Power
855 Central Ave
Suite 200
Ashland, KY 41101
800-572-1113
www.kentuckypower.com
Electric utility systems.
President & COO: Brett Mattison
VP, Regulatory & Finance: Ranie Wohnhas
VP, External Affairs & Customer Service: Cynthia Wiseman
Estimated Sales: $1,000,000,000+
Parent Co: American Electric Power

24829 Kentwood Spring Water Company
100 Stable Drive
Patterson, LA 70392-0743
985-395-9313
Fax: 985-395-2148 www.kentwoodsprings.com
Coffee service filtration systems; also, bottled and distilled spring water
Branch Mgr.: Scott Coy
Branch Manager: Dwayne Duplantis
Estimated Sales: $500,000-$1 Million
Number Employees: 9
Parent Co: Syntori
Type of Packaging: Consumer

24830 Kenyon Press
2850 Walnut Ave
Signal Hill, CA 90755-1834
562-424-6600
Fax: 562-424-7599 800-752-9395
www.kenyonpress.com
Menus; custom designing available
President: Paul Demarco
pauld@kenyonpress.net
Sls.: Dan Reed
Estimated Sales: Below $5,000,000
Number Employees: 20-49

24831 Kepes
9016 58th Pl
Suite 600
Kenosha, WI 53144
262-652-7889
Fax: 262-652-7787 800-345-3653
inquire@kepes.com www.kepes.com
Carton glue erectors, semiautomatic carton gluing machines, hot melt glue application equipment, unit rate and totalizing counters, rubber and urethane covered machine components and permalube lubrication system

President: Wayne Pagel Jr
w.pagel@kepes.com
Estimated Sales: $10-20 Million
Number Employees: 20-49

24832 Kerian Machines Inc
1709 Highway 81 S
Grafton, ND 58237
701-352-0480
Fax: 701-352-3776 sales@Kerian.com
www.kerianmachines.com
Manufacturer and exporter of fruit and vegetable graders and sizers
President: John Kerian
CEO: James Kerian
Estimated Sales: $1-2.5 Million
Number Employees: 10-19
Brands:
Kerian Sizer

24833 Kerrigan Paper ProductsInc
293 Neck Rd
Haverhill, MA 1835
978-374-4797
Fax: 978-521-4067
Corrugated boxes
President: William Law
Estimated Sales: $1 - 2.5 Million
Number Employees: 5-9

24834 Kerry, Inc
Global Technology & Innovation Center
3400 Millington Rd
Beloit, WI 53511
608-363-1200
www.kerry.com
Food ingredients, encapsulation, ingredient sourcing, in-house testing and spray drying services.
CEO/Executive Director: Edmond Scanlon
Global President & CEO: Gerry Behan
Executive Director/Group CFO: Marguerite Larkin
Year Founded: 1972
Estimated Sales: Over $1 Billion
Number Employees: 25,000
Number of Brands: 5
Parent Co: Kerry Group Plc
Type of Packaging: Food Service
Brands:
Big Train
DaVinci Gourmet
Golden Dipt
Island Oasis
Ravifruit

24835 Kesry Corporation
16133 W 45th Dr
Golden, CO 80403-1791
303-271-9300
Fax: 303-271-3645 www.kevey.com
President: Tom Kissinger
Estimated Sales: $5 - 10 Million
Number Employees: 5-9

24836 Kess Industries Inc
130 37th St NE
Auburn, WA 98002
253-735-5700
Fax: 253-735-2851 800-578-5564
Manufacturer of an array of standard and custom equipment for accumulating, chilling, coating, depositing, distributing, drying, dumping, metering, pasteurizing, transferring, washing and weighing products.
President: K Jell Fogelgren
Sales and Estimating: Ray Cassingham
Estimated Sales: Below $5 Million
Number Employees: 10-19
Square Footage: 48000

24837 Kessenich's Limited
131 S Fair Oaks Ave
Madison, WI 53704-5897
608-249-5391
Fax: 608-249-1628 800-248-0555
www.kessenichs.com
Restaurant equipment
President: Robert Kessenich
CEO: Cheri Martin
Estimated Sales: $2.5 - 5 Million
Number Employees: 20-49

24838 Kessler Sign Co
2669 National Rd
Zanesville, OH 43701-8257
740-453-0668
Fax: 740-453-5301 800-686-1870
www.kesslersignco.com
Signs and awnings
President: Bob Kessler
bob@kesslersignco.com
Service Director: Mike Taylor
VP: Rodger Kessler
Vice President-Operations: David Kessler
Account Executive: Doug Gabriel
Estimated Sales: $5 - 10 Million
Number Employees: 20-49

24839 Kett
9581 Featherhill Dr
Villa Park, CA 92861-2633
714-779-8400
Fax: 714-693-2923 800-438-5388
sales@kett.com www.kett.com
Our focus is moisture and organic composition analysis, coating thickness measurement, friction, wear, peel, adhesion and other surface property analyses, rice quality instrumentation and other agricultural test instruments for thegrain and seed marketplace.
Owner: Bob Clark
Number Employees: 1-4

24840 Keurig Dr Pepper
53 South Avenue
Burlington, MA 01803
877-208-9991
www.keurigdrpepper.com
Coffee, hot and cold beverage maker systems, flavored soft drinks, teas, waters, juices, juice drinks, and more.
Chairman/CEO: Robert Gamgort
CFO: Sudhanshu Priyadarshi
Chief Legal Officer/General Counsel: Anthony Shoemaker
Chief Research/Development Officer: Dr. Karin Rotem-Wildeman
Year Founded: 2018
Estimated Sales: $11 Billion
Number Employees: 26,000
Number of Brands: 70+
Number of Products: 530+
Type of Packaging: Consumer, Food Service, Bulk
Other Locations:
Production
Castroville CA
R&D, Professional Services
Burlington MA
Production
Knoxville TN
Production
Windsor VA
Production
Sumner WA
Keurig Canada
Montreal, QC, Canada
Brands:
7UP
A&W Root Beer
Adagio
Bai
Barista Bros
Barista Prima Coffeehouse
Big Red
Brûlerie Mont Royal
Brûlerie St. Denis
Cactus Cooler
Caf, Escapes
Caf, Punta del Cielo
Canada Dry
Caribou Coffee
Cinnabon
Clamato
Coffee People
Cora
Cplus
Crush
Deja Blue
Diedrich Coffee
Diet Rite
Donut House Collection
Dr. Pepper
Emeril
Evian
Forto
Gila Caf,
Gloria Jean's Coffees
Green Mountain Coffee

Hawaiian Punch
High Brew Coffee
Hires
Hollys Coffee
IBC
Kahlúa
Krispy Kreme
Laughing Man
Laura Secord
Margaritaville
Mott's
Nantucker Nectars
Nehi Cola
Neuro
Newmann's Own Organics
Orangina
Orient Express
Panera Bread
Peet's Coffee
Penafiel
ReaLemon
Revv
Rose's
Royal Crown Cola
Schweppes
Snapple
Squirt
Stewart's
Straight Up Tea
Sun Drop
Sunkist
SunnyD
Tahitian Treat
The Original Donut Shop
Timothy's
Tully's Coffe
The Original Donut Shop
Timothy's
Tully's Coffe
Van Houtte
Vernors
Vita Coco

24841 Kevin's Natural Foods
4221 E Mariposa Rd
Stockton, CA 95215
888-638-7083
www.kevinsnaturalfoods.com
Health-forward food products such as refrigerated
protein entr,es, side dishes, sauces, and spices. Prod-
ucts cater to specific diets (paleo, keto, plant-based,
gluten-free, etc.)
Co-Founder & Chief Operating Officer: Kevin
McCray
Co-Founder & Chief Executive Officer: Dan Costa
National Sales Manager: Jesse Isaacs
Year Founded: 2014
Estimated Sales: $280,000
Number Employees: 51-200

24842 Kew Cleaning Systems
1500 N Belcher Road
Clearwater, FL 33765-1301
800-942-1690
High pressure washers and waste water treatment
systems
G.M.: Ed Hilfretz
Number Employees: 12
Brands:
Kew

24843 Kewanee Washer Corporaton
3209 Saint Andrews Court
Findlay, OH 45840-2948
419-435-8269
Fax: 419-425-0512
Commercial pot and pan washing units
Owner: Judith White
GM: C Paul White
Estimated Sales: Less than $500,000
Number Employees: 1-4
Square Footage: 16
Brands:
Kewanee K99

24844 Key Automation
1301 Corporate Center Drive
Suite 113
Eagan, MN 55121-1259
651-455-0547
Fax: 651-686-5232 tgriffith@keyauto.com

Standard and custom designed packaging machinery
including cartoners and case packers for pouches
and bags; also, product handling, orienting and feed-
ing systems
Sls.: David Olson
Estimated Sales: $1 - 5 Million
Number Employees: 8
Square Footage: 8000
Brands:
Ccl

24845 Key Container Company
PO Box 71
South Gate, CA 90280
323-564-4211
Fax: 323-564-5127 custsvc@keycontainer.com
www.keycontainer.com
Shipping containers
President: Robert J Watts
Contact: Wanda East
east@keycontainer.com
Estimated Sales: $20-50 Million
Number Employees: 100-249

24846 Key Industrial
997 Enterprise Way
Napa, CA 94558-6209
707-252-1205
Fax: 707-252-9054 800-812-5258
Wine industry equipment
Owner: John Boyanich
jboyanich@keyindustrial.com
Estimated Sales: $5 - 10 Million
Number Employees: 10-19

24847 Key International Cranbury
4 Corporate Dr # A
Suite A
Cranbury, NJ 08512-3613
609-235-9693
Fax: 732-972-2630 www.keyinternational.com
Packaging and processing equipment
President: Kevin Beenders
CEO: Valerie Ianieri
CEO: Primo Ianieri
VP Sales: Kevin Beenders
Contact: Jocelyn Aguilu
aguilu.jocelyn@keyinternational.com
Purchasing: Bill Howard
Estimated Sales: Less Than $500,000
Number Employees: 1-4

24848 Key Material Handling Inc
4790 Alamo St
Simi Valley, CA 93063-1837
805-520-6007
Fax: 805-520-3007 800-539-7225
www.keyrack.com
Stainless steel and aluminum material handling
equipment, racks, containers, conveyors, lifts,
scales, shelving, tables and trucks; custom fabrica-
tion available
Owner: Rick Galbraith
rick@keymaterial.com
Sls.: John Galbraith
Estimated Sales: Less Than $500,000
Number Employees: 1-4
Square Footage: 40000
Brands:
Interlake
Keyrack
Rapid Rack

24849 Key Packaging Co
15th St E
Sarasota, FL 34243
941-355-2728
Fax: 941-351-8708 webinfo@keypackaging.com
www.keypackaging.com
Manufacturer and exporter of thermoformed plastic
packaging, containers, food trays and blister packs
President: Earl Smith
earl@keypackaging.com
Quality Control: Gifford Quast
Sales Coordinator: Gene Donohue
Sales Director: Karlson Strouse
Manager: Karlson Strouse
Purchasing Manager: Chris Rathbun
Estimated Sales: $10-20 Million
Number Employees: 50-99
Square Footage: 104000
Type of Packaging: Consumer, Food Service, Bulk

24850 (HQ)Key Technology Inc.
150 Avery St.
Walla Walla, WA 99362
509-529-2161
Fax: 509-394-3538 www.key.net
Design, manufacture and market process automation
systems for food and other industries. This technol-
ogy integrates automated optical inspection systems,
specialized conveyor systems, and processing/prepa-
ration systems, as well asresearch, development, and
world-class engineering.
Vice President, Finance: Carson Brennan
Vice President, Global Sales: Daniel Leighty
Vice President, Global Operations: Shawn
Prendiville
Year Founded: 1948
Estimated Sales: $116.33 Million
Number Employees: 500-999
Square Footage: 173000
Other Locations:
Redmond OR
Brands:
Adr
Horizon
Impulse
Iso-Flo
Manta
Oncore
Optyx
Remotemd
Smart Shaker
Spiral-Flo
Symetix
Tegra
Tobacco Sorter 3
Turbo-Flo
Veg-Mix
Veo

24851 (HQ)Key-Pak Machines
1221 Us Highway 22
Suite 1
Lebanon, NJ 8833
908-236-2111
Fax: 908-236-7013 www.key-pak.com
An extension of the specialized packaging equip-
ment manufactured by Research & Development
Packaging Corp. Specializing in vertical
form/fill/seal machines, Key-Pak has consistently
expanded its machinery portfolio over the years
byadding combinational net-weigh scales, cup in-
dexing system, piston liquid fillers and even
conveyors.
CEO: Donald Bogut
Vice President: Chris Wanthouse
Research & Development: Don Bogut
Marketing Director: Christopher Wanthouse
Sales Director: Christopher Wanthouse
Operations Manager: Stan Florey
Estimated Sales: $1 - 3 Million
Number Employees: 5-9
Number of Brands: 1
Square Footage: 17000
Brands:
Key-Pak

24852 Key-Pak Machines
1221 Us Highway 22
Suite 1
Lebanon, NJ 08833
908-236-2111
Fax: 908-236-7013 www.key-pak.com
Vertical form fill seal machines, net weight scale
systems
President: Donald Bogut
Principal: Arthur Bogut
Estimated Sales: $1 - 3 Million
Number Employees: 5-9

24853 Keystone Adjustable CapCo Inc
1591 Hylton Rd # B
Pennsauken, NJ 08110-1381
856-317-9879
Fax: 856-663-6075 800-663-5439
info@keystonecap.com www.keystonecap.com
Disposable sanitary headwear including paper and
cloth chef hats, overseas caps and bouffants, beard
covers, hair nets, etc.; also, aprons, shoe covers,
nonwoven coveralls and sleeves; exporter of overseas caps, chef hats and hairnets
CEO: Andrew Feinstein
afeinstein@keystonecap.com
Estimated Sales: $50-100 Million
Number Employees: 100-249

Number of Brands: 1
Number of Products: 400
Square Footage: 95000
Type of Packaging: Consumer, Food Service, Private Label, Bulk
Brands:
Classy Caps
Cordon Bleu Chef Hats

24854 Keystone Adjustable CapCo Inc
1591 Hylton Rd # B
Pennsauken, NJ 08110-1381

856-317-9879
Fax: 856-663-6075 800-663-5439
info@keystonecap.com www.keystonecap.com
Tin and aluminum continuous thread caps for glass
and plastic containers
President: Dorothy Lynch
CEO: Andrew Feinstein
afeinstein@keystonecap.com
Secy.: Marie Forman
Plant Manager: Rodger Rohebach
Estimated Sales: $2.5-5 Million
Number Employees: 100-249
Square Footage: 18000

24855 Keystone Manufacturing Inc
668 Cleveland St
Rochester, PA 15074

724-775-2227
Fax: 724-775-2739 800-446-7205
sales@keystonemfg.com www.keystonemfg.com
Metal conveyor belting
Owner: Dick Elste
sales@keystonemfg.com
CFO: Richard Elste
Quality Control: Drew Elste
Estimated Sales: $2.5 - 5 Million
Number Employees: 20-49
Number of Products: 7-10

24856 Keystone Packaging Svc Inc
555 Warren St
Phillipsburg, NJ 08865-3230

908-454-8567
Fax: 908-454-7173 800-473-8567
Polyethylene plastic for packaging, printed and
unprinted rolls, sheets and bags
President: John R Schoeneck
jschj@earthlink.net
Estimated Sales: $2.5-5 Million
Number Employees: 10-19
Square Footage: 148000

24857 Keystone Process Equipment
PO Box 446
Philipsburg, PA 16866-446

814-684-5500
Fax: 814-684-7475 sales@keystoneprocess.com
www.keystoneprocess.com
Agitation systems, curd, tank, aseptic processing
system, custom fabrication, processing and
packaging
Manager: Greg Kearney
Estimated Sales: $1 - 3 Million
Number Employees: 1-4

24858 Keystone Rubber Corporation
PO Box 9
Greenbackville, VA 23356

717-235-6863
Fax: 717-235-9681 800-394-5661
Manufacturer and exporter of conveyor belting, rub-
ber sheeting hoses, rubber gaskets and fittings; FDA
approved materials
President: Gloria Lawson
Sales: Mary Baley
Estimated Sales: $5 - 10 Million
Number Employees: 10-19
Parent Co: Maryland Rubber Corporation

24859 Keystone Universal Corp
18400 Rialto St
Melvindale, MI 48122-1946

313-388-0063
Fax: 313-388-6495 ebonex@flash.net
www.ebonex.com
Ammonium carbonate lump, chip powder
President: Michelle Toenniges
ebonex@flash.net
Estimated Sales: $1 - 5 Million
Number Employees: 5-9

24860 Keystone Valve
9100 W Gulf Bank Road
Houston, TX 77240

713-937-5375
Fax: 713-937-5478
Wine industry valves

24861 Khs USA Inc
5501 N Washington Blvd
Sarasota, FL 34243-2249

941-359-4000
Fax: 941-359-4043 877-227-8358
Packaging and special machinery including bag and
carton filling and shrink-banding
President: Reno Cruz
Cio/Cto: Terry Kerns
terry.kerns@khs.com
Executive: Paul Rosile
Estimated Sales: $5 - 10 Million
Number Employees: 100-249
Brands:
Bartelt
Weco

24862 Khs USA Inc
880 Bahcall Ct
Waukesha, WI 53186-1801

262-797-7200
Fax: 262-797-0025 info@khs.com
www.khs.com
Provide filling and packaging services for the bever-
ages and food industries: stainless steel commercial
food processing and beverage bottling machinery,
processing, continual mixing and blending, rinsing,
filling, capping, net weightfillers, aseptic fillers, and
labels.
Director, US Operations: John Turner
Purchasing Manager: Jeff Camargo
Estimated Sales: $106 Million
Number Employees: 250-499
Parent Co: KHS GmbH
Other Locations:
KHS Manufacturing Facility
Sarasota FL

24863 Khs USA Inc
5501 N Washington Blvd
Sarasota, FL 34243-2249

941-359-4000
Fax: 941-359-4043 info@khs.com
Provide filling and packaging services for the bever-
age and food industries.
Cio/Cto: Terry Kerns
terry.kerns@khs.com
Director of Operations: John Turner
Estimated Sales: $20-50 Million
Number Employees: 100-249
Parent Co: KHS GmbH

24864 Kidde Residential & Commercial
1016 Corporate Park Dr
Mebane, NC 27302-8368

919-563-5911
Fax: 919-563-3954 www.kidde.com
Manufacturer and exporter of portable and
hand-held fire extinguishers
Vice President: Bob Amrine
amrine.robert@kiddeus.com
Vice President: Bob Amrine
amrine.robert@kiddeus.com
Number Employees: 250-499
Parent Co: William Holdings
Type of Packaging: Consumer, Food Service, Pri-
vate Label, Bulk

24865 Kidde-Fenwal Inc
400 Main St
Ashland, MA 01721-2100

508-881-2000
Fax: 508-881-6134 www.kidde-fenwal.com
Fire protection products including clean agent sup-
pression systems, pre-engineered systems, high sen-
sitivity smoke detection devices, alarm and
suppression control units, conventional/intelligent
fire sensors, alarm devices and specialhazard fire
and overheat detection
President: John Sullivan
CFO: Michael Cousindau
Quality Control: Robert Lovell
Number Employees: 250-499

24866 Kiefel Technologies
5 Merrill Industrial Dr # -B
Hampton, NH 03842-1963

603-929-3900
Fax: 603-926-1387
Thermoforming and heat sealing equipment
President: Alfred Rak
Estimated Sales: $10-20 Million
Number Employees: 20-49

24867 Kiefer Brushes, Inc
15 Park Dr
Franklin, NJ 07416

Fax: 888-239-1986 800-526-2905
Manufacturer, exporter and importer of brushes in-
cluding oven, floor, window and counter; also,
broom and wax applicators, squeegee mop handles,
paint rollers and brushes
President and CFO: Edward F Boscia
CEO: Gregory Kiefer
Number Employees: 20-49
Square Footage: 100000
Brands:
Dispose a Scrub
Easy Sweep
Lil Wunder-Miniature Scrub
Lok-Tight Handle
Rid-A-Gum

24868 Kikkoman Sales USA Inc.
50 California St
Suite 3600
San Francisco, CA 94111

415-956-7750
www.kikkomanusa.com
President & CEO: Masanao Shimada
Estimated Sales: $100,000,000 - $499,999,999
Number Employees: 100-249

24869 Kilcher Company
1308 Pasadena Avenue S
Apt 11
South Pasadena, FL 33707-3754

727-367-5839
Fax: 727-363-1959
Consultant specializing in sales and marketing for
the barbecue industry
Pres.: James Kilcher
Number Employees: 16

24870 Kildon Manufacturing
192 Thomas Street
Ingersoll, ON N5C 267
Canada

519-485-1593
Fax: 519-485-1084 800-485-4930
Hand cleaners including waterless, lotion and liquid
soap
President: Paul White
Secy./Treas.: Nelda Rumble
Quality Control: Donald Parker
Estimated Sales: Below $5 Million
Number Employees: 3

24871 Kilgore Chemical Corporation
880 Heritage Park Boulevard
Suite 200
Layton, UT 84041-5680

801-546-9909
Fax: 801-775-9468
Environmentally-safe cleaning chemicals
Estimated Sales: $5 - 10,000,000
Number Employees: 5-9
Brands:
Natural Solutions

24872 Killington Wood
ProductsCompany
PO Box 696
Rutland, VT 05702-0696

802-773-9111
Fax: 802-770-3551
Wooden pallets and boxes
President: William H Carris
Opers. Mgr.: Boris Serkalow
Estimated Sales: $1-2.5 Million
Number Employees: 250-499
Parent Co: Carris Reels

24873 Killion Industries Inc
1380 Poinsettia Ave
Vista, CA 92081-8504
760-727-5107
Fax: 760-599-1612 800-421-5352
sales@killionindustries.com
www.killionindustries.com
Manufacturer and exporter of checkstands, and re-
frigerated fixtures
President: Richard W Killion
richard@killionindustries.com
Estimated Sales: $20-50 Million
Number Employees: 100-249
Square Footage: 200000

24874 Kim Lighting
PO Box 60080
City of Industry, CA 91716-0080
626-968-5666
Fax: 626-369-2695 sales@kimlighting.com
www.kimlighting.com
Manufacturer and exporter of lighting fixtures
President: Bill Foley
Regional Sales Manager: Debbie Bell
Estimated Sales: $20-50 Million
Number Employees: 250-499
Parent Co: US Industries

24875 Kimball Companies
75 N Main St
East Longmeadow, MA 01028-2358
413-525-1881
Fax: 413-525-2668
Wood, corrugated and plastic boxes, bulk containers,
foam pads, plastic skids and collapsible storage bins
VP: David Kimball
VP: D Michael Killoran
Manager: Jeanne Matty
Estimated Sales: Below $5 Million
Number Employees: 5-9
Square Footage: 400000
Type of Packaging: Bulk

24876 (HQ)Kimberly-Clark Corporation
351 Phelps Drive
Irving, TX 75038
972-281-1200
www.kimberly-clark.com
Manufacturer and exporter of toilet paper, paper
towels, diapers, feminie products, tissues.
Pres., North America Consumer Business: Kim
Underhill
Chairman & CEO: Michael Hsu
CFO: Maria Henry
President & Chief Operating Officer: Michael Hsu
Chief Growth Officer: Alison Lewis
Year Founded: 1872
Estimated Sales: $18.5 Billion
Number Employees: 42,000
Number of Brands: 31
Type of Packaging: Consumer, Food Service, Pri-
vate Label, Bulk
Brands:
  COTTONELLE
  DEPEND
  DRYNITES
  GREEN FINGERS
  GooDNIites
  HUGGIES
  KLEEN BEBE
  KLEENEX
  KOTEX
  LITTLE SWIMMERS
  PLENTITUD
  POISE
  PULL-UPS
  SCOTTEX
  SNUGGLERS
  VIVA

24877 Kimberly-Clark Professional
1400 Holcomb Bridge Rd
Roswell, GA 30076
800-241-3146
kcpinfo@kcc.com www.kcprofessional.com
Paper and nonwoven products including facial and
bath tissues, hand towels, disposable wipers and
protective garments; also, hand towel dispensers and
bath tissue systems
President: Russ Torres
Estimated Sales: $500,000-$1 Million
Number Employees: 1,000-4,999
Parent Co: Kimberly-Clark Corporation

Brands:
  COTTONELLE
  KIMTECH
  KLEENEX
  KLEENGUARD
  SCOTT
  SMITH & WESSON
  WYPALL

24878 Kincaid Enterprises
PO Box 549
Nitro, WV 25143
304-755-3377
Fax: 304-755-4547 800-951-3377
Manufacturer and exporter of insecticides and other
agricultural chemicals
President: R E Kincaid
VP Production: Brian Kincaid
Estimated Sales: $5 - 10 Million
Number Employees: 5-9
Brands:
  Chloroneb
  Marlate
  Terraneb

24879 Kinder Morgan Inc
6100 Cunningham Rd
Houston, TX 77041-4708
713-466-0496
Fax: 713-896-8830 www.kindermorgan.com
Conveyor systems including overland, radial, stack-
ers and portable screening plants
Manager: Ron Smith
ronald_smith@kindermorgan.com
VP: Ronald Smith
manager: Ronlad Smith
Estimated Sales: $20 - 30 Million
Number Employees: 50-99
Square Footage: 54000

24880 Kinematics & Controls Corporation
15151 Technology Dr.
Brooksville, FL 34604-0690
352-796-0300
Fax: 352-796-4477 800-833-8103
sales@kcontrols.com www.kcontrols.com
Manufacturer and exporter of liquid level sensors
and liquid/powder filling machines
President: John Rakucewicz
Contact: Ricky Clotter
ricky@kcontrols.com
Number Employees: 10
Square Footage: 8000

24881 Kinergy Corp
7310 Grade Ln
Louisville, KY 40219-3437
502-366-5685
Fax: 502-366-3701 kinergy@kinergy.com
www.kinergy.com
Manufacturer, designer, importer and exporter of
bulk solid material handling equipment including
bin and container activators, storage pile and rail car
dischargers, rail car shakers, feeders, conveyors,
deliquefying and deslimingscreens and fluid bed
coolers
President: George Dumbaugh
CEO: Scott Greenwell
CFO: Charles Hays
Manager: Lim Adeline
adeline@kinergy.com.sg
Estimated Sales: $10-20 Million
Number Employees: 20-49
Square Footage: 50000

24882 Kinetic Co
6775 W Loomis Rd
Greendale, WI 53129-2700
414-425-8221
Fax: 414-425-7927
joseph.masters@knifemaker.com
www.knifemaker.com
Manufacturer and exporter of perforating blades,
machine and packaging knives and slitters
President: Kyle Peerenboom
kylepeerenboom@nestlepurinacareers.com
VP: Cash Masters
VP of Sales: Tina Lawton
General Manager: Ian Finkill
Estimated Sales: $10 - 20 Million
Number Employees: 50-99
Type of Packaging: Food Service

24883 Kinetic Equipment Company
2146 W Pershing Street
Appleton, WI 54914-6074
806-293-4471
Fax: 806-293-1103
Cooling, food processing and material handling
equipment and machinery including pump feeders,
blenders, dumpers, mixers, conveyors; also, replace-
ment parts
Owner: Joe Offield
V.P.: Susan Stevenson
Purch. Agt.: Herb Chaney
Estimated Sales: $10 - 20 Million
Number Employees: 5
Brands:
  Cryojet
  Kec I

24884 Kinetico
11015 Kinsman Rd
Newbury, OH 44065-9787
440-564-9111
Fax: 440-564-7641 custserv@kinetico.com
www.kinetico.com
Manufacturer and exporter of water conditioners,
purifiers and filters. Systems are utilized in a wide
variety of residential and commercial applications
that include restaurants, hotels, carwashes, hospitals
and others
President: Toby Thomas
tthomas@kinetico.com
Commercial Sls. Mgr.: George Hohman
CFO: Trevor Wilson
CEO: Shamus Hurley
R&D: Keith Brown
VP Industrial: Chris Hanson
Estimated Sales: $20 - 50 Million
Number Employees: 250-499
Type of Packaging: Bulk
Brands:
  Kinetico

24885 King 888 Company
PO BOX 51360
Sparks, NV 89436
775-530-5718
Fax: 800-785-3674 800-785-3674
www.king888.com
Energy drinks
Sales Representative: Gary Larson
Type of Packaging: Food Service

24886 King Arthur
646 Shelton Ave
Statesville, NC 28677-6104
704-873-0300
Fax: 704-872-4194 800-257-7244
karthur@i-america.net
Manufacturer and exporter of room service carts,
furniture, sternos, chafers and serving equipment
V.P. Sls./Mktg.: Greg Holroyd
Estimated Sales: $10-20,000,000
Number Employees: 1-4
Parent Co: Falcon Products
Brands:
  Sterno

24887 King Badge & Button Company
17792 Metzler Ln
Suite A
Huntingtn Bch, CA 92647
714-847-3060
Fax: 714-841-3380
Promotional products including badges and buttons.
Available with graphic arts engraving
CEO: Dick Dusterhoft
Manager: Mike Kuskie
Estimated Sales: $300,000+
Number Employees: 1-4
Square Footage: 4400

24888 King Bag & Mfg Co
1500 Spring Lawn Ave
Cincinnati, OH 45223-1699
513-541-5440
Fax: 513-541-6555 800-444-5464
mike@kingbag.com www.kingbag.com
Manufacturer, importer and exporter of bulk han-
dling bags, filters bags and curtains, crumb belts
President: Annie Bunn
annie@kingbag.com
VP: Ron Kirsch Jr
Sales Manager: Mike Jennings
Production Manager: Chris Miller

Estimated Sales: $2.5-5 Million
Number Employees: 20-49
Square Footage: 80000

24889 King Company
4830 Transport Drive
Dallas, TX 75247-6310

507-451-3770
Fax: 507-455-7400 king@kingcompany.com
Manufacturer and exporter of air curtains, process
air conditioning, filtration systems and finned coils
Sls. Mgr.: Thomas Heisler
Marketing Manager: Mike Kaler
Sales Manager: Bruce Glover
Estimated Sales: $1 - 5 Million
Number Employees: 100-249
Square Footage: 240000
Parent Co: United Dominion Industries
Brands:
 National

24890 King Electric Sign Co
PO Box 1884
Nampa, ID 83653-1884

208-466-2000
Fax: 208-468-0546
kingelectricsigns@hotmail.com
www.king-electric.com
Neon and plastic signs
President: Ron Harrold
Estimated Sales: Less than $500,000
Number Employees: 10

24891 King Engineering - King-Gage
8019 Ohio River Boulevard
Newell, WV 26050

800-242-8871
www.King-Gage.com
Level measurement systems and compressed air fil-
ters
President: Steve Lefevre
Estimated Sales: Below $5 Million
Number Employees: 20-49
Square Footage: 28000
Type of Packaging: Bulk
Brands:
 King Filters
 King-Gage Systems

24892 King Packaging Co
708 Kings Rd
Schenectady, NY 12304-3665

518-370-5464
Fax: 518-393-5464
Contract packaging of cat litter, ice melt products
and decorative landscape stone.
Owner: Bill Venezio
 bvenezio@kingpackagingcorp.com
Plant Manager: Anthony Farone
Estimated Sales: Less Than $500,000
Number Employees: 5-9
Number of Brands: 6
Number of Products: 24
Square Footage: 240000
Type of Packaging: Consumer, Private Label

24893 King Plastic Corp
1100 N Toledo Blade Blvd
North Port, FL 34288-8694

941-493-5502
Fax: 941-497-3274 800-780-5502
llathrum@kingplastics.com www.kingplastic.com
Manufacturer and exporter of tamper-resistant plas-
tic containers including cups
President: Debra Cunningham
 cunningham@kingplastic.com
VP: Robert King
Marketing Manager: Marjorie Williamson
Sales Manager: Larry Lathrum
Estimated Sales: $10 - 20 Million
Number Employees: 100-249
Square Footage: 200000
Type of Packaging: Bulk
Brands:
 Seal-Top
 Tamp-R-Saf

24894 King Products
1435 Bonhill Road
Unit 25
Mississauga, ON L5T 1V2
Canada

866-454-6757
Fax: 416-850-9828 sales@mzero.com
www.kingproducts.com
Manufacturer and exporter of outdoor plastic signs,
point of purchase displays and furniture
President: Philippe Moulin
CFO: Roger Whitzel
Number Employees: 90
Parent Co: Meridian Kiosks

24895 King Research Laboratory
PO Box 700
Maywood, IL 60153-0700

708-344-7877
Alarm systems including early warning sonic bug
that detects shoplifting, gun shots and break-ins
through any solid material
President/Inventor: John King
Estimated Sales: Less than $500,000
Number Employees: 4

24896 King Sales & EngineeringCompany
2965 Gatlin Road
Placerville, CA 95667-5116

888-546-4725
Fax: 530-644-8279 888-546-4725
Wine industry labelers, label gluers, parts and repair
Estimated Sales: $1-2.5 Million
Number Employees: 10-19

24897 King Sign Company
355 W Thornton St
Akron, OH 44307

330-762-7421
Fax: 330-762-7422
Plastic, wood, metal and cast aluminum signs
President: Wayne V King
Estimated Sales: $500,000-$1 Million
Number Employees: 1-4

24898 (HQ)King of All Manufacturing
PO Box 178
Clio, MI 48420-0178

810-564-0139
Fax: 810-232-6698
Drain/sewer and septic tank cleaners, dishwashing
machine detergents and restaurant cleaners
Estimated Sales: $1-2.5 Million
Number Employees: 5-9
Square Footage: 32000
Brands:
 King of All

24899 Kingery & Assoc
1347 IL Highway 1
Carmi, IL 62821-4929

618-382-3347
Fax: 618-382-3611 888-844-1665
www.grocerytraders.com
Grocery, meat, produce and HBC
President: Ron Kingery
VP: Woodie Pontey
President: Ron Kingery
Public Relations: Bob Estes
Operations: Steve Kemer
IT: Tammy Sisco
 tsisco@yourclearwave.com
Estimated Sales: $10 - 20 Million
Number Employees: 5-9
Square Footage: 33300
Type of Packaging: Consumer, Food Service, Pri-
vate Label, Bulk

24900 Kings River Casting
1350 North Ave
Sanger, CA 93657-3742

559-875-8250
Fax: 559-875-1491 888-545-5157
Sales@KingsRiverCasting.Com
Manufacturer and exporter of tables, chairs and
barstools
President/CEO: Pat Henry
 henry@kingsrivercasting.com
Vice President: Dale Monteleone
Estimated Sales: Below $5 Million
Number Employees: 10-19
Square Footage: 54000
Parent Co: Kings River Casting

Type of Packaging: Food Service

24901 Kingspan Insulated Panels, Ltd.
Langley Office
5202-272nd Street
Langley, BC
Canada

604-607-1101
877-638-3266
Cold storage and blast freezer doors, as well as controlled environment and low temperature doors for
the food and beverage industry. Also a manufacturer
of paneling and roof panels for industrial buildings.

24902 Kingston McKnight
419 Avenue Del Ora
Redwood City, CA 94062

650-462-4900
Fax: 650-268-3733 800-900-0463
Manufacturer, importer and exporter of slip-resistant
safety shoes serving the hospitality industry
Owner: Jeff Mc Knight
VP: Terry Kingston
Contact: Terry Kingston
 tphilipk@yahoo.com
Estimated Sales: $1,000,000
Number Employees: 1-4
Square Footage: 10000
Other Locations:
 Kingston McKnight
 Las Vegas NV
Brands:
 Kingston McKnight

24903 Kinsa Group Inc
9779 S Franklin Dr # 200
Franklin, WI 53132-9566

414-421-2000
Fax: 414-421-6000 www.ihobnob.com
Full-service recruiting firm in the food and beverage
industry
Vice President: Laurie Hyllberg
 laurieh@kinsa.com
Vice President: Michelle Nolan
Estimated Sales: $1-2.5 000,000
Number Employees: 10-19

24904 Kinsley Inc
901 Crosskeys Dr
Doylestown, PA 18902-1025

215-348-7723
Fax: 215-348-7724 800-414-6664
info@kinsleyinc.com www.kinsleyinc.com
Manufacturer and exporter of bottle sorters and un-
scramblers, capping and filling machinery, bottle
conveyors and timing screws.
President: T Mc Carthy
 info@kinsleyinc.com
R&D: James Malloy
Quality Control: James Malloy
Sales: Brandon Concannon
Engineering Manager: David Hansen
Plant Manager: Dan Froehlich
Estimated Sales: Below $5 Million
Number Employees: 5-9
Brands:
 Kinsley Timing Screw
 Roll-Tite

24905 Kinsley Inc
901 Crosskeys Dr
Doylestown, PA 18902-1025

215-348-7723
Fax: 215-348-7724 800-414-6664
www.kinsleyinc.com
Container feed machinery, line combiners, dividers,
cap elevator feeders, screw cap tighteners, custom
changing parts
President: T Mc Carthy
 info@kinsleyinc.com
Senior Engineer: Dave Hanson
Plant Manager: Dan Froehlich
Estimated Sales: $2.5-5 Million
Number Employees: 5-9

24906 Kirkco Corp
2213 Stafford Street Ext
Monroe, NC 28110-9651

704-289-7090
Fax: 704-289-7091 sales@kirkcocorp.com
www.kirkcocorp.com
Food processing, packaging, code dating and case
sealing machinery

President: T W Kirkpatrick
sales@kirkcorp.com
Estimated Sales: $1-2,500,000
Number Employees: 5-9

24907 Kisco Manufacturing
5155 Argyle Street
Port Alberni, BC V9Y 1V3
Canada

604-823-7456
Fax: 250-724-5155 www.kiscomanufacturing.com
Manufacturer and exporter of flour silos and scales, conveyor systems and water meters
Pres.: Svend Kuhr
Svce. Mgr.: Peter Kuhr
Number Employees: 5
Square Footage: 14000
Parent Co: Kisco Foods
Brands:
  Kimac
  Kisco
  Mix Master

24908 Kiss International/Di-tech Systems
965 Park Center Drive
Vista, CA 92081-8312

800-527-5477
Fax: 760-599-0207 800-527-5477
Manufacturer and exporter of reverse osmosis water purification systems; also, components and filter cartridges
VP/General Manager: Theresa Hawks
Sales/Customer Service: Becky Rivera
Sales/Customer Service: Kerri Rivera
Number Employees: 22
Square Footage: 80000
Parent Co: Aqua Care Corporation
Brands:
  Di-Tech

24909 Kisters Kayat
5501 N Washington Boulevard
Sarasota, FL 34243-2249

386-424-0101
Fax: 386-424-0266 parts@kkiusa.com
Manufacturer, importer and exporter of high speed tray and wraparound packers, shrink wrappers, tray stackers and turners and case sealers
VP Finance: Peter Welen
VP Engineering: Gary Hunt
Number Employees: 90
Square Footage: 144000
Parent Co: Kisters Maschinenbau GmbH

24910 Kitchen Equipment Fabricating
7007 Stearns St
Houston, TX 77021-4622

713-747-3611
Fax: 713-747-1892
Stainless steel sinks, tables and counters
President: Lloyd Hartsfield
lloyd@kitchenequipfab.com
Estimated Sales: $5 - 10 Million
Number Employees: 50-99

24911 KitchenRus
1006 S. Milpitas Blvd
Milpitas, CA 95035

408-262-1898
Fax: 408-262-1890 800-796-7797
service@kitchenrus.com www.kitchenrus.com
Cutlery; spreader, salad server set, pepper mill, kitchen utensils, flatware
Estimated Sales: $500,000-$1 Million
Number Employees: 9

24912 Kitchener Plastics
962 Guelph Street
Kitchener, ON N2H 5Z6
Canada

519-742-0752
Fax: 519-742-9247 800-429-5633
Manufacturer and exporter of plastic signs
President: Gabrielle Wolf
Estimated Sales: Below $5 Million
Number Employees: 4

24913 Kitcor Corp
9959 Glenoaks Blvd
Sun Valley, CA 91352-1085

818-767-4800
Fax: 818-767-4658 www.kitcor.com
Custom made stainless steel food processing equipment for hotels, schools, restaurants and hospitals

President: Kent Kitchen
kentkitchen@kitcor.com
Vice President: James Kitchen
Purchasing: Kathleen Anderson
Estimated Sales: $5 Million
Number Employees: 20-49
Type of Packaging: Food Service

24914 Kiva Designs
1350 Hayes St
Suite C-16
Benicia, CA 94510-2945

707-748-1614
Fax: 707-748-1621

24915 Kiwi Coders Corp
265 Messner Dr
Wheeling, IL 60090-6495

847-541-4511
Fax: 847-541-6332 info@kiwicoders.com
www.kiwicoders.com
Marking and coding equipment
Owner: Brent Mc Kay
john.glas@kiwicoders.com
Estimated Sales: $2.5-5 Million
Number Employees: 10-19

24916 Klean Kanteen
3960 Morrow Lane
Chico, CA 95928

530-592-4552
800-767-3173
original@kleankanteen.com
www.kleankanteen.com
Manufactures BPA-free metal bottles as an alternative to plastic and aluminum bottles.
Co-CEO & Co-Owner: Michelle Kalberer
Year Founded: 2004
Estimated Sales: $35 Million
Number Employees: 80
Number of Brands: 1
Brands:
  Klean Kanteen

24917 Kleen Products Inc
8136 SW 8th St
Oklahoma City, OK 73128-4210

405-495-1168
Fax: 405-495-1175 800-392-1792
ken@joeshandcleaner.com
www.joeskleenproducts.com
Manufacturer and exporter of hand, glass and floor cleaners
CEO: Kenneth Newman
CFO: Kenneth Newman
Vice President: Michael Newman
R&D: Kenneth Newman
Quality Control: Joe Brantley
Estimated Sales: $1.5 Million
Number Employees: 5-9
Type of Packaging: Private Label

24918 Kleer Pak
320 S LA Londe Ave
Addison, IL 60101-3309

630-543-0208
Fax: 630-543-0811 888-550-2247
sales@kleerpak.com
Custom bags/pouches for the packaging industry.
President: Gordhan Patel
g.patel@kleerpak.com
Vice President: Kenneth Johnson
Estimated Sales: $3 Million
Number Employees: 10-19

24919 Klever Kuvers
2889 San Pasqual Street
Pasadena, CA 91107-5364

626-355-8441
Fax: 626-355-1331
Indoor and outdoor vinyl table cloths and vinyl aprons
Owner: Mary Ann Froede
CEO: Ruth Breslow
Estimated Sales: $100,000
Number of Brands: 1
Number of Products: 3-5
Type of Packaging: Consumer, Food Service, Private Label, Bulk
Brands:
  Klever Kuvers

24920 Kliklok-Woodman
5224 Snapfinger Woods Dr
Decatur, GA 30035-4023

770-981-5200
Fax: 770-987-7160 www.kliklokwoodman.com
Manufacturer and exporter of flexible packaging machinery for the snack food, confectionery, nut and baking industries including fillers, sealers, weighers, loaders, closers, etc
President: Peter Black
pblack@klikwood.com
CEO: William Crist
Sales Director: T Long
Public Relations: C Kuhr
Estimated Sales: $45 Million
Number Employees: 100-249
Number of Brands: 5
Number of Products: 50
Square Footage: 220000
Parent Co: Kliklok Corporation
Brands:
  Captain
  Certipack
  Clipper
  Concorde
  Cyclone
  Gemini
  Pacer
  Polaris
  Woodman

24921 Kline Process Systems Inc
625 Spring St # 200
Suite 200
Reading, PA 19610-1771

610-371-0300
Fax: 610-371-0300 www.kpsnet.com
Batch control systems, custom fabrication and process control systems for the food and dairy industry
Owner/President: Robert Kline
rob@kpsnet.com
Number Employees: 50-99

24922 Klinger Constructors LLC
8701 Washington St NE
Albuquerque, NM 87113-1680

505-822-9990
Fax: 505-821-0439 www.klingerllc.com
Offers extensive construction and design-build services in commercial, industrial and institutional markets
President: John Gleeson
CEO: Tom Novak
tomn@klingerllc.com
CEO: Tom Novak
Business Development Manager: Shirley Anderson
Estimated Sales: $30 Million
Number Employees: 20-49
Parent Co: Klinger Company

24923 Klippenstein Corp
5399 S Villa Ave
Fresno, CA 93725-8903

559-834-4258
Fax: 559-834-4263 888-834-4258
sales@klippenstein.com www.klippenstein.com
Case sealers, formers and material handling, packaging and conveyor systems
President: Ken Klippenstein
ken@klippenstein.com
President: Richard Klippenstein
General Manager: Ken Klippenstein
Estimated Sales: $1 - 3,000,000
Number Employees: 10-19
Square Footage: 10000

24924 Klockner Filter Products
8314 Tiogawoods Dr
Sacramento, CA 95828-5048

916-689-2328
Fax: 916-689-1035
Wine industry filtration systems, laboratory instruments and supplies
President: Paris Rivera
Estimated Sales: $1 - 5 Million
Number Employees: 20-49

24925 Klockner Packaging Machinery
6767 Forest Hill Avenue
Suite 305
Richmond, VA 23225

804-560-7767
Fax: 804-560-7752

24926 Klockner Pentaplast of America
P.O. Box 500
Gordonsville, VA 22942
540-832-3600
Fax: 540-832-5656 kpainfo@kpfilms.com
www.kpfilms.com
Manufacturer and exporter of rigid vinyl, polyester
and barex films for form/fill/seal, hot fill, trays,
cups, portion packs, rounds, clamshells and modi-
fied atmospheric packaging of food and full body
shrink sleeves for beverages
Chairman: Bruno Deschamps
CFO: Markus Holzl
Vice President: Michael Tubridy
Research & Development: Dean Inman
Marketing Director: Michael Ryan
Sales Director: Bobby Nolan
Communications Manager: Nancy Ryan
Chief Operating Officer: Stefan Brandt
Number Employees: 500-999
Number of Brands: 17
Type of Packaging: Consumer, Food Service
Brands:
Pentafood

24927 Kloppenberg & Co
2627 W Oxford Ave
Englewood, CO 80110-4391
303-761-1615
Fax: 303-789-1741 800-346-3246
klopco@kloppenberg.com www.kloppenberg.com
Ice storage, handling, carting, dispensing and bag-
ging equipment
President: Joseph R Kloppenberg
CEO: Joe Kloppenberg
joklo@kloppenberg.com
Estimated Sales: Below $5 Million
Number Employees: 50-99
Square Footage: 240000

24928 Kloss Manufacturing Co Inc
7566 Morris Ct
Suite 310
Allentown, PA 18106-9247
610-391-3820
Fax: 610-391-3830 800-445-7100
Processor and exporter of flavoring extracts for Ital-
ian ices and slushes; also, concession equipment and
supplies, fountain syrups, popcorn, cotton candy,
nachos and waffles
Owner: Stephen Lloss
skloss@klossfunfood.com
Estimated Sales: $3-5 Million
Number Employees: 10-19
Square Footage: 120000
Type of Packaging: Food Service, Private Label,
Bulk
Brands:
Kloss

24929 Klr Machines Inc
350 Morris St # E
Suite E
Sebastopol, CA 95472-3871
707-823-2883
Fax: 707-823-6954 www.buchervaslin.com
Winery equipment, fruit and vegetable juice process-
ing
Vice President: Scott Wallace
scott.wallace@klrmachines.com
VP: Mike Haswell
Estimated Sales: $5 - 10 Million
Number Employees: 5-9

**24930 (HQ)Kluber Lubrication N
America**
32 Industrial Dr
Londonderry, NH 03053-2008
603-434-7704
Fax: 603-647-4106 800-447-2238
kevin.wylie@us.kluber.com
www.klubersolutions.com
Specialty lubricants designed for extreme conditions
and environments in canning, baking, beverage, confectionery and pasta plants. Kluber offers a full
range of products conforming to USDA H1 and H2
requirements. the stringent qualityassurance in components and production makes Kluber the food and
beverage industry's partner for healthier and safer
world

President: Daniel Alarcon
danielalarcon@klubersolutions.com
CEO: Wolfgang Christandl
North America Marketing Manager: James Sellect,
Jr.
Estimated Sales: $20 Million
Number Employees: 50-99

24931 Kluber Lubrication N America
32 Industrial Dr
Londonderry, NH 03053-2008
603-434-7704
Fax: 603-647-4106 kevin.wylie@us.kluber.com
www.klubersolutions.com
President: Daniel Alarcon
danielalarcon@klubersolutions.com
CEO: Wolfgang Christandl
Estimated Sales: $20 Million
Number Employees: 50-99

24932 Knapp Container
17 Old Turnpike Rd
Beacon Falls, CT 6403
203-888-0511
Fax: 203-881-1817
Corrugated boxes and containers
Owner: George A Meder
Estimated Sales: $10-20 Million
Number Employees: 10-19

24933 Knapp Logistics Automation Inc
2124 Barrett Park Dr NW # 100
Suite 100
Kennesaw, GA 30144-3602
770-426-0067
Fax: 678-388-2893 sales.us@knapp.com
www.knapp.com
Owner: Ingomar Penz
Number Employees: 50-99

24934 Knapp Manufacturing
5227 E Pine Ave
Fresno, CA 93727
559-251-8254
Fax: 559-251-8224 sriley@knappmfg.com
Household and industrial cleaners, laundry deter-
gents, disinfectants, germicides and floor polish
President: Mike Knapp
Technical Director: Doug Banta
Contact: Doug Banta
doug@knappmfg.com
G.M.: Sandra Christino
Estimated Sales: $2.5-5 Million
Number Employees: 5-9
Square Footage: 58000
Parent Co: BouMatic, LLC

24935 Knapp Shoes
2469 State Route 54a
Penn Yan, NY 14527
Fax: 315-536-6909
Slip-resistant and steel toe footwear
Pres./COO: Willie Taaffe
Number Employees: 25
Parent Co: Iron Age Corporation

24936 Knechtel Laboratories Inc
7341 Hamlin Ave
Skokie, IL 60076-3902
847-673-4477
Fax: 847-673-4487 info@knechtel.com
www.knechtel.com
Confectionery, pharmaceutical and foods develop-
ment, troubleshooting and pilot plant operations
support
President: Robert Boutin
rboutin@knechtel.com
CFO: Robert Boutin
Estimated Sales: $1 - 2.5 Million
Number Employees: 10-19
Square Footage: 108000
Type of Packaging: Consumer, Food Service, Pri-
vate Label, Bulk

24937 Knight Equipment Canada
Unit 6
Mississauga, ON L5N 7X8
Canada
949-595-4800
Fax: 905-542-1536 800-854-3764
cs.knight@idexcorp.com www.knightequip.com
Chemical dispensing equipment and dishwashing
machines

Number Employees: 7
Parent Co: Knight Equipment

24938 Knight Equipment International
20531 Crescent Bay Dr
Lake Forest, CA 92630-8825
949-595-4800
Fax: 949-595-4801 800-854-3764
www.knightequip.com
Manufacturer and exporter of low energy dish wash-
ing machines; also, pumps, controls and dispensers
President: George Noa
Pres.: Paul Beldham
Sales/Mktg: George Noa
Contact: Joah Bridwell
jbridwell@kofc9487.com
Estimated Sales: $20-50 Million
Number Employees: 1,000-4,999
Brands:
Ultra Wash

24939 Knight Ind
1140 Centre Rd
Auburn Hills, MI 48326-2602
248-377-4950
Fax: 248-377-2135 literature@knight-ind.com
www.knight-ind.com
Air powered positioning equipment and ergonomic
lifting equipment
CEO: James Zaguroli Jr
Contact: Greg Akey
gakey@knight-ind.com
Estimated Sales: $20-50 Million
Number Employees: 1-4

24940 Knight Paper Box Company
4651 W 72nd St
Chicago, IL 60629-5882
773-585-2035
Fax: 773-585-3824
Paper folding boxes
Contact: Ginnie Glowicki
gglowicki@knightpack.com
Estimated Sales: $10-20 Million
Number Employees: 50-99
Square Footage: 170000

24941 Knight's Electric Inc
11410 Old Redwood Hwy
Windsor, CA 95492-9523
707-433-6931
Fax: 707-431-2342 info@knightselectric.com
www.knightselectric.com
Wine industry service and repair
President: Barbara Ragsdale
barbara@knightselectric.com
CFO: Barbara Ragstale
Administrator: Barbara Ragsdale
Estimated Sales: $5 - 10 Million
Number Employees: 20-49

24942 Knobs Unlimited
13350 Bishop Rd
Bowling Green, OH 43402
419-353-8215
Fax: 419-353-8325
Manufacturer and exporter of plastic replacement
knobs for appliances
Owner/Plt. Mgr.: John Cardenas
R & D: William Anderson
R & D: John Cardinas
Estimated Sales: Below $5 Million
Number Employees: 5-9
Square Footage: 17000

24943 Knott Slicers
290 Pine Street
Canton, MA 02021-3353
781-821-0925
Fax: 781-821-0768
Manufacturer and exporter of slicing machinery for
potato chips, yams, plantains, yuccas, bananas, taro
roots, beets, potatoes, tomatoes and bagel sticks
President: Alan Burgess
VP: Steve Burgess
Quality Control: Doug Merrill
Marketing/Sales: Alan Burgess
Operations: Jim Stratis
Estimated Sales: $10-15 Million
Number Employees: 50-99
Number of Products: 5
Square Footage: 120000
Parent Co: Burgess Brothers
Type of Packaging: Food Service

24944 Koch Container
797 Old Dutch Rd
Victor, NY 14564-8972

585-924-1600
Fax: 585-924-7040 koch1@frontiernet.net
www.kochcontainer.com
Corrugated boxes and displays; wholesaler/distributor of corner boards, edge protectors, plastic bags and fiber tubes
President: Tom Baumgartner
tomb@kochcontainer.com
Mgr. Cust. Svce.: Cheryl Wessells
Estimated Sales: $20 - 50 Million
Number Employees: 50-99
Parent Co: Buckeye Corrugated

24945 (HQ)Koch Equipment LLC
1414 W 29th St
Kansas City, MO 64108-3604

816-931-4557
Fax: 816-753-4976 info@kochequipment.com
www.ultrasourceusa.com
Manufacturer and distributor of processing, packaging and labeling equipment to the meat, poultry, seafood and general food manufacturing markets
CEO: John Starr
Estimated Sales: $38 Million
Number Employees: 100-249
Number of Brands: 10
Number of Products: 30
Square Footage: 180000
Type of Packaging: Consumer, Food Service, Private Label, Bulk
Brands:
 Cook Master
 Crossweb
 Grand Prize
 Injectamatic
 Intact
 Kats
 Koch
 Market Master
 Portion Master
 Ultravac

24946 Koch Equipment LLC
1414 W 29th St
Kansas City, MO 64108-3604

816-931-4557
Fax: 816-753-4976 800-456-5624
info@kochequipment.com
www.ultrasourceusa.com
Owner: Kyle Huff
kyle.huff@kochsupplies.com
CEO and Chairman of the Board: John D. Starr
Estimated Sales: $50 - 100 Million
Number Employees: 100-249

24947 Koch Membrane Systems Inc
850 Main St
Wilmington, MA 01887-3388

978-694-7000
Fax: 978-657-5208 888-677-5624
info@kochmembrane.com
www.kochmembrane.com
Developer and manufacturer of innovative membrane filtration systems.
President: Bill Barber
barberb@kochind.com
Number Employees: 250-499

24948 Kochman Consultants LTD
5545 Lincoln Ave
Morton Grove, IL 60053-3430

847-470-1195
Fax: 847-470-1189 info@kclcad.com
www.kclcad.com
Designer and exporter computer software for the food service industry
President: Ronald Kochman
ron@kclcad.com
R & D: Kevin Kochman
Vice President: Kevin Kochman
Estimated Sales: Below $5 Million
Number Employees: 5-9
Square Footage: 8000
Type of Packaging: Food Service
Brands:
 Kcl Cad Foodservice
 The Kcl Cadalog

24949 Kodex Inc
160 Park Ave # 7
Nutley, NJ 07110-2808

973-235-0606
Fax: 973-235-0132 800-325-6339
sales@kodexray.com www.kodexray.com
Manufacturer, importer and exporter of x-ray inspection systems for detection of contaminants in packaged and fresh food products
President: Gary Korkala
kodex@kodexray.com
General Manager: Don Airey
VP: Gary Korkala
Quality Control: Garrett Sollitto
Sales: Richard Zieminski
Estimated Sales: $3-4 Million
Number Employees: 5-9
Square Footage: 17600
Brands:
 Imagex
 Rapiscan
 Scanvision

24950 Koehler Instrument Co Inc
1595 Sycamore Ave
Bohemia, NY 11716-1732

631-589-3800
Fax: 631-589-3815 800-878-9070
sales@koehlerinstrument.com
www.koehlerinstrument.com
Manufacturer and exporter of lubricant, grease and viscosity testing equipment
President: Roy Westerhaus
rwesterhaus@koehlerinstrument.com
CFO: Peter Brey
R&D: Dr Raj Shah
Marketing: Dr Wayne Goldenberg
Sales: Atul Gautama
Production: Joseph Russo
Estimated Sales: $10-20,000,000
Number Employees: 50-99
Number of Brands: 2
Number of Products: 200
Square Footage: 35000
Brands:
 Okzdata
 Ruler

24951 Koehler-Gibson Marking
875 Englewood Ave
Buffalo, NY 14223-2334

716-838-5960
Fax: 716-838-6859 800-875-1562
sales@kgco.com www.kgco.com
Manufacturer and exporter of marking devices, steel stamps, embossing dies, stencils, etc.; also, printing plates and cutting dies for plastic and corrugated packaging
Owner: David Koehler
ddk@kgco.com
Estimated Sales: $2.5-5 Million
Number Employees: 20-49
Square Footage: 28000

24952 Kofab
300 Kofab Dr
Algona, IA 50511-7317

515-295-7265
Fax: 515-295-7268 sales@kofab.com
www.kofab.com
Custom food processing equipment and stainless steel conveyor belt pulleys
Owner: Brian Schiltz
Vice President: Bill Schiltz
Manager: Bill Schiltz
wjschiltz@kofab.com
Plant Manager: Gray Schiltz
Estimated Sales: $1 - 3 Million
Number Employees: 20-49
Square Footage: 84000

24953 Kohlenberger Associates Consulting Engineering
611 S Euclid St
Fullerton, CA 92838

714-738-7733
Fax: 714-738-3905
kohlenberger@kaceenergy.com
www.kaceenergy.com
Design and engineering consultant specializing in food processing plants and systems, refrigeration and freezing systems and cold storage warehouses

President: M Kohlenberger
CFO: Karl Kohlenberger
Vice President: Ted Kohlenberger
Contact: Karl Kohlenberger
karl@kaceenergy.com
Estimated Sales: $500,000-$1 Million
Number Employees: 1-4
Square Footage: 8800

24954 Kohler Awning Inc
2600 Walden Ave
Buffalo, NY 14225-4736

716-685-3333
Fax: 716-685-0126 800-875-9091
sales@kohlerawning.com
www.kohlerawning.com
Commercial awnings
President: John Martin Kohler Sr
HR Executive: Pat Kuz
pat@kohlerawning.com
Estimated Sales: $10 - 20,000,000
Number Employees: 50-99

24955 Kohler Industries Inc
4925 N 56th St # C
Lincoln, NE 68504-1771

402-465-8845
Fax: 402-465-8841 800-365-6708
info@kohlerequip.com www.kohlerequip.com
Food processing and packaging equipment
President/Owner: Jim Kohler
jim@kohlerequip.com
Marketing: Luke Bundy
Sales: Kirt Borer
Estimated Sales: $3 - 5 Million
Number Employees: 10-19
Square Footage: 54000
Parent Co: Kohler Industries

24956 Kohler Industries Inc
4925 N 56th St # C
PO Box 29496
Lincoln, NE 68504-1771

402-465-8845
Fax: 402-465-8841 800-365-6708
info@kohlerequip.com www.kohlerequip.com
Manufacturer and distributor of freezers, conveyors, bagging equipment and mixers.
President/Owner: Jim Kohler
jim@kohlerequip.com
IT: Scott Jaquez
Sales: Norm Pavlish
Office Mgr./ Inventory Control: Dave Bonczynski
Number Employees: 10-19

24957 Koke Inc
582 Queensbury Ave
Queensbury, NY 12804-7612

518-793-6767
Fax: 518-793-9747 800-535-5303
info@kokeinc.com www.kokeinc.com
Material handling equipment including pallet jacks, dock boards and levelers and fork lifts
Pres.: John Koke
CEO: John Koke
Estimated Sales: Below $5,000,000
Number Employees: 20-49
Square Footage: 60000

24958 Kold Pack
5014 Page Ave
Jackson, MI 49201

517-764-1550
Fax: 517-764-1195 800-824-2661
sales@koldpack.com
Coolers and freezers
President: Glen Stuard
Marketing Manager: Ed Sayles
Contact: Kim Laserra
klaserra@koldpack.com
Purchasing Manager: Kim LaSerra
Estimated Sales: $5 - 10 Million
Number Employees: 10-19
Brands:
 Copeland
 Heatcraft
 Russell
 Tecumseh

24959 Kold-Draft
1525 E Lake Rd
Erie, PA 16511-1088
814-453-6761
Fax: 814-455-6336 tomm@kold-draft.com
www.kolddraft.com
CEO: John Brigham
Contact: Shawn Heifner
sheifner@eriemg.com
Estimated Sales: $5 - 10 Million
Number Employees: 20-49
Parent Co: Uniflow Manufacturing

24960 Kold-Hold
P.O. Box 570
Edgefield, SC 29824-0570
803-637-3166
Fax: 803-637-3046
Manufacturer and exporter of cold plates for refrigeration trucks; used in short delivery
President: Paul Cooper
G.M.: Dave Stasktlunas
Number Employees: 100-249
Square Footage: 440000
Parent Co: Tranter
Brands:
Kold-Hold

24961 Kole Industries
PO Box 20152
Miami, FL 33102
305-633-2556
Fax: 305-638-5821
Manufacturer and exporter of corrugated parts, bins and mailing and shipping room supplies
President: Arthur Kaplan
Contact: Donald Spraque
donald.spraque@koleindustries.com
Estimated Sales: $5 - 10 Million
Number Employees: 15
Parent Co: National Lithographers

24962 Kolinahr Systems
6840 Ashfield Dr
Blue Ash, OH 45242
513-745-9401
Fax: 513-794-3240 sales@geneng.com
www.geneng.cc
Pallet labeling and pallet load stacking equipment
President: Gary Jenkins
Marketing Director: Bill Walker
Contact: Doug Barnhold
dougbarnhold@kolinahrsystems.com
Estimated Sales: $2 Million
Number Employees: 10-19
Number of Products: 9

24963 Kolpak
2915 Tennessee Ave N
Parsons, TN 38363
731-847-6361
Fax: 731-847-5387 800-826-7036
www.kolpak.com
Manufacturer and exporter of walk-in coolers and freezers
General Manager: Gerry Senion
VP: Jack Antell
Contact: Jack Antell
j.antell@kolpak.com
Estimated Sales: $50-100 Million
Number Employees: 100-249
Type of Packaging: Food Service

24964 Kolpak Walk-ins
P.O. Box 550
Parsons, TN 38363-0550
731-847-6361
Fax: 731-847-5387 800-826-7036
www.kolpak.com
Manufacturer and exporter of walk-in coolers, freezers and refrigeration systems
Quality Control: Barry Autry
CFO: Tonny Jordan
VP: Jack Antell
Research & Development: Richard Fahey
Marketing Director: Stephanie Ferrell
Plant Manager: Steve Clayton
Estimated Sales: $50 - 75 Million
Number Employees: 20-49
Parent Co: Manitowoc Foodservice Group
Brands:
Expresso
Kolpak

Polar-Chill
Polar-Pak

24965 Kom International
Place Du Parc, Box 1113
Montreal, QC H2V 4P2
Canada
514-849-4000
Fax: 514-849-8888 www.komintl.com
Managment consulting services in supply chain, warehouse, distribution
President and CEO: Allan Kohl
COO: Keith Swiednicki

24966 Komatsu Forklift USA
1701 Golf Rd # 100
PO Box 5049
Rolling Meadows, IL 60008-4227
847-437-5800
Fax: 770-784-0700
forkliftmarketing@komatsuna.com
www.komatsuforkliftusa.com
Fork lift trucks
President: Motohisa Kai
CFO: David Adea
Contact: Bill Fruland
bfruland@ktmusa.com
Estimated Sales: $5 - 10 Million
Number Employees: 20-49
Square Footage: 250000

24967 Komax Systems Inc
15301 Graham St
Huntington Beach, CA 92649-1110
310-830-4320
Fax: 310-830-4320 800-826-0760
www.komax.com
President: Robert Smith
info@komax.com
Estimated Sales: $3,000,000 - $5,000,000
Number Employees: 10-19

24968 Kombucha Brooklyn
906 State Route 28
Kingston, NY 12401-7264
917-261-3010
Fax: 888-397-6817
Manufacturer of equipment used to brew kombucha.
Founder and CEO: Eric Childs
info@kombuchabrooklyn.com
Co-Founder: Jessica Childs
Number Employees: 1-4

24969 Komline-Sanderson Engineering
12 Holland Ave
Peapack, NJ 7977
908-234-1000
Fax: 908-234-9487 800-225-5457
info@komline.com www.komline.com
Paddle Dryer/Processor for drying, crystallizing, calcining, tooling, heating, reacting, sterilization. Liquid solid separation filters, filtration with cake washing and clarification, vacuum filtration products. Pumps, wastewatertreatment sludge by-product dewatering and drying.
CEO: Russell Komline
rkomline@komline.com
Vice President: Christopher Komline
Purchasing Manager: W Tiger
Estimated Sales: $35-40 Million
Number Employees: 100-249
Square Footage: 85000

24970 Konica Minolta Corp
101 Williams Dr
Ramsey, NJ 07446-1293
201-825-4000
Fax: 201-825-7567 888-473-3637
www.konicaminolta.com
Manufacturer and exporter of color measuring instrumentation including spectrophotometers, colorimeters, light meters, etc.; also, computer software for color formulation and quality control
CEO: Scott Cohen
scohen@mi.konicaminolta.us
CEO: Jun Haraguchi
Marketing Director: Maria Repici
Number Employees: 500-999

24971 Konica Minolta SensingAmericas
101 Williams Drive
Ramsey, NY 07446
201-785-2413
Fax: 201-785-2482 888-473-2656

Sensory machines
President: Hal Yamazaki
Vice President: Grant Hume
Number Employees: 35

24972 Kontane
1000 Charleston Regional Pkwy
Charleston, SC 29492
843-352-0011
Fax: 828-397-3683 info@kontanelogistics.com
www.kontane.com
Manufacturer and exporter of containers: heavy duty wooden, household storage and custom built; also, pallet and export boxes and cleated plywood
President: Ed Byrd
VP: Jason Essenberg
COO: Rusty Byrd
Estimated Sales: $2.5-5 Million
Number Employees: 100-249

24973 Konz Wood Products Co
616 N Perkins St
Appleton, WI 54914-3133
920-734-7770
Fax: 920-734-4811 877-610-5145
info@konzwoodproducts.com
www.konzwoodproducts.com
Pallets, skids and wooden shipping crates
Owner: Lawrence Konz Jr
HR Executive: Bob Beckstrom
info@konzwoodproducts.com
Quality Control: Lawrence A Konz
Estimated Sales: $2.5 - 5 Million
Number Employees: 50-99
Parent Co: Appleton Lumber Company

24974 Koolant Koolers
2625 Emerald Dr
Kalamazoo, MI 49001
269-349-6800
Fax: 269-349-8951 800-968-5665
www.dimplexthermal.com
Custom and standard liquid coolers and water chillers for the removal of heat from industrial and continuous processes
CEO: Mark Rostagno
VP: Spencer Malcolm
Sales Manager: Kristen Ulsh
Vice President of Operations: Spencer Malcolm
Estimated Sales: $20 - 50 Million
Number Employees: 50-99
Square Footage: 60000
Brands:
Koolant Koolers

24975 Kopykake
3699 W 240th St
Torrance, CA 90505-6002
310-373-8906
Fax: 310-375-5275 800-999-5253
sales@kopykake.com www.kopykake.com
Manufacturer and exporter of computerized cake photo printing, edible frosting sheets and edible ink. kartriges, cake decorating equipment and supplies, including drawing projectors, airbrushes and compressors, food colors, disposabledecorating bags, etc
President: Gerry Mayer
gerry@kopykake.com
Vice President: Greg Mayer
Sales Director: Rudy Arce
Estimated Sales: $1-2.5 Million
Number Employees: 20-49
Square Footage: 80000
Type of Packaging: Food Service
Brands:
Airmaster
Kobra
Kopykake
Kopyrite
Kroma Jet
Kroma Kolor

24976 Korab Engineering Company
7727 Beland Avenue
Los Angeles, CA 90045-1128
310-670-7710
Fax: 310-670-7710
Manufacturer, exporter and importer of packaging machinery including liquid fillers, monoblock machinery, automation systems, vertical form fillers, seal machinery, horizontal thermoforming equipment, tray makers, pick and placeequipment, etc

Pres./G.M.: Jacek Zdzienicki
Shop Mgr.: Eric Zuber
Cust. Rel.: Janine Luciano
Number Employees: 5-9
Square Footage: 16000

24977 Korber Medipak Inc
14501 58th St N
Clearwater, FL 33760-2808

727-538-4644
Fax: 727-532-6521 www.kmedipak.com
Specialty molds, dies and packaging machinery
President: Michael DE Collibus
decollibus@kmedipak.com
Estimated Sales: $10-25 Million
Number Employees: 20-49

24978 Kord Products Inc.
325B West Street #200
PO Box 265
Brantford, ON N3T 5M8
Canada

Fax: 519-753-2667 800-452-9070
www.kord.ca
Manufacturer and exporter of plastic injection
molded products including blisters, clamshells and
fiber protective packaging, custom molded products
President: Don Gayford
CEO: Gerry Docksteader
Research & Development: David Penkmann
Marketing Director: Jon Hensen
Plant Manager: Brock Howes
Purchasing Manager: Rachel St. Laurent
Number Employees: 200

24979 Kornylak Corp
400 Heaton St
Hamilton, OH 45011-1894

513-863-1277
Fax: 513-863-7644 800-837-5676
kornylak@kornylak.com www.kornylak.com
Manufacturer and exporter of material handling
equipment including conveyors, multi-directional
and plastic skate wheels and gravity controlled live
storage systems
President: Thomas Kornylak
Staff, Engineering Department: Richard Kornylak
Marketing/Sales Manager: Anne McAdams
IT: Walter Stortz
walter@kornylak.com
Purchasing Director: Ginger Vizedom
Estimated Sales: $5 Million
Number Employees: 20-49
Square Footage: 400000
Brands:
Ags 100
Armorbelt
Mini-Wheel
Palletflo
Superwheel
Transwheel
Ts Conveyor
Zipflo

24980 Kosempel Manufacturing Company
3760 M Street
Philadelphia, PA 19124-5538

215-533-7110
Fax: 215-744-5220 800-733-7122
Custom metal products including bowls, funnels,
hoppers and coating pans
Sls.: Rob Borst
Estimated Sales: $5-10 Million
Number Employees: 50-99
Square Footage: 120000

24981 (HQ)Koser Iron Works
PO Box 133
Barron, WI 54812

715-537-5654
bill@poweram.com
Storage racks; also, custom stainless steel fabrica-
tion available
President: Willian E Koser
Production Manager: David Fall
Purchasing Manager: David Fall
Estimated Sales: Below $5 Million
Number Employees: 20-49
Square Footage: 60800

24982 Kotoff & Company
324 N San Dimas Ave
San Dimas, CA 91773-2601

626-443-7115
Fax: 626-443-7110
Standard and custom plated wire shelving
President: James Kotoff
VP: Mary Ann Kotoff
Manager: Dean Miller
Estimated Sales: $1-2.5 Million
Number Employees: 5-9
Square Footage: 25000

24983 Koza's Inc
2910 S Main St
Pearland, TX 77581-4710

281-485-1462
Fax: 281-485-8000 800-594-5555
sales@kozas.com www.kozas.com
Manufacturer and exporter of advertising novelties
including caps and hats; also, custom cresting
available
Owner: Joseph Koza
jek@kozas.com
Estimated Sales: $6 Million
Number Employees: 50-99
Square Footage: 40000

24984 Kraissl Co Inc
299 Williams Ave
Hackensack, NJ 07601-5289

201-342-0008
Fax: 201-342-0025 800-572-4775
kraissl@aol.com www.strainers.com
Strainers, filters, valves for pipelink service
President/CEO: Richard Michel
richard@moviesunlimited.com
Foreman: Winston Philips
Chairman of the Board: Richard Michel
Tech Sales: Bill Henderson
Office Supervisor: Barbara Punthsecca
Estimated Sales: Below $5,000,000
Number Employees: 50-99
Square Footage: 14000
Type of Packaging: Bulk
Brands:
Kraissl
Sea-View

24985 Kramer
125 Clairemont Ave
Suite 330
Decatur, GA 30030-2551

404-371-1835
Fax: 404-892-8881
Owner: Myron N Kramer
Estimated Sales: $.5 - 1 million
Number Employees: 5-9

24986 Kraus & Sons
215 W 35th St
Suite 300
New York, NY 10001

212-620-0408
Fax: 212-924-4081
Manufacturer and exporter of badges, buttons, flags,
banners and awnings
Owner: Paul Schneider
Estimated Sales: Below 1 Million
Number Employees: 5-9
Type of Packaging: Food Service

24987 Kreative Koncepts
154 W Washington Street
Marquette, MI 49855-4320

906-228-9354
Fax: 906-228-8918 800-638-2019
Microwave accessories
President: Robert Green
Brands:
Rib Chef
Souper 1 Step

24988 Kreissle Forge Ornamental
7947 N Tamiami Trl
Sarasota, FL 34243-1999

941-355-6795
Fax: 941-351-3213
Ornamental iron fixtures
President: Martin Haas
VP: Joey Kreissle
Estimated Sales: Less Than $500,000
Number Employees: 1-4

24989 Krepe-Kraft
1801 Elmwood Ave
Buffalo, NY 14207-2463

716-826-5813
Fax: 716-447-9201 800-637-2536
sales@modpac.com
Specialty paperboard folding cartons, grease-proof
cookie boxes, large takeout tote, upscale valentines'
day designs and gift basket box
President/CEO: Daniel C. Keane
sales@krepekraft.com
CFO: David B. Lupp
VP & Finance: Daniel Geary
Marketing Manager: Chuck Littlecom
Sales Exec: Katie Niedermeier
Estimated Sales: $10-25 Million
Number Employees: 100-249
Number of Products: 500
Square Footage: 300000
Type of Packaging: Consumer, Food Service, Pri-
vate Label
Brands:
Fashionglo

24990 Krewson Enterprises
855 Canterbury Rd
Cleveland, OH 44145-1420

440-871-8780
Fax: 440-871-5127 800-521-2282
airtools@superiorpneumatic.com
www.superiorpneumatic.com
Manufacturer and exporter of adjustable freezer and
cooler alarms
President: Bradley Krewson
Contact: Walter Krewson
pshkol@aol.com
Estimated Sales: $5-10 Million
Number Employees: 5-9
Square Footage: 20000
Parent Co: Superior Pneumatic & Manufacturing
Brands:
Protecto-Freeze
Protecto-Temp

24991 Krimstock Enterprises
1426 Union Ave
Pennsauken, NJ 08110

856-665-3676
Fax: 856-662-8083 krim@bellatlantic.net
Advertising specialties, signs, displays and exhibits;
cutting and engraving services available
Owner: Joseph Crew
Estimated Sales: $1 - 5,000,000
Number Employees: 5-9
Square Footage: 7000

24992 Krispy Kist Company
120 S Halsted Street
Department R8
Chicago, IL 60661-3508

312-733-0900
Fax: 312-733-3508
Manufacturer and exporter of snack food processing
machinery including extruders, fryers, kettles, coat-
ing tumblers, mixers, ovens and peanut roasters
Sales/Operations: J Geiersbach
Office Mgr.: Kevin Coster
Estimated Sales: $1-5 Million
Number Employees: 8
Square Footage: 20000
Type of Packaging: Food Service
Brands:
Krispy
Krispy Kist

24993 Krogh Pump Co
251 W Channel Rd
Benicia, CA 94510-1129

707-747-7585
Fax: 707-747-7599 800-225-7644
Manufacturer and exporter of horizontal and vertical
centrifugal pumps for abrasive, corrosive, food and
sewage services
Owner: Charles O' Brian
Estimated Sales: $2.5-5 Million
Number Employees: 20-49
Square Footage: 30000
Type of Packaging: Food Service, Private Label

24994 Krones
PO Box 321801
9600 S. 58th St.
Franklin, WI 53132-6241
414-409-4000
Fax: 414-409-4100 800-752-3787
www.kronesusa.com
Food processing and packaging machinery including
blenders, fillers, labelers, bottle washers and rinsers,
palletizers, depalletizers, pasteurizers, etc.
CEO: Christoph Klenk
CFO: Norbert Broger
Chief Sales Officer: Thomas Ricker
Year Founded: 1951
Estimated Sales: $4.1 Billion
Number Employees: 15,299
Square Footage: 232000
Parent Co: Krones AG

24995 Krowne Metal Corp
100 Haul Rd
Wayne, NJ 07470-6616
973-305-3300
Fax: 973-872-1129 800-631-0442
customerservice@krowne.com www.krowne.com
Manufacturer and exporter of bar equipment, hand
sinks and faucets
Vice President: James Angood
james.angood@krowne.com
Exec. V.P.: Roger Forman
Vice President: James Angood
james.angood@krowne.com
Estimated Sales: $5-10,000,000
Number Employees: 10-19
Square Footage: 160000

24996 Krueger Food Laboratories
21 Alpha Rd # D
Suite D
Chelmsford, MA 01824-4172
978-256-1220
Fax: 978-256-1222 dkrueger@kfl.com
www.kfl.com
Analytical testing service for pesticide residues and
nutritional labeling; also, microbiology, consultation
and sampling
President: Dana Krueger
Lab Mgr.: Jeanne Maciel
Office Mgr.: Sherida George
Contact: Joe Golemme
jgolemme@kfl.com
Estimated Sales: $5-10 Million
Number Employees: 20-49
Square Footage: 16000

24997 Krueger International Holding
1330 Bellevue St.
Green Bay, WI 54302
800-424-2432
info@ki.com
Tables, stools and chairs.
Chairman/CEO: Richard Resch
President: Brian Krenke
Year Founded: 1941
Estimated Sales: $650 Million
Number Employees: 3,000+
Square Footage: 250000

24998 Krusoe Sign Co
5365 Canal Rd
Cleveland, OH 44125-4808
216-447-1177
Fax: 216-447-1516
Signs including advertising and plastic
President: Dale Krusoe
krusoesigns@aol.com
Estimated Sales: Less Than $500,000
Number Employees: 1-4

24999 Krystal Holographics
555 W 57th St
New York, NY 10019-2925
212-261-0400
Fax: 212-262-0414 800-998-5775
Suppliers of semi-conductors, electro mechanical
components
Owner: Azi Lezi
CEO: Dan Toben
Estimated Sales: $5 - 10 Million
Number Employees: 50-99

25000 Krystatite Films
PO Box 89
Mar Lin, PA 17951-0089
570-621-6097
Fax: 570-622-1037
Flat, centerfolded and tube PVC shrink film for
overwrapping and bundling
Estimated Sales: $1 - 5 Million

25001 Kuecker Equipment Company
801 W Markey Rd
Belton, MO 64012
816-331-7070
Fax: 816-331-7888 info@kuecker.com
www.kuecker.com
President: Stanley Kuecker
CEO: Mike Langdom
CFO: Alice Kuecker
VP Sales: Jim Kuecker
System Sales: Dan Bingaman
Contact: Bev Rhoades
bev.rhoades@kuecker.com
Estimated Sales: Below $5 Million
Number Employees: 10-19

25002 Kuehne Chemical
86 N Hackensack Ave
Kearny, NJ 07032-4673
973-589-0700
Fax: 973-589-4866 info@kuehnecompany.com
www.kuehnecompany.com
Industrial strength bleach including sodium
hypochlorite; wholesaler/distributor of caustic soda,
caustic potash, chlorine and sulfur
President & CEO: Don Nicolai
Estimated Sales: $61 Million
Number Employees: 50-99
Square Footage: 10000

25003 Kuepper Favor Company,
Celebrate Line
P.O. Box 428
Peru, IN 46970-0428
765-473-5586
Fax: 765-472-7247 800-321-5823
www.partydirect.com
Manufacturer and importer of paper party favors, fa-
vor goodie bags, custom imprinted lite-up favors
and novelties
President: Mike Kuepper
VP: Douglas Kuepper
Head of Marketing Department: Jane Grund
Contact: Michael Keeper
mike@partydirect.com
Number Employees: 50-99
Type of Packaging: Consumer, Private Label, Bulk
Brands:
Celebrate Line
K Line
Party Direct

25004 Kuest Enterprise
PO Box 110
Filer, ID 83328-0110
208-326-4084
Fax: 208-326-6604
goldengraingrinder@hotmail.com
Manufacturer and exporter of grain grinders
Founder: Johnnie Kuest
Estimated Sales: $500,000 - $1 Million
Number Employees: 1-4

25005 Kuhl Corporation
39 Kuhl Rd
PO Box 26
Flemington, NJ 8822
908-782-5696
Fax: 908-782-2751 khh@kuhlcorp.com
www.kuhlcorp.com
Industrial washing machines for the food industry
President: Henry Kuhl
CEO: Kevin Kuhl
CFO: Rick Kuhl
Marketing/Public Relations: Michael Vella
Contact: Paul Chou
pchou@kuhlcorp.com
Operations Manager: John Pichell
Plant Manager: Al Fisher
Estimated Sales: $12 Million
Number Employees: 70
Square Footage: 40000

25006 Kuriyama of America Inc
360 E State Pkwy
Schaumburg, IL 60173-5335
847-755-0360
Fax: 847-885-0996 800-800-0320
www.kuriyama.com
Thermoplastic, rubber and metal hose products and
accessories including couplings and fittings for use
in industrial and commerical applications
Marketing: Gary Kammes
Contact: Lauren Allen
lauren.j.allen@moody.edu
Estimated Sales: $70+ Million
Number Employees: 20-49
Type of Packaging: Private Label, Bulk
Other Locations:
Houston TX
Santa Fe Springs CA
Kennesaw GA
New Egypt NJ
Mexico

25007 Kurtz Food Brokers
1028 Peach Street
San Luis Obispo, CA 93401
805-543-3727
Fax: 866-633-2140 800-696-7423
kevin@kurtzinc.net www.kurtzfoodbrokers.com
Broker of confectionery products, industrial ingredi-
ents, rice, rice crackers, raisins, nuts, etc.
President: Ed Kurtz
Diretor Sales/Marketing: Kevin Magon
Sales Coordinator: Vicki Crawford
Contact: Nicole Ansbro
nicole@kurtzinc.net
Estimated Sales: Under $500,000
Number Employees: 3
Square Footage: 1500

25008 Kurtz Oil Company
3305 Healy Dr
Winston Salem, NC 27103-1406
336-768-1515
Fax: 336-722-4634
Industrial lubricants
President: Anne Kiger
Estimated Sales: $1 - 2.5 Million
Number Employees: 1-4
Brands:
Pilot

25009 Kurz Transfer Products LP
11836 Patterson Rd
Huntersville, NC 28078
704-927-3700
Fax: 704-927-3701 800-950-3645
sales@kurzusa.com www.kurzusa.com
Metalized and coated films, hot stamping foils and
plastic printing machinery
CEO: Brian Nowak
Estimated Sales: $28 Million
Number Employees: 1000-4999
Square Footage: 60000

25010 Kusel Equipment Company
PO Box 87
Watertown, WI 53094-0087
920-261-4112
Fax: 920-261-3151 sales@kuselequipment.com
www.kuselequipment.com
Manufactures stainless steel drainage systems and
cheese equipment.
President: Dave Smith
Contact: Clark Derleth
cderleth@kuselequipment.com
Estimated Sales: $10 Million
Number Employees: 1-4

25011 Kwikprint ManufacturingInc
4868 Victor St
Jacksonville, FL 32207-1702
904-737-3755
Fax: 904-730-0349 800-940-5945
www.kwik-print.com
Manufacturer and exporter of foil, gold and hot
stamping equipment; also, custom stamping dies and
foils; wholesaler/distributor of advertising special-
ties and promotional items
Owner: Mike Bulger
mbulger@kwik-print.com
V.P.: Lynn Cann
Estimated Sales: Below $5 Million
Number Employees: 5-9
Square Footage: 48000

Type of Packaging: Food Service, Private Label, Bulk
Brands:
  Kwikprint

25012 Kysor Panel Systems
4201 N Beach St
Fort Worth, TX 76137
817-230-8703
Fax: 817-281-5521 800-633-3426
jburke@kysorpanel.com
Manufacturer and exporter of refrigerated walk-in coolers
President: David Frase
Quotations: Gary Holloway
Contact: Shannon Barnes
  sbarnes@fidelitylifeandhealth.com
Estimated Sales: $20-50 Million
Number Employees: 100-249
Square Footage: 300000
Parent Co: Scotsman Industries
Other Locations:
  Kysor Panel Systems
  Goodyear AZ

25013 Kysor/Kalt
7320 NE 55th Ave
Portland, OR 97214-2138
503-235-0776
Fax: 503-249-8452
Walk-in coolers and freezers
Owner: Kevin Kayser
Estimated Sales: $1 - 3 Million
Number Employees: 1-4
Parent Co: Kysor Industrial Corporation

25014 Kyung Il Industrial Company
10771 El Caballo Avenue
San Diego, CA 92127-3311
858-673-1211
Fax: 858-673-5311
Rotogravure printing, laminated rolls on pouches, flat standup zipper
President: Lee Sung Ho
CEO: Kyo Sun Kim
Quality Control: Sunyu Kim
Partner: Kyosun Kim
Estimated Sales: Below $5 Million
Number Employees: 4

25015 L & C Plastic Bags
500 Dick Minnich Dr
Covington, OH 45318-1263
937-473-2968
Fax: 937-473-5334 sales@LCPlastics.com
www.lcplastics.com
Plastic and polyethylene bags
President: Rodd Sprenkel
  rsprenkel@lcplastics.com
Estimated Sales: Below $5 Million
Number Employees: 10-19

25016 (HQ)L & L Packing Co
527 W 41st St
Chicago, IL 60609
773-285-5400
Fax: 773-285-0366 sales@worldsbeststeak.com
www.landlpacking.com
Established in 1955. Supplier of prime and choice aged beef, pork, veal, lamb and poultry.
President: Joel Lezak
Year Founded: 1955
Estimated Sales: $10.3 Million
Number Employees: 20-49
Type of Packaging: Consumer, Private Label

25017 L & M Food Svc Inc
885 Airpark Dr
Bullhead City, AZ 86429-5886
928-754-3241
Fax: 928-754-2241 info@lmfoodservice.com
www.lmfoodservice.com
Wholesaler/distributor of equipment and fixtures and general merchandise including paper, janitorial and bar supplies; serving the food service market
President: Ron Laughlin
  laughlinrc@lmfoodservice.com
CEO: Andy Roesch
Vice President: Judy Laughlin
Plant Manager: Tom Watkins
Purchasing Manager: Dick Motsinger
Estimated Sales: $14 Million
Number Employees: 20-49
Square Footage: 100000

25018 L & N Label Co
2051 Sunnydale Blvd
Clearwater, FL 33765-1202
727-442-5400
Fax: 727-442-8915 800-944-5401
customerservice@lnlabel.com www.lnlabel.com
Manufacturer and exporter of die cut pressure sensitive labels; blank and printed types and roll, sheet, long and short runs available. Four color process labels, up to 8 colors.
President: Steve Sabadosh
  artdepartment@lnlabel.com
Vice President: Julee Sabadosh
Sales Director: Reyna Martin
IT Executive: John Brand
Production Manager: Curtis Booth
Plant Manager: Dave Gioia
Estimated Sales: $4-5 Million
Number Employees: 20-49
Square Footage: 80000
Type of Packaging: Private Label

25019 L A Cabinet & FinishingCo
810 E Jefferson Blvd
Los Angeles, CA 90011-2593
323-233-7245
Fax: 323-233-7248
Store fixtures
President: Mark Klein
VP: Mark Klein
Estimated Sales: $1-2.5 Million
Number Employees: 10-19

25020 L ChemCo Distribution
3230 Commerce Center Place
Louisville, KY 40211-1900
502-775-8387
Fax: 502-775-5981 800-292-1977
Wholesale distributor of commercial and industrial janitorial cleaning supplies and equipment; also including sell of pesticides, weedicides and herbicides
Estimated Sales: $1.5 Million
Number Employees: 9
Square Footage: 28000

25021 L Cubed Corp
871 Range End Rd
Dillsburg, PA 17019-9463
717-432-9738
Fax: 717-432-8389 800-826-2775
www.tamsystems.com
Bagging machines
Owner: Lin Lobaugh
  llobaugh@tamsystemsonline.com
Estimated Sales: $1 Million
Number Employees: 20-49

25022 L G I Intl Inc
6700 SW Bradbury Ct
Portland, OR 97224-7734
503-620-0528
Fax: 503-620-3296 800-345-0534
sales.usa@lgintl.com www.lgitechnology.com
Manufacturer and exporter of pressure sensitive, front panel, bar code and clean room labels
President: Tim Hartka
  tim.hartka@lionbrothers.com
International Sales: Greg Jarmin
Sales Manager: Dale Gremaux
Estimated Sales: $1 - 5 Million
Number Employees: 20-49
Square Footage: 172000

25023 L T Hampel Corp
W194n11551 Mccormick Dr
Germantown, WI 53022-3000
262-255-4540
Fax: 262-255-9731 800-681-6979
sales@hampelcorp.com www.hampelcorp.com
Manufacturer and exporter of plastic pallets including rugged light weight, steel reinforced, thermoformed, nestable, standard and custom interlocking sleeve pack and double decker
President: Lance Hampel
CEO: Dave Brudvig
  dbrudvig@thermoformpallets.com
Estimated Sales: $10 - 20 Million
Number Employees: 100-249
Brands:
  Calf-Tel
  Intrustor
  Pallid

25024 L&A Engineering and Equipment
PO Box 2997
Turlock, CA 95381-2997
209-668-8107
Fax: 209-668-0636
Wine industry processing equipment
Estimated Sales: $1-5 Million
Number Employees: 3

25025 L&A Process Systems
1704 Reliance St
Modesto, CA 95358
209-581-0205
Fax: 209-581-0194
Manufacturer and exporter of evaporators, distilleries, rotary coil vessels for jam and jelly production, ceramic cross flow micro-filtration and essence/aroma recovery systems
CEO: Don Carter
Estimated Sales: $1-2.5 Million
Number Employees: 5-9

25026 L&H Wood Manufacturing Company
PO Box 441
Farmington, MI 48332-0441
248-474-9000
Fax: 248-474-0269 www.michigancorporates.com
New and used pallets, skids, wood and wirebound boxes, stretch film and machines, steel and synthetic strapping and strapping machines
Sales Manager: Bill Lindbert
Controller: Kris Lindbert
Estimated Sales: $5-10 Million
Number Employees: 1-4
Square Footage: 60000

25027 L&L Associates
S87w27765 Lakeview Lane
Mukwonago, WI 53149-9665
281-221-4994
Fax: 262-363-3940
L&L Associates are experienced, professional, independent Packaging Consultants offering experience in a full complement of packaging disciplines since 1990. All recommendations for packaging equipment, systems, materials and servicesare objective and selected from the entire packaging industry, both domestically and internationally, as required

25028 L&L Engraving Company
40 Old Lake Shore Road
Gilford, NH 03249-6522
603-524-3032
Fax: 603-524-6106 888-524-3032
Manufacture of stamps, rubber stamps, dating and numbering, coding, dating and marking equipment, advertising signs, plastic signs, plastic and metal fabricators
CEO: Melanie Burgess
*Estimated Sales:*less than $500,000
Number Employees: 1-4

25029 L&L Reps
4630 200th Street SW
Lynnwood, WA 98036-6608
425-778-9536
Fax: 425-778-6071
Brewing devices (urns, cleaners, coffeemakers), coffee filters, dispensing equipment, filtration equipment
President: Tracy Tayne
Estimated Sales: $5 - 10 Million
Number Employees: 3

25030 L&M Chemicals
5018 Trenton Street
Tampa, FL 33619-6832
813-247-6007
Fax: 813-247-6473 800-362-3331
lmccbill@gmail.com www.lmcc.com
Industrial chemicals including disinfectants, detergents and hand cleaners
Owner: Robert Pasciuta
Estimated Sales: Less than $500,000
Number Employees: 4
Parent Co: Gator Supply

25031 L&S Pallet Company
15150 Middlebrook Drive
Houston, TX 77058-1210
281-443-6537
Wooden pallets
Secretary/Treasurer: Allan Findley

Estimated Sales: $1-2.5 Million
Number Employees: 5-9

25032 L&S Products
422 Jay St
Coldwater, MI 49036-2112
517-279-9526
Fax: 517-278-8648 info@lsproducts.com
Store fixtures including garment and display racks
and steel tubing products
CEO: Mark Neesley
CFO: Shanayne Neesley
R&D: Shanayne Neesley
Estimated Sales: Below $5 Million
Number Employees: 1-4
Square Footage: 120000

25033 L.A. Darling Co., LLC
1401 U.S. Highway 49B
Paragould, AR 72450-3139
800-682-5730
www.ladarling.com
Modular merchandising systems, store fixtures, gon-
dolas and shelving systems, gourmet racks, check-
outs, service desks and P.O.P. displays, gondolas,
specialty wood and metal fixtures.
Group President: Randy Guthrie
Year Founded: 1897
Estimated Sales: $110.8 Million
Number Employees: 1000-4999
Square Footage: 3000
Parent Co: Marmon Retail Store Equipment LLC

25034 L.C. Thompson Company
1303 43rd St.
Kenosha, WI 53140
262-652-3662
Fax: 262-652-3526 800-558-4018
www.lcthomsen.com
Manufacturer, importer and exporter of dairy pro-
cessing machinery including control systems, filters,
gaskets, hoses, pumps, strainers, thermometers, tub-
ing and valves
President: Wayne Borne
Sls. Mgr.: Mike Dyutka
Service Manager: Mike Dyutka
Sales: Joyce Saftig
Contact: Hose Hooks
hhooks@lcthomsen.com
Number Employees: 20-49
Square Footage: 48000

25035 LA Graphics
15 Ellwood Court
Greenville, SC 29607-5340
864-297-1111
Fax: 864-987-9920
Commercial awnings
Corporate Manager: Nancy Keller
Quality Control: Larry Boeller
Estimated Sales: Below $5,000,000
Number Employees: 50

25036 LA Marche Mfg Co
106 Bradrock Dr
Des Plaines, IL 60018-1967
847-299-1193
Fax: 847-299-3061 www.lamarchemfg.com
Manufacturer and exporter of battery chargers for
forklift trucks and vehicles
President: Stan Burg
agalvan@conversantmedia.com
EVP: Raj Dhiman
CFO: Rick Rutkowski
Vice President: J. Vargas
Research & Development: Vance Pearson
Quality Control Manager: Bob Brewer
Marketing Director: S. Burg
Sales Director: John Pawula
Customer Service Manager: Lacy Zyrkowski
agalvan@conversantmedia.com
Director Purchasing: Bob Lewinski
Estimated Sales: $10-20 Million
Number Employees: 100-249
Square Footage: 170000

25037 LA Monica Fine Foods
PO Box 309
Millville, NJ 08332
info@lamonicafinefoods.com
www.lamonicafinefoods.com
Surf clams and ocean clams from US certified wa-
ters, serving the fresh, canned and frozen markets.
Founder: Peter LaMonica

Number Employees: 20-49
Square Footage: 360000
Type of Packaging: Consumer, Food Service, Pri-
vate Label, Bulk
Brands:
Cape May
Lamonica

25038 LA Motte Co
802 Washington Ave
Chestertown, MD 21620-1015
410-778-3100
Fax: 410-778-6394 800-344-3100
mkt@lamotte.com
Kits, test strips and meters for water analysis, moni-
toring sanitizer and caustic or acid cleaner concen-
trations, process or waste waters and boiler and
cooling tower waters
President: David Lamotte
dlamotte@lamotte.com
CFO: Roland Willis
Quality Control: Susan Franklin
Marketing Director: Sue Byerly
VP Sales: Richard Lamotte
Estimated Sales: $50 - 100 Million
Number Employees: 100-249

25039 LA Rosa Refrigeration &Equip
19191 Filer St
Detroit, MI 48234-2883
313-368-6620
Fax: 313-368-1317 800-527-6723
www.larosaequip.com
Commercial refrigeration equipment including
freezers; also, liquid and portable bars, holding cabi-
nets, holding and warming equipment and steam
tables
Owner, President: Sebastiano Grillo
sgrillo@larosaequip.com
Vice President: Jerry Grillo
Marketing, Administrations: Chelsea Van
Hazenbrouck
Sales and Design Manager: Dan Gudenau
Estimated Sales: $2.5-5 Million
Number Employees: 20-49

25040 LAB Equipment
1326 New Seneca Tpke
Skaneateles, NY 13152
315-685-5781
Fax: 315-685-8106 800-522-5781
service@labequipment.com
www.labequipment.com
Shock, vibration, compression and incline impact
test systems, as well as test data acquisition systems
President: Robert Noonan
Sales Director: Thomas Dunne
Estimated Sales: $1 - 5 Million
Number Employees: 20

25041 LANTECH.COM
11000 Bluegrass Pkwy
Jeffersontown, KY 40299-2399
502-267-4200
Fax: 502-266-5031 800-866-0322
jerryt@lantech.com www.lantech.com
Stretch wrappers, palletizers, conveyor systems
President: Jim Lancaster
jim.l@lantech.com
Estimated Sales: $50 - 75 Million
Number Employees: 250-499

25042 LANXESS Corp.
111 RIDC Park West Dr
Pittsburgh, PA 15275-1112
800-526-9377
lanxess.us
Specialty chemicals
President & CEO: Antonis Papadourakis

25043 LB Furniture Industries
99 S 3rd St
Hudson, NY 12534
518-828-1501
Fax: 518-828-3219 800-221-8752
sales@lbfurnitureind.com
Manufacturer and exporter of tables, chairs and
booths
President: Les Lak
Contact: Penny Abell
penny@lbfurnitureind.com
Estimated Sales: $1-2.5 Million
Number Employees: 10-19
Square Footage: 650000

25044 LBP Manufacturing LLC
1325 S Cicero Ave
Cicero, IL 60804-1404
708-652-5600
Fax: 708-652-5537 sales@lbpmfg.com
www.lbpmfg.com
Manufacturer and exporter of hot cup sleeves,
take-out containers and acrylic displays and dispens-
ers
President: Barry Silverstein
Pricing Manager: Mary Lou Medina
CFO: Mike Schaechter
VP: Matthew Cook
R&D and QC: Barry M
Estimated Sales: $10 - 20 Million
Number Employees: 500-999
Parent Co: Terrace Paper Company
Brands:
Coffee Clutch
Coffee on the Move
Safepak

25045 LCI Corporation
4433 Chesapeake Dr
Charlotte, NC 28216
704-398-7728
Fax: 704-398-7728 info@lcicorp.com
lcicorp.com
Thin-film evaporation systems, agglomeration sys-
tems, pelleting presses and feeder equipment manu-
factures
Manager: Scott Meyers
President: Lacey Hayes
Estimated Sales: $15-30 Million
Number Employees: 100-249
Parent Co: Bacon Industrial Manufacturing

25046 LDC Analytical
28271 Leticia
Mission Viejo, CA 92692-2329
949-586-5340
Fax: 949-586-9373
Wine industry probers and meters

25047 LDI Manufacturing Co
417 North St # 104
Logansport, IN 46947-2775
574-722-3124
Fax: 574-722-7213 800-366-2001
www.ldi-industries.com/LDI.htm
Manufacturer and exporter of exhaust ventilation
equipment including commercial exhaust hoods and
fans. Distribution of complete, pre-engineered heat-
ing and air conditioningequipment system. Custom
stainless steel and metalfabrication. Indoor environ-
ment air quality equipment systems
Manager: Susan Begley
susan@ldimfg.com
VP Finance: Camille Hall
Marketing Director: Susan Erny
VP Customer Services: Susan Erny
Estimated Sales: $5-10 Million
Number Employees: 5-9
Square Footage: 100000
Type of Packaging: Food Service
Brands:
Greese Gobler
Magic Wash
Smart Hood
Sup-Ex
Top Sergent

25048 LDJ Electronics
1280 E Big Beaver
PO Box 219
Troy, MI 48083-0219
248-528-2202
Fax: 248-689-2525
Process control, monitoring and line monitoring sys-
tems; also, computer software systems and services
Public Relations: Derrick Peterman
Estimated Sales: $5-10,000,000
Number Employees: 20-49

25049 LDS Corporation
7900 E Union Ave
Suite 1007
Denver, CO 80237
303-928-1124
Fax: 303-217-7050 866-25 -ARDE
President/CEO: Joe Caston
VP of Finance/CFO: John C. Frank
Estimated Sales: $10 - 20 Million
Number Employees: 20-49

25050 LECO Corp
3000 Lakeview Ave
St Joseph, MI 49085-2319
269-983-5531
Fax: 269-982-8977 800-292-6141
info@leco.com www.leco.com
Analytical instrumentation
President: Robert J Warren
robert_warren@leco.com
Number Employees: 1000-4999

25051 LECO Corp
3000 Lakeview Ave
St Joseph, MI 49085-2319
269-983-5531
Fax: 269-982-8977 800-292-6141
info@leco.com www.leco.com
Analytical instrumentation for primary and secondary analyses of food, ingredients and flavors
President: Robert J Warren
robert_warren@leco.com
Number Employees: 1000-4999

25052 LEESON Electric Corp
1051 Cheyenne Ave
Grafton, WI 53024-9541
262-377-8810
Fax: 262-377-9025 www.leeson.com
Manufacturer and exporter of electric motors, gears and drives for food processing machinery.
CEO: Henry Knueppel
CFO: Dave Barta
VP: Bud Pritchard
Marketing: Philippe De Gail
Sales: Steve Weber
COO: Mark Gliebe
Number Employees: 500-999
Brands:
Leeson
Speedmaster
Washguard

25053 LEWA Inc
PO Box 6820
Holliston, MA 01746-6820
508-429-7403
Fax: 508-429-8615 888-539-2123
www.lewa-inc.com
Manufacturer and exporter of precision metering and mixing pumps and systems for blending and proportioning all liquids; also, seal-less controlled volume pumps for process services and moderate high pressures
President/Owner: Lee Bollow
lbollow@lewa-inc.com
Marketing: Marlis Morse
Estimated Sales: $10 - 20 Million
Parent Co: LEWA GmbH

25054 LIS Warehouse Systems
9201 Southern Pine Boulevard
Suite E
Charlotte, NC 28273-5537
704-926-1700
Fax: 704-926-1799 888-547-9670
Software for warehousing, inventory management, material handling and control
Chairman of the Board: Alok Singh
Senior Vice President, Director of Accou: Andrew Kirkwood
VP Sales/Marketing: Bob Carver
Number Employees: 25
Parent Co: LIS

25055 LIST
42 Nagog Park
Acton, MA 01720-3445
978-635-9521
Fax: 978-263-0570
Food processing machinery for viscous, sticky and crust forming materials including mixers, kneaders, dryers, heaters, melters, coolers, etc
CEO: Klaus List
VP Sales: Hefunt Schildknecht
Estimated Sales: $1-5 Million
Number Employees: 20
Square Footage: 18000
Parent Co: LIST AG

25056 LMC International
893 N Industrial Dr
Elmhurst, IL 60126
630-834-7789
Fax: 630-834-4322 info@Latiniusa.com
www.lmcinternational.com
Equipment for the confectionery and bakery industries
Sales/Marketing: Pat Kiel
Sales Director: Roger Hohberger
Sales: Daniel Herman
Estimated Sales: $15 000,000
Number Employees: 50
Number of Brands: 2
Number of Products: 50
Square Footage: 30000
Brands:
Hohberger Products
Latini Products

25057 LMCO
4705 Highway 36 S
Suite 1
Rosenberg, TX 77471-9254
281-342-8888
Fax: 832-595-5000
Brooms, mops and handles
President: Leslie Moore
Estimated Sales: $500,000-$1 Million
Number Employees: 5-9
Square Footage: 18000

25058 LMH
1714 Colfax St
Suite E
Concord, CA 94520
925-686-6400
Fax: 925-686-3836 800-531-6782
Wine industry pumps, mixers, tanks and process equipment; local service, fabrication and equipment repair
Estimated Sales: $5-10 Million
Number Employees: 10-19

25059 LMK Containers
PO Box 1001
Centerville, UT 84014-5001
626-821-9984
Manufacturer, importer and exporter of glass and plastic bottles, jars, caps and containers
Purchasing Director: Robert Frome
Type of Packaging: Consumer, Food Service, Private Label, Bulk
Brands:
Aastro

25060 LPA Software
400 Linden Oaks
Suite 140
Rochester, NY 14625
866-783-9900
www.lpa.com
Prepackaged software, software development and consulting for a variety of business applications including supply chain, semiconductor, internet and client server systems
President: Donald Soule
Vice President: Katrina Adams
Estimated Sales: $300,000-500,000
Number Employees: 120

25061 LPACK - Loersch Corporation
1530 E Race Sreet
Allentown, PA 18109
610-264-5641
Fax: 610-266-0330 www.lpack.com
Manager: Robert Kreger
Estimated Sales: $1,000,000 - $3,000,000
Number Employees: 5-9

25062 LPI Imports
901 N Kilpatrick Avenue
Chicago, IL 60651-3326
877-389-6563
Fax: 773-379-5616
Shelving, shelf ledges, shelf dividers, posts and casters; also, labels
General Manager: Alan Kaplan
Parent Co: Leggett & Platt
Brands:
Snake Shelving

25063 LPI Information Systems
10020 Fontana Ln
Overland Park, KS 66207-3640
913-381-9118
Fax: 913-381-9118 888-729-2020
www.datasmithpayroll.com
Manufacturer and exporter of payroll software and tax forms
President: David Land
landlines@datasmithpayroll.com
Number Employees: 20-49
Brands:
Datacheck
Datasmith

25064 LPS Industries
10 Caesar Pl
Moonachie, NJ 07074-1701
201-438-3515
Fax: 201-438-1326 800-275-4577
www.lpsind.com
Custom manufaturer of flexible packaging such as stand up pouches, bags and roll stock. They offer eight color printing, micro hook and loop recloseable options, in-house QA and QR departments with testing lab and a solventlesslamination process.
President & CEO: Madeleine Robinson
Chief Financial Officer: Mary Elmer
Vice President, Marketing: Charles Ardman
Vice President, Sales: Domenick Pasqualone
Vice President, Operations: Phil Pasqualone
Estimated Sales: $50-100 Million
Number Employees: 100-249
Square Footage: 250000
Type of Packaging: Consumer, Food Service, Private Label, Bulk
Other Locations:
Cerritos CA
Indianapolis IN
Marietta GA
Moonachie NJ

25065 LPS Technology
1009 McAlpin Court
Grafton, OH 44044-1322
440-355-6992
Fax: 440-355-6998 800-586-1410
Manufacturer and exporter of washers, ovens, compressed air systems, conveyors and air vacuums
President: Dean Burke
General Manager: Dave Bobak
Estimated Sales: $1-2,500,000
Number Employees: 10-19
Parent Co: Eton Fab Company

25066 LRM Packaging
41 James St
South Hackensack, NJ 07606-1438
201-342-2530
Fax: 201-342-4351 info@lrmpackaging.com
www.lrmpackaging.com
Contract packager of snack and dry foods, etc
President: Erika Castro
erikacastro@lrmpackaging.com
Director Sales: John Natali, Jr.
Production Manager: Mike Hoskins
Estimated Sales: Below $5,000,000
Number Employees: 20-49
Square Footage: 200000

25067 LSI Industries Inc
10000 Alliance Rd
Blue Ash, OH 45242-4738
513-793-3200
Fax: 513-984-1335 www.lsi-industries.com
Visual merchandising displays and pressure sensitive signs
President: David McCauley
CEO: Dennis W Wells
dennis.wells@lsi-industries.com
Quality Control: Bruce Soleinger
VP Sales/Marketing: Robert Lux
National Sales Manager: Todd Blandford
Estimated Sales: $1 - 3 Million
Number Employees: 1000-4999

25068 LTI Boyd Corp
600 S Mcclure Rd
Modesto, CA 95357-0520
209-491-4700
Fax: 209-236-0154 888-244-6931
customerservice@boydcorp.com
www.boydcorp.com

Conveyor belting, gaskets, sheet goods, sponge, rubber and cork
Manager: Gregg Mynhier
CEO: Mitch Aiello
  mitch.aiello@boydcorp.com
Sales: Jim Hemingway
General Manager: Lyle Hemingway
Estimated Sales: $5-10 Million
Number Employees: 50-99
Square Footage: 160000
Brands:
  Goodyear
  Klinger

25069 LTI Printing Inc
518 N Centerville Rd
Sturgis, MI 49091-9601
                                        269-651-7574
  Fax: 269-651-3262 www.ltiprinting.com
Manufacturer and exporter of labels and offset cartons
President: Don Frost
  dfrost@ltiprinting.com
Estimated Sales: $20-50 Million
Number Employees: 50-99
Type of Packaging: Consumer, Food Service, Bulk

25070 LVO Manufacturing Inc
808 N 2nd Ave E
Rock Rapids, IA 51246-1759
                                        712-472-3734
  Fax: 712-472-2203 marilyn_lvo@yahoo.com
                                        www.lvomfg.com
Bakery equipment
President: Marilyn Mammenga
  marilyn_lvo@yahoo.com
CFO: Lambert Benno
Estimated Sales: $5 - 10 Million
Number Employees: 20-49

25071 LXE
P.O. Box 926000
Norcross, GA 30010-6000
                                        770-447-4224
  Fax: 770-447-4405 info@lxe.com
RF computer network systems, logistics, transportation, health care
President: Jim Childress
CEO: Alfred Hansen
CEO: Paul B Domorski
VP Sales: B Johnson
Contact: Philippe Bechet
  bechet.p@ems-t.com
Estimated Sales: $50 - 100 Million
Number Employees: 250-499
Parent Co: EMS technologies

25072 La Creme Coffee & Tea
438 W Mockingbird Lane
Dallas, TX 75247
                                        214-352-8190
  Fax: 214-352-8173 877-493-2326
    info@lacremecoffeeandtea.com
    www.lacremecoffeeandtea.com
Tea and coffee brewers
Estimated Sales: $500,000-$1 Million
Number Employees: 9

25073 La Crosse
W6636 L B White Rd
Onalaska, WI 54650
                                        608-783-2800
  Fax: 608-783-6115 800-345-0018
    www.hospitalityinternational.com
Manufacturer and exporter of underbar items including sinks, drain boards, ice chests, cocktail stations and storage units; also, portable bars
CEO: Tony Wilson
CFO: Jack Lauer
Vice President of Development: Ron Provus
Marketing Director: Bridget Crave
Sales Director: Della Indahl
Estimated Sales: $50 - 100 Million
Number Employees: 100-249
Parent Co: Hospitality International
Brands:
  La Crosse
  Stowaway

25074 La Crosse Milling Company
105 Hwy 35
P.O. Box 86
Cochrane, WI 54622
                                        608-248-2222
  Fax: 608-248-2221 800-441-5411
    ghartzell@lacrossemilling.com
    www.lacrossemilling.com
Whole grain, organic and Kosher grain ingredients including oats, barley and wheat, products include conventional and organic oat flakes, oat flour, oat bran, oat fiber, pearled barley, barley flakes, barley flour, rolled wheat andother specialty milled grains.
President/Sales: Glenn Hartzell
Controller/Assistant Treasurer: Teresa Waters
Safety Manager: Bryan Hoch
Quality Manager: Jeff Meyer
Food Sales Assistant: Michelle Kosidowski
Year Founded: 1947
Estimated Sales: $43.43 Million
Number Employees: 85
Type of Packaging: Bulk

25075 La Crosse Sign Co.
2502 Melby St
Eau Claire, WI 54703
                                        715-835-6189
  Fax: 715-835-6868 www.lacrossesign.com
Indoor and outdoor signs including electric, painted, vinyl lettering and neon
VP: Gregory Mitchell
Estimated Sales: $1-2.5 Million
Number Employees: 5-9

25076 La Menuiserie East Angus
25 Rue Willard
East Angus, QC J0B 1R0
Canada
                                        819-832-2746
                                  Fax: 819-832-3474
Wooden pallets
President/CFO: Robert La Pointe
Quality Control/R&D: Robert Lapointe
Estimated Sales: Below $5 Million
Number Employees: 40

25077 La Poblana Food Machines
5952 East Nance Street
Mesa, AZ 85215
                                        480-258-2091
                                  Fax: 480-452-0538
La Poblana Food Machines LLC offers sales and service of commercial-grade tortilla-making equipment. Manufacture their lines as well as custom machinery.
President: Sherrie Soria

25078 La Rinascente Macaroni Company
41 James St
South Hackensack, NJ 07606
                                        201-342-2530
    info@lrmpackaging.com
    www.lrmpackaging.com
Macaroni, flour and packaged food products.
Consultant: John Natali
Estimated Sales: $20-50 Million
Square Footage: 600000
Type of Packaging: Consumer, Food Service, Private Label, Bulk
Brands:
  La Rinascente Pasta Products

25079 LaCrosse Safety and Industrial
18550 NE Riverside Parkway
Portland, OR 97230-4975
                                        503-766-1010
  Fax: 800-558-0188 800-557-7246
Manufacturer and importer of waterproof protective clothing and footwear including vulcanized double coated rubber aprons
President: John McGinnis
Manager: Tammy Woolrage
Sales Director: Ken Furtech
Contact: John Mcginnis
  jmcginnis@lacrossefootwear.com
Number Employees: 100-249
Number of Products: 600
Parent Co: Standalone

25080 Labconco Corp
8811 Prospect Ave
Kansas City, MO 64132-2696
                                        816-333-8811
  Fax: 816-363-0130 800-821-5525
    labconco@labconco.com www.labconco.com
Manufacturer and exporter of scientific laboratory equipment and apparatus including chloride instruments, Kjeldahl nitrogen determination apparatus and fat and fiber apparatus
President: Stephen Gound
  stephengound@labconco.com
Executive VP: Mark Weber
VP Marketing: Debbie Kenny
National Sales Manager: Tom Schwaller
Estimated Sales: $30 Million
Number Employees: 100-249
Brands:
  Centrivap
  Flaskscrubber
  Freezone
  Paramount
  Protector
  Purifier
  Rapidvap
  Steamscrubber
  Waterpro

25081 Label Art
2278 Brockett Rd
Tucker, GA 30084
                                        770-939-6960
  Fax: 770-939-6960 800-652-1072
Manufacturer and exporter of grocery shelf marking products, warehouse picking labels and continuous and sheet fed laser printer products
National Sales Manager: Deborah Goss
Sales Representative: Lisa Wood
Estimated Sales: $20-50 Million
Number Employees: 100-249
Square Footage: 30000

25082 Label Express
1305 S 630 E
American Fork, UT 84003-3375
                                        801-772-0677
  Fax: 801-642-3510 877-639-8600
Labels, shrink bands and folding cartons
CFO: Jeff Sinclair
R&D: Carlene West
General Manager: Mike Kekeegan
Marketing Manager: Derick Sims
Estimated Sales: $20 - 50 Million
Number Employees: 50-99
Parent Co: Impaxx

25083 Label House
503 S Raymond Ave
Fullerton, CA 92831-5026
                                        714-449-0632
  Fax: 714-441-0698 800-499-5858
    sales@labelhouse.com www.labelhouse.net
Pressure sensitive labels and tags; wholesaler/distributor of label dispensers and applicators, thermal transfer ribbons, case coders, bar code printers and software
Owner: Al Jiacomin
owner: Karen Freeman
VP Sales: Leone Grant
Estimated Sales: $1 - 2.5 Million
Number Employees: 10-19

25084 Label Impressions
1831 W Sequoia Ave
Orange, CA 92868-1017
                                        714-634-3466
  Fax: 714-634-3468 info@labelimpressions.com
                    www.labelimpressions.com
High quality customer labels, tags and flexible packaging. Recognized as a quality, green technology manufacturer.
President: Jeff Salisbury
  jeff@labelimpressions.com
CEO: Ted Salisbury
CFO: Carolyn Deyse
VP Sales & Sustainability: Jeff Morrow
R&D: Marie Graham
Quality Assurance: Steve Smith
Operations: Rick Ybarra
Estimated Sales: $8 Million
Number Employees: 20-49
Number of Products: 1000
Square Footage: 40000

Type of Packaging: Consumer, Food Service, Private Label, Bulk

25085 Label Makers
8911 102nd St
Pleasant Prairie, WI 53158-2212
262-947-3300
Fax: 262-947-3301 800-208-3331
www.lmipackaging.com
Manufacturer and exporter of heat seal lidding, flexible packaging solutions, daisychain, rollstock & die cut lidding
Owner: Virginia Moran
CEO: Jean Moran
Vice President of Business Development: Randall Troutman
VP Research & Development: Mike Gorzynski
Director of Marketing: Lea Connelly
National Accounts Manager: Gary Morrison
VP Operations: Vince Incandela
Number Employees: 20-49

25086 Label Mill
2416 Jackson Street
Savanna, IL 61074-2836
815-273-4707
Fax: 815-273-7074 800-273-4707
pmills@labelmill.com www.labelmill.com
Standard and custom label applicators
Owner: Andy Mills
Contact: Jill Holtman
jholtman@labelmill.com
Estimated Sales: $1 - 3 Million
Number Employees: 5-9

25087 Label Products Inc
12571 Oliver Ave S # 700
Suite 700
Burnsville, MN 55337-6664
952-996-0909
Fax: 952-996-0202 877-370-0688
sales@labelproducts.com www.labelproducts.com
Labels including pressure sensitive, UPC and bar code; also, embossed, holographic and computer designed available
President and CFO: Ed Christenson
edc@labelproducts.com
Product Manager: Stu Knilons
Sales Manager: Kevin Peterson
Operations Manager: Kevin Peterson
Production Manager: Stu Knilons
Plant Manager: Kevin Peterson
Estimated Sales: $10 - 20 Million
Number Employees: 20-49
Square Footage: 29000

25088 Label Solutions
151 W Passaic St # 2
2nd Floor
Rochelle Park, NJ 07662-3105
201-599-0909
Fax: 201-599-9888 ilana@labelsolutions.net
www.labelsolutions.net
Wine industry pressure sensitive labels
President: Ilana Weiss
ilana@labelsolutions.net
Estimated Sales: Below $5 Million
Number Employees: 1-4

25089 Label Specialties Inc
704 Dunn Way
Placentia, CA 92870-6805
714-961-8074
Fax: 714-961-8276 800-635-2386
www.labelspec.com
Labels including scale printer, ingredient printer, bar code, plain, pressure sensitive, stock and custom; also, transfer ribbons
Owner: Micheal Gyure
VP: Thomas Wetterhus
Manager: Maria Arellano
marellano@labelspec.com
Estimated Sales: $1-2.5 Million
Number Employees: 10-19
Square Footage: 18000

25090 Label Supply Company
3013 Sherwood Ln
Colleyville, TX 76034
785-256-2488
Fax: 785-256-2582 800-444-8186
Labeling equipment
Estimated Sales: $.5 - 1 million
Number Employees: 5-9

25091 Label Systems
56 Cherry St
Bridgeport, CT 06605-2370
203-333-5503
Fax: 203-336-8570 www.labelsysinc.com
Labels including pressure sensitive, imprintable and holographic for shelf marking applications
President: Michael Zubretsky
mzubretsky@labelsysinc.com
Quality Control: Howard Sands
R&D: George Houston
VP: Rich Zucker
Estimated Sales: $10 - 20 Million
Number Employees: 50-99
Parent Co: Bridgestone Company

25092 Label Systems
1150 Kerrisdale Blvd.
Unit 2
Newmarket, ON L3Y 8Z9
Canada
905-836-7844
Fax: 905-853-9357 m.kirby@label-systems.com
www.label-systems.com
Manufacturer and exporter of pressure sensitive label machinery and equipment.
Sales Director: Matthew Kirby
Number Employees: 5
Square Footage: 44000

25093 Label Systems & Solutions
1430 Church St
Bohemia, NY 11716-5028
631-563-4549
Fax: 631-567-4338 800-811-2560
Badges, printers, advertising specialties, labels, tags and tapes; also, art production services available
Sales Manager: Stacy Moller
Estimated Sales: $500,000-$1 Million
Number Employees: 5-9

25094 Label Systems Inc
4111 Lindbergh Dr
Addison, TX 75001-4345
972-387-4512
Fax: 972-387-4935 800-220-9552
sales@labelsystemsinc.com
www.labelsystemsinc.com
Labels including custom designed, pressure sensitive, plain, printed, die cut on rolls and sheeted; also, decals and metal name plates
Owner: Amy Van Brunt
VP: Amy Van Brunt
Quality Control: Marcia Macias
Sales: Rick Brown
amy@labelsystemsinc.com
Public Relations: Sue Van Brunt
Operations/Production: Bruno Contreaus
Purchasing: Yivan Chenn
Estimated Sales: $2.5-5 Million
Number Employees: 20-49
Number of Products: 150

25095 Label Technology Inc
2050 Wardrobe Ave
Merced, CA 95341-6409
209-384-1000
Fax: 209-384-0322 800-388-1990
www.labeltech.com
Pressure sensitive labels, tags and flexible packaging; also, label imprinters and applicators
President: Quincy Adams
quincy.adams@labeltech.com
VP Product Development: Dennis Deisenroth
VP Sales: Phil Henderson
Estimated Sales: $2.5-5,000,000
Number Employees: 100-249
Square Footage: 126000

25096 Label World
29 Jet View Dr
Rochester, NY 14624
585-235-0200
Fax: 585-235-0398 800-836-8186
Prime labels
President/CEO: John McDermott
CEO: Janet Allardice
allardice@labelworldusa.com
VP Sales & Marketing: Skylar Rote
Estimated Sales: $10-20 Million
Number Employees: 50-99

25097 Label-Aire Inc
550 Burning Tree Rd
Fullerton, CA 92833-1449
714-441-0700
Fax: 714-526-0300 info@label-aire.com
www.label-aire.com
Manufacturer and exporter of pressure-sensitive label applicators and rotary and incline systems
President: George Allen
gallen@label-aire.com
Marketing Manager: William Claproth
Sales: Steve Winders
Operations: Gene Bukovi
Estimated Sales: $20 - 50 Million
Number Employees: 100-249
Square Footage: 60000
Parent Co: Impaxx
Type of Packaging: Consumer, Food Service, Private Label, Bulk

25098 Labelette Company
1237 Circle Avenue
Forest Park, IL 60130-2416
708-366-2010
Fax: 708-366-0226 www.labelette.com
Manufacturer and exporter of semi-automatic and automatic labeling machinery
Estimated Sales: $5 - 10 Million
Number Employees: 20-49
Square Footage: 40000
Brands:
Labelette

25099 Labeling Systems
32 Spruce St
Oakland, NJ 07436
201-405-0767
Fax: 201-405-1179 888-405-4574
lsi@labelingsystems.com
www.labelingsystems.com
Labeling machinery
President: Theodore Zaccheo
Contact: Brian Baker
brian.baker@lsi.com
Estimated Sales: $5 - 10 Million
Number Employees: 20-49

25100 Labeling Systems Clearwater
PO Box 1955
Largo, FL 33779-1955
727-539-7784
Fax: 727-538-5626 800-749-1057
Supplies for DSD route sales, handheld labelers for price marking, promotional labeling, date coding
Estimated Sales: $1-2.5 Million
Number Employees: 5-9

25101 Labelmart
11733 95th Ave N
Maple Grove, MN 55369-5551
763-493-0099
Fax: 763-493-0093 888-577-0141
info@cmsitechnologies.com
Pressure sensitive labels and tags including die cut blank and printed; also, thermal transfer ribbons and printers
Owner: Steve Nelson
steven@labelmart.com
Estimated Sales: $5-10 Million
Number Employees: 20-49
Parent Co: Computerized Machinery Systems

25102 Labelmax Inc
1209 San Dario Ave
Laredo, TX 78040-4505
956-722-6493
Pressure sensitive labels and thermal transfer and laser sheet; consultant specializing in bar coding services
CEO: Jorge Martinez
Finance Manager: Edgar Martinez
Estimated Sales: $3 - 5,000,000
Number Employees: 5-9

25103 Labelprint America
8 Opportunity Way
Newburyport, MA 01950-4043
978-463-4004
Fax: 978-463-9748
accounting@labelprintamerica.com
www.labelprintamerica.com
Labels, decals, tags, pressure sensitive labeling equipment and thermal imprinters

Owner: Tony Yemma
tony@labelprintamerica.com
President Marketing: Tony Yemma
VP Operations: Bob Haley
Estimated Sales: $2.5 - 5 Million
Number Employees: 20-49
Square Footage: 84000

25104 Labelquest Inc
493 W Fullerton Ave
Elmhurst, IL 60126-1404
630-833-9400
Fax: 630-833-9421 800-999-5301
gary@labelquest.net www.labelquest.net
Manufacturer and exporter of labels, decals and heat transfers
President: Pat Vandenberg
Sales Manager: Neil Vandenberg
Estimated Sales: $2.5 - 5 Million
Number Employees: 50-99
Square Footage: 10000

25105 Labels & Decals International
300 Frontier Way
Bensenville, IL 60106
630-227-0500
Fax: 630-227-1016 info@labels-decals.com
www.labels-decals.com
Pressure sensitive labels and decals
Owner: Cliff Bode
Contact: Steve Bartscher
steve@labels-decals.com
Estimated Sales: $2.5-5 Million
Number Employees: 10-19

25106 Labels By Pulizzi Inc
3325 Wahoo Dr
Williamsport, PA 17701-9243
570-326-1244
Fax: 570-326-3453 www.labelsbypulizzi.com
Customized pressure sensitive labels for food products
President: Charline Pulizzi
cpulizzi@labelsbypulizzi.com
R&D: Joseph Pulizzi
VP: Joseph Pulizzi, Jr.
Manager: Mark Porter
Purchasing Executive: Dalbys Kreisher
Estimated Sales: $10 - 20 Million
Number Employees: 50-99
Square Footage: 400000

25107 Labels Plus
2407 106th St SW
Everett, WA 98204-3628
425-745-4592
Fax: 425-523-1973 800-275-7587
sales@labelsplus.com www.labelsplus.com
Custom printed pressure sensitive labels
President: Eric C Phillips
Accountant: James Peterson
Contact: John Bitow
johnb@labelsplus.com
Estimated Sales: $10 - 20 Million
Number Employees: 20-49

25108 Lablynx Inc
1770 the Exchange SE # 240
Atlanta, GA 30339-2038
770-859-1992
Fax: 678-391-6982 800-585-5969
sales@lablynx.com
President: John H Jones
Number Employees: 5-9

25109 Laboratory Devices
PO Box 6402
Holliston, MA 01746-6402
508-429-1716
Fax: 508-429-6583
Manufacturer and exporter of laboratory instruments
Estimated Sales: $1 - 5 Million
Number Employees: 5

25110 Labpride Chemicals
2281 Light St
Bronx, NY 10466-6136
718-547-5757
Fax: 718-994-0494 800-467-1255
Heavy duty degreasers, disinfectants, sanitizers, detergents, brooms, mops, sponges, squeegees, brushes and cleaners including glass, oven, walls, bathrooms, etc

Owner: Ralph Derose
VP: Domenick DeRose
Operations Manager: James Lanfear
Estimated Sales: $5 - 10 Million
Number Employees: 20-49
Square Footage: 8000

25111 Labtech Industries
7707 Lyndon St
Detroit, MI 48238-2465
313-862-1737
Fax: 313-862-1131 800-525-8667
www.brycegroup.com
Industrial cleaners and specialty chemicals
President/Co-Owner: Corey Bryce
Co-Owner: Dennis Bryce
cbryce@labtechcorp.com
Estimated Sales: Less than $500,000
Number Employees: 10-19

25112 Labvantage Solutions
200 Broadway
Troy, NY 12180-3289
518-274-1990
Fax: 518-274-7824 www.labvantage.com
Laboratory Information Management Systems (LIMS), chromatography and a broad spectrum of other applications
Chief Executive Officer: Jeff Ferguson
Vice President of Professional Services: Anuj Uppal
Vice President of Quality: Fernando Casanova
Business Director: Anneli Friberg
Estimated Sales: $1 - 5 Million

25113 Labvantage Solutions Inc
265 Davidson Ave # 200
Suite 220
Somerset, NJ 08873-4120
908-231-6703
Fax: 732-560-0121 888-346-5467
nasales@labvantage.com www.labvantage.com
Developer of laboratory information management systems for sample forecasting, scheduling and login, data calculations, product specification checks, quality control and reporting
Manager: Deborah Washington
Marketing Manager: Heather Maguire
VP Sales/Marketing: Don Seitz
Estimated Sales: $10 - 15 Million
Number Employees: 50-99
Brands:
Labmaestro
Labmaestro Chrom Perfect
Labmaestro Ensemble
Labvantage
Pro-Lims
Seedpak
Trace

25114 Laciny Brothers Inc
6622 Vernon Ave
St Louis, MO 63130-2650
314-862-8330
Fax: 314-862-8332 www.lacinybros.com
Custom fabricated food processing equipment.
President: Timothy Laciny
tlaciny@lacinybros.com
Marketing/Sales/Public Relations: John Ulz
Operations/Production: Rick Gratza
Plant Manager: Don Fitzgerald
Purchasing Manager: Terry Brown
Estimated Sales: $2.5-5 Million
Number Employees: 20-49
Square Footage: 124000

25115 Lacroix Packaging
77 De l'Eglise Street
St-Placide, Quebec, QC J0V 2B0
Canada
450-258-2262
Fax: 450-258-3345
cbouveret@emballagelacroix.com
www.emballagelacroix.com
Customized packaging and labels.

25116 Lacrosse-Rainfair SafetyProducts
3600 S Memorial Dr
Racine, WI 53403-3822
262-554-7000
Fax: 414-554-6619 800-558-5990
Manufactures protective outerware, footwear, aprons and insulated clothing

CEO: Joe Schneider
CFO: Bruce Bartelt
Vice President: Gregg Liederbach
Public Relations: Anna Gardner
Plant Manager: John Schleicher
Purchasing Manager: Cindy Krause
Estimated Sales: $44 Million
Number Employees: 100-249

25117 Ladder Works
1125 E Saint Charles Rd
Lombard, IL 60148-2085
630-629-7154
Fax: 630-268-9655 800-419-5880
Manufacturer and exporter of flag poles and flags
Owner: Ed Reeder
Inside Sales Manager: Lisa Simpson
Estimated Sales: $10-20,000,000
Number Employees: 20-49
Parent Co: Uncommon USA

25118 (HQ)Lady Mary
126 Lady Mary Lane
PO Box 157
Rockingham, NC 28379-4965
910-997-7321
Fax: 910-997-7324
Round, rectangular, round/square, moisture/grease proof and recyclable disposable cake boards
President: Mary Stanley
Estimated Sales: $2.5-5 Million
Number Employees: 10-19
Square Footage: 160000
Other Locations:
Lady Mary
Rockingham NC
Brands:
Dainty Boards
Party Plates
Tuftboard

25119 Lafayette Sign Company
47 Sindle Ave
Little Falls, NJ 07424-1650
973-812-5000
Fax: 973-812-8222 800-343-5366
www.lafayettesign.com
Plastic and neon signs
President: John Scott
Permit Coordinator: Gerald Koczot
Estimated Sales: $1-2.5 Million
Number Employees: 10-19

25120 Lafayette Tent & AwningCo
125 S 5th St
Lafayette, IN 47901-1618
765-742-4277
Fax: 765-742-4462 800-458-2955
www.lafayettetent.com
Commercial awnings and rental tents/full line special event rental firm.
President: Henry Ebershoff
CEO: Craig Ebershoff
lta@lafayettetent.com
CFO: Craig Ebershoff
Vice President: Craig Ebershoff
Research & Development: Craig Ebershoff
Quality Control: Craig Ebershoff
Marketing Director: Craig Ebershoff
Sales Director: Craig Ebershoff
Public Relations: Craig Ebershoff
Operations Manager: Craig Ebershoff
Production Manager: Craig Ebershoff
Plant Manager: Craig Ebershoff
Purchasing Manager: Craig Ebershoff
Estimated Sales: $5-10,000,000
Number Employees: 20-49

25121 Lafitte Cork & Capsule Inc
45 Executive Ct
Napa, CA 94558-6267
707-258-2675
Fax: 707-258-0558 800-343-2675
info@lafitte-usa.com www.lafitte-usa.com
Wine industry corks and capsules
President: Angie Allen
aallen@lafitte-usa.com
VP: Barry Rucker
Estimated Sales: $1-2.5 Million
Number Employees: 10-19

25122 Laggren's LLC
100 Whittingham Dr
Monroe Twp, NJ 08831-2610
609-235-9883
Fax: 908-756-7560 dlasser@comcast.net
Commercial awnings, window treatments, canopies,
custom draperies, flags, flagpoles, banners, and radiator covers and enclosures.
President: David Lasser
Estimated Sales: $1-2,500,000
Number Employees: 10-19
Square Footage: 14000

25123 Laidig Inc
14535 Dragoon Trl
Mishawaka, IN 46544-6896
574-256-0204
Fax: 574-256-5575 sales@laidig.com
www.laidig.com
Manufacturer and exporter of bulk material steel
storage structures and handling systems including
conveyors
President: Wyn Laidig
sales@laidig.com
SVP: Tom J Lindenman
Vice President Marketing/Information: Daniel
Laidig
Vice President Sales: Mike Laidig
VP, Manufacturing: Dan Collins
Estimated Sales: $5-10 Million
Number Employees: 50-99
Parent Co: LIS Corporation

25124 Lail Design Group
1505 Main St
Saint Helena, CA 94574
707-963-1565
Fax: 707-963-4509 www.laildesign.com
Facility planning and design
Principal Architect: S Doug Osborn
Principal Architect: Paul Kelley
Marketing Director: Tim Martin
Contact: Maria Reyes
mreyes@cordblood.com
Manager: Doug Osborn
Estimated Sales: $1.6 Million
Number Employees: 10-19

25125 Laitram LLC
200 Laitram Ln
Harahan, LA 70123-5308
504-733-6000
Fax: 504-733-5257 800-533-8253
www.laitram.com
Manufactures high-quality, stainless steel equipment
for the seafood processing industry. Product line includes shrimp peeling systems, shrimp grading systems, shrimp deveiners, and seafood steam cookers
and chillers
President: Paul Gariepy
CEO: James M Lapeyre Jr
Marketing Director: Albert Esparza
Operations Manager: Albert Wilson
Estimated Sales: $8.7 Million
Number Employees: 1000-4999
Parent Co: Laitram Corporation

25126 Lake City Signs
604 Avenue C
Boulder City, NV 89005-2738
702-293-5805
Fax: 705-293-0624
Electric signs, pennants and banners; also, lettering
service available
Co-Owner: Denise Henderson

**25127 Lake Eyelet Manufacturing
Company**
123 Old Canal Way
Weatogue, CT 06089-9688
860-628-5543
Fax: 860-628-4899
Eyelet machinery products including bottle capping,
ferrules, shells and stampings
Sales Manager: Joseph Ciriello
Estimated Sales: $2.5-5 Million
Number Employees: 50-100

**25128 Lake Michigan Hardwood
Company**
PO Box 265
Leland, MI 49654-0265
231-256-9811

Wooden pallets
Estimated Sales: $2.5-5 Million
Number Employees: 19

25129 Lake Process Systems Inc
27930 W Commercial Ave
Lake Barrington, IL 60010-2442
847-381-7663
Fax: 847-381-7688 800-331-9260
paul@lakeprocess.com www.lakeprocess.com
Cleaning and sanitizing systems, fittings, CIP and
COP units, skid systems and sanitary heat
exchangers; also, design and installation of process
and CIP systems available
President: Paul Harris
Secretary/Treasurer: Rebecca Harris
Estimated Sales: $1-2.5 Million
Number Employees: 10-19

25130 Lake Shore Industries Inc
1817 Poplar St
Erie, PA 16502-1624
814-456-4277
Fax: 814-453-4293 800-458-0463
info@lsisigns.com www.lsisigns.com
Interior and exterior signage; exporter of signs and
markers
President: Leo Bruno
info@lsisigns.com
Estimated Sales: $2.5 - 5 Million
Number Employees: 10-19
Square Footage: 38480
Brands:
Lashimar
Letter-Lites

**25131 Lakeland Rubber Stamp
Company**
PO Box 372
Lakeland, FL 33802-0372
863-682-5111
Fax: 888-465-6373 www.holmesstamp.com
Rubber stamps
President: James Bronson
Quality Control: Hood Thom
VP Marketing: Thomas Hood
Estimated Sales: $10-20 Million
Number Employees: 5-9

25132 Lakeside Container Corp
299 Arizona Ave
Plattsburgh, NY 12903-4429
518-561-6150
Fax: 518-561-4449 www.lakesidecontainer.com
Corrugated boxes and pads
President: George Bouyea
CFO: Paige Raville
Sales: Miki Worden
Plant Manager: Tom Vaughan
Estimated Sales: $1 - 2.5 Million
Number Employees: 20-49

25133 (HQ)Lakeside Manufacturing Inc
4900 W Electric Ave
Milwaukee, WI 53219-1629
414-645-0630
Fax: 414-902-6545 888-558-8565
info@elakeside.com www.elakeside.com
Manufacturer and exporter of mobile material handling and food service equipment including carts,
racks, containers, dispensers, portable beverage bars,
etc
President: Joe Carlson
jcarlson@elakeside.com
Chairman/CEO: Lawrence Moon
Chairman of the Board: Lawrence Moon
VP Sales: Alex Carayannopoulos
Estimated Sales: $10 - 20 Million
Number Employees: 100-249
Brands:
Adjust-A-Fit
Aris
Condi Express
Creation Station
Ergo-One
Extreme Duty
Lakeside
Party Pleaser
Serv 'n Express

25134 Lakeside-Aris Manufacturing
1977 S Allis Street
Milwaukee, WI 53207-1248
414-481-3900
Fax: 414-481-9313 800-558-8565
Manufacturer and exporter of serving carts and culinary display trays
VP: Jon Carlson
VP Sales: Alex Carayannopoulos
Estimated Sales: $10-20 Million
Number Employees: 100-249
Parent Co: Lakeside Manufacturing
Type of Packaging: Consumer, Food Service

25135 Lakeview Rubber Stamp Co
4316 N Lincoln Ave
Chicago, IL 60618-1712
773-539-1525
Fax: 773-539-2718
Rubber stamps
Owner: Terry Lange
lakeviewstamp@aol.com
Estimated Sales: Less Than $500,000
Number Employees: 1-4
Square Footage: 2200

25136 Lakewood Enginerring
501 N Sacramento Blvd
Chicago, IL 60612-1099
773-722-4300
Fax: 773-722-1541 800-621-4277
www.holmesproducts.com
Industrial and portable electric fans and heaters;
also, heavy-duty and ball-bearing swivels, plastic
and metal christmas tree stands
Estimated Sales: $80 Million
Number Employees: 500-999
Square Footage: 750000

25137 Lakewood Processing Machinery
875 Brooks Ave
Holland, MI 49423-5338
Fax: 616-392-8977 800-366-6705
info@lakewoodpm.com www.lakewoodpm.com
Sizers, netweight fillers, checkweighers, washers,
volumetric fillers, color sorters
President: Mike Miedema
VP Sales & Marketing: Denny Schepel
R & D: Dale Miedima
Contact: Scott Avink
scott.avink@lakewoodfabtech.com
Estimated Sales: $5-10 Million
Number Employees: 10-19

25138 Lako Tool & Mfg Inc
7400 Ponderosa Rd
P.O. Box 425
Perrysburg, OH 43551-4857
419-662-5256
Fax: 419-662-8225 800-228-2982
lsmith@lakotool.com www.lakotool.com
Sealing, cutting and punching devices
President: Larry Smith
Sales Manager: Jo Montano
Manager: Lou Montano
lsmith@lakotool.com
Estimated Sales: $2.5-5 Million
Number Employees: 10-19

25139 Lakos Separators & Filtration
1365 N Clovis Ave
Fresno, CA 93727-2282
559-255-1601
Fax: 559-255-8093 800-344-7205
info@lakos.com www.lakos.com
Fluid handling systems
Owner: Claude Laval
Contact: Betty Ava
bettya@lakos.com
Estimated Sales: $10-20 000,000
Number Employees: 50-99

25140 Lamar Advertising Co
5321 Corporate Blvd
Baton Rouge, LA 70808-2506
225-926-1000
Fax: 225-926-1005 www.lamar.com
Advertising signs including outdoor, painted and
poster panel

CEO: Sean E Reilly
 sreilly@lamarhq.com
CEO: Kevin Reilly
CFO: Keith Istre
Executive Vice President: Brent McCoy
Chief Marketing Officer: Thomas Teepell
Vice President, Director of National Sal: John Miller
Vice President of Operations: Robert Switzer
Estimated Sales: Over $1 Billion
Number Employees: 1000-4999

25141 Lamar Advertising Co
405 Country Place Pkwy
Pearl, MS 39208-6774

601-948-3443
Fax: 601-355-6255 800-893-2560
twall@lamar.com www.lamar.com
Outdoor advertising signs
Manager: Marty Elrod
CEO: Kevin Reilly Jr.
CFO: Keith Istre
Executive Vice Prsident: Brent McCoy
Chief Marketing Officer: Thomas Teepell
Vice President, Director of National Sal: John Miller
Manager: Daryl Ainsworth
 dainsworth@lamarhq.com
Vice President of Operations: Robert Switzer
Estimated Sales: $5 - 10 Million
Number Employees: 20-49

25142 Lamb Sign
11979 Falling Creek Dr
Manassas, VA 20112

703-791-7960
Fax: 703-263-1761
Building identification and marking devices includ-
ing metal letters, directory and bulletin boards and
signs
President: Robert W Schneider
VP: R Wiesheier
Estimated Sales: Below $5 Million
Number Employees: 1-4
Square Footage: 61200

25143 Lamb Weston Holdings, Inc.
599 S. Rivershore Ln.
Eagle, ID 83616

208-938-1047
800-766-7783
www.lambweston.com
Frozen potato products.
President/CEO: Tom Werner
Senior VP/CFO: Bernadette Madarieta
Senior VP/General Counsel: Eryk Spytek
Year Founded: 1950
Estimated Sales: $3.9 Billion
Number Employees: 7,600
Number of Brands: 9
Type of Packaging: Consumer, Food Service
Other Locations:
 Lamb Weston Manufacturing Plant
 Weston OR
 Lamb Weston Manufacturing Plant
 Kennewick WA
 Lamb Weston Manufacturing Plant
 Prosser WA
 Lamb Weston Manufacturing Plant
 Boise ID
 Lamb Weston Manufacturing Plant
 Alberta, Canada
Brands:
 Colossal Crisp
 CrispyCoat
 LW Private Reserve
 Lamb Weston
 Lamb's Seasoned
 Lamb's Supreme
 Stealth Fries
 Sweet Things
 Tavern Traditions

25144 Lambert Company
PO Box 740
Chillicothe, MO 64601-0740

660-646-2150
Fax: 660-646-2152 800-821-7667
Manufacturer and exporter of work gloves and
headwear
President: James Lambert
CFO: James Lambert
Estimated Sales: $5 - 10 Million
Number Employees: 6
Type of Packaging: Consumer, Food Service, Pri-
vate Label

25145 (HQ)Lambert Material Handling
6581 Townline Rd
Syracuse, NY 13206-1175

315-471-5103
Fax: 315-478-2804 800-253-5103
Palletizers and conveyor systems
Purchasing: Wendy Lewke
Number Employees: 10-19
Type of Packaging: Consumer
Other Locations:
 Lambert Material Handling
 Baldwinsville NY

25146 Lambertson Industries Inc
1335 Alexandria Ct
Sparks, NV 89434-9597

775-857-1100
Fax: 775-857-3289 800-548-3324
Stainless steel manufacturing
Owner: Jason Weiss
Marketing Director: Justin Pecot
Sales Manager: Ken Hewson
 jasonweiss@lambertson.com
Operations Manager: Joseph McCaslin
Production Manager: Oswaldo Garcia
Estimated Sales: $1.5-3,500,000
Number Employees: 20-49
Square Footage: 60000
Brands:
 L.I. Industries

25147 Lambeth Band Corporation
PO Box 50490
New Bedford, MA 02745-0017

508-984-4700
Fax: 508-984-4780
Manufacturer and exporter of belting including ny-
lon and urethane elastic bands.
President: Braley Gray
CEO: Lisa Larsen
Estimated Sales: $3 - 5 Million
Number Employees: 5-9
Square Footage: 14000
Brands:
 Lambeth Band

25148 Lamco Chemical Co Inc
212 Arlington St
Chelsea, MA 02150-2305

617-884-8470
Fax: 617-889-4207
Floor wax and cleaner
President: Jim Lam
 bonnetto@aol.com
Estimated Sales: $1 - 3 Million
Number Employees: 1-4

25149 Lamcor
8025 South Willow Street
Unit 109
Minneapolis, NH 3103

603-647-6386
Fax: 603-647-6388 info@Lamcor.com
www.lamcor.com
Tea and coffee industry packaging materials
Estimated Sales: $5-10 Million
Number Employees: 45

25150 Lamcraft Inc
4131 NE Port Dr
Lees Summit, MO 64064-1671

816-795-5505
Fax: 816-795-8310 800-821-1333
customer-service@lamcraft.com
www.lamcraft.com
Laminating equipment and supplies including plastic
laminates; also, plastic and paper laminating services for menus, price lists, recipe cards, table tents,
etc
Owner: Bob Sabin
 rsabin@lamcraft.com
Finance Executive: Darlene Rose
Estimated Sales: $10-20 Million
Number Employees: 10-19

25151 Laminated Paper Products
14491 Wyrick Ave
San Jose, CA 95124-3533

408-888-0880
Folding cartons
Owner: P Drake
 pdrake@laminatedpaperproducts.com
Estimated Sales: less than $500,000
Number Employees: 1-4

25152 Laminated Papers
PO Box 351
Holyoke, MA 01041-0351

413-533-3906
Fax: 413-533-2709
Laminated waterproof paper
President: Bernard Adams
Estimated Sales: $20-50 Million
Number Employees: 50-99

25153 Laminating TechnologiesInc
291 N Industrial Way
Canton, GA 30115-8218

770-345-7144
Fax: 770-345-7133 866-704-9992
pstoker@bakenship.com www.bakenship.com
Containers for hot and cold food products
Owner: Pat Haddon
 phaddon@pkgatl.com
Estimated Sales: $1-5 Million
Number Employees: 20-49

25154 Laminations
3010 E Venture Dr
Appleton, WI 54911-8309

920-831-0596
Fax: 920-831-0612 800-925-2626
webgnc@greatnortherncorp.com
www.laminationsonline.com
Uboard edge protectors
President: Jeff Strenger
Estimated Sales: $10-20 Million
Number Employees: 50-99

25155 Lamitech West
115 Post Street
Santa Cruz, CA 95060

831-425-6625
Fax: 831-425-6627 TPocock@lamitech.com
www.lamitech.com
Manufacturer of paperboard products for food pack-
aging, printing products, custom laminating and
other converting services.
Vice President, General Manager: Adam Reiser
Senior Sales Representative: Tim Pocok
Number Employees: 1-4

25156 Lamports Filter Media
777 E 82nd St
Cleveland, OH 44103-1817

216-881-2050
Fax: 216-881-8957 info@lamports.com
www.lamports.com
Manufacturer and exporter of fabricated textiles for
air and liquid filtration
President: Walter Senney
Contact: Jennifer Geraci
 jennifer.geraci@lamports.com
Estimated Sales: $5 - 10 Million
Number Employees: 20-49
Square Footage: 120000

25157 Lampson Tractor Equipment
P.O. Box 85
Geyserville, CA 95441-0085

707-967-3554
Fax: 707-967-3575 jmarcust@sbcglobal.net
Power equipment
Manager: Mark Terrell
Estimated Sales: $5-10 Million
Number Employees: 10-19

25158 Lamson & Goodnow
45 Conway St
Shelburne Falls, MA 01370-1420

413-625-6331
Fax: 413-625-9816 800-872-6564
info@lamsonsharp.com
www.lamsonandgoodnow.com
Manufacturer and exporter of culinary knives in-
cluding butchers' cleavers, bread, cheese and steak
President: Jim Pelletier
 jpelletier@lamsonsharp.com
CFO: David Dunn
Marketing: Kurt Saunders
Sales Manager: Kurt Zanner
Plant Manager: Fran Gipe
Estimated Sales: $10 - 20 Million
Number Employees: 20-49
Type of Packaging: Consumer, Food Service, Pri-
vate Label, Bulk
Brands:
 Lamson
 Lamson Sharp

25159 Lancaster Colony Corporation
380 Polaris Parkway
Suite 400
Westerville, OH 43082
614-224-7141
www.lancastercolony.com
Amenities including glassware, ice and food molds, iced tea dispensers, wood grain serving trays, ice buckets, aluminum cookware and commercial coffee urns, candles and matting. Foodservice products include frozen appetizers, dips, andsalad dressings.
Executive Chairman: John Gerlach

President & CEO: David Ciesinki
Vice President/CFO/Assistant Secretary: Thomas Pigott
General Counsel/Chief Ethics Officer: Matthew Shurte
VP, Corp. Finance/Investor Relations: Dale Ganobsik
Year Founded: 1961
Estimated Sales: $1.13 Billion
Number Employees: 2000
Number of Brands: 5
Type of Packaging: Consumer, Food Service, Bulk
Brands:
  Flatout
  Marzetti
  New York Brand Bakery
  New York Brand Texas Toast
  Sister Schubert's

25160 Lancaster Laboratories
PO Box 12425
Lancaster, PA 17605
717-656-2300
Fax: 717-656-2681 www.lancasterlabs.com
Analytical laboratory providing comprehensive sanitation and pollution testing, microbiology, method development and validation/quality control services
President: J Wilson Hershey
Manager: Art Pezzica
Directory Contact: Anne Osborn
Contact: Kathy Agosto
  kagosto@lancasterlabs.com
Estimated Sales: $20-50 Million
Number Employees: 500-999
Square Footage: 175000

25161 Lancer Corp
100 N Gary Ave
Cuite C
Roselle, IL 60172
847-524-1707
Fax: 847-524-1710 877-814-2271
www.lancercorp.com
Beverage dispensing equipment.
Type of Packaging: Food Service
Other Locations:
  Lancer Corp.
  Beverley

25162 (HQ)Lancer Corp
6655 Lancer Blvd
San Antonio, TX 78219
Fax: 210-310-7250 888-676-5196
generalinfo@lancercorp.com
www.lancerworldwide.com
Beverage dispensing equipment.
President: Wayne Degon
Buyer/Planner: Gerry Law, Jr.
Estimated Sales: $113 Million
Number Employees: 1,500

25163 Landau Uniforms Inc
8410 W Sandidge Rd
Olive Branch, MS 38654-3412
662-895-7200
Fax: 662-895-5099 800-238-7513
Manufacturer, importer and exporter of aprons, shirts and fast-food uniforms
President: Nat Landau
CEO: Bruce Landau
CFO: Nancy Russell
  nrussell@landau.com
Vice President: Gregg Landau
Quality Control: Dale Scott
Estimated Sales: $20 - 50 Million
Number Employees: 250-499
Type of Packaging: Food Service
Brands:
  Landau

25164 Landen Strapping
5050 Prince George Dr
Prince George, VA 23875-2623
804-452-2005
Fax: 804-722-1652 landenservice@gmail.com
plasticstrappingmachines.com
Owner: Margaret Spencer
  margaret.spencer@strapmc.com
Number Employees: 20-49

25165 Landis Plastics
5750 W 118th St
Alsip, IL 60803-6012
708-396-1470
Fax: 708-824-3722
Manufacturer and exporter of injected molded plastic packaging supplies including can lids, jar caps, containers, scoops and pails; exporter of containers and lids
Estimated Sales: $50-100 Million
Number Employees: 300
Square Footage: 102063
Parent Co: Berry Plastics Group, Inc.

25166 Landmark Kitchen Design
1900 W Chandler Blvd # 15-373
Chandler, AZ 85224-6217
602-443-0344
Fax: 623-846-6877 866-621-3192
sean@landmarkphx.com www.landmarkphx.com
Principal: Sean Kellenbarger
Vice President: Sean Kellenbarger
VP R&D: John Andrews
Project Coordinator: Sean P Kellenbarger
Estimated Sales: Below $5 Million
Number Employees: 1-4

25167 Landoll Corp
1900 North St
Marysville, KS 66508-1271
785-562-5381
Fax: 785-562-4891 mhpsales@landoll.com
Manufacturer and exporter of articulated front-wheel steered forklifts and electric forklift trucks for narrow aisle storage applications
Owner: Don Landoll
CEO: Ron Otten
CFO: Dan Caffrry
R&D: Dave Kongs
Quality Control: Henk Crucker
Sales Director: Alan Laney
  don.landoll@landoll.com
Estimated Sales: $30 - 50 Million
Number Employees: 500-999
Number of Brands: 2
Number of Products: 1
Square Footage: 350000
Type of Packaging: Bulk
Brands:
  Bendi
  Pivotmast

25168 Landoo Corporation
331 Maple Avenue
Horsham, PA 19044-2139
785-562-5381
Fax: 785-562-4853
Manufacturer and exporter of lift trucks
President: Jon Landoo
CFO: Dan Caffrey
Quality Control: Hank Burker
R & D: Dave Kongs
Marketing Supporting Manager: Jennifer Reynolds
VP Sales Manager: Kim Wanamaker
Export Sales Manager: Dave Pederson
Estimated Sales: $20-50 Million
Number Employees: 10
Square Footage: 65000

25169 Landsman Foodservice Net
2403 Logan Road
Owing Mills, MD 21117
410-363-7038
Fax: 301-330-4299
Employment agency/executive search firm specializing in selection and placement of food service industry personnel
President: Jeffrey Landsman
Estimated Sales: Less than $500,000
Number Employees: 4
Parent Co: Winston Franchise Corporation

25170 Lane Award Manufacturing
1118 S Central Ave
Phoenix, AZ 85004-2734
602-258-8505
Fax: 602-254-5489 800-843-2581
info@laneaward.com www.laneaward.com
Corporate and personal awards, business gifts, advertising and promotional items
President: John Luvisi
National Sales Manager: David Norgord
Contact: Victor Burnau
  v.burnau@cox.net
General Manager: Mack Gleekel
Purchasing Manager: Mike Abril
Estimated Sales: Below $5 Million
Number Employees: 20-49
Square Footage: 80000

25171 Lang Manufacturing Co
6500 Merrill Creek Pkwy
Everett, WA 98203-5860
425-349-2400
Fax: 425-349-2733 800-882-6368
info@langworld.com www.langworld.com
Offer a quality line of innovative gas and electric commercial cooking equipment to the commercial, retail, marine, correctional, and government foodservice inductries
President: Dave Ek
CEO: Tracy Olson
Executive VP: Steve Hegge
Manager of Marketing: Annette Steinbach
Vice President of Sales and Marketing: Jim Baxter
Purchasing Manager: Mark Johnston
Estimated Sales: $20-50 Million
Number Employees: 5-9
Square Footage: 90000
Type of Packaging: Food Service
Brands:
  Pane Bella

25172 (HQ)Langen Packaging
6154 Kestrel Road
Mississauga, ON L5T 1Z2
Canada
905-670-7200
Fax: 905-670-5291
Manufacturer and exporter of packaging machinery and carton and case packers
President: Stuart Cooper
CFO: Alan Makhan
VP Marketing/Sales: Kevin Walsh
VP Engineering: Peter Guttinger
Purchasing Manager: Elinor Workman
Estimated Sales: $20 - 30 Million
Number Employees: 100
Square Footage: 80000

25173 (HQ)Langer Manufacturing Company
1025 7th Street SW
Cedar Rapids, IA 52404-1918
319-362-1481
Fax: 319-364-7131 800-728-6445
langermfg@aol.com
Manufacturer and exporter of wire products including milk bottle crates, bakery racks, partitioned cases, custom baskets and display racks
President: John R Langer
CEO: James M Langer
Sales: John Langer
Operations: James Langer
Estimated Sales: $2.5 Million
Number Employees: 20-49
Number of Products: 150
Square Footage: 80000

25174 Langer Manufacturing Company
1025 7th Street SW
Cedar Rapids, IA 52404-1918
319-362-1481
Fax: 319-364-7131 800-728-6445
Carriers, racks, P.O.P. displays
President: John R Langer
Estimated Sales: $2 Million
Number Employees: 55

25175 Langsenkamp Manufacturing
1699 South 8th St
Indianapolis, IN 46060
317-773-2100
Fax: 317-585-1715 877-585-1950
www.warnerbodies.com

Manufacturer and exporter of canning and food processing machinery including pumps, finishers, tanks, can openers and crushers, etc
President: Rick Manasek
Sales: Roger McNew
Controller: Bryan Lindsay
Estimated Sales: $2.5-5 Million
Number Employees: 18-25
Number of Brands: 1
Number of Products: 10
Square Footage: 62000

25176 (HQ)Langston Co Inc
1760 S 3rd St
Memphis, TN 38109-7712
901-774-4440
Fax: 901-942-5402 lango@bellsouth.net
www.langstonbag.com
Manufacturer and exporter of bags including burlap, produce and multi-wall paper
CEO: Robert Langston
CEO: Robert Langston
Production Manager: Steve Winston
Estimated Sales: $20-50 Million
Number Employees: 50-99

25177 Lanly Co
26201 Tungsten Rd
Cleveland, OH 44132-2997
216-731-1115
Fax: 216-731-7900 sales@lanly.com
www.lanly.com
Designs and builds custom heat processing equipment for an extensive range of industries.
President: Dennis Hill
mmarincic@lanly.com
Sales Exec: Martin F Marincic
Plant Manager: Tim Brooks
Estimated Sales: $5-10 Million
Number Employees: 20-49
Square Footage: 136000

25178 Lanly Co
26201 Tungsten Rd
Cleveland, OH 44132-2997
216-731-1115
Fax: 216-731-7900 lanly@lanly.com
www.lanly.com
Custom heat process equipment: dryers, ovens, material handling equipment and controls
VP: Dennis Hill
Sales Exec: Martin F Marincic
Plant Manager: Tim Brooks
Estimated Sales: $5-10 Million
Number Employees: 20-49

25179 Lanmar Inc
3160 Doolittle Dr
Northbrook, IL 60062-2409
847-564-5520
Fax: 847-564-4682 800-233-5520
ptfe@lanmarinc.com
PTFE tapes, PTFE fabrics, custom PTFE belts.
President: Martin Jacobs
ttfe@lanmarinc.com
Sales Director: Paul Siegal
Production: Logan Jacobs
Estimated Sales: $1-2.5 Million
Number Employees: 1-4
Type of Packaging: Food Service, Private Label

25180 Lansing Corrugated Products
16248 S Lowell Rd
Lansing, MI 48906-9324
517-323-2752
Fax: 517-323-9322
Corrugated and fiber boxes

25181 Lansmont Corp
17 Mandeville Ct
Monterey, CA 93940-5745
831-655-6600
Fax: 831-655-6606 sales@lansmont.com
www.lansmont.com
Shock, drop, field data recorders, vibration, compression, data acquisition systems.
President: Joe Driscoll
CFO: Patti Monahan
VP: Peter Brown
Vice President Marketing/Business Dvlpmt: Eric Joneson
Customer Support Manager: Eric Whitfield
Customer Support Specialist: Aaron Brown

Estimated Sales: $5 - 10 Million
Number Employees: 50-99

25182 Larco
210 10th Ave NE
Brainerd, MN 56401-2802
218-829-9797
Fax: 218-829-0139 800-523-6996
sales@larcomfg.com www.larco.com
Manufacturer and exporter of switch mats and controls for machine guarding safety
President: B Wilder
bwilder@mulberrymc.com
Sales Manager: Joe Schultz
Estimated Sales: $2.5-5 Million
Number Employees: 50-99
Parent Co: Acrometal Companies

25183 Larien Products
351 Pleasant St
PMB 224
Northampton, MA 01060
413-586-4000
Fax: 413-585-0101 800-462-9237
lsmith@larien.com www.larien.com
Larien is noted for a patented bagel slicing design that safely isolates the user from the slicing action. We manufacture a consumer model and a commercial model
President: Rick Ricard
CEO: Lois Smith
National Sales Manager: Jim Dodge
Operations: Elizabeth DiVito
Estimated Sales: $1 Million
Number Employees: 1-4
Number of Brands: 4
Number of Products: 4
Type of Packaging: Consumer, Food Service
Brands:
Bagel Biter
Bagel Butler
Commerical Bagel Biter
Original Bagel Guillotine
Original Bigfoot Bottle Inversion

25184 Larkin Industries
114 David Green Rd
Birmingham, AL 35244-1648
205-987-1535
Fax: 205-987-0583 800-322-4036
www.larkinhoods.com
Ventilation systems including exhaust hoods and fans, supply fans, heated make-up air units, duct work and roof curbs
Owner: Larkin Strong
larkin.strong@larkinindustries.com
VP: Stephen Ridlespurge
Sales: Thomas Renfroe
Estimated Sales: $2.5 - 5 Million
Number Employees: 20-49
Square Footage: 80000

25185 Laros Equipment Co Inc
8278 Shaver Rd
Portage, MI 49024-5440
269-323-1441
Fax: 269-323-0456 laros@globalcrossing.net
www.laros.com
Manufacturer and exporter of conveyor systems
President: Tim Vanness
Estimated Sales: $10-20 Million
Number Employees: 20-49
Parent Co: George R. Laure Enterprises

25186 Larose & Fils Lte
2255 Industrial Boulevard
Laval, QC H7S 1P8
Canada
514-382-7000
Fax: 450-667-8515 877-382-7001
info@larose.ca www.larose.ca
Cleaning equipment and supplies including sweepers, pressure washers, germicides, disinfectants, drain openers, etc.; industrial floor polishers and waxstrippers; importer of vacuum cleaners

President: Jean Larose
CEO: Manon Larose
CFO: Richard Colerette
VP: Pierre Larose
Research & Development: Andr^ Foisy
Quality Control: Yves Lafrances
Marketing Director: France Morin
Sales Director: Andr^ Foisy
Public Relations: France Morin
Operations Manager: Manon Larose
Purchasing Manager: Anick Murray
Number Employees: 40
Square Footage: 120000
Parent Co: Labchem
Type of Packaging: Consumer, Food Service, Private Label
Brands:
Indo
Rare
Sensas
Sublime

25187 Larry B Newman Printing
2010 Middlebrook Pike
Knoxville, TN 37921-5842
865-524-1338
Fax: 865-524-1377 888-835-4566
info@larrynewmanprinting.com
larrynewmanprinting.com
Mounted and unmounted rubber stamps; also, engraved stationery
Owner: Larry Newman
larry@larrynewmanprinting.com
Manager: Brian McMillan
Estimated Sales: Less Than $500,000
Number Employees: 1-4
Square Footage: 21600
Type of Packaging: Consumer, Private Label, Bulk

25188 Larson Pallet Company
W4995 Bjorklund Rd
Ogema, WI 54459
715-767-5131
Fax: 715-767-5888
Pallets
President: Gerald Larson
Secretary: Gerald Larson
Estimated Sales: $1-2.5 Million
Number Employees: 20-49

25189 Laschober & Sovich Inc
20301 Ventura Blvd # 338
Suite 338
Woodland Hills, CA 91364-0949
818-713-9011
Fax: 818-713-1104 llanier@laschobersovich.com
www.laschobersovich.com
Consultant specializing in commercial kitchen design for quick serve restaurants, hotels and casinos, institutional facilities, prisons, hospitals, schools, etc
President: Larry Lanier
llanier@laschobersovich.com
VP, Global Ideation: Klaus Mager
Project Manager: Jonathan Turnbull
VP, Global Ideation: Joy Shelter
Business Development: Carolyn Nott
Estimated Sales: $1 - 3 Million
Number Employees: 5-9

25190 Lasco Composites
8015 Dixon Dr
Florence, KY 41042-2992
859-371-7720
Fax: 859-371-8466 www.kemlite.com
Composite fiberglass reinforced wall/ceiling panels
Executive VP, Business Development: Jim Simmons
Vice President of Sales: Jack Stambaugh
Plant Manager: Jeff Rasmussen
Estimated Sales: $15 - 20 Million
Number Employees: 100-249

25191 Lasermation Inc
2629 N 15th St
Philadelphia, PA 19132-3904
215-228-7900
Fax: 215-225-1593 800-523-2759
www.lasermation.com
Manufacturer and exporter of brass and mylar stencils, awards, wine holders, pepper grinding mills and wooden back bar displays. Signs, executive gifts and awards
President: Joseph Molines
jmolines@lasermation.com

Estimated Sales: $1-3 Million
Number Employees: 10-19
Square Footage: 50000
Type of Packaging: Private Label

25192 Lasertechnics
80 Colonnade Rd
Nepean, OC K2E 7L2
613-749-4895
Fax: 613-749-8179
webinquiry@lightmachinery.com
CEO: Martin Janiak

25193 Lasertechnics Marking Corporation
80 Colonnade Road
Nepean, ON K2E 7L2
Canada
613-749-4895
Fax: 613-749-8179
webinquiry@lightmachinery.com
Manufacturer and exporter of laser code markers
and date/code marking equipment
CEO: Martin Janiak
Sales/Marketing: Bob Michael
Director Sales Administration: Bob Baker
Estimated Sales: $2.5-5 Million
Number Employees: 20-49
Square Footage: 96000
Parent Co: Quantrad Sensor
Brands:
  Blazer

25194 Lask Seating Company
3700 S Iron Street
Chicago, IL 60609-2118
773-254-3448
Fax: 773-254-1373 888-573-2846
stoolsandchairs@aol.com
Wooden and metal chairs, stools, tabletops and bases
CEO: David Prawer
CFO: Judith Friedman
R&D: Howia Prawer
Estimated Sales: $3 - 5 Million
Number Employees: 25
Square Footage: 168000

25195 Latendorf Corporation
PO Box 205
Brielle, NJ 08730-0205
732-528-0180
Fax: 732-528-6804 800-526-4057
Manufacturer, importer and exporter of bakery machinery
Owner: Malcolm Latendorf
Estimated Sales: $1 - 5 Million
Number Employees: 50-99
Square Footage: 120000

25196 Latendorf Corporation
PO Box 205
Brielle, NJ 08730-0205
732-528-0180
Fax: 732-528-6804
Conveyor systems
Estimated Sales: $10-25 Million
Number Employees: 73

25197 Laticrete International
91 Amity Rd
Bethany, CT 06524
203-393-0010
Fax: 203-393-1684 800-243-4788
support@laticrete.com www.laticrete.com
President: David Rothbert
CFO: Jim Walker
CEO: David Rothberg
R&D: Clodio Nicolini
Quality Control: Dilsa Hawkins
Contact: Steve Aflague
  snaflague@laticrete.com
Estimated Sales: $50 - 100 Million
Number Employees: 100-249

25198 Latini Products Company
893 Industrial Drive
Elmhurst, IL 60126-1117
630-834-7789
Fax: 630-834-4322 www.latini-hohberger.com
Flat and ball lollipop machines, formers and wrapers
Director: Roger Hohberger
Estimated Sales: $3 - 5 Million
Number Employees: 10-19

25199 Latter Packaging Equipment
3206 W Jefferson Blvd
Los Angeles, CA 90018
323-737-0440
Fax: 323-737-4867 800-582-7711
info@latter.com www.latter.com
Modular shrink packaging systems including mini
L-sealer shrink tunnel systems, one arm bar sealer
systems, shrink band tunnels and conveyors and
easy open shrink film tab system
President: Melvin Latter
CFO: Melvin Latter
R&D: Melvin Latter
Estimated Sales: $5 - 10 Million
Number Employees: 10-19

25200 Lattini, Inc.
250 E. Main St.
Ste. 2300
Rochester, NY 14604
lattini.com
Sunflower seed milk - free of dairy, gluten, nuts, and soy.
Founder & CEO: Nicholas Romano
Number of Brands: 1
Number of Products: 3
Brands:
  LATTINI

25201 Laub-Hunt Packaging Systems
13547 Excelsior Dr
Norwalk, CA 90650-5236
562-802-9591
Fax: 562-802-8183 888-671-9338
info@laubhunt.com www.laubhunt.com
Manufacturer and exporter of liquid fillers
Vice President: Jeff Hunt
  info@laubhunt.com
Quality Control: E J Daniel
Vice President: Jeff Hunt
Marketing Director: Jean Pei
Estimated Sales: Below $5 Million
Number Employees: 5-9
Square Footage: 20000

25202 Laucks' Testing Laboratories
940 S Harney St
Seattle, WA 98108
206-767-5060
Fax: 206-767-5063
Laboratory providing nutrient labeling and chemical
and microbiological analyses.and mainly testing labs
President: Mike Owens
Technical Director: Mike Nelson
CFO: Jeff Owens
Chairman: James Owens
Lab Director: Kathy Kreps
Marketing/Sales: Mike Owens
Sr. Project Manager: Hugh Prentice
Estimated Sales: $5 - 10 Million
Number Employees: 55
Square Footage: 75000

25203 Laughlin Sales Corp
3618 N Grove St
Fort Worth, TX 76106-4466
817-625-7756
Fax: 817-625-0687 www.laughlinconveyor.com
Manufacturer and exporter of conveyor systems in-
cluding metal belt, chain, vibrating, magnetic, roller,
etc.; also, custom designing available
President: Matt Laughlin Jr
VP Engineering/Manufacturing: David Laughlin
Sales Manager: Gene Fields
Estimated Sales: $1 - 2.5 Million
Number Employees: 1-4
Square Footage: 200000

25204 Lauhoff Corporation
241 Chene St
Detroit, MI 48207
313-259-0027
Fax: 313-259-2652
Cereal flaking mills and cookers, lab equipment and
special process machinery
CEO: George H Lauhoff
President: Charles Lauhoff
VP: Greg Brecht
Estimated Sales: $20-30 Million
Number Employees: 10-19
Square Footage: 20000

25205 Laundry Aids
602 Washington Ave # A
Carlstadt, NJ 07072-2902
201-933-3500
Fax: 201-933-5193
Cleaning supplies including ammonia, fabric soft-
ener and laundry and dish detergent; contract
packager of liquids in plastic bottles
President: R A Yaffa
VP Sales: Ved Sing
Purchasing Agent: Lou Gagliano
Estimated Sales: $40-60 Million
Number Employees: 250-499
Square Footage: 200000
Brands:
  Fast'n Easy
  Sea Mist

25206 Laundrylux
461 Doughty Blvd
Inwood, NY 11096-1344
516-371-4400
Fax: 516-371-4029 800-645-2205
info@laundrylux.com www.laundrylux.com
Commercial front load washers, dryers and dry
cleaning equipment
Executive Chair: Neil Milch
CEO: John Sabino
CFO: James Fair
VP, Marketing: Dyann Malcolm
EVP, Sales: Gordon Kertland
Chief People Officer: Karishma Israni
Estimated Sales: $9 Million
Number Employees: 50-99
Square Footage: 80000

25207 Laurel Awning Co
1573 Hancock Ave
Apollo, PA 15613-8404
724-567-5689
Fax: 724-568-3152 888-567-5689
sales@laurelawnings.com
www.laurelawnings.com
Commercial awnings
President: Greg Schmieler
  sales@laurelawnings.com
Co-Ownr.: Bonnie Schuster
Estimated Sales: $2.5-5 Million
Number Employees: 10-19

25208 Lauritzen Makin Inc
101 W Felix St
Fort Worth, TX 76115
817-921-0218
Fax: 817-921-3963 info@lmakin.com
www.lmakin.com
Custom restaurant fixtures, bars, hostess stands,
serving lines, benches, stations, cabinets and table
tops
President: J Hatcher James Iii
VP: Bruce Barker
Marketing/Sales Director: Georgia Clarke
General Manager: Robin Irvine
Estimated Sales: $1-2.5 Million
Number Employees: 10-19
Parent Co: Liberty Company

25209 Laval Paper Box
118 Hymus
Pointe Claire, QC H9R 1E8
Canada
450-669-3551
Fax: 514-694-5636
Manufacturer and exporter of cardboard boxes
President: Frank Carbone
Number Employees: 200
Type of Packaging: Bulk

25210 Lavazza Premium Coffees
3 Park Ave # 35
New York, NY 10016-5902
212-725-9196
Fax: 212-725-9475 info@lavazza.it
www.lavazza.com
Manufacturer and importer of Italian coffee and
espresso machines
VP: Ennio Ranaboldo
Contact: Bidya Alie
  balie@sovrana.com
Estimated Sales: $10-20 Million
Number Employees: 20-49
Parent Co: LaVazza Premium Coffee
Type of Packaging: Consumer, Food Service

705

25211 Lavi Industries
27810 Avenue Hopkins
Valencia, CA 91355-3409

661-257-7809
Fax: 661-257-4938 800-624-6225
sales@lavi.com www.lavi.com
Manufacturers of Architectural Metals, Public Guidance Systems,Hospitality Fixtures, Traditional Portable Post for Hospitality, Rope Ends & Snaps, Beltrac Series in many lengths, colors and widths, Sign Frames, Graphics, Sneeze GuardsStemware Racks, Bellman Carts, Trucks, Specialty Hardware Products and much more
President: Gavriel Lavi
  gavriel@lavi.com
Director Sales: Edward Bradford
Estimated Sales: $20 - 50 Million
Number Employees: 100-249
Square Footage: 75000
Type of Packaging: Food Service
Brands:
  Beltrac

25212 Lavo Company
4829 W Mill Rd
Milwaukee, WI 53218-1407

414-353-2140
Fax: 414-353-4917
Distributor of liquid soap; also, liquid and paste floor polish
Manager: Wendy Maus
Estimated Sales: $1 - 2.5 Million
Number Employees: 1-4
Parent Co: Palmer

25213 Lawless Link
7215 Westboro Pl # 100
San Antonio, TX 78229-4178

210-342-8899
Fax: 210-342-8844 lawlessgrp@aol.com
Recruiter specializing in nationwide placement of mid-level and executive personnel for the food industry
President: Kathleen Lawless
CEO: John Lawless
CFO: J P Lawless
Manager: J Lawless
  lawlessgrp@aol.com
Estimated Sales: Less Than $500,000
Number Employees: 5-9

25214 Lawrence Equipment Inc
2034 Peck Rd
South El Monte, CA 91733-3727

626-442-2894
Fax: 626-350-5181 800-423-4500
www.lawrenceequipment.com
Manufacturer and exporter of food processing machinery including corn and flour tortilla systems, corn based snack lines and pizza forming lines; importer of dough processing equipment
President: John Lawrence
  johnlawrence@lawrenceequipment.com
Vice President: Glenn Shelton
International Sales: Dan Woodward
Estimated Sales: $10-20 Million
Number Employees: 100-249
Square Footage: 172000

25215 Lawrence Fabric Structures
3509 Tree Court Industrial Blv
St Louis, MO 63122-6619

636-861-0100
Fax: 636-861-0100 800-527-3840
sales@lawrencefabric.com
www.lawrencefabric.com
Commercial awnings and canopies
President: Mike Bowman
Vice President: Jerry Grimand
Plant Manager: John Hinckley
Purchasing Manager: Matt Roslawski
Estimated Sales: Less Than $500,000
Number Employees: 50-99

25216 Lawrence Glaser Associates
505 S Lenola Rd Ste 202
Moorestown, NJ 8057

856-778-9500
Fax: 856-778-4390
Executive search firm specializing in the selection of sales and marketing managers
President: Lawrence Glaser

Estimated Sales: Less than $500,000
Number Employees: 5-9
Square Footage: 2000

25217 Lawrence Metal ProductsInc
260 Spur Dr S
Bay Shore, NY 11706-3900

631-666-0300
Fax: 631-666-0336 800-441-0019
info@lawrencemetal.com www.tensatorgroup.com
Manufacturer and exporter of brass, chrome and stainless steel bar railings; also, glass racks, food shields and crowd control
President: David Lawrence
CEO: Jeremy Williman
Marketing: Suzanne De Angelo
Director Sales/Marketing: Betty Castro
Estimated Sales: $10-20 Million
Number Employees: 100-249
Square Footage: 160000
Brands:
  Lawrence
  Tensabarrier

25218 (HQ)Lawrence Paper Co
2801 Lakeview Rd
Lawrence, KS 66049-8950

785-843-8111
Fax: 785-749-3904 sales@lpco.net
www.lpco.co
Corrugated boxes
President: Ann Gardner
  agardner@ljworld.com
Sales Manager: Mike Sullivan
Estimated Sales: $20-50 Million
Number Employees: 100-249
Square Footage: 230000

25219 Lawrence Schiff Silk Mills
31 W. 34th Street
Suite 7002
New York, NY 10001

212-679-2185
Fax: 212-696-4565 800-272-4433
Manufacturer and exporter of ribbons, tapes, bindings, webbings and trims
President/CEO: Richard J. Schiff
CFO: Bruce Ershler
VP Sales/Marketing: Nancy Sherman
Estimated Sales: $5 - 10 Million
Number Employees: 10-19

25220 Lawrence Sign
945 Pierce Butler Rte
St Paul, MN 55104-1595

651-488-6711
Fax: 651-488-6715 800-998-8901
Signs and advertising displays
CEO: Rob Walker
  rwalker@lawrencesign.com
CFO: Susan Joos
Sr. Vice President of Sales: Steve Hirtz
General Manager: Shannon King
Vice President of Sales & Marketing: Chuck Hesse
Office Manager: Brenda Aschoff
Production Manager: Joe Longtin
Estimated Sales: $2.5 - 5 Million
Number Employees: 20-49

25221 Lawrence-Allen Group
2031 Fairmont Drive
San Mateo, CA 94402-3925

650-345-2909
800-609-2909
Consultant specializing in food product nutrition analysis and services for food processors and the food service market
Food Technologist: Karen Stiles
Estimated Sales: Below $500,000
Number Employees: 1

25222 Lawson Industries
1320 NW US Highway 50
Holden, MO 64040-9497

816-732-4347
www.lawsonindustries.com
Crates and pallets
Owner: Sergio Gonzalez
  sergio.gonzalez@lawsonindustries.com
Estimated Sales: Less Than $500,000
Number Employees: 1-4

25223 Laydon Company
PO Box 69
Brown City, MI 48416-0069

810-346-2952
Fax: 810-346-2900 laydonco@greatlakes.net
Manufacturer and exporter of precision custom plastic injection molding including long and short run
VP: Sandy Fuller
Sales Manager: Connie Dixon
Estimated Sales: $10-20 Million
Number Employees: 50-99
Square Footage: 70000

25224 Layflat Products
901 Tatum St
Shreveport, LA 71107

318-222-6141
Fax: 318-424-2949 800-551-8515
Manufacturer and exporter of screw-type wet mops, mop heads and handles
Owner: James Beadles
National Sales Manager: Bill Hill
Director Operations: Steve Williams
Estimated Sales: $3 - 5 Million
Number Employees: 20-49
Square Footage: 50000
Type of Packaging: Consumer, Food Service, Private Label
Brands:
  Layflat

25225 Lazer Images Instant Signs
33664 5 Mile Rd
Livonia, MI 48154-2866

734-427-4141
Fax: 734-427-4497 800-875-7446
www.lazerimages.com
P.O.P. sign making equipment including custom signage onto blank or pre-printed stock banners
Owner: Chris Crews
  chris@lazerimages.com
Sales/Marketing: Chris Crews
Estimated Sales: Less Than $500,000
Number Employees: 1-4

25226 Lazy Man Inc
560 Independence St # 100
Belvidere, NJ 07823-2028

908-475-5315
Fax: 908-475-3165 800-475-1950
www.lazyman.com
Commercial and domestic gas-fired barbecue equipment and cast iron burners for urns, steam tables, water heaters, hot dog carts, etc
President: G D Mc Glaughlin
CEO: D Nawrocki
Sales Manager: G Williams
Marketing Director: Garland Williams
Sales Director: Garland Williams
Contact: Brian Haun
  brian@lazyman.com
Estimated Sales: Below $5 Million
Number Employees: 10-19
Square Footage: 40000
Brands:
  Ccc Burners
  Lazy-Man
  Minute Glow

25227 Lazzari Fuel Co LLC
11 Industrial Way
Brisbane, CA 94005-1001

415-467-2970
Fax: 415-468-2298 800-242-7265
info@Lazzari.com www.lazzari.com
Mesquite lump charcoal and wood chips; importer and exporter of mesquite lump charcoal
Owner: Robert Colbert
CEO: Richard Morgan
Estimated Sales: $1 - 3 Million
Number Employees: 10-19
Square Footage: 74000
Type of Packaging: Consumer, Food Service, Private Label, Bulk
Brands:
  Lazzari

25228 Le Fiell Co
5601 Echo Ave
Reno, NV 89506-3207

402-592-9993
Fax: 402-592-7776 meatsys@lefiellco.com
www.lefiellco.com

Manufacturer and exporter of conveyors, meat packing and slaughter house machinery, trolley and trucks, meat house, engineering and overhead track switches, hide pullers and dehairers and restrainers for custom installation
Owner: Joe Gonzales
  j.gonzales@lefiellco.com
CEO: Brandon Camp
COO: Joe Gonzales
Plant Manager: Dave Gomes
Estimated Sales: $2.5 Million
Number Employees: 20-49
Square Footage: 100000
Brands:
  Le Fiell

25229 Le Fiell Co
5601 Echo Ave
Reno, NV 89506-3207
402-592-9993
Fax: 402-592-7776 meatsys@lefiellco.com
www.lefiellco.com
Owner: Brandon Camp
  bcamp@lefiellco.com
Senior Vice President/Co-Owner: Kathlene M. Schmidt
Estimated Sales: $5 - 10 Million
Number Employees: 20-49

25230 (HQ)Le Jo Enterprises
765 Pike Springs Rd
Phoenixville, PA 19460-4743
484-924-9187
Fax: 484-921-9009 www.lejo.com
Manual food preparation machines, grill maintenance tools, safety table lamps and chafing fuel
President: Deirdre D'Ambro
  deirdre@lejo.com
CFO: Lauras Hasan
Quality Control: Rudy Sciubba
VP Sales: Jack Kelly
Estimated Sales: $20 - 50 Million
Number Employees: 20-49
Other Locations:
  Le-Jo Enterprises
  Malvern PA
Brands:
  Diablo
  Dine Aglow

25231 Le Moulin Bakery, Inc.
6913 NE 3rd Ave
Miami, FL 33138-5511
305-756-1414
www.lemoulinbakery.com
Manufacturer/distributor of baguettes, baked goods, sandwiches, and breads.
President: Alain Bitton
Estimated Sales: $893,000
Number Employees: 6-10

25232 Le Smoker
321 Park Avenue
Salisbury, MD 21801-4208
410-677-3233
Fax: 410-677-3234
Stainless steel smokers, fire place, grills, wood chips, chunks and charcoal; exporter of smokers
President: Richard Isaacs
VP: Dominique Isaacs
Number of Brands: 3
Square Footage: 12000
Type of Packaging: Food Service
Brands:
  Le Smoker

25233 (HQ)Le Sueur Cheese Co
719 N Main St
Le Sueur, MN 56058-1404
507-665-3353
Fax: 507-665-2820 800-757-7611
info@daviscofoods.com www.daviscofoods.com
Variety of cheese including low-fat, no-fat, enzyme-modified cheeses and other customer specified varieties
President: Mark Davis
Vice President: Jim Ward
Manager: Mitch Davis
  mitch.davis@daviscofoods.com
Production Manager: Roger Schroder
Purchasing Manager: Gregory Bush
Estimated Sales: $14.90
Number Employees: 100-249

Square Footage: 12000
Parent Co: Davisco Foods International, Inc.
Other Locations:
  Le Sueur Cheese Plant
  Jerome ID

25234 Leader Corporation
3205 Bishop Dr 105
Arlington, TX 76010
817-640-4610
Fax: 817-649-4182
Estimated Sales: $3 - 5 Million
Number Employees: 10-19

25235 Leader Engineering-Fab Inc
695 Independence Dr
PO Box 670
Napoleon, OH 43545-9191
419-592-0008
Fax: 419-592-0340 www.lefusa.com
Filling systems, peelers, peel eliminators and can unscramblers; also, custom design and fabrication available
President: Charles B Leader Jr
CFO: Charles B Leader Jr
Vice President: John Cichocki
  jcichocki@lefusa.com
R&D: Charles B Leader Jr
Quality Control: Charles B Leader Jr
Plant Manager: John Hill
Estimated Sales: $5 - 10 Million
Number Employees: 20-49
Square Footage: 48000
Brands:
  Leader/Fox

25236 Leal True Form Corporation
248 Buffalo Ave
Freeport, NY 11520
516-379-2008
Fax: 516-623-8011 franklintoribio@aol.com
Vacuum formed blisters and trays
Owner: Arnulfo Toribio
Estimated Sales: $1-2.5 Million
Number Employees: 10-19

25237 Leaman Container
5701 E Rosedale St # A
Fort Worth, TX 76112-7732
817-429-2660
Fax: 817-429-2839
customerservice@leamancontainer.com
www.leamancontainer.com
Corrugated boxes
Owner: Steve Leaman
  sleaman@leamancontainer.com
VP Marketing: Perry Haynes
Estimated Sales: $20-50 Million
Number Employees: 20-49

25238 Lear Romec
PO Box 4014
Elyria, OH 44036
440-323-3211
Fax: 440-322-3378
chapman@craneaerospace.com
www.learromec.com
Pumps and fluid handling systems
President: Brendan Curran
Director Marketing: Seamus O'Brien
Number Employees: 100-249
Parent Co: Crane Company

25239 Least Cost FormulationsLTD
824 Timberlake Dr
Virginia Beach, VA 23464-3239
757-467-0954
Fax: 757-467-2947 sales@lcfltd.com
www.lcfltd.com
Manufacturer and exporter of material requirement planning and technical software for the blending industry
Owner: Robert Labudde
  ral@lcfltd.com
VP Marketing: Joy LaBudde
Estimated Sales: $1 Million
Number Employees: 1-4
Brands:
  Least Cost Formulator
  Market Forecaster
  Qc Assistant
  Qc Database Manager

25240 (HQ)Leathertone
2040 Industrial Dr.
Findlay, OH 45840
419-429-0188
Fax: 419-425-2927 www.leathertone.com
Plastic labels and signs
President: James Rubenstein
VP: Howard Rubenstein
Estimated Sales: $2.5-5 Million
Number Employees: 10-19

25241 Leaves Pure Teas
1392 Lowrie Avenue
South San Francisco, CA 94080-6402
650-583-1157
Fax: 650-583-1163
Retail and wholesale premium teas in teabags and loose for grocery, food service and specialty retailers
Estimated Sales: $1 - 5 Million

25242 Leavitt & Parris Inc
256 Read St
Portland, ME 04103-3446
207-797-0100
Fax: 207-797-4194 800-833-6679
contact@leavittandparris.com
www.leavittandparris.com
Awnings; rental company of tents, chairs, tables, etc
President: John Hutchins
Estimated Sales: Below $5,000,000
Number Employees: 10-19

25243 Lebensmittel Consulting
10760 West County Road 18
Fostoria, OH 44830-9623
419-435-2774
Fax: 419-435-9139
Consultant offering laboratory, product development, process development, food testing and genetic engineering services
Owner: Richard Basel
  basel1@bright.net
VP: Margaret Basel
Research & Development: Richard Basel
  basel1@bright.net
Quality Control: Richard Basel
  basel1@bright.net
Number Employees: 10
Square Footage: 20000

25244 Lechler Inc
445 Kautz Rd
St Charles, IL 60174-5301
630-377-6611
Fax: 630-377-6657 800-777-2926
karenberker@lechlerusa.com www.lechlerusa.com
We are one of the largest manufacturers of spray nozzles, accessories and headers. We produce these products in various alloys and plastics to serve a wide variety of fluid applications. From tank washing nozzles and machines which canclean tanks of all sizes to air atomizing nozzles which can coat food or lubricate equipment to standard flat fan and full cone nozzles which can wash food or mix fluids. We have the spraying application products for the food processing industry
President/CEO: Ralph Fish
CEO: Terry Hayden
  terry@lechlerusa.com
Marketing/Sales: Karen Berker
Estimated Sales: $10-20,000,000
Number Employees: 50-99
Square Footage: 45000
Parent Co: Lechler GMBH
Brands:
  Lechler
  Spraco
  Tank Cleaning Systems

25245 Leclaire Packaging Corp
W1351 Elmwood Ave
Ixonia, WI 53036-9437
920-206-9902
Fax: 920-206-9904 stucl@aol.com
Corrugated containers and packaging materials
CEO: Daniel Steuber, Jr.
Vice President: James Steuber
Estimated Sales: Below $5 Million
Number Employees: 10-19
Number of Products: 3
Square Footage: 36000
Type of Packaging: Bulk

25246 Leclerc Foods USA
44 Park Drive
Montgomery, PA 17752-8534
570-547-6295
Fax: 570-547-6719
Cookies, snack bars, crackers, cereals and chocolate
Contact: Tina Baier
 tbaier@leclercfoods.com
Estimated Sales: $8.2 Million
Number Employees: 74

25247 Leco Plastic Inc
130 Gamewell St
Hackensack, NJ 07601-4230
201-343-3330
Fax: 201-343-0558 info@lecoplastics.com
 www.lecosolar.com
Bag and bundle tie, pack handles, die cutting, plastic ties
Owner: Barry Schwartz
 barry.schwartz@lecoplastics.com
Production: Burton Schwartz
Estimated Sales: $1-2.5 Million
Number Employees: 10-19
Square Footage: 28000
Type of Packaging: Bulk

25248 Lee Engineering Company
505 Narragansett Park Drive
Pawtucket, RI 02861-1970
401-725-6100
Fax: 401-728-7840
Material handling equipment including pallet stack-ers and scissor and dock lifts
CEO/President: Bill Sample
Estimated Sales: $10,000,000 - $25,000,000
Number Employees: 100-249
Parent Co: Long Reach Holdings

25249 Lee Financial Corporation
8350 N. Central Expressway
Suite 1800
Dallas, TX 75206
972-960-1001
Fax: 972-404-1123 Info@Leefin.com
 www.leefin.com
Manufacturer and exporter of corn cutters, pea shellers and electric nutcrackers
President: Dana Pingenot
CEO & Founder: Richard Lee
CFO: Blake Decker
VP: Teresa Quinn
Contact: Rebecca Anderson
 randerson@leefin.com
COO & Director of Human Resources: Jeff Ramsey
Estimated Sales: Below $5 Million
Number Employees: 20-49
Square Footage: 14000

25250 Lee Industries
50 W Pine St
Philipsburg, PA 16866
814-342-0461
Fax: 814-342-5660 www.leeind.com
Custom sanitary process equipment.
President/CFO/COO: Joshua Montler
Chairman & CEO: Robert Montler
Vice President, Sales: Gregory Wharton
Year Founded: 1924
Estimated Sales: $100-500 Million
Number Employees: 100-249

25251 Lee Products Co
800 E 80th St
Minneapolis, MN 55420-1396
952-300-2908
Fax: 952-854-7177 info@leeproducts.com
 www.leeproducts.com
Hand cleaning pads
President: John Houle
 info@leeproducts.com
CFO: Rey Lee
Sales Exec: Faye Roy
Estimated Sales: $5-10 Million
Number Employees: 20-49

25252 Lee Soap Company
6620 E 49th Ave
Commerce City, CO 80022
303-289-9041
Fax: 303-289-9042 800-888-1896
orders@leesoap.com www.leesoap.com
Janitorial supplies including compounders, laundry detergent and soap

Owner: Carl Kelley
Sales Manager: Jim Sumner
Contact: Dave Himmelberg
 daveh@leesoap.com
Estimated Sales: $5-10 Million
Number Employees: 10-19

25253 Leedal Inc
3453 Commercial Ave
Northbrook, IL 60062-1818
847-498-0111
Fax: 847-498-0198 sink@leedal.com
 www.consolidateddoorintl.com
Manufacturer, importer and exporter of pot and pan washers, disposers, power scrubbers, wire shelfing, hot dog cookers, and steam tables
President: Aj Levin
 ajlevin@hotmail.com
CFO: Sheldon Levin
Vice President: A Levin
Quality Control: Levin
Sales Director: Josie Negron
Estimated Sales: $5 - 10 Million
Number Employees: 20-49
Square Footage: 28000
Type of Packaging: Consumer, Food Service, Private Label, Bulk

25254 Leedal Inc
3453 Commercial Ave
Northbrook, IL 60062-1818
847-498-0111
Fax: 847-498-0198 www.consolidateddoorintl.com
Stainless steel equipment, custom fabrication, steam tables, sinks, and tanks
President: Aj Levin
 ajlevin@hotmail.com
Vice President: A Levin
Sales Director: Josie Negron
Estimated Sales: $10 - 20 Million
Number Employees: 20-49
Square Footage: 14000
Type of Packaging: Consumer, Food Service, Private Label, Bulk

25255 Leeds Conveyor Manufacturer Company
PO Box 383
Guilford, CT 06437
203-453-5277
Fax: 203-453-6329 800-724-1088
 www.leedsconveyor.com
Conveyor systems including chain and roller in mild and stainless steel, belt conveyors and mesh chain in metal and plastic; also, accumulators and unscramblers
President: Paul Nangle
CFO: Debbie Nancy Nangle
Manufacturing Manager: Sean LeTarte
Number Employees: 10
Square Footage: 64000

25256 Leeman Labs Inc
110 Lowell Rd
Hudson, NH 03051-4806
603-886-8400
Fax: 603-886-4322 800-634-9942
 www.leemanlabs.com
Analytical instrumentation including coupled plasma spectrometers, metal alloy, cyanide and mer-cury analyzers and prep systems
CEO: John Leeman
Director Sales Marketing: Bill Driscoll
Contact: Ed Rau
 leemanlabsinfo@teledyne.com
Director International Operations: Paul Maaskant
Estimated Sales: $10-20 Million
Number Employees: 5-9
Square Footage: 100000
Brands:
 A30
 Ap/Ps 1214
 Ap/Ps200 Ii
 Dre (Direct Reading Echelle Icp)
 Plasma-Pure

25257 Leer Inc
206 Leer St
New Lisbon, WI 53950-1163
608-562-3161
Fax: 608-562-6022 800-237-8350
info@leerlp.com www.leerinc.com
Manufacturer and exporter of self-service ice mer-chandising equipment and block ice-makers

VP: Charlotte Maginnis
CEO and Owner and President: Steve Dolenzel
IT: Kevin Kracht
 kkracht@leerlp.com
Estimated Sales: $500,000 - $1 Million
Number Employees: 100-249
Square Footage: 320000
Parent Co: Leer Manufacturing Partner
Type of Packaging: Bulk
Other Locations:
 Star/Starrett
 Dumas AZ
Brands:
 Leer
 Star
 Starrett

25258 Legacy Plastics
1116 5th St
Henderson, KY 42420-2804
270-827-1318
Fax: 270-831-6510
SCourtney@LegacyPlastics.com
 www.legacyplastics.com
A custom thermoplastic Profile extrusion company offering products such as signage, price channels, dividers, extrusions and plastic components made from materials such as: styrene, acrylic, ABS, PVC, polycarbonate, etc; as well asflexible tubing products.
President: Roger Courtney
CEO: Doug Bray
CFO: John Brooks
Sales Director: Tom Simmering
Production Manager: Sharon Courtney
Purchasing Manager: Barb Claridge
Estimated Sales: $1.5 Million
Number Employees: 10-19
Number of Products: 100+
Square Footage: 40000
Parent Co: Display Specialties

25259 Legal Sea Foods
1 Seafood Way
Boston, MA 02210-2700
617-530-9000
Fax: 617-782-4479 www.legalseafoods.com
Restaurant chain and gourmet seafood gifts
President: Jason Ananda
 jason.a.josephson@williams.edu
CFO: Mark Synott
Quality Control: Steve Martinello
Estimated Sales: $10 - 100 Million
Number Employees: 100-249

25260 Legge & Associates
PO Box 599
Rockwood, ON N0B 2K0
Canada
519-856-0444
Fax: 519-856-0555
Consultant specializing in the design of food service and hospitality facilities
Principal: Scott Legge

25261 Leggett & Platt Inc
1 Leggett Road
Carthage, MO 64836-9649
417-358-8131
Fax: 417-358-5840 www.leggett.com
Manufacturer and exporter of store fixtures includ-ing bakery showcases, cash register stands and checkouts, bulk shelving and storage units and cus-tom wood display equipment
President & COO: J. Mitchell Dolloff
Chair & CEO: Karl Glassman
EVP & CFO: Jeffrey Tate
SVP & General Counsel: Scott Douglas
CIO: Michael Blinzler
Plant Manager: Jim Winters
Director, Procurement: Jeff Mitchell
Estimated Sales: Over $1 Billion
Number Employees: 10000+
Square Footage: 15491
Parent Co: Reflector Hardware Corporation
Type of Packaging: Consumer, Food Service, Bulk
Other Locations:
 Goer Manufacturing Co.
 Union MO

25262 Leggett & Platt Storage
11230 Harland Drive
Vernon Hills, IL 60061-1547
847-816-6246
Fax: 847-968-3899 www.focuspg.com

Manufacturer and exporter of cabinets, racks, mobile
storage equipment, shelving, carts, servingware,
buffetware, utensils, utility trucks, dollies and
tote/bus boxes
President: Keith Jaffee
Number Employees: 10-19
Square Footage: 2000000
Parent Co: SPG International, LLC
Other Locations:
Leggett & Platt
Charlotte NC

25263 Legible Signs
2221 Nimtz Road
Loves Park, IL 61111-3928
815-654-7323
Fax: 815-654-9679 800-435-4177
Polyethylene safety signs, aluminum name plates,
custom decals and menu covers
Customer Service: Trina Bentley
Estimated Sales: $1-2.5 Million
Number Employees: 10-19

25264 Legion Industries Inc
370 Mills Rd
Waynesboro, GA 30830-5360
706-554-4411
Fax: 706-554-2035 800-887-1988
www.legionindustries.com
Food service equipment including steam equipment,
kettles, ovens and braising pans
Manager: Susan Riggs
CEO: Chuck Brown
cbrown@legionindustries.com
Estimated Sales: Below $5,000,000
Number Employees: 20-49
Square Footage: 5000

25265 Legion Lighting Co Inc
221 Glenmore Ave
Brooklyn, NY 11207-3307
718-498-1770
Fax: 718-498-0128 800-453-4466
sales@legionlighting.com
www.legionlighting.com
Manufacturer and exporter of architecturally engi-
neered fluorescent lighting equipment
President: Michael Bellovin
VP Sales: Michael Bellovin
Engineering: Wayne Cowell
Sales: Evan Bellovin
Accountant: Gia Carla Rodriguez
Estimated Sales: $5-10 Million
Number Employees: 50-99
Square Footage: 12000
Brands:
Circledome
Comfort-Lume
Compact Cube
Contempo
Corritempo
Drum-Plex
Excelon
Gemini
Legion-Aire
Lytegress
Mod-Plex
Mod-U-Beam
My-T-Lite
Panelume
Paralume
Prismalier
Securlume
Skylume
Teg-U-Lume
Trimlume
Vandalex
Vaportron

25266 Legumex Walker, Inc.
1345 Kenaston Blvd
Winnipeg, MB R6W 4B3
Canada
204-808-0448
Grains
Investor & Media Relations: Marin Landis

25267 Lehi Mills
833 E Main St
Lehi, UT 84043-2286
877-311-3566
contact@lehimills.com lehirollermills.com

Processor of flour, feed and meal; also, pancake
mixes, cookie mixes, brownie mixes, bread mixes
and preserves.
President: Sherman Robinson
General Manager: Brock Knight
VP, Sales/Marketing: Steve DeJohn
sdejohn@lehirollermills.com
Year Founded: 1906
Estimated Sales: $20-50 Million
Number Employees: 20-49
Number of Brands: 1
Type of Packaging: Food Service, Private Label
Brands:
Lehi Mills

25268 Lehigh Safety Shoe Co LLC
39 E Canal St
Nelsonville, OH 45764-1247
740-753-1951
Fax: 740-753-7240 866-442-5429
clientservices@lehighoutfitters.com
www.lehighsafetyshoes.com
Shoes including steel toe, nonsteel toe and nonslip
CEO: David Sharp
david.sharp@rockybrands.com
Number Employees: 50-99
Brands:
Lehigh

25269 Lehman Sales Associates
3025 Saddle Brook Trl
Sun Prairie, WI 53590
608-575-7712
Fax: 608-837-8421 bob@lehmanequip.com
Manufacturer and exporter of used and rebuilt food
processing and packaging equipment
President: Richard Lehman
Estimated Sales: $1 - 2.5 Million
Number Employees: 1-4

25270 Lehmann Mills Inc
11000 Youngstown Salem Rd
PO Box 1083
Salem, OH 44460-9654
330-332-9951
Fax: 330-332-2208 888-919-9494
info@lehmannmills.com www.lehmannmills.com
Three-roll horizontal mills, Three-roll vertical mills,
Technical field service Installation start-up and su-
pervision, Operator training and maintenance, Con-
sultation services, In-house CAD engineering,
Custom-designed upgrades, Problemsolving
capabilities
Owner: David Hrovatic
info@lehmannmills.com
Estimated Sales: $5-10 Million
Number Employees: 20-49

25271 Leibinger-USA
2702-B Buell Drive
East Troy, WI 53120
262-642-4030
Fax: 262-642-4033 info@leibinger-group.com
www.leibingerusa.com
A family owned business since 1948 and a premier
manufacturer of security, industrial and commerical
printing solutions, introduces the Jet2 Printer -the
only low maintenance continuous in jet (CIJ) printer
on the market today. the Jet2features a retractable
gutter which creates an air tight seal over the nozzle
eliminating ink from drying in the nozzle. This revolutionary design is far superior to traditional flush
nozzle systems.
President: Gunter Leibinger
Vice President: Steve Talbot
Sales Director: Alexander Deuchert
Number of Products: 3
Type of Packaging: Consumer, Food Service, Private Label, Bulk

25272 Leica Microsystems
3362 Walden Ave
Depew, NY 14043
716-686-3000
Fax: 716-686-3085 800-346-4560
analytical@leica-microsystems.com
Refractometers, microscopes and colony counters
Marketing Director: Thomas Ryan
Sales Director: Terry Grant
Contact: Ludger Althoff
ludger@leica-microsystems.com
Estimated Sales: $2.5-5 Million
Number Employees: 20-49
Parent Co: Leica AG

Brands:
Ar200
Ar600
Arias500
Auto Abbe
Brix 15hp
Brix 30
Brix 35hp
Brix 50
Brix 65hp
Brix 90
Brix 90hp
Leica
Mark Ii
Mark Ii Plus
Oe200

25273 Leichtman Ice Cream Company
175 N Vine St Apt 3b
Hazleton, PA 18201
570-454-2428
Fax: 570-454-2540 800-735-4379
Ice Cream Distributors
Estimated Sales: $5-10 000,000
Number Employees: 15

25274 Leidos Engineering
221 3rd St # A
Newport, RI 02840-1087
401-847-4210
Fax: 401-849-1585 800-729-4210
www.saic.com
Inventory and measurement services, package reduc-
tion consulting and customized data managment
software. Global environmental packaging services
President: Anthony Moraco
President, Chief Executive Officer: John Jumper
Executive Vice President of Human Resour: Brian
Keenan
Chief Technical Officer: Amy Alving
Marketing: Janie Harris
Chief Operating Officer: Stuart Shea
IT: Roger Wells
roger.k.wells@saic.com
Estimated Sales: $10-20 Million
Number Employees: 50-99

25275 Leister/Heely-Brown Company
1139 Goodwin Rd NE
Atlanta, GA 30324-2715
404-846-0401
Fax: 404-350-2696 800-241-4628
info@heely-brown.com www.heely-brown.com
Hot air tools provide solutions for customers' pack-
aging, shrinking, drying, heating, forming, stak-
ing,curing, plastic welding, prototyping, soldering
and de-soldering and activating applications
Manager: Nancy Chambers
CFO: Michael Spencer
Estimated Sales: $20 - 50 Million
Number Employees: 1-4

25276 Leister/Malcom Company
207 High Point Avenue
Unit 7B
Portsmouth, RI 2871
401-683-3199
Fax: 401-683-3177 800-289-7505
www.malcom.com
Hot air equipment for various packaging applica-
tions including hand-held heat guns and pallet
shrink guns to large process heaters
Chairman: George Bixby
President: Jonathan Bixby
Sales/Marketing Administrator: Sheila Carpenter
President: Jonathan Bixby
Sales/Technical Support: Mary Bass
Application Engineer: Steve Robertson
Chairman: George Bixby
Estimated Sales: $1 - 3 Million
Number Employees: 1-4

25277 Leister/Uneco Systems
8412 Autumn Drive
Woodridge, IL 60517
630-972-0500
Fax: 630-910-0558 800-700-6894
junewitz@att.net
Plastic weld, packaging, roofing, process heat, dry-
ing SMT electronics, Leister hot air tools and blow-
ers
President: John A Unewitz
CFO: John A Unewitz
Sales Director: John Unewitz

Estimated Sales: $1 - 3 Million
Number Employees: 1-4
Brands:
   Leister Heat Guns

25278 Leland Limited Inc
2614 S Clinton Ave
South Plainfield, NJ 07080-1427
          908-561-2000
Fax: 908-668-7716 sales@lelandltd.com
          www.lelandgas.com
Manufacturer and exporter of food mixing equipment
Owner: Lee Stanford
   lee@lelandgas.com
Engineer: P Bowlin
Customer Service: R Callaway
Estimated Sales: $5-10 Million
Number Employees: 10-19
Brands:
   Leland Southwest

25279 Leland Limited Inc
2614 S Clinton Ave
South Plainfield, NJ 07080-1427
          908-561-2000
Fax: 908-668-7716 800-984-9793
sales@lelandltd.com www.lelandgas.com
Manufacturer, importer and exporter of whipped cream machinery and soda syphons
Owner: Lee Stanford
   lee@lelandgas.com
Estimated Sales: $5,000,000
Number Employees: 10-19
Square Footage: 30000
Type of Packaging: Food Service
Brands:
   Leland
   Mr. Fizz

25280 Lematic Inc
2410 W Main St
Jackson, MI 49203-1099
          517-787-3301
Fax: 517-782-1033 sales@lematic.com
          www.auto-op.com
Manufacturer and exporter of bulk packaging, bagging machinery and dry pan cleaners; also, bakery equipment including garlic and French bread makers and slicers for buns, bagels, croissants, etc
Owner: Dale Lecrone
   dlecrone@lematic.com
CEO: Dale LeCrone
Director Sales: George Arnold
   dlecrone@lematic.com
Estimated Sales: $5-10 Million
Number Employees: 50-99
Square Footage: 60000

25281 Lengsfield Brothers
PO Box 50020
New Orleans, LA 70150-0020
          504-529-2235
       Fax: 504-524-9281
Manufacturer and exporter of candy boxes

25282 Lenkay Sani Products Corporation
473 Wortman Ave
Brooklyn, NY 11208
          718-927-9260
       Fax: 718-257-0461
Custom packaging
President: Frank Drayer
Estimated Sales: Below $5 Million
Number Employees: 5-9
Square Footage: 24000

25283 Lenox Corp
1414 Radcliffe St # 1
Bristol, PA 19007-5496
          267-525-7800
Fax: 267-525-5618 800-223-4311
          www.lenox.com
Manufacturer and exporter of chinaware, stemware, silverplated hollowware, crystal gifts and flatware including stainless and sterling
Owner: Walter S Lenox
   walter.lenox@lenox.com
CFO: James Burwitt
Quality Control: Dave Summers
Number Employees: 1000-4999
Parent Co: Brown-Foreman
Type of Packaging: Food Service

25284 Lenox Locker Company
PO Box 317
Dunmore, PA 18512-0317
          740-375-0730
       Fax: 717-222-4141
Sanitation supplies and equipment

25285 Lenser Filtration
1750 Oak St
Lakewood, NJ 8701
          732-370-1600
Fax: 732-370-8411 www.lenserusa.com
Polypropylene and other thermoplastic filter elements for use in solids and liquid seperation
Sales: Robert Iovino
Production: Tom Van Leet
   tomvanleet@lenserusa.com
Estimated Sales: $5 - 10 Million
Number Employees: 20-49

25286 Lentia Enterprises Ltd.
17733-66th Ave
Surrey, BC V3S 7X1
Canada
          604-576-8838
Fax: 604-576-1064 888-768-7368
Naturally fermented, dehydrated sourdoughs from both wheat and rye flours, specialty malted products such as whole malted rye kernels, aroma malts, colouring malts and clean label bread mixes.
President/Board Member: Karl Eibensteiner
Director: Gertrude Eibensteiner
Estimated Sales: $4.08 Million
Number Employees: 23

25287 Lentz Milling Co
2045 N 11th St
Reading, PA 19604-1201
          610-921-0666
Fax: 610-929-3682 800-523-8132
          www.lentzmilling.com
Owner: Ted Lentz
Sales/Accounts Supervisor: Jane Adams
   tlentz@lentzmilling.com
Estimated Sales: $50-100 Million
Number Employees: 100-249

25288 Lenweaver Advertising
108 W Jefferson St Ste 300
Syracuse, NY 13202
          315-422-8729

25289 Lenze Americas
630 Douglas St
Uxbridge, MA 01569
          508-278-9100
Fax: 508-278-7873 800-217-9100
info.us@lenze.com www.lenze.com/en-us
Manufacturer of electrical and mechanical drives
President, Lenze Americas: Chuck Edwards
Estimated Sales: $100,000,000 - $499,999,999
Number Employees: 1,000-4,999

25290 Leon Bush Manufacturer
1870 Elmdale Avenue
Glenview, IL 60026-1356
          847-657-8888
       Fax: 847-657-9710
Plastic injection molding for wedding cake plates and ornaments; also, industrial baking utensils and deli trays
Sales Manager: David Drew
Estimated Sales: $500,000-$1 Million
Number Employees: 5-9

25291 Leon C. Osborn Company
1020 Bay Area Blvd
Suite 120
Houston, TX 77289-0014
          281-488-0755
Fax: 281-480-9739 www.leoncosborn.com
Washers for fresh pack pickles, brine stock, beets, potatoes, carrots, squash, and other vegetables
President: David S Osborn
Contact: Jim Degreif
   jim@leoncosborn.com
Estimated Sales: $.5 - 1 million
Number Employees: 1-4

25292 Leotta Designers
800 Brickell Ave
Ste 602
Miami, FL 33131
          305-371-4949
Fax: 305-371-2844 www.leottadesigners.com
Interior designer; services include space planning, corporate interior design, site selection and lease negotiation
President: Marc J Leotta
VP: J Kalbach
Estimated Sales: $500,000 - $1 Million
Number Employees: 5-9

25293 Lepel Corp
W227n937 Westmound Dr # 2
Waukesha, WI 53186-1747
          262-782-0450
Fax: 262-782-3299 800-231-6008
          www.lepel.com
Process control systems features motion, linear, alignment and cap height detectors, along with idle control and Windows-compatible software for process control, induction cap sealing
Vice President: Al Peters
Sales Coordinator: Bonnie Leivenger
Manager: Bonnie Leitinger
   bleitinger@lepel.com
Manager: Bonnie Leitinger
Estimated Sales: $2.5 - 5 Million
Number Employees: 1-4
Square Footage: 2500
Parent Co: Lepel Corporation
Brands:
   Cspiust Capsealing System
   Lepakjr Capsealing System

25294 Leprino Foods Co.
1830 W. 38th Ave.
Denver, CO 80211
          303-480-2600
Fax: 303-480-2605 800-537-7466
          www.leprinofoods.com
Mozzarella cheese, cheese blends, and pizza cheese made especially for pizzeria and foodservice operators, frozen food manufacturers and private label cheese packagers.
Chairman/CEO: Jim Leprino
CFO: Ron Klump
Year Founded: 1950
Estimated Sales: $3.5 Billion
Number Employees: 5,000+
Square Footage: 60000
Type of Packaging: Food Service, Bulk
Other Locations:
   Leprino Foods
   Allendale MI
   Leprino Foods
   Fort Morgan CO
   Leprino Foods
   Greeley CO
   Leprino Foods
   Lemoore CA
   Leprino Foods
   Remus MI
   Leprino Foods
   Roswell NM
   Leprino Foods
   Tracy CA
   Leprino Foods
   Waverly NY

25295 Lermer Packaging
202 Washington Avenue
Carlstadt, NJ 07072-3001
          908-789-0900
       Fax: 908-789-0235
Wine industry packaging
Estimated Sales: $10-20 Million
Number Employees: 20-49

25296 Leroy Signs, Inc.
6325 Welcome Ave N
Brooklyn Park, MN 55429
          763-535-0080
Fax: 763-533-2593 info@leroysigns.com
          www.leroysigns.com
Plastic and neon signs
Owner: Leroy Reiter
Contact: Andria Reiter
   andria.reiter@leroysigns.com
Estimated Sales: $2.5-5 Million
Number Employees: 20-49

25297 Leroy's Restaurant Supply
1306 S Grant Ave
Odessa, TX 79761-6844
432-333-2621
Fax: 915-333-2621 reedbbq@aol.com
Wholesaler/distributor of new and used food service
equipment; serving the food service market
Owner: Audrianna Hinojosa
audrianna@wix.com
Estimated Sales: Less than $500,000
Number Employees: 5-9

25298 (HQ)Les Industries Touch Inc
4025 Lesage
Sherbrooke, QC J1L 2Z9
Canada
819-822-4140
Fax: 819-822-2904 800-267-4140
info@industriestouch.com
www.industriestouch.com
Manufacturer and exporter of toothpicks, skewers,
plastic cutlery, straws etc.
President: Gervais Morier
Sales Director: Gerald Bouchard
Operations Manager: Jean-Yves Blouin
Estimated Sales: $10-20 Million
Number Employees: 50-99
Number of Products: 300+
Square Footage: 90000
Type of Packaging: Consumer, Food Service, Private Label, Bulk
Brands:
Touch

25299 Lesco Design & Mfg Co
1120 Fort Pickens Rd
La Grange, KY 40031-9396
502-222-7101
Fax: 502-222-5508 sales@lesco-design.com
www.lescodesign.com
Conveyor belts
President: Lance Kaufman
dkaufman@lescodesign.com
CFO: Steve Herald
VP: Lance Kaufman
VP Sales: Dick Wilder
Estimated Sales: $20-50 Million
Number Employees: 50-99
Square Footage: 115000

25300 Lester Box & Mfg Div
1470 Seabright Ave
Long Beach, CA 90813-1152
562-437-5123
Fax: 562-436-1437 sales@lesterbox.com
www.lesterbox.com
Manufacturer and exporter of wooden boxes and
crates, pallets, skids and foam inserts
Manager: Steve Amato
steve@lesterbox.com
Estimated Sales: $1-2.5 Million
Number Employees: 10-19
Square Footage: 60000

25301 Letica Corp
52585 Dequindre Rd
Rochester Hills, MI 48307-2321
248-652-0557
Fax: 248-608-2153 800-538-4221
www.letica.com
Manufacturer and exporter of plastic shipping containers, paper and plastic cups and containers for
cultured dairy products and freight lines
CEO: Ilija Letica
iletica@letica.com
CEO: Ilija Letica
Sales Director: David Bradwell
Public Relations: David Schueler
Estimated Sales: $5 - 10 Million
Number Employees: 1000-4999
Brands:
Letica
Maui Cup

25302 Letrah International Corp
W7603 Koshkonong Mounds Rd
Fort Atkinson, WI 53538-8709
920-563-6597
Fax: 920-563-7515 doughartel@gmail.com
www.hartelinternational.com
Manufacturer, importer and exporter of process control systems including blending, processing,
clean-in-place, refrigeration, level, load cell, metering, proportioning and packaging.

President: Douglas Hartel
doughartel@gmail.com
Estimated Sales: Less Than $500,000
Number Employees: 1-4
Square Footage: 5332

25303 Letraw Manufacturing Company
200 Quaker Rd
Box 2
Rockford, IL 61104
815-987-9670
Fax: 815-987-9830 rwartell@letraw.com
www.letraw.com
Cleaning supplies including metal scrubbers and
scouring cloths; importer of Mexican vanilla extract
Partner: Ralph Wartell
Estimated Sales: less than $500,000
Number Employees: 5
Square Footage: 8000
Type of Packaging: Consumer, Food Service

25304 Leuze-Lumiflex
55395 Lyon Industrial Drive
New Hudson, MI 48165-8545
973-586-0100
Fax: 973-586-1590 www.leuze-lumiflex.com
Opto-sensors and work safety products including bar
code readers, clear media detection sensors, clear
and opaque label detection sensors, cap orientation
detection sensors, fork sensors, luminescence sensors, laser distance sensingdevices and safety li
President: Vincent Orrico
Contact: Ben Fifield
bfifield@leuzeusa.com
Estimated Sales: $20 - 50 Million
Number Employees: 300

25305 Levelmatic
1135 NW 159th Dr
Miami, FL 33169-5882
305-625-2451
Fax: 305-623-0475 800-762-7565
sales@atlasfoodserv.com www.atlasfoodserv.com
Self leveling dispensers for plates, bowls, racks,
trays, etc
President: David Meade
VP Sales: Howard Bolnar
VP Manufacturing: Mark Siegfriedt
Estimated Sales: $10 - 20 Million
Number Employees: 100-249
Parent Co: Atlas Metal Industries

25306 Levin Brothers Paper
1325 S Cicero Ave
Cicero, IL 60804
708-652-5600
Fax: 708-780-6975 800-545-6200
clutch@idt.net www.lbpmfg.com
Corrugated boxes, tape and packaging materials;
wholesaler/distributor of paper products and restaurant supplies
President: Barry Silverstein
CFO: Mike Schaechter
VP: Matthew Cook
Quality Control: Larry Rosenberg
Contact: Suliman Abdallah
abdallah@lbpmfg.com
Estimated Sales: $10-20 Million
Number Employees: 10-19
Square Footage: 250000
Brands:
Safe-Pack

25307 Lewco Inc
706 Lane St
Sandusky, OH 44870-3846
419-625-4014
Fax: 419-625-1247 sales@lewcoinc.com
www.lewcoinc.com
Conveyor systems including belt, bottle and chain,
stainless steel, gravity and powered roller. Also industrial ovens for drum heating and general thermal
processing applications
President: Pete Gay
peteg@gardeners.com
CFO: Jim Chapman
VP Oven Products: Ron Guerra
Quality Control: Andrews Smith
VP Conveyor Products: Jerry Guerra
Estimated Sales: $10 - 20 Million
Number Employees: 100-249
Square Footage: 270000
Brands:
Heat-Pro

25308 Lewis & Clark Company
111 Main Street
Suite 130
Lewiston, ID 83501
208-799-9083
Fax: 208-799-9082 vvision@lewiston.com
A consulting engineering firm
President: Jim Luper
Vice President: Eddy Chapman
Contact: Cheryl Teed
cteed@valleyvision.org
Estimated Sales: $500,000 - $1,000,000
Number Employees: 1-4

25309 Lewis Label Products Corporation
2300 Race St
Fort Worth, TX 76111
817-834-7334
Fax: 817-834-2210 800-772-7728
cmorvan@lewislabel.com www.lewislabel.com
Pressure sensitive labels
Owner: Gibson Lewis
CFO: Gibson Lewis
VP Sales: George Noah
Contact: Carlos Aguirre
caguirre@lewislabel.com
Manager: Cole Morvan
Estimated Sales: $10 - 20 Million
Number Employees: 20-49

25310 Lewis M Carter Mfg Co Inc
Highway 84 W
Donalsonville, GA 39845
229-524-2197
Fax: 229-524-2531 800-332-8232
lmc@lmcarter.com www.lmcarter.com
Manufacturer and exporter of peanut shellers, cleaners, vibratory conveyors, elevators, sizing shakers,
reclaimers, stoners, gravity separators, belt sizers,
bean polishers, blanchers and bean ladders. Also air
pollution controlequipment
President: Lewis Carter Jr
CFO: Gordon Carpenter
gordon.caarpenter@lmcarter.com
Sales Representative: David Sandlin
Sales Manager: Jack Williams, Jr.
Estimated Sales: $10 - 20 Million
Number Employees: 100-249
Square Footage: 600000
Brands:
Lmc

25311 Lewis Packing Company
17480 Shelley Ave
Sandy, OR 97055-8055
503-668-8122
Packaging
Owner: Kris Jones
Estimated Sales: Under $500,000
Number Employees: 1-4

25312 Lewis Steel Works Inc
613 S Main St
Wrens, GA 30833-4534
706-547-6561
Fax: 706-547-3020 800-521-5239
lewisteel@bellsouth.net
www.lewissteelworks.com
Refuse containers
Owner/President: Brian Lewis
Chairman of the Board: R A Lewis
IT: Sharlene Garner
lewisteel@bellsouth.net
Estimated Sales: $10 - 20 Million
Number Employees: 50-99

25313 Lewisburg Container Co
275 W Clay St
P.O. Box 39
Lewisburg, OH 45338-8107
937-962-0101
Fax: 937-962-4504
Corrugated containers
Estimated Sales: $39 Million
Number Employees: 250-499
Square Footage: 384000
Parent Co: Pratt Properties, Inc.

25314 Lewisburg Printing
170 Woodside Ave
Lewisburg, TN 37091-2866
931-359-1526
Fax: 931-270-3112 800-559-1526
info@lpcink.com www.lpcink.com

Manufacturer and exporter of litho sheet labels, point of purchase advertising brochures, posters and manuals
President: Seawell Brandau
CEO: Thomas Hale Hawkins, IV
CEO: Hale Hawkins
VP Sales: Kirk Kelso
Director of Operations: Brian Tankersley
Estimated Sales: $5-10 Million
Number Employees: 50-99

25315 (HQ)Lewtan Industries Corporation
PO Box 2049
Hartford, CT 06145-2049
860-278-9800
Fax: 860-278-9019 lewtan@snet.net
Manufacturer and exporter of advertising specialties and promotional products including coasters, mighty grips, skimmers, clips, emblems, tape measures, mouse pads, calendars, etc
President: Douglas Lewtan
Estimated Sales: $10 Million
Number Employees: 20-49
Square Footage: 74000

25316 Lexel
2901 Shamrock Avenue
Fort Worth, TX 76107-1314
817-332-4061
lexel@flash.net
Wooden containers for shipping and storage
President: Pat Alexander
VP/Manager: Lee Ray Davis
Estimated Sales: $500,000-$1 Million
Number Employees: 4

25317 Lexidyne of Pennsylvania
PO Box 5372
Pittsburgh, PA 15206-0372
412-661-4526
Fax: 858-815-7346 800-543-2233
General Manager: Rick Simoni
Number Employees: 10-19

25318 Lexington Logistics LLC
N7660 Industrial Rd
Portage, WI 53901-9451
608-742-5303
Fax: 608-742-9153 800-356-8150
hbreezer@trienda.com www.trienda.com
Plastic thermoformed pallets, self-palletizing shipping systems and material handling devices
President: Curtis Zamec
curtis.zamec@trienda.com
VP Sales/Marketing: Rob Klinko
Number Employees: 250-499
Square Footage: 1000000
Brands:
Dc Distribution Center
Enviropal/Recy
Load Locker
Weight Lifter
Wolf Pak

25319 Lexington Logistics LLC
N7660 Industrial Rd
Portage, WI 53901-9451
608-742-5303
Fax: 608-742-9153 800-356-8150
hbreezer@trienda.com www.trienda.com
Plastic, material handling products
President: Curtis Zamec
curtis.zamec@trienda.com
CFO: Jim Masterangelo
VP Marketing: Bob Shimmel
Plant Mgr: David Fiddes
Number Employees: 250-499

25320 Lexington Logistics LLC
N7660 Industrial Rd
Portage, WI 53901-9451
608-742-5303
Fax: 608-742-9153 800-356-8150
bklimko@wilbertinc.com www.trienda.com
President: Curtis Zamec
curtis.zamec@trienda.com
Marketing Manager: Paul Schoeder
Sales Director: Rick Sasse
Estimated Sales: $1 - 5 Million
Number Employees: 250-499
Square Footage: 1200000
Parent Co: Wilbert

25321 Leyman Manufacturing Corporation
10900 Kenwood Rd
Cincinnati, OH 45242
513-891-6210
Fax: 513-891-4901 866-539-6261
www.leymanlift.com
Manufacturer, importer and exporter of trailer and truck loading and unloading equipment, hydraulic lifts, elevators, tailgates, platforms, carts, dollies and van bodies
President: John McHenry
Marketing: Joann Russo
VP Sales: Chip Drews
Contact: Larry Disque
ldisque@leymanlift.com
Estimated Sales: $20-50 Million
Number Employees: 50-99
Type of Packaging: Food Service
Other Locations:
Leyman Manufacturing Corp.
Cincinnati OH

25322 Libbey Inc.
300 Madison Ave.
Toledo, OH 43604
419-325-2100
Fax: 419-325-2749 info@libbey.com
www.libbey.com
Table glassware.
Chairman/CEO: William Foley
william.foley@libbey.com
Senior VP/CFO: Jim Burmeister
Vice President/Chief Information Officer: Dave Anderson
Year Founded: 1818
Estimated Sales: $797.9 Million
Number Employees: 6,230
Number of Brands: 8
Brands:
Crisa
Libbey
Lunita
Pyrorey
Royal Leerdam
Santa Elenita
Syracuse China
World Tableware

25323 Libby Canada
Unit 26
Mississauga, ON L5L 4M1
Canada
905-607-8280
Fax: 905-607-8130 www.libbey.com
China, glassware, flatware and hollowware
CEO: John Mayer
National Accounts Manager: Giulio Accardi
Number Employees: 10
Square Footage: 10400
Parent Co: Libby
Brands:
Syracuse

25324 Liberty Carton Co.
870 Louisiana Ave. S.
Golden Valley, MN 55426
763-540-9600
800-328-1784
www.libertycarton.com
Specialty packaging, displays, promotional items, and gifts.
Year Founded: 1918
Estimated Sales: $100 Million
Number Employees: 100-249
Parent Co: Liberty Diversified International

25325 Liberty Distributing Inc
909 Valley Ave NW
Puyallup, WA 98371-2517
253-922-8506
Fax: 253-922-5107 888-882-8506
www.libertydistributing.com
Distributor of dairy for wholesalers including; milk, cottage cheese, butter, sour cream, ice cream, non-dairy sour cream, cheese, margarine, eggs, yogurt, creamers, chocolate milk & syrups, apple, orange & grape juices, organic milkssoft serve, flavored milk powders, ice cream topper sauces, buttermilk, tea, bread & buns, ice
Owner: Ed Interbitzen
ed@libertydistributing.com
Estimated Sales: $430,000
Number Employees: 20-49

Type of Packaging: Consumer, Food Service, Private Label, Bulk

25326 Liberty Engineering Co
10567 Main St
Roscoe, IL 61073-8830
815-623-7677
Fax: 815-623-7050 877-623-9065
info@libertyengineering.com
www.libertyengineering.com
Manufacturer and exporter of rotary dies, candy molds, starch molding processing equipment and depositing pumps
President: Brian Belardi
bbelardi@libertyengineering.com
Engineering Manager: John Micinski
Quality Control: Rob Klein
Plant Manager: John Akelaitis
Estimated Sales: Below $5 Million
Number Employees: 10-19
Square Footage: 40000
Parent Co: Libco Industries

25327 Liberty Food Svc
1410 Michigan St
Storm Lake, IA 50588-1961
712-732-6379
Fax: 713-732-3325 800-425-1088
www.libertyfoodservice.com
Owner: Tom Agan
Corporate Finance Manager: Liza Gunnerson
Sales/Customer Service Manager: Cindi Daufeldt
tom@libertyfoodservice.com
Estimated Sales: Less Than $500,000
Number Employees: 5-9

25328 Liberty Label
101 W Shrader St
Liberty, MO 64068-2464
816-781-6717
Fax: 620-223-2201 800-783-5285
www.libertylabelsinc.com
Pressure sensitive labels
Estimated Sales: $500,000-$1 Million
Number Employees: 5-9

25329 Liberty Machine Company
125 Derry Court
York, PA 17406-8405
717-848-1493
Fax: 800-745-8150 800-745-8152
Manufacturer and exporter of wire racks and grilles for refrigerators, ovens, etc.; also, wire material handling equipment
President: Brad Stump
Secretary/Treasurer: Patti Miller
Estimated Sales: $3 - 5 Million
Number Employees: 20
Square Footage: 36000
Type of Packaging: Food Service

25330 Liberty Ware LLC
PO Box 160450
Clearfield, UT 84016-0450
801-825-5885
Fax: 801-825-5875 888-500-5885
bbbrisko@aol.com
Manufacturer, importer and exporter of frying and stock pans, flatware, thermometers, disposable gloves and aprons, tongs, ladles, salt and pepper shakers and portion control equipment
Owner: Robert Brisko
rbrisko@libertywareusa.com
Estimated Sales: $1 - 2,500,000
Number Employees: 10-19
Brands:
Libertyware

25331 Libman Co
220 N Sheldon St
Arcola, IL 61910-1616
217-268-4200
Fax: 217-268-3422 877-818-3380
info@libman.com www.libman.com
Cleaning supplies including brushes, brooms, mops, scrubbers, etc
President: Derek Arndt
darndt@libman.com
CFO: William Libman
VP Sales/Marketing: Kim Spafford
Treasurer: William Libman
Estimated Sales: $1 - 2.5 Million
Number Employees: 250-499

Brands:
   Libman

25332 (HQ)Libra Technical Center
101 Liberty St
Metuchen, NJ 08840-1215

732-321-5200
Fax: 32 -21 -203

Manufacturer and marketer of propietary, patented tests for estimation and measurement of chemical characteristics of fats and oils, especially with regard to degradation during deep-fat frying. Kits are correlated with OfficialMethods and are available for measurement fo Total Polar Materials, Free Fatty Acids, and ppm alkaline surfactants/soaps (Water Emulsion Titratables)
President: Michael Blumenthal PhD
Executive VP: Trean Blumenthal
Marketing/Sales: Ken Salzinger
Estimated Sales: $.5 - 1 million
Number Employees: 1-4
Number of Brands: 1
Type of Packaging: Food Service
Other Locations:
   Libra Technologies
   Metuchen NJ
Brands:
   Veri-Fry
   Veri-Fry Pro

25333 Liburdi Group of Companies
2599 Charlotte Highway
Mooresville, NC 28117

704-230-2510
Fax: 704-230-2555 800-533-9353
info@liburdidimetrics.com www.liburdi.com

Orbital welding equipment for tubes and pipes
President: Joe Liburdi
Estimated Sales: $3 Million
Number Employees: 20-49

25334 License Ad Plate Co
13110 Enterprise Ave
Cleveland, OH 44135-5102

216-265-4200
Fax: 216-265-4203 lapco@stratos.net
www.laline.net

Metal and plastic signs, pressure sensitive and thermal die cut decals, vinyls, mylars, scotchlite, frames, etc
President: Richard Russell
Estimated Sales: Below $5 Million
Number Employees: 5-9
Square Footage: 12000

25335 Licker Candy Company
1600 E Second Street
Winslow, AZ 86047-4456

520-289-4815
Fax: 520-289-9415

25336 Lido Roasters
3215 Brooklawn Ter
Chevy Chase, MD 20815-3936

301-718-9719
Fax: 301-718-9735

Tea and coffee roasters

25337 Life Spice & Ingredients LLC
216 W Chicago Ave # 2
Chicago, IL 60654-3100

312-274-0073
www.lifespiceingredients.com

Spices.
President: Peter Garvy
   pgarvy@lifespiceingredients.com
Vice President of Sales & Marketing: Lisa Stern
Vice President of Operations: Michael Mastrangelo
Estimated Sales: $25 Million
Number Employees: 11-50

25338 Lifeline Technology Inc
116 the American Rd
Morris Plains, NJ 07950-2443

973-984-0525
Fax: 973-984-1520 info@temptimecorp.com

Self-adhesive time/temperature indicator labels that monitor the cummulative effect of heat over time
Chairman: Jean-Paul Martin
VP: Ted Prusik
Estimated Sales: $2.5-5 Million
Number Employees: 20-49
Number of Brands: 2

Number of Products: 2
Square Footage: 80000
Type of Packaging: Consumer, Food Service, Private Label, Bulk
Brands:
   Fresh-Check
   Fresh-Scan
   Heatmaker Uvm

25339 (HQ)Lifetime Brands Inc
1000 Stewart Ave
Garden City, NY 11530-4814

516-683-6000
Fax: 516-555-0101
questions@lifetimebrands.com
www.lifetimebrands.com

Exporter, importer and manufacturer of cutlery and gadgets
President: Steven Lizak
Chairman of the Board: Jeffrey Siegel
CFO: Rob Roknznally
VP: Bruce Cohen
VP: Larry Sklute
Number Employees: 1000-4999
Square Footage: 800
Brands:
   Armstrong Forge
   Avanti
   Barclay Geneve
   Carver Aid
   Color Brights
   Color Charms
   Colorgems
   Cordon Bleu
   Country Christmas
   Golden Barclay Geneve
   Heartland
   Jet Cut
   L C Germain
   Marmalade
   Old Homestead
   Paris Splendor
   Pierre Santini
   Pro/Star
   Rack-The-Knife
   Santa Fe
   Southwest
   Sugar Plum
   Tristar
   Welcome Home
   Windy

25340 Lifoam Industries LLC
2 5th St
Peabody, MA 01960-4916

978-278-0008
Fax: 978-278-0015 800-832-4725

Packaging; insulated foam boxes and refrigerated jello packs
President: Bruce Trusdale
Manager: Randy Caraway
   rcar@lifoam.com
Estimated Sales: $10-20 Million
Number Employees: 50-99

25341 Lift Rite
5975 Falbourne Street - Unit 3
Mississauga, ON L5R 3L8
Canada

905-456-2603
Fax: 905-456-1383 www.liftrite.com

Manufacturer and exporter of stackers, pallet trucks, easy lifts and hi-lifters
President: Mel Griffin
Number Employees: 90

25342 Liftomatic Material Handling
700 Dartmouth Ln
Buffalo Grove, IL 60089-6902

847-325-2930
Fax: 847-325-2959 800-837-6540
sales@liftomatic.com www.liftomatic.com

Manufacturer and exporter of drum handlers, lift truck attachments and lifting equipment
President: Todd Berg
   tpberg@liftomatic.com
Sales Manager: E Darren Berg
Inside Sales: Angela Foster
Estimated Sales: $3-5,000,000
Number Employees: 10-19
Square Footage: 34000
Brands:
   Ergo-Matic
   Parrot-Beak

25343 Light Technology Ind
811 Russell Ave # 302
Suite 302
Gaithersburg, MD 20879-3518

301-990-4050
Fax: 301-990-7525 sales@ltindustries.com
www.ltindustries.com

Manufacturer and exporter of control systems and instrumentation for quality control measurements in labs and on line, including, liquid, solid, powders, pellets, etc.
President: Aviva Landa
Marketing Director: Aviva Landa
Estimated Sales: $1-5 Million
Number Employees: 10-19

25344 Light Waves Concept
the Esquire Building 41st St
4100 1st Ave 3rd Floor North
Brooklyn, NY 11232

212-677-5230
Fax: 347-416-6201 800-670-8137
customerservice@lightwavesconcept.com
www.lightwavesconcept.com

Manufacturer, importer and exporter of lighting fixtures and low voltage track lighting
President: Joel Slavis
Estimated Sales: Below $5 Million
Number Employees: 10-19
Square Footage: 12000
Brands:
   Lightwaves

25345 Lighthouse for the Blindin New Orleans
123 State St
New Orleans, LA 70118

504-899-4501
Fax: 504-895-4162 clee@lhb.org
www.lhb.org

Brooms, brushes, cotton and rayon mops, scrubbers and household textile items; also, remanufactured laser printer cartridges
President: Bill Crist
CEO: Bill Price
Contact: Mary Anderson
   manderson@lhb.org
Controller: Ron Wattigny
Estimated Sales: $10 - 20 Million
Number Employees: 50-99
Square Footage: 800000
Brands:
   Lighthouse
   Skilcraft

25346 Lightolier
631 Airport Rd.
Fall River, MA 02720

508-679-8131
Fax: 508-674-4710 www.lightolier.com

Lighting fixtures.
Year Founded: 1904
Estimated Sales: $100-500 Million
Number Employees: 250-499
Parent Co: Genlyte Group

25347 Lights On
1960 Central Park Ave
Yonkers, NY 10710

914-961-0588
Fax: 914-961-0589

Manufacturer, importer and exporter of lighting fixtures
Manager: Glenn Aroni
Estimated Sales: Less than $500,000
Number Employees: 10-19
Square Footage: 6000

25348 Lignetics Inc
31756 Highway 200 E
Sandpoint, ID 83864

208-263-0564
Fax: 208-263-9292 800-544-3834
www.lignetics.com

Barbecue pellets for pellet grills and flavor enhancers for charcoal
President: Ken Tucker
   kent@lignetics.com
General Manager: Lyle Wiese
Regional Manager: Kevin Schaper
VP Sales/Marketing: Bob Wilson
Sales/Traffic Coordinator: Lindsay Turner

Estimated Sales: $2 Million
Number Employees: 20-49
Parent Co: Lignetics
Brands:
  Bbq Pellets
  Grill Master

25349 Lil' Orbits
2850 Vicksburg Ln N
Minneapolis, MN 55447

763-559-7505
Fax: 763-559-7545 800-228-8305
contact@lilorbits.com www.lilorbits.com
Manufacturer and exporter of vending carts, displays
and automatic doughnut and crepe/pancake ma-
chines and accessories
Founder: Ed Anderson
  e.anderon@lilorbits.com
President: Charlie Anderson
Vice President: Brian OGara
Marketing: Mike Foster
Sales: Brian O'Gara
Office Manager: Sue Larson
Service Production Manager: Terry OGara
Purchasing: Terry O'Gara
Estimated Sales: $3 - 5 Million
Number Employees: 10-19
Number of Brands: 2
Number of Products: 10
Square Footage: 100000
Brands:
  Lil' Orbits
  Orbie
  Uni-Matic

25350 Lillsun Manufacturing Co
1350 Harris St
PO Box 767
Huntington, IN 46750-4302

260-356-6514
Fax: 260-356-8337 mail@lillsun.com
www.lillsun.com
Manufacturer and exporter of bakers' woodenware
including pizza and oven peels, paddles and proof-
ing boards
President: Bill Sundermann
  mail@lillsun.com
VP: W Sunderman
Estimated Sales: $1-2.5 Million
Number Employees: 5-9

25351 Lillsun Manufacturing Co
1350 Harris St
PO Box 767
Huntington, IN 46750-4302

260-356-6514
Fax: 260-356-8337 mail@lillsun.com
www.lillsun.com
Baker's woodenware; pizza and oven peels
President: Bill Sundermann
  mail@lillsun.com
CEO: Gregory Williams
VP: Carrie Williams
Estimated Sales: $1-2.5 Million
Number Employees: 5-9

25352 Lima Barrel & Drum Company
1140 Franklin St
Lima, OH 45804

419-224-8916
Fax: 419-227-3424
New and reconditioned steel drums, barrels and con-
tainers
President: Randy Hersh
Estimated Sales: $5 - 10 Million
Number Employees: 10-19

25353 Lima Sheet Metal
1001 Bowman Rd
Lima, OH 45804-3409

419-229-1161
Fax: 419-229-8538 www.limasheetmetal.com
Food processing and canning equipment; also, safety
guards, ladders and platforms; repair service avail-
able
President: Bo Emerick
  emerick_steve@yahoo.com
Vice President and Senior Fabricator: Tom Emerick
Office Manager: Anne Emerick
Estimated Sales: $1-2.5 Million
Number Employees: 10-19
Square Footage: 44000

25354 Limoneira Co
1141 Cummings Rd
Santa Paula, CA 93060-9783

805-525-5541
Fax: 805-525-8761 info@limoneira.com
www.limoneira.com
Packing house for Sunkist Growers, Inc. citrus fruit.
President/CEO: Harold Edwards
VP/Finance & Administration: Don Delmatoff
Senior VP: Alex M Teague
  amteague@limoneira.com
Business Development Manager: David McCoy
Marketing Director: John Chamberlain
Director Packing & Sales: Tomas Gonzales
Director Information Systems: Eric Tovias
Agritourism Operations Manager: Ryan Nasalroad
Estimated Sales: $20 Million
Number Employees: 250-499
Type of Packaging: Food Service

25355 Lin Engineering Inc
16245 Vineyard Blvd
Morgan Hill, CA 95037-7123

408-919-0200
Fax: 408-919-0201 sales@linengineering.com
www.linengineering.com
Supplier of stepping moulder
President: Ted Lin
  tlin@linengineering.com
Accounting: Emma Lin
Quality Control: Rob Carl
Estimated Sales: $1 - 2.5 Million
Number Employees: 5-9

25356 (HQ)Lin Pac Plastics
200 Windrift Court
3
Roswell, GA 30076-3727

770-751-6006
Fax: 770-751-7154
Manufacturer and exporter of plastic egg cartons and
food service packaging containers; also, processing
and packaging trays
Sales/Marketing Manager: James Gullo
Other Locations:
  Lin Pac Plastics
  Sebring FL

25357 LinPac
6842 Templin Ct
San Angelo, TX 76904-4112

325-651-7378
Fax: 325-651-7482 800-453-7393
Manufacturer and exporter of corrugated boxes and
other packaging materials
President: Robert Hanton
Quality Control: Alvin Kennedy
R&D: Sal Flores
President: Nigel Roe
Plant Manager: Danny Lopez
Estimated Sales: $10 - 20 Million
Number Employees: 20-49
Square Footage: 100000
Parent Co: LinPac

25358 Lincoln
One Lincoln Way
St Louis, MO 63120

314-679-4200
Fax: 314-679-4359 www.lincolnindustrial.com
World leader in the manufacturer and sale of lubrica-
tion systems and industrial pumping equipment for
industry
President: Bart Aitke
Contact: Wayne Chew
  wchew@lincare.com
Number Employees: 500-999

25359 Lincoln Coders Corp
2815 Independence Dr
PO Box 8009
Fort Wayne, IN 46808-1326

260-482-8493
Fax: 260-483-2407 800-248-4452
sales@lincolncoders.com www.lincolncoders.com
Carton coders and rubber type and ink rolls
President: Robert Beaver
Estimated Sales: $1-2.5 Million
Number Employees: 10-19

25360 Lincoln Foodservice
1333 East 179th Street
Cleveland, OH 44110

260-459-8200
Fax: 800-285-9511 800-374-3004
www.lincolnfp.com
Designs, manufactures, and markets commercial and
institutional foodservice cooking equipment, serving
systems, and utensils. the company also manufac-
tures and markets a line of electric Fresh-O-Matic
food steamers.
President: Charlie Kingdon
Plant Manager: Jim Muston
Purchasing Manager: Tom Hengy
Number Employees: 250-499
Brands:
  Centurion
  Fresh-O-Matic
  Impinger
  Impinger a La Carte
  Redco
  Traditionalware
  Wear-Ever

25361 Lincoln Suppliers
1225 County Road 45 North
Owatonna, MN 55060

507-451-7410
Fax: 507-451-2968 800-622-8425
www.lincolnsuppliers.com
Agitation systems, milk, silo, tank, aseptic processing equipment, batch control systems, cheese equipment, washer and drier chillers, fillers, milk, steam,
heat exchangers, plate, scraped surface, homogenizers, margarine processingequipment, piping, fi
President: Michael Grunwald
Estimated Sales: $5 - 10 Million
Number Employees: 20-49

25362 Lincoln Tent Inc
3900 Cornhusker Hwy # 1
Suite 1
Lincoln, NE 68504-1581

402-464-1900
Fax: 402-467-4907 800-567-4559
inquiries@lincolntent.com www.lincolntent.com
Commercial awnings
Owner: Tom Miller
  inquiries@lincolntent.com
Estimated Sales: $2.5 - 5 Million
Number Employees: 20-49

25363 Linde North America
575 Mountain Ave
Murray Hill, NJ 07974

908-464-8100
Fax: 908-417-5699 www.linde.com
Gases and whole industrial welding equipment
Executive VP, Americas: Andreas Opfermann
Estimated Sales: $250 Million
Number Employees: 100-249

25364 Line of Snacks Consultants
13220 Castleton Dr
Dallas, TX 75234-5113

972-484-1155
Fax: 972-243-3974
Consultant providing services to the snack industry
worldwide for processing, technology, management,
marketing, distribution and new product
development
President: Donald Petty
Estimated Sales: Below $5 Million
Number Employees: 1-4
Square Footage: 2800

25365 Line-Master Products
PO Box 407
Cocolalla, ID 83813-0407

208-265-4743
Fax: 208-265-9393
Manufacturer and exporter of work benches, push
carts and fixed and mobile material handling racks
President: Jackie Warren
Estimated Sales: $1-2.5 Million
Number Employees: 5-9
Parent Co: Sandefur Engineering Company

25366 LineSource
600 Berkshire Avenue
Springfield, MA 01109-1052

413-747-9488
Fax: 413-746-4498

Food processing equipment; custom design services available
President: William Stotler
Vice President: Ken Bonardi
Sales/Marketing: Les Parkos
Estimated Sales: $1 - 3,000,000
Number Employees: 5-9
Type of Packaging: Consumer, Food Service, Private Label

25367 (HQ)Linear Lighting Corp
3130 Hunters Point Ave
Long Island City, NY 11101-3132
718-361-7552
Fax: 718-937-2747 mike@linearltg.com
Manufacturer and exporter of lighting fixtures
President: Larry Deutsch
larry@linearltg.com
CFO: Lois Shorr
R&D: Kewin Ehrhardt
Estimated Sales: $20 - 50 Million
Number Employees: 100-249

25368 Linett Company
390 Fountain St
Blawnox, PA 15238
412-826-8531
Fax: 800-530-8329 800-565-2165
Strapping dispensers, castered stocking ladders, oily waste cans, special access ladders, crossovers and carts
President: Fred Schwartz
Vice President: Melvin Solomon
Marketing Director: Ronald Schwartz
Contact: Lynn Waxler
lynn@tri-arc.com
Manager Operations: Nick Valore
Purchasing Manager: Chris Gianfrancesco
Estimated Sales: $10-20 Million
Number Employees: 130
Square Footage: 650000
Brands:
Castered Safety
Conveyor Crossovers
Ladder Crossovers
Tri-Arc Manufacturing

25369 Linette
PO Box 212
Womelsdorf, PA 19567-0212
610-589-4526
Fax: 610-589-2706
VP: James P Linette
Number Employees: 100-249

25370 Linker Equipment Corporation
5 Evans Terminal
Hillside, NJ 07205
908-353-0700
Fax: 908-353-1621 www.linkercorp.com
Owner, President: David Linker
Regional Manager: Rungkun Roeksangsri
Contact: Barry Brothers
linkercorp@aol.com
Estimated Sales: $10,000,000 - $25,000,000
Number Employees: 100 - 250

25371 Linker Machines
20 Pine St
Rockaway, NJ 07866-3131
973-983-0001
Fax: 973-983-0011 sales@linkermachines.com
www.linkermachines.com
Manufacturer and exporter of automatic sausage linking and peeling machinery; also, general purpose grease
Owner: Jean Hebrank
sales@linkermachines.com
VP: R Hebrank
General Manager: Rob Hebrank, Jr.
Estimated Sales: $2.5-5 Million
Number Employees: 1-4
Square Footage: 8000
Brands:
Linkerlube
Ty-Linker
Ty-Peeler

25372 Linnea's Cake & Candy Supplies
975 Oak St
San Bernardino, CA 92410-2424
909-885-1446
Fax: 909-383-7201 sales@linneasinc.com
www.linneasinc.com

Candy, cake supplies, candy boxes, molds and all ingredients needed for cake and candy manufacturing
Manager: Mike Peterson
CFO: Polly Holman
Manager: Mike Peterson
Quality Control: Frank Romocean
Manager: Christopher Romocean
cromocean@linneasinc.com
Estimated Sales: Below $5 Million
Number Employees: 5-9
Parent Co: Linnea's Candy & Cake Supplies

25373 Linnea's Candy & Cake Supplies
4149 Karg Industrial Pkwy
Kent, OH 44240-6425
330-678-7112
Fax: 330-678-7133 www.linneasinc.com
Candy and cake supplies
Owner: Linnea Romocean
linnea@linneasinc.com
Estimated Sales: $5 - 10 Million
Number Employees: 10-19

25374 Linpac Materials Handling
3626 N Hall Street
Suite 729
Dallas, TX 75219-5127
214-599-9023
Fax: 214-599-9024 www.linpac.com
Supplier of reusable food containers to the supermarket industry

25375 Linpac Plastics
600 Corporate Drive
Suite 450
Fort Lauderdale, FL 33334-3606
954-492-5481
Fax: 954-489-0512 darin_gregg@linpac.com
www.linpac.com
Vice President of Marketing: Adam Barnett
Number Employees: 9

25376 Linvar
237 Hamilton St
Suite 202
Hartford, CT 6106
860-951-3818
Fax: 860-951-3547 800-282-5288
Manufacturer and exporter of metal shelving systems and plastic containers
Vice President: John Ramondetta
General Manager: John Ahern
Estimated Sales: $5 - 10 Million
Number Employees: 10-19
Square Footage: 50000
Brands:
Linbin's
Linshelf

25377 Linx Xymark
16 Lakeside Drive
Marlton, NJ 08053-2705
856-988-7125
Fax: 856-988-7126
Estimated Sales: $1 - 5 Million

25378 (HQ)Linzer Products Corp
248 Wyandanch Ave
West Babylon, NY 11704-1506
631-253-3333
Fax: 631-253-9750 800-423-3254
www.linzerproducts.com
Manufacturer and exporter of confectioners' and bakers' brushes and rollers
President: Alan Benson
CEO: Mark Aaronson
elliottw@linzerproducts.com
VP Sales: Brent Swenson
VP Production: Sidney Zichvin
Number Employees: 100-249
Type of Packaging: Consumer

25379 Lion Apparel Inc
7200 Poe Ave # 400
Suite 400
Dayton, OH 45414-2798
937-898-1949
Fax: 937-898-2848 800-548-6614
www.lionprotects.com
Uniforms including work clothing, shirts, trousers, outerwear, cashiers' aprons and smocks

CEO: Stephen Schwartz
VP, Finance: Deanna Jensen
Chief Technology Officer: Mark Boyed
VP, Operations: Dave Cook
Estimated Sales: $66 Million
Number Employees: 100-249
Square Footage: 37000
Parent Co: Lion Apparel

25380 Lion Labels Inc
15 Hampden Dr
South Easton, MA 02375-1159
508-230-8211
Fax: 508-230-8116 800-875-5300
epage@lionlabels.com www.lionlabels.com
Manufacturer and exporter of signage, pressure sensitive labels and decals
President: Jerome Berke
jberke@lionlabels.com
CEO: Michael Berke
CFO: Nina Berke
Sales Director: Moe Decelles
Operations Manager: Ed Page
Production Manager: Bruce Boteliao
Estimated Sales: $4.7 Million
Number Employees: 20-49
Square Footage: 58000
Type of Packaging: Consumer, Food Service, Private Label, Bulk

25381 Lion Laboratories
139 Mill Rock Road E
Old Saybrook, CT 06475-4217
860-388-6911
Fax: 860-388-6216
Non-invasive authenticity testing

25382 Lion/Circle Corp
4600 W 72nd St # 1
Chicago, IL 60629-5881
773-284-3666
Fax: 773-284-3654 info@lioncircle.com
Advertising novelties and specialties including buttons, balloons, key tags, etc.
President: Phillip Carollo
pcarollo@lioncircle.com
Sales/Marketing Executive: Rich Carollo
Purchasing Agent: Mike Webber
Estimated Sales: $1 - 5 Million
Number Employees: 20-49
Square Footage: 180000

25383 (HQ)Liqui-Box
901 E. Byrd St.
Suite 1105
Richmond, VA 23219
804-325-1400
www.liquibox.com
Food and industrial plastic packaging and packaging systems.
President/CEO: Ken Swanson
Chief Financial Officer: Ron Lueptow
Chief Operating Officer: Andrew McLeland
Chief Commercial Officer: Kevin Grogan
Year Founded: 1961
Estimated Sales: $128.6 Million
Number Employees: 684

25384 Liqui-Box Corp
901 E Byrd St # 1105
Richmond, VA 23219-4068
804-325-1400
Fax: 614-888-0982 804-325-1400
liquibox@liquibox.com
Manufacturer and exporter of form, fill and seal pouch packaging machinery; also, bag-in-box, retort and dispenser systems
CEO: Terry Barfield
tbarfield@hillcresttransportation.com
Plant Manager: Barry Pritchard
Estimated Sales: $5-10 Million
Number Employees: 500-999
Parent Co: Liqui-Box Corporation

25385 Liquid Assets
1421 Grove Street
Healdsburg, CA 95448-4711
707-527-9308
Fax: 707-527-9306 800-730-1030
Wine industry stainless steel tanks

25386 Liquid Controls LLC

105 Albrecht Dr
Lake Bluff, IL 60044-2242

847-295-1050
Fax: 847-295-8252 800-458-5262
lc-info.lcmeter@idexcorp.com www.lcmeter.com
Blending and batching equipment, flow meters and
process control instrumentation
President: Matt Stillings
General Manager: Fred Niemeier
Global VP Sales & Marketing: John Thompson
VP Sales: Royal Wollberg
Number Employees: 250-499
Parent Co: IDEX Corporation

25387 Liquid Sampling Systems

416 Jacolyn Dr NW
Cedar Rapids, IA 52405-3407

319-365-2259
Fax: 319-365-2259 rob@pro-rata.com
www.pro-rata.com
Fluid sampling instrument sales and manufacturing
Owner: Robert Johnson
Estimated Sales: Below $5 Million
Number Employees: 1-4

25388 Liquid Scale

2033 Old Highway 8 NW
New Brighton, MN 55112

651-633-2969
Fax: 651-633-2969 888-633-2969
Manufacturer and exporter of milk silo air agitators,
liquid level gauges and controls and needlepoint
dividers
Estimated Sales: Under$300,000
Number Employees: 1-4
Square Footage: 6000
Brands:
  Liquid Scale
  Shimp

25389 Liquid Scale

2033 Old Highway 8 NW
New Brighton, MN 55112

651-633-2969
Fax: 651-633-2969 888-633-2969
Liquid level gauges
President: Dale J Tilden
Estimated Sales: Less than $500,000
Number Employees: 1-4

25390 (HQ)Liquid Solids Control Inc

10 Farm St
Upton, MA 01568-1665

508-529-3377
Fax: 508-529-6591
paulb@liquidsolidscontrol.com
www.liquidsolidscontrol.com
Manufacturer and exporter of in-line process control
refractomers for continuous measurement and pro-
duction; also, quality assurance of dissolved food
solids available
President: Paul R Bonneau
usa@liquidsolidscontrol.com
CFO: Paul R Bonneau
VP: Gordon Vandenburg
Estimated Sales: $10 - 20 Million
Number Employees: 10-19
Square Footage: 50000
Other Locations:
  Liquid Solids Control
  Victoria BC
Brands:
  Lsc Model 614
  Lsc Model 725

25391 Liquitane

910 7th Ave
Berwick, PA 18603-1127

570-759-6200
Fax: 570-759-6254 www.ccrllc.com
Plastic bottles and containers
Plant Manager: Bryan Statskey
Estimated Sales: $20-50 Million
Number Employees: 100-249
Parent Co: Liquitane

25392 Lista International Corp

106 Lowland St
Holliston, MA 01746-2094

508-429-1350
Fax: 508-626-0353 800-722-3020
sales@listaintl.com www.listaintl.com
Storage and workbench products.

President: Peter Lariviere
CFO: David Gavlik
Vice President: John Alfieri
Marketing: Anne Swagoriusky
Sales: John Alfieri
Estimated Sales: $50-100 Million
Number Employees: 100-249
Number of Brands: 2
Square Footage: 225000
Parent Co: Stanley Black & Decker
Brands:
  Storage Wall

25393 Listo Pencil Corp

1925 Union St
Alameda, CA 94501-1345

510-522-2910
Fax: 510-522-3798 800-547-8648
sales@listo.com www.listo.com
Manufacturer and exporter of mechanical marking
pencils, carton openers and industrial razor blades
President: Rick Stuart
rick@listo.com
VP: Rick Stuart
Estimated Sales: Less Than $500,000
Number Employees: 1-4
Square Footage: 34000
Brands:
  Listo

25394 Litchfield Packaging Machinery

71 Benedict Rd
Morris, CT 06763-1117

860-567-2011
Fax: 860-567-2012 www.litchfieldpackaging.com
Beverage packaging equipment
President: Ric Edwards
Contact: Rick Edwards
  lpm@litchfieldpackaging.com
Estimated Sales: Below $5 Million
Number Employees: 5-9
Type of Packaging: Bulk

25395 Litco International Inc

1 Litco Dr
Vienna, OH 44473-9600

330-539-5433
Fax: 330-539-5388 800-236-1903
info@litco.com www.litco.com
Supplier of export pallets, seperator sheets and air
bags for the food industry also a supplier of export
and domestic pallet solutions and load securement
products.
President: Gary Trebilcock
  gary@litco.com
CEO: Lionel Trebilcock
VP Sales: Gary Sharon
Estimated Sales: $5 Million
Number Employees: 10-19

25396 Lite-Weight Tool & Mfg Co

8621 San Fernando Rd
Sun Valley, CA 91352-3104

818-767-7901
Fax: 818-767-0010 800-859-3529
info@liteweighttool.com www.liteweighttool.com
Manufacturer and exporter of squeegees including
emulsion spreading, handheld and floor
President: C R Brunson
VP: Andy Brunson
Estimated Sales: $500,000
Number Employees: 1-4
Square Footage: 10000

25397 Litecontrol

65 Spring St
Plympton, MA 02367-1701

781-294-0164
Fax: 781-293-2849 www.litecontrol.com
Manufacturer and exporter of lighting fixtures
President/CEO: Brian Golden
  brian.golden@litecontrol.com
Senior Accountant: Kristen Woods
VP/Sales: Vince Santini
R&D: Paul Duane
Quality Control: James Pierce
Marketing Manager: Cory Passerello
Sales: Vince Santini
Project Manager: Barbara Goodwin
Estimated Sales: $5 - 10 Million
Number Employees: 100-249

25398 Lithibar Matik

13521 Quality Drive
Holland, MI 49424-8465

616-399-5215
Fax: 616-399-4026 800-626-0415
sales@besser.com
Bag and case pallets
Estimated Sales: $10 - 15 Million
Number Employees: 50-100

25399 Lithonia Lighting

1400 Lester Rd NW
Conyers, GA 30012-3908

770-922-9000
Fax: 770-483-2635 comments@lithonia.com
www.lithonia.com
Manufacturer and exporter of electric and fluores-
cent lighting fixtures
President: Vern Nagel
CFO: Wesley Wittich
wes.wittich@acuitybrands.com
Number Employees: 20-49

25400 Little Giant Pump Company

9255 Covedale Rd.
Fort Wayne, IN 46809

260-824-2900
Fax: 260-824-2909 www.littlegiant.com
Decorative and outdoor lighting fixtures, and water
removal and transfer pumps.
Chairman/CEO, Franklin Electric: Gregg Sengstack
Estimated Sales: $100-500 Million
Number Employees: 500-999
Square Footage: 270000
Parent Co: Franklin Electric

25401 Little Rock Broom Works

7710 Jamison Rd
Little Rock, AR 72209-5541

501-562-0311
Fax: 501-562-3887
House and whisk brooms; also, mop heads and
sticks
Owner: Evert Hatcher
Estimated Sales: $2.5-5 Million
Number Employees: 20-49

25402 Little Rock Crate & Basket Co

1623 E 14th St
Little Rock, AR 72202-4296

501-376-6961
Fax: 501-372-6252 800-223-7823
Fruit and vegetable shipping containers, wire bound
crates for shrimp, fish and vegetables and veneer
and novelty fruit baskets
President: William Swann
dbasketman@aol.com
Estimated Sales: $10 - 20 Million
Number Employees: 50-99
Parent Co: Little Rock Crate & Basket Company

25403 Little Rock Sign

1117 Highway 365 S
Conway, AR 72032-9288

501-372-7403
Fax: 501-327-4337
www.littlerockconwaysign.homestead.com
Advertising, electric and plastic signs
Owner: Bob Whitehouse
  bob@littlerockconwaysign.com
General Manager: Laverne Anderson
Estimated Sales: $1 - 2.5 Million
Number Employees: 10-19

25404 Little Squirt

10 Compass Court
Toronto, ON M1S 5R3
Canada

416-665-6605
Fax: 416-665-5631
Portion controlled and refrigerated cream/milk dis-
pensers
President: Garnet Rich
R&D: Bryan Symonds
Number Employees: 40
Brands:
  Little Squirt

25405 Littleford Day

PO Box 128
Florence, KY 41022-0128

859-525-7600
Fax: 859-525-1446 800-365-8555
sales@littleford.com www.littleford.com

Food processing equipment including mixers, granulators, sterilizers, agglomerators, vacuum dryers, liquid dispensers and pressure cookers; importer and exporter of mixers, dryers and sterilizers
President & CEO: Charles Kroeger
Research & Development: Glen Vice
Marketing & Sales: William R Barker
Contact: Steve Grall
 sgrall@littleford.com
Estimated Sales: $50-100 Million
Number Employees: 100-249
Number of Brands: 10
Number of Products: 10
Type of Packaging: Food Service, Private Label

25406 Live Floor Systems
1076 Harrisburg Pike
Carlisle, PA 17013-1615
717-243-6644
Fax: 717-243-9926
Manufacturers of automated loading and unloading systems
Director Sales: Norm Fortney
Number Employees: 20

25407 Livingston-Wilbor Corporation
PO Box 496
Edison, NJ 08818-496
908-322-8403
Fax: 908-322-9230
Manufacturer and exporter of labeler change parts
Purchasing Agent: Chris Haigh
Estimated Sales: $1-2.5 Million
Number Employees: 10-19
Square Footage: 24000
Type of Packaging: Consumer, Food Service, Private Label

25408 Lixi Inc
120 S Lincoln Ave
Carpentersville, IL 60110-1703
847-961-6666
Fax: 847-961-6667 lixi@lixi.com
www.lixi.com
Manufacturer and exporter of inspection systems specializing in automatic detection of defects and rejection from conveyors
President: Brent Burns
 bburns@lixi.com
Sales Manager: Joseph Plevak
Production: Ken Belzey
Estimated Sales: $2.5-5 Million
Number Employees: 10-19
Square Footage: 20000

25409 Lixi, Inc.
11980 Oak Creek Pkwy
Huntley, IL 60142
847-961-6666
Fax: 847-961-6667 lixi@lixi.com
www.lixi.com
Small x-ray imaging systems used for monitoring quality assurance, product malfunctions and fault analysis, security inspection and product tampering.
Contact: Brent Burns
 bburns@lixi.com

25410 Lloyd Disher Company
5 Powers Lane Place
Decatur, IL 62522-3287
217-429-0593
Fax: 217-423-2611 www.manta.com
Manufacturer and exporter of aluminum alloy Teflon coated ice cream scoops
President: Gordan R Lloyd
Sales Manager: Lucy Murphy
Estimated Sales: $1 - 5 Million
Number Employees: 4
Square Footage: 10000
Brands:
 Lloyd

25411 Lloyd's Register QualityAssurance
1330 Enclave Pkwy
Suite 200
Houston, TX 77077
281-578-7995
Fax: 281-398-7337 888-877-8001
info-usa@lrqa.com www.lrqausa.com
Company providing quality system certification; serving the food and dairy industries

President: Paul Huber
CFO: Beverly Simmons
Quality Control: Atul Puri
Contact: Micheal Hatcher
 mhatcher@mail.montcopa.org
Estimated Sales: $5-10 Million
Number Employees: 1-4

25412 Lloyd's of Millville
102 S 8th St # B
Millville, NJ 08332-3415
856-825-0345
Fax: 856-825-7666 www.lloydsofmillville.com
Commercial awnings
President: Benjamin Lloyd Jr
VP: Rick Lloyd
Estimated Sales: Below $5,000,000
Number Employees: 1-4

25413 Lmi Packaging
8911 102nd St
Pleasant Prairie, WI 53158-2212
262-947-3300
Fax: 262-947-3301 800-208-3331
www.lmipackaging.com
Manufacturer and exporter of heat sealing lidding, flexible packaging solutions, daisychain, rollstock & die cut lidding
Owner: Virginia Moran
CEO: Jean Moran
Vice President of Business Development: Randall Troutman
Vp R&D: Mike Gorzynski
Director of Marketing: Lea Connelly
National Accounts Manager: Gary Morrison
Vp Operations: Vince Incandela
Estimated Sales: $5-10 Million
Number Employees: 20-49

25414 LoTech Industries
12136 W Bayaud Ave Ste 120
Lakewood, CO 80228
303-202-6337
Fax: 303-202-9252 800-295-0199
Manufacturer and exporter of catering and food service custom imprinted utensils including plastic spoons, tongs, cake servers, pizza cutters, ladles, spatulas, and pasta forks
Vice President: Bev Whiteside
Estimated Sales: $2 Million
Number Employees: 3
Type of Packaging: Consumer, Food Service, Private Label, Bulk
Brands:
 Lotech

25415 Load King Mfg
1357 W Beaver St
Jacksonville, FL 32209-7694
904-354-8882
Fax: 904-353-1984 800-531-4975
www.loadking.com
Manufacturer and exporter of garbage and waste compactors, cardboard recycling balers, stainless steel tables, sinks, wire racks, carts, salad bars, checkout counters, etc. Manufactures fixtures and equipment worldwide to the supermarket, restaurant and retail industries
CEO: Charlie Chupp Jr
VP Sales: Charles Chupp
Estimated Sales: $10 - 20 Million
Number Employees: 100-249
Square Footage: 600000
Type of Packaging: Consumer, Food Service

25416 LoadBank International
4654 35th St
Orlando, FL 32811-6521
407-957-4000
Fax: 407-957-4175 800-458-9010
Manufacturer and exporter of material handling and distribution equipment including dock staging and cross-docking systems
President: Doug Hughes
Vice President: Mike Willett
Sales Director: Mike Willett
Operations Manager: John Veitch
Estimated Sales: $1-2.5 Million
Number Employees: 20-49
Number of Brands: 12
Number of Products: 12
Brands:
 Air-Trax
 Dock Xpress

 Loadbank
 Xpresslane

25417 Lobsters Alive Company
1447 Five Islands Rd
Georgetown, ME 4548
207-371-2990
Fax: 815-344-4479 keith@fiveislandslobster.com
fiveislandslobster.com
Wholesaler/distributor of lobster tank supplies and parts; also, sales and service of new and reconditioned lobster tanks available; design consultant specializing in large holding systems
General Manager: Joann Baureis
Equipment Specialist: Dennis Baureis
Estimated Sales: $500,000-$1 Million
Number Employees: 1-4
Square Footage: 4000

25418 Lobue's Rubber Stamp Co
1228 Mcgowen St
Houston, TX 77004-1108
713-652-0031
Fax: 713-652-0511
www.lobuesrubberstampco.com
Rubber stamps
President: Grant Gaumer
 lobuestamp@earthlink.net
Estimated Sales: $1-2.5 Million
Number Employees: 5-9

25419 Location Georgia
245 Peachtree Center Avenue NE
Atlanta, GA 30303-1222
800-946-4642
Fax: 404-302-8333
locationgeorgia@meagpower.org
President, Chief Executive Officer: Robert Johnston
Sr. Vice President, Chief Administrative: Scott Jones
Sr. Vice President, Chief Operating Offi: Steven Jackson

25420 Lock Inspection Systems
207 Authoring Dr
Fitchburg, MA 01420-6094
978-343-3716
Fax: 978-343-6278 800-227-5539
sales@lockinspection.com
www.lockinspection.com
Contact: Walter Army
 warmy@lockwoodint.com

25421 Lock Inspection Systems
207 Authority Drive
Fitchburg, MA 01420-6094
978-343-3716
Fax: 978-343-6278 800-227-5539
sales@lockinspection.com
www.lockinspection.com
Manufacturer, importer and exporter of advanced quality control detection systems including metal detectors, checkweighers and conveyors for the packaging and processing industries
President: Mark D'Onofrio
Marketing Director: Michelle Contois
VP of Sales & Marketing: David Arseneault
Contact: Walter Army
 warmy@lockwoodint.com
Production Manager: Brian Clough
Purchasing Manager: John Parker
Estimated Sales: $5-10 Million
Number Employees: 20-49
Square Footage: 120000
Parent Co: Transfer Technology Group PLC

25422 Lockhee Martin Postal Tech Inc
6201 E 43rd St
Tulsa, OK 74135-6562
918-622-2697
Fax: 918-622-2697
Manual, advanced and multiline bar coding and mail sorting machines
President: Bill Dobbs
Estimated Sales: $10-20 Million
Number Employees: 5-9
Parent Co: Lockheed Martin

25423 Locknane
720 132nd St SW
Suite 207
Everett, WA 98204-9359
425-742-5187
Fax: 425-745-0277 800-848-9854

Manufacturer and exporter of nylon apparel and vinyl aprons; also, jackets
President: Duane Locknane
   duane.locknane@locknane.com
Marketing Director: Brent Locknane
Purchasing Manager: Tami Matuizek
Estimated Sales: $3 - 5 Million
Number Employees: 25
Square Footage: 14000
Type of Packaging: Food Service
Brands:
   Jo-Lock

25424 Locknetics
11819 N Pennsylvania St
Carmel, IN 46032-4555

Fax: 860-584-2136
Manufacturer and exporter of electro-magnetic locking systems
Finance Executive: Robert Zdanowski
Sales Manager: George Nortonen
Estimated Sales: $20 - 50 Million
Number Employees: 100-249
Parent Co: Ingersoll-Rand.

25425 Lockwood Greene Engineers
303 Perimeter Ctr N Ste 800
Atlanta, GA 30346
770-829-6500
Fax: 770-818-8100 www.lg.com
Consultant and designer providing plant and production line layout, process and packaging engineering, automation and control systems and environmental services
Manager: Angela Davis
Manager: Barry Hall
Sr. VP: Bill Leslie
VP: Fizool Israel
Estimated Sales: $50 - 100 Million
Number Employees: 250-499
Parent Co: Lockwood Greene Engineers

25426 Lockwood Greene Engineers
1450 Greene St Ste 200
Augusta, GA 30901
706-724-8225
Fax: 706-724-8422
Consultant and designer providing plant and production line layout, process and packaging engineering, automation and control systems and environmental services
Manager: Tom Sickling
Project Manager: Bob Grahl
Director: Lauren Watters
Estimated Sales: $10-20 Million
Number Employees: 50-99
Square Footage: 12000
Parent Co: Lockwood Greene Engineers

25427 Lockwood Greene Engineers
270 Davidson Ave # 4
Somerset, NJ 08873-4140
732-560-5700
Fax: 732-868-2300 www.lg.com
Consultant and designer providing plant and production line layout, process and packaging engineering, automation and control systems and environmental services
Manager: Sherman Schwartz
Project Director: Tom Geffert
Senior Vice President, Chief Human Resou:
Don-Hyung Kang
President, Chief Operating Officer: Jong-Sik Kim
Estimated Sales: $20-50 Million
Number Employees: 100-249
Parent Co: Lockwood Greene Engineers

25428 Lockwood Greene Engineers
4201 Spring Valley Road
Suite 1500
Dallas, TX 75244-3669
972-991-5505
Fax: 972-960-2070 www.lg.com
Consultant and designer providing plant and production line layout, process and packaging engineering, automation and control systems and environmental services
President/COO: Lee McInitre
CEO: Ralph Peterson
Chief Financial Officer: Samuel Iapalucci
Senior Vice President, Chief Human Resou:
Don-Hyung Kang
President, Chief Operating Officer: Jong-Sik Kim

Estimated Sales: $20 - 50 Million
Number Employees: 60
Parent Co: Lockwood Greene Engineers

25429 Lockwood Greene Engineers
2035 Lakeside Center Way
Suite 200
Knoxville, TN 37922-6595
256-533-9907
Fax: 256-533-7476
Consultant and designer providing plant and production line layout, process and packaging engineering, automation and control systems, environmental services and architectural engineering support
Office Manager: Tom Glazener
Estimated Sales: $1-2.5 Million
Number Employees: 19
Parent Co: Lockwood Greene Engineers

25430 Lockwood Greene Engineers
130 Concord Rd
Knoxville, TN 37934-2901
865-218-5377
Fax: 865-777-3834 www.lg.com
Consultant and designer providing plant and production line layout, process and packaging engineering, automation and control systems and environmental services
President: Cathy Neubert
CEO: Ralph Peterson
Senior Vice President, Chief Human Resou:
Don-Hyung Kang
President, Chief Operating Officer: Jong-Sik Kim
Estimated Sales: $10-20 Million
Number Employees: 10-19
Parent Co: Lockwood Greene Engineers

25431 Lockwood Greene Engineers
2035 Lakeside Center Way
Suite 200
Knoxville, TN 37922-6595
251-476-2400
Fax: 251-344-7400
Consultant and designer providing plant and production line layout, process and packaging engineering, automation and control systems and environmental services
Office Manager: David Holland
Estimated Sales: $.5 - 1 million
Number Employees: 5-9
Parent Co: Lockwood Greene Engineers

25432 Lockwood Greene Engineers
7101 Executive Center Drive
Suite 297
Brentwood, TN 37027-3239
615-221-5031
Fax: 615-221-5078 www.lg.com
Consultant and designer providing plant and production line layout, process and packaging engineering, materials handling, automation and control systems and environmental services
President: Lee McIntire
CEO: Ralph Peterson
Senior Vice President, Chief Human Resou:
Don-Hyung Kang
President, Chief Operating Officer: Jong-Sik Kim
Estimated Sales: $1-2.5 Million
Number Employees: 19
Parent Co: Lockwood Greene Engineers

25433 Lockwood Greene Engineers
270 Davidson Ave # 4
Somerset, NJ 08873-4140
732-560-5700
Fax: 732-868-2300 www.lg.com
Consultant and designer providing plant and production line layout, process and packaging engineering, automation and control systems and environmental services
Manager: Sherman Schwartz
Senior Vice President, Chief Human Resou:
Don-Hyung Kang
President, Chief Operating Officer: Jong-Sik Kim
Estimated Sales: $20 - 50 Million
Number Employees: 100-249
Parent Co: Lockwood Greene Engineers

25434 Lockwood Greene Engineers
165 Road Km 10 Pueblo Viejo
Guaynabo, PR 00968
787-781-9050
Fax: 787-781-0177 www.lg.com

Consultant and designer providing plant and production line layout, process, packaging, engineering, automation and control systems, construction management, environmental services and validation services.
Office Manager: Gene Scott
Director Projects: Jorge Alvarez
Senior Vice President, Chief Human Resou:
Don-Hyung Kang
Marketing Director: Mayra Rodriguez
Validations Manager: Victor Batista
Estimated Sales: $64 Million
Number Employees: 178
Square Footage: 13000
Parent Co: Lockwood Greene Engineers

25435 Lockwood Greene Technologies
1450 Greene St Ste 200
Augusta, GA 30901
505-889-3831
Fax: 505-889-3842
Consultant and designer providing plant and production line layout, process and packaging engineering, automation and control systems and environmental services
Estimated Sales: $2.5-5 Million
Number Employees: 19
Parent Co: Lockwood Greene Engineers

25436 Lockwood Manufacturing
31251 Industrial Rd
Livonia, MI 48150-2035
734-425-5330
Fax: 734-427-5650 800-521-0238
customerservice@lockwoodusa.com
www.lockwoodusa.com
Wine racks, wine storage coolers, and food service equipment.
President: David Lamson
   dwlamson@lockwoodusa.com
TBA Sales: David Lawrence
TBA Sales: Chad Buckles
Number Employees: 20-49

25437 Lockwood Packaging
271 Salem Street
Unit G
Woburn, MA 01801-2004
781-938-1500
Fax: 781-938-7536 800-641-3100
Manufacturer and exporter of automatic weighing and bagging equipment and supplies; also, repair and operating services available
President: Richard Gold
VP: Thomas Gold
VP: Hans Van Der Sande
Estimated Sales: $.5 - 1 million
Number Employees: 20-49

25438 Lodal Inc
620 N Hooper St
Kingsford, MI 49802-5400
906-779-1700
Fax: 906-779-1160 800-435-3500
sales@lodal.com www.lodal.com
Manufacturer and exporter of refuse removal systems
President: Bernie Leger
CFO: Bernard Leger
Director Marketing: Darren Tavonatti
Estimated Sales: $10 - 20 Million
Number Employees: 100-249

25439 Lodge Manufacturing Company
503 S Cedar Ave
South Pittsburg, TN 37380
423-837-5919
Fax: 423-837-8279 www.lodgemfg.com
Manufacturer, importer and exporter of cast iron cookware, bakeware and servingware
President: Henry Lodge
CEO: Bob Kellermann
CEO: Robert F Kellermann
R&D: Jeanne Scholze
Quality Control: Lou Zarzaur
VP Sales: Gray Bekurs
Contact: Richard Lodge
   rlodge@lodgemfg.com
VP Production: Mike Whitfield
Estimated Sales: $20 - 50 Million
Number Employees: 100-249
Type of Packaging: Consumer, Food Service

25440 Lodging By Charter
206 E Frazier Ave
Liberty, NC 27298-8289
336-622-2201
Fax: 336-622-5000 800-327-2548
info@loewensteininc.com
www.charterfurniture.com
Chairs, stools, tables and table bases
President: Bruce Albertson
CFO: Winson Tortorici
Quality Control: Beata Kaminiski
Manager: Debbie Thompson
dthompson@brownjordan.com
VP Operations: David Biancofiore
Number Employees: 100-249
Square Footage: 330000

25441 Lodi Metal Tech
P.O. Box 967
Lodi, CA 95241-0967
209-334-2500
Fax: 209-334-1259 800-359-5999
Manufacturer and exporter of racks
Manager: Dean Bender
Estimated Sales: $10-20,000,000
Number Employees: 50-99
Square Footage: 310000

25442 Loeb Equipment
4131 S State St
Chicago, IL 60609-2942
773-496-5720
Fax: 773-548-2608 Sales@loebequipment.com
www.loebequipment.com
Wholesaler/distributor of used packaging and processing equipment.
President/CEO: Howard Newman
howardn@loebequipment.com
Marketing Director: Sara Bogin
howardn@loebequipment.com
Sales Manager: Tom Larson
Number Employees: 20-49
Square Footage: 600000

25443 Loeb Equipment
4131 S State St
Chicago, IL 60609-2942
773-496-5720
Fax: 773-548-2608 800-560-5632
www.loebequipment.com
Buy and sell packaging and processing equipment to food industry. Also specialize in certified appraisels, asset managment and liquidators
President: Howard Newman
howardn@loebequipment.com
Vice President: John Hagist
Marketing Director: Sara Bogin
Sales Manager: Tom Larson
Number Employees: 20-49
Type of Packaging: Food Service, Private Label

25444 Logemann Brothers Co
3150 W Burleigh St
Milwaukee, WI 53210-1999
414-445-3005
Fax: 414-445-1460 logemannbalers@aol.com
Manufacturer and exporter of scrap-metal, liber and refuse bales, also, alligator shears, briquettes and guillotines
Owner: Carl Dieterle
carl@milwpc.com
General Sales Manager: Robert Pichta
Estimated Sales: $2.5 Million
Number Employees: 20-49

25445 Logility
470 E Paces Ferry Rd NE
Atlanta, GA 30305
404-261-9777
Fax: 404-264-5206 800-762-5207
ask@logility.com www.logility.com
President and CEO: J. Michael Edenfield
CFO: Vincent Klinges
VP of Research and Development: Mark A. Balte
Vice President of Marketing: Karin L. Bursa
Estimated Sales: $20 - 25 Million
Number Employees: 100-249

25446 Logility TransportationGroup
1011 East Touhy Avenue
Suite 315
Des Plaines, IL 60018
847-699-6620
Fax: 847-699-6671 www.logility.com

Software for routing, carrier selection, freight audit, order consolidation, freight accounting and transportation management; also, integrated and proven solutions
President, CEO: J. Michael Edenfield
CFO: Vincent Klinges
EVP Sales and Marketing: H. Allan Dow
Vice President of Research and Developme: Mark A. Balte
VP Marketing: Karin L. Bursa
Vice President of Customer Service: Donald L. Thomas
Estimated Sales: $2.5-5 Million
Number Employees: 20-49
Square Footage: 36800
Parent Co: Logility
Brands:
Base Rate
Carrier Select
Dsi Escort
Match Pay
Preshipment Planning
Ship Wise

25447 Logix
10518 NE 68th St # 103
Suite 103
Kirkland, WA 98033-7003
425-828-4149
Fax: 425-828-9682 800-275-8112
www.logix-controls.com
Industrial refrigeration control system for the food, beverage and cold storage industries providing management and facility wide system tracking and reporting. Special fermentation controls available for wineries and alliedindustries
President: Jim Conant
contact@logix-controls.com
CFO: Jim Conant
VP: Micheal Ghan
Sales: Stephen Bowers
Operations: Scott Gillette
Production: Thomas Kulin
Estimated Sales: $2.5 - 5 Million
Number Employees: 10-19
Number of Brands: 2
Number of Products: 6
Square Footage: 1000
Brands:
Logix

25448 Logo Specialty Advertising Tems
PO Box 270544
Tampa, FL 33688-0544
561-429-4725
800-704-0094
roz@everythinglogo.com
www.logospecialtyadvertisingitems.com
Specialty advertising items
Co-Owner: Roz Kodish
Estimated Sales: less than $500,000
Number Employees: 1-4

25449 Logotech Inc
18 Madison Rd
Fairfield, NJ 07004-2309
973-882-9595
Fax: 973-882-0902 800-988-5646
Pressure sensitive label manufacturer
President: Leslie Gurland
labels@logotech-inc.com
CFO: Rodney Schundler
Research & Development: Jamie Fedor
Quality Control: Bruce Wade
Sales: Halley Mechanic
Estimated Sales: $5,000,000 -$15,000,000
Number Employees: 20-49
Square Footage: 56000

25450 Lohall Enterprises
6755 N Range Line Road
Milwaukee, WI 53209-3209
414-351-1270
Fax: 414-351-4531 lohall@execpc.com
Wrapping paper, wet waxed paper roll and sheet
Vice President: Arnold Garber
Purchasing Manager: Mary Anne Garber
Estimated Sales: $1 Million+
Number Employees: 3

25451 Loma International
283 E Lies Rd
Carol Stream, IL 60188-9421
630-588-0900
Fax: 630-588-1394 800-872-5662
www.loma.com
Manufacturer, exporter and importer of metal detectors and weighing equipment
President: Gary Wilson
CFO: Hary Pommier
Technical Director: Mike Nevin
Manager of IT: Brooke Kruger
Marketing Manager: James Chrismas
Sales Manager: Andrey Ivanov
Contact: Carlos Aillon
carlos.aillon@loma.com
Estimated Sales: $20 - 50 Million
Number Employees: 50-99
Square Footage: 21000

25452 Loma Systems
283 E Lies Rd
Carol Stream, IL 60188
630-588-0900
800-872-5662
www.loma.com
Inspection systems-metal detectors, check weighess, x-ray inspection systems.
President: Martin Lymn
CFO: Harold Pommier
Sales: Sandy Stillmaker
Contact: Carlos Aillon
caillon@loma.com
Operations: Craig Scachitti
Estimated Sales: $20-$50 Million
Number Employees: 80

25453 Lomont IMT
1516 E. Mapleleaf Drive
Mt. Pleasant, IA 52641
319-385-1528
Fax: 319-385-1533 800-776-0380
info@lomont.com www.lomontimt.com
Industrial safety signs, equipment tags and labels.
Number Employees: 150
Square Footage: 200000

25454 Lone Peak Labeling Systems
1272 W 2240 S # B
Suite B
West Valley City, UT 84119-1444
801-975-1818
Fax: 801-975-1865 800-658-8599
chrisa@lonepeaklabeling.com
www.lonepeaklabeling.com
Labels
President/Owner: Chris Appelbaum
chrisa@lonepeaklabeling.com
Operations: Jason Halling
Estimated Sales: $3.5 Million
Number Employees: 20-49

25455 Lone Star Container Corp
700 N Wildwood Dr
Irving, TX 75061-8832
972-579-1551
Fax: 972-554-6081 800-552-6937
jphipps@lonestarbox.com
www.lonestarcontainer.com
Manufacturer and exporter of corrugated boxes
President: Jerry C Hardison
jhardison@lonestarbox.com
CEO: John McLeod
Manager: Joe Phipps
Estimated Sales: $500,000-$1 Million
Number Employees: 100-249

25456 Lonestar Banners & Flags
212 S Main St
Fort Worth, TX 76104-1223
817-335-2548
Fax: 817-877-1610 800-288-9625
www.fortworthflag.com
Flags, banners, outdoor advertising displays and pennants; exporter of flags
President: James Eggleston
Vice President: Mark Buechelle
info@abcflag.com
VP Marketing: Pam Engelhardt
Estimated Sales: $5-10 Million
Number Employees: 20-49
Square Footage: 80000

25457 Long Company
20 N. Wacker Drive
Suite 1010
Chicago, IL 60606-2901
312-726-4606
Fax: 312-726-4625 800-400-8615
info@thelongco.com
President: Bill Zimmerman
CEO: Roger Masa
V.P. Operations - Consulting Services: Gary
Swymeler
Director of Quality, R & D: Albert Bachman
Contact: Jo Rustik
jrustik@thelongco.com
Director of Manufacturing Services: Duane Bull
Purchasing Director: Larry Devereux

25458 Long Food Industries
709 Rock Beauty Road
Fripp Island, SC 29920-7344
843-838-3205
Fax: 843-838-3918 www.longfoodindustries.com
Shrimp, cooked/diced chicken, clam (meat and
broth), beef (diced/cooked), lobster, fish and pork
President: Leon Long
Estimated Sales: $10-20 Million
Number Employees: 1
Type of Packaging: Food Service

25459 Long Island Stamp Corporation
5431 Myrtle Ave
Flushing, NY 11385
718-628-8550
Fax: 718-628-8560 800-547-8267
Rubber stamps, signs, labels, daters and seals
Owner: Harriet Pollak
VP: Harry Pollak
Estimated Sales: $1-2.5 Million
Number Employees: 10-19
Square Footage: 9000

25460 Long Range Systems
4550 Excel Pkwy # 200
Suite 200
Addison, TX 75001-5713
214-553-5308
Fax: 214-221-0160 800-577-8101
info@pager.net www.pager.net
A leading innovator of guest and staff paging and
management systems for 14 years. We invented the
popular coaster pager and now offer more pagers
than anyone else. We have over 35 products de-
signed to help you streamline operationsimprove
service and increase sales every day. We provide the
highest quality, most durable products on the mar-
ket, plus we offer exclusive products and services no
other company can.
Owner: Ken Lovgren
CEO: John Weber
jweber@lrsus.com
Marketing Director: Kevin Hosey
Sales Director: Jim Livingston
Number Employees: 50-99
Brands:
Adverteaser
Coaster Call
Cool Blue
Keycall
Lobster Call
Star Pager
The Butler
The Informant
Total Control

**25461 Long Reach
ManufacturingCompany**
136 Main Street
Suite 4
Westport, CT 06880-3304
713-434-3400
Fax: 713-433-9710 800-285-7000
www.longreach.com
Manufacturer and exporter of lift truck attachments
and pallet trucks
Chief Executive Officer: William Masson
Chief Financial Officer: William Masson
Vice President: Pat Poyton
Estimated Sales: $33 Million
Number Employees: 142
Brands:
Rol-Lift

25462 Longaberger Basket Company
701 Chestnut St
Dresden, OH 43821
740-518-8018
Picnic baskets.
Chief Executive Officer: Tami Longaberger
Chief Administrative Officer: Lisa Hittle
lisa.hittle@longaberger.com
Year Founded: 1896
Estimated Sales: $50-100 Million
Number Employees: 6,390
Square Footage: 180000

**25463 Longford Equipment
International**
41 Lamont Avenue
Toronto, ON M1S 1A8
Canada
416-298-6622
Fax: 416-298-6627 888-298-2900
longford@longfordint.com www.longfordint.com
Estimated Sales: $15 Million
Number Employees: 100

25464 Longford Equipment US
938 Manchester Rd
Glastonbury, CT 06033-2629
416-298-6622
Fax: 860-633-8207 feederpro@aol.com
www.longfordint.com
Coupon and leaflet feeding machinery. Also turn-
keys attaching to packaging lines available
Owner: Guy Sanderson
Manager: Guy Sanderson
Estimated Sales: $1-2.5 Million
Number Employees: 1-4

25465 Longhorn Imports Inc
2202 E Union Bower Rd
Irving, TX 75061-8814
972-721-9102
Fax: 972-579-4890 800-641-8348
info@longhornimports.com
www.longhornimports.com
Baskets, gift boxes, specialty containers, glassware,
seasonal items and packaging products
Owner: Bruce Mc Adoo
longhornim@aol.com
VP/VP Finance: Carol Adoo
Marketing: Wendy Mawhee
Estimated Sales: $3.1 Million
Number Employees: 10-19

25466 Longhorn Packaging Inc
110 Pierce Ave
San Antonio, TX 78208-1928
210-222-9686
Fax: 210-226-7511 800-433-7974
www.longhornpackaging.com
Manufacturer and exporter of converted flexible
packaging film and vertical form/fill/seal packaging
machinery; also, contract packaging available
President: Holly Ferguson
hferguson@prosper-isd.net
VP: Bill Green
VP Production: Harold Smith
Estimated Sales: $20-50 Million
Number Employees: 50-99
Square Footage: 40000

25467 Longview Fibre Co
300 Fibre Way
Longview, WA 98632-1199
360-575-5290
Fax: 360-575-5934 800-929-8111
www.longviewfibre.com
Paper, corrugated and fibre containers, cushioning
materials and corrugated pallets
Chairman of the Board: Richard Wollenberg
CEO: Frank V McShane
Sales Manager: Fran Goetz
Contact: John Harris
jmharris@longfibre.com
Plant Manager: Harry Johnson
Estimated Sales: $20 - 50 Million
Number Employees: 1,000-4,999
Square Footage: 400000

25468 Longview Fibre Company
8705 SW Nimbus Ave
Beaverton, OR 97008-4000
503-350-1600
Fax: 323-725-6341 www.longviewfibre.com

Manufacturer and exporter of disposable liquid bulk
bins
Sales Manager: Dennis Dorgan
Vice President of Sales and Marketing: Lou
Loosbrock
Sales Bulk Liquid Packaging: Paul Hansen
Estimated Sales: $1 - 3 Million
Number Employees: 5-9
Type of Packaging: Bulk
Brands:
Drumplex
Liquiplex

25469 Longview Fibre Company
P.O. Box 106
Oakland, CA 94604
510-569-2616
Fax: 510-569-4141 www.longviewfibre.com
Wine industry packaging and design
Vice President of Sales and Marketing: Lou
Loosbrock
Plant Manager: Nathan Dyke
Estimated Sales: $10-20 Million
Number Employees: 50-99
Parent Co: Longview Fibre

25470 Lonza Inc
412 Mount Kemble Ave
Suite 200C
Morristown, NJ 07960
www.lonza.com
BioResearch, pharma and biotech research, water
treatment, agriculture ingredients, and coatings &
composites.
CEO: Pierre-Alain Ruffieux
Year Founded: 1897
Estimated Sales: $350 Million
Number Employees: 69
Number of Products: 100

25471 Loos Machine
205 W Washington St
Colby, WI 54421-9458
715-223-2844
Fax: 715-223-6140 www.loosmachine.com
Custom designed automated food processing equip-
ment for the dairy, meat and poultry industries.
Owner: Dennis Baumgartner
info@loosmachine.com
Number Employees: 20-49

25472 Loprest Co
2825 Franklin Canyon Rd
Rodeo, CA 94572-2116
510-799-3101
Fax: 510-799-7433 888-228-5982
sales@loprest.com www.loprest.com
Water treatment equipment, ion exchange equipment
and resin
President: Randy Richey
CFO: Randy Richey
Contact: Amy Velazquez
avelazquez@buttecounty.net
Estimated Sales: $1 - 2.5 Million
Number Employees: 1-4

25473 Lorac Union Tool Co
97 Johnson St
Providence, RI 02905-4518
401-781-3330
Fax: 401-941-7717 888-680-3236
lorac@loracunion.com www.loracunion.com
Manufacturer and exporter of point of purchase dis-
plays and sign holders
President: Richard Carroll
Estimated Sales: $5 - 10 Million
Number Employees: 10-19
Square Footage: 204000
Parent Co: Lorac Company
Brands:
Sava-Klip

25474 Lord Label Group
2980 Planters Place
Charlotte, NC 28216-4149
704-394-9171
Fax: 704-394-0641 800-341-5225
Manufacturer and exporter of labels and labeling
equipment
Director Marketing: George McCrary
VP Sales Eastern Region: Jim Prendergast
Sales Manager Western Region: Tom Deegan
Number Employees: 250
Parent Co: Mail-Well

Other Locations:
Lord Label Group
Arlington TX

25475 Lord Label Machine Systems
10350A Nations Food Road
Charlotte, NC 28273

704-644-1650
Fax: 704-664-1662 www.satoamerica.com
Manufacturer and exporter of label applicators
General Manager: Les Roisum
Number Employees: 20-49
Square Footage: 72000
Parent Co: Mail Well
Brands:
Label Robotix
Predator 1500-3000
Tr 1000-2000

25476 (HQ)Loren Cook Co
2015 E Dale St
Springfield, MO 65803-4637

417-869-6474
Fax: 417-862-3820 800-289-3267
info@lorencook.com www.lorencook.com
Manufacturer and exporter of fans, blowers and ventilators
President: Gerald Cook
Cmo: Victor Colwell
vcolwell@lorencook.com
Estimated Sales: $77 Million
Number Employees: 1000-4999
Other Locations:
Loren Cook Co.
Ashville NC

25477 Lorenz Couplings
PO Box 1002
Cobourg, ON K9A 4K2
Canada

905-372-2240
Fax: 905-372-4456 800-263-7782
www.lorenz.ca
Manufacturer and exporter of stainless steel gasket
couplings for connection of pipe and tube in bulk
handling conveying and vacuum systems
President: Peter Lorenz
CEO: Stacy Warner
Estimated Sales: Below $5 Million
Number Employees: 30
Square Footage: 80000

25478 Lorenzen's Cookie Cutters
2080 Maple Street
Wantagh, NY 11793-4108

516-781-7116
Fax: 516-781-1110 fclorenzen@aol.com
Custom stainless steel cookie cutters
CEO: Margaret Lorenzen
Estimated Sales: $1 - 5 Million
Number Employees: 2
Square Footage: 1750

25479 Loria Awards
1876 Central Park Ave
Yonkers, NY 10710-2998

914-779-3377
Fax: 914-779-3587 800-540-2927
customerservice@loriaawards.com
www.loriaawards.com
Awards, stemware and name plates; also, imprinting
available
Owner: Roger Loria Sr
VP: Roger Loria Jr
Production Manager: David DiPietro
Estimated Sales: $1-2.5 Million
Number Employees: 10-19
Square Footage: 120000

25480 Lorrich & Associates
11310 Ganesta Road
San Diego, CA 92126-1643

858-586-0823
Fax: 858-586-6210 lorrichusa@aol.com
Consultant specializing in design, marketing and
promotion for the restaurant industry
President: Richard Bartole
VP: Lorraine Bartole
Estimated Sales: Less than $500,000
Number Employees: 1-4

25481 Los Angeles Label Company
6141 Sheila St
Commerce, CA 90040-2406

323-720-1200
Fax: 323-724-1024 800-606-5223
www.lalabel.com
Prime labels, tickets, coupons, variable printing on
tag stock and pressure sensitive materials
Manager: Bruce Frost
President, Chief Executive Officer: Thomas
Waechter
Vice President: John Redgrave
Estimated Sales: $10 - 20 Million
Number Employees: 50-99
Square Footage: 60000

**25482 Los Angeles Paper Box &Board
Mills**
PO Box 60830
Los Angeles, CA 90060-0830

323-685-8900
Fax: 323-724-2181 bill@lapb.com
Chip board and boxes including rigid, folding, set
up, etc
President: William H Kewell Iii
CFO: Knita Chau
VP Sales: Robert Appoloney
Estimated Sales: $20 - 50 Million
Number Employees: 20-49

25483 Louie's Finer Meats
Highway 63 North
2025 Superior Avenue
Cumberland, WI 54829

715-822-4728
Fax: 715-822-3150 800-270-4297
lfm@louiesfinermeats.net
www.louiesfinermeats.com
Smoked sausages
Owner/President: Louie Muench Sr
VP: Louie Muench Jr
Number Employees: 4

25484 Louis A Roser Company
608 W 700 S
Salt Lake City, UT 84104

801-363-8849
Fax: 801-328-9670 800-324-6864
roserinfo@laroser.com www.laroser.com
President: Roy Iversen
Estimated Sales: $5 - 10 Million
Number Employees: 10-19

25485 (HQ)Louis Baldinger & Sons
875 3rd Ave Fl 9
New York, NY 10022-0123

718-204-5700
Fax: 718-721-4986
Manufacturer and exporter of decorative and custom
lighting fixtures
President: Howard Baldinger
Chairman of the board: Daniel Baldinger
Quality Control: Shankar Balmick
VP Sales/Marketing: Linda Senter
Contact: Edison Alulema
ealulema@baldinger.com
Estimated Sales: $10-20 Million
Number Employees: 120
Type of Packaging: Consumer

25486 Louis Jacobs & Son
161 N 4th St
Brooklyn, NY 11211-3279

718-782-3500
Fax: 718-384-1167
Paper table covers, plain, embossed and creped,
sheets and rolls
CEO: Abram Cohen
Estimated Sales: $10 - 20 Million
Number Employees: 5-9
Square Footage: 36000
Type of Packaging: Food Service, Private Label,
Bulk
Brands:
Clothsaver Paper Tabl-Mats
Duo-Stress Place Mats

25487 Louis Roesch Company
289 Foster City Blvd
Suite B
Foster City, CA 94404-1100

415-621-4700
Fax: 415-621-1152
Paper labels; also, label printing services available

President: Michael A Davos
CFO: Mike Davos
Sales Manager: Bob Davos
Pur Mgr: Jason Hong
Estimated Sales: $10-20 Million
Number Employees: 10

25488 Louisville Bedding Co Inc.
10400 Bunsen Way
Louisville, KY 40299

502-813-8059
loubed.com
Chair pads, table cloths and place mats.
President/CEO: Steve Elias
Year Founded: 1889
Estimated Sales: $100-$500 Million
Number Employees: 500-999

25489 Louisville Container Company
4401 W 62nd Street
Indianapolis, IN 46268-4829

502-361-5300
Fax: 317-297-5019 888-539-7225
Plastic and glass bottles and jars; also pails
President: Steve Heidt
Marketing Director: Nancy Heidt
Estimated Sales: $1 Million
Number Employees: 3
Square Footage: 7400

25490 Louisville Dryer Company
1100 Industrial Boulevrd
Louisville, KY 40219

502-969-3535
Fax: 502-962-9028 800-735-3613
mail@louisvilledryer.com
www.louisvilledryer.com
Manufacturer and exporter of rotary drying and
cooling equipment, distillation columns, heat
exchangers, pressure vessels and conveyors
VP Sales: Robin Henry
Process Engineer: John Robertson
Plant Manager: Gary Billion
Estimated Sales: $5-10 Million
Number Employees: 20-49

25491 Louisville Lamp Co
3316 Gilmore Industrial Blvd
Louisville, KY 40213-2173

502-964-4094
Fax: 502-964-1349
customerservice@louisvillelamp.com
www.louisvillelamp.com
Custom fluorescent lighting fixtures
President: Rick Buehner
National Accounts: Mike Davidson
Estimated Sales: $1 - 2.5 Million
Number Employees: 50-99

25492 Loveshaw Corp
2206 Easton Tpke
PO Box 83
South Canaan, PA 18459

570-937-4921
Fax: 570-937-3229 800-572-3434
info@loveshaw.com www.loveshaw.com
Manufacturer and exporter of packaging machinery
including case sealers and formers; also, ink jet
printers, labeling equipment
President: Doug Henry-Om
Cmo: Wes Carpenter
wcarpenter@loveshaw.com
VP: Mark Craddick
Marketing Manager: Valerie Burke
Sales: Chet Metcalf
Estimated Sales: $10-24 Million
Number Employees: 100-249
Parent Co: ITW
Brands:
Little David

25493 Low Humidity Systems
8425 Hazelbrand Road NE
Covington, GA 30014

770-788-6744
Fax: 770-788-6745 Info@dehumidifiers.com
www.dehumidifiers.com
Manufacturer and exporter of desiccant
dehumidifiers
Sales Manager: Debra Adams
Estimated Sales: $2.5-5 Million
Number Employees: 10-19
Square Footage: 60000

25494 (HQ)Low Temp Industries Inc
9192 Tara Blvd
Jonesboro, GA 30236-4913
678-674-1317
Fax: 770-471-3715 lt@lowtempind.com
www.lowtempind.com
Manufacturer and exporter of stainless steel, fiberglass and wood-free standing and hot food counters. Custom stainless steel kitchen equipment, serving lines, buffets and salad bars, portable hot and cold carts and custom millwork
CEO: William Casey
Executive VP: David W Pearson
dpearson@lowtempind.com
VP Sales: Steve Ballard
Director Purchasing: Dan Casey
Estimated Sales: $10-20 Million
Number Employees: 100-249
Square Footage: 500000
Type of Packaging: Food Service
Brands:
Cara
Colorpoint
Low Temp

25495 Lowe Refrigeration Inc
105 Cecil Ct
Fayetteville, GA 30214-7906
770-461-9001
Fax: 770-461-8020 www.lowerental.com
Vice President: Richard Epton
richard@loweusa.com
VP: Richard Epton
Estimated Sales: $1 - 3 Million
Number Employees: 10-19

25496 Lowell Paper Box Company
23 Dumaine Ave
Nashua, NH 03063-4070
603-595-0700
Fax: 603-595-6337
Paper folding cartons
President: Paul Connolly
CEO: Mark Dirico
Estimated Sales: $10-20 Million
Number Employees: 100-249

25497 Lowen Color Graphics
1111 Airport Rd
Hutchinson, KS 67501-1983
620-663-2161
Fax: 620-663-1429 800-545-5505
elainem@lowen.com www.buildersigns.com
Point of sale vinyl graphics for floors and fleet and interior store graphics
Vice President of Sales & Marketing: Darren Keller
Contact: Sergio Desoto
s.desoto@lowen.com
Estimated Sales: Less Than $500,000
Number Employees: 1-4

25498 Lowery's Premium Roast Gourmet Coffee
P.O. Box 1858
Snohomish, WA 98291
360-668-4545
Fax: 360-863-9742 800-767-1783
www.loweryscoffee.com
Coffee and wholesale and custom roasters, espresso machines, espresso accessories
President: Donald Lowery
CFO: Jeanette Zimmerman
Marketing: Mike Lowery
Contact: Don Lowery
dlowery@loweryscoffee.com
Roast/Operations Manager: Jerry Lowery
Estimated Sales: Below $5 Million
Number Employees: 20-49
Number of Brands: 2
Number of Products: 100
Square Footage: 20000
Type of Packaging: Private Label
Brands:
Lowery's Coffee
Pasano's Syrups

25499 Lowry Computer ProductsInc
1607 9th St
St Paul, MN 55110-6717
651-429-7722
Fax: 651-429-6006 800-429-7722
Manager: Karla Bridgeman
Manager: Jim Bergman
jamesb@lowrycomputer.com

Estimated Sales: $20 - 50 Million
Number Employees: 20-49

25500 (HQ)Loy Lange Box Co
222 Russell Blvd
St Louis, MO 63104-4608
314-776-4712
Fax: 314-776-2810 800-886-4712
info@loylangebox.com www.loylangebox.com
Corrugated shipping containers and point of purchase displays
Owner: Larry Mcmahon
Chairman: C McMahon
VP: J Cochran
Estimated Sales: $2.5 - 5 Million
Number Employees: 50-99
Square Footage: 192000
Other Locations:
Loy-Lange Box Co.
Belle MO

25501 Loyal Manufacturing
1121 S Shortridge Rd
Indianapolis, IN 46239-1081
317-359-3185
Fax: 317-353-9284 www.loyalmfg.com
Custom fabricated metal products including storage cabinets, shelving racks, etc.; also, cash drawers, point of sale components and security items
President: Ronald Lambert
CEO: Todd Fox
tfox@loyalmfg.com
Estimated Sales: $2.5-5 Million
Number Employees: 10-19
Square Footage: 26000
Brands:
Loyal

25502 Lozier Corp
6336 John J Pershing Dr
Omaha, NE 68110-1122
402-457-8000
Fax: 402-457-8478 800-228-9882
www.lozier.com
Manufacturer and exporter of store fixtures
CEO: Sheri Andrews
sandrews@lozier.biz
CEO: Allan G Lozier
Estimated Sales: $500,000-$1 Million
Number Employees: 1000-4999
Parent Co: Lozier Corporation

25503 Ltg Inc
105 Corporate Dr
Spartanburg, SC 29303-5045
864-599-6340
Fax: 414-672-8800 sales@itsllcusa.com
www.ltg.de
Manufacturer and exporter of controlled heat processing systems for the metal container industry
President: Gerhard Seyffer
gerhard.seyffer@ltg-inc.net
General Manager: Bill Lawrence
VP: Brian Schofield
Estimated Sales: $20 - 50 Million
Number Employees: 1-4
Square Footage: 180000

25504 Lubar Chemical
1208 Iron Street
Kansas City, MO 64116-4009
816-471-2560
Fax: 816-421-2426
Institutional and industrial chemicals including cleaners, degreasers, detergents, floor care products, disinfectants and deodorants; custom blending and private labeling available
Estimated Sales: $5-10 Million
Number Employees: 20-49

25505 Lubriplate Lubricants
129 Lockwood St
Newark, NJ 07105-4720
419-691-2491
Fax: 973-589-4432 800-733-4755
www.lubriplate.com
Manufacturer and exporter of food grade lubricating oils and grease
President: Richard Mc Cluskey
Vice President, General Manager, Chief M: Jim Girard
Contact: Michael Barto
mbarto@lubriplate.com

Number Employees: 100-249
Parent Co: Fisk Brothers

25506 Lubriquip
P.O. Box 1441
Minneapolis, MN 55440-1441
612-623-6000
Fax: 612-378-3590 www.lubriquip.com
Automatic lubrication systems for food processing machinery and equipment, stainless steel injectors and feeder assemblies, single point centralized lubrication systems and conveyor systems
President: Rick Morgan
Quality Control: Jack Gacka
Vice President, General Counsel, Secreta: Karen Gallivan
Plant Manager: Ryan Eidenschink
Estimated Sales: $20,000,000 - $49,999,999
Number Employees: 1,000-4,999

25507 Lucas Industrial
1445 American Way
PO Box 293
Cedar Hill, TX 75104-8409
972-291-6400
Fax: 972-291-6447 800-877-1720
sales@lucasindustrial.com
www.lucasindustrial.com
Manufacturer, importer and wholesaler/distributor of power transmission products including steel and stainless steel shaft and split collars, linear bearing and shaftings, roller chains and mounted bearing
Owner: Mike Lucas
Sales Manager: Bobby Swann
lucasindustrial@aol.com
Estimated Sales: Below $5 Million
Number Employees: 5-9

25508 Luce Corp
336 Putnam Ave
Hamden, CT 06517-2744
203-787-0281
Fax: 203-230-2753 800-344-6966
Kitchen canisters with moisture absorbing knobs
President: Timothy Pagnam
Estimated Sales: $1 - 3 Million
Number Employees: 5-9
Brands:
Blue Magic
Krispy Kan

25509 Luciano Packaging Technologies
29 County Line Rd
Branchburg, NJ 08876-3417
908-722-3222
Fax: 908-722-5005 lpt@lucianopackaging.com
www.lucianopackaging.com
President: Lawrence W. Luciano
lluciano@lucianopackaging.com
Estimated Sales: $3 - 5 Million
Number Employees: 10-19

25510 Lucie Sable Imports
3349 Howard St
Skokie, IL 60076-4010
847-677-2867
Fax: 847-677-2018 800-582-4326
luciesable@aol.com
Owner: Lucie Sable
CFO: Mike Kacyn
R & D: Madelaine Brown
Estimated Sales: $2.5-5 Million
Number Employees: 5-9

25511 Lucille Farms
PO Box 517
Montville, NJ 07045-0517
973-334-6030
Fax: 973-402-6361 800-654-6844
Cheeses
President: Al Falivene
CEO: Jay Rosengarten
Number Employees: 90

25512 Luckner Steel Shelving
5454 43rd St
Flushing, NY 11378-1028
718-363-0500
Fax: 718-784-9169 800-888-4212
info@karpinc.com www.karpinc.com
Manufacturer and exporter of wire shelving

President: Burt Gold
  bgold@karpinc.com
CFO: Ron Peterson
Marketing: Claudia Holtz
Sales: Chantale Laraque
Estimated Sales: $5 - 10,000,000
Number Employees: 50-99
Square Footage: 45000
Parent Co: Karp Associates
Brands:
  Penco

25513 Lucks Food Equipment Company
21112 72nd Avenue S
Kent, WA 98032-1339
253-872-2180
Fax: 253-872-2013 811-824-0696
info@lucks.com www.lucks.com
Rack ovens, proof boxes, dividers and rounders, revolving tray ovens, spiral mixers, sheeters and moulders
President: Rick Ellison
Chief Financial Officer: Carl Lucks
Senior Vice President of Operations: Dan Elliott
VP Marketing: Kurt Lucks
Contact: Tom Scherer
  tscherer@lucks.com
Estimated Sales: $20-50 Million
Number Employees: 100-250

25514 (HQ)Luco Mop Co
3345 Morganford Rd
St Louis, MO 63116-1805
314-772-5656
Fax: 314-772-5826 800-522-5826
www.lucomop.com
Mops, brooms and accessories
Owner: John Shalhoub
  john@lucomop.com
Estimated Sales: $1-2.5 Million
Number Employees: 10-19

25515 Ludeca Inc
1425 NW 88th Ave
Doral, FL 33172-3017
305-591-8935
Fax: 305-591-1537 info@ludeca.com
Laser tools for machinery alignment and instruments for machine condition monitoring
Manager: Frank Heilemann
CFO: Danny Cermelli
  danny.cermelli@ludeca.com
Estimated Sales: $2.5-5 Million
Number Employees: 20-49

25516 Ludell Manufacturing Co
5200 W State St
Milwaukee, WI 53208-2688
414-476-9934
Fax: 414-476-9864 800-558-0800
sales@ludellmfg.com
www.ludellmanufacturing.com
Manufacturer and exporter of ASME certified heat exchangers, custom engineered wastewater heat recovery systems, direct contact water heaters, and boiler feedwater systems, replacement storage tanks and boiler stack economizers
Owner: Robert Fesmire
  george.simpson@gcmk.org
Chief Executive Officer: Bob Fesmire
CFO: David Arthur
Quality Control: Richard Ogren
Vice President: Robert Fesmire
  george.simpson@gcmk.org
Sales Director: Greg Thorn
  george.simpson@gcmk.org
Plant Manager: Gary Nance
Purchasing Manager: Mark Grosskreutz
Estimated Sales: $8.5 Million
Number Employees: 20-49
Number of Brands: 6
Number of Products: 2
Square Footage: 200000

25517 Luetzow Industries
1105 Davis Ave
South Milwaukee, WI 53172-1195
414-762-0410
Fax: 414-762-0943 800-558-6055
www.luetzow.cc
Manufacturer and exporter of polyethylene bags and film, and sheating
President: Albert Luetzow
VP: Brent Luetzow

Estimated Sales: $10 - 20 Million
Number Employees: 20-49
Square Footage: 160000
Type of Packaging: Consumer, Private Label, Bulk
Brands:
  Luetzow
  Sir Flip Flop

25518 Luhr Jensen & Sons Inc
400 Portway Ave
Hood River, OR 97031-1192
541-386-3811
Fax: 541-386-4917 www.luhrjensen.com
Sausage and brine mixes and seasonings and spices; also, sausage making kits, electric smokers and wood flavor fuels
President: Philip Jensen
  philipjensen@luhrjensen.com
Customer Service: Linda Gordon
Estimated Sales: $10-20 Million
Number Employees: 250-499
Square Footage: 100000

25519 Luke's Almond Acres
11281 S Lac Jac Ave
Reedley, CA 93654
559-638-3483
Fax: 559-637-7788
Wooden crates and gift boxes; packer of dried fruit and nuts
Owner: Ed Esajin
Owner: Lucas Nersesian
  lnersesian@gmail.com
*Estimated Sales:*less than $500,000
Number Employees: 1-4
Square Footage: 10000
Brands:
  Luke's Almond Acres

25520 Luma Sense TechnologiesInc
3301 Leonard Ct
Santa Clara, CA 95054-2054
408-727-1600
Fax: 408-727-1677 800-631-0176
info@lumasenseinc.com www.lumasenseinc.com
Temperature monitoring sensors used in microwave food processing development and gas monitoring systems.
CEO: Michael Chavez
  mchavez@clp.com
CEO: Vivek Joshi
Marketing Director: Mark Reis
Public Relations: Judi Seavers
Estimated Sales: $10-20 Million
Number Employees: 50-99
Square Footage: 74000

25521 Lumaco Inc
9-11 E Broadway
Hackensack, NJ 07601-6821
201-342-5119
Fax: 201-342-8898 800-735-8258
valvinfo@lumaco.com www.lumaco.com
Stainless steel manual and pneumatic valves
Owner: Anita Buxbaum
Sales Manager: Don Kiefer
Estimated Sales: $2.5-5 Million
Number Employees: 5-9
Square Footage: 10000

25522 Lumaco Inc
9-11 E Broadway
Hackensack, NJ 07601-6821
201-342-5119
Fax: 201-342-8898 800-735-8258
valvinfo@lumaco.com www.lumaco.com
Sanitary stainless steel valves
Owner: Anita Buxbaum
Estimated Sales: $2.5-5 Million
Number Employees: 5-9
Square Footage: 10000
Brands:
  Lumaco

25523 Lumacurve Airfield Signs
9115 Freeway Dr
Macedonia, OH 44056
330-467-2030
Fax: 330-467-2076 800-258-1997
www.lumacurve.com
Manufacturer and exporter of porcelain top tables

President: John A Messner
Quality Control: Craig Fussner
R&D: Dane Scholz
Sales: Neil Messner
Contact: Melanie Rostankowski
  melanie@lumacurve.com
Estimated Sales: Below $5,000,000
Number Employees: 20-49
Parent Co: Standard Signs Inc.
Type of Packaging: Food Service
Brands:
  Logotop

25524 Lumax Industries
301 Chestnut Ave
Altoona, PA 16601
814-944-2537
Fax: 814-944-6413 sales@lumaxlighting.com
www.lumaxlighting.com
Manufacturer and exporter of lighting fixtures and H.I.D. luminares including commercial, industrial and custom
CEO: Vineet Sahni
  vineetsahni@lumaxmail.com
CEO: Donald E Snyder
National Sales Manager: Randy Solliday
VP Operations: Ken Merritts
Estimated Sales: $10-20 Million
Number Employees: 100-249
Square Footage: 320000
Type of Packaging: Consumer, Food Service, Private Label
Brands:
  Light Forms

25525 Lumber & Things
PO Box 386
Keyser, WV 26726
304-788-5600
Fax: 304-788-7823 800-296-5656
www.lumberandthings.com
We have been in business for over 30 years. Our customers depend on the standards that we build on: Honesty-Quality-Service. We produce: Reconditioned, Remanufacture and New pallets; Reconditioned, Remanufactured and Recycled tier/slipsheets; Reconditioned, Remanufactured and New top frames; Reconditioned and New can and glass bulk pallets. With an attendant standing by our 24 hour hotline we can provide your company with delivery within 24 hours of your phone call.
President: Jack Amoruso
National Accounts Manager: Victor Knight
Customer Service Specialist: Patricia Davis
Plant Manager: Jack Amoruso
Purchasing Director: Ken Winter
Number Employees: 100-249
Square Footage: 150000
Type of Packaging: Consumer, Food Service, Private Label, Bulk

25526 Lumenite Control Tech Inc
2331 17th St
Franklin Park, IL 60131-3432
847-455-1450
Fax: 847-455-0127 800-323-8510
customerservice@lumenite.com
www.lumenite.com
Manufacturer, importer and exporter of blending and batching equipment, flow meters, level detectors and temperature indicators and controllers
Owner: Ron Calabrese
  roncalabrese@lumenite.com
Office Manager: Craig Meixner
V.P. Engineering: Ronald Calabrese
Sales manager: David Calabrese
Advertising Manager: Carol Calabrese
Service Representative: Rosa Furio
Estimated Sales: $2.5-5 Million
Number Employees: 10-19
Square Footage: 40000
Brands:
  Industrialeveline
  Paneleveline

25527 Luminiere Corporation
4269 Park Ave
Bronx, NY 10457-4207
718-295-5450
Fax: 718-295-5451
Manufacturer, importer and exporter of crystal and bronze chandeliers, electric lamps, lighting fixtures and display lighting

Owner: Herbert Leggan
VP: A Langsam
VP: N Gussack
Estimated Sales: $3 - 5 Million
Number Employees: 5-9
Square Footage: 100000

25528 Lumsden Corporation
PO Box 4647
Lancaster, PA 17604

717-394-6871
Fax: 717-394-1640 800-367-3664
sales@lumsdencorp.com www.lumsdencorp.com
CEO: Glenn Farrell
Contact: Kim Le
kle@lumsdencorp.com
Estimated Sales: $10-20 Million
Number Employees: 20-49

25529 Lumsden Flexx Flow
PO Box 4647
Lancaster, PA 17604

717-394-6871
Fax: 717-394-1640 800-367-3664
sales@lumsdenbelting.com
www.lumsdencorp.com
Wire and mesh conveyor belting, chain driven belts,
positive drive pin rolls, furnace curtains and wire
straightening devices; exporter of conveyor belting
President: Glenn Farrell
Quality Control: Glenn Farrell
Sales Manager: Pete Moore
Contact: Clayton Farrell
cfarrell@lumsdencorp.com
Estimated Sales: Below $15 Million
Number Employees: 20-49
Brands:
Flexx Flow

25530 Lunn Industries
1 Garvies Point Road
Glen Cove, NY 11542-2821

516-671-9000
Fax: 516-671-9005
Fiberglass and reinforced plastic containers
President: Bob Robinson
Sales Manager: Don Trachta Reda
Number Employees: 10

25531 Luseaux Labs Inc
16816 Gramercy Pl
Gardena, CA 90247-5282

323-321-0562
Fax: 310-538-3889 800-266-1555
detergents@luseaux.com www.luseaux.com
Manufacturer, importer and exporter of cleaners,
sanitizers and detergents including liquid and
powder
Vice President: Kathy Kalohi
kathy@luseaux.com
Chief Information Officer: Charles Edwards
Office Manager: Kathleen Kalohi
Estimated Sales: $810,000
Number Employees: 5-9
Square Footage: 180000
Type of Packaging: Food Service, Private Label,
Bulk
Other Locations:
Kingman AZ
Brands:
Luseaux

25532 Lustrecal
715 S Guild Ave
Lodi, CA 95240-3153

209-370-1600
Fax: 209-370-1690 800-234-6264
rbeckler@lustrecal.com www.lustrecal.com
Manufacturer and exporter of color anodized and
etched aluminum nameplates and labels
CEO: Clydene Hohenrieder
chohenrieder@lustrecal.com
Estimated Sales: $20-50 Million
Number Employees: 50-99

25533 Luthi Machinery Company, Inc.
1 Magnuson Avenue
Pueblo, CO 81001

719-948-1110
Fax: 719-948-9540 sales@atlaspacific.com
www.luthi.com
Manufacturer and exporter of can filling and dicing
machinery for tuna, salmon, chicken, turkey, pork
and beef

President: Erik Teranchi
CFO/VP: Don Freeman
V.P. & General Manager: Craig Furlo
Marketing/Sales: Robb Morris
Sales: Gini Fisher
Contact: Juan Monroy
jmonroy@luthi.com
Production: Vern Brown
Number Employees: 50
Square Footage: 136000

25534 Luxfer Gas Cylinders
3016 Kansas Ave # 1
Riverside, CA 92507-3445

951-684-5110
Fax: 951-328-1117 www.luxfercylinders.com
President: Andy Butcher
CFO: Micheal Edwards
R&D: Hendy Holrowd
Quality Control: Rick Willson
Estimated Sales: $20 - 50 Million
Number Employees: 250-499

25535 Luxo Corporation
Ste 105
5 Westchester Plz
Elmsford, NY 10523-1645

914-937-4433
Fax: 914-937-7016 800-222-5896
www.luxous.com
Manufacturer and importer of magnification, ambi-
ent and task lighting fixtures
Regional Sales Manager: Doug Benway
Estimated Sales: $10-20 Million
Number Employees: 50-99
Square Footage: 120000
Parent Co: Luxo ASA
Type of Packaging: Food Service

25536 Lyco Manufacturing
PO Box 2022
Wausau, WI 54402-2022

715-845-7867
Fax: 715-842-8228 info@lyco.com
www.lycowausau.com
Stainless steel liquid ring vacuum pumps for food,
pharmaceutical, chemical, medical, laboratory and
general industrial applications where corrosion resistance is beneficial.
President: Thomas Frane
Number Employees: 50-99

25537 Lyco Manufacturing Inc
115 Commercial Dr
Columbus, WI 53925-1008

920-623-4152
Fax: 920-623-3780 sales@lycomfg.com
www.lycomfg.com
Commercial food processing equipment manufacturer specializing in the areas of heating/cooling, liq-
uid/solid separation, root crop preparation and snap
bean processing equipment
CEO: Steve Hughes
steve.hughes@lycomfg.com
Estimated Sales: $4.5 Million
Number Employees: 50-99

25538 Lyco Wausau
P.O. Box 2022
Wausau, WI 54402-2022

715-845-7867
Fax: 715-842-8228 www.lycowausau.com
Manufacturer and exporter of stainless steel liquid
ring vacuum pumps and systems for filling,
deaerating, cooking, dewatering, conveying, evapo-
rating and packaging
President: Thomas Frane
Estimated Sales: $3 - 5 Million
Brands:
Lyco
Vaqmer

25539 Lydall
PO Box 2002
Doswell, VA 23047-2002

804-266-9611
www.lydall.com
Packaging products and wooden pallet replacements

President, CEO: Dale G. Barnhart
EVP, CFO: Robert K. Julian
Vice President, Chief Accounting Officer: James V.
Laughlan
VP Sales: P Mullins
Vice President, Human Resources: William M.
Lachenmeyer
Plant Manager: E Smith
Estimated Sales: $1 - 5 Million
Number Employees: 100
Parent Co: Lydall

25540 Lyman-Morse Fabrication
19 Elltee Cir
Thomaston, ME 04861-3218

207-594-7655
Fax: 207-594-7790 www.lymanmorse.com
Manager: Johnathan Egan
jegan@lymanmorse.com
General Manager: Mike Young
Manager: Dave Wyllie
Estimated Sales: $3 - 5 Million
Number Employees: 10-19

25541 (HQ)Lynch Corp
140 Greenwich Ave # 4
Suite 4
Greenwich, CT 06830-6560

203-340-2590
Fax: 401-453-2009
Manufacturer and exporter of glass forming and
packaging machines
President: Richard E McGrail
CEO: Ralph R Papitto
ralphp@gemini-cap.com
CFO: Raymond Keller
Estimated Sales: $20 - 30 Million
Number Employees: 1-4

25542 Lynch-Jamentz Company
5150 Candlewood Street
Lakewood, CA 90712-1925

562-630-6798
Fax: 562-630-5901 800-828-6217
Skewers, hot pan grips, spoons and racks including
roasting, baking and broiling
CEO: Ron Trepte, Sr.
Marketing Director: Ron Trepte, Sr.
Secretary: E Trepte
Purchasing Manager: Ron Trepte, Sr.
Estimated Sales: $1-2.5 Million
Number Employees: 10
Square Footage: 48000
Parent Co: Trepte's Wire & Metal Works

25543 Lynden Meat Co
1936 Front St
Lynden, WA 98264-1708

360-354-2449
Fax: 360-354-7687
Livestock slaughtering services, herd managemnt,
livestock breeding and grooming, livestock manage-
ment, livestock selection, ice cube makers, ice block
makers, industrial freezers.
Owner: Rick Biesheuvel
Estimated Sales: $3 - 5 Million
Number Employees: 5-9
Type of Packaging: Consumer

25544 (HQ)Lynn Sign Inc
8 Gleason St
Andover, MA 01810-3324

978-470-1194
Fax: 978-346-8197 800-225-5764
lynnsign@aol.com
Manufacturer and exporter of changeable plastic let-
ters and signs, menu boards, building directories,
bulletin boards, display cases, engraving stock and
sign holders
Owner: R Rand Richmond
Public Relations: Darlene Reiss
Manager: Lynn Sullivan
Estimated Sales: Less Than $500,000
Number Employees: 1-4
Number of Brands: 1
Square Footage: 34000
Type of Packaging: Bulk
Brands:
Lynnply

25545 Lyon LLC
420 N Main St
Montgomery, IL 60538-1367
630-892-8941
Fax: 630-264-4542 www.lyonworkspace.com
Manufacturer and exporter of metal storage equipment including shelving, cabinets, etc
CEO: R Peter Washington
CEO: R Peter Washington
Marketing Director: Robert Bell
Estimated Sales: $50-100 Million
Number Employees: 1000-4999

25546 Lyons Falls Pulp & Paper
77 E Crystal Lake Avenue
Crystal Lake, IL 60014-6171
815-455-0981
Fax: 815-455-0997
Tea and coffee industry pouch materials (cellophane, paper, films)
Estimated Sales: $1-2.5 Million
Number Employees: 1-4

25547 M & D Specialties Inc
17301 NW Oak Ridge Rd
Yamhill, OR 97148-8119
503-662-4516
Fax: 503-662-3629
Wine industry labelers, pumps
Manager: Kathy Aplin
mdspec@msn.com
Estimated Sales: Less Than $500,000
Number Employees: 1-4

25548 M & E Mfg Co Inc
19 Progress St
Kingston, NY 12401-3611
845-331-2110
Fax: 845-331-4143
customerservice@zframerack.com
Manufacturer and exporter of shelving, racks, tables, cutting boards, trucks, platters, dollies and carts
President: Conor Curley
conor.curley@digicelgroup.com
Executive VP: Don Hall
Estimated Sales: $20 - 50 Million
Number Employees: 50-99
Square Footage: 40000
Brands:
Butcher Buddy
Deli Buddy

25549 M & G Packaging Corp
22610 Jamaica Ave
Floral Park, NY 11001-3812
718-343-0343
Fax: 516-488-3181 800-240-5288
charles@mgpackaging.com
www.mgpackaging.com
Boxes, cartons, foam, packaging material and plastic bags
President: Charles Rick
VP: Charles Rick
Estimated Sales: $20-50 Million
Number Employees: 5-9
Brands:
Avi

25550 M & H Crate Inc
4022 Fm 347 N
Jacksonville, TX 75766-6696
903-683-5351
Fax: 903-683-9593
Wooden pallets and shipping crates
CEO: Davy Sanders
dfsanders@mhcrates.com
Supervisor: Andy McCown
Estimated Sales: $10-20 Million
Number Employees: 100-249
Square Footage: 40000

25551 M & M Display
7700 Brewster Ave
Philadelphia, PA 19153-3299
215-492-1963
Fax: 215-365-5610 800-874-7171
bobdigiorgio@mmdisplays.com
www.mmdisplays.com
Screen printing, digital printing, p.o.p. displays, metal sign frames, banners, decals, interior graphics, and several patented items including nozzle talkers brand
CEO: Michael Sell
Sales Exec: Robert Digiorgio
Production Manager: Chris Mace
Purchasing Manager: William Gonzacez
Estimated Sales: $11 Million
Number Employees: 50-99
Square Footage: 160000

25552 M & M Equipment Corp
7355 Monticello Ave
Skokie, IL 60076-4024
847-673-0350
Fax: 847-673-0350 sales@mmequip.com
www.mmequip.com
Cutting and boning devices, slaughtering equipment
Owner: Marc Newman
sales@mmequip.com
Estimated Sales: $1 - 2.5 Million
Number Employees: 10-19

25553 M & M Industries Inc
316 Corporate Pl
Chattanooga, TN 37419-2339
423-821-3302
Fax: 423-821-9017 800-331-5305
cstone@mmcontainer.com www.ultimatepail.com
Life Latch plastic pails suitable for a variety of purposes including the food industry. Uses include livestock feed and grains; pet food storage; seeds; vitamin supplements, etc.
VP: Glenn H Morris Jr
gmorris@m-m-industries.com
Regional Accounts Manager: Rae Green
Regional Accounts Manager: Cindy Stone
Regional Accounts Manager: Tiffany King
Regional Accounts Manager: Janet Rogers
Estimated Sales: $10-25 Million
Number Employees: 100-249

25554 M & M Poultry EquipmentInc
296 Carlton Rd
Hollister, MO 65672-5156
417-334-6641
Fax: 417-332-2881 800-872-9687
drew.horst@mandmpoultry.com
www.mandmpoultry.com
Poultry processing equipment, overhead conveyor chain, picking fingers, misc, spare parts, and feather picker.
President: Rob L Middleton
middletonr@middletongroup.com
Marketing: Larry McGriff
Sales: Sloan Houston
Production: Jason Burkett
Number Employees: 50-99

25555 M & O Perry Industries
412 N Smith Ave
Corona, CA 92880-6903
951-273-1534
Fax: 951-734-2454 sales@moperry.com
www.moperry.com
Filling equipment for the animal health, biotech, diagnostic, medical device, ophthalmic and pharmaceutical markets. liquid and powder filling technologies
President: Phillip Osterhaus
posterhaus@moperry.com
Estimated Sales: $5-10 Million
Number Employees: 20-49

25556 M & O Perry Industries
412 N Smith Ave
Corona, CA 92880-6903
951-273-1534
Fax: 951-734-2454 sales@moperry.com
www.moperry.com
Powder fillers, liquid fillers
President: Phillip Osterhaus
posterhaus@moperry.com
Estimated Sales: $5-10 Million
Number Employees: 20-49

25557 M & Q Packaging Corp
1120 Welsh Rd
North Wales, PA 19454-3794
267-498-4000
Fax: 267-498-0030 www.mqplastics.com
High quality plastic products.
President: David Carlin
Contact: Chris Duplisea
chris@mqplastics.com
Estimated Sales: $26 Million
Number Employees: 10-19
Parent Co: M&Q Plastics Products
Type of Packaging: Food Service

25558 M & R Sales & Svc Inc
1n372 Main St
Glen Ellyn, IL 60137-3576
630-858-6101
Fax: 630-858-6134 800-736-6431
www.mrprint.com
Manufacturer and exporter of belting, switches, etc
CEO: Richard Hoffman
Estimated Sales: $1-2.5 Million
Number Employees: 20-49
Parent Co: M&R Printing Equipment

25559 M & S Automated FeedingSysts
1194 Cliff Rd E
Burnsville, MN 55337-1577
952-894-3263
Fax: 952-895-9910 masafs@msautomated.com
www.msautomated.com
President: Mark Grinager
mark@msautomated.com
Estimated Sales: $3,000,000 - $5,000,000
Number Employees: 10-19

25560 M & W Protective Coating LLC
2239 16 3/4 Ave
Rice Lake, WI 54868-8786
715-234-2251
Protective coating
Manager: Douglas Winkel
Manager: Douglas Winkel
Estimated Sales: Less Than $500,000
Number Employees: 1-4

25561 (HQ)M D Stetson Co
92 York Ave
Randolph, MA 02368-1892
781-986-6161
Fax: 781-961-1764 800-255-8651
service@mdstetson.com www.mdstetson.com
Cleaning, degreasing and sanitizing chemicals, liquid hand soap and furniture and floor polish; wholesaler/distributor of maintenance equipment and supplies, industrial sweepers and scrubbers
President: Michael Glass
michael.glass@mdstetson.com
Treasurer and R&D and Quality Control: Andrea Adams
Estimated Sales: $15 - 20 Million
Number Employees: 20-49
Square Footage: 104000

25562 M F & B Restaurant Systems Inc
133 Icmi Rd
Dunbar, PA 15431-2309
724-628-3050
Fax: 724-626-0247
Remanufacture conveyor pizza ovens, sell new and used parts
Owner: Mike French
mfrench@edgeoven.com
Vice President: Michael French
Estimated Sales: $400,000
Number Employees: 5-9
Number of Brands: 5
Square Footage: 24000
Brands:
Lincoln Ovens
Middleby Marshall Ovens

25563 M F G Inc
5620 19th Ave
Kenosha, WI 53140-3935
262-652-3336
Fax: 262-652-3322 mfgincorp@aol.com
www.mfginc.info
Packaging machinery
President: George Roders
mfgincorp@aol.com
Estimated Sales: $1-5 Million
Number Employees: 5-9

25564 M G America Inc
31 Kulick Rd
Fairfield, NJ 07004-3307
973-575-2509
Fax: 973-808-8421 cradossi@mgamerica.com
www.mgamerica.com

Capsule fillers, liquid and powder fillers, tube fillers, capsule checkweighers, cartoners, case packers and palletizers
President: Fabio Trippodo
Estimated Sales: $2.5 - 5 Million
Number Employees: 10-19

25565 M G Newell Corp
301 Citation Ct
Greensboro, NC 27409-9027
336-393-0100
Fax: 336-393-0140 800-334-0231
sales@mgnewell.com www.mgnewell.com
We provide equipment and engineered solutions in automation and control, CIP and custom washing systems, field service, calibration, maintenance, repair, fluid handling, heat exchange, installation, material handling, mixing andblending, process design, skidded system fabrication
President: John Sherrill
john.sherrill@mgnewell.com
CFO: Julie Hart
Vice President: Julie Hart
VP Engineering: Tony Saenz
Marketing Director: Gray Sherrill
Human Resources: Deb Gaither
VP/Chief Operating Officer: Michael Sherrill
Estimated Sales: $10 - 20 Million
Number Employees: 20-49

25566 M J D Trucking
2055 Demarco Dr
Vineland, NJ 08360-1554
856-205-9490
Fax: 856-205-9491 800-458-0439
www.mjdtrucking.net
Owner: John Davey
john@mjdtrucking.net
Estimated Sales: $3 - 5 Million
Number Employees: 20-49

25567 M M Industries Inc
36135 Salem Grange Rd
P.O. Box 720
Salem, OH 44460-9442
330-332-4958
Fax: 330-332-1543 800-227-7487
info@vorti-siv.com www.vorti-siv.com
Serving and filtration equipment. Manufacturer of sieving, straining and self-cleaning in-line filtration systems. Commonly used for ingredient sifting; particle separation and classification; liquid/solid separation and liquidfiltration
President: Barbara Maroscher
info@vorti-siv.com
VP: Vic Maroscher
Public Relations: Dennis Ulrich
Estimated Sales: $2.5 - 5 Million
Number Employees: 10-19
Square Footage: 160000

25568 M O Industries Inc
9 Whippany Rd # B1-2
Unit B1-2
Whippany, NJ 07981-1530
973-386-9228
Fax: 973-428-0221 sales@moindustries.com
www.moindustries.com
Manufacturer importer and exporter of movable and stationary drum lifters/positioners; also, dust control blending, crushing and milling size reducers, pallets, stainless steel funnels, quick-release valves, viscous materialdischargers, and stainless steel drums
President: German Leiva
gleiva@moindustries.com
Estimated Sales: $4 Million
Number Employees: 5-9
Brands:
 M.O.-Lift
 Robusto
 Vispro

25569 M S Plastics & Packaging Inc
10 Park Pl # 11
Building 2-1A2
Butler, NJ 07405-1370
973-492-2400
Fax: 973-492-7801 800-593-1802
Polyethylene bags, liners, sheets, stretch wrap, printed bags, tubing, stretch and shrink film and bands; importer of plastic shrink films and bands
Owner: Ellen Saraisky
info@msplastics.com
CFO: Al Saraisky

Estimated Sales: $3 - 5 Million
Number Employees: 20-49
Brands:
 Banderwrapper
 Disposawrapper
 Freightwrap
 Polybander

25570 M S Willett Inc
220 Cockeysville Rd
Cockeysville, MD 21030-4367
410-771-0460
Fax: 410-771-6972 info@mswillett.com
www.mswillett.com
Manufacturer and exporter of precision equipment to produce stamped and formed metal food, shallow drawn and specialty containers and easy open can ends
President: Gabriel Gauzon
pgauzon@worldbank.org
R&D: Gary Ruby
Quality Control: Robert Burns
Sales Director: Gary Ruby
Public Relations: Linda Ambrose
Plant Manager: Larry Felty
Purchasing Director: Jack Kersch
Estimated Sales: $5 Million
Number Employees: 50-99
Square Footage: 240000

25571 M S Willett Inc
220 Cockeysville Rd
Cockeysville, MD 21030-4367
410-771-0460
Fax: 410-771-6972 info@mswillett.com
www.mswillett.com
Turnkey systems and tooling for the production of light metal packaging components, easy open ends, shallow drawn cans and food tray, hinge cover boxes, and small deep drawn parts
President: Gabriel Gauzon
pgauzon@worldbank.org
Engineering, Development & Sales: Gary Ruby
Quality & Safety: Robert Burns
Public Relations: Linda Ambrose
Manager Manufacturing Serv.: Jack Kersch
T&D Manager: Larry Felty
Estimated Sales: $5-10 Million
Number Employees: 50-99
Square Footage: 292000

25572 M&C Sweeteners
650 Industrial Road
Blair, NE 68008-2649
402-533-1843
Fax: 402-433-1831

25573 M&L Plastics
150 Pleasant St
Easthampton, MA 01027-1887
413-527-1330
Fax: 413-527-8621
Manufacturer and exporter of plastic display containers
Number Employees: 10-19
Parent Co: Paragon Rubber Corporation

25574 M&Q Plastic Products
1120 Welsh Rd
Suite 170
North Wales, PA 19454
267-498-4000
Fax: 267-498-0030 877-726-7287
High Temperture flexible, packaging products ideal for use in oven, microwave, and steamtable applications
Director Sales/Marketing: Tim Blucher
Contact: Ernie Bachert
ebachert@pansaver.com
Product Manager: George Schmidt
Estimated Sales: $2.5-5 Million
Number Employees: 75
Square Footage: 80000
Brands:
 Monolyn
 Pansaver

25575 M&R Flexible Packaging
PO Box 907
Springboro, OH 45066-0907
937-298-7272
Fax: 937-298-7388 800-543-3380

Manufacturer, importer and exporter of plastic bags, industrial packaging materials, plastics and shipping room supplies
President/Owner: Ronald Morris
Estimated Sales: $2.5-5,000,000
Number Employees: 10-19

25576 M&S Manufacturing
3728 Telegraph Rd
Arnold, MO 63010
636-464-2739
Fax: 636-464-5923
Hot food wells, refrigerated bases, hoods, walk-in coolers and tables including steam, salad, dish and soil
Owner: Darlene Spink
VP Secretary: Darline Spink
Estimated Sales: $500,000-$1 Million
Number Employees: 5-9
Square Footage: 5600

25577 M&S Miltenberg & Samton
2 Hollyhock Road
Wilton, CT 06897-4438
203-834-0002
Fax: 203-834-1002 www.miltsam.com
Carton machines: closing, filling, handling, sealing; coaters, cooling equipment: cooling tunnels, tables; cut and wrap equipment, extruders: chewing gum, coconut candy, confectionery; feeder belts, automatic, batch, rope, screw;feeding and placement system; flow-pack machines, glazing machines, gum sanders, kettles, licorice machines
Contact: Frank Franze
ffranze@miltsam.com
Estimated Sales: $2.5-5 Million
Number Employees: 5-9

25578 M-E-C Co
1400 Main St
Neodesha, KS 66757-1679
620-325-2673
Fax: 620-325-2678
Manufacturer and exporter of dryer systems for nonedible biological materials and foodwastes including convection, total, rotary, and flash tube
President: John Quick
jquick@m-e-c.com
CFO: Jerry Creekmore
R&D: Mike Hudson
Quality Control: Kent Shields
Sales Manager: Gary Follmer
Purchasing: John George
Estimated Sales: $20 - 50 Million
Number Employees: 100-249
Square Footage: 170000

25579 M-One Specialties
974 W 100 S
Salt Lake City, UT 84104-1198
801-596-2500
Fax: 801-521-6502 800-525-9223
mone@moneplumbing.com
www.m-oneplumbing.com
Faucet and plumbing repair and replacement parts-bathroom hardware and ada parts
President/Owner: George Mattena
mone@moneplumbing.com
Estimated Sales: $5 - 10,000,000
Number Employees: 10-19
Number of Brands: 164
Number of Products: 2800
Type of Packaging: Bulk

25580 M-TEK Inc
1675 Todd Farm Dr
Elgin, IL 60123
847-741-3500
Fax: 847-741-3569 847-741-3500
mtek@mtekcorp.com www.mtekcorp.com
Vacuum packaging machinery
President: Richard Maskell
VP Marketing/Sales: Rick Tkaczyk
Contact: Norm Buggele
nbuggele@mtekcorp.com
Operations Manager: Alan Wojak
Production Manager: Mark Evans
Purchasing Manager: Jason Aleo
Estimated Sales: $5-10 Million
Number Employees: 20-49
Number of Brands: 2
Type of Packaging: Consumer, Food Service, Private Label, Bulk

25581 M-Tech & Associates
4323 Stonewall Avenue
Downers Grove, IL 60515-2654
630-810-9714
Fax: 630-810-9712
Consultant specializing in implementing MRP
scheduling, training, production and process
monitoring
Number Employees: 5
Square Footage: 2000

25582 M-Vac Systems Inc
14621 S 800 W # 100
Suite 100
Bluffdale, UT 84065-4863
801-523-3962
www.m-vac.com
the m-vac is a dry or wet vacuuming collection/con-
tainment device used to detect and recover surface
pathogens.
Owner: Dr. Bruce Bradley
Parent Co: MSI

25583 (HQ)M.E. Heuck Company
1111 Western Row Road
Mason, OH 45040-2649
513-681-1774
Fax: 513-681-2329 800-359-3200
Manufacturer, importer, exporter of kitchen utensils
including barbecue tools, nut crackers, shellfish
crackers, etc
President: Ramesh Malhotra
CFO: Tim Omelia
VP: Bill Dickmann
R&D: Tim Omelia
Manager: Linda Brandt
Contact: Chris Carthy
c.carthy@heuck.com
Estimated Sales: $20 - 50 Million
Number Employees: 30
Square Footage: 90000
Brands:
Burpee
H.M. Quackenbush
Mr. Food

25584 M.H. Rhodes Cramer
105 Nutmeg Rd S
South Windsor, CT 6074
860-291-8402
Fax: 860-610-0120 877-684-6464
customer-service@mhrhodes.com
www.mhrhodes.com
Manufacturer, importer and exporter of timers in-
cluding audible signal and electronic as well as me-
chanical timers/time switches for OEM's
President: Ken Mac Cormac
Founder: Mark Rhodes, Sr.
Manager Sales: Jim Kline
Customer Service: Bernie Rodrigues
Purchasing Manager: Jeff Carlson
Estimated Sales: $10-20 Million
Number Employees: 100-249
Square Footage: 170000
Type of Packaging: Consumer, Food Service, Pri-
vate Label, Bulk
Brands:
Mark-Time

25585 MAC Equipment
7901 NW 107th Ter
Kansas City, MO 64153-1910
816-891-9300
Fax: 816-891-8336 sales@macequipment.com
www.macequipment.com
President: Jay Brown
Contact: Mike Althouse
althousem@macequipment.com
Estimated Sales: Below $5 Million
Number Employees: 250-499

25586 MAC Equipment
7901 NW 107th Ter
Kansas City, MO 64153-1910
816-891-9300
Fax: 816-891-8336 800-821-2476
sales@macequipment.com
www.macequipment.com
Equipment: pneumatic conveying and dust collection
President: Jay Brown
Food Group Manager: Stuart Carrico
Contact: Mike Althouse
althousem@macequipment.com

Estimated Sales: $10-20 Million

25587 MAC Tac LLC
4560 Darrow Rd
Stow, OH 44224-1898
330-688-1111
Fax: 330-688-2540 866-262-2822
mactac.americas@mactac.com www.mactac.com
Manufacturer and exporter of pressure sensitive pa-
per, film and foil products
President: Jim Peruzzi
Cmo: Jennifer Bowman
jmbowman@bemis.com
Executive VP: Robert Hawthorne
Purchasing Agent: Hank Cardarelli
Number Employees: 500-999
Parent Co: Bemls Company
Brands:
Copyback
Durascan
Eze-Gloss
Eze-Therm
Mac-Copy
Mac-Gloss
Mac-Jet
Optichrome
Opticlear
Optiscan
Pharmaclear
Pharmalite
Pharmasoft
Polyfilm
Trans Label
Ultrascan

25588 MAF Industries Inc
36470 Highway 99
PO Box 218
Traver, CA 93673
559-897-2905
Fax: 559-897-3422 mafusa@aol.com
www.mafindustries.com
Manufacturer, importer and exporter of packaging
equipment including sizers, color sorters, box fillers,
robotic bin dumpers, washers, waxers, etc
CEO: Jack Kraemer
CFO/Controller: Raul Mejia
Sales Manager: Leendert Van Der Tas
Manager: Raul Mejia
rmejia@mafindustries.com
Estimated Sales: $10-20 Million
Number Employees: 50-99
Square Footage: 100000
Parent Co: SMCM
Brands:
Agrobotic Technology

25589 MAK Wood Inc
1235 Dakota Dr # E
Unit E
Grafton, WI 53024-9477
262-387-1200
Fax: 262-387-1400 info@makwood.com
www.makwood.com
Novelty sugars, cranberry, probiotics, lactobacillus
and bifidobacterium. Supplier of L-arabinose,
L-fucose, L-rhamnose, lactates, and of other
probiotics.
Owner: Mark Brudnak
Secretary/Treasurer: Joseph Brudnak
Sr Executive VP: Mark Brudnak
Manager, Technical Sales Services: Eric Baer
mark@makwood.com
Estimated Sales: $380,000
Number Employees: 5-9
Type of Packaging: Private Label, Bulk

25590 MAP Systems International
300 E Touhy Avenue
Des Plaines, IL 60018-2669
847-299-7800
Fax: 847-299-8330
Modified atmospheric packaging, vacuum packaging equipment, blenders, choppers, smokehouses,
stuffers, slicers and plant supplies. Products and services for" industrial food processing equipment; industrial food packaging equipment;grocery and
restauran equipment; and also butcher supplies and
food processing supplies.
Number Employees: 30

25591 MAP Tech Packaging Inc
145 Dillon Rd
Hilton Head Isle, SC 29926-3705
843-342-5900
Fax: 843-342-5924
gfoulke@maptechpackaging.com
www.maptechpackaging.com
Gas sensors that monitors the intake of ammonia,
carbon monoxide, chlorine, chlorine dioxide, hydrogen sulfide, hydrogen, oxygen, etc.
President & CEO: Gary Bert
gbert@maptechpackaging.com
Estimated Sales: $1 - 3 Million
Number Employees: 10-19

25592 MAP Tech Packaging Inc
145 Dillon Rd
Hilton Head Isle, SC 29926-3705
843-342-5900
Fax: 843-342-5924
gfoulke@maptechpackaging.com
www.maptechpackaging.com
President & CEO: Gary Bert
gbert@maptechpackaging.com
Estimated Sales: $1 - 3 Million
Number Employees: 10-19

25593 MAPS Software
P.O. Box 821
Columbus, MS 39703-0821
662-328-6110
Fax: 662-329-9799
Computer software including point of sale, free and
reduced application, purchasing and financial
President: Victor Fuqua
CFO: Sandy David
Representative: Jenny Taylor
Office Manager: Sandy Robinson
Estimated Sales: Below $5 Million
Number Employees: 4

25594 MBC Food Machinery Corp
78 Mckinley St
Hackensack, NJ 07601-4009
201-489-7000
Fax: 201-489-0614
jbattaglia@mbcfoodmachinery.com
www.mbcfoodmachinery.com
Manufacturer and exporter of filling pumps and automatic frozen pasta processing machinery including
ravioli, manicotti and cavatelli
President and CFO: John Battaglia
Estimated Sales: Less than $500,000
Number Employees: 5-9

25595 MBX Packaging Specialists
207 N 1st Ave
Wausau, WI 54401-4403
715-845-1171
Fax: 715-848-1054 randy@mbxpkg.com
www.mbxpkg.com
Recycled plastic pallets in custom sizes and styles
President: Gary Yonke
gary@mbxpkg.com
CEO: Harvey H Scholfield Jr
VP Sales: Randy Haupt
Estimated Sales: $10-20 Million
Number Employees: 100-249
Square Footage: 200000
Parent Co: MBX Packaging
Other Locations:
MBX Packaging
Beloit WI
Brands:
Enviro-Board

25596 MC Creation
1550 Bryant Street
Suite 760
San Francisco, CA 94103-4877
415-775-1135
Consultant specializing in home meal replacement
concepts and food culture development promoting
sushi
Estimated Sales: $300,000-500,000
Number Employees: 1-4

25597 MCD Technologies
2515 South Tacoma Way
Tacoma, WA 98409-7527
253-476-0968
Fax: 253-476-0974 www.mcdtechnologiesinc.com
Manufacturer and exporter of food dryers and evaporators; also, contract toll drying

President: Karin Bolland
 info@mcdtechnologiesinc.com
VP: Richard Magoon
Marketing: Leo Schultz
Estimated Sales: $1-2.5 Million
Number Employees: 10-19
Square Footage: 36000
Brands:
 Refractance Window

25598 MCM Fixture Co
21306 John R Rd
Hazel Park, MI 48030-2211
 248-547-9280
 Fax: 248-547-9270 tawny@mcmstainless.com
Stainless steel food service equipment including cafeteria counters, sinks, tables, hoods and refrigerators; custom fabrication available, custom wall panels, both smooth and quilted, as well as corner guards in all sizes to order.
President: Gary Brown
 gary@mcmstainless.com
Vice President: Eric Brown
Estimated Sales: $1-2.5 Million
Number Employees: 10-19

25599 MCNAB Inc
383 E 29th St # 2
Suite 2
Buena Vista, VA 24416-1293
 540-261-1045
 Fax: 540-261-1268 info@themcnab.com
Owner: Garnette Teass
 sales@themcnab.com
Quality Control: Brad Witt
Estimated Sales: $3 - 5 Million
Number Employees: 10-19

25600 MCR Technologies Group Inc
13420 Galt Rd
PO Box 1016
Sterling, IL 61081-8913
 815-622-3181
 Fax: 815-622-0819 877-622-3181
 sales@weighshark.com
 www.mcrtechnologiesgroup.com
Metal detectors
President: Mark Humphreys
 mhumphreys@weighshark.com
Estimated Sales: $1.5 Million+
Number Employees: 5-9
Number of Brands: 4
Number of Products: 9
Square Footage: 4000
Type of Packaging: Food Service

25601 MDE Corp
11965 Brookfield St
Livonia, MI 48150-1736
 734-744-5480
 Fax: 313-931-2015 800-482-3393
 mielsen@mdecorp.com www.mdecorp.com
Fillers, air, milk, filtration equipment, heat exchangers, plate, scraped surface, homogenizers, ice and ice cream equipment, ingredient feeders, meters, flow, milk, solids, aseptic processing equipment, batch control systems, andcentrifuges
President: Veronica Burnett
 vburnett@mdecorp.com
VP: Robert Nielson Jr
Estimated Sales: $5-10 Million
Number Employees: 20-49

25602 MDH Packaging Corporation
101 Miller Drive
Crittenden, KY 41030-7560
 859-746-0993
 Fax: 859-746-0933 www.ripnzip.com
Contact: Rainer Garger
 rgarger@ripnzip.com
Estimated Sales: $3,000,000 - $5,000,000
Number Employees: 10-19

25603 MDI Worldwide
38271 W 12 Mile Rd
Farmington Hills, MI 48331-3041
 248-553-1900
 Fax: 248-488-5700 800-228-8925
 sales@mdiworldwide.com
 www.mdiworldwide.com
Designs and manufactures marketing displays, retail displays, commercial sign holders, POP displays and merchandising displays

President: Lisa Sarkisian
 lsarkisian@mdiworldwide.com
Number Employees: 100-249
Type of Packaging: Food Service
Brands:
 Postergrip
 Storeworks

25604 MDR International
14861 NE 20th Ave
North Miami, FL 33181
 305-944-5019
 Fax: 305-949-4136 mdrinc@bellsouth.com
 www.mdrinternational.com
Glassware, hurricane glasses, plastic beer mugs, tumblers and mason jar mugs
Owner: Bernard Ghelbendorf
VP Marketing: Gary Fein
Estimated Sales: $2.5-5,000,000
Number Employees: 10-19

25605 MDS Nordion
447 March Road
Ottawa, ON K2K 1X8
Canada
 613-592-2790
 Fax: 613-592-6937 800-465-3666
Supplies patented food irradiation solutions for the meat, poultry and produce industry. Our equipment and process eliminates food-borne pathogens such as E. coli, Salmonella and Listeria from food, prolongs shelf life and treatsproduct for quarantine and bio-security after harvest
President: Steve West
CFO: Micheal Thomas
Senior Vice President, General Counsel,: Andrew Foti
Product Manager Food and Radiation: Joseph Borsa Ph D
R&D and Director: Pierre Lahaie
Marketing Director: Carolin Vandenberg
Senior Vice President of Sales and Marke: Kevin Brooks
Number Employees: 800
Parent Co: MDS
Brands:
 Centurion

25606 MDS-Vet Inc
3429 Stearns Rd
Valrico, FL 33596-6450
 813-653-1180
 Fax: 813-684-5953 tbattle@mdsincorporated.com
 www.mdsvet.com
Manufacturer and exporter of scopes used to check bacteria in pipes and tubes
Owner: Jayson Fitzgerald
 jfitzgerald@seminolecountyfl.gov
Director Marketing: Trudi Battle
Estimated Sales: Less than $500,000
Number Employees: 5-9

25607 MDT
971 Dogwood Trl
Tyrone, GA 30290-2708
 770-631-9074
 Fax: 770-486-9903 info.us@mdt-tex.com
Shades,structures and umbrellas for commercial purposes
Manager: Enlai Hooi
 enlai.hooi@mdt-tex.com
Estimated Sales: $1-2.5 Million
Number Employees: 1-4

25608 MEPSCO
1888 E Fabyan Pkwy
Batavia, IL 60510-1498
 Fax: 630-231-9372 800-323-8535
 www.mepsco.com
Estimated Sales: $9 Million
Number Employees: 20-49

25609 MERRICK Industries Inc
10 Arthur Dr
Lynn Haven, FL 32444-1685
 850-522-4300
 Fax: 850-265-9768 800-271-7834
 info@merrick-inc.com www.merrick-inc.com
Manufacturer and exporter of process weighing and control equipment, belt feeders and loss-in-weight feeders

CEO: Larry Adams
 ladams@acistudios.com
CEO: Joe K Tannehill Sr
Purchasing Manager: Steve Rhinehart
Estimated Sales: $10-20,000,000
Number Employees: 100-249
Square Footage: 55000
Brands:
 Gravimerik
 Mc2
 Mc3
 Superbridge

25610 MGF.com
2700 Cumberland Parkway
Suite 500
Atlanta, GA 30339
Canada
 770-444-9686
Cleaning compounds, detergents and disinfectants
Founder, CEO: Mitch Free
Number Employees: 20
Square Footage: 60000

25611 MGM Instruments
925 Sherman Ave
Hamden, CT 06514-1150
 203-248-4008
 Fax: 203-288-2621 800-551-1415
 sales@mgminstruments.com
 www.mgminstruments.com
Analyzes and tests plant operations, wastewater
President: Patrick Harewood
Chairman and CEO: George Mismas
 georgem@mgminstruments.com
Number Employees: 20-49

25612 MGP Ingredients Inc
100 Commercial St
Atchison, KS 66002-2514
 913-367-1480
 Fax: 913-367-0192 800-255-0302
 selmak@mgpingredients.com
 www.mgpingredients.com
CEO: Augustus C Griffin
 augustus.griffin@mgpingredients.com
Number Employees: 250-499

25613 MGS Machine Corp
9900 85th Ave N
Maple Grove, MN 55369-6801
 763-425-8808
 Fax: 763-493-8818 800-790-0627
 info@mgsmachine.com www.mgsmachine.com
Packaging machinery manufacturing; feeding and cartoning
President: Richard Bahr
 richard.bahr@mgsmachine.com
Estimated Sales: $10-20 Million
Number Employees: 100-249

25614 MGS Machine Corp
9900 85th Ave N
Maple Grove, MN 55369-6801
 763-425-8808
 Fax: 763-493-8818 800-790-0627
 info@mgsmachine.com www.mgsmachine.com
Vibratory feeders, centrifugal feed systems
President: Richard Bahr
 richard.bahr@mgsmachine.com
Estimated Sales: $1-5 Million
Number Employees: 100-249

25615 MIFAB Inc
1321 W 119th St
Chicago, IL 60643-5109
 773-341-3030
 Fax: 773-341-3047 800-465-2736
 sales@mifab.com www.mifab.com
Manufacturer, importer and exporter of grease traps, oil, sediment and lint interceptors, floor drains, access doors, etc
President: Michael Whiteside
 mwhiteside@mifab.com
Accounting Manager: Daniel ODekirk
Vice President of Division: Paul Lacourciere
Engineering Manager: Jason Gremchuk
Quality Control Manager: John Murphy
National Sales Manager: Andrew Haines
Purchasing Manager: Alice OConnor
Number Employees: 50-99
Square Footage: 180000
Brands:
 Mifab

25616 MILLIPORE Sigma
290 Concord Rd
Billerica, MA 01821-3405
978-715-4321
Fax: 978-715-1393 www.emdmillipore.com
Wine and food industry filtration equipment.
Multiscreen filter plates, Montage Plasmid Miniprep
kit, Opticap Gamma sterilizable capsules, Ezpak
membranes and membrane dispenser
Chairman: Fran Lunger
CFO: Anthony L Mattacchione
anthony_mattacchione@millipore.com
Number Employees: 500-999

25617 MISCO Refractometer
3401 Virginia Road
Cleveland, OH 44122
216-831-1000
Fax: 216-831-1195 866-831-1999
www.misco.com
Manufacturer and exporter of digital hand-held
abbe/labprator, inline/process refractometers. Estab-
lished in 1949 in Cleveland, Ohio and is recognized
as a world leader in the refractometer industry.
CEO: Michael Rainer
Contact: Tosha Hudson
thudson@misco.com
Number Employees: 10-19
Type of Packaging: Food Service, Bulk
Brands:
Abbe

25618 MIT Poly-Cart Corp
211 Central Park W # 14j
New York, NY 10024-6020
212-724-7290
Fax: 212-721-9022 800-234-7659
info@mitpolycart.com www.mitpolycart.com
Industrial polyethylene hand carts and trucks
President: Daniel Moss
danielmoss@aol.com
Vice President: Isaac Rinkewick
Research & Development: Isaac Rinkewick
Marketing Director: Sandy Divack
Sales Director: Marty Winnick
Customer Service: Marty Winnick
Estimated Sales: $1-2.5 Million
Number Employees: 10-19
Number of Brands: 1
Number of Products: 50
Type of Packaging: Bulk

25619 MIWE USA
54 Jamestown Road
Belle Mead, NJ 08502-5222
908-904-0221
Fax: 908-904-0241 miweusa@aol.com
www.miwe.de
President: Hary Jacoby
CFO: Hary Jacoby
Quality Control: Hary Jacoby
R&D: Hary Jacoby
Estimated Sales: $5 - 10 Million
Number Employees: 4

25620 MJ Puehse & Company
P.O. Box 2043
Carefree, AZ 85377
530-677-8863
Fax: 530-683-4011 www.mjpuehse.com
Sales and Marketing Agency selling ingredients to
food and beverage companies.
President: Michael Puehse

25621 MLS Signs Inc
25733 Dhondt Ct
Chesterfield, MI 48051-2601
586-948-0200
Fax: 586-948-0300 www.phillipssign.com
Neon, acrylic, metal and vinyl letters, illuminated
signs and cake stands; also, crane truck service and
installation available
President: William Siewert
mlssigns@ameritech.net
Estimated Sales: $1-2.5 Million
Number Employees: 10-19
Square Footage: 8000

25622 MMLC
12403 Wellington Park
Houston, TX 77072-3954
281-983-0315
Fax: 713-868-8041 800-727-5700
info@mmldesign.com www.mmldesign.com

President: Jerry Lecontte
Quality Control: Ray Nevill
Estimated Sales: $300,000-500,000
Number Employees: 1-4

25623 MMR Technologies
1400 N Shoreline Blvd Ste A5
Mountain View, CA 94043-1346
650-962-9620
Fax: 650-962-9647 855-962-9620
www.mmr-tech.com
Manufacturer and exporter of microminiature refrig-
eration equipment for materials research
CEO: William Little
Sales VP: Robert Paugh
Contact: Lee Asplund
leea@mmr.com
Estimated Sales: $2.5-5 Million
Number Employees: 10-19
Square Footage: 36000

25624 MOCAP Inc
409 Parkway Dr
Park Hills, MO 63601-4435
573-431-4610
Fax: 314-543-4111 800-633-6775
sales@mocap.com www.mocap.com
Transparent tubing
President: Joseph Miller
jmiller@mocap.com
Estimated Sales: $10-20 Million
Number Employees: 50-99

25625 MOCON Inc
7500 Mendelsohn Ave N
Minneapolis, MN 55428-4045
763-493-6370
Fax: 763-493-6358 www.mocon.com
Scientific testing and equipment, permeation, leak
detection, headspace, weighing,testing
President/CEO: Robert Demorest
rdemorest@mocon.com
Estimated Sales: $37 Million
Number Employees: 250-499

25626 MODAGRAPHICS
5300 Newport Dr
Rolling Meadows, IL 60008-3797
847-392-3980
Fax: 847-392-3989 marketing@modagrafics.com
www.modagrafics.com
Manufacturer and exporter of graphics for food
stores and truck fleets
President/CEO: Neil Macleod
Estimated Sales: $12 Million
Number Employees: 100-249
Square Footage: 80000

25627 MPBS Industries
2820 E Washington Blvd
Los Angeles, CA 90023-4217
323-268-8514
Fax: 323-268-6305 800-421-6265
www.mpbs.com
Modified atmospheric packaging, vacuum packaging equipment, blenders, choppers, smokehouses,
stuffers, slicers and plant supplies. Products and services for: industrial food processing equipment; industrial food packaging equipment;grocery and
restaurant equipment; and also butcher supplies and
food processing supplies.
President: Michael Dernburg
Manager: Bob Maxwell
bob@mpbs.com
Estimated Sales: $2.5 - 5 Million
Number Employees: 10-19

25628 MPE Group
6981 N Park Drive
Pennsauken, NJ 08109-4205
856-317-9960
Fax: 856-317-9963 www.mpe.nl
Scraped surface heat exchangers, unique bottom
driven processing veessels, crystallization tanks,
complete processing systems, aseptic processing
systems, vacuum gas packaging systems, vacuum
drying
Estimated Sales: $55 Million
Number Employees: 275

25629 MPI Label Systems
450 Courtney Rd
P.O. Box 70
Sebring, OH 44672-1339
330-938-2134
Fax: 330-938-9878 800-837-2134
info@mpilabels.com www.mpilabels.com
labels and equipment. Some of their products in-
clude flexible packaging, pressure-sensitive labels,
automatic labeling equipment, RFID labels/tags,
roll-fed wrap labels, shrink products, thermal print-
ers, barcode scanners, labelingsoftware and more.
President: Randy Kocher
Marketing Manager: Linda Buttermore
Account Manager Sales: Michele Beckett-Carver
Estimated Sales: $20 - 50 Million
Number Employees: 500+
Square Footage: 110000
Parent Co: Miller Products
Other Locations:
Alliance OH
Baltimore MD
Charlotte CT
Danielson CT
Grand Prairie TX
Norwich NY
Stockton CA
University Park IL
Wadsworth OH
Whites Creek TN
Brands:
Anchorseal
Mpi 90
Mpi-L
Prime Label
Prime Plus Irc
Scannable Bar Code Hologram

25630 MPI Simgraph
210 Meijer Dr
Suite B
Lafayette, IN 47905-4694
765-449-4100
Fax: 765-449-1703
Visual packaging software products including Leap-
frog graphic database manager, Imagepak for creat-
ing visual packaging instruction sheets and
Iconworker for creating visual assembly and process
instruction sheets
Estimated Sales: $1 - 5 Million

25631 MPS North America, Inc.
8236 Nieman Road
Lenexa, KS 66214
913-310-0055
Fax: 913-310-0088 www.mps-group.nl
Food products machinery
President: Serge Cramer
VP: Jerry Frizzell
Operations Manager: John Estrada
Estimated Sales: $2 Million
Number Employees: 1-4
Parent Co: MPS meat processing systems

25632 MRC Bearing Services
1510 Gehman Rd
Harleysville, PA 19438
215-513-4400
Fax: 215-513-4736 800-672-7000
Bearings for the food industry
President: Don Poland
Sales Director: Jay Carlson
Public Relations: Wendy Garle
Estimated Sales: $1 - 5 Million

25633 MRC Bearing Services
1510 Gehman Road
Kulpsville, PA 19443
215-513-4726
Fax: 888-322-4672 800-672-7000
Bearings
President: Tom Johnstone
Number Employees: 10

25634 MRI Upper Westchester
118 N Bedford Road
Suite 103
Mount Kisco, NY 10549-2554
914-241-2788

25635 MSK Covertech
4170 Jvl Industrial Park Dr
Marietta, GA 30066
770-928-1099
Fax: 770-928-3849 info@msk.us
www.mskcovertech.com
Packaging machinery
Marketing: Marcela Leano
General Manager: Braden Camp
Estimated Sales: $1-5 Million
Number Employees: 8
Parent Co: MSK Covertech Group
Brands:
Econotech
Powertech
Recotech

25636 MSSH
901 N Carver St
Greensburg, IN 47240-1014
812-663-2180
Fax: 812-663-5405 ashleymachine@yahoo.com
Manufacturer and exporter of eviscerating tables,
poultry pickers and scalders
Manager: Jim Israel
CFO: Jim Israel
Estimated Sales: $30-50 Million
Number Employees: 5-9
Square Footage: 8000

25637 MTL Etching Industries
861 Fiske St
Woodmere, NY 11598-2429
516-295-9733
Fax: 516-295-9733
Manufacturer and exporter of advertising specialties,
nameplates, dials, scales, rulers, etc
CEO: Alan Stern
Estimated Sales: $1 - 3 Million
Number Employees: 10-19

25638 MTP Custom Machinery Corporation
3857 Hyde Park Boulevard
Niagara Falls, NY 14305-1701
716-282-5705
Fax: 716-282-5741 mtpcorp@aol.com
Accumulating conveyors
Estimated Sales: $1-5 Million
Number Employees: 29

25639 Mac Papers Inc
8370 Philips Hwy
Jacksonville, FL 32256-8204
904-733-9660
Fax: 904-733-9622 800-334-7026
www.macpapers.com
Envelopes and die cut paper
Manager: Bob Tees
Vice President: Darnell Babbit
dbabbit@macpapers.com
Plant Manager: Ted Towner
Estimated Sales: $20-50 Million
Number Employees: 100-249
Parent Co: MAC Paper

25640 MacDonald Steel Ltd
200 Avenue Road
Cambridge, ON N1R 8H5
Canada
519-620-0400
Fax: 519-621-4995 800-563-8247
Sales@HDPCANADA.COM
www.hdpcanada.com
Number Employees: 10
Parent Co: HDP

25641 MacMillan Bloedel Packaging
4001 Carmichael Rd
Montgomery, AL 36106-3613
334-244-0562
Fax: 334-213-6199 800-239-4464
Manufacturer and exporter of corrugated shipping
containers
VP: J Tignor
Director Marketing: Stewart Williams

25642 Macdonald Signs & Advertising
6364 E State Highway 107
Edinburg, TX 78542-7295
956-787-0016
Fax: 956-787-8466
Magnetic signs

Owner: Lupette Mac Donald
macdonald_printing@yahoo.com
Estimated Sales: Less Than $500,000
Number Employees: 1-4

25643 Machanix Fabrication Inc
13929 Magnolia Ave
Chino, CA 91710-7032
909-590-9700
Fax: 909-590-3932 800-700-9701
www.machanixfab.com
Food processing equipment and supplies including
blenders, mixers, slicers, toasters, etc
CEO: Craig Broswell
machanixfab@gmail.com
Estimated Sales: Less Than $500,000
Number Employees: 1-4
Square Footage: 12000

25644 (HQ)Machem Industries
1607 Derwent Way
Delta, BC V3M 6K8
Canada
604-526-5655
Fax: 604-526-1618
Manufacturer and exporter of alkaline, acid and spe-
cialty cleaners, sanitizers, chain lubes, defoamers,
descalers and chlorine dioxide
General Manager: Paul Grehen
Other Locations:
Machem Industries
Regina SK
Brands:
Dairi-San
Kloriclean
Optimum
Orbit
Progress
Rinsol
Topsan
Tuff Stuff

25645 Machine Applications Corp
3410 Tiffin Ave
Sandusky, OH 44870-9752
419-621-2322
Fax: 419-621-2321 info@macinstruments.com
www.macinstruments.com
Steam flow meters and high temperature humidity
analyzers
President: James Weit
info@macinstruments.com
Sales Manager: Janet Jarrett
Estimated Sales: Below $5 Million
Number Employees: 5-9
Square Footage: 16000

25646 Machine Builders & Design Inc
806 N Post Rd
Shelby, NC 28150-4247
704-482-3456
Fax: 704-482-3000 www.machinebuilders.com
Manufacturer and exporter of cookie packaging ma-
chinery
President/Owner: Darryl Mims
Finance Manager: Steve Hyde
Vice President: Brad Hogan
Service Manager: Phillip Cannon
Sales Manager: Rick MaDaniel
Engineering Manager: Eric Grayson
Estimated Sales: $5-10,000,000
Number Employees: 20-49

25647 Machine Builders & Design Inc
806 N Post Rd
Shelby, NC 28150-4247
704-482-3456
Fax: 704-482-3000
mbdusa@machinebuilders.com
www.machinebuilders.com
Bakery equipment
President: Darryl Mims
Finance Manager: Steve Hyde
Vice President: Brad Hogan
Sales Manager: Rick McDaniel
Service Manager: Phillip Cannon
Estimated Sales: $5-10 Million
Number Employees: 20-49
Type of Packaging: Bulk

25648 Machine Electronics Company
9 Devoe St
Brooklyn, NY 11211
718-384-3211

Manufacturer and exporter of packaging, wrapping
and bag filling machinery
Manager: Tom Costello
Number Employees: 44

25649 Machine Ice Co
8915 Sweetwater Ln
Houston, TX 77037-2706
281-448-7823
Fax: 713-868-4424 800-423-8822
www.machineice.com
Wholesaler/distributor and exporter of mobile ice
centers, ice plants, ice machines and refrigeration
equipment; also, walk-in and reach-in coolers, cold
storage facilities, ice cream makers, etc.; serving the
food service market
President: Dan Celli
Sales Manager: Walter Felix
Estimated Sales: Less Than $500,000
Number Employees: 1-4
Square Footage: 88000

25650 Machine Ice Co
8915 Sweetwater Ln
Houston, TX 77037-2706
281-448-7823
Fax: 713-868-4424 800-423-8822
www.machineice.com
Manufacturer and exporter of ice equipment includ-
ing automatic ice cube makers, dispensers, crushers
and storage bins; also, air conditioning units
President: Dan Celli
Sales Manager: Walter Felix
Estimated Sales: Less Than $500,000
Number Employees: 1-4
Square Footage: 200000

25651 Machinery & Equipment Corp
3401 Bayshore Blvd
Brisbane, CA 94005-1498
415-467-7010
Fax: 415-467-2639 800-227-4544
info@machineryandequipment.com
www.machineryandequipment.com
Buy and sell used processing and packaging equip-
ment. Manufacture sanitary ribbon mixes and sell
new dicers
President: Mike Ebert
CFO: Bryant Caston
Food Division Manager: Don Riochet
Estimated Sales: $4 Million
Number Employees: 10-19

25652 Machinery & Equipment Company, Inc.
PO Box 7632
San Francisco, CA 94120
415-467-3400
Fax: 415-467-2639 800-227-4544
info@machineryandequipment.com
www.machineryandequipment.com
President: Mike Ebert
CFO: Bryan Caston
Estimated Sales: $5,000,000 - $9,999,999
Number Employees: 20

25653 Machinery Corporation ofAmerica
4401 Capitola Road
Suite 3
Capitola, CA 95010-3572
831-479-9901
Fax: 831-479-4443
Supplier of rebuilt food processing equipment
Contact: Rick Bakanoff
rick.bakanoff@mca-america.com
Estimated Sales: $1 Million
Number Employees: 5

25654 Machinery Engineering Technology
2629 E County Road O
Janesville, WI 53546
608-758-0506
Fax: 608-758-1343 877-758-0506
met-llc@execpc.com
Stainless steel equipment for food filling, sealing
and lidding
Estimated Sales: $3 Million
Number Employees: 5-9

25655 Mack-Chicago Corporation

2555 S Leavitt St
Chicago, IL 60608-5202

773-376-8100
Fax: 773-376-0883 800-992-6225

Point-of-purchase displays, gift boxes and corrugated shipping containers; also, fire retardant and corrugated disposable chafing dishes available
President: Alwin J Kolb
CFO: Alwin J Kolb
Quality Control: Jerry Santeford
Sales Manager: Dale Arnold
Contact: George Pluta
  george@mackltd.com
General Manager: Ron Praun
Plant Manager: Ken Kruger
Estimated Sales: $20 - 50 Million
Number Employees: 100-249
Square Footage: 425000
Parent Co: Mack Packaging Group

25656 Mackenzie Creamery

6722 Pioneer Trl
Hiram, OH 44234-9714

330-569-3368
Fax: 330-569-3387 info@mackenziecreamery.com
  www.mackenziecreamery.com
Organic Artisan goat cheeses
Founder/President: Jean Mackenzie
  jeanniegoat@yahoo.com
Estimated Sales: Less Than $500,000
Number Employees: 10-19

25657 Mackie International. Inc.

719 Palmyrita Avenue
Riverside, CA 92507

951-346-0530
Fax: 951-346-0541
carmel@mackieinternational.net
  www.mackieinternational.net
Stabilizers
President: Ernesto U Dacay
Contact: Amando Briones
  a.briones@mackieinternational.net
Estimated Sales: $1 Million
Number Employees: 50-99

25658 Maco Bag Corp

412 Van Buren St
Newark, NY 14513-9205

315-226-1000
Fax: 315-226-1050 www.macopkg.com
Plastic bags and barrier packaging
President: Craig Miller
  craig.miller@macobag.com
CEO: J Scott Miller
Number Employees: 100-249
Square Footage: 100000
Type of Packaging: Consumer, Food Service, Private Label, Bulk

25659 Macon Awning & Canvas Prod

230 South St
Macon, GA 31206-1066

478-743-2684
Commercial awnings
President: David B Redding Jr
  dr@maconcanvas.com
Estimated Sales: $1-2.5 Million
Number Employees: 10-19

25660 Macrie Brothers

750 S 1st Rd
Hammonton, NJ 08037-8407

609-561-6822
Fax: 609-561-6296 bluebuck@bellatlantic.net
Blueberries
Owner/CEO: Paul Macrie III
Superviser: Al Macrie
Operations: Nicholas Macrie
Production: Michael Macrie
Estimated Sales: Below $5 Million
Number Employees: 5
Square Footage: 120000
Type of Packaging: Consumer, Food Service, Private Label, Bulk
Brands:
  Blue Buck

25661 Macro Plastics Inc

2250 Huntington Dr
Fairfield, CA 94533-9732

707-437-1200
Fax: 707-437-1201 800-845-6555
  www.macroplastics.com
Manufacturer high pressure injection molded products for food and agriculture
CEO: Warren Macdonald
  wmacdonald@macroplastics.com
CEO: Pat Brandt
Estimated Sales: $10 - 20 Million
Number Employees: 20-49

25662 Maddox/Adams International

1421 SW 107th Ave
Suite 213
Miami, FL 33174

305-592-3337
Fax: 305-591-2591 alina@maddoxadams.com
  www.maddoxmetalworks.com
Food processing equipment for snack foods including tortillas, corn chips and popcorn; also, bake and fry extrusion equipment and nut roasters
Sales: Alina Del Rivero
Estimated Sales: $300,000-500,000
Number Employees: 1-4
Parent Co: Beatrice Companies

25663 MadgeTech, Inc.

879 Maple Street
Contoocook, NH 03229

603-456-2011
Fax: 603-456-2012 info@madgetech.com
  www.madgetech.com
Data logging instrumentation used for reading and monitoring temperatures both during and after the cooking process.
Contact: Ann Battles
  ann@madgetech.com

25664 Madison County Wood Products

4597 Highway C
Fredericktown, MO 63645

314-584-1802
  www.mcwp.com
New and used hard and soft wood pallets
President: James Kesting
Estimated Sales: $12 Million
Number Employees: 100-249
Square Footage: 50000

25665 Madix Inc

1537 S Main St
Goodwater, AL 35072-6620

256-839-6354
Fax: 256-839-5608 www.madixinc.com
Supermarket fixtures and food service showcases
CFO: Justin Saunders
Plant Manager: Phillip Whitley
Purchasing Director: Kim Wright
Estimated Sales: $50-100 Million
Number Employees: 250-499
Square Footage: 91730

25666 Madsen Wire Products Inc

101 Madsen St
Orland, IN 46776-5417

260-829-6561
Fax: 260-829-6652 bsnyder@madsenwire.com
  www.madsenwire.com
Manufacturer and designer of wire baskets, bases, containers, carts, displays, grids, stands, trays, fan and clamp guards, shelving, cages, etc. Constructed out of cold roll steel or stainless steel
President: Steve Cochran
  scochran@generalcage.com
Estimator/Customer Service: Gwen Wheaton
Account Manager: Kim Straley
Estimated Sales: $10-20 Million
Number Employees: 20-49
Square Footage: 84000
Type of Packaging: Food Service, Private Label, Bulk

25667 Magi Kitch'n

10 Ferry St
Concord, NH 03301-5022

603-225-6684
Fax: 603-230-5548 800-441-1492
sales@pitco.com www.magikitchn.com

Manufacturer and exporter of commercial cooking equipment including mobile outdoor units and gas, electric and charcoal broilers; also, broiler-griddles including mesquite and charcoal
President: Robert Bosa
  bosa@magikitchn.com
CFO: Bob Granger
Vice President, General Manager: Greg Moyer
VP: George McMahon
Quality Control: Ray Amitrano
Senior Manager of Sales: Bonnie Bolster
Public Relations: Thomas Cassin
VP Operations: Robert Granger
Vice President of Operations: Steve Reale
Purchasing Manager: Terri Miller
Estimated Sales: $30 - 50 Million
Number Employees: 20-49
Parent Co: Middleby Corporation
Type of Packaging: Food Service
Brands:
  Magicater
  Magikitch'n

25668 Magic American Corporation

23700 Mercantile Road
Cleveland, OH 44122-5900

216-464-2353
Fax: 216-464-5895 800-321-6330
  www.magicamerican.com
Manufacturer and exporter of household cleaning products including stain removers and floor polish
President: Ross Chawson
VP: Scott Zeilinger
Sales Manager: Bob Beebe
Contact: James Zeilinger
  jimmyze@aol.com
Estimated Sales: $10 - 20 Million
Number Employees: 50
Square Footage: 110000
Brands:
  Goo Gone
  Magic

25669 Magic Seasoning Blends

720 Distributors Row
Po Box 23342
New Orleans, LA 70123-3208

504-731-3590
Fax: 504-731-3576 800-457-2857
  www.magicseasoningblends.com
Dry spices, rubs, bottled sauces and marinades.
Owner: Paul Prudhomme
  pprudhomme@chefpaul.com
President/CEO: Shawn McBride
CFO: Paula LaCour
R&D Director: Sean O'Meara
VP Sales/Marketing: John McBride
Director of Sales and Marketing: Anna Zuniga
  pprudhomme@chefpaul.com
Human Resources Director: Naomi Roundtree
Director of Operations: Joey Duplechain
Vice President of Manufacturing: David Hickey
Purchasing Director: Patricia Cantrelle
Estimated Sales: $9.6 Million
Number Employees: 50-99
Number of Brands: 3
Number of Products: 29
Square Footage: 260000
Type of Packaging: Consumer, Food Service, Private Label, Bulk
Brands:
  Barbecue Magic
  Blackened Redfish Magic
  Blackened Steak Magic
  Breading Magic
  Gravy & Gumbo Magic
  Magic Pepper Sauce
  Magic Sauce & Marinades
  Meat Magic
  Pizza & Pasta Magic
  Pork & Veal Magic
  Poultry Magic
  Salmon Magic
  Seafood Magic
  Shrimp Magic
  Sweetfree Magic
  Vegetable Magic

25670 Magline Inc
1205 W Cedar St
Standish, MI 48658-9563
989-512-1000
Fax: 989-879-5399 800-624-5463
customerservice@magliner.com
www.magliner.com
Aluminum material handling equipment including 2
and 4 wheel hand trucks and delivery ramps; also,
dock equipment
CEO: D Brian Law
Marketing: Carol Sundeck
Sales Manager: Joe Howeth
Number Employees: 50-99
Brands:
Brake
Equalizer
Gemini

25671 Magna Industries Inc
1825 Swarthmore Ave # 1
Suite 1
Lakewood, NJ 08701-4570
732-905-0957
Fax: 732-367-2989 800-510-9856
sales@magnaindustries.com
www.magnaindustries.com
Racks and carts for bakery and food industries
Owner: Jerry Crominski
sales@magnaindustries.com
Estimated Sales: $10-20 Million
Number Employees: 20-49

25672 Magna Machine Co
11180 Southland Rd
Cincinnati, OH 45240-3295
513-851-6900
Fax: 513-851-6904 800-448-3475
sales@magna-machine.com
www.magna-machine.com
Bakery machinery including horizontal mixers and
depositors
President: Paul Kramer
pkramer@magna-machine.com
VP: Rob Baur
Estimated Sales: $2.5-5 Million
Number Employees: 50-99

25673 Magna Machine Co
11180 Southland Rd
Cincinnati, OH 45240-3295
513-851-6900
Fax: 513-851-6904 800-448-3475
sales@magna-machine.com
www.magna-machine.com
Horizontal, batch, dough, bakery, adhesives, high
viscosity, paint color dye, vacuum and pharmaceuti-
cal chemical mixers
President: Paul Kramer
pkramer@magna-machine.com
VP: Baur
CFO: Windy Willey
Estimated Sales: $2.5 - 5 Million
Number Employees: 50-99

25674 Magna Power Controls
P.O. Box 13615
Milwaukee, WI 53213-0615
262-783-3500
Fax: 262-783-3510 800-288-8178
lbostrom@magnetek.com www.magnetek.com
Manufacturer and exporter of material handling
equipment including control, electrification and
automation
President: Andy Glass
CFO: Ryan Gyle
CEO: Peter M McCormick
Quality Control: Mark Logic
R & D: Ban Beilfuss
Marketing/Sales: Perry Pabich
Estimated Sales: $20 - 50 Million
Number Employees: 250-499
Type of Packaging: Bulk

25675 Magnaform Corp
2685 S 4th St
Van Buren, AR 72956-6024
479-474-7569
Fax: 479-474-2641 www.magnaform.com
Owner: Edward Boyd
ed@magnaform.com
Estimated Sales: $1 - 3 Million
Number Employees: 5-9

25676 Magnatech Corp
6 Kripes Rd
East Granby, CT 06026-9645
860-653-2573
Fax: 860-653-0486 888-393-3602
info@magnatechllc.com www.magnatechllc.com
Sanitary processing tubes and fittings for food processing and dairy industries.
Executive VP: Garry Mccabe
gmccabe@magnatech-lp.com
Number Employees: 20-49

25677 MagneTek
16555 W Ryerson Rd
New Berlin, WI 53151-3633
262-782-0200
Fax: 262-782-1283 www.yaskawa.com
Fractional and integral horsepower AC/DC motors
and speed controls
President & COO, Drives & Motion Divisio: Mike
Knapek
President & COO, Drives & Motion Divisio: Mike
Knapek
Contact: Shankar Rao
shrao@magnetek.com
Estimated Sales: $50 - 100 Million
Number Employees: 100-249

25678 Magnetic Products Inc
683 Town Center Dr
Highland, MI 48356-2965
248-887-5600
Fax: 248-887-6100 800-544-5930
info@mpimagnet.com www.mpimagnet.com
Magnetic separators, metal detectors and check
weighers
President: Keith Rhodes
keith.rhodes@mpimagnet.com
R&D: Ron Kwaz
Marketing: Ellen Kominars
Sales: Del Butler
Estimated Sales: $6 Million
Number Employees: 20-49
Square Footage: 160000

25679 Magnetic Technologies LTD
43 Town Forest Rd
P.O. Box 257
Oxford, MA 01540-2845
508-987-3303
Fax: 508-987-2875 sales@magnetictech.com
www.magnetictech.com
Magnetic clutches for bottle capping
President: John Deluca
VP: Greg Podstanka
Sales: Howard Schwerdlin
Estimated Sales: $1,000,000 - $5,000,000
Number Employees: 10-19

25680 Magnetool Inc
505 Elmwood Dr
Troy, MI 48083-2755
248-588-5400
Fax: 248-588-5710 sales@magnetoolinc.com
www.magnetoolinc.com
Manufacturer and exporter of magnetic separation
equipment
President: A T Churchill
atchurchill@magnetoolinc.com
Engineer: Mike Wright
VP: C Sulisz
Estimated Sales: $20 - 50 Million
Number Employees: 20-49
Square Footage: 40000

25681 Magnum Coffee Packaging
16800 Java Boulevard
Nunica, MI 49448
616-837-0333
Fax: 616-837-0777 www.magnumcoffee.com
Tea and coffee industry packaging materials and ma-
chines
Owner: Kevin Kihnke
Estimated Sales: $2.5 - 5 Million
Number Employees: 20-49

**25682 Magnum Custom Trailer &BBQ
Pits**
10806 Hwy 620 N
Austin, TX 78726
512-258-4101
Fax: 512-258-2701 800-662-4686
sales2@magnumtrailers.com
www.magnumtrailers.com

Manufacturer and exporter of barbecue and catering
trailers, custom kitchens and mobile concession
stands
President: Charles Mc Lemore
Sales: Todd McLemore
Sales: Richard Westlund
Plat Manager: Jeff Israel
Estimated Sales: $15 Million
Number Employees: 50-99
Square Footage: 200000
Brands:
Magnum

25683 Magnum Systems Inc
1250 Seminary St
Kansas City, KS 66103-2515
913-362-1710
Fax: 913-362-7863 800-748-7000
www.magnumsystems.com
Automated packaging machinery
President: Brian Klughardt
Contact: Shannon Beal
sbeal@magnumsystems.com
Estimated Sales: $500,000-$1 Million
Number Employees: 50-99
Parent Co: Taylor Products

25684 Magnuson
1 Magnuson Ave
Pueblo, CO 81001-4889
719-948-9500
Fax: 719-948-9540 sales@magnusoncorp.com
www.magnusoncorp.com
Manufacturer and exporter of processing and pack-
aging machinery including vegetable cutters and
peelers, washers and feeders; also, full can
palletizers
Owner: Bob Smith
bsmith@magnusoncorp.com
VP/General Manager: Craig Furlo
Estimated Sales: $2.5-5 Million
Number Employees: 20-49
Parent Co: Atlas Pacific Engineering

25685 Magnuson Industries
3005 Kishwaukee St
Rockford, IL 61109-2061
815-229-2970
Fax: 815-229-2978 800-435-2816
www.posi-pour.com
Manufacturer, importer and exporter of portion con-
trol liquor pourers and bar supplies
Vice President: Stewart Magnuson
smagnuson@posi-pour.com
VP: Stewart Magnuson
Director Sales: Robert Gough
Estimated Sales: $5-10 Million
Number Employees: 10-19
Square Footage: 80000
Brands:
Posi-Pour

25686 Magnuson Products
66 Brighton Rd
Clifton, NJ 07012-1600
973-472-9292
Fax: 973-472-5686
Industrial cleaning compounds for bottles, dairy,
glass, pipes, dishwashers, etc
President: Al Reisch
info@sergeantthem.com
Estimated Sales: $10 - 20 Million
Number Employees: 1-4

25687 Magpowr
1626 Manufacturers Dr
Fenton, MO 63026-2839
636-343-5550
Fax: 636-326-0608 800-624-7697
magpowr@magpowr.com www.magpowr.com
Equipment components, tension and torque control
and capping clutches
Owner: Benson Portnoy
VP: Jeff Hutchings
CEO: Bruce Ryen
Estimated Sales: $10 - 20 Million
Number Employees: 50-99
Brands:
Magpowr

25688 Magsys Inc
4144 S 112th St
Milwaukee, WI 53228-1914
414-543-2177
Fax: 414-541-9203
Manufacturer and exporter of stainless steel magnetic conveyor equipment for transport of ferrous crowns, caps and closures
President: Rudy Zwiebel
Estimated Sales: Below $5 Million
Number Employees: 1-4
Square Footage: 10000
Brands:
Magsys

25689 Mahaffy & Harder Engineering Company
140 Clinton Road
Fairfield, NJ 07004-0002
973-227-4004
Fax: 973-227-3634
President: A Mahaffy-Berman
Vice President of Engineering: Henry Nixon
Vice President of Sales/Marketing: Russ Garofalo
Vice President of Operations: Mike Summersett
Estimated Sales: $5 - 10 Million
Number Employees: 50-99

25690 (HQ)Mahoney Environmental
712 Essington Rd
Joliet, IL 60435-4912
815-725-2056
Fax: 815-730-2087 800-892-9392
info@mahoneyenvironmental.com
Grease handling equipment; also, grease collection, recycling and rendering services available
President: Rick Sabol
ricksabol@mahoneyenvironmental.com
Partner: John Mahoney
VP Marketing: Brad Schofield
Equipment Sales Manager: Kyle Taylor
Estimated Sales: $2.5 - 5,000,000
Number Employees: 50-99
Other Locations:
Mahoney Environmental
Mendota IL
Brands:
The Recycler

25691 Maier Sign Systems
515 Victor Street
Saddle Brook, NJ 07663-6118
201-845-7555
Fax: 201-845-3336
Manufacturer and exporter of bulletin and menu boards, directories, awnings and signs including plastic, metal and neon
President/CEO: Stuart Brown
Estimated Sales: Less than $500,000
Number Employees: 4
Square Footage: 32000
Parent Co: Elms Industries

25692 Mail-Well Label
295 Lillard Dr
Sparks, NV 89434-8902
775-359-1703
Fax: 775-359-1736
Glue-applied paper and metallized and foil labels for wine, beer, beverage products, canned vegetables, fruit and seafood
Site Manager: John Brandoff
VP: Cameron Beddome
Estimated Sales: $50-100 Million
Number Employees: 100-249
Parent Co: Lawson Mardon Group

25693 Mail-Well Label
6901 Rolling Mill Road
Baltimore, MD 21224-2030
410-282-4500
Fax: 410-288-3509 800-637-4879
Paper labels including litho-printed, square or die cut, high gloss and product resistant; also, aqueous coated laminates for corrugated containers
Community Manager: Richard Dix
General Manager: Russell Hoffman
Operations Manager: John Rixham
Estimated Sales: $20-50 Million
Number Employees: 250-499
Square Footage: 85000
Parent Co: Lawson Mardon Packaging

25694 Main Course Consultants
8629 Avers Avenue
Skokie, IL 60076-2201
847-869-7633
Fax: 847-866-0898
Consultant specializing in concept and menu development for restaurants; also, cost analysis, business plans and mystery shopping services available
President: Lee Michaels
Number Employees: 27

25695 Main Lamp Corp
1073 39th St
Brooklyn, NY 11219-1017
718-436-8500
Fax: 718-438-6836
price@nationwidelighting.com
www.mainlampwarehouse.com
Lighting fixtures, table lamps and ceiling fans
President: William Ain
price@nationwidelighting.com
CFO: Misses Ains
Salesperson: J Piccozino
Manager Operations: R Dabideen
Estimated Sales: $2.5 - 5 Million
Number Employees: 1-4
Square Footage: 200000
Brands:
Casablanca
Stiffel
Weinstock

25696 Mainca USA Inc
411 Eichelberger St
St Louis, MO 63111-1914
314-351-4677
Fax: 314-353-6655 877-677-7761
maincausa@maincausa.com www.maincausa.com
Meat processing equipment; including: mixers, choppers, saws, grinders, moulders and sausage stuffers
President: Dale Schmidt
maincausa@aol.com
Estimated Sales: Under $500,000
Number Employees: 10-19

25697 Maine Industrial Plastics & Rubber Corporation
21 Teague Street
P.O. Box 381
Newcastle, ME 04553
207-563-5532
Fax: 207-563-8457 800-540-1846
www.miprcorp.com
Conveyor belting, rubber and plastic sheet
President: Henry Lee
Vice President: Whitney Lee
Estimated Sales: $1 - 3 Million
Number Employees: 9
Square Footage: 48000
Parent Co: Maine Industrial Corp.

25698 Maine Poly Aquisition
PO Box 1385
Windham, ME 04062-1385
207-946-7440
Fax: 207-946-5102
Plastic bags
President: Kimball H Dunton
CFO: Jackie Cooutier
Public Relations: Steve Spencer
Estimated Sales: $10-20 Million
Number Employees: 10

25699 Mainline Industries Inc
1 Allen St # 1
Suite 1
Springfield, MA 01108-1953
413-733-5771
Fax: 413-733-5929 800-527-7917
www.mainlineind.com
Manufacturer and exporter of disposable wipers, cleaning towels and scuff pads
President: Paul Motter
paumotter@mainlineind.com
VP: Carlo Rovelli
Quality Control: Angie Smith
Marketing Support: Lee Albert
Estimated Sales: $2.5-5 Million
Number Employees: 5-9
Brands:
Aquawipes
Hydroscrubs
Hydrowype

25700 Mainstreet Menu Systems
1375 N Barker Rd
Brookfield, WI 53045-5215
262-782-6000
Fax: 262-782-6515 800-782-6222
info@mainstreetmenus.com
Manufacturer and exporter of point of purchase displays, menu boards and order racks. Design, engineer, produce & install menu boards, graphics & displays.
President: Doug Watson
CFO: Bill Hintz
Research & Development: Paul Steinbrenner
Marketing: Angie Herrmann
Estimated Sales: $10 - 20 Million
Number Employees: 20-49
Parent Co: Howard Company
Type of Packaging: Food Service
Brands:
Mainstreet

25701 Maja Equipment Company
6005 N 9th Street
Omaha, NE 68110-1121
402-346-6252
Fax: 402-346-6953
Skinning and derinding machinery for fish, poultry, pork and beef; also, rotating evaporators
Product Manager: Steven Lemke
Sales: Kent Rounds
Sales: Aaron Borns
Estimated Sales: $1 - 5 Million
Number Employees: 20-50

25702 Majestic
60 Cherry Street
Bridgeport, CT 06605-2395
203-367-7900
Fax: 203-335-6973
Manufacturer, importer and exporter of plastic serving and tabletop accessories including beverage glasses, pitchers, bowls, mugs, stemware, ice buckets, plates, trays and coasters; manufacturer of electric lamps and plastic kitchentools and gadgets
Contact: Elliott Zivin
ezivin@majesticgifts.com
Estimated Sales: $2.5-5 Million
Number Employees: 10-19
Parent Co: Zivco
Brands:
Basket Weave
Chroma Lamps
Diner Mug
Facets
Ice-Stir-Cools
Koziol
Seaglass
Transitions

25703 Majestic Coffee & Tea
3870 Charter Park Dr
San Jose, CA 95136-1388
408-448-6370
Fax: 408-448-8537
Brewing devices, roasting machines
Estimated Sales: less than $500,000
Number Employees: 1-4

25704 Majestic Flex Pac
3337 Grapevine Street
Mira Loma, CA 91752
951-361-0247
Fax: 951-361-0260
Majestic Flex PAC is a manufacturer and supplier of shrink sleeves, pouches, laminations, and custom bags to numerous industries including that of food and beverage, dairy, bakery and snack, candy and confection.
President: Leonardo Gutierrez
Type of Packaging: Consumer

25705 Majestic Industries Inc
15378 Hallmark Ct
Macomb, MI 48042-4017
586-786-9100
Fax: 586-786-9105 www.majesticind.net
Manufacturer and exporter of treated dusting cloths and wet and dust mops
President: Gavonna Agnew
gagnew@majesticind.com
CEO: Gary Potashnick
Estimated Sales: $1 - 3 Million
Number Employees: 50-99
Number of Brands: 10

Number of Products: 250
Square Footage: 128000
Type of Packaging: Consumer, Food Service, Private Label, Bulk
Brands:
  Monarch
  Sir Dust-A-Lot
  Sweeping Beauty
  Velva-Sheen

25706 Makat
500 Tillessen Boulevard
Ridgeway, SC 29130-8543
803-337-4700
Fax: 803-337-4701 makatusa@infoave.net
Extruding and depositing machines for confectionery and baking industries, starch and starchless moulded goods as well as center-in-shell, nougat, fondant, fudge, truffles, chocolate, hard candy, and caramel products
Estimated Sales: $2.5-5 Million
Number Employees: 5-9

25707 Mako Services
4297 Buford Dr
Suite 2A
Buford, GA 30518-3400
770-932-3292
Fax: 770-932-3290
Full line seafood, meats
Owner: Joe Connor
Estimated Sales: $10 - 20 Million
Number Employees: 10-19

25708 Malaysian Palm Oil Board
3516 International Court N.W.
Washington, DC 20008-3022
202-572-9719
Fax: 202-572-9783 mpobtas@aol.com
www.mpob.gov.my
Offers customer support and technical advisory services to users and potential users of Malaysian palm and palm kernel oil products in the US, Canada, and Latin America
Regional Manager: Rosidah Radzian
Director General: Datuk Dr. Choo Yuen May
Deputy Director General: Dr. Hj. Ahmad Kushairi Din
Estimated Sales: $1-2.5 Million
Number Employees: 1-4

25709 Malco Manufacturing Co
13917 S Main St
Los Angeles, CA 90061-2151
310-366-7696
Fax: 310-366-7694 866-477-7267
info@malcomfg.com www.malcomfg.com
Bun and pie pans, foil containers and aluminum bakery racks
VP: Steve Goodman
Manager: Patricia Hansen
  patricia@malcomfg.com
Estimated Sales: $5 Million
Number Employees: 5-9

25710 Malcolm Stogo Associates
41 Tudor Lane
Scarsdale, NY 10583-4909
914-472-7255
Fax: 914-472-8861
International dairy and food consultant specializing in ice cream product development and marketing concept strategies
President: Malcolm Stogo
VP/Treasurer: Barbara Stogo
Number Employees: 7
Square Footage: 6000

25711 Mali's All Natural Barbecue Supply Company
161 Bramblewood Ln
East Amherst, NY 14051-1417
716-688-2210
Fax: 716-688-2795 800-289-6254
buymali@localnet.com
Manufacturer, importer and exporter of lump charcoal, briquettes and wood for smoking and cooking; also, grilling woods
President: James Maliszewski
CEO: Frances Maliszewski
Estimated Sales: $1 - 3 Million
Number Employees: 1-4
Number of Brands: 1

Brands:
  Mali's

25712 Mall City Containers Inc
2710 N Pitcher St
Kalamazoo, MI 49004-3490
269-381-2706
Fax: 269-381-7878 800-643-6721
info@mallcitycontainers.com
www.mallcitycontainers.com
Corrugated boxes and point of purchase displays
Owner: Ben Boeresma
CEO: Ben Boersma
Sales Manager: Tom Vandenberg
Estimated Sales: $10 - 15 Million
Number Employees: 50-99

25713 (HQ)Malnove of Nebraska
13434 F St
Omaha, NE 68137-1181
402-330-1100
Fax: 402-330-2941 800-228-9877
www.malnove.com
Manufacturer and exporter of folding paperboard cartons
President, CEO: Paul Malnove
CFO: Jim Belcher
VP: Dick Lawson
VP Sales: Michael Querry
Operations: Steve Maynar
Plant Manager: Craig Beaber
Estimated Sales: $500,000 - $999,999
Number Employees: 500-999
Square Footage: 800000
Type of Packaging: Consumer, Food Service, Private Label

25714 Malo Inc
12111 E 51st St # 106
Tulsa, OK 74146-6005
918-583-2743
Fax: 918-583-6208 sales@maloinc.com
www.maloinc.com
Manufacturer and exporter of crateless and overpressure retort systems for low-acid foods in metal and flexible containers
President: Chuck Clugston
  cclugston@maloinc.com
VP: Allen Stucky
Marketing/Sales: Rick Holsted
Estimated Sales: $2.5-5 Million
Number Employees: 10-19
Square Footage: 80000
Brands:
  Malo

25715 Malo Inc
12111 E 51st St # 106
Suite 106
Tulsa, OK 74146-6005
918-583-2743
Fax: 918-583-6208 sales@maloinc.com
www.maloinc.com
President: Chuck Clugston
  cclugston@maloinc.com
Estimated Sales: $3 - 5 Million
Number Employees: 10-19

25716 Malpack Polybag
120 Fuller Rd
Ajax, ON L1S3R2
Canada
905-428-3751
Fax: 416-297-9874
Low and high density polyethylene t-shut carry-out sacks and bread and bagel bags
President: Guy DiPietro
General Manager: Jim Leo
Secretary: Joe Galea
Number Employees: 210
Square Footage: 240000
Parent Co: Malkpack
Other Locations:
  Malpack Polybag
  Ajax ON

25717 Maltese Signs
5550 Peachtree Industrial Blvd
Norcross, GA 30071-1450
770-368-0911
Fax: 770-454-7383
Signs

President: Eloi Duguay
CFO: Rejean Pelletiar
VP: Michael Maltese
Estimated Sales: $10 Million
Number Employees: 100-249
Square Footage: 130000

25718 Malteurop North America
3830 W Grant St
Milwaukee, WI 53215
414-671-1166
www.malteurop.com
Processor and exporter of malt, also offers several modes of commercial collaboration, as well as consulting, engineering, and training services.
CEO: Olivier Parent
President, North America: Kevin Eikerman
Chief Commercial & Innovation Officer: Alain Caekaert
Year Founded: 1984
Estimated Sales: $31.5 Million
Number Employees: 1,100+
Parent Co: Malteurop
Type of Packaging: Food Service, Bulk

25719 Malthus Diagnostics
35888 Centre Ridge Road
North Ridgeville, OH 44039
440-327-2585
Fax: 440-327-7286 800-346-7202
Automated microbiological analyzers; manufacturer, importer and exporter of incubators and growth media
Director Marketing/Sales: Joseph Carney
Director US Operations: Joseph Carney
Estimated Sales: $1-2.5 Million
Number Employees: 25
Square Footage: 2000
Parent Co: IDG
Brands:
  Lab M Media
  Malthus System V

25720 Man-O Products
811 Ridgeway Ave
Cincinnati, OH 45229
513-281-5959
Fax: 513-936-6555 888-210-6266
Manufacturer and exporter of protective hand creams and soap products
President: Steve Seltzer
Quality Control: Andy Joseph
Sales Manager: Tom Joseph
Estimated Sales: $5 - 10 Million
Number Employees: 5-9

25721 Man-Tech Associates
600 Main St
Tonawanda, NY 14150-3723
716-743-1320
Fax: 519-763-2205 800-206-8116
literature@mantech.ca
Laboratory and analytical equipment including PC controlled automated ion analysis and titration systems
President: Edward Godman
Marketing Supervisor: Richard Veilans
Contact: Robert Middleton
  rmenegotto@mantech-inc.com
Estimated Sales: Less than $500,000
Number Employees: 1-4

25722 Manabo
501 Main Street
Platte City, MO 64079-8460
816-431-3948
Fax: 816-431-3951
Cutting and boning equipment, sharpening machines and services; safety apparel; sanitation supplies and equipment

25723 (HQ)Management Insight
33 Boston Post Road West
Suite 220
Malborough, MA 1752
508-485-2100
Fax: 508-485-1388 www.mgtinsight.com
Restaurant and food service consultant providing stratigic planning, facility programming, pre-opening planning, market and financial feasibilty studies, audits, menu development, and restaurant revitalization

President/CEO: Jack Mandelbaum
Vice President: Elizabeth Michalski
Director of Operations: Lisa Stone
Estimated Sales: $.5 - 1 million
Number Employees: 3
Square Footage: 3150

25724 Management Recruiters
1801 Market St, 13th Floor
Philadelphia, PA 19103
941-756-3001
Fax: 215-751-1757 800-875-4000
admin@mriflorida.com www.mrinetwork.com
Consultant specializing in employment search and recruitment
President: R Rush Oster
Contact: Edward Billigmeier
edward.billigmeier@mrinetwork.com
General Manager: Robert Boal
Estimated Sales: less than $500,000
Number Employees: 1-4
Parent Co: Management Recruiters International

25725 Management Tech of America
4742 N 24th Street
Suite 410
Phoenix, AZ 85016-4862
602-381-5800
Fax: 602-251-0903
Manufacturer and exporter of software for the control of material handling systems
Estimated Sales: $10-20 Million
Number Employees: 50-99

25726 Manchester Tool & Die Inc
601 S Wabash Rd
North Manchester, IN 46962-8148
260-982-8524
Fax: 260-982-4575
www.manchestertoolanddie.com
Manufacturer and exporter of packaging equipment and machinery; also, prototype development available
President: Barry Blocher
bablocher@manchestertoolanddie.com
Sales/Supervisor: Robin Brubaker
Production Manager: Steve Music
Plant Manager: Josh Berry
Estimated Sales: $2.5-5 Million
Number Employees: 50-99
Square Footage: 34000

25727 Mancini Packing Co
3500 Mancini Pl
Zolfo Springs, FL 33890-4710
863-735-2000
Fax: 863-735-1172 800-741-1778
rmancini@mancinifoods.com
www.mancinifoods.com
Peppers and olive oil
Chairman/President: Frank Mancini
fmancini@mancinifoods.com
VP: Alan Mancini
Estimated Sales: $11 Million
Number Employees: 50-99
Type of Packaging: Consumer, Food Service, Private Label, Bulk
Brands:
Mancini

25728 Mandarin Soy Sauce Inc
4 Sands Station Rd
Middletown, NY 10940-4415
845-343-1505
Fax: 845-343-0731 info@wanjashan.com
www.wanjashan.com
Soy sauce, asian sauce, rice and vinegar
President: Alvin Lam
alvin.c.lam@chase.com
VP: Mike Shapiro
Estimated Sales: $165 Million
Number Employees: 20-49
Square Footage: 170000
Brands:
Wan Ja Shan

25729 Mandeville Company
2800 Washington Ave N
Minneapolis, MN 55411-1683
612-521-3671
Fax: 612-521-3673 800-328-8490

Manufacturer and wholesaler/distributor of equipment for meat processors, delis and restaurants including saws, grinders, mixers, tumblers, marinators, knives, scales, juicers and slicers; also, reconditioned equipment; serving the food service market
President: Julie Lane
Secretary: Phyllis Stellmaker
Estimated Sales: $2.5-5 Million
Number Employees: 10-19
Square Footage: 40000

25730 Mane, Inc.
2501 Henkle Dr.
Lebanon, OH 45036
513-248-9876
Fax: 513-248-8808 requests@mane.com
www.mane.com
Flavors/fragrances.
President/CEO: Jean Mane
Year Founded: 1871
Estimated Sales: $105 Million
Number Employees: 50-99
Square Footage: 65000

25731 Manhattan Truck Lines
91 Michigan Ave
Paterson, NJ 07503-1807
973-278-0190
Fax: 973-278-0582 800-370-7627
info@pariserchem.com www.pariserchem.com
Manufacturer and exporter of warewashing detergents, water-treatment chemicals and institutional maintenance products. Products include laundry chemicals, soaps and detergents
Owner: Bill Moakley
bmoakley@pariserchem.com
VP: Andrew Pariser
VP: Scott Pariser
Estimated Sales: $10-20 Million
Number Employees: 10-19
Type of Packaging: Consumer, Food Service, Private Label, Bulk

25732 Manitowoc Foodservice
2100 Future Drive
Sellersburg, IN 47172
818-637-7200
Fax: 818-637-7222 800-367-4233
www.manitowocbeverage.com
Manufacturer, importer and exporter of automatic ice transportation systems, beverage and ice dispensers, faucets, fluid control devices, pumps, timers, bar guns and carbonators
Manager: Andrew Nelson
CEO: G McCann
Contact: Paul Hanniffy
hanniffypaul@gmail.com
Estimated Sales: $3 - 5 Million
Number Employees: 5-9
Square Footage: 480000

25733 Manitowoc Ice Machine
2110 S 26th St
Manitowoc, WI 54220-6321
920-682-0161
Fax: 920-683-7589 800-545-5720
www.manitowocice.com
Manufacturer and exporter of ice machines, ice storage bins and reach-in refrigerators and freezers
Vice President: Lee Wichlacz
lee.wichlacz@manitowoc.com
Executive Vice President: Larry Bryce
Vice President of Sales: Kevin Clark
VP International Operations: Mark Kreple
Estimated Sales: $1 - 5 Million
Number Employees: 250-499
Square Footage: 365000
Parent Co: Manitowoc Foodservice Group

25734 Mankato Tent & Awning Co
1021 Range St
North Mankato, MN 56003-2238
507-625-5115
Fax: 507-625-5111 866-747-3524
www.mankatotent.com
Industrial curtains
President: Charles D Gasswint
Sales/Marketing Executive: Devin Gasswint
Purchasing Manager: Jesse Spiess
Estimated Sales: $1-2,500,000
Number Employees: 5-9
Square Footage: 20000
Type of Packaging: Consumer, Food Service

25735 Mankuta Bros Rubber Stamp Co
1395 Lakeland Ave # 16
PO Box 240
Bohemia, NY 11716-3319
631-589-6880
Fax: 516-694-6063 800-223-4481
info@mankuta.com www.mankuta.com
Rubber stamps and engraved signs; wholesaler/distributor of marking devices and pre-inked stamps; embossers; seals; time stamps; etc
Co-Owner: Fred Mankuta
Estimated Sales: Less than $500,000
Number Employees: 20-49
Square Footage: 6000
Brands:
Justrite

25736 Mannhardt Inc
3209 S. 32nd Street
Sheboygan Falls, WI 53082
920-467-1027
Fax: 773-625-5639 800-423-2327
mannhardt1@aol.com mannhardtice.com
Ice storage dispensers and bagging equipment
President: John Williams
Sales: Lori Justinger
Number Employees: 10-19

25737 Mannhart
4401 Blue Mound Rd
Fort Worth, TX 76106
817-421-0100
Fax: 817-421-0246
Commercial vegetable cutters and salad dryers.
President: Edwin Mannhart
Marketing: Christa Mannhart
Sales: Christa Mannhart
Purchasing: Pat Mannhart
Estimated Sales: $3 - 5 Million
Number Employees: 10-19
Number of Brands: 1
Number of Products: 2
Square Footage: 30000
Brands:
Mannhart

25738 (HQ)Manning Lighting Inc
1810 North Ave
Sheboygan, WI 53083-4619
920-458-2184
Fax: 920-458-2491 info@manningltg.com
www.digitalspeck.com
Manufacturer and exporter of lighting equipment including institutional decorative chandeliers
Owner: Andy Manning
Controller: Mary Kuhfuss
Sales: Liz Manning
amanning@manningltg.com
Estimated Sales: $10 - 20 Million
Number Employees: 20-49
Type of Packaging: Food Service

25739 Manning Systems
405 Barclay Blvd
Lincolnshire, IL 60069
913-712-5576
Fax: 913-712-5580 800-444-9935
manning@honeywell.com
Portion control trays, polysheets, poly bags
National Sales Manager: Chuck Linn
Estimated Sales: $1-$3 Million
Number Employees: 5-9
Parent Co: Honeywell

25740 Mannkraft Corporation
100 Frontage Rd
Newark, NJ 07114
973-589-7400
Fax: 973-465-6851
Corrugated boxes and point of purchase displays
President: Dennis Mehiel
Marketing Executive: John Prentiss
Sales Manager: Mark Taylor
Contact: Terence Mcnealy
tbmcnealy@yahoo.com
Estimated Sales: $20-50 Million
Number Employees: 100-249

25741 Mansfield Rubber Stamp
174 S Mulberry St
Mansfield, OH 44902-7423
419-524-1442
Fax: 419-524-7083 stamp174@aol.com
www.mansfieldrubberstamp.com

Rubber and pre-inked stamps, engraved plastic and wood signs and magnetic signs
Owner: Jerry Parrella
stamp174@aol.com
Estimated Sales: Less Than $500,000
Number Employees: 1-4

25742 Manta Ray
N60w14551 Kaul Avenue
Menomonee Falls, WI 53051-5907
888-931-2207
Fax: 262-252-4382
Carton taping, randon carton sealers

25743 Manufacturers Agents forthe Foodservice Industry
1199 Euclid Ave
Atlanta, GA 30307
404-214-9474
Fax: 770-433-2450 info@mafsi.org
www.mafsi.org
Represents the professionalism of our outsourced sales reps to the industry by providing business information for manufacturers and foodservice industries.
VP: M Jeffrey Hessel
Contact: Ambrus Amanda
aambrus@mafsi.org
Number Employees: 1-4

25744 Manufacturers CorrugateBox
5830 57th St
Flushing, NY 11378-3110
718-894-7200
Fax: 718-894-2567
Corrugated boxes
Manager: Sheldon Baim
mcc@maspethchamberofcommerce.org
Manager: Steven Etra
Plant Manager: Curatola
Estimated Sales: $20 - 50 Million
Number Employees: 10-19

25745 Manufacturers Railway Company
One Arsenal Street
Saint Louis, MO 63118
314-577-1775
Fax: 314-577-1810
amund.whittley@anheuser-busch.com
www.trainweb.org
Provides terminal rail-switching services to industries in St. Louis over 42 miles of track and repairs and rebuilds locomotives for the railroad industry. Insulated beverage and hopper railcars. Its two trucking subsidiaries, with afleet of 170 specialty designed trailers, furnish cartage and warehousing services at four locations to serve Anheuser-Busch and other beverage container customers.
President: Kurt Andrew
Number Employees: 100-249
Parent Co: Anheuser-Busch Companies

25746 (HQ)Manufacturers Wood Supply Company
1936 Scranton Road
Cleveland, OH 44113-2429
216-771-7848
Fax: 216-771-7848
Manufacturer, importer and exporter of specialty and industrial wood products including plywood and masonite boxes, packaging inserts and basket bases; custom sizing available
Plant Manager: Joseph Rielinger
Estimated Sales: $1-2.5 Million
Number Employees: 6
Square Footage: 40000

25747 Manufacturing Business Systems
100 N Brand Blvd Ste 600
Glendale, CA 91203
818-551-1758
Fax: 253-399-6201 info@formulas.com
www.formulas.com
Wholesaler/distributor of process manufacturing software
President: Herbert Molano
Estimated Sales: $500,000 - $1,000,000
Number Employees: 5-9

25748 Manufacturing Warehouse
110 NW 24th Avenue
Miami, FL 33125-5260
305-635-8886
Fax: 305-633-2266
Manufacturer and exporter of freezers including walk-in, ice cream and quick freezing; also, walk-in coolers and doors: strip, supermarket and cold storage
Estimated Sales: $1 - 5 Million
Number Employees: 4
Square Footage: 20000

25749 MapFresh
20 Palmetto Pkwy
Suite F
Hilton Head Isle, SC 29926-2459
843-681-5900
Fax: 843-681-5924
Modified atmospheric packaging, trays, conveyor merge units and accessories, gas packaging equipment, vacuum packaging equipment
Estimated Sales: $1 - 5 Million

25750 Maple Hill Farms
12 Burr Rd
PO Box 767
Bloomfield, CT 06002-2204
860-242-9689
Fax: 860-243-2490 800-842-7304
www.mhfct.com
Milk and ice cream vending machines
President: William Miller
info@maplehillfarm.com
General Manager: Edward Jones
Estimated Sales: $5-10 Million
Number Employees: 10-19

25751 Maple Leaf Awning & Canvas Co
8100 Warden Rd
Sherwood, AR 72120-4214
501-834-8891
Fax: 501-834-5397 800-947-4233
awnings@mapleleafcanvas.com
Commercial awnings
Owner: Jim Wilson
awnings@mapleleafcanvas.com
Estimated Sales: $1-2,500,000
Number Employees: 5-9
Parent Co: Custom Canvas Products
Brands:
Maple Leaf

25752 Mar-Boro Printing & Advertising Specialties
1219 Gravesend Neck Rd
Brooklyn, NY 11229-4209
718-336-4051
Fax: 718-336-7996
Advertising specialties, labels, boxes and bags; also, business cards, commercial printing and typesetting services available
VP: James Bruno
Estimated Sales: $500,000-$1,000,000
Number Employees: 5-9

25753 Mar-Con Wire Belt
2431 Vauxhall Place
Richmond, BC V6V 1Z5
Canada
604-278-8922
Fax: 604-278-8938 877-962-7266
www.metalbelt.com
Manufacturer and exporter of wire mesh conveyor belting, food processing equipment, conveyors and sheet metal fabrications including stamping
President: Michael Chiu
CFO: Michael Chiu
R&D: Michael Chiu
Sales Director: Krey Miller
Production/Purchasing: Nathan Chiu
Estimated Sales: $5 Million
Number Employees: 25
Square Footage: 10000
Brands:
Mar-Con

25754 Mar-Khem Industries
PO Box 2266
Cinnaminson, NJ 8077
Fax: 856-829-9203
Supplier, exporter of closeouts; also, investment recovery and used equipment available

President: Anthony Corradetti
a_corradetti@mar-khem.com
Number Employees: 5-9
Number of Brands: 200
Number of Products: 800
Square Footage: 500000
Type of Packaging: Consumer, Food Service, Private Label, Bulk

25755 Mar-Len Supply Inc
23159 Kidder St
Hayward, CA 94545-1630
510-782-3555
Fax: 510-782-2032 mark@marlensupply.com
www.marlensupply.com
Manufacturer and exporter of biodegradable oil and grease dispersing and removing compounds
Owner/President/office Manager: Shirley Winter
marlensupply@aol.com
Technical Director: Frank Winter
Production/Sales Manager: Mark Wieland
Production Engineer: Curt Winter
Estimated Sales: $500,000-$1 Million
Number Employees: 1-4

25756 Marathon Equipment Co
P.O. Box 1798
Highway 9 S
Vernon, AL 35592-1798
205-695-9105
Fax: 205-695-8813 800-269-7237
www.marathonequipment.com
Commercial waste and recycling equipment including balers and self-contained and stationary compactors.
President/General Manager: Vic Ujihara
Estimated Sales: $47 Million
Number Employees: 250-499
Parent Co: Dover Corporation
Brands:
Bale Tech
Eliminator
Jobmaster
Ram-Jet
Rampro

25757 Marathon Products Inc
627 Mccormick St
San Leandro, CA 94577-1109
510-562-6450
Fax: 510-562-5408 800-858-6872
marathon@marathonproducts.com
www.marathonproducts.com
Environmental monitors
CEO: Jon Nakagawa
jnakagawa@marathonproducts.com
Executive Vice President: Kevin Flynn
Number Employees: 10-19

25758 Marazzi USA
359 Clay Road E
Sunnyvale, TX 75182
972-232-3801
contact.us@marazzitile.com
www.marazziusa.com
Tile manufacturer
Estimated Sales: $100,000,000 - $499,999,999
Number Employees: 6,000

25759 Marble Manor
37231 SE Louden Rd
Corbett, OR 97019-8810
503-695-5531
Fax: 503-695-5534 www.marblemanor.com
Owner: William Marble
Estimated Sales: Less Than $500,000
Number Employees: 1-4

25760 Marburg Industries Inc
1207 Activity Dr
Vista, CA 92081-8510
760-727-3762
Fax: 760-727-5502 marburgind@aol.com
www.marburgind.com
Manufacturer and exporter of tamper evident packaging machinery
VP Marketing: Barbara Paschal
Manager: Barbara Paschal
Estimated Sales: $1-2.5 Million
Number Employees: 10-19
Square Footage: 20000
Type of Packaging: Food Service, Private Label, Bulk

Brands:
Autocapsealer

25761 Marc Refrigeration Mfg Inc
7453 NW 32nd Ave
Miami, FL 33147-5877
305-691-0500
Fax: 305-691-1212 info@marcrefrigeration.com
www.marcrefrigeration.com
Manufacturer and exporter of commercial refrigerators and ice cream freezers
President: Hy Widel
Vice President: Loretta Widelitz
lwidelitz@marcrefrigerationmfginc.com
Treasurer: Hal Videlitz
Secretary: Robert Gordon
Estimated Sales: $5-10 Million
Number Employees: 20-49
Square Footage: 228000
Type of Packaging: Food Service

25762 (HQ)Marcal Paper Mills
1 Market St
Elmwood Park, NJ 07407
201-796-4000
Fax: 201-796-0470 800-631-8451
www.marcalpaper.com
Tissues, napkins and towels made from recycled paper
President & CEO: Rob Baron
CFO: Scott Dicus
VP, Opertions: Stacy Lee
Estimated Sales: $80 Million
Number Employees: 800
Other Locations:
Marcal Paper Mills
Augusta GA
Brands:
Aspen
Bella
Fluff Out
Sani-Hanks
Snowlily
Sst
Sunrise

25763 Marcel S. Garrigues Company
560 3rd St
San Francisco, CA 94107
415-421-0371
Fax: 415-957-2638
Tea and coffee industry reconditioners, samplers and weighers
Manager: Lana Jow
Estimated Sales: $500,000-$1 Million
Number Employees: 5-9

25764 Marchant Schmidt Inc
24 W Larsen Dr
Fond Du Lac, WI 54937-8518
920-921-4760
Fax: 920-921-9640 sales@marchantschmidt.com
www.marchantschmidt.com
Manufacturers stainless steel products and equipment for the food and dairy industry
Vice President: Richard F Schmidt
rschmidt@marchantschmidt.com
CEO: Myleen Schmidt
Vice President: Lyle Schmidt
Sales Director: Jeno Thuecks
Estimated Sales: $11 Million
Number Employees: 100-249
Square Footage: 48000

25765 Marchesini Packaging Machinery
43 Fairfield Pl
West Caldwell, NJ 07006-6206
973-575-7445
Fax: 973-575-4051 info@marchesiniusa.com
www.marchesiniusa.com
Bag filling and sealing machines, bag forming machines, bundling machines, carton machines: closing, filling, handling, sealing, casing equipment: packers
President: Roger Toll
roger.toll@marchesiniusa.com
Controller: Elaine Miller
Estimated Sales: $2.5 - 5 Million
Number Employees: 20-49

25766 Marco Products
923 S Main St
Adrian, MI 49221-3709
517-265-3333
Fax: 517-265-3650
Plastic containers
Manager: Norman Double
Estimated Sales: $2.5-5 Million
Number Employees: 10-19
Square Footage: 108000

25767 Marcus Carton Company
324 S Service Rd
Melville, NY 11747-3270
631-752-4200
Fax: 631-752-0022
Folding paper boxes
Vice President: Nancy Simon
Director Marketing: Douglas Campbell
Estimated Sales: $1 - 5 Million
Number Employees: 10-19
Square Footage: 74000

25768 Marden Edwards
1866 Verne Roberts Cir
Antioch, CA 94509
925-777-1403
Fax: 925-777-1406 800-332-1838
usasales@mardenedwards.com
www.mardenedwards.com
Packaging
Contact: David Aimson
d.aimson@mardenedwards.com
Estimated Sales: Below 1 Million
Number Employees: 1-4

25769 Marel Food Systems, Inc.
8145 Flint Street
Lenexa, KS 66214
913-888-9110
Fax: 913-888-9124 info@marel.com
www.marel.com
Manufacturer of meat hoppers, checkweighers, scales and end line scales. Also manufacture batter mixers, flour and bread applicators, spiral and linear ovens and steam cookers.
CEO: Theo Hoen
CFO: Eric Kaman
Regional Sales Manager: David Bertelsen
Contact: Debra Bernas
dbernas@marel.com

25770 Marel Stork Poultry Processing
1024 Airport Pkwy
Gainesville, GA 30501-6814
770-532-7041
Fax: 770-532-5672
Manufacturer and exporter of poultry processing equipment
President: Frank Nicoletti
frank.nicoletti@stork.com
Executive VP: Frank Nicoletti
Manager Domestic Sales: Bryon Lovingood
Estimated Sales: $20-50 Million
Number Employees: 100-249
Square Footage: 145000

25771 Marel Stork Poultry Processing
1024 Airport Pkwy
Gainesville, GA 30501-6814
770-532-7041
Fax: 770-532-5672 800-247-8609
info.us@marel.com www.marel.com/poultry
Poultry processing equipment
President: Frank Nicoletti
frank.nicoletti@stork.com
Director: Bob Conklin
Number Employees: 100-249
Parent Co: Marel

25772 Marel Townsend
2425 Hubbell Ave
Des Moines, IA 50317
515-265-8181
Fax: 515-263-3333 800-247-8609
info.townsendusa@stork.com www.marel.com
Processing equipment for meat processing; including single scales, production lines and turnkey systems
Contact: Maria Bozaan
maria.bozaan@marel.com
Parent Co: Marel

25773 Marel USA
9745 Widmer Road
Lenexa, KS 66215-1260
913-888-9110
Fax: 913-888-9124 888-888-9107
info@marelusa.com www.marel.com
Complete range of super fast scales, software, monitoring equipment intelligent portioning, grading modules, intergrated systems, flatteners, shish-kebab machines and service contracts
President: Noel Whitten
CFO: Noel Whitten
VP Service: Petur Petursson
Marketing Director: Heather MacKenzie
VP Sales: Larry Campbell
Contact: Michael Jusseaume
michael.jusseaume@marelusa.com
Estimated Sales: $2.5 - 5 Million
Number Employees: 35
Square Footage: 41600
Parent Co: Marel Hf.

25774 Maren Engineering Corp
111 W Taft Dr
South Holland, IL 60473-2049
708-333-6250
Fax: 708-333-7507 800-875-1038
sales@marenengineering.com
www.marenengineering.com
Manufacturer and exporter of vertical and horizontal balers for corrugated paper and other applications; also, shredders, drum crushers and packers
CFO: Lee Norbeck
Vice President: Charles Brown
R & D: David Rudofski
Manager: Greg Hermdon
Estimated Sales: $5-10 Million
Number Employees: 20-49
Parent Co: Kine Corporation

25775 (HQ)Marfred Industries
12708 Bradford St
Sun Valley, CA 91353
818-896-3449
Fax: 818-889-4239 800-529-5156
Corrugated boxes and folding cartons
President: Marvin Fenster
CFO: Marc Fenster
Quality Control: John Ramirez
Marketing: Brian Mallay
Sales/Marketing Manager: Chris Gaff
Operations: Marc Fenster
Plant Manager: Randy Phares
Estimated Sales: $500,000-$1 Million
Number Employees: 100-249
Number of Brands: 50
Number of Products: 5000
Square Footage: 930000
Type of Packaging: Consumer, Food Service, Private Label, Bulk

25776 Margia Floors
270 Bellevue Ave.
Newport, RI 2840
401-489-7805
Fax: 228-822-0096 info@margiafloors.com
www.margiafloors.com
Floor and wall coating materials, flooring, floor grating, building and construction consultants
Estimated Sales: $1 - 5 Million
Number Employees: 2

25777 Marin Cleaning Systems
3239 Monier Cir
Suite 1
Rancho Cordova, CA 95742-6833
916-635-6861
Wine industry tank cleaners
Owner: Nathan Bari
Estimated Sales: $300,000-500,000
Number Employees: 1-4

25778 Marineland Commercial Aquariums
3001 Commerce St.
Blacksburg, VA 24060-6671
805-529-0083
Fax: 805-529-0852 800-322-1266
consumersupport@unitedpetgroup.com
www.marineland.com
Manufacturer and exporter of display tanks for lobsters and fish

President: Gary Smith
CFO: John McGreevy
Vice President: Bill Sheweloff
Quality Control: Fred Bohmour
Sales Manager (West Coast): Jay Dersahagian
Contact: Keri Barton
  barton@marineland.com
Estimated Sales: $5 - 10 Million
Number Employees: 250-499

25779 Marion Body Works Inc
211 W Ramsdell St
Marion, WI 54950-9683
715-754-5261
Fax: 715-754-5776 contactus@marionbody.com
www.marionbody.com
Dry, refrigerated and curtainside vans; also, structural platforms and glasshaulers
President: James Simpson
  jsimpson@marionbody.com
Sales Manager: Mike Foley
Production Manager: Kent Cournoyer
Estimated Sales: $10 - 20 Million
Number Employees: 100-249
Square Footage: 240000
Brands:
  Marion

25780 Marion Pallet Company
281 Copeland Ave
Marion, OH 43302
740-382-5063
Fax: 740-387-9478 800-432-4117
New and rebuilt wooden pallets
Owner: Devin Needles
Contact: Ashley Karg
  akarg@marionstar.com
Estimated Sales: $10-20 Million
Number Employees: 10-19
Square Footage: 20000

25781 Marion Paper Box Co
600 E 18th St
Marion, IN 46953-3304
765-664-6435
Fax: 765-664-6440 sales@marionbox.com
www.marionpaperboxco.com
Manufacturer and exporter of folding and set-up paper boxes; also, die cutting and partitions available. Also manufactures pads
Owner: Joe Mc Coy
Sales: Jason Priest
  marionpaperbox2004@yahoo.com
Manager Operations: David Wilson
Estimated Sales: $2.5 - 5 Million
Number Employees: 5-9
Square Footage: 30000

25782 Mark Container Corporation
1899 Marina Blvd
San Leandro, CA 94577-4225
510-483-4440
Fax: 510-352-1524 www.wellsfargo.com
Manufacturer and exporter of corrugated boxes
Manager: Shuzair Malik
Estimated Sales: $10-20 Million
Number Employees: 10-19

25783 Mark Products Company
46 Rainbow Trl
Denville, NJ 7834
973-983-8818
Fax: 973-627-6273
Manufacturer and exporter of packaging equipment and materials including shrink and pallet wrappers and wrapping films; importer of shrink PVC films
President: Doug Mark
VP: Charles Scweizer
Number Employees: 1-4
Number of Brands: 1
Number of Products: 10
Square Footage: 4000
Type of Packaging: Food Service, Bulk

25784 Mark Slade ManufacturingCompany
PO Box 325
Seymour, WI 54165-0325
920-833-6557
Fax: 920-833-7456 drhandles@new.rr.com
Wood dowels, core plugs, cant hooks, pallets and displays

Estimated Sales: less than $300,000
Number Employees: 2
Square Footage: 20100

25785 Mark-It Rubber Stamp & Label Company
912 Hope St
Stamford, CT 06907-0031
203-348-3204
Fax: 203-323-7846
Manufacturer and converter of self-stick labels, rubber stamps and marking devices
President: Archie Dean
Executive VP: Archie Dean
Quality Control: Archie Dean
Sales Manager: Jack O'Neil
Estimated Sales: Below $5 Million
Number Employees: 5-9

25786 MarkeTeam
Corporate Office
PO Box 850
Vancouver, WA 98666
360-696-3984
Fax: 360-693-0192 www.marketeamnw.com
Manufacturers' representative for food service equipment including supplies and furniture
President: Daniel Miles
CEO: Jim Mincks
CFO: David Mincks
VP: William Kelly
Estimated Sales: Below $5 Million
Number Employees: 10-19

25787 Market Forge IndustriesInc
35 Garvey St
Everett, MA 02149-4403
406-209-1300
Fax: 617-387-4456 866-698-3188
custserv@mfii.com www.mfii.com
Comerical food service equipment
President & CEO: David Zappala
Estimated Sales: $13 Million
Number Employees: 10-19
Square Footage: 14859
Type of Packaging: Food Service

25788 Market Sales Company
PO Box 590639
Newton, MA 02459-0639
617-232-0239
Fax: 617-232-0239
Vacuum packaging equipment, vaccum bags and films.
Vice President: Linda Pollino
Sales Manager: Edward Pollino

25789 Market Sign Systems
75 W Commercial St
Portland, ME 04101-4797
207-773-7585
Fax: 207-773-3151 800-421-1799
info@nimlok-maine.com
Point of purchase aluminum sign holders
Owner: Ken Janson
VP: Marc Breton
Number Employees: 1-4
Square Footage: 2400
Brands:
  Casemate

25790 Marketing & Technology Group
1415 N Dayton St # 115
Chicago, IL 60642-7033
312-274-2200
Fax: 312-266-3363 info@meatingplace.com
www.meatingplace.com
Computer systems and software, meat industry publications and information
Owner: Mark Lefens
  jfranklin@meetingplace.com
Chairman: Jim Franklin
Vice President of Information Systems: Annica Burns
Director of Marketing: Laurie Hachmeister
Account Executive: Dave Lurie
  jfranklin@meetingplace.com
Production Manager: Shirleen Kajiwara
Estimated Sales: $5 - 10 Million
Number Employees: 20-49

25791 Marketing & Technology Group
1415 N Dayton St
Suite 115
Chicago, IL 60642
312-266-3311
Fax: 312-266-3363 amcguire@meatingplace.com
www.meatingplace.com
Computer systems and software, meat industry publications and information, sales and advertising promotions and materials
Owner: Mark Lefens
VP Editorial: Bill McDowell
Circulation/Marketing Manager: Steve Gardberg
Sales Manager: Mary Lea
Contact: Delorian Allen
  dallen@meatingplace.com
Chairman Operations: Jim Franklin
Production Manager: Bernie Schlameuss
Estimated Sales: $5-10 Million
Number Employees: 20-49
Parent Co: Marketing & Technology Group

25792 Marketing Concepts
34 Hinda Blvd
Riverhead, NY 11901-4804
631-727-8886
Fax: 631-369-3903 www.auto-matetech.com
Tea and coffee industry conveying equipment (elevators, machiners and buckets), cappers, cleaners and closers (for coffee jars)
Owner: Kenneth Herzog
Estimated Sales: $10 - 20 Million
Number Employees: 20-49

25793 Marketing Management Inc
4717 Fletcher Ave
Fort Worth, TX 76107-6826
817-731-4176
Fax: 817-732-5610 800-433-2004
sales@mmibrands.com www.mmibrands.com
Retail & merchadising marketing, brand development, quality assurance, consumer research, consumer response, procurement, inventory management, category development, package design, information technology, networking and e-commercemulti media and more
President: Randy Hurr
CEO: Herb Pease Jr
VP, CFO: Donna Smith
Vice President: Ed Mieskoski
R&D: Bill Bradshaw
VP, Market Solutions: Steve Thomas
Sales: Bill Bradshaw
Public Relations: Joni Grulke
Operations: H Pease Jr
Estimated Sales: $10 - 20 Million
Number Employees: 50-99
Square Footage: 130000

25794 Marking Devices Inc
3110 Payne Ave
Cleveland, OH 44114-4504
216-861-4498
Fax: 216-241-1479 mdinc@en.com
www.realtyappreciation.com
Manufacturer and exporter of rubber and polymer printing plates and rubber and steel stamps
Owner: John Enci
VP: John Wacker
Sales Manager: Dave Tully
  johne@royalacme.com
Estimated Sales: $2.5-5 Million
Number Employees: 20-49
Square Footage: 22000

25795 Marking Methods Inc
301 S Raymond Ave
Alhambra, CA 91803-1531
626-308-5800
Fax: 626-576-7564
experts@markingmethods.com
www.markingmethods.com
Permanent stress-free marking equipment including electro-chemical hot stamping for plastics, laser, dot peen for metal parts and equipment; exporter of electro-chemical marking equipment, etc
President: Nataly Baltazar
  natalyb@markingmethods.com
CEO: A Bennett
CFO: Susan Chu
Sales Director: Victor Amorim
Estimated Sales: Below $5 Million
Number Employees: 20-49
Square Footage: 40000

Brands:
Mark-300a
Marking Methods, Inc.

25796 Marklite Line
34 Davis Dr
Bellwood, IL 60104-1047
708-668-4900
Fax: 630-668-4906
Advertising and pressure sensitive tapes and labels;
also, custom printing available
Customer Service: Agnes Vincenzo
Advertising: Maryann Mueller
Estimated Sales: $3 - 5 Million
Number Employees: 10-19

25797 Marko Inc
1310 Southport Rd
Spartanburg, SC 29306-6199
864-585-2259
866-466-2726
rmeehan@markoinc.com www.markoinc.com
Janitorial cleaners, disinfectants and waxes; whole-
saler/distributor of paper supplies and janitorial
equipment including aerosols and mops
Owner: Anne Meehan
ameehan@markoinc.com
CEO: Ann Meehan
VP Marketing: Richard Meehan, Jr.
Purchasing Manager: Melanie Meehan
Estimated Sales: 800000
Number Employees: 5-9
Number of Brands: 10
Number of Products: 450
Square Footage: 24000
Type of Packaging: Private Label
Brands:
Marko

25798 Marko Inc
1310 Southport Rd
Spartanburg, SC 29306-6199
864-585-2259
Fax: 864-585-0750 866-466-2756
www.markoinc.com
Manufacturer and exporter of table cloths and skirt-
ing; also, napkins, aprons and place mats
Owner: Anne Meehan
ameehan@markoinc.com
VP Sales/Marketing: Tony La Porte
VP Manufacturing: Rob James
Estimated Sales: $10-20 Million
Number Employees: 5-9
Type of Packaging: Food Service
Brands:
Marko Intl.
Markoated
Midwest Marko

25799 Markwell Manufacturing Company
692 Pleasant St
Norwood, MA 2062
781-769-6610
Fax: 781-769-7060 800-666-1123
info@mrkwll.com www.mrkwll.com
Manufacturer, importer and exporter of plier, box
and hand, foot and air operated staplers, tackers and
carton sealers; also, staples, collated nails, marking
crayons, tapes, strech-wrap, and spray ashesives
President: Sam Opland
Contact: Jeff Cobb
markwellusa@gmail.com
Estimated Sales: $1-2.5 Million
Number Employees: 5-9
Square Footage: 27000
Brands:
Markwell
Sta-Plyer
Tackmaster

25800 Marland Clutch Products
PO Box 308
La Grange, IL 60525-0308
708-352-3330
Fax: 877-216-3001 800-216-3515
info@marland.com www.marland.com
Heavy duty, industrial free wheeling clutches and
conveyor back stops
President: Charlie Nins
CFO: John Young
Estimated Sales: $5 - 10 Million
Number Employees: 3

25801 Marlen
4780 NW 41st Street
Ste 100
Riverside, MO 64150
913-888-3333
Fax: 913-888-5471 www.marlen.com
Portioning and forming equipment, in-line grinders,
pumping equipment and material handling products.
President: Richard Schneider
CEO: Jim Anderson
Regional Sales Manager: Fernando Casado
Contact: Jeff Blansit
jeff.blansit@marlen.com

25802 Marlen International
9202 Barton St
Overland Park, KS 66214
913-888-3333
Fax: 913-888-6440 800-862-7536
Food processing equipment, including: pumps,
portioners, formers and in-line grinders
Vice President: Bill Faivre
Sales Manager: Jarrod McCarroll
Contact: Grant Beck
grant.beck@marlen.com
Estimated Sales: $35 Million
Number Employees: 85
Parent Co: Pfingsten Partners

25803 Marlen International
441 30th St
Astoria, OR 97103-2807
503-861-2273
Fax: 913-888-6440 800-862-7536
www.marlen.com
Continuous flow slicers, dicers, strip cutters, shred-
ders, volumetric rotary/piston fillers, pak-shapers,
specialty conveyors, etc
Manager: Pete Johnson
CFO: Irene Codonau
Vice President: Jarrod McCarroll
Research & Development: Robert Zschoche
Quality Control: David Bogih
Marketing/Sales: Pete Johnson
Regional Sales Manager: Mike Leiker
Public Relations: Jack Walls
Inside Sales: Jack Walls
Production Manager: David Bogh
Plant Manager: Rusty Price
Purchasing Manager: Mark Ross
Estimated Sales: $10-20 Million
Number Employees: 20-49
Square Footage: 120000
Brands:
Auto-Logger
Auto-Shredder
Auto-Slicer
Automated Boxing Line
Home-Style
Mega-Slicer
Nu-Pak Performance F-Series
Nu-Pak Portion
Pak-Shaper
Pathfinder
Performance
Q-Ber
Table Top

25804 Marlen International
441 30th St
Astoria, OR 97103-2807
800-862-7536
Fax: 913-888-5471 sales@marlen.com
www.marlen.com
Manufactures dicing, filling, slicers and shredding
machinery
Vice President: Jarrod McCarroll
Estimated Sales: $10-20 000,000
Number Employees: 20-49

25805 Marlen Research
P.O. Box 457
Hutchinson, KS 67504-457
316-683-6542
Fax: 316-665-6793 www.marlen.com
Elevators, loaders, lifters, dumpers, tubs, drums,
tanks, vats and buckets for materials handling, pro-
cessing equipment includes ham presses, molds and
accessories, temperature controls, contact plate and
belt freezers
Estimated Sales: $10-20 Million
Number Employees: 50-99
Parent Co: Marlen Research Corporation

25806 Marlen Research Corporation
9202 Barton St
Shawnee Mission, KS 66214
913-888-3333
Fax: 913-888-6440 sales@marlen.com
www.marlen.com
Designer and manufacturer of food processing
equipment such as pump/vacuumizer, sizers, grind-
ers, exact weight portioners, product racks, dumpers,
vats, continous mold systems, thermal processing
equipment and custom designed tanks andhoppers
President: Adam Anderson
VP: Bill Faivre
Marketing/Sales: Teresa Kem
Sales Manager: Fernando Casado
Contact: James Andrson
sales@marlen.com
Estimated Sales: $6-$7 Million
Number Employees: 50-99
Square Footage: 40000
Brands:
Gbc
Marlen
Reno

25807 Marlen Research Corporation
9202 Barton St
Shawnee Mission, KS 66214
913-888-3333
Fax: 913-888-5471 800-862-7536
sales@marlen.com www.marlen.com
President: Adam Anderson
CFO: Larry Dearmond
Contact: James Andrson
sales@marlen.com
Estimated Sales: $20 - 50 Million
Number Employees: 50-99

25808 Marley Engineered Products LLC
470 Beauty Spot Rd E
Bennettsville, SC 29512-2770
843-479-4006
Fax: 843-479-5205 800-327-4328
www.marleymep.com
Blowers and fans
President: Tom Blashill
tom.blashill@spx.com
Estimated Sales: $5-10 Million
Number Employees: 500-999

25809 Marlin Steel Wire Products
2640 Merchant Dr
Baltimore, MD 21230-3307
410-644-7456
Fax: 410-644-7457 877-762-7546
sales@marlinwire.com www.marlinwire.com
Steel wire shelving and racks
President: Chris Elwood
chris.elwood@marlinsteel.com
CFO: Susan Fuller
Estimated Sales: $20 - 50 Million
Number Employees: 20-49
Number of Products: 450
Square Footage: 25000

25810 Marlite
1 Marlite Dr
Dover, OH 44622
330-343-6621
Fax: 330-343-7296 800-377-1221
info@marlite.com www.marlite.com
Manufacturer and exporter of sanitary wall and ceil-
ing panel systems, decorative wall panel systems,
doors/frames, restroom partitions, korelock panels,
retail merchandising display systems, etc
CFO: Kimberly McBride
VP, Sales & Marketing: Greg Triplett
Contact: Nini Abreu
nabreu@marlite.com
Estimated Sales: $21 Million
Number Employees: 251-500
Square Footage: 450000
Brands:
Accents Frp
Borders
Displawall
Firetest
Korelock
Marlite
Marlite Brand Frp
Marlite Modules
Plank
Surface Systems
Symmetrix Frp

25811 Marlo Manufacturing
301 Division St
Boonton, NJ 07005-1826
973-423-0226
Fax: 973-423-1638 800-222-0450
Manufacturer, importer and exporter of stainless steel food service equipment
Founder: Sal Pirruccio
Partner: Larry Dubov
larry@marlomfg.com
VP, Manufacturing: Paul Pirruccio
VP, Sales & Marketing: Larry Dubov
VP, Operations: Paul Tommasi
Plant Manager: Paul Pirruccio
Estimated Sales: $4-6 Million
Number Employees: 1-4
Square Footage: 60000
Type of Packaging: Food Service

25812 Marlow Watson Inc
37 Upton Dr # 1
Wilmington, MA 01887-4452
978-658-0041
Fax: 978-658-0041 800-282-8823
www.watson-marlow.com
Peristaltic hose pumps for metering, transferring and dispensing
CEO and CFO: James Whalen
Contact: Joakim Cederqvist
jcederqvist@wmbpumps.com
Estimated Sales: $20 - 50 Million
Number Employees: 5-9
Parent Co: Spirax Sarco Engineering Group
Brands:
Bioprene
Marprene
Watson-Marlow

25813 Maro Paper Products Company
333 31st Ave
Bellwood, IL 60104-1527
708-649-9982
Fax: 708-649-9986 www.marocarton.com
Folding cartons and blister cards
Owner: Joseph Maro
VP: J Maro
Estimated Sales: $5-10 Million
Number Employees: 100-249

25814 (HQ)Marpac Industries
PO Box 784
Philmont, NY 12565-0784
845-336-8100
Fax: 845-336-5006 888-462-7722
Plastic bottles and containers
VP Sales: B Williams
Operations: Gen Gendrow
Estimated Sales: $10-20 Million
Number Employees: 50-99
Square Footage: 68000
Type of Packaging: Consumer, Food Service
Other Locations:
Marpac Industries
Kingston NY
Brands:
E-Z Access

25815 (HQ)Marq Packaging Systems Inc
3801 W Washington Ave
Yakima, WA 98903-1181
509-966-4300
Fax: 509-452-3307 800-998-4301
info@marq.net
Case sealers, product settling & sealing, tray formers and case erector bottom sealers
President: Rocky Marquis
CFO: Diahann Curtis
dcurtis@marq.net
VP: Kelli Barton
Sales Co-coordinator: Jim Hansen
Operations: G W Walker
Estimated Sales: $5-10 Million
Number Employees: 20-49
Square Footage: 135000
Type of Packaging: Food Service, Bulk

25816 Marq Packaging Systems Inc
3801 W Washington Ave
Yakima, WA 98903-1181
509-966-4300
Fax: 509-452-3307 800-998-4301
info@marq.net
Wine industry Bag in Box, case sealing

President: Rocky Marquis
CEO: Ted Marquis Sr
CFO: Diahann Curtis
dcurtis@marq.net
Chairman of the Board: Theodore Marquis Sr
Number Employees: 20-49

25817 Marquip Ward United
1300 N Airport Rd
Phillips, WI 54555-1527
715-339-2191
www.marquipwardunited.com
Machinery for corrugated containers
Estimated Sales: $1 - 5 Million
Number Employees: 500-999
Parent Co: Barry-Wehmiller

25818 Marquis Products
91 Pipin Road
Concord, ON L4K 4J9
Canada
905-738-2082
Fax: 905-738-2417 800-268-1282
Refrigeration equipment including walk-in, reach-in coolers, sliding and glass doors and freezers
President: Vincent Melfi
Number Employees: 30

25819 Marriott Walker Corporation
925 E Maple Rd
Bingham Farms, MI 48009
248-644-6868
Fax: 248-642-1213 mwc@marriottwalker.com
www.marriottwalker.com
Manufacturer and exporter of evaporators, spray dryers, etc
President: Winthrop Walker
VP Engineering: Mark Price
Contact: Mary Ayotte
mayotte@marriottwalker.com
Estimated Sales: $1-2.5 Million
Number Employees: 5-9
Square Footage: 13200
Brands:
Marriott Walker

25820 Marron Foods
327 Woodlands Rd
Box 15
Harrison, NY 10528
914-967-2442
Fax: 914-967-2220 info@marronfoods.com
www.marronfoods.com
Agglomeration/instantizing ,spray drying, blending, industrial, food serice, consumer pouch/canister packaging
President: Matt Pearson
Number Employees: 100
Brands:
80WheyUSA
MaltoPure
Milkman
SlimMilk
SlimMilk LF

25821 (HQ)Mars Air Products
14716 S Broadway
Gardena, CA 90248-1814
310-532-1555
Fax: 310-324-3030 800-421-1266
info@marsair.com www.marsair.com
Manufacturer and exporter of air purifiers and heated and unheated air curtains in electric, gas, steam and hot water for insect control and environmental separation; also, packaged make-up air, cooling, heating and ventilatingsystems
Owner: Jimmy Johnson
johnson@skycatch.com
Vice President: Steve Rosol
Quality Control: Michael Goldman
Marketing Director: Dana Agens
Plant Manager/Purchasing Director: Frank Cuaderno
Estimated Sales: Below $5 Million
Number Employees: 50-99
Square Footage: 392000
Brands:
Ares
Combi
Mars
Whispurr Air
Windguard

25822 Mars Systems
1140 Empire Central Dr
Dallas, TX 75247-4322
214-634-7441
Fax: 972-252-9566
Restaurant entertainment systems
Owner: Robert Morris
Account Executive: Sheila Bellucci
Estimated Sales: $500,000-$1 Million
Number Employees: 5-9

25823 Marsch Pacific Cork & Foil
2427 Pratt Avenue
Hayward, CA 94544-7829
510-429-3200
Fax: 510-429-3200
Wine industry cork and capsule supplies
Estimated Sales: $5-10 Million
Number Employees: 10-19

25824 (HQ)Marsh Company
PO Box 388
Belleville, IL 62222-0388
618-234-1122
Fax: 618-234-1529 800-527-6275
marshco@marshco.com www.marshco.com
Manufacturer, exporter and importer of large and small character ink jet coding systems, marking and sealing machines and supplies
President: Robret Willett
CEO/Chairman: John Marsh
CFO: Mark Kuhn
Quality Control: Mark Wilmsen
R&D: Jerry Robertson
VP Sales/Marketing: P Wagner
Estimated Sales: $20 - 50 Million
Number Employees: 500
Other Locations:
Marsh Co.
S.A, Geneva
Brands:
Contact Marking
Dial Taper
Lcp/Dl
Lcp/Ml8
Mini-Mark
Symbol Jet
Touch Taper
Twin Taper
Ultra Taper
Unicorn

25825 Marshakk Smoked Fish Company
6980 75th St
Flushing, NY 11379-2531
718-326-2170
Fax: 718-384-6661
Specialty foods
President: Marie Cook
Vice President: Gary Cook
Sales Director: Sean Cook
Estimated Sales: $10-24.9 000,000
Number Employees: 50-99
Type of Packaging: Private Label
Brands:
Almondina
Aunt Jenny's
Babcock
Boone Maman
Bovril
Breadshop
Brianna's
Carapelli
Carr's
Celestial
Coco Pazzo
Colavita
Consorzio
Dececco
Del Verde
Dell Amore's
Delouis
Dessvilie
Dickinson
Droste
Dutch Gold
Eden
El Paso
Finncrisp
French Market
Green Mountain
Grielle
Guiltless Gourmet
Hero

Highland Sugar Vermont
Holgrain
Illy
Knorr
Konriko
La Marne Champ
La Posada
La Preferida
Langnese
Lindt
Maille
Marmite
McCann's
Melba
Melitta
Monnini
New York Flatbread
Old Monk
Poell
Pommery
Pritikin
Qugg
Rao's
Romanoff
Spice Hunter
Spice Island
St. Dalfour
Sunbrand
Texmati
Timpone's
Tip Tree
Tropical Bee
Twinings

25826 Marshall Air Systems Inc
419 Peachtree Dr S
Charlotte, NC 28217-2098

704-525-6230
Fax: 704-525-6229 800-722-3474
customerservice@marshallair.com
www.marshallair.com
Manufacturer and exporter of food warming and
conveyorized cooking systems including broilers;
also, ventilation systems including hoods and fans
Chairman: Robert Stuck
Chairman: Marina Flick
mflick@marshallair.com
Estimated Sales: $20-50 Million
Number Employees: 50-99
Type of Packaging: Food Service
Brands:
Autobake
Autobroil
Autobroil Omni
Autogrill
Automelt
Autoroast
Thermoglo

25827 (HQ)Marshall Boxes Inc
715 Lexington Ave
Rochester, NY 14613-1807

585-458-7432
Fax: 585-458-6302 info@marshallboxes.com
www.marshallboxes.com
Wooden boxes, pallets and plywood parts
President: John Skuse
jskuse@marshallboxes.com
Estimated Sales: $2.5-5 Million
Number Employees: 10-19
Square Footage: 44000
Other Locations:
Marshall Boxes
Rancho Cucomonga CA

25828 Marshall Ingredients
5740 Limekiln Rd
Wolcott, NY 14590

800-796-9353
Fruits and vegetables in different forms such as fi-
ber, pellet, whole, diced, sliced, powder, seeds,
pomace
National Sales Manager: Casey Koehnlein
Contact: Scott Edwards
sedwards@marshallingredients.com
Type of Packaging: Bulk

25829 Marshall Instruments Inc
2930 E LA Cresta Ave
Anaheim, CA 92806-1833

714-632-8565
Fax: 714-666-2326 800-222-8476
info@marshallinstruments.com
www.marshallinstruments.com
Bi-metallic dial thermometers, distributor of high
performance shock proof pressure gauges
President: Nancy Lynch
info@marshallinstruments.com
VP: Nancy Lynch
Product Manager: Tim Bowers
Estimated Sales: $2.5-5 Million
Number Employees: 20-49
Square Footage: 24000

25830 (HQ)Marshall Paper Products
PO Box 267
East Norwich, NY 11732

Fax: 718-821-5779
Corrugated paper
VP: Brian Sadowsky
Estimated Sales: $1-2.5 Million
Number Employees: 5

25831 Marshall Plastic Film Inc
904 E Allegan St
Martin, MI 49070-9797

269-672-5511
Fax: 269-672-5035 www.marshallplastic.com
Manufacturer and exporter of form, fill, seal and
shrink plastic films and bags
President: Rich Bowman
rbowman@marshallplastic.com
VP: Casey McCarthy
Customer Service: William Rackley
Customer Service: Sylvia Davis
Estimated Sales: $20-50 Million
Number Employees: 20-49
Square Footage: 45500
Brands:
Marshall Blue
Marshall Pink Under the Sink

25832 Marshfield Food Safety
1100 N. Oak Avenue
Marshfield, WI 54449

888-780-9897
www.marshfieldfoodsafetyllc.com
Food safety testing facility.
Quality Manager: Debbie Chilson
Marketing: Marsha Barwick
Chief Scientific Officer: Roy Radcliff

25833 (HQ)Marston Manufacturing
13700 Broadway Ave
Cleveland, OH 44125-1945

216-587-3400
Fax: 216-587-0733 www.tomlinsonind.com
Wooden tray stands and oak chairs including high
and booster; also, condiment holders, cast iron cook-
ware, bread boards, sandwich tartans and
underliners
President: H Meyer
CEO: Mike Figas
CFO: Don Calkins
Sales: John DiNapoli
Estimated Sales: $2.5-5 Million
Number Employees: 100-249
Square Footage: 160000
Other Locations:
Marston Manufacturing
Richmond VA

25834 Mart CART-Smt
112 E Linden St
Rogers, AR 72756-6035

479-636-5776
Fax: 479-246-6473 800-548-3373
apc@assembledproducts.com
www.assembledproducts.com
Manufacturer and exporter of pressure washers
President: George Panter
Vice President: Bob Sage
Marketing Director: Steve Scroggins
Sales Director: Kent Langum
Plant Manager: R Smith
Purchasing Manager: Don McKenzie
Estimated Sales: $20 - 30 Million
Number Employees: 100-249
Square Footage: 123000
Parent Co: Assembled Pro Corporation
Brands:
Spraymaster

25835 Mart CART-Smt
112 E Linden St
Rogers, AR 72756-6035

479-636-5776
Fax: 479-246-6473 800-548-3373
www.assembledproducts.com
President: George Panter
Estimated Sales: $1 - 5 Million
Number Employees: 100-249

25836 Martco Engravers
792 Main Street
Fremont, NH 03044-3506

603-895-3561
Fax: 603-895-3717
Badges, ribbons, plaques, awards, trophies and rub-
ber stamps
Partner: Arthur Courteau
Estimated Sales: Less than $500,000
Number Employees: 4

25837 Martech Research
15 Myrtle Dr
Bishopville, SC 29010-1764

803-428-2000
Fax: 803-428-1598
bmaresca@martechresearch.com
www.martechenvironmental.com
Custom manufacturing, formulation, private labeling
and toll blending. Shelf life extension products for
fruits, vegetables, oils and beverages.
Founder & President: Amie Maresca
Manager: Benny Maresca
bmaresca@martechresearch.com
Estimated Sales: $3.7 Million
Number Employees: 1-4
Square Footage: 84000
Type of Packaging: Consumer, Private Label, Bulk

25838 Martin Brothers Inc
3057 Cajun Dr
Winnsboro, LA 71295-6849

318-435-4581
Fax: 318-435-4581 800-652-2532
kmartin@teammartinbrothers.com
www.teammartinbrothers.com
Heat exchangers, ice cream equipment, ingredient
feeders, piping, fittings and tubing, sanitary
President: W K Martin
wmartin@teammartinbrothers.com
VP Sales & Marketing: Conrad L. Gaither
Sales: Lamar Johnson
Sales: Kelly Martin
Sales: Dwayne Long
Estimated Sales: $5-10 Million
Number Employees: 10-19

25839 Martin Cab Div
7108 Madison Ave
Cleveland, OH 44102-4093

216-377-8200
Fax: 216-651-2079 www.martincab.com
Manufacturer and exporter of cab enclosures, in-
cluding freezer cabs
President: James Martin
CFO: Jim Markin
Chairman: Pauline Martin
VP Sales/Marketing: James Girard
Estimated Sales: $20 - 50 Million
Number Employees: 5-9
Parent Co: Martin Sheet Metal

25840 Martin Control Systems Inc
5955 Wilcox Pl
Suite B
Dublin, OH 43016

614-761-5600
Fax: 614-761-5601 SalesEng@MartinCSI.com
www.martincsi.com
Designs, executes and completes industrial control
system and data collection projects to automate man-
ufacturing and process facilities.
President/Owner: Joe Martin
Principal Project Engineer: Rick Derthick
Marketing & Sales Manager: James Sellitto
Contact: Karen Martin
kmmartin@martincsi.com

25841 Martin Electric Plants
280 Pleasant Valley Rd
Ephrata, PA 17522-8620

717-733-7968
Fax: 717-733-1981 800-713-7968
office@martinsice.com www.martinsice.com

Ice
Owner: Isaac Martin
  james@martinselectricplants.com
Sales Manager: Randy Martin
Site Manager: James Martin
  james@martinselectricplants.com
Manager: Jerry Martin
Estimated Sales: $500,000-$1 Million
Number Employees: 5-9
Square Footage: 16800

25842 (HQ)Martin Engineering
1 Martin Pl
Neponset, IL 61345-9766

309-852-2384
Fax: 309-594-2432 800-766-2786
info@martin-eng.com www.martin-eng.com
Manufacturer and exporter of belt conveyors and
cleaners, transfer point skirting systems and electric,
hydraulic and pneumatic vibrators; importer of elec-
tric vibrators
Owner: E H Peterson
CEO: Scott Hutter
CFO: Ron Vick
CTO: R Todd Swinderman
VP: Jim Turner
Public Relations: AD Marti
Estimated Sales: $20 - 50 Million
Number Employees: 100-249
Square Footage: 130000
Other Locations:
  Martin Engineering
  Walluf
Brands:
  Durt Howg
  Durt Tracker
  Martin

25843 Martin Engineering
1 Martin Pl
Neponset, IL 61345-9766

309-852-2384
Fax: 800-814-1553 800-544-2947
info@martin-eng.com www.martin-eng.com
Vibration systems and solutions to boost material
flow, linear and rotary vibrators keep material mov-
ing while reducing noise and air consumption, in-
cludes vibratory feeders, conveyors and compaction
tables for metering transportingand compacting
powder.vibrators in pneumatic, electric and
hydraulic power
President: Scott Hutter
Chief Executive Officer: R Todd Swinderman
Vice President of Sales and Marketing: James
Turner
Vice President of Operations: Robert Nogaj
Number Employees: 100-249

25844 Martin Laboratories
PO Box 1873
Owensboro, KY 42302-1873

270-685-4441
Fax: 270-684-7859 800-345-9352
Manufacturer and exporter of hand cleaners and
soaps including liquid and waterless
President: Harold C Martin
National Sales Manager: Art Wilbert
Contact: Clifford Martin
  rwatson@tqsinc.com
Customer Service: Stacia Jarvis
Estimated Sales: $10-20 Million
Number Employees: 5-9
Square Footage: 60000
Brands:
  M30

25845 Martin Sprocket & Gear Inc
3100 Sprocket Dr
Arlington, TX 76015-2898

817-258-3000
Fax: 817-258-3333 mail@martinsprocket.com
  www.martinsprocket.com
Wine industry conveyors and screws, power transmission and bulk material handling products,
sprockets, sheaves, gears, couplings, timing pulleys,
interchangeable bushings, screw conveyors (steel
and plastic), bucket elevators, verticalscrew
elevators
President/Owner: Reid Martin
  rmartin@martinsprocket.com
CFO: Chuck Reynolds
Estimated Sales: $50-100 Million
Number Employees: 1000-4999

25846 Martin Vibration Systems
990 Degurse Ave
Marine City, MI 48039

810-765-7460
Fax: 810-765-7461 800-474-4538
felcom@pobox.com www.shake-it.com
Feeders, vibrators, dry bulk material handling equip-
ment
President: Mike Lindbeck
Contact: Jay Valuet
  valuetj@shake-it.com
Type of Packaging: Bulk

25847 Martin/Baron
5454 2nd St
Irwindale, CA 91706-2000

626-960-5153
Fax: 626-962-1280 www.mbicryo.com
Manufacturer and exporter of food processing
equipment, stainless steel conveying systems, cryo-
genic and mechanical coolers and freezers, steam
and radiant heat cookers, spirals, tunnels, cabinets
for heat transfer and vertical pizzaovens
President: Jonathan Martin
VP: David Baron
Sales: Allan Weiner
Operations: Carl Gumber
Estimated Sales: $3 - 5 Million
Number Employees: 10-19
Square Footage: 48000
Brands:
  Martin/Baron
  Mbi

25848 Martingale Paper Company
3022 N 16th St
Philadelphia, PA 19132

215-225-7070
Fax: 215-660-0822
Paperboard boxes and paper stationery products
Owner: Martin Grossman
Estimated Sales: $5-10 Million
Number Employees: 5-9

25849 Martini SRL
20 Industrial Street W
Clifton, NJ 07012-1712

973-778-4927
Fax: 973-778-9820
Estimated Sales: Below 1 Million
Number Employees: 10

25850 Marv Holland Industries
10939-120 Street
Edmonton, AB T5H 3R3
Canada

780-453-5044
Fax: 800-361-0263 800-661-7269
  custserv@marvholland.com
Manufacturer and distributor of apparel such as
business uniforms and flame resistant safety wear
for industry and casual clothing.
President: Gene Fyzenky
Number Employees: 100-249

25851 Marvell Packaging Company
490 Us Highway 46
Fairfield, NJ 07004-1906

973-822-9339
Fax: 973-575-6637 800-445-8947
Contract packaging service
Vice President: Barry Berman
Estimated Sales: $10 Million
Number Employees: 50-99
Number of Products: 20
Square Footage: 65000
Type of Packaging: Private Label

25852 Marygrove Awnings-Toledo
3217 Genoa Rd
Perrysburg, OH 43551-9703

419-241-9181
Fax: 419-837-2814 www.marygrove.com
Commercial awnings
President: Don Reinbolt
Manager: Ken Cruzel
  kcruzel@marygrove.com
Estimated Sales: Less Than $500,000
Number Employees: 5-9
Parent Co: Toledo Tarp Service

25853 Maryland Packaging Corporation
7030 Troy Hill Dr
Elkridge, MD 21075

410-540-9700
Fax: 410-540-9789 www.marylandpackaging.com
Manufacturer and exporter of shrink wrapping,
sleeve bundling, horizontal form/fill/seal,
overwrapping and horizontal bagging machinery,
also have a contract packaging division
President: John Voneiff II
CEO: Marwan Moheyeldien Sr.
Quality Control Manager: Drexel Nelson
Sales Director: Jay Gibson
HR: Mari Cruz Abarca
Estimated Sales: $5 - 10,000,000
Number Employees: 60
Square Footage: 50000
Type of Packaging: Consumer, Food Service, Pri-
  vate Label, Bulk
Brands:
  Tpa

25854 Maryland Plastics Inc
251 E Central Ave
Federalsburg, MD 21632-1313

410-754-5566
Fax: 410-754-8882 800-544-5582
  sales@marylandplastics.com
  www.marylandplastics.com
Accessories/supplies i.e. picnic baskets, cooking im-
plements/housewares.
President: John Soper
  jsoper@marylandplastics.com
Marketing: John Bucchioni
Manager: Jerry Dickerson
Number Employees: 50-99

25855 Maryland Wire Belts
8000 Hub Parkway
Cleveland, OH 44125

216-642-9100
Fax: 216-642-9573 800-677-2358
  salessupport@bdi-usa.com www.bdi-usa.com
Manufacturer and Exporter of conveyor belting,
conveyors and conveyor services
President: William Weber
CEO: Duane Marshall
CEO: Bill Colson
Number Employees: 100-249
Square Footage: 400000
Brands:
  Bfs
  Curve Flex
  Curve Mesh
  Elevayor
  Flat Seat
  Obfs
  Pactite
  Pos-A-Trak
  Precision Belt Series
  Shove-It Rods
  Spun Head

25856 (HQ)Maselli Measurements Inc
7746 Lorraine Ave # 201
Stockton, CA 95210-4234

209-474-9178
Fax: 209-474-9241 800-964-9600
daveodum@maselli.com www.maselli.com/en
Process & laboratory refractometers
President: Mario Maselli
  mariomaselli@maselli.com
Quality Control: Mario Maselli
Sales: Dave Odum
Estimated Sales: $2.5-5 Million
Number Employees: 5-9
Number of Brands: 1
Number of Products: 10
Other Locations:
  Maselli Measurements
  Leon, GTO
Brands:
  Lr01 Laboratory Refractometer
  Ur20 Process Refractometer

25857 Maselli Measurements Inc
7746 Lorraine Ave # 201
Stockton, CA 95210-4234

209-474-9178
Fax: 209-474-9241 800-964-9600
daveodum@maselli.com www.maselli.com/en
Liquid analysis machines such as carbonated beverage analysis systems, automatic and in-line refractometers

President: Mario Maselli
mariomaselli@maselli.com
Sales Manager: Dave Odum
Number Employees: 5-9

25858 Mason Candlelight Company
PO Box 59
New Albany, MS 38652-0059

310-338-6987
Fax: 310-348-0135 800-556-2766
Manufacturer and exporter of tabletop lighting including lamps and candles
VP/General Manager: Robert Gasbarro
Plant Supervisor: Robert Bacher
Estimated Sales: $2.5-5 Million
Number Employees: 9
Square Footage: 180000
Parent Co: Standex International Corporation

25859 Mason City Tent & Awning Co
408 S Federal Ave
Mason City, IA 50401-3837

641-423-0044
Fax: 641-423-8566 customercare@ripflag.com
www.ripflag.com
Commercial awnings and industrial curtains
Manager: Russalyn Davis
customercare@ripflag.com
Estimated Sales: Less Than $500,000
Number Employees: 1-4
Square Footage: 20000
Parent Co: ITF Industries

25860 (HQ)Mason Transparent Package Company
PO Box 852
Armonk, NY 10504-0852

718-792-6000
Fax: 718-823-7279
Printed and converted films and bags including polyethylene, clysar, polypropylene, linear low density, co-extruded, etc.; importer of film
President: Richard Cole
VP: Kevin O'Connell
Estimated Sales: $2.5 - 5 Million
Number Employees: 10-19
Square Footage: 100000

25861 Mason Ways Indestructible
580 Village Blvd # 330
West Palm Beach, FL 33409-1953

561-478-8838
Fax: 800-693-7745 800-837-2881
www.masonways.com
Materials handling equipment; pallets and accessories, tubs, drums, tanks, vats, buckets
Owner: Judd Ettinger
judd.ettinger@masonways.com
CEO: Allen Mason
Marketing Director: Ira Brichta
Operations Manager: Debbie Shrake
Estimated Sales: $1 - 5 Million
Number Employees: 1-4
Number of Brands: 6
Number of Products: 60
Type of Packaging: Food Service, Private Label, Bulk

25862 Massachusetts ContainerCorporation
455 Sackett Point Road
North Haven, CT 6473

203-248-2161
Fax: 203-248-0241 www.unicorr.com
Corrugated boxes
VP: Jack Aundre
Contact: Larry Caron
lcaron@unicorr.com
Estimated Sales: $10-20 Million
Number Employees: 100-249
Parent Co: Connecticut Container Corporation
Other Locations:
Massachusetts ContainerCorp.
Sharon VT

25863 Massillon Container Co
49 Ohio St SW
Navarre, OH 44662-1183

330-879-5653
Fax: 330-879-2772 benv@vailpkg.com
www.vailpkg.com
Corrugated shipping containers

President: Jodi Frkuska
jodif@vailpkg.com
Quality Control: Cliff Robertson
Accounting: Donna Winter
Estimated Sales: $9 Million
Number Employees: 50-99
Parent Co: Vail Industries

25864 Master Air
415 S Grant St
Lebanon, IN 46052-3605

317-375-7600
Fax: 317-375-7607 800-248-8368
Manufacturer and exporter of commercial kitchen ventilation equipment including hood systems and fan controls
President: Loren Gard
Sales Engineer: Jim Rader
Office Manager: Sharon Amack
Engineer: Kevin Blandford
Estimated Sales: $2.5-5 Million
Number Employees: 20-49
Square Footage: 118000
Brands:
Mastertech
Mastertech Direct Fired

25865 Master Containers
209 SW Phosphate Blvd
Mulberry, FL 33860

863-425-5571
Fax: 978-964-1552 800-881-6847
Foam cups and containers
President: Thomas Lyons
VP: Richard Lyone
Marketing Manager: Rachael Pantely
Sales Manager: Elaine Karau
Estimated Sales: $10 - 20 Million
Number Employees: 50-99

25866 Master Disposers
PO Box 27186
Cincinnati, OH 45227-0186

513-271-1861
Fax: 513-271-1867 www.masterdisposers.com
President: Mary Grogan
R&D: Rich Grogan
Estimated Sales: $3 - 5 Million
Number Employees: 10

25867 Master Magnetics
747 South Gilbert Street
Castle Rock, CO 80104

303-688-3966
Fax: 303-688-5303 800-525-3536
magnet@magnetsource.com
www.magnetsource.com
Magnetic products for food purification systems including ceramic plate, permanent pulleys and hopper grates; also, shelf marking systems
President: John E Nellessen
Marketing Manager: Jennifer Brown
Contact: Lora Allen
loraa@magnetsource.com
General Manager: Pat Orcutt
Estimated Sales: $3 - 5 Million
Number Employees: 7
Square Footage: 88700

25868 Master Package Corporation
142 Indianhead Drive
Menomonie, WI 54751

715-229-2156
Fax: 715-229-2689 800-347-4144
mpabich@masterpackage.com
www.masterpackage.com
Fiber board, cylindrical and metal bound containers
President: Mark Pabich
Office Manager: Carole Buss
Estimated Sales: $5-10 Million
Number Employees: 20-49

25869 Master Paper Box Co
3641 S Iron St
Chicago, IL 60609-1322

773-927-0252
Fax: 773-927-8086 877-927-0252
musser@masterpaperbox.com
www.masterpaperbox.com
Set-up and heart paper boxes

Owner: Bill Farago
bfarago@masterpaperbox.com
VP/ Sales: Michael Musser
Operations Manager: Bill Farago Jr.
Secretary/Treasurer: Angela Sears
Estimated Sales: $2.5-5 Million
Number Employees: 20-49
Square Footage: 220000

25870 Master Printers
308 Main St
Canon City, CO 81212-3732

719-275-8608
Fax: 719-275-8106
Advertising signs
Owner: Susie Smith
masterprinters@brefman.net
VP: Susie Pacheco
Estimated Sales: Less Than $500,000
Number Employees: 1-4

25871 Master Signs-Div of Masterco
5545 Parkdale Dr
Dallas, TX 75227-3205

214-381-6207
Fax: 214-381-1090
Plastic, electric, fluorescent and neon signs; also, illuminated awnings and interior graphics
President: Robert Green
masterco@aol.com
CFO: Brenda Green
Estimated Sales: $1 - 2.5 Million
Number Employees: 20-49
Parent Co: Masterco

25872 Master Tape & Label Printers
4517 N Elston Ave
Chicago, IL 60630-4420

773-685-4100
Fax: 773-685-1555 800-621-5801
www.mastertapeprinters.com
Adhesive, gummed, marking and pressure sensitive tapes and labels
Owner: Malcolm Grant
malcolm.grant@shaffstall.com
CEO: Melcon Grant
CFO: Malcolm Grant
VP: Andy Casey
Quality Control: Robert Wren
Marketing Director: Bob Wern
Estimated Sales: Below $5 Million
Number Employees: 20-49

25873 Master-Bilt
908 State Highway 15 N
New Albany, MS 38652-9507

662-534-9061
Fax: 662-534-6049 800-647-1284
www.master-bilt.com
Manufacturer and exporter of commercial refrigeration products including refrigeration and freezer cabinets, walk-in and reach-in units, etc; also, merchandising units for dairy items and deli cabinets
President: Craig Masters
Purchasing: Larry Fry
Estimated Sales: $50-100 Million
Number Employees: 500-999
Square Footage: 64006
Parent Co: Standex International Corporation

25874 (HQ)Masterbuilt Manufacturing Inc
1 Masterbuilt Ct
Columbus, GA 31907-1313

706-327-5622
Fax: 706-327-5632
customerservice@masterbuilt.com
www.masterbuilt.com
Grills, smokers, fryers, spices, marinades, wheel free cargo carriers, and bike carriers
Owner: John Mclemore
VP Sales/Marketing: Ben Garnto
jmclemore@masterbuilt.com
Estimated Sales: $10 - 20,000,000
Number Employees: 50-99
Number of Brands: 4
Type of Packaging: Consumer, Food Service, Private Label

25875 Mastercraft
234 W Northland Ave
Appleton, WI 54911

920-739-7682
Fax: 920-739-3208 800-242-6602

Paper products including menus, place mats, menu covers and presentation folders
General Manager: Rick Kerr
Estimated Sales: $1-2.5 Million
Number Employees: 10-19
Square Footage: 25600

25876 Mastercraft Industries Inc
777 South St
Newburgh, NY 12550-4159
845-565-8850
Fax: 845-565-9392 800-835-7812
www.mastercraftusa.com
Manufacturer, importer and exporter of industrial vacuum cleaners, parts, floor machines, carpet extractors, automatic scrubbers, steamers, marble/stone maintenance equipment and chemicals
President: Howard Goldberg
Community Director: Jay Goldberg
Executive VP: Carol Andreasian
Quality Control: Jay Goldberg
Estimated Sales: $10 - 20 Million
Number Employees: 50-99
Square Footage: 200000
Brands:
Dynavac
Quarrymaster
Sootmaster

25877 Mastercraft International
PO Box 668407
Charlotte, NC 28266-8407
704-392-7436
Fax: 704-395-1600
Manufacturer and exporter of packaging machinery including vertical and horizontal cartoners
President: Dan Rothwell
Engineer: A Christopher
Estimated Sales: $1 - 2.5 Million
Number Employees: 9
Square Footage: 40000
Brands:
Mastercraft International
Memco

25878 Mastercraft Manufacturing Co
3715 11th St # B1
Long Island City, NY 11101-6006
718-729-5620
Fax: 718-729-5620
Awards, badges, medals, incentives, premiums and plaques; exporter of badges; importer of pins and patches
Owner: Murray Wiener
mwiener@mastercraft-boats.net
General Manager: Peter Borsits
General Manager: Peter Borsits
Estimated Sales: $500,000 - $1,000,000
Number Employees: 5-9
Square Footage: 2000

25879 Mastermark
19017 62nd Ave S
Kent, WA 98032
206-762-9610
Fax: 206-763-8492
customerservice@mastermark.net
www.mastermark.net
Food packaging, rubber pre-ink and self-inking stampss, interior and exterior architecural signage, printing coder dies and stencils products
President: Cindy Hutter
CFO: C G
Marketing/Sales: Brian Carter
Contact: David Alldredge
dave@mastermark.net
Operations: CG Gambling
Production: CG Gambling
Estimated Sales: Below $5 Million
Number Employees: 1-4
Square Footage: 100000
Type of Packaging: Consumer, Private Label, Bulk
Brands:
Mastermark

25880 Masternet, Ltd
690 Gana Court
Mississauga, ON L5S 1P2
Canada
905-295-0005
Fax: 905-795-9293 800-216-2536
www.masternetltd.com

Plastic net, nettingon rolls, net bags, mesh liners, packaging products, wattle nets, protection packaging.
VP: Linda Hartman
Number Employees: 40
Square Footage: 240000

25881 Masterpiece Crystal
96 Trolley St
Jane Lew, WV 26378
304-884-7841
Fax: 304-884-7842 deba@access.mountain.net
Hand blown table and glassware
Owner: Bill Hogan
deba@wvdsl.net
Marketing Director: William Hogan
Sales Manager/Customer Service: Debbie Bailey
Estimated Sales: $5-10 Million
Number Employees: 20-49

25882 Mastex Industries
2035 Factory Ln
Petersburg, VA 23803
804-732-8300
Fax: 804-732-8395
Manufacturer and exporter of electric and thermostatically controlled dish warmers and cooking utensils
President: Frank Mast
National Sales Manager: Paul Christian
Estimated Sales: $1 - 5 Million
Number Employees: 10-19
Square Footage: 100000
Type of Packaging: Consumer

25883 Mastio & Co
2921 N Belt Hwy # M14
Suite M-14
St Joseph, MO 64506-2070
816-364-6200
Fax: 816-364-3606 info@mastio.com
www.mastio.com
Consultant for the packaging industry providing market research and information, customer satisfaction benchmarking, databases and re-engineering solutions
Owner: Bart Thedinger
Executive VP: Kristina Hidy
khidy@mastio.com
Sales/Marketing Executive: Bart Thedinger
Sales: Kevin Huntsman
MIS Manager: Steve Nash
Estimated Sales: Below $5 Million
Number Employees: 10-19
Square Footage: 34000

25884 Matcon Americas
832 N Industrial Dr
Elmhurst, IL 60126-1132
856-256-1330
Fax: 856-256-1329 druble@idexcorp.com
www.matconibc.com
Matcon is a supplier of processing equipment for dry materials. They use portable containers (Intermediate Bulk Containers or IBSs) in their production. Matcon specializes in recipe batching, powder blender and packaging operations.
Vice President: Dan Ruble
Service Account Manager: Dan Veilleux
Senior Applications Specialist: Phil Spuler
Estimated Sales: $5-10 Million
Number Employees: 5
Square Footage: 11000
Parent Co: Matcon Ltd.

25885 Mateer Burt
700 Pennsylvania Drive
Exton, PA 19341-1129
610-321-1100
Fax: 610-321-1199 800-345-1308
www.mateerburt.com
Manufacturer and exporter of filling and labeling machinery and parts; installation available
Marketing Manager: April Koss
Estimated Sales: $1 - 5 Million
Number Employees: 50-99
Number of Brands: 7
Number of Products: 4
Square Footage: 320000

25886 (HQ)Material Control
P.O. Box 308
North Aurora, IL 60542
630-892-4274
Fax: 630-892-4931 800-926-0376
www.materialcontrolinc.com
Conveyor safety stop switches, belt cleaners and hood covers, bin aerators; distributor of plastic bins and totes, shelving, cabinets, mats, matting, fans, measurement and gas monitoring instruments and ventilation equipment
Manager: Jack Pierce
Sales Director: Bob Hutchins
Plant Manager: Jim Pierce
Estimated Sales: $3 - 5,000,000
Number Employees: 5-9
Other Locations:
Material Control
Aurora IL

25887 Material Handling Technology, Inc
113 International Drive
Morrisville, NC 27560
919-388-0050
Fax: 919-388-0051 800-779-2475
mht@mht1.com materialhandlingtech.com
Conveyors, material handling equipment, sortation equipment

25888 Material Storage Systems
8827 Will Clayton Pkwy
Humble, TX 77338-5821
281-446-7144
Fax: 281-446-7391 800-881-6750
info@msshouston.com www.msshouston.com
Manufacturer and exporter of storage and material handling equipment
Owner: Mike Gonzales
Plant Manager: Paul Eye
Estimated Sales: $1 - 2.5 Million
Number Employees: 20-49
Brands:
Webblock

25889 Material Storage Systems
PO Box 1010
Gadsden, AL 35902
256-543-2467
Fax: 256-547-6725 877-543-2467
Exclusive rights to the Lemanco product line. Major products are modular bolted storage bins, welded silos and refuse containers. Many accessory items are also available
President: Barney Leach
CFO: Cindi Graves
Vice President: Craig Graves
R&D: Randall Wright
Quality Control: Robert Bellow
Marketing Director: Dawn Howell
VP Sales: Craig Graves
Operations Manager: Paul Allen
Production Manager: Paul Allen
Plant Manager: Randal Wright
Purchasing Manager: Robert Bellow
Estimated Sales: $1 Million
Number Employees: 30
Number of Brands: 1
Number of Products: 3
Square Footage: 90000
Brands:
Lamanco

25890 Material Systems Engineering
P O Box 115
Stilesville, IN 46180
317-745-7263
Fax: 317-203-0748 800-634-0904
Bulk conveying systems including pneumatic dust collecting and drag chain; also, designing, engineering and fabrication services available
Owner: George Mc Comb
Purchasing/Office Manager: Rona Campbell
Estimated Sales: $1-2.5 Million
Number Employees: 5-9
Square Footage: 23200

25891 Materials Handling Equipment Company
3800 Quentin St
Denver, CO 80239
303-573-5333
Fax: 303-893-3854

Wholesaler/distributor of material handling equipment
Manager: Jenett Garcia
CFO: Ron Conrad
Estimated Sales: $50 - 100 Million
Number Employees: 100-249
Square Footage: 60000

25892 Materials Handling Systems
20763 Bollman Place
Savage, MD 20763

410-379-0070

Fax: 410-379-0037 MHSUSA@aol.com
Conveyors, hand trucks, casters and materials handling equipment
Estimated Sales: $10-20 Million
Number Employees: 50-99

25893 Materials Storage Systems
PO Box 1010
Gadsden, AL 35902-1010

256-543-2467

Fax: 256-547-6725 877-543-2467
Bolted nuts
Estimated Sales: $2.5-5 Million
Number Employees: 20-49

25894 Materials Transportation Co
1408 Commerce Dr
PO Box 1358
Temple, TX 76504-5134

254-298-2900

Fax: 254-771-0287 800-433-3110
info@mtcworldwide.com
Manufacturer and exporter of food processing equipment, cookers, dumpers, blenders and screw and belt conveyors
President & CEO: Jim Granfor
CEO: Reg Ackerman
r.ackerman@mtcworldwide.com
VP Sales: Stephen Hicks
Estimated Sales: $23.4 Million
Number Employees: 100-249
Number of Brands: 6
Number of Products: 6

25895 Matfer Inc
16150 Lindbergh St
Van Nuys, CA 91406-1707

818-782-0792

Fax: 818-782-0799 800-766-0333
contact@matferinc.com
www.matferbourgeatusa.com
Manufacturer, importer and exporter of kitchen and bakery utensils including molds, nonstick baking sheets, pastry bags, thermometers, food mills, juicers, casserole dishes, commercial mixers, mandolines, saute pans, etc
Manager: Jean Paul Riou
CEO: Jean Paul Rio
VP: Pierre Perisot
National Sales Manager: Dominique Besson
Manager: Sergey Perevalov
sperevalov@matferinc.com
Estimated Sales: $8 Million
Number Employees: 10-19
Square Footage: 30000
Parent Co: Matfer France

25896 Mathason Industries
6659 Sanzon Rd
Baltimore, MD 21209

410-484-5935

Fax: 410-484-0334 imathason@hotmail.com
Supplier of bakery equipment
President: Susan Mathason
Comptroller: I Mathason
Sales Director: I Mathason
Contact: Irwin Mathason
imathason@hotmail.com
Estimated Sales: $250000
Number Employees: 1-4

25897 Mathews Conveyor
1524 Lebanon Rd
Danville, KY 40422-9601

859-236-9400

Fax: 859-238-7443 800-628-4397
crodgers@mathewsconveyor.com
Conveyor systems and palletizers

President: Chuck Waddle
Chief Executive Officer: Chris Cole
CFO: Bob Duplain
Vice President of Project Management: Alfred Rebello
Chief Technical Officer: Ray Neiser
Marketing Coordinator: Beverly Cooper
Senior Vice President of Sales and Marke: Jim McKnight
Contact: Dave Gooch
dave@mathewsconveyor.com
Vice President of Operations: Chris Arnold
Purchasing Agent: Anna McClellan
Estimated Sales: $85 Million
Number Employees: 250-499
Square Footage: 300000
Parent Co: FKI Logistex

25898 Matik North America
33 Brook St
West Hartford, CT 06110-2350

860-232-2323

Fax: 860-233-0162 sales@matik.com
www.matik.com
President: Jarrett Chouinard
jchouinard@matik.com
Estimated Sales: $3 - 5 Million
Number Employees: 10-19

25899 Matiss
8800 25th Avenue
St Georges, QC G6A 1K5
Canada

418-227-9141

Fax: 418-227-9144 888-562-8477
doris.boily@matiss.com www.matiss.com
Manufacturer and exporter of bakery processing equipment including greasers, depositors, fillers, cutting and batching systems; also, snack food and pizza processing and packaging equipment; laboratory testing available
President: Jacques Martel
CFO: Pierre Martel
Sales Manager: Francois Henault
Sales Engineer: Patrice Painchaud
General Manager: Jacques Martel
Estimated Sales: Below $5 Million
Number Employees: 90
Square Footage: 80000

25900 Matot - Commercial GradeLift Solutions
2501 Van Buren
Bellwood, IL 60104-2459

708-547-1888

Fax: 708-547-1608 800-369-1070
sales@matot.com www.matot.com
Manufacturer and exporter of electric dumbwaiters
Co-President/ Owner: Anne B. Matot
Co-President: Cathryn Matot
Executive Vice President: Jim Piper
Senior Vice President, Sales: Jim Peskuski
Estimated Sales: $1-2.5 Million
Number Employees: 5-9
Square Footage: 32000

25901 Matrix Engineering
P.O. Box 650728
Vero Beach, FL 32965-0728

772-461-2156

Fax: 772-461-7185 800-926-0528
www.griprock.com
Manufacturer and exporter of safety and slip resistant floor mats and flooring
President: Thomas Hayes
CEO: Edward Saylor
Vice President: Thomas Hayes
Operations Manager: Randi McManus
Number Employees: 19
Number of Brands: 4
Number of Products: 4
Square Footage: 40000
Brands:
Grip Rock
Matrix
Super G

25902 Matrix Group Inc.
16 Yantecaw Ave
Bloomfield, NJ 07003

973-338-5638

Fax: 973-338-0164 info@m8trix.com
www.m8trix.com

Consulting to natural foods maraketplace; master broker
President: Ray Wolfson
rwolfson@m8trix.com
VP: Irene Sherman
Sales: Ray Wolfson
rwolfson@m8trix.com
Estimated Sales: $2.5-5 Million
Number Employees: 5
Number of Brands: 3-6
Type of Packaging: Consumer

25903 Matrix Packaging Machinery
650 N Dekora Woods Blvd
Saukville, WI 53080-1674

262-268-8300

Fax: 262-268-8301 888-628-7491
sales@matrixpm.com www.matrixpm.com
Manufacturer and exporter of vertical form/fill/seal machinery
Gen Mgr/R&D/Quality Control: Marc Willden
Marketing: Lori Stein
Sales Exec: Matt Lanfrankie
Public Relations: John LaBouve
sales@matrixpm.com
Operations: Jane Barnett
Production/Plant Manager: Tim Marchant
Purchasing: Lori Klandrud
Estimated Sales: $15-20 Million
Number Employees: 50-99
Square Footage: 80000
Parent Co: Pro Mach Inc
Brands:
Matrix 916
Matrix1000

25904 Matson LLC
45620 SE North Bend Way
North Bend, WA 98045

425-888-6212

Fax: 425-888-6216 800-308-3723
www.corrys.com
Manufacturer and exporter of insecticides
President: Ken Matson
matson@corrys.com
Sales Representative: Dave Grasmann
Estimated Sales: $5 - 10 Million
Number Employees: 5-9

25905 Mattec Corp
1301 Mattec Dr
Loveland, OH 45140-7300

513-683-1802

Fax: 513-683-1619 800-966-1301
www.epicor.com
Control systems. manufacturers of blow molding, extrusion, blown film applications and related plastic processes. Printing, metal stamping, packaging, assembly and secondary operations
President: Mick Thiel
VP Sales/Marketing: David Monroe
Contact: Lysa Whitt
l.whitt@mattec.com
Estimated Sales: $10-20 Million
Number Employees: 50-99

25906 Matthews Marking Systems Div
6515 Penn Ave
Pittsburgh, PA 15206-4407

412-665-2500

Fax: 412-665-2550 800-625-2500
www.matthewsmarking.com
Manufacturer and exporter of marking equipment for identification of products and packaging; also, turnkey systems available
President: Annette Aranda
aaranda@matthewsinternational.com
Vice President: Peter Hart
Marketing Director: Michelle Staulding
Estimated Sales: $10-20 Million
Number Employees: 100-249
Parent Co: Matthew International Corporation
Other Locations:
Matthews International Corp.
10156 Torino
Brands:
Indent-A-Mark
Jet-A-Mark
Jet-A-Mark/Linx
Print-A-Mark

25907 Matthiesen Equipment

566 N Ww White Rd
San Antonio, TX 78219-2816

210-333-1510
Fax: 210-333-1563 800-624-8635
ctorres@matthiesenequipment.com
www.matthiesenequipment.com
Manufacturer and exporter of material handling processing machinery for ice including bins, baggers, belt and screw conveyors, crushers, bag closers, drying belts, etc.; exporter and wholesaler/distributor of ice machinery
Office Manager: Claudia Torres
Research & Development: Stephen Niestroy
National Sales Manager: Diane Hardekopf
Sales Engineer: Jerry Bosma
Production Manager: Pete Ruiz
Purchasing: John Barratachea
Estimated Sales: $2.5-5 Million
Number Employees: 5-9
Square Footage: 80000
Parent Co: Tour Ice National
Brands:
  Arrow
  Clinebell
  Hamer
  Kasten/Kamco
  Mannhardt
  Matthiesen
  Mgr
  Turbo
  Vogt

25908 Maui Wowi Fresh HawaiinBlends

5445 DTC Parkway
Suite 1050
Greenwood Village, CO 80111-3142

303-781-7800
Fax: 303-781-2438 877-849-6992
hula@mauiwowi.com www.mauiwowi.com
A Entrepreneur 500 ranked gourmet smoothie and espresso cart franchise.
President: Mark Challis
CEO: Michael Haith
CEO: Michael Haith
Contact: Wei Frank
  wei.frank@mauiwowi.com
Estimated Sales: $1 - 3 Million
Number Employees: 20-49
Number of Brands: 1
Number of Products: 3
Square Footage: 20000
Type of Packaging: Food Service

25909 Maull-Baker Box Company

16685 Lower Valley Ridge Drive
Brookfield, WI 53005-5557

414-463-1290
Fax: 414-463-5975
Manufacturer and exporter of wooden boxes, crates, pallets and skids
President: Jerry Maull
Estimated Sales: $2.5-5 Million
Number Employees: 9

25910 Maurer North America

6324 N Chatham Avenue
Kansas City, MO 64151-2473

816-914-3518
Fax: 816-746-5011
Manufacturer and importer of food processing equipment
President: Rolf Hammann
Parent Co: A.G. Maurer
Brands:
  Atmos
  Maurer

25911 (HQ)Mauser Packaging Solutions

1515 W 22nd St
Suite 1100
Oak Brook, IL 60523

800-527-2267
www.mauserpackaging.com
Recyclable bulk packaging, bulk handling and shipping, and warehouse storage of both liquids and solids.
President & CEO: Kenneth Roessler
Chief Financial Officer: Tom De Weerdt
EVP, Procurement & Logistics: Leslie Bradshaw
Chief Information Officer: Ed DePrimo
EVP/General Counsel/CCO: Patrick Sheller

Year Founded: 2018
Estimated Sales: Over $1 Billion
Number Employees: 11,000
Type of Packaging: Bulk

25912 Mauser, Schindler & Wagner

3102 Wilderness Boulevard E
Parrish, FL 34219-8419

941-776-2230
Fax: 941-776-2239 ken@mauserinc.com
www.schiwa.de/en/international
Weight control systems, slicers
President: Kem Mauser
CFO: Linda Mauser
VP: Linda Mauser
Number Employees: 4
Square Footage: 4800

25913 Maverick Enterprises Inc

751 E Gobbi St
Ukiah, CA 95482-6205

707-463-5591
Fax: 707-463-0188 www.maverickcaps.com
Wine closures and caps
President: Steve Otterbeck
CEO: Charles Sawyer
  csawyer@maverickcaps.com
Executive Vice President of Business Dev: Jon Henderson
Vice President of Operations: Fred Koeppel
Estimated Sales: $5-10 Million
Number Employees: 50-99

25914 Maves International Software Corp.

100 York Boulevard
Suite 404
Richond Hill, ON L4B 1J8
Canada

905-882-8300
Fax: 905-882-1550 www.maves.com
President: Aaron Laird
CFO: Audrey Badb
Estimated Sales: $1,000,000 - $2,499,999
Number Employees: 60

25915 Max Packaging

109 6th Ave NW
Attalla, AL 35954-2049

256-538-2233
Fax: 256-538-1929 800-543-5369
info@maxpackaging.com
www.maxpackaging.com
Manufacturer and contract packager of disposable plastic cutlery
Owner: Gary Mcfarland
  gary@maxpackaging.com
General Manager: D McFarland
Plant Manager: Jay Bailey
Estimated Sales: $5-10 Million
Number Employees: 100-249
Square Footage: 40000
Parent Co: Gadsen Coffee Company

25916 Maxco Supply

605 S Zediker Ave
Parlier, CA 93648

559-646-6700
Fax: 559-646-6710 markf@mx2co.com
www.maxcopackaging.com
Case erectors and tray and bliss box formers for corrugated boxes
President: Max Flaming
CFO: David Bryant
Sales Manager: Paul Flaming
Contact: Louise Arroyo
  louise@maxco.com
Estimated Sales: $20 - 50 Million
Number Employees: 250-499

25917 Maxi-Vac Inc.

PO Box 688
Dundee, IL 60118

855-629-4538
sales@maxi-vac.com
www.maxi-vac.com
Manufacturer and exporter of pressure washers and steam cleaning equipment
President: Jim Nolan
Secretary and Treasurer: Janice Nolan
Estimated Sales: $1-2.5 Million
Number Employees: 1-4
Brands:
  Jet Streamer

25918 Maximicer

4175 Country Road 268
Georgetown, TX 78628

512-259-0500
Fax: 512-258-8804 800-289-9098
info@Maximicer.com
Manufacturer and exporter of optimizers for ice making machinery
President: J L Love
VP Manufacturing & Product Dev: Daniel L Welch
Contact: J Love
  j.love@maximicer.com
Estimated Sales: $1 - 3,000,000
Number Employees: 1-4
Type of Packaging: Food Service, Private Label
Brands:
  Maximicer

25919 Maximus Systems

1250, rue Marie-Victorin
St-Bruno-de-Montarville, QC J3V 6B8
Canada

877-445-6556
info@maximus-systems.com
www.maximus-solution.com
Offers solutions for manufacturing poultry, hog, and dairy.
Business Development: Nizar Barrou
VP, International Sales: Marc Boivin
Year Founded: 2010
Number Employees: 35-50

25920 Maxitrol Company

P.O. Box 2230
Southfield, MI 48037-2230

248-356-1401
Fax: 248-356-0829 info@maxitrol.com
www.maxitrol.com
Owner: Bonnie Kern-Koskela
CFO: Christopher Kelly
Estimated Sales: $20 - 50 Million
Number Employees: 50-99

25921 Maxwell House & Post

800 Westchester Ave
Rye Brook, NY 10573-1354

914-335-2500
Fax: 914-335-2706
Coffee and breakfast foods
President: Ann Fudge
Estimated Sales: Under $500,000
Number Employees: 1-4
Parent Co: Kraft Foods

25922 May-Wes Manufacturing Inc

120 Eastgate Dr SE
Hutchinson, MN 55350-1929

320-587-2322
Fax: 320-587-6112 800-788-6483
techsupport@maywes.com www.maywes.com
Grain hoppers and crop dividers; also, plastic combine skids
VP: Mark Bruns
Sales Exec: Daryl Peterson
Manager: Connie Lindbeck
Estimated Sales: $2.5-5 Million
Number Employees: 20-49

25923 Maya Overseas Food Inc

4885 Maspeth Ave
Flushing, NY 11378-2109

718-894-5145
Fax: 718-894-5178 888-289-6292
maya.foods@verizon.net
Supplier of South East Asian groceries to retail stores, restaurants and distributors throughout America.
President/Owner: Umesh Mody
  maya.foods@verizon.net
Estimated Sales: $17.4 Million
Number Employees: 10-19

25924 Mayco Inc

2811 Mican Dr
Dallas, TX 75212-4602

214-638-4848
Fax: 214-638-4850 www.maycopallet.com
Wooden pallets
President: David Gwinn
  david@maycopallet.com
Office Manager: Melba Gwinn
Corporate Controller: Ricky Thomason

Estimated Sales: Below $5 Million
Number Employees: 10-19
Square Footage: 120000

25925 Mayekawa USA, Inc.
8750 West Bryn Mawr Avenue
Suite 190
Chicago, IL 60631
773-516-5070
www.mayekawausa.com
Freezing, thawing and heating units.
Contact: Bryan Arevalo
barevalo@mayekawausa.com

25926 Maypak Inc
5 Mansard Ct
Wayne, NJ 07470-6040
973-696-0780
Fax: 973-633-8621 info@maypakinc.com
www.maypakinc.com
Fabricated polyethylene, expanded polystyrene and polyurethane foam; also, wooden boxes and fiberboard cartons, cooler packs, die cutting, insulated containers, custom designed cases and inserts.
President: Paul Palombi
paul@maypakinc.com
Number Employees: 10-19

25927 Mayr Corporation
4 North St
Suite 300
Waldwick, NJ 07463
201-445-7210
Fax: 201-445-8019 800-465-6297
info@mayrcorp.com www.mayrcorp.com
Real-time production and process monitoring systems, plant scheduling systems, full bar coding and product traceability and genealogy systems
President: Augie Mustardo
CFO: August Mustardo
Contact: Ken Meli
meli@mayrcorp.com
Estimated Sales: Below $5 Million
Number Employees: 10-19

25928 Mays Chemical Co
5611 E 71st St
Indianapolis, IN 46220-3920
317-842-8722
Fax: 317-576-9630 info@mayschem.com
www.mayschem.com
Chemical ingredients and related products
President: William Mays
williamm@mayschem.com
CFO: Deric Gillispie
Quality Control: Phill Poehler
Marketing Representative: Gloria Yuan
Estimated Sales: $.5 - 1 million
Number Employees: 50-99

25929 Maytag Corporation
553 Benson Rd.
Benton Harbor, MI 49022
800-344-1274
www.maytag.com
Ranges and stoves.
Chairman/CEO: Marc Bitzer
Executive VP/CFO: Jim Peters
Senior VP/General Counsel: Kirsten Hewitt
Year Founded: 1893
Estimated Sales: $4.7 Billion
Number Employees: 2,500
Square Footage: 116393
Parent Co: Whirlpool Corporation
Brands:
 Admiral
 Hardwick
 Jennair
 Magic Chef
 Maytag

25930 Maywood Furniture Corp
23 W Howcroft Rd
Maywood, NJ 07607-1022
201-845-6517
Fax: 201-845-4586 800-238-6797
sales@maywood.com www.maywood.com
President: Tom McMullen
CEO: Bill DeSaussure
CFO: Barbara Jenkins
Operations Manager: Jack DeSaussure
Plant Engineer: Toni Ljekocevic
Estimated Sales: $10 - 20 Million
Number Employees: 50-99

25931 Mayworth Showcase WorksInc
1711 W State St
Tampa, FL 33606-1043
813-251-1558
Fax: 813-251-1558
Display cases
Owner: Jack Mayworth
Estimated Sales: $1 - 3 Million
Number Employees: 5-9

25932 Mba Suppliers Inc.
1000 Fort Crook Rd N
Suite 100
Bellevue, NE 68005-4573
402-597-5777
Fax: 402-597-2444 800-467-1201
www.mbasuppliers.com
New, reconditioned, used and pre-owned food processing and meat equipment and supplies.
Contact: Kevin Hammerle
khammerle@mbasuppliers.com

25933 Mc Call Co
4013 Tennessee Ave
PO Box 2033
Chattanooga, TN 37409-1322
423-821-4583
Fax: 423-821-5950 sales@mccallcompany.com
Wholesaler/distributor of packaging materials
Owner: P Henze
Office Manager: Helen Lemacks
Purchasing: Mike Henze
Estimated Sales: $1-2.5 Million
Number Employees: 1-4

25934 Mc Court Label Co
20 Egbert Ln
Lewis Run, PA 16738-3802
814-362-3851
Fax: 814-362-9764 800-458-2390
mccourt@mccourtlabel.com
Pressure sensitive labels for thermal and laser imprinting
President: David G Ferguson
dferguson@mccourtlabel.com
Quality Control: June Wegner
Operations Manager: Bert Clark
Estimated Sales: $10-20 Million
Number Employees: 50-99
Square Footage: 86000

25935 Mc Lean Packaging
1504 Glen Ave
Moorestown, NJ 08057-1104
856-359-2600
Fax: 856-359-2910 800-923-7801
dave@mcleanpackaging.com
www.mcleanpackaging.com
Manufacturers of Corrugated displays,containers, mini flute single face laminated boxes, vinyl and set-up rigid paper boxes, plastic folding boxes, transperent boxes and cylinders, vacuum forming
President of Corrugated Division: Stuart Fenkel
Contact: Gary Buchert
gary.buchert@mcleanpackaging.com
Estimated Sales: $30 - 50 Million
Number Employees: 50-99
Square Footage: 400000

25936 McBrady Engineering Inc
1251 S Larkin Ave
PO Box 2549
Violet, IL 60434
815-744-8900
Fax: 815-744-8901 mcbrady@sbcglobal.net
www.mcbradyengineering.com
Bottle cleaning machinery
President: Garrett McBrady
Sales: David Anderson
Purchasing: Gina Wharrie
Number Employees: 18
Type of Packaging: Consumer, Food Service
Brands:
 Duster
 Gripper
 Model #10
 Orbit
 Unscrambler
 Vial Washer

25937 McCain Produce Inc.
8734 Main Street
Florenceville-Bristol, NB E7L 3G6
Canada
506-392-3036
www.mccainpotatoes.ca
Potato grower and processor
Parent Co: McCain Foods Ltd.
Type of Packaging: Consumer, Food Service

25938 McCarter Corporation
PO Box 351
Norristown, PA 19404-0351
610-272-3203
Fax: 610-275-5120
Manufacturer and exporter of paste and confectionery mixing equipment
President: H Craig McCarter
Number Employees: 17
Square Footage: 150000

25939 McClier
401 E Illinois St # 2
Chicago, IL 60611-4319
312-321-8900
Fax: 312-755-2750
Architects and engineers, building and construction consultants
President: Kenneth Terpin
CFO: Nino Conti
CEO: Daniel McLean
Estimated Sales: $20 - 50 Million
Number Employees: 250-499

25940 McCormack ManufacturingCompany
PO Box 1727
Lake Oswego, OR 97035
503-639-2137
Fax: 503-639-1800 800-395-1593
Manufacturer and exporter of industrial refrigeration equipment including quick freezing and sub-zero freezers
CEO: Gary Montgomery
VP Engineering: Tom Resseler
Estimated Sales: $10-20 Million
Number Employees: 1-4
Square Footage: 50000

25941 (HQ)McCormick Enterprises
729 S Grove St
Post Office Box 577
Arlington Heights, IL 60006
847-398-8680
Fax: 847-398-8625 800-323-5201
sales@mccormicksnet.com
www.mccormicksnet.com
Processing and conveying equipment; installation services available
Owner: Bill Mc Cormick
CEO: B McCormick
CFO: C Palanca
Estimated Sales: $10-20 Million
Number Employees: 50-99
Other Locations:
 McCormick Enterprises
 Delton MI

25942 McDowell Industries
PO Box 2087
Memphis, TN 38101-2087
901-527-6596
Fax: 901-525-6596 800-622-3695
Manufacturer and importer of textile bags for vegetables and grain
Manager Customer Service: Scott Feuer
Plant Superintendent: Rod Johnston
Number Employees: 100-249
Square Footage: 500000
Type of Packaging: Consumer, Food Service, Private Label, Bulk
Brands:
 McKnit
 Softweve McKnit

25943 McGlaughlin Oil Co
3750 E Livingston Ave
Columbus, OH 43227-2282
614-231-2518
Fax: 614-231-7431 800-839-6589
teresa@mcglaughlinoil.com www.faslube.com
Lubricants food grade

CEO: Steve Theodor
steve@faslube.com
Vice President: Dick Green
Sales Director: Dick Green
Estimated Sales: $5-10 Million
Number Employees: 10-19
Type of Packaging: Consumer, Food Service, Private Label, Bulk

25944 McGraw Box Company
PO Box 652
Mc Graw, NY 13101-0652
607-836-6465
Fax: 607-836-6413
Silverware chests and wooden boxes
Owner: Harold J Ousby Iii
Number Employees: 100-249

25945 McGraw Hill/London House
1030 Higgins Rd
Suite 205
Park Ridge, IL 60068-5760
847-292-1900
Fax: 847-292-1906 800-221-8378
Personnel service providing human resource testing and evaluation programs
President: Sam Maurice
Parent Co: MacMillan/McGraw Hill Educational Publishing Company

25946 McGunn Safe Company
29 S La Salle St # 425
Chicago, IL 60603-1599
312-782-3668
Fax: 312-782-4502 800-621-2816
Manufacturer and exporter of safes and other security devices
Partner: Maureen J Mc Gann
Sales/Marketing: Pat McGunn
Estimated Sales: $.5 - 1 million
Number Employees: 1-4
Square Footage: 100000
Brands:
Cash Handler
Quick Drop
Smart Lock
Smart Safe 2000

25947 McKearnan Packaging
PO Box 7281
Reno, NV 89510-7281
775-356-6111
Fax: 775-356-2181 800-787-7857
surplus@mckernan.com www.mckernan.com
Surplus packaging components
General Manager: Maurice Oschlog
Chief Operating Officer: Frank Maggio

25948 McMillin Manufacturing Corporation
2835 E Washington Blvd
Los Angeles, CA 90023
323-268-1900
Fax: 323-262-5144 www.mcmillinwire.com
Wire products including display and bakery racks and shelving
President: Bruce Goodman
bruceg@mcmillin-mfg.com
Quality Control: Bell Harmon
Estimated Sales: Below $5 Million
Number Employees: 20-49
Square Footage: 120000
Brands:
McMillin Wire

25949 McNeil Food Machinery
1881 E Market Street
Stockton, CA 95205-5673
209-463-4343
Fax: 785-874-4241
Dealer and autioner of used food processing and packaging equipment
Estimated Sales: $10 - 20 Million
Number Employees: 50-99

25950 McNeil Nutritionals
7050 Camp Hill Rd
Fort Washington, PA 19034
215-273-7000
Fax: 908-874-1120 www.splenda.com
Artificial sweetners

President: Peter Luther
Vice President: Sheila Bergey
Contact: Joan Anton
janton@mcnus.jnj.com
Estimated Sales: $10-20 Million
Parent Co: Johnson & Johnson

25951 McNeil Specialty Products Company
PO Box 2400
501 George St.
New Brunswick, NJ 08903-2400
732-524-3799
Fax: 732-524-3303
artifical sweetners.such as sucralose.
President: Stephen Fanning
Director Sales (North America): Jim Thornton
Director International Sales: Joseph Zannoni
Contact: Donna Fernandez
donna@sucralose.com
Estimated Sales: $10-25million
Number Employees: 20-49
Parent Co: Johnson & Johnson

25952 McNew & Associates, William B.
225 San Marino Drive
San Rafael, CA 94901-1583
415-457-3940
Fax: 415-457-3142
Wine industry tank vents
Owner: William McMill
Sales Engineer: Kevin McMill
Estimated Sales: $1-2.5 Million
Number Employees: 1-4
Square Footage: 2000
Type of Packaging: Private Label

25953 McNichols Company
251 Wille Rd # C
Des Plaines, IL 60018-1861
847-376-5848
Fax: 847-635-1115 800-237-3820
www.mcnichols.com
Grip strut safety grating, grate lock grating, fiberglass grating, safety flooring, bar grating, perforated metal and screens, decorative perforated patterns, wire cloth and screens, filter cloth, testing sieves, hardware cloth andsecurity screens
Manager: Kevin Shrout
Contact: Janet Aleksiak
jaleksiak@mcnichols.com
Estimated Sales: Below $5 Million
Number Employees: 20-49

25954 McNichols Conveyor Company
21411 Civic Center Drive
Suite 204
Southfield, MI 48076
248-357-6077
Fax: 248-357-6078 800-331-1926
sales@mcnicholsconveyor.com
www.mcnicholsconveyor.com
Manufacturer, exporter and designer of conveyors including power roller, gravity roller and belt
President: Robert Iwrey
General Manager: Vince Giannone
Estimated Sales: $2.5-5 Million
Number Employees: 5-9
Brands:
F.E.I., Inc.
Gregory-Adams
New London Engineering
Omni-Metalcraft
Rapid Flex
Roach

25955 McQueen Sign & Lighting
1017 12th Street NE
Canton, OH 44704-1398
330-452-5769
Fax: 330-452-5792 68262mcqsign@cannet.com
Signs including neon, plastic, interchangeable and illuminated letters; also, interior graphics available
Estimated Sales: $500,000-$1 Million
Number Employees: 5-9

25956 (HQ)Mcbrady Engineering Co
1251 S Larkin Ave
Rockdale, IL 60436-9326
815-744-8900
Fax: 815-744-8901 www.mcbradyengineering.com
Manufacturer and exporter of container cleaning equipment

Owner: Garrett Mc Brady
Vice President: Garrett McBrady
Sales: David Anderson
Estimated Sales: $2 Million
Number Employees: 10-19
Number of Brands: 7
Number of Products: 3
Square Footage: 60000
Brands:
Bottle Air
Bottle Duster
Orbit
Vial Washer-Dryer

25957 Mcbride Sign Co
5493 S Amherst Hwy
Madison Heights, VA 24572
434-847-4151
Fax: 434-845-6980 info@mcbridesigns.com
www.mcbridesigns.com
Signs including advertising, changeable letter, electric, interchangeable, luminous tube, plastic and point of purchase; also, installation and service available
Owner: Tony Mc Bride
tg@mcbridesigns.com
General Manager: Lawrence Bryant
Vice President: Tony McBride
Estimated Sales: $1.25 Million
Number Employees: 10-19
Square Footage: 89000
Type of Packaging: Private Label

25958 Mcclancy Seasonings Co
1 Spice Rd
Fort Mill, SC 29707
803-548-2366
Fax: 803-548-2379 800-843-1968
info@mcclancy.com www.mcclancy.com
Processor and exporter of spices, seasonings and dry food mixes including salad dressing, dips, breadings, batters, gravies, soups, sauces and meat marinades, snack food seasonings, nut and pretzel coatings, whole and ground spices;custom blending available.
President: Reid Wilkerson
Year Founded: 1947
Estimated Sales: 10 Million
Number Employees: 50-99
Number of Brands: 3
Type of Packaging: Consumer, Food Service, Private Label, Bulk
Brands:
Continental Chef
Southern Sweetener
Spice Trader

25959 Mccrone Microscopes & Acces
850 Pasquinelli Dr
Westmont, IL 60559-5594
630-288-7087
Fax: 630-887-7764 www.mccrone.com
Consultant providing microscopy and ultramicro-analytical services including materials analysis, characterization and identification; wholesaler/distributor of microscopes and microscopy supplies
CEO/President: Donald Brooks
VP: Richard Bisbing
Manager: David Wiley
mccrone@mccrone.com
VP/Director Operations: Bonnie Betty
Estimated Sales: $5-10 Million
Number Employees: 50-99
Square Footage: 75000
Parent Co: McCrone Group

25960 Mccullough Industries Inc
13047 County Road 175
P.O. Box 222
Kenton, OH 43326-9022
419-673-0767
Fax: 419-673-8176 800-245-9490
sales@mcculloughind.com
www.mcculloughind.com
Manufacturer and exporter of self dumping hoppers
Owner: Steve Mc Cullough
smm@mcculloughind.com
Owner: W McCullough
Number Employees: 20-49

25961 Mcguckin & Pyle Inc
227 Brandywine Ave
Downingtown, PA 19335
610-269-9770
Fax: 610-873-8970 DConnolly@mcg-pyle.com
www.mcg-pyle.com
Packaging and process equipment
President: Keith Connolly
Chief Executive Officer: Dennis Connolly
Research: Brian Sproul
Operations: Tom Blam
Estimated Sales: $5-10 Million
Number Employees: 20-49

25962 Mcintosh Box & Pallet Co
5864 Pyle Dr
East Syracuse, NY 13057-9459
315-446-9350
Fax: 315-446-5427 800-219-9552
info@mcintoshbox.com www.mcintoshbox.com
Wooden boxes, pallets and skids
President: Rich Huftalen
Accounts Manager/Sales: Brian Hotchkin
Estimated Sales: $2.5-5 Million
Number Employees: 20-49
Square Footage: 200000

25963 Mcintyre Metals Inc
310 Kendall Mill Rd
Thomasville, NC 27360-5524
336-476-3646
Fax: 336-476-3622 800-334-0807
www.mcmetals.com
Manufacturer and exporter of point-of-purchase dis-
plays including stock and special designs, powder
coated and wire formed
President: Jeff Mc Intyre
jeff@mcmetals.com
VP: Gilbert Luck
Sales Manager: Jim Plumb
VP, Operations: Mike Smith
Estimated Sales: $2.5-5 Million
Number Employees: 20-49

25964 Mckey Perforating Co Inc
3033 S 166th St
New Berlin, WI 53151-3555
262-786-2700
Fax: 262-786-7673 800-345-7373
jmckey@mckey.com
www.mckeyperforatingco-inc.com
Manufacturer and exporter of component parts for
food handling equipment and perforated metals and
plastics
President/CEO: Jean Mc Key
General Manager: Don Pirlot
dpirlot@mckey.com
Product Development Manager: Tony Elsinger
VP Marketing: Jim Thurman
VP, Sales: Jim Thurman
Director of Operations: James Kuehn
Purchasing Manager: Wayne Schowalter
Estimated Sales: $4700000
Number Employees: 50-99
Square Footage: 280000

25965 (HQ)Mclaughlin Gormley KingCo
8810 10th Ave N
Minneapolis, MN 55427-4372
763-544-0341
Fax: 763-544-6437 800-645-6466
www.mgk.com
Manufacturer and exporter of insecticide concen-
trates and repellents
President: William D Gullickson Jr
CEO: Steve Gullickson
steve.gullickson@mgk.com
CFO: Tom Majpor
Quality Control: Michael Lunch
Director Marketing: Dan Untiedt
Production Manager: Don Sundquist
Estimated Sales: $20-50 Million
Number Employees: 50-99
Square Footage: 100000
Other Locations:
McLaughlin Gormley KingCo.
Baltimore MD

25966 Mclaughlin Paper Co Inc
61 Progress Ave
West Springfield, MA 01089-3323
413-736-6066
Fax: 413-730-6604 800-842-6656
sales@mclaughlinpaper.com
www.mclaughlinpaper.com
Paper, paper board, specialty grades: tissue, foils,
metallized paper, release papers, foil board, holographic, heat seal, laminates, velours, papefilm, imports, folding cartons, rigid boxes, corrugated
laminates, gift wrap, retail orprivate label, pict
Owner: Daniel Mc Laughlin
Contact: Dan Mclaughlin
dan.mclaughlin@mclaughlinpaper.com
Estimated Sales: $1-2.5 Million
Number Employees: 10-19

25967 Mcmahon's Farm
305 Jackson Rd
Hopewell Jct, NY 12533-8615
845-227-0120
Fax: 845-227-9282 orders@mcmahonsfarm.com
www.mcmahonsfarm.com
Wholesale distributor of organic, natural and specialty foods as well as eggs, dairy and other food
products
Owner: Tom Mc Mahon
colette@mcmahonsfarm.com
Owner: Colette McMahon
Number Employees: 20-49

25968 Mcnairn Packaging
6 Elise St
Westfield, MA 01085-1414
413-568-1989
Fax: 413-562-1903 800-867-1898
sales@mcnairnpackaging.com
Packaging paper for the food industry
President: Ken Miller
CFO: Dennis Czosnek
Manager: Roger Pietras
rpietras@mcnairnpackaging.com
COO: Bart Gogarty
Estimated Sales: $19 Million
Number Employees: 50-99

25969 Mcneill Signs Inc
555 S Dixie Hwy E
Pompano Beach, FL 33060-6985
954-946-3474
Fax: 954-946-8051 sales@mcneillsigns.com
www.mcneillsigns.com
Signs including plastic, neon and metal
President: J R Mc Neill
jmcneillsigns@mcneillsigns.com
CFO: Jay R McNeill
R&D: Jay R McNeill
Quality Control: Jay R McNeill
Estimated Sales: $1 - 2.5 Million
Number Employees: 20-49

25970 Mcneilly Wood Products Inc
120 Neelytown Rd
Campbell Hall, NY 10916-2807
845-457-9651
Fax: 845-457-4220
dan@mcneillywoodproducts.com
www.mcneillywoodproducts.com
Wooden and used pallets and skids
Owner: Dan Mc Neilly
dan@mcneillywoodproducts.com
Vice President: Dan McNeilly
President: Tim McNeilly
Estimated Sales: $5-10 Million
Number Employees: 20-49
Square Footage: 40000

25971 Mcroyal Industries Inc
1421 Lilac St
Youngstown, OH 44502-1339
330-747-8655
Fax: 330-747-3331 800-785-2556
www.mcroyal.com
Manufacturer and exporter of laminated restaurant
fixtures including counters, booths, tables, kiosks,
etc.; also, point of purchase displays
CEO: John N Lallo
jklallo@mcroyal.com
Purchasing Agent: Don Ceo
Estimated Sales: $2.5-5 Million
Number Employees: 5-9
Square Footage: 56000

Brands:
Formica
Nevamar
Pionite
Wilson Art

25972 MeGa Industries
5109 Harvester Road, Unit 3A
Burlington, ON L7L 5Y9
Canada
905-631-6342
Fax: 905-631-6341 800-665-6342
sales@megaindustries.com
www.megaindustries.com
Manufacturer, importer, exporter and wholesaler/dis-
tributor of material and bulk handling equipment in-
cluding vibrating tables, conveyors, bins, feeders,
vibrators and bin level controls and indicators
President: Mel Gallagher
Sales: Steve Atkinson
Number Employees: 5-9
Square Footage: 12000
Brands:
Dynapac

25973 Mead & Hunt Inc
6501 Watts Rd # 101
Madison, WI 53719-1397
608-273-6380
Fax: 608-273-6391 888-364-7272
madison@meadhunt.com www.meadhunt.com
Consultant specializing in the design of plant lay-
outs, processing, refrigeration, wastewater treatment
and environmental systems; also, cold storage and
warehouse and office/labs facilities
President: Rajan Sheth
rajan.sheth@meadhunt.com
Quality Control: Carry Rossa
Vice President: Doug Green
Marketing Director: Mike Pankratz
Food/Dairy Facilities Manager: Scott Freye
Estimated Sales: $20 - 50 Million
Number Employees: 100-249
Parent Co: Mead & Hunt
Other Locations:
Mead & Hunt
Modesto CA

25974 (HQ)Meadows Mills Inc
1352 W D St
PO Box 1288
North Wilkesboro, NC 28659-3506
336-838-2282
Fax: 336-667-6501 800-626-2282
sales@meadowsmills.com
www.meadowsmills.com
Manufacturer and exporter of stone burr and ham-
mer mills, grits separators, bolters, eccentric sifters,
elevating fans, collectors, elbows, piping, self rising
corn meal mixer, and hand boggers, christmas tree
palletizers
Vice President: Corey Sheets
csheets@meadowsmillscoinc.com
CFO: June Hege
Senior VP: Corey Sheets
VP Sales/Marketing: Brian Hege
VP Product Engineering: Robert Miller
Purchasing: Corey Sheets
Estimated Sales: $5 Million
Number Employees: 20-49
Number of Brands: 4
Square Footage: 210000
Type of Packaging: Consumer, Food Service, Pri-
vate Label, Bulk
Other Locations:
Meadows Mills
Tynda, Amur
Brands:
Meadows
Stone Burr Mills

25975 Meadwestvaco Corp
501 S 5th St
Richmond, VA 23219-0501
804-444-7939
Fax: 843-745-3028 804-444-1000
Manufacturer and exporter of kraft paper
Chairman and Chief Executive Officer: John A.
Luke, Jr.
SVP and Chief Financial Officer: E. Mark
Rajkowski
Chief Marketing & Innovation Officer: Diane Teer
Contact: Suzanne Abbot
suzanne.abbot@mwv.com
EVP, Global Operations: Robert A. Feeser

Estimated Sales: $5-10 Million
Number Employees: 1-4
Type of Packaging: Consumer, Food Service, Private Label, Bulk

25976 Measurement Systems Intl
14240 Interurban Ave S # 200
Tukwila, WA 98168-4661

206-433-0199
Fax: 206-244-8470 800-874-4320
info@msiscales.com www.msiscales.com
Manufactures and markets integrated systems solutions for industrial wieghing and process control
President: Ron Wenzel
rwenzel@msiscales.com
CFO: Ronald Wenzel
Quality Control: Rodney Rodems
Product Marketing Manager: Jeff Brandt
Sales Director: Tim Carroll
Purchasing Manager: David Bannister
Estimated Sales: $5 - 10 Million
Number Employees: 20-49
Brands:
Cellscale
Check-Weigh
Dyna-Link
Msi-6000
Msi-9000
Port-A-Weigh
Porta-Weigh-Plus

25977 Measurex/S&L Plastics
2860 Bath Pike
Nazareth, PA 18064-8898

610-759-0280
Fax: 610-759-0650 800-752-0650
Plastic measuring scoops, plastic apothecary jars and clear plastic cubes
President: John Bungert
Marketing/Sales: Denise Yonney
Purchasing Manager: Ron Timura
Estimated Sales: $10-20 Million
Number Employees: 100-249
Square Footage: 380000
Brands:
Dynagro
Measurex

25978 Meat & Livestock Australia
1401 K Street NW, Ste 602
Washington DC, DC 20005

202-521-2555
Fax: 202-521-2699 www.australian-meat.com
Beef, lamb and goatmeat
Regional Manager: Stephen Edwards
Marketing: Elise Garling
Retail Development: Linden Cowper
Contact: Peter Barnard
pbarnard@mla.com.au
Estimated Sales: $4 Million
Number Employees: 5

25979 Meat Marketing & Technology
1415 N Dayton St
Chicago, IL 60642-2643

312-266-3311
Fax: 312-266-3363 www.meatingplace.com
Computer systems and software, meat industry publications and information, sales and advertising promotions and materials
President: Mark Lefens
Chairman: Jim Franklin
Vice President of Information Systems: Annica Burns
Director of Marketing: Laurie Hachmeister
Account Executive: Dave Lurie
Production Manager: Shirleen Kajiwara
Estimated Sales: $5 - 10 Million
Number Employees: 20-49

25980 Meat Quality
713 W Prospect Avenue
Springfield, IL 62704-5026

217-744-0150
Fax: 217-744-0630 agmed@msn.com
Quality control instruments, analyzing fat testing
Estimated Sales: $1 - 5 Million

25981 Meatlonn
2035 Lemoine Avenue
2nd Floor
Fort Lee, NJ 07024-5704

201-944-6814
Fax: 888-510-2350 800-965-5144
www.taikoh-usa.com
Casings
President: Masaki Nomura
Estimated Sales: $5 - 10 Million
Number Employees: 1-4

25982 Mecco Marking & Traceability
290 Executive Drive
PO Box 307
Cranberry Township, PA 16066

724-779-9555
Fax: 724-779-9556 888-369-9190
info@mecco.com www.mecco.com
For over 100 years MECCO Marking Systems has partnered with a variety of industries for permanent marking solutions. Products range from high quality hand - held marking devices, portable marking tools, and computer - controlledmarking systems. the lates technology of bumpy barcode marking systems enhance MECCO's position as an industry leader and innovator for marking solutions
CEO: Dean Frenz
CFO: Christine Grabowski
R&D: Eric McElnoy
Marketing: Todd Hockenberry
VP Sales: Todd Hockenberry
Purchasing: Frank Zowojski
Estimated Sales: $3 - 5 Million
Number Employees: 20-49
Brands:
Code-A-Can
Code-A-Plas
Code-A-Top

25983 Mechtronics International
705 Old Westtown Rd
Suite E
West Chester, PA 19382-4988

610-431-3655
Fax: 610-431-3774
Waxed paper-single ply and 2-ply rollstock and cut sheets, bacon layout paper, bakery and cheese interleaf papers, polypropylene film, high density polyethylene film and pasta interleaf.
President: Jonathan Kent
VP: Karen Kent
Contact: Donna Kasznel
donna.kasznel@mechtronicsinternational.com
Estimated Sales: Below $5 Million
Number Employees: 10-19
Type of Packaging: Consumer, Food Service, Private Label, Bulk

25984 Mechtronics Paper Corp
1504 Mcdaniel Dr
West Chester, PA 19380-6670

610-429-9860
Fax: 610-429-9864 ericrich1@aol.com
Interleaf paper and film waxed papers, grease proof, grease-resistant, patty paper, film, no-zorb moisture and grease resistant paper, 2 ply waxed paper
President/Owner: Eric Osner
ericrich@aol.com
Vice President: Karen Kent
Sales/Marketing Director: Karen Kent
Purchasing: Eric Osner
Estimated Sales: $1-2.5 Million
Number Employees: 1-4
Type of Packaging: Consumer, Food Service, Private Label, Bulk

25985 Mectra USA
P.O. Box 350
Bloomfield, IN 47424-0350

812-384-3521
Fax: 812-384-8518 www.mectralabs.com
Fully automatic, floor level, bulk palletizer for round and nonround containers, intelligent bottle stacker, automatic layer pad, top frame and empty pallet inserters
President: Tom Clement
Estimated Sales: $1 - 3 Million
Number Employees: 10-19

25986 Medallion Laboratories
9000 Plymouth Ave N
Minneapolis, MN 55427-3870

763-764-4453
Fax: 763-764-4010 800-245-5615
info@medlabs.com www.medallionlabs.com
Testing laboratory providing analytical and microbiological services to the food industry including nutrition labeling support, physical testing, shelf life studies, pesticides and special projects
President: Mike Baim
General Manager: Lisa Povolny
Quality Manager: Sandy Zinn
Marketing Director: Dereen Rief
Sales Director: Ann Diesen
Business Development Manager: Sarah Klaus-Ryan
Operations Manager: Todd Jensen
Technical Manager: David Plank
Estimated Sales: Less than $500,000
Number Employees: 5-9
Parent Co: General Mills

25987 Medallion Laboratories
9000 Plymouth Ave N
Minneapolis, MN 55427-3870

763-764-4453
Fax: 763-764-4010 800-245-5615
info@medlabs.com www.medallionlabs.com
Chemical, physical and microbiological testing
General Manager: Petros Levis
Technical Manager: David Plank
Business Development Manager: Lisa Povolny
Manager: Lisa Povolny
lisa.povolny@medslab.com
Operations Manager: Kelly Schwenn
Number Employees: 5-9

25988 Medical Packaging Corporation
941 Avenida Acaso
Camarillo, CA 93012-8755

805-388-2383
Fax: 805-388-5531 info@medicalpackaging.com
www.medicalpackaging.com
Industrial and medical device manufacturer specializing in specimen collection, custom reagent packaging, and test device design.
CEO: Fred Nason
Director of Operations: Darren Davidson
Estimated Sales: $10-20 Million
Number Employees: 50-99
Type of Packaging: Private Label

25989 (HQ)Mednik Wiping MaterialsCo
6740 Romiss Ct
St Louis, MO 63134-1037

314-524-2200
Fax: 314-524-2221 800-325-7193
isales@riverbendtextiles.com
www.riverbendtextiles.com
Cheesecloths, dish and dusting cloths and paper towels; also, disposable nonwoven and paper wipers
Owner: Jim Mednik
jmednik@riverbendtextiles.com
Secretary: Nancy Mednik
VP: Richard Wolf
Estimated Sales: $10-20 Million
Number Employees: 20-49

25990 Mee Industries
204 W Pomona Ave
Monrovia, CA 91016

626-359-4550
Fax: 626-359-4660 www.meefog.com
Wine industry fog humidifers
CEO: Eric Adamson
eric.adamson@meefog.com
CEO: Thomas Mee Iii
Estimated Sales: $20-50 Million
Number Employees: 5-9

25991 Meech Static Eliminators USA
2915 Newpark Dr
Barberton, OH 44203-1049

330-564-2000
Fax: 330-564-2005 800-232-4210
info@meech.com www.meech.com
Static control equipment for the packaging industry
Vice President: Matt Fyffe
matt.fyffe@meechusa.com
VP: Matt Fyffe
Estimated Sales: $2.5-5 Million
Number Employees: 10-19

25992 Meguiar's Inc
17991 Mitchell S
Irvine, CA 92614-6015
949-752-8000
Fax: 949-752-5784 www.meguiars.com
Manufacturer and exporter of furniture and floor
cleaning products including polish
CEO: Barry Meguiar
barry.meguiar@meguiars.com
CEO: Barry Meguiar
Estimated Sales: $20 - 50 Million
Number Employees: 100-249
Brands:
Meguiar's
Meguiar's Mirror Glaze

25993 Meheen Manufacturing Inc
325 N Oregon Ave
Pasco, WA 99301-4236
509-547-7029
Fax: 509-547-0939 www.meheen-mfg.com
Computer automated carbonated beverage bottling
machines
Owner: Stephanie Cartagena
scartagena@meheen.com
CFO: Dave Meheen
Quality Control: Dave Meheen
R&D: Dave Meheen
Estimated Sales: Less Than $500,000
Number Employees: 1-4
Square Footage: 10000

**25994 Meil Electric Fixture
Manufacturing Company**
1045 W Glenwood Ave
Philadelphia, PA 19133
215-228-8528
Fax: 215-228-3898
Fluorescent lighting fixtures
President: Stephen Dinerman
CFO: Stanley Neil
Estimated Sales: $1 - 2.5 Million
Number Employees: 5-9

25995 Meilahn Manufacturing Co
5900 W 65th St
Chicago, IL 60638-5499
773-581-5204
Fax: 773-581-5404 www.meilahnmfg.com
Furniture, custom cabinetry and point of purchase
displays
President: Gary Clarin
g.clarin@meilahnmfg.com
VP: Dave Sawyer
Estimated Sales: $5-10 Million
Number Employees: 10-19
Square Footage: 44000

25996 Melcher Manufacturing Co
6017 E Mission Ave
Spokane Valley, WA 99212-1264
509-535-7626
Fax: 509-536-3931 800-541-4227
sales@melcher-ramps.com
www.melcher-ramps.com
Manufacturer and exporter of fiberglass truck-load-
ing ramps
President: Wayne Hardan
Sales Manager: Wendell Anglesey
Plant Manager: Dick Colby
Estimated Sales: Below $5 Million
Number Employees: 10-19

25997 Melco Steel Inc
1100 W Foothill Blvd
Azusa, CA 91702-2818
626-334-7875
Fax: 626-334-6799 info@melcosteel.com
www.melcosteel.com
Canned food sterilizing and cooking equipment in-
cluding pressure vessels, retorts, quick opening
doors, reaction chambers; manufacturer and exporter
of autoclaves
President: Michel Kashou
michelkashou@melcosteel.com
VP: Joe Varela
Chief Engineer: Jeff Cowan
Estimated Sales: $2.5-5 Million
Number Employees: 20-49
Square Footage: 50000
Brands:
Harris

25998 Melitta Canada
10-6201 Highway #7
Vaughan, ON L4H 0K7
Canada
416-243-8979
Fax: 416-243-1808 800-565-4882
mjohnston@melitta.ca www.melitta.ca
Coffee filters; processor of coffee
Estimated Sales: $1 - 5 Million
Number Employees: 10-20
Parent Co: Melitta North America
Type of Packaging: Consumer

25999 Melitta North America, Inc.
13925 58th St N
Clearwater, FL 33760
727-535-2111
Fax: 727-535-7376 888-635-4880
info@melitta.com www.melitta.com
Processor, importer and exporter of coffee; also, cof-
fee machines and filters
President/CEO: Marty Miller
Quality Assurance Manager: Mark Kiczalis
VP, Marketing: Chris Hillman
VP, Sales: Ed Mitchell
Estimated Sales: $27 Million
Number Employees: 100-249
Number of Brands: 1
Square Footage: 104000
Type of Packaging: Consumer, Food Service
Brands:
Melitta

26000 Mell & Co
6700 W Touhy Ave
Niles, IL 60714-4518
Canada
847-647-0100
Fax: 847-470-0581 800-262-6355
customerservice@restaurantdiscountwarehouse.co
m
Sherbrooke OEM Ltd is an innovative company spe-
cializing in the design, fabrication and installation of
bulk handling equipment for various industries
Owner: Douglas Warshauer
douglas@mellandengineering.com
Owner: Doug Warshauer
Marketing: Doug McCreight
Estimated Sales: $6.5 Million
Number Employees: 10-19
Brands:
Sherbrooke Oem

26001 Mello Smello LLC
6010 Earle Brown Dr # 100
Minneapolis, MN 55430-4516
763-504-5400
Fax: 763-504-5493 888-574-2964
Mealbags, trayliners and kids premiums, stickers,
tattoo's, static cling
President: Joe Morris
jmorris@mellosmello.com
Estimated Sales: $24.4 Million
Number Employees: 50-99
Square Footage: 70000
Parent Co: Miner Group International
Type of Packaging: Food Service, Private Label
Brands:
Pizza Pozze

26002 Melmat Inc
5333 Industrial Dr
Huntington Beach, CA 92649-1516
714-379-4555
Fax: 714-379-4554 800-635-6289
info@melmat.com
Manufacturer and wholesaler/distributor of plastic,
bulk and custom molded containers, tote boxes,
tubs, tanks and insulated and single-wall bins
Owner: John Melmat
john@mailmat.com
CEO: Laura Kreisberg
CFO: Vera Moeder
Vice President: David Kriegt
Estimated Sales: $1-2.5 Million
Number Employees: 10-19
Square Footage: 44000
Brands:
Kudl-Pak
Space Case

26003 Melrose Displays
2 Brighton Avenue
Passaic, NJ 07055-2002
973-471-7700
Fax: 973-471-6885
Custom point-of-purchase displays and store fixtures
in wire, wood, metal, tubing and plastic; also, front
end check out fixtures
President: Richard Cohen
CEO: Melvin Cohen
Sr. VP: Gerry Turk
Estimated Sales: $10 - 20 Million
Number Employees: 150
Square Footage: 450000
Brands:
Quick Step...The Produce Manager

26004 Melsur Corporation
7752 Us Route 5
Westminster, VT 05158-9683
802-463-3969
Fax: 802-463-1353

26005 Melton Hot Melt Applications
745 West Winder Industrial Pkwy
Winder, GA 30680
770-307-0942
Fax: 770-307-0955 888-357-9317
Owner: Tony Laniewicz
Estimated Sales: Below $5 Million
Number Employees: 5-9

26006 Meltric Corporation
4640 W Ironwood Dr
Franklin, WI 53132
414-817-6160
Fax: 414-817-6161 800-824-4031
www.meltric.com
Switch related plugs and receptacles that ensures
electrical safety
CEO: Paul Barnhill
Contact: John Baranowski
jbarnowski@meltric.com
Manager: Mark Rasmussen

26007 Melville Plastics
943 Trollingwood Rd
Haw River, NC 27258-8757
336-578-5800
Fax: 336-578-5402 www.ckspackaging.com
Plastic containers for dairy products
Operations Manager: Ken Pierceson
Plant Manager: Dave Sebastian
Estimated Sales: $20 - 50 Million
Number Employees: 100-249

26008 Melvina Can Machinery Company
30 Casey Rd
Hudson Falls, NY 12839
518-743-0606
Fax: 631-391-9039
Manufacturer, importer and exporter of compound
liners, can machinery and oil filter equipment, in-
cluding can seamers and closers
President: Thomas Cahill
Estimated Sales: $5-10 Million
Number Employees: 10-19
Parent Co: Can Industries

26009 Membrane Process & Controls
922 N 3rd Ave
Edgar, WI 54426-9013
715-352-3206
Fax: 715-352-2194 jstencil@membranepc.com
www.membranepc.com
Membrane filtration, instrumentation and control en-
gineering for the food and dairy industry
President: Joel Stencil
jstencil@membranepc.com
Process/Control Engineer: Joel Stencil
Estimated Sales: $500,000-$1 Million
Number Employees: 10-19

26010 Membrane System Specialist Inc
1430 2nd St N
PO Box 998
Wisconsin Rapids, WI 54494-2914
715-421-2333
Fax: 715-423-6181
membrane@mssincorporated.com
www.mssincorporated.com

Manufacturer and exporter of brine and control systems, evaporators, condensers, filtration and membrane processing equipment, separators, clarifiers, waste water treatment systems and whey processing equipment for dairy industry
Owner: Greg Pesko
  membrane@mssincorporated.com
Regional Sales Manager: Marian Oehme
Production Manager: Derek Hibbard
Estimated Sales: Below $5 Million
Number Employees: 5-9
Square Footage: 20840

26011 Memor/Memtec America Corporation
2118 Greenspring Dr
Timonium, MD 21093-3112
                    410-252-0800
      Fax: 410-560-2857 www.pall.com
Wine industry filtration equipment
President, Life Sciences: Yves Baratelli
Chairman & Chief Executive Officer: Lawrence D. Kingsley
Chief Financial Officer: Akhil Johri
Senior Vice President, Operations: Richard Jackson
Chief Technology Officer: Michael Egholm, Ph.D.
Estimated Sales: $1 - 5 Million
Number Employees: 250-499

26012 Memphis Delta Tent & Awning
296 East St
Memphis, TN 38126-2414
                    901-522-1238
      Fax: 901-522-1241 www.mdtna.com
Aluminum and canvas awnings, tarpaulins and tents; also, bags including canvas, cotton duck, vinyl, nonwoven and filter
Owner: Chuck Cross
  memphisdelta@aol.com
Owner & Sales Manager: Paul Gatti
Estimated Sales: $500,000-$1 Million
Number Employees: 10-19
Brands:
  Delta

26013 Menasha Corp
1645 Bergstrom Rd
Neenah, WI 54956-9766
                    920-751-1000
      Fax: 920-751-1236 800-558-5073
                info@menasha.com
          www.menashacorporation.com
Corrugated containers
President/CEO: James Kotek
SVP/CFO: Thomas Rettler
VP/General Counsel/Corporate Secretary: Mark Fogarty
Estimated Sales: Over $1 Billion
Number Employees: 5000-9999
Square Footage: 12523

26014 Menasha Packaging Co LLC
1645 Bergstrom Rd
Neenah, WI 54956-9701
                    920-751-1000
      Fax: 920-751-1236 877-818-2016
      info@menasha.com www.menasha.com
Food packaging, packaging for in-store supermarket bakeries
CEO: Michael K Waite
  michael.waite@menahsa.com
Sales Director: Scott Sanders
Estimated Sales: $10 - 25 Million
Number Employees: 1000-4999
Parent Co: Menasha Corporation
Type of Packaging: Consumer, Food Service, Private Label, Bulk
Brands:
  The Sunbrite Line

26015 Mengibar Automation
103 Steam Whistle Dr
Warminster, PA 18974
                    215-396-2200
      Fax: 215-396-6774 info@penntech-corp.com
                www.penntech-corp.com
Manufacturers of packaging machinery for the pharmceutical industry
President: Ger Smit
  gersmit@mai-jp.net
General Manager: David Mohl
Estimated Sales: $10-20 Million
Number Employees: 1-4
Square Footage: 20000

26016 Menke Marking Devices
13253 Alondra Blvd
Santa Fe Springs, CA 90670-5574
                    562-921-1380
      Fax: 562-921-1184 800-231-6023
          sales@menkemarking.com
          www.menkemarking.com
Manufacturer and exporter of large and small character ink jet printers, roller coders and rubber and steel codes
President: Stephen Menke
VP: Rocco Falatico
Sales Manager: Paul Carrocino
Estimated Sales: $1-2.5 Million
Number Employees: 10-19
Square Footage: 21000

26017 Mennekes Electrical Products
277 Fairfield Rd # 6
Fairfield, NJ 07004-1931
                    973-882-0224
      Fax: 973-882-5585 800-882-7584
          info@mennekes.com
20A - 100A power plugs, cord drop connectors for portable equipment applications, HP rated NEMA 4X motor disconnects and receptacles with interlocking for OSHA lockout, tagout requirements
President: Tom Bodner
  tbodner@mennekes.com
VP: Thomas Bodnar
Vice President of Sales and Marketing: Paul DiAntonio
Vice President of Operations: AnnaMarie Fusaro
Estimated Sales: $20 - 50 Million
Number Employees: 20-49

26018 Mennel Milling Company
319 S Vine Street
Fostoria, OH 44830
                    419-435-8151
      Fax: 419-436-5150 800-688-8151
          info@mennel.com www.mennel.com
Processor of flour used in cake mixes, cookies, snack crackers, breadings, batters, gravies, soups, ice cream cones, pretzels and oriental noodles.
President: D. Ford Mennel
Controller: Lori Kitchen
Senior Technical Advisor: C J Lin
Vice President of Operations: David Marty
Corp Milling Engineer: Joel Hoffa
Year Founded: 1886
Estimated Sales: Below $5 Million
Number Employees: 100-249
Type of Packaging: Bulk

26019 Menu Graphics
PO Box 38397
Olmsted Falls, OH 44138-0397
                    216-696-1460
      Fax: 216-696-1463
Manufacturer and designer of menus and menu accessories
Director: Felicia West
Estimated Sales: $1-2.5 Million
Number Employees: 10-19
Parent Co: AD Art Litho

26020 Menu Men
PO Box 1172
Palm Harbor, FL 34682-1172
                    727-934-7191
      Fax: 727-937-0267
Menus and menu boards, covers, holders and displays
Number Employees: 5-9
Parent Co: Menu Men

26021 Menu Promotions
4510 White Plains Rd
Bronx, NY 10470-1609
                    718-324-3800
      Fax: 718-324-5598
Menu covers
President: Andrea Bongiovanni
  andrea@menucovers.biz
Estimated Sales: Less than $500,000
Number Employees: 5-9
Parent Co: Mona Slide Fasteners

26022 Menu Solution Inc
4510 White Plains Rd
Bronx, NY 10470-1609
                    718-994-9049
      Fax: 718-994-6913 800-567-6368
          sales@menucovers.biz www.menucovers.biz
Owner: Joel Varrocas
Contact: Jaclyn Barrocas
  jaclyn@menucovers.biz
Estimated Sales: $5 - 10 Million
Number Employees: 20-49

26023 MenuMark Systems
5700 W Bender Court
Milwaukee, WI 53218-1608
                    414-228-4350
      Fax: 414-228-4373

26024 Menulink
7777 Center Ave # 600
Huntington Beach, CA 92647-3099
                    714-934-6368
      Fax: 714-895-2332
Computer software including food cost, inventory, human resources, accounting and labor scheduling
Manager: Bob Thomas
CFO: Ronald Whitaker
Estimated Sales: $5 - 10 Million
Number Employees: 20-49
Brands:
  Back Office Assistant
  Menulink

26025 Mepsco
1888 E Fabyan Pkwy
Batavia, IL 60510-1498
                    630-231-4130
      Fax: 630-231-9372 800-323-8535
                www.mepsco.com
Manufacturer and exporter of mechanical tenderizers and pickle injector machinery for the curing of pork and beef, marinating of chicken and the basting of turkey
President: Robert Benton
Estimated Sales: $9,000,000
Number Employees: 20-49
Square Footage: 32000
Brands:
  Mepsco

26026 Merchandising FrontiersInc
1300 E Buchanan St
Winterset, IA 50273-9589
                    515-462-4965
      Fax: 515-462-4962 800-421-2278
          sales@mfi4u.com www.mfi4u.com
Manufacturer and exporter of indoor/outdoor carts, displays and kiosks
Owner: Jerry Mayer
  jmayer@merchandisingfrontiers.com
Co-Owner And CEO: Janet Mayer
Estimated Sales: $2.5-5,000,000
Number Employees: 20-49
Square Footage: 62000

26027 Merchandising Inventives
1665 S Waukegan Rd
Waukegan, IL 60085
                    847-688-0591
      Fax: 847-688-0748 800-367-5653
                www.merchinv.com
Manufacturer and exporter of point of purchase advertising display hardware components including mobile kits, ceiling fixtures, pole displays, banner hangers, shelf fixtures, display fasteners, etc
CEO: Ethan Berger
CFO: Diane Johnson
Vice President: Dan Jezierny
Quality Control: Aier Torres
Public Relations: Kay Berger
Operations Manager: Dan Jezierny
Production Manager: Jose Gayton
Plant Manager: Sue Kradwitz
Purchasing Manager: Sue Kradwitz
Estimated Sales: $12 Million
Number Employees: 20-49
Number of Products: 2000
Square Footage: 90000
Parent Co: DisplaWerks

26028 Merchandising Systems Manufacturing
2951 Whipple Rd
Union City, CA 94587-1207
650-324-8324
Fax: 650-324-4584 800-523-1468
Manufacturer and exporter of store displays and fixtures
President/Owner: Kyle Robinson
National Account Manager: Carol Sauceda
Contact: Kumar Gaurav
kumar@wireline.net
Estimated Sales: $5 - 10 Million
Number Employees: 20-49
Square Footage: 176000

26029 Merchants Publishing Company
20 Mills St
Kalamazoo, MI 49048
269-345-1175
Fax: 269-345-6999
Labels, tags and folding cartons
President: M Jack Fleming
CFO: Dick Nagle
VP Sales / Marketing: Ben Behrman
National Sales Manager (Label Division): Frank Brady
Estimated Sales: $10-20 Million
Number Employees: 50-99

26030 Merco/Savory
980 South Isabella R
Mt. Pleasant, MI 48858
989-773-7981
Fax: 800-669-0619 800-733-8821
Manufacturer and exporter of rotisseries, broilers, toasters, hot dog grilling systems, convection, pizza and cookie ovens, heated display cases and food warmers
President: Stephen Whiteley
COO: Marion Antonini
Director Marketing: Barbara Wolf
Director Sales: Alan Oates
Number Employees: 250-499
Square Footage: 30000
Parent Co: ENODIS
Type of Packaging: Food Service

26031 Mercury Equipment Company
15023 Sierra Bonita Lane
Chino, CA 91710-8902
909-606-8884
Fax: 909-606-8885 800-273-6688
Manufacturer and exporter of doughnut making equipment and bakery display cases and fixtures
President: Mike Campbell
Vice President: Joe Campbell
Estimated Sales: $1 - 3 Million
Number Employees: 6
Square Footage: 20000
Brands:
Belshaw
Dca
Mercury

26032 Mercury Floor Machines Inc
110 S Van Brunt St
Englewood, NJ 07631-3494
201-568-4606
Fax: 201-568-7962 888-568-4606
mrbill@mercuryfloormachines.com
www.mercuryfloormachines.com
Floor scrubbers, vacuums and carpet extractors
President/CEO: William Allen
Quality Control: William Parker
General Manager: Bill Bacich
Estimated Sales: $2.5-5 Million
Number Employees: 10-19
Square Footage: 16000

26033 Mercury Plastic Bag Company
168 7th St
Passaic, NJ 7055
973-778-7200
Fax: 973-778-0549
Polyethylene and polypropylene packaging bags
President: Marvin Rosen
VP Sales: Stuart Rosen
Estimated Sales: $5-10 Million
Number Employees: 20-49

26034 Meriden Box Company
321 Blue Hills Drive
Southington, CT 06489-4605
860-621-7141
Fax: 860-621-7141
Hard and soft wood boxes and pallets

26035 Merieux Nutrisciences
2057 Builders Pl
Columbus, OH 43204-4886
614-486-0150
Fax: 614-486-0151 silliker@silliker.com
www.merieuxnutrisciences.com
Consultant offering analytical services for food processors
Manager: Amitha Miele
Estimated Sales: $5 - 10 Million
Number Employees: 20-49
Parent Co: Silliker Laboratories

26036 Meritech
600 Corporate Circle
Suite H
Golden, CO 80401-5643
303-790-4670
Fax: 303-790-4859 800-932-7707
www.meritech.com
No-touch automated hygiene equipment to the food processing, food service, medical, cleanroom, daycare, school and prison industries.
President/CEO: Jim Glenn
Sales: Michele Colbert
Contact: Samantha Dill
samanthadill@wiradcom.com
Estimated Sales: $5-10 Million
Number Employees: 10-19
Square Footage: 40000
Type of Packaging: Food Service
Brands:
Chg 2%
Chg 4%
Machine Mochers
Quat E-2
Quat F-5
Shelf Clean A-1

26037 Meriwether Industries
12 Prospect St
Bloomfield, NJ 7003
973-743-0463
Fax: 973-743-0614 800-332-2358
Power transmission and conveyor belts
President: Samuel Wolosin
CFO: Samuel Wolosin
Estimated Sales: $1 - 2.5 Million
Number Employees: 3
Square Footage: 6000
Brands:
Extremultus
Transilon

26038 Merix Chemical Company
230 W Superior St
Chicago, IL 60654-3595
312-573-1400
Fax: 773-221-3047 www.marxsaunders.com
Manufacturer and exporter of anti-static coatings for polyethylene films; also, anti-fog coatings to prevent moisture and condensation on food display cases
Owner: Bonnie Marx
Manager: Z Blowert
Estimated Sales: $1 - 5 Million
Number Employees: 5-9
Square Footage: 6000
Brands:
Merix

26039 Merlin Development Inc
181 Cheshire Ln N # 500
Minneapolis, MN 55441-8715
763-475-0224
Fax: 763-475-1626 merlin@merlindev.com
www.merlindevelopment.com
Consultant providing contract research and product development services to the food industry
President: Paul Thompson
General Manager: Paul Thompson
Manager: Kellie Fischer
kfischer@merlindev.com
Estimated Sales: $3 - 5 Million
Number Employees: 5-9
Square Footage: 17880

26040 Merlin Process Equipment
700 Louisiana St
Houston, TX 77002-2700
713-221-1651
Fax: 713-690-3353
Manufacturer and exporter of mixers
Estimated Sales: $300,000-500,000
Number Employees: 1-4

26041 Merric
4742 Earth City Expy
Bridgeton, MO 63044
314-770-9944
Fax: 314-770-1440 www.merric.com
Tabletops, booths, cabinets and point of sale counters
Owner: Dan Claypool
Administration: Tricia Weiss
Accounts Manager: Karrie Dyas
AutoCAD Engineer: Greg Koets
Engineer/IT: Aaron Pattillo
Sr. Project Manager: Amy DeVries
VP Operations: Tom Boylan
Project Manager: Chris Robertson
Estimated Sales: $2.5-5,000,000
Number Employees: 20-49

26042 Merrill Distributing Inc
1301 N Memorial Dr
Merrill, WI 54452-3188
715-536-4551
Fax: 715-536-5757 800-677-6320
www.merrilldistributing.com
Food service distributor
President: John Schewe
jschewe@merrilldistributing.com
Estimated Sales: Below $5 Million
Number Employees: 50-99

26043 Merrillville Awning Co
1420 E 91st Dr
Merrillville, IN 46410-7174
219-736-9800
Fax: 219-736-9100 800-781-6100
www.awningguy.com
Commercial awnings
Owner: Mike Blessing
mike@awningguy.com
Estimated Sales: $2.5-5,000,000
Number Employees: 10-19

26044 Merryweather Foam Inc
1212 Wynette Rd
Sylacauga, AL 35151-4601
256-249-8546
Fax: 256-249-8548 sales@merryweather.com
www.merryweather.com
Plastic foam parts and pressure-sensitive tapes
General manager: Bellaire Riley
IT: Ed Spraley
ed@merryweather.com
Plant Manager: Cliff Shelnut
Estimated Sales: $5-10 Million
Number Employees: 20-49
Parent Co: Merryweather Foam

26045 (HQ)Merryweather Foam Inc
1212 Wynette Rd
Sylacauga, AL 35151-4601
256-249-8546
Fax: 256-249-8548 www.merryweather.com
Plastic foam parts; fabricator/convertor of polyurethane and polyethylene foams with and without pressure sensitive adhesives and coatings
Director Sales/Marketing: Don Sweigert
Sales Administrator: Tina Rockhold
Customer Service Manager: Theresa Karabinus
IT: Ed Spraley
General manager: Bellaire Riley
Estimated Sales: $10 - 20 Million
Number Employees: 20-49
Square Footage: 200000
Other Locations:
Merryweather Foam
Sylacauga AL

26046 Mertz L. Carlton Company
6147 W 65th Street
Bedford Park, IL 60638-5303
708-594-1050
Fax: 716-626-1616
Cleaning compounds
Estimated Sales: $2.5-5 Million
Number Employees: 10-19

26047 Mesa Laboratories Inc

12100 W 6th Ave
Lakewood, CO 80228-1252

303-987-8000
Fax: 303-987-8989 800-525-1215
www.mesalabs.com

Manufacturer, importer and exporter of temperature, pressure and humidity monitoring products for processing, distribution and transportation; also, ultrasonic composition analyzers and flow meters
President: Luke Schmieder
CEO: John J Sullivan
john@mesalabs.com
CFO: Steven Peterson
Research And Development: Preston Graves
Quality Control: Jeff Zepp
Marketing: David Price
Sales: Owen Israelsen
Operations: Clint Englehart
Production: Rex Trout
Estimated Sales: $9 Million
Number Employees: 250-499
Number of Brands: 7
Square Footage: 79232
Parent Co: Mesa Laboratories
Brands:
Datatrace

26048 Mesler Group

3725 Okemos Road
Okemos, MI 48864-3929

517-349-7066
Fax: 517-349-7069 mgi@voyager.net
Consulting for the food ingredient industry
President: Fred Mesler

26049 Messina Brothers Manufacturing Company

1065 Shepherd Avenue
Brooklyn, NY 11208-5713

718-345-9800
Fax: 718-345-2441 800-924-6454
Manufacturer, importer and wholesaler/distributor of mops, brooms and brushes
Sales Representative: Robert Messina
General Manager: Lawrence Mirro
Number Employees: 15
Square Footage: 90000
Parent Co: Howard Berger Company

26050 Met-Pro Corp

1550 Industrial Dr
Owosso, MI 48867-9775

989-725-8185
Fax: 989-725-8188 800-392-7621
info@mpeas.com www.mpeas.com
Pumps including fiber glass reinforced, vinyl ester, epoxy and chemical process
Controller: Dave Mogg
COO: Greg Kimmer
greg.kimmer@dualldiv.com
VP/General Manager: R De Hont
Sales/Marketing Manager: E Murphy
Engineering Manager: R Petersen
Estimated Sales: $5 Million
Number Employees: 20-49
Square Footage: 200000

26051 Met-Pro Corp

1550 Industrial Dr
Owosso, MI 48867-9775

989-725-8185
Fax: 989-725-8188 info@dualldiv.com
www.dualldiv.com
Air pollution controls for food processing plants
Controller: Dave Mogg
COO: Greg Kimmer
greg.kimmer@dualldiv.com
Sales Manager: Rob Teich
Estimated Sales: $5 - 10 Million
Number Employees: 20-49
Square Footage: 240000
Parent Co: Met-Pro Corporation

26052 Metal

141 Metal Park Dr
Columbia, SC 29209-5072

803-776-9252
Fax: 803-776-9610
Restaurant equipment including metal sinks and tables
President: Frances Smoak
fsmoak@mef-inc.com

Estimated Sales: Below $5 Million
Number Employees: 5-9
Square Footage: 120000

26053 Metal Container Corporation

3636 S Geyer Rd # 400
St Louis, MO 63127-1218

314-957-9500
Fax: 314-957-9515 www.budlight.com
More than 20 billion cans and 20 billion lids annually at its 11 can and lid manufacturing facilities. Supplies about 60% of Anheuser-Bussch's container and lid requirements and is a signifcant supplier to the US soft-drink containermarket
President/Owner: Tony Bhalla
CEO: Joe Sellinger
Contact: Mike Balassi
mike.balassi@anheuser-busch.com
Number Employees: 100-249
Parent Co: Anheuser-Busch Companies

26054 Metal Equipment Company

600 Dover Center Rd
Cleveland, OH 44140-3310

440-835-3100
Fax: 440-835-1780 800-700-6326
Manufacturer, importer and exporter of custom metal industrial carts, storage racks, industrial bottle washers, waste management tanks, guards, platform trucks and pallet carriers
Manager: Bill Reilly
General Manager: Paul Drda
VP: Robert Walzer
Estimated Sales: Below $5 Million
Number Employees: 5-9
Square Footage: 110000

26055 Metal Kitchen Fabricators Inc

5121 April Ln
Houston, TX 77092-3499

713-683-8375
Fax: 713-683-8378
Custom manufacturer of food service equipment including stainless steel shelves, countertops and sinks
Owner: Glen Propes
mks@metalkitchens.net
Estimated Sales: Below $5 Million
Number Employees: 10-19

26056 Metal Master Sales Corp

1159 N Main St
Glendale Heights, IL 60139-3509

630-858-4750
Fax: 630-858-4735 800-488-8729
sales@metalmaster.com www.metalmaster.com
Manufacturer and exporter of food processing equipment and parts, cabinets, hoods, trays, tables, sinks, carts, tableware, canopies, fixtures, art metal, serving lines, bartops and countertops, etc
Owner: Jim Jensen
jjensen@metalmaster.com
VP: Bob Lonrod
Estimated Sales: $2.5 - 5 Million
Number Employees: 10-19
Square Footage: 104000
Parent Co: Richards Manufacturing & Services Corporation
Brands:
Biltrite
Caterware

26057 Metal Masters Northwest

20926 63rd Ave W
Suite A
Lynnwood, WA 98036-7402

425-775-4481
Fax: 425-775-2618 www.metalmastersnw.com
Custom fabricated stainless steel restaurant products including cooking, heating and serving equipment
Owner: Craig Jeppesen
craig.jeppesen@metalmastersnw.com
VP: Timothy Eaves
Estimated Sales: $1-2.5 Million
Number Employees: 10-19
Square Footage: 20000

26058 Metalcretye Manufacturing Company

4133 Payne Ave
Cleveland, OH 44103-2324

440-526-5600
Fax: 440-526-5601 800-526-5602
sales@metalcreteindustries.com
www.metalcreteindustries.com

Owner: Ron Stankie
Estimated Sales: $3 - 5 Million
Number Employees: 10-19

26059 Metaline Products Co Inc

101 N Feltus St
South Amboy, NJ 08879-1529

732-721-1373
Fax: 732-727-0272 sales@metalineproducts.com
www.metalineproducts.com
Manufacturer and exporter of wood, wire, plastic and corrugated display racks, shelving and point of purchase displays
President: Natalie Papailiou
natalie@mstudio.com
VP: August Zilincar
Estimated Sales: $2.5-5 Million
Number Employees: 20-49
Square Footage: 50000

26060 Metalloid Corp

504 Jackson St
Huntington, IN 46750

260-358-4610
Fax: 260-356-3201 800-686-3201
sales@metalloidcorp.com
www.metalloidcorp.com
Manufacturer and exporter of cutting fluids, tapping compounds and hand cleaners
President: Gary Russ
gruss@metalloidcorp.com
VP Marketing: William Fair
Estimated Sales: $2.5-5 Million
Number Employees: 10-19

26061 Metcalf & Eddy

701 Edgewater Dr Ste 200
Wakefield, MA 1880

781-246-5200
Fax: 781-245-6293
Consultant providing water and wastewater treatment services; also, engineering, design, construction, operations and maintenance available
President: Micheal S Burke
Chairman/CEO: John M Dionisio
Contact: Robert Adams
robert.adams@m-e.aecom.com
Number Employees: 20-49
Parent Co: Air & Water Technology

26062 Metcraft

13910 Kessler Drive
Grandview, MO 64030-5312

816-761-3250
Fax: 816-761-0544 800-444-9624
info@powersoak.com
Stainless steel custom fabricated food processing equipment, plumbing fixtures and power soak pot washing systems
President: John Cantrell
President: John Cantrell
Vice President of Distribution: Barry Bergstein
Marketing Director: Virginia Black
President: John Cantrell
Vice President of Operations: John McCreight
Manufacturing Manager: Monty Patton
Estimated Sales: $5 - 10 Million
Number Employees: 60
Square Footage: 60000
Parent Co: Emco
Brands:
Power Soak

26063 Metko Inc

1301 Milwaukee Dr
New Holstein, WI 53061-1443

920-898-4221
Fax: 920-898-1389 sales@metko.com
www.metko.com
Full-service precision custom metal fabricator offering engineering support, parts, subassemblies and complete assembled parts in a large range of metals and custom finishes.
President: Michael Mc Carthy
CEO/Founder: David McCarthy
Marketing: Jim Kreger
Sales: Jim Kreger
Public Relations: Jim Kreger
Human Resources: Diane McCarthy
Production: Mike Lider
Plant Manager: Mike Lider
Purchasing: Scott Lynch

Estimated Sales: $5-10 Million
Number Employees: 50-99
Square Footage: 42000
Brands:
  Custom Metal Fabricator

26064 Metl-Span I Ltd
1720 Lakepointe Drive
Suite #101
Lewisville, TX 75057-2650
972-221-6656
Fax: 972-420-9382 877-585-9969
www.metalspan.com
CEO: Karl F Hielscher
Estimated Sales: $5 - 10 Million
Number Employees: 100-249

26065 Metlar Us
2248 Roanoke Ave
Riverhead, NY 11901-1822
631-252-5574
Fax: 828-253-7773 www.metlar-us.com
Manufacturer, importer and exporter of fine pore filters
Office Manager: Anne Ogg
Contact: Doreen Kula
  dkula@metlar-us.com
Estimated Sales: $1 - 5 Million
Number Employees: 1-4
Parent Co: US Filter/Schumacher

26066 Meto
P.O. Box 518
Morris Plains, NJ 07950-0518
973-606-5660
Fax: 973-606-5661 800-645-3290
www.meto.com
Barcode printers, applicators, labels
Manager: William E Staehle
Estimated Sales: $5 - 10 Million
Number Employees: 20-49

26067 Metro Corporation
P.O. Box A
Wilkes Barre, PA 18705
570-825-2741
800-992-1776
www.intermetro.com
Supplier of food service storage, warehandling and transport solutions. the complete range of Metro products puts space to work in virtually avery area - cooler, freezer, dry storage, food preparation, catering and front of thehouse.
President & CEO: John Nackley
Vice President, Sales: Bill O'Donoghue
Year Founded: 1929
Estimated Sales: $100-500 Million
Number Employees: 1000-5000
Type of Packaging: Food Service
Brands:
  Flavor Lock
  Metromax
  Metromax Q
  Sani-Stack
  Smart Single
  Smart Track
  Smart Wall
  Super Adjustable Super Erecta
  Super Erecta
  Top Truck

26068 Metro Signs
4224 Losee Road
Suite J
N Las Vegas, NV 89030
702-649-9333
Fax: 702-649-9336 www.sbn.com
Signs; lettering service available
President: Frank Gaskill
Estimated Sales: Less than $500,000
Number Employees: 4

26069 Metron Instruments, Inc
Dock 3 or 4
23103 Miles Road
Cleveland, OH 44128
216-332-0592
Fax: 216-274-9262
sanderson@metroninstruments.com
www.metroninstruments.com
Heat exchangers, plate, centrifuges, milk tester, milk standardizer
Owner: Robert P Carter

Estimated Sales: $1-2.5 Million
Number Employees: 5-9

26070 Metroplex Corporation
PO Box 681987
Houston, TX 77268
281-257-8570
Fax: 281-257-8572
Consultant for corporate and private outplacement including professional services
President: Willard Jackson
Principal: Reid Matthews
CFO: Bob Stevens
CEO: Zia Qureshi
R & D: Howard Davis
Estimated Sales: $10 - 20 Million
Number Employees: 50-99

26071 Metropolitan Flag & Banner Co
3237 Amber St # 5
Philadelphia, PA 19134-3227
215-426-2775
Fax: 215-426-5106 Sales@metflag.com
www.metflag.com
Flags and banners
President: Robert Snyder
  rob@metflag.com
CFO: Robert Snyder
Quality Control: Robert Snyder
R&D: Robert Snyder
Estimated Sales: Below $5 Million
Number Employees: 10-19

26072 Metrovock Snacks
6116 Walker Avenue
Maywood, CA 90270-3447
323-771-3221
Fax: 323-771-2429 800-428-0522
www.giftbasketsupplies.com
Themed gift baskets
President and QC: Paul Popcorn
Contact: Carol Gregory
  csnacks1@aol.com
Estimated Sales: $500,000 - $1 Million
Number Employees: 20

26073 Metspeed Labels
6300 Mcpherson St
PO Box 850
Levittown, PA 19057-4728
215-956-9101
Fax: 215-946-7201 888-886-0638
info@metspeedlabel.com
www.metspeedlabel.com
Pressure sensitive tags and labels
President: Joe Felix
  joe@metspeedlabel.com
VP: Joe Felix
Marketing: Bob Reeder
Estimated Sales: Less Than $500,000
Number Employees: 1-4

26074 Metsys Engineering
9855 W 78th Street
Suite 10
Eden Prairie, MN 55344-8003
952-944-1081
Fax: 952-944-1431
Solutions to consumer product manufacturers through system engineering, development of operating documentation and technical training
Sales/Marketing Administrator: Mary Sandler
Estimated Sales: $2.5-5 Million
Number Employees: 20-49

26075 Mettler-Toledo Hi-Speed
1571 Northpointe Pkwy
Lutz, FL 33558
800-447-4439
hispeed@mt.com www.mt.com
Checkweighers, weighing and material handling.
Head of Product Inspection Division: Jonas Greutert
Regional Sales Director: John Fletcher
Estimated Sales: $20 - 50 Million
Number Employees: 100-249
Type of Packaging: Food Service, Bulk

26076 Mettler-Toledo Process Analytics, Inc
900 Middlesex Turnpike
Building 8
Billerica, MA 01821
800-352-8763
mtprous@mt.com www.mt.com/pro

Manufacturer, importer and exporter of process measurement equipment including pH and dissolved oxygen probes, transmitters and head space analyzers.
Head of Process Analytics Division: Gerry Keller
Estimated Sales: $10-20 Million
Number Employees: 50-99
Square Footage: 20000
Brands:
  Infit
  Ingold
  Inpro
  Intrac
  Xerolyt

26077 Mettler-Toledo SafelineInc
1571 Northpointe Pkwy
Lutz, FL 33558
800-638-8537
www.mt.com
Metal detectors and x-ray equipment for food products (including bulk, pakced, liquid, slurry and powder) and for pharmaceutical products.
National Sales Manager: Oscar Jeter
Market Communications Specialist: Sarrina Crowley
Estimated Sales: $5 Million
Number Employees: 100-249
Square Footage: 276000
Brands:
  Safeline

26078 (HQ)Mettler-Toledo, LLC
1900 Polaris Pkwy
Columbus, OH 43240
800-638-8537
www.mt.com
Manufacturer and exporter of stainless steel scales and printing devices for processing applications including portion control, sorting, box weighing, shipping/receiving and in-motion weighing.
Chief Executive Officer: Olivier Filliol
  olivier.filliol@mt.com
Chief Financial Officer: Shawn Vadala
Head of Supply Chain & IT: Oliver Wittorf
Head of Divisions & Operations: Peter Aggersbjerg
Head of Process Analytics Division: Gerry Keller
Head of Industrial Division: Elena Markwalder
Head of Product Inspection Division: Jonas Greutert
Head of Human Resources: Christian Magloth
Year Founded: 1946
Estimated Sales: Over $2 Billion
Number Employees: 10,000

26079 Metz Premiums
250 W 57th St # 25
New York, NY 10107-0001
212-315-4660
Fax: 212-541-4559 metzpremiums@yahoo.com
Manufacturer and importer of uniforms; also advertising specialties including metal pins and key rings, tote bags, picture frames and ceramic products
VP Sales: Laurie Zelen
Purchasing Manager: Gerry Kroll
*Estimated Sales:*less than $500,000
Number Employees: 1-4

26080 Metzgar Conveyors
901 Metzgar Dr NW
Comstock Park, MI 49321-9758
616-784-0930
Fax: 616-784-4100 888-266-8390
sales@metzgarconveyors.com
Manufacturer and exporter of conveyors and package and pallet handling systems
President: D R Metzgar
  dr.metzgar@metzgarconveyor.com
VP: Roger Scholten
R & D: Tom Dewey
Marketing: Roger Schotten
Production: Jon Goeman
Purchasing Manager: David Stevens
Estimated Sales: $10 Million
Number Employees: 50-99
Square Footage: 100000

26081 Mex-Char
1119 E 10th St
Douglas, AZ 85607-2301
520-364-2138
Fax: 520-364-2138
Mesquite, horticultural, avicultural, industrial and granulated charcoal
Owner: Oscar Teran

Estimated Sales: $1 - 5 Million
Number Employees: 1-4
Square Footage: 80000
Type of Packaging: Bulk

26082 Meyer & Garroutte Systems
P.O. Box 5460
San Antonio, TX 78201-0460
210-736-1811
Fax: 210-736-9452 www.meyer-industries.com
CEO: Eugene W Teeter
Estimated Sales: $10 - 20 Million
Number Employees: 50-99

26083 Meyer Industries
3528 Fredericksburg Rd
San Antonio, TX 78201-3849
210-736-1811
Fax: 210-736-9452 sales@meyer-industries.com
www.meyer-industries.com
Food processing equipment
CEO: Eugene Teeter
eteeter@meyer-industries.com
CFO: Larry Marek
Number Employees: 50-99

26084 Meyer Label Company
15143 Winkler Rd
Fort Myers, FL 33919
239-489-0342
Fax: 201-894-8867
Manufacturer and exporter of pressure sensitive and
roll labels
Owner: Kurt Meyer
VP Sales: Bob Reineke
Estimated Sales: $2.5-5 Million
Number Employees: 1-4
Square Footage: 50000

26085 Meyer Machine & Garroutte Products
3528 Fredericksburg Rd.
P.O. Box 5460
San Antonio, TX 78201-0460
210-736-1811
Fax: 210-736-4662 www.meyer-industries.com
Manufacturer and exporter of belt and vibratory con-
veyors and feeders, pivoting bucket elevators, spiral
lowerators, fryers, broilers, ovens, live bottom and
bin storage and food seasoning equipment.
President: Eugene Teeter
Quality Control and CFO: Larry Marek
North & South Central Regional Sales Mgr: Roland
Metivier
Northeast/Southeast Regional Sales Mgr: Scott
Carter
Western Regional Sales Mgr: Jim Lassiter
VP Manufacturing: Carroll Fries
Estimated Sales: $10 - 20 Million
Number Employees: 50-99
Square Footage: 200000
Parent Co: Meyer Industries
Other Locations:
  Meyer Machine Co.
  West Midlands
Brands:
  Dynaflex
  Magneflex
  Simplex
  Vibraflex

26086 Meyer Packaging
PO Box 232
Palmyra, PA 17078-0232
717-838-6300
Set-up paper boxes
VP: Stephen Meyer
Estimated Sales: $10 - 15 Million
Number Employees: 50-100
Square Footage: 200000

26087 (HQ)Meyers Printing Co
7277 Boone Ave N
Minneapolis, MN 55428-1539
763-533-9730
Fax: 763-531-5771 info@meyers.com
www.meyers.com
Pressure sensitive and roll labels; lithographic, large
format printing and printing on plastics available
CEO: Michael Lane
Estimated Sales: $50-100 Million
Number Employees: 250-499

26088 Meyhen International
556 Industrial Way West
Eatontown, NJ 07724
732-363-2333
Fax: 732-905-7696 www.meyhenfingers.com
Food Processing equipment; rubber products
Owner: Meir Toshav
CEO: Henry Stern
Number Employees: 30

26089 Meyn America LLC
1000 Evenflo Dr
Ball Ground, GA 30107-4544
770-967-0532
Fax: 770-967-1318 888-881-6396
sales.usa@meyn.net www.meyn.com
Meat industry processing equipment
President: Heath Jarrett
heath.jarrett@meyn.net
Principal: David McNeal
Sales Director: Rick Boze
Number Employees: 100-249
Parent Co: Cooperatieve Meyn

26090 Mezza
222 E Wisconsin Avenue
Suite 300
Lake Forest, IL 60045-1723
847-735-2516
Fax: 415-727-4471 888-206-6054
Suppliers to the finest kitchens in America with a
worldwide selection of gourmet pantry items
Type of Packaging: Food Service, Private Label

26091 Mia Rose Products
177 Riverside Ave Ste F
Newport Beach, CA 92663
714-662-5465
Fax: 714-662-5891 800-615-2767
www.miarose.com
Manufacturer and exporter of natural, biodegradable
air fresheners, deodorizing mists and home cleaners
made with real citrus
President/CEO: Mia Rose
Marketing/Sales: Carolena Hidalgo
Contact: Carmen Arzate
c.arzate@morrisrose.com
Estimated Sales: $2 Million
Number Employees: 10-19
Square Footage: 8000
Type of Packaging: Consumer, Private Label
Brands:
  Air Therapy
  Citri-Glow
  Pet Air

26092 Miami Awning
3905 NW 31st Ave
Miami, FL 33142-5122
786-615-6503
Fax: 305-576-0514 800-576-0222
sales@miamiawning.com www.miamiawning.com
Commercial awnings
Manager: Joan Garvey
Vice President: Rick Lassiter
rlassiter@dolphins.nfl.com
Estimated Sales: $5-10,000,000
Number Employees: 50-99

26093 Miami Metal
255 NW 25th Street
Miami, FL 33127-4329
305-576-3600
Fax: 305-576-2339
Manufacturer and exporter of chairs, cushions, pads,
table legs and bases and booths
Sales Manager: Carol Sieger
Estimated Sales: $20-50 Million
Number Employees: 100-249
Type of Packaging: Food Service
Brands:
  Pompeii Furniture

26094 Miami Systems Corporation
10001 Alliance Rd
Blue Ash, OH 45242
513-793-0110
Fax: 513-793-1140 800-543-4540
info@miamisystems.com
Business forms, salesbooks, cut sheets, unitsets,
continuous register forms, mailers, cardsets, ATM
forms, envelopes, checks, guest checks, gift certificates, labels, etc

President: Samuel Peters
CFO: Jim Enright
Executive VP: Henry Peters
VP Sales/Marketing: Tim Scully
Contact: Kathye Buyok
kathye_buyok@trihealth.com
Estimated Sales: $18 Million
Number Employees: 1,000-4,999

26095 (HQ)Mic-Ellen Associates
1173 Collegeville Rd
Collegeville, PA 19426
610-454-1582
Fax: 610-454-1583 800-872-1252
Consultant specializing in marketing natural prod-
ucts to the health food industry
President: Michael Molyneaux
Number Employees: 5-9
Square Footage: 12000

26096 Micelli Chocolate Mold Company
135 Dale St
West Babylon, NY 11704
631-752-2888
Fax: 631-752-2885 micelliusa@aol.com
www.micelli.com
Manufacturer and exporter of plastic and metal
molds for chocolate products
President: Joseph Micelli
Vice President: John Micelli
Sales Director: John Micelli
Contact: Mike Daly
mike_daly@micelli.com
Plant Manager: John Micelli
Estimated Sales: $3-5 Million
Number Employees: 10-19
Square Footage: 20000

26097 Michael Blackman & Assoc
1106 Broadway
Santa Monica, CA 90401-3008
310-656-1010
Fax: 310-393-9397 800-889-4925
www.michaelblackmanandassociates.com
Consultant providing design services
President: Micheal Blackman
Contact: Adrienne Blackman
adrienne@mbaassoc.com
Estimated Sales: $12,000,000 - $15,000,000
Number Employees: 10-19
Square Footage: 8000

26098 Michael Distributor Inc
PO Box 8681
Fountain Valley, CA 92728-8681
Fax: 714-966-1361
Food distributor and related products provider - gro-
cery, cooking oil, meat, sugar, canned foods, pro-
duce, dairy, candy & paper goods. Services to Food
service and retail industries.
President: Miguel Ortega
Estimated Sales: $8 Million
Type of Packaging: Food Service, Private Label

26099 Michael G. Brown & Associates
311 Society Pl
Newtown, PA 18940
215-860-4540
Fax: 215-579-7355
Texture analyzers
Contact: Michael Brown
mgba@voicenet.com
Estimated Sales: $1 - 5 Million

26100 Michael Leson Dinnerware
P.O. Box 5368
Youngstown, OH 44514
330-726-4788
Fax: 330-726-2274 800-821-3541
www.americanrails.com
Manufacturer, exporter and importer of dinnerware,
flatware, glassware, mugs, plate covers, platters, pre-
miums, incentives, salt and pepper shakers, etc
CEO: Michael Leson
Estimated Sales: $500,000-$1,000,000
Number Employees: 1-4
Parent Co: MLD Group

26101 Michaelo Espresso
309 S Cloverdale St # D22
Ste D22
Seattle, WA 98108-4572
206-695-4950
Fax: 206-695-4951 800-545-2883
info@michaelo.com
Kiosks, carts and vending equipment; importer and
wholesaler/distributor of espresso and granita ma-
chinery and panini grills; serving the food service
market
President: Michael Myers
info@michaelo.com
General Manager: Russ Myers
National Sales Manager: Douglas Pratt
Estimated Sales: $5-10 Million
Number Employees: 10-19
Square Footage: 40000
Type of Packaging: Food Service

26102 Michelman Inc
9080 Shell Rd
Blue Ash, OH 45236-1232
513-793-7766
Fax: 513-793-2504 800-333-1723
general@michem.com www.michelman.com
Water-based performance coatings and coating ap-
plication equipment for the corrugated and pa-
per-converting industries,including floor
polishes,inks,fibre glass,snack food packing
President: Steven Shifman
CFO: Jeff Rodgers
jeff.rodgers@michemprime.com
Vice President: Bob Poletti
Estimated Sales: $20 - 50 Million
Number Employees: 100-249
Parent Co: Michelman World
Type of Packaging: Bulk

26103 Michelson Laboratories Inc
6280 Chalet Dr
Commerce, CA 90040-3761
562-928-0553
Fax: 562-927-6625 888-941-5050
info@michelsonlab.com www.michelsonlab.com
Testing and analysis including microbiological anal-
ysis, pesticide residues, nutritionals, herbal analysis,
vitamins, FDA import alert analysis, drinking water,
wastewater and HACCP audits,meat processing, sea-
food, poultry, dairyproduce, bakery, spices and sea-
sonings, wastewater and effluent
President: Grant Michealson
grant@michelsonlab.com
Laboratory Director: Stephen Roesch
Instrumentation Manager: Maria Lopez
Chemistry Operations Manager: Roy Lung
Microbiology Asst Manager: Nolberto Colon-Droz
Estimated Sales: $5-10 Million
Number Employees: 50-99
Square Footage: 80000

26104 (HQ)Michiana Box & Crate
2193 Industrial Dr
Niles, MI 49120-1254
269-683-6372
Fax: 269-684-7860 800-677-6372
www.kampsinc.com
GMA and can pallets, bulk bins, export boxes, crates
and skids; exporter of bulk bins
President: Gary Cehovic
CEO: Thomas Kiehl
CFO: Dan Searfoss
Production Manager: Bog Modlin
Estimated Sales: $27 Million
Number Employees: 100-249
Number of Products: 205
Square Footage: 76000
Type of Packaging: Bulk

26105 Michiana Corrugate Products
110 N Franks Ave
Sturgis, MI 49091-1582
269-651-5225
Fax: 269-651-5799 www.michianacorrugated.com
Corrugated and die cut boxes; also, pads, partitions
and chipboard
President: Eric Jones
mcpcust@michianacorrugated.com
Sales Service: Patricia Vanzile
Estimated Sales: $20-50 Million
Number Employees: 20-49
Square Footage: 40000

**26106 Michigan Agricultural
Cooperative Marketing
Association**
P.O. Box 30960
Lansing, MI 48909-8460
517-323-7000
Fax: 517-323-6793 800-824-3779
www.michiganfarmbureau.com
Consultant for apple, cherry, asparagus and plum
processors
President: Wayne Wood
Div. Manager: Jerry Campbell
CFO: John Vancermolen
Vice President: Mike Fusilier
Number Employees: 100-249
Parent Co: Michigan Farm Bureau Family of Com-
panies

26107 Michigan Apple Res Committee
13750 S Sedona Pkwy # 3
Suite 3
Lansing, MI 48906-8101
517-669-8353
Fax: 517-669-9506 800-456-2753
Staff@MichiganApples.com
www.michiganapples.com
Offers marketing, communications, consumer educa-
tion and research on behalf of Michigan apple
growers.
Executive Director: Diane Smith
Account Manager: Mike Bardon
Account Manager: Cam Harrington
Communications and Marketing Manager: Gretchen
Mensing, APR
Office/Marketing Coordinator: Esther Haviland
Estimated Sales: $1-2.5 Million
Number Employees: 1-4

26108 (HQ)Michigan Box Co
1910 Trombly St
Detroit, MI 48211-2130
313-873-8084
Fax: 313-873-8084 888-642-4269
info@michiganbox.com www.michiganbox.com
Manufacturer and exporter of corrugated and pizza
boxes, point of purchase displays, crates and pallets;
also, custom printed and corrugated carry-out food
containers available
President: Elaine Fontana
efontana@michiganbox.com
Sales Manager: Scott Keech
Operations: Ralph Betzler
Estimated Sales: $10-20 Million
Number Employees: 50-99
Square Footage: 400000
Other Locations:
Michigan Box Co.
Detroit MI

26109 Michigan Brush Mfg Co
7446 Central St
Detroit, MI 48210-1037
313-834-1070
Fax: 313-834-1178 800-642-7874
sales@mi-brush.com www.michiganbrush.com
Manufacturer and exporter of brushes, brooms,
mops, and paint rollers, also squeegees for food pro-
cessing and food services.
President: Bruce Gale
mmfgcoinc@aol.com
CFO: Bruse Gale
Estimated Sales: $1 - 3 Million
Number Employees: 10-19
Number of Brands: 4
Number of Products: 1001
Square Footage: 220000
Type of Packaging: Private Label, Bulk
Brands:
Dorden
Mibco
Mibrush
Rol-Brush

26110 Michigan Desserts
10750 Capital St
Oak Park, MI 48237-3134
248-544-4574
Fax: 248-544-4384 800-328-8632
sales@midasfoods.com www.midasfoods.com
Sweet dry mix items
President: Richard Elias
relias@midasfoods.com
Sr VP Sales/Marketing: Gary Freeman
Estimated Sales: $7 Million
Number Employees: 20-49
Square Footage: 180000
Parent Co: Midas Foods India
Type of Packaging: Consumer, Food Service, Pri-
vate Label, Bulk
Brands:
American Savory
Michigan Dessert
Sin Fill

26111 Michigan Food Equipment
8155 Fieldcrest Dr
Brighton, MI 48116-8316
810-231-5132
Fax: 810-231-5132
Shrink tunnels, bacon processing equipment and ac-
cessories, blenders, frozen meat slicers, flakers and
breakers, grinders, stuffers and accessories
Owner: Gary Radtke
Estimated Sales: $1 - 2.5 Million
Number Employees: 1-4

26112 Michigan Industrial Belting
31617 Glendale St
Livonia, MI 48150-1828
734-427-7700
Fax: 734-427-0788 800-778-1650
marty@mibelting.com www.mibelting.com
Conveyor belts and power transmission conveyor
systems; wholesaler/distributor of conveyor belts,
bearings, motors and controls
Owner: Bill Kohler
bill@mibelting.com
Estimated Sales: Below $5 Million
Number Employees: 10-19
Square Footage: 240000

26113 Michigan Maple Block Co
1420 Standish Ave
Petoskey, MI 49770-3049
231-347-4170
Fax: 231-347-7975 800-447-7975
mmb@mapleblock.com www.butcherblock.com
Manufacturer, importer and exporter of cutting
boards, tabletops, carving boards and preparation
and bakery tables
President: James Reichart
VP Sales & Marketing: Pat Stanley
VP Sales/Marketing: Russell Foth
Estimated Sales: $5-10 Million
Number Employees: 50-99
Parent Co: Bally Block Company
Type of Packaging: Food Service
Brands:
Wood Welded

26114 Michigan Pallet Inc
1225 N Saginaw St
St Charles, MI 48655-1024
989-865-9915
Fax: 989-865-9037
Wooden skids, pallets and boxes
President: Rick Lorentzen
Sales: Duane Schneider
Sales: Dan McGee
Estimated Sales: $5-10 Million
Number Employees: 50-99

26115 Micor Co Inc
3232 N 31st St
Milwaukee, WI 53216-3828
414-873-2071
Fax: 414-873-3904 800-284-4308
micorox@execpc.com www.micorco.com
Floors, floor sealers, protective coatings, epoxy
floors, floor resurfacers
President: Barbara Greenberg
patricknap@aol.com
Sales Exec: Patrick Cox
Estimated Sales: $1-2.5 Million
Number Employees: 5-9

26116 Micro Affiliates
3986 Ballynahown Cirle
Fairfax, VA 22030-2497
301-881-4115
Fax: 301-881-0340 800-430-1099
www.joesdata.com
Four-way security door viewers
Estimated Sales: $2.5 - 5 Million
Brands:
Door Spy

26117 Micro Filtration Systems
PO Box 367
Elon College, NC 27244-0367
336-570-1933
Fax: 336-570-1933
Wine industry laboratory equipment

26118 Micro Matic
19761 Bahama St
Northridge, CA 91324
818-701-9765
Fax: 818-341-9501 sac@micro-matic.com
www.micro-matics.com
Manufactures liquid transfer valves and related
equipment
President: Peter Muzzonigro
CFO: Jim Motush
Sales Manager: Barry Broughton
Contact: Allen Cossairt
allen@micro-matics.com
Estimated Sales: $20 - 50 Million
Number Employees: 50-99
Parent Co: Micro Matic AIS
Type of Packaging: Bulk

26119 Micro Qwik
1017 Park St
Cross Plains, WI 53528-9631
608-798-3071
Fax: 608-798-4452
webmaster@plasticingenuity.com
www.plasticingenuity.com
Dual-ovenable plastic containers
President: Thomas Kuehn
Sales Manager: Denny McGuigan
Sales: Janet Erdman
Estimated Sales: $20 - 50 Million
Number Employees: 250-499
Parent Co: Plastic Ingenuity

26120 Micro Solutions Ent Tech & Dev
8201 Woodley Ave
Van Nuys, CA 91406-1231
818-718-0911
Fax: 818-407-7575 800-673-4968
info@mse.com www.mse.com
Packaging equipment including specialties, metal
parts, cartoners, conveyors, collators and assembly
equipment
President: Martha Sherman
CEO: John Sherman
VP: Scott Sherman
Marketing Manager: Scott Sherman
Contact: Oscar Aguilar
oaguilar@mse.com
Estimated Sales: $1-2.5 Million
Number Employees: 5-9
Square Footage: 100000

26121 Micro Wire Products Inc
120 N Main St
Brockton, MA 02301-3911
508-584-0200
Fax: 508-584-1188 jwmwp@aol.com
www.microwire-products.com
Manufacturer and importer of welded wire baskets,
store diplays and fixtures and dishwasher and tray
racks
Owner: Jeff Weafer
jwmwp@aol.com
Controller: Linda Weaver
Treasurer: Arnold Wilson
Estimated Sales: $5 - 10 Million
Number Employees: 20-49
Square Footage: 280000

26122 Micro-Blend
2550 4th Street
Ingleside, TX 78362-5911
361-776-0179
Fax: 361-776-3787 microblend@aol.com
Number Employees: 80

26123 Micro-Brush Pro Soap
1830 E Interstate 30
Rockwall, TX 75087-6241
972-722-1161
Fax: 972-722-1584 800-776-7627
www.prosoap.com
Manufacturer and exporter of hand cleaning scrubs
and pastes for removing inks, food coloring and
food odors; also, soap dispensers
President: Scott L Self
VP Operations: James Wilkins, III

Estimated Sales: $10-20 Million
Number Employees: 5-9
Square Footage: 36000
Parent Co: Texas Nova-Chem Corporation
Type of Packaging: Food Service
Brands:
Micro-Brush
Pro Soap

26124 Micro-Chem Laboratory
Building A, Unit 16
Mississauga, ON L5T 2L5
Canada
905-795-0490
Fax: 905-795-0491 info@micro-chem.com
Consulting laboratory providing microbiological,
nutritional and product development services
President: Ash Mathur
Lab Manager: Nancy Reynolds
Number Employees: 10
Square Footage: 20000

26125 Micro-Strain
291 Stony Run Rd
Spring City, PA 19475
610-948-4550
Manufacturer and exporter of digital and analog
electronic measuring systems and devices including
scales and weighing systems
President: Rolf Jespersen
Estimated Sales: Less than $500,000
Number Employees: 1-4
Square Footage: 10000

26126 MicroAnalytics
4500 140th Avenue
Ste. 101
Clearwater, FL 33762
727-483-5562
Fax: 727-538-4237 info@mapmechanics.com
www.bestroutes.com
Computer software, routing and scheduling software
distribution planning and translation of distribution
logistics
President: J Michael Hooban
Director Sales: Ted Hooban
Estimated Sales: Below $5 Million
Number Employees: 10-19
Brands:
Bustops
Truckstop

26127 MicroFlo Company
530 Oak Court Dr # 100
Memphis, TN 38117-3722
901-432-5000
Fax: 901-432-5100 www.arysta-na.com
Wine industry pheromones
VP: John Reid
Estimated Sales: $20-50 Million
Number Employees: 20-49

26128 MicroThermics, Inc.
3216-B Wellington Ct
Raleigh, NC 27615
919-878-8045
Fax: 919-878-8032 info@microthermics.com
www.microthermics.com
Manufacturer and exporter of laboratory and food
processing equipment for pasteurization and aseptic
purposes.
President: John Miles
Executive Vice President: David Miles
VP Sales, Marketing, Business Operations: David
Miles
Estimated Sales: $5-10 Million
Other Locations:

26129 Microbac Laboratories
101 Bellevue Rd # 301
Suite 301
Pittsburgh, PA 15229-2132
412-459-1060
Fax: 866-515-4668 866-515-4668
microbac_info@microbac.com
www.microbac.com
Consultant/laboratory firm providing environmental
air, water and waste testing for EPA and OSHA compliance; also, food testing for nutritional value, bacteria, quality control, etc

President/CEO: J Trevor Boyce
Chairman: A Warne Boyce
Executive Vice President: Warne Boyce
Technical Director: Bryan Hauger
Chief Operating Officer: Sean Hyde
Estimated Sales: $10-20 Million
Number Employees: 10
Square Footage: 30000
Parent Co: Microbac Laboratories

26130 Microbac Laboratories
2000 Corporate Drive
Wexford, PA 15090-7611
724-934-5030
Fax: 724-934-5088 cearle@microbac.com
www.microbac.com
Analytical services and consulting
Executive Vice President: Warne Boyce
Technical Director: Bryan Hauger
Technical Service/Market Development: Thomas
Zierenberg
Contact: Wade Delong
wade.delong@microbac.com
Chief Operating Officer: Sean Hyde
Estimated Sales: $10-20 Million
Number Employees: 250-499

26131 Microbac Laboratories Inc
101 Bellevue Rd # 301
Suite 301
Pittsburgh, PA 15229-2132
412-459-1060
Fax: 866-515-4668 microbac_info@microbac.com
www.microbac.com
Laboratory consultant providing nutritional labeling,
sanitation inspections, plastic container/wrap analy-
sis, shelf-life studies and pathogen testing services
Chairman, President & CEO: J Trevor Boyce
Senior Vice President: Robert S. Crookston
Technical Director: Bryan Hauger
Chief Operating Officer: Sean Hyde
IT: Lynette Bauer
lbauer@microbac.com
Estimated Sales: $500,000 - $1 Million
Number Employees: 250-499
Parent Co: Microbac Laboratories

26132 Microbac-Wilson Devision
3809 Airport Dr NW
Wilson, NC 27896-8649
252-237-4175
Fax: 252-237-9341 www.microbac.com
Analytical laboratory specializing in chemical and
microbiological analysis of food samples. Nutri-
tional label analysis, nutraceutical analysis, and
camera ready nutirtional labels
Executive Director: Robert Dermer
CAO: Jeff Taylor
jeff.taylor@microbac.com
Marketing/Sales: Walter Nogg
Department Manager: Martin Donenco
Estimated Sales: $10 - 20 Million
Number Employees: 50-99
Square Footage: 42000
Parent Co: Microbac Laboratories

26133 Microbest Inc
670 Captain Neville Dr # 1
Waterbury, CT 06705-3855
203-597-0355
Fax: 203-597-0655 800-426-4246
www.microbest.com
Manufacturer and exporter of cleaning supplies and
equipment including microbial floor cleaners, de-
greasers, treatment products, etc
President: Ed Mc Nerney
emcnerney@microbest.com
CEO: Michael Troup
VP Sales/Marketing: Gary Garavaglin
Estimated Sales: $1 - 5 Million
Number Employees: 50-99
Brands:
Bio Cleansing Systems
Microbest, Inc.

26134 Microbiologics Inc
200 Cooper Ave N
St Cloud, MN 56303-4440
320-253-7400
Fax: 320-253-6250 800-599-2847
info@microbiologics.com
www.microbiologics.com

CEO: Bradley D Goskowicz
    bgoskowicz@mbl2000.com
CEO: Robert Corborn
National Sales Manager: Julie Sundgaard
Estimated Sales: $1 - 5 Million
Number Employees: 50-99

26135 Microbiology International
5111 Pegasus Ct
Suite H
Frederick, MD 21704-8318

                              301-662-6835
    Fax: 301-662-8096 800-396-4276
info@800ezmicro.com www.800ezmicro.com
Supply systems that automate sample preparation,
bacterial enumeration and media preparation/plate
and tube filling; provides complete media prepara-
tion services
Owner: Kevin Klink
Contact: Lauren Axline
    lauren.axline@800ezmicro.com
Product Manager: Bill Richman
Estimated Sales: Below $5 Million
Number Employees: 10-19

26136 Microcheck Solutions
9777 West Gulf Bank Ste C-5
PO Box 984
Humble, TX 77347

                              713-856-9801
    Fax: 713-460-0240 800-647-4524
www.microchecksolutions.com
Point of sale equipment
Marketing Manager: Barbara Collins
Sales Manager: Barbara Collins
Estimated Sales: $1 - 3 Million
Number Employees: 1-4
Square Footage: 20000

26137 Microcool
30670 Hill St
Thousand Palms, CA 92276-2618

                              760-322-1111
    Fax: 760-343-1820 800-322-4364
info@microcool.com www.microcool.com
Wine industry temperature and humidity control sys-
tems, patio misting and cooling
Owner: Mike Lemche
    mlemche@microcool.com
Marketing: Mark Stanley
Sales: Jim Murphy
Estimated Sales: $3 - 5 Million
Number Employees: 10-19

26138 Microdry
5901 W Highway 22
Crestwood, KY 40014-7217

                              502-241-8933
    Fax: 502-241-5907 engineering@microdry.com
                www.nemeth-engineering.com
Manufacturer and exporter of industrial microwaves
Owner: Peter Nemeth
    info@nemethengineering.com
Systems Specialist: Mark Isgryg
Plant Manager: Herb Bullis
Estimated Sales: $2.5-5 Million
Number Employees: 20-49
Square Footage: 100000

26139 Microflex Corp
2301 Robb Dr
Reno, NV 89523-1901

                              775-746-6600
    Fax: 775-746-6577 800-876-6866
                jfarris@microflex.com
Food handling gloves
President: Mike Mattos
CEO: Lloyd Rogers
Director Sales: Chris Verhulst
Contact: Brian Sublett
    brians@microflex.com
Manager West Coast Food Service: Karen Baum
Manager Industrial Division: Mike Williamson
Estimated Sales: $20 - 50 Million
Number Employees: 1-4
Brands:
    Micro Flex

26140 Microfluidics International
90 Glacier Dr # 1000
Suite 1000
Westwood, MA 02090-1818

                              617-969-5452
    Fax: 617-965-1213 800-370-5452
                www.microfluidicscorp.com
Manufacturer and exporter of high pressure mixing
equipment for processing emulsions, dispersions,
liposomes, particle size reduction, deagglomeration,
high end food, flavorings and colorants
President: Robert Bruno
CEO: Irwin Gruverman
Controller: Dennis Riordan
Marketing Communications Manager: Wendy
Rogalinski
Number Employees: 20-49
Square Footage: 60000
Brands:
    Microfluidizer Pro.Equipment

26141 Micromeritics
4356 Communications Dr
Norcross, GA 30093-2901

                              770-638-7569
    Fax: 770-662-3696 www.micromeritics.com
Manufacturer and exporter of analytical instruments
for production and process control application
President: Preston Hendrix
Estimated Sales: $20-50 Million
Number Employees: 100-249
Type of Packaging: Bulk

26142 Micron Automation
4516 W North a St
Tampa, FL 33609-2039

                              813-637-8810
    Fax: 813-637-8819 www.morrisautomation.com
President: Peter Buczynsky
Vice President Technical Operations: Ingo Federle
Vice President Sales And Service: Ben Brower

26143 Micron Separations
135 Flanders Rd
Westborough, MA 01581-1031

                              508-366-8212
    Fax: 508-366-5840 800-444-8212
Wine industry filtration equipment
Estimated Sales: $5-10 Million
Number Employees: 50-99

26144 Microplas Industries
2364 Brookhurst Dr
Dunwoody, GA 30338

                              770-234-0600
    Fax: 770-234-0601 800-952-4528
Manufacturer and importer of polyethylene shrink
film and black conductive and antistat LDPE and
HDPE bags
President: John J Cawley
Estimated Sales: Below $500,000
Number Employees: 1-4
Square Footage: 10000
Brands:
    Hi Shrink
    Micorduct
    Microstat

26145 Micropoint
1077 Independence Ave # B
Mountain View, CA 94043-1601

                              650-969-3097
    Fax: 650-969-2067 www.microfit.com
Manufacturer, importer and exporter of writing and
marking pens
President: Paul Vodak
Estimated Sales: less than $500,000
Number Employees: 1-4
Brands:
    Art-Stik
    Color Brush
    Color-Craft
    Facts Finder
    Fine-Stik
    Fits All
    Gripper
    Ink Stik
    Ink-Stik 'n' Holder
    Micro-Mini
    Mustang
    Perma-Mark
    Phone Pen
    Pinto
    Premier

    Super Marker
    Unimark
    White Board Marker
    Wik Stik
    Win Pen

26146 Micropub Systems International
10 Milford Rd
Rochester, NY 14625

                              585-385-3990
    Fax: 585-385-4387 www.micropub.com
Manufacturer and exporter of beer brewing systems;
processor of brewing ingredients
Manager: Barb Smith
Estimated Sales: Below $500,000
Number Employees: 10-19
Square Footage: 80000
Brands:
    Micropub

26147 Micropure Filtration Inc
1100 Game Farm Cir
Mound, MN 55364-7900

                              952-472-2323
    Fax: 952-472-0105 800-654-7873
tsenney@micropure.com www.micropure.com
Manufacturer, importer and exporter of food and
beverage filtration and regulating devices including
segmented stainless steel, cartridge, air, processing,
sampler, trap filter removers and air filters, culinary
steam.
President: Trey Senney
Estimated Sales: Less Than $500,000
Number Employees: 1-4
Square Footage: 4000
Brands:
    Glas-Flo
    Mem-Pure
    Micro-Pure
    Pro-Flo
    Segma-Flo
    Segma-Pure

26148 Microscan Systems Inc
700 SW 39th St # 100
Renton, WA 98057-2316

                              425-226-5700
    Fax: 425-226-8250 800-762-1149
info@microscan.com www.microscan.com
Bar code scanning equipment
President: Steve Holahan
    sholahan@microscan.com
CFO: Mark Milburn
Marketing Director: Laura Hoffman
Sales Director: Bill Westgate
Public Relations: Susan Snyder
Operations Manager: Jerry Naumcheff
Production Manager: Jim Murray
Purchasing Manager: Mike Moritz
Estimated Sales: $10-20,000,000
Number Employees: 100-249
Number of Brands: 1
Number of Products: 9
Type of Packaging: Private Label
Brands:
    Microscan

26149 Microtechnologies
123 Whiting St. Ste 1A
Plainville, CT 6062

                              860-829-2710
    Fax: 860-516-1549 888-248-7103
support@temperatureguard.com
                www.temperatureguard.com
Manufacturer and exporter of HVAC controls
President: Frank Geissler
Estimated Sales: Below $5,000,000
Number Employees: 5-9
Square Footage: 8000

26150 Microthermics
3216 Wellington Ct # 102
Raleigh, NC 27615-4122

                              919-878-8045
    Fax: 919-878-8032 info@microthermics.com
                www.microthermics.com
Specializes in the simulation, scale up, and scale
down of UHT, HTST, Aseptic, continuos cooking
and hot-fill process
President: John Miles
Vice President: David Miles
Regional Technical Sales Manager: Edgardo Vega
Manager: Mike Gregory

Estimated Sales: $1 - 3 Million
Number Employees: 20-49

26151 Microtouch Systems Inc
501 Griffin Brook Dr
Methuen, MA 01844-1870

978-659-9000
Fax: 978-659-9100 touch@mmm.com
Point of sale touch screen systems
Contact: Ricardo Alcantara
ralcantara@mmm.com
Number Employees: 500-999
Brands:
Microtouch

26152 Microtron Abrasives
10424 Rodney St
Pineville, NC 28134

704-889-7256
Fax: 704-889-5102 800-476-7237
www.glit-microtron.com
Abrasive and nonabrasive handpads, metal sponges, cellulose sponge products, griddle screens, soap impregnated abrasive pads, nonwoven floor maintenance pads and related accessories
Manager: Jeff Dean
VP/COO: Robert Quigley
Contact: David Blackington
fmcclure@u.washington.edu
Estimated Sales: $20-50 Million
Number Employees: 5-9
Square Footage: 100000
Parent Co: Katy Industries
Brands:
Hef-T-Clean
Jif-Y-Clean
Pot-N-Pan Handler
Soap-N-Scrub

26153 Microwave Research Center
3856 Princeton Cir
Eagan, MN 55123-1520

651-456-9190
Fax: 651-454-6480
Consultants specializing in microwave technology, products and strategies; also, development of single and 2-mode applicators and related switch-mode power supplies
Project Director: Jan Claesson
VP: Per Risman
Estimated Sales: $.5 - 1 million
Number Employees: 1-4
Square Footage: 10000
Parent Co: Rubbright Group
Brands:
Microduction
Thermalizer

26154 Microworks Pos Solutions Inc
2112 Empire Blvd # 2a
Suite 2A
Webster, NY 14580-1935

585-787-2058
Fax: 585-787-2289 800-787-2068
www.microworks.com
Point of sale hardware and software for dine-in, carry out and delivery restaurants,prism for windows,prism classictouch,prism classiclite
Manager: Tim Freida
timf@microworks.com
Estimated Sales: Less than $500,000
Number Employees: 10-19

26155 Mid Atlantic Packaging Co
14 Starlifter Ave
Dover, DE 19901-9200

302-734-8833
Fax: 302-734-8698 800-284-1332
sales@midatlanticpackaging.com
www.midatlanticpackaging.com
Bags, boxes, fill material, labels, ribbons and bows
Owner: Herb Glanden
Marketing: Don Glanden
Sales Director: Donald Glanden
hgmap@dmv.com
Estimated Sales: $3-7 Million
Number Employees: 20-49
Number of Brands: 50
Number of Products: 25
Square Footage: 60000

26156 Mid Cities Paper Box Company
7661 Fostoria Street
Downey, CA 90241-3240

562-927-1431
Fax: 562-927-3271 877-277-6272
Paper boxes, folding cartons, laminate, foil stamp, window in-house and displays
President/CEO: Ken Sipple
Owner: Norm Sipple
Marketing Director: Angie Saavedra
Sales Director: Mike Sipple
Purchasing Manager: Letha Lands
Estimated Sales: $12 Million
Number Employees: 85
Square Footage: 220000
Type of Packaging: Consumer, Food Service, Private Label

26157 Mid South Graphics
PO Box 110889
Nashville, TN 37222-0889

615-331-4210
Fax: 615-331-4367
Pressure sensitive labels and tags
Customer Service Manager: Patricia Davenport
Estimated Sales: $4 Million
Number Employees: 20-50
Square Footage: 60000

26158 Mid West Quality GlovesInc
835 Industrial Rd
Chillicothe, MO 64601-3218

660-646-2165
Fax: 660-646-6933 800-821-3028
www.midwestglove.com
Manufacturer and exporter of work, garden and sports protective gloves
Chairman of the Board: Stephen Franke
sfranke@midwestglove.com
Marketing Manager: Shirley Fisher
Sales Manager: Clark Carlton
Estimated Sales: $20-50 Million
Number Employees: 100-249
Brands:
Smart Hands
Wolverine

26159 Mid-Lands Chemical Company
1202 S 11th St
Omaha, NE 68108-3611

402-346-8352
Fax: 402-346-7694 800-642-5263
orders@midlandsci.com www.midlandsci.com
Manufacturer and exporter of ice packs
Account Manager: Brian Plautz
Operations Manager: Matt Sutej
Estimated Sales: $1-2,500,000
Number Employees: 10-19
Type of Packaging: Food Service, Private Label
Brands:
Polar Pack

26160 Mid-Southwest Marketing
3900 S Broadway
Edmond, OK 73013-4115

405-341-3962
Fax: 405-359-9043
Bubble gum dispensers; also, maintenance available
Manager: Teresa Brown
Estimated Sales: Less than $500,000
Number Employees: 1-4

26161 Mid-State Awning & Patio Co
113 Musser Ln
Bellefonte, PA 16823-9163

814-355-8979
Fax: 814-355-1405 tepawning@aol.com
www.midstateawning.com
Commercial awnings
President: Terry Phillips
tepawning@aol.com
Estimated Sales: $400,000
Number Employees: 5-9

26162 Mid-State Metal Casting& Mfg
2689 S 10th St
Fresno, CA 93725-2041

559-445-1974
Fax: 559-445-1320
Aluminum casters
President: Dave Pittman
Estimated Sales: Less Than $500,000
Number Employees: 1-4

26163 Mid-States Mfg & Engr Co Inc
509 E Maple St
PO Box 100
Milton, IA 52570-9636

641-656-4271
Fax: 641-656-4225 800-346-1792
www.mid-states1.com
Manufacturer and exporter of steel shipping containers, hand and platform trucks and nonpowered material handling equipment
Cio/Cto: Kevin Early
kevinearly@mid-states1.com
COO: Kevin Early
Purchasing Director: Suzie Lister
Estimated Sales: $5 Million
Number Employees: 20-49
Square Footage: 280000
Type of Packaging: Bulk

26164 Mid-West Wire Products
800 Woodward Hts
Ferndale, MI 48220-1488

248-548-3200
Fax: 248-542-7104 800-989-9881
schargo@midwestwire.com
Manufacturer and exporter of wire baskets and specialties including display, transporter and merchandising trays
President: Richard Geralds
VP: Steven Chargo
Vice President: Christopher Wozniacki
cwozniacki@midwestwires.com
VP Sales: Steven Chargo
VP Manufacturing: William Klein
Estimated Sales: $5 - 10 Million
Number Employees: 20-49

26165 Midbrook Inc
1300 Falahee Rd # 51
Jackson, MI 49203-4700

517-787-3481
Fax: 517-787-2349 800-966-9274
sales@midbrook.com
www.midbrookmetalfab.com
Manufacturer and exporter of washing, drying and wastewater treatment equipment
CEO: Mick Lutz
mlutz@midbrook.com
CEO: Mick Lutz
Manufacturing Manager: E Houghton
Estimated Sales: $20-50 Million
Number Employees: 100-249
Brands:
Hurricane Systems

26166 Midco Plastics
800 S Bluff St
Enterprise, KS 67441-9112

785-263-8999
Fax: 785-263-8231 800-235-2729
jjahn@midcoplastics.com
www.midcoplastics.com
Plastic bags, covers and linings including printed or plain
President: Mike Carney
General Manager/VP: Michael Carney
Treasurer: Jeff Jahn
Estimated Sales: $10-20 Million
Number Employees: 20-49
Square Footage: 54000

26167 Middleby Corp
1400 Toastmaster Dr
Elgin, IL 60120-9272

847-741-3300
sales@middleby.com
www.middleby.com
Manufacturer, importer and exporter of conveyor and convection ovens, ranges, fryers, toasters and steamers.
Chief Executive Officer: Timothy Fitzgerald
Chief Operating Officer: Devid Brewer
Corporate Treasurer: Martin Lindsay
Estimated Sales: #2.72 Billion
Number Employees: 5000-9999
Other Locations:
Middleby Corp.
Miramar FL
Brands:
Middlebe Marshal
Rofry
South Bend
Toast Master

26168 Middleby Marshall Inc
1400 Toastmaster Dr
Elgin, IL 60120-9272

847-741-3300
www.middmarshall.com
Manufacturer and exporter of high speed conveyor ovens for pizza, bagels, pretzels and full service restaurants; also, ranges, broilers, combi ovens, toasters, hot food warmers and steam equipment
President: John Kania
Year Founded: 1888
Estimated Sales: $50 - 75 Million
Number Employees: 100-249
Square Footage: 285000
Parent Co: Middleby Corporation
Type of Packaging: Food Service
Other Locations:
Middleby Marshall, CTX
Elgin IL
Brands:
Ctx
Middleby Marshall
Southbend
Toastmaster

26169 Middleton Printing & Label Co
200 32nd St SE # A
Grand Rapids, MI 49548-2269

616-247-8742
Fax: 616-247-1352 800-952-0076
www.gomiddleton.com
Pressure sensitive roll and sheet labels, tags, name plates, commerical printing, booklets, forms, custom laser labels, etc.
President: Blake Middleton
blake@gomiddleton.com
Estimated Sales: $1-3 Million
Number Employees: 5-9
Square Footage: 40000

26170 Middough Inc
1901 E 13th St # 300
Suite 400
Cleveland, OH 44114-3542

216-367-6000
Fax: 216-367-6020 contactus@middough.com
www.middough.com
Middough's full service, single-source organization, provides food processors and distributors with professionals versed in HACCP, FDA, GMP, AIB, BISSIC, USDA, 3A Dairy and cGMP, as well as state-of-the-art technology, sanitary andsafety design practices for civil, structural, mechanical, electrical and controls. Applicable products in the food industry includes that of commodities/ingredients; processed foods and beverages.
President/CEO: Ronald Ledin
VP: Paul W. Jahn
Business Development Director: James Bingham
Number Employees: 250-499

26171 Midland Manufacturing Co
101 E County Line Rd
Monroe, IA 50170-7950

641-259-2625
Fax: 641-259-3216 800-394-2625
marianne@midlandmfgco.com
www.midlandmfgco.com
Blow molded plastic containers
President: Terry Vriezelaar
terry@midlandmfgco.com
Vice President: Jeff Vriezelaar
Estimated Sales: $5 Million
Number Employees: 20-49
Square Footage: 100000

26172 Midland Research Labratories
851 N Martway Drive
Olathe, KS 66061-7053

913-888-0560
Fax: 913-492-7860
Boiler water and cooling water treatment, food process chemicals for prevention of can corrosion and spotting plus chlorine dioxide
President: John Opelka
R & D: James Rauh
Quality Control: Fred Hopkins
Estimated Sales: $5-10 Million
Number Employees: 10

26173 Midlands Packaging Corp
4641 N 56th St
Lincoln, NE 68504-1795

402-464-9124
Fax: 402-464-6720
midlandspkg@midlandspkg.com
www.midlandspkg.com
Folding cartons, corrugated containers, and thermoformed plastics.
President: Steven Warman
warmans@midlandspkg.com
Quality Assurance Manager: Pat Moser
Production Services Manager: Doug Smith
Plant Manager: Gary Riecke
Estimated Sales: $20-25 Million
Number Employees: 100-249
Square Footage: 235000

26174 Midmac Systems
590 Hale Ave N
Saint Paul, MN 55128

651-739-1700
Fax: 651-739-1777
Custom machinery, robotics, systems integration, automatic assembly
Contact: Larry Kopacek
midmac@midmac.net
Estimated Sales: $10-20 Million
Number Employees: 50-99

26175 Midvale Paper Box
19 Bailey St
Wilkes Barre, PA 18705-1907

570-824-3577
Fax: 570-824-4639 midvalebox@hotmail.com
www.midvalebox.com
Set-up and folding boxes including pizza boxes, bakery boxes, frozen food boxes, beer 6-packs and 4-packs. stadium trays and meat boxes
President: David Frank
dfrank@midvalebox.com
Estimated Sales: Below $5 Million
Number Employees: 20-49
Number of Products: 150
Square Footage: 200000

26176 Midwest Aircraft Products Co
125 S Mill St
Lexington, OH 44904-9571

419-884-2164
Fax: 419-884-2331 www.midwestaircraft.com
Manufacturer and exporter of food handling equipment including liquid containers, ice drawers, oven racks and beverage drawers and carts for airline food services
Owner: Jerry Miller
j.miller@midwestaircraft.com
CFO: Gayle Gorman Freeman
Engineering Manager: Matt Marles
CEO: Gayle Gorman Freeman
Sales: Richard Baker
Manufacturing: Lee Craii
Production: Gene Wheitner
Purchasing Manager: Chuck Kumisarek
Estimated Sales: $10 - 20 Million
Number Employees: 10-19
Square Footage: 26000

26177 Midwest Badge & NoveltyCo
3337 Republic Ave
Minneapolis, MN 55426-4108

952-927-9901
Fax: 952-927-9903
Manufacturer, importer and wholesaler/distributor of name badges, buttons and advertising specialties
President: Kevin Saba
kevin.saba@mgincentives.com
Estimated Sales: Less than $500,000
Number Employees: 1-4
Square Footage: 16000
Type of Packaging: Consumer, Private Label, Bulk

26178 Midwest Box Co
9801 Walford Ave # C
Suite C
Cleveland, OH 44102-4788

216-281-3980
Fax: 216-281-5707 www.midwestboxco.com
Corrugated containers
Owner: Suzy Remer
Manager: Susie Remer
susie@midwestboxco.com
Estimated Sales: $10 - 20 Million
Number Employees: 20-49

26179 Midwest Fibre Products Inc
2819 95th Ave
Viola, IL 61486-9527

309-596-2955
Fax: 309-596-2901
Boxes including corrugated and folding
Owner: Domenico Dulio
Estimated Sales: $5-10 Million
Number Employees: 20-49

26180 Midwest Folding Products
1414 S Western Ave
Chicago, IL 60608

312-666-3366
Fax: 312-666-2606 800-344-2864
sales@midwestfolding.com
www.midwestfolding.com
Banquet and meeting room tables in lighweight plastic, steel edge plywood and high-pressure plastic laminate with plywood core tops. Comfort Leg meeting room tables afford your guests unobstructed knee space and increase seatingcapacity, dual-height cocktail tables, table storage and handling systems are also available
CEO: Darryl Rossen
CFO: Len Farrell
Vice President: Chuck Pineau
Marketing Director: Ken Hufstater
Sales Director: Bob Bishop
Plant Manager: Sam Thomas
Purchasing Manager: Oscar Ortiz
Estimated Sales: $35 Million
Number Employees: 100-249
Number of Brands: 1
Square Footage: 200000
Type of Packaging: Bulk
Brands:
Midwest

26181 Midwest Foodservice News
2736 Sawbury Boulevard
Columbus, OH 43235-4579

614-336-0710
Fax: 614-336-0713
A regional food service publication with more than 28,000 readers in Ohio, Michigan, Indiana, Kentucky, Pennsylvania, and West Virginia

26182 Midwest Industrial Packaging
PO Box 1927
Spartanburg, SC 29304-1927

864-503-2200
Fax: 864-503-2430 800-910-5592
millichem@milliken.com
www.millikenchemical.com
Packaging tools
President: Thomas J Malone
Estimated Sales: $5-10 Million
Number Employees: 50

26183 Midwest Juice
3993 Roger B Chaffee Mem SE #F
Suite F
Grand Rapids, MI 49548-3404

616-774-6832
Fax: 616-774-0373 877-265-8243
info@midwestjuice.com www.midwestjuice.com
Beverages, coffee dispensers, aseptic portion cups
President: Mike Luhn
Owner: Noel Luhn
Number Employees: 5-9
Type of Packaging: Food Service, Private Label, Bulk
Brands:
Triarc Beverages
Veryfine

26184 Midwest Laboratories
13611 B St
Omaha, NE 68144-3693

402-334-7770
Fax: 402-334-9121 info@midwestlabs.com
www.midwestlabs.com
Consultant specializing in sanitation, analysis and testing services
President: Ken Pohlman
Estimated Sales: $500,000-$1 Million
Number Employees: 100-249

26185 Midwest Laboratories
13611 B St
Omaha, NE 68144-3693

402-334-7770
Fax: 402-334-9121 getinfo@midwestlabs.com
www.midwestlabs.com
Laboratory specializing in the testing of food and agricultural products; also complete nutritional labeling, environmental and microbiological services available
CEO: Ken Pohlman
Finance Ex: Laura Honeycutt
Quality Control: Jerry King
Marketing: Brent Pohlman
Estimated Sales: $5-10 Million
Number Employees: 100-249
Square Footage: 130000

26186 Midwest Metalcraft & Equipment
200 Industrial Dr
Windsor, MO 65360

660-647-3167
Fax: 660-647-5580 800-647-3167
sales@4mmc.com www.4mmc.com
Stainless steel food processing equipment including vats, hoppers, screw conveyors, dumpers, mixers, blenders, liquid chilling systems, bel conveyors, spiral ham slicers an multi-blade band saw.
President: Dennis Brown
Contact: Ed Barnhart
ebarnhart@4mmc.com
General Manager: Jay Warren
Production Manager: Alan Cooper
Estimated Sales: $5-10 Million
Number Employees: 20-49
Number of Brands: 1
Number of Products: 10
Square Footage: 56000

26187 Midwest Paper Products Company
1237 S 11th St
Louisville, KY 40210

502-636-2741
Corrugated boxes
Sales Manager: Woody Heckenkomp
Estimated Sales: $20-50 Million
Number Employees: 20-49
Square Footage: 50000

26188 Midwest Paper Tube & CanCorporation
2800 S 163rd St
New Berlin, WI 53151

262-782-7300
Fax: 262-782-7330
Paper cans and tubes
Owner: Ron Karani
CFO/QC: Sharon Mahoney
Estimated Sales: $5 - 10 Million
Number Employees: 10-19

26189 Midwest Promotional Group
2011 S Frontage Rd
Summit, IL 60527

708-563-0600
Fax: 708-563-0603 800-305-3388
sales@midwestgrp.com www.midwestgrp.com
Manufacturer and wholesaler/distributor of advertising calendars, embroidered aprons, uniforms, shirts, etc.; also, silk screening available
President: David Lewandowski
CEO: Don Lewandowski
VP: Keith Vacey
Chairman: Don Lewandowski
Sales Director: Rick Dignault
Operations Manager: Roger Wilson
Accounting Executive: Jeff Feichtinger
Estimated Sales: $5-10 Million
Number Employees: 50-99
Square Footage: 33000

26190 (HQ)Midwest Rubber Svc & Supply
14307 28th Pl N
Minneapolis, MN 55447-4867

763-559-2551
Fax: 763-559-4429 800-537-7457
Standard conveyor belts, cleated flexible vanner edges, center guides and die cut rubber collapsible containers; also, custom fabrication, design and field vulcanizing available
Owner: Kathy Kroah
Cio/Cto: John Briesch
jbriesch@midwestrubber.com
Inside Sales Manager: Dave Newell
Purchasing Agent: Todd Winn
Estimated Sales: $300,000-500,000
Number Employees: 20-49
Square Footage: 120000

26191 Midwest Stainless
408 3M Drive NE Suite B
Menomonie, WI 54751

715-235-5472
Fax: 715-235-5484
Manufacturer and exporter of dairy tanks, CIP systems, heat exchangers, cheese presses, pumps, valves, fittings and complete turn-key process systems for the food, dairy and biotechnical industries
President : Joe Maxfield
VP & General Manager: Josh Hoover
Sales Engineer: Tim Jenneman
Operations Manager : Rob Hesse
Estimated Sales: $10-20 Million
Number Employees: 20-49
Square Footage: 38000

26192 Midwest Wire Products LLC
649 S Lansing Ave
Sturgeon Bay, WI 54235-2853

920-743-6591
Fax: 920-743-3777 800-445-0225
mwp@wireforming.com www.wireforming.com
Wire forms, grills, racks, shelves, baskets, etc.; contact services available
President: Eric Vollrath
CFO: Judy Weber
HR Executive: Sally Beisner
mwp@wireforming.com
Engineering: John Buhk
Quality Control: Wendy Woodgate
Marketing/Sales: Dirk Huenink
Production Manager: Mike Noble
Plant Manager: Steve Culver
Purchasing Manager: Judy Weber
Estimated Sales: $7 Million
Number Employees: 50-99
Square Footage: 170000

26193 Midwest Wire Specialties
4545 W Cortland St
Chicago, IL 60639-5104

773-292-6300
Fax: 773-292-6304 800-238-0228
info@midwestwirechicago.com
www.midwestwirechicago.com
Custom point of purchase displays, material handling and filter baskets, guards, wire forms, oven racks and smoke sticks
President: Chris Sitkiewicz
Plant Manager: Charles Schlismann
Estimated Sales: $50-100 Million
Number Employees: 20-49
Square Footage: 55000

26194 Midwestern Bulk Bag
3230 Monroe St
Toledo, OH 43606-4519

419-241-3112
Fax: 419-241-0080 800-448-6494
New and reconditioned bulk bags, standard and custom made containment racks , polyethylene bags
CEO: Tony O'Neal
VP: Paula Lalor
Production Manager: T King
Estimated Sales: $2.5-5 Million
Number Employees: 5-9
Square Footage: 45000

26195 Midwestern Industries Inc
915 Oberlin Ave SW
Massillon, OH 44647-7661

330-837-4203
Fax: 330-837-4210 info@midwesternind.com
www.midwesternind.com
Round and rectangular vibrating screening equipment, replacements parts and screens, electric screen heating products for rectangular vibrating machines
President: Barb Sylvester
info@midwesternind.com
Estimated Sales: $10 - 20 Million
Number Employees: 50-99

26196 Mies Products
505 Commerce St
West Bend, WI 53090-1698

262-338-0676
Fax: 262-338-1244 800-480-6437
info@miesproducts.com www.miesproducts.com
Processor and exporter of breading for chicken, fish, meats and vegetables; also, holding and display warmers and electric pressure fryers and filter machines for fats and oils
President: Mike Mies
VP: Mike Mies
Sales: Mark Mey
Purchasing Director: Ed Casey
Estimated Sales: $3 - 5 Million
Number Employees: 10-19
Number of Brands: 1
Number of Products: 10
Square Footage: 135040
Type of Packaging: Food Service, Private Label
Brands:
　Karbonaid Xx
　Mies

26197 Migali Industries
516 Lansdowne Ave
Camden, NJ 08104-1198

856-963-3600
Fax: 856-963-3604 800-852-5292
contact@migali.com www.migali.com
Manufactures a complete line of G3 reach-in refrigerators and freezers, glass door merchandisers, sandwich tables, pizza preparation tables, and beer equipment. Also distributes Brema Ice Cream Makers, high quality machines inclusingundercounter and modular cubes and flakers.
President: Ernest Migali
Estimated Sales: $5-10 Million
Number Employees: 20-49

26198 Migatron Corp
935 Dieckman St # A
Suite A
Woodstock, IL 60098-9203

815-338-5800
Fax: 815-338-5803 888-644-2876
info@migatron.com www.migatron.com
Manufacturer, exporter and importer of ultrasonic sensors
President: Frank Wroga
info@migatron.com
Estimated Sales: $2.5 - 5 Million
Number Employees: 10-19
Brands:
　Tubular Sonics

26199 Mikasa Hotelware
1 Mikasa Drive
Secaucus, NJ 07094-2581

201-867-9210
Fax: 201-867-2385 866-645-2721
gwen_opfell@mikasa.com www.mikasa.com
Manufacturer, exporter and importer of china, dinnerware and crystal
VP: Neil Orzeck
Contact: John Beaupre
jbeaupre@mikasa.com
Number Employees: 100-249

26200 Miken Cosmpanies
PO Box 178
Buffalo, NY 14231-0178

716-668-6311
Fax: 716-668-7630
Packaging machinery including pressure sensitive label, adhesive coating, die cutting and foil stamping
President: Michael Bolas
President: M Bolas
Estimated Sales: $20 - 50 Million
Number Employees: 100-249
Other Locations:
　Miken Cos.
　Buffalo NY

26201 Mil-Du-Gas Company/StarBrite
4041 SW 47th Ave
Fort Lauderdale, FL 33314-4031

954-587-6280
Fax: 954-587-2813 800-327-8583
peter@starbrite.com www.starbrite.com
Manufacturer and exporter of mildew preventers with air fresheners and maintenance and cleaning chemicals

CEO: Peter Dornau
CFO: Jeff Barocas
Executive Vice President: Gregor Dornau
Vice President, Technology: Justin Gould
VP of Marketing / Art Dept & Literature: Bill Lindsey
Senior Vice President, Sales: Marc Emmi
Vice President, Sales: Dennis Torok
Vice President, Operations/Manufacturing: Will Dudman
Number Employees: 20-49
Square Footage: 560000
Parent Co: Ocean Bio-Chem
Other Locations:
 Mil-Du-Gas Co./Star Brite
 Montgomery AL
Brands:
 Extend-A-Brush
 M-D-G Formula-2
 Star Brite

26202 Milan Box Corporation
2090 West Van Hook Street
P.O. Box 30
Milan, TN 38358

731-686-3338
Fax: 731-686-3330 800-225-8057
andrew@milanbox.com www.milanbox.com
Plywood pallet boxes, crates and wirebound and wooden boxes; exporter of wirebound boxes
President: Franklin Dedmon
 franklin@milanbox.com
Finance Manager: Donna Hardy
VP: Andrew Dedmon
President/Head Sales/Marketing: Franklin Dedmon
Head of Operations: Freddy McCartney
Head of Production: Rudy Graves
Estimated Sales: $10 - 20 Million
Number Employees: 50-99
Brands:
 Mylanbox Ibc

26203 Milburn Company
520 Bellevue Street
Detroit, MI 48207-3733

313-259-3410
Fax: 313-259-3415
Manufacturer and exporter of soap and soap dispensers, manufacturing, skincreams and lotions
VP/Marketing: Frank Newman
Estimated Sales: Less than $500,000
Number Employees: 1-4
Square Footage: 20000
Brands:
 Ply Skin Cream

26204 Mile Hi Express
1335 40th St
Denver, CO 80205-3310

303-296-8465
Fax: 303-296-8468 800-332-2064
www.milehiexpress.com
President: Brit Schabacker
 dispatch@milehiexpress.com
Comptroller/Operations: Diana Troute
Estimated Sales: $3 - 5 Million
Number Employees: 10-19

26205 Miles Willard Technologies
655 W Sunnyside Rd
Idaho Falls, ID 83402-4707

208-523-4741
Fax: 208-529-8236 mwt@snackteam.com
www.snackteam.com
Research and development consultant for snack foods and potato processing
Managing Partner: Randy Kern
Research Manager: Veldon Hix
Estimated Sales: $10-20 Million
Number Employees: 10-19
Square Footage: 60000

26206 Military Club & Hospitality
825 Old Country Rd
Westbury, NY 11590-5501

516-334-3030
Fax: 516-334-3059 ebm-mail@ebmpubs.com
www.ebmpubs.com
President: Murry Greenwald
Estimated Sales: $10 - 20 Million
Number Employees: 1-4

26207 Miljoco Corp
200 Elizabeth St
Mt Clemens, MI 48043-1643

586-777-4280
Fax: 586-777-7891 888-888-1498
www.miljoco.com
Manufacturers standard and custom thermometers.
President: Howard M Trerice
 htrerice@miljoco.com
Reaserch Development: Heath Trerice
Quality Control: Bruce Trerice
Marketing: Mike Mroz
Sales: Tom Adams
Public Relations: Mike Mroz
Plant Manager: Alex Jakob
Purchasing: Kimberly Trerice
Estimated Sales: $10-20 Million
Number Employees: 20-49
Square Footage: 94000
Brands:
 Miljoco

26208 Mill Engineering & Machinery Company
727 66th Avenue
Oakland, CA 94621-3713

510-562-1832
Barley grain roller mills
Estimated Sales: $500,000-$1 Million
Number Employees: 4

26209 Mill Equipment Co Inc
124 S Dodge St # 3
Burlington, WI 53105-1900

262-763-9101
Fax: 262-763-9102 800-551-9101
skippercad@aol.com www.milleqp.com
Bins: bulk storage, hoppers; bulk handling systems: conveying, conveyor accessories, conveyor componenets, conveyors, feeder belts
Estimated Sales: $500,000-$1 Million
Number Employees: 1-4

26210 Mill Wiping Rags Inc
1656 E 233rd St
Bronx, NY 10466-3306

718-994-7100
Fax: 718-994-1973 ragmaster67@optonline.net
www.millwipingrags.com
Manufacturer and exporter of wiping rags, cheesecloth and paper wipes, bar towels
President: F Scifo
 millrags@optimaline.net
Quality Control: A Pimento
Marketing Director: Eric Saltzman
Sales Director: Eric Saltzman
Plant Manager: F Scifo
Purchasing Manager: Eric Saltzman
Estimated Sales: $2 Million
Number Employees: 50-99
Number of Brands: 3
Number of Products: 100
Parent Co: D. Benedetto
Type of Packaging: Private Label, Bulk

26211 Mill-Rose Co
7995 Tyler Blvd
Mentor, OH 44060-4896

440-946-5727
Fax: 440-255-5039 800-321-3598
www.millrose.com
Manufacturer and exporter of grill and basting brushes
President: Paul Miller
 millrose@en.com
CFO: Vincent Pona
Sales Manager: Gregory Miller
Purchasing Manager: Susan Stallknict
Estimated Sales: $20 Million
Number Employees: 100-249
Brands:
 Clean Fit

26212 Millard Manufacturing Corp
10602 Olive St
La Vista, NE 68128-2993

402-331-8010
Fax: 402-331-0909 800-662-4263
sales@millardmfg.com www.millardmfg.com
Conveyors and food processing equipment for canners, poultry and frozen food processors; also, walk surfaces available

Vice President: Mike Price
 mprice@millardmfg.com
VP: Mike Price
VP Administration: Mike Price
VP Sales: Harold Ellis
Purchasing Agent: Lynn Hedell
Estimated Sales: $5 - 10 Million
Number Employees: 50-99
Square Footage: 130000
Brands:
 Optigrip

26213 Millenia Industries Corp
PO Box 953909
Lake Mary, FL 32795-3909

407-804-1193
Fax: 407-804-1934
Manager: Frank Benevento
 beneventofrank@milleniahope.com
Estimated Sales: Less Than $500,000
Number Employees: 1-4

26214 Miller Group Multiplex
1610 Design Way
Dupo, IL 62239-1826

636-343-5700
Fax: 618-286-6202 800-325-3350
info@miller-group.com www.otpracks.com
Manufacturer and exporter of store fixtures and display systems including point of purchase
President: Randy Castle
CFO: Roger Lovejoy
Director Marketing: Tony Evans
Marketing: Catherine Lafarth
Marketing Services: Cathy Berding
Estimated Sales: $10 - 20 Million
Number Employees: 20-49
Square Footage: 80000
Parent Co: Miller Multiplex
Brands:
 Multiplex

26215 Miller Hofft Brands
PO Box 1323
Indianapolis, IN 46206-1323

317-638-6576
Fax: 317-638-9438
Conveying systems, bulk material bins, hoppers and screw conveyors
President: James Kuester
Estimated Sales: $1 - 5,000,000

26216 Miller Manufacturing Co
2032 Divanian Dr
Turlock, CA 95382-9501

209-632-3846
Fax: 209-632-1369 miller@thevision.net
www.miller-mfg.com
Recycling machines
President: Richard Veeck
R&D: George Lazich
Estimated Sales: Below $5 Million
Number Employees: 5-9

26217 Miller Metal Fabrication
16356 Sussex Hwy # 2
Bridgeville, DE 19933-3056

302-337-2291
Fax: 302-337-2290 www.millermetal.com
U.S.D.A. approved conveyors, poultry chill tanks and hand carts; also, parts available
Owner: Marty Miller
 marty@millermetal.com
VP: H Thompson
Estimated Sales: $5 Million
Number Employees: 20-49

26218 (HQ)Miller Studio
734 Fair Ave NW
PO Box 997
New Philadelphia, OH 44663-1589

330-339-1100
Fax: 330-339-4379 800-332-0050
www.miller-studio.com
Manufacturer and exporter of pressure sensitive double-coated tape for decorative trim, mounting, fastening, etc.; also, adhesive systems
President: John Basiletti
Purchasing Manager: Tina Schlemmer
Sales: Mark Gazdik
Estimated Sales: $5 - 10 Million
Number Employees: 50-99
Type of Packaging: Consumer

Brands:
   Magic-Mounts

26219 Miller Technical Svc
47801 W Anchor Ct
Plymouth, MI 48170-6018

734-414-1769
Fax: 734-738-1975 millerstec@cs.com
www.nextmobilitynow.com
Manufacturer and exporter of rebuilt and used packaging and food processing equipment; also, machinery parts; repair and rebuilding services available
President: James Miller
CEO: Patrick Miller
   pmiller@mtsmedicalmfg.com
Estimated Sales: $.5 - 1 million
Number Employees: 20-49
Square Footage: 6000
Type of Packaging: Food Service

26220 Millerbernd Systems
330 6th St S
P.O. Box 37
Winsted, MN 55395-1102

320-485-2685
Fax: 320-485-3900
Design, manufacture and install processing equipment for the dairy and cheese industries such as pasteurization and heat transfer units, controls and automation systems, agitating tanks, batching/blending and barrel handlingsystems.
President: Brad Millerbernd
   bmillerbernd@millerbernd.com
VP: Terry Voight
National Sales Manager: Lisa Stanger
Product Manager: Frank Bruggman
Purchasing: Sam Zimmerman
Number Employees: 100-249

26221 Millhiser
1125 Commerce Road
Richmond, VA 23224-7505

804-233-9886
Fax: 804-233-1931 800-446-2247
Plastic and cloth bags
President: Willard Foster
VP Sales/Marketing: James Bledsoe
Estimated Sales: $10-20,000,000
Number Employees: 100-249

26222 Milligan & Higgins
PO Box 506
Johnstown, NY 12095

518-762-4638
Fax: 518-762-7039 info@milligan1868.com
www.milligan1868.com
Manufacturer, importer and exporter of kosher edible and technical gelatins.
Year Founded: 1868
Parent Co: Hudson Industries Corporation
Type of Packaging: Bulk

26223 Milliken & Co
P.O. Box 1926
Spartanburg, SC 29304

864-503-2020
brand@milliken.com
www.milliken.com
Aprons, table cloths and skirting and place mats.
Chief Executive Officer: J. Harold Chandler
Year Founded: 1865
Number Employees: 7,000
Brands:
   Ambassador
   Embassy
   Visa

26224 Milltronics
734 W North Carrier Pkwy
Grand Prairie, TX 75050-1001

817-277-3543
Fax: 817-277-3894 www.milltronics.com
Wine industry measuring devices
Estimated Sales: $10-20 Million
Number Employees: 50-99

26225 Millwood Inc
3708 International Blvd
Vienna, OH 44473-9796

330-393-4400
Fax: 330-393-4401 lwilliamson@citynet.net
www.millwoodinc.com
Pallets and industrial blockings

President: Keith Ainsley
   kainsley@millwoodinc.com
CEO: Larry Supple
CPA/Controller: Mark Price
Estimated Sales: $5 - 10 Million
Number Employees: 20-49

26226 Milprint
PO Box 2968
Oshkosh, WI 54903-2968

920-303-8600
Fax: 920-303-8610
Printed flexible packaging materials for the confectionery industry, including coatings, laminations, films and adhesives for foil, cellophane, glassine and paper
President: Robert Hawthorne
Alliance Manager: Karen Cverko
CFO: Stephanie Rucinski
Quality Control: Dennis Howard
Marketing Manager: Mike Miller
Contact: Dan Kearny
   d.kearny@milprint.com
Estimated Sales: $10-20 Million
Number Employees: 10
Parent Co: Bemis Company

26227 Milsek Furniture PolishInc.
5525 E Pine Lake Rd
North Lima, OH 44452

330-542-2700
Fax: 330-542-1059 www.milsek.com
Manufacturer, exporter and wholesaler/distributor of furniture polish and cleaner
President: Jean Hamilton
VP: Susan Bender
Estimated Sales: Under $1 Million
Number Employees: 5-9
Number of Brands: 1
Number of Products: 2
Square Footage: 108000
Brands:
   Milsek

26228 Miltenberg & Samton
4 High Street
Suite 7
Stamford, CT 06902-4923

203-834-0002
Fax: 203-321-1348
High speed flow wrapper, confectionery wrapping machinery, extruders and cooling tunnels for cut and wrap products, complete infeed and discharge systems, flexible packaging films
President: Ronald Kehle
Estimated Sales: $3 - 5 Million
Number Employees: 8
Square Footage: 200

26229 Milton A. Klein Company
PO Box 363
New York, NY 10021-0006

516-829-3400
Fax: 516-829-3427 800-221-0248
President: Irene Klein
VP: Allen Klein
Number Employees: 15
Square Footage: 6800

26230 Milton Can Company
PO Box 1100
Elizabeth, NJ 07207-1100

908-289-8100
Fax: 908-355-2397
Tea and coffee cans, papers (electrolytic)
Estimated Sales: $25-50 Million
Number Employees: 70

26231 Milvan Food Equipment Manufacturing
Units #1-3
Rexdale, ON M9W 5S5
Canada

416-674-3456
Fax: 416-674-2386
Commerical kitchen equipment including tables, exhaust canopies and back bars
President: Rocco Mazziotta
Number Employees: 10

26232 Milwaukee Dustless Brush Co
1632 Hobbs Dr
Delavan, WI 53115-2029

323-724-7777
Fax: 323-724-1111 sales@milwaukeedustless.com
www.milwaukeedustless.com
Manufacturer, importer and exporter of floor brushes, squeegees, sponge mops, utility brushes and related janitorial maintenance tools
National Sales Manager: Jeff Feder
Estimated Sales: $5-10 Million
Number Employees: 50-99
Brands:
   Speed Squeegy
   Speed Sweep
   Speedy Mop

26233 Milwaukee Sign Company
2076 1st Ave
Grafton, WI 53024

262-375-5740
Fax: 262-376-1686
Manufacturer and exporter of internally illuminated signs and menu systems
President: Kevin Sutherby
R&D: Rick Richards
Contact: Nancy Stansy
   rcarlson@kdhe.state.ks.us
Estimated Sales: $20 - 30 Million
Number Employees: 100-249
Type of Packaging: Food Service, Bulk

26234 Milwaukee Tool & MachineCompany
PO Box 94
Okauchee, WI 53069-0094

262-821-0160
Fax: 262-821-0162 mtmco@execpc.com
Manufacturer and exporter of packaging machinery
President: Richard Mumper
VP: Ralph Mumper
Estimated Sales: $5-10 Million
Number Employees: 10

26235 Mimi et Cie
P.O. Box 80157
Seattle, WA 98108-0157

206-545-1850
Fax: 800-284-3834 www.mimietcie.com
Manufacturer, importer and exporter of decorative packaging including shrink and printed basket wrap and food bags for cookies, candy, etc. Also waxed tissue paper, food containers and custom products including bags, totes andribbons
President: Mark Revere
Estimated Sales: $1-2.5 Million
Number Employees: 50-99
Square Footage: 80000
Type of Packaging: Consumer, Food Service, Private Label, Bulk
Brands:
   Bagskets
   Blooming Bags
   Goodie Bags
   Shimmer

26236 Minarik Corporation
905 East Thompson Avenue
Glendale, CA 91201

800-646-2745
Fax: 800-394-6334 888-646-2745
Contact: Adam Abrahamson
   adam.abrahamson@minarik.com
Parent Co: Kaman Corporation

26237 Mince Master
6530 W Dakin St
Chicago, IL 60634-2412

773-282-0722
Fax: 773-282-9744 888-646-2362
tech@mincemaster.com www.mincemaster.com
Emulsifiers, accessories, grinder plates and knives
Owner: Mike Mihailovic
Estimated Sales: $1 - 3 Million
Number Employees: 10-19

26238 Minges Printing & Advg Specs
323 S Chestnut St
Gastonia, NC 28054-4542

704-867-6791
Fax: 704-867-3596 mingesco@belsouth.net
www.mingesprinting.com
Advertising specialties

President: Gene Minges Sr
sedcbfox@aol.com
Estimated Sales: $500,000 - $1 Million
Number Employees: 5-9
Square Footage: 12000

26239 Mini-Bag Company
83 Rome Street
Farmingdale, NY 11735-6699
631-694-3325
FDA approved polyethylene and plastic bags
Estimated Sales: $1-2.5 Million
Number Employees: 4

26240 Minipack
1832 N Glassell Street
Orange, CA 92865
714-283-4200
Fax: 714-283-4268 minipack@spm.it
www.minipack-america.com
Owner: Joe Sielski
Member: Joseph Sielski
Estimated Sales: $1 - 3 Million
Number Employees: 5-9

26241 Minners DesignsInc.
7 W 34th St
Suite 929
New York, NY 10001
212-688-7441
Fax: 212-980-6309 www.minners.com
Glassware and chinaware for the food service market
President: Maureen K Cole
Director Sales: Bernard Durkin
Director Purchasing: Maureen Cole
Estimated Sales: $1 - 2.5 Million
Number Employees: 5-9

26242 Minnesota Automation
975 3rd St SW
Crosby, MN 56441
218-546-2222
Fax: 218-546-2104 888-800-6861
Packaging machinery, pick and place machines
Manager: Greg Mangan
Marketing/Sales: Ken Campbell
Contact: Stephen Humphrey
sales@graphicpkg.com
Plant Manager: Greg Maegan
Estimated Sales: $25-50 Million
Number Employees: 100-249
Parent Co: Riverwood International Corporation
Brands:
Minnesota Automation

26243 Minnesota Valley Testing Lab
1126 N Front St
New Ulm, MN 56073-1176
507-354-8517
Fax: 507-359-2890 800-782-3557
crc@mvtl.com www.mvtl.com
Turnkey liquid nitrogen systems
Owner/CEO/President: Thomas R Berg
CEO: Tom Berg
tberg@mvtl.com
Marketing: Rob TRUE
Sales: John Gray
Estimated Sales: $10-20 Million
Number Employees: 100-249
Square Footage: 78000

26244 Minnesuing Acres
8084 South Minnesuing Acres Drive
Lake Nebagamon, WI 54849
715-374-2262
Fax: 715-374-2118 jpolinsky@radisson.com
www.minnesuingacres.com
Consultant providing loyalty reward programs including electronic card and data based marketing, trading stamps, controlled markdowns, sweepstakes and related services
General Manager: Jim Polinsky
CFO: Tim Hennessy
VP/General Manager: Steve Aase
Director Marketing: Curt Lund
National Sales Manager: Brent Christiansen
Contact: Gregg Basset
gbasset@minnesuingacres.com
Estimated Sales: $3 - 5 Million
Number Employees: 20-49

26245 Minsa Southwest Corp
Hwy 84 E
Muleshoe, TX 79347
806-272-5545
Fax: 806-272-5135
Products for preparation of hot rack table tortillas, fresh or refrigerated, frozen tortilla or enchilada, hand feed tacos, in-line tacos and tortilla chips, extruded corn chips, tamales, and taquitos and/or enchiladas
President: Raul Ayala
raul.ayala@minsa.com
President: Jorge Arturo
CFO: Teresa Sitz
R&D: Jim Barne
Quality Control: Veronica Arroyo
Customer Service Head: Gina Smith
Estimated Sales: $5 - 10 Million
Number Employees: 50-99

26246 Minuteman Power Boss
175 Anderson St
Aberdeen, NC 28315
314-283-7304
Fax: 910-944-7409 800-323-9420
info@minutemanintl.com www.powerboss.com
Manufacturer and exporter of power sweepers and scrubbers
President: Greg Rau
VP: Gregory Rau
Advertising Manager: Krista Harris
Estimated Sales: $5 - 10 Million
Number Employees: 100-249
Square Footage: 200000
Parent Co: Minuteman International
Other Locations:
Minuteman PowerBoss
Villa Park IL
Brands:
Armadillo
Badger
Otter
Prowler

26247 Minuteman Power Box Inc
175 Anderson Street
Aberdeen, NC 800-323-94
910-944-2105
Fax: 910-944-7409 info@minutemanintl.com
www.powerboss.com
CEO: Greg Rau
Number Employees: 100-249

26248 Mione Manufacturing Company
51 Democrat Rd
Mickleton, NJ 8056
856-423-1374
Fax: 856-423-6522 800-257-0497
Industrial and consumer use hand soap and laundry detergent
Manager: Benny Sorbello
Estimated Sales: $500,000-$1 Million
Number Employees: 1-4
Square Footage: 24000
Brands:
Mione W P-1

26249 Miracle Exclusives
PO Box 2508
Danbury, CT 06813-2508
203-796-5493
Fax: 203-648-4871 info@miracleexclusives.com
www.miracleexclusives.com
Home applicance pressure cooker
Vice President: Burn Wick
Estimated Sales: $500,000-$1 Million
Number Employees: 5

26250 Miroil
602 Tacoma St
Allentown, PA 18109-8103
610-437-4618
Fax: 610-437-3377 800-523-9844
hgos1946@gmail.com www.miroil.com
Manufacturer and exporter of frying oil stabilizer, filter aids and clean and reusable filters for fryers; also, testing for polar and alkaline contaminants
President: Bernard Friedman
Manager: J Wessner
Contact: Bernard Firedman
bfiredman@miroil.com
Estimated Sales: $5 - 10 Million
Number Employees: 1-4
Square Footage: 140000

Brands:
Ez Flow
Frypowder
Miroil

26251 Miron Construction Co.
1471 McMahon Dr.
Neenah, WI 54956
920-969-7000
Fax: 920-969-7393
business.development@miron-construction.com
www.miron-construction.com
Pre-construction, construction management, design-build, general construction and industrial services to numerous markets, including the food processing industry.
President/CEO: David Voss

Vice President/COO: Tim Kippenhan
Secretary/Treasurer/CFO: Dean Basten
Year Founded: 1918
Estimated Sales: $500 Million
Number Employees: 1,500+
Square Footage: 112000

26252 Mirro Company
1115 W 5th Ave
Lancaster, OH 43130
800-848-7200
Fax: 920-684-1929
Cookware, bakeware, tools and gadgets
Owner: Dave Moore
Estimated Sales: $1 - 5 Million
Number Employees: 1-4
Parent Co: Newell Companies
Type of Packaging: Food Service
Brands:
Mirro Foley
Rema
Wearever

26253 Mirro Products Company
PO Box 2243
High Point, NC 27261
336-885-4166
Fax: 336-885-1066
Plastic displays, vacuum-formed snack racks, plastic and electric signs
President: David Horney
Estimated Sales: $5 - 10 Million
Number Employees: 10-19

26254 Mirror Tech Mfg Co Inc
286 Nepperhan Ave
Yonkers, NY 10701-3403
914-423-1600
Fax: 914-423-1667 mirrortech@verizon.net
www.mirror-tech.com
Glass, metal and acrylic observation convex mirrors
President: Richard Cleary
mirrortech@verizon.net
Treasurer and CFO: D Barnett
Quality Control: Frank Serine
Estimated Sales: Below $5 Million
Number Employees: 20-49
Square Footage: 28000

26255 Mission Laboratories
2433 Birkdale St
Los Angeles, CA 90031
323-223-1405
Fax: 323-223-9968 888-201-8866
srose@missionlabs.net www.missionlabs.net
Commercial and household cleaning and sanitary supplies including floor finish and strippers, carpet cleaners, disinfectants, hand soaps, heavy duty cleaners/degreasers, sweeping compounds, etc. Supplier to the food industry andsuppliers to food service
President: Robert Rosenbaum
CFO: Robert Rosenbaum
Quality Control: David Schultz
Executive VP Sales/Marketing: Jim Ryan
Contact: Margarita Arzate
m.arzate@missionlabs.net
Estimated Sales: $20 - 50 Million
Number Employees: 20-49
Square Footage: 75000
Type of Packaging: Consumer, Food Service, Private Label, Bulk

26256 Missouri Equipment
2222 N 9th St
St Louis, MO 63102-1412
314-621-0144
Fax: 314-621-4170 800-727-6326
meco2222@sbcglobal.net
Sink tops, counters and tables
President: Gregory Klapp
VP: C Klapp
Estimated Sales: $5 Million
Number Employees: 20-49
Square Footage: 120000

26257 Missouri Grocers Assn
315 N Ken Ave
Springfield, MO 65802-6213
417-831-6662
Fax: 417-831-3907 www.missourigrocers.com
A non-profit, state-wide organization representing retailers, wholesalers, distributors, brokers, suppliers, vendors and manufacturters that formulate the grocery industry in the State of Missouri.
State Director: Dan Shaul
Estimated Sales: $5-10 Million
Number Employees: 5-9

26258 Mister Label, Inc
PO Box 326
Bluffton, SC 29910
843-815-2222
Fax: 843-815-5488 800-732-0439
misterlabel@msn.com www.misterlabel.com
Manufacturer and exporter of labels including pressure sensitive, heat seal, gummed, tyvek and tag-stock
President: Todd Elliot
Chief Operating Officer: Kelly Elliot
Estimated Sales: $5-10 Million
Number Employees: 11
Square Footage: 30000
Type of Packaging: Food Service, Private Label, Bulk

26259 Mitec
2445 Meadowbrook Pkwy
Duluth, GA 30096-4636
770-813-5959
Fax: 770-813-1818 888-854-1851
www.mitec.com
Manufacturers of insulated metal panels for commercial, industrial and cold storage buildings.
President: Bryan A. Shaver
bshaver@mitecnet.com
Estimated Sales: $1 - 5 Million
Number Employees: 100-249

26260 Mitsubishi Caterpillar Mcfa
2121 W Sam Houston Pkwy N
Houston, TX 77043-2316
713-365-1000
Fax: 713-365-1441 800-228-5438
www.mcfa.com
Lift trucks and tires
CEO: Shigeru Tanemura
Mktg Head: Jennifer Evans
Estimated Sales: $3 - 5 Million
Number Employees: 500-999

26261 Mitsubishi Fuso Truck of America
2015 Center Square Rd
Swedesboro, NJ 08085-1683
856-467-4500
Fax: 856-467-4695 877-829-3876
R&D: Jim Peary
CEO: Jecka Glasman
jglasman@mitfuso.com
CEO: Bob Mc Dowell
Estimated Sales: $10 - 20 Million
Number Employees: 50-99

26262 Mitsubishi Gas ChemicalAmerica
655 Third Avenue
24th Floor
New York, NY 10017
212-687-9030
Fax: 212-687-2812 888-330-6422
contact@mgc-a.com www.mgc-a.com
Contact: Satoshi Hayashi
satoshi.hayashi@mitsubishicorp.com
Estimated Sales: $1,000,000 - $2,499,999
Number Employees: 250-499

26263 (HQ)Mitsubishi Intl. Corp.
520 Madison Avenue
Floor 18
New York, NY 10022-4327
212-759-5605
Fax: 212-605-1810 800-442-6266
Food commodities: coffee, cocoa, dairy products, fruits, vegetables and frozen juice concentrates. Food ingredients, enzymes, emulsifiers, baking agents.
President: James Brumm
CFO: Yasuyuki Sugiura
Executive VP/COO: Yoshihiko Kawamura
Sales/Purchasing Representative: Patrick Welch
Contact: Keigo Ando
keigo.ando@mitsubishicorp.com
Number Employees: 250-499
Other Locations:
Seattle WA

26264 Mitsubishi Polyester Film, Inc.
2001 Hood Rd.
PO Box 1400
Greer, SC 29652
864-879-5000
Fax: 864-879-5006 contact@m-petfilm.com
www.m-petfilm.com
Biaxially oriented polyester films, and copolyester shrink sleeve film.
President/CEO: Dennis Trice
Year Founded: 1991
Estimated Sales: $61 Million
Number Employees: 600
Number of Brands: 1
Number of Products: 100
Square Footage: 24239
Parent Co: Mitsubishi Chemical Corporation
Brands:
Hostaphan

26265 Mity Lite Inc
1301 W 400 N
Orem, UT 84057-4442
801-224-0589
Fax: 801-224-6191 800-909-8034
info@mitylite.com www.mitylite.com
Lightweight and durable folding chairs, folding chairs, stacking chairs, carts, lecterns, portable partitions and portable dance floors.
CEO: John Dudash
johnd@mitylite.com
Marketing Manager: Michael Peterson
Sales/Marketing Director: Kevin Stoker
Number Employees: 10-19
Square Footage: 108850
Brands:
Myti Host Chair
Myti Lite Tables
Myti Taff Chair
Summit Lectern
Swift Set Folding Chairs

26266 (HQ)Miura Boilers
1900 the Exchange SE # 330
Suite 330
Atlanta, GA 30339-2050
Canada
770-916-1695
Fax: 770-916-1858 atlanta@miuraz.com
Steam and hot water boilers for the food processing plant.
President: Masashi Hirose
President: Mark Utzinger
Sales: Mike Mazzei
Manager: Yo Nakagawa
Estimated Sales: $1-2.5 Million
Number Employees: 5-9

26267 Mlp Seating
950 Pratt Blvd
Elk Grove Vlg, IL 60007-5119
847-956-1700
Fax: 847-956-1776 800-723-3030
www.mlpseating.com
Manufacturer and exporter of chairs, tables and bar stools
President: Ralph D Samuel
rdsamuel@mlpseating.com
R&D: Ralph D Samuel
Quality Control: Goerge Stembridge
Sales: Steven Seres
Estimated Sales: $5 - 10 Million
Number Employees: 20-49

26268 Mmi Engineered Soultions Inc
1715 Woodland Dr
Saline, MI 48176-1614
734-429-4664
Fax: 734-429-4664 800-825-2566
info@moldedmaterials.com www.mmi-es.com
Manufacturer and exporter of custom molded totes and trays for processing and shipping
Manager: Mike Wolf
COO: R Campbell
VP Engineering: T Elkington
Estimated Sales: Below $5 Million
Number Employees: 50-99
Square Footage: 160000

26269 Mobern Electric Corporation
8200 Stayton Dr.
Suite 500
Jessup, MD 20794
301-725-3030
Fax: 301-953-9310 800-444-9288
sales@mobern.com www.mobern.com
Lighting fixtures
Estimated Sales: $5-10 Million
Number Employees: 50-99

26270 Mobil Composite Products
PO Box 5445
Norwalk, CT 06856-5445
203-831-4200
Fax: 203-831-4222 800-BUY-TREX

26271 Mocon Inc
7500 Boone Ave N # 110
Minneapolis, MN 55428-1026
763-493-7229
Fax: 763-493-6358 info@mocon.com
www.mocon.com
Manufacturer and exporter of instrumentation, consulting, and laboratory services to medical, pharmaceutical, food and other industries worldwide. Develops and manufactures high technology instrumentation and provides consulting andanalytical service to research laboratories, manufacturers and quality control departments in the life sciences, food/beverage, polymer/adhesives, electronic and other industries
CEO: Robert Demorest
CFO: Darrell Lee
VP: Doug Lindemann
Research And Development: Dan Mayer
Marketing: Guy Wray
Sales: Betty Kauffman
Public Relations: Sophia Dilberakis
Production: Tim Ascheman
Estimated Sales: $25 Million
Number Employees: 120
Square Footage: 50000
Brands:
Gsa
Oxtran
Pac Check
Pac Guard
Permatran
Profiler
Skye

26272 Modar
1394 E. Empire Ave.
Benton Harbor, MI 49022
269-925-0671
Fax: 269-925-0020 800-253-6186
modar@qtm.net
Manufacturer and exporter of ready-to-assemble store fixtures, shelving, point-of-purchase displays, furniture and storage cabinets; also, particle board laminating services available
President: Dennis Rousseau
Sales Manager: Gary Cichon
Inside Sales Manager: Jim Hendrix
Estimated Sales: $12.7 Million
Number Employees: 90
Square Footage: 300000
Other Locations:
Warehousing
Bridgman MI
Sales, Marketing, Design
Middletown CT

26273 Modern Baking Magazine
Ste 2300
330 N Wabash Ave
Chicago, IL 60611-7619
847-299-4430
Fax: 847-296-1968

Baking Inustry information
Estimated Sales: $1 - 3 Million
Number Employees: 10-19

26274 Modern Brewing & Design
3171 Guerneville Road
Santa Rosa, CA 95401-4028
707-542-6620
Fax: 707-542-3147

Manufacturer and exporter of barrel microbrewing
and brewpub equipment; also, support tanks and
stainless steel wine storage vessels
President: Daniel Shulte
Secretary: Russell Kargell
VP: Robert Kral
Number Employees: 32

26275 Modern Electronics Inc
280 Independence Ave
Grand Cane, LA 71032-5171
318-872-4764
Fax: 318-872-4768 www.me-equip.com

Pecan processing equipment
President: Richard M Oliver
Quality Control: Richard Oliver
Estimated Sales: $1 - 2.5 Million
Number Employees: 5-9

26276 Modern Metalcraft
1257 East Wackerly Rd.
Midland, MI 48642
989-835-3291
Fax: 989-835-8431 800-948-3182
www.modernmetalcraft.com

Metal products including displays
President/CEO: John D. McPeak
Product Group Manager: Frank Robison
Estimated Sales: Below $5 Million
Number Employees: 10-19
Square Footage: 60000

26277 Modern Metals Industries
128 Sierra St
El Segundo, CA 90245
310-516-0851
Fax: 310-322-8617 800-437-6633

Metal cabinets, industrial carts and material han-
dling equipment
VP: Robert Lee Sherrill
Estimated Sales: $1-2,500,000
Number Employees: 19

26278 Modern Packaging
3245 N Berkeley Lake Rd NW
Duluth, GA 30096
770-622-1500
Fax: 770-814-0046
www.modernpackaginginc.com

Contract packager of condiments and liquid food
items; warehouse providing dry, cooler and humid-
ity-controlled storage of foodstuffs, liquid packaging
products and seasonal sales items; also, pick and
pack and rail siding available
President: Herb Sodel
VP: Nancy Sodel
Estimated Sales: $3.6 Million
Number Employees: 50-99
Square Footage: 400000

26279 Modern Packaging Inc
505 Acorn St
Deer Park, NY 11729-3601
631-595-2437
Fax: 631-595-2742
info@modernpackaginginc.com
www.modernpackaginginc.com

Designs and manufactures precision packaging sys-
tems for the food, dairy, cosmetic and drug indus-
tries
President: Golam Alam
purchasing@modernpackaginginc.com
Estimated Sales: Less Than $500,000
Number Employees: 1-4
Square Footage: 120000

26280 Modern Paper Box Company
166 Valley Street
Bldg 3
Providence, RI 02909-2458
401-861-7357
Fax: 401-272-2040

Paper boxes
Contact: Krista Olson
kolson@polygon.net
Number Employees: 10

26281 Modern Plastics
88 Long Hill Cross Rd # 4
Shelton, CT 06484-4783
203-333-3128
Fax: 203-333-4625 800-243-9696
customerservice@modernplastics.com
www.modernplastics.com

Plastic films.distributors of plastic sheets, tubes and
films,provide custom fabrication. brands - ABS,
Acetal, Ardel, Arlon, Acetron, Acculum, Acrylic,
Benelex, ceanese, celazole PBI, Ensitep, hyzod
sheets, isoplat, kel-F, Kydexkynar, lexan, MD nylon,
Macrolux, Merlon, nylon, PAS, Peek, PCTFE,
Phenolics, PET, PVDF, Radel, PVC, Rexolite,
Rulon, Sanalite, Sintra, Sintimid, Surlyn, Teflon,
Torlon, TPX, Valox, Victrex, Vespel, Warps, Xenoy,
Zelux, Zytel
President: Bing Carbone
bcarbone@modernplastics.com
CEO: James Carborne
CFO: Patrick Roderick
Corporate VP: Robert Carbone
Quality Control: Daryl Guberman
Distribution Plastic Sales: Raymond Aneiro
VP Operations: Patrick Roderick
Fabrication/Production: Mark Moriarty
Corporate Purchasing Manager: John Fucci
Estimated Sales: $2.5-5 Million
Number Employees: 20-49

26282 Modern Process Equipment Inc
3125 S Kolin Ave
Chicago, IL 60623-4890
773-254-3929
Fax: 773-254-3935 solutions@mpechicago.com
www.mpechicago.com

Manufacture and market size reduction equipment
for the coffee, food, chemical, mineral and pharma-
ceutical industry
President: Daniel Ephraim
daniel@mpechicago.com
Vice President: Phil Ephraim
Sales Director: Scott Will
Estimated Sales: $5-10 Million
Number Employees: 20-49

26283 Modern Stamp Company
1305 Saint Paul St
Baltimore, MD 21201
410-685-0505
Fax: 410-727-2146 800-727-3029
baumstamps@aol.com

Stamps, checks, seals, stencils, signs, trophies,
awards, badges, labels, inks, printing dies, date and
lot coding equipment and ink jet coders
Sales Manager: Dennis Burns
Manager: George Pagels
Estimated Sales: $1-2.5 Million
Number Employees: 5-9
Square Footage: 20000

26284 Modern Store Fixtures Company
1359 Medical District Drive
Dallas, TX 75207
214-634-2505
Fax: 214-634-2543 800-634-7777
customerservice@modernstore.com
www.modernstore.com

Glass display cases and store fixtures
VP: Lillian Knopf
General Manager: Bruce Meltzer
Estimated Sales: $5-10 Million
Number Employees: 10-19
Square Footage: 62000

26285 Modesto Tent & Awning
4448 Sisk Rd
Modesto, CA 95356-8729
209-545-6150
Fax: 209-545-6152
signs1@modestotentandawning.com
www.midvalleytarp.com

Awnings, canopies, tarps and tents

Owner: Suzanne Caragan
suzanne.caragan@kp.org
Secretary and Treasurer: Leonard Rigg
VP: Barney Valk
Estimated Sales: $1-2,500,000
Number Employees: 10-19
Square Footage: 36000

26286 Modular Packaging
6 Aspen Dr
Randolph, NJ 07869-1103
973-970-9393
Fax: 973-970-9388
customer.services@modularpackaging.com
www.modularpackaging.com

Packaging machinery including unscrambler
desiccant feeders, shrink bundlers, cottoners, blister
and case packers, cappers, etc.; importer of
cartoners, case and blister packers, counters, etc.;
exporter of liquid fillers, tube fillersand cottoners
President: Clifford Smith
cliffs@modularpackaging.com
Vice President: Bradford Smith
Estimated Sales: $3 - 5,000,000
Number Employees: 10-19
Square Footage: 36000
Brands:
Eclipse
Modular Kt
Omega

26287 Modular Packaging
6 Aspen Dr
Randolph, NJ 07869-1103
973-970-9393
Fax: 973-970-9388
customer.service@modularpackaging.com
www.modularpackaging.com

Packaging line design, integration and service support, liquid filling lines, filling, blister packaging,
closing and labeling machines
President: Clifford Smith
cliffs@modularpackaging.com
Estimated Sales: $3 - 5 Million
Number Employees: 10-19

26288 Modular Panel Company
63 David Street
New Bedford, MA 02744-2320
508-993-9955
Fax: 508-993-9957

Manufacturer and exporter of insulated panels for
freezers and coolers
President: James Chadwick
Drafting Engineer: Pasquale Sbardella
Estimated Sales: Below $5 Million
Number Employees: 10

26289 Modularm Corporation
61 Mall Dr
Commack, NY 11725
631-864-3860
Fax: 631-864-3863

A temperature and refrigeration monitoring systems
manufacturer with innovative products designed to
protect perishables, save energy and increase
operator safety.
President: Donald Olsen
Marketing Director: Bryan Barash
Sales Director: Marci Norwood

26290 Modulightor Inc
246 E 58th St
New York, NY 10022-2011
212-371-0336
Fax: 212-371-0335 www.modulightor.com

Manufacturer, importer and wholesaler/distributor of
lighting fixtures
Owner: Ernst Wagner
ernst@modulightor.com
Estimated Sales: $1-2.5 Million
Number Employees: 10-19
Square Footage: 26000
Brands:
Modulator

26291 Modutank Inc
4104 35th Ave
Long Island City, NY 11101-1410
718-392-1112
Fax: 718-786-1008 800-245-6964
info@modutank.com www.modutank.com

Above-ground, modular bolted steel tanks, liquid storage tanks, settling tanks, containment for earthen materials and slurries as well as a wide range of secondary containment systems for sanitary applications, tanker trucks and wheeled vehicles.
President: Reed Margulis
info@modutank.com
Estimated Sales: $1 - 5 Million
Number Employees: 10-19
Number of Products: 10

26292 Moeller Electric
4140 World Houstn Pkwy Ste 100
Houston, TX 77032
832-613-6250
Fax: 832-613-6225 800-394-5687
www.moellerusa.net
Motor controls, miniature and standard circuit breakers and custom control panels; also, switches including cam, PLC, pushbutton and safety limit
President: John Hamm
VP Marketing: Tom Thornton
Estimated Sales: $20-50 Million
Number Employees: 5-9

26293 Moen Industries
10330 Pioneer Blvd
Suite 230
Santa Fe Springs, CA 90670
562-946-6381
Fax: 562-946-3200 800-732-7766
rstorms@moenindustries.com
Manufacturer and exporter of corrugated box forming and sealing equipment
Owner: Carl Moen
Sales Co-coordinator: Iris Walker
Contact: Noreen Boos
boos@moenindustries.com
Purchasing Manager: Lori Maxey
Estimated Sales: $5-10 Million
Number Employees: 50-99
Square Footage: 76000
Brands:
Blissmaster
Lamo-Bliss
Lamo-Tray

26294 Moffat
12000 Crownpoint Drive
Suite 100
San Antonio, TX 78233-5315
210-590-9381
Fax: 210-590-9479 866-589-0664
start.cortera.com
Half and full size electric and gas infrared convection ovens; also, proofers
Estimated Sales: $.5 - 1 Million
Number Employees: 5-10
Parent Co: Moffat
Brands:
Bakbar
Turbofan

26295 Mohawk Northern Plastics
PO Box 583
Auburn, WA 98071
253-939-8206
Fax: 253-939-4015 800-426-1100
Extruded and printed flexible polyethylene packaging including bags and film
President: Dan Mc Farland
CFO: Dan McFarlan
Sales Manager: Tom Couples
Estimated Sales: $20-50 Million
Number Employees: 100-249

26296 Mohawk Paper Mills
1400 Crescent Vischer Ferry Road
Clifton Park, NY 12065
518-371-6700
www.mohawkterrace.com
Coated and uncoated printing paper
Estimated Sales: $50-100 Million
Number Employees: 250-499

26297 Mohawk Western PlasticsInc
1496 Arrow Hwy
P.O. Box 463
La Verne, CA 91750-5297
909-593-7547
Fax: 909-596-8691
jhenderson@mohawkwestern.com
www.mohawkwestern.com
Polyethylene bags

President: Chris Mordoff
CEO: John Mordoff
cmordoff@mohawkwestern.com
Estimated Sales: $5-10 Million
Number Employees: 20-49

26298 Moisture Register Products
9567 Arrow Route
Suite E
Rancho Cucamonga, CA 91730
909-941-7776
Fax: 909-941-1830 800-966-4788
www.moistureregisterproducts.com
Manufacturer and exporter of computers for measuring moisture content in solids for the food processing industry
Owner: John Lundstrom
Sales: Gabriel Cote
craig.mitchell@bankofamerica.com
Contact: Craig Mitchell
craig.mitchell@bankofamerica.com
Estimated Sales: $3 - 5 Million
Number Employees: 10-19
Parent Co: Aqua Measure Instrument Company
Brands:
Bsp901
Smart Ii

26299 Mol Belting Co
2532 Waldorf Ct NW
Grand Rapids, MI 49544-1478
616-453-2484
Fax: 616-453-2008 800-729-2358
sales@molbelting.com www.molbelting.com
Materials handling equipment, conveyors and accessories
President: Rick Mol
rmol@molbelting.com
Estimated Sales: $10-20 Million
Number Employees: 50-99

26300 Mold-Rite Plastics LLC
2222 Highland Rd
Twinsburg, OH 44087-2231
330-425-4206
Fax: 330-425-4586 marketing@weatherchem.com
www.weatherchem.net
A packaging company that designs, develops, and delivers innovative dispensing closures.
CEO: Jennifer Altstadt
CFO: Bill Wolf
Research & Development: Barry Daggett
VP Marketing: Anna Fedova-Levi
Director of Sales: Jack Hotz
VP Operations: Carol Rinder
Estimated Sales: $10-20 Million
Number Employees: 100-249
Square Footage: 80000
Parent Co: Weatherhead Industries
Type of Packaging: Consumer, Food Service, Private Label
Brands:
Agricap
Flapper
Tec-Loc
Top-Squeeze

26301 Molded Container Corporation
1622 N Lombard St
Portland, OR 97217-5534
503-233-8601
Fax: 503-233-0621
Plastic containers and lids
Manager: Rick Copes
Estimated Sales: $16 Million
Number Employees: 100-249
Square Footage: 160000

26302 Molded Fiber Glass TrayCompany
6175 Highway 6
Linesville, PA 16424
814-683-4500
Fax: 814-683-4504 800-458-6050
info@mfgtray.com www.mfgtray.com
Manufactures reinforced composite trays, containers, and flats used in the confectionary, bakery, food service, pharmaceutical, and electronics industries as well as many other markets for in-process handling of goods.
Manager: Ron Orr
Contact: Eric Bennett
ebennett@moldedfiberglass.com

Estimated Sales: $20-50 Million
Number Employees: 100-249

26303 Molded Pulp Products
1780 Dreman Avenue
Cincinnati, OH 45223-2456
513-681-3016
Fax: 513-681-5121
Custom molded products
Estimated Sales: $20-50 Million
Number Employees: 50-99

26304 Molding Automation Concepts
1760 Kilkenny Ct
Woodstock, IL 60098
815-337-3000
Fax: 815-337-3020 800-435-6979
sales@macautomation.com
www.macautomation.com
Manufacturer and exporter of horizontal, incline and elevator belt conveyors for automatic box, tote bag and tray filling systems
President: Frank Altvedt
R&D: Frank Altvedt
Sales Manager: Randy Artheid
Contact: April Booze
april@centerforenrichedliving.org
Estimated Sales: $10 - 20,000,000
Number Employees: 50-99
Type of Packaging: Bulk

26305 Moli-International
1150 W Virginia Ave
Denver, CO 80223-2026
303-777-0364
Fax: 303-777-0658 800-525-8468
sales@moliinternational.com
Manufacturer and exporter of displays, sampling and merchandising covers, pans, trays, clear plexiglass, service carts, ice bins, water stations, sinks and sneeze guards
Owner: Larry Larson
llarson@moliinternational.com
Secretary/Treasurer: Larry Larson
Estimated Sales: $500,000-$1 Million
Number Employees: 5-9
Square Footage: 25000
Type of Packaging: Food Service
Brands:
Merchant & Moli-Shields

26306 Moline Machinery LLC
114 S Central Ave
PO Box 16308
Duluth, MN 55807-2302
218-624-5734
Fax: 218-628-3853 800-767-5734
sales@moline.com www.moline.com
Manufacturer and exporter of proofing, frying and dough processing systems for doughnuts, specialty breads, snack foods and yeast raised products
President: Gary Moline
gmoline@moline.com
Sales Manager: Terry King
Engineering Director: Larry Meyer
Estimated Sales: $10-20 Million
Number Employees: 50-99
Square Footage: 190000
Brands:
Moline

26307 Molins/Sandiacre Richmond
8191 Brook Rd # G
Richmond, VA 23227-1334
804-421-8795
Fax: 804-421-8798 864-486-4000
sandiacre.usa@molins.com
Manufacturer, importer and exporter of packaging machinery
Founder: Herman Hayssen
Vice President of Sales and Marketing: Dan Minor
Estimated Sales: $10 - 20 Million
Number Employees: 1-4

26308 Moll-Tron
1457 Ammons St
Lakewood, CO 80214-6108
303-969-8888
Fax: 303-969-8110 800-525-9494
www.molitron.com

Manufactures complete line of commercial kitchen exhaust equipment including restaurant wet scrubbers, water scrubbing ventilators and restaurant odor control systems for restaurants and other commercial kitchens.
President: Scott Airhart
scott@molitron.com
Estimated Sales: Less Than $500,000
Number Employees: 1-4
Brands:
Moli-Tron

26309 Mollenberg-Betz Inc
300 Scott St
Buffalo, NY 14204-2293
716-614-7473
Fax: 716-614-7465 vmollen@mollenbergbetz.com
www.mollenbergbetz.com
Cold storage facilities, freezers, refrigeration equipment and parts; also, design and installation services available. Design and installation of refrigeration systems, suppliers of refrigeration equipment and parts-service
Owner: Knut Lerdal
klerdal@hotmail.com
Quality Control: John Paytash
Executive VP: Joe Kilijanski
Purchasing: Gene Kaderbeck
Estimated Sales: $30 Million
Number Employees: 50-99
Square Footage: 30000

26310 Mollers North America Inc
5215 52nd St SE
Grand Rapids, MI 49512-9702
616-942-6504
Fax: 616-942-8825 www.mollersna.com
Designers and manufacturers of valve packing equipment, bag handling conveyors, automatic bag palletizers, pallet handling conveyors, stretch-hooders and shrinkwrapping systems
Executive VP: Tom Wagner
Executive VP: Carlos Saenz
Contact: Brandi Ackerman
b.ackerman@mollersna.com
Estimated Sales: $10 Million
Number Employees: 50-99
Square Footage: 100000
Parent Co: Maschinenfabrik Mollers GmbHu Company

26311 Moly-XL Company
Ih 295 Business Ctr
Westville, NJ 8093
856-848-2880
Fax: 856-848-2799
Industrial greases, oils and lubricants
President: Frank Iacovone
VP: Kenneth Kunz
Number Employees: 5-9
Square Footage: 20000
Parent Co: Master Lubricants Company
Brands:
Moly-Xl

26312 Momar
1830 Ellsworth Industrial Drive NW
Atlanta, GA 30318-3746
800-556-3967
info@momar.com www.momar.com
Manufacturer and exporter of industrial maintenance chemicals, water treatment products, lubricants and cleaning chemicals for the food processing industry
Estimated Sales: $34 Million
Number Employees: 300
Square Footage: 50000
Brands:
Aquatrol
Lubest
Mochem
Momarket

26313 Momence Pallet Corp
11414 E State Route 114
Momence, IL 60954-3882
815-472-6451
Fax: 815-472-6453 www.momencepallet.com
Wooden pallets
President: Andrew Cryer
Secretary/Treasurer: Norm Cryer
Estimated Sales: $2.5-5 Million
Number Employees: 20-49
Square Footage: 100000

26314 Monadnock Paper Mills Inc
117 Antrim Rd
Bennington, NH 03442-4205
603-588-3311
Fax: 603-588-3158 mpm.com
Manufacturer and exporter of paper including uncoated cover, text, technical specialty and converting, nonwovens
President/Chairman/CEO: Richard Verney
Estimated Sales: $68 Million
Number Employees: 100-249
Square Footage: 300000

26315 Monarc Group
2928 41st Avenue
Suite 910b
Long Island City, NY 11101-3303
866-848-4283
Fax: 866-873-8625

26316 Monarch-McLaren
329 Deerhide Crescent
Weston, ON M9M 2Z2
Canada
416-741-9675
Fax: 416-741-2873
Manufacturer, importer and wholesaler/distributor of conveyor and transmission belting, V-belts, timing belts, variable speed belts, hoses, pulleys, chains, sprockets, bearings, speed reducers, casters, motors, couplings, belt lacingleather packings, etc
President: Terence Whitfield
Sales Manager: Brian Flint
Estimated Sales: Below $5 Million
Number Employees: 10
Square Footage: 72400
Brands:
Monarch-Mclaren
Polyplast
Yorkcord
Yorkedge
Yorkflex
Yorkgrip
Yorklink
Yorklon
Yorkmate
Yorkpack
Yorktex
Yorktex Leather

26317 Monastary Mustard
840 South Main Street
Angel, OR 97362
503-949-6321
monasterymustard.com
Mustard
Mustard Flavor Creator: Sister Terry Hall

26318 Monitor Company
P.O. Box 4411
Modesto, CA 95352-4411
209-523-0500
Fax: 209-523-4267 800-537-3201
Manufacturer and exporter of temperature recorders
Estimated Sales: $1 - 5 Million
Number Employees: 15
Brands:
Temprecord

26319 Monitor Technologies LLC
44W320 Keslinger Rd
Elburn, IL 60119
630-365-9403
Fax: 630-365-5646 800-601-6204
monitor@monitortech.com www.monitortech.com
Level and flow monitoring products for powder and bulk solids
President/Owner: Craig Russell
Estimated Sales: $5+ Million
Number Employees: 20-49
Type of Packaging: Private Label
Brands:
Bulksonics
Dustalarm

26320 MonoSol
707 E 80th Pl
Merrillville, IN 46410
219-762-3165
Fax: 219-755-4062 www.monosol.com
Manufacturer of water-soluble films that can be used in the food manufacturing process.

Senior Manager, New Business Development: Dorota Bartosik
Marketing & Sales Administrator: Kate Triemstra
Contact: Chris Addis
caddis@monosol.com
Parent Co: Kuraray
Other Locations:
Production Facility
Portage IN
Production Facility
La Porte IN
Production Facility DuneLand
Portage IN
UK Production Facility
Hartlebury, UK
Production Facility
Saijo, Japan

26321 Monoflo International Inc
882 Baker Ln
Winchester, VA 22603-5722
540-665-1691
Fax: 540-665-9785 800-446-6693
sales@miworldwide.com
Collapsible plastic containers
Owner: Gus Nusu
monoflo@miworldwide.com
Estimated Sales: $10-20 Million
Number Employees: 100-249

26322 Monon Process EquipmentCo
6289 N 150 E
Monon, IN 47959-8010
219-253-7777
Fax: 219-253-8580 www.mononprocess.com
President and CEO: Troy Paluchniak
sales@mononprocess.com
Estimated Sales: Below $5 Million
Number Employees: 1-4

26323 Monroe Environmental Corp
810 W Front St
Monroe, MI 48161-1627
734-242-7654
Fax: 734-242-5275 800-992-7707
sales@mon-env.com www.mon-env.com
Manufacturer oil mist, smoke and vapor collectors, venturi scrubbers, dust collectors, water & wastewater clarifiers.
Owner: Gary Pashaian
gpashaian@monroeenvironmental.com
Sales Manager: Adam Pashaian
Operations Manager: Rob Cardella
Estimated Sales: $15 Million
Number Employees: 50-99
Square Footage: 70000

26324 (HQ)Monroe Extinguisher Co Inc
105 Dodge St
Rochester, NY 14606-1503
585-235-3310
Fax: 585-235-7312 tcurtain@monroekitchen.com
www.monroeextinguisher.com
Custom stainless steel kitchen equipment: sinks, tables and hoods
President: Thomas Curtin
tcurtin@monroeextinguisher.com
Sales: Anthony Salemme
Plant Manager: Craig Mackey
Purchasing: Adam Curtain
Estimated Sales: Below $5 Million
Number Employees: 10-19
Square Footage: 50000
Other Locations:
Monroe Kitchen Equipment
Rochester NY

26325 Monsol
1701 County Line Road
Portage, IN 46368-1234
219-762-3165
Fax: 219-763-4477 800-237-9552
info@monosol.com www.monosol.com
Packaging water soluble film
General Manager: P Scott Bening
Product Development Manager: Jonathan Gallagher
Contact: Marianne Austin
marianneaustin@monosol.com
Clerk: Darlene Taylor
Estimated Sales: $1 - 5 Million
Number Employees: 50-99

26326 Montague Co
1830 Stearman Ave
Hayward, CA 94545-1018
510-785-8822
Fax: 510-785-3342 800-345-1830
www.montaguecompany.com
Manufacturer and exporter of commercial gas and electric cooking equipment. Products include convection ovens, deluxe griddles, heavy duty & medium duty ranges, counter equipment, fryers, over-fired and under-fired broilers, deckovens, chinese ranges, induction cooking equipment, under-counter refrigeration, and custom island suites.
President: Thomas Whalen
  twhalen@montague-inc.com
VP Finance: R Erickson
VP Sales/Marketing: Gary Rupp
Purchasing: Lisa Catanzano
Estimated Sales: $30-30 Million
Number Employees: 100-249
Type of Packaging: Food Service
Brands:
  Grizzly
  Hearthbake
  Legend
  Vectaire

26327 Montalbano Development Inc
3275 Veterans Meml Hwy # B15
Ronkonkoma, NY 11779-7665
631-737-2236
Fax: 631-467-1035 800-739-9152
www.montalbanoinc.com
Provider of computer services for the food industry including
Owner: Chris Montalbano
  chrism@montalbanoinc.com
VP: Chris Montalbano
Manager: Steghen Naroney
Estimated Sales: $2.5-5,000,000
Number Employees: 20-49

26328 Monte Glove Company
1208 Industrial Park Road
Wilkesboro, NC 28697-8490
662-263-5353
Fax: 662-263-5771
Work gloves, oven mitts, hand pads, sleeves
President: Glenn Clarke
Sales Manager: Theresa Lewis
Production: John Hall
Estimated Sales: $10-20 Million
Number Employees: 50-99
Parent Co: Golden Needles Knitting
Type of Packaging: Food Service, Private Label

26329 Monte Package Co
3752 Riverside Rd
Riverside, MI 49084-5101
269-849-1722
Fax: 269-849-0185 800-653-2807
www.montepkg.com
Packaging materials including boxes
President: Tony Monte
  tonym@montepkg.com
Owner: Sam Monte
Estimated Sales: $10-20 Million
Number Employees: 10-19

26330 Montebello Container Corp
14333 Macaw St
La Mirada, CA 90638-5208
714-994-2351
Fax: 714-994-3875 www.montcc.com
Corrugated containers
President: R. Anthony Salcido
Vice President: John Salcido
Production Superintendent: Roger Esquer
Estimated Sales: $5-10 Million
Number Employees: 100-249

26331 Montebello Packaging
1036 Aberdeen St
Hawkesbury, ON K6A 1K5
Canada
613-632-7096
Fax: 613-632-9638 bpilon@montebellopkg.com
www.montebellopkg.com
Aluminum aerosol cans & aluminum/laminate tubes.
President: Jean-Fran‡ois Leclerc
Director, Finance: Caroline Leblanc
Vice President, Sales/Marketing: Steven MacPhail
Director, Quality Operations: Joe Browning
Vice President, Operations: Emmanuel Piec

Year Founded: 1952
Estimated Sales: $20-50 Million
Number Employees: 240
Number of Brands: 3
Parent Co: the Jim Pattison Group
Brands:
  M-Bond
  M-Purity Ring
  M-Purity Seal

26332 Montello Inc
6106 E 32nd Pl # 100
Suite 100
Tulsa, OK 74135-5495
918-665-1170
Fax: 918-665-1480 800-331-4628
www.montelloinc.com
Specialty industrial chemicals
President: Allen Johnson
  allenj@montelloinc.com
Estimated Sales: $2.5 Million
Number Employees: 5-9

26333 Monterey Bay Food Group
661 Meadow Rd
Aptos, CA 95003-9786
831-685-8600
Fax: 831-685-8656
Consultant providing strategic planning, marketing and product management; also, assessment of products and business opportunities
Market Research Manager: Amy Seibert
Contact: Charles Dyer
  charley@mbfoodgroup.com
Operations Manager: Lora Keyte
Estimated Sales: $1-2.5 Million
Number Employees: 5-9

26334 Monument Industries Inc
159 Phyllis Ln
Bennington, VT 05201-1663
802-442-8187
Fax: 802-442-8188
Manufacturer and exporter of polyethylene bags
Vice President: Jay L Whitten
VP: Jay L Whitten
Estimated Sales: $5-10 Million
Number Employees: 20-49

26335 Moog Components Group
1501 N Main St
Blacksburg, VA 24060-2523
540-552-0382
Fax: 540-951-3832 800-382-5366
sales@electro-tec.com www.moog.com
Sliprings
Manager: Michelle Layne
  mlayne@moog.com
Estimated Sales: $50-100 Million
Number Employees: 250-499

26336 Moog Inc
400 Jamison Rd # 26
East Aurora, NY 14052
716-652-2000
Fax: 716-687-4457 800-272-6664
www.moog.com
Brushless servo motors and drives
President/COO/CEO: John Scannell
Chairman: Robert T. Brady
CFO: Donald Fishback
Manager: Kelly Lalley
Estimated Sales: Over $1 Billion
Number Employees: 10000+

26337 Moon Valley Circuits
12350 Maple Glen Rd
Glen Ellen, CA 95442
707-996-4157
jill@moonvalleycircuits.com
www.moonvalleycircuits.com
Wine industry temperature controls
Owner: Mike Miller
  mike@moonvalleycircuits.com
Quality Control: Michael Miller
CFO: Michael Miller
R&D: Michael Miller
Estimated Sales: Less Than $500,000
Number Employees: 1-4

26338 Moore Efficient Communication Aids
PO Box 11023
Denver, CO 80211
303-433-8456
Fax: 303-433-8450
Marking devices, rubber stamps and sign systems
Owner: Ed Moore
Executive Secretary: Pam Craig
Production Manager: Leroy Eddy
Estimated Sales: $1-2.5 Million
Number Employees: 5-9
Square Footage: 30000
Type of Packaging: Private Label, Bulk
Brands:
  Lifetime
  Trodat
  X Stamper

26339 Moore Paper Boxes Inc
2916 Boulder Ave
Dayton, OH 45414-4834
937-278-7327
Fax: 937-278-5932
Manufacturer and exporter of paper boxes
President: Charles Moore
Estimated Sales: $10-20 Million
Number Employees: 5-9

26340 Moore Production Tool Spec Inc
37531 Grand River Ave
Farmington Hills, MI 48335-2879
248-476-1200
Fax: 248-476-6887
Manufacturer and exporter of sealing jaws, knives, anvils and packaging tooling
President: Durk Moore
CEO: Richard Moore
President: Richard Moore
Sales: Brian Carfango
Estimated Sales: $2.5-5 Million
Number Employees: 20-49
Square Footage: 56000

26341 Moore Push-Pin Co
1300 E Mermaid Ln
Glenside, PA 19038-7696
215-233-5700
Fax: 215-233-0660 www.push-pin.com
Converting and batching equipment, specialty fasteners
President: Alice Cataldi
  alicecataldi@push-pin.com
Estimated Sales: $5-10 Million
Number Employees: 50-99

26342 Moorecraft Box & Crate
101 Royster Street
PO Box 1528
Tarboro, NC 27886-1528
252-823-2510
Fax: 252-823-2228 steve@moorecraft.com
www.moorecraft.com
Wood and plywood shipping boxes and crates and custom pallets
Owner: Stephen Redhage
VP: Sharon Redhage
Contact: Steve Redhage
  steve@moorecraft.com
Estimated Sales: $1-2.5 Million
Number Employees: 50-99
Square Footage: 9000

26343 Moran Canvas Products Inc
8135 Center St
La Mesa, CA 91942-2907
619-462-7778
Fax: 619-462-7776 800-515-1130
morancanvas@sbcglobal.net
www.morancanvas.com
Commercial awnings
Owner: Don Bell
CFO: Paulette Moran
Sales Manager: Roger Smith
  don@myshadydesigns.net
Estimated Sales: Below $5,000,000
Number Employees: 10-19

26344 (HQ)Morgan Brothers Bag Company

PO Box 25577
Richmond, VA 23260-5577

804-355-9107
Fax: 804-355-9100

Textile bags for hams, peanuts, citrus fruits, scallops and crops
Owner: Jim Edge
VP: Annabel Lewis
Estimated Sales: $20-50 Million
Number Employees: 50-99
Square Footage: 37800

26345 Morgan Corp

111 Morgan Way
PO Box 588
Morgantown, PA 19543-7714

610-286-5025
Fax: 610-286-0581 800-666-7426

info@morgancorp.com www.morgancorp.com
President: James Youse
james.youse@morgancorp.com
Estimated Sales: $1 - 5 Million
Number Employees: 1000-4999
Parent Co: J.B. Poindexter & Co

26346 Morning Star Coffee, Inc.

207 Carter Dr Ste E
West Chester, PA 19382-4506

610-701-7022
Fax: 610-701-7032 888-854-2233

Specialty coffee roasters
President: Thomas Gaspar
Contact: Charles Streitwieser
cmarks@citymission.org
VP, Operations: Antonio Sordi
Estimated Sales: $75 - 100 Million
Number Employees: 5-9

26347 Morning Star Foods

8 Joanna Court
East Brunswick, NJ 08816-2108

800-237-5320
Fax: 732-432-3928

Manufacturer and marketer of consumer packaged goods
President/CEO: Herman Graffinder
CFO: Craig Miller
Sr. VP Marketing: Toby Purdy
Sr. VP Operations: Samuel Hillin
Parent Co: Dean Foods Company
Type of Packaging: Private Label, Bulk

26348 Morphy Container Company

17 Woodyatt Drive
Brantford, ON N3R 7K3
Canada

519-752-5428
Fax: 519-752-2260

Packaging containers including corrugated boxes
Office Manager: Barbara Shaw
Production Manager: Peter Hird
Square Footage: 12000

26349 Morris & Associates

803 Morris Dr
Garner, NC 27529

919-582-9200
Fax: 919-582-9100 info@morris-associates.com
www.morris-associates.com

Custom refrigeration equipment for the foodprocessing industry. Specializing in industrial ice makers and storage and delivery systems.
CEO: Bill Morris III
Research & Development: John Shell
Marketing Director: Virginia Arello
Sales Director: Bobby Cathey
Operations Manager: David Maw
Production Manager: Ron Correia
Purchasing Manager: Tomc Patterson
Estimated Sales: $5 - 10 Million
Number Employees: 10-19
Number of Products: 20+
Square Footage: 100000
Brands:
Chill Master
Ice Master

26350 Morris Industries

8130 Cryden Way
Forestville, MD 20747

301-568-5005
Fax: 301-420-4140 www.morris-industries.com

Pressure sensitive labels
President: Dave Morris
CEO: Dave Shotland
Estimated Sales: $3 - 5 Million
Number Employees: 10-19
Square Footage: 18000

26351 Morris Transparent Box Co

945 Warren Ave
East Providence, RI 02914-1423

401-438-6116
Fax: 401-434-9779 MorrisBox@aol.com
www.morristransparentbox.com

Plastic wedding cake boxes and covers
President: Alfred T Morris Jr
VP: Jean Morris
Estimated Sales: $2.5-5 Million
Number Employees: 20-49

26352 Morrison Timing Screw Co

335 W 194th St
Glenwood, IL 60425-1501

708-331-6600
Fax: 708-756-6620 info@morrison-chs.com
www.morrison-chs.com

Manufacturer and exporter of timing screws and automatic can opening systems
President: Nick Wilson
CEO: Nancy Wilson
Vice President: Lois Hayworth
Vice President of Operations: Chris Wilson
IT: Tim Dupin
tim.dupin@morrison-chs.com
Estimated Sales: $10-20 Million
Number Employees: 20-49

26353 Morrison Weighing Systems Inc

7605 50th St
Milan, IL 61264-3272

309-799-7311
Fax: 309-799-7313 www.morrisonweighing.com

Checkweighing devices, weight control systems, scales, weigh-convey systems
President: Donald G Morrison
don-morrison@mchsi.com
Estimated Sales: $1-2.5 Million
Number Employees: 5-9

26354 Morrissey Displays & Models

20 Beverly Rd
Port Washington, NY 11050

516-883-6944
Fax: 516-767-2379

Manufacturer and exporter of display booths
Owner: Stuart Morrissey
Estimated Sales: $500,000-$1 Million
Number Employees: 1-4

26355 Morrow Technologies Corporation

12000 28th Streett North
St Petersburg, FL 33716

727-531-4000
Fax: 727-531-3531 877-526-8711

sales@janusdisplays.com www.janusdisplays.com
Manufacturer and exporter of interior electronic signs including Leo, LCD and Plasma
Owner: Sharon Morrow
CEO: John Morrow
Controller: Kathy Naranjo
Marketing: Rhonda Candreva
Sales Manager: Steve Asbrand
Number Employees: 20-49
Brands:
Janus

26356 Morse Manufacturing Co Inc

727 W Manlius St
East Syracuse, NY 13057-2145

315-437-8475
Fax: 315-437-1029 inquiry@morsedrum.com
www.morsemfgco.com

Drum handling equipment, fork attachments for drum moving and drum mixers; exporter of drum handling equipment including rotators, handlers and tumblers
President: Nate Andrews
Chairman of the Board: Robert Andrews
randrews@morsedrum.com
Marketing: Ralph Phillips
Sales Manager: Phil Mulpagano
Number Employees: 20-49
Number of Brands: 1
Number of Products: 100

26357 Mortec Industries Inc

29240 County Road R
P.O. Box 977
Brush, CO 80723-9444

970-842-5063
Fax: 970-842-5061 800-541-9983

joe@mortecscales.com www.mortecscales.com
Manufacturer and exporter of electronic weighing scales; wholesaler/distributor of computer hardware and software; serving the food service market
Owner: Joe Kral
mortecscales@gmail.com
Estimated Sales: $1-2.5 Million
Number Employees: 1-4
Type of Packaging: Consumer, Food Service

26358 (HQ)Moseley Realty LLC

31 Hayward St # A2
Franklin, MA 02038-2166

508-520-6915
Fax: 508-520-6915 800-667-3539
www.moseleycorp.com

Modular merchandising systems including carts, kiosks, point of purchase displays and store systems; also, design and architectural consulting services available
President: Thomas C Moseley Jr
tmoseley@moseleycorp.com
COO: Richard Kerley
Sr. VP: Christine Milloff
Estimated Sales: $10 - 20 Million
Number Employees: 10-19
Square Footage: 100000
Other Locations:
Moseley Corp.
Dallas TX

26359 Moser Bag & Paper Company

32485 Creekside Drive
Cleveland, OH 44124-5221

216-341-4111
Fax: 216-341-6507 800-433-6638

Specialty bags including paper, glassine and kraft
President: Ted Welles
Estimated Sales: $5-10 Million
Number Employees: 20-49
Type of Packaging: Food Service
Brands:
Stubby Clear-Vue
Stubby Less Crush

26360 Moss Inc

2600 Elmhurst Rd
Elk Grove Vlg, IL 60007-6312

847-238-4200
Fax: 847-238-4604 800-341-1557
www.mossinc.com

Custom labels including pressure sensitive, multi-panel and on-pack for recipes, coupons, product information, etc
President and CEO: Dan Patterson
CEO: Meagan Alwert
malwert@mossinc.com
EVP and CFO: Mark Ollinger
Executive Vice President of Research and: Bob Frey
Executive Vice President of Operations: Vince Marler
VP Production Logistics: Joe Donley
Number Employees: 100-249
Brands:
Fix-A-Form

26361 Mosshaim Innovations

13901 Sutton Park Drive S
Suite 120
Jacksonville, FL 32224-0229

614-985-3000
Fax: 614-985-0703 888-995-7775

Portable, 120 volt, vitro ceramic glass stovetops. Also produces 120 volt drop-in stovetops. Patented technology will replace gas and induction portables
President: James Sarvadi
Quality Control: Tom Dorothy
R & D: James Sarvadi
VP Marketing: Donald Lewis
VP Operations: James Sarvadi
Estimated Sales: Below $5 Million
Number Employees: 10
Number of Brands: 2
Square Footage: 40000
Parent Co: Mosshaim Innovations
Brands:
Le Gourmates
Series S

26362 Mosuki
105 Bridge Road
Islandia, NY 11749-5207
631-234-4111
Fax: 631-234-2940 varduino@aol.com
Espresso machines/accessories

26363 Motion Industries Inc
1605 Alton Rd
Birmingham, AL 35210-3770
205-956-1122
Fax: 205-951-1172 877-609-7975
www.motionindustries.com
Equipment parts and supplies.
CEO: Timothy P Breen
timothy.breen@motion-ind.com
Manager: Matt McComb
Estimated Sales: Over $1 Billion
Number Employees: 5000-9999

26364 Motion Technologies
10 Forbes Rd
Northborough, MA 01532-2501
508-460-9800
Fax: 508-460-5090 800-468-2976
www.autofry.com
Ventless, enclosed, automated deep fryers
President: William Mc Mahon
wmcmahon@motiontechnology.com
Sales: Jamie Fisher
National Sales Manager: James Hall
Estimated Sales: $2.5-5 Million
Number Employees: 20-49
Square Footage: 17000
Brands:
Autofry

26365 Motom Corporation
631 Il Route 83
Suite 180
Bensenville, IL 60106-1342
630-787-1995
Fax: 630-787-1795
Manufacturer and exporter of drying and baking ovens, cleaning and automated material handling equipment
President: T Teshigawara
VP: W Kojima
Number Employees: 16
Parent Co: Tsukamoto Industrial Trading Company

26366 Motoman
805 Liberty Ln
West Carrollton, OH 45449
937-847-6200
Fax: 937-847-6277
customerservice@motoman.com
www.motoman.com
Robotic automation including packaging and palletizing
President: Steve Barhorst
Contact: Chris Anderson
chris.anderson@motoman.com
Estimated Sales: $45 Million
Number Employees: 250-499
Square Footage: 182000
Parent Co: Yaskawa Company
Type of Packaging: Consumer, Food Service
Brands:
Motoman

26367 Mouli Manufacturing Corporation
1 Montgomery Street
Belleville, NJ 07109-1305
201-751-6900
Fax: 201-751-0345 800-789-8285
moulimfg@aol.com
Manufacturer, importer and exporter of stainless steel food service equipment including cheese shredders, choppers, cutter, peelers, pots, pans and vegetable processors, etc
VP: P Varkala
Sales: Chris Varkala
Estimated Sales: $1 - 5 Million
Number Employees: 5-9
Square Footage: 60000
Brands:
Mouli

26368 Mound Tool Co
9301 Watson Industrial Park
St Louis, MO 63126-1578
314-968-3991
Fax: 314-968-1240 info@moundtool.com
President: R Osborne
Manager: Edward Simo
info@moundtool.com
Estimated Sales: Below $5 Million
Number Employees: 10-19

26369 Mount Hope Machinery Company
1 Technology Dr
Westborough, MA 01581-1786
508-616-9458
Fax: 508-616-9479
Web control equipment for textiles, paper, plastics, film and foil
President: Bertram Staudenmaier
President: Doug Milner
Director Applications: Carl Wertz
Sales Director: Kevin Frank
Customer Service Support Manager: Ed Gaudette
Estimated Sales: $10 - 20 Million
Number Employees: 50-99
Parent Co: BTR Paper Group

26370 Mount Vernon Plastics
460 Ogden Avene
Mamaroneck, NY 10543
914-698-1122
Fax: 914-698-1707 info@mtvernonplastics.com
www.mtvernonplastics.com
Plastic bags
Manager: Michael Dino
Estimated Sales: $2.5-5 Million
Number Employees: 10-19

26371 Mountain Pacific Machinery
515 S 9th St
Boise, ID 83702-7006
208-345-9033
Fax: 208-345-9037 877-466-9031
parts@mountpac.com www.mountpac.com
Dealers of food processing, packaging and material handling equipment
Sales: Josh Wiechman
Manager: Jeff Wiechman
jwiechman@mountpac.com
Manager: Jeff Wiechman
Estimated Sales: $10-20 Million
Number Employees: 1-4

26372 Mountain Pride
421 Bell Dr
PO Box 6077
Ketchum, ID 83340
208-725-5600
Fax: 208-725-5601
President: Stuart Siderman
Estimated Sales: $.5 - 1 million
Number Employees: 1-4

26373 Mountain Safety Research
4000 1st Avenue South
Seattle, WA 98134
206-505-9500
Fax: 206-682-4184 800-877-9677
info@msrgear.com www.cascadedesigns.com
Manufacturer, importer, and exporter of camp stoves, fuel bottles, water filtration products and cook sets
President: Joe Mc Sweeney
Research & Development: Kevin Gallagher
Manager Marketing/Sales: Michael Glavin
Director, Government Sales: Tim Davis
Contact: Dave Bartholomew
dbartholomew@msrgear.com
VP Operations/Engineering: R Michael Ligrano
Manager Product: Gail Snyder
Estimated Sales: $10-20 Million
Number Employees: 1-4
Number of Brands: 1
Number of Products: 250
Square Footage: 160000
Parent Co: Recreational Equipment
Type of Packaging: Consumer
Brands:
Alpine/Xpd
Cloudliner
Denali
Miniworks
Msr
Msr Carabiners

Rapid Fire
Superfly
Water Works
Whisperlite
X-Gk

26374 Mountain Secure Systems
1350 Kansas Ave
Longmont, CO 80501-6546
303-678-9898
Fax: 303-651-7171 800-MSI-PEAK
www.mountainsecuresystems.com
Software MES, specification
Manager: Ken Dickson
ken.dickson@mountainsecuresystems.com
Estimated Sales: $5-10 Million
Number Employees: 20-49

26375 Mountain States Processing
1293 Denver Ave
Fort Lupton, CO 80621-2649
303-857-0380
mtnstatespr@aol.com
Industrial equipment and machinery
President: David Morgan
Estimated Sales: $1 Million
Number Employees: 1-4
Square Footage: 12000

26376 Mountain View Estates Coffee
1260 Martin Grove Rd
Etobicoke, ON M9W 4X3
Canada
416-694-5455
www.estatescoffee.com
Wholesale food service distributor of roasted coffee, as well as sleeves/cups, syrups, and cleaning supplies.
Type of Packaging: Food Service, Private Label

26377 Mountain-Pacific Machinery
11705 SW 68th Ave # 200
Portland, OR 97223-8694
503-639-7635
Fax: 503-639-7707 877-466-9031
parts@mountpac.com www.mountpac.com
Dealers of food processing, packaging and material handling equipment
President: Dean Smith
jchilson@mountpac.com
Sales: Josh Wiechman
Estimated Sales: $3 - 5 Million
Number Employees: 5-9

26378 Mountaingate Engineering
540 Division Street
Campbell, CA 95008-6906
408-866-5100
Fax: 408-866-8896
Can and end drying, curing and sterilizing systems
Estimated Sales: $1 - 5 Million
Parent Co: Nordson Corporation Container Systems

26379 (HQ)Mouron & Co Inc
1025 Western Dr
Indianapolis, IN 46241-1436
317-243-7955
Fax: 317-243-2514 info@mouronandco.com
www.mouronstainless.com
Stainless steel tables and counters
President: T H Mouron
tom@mouronandco.com
VP: G Mouron
Engineer: P Skrojane
General Manager: Phil Skorjanc
Accounting: Mark Bryant
Estimated Sales: $2.5-5 Million
Number Employees: 10-19

26380 MovinCool/DENSO Products and Services Americas
3900 Via Oro Ave
Long Beach, CA 90810-1868
Fax: 310-513-7319 800-264-9573
info2@movincool.com movincool.com
Supplier of portable spot air conditioning.
Marketing Communications Manager: Eddie Stevenson
Estimated Sales: $50 - 75 Million
Number Employees: 100-249
Brands:
Movincool

26381 Moyer Diebel
3765 Champion Blvd
Winston Salem, NC 27105-2667
336-661-1992
Fax: 336-661-1979 info@moyerdiebel.com
www.moyerdiebel.com
Manufacturer and exporter of commercial dishwashers
President: Lin Senseing
lsenseing@championindustries.com
Sales Associate: Robert Croker
Estimated Sales: $20-50 Million
Number Employees: 100-249

26382 Moyer Packing Co.
741 Souder Rd.
Elroy, PA 18964
Fax: 970-346-4611 800-967-8325
www.mopac.com
Boxed and ground beef, and fresh and frozen boxed beef.
Year Founded: 1877
Estimated Sales: Less Than $500,000
Parent Co: JBS USA
Type of Packaging: Consumer, Private Label, Bulk
Brands:
Mopac

26383 Moyno
PO Box 960
Springfield, OH 45501
937-327-3111
Fax: 937-327-3177 www.moyno.com
Manufacturer and exporter of progressing cavity pumps and pinch valves
VP Operations: Norman Shearer
Product Manager: Andy Kosiak
VP Sales: Bob Lepera
Contact: Paul Reiss
paul.reiss@nov.com
Engineering Manager: Dale Parrett
Plant Manager: Todd Brown
Estimated Sales: $20-30 Million
Number Employees: 250-499
Square Footage: 240000
Parent Co: National Oilwell Varco
Brands:
Moyno
R&M

26384 Mp Equip. Co.
4305 Hamilton Mill Rd
Suite 400
Buford, GA 30518
770-614-5355
Fax: 770-614-5303 www.mpequipment.com
Designer and manufacturer of new equipment for the poultry, meat and seafood industries. Also sell pre-owned equipment such as batter mixers and applicators, frying systems, breaders, ovens, formers and reject conveyors.
President: Jerrill Sprinkle
General Manager: Jeff Sprinkle

26385 Mpp Inc
346 Huntingdon Ave
Waterbury, CT 06708-1430
203-574-5400
Fax: 203-597-9448 chromerolls@mpp.net
www.mpp.net
Chromium roll fabricating and surface finishing company that provides rebuilding, grinding, plating and finishing services for all web processing applications used in the manufacturing of plastic sheet & film, paper, non-woven fabricsand food processing industries.
President: Gary Nalband
gnalband@mpp.net
Vice President Sales & Marketing: Rimas Kozica
Operations Manager: Carlos Pacheco
Plant Manager: Richard Hall
Number Employees: 50-99

26386 (HQ)Mr Ice Bucket
345 Sandford St
New Brunswick, NJ 08901-2320
732-545-0420
Fax: 732-846-3383 www.mricebucket.com
Manufacturer and exporter of vinyl ice buckets and plastic trays and tumblers

President/CEO: Fred Haleluk
fhaleluk@mistericebucket.com
Information Systems Manager: Elaine Herman
Sales Manager: Sudesh Rajpal
Estimated Sales: $1-2.5 Million
Number Employees: 5-9
Square Footage: 40000
Brands:
Mr. Ice Bucket

26387 Mr. Bar-B-Q
5650 University Parkway
Suite 400
Winston-Salem, NC 27105
516-752-0670
Fax: 516-752-0683 800-333-2124
mzemel@mrbarbq.com
Manufacturer and importer of portable butane stoves, lighters, cookers and buffet and omelet stations
President/CEO: Marc Zemel
Senior VP: Adam Schillen
Director - Sales & Marketing: Wendy Sender
Senior VP -Sales: Jeff Lynch
VP operations: Michael Guadagno
Estimated Sales: $10 - 20 Million
Number Employees: 20-49
Square Footage: 68000
Brands:
Chef Master

26388 (HQ)Mrs Clark's Foods
740 SE Dalbey Dr
Ankeny, IA 50021-3908
515-964-8036
Fax: 515-964-8397 800-736-5674
info@mrsclarks.com www.mrsclarks.com
Shelf-stable beverages, sauces and dressings
President: Ron Kahrer
QC: Ned Williams
Sales: Julie Southwick
Plant Manager: John Weber
Purchasing: Ron Mathis
Estimated Sales: $450,000
Number Employees: 100-249
Number of Brands: 12
Number of Products: 50
Square Footage: 240000
Parent Co: AGRI Industries
Type of Packaging: Consumer, Food Service, Private Label
Brands:
Alljuice
Nature's Choice

26389 Mrs. Smith's Bakeries
7001 Asheville Hwy
Spartanburg, SC 29303-1875
864-503-9101
Fax: 864-503-9129
Pies and cobblers
Founder: Amanda Smith
Parent Co: Schwan's Consumer Brands
Brands:
MRS. SMITH'S

26390 Mt Valley Farms & Lumber Prods
1240 Nawakwa Rd
Biglerville, PA 17307-9728
717-677-6166
Fax: 717-677-9283 admin@mtvalleyfarms.com
www.mtvalleyfarms.com
Hardwood bins, skids and pallets; also, sawdust
President: Henry L Taylor
CFO: Patrick McCreary
VP/Operations: H Michael Taylor
R & D: Jemay Lua
Estimated Sales: Below $5 Million
Number Employees: 50-99
Square Footage: 208000
Other Locations:
Mountain Valley Farms &Lumbe
Biglerville PA
Brands:
Enviro-Logs

26391 Mt Vernon Neon Inc
1 Neon Dr
Mt Vernon, IL 62864-6723
618-242-0645
Fax: 618-244-6926 www.everbrite.com
Neon signs
Founder: Charles Wamser
Plant Manager: Steve Porter

Estimated Sales: $10-20 Million
Number Employees: 100-249
Parent Co: Everbright Electric Signs

26392 Mt Vernon Packaging Inc
135 Progress Dr
Mt Vernon, OH 43050-4772
740-397-3221
Fax: 740-393-2002 888-397-3221
Tommy@mountvernonpackaging.com
mountvernonpackaging.com
Paper boxes
President: Donald Nuce
dnuce@mountvernonpackaging.com
Estimated Sales: $5-10 Million
Number Employees: 5-9

26393 Mt. Lebanon Awning & Tent Company
P.O. Box 27
Presto, PA 15142
412-221-2233
Fax: 412-221-0204 info@mtlebanonawning.com
www.mtlebanonawning.com
Commercial awnings
President: Robert Campbell
Estimated Sales: $1-2,500,000
Number Employees: 10-19

26394 Mtc Food Equipment
17708 Widme Rd NE
Unit D
Poulsbo, WA 98370
360-697-6319
Fax: 360-697-6738 mtc@mtcfoodequipment.com
www.mtcfoodequipment.com
De-boning machines, bowl choppers, vacuum packers, slicers, grinders, meat saws, ice machines, stuffing machines, freezing equipment, smokehouses, filleting machines, skinning machines, and many other types of food processmachinery.
Owner: Todd Comstock
Estimated Sales: $500,000
Number Employees: 1-4
Square Footage: 2367

26395 Mts Seating
7100 Industrial Dr
Temperance, MI 48182-9105
734-847-3875
Fax: 734-847-0993 info@mtsseating.com
www.mtsseating.com
Manufacturer and exporter of metal stack chairs, bar stools, pedestal tables and bases and a complete line of hospitality and food service seating
President: Bart Kulish
Marketing Manager: Eric Foster
Sales VP: Greg Piper
Estimated Sales: $20 - 50 Million
Number Employees: 250-499
Square Footage: 200000
Parent Co: Michigan Tube Swagers Fabricators
Type of Packaging: Food Service

26396 Muckler Industries, Inc
355 Leesmeadow Rd.
Suite 207
Saint Louis, MO 63125
314-631-7616
Fax: 314-631-7409 800-444-0283
ktechinfo@mucklertech.com
Manufacturer and exporter of commercial kitchen hoods, baffle filters, waterwash and grease extractors, engineered commercial ventilation and utility distribution systems
National Sales Manager: Douglas Muckler
Sales: Sean Wood
Estimated Sales: $2.5-5 Million
Number Employees: 10
Square Footage: 60000
Type of Packaging: Food Service
Brands:
Challenger
Contender
Edc
Finalist
Performer

26397 (HQ)Muellermist Irrigation Company
2612 S. 9th Ave.
P.O. Box 6307
Broadview, IL 60155
708-450-9595
Fax: 708-450-1403 info@muellermist.com
www.muellermist.com
Manufacturer and exporter of underground lawn sprinkling and solar roof cooling systems
President: Tammy Boralli
Contact: Tammy Buralli
tburalli@muellermist.com
Estimated Sales: $10 - 20 Million
Number Employees: 50-99
Square Footage: 36000
Type of Packaging: Bulk
Brands:
Fanjet

26398 Mugnaini Imports
11 Hangar Way
Watsonville, CA 95076
831-761-1767
Fax: 831-728-5570 888-887-7206
mugnaini@mugnaini.com www.mugnaini.com
Supplier and importer of wood burning ovens and gas fire
Owner: Andrea Smith
Contact: Curt Corcoran
curt@mugnaini.com
Manager: Ken Belardi
Estimated Sales: Less than $500,000
Number Employees: 1-4

26399 Mulholland Co
1332 N Main St
Fort Worth, TX 76164-9117
817-624-1153
Fax: 817-624-1445 www.mulhollands.com
Plastic signs and nameplates
Manager: Dean Brown
Cmo: Nick Griffin
ngriffin@mulhollands.com
Marketing Manager: Sonny Muholland
Estimated Sales: $10-20 Million
Number Employees: 50-99

26400 Mulholland-Harper Company
PO Box C
Denton, MD 21629-0298
410-479-1300
Fax: 410-479-0207 800-882-3052
Manufacturer and exporter of electric fixtures and signs including electric, plastic, metal and outdoor and exterior identification
President: Patrick Hanrahan
Manufacturing Manager: Michael Conner
Estimated Sales: $5-10 Million
Number Employees: 50-99
Square Footage: 200000

26401 Mulligan Associates
286 Barbados Dr
Mequon, WI 53092
414-305-0840
Fax: 262-242-3944 800-627-2886
gene@mulliganassociates.com
Manufacturer, importer and exporter of high and low volume citric and noncitric juicers, fruit and vegetable peelers, water vending machines and sugar cane and wheat grass extractors
President: Gene Mulligan
CFO: Gene Mulligan
Quality Control: Gene Mulligan
Marketing: Gene Mulligan
Sales Director: Gene Mulligan
General Manager: Bonnie Mulligan
Estimated Sales: $2 Million
Number Employees: 50-99
Square Footage: 30000
Parent Co: AOJ Manufacturing
Type of Packaging: Food Service

26402 Mulligan Sales
P.O. Box 90008
City of Industry, CA 91715-0008
626-968-9621
Fax: 626-369-8452
Dairy, preservatives, acids, bakery, gums, stabilizers, dehydrated fruits and vegetables
President: Jeff Mulligan
Sales Manager: Dean Lenz

Estimated Sales: $20-50 Million
Number Employees: 10-19
Square Footage: 30000

26403 Mullnix Packages Inc
3511 Engle Rd
Fort Wayne, IN 46809-1117
260-747-3149
Fax: 260-747-1598
Plastic containers for frozen foods, prepared salads and fresh, refrigerated and controlled atmosphere products
President: Luke Gross
President, Chief Executive Officer: Gene Gentili
VP Sales/Marketing: Tim Love
Regional Sales Manager, Central US: Brian Schmitz
Operations Manager: Carey Edwards
Estimated Sales: $20-50 Million
Number Employees: 500-999
Square Footage: 118000

26404 Multi-Color Corp
1836 Sal St
Green Bay, WI 54302-2114
920-468-1269
Fax: 920-468-6793 800-236-8208
www.multicolorcorp.com
Labels including flexo, pressure sensitive and glue applied; also, pressure sensitive films and tags
President: Andrew Walker
Controller: Jim Gombar
CFO: James Gombar
Operations: Gary Karnopp
Quality Control: Greg Liplante
Estimated Sales: $10 - 20 Million
Number Employees: 50-99
Square Footage: 80000
Parent Co: NorthStar Print Group

26405 Multi-Fill Inc
4343 W 7800 S Ste B
West Jordan, UT 84088
801-280-1570
Fax: 801-280-4341 info@multi-fill.com
www.multi-fill.com
Volumetric filling equipment for the food processor. Line configurations for cooked rice, short/long pasta, vegetables, fruits, ready-to-eat salads (cut, sliced, IQF, blanched, or raw). New technology for the MPF fillers allows forfaster changeover, tighter accuracy's, increased cleanliness of fill, and results in less down time.
President: Richard Price
rt72@netzero.net
Sales Director: Bill Allred
Estimated Sales: Below $5 Million
Number Employees: 10-19
Square Footage: 22000

26406 Multi-Pak
180 Atlantic St
Hackensack, NJ 07601-3301
201-342-7474
Fax: 201-342-6525 www.multipakcorp.com
Manufacturer and exporter of refuse compactors for multi-dwelling units, hotels, hospitals and restaurants; also, attaching containers, odor control equipment and other collection systems. Hopper door repairs, chute cleaning, recyclingsystem
President: Niel Cavanaugh
ncavanaugh@multipak.com
Chairman of the Board/CFO/R&D: Niel Cavanaugh
Estimated Sales: $2.5 - 5 Million
Number Employees: 20-49
Square Footage: 24000

26407 Multi-Panel Display Corporation
107 Georgia Ave
Brooklyn, NY 11207-2401
718-495-3800
Fax: 718-346-0871 800-439-0879
Display racks and swing type display boards and panels; exporter of display units
President: Tommy Weber
VP: Zipora Weber
Contact: Daniel Weber
multipanel@aol.com
Estimated Sales: Less than $500,000
Number Employees: 5-9
Square Footage: 40000

26408 Multi-Plastics Extrusions Inc
600 Dietrich Ave
Hazleton, PA 18201-7754
570-455-2021
Fax: 570-455-0178 www.multi-plastics.com
Manufacturer and exporter of transparent biaxially oriented polystyrene sheets used for pressure and vacuum forming
Cmo: Paul Hinspeter
paul.hinspeter@alcoa.com
VP/General Manager: Eugene Whitacre
Plant Manager: Juan Escobar
Estimated Sales: $20-50 Million
Number Employees: 100-249

26409 MultiFab Plastics
60B Tenean Street
Boston, MA 02122-2738
617-287-1411
Fax: 617-287-0299 888-293-5754
Bagel and bulk food bins, acrylic displays, cases, table tents and sign holders
President: Stan Lisowski
Vice President: David Lisowski
Estimated Sales: $1-2.5 Million
Number Employees: 10-19

26410 MultiMedia Electronic Displays
11370 Sunrise Park Dr
Rancho Cordova, CA 95742-6542
916-852-4220
Fax: 916-852-8325 800-888-3007
www.multimedialed.com
Manufacturer and exporter of programmable electronic signs
President: William Y Hall
CEO: Rex Williams
Marketing Director: Karen Klueh
Contact: Steven Craig
scraig@multimedialed.com
Operations Manager: Paul Selems
Plant Manager: George Pappas
Estimated Sales: $5 - 10 Million
Number Employees: 20-49
Number of Brands: 5
Number of Products: 200
Parent Co: SignUp
Type of Packaging: Food Service

26411 Multibulk Systems International
6 W 3rd Street
Wendell, NC 27591-8086
919-366-2100
Fax: 919-676-7716
Manufacturer and exporter of bulk bag flexible containers
Sales Manager: John Watson
Estimated Sales: $500,000-$1,000,000
Number Employees: 5-9
Type of Packaging: Private Label
Brands:
Multibulk

26412 Multifeeder Technology Inc
4821 White Bear Pkwy
St Paul, MN 55110-3325
651-407-3100
Fax: 651-407-3199 info@multifeeder.com
www.multifeeder.com
Friction Feeders
President: Neal Nordling
Estimated Sales: Less Than $500,000
Number Employees: 1-4

26413 Multifilm Packaging Corp
1040 N Mclean Blvd
Elgin, IL 60123-1709
847-695-7600
Fax: 847-695-7645 800-837-9727
info@multifilm.com
Constantia Multifilm is an integrated manufacturer of flexible packaging solutions for the food, beverage, and confectionery industries.
President: Chris Rogers
chris.rogers@constantia-multifilm.com
Vice President Finance: Robert Tate
Graphics Manager: Terry Piatkowski
New Business Development Manager: Marcus Magnusson
Vice President Sales and Marketing: Chris Rogers
Customer Service: Nancy Jung
Production Manager: Mike Huey
Plant Manager: Dave Rohrschneider

Estimated Sales: Below $5 Million
Number Employees: 50-99
Type of Packaging: Consumer

26414 Multigrains Bread Co
117 Water St
Lawrence, MA 01841-4720
978-691-6100
Fax: 978-373-4801 www.multigrainsbakeries.com
Multigrain breads
President: Joseph Faro
joseph@multigrainsbakeries.com
EVP/Director R&D: Chuck Brandano
Director of Quality: Adam Gabour
Director of Purchasing: Darren Gaiero
Number Employees: 100-249

26415 Multikem Corp
700 Grand Ave
Ridgefield, NJ 07657-1524
201-941-4520
Fax: 201-941-5239 800-462-4425
www.multikem.com
President: Larry Muhlberg
multikem@mindspring.com
Estimated Sales: $5 - 10 Million
Number Employees: 5-9

26416 Multiplex Co Inc
2100 Future Dr
Sellersburg, IN 47172-1874
812-256-7777
Fax: 636-527-4313 800-787-8880
www.google.com
High capacity dispensing systems for beverages including beer; also, water filtration systems
President & Chief Operating Officer: J. Kisling
Chief Executive Officer: Terry Growcock
Contact: John Bell
jbell@manitowocfsg.com
Estimated Sales: $34.6 Million
Number Employees: 1-4
Square Footage: 10000000
Parent Co: Manitowoc Foodservice Group
Brands:
Beermaster
Computap
Intercept
Pr/O-Rox
Re-Fresh

26417 Multipond America Inc
2301 Hutson Rd
Green Bay, WI 54303-4712
920-490-8249
Fax: 920-490-8482 sales-us@multipond.com
Multipond America Inc, is a wholly owned subsidiary of Multipond, Germany which is the sales and service division of the German based manufacturing company ATOMA. Mutlipond Weighing Technology and mutlihead weigher systems for thepackaging industry stands for the maximum accuaracy, performance, and reliability. We work closely with our customers on continuous improvement in all aspects of our design. We develop and produce customized multihead weigher systems for ourcustomers.
Vice President: Fred Horn
fwd@multipondamerica.com
Controller: Paul Plutz
Project Manager: Keven Diederich
Research/Development: John Tuchscherer
VP Sales/Marketing: Frederick Horn
Technical Sales Engineer: Jerry Van Lannen
Estimated Sales: $10 Million
Number Employees: 5-9

26418 (HQ)Multisorb Technologies Inc
325 Harlem Rd
Buffalo, NY 14224-1893
716-824-8900
Fax: 716-824-4128 800-445-9890
info@multisorb.com www.multisorb.com
Manufacturer and exporter of active packaging technologies for food packaging, including odor absorbers, desiccants, and moisture regulators, and odor and other volatile absorbers.
President: James Renda
jrenda@multisorb.com
Marketing: Tom Powers
Marketing Communications Coordinator: Kay Krause
Number Employees: 500-999
Square Footage: 340000

Other Locations:
Multisorb Technologies
Orchard Park NY
Brands:
Freshmax
Freshpax
Minipax
Natrasorb
Sorbicap

26419 Multisorb Technologies Inc
325 Harlem Rd
Buffalo, NY 14224-1893
716-824-8900
Fax: 716-824-4128 info@multisorb.com
www.multisorb.com
President: James Renda
jrenda@multisorb.com
Estimated Sales: $1 - 3 Million
Number Employees: 500-999

26420 Multivac
21209 Durand Ave
Union Grove, WI 53182-9711
262-878-0366
Fax: 262-878-4019 800-640-4213
www.multivacinc.com
Stainless steel material handling equipment; also, industrial vacuum equipment and dust collectors
Owner: Wally Haag
multivac@wi.net
V.P.: Margaret Haag
Plant Manager: Dwane Hartlage
Estimated Sales: Below $5 Million
Number Employees: 20-49
Square Footage: 60000
Parent Co: M&W Shops

26421 Multivac Inc
11021 N Pomona Ave
Kansas City, MO 64153-1146
816-891-0555
Fax: 816-891-0622 800-800-8552
muinc@multivac.com
Wholesaler/distributor, importer and exporter of thermoform, fill and seal packaging equipment; also, tray sealers, chamber vacuum packaging and labeling equipment; sales support services available
President: Michel Defenbau
CEO: Werner Britz
werner.britz@multivacsa.com
CEO: Jan Erik Kuhlmann
CFO: Danny Liker
Sales Director: Norm Winkel
Estimated Sales: $50 - 60Million
Number Employees: 100-249
Square Footage: 60000
Parent Co: Multivac Export AG

26422 Mumper Machine Corporation
5081 N 124th St
Butler, WI 53007
262-781-8908
Fax: 262-781-1253
Manufacturer and exporter of vegetable topping and conveying equipment
President: Jordy Mumper
Estimated Sales: $500,000-$1 Million
Number Employees: 5-9

26423 Mundial
63 Broadway # 1
Norwood, MA 02062-3558
781-762-0053
Fax: 781-762-0364 800-487-2224
info@mundial-usa.com www.mundialusa.com
Manufacturer, importer and exporter of knives, scissors and shears
President: Adilson Delatorre
CFO: John Keese
Sales VP: Rich Zirpolo
Estimated Sales: $1-2.5 Million
Number Employees: 1-4
Square Footage: 200000
Parent Co: Zivi-Hercules
Type of Packaging: Consumer, Food Service, Bulk

26424 Munson Machinery Co
210 Seward Ave
PO Box 855
Utica, NY 13502-5750
315-797-0090
Fax: 315-797-5582 800-944-6644
info@munsonmachinery.com
www.munsonmachinery.com
Mixers, blenders and size reduction equipment for bulk solid materials.
Partner/VP/COO: Thomas Dalton III
Marketing Manager: Charles Divine
Regional Sales Manager: Darren Woods
Estimated Sales: $5 - 10 Million
Number Employees: 20-49
Square Footage: 90000

26425 Munters Corp
79 Monroe St
Amesbury, MA 01913-3204
978-388-0600
Fax: 978-241-1219 800-843-5360
www.munters.com
Manufacturer and exporter of continuous desiccant dehumidification systems
President: Mike Mc Donald
Cmo: Scott Haynes
shaynes@munters.com
Estimated Sales: $20-50 Million
Number Employees: 250-499
Square Footage: 175000
Parent Co: Munters Corporation

26426 Murata Automated Systems
PO Box 667609
2120 Queen City Drive
Charlotte, NC 28266
704-573-2250
Fax: 704-394-2001 800-428-8469
info@muratec-usa.com www.muratec-usa.com
Automated material handling and control systems including storage and retrieval, guided vehicles, conveyors, monorails, etc.; also, software
President: Masaharu Nishio
Manager Projects: Masato Ohzawa
CFO: Dale Mitchell
Quality Control: Gary Reynoles
Estimated Sales: $.5 - 1 million
Number Employees: 100
Parent Co: Murato Machinery

26427 Murk Brush Company
P.O. Box 726
New Britain, CT 06050-0726
860-249-2550
Fax: 860-249-2550
Brushes for the food and beverage industry, FDA approved brush construction; specialist in OEM Brush Design
Sales: Dave Hames
Estimated Sales: 500000
Number Employees: 1-4
Number of Products: 2600
Square Footage: 28000
Type of Packaging: Bulk

26428 Murnane Co
607 Northwest Ave
Northlake, IL 60164-1398
708-449-1200
Fax: 708-449-1231 www.murnanecompanies.com
Packaging materials and paperboard boxes
President: Frank J Murnane Jr
Vice President: Patrick J Murnane
pjmurnane@murnanecompanies.com
Estimated Sales: $20-50 Million
Number Employees: 50-99

26429 Murnell Wax Company
237 Memorial Drive
Springfield, MA 01104-3228
781-395-1323
Fax: 781-395-8160
Floor polish and cleaners
Estimated Sales: $1-2.5 Million
Number Employees: 6

26430 Murotech
550 Mckinley Rd
St Marys, OH 45885-1803
419-394-6529
Fax: 419-394-6820 800-565-6876
muropeeler@aol.com www.murotech.com

Manufacturer, exporter and importer of semi-automatic peeling machines for fruits and vegetables including oranges, apples, mangos, cantaloupes and rutabegas
President: Naonobu Kenmoku
Quality Manager: Rick Wiley
Sales Manager: S. Sugimoto
Production Manager: Koichi Uchida
Estimated Sales: $500,000-$1 Million
Number Employees: 100-249
Square Footage: 4000
Parent Co: Muro Corporation
Brands:
    Muro

26431 (HQ)Murray Envelope Corporation
1500 N Main St
Suite C
Hattiesburg, MS 39401-1911
601-583-8292
Fax: 800-423-7589   murray@netdoor.com
Manufacturer and exporter of filing folders and envelopes
Owner: Marvin Murry
CFO: Joae Comprtallo
R & D: Lenda Wisa
Estimated Sales: Below $5 Million
Number Employees: 1-4

26432 Murray Runin
531 Cascade Court
Mahwah, NJ 07430-2750
201-512-3885
Fax: 201-512-3850   consultrun@aol.com
Management consultant specializing in operational and distribution problem solving
Owner: Murray Runin

26433 Murtech Manufacturing
835 Fairfield Avenue
Kenilworth, NJ 07033-2059
908-245-1556
Fax: 908-245-8707
Grids for bottle tanking
Owner: Mike Blazinsky
Estimated Sales: Less than $500,000
Number Employees: 4

26434 (HQ)Murzan Inc
2909 Langford Rd # A700
Rd. 1-700
Peachtree Cor, GA 30071-1512
770-448-0583
Fax: 770-448-0967   murzan@murzan.com
www.murzan.com
Manufacturer and exporter of food processing pumps and drum unloading, turnkey and bag-in-box blending/batching systems
Owner: Alberto Bazan
    murzan@aol.com
CEO: Alberto Bazan
Estimated Sales: $2,600,000
Number Employees: 50-99

26435 Music City Metals Inc
2633 Grandview Ave
Nashville, TN 37211-2202
615-255-4481
Fax: 615-255-4482   800-251-2674
musiccitymetals@musiccitymetals.net
www.musiccitymetals.net
Cast iron hot plates, gas burners, cooking grids, cast iron and stainless steel burners, grids and grates for gas grills.
President: Bo Richardson
    musiccitymetals@musiccitymetals.net
Estimated Sales: $1 - 2.5 Million
Number Employees: 10-19
Brands:
    Kings Kooker

26436 Muskegon Awning & Fabrication
2333 Henry St
Muskegon, MI 49441-3097
231-759-0911
Fax: 231-759-3200   800-968-3686
www.muskegonawning.com
Awnings and canvas related products
President: David Bayne
    dbayne@muskegonawning.com
CEO: Gordon Moen
President: Lora Davis
Sr. Sales Representative: Peter Yonkavit

Estimated Sales: Below $5 Million
Number Employees: 5-9
Square Footage: 57200

26437 Muskogee Rubber Stamp &Seal Company
23549 S 450 Rd
Fort Gibson, OK 74434
918-478-3046
Seals, daters, magnetic signs, price marking inks and rubber stamps
Owner: Sarah Turner
Owner: Paul Owen
Estimated Sales: Less than $500,000
Number Employees: 1-4

26438 Muth Associates
53 Progress Ave
Springfield, MA 01104-3266
413-734-2107
Fax: 413-734-2107   800-388-0157
info@muthassociates.com   muthassociates.com
Wholesaler/distributor of adsorbent materials
President: Cis Lafond
    cislafond@muthassociates.com
CEO: Doug Muth
CFO: Sandra Peterson
Estimated Sales: $5-10 Million
Number Employees: 10-19
Number of Products: 300
Square Footage: 52000
Type of Packaging: Private Label, Bulk
Brands:
    Desi-Pak
    Sorb-It
    Tri-Wall

26439 Mutual Stamping & Mfg Co
655 Plains Rd
P.O. Box 5060
Milford, CT 06461-1736
203-877-3933
Fax: 203-877-1822   800-735-3933
Wine industry stainless steel barrels
Owner: Jay Fox
    info@drumsofsteel.com
Estimated Sales: $500,000 - $1 Million
Number Employees: 5-9

26440 My Serenity Pond
15009 Held Cir
Cold Spring, MN 56320
320-363-0411
Fax: 320-363-0339   www.myserenitypond.com
Identification products including nameplates, and stamp business forms
President: Marlin Boeckmann
Estimated Sales: $300,000-500,000
Number Employees: 1-4
Square Footage: 40000

26441 My Style
614 NW Street
Raleigh, NC 27603
919-832-2526
Fax: 919-832-1546   800-524-8269
Wholesaler/distributor, importer and exporter of teak, cast aluminum, stainless steel and hardwood outdoor furniture; also, wooden and market umbrellas
Director: Ward Usmar
Owner: Klaus Weihe
Owner: Eik Niemann
Marketing Administrator: Ceri Usmar
Number Employees: 1-4
Square Footage: 13500
Brands:
    Caribbean Shade Market Umbrellas
    Lingot Stainless & Hardwood Floors
    Siesta Shade Market Umbrellas
    Teake Furniture

26442 Mycom Group
110-6620 McMillan Way
Richmond, BC V6W 1J7
Canada
604-270-1544
Fax: 604-270-9870
Refrigeration equipment and supplies
President: Yasushi Sasaki

26443 Mycom Sales
210 Summit Ave
Suite C12
Montvale, NJ 07645
201-307-9199
Fax: 201-307-1566
Estimated Sales: $1 - 3 Million
Number Employees: 1-4

26444 Mycom/Mayekawa Manfacturing
16825 Ih 35 N
Selma, TX 78154-1223
210-599-4536
Fax: 210-599-4538
Manager: Pete Valdez
Estimated Sales: $1 - 3 Million
Number Employees: 1-4

26445 Myers Container
21301 Cloud Way
Hayward, CA 94545-1216
510-785-8235
Fax: 510-271-6215   jcutt@myerscontainer.com
www.myerscontainer.com
Manufacturer, exporter and reconditioner of steel drums including aseptic, hot pack food, conical and vegetable oil
President: John Cutt
Chief Executive Officer: Kyle Stavig
CFO: Thomas Holmes
Quality Control: Dana Zanone
Manager Food Sales: Roger Thornton
Manager: Benjamin Rivera
    brivera@myerscontainer.com
Estimated Sales: $50-100 Million
Number Employees: 10-19
Square Footage: 500000
Parent Co: IMACC Corporation
Brands:
    Pureliner
    Purestack
    Purevac

26446 Myers Ice Company
102 N 9th St
Garden City, KS 67846-5350
620-275-5751
Fax: 620-275-8574   800-767-5751
Ice
Co-Owner: Craig Myers
    c.myers@myersice.com
Co-Owner: Carl Myers
Estimated Sales: $1-2.5 Million
Number Employees: 10-19
Brands:
    Myers Ice Co.

26447 Myers Restaurant SupplyInc
1599 Cleveland Ave
Santa Rosa, CA 95401-4280
707-570-1200
Fax: 707-542-0350   800-219-9426
brett@myersrestaurantsupply.com
www.myersrestaurantsupply.com
Wholesaler/distributor of restaurant and bar equipment and supplies; serving the food service market
Owner: Rob Myers
CEO: Jon Myers
CFO: Brett Livingstone
Estimated Sales: $2.5 - 5 Million
Number Employees: 20-49
Square Footage: 44000

26448 N & A Mfg
203 Inman St
Mallard, IA 50562-7509
712-425-3512
Fax: 712-425-3308   spraymatic@iowatelecom.net
www.pressuresprayers.net
Agricultural high pressure hot and cold washers, power scrapers and accessories for high pressure washer systems
President: Virgil Auten
Sales Manager: Troy Auten
Estimated Sales: $1 - 2.5 Million
Number Employees: 1-4
Square Footage: 13400
Brands:
    Spraymatic
    Vibramatic

26449 N A P Engineering
10965 Harborside Dr
Largo, FL 33773-4428
727-544-3118
www.napengineering.com
Manufacturer of Rotary Fillers and Sealers, Inline
Tray Fillers and Sealersand Specialty Parts.
President: Paul Desocio
glouli@tampabay.rr.com
Estimated Sales: Less Than $500,000
Number Employees: 1-4

26450 N.A. Krups
7 Reuten Dr
Closter, NJ 07624-2120
201-767-5500
Fax: 201-784-3710 www.krupsusa.com
Brewing devices
President: Mark Navarre
Estimated Sales: $10-20 Million
Number Employees: 50-99

26451 N.G. Slater Corporation
42 W 38th St Rm 200
Suite 1002
New York, NY 10018
212-768-9434
Fax: 212-869-7368 800-848-4621
info@ngslater.com www.ngslater.com
Manufacturer and distributors of custom imprinted
and specialties, badges, buttons and emblems
Owner: Robert Slater
VP: Alan Slater
Estimated Sales: $1 - 3,000,000
Number Employees: 5-9

26452 NACCO Industries Inc.
5875 Landerbrook Dr
Suite 220
Cleveland, OH 44124
440-229-5151
www.nacco.com
Manufacturer and exporter of forklift trucks
President & CEO: J.C. Butler

Estimated Sales: $50-100 Million
Number Employees: 141
Square Footage: 68384

26453 NAP Industries
667 Kent Ave
Brooklyn, NY 11249-7500
718-625-4948
Fax: 718-596-4342 877-635-4948
info@napind.com www.napind.com
Manufacturer and exporter of bags including heat
sealed, meat, plastic, polyethylene and shopping;
also, pressure sensitive tapes
President: Leo Lowy
morris@napind.com
Sales Exec: Morris Lowy
Estimated Sales: $5-10 Million
Number Employees: 20-49

26454 NB Corporation of America
46750 Lakerville Blvd.
Fremont, CA 94538
510-490-1420
Fax: 510-490-1733 888-562-4175
info@nbcorporation.com www.nbcorporation.com
President: Toru Yamazaki
Estimated Sales: $3 - 5 Million
Number Employees: 10-19

26455 NCC
21005 Obrien Rd
Groveland, FL 34736-9590
352-429-9036
Fax: 352-429-9039 800-429-9037
novelty@aol.com www.partyplasticsplus.com
Hotel and restaurant supplies including catering and
buffet trays, plastic drinkware, pitchers, bowls and
serving utensils
President: Sara Michaeli
sara@global-nation.com
CEO: Asher Michaeli
CFO: Joe Michaeli
VP: Sara Coslett
R&D: Joe Michaeli
Marketing: Ed Coslett
Sales Manager: Ed Coslett
Public Relations: Sara Coslett
Manager: Sara Michaeli
Plant Manager: Paul Patin

Estimated Sales: $1-2.5 Million
Number Employees: 20-49
Square Footage: 125000
Parent Co: Novelty Crystal Corporation
Type of Packaging: Food Service

26456 NCR Corp
Atlanta, GA 30308
937-445-1936
800-225-5627
www.ncr.com
Point-of-sale systems including self-ordering kiosks,
guest and table management, kitchen production and
payment processing.
Executive Chairman: Frank Martire
President & CEO: Michael Hayford
EVP/CFO: Andre Fernandez
EVP/General Counsel: Jim Bedore
EVP, NCR Hospitality: Dirk Izzo
SVP & GM, NCR Retail: David Wilkinson
SVP/Chief Information Officer: William (Bill)
Vancuren
EVP, NCR Global Sales: Dan Campbell
EVP, Global Customer Services: J. Robert Ciminera
Chief Operating Officer: Owen Sullivan
Year Founded: 1884
Estimated Sales: $6.4 Billion
Number Employees: 34,000

26457 NCR Counterpoint
4325 Alexander Dr
Alpharetta, GA 30022
800-852-5852
www.counterpointpos.com
Consultant providing point of sale, back office and
headquarter solutions for quick and full service es-
tablishments.
President & CEO: Michael Hayford
Chief Operating Officer: Paul Laungenbahn
EVP, CFO & Chief Accounting Officer: Bob
Fishman
EVP, CAO & Chief Human Resources Officer:
Andrea Ledford
SVP & Chief Information Officer: William
Vancuren
SVP, General Counsel & Secretary: Edward
Gallagher

26458 NDC Infrared EngineeringInc
5314 Irwindale Ave
Irwindale, CA 91706
626-960-3300
Fax: 626-939-3870 info@ndcinfrared.com
www.ndcinfrared.com
Manufacturer and exporter of on-line instrumenta-
tion for measurement of moisture, fat/oil, protein
and caffeine including testers and analyzers
President: Bromley Beadle
Marketing Manager: Raymond Shead
Sales/Marketing Executive: Bill Diltz
Contact: Drew Cheshire
jhazlett@verrents.com
Estimated Sales: $20 - 50 Million
Number Employees: 50-99
Square Footage: 50000
Parent Co: Fairey Group
Brands:
  Mm710
  Tm710

26459 NECO/Nebraska Engineering
9364 N 45th St
Omaha, NE 68152-1328
402-453-6912
Fax: 402-453-0471 800-367-6208
www.necousa.com
Manufacturer and exporter of grain processing and
handling equipment including cleaners, augers,
spreaders, conveyors, dryers and aeration fans
President: Steve Campbell
VP: Bryan Hayes
Marketing Director: Steve Campbell
Sales Manager: Pat McCarthy
Manager: William Hiltgen
Plant Manager: Rick Wulf
Purchase Head: Rick Wuls
Estimated Sales: Below $5 Million
Number Employees: 50-99
Square Footage: 300000
Parent Co: GLOBAL Industries

26460 NEPA Pallet & ContainerCo
12027 3 Lakes Rd
Snohomish, WA 98290-5502
360-568-3185
Fax: 360-568-9135 www.nepapallet.com
Manufacturer and exporter of pallets and bins
President: Denton Sherry
dsherry@nepapallet.com
Estimated Sales: $5 - 10 Million
Number Employees: 100-249

26461 NIMCO Corp
1000 Nimco Dr
Crystal Lake, IL 60014-1704
815-459-4200
Fax: 815-459-8119 info@nimco.com
www.nimco.com
Form, fill seal for gable-top cartons
President: Jerry Bachner
nimco@nimco.com
Estimated Sales: $5-10 Million
Number Employees: 20-49

26462 NJM Packaging
56 Etna Rd
Lebanon, NH 03766-1419
603-448-0300
Fax: 603-448-4810 800-432-2990
info@njmpackaging.com www.njmpackaging.com
Packaging equipment and labeling equipment
President/CEO: Michel Lapierre
Director International Sales: Marc Lapierre
CFO: Jim Moretti
moretti@njmpackaging.com
Vice President Operations Finances: Andre
Caumartin
Vice President: Daniel Lapierre
Marketing Director: Marla Stallmann
VP Sales: Mark LaRoche
Human Resources: Todd Savage
Number Employees: 10-19

26463 NJM Packaging
56 Etna Rd
Lebanon, NH 03766-1419
603-448-0300
Fax: 603-448-4810 800-432-2990
info@njmpackaging.com www.njmpackaging.com
Wine industry labeling equipment
President & CEO: Michel Lapierre
CFO: Jim Moretti
moretti@njmpackaging.com
VP: Daniel Lapierre
Marketing: Marla Stallman
Director International Sales: Marc Lapierre
Estimated Sales: $5-10 Million
Number Employees: 10-19

26464 NJM/CLI
8 Plateau Street
Pointe Claire, QC H9R 5W2
Canada
514-630-6990
Fax: 514-695-0801
Manufacturer, exporter and importer of packaging
machinery including fillers, cappers, labelers, tablet
and capsule counters, etc
President: Michel LaPierre
Director: Charles Lapierre
VP: Dan Lapierre
Marketing: Louise Lafleur
VP Sales: Mark Laroche
Number Employees: 150
Square Footage: 80000
Parent Co: NJM/CLI Packaging Systems Interna-
tional
Brands:
  Blipack
  Cli
  Cremer
  New Jersey Machine

26465 (HQ)NOVOLEX
5160 W Missouri Ave
Glendale, AZ 85301-6002
623-842-2236
Fax: 623-930-9406 800-243-0306
www.novolex.com
Polyethylene food and utility bags, printed bags,
trash can liners, sleeves, tubing, interfold and sheeting
Manager: Ron Shaw
rshaw@fortuneplastics.com
VP Sales/Marketing: Ed Gillespie

Estimated Sales: $20-50 Million
Number Employees: 20-49
Other Locations:
   Fortune Plastics
   Phoenix AZ
Brands:
   Duraliner
   Dynaplas
   Enviroplas
   Hid-Tuff

26466 NPC Display Group
105 Avenue L
Newark, NJ 7105

    973-589-2155
    Fax: 973-589-2414
Containers including paper, corrugated and solid fiber
President: Dennis Mehiel
CFO: Allen Edelman
Contact: Donna Wiggs
  donna.wiggs@usdisplaygroup.com
Number Employees: 100-249

26467 NS International
800 Kirts Blvd # 300
Troy, MI 48084-4880

    248-362-8570
    Fax: 248-352-9125 george@nsusa.com
    www.ns-international.net
High speed, vertical 3 or 4 sided fill and seal machine for liquids and paste with multi-task programmable control
President: Arthur McMillen
Contact: Yoshi Ida
  yoshi@nsusa.com
Estimated Sales: $20-50 Million
Number Employees: 1,000-4,999

26468 NSF International
789 N Dixboro Rd
Ann Arbor, MI 48105

    734-769-8010
    Fax: 734-769-0109 800-673-6275
    info@nsf.org www.nsf.org
Organization sets public health standards and tests and certifies products and systems
CEO: Kevan Lawlor
  lawlor@nsf.org
Number Employees: 2800

26469 NST Metals
721-723 East Main Street
Louisville, KY 40202

    502-584-5846
    Fax: 502-584-3481
Manufacturer and exporter of food processing equipment, pressure vessels, hoppers, bins and silos
President: Joe Harvey
VP: Kenneth Harvey
VP: Brian Harvey
Estimated Sales: $1-2.5 Million
Number Employees: 5-9
Square Footage: 28000
Type of Packaging: Consumer, Bulk

26470 NTN Wireless
6080 Northbelt Dr.
Norcross, GA 30071

    770-277-2760
    Fax: 770-277-2765 800-637-8639
    james.frakes@ntn.com
Manufacturer and exporter of wireless server call systems and in-house server, guest and table ready paging systems
President: Mark Degortor
Number Employees: 20-49
Square Footage: 16000
Parent Co: Hysen Technologies
Brands:
   Beck 'n Call
   Economy Pager
   Perfect Pager
   Serv 'r Call
   Table Turner

26471 NTS
126 Peach State Court
Suite A-C
Tyrone, GA 30290-2744

    770-631-0203
    Fax: 770-631-0718

CFO: Philippe Jafflin

Estimated Sales: $10 - 20 Million
Number Employees: 20-49

26472 NYP
10 Site Rd
Leola, PA 17540-1849

    717-656-0299
    Fax: 717-656-0350 800-541-0961
    padiv@nyp-corp.com www.nyp-corp.com
Plain and printed bags including multi-wall, paper, polyethylene, woven polypropylene, burlap, cotton and mesh; importer of woven polypropylene bags
VP: Christopher LaBelle
VP Sales: Gerald LaBelle
Sales/Customer Service: Don Ament
  dament@nyp-corp.com
Manager: Beverley Campbell
Division Manager: Robert Ellis
Purchasing Manager: Katie Gorsuch
Estimated Sales: less than $500,000
Number Employees: 1-4
Square Footage: 30000
Parent Co: NYP Corporation
Type of Packaging: Private Label, Bulk

26473 Nagel Paper & Box Company
3286 Industrial Drive
Saginaw, MI 48601

    989-753-4405
    Fax: 989-753-2493 800-292-3654
    info@nagelpaper.com www.nagelpaper.com
Fiber tubes, caps and plugs
Contact: James Baker
  james@nagelpaper.com
Estimated Sales: $1 - 3 Million
Number Employees: 18
Square Footage: 80000
Type of Packaging: Food Service

26474 Nalco Water
1601 W Diehl Rd
Naperville, IL 60563-1198

    Fax: 800-288-0878 800-288-0879
    customerservice.us@nalco.com www.ecolab.com
Process chemicals, water treatment, waste water treatment.
EVP & President, Global Industrial: Darrell Brown
EVP & GM, Global Food & Beverage: Nicholas Alfano
Year Founded: 1928
Estimated Sales: $4.2 Billion
Number Employees: 11,500
Parent Co: Ecolab Inc

26475 Nalge Process Technologies Group
75 Panorama Creek Dr
Rochester, NY 14625-2385

    585-586-8800
    Fax: 585-586-8431 nnitech@nalgenunc.com
    www.nalgenunc.com
Manufacturer and exporter of blowers, fans, fittings, hoses, liquid mixers, pipe tube and hose clamps, safety equipment and tanks
Marketing: Karen Dally
Sales Manager: John Cooling
Contact: Charlie Amico
  camico@nalgenunc.com
Product Manager: Greg Felosky
Number Employees: 500-999
Parent Co: Sybron Corporation

26476 Nalge Process Technologies Group
29 Brookfield Drive
Lafayette, NJ 07848-2006

    973-579-1313
    Fax: 973-579-3908 800-988-4876
Bins
Estimated Sales: $5-10 Million
Number Employees: 38

26477 Naltex
220 E Saint Elmo Rd
Austin, TX 78745

    512-447-7000
    Fax: 512-447-7444 800-531-5112
    www.delstarinc.com
Manufacturer and exporter of plastic mesh, heat sealing and header bags; also, case liners
Marketing: Marjorie Wilcox
Product Manager: Susan Emory
  semory@delstarinc.com
Plant Manager: Scott Mc Henry

Estimated Sales: $20-50 Million
Number Employees: 100-249
Square Footage: 110000
Brands:
   Flex Net
   Mari-Net
   Naltex
   Shur-Grip
   Softliner
   Texliner

26478 Naman Marketing
9870 Pineview Avenue
Theodore, AL 36582-7403

    251-438-2617
    Fax: 251-433-5032

President: George Naman

26479 Namco Controls Corporation
760 Beta Dr # F
Cleveland, OH 44143-2334

    440-460-1360
    Fax: 440-460-3800 800-626-8324
    www.namcocontrols.com
Manufacturer and exporter of packaging and material handling presence and position sensors including photoelectric, laser scanner, rotary cam switch and proximity
President: Alex Joseph
Marketing Manager: Chuck Juda
VP Sales/Marketing: Bob Joyce
Plant Manager: Jamy Robins
Number Employees: 1-4
Parent Co: Danaher Corporation
Other Locations:
   Namco Controls Corp.
   Herzhorn
Brands:
   Cylindicator
   Lasernet
   Namco
   Snap-Lock

26480 Namco Machinery
5421 73rd Pl
Maspeth, NY 11378

    Fax: 718-803-0165
Manufacturer and exporter of bottle washing machinery for laboratory glassware
President: Manning E Cole
  jackjackson54@aol.com
Sales Manager: R Jackson
Estimated Sales: $3 - 5 Million
Number Employees: 5-9

26481 Nameplate
87 Empire Dr
St Paul, MN 55103-1856

    651-228-1522
    Fax: 651-228-1314 www.nameplatesdiv.com
Badges, medals, name plates, signs, stamps, tags and labels
President: G Mellgren
  g.mellgren@dmpolystamps.com
Estimated Sales: $2.5-5 Million
Number Employees: 50-99
Parent Co: St. Paul Stamp Works

26482 Napa Fermentation Supplies
575 Third St # A
Napa, CA 94559-2701

    707-255-6372
    Fax: 707-255-6462 napafermentation@aol.com
    www.northnaparotary.org
Wine industry fermentation supplies
Owner: Pat Watkins
Manager: Megan Furth
Estimated Sales: less than $500,000
Number Employees: 5-9

26483 Napa Valley Bung Works
151 Camino Dorado
Napa, CA 94558-6213

    707-963-0241
    Fax: 707-963-0241
Bung hole stoppers
Estimated Sales: $1 - 5 Million
Number Employees: 5-9

26484 Napa Wooden Box Co
369 S Kelly Rd
American Canyon, CA 94503-9647
707-224-6447
Fax: 707-224-1613 www.napawoodenbox.com
Wooden gift boxes, wooden specialty packaging,
wooden displays
President: Greg Chase
greg@napawoodenbox.com
Estimated Sales: $5-10 Million
Number Employees: 20-49

26485 Napco Graphics Corporation
200 Covington Drive
Bloomingdale, IL 60108-3105
630-529-2900
Fax: 630-529-4395 www.napco.com
Flexographic printing, four-color process labels,
thermal labels, thermal ribbons, custom pres-
sure-sensitive labels
President: Geno Napolitano
Estimated Sales: $10-20 Million
Number Employees: 50-99

26486 Napco Security Systems Inc
333 Bayview Ave
Amityville, NY 11701-2800
631-842-0253
Fax: 631-789-9292 salesinfo@napcosecurity.com
www.napcosecurity.com
Manufacturer and exporter of electronic security
systems and accessories including control panels
President/Chairman/CEO: Richard Soloway
Estimated Sales: $71 Million
Number Employees: 5-9
Square Footage: 90000
Brands:
Magnum Alert

26487 Napoleon Appliance Corporation
214 Bayview Drive
Barrie, ON L4N 4Y8
Canada
705-726-4278
Fax: 705-725-2564 866-820-8686
wecare@napoleonproducts.com
www.napoleongrills.com
Manufacturer and exporter of gas grills
President: Wolfgang Schroeter
VP: Ingrid Schroeter
Research & Development: Steve Schwartz
Quality Control: Steve Taylor
Marketing/Sales: David Blain
Plant Manager: Michael Pulfer
Purchasing Manager: Lynda Allen
Number Employees: 100
Number of Brands: 11
Square Footage: 600000
Parent Co: Wolf Steel
Brands:
Elegance
Emerald
Horizon
Lifestyle
Napoleon
Premiere
Prestige
Signature
Ultrachef

26488 NaraKom
PO Box 368
Peapack, NJ 07977-0368
908-234-1776
Fax: 908-234-0964
Distributor of Nara milling, sizing, coating, and
powder surface modification technology in the
Americas
President: C Komline
Number Employees: 20-49
Parent Co: Komline-Sanderson Engineering Corpo-
ration

26489 Nashua Corporation
250 S. Northwest Highway
Suite 203
Park Ridge, IL 60068
402-397-3600
Fax: 402-392-6080 800-323-4265
www.nashua.com
Manufacturer and exporter of computer and pressure
sensitive labels

President: Andrew Albert
CFO: John Patenaude
VP: Michael Jarrett
VP: Mike Jarrutt
Contact: Charles Bonnier
cbonnier@nashua.com
Number Employees: 100-249

26490 Nashua Corporation
44 Franklin Street
Nashua, NH 03064-2665
603-661-2004
Fax: 603-880-5671 info@amstock.com
Manufacturer and exporter of industrial tape and la-
bels
President: Andrew Albert
CFO: John Petenaude

**26491 Nashville Display Manufacturing
Company**
306 Hartmann Drive
Lebanon, TN 37087
615-743-2900
Fax: 615-743-2901 888-743-2572
dissales@nashvillewire.com
www.nashvilledisplay.com
Manufacturer and exporter of displays and merchan-
disers for retail products
President: David L Rollins
CFO: Jeff McCeann
VP: E White
Quality Control: Charles Brittain
R & D: Juris Leikartt
Sales Manager: Richard Hornsay
Office Manager: Jere Lane
Estimated Sales: $10-20 Million
Number Employees: 20-49
Square Footage: 1600000

26492 Nashville Wire Products
295 Driftwood Dr
Nashville, TN 37210
615-743-2480
Fax: 615-255-8349 www.nashvillewire.com
Wire oven and warming racks and barbecue grids
President: David L Rollins
Shipping Manager: Levon Mathis
Division Manager: Steven Rollins
Plant Manager: Roy Binkley
Estimated Sales: $20-50 Million
Number Employees: 10-19
Square Footage: 140000
Parent Co: Nashville Wire Products Manufacturing
Company

26493 Nashville Wraps LLC
242 Molly Walton Dr
Hendersonville, TN 37075-2154
615-431-5000
Fax: 800-646-0046 800-547-9727
info@nashvillewraps.com
www.nashvillewraps.com
Bags and bows, gift wrap, tissue paper, ribbon,
candy boxes, food packaging, custom printing and
eco-friendly retail packaging
Marketing Director: James Meadows
Estimated Sales: Less Than $500,000
Number Employees: 1-4

26494 Natale Machine & Tool Co Inc
339 13th St
Carlstadt, NJ 07072-1917
201-933-5500
Fax: 201-933-8146 800-883-8382
www.circle-d.com
Manufacturer and exporter of emergency lighting in-
cluding flash, flood and spot lights; also, HID,
quartz and commercial lighting available
CEO: Dominick Natale
VP: Lynn Natale
Sales: John Cocozzo
Production/Plant Manager/Purchasing: John
Cocozzo
Estimated Sales: $3 - 5 Million
Number Employees: 10-19
Square Footage: 30000
Brands:
Circle D Lights
Streamlight

26495 Nation/Ruskin
206 Progress Dr
Montgomeryville, PA 18936
267-654-4000
Fax: 267-654-4010 800-523-2489
Natural and synthetic sponges; also, cloths and
brushes
President: Raymond Adolf
VP Sales: John Holcombe
VP Sales: Stan Ruskin
Contact: Sandy Adolf
sadolf@nationalhardwareshow.com
Estimated Sales: $1 - 3 Million
Number Employees: 10-19
Brands:
Ez-One

26496 National Ammonia Co
735 Davisville Rd # 3
Southampton, PA 18966-3277
215-322-1238
Fax: 215-322-7791 800-643-6226
sales@tannerind.com www.tannerind.com
Anhydrous ammonia and aqua ammonia for uses including refrigeration applications, metal treating,
chemical, pharmaceutical and petroleum industries,
agriculture, reprographincs, resins, polymers, acid
neutralization, water treatmentand explosives
CEO: Raymond Tanner
VP: Greg Tanner
Estimated Sales: $30 - 50 Million
Number Employees: 100-249

26497 National Band Saw Co
25322 Avenue Stanford
Santa Clarita, CA 91355-1214
661-294-9552
Fax: 661-294-9554 800-851-5050
harley@nbsparts.com www.nbsparts.com
Manufacturer, exporter and wholesaler/distributor of
replacement parts for meat slicing and cutting ma-
chinery; importer of slicing knives, tenderizers and
bread slicing and patty-making machines; whole-
saler/distributor of office andshipping supplies
Owner: Enrique Barbosa
enriqueb@nbarizona.com
VP: Chris Tuttle
R & D: Ron Voytek
Director of IT Computer Services: Jason Jasperson
Production: Ron Voytek
Estimated Sales: Below $5 Million
Number Employees: 10-19
Square Footage: 12200
Type of Packaging: Consumer, Food Service, Pri-
vate Label, Bulk

26498 National Bar Systems
16571 Burke Lane
Huntington Beach, CA 92647-4537
714-848-1688
Fax: 714-848-2788 www.nbsmfg.com
Manufacturer and exporter of stainless steel un-
der-bar equipment including sinks, work tables and
ice storage equipment
President: Johnny Lee
VP: John Ashkarian
CFO: Joe Kim
Contact: Joe Kim
joek@nbsmfg.com
Estimated Sales: $5 - 10 Million
Number Employees: 5-9

26499 National Cart Co
3125 Boschertown Rd
St Charles, MO 63301-3263
636-947-3800
Fax: 636-723-4477 sales@nationalcart.com
www.nationalcart.com
Manufacturer and exporter of oven racks, bun pans
and pan tray carts
CEO: Brian Gillis
zroach@kumc.edu
CEO: Robert Unnerstall
Estimated Sales: $20-50 Million
Number Employees: 100-249
Square Footage: 100000

26500 National Chemicals Inc
105 Liberty St
PO Box 32
Winona, MN 55987-3706
507-494-8848
Fax: 507-454-5641 800-533-0027

Detergents, sanitizers and cleaners for food service use
Chairman of the Board: Louis Landman
 clandman@natlchem.com
Estimated Sales: $10-20 Million
Number Employees: 10-19
Number of Brands: 21
Number of Products: 46

26501 National Computer Corporation
211 Century Drive
Suite 100-B
Greenville, SC 29607
866-944-5164
Fax: 864-235-7688 www.nccusa.com
Manufacturer, importer and exporter of point of sale systems
President: Douglas Harris Jr
Contact: Mary Harris
 mharris@nccusa.com
Estimated Sales: $5 - 10,000,000
Number Employees: 10-19

26502 National Construction Services
PO Box 820
Frazer, PA 19355
610-647-8050
Fax: 610-647-8540 800-557-8050
President: Lee Krow
 krow@krbassociates.com
CFO: Lee Krow
R&D: Lee Krow
Quality Control: Lee Krow
Estimated Sales: $5 - 10 Million
Number Employees: 10-19

26503 National Construction Technologies Group
4967 Kensington Gate
Excelsior, MN 55331-9345
952-474-7126
Fax: 952-474-7370
Specialized concrete surfaces including surface preparation, surface coatings, concrete construction
Estimated Sales: $1 - 5 Million

26504 (HQ)National Conveyor Corp
2250 Yates Ave
Commerce, CA 90040-1914
323-725-0355
Fax: 323-725-1440 info@natconcorp.com
Manufacturer and exporter of utensil washers, conveyor equipment, dish handling systems and waste reduction systems
Owner: Frank Bargas
Customer Service Manager: Luis Vargas
 fra_cie@netzero.com
Engineer Manager: Joseph Marin
Estimated Sales: $2.5 - 5 Million
Number Employees: 10-19
Square Footage: 60000
Type of Packaging: Food Service
Brands:
 Power Dishtable
 Roto-Stak
 Uni-Band

26505 National Datacomputer
900 Middlesex Tpke
Suite 5-1
Billerica, MA 01821
978-663-7677
Fax: 978-667-1869
Computer systems: handheld systems, route accounting, sales automation
CEO: William B Berens
Contact: Carla Bacucci
 carla.bacucci@ndcomputer.com
Estimated Sales: $10-25 Million
Number Employees: 5-9

26506 National Discount Textile
2210 Defoor Hills Rd NW
Atlanta, GA 30318-2200
404-351-1630
Fax: 404-351-1631
www.national-discount-textiles.com
Owner: Murray Shelton
 nina@buccaneerinc.com
Number Employees: 10-19

26507 National Distributor Services
3033 S Parker Road
Suite 400
Aurora, CO 80014-2921
303-755-4411
Fax: 303-755-4545
Manufacturer and exporter of forklifts
President: B Anthony Reed
CEO: Tony Reed
Number Employees: 50

26508 National Drying Machry Co Inc
2190 Hornig Rd
Philadelphia, PA 19116-4202
215-464-6070
Fax: 215-464-4096 info@nationaldrying.com
www.nationaldrying.com
Manufacturer and exporter of thermal processing equipment including dehydrators, dryers, ovens, roasters, blanchers, coolers and multi-tier and multi-pass conveyor systems and feeders
President: Richard Parkes
Director Marketing/Sales: Paul Branson
Director: Richard Eckard
Estimated Sales: $20-50 Million
Number Employees: 5-9
Square Footage: 80000
Parent Co: Apollo Sheet Metal

26509 National Emblem
PO Box 5325
Carson, CA 90749-5325
310-515-5055
Fax: 310-515-5966 800-877-5325
www.nationalemblem.com
Embroidered and screen printed emblems, caps, keyrings and woven labels
President: Milton Lubin Sr
CFO: Alicia Bsiez-Sounds
National Sales Manager: Marvin Grimm
Sales Director: Milton Lobin, Jr.
Estimated Sales: $20 - 50 Million
Number Employees: 250-499

26510 National Embroidery SvcInc
3390 E Main Rd # 1
Portsmouth, RI 02871-4240
401-683-4724
Fax: 401-683-0012 800-227-1451
sales@nationalembroidery.com
www.nationalembroidery.com
Custom embroidered uniforms, hats, shirts, vests, chef coats and aprons
President and R&D: Dale Wood
Quality Control: Eileen Wood
CEO and CFO: Dale B Wood
Estimated Sales: Less than $500,000
Number Employees: 5-9
Square Footage: 10000

26511 National Energy Consultants
PO Box 562
Cedar Falls, IA 50613-0027
319-231-0857
Fax: 877-553-0187 888-841-6987
info@nationalenergyconsultants.com
www.nationalenergyconsultants.com
Energy consulting, procurement, management and consolidated billing capabilities
Number Employees: 10-19

26512 (HQ)National Equipment Corporation
801 E 141st St
Bronx, NY 10454
718-585-0200
Fax: 718-993-2650 800-237-8873
sales@unionmachinery.com
www.unionmachinery.com
Manufacturer, importer and exporter of used and reconditioned food processing and packaging equipment
VP: Arthur Greenberg
VP: Richard Greenberg
VP: Charles Greenberg
Contact: David Feinne
 dfeinne@unionmachinery.com
Number Employees: 20-49
Square Footage: 1800000
Other Locations:
 National Equipment Corp.
 Naucalpan

26513 National FABCO Manufacturing
12927 Gravois Rd
St Louis, MO 63127-1714
314-842-4571
Fax: 314-842-8088
Custom designed food serving equipment including counters, sinks, refrigerated carts, hoods, countertops and tables
President: John Gates
 john.gates@sefa.com
VP: Frank Ruggeri
Estimated Sales: $10 - 20 Million
Number Employees: 20-49
Square Footage: 11000
Type of Packaging: Food Service, Private Label
Brands:
 Cleveland
 Groen
 Hatc
 Hubort
 Southbend
 Thermobend
 Traulsen
 Victory

26514 National Foam
180 Sheree Blvd # 3900
Exton, PA 19341-1272
610-363-1400
Fax: 610-524-9073 www.kidde-fire.com
Manufacturer and exporter of foam fire extinguishing chemicals and equipment
Manager: Bobby Nelson
CFO: Larry Mansfield
Contact: Herbert Cooper
 herbert.cooper@nationalfoam.com
Estimated Sales: $20 - 50 Million
Number Employees: 100-249
Parent Co: Racal-Chubb

26515 National Food Laboratories Inc
365 N Canyons Pkwy # 101
Suite 201
Livermore, CA 94551-7703
925-828-1440
Fax: 925-243-0117 www.covance.com
Consulting laboratory specializing in market research, sensory analysis, process and product development, analytical services and pilot plant services
President: Kevin Buck
 buckk@thenfl.com
VP, Finance & Administration: Mindy Hungerman
Quality Assurance and Safety Manager: Bob Takens
Division Manager: Rupinder Jaura
VP, Business Development: Angie McKenzie
Estimated Sales: $10 - 20 Million
Number Employees: 50-99
Square Footage: 120000
Parent Co: National Food Processors Association

26516 National Food Product Research Corporation
318 Main Street
P.O. Box 419
West Newbury, MA 01985-0519
978-363-2144
Fax: 978-363-2073 800-363-2144
Consultant providing marketing research for food, products, equipment and services
Owner: John Sibley
 nfpsib@greennet.net
Executive VP: John Sibley
Estimated Sales: Below $5 Million
Number Employees: 10-19

26517 National Honey Board
11409 Business Park Cir # 210
Suite # 210
Firestone, CO 80504-9203
303-776-2337
Fax: 303-776-1177 800-553-7162
honey@nhb.org
Educates consumers about the benefits and uses for honey and honey products.
Chairperson, Board Member: Brent Barkman
CEO, Board Member: Bruce Boynton
Vice Chairperson, Board Member: Mark Mammen
Director Scientific Affairs: Marcia Cardetti
Marketing Director: Tami Yanosk
IT Administrator and Webmaster: Darren Brown
Number Employees: 5-9

26518 National Hotpack
3538 Main Street
Stone Ridge, NY 12484
845-255-5000
Fax: 845-687-7481 800-431-8232
www.hotpack.com
Hotpack manufactures and sells enviromental rooms
and chambers, stability rooms and chambers, humid-
ity rooms and chambers, glassware washers and dry-
ers, vacuum ovens, sterilizers and autoclaves, C-O2
incubators, general purposeincubators, ovens, refrig-
erators, freezers
President/CEO: Bill Downs
CFO: Michael Bonner
Marketing: Shireen Scott
Sales: James Shiever
Estimated Sales: $65 Million
Number Employees: 100-249
Square Footage: 70000
Parent Co: SP Industries
Brands:
  Heinicke
  Hotpack
  National Labortory Products
  Oem Products

26519 National Instruments
4119 Fordleigh Rd
Baltimore, MD 21215-2292
410-764-0900
Fax: 410-951-2093 866-258-1914
jrosen@filamatic.com www.filamatic.com
Manufacturer and exporter of liquid filling, capping
and turnkey packaging equipment
CEO: Robert Rosen
VP Marketing/Sales: Jim Striese
Manager: Mark Evans
  mark.evans@filamatic.com
Estimated Sales: $10-20 Million
Number Employees: 50-99
Brands:
  Capamatic
  Dial-A-Fill
  Econofil
  Filamatic
  Synchromat

26520 National Interchem Corporation
13750 Chatham Street
Blue Island, IL 60406-3218
773-638-5100
Fax: 773-638-8769 800-638-6688
www.nichemical.com
Manufacturer and exporter of industrial cleaning and
maintenance chemicals
Director Sales: Greg Fishman
Estimated Sales: $2.5-5 Million
Number Employees: 10-19

26521 National Label Co
2025 Joshua Rd
Lafayette Hill, PA 19444-2426
610-825-3250
Fax: 610-834-8854 www.nationallabel.com
Manufacturer and exporter of pressure sensitive la-
beling equipment and labels
Exec VP: James Shacklett IV
Estimated Sales: $50-100 Million
Number Employees: 250-499
Type of Packaging: Bulk

26522 National Marker Co Inc
100 Providence Pike
North Smithfield, RI 02896-8046
401-762-9700
Fax: 401-762-1010 800-453-2727
sales@nationalmarker.com
www.nationalmarker.com
Plastic safety signs
President: Michael Black
  mblack@nationalmarker.com
Marketing Director: Patricia O'Hara
Estimated Sales: $5 - 10 Million
Number Employees: 50-99

26523 National Marking Products Inc
5606 Greendale Rd
Henrico, VA 23228-5816
804-266-7691
Fax: 804-266-6110 800-482-1553
www.nationalmarking.com
Promotional items including rubber stamps, plastic
signs, shipping supplies, bronze tablets, labels, tags
and awards

President/Owner: Richard Reinhard
ric@nationalmarkingproducts.com
Manager: Brenda Puryear
Estimated Sales: Below $5 Million
Number Employees: 10-19
Square Footage: 30000

26524 National Menuboard
4302 B St NW # D
Auburn, WA 98001
253-859-6068
Fax: 253-859-8412 800-800-5237
Menu boards including illuminated, nonilluminated,
indoor and outdoor
President: Dave Medzegian
  dave@nationalmenuboard.com
Sales Representative: Wendi Adsley
Estimated Sales: Below $5 Million
Number Employees: 5-9
Square Footage: 40000

26525 National Metal Industries
203 Circuit Avenue
West Springfield, MA 01089-4016
413-785-5861
Fax: 413-737-2309 800-628-8850
www.national-metal.com
Manufacturer and exporter of metal stamps and parts
for food processing equipment
Sales Manager: Bryan Costello
Estimated Sales: $10-20 Million
Number Employees: 50-99
Parent Co: Standex International Corporation

26526 (HQ)National Novelty Brush Co
505 E Fulton St
Lancaster, PA 17602-3022
717-299-5681
Fax: 717-397-0991 www.nnbc-pa.com
Manufacturer and exporter of brushes, applicators
and metal screw caps
President: Richard Seavey
  rseavey@nnbc-pa.com
CFO: Bryan Howett
Quality Control: Sandy Donley
Sales Manager: Ronald Vellucci
Customer Service: Marianne Walsh
Estimated Sales: $20 - 50 Million
Number Employees: 100-249

26527 National Oilwell Varco
125 Flagship Dr
North Andover, MA 01845-6119
978-687-0101
Fax: 978-687-8500 800-643-0641
inquiry@kenics.com www.chemineer.com
Processing equipment: static and high shear mixers
and heat exchangers
Manager: Mark Raymond
Quality Control: John Cercone
Marketing Director: Dave Ryan
Manager: George Hanna
  ghanna@kenics.com
Purchasing Manager: Laura Parker
Estimated Sales: $20 - 50 Million
Number Employees: 20-49
Parent Co: Robbins & Meyers
Brands:
  Greerco
  Kenics

26528 National Package SealingCompany
10791 SE Skyline Drive
Santa Ana, CA 92705-7413
714-630-1505
Fax: 714-632-3217
Manufacturer and exporter of electric and manual
dispensers for gummed carton sealing tapes and
labels
President: William Amneus
Marketing Director: Fay Amneus
Estimated Sales: $2.5-5 Million
Number Employees: 19
Square Footage: 80000

26529 National Packaging
PO Box 4798
Rumford, RI 02916-0798
401-434-1070
Fax: 401-438-5203 www.multiwall.com
Manufacturer and exporter of cloth winding reels
and single faced corrugated paper
President: Charles M Dunn

Estimated Sales: $20-50 Million
Number Employees: 10-19
Parent Co: Real Reel Corporation

26530 (HQ)National Pen Co
12121 Scripps Summit Dr # 200
San Diego, CA 92131-4609
858-675-3000
Fax: 858-675-3030 info@nationalpen.com
www.nationalpen.com
Ink pens
President: Thomas Liguorii
Chief Executive Officer: Dave Thompson
Chief Financial Officer: Rich Obrigawitch
SVP, North America Direct: Ron Childs
Number Employees: 100-249

26531 National Plastics Co
15505 Cornet St
Santa Fe Springs, CA 90670-5511
562-926-4511
Fax: 562-926-0222 800-221-9149
mra@natcos.com www.menucovers.com
Menu covers, loose leaf binders, wine lists, check
presenters, transparent price card holders and pad
holders; exporter of menu covers
President: Gregory Mitchell
  gregm@natcos.com
Marketing Director: Mark Anderson
Sales Director: Brian Bromm
Office Manager: Bryan Carr
Plant Manager: Benjamin Jimenez
Estimated Sales: $5-10 Million
Number Employees: 50-99
Square Footage: 36000
Parent Co: National Plastic Company of California

26532 National Poly Bag Manufacturing Corporation
220 West Street
Brooklyn, NY 11222-1350
718-629-9800
Fax: 718-629-0265
Plastic bags and film
Estimated Sales: $1 - 5 Million
Number Employees: 12

26533 National Polymers
7920 215th St W
Lakeville, MN 55044-9015
952-469-4977
Fax: 952-469-2051 800-328-4577
scoops@nationalmeasures.com
Plastic measures for powdered and liquid products
President: Dennis Anderson
CFO: Mac Moore
Sales Manager: Mac Moore
Manager: Paul Kinney
Production/Advertising: Wes Anderson
Estimated Sales: Less Than $500,000
Number Employees: 1-4
Type of Packaging: Bulk

26534 National Printing Converters
4310 Bonavita Dr
Encino, CA 91436
818-906-7936
Manufacturer and exporter of data processing
printed, pressure sensitive, laser, on-line pattern ad-
hesive and vinyl shelf marking labels and shelf
talkers
President: Brain Buckley
Chairman: Robert Buckley
Operations Manager: Richard Atkins
Estimated Sales: $.5 - 1 million
Number Employees: 1-4
Square Footage: 110000
Brands:
  Label Data-Set

26535 National Provisioner
7300 N. Linder Ave.
Skokie, IL 60077-3217
847-763-9534
Fax: 847-763-9538 NP@halldata.com
www.provisioneronline.com

26536 National Purity LLC
6840 Shingle Creek Pkwy # 23
Brooklyn Center, MN 55430-1459
612-672-0022
Fax: 612-672-0027 www.nationalpurity.com
Soaps, detergents, cleaning agents and soap based
industrial lubricants

President: Sean Spillane
 sspillane@nationalpurity.com
National Account Manager: Bill Stark
Field Account Manager: Sean Spillane
Estimated Sales: $20-50 Million
Number Employees: 5-9
Square Footage: 52000

26537 National Restaurant Supply Company
2513 Comanche Rd NE
Albuquerque, NM 87107

877-654-6554
sales@nrsupply.com www.nrsupply.com
Wholesaler/distributor of equipment, supplies,
china, silverware, tabletop items, furniture and stainless steel fabrication; serving the food service
market.

26538 National Scoop & Equipment Company
PO Box 325
Spring House, PA 19477-0325

215-646-2040
Manufacturer, wholesaler/distributor and importer of
pails, buckets, scales, scoops, skimmers, dippers,
disposable paper clothing, sinks and trucks
Manager: Ken Johnson

26539 National Sign Corporation
1255 Westlake Ave N
Seattle, WA 98109-3531

206-282-0700
Fax: 206-285-3091 info@nationalsigncorp.com
www.nationalsigncorp.com
Manufacturing, installation and servicing of interior
and exterior signage, including ADA signs.
President: Timothy Zamberlin
Estimated Sales: $5-10 Million
Number Employees: 35
Square Footage: 60000

26540 National Sign Systems
4200 Lyman Ct
Hilliard, OH 43026-1213

614-529-6628
Fax: 614-850-2552 800-544-6726
sales@natsignsys.com www.natsignsys.com
Signs, menu systems, copy strips and HVAC equip-
ment screens
President: James Cullinan
 jcullinan@natsignsys.com
CFO: Paul Saokendach
VP Sales/Marketing: Paul Falkenbach
Estimated Sales: $10 - 20,000,000
Number Employees: 100-249
Square Footage: 310920

26541 National Stabilizers
1846 Business Center Dr
Duarte, CA 91010-2997

626-359-4584
Fax: 626-359-4586
Stabilizers
President: Robert Burger
Quality Control: Raivo Partma
VP Sales: Robert Burger
Sales/Purchasing: Tomas Martinez
Estimated Sales: $2.5-5 Million
Number Employees: 5 to 9
Brands:
 Stabak
 Stacol

26542 National Steel Corporation
100 Quality Drive
Ecorse, MI 48229-1850

734-953-3603
Fax: 734-953-3601
Tin plate and chromium coated steel for production
of containers, ends, closures and crowns

26543 National Stock Sign Co
1040 El Dorado Ave
Santa Cruz, CA 95062-2825

831-476-2020
Fax: 831-476-1734 800-462-7726
nationalstock@sbcglobal.net
Safety, parking and no smoking signs
President: Henrietta Cooper
Marketing Manager: Lorraine Kirkpatrick
General Manager: Joel Kirkpatrick

Estimated Sales: $1 - 3 Million
Number Employees: 10-19
Square Footage: 30000
Brands:
 Nassco

26544 National Sunflower Assn
2401 46th Ave SE # 206
Suite 206
Mandan, ND 58554-4829

701-328-5100
Fax: 701-328-5101 888-718-7033
johns@sunflowernsa.com www.sunflowernsa.com
Non-profit corporation designed to advance the sun-
flower industry.
Executive Director: John Sandbakken
Meeting Planner & Advertising Sales: Lerrene Kroh
BusinessOffice Manager: Tina Mittelsteadt
Number Employees: 5-9

26545 National Tape Corporation
5128 Storey Street
New Orleans, LA 70123-5320

504-733-8020
Fax: 504-734-8751 800-535-8846
Manufacturer and exporter of pressure sensitive la-
bels and tapes including masking, duct, electrical,
pressure sensitive and marking
VP Sales: Joel Teachworth
VP: Robert Wiswall
Number Employees: 100
Square Footage: 520000

26546 National Time RecordingEqpt
64 Reade St # 2
New York, NY 10007-1870

212-227-3310
Fax: 212-227-5353 info@nationaltime.net
www.nationaltime.net
Manufacturer and exporter of time clocks, time
stamps and thermometers
VP: K Kelly
Estimated Sales: $5-10 Million
Number Employees: 10-19

26547 National Towelette
1726 Woodhaven Dr
Bensalem, PA 19020-7108

215-245-7300
Fax: 215-245-7390 info@towelettes.com
www.flexwipes.com
Individually wrapped moist towelettes
President: Tim Brock
 brock@towelettes.com
CFO: Tim Bro
Number Employees: 50-99
Square Footage: 50000

26548 National Velour Corp
36 Bellair Ave
Warwick, RI 02886-2206

401-737-8300
Fax: 401-738-7418 800-556-6523
service@nationalvelour.com
www.nationalvelour.com
Manufacturer and exporter of flock for packaging
and displays; also, custom flocking and stock lines
available
President: Oscar Der Manouelian
Estimated Sales: $5-10 Million
Number Employees: 10-19

26549 National Wooden Pallet & Container Association
1421 Prince Street
Suite 340
Alexandria, VA 22314-2805

703-519-6104
Fax: 703-519-4720 palletcomm@aol.com
www.palletcentral.com
Manufacture, repair and distribute pallets and wood
packaging in unit-load solutions.
President/CEO: Brent J. McClendon, CAE
Vice President of Operations and Events: Isabel
Sullivan
Sales Director: Joni Leonardo
Contact: Patrick Atagi
 patrick@palletcentral.com
Number Employees: 10-19

26550 Nationwide Boiler Inc
42400 Christy St
Fremont, CA 94538-3141

510-490-7100
Fax: 510-490-0571 800-227-1966
info@nationwideboiler.com www.catastak.com
President/Owner: Jeff Shallcross
 jeff@nationwideboiler.com
Chairman of the Board: Richard Bliss
Estimated Sales: $5 - 10 Million
Number Employees: 20-49

26551 Nationwide Pennant & Flag Mfg
7325 Reindeer Trl
San Antonio, TX 78238-1214

210-684-3524
Fax: 210-680-2329 800-383-3524
sales@napmfg.com www.napmfg.com
Manufacturer and exporter of pennants, flags, flag-
poles, banners and decals
President: Donald W Engelhardt
CEO: Rick Sutton
Sales: Joe Pyland
Estimated Sales: $10-20 Million
Number Employees: 50-99
Square Footage: 120000

26552 Nationwide Wire & BrushManufacturing
411 Evergreen Drive
Lodi, CA 95242-4629

209-334-9660
Fax: 209-334-9432
Power brooms and brushes for the food industry
President: Richard Savage
Sales Manager: Jim Olvera
Estimated Sales: Below $5 Million
Number Employees: 35

26553 Native Lumber Company
8 N Branford Road
Wallingford, CT 06492-2712

203-269-2625
Wooden pallets
Co-Owner: Dick Smith
Estimated Sales: $2.5-5 Million
Number Employees: 9

26554 Natural Fuel Company, LLC
899 Northgate Dr.
Ste. 408
San Rafael, CA 94903

415-491-4944
mark@naturalfuelco.com
www.naturalfuelco.com
Lump mesquite charcoal and firewood from Mexico
for distribution in the US to foodservice distributors.
President & Director, Sales & Marketing: Mark
Schulz

26555 Natural Marketing Institute
272 Ruth Rd # 1
Harleysville, PA 19438-1927

215-513-7300
Fax: 215-513-1713 www.nmisolutions.com
Consultant to food industry specializing in consumer
research, market analysis and brand and product de-
velopment.
Owner: Sandra Carrow
 sandra.carrow@nmisolutions.com
Managing Partner: Steve French
Public Relations: Dana Marinari
Number Employees: 1-4
Square Footage: 20000
Parent Co: Mic-Ellen Associates

26556 Nature Knows, Inc.
7050 Telford Way
Unit 100 B
Mississauga, ON L5S 1V7
Canada

905-612-0085
Contact@NatureKnows.ca
natureknows.ca
Provider of plant-based snacking products.
Founder & Chief Brand Ambassador: Andrea
Watson
Year Founded: 2016
Number Employees: 2-10
Type of Packaging: Food Service

26557 Nature Most Laboratories
Trigo Business Park
60 Trigo Drive
Middletown, CT 06457-6157
860-346-8991
Fax: 860-347-3312 800-234-2112
sales@naturemost.com
Manufacturer, importer and exporter of products, vitamins, oils, minerals, herbal supplements
President: Robert Trigo
Marketing: Sam Schwartz
Sales: Donna Platnum
Operations: Fred Wuschner
Estimated Sales: $5 - 10 Million
Number Employees: 20-49
Number of Brands: 3
Number of Products: 300
Square Footage: 80000
Type of Packaging: Consumer, Private Label
Brands:
    Naturemost Labs
    Trigo Labs

26558 Nature Soy Inc
713 N 10th St
Philadelphia, PA 19123-1902
215-765-3289
Fax: 215-765-3266 support@naturesoy.com
Manufacturer/supplier of healthy soy and vegetarian products to the ethnic market
President: Yat Wen
CEO: Gene He
he@naturesoy.com
EVP: Fenjin He
Estimated Sales: $2.4 Million
Number Employees: 20-49
Square Footage: 35000

26559 Nature's Own
11 Fred Roddy Avenue
Attleboro, MA 2703
508-399-8690
Fax: 508-399-8693 www.naturesown.com.au
Natural hardwood charcoal and grilling/smoking woods; importer of herbwoods; exporter of hardwood charcoal
President/Owner: Don Hysko
VP: Holly Hysko
Sales Manager: Dana Bracket
Estimated Sales: $2.5-5 Million
Number Employees: 5-9
Square Footage: 50000
Brands:
    Loon
    Nature's Own
    Pfb (Produits Forresters Baasques)
    Treestock

26560 Naughton Equipment Sales
1203 Madison St
Fort Calhoun, NE 68023-3524
402-468-4682
Fax: 402-468-4683 866-858-4682
sales@naughtonequipment.com
www.naughtonequipment.com
Foof processing equipment for the meat, poultry, and fisch industries
President: Daniel Naughton
VP: Kathy Naughton
R & D: Ed Kermeen
Marketing: Jerry Naughton
Estimated Sales: $1 - 3 Million
Number Employees: 1-4
Square Footage: 60000
Brands:
    Carcos Splutting Saw
    Ez Splitter Ii

26561 Navco
11929 Brittmoore Park Dr
Houston, TX 77041-7226
832-467-3636
Fax: 832-467-3800 800-231-0164
sales@navco.us www.navco.us
Manufacturer and exporter of material handling equipment including pneumatic and electric vibrators
President: Mark Neundorfer
Marketing Manager: Ben Snider
Number Employees: 10-19

26562 Navy Brand
3670 Scarlet Oak Blvd
St Louis, MO 63122-6606
636-861-5500
Fax: 636-861-5509 800-325-3312
navybrand@navybrand.com www.navybrand.com
Manufacturer and wholesaler/distributor of industrial degreasers, cleaners and water treatment systems for boilers and cooling towers
President: Ed Schooling
CEO: Edwin Schooling
Director Sales: Jack Julier
IT: Edwin Schooling
eschooling@navybrand.com
Estimated Sales: $1.5 Million
Number Employees: 10-19
Square Footage: 200000

26563 Naylor Association Solutions
5950 NW 1st Pl
Gainesville, FL 32607-6060
352-332-1252
Fax: 352-331-3525 www.naylor.com
Publications
Manager: Jason Dolder
jdolder@naylor.com
Number Employees: 250-499

26564 Neal Walters Poster Corporation
PO Box 480
Bentonville, AR 72712-0480
501-273-2489
Fax: 501-271-2132
Manufacturer and exporter of billboard and point of purchase posters, product markings, decals, bar code and pressure sensitive labels, business and computer forms, etc
President: James Walters
Secy./Treas.: Thomas Walters
V.P.: John Walters
Estimated Sales: $500,000-$1 Million
Number Employees: 9
Square Footage: 60000

26565 Nebraska Bean
85824 519th Ave
Clearwater, NE 68726-5239
402-887-5335
Fax: 402-887-4709 800-253-6502
brett@nebraskabean.com www.nebraskabean.com
Experienced grower, processor and packager of quality popcorn. the fully integrated operation offers microwave, bulk, private label and poly bags of popcorn
President: Brett Morrison
brett@nebraskabean.com
VP: Brett Morrison
Sales: Michelle Steskal
Estimated Sales: $10 - 20 Million
Number Employees: 20-49
Number of Brands: 1
Square Footage: 10000
Type of Packaging: Consumer, Food Service, Private Label, Bulk
Brands:
    Morrison Farms

26566 Nebraska Neon Sign Co
1140 N 21st St
Lincoln, NE 68503-1698
402-476-6563
Fax: 402-476-3461 nesignco@gmail.com
www.nebraskaneonsign.com
Signs including neon, wooden, illuminated, etc
President: Robert Norris
bnorris@nebraskasign.com
Estimated Sales: $2.5-5 Million
Number Employees: 20-49

26567 Necedah Pallet Co Inc
703 N Harvey St
Necedah, WI 54646-8179
608-565-2619
Fax: 608-565-2979 800-672-5538
Wooden pallets and skids
Sales/Marketing: Steve Schultz
General Manager: Terry Hess
Estimated Sales: $2.5-5 Million
Number Employees: 20-49
Square Footage: 40000
Parent Co: Northern Pallet & Supply
Type of Packaging: Bulk

26568 Nederman
102 Transit Ave
Thomasville, NC 27360-8927
336-821-0800
Fax: 336-821-0890 800-533-5286
www.nederman.com
Manufacturer and importer of dust collection filters, cyclones, grinders, pipe clamps and ducts
President: Tom Ballus
tom.ballus@nederman.com
Marketing Director: Tarey Cullen
VP Sales: Steve McDaniel
Estimated Sales: $20-50 Million
Number Employees: 100-249
Brands:
    Clean-Sweep
    Quick-Fit
    Vortex

26569 Nederman
102 Transit Ave
Thomasville, NC 27360-8927
336-821-0800
Fax: 336-821-0890 800-533-5286
www.nederman.com
Nederman LLC is a leading manufacturer of state of the art Dust, Fume, and Mist Collection Systems for the paper industry and recycling processes. Our products deliver consistent reliability, low energy consumption and compliance withOSHA and NFPA combustible dust requirements. Our experience and proven techniques have allowed us to save customers up to 80 percent on their energy costs.
President: Tom Ballus
tom.ballus@nederman.com
Sales: Rob Williamson
Estimated Sales: $3 - 5 Million
Number Employees: 100-249

26570 Nefab
204 Airline Drive
Suite 600
Coppell, TX 75019
469-444-5320
Fax: 847-985-3200 800-536-7261
www.nefab.com
No-nail, lightweight, collapsible export containers made from plywood and steel
President: Lars-ake Rydh
President, Chief Executive Officer: David MArk
Executive Vice President: Anders M"rk
Contact: Brad Ackerman
brad.ackerman@nefab.com
Estimated Sales: $2.5-5 Million
Number Employees: 5-9

26571 Nefab Packaging Inc
850 Mark St
Elk Grove Vlg, IL 60007-6704
847-787-0340
Fax: 630-595-7230 www.nefab.us
Plywood, no-nail, foldable and reusable packaging systems for transport, storage and internal distribution
President, Chief Executive Officer: David MArk
Executive Vice President: Anders M"rk
Estimated Sales: $2.5-5 Million
Number Employees: 100-249
Parent Co: Nefab A.B.
Brands:
    Repak

26572 Nefab Packaging Inc
850 Mark St
Elk Grove Vlg, IL 60007-6704
847-787-0340
Fax: 630-595-7230 800-536-7261
www.nefab.com
No-nail, collapsible, export and reusable containers, easy to assemble and available in custom and stock sizes - made from a combination of plywood and steelContainers are delivered flat and designed to customer's specification.providing packaging solutions.cost effective transport containers
President, Chief Executive Officer: David MArk
Executive Vice President: Anders M"rk
Sales Director: Lori Brownstein
Estimated Sales: $2.5-5 Million
Number Employees: 100-249
Type of Packaging: Consumer

26573 (HQ)Nefab Packaging Inc.
204 Airline Dr
Suite 100
Coppell, TX 75019

Fax: 469-444-5308 800-322-4425
www.nefab.com
Industrial crates material handling products including pallets
Contact: Stephanie Carreon
scarreon@nefab.us
Estimated Sales: $5 - 10 Million
Number Employees: 10
Square Footage: 92000

26574 Nefab Packaging, Inc.
204 Airline Drive
Suite 100
Coppell, TX 75019

469-444-5308
Fax: 603-367-4329 800-322-4425
www.nefab.us
Manufacturer and exporter of wooden industrial packaging and distribution equipment including pallets, skids, crates and boxes; also, milling services available
Director of Global Business Development: Ken Wilson
Chief Executive Officer: Brian Bulatao
VP: Andi Wilson
Executive Vice President: Eric Howe
Contact: Stephanie Carreon
scarreon@nefab.us
Number Employees: 400

26575 Neff Packaging
10 Kingbrook Pkwy
Simpsonville, KY 40067-5625

502-722-5020
Fax: 502-722-5070 800-445-4383
rdneff@neffpackaging.com
www.neffpackaging.com
Folding paper boxes and cartons
Owner: Robert D Neff
CEO: R Neff
rdneff@neffpackaging.com
Marketing Director: R Neff
Estimated Sales: $1-2.5 Million
Number Employees: 50-99
Parent Co: Neff Courier Group

26576 Neilson Canvas Company
715 W Washington St
Sandusky, OH 44870-2334

419-625-0581
Fax: 419-625-4315
Commercial awnings
President: Robert Nielsen
VP: Darcy Neilson
Estimated Sales: $1-2,500,000
Number Employees: 10-19

26577 (HQ)Nelipak
3720 W Washington St
Phoenix, AZ 85009-4765

602-269-7648
Fax: 602-269-7640 www.nelipak.com
Thermoformed products including shelf organizers, freezer trays, point of purchase displays and shipping and handling trays; also, contract packaging including club packs, assembly, shrink packaging, display packout, bagging andlabeling
President: Donald Bond
qstein@flexpak.net
CFO: Steve Merray
Quality Control: Carlos Pineda
Marketing Director: Don Richardson
Operations Manager: Rick Colton
Purchasing Manager: Jim Boley
Estimated Sales: $20 - 50 Million
Number Employees: 100-249
Square Footage: 82000
Type of Packaging: Consumer, Food Service, Private Label, Bulk

26578 (HQ)Nella Cutlery Toronto, Inc.
148 Norfinch Dr
Toronto, ON M3N 1X8
Canada

416-740-2424
Fax: 416-740-9363 www.nellaonline.com
Importer, manufacturer, and distributor of food service equipment used in restaurants, supermarkets, delicatessens, and convenience stores.

President: Rob Nella
CEO: Jim Nella
Year Founded: 1951
Number Employees: 101-250

26579 Nella Cutlery Toronto, Inc.
433 Queen St E
Toronto, ON M5A 1T5
Canada

416-847-1112
Fax: 416-847-1115 www.nellaonline.com
Importer, manufacturer, and distributor of food service equipment.

26580 Nella Cutlery Toronto, Inc.
1164 Ellesmere Road
Scarborough, ON M1P 2X4
Canada

416-292-0828
www.nellaonline.com
Importer, manufacturer, and distributor of food service equipment.

26581 Nelles Automation
7000 Hollister St
Houston, TX 77040-5617

713-939-9399
Fax: 713-939-0393
tom.christopher@telvent.abengoa.com
www.telvent.com
Manufacturer and exporter of automated control systems and circuit boards for electric utility
President: Dave Jardine
CFO: Manuel Fanchez
VP: Tom Christopher
Estimated Sales: $1 - 3 Million
Number Employees: 5-9
Parent Co: Valmet

26582 Nelson & Associates Recruiting
PO Box 2686
Kirkland, WA 98083

425-823-0956
Fax: 425-820-4541 www.foodrecruiter.com
Personnel recruiter specializing in executive, managerial and technical food industry positions
President: Kenneth Nelson
Estimated Sales: Below $5 Million
Number Employees: 1-4

26583 Nelson Co
4517 North Point Blvd
Sparrows Point, MD 21219-1798

410-477-3000
Fax: 410-388-0246 info@nelsoncompany.com
www.nelsoncompany.com
Wooden pallets and skids; wholesaler/distributor of plastic and metal pallets, shrink and stretch wraps, angleboards and void fillers
President: Arthur Caltrider
IT Executive: John Williams
jack.williams@nelsoncompany.com
Estimated Sales: $5 - 10 Million
Number Employees: 50-99
Parent Co: Nelson Company

26584 Nelson Container Corp
W180n11921 River Ln
Germantown, WI 53022-6308

262-250-5000
Fax: 262-250-5015 contact@nelsoncontainer.com
www.nelsoncontainer.com
Containers and corrugated boxes
President: Thomas Nelson
President: Tom Nelson
Estimated Sales: $20-50 Million
Number Employees: 20-49

26585 Nelson Custom Signs
1199 S Sheldon Rd
Plymouth, MI 48170-2192

734-455-0500
Fax: 734-455-0800
Signs including neon, painted, wooden, etc
Manager: Pete Nelson
Estimated Sales: Less than $500,000
Number Employees: 1-4

26586 Nelson, Gene
12786 Old Redwood Hwy
Healdsburg, CA 95448-9512

707-433-5138
Fax: 707-433-9214
Wine industry wood bungs

Owner: Gene Nelson
Contact: Mike Parker
mike@abwoodtech.com
Estimated Sales: less than $500,000
Number Employees: 5-9

26587 Nelson-Jameson Inc
2400 E 5th St
Marshfield, WI 54449-4661

715-387-1151
Fax: 715-387-8746 800-826-8302
sales@nelsonjameson.com
www.nelsonjameson.com
Wholesale distributor serving food and beverage processors. Wide-line distributor of sanitation, maintenance, laboratory, processing and flow control, personnel and safety supplies
President: Jerry Lippert
j.lippert@nelsonjameson.com
CEO: John Nelson
CEO: Bruce Lautenschlager
Estimated Sales: $50 - 75 Million
Number Employees: 50-99
Number of Brands: 750+
Other Locations:
Nelson-Jameson
Twin Falls ID
Nelson-Jameson
Turlock CA

26588 Nemco Electric Company
207 S Horton St
Seattle, WA 98134-1929

206-622-1551
Fax: 206-622-4449
Lighting equipment including custom chandeliers for hotel lobbies and banquet rooms and portable fluorescent work lights; also, custom lighting fixtures available
President: Arnold Larson
VP: Judy Larson
Estimated Sales: $1-2.5 Million
Number Employees: 1-4
Square Footage: 80000

26589 Nemco Food Equipment
301 Meuse Argonne St
PO Box 305
Hicksville, OH 43526-1143

419-542-7751
Fax: 419-542-6690 800-782-6761
mwibel@nemcofoodequip.com
Manufacturer and exporter of vegetable slicers and cutters
President: Jarod Martenies
vanney75@yahoo.com
Estimated Sales: $10-20 Million
Number Employees: 50-99
Type of Packaging: Food Service

26590 Nemeth Engineering Assoc
5901 W Highway 22
Crestwood, KY 40014-7217

502-241-1502
Fax: 502-241-5907
info@nemeth-engineering.com
www.nemeth-engineering.com
Manufacturer and exporter of radio frequency heating systems for drying, baking, moisture leveling, proofing, thawing, tempering and deinfestation
President: Peter Nemeth
pnemeth@nemeth-engineering.com
Sales Manager: Ned Snow
Sales Associate: Bobbie Gardner
Estimated Sales: $5-10 Million
Number Employees: 20-49
Square Footage: 150000

26591 Neo-Image Candle Light
1331 Blundell Road
Mississauga, ON L4Y 1M6
Canada

905-273-3020
Fax: 905-273-6905 800-375-8023
info@candlesjustonline.com www.neo-image.com
Candles and accessories
Sales Manager: Ric Jones
General Manager: Steve Stratakos
Estimated Sales: $15 Million
Number Employees: 25-49
Parent Co: North America Candle
Brands:
Neo-Image

26592 Neo-Ray Products
537 Johnson Avenue
Brooklyn, NY 11237-1304
718-456-7400
Fax: 718-456-5492 800-221-0946
Manufacturer and exporter of architectural grade
fluorescent lighting systems
National Sales Manager: Andrew Gross
Estimated Sales: $20-50 Million
Number Employees: 100-249

26593 Neogen Corp
620 Lesher Pl
Lansing, MI 48912-1509
517-372-9200
Fax: 517-372-2006 800-234-5333
foodsafety@neogen.com www.neogen.com
Manufacturer, importer and exporter of food patho-
gen testing kits
CEO: John Adent
Marketing Manager: Margaret Cyr
General Manager: Mark Mozola
Estimated Sales: $2.5-5 Million
Number Employees: 1000-4999
Parent Co: Vysis
Brands:
   Gene-Trak

26594 (HQ)Neokraft Signs Inc
686 Main St
Lewiston, ME 04240-5800
207-782-9654
Fax: 207-782-0009 800-339-2258
www.neokraft.com
Aluminum, neon and plastic signs; also wide format
digital thermal printing
President: Peter Murphy
Partner: Peter Murphy
VP: Phil Bolduc
Marketing Director: Paul Lessard
Estimated Sales: Below $5 Million
Number Employees: 20-49
Square Footage: 20000

26595 (HQ)Neon Design-a-Sign
26022 Cape Dr Bldg H
Laguna Niguel, CA 92677
949-348-9223
Fax: 949-348-1736 888-636-6327
Manufacturer and exporter of signs including
changeable, fiber-optic neon and programmable
LED message displays. Also have a full line of LED
lighting.
President: Timothy Piper
CEO: Christine Busnardo
Contact: Tim Piper
piper@neon-das.com
Estimated Sales: $600,000
Number Employees: 1-4
Square Footage: 8000
Brands:
   Logo River
   Neon Design-A-Sign
   Neon Light Pegs

26596 Neonetics Inc
900 S Main St
Hampstead, MD 21074-2202
410-374-8057
Fax: 410-374-8056 AlanObligin@yahoo.com
Manufacturer, importer and exporter of neon signs
Owner: Allen Obligen
neonman@neonetics.com
CFO: Brad Sogollss
VP: Brad Sotoloff
Estimated Sales: Less Than $500,000
Number Employees: 1-4
Brands:
   Ne-On the Wall
   Neonetics

26597 Neos
12797 Meadowvale Road NW
Suite B
Elk River, MN 55330-1171
763-441-0705
Fax: 763-441-0706 888-441-6367
neosinc@att.net www.neos-server.org
Manufacturer and exporter of packaging machinery
for rigid plastic containers; also, burrito and sliced
bread dispensers, conveyors with filler depositers,
folding tables for assembly and fillers

President: Jack T Mowry
CFO: Greg Erlandson
National Sales Manager: Joe Gibbs
Estimated Sales: $1-2.5 Million
Number Employees: 5-9
Square Footage: 48000

26598 (HQ)Nercon Engineering & Manufacturing
PO Box 2288
Oshkosh, WI 54903-2288
920-233-3268
Fax: 920-233-3159
Manufacturer and exporter of table top, belt and case
conveyors, bi-directional tables, vertical accumula-
tors, label removers, twist rinsers, bottle emptiers,
can coolers, etc
President: Jim Nerenhausen
CEO: Jay Nerenhausen
Marketing: Jim Streblow
Estimated Sales: $10 - 20 Million
Number Employees: 100-249
Square Footage: 166500
Other Locations:
   Nercon Engineering & Manufact
   Oconto WI
Brands:
   Easy-Rol

26599 Net Material Handling
1300 W Fond Du Lac Ave
Milwaukee, WI 53205
414-263-1300
Fax: 414-263-7544 800-558-7260
Two and four-wheel hand trucks, two-wheel electric
trucks, dollies, carts, ramps, etc
President: Wendy Alzell
VP: Wayne Kappel
Contact: Mike Kappel
victor@runningrebels.org
Estimated Sales: $1-2.5 Million
Number Employees: 1-4
Square Footage: 28000
Brands:
   Escalera
   Magline
   Yeats

26600 Net Pack Systems
36 Oak Street
Oakland, ME 04963-5019
207-465-4531
Fax: 207-465-9662
Bags including netting, open mesh, heat sealed,
plastic and polyethylene for cooking, fruits, vegeta-
bles, poultry, meat and refrigeration
President: Edward Johnson
Operations Manager: Douglas Johnson
General Manager: Edward Johnson
Estimated Sales: $1 - 2.5 Million
Number Employees: 5-9

26601 Netzsch Pumps North America
119 Pickering Way
Exton, PA 19341-1311
610-363-8010
Fax: 610-363-0971 netzsch@netzschusa.com
www.pumps.netzsch.com
Manufacturer and exporter of pumps, filter presses
and grinding mills
CEO: Dr Tilo Stahl
CFO: Mark Vitcov
VP: John Maguire
R&D: Harry Way
Quality Control: Bill Pye
Marketing: Kelly Rismiller
Public Relations: Kelly Rismiller
Production: Bob Hopple
Plant Manager: Bob Maxwell
Purchasing: Bob Hoffman
Estimated Sales: $30 Million
Number Employees: 50-99
Square Footage: 85000
Parent Co: Netzsch

26602 Neugart
3047 Industrial Blvd # 12
Bethel Park, PA 15102-2537
412-835-4154
Fax: 412-835-4194 sales@neugartusa.com
www.neugartusa.com
Planetary gearboxes, angle gearboxes, custom made
gears, honing, motor mounting

President: Gerhard Antony
VP sales: Tim Francis
Estimated Sales: $1 - 3 Million
Number Employees: 5-9

26603 Neupak
4607 Dovetail Drive
Madison, WI 53704
608-241-1118
Fax: 608-241-4448 800-383-1128
sales@ideal-pak.com www.neupak.com
Manufacture liquid filling machines
President, Chief Executive Officer: Steve Bethke
Vice President: Bruce Bierman
Marketing Manager: Steven Meyer
National Sales Manager: Robert Whetstone
Estimated Sales: $1 - 5 Million
Number Employees: 17

26605 Neutec Group
1 Lenox Ave
Farmingdale, NY 11735
516-870-0877
Fax: 516-977-3774 888-810-5179
info@neutecgroup.com www.neutecgroup.com
Manufacturer of technologies for the quality control
and research and development laboratory.
Founder & CEO: Ronen Neutra
VP: Orna Zohar-Neutra

26606 Nevlen Co. 2, Inc.
96 Audubon Road
Wakefield, MA 01880-1200
978-462-7777
Fax: 978-462-7774 800-562-7225
nevlen@nevlen.com
Manufacturer and exporter of van equipment includ-
ing roof racks, shelving, drawer units and partitions
VP: James Capomaccio
VP: M Nickerson
Executive VP/Treasurer: J Capomaccio
Estimated Sales: $2.5-5 Million
Number Employees: 20-49
Square Footage: 208000
Brands:
   Nevlen

26607 (HQ)Nevo Corporation
50 Hayney Ct
PO Box 601
Ronkonkoma, NY 11779-7220
631-585-8787
Fax: 631-585-9285
Manufacturer and exporter of roll-in and rotating
rack convection ovens
President: Richard Gehnrich
Treasurer: Leon Pedigo
VP: Wayne Pedigo
Estimated Sales: $1 - 3 Million
Number Employees: 20-49
Square Footage: 46000

26608 New Age Industrial
16788 US Highway 36
PO Box 520
Norton, KS 67654-5488
785-877-5121
Fax: 785-877-2616 800-255-0104
janet@newageindustrial.com
www.newageindustrial.com
Manufacturer and exporter of aluminum backroom
equipment including mobile platters, lug carts,
racks, shelving, dollies and tables
President: Dakota Criqui
dcriqui@newagefoodserviceequipment.com
VP: Tom Sharp
Sales Director: Allen Hasken
Estimated Sales: $10 - 20 Million
Number Employees: 100-249
Type of Packaging: Food Service

26609 New Attitude Beverage Corporation
PO Box 117385
Burlingame, CA 94011-7385
310-414-6501
Fax: 310-414-6547 newattbev@aol.com
Unique package designs and products beverages for
the industry
Estimated Sales: $2 Million
Number Employees: 22
Type of Packaging: Consumer, Food Service

26610 New Brunswick Intl Inc
76 Veronica Ave
Somerset, NJ 08873-3417
732-828-3633
Fax: 732-828-4884 marketing@nbidigi.com
www.nbidigi.net
Scales, labels, wrapping and overwrap machines
President: John Baumann
john.baumann@nbi-digi.com
CFO: Victor Liras
R & D: Ed Hearon
Estimated Sales: $5-10 Million
Number Employees: 20-49

26611 New Carbon Company
PO Box 71
Buchanan, MI 49107-0071
574-247-2270
Fax: 574-247-2280 newcarbon@qtm.net
www.goldenmalted.com
This company has 4 separate entries all of which are
duplicates. Three of the entries are to be deleted and
only one kept.

26612 New Castle Industries Inc
1399 County Line Rd
New Castle, PA 16101-2955
724-654-2603
Fax: 724-656-5620 800-897-2830
info@nordsonxaloy.com
CEO: Walter Cox
Contact: Walter Cox
wcoxjr@xaloy.com
Estimated Sales: $1 - 5 Million
Number Employees: 10-19
Parent Co: Nordson XALOY Incorporated

26613 New Centennial
P.O. Box 708
Columbus, GA 31902-0708
706-323-6446
Fax: 706-327-9921 800-241-7541
Non-refrigerated and refrigerated side and rear- ac-
cess truck bodies and trailers for the beverage and
food distribution industry
Manager: Bob Hudak
Marketing Director: Wes Hauglie
Sales Director: Dan Burt
Plant Manager: Bob Hudak
Purchasing Manager: Tim Fitzpatrick
Estimated Sales: $10-20 Million
Number Employees: 50-99

26614 New Chief Fashion
3223 E 46th St
Vernon, CA 90058-2407
323-582-5322
Fax: 323-581-0077 800-639-2433
www.newchef.com
Manufacturer and exporter of aprons, uniforms and
chef hats
Owner: Lucien Salama
lucien@newchef.com
Estimated Sales: Less Than $500,000
Number Employees: 1-4
Type of Packaging: Food Service

26615 New Court
3200 Court St
Texarkana, TX 75501-6619
903-838-0521
Fax: 903-838-9452
Laminated sanitary insulated and noninsulated wall
and ceiling panels including fiberglass, painted alu-
minum and stainless steel
President: Calvin Court
ctcourt@msn.com
VP Marketing: Melvin Court
Sales Director: Jodi Shewmaker
Estimated Sales: $20 - 50 Million
Number Employees: 100-249
Brands:
New-Glass
Poly-Liner

26616 New Data Systems Inc
19 Claremont Ln
Suffern, NY 10901-7011
845-357-7744
Fax: 845-357-7933
Accounting and trading position software for importers, exporters and commodity traders
Owner: Peter Bellin
peter@catstoday.com

Estimated Sales: $1-2.5 Million
Number Employees: 1-4

**26617 New England Cheese Making
Supply Company**
54 Whately Rd
Suite B
South Deerfield, MA 01373
413-397-2012
Fax: 413-397-2014 info@cheesemaking.com
www.cheesemaking.com
Ingredients and supplies for cheesemaking and home
dairy needs
Owner: Ricki Carroll
ricki@cheesemaking.com
Estimated Sales: Below $5 Million
Number Employees: 1-4

26618 New England Label
1213 US Route 302
Barre, VT 5641
802-476-6393
Fax: 802-476-7159 800-368-3932
salesoffice@wnpinc.com www.wnpinc.com
Pressure sensitive labels
Sales Representative: Vicki Adams
Contact: Randy Ensminger
rensminger@newenglandlabel.com
General Manager: Jim Veness
Production Manager: Chris Rivers
Estimated Sales: $500,000-$1 Million
Number Employees: 5-9
Square Footage: 7626
Parent Co: Willington Company

26619 New England Machinery Inc
2820 62nd Ave E
Bradenton, FL 34203-5305
941-755-5550
Fax: 941-751-6281 info@neminc.com
www.neminc.com
Manufacturer and exporter of hopper/elevators and
bottling machinery including unscramblers,
orienters, cappers, lidders, puckers, de-puckers, gap
transfers and more
Owner: Pat Charles
pat.charles@jacksonhealth.org
Director Sales/Marketing: Marge Bonura
VP Manufacturing: Geza Bankuty
Number Employees: 100-249
Square Footage: 160000
Brands:
N.E.M.

26620 New England Overshoe Company
1193 S Brownell Rd
Williston, VT 05495-7416
802-846-8880
Fax: 802-863-6888 888-289-6367
Neos@overshoe.com
Footwear for the food and pharmaceutical industry,
soles that keep particles from being spread, a Poly
Urethane Upper that does not harbor bacteria and
can be cleaned both inside and out reducing
biohazard contamination
President: Scott Hardy
Marketing Coordinator: Robyn Terranova
Estimated Sales: $2.4 Million
Number Employees: 5-9
Parent Co: Linckia Development

26621 New England Pallets & Skids
250 West St
Ludlow, MA 01056-1248
413-583-6628
Fax: 413-583-5187 www.nepallets.com
Wooden pallets
President: Cynthia Kawie
Estimated Sales: $1-2.5 Million
Number Employees: 10-19
Square Footage: 200000
Type of Packaging: Consumer, Food Service

26622 (HQ)New England Wooden Ware
205 School St # 201
Suite 201
Gardner, MA 01440-2781
978-630-3600
Fax: 978-630-1513 800-252-9214
www.newoodenware.com
Manufacturer, importer and exporter of corrugated
paper boxes

President: David Urquhart
VP Sales: R Goguen
Quality Control Manager: Don Broderick
Sales Manager: Mark Salisbury
Contact: Judith Berman
judithb@mediatemanagement.com
VP Production: D Urquhart
Estimated Sales: Less Than $500,000
Number Employees: 1-4
Square Footage: 386000
Other Locations:
New England Wooden WareCorp.
Fitchburg MA

26623 New Era Label Corporation
51 Valley St
Belleville, NJ 07109-3011
973-759-2444
Fax: 973-759-2993
Seals, stickers and labels including paper, pressure
sensitive, spot carbon, carbon interleaved and con-
secutively numbered
Sales: Fred Iannone
Manager: Tom Savano
Estimated Sales: $1 - 5 Million
Number Employees: 10-19

26624 New Generation SoftwareInc
3835 N Freeway Blvd # 200
Suite 200
Sacramento, CA 95834-1954
916-920-2200
Fax: 916-920-1380 800-824-1220
admin@ngsi.com www.ngsi.com
Financial, distribution and business intelligence
software solutions
President: Bernard B Gough
bgo@ngsi.com
Estimated Sales: $10 - 20 Million
Number Employees: 50-99

26625 New Hatchwear Company
Bay 104, 4711
13th Street N.E.
Calgary, AB T2E 6M3
Canada
403-291-2525
Fax: 403-291-2521 800-661-9249
Uniform apparel including skirts, blouses, dresses,
aprons, tunics, slacks, smocks, vests, jackets, tai-
lored blazers, formals, kitchen whites, service coats,
industrial clothing and outerwear, security, law en-
forcement and military.
Purchasing Manager: Sandra Dimitrijevic
Number Employees: 50-99
Type of Packaging: Consumer, Food Service, Pri-
vate Label

26626 New Haven Awnings
178 Chapel St
New Haven, CT 06513-4209
203-562-7232
Fax: 203-624-4124 800-560-5650
info@nhawning.com www.nhawning.com
Commercial awnings
President: Dan Barnick
Partner: Tom Gumkowski
Estimated Sales: $5-10,000,000
Number Employees: 10-19

26627 New High Glass
12713 SW 125th Ave
Miami, FL 33186-5404
305-232-0840
Fax: 305-251-7622 800-GLA-SSUS
sales@newhigh.com www.newhighglass.com
Wine industry bottles and closures
President: Enrico Raccah
len@newhigh.com
Estimated Sales: $10-20 Million
Number Employees: 20-49

26628 New Horizon Foods
33440 Western Ave
Union City, CA 94587-3202
510-489-8600
Fax: 510-489-9797
Dough conditioners, bread bases, natural mixes,
beverage, cake, muffin, pudding, meat spices, spice
blends, snack and chip seasonings, custard, ice
cream, waffle cone and sauce mixes and bases; exporter of dough conditioners and cakeand muffin
mixes

Owner: Ken Crawford
kenc@newhorizonfoodsinc.com
Senior Vice President: Yael Melzer
Number Employees: 10-19
Parent Co: Tova Industries
Type of Packaging: Consumer, Food Service, Private Label, Bulk

26629 New Horizon Technologies
3100 Geo Washntn Way
Richland, WA 99354
509-372-4868
Fax: 509-372-4869 www.feandc.com
Food irradiation processing facility specializing in fresh fruits and vegetable, poultry, meat and seafood for R&D applications
President/ CEO: Richard T French
EVP/ CEO: DeVerne Dunnum
CFO: Bassel Younes
VP Market Development: Carl Holder
EVP, Business Development: Richard French Jr.
VP Operations: Dave Eakin
Estimated Sales: $500,000-$1,000,000
Number Employees: 1-4

26630 New Jersey Department OfAgriculture
Po Box 330
Trenton, NJ 08625
609-292-8856
logan.brown@ag.state.nj.us
www.state.nj.us
Agriculture
Secretary of Agriculture: Douglas Fisher
Contact: Patricia Gray
patricia.gray@dhs.state.nj.us

26631 New Jersey Wire Stitching Machine Company
1841 Old Cuthbert Road
Cherry Hill, NJ 08034
856-428-2572
Fax: 856-428-3069 sales@newjerseywire.com
www.newjerseywire.com
Manual and auto bag closers for poly, mesh and drawstring bags at high speeds; also, wire stitchers for fiber and corrugated containers, trays, metals, display boxes and plastics
Manager: Mike Menaquala
CEO: Fred Rexon
Contact: Mike Menquale
info@newjerseywire.com
General Manager: Michael Menaquale
Estimated Sales: $500,000-$1 Million
Number Employees: 1-4
Square Footage: 40000
Parent Co: Precision Automation Company

26632 New Klix Corporation
551 Railroad Avenue
South San Francisco, CA 94080-3450
650-761-0622
Fax: 650-589-6735 800-522-5544
Manufacturer and exporter of warewash, laundry detergents and cleaning compounds
President: Rodrigo Ortiz
VP: Lautaro Ortiz
Estimated Sales: $2.5-5 Million
Number Employees: 19
Square Footage: 110000
Type of Packaging: Food Service, Private Label
Brands:
Klix

26633 New Lisbon Wood ProductsManufacturing Company
1127 S Adams St
New Lisbon, WI 53950
608-562-3122
Fax: 608-562-3221 acewoodproducts@excite.com
www.acewoodproducts.com
Custom wooden pallets, skids and crates
Owner: David Brinkman
Marketing: Linda Brinkman
Sales: Sonya Brach
Plant Manager: Dan Batten
Estimated Sales: $1-2.5 Million
Number Employees: 10-19
Square Footage: 40000
Parent Co: Ace Wood

26634 New London Engineering
1700 Division St
New London, WI 54961-9137
920-982-4030
Fax: 920-982-6800 800-437-1994
nlesales@nleco.com www.nleco.com
Conveyors including line and table top chain
President: Martin Bonneson
CEO: Frank Ferdon
Quality Control: Dale Turdell
Director Sales/Marketing: Dale Trudell
Estimated Sales: $10 - 20 Million
Number Employees: 50-99
Square Footage: 100000
Parent Co: Bonntech International

26635 New Mexico Products Inc
503 Vineyard Rd NE
Albuquerque, NM 87113-1020
505-345-7864
Fax: 505-344-2581 877-345-7864
Wooden boxes, crates and custom pallets including softwood only
President: David St John
nmpoffice@flash.net
Sales Director: Matt Walker
Office Manager: Stella Torres
Estimated Sales: Less Than $500,000
Number Employees: 1-4
Square Footage: 12000

26636 New Pig Corp
1 Pork Ave
PO Box 304
Tipton, PA 16684-9001
814-684-0101
Fax: 814-684-0961 800-468-4647
salesdept@newpig.com www.newpig.com
Industrial leak, spill, safety, maintenance, storage, handling and repair products
President: Nino Vella
CEO: Charlie Craig
charlie.craig@transedgetruck.com
CFO: Jim Crlin
Executive VP: Doug Hershey
Quality Control: Steve Klling
R & D: Mark Woytowich
Director of Public Relations: Carl DeCaspers
Purchasing Manager: Bill Lidwell
Estimated Sales: Below $5 Million
Number Employees: 250-499

26637 New Resina Corporation
27455 Bostik Court
Temecula, CA 92590
951-296-6585
Fax: 951-296-5018 800-207-4804
sales@resina.com www.resina.com
President: Michael Tom
CEO: Andy Lask
Number Employees: 10-19

26638 New Tiger International
117 State Street,
Westbury, NY 11590
516-942-9312
Fax: 516-942-9306 newtiger6688@yahoo.com
www.greatporcini.com
Dried, frozen, fresh and canned mushrooms
Marketing: Richard Lin
Contact: Shari Baldwin
sbaldwin@greatporcini.com

26639 New Way Packaging Machinery
PO Box 467
Hanover, PA 17331
717-637-2133
Fax: 717-637-2966 800-522-3537
sales@labeler.com
Manufacturer and exporter of labeling machinery
President: Edward Abendschein
Contact: Merle Mcmaster
merle@labeler.com
Estimated Sales: $10-20 Million
Number Employees: 5-9

26640 New York Corugated Box Co
239 Lindbergh Pl # 1
Paterson, NJ 07503-2821
973-742-5000
Fax: 973-742-7666 www.nycorrugatedbox.net
Corrugated cartons and inserts
President: Robert Rosner
General Manager: Robert Rosner

Estimated Sales: $2.5-5 Million
Number Employees: 5-9
Square Footage: 28000

26641 New York Folding Box CoInc
20 Continental Dr
Stanhope, NJ 07874-2658
973-347-6932
Fax: 973-347-2303 ken@nyfoldingbox.com
www.nyfoldingbox.com
Folding boxes
President: Harry Kaplan
Chairman of the Board: Jerome Joseph Kaplan
VP: Robert Kaplan
Sales Manager: Sal Vassallo
Estimated Sales: $5-10 Million
Number Employees: 5-9

26642 New York State Electric& Gas
1 Corporate Dr
Binghamton, NY 13902
607-762-7200
Fax: 607-762-8614 800-572-1111
www.nyseg.com
President: Jim Laurito
Senior VP: Jeffrey K Smith
gsmith@nyseg.com
Estimated Sales: $1 - 5 Million
Number Employees: 1000-4999

26643 New-Ma Co. Llc
4618 44th St SE
Grand Rapids, MI 49512
616-942-5500
Fax: 616-942-5511 www.newma.it
Horizontal and vertical packaging machines, counting and weighing systems.
Contact: Nico Nicoletti
n.nicoletti@newmapackaging.com

26644 Newark Wire Cloth Co
160 Fornelius Ave
Clifton, NJ 07013-1844
973-778-4478
Fax: 973-778-4481 800-221-0392
info@newarkwire.com www.newarkwire.com
Manufacturer, exporter and importer of wire cloth, filters, strainers, testing sieves, etc. Manufacturers of the Sani Cloan Strainer product line. Consisting of: inline, side inlet, and hi-capacity basket strainers. Custom fabricationsare a specialty.
President/Owner: Richard Campbell
rcampbell@newarkwire.com
Estimated Sales: $5 - 10 Million
Number Employees: 20-49
Square Footage: 120000
Type of Packaging: Food Service

26645 Newcastle Co Inc
3812 Wilmington Rd
New Castle, PA 16105-6134
724-658-4516
Fax: 724-658-5100 ncco@newcastleco.com
www.newcastleco.com
Manufacturer and integrator of load transfer systems, palletizers, pallet dispensers, sheet dispensers, and conveyors.
Owner: Dennis Alduk
ncco@losch.net
Number Employees: 5-9
Brands:
Floor Level
Palavator

26646 Newco Enterprises Inc
3650 New Town Blvd
St Charles, MO 63301-4357
636-946-1330
Fax: 314-925-0029 800-325-7867
www.newcocoffee.com
Coffee and tea brewing equipment and water treatment systems; exporter of commercial coffee brewers
Owner: Karen Enke
CFO: Mcenke Karen
VP Marketing: Anthony Westcott
VP, Sales: Jason College
s.murthy@trafinfo.com
Estimated Sales: $10 - 20 Million
Number Employees: 100-249
Square Footage: 160000

26647 Newco Inc
1 Hicks Ave # A
Newton, NJ 07860-2629
973-383-7777
Fax: 973-383-0506 www.newco.com
Decorative facing for paneling and wall coverings
President: James Berezny
Estimated Sales: $20-50 Million
Number Employees: 20-49

26648 Newcourt, Inc.
PO Box 182
Madison, IN 47250-0182
800-933-0006
Fax: 812-265-6455
Composite laminated floorings for mezzanines
Sales Director: John Gramke
Number Employees: 2

26649 Newell Brands
6655 Peachtree Dunwoody Rd
Atlanta, GA 30328
consumer.inquiries@newellco.com
www.newellbrands.com
Manufacturer and exporter of food service, sanitary
maintenance and material handling products.
President & CEO: Ravi Saligram
Unit CEO, Appliances & Cookware: David Hammer
Unit CEO, Food: Kris Malkoski
CFO & President, Business Operations: Christopher
Peterson
Chief Legal & Administrative Officer: Bradford
Turner
Chief Human Resources Officer: Steve Parsons
Chief Customer Officer: Mike Hayes
Chief Procurement Officer: Steve Nikolopoulos
Year Founded: 1903
Estimated Sales: $14.7 Billion
Number Employees: 49,000
Type of Packaging: Consumer, Food Service

26650 Newlands Systems
602-30731 Simpson Road
Abbotsford, BC V2T 6Y7
Canada
604-855-4890
Fax: 604-855-8826 mail@nsibrew.com
Manufacturer and exporter of brewing equipment
and machinery
President: Brad McQuhae
Director Marketing: Loch McJannett
Number Employees: 10
Square Footage: 80000
Type of Packaging: Food Service

26651 (HQ)Newly Weds Foods Inc
2501 N Keeler Ave
Chicago, IL 60639-2131
773-489-6224
Fax: 773-489-2799 800-621-7521
nwfnorthamerica@newlywedsfoods.com
www.newlywedsfoods.com
Processor and exporter of breadings, batters, season-
ing blends, marinades, glazes and capsicum products
President: Charles T. Angell
CFO: Brian Johnson
SVP Sales & Marketing: Bruce Leshinski
R&D: Jim Klein
Sales Director: Jim Chin
Contact: Mary Adderhold
madderhold@newlywedsfoods.com
VP Manufacturing: Mike Hopp
Plant Manager: Leo Vogler
Director of Purchasing: Tom Lisack
Estimated Sales: $959 Million
Number Employees: 1-4
Square Footage: 1500000
Other Locations:
Newly Weds Foods
Bethleham PA
Newly Weds Foods
Chicago IL
Newly Weds Foods
Cleveland TN
Newly Weds Foods
Watertown MA
Newly Weds Foods
Yorkville IL
Newly Weds Foods
Horn Lake MS
Newly Weds Foods
Edmonton AB
Newly Weds Foods
Montreal QC

Newly Weds Foods
Toronto ON
Brands:
Batter Blends
Blended Breaders
Newly Weds

26652 Newman Labeling Systems
4400 Route 9 South
Suite 1000
Freehold, NJ 07728
609-597-8722
Fax: 609-597-8755 newmanmps@aol.com
www.newmanlabeling.com
President: John W Clayton
Vice President Operations: Michael Semiraro
Estimated Sales: $1 - 5 Million
Number Employees: 10-19

26653 Newman Sanitary Gasket Co
964 W Main St
P.O. Box 222
Lebanon, OH 45036-9173
513-932-7379
Fax: 513-932-4493 customer@newmangasket.com
www.newmangasket.com
Manufacturer and exporter of foodgrade sanitary
process piping gaskets, seals and F.D.A. O-rings.
Also custom molded rubber parts
President: David W Newman
davidn@newmangasket.com
CEO: Tom Moore
VP: Betsy Newman
Marketing Director: Larry Hensel
Customer Service Manager: Cindy Swagler
Plant Manager: Matt Agricola
Estimated Sales: $1-5,000,000
Number Employees: 50-99
Square Footage: 65000
Type of Packaging: Private Label, Bulk
Brands:
Newman

26654 Newmarket Corp
135 Commerce Way
Portsmouth, NH 03801-3243
804-788-5555
Fax: 603-436-1826 888-829-8871
www.newmarket.com
Windows based sales, marketing and catering soft-
ware
CEO: Sean O Neill
CFO: Ken Smaha
Contact: Kristen Acheson
kacheson@newmarketinc.com
Estimated Sales: $33.4 Million
Number Employees: 380
Square Footage: 27000
Brands:
Breeze
Ccbreeze
Cvbreeze
Delphi
Delphi 7.0
Global Sfa
Regional Delphi

26655 Newport Electronics Inc
2229 S Yale St
Santa Ana, CA 92704-4401
714-540-4914
Fax: 714-968-7311 800-639-7678
info@newportus.com www.microinfinity.com
NEWPORT is known for designing and manufactur-
ing the world's most accurate industrial
intrumentation. Prestotek brand of products in-
cludes: pH, ORP, conductivity, Resistivity, salt, and
much more. Offered as panel mount ofhandheld
instruments.
President: Milton Hollander
Manager: Dick Hollander
Estimated Sales: $1 - 3 Million
Number Employees: 50-99
Parent Co: Newport Electronics
Type of Packaging: Private Label
Brands:
Pocket Pal
Presto-Tek

26656 Newstamp Lighting Factory
227 Bay Rd
P.O. Box 189
North Easton, MA 02356-2673
508-238-7073
Fax: 508-230-8312 www.newstamplighting.com
Wall and ceiling lights
Owner: Robert Zeitsiff
bob@newstamplighting.com
VP Marketing: Charles Edwards
Estimated Sales: $1-2.5 Million
Number Employees: 20-49

26657 Newstamp Lighting Factory
227 Bay Rd
PO Box 189
North Easton, MA 02356-2673
508-238-7073
Fax: 508-230-8312 www.newstamplighting.com
Electric lighting fixtures, metal stamping equipment,
plumbing products and security windows; exporter
of electric lighting fixtures
President: Robert Zeitsiff
bob@newstamplighting.com
VP: Sandra Zeitstiff
Clerk: Charlotte Zeitstiff
Estimated Sales: $2.5-5 Million
Number Employees: 20-49
Square Footage: 68000

26658 Newtech Inc
11 Hedding Dr
Randolph, VT 05060-1032
802-728-9170
Fax: 802-728-9163 800-210-2361
dewater91@msn.com
www.newtechdewatering.com
Manufactures dewatering systems for wastewater
President: Robert Dimmick
robert@dimmickservices.com
Estimated Sales: $3 Million
Number Employees: 10-19

26659 Newton Broom Co
1508 W Jourdan St
PO Box 358
Newton, IL 62448-2006
618-783-4424
Fax: 618-783-2442 sales@newtonbroom.com
www.newtonbroom.com
Brooms, mops and staple brushes
Manager: Don Leventhal
don@newtonbroom.com
Manager: Becky Shamhart
Estimated Sales: Below $5 Million
Number Employees: 20-49

26660 Newton OA & Son Co
16356 Sussex Hwy
Bridgeville, DE 19933-3056
302-337-3782
Fax: 302-337-3780 800-726-5745
solutions@oanewton.com www.oanewton.com
Manufacturer and exporter of weighing equipment
and pneumatic and mechanical material handling
systems including dust collection
President: Rob Rider
Number Employees: 20-49

26661 Newwaveenviro
6595 S Dayton St # 3100
Greenwood Vlg, CO 80111-6189
303-221-3232
Fax: 303-221-3233 800-592-8371
customerservice@newwaveenviro.com
Water filtration systems and accessories
President: Virgil Archer
Manager: Sheri Archer
sheri.archer@newwaveenviro.com
Estimated Sales: $1 - 3 Million
Number Employees: 20-49

26662 Nexel Industries Inc
11 Harbor Park Dr
Port Washington, NY 11050-4656
516-484-5225
Fax: 516-625-0084 800-245-6682
nexelinfo@nexelwire.com www.nexelwire.com
Manufacturer, importer and exporter of material
handling and storage systems including solid steel
and wire shelving, trucks and carts

Vice President: Dibuseng Moloi
dmoloi@businessmonitor.com
VP: John Svitek
Inside Sales Manager: Howard Ziporkin
National Sales Manager: Jerry Mark
Number Employees: 100-249
Square Footage: 2400000
Type of Packaging: Food Service, Private Label
Brands:
Loadmaster
Nexel
Nexelite
Nexelon
Poly-Z-Brite
Space-Trac

26663 Nexen Group
560 Oak Grove Pkwy
St Paul, MN 55127-8500

651-484-5900
Fax: 651-286-1099 800-843-7445
info@nexengroup.com www.nexengroup.com
Producer of precision motion control equipment.
Products include industrial clutches, brakes, web
guides, tension and automated assembly tools.
CEO: Hutch Schilling
VP, Sales & Marketing: Tim Dillon
Estimated Sales: $20 - 50 Million
Number Employees: 200 - 500
Other Locations:
Webster WI

26664 Nexeo Solutions
5200 Blazer Pkwy
Dublin, OH 43017-3309

614-790-3333
Fax: 614-790-4427 877-343-3278
csr@ashchem.com www.nexeosolutions.com
President: Charlie Brown
crbrown@ashland.com
Chairman, Chief Executive Officer: Jim OBrien
Vice President: Blair Boggs
Senior Vice President of Research and De: Fran
Lockwood
Director of Marketing: John Stotz
Director of Corporate Communications: Gary
Rhodes
Estimated Sales: Over $1 Billion
Number Employees: 1000-4999

26665 Nexira
15 Somerset St
Somerville, NJ 08876-2828

908-707-9400
Fax: 908-707-9405 800-872-1850
info-usa@nexira.com www.nexira.com
Nexira is a global leader in natural ingredients and
botanical extracts for food nutrition and dietary supplements. Nexira built its reputation as the world
leader in acacia gum and now manufactures a wide
range of functional andnutritional ingredients, anti-
oxidants, and active botanicals for weight manage-
ment, sports nutrition, digestive and cardiovascular
health. It manufactures the following ingredients for
the food and health industry: acacia gun, botanical
extracts andpowders.
President: Stephane Dondain
heese@cnius.com
VP: Teresa Yazbek
Marketing/Logistics Specialist: Nina Segura
Sales: Bob Bremer
Estimated Sales: $14 Million
Number Employees: 10-19
Number of Brands: 25
Number of Products: 100
Type of Packaging: Bulk
Brands:
CACTi-NEA
EFICACIA
EQUACIA
EXOCYAN
FIBREGUM
ID-ALG
INSTANTGUM
NEOPUNTIA
SPRAYGUM
THIXOGUM
VINITROX

26666 Nexthermal
1045 Harts Lake Rd
Battle Creek, MI 49037-7357

269-964-0271
Fax: 269-964-4526 800-937-4681
sales@hotset.com
Cartridge, coil, band, strip and tubular heaters, tem-
perature controls, thermocouples, connectors
President: Srekumar Bandyopadhyay
kumar@nexthermal.com
Estimated Sales: $5-10 000,000
Number Employees: 100-249

26667 Nhs Labs Inc
11665 W State St
Star, ID 83669-5223

208-939-5100
Fax: 208-939-5100 888-546-8694
www.nutritionmanufacturer.com
Private label sports drinks, supplements, and energy
drinks
CEO: Larry Leach
Number Employees: 50-99
Square Footage: 74000

26668 Ni Source Inc
801 E 86th Ave
Merrillville, IN 46410-6272

219-647-5990
Fax: 219-853-5161 www.nisource.com
Air pollution control, chilling units, heating systems,
recording and monitoring devices and controls
Chairman of the Board: Gary L Neale
CEO: Joseph Hamrock
hamrock@nisource.com
CEO: Eileen O Odum
Estimated Sales: Over $1 Billion
Number Employees: 5000-9999

26669 Niagara Blower Company
673 Ontario St
Buffalo, NY 14207

716-875-2000
Fax: 716-875-1077 800-426-5169
sales@niagarablower.com
www.niagarablower.com
Manufacturer and exporter of custom refrigeration
systems including bacteria-free, frost-free moisture
management, evaporators, condensers and
dehumidification
President: Peter Demakos
Marketing Assistant: Jen Dorman
Sales Manager: Phil Rowland
Contact: David Anderson
danderson@niagarablower.com
COO: Peter Demakos
Estimated Sales: $10 - 20 Million
Number Employees: 50-99
Square Footage: 200000
Brands:
Aero Heat Exchanger
Hygrol
No Frost

26670 Niantic Awning Company
PO Box 864
Windham, NH 3087

978-225-0108
Fax: 860-739-0168 info@necpa.org
www.necpa.org
Commercial awnings
President: Scott Massey
Vice President: Cheryl Yennaco
Vice President: Mike Cornell
Estimated Sales: Less than $500,000
Number Employees: 5-9

26671 (HQ)Nice-Pak Products Inc
2 Nice-Pak Park
Orangeburg, NY 10962-1376

845-365-1700
800-444-6725
www.nicepak.com
Manufacturer and exporter of cleaning and sanitizing supplies including moist towelettes, disposable
wash cloths, surface disinfectants and hand
sanitizers.
Chief Executive Officer: Robert Julius
Chief Operating Officer: Ron Gordon
Analytic Chemist: Elmira Abdelnasser
eabdelnasser@nicepak.com
Year Founded: 1955
Estimated Sales: $165.5 Million

Number Employees: 2,500
Square Footage: 28000
Type of Packaging: Consumer, Food Service, Pri-
vate Label
Brands:
Alcohol Prep Pads 100's
Nice-N-Clean
Pdi
Rub a Dubs
Sani-Cloth
Sani-Hands
Sani-Wipe
Wet-Nap 1000-Pak

26672 Nicholas Machine and Grinding
7500 San Felipe St
Suite 600
Houston, TX 77063-1790

713-914-8077
Fax: 713-972-1164 800-747-1256
Owner: James Nail

26673 Nicholas Marketing Associates
179 Larch Ave
Bogota, NJ 07603-1222

201-343-9414
Fax: 201-343-3256
Consultant specializing in marketing and promotion
Director: Gary Fermature
Managing Director: Nicholas Zampetti, Jr.
Estimated Sales: $1-2.5 Million
Number Employees: 2

26674 Nichols Specialty Products
10 Parker Street
Southborough, MA 01772-1949

508-481-4367
Fax: 508-481-7806
Manufacturer and exporter of bottle and can capping
machinery
President: Larry Quinlan
CEO: Janet Wellman
CFO: Shannon Quinlan
Number Employees: 10
Brands:
Kinex

26675 Nichols Wire
1547 Helton Dr
Florence, AL 35630

256-764-4271
Fax: 256-767-5152
Teabag wire
President: Earl D Thomason
Contact: Francesca Cohen
fcohen@nicholswire.com
Estimated Sales: $25 - 50 Million
Number Employees: 100-249

26676 Nickel 9 Distillery
90 Cawthra Ave
Unit #100
Toronto, ON M6N 3C2
Canada

647-341-5959
www.nickel9distillery.com
Spirits, including rum, vodka, gin, brandy, and or-
ange liqueur, cocktail kits, and bar equipment.
Owner & Operator: Chris Jacks
Director, Marketing: Michael Pez
Year Founded: 2017
Number Employees: 11-50
Number of Brands: 10
Brands:
Crazy
Golden Temple
Gubiani Maple Espesso Anice
Hidden Temple
Island Diaz
Jacky Apple Jack
Monkey
Ni9
Northern Temple
Top Secret

26677 Nicol Scales & Measurement LP
7239 Envoy Ct
Dallas, TX 75247-5103

214-428-8181
Fax: 214-428-8127 800-225-8181
sales@nicolscales.com www.nicolscales.com
Manufacturer and exporter of industrial scales and
force measuring equipment; also, leasing available

President, CEO: Ted Tabolka
ted@nicolscales.com
Director of Finance: Oliver Jackson
Vice President, Service: Steve Ford
Director of Sales and Marketing: Jim Budke
Estimated Sales: $5 - 10 Million
Number Employees: 20-49

26678 Nicomac Inc
80 Oak St # 201
Norwood, NJ 07648-1342

201-768-9501
Fax: 201-768-9504 800-628-0006
sales@nicosgroup.com www.nicomac.com
Autoclaves, coaters, ceiling grid systems, ceiling
panels, coatings, tableaquous, design services,
doors, automatic and manual, floor finishes, modular
rooms, ovens, steam generators, sterilizers, auto-
clave, stopper sterilizing tablet hoppers
President: Francesco Nigris
Manager: Rosanne Cangialosi
rosannec@nicomac.com
Manager: Rosanne Cangialosi
Estimated Sales: $5 Million
Number Employees: 1-4

26679 (HQ)Nicosia Creative Expresso
355 W 52nd St Fl 8
New York, NY 10019

212-515-6600
Fax: 212-265-5422 info@niceltd.com
www.niceltd.com
Consultant to the food industry; packaging design
services available
President: Davide Nicosia
Contact: David Balch
balch@niceltd.com
Estimated Sales: Below $5,000,000
Number Employees: 20-49
Square Footage: 8000
Type of Packaging: Consumer, Food Service, Pri-
vate Label, Bulk
Other Locations:
Nicosia Creative Expresso
Madrid

26680 Nidec Minster Corp.
240 West Fifth Street
Minster, OH 45865

www.minster.com
Presses for production of food and beverage cans,
ends, and easy open ends
CEO: David Winch
Estimated Sales: $118 Million
Number Employees: 500

26681 Nieco Corporation
7950 Cameron Drive
Windsor, CA 95492

707-284-7100
Fax: 707-284-7430 800-643-2656
sales@nieco.com www.nieco.com
Manufacturer and exporter of automatic bun grilling
and meat broiling machines for hamburgers, steaks,
chicken and fish
President: Ed Baker
Executive VP: John Brown
Contact: Steve Alcocer
salcocer@nieco.com
Estimated Sales: $10-20 Million
Number Employees: 50-99
Square Footage: 150000
Type of Packaging: Food Service

26682 Nifty Packaging
4 Jocama Blvd
Old Bridge, NJ 08857-3513

732-591-1140
Fax: 732-591-8477 800-631-2172
contactus@niftypack.com www.niftypack.com
Shipping room products, tape, tape and label dis-
pensers, stretch film, strapping and tools and enve-
lopes
President: Norman Ferber
Estimated Sales: $10-20 Million
Number Employees: 5-9

26683 Nigrelli Systems Purchasing
16024 County Road X
Kiel, WI 53042-9741

920-693-3165
Fax: 920-693-3634 800-693-3144
www.aquamasterfountains.com

Manufacturer and exporter of continuous motion
case and tray packing systems, tray formers, plastic
tray denesting systems, bulk container and bottled
water packers, wrap around packers and
shrinkwrapping equipment
President: Nicholas Nigrelli
VP Sales: David O'Keefe
Estimated Sales: Less Than $500,000
Number Employees: 1-4

26684 Nijal USA
1920 S 1st St
Minneapolis, MN 55454-1055

651-353-6702
Fax: 612-395-5257
Meat and bakery processing equipment
President: Michael Halbaut

26685 Nijhuis Water Technology
560 W Washington Blvd
Unit 320
Chicago, IL 60661-2693
Canada

312-466-9900
Fax: 312-300-4105 info@nijhuis-water.com
www.nijhuis-water.nl
Provides complete wastewater treatment systems
and installation services
Vice President: Adriaan Van Der Beck
Parent Co: Nijhuis Water Technology B.V.

26686 Nikka Densok
610 Garrison St # D
Lakewood, CO 80215-5882

303-202-6190
Fax: 303-202-6195 800-806-4587
sales@nikkadensok.com www.nikkadensok.com
Leak detection systems for food product packaging
President: Brian Ball
Estimated Sales: $5 - 10 Million
Number Employees: 5-9
Parent Co: Nikka Densok

26687 Nilfisk, Inc.
740 Hemlock Rd
Suite 100
Morgantown, PA 19543

Fax: 610-286-7350 800-645-3475
www.nilfiskcfm.com
Powered cleaning equipment
Exec. VP, Americas: Andrew Ray

26688 Nimbus Water Systems
41840 McAlby Ct # A
Murrieta, CA 92562-7080

951-894-2800
Fax: 760-591-0106 800-451-9343
www.nimbuswater.com
Manufacturer and exporter of water treatment equip-
ment; also, consultant providing water and water re-
cycle systems design services
Founder: Donald Bray
CEO: Mike Faulkner
VP Marketing/Sales: Tony Pagliano
Contact: Sid Brandhuber
sid@nimbuswater.com
Purchasing Manager: Bree Ann Plange
Estimated Sales: $2.5-5 Million
Number Employees: 1-4
Number of Products: 50
Square Footage: 140000
Brands:
Nimbus Cs
Nimbus Fs
Nimbus N
Nimbus Sierra
Nimbus Watermaker

26689 Nina Mauritz Design Service
603 W Park Avenue
Libertyville, IL 60048-2664

847-968-4438
Fax: 847-816-8618
Consultant specializing in space allocation, traffic
flow, design and specification of food service equipment and interior finishes for commercial kitchens,
cafeterias and dining areas
Principal: Nina Mauritz

26690 Niro
1600 Okeefe Rd
Hudson, WI 54016

715-386-9371
Fax: 715-386-9376 www.niroinc.com
Custom fabrication, filtration equipment, aseptic
processing equipment, heat recovery systems,
deaerators, dryers, fluid bed, spray, pilot plants, pro-
cess control, high pressure pumps and homogenizers
President: Steve Kaplan
VP: Eric Bryars
VP: Christian Svensgaard
Marketing Coordinator: Heather Szymanski
Contact: Tim Huntley
thuntley@nilpeter.net
Manager Food/Dairy Evaporators: Bo Bjarekull
Estimated Sales: $20 - 50 Million
Number Employees: 100-249
Parent Co: GEA Group
Other Locations:
Niro
Columbia MD

26691 Niro Inc
1600 Okeefe Rd
Hudson, WI 54016

715-386-9371
Fax: 715-386-9376 www.niroinc.com
Powder handling and packing systems
VP: Eric Bryars
Contact: Tim Huntley
thuntley@nilpeter.net
Estimated Sales: $20 - 50 Million
Number Employees: 100-249

26692 Niroflex, USA
PO Box 90
Deerfield, IL 60015

847-400-2638
Fax: 847-919-3809 metalmesh@niroflex.com
www.niroflex.com
Maker of stainless steel mesh gloves and apparel
that is designed to protect workers in the meat and
poultry food processing industry.
Vice President: Loren Rivkin

26693 Nita Crisp Crackers LLC
454 S. Link Lane
Fort Collins, CO 80524

970-482-9090
Fax: 970-482-1043 866-493-4609
www.nitacrisp.com
Artisan flatbreats in small batches or in bulk to natu-
ral grocers, specialty food stores, and restaurants
from coast to coast
Managing Partner: Steve Landry
CEO: Paul Pellegrino
Customer Service / Sales: Michele Hattman
Estimated Sales: $170,000
Number of Products: 1
Square Footage: 5614
Type of Packaging: Consumer, Food Service, Bulk
Brands:
Nita Crisp

26694 Nitech
911 E 23rd St
Columbus, NE 68601-3736

402-563-3188
Fax: 402-563-2792 800-237-6496
info@nitechIPM.com www.nitechpm.com
Turntables and stretch wrapping equipment
Owner: Roger Bettenhousen
rogerb@nitechindustries.com
Sales Director: Chris Bettenhausen
Estimated Sales: $2.5-5,000,000
Number Employees: 20-49
Type of Packaging: Bulk

26695 Nitsch Tool Co Inc
1715 Grant Blvd
Syracuse, NY 13208-3017

315-472-4044
Fax: 315-472-4051
Manufacturer and exporter of machine knives for
baking
Owner: Leonard Nitsch
Estimated Sales: Less than $500,000
Number Employees: 1-4

26696 Nitta Corp of America
7605 Nitta Dr
Suwanee, GA 30024-6666
770-497-0212
Fax: 770-623-1398 800-221-3689
www.nitta.com
Urethane and PVC conveyor belts, rubber covered, leather power transmission belts
Vice President: Tracy Mc Soley
tmcsoley@nitta.com
VP: Tracy Mc Soley
Marketing/Sales: Bruce Cooper
VP Operations: Kim Millsaps
Estimated Sales: $5-10 Million
Number Employees: 50-99

26697 Nolon Industries
PO Box T
Mantua, OH 44255
330-274-2283
Fax: 330-274-2283
Manufacturer and exporter of fiberglass reinforced plastic boxes
President: Nick Nicolanti
Type of Packaging: Bulk

26698 Nolu Plastics
30152 Aventura
Rancho Santa Margarita, CA 92688-2019
866-765-8744
Fax: 866-447-6587 800-346-7822
solusteam@solusii.com www.solusii.com
Plastic conveyor components, guide rails, chain supports, PVC conveyor rollers
Inside Sales: Kathy Yakas
District Manager: Kevin Dahill
Number Employees: 35
Number of Products: 15

26699 Nomaco
501 Nmc Dr
Zebulon, NC 27597-2762
919-655-0801
Fax: 919-269-7936 info@nomaco.com
www.nomaco.com
Plastic foam extrusions
President: Julian Young
jyoung@nomaco.com
CEO: Mick Dannin
Estimated Sales: $10 - 20 Million
Number Employees: 1-4

26700 Nomafa
975 Old Norcross Rd # A
Lawrenceville, GA 30045-4321
770-338-5000
Fax: 770-338-5024 www.albanydoorsystems.com
Plant Manager: Dan Garrau
Estimated Sales: $20 - 50 Million
Number Employees: 100-249
Parent Co: Albany International

26701 Nook Industries
4950 E 49th St
Cleveland, OH 44125-1016
216-271-7900
Fax: 216-271-7020 800-321-7800
www.nookindustries.com
Ball bearing screws, thread screw products, worm gear actuators, splines and mechanical power jacks
President & CEO: Joseph Nook III
Estimated Sales: $10 - 25 Million
Number Employees: 100-249

26702 (HQ)Nor-Lake
727 Second St
Hudson, WI 54016
715-386-2323
www.norlake.com
Refrigeration systems including walk-in coolers, walk0in freezers, milk coolers, ice cream freezers, environmental rooms, plasma refrigerators and chromatography refrigerators.
CEO: Jim Markus
Estimated Sales: $26 Million
Number Employees: 300
Square Footage: 20000
Parent Co: Standex International Corporation
Type of Packaging: Food Service
Brands:
　Barrier
　Classic
　Fineline
　Foodbank

Kold Locker
Nova Ii
Thermo Flow

26703 NorCrest Consulting
2044 County Road 512
Divide, CO 80814
719-687-7635
Consultant specializing in business management and technical information on fermentation, yeast products and genetic engineering for the food ingredient and biotechnology industries
President: John Norell
VP: Beverly Norell
Number Employees: 14
Square Footage: 8000

26704 (HQ)Noral
88 Pleasant Street S.,
Natick, MA 01760-563
508-653-5574
Fax: 508-653-1828 800-348-2345
Manufacturer and exporter of portable digital thermometers and probes including temperature measurement griddle probes, insertion, handheld and compact
President: Albert Ladanyi
CEO: Dr Deszo Ladanyi
VP Sales: Vincent Passiatore
Contact: Harry Erickson
harrye@noral.com
Operations: Dave Gilgenback
Purchasing Director: Mark O'Malley
Estimated Sales: $1-2.5 Million
Number Employees: 20
Square Footage: 80000

26705 Norand Aluminum
801 Crescent Centre Drive
Suite 600
Franklin, TX 37067
615-771-5700
Fax: 615-771-5701 www.norandaaluminum.com
Manufacturer and exporter of laminated foil and aluminum foil pie plates
CEO: Kip Smith
Estimated Sales: $97 Million
Number Employees: 820
Parent Co: Noranda
Type of Packaging: Private Label, Bulk

26706 Norback Ley & Assoc
3022 Woodland Trl
Middleton, WI 53562-1900
608-233-3814
Fax: 608-233-3895 www.norbackley.com
Manufacturer and exporter of food safety, HACCP and thermal processing software in English, Spanish, French, and Japanese
Owner: Kathleen A Ley
Chief Executive Officer: Sebastian Norback
CFO: Kathryn Olszewski
Estimated Sales: Less Than $500,000
Number Employees: 1-4
Number of Brands: 9
Number of Products: 14
Brands:
　Aprenda Haccp
　Do Haccp
　Do Sop
　Learn Haccp
　Record Haccp
　Tform
　Tpro

26707 Norback Ley & Assoc
3022 Woodland Trl
Middleton, WI 53562-1900
608-233-3814
Fax: 608-233-3895 www.norbackley.com
Provider of software tools for the food safety industry
President: Kathleen Ley
CFO: John Norback
R&D: John Norback
Quality Control: Kathleen Ley
Estimated Sales: Less Than $500,000
Number Employees: 1-4

26708 Norcal Beverage Co
2150 Stone Blvd
West Sacramento, CA 95691
916-372-0600
Fax: 916-374-2605 www.ncbev.com

Producer and wholesaler/distributor of beers, hard ciders, and nonalcoholic beverages. Also contract manufacturing and equipment solutions.
President & CEO: Shannon Deary-Bell
Chairman: Donald Deary
EVP, Marketing & External Affairs: Roy Grant Deary III
EVP, Transportation & Logistics: Timothy Deary
Year Founded: 1937
Estimated Sales: $36.7 Million
Number Employees: 500-999
Square Footage: 152000
Type of Packaging: Consumer, Food Service, Bulk
Brands:
　Activate Drinks
　Alaskan Brewing Company
　Anheuser-Busch Inbev
　Arizona Iced Tea
　Arrowhead Spring Water
　Bacardi Silver
　Bass
　Beach Bum Blonde Ale
　Beck's
　Black Diamond Brewing Company
　Boddingtons Pub Ale
　Budweiser
　Busch
　Calistoga Water
　Crispin Cider
　Crown Imports
　Czechvar Lager
　Dominion
　Firestone Walker Brewery
　Fordham
　Fox Barrell Hard Cider
　Go Girl Energy Drink
　Goose Island Honker's Ale
　Hoegaarden
　Hurricane
　Icelandic Glacial Water
　Icelandic Spring Water
　Illy Chilled Coffee
　Jack's Pumpkin Spice
　King Cobra
　Kirin Ichiban
　Kokanee
　Kona Pale Ale
　Land Shark Lager
　Leffe Blonde
　Lost Energy
　Margaritaville Paradise Key Teas
　Michelob Light
　Monster Energy
　Natural Light
　Nestle Nesquick
　O'Doul's
　Redbridge
　Redhook Esb
　Rogue Brewery
　Rolling Rock
　Rumba Energy Juice
　Shock Top Belgian White
　Sierra Nevada
　Speed Energy Drink
　Starr Hill Amber Ale
　Stella Artois
　Tilt
　Unbound Energy
　Widmer Hefeweizen
　Wild Blue
　Wyders Cider
　Ziegenbock

26709 Norden Inc
230 Industrial Pkwy # A
Branchburg, NJ 08876-3580
908-252-9483
Fax: 908-707-0073 www.nordenmachinery.com
Tube filling and cartoning machinery; also, automatic tube feeders
President: Geron Adolffon
Sales Director: Fredrik Nusson
Estimated Sales: $5 - 10 Million
Number Employees: 5-9
Parent Co: Norden Pac International AB

26710 Nordic Doors
PO Box 20
Dumas, AR 71639-0020
800-827-0326
Fax: 870-382-6140

26711 Nordic Printing & Packaging
5017 Boone Ave N
New Hope, MN 55428

763-535-6440
Fax: 763-535-1821 moneta.lv
Lithographic printed and folding cartons
Owner: Dee Dee Foster
CFO: Dee Dee Faster
Quality Control: Mary Rubink
Sales Director: Rick Parkin
Contact: Dee Foster
  dee.foster@marcomnordic.com
Office Manager: Lee Thomson
Purchasing Manager: Jeff Vander Plaats
Estimated Sales: $10 - 20 Million
Number Employees: 50-99
Type of Packaging: Consumer, Food Service, Private Label, Bulk

26712 Nordson Corp
11475 Lakefield Dr
Duluth, GA 30097-1557

770-497-8971
Fax: 866-667-3329 800-683-2314
pkgwebcontacts@nordson.com www.nordson.com
Manufacturer and exporter of adhesive dispensers
and applicators, adhesives, coatings, heat sealers and
coating, gluing, labeling and packaging machinery
President: John Raven
VP: John Keane
Manager Marketing Communication: Dave Grgetic
Business Developmental Specialist: Salieta Stone
Estimated Sales: $20-50 Million
Number Employees: 250-499

26713 Nordson Sealant Equipment
45677 Helm St
PO Box 701460
Plymouth, MI 48170-6025

734-459-8600
Fax: 734-459-8686 sales@sealantequipment.com
  www.sealantequipment.com
Manufacturer and exporter of adhesive and food dispensing machinery
President/Chairman: Carl Schultz
Sales/Marketing/Public Relations: James Schultz
Contact: Randy Cochran
  r.cochran@sealantequipment.com
Estimated Sales: $10-20 Million
Number Employees: 50-99

26714 Noren Products Inc
1010 Obrien Dr
Menlo Park, CA 94025-1409

650-322-9500
Fax: 650-324-1348 866-936-6736
  sales@norenproducts.com
  www.norenproducts.com
Manufacturer and exporter of heat pipes, compact
cabinet coolers, thermal pins, AcoustiLock, and
HyTec Coolers.
Owner: Kimberely Dawn
Estimated Sales: $10-20,000,000
Number Employees: 50-99
Brands:
  Compact

26715 Norgren Inc.
5400 S Delaware St
Littleton, CO 80120

800-514-0129
  www.imi-precision.com
Pneumatic and fluid control products such as filters,
regulators, lubricators, fittings and valves
President, Americas Region: Ryan Schroeder
Estimated Sales: $100 - 200 Million
Number Employees: 5,000-9,999

26716 Norgus Silk Screen Co Inc
58 Sylvan Ave
Clifton, NJ 07011-2736

973-365-0600
Fax: 973-365-2749 www.gasolineadvertising.com
Shelf tackers, dividers, point of purchase signs, window banners and signage
President: Sanjay Thakker
  s.thakker@gasolineadvertising.com
Estimated Sales: $30-50 Million
Number Employees: 5-9
Square Footage: 8000

26717 Norland International
PO Box 67189
Lincoln, NE 68506

402-441-3737
Fax: 402-441-3735 bk@norlandintl.com
  www.norland-intl.com
Bottled water plants, water distillation systems,
small bottle filler options, ozone generating systems,
pre-treatment systems, blow molding equipment
Owner: Mike Mc Farland
Estimated Sales: $1 - 2.5 Million
Number Employees: 20-49

26718 Norman International
4501 S Santa Fe Ave
Vernon, CA 90058-2129

323-582-7132
Fax: 323-582-3464 800-289-8644
un4g@yahoo.com www.normaninternational.com
Manufactures vinyl radio frequency heat seald bags,
is also an importer of vinyl zipper bags for retail
packaging.
President: Norman Levine
Vice President: Chris Werner
  chris@normaninternational.com
Estimated Sales: $20-50 Million
Number Employees: 20-49

26719 Normandie Metal Fabricators
55 Channel Drive
Port Washington, NY 11050-2216

516-944-9141
Fax: 516-944-3670 800-221-2398
Cabinets, carts, dollies, racks, tables, pizza ovens
and transport equipment
VP Sales: Jordan Klein
VP Operations: Bill Koines
Number Employees: 20-49

26720 Norpak Corp
70 Blanchard St
Newark, NJ 07105-4702

973-589-4200
Fax: 973-578-8845 800-631-6970
  sales@norpak.net www.norpak.net
Manufacturer, importer and exporter of plain and
printed food wrap including foil laminated, waxed
and freezer paper; also, baking pan liners and
interfolded deli sheets
President: Anthony Coraci
CFO: Lidia Gelasmagas
VP/General Manager: Robert Godown
Sales Manager: Michael Pacyna
Manager: Pedro Oliveira
  poliveira@norpak.com
Estimated Sales: $20 - 30 Million
Number Employees: 20-49
Square Footage: 10000
Brands:
  Delwrap
  Lightning Wrap
  Meat Pak
  Mica Wax
  Nuparch
  War Wrap

26721 Norris Products Corporation
675 Cincinnati Batavia Pike
Cincinnati, OH 45245

513-688-7300
Fax: 513-688-0042 877-543-2278
service@norriscorp.com www.norriscorp.com
Two-wheel portable hand carts
Owner: Paul Wilhelm
CFO: Rose Mappin
Marketing Director: Mark Glassmeyer
Estimated Sales: $10 - 20 Million
Number Employees: 20-49
Brands:
  Caddy-All
  Jet Set
  Super Cart

26722 Norristown Box Company
PO Box 377
Norristown, PA 19404-0377

610-275-5540
Fax: 610-275-6585
Set-up and folding paper boxes for pharmaceutical,
glass, confectionery and industrial instruments
President: John P Eliff
Office Manager: S Fryer
Estimated Sales: $2.5-5 Million
Number Employees: 5-9

Brands:
  Norrbox

26723 Norristown Box Company
PO Box 377
Norristown, PA 19404-0377

610-275-5540
Fax: 610-275-6585
Posters, paperboard, folding and set-up boxes
President: John P Eliff
Estimated Sales: $2.5-5 Million
Number Employees: 5-9

26724 Norse Dairy Systems
1740 Joyce Ave
Columbus, OH 43219-1026

614-294-4931
Fax: 614-299-0538 800-338-7465
  kmcgrath@norse.com www.norse.com
Filling equipment for the ice cream industry; also,
ice cream cones and push-up tubes
President: Scott Fullbright
CEO: Scot Fulbright
  sfulbr@norse.com
CFO: Randy Harvey
R & D: Gunther Brinkman
Director Operations: John Deininger
Estimated Sales: $1 million
Number Employees: 250-499
Parent Co: George Weston Ltd.

26725 North American Container Corp
1811 W Oak Pkwy # D
Suite D
Marietta, GA 30062-2279

770-431-4858
Fax: 770-431-6957 800-929-0610
  www.nacontainer.com
Custom manufactured bulk boxes and fibercore
wood replacement material
President: Michael Grigsby
  mgrigsby@nacontainer.com
Estimated Sales: $10-20,000,000
Number Employees: 10-19
Type of Packaging: Bulk

26726 North American DeerFarmers Association
9301 Annapolis Road
Suite 206
Lanham, MD 20706-3132

301-459-7708
Fax: 301-459-7864 info@nadefa.org
  www.nadefa.org
Committed to promoting deer farming and ranching.
President: Jill Bryar Wood
Executive Director: Barbara Fox
Number Employees: 1-4

26727 North American Packaging Corp
140 E 30th St
New York, NY 10016-7319

212-213-4141
Fax: 212-213-4145 800-499-3521
  info@packagingonline.com
  www.packagingonline.com
Manufacturer and importer of shopping, paper and
plastic bags, gift boxes and stationery including letterhead, business cards, gift certificates, roll and
sheet labels, press kits, catalogs, fliers, etc
Manager: John Destefano
Manager: John DeStefano
Estimated Sales: Below $5,000,000
Number Employees: 1-4

26728 North American Plastic Manufacturing Company
8 Park Lawn Dr
Bethel, CT 6801

203-794-1310
Fax: 203-598-0068 800-934-7752
  www.napcomfg.com
Self-adhesive plastic hangers, hang tabs and point of
purchase hangstrip systems for display packaging
Owner: Robert Laperriere
Sales Manager: Dean Kyburz
Estimated Sales: $1 - 5 Million
Number Employees: 1-4
Square Footage: 18000
Brands:
  Pop Strip

26729 North American Roller Prod Inc
PO Box 2142
Glen Ellyn, IL 60137-6342
630-858-9161
Fax: 630-858-9103 info@narp-trapo.com
www.narp-trapo.com
Conveyor rollers and specialty conveyors
President: Jerry Miller
info@narp-trapo.com
General Manager: Jerry Miller
Year Founded: 1981
Estimated Sales: Less than $500,000
Number Employees: 5-9

26730 North American Signs
3601 Lathrop St
South Bend, IN 46628-6108
574-234-5252
Fax: 574-289-8118 800-348-5000
POBox30@northamericansigns.com
www.northamericansigns.com
Electric and neon signs
President: John Yarger
jmy1@northamericansigns.com
CEO: Noel Yarger
CFO: Tom Yarger
Production Manager: Doug McCoigge
Estimated Sales: $10-20 Million
Number Employees: 50-99

26731 North Atlantic Equipment Sales
Route 376
Hopewell Jct, NY 12533
845-221-2201
Fax: 845-227-7795
Analyzes and tests plant operations, infrared, total
solids, fat, protein, process control
President: Varick Stringham
CFO: Varick Stringham
R&D: Varick Stringham
Quality Control: Varick Stringham
Estimated Sales: $500,000 - $1 Million
Number Employees: 5-9

26732 North Carolina's Southeast
707 West Broad Street
P.O. Box 2556
Elizabethtown, NC 28337
800-787-1333
Fax: 910-862-1482 www.ncse.org
President: Steve Yost
Finance and Office Manager: Tammy Etheridge
Director: Paul G Butler Jr
Director of Business Development: Joe Melvin
Plant Manager: Derek Pringle
Estimated Sales: $1 - 3 Million
Number Employees: 5-9

26733 North Company
E1683 Larson Road
Waupaca, WI 54981-8734
715-258-6104
Fax: 715-258-4986 foodjobs@execpc.com
Executive search firm specializing in research and
development
Executive Recruiter: Henry Warmbier, Ph.D.
Recruiter: Lori Warmbier
Number Employees: 2

26734 North Fork Weld & SteelSupl
68230 Main Rd
Greenport, NY 11944
631-477-0671
Fax: 631-477-0702 sales@nfwss.com
www.nfwelding.com
Wine industry netting reels
President: Joseph Schoenstein
sales@nfwss.com
VP: Fred Shonestein
Estimated Sales: $1-2.5 Million
Number Employees: 10-19

26735 North Side Packing Co
2200 Rivers Edge Dr
New Kensington, PA 15068-4542
724-335-4666
Fax: 724-335-2249
customerservice@northsidefoods.com
www.northsidefoods.com
Processing

President: Robert G Hofmann Ii
CFO: Robert Muhl
R&D: Paula McDaniel
Quality Control: John Stavencon John
Contact: Deborah Rihs
deborah.rihs@northsidefoods.com
Estimated Sales: Less Than $500,000
Number Employees: 1-4

26736 North Star
2120 Hewitt Avenue
Everett, WA 98201-3616
425-252-9600
Fax: 425-252-7598 www.northstarinc.com
Espresso carts, coffee grinders
President: Craig Bunney
craigbunney@gmail.com
Estimated Sales: $1-2.5 Million
Number Employees: 5-9

26737 North Star Engineered Products
28905 Glenwood Rd
Perrysburg, OH 43551-3020
419-726-2645
Fax: 419-666-1549
Manufactures equipment to process fresh cut vegeta-
bles and fruit, including fruit processing centrifuges
Owner: Tom Ziems
tsz@glassline.com
CFO: John K Clement
Sales Manager: Joe Moroni
Technical Services: Buddy Santus
Estimated Sales: $2.5 - 5 Million
Number Employees: 10-19
Type of Packaging: Bulk
Brands:
Helical
Mini Brute
Six Shooter
Tornado

26738 North Star Ice EquipmentCorporation
8151 Occidental Ave S
P.O. Box 80227
Seattle, WA 98108-4210
206-763-7300
Fax: 206-763-7323 800-321-1381
info@northstarice.com www.northstarice.com
Manufacturer and exporter of industrial ice makers
and related handling equipment. Products include
Flake Ice Makers, Liquid Ice Generators, Ice Storage
Systems, Ice Delivery Systems and more.
President: Logan Shepardson
Vice President Sales & Marketing: Tom Crawford
Sales & Marketing Administrator: Jennifer Ward
Director of Operations & Finance: Rachel Camarillo
Estimated Sales: $10 - 20 Million
Number Employees: 11 - 50
Square Footage: 60000
Brands:
Cold Spell
Coldisc

26739 NorthStar Print Group
1222 Perry Way
Watertown, WI 53094
920-206-8626
Fax: 920-262-8582 www.multicolorcorp.com
Label production
CEO: Richard Gasper
CFO: Jim Gombar
R&D: Jerry Fowler
Quality Control: Grieg Petere
Marketing: Terry Fowler
Sr. VP Manufacturing: Andy Walker
Plant Manager: Greg Petre
Estimated Sales: $60 Million
Number Employees: 100-249
Parent Co: Journal Communications

26740 Northbrook Laboratories
1818 Skokie Boulevard
Northbrook, IL 60062-4106
847-272-8700
Fax: 847-272-2348 877-366-3522
djalw@northlandlabs.com
www.northlandlabs.com
Laboratory analysis for food, feed and environmental applications
President: Jamal Alwattar
Contact: Zeek Agosto
zagosto@northlandlabs.com

Estimated Sales: $5 - 10 Million
Number Employees: 50-99

26741 Northcoast Woodworks
381 Buffalo Street
Conneaut, OH 44030-2451
440-593-6249
Fax: 440-593-6249
Wine industry wooden gift boxes

26742 Northeast Box Co
1726 Griswold Ave
Ashtabula, OH 44004-9213
440-992-5500
Fax: 440-992-7820 800-362-8100
www.northeastbox.com
Corrugated boxes, shipping containers and point of
purchase displays; consultant specializing in J.I.T.
warehousing manufactured to specifications
Owner: Ron Marchewka
ron@northeastbox.com
CFO: Peter Adano
VP/Secretary/Treasurer: Paul Seibert
General Manager: Billy Powers
Estimated Sales: $20-50 Million
Number Employees: 50-99
Square Footage: 60000

26743 Northeast Container Corporation
125 Washington Ave
Dumont, NJ 07628-3066
201-385-6200
Fax: 201-385-7356
Corrugated shipping containers
President: John Payne
Estimated Sales: $8-9 Million
Number Employees: 50-99
Square Footage: 130000

26744 Northeast Distributors Inc
210 Essex St # 3
Suite 3
Whitman, MA 02382-1514
781-447-0073
Fax: 781-447-6337 sales@nedinc.com
www.nedinc.com
Ice equipment, piping, fittings and tubing
CEO: Kenneth G Peterson
Quality Control: Linda Mahoney
Sales Exec: Philip Mohan
Estimated Sales: Below $5 Million
Number Employees: 20-49

26745 Northeast Fresh Foods Alliance
20 Scanlon Drive
2nd Floor
Randolph, MA 02368-1745
781-963-9726
Fax: 781-963-9728 neffa1@aol.com
Executive Director: Andrea Walker
Director Sales/Show Manager: John Scolponeti
Number Employees: 1-4

26746 Northeast Laboratory Svc
289 China Rd
Winslow, ME 4901
207-873-7711
Fax: 207-873-7022 866-591-7120
bmears@binax.com www.binax.com
Food technology laboratory service specializing in
USDA certified listeria-salmonella and KAB/nutri-
tional analysis and food-born illness investigations;
also, product development and shelf life
determination
President: Roger Piasio
Production Planning Manager: Eva Chase
Administration Manager: Vicki Massey
Lab Manager: Pam Doughty
Estimated Sales: $6-8 Million
Number Employees: 50-99
Square Footage: 108000
Parent Co: BINAX
Type of Packaging: Consumer, Food Service, Pri-
vate Label, Bulk

26747 Northeast Packaging Co
875 Skyway St
Presque Isle, ME 04769-2063
207-764-6271
Fax: 207-496-3171 www.nepcobags.com
Paper and poly bags

President: Robert Umphrey
rumphrey@mfx.net
Sales Representative: Ken Joy
General Manager: Chris Burtchell
Production Manager: Jesse Harris
Number Employees: 50-99
Type of Packaging: Consumer, Private Label

26748 Northeast Packaging Materials
20 Robert Pitt Dr # 202
Monsey, NY 10952-3340
845-426-2900
Fax: 845-426-3700 www.nepack.com
Manufacturer and exporter of barrier films; available
in roll stock and pouches
President and QC: Stewart Braun
Estimated Sales: Below $5,000,000
Number Employees: 1-4

26749 Northeastern Products Corp
115 Sweet Rd
PO Box 98
Warrensburg, NY 12885-4754
518-623-3161
Fax: 518-623-3803 800-873-8233
info@nep-co.com www.nep-co.com
Manufacturer and exporter of meat smoking sawdust
including hickory, maple, cherry and alder
President: Gary Shiavi
CEO: Paul Schiavi
Marketing Director: Richard Morgan
Estimated Sales: Below $5 Million
Number Employees: 50-99
Square Footage: 80000

26750 Northern Berkshire Tourist
121 Union St
North Adams, MA 01247-3533
413-663-9204
Marking devices, rubber stamps, pads, ink, decals,
engraved nameplates,architectural signs,etc
President: John Luczynsky
Estimated Sales: $300,000-500,000
Number Employees: 1-4
Parent Co: JPDS

26751 Northern Box Co Inc
1328 Mishawaka St
Elkhart, IN 46514-1809
574-264-2161
Fax: 574-262-8943
Corrugated shipping boxes
President: Heidi Linder
VP: Tina Linder
Manager: Dick Scheve
northernboxco@aol.com
Estimated Sales: $5-10 Million
Number Employees: 20-49

26752 Northern Metal Products
6601 Ridgewood Road
St Cloud, MN 56303
320-252-3442
Fax: 320-252-2832 800-458-5549
www.northernmetalproducts.com
Wire and tubing point of purchase merchandising
displays and fixtures
President: Larry Leutt
CEO and President: Larry Lautt
Sr. Sales Engineering: Chuck Lauer
Contact: Kenneth Arceneau
k.arceneau@norwire.com
General Manager: Marc Illies
Estimated Sales: $10 - 20 Million
Number Employees: 100-249
Square Footage: 300000
Parent Co: St. Cloud Industry

26753 Northern Metals & Supply
2100 Llano Rd # N3
Santa Rosa, CA 95407-6430
707-575-0555
Fax: 707-575-4088
Wine and food industry stainless sanitary fittings,
butterfly valve, ball valves, stainless pipe and tub-
ing, pipe fittings, and stainless and aluminum raw
material
President: Thomas F Obuchowski
Estimated Sales: $5-10 Million
Number Employees: 1-4

26754 Northern Package Corporation
201 W 86th Street
Minneapolis, MN 55420-2784
952-881-5861
Fax: 952-881-6758
Corrugated paper boxes
General Manager: Joe Gerow
Number Employees: 55
Parent Co: Liberty Diversified Industries

26755 Northern Stainless Fabricating
P.O. Box 6715
Traverse City, MI 49696-6715
231-947-4580
Fax: 231-947-9074
Manufacturer and exporter of custom made stainless
steel kitchen equipment for food service and institu-
tional use including salad bars, dish tables and prep
tables
President: Mike Fisher
Chief Estimator: Harry Muse
CFO: Michael J Fisher
VP Production: Bruce Muzzarelli
Estimated Sales: $10-20 Million
Number Employees: 50-99
Square Footage: 60000

26756 Northfield Freezing Systems
PO Box 98
Northfield, MN 55057-0098
507-645-9546
Fax: 507-645-6148 800-426-1283
Manufacturer and exporter of freezers, coolers, chill-
ers, hardeners and spiral conveying freezing systems
President: Tim Colies
Sales/Marketing Executive: Larry Deboer
Purchasing Agent: Bill Westby
Estimated Sales: $20 - 50 Million
Number Employees: 120
Parent Co: Frigo Schndia

26757 Northland Consultants
3741 Highway 556
RR2
Sault Ste. Marie, ON P6A 5K7
Canada
705-541-8490
www.northlandconsultants.ca
Marketing consultant specializing in brand develop-
ment for food products
Managing Partner: Marko Koskenoja
Estimated Sales: Less than $500,000
Number Employees: 1-4

26758 Northland Corp
1260 E Van Deinse St
Greenville, MI 48838-1400
616-754-5601
Fax: 616-754-0970 800-223-3900
sales@northlandnka.net
www.documentofconformity.com
Custom refrigeration, commercial and residential
President: Mike Bufton
CFO: Karen Braund
Vice President: Brad Stauffer
Research & Development: Jim Holland
Quality Control: Rick Waldorf
Marketing Director: Gerry Reda
Public Relations: Sindy Angi
Operations/Plant Manager: Kent Coon
Plant Manager: Kent Coon
Purchasing Manager: Richard Burns
Estimated Sales: $10 - 20 Million
Number Employees: 100-249
Square Footage: 440000
Parent Co: AGA Food Service Group
Brands:
Imperial

26759 Northland Corp
1260 E Van Deinse St
Greenville, MI 48838-1400
616-754-5601
Fax: 616-754-0970 800-223-3900
customerservice@northlandnka.net
www.documentofconformity.com
President: Gordon Stauffer
CFO: Brad Stauffer
R & D: Jim Holland
Quality Control: Jim Nielsen
Plant Manager: Kent Coon
Estimated Sales: Below $5 Million
Number Employees: 100-249
Parent Co: Aga Rangemaster Group

26760 Northland Labs
1818 Skokie Blvd
Northbrook, IL 60062-4106
847-272-8700
Fax: 847-272-2348 800-366-3522
djalw@northlandlabs.com
www.northlandlabs.com
Consultant specializing in food testing and analysis
services for microbiological contamination, chemi-
cal analysis/composition and nutritional labeling
President: Jamal Alwattar
Contact: Ezequiel Agosto
zagosto@northlandlabs.com
General Manager: D Alwatter
Estimated Sales: $1 - 5 Million
Number Employees: 5-9
Square Footage: 28000

26761 Northland Process Piping
1662 320th Ave
Isle, MN 56342-4303
320-679-2119
Fax: 320-679-2785 mnoffice@nppmn.com
www.nppmn.com
Brine and clean-in place systems, floor plates and
drains, platforms, walkways and stairs, pumps,
tanks, tubing and valves
Owner: Jennifer Hawk
CFO: Kathy Tramm
Project Sales/Customer Service: Dan Tramm
jennifer.hawk@kellogg.com
Human Resources: Natalie Geist
Foreman: Eirik Andersen
Purchasing/Customer Service: Bruce Richards
Number Employees: 100-249
Other Locations:
Roswell GA
Lemoore CA
Horseheads NY

26762 Northview Laboratories
616 Heathrow Dr
Lincolnshire, IL 60069
847-564-8181
Fax: 847-564-8269
Independent testing laboratory offering microbiolog-
ical, sterility assurance, chemistry & toxicology ser-
vices. Specialized services including water system
validation and monitoring, environmental chamber
storage and feeding studies
Manager: Martin Spalding
Quality Control: Leonart Wojtowicz
CEO: Martin J Spalding Sr
Marketing Director: Laura Ritter
Sales Director: Trisha Daugherty
Contact: Meredith Puljung
meredith.puljung@sgs.com
Plant Manager: Richard Harrington
Estimated Sales: $20 - 50 Million
Number Employees: 100-249
Square Footage: 23000

26763 Northview Laboratories
106 Venture Boulevard
Spartanburg, SC 29306-3805
864-574-7728
Fax: 864-574-7873
Independent testing laboratory offering microbiolog-
ical, sterility assurance, chemistry and toxicology
services
President: Delores Bruce
CFO: Ed Kelley
Vice President of Leasing: David Happ
Chief Operating Officer: Rolland Baribeau
Estimated Sales: $1 - 2.5 Million
Number Employees: 15
Square Footage: 92000
Other Locations:
Northview Laboratories
Spartanburg SC
Northview Laboratories
Hercules CA

26764 (HQ)Northview Pacific Laboratories
1880 Holste Rd
Northbrook, IL 60062
847-564-8181
Fax: 510-964-0551 www.ndt.org
Consultant offering food testing services
Manager: Mario Sotelo
Quality Control: Sarah Khan
VP: Thomas Spalding
R & D: Lonny Barish

Estimated Sales: $10-20 Million
Number Employees: 50-99
Parent Co: Northview Labs
Other Locations:

26765 Northville LaboratoriesInc
100 Rural Hill St
Northville, MI 48167-1538
248-349-1500
Fax: 248-349-1505 sales@jogue.com
www.jogue.com
Flavors
President: Dattu Sastry
  chamber@northville.org
Estimated Sales: $10-20 Million
Number Employees: 20-49

26766 Northwest Analytical Inc
111 SW 5th Ave # 800
Portland, OR 97204-3606
503-224-7727
Fax: 503-224-5236 888-692-7638
nwa@nwasoft.com www.nwasoft.com
Manufacturer and exporter of SPC charting workstation and statistical quality control (SQC) software for control charting, process capability analysis and plant floor data collection
Chairman: Clifford S L Yee
CEO: Bob Ward
  bward@nwasoft.com
CFO: T Olin Nichols
VP: Jeff Cawley
R&D: Louis Halvorsen
VP Marketing: Peter Guilfoyle
VP Sales: Jim Petrusich
Estimated Sales: $10-20,000,000
Number Employees: 20-49

26767 Northwest Art Glass
9003 151st Ave NE
Redmond, WA 98052-3513
425-861-9600
Fax: 425-861-9300 800-888-9444
www.nwartglass.com
Manufacturer and importer of etched glass separators and screens, brass posts, traffic control systems, liscourts and sneeze guards
Owner: Richard Mesmer
  richard@cascadegac.com
Metal Sales/Operations: Steve Bolens
  richard@cascadegac.com
Estimated Sales: $1-2.5 Million
Number Employees: 10-19
Square Footage: 17000
Type of Packaging: Bulk

26768 Northwest Cherry Growers
105 S.18th Street
Suite 205
Yakima, WA 98901-2176
509-453-4837
Fax: 509-453-4880 info@nwcherries.com
www.nwcherries.com
Provides educational information of the health benefits of cherries.
President: B.J. Thurlby
Promotion Director: James W. Michael
International Marketing Director: Keith Hu
International Program Coordinator: Teresa Baggarley
VP International Marketing: Eric Melton
Contact: Teresa Baggarley
  teresa@nwcherries.com
Office Manager/Controller: Joanne Daniels
Estimated Sales: $1 - 3 Million
Number Employees: 5-9

26769 Northwest Food Processors Assn
8338 NE Alderwood Rd # 160
Portland, OR 97220-6811
503-327-2200
Fax: 503-327-2201 www.nwfpa.org
Promotes the food processing industry by including events, membership application, advocacy and issues.
President: David Mcgiverin
  dmcgiverin@nwfpa.org
Executive VP: David Klick
Events & Marketing Mgr.: Karen Waggoner
Sales Coordinator: Sarah Emerson
Accounting & Operations Dir.: Patty Pepin
Number Employees: 10-19

26770 Northwest Laboratories
241 S Holden St
Seattle, WA 98108-4359
206-763-6252
Fax: 206-763-3949 postmaster@nwlabs1896.com
www.nwlabs1896.com
Consultant offering analysis, testing and food research services
CEO: Richard Schefsky
Estimated Sales: $1 - 3 Million
Number Employees: 5-9
Square Footage: 63000

26771 Northwest Molded Products Classic Line
4915 21st Street
Racine, WI 53406-5028
262-554-4412
Fax: 262-554-8370
Small, rigid molded plastic boxes, hot stamp decorating, foam inserts and custom molding
Estimated Sales: $5-10 Million
Number Employees: 20-49

26772 Northwest Products
600 Oak St
Archbold, OH 43502-1579
419-445-1950
Fax: 419-446-2984 www.quadcorehab.org
Wooden pallets
COO: Philip Zuver
COO: Philip Zuver
Executive Director: Bruce Abell
Sales Representative: John Miller
Executive Director: Phillip Zuver
Estimated Sales: $20 - 50 Million
Number Employees: 50-99
Parent Co: Quadco Rehabilitation Center

26773 Northwestern
15054 Oxnard St
Van Nuys, CA 91411
818-786-1581
Fax: 818-786-5063 russbrown@northwestern.com
Display cases and store fixtures
President: C Wayne Noecker
CFO: Rughann Etz
VP: Douglas Noecker
Contact: Audrie Chun
  audrie@northwestern.com
Estimated Sales: $10 - 20 Million
Number Employees: 50-99

26774 Northwestern Corp
922 Armstrong St
PO Box 490
Morris, IL 60450-1921
815-942-1300
Fax: 815-942-4417 800-942-1316
Manufacturer and exporter of vending machinery
President: Richard Bolen
  nwsales@nwcorp.com
CFO: Angie Stropel
R&D: Angie Stropel
Quality Control: Angie Stropel
Sales Director: Diane Olson
Estimated Sales: $10 - 20 Million
Number Employees: 20-49
Square Footage: 100000

26775 Northwind Inc
13300 Maple Hill Rd
Alpena, AR 72611-3008
870-437-5360
Fax: 870-437-2595 877-937-2585
nw@northwindinc.com www.northwindinc.com
Sanitary conveyors, wash stations, meat hoppers, tanks, catwalks and support equipment
President: Mark Ogier
  nw@northwindinc.com
Quality Control: Tim Ogier
Secretary: Tim Ogier
Estimated Sales: Below $5,000,000
Number Employees: 10-19

26776 Norvell Co Inc
4002 Liberty Bell Rd
Fort Scott, KS 66701-8638
620-223-3110
Fax: 620-223-3115 800-653-3147
www.norvellco.com
Manufacturer and exporter of flour mill sifters for the processing of flour, spices, cereals, etc.; also, agitators for blending

Office Manager: Barbara Fitts
General Manager: Mark Shank
Manager: Mark Shank
Estimated Sales: $5-10 Million
Number Employees: 20-49
Square Footage: 80000
Type of Packaging: Food Service
Brands:
  Jet Sifter
  Santare
  Super Drive Sifter

26777 Norwalt Design Inc
961 State Route 10 # 2a
Randolph, NJ 07869-1921
973-927-3200
Fax: 973-927-2841 norwalt@norwalt.com
www.norwalt.com
Bottle capping and plugging equipment, rotary disc and parts feeders, unscramblers, elevator hoppers and assembly machines
President: Walter McDonald
Director Marketing: Anthony Conte
Manager: Michael Seitel
  mike@norwalt.com
Estimated Sales: $2.5 - 5 Million
Number Employees: 20-49
Square Footage: 60000

26778 Norwood Marking Systems
2538 Wisconsin Ave
Downers Grove, IL 60515
630-968-0646
Fax: 630-968-7672 800-626-3464
Manufacturer and exporter of coding systems and accessories including hot stamp imprinters, thermal transfer printers, embossers, hot stamp and thermal transfer ribbon supplies and steel type
General Manager: Larry Kulik
Sales Director: Cliff Vanwey
Estimated Sales: $20-50 Million
Number Employees: 50-99
Parent Co: Illinois Tool Works

26779 Norwood Paper Inc
7001 W 60th St
Chicago, IL 60638-3101
773-788-1528
Fax: 708-656-5310 www.norwoodpaper.com
Paper boards, box fillers and layering sheets
Owner: Mike Bayne
  mike@norwoodpaper.com
Sales Manager: Darin Rakowsky
Sales Manager: Matt Zeman
  mike@norwoodpaper.com
Estimated Sales: $10-20,000,000
Number Employees: 5-9

26780 Nosaj Disposables
PO Box 1290
Paterson, NJ 7509
973-279-4190
Fax: 973-279-6929 800-631-3809
Trash liners, hand cleaners, disposable industrial paper towels and cloth wipers
President: Stanley Slosberg
Sales Director: Harold Gelvan
Estimated Sales: $5 - 10 Million
Number Employees: 10-19
Square Footage: 80000

26781 Nosco
651 S Martin Luther King Jr
Waukegan, IL 60085-7500
847-360-4806
Fax: 847-360-4924 rxquality@nosco.com
www.nosco.com
Folding cartons and labels including roll and cut; also, instructional enclosures and printing of promotional literature available
President: Russell Haraf
CFO: Michael Biesboar
Estimated Sales: $20 - 50 Million
Number Employees: 250-499
Square Footage: 200000

26782 Noteworthy Company
100 Church St
Amsterdam, NY 12010
800-696-7849
Fax: 518-842-8317
Bags including polyethylene, take home, patch, soft loop and molded handle, etc.; also, holiday

Owner: Carol Constigino
CFO: John Cloanglo
Contact: Debi Crisalli
  dcrisalli@noteworthyinc.com
Estimated Sales: $10 - 20 Million
Number Employees: 250-499

26783 Nothum Food Processing Systems
631 S Kansas Ave
Springfield, MO 65802
417-831-2816
Fax: 417-866-4781 800-435-1297
nothum@nothum.com www.nothum.com
Manufacturer and exporter of batter applicators,
breaders, pre-dusters, fryers, shuttle conveyors, char
markers, coaters, blanchers, filters, ovens, polar
therm and stack freezers, etc.
President/Chief Executive Officer: Robert Nothum
  nothum@nothum.com
Sales & Marketing: Robert Nothum
Number Employees: 30

26784 Nottingham Spirk
2200 Overlook Rd
Cleveland, OH 44106-2326
216-231-7830
Fax: 216-231-6275 www.nottinghamspirk.com
Custom designed packaging and displays
President: John Nottingham
  phil_stewart1224@yahoo.com
Manager: Jeff Kalman
Facilities: Phil Stewart
Estimated Sales: $5-10 Million
Number Employees: 50-99

26785 Nova Hand Dryers
12801 Worldgate Drive
Suite 500
Herndon, VA 20170
Canada
703-615-3636
Fax: 877-385-1291
Manufacturer and exporter of warm air hand dryers
Sales Manager: Maurine Cohen
Number Employees: 45
Parent Co: Avmor
Brands:
  Nova

26786 Nova Industries
999 Montague St
San Leandro, CA 94577
510-357-0171
Fax: 510-357-3832 www.bordenlighting.com
Manufacturer and exporter of glare control devices
and lighting fixtures including custom made and in-
candescent
President: James Borden
VP: Floyd Shreeve
Contact: Bobby Aquino
  baquino@bordenlighting.com
Estimated Sales: $2.5-5 Million
Number Employees: 20-49
Square Footage: 28000

26787 Novacart Inc
512 W Ohio Ave
Richmond, CA 94804-2040
510-215-8999
Fax: 510-215-9175 877-896-6682
info@novacartusa.com www.novacartusa.com
President: Giorgio Anghileri
Manager: Joe Miglia
  joe@novacartusa.com
Estimated Sales: $3 - 5 Million
Number Employees: 10-19
Parent Co: Novacart Italy

26788 Novamex
500 W Overland Ave
Suite 300
El Paso, TX 79901
www.novamex.com
Markets and exports a variety of foods and bever-
ages from Mexico.
CEO: Luis Fernandez
COO: Ramon Carrasco
Year Founded: 1986
Estimated Sales: $150 Million
Number Employees: 250-499
Type of Packaging: Food Service
Brands:
  Cholula Hot Sauce
  D'Gari Gelatin

26789 Novar
6060 Rockside Woods Bl N # 400
Suite 400
Cleveland, OH 44131-2378
216-682-1600
Fax: 216-682-1614 800-348-1235
customerservice@novar.com www.novar.com
Computerized control systems for rack and case re-
frigeration, store heating and cooling
President: Paul J Orzeske
VP: Dean Lindstorm
Executive VP: David Weber
Number Employees: 10-19
Square Footage: 280000
Brands:
  Spectrum

26790 Novax Group/Point of Sales
42 Broadway
New York, NY 10004-1617
212-684-1244
Fax: 212-684-2337
Point of sale systems and software
Manager: Reggie Menof
Manager: Charles Chen
Estimated Sales: $1-2.5 Million
Number Employees: 5-9
Parent Co: POS Technology

26791 Novelis Foil Products
3560 Lenox Road
Atlanta, GA 30326
404-760-4000
Fax: 706-812-2039 800-776-8701
www.novelis.com
Aluminum foil, rolls, sheets and disposable contain-
ers
Manager: Charlie Aheran
Marketing Director: Beverly Duncan
Sales Director: Charlie Ahern
Contact: Christina Abdelnour
  christina.abdelnour@novelis.com
Controller: Ed McGee
Number Employees: 10-19
Type of Packaging: Consumer, Food Service, Pri-
  vate Label, Bulk
Brands:
  Alcan

26792 (HQ)Novelty Advertising
1148 Walnut St
Coshocton, OH 43812-1769
740-622-3113
Fax: 740-622-5286 800-848-9163
Manufacturer and exporter of calendars and adver-
tising specialties
President: Gregory Coffman
  gcoffman@noveltyadv.com
Owner: Greg Coffman
Owner: Thad Coffman
VP: Jim McConnell
Estimated Sales: $5-10 Million
Number Employees: 20-49
Type of Packaging: Consumer, Food Service, Bulk

26793 Novelty Baskets
PO Box 1481
Hurst, TX 76053-1481
817-268-5426
Fax: 817-423-6693
A manufacturer of wire basket displays for use in ice
cream convenience stores
Owner: Ken Miller
Operations Manager: Ken Miller
Number Employees: 10

26794 Novelty Crystal
3015 48th Ave
Long Island City, NY 11101-3419
718-458-6700
Fax: 718-458-9408 800-622-0250
joe@noveltycrystal.com www.noveltycrystal.com
Plastic caterware which includes; plastic serving
trays, plastic bowls, plastic bowls, plastic tumblers,
plastic pitchers, plastic stemware and plastic serving
accessories.
Owner: Ed Coslett
  e.coslett@noveltycrystal.com
VP: Asher Michaeli
VP: Joseph Michaeli
CFO: Ashur Michaeli
Estimated Sales: $2.5 - 5 Million
Number Employees: 20-49
Square Footage: 240000

Type of Packaging: Consumer, Food Service

26795 Noveon Inc
9911 Brecksville Rd
Cleveland, OH 44141-3247
216-447-5000
Fax: 216-447-5740
Piping components for touch industrial fluid appli-
cations and a superior balance of properties that pro-
vide longer service in hot corrosive environments
President: Stephen Kirk
CEO: Kan Kim
  kan.kim@noveon.com
Estimated Sales: Over $1 Billion
Number Employees: 500-999

26796 Novolex
101 E Carolina Ave
Hartsville, SC 29500
843-857-4800
800-845-6051
supplier.hotline@novolex.com www.novolex.com
Tea and coffee industry bags (flexible); bags for gro-
cery stores; carryout bags; tortilla steam bags.
Chairman & CEO: Stanley Bikulege
CFO: Paul Palmisano
VP & Corporate Treasurer: Janet Gibbons
SVP, Innovation: Adrianne Tipton
Year Founded: 2003
Estimated Sales: $2.3 Billion
Number Employees: 7,000
Brands:
  BAGCRAFT PACKAGING
  BURROWS PACKAGING
  DE LUXE PACKAGING
  DURO BAG
  GENERAL PACKAGING PRODUCTS
  HERITAGE BAG
  HILEX POLY
  INTERNATIONAL CONVERTER
  SHIELDS

26797 Novus
650 Pelham Blvd
Suite 100
St. Paul, MN 55114
952-944-8000
Fax: 952-944-2542 800-328-1117
www.novusglass.com
Manufacturer and exporter of plastic polish and
scratch remover and auto glass replacement products
President: Keith Beverige
Contact: Allan Dmore
  dmore.allan@novuspolish.com
Number Employees: 1,000-4,999
Square Footage: 40000
Parent Co: TCG International
Type of Packaging: Consumer
Brands:
  Novus Plastic

26798 Now Plastics Inc
136 Denslow Rd
East Longmeadow, MA 01028-3188
413-525-1010
Fax: 413-525-8951 info@nowplastics.com
www.nowplastics.com
NOW Plastics offers an extensive line of high per-
formance film sustracts including but not limited to;
PET, BOPP, CPP, PVC, MOPP, FOPP, OPS, Nylon,
Non Woven, Synthetic Paper, Skin Film, Retort
films and Co-extrusions. AdditionallyNOW Plastics
supplies various types of micro-perforated, laser per-
forated or high clarity bags and films for bakery and
produce packaging.
President: Oded Edan
CEO: Larry Silverstein
  ls@nowplastics.com
CEO: Larry Silverstein
Estimated Sales: $10 - 20,000,000
Number Employees: 10-19
Square Footage: 40000
Type of Packaging: Bulk

26799 Nowakowski
9909 S 57th St
Franklin, WI 53132-8685
414-423-9900
Fax: 414-423-6300 800-394-5866
Stainless steel fabricated food processing equipment
and other metal products

President: Jeff Nowakowski
Vice President: James Nowakowski, Sr.
Sales Director: Bill Redmond
Plant Manager: James Nowakowski, Jr.
Estimated Sales: $2-5 Million
Number Employees: 20-49
Square Footage: 74600

26800 Nozzle Nolen Inc
3975 Coconut Rd
Palm Springs, FL 33461-4003
561-964-6200
Fax: 561-272-2623 800-226-6536
www.nozzlenolen.com
Pest control systems
Manager: Mike Antropoli
mikea@nozzlenolen.com
Estimated Sales: $1 - 2.5,000,000
Number Employees: 20-49
Parent Co: Nozzle Nolen

26801 Nrd LLC
2937 Alt Blvd
P.O. Box 310
Grand Island, NY 14072-1292
716-773-7634
Fax: 716-773-7744 800-525-8076
sales@nrdinc.com www.nrdinc.com
Manufacturer and exporter of static control products
to increase safety, productivity and product quality
including ionizers.
President: Doug Fiegel
dfiegel@nrdinc.com
Chairman: Sal Alfiero
Director Sales & Marketing: Greg Gumkowski
Production Manager: Kathleen Kowalik
Purchasing Manager: Jim Zoldowski
Number Employees: 20-49
Type of Packaging: Bulk

26802 Nrd LLC
2937 Alt Blvd
PO Box 310
Grand Island, NY 14072-1292
716-773-7634
Fax: 716-773-7744 800-525-8076
sales@nrdinc.com www.nrdinc.com
Self-powered static control equipment for labeling,
printing, coating and converting
President: Doug Fiegel
dfiegel@nrdinc.com
Marketing Manager: Colleen Coancy-O'Donnell
Sales Manager: Mike Grimaldi
Number Employees: 20-49

26803 Nrd LLC
2937 Alt Blvd
P.O. Box 310
Grand Island, NY 14072-1292
716-773-7634
Fax: 716-773-7744 800-525-8076
sales@nrdinc.com www.nrdinc.com
President: Doug Fiegel
dfiegel@nrdinc.com
Number Employees: 20-49

26804 Nu CO2 LLC
2800 SE Market Pl
Stuart, FL 34997
772-221-1754
Fax: 772-781-3500 800-472-2855
www.nuco2.com
CO2 systems for fountains; also, service available.
President: Susan Stevenson
VP, Finance: Felicia Gallagher
General Counsel: David Markatos
VP, Sales: John Templin
VP, Human Resources: Annette DiPiero
VP, Field Operations: Derek Burton
Year Founded: 1995
Estimated Sales: $100-500 Million
Number Employees: 1,100
Brands:
Nuco2

26805 Nu-Con Equipment
1610 Lake Dr W
Chanhassen, MN 55317
952-279-5205
Fax: 952-279-5206 877-939-0510

Turnkey sanitary process, conveying, and packaging
solutions from raw material handling to consumer
packaged goods. Sanitary and USDA approved pro-
cess equipment and systems with easy to clean
features
President: Marv Deam
Vice President: Mike Salvador
Marketing/Sales Executive: Marvin Deam
Contact: Bob Mortenson
bmortenson@nucon.com
Purchasing Manager: Tom Haider
Estimated Sales: $20 - 50 Million
Number Employees: 20-49
Square Footage: 30000
Parent Co: Nu-Con

26806 Nu-Dell Manufacturing
2250 E Devon Ave # 349
Des Plaines, IL 60018-4507
847-803-4500
Fax: 847-803-4584 sales@nudell.com
www.posterframescentral.com
Electric blackboards and signs, point of purchase
displays, easels, rope lights, changeable message
and marker boards and other indoor signage
Owner: David Block
Sales Director: Mari Carmona
Customer Service: Janis Vazquez
Estimated Sales: $10 - 20 Million
Number Employees: 5-9
Parent Co: Nu-Dell Manufacturing Company
Type of Packaging: Food Service
Brands:
Ad-Lite
Glo-Glaze
Glo-Ons
Glolite

26807 Nu-Meat Technology
PO Box 599
Scotch Plains, NJ 07076-0599
908-232-7342
Fax: 908-232-5534
Choppers, chub separators, massagers and tumblers,
meat tenderizers, mechanical, pickle injectors,
slicers
Estimated Sales: $20-50 Million
Number Employees: 20-49

26808 Nu-Star Inc
1425 Stagecoach Rd
Shakopee, MN 55379-2798
952-445-8295
Fax: 952-445-0231 800-800-9274
jadams@nustarinc.com
Manufacturer and exporter of carts for lifting, push-
ing and pulling
President: Scott Lorch
slorch@nustarinc.com
CFO: James Coan
VP Power Pusher Division: Scott Lorch
VP Sales & Marketing: John D Adams
Estimated Sales: $5 - 10,000,000
Number Employees: 20-49
Type of Packaging: Bulk

26809 Nu-Tex Styles, Inc.
285 Davidson Ave # 104
Somerset, NJ 08873
732-485-5456
Fax: 732-873-0854 info@nu-tex.com
www.nu-tex.com
Manufacturer, importer and exporter of industrial
fabrics and wiping rags including cheesecloth and
dusting cloth
President: Howard Bromwich
howard@nu-tex.com
Estimated Sales: $1-2.5 Million
Number Employees: 1-4
Number of Brands: 3
Number of Products: 57
Square Footage: 360000

26810 Nu-Towel Co
208 Bennington Ave
Kansas City, MO 64123-1914
816-842-2909
Fax: 816-842-8679 800-800-7247
Disposable wipers, towels and rags
Owner: Dennis Wacknov
CEO: Paul Wacknov
Quality Control: Jason Wacknov
Director Operations: Pat Isbell

Estimated Sales: $1-2.5 Million
Number Employees: 10-19
Square Footage: 140000
Parent Co: American Textile Mills
Brands:
Alabama Rag
Arkansas Rag
California Rag
Carolina Rag
Colorado Rag
Georgia Rag
Illinois Rag
Indiana Rag
Iowa Rag
Kansas City Rag
Kansas Rag
Kentucky Rag
Louisiana Rag
Michigan Rag
Minnesota Rag
Mississippi Rag
Missouri Rag
Nebraska Rag
New Mexico Rag
Ohio Rag
Oklahoma Rag
Pennsylvania Rag
Tennessee Rag

**26811 (HQ)Nu-Trend Plastics
Thermoformer**
119 Sewald St
Jacksonville, FL 32204-1731
904-353-5936
Fax: 904-353-2035
Manufacturer and exporter of thermoformed plastic
containers, trays and inserts
CEO: Michael Corrigan
CFO: Mike Corrigan
Estimated Sales: $2-2.5 Million
Number Employees: 5-9
Square Footage: 30000
Type of Packaging: Consumer, Food Service, Pri-
vate Label

26812 Nu-Vu Food Service Systems
5600 13th Street
Menominee, MI 49858
906-863-4401
Fax: 906-863-5889 800-338-9886
sales@nu-vu.com www.nu-vu.com
Ovens,proofers, oven/proofers, carts,racks,and
roll-in rack ovens.
President: Najib Maalouf
Research & Development: Matt Deming
Sales Director: Reza McDaniel
Contact: Matt Deming
mdeming@nu-vu.com
Director of Purchasing: Wendy Swanson
Estimated Sales: $1 - 5 Million
Number Employees: 100-249

26813 NuTone
9825 Kenwood Rd
Suite 301
Cincinnati, OH 45242
513-527-5100
Fax: 513-527-5177 888-336-3948
www.nutone.com
Manufacturer and exporter of range hoods, exhaust
fans, heaters, central cleaning systems, etc.
CEO: David Pringle
CFO: Bill Kissell
Quality Control: Gloria Wrenn
Contact: Jimmie Cheek
jcheek@nutone.com
Manager: Fabio Fronda
Number Employees: 500-999
Parent Co: Nortek

26814 Nuance Solutions Inc
1140 E 103rd St
Chicago, IL 60628-3010
773-785-2300
Fax: 800-621-1276 800-621-8553
cjh@nuancesol.com www.nuancesolutions.com
Manufacturer and exporter of liquid and jelly hand
soap, degreasers, disinfectants, pine oil germicide,
sanitizers and hard surface cleaners
Owner: James Flanagan
jflana1@nuancesol.com
VP Marketing: Neil Houtsma
Estimated Sales: $20 - 50 Million
Number Employees: 50-99

Square Footage: 150000
Parent Co: Bullen Metawest
Type of Packaging: Bulk

26815 Nucon Corporation
111 S Pfingsten Ste 100
Deerfield, IL 60015

847-564-3505
Fax: 847-509-0011 877-545-0070
customersupport@brightsparktravel.com
www.brightsparktravel.com
Manufacturer and exporter of plastic pallets
Owner: Mitchell Slotnick
VP Sales/Marketing: Allan Wasserman
Estimated Sales: $2.5-5,000,000
Number Employees: 20-49

26816 Nulco Lighting
123 Dyer St
Suite 2
Providence, RI 2903

401-728-5200
Fax: 401-728-8210
Decorative electric lighting fixtures
President: Kent Nulman
CEO: Robert Delogo
CFO: Robert Geloge
R & D: Richard Ruggeri
Quality Control: Joe Lenk
National Sales Manager: Stephen Rice
Estimated Sales: $5-10 Million
Number Employees: 100-249

26817 Numatics Inc
46280 Dylan Dr # 100
Novi, MI 48377-4910

248-596-3200
Fax: 248-596-3201 insidesales@numatics.com
www.numatics.com
Cmo: David K Dodds
 david.dodds@numatics.com
VP: David K Dodds
Estimated Sales: $1 - 5 Million
Number Employees: 500-999

26818 Numeric Computer Systems Inc
275 Oser Ave
Hauppauge, NY 11788-3609

631-486-9000
Fax: 631-486-9032 800-321-7822
www.numericcomputersystems.com
President / CEO: Robert Hochberg
 robert.hochberg@ncssuite.com
Managing Director: Pedro Toro
CFO: Wayne Hochberg
Executive VP-Strategy and Business Devel: Allen Dickason
COO: Mark Hochberg
Estimated Sales: $5 - 10 Million
Number Employees: 1-4

26819 Nuova Distribution Centre
6940 Salashan Pkwy
Bldg - A
Ferndale, WA 98248-8314

360-366-2226
Fax: 360-366-4015 info@nuovadistribution.com
www.nuovadistribution.com
Manufacturer and importer of coffee and espresso grinders, sandwich grills and espresso, cappuccino and Italian slush/granita machines
President: Roberto Bresciani
 roberto@nuovadistribution.com
Coordinator: Vic Bialas
Estimated Sales: $1 - 3 Million
Number Employees: 10-19
Brands:
 Nuova Simonelli

26820 Nuova Simonelli USA
1915 1st Ave S
Seattle, WA 98134-1405

206-223-5533
Fax: 206-223-5525 info@nuovadistribution.com
www.nuovadistribution.com
Espresso machines and accessories, grinders
Member: Robert Bresciani
Estimated Sales: $1 - 3 Million
Number Employees: 1-4

26821 Nutec Manufacturing Inc
908 Garnet Ct
New Lenox, IL 60451-3569

815-722-2800
Fax: 815-722-2831 815-722-5348
sales@nutecmfg.com www.nutecmfg.com
Manufacturer, importer and exporter of food forming equipment including patties formers, cubers and conveyors
President: Ken Sandberg
CEO: Zibe Gibson
 bids@nutecmfg.com
Vice President: Mike Barnett
Research & Development: Bob Nard
Marketing Director: Mike Barnett
Sales Director: Mike Barnett
IT: Jeff Regan
Production Manager: John Goetzinger
Plant Manager: Ken Galloy
Purchasing: John Goetzinger
Estimated Sales: $2.5-5 Million
Number Employees: 10-19
Square Footage: 20000
Brands:
 Nutec
 Provatec

26822 Nutec Manufacturing Inc
908 Garnet Ct
New Lenox, IL 60451-3569

815-722-2800
Fax: 815-722-2831 suggestions@nutecmfg.com
www.nutecmfg.com
Food forming and depositing equipment
President: Ken Sandberg
IT: Jeff Regan
 bids@nutecmfg.com
Estimated Sales: $10 - 20 Million
Number Employees: 10-19

26823 Nutec Manufacturing Inc
908 Garnet Ct
New Lenox, IL 60451-3569

815-722-2800
Fax: 815-722-2831 sales@nutecmfg.com
www.nutecmfg.com
Food processing equipment
President: Ken Sandberg
IT: Jeff Regan
 bids@nutecmfg.com
Estimated Sales: $5-10 Million
Number Employees: 10-19

26824 Nutra Food Ingredients, LLC
4683 50th Street SE
Kentwood, MI 49512

616-656-9928
Fax: 419-730-3685
sales@nutrafoodingredients.com
www.nutrafoodingredients.com
Functional and nutritional ingredients supplier to the food, beverage, nutraceutical and cosmetics industries
President: Bryon Yang
Director of Business Development: Tim Wolffis
Quality Control: Monica Mylet
 monica.mylet@nutrafoodingredients.com
Director of Sales and Marketing: Clarence Harvey
Year Founded: 2004
Estimated Sales: Under $500,000
Number Employees: 1-4
Other Locations:
 Distribution Center
 Edison NJ
 Distribution Center
 Carson CA

26825 (HQ)Nutraceutical International
222 S. Main Street
16th Floor
Salt Lake City, UT 84101

435-655-6000
800-538-5888
info@nutraceutical.com www.nutraceutical.com
Supplements.
CEO: Monty Sharma
Chief Administrative Officer: Cory McQueen
Chief Marketing Officer: John D'Alessandro
Chief Operating Officer: Camilla Shumaker
Year Founded: 1993
Estimated Sales: $188.07 Million
Number Employees: 810
Number of Brands: 35
Square Footage: 6103

Type of Packaging: Consumer, Food Service, Bulk
Brands:
 Allvia
 BuckPower
 Complimed
 Dowd & Rogers
 Food Source
 FunFresh Foods
 Herbs for Kids
 Homeopathy for Kids
 Honey Gardens
 KAL
 Miztique
 Montana Big Sky
 NatraBio
 Natural Balance
 Natural Sport
 NaturalCare
 Nature's Herbs
 Nutra BioGenesis
 Oakmont Labs
 Paleo Planet
 Pioneer
 Premier One
 Refrigerator Fresh
 Solaray
 Spring Drops
 Sunny Green
 Sweet Moose
 Taste Waves
 The Real Food Trading Co.
 VAXA
 VegLife
 Veglife
 World Berries
 Zand
 Zylicious
 bioAllers

26826 Nutri-Bake Inc
1208 Rue Bergar
Laval, QC H7L 5A2
Canada

450-933-5936
Fax: 888-263-3208 info@nutri-bake.com
www.organic-baked-goods.com
Manufacturer and wholesaler of baked goods
President: Peter Tsatoumas

26827 Nutrifaster Inc
209 S Bennett St
Seattle, WA 98108-2226

206-767-5054
Fax: 206-762-2209 800-800-2641
Sales@Nutrifaster.com www.nutrifaster.com
Manufacturer and exporter of centrifugal juice extractors
President: Bert Robins
Sales/Service: Fred Davies
Manager: Rocco Robins
 sales@nutrifaster.com
Estimated Sales: Less than $500,000
Number Employees: 5-9
Type of Packaging: Food Service
Brands:
 Nutrifaster N-350

26828 Nutrin Distribution Company
1627 Connecticut Ave NW
Suite 3
Washington, DC 20009

Fax: 815-301-9184 888-718-3235
adam@nutrin.com www.nutrin.com
Supplier of peanut products, importer with just-in-time deliver in the US and Canada. Products include peanut flour, butter, oil, extract, and essence as well as roasted and chopped peanuts.
President: Adam Benado

26829 Nutrinfo Corporation
108 Water Street
Watertown, MA 02472-4696

617-923-2377
Fax: 617-926-6360 800-676-6686
Consultant to the U.S. food and dietary supplement industries providing services including design, food technology, marketing, promotion, sanitation, testing, nutritional analysis and international food labeling
President: Richard Litner
VP: Sanjeev Mohanti
Director Science: Thomas Hansen

Number Employees: 11
Square Footage: 6000

26830 Nutrinova
1601 Lbj Fwy
Dallas, TX 75234-6034
972-443-4000
Fax: 972-443-4994 800-786-3883
www.nutrinova.com
A global technology and specialty materials company that engineers and manufacturers a wide variety of products essential to everyday living.
President: Graham Hall
cheryl.colline@nutrinova.com
Chairman, Chief Executive Officer: Mark Rohr
Vice President: Jiro Okada
Marketing Manager North America: Patricia Hanley
Contact: Colline Cheryl
cheryl.colline@nutrinova.com
Chief Operating Officer: Doug Madden
Number Employees: 5-9
Parent Co: Nutrinova Nutrition Specialists & Food Ingredients GmbH

26831 Nutrisciences Labs
70 Carolyn Boulevard
Farmingdale, NY 11735
631-247-0600
855-492-7388
info@nutricaplabs.com
www.nutrasciencelabs.com
Nutritional supplements including vitamins, minerals, and sports supplements.
Executive Vice President: Vincent Tricario
VP Digital Marketing: Andrew Goldman
VP Sales: Blayney McEneaney
Operations Manager: Dana Roveto
Estimated Sales: $45 Million
Number Employees: 40
Parent Co: Twinlab Consolidation Corporation

26832 Nutrition & Food Associates
PO Box 47007
Plymouth, MN 55447
763-550-9475
Fax: 763-559-3675 info@nutriform.com
www.nutriform.com
Manufacturer and exporter of computer software for product development, nutrition labeling, recipe and menu analysis
President: Patricia Godfrey
Estimated Sales: Below $5 Million
Number Employees: 1-4
Type of Packaging: Food Service
Brands:
Nutriform

26833 Nutrition Network
4199 Campus Drive
Suite 550
Irvine, CA 92612-4694
949-753-7998
Fax: 949-497-8991
Nutrition support consultant providing services to food producers, dietitians and consumers
CEO: Charlene Rainey
Director Technical Services: Leslie Nyquist
Estimated Sales: $500,000-$1 Million
Number Employees: 5-9
Square Footage: 6000

26834 Nutrition Research
504 S 13th St
Livingston, MT 59047
406-222-3541
Fax: 406-823-6499 www.livingstonhealthcare.org
Research and development firm offering turnkey assistance in the design and processing of natural foods, vitamin, mineral and herbal supplements, etc
President: Lee Dreyer
CEO: Bren Lowe
Human Resources Director: Connie Dunn

26835 Nutsco Inc
1115 S 2nd St
Camden, NJ 08103-3232
856-966-6400
Fax: 856-966-6544 www.nutsco.com
Supply chain management for high quality raw cashews

President: Fransisco A Neto
VP: Patricio Assis
Marketing: Sueli Vieira
Sales: Sueli Vieira
Plant Manager: Steve McCall
Estimated Sales: $5-10 Million
Number Employees: 10-19
Square Footage: 50800
Parent Co: Usibras (Brazil)

26836 Nutty Bavarian
305 Hickman Dr
Sanford, FL 32771-6905
407-444-6322
Fax: 407-444-6335 800-382-4788
bruno@nuttyb.com www.nuttyb.com
Cinnamon nut glaze syrup and fresh roasted gourmet nuts; Manufacturer of nut roasting carts and warmers as well as paper and plastic cones and gift tins for nuts
Owner: David Brent
bruno@nuttyb.com
Customer Service Manager: Amber Stefanisko
Controller: Keya Morgan
Vice President of Sales: David Zangenberg
bruno@nuttyb.com
Production Manager: Ed Conrado
Estimated Sales: $500,000-$1 Million
Number Employees: 10-19
Square Footage: 28800
Type of Packaging: Consumer, Bulk
Brands:
Nbr 2000
Nutty Bavarian

26837 Nyco Products Co
5332 Dansher Rd
Countryside, IL 60525-3124
708-579-8100
Fax: 708-579-9898 800-752-4754
bstahurski@nycoproducts.com
www.nycoproducts.com
Cleaning and sanitation supplies including deodorants, detergents, emulsifying agents, metal polish and glass, pipe, toilet bowl and drain cleaners
President: Robert Stahurski
jwunderlich@nycoproducts.com
VP Sales: John Wunderlich
Sales Exec: John Wunderlich
VP Operations: Robert Houston
Estimated Sales: $5-10 Million
Number Employees: 50-99
Square Footage: 150000
Parent Co: NYCO Products Company

26838 Nydree Flooring
1115 Vista Park Dr # C
Ste D
Forest, VA 24551-4686
434-525-5252
Fax: 434-525-7437 800-682-5698
www.nydreeflooring.com
Commercial flooring
Owner: Barry Brubaker
VP Radiation: James Myron
Estimated Sales: $500,000-$1 Million
Number Employees: 50-99
Square Footage: 72000
Parent Co: Appliant Radian Energy Corporation
Brands:
Packing House

26839 Nyman Manufacturing Company
275 Ferris Ave
Rumford, RI 02916-1033
401-438-3410
Fax: 401-438-5975
Manufacturer and exporter of plastic cups, dinnerware, lids, caps and covers; also, paper cups
Marketing Director: Laura Coupal
General Manager (Paper): Walter Bennett
General Manager (Plastic): Al Domenici
Type of Packaging: Food Service
Brands:
First Choice
Natural Choice
Popular Choice

26840 O A Newton & Son Co
16356 Sussex Hwy # 1
PO Box 397
Bridgeville, DE 19933-3056
302-337-8211
Fax: 302-337-3780 800-726-5745
solutions@oanewton.com www.oanewton.com
Materials handling and control, feed and grain handling, irrigation
President: Rob F Rider Jr
Chairman of the Board: Robert Rider
Estimated Sales: $10 - 20 Million
Number Employees: 20-49

26841 O K Mfg
2340 S 900 W # A
South Salt Lake, UT 84119-1553
801-974-9116
Fax: 801-974-5458 800-748-5480
okmfgsales@gmail.com www.gumball-depot.com
Bubble gum and novelty vending equipment and plush cranes
President: Jeff Ostler
k_ausler@okmfg.net
Sales Exec: Kurt Ausler
Owner/Production: Jeff Ostler
Estimated Sales: $5-10 Million
Number Employees: 5-9
Square Footage: 208000
Brands:
Ok

26842 O'Brian Tarping SystemsInc
2330 Womble Brooks Rd E
Wilson, NC 27893-7947
252-291-2141
Fax: 252-291-1416 800-334-8277
sales@obriantarping.com www.obriantarping.com
Commercial awnings, unautomatic tarting systems
President: Woody O'Brian
woody@obriantarping.com
Estimated Sales: $3 - 5 Million
Number Employees: 20-49

26843 O'Brien Bros Inc
51 Doty Cir
West Springfield, MA 01089-1307
413-734-7121
Fax: 413-737-1642 800-343-0949
www.obrienbrothersinc.com
Locks and locksmith supplies
Owner: Joe O'Brien
joeobrien@obrienbrothersinc.com
Estimated Sales: $.5 - 1 million
Number Employees: 1-4

26844 O'Brien Installations
4435 Corporate Drive
Burlington
Ontario, CA L7L 5T9
Canada
905-336-8245
Fax: 905-331-6494 info@obrieninstall.com
www.obrieninstall.com
Manufacturer and exporter of cranes
President: George O'Brien
Marketing Coordinator: John Marchetti
Sales Director: Wayne Davis
Production Manager: Randy Mullin
Purchasing Manager: Krys Klain
Estimated Sales: $1-10 Million
Number Employees: 50-99
Square Footage: 80000
Parent Co: O'Brien Material Handling
Other Locations:
O'Brien Material Handling
Memramock, NB

26845 O'Dell Corp
13833 Indian Mound Rd
Ware Shoals, SC 29692-3533
864-861-2222
Fax: 864-861-3171 800-342-2843
www.odellcorp.com
Manufacturer, importer and exporter of household and janitorial mops, brooms, brushes and handles
CEO: Wh O'Dell
who@odellcorp.com
VP: Paul O'Dell
Customer Service: Gayle O'Dell
Estimated Sales: $10-20 Million
Number Employees: 100-249
Square Footage: 170000

Brands:
Kitchen Queen

26846 O-Cedar
2188 Diehl Road
Aurora, IL 60502

217-379-2377
Fax: 217-379-9901 800-543-8105
www.ocedar.com
Brooms including corn, rattan, bamboo, etc
President: Stanley Koschnick
General Manager: Stanley Kochnick
Estimated Sales: $1 - 5 Million
Number Employees: 50-99
Parent Co: Freudenberg Household Products LP

26847 O-Cedar
2188 Diehl Road
Aurora, IL 60502

219-726-8128
800-543-8105
www.ocedar.com
Manufacturer and exporter of industrial brooms and brushes
Plant Manager: Mike White
Parent Co: O'Cedar Vining

26848 O.B.S. Trading
2370 N High
Suite 3
Jackson, MO 63755

573-243-6999
Fax: 573-243-8723 www.obstrading.com
Planning and designing to finding the best machines for meat processing
President: Henning Bollerslev

26849 (HQ)O.C. Adhesives Corporation
PO Box 3058
Ridgefield, NJ 07657-3058

973-279-8134
Fax: 973-279-0338 800-662-1595
Industrial water based adhesives for plastic film laminating, bottle labeling and difficult to stick surfaces and UV coated stock
President: Stanley Meyers Phd
Technology Director: Leonard Gross
Director Marketing: Sy Eckstein
Estimated Sales: $2.5-5 Million
Number Employees: 10-19
Square Footage: 50000

26850 O.D. Kurtz Associates
242 Hurst Road NE
Palm Bay, FL 32907-1566

321-723-0135
Fax: 321-723-0151 www.odk.com
Laboratory specializing in extraneous analysis, sanitation appraisals and AOAC food testing
Estimated Sales: $500,000-$1 Million
Number Employees: 5-9

26851 O.K. Marking Devices
1358 Cornwall Street
Regina, SK S4R 2H5
Canada

306-522-2856
Fax: 306-569-3566
Stencils, engraved signs, tags, corporation seals and rubber and photopolymer stamps
President: Fl Clark
Estimated Sales: Below $5 Million
Number Employees: 7
Square Footage: 4000

26852 O/K International Corporation
73 Bartlett Street
Marlborough, MA 01752-3071

508-303-8286
Fax: 508-303-8207 800-521-2908
sales@okcorp.com www.okcorp.com
Hot-air sealers, case erectors, case liners and conveyor systems, strech wrappers
Marketing Director: Ann Marie Kellett
Contact: Marcela Barragan
mbarragan@okcorp.com
Plant Manager: Hans Mentink
Estimated Sales: $5 - 10 Million
Number Employees: 25-49
Type of Packaging: Consumer, Bulk

26853 OCS Checkweighers Inc
2350 Hewatt Road
Snellville, GA 30039

678-344-8300
Fax: 678-344-8030 info.usa@ocs-cw.com
www.ocs-cw.com
Packaging machinery
President: Ingolf Latz
CEO/CFO: Theo Dueppre
Sales Manager: Rachel Edwards
Contact: Jeff Borrelli
jeff.borrelli@ocs-cw.com
Estimated Sales: $1.5 Million
Number Employees: 13

26854 OI Analytical
151 Graham Rd
College Station, TX 77845-9654

979-690-1711
Fax: 979-690-0440 oimail@oico.com
www.oianalytical.com
Cmo: Gary Englehart
genglehart@oico.com
CEO: J Bruce Lancaster
Estimated Sales: $20,000,000 - $49,999,999
Number Employees: 50-99

26855 OK Stamp & Seal Company
1608 Linwood Blvd
Oklahoma City, OK 73106-5052

405-235-7853
Fax: 405-232-4139
Rubber stamps
President: Steve Fagundes
Estimated Sales: Less than $500,000
Number Employees: 1-4

26856 OMNOVA Solutions
175 Ghent Road
Fairlawn, OH 44333

330-869-4200
www.omnova.com
Plastic, calendered, plain and printed vinyl film
CEO: Anne Noonan
Plant Manager: Lee Szwast
Purchasing Director: Robert Culp
Estimated Sales: $1.13 Billion
Number Employees: 2,390
Square Footage: 10124
Parent Co: GenCorp

26857 OMRON Systems LLC
55 Commerce Dr
Schaumburg, IL 60173-5302

224-520-7650
Fax: 847-843-7686 www.omron.com
Electronic cash registers with software for fast food, fine dining and cafeteria markets; also, touch screen systems for restaurants and hospitality
President, CEO: Yoshihito Yamada
jcornet@omronost.com
CFO: Yoshinori Suzuki
Director, EVP: Akio Sakumiya
Sales Exec: Jac Cornet
Estimated Sales: $15 - 20 Million
Number Employees: 1-4

26858 OMRON Systems LLC
55 Commerce Dr
Schaumburg, IL 60173-5302

224-520-7650
Fax: 847-843-7686 800-556-6766
omroninfo@omron.com www.omron.com
Instrumentation and control products including PLCs, sensors and temperature controllers
President: Craig Bauer
jcornet@omronost.com
CEO: Tastu Goto
Sales Exec: Jac Cornet
Estimated Sales: $4.6 Million
Number Employees: 1-4
Square Footage: 30000
Parent Co: Omron Corporation
Brands:
Smart Factory

26859 OMYA, Inc.
9987 Carver Rd
Suite 300
Cincinnatti, OH 45242

513-387-4600
800-749-6692
www.omya.com
Fillers and pigments from calcium carbonate and dolomite, and distributor of chemical products.
President: Anthony Colak
CFO: Michael Phillips
Secretary: Leonard Eisenberg
Asst Sec: Patricia Kirkendall
Manager Technology Services: Michael Roussel
Sales Manager: Maria Burt
Contact: Hilary Allard
hilary.allard@omya.com
Manager: Scott McCalla
Manager Projects Engineering: Scott Schaffner
Director of Engineering: Rob Tikoft
Director Purchasing: Derrell Riley
Estimated Sales: $4.3 Million
Other Locations:
Proctor VT
Cincinnati OH
Woodland WA
Kingsport TN
Lucerne Valley CA
Johnsonburg PA
Florence VT
Hawesville KY
Sylacauga AL
Superior AZ
Long Beach CA

26860 ORB Weaver Farm
3406 Lime Kiln Road
New Haven, VT 05472

802-877-3755
marjorie@orbweaverfarm.com
www.orbweaverfarm.com
Fresh fruits and vegetables, and fine cheeses
President: Marjorie Susman
marjorie@orbweaverfarm.com

26861 ORBIS
1055 Corporate Center Dr
Oconomowoc, WI 53066-4829

262-560-5000
Fax: 262-560-5841 800-890-7292
info@orbiscorporation.com
www.orbiscorporation.com
Plastic containers, hand-held and bulk and pallets
CEO: Jim Kotek
Marketing Director: Pete Budney
Public Relations: Samantha Goetz
Purchasing Manager: Robert Kroening
Number Employees: 100-249
Parent Co: Menasha Corporation
Type of Packaging: Food Service, Bulk

26862 ORBIS
1055 Corporate Center Dr
Oconomowoc, WI 53066-4829

262-560-5000
Fax: 262-560-5841 info@orbiscorporation.com
www.orbiscorporation.com
Plastic pallets and containers
President: William F Ash
Sales Manager: Jo Ann Bahling
Sales Manager: Sherri Brigowatz
Sales Manager: Sally Meyers
Estimated Sales: $20-50 Million
Number Employees: 100-249
Parent Co: Menasha Corporation Convoy Plastic Pallets

26863 ORBIS
1055 Corporate Center Dr
Oconomowoc, WI 53066-4829

262-560-5000
Fax: 262-560-5841 800-999-8683
info@orbiscorporation.com
www.orbiscorporation.com
Total returnable packaging systems, containers, pallets, interiors
President: Linda Balwinski
linda.balwinski@orbiscorporation.com
CEO: Dave Schopp
Estimated Sales: $20-50 million
Number Employees: 100-249

26864 ORBIS
1055 Corporate Center Dr
PO Box 389
Oconomowoc, WI 53066-4829

262-560-5000
Fax: 262-560-5841 800-890-7292
info@orbiscorporation.com
www.orbiscorporation.com

Provides reusable packaging for the bakery, dairy, beverage, red meat/poultry and general food processing industry.
President: William F Ash
VP Finance: Mark Gorzek
VP Marketing/Sales: James Solum
VP Sales: Tim Henkel
VP Human Resources: Tom Bissell
VP Operations: Mike McKay
Number Employees: 100-249
Square Footage: 15011
Parent Co: Menasha Corporation

26865 ORBIS RPM
5250 E Terrace Drive
Suite 106
Madison, WI 53718

608-852-8840
Fax: 608-237-8162 www.corbiplastics.com
Packaging materials including plastic reusable pallets, divider sheets/layer pads and top frames.
President: Jack Graham
General Manager: Chad Feehan
Parent Co: Menasha Corporation
Type of Packaging: Food Service

26866 (HQ)OSF
650 Barmac Drive
Toronto, ON M9L 2X8
Canada

416-749-7700
Fax: 416-740-6365 800-465-4000
Manufacturer and exporter of store fixtures, showcases and displays; also, steel shelving
CEO: Harry Shier
Co-Chairman: Milton Shier
Number Employees: 2100
Square Footage: 8800000
Other Locations:
  OSF
  Blackstone VA
Brands:
  Century Line
  Tufkote
  Vista Classic Line

26867 OSRAM SYLVANIA
100 Endicott Street
Danvers, MA 01923

978-777-1900
Fax: 978-750-2152 800-544-4828
www.sylvania.com
President: Charles Jerabeck
President, Chief Executive Officer: Rick Leaman
Contact: Michael Abbott
  michael.abbott@sylvania.com
Number Employees: 10,000

26868 OTD Corporation
P.O. Box 510
Hinsdale, IL 60522-0510

630-321-9232
Fax: 574-254-5092
Manufacturer and exporter of aluminum containers, racks and pallets
President: James Ogle
Controller: Jean Chatman
Estimated Sales: $20-30 Million
Number Employees: 1-4

26869 OTP Industrial Solutions
3601 N Fruitridge Ave
Terre Haute, IN 47804-1756

812-466-2734
Fax: 812-466-2831 860-953-7632
www.otpnet.com
Manufacturer and exporter of overhead bridge cranes, wire rope winches, conveyors and reciprocating feeders
Manager: Walt Tompkins
CEO/Engineer: Steve White
CFO: Jim Bennett
Vice President: Joe Goda
Marketing Director: Dave Parks
Sales Director: Tom Bland
Public Relations: Tom Bland
Plant Manager: Steve Rowe
Purchasing Manager: Jerry Taylor
Estimated Sales: $16.5 Million
Number Employees: 10-19
Square Footage: 40000

26870 (HQ)OWD
PO Box 1260
Tupper Lake, NY 12986-0260

518-359-2944
Fax: 518-359-2994 800-836-1693

www.jarden.com/phoenix.zhtml?c=72395&p=irol..
.ID.
Manufacturer and exporter of plastic spoons, forks, knives, straws, cups and plates
CEO: James E. Lillie
CFO: John Breshahan
Vice President: Rachel Wilson
R & D: Allison Malkin
VP Sales: Al Huggins
Estimated Sales: Less than $500,000
Number Employees: 100-249
Square Footage: 260000
Parent Co: Jarden Corporation
Other Locations:
  O.W.D.
  La Fayette GA
Brands:
  Lady Dianne

26871 OXO International
601 West 26th St
Suite 1050
New York, NY 10001

212-242-3333
Fax: 717-709-5350 www.oxo.com
Manufacturer of kitchen utensils and appliances
President: Edward Ahn
  eahn@oxo.com
VP, Sales: Michael Cleary
Estimated Sales: $2.5-5 Million
Number Employees: 50-99
Number of Products: 1000
Type of Packaging: Consumer
Brands:
  Oxo Goodgrips

26872 Oak Barrel Winecraft
1443 San Pablo Ave
Berkeley, CA 94702-1045

510-849-0400
Fax: 510-528-6543 info@oakbarrel.com
www.oakbarrel.com
Oak barrels for wine and beer making, bottles and stoppers for wine, vinegar starter culture and bottling and brewery machinery; importer of wine presses, crushers and barrels; also, wholesaler/distributor of vinegar starter cultureand barrels
President and CFO: Bernard Rooney
  info@oakbarrel.com
Vice President: Homer Smith
Estimated Sales: $5 - 10 Million
Number Employees: 1-4
Square Footage: 12000

26873 Oak Creek Pallet Company
5059 N 119th Street
Milwaukee, WI 53225-3607

414-762-7170
Fax: 414-762-3070
Wooden pallets, boxes and crates
President: Gary LaMaster
Number Employees: 90

26874 Oak International
1160 White St
Sturgis, MI 49091

269-651-9790
Fax: 269-651-7849 www.cimcool.com
Manufacturer and exporter of FDA approved cutting, stamping and drawing oils; also, grinding coolants and cleaners
Sr. VP Sales/Operations: F Edwards
Contact: Michelle Dressler
  michelle_dressler@milacron.com
Plant Manager: Jim Phillips
Estimated Sales: $5 - 10 Million
Number Employees: 10-19
Square Footage: 52000
Brands:
  Oak Draw
  Oak Kleen
  Oak Kool
  Oak Kote
  Oak Protect
  Oil Rids

26875 Oak Street Manufacturing
255 Welter Dr
Monticello, IA 52310

319-465-4042
Fax: 877-465-4042 877-465-4344
www.oakstreetmfg.com
Manufacturer and distributor of restaurant furnishings
President/Owner: Cindy Bagge *Year Founded:* 1995

26876 Oakes & Burger
PO Box 665
Niles, OH 44446-0665

800-321-0106
Fax: 330-652-2617
Aseptic processing equipment, batch control systems, chillers, clean rooms and equipment, custom fabrication, deaerators, homogenizers, ice equipment, ingredient feeders, meters, expert systems, filters

26877 Oakes Carton Co
5575 Collingwood Ave
Kalamazoo, MI 49004-1525

269-381-6022
Fax: 269-381-2948 www.oakescarton.com
Paper folding cartons
Owner: Judy Day
VP Sales Manager: James Savage
  judyd@oakescarton.com
Customer Service: Oakes Carton
Office Manager / Accounting / Human Reso: Judee Buckhout
Estimated Sales: $2.5-5 Million
Number Employees: 20-49

26878 Oakite Products
P.O. Box 7
New Providence, NJ 07974-0007

908-464-6900
Fax: 908-464-5354 800-526-4473
Developer. manufacturer and supplier of state-of-the-art specialty chemical products.
President: Don LeBart
CEO: Ron Felber
Estimated Sales: $75-$80 Million
Number Employees: 50-99

26879 Oaklee International
125 Raynor Ave
Ronkonkoma, NY 11779-6666

631-436-7900
Fax: 631-436-7985 800-333-7250
service@oaklee.com www.oaklee.com
Shrink film, sleeve labels, promotional packaging, protective packaging
Executive Director: Alice Zebrowski
  alice@oaklee.com
Sales Exec: Alice Zebrowski
Number Employees: 100-249

26880 Oaklee International
125 Raynor Ave
Ronkonkoma, NY 11779-6666

631-436-7900
Fax: 631-436-7985 800-333-7250
service@oaklee.com www.oaklee.com
Executive Director: Alice Zebrowski
  alice@oaklee.com
Sales Exec: Alice Zebrowski
Estimated Sales: $5 - 10 Million
Number Employees: 100-249

26881 Oakton Instruments
PO Box 5136
Vernon Hills, IL 60061-5136

888-462-5866
Fax: 847-247-2984 888-462-5866
info@4oakton.com www.4oakton.com
Provides pH, ORP, conductivity/TDS, dissolved oxygen, relative humity, time, temperature, and barometric pressure instrumentation, baths, ovens, vacuum pumps, desiccators, clamps and magnifiers
Marketing Director: Bob Langie
Estimated Sales: $1 - 5 Million
Brands:
  Oakton

26882 Oates Flag Co Inc
10951 Electron Dr
Louisville, KY 40299-6410

502-267-8200
Fax: 502-267-8246 sales@oatesflag.com
www.oatesflag.com

801

Flags and pennants; silk screening, athletic lettering and embroidery available
Owner: C R Oates
  randy@oatesflag.com
Marketing Director: Reggie Oates
Estimated Sales: Below $5 Million
Number Employees: 10-19

26883 Obergurg Engineering
1814 Empire Industrial Court
Suite G
Santa Rosa, CA 95403-1946
                707-542-4153
          Fax: 707-542-4152
Wine industry label design
Manager: Joan Murphy
Number Employees: 7

26884 Oc Lugo Co Inc
15 Third St # 2
New City, NY 10956-4946
                845-480-5121
        Fax: 845-480-5122 info@oclugo.com
                www.oclugo.com
Supplier of chemicals, vitamins, minerals, gelatins and food ingredients. OC Lugo's other division is Critical Filtration supplies
President: Richard Lugo
  rlugo@oclugo.com
Estimated Sales: $830,000
Number Employees: 5-9

26885 Occidental Chemical Corporation
5 Greenway Plaza
P.O. Box 27570
Houston, TX 77046-0506
                713-215-7000
        Fax: 716-278-7880 www.oxy.com
Chemicals including bottle cleaning compounds; processor of soda for carbonated soft drinks
President and CEO: Stephen I. Chazen
Contact: Alison Frey
  alison_frey@oxy.com
Plant Manager: Candace Jaunzemis
Director Purchasing: Tony Orbegoso
Estimated Sales: $.5 - 1 million
Number Employees: 1-4
Parent Co: Occidental Petroleum

26886 Occidental Chemical Corporation
5005 L B J Fwy
Suite 2200
Dallas, TX 75244
                972-404-3800
        Fax: 972-448-6631 800-733-3665
                www.oxychem.com
Basic chemicals concentrated in the chloro-vinyls including chlorine, caustic soda, ethylene dichloride and polyvinylchloride
President: James Lienert
CFO: Dennis Blake
Site Manager: Rick Zelley
Number Employees: 3000
Parent Co: Occidental Petroleum Corporation

26887 Oceanpower America
222 Meadows Lane NE
Leesburg, VA 20176
                305-721-7823
        info@email.oceanpower.com
        www.oceanpoweramerica.com
Manufacturer of ice cream machines*Year Founded:* 1996

26888 (HQ)Ockerlund Industries
1555 Wrightwood Court
Addison, IL 60101
                708-771-7707
        Fax: 708-620-1630 guyo@ockerlund.com
Corrugated, plastic and wooden boxes
President: Stan Joray
  jjoray@oxbox.biz
CEO: Guy Ockerlund
Estimated Sales: $10 - 20 Million
Number Employees: 100-249

26889 Ocme America Corporation
2200 N Susquehanna Trail
York, PA 17404-1652
                717-843-6263
        Fax: 717-843-6748 tsnelbaker@ocmeusa.com
                www.ocme.it

Packaging machinery including fillers, depalletizers, wrap-around case packers, shrink wrap machines and palletizers
President: Emmanuel Gattescht
  egattescht@ocme.it
President: Tony Intriona
R&D: Anthony Trona
Sales Coordinator: Thelma Snelbaker
Estimated Sales: $5 - 10 Million
Number Employees: 10
Square Footage: 16000
Parent Co: Ocme SRL

26890 Ocs Checkweighers, Inc.
2350 Hewatt Rd
Snellville, GA 30039
                678-344-8030
        Fax: 678-344-8030 info.usa@ocs-cw.com
                www.ocs-cw.com
High-speed weighing systems.
Contact: Jeff Borrelli
  jeff.borrelli@ocs-cw.com

26891 Odell's
Reno, NV
                800-635-0436
        odellscustomerservice@venturafoods.com
                www.popntop.com
Popping oils and popcorn toppings.
Co-owner: Arthur Anderson
Co-owner: Vikki Anderson

26892 Oden Machinery
199 Fire Tower Dr
Tonawanda, NY 14150-5813
                716-874-3000
        Fax: 716-874-1589 800-658-3622
        sales@odencorp.com www.odencorp.com
Manufacturer and exporter of volumetric and net weight filling machinery for liquid and semi-l;iquid products.
President: Gary Gellerson
  ggellerson@odenmachinery.com
Marketing Director: Phyllis Phallen
Sales Director: Gary Laidman
Number Employees: 20-49
Brands:
  Grav/Tronic
  Mega/Fill
  Net/Mass
  Pro/Fill
  Pro/Matic
  Servo/Fill

26893 Odenberg Engineering
4038 Seaport Blvd
West Sacramento, CA 95691
                916-371-0700
        Fax: 916-371-5471 800-688-8396
                sales@odenberg.com
Manufacturer and exporter of batch steam peelers, chillers/freezers and sorters
President: Maurice Moynihan
VP: Ashley Hunter
Contact: Noel Basquel
  noel.basquel@odenberg.com
Production Sales Manager: Diamond Meagher
Estimated Sales: $10 - 20,000,000
Number Employees: 20-49
Parent Co: Odenberg Engineering

26894 Odessa Packaging Services
202 N Bassett St
Clayton, DE 19938
                302-653-8474
        Fax: 302-653-8612 800-633-7726

26895 Odor Management
1 Corporate Dr # 100
Suite 100
Long Grove, IL 60047-8887
                847-304-9111
        Fax: 847-304-0989 800-662-6367
                www.odormanagement.com
President: Phil Coffey
  coffey@omiindustries.com
Lead Scientist, Research and Development: Laura Haupert
Director of Marketing and Brand Developm: Melinda Adamec
National Sales Director: Tom Minett
Chief Operating Officer and Director of: Charles Timcik
Director of Operations: Stephen Lattis

Estimated Sales: Less Than $500,000
Number Employees: 1-4

26896 Oenophilia
1713 Legion Road
Chapel Hill, NC 27517-2359
                919-942-1250
          Fax: 919-942-5718
Wine and bar accessories

26897 Oerlikon Balzers Coating USA
1181 Jansen Farm Ct
Rogers Business Park
Elgin, IL 60123-2595
                847-695-5200
        Fax: 847-695-4051 info.balzers.us@oerlikon.com
                www.oerlikon.com/balzers/us
President: Kristen Kunz
CEO: Hans Br,,ndle
CFO: Volker Dostmann
Manager: Gary Cunningham
  gary.cunningham@oerlikon.com
Number Employees: 20-49

26898 Oerlikon Leybold Vacuum
5700 Mellon Rd
Export, PA 15632-8900
                724-327-5700
        Fax: 724-325-3577 www.oerlikon.com
Manufacturer, importer and exporter of vacuum pumps and systems
Chief Executive Officer: Andreas Widl
Vice President: P Albert
Manager of Technical Services: Joachim GstAhl
Marketing Director: M Vitale
Head of Sales: Werner SchAdler
Manager: Jim Hupp
Chief Operating Officer, Chief Operating: Wolfgang Ehrk
Plant Manager: Dennis Pellegrino
Number Employees: 1-4
Square Footage: 596000
Parent Co: Leybold AG
Brands:
  Sogevac

26899 Oerlikon Leybold Vacuum
5700 Mellon Rd
Export, PA 15632-8900
                724-327-5700
        Fax: 800-215-7782 www.oerlikon.com
Packaging machinery
Owner: Lori Arola
VP: Maura Powers
Marketing Director: Mario Vitale
Human Resources Manager: Valerie Mooney
Estimated Sales: $60 Million
Number Employees: 1-4
Square Footage: 62000

26900 Oetiker Inc
6317 Euclid St
Marlette, MI 48453-1426
                989-635-3621
        Fax: 989-635-2157 800-959-0398
        info@us.oetiker.com www.oetiker.com
Supplier of hose clamps and rings
CEO: Chris Parker
Quality Control: Dan Roche
Marketing Coordinator: Christine Lowe
Sales Director: Brian Milek
Account Manager: Brent Christenen
Production Manager: Bruce Christensen
Purchasing Manager: Shelly Davies
Estimated Sales: $10 - 20 Million
Number Employees: 100-249
Parent Co: Hans Oetiker AG

26901 Ogden Manufacturing Company
103 Gamma Drive
Pittsburgh, PA 15238
                412-967-3906
        Fax: 412-967-3930 cs@ogdenmfg.com
                www.ogdenmfg.com
Manufacturer and exporter of electric heating elements and microprocessor-based temperature controls
VP: Randy Lee
Marketing Manager: Gordon Hollander
Contact: Barbara Lee
  cs@ogdenmfg.com
Estimated Sales: $5-10 Million
Number Employees: 150-250
Square Footage: 260000

Brands:
Etr
Mighty Blade

26902 Ohaus Corp
7 Campus Dr # 300
Parsippany, NJ 07054-4413
973-377-9000
Fax: 973-593-0359 800-672-7722
marla.bormann@ohaus.com
Manufacturer and exporter of electronic, analytical, precision top loading and moisture balances; also, portable and bench scales
President: Ted Xia
ted.xia@ohaus.com
CFO: Peter Minder
Estimated Sales: $25 - 50 Million
Number Employees: 250-499
Brands:
Ohaus

26903 Ohio Conveyor & Supply Inc
1310 N Main St
Findlay, OH 45840-3703
419-422-3825
Fax: 419-422-4490
Conveyors and wholesaler/distributor of conveyor belts
President: John R Snyder
jrsnyder@ohioconveyorsupply.com
Estimated Sales: $1 - 2.5 Million
Number Employees: 5-9

26904 Ohio Magnetics Inc
5400 Dunham Rd
Maple Heights, OH 44137-3653
216-662-8484
Fax: 216-662-2911 800-486-6446
sales@ohiomagnetics.com
www.ohiomagnetics.com
Manufacturer and exporter of magnetic separators, metal detectors and conveyors
Manager: John Wohlgemuph
Sales Manager: Ken Richendollar
General Manager: John Wohlgemuth
Plant Manager: Tim Essick
Purchasing: Bob Zajc
Estimated Sales: $10-20 Million
Number Employees: 20-49
Square Footage: 288000
Parent Co: Ohio Magnetics
Brands:
Stearns

26905 Ohio Medical Corp
1111 Lakeside Dr
Gurnee, IL 60031-2489
847-855-0500
Fax: 847-855-6300 800-448-0770
www.ohiomedical.com
Filters, air
President: James Koppa
CEO: Halden Zimmermann
halden.zimmermann@ohiomedical.com
Chairman of the Board: Craig R Schifter
Sales: Martin Jindra
Estimated Sales: $20-50 Million
Number Employees: 100-249

26906 Ohio Rack Inc
1405 S Liberty Ave
PO Box 3517
Alliance, OH 44601-4231
330-823-8200
Fax: 330-823-8136 800-344-4164
ohiorack@cannet.com www.ohiorack.com
Wholesaler/distributor of used portable stack racks and pallet rack systems; manufacturer of new portable stack racks
President: George Pilla
ohiorack@cannet.com
Estimated Sales: Below $5,000,000
Number Employees: 5-9

26907 Ohio Soap Products Company
1340 E 289th St
Wickliffe, OH 44092
440-585-1100
Fax: 216-341-9900 www.diamondshine.com
Industrial soap
VP Sales: Scott Soble
Estimated Sales: $10-20 Million
Number Employees: 19

Brands:
Ohio

26908 Ohlson Packaging
490 Constitution Dr
Taunton, MA 02780-7389
508-977-0004
Fax: 508-977-0007 sales@ohlsonpack.com
www.ohlsonpack.com
Manufacturer and exporter of automatic stainless steel weighing machinery for bagging or boxing pasta, frozen foods, candy, produce, etc
Owner: John Ohlson Jr
Vice President: John Ohlson
Estimated Sales: $7 Million
Number Employees: 10-19

26909 Ohly Americas
35 Adams St NE
Hutchinson, MN 55350
320-587-2481
Fax: 320-587-8617 800-321-2689
info@ohly.us www.ohly.com
Yeast, dry condiments such as sweeteners and sauce powders.
CEO: Ralf Fink
Global CFO: Christian Hoika
Global Innovations Director: Raphael Levesque
Marketing & Supply Chain Director: Frank Kahler
Global Sales Director: Rainer Huttermann
Global HR Director: Lene Kruse
Global Operations Director: Marc Gerigk
Estimated Sales: $100-500 Million
Parent Co: ABF Ingredients - Division of Associated British Foods

26910 Oil Skimmers Inc
12800 York Rd # G
Cleveland, OH 44133-3682
440-237-4600
Fax: 440-582-2759 800-200-4603
info@oilskim.com www.oilskim.com
Waste oil removal
President: Jeff Mann
jeff@oilskim.com
President/CEO: William Townsend
VP: Jim Petrucci
Marketing Director: Mary Petit
CIO/Sales Manager: Rob Fiorilli
Estimated Sales: $2.7 Million
Number Employees: 20-49
Square Footage: 100000

26911 Oil-Dri Corporation of America
410 N Michigan Ave
Suite 400
Chicago, IL 60611
800-233-9802
info@oildri.com www.oildri.com
Developer of products for consumer, industrial and automotive, agricultural, sports fields and fluids purification markets.
President & CEO: Daniel Jaffee
CFO: Susan Kreh
VP, General Counsel: Laura Scheland
COO: Molly Vandenheuvel
Year Founded: 1941
Estimated Sales: $262 Million
Number Employees: 500-999
Brands:
Oil-Dri

26912 Ojeda USA
460 Southport Commerce Blvd
Spartanburg, SC 29306
864-574-6004
Fax: 864-574-6005 www.ojedausa.com
Commercial refrigeration equipment, specializing in novelty freezers and open air display cases
VP: Mark Thompson *Year Founded:* 2005

26913 Ok Kosher Certification
391 Troy Ave
Brooklyn, NY 11213-5322
718-756-7500
Fax: 718-756-7503 info@ok.org
www.ok.org
Consultant specializing in kosher certification services

Owner: Don Levy
rdylevy@ok.org
Chief Customer Relations Officer: Eli Lando
CFO: Thelma Lezy
Manager: Levi Marmulsteyn
R&D: Rikal Fogelman
Director: Chaim Fogelman
Operations Manager: Rikal Fogelman
Estimated Sales: $2.5 - 5 Million
Number Employees: 20-49

26914 Ok Kosher Certification
391 Troy Ave
Brooklyn, NY 11213-5322
718-756-7500
Fax: 718-756-7503 info@ok.org
www.ok.org
Manufacturers and suppliers of Kosher food, wine and utensils
Owner: Don Levy
rdylevy@ok.org
Estimated Sales: $2.5 - 5 Million
Number Employees: 20-49

26915 Ok Uniform Co Inc
253 Church St # B
New York, NY 10013-3438
212-791-9789
Fax: 212-791-9795 866-700-5765
www.okuniform.com
Manufacturer and exporter of uniforms including restaurant wear, formal wear and work/industrial wear; a complete line of anywhere shoes/clogs; full line of tuxedos and formal wear for men and women. We also carry disposable uniformscoveralls, etc
CEO: Ellie Cohen
CFO: Ezra Cohen
Sales Manager: Ivan Cohen
Public Relations: Taimara K
Manager: George Gross
Estimated Sales: $1-2.5 Million
Number Employees: 5-9
Number of Brands: 4
Brands:
Big Ben
Car Hartt
Dickies
Red Kap

26916 Oklabs
921 NW 72nd Street
Oklahoma City, OK 73116-7107
405-843-6832
Fax: 405-843-6832
Laboratory providing microbiological, protein, fat, moisture and salt analysis; consultant specializing in product and process development
President: Walter Seideman
Estimated Sales: $500,000-$1 Million
Number Employees: 5-9

26917 Oklahoma Neon
6550 E Independence Street
Tulsa, OK 74115-7861
918-835-1548
Fax: 918-835-0528 888-707-6366
Awnings, channel letters and architectural, plastic, neon and electric signs; also, service and installation
President: Randy Olmstead
Vice President: Gene Russell
Estimated Sales: $5-10 Million
Number Employees: 50-99

26918 Okura USA Inc
9970 Lakeview Ave
Lenexa, KS 66219-2502
913-599-1111
Fax: 913-599-0096 800-772-1187
www.vanguardshrinkfilms.com
Manufacturer and importer of polyolefin heat shrinkable packaging films
President: John Campbell
john.campbell@okura-usa.com
Sales Manager: Mike Coyle
Sales Manager: Bill Filer
Estimated Sales: $1 - 2.5 Million
Number Employees: 5-9
Square Footage: 50000
Parent Co: Okura Industrial Company

26919 Olam Spices
205 East River Park Pl
Suite 310
Fresno, CA 93720
559-447-1390
USA@olamnet.com
www.olamgroup.com
Edible nuts, cocoa, coffee, cotton and spices and
vegetable ingredients
Co-Founder/Group CEO/Executive Director: Sunny
Verghese
Managing Director/Group CFO: N. Muthukumar
Year Founded: 2002
Estimated Sales: $13.9 Billion
Number Employees: 5,000+
Number of Products: 47
Parent Co: Olam International
Type of Packaging: Bulk
Other Locations:
   USA Head Office
   Fresno CA
   Branch Office
   Buckeye AZ
   Firebaugh CA
   Fresno CA
   HighwayGilroy CA
   Hanford CA
   Healdsburg CA
   Lemoore CA
   Williams CA
   Blakely GA
   Sylvester GA
   Chicago IL
   Willowbrook IL

26920 Olcott Plastics
95 N 17th St
St Charles, IL 60174-1636
630-584-0555
Fax: 630-584-5655 888-313-5277
sales@olcottplastics.com www.olcottplastics.com
Manufacturer, importer and exporter of plastic con-
tainers, jars and jar closures.
President: Joe Brodner
joe.brodner@olcottplastics.com
CFO: Mark Herzog
Quality Manager: Perry Norsworthy
Sales Manager: Troy Rusch
Human Resources Director: Sandy Allen
Purchasing: Teresa Casey
Estimated Sales: $12.6 Million
Number Employees: 50-99
Square Footage: 120000
Type of Packaging: Consumer, Private Label, Bulk

26921 Old Dominion Box
190 Norman Court
Des Plaines, IL 60016-2437
847-342-8760
Fax: 847-870-8179
Boxes

26922 (HQ)Old Dominion Box Co Inc
186 Dillard Rd
Madison Heights, VA 24572-2530
434-929-6701
Fax: 434-929-6354 www.olddominionbox.com
Boxes, cartons, containers and packaging machinery
President: Mike Buhler
Sales Engineer: Kurt Franke
Estimated Sales: $50-100 Million
Number Employees: 1-4

26923 Old Dominion Box Company
PO Box 77
Burlington, NC 27216-0077
336-226-4491
Fax: 336-570-1217
Manufacturer and exporter of small paper and set-up
boxes
Estimated Sales: $500,000-$1 Million
Number Employees: 4
Parent Co: Mark IV Industries

26924 Old Dominion Wood Products
800 Craddock St
PO Box 11226
Lynchburg, VA 24501-1700
434-846-3019
Fax: 434-846-1213 800-245-1632
csodwp@att.net www.olddominionwood.net
Manufacturer, importer and exporter of chairs, tray
stands, laminated trash receptacles, booths, tabletops
and table bases
Owner: George R Harris
Customer Service: Sherri Stilwell
Sales Director: Dennis Hunt
IT: Cindi Rice
crice@olddominionwoodproducts.com
Estimated Sales: $3 - 5 Million
Number Employees: 10-19
Number of Products: 1000
Square Footage: 120000

26925 Old English Printing & Label Company
13661 Sandy Malibu Pt
Delray Beach, FL 33446
561-997-9990
Fax: 610-668-7920
Labels and forms; also, printing services available
President: H Brooks
Estimated Sales: $1-2.5 Million
Number Employees: 1-4

26926 Old Mansion Inc
3811 Corporate Rd
PO Box 1839
Petersburg, VA 23805
804-862-9889
800-476-1877
www.oldmansion.com
Quality spices, seasonings, coffee and teas
Sales: Tom Mullen
Number Employees: 20-49
Type of Packaging: Consumer, Food Service, Pri-
vate Label, Bulk

26927 Olde Country Reproductions Inc
145 N Hartley St
York, PA 17401-3334
717-848-1859
Fax: 717-845-7129 800-358-3997
pewtarex@epix.net
Manufacturer and exporter of pewter plates, mugs,
goblets, trays, skillets, platters, bowls, servers, can-
dle sticks, ice coolers, ladles, pans and kettles
President: W Swartz
VP Sales: Chris Kiehl
Manager: Chris Kiehl
ckiehl@pewtarex.com
Estimated Sales: $20 - 50 Million
Number Employees: 20-49
Number of Brands: 2
Number of Products: 2000
Square Footage: 50000
Type of Packaging: Bulk
Brands:
   Pewtarex
   York Pewter

26928 Olde Thompson Inc
3250 Camino Del Sol
Oxnard, CA 93030-8998
805-983-0388
Fax: 805-983-1849 800-827-1565
jshumway@oldethompson.com
www.oldethompson.com
Wood, metal and plastic kitchenware; also, alumi-
num platters and peppermills
VP: Jeff Shumway
Contact: Anne Kerwien
Estimated Sales: $5-10 Million
Number Employees: 100-249
Brands:
   Olde Thompson

26929 Ole Hickory Pits
333 N Main St
Cape Girardeau, MO 63701-7205
573-334-3377
Fax: 573-334-3377 800-223-9667
main@olehickorypits.com
www.olehickorypits.com
Manufacturer and exporter of commercial barbecue
pits
President: David Knight
main@olehickorypits.com
CFO: David Scherer
Sales Coordinator: Margaret Wiggins
Estimated Sales: Below $5 Million
Number Employees: 20-49
Square Footage: 40000
Type of Packaging: Consumer, Food Service, Pri-
vate Label, Bulk
Brands:
   Ole Hickory Pits

26930 Oles De Puerto Rico Inc
350 Calle D
Bayamon, PR 00959-1927
787-786-1700
Fax: 787-740-3222 oles@poque.com
Envelopes and continous forms
President: John R Young
CFO: Moreno
Quality Control: Megiul Medina
General Manager: Raphael Moreno
Director Manufacturing: Roberto Soltero
Plant Manager: Miguel Medina
Estimated Sales: $5 - 10 Million
Number Employees: 1-4
Parent Co: Oles Envelope Corporation

26931 Olive Can Company
1111 Bowes Rd
Elgin, IL 60123
847-468-7474
Fax: 847-468-7695
Manufacturer and exporter of decorative custom tins
and trays
Executive VP/General Manager: Virginia Price
National Sales Manager: Tom Doyle
Trade Show Manager: Carolyn Wisniewski
Number Employees: 125
Square Footage: 288000

26932 Oliver Bentleys
13 W York St
Savannah, GA 31401-3703
912-201-1688
Fax: 877-395-7335 ollieb@oliverbentleys.com
www.oliverbentleys.com
Maker of dog treats.
Contact: Eric Zimmerman
ezimmerman@eastdilsecured.com
Number Employees: 5-9

26933 Oliver Manufacturing Company
17777 Us Highway 50
Rocky Ford, CO 81067
719-254-7813
Fax: 719-254-6371 888-254-7813
contactus@olivermanufacturing.com
www.olivermanufacturing.com
Cleaners (green coffee), graders (automatic and
pneumatic), reclaiming machinery
President/CEO: Brian Burney
Chief Engineer: Shane Pritchard
Director of Sales/ Marketing: Jon Moreland
Sales Director: Thomas Helman
Contact: Scott Blakley
scott.blakley@olivermanufacturing.com
Chief Operating Officer: Joe Pentlicki
Material Control Manager: Jeffrey Fawcett
Estimated Sales: $5-10 Million
Number Employees: 20-49
Square Footage: 60000
Brands:
   Fluid Dryer
   Hi-Cap
   Linear Separator
   Maxi-Cap

26934 Oliver Packaging & Equipment Co.
3236 Wilson Dr NW
Walker, MI 49534
616-356-2950
Fax: 616-233-1132 800-253-3893
oliver-info@oliverquality.com
www.oliverquality.com
Bakery and meal packaging equipment
President/Owner: Chadd Floria

26935 Oliver Products Company
511 6th St NW
Grand Rapids, MI 49504
616-456-5290
Fax: 616-456-5820 www.oliverproducts.com
President: John R Green
CFO: Jim Johnson
R&D: Jack Knodlauch
Quality Control: Loura Keena
Contact: Lisa Miller
lmiller@oliverquality.com
Estimated Sales: $50 - 100 Million
Number Employees: 100-249

26936 Olivina. LLC
4555 Arroyo Road
Livermore, CA 94550
925-455-8710
charles@theolivina.com
www.theolivina.com
Olive oils.
Year Founded: 1881
Estimated Sales: $25 Million
Number Employees: 20

26937 Olmarc Packaging Company
Ste 1100
350 N La Salle Dr
Chicago, IL 60654-5131
708-562-2000
Fax: 708-562-9044
Packaging service
President: Cain Olmarc
VP: Mark Olmarc
CEO: Kenneth Marchetti
Estimated Sales: $20 - 50 Million
Number Employees: 900

26938 Olney Machinery
9057 Dopp Hill Road
PO Box 280
Westernville, NY 13486
315-827-4208
Fax: 315-827-4249 info@olneymachinery.com
www.olneymachinery.com
Manufacturer, importer and exporter of canning and
food packing machinery
President: W Floyd Olney
Secretary and Treasurer: J Olney
Estimated Sales: $2.5-5 Million
Number Employees: 20-49

26939 Olson Wire Products Co
4100 Benson Ave
Baltimore, MD 21227-1487
410-242-7900
Fax: 410-247-4206
randy@olsonwireproducts.com
Racks including bakery, bottle, display, refrigerator
and wire. Also refrigerator shelves and trays
President: Randy Olson
randy@olsonwireproducts.com
Estimated Sales: $20-50 Million
Number Employees: 50-99

26940 Olympia International
4203 Pan American Blvd
P.O. Box 6836
Laredo, TX 78045-7954
956-725-8558
Fax: 956-723-6968 www.olympiaintl.com
Tea and coffee samplers and weighers
President: Sergio Velasquez
sergio@olympiaintl.com
Vice President: Patsy Gonzalez
Estimated Sales: $1-2.5 Million
Number Employees: 10-19

26941 Olympus America Inc
3500 Corporate Pkwy
Center Valley, PA 18034-8229
484-896-5000
Fax: 631-844-5620 800-446-5260
www.olympusamerica.com
Testing and inspection equipment: industrial
videoscopes, fiberscopes and rigid boroscopes,
video cameras, packaging and assembly line
equipment
President: Mark Gumz
CFO: Harryirnob Kawamata
Quality Control: Timothy Sullivan
Contact: Chris Abbott
chris.abbott@olympus.com
Estimated Sales: $1,000,000 - $2,499,999
Number Employees: 50-99

26942 Omaha Fixture Mfg
10320 J St
Omaha, NE 68127-1018
402-331-8692
Fax: 402-593-5716 800-637-2257
Service@OmahaFixture.com
www.omahafixture.com
Store fixtures
Sales Manager: Dan Gould
Catalog Sales Manager: Roger King
Contact: Joel Alperson
alperson.joel@omahafixture.com

Number Employees: 10-19

26943 Omaha Neon Sign Co
1120 N 18th St
Omaha, NE 68102-4192
402-341-6077
Fax: 402-341-7654 800-786-6366
sales@omahaneon.com www.omahaneon.com
Signs including changeable letter, electric, luminous
tube, neon and plastic
President: Samuel J Marchese
Cio/Cto: Sean Cornett
seancornett@omahaneon.com
Estimated Sales: $5-10 Million
Number Employees: 50-99

26944 Omar Awnings & Signs
202 Wesley St
Johnson City, TN 37601-1720
423-282-9180
Fax: 423-282-3970 800-274-6627
info@omarawning.com www.omarawning.org
Commercial awnings
Owner: Susan Snowden
Production Manager: Bobenn Ette
Estimated Sales: $1-2,500,000
Number Employees: 20-49

26945 Omcan Inc.
3115 Pepper Mill Court
Mississauga, ON L5L 4X5
Canada
800-465-0234
Fax: 905-607-0234 sales@omcan.com
www.omcan.com
Manufacturer and importer of food processing ma-
chinery
Estimated Sales: $500,000 - $1 Million
Number Employees: 1-4
Square Footage: 600000

**26946 Omcan Manufacturing &
Distributing Company**
3115 Pepper Mill Court
Mississauga, ON L5L 4X5
Canada
905-607-0234
Fax: 905-828-0897 800-465-0234
sales@omcan.com www.omcan.com
Manufacturer and exporter of butcher knives; per-
sonalized knives available; wholesaler/distributor of
food service equipment and supplies including cut-
ters, slicers, choppers, bowls, vegetable processors,
mixers, etc.; serving the foodservice market
Owner: Tar Nella
General Manager: Tarcisio Nella
Number Employees: 30
Square Footage: 600000

26947 Omega Company
P.O. Box 4047
Stamford, CT 06907-0047
203-359-1660
Fax: 203-359-7700 800-848-4286
www.omega.com
Consultant providing food process, architectural de-
sign and engineering services
Contact: Edward Maahoney
vanzetti@msn.com
Estimated Sales: $1-2.5 Million
Number Employees: 2
Type of Packaging: Bulk

26948 Omega Design Corp
211 Philips Rd
Exton, PA 19341-1336
610-363-6555
Fax: 610-524-7398 800-346-0191
sales1@omegadesign.com
www.omegadesign.com
Manufacturer and exporter of secondary orienters,
desiccant feeders, plastic bottle unscramblers, wrap
around case packers and shrink bundling, tray loading and wrapping equipment; importer of wrap
around case packers and tray loadingand wrapping
equipment
President: Glenn Siegele
gsiegele@omegadesign.com
VP Sales/Marketing Manager: Randy Caspersen
International Sales Manager: Niall McDermott
Food/Beverage Manager: Paul Sherman
Estimated Sales: $10 - 20 Million
Number Employees: 50-99
Square Footage: 90000

26949 Omega Industrial Products Inc
795 N Progress Dr
Saukville, WI 53080-1613
262-284-4184
Fax: 262-284-4199 800-279-6634
omega@omegaindl.com www.omegaindl.com
Manufacturer and exporter of conveyor and wall
guards, handrails and steel safety barriers stairs
President: John Weber
omega@omegaindl.com
CFO: John Weber
Operations Manager: James Pautmann
Number Employees: 10-19
Square Footage: 27000
Brands:
Omega Protective Systems
Quick-Step Stair Systems
Trak-Shield

26950 Omega Industries
1011 Hanley Industrial Ct
St Louis, MO 63144-1907
314-961-1668
Fax: 314-961-8172 omegaiijtm@msn.com
www.omegaindinc.com
Acrylic food bins, oak and plastic bakery racks,
floor and counter bakery bins, vacuum formed trays
and wood, wire and plastic point of purchase dis-
plays
President: Joseph T Mort
Vice President: Linda Mort
Quality Control: Adam Mort
Sales Director: Jackie Williams
Production Manager: Joseph Howard
Plant Manager: Danny Astroth
Estimated Sales: $1-2 Million
Number Employees: 5-9
Square Footage: 50000
Type of Packaging: Consumer, Bulk

26951 Omega Products Inc
6291 Lyters Ln
Harrisburg, PA 17111-4622
717-561-1105
Fax: 717-561-1298 800-633-3401
omega@omegajuicers.com
www.omegajuicers.com
Manufacturer and exporter of fruit and vegetable
juice extractors
President: Rob Boyd
rboyd@omegajuicers.com
VP Sales: James Pascotti
Estimated Sales: $1600000
Number Employees: 10-19
Square Footage: 80000
Brands:
Omega

26952 Omega Thermo Products
205 S Wisconsin Ave
Stratford, WI 54484
715-687-8102
Fax: 715-687-8053 800-470-1126
omega@laser-plate.com
www.omegathermoproducts.com
President: Phillip Kraft
Vice President: Martin Reuter
mreuter@laser-plate.com
Insider Sales Manager: Chuck Knetter
Engineering Manager: Don Hessefort
Plant Manager: Patrick Jenkins
Purchasing Agent: Matt Mackie
Estimated Sales: Below $5 Million
Number Employees: 20-49

26953 Omicron Steel Products Company
11701 Park Lane S
Jamaica, NY 11418-1014
718-805-3400
Fax: 718-805-3401
Manufacturer, importer and exporter of shelving,
worktables, benches, counters, racks, storage cabi-
nets, carts, hand trucks, conveyors, store fixtures,
chairs and stools
Sales Manager: Jerry Czajowski
Estimated Sales: $1 - 5 Million
Number Employees: 6
Parent Co: Omicron Group

26954 Omni Apparel
113 Kingsbridge Dr
Carrollton, GA 30117-5246

770-838-1008
Fax: 770-838-1038 oapparel@bellsouth.com
www.omniapparel.com
Butcher frocks, aprons, sweatshirts, t-shirts, golf
shirts and hats which can be custom embroidered
with your company logo.
Owner: Brenda Horsley
brendahorsley@omniapparel.com
Number Employees: 10-19

26955 Omni Controls Inc
5309 Technology Dr
Tampa, FL 33647-3523

813-971-5001
Fax: 813-960-4779 800-783-6664
sales@omnicontrols.com www.omnicontrols.com
Manufacturer and exporter of pressure, flow, tem-
perature and sanitary transmitters
President: Bryan Nye
zacharyillare@aforesearch.com
Accountant: Dianne Delarenzo
Sales Director: Frank Most
Estimated Sales: $2.5-5 Million
Number Employees: 1-4
Square Footage: 2000
Brands:
Omni Controls

26956 Omni Craft Inc
5640 Feltl Rd
Hopkins, MN 55343-7911

952-988-9944
Fax: 952-938-2035
Manufacturer, exporter and designer of exhibits and
displays
Owner: Mike Rendahl
mrendahl@omnicraft.com
Estimated Sales: Less Than $500,000
Number Employees: 1-4
Square Footage: 120000
Type of Packaging: Consumer, Food Service

26957 Omni Facility Resources
2105 W Belmont Avenue
Chicago, IL 60618-6413

800-905-5061
Fax: 773-248-9791
Plant sanitation services

26958 Omni International
935 Cobb Place Blvd NW # 110
Kennesaw, GA 30144-6802

770-421-0058
Fax: 770-421-0206 800-776-4431
omni@omni-inc.com www.omni-inc.com
Manufacturer and exporter of mechanical shear ho-
mogenizers and dispersers suited for R/D, QA/QC,
content analysis, fat replacement, beverages, dairy,
etc
President: Karl Jahn
omni@omni-inc.com
Vice President: James Partridge
Quality Control: Eric Ruwe
Manufacturing Manager: Pete Tortorelli
Estimated Sales: Below $5 Million
Number Employees: 20-49
Square Footage: 40000
Type of Packaging: Food Service, Private Label
Brands:
Omni-Glh
Omni-Macro
Omni-Mixer
Omni-Th
Omni-Uh
Shear Flow

26959 Omni Lift Inc
1485 S 300 W
Salt Lake City, UT 84115-5137

801-486-3776
Fax: 801-486-3780 omnibelt@aol.com
www.omni-lift.com
Conveyor belts and belt cleaners
Manager: Jim Gillett
omnibelt@aol.com
VP Operations: Jim Gilett
Estimated Sales: $500,000-$1,000,000
Number Employees: 1-4

26960 Omni Metalcraft Corporation
4040 Us Highway 23 N
Alpena, MI 49707

989-358-7000
Fax: 989-358-7020 info@omni.com
www.omni.com
Manufacturer and exporter of skatewheel, belt,
roller, vertical and chain conveyors
Chairman of the Board: Ronald W Winter
VP Sales/Marketing: Paul Diamond
Contact: Leeck Austin
austinl@omni.com
Estimated Sales: $20-50 Million
Number Employees: 50-99
Square Footage: 130000

26961 Omni Technologies Inc
779 Rudolph Way
Greendale, IN 47025-8378

812-539-4144
Fax: 812-539-4437 www.omnitechnologies.com
Packaging machinery, custom compression molded
polyurethane parts and small quantities, runs of in-
jection molded parts
President: Steve Geiser
sgeiser@omnitechnologies.com
Estimated Sales: $4 Million
Number Employees: 50-99

26962 Omnimark Instrument Corporation
1320 S Priest Dr # 4
Tempe, AZ 85281-6959

480-784-2200
Fax: 480-784-4738 800-835-3211
Moisture analyzers
President: Brian Taylor
Contact: Charlene Byers
chbyers@yahoo.com
Estimated Sales: $2.5 - 5 Million
Number Employees: 10-19

26963 Omnion
185 Plain St Rockland
Rockland, MA 02370-0614

781-878-7200
Fax: 781-878-7465 omnion@world.std.com
Manufacturer and exporter of oxidative stability an-
alytical instrumentation for the food industry
President: Frank Mcgovern McGovern
Technical Specialist: Cheryl Porter
Estimated Sales: $1 - 3,000,000
Number Employees: 5-9
Type of Packaging: Bulk

26964 Omnipak Import Enterprises Inc
2916 120th St
Flushing, NY 11354-2506

718-353-3741
Fax: 718-353-3741 800-348-6664
info@omnipakimport.com
www.omnipakimport.com
Coffee, espresso coffee, espresso equipment, spring
water, espresso bar furniture, espresso machine parts
Owner: Gregory Di Mattino
gregory@omnipak.com
CEO: Kathy Tuschetpa
Estimated Sales: $10 - 20 Million
Number Employees: 10-19

26965 Omnitech International
2715 Ashman Street
Midland, MI 48640

989-631-3377
Fax: 989-631-0812 info@omnitechintl.com
www.omnitechintl.com
Manufacturer and exporter of turnkey can and can
end systems for domestic and international installa-
tion
CEO: Lee Rouse
Vice President/Business Manager, Plastic: Phil
Sarnacke
Operations Manager/Controller: Carolyn Owen
Estimated Sales: $5 - 10 Million
Number Employees: 10-19
Square Footage: 24000

26966 Omnitemp Refrigeration
9300 Hall Road
Downey, CA 90241-5309

562-923-9660
Fax: 562-862-7466 800-423-9660
www.omniteaminc.com
Manufacturer and exporter of display cases and heat
recovery and refrigeration equipment
Owner: Don Hyatt
CEO, President: Mr. Haasis
Plant Manager: Jess McKeoun
Estimated Sales: $1 - 5 Million
Number Employees: 50-99
Type of Packaging: Food Service

26967 On Assignment Inc
6230 Jonestown Rd # A
Suite A
Harrisburg, PA 17112-6257

717-545-6530
Fax: 717-652-8914 800-998-3411
harrisburg@labsupport.com
www.onassignment.com
Consulting services
Account Executive: Chris Quevedo
Manager: Craig Miller
craig.miller@onassignment.com
Estimated Sales: Less Than $500,000
Number Employees: 5-9
Parent Co: On Assignment

26968 On Site Gas Systems Inc
35 Budney Rd
Newington, CT 06111-5133

860-667-8888
Fax: 860-667-2222 888-748-3429
info@onsitegas.com www.onsitegas.com
On Site Gas designs and manufactures PSA, mem-
brane and combustion based oxygen and nitrogen
gas generation systems. Applications within the
food industry utilizing food and beverage nitrogen
include that of: beveragemixing/dispensing; coffee
producers/packers; fruit orchards/storage; perishable
transportation; winemakers; and kiln/grain drying.
Snack food packaging.
President/Founder: Frank Hursey
CEO: Guy Hatch
Chief Engineer: Sanh Phan
Vice President Sales: Bob Wolff
PR: Maylin O Conner
Vice President Manufacturing: Sean Haggerty
Number Employees: 20-49

26969 On-Campus Hospitality
P.O. Box 1500
Westbury, NY 11590-0812

516-334-3030
Fax: 516-334-3059 ebm-mail@ebmpubs.com
www.ebmpubs.com
President: Murry Greenwald
Estimated Sales: $10 - 20 Million
Number Employees: 20-49

26970 On-Hand Adhesives
940 Telser Rd
Lake Zurich, IL 60047-6714

847-437-7773
Fax: 847-437-8006 800-323-5158
www.gluguru.com
Hot melt equipment and adhesives for case sealing
and palletizing rebuilding machinery
Owner, President & Secretary: Mike Cooper
Chairman, Treasurer: George Cooper
Vice President: Lin Sliwa
Vice President: Margaret Cooper
Estimated Sales: $2.5 - 5 Million
Number Employees: 10-19
Square Footage: 27600

26971 OnTrack Automation Inc
592 Colby Drive
Waterloo, ON N2V 1A2
Canada

519-886-9090
Fax: 519-886-9306 ontrack@psangelus.com
www.ontrack-inc.com
Manufacturer and exporter of bottling machinery in-
cluding orienters line conveyors, labeling change
parts, feedscrews
President: Ward Flannery
Plant Manager: Ed Gardiner
Purchasing Manager: Daren Ste. Marie
Number Employees: 20-49
Parent Co: Joseph E. Seagram & Sons

26972 Oneida Food Service
200 S Civic Center Dr
Columbus, OH 43215

Fax: 315-361-3745 800-828-7033
FSCustomerService@oneida.com
www.oneida.com
Manufacturer, importer and exporter of stainless
steel and silver plated hollowware and flatware;
also, dinnerware, glassware, crystal and china.
CEO: Scott McDaniel
Year Founded: 1848
Estimated Sales: $100,000,000 - $499,999,999
Number Employees: 1,000-4,999
Number of Brands: 9
Parent Co: Oneida
Brands:
  Buffalo
  Calp
  D.J.
  Noritake
  Oneida
  Rego
  Sant' Andrea
  Schonwald
  Schott

26973 Oneida LTD Silversmiths
163 Kenwood Ave # 181
Oneida, NY 13421-2829
Canada

315-361-3000
Fax: 315-361-3700 888-263-7195
sales@oneida.com www.oneida.com
Distrubutor of tabletop supplies including flatware,
china, glassware and hollowware
Senior VP: Paul E Gebhardt
  paul.gebhardt@oneida.com
Sales Manager: Frank Fan
Number Employees: 5-9
Number of Brands: 15
Number of Products: 8000
Square Footage: 400000
Parent Co: Oneida
Type of Packaging: Food Service
Brands:
  D.J.
  Delco Buffalo
  Oneida
  Rego
  Sant Andrea
  Schonwald
  Schott Zwiesel

26974 (HQ)Onevision Corp
5805 Chandler Ct # A
Westerville, OH 43082-9076

614-794-1144
Fax: 614-794-3366 neil@onevisioncorp.com
www.craftbrewquality.com
Can inspection systems
President: Neil Morris
  neil@onevisioncorp.com
Quality Control: Matt Allaire
Director Sales: Mike Raczynski
Estimated Sales: Below $5 Million
Number Employees: 5-9
Square Footage: 9000
Other Locations:
  OneVision Corp.
  Riverside CA

26975 Onguard Industries LLC
1850 Clark Rd
Havre De Grace, MD 21078-4000

410-272-2000
Fax: 410-272-3346 800-365-2282
sales@onguardindustries.com
www.onguardindustries.com
CEO/Chairman: Douglas Ramer
CEO: Chris Maistros
  cmaistros@onguardindustries.com
Chief Financial Officer: Dennis Wessel
CEO: Chris Maistros
Quality Coordinator: Jim Gorham
VP Operations: Chris Maistros
Number Employees: 100-249

26976 Onguard Industries LLC
1850 Clark Rd
Havre De Grace, MD 21078-4000

410-272-2000
Fax: 410-272-3346 800-304-2282
sales@onguardindustries.com
www.onguardindustries.com
Protective clothing and non-slip boots.
CEO: Chris Maistros
  cmaistros@onguardindustries.com
Number Employees: 100-249

26977 Onset Computer Corp
470 Macarthur Blvd
Bourne, MA 02532-3838

508-743-3100
Fax: 508-759-9100 800-564-4377
sales@onsetcomp.com www.onsetcomp.com
Design and manufacturing of miniature, bat-
tery-powered data loggers
President: Justin Testa
  justin_testa@onsetcomp.com
Product Application Specialist: Herman Gustafson
Estimated Sales: $13 Million
Number Employees: 100-249
Square Footage: 40000

26978 Onsite Sycom Energy Corporation
1010 Wisconsin Avenue NW
Suite 340
Washington, DC 20007-3680

202-625-4126
Fax: 202-625-1067

26979 Ontario Glove and Safety Products
5 Washburn Drive
Kitchener, ON N2R 1S1
Canada

519-886-3590
Fax: 519-886-3597 800-265-4554
sales@ontarioglove.com www.ontarioglove.com
Manufacturer and importer of gloves including
PVC, cotton, latex and neoprene; wholesaler/distrib-
utor and exporter of leather and synthetic aprons
President: John McCarthy
CFO: Randell Moore
Quality Control: Truedy Henric
Number Employees: 10

26980 Ontario Popping Corn Co.
319 Norfolk County Road 60
Walsingham, ON N0E 1X0
Canada

www.ontariopoppingcorn.com
Grower and producer of popping corn kernels.
Owner: Blair Townsend
Year Founded: 1985
Estimated Sales: $6.2 Million
Number Employees: 2-10
Number of Brands: 1
Type of Packaging: Food Service
Brands:
  Marque Uncle Bob's Brand

26981 Op Sec Security
2 Applegate Dr
Trenton, NJ 08691-2342

609-632-0800
Fax: 609-632-0850 www.jdsu.com
Holograms
President: Kenneth Traub
Number Employees: 50-99
Parent Co: JDS Uniphase Corporation

26982 (HQ)Opal Manufacturing Ltd
10 Compass Court
Toronto, ON M1S 5R3
Canada

416-646-5232
Fax: 416-646-5242 rosa@nrttech.com
www.customvendingmachines.com
Manufacturer and exporter of custom vending ma-
chines and refrigerated liquid portion control cream
dispensers
Sales: Brian Simon
Number Employees: 10
Brands:
  Little Squirt
  Opal

26983 Open Date Systems
Georges Mill Rd
Sunapee, NH 3782

603-763-3444
Fax: 603-763-4222 877-673-6328
sales@opendate.com www.opendate.com
Coding systems including hot stamp, thermal trans-
fer and fully and semi-automatic carton; feeding
systems
President/CEO: Thierry Brousse
CFO: Nikki MacLennan
Vice President: Rick Berquist
Marketing/Sales: Don Morong
Contact: James Poitras
  james@opendate.com
Production Manager: Terry Bartlett
Purchasing: Marcia Crawford
Estimated Sales: $3,000,000
Number Employees: 5-9
Square Footage: 6000
Parent Co: Open Date Equipment
Brands:
  Eurocode
  Printmaster
  Sprint
  Thermocode

26984 Opie Brush Company
16400 E Truman Rd
Independence, MO 64050-4161

816-246-6767
Fax: 816-833-8955 800-877-6743
Manufacturer and exporter of custom made and in-
dustrial brushes including flour milling
Marketing: Connie Dulin
General Manager: Connie Dulin
Plant Manager: James Dulin
Estimated Sales: $500,000-$1 Million
Number Employees: 5-9
Number of Brands: 1
Square Footage: 24000

26985 Optek Inc
5229 Cheshire Rd
Galena, OH 43021-9407

740-548-4700
Fax: 740-548-4999 800-533-8400
wtkavage@optek-inc.com www.optek-inc.com
Manufacturer and exporter of volume flow measure-
ment systems for belt conveyors, tablet counting
systems and control systems including moisture,
temperature and fill level
President/CFO: Dr. Marvin E. Monroe
VP: William Kavage
Estimated Sales: Below $5 Million
Number Employees: 1-4
Square Footage: 30000
Brands:
  Check Fill

26986 Optek-Danulat
N118w18748 Bunsen Dr
Germantown, WI 53022-6322

262-437-3600
Fax: 262-437-3699 888-551-4288
info@optek.com www.optek.com
High performance inline photometric analyzers for
industrial liquid and gas processing applications,
and photometric measuring systems for the food,
beverage and dairy industries.
CEO: Juergen Danulat
Vice President: Rik Meyer
  rmeyer@optek.com
Marketing & Sales Communications Manager:
Aleah Schmitz
Number of Products: 50
Square Footage: 27000

26987 Optel Vision
2680 Boul Du Parc Technologique
Quebec, QC G1P 4S6
Canada

418-688-0334
Fax: 418-688-9397 866-688-0334
www.optelvision.com
Packaging line inspection systems. Label inspector,
barcode inspector, date code inspector, blister pack
inspector
President: Louis Roy
CFO: Nancy Houley
Vice President: Jean Lafortune
R&D: Mathew Kowalcyk
Marketing/Public Relations: Jenny Normandeau
Sales Director: Pierre Turcotte

Estimated Sales: Below $5 Million
Number Employees: 40
Square Footage: 12000

26988 **Optex**
13661 Benson Ave
Chino, CA 91710

909-993-5770
Fax: 310-533-5910 800-966-7839
www.optexamerica.com
Manufacturer and exporter of alarm systems and
sensors
President: Robert Blair
VP Marketing/Sales: Jay Kessel
Contact: Norma Armstrong
narmstrong@optexamerica.com
Estimated Sales: $20 - 50 Million
Number Employees: 25-30
Parent Co: Optex
Brands:
Morse
Optex

26989 **Optical Security Group**
1932 Valley View Lane
Dallas, TX 75234

972-247-1288
Fax: 303-534-1010 osllc@sbcglobal.net
Manufactures lenticular products
President: Mark Turange
CEO: Mark Turnage
Contact: Koko Katanjian
kkatanjian@opticalsecurityllc.com
Estimated Sales: $1-5 Million
Number Employees: 50-99

26990 **Optima Corp**
1330 Contract Dr
Green Bay, WI 54304-5681

920-339-2222
Fax: 920-339-2233 www.optima-packaging.com
Filling and packaging machines
President: Tom Seifert
thomas.seifert@optima-usa.com
Marketing Director: Cathy Hendricks
Estimated Sales: $5 - 10 Million
Number Employees: 50-99
Parent Co: Optima Packaging Group

26991 **Optima International**
10601 Jefferson Chemical Rd
Conroe, TX 77301

936-441-1333
Fax: 936-760-1141
info@optima-international.co.uk
www.optima-international.com
President: Simon Spiller
Quality Control: Christie Coites
Number Employees: 10

26992 **Optimal Automatics**
120 Stanley St
Elk Grove Village, IL 60007

847-439-9110
Fax: 847-439-9115 www.autodoner.com
Vertical broiler manufacturer
President/Owner: John Georgis

26993 **Optipure**
2605 Technology Drive
Bldg 300
Plano, TX 75074

972-422-1212
Fax: 972-422-6262 www.procamcontrols.com
Water filters and water filtration equipment; full line
of filtration products for foodservice applications
(ice machines, steam equipment, coffee./tea,
espresso, balers, fountain, beverages).
Owner: Roy Sebert
Director Sales/Marketing: Keefe Aldstadt
Contact: Keese Aldstadt
keefe@filterxpress.com
Estimated Sales: $2.5-5 Million
Number Employees: 10-19
Number of Brands: 1
Number of Products: 50+
Parent Co: Procam Controls Inc
Type of Packaging: Consumer, Food Service, Private Label, Bulk
Brands:
Opti Pure

26994 **Oracle Hospitality**
500 Oracle Pkw
Redwood, CA 94065

650-506-7000
800-392-2999
www.oracle.com/industries/hospitality
Manufacturer and exporter of management system
software for hospitality, food and beverage, table
seating for hotels, motels, casinos and other leisure
and entertainment businesses.
Chairman & Chief Technology Officer: Lawrence
Ellison
Vice Chairman: Jeffrey Henley
Chief Executive Officer: Safra Catz
Chief Corporate Architect: Edward Screven
Year Founded: 1977
Estimated Sales: $39.50 Billion
Number Employees: 136,000
Parent Co: Oracle Corporation
Type of Packaging: Food Service
Other Locations:
Micros Systems/Fidelio Softwa
Elk Grove Village IL
Brands:
Fidelio
Micros

26995 **Oracle Packaging**
220 Polo Rd
Winston Salem, NC 27105-3441

336-777-5000
Fax: 336-777-5440 800-952-9536
Folding cartons for the dairy industry
President: Ted McLaren
CEO: Scott Dickman
scottdickman@oraclepkg.com
Plant Manager: Berkley Cooke
VP: Lou Carozza
Estimated Sales: $10-20 Million
Number Employees: 250-499
Square Footage: 110000

26996 **Orange Plastics**
1825 S Acacia Ave
Compton, CA 90220

310-609-2121
Stretch film, pallet wrap and produce and grocery
bags
National Sales Manager: Michael Kopulsky
Estimated Sales: $20-50 Million
Number Employees: 100-249

26997 **Orangex**
104 E 40th Street
New York, NY 10016-1801

212-986-9353
Fax: 212-986-9357 sales@orangex.com
www.orangex.net

26998 **Oration Rubber Stamp Company**
RR 94
Columbus, NJ 8022

908-496-4161
Fax: 908-496-4989
Rubber stamps for food packaging
Customer Representative: Carole Vorhis
Manager: Chris Baier
Parent Co: Cosco

26999 **Orber Manufacturing Co**
1655 Elmwood Ave # 30
Cranston, RI 02910-4933

401-781-0050
Fax: 401-781-7720 800-761-4059
Metal specialties including badges, medals, emblems and key chains
Vice President: Larry Shwartz
Estimated Sales: $1 - 3 Million
Number Employees: 10-19

27000 **Orbis Corp.**
39 Westmore Drive
Rexdale, ON M9V 4Y6
Canada

416-745-6980
Fax: 416-745-1874 800-890-7292
info@orbiscorporation.com
www.orbiscorporation.com
Injection moulding
President: Howard Walton
Sales: Relph Kert
Number Employees: 250-499
Brands:
Norseman

27001 **Orbisphere Laboratories**
3 W Main St
Buford, GA 30518

770-932-1400
Fax: 770-932-1230 gthomas@hachultra.com
Gas analyzers for in-lines process and laboratory use
Contact: John Franklin
fjohn@orbisphere.com
Estimated Sales: $500,000-$1 Million
Number Employees: 1-4

27002 **Orca Inc**
199 Whiting St
New Britain, CT 06051-3146

860-223-4180
Fax: 860-826-1729 www.orca-mfg.com
Manufacturer and exporter of custom caps including
can, glass and screw neck ends
Owner: Brian Melanson
bmelanson@orca-mfg.com
Estimated Sales: $5-10 Million
Number Employees: 50-99
Square Footage: 60000

27003 **Orchard Gold**
1762 Hester Avenue
PO Box 28481
San Jose, CA 95159

408-279-8822
Fax: 209-835-2044
President: Ron Ruscigno
Brands:
Corral Hollow Ranch
Orchard

27004 **Orchem Corporation**
4293 Mulhauser Rd
Fairfield, OH 45014

513-874-9700
Fax: 513-874-3624
craig.feltner@orchemcorp.com
www.orchem.com
Food and beverage cleaning and sanitation.
President: Oscar Robertson
General Manager: Craig Feltner
craig.feltner@orchemcorp.com
Estimated Sales: $5-10 Million
Number Employees: 20-49

27005 **Order-Matic Corporation**
PO Box 25463
Oklahoma City, OK 73125-0463

405-672-1487
Fax: 405-672-5349 800-767-6733
www.ordermatic.com
Electronic restaurant equipment including communication systems and POS systems for fast food and
drive-thru restaurants
President: William B Cunningham
CFO: Dan Webb
Vice President: Greg Cunningham
National Sales Manager: Paul Barron
Contact: Stanley Chandy
chandy@ordermatic.com
Estimated Sales: $20-50 Million
Number Employees: 100-249

27006 **(HQ)Ore-Cal Corp**
634 Crocker St
Los Angeles, CA 90021-1002

213-623-8493
Fax: 213-228-6557 800-827-7474
CustomerService@ore-cal.com www.ore-cal.com
Shrimp, pangasius, mahi mahi, swordfish, calamari,
breaded shrimp, and ready mixed entree dishes such
as; shrimp scampi, seafood gumbo, cioppino, shrimp
pad thai, and shrimp tom kha soup.
President: William Shinbane
Human Resources: Josephine Davif
Controller/Vice President Finance: Mark Feldstein
Vice President: Mark Shinbane
Lab Director: Avito Moniz
Human Resources Compliance & Regulatory:
Wendy Gomez
Manager of National Sales: Shelley Gee
Manufacturing Supervisor: Rick Kanase
Estimated Sales: $10.9 Million
Number Employees: 50-99
Number of Brands: 1
Number of Products: 11+
Square Footage: 240000
Type of Packaging: Consumer, Food Service, Private Label, Bulk

Brands:
Harvest of the Sea

27007 Oreck Manufacturing Co
1400 Salem Rd
Cookeville, TN 38506-6221

504-733-8761
Fax: 504-733-6709 800-989-3535
www.oreck.com
Industrial vacuum cleaners
President: Thomas A Oreck
CEO: David Oreck
CFO: San Eilers
Quality Control: Scott Dessen
Marketing Director: Nancy Willy
Estimated Sales: Less Than $500,000
Number Employees: 1-4
Brands:
Oreck

27008 Oregon Pacific Bottling
93487 Sixes River Road
Sixes, OR 97476-9713

541-332-7307
Fax: 541-332-1603
Bottling,labeling
Number Employees: 10

27009 Orelube Corp
20 Sawgrass Dr
Bellport, NY 11713-1549

631-205-9700
Fax: 631-205-9797 800-645-9124
info@orelube.com www.orelube.com
Manufacturer and exporter of lubricants including
aluminum complex EP grease, chain oil and syn-
thetic grease
Owner: Robert Silverstin
robert@orelube.com
Purchasing Agent: Donna Klempka
Estimated Sales: $5-10 Million
Number Employees: 10-19
Square Footage: 132000
Brands:
Bakesafe 500
Boelube Aerospace
Et-2a
Et-2s
Ht-1001
Ht-500
Ocean 7
Orelube Industrial

27010 Organic Products Co
1963 E Irving Blvd
Irving, TX 75060-4555

972-438-7321
Fax: 972-438-7321 ink@opcompany.com
www.opcompany.com
Marking inks
General Manager: Arthur Botvin
ink@opcompany.com
Estimated Sales: Less Than $500,000
Number Employees: 1-4
Brands:
Opco
Organic Products
Sentry Seal
Torgue Seal

27011 Orics Industries
240 Smith St
Farmingdale, NY 11735

718-461-8613
Fax: 718-461-4719 info@orics.com
www.orics.com
Manufacturer and exporter of tray sealers for vac-
uum gas flush map packaging
Owner: Ori Cohen
Contact: Staci Banta
staci_banta@orics.com
Number Employees: 20-49

27012 Oriental Motor USA Corporation
2580 W 237th Street
Torrance, CA 90505-5217

310-325-0040
Fax: 310-257-0297 800-816-6867
techsupport@orientalmotor.com
www.orientalmotor.com
President: Manatoshi Yamauchi
Contact: Gulay Yildirim
gulayyildirim@moeller.com

Estimated Sales: $20 - 50 Million
Number Employees: 80

27013 Original Lincoln Logs
5 Riverside Dr
PO Box 135
Chestertown, NY 12817

518-494-5500
Fax: 518-494-7495 800-833-2461
info@lincolnlogs.com www.lincolnlogs.com
Wooden pallets, boxes, crates and skids; also, used
and reconditioned pallets and crates
Owner: Andrea Demetriou
andreademetriou@lincolnlogs.com
Plant Manager: Robert Rust
Estimated Sales: $500,000-$1 Million
Number Employees: 50-99
Square Footage: 24000

27014 Original Packaging & Display Company
4161 Beck Avenue
Saint Louis, MO 63116-2632

314-772-7797
Fax: 314-772-7271
Solid and set-up paper boxes
Member: Herbert J Strather
Sales Director: Ken Monschein
General Manager: Ed Taylor
Plant Manager: Mark Nehhans
Purchasing Manager: Todd Brock
Estimated Sales: $300,000-500,000
Number Employees: 20
Type of Packaging: Consumer, Food Service

27015 Original Wood Seating
PO Box 48393
Atlanta, GA 30362

678-966-0406
Fax: 678-894-3886 www.owseating.com
Custom restaurant seating

27016 Orion Packaging SystemsInc
4750 County Road 13 NE
Alexandria, MN 56308-8022

901-888-4170
Fax: 901-365-1071 800-333-6556
sales@orionpackaging.com
www.orionpackaging.com
Manufacturers a wide range of high-quality stretch
wrapping machines for virtually any pallet load of
product unitizing application. Machines ore avail-
able in rotary tower, turntable or orbital ring styles.
Orion equipment features allstructural steel con-
struction, high-efficiency powered prestretch film
delivery with easy threading, and the best warrenty
in the industry
Manager: Glenn Greene
CFO: Marsha Greene
Advertising Manager: Peter Vilardi
Contact: Dennis Alexander
dalexander@orionpackaging.com
Operations Manager: Glenn Greene
Plant Manager: Andre LaVigne
Estimated Sales: Less Than $500,000
Number Employees: 1-4
Number of Brands: 10
Number of Products: 34
Square Footage: 200000
Parent Co: Pro Mach
Other Locations:
Orion
Laval Quebec, Canada

27017 Orion Research
100 Cummings Ctr
Beverly, MA 01915

978-232-6000
www.scientificcomputing.com
Manufacturer and exporter of analytical instruments
for the measurement of sodium, pH chemical species
in solutions and moisture in foods.
Estimated Sales: $100-500 Million
Parent Co: Scientific Computing
Brands:
Orion
Perphect
Ross

27018 Orkin LLC
2170 Piedmont Rd NE
Atlanta, GA 30324-4135

844-512-4777
www.orkin.com

Pest control, fly control, rodent control, bird control,
odor control.
President: Eugene Iarocci
CEO/COO: Glen Rollins
Year Founded: 1901
Estimated Sales: $100-500 Million
Number Employees: 8,000

27019 Orr's Farm Market
Po Box 906
Martinsburg, WV 25402-0906

304-263-1027
Fax: 304-263-1153
dondove@orrsfarmmarket.com
www.orrsfarmmarket.com
Farm market

27020 Ortemp
11889 Creek Hollow Rd
Healdsburg, CA 95448

707-433-4459
Fax: 707-433-4450
Wine industry temperature warning devices

27021 Orthodox Union
11 Broadway # 13
New York, NY 10004-1587

212-563-4000
Fax: 212-564-9058 koegelp@ou.org
World's largest and most respected kosher certifica-
tion, over 400,000 products.
President: Martin Nachimson
nachimsonm@ou.org
CEO: Eli Edelman
Marketing: Phyllis Koegel
Number Employees: 100-249

27022 (HQ)Ortmayer Materials Handling
926 Bedford Ave
Corner Willoughby
Brooklyn, NY 11205-3913

718-875-7995
Fax: 718-875-6385 goldy@ortmayer.com
www.ortmayer.com
Material handling equipment including hand carts,
semi line skids, stock trucks, lockers and shelving,
also distributors of Magline and B&P alum hand
trucks
President: Mendel Gross
mendel@ortmayer.com
Vice President: Noson Schelhter
Estimated Sales: $4 Million
Number Employees: 5-9
Square Footage: 20000

27023 Orwak
10820 Normandale Boulevard
Minneapolis, MN 55437-3112

612-881-9200
Fax: 612-881-8578 800-747-0449
www.orwak.us
Manufacturer and exporter of trash compactors and
recycling balers
Estimated Sales: $500,000-$1 Million
Number Employees: 4
Brands:
Orwak

27024 Osage Food Products Inc
120 W Main St # 200
Washington, MO 63090-2121

636-390-9477
Fax: 636-390-9485 sales@osagefood.com
www.osagefood.com
Osage is a multi-dimensional company supplying ingredients and food products. Our ingredients for
manufacturing. Our packaged goods division supplies national brands and private label products for
food service and retail. Our specialtyproducts division works with manufacturers, marketing residual
ingredients and finished goods that are needed to
sell
President: William Dickinson
Estimated Sales: $2.5 - 5,000,000
Number Employees: 5-9
Type of Packaging: Consumer, Food Service, Private Label, Bulk
Brands:
Central Volky
Oven Gem

27025 Oscartek
361 - 367 Beach Rd
Burlingame, CA 94010
650-342-2400
Fax: 650-342-7400 855-885-2400
www.oscartek.com
Display cases
CEO: Rabih Ballout

27026 Oscartielle Equipment Company
855 Mahler Road
Burlingame, CA 94010-1603
650-827-3510
Fax: 650-827-3511 800-672-2784
Gelato and ice cream displays
President: Rabih S Ballout
rballout@otl-usa.com
Number Employees: 10

27027 Osgood Industries
601 Burbank Rd
Oldsmar, FL 34677-4903
813-855-7337
Fax: 813-855-3068 sales@osgoodinc.com
Fillers and heat sealers for containers
President: Martin Mueller
mmueller@osgoodinc.com
Executive VP: Richard Mueller
Estimated Sales: $20-50 Million
Number Employees: 100-249
Type of Packaging: Food Service, Private Label,
Bulk

27028 Osgood Industries
601 Burbank Rd
Oldsmar, FL 34677-4903
813-855-7337
Fax: 813-855-3068
Manufactureer of trays, containers and packaging
for the dairy and food industries.
President: Martin J Mueller
mmueller@osgoodinc.com
Number Employees: 100-249

27029 Oshikiri Corp of America
10425 Drummond Rd
Philadelphia, PA 19154-3898
215-637-8112
Fax: 215-637-6041 www.oshikiri.com
Bakery mixers, molders and proofers
Estimated Sales: $2.5-5 Million
Number Employees: 20-49

27030 Osram Sylvania
129 Portsmouth Ave
Exeter, NH 03833-2105
603-772-4331
Fax: 603-772-1072 www.sylvania.com
Quartz tubing, sockets, infrared heaters
President: Charles Jerabek
President, Chief Executive Officer: Rick Leaman
Quality Control: Lake Patterson
Manager of Corporate Communications: Anne
Guertin
Plant Manager: Michael Huelsemann
Estimated Sales: $25 - 50 Million
Number Employees: 250-499

27031 Osram Sylvania
100 Endicott St # 1
Danvers, MA 01923
978-777-1900
Fax: 978-750-2152 800-544-4828
communications@sylvania.com
www.sylvania.com
Lamps and ballasts
President: Charles Jerabeck
President, Chief Executive Officer: Rick Leaman
CFO: Martin Goetzeler
Quality Control: Russell Liddle
R&D and Executive Director: John Gustafson
Manager Sales/Marketing: Bob Nigrello
Contact: Debra Barshinger
debra.barshinger@sylvania.com
Number Employees: 10,000
Brands:
Capsylite
Dulux
Lumalux
Metalarc
Octron

27032 Oss Food Plant Sanitation Services
1050 Tower Lane
Bensenville, IL 60106
Fax: 630-521-0092 800-905-5061
www.ossfoodplantsanitation.com
Sanitation cleaning, environmental cleaning, staffing
for maintenance and operation

27033 Ossid Corp
4000 College Rd
PO Drawer 1968
Battleboro, NC 27809-8500
252-446-6177
Fax: 252-442-7694 800-334-8369
sales@ossid.com www.ossid.com
Food packaging equipment.
Owner/President: Bud Lane
Principal/VP Finance: Kim Brewer
VP/General Manager: Ernie Newell
Sales Director: Jason Angel
Number Employees: 50-99
Square Footage: 80000

27034 (HQ)Osterneck Company
Highway 72 E
Lumberton, NC 28358
910-738-2416
Fax: 910-739-2881 800-682-2416
Manufacturer and exporter of plastic bags and wo-
ven polypropylene products
Vice President: Leroy Freeman
Estimated Sales: $1 - 5 Million
Number Employees: 50-99
Square Footage: 400000
Brands:
O-Tex

27035 Ostrem Chemical Co. Ltd
2310-80 Avenue
Edmonton, AB T6P 1N2
Canada
780-440-1911
Fax: 780-440-1241 inquiries@ostrem.com
www.ostrem.com
Industrial cleaning compounds
President: Roar Tungland
CFO: Ben Tungland
Marketing Director: Ken Sagan
Number Employees: 40
Square Footage: 160000
Type of Packaging: Private Label

27036 Ott Packagings
719 Route 522
Selinsgrove, PA 17870-1298
570-374-2811
Fax: 570-374-2891
Set-up boxes
Chairman of the Board: Robert McNeil
Quality Control Manager: Bob Vanhorn
Sales Manager: Steve Stancaco
Contact: Doug Marshall
dmarshall@ottpkg.com
Operations Manager: Wes Craig
Purchasing Mgr: John Clark
Estimated Sales: $5-10 Million
Number Employees: 50-99

27037 Ottenheimer Equipment Company
PO Box 4395
Lutherville Timonium, MD 21094-4395
410-597-9700
Fax: 410-252-7775
Wholesaler/distributor of food service equipment;
serving the food service market; also, consultant for
the design of food facilities
Estimated Sales: $.5 - 1 million
Number Employees: 1-4

27038 Otterbine Barebo Inc
3840 Main Rd E
Emmaus, PA 18049-9598
610-965-6018
Fax: 610-965-6050 800-237-8837
info@otterbine.com www.otterbine.com
Water aeration systems
Owner: Charles Barebo
charliebarebo@otterbine.com
Sales Manager: Charlie Barebo
Estimated Sales: $1 - 3 Million
Number Employees: 20-49

Brands:
Concep2

27039 Otto Braun Bakery Equipment
115 Dingens Street
Buffalo, NY 14206-2304
716-824-1252
Fax: 716-824-6076
Bakery racks, proofers, coaters, frying screens,
doughnut fryers and hand trucks
President: Rudolph Hug
Secretary/Treasurer: Arthur Karneth
Estimated Sales: $1-2.5 Million
Number Employees: 4

27040 Otto Material Handling
14609 Sorrel Ct
Charlotte, NC 28278-8322
704-587-1055
Fax: 704-587-9368 800-942-2758
info@otto-usa.com
Plastic waste containers
President: R Otto
Sales/Marketing Coordinator: Meredith Burris
Estimated Sales: $10-20 Million
Number Employees: 10-19

27041 Ottumwa Tent & Awning Co
635 W 2nd St
P.O. Box 494
Ottumwa, IA 52501-2312
641-682-2257
Fax: 641-682-4357
www.ottumwatentandawning.com
Commercial awnings
President: Jim Cagwin
j.cagwin@kyoutv.com
Estimated Sales: Less Than $500,000
Number Employees: 1-4

27042 Ouachita Machine Works
120 N Hilton St
West Monroe, LA 71291-7499
318-396-1468
Fax: 318-396-1668
Manufacturer and exporter of packaging machinery
including automatic and stretch balers
President: Jimmy Dulaney
jdulaney@omwinc.com
CFO: Jimmy Dulaney
R&D: Don Hudson
Quality Control: Jimmy Dulaney
Estimated Sales: Below $5 Million
Number Employees: 20-49
Parent Co: Ouachita Machine Works

27043 Ouellette Machinery Systems
1761 Chase Dr
Fenton, MO 63026-2037
636-343-7200
Fax: 636-326-0249 800-545-7619
sales@omsinc.net www.omsinc.net
Bulk palletizers and depalletizers; case, drum, pail
palletizers; pallet and container conveyors, pallet
stackers and unstackers, sheet stackers and
unstackers .
President: Joseph Ouellette
sales@omsinc.net
VP Design: Richard Ouellette
Purchasing: Robert Del Pietro
Estimated Sales: $10-20 Million
Number Employees: 20-49
Square Footage: 146460

27044 Our Name is Mud
224 W 29th St
New York, NY 10001-5204
212-244-4711
Fax: 800-972-9982 877-683-7867
www.ournameismud.com
Emphasizing engineering for bulk material handling,
process, bag opening and disposal systems
Owner: Lorrie Veasey
CEO: Kip Veasey
CFO: John Nelsen
Marketing: Victoria Compton-Jorasch
Sales: Jill Bukzin
Public Relations: Victoria Compton-Jorasch
Estimated Sales: $3 - 5 Million
Type of Packaging: Bulk

27045 Outlook Packaging
PO Box 775
Neenah, WI 54957-0775
920-722-1666
Fax: 920-722-0008
Manufacturer, importer and exporter of flexible packaging materials for meat, cheese, candy, frozen food, fish, poultry and other various industrial applications
President: Joe Baksha
Contact: Dennis Grabski
Estimated Sales: $20,000,000 - $49,999,999
Number Employees: 250-499
Square Footage: 83000
Parent Co: Flexible Technology
Type of Packaging: Bulk

27046 Outotec USA Inc
8280 Stayton Dr # M
Suite M
Jessup, MD 20794-9609
301-543-1200
Fax: 301-543-0002 www.outotec.com
Manufacturer and exporter of energy recovery systems including waste incinerators and waste disposal equipment; also, fluidized bed systems and fabrication services available
President & CEO: Pekka Vauramo
Plant Manager: Mark Castle
Purchasing Manager: Joe Malloy
Estimated Sales: $50 Million
Number Employees: 10-19
Number of Brands: 1
Square Footage: 30000
Parent Co: Idaho Energy Partnership

27047 Outside the Lines, Inc
640 Michael Drive
Sonoma, CA 95476
707-933-0687
Consulting for the Wine & Hospitality Industry: executive search, onine sexual harassment prevention training, customer satisfaction surveys, employee satisfaction surveys, training progrm development.
President: Margie Tosch

27048 Outterson, LLC
7747 Woodstone Drive
Cincinnati, OH 45244-2855
513-474-3521
Specializes- brew pubs, wineries and microdistilleries
Estimated Sales: $1.5 Million
Number Employees: 1

27049 Ovalstrapping Inc
120 55th St NE
Fort Payne, AL 35967-8140
256-845-1914
Fax: 256-845-1493 info@ovalstrapping.com
Strapping and strapping machines
Marketing Assistant: Jolie Martin
Sales Exec: Ronnie Berry
Plant Manager: Howard G Owen
Estimated Sales: $5-10 Million
Number Employees: 20-49

27050 Oven Deck Shop
11560 184th Pl
Orland Park, IL 60467-4904
708-478-6032
Fax: 708-849-3186
Baking stones for deck pizza ovens and revolving pizza and bagel ovens
Sales Director: Mike Casey
Manager: Mark Otoole
Estimated Sales: Below $5 Million
Number Employees: 1-4
Number of Brands: 2
Number of Products: 1
Square Footage: 8000
Type of Packaging: Private Label

27051 Ovention
635 South 28th Street
Milwaukee, WI 53215
855-298-6836
connect@oventionovens.com oventionovens.com
Commercial oven manufacturer
Marketing: Jordan Robinson-Delaney
General Manager: Steve Everett

27052 Ovenworks
8300 Austin Avenue
Morton Grove, IL 60053-3209
847-965-3700
Fax: 847-965-8585 800-899-OVEN
www.ovenworkspizza.com
Revolving tray ovens, rotating rack ovens, small specialty oven proofers
Estimated Sales: $10-20 Million
Number Employees: 50-99

27053 (HQ)Overhead Conveyor Co
1330 Hilton Rd
Ferndale, MI 48220-2898
248-547-3800
Fax: 248-547-8344 800-396-2554
www.occ-conveyor.com
Supplier/mfg of material handling (conveyor) systems and (spurgeon) stacking machines for non-ferrous metals
President: Thomas Woodbeck
CEO: M Woodbeck Jr
Marketing & Sales Manager: Catherine Nall
Estimated Sales: $10-30 Million
Number Employees: 50-99
Square Footage: 200000
Parent Co: Spurgeon Company

27054 Overnight Labels Inc
151 W Industry Ct # 15
Deer Park, NY 11729-4600
631-242-4240
Fax: 631-242-4385 800-472-5753
custservice@overnightlabels.com
www.overnightlabels.com
US-based manufacturer specializing in labels, shrink sleeves, and flexible packaging. Multiple award winner, including awards for print and environmental excellence
Co-Owner: Don Earl
Co-Owner: Diane Pannizzo
Number Employees: 50-99
Type of Packaging: Consumer, Food Service, Private Label, Bulk

27055 Owens-Illinois Inc
1 Michael Owens Way
Perrysburg, OH 43551-2999
567-336-5000
glass@o-i.com
www.o-i.com
Manufacturer and exporter of plastic bottles, containers, closures and carriers including HDPE, PVC, PET, LDPE, multilayer and barex
Chairman and Chief Executive Officer: Al Stroucken
CEO: Andres A Lopez
andres.lopez@o-i.com
SVP and CFO: Steve Bramlage
SVP and General Counsel: Jim Baehren
SVP and Chief Administrative Officer: Paul Jarrell
Estimated Sales: Over $1 Billion
Number Employees: 10000+

27056 Oxbo International Corp
100 Bean St
Clear Lake, WI 54005-8400
715-263-2112
Fax: 715-263-3324 800-628-6196
www.oxbocorp.com
Manufacturer and exporter of pea, bean and sweet and seed corn harvesting machinery and vibratory sorting tables
President: Andy Tallobt
Cmo: Doug Aherns
daherns@oxbocorp.com
VP Sales: Andrew Talbott
Inside Sales: Doug Ahrens
Human Resources: Deborah Arcand
Estimated Sales: $10 - 20 Million
Number Employees: 100-249
Square Footage: 220000
Brands:
One Row Trac-Pix
Pixall Big Jack Mark Ii
Pixall Corn Puller
Pixall Cornstalker Db18
Pixall Cornstalker El20
Pixall One-Row Pull-Pix
Pixall Super Jack
Pixall Vst

27057 Oxidyn
3712 Summer Pl
Raleigh, NC 27604-4252
919-790-6767
Fax: 919-790-6768
Custom contract assembling
Owner: Melvin Rogers
Estimated Sales: $500,000-$1 Million
Number Employees: 5-9

27058 Oxoid
Suite 100
Nepean, ON K2G 1E8
Canada
613-226-1318
Fax: 613-226-3728 800-567-8378
webinfo.ca@oxoid.com
A manufacturer and distributor of diagnostic test and control in microbiology
Marketing Director: Brian Kemp
Sales Director: Jeff Crawford
Estimated Sales: $15 Million
Number Employees: 50-100
Parent Co: Oxoid

27059 Oystar North America
523 Raritan Center Parkway
Raritan Center
Edison, NJ 08837
732-343-7600
Fax: 732-343-7601 www.oystar-group.com
Solutions for packaging machines.
President/CEO: Barry Shoulders
VP Finance: Suzanne Zeitler
VP Sales/Marketing: Tom Riggins
VP Manufacturing Operations: Frederick Priester
VP Purchasing: Linda Petersen
Number Employees: 235
Square Footage: 10228

27060 Oyster Bay Pump Works Inc
78 Midland Ave # 1
PO Box 725
Hicksville, NY 11801-1537
516-933-4500
Fax: 516-933-4501 info@obpw.com
www.obpw.com
Manufacturer and exporter of dispensers including single channel, multi-channel and conveyor systems for metering fluids
President: Eyal Angel
eangel@obpw.com
Sales/Marketing: Michael Dedora
Estimated Sales: $5 - 10 Million
Number Employees: 20-49
Square Footage: 40000
Type of Packaging: Consumer, Food Service, Private Label, Bulk

27061 Ozark Tape & Label Co
2061 E Mcdaniel St
Springfield, MO 65802-2926
417-831-1444
Fax: 417-831-1424
Printed pressure sensitive tapes, tags and labels
R&D: Steve Lane
Manager: Steve Lane
Manager: Steve Lane
Production Manager: Steve Lane
Estimated Sales: $1 - 2.5 Million
Number Employees: 10-19
Square Footage: 10000

27062 Ozarka Drinking Water
4718 Mountain Creek Pkwy
Dallas, TX 75236
817-354-9526
www.ozarkawater.com
Bottled water.
Estimated Sales: $20-50 Million
Number Employees: 100-249
Number of Brands: 1
Parent Co: Ozarka Houston Water Company
Brands:
Ozarka

27063 Ozotech Inc
2401 E Oberlin Rd
Yreka, CA 96097-9577
530-842-4189
Fax: 530-842-3238 ozotech@ozotech.com
www.ozotech.biz

Manufactures ozone generators, air preparation and water treatment systems for commercial, industrial and home uses
President: Ken Mouw
  km@ozotech.com
Administration Director: Nancy Mouw
Marketing Director: Kat Hoag
Sales Manager: Steve Christopher
Purchasing Manager: Cari Burke
Number Employees: 20-49
Type of Packaging: Consumer, Private Label

27064 P & A Food Ind Recruiters
188 Liberty Way
Woodbury, NJ 08096-6822
    856-384-4774
  Fax: 856-384-8074 foodrecruit@comcast.net
    www.pandafoodrecruit.com
Executive search firm specializing in permanent selection and placement of executive, managerial and technical personnel in the food industry only
President: Paul Sundstrom
  foodrecruit@comcast.net
VP and Partner: Andrew Sundstrom
Operations Manager: Dieter Sievers
Estimated Sales: Less Than $500,000
Number Employees: 1-4
Parent Co: Winston Franchise Corporation

27065 P & F Machine
301 S Broadway
Turlock, CA 95380-5414
    209-667-2515
  Fax: 209-667-4945 eparker@pfmetals.com
    www.pfmetals.com
Manufacturer and exporter of custom engineered and fabricated food, poultry and wine processing equipment
Contact: Brian Alves
  balves@pfmetals.com
Purchasing Agent: Jim Wells
Estimated Sales: less than $500,000
Number Employees: 50-99

27066 P & L Specialties
1650 Almar Pkwy
Santa Rosa, CA 95403-8253
    707-573-3141
  Fax: 707-573-3140 888-313-7947
sales@pnlspecialties.com www.pnlspecialties.com
Winery equipment
President: Edwin L Barr
  ebarr@pnlspecialties.com
Estimated Sales: $10-20 Million
Number Employees: 20-49

27067 P & L System
819 Pickens Industrial Drive
Suite 5
Marietta, GA 30062-3159
    678-355-9809
  Fax: 678-354-7253 nstyrin@hotmail.com
    www.pandl.co.uk
CEO: Chris Lee
Estimated Sales: Below $5 Million
Number Employees: 6

27068 P M Plastics
627 Capitol Dr
Pewaukee, WI 53072-2514
    262-691-1700
  Fax: 262-691-4405 jkildow@pmplastic.com
    www.pmplastic.com
Molded plastic signs, diplays and packaging products
HR Executive: Rhonda Schmitt
  rschmitt@pmplastic.com
Engineering: John Matejcik
Quality Control: Ryan Ford
Sales: Jeff Kildow
Manager: William E Ford Jr
Plant Manager: William Ford, Jr.
Estimated Sales: $10-20 Million
Number Employees: 100-249

27069 P R Farms Inc
2917 E Shepherd Ave
Clovis, CA 93619-9152
    559-299-0201
  Fax: 559-299-7292 pat@prfarms.com
    www.prfarms.com
President: Pat V Ricchiuti
  pat@prfarms.com
CEO: Pat V Ricchiuti

Estimated Sales: $10-20 Million
Number Employees: 100-249

27070 P&E
108 Marcia Dr
Altamonte Spgs, FL 32714-2913
    407-857-3888
  Fax: 407-857-0900 800-438-0674
Packaging equipment including bag-in-box and cases
Office Manager: Beverly Smith
Estimated Sales: $5-10,000,000
Number Employees: 50-99

27071 P&H Milling Group
1060 Fountain Street North
Cambridge, ON N3E 0A1
Canada
    519-650-6400
  Fax: 519-650-6429 info@dovergrp.com
Baking ingredients and flours
President: Sheila LaLang

27072 P.F. Harris Manufacturing Company
PO Box 1122
Alpharetta, GA 30009
    904-389-5686
  Fax: 904-384-0979 800-637-0317
  info@pfharris.com www.pfharris.com
Manufacturer, importer and exporter of insecticides and pest control devices including roach tablets
General Manager: Franklin Goodman
Contact: Beth Cline
  beth@pfharris.com
Estimated Sales: $300,000-500,000
Number Employees: 4
Square Footage: 24000
Brands:
  Harris Bug Free
  Harris Famous

27073 P.L. Thomas & Company
119 Headquarters Plaza
Morristown, NJ 07960
    973-984-0900
  Fax: 973-984-5666 www.plthomas.com
Supplier of extracts, natural color and flavorings, herbs and probiotics.
President: Paul Flowerman

27074 PAC Equipment Company
PO Box 8
Garfield, NJ 07026-0008
    973-478-1008
  Fax: 973-478-1008
Solid waste equipment, compactors and roll offs
President: Walter Johns
Number Employees: 10

27075 PAL Marking Products
10 Princess Street
Sausalito, CA 94965-2210
    415-332-2596
  Fax: 415-332-2598
Wine industry labelers
Estimated Sales: less than $500,000
Number Employees: 1-4

27076 PAM Fastening Technology Inc
1108 Continental Blvd # A
Charlotte, NC 28273-6485
    704-583-2425
  Fax: 704-394-9339 800-699-2674
Hot-melt adhesives and hot-melt applicators, autofeed system
Owner: Ted Minchew
VP: Edward Minchew
Estimated Sales: $5 - 10 Million
Number Employees: 5-9

27077 PAR Tech Inc
8383 Seneca Tpke
New Hartford, NY 13413
    800-448-6505
    www.partech.com
Manufacturer and exporter of computerized cash registers.
President & CEO: Savneet Singh
CFO: Bryan Menar
VP/General Counsel/Corporate Secretary: Cathy King
VP, Business Development: Chris Byrnes
Chief Human Resources Officer: Darla Haas

Year Founded: 1978
Estimated Sales: $118 Million
Number Employees: 500-999
Type of Packaging: Food Service

27078 PAR Visions Systems Corporation
8375 Seneca Tpke
New Hartford, NY 13413-4957
    703-433-6300
  Fax: 315-768-3838 800-448-6505
    www.parlms.com
X-ray inspection systems
VP: John W Sammon Iii
Estimated Sales: $1 - 5 Million
Number Employees: 10-19

27079 PAR-Kan
2915 W 900 S
Silver Lake, IN 46982-9300
    260-352-2141
  Fax: 260-352-0701 800-291-5487
  info@par-kan.com www.par-kan.com
Manufacturer and exporter of recycled grease containers, lids, screens and caster frames
President: David Caldwell
CFO: Richard Burton
  rburton@par-kan.com
Marketing: Todd Sheets
Sales: Carolyn Montel
Estimated Sales: $10 - 20 Million
Number Employees: 50-99
Brands:
  Par-Kan

27080 PASCO
2600 S Hanley Rd # 450
St Louis, MO 63144-2593
    314-781-2212
  Fax: 314-781-9986 800-489-3300
    pasco@pascosystems.com
    www.pascosystems.com
Manufacturer and exporter of packaging machinery including slipsheet and pallet dispensers and bag, drum, pail and case palletizers
President: Dominic Spitalieri
  spitalierid@pasco-group.com
CFO: Teresa Ovelgoenner
Executive VP: Sandy Elfrink
Sales Manager: Darin Everett
Estimated Sales: $10-20,000,000
Number Employees: 20-49
Square Footage: 50000

27081 PBC
185 Route 17 North
Mahwah, NJ 07430
    201-512-0387
  Fax: 201-512-1459 800-514-2739
brewing@pubbrewing.com www.pubbrewing.com
Stainless steel tanks; importer of beer and wine filters; exporter of microbrew systems
President: Erwin Eibert
CFO: David Generso
VP: Ralph Eibert
Design Engineer: Dino Benvenuto
Estimated Sales: $3.5 Million
Number Employees: 10-19

27082 PBC Manufacturing
185 Route 17 North
Mahwah, NJ 07430-1212
    201-512-0387
  Fax: 201-512-1459 800-514-2739
    www.pubbrewing.com
Wine industry SS vessels, packaging, filtration
Owner: Erwin Eibert
Manager: Mat Swanson
Production Manager: Ralph Eivert
Estimated Sales: $1 - 5 Million
Number Employees: 10-19

27083 PBI Dansensor America
139 Harristown Rd # 102
Glen Rock, NJ 07452-3326
    201-251-6490
  Fax: 201-251-6491 www.pbi-dansensor.com
President: Jim Margiotta
Chief Executive Officer, Managing Direct: Jesper Bilde
Marketing Director: Karsten Kejlhof
Estimated Sales: Below $5 Million
Number Employees: 10-19

27084 PBM Inc
1070 Sandy Hill Rd
Irwin, PA 15642-4747
724-863-0550
Fax: 724-863-3283 800-967-4PBM
info@pbmvalve.com www.pbmvalve.com
Valve manufacturing
CEO: Stuart Zarembo
Controller: Nancy Mayer
Engineering/Manufacturing Manager: Jeff Kerr
Quality Control: Ed Docherty
Marketing/Sales Manager: Jay Giffen
COO: Mark Nahorski
Plant Manager: Mark Nahorski
Purchasing Manager: Phil Kochasic
Estimated Sales: $15 Million
Number Employees: 50-99

27085 PC/Poll Systems
3162 Cedar Crest Rdg
Suite B
Dubuque, IA 52003
563-556-3556
Fax: 563-556-0405 800-670-1736
www.pcpoll.com
Manufacturer and exporter of software providing the ability to connect a PC to a cash register; compatible with all Casio ECR's NCR 2170, 2113, CRS 2000 and 3000 and Samsung 6500; also, provides collection, display, printing, export ofreports, etc
Support: Gary Bishop
Estimated Sales: $2.5-5 Million
Number Employees: 5-9
Square Footage: 2400

27086 PCI Inc
10800 Baur Blvd
St Louis, MO 63132-1629
314-872-9333
Fax: 314-872-9104 800-752-7657
sales@pcistl.com www.pcistl.com
Toilet bowl cleaners and drain openers
President: Stephen Mclaughlin
smclaughlin@pcistl.com
Technology: Scott Kretzer
Estimated Sales: $5-10 Million
Number Employees: 20-49
Square Footage: 84000
Brands:
Acid Free
Brite Bowl
Chief 90
Drain Power
Jet White
Scout 20

27087 PCM Delasco Inc
11940 Brittmoore Park Dr
Houston, TX 77041-7225
713-896-4888
Fax: 713-896-4806 www.pcmusainc.com
Designer and manufacturer in Progressive Cavity, Peristaltic and hose pump and offers solutions for a wide range of applications
President: Bruno Lafont
Estimated Sales: Less than $500,000
Number Employees: 1-4

27088 (HQ)PDC International
1106 Clayton Ln # 521w
Austin, TX 78723-2489
512-302-0194
Fax: 512-302-0476 sales@pdc-corp.com
www.pdceurope.com/
Manufacturer and exporter of heat shrinkable tamper-evident seal and sleeve label machinery.
President: Neal Konstantin
Chief Executive Officer: Anatole Konstantin
VP: Alcyr Coelho
Marketing & Sales Director North America: Alcyr Coelho
Sales Representative: Reid Vail
Purchasing: Paul Strauss
Estimated Sales: $20 - 50 Million
Number Employees: 50-99
Square Footage: 17000
Other Locations:
PDC International Corporation
Austin TX

27089 PDMP
105 Loudoun St SW
Leesburg, VA 20175-2910
703-777-8400
Fax: 703-777-8430 wmt@pdmpinc.com
www.pdmpantiqueprints.com
Contract manufacturer of packaging materials including foam extrusions and molding
President: William Teringo
Estimated Sales: Less Than $500,000
Number Employees: 5-9

27090 PDQ Plastics Inc
7 Hook Rd # T
Bayonne, NJ 07002-5006
201-823-0270
Fax: 201-823-0345 800-447-7141
hartson@pdqplastics.com www.pdqplastics.com
Plastic pallets
President: Barry Nathans
VP/General Manager: Harston Poland
Estimated Sales: $1-2.5 Million
Number Employees: 10-19
Square Footage: 200000

27091 PEAK Technologies, Inc.
10330 Old Columbia Rd
Columbia, MD 21046
410-312-6000
Fax: 410-309-6219 800-926-9212
www.peaktech.com
Systems integrator of automatic identification and data collection equipment and systmes
Contact: Steve Arcidiacono
steve.arcidiacono@peak-ryzex.com
Estimated Sales: $52 Million
Number Employees: 777
Square Footage: 7350
Parent Co: Moore Corporation
Other Locations:
PEAK Technologies-North East
Hasbrouck Heights NJ
PEAK Technologies
Dover NH
PEAK Technologies NYC
New York NY
PEAK Technologies-North Central
Itasca IL
PEAK Technologies-New England
Nashua NH
PEAK Technologies Canada Limited
Mississauga, ON, Canada

27092 PFI Displays Inc
40 Industrial St
PO Box 508
Rittman, OH 44270-1525
330-925-9015
Fax: 330-925-8520 800-925-9075
jtricomi@pfidisplays.com www.pfidisplays.com
Manufacturer and exporter of point of purchase displays, exhibits and store fixtures
President: Anthony R Tricomi
Chairman of the Board: Vincent Tricomi
Vice President of Sales: Jim Tricomi
Estimated Sales: $5 - 10 Million
Number Employees: 20-49
Square Footage: 140000

27093 PFM Packaging MachineryCorporation
1271 Ringwell Drive
Newmarket, ON L3Y 8T9
Canada
905-836-6709
Fax: 905-836-7763 info@pfmnorthamerica.com
www.pfmnorthamerica.com
PFM has over 40 years of experience in manufacturing over 35 different models of flow wrappers - both vertical and horizontal.
President: Elizabeth Fioravanti
Engineering Manager: Mike Borza
Marketing Director: Jackie Pineau
Sales Director: Lana Pratt
Estimated Sales: $4.5 Million
Number Employees: 40
Square Footage: 200000

27094 PHD Inc
9009 Clubridge Dr
Fort Wayne, IN 46809-3000
260-747-6151
Fax: 260-479-2312 800-324-8511
phdinfo@phdinc.com www.phdinc.com

Grippers, cylinders, escapements, slides, rotary actuators, sheet metal clamps
CEO: Harry Neff
CEO: Harry Neff
Estimated Sales: $40 Million+
Number Employees: 100-249

27095 PHF Specialists
P.O. Box 7697
San Jose, CA 95150-7697
408-275-0161
Fax: 408-280-0979 phfspec@pacbell.net
www.phfspec.com
HACCP programs for vegetables, meats, seafood and food service, thermal process design and validation and third party audits
Owner: Pamela Hardt-English
Estimated Sales: Below 1 Million
Number Employees: 1-4

27096 PHI Enterprises
12832 Garden Grove Boulevard
Suite E
Garden Grove, CA 92843-2014
714-537-7858
Fax: 714-537-8228 800-971-9955
phienterprises@aol.com www.phienterprises.com

27097 PIAB Vacuum Conveyors
65 Sharp Street
Hingham, MA 02043-4311
781-792-0003
Fax: 781-337-6864 800-321-7422
info@piab.com www.piab.com
Material handling/processing systems: pneumatic vacuum conveyor
Vice President of Business Development: Ed McGovern
CEO: Donald Spradlin
Contact: Linda Bearce
lbearce@piab.com
Estimated Sales: $10 - 20 Million
Number Employees: 45

27098 PLM Trailer Leasing
5722 S Naylor Rd
Livermore, CA 94551-8300
925-245-0056
Fax: 925-245-0185 877-736-8756
www.plmtrailer.com
President, Chief Executive Officer: Keith Shipp
acapone@plmtrailer.com
CEO: Hugh Fehrenbach
Vice President of Sales: Mark Domzalski
Site Manager: Anthony Capone
acapone@plmtrailer.com
Estimated Sales: $3 - 5 Million
Number Employees: 1-4

27099 PM Chemical Company
5319 Grant Street
San Diego, CA 92110-4010
619-296-0191
Manufacturer and exporter of detergents, soaps and food processing cleaners
President: John Mehren
soapies@pacbell.net
CEO: Bernard Mehren
Estimated Sales: $1-2.5 Million
Number Employees: 5-9
Square Footage: 40000
Brands:
Astro
Pure Chem
Red X
Sofwite

27100 PM Plastics
3970 Parsons Rd
Howell, MI 48855-9617
517-546-9900
Fax: 517-546-7097 800-854-2920
www.pmpnet.com
President: Don Verna
Estimated Sales: $10-20 Million
Number Employees: 50-99

27101 PMC Global Inc.
12243 Branford St.
Sun Valley, CA 91352
818-896-1101
Fax: 818-897-0180 info@pmcglobalinc.com
www.pmcglobalinc.com

Custom cutlery, chemical intermediates and packing services.
Founder/CEO/President: Philip Kamins
   pkamins@pmcglobal.com
EVP/Chief Financial Officer: Thian Cheong
Year Founded: 1974
Estimated Sales: $1.3 Billion
Number Employees: 5000-9999
Type of Packaging: Consumer, Food Service

27102 PME Equipment
230 Route 206
Suite 405
Flanders, NJ 07836
973-927-2700
   Fax: 973-927-4411 www.pmeequipment.com
Representatives
Estimated Sales: $1-2.5 Million
Number Employees: 5-9
Square Footage: 1200

27103 PMI Cartoning Inc
850 Pratt Blvd
Elk Grove Vlg, IL 60007-5117
847-593-0876
   Fax: 847-437-1627 btisma@pmicartoning.com
                    www.pmicartoning.com
Custom designed carton packaging machinery and systems
President: Branko Tisma
   btisma@pmicartoning.com
Vice President of Sales: Tony BLESS
Vice President of Sales: Tony Bless
Estimated Sales: $2.5 - 5 Million
Number Employees: 50-99

27104 PMI Food Equipment Group
701 S Ridge Ave
Troy, OH 45374-0001
937-332-3000
   Fax: 937-332-2852 www.hobartcorp.com
Equipment and systems including ovens, salad bars, electronic weighing, wrapping and labeling systems, etc
President: John McDonough
VP: Ken Kessler
Vice President: Jack Gridley
Research Director of Research: David Sprinkle
Business Development Manager: John Davis
Contact: Jennifer Monnin
   jennifer.monnin@hobartcorp.com
Number Employees: 1,000-4,999
Parent Co: Premark International
Brands:
   Adamatic
   Foster
   Hobart
   Stero
   Tasselli
   Vulcan
   Wolf

27105 PMMI Bookstore
11911 Freedom Drive
Suite 600
Reston, VA 20190
571-612-3200
   Fax: 703-243-8556 888-275-7664
   pmmiwebhelp@PMMI.org www.pmmi.org
Packaging and processing
President and CEO: Charles D. Yuska
Executive Assistant: Corinne G Mulligan
CAE, Vice President, Finance: Craig Silverio
Director, Technical Services: Fred Hayes
Vice President, Market Development: Jorge Izquierdo
Contact: Monjur Alum
   monjur@pmmi.org
Director, Operations: Caroline Abromavage
Number Employees: 20-49

27106 (HQ)POS Pilot Plant Corporation
118 Veterinary Road
Saskatoon, SK S7N 2R4
Canada
306-978-2800
   Fax: 306-975-3766 800-230-2751
                    www.pos.ca

Wide variety of industries served, including food and ingredients, fats and oils, nutraceutical and functional food, cosmetics, cosmeceuticals and fragrances, feeds and biotechnology. Total capability under one roof, including fullsolvent extraction, algae and yeast based biomass extraction,analytical services and custom processing. services supported by in-house analytical,methods, development, logistics, and information research.
President & CEO: D.A. Kelly
VP: Paul Fedec
Manager of Quality: Grace Varga
VP, Operations and Corporate Affairs: Heather Ryan
Public Relations: Marilyn Huber
VP, Operations: Grace Varga
Purchasing: Sandra Bodnar
Number Employees: 87

27107 POSitively Unique
591 Boxford Lane
Columbus, OH 43213-2603
614-755-2469
Fax: 614-575-2578
Windows based POS Systems for the hospitality industry
President: Gary Zomonski
Number Employees: 6

27108 PPC Perfect Packaging Co
26974 Eckel Rd
PO Box 286
Perrysburg, OH 43551-1214
419-874-3167
Fax: 419-874-8044
Manufacturer and exporter of custom wooden boxes for machinery and related equipment and domestic, export and military packaging; also, heated warehousing available
Owner: Anil Sharma
Estimated Sales: Less Than $500,000
Number Employees: 1-4
Square Footage: 28000

27109 PPG Industries Inc
500 Techne Center Dr
Milford, OH 45150-2763
513-576-0360
   Fax: 513-576-3053 www.ppg.com/packaging
Pretreatment chemicals, interior and exterior coatings for the metal packaging industry
President: Michael Horton
Human Resources: Casandra Tembo
Vice President of Research and Developme: Charles Kahle
Vice President of Operations: John Richter
Vice President of Purchasing: Stephen Lampe
Estimated Sales: $20-50 Million
Number Employees: 50-99

27110 PPI
11800 Industriplex Blvd
#9
Baton Rouge, LA 70809-5187
225-330-4602
   Fax: 225-752-1163 sales@podpack.com
                    www.podpack.com
Co-packer for single serve coffee and tea products, includes espresso pods, Cups, Cold Brew One pods, quick serve restaurant pods, OCS coffee and tea pods, and hotel in-room pods. Also offer custom packaging services.
CEO: William Powell
Quality Control: Gary Kennington
Executive VP/Chief Operating Officer: Tom Martin
Customer Service Supervisor: Priscilla Short
Supply Chain Manager: Drew Brown
Estimated Sales: Less Than $500,000
Number Employees: 1-4
Type of Packaging: Food Service, Private Label

27111 PPI Printing Press
3008 Main St
Union Gap, WA 98903-1758
509-453-6130
Fax: 509-453-4159
Manufactures thermoform packaging— blisters, blisterboard and skinboard, clamshells, food trays and printed inserts
Manager: Jim Burde
Estimated Sales: $5-10 Million
Number Employees: 50-99

27112 PPI Technologies Group
1610 Northgate Blvd
Sarasota, FL 34234
941-359-6678
   Fax: 941-359-6804 rcmpp@aol.com
                    www.ppitechnologies.com
Manufacturer and supplier of stand up pouch machinery
President: Stuart Murray
CEO: R Charles Murray
CFO: Karena Thomas
Vice President: Sandra Christensen
Research & Development: Rudi Kleer
Quality Control: Gary Bush
Marketing: Richard Murray
Marketing/Sales: Robert Libera
Contact: Andre Beukes
   abeukes@redi2drinqgroup.com
Operations Manager: Peter Aeberhard
Production Manager: Pete Ceconci
Plant Manager: Sean Reed
Purchasing Manager: Tom Richard
Estimated Sales: $20 Million
Number Employees: 40
Number of Brands: 7
Number of Products: 10
Square Footage: 60000
Parent Co: Profile Packaging Inc - Paksource Group LLC
Type of Packaging: Food Service
Brands:
   Laudenberg
   Nishibe
   Psgjme
   Psglee

27113 PQ Corp
300 Lindenwood Dr
Malvern, PA 19355-1740
610-651-4200
   Fax: 610-651-4504 ed.myszak@pqcorp.com
                    www.pqcorp.com
President: Stanley W Silverman
CEO: George J Biltz
   george.biltz@pqcorp.com
CEO: Michael R Boyce
Number Employees: 1000-4999

27114 PROCON Products
869 Seven Oaks Blvd # 120
Suite 120
Smyrna, TN 37167-6482
615-355-8000
   Fax: 615-355-8001 mail@proconpump.com
                    www.proconpumps.com
Manufacturer and exporter of positive displacement rotary vane pumps
President: Paul Roberts
   proberts@proconpump.com
VP, Sales & Business Development: Jim Kelly
Product Manager: Jeff Kulikowski
Purchasing Agent: Tracy Harris
Estimated Sales: $10-25 Million
Number Employees: 20-49
Parent Co: Standex International
Type of Packaging: Food Service

27115 PROMA Technologies
24 Forge Pkwy
Franklin, MA 02038
508-541-7700
   Fax: 508-541-7777 800-343-6977
Holographic metallized paper
President: Frank Sereno
CFO: Robert Kynoch
Marketing Director: Harry Mann
Estimated Sales: $20 - 50 Million
Number Employees: 1-4
Square Footage: 140000

27116 PSI
1901 S Meyers Rd # 400
Suite 400
Oakbrook Terrace, IL 60181-5260
630-705-9290
   Fax: 800-548-7901 www.psiusa.com
Consultant specializing in nutritional labeling testing, sanitation audits and microbiological and chemical food testing

Cmo: David Albee
  dalbee@periph.net
Executive Vice President: Tom Boogher
Manager: Rodney Ortega
Sales Manager: Sharon Winders
District Manager: John Southerland
Number Employees: 60
Square Footage: 40000
Parent Co: PSI

27117 PSI Preferred Solutions
7819 Broadview Road
Cleveland, OH 44131-6146
  216-642-1200
  Fax: 216-642-1166 800-522-4522
  www.stayflex.com
Fiberglass wall and ceiling paneling, floor and wall
coating materials, paints, enamels and coating, insulated building panels, insulation-floors, ceilings, refrigerated structures and corrosion control
President: John Stahl
Contact: Connie Thompson
  cthompson@blueskysolution.co.uk
Estimated Sales: $500,000-$1 Million
Number Employees: 5-9

27118 PTI Packaging
1055 Saddle Rdg
Portage, WI 53901
  920-623-3566
  Fax: 920-623-5659 800-501-4077
  protech@powerweb.net
Manufacturer and exporter of palletizers, conveyors,
sheet dispensers, pallet dispensers/conveyors and
package accumulators
President: John Wildner
  jwildner@ptipackaging.com
Estimated Sales: $2.5-5,000,000
Number Employees: 1-4

27119 PTR Baler & Compactor Co
2207 E Ontario St
Philadelphia, PA 19134-2615
  267-345-0490
  Fax: 215-533-8907 800-523-3654
  sales@ptrco.com www.ptrco.com
Manufacturer and exporter of vertical recycling
balers and waste compaction systems
President/CEO: Michael Savage
IT: Joseph Bennett
  jbennett@tramrail.com
Estimated Sales: $30 Million
Number Employees: 100-249
Number of Brands: 3
Square Footage: 135000
Parent Co: RJR Enterprises
Brands:
  Trampak

27120 PURA
9848 Glenoaks Boulevard
Sun Valley, CA 91352-1045
  818-768-0451
  Fax: 661-257-6385 800-292-7872
Manufacturer and exporter of ultraviolet and filtra-
tion water treatment products
Vice President: Edwin Roberts
Regional Sales Manager: Brad Hess
Estimated Sales: $1-2.5 Million
Number Employees: 10-19
Square Footage: 320000
Parent Co: Hydrotech
Brands:
  Pura

27121 PURAC America
111 Barclay Blvd
Lincolnshire, IL 60069
  608-752-0449
  Fax: 847-634-1992 pam@purac.com
  www.purac.com
President: Gerrit Vreeman
Contact: Lisette Nanning
  l.nanning@puracaps.com
Estimated Sales: $20 - 50 Million
Number Employees: 20-49

27122 PVI Industries LLC
3209 Galvez Ave
Fort Worth, TX 76111-4509
  817-335-9531
  Fax: 817-332-6742 800-784-8326
  pbothner@pvi.com www.pvi.com
Hot water generation for sanitation and process

President: Craig Adams
CEO: Chris Bollas
  cbollas@pbi.com
CFO: Lynn Meadows
R & D: Frank Myers
Quality Control: John Calland
Sales: Chris Bollas
Number Employees: 20-49

27124 Pa R Systems Inc
707 County Road E W
St Paul, MN 55126-7007
  651-528-5200
  Fax: 651-483-2689 800-464-1320
  info@par.com www.par.com
A leader in the design, construction, installation and
support of large-scale, as well as small and precise,
high-precision robotic and matieral handling equip-
ment and systems.
President: Mark A Wrightsman
CEO: Mark Wrightsman
  mwrightsman@par.com
CFO: Brad Yopp
Research & Development: Albert Sturm
Quality Control: Jenny Conlin
Marketing Director: Karen Knoblock
Sales Director: Brian Behm
Production Manager: Wayne Skiba
Purchasing Manager: Kallie Swartz
Estimated Sales: $80 Million
Number Employees: 100-249
Square Footage: 60000
Brands:
  Cimroc
  Ederer
  Jered
  Mec
  M"Zak
  Nr
  Pr
  Ssi Robotics
  Tr
  Vector
  Xr

27125 Pac Strapping Products
307 National Rd
Exton, PA 19341-2647
  610-363-8805
  Fax: 610-363-7349 800-523-7752
  info@strapsolutions.com www.strapsolutions.com
Plastic strapping and accessories for strapping
President: Edwin A Brownley Jr
CFO: Pete Sylvester
  ps@strapsolutions.com
Estimated Sales: $20 - 50 Million
Number Employees: 20-49

27126 PacTech Engineering
4444 Carver Woods Drive
Cincinnati, OH 45242-5532
  513-792-1090
  Fax: 513-891-4232 www.pactech.com
Engineering consultant specializing in packing sys-
tems including feasibility, conceptual, design, instal-
lation, etc
CEO: Sam Pantano
Business Development Manager: Tina Eckert
Contact: Richard Mckee
  mckee@pactech.com
Estimated Sales: $1 - 5 Million
Number Employees: 20-49
Square Footage: 20000

27127 Pace Labels Inc
104 Twenty Nine Ct
Williamston, SC 29697-9497
  864-840-9511
  Fax: 864-855-3637 800-789-1592
Pressure sensitive labels
Owner: Stuart Pace
  pacepres@aol.com
CEO: W Stuart Pace
Estimated Sales: $1-2.5 Million
Number Employees: 5-9
Square Footage: 40000
Type of Packaging: Consumer, Food Service, Pri-
vate Label, Bulk

27128 Pace Packaging Corp
3 Sperry Rd
Fairfield, NJ 07004-2004
  973-227-1040
  Fax: 973-227-7393 800-867-2726
  sales@pacepackaging.com
  www.pacepackaging.com
Manufacturer and exporter of high speed plastic bot-
tle unscramblers
President/CFO: Kenneth F Regula
Vice President-Sales: Glenn G. Kelley
Quality Control: Mike Regula
Sales Manager: Glenn Kelley
Manager: Sam Jarkas
  jarkas@pacepkg.com
VP Manufacturing: Ken Regula
Estimated Sales: $5 - 10 Million
Number Employees: 20-49
Square Footage: 60
Brands:
  Omni-Line

27129 Pace Products
2764 N.Green Valley Pkwy
Henderson, NV 89014
  702-272-0048
  Fax: 702-272-0668 800-796-2675
  pacecork@msn.com
Special packaging
Owner: Michael Piluso
Estimated Sales: $1-5 Million
Number Employees: 1-4

27130 Pacemaker Packaging Corp
7200 51st Rd
Woodside, NY 11377-7631
  718-458-1188
  Fax: 718-429-2907
Bag closers and fillers
President: Emil Romotzki
  mmromotzki@aol.com
Sales Coordinator: Gene Cignoli
Estimated Sales: $1-2.5 Million
Number Employees: 5-9
Brands:
  Pacemaker
  Unibagger

27131 Pacer Pumps
41 Industrial Cir
Lancaster, PA 17601-5927
  717-656-2161
  Fax: 717-656-0477 800-233-3861
  sales@pacerpumps.com www.pacerpumps.com
Manufacturer and exporter of pumps including
self-priming centrifugal nonmetallic, hand operated
and powered drum
Manager: Glenn Geist
  sales@pacerpumps.com
General Manager: Denzel Stoops
Marketing: Art Foster
Sales: Ron Hock
Manager: Glenn Geist
  sales@pacerpumps.com
Purchasing Manager: Ernie Stoltzfus
Estimated Sales: $5 - 10 Million
Number Employees: 20-49
Square Footage: 144000
Parent Co: Serfilco
Brands:
  Camelot
  Pacer

27132 Pacific Bag
15300 Woodinville Redmond Road NE
Suite A
Woodinville, WA 98072
  425-455-1128
  Fax: 425-455-1886 800-562-2247
  bags@pacificbag.com www.pacificbag.com
Flexible packaging and packaging equipment
CEO: Mark Howley
Estimated Sales: $5-10 Million
Number Employees: 20-49

27133 Pacific Bearing Company
P.O. Box 6980
Rockford, IL 61125-1980
  815-389-5600
  Fax: 815-389-5790 800-962-8979
  marketing@pacific-bearing.com

CEO: Robert Schroeder
President: Glen Michalske
Quality Control: Paul Bertolasi
Contact: Shawn Anderson
shawn.anderson@pacific-bearing.com
Estimated Sales: $10 - 20 Million
Number Employees: 100-249

27134 Pacific Bottleworks Co.
202-9188 Glover Road
Box 490
Fort Langley, BC V1M 2R8
Canada

855-371-1011
info@pbwc.ca www.pbwc.ca
Beverages, including craft soda, iced tea, kombucha,
lemonade, and coffee.
Co-Founder: James Colburn
Controller: Claire Druce
Creative Director: Shayla Colburn
National Sales Director: Reece Keeler
Year Founded: 2004
Estimated Sales: $4.6 Million
Number Employees: 11-50
Number of Brands: 10
Type of Packaging: Food Service
Brands:
Boylan Soda
Brew Dr. Kombucha
Cabana Lemonade
Goodrink Tea
Goodwater
Mash
Organic Spritzer
Powza
Proud Source
Stumptown Coffee

27135 Pacific Coast Container
11010 NE 37th Cir
Suite 110
Vancouver, WA 98682

360-892-3451
Fax: 360-892-4955 www.saxco.com
Wine industry glass containers
Manager: Mark Petays
Estimated Sales: $2.5-5 Million
Number Employees: 10-19

27136 Pacific Expresso
716 Frederick St
Santa Cruz, CA 95062-2205

831-429-1920
Fax: 831-459-0798 888-429-1920
info@pacificespresso.com
www.pacificespresso.com
Artisan Coffees Roasted to Order. Pacific Espresso
has a long standing tradition of excellent customer
service to supplement their high quality coffees, teas
and espresso machines.
President: Tim O'Connor
tim@pacificespresso.com
Operations: Paula Berman
Estimated Sales: $500,000 - $1 Million
Number Employees: 5-9

27137 Pacific Handy Cutter Inc
2968 Randolph Ave
Costa Mesa, CA 92626-4312

714-662-1033
Fax: 714-662-7595 800-229-2233
info@pacifichandycutter.com www.go-phc.com
Tool and blade manufacturer: safety carton cutters,
point blades, and specialized hook knives
President/CEO: Mark Marinovich
Sales: Dave Puglisi
Contact: Joe Garavaglia
joe@pacifichandycutter.com
Estimated Sales: $10-20 Million
Number Employees: 1-4

27138 Pacific Harvest Products
13405 SE 30th Street
Bellevue, WA 98005-4454

425-401-7990
Dry blends, sauces, dressings, bases
Contact: Nicholas Ade
n.ade@pnb.org
Number Employees: 20-49
Type of Packaging: Consumer, Food Service, Private Label, Bulk
Brands:
Firmenich

27139 Pacific Isles Trading
465 Monroe Avenue
Township of Washington, NJ 07676-4928

201-666-8849
Fax: 201-666-6053 jzberkman@aol.com
Gift containers and specialty packaging made of
abaca

27140 Pacific Merchants
149 S Burlington Avenue #507
Los Angeles, CA 90049

818-988-8999
Fax: 818-988-6999 888-207-8999
info@pacificmerchants.com
www.pacificmerchants.com
Hard wood kitchen utensils
Marketing: Bruce Mannis

27141 Pacific Northwest Canned Pear
105 S 18th St # 205
Yakima, WA 98901-2176

815-263-6259
Fax: 509-453-4880 www.eatcannedpears.com
Provides information to retail and foodservice customers about canned pears.
President: B J Thurlby
Business Manager: Ken Severn
Estimated Sales: $1-2.5 Million
Number Employees: 20-49

27142 Pacific Northwest Wire Works
3250 International Pl
Dupont, WA 98327-7707

Fax: 425-656-9090 800-222-7699
Wire shelving for refrigerators, stoves, etc
Manager: James Bennett
Estimated Sales: Below $5 Million
Number Employees: 10-19

27143 Pacific Oasis Enterprise Inc
8413 Secura Way # B
Santa Fe Springs, CA 90670-2297

562-698-9146
Fax: 562-698-9147 800-424-1475
POEUS@PacificOasis.com
Manufacturer, importer and exporter of stainless
steel scouring pads for the cleaning of pans, grills,
ovens, etc.; also, disposables including aprons and
gloves
President: S C Chen
scchen@pacificoasis.com
Quality Control: Nick Sumgsun
General Manager: Daisy Reyes
Manager: Nely Go
Estimated Sales: $2.5 - 5 Million
Number Employees: 1-4

27144 Pacific Ozone Technology
6160 Egret Ct
Benicia, CA 94510-1269

707-747-9600
Fax: 707-747-9209 www.pacificozone.com
Pacific Ozone is the leading manufacturer of advanced disinfection air-cooled ozone generators and
packaged ozone systems for industrial applications
including precision dissolved ozone control, instruments and UL control panelsresponse now service
and over 9,000 installations worldwide.
Director: Brian Johnson
Sales Administration Manager: Michelle McHale
Estimated Sales: $500,000 - $1 Million
Number Employees: 25

27145 Pacific Packaging Machinery
1284 Puerta Del Sol
San Clemente, CA 92673

949-369-2425
Fax: 949-369-2429 sales@pacificpak.com
www.pacificpak.com
Packaging machinery liquid fillers for all industries
Contact: Pete Carpino
information@pacificpak.com
Estimated Sales: $5-10 Million
Number Employees: 20-49

27146 Pacific Packaging Systems
2125 Williams St
San Leandro, CA 94577-3224

510-352-1070
Fax: 510-352-8535 800-272-7774
Wine industry shrink wrap equipment
Estimated Sales: $5 - 10 Million
Number Employees: 5-9

27147 Pacific Paper Box Co
4916 Cecilia St
Cudahy, CA 90201-5994

323-771-7733
Fax: 323-562-0934
Rigid paper and plastic boxes
President: Joseph Erhardt
VP: Craig Harrison
Estimated Sales: $5-10 Million
Number Employees: 20-49
Square Footage: 140000
Parent Co: Pacific Paper Box Company

27148 Pacific Pneumatics
8576 Red Oak Avenue
Rancho Cucamonga, CA 91730-4822

909-481-8300
Fax: 909-481-8308 800-221-0961
sales@pacpneu.com www.pacpneu.com
Chillers, pneumatic and portable conveyors, vacuum
pumps, dryers and material handling equipment
Estimated Sales: $1 - 5 Million
Number Employees: 6

27149 Pacific Press Company
1215 Fee Ana St.
Anaheim, CA 92807

714-525-0630
Fax: 714-525-2664 800-878-8029
sales@pacpress.com www.pacpress.com
Wine industry frame filters
Owner: Sean Duby
Contact: Steve Bender
stevebender@pacpress.com
Estimated Sales: $2.5-5 Million
Number Employees: 20-49

27150 Pacific Process Machinery
2062 Stonefield Lane
Santa Rosa, CA 95403-0951

707-523-4122
Fax: 707-523-4418
Dealer of rebuilt and used centrifuges dryers, evaporators, presses, and other processing equipment
Estimated Sales: $1 - 5 Million

27151 Pacific Process Technology
7370 Cabrillo Avenue
La Jolla, CA 92037-5201

858-551-3298
Fax: 858-459-2362
Filtration and pasteurization systems, separators,
clarifiers, pump feeders/stuffers and cheese processing equipment including grinders and mixers
President: Bill Loy
VP Engineering: John Perlman
VP Marketing: Jeff Campbell

27152 Pacific Refrigerator Company
328 S Mountain View Avenue
San Bernardino, CA 92408-1415

909-381-5669
Fax: 909-888-1203
Manufacturer and exporter of walk-in cooler and
freezers
President: John Gomez
Estimated Sales: Below $5 Million
Number Employees: 10

27153 Pacific Scale Company
16002 SE 106th Ave
P.O. Box 1606
Clackamas, OR 97015

503-657-7500
Fax: 503-657-5561 800-537-1886
psco@pacifier.com www.pacificscale.com
Steel, stainless steel and aluminum platform floor,
livestock and lift truck scales; also, tank mounts and
batching meters
President: Harry Baughn
VP: Joel Offield
Secretary: Lee Offield
Estimated Sales: $2.5-5 Million
Number Employees: 5-9
Square Footage: 14600
Brands:
Lift-N-Weigh
Tuf-N-Low

27154 Pacific Scientific Instrument
481 California St
Grants Pass, OR 97526
541-479-1248
Fax: 541-479-3057 800-866-7889
infogp@hachultra.com
Manufacturer and exporter of instruments for detecting and measuring minute particles
Estimated Sales: $50-100 Million
Number Employees: 100-249
Square Footage: 10000
Brands:
  Hiac Royco

27155 Pacific Sign Construction
12339 Oak Knoll Rd
Poway, CA 92064-5319
858-486-8006
Fax: 858-486-8124 pacsign@pacificsign.com
Manufacturer and exporter of luminous signs
President: Roy Flahive
  flahive@pacificsign.com
Estimated Sales: $500,000-$1 Million
Number Employees: 5-9

27156 Pacific Southwest Container
P.O. Box 3351
Modesto, CA 95353-3351
209-526-0444
Fax: 209-522-8746 800-772-0444
bsmith@teampsc.com www.teampsc.com
Wine industry point of purchase packaging
President/Owner: John Mayol
Executive Vice President of Sales and Ma: Bryan Smith
Contact: Marc Crandall
  mcrandall@teampsc.com
Estimated Sales: $20 - 50 Million
Number Employees: 250-499

27157 Pacific Spice Company Inc.
6430 E Slauson Ave
Commerce, CA 90040-3108
323-726-9190
info@pacificspice.com
www.pacspice.com
Spices and herbs.
President: Gershon Schlussel
Year Founded: 1966
Estimated Sales: 22 Milliom
Number Employees: 100-249
Number of Brands: 1
Square Footage: 150000
Type of Packaging: Consumer, Food Service, Private Label, Bulk
Brands:
  Pacific Natural Spices

27158 Pacific Steam Equipment, Inc.
10648 Painter Ave
Santa Fe Springs, CA 90670
562-906-9292
Fax: 562-906-9223 800-321-4114
sales@pacificsteam.com
Manufacturer and exporter of boilers; distributor of food processing machinery
Owner: David Ken
President: William Shanahan
Vice President: Shin King
Marketing Manager: Simon Lee
Sales Manager: Santiago Kuan
Contact: Dave Kang
  res@pacificsteam.com
Estimated Sales: $2.9 Million
Number Employees: 25
Square Footage: 90000

27159 Pacific Store Designs Inc
11781 Cardinal Cir
Garden Grove, CA 92843-3815
714-636-4440
Fax: 714-636-4442 800-772-5661
psd4cmiller@sbcglobal.net
www.pacificstoredesigns.com
Manufacturer and exporter of retail store fixtures including shelving, general contractor, architectuer and desgin services trade show exhibits and custom woodworking items specializing in small to medium sized convenience, gourmetand health food stores; also, installation services available

President: Chris Miller
Sr. Vice President: James Raynor
Research & Development: Sonia Quintana
Quality Control: Erv Miller
Plant Manager: Ken Kasper
Estimated Sales: Less Than $500,000
Number Employees: 1-4
Square Footage: 13200
Type of Packaging: Private Label

27160 Pacific Tank
17177 Muskrat Ave
Adelanto, CA 92301
760-246-6136
Fax: 760-246-6062 800-449-5838
pactankltd@aol.com
Double wall, fiberglass and storage tanks, food processing equipment and material handling equipment
President: Norvald Farestveit
CFO: Robert Clanton
Estimated Sales: Below $5,000,000
Number Employees: 10-19
Square Footage: 10000

27161 Pack & Process
309 136th Ct E
Bradenton, FL 34212
Fax: 302-658-6928 877-777-8425
Contract packaging for food, ingredients. Horizontal and vertical form-fill, standup pouching, sachet
President: Steven A Ames
Estimated Sales: Less than $500,000
Number Employees: 10

27162 Pack Air Inc
449 S Green Bay Rd
Neenah, WI 54956-2374
920-727-3000
Fax: 920-727-3010 salesis@packairinc.com
www.packairinc.com
Accumulating conveyors
President: Rob Mc Carry
  rob_m@packairinc.com
CEO: Pete Clater
Sales Manager: Rob McCarry
Manager: Ron Mc Carry
Estimated Sales: $10 Million
Number Employees: 50-99

27163 Pack All
3003 W Hirsch St
Melrose Park, IL 60160-1738
708-410-1140
Fax: 708-410-1137 888-806-9800
laurac@pack-all.com www.pack-all.com
Packaging equipment: shrink packaging machinery and tamper evident neck banding
President: Dennis Favale
  dennis@pack-all.com
Office Administrator: Laura Cannata
Estimated Sales: $1 - 3 Million
Number Employees: 5-9

27164 Pack Line Corporation
3026 Phillips Ave
Racine, WI 53403
262-635-6966
Fax: 262-634-0512 800-248-6868
packrite@packrite.com www.packrite.com
Manufacturer, importer and exporter of semi-automatic and automatic fillers and capping, and sealing machinery
Manager: Dave Bornhuepter
CFO: Michael Beilinson
Vice President: Nick Maslovets
Marketing Director: Erica Kosinski
Estimated Sales: $1 Million
Number Employees: 5-9
Square Footage: 8000
Parent Co: Pack Line

27165 Pack Process Equipment
17025 N Scottsdale Rd # 100
Scottsdale, AZ 85255-5887
480-513-7676
Fax: 480-513-7677
Agitators, bag forming machines, bar formers, batch kneaders, blanchers, blenders, brushes, wrapping, foiling, carton machines: closing, filling, forming, handling, sealing, chocolate equipment
Manager: Lisa Smoke
Estimated Sales: $3 - 5 Million
Number Employees: 10-19

27166 Pack Rite Machine Mettler
3026 Phillips Ave
Mt Pleasant, WI 53403-3585
262-635-6966
Fax: 262-634-0521 800-248-6868
packrite@packrite.com www.packrite.com
Manufacturer and exporter of bag closing, and packaging machinery
Manager: Dave Bornhuepter
  dave.bornhuepter@mt.com
General Manager: Dave Bornhuetter
Estimated Sales: $3 - 5 Million
Number Employees: 5-9
Square Footage: 24000
Parent Co: Mettler-Toledo
Brands:
  Pack Rite

27167 Pack Rite Machine Mettler
3026 Phillips Ave
Mt Pleasant, WI 53403-3585
262-635-6966
Fax: 262-634-0521 800-248-6868
packrite@packrite.com www.packrite.com
Manufactures and distributes sealing and handling products including poly sealers, thermo sealers, band sealers, conveyors & accumulating tables.
Marketing Executive/General Manager: Dave Bornhuetter
Manager: Dave Bornhuepter
  dave.bornhuepter@mt.com
Manufacturing Supervisor: Dale Klinkhammer
Number Employees: 5-9
Square Footage: 10410
Parent Co: Mettler-Toledo, Inc

27168 Pack Star
220 S. 5th Ave
City of Industry, CA 91746
626-922-0537
Fax: 626-330-8658
Packaging Machinery and Materials
Estimated Sales: $3 - 5 Million
Number Employees: 5-9

27169 Pack West Machinery
5316 Irwindale Ave # B
Baldwin Park, CA 91706-2034
626-814-4766
Fax: 626-814-1615 www.ratioflo.com
Manufacturer and exporter of packaging machinery including top driven and in-line cappers
Owner: Bill Ellison
Marketing/General Manager: Loren Lauxen
Estimated Sales: $2.5-5,000,000
Number Employees: 20-49

27170 Pack'R North America
1921 W Wilson Street
Suite A171
Batavia, IL 60510-1680
630-761-3104
Fax: 630-761-3105 www.filling-equipment.com
Net weight liquid fillers and software
General Manager: Pierre Guillon
Estimated Sales: $1 - 5 Million
Number Employees: 1-4

27171 Pack-A-Drum
862 Hawksbill Island Dr
Satellite Beach, FL 32937-3850
321-773-1551
Fax: 321-779-3816 800-694-6163
profits@packadrum.com www.pack-a-drum.com
Manufacturer and exporter of manually operated trash compactors/deflators, waste containers and platform carts with free waste management consulting for customers.
President: William E Wagner
  pack-a-drum@cfl.rr.com
CFO: Kelli Wagner
VP Marketing: Erik Wagner
VP Sales: Mark Wagner
Director Customer Service: Kirk Wagner
Estimated Sales: $2 Million
Number Employees: 5-9
Number of Brands: 1
Number of Products: 10
Square Footage: 200000
Brands:
  Pack-A-Drum

27172 Pack-Rite
95 Day Street
Newington, CT 06111-1299

860-953-0120
Fax: 860-953-3354

Wooden boxes; also, packaging services available
Sales Manager: Oleg Ouchakof
Estimated Sales: $1-2.5 Million
Number Employees: 10-19

27173 Package Automation Corporation
53016 Highway 60, Acheson Industrial
Spruce Grove, AB T7X 3L3
Canada

780-962-6265
Fax: 780-962-6215 sales@pacauto.com
www.packageautomation.com

27174 Package Concepts & Materials Inc
1023 Thousand Oaks Blvd
Greenville, SC 29607-5642

864-458-7291
Fax: 864-458-7295 800-424-7264
sales@packageconcepts.com
www.packageconcepts.com
Cook-in casings for meat and poultry processing
President: Peter Bylenga
Estimated Sales: $10 - 20 Million
Number Employees: 50-99
Square Footage: 100000
Type of Packaging: Food Service

27175 Package Containers Inc
777 NE 4th Ave
Canby, OR 97013-2398

503-266-2721
Fax: 503-266-8650 800-266-5806
sales@packagecontainers.com
www.packagecontainers.com
Specialty paper converting. Produce merchandising
paper totes and wire ties. Importer/distributor of
poly products.
President/CEO: Robert Degnan
Director of Operations: John Stupfel
CFO/Controller: Rolland Royce
MW Regional Sales: Mary Pytko
NE Regional Sales: P R Morris
Director of Sales & Marketing: Scott Koppang
Estimated Sales: $10,000,000 - $19,999,999
Number Employees: 50-99
Number of Brands: 6
Number of Products: 5
Square Footage: 80000
Type of Packaging: Food Service, Private Label
Brands:
Adver-Tie
Home Toter
Insta-Tie
Skirt Tie

27176 Package Converting Corp
380 Dwight St
Holyoke, MA 01040-5891

413-533-2992
Fax: 413-533-5201
Flexible packages, vacuum packaging materials,
vacuum packaging equipment, beef, lamb, meat
Estimated Sales: $1-2.5 Million
Number Employees: 50-99

27177 Package Conveyor Co
123 S Main St
Fort Worth, TX 76104-1222

817-332-7195
Fax: 817-334-0855 800-792-1243
wapowers@flash.net
Manufacturer and exporter of conveying equipment
including flat, inclined and floor-to-floor belts
Owner: Jack Powers
pcco@flash.net
President: Doyle Powers
Estimated Sales: $2.5-5 Million
Number Employees: 10-19
Parent Co: W.A. Powers Industries

27178 (HQ)Package Machinery Co Inc
80 Commercial St
Holyoke, MA 01040-4704

413-315-3801
Fax: 413-732-1163
customerservice@packagemachinery.com
www.packagemachinery.com
Manufacturer and exporter of rebuilt packaging and
injection molding equipment; also, parts

President: Katherine E Putnam
kputnam@packagemachinery.com
Marketing Manager: Meg Cook
General Manager: Paul Stiebel
Estimated Sales: $2.5-5 Million
Number Employees: 20-49
Square Footage: 44000
Brands:
Package

27179 Package Nakazawa
16233 Hartsook Street
Encino, CA 91436-1304

818-708-3771
Fax: 818-907-9756
yokuaki@americanaccessusa.com
www.packagenakazawa.com
President: Yokoaki Nazakwa
Sales Contact: Yoko Okuaki
Estimated Sales: $300,000-500,000
Number Employees: 3

27180 Package Products
3126 Preble Avenue
Pittsburgh, PA 15233-1084

412-766-1234
Fax: 412-766-6335
Estimated Sales: $10 - 20 Million
Number Employees: 50-99

27181 Package Service Company of Colorado
1800 NW Vivion Rd
Northmoor, MO 64150-9611

816-891-8300
Fax: 816-891-9032 800-748-7799
Pressure sensitive labels, printed packaging and pro-
motional coupons
Chairman: Jeff Nedblake
Quality Control: Bill Krumrei
R & D: Larry Johnson
Marketing Director: Mike Steczak
VP Sales: Dennis Shannon
Estimated Sales: $20-50 Million
Number Employees: 100-249
Square Footage: 57000

27182 Package Supply Equipment
P.O. Box 19021
Greenville, SC 29602

404-344-8551
Fax: 864-277-0957
Wine industry corks and closures
President: Gary Daniels
CEO: Gary Daniels Sr
Estimated Sales: $50-75 Million
Number Employees: 5-9

27183 Package Systems Corporation
109 Connecticut Mills Avenue
Danielson, CT 06239-1653

860-774-0363
Fax: 860-774-5326 800-522-3548
Pressure sensitive rolls and sheets, labels, label ma-
chinery and grease proof polystyrene inserts for
meats, poultry, etc.; importer of cellophane; exporter
of labels
Sales/Marketing Executive: Charles Pingeton
VP Sales: Randall Duhaime
Estimated Sales: $2.5-5 Million
Number Employees: 20-49
Square Footage: 132000

27184 Packagemasters
52 Sindle Avenue
Little Falls, NJ 07424-1619

973-890-7511
Fax: 973-890-0470
Tea and coffee bags and packaging film supplies,
pouch materials

27185 (HQ)Packaging & Processing Equipment
121 Earl Thompson Road
Ayr, ON N0B 1E0
Canada

519-622-6666
Fax: 519-622-6669
Manufacturer and exporter of new, used, rebuilt and
custom built blister packagers, bottle sorters,
cappers, cartoners, case packers and sealers, cleaners, conveyors, fillers, heat sealers, kettles, labelers,
mixers, palletizerstanks, etc

President: P Wiese
CEO: Peter Weise
Other Locations:
Packaging & Processing Equipm
Windhagen

27186 Packaging Aids Corporation
P.O. Box 9144
San Rafael, CA 94912-9144

415-454-4868
Fax: 415-454-6853 sales@pacaids.com
www.pacaids.com
Manufacturer, importer and exporter of sealing ma-
chinery for meat, produce, poultry and seafood; also,
vacuum chambers and form/fill machinery
President: Serge Berguig
Quality Control: Dana McDaniel
National Sales/Marketing Manager: R Perrone
Sales Manager (Eastern Region): Jerry Henry
Estimated Sales: $5-10 Million
Number Employees: 20-49
Brands:
Audion

27187 Packaging Associates
4 Middlebury Boulevard
Randolph, NJ 07869-1121

973-252-8890
Fax: 973-252-8894 cliffbridge@msn.com
Tamper-evident and CT plastic closures and bottles
including PET, PP and HDPE; also, contract packag-
ing of powders and liquids available
President: Stu Weinshanker
Business Development Manager: Paul Ludgate
Sales Manager: Jim Lawson
Estimated Sales: $3 - 5 Million
Number Employees: 15
Square Footage: 20000
Type of Packaging: Consumer, Food Service, Pri-
vate Label, Bulk

27188 Packaging By Design of Il
1460 Bowes Rd
Elgin, IL 60123-5539

847-741-5600
Fax: 847-741-5666
mike@packaging-by-design.com
www.packaging-by-design.com
Flexographic packaging for the food industry prod-
uct line of which includes roll-stock surface printed
films; roll-stock custom laminations; roll-stock re-
verse printed and laminated, and preformed bags
VP: Charles Graziano
Sales Manager: Michael Graziano
Manager: Steve Madeck
smadeck1207a@aol.com
General Manager: Ira Krakow
Number Employees: 20-49
Type of Packaging: Consumer

27189 Packaging Concept Company
1801 N Kentucky Avenue
Evansville, IN 47711-3853

812-464-2525
Fax: 812-464-8080
Design and development of plastic bottle closure
President: Bruno Zumbuhl
Estimated Sales: Below $5 Million
Number Employees: 10

27190 Packaging Consultants Associated Inc
7820 Airport Hwy
Pennsauken, NJ 08109

856-488-0277
Fax: 856-488-0957 info@thenewpca.com
Packaging equipment, heat seal
President: Joseph R Morgan
CFO: Vincent Giannetti
Estimated Sales: $2.5 - 5 Million
Number Employees: 5-9

27191 (HQ)Packaging Corporation of America
1 N Field Court
Lake Forest, IL 60045

800-456-4725
www.packagingcorp.com
Boxes of all sizes.

Chairman & CEO: Mark Kowlzan
mkowlzan@packagingcorp.com
SVP & Chief Financial Officer: Robert Mundy
EVP, Corrugated Products: Thomas Hassfurther
SVP, Mill Operations: Charles Carter
SVP/General Counsel/Secretary: Kent Pflederer
SVP, Sales & Marketing, Corrugated Prod.: Thomas
W.H. Walton
Estimated Sales: Over $1 Billion
Number Employees: 14,600
Parent Co: Packaging Corporation of America

27192 Packaging Design Corp
101 Shore Dr
Burr Ridge, IL 60527-5887
630-323-1354
Fax: 630-323-2802 info@pack-design.com
www.pack-design.com
Corrugated boxes
President: Scott Jones
sjones@pack-design.com
Vice President: Scott Jones
Sales Director: Benjamin Gercone
Production Manager: Don Hlavac
Estimated Sales: $6 Million
Number Employees: 20-49
Square Footage: 70000

27193 Packaging Distribution Svc
2308 Sunset Rd
Des Moines, IA 50321-1141
515-243-3156
Fax: 515-243-1741 mail@pdspack.com
www.pdspack.com
Wiping cloths
Owner: Bruce Sherman
bsherman@pdspack.com
Number Employees: 20-49

27194 (HQ)Packaging Dynamics
PO Box 5332
Walnut Creek, CA 94596-1332
925-938-2711
Fax: 925-938-2713 dlehm19148@aol.com
Manufacturer, importer and exporter of packaging
machinery including horizontal and vertical
form/fill/seal machinery, liquid fillers and bottling
lines, cartoners, wrappers, bundlers and tea baggers
President: Richard Novak
Engineering Manager: Mike Sanchez
Marketing: Banchez
Sales Manager: Fred Wermuth
Estimated Sales: $2.5-5 Million
Number Employees: 5-9
Square Footage: 20000

27195 Packaging Dynamics
35B Carlough Rd
Bohemia, NY 11716
631-563-4499
Fax: 631-563-4893 dlehm19148@aol.com
www.packagingdynamics.com
Liquid filling and packaging equipment
Owner: Eric Lehmann
Estimated Sales: $2.5-5 Million
Number Employees: 10-19

27196 (HQ)Packaging Dynamics Corp
3900 W 43rd St
Chicago, IL 60632-3421
773-843-8000
Fax: 773-254-8136
Manufacturer and exporter of packaging machinery
including liquid filling
CEO: Patrick T Chambliss
pchambliss@pkdy.com
Vice President of Human Resources: Paul
Christensen
Estimated Sales: $2.5-5 Million
Number Employees: 1000-4999
Square Footage: 40000
Other Locations:
Packaging Dynamics Ltd.
Hartwell GA

27197 Packaging Dynamics International
17153 Industrial Hwy
Caldwell, OH 43724-9779
740-732-5665
Fax: 740-732-7515
laminations@ici-laminating.com
Manufacturer and exporter of aluminum beverage
and can liners, containers for biscuits and sandwich
wrap; also, laminated paper

President: Darin Barton
VP: Gerry Medlin
Estimated Sales: $15 - 20 Million
Number Employees: 50-99
Parent Co: Alupac
Brands:
I-Rap

27198 Packaging Enterprises
12 N. Penn Ave
Rockledge, PA 19046
215-379-1234
Fax: 215-379-1166 800-453-6213
fillers@packagingenterprises.com
www.packagingenterprises.com
Manufacturer and exporter of plastic bags and
pouches
President: Lee Sanford
Contact: Terry Geyer
terry@packagingenterprises.com
Estimated Sales: $1-2.5 Million
Number Employees: 1-4
Square Footage: 72000
Type of Packaging: Private Label, Bulk
Brands:
Sobo

27199 Packaging Enterprises
12 N. Penn ave.
Rockledge, PA 19046
215-379-1234
Fax: 215-379-1166 800-453-6213
fillers@packagingenterprises.com
www.packagingenterprises.com
Manufacturer and exporter of filling machinery for
liquids and viscous food products
President: Terrence Geyer
VP: Timothy Geyer
Contact: Terry Geyer
terry@packagingenterprises.com
Estimated Sales: $2.5-5 Million
Number Employees: 10-19
Number of Products: 15
Square Footage: 13600
Type of Packaging: Private Label
Brands:
Geyer

27200 Packaging Equipment & Conveyors, Inc
52853 County Road 7
Elkhart, IN 46514-9522
574-266-6995
Fax: 574-264-6210
Manufacturer and exporter of liquid and aerosol fill-
ing line equipment; also, modular conveying sys-
tems, bi-directional accumulation tables, flight-bar
sorters, tube taping machines, orienting systems,
de-palletizers, can de-elevatorsand product hoppers
Manager: Dennis Kline
Vice President: Brenda Arbogast
Research & Development: Brad Wegner
Sales Director: Chuck Reed
Operations Manager: Dennis Kline
Estimated Sales: $3 Million
Number Employees: 5-9
Number of Products: 16
Square Footage: 40000
Type of Packaging: Private Label
Brands:
Connect-A-Veyor

27201 Packaging Graphics LLC
60 Delta Dr
Pawtucket, RI 02860-4556
401-725-7700
Fax: 401-727-2700
Blister cards
Manager: Gary Stiffler
Estimated Sales: $20-50 Million
Number Employees: 100-249
Square Footage: 250000

27202 Packaging Group
360 Spinnaker Way
Concord, ON L4K 4W1
Canada
905-761-7040
Fax: 905-761-7266
Supplier of flexible packaging materials. Cello-Foil
Holdings has acquired the company as of September
2005
President: Ted Hue
CFO: Frank Petti

Parent Co: Cello-Foil Holdings, Corp

27203 Packaging Machine Service Company
2260 Lithonia Industrial Boulevard
Suite C
Lithonia, GA 30058-4668
770-482-4808
Fax: 770-482-9371 800-871-4764
pmscom@aol.com
Glueformer, in-line tri-seal closer, autoload end load
cartoner
Estimated Sales: $1-2.5 Million
Number Employees: 10-19

27204 Packaging Machinery
2303 W Fairview Ave
Montgomery, AL 36108-4158
334-265-9211
Fax: 334-265-9218
Manufacturer and exporter of material handling
equipment, designer packaging machinery, convey-
ors, etc
Finance/Treasurer: Bruce Murchison
Estimated Sales: $1-2.5 Million
Number Employees: 5-9
Type of Packaging: Bulk

27205 Packaging Machinery & Equipment
179-181 Watson Ave
West Orange, NJ 7052
973-325-2418
Fax: 973-325-6937 packmach@aol.com
www.packagingmachineryandequipment.com
Manufacturer and exporter of cartoners and machin-
ery including marking, printing, dating and coding;
also, rebuilding of packaging equipment available
President: James Lyle Clark
Secretary: Mary Cameron
Quality Control: Dennis McDermott
Estimated Sales: Below $5 Million
Number Employees: 1-4

27206 Packaging Machinery International
1260 Lunt Avenue
Elk Grove Village, IL 60007-5618
847-640-1512
Fax: 847-640-8732 800-871-4764
www.pmi-intl.com
Manufacturer and exporter of packaging machinery
and equipment including shrink wrappers and
bundlers
President: Branko Vukotic
CFO: Branko Vukotic
VP: Randy Spahr
Estimated Sales: $5 - 10 Million
Number Employees: 20-49
Square Footage: 56000

27207 Packaging Machinery Svc
4217 E Jefferson Ave
Fresno, CA 93725-9707
559-834-4400
Fax: 559-834-4835 877-402-1404
pmsc@bellsouth.net
www.packagingmachineryservices.com
Owner: Doug Bridger
tbri591434@aol.com
Estimated Sales: $1 - 5 Million
Number Employees: 1-4

27208 Packaging Machines International
9511 River St
Schiller Park, IL 60176-1019
847-640-1512
Fax: 847-640-8732 800-871-4764
President: Branko Vukotic
CFO: Randy Swpahr
Estimated Sales: $5 - 10 Million
Number Employees: 10

27209 Packaging Materials Co
6995 Industrial Ave
El Paso, TX 79915-1116
915-772-9012
Fax: 915-779-8751 800-325-4195
dbarron@writeme.com
www.packagingmaterials.com
Pressure sensitive labels including heat seal, dry
gum and bar code

President: Armando Barron
  abarron@packagingmaterials.com
VP: Larry Muther
Estimated Sales: Less Than $500,000
Number Employees: 1-4
Square Footage: 64000

27210 Packaging Materials Inc
62805 Bennett Ave
Cambridge, OH 43725-9490

740-432-6337
Fax: 740-439-4718 800-565-8550
Polyethylene film and bags including shrink, bundle wrap, form-fill-seal, on rolls, etc.; also, six color printing available
President: Ron Funk
CFO: Amanda Johnson
VP Manufacturing: Ron Funk
VP Sales: Bill Funk
VP Production: Ron Funk
Estimated Sales: $5 - 10 Million
Number Employees: 20-49
Type of Packaging: Food Service, Private Label, Bulk

27211 Packaging Partners, Ltd.
951 Thorndale Avenue
Bensenville, IL 60106-1139

630-238-1964
Fax: 630-238-2801
Founder: Grover L. Foote
Sales Representative: Hoyt Diehl
Type of Packaging: Consumer

27212 Packaging Parts & Systems
22831 Avenida Empresa
Rcho Sta Marg, CA 92688

949-888-7221
Fax: 949-888-7112 www.extremepkg.com
Owner: Ray Uttaro
Estimated Sales: $1 - 3 Million
Number Employees: 1-4

27213 (HQ)Packaging Products Corp
6820 Squibb Rd
Mission, KS 66202-3224

913-262-3033
Fax: 913-789-8698
Manufacturer and exporter of printed and converted flexible packaging materials including sheet and roll
President: Jack Joslin
CEO: Laird Dowgray
  dlaird@packagingcorp.com
Sales/Marketing: Laird Dowgray
Sales Manager: Tom Zammit
COO: Jack Joslyn
Billing & Accounts Receivable: Cindy Hansen
Number Employees: 50-99
Square Footage: 74000
Other Locations:
  Packaging Products Corp.
  Rome GA

27214 Packaging Progressions
102 G P Clement Dr
Collegeville, PA 19426-2044

610-489-9096
Fax: 610-489-8394 sales@pacproinc.com
www.pacproinc.com
A full line of stainless steel packaging/processing equipment for the food industry; alignment, centralizer, interleaver, counter stacker
President: Larry Ward
  lward@pacproinc.com
Sales Director: Drew Ward
Estimated Sales: $2.5-5,000,000
Number Employees: 20-49
Type of Packaging: Food Service, Private Label, Bulk

27215 Packaging Service Co Inc
1904 Mykawa Rd
Pearland, TX 77581-3210

281-485-4320
Fax: 281-485-3242 800-826-2949
sales@packserv.com www.packserv.com
Contract packager and exporter of charcoal starter, all-purpose cleaners, lamp oil and household chemicals; private labeling available

President: Gean-Pierre Baizan
  websales@packserv.com
Quality Control: Carl Caldwell
VP/General Manager: Jean-Pierre Baizan
Manager Grocery/Sales: Larry Lubs
Export Manager: George Foster
Plant Manager: Luis Dela Cruz
Estimated Sales: $20-25 Million
Number Employees: 100-249
Square Footage: 150000

27216 Packaging Solutions
11600 Magdalena Avenue
Los Altos Hills, CA 94024-5150

650-917-1022
Fax: 510-791-7606
Trays, cartons, labels, inserts and cold temperature shippers
President: Clayton Bussey
Co-Owner: Jerry Chaine
Estimated Sales: $1-2.5 Million
Number Employees: 5-9

27217 Packaging Specialties Inc
1663 S Armstrong Ave
Fayetteville, AR 72701-7232

479-521-2580
Fax: 479-521-2748 800-247-3446
gmathews@psi-ark.com
Flexographic printing
President: Kaaren Biggs
CEO: Robert Farrell
  rfarrell@psi-ark.com
Estimated Sales: $20-50 Million
Number Employees: 100-249

27218 Packaging Store
1255 Howard St
San Francisco, CA 94103

415-558-8100
Fax: 415-558-0625 www.the-packaging-store.com
Wine industry foam carriers
President: Richard Neill
Contact: Arlen Jenkins
  arlen.jenkins@thepackagingstore.com
Estimated Sales: $1-2.5 Million
Number Employees: 20-49

27219 Packaging Systems Automation
2200 Niagara Ln N
Plymouth, MN 55447

763-473-1032
Fax: 763-473-1204
Continuous motion cartoner, pouch flattener
Owner: Steven Swanlund
Estimated Sales: $20-50 Million
Number Employees: 20-49

27220 (HQ)Packaging Systems Intl
4990 Acoma St
Denver, CO 80216-2030

303-244-9000
Fax: 303-298-1016 www.pkgsys.com
Manufacturer and exporter of bag filling and weighing machinery, portable flexible conveyors, bag openers, stackers, palletizers and material handling machinery
President: Michael Lott
  mlott@pkgsys.com
Chairman of the Board: H Lott
Quality Control: Jenee Jenee
Sr. VP Sales/Marketing: A Guyton
Estimated Sales: $5-10 Million
Number Employees: 20-49
Square Footage: 150000
Parent Co: St. Regis Paper Company

27221 Packaging Technologies
145 Main St
Tuckahoe, NY 10707-2906

914-337-2005
Fax: 914-337-8519 800-532-1501
info@ptiusa.com www.ptiusa.com
Food packaging, filling, sealing equipment and inspection systems, both visual and package integrity systems. Also, leak testing equipment for filled and empty packages, off-line/SPC and 100% on-line systems, vision inspectionequipment for packages and air-borne ultrasonic systems for seal integrity

President and CEO: Tony Stauffer
R & D: Mike Noller
Vice President: Oliver Stauffer
Marketing Director: Sylvia Stauffer
Sales Manager: Jesse Sklar
Manager: Oliver Stauffer
  ostauffer@pti.com
Operations Manager: Heinz Wof
Estimated Sales: $5-10 Million
Number Employees: 20-49

27222 Packaging Technologies
P.O. Box 3848
Davenport, IA 52808-3848

563-391-1100
Fax: 563-391-4951 800-257-5622
sales@packt.com www.ptipacktech.com
Manufacturer and exporter of packaging, food processing and analyzing machinery
President: Barry Shoulders
Marketing: Julie Doty
Sales: Tom Riggins
Contact: Mary Baltzell
  mary.baltzell@packt.com
Estimated Sales: $37 Million
Number Employees: 100-249
Square Footage: 200000
Parent Co: WKA

27223 Packaging Technologies
145 Main St
Tuckahoe, NY 10707-2906

914-337-2005
Fax: 914-337-8519 info@ptiusa.com
www.ptiusa.com
President: Tony Stauffer
Vice President: Oliver Stauffer
Sales Manager: Jesse Sklar
Manager: Oliver Stauffer
  ostauffer@pti.com
Estimated Sales: $10 - 20 Million
Number Employees: 20-49

27224 Packaging and Converting Hotline
809 Central Ave Suite 200
PO Box 1052
Fort Dodge, IA 50501-1052

515-955-1600
Fax: 515-955-1668 800-247-2000
www.packaginghotline.com
Packing supplies
CEO: Gale W McKinney Ii
Estimated Sales: $50 - 100 Million
Number Employees: 100-249

27225 Packexpo.Com
11911 Freedom Drive
Suite 600
Reston, VA 20190

703-243-8555
Fax: 703-243-8556 expo@pmmi.org
www.pmmi.org
President: Charles Yuska
Executive Assistant: Corinne Mulligan
CFO: Marry N Japour
Director, Tradeshow Marketing: Jeannine Gibson
Director, Business Intelligence: Paula Feldman
Senior Director, PR/Communications: Julie Ackerman
Director, Operations: Caroline Abromavage
Vice President, Administration: Katie Bergmann
Number Employees: 20

27226 Packing Material Company
PO Box 252
Southfield, MI 48037

248-489-7000
Fax: 248-489-7009
Manufacurer of boxes, cases, skids, wooden pallets, packaging films and foams used for temperature sensitivity. Also corrugated products, forest products, strapping, plastic fabrication and thermal pak
President: James Foster
VP: Gary Turnbull
VP: Gary Turnbull
General Manager: Jack Smylie
Controller: James Gross
Estimated Sales: $1 - 2.5 Million
Number Employees: 10-19
Number of Products: 11
Type of Packaging: Private Label, Bulk
Brands:
  Thermalpak

27227 Packing Specialties
11350 Kaltz Ave
Warren, MI 48089
586-758-5240
Fax: 586-758-3557 sales@packspec.net
www.packspec.net
Corrugated containers
President: Kurt Tabor
Contact: Brian Bazick
bbazick@packspec.net
Manager: Joe Zehel
Estimated Sales: $5-10 Million
Number Employees: 20-49
Parent Co: Ecorse Packaging Specialties

27228 PacknWood
213 W 35th Street
14th Floor
New York, NY 10001
201-604-3840
Fax: 201-604-3863 contact@packnwood.com
www.packnwood.com
Eco-friendly food service products
CEO: Adam Merran
Number Employees: 11-50

27229 Packotronics
1813 Elmdale Avenue
Glenview, IL 60026-1355
947-487-1281
Ovens, makeup lines, depositors, packaging
President: Roger Hollando

27230 Packrite Packaging
3900 Comanche Drive
Archdale, NC 27263
336-431-1111
Folding boxes
General Manager: Hollis Kelley, Sr.
Estimated Sales: $5-10 Million
Number Employees: 50-99
Square Footage: 150000
Parent Co: Caraustar Industries

27231 Packworld USA
539 S Main St
Nazareth, PA 18064-2728
610-746-2765
Fax: 610-759-1766 sales@packworldusa.com
www.packworldusa.com
Sealing machinery including heatseal presses for
tray lidding and irregular shapes, bag/pouch, rotary
belt, etc
President: Charles H Trillich
kfeyti@packworldusa.com
CFO: Kathy Feyti
VP: Helma Young
Quality Control and R&D: Gabe Munoz
General Manager: Frank Welles
Estimated Sales: Below $5 Million
Number Employees: 10-19
Number of Products: 10

27232 Packworld USA
539 S Main St
Nazareth, PA 18064-2728
610-746-2765
Fax: 610-759-1766 sales@packworldusa.com
www.packworldusa.com
Precision validatable heat sealers for accurate tem-
perature control
President: Charles Trillich
kfeyti@packworldusa.com
Estimated Sales: $5-10 Million
Number Employees: 10-19

27233 Pacmac Inc
1501 S Armstrong Ave
Fayetteville, AR 72701-7230
479-521-0525
Fax: 479-521-2448 800-834-1544
fterminella@pacmac.com www.pacmac.com
Manufacturer and exporter of vertical form/fill/seal
machinery
Administrator: Joe Terminella
Manager: Frank Terminella
terminella@pacmac.com
Estimated Sales: $2.5-5,000,000
Number Employees: 20-49
Square Footage: 200000
Brands:
Ter-A-Zip

27234 Pacmaster by Schleicher
130 Wicker St
Sanford, NC 27330-4265
919-775-7318
Fax: 919-774-8731 800-775-7570
soa@interpath.com www.intimus.com
President: Jack Costelloe
Sales: Kathy Ainsworth
Estimated Sales: $10 - 20 Million
Number Employees: 50-99

27235 Pacmatic Corporation
8325 Green Meadows Drive N
Lewis Center, OH 43035-9451
740-657-8283
Fax: 740-657-8483 800-468-0440
uspacmatic@aol.com
Automatic horizontal bagger from film roll, pallet
stretch wrapper, flowpack wrapping machine
Estimated Sales: $5-10 Million
Number Employees: 10-19

27236 Pacmoore Products
1844 Summer St
Hammond, IN 46320-2236
219-932-2666
Fax: 219-932-3344 866-610-2666
solutions@pacmoore.com www.pacmoore.com
Ingredient processing services
President: Brittany Lewis
britt_cheese@hotmail.com
Corporate Controller: Lee Randall
VP Quality Assurance: Giri Veeramuthu
VP Sales & Marketing: Chris Bekermeier
National Sales Director: Tony Weber
VP Human Resources: Susan Bondy
VP Operations: Scott Reid
VP Engineering: Brent Ness
Estimated Sales: $3.4 Million
Number Employees: 100-249
Type of Packaging: Consumer, Food Service, Pri-
vate Label, Bulk

27237 Paco Label Systems Inc
1 Hombre Dr
Tyler, TX 75707
903-561-2125
Fax: 903-561-3455 800-346-4185
www.pacolabel.com
Labels
Owner: Rowe Anderson
randerson@pacolabel.com
General Manager: Rowe Anderson
Office Manager: Mary June Goodson
Estimated Sales: Below $5 Million
Number Employees: 10-19
Type of Packaging: Bulk

27238 Paco Manufacturing
2120 Addmore Ln
Clarksville, IN 47129-9151
812-283-7963
Fax: 812-283-7992 www.pacomanufacturing.com
Stretch wrap
General Manager/VP: G Morris
Contact: Sue Foulks
mmikes@multisy.com
Estimated Sales: $10-20 Million
Number Employees: 20-49
Square Footage: 70000
Parent Co: Precision Automation Company

27239 Pacosy
8480 Darnley
Mount Royal, QC H4T 1M4
Canada
514-738-4894
Fax: 514-738-8633 contact@pacosy.com
www.pacosy.com
Hand dryers

27240 Pacquet Oneida
1600 Westinghouse Boulevard
Charlotte, NC 28273-6327
973-777-5600
Fax: 973-777-2155 800-631-8388
Laminations for snack food, confectionery, pasta,
bakery and coffee markets
President: Pet Matthais
Number Employees: 200
Parent Co: Butler & Smith
Brands:
Ful-Lok

27241 Pactiv
2023 Encino Vista Street
San Antonio, TX 78259-2431
210-481-3280
Fax: 210-481-3281
Territory Manager: Lawrence Treger
Type of Packaging: Consumer

27242 Pactiv LLC
1900 W Field Ct
Lake Forest, IL 60045
800-476-4300
www.pactiv.com
Manufacturer and exporter of bags, cartons, contain-
ers, film, trays, etc.
Chief Executive Officer: John McGrath
Year Founded: 1965
Estimated Sales: $7.3 Billion
Number Employees: 11,000
Parent Co: Reynolds Group Holdings, LLC

27243 Pacur
3555 Moser St
Oshkosh, WI 54901-1270
920-236-2888
Fax: 920-236-2882
Manufacturer and exporter of packaging materials;
extruder of PET, PP, PETG, CPET, APET, RPET and
recycled materials
President: Ron Johnson
rjohnson@pacur.com
R&D: Tim Wiycha
Director Sales/Marketing: Richard Knapp
Estimated Sales: $20 - 50 Million
Number Employees: 100-249
Square Footage: 80000
Parent Co: Rexham

27244 Paddington Corporation
400 Kelby St
Suite 8
Fort Lee, NJ 07024-2938
201-461-7800
Fax: 201-461-2677 www.paigecompany.com
Storage boxes
Owner: Allan Levine
VP National Accounts: Larry McGinn
VP Sales: Gary Ruvo
Group Brand Manager: Scott Green
Sales Director: Richard Ambler
Brand Manager: John Shavlen
Group Brand Manager: Jaime Friedman
Purchasing Manager: Elaine Griffith
Estimated Sales: $20-50 Million
Number Employees: 1-4
Parent Co: Diageo United Distillers and Vinters

27245 Padinox
489 Brackley Point Road
P.O. Box 20106
Winsloe, PE C1A 9E3
Canada
902-629-1500
Fax: 902-629-1502 800-263-9768
paderno@padinox.ca www.paderno.com
Manufacturer and exporter of stainless steel cook-
ware including pots, pans, gadgets, utensils and
bakeware
President: Jim Casey
VP: Tim Casey
Marketing: Scott Chandler
Production: Ernie Bremman
Number Employees: Oover 200
Brands:
Chaudier
Paderno

27246 Pafra/Veritec
260 Us Highway 46
Fairfield, NJ 07004-2324
973-575-2752
Fax: 973-575-2649 800-357-2372
Hot and cold adhesive equipment, noncontact gun
assemblies, glue detection, bar code verification
Estimated Sales: $1 - 5 Million
Number Employees: 20-49

27247 Page Slotting Saw Co Inc
3820 Lagrange St
Toledo, OH 43612-1425
419-476-7475
Circular blade machine knives, perforators and
slitters for paper, leather and plastic food packaging

President: James Bouldin
General Manager: Bill Gibbons
Estimated Sales: $5-10 Million
Number Employees: 20-49
Square Footage: 16000

27248 Paget Equipment Co
417 E 29th St
Marshfield, WI 54449-5312
715-384-3158
Fax: 715-387-0720 paget@northsidecomp.com
www.pagetequipment.com
Manufacturer and exporter of process control systems, spray dryers, evaporators, tanks, heat exchangers, wet separators, blenders and conveyors
President: James Reigel
jimr@pagetequipment.com
CFO: James Reigel
Quality Control: Steve Desmet
Sales: Richard Wermersen
Project Engineer: Brian Johnson
Estimated Sales: $5 - 10 Million
Number Employees: 50-99
Square Footage: 88000
Parent Co: JBL International

27249 Pagoda Industries Inc
777 Commerce St
Reading, PA 19608-1308
610-678-8096
Fax: 610-678-8036
Industrial detergents and degreasers including floor cleaners and equipment cleaners
Owner: Dave Weaver
VP Sales: Blair Weaver
ppidave@dejazzd.com
Estimated Sales: Below $5 Million
Number Employees: 1-4
Number of Products: 50
Square Footage: 8000

27250 Pak 2000 Inc
189 Governor Wentworth Hwy
Mirror Lake, NH 3853
603-569-3700
Fax: 603-569-5478
World's leading producer of high quality shopping bags and tamper evidence security bags targeting major brands in sectors such as luxury, cosmetics, fashion & retail, fine food and beverage worldwide. We are equipped to provide acomplete service from concept development through to production, logistics and customer support worldwide
Vice President: William B Gram
CEO: Nina Virga
Vice President: William B Gram
Marketing Director: Veronique Aboohe
VP Sales/Marketing: Mary Sieninmer
Estimated Sales: $20-50 Million
Number Employees: 50-99
Number of Products: 56
Parent Co: Asia Pulp and Paper
Brands:
  Cartier
  Chanel
  Estee Lauder
  Guerlain
  Nordstrom
  Tiffany

27251 Pak Technologies
7025 W Marcia Rd
Milwaukee, WI 53223
414-438-8600
Fax: 414-977-1458
Packager and distributer
Owner: Kevin Scheule
Contact: Jim Barringer
jbarringer@paktech.com

27252 Pak-Rapid
1050 Colwell Ln Bldg 4
Conshohocken, PA 19428
610-828-3511
Fax: 610-828-4290 www.pakrapid.com
Vertical and horizontal packaging machinery for vitamins, liquids and powders
Sales: Jim Wallace
Sales: Lisa Crawford
Estimated Sales: $1-2.5 Million
Number Employees: 10-19
Square Footage: 20000

27253 Pak-Sak Industries I
122 S Aspen St
Sparta, MI 49345-1442
616-887-8837
Fax: 616-887-7411 800-748-0431
www.packagingpersonified.com
Plain and printed polyethylene film and plastic bags
Marketing: Dave Rimer
Marketing Manager: Tom Wright
Business Manager: Doug Dolder
IT Executive: Mark Christensen
paksakacct@voyager.net
Estimated Sales: $20 - 50 Million
Number Employees: 100-249
Square Footage: 80000
Parent Co: Maxco

27254 Pak-Sher
2500 N Longview St
Kilgore, TX 75662-6840
903-984-8596
Fax: 903-984-1524 www.paksher.com
Carry out, deli, bakery, seafood and hot food bags, interfolded sheets, drink carriers and sine wave bags; also, custom packaging available
President: John Decker
jdecker@att.eu
VP Sales/Marketing: Tom Croninn
Estimated Sales: $20-50 Million
Number Employees: 100-249

27255 Paket Corporation
9165 S Lake Shore Dr
Chicago, IL 60617
773-221-7300
Fax: 773-221-7316 info@paketcorp.com
www.paketcorp.com
Contract packager of private label items.
President: Mark O'Malley
Vice President Sales: Carvel Massengale
Estimated Sales: $8 - 10 Million
Square Footage: 210000
Type of Packaging: Private Label

27256 Paket Corporation/UniquePack
9165 S. Harbor Avenue
Chicago, IL 60617-4436
773-221-7300
Fax: 773-221-7316 www.paketcorp.com
Packaging service
President: Mark O'Malley
Controller: Stella Diaz
Vice President of Manufacturing: Mike Hintz
Estimated Sales: $3 - 5 Million
Number Employees: 20-49

27257 Pakmark
PO Box 228
Chesterfield, MO 63006-0228
636-532-7877
Fax: 636-532-9634 800-423-1379
pakmark@pakmark.com
Manufacturer and exporter of decorative pressure sensitive labels and tapes; also, hot-stamped and embossed foil
Estimated Sales: $1-2.5 Million
Number Employees: 10-19
Brands:
  Signette

27258 Paktronics Controls
23555 Telegraph Road
Southfield, MI 48033-4129
248-356-1400
Fax: 248-356-0829 info@maxitrol.com
www.maxitrol.com
Manufacturer, importer and exporter of temperature controls
President: David Sundberg
Inside Sales: Toni Thompson
Purchasing Manager: Linda McCleskey
Estimated Sales: $2.5-5 Million
Number Employees: 10
Square Footage: 21600
Parent Co: Maxitrol Company
Brands:
  Beta Series
  Pakstat
  Paktronics
  Trakstat

27259 Palace Packaging Machines Inc
4102 Edges Mill Rd
Downingtown, PA 19335-1954
610-873-7252
Fax: 610-873-7384 palace@unscramblers.com
www.unscramblers.com
Plastic bottle handling and cap/lid feeding systems. Component feeding and counting systems also available for food, beverage, and medical applications
President: Stephen Taraschi
cserve@unscramblers.com
Marketing: Stephen Taraschi
Estimated Sales: $5-10 Million
Number Employees: 20-49
Square Footage: 70000

27260 Paley-Lloyd-Donohue
125 Bayway Ave
Elizabeth, NJ 07202-3006
908-352-5835
Fax: 908-352-8042
Janitorial supplies including cheesecloth and germicidal multi-purpose cleaners
President: Bill Paley
CFO: Bill Paley
VP: Rick Paley
Estimated Sales: $5 - 10 Million
Number Employees: 5-9
Square Footage: 40000
Brands:
  Lemon Kleen 32

27261 Palintest USA
1455 Jamike Ave # 100
Suite 100
Erlanger, KY 41018-3147
859-341-7423
Fax: 859-341-2106 info@palintestusa.com
www.palintest.com
Water testing equipment
Vice President: Ken Kershner
ken.kershner@palintestusa.com
VP: David Miller
VP: David Miller
Estimated Sales: $1-2.5 Million
Number Employees: 10-19
Parent Co: the Halma Group

27262 Pall Corp
25 Harbor Park Dr
Port Washington, NY 11050-4664
516-484-5400
Fax: 516-484-5228 866-905-7255
foodandbeverage@pall.com www.pall.com
the largest and most diverse filtration, separations and purifications company in the world. For the food and beverage industries, Pall has developed filtration and advanced filtration systems that meet market needs for reliability andcost effectiveness.
President/CEO/CFO: Lawrence D. Kingsley
President, Life Sciences: Yves Baratelli
President, Industrial: Ruby Chandy
Vice President, Finance & Treasurer: R. Brent Jones
Chief Technology Officer: Michael Egholm, Ph.D
Senior Vice President, Business Developm: H. Alex Kim
Chief Human Resources Officer: Linda Villa
Senior Vice President, Global Operations: Kenneth V. Camarco
Estimated Sales: Over $1 Billion
Number Employees: 10000+

27263 Pall Corp
25 Harbor Park Dr
Port Washington, NY 11050-4664
516-484-5400
Fax: 516-484-5228 866-905-7255
foodandbeverage@pall.com www.pall.com
Researching and developing filtration and advanced separation systems that will help improve the quality of products for the food and beverage processor.
Chairman & Chief Executive Officer: Lawrence Kingsley
CEO: Rainer Blair
rainer_blair@pall.com
Chief Financial Officer: Akhil Johri
CEO: Eric Krasnoff
Chief Technology Officer: Michael Egholm
SVP, Corporate Strategy: H. Alex Kim
Market Sales Manager: Kathleen Berry
Senior Vice President, Operations: Richard Jackson
Estimated Sales: Over $1 Billion
Number Employees: 10000+

27264 Pall Corp
25 Harbor Park Dr
Port Washington, NY 11050-4664
516-484-3600
Fax: 516-801-9754 foodandbeverage@pall.com
www.pall.com
Filtration, seperations, and purification products.
President: Jennifer Honeycutt
SVP, Finance General & Administrator: Jeffrey Figg
SVP & General Counsel: Cathleen Colvin
Chief Technology Officer: Martin Smith
SVP, Global Operations: Wayne Hewitt
VP, Business Development & Strategy: Martin Wirtz
President, Pall Industrial: Naresh Narasimhan
Year Founded: 1946
Estimated Sales: $2.7 Billion
Number Employees: 10,000+

27265 Pall Filtron
50 Bearfoot Rd # 1
Northborough, MA 01532-1551
508-393-1800
Fax: 508-393-1874 800-345-8766
piannucci@pall.com www.pall.com
Filtration and separation systems for food and beverage applications
Sr. VP: Jamie Monat
VP Sales: Piers O'Donnell
Contact: Engin Ayturk
engin_ayturk@pall.com
Estimated Sales: $20 - 50 Million
Number Employees: 50-99
Parent Co: Pall Group
Other Locations:
Pall Filtron
Shinagawa-Ku
Brands:
Emflon
Fluorodyne
Hdc Ii
Pallcell
Pallsep
Profile Ii Plus
Ultipleat
Ultipor Gf/Gf Plus
Ultipor N66

27266 Pallet Management Systems
PO Box 339
Lawrenceville, VA 23868-0339
804-848-2164
Fax: 804-848-4888 800-446-1804
New and used wooden, metal and plastic pallets; also, pallet repair, management, distribution and recovery services available
Chairman/CEO: Johnary Lucy
Director: Donald Norwood
Estimated Sales: $20-50 Million
Number Employees: 100-249
Square Footage: 63000

27267 Pallet Masters
655 E Florence Ave
Los Angeles, CA 90001-2319
323-758-1713
Fax: 323-758-9600 800-675-2579
Pallets
Owner: Steve Anderson
Inside Sales Manager: Bridgette Lathem
sanderson@palletmasters.com
General Manager/Controller: Tim Hwang
Estimated Sales: Below $5 Million
Number Employees: 20-49
Parent Co: Trojan Transportation

27268 Pallet One Inc
1470 US Highway 17 S
Bartow, FL 33830-6627
863-533-1147
Fax: 863-533-3065 800-771-1148
sales@PalletOne.com www.palletone.com
Pallets
Chairman, President, CEO: Howe Wallace
CFO: Casey A Fletcher
cfletcher@palletone.com
VP and CFO: Casey Fletcher
Vice President of Sales: Keith Reinstetle
Chief Operating Officer: Al Holland
Estimated Sales: Less than $500,000
Number Employees: 1000-4999
Square Footage: 160000

27269 Pallet One Inc
1470 US Highway 17 S
Bartow, FL 33830-6627
863-533-1147
Fax: 863-533-3065 800-771-1148
www.palletone.com
Manufacturer and exporter of wooden pallets and harvesting bins
CEO/President/Chairman: Howe Q. Wallace
CFO: Casey A Fletcher
cfletcher@palletone.com
Vice President: Donnie Isaacson
Vice President of Sales: Keith M. Reinstetle
COO: Matt B. Sheffield
Estimated Sales: $10 - 20 Million
Number Employees: 1000-4999
Parent Co: IFCO

27270 Pallet One Inc
165 Turkey Foot Rd
Mocksville, NC 27028-5930
336-492-5565
Fax: 336-492-5682
Wooden pallets and skids
Cmo: Ed Cartner
ecartner@palletone.com
Estimated Sales: $1 - 5 Million
Number Employees: 100-249
Parent Co: Palex Company

27271 Pallet Pro
9980 Clay County Hwy
Moss, TN 38575-6333
931-258-3661
Fax: 931-258-3280 800-489-3661
barkybeaver@info-ed.com
Pallets
Manager: Mary Strong
CEO: J Smith
Quality Control: Jackie Trent
VP Manufacturing: J Wix
VP Marketing: K Donaldson
Estimated Sales: $10 - 20 Million
Number Employees: 20-49
Square Footage: 30000

27272 Pallet Reefer International LLC
4000 Highway 56
Houma, LA 70363-7817
731-616-2219
Fax: 985-868-3715 800-259-3693
lsaia@palletreefer.com
Member of the Board: Louis P Salia III
Number Employees: 10,000+

27273 Pallet Service Corp
11201 90th Ave N
Maple Grove, MN 55369-4048
763-391-8020
Fax: 763-391-8026 888-391-8020
www.palletservice.com
Pallets; also, recycling of cardboard available
President: Robert Wenner
palletserv@aol.com
Sales: Tom Saari
Manager: Scott Wicklund
Estimated Sales: $5-10 Million
Number Employees: 50-99

27274 Pallets Inc
99 1/2 East St
PO Box 326
Fort Edward, NY 12828-1813
518-747-4177
Fax: 518-747-3757 sales@pltsinc.com
www.palletsincorporated.com
Wooden pallets, skids and crates
President: Clint Binley
cbinley@palletsincorporated.com
Sales Manager: Clinton Binley
Estimated Sales: $2.5-5 Million
Number Employees: 20-49

27275 Pallister Pallet
14035 70th Street
Wapello, IA 52653-9596
319-523-8161
Fax: 319-523-5429
Wooden pallets
Secretary/Treasurer: Heather Pallister
VP: Ted Pallister
Estimated Sales: $3 Million
Number Employees: 20-49
Square Footage: 90000

27276 Pallox Incorporated
7221 Hickory Ln
Onsted, MI 49265
517-456-4101
Fax: 517-456-7821
Manufacturer and exporter of wooden pallets, skids and boxes; also, pallet repair and design available; also heat treat pallets for ISPM-15 standard
President: R J Moore
Estimated Sales: $2.5 Million
Number Employees: 20-49
Number of Products: 100
Square Footage: 36000

27277 Palm Bay Imports
301 Yamato Road
Suite 1150
Boca Raton, FL 33487-4917
561-362-9642
Fax: 561-362-7296 800-872-5622
Wines
Logistics: Frank Vella
Marketing Director: Dana Friedman
Sales Manager: Patty Becker
Human Resources Manager: Rosemary Olenick
Estimated Sales: $38 Million
Number Employees: 100-249
Type of Packaging: Consumer, Bulk
Brands:
Alexander Grappa
Aneri
Anselmi
Bauchant
Bertani
Blue Fish
Bodegas Campillo
Boissiere
Bottega Vinaia
Boulard
Brown Brothers
Candido
Cavit
Circus
Citra
Col Dorcia
Ey
Firstland
Frapin
Frotious
Santana
Sella & Mosca

27278 (HQ)Palmer Distributors
23001 W Industrial Dr
St Clair Shores, MI 48080-1187
586-498-2900
Fax: 586-772-4627 800-444-1912
sales@palmerpromos.com
www.palmerpromos.com
Manufacturer and exporter of display cases, card holders, bowls, tray covers, light boxes and syrup bottles
President: Jim Palmer
jpalmer@palmerpromos.com
VP: Mark Armstrong
Food Service Sales Manager: Michael Lacoursiere
Estimated Sales: $10 - 20 Million
Number Employees: 50-99
Square Footage: 100000
Type of Packaging: Food Service
Brands:
Pdi
Ppp

27279 Palmer Fixture Company
1255 Winford Ave
Green Bay, WI 54303-3707
950-884-8698
Fax: 920-884-8699 800-558-8678
info@palmerfixture.com www.palmerfixture.com
Manufacturer, importer and exporter of paper towel, tissue, and napkin dispensers including a universal hands-free towel dispenser
Owner: Bill Palmer
Vice President: Greg Kampschroer
Contact: Siggi Witt
siggi@palmerfixture.com
Purchasing Manager: Chris Worth
Estimated Sales: $820,000
Number Employees: 7
Square Footage: 44000
Brands:
Economy

Holdit
Natures Plumber

27280 Palmer Snyder
400 N Executive Drive
Brookfield, WI 53005-6068
262-780-8780
Fax: 262-780-8790 800-762-0415
www.palmersnyder.com
Manufacturer and exporter of plywood and plastic folding tables, wooden folding chairs maintenence free, galerie series chairs and transport cars for tables and chairs
CEO: Richard Bibler
VP Sales: Craig Clarke
Sales Representative: Chelsea Stecker
Estimated Sales: $1-2.5 Million
Number Employees: 100-250
Square Footage: 600000
Parent Co: Palmer Snyder
Other Locations:
    Palmer Snyder
    Elkhorn WI
Brands:
    Palmer Snyder

27281 Palmer Wahl
234 Old Weaverville Rd
Asheville, NC 28804-1260
828-658-3131
Fax: 828-658-0728 800-421-2853
info@palmerwahl.com
Manufactures temperature and pressure instrumentation. Process Industrial and RTD thermometers, Bimetal, Dial and Sanitary thermometers, infrared thermal imagers, Temperature Recording Labels and Chart Recorders, Pressure gauges andThermowells.
Owner: Stephen Santangelo
Vice President: Schuyler Tilly
Quality Control: Paul Lankford
VP Sales: Gary Lux
Brands:
    All Star
    Cleanliners
    Digi-Stem
    Heat Prober
    Heat Spy
    Temp-Plate

27282 Palmetto Canning
3601 US Highway 41 N
Palmetto, FL 34221
941-722-1100
pcrbaggs@tampabay.rr.com
palmettocanning.com
Canning and packaging sauces and beverage
Estimated Sales: $5-10 Million
Number Employees: 1-4
Square Footage: 128000
Type of Packaging: Consumer, Private Label
Brands:
    Palmalito

27283 Palmetto Packaging
1131 Edwards Cir
Florence, SC 29501-2838
843-662-5800
Fax: 843-662-5668
CustomerService@palmettopackaging.com
Corrugated and fiber boxes
President: David Searcy
HR Executive: John Taylor
    jtaylor@palmettopackaging.com
Estimated Sales: $5-10 Million
Number Employees: 50-99

27284 Palmland Paper Company
708 NE 2nd Ave
Fort Lauderdale, FL 33304
954-764-6910
Fax: 954-779-3849 800-266-9067
Paper place mats, dinner and cocktail napkins, etc
Chairman of the Board: Bernard Beauregard
Secretary: Linda Dunn
Estimated Sales: $2.5-5 Million
Number Employees: 5-9
Square Footage: 16000

27285 Palo Alto Awning
750 W San Carlos
San Jose, CA 95126
650-968-4270
Fax: 650-968-3676 800-400-4270
info@PaloAltoAwning.com
www.paloaltoawning.com
Commercial awnings
President: John Ashman
Estimated Sales: $1-2.5 Million
Number Employees: 10-19

27286 Paltier
1701 Kentucky St
Michigan City, IN 46360
219-872-7238
Fax: 219-872-9480 800-348-3201
Manufacturer and exporter of engineered storage rack systems including cantilever and drive-in/drive-thru
VP/General Manager: James Washington
Plant Manager: Glenn Clark
Estimated Sales: $20-50 Million
Number Employees: 100-249
Square Footage: 110000
Parent Co: Lyon Metal Products
Type of Packaging: Food Service
Brands:
    Interchange
    Pal Dek
    Pal Gard
    Paltier

27287 Pamco Label Co Inc
2200 S Wolf Rd
Des Plaines, IL 60018-1934
847-803-2200
Fax: 847-803-2209 info@pamcolabel.com
www.resourcelabel.com
Pressure sensitive tape and labels
Cmo: Danny Fishbein
    dfishbein@pamcolabel.com
Controller: Maureen Brandes
CEO: Alan M Berkowitz
Vice President of Operations: Dave Heaster
Estimated Sales: $10 Million
Number Employees: 100-249
Square Footage: 52000

27288 Pan American Papers Inc
5101 NW 37th Ave
Miami, FL 33142-3232
305-635-2534
Fax: 305-635-2538 jvl@panampap.com
www.panampap.com
Distributors of paper
Sr. VP: Jesus Roca
    panampap@bellsouth.net
Executive VP: Francisco Valdes
Estimated Sales: $20-50 Million
Number Employees: 10-19
Square Footage: 80000

27289 Pan Pacific Plastics Inc
26551 Danti Ct
Hayward, CA 94545-3917
510-785-6888
Fax: 510-785-6886 888-475-6888
panpacplastics@aol.com
Manufacturer, exporter and importer of plastic bags
President: Ying Wang
    mtan@pppmi.com
Marketing/Sales: Mike Tan
Sales Exec: Mike Tan
Estimated Sales: $20-50 Million
Number Employees: 20-49
Square Footage: 40000
Parent Co: Pan Pacific Group Companies
Type of Packaging: Consumer, Food Service, Private Label, Bulk

27290 Panamerican Logistics
1270 Woolman Pl
Atlanta, GA 30354-1392
404-767-1700
Fax: 404-559-4380
Handling facitility
Owner: Camilo Bundia
    operations@panamlogistics.com
Estimated Sales: $3 - 5 Million
Number Employees: 10-19

27291 Panasonic Commercial Food Service
2 Riverfront Plaza
Newark, NJ 07102
na.panasonic.com/us/industries/food-service-technology
Commercial microwave ovens, vacuum cleaners, compact fluorescent light bulbs and ventilating fans; importer of rice cookers.
CEO, US Company: Mototsugu Sato
Year Founded: 1918
Estimated Sales: $79 Billion
Number Employees: 257,533
Brands:
    Panasonic

27292 Panhandler, Inc.
PO Box 1329
Cordova, TN 38088-1329
800-654-7237
Fax: 901-336-6377 panhandlerpads@yahoo.com
www.panhandlerinc.com
Manufacturer and exporter of pot holders, bakers' gloves and bakery oven pads
Owner: Don White
CEO: Sherrie Nischwitz
Vice President: Christy Graves
Number Employees: 8
Square Footage: 24000
Type of Packaging: Food Service
Brands:
    Panhandler Safety-Wall
    Panhandler Twin-Terry

27293 Panoramic Inc
1500 N Parker Dr
Janesville, WI 53545-0732
608-754-8850
Fax: 608-754-5703 800-333-1394
packages@panoramicinc.com
www.panoramicinc.com
Food, Retail and Industrial Packaging, Stock PET Food Tubs/Containers. Thermoformed Plastic Clamshells, Blisters, Trays, Containers, Custom Packaging Designs, Rigid Set-Up Boxes (Box/Tray Combinations). Contract Packaging/Fulfillment.In-House Design, Tooling, Prototypes
Cio/Cto: Charlie Miller
    charlie.miller@panoramic.com
CEO: Rick Holznecht
Estimated Sales: $20-50 Million
Number Employees: 100-249

27294 Panther Industries Inc
8990 Barrons Blvd # 101
Highlands Ranch, CO 80129-2347
303-703-9876
Fax: 720-283-9462 800-530-6018
sales@print-n-apply.com www.print-n-apply.com
Supplies labeling equipment for the food industry
President: James Thompson
    jthompson@print-n-apply.com
CFO: James Thompson
R&D: James Thompson
Quality Control: Jim Thompson
Estimated Sales: $1 Million
Number Employees: 5-9

27295 Paoli Properties
2531 11th St
Rockford, IL 61104-7219
815-965-0621
Fax: 815-965-5393
Manufacturer and exporter of one-step deboners and desinewers for meat, poultry and seafood
President: Louis Paoli
    info@stephenpaoli.com
CFO: Louis Paoli
Sales: Neal Ryan
General Manager: Shawn Lee
Estimated Sales: $5 - 10 Million
Number Employees: 10-19
Square Footage: 760000
Brands:
    Paoli One Step

27296 Papelera Puertorriquena
PO Box 119
Utuado, PR 00641-0119
787-894-2098
Fax: 787-894-0517
Paper and plastic bags
President: Jose A Rios Montalvo
Manager: Jose Rios

Number Employees: 80
Parent Co: All Plastic Products

27297 Paper Box & Specialty Co
1505 Sibley Ct
Sheboygan, WI 53081-2456
920-459-2440
Fax: 920-459-2463 888-240-3756
Linda.quast@paperboxandspecialty.com
www.paperboxandspecialty.com
Manufacturer and exporter of set-up and folding cartons, poly-coated cheese liners and gift boxes
President: David Van Der Puy
Contact: Nicole Spielvogel
tgesch@pathconit.com
Estimated Sales: $2.5 - 5 Million
Number Employees: 20-49
Square Footage: 150000

27298 (HQ)Paper Converting MachineCompany
2300 S Ashland Ave
Green Bay, WI 54304
920-494-5601
Fax: 920-494-8865 www.pcmc.com
Printing presses print narrow to wide flexographic printing on film, paper, labels, non-woven board stock.
President: Steve Kemp
Vice President of Sales: Mark Zastrow
Sales Engineer: Mike Callahan
mikecallahan@pcmc.com
Year Founded: 1919
Estimated Sales: $237 Million
Number Employees: 1,000
Parent Co: Barry-Wehmiller Companies, Inc.

27299 Paper Converting Machine Company
1163 Glory Rd
Green Bay, WI 54304
920-494-5601
Fax: 920-494-8865 www.pcmc.com
Printing presses print narrow to wide flexographic printing on film, paper, labels, non-woven board stock.
Square Footage: 880000
Parent Co: Barry-Wehmiller Companies Inc
Other Locations:
Aquaflex
Boucherville, PQ Canada
Brands:
Aquaflex
Chromas
Els
Fpc
Instaprep

27300 Paper Machinery Corp
8900 W Bradley Rd
Milwaukee, WI 53224-2822
414-354-8050
Fax: 414-354-8614 info@papermc.com
www.papermc.com
Paperboard cup and package forming machines
Owner: Donald W Baumgartner
donaldbaumgartner@papermc.com
CFO: Scott Koehler
CEO: Donald W Baumgartner
Estimated Sales: $20 - 50 Million
Number Employees: 100-249

27301 Paper Pak Industries
1941 N White Ave
La Verne, CA 91750-5663
909-392-1750
Fax: 909-392-1732 www.paperpakindustries.com
Meat and poultry absorbent pads
COO: Dennis Murphy
VP Packing Products: Jim Gillispie
Manager: Bob Schindel
bschindel@paperpakindustries.com
Estimated Sales: $20-50 Million
Number Employees: 50-99
Brands:
Dri-Sheet
Securely Yours
Zap Soakers

27302 (HQ)Paper Pak Industries
1941 N White Ave
La Verne, CA 91750-5663
909-392-1750
Fax: 909-392-1760
salesinfo@paperpakindustries.com
Supplier of absorbent product packaging to the leading food processors, supermarket chains, and packaging manufacturers and distributors
President/CEO: Ron Jensen
VP/General Counsel: Marty Michael
Director of Technology: Sayandro Versteylen
VP Sales/Marketing: John Terrien
Manager: Bob Schindel
bschindel@paperpakindustries.com
Estimated Sales: $15-$18 Million
Number Employees: 50-99
Type of Packaging: Food Service, Bulk

27303 Paper Product Specialties
PO Box 363
Waukesha, WI 53187-0363
262-549-1730
Fax: 262-549-3614 www.lauterbachgroup.com
Pressure sensitive labels and tags; also, heat seal paper and flexible packaging
President: Shane Lauterbach
Marketing/Sales: Dean Dimitriou
Estimated Sales: $20-50 Million
Number Employees: 50-99
Square Footage: 50000

27304 Paper Products Company
1543 Queen City Ave
Cincinnati, OH 45214
513-921-4717
Fax: 513-251-5553
info@paperproductscompany.com
Folding cartons and foil laminated, poly coated nested bakers' trays
President: Dennis Smith
Sales Manager: Jim Davis
Contact: Karen Campbell
karen@paperproductscompany.com
Estimated Sales: $5 - 10 Million
Number Employees: 20-49
Brands:
Bakers' Gold

27305 Paper Service
PO Box 45
Hinsdale, NH 03451-0045
603-239-6344
Fax: 603-239-8861 www.paperservice.com
Manufacturer and exporter of paper napkins, wrapping and tissue paper
CEO: G O'Neal
Operations Manager: R O'Neal
Estimated Sales: $10-20 Million
Number Employees: 20-49
Square Footage: 400000
Type of Packaging: Food Service, Private Label

27306 Paper Systems Inc
6127 Willowmere Dr
Des Moines, IA 50321-1230
515-280-1111
Fax: 515-280-9219 800-342-2855
nate@paper-systems.com
Manufacturer and exporter of pallets and disposable and returnable bulk containers for food grade liquids and powders
Owner: William Chase
psi@paper-systems.com
Estimated Sales: Below $5 Million
Number Employees: 10-19
Type of Packaging: Bulk
Brands:
Ez-Bulk
Ez-Flow
Ez-Pak
Ez-Pallet
Stack-Sack

27307 Paper Tubes Inc
15900 Industrial Pkwy
PO Box 35140
Cleveland, OH 44135-3322
216-362-2964
Fax: 216-362-2980 800-343-8823
sales@custompapertubes.com
www.custompapertubes.com
Produce custom containers for the food industry.
Samples available upon request

President: Jodi Lombardo
jlombardo@custompapertubes.com
Founder: Luther Stevens
Sales Director: Phil VanDuyn
Vice President of Sales & Marketing: Kevin Kline
Marketing Manager: Emily Miller
Assistant Sales Manager: David Esper
Manufacturing Director: Paula Murad
Estimated Sales: Below $5 Million
Number Employees: 20-49
Square Footage: 30000
Type of Packaging: Consumer, Private Label

27308 Paper Tubes Inc
15900 Industrial Pkwy
PO Box 35140
Cleveland, OH 44135-3322
216-362-2964
Fax: 216-362-2980 800-343-8823
sales@custompapertubes.com
www.custompapertubes.com
Cosmetic pakaging, food grade packaging and see through packaging
President: Jodi Lombardo
jlombardo@custompapertubes.com
Founder: Luther Stevens
Vice President of Sales/Marketing: Kevin Kline
Marketing Manager: Emily Miller
Assistant Sales Manager: David Esper
Manufacturing Director: Paula Murad
Number Employees: 20-49

27309 Paper Works Industries Inc
8800 Sixty Rd
Baldwinsville, NY 13027-1235
315-638-4355
Fax: 315-638-8421 800-847-5677
www.paperworksindustries.com
High barrier rotogravure printed folding cartons made from recycled boxboard; also, can and bottle carriers
CEO: Carlton Highsmith
Logistics: Leo Basciano
Manufacturing: Robert Derby
Plant Manager: Leo Basciano
Estimated Sales: $50 - 100 Million
Number Employees: 100-249
Parent Co: Lawson Mardon Group

27310 Paper-Pak Products
9740 Canterbury Street
Leawood, KS 66206-2106
913-341-7524
Fax: 913-341-7553 rcrossland@paperpak.com
Regional Sales Manager: Robin Crossland

27311 Paperbag Manufacturers Inc
4131 NW 132nd St
Opa Locka, FL 33054-4510
305-685-1100
Fax: 305-685-2200 888-678-2247
baglady@paperbag.com www.paperbag.com
Bags for packaging tea, coffee and more
Vice President: Susan Hernandez
baglady@paperbag.com
Owner: Adam Cohen
VP: Susan Hernandez
Estimated Sales: $1 Million
Number Employees: 10-19

27312 Papertech
108-245 Iell Avenue
North Vancouver, BC V7P 2K1
Canada
604-990-1600
Fax: 604-990-1606 877-787-2737
info@papertech.ca www.papertech.ca
Manufacturer and exporter of dairy processing equipment including clean-in-place systems, milk processors and process control instruments
President: Kari Hilden
Marketing Coordinator: Tanja Kannisto
Number Employees: 30
Brands:
Optec

27313 Paperweights Plus
3661 Horseblock Road
Suite Q
Medford, NY 11763-2232
631-924-3222
Fax: 631-345-0752

Manufacturer, importer and exporter of advertising specialties including emblems, ID badges, name plates, lapel pins, key rings and paperweights
President: Darlene Reynolds
Estimated Sales: Less than $500,000
Number Employees: 1-4
Square Footage: 1700

27314 Papillon Ribbon & Bow
35 Monhegan Street
Clifton, NJ 07013
973-928-6128
Fax: 973-246-1065 800-229-2998
sales@papillonusa.com www.papillonusa.com
Packaging ribbons and bows
President: Wong Vinci
Vice President Finance: Jimmy Cheung
Marketing: Dan Schwatzbach
Contact: Jimmy Cheung
j.cheung@papillonusa.com
Estimated Sales: $7.6 Million
Number Employees: 40

27315 Pappas Inc.
575 E Milwaukee St
Detroit, MI 48202
313-873-1800
Fax: 313-875-7805 800-521-0888
info@pappasinc.com www.pappasinc.com
Makers of fine cutlery, emulsifying equipment, blades, parts and supplies.
Contact: John Pappas
john@pappasinc.com

27316 Paques ADI
182 Main St
Unit 6
Salem, NH 03079
603-890-5434
Fax: 603-898-3991
Supplier of wastewater treatment systems:, anaerobic, UASB, aerobic, hybrid
VP: Al Cocci
Estimated Sales: $1 - 5 Million
Number Employees: 5-9

27317 Par-Pak
3450 Lang Rd
Houston, TX 77092
713-686-6700
Fax: 713-686-5553 www.parpak.com
Rigid plastic containers
Owner: Mohammed Ebrahim
VP Sales: David Goralski
Contact: Courtney Adkinson
courtneyadkinson@gmail.com
Operations Manager: Ali Virani
Estimated Sales: $5-10 Million
Number Employees: 20-49
Square Footage: 96000
Parent Co: Par-Pak

27318 (HQ)Par-Pak
14345 Northwest Freeway
Houston, TX 77040
713-686-6700
Fax: 713-686-5553 888-727-7252
www.parpak.com
Manufacturer and exporter of clear plastic containers for food packaging; also, catering trays
President: Sajjad Ebrahim
VP Technical: Dominic DiDomizio
VP Sales: David Goralski
Estimated Sales: $5 - 10 Million
Number Employees: 20-49
Square Footage: 210000
Brands:
Cake-Mix
Ebony
Invisi-Bowl
Invisible Packaging
Quartz Collection

27319 Parachem Corporation
2733 6th Ave
Des Moines, IA 50313
515-280-9445
Fax: 515-280-7600
Manufacturer and exporter of hand soap, hand soap dispensers, anti-bacterial soap systems in leaf form, etc

President: Beryl Halterman
Marketing Manager: Carla Stephens
Office Manager: Dean Blum
Purchasing Manager: Dean Blum
Estimated Sales: Below $5 Million
Number Employees: 1-4
Square Footage: 48000
Parent Co: Flightags
Brands:
Cleaf
Jardin Savon

27320 Paraclipse
2271 E 29th Ave
Columbus, NE 68601-3166
402-563-3625
Fax: 402-564-2109 800-854-6379
www.paraclipse.com
Manufacturer and exporter of decorative indoor lighted fly traps and industrial fly traps for public dining areas, kitchen and food preparation areas. Outdoor lighted mosquito trap for restaurant outside serving areas and patios.
CFO: Cheryl Ditter
Sales Manager: Len Jochens
Manager: Abby Cremers
acremer@paraclipse.com
Estimated Sales: $3-6 Million
Number Employees: 10-19
Square Footage: 216000
Brands:
Insect Inn Iv

27321 Parade Packaging
333 Washington Blvd
Mundelein, IL 60060
847-566-6264
Fax: 847-566-2017
Plastic bags and films
General Manager: Jerry Alexander
Manager: Scott Silverstein
s.silverstein@fortuneplastics.com
Estimated Sales: $10-20 Million
Number Employees: 50-99
Parent Co: Parade Packaging Materials

27322 (HQ)Paradigm Packaging Inc
1252 E Seventh Ave
Upland, CA 90786
909-985-2750
Fax: 909-985-8463
Injection blow-molded plastic containers and injection molded closures
President: Robert Donnahoo
VP: Mike Mc Allister
Customer Service: Sophia Ibara
Estimated Sales: $10-20 Million
Number Employees: 1-4
Other Locations:
Trans Container Corp.
West Valley City UT
Brands:
Trc

27323 Paradigm Technologies
PO Box 25540
Eugene, OR 97402-0457
541-345-5543
Fax: 541-345-5549 paratech@presys.com
Food and dairy processing equipment and material handling equipment
Owner: Charles Nutter
Brands:
Alan Bradley
Ge

27324 Paradise Inc.
10150 Highland Manor Drive
Suite 200
Tampa, FL 33610
813-752-1155
Fax: 941-754-3168 paradisefruitco@hotmail.com
www.paradisefruitco.com
Candied fruits.
VP, Sales: Tracy Schulis
Year Founded: 1961
Estimated Sales: $21 Million
Number Employees: 100-249
Number of Brands: 6
Square Footage: 275000
Parent Co: Seneca Foods
Type of Packaging: Consumer, Food Service, Private Label, Bulk

Brands:
Dixie Brand
Mor-Fruit
Paradise
Pennant
Sunripe
White Swan

27325 Paradise Plastics
116 39th St
Brooklyn, NY 11232-2712
718-788-3733
Fax: 718-965-4030
www.f.t.domdex.com/fc14kparadisepictures
Plastic garbage bags
President: Kathy Cooper
kcooper@paradiseplastics.com
Estimated Sales: $20 - 50 Million
Number Employees: 20-49

27326 Paradise Products
PO Box 568
El Cerrito, CA 94530-0568
510-524-8300
Fax: 510-524-8165 800-227-1092
100 page catalog of theme decorations and party supplies for special events and sales promotions cateterias and clubs
Controller: Alice Rickey
Sales: Shirley Imai
Number Employees: 14
Number of Products: 3000
Square Footage: 80000
Brands:
Fling Decorating Kits

27327 Paragon Electric Company
PO Box 28
Two Rivers, WI 54241-0028
920-793-1161
Fax: 920-793-3736
Refrigeration defrost controls for walk-in and reach-in coolers and refrigerated display cases
VP/General Manager: Bob Stalder
Sales Manager: Mike Simino
Estimated Sales: $20 - 50 Million
Number Employees: 500

27328 Paragon Films Inc
3500 W Tacoma St
Broken Arrow, OK 74012-1164
918-250-3456
Fax: 918-355-3456 800-274-9727
jpt@paragon-films.com www.paragonfilms.com
Manufacturer and exporter of packaging materials including stretch and specialty films and hand applied and pallet stretch wrap
President: Mike Baab
mbaab@paragon-films.com
Estimated Sales: $20 - 50 Million
Number Employees: 100-249

27329 Paragon Group USA
3433 Tyrone Boulevard N
St Petersburg, FL 33710-1136
727-341-0547
Fax: 727-302-9816 800-835-6962
Manufacturer and exporter of ozone generators designed to electronically eliminate odors without the use of chemicals; also, food preservation equipment
President: David Kocksten
R & D: Phillip Rod
VP Sales: Susan Duffy
Purchasing Manager: Chuch Pacino
Estimated Sales: $1-2.5 Million
Number Employees: 10
Square Footage: 20800
Brands:
Zontec

27330 Paragon International
731 W 18th St
Nevada, IA 50201-7847
515-382-8000
Fax: 515-382-8001 800-433-0333
www.manufacturedfun.com
Manufacturer and exporter of popcorn machines and carts
Owner: Dave Swegle
Quality Control: Bill Tierce
VP Sales/Marketing: Tom Berger
Manager Customer Service: Sandra Holubar

Estimated Sales: $3 - 5,000,000
Number Employees: 20-49
Square Footage: 25000
Brands:
  1911 Originals
  Thrifty Pop

27331 Paragon Labeling
1607 9th St
St Paul, MN 55110-6717
651-429-7722
Fax: 651-429-6006 800-429-7722
info@paragonlabeling.com
www.paragonlabeling.com
Manufacturer and exporter of printing machines and supplies and custom labeling systems
Director of Label Manufacturing Operatio: Karla Bridgeman
CFO: Ed Clarke
Vice President: Craig Blonigen
VP: Craig Blonigen
Sales/Marketing: Craig Blonigen
Contact: Randy Black
  randyb@lowrycomputer.com
Operations Manager: Ken Koehler
Production Manager: Matt Thoreson
Plant Manager: Ken Koehler
Estimated Sales: $5 Million
Number Employees: 5-9
Square Footage: 160000
Parent Co: Lowry Computer Products Company
Brands:
  Paragon

27332 Paragon Labeling
1607 9th St
St Paul, MN 55110-6717
651-429-7722
Fax: 651-429-6006 800-429-7722
info@paragonlabeling.com
www.paragonlabeling.com
Labels, labeling machines, print and apply labelers, ribbons, printers, and scanners
Director of Label Manufacturing Operatio: Karla Bridgeman
Sr. VP: David Heiff
VP: Craig Boligen
Contact: Randy Black
  randyb@lowrycomputer.com
Estimated Sales: $12 Million
Number Employees: 5-9

27333 (HQ)Paragon Packaging
7700 Centerville Rd
Ferndale, CA 95536
707-786-4004
Fax: 707-786-4014 888-615-0065
Rfcohn@gmail.com
Gift packaging including boxes and plastic containers
Owner: Ron Cohn
Production Manager: Ed Davis
Estimated Sales: $1-2.5 Million
Number Employees: 1-4
Square Footage: 3000

27334 Parallel Products Inc
401 Industry Rd
Louisville, KY 40208-1692
502-471-2444
Fax: 813-289-4283 800-883-9100
CustomerServices@parallelproducts.com
www.parallelproducts.com
Processing technologies for food wastes
President: Gene Keisel
  genek@parallelproducts.com
Controller: David Kenney
Vice President of Business Development: Tim Cusson
Vice President Sales and Marketing: Ken Reese
National Sales Manager: Ed Stewart
Corporate HR Manager, Director of Corpor: Hal Park
Vice President of Operations: Bob Pasma
National Customer Service Manager: Denise Gibson
Plant Manager: Russ Hohn
Number Employees: 10-19

27335 Paramount Industries
304 N Howard Ave
PO Box 259
Croswell, MI 48422
810-679-2551
Fax: 810-679-4045 800-521-5405
piisales@paramountlighting.com
www.paramountlighting.com
High performance lighting for specialized environments
President: Craig Bailey
  piiadv@paramountlighting.com
VP Sales: Derryl Fewins
Sales: Angie Smiley
Plant Manager: Jim Jarchow
Estimated Sales: Below $5 Million
Number Employees: 50-99
Square Footage: 90000
Brands:
  Aerolux
  Cleanroom
  Craft Lite
  Guardcraft
  Techniseal
  Vandalume

27336 (HQ)Paramount ManufacturingCompany
353 Middlesex Ave
Wilmington, MA 1887
978-657-4300
Fax: 978-658-5215
Store fixtures, cafeteria counters and table and wall units
Owner: Louis Tarantino
Contact: Joseph Chinnis
joseph.chinnis@paramountmfg.com
Estimated Sales: $2.5-5 Million
Number Employees: 10-19

27337 Paramount Packaging Corp
1221 Walt Whitman Rd
Melville, NY 11747-3010
516-333-8100
Fax: 516-333-9720 ppc735@aol.com
www.paramountcontainer.com
Designer and builder of custom food equipment and machinery that include sanitary conveyor system, reciprocating nose conveyor/feeder system, high speed bread product slicing and separating, and band saw bread products slicing andseparating
Owner: Shawn Murphy
  dave@nyli.com
Number Employees: 10-19

27338 Paramount Packing & Rubber Inc
4012 Belle Grove Rd
Baltimore, MD 21225-2699
410-789-2233
Fax: 410-789-2238 866-727-7225
www.paramountpacking.com
Gaskets
President: Jay Huber
  info@paramountpacking.com
CEO: James Huber
Vice President: Byron Huber
Quality Control: Joe Kammerzel
Sales Director: Joel Hayer
Estimated Sales: $500,000-$1 Million
Number Employees: 5-9
Number of Brands: 100
Number of Products: 85
Square Footage: 15000
Type of Packaging: Consumer

27339 Parasol Awnings
4834 Hickory Hill Rd
Memphis, TN 38141
901-368-4477
Fax: 901-368-1798 sales@parasolawnings.com
Commercial awnings
Manager: Michael Folk
Contact: Marie Anthony
  manthony@parasolawnings.com
Chief Manager: Michael Fold
Estimated Sales: $2.5-5 Million
Number Employees: 10-19

27340 Paratherm Corporation
31 Portland Rd
Conshohocken, PA 19428
610-941-4900
Fax: 610-941-9191 800-222-3611
info@paratherm.com www.paratherm.com

Manufacturer and exporter of food-grade heat transfer fluids for precise and uniform temperature control in food processing applications
President: John Fuhr
Research & Development: Jim Oetinger
Marketing Director: Andy Andrews
Sales Director: Jim Oetinger
Contact: Andy Andrews
  aandrews@paratherm.com
Purchasing Manager: Anne Grabowski
Estimated Sales: $2.5-5 Million
Number Employees: 1-4
Number of Brands: 1
Number of Products: 9
Square Footage: 20000
Brands:
  Paratherm Nf
  Paratherm Or

27341 Parish Manufacturing Inc
7430 New Augusta Rd
Indianapolis, IN 46268-2291
317-872-0172
Fax: 317-872-1242 800-592-2268
www.parishmfg.com
Manufacturer and exporter of bag-in-box liquid packaging systems
President: Richard Smith
  rsmith@parishmfg.com
Estimated Sales: $10-20 Million
Number Employees: 20-49
Square Footage: 56000
Type of Packaging: Consumer, Food Service, Bulk

27342 Parisi Inc
305 Pheasant Run
Newtown, PA 18940-3423
215-968-6677
Fax: 215-968-3580
Manufacturer and exporter of bars, booths, counters, tabletops and buffet equipment; also, bakery, confectionery and deli display cases
President: Ron Germain
  rgermain@parisi-royal.com
CFO: Gary Graf
Marketing Director: Eleanor Parisi
Sales Director: Dave Moore
Sales: Bill Matnias
Operations Manager: Steve Dickier
Estimated Sales: $10 - 20 Million
Number Employees: 50-99
Square Footage: 180000

27343 (HQ)Parisian Novelty Company
17859 Tipton Ave
Homewood, IL 60430
773-847-1212
Fax: 773-847-2608
Printed plastic signs and labels
General Manager: Norman Weinberg
Estimated Sales: less than $500,000
Number Employees: 50-100

27344 Parity Corp
11812 N Creek Pkwy N # 204
Bothell, WA 98011-8202
425-487-0997
Fax: 425-487-2317 www.paritylink.com
Manufacturer and exporter of accounting, systems integration and inventory control software
Owner: Arvid Tellevik
  atellevik@paritycorp.com
R & D: John Ratliff
VP: George Fletcher
Office Administrator: Cindy Kouremetis
Estimated Sales: $5-10,000,000
Number Employees: 20-49
Square Footage: 4000

27345 Parity Corp
11812 N Creek Pkwy N # 204
Suite 204
Bothell, WA 98011-8202
425-487-0997
Fax: 425-487-2317 Info@ParityCorp.com
Develops specialized software and related services for the food industry; industry specific business management tools
Owner: Arvid Tellevik
  atellevik@paritycorp.com
Estimated Sales: $5-10 Million
Number Employees: 20-49

27346 Park Custom Molding
940 S Park Avenue
Linden, NJ 07036-1646
908-486-8882
Fax: 908-486-1376
Plastic packaging products
VP Sales: Edward Joffe
Estimated Sales: $2.5-5 Million
Number Employees: 20-49

27347 Parker Sales & Svc
69 Parker Ln
Sparta, NC 28675-8341
336-372-2812
Fax: 336-372-4119 filtersrus@skybest.com
www.psasinc.com
Dust collection filters
Owner: Charles Moyer
chuckm@psasinc.com
Estimated Sales: $5-10 Million
Number Employees: 20-49
Square Footage: 40000

27348 (HQ)Parker-Hannifin Corp
6035 Parkland Blvd
Cleveland, OH 44124
216-896-3000
Fax: 216-896-4000 800-272-7537
c-parker@parker.com www.parker.com
Motion control technologies and systems, providing
precision-engineered solutions.
President & Chief Operating Officer: Lee Banks
Chairman & Chief Executive Officer: Thomas
Williams
twilliams@parker.com
Executive VP Finance/Admin. & CFO: Catherine
Suever
VP/General Counsel/Secretary: Joseph Leonti
Year Founded: 1917
Estimated Sales: $14.3 Billion
Number Employees: 57,170

27349 Parker-Hannifin Corp
HVAC Filtration Division
100 River Ridge Circle
Jeffersonville, IN 47130
Fax: 866-601-1809 866-247-4827
www.parker.com
Filtration products including filter bags, cartridges
and systems.
President & Chief Operating Officer: Lee Banks
Chairman & Chief Executive Officer: Thomas
Williams
Brands:
Fulflo

27350 Parker-Hannifin Corp
Electromechanical & Drives Division
1140 Sandy Hill Rd
Irwin, PA 15642
Fax: 707-584-8015 800-358-9070
www.parker.com
PC-based control, HMI software, industrial PCs, OI
workstations.
President & Chief Operating Officer: Lee Banks
Chairman & Chief Executive Officer: Thomas
Williams

27351 Parker-Hannifin Corp
Gas Separation & Filtration Division
4087 Walden Ave
Lancaster, NY 14086
978-858-0505
Fax: 978-478-2501 800-343-4048
www.balstonfilters.com
Parker Balston filters, compressed air dryers, and ni-
trogen generators.
President & Chief Operating Officer: Lee Banks
Chairman & Chief Executive Officer: Thomas
Williams

27352 Parker-Hannifin Corp
Hose Products Division
30242 Lakeland Dr
Wickliffe, OH 44092
440-943-5700
Fax: 440-943-3129 ihporders@parker.com
Food and beverage hoses with internally expanded
couplings; internal expansion crimpers available.

President & Chief Operating Officer: Lee Banks
Chairman & Chief Executive Officer: Thomas
Williams

27353 Parkland
PO Box 266342
Houston, TX 77207-6342
713-926-5055
Fax: 713-926-7358
Manufacturer and exporter of air conditioners, re-
frigerators and heating and ventilation equipment
President: J P Landers
Office Manager: John Rosales
Number Employees: 10
Type of Packaging: Food Service

27354 (HQ)Parkson Corp
1401 W Cypress Creek Rd # 100
Fort Lauderdale, FL 33309-1969
908-464-0700
Fax: 954-974-6182 www.parkson.com
Manufacturer and exporter of bulk material convey-
ors, bucket elevators and slide and diverter gates;
importer of shaftless spirals
Owner: Steven Lombardi
CEO: Zain Mahmood
Director Marketing: Charlene Low
Estimated Sales: $1-2.5 Million
Number Employees: 250-499
Square Footage: 120000
Parent Co: Conelco
Brands:
Corra-Trough

27355 Parkson Corp
562 Bunker Ct
Vernon Hills, IL 60061-1831
847-816-3700
Fax: 847-816-3707 technology@parkson.com
www.parkson.com
Provider of equipment and systems for water/pro-
cess water and wastewater treatment including
screens, sand filters, dewatering presses, inclined
plate clarifiers, conveyors, filter presses, sludge
thickeners and thermodryers andaeration
President: Axel Johnson, Inc
CEO: William Acton
Marketing Director: Charlene Low
Sales Director: Michael Miller
Number Employees: 10-19
Parent Co: Parkson Corporation
Brands:
American Bulk Conveyors
Hycor Screening & Dewatering Equip.
Parkson Dynasand Gravity Filters
Parkson Lamella Plate Settlers

27356 Parkson Corporation
PO Box 408399
Fort Lauderdale, FL 33340-8399
954-974-6610
Fax: 954-974-6182 www.parkson.com
Supplier of innovative, cost effective solutions for
potable water, process water, and industrial and mu-
nicipal wasterwater problems.
President/CEO: Zain Mahmood
Estimated Sales: $20,000,000 - $49,999,999
Number Employees: 250-499
Parent Co: Axel Johnson Company

27357 Parkway Plastic Inc
561 Stelton Rd
Piscataway, NJ 08854-3868
732-752-3636
Fax: 732-752-2192 800-881-4996
sales@parkwayjars.com
www.store.parkwayjars.com
Manufacturer and exporter of polystyrene, linear
polyethylene and polypropylene jars, bottles, boxes
and caps
President: Debbie Coyle
dcoyle@parkwayproducts.com
Estimated Sales: $10 - 20 Million
Number Employees: 50-99

27358 Parlor City Paper Box Co Inc
2 Eldredge St
Binghamton, NY 13901-2600
607-772-0600
Fax: 607-772-0806 parcitybox@aol.com
Manufacturer and exporter of trays and printed folding boxes

President: David Culver
Sales/Marketing: Jeffrey Culver
Office Manager: Juanita Mendez
Estimated Sales: $5-10 Million
Number Employees: 20-49
Square Footage: 204000

27359 Parrish's Cake Decorating
225 W 146th St
Gardena, CA 90248-1803
310-324-2253
Fax: 310-324-8277 800-736-8443
Aluminum cake pans, cookie cutters, artificial icing,
candy molds, plates and pillars, pastry bags, food
colors and flavorings
President: Bob Parrish
customerservice@parrishsmagicline.com
VP: Norma Parrish
Estimated Sales: $1 - 3 Million
Number Employees: 10-19
Number of Products: 4000
Square Footage: 180000
Type of Packaging: Consumer, Food Service, Pri-
vate Label, Bulk
Brands:
Magic Line
Magic Mist
Magic Mold
Perma-Ice

27360 Parsons Manufacturing Corp.
1055 Obrien Dr
Menlo Park, CA 94025
650-324-4726
Fax: 650-324-3051
Manufacturer and exporter of sample cases, tote
boxes, travel cases and shipping cases
Owner: Alan Parsons
VP Sales/Marketing: Steve Wurzer
Contact: Alan Hall
alan.hall@parsons.com
Estimated Sales: $20-50 Million
Number Employees: 20-49

27361 Parta
2000 Summit Rd
Kent, OH 44240-7140
330-678-7745
Fax: 330-676-6310 800-543-5781
www.partaonline.org
Set-up paper boxes, vacuum formed parts, plastic
lids and folding cartons
Secretary, Treasurer, General Manager, P: John
Drew
jdrew@partaonline.org
Estimated Sales: $5-10 Million
Number Employees: 100-249
Square Footage: 200000

27362 Partex Corporation
G-4415 Richfield Road
Flint, MI 48506
810-736-5656
Fax: 810-736-5100
Parts for ice cream dispensing equipment
Number Employees: 5

27363 Particle Sizing Systems
8203 Kristel Circle
Port Richey, FL 34668
727-846-0866
Fax: 727-846-0865 sales@pssnicomp.com
www.pssnicomp.com
Particle sizers
President: David Nicoli
Finance Manager: Carrey Hasapidis
Bookkeeper: Inge Griffith
Head Marketing: Patrick Ohagen
Contact: Heather Belfi
belfi@pssnicomp.com
Head Production: Chris Rowan
Purchasing Manager: Ray Ruttan
Estimated Sales: $2.5 - 5 Million
Number Employees: 20-49
Square Footage: 12000

27364 Partner Pak
5322 Oceanus Dr # 101
Huntington Beach, CA 92649-1031
714-799-7879
Fax: 714-799-2858 info@partnerpak.com
www.partnerpak.com
Owner: Gary Eddington
gary@partnerpak.com

Estimated Sales: $1 - 3 Million
Number Employees: 5-9

27365 Partners International
PO Box 27
Hanover, NH 03755-0027

      603-643-8574
      Fax: 603-643-3835
Consultant specializing in international acquisitions
and export development
VP: Joan Drape
Estimated Sales: $1 - 5 Million

27366 Partnership Resources
1069 10th Ave SE
Minneapolis, MN 55414-1388

      612-331-2075
Fax: 612-331-2887 www.partnershipresources.org
Manufacturer and exporter of electric infrared heat-
ing systems and based power controllers
Manager: Dan Mc Calister
  danmccalister@partnershipresources.org
Chief Executive Officer: Norm Munk
Marketing Manager: James Lee
Manager: Dan Mc Calister
  danmccalister@partnershipresources.org
Chief Operating Officer: Julie Zbaracki
Number Employees: 50-99
Square Footage: 360000
Brands:
  Chambir
  Controlir
  Hi-Tempir
  Lineir
  Paneir
  Spotir
  Stripir

27367 Party Linens
7780 S Dante Ave
Chicago, IL 60619

      773-731-9281
    Fax: 773-731-7669 800-281-0003
      www.partylinens.com
Manufacturer and importer of specialty linens and
table skirting for various table shapes
Owner: Ed Denormandie
Estimated Sales: $2.5-5 Million
Number Employees: 10-19
Square Footage: 20000
Parent Co: DeNormandie Towel & Linen

27368 Party Perfect Catering
3030 Audley Street
Houston, TX 77098-1926

      713-522-3932
    Fax: 713-522-1746 800-522-5440
Catering, event and kitchen production software
Owner: Ruth Meric
Sales Manager: Kelly Folk

27369 Party Yards
950 S Winter Park Drive
Suite 101
Casselberry, FL 32707-5451

      407-696-9440
    Fax: 407-696-6963 877-501-4400
  partyyards@aol.com www.partyyards.com
Manufacturer, importer and exporter of plastic cups
VP: Andrew Baron
Sales Contact: Peter Dorney
Estimated Sales: $2.5-5 Million
Number Employees: 5-9
Square Footage: 48000
Parent Co: Party Yards
Brands:
  Glow
  Glow Shots
  Party Yards

27370 Parvin Manufacturing Company
6033 W Century Blvd # 1180
Los Angeles, CA 90045-6424

      310-645-4411
    Fax: 323-585-0427 800-648-0770
Manufacturer, importer and exporter of protective
clothing and supplies including oven/barbecue mitts,
aprons, skillet handle covers and insulated pizza
delivery bags
Owner: Michael Provan
VP: Rick Resnick
Estimated Sales: $10-20 Million
Number Employees: 5-9
Square Footage: 68000

Brands:
  Flameguard
  Footguard
  Pro-Cut

27371 Pasco Poly Inc
407 River Dock Rd
Weiser, ID 83672-5819

      208-549-1861
  Fax: 208-549-0530 www.pascopoly.com
Wine industry tanks
Chairman of the Board: David D Rule
Estimated Sales: Less Than $500,000
Number Employees: 1-4

27372 Pasquini Espresso Co
1501 W Olympic Blvd
Los Angeles, CA 90015-3803

      213-739-8826
    Fax: 213-385-8774 800-724-6225
      www.pasquini.biz
Manufacturer and exporter of commercial espresso
equipment
President: Ambrose Pasquini
  pasquini@pasquini.com
VP: Guy Pasquini
National Sales Manager: Sergio Laganiere
Estimated Sales: Below $5 Million
Number Employees: 20-49
Square Footage: 24000
Type of Packaging: Food Service

27373 Pasta Filata International
154 Pine Street
Montclair, NJ 07042-4910

      973-744-6640
      Fax: 973-744-1488
Estimated Sales: $1 - 5 Million
Number Employees: 2

27374 Pasta Life
New York, NY 10014

      754-253-3683
      sales@pasta.life
      pasta.life
Gluten-free and 100% biodegradable pasta straws.
Co-Founder: David Sedacca
Year Founded: 2019
Number of Brands: 1
Number of Products: 5
Type of Packaging: Food Service
Brands:
  PASTA LIFE

27375 Pastabiz Pasta Machines
2129 Harrison St
San Francisco, CA 94110-1321

      415-431-5049
    Fax: 415-621-4613 www.brickovens.biz
Pasta machines
Owner: Emilio Mitidieri
  info@pastabiz.com
Estimated Sales: $300,000-500,000
Number Employees: 5-9

27376 Pastry Art & Design
12 W 37th St # 9
New York, NY 10018-7480

      212-239-0855
      Fax: 212-967-4184
Magazine
President: Michael Schneider
Estimated Sales: $3 - 5 Million
Number Employees: 10-19

27377 Patchogue - Medford Library
54-60 East Main Street
Patchogue, NY 11772

      631-654-4700
    Fax: 631-289-3999 www.pmlib.org
Information source
Manager: Dina M Chrils
Contact: John Marcozzi
  jmarcozzi@seds.org
Number Employees: 100-249

27378 Pate International
2350 Taylor St # 1
Suite 1
San Francisco, CA 94133-1818

      415-928-4400
Fax: 415-928-0690 info@pateinternational.com
      www.pateinternational.com
Wine industry packaging

President: Susan Pate
  susan@pateinternational.com
Estimated Sales: Less Than $500,000
Number Employees: 1-4

27379 Pater & Associates
P.O. Box 54884
Cincinnati, OH 45254

    Fax: 513-474-4829 payday11@aol.com
Printed and plain flexible packaging films, pouches,
and bags; folding paperboard cartons; bag closing
equipment and loks
Owner: James Pater Jr
CFO: James Pater Jr
Sales: James Pater Jr
Purchasing Director: James Pater Jr

27380 Patio Center Inc
1507 Eraste Landry Rd
Lafayette, LA 70506-1996

      337-233-9896
  Fax: 337-232-7178 patiocenter@patiocenter.com
Commercial awnings
President: Herman D Richard
VP: Ryan Richard
Estimated Sales: Below $5 Million
Number Employees: 20-49

27381 Patio King
10744 SW 190th St
Cutler Bay, FL 33157-7616

      305-316-7508
      www.patioking.com
Gas and charcoal outside and commercial barbecues
for restaurants
Contact: King Patio
Secretary: Edith Garcia
Estimated Sales: $1-2.5 Million
Number Employees: 1-4
Square Footage: 6000

27382 Patlite Corp
20130 S Western Ave
Torrance, CA 90501-1307

      310-328-3222
    Fax: 310-328-2676 888-214-2580
    sales@patlite.com www.patlite.com
Visual and audible warning devices
President: Fumio Sawamura
Sales: Sandra Rodriguez
Number Employees: 10-19

27383 Patrick & Co
2100 N Stemmons Fwy # Tm2927
Suite 2927
Dallas, TX 75207-3001

      214-761-0900
Fax: 214-761-1985 info@patrickandcompany.com
Metal signs, name plates, badges, office supplies,
stationery and furniture
Owner: Patrick Ongena
Sales Manager: Mark Rodby
Estimated Sales: $500,000-$1 Million
Number Employees: 1-4

27384 Patrick E. Panzarello Consulting Services
8001 Grove Street
Sunland, CA 91040-2111

      818-353-0431
      Fax: 818-951-6638
Consultant specializing in architectural design ser-
vices, health department permits
President: Patrick Panzarello
CEO: Mike Hess
CFO: Ed Navaratte
Estimated Sales: 200000

27385 Patrick Signs
5411 Randolph Rd
Rockville, MD 20852

      301-770-6200
    Fax: 301-770-0083 jpn123@prodigy.net
Signs; also, installation services available
Owner: Constance Nusbaum
Estimated Sales: $1 - 5 Million
Number Employees: 20-49

27386 Patterson Fan Co Inc
1120 Northpoint Blvd
Blythewood, SC 29016-8873
803-691-4750
Fax: 803-691-4751 800-768-3985
info@pattersonfan.com www.pattersonfan.com
Industrial fans, air movement equipment
President: Vance Patterson
Regional Manager: Albert Howell
Vice President, Chief Operating Officer: Thomas Salisbury
Estimated Sales: $10-20 Million
Number Employees: 50-99

27387 Patterson Industries
250 Danforth Road
Scarborough, ON M1L 3X4
Canada
416-694-3381
Fax: 416-691-2768 800-336-1110
process@pattersonindustries.com
www.pattersonindustries.com
Designers, engineers and manufacturers of quality time proven equipment for the food industries; Ribbon and Paddle mikers, ThoroBlender Double Cone Blenders, Conaform Double Cone Vacuum Dryers, Ribbon and Paddle type round bodydryers, pressure vessels and heat exchangers and general mixing and agitation equipment
President: H Haischt
CFO: Seth Mendonza
Research & Development: Mike Lindsey
Sales Director: M Lindsey
Estimated Sales: $2,500,000
Number Employees: 10-20
Square Footage: 120000
Brands:
Conaform
Thoroblender

27388 (HQ)Patterson Laboratories
11930 Pleasant Street
Detroit, MI 48217-1620
313-843-4500
Fax: 313-843-9416
Industrial chemicals and cleaners including bottled ammonia, bleaches, window cleaners and detergents
VP Produce: Darrell Cardwell
Administration: Richard Hodgkinson
Estimated Sales: $1 - 5 Million
Number Employees: 50-99
Square Footage: 180000
Brands:
Blue Ribbon
Ful-Value
Steer Clear

27389 (HQ)Patterson-KelleyHars Company
PO Box 458
East Stroudsburg, PA 18301-0458
570-421-7500
Fax: 570-421-8735 www.patkelco.com
Batch and continuous blenders, dryers, compact water heaterand gas fired boilers for commercial, institutional and industrial applications
Manager: Mark Lasewicz
Marketing Director: Ruth Ann Rocchio
Sales Manager: Jef Potters
Contact: Christine Bushta
c.bushta@patkelco.com
Estimated Sales: $35 Million
Number Employees: 100-249
Square Footage: 200000
Brands:
Cross-Flow
Twin-Shell
Zig-Zag

27390 Patty O Matic Machinery
185 Squankum Rd
Farmingdale, NJ 07727-3753
732-938-2757
Fax: 732-938-5809 877-938-5244
info@pattyomatic.com www.pattyomatic.com
Molding equipment for meat, seafood, vegetables, etc.; also, meat preparation machinery, portion control equipment and weight control equipment
Owner: Daniel Miles
Sales Director: Daniel Miles
daniel.miles@wtwinter.com
Estimated Sales: $1-2.5 Million
Number Employees: 5-9

Brands:
Patty-O-Matic

27391 Patty Paper Inc
1955 N Oak Dr
Plymouth, IN 46563-3412
574-935-8439
Fax: 574-936-6053 800-782-1703
www.pattypaper.com
Manufacturer and supplier of specialty papers for wrapping meat, cheese and deli items, bakery style picking paper and waxed paper.
Manager: Sherry Simmons
Number Employees: 1-4

27392 Paul G. Gallin Company
222 Saint Johns Avenue
Yonkers, NY 10704-2717
914-964-5800
Fax: 914-964-5293
Manufacturer and exporter of uniforms and accessories
Estimated Sales: $25-50 Million
Number Employees: 18
Square Footage: 12000
Type of Packaging: Bulk

27393 Paul Hawkins Lumber Company
RT 2 Box 387A
Mannington, WV 26582
304-986-2230
Wooden lift truck pallets
Owner: Paul Hawkins
Estimated Sales: $2.5-5 Million
Number Employees: 1-4

27394 Paul Mueller Co Inc
1600 W Phelps St
Springfield, MO 65802
417-575-9000
800-683-5537
contact@paulmueller.com www.paulmueller.com
Stainless steel processing systems and equipment for the food, dairy, beverage, chemical, pharaceutical, biotechnology, and pure water industries. Also the erection of vessels in the field, expanded scope, transportation and electricalcontrols.
President & CEO: David Moore
CFO: Ken Jeffries
Global Marketing Manager: Jay Holden
Director, Operations: Michael Payne
Year Founded: 1940
Estimated Sales: $200 Million
Number Employees: 1000-4999
Square Footage: 975000
Other Locations:
Osceola IA
Brands:
Accu-Therm
Avalanche
Maximice
Pyropure
Sentry Ii
Temp Plate
Vapure

27395 Paul N. Gardner Company
316 NE 1st St
Pompano Beach, FL 33060-6608
954-946-9454
Fax: 954-946-9309 800-762-2478
gardner@gardco.com www.gardco.com
Producer of physical testing instruments. Their brands include Gardco and EZ Zahn Viscosity Cup.
President: Paul Gardner
tjohns@gardco.com
Vice President, International Sales: Sandra Bride
Marketing: Sherri Thompson
Sales Manager: Bill Bride
Manager, Customer Service: Cheryl Wilson
Manager & Director: Lisa Richards
Estimated Sales: $7 Million
Number Employees: 33

27396 Paul O. Abbe
P.O. Box 80
Bensenville, IL 60106-0080
630-350-2200
Fax: 630-350-9047 sales@pauloabbe.com
www.aaronequipment.com
Manufacturer and exporter of tumble and agitated mixers and blenders for powders and solids; also, batch vacuum and fluidized dryers and ball and pebble mills

VP: Alan Cohen
Vice President of Business Development: Bruce Baird
Estimated Sales: $5-10 Million
Number Employees: 20-49
Square Footage: 140000
Brands:
Fluidized
Forberg Ii
Rota-Blade
Rota-Cone

27397 Paul O. Abbe
139 Center Avenue
Little Falls, NJ 07424-2220
973-256-4242
Fax: 973-256-0041 sales@pauloabbe.com
www.pauloabbe.com
Chemical processing equipment: ball and pebble mills, vacuum dryers, blenders and mixers
VP: Allen Cohen
Estimated Sales: $10-20 Million
Number Employees: 4

27398 Paul T. Freund Corporation
P.O. Box 130
Palmyra, NY 14522
315-597-4873
Fax: 315-597-4188 800-333-0091
Set-up, paper covered and candy boxes
CEO: Paul Freund Jr
VP Marketing: Thomas Farnham
Estimated Sales: $10-20 Million
Number Employees: 100-249

27399 Pavailler Distribution Company
232 Pegasus Avenue
Northvale, NJ 07647-1904
201-767-0766
Fax: 201-767-1723
Bakery equipment
Estimated Sales: $2.5-5 Million
Number Employees: 9
Square Footage: 22400

27400 Pavan USA Inc
Connelly Rd
Emigsville, PA 17318
717-767-4889
Fax: 717-767-4656 www.pavan.com
Design and engineering of technologies and intergrated product lines for cereal base food.
President: Dave C Parent
VP/General Manager: David Parent
Estimated Sales: $1-3 Million
Number Employees: 1-4
Square Footage: 20000
Parent Co: Pavan SrL
Brands:
Mapimpianti
Pavan
Toresani

27401 Paxall
7300 Monticello Ave
Skokie, IL 60076-4025
847-677-7800
Fax: 847-677-7139
Tea and coffee industry packaging machines
Estimated Sales: $1 - 5 Million
Number Employees: 1-4

27402 Paxar
500 E 35th Street
Paterson, NJ 07504-1720
973-684-6564
Fax: 973-684-0235
Woven labels
Estimated Sales: $20-50 Million
Number Employees: 20-49

27403 Paxon Polymer Company
Baton Rouge
Baton Rouge, LA 70892
225-775-4330
Fax: 225-774-6632
Estimated Sales: $1 - 5 Million

27404 Paxton Corp
86 Tupelo St # 5
Unit 5
Bristol, RI 02809-2837
401-396-9062
Fax: 203-925-8722 paxton@paxtoncorp.com

Food processing machines such as cutters, slicers, shredders, dicers, graters, and strip cutters, for vegetables, fruits, cheeses, and nuts
President: Leif Jensen
  paxton@paxtoncorp.com
CFO: Monica Wingard
Sales Director: Steven King
Estimated Sales: $3 - 5 Million
Number Employees: 1-4
Square Footage: 30000
Brands:
  Alexanderwerk
  Hallde
  Paxton

27405 Paxton North America
5300 Port Royal Road
Springfield, VA 22151
          703-321-7600
  Fax: 703-321-9426 800-336-4536
  info@paxton.com www.paxton.com
Plastic tote containers and bulk boxes
Estimated Sales: Below $500,000
Number Employees: 7

27406 Paxton Products Inc
10125 Carver Rd
Blue Ash, OH 45242-4798
          513-891-7474
  Fax: 513-891-4092 800-441-7475
  sales@paxtonproducts.com
  www.paxtonproducts.com
A leader in energy saving, application-specific air systems. Designs and manufactures compact, energy-efficient compressors, blowers, air knives and drying systems.
General Manager: Barbara Stefl
Engineering Manager: Steve Pucciani
Quality Control: Charlie Hertel
International Sales Manager: Rick Immell
Customer Service: Anne Tomsic
Operations Manager: Stan Coley
Buyer: Sherry Driskell
Number Employees: 20-49

27407 Payne Controls Co
Rocky Step Rd
Scott Depot, WV 25560
          304-757-7353
  Fax: 304-757-7305 800-331-1345
  info@PaynEng.com www.payneng.com
Manufacturer and exporter of motor controls for material handling equipment and SCR controls for ovens and process temperature controls
President: Roger Westfall
  roger@payneng.com
Manager Marketing Services: Jean Miller
Estimated Sales: $5-10 Million
Number Employees: 10-19
Square Footage: 72000
Brands:
  Sentrol 31
  Sentrol Em3

27408 Pci Membrane Systems Inc
1615 State Route 131
Milford, OH 45150-2667
          513-575-3500
        Fax: 513-575-7393
Membrane filtration
CEO: Sandy Maxwell
Vice President: David Pearson
Estimated Sales: $500,000-$1 Million
Number Employees: 5-9

27409 Peace Industries
1100 Hicks Rd
Rolling Meadows, IL 60008-1016
          847-259-1620
  Fax: 847-259-9236 800-873-2239
        www.spotnails.com
Manufactures a wide range of industrial fastening products including nails, staples, pins, brads and tools for use in packaging, furniture/woodworking, construction, factory-built housing and many other industries.

President: Mark R Wilson
CFO: Rex Janderman
Vice President: Win Waterman
Marketing Director: Candi Mortenson
Sales Director: Win Waterman
Contact: Leon Larosa
  llarosa@spotnails.com
Plant Manager: Sy Akbari
Purchasing Manager: Alice Mortenson
Estimated Sales: $10 - 20 Million
Number Employees: 50-99
Type of Packaging: Bulk

27410 (HQ)Peacock Crate Factory
225 Cash St
PO Box 1110
Jacksonville, TX 75766
          903-586-0988
  Fax: 903-586-7476 800-657-2200
Manufacturer and exporter of wood veneer gift, fruit and vegetable baskets; also, store fixtures and displays
President: Richard S Peacock
CFO: Claudia Vastal
Vice President: Speedy Peacock
Estimated Sales: Below $5 Million
Number Employees: 20-49
Other Locations:
  Peacock Crate Factory
  Jacksonville TX

27411 Pearson Packaging Systems
8120 W Sunset Hwy
Spokane, WA 99224-9048
          509-838-6226
  Fax: 509-747-8532 800-732-7766
  info@pearsonpkg.com www.pearsonpkg.com
Manufacturer and exporter of case forming, case packing, tray forming, bottom, top or end sealing, carrier erecting, multipacking, partition and bag inserting machinery, and magazine feeding machinery
CEO: Michael Senske
  psenske@pearsonpkg.com
CFO: Randy Bell
Vice President of Engineering: Leo Robertson
Marketing/Sales: Mark Ewing
Vice President of Sales and Marketing: Randy Denny
Estimated Sales: $10 - 20 Million
Number Employees: 100-249
Square Footage: 220000
Type of Packaging: Food Service, Private Label, Bulk

27412 Pearson Packaging Systems
8120 W Sunset Hwy
Spokane, WA 99224-9048
          509-838-6226
  Fax: 509-747-8532 800-732-7766
  sales@goodmanpkg.com www.pearsonpkg.com
Case/tray packaging equipment
CEO: James A Goodman
President, Chief Executive Officer: Michael Senske
  psenske@pearsonpkg.com
Vice President of Engineering: Leo Robertson
President: Billy Goodman
Vice President of Sales and Marketing: Randy Denny
Number Employees: 100-249

27413 Pearson Research Assoc
PO Box 1778
Santa Cruz, CA 95061-1778
          831-429-9797
  Fax: 831-426-7010 info@pearsonresearch.com
        www.pearsonresearch.com
Consultant specializing in market research, survey design, consumer tests, sensory evaluation, focus groups, etc
Owner: Adrian Pearson
  adrian@pearsonresearch.com
Number Employees: 1-4

27414 Pearson Signs Service
2031 Hanover Pike
Hampstead, MD 21074-1336
          410-239-3838
        Fax: 410-239-3848
Signs including metal, wood, paper, plastic and neon
Owner: Herb Shaffer
Estimated Sales: $1 - 5 Million
Number Employees: 5-9
Square Footage: 6000

27415 Pease Awning & Sunroom Co
21 Massasoit Ave
East Providence, RI 02914-4439
          401-438-2850
  Fax: 401-434-6520 president@necpa.org
        www.peasecompany.com
Commercial awnings; also, installation services available
President: Ted Franklin
  sales@peasecompany.com
VP: Donald Franklin
Purchasing Manager: Edwin Franklin
Estimated Sales: $1 - 5 Million
Number Employees: 10-19
Square Footage: 84000

27416 Pecan Deluxe Candy Co
2570 Lone Star Dr
Dallas, TX 75212-6308
          214-631-3669
          800-733-3589
  pdcc_info@pecandeluxe.com
        www.pecandeluxe.com
Dessert and baked goods ingredients: toffees, nuts, chocolate coated items, flavor bases and sauces.
President/CEO: Jay Brigham
Estimated Sales: $20-50 Million
Number Employees: 250-499
Number of Products: 2000
Square Footage: 63000
Type of Packaging: Bulk

27417 Pechiney Plastic Packaging
716 Tanager Lane
West Chicago, IL 60185-5949
          630-293-8050
        Fax: 630-293-8064
Food Sales/Marketing: David Quinn
Estimated Sales: $1 - 5 Million
Type of Packaging: Consumer

27418 Pechiney Plastic Packaging
8770 W Bryn Mawr Ave
Chicago, IL 60631
          773-399-0255
        Fax: 773-399-8549
Flexible packaging and plastic bottles
President: Ilene Gordon
CFO: Robert Mosesian
Quality Control: Rey Brunelle
Contact: Eileen Lerum
  eileen.lerum@alcan.com
Estimated Sales: $20 - 50 Million
Number Employees: 250-499

27419 (HQ)Peco Controls Corporation
1439 Emerald Ave
Modesto, CA 95351
          510-226-6686
  Fax: 510-226-6687 800-732-6285
  info@pecocontrols.com www.pecocontrols.com
Manufacturer and exporter of monitors for inspecting fill and vacuum/pressure levels, contents and labels of packages; also, automatic container sampling systems and two-piece can metrology systems
President: F Allan Anderson
Vice President: Aslam Khan
Quality Control: Cheong Chan
Contact: Allan Anderson
  a.anderson@pecocontrols.com
Estimated Sales: $3 - 5 Million
Number Employees: 35
Square Footage: 64000
Type of Packaging: Consumer, Private Label
Other Locations:
  Peco Controls Corp.
  Pershore, Wozos
Brands:
  Criterion
  Gamma 101p
  Sample Trac
  Vac Trac
  Valv-Chek

27420 Pecora Nera, Inc.
Vaughan, ON L4K 3W7
Canada
        hello@pecoranerafinepasta.ca
        www.pecoranerafinepasta.ca
Pasta, bread, and dough.
Founder: Tom Bielecki *Year Founded:* 2020
Type of Packaging: Food Service

27421 Peekskill Hair Net
201 S Division Street
Peekskill, NY 10566-3611
914-737-1524
Fax: 914-788-3890
Acetate, nylon and rayon protective hair nets and
caps
President: John Kotowski
Secretary/Bookkeeper: Gertrude DeFazio
Treasurer: John Kotowski
Number Employees: 10
Square Footage: 12000

27422 Peerless Cartons
1073 Martingale Drive
Bartlett, IL 60103-5676
312-226-7952
Fax: 312-226-6861
Folding cartons
President: Larry Mitchell
Estimated Sales: $2.5-5 Million
Number Employees: 19

27423 Peerless Conveyor & MfgCorp
201 E Quindaro Blvd
Kansas City, KS 66115-1424
913-342-2240
Fax: 913-342-2237 www.peerlessconveyor.com
Conveyors and conveying equipment for bulk mate-
rials including grain sugar
President: William S Walker
wwalker@peerlessconveyor.com
Sales Director: Chuck Leonard
Production Manager: Seth Rodriquez
Estimated Sales: $2.5 - 5 Million
Number Employees: 20-49
Square Footage: 80000

**27424 Peerless Dough Mixing and
Make-Up**
P.O. Box 769
Sidney, OH 45365-0769
937-492-4158
Fax: 937-492-3688 800-999-3327
www.thepeerlessgroup.us
Dough machinery
President: Dane Belden
Chairman/CEO: Robert Zielsdorf
Estimated Sales: $20 - 50 Million
Number Employees: 100-249

27425 Peerless Food Equipment
500 S Vandemark Rd
Sidney, OH 45365-8991
937-492-4158
Fax: 937-492-3688 www.peerlessfood.com
Manufacturer and exporter of snack food and bakery
processing equipment including conveyors, coolers,
depositors, icers, mixers, pumps, topping applicators
and bagel machinery
General Manager: George Hoff
Director of Marketing: Sherri Swabb
Director of Sales: Richard Taylor
Estimated Sales: 5-10 Million
Number Employees: 100-249
Square Footage: 208000

27426 Peerless Food Equipment
500 S Vandemark Rd
Sidney, OH 45365-8991
937-492-4158
Fax: 937-492-3688 info@petersmachinery.com
www.peerlessfood.com
Manufacturer and exporter of food processing ma-
chinery including stackers and cookie sandwiching
and wrapping equipment
General Manager: George Hoff
Controller: David Alexander
Director, Marketing And Customer Support: Sherri
Swabb
Sales Director: Richard Taylor
Human Resource Manager: Kathy Weldy
Plant And Materials Manager: Mike Gniazdowski
Estimated Sales: $7 Million
Number Employees: 100-249
Parent Co: Peerless Group

27427 Peerless Gouet LLC
2039 Clipper Drive
Lafayette, CO 80026-3160
720-890-7306
Fax: 720-890-1286 jwp@indra.com
President: John Parr

27428 Peerless Lighting Corporation
PO Box 2556
Berkeley, CA 94702-0556
510-845-2760
Fax: 510-845-2776 www.peerless-lighting.com
Manufacturer and exporter of institutional and com-
mercial fluorescent lighting fixtures
President: Douglas Herst
VP: Jim Young
Manager Marketing Services: Margaret Einhorn
Contact: Michael Brunasso
michael.brunasso@peerless-lighting.com
Estimated Sales: $10-20 Million
Number Employees: 50-99

27429 Peerless Machine & ToolCorp
1804 W 2nd St
Marion, IN 46952-3362
765-662-2586
Fax: 765-662-6067
peerlessmt@peerlessmachine.com
www.peerlessmachine.com
Paper converting machinery, paper plates and trays
Owner: Jeff Carson
jeffreycarson@peerlessmachine.com
Estimated Sales: $2.5-5 Million
Number Employees: 20-49

**27430 (HQ)Peerless Machinery
Corporation**
PO Box 769
Sidney, OH 45365
937-492-4158
Fax: 937-492-3688 800-999-3327
www.thepeerlessgroup.us
Manufacturer and exporter of bakery mixers, divid-
ers, blenders and rounders
President: Dane Belden
Director Marketing: Terry Bartsch
VP Sales: Michael Booth
Contact: David Alexander
dalexander@thepeerlessgroup.us
Estimated Sales: $20-50 Million
Number Employees: 100-249
Square Footage: 75000
Other Locations:
Peerless Machinery Corp.
Odessa FL
Brands:
Hallmark
Peerless
Royal
Supergrain

27431 Peerless Ovens
334 Harrison St
Sandusky, OH 44870
419-625-4514
Fax: 419-625-4597 800-548-4514
www.peerlessovens.com
Manufacturer and exporter of bakery and pizza ov-
ens, griddles and ranges
President: Bryan Huntley
peerless@lrbcg.com
Estimated Sales: $1-2.5 Million
Number Employees: 10-19
Square Footage: 200000
Type of Packaging: Food Service

27432 Peerless Packages
23600 Mercantile Rd # A
Cleveland, OH 44122-5971
216-464-3620
Fax: 216-464-3440
Plastic and paper bags and boxes
Sales: Lynn Harmon
Sales Manager: Lynn Harmon
Estimated Sales: $1-2.5 Million
Number Employees: 5-9

27433 Peerless of America
109 Schelter Rd
Lincolnshire, IL 60069-3603
847-634-7500
Fax: 847-634-7506
Manufacturer and exporter of refrigeration and air
conditioning equipment including evaporators,
finned coils, heat transfer products and unit and
flash coolers
Owner: Igor Gordon
VP Sales/Marketing: Michael Schopf
Estimated Sales: $20-50 Million
Number Employees: 100-249
Square Footage: 395000

27434 Peerless-Premier Appliance Co
119 S 14th St
Belleville, IL 62220-1715
618-233-0475
Fax: 618-235-1771 info@premierrange.com
www.premierrange.com
Manufacturer and exporter of gas and electric ranges
President: Joseph Geary
CEO: Robert Burggraf
burggraf@premierrange.com
CEO: Alex Volansky
Chairman of the Board: William T Sprague
VP Marketing: Allan Gramlich
National Sales Manager: Robert Volkmann
Estimated Sales: $20 - 50 Million
Number Employees: 100-249
Square Footage: 300000
Brands:
Eagle
Heritage By Orbon
Mark Royal
Modern Chef
Premier

27435 Peerless-Winsmith Inc
172 Eaton St
Springville, NY 14141
716-592-9310
Fax: 716-592-9546 www.winsmith.com
Manufacturer and exporter of worm gear speed re-
ducers for material handling conveyors and machin-
ery; also, food processing and bottling machinery.
Year Founded: 1901
Estimated Sales: $100-500 Million
Number Employees: 100-249

27436 Pel-Pak Container
1107 Dowzer Ave
Pell City, AL 35125
205-338-2993
Fax: 205-338-6120 800-239-2699
Corrugated boxes
President: Jeanette L Chasteen
Plant Manager: Mike Richerzhagen
Number Employees: 19

27437 Pelco Packaging Corporation
269 Mercer St.
Stirling, NJ 07980
908-647-3500
Fax: 908-647-1868
customerservice@pelcopackaging.com
www.pelcopackaging.com
Plastic material handling equipment and packaging
including boxes
President: Arthur J Brinker
Estimated Sales: $1 - 2.5 Million
Number Employees: 15

27438 Pelican Displays
109 E 1st St
Homer, IL 61849-1101
217-896-2628
Fax: 217-896-2628 800-627-1517
Wood, polyethylene and acrylic bulk food display
bins
Owner: David Lucas
Estimated Sales: $1 - 5 Million
Number Employees: 1-4
Square Footage: 17000

27439 Pelican Marine Supply LLC
2911 Engineers Rd
Belle Chasse, LA 70037-3150
504-392-9062
Fax: 504-394-5528 www.pelicanmarinedist.com
Beef, pork, poultry, fish, seafood and general groceri-
ies
President: Peter Bretchel
Manager: James Lutz
jameyl@pelicanmarinedist.com
Estimated Sales: $10 - 20 Million
Number Employees: 5-9

27440 Pelican Products Inc
1049 Lowell St
Bronx, NY 10459-2608
718-860-3220
Fax: 718-860-4415 800-552-8820
info@pelicanproducts.com
www.pelican.com
Manufacturer and exporter of molded plastic advertising specialties, imprinted premiums and promotional give-aways including coasters, stirrers,
cocktail forks, corkscrews and ball point pens

Vice President: David Silver
david@pelicanproducts.com
CEO: Harold Silver
Vice President: Dave Silver
Estimated Sales: $2.5 - 5 Million
Number Employees: 10-19
Square Footage: 40000

27441 Pell Paper Box Company
PO Box 584
Elizabeth City, NC 27907-0584
   252-335-4361
Fax: 252-335-9639 murry@series2000.com
Set-up and folding boxes for frozen foods, baked
goods and promotional and specialty products
COO: P Murry Pitts
General Manager: Tony Rossi
Estimated Sales: $10-20 Million
Number Employees: 50-99
Square Footage: 170000

27442 Pellenc America
955 S Virginia Street
Suite 116
Reno, NV 89502-0413
   702-853-3455
Fax: 702-853-4554
Wine industry pruning equipment

27443 Pellerin Milnor Corporation
700 Jackson St
P.O. Box 400
Kenner, LA 70063-0400
   504-467-9591
   800-469-8780
milnorinfo@milnor.com www.milnor.com
A leading commercial and industrial laundry equip-
ment manufacturer. Washer-extractors range in size
from 25 lb to 700 lb capacity; dryers from 30-550 lb.
These models are available with a variety of controls
from very simple to quitesophisticated, depending
upon your food and beverage linen needs.
President: James Pellerin
Vice President: Russ Poy
Year Founded: 1947
Estimated Sales: $100+ Million
Number Employees: 530
Square Footage: 400000
Brands:
  E-P Plus
  System 7

27444 Pelouze Scale Company
7400 W 100th Place
Bridgeview, IL 60455-2438
   708-430-8330
Fax: 800-654-7330 800-323-8363
www.pelouze.com
Manufacturer and exporter of mechanical and elec-
tronic timers, food thermometers and food portion,
dietetic, electronic digital and shipping and
receiving scales
VP: Dan Maeir
VP: Dan Maeir
National Sales Manager: Jack Kramer
Customer Service Manager: Laura Anton
Estimated Sales: $50 - 100 Million
Number Employees: 140
Parent Co: Sunbeam
Type of Packaging: Consumer, Food Service

27445 Pemberton & Associates
3610 Nashua Drive
Mississauga, ON L4V 1X9
Canada
   905-678-8900
Fax: 905-678-8989 800-668-6111
pemco@pemcom.com www.pemcom.com
President: Dennis Hicks
R&D: Keith Tse
Vice President: Bill Froggatt
Number Employees: 20

27446 Pemberton & Associates
152 Remsen Street
Brooklyn, NY 11201
Canada
   718-923-1111
Fax: 718-923-6065 800-736-2664
career@pemcom.com www.pemcom.com
Manufacturers full service representative of meat
and poultry processing, and packaging equipment
Founder, President: Wade Saadi
Vice President of Operations: Jim Kenner

Number Employees: 15

27447 Penasack Co Inc
49 Sanford St
PO Box 396
Albion, NY 14411-1117
   585-589-5873
Fax: 585-589-0046 penasack@rochester.rr.com
www.penasack.com
Manufacturer and fabricator of stainless steel prod-
ucts
President: Gerard Da More
penasack@rochester.rr.com
Engineering Manager: Jeff Kinser
Operations: Mike Hrycelak
Estimated Sales: $3-5 Million
Number Employees: 20-49
Square Footage: 80000
Parent Co: GDM Enterprises
Type of Packaging: Food Service, Private Label,
Bulk

27448 Penco Products
P.O. Box 158
Skippack, PA 19474
   610-666-0500
Fax: 610-666-7561 800-562-1000
customerservice@pencoproducts.com
www.pencoproducts.com
Manufacturer and exporter of shelving, work
benches, storage cabinets, pallet racks and lockers
President: Greg Grogan
VP Sales/Marketing: Bill Vain
Estimated Sales: $20-50 Million
Number Employees: 250-499
Brands:
  Clipper
  Erectomatic
  Hi-Performance
  Rivit Orite

27449 Penda Form Corp
200 S Friendship Dr
New Concord, OH 43762-9641
   740-826-5000
Fax: 740-826-5001 800-837-2574
Material handling equipment including trays, pallets
and covers; exporter of electrical components
President: John Knight
jknight@fabri-form.com
VP Sales: Larry Howard
Manager Customer Service: Dennis Hardin
jknight@fabri-form.com
Plant Manager: Jerry Andrech
Number Employees: 50-99

27450 Pengo Attachments Inc
13369 60th St SW
Cokato, MN 55321-4210
   320-286-5581
Fax: 320-286-5583 800-599-0211
pengosales@pengoattachments.com
www.pengoattachments.com
Custom fabricated conveyor screws for food appli-
cations
Cio/Cto: Dave Bailey
dbailey@paladinbrands.com
VP/ General Manager: Brian Rickards
Engineering Manager: Eric Matthias
Vice President-Sales/Marketing: Dana Scudder
HR Business Partner: Ray Waite
Operations Manager: Jim Groat
Product Manager: Mary Pohlman
Division Controller: John Ricke
Estimated Sales: $10-20 Million
Number Employees: 100-249
Square Footage: 84000
Parent Co: Crown Holdings

27451 Penguin Natural Foods, Inc.
4400 Alcoa Ave
Vernon, CA 90058
   323-727-7980
Fax: 323-727-7983 www.penguinfoods.com
Rice, baking mixes, potato mixes, cornbreads, pastas
and rice blends.
President: Scott Nairne
Year Founded: 1991
Estimated Sales: $25 Million
Number Employees: 132
Type of Packaging: Consumer, Food Service, Pri-
vate Label

27452 Peninsula Plastics
2800 Auburn Ct
Auburn Hills, MI 48326-3203
   248-852-3731
Fax: 248-852-5482 800-394-8698
www.peninsulaplastics.com
Custom vacuum formed packaging products
President: Richard Jositas
Controller/CFO: Grace McKinney
Vice President: Ryan Victory
ryanvictory@peninsulaplastics.com
General Manager: Roderick Zielinski
Estimated Sales: $10 - 20 Million
Number Employees: 50-99
Square Footage: 60000

27453 Penley Corporation
PO Box 277
West Paris, ME 04289-0277
   207-674-2501
Fax: 207-674-2510 800-368-6449
Manufacturer, importer and exporter of wooden
toothpicks, matches, chopsticks, etc.; also, plastic
cutlery and drinking straws
Owner: Richard Penley
Director Sales/Marketing: Stephen Gilman
Director Manufacturing: Robert Warrington
Estimated Sales: $5-10 Million
Number Employees: 10-19

27454 Penn Barry
605 Shiloh Rd
Plano, TX 75074-7210
   972-212-4700
pennbarrysales@pennbarry.com
www.pennvent.com
Fans and ventilation equipment
President: Scott Adamson
sadamson@pennbarry.com
Number Employees: 50-99
Parent Co: Air System Components, Inc.

27455 Penn Barry
605 Shiloh Rd
Plano, TX 75074-7210
   972-212-4700
Fax: 972-212-4701
pennbarrysales@pennbarry.com
www.pennbarry.com
Single source for commercial and industrial ventila-
tion product solutions.
President: Scott Adamson
sadamson@pennbarry.com
Number Employees: 50-99
Square Footage: 120000
Parent Co: Air System Components, Inc.
Brands:
  Barry Blower
  Bayley Fan
  Industrial Air
  Penn Ventilation
  Supreme

27456 Penn Bottle & Supply Company
7150 Lindbergh Boulevard
Philadelphia, PA 19153-3008
   215-365-5700
Fax: 215-365-2320
Plastic and glass bottles
CEO and President: Richard Probinsky
VP Finance and Administration: Paul Silverman

27457 Penn Products
91 Main Street
Portland, CT 6480
   860-342-2500
Fax: 860-342-5563 800-490-7366
service@pennproducts.com
www.pennproductsusa.com
Custom injection molded plastic boxes and contain-
ers
VP Operations: Ray Pennoyer
Administrator: Raymond Pennoyer Iii
Estimated Sales: $2.5-5 Million
Number Employees: 20-49
Number of Brands: 1
Square Footage: 40000
Type of Packaging: Private Label, Bulk

27458 Penn Refrigeration Service Corporation
P.O. Box 1261
Wilkes Barre, PA 18703-1261
570-825-5666
Fax: 570-825-5705 800-233-8354
sales@pennrefrig.com
Manufacturer and exporter of refrigeration equipment and systems including walk-in coolers and freezers
President: Albert Finarelli Jr
afinarelli@pennrefrig.com
Plant Manager: John Gosciewski
Estimated Sales: $5 - 10 Million
Number Employees: 50-99

27459 Penn Scale ManufacturingCompany
150 W Berks St
Philadelphia, PA 19122
215-739-9644
Fax: 215-739-9640 sales@pennscale.com
www.pennscale.com
Scales and scoops
President: Larry Biren
Owner: Andy Levin
Quality Control: Andy Levin
Contact: Mary Biren
mary.biren@pennscale.com
Estimated Sales: $300,000
Number Employees: 5-9
Square Footage: 24000
Brands:
Penn Scale

27460 PennPac International
8200 Flourtown Avenue
Suite 6b
Wyndmoor, PA 19038-7969
215-836-1380
Fax: 215-836-7885
Plastic containers
Estimated Sales: less than $500,000
Number Employees: 1

27461 Pennsylvania Food Merchants Association
P.O. Box 870
Camp Hill, PA 17001-0870
717-731-0600
Fax: 717-731-5472 800-543-8207
pfma@aol.com www.pfma.org
Our mission is to improve the profitability of companies in the retail and wholesale food distribution industry.
President/CEO: David Mc Corkle
CFO: Dwight Cromer
Sr. VP Association Services: Randolph St.John
Vice President, Sales & Marketing: Autumn Thomas
Sales Support Specialist: Michele Weaver
Contact: Steve Halterman
shalterman@memoco.com
Administrative Assistant: Jennifer Hamelin
Number Employees: 50-99

27462 Penny Plate
PO Box 3003
Haddonfield, NJ 08033
856-429-7583
Fax: 856-429-7166 mmiller@pennyplate.com
www.pennyplate.com
Aluminum food service containers
Assistant to CEO: George Buff
CEO: George Buff
Contact: Nancy Arno
narno@pennyplate.com
Estimated Sales: $30 - 50 Million
Number Employees: 100-249

27463 Pensacola Rope Company
PO Box 1926
Slidell, LA 70459-1926
850-968-9760
Fax: 850-968-1669
Solid braided nylon cord and rope
President: Thomas Fields
Estimated Sales: $500,000-$1 Million
Number Employees: 4

27464 Penske Truck Leasing Corp
2675 Morgantown Rd
Reading, PA 19607-9676
610-775-6000
844-376-4095
www.gopenske.com
Truck leasing service.
President: Brian Hard
brian.hard@penske.com
Year Founded: 1969
Estimated Sales: $8.4 Billion
Number Employees: 36,000
Parent Co: Penske Corp

27465 Pentad Group Inc
7234 Francisco Bend Dr
Delray Beach, FL 33446
561-362-8678
Fax: 561-495-9777 labelsaver@aol.com
www.labeloff.com
Logos on any item, wine related products such as wine label removers, wine label albums, glassware, coolers, aprons, posters, etc
CEO: Marvin Pesses
Vice President: Marvin Pesses
Contact: Elaine Pesses
mpesses@yahoo.com
Estimated Sales: $2.5-5 Million
Number Employees: 5
Number of Products: 46
Type of Packaging: Consumer, Private Label
Brands:
Labeloff Wine Label Removers

27466 Pentair Valves & Controls
3950 Greenbriar Dr
Stafford, TX 77477-3919
281-274-4400
Fax: 281-240-1800 www.pentair.com
Manager: Frank Hoban
frank.hoban@pentair.com
Plant Manager: Andy Masullo
Number Employees: 500-999

27467 Pentwater Wire ProductsInc
474 S Carroll St
Pentwater, MI 49449-8772
231-869-6911
Fax: 231-869-4020 877-869-6911
pwp@pentwaterwire.com
www.pentwaterwire.com
Racks, displays, containers, assemblies, shelving and baskets
President: Ivan Ewing
iewing@pentwaterwire.com
Vice President: Dwight Swanson
Sales Director: Mike Piper
Estimated Sales: $5-10 Million
Number Employees: 50-99
Square Footage: 200000
Brands:
On Guard

27468 Peoria Meat Packing
1300 W Lake St
Chicago, IL 60607-1512
312-738-1800
Fax: 312-738-1180 www.peoriapacking.com
Packaging
Owner: Harry Katsiavlos
Estimated Sales: $10 - 20 Million
Number Employees: 1-4

27469 Peoria Tent & Awning
3012 W Farmington Road
Peoria, IL 61604
309-674-1128
Fax: 309-697-9871 www.peoriaawning.com
Commercial awnings
Owner: Mark Hutchison
Estimated Sales: $1-2,500,000
Number Employees: 20-49
Parent Co: PAMA Group

27470 Pepetti's Hygrade Egg Product
100 Trumbull Street
Elizabeth, NJ 07206-2105
908-351-9618
Fax: 908-351-7528 www.papetti.com
Estimated Sales: $.5 - 1 million
Number Employees: 1-4

27471 Pepper Mill
558 S Broad St
Mobile, AL 36603-1124
251-433-7919
Fax: 251-433-3364 800-669-5175
Trivet boards and brushes including wire and bristle
President: Scott Gonzalez
scott@3geroges.com
VP Finance: Siobhan Gonzalez
Estimated Sales: $.5 - 1 million
Number Employees: 1-4
Square Footage: 2000
Brands:
Fajita Trivet
Monster
Roughneck

27472 (HQ)Pepper Source Inc
2720 Athania Pkwy
Metairie, LA 70002-5904
504-885-3223
Fax: 504-885-3187 www.peppersource.com
Sauces and glazes, dry blends, custome rubs and packaging services.
President: Joe Morse
Contact: Shannon Glover
sglover@peppersource.com
Vice President of Operations: Paul Liggio
Production Supervisor: Mike Bartels
Estimated Sales: $15 Million
Number Employees: 5-9
Type of Packaging: Food Service, Private Label, Bulk
Other Locations:
Pepper Source
Van Buren AR
Pepper Source
Rogers AR

27473 PepperWorks
303 Industrial Way
Suite 5
Fallbrook, CA 92028
760-723-0202
Fax: 760-723-2227 info@wine-master.com
Wine industry tasting room supplies
Manager: Biby Zeledon

27474 Pepperell Paper Company
9 S Canal Street
Lawrence, MA 01843-1412
978-433-6951
Fax: 978-433-6427
Manufacturer and exporter of specialty papers including acid free, beater dyed colors, packaging, supercalendered, grease, mold and flame resistant, crepe, flour bag, kraft, etc
Sales Manager: Steve Ulicny
Number Employees: 4
Square Footage: 400000
Parent Co: James River Corporation
Brands:
Strypel
Styprint
Stysorb

27475 Pepperl & Fuchs Inc
1600 Enterprise Pkwy
Twinsburg, OH 44087-2245
330-425-3555
Fax: 330-425-4607 sales@us.pepperl-fuchs.us
www.pepperl-fuchs.us
Industrial controls and sensors
President: Wolfgang Mueller
wmueller@us.pepperl-fuchs.us
R&D: Hurman Witch
CEO: Wolfgang Mueller
Estimated Sales: $20 - 50 Million
Number Employees: 100-249

27476 PepsiCo.
700 Anderson Hill Rd.
Purchase, NY 10577
914-253-2000
www.pepsico.com
Global brands food, snack and beverage company.
Chairman/CEO: Ramon Laguarta
President, Global Foodservice: Anne Fink
Vice Chairman/CFO: Hugh Johnston
EVP/Chief Scientific Officer: Ren, Lammers
Year Founded: 1965
Estimated Sales: $79.5 Billion
Number Employees: 291,000

Number of Brands: 54
Square Footage: 40000
Type of Packaging: Consumer
Brands:
  AMP ENERGY Organic
  Aquafina
  Bare
  Brisk
  Bubly
  Cap'n Crunch
  Cheetos
  Cracker Jack
  Doritos
  Frito-Lay
  Fritos
  Funyuns
  Gatorade
  Grandma's
  IZZE
  Imag!ne
  Kevita
  Life
  Life WTR
  Lipton
  Maker
  Matador
  Maui Style
  Miss Vickies
  Mountain Dew
  Mug Root Beer
  Munchos
  Naked
  Near East
  Nut Harvest
  O.N.E
  Off the Eaten Path
  Pasta Roni
  Pearl Milling Company
  Pepsi
  Propel
  Pure Leaf
  Quaker
  Red Rock Deli
  Rice A Roni
  Rold Gold
  Ruffles
  SOBE
  Sabra
  Sabritones
  Santitas
  Sierra Mist
  Smartfood
  Stacy's Pita Chips
  Starbucks Frappacino
  Stubborn Soda
  Sun Chips
  Tostitos
  Tropicana

27477 Per Pak/Orlandi
131 Executive Boulevard
Farmingdale, NY 11735
631-756-0110
Fax: 631-756-0256 www.orlandi-usa.com
Contract packager offering high-speed over wrapping, form fill and seal for liquids, powders and cartoning
President: Sven Dobler
COO: Per Dobler
Controller: David Hays
VP Marketing: Dale Beal
Plant Manager: Mike Cheff
Estimated Sales: $5 - 10 Million
Number Employees: 50-99
Parent Co: Jefferson Smurfit Corporation

27478 Per-Fil Industries Inc
407 Adams St
Riverside, NJ 08075-3098
856-461-5700
Fax: 856-461-0741 www.per-fil.com
Manufacturer and exporter of filling machinery for liquids, powder, paste, granules and food products
President: Shari Becker
Director/Chairman: Horst Boellmann
  per-fil@sales.com
Service Manager: Tobin Wrice
National and International Sales: Shari Becker
Estimated Sales: Below $5 Million
Number Employees: 20-49
Square Footage: 29000
Brands:
  Micro-Recharger
  Rotary Recharger

27479 Perception
3307 S College Avenue
Unit 113
Fort Collins, CO 80525-4196
970-226-1941
Fax: 970-221-4809

27480 Peregrine Inc
5301 N 57th St # 102
Lincoln, NE 68507-3164
402-466-4011
Fax: 402-466-1639 800-777-3433
info@peregrine-inc.com www.peregrine-inc.com
Manufacturer and exporter of material handling equipment including four-wheel steering trailers
President: Troy Rivers
  troy@peregrine-inc.com
Office/Sales Manager: Joyce Schiermann
Estimated Sales: $1 - 2,500,000
Number Employees: 5-9
Type of Packaging: Bulk
Brands:
  Quad-Steer

27481 Perfecseal
9800 Bustleton Ave
Philadelphia, PA 19115
215-673-4500
Fax: 215-676-1311 800-568-7626
www.perfecseal.com
Heat seal coated materials, coated paper and laminations, laminated films, tubing, header bag packaging
President: Paul Verbeten
CEO: Alan McClure
R&D: Richard Craig
Quality Control: Gail Turner
CFO: Ben Travey
Contact: Janet Voegele
  jvoegele@bemis.com
Plant Manager: Gail Turner
Estimated Sales: $83.8 Million
Number Employees: 100-249

27482 Perfect Equipment Inc
4259 Lee Ave
Gurnee, IL 60031-2175
847-244-7200
Fax: 847-244-7205 800-356-6301
info@perfectequip.com www.perfectequip.com
Manufacturer and exporter of beverage and condiment dispenser systems, custom fabricated stainless steel bar and restaurant equipment including underbar and portable and back bar units, glycol units and water chillers
President: Sanford Hahn
  sandy@perfectequip.com
CEO: Kay Hahn
Sales/ Administration: Kathy Pino
Operations Manager/ R&D: Alan Hale
Plant Manager: Alan Hale
Purchasing: Gene Wood
Estimated Sales: $5-10,000,000
Number Employees: 20-49
Square Footage: 28000
Type of Packaging: Food Service

27483 Perfect Fit Glove Company
85 Innsbruck Dr
Cheektowaga, NY 14227
716-668-2000
Fax: 716-668-3224 800-245-6837
perfectfitglove@perfectfitglove.com
Safety equipment and hand protection
Manager: Greg Wall
Estimated Sales: $50 - 75 Million
Number Employees: 50-99

27484 Perfect Fry Company
615 71st Avenue SE
Calgary, AB T2H 0S7
Canada
403-255-7712
Fax: 403-255-1725 800-265-7711
profits@perfectfry.com www.perfectfry.com
Manufacturers ventless countertop deep fryers designated for commercial deep-frying without the instalation of hoods and vents

Vice President of Business Development: Gary Calderwood
CFO: Sharon Hyasdick
Vice President, General Manager: Greg Moyer
Research & Development: Shaun Calderwood
Senior Manager of Sales: Bonnie Bolster
Vice President of Operations: Steve Reale
Plant Manager: Jeff Scott
Estimated Sales: Below $5 Million
Number Employees: 20
Square Footage: 60000
Parent Co: Perfect Fry Corporation
Type of Packaging: Food Service
Brands:
  Perfect Fry

27485 Perfect Plank Co
2850 S 5th Ave
Oroville, CA 95965-5851
530-533-7606
Fax: 530-533-2814 800-327-1961
www.perfectplank.com
Laminated wood countertops, butcher blocks, tabletops and sign blanks
Sales Manager: Terry Horne
Manager: Terry Horne
  perfectplank@att.net
General Manager: Jim Horne
Production Manager: Bob Horne
Sales and Accounts Payable: Adam Horne
Estimated Sales: $1-2.5 Million
Number Employees: 10-19
Square Footage: 120000

27486 Perfect Score Company
9326 Garfield Blvd
Cleveland, OH 44125-1313
216-883-8000
Fax: 216-883-8800 sales@theperfectscore.com
www.theperfectscore.com

27487 Perfex Corporation
32 Case St
Poland, NY 13431
315-826-3600
Fax: 315-826-7471 800-848-8483
perfex@perfexonline.com www.perfexonline.com
Manufacturer and exporter of PVC floor and neoprene rubber squeegees, polypropylene, chemical resistant and hygienic brooms and brushes, shovels and stainless steel clean room flat mopping systems
President: Michael Kubick
Marketing Manager: Mike Dougherty
Sales: Irene Gouthier
Customer Service Supervisor: Trudy Pickerd
Estimated Sales: $1-2.5 Million
Number Employees: 10-25

27488 Performance Contracting
11145 Thompson Ave.
Lenexa, KS 66219
913-888-8600
800-255-6886
info@pcg.com www.performancecontracting.com
Construction of specialized facilities for cold storage, food processing and distribution.
President/CEO: William Massey
Vice President/CFO: Alan Clayton
Vice President/General Counsel: Rod Eisenhauer
Chief Operating Officer: Jason Hendricks
Year Founded: 1984
Estimated Sales: $871 Million
Number Employees: 7,000
Square Footage: 36000

27489 Performance Imaging Corp
5392 Leon St
Oceanside, CA 92057-3654
760-721-2925
Fax: 760-721-2925 800-266-5742
www.performanceimaging.com
Specializing in machine vision inspection systems offering complete package inspection. Capabilities include label inspection, character recognition and verification, cap inspection and fill level; custom application softwareavailible
Contact: Michael Russe
  m.russe@performanceimaging.com
Estimated Sales: $2.5-5 Million
Number Employees: 10-19

27490 Performance Packaging
6430 Medical Center St # 102
Suite 102
Las Vegas, NV 89148-2403
702-240-3457
Fax: 702-240-3453 ppsales@pplv.co
www.pplv.co
President: Robert Reinders
  robreinders@performace-packaging.com
CFO: Bruce Moore
Estimated Sales: Below $5 Million
Number Employees: 5-9

27491 Performance Packaging
251 N Roeske Avenue
Trail Creek, IN 46360-5072
219-874-6226
Fax: 219-874-3011
Corrugated boxes and packaging materials
VP Sales/Marketing: Will Childers
Contact: Dotti Kasten
  dotti.kasten@plastipak.com
Estimated Sales: $5-10 Million
Number Employees: 2
Square Footage: 200000

27492 Perl Packaging Systems
80 Turnpike Dr # 2
Middlebury, CT 06762-1830
203-598-0066
Fax: 203-598-0068 800-864-2853
Manufacturer and exporter of straight line liquid fill-
ing machines, piston fillers, portable cappers, rotary
unscramblers, cap and bottle orienter feeders and
labelers
President: David Baker
Estimated Sales: $3 - 5 Million
Number Employees: 5-9
Square Footage: 40000

27493 Perley-Halladay Assoc
1037 Andrew Dr
West Chester, PA 19380-4293
610-840-6300
Fax: 610-647-1711 800-248-5800
  sales@perleyhalladay.com
  www.perleyhalladay.com
Manufacturer and exporter of refrigerated buildings,
walk-in coolers and process freezers
Owner: Boone Flint
  bf@perleyhalladay.com
Office Mngr.: Jim Sonvogni
Estimated Sales: $2.5-5 Million
Number Employees: 1-4

27494 Perlick Corp
8300 W Good Hope Rd
Milwaukee, WI 53223-4524
414-353-7060
Fax: 414-353-7069 800-558-5592
  perlick@perlick.com www.perlick.com
Manufactuer of bar and beverage dispensing equip-
ment for the foodservice industry.
President, CEO: Paul Peot
  pap@perlick.com
CFO: Mike Pitialip
VP of Manufacturing: Tim Carpenter
VP of Marketing & Business Development: Tim
Ebner
VP of Commercial Sales: Jim Koelbl
Number Employees: 250-499
Square Footage: 1112000
Type of Packaging: Food Service

27495 Permacold Engineering Inc
3005 NE Argyle St
Portland, OR 97211-1946
503-249-8190
Fax: 503-249-8322 800-455-8585
  info@permacold.com www.permacold.com
Refrigeration contractors: parts, service, overhaul
and construction
Owner: Steve Jackston
  steve.jackson@permacold.com
Vice President: Randy Clelokit
Marketing: Lindsay Jackson
Sales Director: Randy Cieldna
Operations Manager: Steve Jackson
Estimated Sales: $20 - 50 Million
Number Employees: 50-99

27496 Permaloc Security Devices
PO Box 4699
Silver Spring, MD 20914
301-681-6300
Fax: 301-681-7552
Installation and monitoring of alarm systems
Owner: James Wolfe
Secretary/Treasurer: John Goetz
Vice President: Berthol Harbrant
Estimated Sales: $500,000-$1 Million
Number Employees: 20-49
Square Footage: 7000

27497 Permul Ltd.
3397 American Drive
#5
Mississauga, ON L4V 1T8
Canada
800-567-4432
  info@permul.com permul.com
Wholesale distributor and manufacturer of commer-
cial restaurant equipment.
President: Stephanie Perry
VP, Finance & Operations: Jay Nimigon
Operations Manager: Janet Magno
Year Founded: 1985
Estimated Sales: $7.5 Million
Number Employees: 11-50
Number of Brands: 20
Brands:
  Carter-Hoffmann
  Cooler Concepts
  Dormont
  Doyon
  Franke
  Hoshizaki
  Imperial
  Jackson WWS
  Kitchen Brains
  Lacor
  Lang
  Mars
  OptiPure
  Panasonic
  Perlick
  Sammic
  Star
  Toastmaster
  Watts
  Wells

27498 Perna USA
2129 Center Park Dr
Charlotte, NC 28217-2904
704-357-0264
Fax: 704-377-3106 800-997-3762
  info@permausa.com www.permausa.com
Manager: Kevin Keating
Contact: Joanna Adkins
  jadkins@permausa.com
Estimated Sales: $5 - 10 Million
Number Employees: 5-9
Parent Co: perma-tec GmbH u. Co. KG

27499 Perplas
4073 Shoreside Cir
Tampa, FL 33624-2373
610-268-1620
Fax: 610-268-1621 800-898-0378
  sales@perplascorp.com www.perplascorp.com
Estimated Sales: $1 - 5 Million

27500 Perry Videx LLC
25 Mount Laurel Rd
Hainesport, NJ 08036-2711
609-267-1600
Fax: 609-267-4499 info@perryvidex.com
www.perryvidex.com
Wholesaler/distributor, importer and exporter of
used food processing equipment; serving the food
service market
President/ CEO: Gregg Epstein
  gepstein@perryvidex.com
VP-Finance: Bob Bowdoin
VP- Production: Ron Mueller
Sales: Pete D'Angelo
Estimated Sales: $5-10 Million
Number Employees: 20-49

27501 Perten Instruments
6444 S 6th Street Rd # A
Springfield, IL 62712-6882
217-585-9440
Fax: 217-585-9441 888-773-7836
  lblack@perten.com www.perten.com
Manufacturer, importer and exporter of spectrome-
ters, gluten and alpha analysis testing equipment,
laboratory sample mill grinders and NIR analyzers
President: Gavin O'Reilly
  goreilly@perten.com
Manager Western: Carl Meuser
Manager Eastern: Walter Munday
Sales/Marketing Manager: Wes Shadow
Estimated Sales: $2.5-5 Million
Number Employees: 20-49
Square Footage: 16000
Parent Co: Perten Instruments AB
Brands:
  Da 7000
  Skcs

27502 Perten Instruments
6444 S 6th Street Rd # A
Springfield, IL 62712-6882
217-585-9440
Fax: 217-585-9441 jpowers@perten.com
www.perten.com
Analytical laboratory services, analyzing fat testing
President: Gavin O'Reilly
  goreilly@perten.com
CEO: Sven Holmlund
Manager: Gavin O'Reilly
Estimated Sales: $2.5 - 5 Million
Number Employees: 20-49

27503 Perten Instruments
PO Box 7398
Reno, NV 89510-7398
702-829-8199
Fax: 775-829-8196 info@perten.com
www.perten.com
Tea and coffee industry moisture analyzers, quality
control instruments
Chief Executive Officer: Sven Holmlund
Sales/Marketing Manager: Wes Shadow
Number Employees: 110

27504 Peryam & Kroll Research
6323 N Avondale Ave # 211
Suite 211
Chicago, IL 60631-1930
773-774-3100
Fax: 773-774-7956 800-747-5522
  info@pk-research.com
  www.pcmrewardcenter.com
President/CEO: James M. Ondyak
  ondyak@pk-research.com
Chairman of the Board: Beverley J. Kroll
CFO: Eric Maddux
Senior Vice President: Dr. Richard Popper
Estimated Sales: $5 - 10 Million
Number Employees: 250-499

27505 Peskin Sign Co
3991 Simon Rd
Youngstown, OH 44512-1390
330-783-2470
Fax: 330-783-9704
Plastic and neon signs
President: Gerry Peskin
VP: Jerry Peskin
Estimated Sales: Less Than $500,000
Number Employees: 5-9

27506 Pestcon Systems Inc
1808 Firestone Pkwy NE
Wilson, NC 27893-7991
252-237-7923
Fax: 252-243-1832 800-548-2778
  www.degeschamerica.com
Marketer of stored commodity pesticide protection
products
Sales Exec: George Hunt
Estimated Sales: $1 - 5 Million
Number Employees: 10-19
Other Locations:
  Pestcon Systems
  Wilson NC

27507 Pester-USA
110 Commerce Drive
Allendale, NJ 07401-1656
201-327-7009
Fax: 201-327-7824 pester-usa@pester.com
www.pester.com/en
End-of-line equipment, overwrapping, stretch/shrink
bundling, case packing, palletizing
Vice President: Joachim Eckart
Contact: Walter Berghahn
walter-berghahn@pester.com
Estimated Sales: $5 - 10 Million
Number Employees: 10-19

27508 Petal
30 W 31st St
New York, NY 10001
212-947-3662
Fax: 212-279-5107
Consultant specializing in research and development
for beverage flavors
Estimated Sales: Below $500,000
Number Employees: 1-4

27509 Peter Drive Components
5148 Kennedy Rd
Suite 600
Fayetteville, GA 30214
678-904-0853
Fax: 770-371-5063
Solutions for shaft/hub connections
Estimated Sales: $1 - 3 Million
Number Employees: 1-4

27510 Peter Dudgeon International
740 Kopke St
Honolulu, HI 96819-3315
808-841-8211
Fax: 808-842-5093
Plastic materials
President: Peter Dudgeon
Treasurer: Shawn D Badham
Vice President: Andrew W Dudgeon
Contact: Jorge Delgado
jdelgado@gourmetfoodsinc.com
Estimated Sales: $5 - 10 Million
Number Employees: 5-9

27511 Peter Gray Corporation
44 Park St
Andover, MA 01810-3692
978-470-0990
Fax: 978-475-6663
Stainless steel stampings, deep drawn parts, cylin-
ders, pans, burners, barbecue housings and
thermoset molded plastics, etc
Chairman, President, Chief Executive Off: Michael
Strianese
Executive Vice President of Corporate St: Curtis
Brunson
Director Sales: Mark Marchessault
Senior Vice President of Operations: Richard Cody
Estimated Sales: $1 - 5 Million
Number Employees: 1-4
Square Footage: 320000
Parent Co: Peter Gray Corporation

27512 Peter Kalustian Associates
239 Reserve Street
Boonton, NJ 07005-1301
973-334-3008
Fax: 973-334-2757
Consultant specializing in manufacturing manage-
ment, engineering, construction and marketing for
the fat, margarine, shortening, cocoa butter substi-
tute, fatty acid and derivative industries
President: Peter Kalustian
Number Employees: 3
Square Footage: 2700

27513 Peter Pan Sales
PO Box 8658
St. John's, NL A1B 3T1
Canada
709-747-1990
Fax: 709-747-1482 800-563-9090
peterpan@nfld.com
Paper and plastic distributor
President: D Spurrell
Vice President: Chris Spurrell
Number Employees: 15
Square Footage: 88000

27514 Peter Pepper Products Inc
17929 S Susana Rd
Compton, CA 90221-5597
310-639-0390
Fax: 310-639-6013
customerservice@peterpepper.com
www.peterpepper.com
Trash receptacles, reusable containers, displays,
store fixtures and tables
President: Sigi Pepper
sigipepper@peterpepper.com
CFO: Michael Pepper
Quality Control: Bob Caceres
Marketing/Sales: Kip Pepper
Purchasing Manager: Chuck Martlaro
Estimated Sales: $10 - 20 Million
Number Employees: 50-99
Brands:
Minimint
Peppermint
Tasque

27515 (HQ)Peterboro Basket Co
130 Grove St
PO Box 120
Peterborough, NH 03458-1756
603-924-3861
Fax: 603-924-9261 www.peterborobasket.com
Insulated coolers and baskets including fruit, vegeta-
ble and shopping
CEO: Russell E Dodds
rdodds@peterborobasket.com
Estimated Sales: $10-20 Million
Number Employees: 50-99
Square Footage: 72000

27516 Peterson Fiberglass Laminates
PO Box 158
Shell Lake, WI 54871-0158
715-468-2306
Fax: 715-468-7923
Brine tanks, flume and canal brining systems, cheese
conveyors and fiberglass tanks for live fish transport
Vice President: Wayne Peterson
Estimated Sales: $500,000-$1 Million
Number Employees: 9
Square Footage: 32000

27517 Peterson Manufacturing Company
24133 W 143rd St
Plainfield, IL 60544
815-436-9201
Fax: 815-436-2863 800-547-8995
callpmc@peterson-mfg.com
www.peterson-mfg.com
Manufacturer and exporter of metal storage racks
President: Gerry Kusiolek
CFO: Dicks Jenkins
Chairman of the Board: David Peterson
Estimated Sales: $5 - 10 Million
Number Employees: 50-99

27518 Peterson Sign Co
660 Mapunapuna St
Honolulu, HI 96819-2031
808-521-6785
Fax: 808-836-1496 petersonsignco@cs.com
www.petersonsign.com
Signs including magnetic, engraved and silk
screened
President: Chito Batoon
cbatoon@petersonsign.com
Estimated Sales: $1-2.5 Million
Number Employees: 100-249

27519 Petoskey Plastics
5725 Commerce Blvd
Morristown, TN 37814-1096
423-586-8917
Fax: 423-587-1524 www.petoskeyplastics.com
Open zipper/recloseable and take-out food bags
President: Paul Keiswetter
General Manager (Morristown): Gary Ramsey
General Manager (Santa Fe Springs): Dennis
Waggoner
Vice President of Sales and Marketing: Charles Lee
Director of Operations: Steven Smith
Plant Manager: Gordon Thompson
Number Employees: 100-249

27520 (HQ)Petro Moore Manufacturing Corporation
3641 Vernon Blvd
Long Island City, NY 11106-5123
718-784-2516
Fax: 718-784-7099
Manufacturer and exporter of steel folding legs and
folding and stackable tables
President: Robert Murphy
Secretary: Jan DeRosa
Estimated Sales: Below $5 Million
Number Employees: 5-9
Square Footage: 40000
Type of Packaging: Food Service

27521 Petro-Canada Lubricants
2310 Lakeshore Road
Mississauga, ON L5J 1K2
Canada
866-335-3369
Fax: 905-822-7450 www.petro-canada.ca
Petro-Canada is a world class producer of more than
350 advanced lubricants, specialty fluids, food grade
grease and lubricants
Number Employees: 10
Number of Products: 350
Parent Co: Suncor Energy Inc
Type of Packaging: Consumer, Food Service, Pri-
vate Label, Bulk

27522 Petrochem Insulation
110 Corporate Pl
Vallejo, CA 94590
707-644-7455
Fax: 707-644-4908 800-520-2705
www.petrocheminc.com
Petrochem is your premier single source specialty
contractor.providing mechanical isulation,heat trac-
ing, removable pad fabrication, fireproofing, scaf-
folding,floor coatings and abatement services.
working nationwide fromsevenregional offices.
President: Art Lewis
Marketing Director: Brian Benson
Sales Director: Brian Benson
Contact: Paul Aceto
paul@silverspoonevents.com
Estimated Sales: $1 - 5 Million
Number Employees: 250-499

27523 (HQ)Petroleum Analyzer Co LP
8824 Fallbrook Dr
Houston, TX 77064-4855
281-940-1803
Fax: 281-580-0719 800-444-8378
sales@paclp.com www.paclp.com
Manufacturer and exporter of analyzers including
total nitrogen, sulfur and fluoride; sulfur-selec-
tive and nitrogen-specific GC and HPLC detectors
President: Jereon Schmits
jereon@paclp.com
CEO: Randy Wreyford
Marketing Director: Cindy Goodman
Sales Manager: Emmanuel Filaudeau
Number Employees: 500-999
Square Footage: 120000
Other Locations:
Antek Instruments
Dusseldorf

27524 Pexco Packaging Corporation
PO Box 6540
Toledo, OH 43612
419-470-5935
Fax: 419-470-5940 800-227-9950
www.pexcopkg.com
Bags including plain and printed polyethylene, poly-
propylene and styrene recloseable; also, roll stock
available
President: William Buri
Controller: Gene Roach
Production Manager: Thomas Jesionowski
Estimated Sales: $5-10 Million
Number Employees: 20-49
Square Footage: 80000

27525 Pez Candy Inc
35 Prindle Hill Rd
Orange, CT 06477-3616
203-795-0531
Fax: 203-799-1679
Candy and dispensers

President: Joseph Vittoria
CEO: Christian Jegen
  jegen@pezcandyinc.com
CFO: Brian Fry
VP Marketing: Peter Vandall
VP Sales: Dan Silliman
VP Operations: Mark Morrissey
Estimated Sales: $3,100,000
Number Employees: 100-249
Type of Packaging: Consumer
Other Locations:
  PEZ Candy
  Orange CT
Brands:
  Pez

27526 Pfankuch Machinery Corporation
5885 149th St W Ste 101
Apple Valley, MN 55124
                                    952-891-3311
  Fax: 952-891-5168 pfankuchmachine@msn.com
Manufacturer, importer and exporter of packaging
machinery including feeders, collators, counters and
wrappers
CEO: Claus Pfankuch
Estimated Sales: $3 - 5,000,000
Number Employees: 5-9
Square Footage: 22000
Parent Co: Pfankuch Maschinen

27527 Pfeil & Holding Inc
5815 Northern Blvd
Woodside, NY 11377-2297
                                    718-545-4600
  Fax: 718-932-7513 800-247-7955
  info@cakedeco.com www.cakedeco.com
Bakers' equipment and utensils, cake decorations,
pastry bags, pans, tubes, tier separators, flavors and
ingredients
President: David Gordils
  davidg@cakedeco.com
CEO: Sy Stricker
Sales Director: Jenn Covalluzzi
Estimated Sales: $5-10 Million
Number Employees: 20-49
Number of Products: 7000
Square Footage: 200000
Brands:
  PFEIL

27528 PhF Specialist
P.O. Box 7697
San Jose, CA 95150-7697
                                    408-275-0161
  Fax: 408-280-0979 www.phfspec.com
Owner: Pamela Hardt-English
Estimated Sales: $300,000-500,000
Number Employees: 1-4

27529 Pharmaceutic Litho & Label Co.
3990 Royal Ave
Simi Valley, CA 93063
                                    805-285-5162
  Fax: 805-285-5182 800-882-9743
  www.pharmaceuticlitho.com
Label printer
President/Owner: Jason Laurence
CEO: Bill Burch
Sales: Ken Zaves
Operations: Ed Bergmann
Year Founded: 1964
Number Employees: 51-100
Square Footage: 75000

27530 Pharmaceutical & Food Special
P.O. Box 7697
San Jose, CA 95150-7697
                                    408-275-0161
  Fax: 408-280-0979 phfspec@pacbell.net
  www.phfspec.com
Importer and exporter of temperature sensing equip-
ment; also, consulting services available including
plant and process design, training, seminars and
FDA/USDA regulation compliance packaging
design
President: Pamela Hardt-English
Quality Control: Peter Cocotas
Vice President: Peter Cocotas
Food Tecnologist: Kim Cortes
Estimated Sales: Below $5 Million
Number Employees: 1-4
Square Footage: 10000

27531 Phase Fire Systems
2685 S Melrose Drive
Vista, CA 92081
                                    760-741-2341
  Fax: 760-741-2218 888-741-2341
  www.phasefiresystems.com
Shrink packaging machinery including sleevers and
banders; also, tunnel ovens
President: Noel Perez
Secretary/Accounts Payable: Nicole Perez
Purchasing Manager: John Edgar
Estimated Sales: $1-2.5 Million
Number Employees: 9

27532 Phase II Pasta Machine Inc
55 Verdi St
Farmingdale, NY 11735-6316
                                    631-293-4259
  Fax: 631-293-4572 800-457-5070
  pastamachine@aol.com
Manufacturer, exporter and importer of commercial
pasta equipment
President: Michael Wilson
  pastamachines@aol.com
Estimated Sales: Less Than $500,000
Number Employees: 1-4
Square Footage: 11000
Brands:
  Pastamagic
  Pastamatic

27533 Phelps Industries
P.O. Box 190718
Little Rock, AR 72219-0718
                                    501-568-5550
  Fax: 501-568-3363 www.phelpsfan.com
Manufacturer and exporter of platform dump trucks
and live floor hoppers for bulk handling
Owner: Donald Phelps
Vice President: John Phelps
Estimated Sales: $10 - 20 Million
Number Employees: 50-99

27534 Phenix Label Co
11610 S Alden St
Olathe, KS 66062-6923
                                    913-327-7000
  Fax: 913-327-7010 800-274-3649
  info@phenixlabel.com www.phenixlabel.com
Manufacturer and exporter of custom printed labels
President: Hans Peter
  hpeter@phenixlabel.com
CFO: Mark Volz
VP: Mike Darpel
Quality Control: Gina Waltmire
Estimated Sales: $10-20 Million
Number Employees: 100-249
Square Footage: 70000
Parent Co: Phenix Box & Label Company
Type of Packaging: Consumer, Food Service, Pri-
vate Label

27535 Philadelphia Glass Bending Company
2520 Morris Street
Philadelphia, PA 19145-1716
                                    215-726-8468
  Fax: 215-336-3002
Lighting fixtures
Estimated Sales: $20-50 Million
Number Employees: 50-99
Parent Co: Seagull Lighting Products

27536 Philipp Lithographing Co
1960 Wisconsin Ave
PO Box 4
Grafton, WI 53024-2623
                                    262-377-1100
  Fax: 262-377-6660 800-657-0871
  help@philipplitho.com www.philipplitho.com
Manufacturer and exporter of labels and point of
purchase displays
President/CEO: Peter Buening
  pbuening@philipplithographing.com
CFO/Treasurer: Dave Kaehny
Vice President/General Counsel: Stacy Buening
Estimated Sales: $5-10 Million
Number Employees: 50-99
Square Footage: 70000
Type of Packaging: Private Label

27537 Philips Lighting Company
PO Box 6800
Somerset, NJ 08875-6800
                                    732-563-3000
  Fax: 732-563-3641 www.lighting.philips.com
Manufacturer and exporter of lamps including in-
candescent, fluorescent, HID, specialty, miniature,
etc
CEO: Ed Crawford
Director Channel Marketing: Paul Lienesch
Contact: Koen Joosse
  koen.joosse@philips.com
Estimated Sales: $30 - 50 Million
Number Employees: 10,000

27538 Phillips Gourmet Inc
1011 Kaolin Rd
PO Box 190
Kennett Square, PA 19348-2605
                                    610-925-0520
  Fax: 610-925-0527 info@phillipsgourmet.com
  www.phillipsmushroomfarms.com
Mushrooms
President: Marshall Phillips
  marshall@phillipsgourmet.com
Number Employees: 100-249
Parent Co: Phillips Mushroom Farms
Type of Packaging: Consumer, Food Service
Brands:
  Bella

27539 Phillips Plastics and Chemical
3200 Southwest Fwy
suite 3200
Houston, TX 77027-7538
                                    713-552-9595
  Fax: 713-552-0231 800-537-3746
  www.phillipsakers.com
Food packaging, industrial packaging, clear rigid
and flexible packaging, conventional equipment
Contact: Harris Gregory
  harris.clm@phillipsakers.com
Number Employees: 100-249

27540 Phillips Refrigeration Consultants
4014 Balmoral Drive
Champaign, IL 61822-8552
                                    217-355-0319
                                    Fax: 217-355-0324
President: John Phillips
Number Employees: 3

27541 (HQ)Philmont Manufacturing Co.
370 Overpeck Pl
Englewood, NJ 07631
                                    201-816-5867
  Fax: 201-569-3426 888-379-6483
Table padding and tablecloths
President: Bruce Strongwater
Quality Control: Jason Strongwater
Executive VP: Michael Rattner
CFO: Catherine Maren
VP Marketing: Adrian Trautman, Jr.
National Sales Manager: Bill Sarna
Estimated Sales: $20 - 30 Million
Number Employees: 100
Square Footage: 35000

27542 Phoenix & Eclectic Network
172 N York St
Elmhurst, IL 60126-2762
                                    630-530-4373
                                    Fax: 630-530-0651
Consultant providing packaging design services to
food processors
Estimated Sales: $1 - 5 Million
Number Employees: 5-9

27543 Phoenix Closures Inc
1899 High Grove Ln
Naperville, IL 60540-3996
                                    630-544-3475
                                    Fax: 630-420-4774
  greatcaps@phoenixclosures.com
  www.phoenixclosures.com
Manufacturer and exporter of caps and seals
President: Bert Miller
CFO: Rich Classen
Quality Control: Jim Twohij
VP Sales/Marketing: Jeff Davis
Sales Director: Tim Ferrel
Estimated Sales: $20 - 50 Million
Number Employees: 250-499

Number of Products: 1000
Square Footage: 100000
Brands:
Accugard
Accuseal
Sealgard
Softseal
Sureseal
Torkgard
Tritab

27544 Phoenix Coatings
19893 Berenda Blvd
Madera, CA 93638
559-675-8122
Fax: 559-673-2571 800-464-1958
Decorative wine bottles
President/CEO: Tom Burk
Owner: Bob Pricer
Controller: Gordon Begman
Contact: Gordon Begeman
gman@phoenixcoatings.com
Office Manager: Craig Alton
Safety Officer: Mark Pankratz
Estimated Sales: $500,000-$1 Million
Number Employees: 5-9

27545 Phoenix Contact Inc
586 Fulling Mill Rd
Middletown, PA 17057-2966
717-944-1300
Fax: 717-944-1625 800-586-5525
info@phoenixcon.com www.phoenixcontact.com
President & CEO: Jack Nehlig
jnehlig@phoenixcon.com
Estimated Sales: $50 - 100 Million
Number Employees: 500-999

27546 Phoenix Engineering
8162 Market St # H
Suite H
Youngstown, OH 44512-6200
330-726-3477
Fax: 608-827-5898 www.phoenixdesigneng.com
Filling and heat sealing equipment
Owner: Christopher Jones
cjones@phoenixdesigneng.com
Number Employees: 5-9

27547 Phoenix Engineering
13208 Arctic Circle
Santa Fe Springs, CA 90670-5510
562-407-0512
Fax: 562-407-0518 800-991-1395
sales@pouchmachines.com
www.pouchmachines.com
Resins for cast and blown films for food packaging
President and CFO: Lynn Worthington
Contact: Brian Dykema
sales@pouchmachines.com
Estimated Sales: $1 - 2.5 Million
Number Employees: 1-4

27548 Phoenix Industries Corp
114 N Bedford St
Madison, WI 53703-2610
608-251-2533
Fax: 608-256-2604 888-241-7482
www.negusboxnbag.com
Manufacturer and exporter of corrugated ice cream containers; wholesaler/distributor and exporter of packaging supplies including bags
President: Rod Shaughnessy
contact.nequs@negusboxnbag.com
Sales: Greg Koch
Operations: Al Baler
Estimated Sales: $1-5 Million
Number Employees: 5-9
Square Footage: 40000
Parent Co: Phoenix Industries Corporation
Brands:
Negus Octapak
Negus Square Pak

27549 Phoenix Process Equipment
2402 Watterson Trl
Louisville, KY 40299-2536
502-499-6198
Fax: 502-499-1079 phoenix@dewater.com
www.dewater.com
President: Gary L Drake
CFO: Stephen Kovaka
Manager: Vlad Zalmanov
vzalmanov@phoenixprocess.com

Estimated Sales: $5 - 10 Million
Number Employees: 20-49

27550 Phoenix Sign Company
112 Clemons Rd
Aberdeen, WA 98520-0112
360-532-1111
Fax: 360-637-8557
Neon, electric, wooden and plastic signs
Owner: Faron Lash
Estimated Sales: $.5 - 1 million
Number Employees: 1-4

27551 Phoenix Wholesale Foodservice
16 Forest Pkwy
Building J
Forest Park, GA 30297-2015
404-363-9800
Fax: 404-363-4562 800-613-1998
sales@coboco.net www.phoenixwfs.com
Fruits, vegetables, dairy, eggs, dressings, prepared meals, oil, tofu and bottled water
Vice President: Carol Peterman
carolp@coboco.net
VP: Richard Monahan
Manager of Sales: David Cowart
Specialty Buyer: Billy Sowers
Estimated Sales: $9.5 Million
Number Employees: 250-499
Square Footage: 320000

27552 Photo Graphics Co
5100 Martha Truman Rd # C
Grandview, MO 64030-1172
816-761-3333
Fax: 816-761-3032 www.nameplates-labels.com
Industrial name plates and labels
Manager: Andy Ortbals
andy@pgnameplates.com
Production Manager: Andrew Ortbals
Estimated Sales: Less Than $500,000
Number Employees: 1-4
Square Footage: 19200
Brands:
Metalphoto

27553 Phytopia Inc
6947 Forest Glen Dr
Dallas, TX 75230-2358
214-750-7322
Fax: 214-750-7910 888-750-9336
barbara@phytopia.com www.phytopia.com
Culinary trained registered dietitian specializing in low-fat recipe development and nutritional analysis
Owner: Barbara Gollman, MS, RD
bgollman@phytopia.com
Estimated Sales: Less Than $500,000
Number Employees: 1-4

27554 Phytotherapy Research Laboratory
W Fourth S
PO Box 627
Lobelville, TN 37097-0627
931-593-3780
Fax: 931-593-3782 800-274-3727
Herb extracts
President: Brent Davis
Estimated Sales: $500,000-$1 Million
Number Employees: 1-4
Square Footage: 50000
Type of Packaging: Private Label
Brands:
Forest Center
Hahg
Prl

27555 Piab USA Inc
65 Sharp St
Hingham, MA 02043-4311
781-337-7309
Fax: 781-337-6864 800-321-7422
info@piab.com www.piab.com
Vice President: Greg Anderson
andersong@piab.com
Vice President of Business Development: Ed McGovern
Estimated Sales: $10 - 20 Million
Number Employees: 20-49

27556 Piab USA Inc
65 Sharp St
Hingham, MA 02043-4311
781-337-7309
Fax: 781-337-6864 800-321-7422
info-usa@piab.com www.piab.com
N.A. distributor and manufacturer of vacuum conveyors and pumps for company based in Sweden
President: Chuck Weilbrenner
Vice President: Greg Anderson
andersong@piab.com
Estimated Sales: $10 - 20 Million
Number Employees: 20-49

27557 Piab Vacuum Products
65 Sharp St
Hingham, MA 2043
781-792-0003
Fax: 781-337-6864 800-321-7422
info@piab.com www.piabusa.com
Vacuum pumps, suction cups, vacuum filters, pneumatic conveyors, etc
President: Chuck Weilbrenner
CEO: Don Spradlin
Marketing Director: Ed McGraven
Sales: Jack Gray
Contact: Jaime Bohorquez
jbohorquez@piab.com
Estimated Sales: $10 - 20 Million
Number Employees: 50-99

27558 Piacere International
1101 Air Way
Glendale, CA 91201-2403
818-240-7335
Fax: 818-240-0558 800-432-3288
Espresso machines and accessories, pre-brewed espresso, roasters, powders
Manager: Dick Forque
Estimated Sales: $1.5 Million
Number Employees: 30

27559 Picard Bakery Equipment
1325 E Notre-Dame Estate
Victoriaville, QC G6P 4B8
Canada
819-758-1883
Fax: 819-758-1465
Picard Ovens, Inc is the proud manufacturer of the REVOLUTION HYBRID OVEN, moduler deck oven, LP200 baking stone, SPITFIRE pizza oven, PRG rotisserie ovenm and much more.
President: Gilles Picard
Chief Financial Officer: Isabella Dupua
Vice President: Guy Picard
Research: Phillipe Lamay
Quality Control: Francis Picard
Marketing: Kristina Marchelli
Sales: Eric Ambrosio
Public Relations: Kristina Marchelli
Operations: Francis Picard
Estimated Sales: $5-10 Million
Number Employees: 10

27560 Pick Heaters
P.O. Box 516
West Bend, WI 53095
262-338-1191
Fax: 262-338-8489 800-233-9030
info1@pickheaters.com www.pickheaters.com
Manufacturer and exporter of direct steam injection liquid heating systems including heat exchangers, water heaters, hose stations and clean-in-place; also, cookers including food/starch, fruit and vegetable purees, etc
CEO: Prudence Hway
Executive VP: Michael Campbell
Estimated Sales: $2.5 - 5 Million
Number Employees: 25
Brands:
Constant Flow
Pick
Sanitary
Variable Flow

27561 Pickard China
782 Pickard Ave
Antioch, IL 60002-1574
847-395-3800
Fax: 847-395-3827 finest@pickardchina.com
www.pickardchina.com
Manufacturer and exporter of stock and custom fine china

President: Andrew P Morgan
  amorgan@pickardchina.com
International Sales VP: Larry Smith
Estimated Sales: $5-10 Million
Number Employees: 20-49
Square Footage: 120000
Brands:
  Pickard

27562 Pickle Packers International Inc.
1101 17th Street NW
Suite 700
Washington, DC 20036

202-331-2456
www.ilovepickles.org
Sponsors research, representing industry before government agencies, educational materials and providing networking opportunities to its members.
Contact: Dennis Beal
  dbeal@robgroup.com
Estimated Sales: $.5 - 1 million
Number Employees: 1-4

27563 Pickney Molded Plastics
3970 Parsons Rd
Howell, MI 48855-9617

517-546-9900
Fax: 517-546-7097 800-854-2920
www.pmpnet.com
Food transport systems
President: Don Verna
Estimated Sales: $10-20 Million
Number Employees: 50-99

27564 Pickwick Manufacturing Svc
4200 Thomas Dr SW
Cedar Rapids, IA 52404-5055

319-393-7443
Fax: 319-393-7456 800-397-9797
www.pickwick.com
Manufacturer and exporter of poultry processing equipment including batch scalders, pickers and conveyorized eviscerating lines
President: Walter F Corey
  wcorey@pickwick.com
CEO: Walter F Corey
Estimated Sales: $20-50 Million
Number Employees: 100-249
Square Footage: 100000
Brands:
  Dunkmaster
  Econo System
  Hom-Pik
  Pickwick
  Spin-Pik

27565 Picnic Time Inc
5131 Maureen Ln
Moorpark, CA 93021-1783

805-529-4500
Fax: 805-529-7474 888-742-6429
info@picnictime.com www.picnictime.com
Picnic baskets
President: Mario Tagliati
  picnictime@picinctime.com
Managing Partners: Paul Cosaro
Managing Partners: Danny Corbucci
Vice President/Founder: Gustavo Cosaro
Marketing: Danny Corbucci
Sales Exec: Scott Mccormick
Estimated Sales: $5.4 Million
Number Employees: 50-99

27566 Pieco
2179 145th Ave
Manchester, IA 52057-8935

563-927-3352
Fax: 563-927-2310 800-334-3929
sales@pieco.com www.pieco.com
Cutting and boning devices, sharpening machines and services, sharpening and overhaul equipment, bone chips and cartilage removal, emulsifiers, accessories
Owner: Jerry York
  jerry@pieco.com
Estimated Sales: $1-2.5 Million
Number Employees: 5-9

27567 Pieco
2179 145th Ave
Manchester, IA 52057-8935

563-927-3352
Fax: 563-927-2310 800-334-3929
www.pieco.com

Circular blade sharpeners and rotary surface grinders, grinder parts, wheels, knives and also recondition mechanical deboning equipment.
Owner: Jerry York
  jerry@pieco.com
Number Employees: 5-9

27568 Piepenbrock Enterprises
919 State Route 33
Freehold, NJ 07728-8454

732-683-0991
Fax: 732-683-0992 800-942-0052
www.siebler.de
Pouching machine for tablets, caplets and capsules
Estimated Sales: $1 - 5 Million

27569 Pieper Automation
825 Ontario Rd
Green Bay, WI 54311-8017

920-465-4600
Fax: 920-465-4601 sales@pieper-automation.com
www.pieper-automation.com
Control systems integration, design and build custom automation machinery and control panels
Director of Sales: Paul Wenner
Number Employees: 100-150

27570 Pier 1 Imports
453 Chestnut Ridge Rd
Woodcliff Lake, NJ 07677-7679

201-666-4500
Fax: 201-666-8525 800-448-9993
www.pier1.com
Espresso machines, wood burning ovens and pasta equipment; importer of pasta and espresso equipment
Manager: Lauren Sanders
Estimated Sales: $1 - 3 Million
Number Employees: 10-19
Type of Packaging: Food Service
Brands:
  Cap-O-Mat

27571 Pierce Laminated Products Inc
2430 N Court St
Rockford, IL 61103-3999

815-968-9651
Fax: 815-968-7601 www.piercelaminated.com
Countertops and store fixtures
President: Eric Lindroth
  eric@piercelaminated.com
Vice President: Eric Lindroth
Estimated Sales: $2.5-5 Million
Number Employees: 20-49
Square Footage: 70000

27572 Pierrepont Visual Graphics Inc
15 Elser Ter
Rochester, NY 14611-1607

585-235-5620
Fax: 585-235-8376 info@pvgrochester.com
www.pvgrochester.com
Signs, directory boards, vinyl letters, pressure sensitive decals, banners, posters and T-shirts
President: Scott Zappia
  scott@pierrepont.com
Vice President: Terry Zappia
Estimated Sales: $1-2.5 Million
Number Employees: 10-19
Square Footage: 68000
Type of Packaging: Private Label

27573 Pike Awning Co
7300 SW Landmark Ln
Portland, OR 97224-8029

503-624-5600
Fax: 503-968-5440 800-866-9172
sales@pikeawning.com www.pikeawning.com
Commercial awnings
Owner: Tony Spear
Vice President: Ken Spearing
Estimated Sales: $2.5-5 Million
Number Employees: 20-49

27574 (HQ)Pilant Corp
4100 W Profile Pkwy
Bloomington, IN 47404-2546

812-334-7090
Fax: 317-392-4772 800-366-3525
Manufacturer and exporter of custom and stock recloseable and polyethylene bags

Manager: Peter Lenzen
Executive VP: Ronald Thieman
VP Sales: Dick Zurich
Manager: Curt Howard
  howard@pliantcorporation.com
Estimated Sales: $3 - 5 Million
Number Employees: 5-9
Square Footage: 1400000
Other Locations:
  KCL Corp.
  Dallas TX

27575 Pilgrim Plastics
1200 W Chestnut St
Brockton, MA 02301-5574

508-436-6300
Fax: 508-580-0829 800-343-7810
www.pilgrimplastics.com
Manufacturer and exporter of plastic point of purchase displays, including window displays, door displays, counter change mats, shelf displays, membership cards, change cashing cards, promotional items, rulers, luggage tags, etc
President: Mark Abrams
  mabrams@starprintingcorp.com
CFO: Mark Abrams
Quality Control: Jason Abrams
Estimated Sales: Below $5 Million
Number Employees: 50-99
Square Footage: 320000

27576 Pillar Technologies
475 E Industrial Dr
PO Box 110
Hartland, WI 53029-2336

262-912-7200
Fax: 262-912-7272 888-PIL-LAR6
www.pillartech.com
Induction sealers
Sales: Brad Budde
Manager: Tammy Wentlandt
  tammyw@tastefullysimple.com
General Manager: Mark Stohl
Number Employees: 20-49
Parent Co: Illinois Tool Works Inc

27577 Pilot Brands
PO Box 10107
Zephyr Cove, NV 89448

775-588-8850
Fax: 775-588-8380 800-621-5262
info@pilotbrands.com www.pilotbrands.com
President: Kitt Barkley

27578 Pilz Automation Safety LP
7150 Commerce Blvd
Canton, MI 48187-4289

734-354-0272
Fax: 734-354-3355 888-650-7450
info@pilzusa.com www.pilzusa.com
CEO: Thomas Pilz
Manager: Michael Beerman
  m.beerman@pilzusa.com
Estimated Sales: Below $5 Million
Number Employees: 20-49

27579 Pinckney Molded Plastics
3970 Parsons Rd
Howell, MI 48855

517-546-9900
Fax: 517-546-7097 800-854-2920
Cases, crates, dollies, trays, totes, pallets
President: Don Verna
Chairman of the Board: Leland Blatt
Sales Manager: Dave Heyink
Contact: Rich Kruyer
  rkruyer@pmpnet.com
Estimated Sales: $10 - 20 Million
Number Employees: 50-99

27580 Pine Bluff Crating & Pallet
2600 S Persimmon St
Pine Bluff, AR 71603-3667

870-879-2287
Fax: 870-879-1190 866-415-1075
www.pinebluffcrating.com
Wooden pallets and skids
President: Mark Thicksten
Operations Manager: Zach Thicksten
Pallet Production Manager: Robert Ferguson
Customer Accounts/office operations: Mark Thicksten
Estimated Sales: $2.5 - 5 Million
Number Employees: 20-49

27581 Pine Point Fisherman's Co-Op
96 King St.
Scarborough, ME 04074
207-883-3588
Fax: 207-883-6772 lobsterco-op.com
Lobsters
Estimated Sales: $1 - 3 Million
Number Employees: 5-9

27582 Pine Point Wood Products Inc
19380 CO Rd 81
Osseo, MN 55311
763-428-4301
Fax: 763-428-4304 pineptwood@msn.com
Custom cut wooden pallets, skids, crates and containers
Owner: Jay Talbot
Quality Control: Larry Corbin
Sales Manager: Don Lenz
Sales: Larry Corbin
Estimated Sales: $10 - 20 Million
Number Employees: 10-19

27583 Pinn Pack Packaging LLC
1151 Pacific Ave
Oxnard, CA 93033-2472
805-385-4100
Fax: 805-981-0444 www.pinnpack.com
Custom thermoformed blisters, clamshells and trays; also, cups and cookie containers
President: Samuel Hong
General Manager: Brian Yamaguchi
Vice President: Dale Hong
daleh88567@aol.com
VP Operations: Sam Hong
Estimated Sales: $20 - 50 Million
Number Employees: 100-249
Square Footage: 43000

27584 Pinnacle Foods Inc.
222 W Merchandise Mart Plaza
Chicago, IL 60654
312-549-5000
877-266-2472
www.pinnaclefoods.com
Packaged and frozen foods.
President & CEO, Conagra: Sean Connolly
Year Founded: 1998
Estimated Sales: $3.14 Billion
Number Employees: 4,900
Parent Co: Conagra Brands
Type of Packaging: Consumer
Brands:
Armour
Bernstein's
Birds Eye
Brooks
Celeste
Comstock Wilderness
Duncan Hines
Earth Balance
El Restaurante
Erin's
Evol
Gardein
Glutino
Hawaiian
Husman's
Lender's
Log Cabin
Mrs. Butterworth's
Mrs. Paul's
Nalley
Open Pit
Pearl Milling Company
Smart Balance
Snyder
Tim's Cascade Snacks
Udi's
Van de Kamp's
Vlasic

27585 Pinnacle Furnishing
10564 Nc Highway 211 E
Aberdeen, NC 28315
910-944-0908
Fax: 910-944-0920 866-229-5704
www.pinnaclefurnishings.com
Manufacturer and exporter of chairs and tables for restaurants, casinos, hotels and banquets

President: Jack Berggren
R&D: Jack Berggren
Vice President: Steve Laufer
Quality Control: Sarah Swanson
Regional Sales Representative: Bunnie Strauh
Estimated Sales: $2.5 - 5,000,000
Number Employees: 20-49
Square Footage: 80000

27586 Pino's Pasta Veloce
1903 Clove Road
Staten Island, NY 10304-1607
718-273-6660
Fax: 718-720-5906
Pasta sauce, pasta heaters
Manager Marketing: Joe Klaus
VP Operations: Al Cappillo
Estimated Sales: $2.5-5,000,000
Number Employees: 1-4
Parent Co: AEI
Type of Packaging: Consumer, Food Service
Brands:
Pino's Pasta Veloce

27587 Pinquist Tool & Die Company
63 Meserole Avenue
Brooklyn, NY 11222
718-389-3900
Fax: 718-349-3168 800-752-0414
www.pinquisttool.com
Metal stampings, display hardware, banner stands and wire and tubing racks
President: Richard Pinquist
Sales Director: C Oshinsky
Estimated Sales: Below $5 Million
Number Employees: 20-49
Square Footage: 20000

27588 Pioneer Chemical Co
13717 S Normandie Ave
Gardena, CA 90249-2609
310-366-7393
Fax: 310-366-7193
customerservice@pioneerchem.com
www.pioneerchem.com
Janitorial supplies, disinfectants, soaps and cleaning equipment
President: Jose Alvarez
jose@pioneerchem.com
Manager: Mary Alvarez
Estimated Sales: Below $5 Million
Number Employees: 10-19

27589 Pioneer Labels Inc
1195 S Lipan St # C
Suite C
Denver, CO 80223-3094
303-744-1606
Fax: 303-744-2443 877-744-1606
kevin@pioneerlabels.com www.pioneerlabels.com
Labels
President: Kevin Daly
kevin@pioneerlabels.com
Estimated Sales: Less Than $500,000
Number Employees: 1-4

27590 (HQ)Pioneer Manufacturing Co Inc
4529 Industrial Pkwy
Cleveland, OH 44135-4505
216-671-5500
Fax: 216-671-5502 800-877-1500
www.pioneerathletics.com
Aerosol insecticides, dustless chemical floor polishing mops, liquid quick drying floor wax and patching material for freezer and cooler floors
Owner: Doug Schattinger
dschat@aol.com
Estimated Sales: $20 - 50 Million
Number Employees: 100-249
Square Footage: 68000
Brands:
Advance
Kent

27591 Pioneer Marketing International
188 Westhill Drive
Los Gatos, CA 95032-5032
408-356-4990
Fax: 408-356-2795 www.pioneer.com
Corn, soybeans, alfalfa, canola, wheat, sunflowers; marketing, sales and product promotion
Partner: Russ Tritomo
Director Sales: Ed DeSoto

Estimated Sales: $1 - 5 Million
Number Employees: 4
Brands:
Encirca
Nutrivail
Pioneer

27592 Pioneer Packaging
220 Padgette St
Chicopee, MA 1022
413-378-6930
Fax: 413-378-6963
info@pioneerpackaginginc.com
Vacuum formed folding cartons
Owner: Jeffrey Shinners
Contact: Scott Anschuetz
sanschuetz@pioneerpackaginginc.com
Estimated Sales: $5-10 Million
Number Employees: 50-99

27593 Pioneer Packaging & Printing
1220 Lund Blvd
Anoka, MN 55303-1092
763-323-8308
Fax: 763-323-8207 800-708-1705
Folding paper boxes
President: Greg Polack
President/CEO: Greg Pollack
CFO: Richard Hall
Quality Control: Jon Maguessen
Contact: Sherry Tollefson
stollefson@pioneerpackaging.com
Estimated Sales: $10 - 20 Million
Number Employees: 100-249

27594 Pioneer Packaging Machinery
135 Farrs Bridge Rd
Pickens, SC 29671
864-878-4999
Fax: 864-878-8642
President: Howard Frist
Estimated Sales: $5 - 10 Million
Number Employees: 10

27595 Pioneer Plastics Inc
1584 US Highway 41a N
Dixon, KY 42409-9328
270-639-9133
Fax: 270-639-5882 800-951-1551
sales@pioneerplastics.com
www.pioneerplastics.com
Manufacturer and exporter of rigid molded clear plastic containers including round, square, oval and rectangular
President: Edward Knapp
CFO: Edward Knapp Jr
Marketing Manager: Wayne Fiester
Customer Service: David Fiester
Estimated Sales: $5 - 10 Million
Number Employees: 50-99
Type of Packaging: Consumer, Food Service

27596 Pioneer Sign Company
PO Box 583
Lewiston, ID 83501-0583
208-743-1275
Signs; crane installation service available
Owner: Bradley Keller
Estimated Sales: $1-2.5 Million
Number Employees: 19
Parent Co: Pioneer Sign Company

27597 (HQ)Piper Products Inc
300 S 84th Ave
Wausau, WI 54401-8460
715-842-5382
Fax: 715-848-1870 800-544-3057
info@piperonline.net www.piperonline.net
Aluminum racks, transport cabinets, dollies, proofer cabinets, hot boxes, pans and accessories; exporter of aluminum racks and transport cabinets
President: Roger D Sweeney
CEO: Tony Sweeney
National Sales Manager: R Joseph Graf
Customer Service: Evelyn Yakich
Estimated Sales: $10 - 20 Million
Number Employees: 50-99
Type of Packaging: Food Service
Other Locations:
Piper Products
Wausau WI

27598 Piper Products Inc
300 S 84th Ave
Wausau, WI 54401-8460

715-842-5382
Fax: 715-848-1870 800-544-3057
www.piperonline.net
Manufacturer and exporter of ovens, proofers, combination oven/proofers, transport and heated cabinets and bakery racks, cafeteria, buffet lines, tray delivery carts and support equipment
CEO: Tony Sweeney
CEO: Tony Sweeney
Estimated Sales: $10 - 20 Million
Number Employees: 50-99
Type of Packaging: Food Service
Brands:
Piper Products
Super Systems

27599 Piqua Paper Box Co
616 Covington Ave
PO Box 814
Piqua, OH 45356-3205

937-773-0313
Fax: 937-773-0142 800-536-2136
www.piquapaperbox.com
Rigid and folding cartons, vinyl and specialty packaging
President: Brian T Gleason
Estimated Sales: $5-10 Million
Number Employees: 50-99
Square Footage: 170000

27600 Pitco Frialator Inc
509 Route 3a
Bow, NH 03304-3102

603-225-6684
Fax: 603-230-5548 800-258-3708
dpacka@maytag.com www.pitco.com
Manufacturer and exporter of commercial cooking equipment including standard, high capacity, doughnut/bakery and high efficiency fryers, pasta cookers, frying filters and baskets
President: Scott Blasingame
sblasingame@pitco.com
Director Materials: Steve Karas
VP/General Manager: Robert Granger
VP Engineer: George McMahon
Estimated Sales: $20-50 Million
Number Employees: 20-49
Parent Co: G.S. Blodgett Corporation
Type of Packaging: Food Service
Brands:
Frialator
Pitco

27601 Pittsburgh Corning Corp
800 Presque Isle Dr
Pittsburgh, PA 15239-2799

724-327-6100
Fax: 724-387-3805
Manufacturer and exporter of moisture resistant glass insulation for floors, walls and roofs of food and beverage buildings, coolers and freezers
Estimated Sales: $45 Million
Number Employees: 20-49
Parent Co: Owens Corning
Brands:
Foamglas

27602 Pittsburgh Tank Corp
1500 Industrial Dr
Monongahela, PA 15063-9753

724-258-0200
Fax: 724-258-7350 800-634-0243
sales@pghtank.com www.pghtank.com
Aluminum, carbon steel and stainless steel storage tanks
President: James Bollman
sales@pghtank.com
Vice President: Phil Duvall
Research & Development: Jeff Farrar
Sales Director: John Thompson
Purchasing Manager: Tracie Doman
Estimated Sales: 5-10 Million
Number Employees: 50-99
Number of Products: 6
Square Footage: 70000
Type of Packaging: Bulk

27603 Pittsfield Weaving Company
PO Box 8
Pittsfield, NH 3263

603-435-8301
Fax: 603-435-6753
Woven labels
President: Gilbert Bleckmann
Controller: Robert Russell
Estimated Sales: $10-20 Million
Number Employees: 50-99

27604 Pizzamatic USA
130 E 168th St
South Holland, IL 60473-2836

708-331-0660
Fax: 708-331-0663 888-749-9279
sandy@pizzamaticusa.com www.pizzamatic.com
Pizza production systems and pizzeria equipment
Co-founder: Clifford E. Fitch Jr
Sales: Sandy Johnson
Estimated Sales: $1-5 Million
Number Employees: 10-19

27605 Placemat Printers
Old Rt. 22 & 863
P.O. Box 699
Fogelsville, PA 18051-0699

610-285-2255
Fax: 610-285-2607 800-628-7746
www.mastercraftprinting.com
Full scale commercial print e-design shop
President: Darlene Pinto
Estimated Sales: Below $5 Million
Number Employees: 10-19

27606 Placon Corp
6096 Mckee Rd
Fitchburg, WI 53719-5103

608-271-5634
Fax: 608-271-3162 800-541-1535
betterdesign@placon.com www.placon.com
Thermoformed plastic packages, blister packages, box inserts, medical disposables and food container trays
President: Jan Acker
CEO: Dan Mohs
dmohs@placon.com
CEO: Dan Mohs
CFO: Rick Terrin
Estimated Sales: $50 - 75 Million
Number Employees: 250-499

27607 Placon Corp
1227 Union Street Ext
PO Box 548
West Springfield, MA 01089-4022

413-785-1553
Fax: 413-731-5952 800-342-2011
info@plasticpkg.com www.placon.com
Injection molded plastic food containers and lids
President: Susan Weiss
sweiss@plasticpkg.com
CFO: Edd Katotlam
Estimated Sales: $10-25 Million
Number Employees: 100-249

27608 (HQ)Plainview Milk Products
130 2nd St SW
Plainview, MN 55964-1394

507-534-3872
Fax: 507-534-3992 800-356-5606
www.plainviewmilk.com
Butter, whey and milk; custom agglomeration and spray drying
General Manager: Dallas Moe
dmoe@plainviewmilk.com
Controller: Janna Van Rooyen
Sales Manager: Darrell Hanson
Plant Manager: Donny Schreiber
Number Employees: 50-99
Square Footage: 18060
Type of Packaging: Consumer, Food Service, Private Label, Bulk
Brands:
Greenwood Prairie

27609 Planet Products Corp
4200 Malsbary Rd
Blue Ash, OH 45242-5598

513-984-5544
Fax: 513-984-5580 info@planet-products.com
www.planet-products.com
Manufacturer and exporter of sausage and frankfurter loading, cheese stick equipment. Manufacturer of turnkey systems in automating sandwich assembly and other ready to eat products
Owner: Kathy Randolph
krandolph@planet-products.com
CEO: Mike F
VP: John Abraham
Marketing: Jennifer Coromel
Estimated Sales: $10-20 Million
Number Employees: 20-49
Brands:
Link N Load
Servo-Pak

27610 Plas-Ties Co
14272 Chambers Rd
Tustin, CA 92780-6994

714-542-4487
Fax: 714-972-2978 800-854-0137
info@plasties.com www.plastictyer.com
Strip and air curtains and food service doors
Owner: Lou Contreras
Sales Manager: Jesse Garcia
Estimated Sales: $5-10 Million
Number Employees: 20-49
Square Footage: 240000

27611 Plascal Corp
361 Eastern Pkwy
PO Box 590
Farmingdale, NY 11735-2713

516-249-2200
Fax: 516-249-2256 800-899-7527
plascal@aol.com www.plascal.com
Manufacturer and exporter of plain, printed, laminated and PVC plastic film and sheeting
CEO: Mark Hurd
President: Fred Hurd
Estimated Sales: $10-20 Million
Number Employees: 100-249

27612 Plaskid Company
PO Box 162841
Austin, TX 78716-2841

512-328-7785
Fax: 714-972-2978 800-854-0137
Coatings to frictionize plastics, application systems for films and foam

27613 Plassein International
200 S Biscayne Boulevard
Suite 900
Miami, FL 33131-5344

860-429-5070
Fax: 860-429-5071 866-752-7734

27614 Plasseint International
920 Wilshire Drive
Libertyville, IL 60048-1858

847-680-5835
Fax: 847-680-1478 rickk101@aol.com
A packaging firm, manufacture plastic packaging materials in US and Canada

27615 Plast-O-Matic Valves Inc
1384 Pompton Ave # 1
Suite 1
Cedar Grove, NJ 07009-1095

973-256-9344
Fax: 973-256-4745 info@plastomatic.com
www.plastomatic.com
Thermoplastic valves
VP: Bob Sinclair
Estimated Sales: $10-25 Million
Number Employees: 50-99

27616 Plastech
205 W Duarte Rd
Monrovia, CA 91016-4529

626-358-9306
Fax: 626-303-6288
Manufacturer and exporter of plastic point of purchase displays
Owner: Pat Delaney
CFO: Pat Delaney
Contact: Laurie Castro
jauthier@solarcity.com
Estimated Sales: Below $5 Million
Number Employees: 10-19
Type of Packaging: Consumer, Bulk

27617 Plastech Corp
2080 General Truman St NW
Atlanta, GA 30318-2010
404-355-9682
Fax: 404-355-5410 info@plastech.com
www.plastech.com
Thermoformed plastic products including blister and
clamshell packaging, trays and signs; also, in-house
product design and tool making, computerized trimming, finishing and decorating, assemblies and
prototypes available
President: Larry W Lee
accounting@plastech.com
Quality Control: Darius Lee
Sales/Marketing: David Lee
Estimated Sales: Below $5 Million
Number Employees: 20-49

27618 Plasti Print Inc
1620 Gilbreth Rd
Burlingame, CA 94010-1405
650-652-4950
Fax: 650-652-4954 www.plasti-print.com
Plastic pressure-sensitive labels and shelf strips
President: Michael Magpantay
mom@truecar.com
CEO: Helen Vigil
VP: Rodney Vigil
Estimated Sales: Below $5 Million
Number Employees: 5-9
Square Footage: 9000

27619 Plasti-Clip Corp
38 Perry Rd
Milford, NH 03055-4308
603-672-1166
Fax: 603-672-6637 800-882-2547
sales@plasticlip.com www.plasticlip.com
Manufacturer and exporter of point of purchase clips
and fasteners including displays, price tags, tickets,
etc; also, coupon holders, employee (and visitor) ID
badging software and supplies
President: Daniel Faneuf
sales@plasticlip.com
Estimated Sales: $1-2.5 Million
Number Employees: 5-9
Number of Brands: 50
Number of Products: 1000
Square Footage: 14000
Brands:
3m
Anchor
Arrow Clip
Crystal View
Dc Uni-Clip
E-Z Rak-Clip
Flex-Holder
Grip Clip
Gt Uni-Clip
Magnaclamp
Mid-Trak
Plasti-Rivet
Premium Trak-Clip
Presto Galaxy
Snap'n Clip
Springrip
Take-1
The Messenger
Thum-Screw
Trak Clip
Uni-Badge
Uni-Strap
Wobblers

27620 Plasti-Line
445 S Gay Street
Suite 100
Knoxville, TN 37902-1133
865-938-1511
Fax: 865-947-8531 800-444-7446
Manufacturer and exporter of plastic, metal, interior
and exterior illuminated signs including menu
boards and point of purchase displays
VP Marketing: Mickey Davis
Marketing Manager: Mary Ann Herrick
Estimated Sales: $20 - 50 Million
Number Employees: 500-999

27621 Plasti-Mach Corporation
704 Executive Blvd # G
Valley Cottage, NY 10989-2023
845-267-2985
Fax: 845-267-2825 800-394-1128
plastimach@plastimach.com
www.plastimach.com
Manufacturer and exporter of used equipment in-
cluding thermoforming, extrusion and heat sealing
President: Robert Rosen
VP: Jerry Hammerman
Contact: Tammy Sabat
tammysabat@plastimach.com
Estimated Sales: $1 - 5 Million
Number Employees: 5-9
Square Footage: 40000

27622 Plastic Art Signs
3931 W Navy Blvd
Pensacola, FL 32507-1256
850-455-4114
Fax: 850-455-5033 866-662-7060
www.plasticartssigns.com
Neon and plastic signs
President: Jon Navarro
jon@plasticartssigns.com
Estimated Sales: $500,000-$1 Million
Number Employees: 10-19

27623 Plastic Assembly Corporation
1 Sculley Rd. Unit A
Ayer, MA 01432-632
Fax: 978-772-6096 patrickmagnus@aol.com
Plastic containers
President: Regis M Magnus
R & D: Patric Magnus
Estimated Sales: Below $5 Million
Number Employees: 10
Square Footage: 150000
Brands:
Blinky

27624 Plastic Container Corp
2508 N Oak St
Urbana, IL 61802-7207
217-352-2722
Fax: 217-352-2822 jgentles@netpcc.com
www.netpcc.com
Plastic bottles
President & CEO: Ron Rhoades
Sales Manager: Jo Ellen Gentles
Sales Representative: John Foote
Number Employees: 50-99
Square Footage: 500000
Type of Packaging: Consumer

27625 Plastic Craft Products Corp
744 W Nyack Rd
PO Box K
West Nyack, NY 10994-1998
845-358-3010
Fax: 845-358-3007 800-627-3010
pc@plastic-craft.com www.plastic-craft.com
Plastic film and acrylic signs
President: Mark Brecher
pc@plastic-craft.com
VP Sales: Mark Brecher
Operations Manager: Yung Nguyen
Estimated Sales: $2.5-5 Million
Number Employees: 20-49
Square Footage: 66000

27626 Plastic Equipment
305 Rock Industrial Park Drive
Bridgeton, MO 63044-1214
800-645-5439
Fax: 314-739-3240 800-270-6225

27627 Plastic Fantastics/BuckSigns
823 Siskiyou Boulevard
Ashland, OR 97520-2168
541-482-2223
Fax: 541-482-2223 800-482-1776
Push-type portion control food dispensers, brochure
holders, picture frames, signs, magazine holders,
grocery displays, medical appliances, bulk food dispensers, display boxes, acrylic wine racks, engraved
and sand blasted woodsigns
Owner: Michael Buckley
CEO: Barbara Buckley
CFO: Issac Reed

Estimated Sales: $2.5-5 Million
Number Employees: 4
Square Footage: 2800

27628 Plastic Ingenuity
1017 Park St
Cross Plains, WI 53528-9631
608-798-3071
Fax: 608-798-4452 www.plasticingenuity.com
Thermoformed packaging, tooling & extrusion ser-
vices for the food packaging industry.
President: Tom Kuehn
tom@plasticingenuity.com
Number Employees: 250-499

27629 Plastic Packaging Technologies
750 S 65th St
Kansas City, KS 66111-2301
913-287-3383
Fax: 913-287-9420 800-468-0029
info@plaspack.com www.plaspack.com
President: David Staker
CFO: Deena Staus
Quality Control: John Seevers
R&D: John Seevers
Number Employees: 100-249

27630 Plastic Printing LLC
320 Clay St
Dayton, KY 41074-1256
859-581-5700
Fax: 859-291-2112 877-581-7748
Plastic advertising items
President: Barry Henry
plasticprt@yahoo.com
Manager: Shawn Davis
Estimated Sales: Below $5 Million
Number Employees: 1-4
Square Footage: 12654

27631 Plastic Suppliers Inc
2400 Marilyn Ln
Columbus, OH 43219
614-471-9100
800-722-5577
www.plasticsuppliers.com
Complete line of unsupported film substracts for the
label market including Labelflex, a biaxially
oreinted polysterne label stock film, polyester film,
polypropylene films for labeling, packaging and
lamination applications, PVC andsynthetic papers;
also new shrink label films. Whether your products
call for durability, printability or over all appear-
ance, Plastic suppliers is your total films solution
President & CFO: Michael DuFrayne
CEO: George Thomas
Director, R&D/New Product Development: Ed
Tweed
VP, Sales & Markting for the Americas: Brad
Bastion
VP, Manufacturing: Erich Emhuff
COO: Tom Bowden
Year Founded: 1949
Estimated Sales: $100-500 Million
Number Employees: 250-499
Brands:
Labelflex
Polyflex
Tip-On

27632 Plastic Supply Inc
8 Liberty Dr
Londonderry, NH 03053-2251
603-260-6101
Fax: 603-668-1691 800-752-7759
sales@plasticsupply.com www.plasticsupply.com
Lobster tanks
President: John Murphey
sales@plasticsupply.com
General Manager: Bill Johnson
Estimated Sales: $2.5-5 Million
Number Employees: 10-19
Square Footage: 23000
Parent Co: Plastic Supply Inc
Brands:
Atlantic Lobster

27633 Plastic Systems Inc
465 Cornwall Ave
Buffalo, NY 14215-3125
716-835-7555
Fax: 716-835-7776 800-604-7159
www.plasticsystems.com
Custom molding of vacuum formed parts

843

President: Daniel E Mcnamara
daniel@plasticsystems.com
Estimated Sales: $1-2.5 Million
Number Employees: 5-9

27634 Plastic Tagtrade Check
1201 Woodside Ave
Essexville, MI 48732-1285

989-892-7913
Fax: 989-892-7988

Plastic badges and tags
President: Earl J Mast
President: Earl J Mast
Office Manager: Alice Brennan
Estimated Sales: $10-20 Million
Number Employees: 10-19

27635 Plastic Turning Company
331 Hamilton Street
Leominster, MA 01453-2313

978-534-8326

Plastic signs and canopies
Proprietor: Ruth Nickel
Estimated Sales: Less than $500,000
Number Employees: 4
Square Footage: 5000

27636 Plastican Corporation
271 Us Highway 46
Suite G110
Fairfield, NJ 07004-2489

973-227-7817
Fax: 973-227-6821

Plastic containers
President: John Carrico
Manager: Kathy Gaiser
Estimated Sales: $5-10 Million
Number Employees: 5-9

27637 Plasticard-Locktech Intl
605 Sweeten Creek Ind Park
Asheville, NC 28803-1774

828-210-4754
Fax: 828-210-4755 800-752-1017
www.plicards.com

Key cards and lock systems
CEO: Mark Goldberg
mgoldberg@plicards.com
Sales Representative: Tom Smith
Estimated Sales: $2.5-5 Million
Number Employees: 250-499

27638 Plastics Inc
9249 Highway 14 W
Greensboro, AL 36744

334-624-8801
Fax: 334-624-4889 www.plasticsinc.com

Plastic milk containers
President: W E Burt
Estimated Sales: $10-20 Million
Number Employees: 20-49

27639 Plastics Industries
213 Dennis St
Athens, TN 37303-2995

423-745-6213
Fax: 951-894-0124 800-894-4876
www.pi-inc.com

Blowmolded plastic bottles
President: Nicholas Rende
VP Sales/Marketing: Dennis Niles
Contact: Jones Dean
jdean@plastecproducts.com
Estimated Sales: $10 - 20 Million
Number Employees: 20-49
Square Footage: 130000

27640 Plastilite Corporation
P.O. Box 12457
Omaha, NE 68112

402-453-7500
Fax: 402-571-6739 800-228-9506
info@plastilite.com www.plastilite.com

Foam coolers designed to keep products frozen during shipping
Sales Representative: Greg Montgomery
Contact: Tom Colligan
tcolligan@plastilite.com
Principal: Tom Colligan
Estimated Sales: $10+ Million
Number Employees: 50-99
Square Footage: 150000
Brands:
Chubby 7 Day Cooler

27641 Plastimatic Arts Corporation
3622 N Home St
Mishawaka, IN 46545

574-254-9000
Fax: 574-254-9001 800-442-3593
sales@pacbannerworks.com
www.pacbannerworks.com

Coding, dating and marking equipment and plastic signs
Owner: Tim Rink
Contact: Dan Clark
dan@pacbannerworks.com
Estimated Sales: $5-10 Million
Number Employees: 20-49
Parent Co: Rink Riverside Printing

27642 (HQ)Plastipak Industries
30 Taschereau Boulevard
Suite 210
La Prairie, QC J5R 5H7
Canada

800-387-7452
Fax: 450-619-1444 www.plastipak.ca

Rigid plastic packaging
President: Normand Tanguay
CFO: Guy Bellemare
Vice President: Yves Gosselin
Estimated Sales: $80,000,000
Number Employees: 400
Number of Products: 5000
Type of Packaging: Food Service, Private Label

27643 Plastipak Packaging
41605 Ann Arbor Road
Plymouth, MI 48170

734-354-3510
Fax: 734-455-0556 info@plastipak.com
www.plastipak.com

Manufacturer and exporter of PET and HDPE bottles and containers
President/CEO: William C Young
Estimated Sales: $5-10 Million
Number Employees: 100-249

27644 Plastipro
5200 W Century Blvd
Los Angeles, CA 90045

417-325-7182
Fax: 310-693-8620 800-779-0561
www.plastproinc.com

Plastic insulated jacketing systems for pipes, tanks, vessels, walls, etc
General Manager: Bill Bitterman
VP: Christy Gonzales
Estimated Sales: $2.5-5,000,000
Number Employees: 19
Square Footage: 30000
Brands:
P.I.C. Plastics, Inc.

27645 Plastiques Cascades Group
Suite 400
Montreal, QC H3A 1G1
Canada

514-284-9850
Fax: 514-284-9866 888-703-6515
www.cascadesreplast.com

Manufactures meat trays, pre-padded trays, plates and ProZorb meat pads. Specializes in plastic thermoforming and operates in the retail and industrial markets under the brand names of Plastichange Benpac and Deli-Tray.
President: Mario Plourve
General Manager: Mario Lacharite
R & D: Claude Cossette
Marketing Assistant: Barbara Hogg
Sales/Marketing Executive: Sandra Hudon
Estimated Sales: $30-50 Million
Number Employees: 10
Parent Co: Plastiques Cascades
Type of Packaging: Consumer, Food Service, Private Label, Bulk
Brands:
Frig-O-Seal
Gourmet
Maxima
Plastichange
Pro-Zorb

27646 Plastocon
1200 W 2nd St
Oconomowoc, WI 53066-3403

262-569-3131
Fax: 262-569-3135 800-966-0103
hottray@plastocon.com www.plastoconinc.com

Manufacturer and exporter of temperature-maintaining meal delivery systems including insulated food trays, mugs, delivery carts, bowls, tray inserts, lids and hot and cold carts; also, rethermalizers and drying and storage racks
President: Joe Camielewski
CEO: Joe Chmielewski
joe.chmielewski@plastoconinc.com
National Sales Manager: Jerry L. Marks
Number Employees: 50-99
Type of Packaging: Food Service, Private Label
Other Locations:
Hot Tray Division
Columbia SC
Brands:
Hot Tray

27647 Plaxall Inc
546 46th Ave
Long Island City, NY 11101-5248

718-784-4800
Fax: 718-784-4611 800-876-5706
info@plaxall.com

Custom thermoformed plastic clamshells, cups and trays; also, experimental model workshop, machine shop and in-plant sheet extrusion of plastic materials
President: James M Pfohl
CEO: Ray Schiffner
rschiffner@plaxall.com
Vice President: Andrew Kirby
Estimated Sales: $10-20 Million
Number Employees: 100-249
Square Footage: 180000
Parent Co: Design Center

27648 Playtex Products, LLC
890 Mountain Ave.
New Providence, NJ 07974

888-310-4290
www.playtexproductsinc.com

Protective neoprene and latex gloves
CEO: Michael Gallagher
Contact: Edward Bleistein
ebleistein@playtex.com
Estimated Sales: $1 - 5 Million
Number Employees: 1750

27649 Plaze Inc
105 Bolte Ln
St Clair, MO 63077-3219

636-629-3400
800-986-9509
info@plaze.com www.plaze.com

Contract packager of aerosol and liquid pan coating products
President: Shelly Anderson
sanderson@plzaeroscience.com
VP Sales: Hugh Davison
VP Manufacturing: Dennis Bullock
Plant Manager: Bob Thornton
Purchasing Manager: Denise Steen
Number Employees: 100-249
Square Footage: 400000
Type of Packaging: Private Label

27650 PlexPack Corp
1160 Birchmount Road
Unit 2
Toronto, ON M1P Z08
Canada

416-291-8085
Fax: 416-298-4328 855-635-9238
info@emplex.com www.plexpack.com

Bag sealing and automated bagging equipment and the bamark line of shrink and sleeve wrapping equipment
President/CEO: Paul Irvine
Vice President: John Lewitt
Number Employees: 20-49
Type of Packaging: Consumer, Food Service, Private Label

27651 Plicon Corporation
4949 Schatulga Road
Columbus, GA 31907-1945

706-561-9999
Fax: 706-563-0567

Coffee industry pouch materials (cellophane, paper, films)
Estimated Sales: $10-30 Million
Number Employees: 20-50

27652 Plitek LLC
69 Rawls Rd
Des Plaines, IL 60018-1326
847-827-6680
Fax: 847-827-6733 800-966-1250
sales@plitek.com
Tea and coffee industry valve applications
President: Rich Andracki
rich.andracki@plitek.com
Estimated Sales: $10 - 20 Million
Number Employees: 50-99

27653 Plus Pharma
2460 Coral St
Vista, CA 92081-8430
760-597-0200
Fax: 760-597-0734 info@pluspharm.com
www.pluspharm.com
Herbs, gelatin and vegetarian capsules
President: Bill Roberts
Estimated Sales: Less Than $500,000
Number Employees: 1-4

27654 Pluto Corporation
PO Box 391
French Lick, IN 47432
812-936-9988
Fax: 812-936-2828 alan.friedman@plutocorp.com
www.plutocorp.com
Contract packager and exporter of household cleaners; also blowmold HDPE plastic bottles
President: Alan J Friedman
Plant Manager: Dennis Kaiser
Estimated Sales: $5-10 Million
Number Employees: 100-249
Square Footage: 240000
Parent Co: AHF Industries

27655 Plymold
615 Centennial Dr
Kenyon, MN 55946-1297
507-789-5111
Fax: 507-789-8315 800-759-6653
seating@plymold.com www.foldcraft.com
Manufacturer and exporter of tabletops, booths, indoor/outdoor clusters, millwork, tables, chairs, waste receptacles, salad bars and cabinets
Founder: Harold Nielsen
CEO: Chuck Mayhew
Marketing Coordinator: John Price
Contact: Jodie Anderson
andersonjodie@plymold.com
Estimated Sales: $20 - 50 Million
Number Employees: 100-249
Square Footage: 275000
Parent Co: Foldcraft
Brands:
Dur-A-Edge
Plymold

27656 (HQ)Plymouth Tube Company
2061 Young St
East Troy, WI 53120
262-642-8201
Fax: 262-642-8486 sales@plymouth.com
www.trent-tube.com
Specialty manufacturer of precision steel tubing, steel and titanium near-net shapes, and steel and titanium cold drawn shapes.
President: Donald Van Pelt
VP Development: Scott Curnel
VP Marketing/Sales: Steve Bohnenkamp
Contact: Mike Kennerson
mkennerson@plymouth.com
Number Employees: 250-499

27657 Pneucon
4802 Industry Dr
Central Point, OR 97502-3286
541-690-1700
Fax: 541-690-1713 800-545-1355
info@pneucon.com www.pneucon.com
Orifices
President: Wayland Gillrspie
Contact: Brian Miner
miner@pneucon.com
Estimated Sales: Less Than $500,000
Number Employees: 1-4

27658 Pneumatic Conveying Inc
960 E Grevillea Ct
Ontario, CA 91761-5612
909-923-2901
Fax: 909-923-4491 800-655-4481
sales@pneu-con.com
www.pneumaticconveyingsolutions.com
Manufacturer and exporter of customized pneumatic conveying equipment
President: Wayland Gillrspie
Sales Engineer: David Gordon
Sales Administrator: Jennifer Edmondson
Estimated Sales: $2.5-5 Million
Number Employees: 20-49
Square Footage: 120000
Parent Co: Pneumatic Conveying
Brands:
Pneu-Con

27659 Pneumatic Scale Angelus
10 Ascot Pkwy
Cuyahoga Falls, OH 44223-3325
330-923-0491
Fax: 330-923-5570 sales@pneumaticscale.com
www.pneumaticscale.com
Manufacturer and exporter of liquid and dry fillers, cappers, and can seamers
President: William Morgan
Marketing Director: Bethany Hilt
Sales Director: Paul Kearney
Contact: Karl Barkhurst
kbarkhurst2@master-lighting.com
Operations Manager: Paul Kelly
Purchasing Manager: Dave Bellet
Estimated Sales: Less Than $500,000
Number Employees: 1-4
Square Footage: 130000
Parent Co: Barry-Wehmiller Company
Type of Packaging: Consumer, Food Service, Private Label, Bulk

27660 Poblocki Sign Co
922 S 70th St
Milwaukee, WI 53214-3163
414-453-4010
Fax: 414-453-3070 www.poblocki.com
Exhibition cases, exterior and interior custom signs and message boards; custom design services available
President: David Drury
CEO: Brian Johnson
bjohnson@poblocki.com
VP: Mark Poblocki
Estimated Sales: $10-20 Million
Number Employees: 100-249
Square Footage: 200000

27661 Pocantico Resources Inc
55 S Broadway # 1
Tarrytown, NY 10591-4004
914-631-1760
Fax: 914-631-7863 info@pocanticoresources.com
www.pocanticoresources.net
Nutritional ingredients supplier.
Owner: Chris Dilorenzo
chris@pocanticoresources.net
Estimated Sales: $10-20 Million
Number Employees: 5-9

27662 Podnar Plastics Inc
1510 Mogadore Rd
Kent, OH 44240-7599
330-673-2255
Fax: 330-673-2273 800-673-5277
www.rez-tech.com
Manufacturer and exporter of injection blow-molded plastic products including bottles and point-of-purchase containers
President: Jack Podnar
Marketing Director: Jack Podnar
Sales Director: C Allen Clarke
Plant Manager: Scott Podnar
Estimated Sales: $5-10 Million
Number Employees: 20-49
Square Footage: 94000
Type of Packaging: Bulk

27663 Pohlig Brothers
8001 Greenpine Rd
N Chesterfield, VA 23237-2259
804-275-9000
Fax: 804-275-9900 info@pohlig.com
www.pohlig.com
Custom folding and rigid set-up paper boxes

President: Susan Gaffney
rpittman@foodlion.com
Estimated Sales: $9 Million
Number Employees: 50-99
Square Footage: 220000

27664 Pointing Color
2526 Baldwin Street
Saint Louis, MO 63106-1949
651-770-7888
Fax: 651-770-7999
Dyes, dispersions for food products

27665 Polanis Plastic of America
820 Freeway Drive N
Suite 208
Columbus, OH 43229-5404
614-848-5560
Fax: 614-848-5570 www.polinas.com
Biaxially oriented polypropylene films, food and confectionery films, antifog films, metallized films, lamination and tape base films

27666 (HQ)Polar Bear
2695 Pine Grove Rd
Cumming, GA 30041
770-292-9222
Fax: 888-776-5598 888-438-7924
polarbear@usa.net www.polarbearcoolers.com
Distributor of commercial refrigeration freezers, ice cubers, ice dispensers and ice storage bins
Owner: Michael Kennis
General Manager Sales/Distribution: Vic Lemieux
Contact: Geoff Cole
geoff@polarbearcoolers.com
General Manager Production Plant: Dwayne Whitehill
Estimated Sales: $5-10,000,000
Number Employees: 5-9
Type of Packaging: Private Label

27667 Polar Beer Systems
26035 Palomar Rd
Sun City, CA 92585-9710
951-928-8174
Fax: 619-449-0464
Manufacturer and exporter of food service equipment including beverage dispensers, servers and preparation equipment; also, carts
Owner: Sandy Blais
admin@polarbeersystems.com
Estimated Sales: $2.5-5 Million
Number Employees: 10-19
Type of Packaging: Food Service

27668 Polar Hospitality Products
2046 Castor Ave
Philadelphia, PA 19134
215-535-6940
Fax: 215-535-6971 800-831-7823
bradk@the-polar.com www.the-polar.com
Manufacturer and exporter of menu covers and wine list covers, check presenters and coasters
President: Brad Karasik
National Sales Manager: Lisa Dale
Customer Service Manager: Arlinda Candelaria
Estimated Sales: $1 Million
Number Employees: 20-49
Square Footage: 72000
Parent Co: Polar Manufacturing
Brands:
Polar

27669 Polar Ice
2423 W Industrial Park
Bloomington, IN 47404-2601
812-333-1528
Fax: 812-333-1591 800-733-0423
Packaged ice
President: Don Kinser
Treasurer: Pam Kinser
Number Employees: 10
Square Footage: 20000

27670 Polar King Transportation
4410 New Haven Ave
Fort Wayne, IN 46803-1650
260-428-2575
Fax: 260-428-2533 888-541-8330
www.polarking.com
Constructed and ready to operate walk-in coolers and freezers for outdoor use

Marketing Director: Kris Markham
Manager: Mike Lovett
  mikel@polarking.com
Manager: Mike Lovett
Number Employees: 5-9
Square Footage: 150000
Brands:
  Polar King

27671 Polar Peaks
16845 N 29th Avenue
Suite I-303
Phoenix, AZ 85053-3053
480-949-4787
Fax: 602-547-8939

27672 Polar Plastics
4210 Thimens Blouevard
St Laurent, QC H4R 2B9
Canada
514-331-0207
Fax: 514-331-7604 info@polarplastic.ca
www.polarplastic.ca
Manufacturer and exporter of disposable plastic tableware including plates, cups, utensils and dish covers
President: David Stevenson
Plant Manager: Claude Jacques
Estimated Sales: $30 - 50 Million
Number Employees: 250
Type of Packaging: Consumer, Food Service

27673 Polar Process
PO Box 190
Plattsville, ON N0J 1S0
Canada
519-896-8077
Fax: 519-896-1850 877-896-7077
Manufactures sanitary equipment meeting 3A/USDA standards. Pumps, pump feeders, extruders, depositors, and on-line blenders for viscous products. Ultrasonic cutting systems. Conveyors, rental units available. Free testing.
CEO/President: Roger Venning
Sales: Tim Venning
Operations: Peter Solomon
Plant Manager: Mark Karlsen
Estimated Sales: $1-5 Million
Number Employees: 20-49
Number of Products: 10
Brands:
  P0lar Pump
  Polar Extruder
  Polar Ultrashear

27674 Polar Tech Industries Inc
415 E Railroad Ave
Genoa, IL 60135-1200
815-784-9000
Fax: 815-784-9009 800-423-2749
info@polar-tech.com www.polar-tech.com
At the forefront of temperature controlled and protective packaging innovation since 1984. Polar Tech industries is the largest manufacturer of temperature assured packaging materials. Offering over 100 sizes of insulated containersnew dry ice making equipment, a complete line of ICE-BRIX refrigerants and cold packs, insulated totes and wine shippers, specialized cakes, candy, sausage and meat shippers, large insulated transports, pallet covers, packaging tape, labels andshipping supplies.
General Manager: Autumn Santeler
Account Representative: Leann Schuman
Account Representative: Liz Suobata
Account Representative: Allen Cole
Customer Service Manager: Lora Evans
Inside Sales: Angie Dellinger
IT: Donald Santeler
  dons@polar-tech.com
Estimated Sales: $5,000,000 - $9,999,999
Number Employees: 10-19

27675 Polar Ware Company
2806 N 15th St
Sheboygan, WI 53083-3943
920-458-3561
Fax: 920-458-2205 800-237-3655
customerservice@polarware.com
www.polarware.com
Manufacturer and exporter of deep drawn and stainless steel items including steam table pans and covers, trays, pans, pots, bowls, containers, smallwares, bar supplies, etc.; importer of smallwares, barware, chafers, beverage serversaccessories and sinks

CEO: Jerry Baltus
Executive VP: Rick Carr
Marketing Director: Steph Wittmus
National Sales Manager: Dick Ballwahn
Contact: Tom Dinolfo
  tom_sharp@sharp-residential.com
Production Manager: Peter Hansen
Purchasing Manager: Tom Kennedy
Estimated Sales: $20-50 Million
Number Employees: 100-249
Square Footage: 250000
Brands:
  Polar Ware
  Yukon

27676 Polibak Plastics America Inc
113 Executive Dr # 116
Suite 116
Sterling, VA 20166-9559
703-964-0339
Fax: 703-709-1012 888-765-4225
info@polibakusa.com www.polibakusa.com
Bioriented polypropylene film, cast polypropylene film, metalized films, polyethylene.
Vice President: Tolga Baki
  tbaki@polybakusa.com
VP: Tolga Baki
Sales Manager: Erdogan Alkan
Estimated Sales: Over $1 Billion
Number Employees: 1000-4999

27677 Poliplastic
415 Rue Saint-Valier
Granby, QC J2G 7Y3
Canada
450-378-8417
Fax: 450-378-0220
Plastic bags including plain, printed and shopping
President: Michael Friedman
Number Employees: 70

27678 Pollard Brothers
5504 N Northwest Hwy
Chicago, IL 60630-1188
773-763-6868
Fax: 773-763-4466 info@pollardbros.com
www.pollardbros.com
Individual lunch tables
President: Jason Hein
  info@pollardbros.com
Marketing Director: Will Hein
Estimated Sales: Below $5 Million
Number Employees: 10-19

27679 Pollinger Company
8100 Nathanael Greene Lane
Charlotte, NC 28227-0654
704-535-2177
Fax: 704-535-4572 pollingerd@aol.com
Batching and blending systems
President: Don Pollinger
Contact: Elliot Schnitzer
  eschnitzer@polingerco.com
Estimated Sales: $30-50 Million
Number Employees: 10

27680 Poly One Corp
33587 Walker Rd
Avon Lake, OH 44012-1145
Canada
440-930-1000
Fax: 440-930-3799 866-765-9663
www.polyone.com
Buckets, pails and containers
President: Robert Hanlin
CEO: Robert M Patterson
  robertmpatterson@polyone.com
VP: Bob Connely
Estimated Sales: Over $1 Billion
Number Employees: 5000-9999
Parent Co: Hamlin

27681 Poly Plastic Products Inc
21 Schultz Dr
PO Box 220
Delano, PA 18220
570-467-3000
Fax: 570-467-3001 www.polyplasticproducts.com
Plastic bags and film

President: Steven Redlich
  stevenredlich@polyplasticproducts.com
Chairman of the Board: Alfred Teo
Accounting Manager: Donna Petri
VP Sales: Vince Oberto
Vice President of Operations: Tim McGowan
Production Manager: Brad Smith
Plant Manager: John Boyer
Purchasing Manager: Donna McGowan
Number Employees: 100-249
Square Footage: 312000

27682 Poly Processing Co
8055 Ash St
French Camp, CA 95231-9667
209-982-4904
Fax: 209-982-0455 877-325-3142
sales@polyprocessing.com
www.polyprocessing.com
Manufacturer and exporter of molded plastic tanks
Quality Control: John Bnnlanco
Sales Manager: Del Mann
Manager: John Blanco
Estimated Sales: $2.5 - 5 Million
Number Employees: 50-99

27683 Poly Shapes Corporation
41740 Schadden Rd
Elyria, OH 44035
Fax: 847-428-8869 800-605-9359
Printed and plain plastic bags including custom shaped
Vice President: Don Harreld
Sales Manager: Tom Drake
Operations Manager: Don Paulson
Estimated Sales: $5-10 Million
Number Employees: 20-49
Square Footage: 90000

27684 Poly-Clip System Corp
1000 Tower Rd
Mundelein, IL 60060-3816
224-778-7533
Fax: 847-949-2815 800-872-2547
gil@polyclip-usa.com www.polyclip.com
Package closure systems
President: Gil Williams
  contact@polyclip.us
Senior Executive Assistant: Pat Mangioni
VP Sales/Marketing: Gil Williams
Estimated Sales: $20 - 50 Million
Number Employees: 50-99

27685 PolyConversions, Inc.
505 E Condit Dr
Rantoul, IL 61866-3604
217-893-3330
Fax: 217-893-3003 888-893-3330
info@polycoUSA.com www.polycousa.com
Supplier of personal protective apparel for industrial safety, food processing, controlled environments, etc.
President: Ronald Smith
Sales Manager: Scott Carlson
Estimated Sales: $10-20 Million
Number of Brands: 2
Number of Products: 15
Square Footage: 47000
Brands:
  Diposables
  Polywear
  Protecting Wear
  Vr

27686 PolyMaid Company
PO Box 1466
Largo, FL 33779-1466
727-507-9321
Fax: 727-524-8271 800-206-9188
www.polymaid.com
Manufacturer and exporter of food mixers and coffee flavoring tumble mixers with removable plastic liners
President: Ken Orthner
VP Operations: Susan Orthner
Number Employees: 4
Square Footage: 20000
Brands:
  Polymaid

27687 Polyair
330 Humberline Drive
Toronto, ON M9W 1R5
Canada
416-679-6600
Fax: 416-679-6610 888-765-9847
marketing@polyair.com www.polyair.com
Estimated Sales: $1 - 5 Million

27688 Polyair Packaging
808 E 113th St
Chicago, IL 60628-5150
773-995-1818
Fax: 773-995-7725 888-pol-yair
marketing@polyair.com www.polyair.com
Protective packaging and insulation
President: Alan Castle
CFO: Henry Schriback
Plant Manager: Carl Honaker
Estimated Sales: $20-50 Million
Number Employees: 50-99

27689 Polybottle Group
7464 132nd Street
Surrey, BC V3W 4M7
Canada
604-594-4999
Fax: 604-594-3257 www.polybottle.com
Stock and custom plastic containers including wide
and narrow mouth
CEO: Chris Hornsby
Sales Manager: Don Kendall
Human Resources: Maggie Pederson
Number Employees: 205
Square Footage: 160000
Parent Co: ABC Group

27690 Polyclutch
457 State Street
North Haven, CT 06473-3094
203-248-6397
Fax: 262-786-3280 800-298-2066
sales@aaman.com www.polyclutch.com
Mechanical and pneumatic slip clutches for overload
protection and torque control
President: Gerald H Shaff
CEO: Gerald Shaff
Contact: Ken Kraynak
ken@polyclutch.com
Number Employees: 20-49

27691 Polycon Industries
1001 E 99th Street
Chicago, IL 60628-1693
773-374-5500
Fax: 773-374-9805
Manufacturer and exporter of plastic bottles and
containers; also, various types of labeling and silk
screening available
VP: Dan Faro
Plant Manager: Fred Palmer
Estimated Sales: $1 - 5 Million
Number Employees: 100-250
Square Footage: 210000

27692 Polyfoam Corp
2355 Providence Rd
PO Box 906
Northbridge, MA 01534-1085
508-234-6323
Fax: 508-234-2123
Plastic foam products
President: Thomas L Coz
CEO: Tom Coz
tcoz@pollyfoamcorp.com
Estimated Sales: $5-10 Million
Number Employees: 100-249

27693 Polymer Solutions International
15 Newtown Woods Road
PO Box 310
Newtown Square, PA 19073
877-444-7225
info@prostack.com www.prostack.com
Bottled water racks
President: Daniel Kelly
Estimated Sales: $170,000
Number Employees: 1
Square Footage: 1706

27694 Polymercia
609 Fertilla Street
Carrollton, GA 30117-3927
770-830-7434
Fax: 770-830-7377 800-762-1678
info@polymerica.com www.polymerica.com
Estimated Sales: $1 - 5 Million
Number Employees: 10-19

27695 (HQ)Polypack Inc
3301 Gateway Centre Blvd
Pinellas Park, FL 33782-6108
727-578-5000
Fax: 727-578-1300 info@polypack.com.com
www.polypack.com
Engineer and manufacturer of shrink packaging
equipment including shrink-wrap robotic infeeds
and collation, continuous motion form fill seal
machines
President/Founder: Alain Cerf
Estimated Sales: $10-20 Million
Number Employees: 50-99
Type of Packaging: Consumer, Food Service, Private Label, Bulk
Other Locations:
Polypack
Shanghai

27696 Polyplastic Forms Inc
49 Gazza Blvd
Farmingdale, NY 11735-1494
631-249-5011
Fax: 631-249-8504 800-428-7659
sales@polyplasticforms.com
www.polyplasticforms.com
Advertising signs and letters including plastic, foam,
wood, metal, vinyl, etc
President: Nancy Behrens
n.behrens@polyplasticforms.com
CEO: Diane Garrett
Marketing Director: Richard Garrett
Sales Director: Wayne Maciura
Plant Manager: Jim Dietz
Estimated Sales: $2.5-5 Million
Number Employees: 20-49

27697 Polyplastics
10201 Metropolitan Dr
Austin, TX 78758-4944
512-339-9293
Fax: 512-339-9317 800-753-7659
sales@1polyplastics.com www.polyplastics.com
Manufacturer, exporter and wholesaler/distributor of
rigid and flexible foamed plastics
President: Dave McArthur
VP: Tim Buckley
Sales Director: Tim Buckley
Manager: Tito Robledo
trobledo@1polyplastics.com
Manufacturing Manager: Harry Stevens
Estimated Sales: $2.5-5 Million
Number Employees: 5-9
Square Footage: 56000
Parent Co: Buckley Industries
Brands:
Avi
Monarch
Rubatex
Sealed Air
Sentinel
Specialty Composites Ear
Uniroyal Ensolite

27698 Polypro International Inc
7300 Metro Blvd
Suite 570
Edina, MN 55439-2346
952-835-7717
Fax: 952-835-3811 800-765-9776
www.polyprointl.com
Guar and cellulose gums
President: Mark Kieper
polypro@polyprointl.com
Controller: Jennifer Jansson
Senior Account Manager, Sales/Technical: Louise
Polizzotto
Customer Service/Logistics: Janet Burger
Estimated Sales: $2.5-5 Million
Number Employees: 1-4
Type of Packaging: Bulk
Brands:
Procol
Progum
Viscol

27699 Polyscience
6600 W Touhy Ave
Niles, IL 60714-4516
847-647-0611
Fax: 847-647-1155 800-229-7569
culinary@polyscience.com www.polyscience.com
Producer of constant temperature control equipment
President: Philip Preston
HR Executive: Pat Shamburg
pshamburg@polyscience.com
Marketing: Bob Bausone
Sales: Jason Sayers
Operations: Wayne Walter
Estimated Sales: $10-20 Million
Number Employees: 100-249
Square Footage: 128000
Parent Co: Preston Industries

27700 Polysource Inc
555 E Statler Rd
PO Box 916
Piqua, OH 45356
937-381-0001
Fax: 937-778-9300 800-290-6323
ewehtje@polysource.com www.polysource.com
Innovative plastic foam solutions for applications
President: Erick Wehtje
CEO: Andrew Palmer
apalmer@polysource.com
Sales/Product Development Manager: Randy
Dickerson
Number Employees: 20-49

27701 Polyspec
6614 Gant Rd
Houston, TX 77066
281-397-0033
Fax: 281-397-6512 888-797-0033
www.polyspec.com
Contact: Monica Bohannon
mbohannon@itw.com
Estimated Sales: $5 - 10 Million
Number Employees: 20-49

27702 (HQ)Polytainers
197 Norseman Street
Toronto, ON M8Z 2R5
Canada
416-239-7311
Fax: 416-239-0596 800-268-2424
www.polytainersinc.com
Designer and manufacturer of thinwall rigid plastic
containers for the food and dairy industry
President: Robert Barrett
Number Employees: 600
Square Footage: 1000000

27703 Polytarp Products
11 Lepage Court
Toronto, ON M3J 2AE
Canada
416-633-2231
Fax: 416-633-1685 800-606-2231
www.polytarp.com
Polyethelene film, sheeting, bags and food grade
President: Steve Ghantous
Estimated Sales: $21 Million
Number Employees: 150
Square Footage: 19106

27704 Polytemp Corp
1116 Middle River Rd
Middle River, MD 21220-2412
410-687-9000
Fax: 410-687-9629 info@polytempcorp.com
www.polytempcorp.com
A leader in the cold storage construction field, specializing in design, furnishing and installation of insulated panels, cold storage doors, floor insulation
and vapor barriers
Vice President: Brian Clarke
info@polytempcorp.com
VP: Brian Clarke
Estimated Sales: $.5 - 1 million
Number Employees: 1-4

27705 Polytop Corporation
P.O. Box 68
Slatersville, RI 02876
401-767-2400
Fax: 401-765-2694
Dispensing closures
President: Steve B Wilson
CFO: Kevin Rowles

847

Estimated Sales: $20 - 50 Million
Number Employees: 250-499

27706 Polytype America Corporation
10 Industrial Ave
Suite 4
Mahwah, NJ 07430-3530
        201-995-1000
    Fax: 201-995-1080 www.wifag-polytype.com
Dry offset printing equipment for plastic containers,
cups, lids, tubes, jars, vials, metal cans and can ends.
President: Pieter S Vander Griendt
VP Sales Converting North America: Glenn
Whitmore
Senior Sales Representative: Rod Brynildsen
VP Sales Wifag USA: Joseph Ondras
Operations Manager: Jim Dominico
Sales Manager Decorating: Felix Gomez
Number Employees: 1000
Parent Co: wifag//polytype

27707 (HQ)Pomona Service & Pkgng Co LA
2733 Central Sta
Yakima, WA 98902
        509-452-7121
    Fax: 509-576-3942
Manufacturer and exporter of produce handling and
packaging equipment
President: John Muller
  pomonasvc@aol.com
Estimated Sales: $1-2.5 Million
Number Employees: 5-9

27708 Ponce Carribian Distributors
PO Box 11946
San Juan, PR 00922-1946
        787-840-0404
    Fax: 787-840-9474 info@ablesales.com
           www.ablesales.com
Candy
General Manager: Luis Bornes
Estimated Sales: Under $500,000
Number Employees: 20-49

27709 Pop Tops Co Inc
10 Plymouth Dr
South Easton, MA 02375-1192
        508-238-8585
    Fax: 508-230-2851 800-647-8677
      sales@poptopssportswear.com
      www.poptopssportswear.com
Sportswear for employee uniforms and advertising
promotions; also, canvas bags; screenprinting and
embroidering available
President: James Fine
VP Marketing: Jim Fine
Manager: Jonathan Fine
  jonathan@poptopssportswear.com
Estimated Sales: $2.5 - 5 Million
Number Employees: 20-49

27710 Pop n Go
12429 East Putnam St
Whittier, CA 90602
        562-945-9351
    Fax: 562-945-6341 888-476-7646
Popcorn vending machines
CEO: Melvin Wyman
Contact: Pop Go
  sportmel@msn.com
Estimated Sales: Below $500,000
Number Employees: 10-19
Brands:
  Pop N Go

27711 Popcorn Connection
7615 Fulton Avenue
North Hollywood, CA 91605-1805
        818-764-3279
    Fax: 818-765-0578 800-852-2676
Popcorn and nuts
Owner: Kevin Needle
VP: Ross Wallach
Estimated Sales: $300,000
Number Employees: 3
Number of Products: 20
Square Footage: 14000
Type of Packaging: Consumer, Food Service, Private Label, Bulk
Brands:
  Corn Appetit
  Corn Appetit Ultimate

  Fruit Corn Appetit
  Video Munchies

27712 Porcelain Metals Corporation
400 South 13th Street
PO Box 7069
Louisville, KY 40210
        502-635-7421
    Fax: 502-635-1200
Manufacturer and exporter of cooking equipment in-
cluding barbecue and charcoal grills, domestic
cooktops and accessories
Manager: Randy Smitley
OEM Sales Management: Bob Miller
Estimated Sales: $10-20 Million
Number Employees: 20-49
Square Footage: 350000
Type of Packaging: Consumer, Private Label
Brands:
  Barbecue Bucket
  Gourmet Grid
  Kingsford

27713 Port Canaveral Authority
445 Challenger Rd # 301
Suite 301
Cape Canaveral, FL 32920-4100
        321-783-7831
    Fax: 321-783-4651 www.portcanaveral.com
Transportation
Chief Executive Officer: John Walsh
  jwalsh@portcanaveral.org
Deputy Executive Director, Chief Financi: Roger
Rees
CEO: Stanley Payne
Sr. Director, Information Systems: Mark Lorusso
Chief of Police & Public Safety: Joe Hellebrand
Sr. Director of Business Development: Robert
Giangrisostomi
Deputy Director, Human Resources: Brenda Morrish
Sr. Director, Cruise and Port Operations: Mike
Meekins
Number Employees: 100-249

27714 Port Erie Plastics Inc
909 Troupe Rd
Harborcreek, PA 16421-1018
        814-899-7602
    Fax: 814-899-7854 jconnole@porterie.com
          www.porterie.com
Lightweight plastic pallets and custom modling
President: John Johnson
CEO: Robert Batcho
  rbatcho@athenaswc.com
Quality Control: Mike Malin
CEO: William C Witkowski
Marketing/Sales Manager: John Connole
Estimated Sales: $20 - 50 Million
Number Employees: 250-499
Parent Co: Port Erie Plastics

27715 Port of Pasco
1110 Osprey Pointe Blvd
Suite 201
Pasco, WA 99301-5827
        509-547-3378
    Fax: 509-547-2547 portofpasco@portofpasco.org
          www.portofpasco.org
Director of Finance & Administration: Linda
O'Brien
Executive Director: James Toomey
Executive Assistant & Public Information: Vicky
Keller
Number Employees: 5-9

27716 Portable Cold Storage
860 Us Route One
Edison, NJ 08540
        609-252-1105
    Fax: 609-252-1107 800-535-2445
      www.portablecoldstorage.com
Rent refrigerated trailers and containers. All electric
three phase equipment. -15°F to +75F indoors or
outdoors
Operations Manager: N Kewley
Estimated Sales: $1 Million+

27717 Portco Corporation
3601 SE Columbia Way Ste 260
Vancouver, WA 98661
        360-696-4167
    Fax: 360-695-4849 800-426-1794
  info@portco.com www.portco.com

Paper and polyethylene bags for fruit, vegetables,
grains, pasta products and fish; also, printed film
rollstock for form and fill; custom printing available
President: Howard M Wall Jr
CEO: Andy Stewart
Controller: Chip Nipschke
VP: Brian Williamson
Estimated Sales: $20-50 Million
Number Employees: 100-249
Square Footage: 240000

27718 Portec Flowmaster
PO Box 589
Canon City, CO 81215-0589
        719-275-7471
    Fax: 719-269-3750 800-777-7471
Curved belt conveyors, curved spiral conveyors,
chutes, straight conveyors.Rollers for conveyors mo-
torized pulleys for conveyors
President/CEO: Lawrence Weber
CEO: Kirk Mortin
Marketing: Dick Watkins
Sales: Ken Cline
Contact: Dick Alter
  dick.alter@portec.com
Estimated Sales: $20 - 50 Million
Number Employees: 100-249
Square Footage: 80000
Parent Co: J. Richard Industries
Brands:
  Portec Flowmaster
  Portec Pathfinder

27719 Porter & Porter Lumber
PO Box 157
Fort Gay, WV 25514
        304-648-5133
    Fax: 304-648-7283
Wooden pallets and skids
Owner: H S Porter Iii
Estimated Sales: $1 - 5 Million
Number Employees: 10-19

27720 (HQ)Porter Bowers Signs
3300 101st Street
Des Moines, IA 50322-3866
        515-253-9622
    Fax: 515-253-9915
Manufacturer and exporter of signs including neon,
painted, indoor and outdoor
Estimated Sales: $1-2.5 Million
Number Employees: 5-9

27721 Portion-Pac Chemical Corp.
400 N Ashland Ave
Suite 1
Chicago, IL 60622
        312-226-0400
    Fax: 312-226-5400 info@portionpaccorp.com
        www.portionpaccorp.com
Manufacturer/exporter of cleaning products includ-
ing pre-measured floor cleaners and detergents,
bathroom and glass cleaner, air freshener odor
counteractant, carpet shampoo, final rinse sanitizers,
extraction detergent andstrippers/degreasers
President: Marvin Klein
Vice President: John Miller
SFS Pac Division Manager: Chuck Ainsworth
Estimated Sales: $10-20 Million
Number Employees: 20-49
Type of Packaging: Consumer, Food Service
Brands:
  Base Pac
  Bowlpack
  Depotpac
  Foam Pac
  Germicidal
  Glass Pac
  Mop Pac
  Mop Paclite
  Neutrapac
  Pot & Pan Pac
  Restore Pac
  Sani Pac
  Scrub Pac
  Steam Pac
  Strip Pac

27722 Portland Paper Box Company
226 SE Madison St
Portland, OR 97214-3317
        503-233-6271
    Fax: 503-232-4922 800-547-2571
Folding paper boxes

Estimated Sales: $5-10 Million
Number Employees: 20-49

27723 Portola Allied
275 Commerce Ave
New Castle, PA 16101-7625
724-658-4306
Fax: 724-657-8597 800-521-1368
Molds for blow molding
Manager: John Piezer
R&D: Pat Taylor
CFO: Bill Stoewer
Estimated Sales: $50 - 100 Million
Number Employees: 50-99

27724 Portugalia Imports
23 Tremont St
Fall River, MA 02720-4821
508-679-9307
Fax: 508-673-1502 portugaliaimports.com
Seafood, breads, vegetables, and other specialty
foods
President/Owner: Fernando Benevides
benevidesf@portugaliaimports.com
Vice President: Michael Benevides *Year Founded:*
1988

27725 Poser Envelope
1999 Harrison St # 100
Oakland, CA 94612-3517
510-251-6100
Fax: 510-444-5253 800-208-6100
Die cut envelopes; also, printing services available
Manager: Heidi Crouch
Sales/Marketing Manager: Doug Drendel
Production Manager: Rick Pallas
Plant Manager: Brain Stee
Estimated Sales: $3 - 5 Million
Number Employees: 10-19

27726 Posimat S A
1646 NW 108th Ave
Miami, FL 33172-2007
305-477-2029
Fax: 305-477-8044 888-767-4628
miami@posimat.com www.posimat.com
Bottle unscramblers, storage silos and bulk convey-
ors
President: Jaime Marti
Estimated Sales: Below $5 Million
Number Employees: 5-9
Number of Brands: 10
Number of Products: 5
Square Footage: 1600

27727 Positech Corp
191 N Rush Lake Rd
Laurens, IA 50554-1299
712-841-4548
Fax: 712-841-4765 800-831-6026
Material handling machinery including manipula-
tors, rotary manifolds and torque arms; exporter of
manipulators
President: Peter Hong
CEO: Mike Olson
CFO: Kent Radford
Quality Control: Kent Radford
Sales/Marketing Manager: Brett Stumbo
Purchasing Agent: Kay Anderson
Estimated Sales: $50 - 75 Million
Number Employees: 50-99
Square Footage: 65000
Parent Co: Columbus McKinnon Corporation
Brands:
    Reaction Arm
    Sam
    Taurus

**27728 (HQ)Positive Employment
Practice**
1 Muller Court
New City, NY 10956-3508
845-638-6442
Consultant specializing in business coaching and
problem solving support including project design,
marketing strategies, organization building, financial
performance, etc
Business Coach: Steven Caccavo
Contact: Karen Caccavo
steve@constructivebusiness.info
Number Employees: 1-4

27729 Poss USA
6643 Cupecoy Drive
Salt Lake City, UT 84121-3242
801-453-1996
Fax: 801-943-1670

27730 Posterloid Corporation
4862 36th St
Long Island City, NY 11101-1918
718-729-1050
Fax: 718-786-9310 800-651-5000
Manufacturer and exporter of menu boards and dis-
plays
President: Robert Sudack
Sales Manager: Allied Collins
Contact: Basil Mcpherson
bmcpherson@posterloid.com
Estimated Sales: $10 - 20 Million
Number Employees: 100-249

27731 Potdevin Machine Co
26 Fairfield Pl
West Caldwell, NJ 07006-6207
973-227-8828
Fax: 201-288-3770 sales@potdevin.com
www.potdevin.com
Wine industry labeling machines
President: Robert S Potdevin
rsp@potdevin.com
Director/Sales: James Barnes
Estimated Sales: $5-10 Million
Number Employees: 20-49

27732 Potlatch Corp
601 W 1st Ave # 1600
Suite 1600
Spokane, WA 99201-3807
509-835-1500
Fax: 509-835-1555 www.potlatchcorp.com
Manufacturer and exporter of paper products includ-
ing napkins, toilet paper, paper towels and facial
tissues
President & CEO: Eric Cremers
VP & CFO: Jerald Richards
VP, General Counsel: Michele Tyler
VP, Public Affairs: Anne Torma
Estimated Sales: $50-100 Million
Number Employees: 500-999
Parent Co: Potlatch Corporation
Brands:
    Potlatch
    Spa
    Velure

27733 Powdersize Inc
20 Pacific Dr
Quakertown, PA 18951-3601
215-536-5605
Fax: 215-536-6630
Contract micronizing, milling and classification and
processing of pharmaceutical, food, cosmetic, and
industrial dry powders in compliance with current
Good Manufacturing Practices, and adherence to the
principles of Total QualityManagement
President: Wayne Sigler
wsigler@powdersize.com
Founder: Lowell Histand
Partner: Thomas Moran
Estimated Sales: $1 - 5 Million
Number Employees: 10-19
Number of Products: 30
Square Footage: 40000
Type of Packaging: Private Label

27734 Powell Systems
162 Churchill Hubbard Rd
Youngstown, OH 44505-1321
330-759-9220
Fax: 330-759-9434 leah@powell-systems.com
www.powellsystems.com
Materials handling containers, metal stampings, bulk
packaging equipment and scales
President: Bill Powell
bill@powell-systems.com
Founder: William J. Powell
Manager: Bill Powell
bill@powell-systems.com
Estimated Sales: Less Than $500,000
Number Employees: 1-4

27735 Power Brushes
756 S Byrne Rd # 1
Toledo, OH 43609-1062
419-385-5725
Fax: 419-382-0756 800-968-9600
president@powerbrushes.com
www.powerbrushes.com
Manufacturer and exporter of custom designed
brushes for harvesting, cleaning, peeling and pack-
ing of fruits and vegetables
President: Tom Parseghian
Sales Director: Scott Dunckel
Manager: Paul Sneider
tafttool@aol.com
Estimated Sales: $3 Million
Number Employees: 20-49

27736 Power Electronics Intl Inc
561 Plate Dr # 8
East Dundee, IL 60118-2467
847-836-2071
Fax: 847-428-7744 800-362-7959
www.peinfo.com
Manufacturer and exporter of variable speed and AC
powered drives
President: Victor Habisohn
Sales Manager: Michael Habisohn
Service Manager: Adam Jezek
Estimated Sales: $20 - 50 Million
Number Employees: 50-99

27737 Power Flame Inc
2001 S 21st St
P.O. Box 974
Parsons, KS 67357-4911
620-421-0480
Fax: 620-421-0948 800-862-4256
csd@powerflame.com www.powerflame.com
Small immersion tube gas, drier and oven burners
President: Chris Allen
callen@powerflame.com
Sales/Marketing Executive: Bob Rizza
Customer Service Manager: Mark Dunlap
callen@powerflame.com
Purchasing Agent: Jerry Cruz
Estimated Sales: $10-20 Million
Number Employees: 250-499
Square Footage: 200000

27738 (HQ)Power Group
40w222 Old Lafox Rd
St Charles, IL 60174
630-587-3770
Fax: 630-377-4603
Dedicated and multi-customer manufacturing, pack-
aging and logistics facilities in the food industry.
Operates 25 facilities in four countries and has been
providing manufacturing outsourcing and integrated
supply chain solutions toFortune 100 customers
since 1968
CEO: Wayne Sims
Sr. VP: Ken Battista
VP Sales: Jay Toelkes
Estimated Sales: $.5 - 1 million
Number Employees: 1-4
Square Footage: 14000000
Type of Packaging: Consumer, Food Service, Pri-
vate Label, Bulk
Other Locations:
    Power Group
    Guildford Surrey

27739 Power Industrial Supply
80 Sebastopol Road
Santa Rosa, CA 95407-6929
707-544-3994
Fax: 707-544-3996
Boiler, control and process piping equipment
Contact: Cheryl Peterson
cpeterson@powerindustries.com
Estimated Sales: $2 Million
Number Employees: 16

27740 Power Industries Inc
520 Barham Ave
Santa Rosa, CA 95404-5934
707-545-7904
Fax: 707-541-2200 sales@powerindustries.com
www.powerindustries.com
Wine industry hoses, pipes, fittings, stainless steel
tanks and construction
President: Rick Call
rickc@powerindustries.com
CFO: Kem Thangvall

Estimated Sales: $20 - 50 Million
Number Employees: 10-19

27741 Power Logistics
1200 Internationale Pkwy
Suite 300
Woodridge, IL 60517-4976

815-936-1800
Fax: 815-936-1970 www.powergroup.com
Warehouse offering cooler, freezer and dry storage for frozen, refrigerated and nonperishable food products
VP Business Development: Ken Battista
Director Operations: Drew Walker
Estimated Sales: $1-2.5 Million
Number Employees: 19
Parent Co: Power Group

27742 Power Machine Company
118 Brookfield Drive
Moraga, CA 94556-1747

510-658-9661
Fax: 510-653-3848
Wine industry pumps and compressors
VP: Christopher Adam
CEO: Elfriede Knight
VP/General Manager: Christopher Adam
Marketing Manager: Henry Zacata
Public Relations Manager: Caral Frawman
Estimated Sales: $5-10 Million
Number Employees: 10-19

27743 (HQ)Power Packaging Inc
525 Dunham Rd
St Charles, IL 60174

630-377-3838
www.powerpackaging.com
Full-service contract manufacturer for dry foods, beverage mixes, bulk blending and filling, hot fill, organic, nutraceuticals, aseptic and commissary. Designs, owns and operates multi-customer and dedicated food manufacturingfacilities nationwide.
President: Gordon Gruszka
Senior Director, Quality Assurance: Keith Schafer
Executive Director, Sales & Marketing: Chuck Woods
Senior Director, Engineering: Gary Gross
Estimated Sales: $50-100 Million
Number Employees: 1000-4999

27744 Power Packaging Inc
401 N Main Hwy 26
Rosendale, WI 54974

920-872-2181
www.powerpackaging.com
Full-service contract manufacturer for dry foods, beverage mixes, bulk blending and filling, hot fill, organic, nutraceuticals, aseptic and commissary. Designs, owns and operates multi-customer and dedicated food manufacturingfacilities nationwide.
Estimated Sales: $50-100 Million
Number Employees: 1,600

27745 Power Soak by Metcraft
13910 Kessler Drive
Grandview, MO 64030-2810

816-761-3250
Fax: 816-761-0544 info@powersoak.com
www.powersoak.com
President: John Cantrell
Vice President of Distribution: Barry Bergstein
Sales Manager: Mary Cunningham
Vice President of Operations: John McCreight
Manufacturing Manager: Monty Patton
Estimated Sales: $10 - 15 Million
Number Employees: 50-100

27746 Power-Pack Conveyor Co
38363 Airport Pkwy
Willoughby, OH 44094-7562

440-975-9955
Fax: 440-975-0505
ppcc@power-packconveyor.com
www.power-packconveyor.com
Belt conveyors
President: Kevin Ensinger
ppcc@power-packconcp.com
CFO: Jim Ensinger
VP: Jim Ensinger
R&D: Jim Ensinger
Estimated Sales: $5 - 10 Million
Number Employees: 20-49

27747 Poweramp
W194n11481 Mccormick Dr
Germantown, WI 53022-3035

262-255-1510
Fax: 262-255-4199 800-643-5424
sales@poweramp.com www.docksystemsinc.com
Manufacturer and exporter of dock levelers including pit-style, edge of dock, truck, truck restraining systems, dock seals and shelters, etc
Owner: Ed Mguire
Vice President: Mike Pilgrim
Estimated Sales: $25 Million
Number Employees: 50-99
Square Footage: 100000
Parent Co: Systems

27748 Powertex Inc
1 Lincoln Blvd # 101
Suite 101
Rouses Point, NY 12979-1087

518-297-2634
Fax: 518-297-2634 800-769-3783
seabulk@powertex.com www.powertex.com
Manufacturer and exporter of dry powder and bulk plastic liners for use in ocean containers and truck trailers
President: Stephen Podd
stephen@powertex.com
Chairman/CEO: Victor Podd
Sales Manager: Patricia Olsen
Estimated Sales: $10 - 20 Million
Number Employees: 50-99
Square Footage: 130000
Brands:
Powerbulk
Powerliner
Powertex Meatstrap
Seabulk Powerliner

27749 Powertex Inc
1 Lincoln Blvd # 101
Suite 101
Rouses Point, NY 12979-1087

518-297-2634
Fax: 518-297-2634 seabulk@powertex.com
www.powertex.com
Tea and coffee container liners
President: Stephen Podd
stephen@powertex.com
Sales/Marketing: Patricia Olsen
Estimated Sales: $10-20 Million
Number Employees: 50-99

27750 Poynette Distribution Center
W8070 Kent Rd
Poynette, WI 53955-9713

608-635-4396
Fax: 608-635-7308 lakesidefoods.com
Peas, green beans, tomatoes, corn and sauerkraut
Sr. VP Operations: Daniel C Cavanaugh
VP Customer Service: James I Ferguson
General Manager: Ross Moland
Plant Manager: Mike Hull
Estimated Sales: $10 - 20 Million
Number Employees: 20-49
Parent Co: Stokely USA
Type of Packaging: Consumer, Private Label

27751 Ppm Technologies LLC
500 E Illinois St
Newberg, OR 97132-2307

503-538-3141
Fax: 503-538-8575 800-246-2034
www.ppmtech.com
Vibratory and belt conveyors, bucket elevators, optical sorters, controls and ingredient application and storage systems
Manager: Mark Eaton
CEO: Robert Petersen
robert.petersen@ppmtech.com
VP: Mark Eaton
Marketing: Neil Anderson
Regional Sales Manager: Ellen Hao
Estimated Sales: $1 - 5 Million
Number Employees: 100-249
Square Footage: 600000
Parent Co: FMC Technologies
Brands:
Allen
Fmc

27752 Ppm Technologies LLC
500 E Illinois St
Newberg, OR 97132-2307

503-538-3141
Fax: 503-538-8575
Manager: Mark Eaton
CEO: Robert Petersen
robert.petersen@ppmtech.com
Regional Sales Manager: Ellen Hao
Estimated Sales: $1 - 5 Million
Number Employees: 100-249

27753 Prairie Packaging Inc
314 Mooresville Blvd
Mooresville, NC 28115-7909

704-660-6600
Fax: 704-660-7604 info@polarplastic.ca
www.wincup.com
Plastic cutlery, plates, bowls, tumblers, stemware and take-out containers; also, custom molded items for the food service and consumer markets
Director: Don Towne
CEO: Eric Cohen
VP Marketing: Dave Hicks
Plant Manager: Philip Goudreault
Estimated Sales: $31.1 Million
Number Employees: 250-499
Brands:
Alpha
Belle
Gild
Infinity
Legend
Perfection
Polar Pal
Polaronde
Pro
Prodigy
Signature
Xl

27754 Prairie View Industries
2620 Industrial Ave
Fairbury, NE 68352-1355

402-729-4055
Fax: 402-729-4058 800-554-7267
info@pvifs.com www.pvifs.com
Accessories, benches, can racks, carts, dollies, drip catcher, dunnage racks, equipment stands, hotshelves, organizers, pan racks, picnic table, pizza racks, platform trucks, ramps, shelving carts, sinks, tables
Owner: Richard Allen
rallen@pviramps.com
Number Employees: 50-99

27755 (HQ)Prater Industries
2 Sammons Ct
Bolingbrook, IL 60440-4995

630-759-9595
Fax: 630-759-6099 877-247-5625
info@praterindustries.com
www.praterindustries.com
Sizing, separation, particle reduction/enlargement equipment
President/CEO: R Scott Prater
Chairman: Robert Prater
rprater@praterindustries.com
CFO: David Utterback
Marketing: Katie Meyers
Estimated Sales: $5-10 Million
Number Employees: 50-99
Square Footage: 110000
Other Locations:
Prater Industries
Sterling IL
Brands:
Mega-Mill
Rota-Sieve

27756 Pratt Industries
5620 Departure Dr
Raleigh, NC 27616-1841

919-334-7400
Fax: 919-850-9353 www.prattindustries.com
Corrugated boxes
Manager: Pam Blackwell
Quality Control: Ed Allen
Sales Manager: Rick White
Manager: Tony Dilbeck
Estimated Sales: $20-50 Million
Number Employees: 50-99
Parent Co: Pratt Industries

27757 Pratt Industries
1975 Sarasota Business Pkwy NE
Conyers, GA 30013-5745
678-607-1433
Fax: 678-607-1473 800-428-9269
www.prattindustries.com
Corrugated boxes
Sales: Michael Wilkie
Estimated Sales: $20-50 Million
Number Employees: 50-99

27758 Pratt Industries
220 Plantation Rd
New Orleans, LA 70123-5312
504-733-7292
Fax: 504-734-8920 www.prattindustries.com
Manufacturer and marketer of advanced intermodal
equipment
President: Jim Hale
CFO: Gary Byrd
R&D: Mark Nay
Manager: Heidi Lecair
hlecair@mhm-inc.com
Estimated Sales: $10 - 20 Million
Number Employees: 50-99

27759 (HQ)Pratt Poster Company
3001 E 30th Street
Indianapolis, IN 46218-2850
317-545-0842
Fax: 317-927-0653 800-645-1012
tpratt@prattcorp.com
Point of purchase advertising signs, flags, pennants
and banners
CEO: Sarah Pratt
National Sales Manager: Thomas Pratt
Contact: Ron Huckabee
rhuckabee@prattcorp.com
Estimated Sales: $10-20 Million
Number Employees: 100-249
Type of Packaging: Bulk

27760 Prawnto Systems
4770 Interstate 30 W
Caddo Mills, TX 75135-7634
903-527-4149
Fax: 903-527-4951 800-426-7254
sales@prawntomachine.com www.prawnto.net
Manufacturer and exporter of shrimp processing
equipment including cutters, processing stations and
deveiners
CEO: Don Morris
sales@prawntomachine.com
VP: Derrell Sawyer
Sales: Derrell Sawyer
Estimated Sales: $1,000,000
Number Employees: 1-4
Number of Brands: 2
Number of Products: 7
Square Footage: 7000
Brands:
Prawnto
Shrimperfect

27761 Prawnto Systems
4770 Interstate 30 W
Caddo Mills, TX 75135-7634
903-527-4149
Fax: 903-527-4951 800-426-7254
sales@prawntomachine.com
President: Don Morris
sales@prawntomachine.com
Estimated Sales: Below $5 Million
Number Employees: 1-4

27762 Praxair Inc
10 Riverview Dr
Danbury, CT 06810
716-879-4077
Fax: 800-772-9985 800-772-9247
info@praxair.com www.praxair.com
Manufacturer and exporter of nitrogen freezing sys-
tems for food packaging.
Chairman & CEO: Steve Angel
SVP & Chief Financial Officer: Matthew White
Executive Vice President: Eduardo Menezes
Executive Vice President: Anne Roby
VP/General Counsel/Corporate Secretary: Guillermo
Bichara
Year Founded: 1907
Estimated Sales: $11.44 Billion
Number Employees: 26,000
Parent Co: Linde plc

Brands:
Linde

27763 Precision
1135 NW 159th Dr
Miami, FL 33169-5882
305-625-2451
Fax: 305-623-0475 800-762-7565
sales@atlasfoodserv.com www.atlasfoodserv.com
Food transport carts, heated and refrigerated convey-
ors, buffet equipment, milk and ice cream units and
modular serving systems
President: David Meade
VP Sales: Howard Bolner
VP Manufacturing: Mark Siegfriedt
Estimated Sales: $10 - 20 Million
Number Employees: 100-249
Parent Co: Atlas Metal Industries

27764 Precision Automation CoInc
1841 Old Cuthbert Rd
Cherry Hill, NJ 08034-1478
856-428-7400
Fax: 856-428-1270
sales@precisionautomationinc.com
www.precisioncovert.com
Chairman of the Board: G Frederick Rexon Sr
Cio/Cto: Dan Pamonio
dpp@precisionautomationinc.com
Estimated Sales: $10-20 Million
Number Employees: 50-99

27765 Precision Automation Co
2120 Addmore Ln
Clarksville, IN 47129-9166
812-283-7963
Fax: 812-283-7992
www.precisionautomationinc.com
President: G Mooris
Estimated Sales: $1 - 3 Million
Number Employees: 20-49

27766 Precision Automation CoInc
1841 Old Cuthbert Rd
Cherry Hill, NJ 08034-1478
856-428-7400
Fax: 856-428-1270
sales@precisionautomationinc.com
President: Glen A Morris
Founder: Fred. Rexon Sr
Chairman: Fred Rexon Sr
Estimated Sales: $3.5 Million
Number Employees: 50-99
Square Footage: 45

27767 Precision Brush
6700 Parkland Blvd
Cleveland, OH 44139-4341
440-498-0140
Fax: 800-252-0834 800-252-4747
info@precisionbrush.com www.brushes.info
Manufacturer and exporter of custom metal channel
strip brushes in various shapes and sizes
President: Jim Benjamin
jim@precisionbrush.com
General Manager: Mike Porter
Estimated Sales: $2.5-5 Million
Number Employees: 10-19
Square Footage: 36000

27768 Precision Component Industries
5325 Southway St SW
Canton, OH 44706-1943
330-477-6287
Fax: 330-477-1052
tricia@precision-component.com
www.precision-component.com
Manufacturer and exporter of special production ma-
chinery, tools, dies, fixtures, short and long run pro-
duction machining, stamping services and cans
President: Tricia Gerak
tfino@saralee.com
CEO: Patricia Gerak
President: Tony Gerak
Sales Manager: Lewis Page
Purchase Manager: George Melson
Estimated Sales: Below $5 Million
Number Employees: 20-49
Parent Co: Brennan Industrial Group
Type of Packaging: Bulk

27769 Precision Micro Control
2075 Corte Del Nogal # N
Carlsbad, CA 92011-1415
760-930-0101
Fax: 760-930-0222 info@pmccorp.com
www.pmccorp.com
Four axis packaged controller with motion control
features
Head Marketing Team: David Clark
Number Employees: 50-99

27770 Precision Plastics Inc
6405a Ammendale Rd # A
Beltsville, MD 20705-1203
301-937-8001
Fax: 301-937-4184 800-922-1317
www.precisionplastics.com
Plastic food service products including sneeze
guards, heat shields, condiment racks, menu/card
holders, ice trays, buffet bars, signage, etc. Also a
3M product distributor
Owner: Oliver Hofe
oliver@precisionplastics.com
Administrator Assistant: Vicki Juneau
Marketing Manager: Chris Marshall
Estimated Sales: $2.5-5 Million
Number Employees: 20-49
Square Footage: 30000

27771 Precision Plus
6416 Inducon Dr W
Sanborn, NY 14132-9019
716-297-2039
Fax: 716-297-8210 800-526-2707
info@precisionplus.com www.precisionplus.com
Vacuum pump replacement parts
Manager: Joseph Miller
joseph.miller@precisionplus.com
Estimated Sales: $7 Million
Number Employees: 20-49
Number of Brands: 15
Number of Products: 2000
Square Footage: 80000
Parent Co: BOC Group, Inc.
Type of Packaging: Food Service
Brands:
Alcatel
Boc Edwards
Boce Stokes
Busch
Ebara
Kinney
Leybold
Precision Scientific
Ristschic
Varian
Welch

27772 Precision Pours
12837 Industrial Park Blvd
Minneapolis, MN 55441-3910
763-694-9291
Fax: 763-694-9343 800-549-4491
ricksandvik@precisionpours.com
Manufacturer and exporter of pour spouts for liquor,
syrups and cooking oils; wholesaler/distributor of
pour cleaning systems
President: Rick Sandvik
ricksandvik@precisionpours.com
Accounting: Patrick Sandvik
VP Sales: Duane Nording
Estimated Sales: Below $5,000,000
Number Employees: 10-19
Square Footage: 9600
Brands:
Rack & Pour
Sure Shot

27773 Precision Printing & Packaging
801 Alfred Thun Rd
Clarksville, TN 37040-5348
931-906-0798
Fax: 931-920-9001 800-500-4526
Metallized and paper glue-applied labels
Chairman of the Board: Joseph Sellinger
National Sales Manager: Reba Meek
Contact: April Sizemore
sizemore.april@anheuser-busch.com
Plant Manager: Rod Stough
Estimated Sales: $50 - 100 Million
Number Employees: 1-4
Parent Co: Anheuser-Busch Companies

27774 Precision Solutions Inc
2525 Tollgate Rd
Quakertown, PA 18951-5306
215-536-4400
Fax: 215-536-4096
info@precisionsolutionsinc.com
www.precisionsolutionsinc.com
Representative for many manufacturers of scale and measurement equipment
Owner: Dan Kendra
dan_kendra@precisionsolutionsinc.com
Technical Service Consultant: Trevor Filipowicz
Number Employees: 10-19

27775 Precision Stainless Inc
501 N Belcrest Ave
Springfield, MO 65802-2504
417-865-8724
Fax: 417-865-0906
Wine industry aseptic processing equipment, bins and blenders and equipment fabrication
Sales Engineer: Bert Adams
Estimated Sales: $25-50 Million
Number Employees: 50-99

27776 Precision Systems Inc
16 Tech Cir # 100
Suite 100
Natick, MA 01760-1038
508-655-7010
Fax: 508-653-6999 precisionsystems@msn.com
www.precisionsystemsinc.com
Milk cryoscopes manufacturing, testing, incoming inspection and final Q.C oeomerers and chemistry analyzers
President: Charles Bell
CFO: Ann Rogers
VP: Jennifer Knapp
Quality Control: Bob Atwood
Estimated Sales: $1-5 Million
Number Employees: 20-49
Number of Brands: 20
Number of Products: 100
Square Footage: 45600
Type of Packaging: Private Label
Brands:
Analette
Cryoscopes
Osmette

27777 Precision Temp Inc
11 Sunnybrook Dr
Cincinnati, OH 45237-2103
513-641-4446
Fax: 513-641-0733 800-934-9690
service@precisiontemp.com
www.precisiontemp.com
Manufacturer and exporter of gas booster heaters for high temperature water
Vice President: Steve Aldrich
aldrich@precisiontemp.com
CEO: Rick Muhlhauser
Vice President: Fred Rohtzeid
Estimated Sales: $2-4,000,000
Number Employees: 10-19
Square Footage: 40000
Type of Packaging: Food Service
Brands:
Precision Temp

27778 (HQ)Precision Wood Products
PO Box 529
Vancouver, WA 98666-0529
360-694-8322
Fax: 360-696-1530 palletmfg@aol.com
Manufacturer and exporter of wooden pallets and containers
President: Marley Petersen Jr
Contact: Tim Darrow
info@palletpricing.com
Estimated Sales: $5-10 Million
Number Employees: 50-99

27779 Precision Wood of Hawaii
PO Box 529
Vancouver, WA 98666-0529
808-682-2055
Fax: 808-682-2465
Pallets, wooden boxes and crates; also, rebuilder of recycled wooden pallets
VP/General Manager: T Ross
Estimated Sales: $1-2.5 Million
Number Employees: 50-100

27780 Precit
710 Tech Park Drive
La Vergne, TN 37086-3622
615-287-8255
Fax: 615-287-8355 800-338-4585
jeff.watson@franke.com
Parent Co: Franke

27781 Preco Inc
500 Laser Dr
Somerset, WI 54025-9774
715-247-3285
Fax: 715-247-5650 800-775-2737
sales@precoinc.com www.precoinc.com
President/CEO: Tim Burns
Manager: Mary Amos
mamos@precoinc.com
Estimated Sales: $1 - 5 Million
Number Employees: 100-249

27782 Preferred Machining Corporation
3730 S Kalamath Street
Englewood, CO 80110-3493
303-761-1535
Fax: 303-789-9300
Manufacturer and exporter of fillers, pumps/stuffers, formers and vacuumizers for poultry, beef, etc. As well as end liners and accessories for the can making industry
Vice President: Jim Abbott
Marketing Director: Tom Hoffmann
Estimated Sales: $10 - 20 Million
Number Employees: 50
Brands:
Prc Weight Control Filler
Versaform

27783 Preferred Packaging
PO Box 700
Mount Gilead, NC 27306
336-884-0792
Fax: 336-884-5829
preferredmichael@northstate.net
Folding paper boxes
President: William H Drummond
VP Sales/Marketing: Michael Drummond
Estimated Sales: $5 - 10 Million
Number Employees: 30
Square Footage: 43000
Type of Packaging: Consumer, Food Service, Private Label

27784 Preferred Packaging Systems
440 S Lone Hill Avenue
San Dimas, CA 91773
Fax: 909-592-5640 800-378-4777
www.ghlpackaging.com
Manufactures, engineers and designs packaging equipment.
Estimated Sales: $10-15 Million
Number Employees: 15
Square Footage: 30000

27785 Premier
5721 Dragon Way
Suite 113
Cincinnati, OH 45227-4518
513-271-0600
Fax: 859-581-5525 800-354-9817
www.excellead.com
Manufacturer and exporter of paper plates, hot dog holders, food trays and foil laminated ashtrays
Owner: Thomas P Santen
VP/General Manager: J Paul Taylor
Sales: Lori Roberts
VP Operations: Viea Gerwin
Plant Manager: Mike McCann
Estimated Sales: $5-10 Million
Square Footage: 80000
Type of Packaging: Private Label
Brands:
Teddy Bear

27786 Premier Brass
255 Ottley Dr NE Ste A
Atlanta, GA 30324-3926
404-873-6000
Fax: 404-873-9993 800-251-5800
info@premierbrass.com www.premierbrass.com
Manufacturer, importer and exporter of brass and chrome components for custom foodguards, display cases and railing systems

President: Alex Mazingue
Vice President: Pep Matus
General Manager: Fred Boyajian
Estimated Sales: $1-2.5 Million
Number Employees: 10-19
Square Footage: 50000
Parent Co: Great Eastern Distributors
Type of Packaging: Food Service
Brands:
Premier Brass

27787 Premier Foods
871 Harbour Way S
Richmond, CA 94804-3612
707-554-4623

27788 Premier Glass & Package Company
PO Box 5612
Napa, CA 94581
707-224-1660
Fax: 707-224-1660
Wine bottles and packaging
President: Kent Robert
Owner: Stuart Humpert
Estimated Sales: Less than $500,000
Number Employees: 1-4

27789 (HQ)Premier Packages
9438 Watson Industrial Park
Saint Louis, MO 63126-1523
314-961-6588
Fax: 314-961-6589 800-466-6588
info@premierpackages.com
Bakery boxes, folding cartons and trays; also, die cutting available
Co-Owner: Jeff Petroski
Estimated Sales: $1-2.5 Million
Number Employees: 5-9
Square Footage: 32000

27790 Premier Plastics Inc
4880 S 134th St
Omaha, NE 68137-1614
402-346-2998
Fax: 402-346-7679 866-446-2998
www.premierplasticsinc.com
Thin gauge packaging for short runs
President: Wayne Alter
walter@premierplasticsinc.com
Sales Manager: Franklin Berry
Customer Service Manager: Elizabeth Laska
walter@premierplasticsinc.com
Estimated Sales: $3 - 5 Million
Number Employees: 20-49
Square Footage: 30000

27791 Premier Restaurant Equipment
7120 Northland Ter N
Brooklyn Park, MN 55428-1573
763-544-8800
Fax: 763-544-7949 info@premiereq.com
www.boelterpremier.com
Provider of design and production services
Owner: James Hara
info@premiereq.com
Estimated Sales: $5 - 10,000,000
Number Employees: 20-49

27792 Premier Skirting Products
241 Mill St
Lawrence, NY 11559-1209
516-239-6581
Fax: 516-239-6810 800-544-2516
info@premierskirting.com
www.premierskirting.com
Manufacturer and exporter of table and skirting cloths, napkins, chair covers and place mats
Owner: Ross Yudin
ross@premeirskirting.com
CEO: C VanDewater
CFO: Linda Ehrlich
Manager: Ross Yudin
ross@premeirskirting.com
Plant Manager: Wayne Rizzo
Estimated Sales: $1 - 2.5 Million
Number Employees: 10-19
Square Footage: 20000

27793 Premier Southern TicketCo
7911 School Rd
Cincinnati, OH 45249-1596

513-489-6700
Fax: 513-489-6867 800-331-2283
sales@premiersouthern.com
Coupons and numbered pressure sensitive labels
President: Kirk Schulz
kirks@premiersouthern.com
Sales Manager: Bill Reilly
Estimated Sales: $5 - 10 Million
Number Employees: 20-49
Parent Co: Price Chopper

27794 Premium Air Systems Inc
1051 Naughton Dr
Troy, MI 48083-1911

248-680-8800
Fax: 248-680-8808 877-430-0333
leonardf@premiumair.net www.premiumair.net
Custom stainless steel food service tables, sinks,
hoods, custom ventilation systems, refrigeration and
HV/AC equipment; also, installation available
President: Leonard Framalin
leonardf@premiumair.net
Sales Manager: Gilbert St.Louis
Engineer Manager: Ken Comito
Estimated Sales: $5-10 Million
Number Employees: 50-99

27795 Premium Foil Products Company
PO Box 32309
Louisville, KY 40232

502-459-2820
Fax: 502-454-5488
Manufacturer and exporter of aluminum foil con-
tainers
President: A J Kleier
VP/General Manager: Robert Moses
Contact: Robert Moses
musherone@aol.com
Estimated Sales: $5-10 Million
Number Employees: 20-49
Type of Packaging: Food Service, Bulk

27796 Premium Pallet
5000 Richmond Street
Philadelphia, PA 19137-1815

215-535-2559
Fax: 215-535-2570 800-648-7347
Skids and pallets
President: Erik Bronstein
Number Employees: 40
Square Footage: 1980

27797 Prengler Products
14865 State Highway 56
Sherman, TX 75092-4621

903-892-9791
Fax: 903-893-9536 craig@prenglerproducts.com
www.prenglerproducts.com
Point of purchase displays
President: Craig S Prengler
craig@prenglerproducts.com
Estimated Sales: $500,000-$1 Million
Number Employees: 10-19
Square Footage: 56000

27798 Prent Corp
2225 Kennedy Rd
Janesville, WI 53545-0885

608-754-0276
Fax: 608-754-2410 prent@prent.com
www.prent.com
Custom thermal former
Owner: Joe Pregont
jpregont@prent.com
Marketing Director: Vicki Damron
Estimated Sales: $50-100 Million
Number Employees: 500-999

27799 Prentiss
3600 Mansell Rd Ste 350
Alpharetta, GA 30022

770-552-8072
Fax: 770-552-8076 info@prentiss.com
www.prentiss.com
Manufacturer, importer and exporter of pesticides,
insecticides and rodenticides
President: Richard A Miller
VP/Purchasing: Jeffery Miller
Sales Director: Larry Eichler

Estimated Sales: $10 - 20 Million
Number Employees: 5-9
Square Footage: 150000
Type of Packaging: Private Label, Bulk
Brands:
Prentox

**27800 Prepared Foods Magazine& Food
Engineering Magazine**
2401 W. Big Beaver Rd
Suite 700
Troy, MI 48084

248-362-3700
Fax: 303-431-0193
Magazine source

27801 Pres-Air-Trol Corporation
704 Bartlett Ave.
Altoona, WI 54720

715-831-6353
Fax: 419-818-0897 800-431-2625
info@senasys.com www.presair.com
Manufacturer and exporter of foot pedals and
switches including pneumatic/electric and shock, ex-
plosion and water-proof; pressure and vacuum
switches, thermometers, thermostats
President: Arthur Blumenthal
Vice President: Doreen Bassin
Sales: Juana Magana
Contact: Ivon Graner
ivong@presair.com
Production/Plant Manager: Chris Felon
Purchasing: Marie Schuartz
Estimated Sales: $10 - 20 Million
Number Employees: 20-49
Square Footage: 24000
Brands:
Control Safe
Disposertrol
Magictrol
Pres-Air-Trol
Tinytrol

27802 Pres-On Products
21 W Factory Rd
Addison, IL 60101

630-543-9370
Fax: 630-628-8025 800-323-7467
Manufacturer and exporter of liners including induc-
tion seal, PE, styrene and self-sealing
Division VP: Tom Cummins
Contact: John Lesavage
johnl@preson.com
VP Manaufacturing: Frank Edes
Estimated Sales: $20-50 Million
Number Employees: 15

27803 Pres-On Tape & Gasket Corp
2600 E 107th St
Bolingbrook, IL 60440-3196

630-628-2255
Fax: 630-628-8025 800-323-7467
www.pres-on.com
Induction and pressure sealed cap liners, gasketing
tapes of vinyl foam
Founder: Henry L. Gianatasio
Executive VP: Kat Liepins
kliepins@preson.com
Estimated Sales: $10 Million
Number Employees: 20-49

27804 Prescolite
695 Walnut Ave
Vallejo, CA 94592-1134

707-562-3500
Fax: 510-577-5022 www.prescolite.com
Manufacturer and exporter of lighting fixtures in-
cluding electric, incandescent, mercury and outdoor
Marketing Manager: John Taylor
Estimated Sales: $20-50 Million
Number Employees: 250-499
Parent Co: US Industries

27805 Presence From Innovation LLC
2290 Ball Dr
St Louis, MO 63146-8602

314-423-9777
Fax: 314-423-0420 info@pfinnovation.com
www.pfinnovation.com
Manufacturer and exporter of universal gravity feed
systems, ice barrel coolers and display and merchan-
dising equipment
President: Jim Watt
Number Employees: 250-499

Brands:
Iceman
Ultra Glide

27806 Presentations South
4748 Jetty St
Orlando, FL 32817-3183

407-657-2108
Fax: 407-849-0930
Manufacturer, designer and exporter of industrial
displays, attraction exhibits, etc
Estimated Sales: $2.5-5 Million
Number Employees: 1-4
Square Footage: 120000

27807 President Container Inc
200 W Commercial Ave
Moonachie, NJ 07074-1684

212-244-0345
Fax: 201-933-9574
pcsales@presidentcontainer.com
www.presidentcontainer.com
Corrugated boxes
President: Lucia Sannicandro
forzals@aol.com
Vice President: Richard Grossbard
General Manager: Larry Grossbard
Vice President of Production: Joe Restifo
Estimated Sales: $20 - 50 Million
Number Employees: 50-99
Square Footage: 200000

27808 Presque Isle Wine Cellars
9440 W Main Rd
North East, PA 16428-2699

814-725-1314
Fax: 814-725-2092 800-488-7492
info@piwine.com www.piwine.com
Wines and wine-making supplies
Owner: Doug Moorhead
doug@piwine.com
Co-Owner: Laury Bouttcher
Estimated Sales: Below $5 Million
Number Employees: 10-19
Type of Packaging: Private Label
Brands:
Presque Isle Wine

**27809 Pressed Paperboard Technologies
LLC**
30400 Telegraph Rd
Bingham Farms, MI 48025-4537

248-646-6500
Fax: 248-646-6532 sales@papertrays.com
www.papertrays.com
Press formed, dual-ovenable paperboard trays for
the frozen food, school and institutional feeding and
pizza industries.
Owner: Lawrence Epstein
Vice President Sales: Al Fotheringham
Contact: Michelle Frasure
michellefrasure@papertrays.com

27810 Pressure Pack
PO Box 3007
Williamsburg, VA 23187-3007

757-220-3693
Fax: 757-229-7612
Asceptic, food processing, heat sealing and can fill-
ing machinery
Owner: Robert Fox
VP Technology: Joseph Marcy
Estimated Sales: $1 - 5,000,000
Number Employees: 1-4

27811 Prestige Label Company
151 Industrial Dr
Burgaw, NC 28425

910-259-3600
Fax: 910-259-6312 800-969-4449
www.prestigelabelsco.com
Labels including thermal, thermal transfer, laser,
computer, styrene inserts, prime, bar code and con-
secutive numbers
Manager: Terie Syme
Estimated Sales: $5-10 Million
Number Employees: 20-49
Square Footage: 36000
Type of Packaging: Private Label

27812 Prestige Metal ProductsInc
885 Anita Ave
PO Box 700
Antioch, IL 60002-2462

847-395-0775
Fax: 847-395-0792 rfq@prestigemetals.com
www.prestigemetals.com
Custom sheet metal fabrication
President: Gordon Miller
info@prestigemetals.com
Estimated Sales: $2.5-5 Million
Number Employees: 20-49
Square Footage: 38000

27813 Prestige Plastics Corporation
8207 Swenson Way
Delta, BC V4G 1J5
Canada

604-930-2931
Fax: 604-930-2936
Manufacturer, importer and exporter of bins, tote
and plastic boxes, cartons, point of purchase dis-
plays and signs; also, die cutting and design services
available
President: Bill Schoenbaum
Sales Manager: James Berry
Estimated Sales: $10-20 Million
Number Employees: 10-19

27814 Prestige Skirting & Tablecloths
60 Dutch Hill Rd # 4a
Orangeburg, NY 10962-1722

845-358-6900
Fax: 845-359-2287 800-635-3313
prestigeskirting@aol.com
Manufacturer and exporter of tablecloths, napkins,
banquet skirting, clips with Velcro, skirt hangers,
chair covers, working racks and custom made linens
President: Marilyn Enison
Office Manager: Emily Valerie Ross
Sales Manager: Paul Tessler
Customer Service: Jane Smithers
Estimated Sales: $5-10 Million
Number Employees: 10-19
Square Footage: 20000
Brands:
    Hangars

27815 Prestolabels.Com
31 Industry Park Court
Tipp City, OH 45371

Fax: 937-667-5687 800-201-7120
andy.heinl@prestolabels.com
www.prestolabels.com
Digital labels and tags
President: Tony Heinl
CEO: Rick Heinl
CFO: Gene Harris
R&D/Sales: Andy Heink
QControl/Operations/Plant Manager: Gary Packott
Marketing/Public Relations: Pat Larson
Contact: Andy Heink
andy@repacorp.com
Production: Rob Sloan
Purchasing: Heidi Ponlman
Estimated Sales: $35 Million
Number Employees: 160
Parent Co: Repacorp, Inc
Type of Packaging: Consumer, Food Service, Pri-
vate Label, Bulk

27816 Preston Scientific
1450 N Hundley St
Anaheim, CA 92806-1322

714-632-3700
Fax: 714-632-7355
Manufacturer and exporter of computer systems in-
cluding data acquisition sub-systems
President and CEO: Bernard Spear
Executive VP: Phillip Halverson
President: Bill Boston
Sales Manager: Charles McGuire
Plant Manager: Amber Brideisca
Purchasing Manager: Robert Exley
Estimated Sales: $1 - 2.5 Million
Number Employees: 1-4
Square Footage: 48000
Parent Co: Halear
Brands:
    Presys1000

27817 Pretium Packaging
200 W 20th St
Hermann, MO 65041-1602

573-486-2811
Fax: 573-486-2443 www.pretiumpkg.com
Manufacturer and exporter of custom packaging and
mustard bottles
President: Keith Harbison
Plant Manager: Bob Gillig
Estimated Sales: $20 - 50 Million
Number Employees: 50-99

27818 Pretium Packaging
512 Forest Rd
Hazle Twp, PA 18202-9389

570-459-1800
Fax: 570-459-6462 petjars@aol.com
www.pretiumpkg.com
Clear polyester food jars and bottles
President: Keith Harbison
Cmo: Tom Marchetto
Human Resources: Jane Mindler
Sales Manager: Bob Plesnicher
VP Manufacturing: Raymond Eble
Estimated Sales: $20 - 50 Million
Number Employees: 50-99
Square Footage: 63000
Parent Co: Pretium Packaging

27819 Pretium Packaging
15450 South Outer Forty Drive
Suite 120
Chesterfield, MO 63017

812-522-8177
Fax: 314-727-8200 314-727-8673
customerservice@pretiumpkg.com
www.pretiumpkg.com
Blow molded plastic bottles in HDPE, PVC, LPDE
and EPET; also, labeling and decorating available
CFO: Bob Mohrmann
Contact: Daniel Lally
dlally@harbison.com
Manager: John Cannaday
Plant Manager: Joe Wolf
Estimated Sales: $10-20 Million
Number Employees: 50-99

27820 Pretium Packaging, LLC.
15450 S Outer Forty
Suite 120
Chesterfield, MO 63017

314-727-8200
pretiumpkg.com
Manufacturer and exporter of plastic bottles and
containers used for syrup.
President/CEO: Paul Kayser
Year Founded: 1992
Estimated Sales: $232.23 Million
Number Employees: 1200
Square Footage: 300
Parent Co: Harrison
Type of Packaging: Bulk

27821 Pretty Products
1255 Karl Ct
Wauconda, IL 60084-1098

847-526-5505
Fax: 847-526-5271 800-726-4849
sales@purdyproducts.com
www.purdyproducts.com
Chemicals, sanitizers, cleaners and degreasers for
food service equipment
President: Robert D Husemoller
rdh@purdyproducts.com
Estimated Sales: $5-10 Million
Number Employees: 5-9

27822 Pri-Pak Inc
2000 Schenley Pl
Greendale, IN 47025-1593

812-537-7300
Fax: 812-537-7310 www.pripak.com
Wine coolers
CFO: Diane Tidwell
dtidwell@pripak.com
Plant Manager: Gary Dunn
Estimated Sales: $50 - 75 Million
Number Employees: 100-249

27823 Pride Container Corporation
4545 W Palmer St
Chicago, IL 60639

773-227-6000
Fax: 773-227-2645

Corrugated containers
President: Jeff Sharfstein
CFO: Jeff McReynolds
Chairman of the Board: Richard Sharfstein
VP Sales: Michael Weiss
Estimated Sales: $20-50 Million
Number Employees: 100-249

27824 Pride Neon Inc
3010 W 10th St
Sioux Falls, SD 57104-6204

605-336-3561
Fax: 605-336-6938 signs@prideneon.com
www.prideneon.com
Indoor and outdoor signs including neon and
back-lit; also, awnings
President: George Menke Jr
bret@prideneon.com
Secretary/Treasurer: Dick Menke
Vice President: Bob Menke
R&D: Nike Menke
Service Manager: Mitch Menke
Sales Exec: Bret Menke
Assistant Financial Manager: Dan Menke
Production Manager: Nick Menke
Estimated Sales: $1,800,000
Number Employees: 20-49

27825 Pride Polymers LLC
1111 N 20th Ave
Yakima, WA 98902-1207

509-452-3330
Fax: 509-452-8850 info@pridepolymers.com
www.pridepolymers.com
Owner: Joe O'Malley
joeo@pridepolymers.com
Estimated Sales: Less Than $500,000
Number Employees: 1-4

27826 Prima-Wawona
7108 N Fresno St
Suite 450
Fresno, CA 93720

559-787-8780
info@prima.com
prima.com
Tree fruits, including peaches, plums, nectarines and
apricots.
CEO: Eric Beringause
Director of Marketing: Lisa Corrigan
Year Founded: 1938
Estimated Sales: Over $1 Billion
Number Employees: 500-999
Number of Brands: 1
Brands:
    PRIMA-WAWONA

27827 Primary Liquidation
80 Orville Dr
Bohemia, NY 11716-2534

631-244-1410
Fax: 516-229-2741
Supplier of surplus closeout liquidation inventories
of a food and grocery nature. Over 29 years of expe-
rience
President: Paul Klein
Estimated Sales: Less Than $500,000
Number Employees: 1-4
Type of Packaging: Consumer, Food Service

27828 Prime Equipment
10201 E Buckeye Ln
Spokane Valley, WA 99206-4270

509-928-8947
Fax: 509-928-0690
Packaging machinery
Contact: Bart Triesch
btriesch@primeequipusa.com
Estimated Sales: $1-2.5 Million
Number Employees: 5-9

27829 Prime Inc.
2740 N. Mayfair Ave.
Springfield, MO 65803

417-866-0001
Fax: 417-521-6878 800-321-4552
www.primeinc.com
Refrigerated, flatbed, and tanker carrier services to
an international customer base.

President/Founder: Robert Low
  rlow@primeinc.com
Director, Finance: Dean Hoedl
General Counsel: Steve Crawford
Director, Technology: Rodney Rader
Director, Marketing: Keith McCoy
Vice President, Sales & Marketing: Steve Wutke
Director, Operations: Pat Leonard
Year Founded: 1970
Estimated Sales: $500 Million
Number Employees: 500-999

27830 Prime Label ConsultantsInc
536 7th St SE
Washington, DC 20003-2737

202-546-3333
Fax: 202-543-4337 800-766-5225
info@primelabel.com www.primelabel.com
Consulting services to processors affected by Federal food labeling regulations
President: Joe Bechtold
Owner/CEO: Elizabeth Bechtold
  liz@primelabel.com
Director, Software Development: Fred Mosher
Food Technologist: Ames Perry
Office Manager: Pat Yingling
Estimated Sales: $1-2.5 Million
Number Employees: 5-9

27831 Prime ProData
800 N Main St
North Canton, OH 44720

330-497-2578
Fax: 330-497-7206 877-497-2578
www.primepro.com
Accounting systems software with consultants specializing in computer systems software analysis
President: Susan Caghan
Contact: Sean Buck
  sbuck@primepro.com
Estimated Sales: $1 - 3 Million
Number Employees: 5-9
Brands:
  Pcas
  Prime Prodata

27832 Prime Tag & Label
1516 F Ave SE
Hickory, NC 28602

828-327-4012
Fax: 828-327-4018 887-710-7771
Manager: Monica Commisso
Estimated Sales: Below 1 Million
Number Employees: 5-9

27833 PrimeSource Equipment
PO Box 2389
Addison, TX 75001-2389

214-273-4900
Fax: 214-273-4999 800-737-8567
sales@primesourcefse.com
A wholesale food service distribution company
CEO: Charles James

27834 Primera Technology
2 Carlson Pkwy N # 375
Plymouth, MN 55447-8800

763-475-6676
Fax: 763-475-6677 800-797-2772
sales@primeralabel.com www.primera.com
Labels
President: Chris Lange
  fsouthward@southward.com
Estimated Sales: $13.3 Million
Number Employees: 10-19

27835 Primex Plastics Corp
1235 N F St
Richmond, IN 47374-2448

765-966-7774
Fax: 765-935-1083 800-222-5116
sales@primexplastics.com
www.primexplastics.com
Rolls and sheets of polystyrene
President: Michael Cramer
  mcramer@primexplastics.com
VP: John Kittner
Estimated Sales: $75 - 100 Million
Number Employees: 500-999

27836 Primlite Manufacturing Corporation
407 S Main St
Freeport, NY 11520

516-868-4411
Fax: 516-868-4609 800-327-7583
sales@primelite-mfg.com
www.primelite-mfg.com
Manufacturer and exporter of outdoor lighting fixtures, plastic globes and store fixtures including custom designed prismatic glass ceiling and wall fixtures
President: Benjamin Heit
Quality Control Manager: Joanne Heit
Estimated Sales: $3 - 5 Million
Number Employees: 10-19
Square Footage: 60000

27837 Primo Roasting Equipment
1309 S Lyon St
Santa Ana, CA 92705-4608

714-556-5259
Fax: 714-556-5690 800-675-0160
dion@primoroasting.com
www.primoroasting.com
Coffee roaster manufacturing
CEO: Dion Humpreys
Manager: Dion Humphreys
  dion@primoroasting.com
Estimated Sales: $500,000-$1 Million
Number Employees: 5-9

27838 Primo Water Corporation
200 Eagles Landing Boulevard
Lakeland, FL 333810

844-237-7466
primowater.com
Water dispensers, purified bottled water, self-service refill drinking water.
President, International: Steven Kitching
Chief Executive Officer: Thomas Harrington
Chief Financial Officer: Jay Wells
Chief Accounting Officer: Jason Ausher
Chief Legal Officer/Secretary: Marni Morgan-Poe
Chief Operating Officer: Cate Gutowski *Year Founded:* 1952
Type of Packaging: Consumer, Food Service, Private Label, Bulk
Other Locations:
  Cliffstar Manufacturing Plant
  East Freetown MA
  Cliffstar Manufacturing Plant
  Fontana CA
  Cliffstar Manufacturing Plant
  Fredonia NY
  Cliffstar Manufacturing Plant
  Greer SC
  Cliffstar Manufacturing Plant
  Joplin MO
  Cliffstar Manufacturing Plant
  N East PA
  Cliffstar Manufacturing Plant
  Walla Walla WA
  Cliffstar Manufacturing Plant
  Warrens WI
  Cott Beverage Manufacturing Plant
  Calgary, Alberta, Canada
  Cott Concentrate Manufacturing
  Columbus GA
Brands:
  AIMIA FOODS
  ALHAMBRA
  ATHENA
  BELMONT SPRINGS
  CANADIAN SPRINGS
  CRYSTAL SPRINGS
  DEEP ROCK WATER
  HINCKLEY SPRINGS
  JAVARAMA
  KENTWOOD SPRINGS
  RCCI
  S&D COFFEE & TEA
  SIERRA SPRINGS
  SPARKLETTS
  STANDARD COFFEE
  TERRAZA

27839 Primus Laboratories
2810 Industrial Parkway
Santa Maria, CA 93455-1880

805-922-0055
Fax: 805-922-2462 800-779-1156
www.primuslabs.com
Wine industry analytical services
President: Bob Stovicek

Estimated Sales: $5 - 10 Million
Number Employees: 250-499

27840 Prince Castle Inc
355 Kehoe Blvd
Carol Stream, IL 60188-1833

630-462-8801
Fax: 630-462-1460 800-722-7853
info@princecastle.com www.princecastle.com
Manufacturer and exporter of preparation and holding equipment including warming and toasting equipment, electronic cooking timers and computers, grill tools, high chairs, fry baskets and shortening filters, dispensers, drink mixerscutters and slicers
President: Ted Bethke
  ted@aviation-schools.com
Product Marketing Manager: Richard Blauvelt
VP Sales/Marketing: William Kinney
Number Employees: 100-249
Square Footage: 240000
Parent Co: Marmon Group
Type of Packaging: Food Service
Brands:
  Comfortline
  Excalibur
  Fasline
  Frequent Fryer
  Merlin
  Multi Mixer
  Portion-All
  Redi-Grill

27841 Prince Industries Inc
5635 Thompson Bridge Rd
Murrayville, GA 30564-1209

770-536-3679
Fax: 770-535-2548 800-441-3303
www.princeindustriesinc.com
Manufacturer and exporter of poultry processing equipment including deboners, grinders and meat pumps
President: Jesse Prince
  prinind@bellsouth.net
CFO: Jesse Prince
Vice President: Dottie Prince
National Sales Manager: Jesse Prince
General Manager: Kam Singh
Estimated Sales: $2.5 - 5 Million
Number Employees: 5-9
Square Footage: 24000

27842 Prince Seating Corp
1355 Atlantic Ave
Brooklyn, NY 11216-2810

718-363-2300
Fax: 718-363-9800 800-577-4623
info@PrinceSeating.com www.princeseating.com
Wood and metal chairs, tables and barstools
Owner: Abe Belsky
  abe.belsky@chairfactory.net
VP: Abe Belsky
Contract Sales: Peri Lissauer
Estimated Sales: $5 Million
Number Employees: 50-99
Square Footage: 260000

27843 Princeton Shelving
873 Center Point Road NE
Cedar Rapids, IA 52402-4664

319-369-0355
Fax: 319-369-0387
Dealer rep. and distributor of pallet racks, wire decking and containers, POP displays, carts (hand, service), racks, steel and wire shelving. Over 500 different companies
Estimated Sales: $1 - 5,000,000

27844 Prinova
285 Fullerton Ave
Carol Stream, IL 60188-1886

630-868-0300
Fax: 630-868-0310 info@prinovausa.com
www.prinovausa.com
Ascorbic acid, B vitamins and amino acids
Owner: Donald Thorp
  sales@premiumingredients.com
Number Employees: 10-19

27845 Prinova
6525 Muirfield Drive
Hanover Park, IL 60133
630-868-0300
Fax: 630-868-0310 info@prinovausa.com
www.prinovausa.com
Food ingredients and aroma chemicals.
President: Donald Thorp
CEO: Richard Thorp
CFO: Donald Cepican
VP: Daniel Thorp
Research/Development Director: Suzanne Johnson
VP Sales/Marketing: Richard Calabrese
Contact: Kim Sean
  kim.sean@prinovausa.com
Estimated Sales: $30-35 Million
Number Employees: 1,000+
Parent Co: AMC Chemicals
Other Locations:
  Premium Ingredients International
  Holladay UT
  Premium Ingredients International
  Ellisville MO
  Premium Ingredients International
  Cranford NJ
  Premium Ingredients Int'l(UK)
  London, England

27846 Print & Peel
620 12th Ave
New York, NY 10036-1004
212-226-7007
Fax: 212-226-7174 800-451-0807
Printed and nonprinted pressure sensitive paper labels, film, paper, etc
President: Linda Owen
VP/Sales: Ronald Steinberg
Contact: Steve Owen
  steveo@lvadhesive.com
Estimated Sales: $5 - 10 Million
Number Employees: 20-49

27847 Print Ons/Express Mark
505 Cuthbertson St
Monroe, NC 28110-3809
704-289-8261
Fax: 704-289-2158
Printed and embroidered shirts
Director Sales Marketing: John Schnader
Estimated Sales: $500,000-$1,000,000
Number Employees: 1-4
Brands:
  Express Mark
  Print Ons

27848 Print-O-Tape Inc
755 Tower Rd
Mundelein, IL 60060-3817
847-362-1476
Fax: 847-949-7449 800-346-6311
customerservice@printotape.com
www.printotape.com
Pressure sensitive labels and tapes
President: Carl J Walliser
CFO: Marty Justin
R&D: Roger Haase
Quality Control: Ron Quba
Marketing Manager: Eddie Walschner
Estimated Sales: $10 - 20 Million
Number Employees: 50-99

27849 Print-Tech
330 E Kilbourn Avenue
Suite 1085
Milwaukee, WI 53202-3146
608-241-5027
Fax: 608-249-7760 800-682-7746
President: Ryan Simons
R&D: Ryan Simons
Quality Control: Randy Agisv
Contact: Randy Heisz
  rheisz@bcblaw.net
Estimated Sales: $5 - 10 Million
Number Employees: 50

27850 Printape Corporation ofAmerica
174 Passaic St
Garfield, NJ 07026-1358
973-815-1880
Fax: 973-815-1882
Printed, pilfer proof, carton sealing, paper tapes
President: Jerry Bialick
Estimated Sales: $20-50 Million
Number Employees: 50-99

27851 Printcraft Marking Devices Inc
1193 Military Rd
Buffalo, NY 14217-1845
716-873-8181
Fax: 716-873-2751 pmdinc@banet.net
Engraved and rubber stamps
Owner: Lynn Wuertzer
  printcraft@verizon.net
Manager: Ruff Wuertzer
Estimated Sales: Less Than $500,000
Number Employees: 1-4

27852 Printex Packaging
555 Raymond Dr
Islandia, NY 11749-4844
631-234-4300
Fax: 631-234-4840 info@printexpackaging.com
www.printexpackaging.com
President: Barbara Colangelo
  valerie.bernard@ubs.com
R & D: Joe Heller
Estimated Sales: $20-30 Million
Number Employees: 50-99

27853 (HQ)Printpack Inc.
2800 Overlook Pkwy. NE
Atlanta, GA 30339
404-460-7000
info@printpack.com
www.printpack.com
Printed, coated, laminated and flexible film, rolls, sheets and heat sealing paper; also, candy bar and meat wrappers.
Chairman/President/CEO: Jimmy Love
Senior VP/CFO: Tripp Seitter
Year Founded: 1956
Estimated Sales: Over $1 Billion
Number Employees: 3,200
Other Locations:
  Bloomington IN
  Elgin IL
  Grand Prairie TX
  Hendersonville NC
  Jackson TN
  Marshall NC
  New Castle DE
  Newport News VA
  Prescott Valley AZ
  Rhinelander WI
  Villa Rica GA
  Williamsburg VA

27854 Printpack Inc.
2121 North Angelina Lane
Bloomington, IN 47404
812-334-5500
info@printpack.com
www.printpack.com
Polyethylene bags for bakeries
Parent Co: Printpack

27855 Printpak
14651 Dallas Pkwy
Suite 320
Dallas, TX 75254-1639
972-392-3101
Fax: 972-392-1129 www.printpakllc.com
President: Dennis Love
Estimated Sales: $1 - 3 Million
Number Employees: 1-4
Type of Packaging: Consumer

27856 Printpak
14651 Dallas Pkwy
Suite 320
Dallas, TX 75254-1639
972-392-3101
Fax: 404-691-8143 800-451-9985
www.printpak.com
President: Dennis Love
Estimated Sales: $1 - 3 Million
Number Employees: 1-4

27857 Printsafe Inc
12125 Kear Pl
Poway, CA 92064-7131
858-748-8600
Fax: 858-748-8640 info@printsafe.com
www.wireandcablemarking.com
President: Tom Hittle
CEO: Alan Anderson
  aanderson@imbee.com
Estimated Sales: $5 - 10 Million
Number Employees: 20-49

27858 Printsource Group
128 Main St
Wakefield, RI 02879-3567
401-789-9339
Fax: 401-789-1750 csr@printsource.com
www.printsourceri.com
Decals, labels, name plates and advertising signs including magnetic, vinyl and hot die cut, printing on plastic containers
President, Chief Executive Officer: Donald Shortman
Sr. Account Manager: Deb Saccoccio
Manager: Mary Lungwitz
  mary@printsource.com
Production Manager: Bruce Gibbs
Estimated Sales: Less Than $500,000
Number Employees: 5-9
Square Footage: 140000
Type of Packaging: Private Label, Bulk

27859 Priority Food Processing
635 Oakwood Rd
Lake Zurich, IL 60047
847-438-1338
Fax: 847-438-1599
Contract dry food blending and packaging
President: Andy Burke
Quality Control: Rodney Hart
Contact: Charles Trinchetilla
  charles@conagrafoods.com
Estimated Sales: $50 - 100 Million
Number Employees: 100-249

27860 Priority One America
3255 Medalist Drive
PO Box 2408
Oshkosh, WI 54903
Canada
920-235-5562
Fax: 866-580-2312
www.priorityonepackaging.com
Manufacturer, exporter and importer of palletizers, conveyors, depalletizers and packaging machinery
President: Colin Cunningham
Controller: Carolyn Schnefer
Estimated Sales: $10 - 20 Million
Number Employees: 100
Square Footage: 30000
Parent Co: Priority One Packaging

27861 Priority One Packaging
815 Bridge Street
Waterloo, ON N2V 2M7
Canada
519-746-6950
Fax: 519-746-3578 800-387-9102
products@priorityonepackaging.com
www.priorityonepackaging.com
Priority One is a manufacturer of palletizing and depalletizing equipment. Included in the product range are both high and low level palletizers, small footprint palletizers, multi-line (shuttle and rotary) palletizers, pailpalletizers, bulk palletizers, high and low depalletizers, table-top and mat-top conveyor systems, pressured and pressureless single filers, bottle and case elevators/lowerators, rinsers, magnetic elevators, cable track, full load stackers, labellersand line integration
Owner/CEO: Colin Cunningham
President: Brian Webster
VP: Drew Cameron
Estimated Sales: $30 Million
Number Employees: 120
Square Footage: 100000
Brands:
  Langguth
  Pro-Pal

27862 Priority One Packaging Machinery
124 N Columbus Street
Randolph, WI 53956
Canada
800-882-4995
Fax: 920-326-6551 800-387-9102
inquiry@arrowheadsystems.com
www.priorityonepackaging.com

27863 Priority Plastics Inc
704 Pinder Ave
Grinnell, IA 50112-9700
641-236-4798
Fax: 641-236-3478 800-798-3512
www.showme.com

Custom silk screened printed plastic canisters and plastic bottles; exporter of plastic bottles
President: Lawrence Den Hartog
Plant Manager: Gary Vowels
Estimated Sales: $20 - 50 Million
Number Employees: 20-49
Square Footage: 28000
Brands:
    Sho-Me

27864 Prism
3180 Presidential Drive
Suite C
Atlanta, GA 30340-3900
770-455-4544
Fax: 770-454-7876
Business solutions

27865 Prism
8300 NW 53rd St
Suite 103
Miami, FL 33166-7710
305-599-9033
Fax: 305-594-9280
Sanitation supplies and services
Manager: Manny Gonzalez
Estimated Sales: Less than $500,000
Number Employees: 1-4

27866 Prism Visual Software Inc
1 Sagamore Hill Dr
Port Washington, NY 11050-2135
516-944-5920
Fax: 516-944-5243 info@prismvs.com
www.prismvs.com
Routing/scheduling software
Owner: David Cullen
CEO: Marc J. Eisenberg
CFO: Robert G. CostantiniVP: John J Stolte, Jr
VP Marketing: Lynn Keating
Vice President of Sales: Andrew Kuneth
Estimated Sales: $3 Million
Number Employees: 10-19

27867 Prism Visual Software Inc
1 Sagamore Hill Dr
Port Washington, NY 11050-2135
516-944-5920
Fax: 516-944-5243 sales@prismvs.com
www.prismvs.com
Readquest, Prisms route management/palm pilot solution for food and beverage companies
Owner: David Cullen
CEO: Lorraine Keating
    lorrainek@prismvs.com
CEO: Lorraine Keating
Marketing: Lynn Keating
Sales Director: Michael Del Colle
Operations: Chris Heinrich
Estimated Sales: $1.5 Million
Number Employees: 10-19

27868 Pro Active Sltns Chaska
12502 Xenwood Ave
Savage, MN 55378-1225
952-890-1820
Fax: 952-890-3844 800-788-7449
www.proactivesolutionsusa.com
Industrial cleaners
President: Sean Teske
CEO: Paul Moe
General Manager: Monica Tucker
Manager: Wade Hustad
    wade.hustad@chaskachem.com
Director Production Deptartment: Jeff Gray
Plant Manager: Jeff Gray
Estimated Sales: Below $5 Million
Number Employees: 10-19

27869 Pro Active Solutions USA LLC
301 Bridge St
Green Bay, WI 54303-1511
920-437-8658
Fax: 920-437-4006 800-411-6734
www.prochemicals.com
Rapid method for microbial contamination detection
Owner: Doug Storhoff
    doug@prochemicals.com
Estimated Sales: $2.5-5 Million
Number Employees: 20-49

27870 Pro Bake Inc
2057 E Aurora Rd # P
Suite Pq
Twinsburg, OH 44087-1938
330-425-4427
Fax: 330-425-9742 800-837-4427
probake@probake.com www.probake.com
Bakery equipment reconditioning
President: Maureen Jarvis
    maureenj@probake.com
Sales Promotion Manager: Jeff Salenger
Estimated Sales: $5-10 Million
Number Employees: 10-19

27871 Pro Controls Inc
1312 Gordon Rd # 1
Yakima, WA 98901-1725
509-457-3386
Fax: 509-457-3491 800-488-3386
Process control systems
Owner: Paula O'Brien
    brien@procontrolsinc.com
Estimated Sales: $1-2,500,000
Number Employees: 10-19

27872 Pro Line Co
10 Avco Rd # 1
Haverhill, MA 01835-6997
978-521-2600
Fax: 978-374-4885 bench@1proline.com
www.1proline.com
Manufacturer and exporter of ergonomic workstations for production and lab areas
Owner: Derek Coughlin
President, Chief Executive Officer: Robert W Hatfield
    bench@1proline.com
Sr. VP: Bob Simmons
Estimated Sales: $3 - 5 Million
Number Employees: 20-49
Type of Packaging: Bulk

27873 Pro Media Inc
W127n8690 Westbrook Xing
Menomonee Falls, WI 53051-3342
262-532-2600
Fax: 262-532-2627 800-328-0439
sales@promediaus.com
Specializing in manufacturer, distributor, and operator frequency programs
President: Tom Collier
    info@promediaus.com
Executive VP: Rick Stolowski
VP Incentive Sales: Jim Egan
Estimated Sales: $10-20,000,000
Number Employees: 10-19
Square Footage: 18000

27874 Pro Pack Systems Inc
1354 Dayton St # A
Salinas, CA 93901-4426
831-771-1300
Fax: 831-771-1303
Adhesive systems, wax systems for wineries, ink jet coding, cave/tray packing
Owner: Mike Armento
    mikea@propacksystems.com
Estimated Sales: Below $5 Million
Number Employees: 5-9
Square Footage: 8

27875 Pro Refrigeration
326 8th St SW
Auburn, WA 98001-5914
253-735-1189
Fax: 253-735-2631 www.prochiller.com
Refrigeration equipment
VP/CEO/General Manager: Jim Vander Giessen
    info@prorefrigeration.com
Chief Financial Officer: Gary Duim
Operations Manager: Matthew Perala
Inventory Control: Kelly Phelps
Purchasing Manager/Technical Support: Rande Routledge
Number Employees: 20-49

27876 Pro Scientific
PO Box 448
Monroe, CT 06468-0448
203-452-9431
Fax: 780-452-9753 prosci@aol.com
www.proscientific.com/chef.html
Handheld and bench top mechanical homogenizers, laboratory and custom homogenizers

Estimated Sales: $1-2.5 Million
Number Employees: 10-19

27877 Pro Scientific Inc
99 Willenbrock Rd
Oxford, CT 06478-1032
203-267-4600
Fax: 203-267-4606 800-584-3776
sales@proscientific.com www.proscientific.com
Manufactures laboratory homogenizers from handheld to larger benchtop programmable models. North American distributor of Andreas Hettich Centifuges which range in size from micro to floor-model. Also distribute a full line ofincubators, water and oil baths and ovens
Owner: Donald Peronace
    don@madisonavecreative.com
Sales/Marketing: Holly Yacko
Estimated Sales: $5 - 10 Million
Number Employees: 10-19
Number of Brands: 3
Number of Products: 40
Brands:
    Hettich
    Memmert
    Pro
    Riebosam

27878 Pro Sheet Cutter
705 S Electric Avenue
Alhambra, CA 91803-1639
626-576-0785
Fax: 626-576-8895
Extrusion fabrication systems, sawing systems, low-level radioactive and mixed waste containers, transloader, grinders, computer controlled slit mask fabricator and electronically integrated control system bandsaw

27879 Pro-Ad-Co Inc
655 N Tillamook St
Portland, OR 97227-1886
503-288-5885
Fax: 503-281-8725 800-287-5885
www.proadco.com
Labels, screen printed decals, signs, point of purchase displays, bumper stickers and metal and engraved name plates
Owner: Cliff Overholt
    sales@proadco.com
Estimated Sales: $5-10 Million
Number Employees: 10-19

27880 Pro-Com Security Systems
2975 W Executive Parkway
STE 156
Lehi, UT 84043
801-770-7233
Fax: 801-770-7233 877-776-2669
procomsecurity.com
Long range radio security systems
Parent Co: Sonitrol Company

27881 Pro-Dex Inc
2361 Mcgaw Ave
Irvine, CA 92614-5831
949-769-3200
Fax: 949-769-3281 800-562-6204
sales@omsmotion.com www.pro-dex.com
Motion controllers, motors, drives
VP: Phil Brown
Chief Executive Officer, President: Michael Berthelot
Vice President of Regulatory Affairs: Joseph Rotino
Marketing: Julie Kealy
Vice President of Sales and Marketing: Frank Noone
Estimated Sales: $5-10 Million
Number Employees: 50-99

27882 Pro-Flo Products
30 Commerce Rd
PO Box 390
Cedar Grove, NJ 7009
973-239-2400
Fax: 973-239-5817 800-325-1057
Manufacturer, importer and exporter of water treatment and filtration equipment, drinking water coolers, chillers and dispensers
President: Louis Reyes
Quality Control: Nicaolas Iannaccio
Estimated Sales: $657,000
Number Employees: 5-9
Square Footage: 8400

27883 Pro-Gram Plastics Inc
700 Pro Gram Pkwy
Geneva, OH 44041-1168
440-466-8080
Fax: 440-466-8099 sales@programplastics.com
www.programplastics.com
Blow-molded plastic bottles
President: Walter Sargi
sw@programplastics.com
Sales Exec: Robert Sweitzer
Production Manager: Robert Sweitzer
Estimated Sales: $5-10 Million
Number Employees: 20-49
Square Footage: 128000

27884 Pro-Tex-All Co
210 S Morton Ave
Evansville, IN 47713-2448
812-424-8268
Fax: 812-424-8330 800-755-5458
drm@protexall.com www.protexall.com
Facility maintenance chemicals, supplies and equipment for industry and commerce
Owner: Jim Kuhn
jkuhn@protexall.com
President: James Kuhn
Vice President: Mike Kuhn
Customer Service: Carla Richards
Estimated Sales: $5 - 10 Million
Number Employees: 10-19
Square Footage: 59000

27885 Pro-Western Plastics
30 Riel Drive
PO Box 261
St Albert, AB T8N3Z7
Canada
780-459-4491
Fax: 800-428-4756 800-661-9835
wayne.hunt@pro-westernplastics.com
www.pro-westernplastics.com
President: Wall Lacroix
Quality Control: Trevor Hansen
CFO: Wall Lacroix
R&D: Wall Lacroix
Number Employees: 275

27886 ProAmpac
12025 Tricon Rd.
Cincinnati, OH 45246
513-671-1777
800-543-7030
www.proampac.com
Polythylene and paper bags, and specialty films.
Custom plastic and paper shopping bags,
polymailers and specialty films. (Blown film with
six monolayer lines, two 3-layer lines and on 7-layer
line.)
CEO: Gregory Tucker
Year Founded: 1966
Estimated Sales: $121.7 Million
Number Employees: 1,100
Square Footage: 815000
Parent Co: PPC Partners
Type of Packaging: Consumer, Food Service, Private Label

27887 (HQ)ProBar Systems Inc.
92 Caplan Ave.
Suite 607
Barrie, ON L4N 0Z7
Canada
800-521-7294
info@probarsystems.com
www.probarsystems.com
Manufacturer and exporter of beverage dispensing
machines including computer controlled bar pouring
and inventory systems, juice dispensers and soft
drink machines
President: Charles M Stimac Jr
CFO: John Hornbeck
Research & Development: Mike Smith
Quality Control: Greg Gemmell
Marketing: Chris Burden
Sales Director: Kris Croft
Operations Manager: Carlos DeMelo
Production/Plant Manager/Purchasing: Jimmy
Neuman
Estimated Sales: $300,000-500,000
Number Employees: 1-4
Number of Brands: 3
Number of Products: 3
Type of Packaging: Private Label

Brands:
Ultra Bar

27888 ProMach
50 East Rivercenter Blvd
Suite 1800
Covington, KY 41011
513-831-8778
Fax: 513-831-5795 866-776-6224
www.promachbuilt.com
Packaging products and machinery
President & CEO: Mark W. Anderson

27889 ProRestore Products
1016 Greentree Road
Suite 115
Pittsburgh, PA 15220
412-264-8340
Fax: 412-920-2905 800-332-6037
sales@prorestoreproducts.com
www.prorestoreproducts.com
Manufacturer and exporter of deodorants, cleaners
and disinfectants
President: Cliff Zlotnik
Contact: Mike Kerner
mikek@prorestoreproducts.com
Estimated Sales: $5 - 10 Million
Number Employees: 20-49
Parent Co: RPM International Inc.
Type of Packaging: Food Service, Private Label,
Bulk
Brands:
Mediclean
Microban
Unikleen
Unsmoke

27890 ProTeam
12438 W Bridger Street
Boise, ID 83713
208-377-9555
Fax: 208-377-8444 800-541-1456
customerservice.proteam@emerson.com
www.pro-team.com
ProTeam became a global phenomenon in the commercial cleaning world after introducing a
game-challenging design innovation, the lightweight
backpack vacuum. Today ProTeam offers a full
range of innovative vacuums, including the
newProGuard wet/dry line.
CEO: Matt Wood
Contact: Richard Coombs
r.coombs@pro-team.com
Estimated Sales: $50-100 Million
Number Employees: 50
Square Footage: 5000

27891 ProVisions Software
36 Thurber Boulevard
Smithfield, RI 02917
401-232-2600
Fax: 401-232-7778 800-422-4782
info@caisoft.com www.caisoft.com/provisions
Software

27892 Proact Inc
3195 Neil Armstrong Blvd
Eagan, MN 55121-2256
651-289-3158
Fax: 651-686-0312 877-245-0405
info@proactinc.org www.proactpackaging.com
Sub-contract packager of food products
President,CEO: Steven Ditschler
sditschler@proactinc.org
Controller: Pat McGuire
Director of Production: David Cavalier
Estimated Sales: $$2.5-5 Million
Number Employees: 100-249
Square Footage: 120000

27893 Probat Inc
601 Corporate Woods Pkwy
Vernon Hills, IL 60061-3111
847-415-5253
Fax: 847-793-8611 877-683-8113
info@probatburns.com www.probatburns.com
Bin silo systems, bin vibrators, blending and mixing
equipment, cleaners, afterburners, augers, automatic
controls, bag emptier, bulk silo servicees, magnetic
separation, moisture analyzers, quality control instruments and cuppingequipment.
President: Karl Schmidt
Vice President of Sales & Marketing: Launtia
Taylor

Estimated Sales: $5-10 Million
Number Employees: 20-49

27894 Probiotic Solutions
1331 W Houston Ave
Gilbert, AZ 85233-1816
480-961-1220
Fax: 480-961-3061 800-961-1220
info@probiotic.com www.probiotic.com
President: Lyndon Smith
Sales Director: Diana Burtrum
probiotic@probiotic.com
Estimated Sales: $1 - 5 Million
Number Employees: 10-19
Parent Co: Bio Huma Netics, Inc.

27895 Procedyne Corp
11 Industrial Dr
New Brunswick, NJ 08901-3657
732-249-8347
Fax: 732-249-7220 mail@procedyne.com
www.procedyne.com
Manufacturer and exporter of fluidized bed systems
including dryers, granulators and thermal processors. Engineering and research and development facility with laboratory and pilor plant. Offer process
design, process development andscale-up testing
President: H Kenneth Staffin
CEO: Kenneth Staffin
kstaffin@procedynecorp.com
VP Process Technology: Thomas Parr
VP Products: Bob Archibald
Chairman of the Board: Dr H Kenneth Staffin
Estimated Sales: $10 - 20 Million
Number Employees: 50-99
Square Footage: 120000
Type of Packaging: Bulk
Brands:
Mikrodyne

27896 Procell Polymers
PO Box 33
Baton Rouge, LA 70821-0033
225-978-8069
Fax: 866-860-1269
Cellulose gum, guar gum, xanthan gum and other
specialty products.
Manager: David Hatcher
Manager: Harry Steeghs
Type of Packaging: Bulk

27897 Procesamiento De Carne
122 S Wesley Ave
Mt Morris, IL 61054-1451
815-734-4171
Fax: 815-734-4201 www.wattnet.com
Equipment for meat processors
President: Gregory A Watt
Estimated Sales: $15 Million
Number Employees: 50-99

27898 Process Automation
P.O. Box 457
Hurst, TX 76053
817-488-9546
Fax: 817-283-1813 800-460-9546
www.processauto.net
Process controls and stainless steel manufacturing
for food and beverage industries
President: Scott Carlson
CFO: Steppnie Duelm
Estimated Sales: $30-50 Million
Number Employees: 20-49

27899 Process Displays
5800 S Moorland Rd
New Berlin, WI 53151
262-782-3600
Fax: 262-782-3857 800-533-1764
Manufacturer and exporter of point of purchase displays, vacuum form trays, case dividers, rail strips,
counter mats, menu board and deli signs and decals
President: Bob Zanotti
Vice President: Brendon Rowan
Contact: Lori Gebhard
gebhard@pdisplays.com
Estimated Sales: $2.5 - 5 Million
Number Employees: 50-99
Square Footage: 200000
Parent Co: Process Retail Group

27900 Process Engineering & Fabrication

20 Hedge Ln
Afton, VA 22920

540-456-8163
Fax: 540-456-8171 800-852-7975
www.processengineeringinc.com
Manufacturer and exporter of custom industrial refrigeration systems, spiral conveyor systems and stainless steel food processing equipment; also, installation services available
President: Bart Shellabarger
CEO: Bob Amacker
CFO: Bruce Neidlinger
Chief Freezing Officer: Charley Marckel
Sales: Jimmy Sokora
Contact: Bruce Neidlinger
  bruce@processengineeringinc.com
Estimated Sales: Below $5 Million
Number Employees: 10
Square Footage: 40000

27901 Process Heating Co

2732 3rd Ave S
PO Box 84585
Seattle, WA 98134-1983

206-682-3414
Fax: 206-682-1582 866-682-1582
inquire@processheating.com
www.processheating.com
Manufacturer and exporter of industrial immersion heaters, circulation heating systems and fuel oil preheaters
President: Rick Jay
  rick@processheating.com
CEO: Ron Jay
Marketing: Mike Peringer
Sales/Industrial: Eric Olden
Estimated Sales: $3 - 5 Million
Number Employees: 10-19
Number of Products: 15
Square Footage: 15000
Brands:
  Lo-Density

27902 Process Heating Corp

547 Hartford Tpke
Shrewsbury, MA 01545-4002

508-842-5200
Fax: 508-842-9418 proheat@gis.net
www.proheatcorp.com
Manufacturer and exporter of ovens, furnaces, air pollution control incinerators and process heating equipment; also, rebuilding and remodeling available
President: Brad Green
  proheat@gis.net
Estimated Sales: Below $5,000,000
Number Employees: 5-9

27903 Process Plus

5320 S 39th Street
Phoenix, AZ 85040

602-470-8051
Fax: 602-470-1654
President: Gerald Schneerer

27904 Process Sensors Corp

113 Cedar St # S1
Milford, MA 01757-1192

508-473-9901
Fax: 508-473-0715 www.processsensors.com
Manufacturer, importer and exporter of moisture measuring instruments
President: Robert Winson
  robertwinson@outback.com
Estimated Sales: $5 - 10,000,000
Number Employees: 20-49

27905 Process Solutions

6701 Garden Rd # 1
Riviera Beach, FL 33404-5900

561-840-0050
Fax: 561-840-0070 sales@processsolutions.net
www.processsolutions.net
Manufacturer and exporter of drum lifters and inverters, stainless steel drums, bins, tanks, control panels and systems, etc.; importer of stainless steel bins and butterfly valves
President: Howard Rosenkranz
Vice President: H Rosenkranz
Estimated Sales: $5-10 Million
Number Employees: 20-49

Brands:
  Ergoscoop
  Omegalift
  Pharmaseal

27906 Process Systems

102 Covington Drive
Barrington, IL 60010-6611

847-842-8618
Fax: 847-842-8619 IlliniPick@aol.com
Sanitary process equipment including modelsam steam jacketed and vacuum/pressure kettles, high and low shear mixers
Estimated Sales: $3-5 Million
Number Employees: 20-50
Square Footage: 30000
Brands:
  Model Sam

27907 Processors Co-Op

1110 Powers Pl
Alpharetta, GA 30009-8389

770-664-1516
Fax: 770-636-3006
Seafood, meats, poultry
President, CEO: Alan Brown
  alanjr@cutyourfoodcost.com
Director of Marketing: Terrie Bradley
Operations Manager: Robert Bragg
Director of Purchasing: Bill Larsen
Estimated Sales: $10 - 20 Million
Number Employees: 10-19

27908 Prodo-Pak Corp

77 Commerce St
Garfield, NJ 07026-1811

973-777-7770
Fax: 973-772-0471
Manufacturer, importer and exporter of form/fill/seal packaging machines for pouches and tube fillers; also, conveyor systems and labeling equipment
President: John Mueller
  sales@prodo-pak.com
Research & Development: Rudy Degenars
Operations/Plant/Purchasing Manager: Ralph Isler
Estimated Sales: $5 - 10 Million
Number Employees: 20-49
Number of Brands: 1
Number of Products: 10
Square Footage: 20000

27909 Product Dynamics

10608 163rd Pl
Orland Park, IL 60467-8858

708-364-7060
Fax: 708-349-0488
www.productdynamicsdivision.com
Product Dynamics offers Product design and formulation, consumer and product research, qualitative insight and analytical sensory testing. They collabrate with your marketing business planning and research and development teams toaddress your strategic and tatical product issues.
President: Lawrence Platt
CEO: Jeff Widdowson
  j.widdowson@rqa-inc.com
Executive Vice President: Mary Ann Platt
Vice President/General Manager: Judy Lindsey
Estimated Sales: $1 - 3 Million
Number Employees: 10-19
Parent Co: RQA, Inc

27910 Product Saver

12838 Stainless Drive
Holland, MI 49424

616-399-2220
Fax: 616-399-7365 jswiatlo@nbe-inc.com
www.productsaver.com
Bag openers, fillers and closers, reclaiming machinery and recovery systems
President: Ed Swiatlo
General Manager: Jess Swiatlo
Estimated Sales: $1 - 5 Million
Number Employees: 10-19

27911 Product Solutions

N Street
220
Wilkes Barre, PA 18701-1706

570-825-0600
Fax: 570-825-0600 888-776-3765
prodsol@aol.com

Consultant providing design and engineering of food service equipment; also, aesthetic and engineering improvements to existing equipment available
President: Robert Cohn
Sales Director: Sandee Cohn
Estimated Sales: $1-2.5 Million
Number Employees: 1-4
Square Footage: 10000

27912 Production Equipment Co

401 Liberty St
Meriden, CT 06450-4500

203-235-5795
Fax: 203-237-5391 800-758-5697
www.productionequipmentcompany.com
Manufacturer and exporter of overhead cranes and hoists; also, steel fabricators
Owner: Bud Davis
VP Sales/Marketing: Rosewell Davis
  bdavis@productionequipment.com
Estimated Sales: $5-10 Million
Number Employees: 20-49

27913 Production Packaging & Processing Equipment Company

1713 East Victory Drive
Savannah, GA 31404

912-856-4281
Fax: 912-354-4615 www.kettles.com
Manufacturer, exporter and wholesaler/distributor of new and rebuilt packaging and processing equipment including mixers, fillers, cap tighteners, labeling, cappers, kettles and tanks
President: Louis R Klein
CEO: Jeff Klein
Estimated Sales: $2.5-5 Million
Number Employees: 5-9
Square Footage: 100000
Brands:
  P3

27914 Production Systems

850 Mountain Industrial Dr NW
Marietta, GA 30060

770-424-9784
Fax: 770-424-8392 800-235-9734
Manufacturer and exporter of package and case conveyors and packaging and palletizing systems; also, integrated control systems for production and processing plants
President: Michael Anderson
Manager Marketing Series: Sharon Phillips
Engineer Manager: Wayne Marlow
Estimated Sales: $5-10 Million
Number Employees: 20-49
Square Footage: 100000
Brands:
  Package To Pallet

27915 Production Techniques Limited

18 Echelon Place, East Tamaki
PO Box 58-874 Greenmount
Auckland, NZ 2013
New Zealand

649-274-3514
Fax: 649-274-3515 sales@ptl.co.nz
www.ptl.co.nz
Provides manufacturing and processing equipment for the chocolate, candy, confectionery and bakery industries. Specialized plant manufacturing covers a wide range of plant applications including standard pieces of equipment such asmelters, depositors, enrobers, moulding plants, cooling tunnels, temperers and decorators.
Managing Director: Jim Halliday
Technical Director: Mike Nevines
Director of Sales and Marketing: Nick Halliday

27916 Productos Familia

1511 Calle Loiza
Santurce, PR 00911-1846

787-268-5929
Fax: 787-268-7717 www.nosotrasonline.com
Supplier of soft paper tissues; wholesaler/distributor, importer and exporter of toilet paper, paper towels and napkins; serving the food service market
President: Fabio Posada
VP: Carlos Upegui
Number Employees: 7
Square Footage: 12000
Parent Co: Productos Familia SA
Type of Packaging: Food Service

27917 Products A Curtron Div
5350 Campbells Run Rd
Pittsburgh, PA 15205-9738

412-787-9750
Fax: 412-787-3665 800-888-9750
info@tmi-pvc.com www.curtronproducts.com
Manufacturer and exporter of leading food safety products such as strip doors, air doors, rack covers, swinging doors, hood enclosures, display cooler curtains, milk cooler curtains and eutectic packs
Manager: Joseph Klaynjans
Contact: Steve Battaglia
stevebattaglia@curtronproducts.com
Estimated Sales: Less Than $500,000
Number Employees: 1-4
Square Footage: 100000
Parent Co: TMI
Brands:
Save-T

27918 Profamo Inc
7506 Albert Tillinghast Dr
Sarasota, FL 34240

941-379-8155
Fax: 941-379-8699 info@profamo.com
www.profamo.com
Provides sales and services for manufacturers of quality assurance and process control equipment for the brewing and beverage industries.
President: Klaus Nimptsch
Technical Information Specialist: Chris Nimptsch
Contact: Chris Nimptsch
chris@profamo.com
Estimated Sales: $300,000-500,000
Number Employees: 1-4

27919 Professional Bakeware Company
11739 N Highway 75
Willis, TX 77378-5740

866-710-1936
Fax: 936-890-8760 800-440-9547
Bakeware, cookware, servingware, displayware and indestructable alumaware
President: David Beauregard
Vice President: Jennifer Beauregard
Marketing/Design: Judy Beck
Public Relations: Stephanie Samudio
Plant Manager: Sterling Samudio
Estimated Sales: $10 - 20,000,000
Number Employees: 20-49
Number of Brands: 5
Number of Products: 500
Square Footage: 15000
Type of Packaging: Food Service, Bulk

27920 Professional Engineering Assoc
8007 Vine Crest Ave # 5
Suite 5
Louisville, KY 40222-8661

502-429-0432
Fax: 502-429-0552
Automated parts feeding systems, feeders, conveyors, screens and process system dryers/coolers
President: Virgil Plummer
Sales Manager: Neal Plummer
Estimated Sales: $2.5-5 Million
Number Employees: 5-9

27921 Professional Image
12437 E 60th St
Tulsa, OK 74146-6906

918-461-0609
Fax: 918-615-1836 800-722-8550
sales@calvertco.com
www.professionalimagepackaging.com
Printing and packaging
President/Owner: Cynthia Calvert-Copeland
Marketing: Jennifer Giebel
Estimated Sales: $8 Million
Number Employees: 20-49

27922 Professional Marketing Group
912 Rainier Avenue S
Seattle, WA 98144-2840

206-322-7303
Fax: 206-322-4351 800-227-3769
www.vacuumpackers.com
Importer, exporter and wholesaler/distributor of commercial grade flush and nonflush vacuum packing machinery
Owner: Thom Dolder
Estimated Sales: $2.5-5 Million
Number Employees: 5-9

27923 Proffitt Manufacturing Company
404 Mitchell Street
Dalton, GA 30721-2705

706-278-7105
Fax: 706-225-4419 800-241-4682
Manufacturer and exporter of dust control mats
CEO: John R Proffitt Jr
VP: W Masters
Manager: Fred Lester
Estimated Sales: $3 - 5 Million
Number Employees: 50
Square Footage: 132000
Brands:
Endurance
Master Turf
New Age
Rib Tred
Ruff N Tuff

27924 Profire Stainless Steel Barbecue
9621 S Dixie Hwy
Miami, FL 33156

305-665-5313
Fax: 305-666-3315 info@profirebbq.com
Outdoor barbecues, built-in-grills, portable grills and other accessories
President and CFO: David Zisman
Contact: Alex Alonzo
lester.perdomo@profirebbq.com
Estimated Sales: $10 - 20 Million
Number Employees: 10

27925 Progress Lighting
101 Corporate Dr # L
Spartanburg, SC 29303-5043

864-599-6000
Manufacturer and exporter of commercial, interior and exterior lighting
Estimated Sales: $77 Million
Number Employees: 5-9
Square Footage: 35000
Parent Co: Hubbell Incorporated
Type of Packaging: Bulk

27926 Progressive Flexpak
1138 Pond Road
Glencoe, MO 63038-1322

800-565-3407
Bottle label, snack, candy, coffee printing films, process, flexo, roto and bag making

27927 Progressive Packaging Inc
14700 28th Ave N # 35
Suite 35
Minneapolis, MN 55447-4876

763-541-1440
Fax: 763-541-1510 800-844-7889
info@progressivepackaging.com
www.progressivepackaging.com
Packaging materials and equipment
President: John Mork
jmork@progressivepackaging.com
VP: C J Mork
Estimated Sales: $1.4 Million
Number Employees: 10-19
Square Footage: 12000

27928 Progressive Plastics
14801 Emery Ave
Cleveland, OH 44135

216-252-5595
Fax: 216-252-6327 800-252-0053
marketing@progressive-plastics.com
www.progressive-plastics.com
Manufactures and design plastic containers for the food and beverage industries. PET, HDPE, PP, PVC, FDA, CGMP, 150 9001 compliant
President & CEO: David Spence
Quality Control: Mary Anne Golba
Contact: Robert Bell
robert@progressive-plastics.com
Operations Manager: Jason Castro
Purchasing Manager: Glen Maringer
Estimated Sales: $20 - 50 Million
Number Employees: 250-499
Square Footage: 300000
Type of Packaging: Bulk

27929 Progressive Software
6836 Morrison Blvd Ste 104
Charlotte, NC 28211

704-295-7000
Fax: 704-849-6401 info@xpient.com
Point of sale and back office software

Marketing Manager: Ryan Willis
VP Global Sales/Marketing: Karen Holick
Contact: Jonathan Kaufman
jonathan.kaufman@xpient.com
Estimated Sales: $1 - 3,000,000
Number Employees: 50-99
Parent Co: Tridex Corporation
Brands:
Iris

27930 Progressive Technology International
3826a Branch River Road
Manitowoc, WI 54220-9479

920-683-2000
Fax: 920-683-9276 888-683-2003
Food processing equipment manufacturers
President: Dale Gehrig
Vice President: Mark Kugsh
Sales Director: Julio Rivera
Estimated Sales: $1-2.5 Million
Number Employees: 4

27931 (HQ)Progressive Tractor &Implement Co.
4947 Bridge Street Hwy
PO Box 2869
Parks, LA 70582

337-845-5080
Fax: 337-845-5090 www.ptieq.com
Sugar cane loaders and harvesters
President: V Kenneth Broussard
Purchasing Manager: Trisha Brasseaux
Estimated Sales: $1 - 3 Million
Number Employees: 5-9
Square Footage: 56000
Brands:
Broussard

27932 Proheatco Manufacturing
3427 Pomona Boulevard
Suite D
Pomona, CA 91768-3260

909-598-7445
Fax: 909-598-3514 800-423-4195
Manufacturer and exporter of ovens, heaters and steam heated systems; exporter of heaters
President: Ralph J Schaefer
Estimated Sales: $1-2.5 Million
Number Employees: 10-19
Square Footage: 24000

27933 Prolamina
975 Broadway St
Wrightstown, WI 54180-1067

920-996-1900
Fax: 920-996-1905 800-765-9283
tbauer@coating-excellence.com
www.coatingexcellence.com
CEO: Rita Cox
rcox@coating-excellence.com
Estimated Sales: $50 - 75 Million
Number Employees: 500-999

27934 Prolon
305 Industrial Ave
Port Gibson, MS 39150-2868

601-437-0061
Fax: 601-437-3068 888-480-9828
www.prolon.biz
Melamine dinnerware, tote boxes, food storage containers, school trays, etc
VP: Steve Gluck
Sales/Marketing: Sylvia Saxon
Estimated Sales: $20-50 Million
Number Employees: 50-99
Square Footage: 116000
Parent Co: Perstorp
Brands:
Prolon Products

27935 Proluxe
PO Box 869
Paramount, CA 90723-0869

562-531-0305
Fax: 562-869-7715 800-594-5528
www.proluxe.com
Manufacturer and exporter of pizza and tortilla presses, dough and vending carts, pizza slicing guides, clam shell and tortilla warming grills, pan racks, conveyor and tray ovens and sauce rings; also, custom stainless steelfabrication available

President: Eugene Raio
VP/General Manager: Daniel Raio
Director of Marketing: Michael Cole
Vice President of Sales: Mike Cervantes
Number Employees: 50
Square Footage: 180000
Brands:
  Doughcart
  Doughpro
  Hotslot
  Personnal
  Pizzacart

27936 Promac
PO Box 9818
Fresno, CA 93794-0818
559-271-9222
Fax: 559-271-9312 888-776-6220
Wine, food and beverage industry process machinery
Estimated Sales: $20-50 Million
Number Employees: 20-49

27937 Promarks
1915 E Acacia St
Ontario, CA 91761-7921
909-923-3888
Fax: 909-923-3588 www.promarksvac.com
Vacuum sealing and vacuum packaging machines.
Also manufacture dicer, stuffer, tumbling and brine
injector machines.
Owner: Karen Chiu
  karen@promarksvac.com
Number Employees: 10-19

27938 Promega
2800 Woods Hollow Rd
Madison, WI 53711
608-274-4330
Fax: 608-277-2516 800-356-9526
www.promega.com
Manufacturer of a kit for testing genetically modi-
fied organisms in food
Chairman & CEO: Dr. William Linton
Estimated Sales: $300 Million
Number Employees: 1200

27939 Promens
100 Industrial Drive
PO Box 2087
St. John, NB E2L 3T5
Canada
506-633-0101
Fax: 506-658-0227 800-295-3725
Trays, cups, jars and plastic packaging for the food
and beverage industry. Also manufacture bins, bin
liners, ingredient bins and dump tubs.

27940 Prominent Fluid Controls Inc
136 Industry Dr
R.I.D.C. Park West
Pittsburgh, PA 15275-1014
412-787-2484
Fax: 412-787-0704 sales@prominent.us
www.prominent.us
Manufacturer disinfection equipment, chlorine diox-
ide and ozone generators
General Manager: Mike Weber
Finance Director: Fran Perfett
VP: Garth Debruyn
Marketing Director: Noel Twyman
National Sales Manager: Mike St Germain
Manager: Mark Botticello
  markb@prominent.us
Operations Director: Jim DiNardo
Estimated Sales: $34 Million
Number Employees: 100-249
Number of Products: 25
Square Footage: 32500

27941 Prominent Fluid Controls Inc
136 Industry Dr
Pittsburgh, PA 15275-1014
412-787-2484
Fax: 412-787-0704 www.prominent.us
Manufacture chemical feed equipment, metering
pumps, process controllers, sensors, desinfection
equipment

President: Victor Dulger
President, Chief Executive Officer: Andreas Dulger
Executive Vice President of Manufacturin: Rainer
Dulger
CFO: Fran Persett
Director of Marketing: Noel Twyman
Director of Sales and Marketing: Mike St
Manager: Mark Botticello
  markb@prominent.us
Director of Operations: Jim DiNardo
Estimated Sales: $10 Million
Number Employees: 100-249
Number of Products: 75
Parent Co: ProMinent DosierTechnick GmbH

27942 Promo Edge
5029 Industrial Road
Wall Township, NJ 07727-3651
732-938-4242
Fax: 732-938-3301
Pressure sensitive labels
Customer Relations: Joanne Switzer
Plant Manager: Ray Mass

27943 Promotion in Motion Companies
PO Box 558
Closter, NJ 07624-0558
201-784-5800
800-369-7391
mail@promotioninmotion.com
www.promotioninmotion.com
Brand name confections, fruit snacks and other fine
foods
President/CEO: Michael Rosenberg
  mrosenberg@promotioninmotion.com
Executive Director: Frank McSorley
COO: Basant Dwivedi
Number Employees: 250-499
Type of Packaging: Private Label

27944 Pronova Biopolymer
135 Commerce Way
Suite 201
Portsmouth, NH 03801-3200
603-433-1231
Fax: 603-433-1348 800-223-9030
bess.mosley@pronova.com www.pronova.com
Processor, importer and exporter of industrial ingre-
dients including alginates, propylene glycol
alginates, chitin and chitosan
General Manager: Sandra Platt
Manager Customer Service: Bess Mosley
Number Employees: 5-9
Parent Co: Pronova Biopolymer
Brands:
  Pro Floc
  Seacure

27945 Pronova Biopolymer
1735 Market Street
Philadelphia, PA 19103-7501
603-433-1231
Fax: 603-433-1348 800-223-9030
www.pronova.com
Solutions for the world's food and pharmaceutical
markets (Omega-3 fatty acids and ultra pure, high
concentrate alginates); onsite electrolytic hydro-
gen/oxygen gas supply systems and cooling/heating
solutions based on Transcritical C-2technology
Information and Internet and HES: Age Wik
Finance/IT: Richard Clemm
Business Development: Kenneth Bern
Business Development: Carl Christian Bachke
Business Development: Bjorn Poul Ringvold
Finance/Divisional Accounting: Kirsti Botheim
Number Employees: 200

27946 Pronto Products Company
11765 Goldring Rd
Arcadia, CA 91006
626-358-5718
Fax: 626-358-9194 800-377-6680
www.prontoproducts.com
Wire products including chrome and stainless steel
dispensers and frying baskets
President: William Parrott
VP: Martha Wagner
Estimated Sales: $20-50 Million
Number Employees: 20-49

27947 Propac Marketing Inc
4556 Sunbelt Dr
Addison, TX 75001-5131
972-733-3199
Fax: 972-733-3790
karen_johnson@propacmarketing.com
www.marsmilitary.com
Packaging for promotional materials including mar-
keting materials, coupons, literature, table tents, etc.;
also, demonstration kits
President: Charles Daigle
Senior Account Director: Arthur Kaplan
Account Executive: Charles Daigle
Estimated Sales: $1 - 2.5 Million
Number Employees: 20-49

27948 Propak
5230 Harvester Road
Burlington, ON L7L 4X4
Canada
905-681-2345
Fax: 905-681-1023 800-263-4872
Sheets, cookie liners, displays and containers includ-
ing point of purchase and corrugated shipping
President: H Keith Munt
CFO: Cris Gumbs
Sales Director: John Nadon
Plant Manager: Colin Carr
Number Employees: 100
Square Footage: 314000

27949 Prospero Equipment Corp
123 Castleton St
Pleasantville, NY 10570-3405
914-769-6252
Fax: 914-769-6786 888-732-1222
President: Tony Prospero
  prospero@cloud9.net
Estimated Sales: $10 - 20 Million
Number Employees: 10-19

**27950 Prosys Innovative Packaging
Equipment**
422 E 17th Street
Webb City, MO 64870-2956
417-673-3870
Fax: 417-673-7971 800-231-3455
info@prosysfill.com www.prosysfill.com
Cartridges, squeeze tubes and containers, automatic
filling equipment, automatic metal tube filler
Division Manager: Don Sonntag
Estimated Sales: $10-20 Million
Number Employees: 20-49

27951 Protectowire Co Inc
60 Washington St
Pembroke, MA 02359-1833
781-924-5384
Fax: 781-826-2045 pwire@protectowire.com
www.protectowire.com
Manufacturer and exporter of fire detection systems
for refrigerated storage
President: Andrew Sullivan
  asullivan@protectowire.com
CFO: Steve Loughlin
VP North American Sales: John Whaling
Chairman of the Board: Carol M Sullivan
Quality Assurance Manager: Richard Twigg
Sales Engineer: John Whaling
Sales Engineer: James Roussel
Estimated Sales: $5-10 Million
Number Employees: 20-49
Brands:
  Firesystem 2000
  Protectowire

27952 Protein Research
1852 Rutan Dr
Livermore, CA 94551-7635
925-243-6300
Fax: 925-243-6308 800-948-1991
info@proteinresearch.com
www.proteinresearch.com
Amino acid, vitamin and mineral supplements
Owner: Robert Matheson
  robert@proteinresearch.com
Director: Theodore Aarons
VP Operations: Daniel Aarons
Estimated Sales: $5-10 Million
Number Employees: 50-99
Number of Products: 12
Square Footage: 132000
Type of Packaging: Private Label, Bulk

27953 Protex International Corp.
180 Keyland Ct
Bohemia, NY 11716-2657
631-563-4250
Fax: 631-563-4206 800-835-3580
b.kennedy@protex-intl.com www.protex-intl.com
Camera domes, simulated surveillance and cash
boxes, safety and detection mirrors, high security
locks and annunciators
President: David Wachsman
CFO: Bill Ciccareli
CEO: Steve Migliorino
VP Sales: Bob Frazier
Contact: Chris Kelsch
   c.kelsch@vanguardprotexglobal.com
Estimated Sales: $20 - 50 Million
Number Employees: 50-99
Square Footage: 34000

27954 Protexall
1025 S. Fourth St
Greenville, IL 62246
618-664-6990
Fax: 877-776-8397 800-334-8939
Manufacturer and exporter of uniforms
President: Wayne Williams
CEO: Lois Williams
Vice President: Wade Williams
Sales Rep Coordinator: Dona Tredge
Operations Head: Randy Woods
Estimated Sales: $5-10 Million
Number Employees: 50-99
Square Footage: 200000
Parent Co: DeMoulin Bros. and Co.

27955 Prototype Equipment Corporation
1081 S Northpoint Blvd
Waukegan, IL 60085-8215
847-596-9000
Fax: 847-596-9001 sales@goodmanpkg.com
Custom packaging machinery, case erectors, case
and tray packers and sealers, packaging integration,
electronic equipment and supplies
President: James Goodman
President, Chief Executive Officer: Michael Senske
Vice President of Engineering: Leo Robertson
Vice President of Sales and Marketing: Randy
Denny
Contact: Becky Kendall
   bgkendall@pearsonpkg.com
Estimated Sales: $10-25 Million
Number Employees: 50-99

**27956 (HQ)Prototype Equipment
Corporation**
1601 Northwind Blvd
Libertyville, IL 60048-9613
847-680-4433
Fax: 847-816-6374
Manufacturer, exporter and importer of robotic
packaging equipment including flexible bag packers,
case formers, pick and place packers, bulk case
packers, top sealers and vertical snack food packers
Owner: Matthew Clatch
Director Sales/Marketing: Bruce Larson
VP Production: William Goodman
Estimated Sales: $300,000-500,000
Number Employees: 5-9
Square Footage: 168000
Brands:
   Goodman
   Pouch Pak
   Universal

27957 Providence Packaging
143 Barley Park Ln
Mooresville, NC 28115-7912
704-660-1469
Fax: 704-660-0988 866-779-4945
Molded foam containers, reflective foil packaging,
refrigerants (ice packs), corrugated shipping con-
tainers, paper products, tapes, poly, plastic and
supplies
Secretary: Deby King
Marketing: David Vance
Contact: Ryan Corbin
   ryan@providencepackaging.com
Estimated Sales: Less Than $500,000
Number Employees: 1-4

27958 Provisioner Data Systems
3467 W Hillsboro Boulevard
Suite 6
Deerfield Beach, FL 33442-9473
800-611-6592
Fax: 954-427-7007 800-611-6592
Computer systems for the food industry. Meat and
seafood processing systems
Number Employees: 15

27959 Provisur Technologies
9150 W 191st St
Mokena, IL 60448-8727
708-479-3500
Fax: 708-479-3598 815-485-4400
info@provisur.com
Food processing equipment: forming machines,
multi-loaf slicers and automatic transport equipment
Contact: Chris Blodgett
   chris@formax.us
Number Employees: 5-9

27960 Provisur Technologies
9150 W 191st St
Mokena, IL 60448-8727
708-479-3500
Fax: 708-479-3598 marketing@formaxinc.com
Advanced forming and slicing systems for the food
processing industry. Also provide tooling, filling
systems and packaging supplies.
VP N. American Sales/Marketing/Service: Kevin
Howard
Contact: Chris Blodgett
   chris@formax.us
Number Employees: 5-9

27961 Provisur Technologies
1116 E Main St
Whitewater, WI 53190-2103
262-473-5254
Fax: 262-473-5867 800-558-9507
www.provisur.com
Poultry & meat grinders, mixers and food processing
equipment.
President & CEO: Mel Cohen
HR Executive: Nancy Blum
   nblum@idcnet.com
Vice President, Sales & Marketing: Kevin Howard
Number Employees: 100-249

27962 Provisur Technologies, Inc.
9150 W 191st St
Mokena, IL 60448-8727
708-479-3500
Fax: 708-479-3598 info@provisur.com
www.provisur.com
Food processing equipment: ground, formed and
further processed; freezing; separation; slicing for
bacon and ready to eat; material handling systems;
paper converting; complete systems
Other Locations:
   Mokena IL
   Tinley Park IL
   Whitewater WI
   Badhoevedorp, Netherlands
   Cocarneau, France
   Indaiatuba, Brazil
   Bangkok, Thailand
   Shanghai, China

27963 (HQ)Prudential Lighting
1737 E 22nd St
Vernon, CA 90058-1008
213-746-0360
Fax: 213-746-8838 800-421-5483
info@prulite.com www.plpsocal.com
Custom and standard fluorescent lighting fixtures
with wet, damp and clean room applications; also,
linear systems
Owner: Jeff Ellis
   ejeff@prulite.com
Vice President: Jeff Ellis
Quality Control: Albert Pastina
Sales Director: Jon Steele
   ejeff@prulite.com
Manager: Alice Elliott
Estimated Sales: $10-20 Million
Number Employees: 500-999
Square Footage: 200000
Brands:
   Galv
   Pru Lites

27964 Pruitt's Packaging Services
2201 Kalamazoo Avenue SE
Grand Rapids, MI 49507-3783
616-243-0553
Fax: 616-243-4424 800-878-0553
Wooden pallets and boxes, watermelon bins, skids
and grocery wraparounds
President: John Pruitt
Secretary/Treasurer: Ruby Gilewski
Sales/Marketing Executive: Brian Hager
Supervisor: James McNitt
Estimated Sales: Below $5 Million
Number Employees: 8
Square Footage: 32000

27965 Prystup Packaging Products
101 Prystup Drive
PO Box 1039
Livingston, AL 35470-1039
205-652-9583
Fax: 205-652-2696 info@prystup.com
www.prystup.com
Folding boxes
President: J Leslie Prystup
CFO: Kathryn Prystrup
VP: James Emroy
R&D: Ronald Harwell
Quality Control: Jason Guin
Marketing: Rick Framer
Sales: Paul Sparkman
Public Relations: Suzanne McGahey
Production: Roy Rainer
Plant Manager: Craig Ray
Purchasing: Rickey Rogers
Estimated Sales: $10 - 20 Million
Number Employees: 100-249
Number of Brands: 6
Square Footage: 220000
Type of Packaging: Consumer, Private Label

27966 Psc Floturn Inc
1050 Commerce Ave # 1
Union, NJ 07083-5080
908-687-3225
Fax: 908-687-1715 sales@flow-turn.com
www.stainlessbeltcurves.com
Manufacturer, importer and exporter of USDA listed
powered belt curve and custom straight conveyors
President: Herman Migdel
Product Manager: J Grabowski
Vice President: Larry Cerpetier
   danotsc@aol.com
Operations Manager: Dan Otero
Estimated Sales: $2.5-5 Million
Number Employees: 10-19
Square Footage: 144000
Brands:
   Floturn

27967 Psion Teklogix
1810 Airport Exchange Blvd
Erlanger, KY 41018-3196
859-372-4100
Fax: 859-371-6422 800-322-3437
President: Ron Caines
Chief Executive Officer: John Conoley
Vice President of Human Resources: Maija Michell
Chief Technical Officer: Mike Doyle
Chief Marketing Officer: Nick Eades
Vice President of Operations: Rob Gayson
Estimated Sales: $50 - 75 Million
Number Employees: 100-249

27968 Psyllium Labs
1701 E Woodfield Road
Suite 636
Schaumburg, IL 60173
888-851-6667
info@psyllium.com www.psylliumlabs.com
Psyllium, chia and quinoa
Operations Executive: Drew West
Other Locations:
   Manufacturing Facility
   North Gujarat, India
   Manufacturing Facility
   Santa Cruz, Bolivia

**27969 Public Service Company of
Oklahoma**
212 E 6th St
Tulsa, OK 74119
888-216-3523
www.psoklahoma.com
Electric utility systems.

President & COO: Peggy Simmons
VP, Regulatory & Finance: Matthew Horeled
VP, External Affairs: Tiffini Jackson
Year Founded: 1913
Estimated Sales: $1,000,000,000+
Parent Co: American Electric Power

27970 Publix Super Market
PO Box 407
Lakeland, FL 33802-0407

800-242-1227
www.publix.com
Groceries, produce, meat, seafood, deli, floral, beer, wine and dairy.
President/CEO: Todd Jones
Chairman: Ed Crenshaw
CFO: David Phillips
Year Founded: 1930
Estimated Sales: $41.1 Billion
Number Employees: 230,000
Other Locations:
Bakery Manufacturing
Atlanta GA
Dairy/Fresh Foods Manufacturing
Deerfield Beach FL
Fresh Foods Manufacturing
Jacksonville FL
Bakery/Deli/Dairy Manufacturing
Lakeland FL
Dairy Manufacturing
Lawrenceville GA

27971 Pucel Enterprises Inc
1440 E 36th St
Cleveland, OH 44114-4117

216-881-4604
Fax: 216-881-6731 800-336-4986
www.pucelenterprises.com
Manufacturer and exporter of material handling equipment, stock carts, drum lifters and hand, shop and platform trucks, benches and cabinets
President: M Ann
amleissa@pucelenterprises.com
Vice President: Robert Mlakar
Plant Manager: Ronald Cook
Estimated Sales: $5-10,000,000
Number Employees: 50-99
Square Footage: 105000

27972 Puget Sound Inline
300 Chestnut Ridge Road
Woodcliff Lake, NJ 07677-7731

253-983-9390
Fax: 253-627-2029 800-831-1117
sales@pugetsoundinline.com
www.pugetsoundbmw.com
Manufactures thermoforming blister packaging—trays, computer, clamshell packaging, electrical, retail display and food
President: Bob Shupe
Estimated Sales: $1-2.5 Million
Number Employees: 10-19

27973 Pulse Systems
422 Connie Avenue
Los Alamos, NM 87544

505-662-7599
Fax: 505-662-7748 www.psilasers.com
Manufacturer and exporter of laser marking and coding systems
President: Edward J McLellan
VP: Linda McLellan
Contact: Holly Page
hpage@pulsesystem.com
Chief Operating Officer: Linda Mclellan
Estimated Sales: $1 - 3 Million
Number Employees: 1-4
Type of Packaging: Consumer, Private Label, Bulk
Brands:
Pulseprint

27974 Pulsetech Products Corp
1100 S Kimball Ave
Southlake, TX 76092-9009

817-329-6099
Fax: 817-329-5914 800-580-7554
ppc@pulsetech.net www.pulsetech.net
Battery maintenance systems, digital battery analyzers, battery chargers and conditioning systems

President: Pete Smith
petesmith@specialized.net
VP/Sales/Marketing: Scott Schilling
Business Manager: Rick Gregory
Business Development Manager: Rick Gregory
Manager: Shawn Doonan
Public Relations: Kevin Hosey
VP/Military Programs: Mark Witt
Director Military Programs: Mark Abelson
Estimated Sales: $500,000-$1 Million
Number Employees: 100-249

27975 Pulva Corp
105 Industrial Dr W
Valencia, PA 16059-3321

724-898-2555
Fax: 724-898-3192 800-878-5828
sales@pulva.com www.pulva.com
Grinding mills, parts and feeders
Owner: Ed Ferree
R&D: Bruce Dene
Quality Control: Bruce Dene
Sales Director: L Ward
ed@pulva.com
Estimated Sales: $20 - 50 Million
Number Employees: 20-49

27976 Pump Solutions Group
1815 S. Meyers Road
Oakbrook Terrace, IL 60181

630-487-2240
Fax: 630-487-2250 info@psgdover.com
www.psgdover.com
Pumps used to assist manufacturers and ingredients users to improve production yields while preserving color, aroma, texture, viscosity, purity and safety.
VP of Marketing: Walter Bonnett
Contact: Gajendra Aggarwalregional
gajendra@psgdover.com
Other Locations:
Grand Rapids MI
Grand Terrace CA
North Wales PA

27977 Purac America
111 Barclay Blvd
Lincolnshire, IL 60069

608-752-0449
Fax: 847-634-1992 pam@purac.com
www.purac.com
Producer of lactic acid, lactates and lactitol
President: Gerrit Vreeman
Vice President: Peter Kooijman
Marketing Manager: Casper Ravesteijn
VP Sales: Peter Hooijman
Contact: Lisette Nanning
l.nanning@puracaps.com
Estimated Sales: $20 - 50 Million
Number Employees: 20-49
Type of Packaging: Bulk

27978 Puratos Corp
1941 Old Cuthbert Rd
Cherry Hill, NJ 08034-1417

856-428-4300
Fax: 856-428-2939 800-654-0036
info@puratos.com www.puratos.com
Baking ingredients
President: Denis Wellington
Cmo: Matt Crumpton
matt.crumpton@puratos.com
Marketing Manager: Sheila Caufield
Estimated Sales: $500,000-$1 Million
Number Employees: 100-249

27979 Pure & Secure LLC-Cust Svc
4120 NW 44th St
Lincoln, NE 68524-1623

402-467-9300
Fax: 402-467-9393 800-875-5915
info@mypurewater.com www.mypurewater.com
Manufacturer and exporter of water treatment equipment; also, bottling and molding equipment
President: A E Meder
ae@pureandsecure.com
Sales Manager: Jason Harrington
Sales Manager: Alan Billups
Estimated Sales: $5-10 Million
Number Employees: 20-49
Square Footage: 90000
Brands:
Pure Water
Ultima

27980 Pure Fit Nutrition Bars
216 Technology Dr # E
Irvine, CA 92618-2416

949-679-7997
Fax: 949-679-7998 866-787-3348
info@purefit.com www.purefit.com
Manufacturer and exporter of fittings, hoses and assemblies
Founder/ CEO: Robb Dorf
robbdorf@purefit.com
Vice President: Robert Elbich
Sales Manager: John Cooling
Number Employees: 1-4
Parent Co: Nalge Process Technologies

27981 Pure Life Organic Foods
6625 W Sahara Ave
Suite 1
Las Vegas, NV 89146

708-990-5817
info@purelifeorganicfoods.com
www.purelifeorganicfoods.com
Organic sugars, coconut milk and coconut oil
Managing Director: Pradeep Mathur
Sales and Marketing Head: Sayida Bano
Parent Co: Pure Diets Intl. Ltd.
Type of Packaging: Bulk

27982 Pure Process Systems
5440 Alder Dr
Houston, TX 77081-1704

713-663-1677
Fax: 713-664-6444 800-879-2326
Pure Process Systems is a design-build environmental engineering and technology application company that utilizes current and innovative technologies to treat, reclaim, and reuse water and residuals for a variety of industriesincluding the food and beverage market.
CEO: Dan Curry
dcurry@ceconet.com
Vice President: Jim Revel
Vice President, Information Systems: Bill Zeis
Senior Project Engineer: Hoon Chung
Project Manager: Marc Thomas
Vice President of Sales: Joe Miniot
Vice President of Operations: Dale Thompson
Number Employees: 5-9

27983 Pure-1 Systems
25 Coligni Ave
New Rochelle, NY 10801-2605

914-576-5800
Fax: 914-235-8849 sales@pure1.com
www.pure1.com
Plumbed water colors, point-of-use water color products, hot and cold bottled water colors with patented Everfull self-filling bottle
Owner: Frank Pisano
Estimated Sales: $1 - 5 Million
Number Employees: 1-4

27984 Pure-Chem Products Company
8371 Monroe Ave
Stanton, CA 90680

714-995-4141
Fax: 714-527-7802
President: Bill King
Contact: Bruce Bereiter
cren@hoaghospital.org
Estimated Sales: $2.5-5 Million
Number Employees: 10-19

27985 PureCircle USA
5 Westbrook Corporate Center
Westchester, IL 60154

708-551-2600
info.usa@purecircle.com
purecircle.com
Stevia
Chairman: John Slosar
CEO: Maga Malsagov
Year Founded: 2001
Estimated Sales: $131 Million
Parent Co: PureCircle Limited
Type of Packaging: Bulk

27986 PureWine Inc
P.O. Box 100
Grapevine, TX 76099

service@drinkpurewine.com
www.drinkpurewine.com
Wine filters that eliminate wine headaches and other negative side effects.

Co-Founder: Dr. David Meadows
Co-Founder: Derek Meadows
Year Founded: 2014
Number Employees: 2-10
Number of Brands: 3
Number of Products: 3
Brands:
  The Phoenix
  The Wand
  The Wave

27987 Purico USA
497 Bramson Ct # 202
Suite 202
Mt Pleasant, SC 29464-8325

843-881-6684
Fax: 843-881-6492 sales@puricousa.com
www.purico.com
Complete range of papers for all types of tea and
coffee bags
Manager: Joe Szorc
Estimated Sales: $5-10 Million
Number Employees: 5-9

27988 Puritan Manufacturing Inc
1302 Grace St
Omaha, NE 68110-2591

402-341-3793
Fax: 402-341-4508 800-331-0487
purmfg@ixnetcom.com www.purmfg.com
Custom fabricated conveyors, mixers, hoppers,
tanks, cereal puffing machinery and catwalks; ex-
porter of cereal puffing machinery
President/Owner: Bill Waters
VP & General Manager: Dave Waters
Estimated Sales: $5-10 Million
Number Employees: 20-49
Square Footage: 350000
Brands:
  Puritan

27989 Puritan/Churchill Chemical Company
1341 Capital Circle SE
Suite E
Marietta, GA 30067-8718

404-875-7331
800-275-8914
Manufacturer and exporter of deodorants, warewash
systems and chemicals, disinfectants and cleaners
including kitchen, industrial laundry and window
President: Richard Bruce
VP Finance: Regina Crothers
Director Marketing: Adam Gould
Number Employees: 240
Parent Co: Gibson Chemical Industries

27990 Purity Foods Inc
417 S Meridian Rd
Hudson, MI 49247-9709

517-448-2050
Fax: 517-448-2070 800-997-7358
info@purityfoods.com
www.natureslegacyforlife.com
Beans, grains, seeds, cereals, cookbooks, flours, gra-
nola, pastas, pretzels and sesame sticks.
President: Donald Stinchcomb
Regional Sales Manager: Hezeden Graye
Manager: Gabby Williamson
  gabby.williamson@purityfoods.com
Estimated Sales: Less Than $500,000
Number Employees: 1-4
Square Footage: 60000

27991 Purity Laboratories
17387 63rd Ave
Lake Oswego, OR 97035-5205

503-297-3636
Fax: 503-297-3738 800-977-3636
www.puritylabsinc.com
Food analyst consultant that determines cleanliness
and nutritional value
VP: Ken Ayers
Manager: Bernd Scholz
  bscholz@kirkmangroup.com
Estimated Sales: Below $5 Million
Number Employees: 10-19
Square Footage: 5400

27992 Purity Products
200 Terminal Dr
Plainview, NY 11803-2312

516-767-1967
Fax: 516-767-1722 800-256-6102
customercare@purityproducts.com
www.puritypgoducts.com
Sauces, mayonnaise, vinegar, mustard, salad dress-
ings, vegetable oils, jellies, pickles
President: William Schroeder
President, Chief Executive Officer: Jahn Levin
  jahn@purityproducts.com
CFO: Bruce Morecroft
Vice President of Quality Assurance: Richard
Conant
Marketing: Al Rodriquez
Operations: Ricky Montejo
Purchasing Director: Charles Menezes
Estimated Sales: Less Than $500,000
Number Employees: 20 - 49
Square Footage: 400000
Parent Co: Sea Specialties Company
Type of Packaging: Food Service, Private Label,
  Bulk
Brands:
  Chef's Choice
  Cheryl Lynn
  Ideal
  Purity

27993 Purolator Facet Inc
8439 Triad Dr
Greensboro, NC 27409-9018

336-668-4444
Fax: 336-668-4452 800-852-4449
info@purolator-facet.com
www.purolator-facet.com
Manufacturer and exporter of self-cleaning and
sterilizable stainless steel filters for viscous fluids,
food and steam
President: Russ Stellfox
  rstellfox@purolator-facet.com
Program Manager: Mark Willingham
Director Sales/Marketing: Kevin Nelson
Number Employees: 100-249
Square Footage: 360000
Parent Co: Dayco Products
Brands:
  Metaledge
  Poromesh
  Poroplate

27994 Puronics Water Systems Inc
5775 Las Positas Rd
Livermore, CA 94551-7819

925-456-7000
Fax: 925-456-7010
Water treatment systems for the consumer and commercial markets. Puronics solutions include technologies such as water conditioning, filtering,
micro-filtration, filtration, carbon filtration, reverse
osmosis and ultra violetdisinfection.
Chief Financial Officer: Mark Cosmez
  esparzaroyr@puronics.com
Director of Commercial Sales: Roy Esparza
  esparzaroyr@puronics.com

27995 Put-Ons USA
7308 Aspen Lane N
Suite 149
Brooklyn Park, MN 55428-1020

763-425-9216
Fax: 763-425-9211 888-425-1215
Uniforms
President: Brian Peterson
Sales Director: Varlerie Peterson
Estimated Sales: Less than $500,000
Number Employees: 4
Square Footage: 6000
Brands:
  Put-Ons U.S.A.

27996 Putnam Group
35 Corporate Dr
Trumbull, CT 06611-6319

203-452-7270
Fax: 203-268-8071
Importer and wholesaler/distributor of promotional
items; also, marketing consultant services available
VP: Ann Rerat
Estimated Sales: Less than $500,000
Number Employees: 1-4

27997 Putsch & Co Inc
354 Cane Creek Rd
Fletcher, NC 28732

828-684-0671
Fax: 828-684-4894 800-847-8427
info@putschusa.com www.putschusa.com
Beet refinery equipment
CFO/R&D: Dieter Mergner
Engineering: Henning Wedemeyer
Sales: Jon E. DeBuvitz
Customer Service: Jeanne West
Manager: Dieter Mergner
Parts/ Supply Chain: Olav Seimer
Plant Superintendent: Dieter Mergner
Estimated Sales: $2.5 - 5 Million
Number Employees: 20-49
Parent Co: H. Putsch & Company

27998 Pyramid Flexible Packaging
120 E La Habra Boulevard
La Habra, CA 90631-5475

562-690-2208
Fax: 562-690-7892
Contact: Darryl Shimada
  dshimada@pyramidhotelgroup.com
Estimated Sales: $1 - 3 Million
Number Employees: 30

27999 Pyro-Chem
1 Stanton St
Marinette, WI 54143

715-732-3465
Fax: 715-732-3569 800-526-1079
charding@tycoint.com www.pyrochem.com
Manufacturer and exporter of pre-engineered fire
fighting systems
CEO: John Fort
Technical Services Engineer: Curt Harding
Technical Services Engineer: Brian Chernetski
General Manager Sales/Marketing: William Vegso
Contact: Edgar Alvarez
  ealvarez@tycoint.com
Product Manager: Katherine Adrian
Estimated Sales: $1 - 5 Million
Number Employees: 12
Square Footage: 60000
Parent Co: Borg-Warner/Wells Fargo Alarm
Brands:
  Kitchen Knight

28000 Pyromation Inc
5211 Industrial Rd
Fort Wayne, IN 46825-5152

260-484-2580
Fax: 260-482-6805 sales@pyromation.com
www.pyromation.com
Manufacturer and exporter of 3A compliant CIP
thermocouples. RTDs, temperature sensors,
thermowells, transmitters, connection heads, wire
and cable
President: Peter Wilson
  kim@pyromation.com
Marketing Manager: Greg Craghead
Sales Manager: Scott Farnham
Estimated Sales: $25-30 Million
Number Employees: 100-249
Square Footage: 40000

28001 Pyrometer Instrument CoInc
92 N Main St # 18
PO Box 479
Windsor, NJ 08561-3209

609-443-5522
Fax: 201-768-2570 800-468-7976
information@pyrometer.com www.pyrometer.com
Manufacturer, importer and exporter of controllers,
sensors, chart recorders, indicators, alarms and por-
table pyrometers; also, pressure transmitters and
temperature measurement systems
Owner: Dave Crozier
  sales@pyrometer.com
CEO: D Crozier
Marketing: Mickey Otto
Estimated Sales: $2.4 Million
Number Employees: 10-19
Number of Brands: 2
Number of Products: 12
Square Footage: 30000
Brands:
  Philips/Pma
  Pyro

28002 Q & B Foods
Irwindale, CA

626-334-8090
Fax: 626-969-1587
customerservice@qbfoods.com
www.qbfoods.com
Dressings, marinades, sauces and mayonnaise
President/Owner: Jerry Shepherd
Estimated Sales: $20-50 Million
Number Employees: 50-99
Square Footage: 50000
Type of Packaging: Private Label
Brands:
    Kewpie
    Rice Road
    The Ojai Cook

28003 Q A Supplies LLC
1185 Pineridge Rd
Norfolk, VA 23502-2043

757-855-3094
Fax: 757-855-4155 800-472-7205
info@QAsupplies.com
Supplier of insulated refrigiwear insulated clothing,
boots and gloves, hot/cold transport bags & covers,
temperature measurements, thermometers and
alarms.
President: David Cowles
    dcowles@qasupplies.com
Sales: Russ Holt
Number Employees: 10-19

28004 Q C Industries
4057 Clough Woods Dr
Batavia, OH 45103-2587

513-753-6000
Fax: 513-753-6001 www.qcconveyors.com
Conveyors, washdowns, timing belts
President: David Dornbach
    ddornbach@qcindustries.com
Marketing Supervisor: Chris Thompson
Estimated Sales: $10-20 Million
Number Employees: 20-49

28005 Q Laboratories
1400 Harrison Ave
Cincinnati, OH 45214-1606

513-471-1300
Fax: 513-471-5600 office@qlaboratories.com
www.qlaboratories.com
Consultant providing laboratory testing services in-
cluding microbiology and analytical chemistry sup-
port, QC/release, antimicrobial efficacy and GMP
testing, plant sanitation audits, nutrition labeling and
preservative analysis
President: David Goins
    dgoins@qlaboratories.com
Microbiology Group Leader: Meghan McDonough
Vice President of Sales & Marketing: Michelle
Kelly
Director of Business Development: Mark Goins
Estimated Sales: $2.5-5 Million
Number Employees: 100-249
Square Footage: 26000

28006 Q Pak Inc
2145 Mccarter Hwy
Newark, NJ 07104-4407

973-483-4404
Fax: 973-484-7896 qpak@earthlink.net
www.qpakcorp.com
Plastic bottles
President: Michael Formica
Contact: Justin Formica
    jformica@qpakcorp.com
Estimated Sales: $2.5-5 Million
Number Employees: 20-49

28007 Q Vac
1973 E. Via Arado
Rancho Dominguez, CA 90220

310-898-3400
Fax: 310-898-3430 888-879-7822
Sales@Newaypkg.com www.qvac.com
Skin packaging machines, roller press die cutting,
automatic conveyor belt blistering sealers, and vac-
uum forming machines
Estimated Sales: $1-2.5 Million
Number Employees: 5-9

28008 Q-Matic Technologies
355 East Kehoe Boulevard
Carol Stream, IL 60188-1817

847-263-7324
Fax: 847-263-7367 800-880-6836
Manufacturer and exporter of conveyor ovens
Sales Manager: David Cook
Production Manager: Frank Agnello
Estimated Sales: $1-2.5 Million
Number Employees: 7
Square Footage: 20000
Type of Packaging: Food Service
Brands:
    Q-Matic

28009 QAD Inc
100 Innovation Pl
Santa Barbara, CA 93108-2268

805-566-6000
Fax: 805-565-4202 www.qad.com
Meat industry computer systems, software, consul-
tants, data processing
CEO: Nolan Adams
    nadams@thecenter.nasdaq.org
CEO: Karl F Lopker
Estimated Sales: $20-50 Million
Number Employees: 1000-4999

28010 (HQ)QBD Modular Systems
5255 Steven Creeks Blvd
#187
Santa Clara, CA 95051

408-890-8924
Fax: 905-459-1478 800-663-3005
daryl@qpd.com www.qpd.com
Manufacturer and exporter of merchandising coolers
and modular display cases
President: Jeff Jaffer
CFO: Mohammed Chowdhary
Number Employees: 40
Brands:
    Qbd

28011 QC
P.O. Box 514
Southampton, PA 18966-0514

215-355-3900
Fax: 215-355-7231 www.qclaboratories.com
Consultant specializing in the testing of food and
dairy products; also, environmental testing available
President: Thomas Heins
Quality Control: Rich Royer
Contact: Schopbach Allen
    schopbach@qclaboratories.com
Estimated Sales: $20 - 50 Million
Number Employees: 100-249
Square Footage: 30000
Parent Co: Land O'Lakes

28012 QDC Plastic Container Co
111 W Mount Hope Ave
Lansing, MI 48910-9093

517-319-4194
Fax: 517-319-4304 800-652-2330
qdcplastics@acd.net www.qdcplastics.com
Supplier of plastic bottles for beverages
President: Stan Martin
    qdcplastics@acd.net
Operations Manager: Ken David
Estimated Sales: $10-20 Million
Number Employees: 50-99
Type of Packaging: Bulk

28013 QMI
426 Hayward Ave N
St Paul, MN 55128-5379

651-501-2337
Fax: 651-501-5797 qmi2@aol.com
Manufacturer and exporter of aseptic sampling and
transfer systems for liquids; also, sampling system
for bioreactors
President: Darrell Bigalke
Manager: Gwen Raddatz
Estimated Sales: Below $5 Million
Number Employees: 1-4
Square Footage: 8000
Parent Co: Quality Management
Brands:
    Qmi
    Qmi Safe Septum

28014 QMS International, Inc.
1833 Folkway Drive
Mississauga, Ontario, ON
Canada

905-820-7225
Fax: 905-820-7021 info@qmsintl.com
www.qmsintl.com
Manufacturer and supplier of new and refurbished
tying machines and supplies for the meat, poultry
and seafood industries.

28015 QNC Inc
12021 Plano Rd # 160
Dallas, TX 75243-5400

972-669-2948
Fax: 972-669-8990 888-668-3687
sales@q-n-c.com www.q-n-c.com
Hot air ovens
President: Paul Artt
    paul@q-n-c.com
Estimated Sales: Below $5,000,000
Number Employees: 5-9
Brands:
    Quik 'n Crispy

28016 QSR Industrial Supply
1888 W Point Drive
Cherry Hill, NJ 08003-2850

856-427-4270
Fax: 856-427-6736 800-257-8282
sales@qsrind.com
Industrial lighting with shatter-resistant and protec-
tive coated bulbs including fluorescent, incandescent
and outdoor
President: David Diamondstein
Manager: Dave Drake
Sales Manager: Rick Jackson
Estimated Sales: $5-10 Million
Number Employees: 20-49
Square Footage: 7000
Brands:
    Permalux Shatter-Kote

28017 QUIKSERV Corp
11441 Brittmoore Park Dr
PO Box 40466
Houston, TX 77041-6919

713-849-5882
Fax: 713-849-5708 800-388-8307
sales@quikserv.com www.quikservtest.com
Manufacturer and exporter of food service
drive-thru windows, security transaction drawers,
BR glass, and air curtains; custom fabrications
available
CEO: Jason T. Epps
    sales@quikserv.com
Marketing/Sales: Ray Epps
Sales Director: Sophia Navarro
Plant Manager: Jack Weaver
Purchasing Manager: Jason Epps
Number Employees: 20-49
Square Footage: 152000
Brands:
    Quikserv

28018 Qosina Corporation
2002-Q Orville Dr. N.
Ronkonkoma, NY 11779

631-242-3000
Fax: 631-242-3230 info@qosina.com
www.qosina.com
OEM components supplier to the medical, cosmetic,
cleanroom, veterinary and pharmaceutical industries.
President/CEO: Scott Herskovitz
Year Founded: 1980
Estimated Sales: $100+ Million
Number Employees: 50-99

28019 Qst Industries Inc
550 W Adams St # 200
Suite 200
Chicago, IL 60661-3665

312-930-9400
Fax: 312-930-0118 carlevato.jeff@qst.com
www.qst.com
CEO: Terra Bobadilla
    niyaz.mulla@nuveen.com
Regional Sales Manager: Sue Wech
Number Employees: 50-99
Type of Packaging: Consumer

28020 (HQ)Qsx Labels
220 Broadway
Everett, MA 2149

617-389-7570
Fax: 617-381-9280 800-225-3496
rkaress@qsxlabels.com www.qsxlabels.com
Manufacturer and exporter of labels including thermal, laser, pin feed, graphic, bar code, etc.; also, label applicators and dispensers
President and CEO: Mike Karess
CFO: Robert Karess
Vice President: Robert Karess
Marketing: Robert Karess
Plant Manager: Peter Kozowylt
Estimated Sales: $5-10 Million
Number Employees: 20-49
Square Footage: 120000
Type of Packaging: Private Label
Brands:
    Quikstik

28021 Quadra-Tech
864 E Jenkins Avenue
Columbus, OH 43207-1317

614-443-0630
Fax: 614-737-5429 800-443-2766
info@quadra-techinc.com
www.quadra-techinc.com
Work tables, fry baskets and specialty smallwares
Manager: Tim Mc Cormick
General Manager: Tim McCormick
Sales Director: Rob Zigler
Contact: Max Barr
    maxbarr@quadra-techinc.com
Estimated Sales: $10-20,000,000
Number Employees: 100-249

28022 Quadrant Epp USA Inc
2710 American Way
PO Box 9086
Fort Wayne, IN 46809-3011

260-479-4100
Fax: 260-478-1074 800-628-7264
americas.epp@qplas.com
www.quadrantplastics.com
Standard and custom food grade components and wear resistant UHMW-PE conveying equipment
President: Roland Finch
Vice President: Mark Edele
Marketing Communication Manager: Connie Brown
National Sales Manager: Robert Blackwood
Manager: Ron Niebel
    ron.niebel@qplas.com
Plant Manager: Lonnie Crump
Number Employees: 50-99
Square Footage: 337712
Other Locations:
    Scranton PA
    Delmont PA
    Reading PA
    Wytheville VA
Brands:
    Redirail
    Tivar

28023 Quadrel Labeling Systems
7670 Jenther Dr
Mentor, OH 44060-4872

440-602-4700
Fax: 440-602-4701 800-321-8509
labeling@quadrel.com www.quadrel.com
Manufacturer and exporter of labeling equipment
President: Lon Deckard
VP/General Manager: Charles Wepler
Marketing: Joe Uhlir
Sales: Christine Burrier
Operations: Shirley Chambers
Estimated Sales: $15-20 Million
Number Employees: 50-99
Square Footage: 80000
Type of Packaging: Consumer, Food Service
Brands:
    Moduline
    Premier
    Q31
    Q32
    Rotary
    Table Line
    Versaline

28024 Quadro Engineering
613 Colby Drive
Waterloo, ON N2V-1A1
Canada

519-884-9660
Fax: 519-884-0253 quadrosales@idexcorp.com
www.quadro.com
Manufactures and markets an innovative line of size reduction mills, emulsifiers, powder dispertion units and vacuum conveyors for the food industry
President: Keith McIntosh
Marketing Manager: Richard Franzke
Number Employees: 100
Number of Brands: 3
Number of Products: 6
Other Locations:
    Millburn NJ
Brands:
    Quadro

28025 Quaker Chemical Company
PO Box 554
Columbia, SC 29202-0554

803-765-9520
Fax: 803-765-9522 800-849-9520
www.quakerchem.com
Janitorial supplies and equipment including mops and floor finish-acrylics for high speed buffers and general use; exporter of cleaning chemicals
President: Josie Hendrix
Contact: Joseph Anderson
    anderson@quakerchem.com
Estimated Sales: $5-10 Million
Number Employees: 5-9
Square Footage: 40000
Brands:
    Fibercare 5000
    Panther Power
    Perma Glo
    Sunburst
    Superwear

28026 (HQ)Quaker Oats Company
555 W. Monroe St.
Suite 1
Chicago, IL 60661

800-367-6287
www.quakeroats.com
Cookies, oats, oatmeal, farina, granola bars, puffed wheat, puffed rice, barley, groats, shredded wheat, pancake syrups and mixes, flour, corn syrups, baking mixes, pasta and corn meal.
Senior VP/General Manager: Robbert Rietbroek
Senior Consultant, IT/OM: Mike Lyons
Year Founded: 1877
Estimated Sales: Over $1 Billion
Number Employees: 10,000+
Number of Brands: 4
Number of Products: 195
Parent Co: PepsiCo
Type of Packaging: Consumer, Food Service
Brands:
    Chewy
    Life
    Quaker
    Real Medleys

28027 Quali-Tech Tape & Label
6695 Grove St
Denver, CO 80221-2126

Fax: 303-431-4405
Grocery store and pressure sensitive labels; also, paper tape
President: Gloria Schlaht
Contact: Tony Pontious
    tpontious@qualitechscan.com
Estimated Sales: $500,000 - $1 Million
Number Employees: 1-4

28028 Qualicon
PO Box 80357
Wilmington, DE 19880-0357

302-695-5300
Fax: 302-695-5301 800-863-6842
Automated instruments that performs ribotyping to get genetic fingerprints that can identify an organism below species level, microbial charecterization, gmo detection and measurement, food safety and quality management services

President: Kevin Huttman
Chief Executive Officer: Eldon Roth
CFO: Beth Peck
Senior Vice President, General Counsel: Thomas Sager
R & D: Lance Bolton
Quality Control: Shawn Anderson
Marketing Manager: Megan DeStefano
Director of Sales: Craig Drinkwater
Number Employees: 10

28029 Qualiform, Inc
689 Weber Drive
Wadsworth, OH 44281

330-336-6777
Fax: 330-336-3668
www.qualiformrubbermolding.com
Manufacturer and exporter of custom molded rubber stoppers
President: Nick Antonino
CFO: Andy Antonino
Quality Control: Duane Lawrence
Contact: Andy Antonino
    aantonino@qualiforminc.com
Estimated Sales: Below $5 Million
Number Employees: 10

28030 Qualita Paper Products
3101 W Macarthur Blvd
Santa Ana, CA 92704-6907

714-540-0994
Fax: 714-540-1077 800-611-4010
www.qualitapaper.com
Paper baking molds, baking cups, carboard trays, doilies, cake boxes, ice cream containers and cups, cake boards, panettone molds and boxes, hard-bottom bags
President: Homar Aguirre
Vice President: Fabrice Clement
Estimated Sales: $860,000
Number Employees: 5-9
Parent Co: A.B.M. Inc.

28031 Quality Aluminum & Hm Imprvmt
1514 Gardner Blvd
Columbus, MS 39702-2802

662-329-2525
Fax: 662-329-3725
Commercial awnings
Owner: Sarah Mattison
    smattison@cableone.net
Estimated Sales: $1-2,500,000
Number Employees: 5-9

28032 Quality Assured Label Inc
1600 5th St S
Hopkins, MN 55343-7814

952-933-7800
Fax: 952-930-1505 sales@qal.com
www.qal.com
Custom pressure sensitive labels
Chairman: Robert Westmeyer
CEO: Robert Westnever
VP: Joe Farnko
Research & Development: Joe Farnko
Marketing Head: Petero Cattori
Estimated Sales: $20 - 50 Million
Number Employees: 20-49

28033 Quality Assured Packing
568 S Temperance Avenue
Fresno, CA 93727-6601

209-931-6700
Fax: 209-931-0286
Industrial tomato ingredient processor and supplier
Estimated Sales: $10-25 Million
Number Employees: 60

28034 Quality Bakers of America
1275 Glenlivet Drive
Suite 100
Allentown, PA 18106-3107

973-263-6970
Fax: 973-263-0937 www.qba.com
Wholesale bakers' cooperative providing consulting services including marketing, sales, product development, research and development, nutritional analysis, etc

Chairman: Sherman Strider
President/Manager: Norman Trapp
VP/Finance: Donald J. Cummings
Director: Judith Moderacki
Research & Development: Andrew Maier
Contact: Don Cummings
  dcummings@qba.com
Estimated Sales: $1.6 Million
Number Employees: 20-49
Brands:
  Sunbeam

28035 (HQ)Quality Cabinet & Fixture Co
885 Gateway Center Way # 201
San Diego, CA 92102-4538
619-266-1011
Fax: 619-266-0878 quality1@qcfc.com
www.qcfc.com
Manufacturer, exporter and importer of store fixtures and wood cabinets
President: Tim Paradise
  tpa@qcfc.com
Sales/Marketing: Laura Cohen
Estimated Sales: $10-20 Million
Number Employees: 100-249

28036 Quality Chekd Dairies Inc
901 Warrenville Rd
Suite 405
Lisle, IL 60532-4309
630-717-1110
Fax: 630-717-1126 mmurphy@qchekd.com
www.qchekd.com
Services for dairy market: food safety, training, procurement and marketing, lab sampling and consultation.
President: Peter Horvath
Director, Accounting: Mary DeMarco
Director, Quality & Food Safety: Chuck Yarris
Estimated Sales: $100-500 Million
Number Employees: 10-19
Brands:
  Quality Chekd Dairy Products

28037 Quality Container Company
1236 Watson St
Ypsilanti, MI 48198
734-481-1373
Fax: 734-481-8790 www.qualitycontainer.com
Manufacturer and exporter of high density polyethylene containers
Manager: Rob Salemi
CFO: Jamie Barche
Quality Control: Robert Johnson
VP Sales/Marketing: Robert Bell
Contact: Jamie Barche
  jbarche@alphap.com
Estimated Sales: $20 - 50 Million
Number Employees: 50-99
Square Footage: 160000
Other Locations:
  Quality Container Company
  Thomasville GA

28038 Quality Containers
128 Milvan Drive
Weston, ON M9L 1Z9
Canada
416-749-6247
Fax: 416-749-3293
Manufacturer and exporter of tin cans and slip cover, friction top and open top containers
President: Patrick Henry
Number Employees: 20
Square Footage: 32000

28039 Quality Containers of New England
83 Portland St
Yarmouth, ME 04096
207-846-5420
Fax: 207-846-3755 800-639-1550
Packaging and containerizing products
President: Gregory H Leonard
VP/Treasurer: Kevin Burns
Plant Manager: David Holub
Estimated Sales: $1-2.5 Million
Number Employees: 10-19
Square Footage: 12000

28040 Quality Control Equipment Co
4280 E 14th St
Des Moines, IA 50313-2604
515-266-2268
Fax: 515-266-0243 www.qcec.com
Manufacturer and exporter of automatic wastewater and dry material samplers, open channel flow meters and flumes
President: Richard Miller
  rmiller@qualitycontrolequipmentco.com
Quality Control: Tim Johnston
Sales Director: Joyce Hanson
Manager: Mike Wright
Purchasing Manager: Tim Johnston
Estimated Sales: $1-3 Million
Number Employees: 20-49
Type of Packaging: Bulk

28041 Quality Controlled Services
11971 Westline Industrial Drive
Suite 200
St. Louis, MO 63146
314-851-3100
Fax: 636-827-6761 800-325-3338
postmaster@delve.com
Data collection firm for marketing and sensory research
President: Laura Livers
CEO: Noel Sitzmann
Controller: Doug Ortwerth
Senior Vice President, Operations: Kim Reale
Account Manager: Jessica Lynch
Senior Vice President of Operations: Kim Reale
Estimated Sales: $1 - 5 Million

28042 Quality Corporation
2401 S Delaware St
Denver, CO 80223
303-777-6608
Fax: 303-777-6488 800-383-3018
Manufacturer and exporter of truck-carried forklifts
President: Kc Ensor
CFO: Kenton C Ensor Jr
Contact: Daniel Collins
  dcollins@qscorp.net
Estimated Sales: $10 - 20 Million
Number Employees: 50-99
Type of Packaging: Bulk

28043 Quality Croutons
4031 S Racine Ave
Chicago, IL 60609
773-890-2343
Fax: 773-927-8228 800-334-2796
Croutons and packaging services
President: David M Moore
Marketing/Sales: Deadra Ashford
Contact: Brandon Beavers
  bbeavers@infomatrix.com
Production Manager: Keith Taylor
Estimated Sales: $1900000
Number Employees: 20-49
Square Footage: 140000
Type of Packaging: Food Service, Private Label, Bulk

28044 Quality Cup Packaging Machinery Corporation
5408 3M Drive N.E.
Menomonie, WI 54751
800-732-4624
Fax: 715-235-1111 info@qualitycup.com
www.qualitycup.com
President: Jeff James
Estimated Sales: $300,000-500,000
Number Employees: 2

28045 Quality Fabrication & Design
955 Freeport Pkwy # 400
Coppell, TX 75019-4455
972-304-3266
Fax: 972-745-4244
AlexPier@quality-fabrication.com
www.quality-fabrication.com
Manufacturer and exporter of stainless steel food processing equipment including corn handling, fryers, seasoning systems, corn cooking systems, conveyors, etc
President: Alex Pier
  alexpier@quality-fabrication.com
VP: Vondel Kremeier
Technical Sales: Harvey Norman
Operations Manager: Roger Pier

Estimated Sales: $12-15 Million
Number Employees: 50-99
Square Footage: 170600

28046 Quality Films
19459 Thompson Ln
Three Rivers, MI 49093-9089
269-679-5263
Fax: 616-679-4261
Polyolefin packaging film
President: Blaine Rabbers
Assistant General Manager: Carol Huskey
Marketing/Sales: Bowie Grant
VP Operations: Richard Rabbers
Estimated Sales: $5 - 10 Million
Number Employees: 10
Square Footage: 132000

28047 Quality Food Equipment
10935 Weaver Ave
South El Monte, CA 91733
626-442-9281
Fax: 626-442-8386 800-423-3744
Blenders, grinders, massagers and tumblers, pickle injectors and slicers
Sales/Marketing Manager: Mo Fikry
Contact: Mike Anderson
  manderson@qualityfoodequipment.com
Manager: Bob Maxwell
Estimated Sales: $1 - 2.5 Million
Number Employees: 5-9

28048 Quality Food Products Inc
172 N Peoria St
Chicago, IL 60607-2311
312-666-4559
Fax: 312-666-7133
Eggs
President: George Aralis
Owner: Jim Aralis
  qfp@earthlink.net
Estimated Sales: $10 - 20 Million
Number Employees: 10-19

28049 Quality Highchairs
13461 Van Nuys Blvd
Pacoima, CA 91331-3059
818-896-3620
Fax: 818-896-3532 800-969-9635
qualityhighchairs12@sbcglobal.net
Hardwood high/youth chairs, booster seats, and tray stands
President: Gilbert Raynosa
Estimated Sales: Less than $500,000
Number Employees: 1-4
Square Footage: 20000
Brands:
  Classi-Tray Stand
  His-470
  Saferstep
  Versa-Chair

28050 Quality Industries
3716 Clark Ave
Cleveland, OH 44109
216-961-5566
Fax: 216-961-5569 qirolls@stratos.net
Rolls and precision parts for packaging and processing equipment
President: Jerald Kaplan
Vice President: Jim Kaplan
Contact: Christel Cooper
  ccooper@mytqg.com
Estimated Sales: $500,000-$1 Million
Number Employees: 5-9
Square Footage: 20000

28051 (HQ)Quality Industries Inc
130 Jones Blvd
La Vergne, TN 37086-3227
615-793-3000
Fax: 615-793-2347 www.qualityindustries.com
Manufacturer and exporter of food service equipment, stainless steal sifter cabinets; also, custom metal fabrication available
President: Fred Apple
CEO: Stanley Bryan
  stanley.bryan@qualityindustries.com
CFO: Jeff Mayfield
CEO: Jeff Mayfield
Quality Control: Terry Tidwell
R&D: Micheal Taylor

Estimated Sales: $20 - 50 Million
Number Employees: 250-499
Square Footage: 190000

28052 Quality Ingredients
14300 Rosemount Dr
Burnsville, MN 55306-6925

952-898-4002
Fax: 952-898-4421 info@qic.us
www.qic.us

Powders: shortening, cream, whip, cheese, lemon.
Services: spray drying, chilling and product development.
Director, Strategy/Marketing: Valorie Klemz
Manager: Stewart Flanery
sflanery@qic.us
Chief of Operations: Robert St.Louis
Estimated Sales: 19 Million
Number Employees: 50-99
Number of Brands: 2
Square Footage: 50000
Type of Packaging: Consumer, Food Service, Private Label, Bulk
Brands:
QuIC-CHEESE
QuIC-FLAVOR

28053 Quality Mop & Brush Manufacturers
341 Great Plain Avenue
Needham, MA 02492-4130

617-884-2999
Fax: 617-884-3999

Mops, brooms, brushes, mop/broom handles and gloves
President: Donald Ferris
Estimated Sales: $1-2.5 Million
Number Employees: 5-9
Brands:
Telescopic

28054 Quality Natural Casing
2431 Wright Blvd
Hebron, KY 41048-8123

859-689-5311
Fax: 859-689-5177 800-328-8701
www.qualitycasing.com

Casings: collagen, fibrous, natural
President: Robert Novachich
Estimated Sales: $5-10 Million
Number Employees: 10-19

28055 Quality Packaging Inc
851 Sullivan Dr
PO Box 1720
Fond Du Lac, WI 54935-9106

920-923-3633
Fax: 920-924-3830 800-923-3633
www.qpack.com

Offers experience in package design, materials and equipment for various types of packaging.
President: Larry Wills
lwills@qpack.com
Plant Manager: Kevin Graham
Estimated Sales: $14.1 Million
Number Employees: 50-99

28056 Quality Plastic Bag Corporation
3430 56th Street
Flushing, NY 11377-2122

718-429-1632
Fax: 718-429-1634 800-532-2247

Plastic bags
Estimated Sales: $2.5-5 Million
Number Employees: 10-19
Square Footage: 30000
Type of Packaging: Bulk

28057 Quality Seating Co
4136 Logan Way
Youngstown, OH 44505-5703

330-747-0181
Fax: 330-747-0183 800-323-2234
www.gasserchair.com

Manufacturer and exporter of furniture including booths, chairs and tables

President: Jay Buttermore
jbuttermore@taylorseating.com
CEO: Roger Gasser
CFO: Frank Joy
Vice President: Marylou Joy
Research & Development: Mel Textoris
Marketing Director: Anthony Johntony
Sales Director: Paula Rapone
Operations Manager: Jim Humparies
Purchasing Manager: Paula Rapone
Estimated Sales: $2.5-5 Million
Number Employees: 20-49
Number of Brands: 1
Number of Products: 100
Square Footage: 200000
Parent Co: Quality Upholstering Company

28058 Quality Transparent BagCo
110 Mcgraw St
Bay City, MI 48708-8276

989-893-3561
Fax: 989-893-3004 bagcentral@aol.com

Polyethylene bags
President: Steve Kessler
bagcentral@aol.com
CEO: Leonard Kessler
Director Corporation Services: Tony Bloenk
Quality Control: Mery Carey
Estimated Sales: $5 - 10 Million
Number Employees: 10-19
Square Footage: 248000
Other Locations:
Quality Transparent Bag
Lawrenceburg TN
Brands:
Best Buy
Valu Pak

28059 Qualtech
1880, Rue L,on-Harmel
Quebec, QC G1N 4K3
Canada

418-686-3802
Fax: 418-686-3801 888-339-3801
info@qualtech.ca www.qualtech.ca

Specializing in stainless steel components and fabrications equipment
President: Andre Giguere
Customer Service: Andre Turcotte
Other Locations:
Saint-Laurent, QC
Scarborough, ON

28060 Qualtrax Inc
105 Industrial Dr
Christiansburg, VA 24073-2536

540-382-4234
Fax: 540-382-4701 800-277-3077
www.qualtrax.com

Computer software
CEO: Marty Muscatello
VP Sales/Marketing: Gary Overstreet
Manager: Megan Hash
mhash@ccs-inc.com
Estimated Sales: $930,000
Number Employees: 5-9
Square Footage: 8204

28061 Quanex Building Products Corp
1800 West Loop S # 1500
Suite 1500
Houston, TX 77027-3246

713-961-4600
Fax: 713-439-1016 www.quanex.com

Glass doors and display units designed to improve thermal performance for refrigerated products, also glass sealant for same
Vice President: Larry Johnson
ljohnson@homeshield.com
President, Chief Executive Officer: Dave Petratis
Vice President, Controller: Deborah Gadin
Quality Manager: Christoph Rubel
Director of Marketing: Erin Johnson
Sales Manager: Andreas Schultheiss
Executive Vice President, Chief Operatin: Curtis Stevens
Estimated Sales: $5-10 Million
Number Employees: 1000-4999

28062 Quantek Instruments
183 Magill Dr
Grafton, MA 01519-1327

508-839-3940
Fax: 508-393-1877
sales@quantekinstruments.com
www.quantekinstruments.com

Oxygen and carbon dioxide analyzers
Contact: Larry Davis
sales@quantekinstruments.com
Estimated Sales: $3 - 5 Million
Number Employees: 20-49

28063 Quantem Corp
1457 Lower Ferry Rd # 1
Ewing, NJ 08618-1493

609-883-9191
Fax: 800-800-1531 609-883-9879
info@quantemcorp.com www.quantemcorp.com

Production Manager: S Sunderland
Estimated Sales: $2 Million
Number Employees: 20-49
Square Footage: 15000
Brands:
Analog Thermostats
Data Loggers
Defrost Controllers
Digital (Appliance) Thermometers
Digital Thermostats
Temperature Sensors
Ventilation Controllers

28064 Quantis Secure Systems
7255 Standard Drive
Hanover, MD 21076-1389

410-712-6020
Fax: 410-712-0329 800-325-6124

Security, fire alarm and intercom systems
President: Kevin Robison
Estimated Sales: $2.5-5 Million
Number Employees: 20-49
Parent Co: BET

28065 Quantum Net
PO Box 49
Sewickley, PA 15143

704-376-0509
Fax: 704-551-0941

Netting plastics, netting and tying machines
President: George Seal
Estimated Sales: $500,000-$1 Million
Number Employees: 6

28066 Quantum Performance Films
601 E Lake St
Streamwood, IL 60107-4101

630-289-5237
Fax: 630-213-6209 800-323-6963

Manufacturer and exporter of flexible polypropylene films
CEO: Robert Dea
Director Marketing: Mark Montsinger
Director Sales: Bill Rowe
Number Employees: 100-249
Square Footage: 1800000
Parent Co: Hood Industries
Brands:
Mirage
Qlam
Qpet

28067 Quantum Storage SystemsInc
15800 NW 15th Ave
Miami, FL 33169-5606

305-687-0405
Fax: 305-688-2790 800-685-4665
sales@quantumstorage.com
www.quantumstorage.com

Plastic storage containers, metal shelving and mobile storage cabinets and carts
President: Hose Babani
ed@quantumstorage.com
VP: Dean Cohen
Marketing: Jose Babani
Sales: Elizabeth Faller
Estimated Sales: $3 - 5,000,000
Number Employees: 10-19
Square Footage: 300000
Parent Co: M&M Plastics
Type of Packaging: Consumer

28068 Quantum Topping Systems Quantum Technical Services Inc
9524 West Gulfstream Road
Frankfort, IL 60423
815-464-1540
Fax: 815-464-1541 888-464-1540
information@q-t-s.com www.q-t-s.com
Manufacturer and designer of manual and automated portion control, cheese, IQF meat, and IQF vegetable. Topping application equipment and pepperoni slicing equipment
President: David White
CEO: Mark Freudinger
Sales Manager: Jim Machura
Contact: John Bautz
jbautz@q-t-s.com
Estimated Sales: $3 - 5 Million
Number Employees: 20
Square Footage: 76000

28069 Quasar Industries
1911 Northfield Dr
Rochester Hills, MI 48309-3824
248-852-0300
Fax: 248-852-0442 sales@quasar.com
www.quasar.com
Microwave ovens
President: Shane Majesky
shanemajesky@hotmail.com
CEO: Denise Higgins
VP Sales: Dave Bearden
Number Employees: 50-99

28070 Queen City Awning
7225 E Kemper Rd
Cincinnati, OH 45249-1030
513-530-9660
Fax: 513-530-0662 info@queencityawning.com
Commercial awnings
Owner: Pete Weingartner
qca_pete@fuse.net
Estimated Sales: Below $5,000,000
Number Employees: 20-49

28071 Quest
PO Box 73381
San Clemente, CA 92673-0113
949-643-1333
Fax: 949-362-4937 foods4you@aol.com
Consultant specializing in nutrition analysis and labeling services for dry, frozen and refrigerated products
President: Harry Messersmith

28072 Quest Corp
12900 York Rd
North Royalton, OH 44133-3623
440-230-9400
Fax: 440-582-7765 info@2quest.com
www.2quest.com
Electronic scales, weighing and batching systems and data acquisition/transmission systems; exporter of weighing and batching systems
Owner: David Fischer
dfischer@2quest.com
Sales/Marketing Manager: Daniel Donovan
Operations Manager: Jerome Kelly
Estimated Sales: $2.5-5 Million
Number Employees: 19

28073 Quetzal Foods International Company
3419 Iberville Street
New Orleans, LA 70119-5322
504-486-0830
Fax: 504-486-0830

28074 Quick Judith & Assoc
13944 Roberts Rd
P.O. BOX 188
Hancock, MD 21750-1620
301-678-5737
Fax: 301-678-5730 www.whereorg.com
Consulting firm specializing in regulatory and quality control, labeling, etc
President: Judith Quick
judyquick@hughes.net
Estimated Sales: Less Than $500,000
Number Employees: 1-4
Square Footage: 800

28075 Quick Label Systems
600 E Greenwich Ave
West Warwick, RI 02893-7526
401-828-4000
Fax: 401-822-2430 877-757-7978
info@quicklabel.com www.quicklabel.com
CFO: Joseph Oconnell
CEO: Everett V Pizzuti
epizzuti@astromed.com
CEO: Albert W Ondis
Estimated Sales: $20,000,000 - $49,999,999
Number Employees: 250-499

28076 Quick Label Systems
600 E Greenwich Ave
West Warwick, RI 02893-7526
401-828-4000
Fax: 401-822-2430 877-757-7978
info@quicklabel.com www.quicklabel.com
Specialty food packaging i.e. gift wrap/labels/boxes/containers.
Principal: Kevin Pizzuti
CEO: Everett V Pizzuti
epizzuti@astromed.com
Estimated Sales: $45,000
Number Employees: 250-499

28077 Quick Point Inc
1717 Fenpark Dr
Fenton, MO 63026-2939
636-343-9400
Fax: 636-343-3587 800-638-1369
www.quickpoint.com
Manufacturer, supplier and exporter of advertising specialties
CEO: John Goessling
CFO: Doug Bozler
Vice President: Duane Mayer
Marketing Director: Duane Mayer
Sales Director: Joe Keely
Operations Manager: Rick Smith
Production Manager: Bryan Frenzel
Purchasing Manager: Dave Miller
Number Employees: 100-249

28078 Quick Stamp & Sign Mfg
805 General Mouton Ave
P. O. Box 3272
Lafayette, LA 70501-8509
337-232-2171
Fax: 337-232-4561 sales@qrstamp.com
www.qrstamp.com
Manufacturer and wholesaler/distributor of regular and self-inking rubber stamps, grocery marking ink, price markers for deposit stamps, daters and numberers
President: Patrick Gaubert
sales@qrstamp.com
Estimated Sales: Less Than $500,000
Number Employees: 1-4
Square Footage: 7200

28079 QuickLabel
600 E Greenwich Ave
West Warwick, RI 02893-7526
401-828-4000
Fax: 401-822-2430 877-757-7978
info@quicklabelsystems.com
www.quicklabel.com
Digital color thermal transfer printers, barcode label printers, labelers, print and apply systems, labels, thermal transfer ribbon
President & CEO: Gregory Woods
CFO: David Smith
Estimated Sales: $50 Million
Number Employees: 250-499
Square Footage: 125000
Parent Co: AstroNova
Type of Packaging: Consumer, Food Service, Private Label, Bulk
Other Locations:
Astro-Med
Longucuil, Quebec
Astro-Med
Slough, United Kingdom
Astro-Med
Trappes, France
Astro-Med
Rodgau, Germany
Astro-Med
Milano, Italy

28080 Quickdraft
1525 Perry Dr SW
Canton, OH 44710-1098
330-477-4574
Fax: 330-477-3314 www.quickdraft.com
Hot dog/sausage casing removal systems, draft inducer's to vent out the heat produced from ovens & boilers and food conveying systems.
Manager: Joseph Ovnic
joe.ovnic@quickdraft.com
Number Employees: 20-49

28081 Quickie Manufacturing Corp
1150 Taylors Ln # 2
Suite 2
Cinnaminson, NJ 08077-2577
856-829-7900
Fax: 856-786-9318 help@quickie.com
www.quickie.com
Mops, brushes, brooms, sponges and scourers
President: Peter Vosbikian
Sr. VP Sales: David Vosbikian
Executive VP Sales/Marketing: Vince Cella
Estimated Sales: $10-20 Million
Number Employees: 50-99

28082 Quikwater Inc
8939 W 21st St
Sand Springs, OK 74063-8515
918-241-8880
Fax: 918-241-8718 sales@quikwater.com
www.quikwater.com
QuikWater manufactures a 99% thermal efficient direct contact water heater that provides potable hot water on demand. Water heated with a QuikWater can be used for domestic purposes, as a food ingredient and for sterilization andsanitation processes. With tremendous thermal efficiency, QuikWater can create up to 40% fuel savings compared to traditional methods.
President: Dana Weber
Marketing: Kay Weiman
Sales: Tammy Collins
Manager: Melissa Arms Trong
marmstrong@hot-water-heater.com
Number Employees: 10-19
Number of Brands: 3
Number of Products: 1
Brands:
Econowater
Quikwater
Twintower

28083 Quintex Corp
205 25th Ave S
Nampa, ID 83686-7399
208-467-1113
Fax: 509-924-7991 www.qntx.com
Custom and stock plastic bottles; also, printing services available
President: Dorothea Christiansen
Regional Sales Manager: Bruce McElwain
Customer Service: George Ferriola
Estimated Sales: $10-20 Million
Number Employees: 10-19
Square Footage: 144000

28084 Quintex Corp
3808 N Sullivan Rd # 8a
Spokane Valley, WA 99216-1618
509-924-7900
Fax: 509-924-7991 www.qntx.com
Manufactures blow mold plastic containers
President: Dorochea Christiansen
CFO: Bob Pullis
Quality Control: Bill Masscy
Estimated Sales: $10 - 20 Million
Number Employees: 50-99

28085 Quipco Products Inc
1401 Mississippi Ave
Suite 5
Sauget, IL 62201-1084
314-993-1442
Fax: 618-271-2311
Manufacturer and exporter of custom and standard service food equipment including counters, racks, sinks and tables; also, custom stainless steel fabrication available
President: James Nations
nations@nationsfoodservice.com
VP/Owner: Jerry Chervitz
Office Manager: Tena Holmes

Estimated Sales: $1 - 3 Million
Number Employees: 5-9
Square Footage: 40000

28086 Qwik Pack Systems
16571 Saddlebrook Ln
Moreno Valley, Mo 92551
951-232-2507
Fax: 909-242-6019
qwikpacksystemsinc@yahoo.com
Automatic and semiautomatic carton sealing and
taping machines. Robotics, L-Sealers, automatic
stretch wrap machines, strapping machines and
adhesive tapes
President: James Mahoney
Estimated Sales: $10-20 Million
Number Employees: 1-4
Number of Brands: 1
Number of Products: 31
Square Footage: 500000
Type of Packaging: Food Service
Brands:
  Qwik Pack Systems

28087 Qyk Syn Industries
8527 NW 66th Street
Miami, FL 33166-2636
305-594-3366
Fax: 305-594-0075 800-354-5640
bobbiebridge@aol.com
Formed plastic and custom neon signs, faces, let-
ters,architectural panels and menu boards
CEO: Ernest Hunt
Estimated Sales: $1 - 5 Million
Number Employees: 10
Square Footage: 7200

28088 R & D Brass
25 Sprout Creek Ct
Wappingers Falls, NY 12590-6342
845-223-6104
Fax: 845-223-6195 800-447-6050
RDBRASSINC@AOL.COM
Brass sneeze guards, booth dividers, railings, glass
racks and crowd control products
Owner: Ed Davis
rdbrassinc@aol.com
Estimated Sales: Less Than $500,000
Number Employees: 1-4
Square Footage: 20000

28089 R A Jones & Co Inc
2701 Crescent Springs Pike
Ft Mitchell, KY 41017-1591
859-341-1807
Fax: 859-341-0519 www.rajones.com
Manufacturer and exporter of automatic carton loading machines, case and tray packers, continuous web
form, fill and seal machinery, bottle uncasers, pouch
makers, fillers and robotic solutions; also provide
complete partial lineintegration services
CEO: Barry Shoulders
shoulders.b@rajones.com
Estimated Sales: $300,000-500,000
Number Employees: 250-499
Parent Co: the Coesia Group

28090 R C Molding Inc
19 Freedom Ct
Greer, SC 29650-4525
864-879-7279
Fax: 864-879-7309
customerservice@rcmolding.com
www.rcmolding.com
Thermoplastic injection molded parts for boxes
President: William Humphrey
whumphrey@rcmolding.com
Estimated Sales: $1-2.5 Million
Number Employees: 10-19
Square Footage: 80000

28091 R C Musson Rubber Co
1320 E Archwood Ave
PO Box 7038
Akron, OH 44306-2825
330-773-7651
Fax: 330-773-3254 800-321-2381
info@mussonrubber.com www.mussonrubber.com
Floor mats
President: Bennie D Segers
bsegers@mussonrubber.com
Vice President: Robert Segers
Research & Development: Joe Kostko

Estimated Sales: $5-10 Million
Number Employees: 20-49

28092 R C Smith Co
14200 Southcross Dr W
Burnsville, MN 55306-6973
952-854-0711
Fax: 952-854-8160 800-747-7648
info@rcsmith.com www.rcsmith.com
Store fixtures
President: Peter Smith
psmith@rcsmith.com
Marketing Manager: Sarah Dunne
Estimated Sales: $2.5-5 Million
Number Employees: 20-49
Square Footage: 40000

28093 R F Hunter Co Inc
113 Crosby Rd # 9
Dover, NH 03820-4389
603-742-9565
Fax: 603-742-9608 800-332-9565
info@rfhunter.com www.rfhunter.com
Manufacturer and exporter of filtration equipment
for edible oils
President: Paul Santoro
sales@rfhunter.com
Estimated Sales: $500,000 - $1 Million
Number Employees: 5-9
Brands:
  Ecco One
  Hunter Filtrator Hf Series
  Mini Max Iii

28094 R F Mac Donald Co
10261 Matern Pl
Santa Fe Springs, CA 90670-3249
714-257-0900
Fax: 714-257-1176
jim.macdonald@rfmacdonald.com
www.rfmacdonald.com
Wine industry pumps
Manager: Christopher Sentner
VP Pump Division: Robert Sygiel
VP Boiler Division: Chris Sentner
Co-President: James T McDonald
Estimated Sales: $20 - 50 Million
Number Employees: 20-49

28095 (HQ)R F Schiffmann Assoc.
149 W 88th St
Suite 1
New York, NY 10024-2424
212-362-7021
microwaves@juno.com
www.microwaveinnovations.com
Consultant specializing in microwave technology
applications
President: Robert Schiffmann
microwaves@juno.com
CFO: Ernest Stein
VP: Marilyn Schiffmann
Estimated Sales: Less Than $500,000
Number Employees: 1-4
Square Footage: 8000

28096 R F Technologies Inc
330 Lexington Dr
Buffalo Grove, IL 60089
800-598-2370
info@rftechno.com www.rftechno.com
Drive thru system sales, repairs, POS, Big Dog Sur-
veillance systems, timers, order confirmation, digital
signage, customer music entertainment and wired in-
tercom systems.
Director of IT: Steve Combs
Vice President, Marketing: Dan Wenger
Year Founded: 1989
Estimated Sales: $50-100 Million
Number Employees: 50-99

28097 R H Saw Corp
28386 W Main St
Barrington, IL 60010-1830
847-381-8777
Fax: 847-381-9492 rhsaw@aol.com
Manufacturer, importer and exporter of cutlery,
blades, grinder plates and knives including metal,
wood and plastic
President: Ralph Hirsch
rhsaw@aol.com
CEO: Larry Adler
Estimated Sales: $500,000-$1 Million
Number Employees: 1-4

28098 R J Mc Cullough Co
1980 Old Philadelphia Pike # A
Rte 340
Lancaster, PA 17602-3431
717-735-8772
Fax: 717-735-8774
Commercial awnings
Owner: J R Mc Cullough
Estimated Sales: Less Than $500,000
Number Employees: 5-9

28099 R K Electric Co Inc
7405 Industrial Row Dr
Mason, OH 45040-1301
513-204-6060
Fax: 513-204-6061 800-543-4936
www.rke.com
Manufacturer and exporter of relays and voltage
suppressors for HVAC applications
President: John L Keller
jkeller@rke.com
Estimated Sales: $5 - 10 Million
Number Employees: 10-19

28100 R Murphy Co Inc
13 Groton Harvard Rd
Ayer, MA 01432-1846
978-772-3481
Fax: 978-772-7569 888-772-3481
sales@rmurphyknives.com
www.murphyknives.com
Industrial knives including carving, butchers', fish
scaling and slitting
President: Douglas Bethke
dbethke@rmurphyknives.com
Plant Manager: Charles Liebfried
Estimated Sales: $2.5 - 5 Million
Number Employees: 10-19

28101 R P Adams
225 E Park Dr
Tonawanda, NY 14150-7813
716-877-2608
Fax: 716-877-9385 800-896-8869
info@rpadams.com www.rpadams.com
President: Richard Adams
rba@rpadams.com
VP: Dan Petko
Estimated Sales: $9 Million
Number Employees: 50-99

28102 R R Donnelley
111 E Wacker Dr
Chicago, IL 60601-3713
312-565-2727
Fax: 312-326-8001 800-742-4455
www.rrdonnelley.com
Signs including permanent point of purchase, plastic
and neon; also, displays and merchandising systems,
pressure sensitive labels, rotary letterpress and
screens
President, CEO: Thomas J. Quinlan, III
Contact: Leonard Abel
leonard.abel@rrd.com
Number Employees: 50-99
Square Footage: 800000
Other Locations:
  Banta Specialty Converting
  Sturtevant WI

28103 R R Street & Co
215 Shuman Blvd # 403
Naperville, IL 60563-5100
630-416-4244
Fax: 630-416-4150 www.4streets.com
Manufacturer and exporter of dry cleaning deter-
gents, fabric finishes, spotters and filtration products
President: L R Beard
lbeard@4streets.com
CFO: James Beecher
Estimated Sales: $5 - 10 Million
Number Employees: 5-9

28104 R T C
2800 Golf Rd
Rolling Meadows, IL 60008-4023
847-640-2400
Fax: 847-640-5175 gcohen@rtc.com
Manufacturer and exporter of merchandising displays, signs, nonmechanical coolers and interactive,
electronic, in store point of purchase displays

President: Bruce Vierck
CEO: Richard Nathan
 rnathan@rtc.com
Sr VP: Howard Topping
Estimated Sales: $500,000-$1 Million
Number Employees: 250-499
Square Footage: 700000

28105 (HQ)R Wireworks Inc
517 Baldwin St
Elmira, NY 14901-2225

607-733-7169
Fax: 607-734-8859 800-550-4009
sales@rwireworks.com www.shoprwireworks.com
Point of purchase displays and fixtures
President: Ned Rubin
 nrubin@rwireworks.com
Quality Control: Terry Cosgelo
Marketing Manager: Deb Eighmey
Estimated Sales: $2.5 - 5 Million
Number Employees: 20-49

28106 R X Honing Machine Corp
1301 E 5th St
Mishawaka, IN 46544-2899

574-259-1606
Fax: 574-259-9163 800-346-6464
www.rxhoning.com
Manufacturer and exporter of honing and sharpening
machines for restaurant knives
President: R J Watson
Estimated Sales: $5-10 Million
Number Employees: 5-9
Square Footage: 11000
Brands:
 Mini Rx Hone

28107 R&C Pro Brands
1655 Sally Road
Wayne, NJ

973-633-7374
Disinfectants, washing compounds, polishes and
cleaners including glass, hand, carpet and windows
President: John Culligan
VP Marketing: Karen Messer
National Sales Manager: Michael Tracy
Parent Co: Reckitt & Colman PLC

28108 R&D Glass Products
1808 Harmon Street
Berkeley, CA 94703-2496

510-547-6464
Fax: 510-547-3620 www.angelfire.com
Wine industry labware
President: Doug Dobson
Estimated Sales: Below $5 Million
Number Employees: 10-19

28109 R&G Machinery
7204 Beckwith Road
Morton Grove, IL 60053-1723

847-966-1530
Fax: 773-265-6311
Tanks, kettles
President: Sofi Rahmon
Estimated Sales: $1-2.5 Million
Number Employees: 4
Square Footage: 100000

28110 R&R Corrugated Container
PO Box 399
Terryville, CT 06786-0399

860-584-1194
Fax: 860-582-5051
Corrugated boxes
President: Richard Braverman
CFO: Wayne
Estimated Sales: $10 - 20 Million
Number Employees: 50-99

28111 R&R Industries
1000 Calle Cordillera
San Clemente, CA 92673

949-361-9238
Fax: 949-361-9360 800-234-1434
rrosen@rrind.com www.rrind.com
Embroidered and printed promotional clothing
President: Richard Rosen
Marketing Manager: Richard Rosin
Production Manager: Robin Grohman
Estimated Sales: $20-50 Million
Number Employees: 50-99

28112 R-Biopharm Inc
870 Vossbrink Dr
Washington, MO 63090-1067

269-789-3033
Fax: 866-922-5856 info@r-biopharm.com
www.r-biopharm.com
Mycotoxin test kits, enzymatic and microbiological
test kits for the detection of residues, food constituents and microbiological contaminnts. Screen for
hormones, antibiotics, genetically modified materials, specified risk materialsallergens and pathogens
in a reliable and cost-effective manner.
President: Kurt Johnson
Vice President: Sean Tinkey
Contact: Carol Donnelly
 carol@r-biopharmrhone.com
Estimated Sales: $1.3 Million

28113 R. Markey & Sons
5 Hanover Sq
Rm 1202
New York, NY 10004

212-482-8600
Fax: 212-344-5838
rmarkeycoffee@compuserve.com
Tea and coffee samplers and weighers
President: Michael Steele
Contact: Joseph Aglione
 aglione@rmarkey.com
Estimated Sales: $1 - 2.5 Million
Number Employees: 20-49
Parent Co: R Markey & Sons

28114 (HQ)R.C. Keller & Associates
14 Passage Lane
Suite 110
Barnegat, NJ 08005-3340

973-694-8810
Fax: 973-649-3535
Consultant specializing in packaging, processing
and automation systems integration, facilities de-
sign, project management, industrial engineering
and operations research
Estimated Sales: $1 - 5 Million
Number Employees: 1

28115 R.G. Stephens Engineering
707 W 16th Street
Long Beach, CA 90813-1410

562-435-6244
Fax: 562-435-1664 800-499-3001
Food processing equipment and supplies, conveyor
systems, waste handling equipment and systems and
process control systems; also, engineering, design,
fabrication and installation services available
General Manager: Ralph Stephens
Manager: Ken Diehl
VP: Diane Stephen
Number Employees: 6

28116 R.H. Chandler Company
1040 Claridge Pl
Saint Louis, MO 63122-2431

314-962-9353
Fax: 314-962-1661
Manufacturer and importer precision machined parts
President: Robert H Chandler
Number Employees: 7
Square Footage: 23200

28117 R.I. Enterprises
PO Box 351
Hernando, MS 38632-0351

662-429-7863
Fax: 662-429-2561
Wire display racks
President: R Gates
Secretary/Treasurer: B Gates
VP: L Gates
Estimated Sales: $500,000-$1 Million
Number Employees: 19
Square Footage: 44000

28118 R.L. Instruments
16009 Arminta Street
Van Nuys, CA 91406

818-780-1800
Fax: 818-780-1978
Refractometer products, spectrophotometers, pH
meters and related products, and microwave mois-
ture and solids analyzer
Owner: April Hodges
Estimated Sales: Below $5 Million
Number Employees: 1-4

28119 R.N.C. Industries
3105 Sweetwater Road
Suite 220
Lawrenceville, GA 30044-8547

770-368-8453
Fax: 770-368-8490 888-844-3864
sales@rncind.com www.rncind.com
Packaging supplies: gift wrap, labels, boxes and
containers.
President: Lawrence Clark
Cfo: Charlotta Clark
Marketing: Taylor Clark
Contact: Salma Abdullahi
 salma@rncind.com
Estimated Sales: $4.9 Million
Number Employees: 46

28120 R.P. Childs Stamp Company
161 Prokop Av
Ludlow, MA 1056

413-733-1211
Fax: 413-737-6865
Marking devices, rubber stamps, parts, pads, num-
bering machines and time recorders
President: Roland Stebbins
Estimated Sales: Below $5 Million
Number Employees: 2 to 4

28121 R.R. Scheibe Company
29 Westgate Rd
Newton Center, MA 2459

508-584-4900
Fax: 508-580-2644 www.scheibeco.com
Serving trays, snack tables and tray stands
Owner: Alan Hackel
Estimated Sales: Below $5 Million
Number Employees: 30

28122 RA Jones & Company
7800 Cooper Rd # 102
Cincinnati, OH 45242-7733

513-891-7800
Fax: 859-341-0519 www.rajones.com
Cartoners, pouch/sachet machines, multipackers,
case packers, robotics, integrated systems
President: Bonsild Gordon
Contact: Tanja Bruner
 tbruner@rajones.com
Estimated Sales: $80 Million
Number Employees: 1-4

28123 RAK Porcelain USA, Inc.
251 Solar Dr.
Suite 1000
Imperial, PA 15126

866-552-6980
Fax: 866-552-6980 info@rakporcelainusa.com
www.rakporcelain.com
Manufacturer and supplier of porcelain tableware.
Horeca & Co. Inc. is the official distributor in
Canada.
President & CEO, RAK Porcelain USA: John
Marino
Year Founded: 2006
Number Employees: 1,000-5,000
Square Footage: 1614500
Parent Co: Horeca & Co. Inc.

28124 RAM Center
5140 Moundview Dr
Red Wing, MN 55066

651-385-2271
Fax: 651-385-2180 800-309-5431
info@autoequipllc.com www.autoequipllc.com
Manufacturer and exporter of systems for robotic
packaging and material handling; including
palletizers for cold room and washdown applications
General Manager: Steve Halverson
R&D: Cory Doln
Executive VP: Dave Muelken
Quality Control: Dave Mulken
Director Sales/Marketing: Steve Valade
Estimated Sales: $10 - 20 Million
Number Employees: 20-49
Parent Co: RAM Center
Brands:
 Ram Center

28125 RAO Contract Sales Inc
94 Fulton St # 4
Paterson, NJ 07501-1200

201-652-1500
Fax: 973-279-6448 888-324-0020
info@rao.com www.rao.com

Manufacturer and exporter of menu and bulletin
boards, pedestal displays, etc
Owner: Brian Bergman
 brian@rao.com
Account Executive: George Cross
Account Executive: Marsha Holland
Estimated Sales: $1 - 5 Million
Number Employees: 5-9
Square Footage: 40000
Brands:
 Tak-Les

28126 RAO Design Intl
9451 Ainslie St
Schiller Park, IL 60176-1139
 847-671-6182
 Fax: 847-671-9276 raodesign@aol.com
 www.blow-fill-sealassociates.com
Turn-key operation setup, PET machines, engineer-
ing and consulting, blow mold making, blow-fill
seal machines, blow molding
CEO: Kumar Murkurthy
Marketing Director: David Muiukurthy
Manager: M Surya
 aptbfs@aol.com
Estimated Sales: $5-10 Million
Number Employees: 20-49

28127 RAPAC Inc
65 Industrial Park
Oakland, TN 38060-4048

 Fax: 901-465-1183 800-280-6333
 rapac.com
Plastic bottles and jars
Estimated Sales: $32 Million
Number Employees: 1-4
Square Footage: 50000

28128 RAS Process Equipment Inc
324 Meadowbrook Rd
Trenton, NJ 08691-2503
 609-371-1220
 Fax: 609-371-1200 www.ras-inc.com
Manufacturer and exporter of process equipment in-
cluding pressure vessels, heat exchangers, reactors,
columns and storage tanks
Owner: John Bonacorda
 jbonacorda@ras-inc.com
Director: John Bonacorda
VP: John Bonacorda
Estimated Sales: $5 - 10 Million
Number Employees: 20-49
Square Footage: 80000

**28129 RBA-Retailer's Bakers
Association**
14239 Park Center Drive
Laurel, MD 20707-5261
 301-725-2149
 Fax: 301-725-2187 301-725-2187
Communications Director: Dawn Rivera
Estimated Sales: $1 - 5 Million
Number Employees: 15

28130 RBM Manufacturing Co
1570 W Mission Blvd
Pomona, CA 91766-1247
 909-620-1333
 Fax: 909-620-6119 info@rbmcsi.com
Art technology for the bulk material handling industry; conveying, surge and distribution systems, vibratory conveyors, belt conveyors, bucket elevators,
controlled by the most advanced electronic instrumentation, either withconventional or computerized
President: Roobik Kureghian
 info@rbmcsi.com
Estimated Sales: Below $5 Million
Number Employees: 10-19

28131 RBS Fab Inc
230 N Hoernerstown Rd
Hummelstown, PA 17036-9562
 717-566-9513
 Fax: 717-566-9268 www.rbsfab.com
Custom designed food processing equipment
Owner: Terry Smith
 rbssabinc@verizon.net
CEO: Joann Smith
Office Manager: Denise Ajala
Production: Edward Rupp
Estimated Sales: $2.5-5 Million
Number Employees: 5-9
Square Footage: 48000

28132 RCS Limited
1301 Commerce Street
Birmingham, AL 35217-3603
 205-841-9955
 Fax: 205-841-2106
Designs and builds contractor for cold storage ware-
houses
Marketing/Sales: Laura Williams

28133 RDA Container Corp
70 Cherry Rd
Gates, NY 14624-2592
 585-247-2323
 Fax: 585-247-5680 www.rdacontainer.com
Corrugated boxes
President: Alan Brant
 alan@yahoo.com
Founder: Peter R. Brant
President: Peter R Brant
Sales Manager: Jack Fennell
Mngr.: Bob Bardeen
Estimated Sales: $10-20 Million
Number Employees: 50-99

28134 RDM International
11643 Otsego Street
North Hollywood, CA 91601-3628
 818-985-7654
 Fax: 818-760-2376 bobmoore@rdmintl.com
 www.rdmintl.com
Processor, importer and exporter of fruits including
frozen, dried, powderes, flakes and canned; also,
fruit concentrates and purees, oils, nuts, pumpkin,
sweet potatoes/yams and coconut
President/Sales: Bob Moore
Operations: Peri Abel
Number of Brands: 135
Number of Products: 280
Square Footage: 276000
Type of Packaging: Food Service, Private Label,
 Bulk
Brands:
 Beesweet Blueberries
 Berry Fine Raspberries
 Big Banana Perfet
 Big Boy Blazin Berries
 Big Red Rhubarb
 Bubba's Yams
 Fruit To the World
 Gourmet Brand Blackberries
 Mountain Mats' Apples
 Pacific Coconut
 Perfect Peach
 Petes Pumpkin
 Rain Sweet
 Rippin Cherries
 Tru Blue Blueberries

28135 RDM Technologies
4711 East 355 Street
Willoughby, OH 44094
Canada
 440-954-3500
 Fax: 440-954-3501 sales@bevcorp.com
 www.bevcorp.com
Estimated Sales: $1,000,000 - $2,499,999
Parent Co: Bevcorp LLC

28136 RDM-Sesco
4711 East 355 Street
Willoughby, OH 44094
 440-954-3500
 Fax: 440-954-3501 sales@bevcorp.com
 www.bevcorp.com
President: David Kemp Sr
CFO: Tim Frantz
Quality Control: Jim Hannah
Number Employees: 60

28137 RDS of Florida
6861 SW 196th Ave
Suite 203-204
Fort Lauderdale, FL 33332
 305-994-7756
 Fax: 305-772-1090 sales@rdsflorida.com
 www.rdsflorida.com
Restaurant point of sale systems including table and
quick service, wireless headsets and close circuit t.v
President: Joe Pollock
General Manager: Matt Sutton
Account Manager: David Henderson
Estimated Sales: $5 - 10 Million
Number Employees: 10-19

28138 REA Elektronik
7307 Young Dr
Suite B
Cleveland, OH 44146-5369
 440-460-0552
 Fax: 440-232-5335 www.rea-systeme.com
Owner: Ray Turchi
Contact: Gary Carr
 gary.carr@goarmy.com
Estimated Sales: $.5 - 1 million
Number Employees: 1-4

28139 REI Systems Inc
45335 Vintage Park Plz # 100
Sterling, VA 20166-6721
 703-256-2245
 Fax: 703-256-9372 info@reisystems.com
Custom-designed conveyor equipment and systems
CEO: Shyam Salona
 salona@reisys.com
Estimated Sales: $1 - 5 Million
Number Employees: 500-999

28140 REM Ohio Inc
11530 Century Blvd
Cincinnati, OH 45246-3305
 513-381-3700
 www.rem-oh.com
Chemical cleaners, sanitizers and detergents
President: Gary Farraria
VP: B Nelson
Controller: Larry Schirmann
Sales Manager: E Newman
Estimated Sales: $2.5 - 5 Million
Number Employees: 10-19
Square Footage: 200000

28141 RES & Associates
300 N Wolf Rd
Suite B
Wheeling, IL 60090-2900
 847-541-0080
 Fax: 847-541-0212 800-741-5919
President: Ralph E Squaglia Jr
Contact: Robert Seddon
 rseddon@res-associates.com
Estimated Sales: $500,000-$1 Million
Number Employees: 1-4

28142 RETROTECH, Inc
127 John Street
Suite 400
West Henrietta, NY 14586-9120
 585-924-6333
 Fax: 585-924-6334 866-915-2777
 www.retrotech.com
Automated warehousing systems
Vice President: Len DeWeerdt
Tactical Marketing Specialist: Cynthia Hamann
VP Operations: Peter Hartman
Estimated Sales: $10-20 Million
Number Employees: 100-249
Number of Brands: 2
Number of Products: 3

28143 REX Pure Foods
2121 Chartres St
New Orleans, LA 70116
 504-525-7305
 800-344-8314
 info@rexfoods.com www.rexfoods.com
Seafood spices and seasonings, sauces, blends, vine-
gar and mustard; packaging services
President: J Geldart
CEO: Jenni Ratliff
VP, Chief Marketing Officer: Gene Ratliff
Estimated Sales: $2.5 Million
Number Employees: 1-4
Type of Packaging: Consumer, Food Service, Bulk
Brands:
 Rex

28144 RFC Wire Forms Inc
525 Brooks St
Ontario, CA 91762-3702
 909-984-5500
 Fax: 909-984-2322 800-334-0937
 rfcmark@verizon.net www.rfcwireforms.com
Soft drink backs, displays and display cases, cooler
displays, cooler racks, custom design and manufacturing of displays and racks

President: Donald Kemby
rfcdon@aol.com
CFO: Jay Munoz
Vice President: Don Kemby
Research & Development: Greg Lunsmann
Quality Control: Donald Kemby
Sales Director: Mark Arriola
Production Manager: Jesse Dunn
Purchasing Manager: Mike Manning
Estimated Sales: $20-30 Million
Number Employees: 20-49
Square Footage: 30000

28145 RGF Environmental GroupInc

1101 W 13th St
Riviera Beach, FL 33404-6701

561-848-1826
Fax: 561-848-9454 800-842-7771
requests@rgf.com www.rgf.com
CEO: Ronald G Fink
rfink@rgf.com
Estimated Sales: $1 - 5 Million
Number Employees: 50-99

28146 RGN Developers

44 Gales Dr Apt 4
New Providence, NJ 7974

Fax: 908-665-6901 rgnsoft@aol.com
Design engineer specializing in software development, technology transfers, engineering specifications and start-up in food, dairy and pharmaceutical plants
President: Raja Nori
Estimated Sales: $2.5-5 Million
Number Employees: 4

28147 RH Forschner

P.O. Box 1212
Monroe, CT 06468-8212

203-929-6391
Fax: 203-925-2933 800-243-4032
web.orders@swissarmy.com www.swissarmy.com
Cutlery, knives, scabbards for cutting and deboning, safety apparel professional swiss knives
President: Susanne Recher
CEO: Carl Elsener
CFO: Thomas M Lupinski
CEO: Rick Taggart
Estimated Sales: $1-2.5 Million
Number Employees: 100-249

28148 RHG Products Company

599 Topeka Way
Suite 200
Castle Rock, CO 80109

303-663-1779
Fax: 319-366-7792 800-553-8131
www.tuckerusa.com
High level window washers, aluminum telescoping handles, brushes, detergent tablets, window and awning cleaning systems, spot free water
President: Irvin Lee Tucker
VP/General Manager: Robin Bradley Tucker
CFO: Robin Tucker
R&D: Robin Tucker
Quality Control: Robin Tucker
Estimated Sales: $5 - 10,000,000
Number Employees: 10-19
Brands:
Tucker

28149 RJ Jansen Company

10831 1st St
Highway KR
Sturtevant, WI 53177

262-884-0511
Fax: 262-884-0512
Chocolate equipment: decorating, enrobing, pumping systems. Cluster machine, coaters, cutting machines: carmel, cream centers; depositors: chocolate, liquid, portable, wire-cut
President: Richard Jansen
Estimated Sales: $3 - 5 Million
Number Employees: 5-9

28150 RJ Jansen Confectionery

10831 1st Street
Sturtevant, WI 53177-3338

262-884-0511
Fax: 262-884-0512 richard@rjjansen.com
www.rjjansen.com

Enrobers, depositors, coaters and packaging equipment, bag and pouch sealers, bag filling and sealing machines, bag forming machines
President: Richard Jansen
richard@rjjansen.com
Estimated Sales: Below 1 Million
Number Employees: 5-9

28151 RJ Wetrz Products Company

519 Austin Avenue
Pittsburgh, PA 15243-2027

724-926-4566
Manufacturer of kits, accessories

28152 RJO Produce Distr Inc

1177 W Shaw Ave
Fresno, CA 93711-3704

559-222-7200
Fax: 559-222-7277 www.rjoproduce.com
Procurement, inspection and delivery of fruits and berries. Also market analyses reports, marketing, and inventory control
Owner: John O'Rourke
sales@rjoproduce.com
Estimated Sales: $3 - 5 Million
Number Employees: 5-9

28153 RJR Executive Search

11999 Katy Freeway
Suite 585
Houston, TX 77079

281-368-8550
Fax: 281-368-8560 sschorejs@rjrsearch.com
www.rjrsearch.com
Executive search firm specializing in selection and placement of consumer packaged goods and services personnel
Research Assistant: Sherry Schorejs
VP: Ray Schorejs
VP: Bob O Dell
Industrial Sales / Operations: Vince Lyden
vlyden@rjrsearch.com
Estimated Sales: $1 - 3 Million
Number Employees: 5-9

28154 RL Instruments

9 Main St # 2e
Douglas, MA 01516

508-476-1935
Fax: 508-476-1927 800-427-4361
www.rlinstruments.com
Refractometers, spectrophotometers, moisture balances, pH meters, and parts and service
Owner: April Hodges
Sales Manager: Todd Hodges
Estimated Sales: Below $5 Million
Number Employees: 5-9

28155 RLS Equipment Company

PO Box 282
Egg Harbor City, NJ 08215-0282

609-965-0074
Fax: 609-965-2509 800-527-0197
www.rlsequipment.com
Winery and fruit processing equipment
President: Robert L Stollenwerk
Estimated Sales: $.5 - 1 million
Number Employees: 7

28156 RLS Logistics

Rosario Leo Building
2185 Main Road
Newfield, NJ 08344

856-694-2500
800-579-9900
info@rlslogistics.com www.rlslogistics.com
Transportation, warehousing and fulfillment to the frozen and refrigerated food industry.
Chief Executive Officer, President: Anthony Leo
Vice President of Development: John Gaudet
Director of Operations: Greg Deitz

28157 RM Waite Inc

45 6th Street
Clintonville, WI 54929

715-823-4327
Fax: 715-823-7311 rmwaite@frontiernet.net
Replacement parts and rebuiling machinery for meat processors
President: Rick Waite
VP: Marsha Waite
Estimated Sales: $768,000
Number Employees: 6
Square Footage: 400

28158 (HQ)RMF Companies

4417 Martha Truman Rd
Grandview, MO 64030-1119

816-839-9258
info@rmfworks.com
www.rmfworks.com
Manufacturer and exporter of food processing equipment focusing on flow-thru massaging, marinating, deboning and portioning; vacuum packaging equipment; freezers and chilling equipment; and engineering services, including turnkeysystems and plant design. Parent company of RMF Steel, Challenge RMF & RMF Freezers.
President/CEO: Jeff Brauner
Estimated Sales: $50-100 Million
Number Employees: 50-99

28159 RMI-C/Rotonics Manaufacturing

736 Birginal Dr
Bensenville, IL 60106-1213

630-773-9510
Fax: 630-773-4274 chicago@rotonics.com
www.rotonics.com
Manufacturer and exporter of polyethylene containers molded from FDA/USDA approved resin including material handling, shipping and storage; also, barrels, drums, tilt trucks, mobile bins, totes and custom molded parts available
Manager: Jay Rule
Sales Director: Michael Morrison
Estimated Sales: $20 - 50 Million
Number Employees: 50-99
Square Footage: 38000
Parent Co: Rotonics Manufacturing
Type of Packaging: Bulk
Brands:
Bulkatilt
Bulkitank
Gripper
Tabletote

28160 RMX Global Logistics

35715 U.S.
Highway 40 Building B
Evergreen, CO 80439

888-824-7365
Fax: 303-674-3803 888-824-7365
www.rmxglobal.com
Shelf stable, high barrier food packaging
President: Steve Whaley

28161 ROI Software, LLC

P.O. Box 2747
Knoxville, TN 37901-2747

865-522-2211
Fax: 865-522-7907 www.resourceopt.com
Software; also, consulting services available
President: T Brient Mayfield
Estimated Sales: Below $5 Million
Number Employees: 10-19

28162 RPA Process Technologies

PO Box 1087
Marblehead, MA 01945-5087

781-631-9707
Fax: 781-631-9507 800-631-9707
www.rosedisplays.com
Manufacturer and exporter of displays including 3-D hanging, hanging sign, window and hall; also, price card holders
President: Michael Hoffman
Assistant to President: Carol Jones
Sales Manager: Tracy Hatfield
Number Employees: 15
Square Footage: 12800
Brands:
Biclops Installation Tool
Clearly Invisible Hooks
Gotcha - Sure Snap Sign Holder
One-Up
Perfect Hanging System
Ropole
Smartbox
Supergotcha

28163 RSI ID Technologies

I-94 at McKnight Road
St. Paul, MN 55144-1000

619-656-2515
Fax: 619-872-0662 888-364-3577

solutions.3m.com/wps/portal/3M/en_US/WW3/Country/

President: John Freund
CEO: Wolff Bielas
Chief Technical Officer: Bruce Roesner
Estimated Sales: $1 - 5 Million
Number Employees: 50-99
Parent Co: 3M

28164 RTG Films
120 New Britain Blvd
Chalfont, PA 18914-1832

215-822-0600
Fax: 215-822-0662 film@rtgpkg.com
www.rtgpkg.com
Flexible Packaging Films consisting of Polypropylene, Polyethylene, Lidding, Forming, Printed, Laminations
Sales: Tom Cheatle
Estimated Sales: Below $5 Million
Number Employees: 10-19
Parent Co: Roberts Technology Group, Inc.

28165 RTI Inc
1325 Williams Dr
Marietta, GA 30066

770-590-4300
Fax: 770-590-4313 800-937-1290
info@internetRTI.com
Point of purchase and inventory software
Owner: James Clutter
Sales/Marketing Executive: Greg Waddell
Contact: Lane Alexander
alexander.lane@internetrti.com
Estimated Sales: $10-20 Million
Number Employees: 20-49

28166 RTI Laboratories
31628 Glendale St
Livonia, MI 48150-1827

734-422-5342
Fax: 734-422-5342 information@rtilab.com
www.rtilab.com
Laboratory facility specializing in environmental, chemical, metallurgical, and industrial hygiene analyses
President: Jerry Singh
CFO: Ralph Davis
VP: Fred Hoitash
Quality Control: Charles O'Bryan
Sales Director: Patricia Jennings
Number Employees: 20-49
Square Footage: 36000

28167 RTI Shelving Systems
40-19 80th Street
Elmhurst, NY 11373

212-279-0435
Fax: 212-465-1795 800-223-6210
info@rtishelving.com www.rtishelving.com
Manufacturer and exporter of steel filing systems, steel and wire shelving, racks, bins and storage systems
Owner: Bhim Motilal
Office Manager: Darryl Buyckes
Estimated Sales: $5 - 10 Million
Number Employees: 10-19

28168 RTS Packaging
250 N Mannheim Rd
Hillside, IL 60162-1835

708-338-2800
Fax: 708-338-2882 webmaster@rocktenn.com
www.rocktenn.com
Corrugated paper and fiberboard box partitions
Manager: Mary Sachs
CFO: Nancy Garner
Estimated Sales: $20 - 50 Million
Number Employees: 100-249
Parent Co: Sonoco Products Company

28169 RTS Packaging
869 State Route 12
Frenchtown, NJ 08825-4223

908-782-0505
Fax: 908-782-0583 www.rocktenn.com
Wine industry corrugated partitions
Manager: Jeff Connlain
Manager: Greg Lawrence
glawrence@rocktenn.com
Estimated Sales: $25-50 Million
Number Employees: 100-249

28170 RTS Packaging
250 N Mannheim Rd
Hillside, IL 60162-1835

708-338-2800
Fax: 708-338-2882 800-558-6984
webmaster@rocktenn.com
Wine industry fiber partitions
Manager: Mary Sachs
Manager: Betch Cambell
Estimated Sales: $20 - 50 Million
Number Employees: 100-249

28171 RTS Packaging
16 Washington Ave
Scarborough, ME 04074-8311

207-883-8921
Fax: 207-883-5189 www.rtspackaging.com
Packaging
General Manager: David Boudreau
Estimated Sales: $20 - 50 Million
Number Employees: 50-99

28172 RVS
5151 Allendale Lane
Taneytown, MD 21787-2155

410-756-2600
Fax: 410-756-6450 www.evapco.com
Architecture and engineering firm providing facility planning, design and construction services to the food and beverage industries.we ofer architecture planning and design and civil structural mechanical and electrical design formanufacture warehouse and distribution facilities.
President: Bill Bartley
Estimated Sales: $5,000,000 - $9,999,999
Number Employees: 5-9

28173 (HQ)RW Products
101 Heartland Blvd
Edgewood, NY 11717-8315

631-349-8400
Fax: 516-349-8407 800-345-1022
www.rwproducts.com
Retail displays, racks and fixtures
General Manager: Jon Scott
VP Sales: Martin Baum
Estimated Sales: $.5 - 1 million
Number Employees: 1-4

28174 RWH Packaging
PO Box 6335
Oakland, CA 94603-0335

510-535-0700
Fax: 510-535-0702
Wine industry packaging
President: Randy Haight
Estimated Sales: Below $5 Million
Number Employees: 10

28175 RWI Resources
3401 Old Wagon Rd
Marietta, GA 30062-5513

770-977-3950
Fax: 770-973-4299 866-545-4794
Developer and marketer of carbonated beverage
Estimated Sales: Below $500,000
Number Employees: 5-9

28176 RXI Silgan Specialty Plastics
541 Technology Dr
Triadelphia, WV 26059-2711

304-547-9100
Fax: 304-547-9200
silgan_sales@silganplastics.com
www.silganplastics.com
Manufacturer and exporter of plastic caps, jar covers, sifter and plug fitments and bottles; custom injection molding available
VP Engineering: Vice Exner
VP Sales: Tony Marceau
Operations Manager: Phil Sanderson
Estimated Sales: $36 Million
Number Employees: 100-249
Square Footage: 168400
Parent Co: Silgan Plastics
Type of Packaging: Consumer, Food Service, Private Label, Bulk
Other Locations:
 RXI Plastics
 Richmond VA
Brands:
 Cs Assembled

28177 Rabbeco
22900 Miles Rd
Cleveland, OH 44128

212-564-0664
Fax: 973-529-0224 mb@packlinecorp.com
www.packline.com
Automatic and semiautomatic filling, sealing and capping systems, cup filling and sealing, bag forming, filling and sealing, bottle lines, shrink wrapping machines, fillers for liquid and paste products
President: Michael Beilinson
Estimated Sales: $.5 - 1 million
Number Employees: 1-4

28178 Rabin Worldwide
731 Sansome St
2nd Floor
San Francisco, CA 94111

415-522-5700
Fax: 415-522-5701 info@rabin.com
www.rabin.com
Owner: Irving Rabin
Estimated Sales: $15 Million
Number Employees: 20-49

28179 Raburn
1060 Thorndale Ave
Elk Grove Vlg, IL 60007-6747

847-350-2229
Fax: 847-350-2657 www.ecolab.com
Manager: Mark Swisher
Estimated Sales: $50 - 100 Million
Number Employees: 50-99
Parent Co: ECOLAB

28180 Racine County Court Cmmssnr
730 Wisconsin Ave
Racine, WI 53403-1238

262-636-3181
Fax: 262-636-3689 800-242-4202
www.wicourts.gov
Labels including litho printed, pressure sensitive, die-cut and gummed; also, commercial printing services available
President: James A. Ladwig
Manager: Anisa Dunn
anisa.dunn@goracine.org
Estimated Sales: Below $5 Million
Number Employees: 10-19

28181 Racine Paper Box Manufacturing
3522 W Potomac Ave
Chicago, IL 60651

773-227-3900
Fax: 773-227-3983
Manufacturer and exporter of boxes including set-up, fancy and folding
President: Navnit Patel
Contact: Atul Patel
atul.patel@ipaksolutions.com
Estimated Sales: $1-2.5 Million
Number Employees: 10-19

28182 Racket Group
713 Walnut St
Kansas City, MO 64106-1615

816-283-0490
Fax: 816-842-8998 mail@racketgroup.com
www.racketgroup.com
Tableware for the airline catering industry
President and CFO: Joseph Hoagland
mail@michadamenities.com
Estimated Sales: $5 - 10 Million
Number Employees: 10-19

28183 Racks
7684 St. Andrews Avenue
San Diego, CA 92154

619-661-0987
Fax: 619-661-0988 www.racksinc.com
Point of Purchase displays.
President: Doug Wall
CFO: Don Wall
VP: Doug Wall
Sales: William Schiffman
Contact: Rick Kniffin
rkniffin@racksinc.com
Production Manager: Mark Kleffel
Estimated Sales: $20-50 Million
Square Footage: 100000

28184 Raco Mfg & Engineering Co
1400 62nd St
Emeryville, CA 94608-2099
510-658-6713
Fax: 510-658-3153 800-722-6999
sales@racoman.com www.alarmagent.com
Controlled atmosphere monitors, alarms, controls
and probes
President: Constance Brown
cbrown@racoman.com
VP Sales/Marketing: James Brown
Estimated Sales: $20 - 50 Million
Number Employees: 100-249
Brands:
Chatterbox
Verbatim

28185 Radcliffe System
Suite 305
Toronto, ON M2J 4R4
Canada
416-493-3844
Fax: 416-493-1616
Estimated Sales: $1 - 5 Million
Number Employees: 5-9

28186 Radding Signs
PO Box 4653
Springfield, MA 1101
413-736-5400
Fax: 413-736-1866
Illuminated and nonilluminated signs including cus-
tom made electric, office building, directional, ga-
rage and outdoor advertising
Estimated Sales: $1-2.5 Million
Number Employees: 10-19
Parent Co: Rador

28187 Rademaker USA
5218 Hudson Dr
Hudson, OH 44236-3738
330-650-2345
Fax: 330-656-2802
rademaker@rademakerusa.com
www.rademaker.com
President: Ronald Gates
rgates@rademaker.com
Vice President: William Palumbo
Estimated Sales: $5 - 10 Million
Number Employees: 10-19

28188 Radiant Industrial Solutions
2121 Brittmoore Rd # 3900
#3900
Houston, TX 77043-2227
713-972-0196
Fax: 713-974-0253 sales@radiantuv.com
www.radiantuv.com
Waste water throught the use of ultravi-
olet light.
President: Troy Smith
Director Business Strategy: Mike Guettette
Manager: Collin Brack
cbrack@radiantuv.com
Technical Manager: John Shol
Number Employees: 10-19

28189 Radiation Processing Division
P.O. Box 5064
Parsippany, NJ 07054-6064
973-267-5660
Fax: 973-267-5667 800-442-1969
Manufacturer and exporter of radiation sanitation
and pathogen elimination equipment for the removal
of bacteria from raw materials and food ingedients
President: Robert Solotist
President: Bruce Welt PhD
Estimated Sales: $1 - 5 Million
Number Employees: 20-49
Square Footage: 120000
Parent Co: Alpha Omega Technology

28190 Radio Cap Company
1331 N Pine St
San Antonio, TX 78202-1219
210-472-1649
Fax: 800-766-4812
Advertising promotion caps
VP: Christopher Edelen
VP Sales: Eileen Guina
Estimated Sales: $1 - 5 Million
Number Employees: 1-4
Parent Co: Norwood Promotional Products

28191 Radio Frequency Co Inc
150 Dover Rd
Millis, MA 02054-1335
508-376-9555
Fax: 508-376-9944 rfc@radiofrequency.com
www.radiofrequency.com
Manufacturer and exporter of radio frequency
post-baking dryers and pasteurization equipment.
President: Tim Clark
tclark@radiofrequency.com
Estimated Sales: $5 - 10 Million
Number Employees: 20-49
Square Footage: 26
Parent Co: Radio Frequency Company
Brands:
Macrowave

28192 Radius Display Products
800 Fabric Xpress Way
Dallas, TX 75234-7260
972-406-1221
Fax: 972-406-1321 888-322-7429
info@radiusdp.com www.radiusdp.com
Manufacturer and exporter of table skirting and
clips.
President: Darla Andrews
dandrews@radiusdisplay.com
CEO: Michelle Stacy
VP Sales: Sherry Day
Estimated Sales: $2.5 - 5 Million
Number Employees: 50-99
Brands:
Omniclip Ii

28193 Rafael Soler
135 Walworth Avenue
White Plains, NY 10606-2720
914-761-4609
Fax: 914-683-3755 info@deprosa.dk
www.derprosa.es
Laminations, labels, acrylic and PVDC coatings,
bottle labels, food packing
President: Raphael Hernandez Soler

28194 Ragtime
4218 Jessup Rd
Ceres, CA 95307-9604
209-667-5525
Fax: 209-634-2667 ragtimewest@earthlink.net
www.ragtimewest.com
Manufacturer and exporter of coin and floppy disk
operated pianos, monkey organs, animated food dis-
pensers and dioramas and calliopes; importer of dec-
orative plastic pipe
Owner: Ken Caulkins
ken@ragtime.com
Manager: Glenn Kern
Estimated Sales: $1-2.5 Million
Number Employees: 5-9
Square Footage: 40000
Brands:
Active Magnetics

**28195 Rahmann Belting & Industrial
Rubber Products**
3100 Northwest Blvd
Gastonia, NC 28052-1167
704-864-0308
Fax: 704-868-4651 888-248-8148
Manufacturer and exporter of industrial conveyors
and transmission belting including oriented nylon,
monofilament and food, etc
Owner: Ron Dayton
CEO: Ronald Dayton
Estimated Sales: $2.5 - 5 Million
Number Employees: 5-9
Square Footage: 60000

28196 Rahr Malting Co
800 West First Ave
Shakopee, MN 55379
952-445-1431
info@rahr.com
www.rahr.com
Malt and brewing supplies.
President: Ron Johnson
Contact: April Abbott
aabbott@rahr.com
Year Founded: 1847
Estimated Sales: $43.6 Million
Number Employees: 100-249
Type of Packaging: Bulk

28197 Railex Corp
8902 Atlantic Ave
Ozone Park, NY 11416-1497
718-845-5454
Fax: 718-738-1020 800-352-3244
tech@railexcorp.com www.railexcorp.com
Supplier and exporter of electric and stationary coat
and hat check equipment; also, garment racks
President: Abe Rutkovsky
railex@railexcorp.com
VP: Sam Rutkovsky
Sales: Bill Quirke
Estimated Sales: $10 - 20 Million
Number Employees: 20-49
Square Footage: 70000
Brands:
Railex

28198 RainSoft Water Treatment System
2080 E. Lunt Ave
Elk Grove Vlg, IL 60007
847-437-9400
Fax: 847-437-1594 comments@rainsoft.com
www.rainsoft.com
Manufacturer and exporter of water treatment equip-
ment including filters, purifiers, reverse osmosis sys-
tems and ultraviolet
President: Robert Ruhstorfer
Commercial Department: Bob Krinner
Estimated Sales: $1 - 5 Million
Number Employees: 100-249
Square Footage: 280000
Brands:
Amazon
Classic Apollo
P-12 Hydefiner
Ultrefiner

28199 Rainbow Industrial Products
825 Morgantown Rd
Reading, PA 19607-9533
610-373-1400
Fax: 610-373-7448 800-426-5751
Manufactures modular plastic belt and flat top
chains and markets a full line of stainless/carbon
steel, case conveyor and multi-flex chains, custom
molded rubber inserts
President: Christopher Nigon
Estimated Sales: $5-10 Million
Number Employees: 500-999

28200 Rainbow Neon Sign Company
202 S Lockwood Dr
Houston, TX 77011-3198
713-923-2759
Fax: 713-923-2875
Advertising signs including neon, plastic and flex
face lighted
President: Louis Freund
VP/Secretary: Naida Freund
Estimated Sales: $500,000-$1 Million
Number Employees: 5-9
Square Footage: 18000

28201 Rainbow Sign Co
257 W 3300 S
Salt Lake City, UT 84115-3432
801-466-7856
Fax: 801-466-1144 www.rainbowsign.com
Neon signs
Owner/Sales: Vincent Coley
Owner/ Sales: Vince Coley
Office Manager: Barbara Barnes
Estimated Sales: $1 - 2.5 Million
Number Employees: 5-9

28202 Rairdon Dodge Chrysler Jeep
12828 NE 124th St
Kirkland, WA 98034-8309
425-821-1777
Fax: 425-814-3180
www.dodgechryslerjeepofkirkland.com
Manufacturer and exporter of checkstands and dis-
play fixtures
Owner: Jack Carroll
Director Sales: Ginny Hansen
Estimated Sales: $5-10 Million
Number Employees: 50-99
Square Footage: 680000

28203 Ralph L. Mason
8344 Patey Woods Rd
Newark, MD 21841
410-632-1766
Fax: 410-632-1142
Wooden pallets
VP: Tom Mason
Plant Manager: Bruce Wood
Estimated Sales: $1 - 5 Million
Number Employees: 10-19
Square Footage: 120000

28204 Ralph's Grocery Company
1014 Vine Street
Cincinnati, OH 45202-1100
310-884-9000
Fax: 310-884-2601 888-437-3496
www.ralphs.com
General groceries: bakery products, beverages,
meats, deli and seafood.
President: Donna Giordano
Estimated Sales: $100-500 Million
Number Employees: 500-999
Parent Co: the Kroger Company
Brands:
Ralphs

28205 Ralphs Pugh Conveyor Rollers
3931 Oregon St
Benicia, CA 94510-1101
707-745-6363
Fax: 707-745-3942 800-486-0021
sales@ralphs-pugh.com www.ralphs-pugh.com
Manufacturer and exporter of rollers, idlers and
bearings for conveyors
President: William Pugh
williamg@ralphs-pugh.com
Vice President: Tom Anderson
Estimated Sales: $5 - 10 Million
Number Employees: 20-49

28206 Ram Equipment Co
W227N913 Westmound Dr
Waukesha, WI 53186-1700
262-513-1114
Fax: 262-513-1115 tiefmach@execpc.com
www.tiefmach.com
Manufacturer and exporter of baking, blending and
batching equipment, bins, control systems, enrobers,
extruders and feeders; manufacturer of custom,
pump feeding systems for pumping high viscosity
products for food and industrialapplications
President: James E Tiefenthaler
jtief@tiefmach.com
VP: Norman Searle
Estimated Sales: Less Than $500,000
Number Employees: 1-4
Number of Brands: 2
Number of Products: 20
Square Footage: 4800

28207 Ram Industries
PO Box 610
Erwin, TN 37650-0610
423-743-6126
Fax: 423-743-6128 800-523-3883
Heat sealed plastic and vinyl products including ad-
vertising novelties, bags, date code label pouches,
3-ring binders, menu covers and ticket, notepad and
guest check holders
VP: Keith Patton
Director Sales: Jack Degatis
Estimated Sales: $1 - 5 Million
Parent Co: Plasco Products

28208 Ram Machinery Corp
11 Cricket Ln
Burlington, CT 06013-1301
860-673-5511
Fax: 860-675-9419
miller@rammachinerycorp.com
Used packaging and production equipment
President: Richard Miller
Estimated Sales: $1-2.5 Million
Number Employees: 5-9

28209 Ramco Innovations Inc
1207 Maple St
West Des Moines, IA 50265-4497
515-225-6933
Fax: 515-225-6933 800-280-6933
www.ramcoi.com
President: Hank Norem
hnorem@ramcoinnovations.com

Estimated Sales: $10 - 20 Million
Number Employees: 20-49

28210 (HQ)Ramco Systems Corp
3150 US Highway 1 # 206
Lawrence Twp, NJ 08648-2420
609-620-4800
Fax: 609-620-4860 800-472-6461
www.ramco.com
Computer software services and prepackaged soft-
ware
Vice Chairman/Managing Director/CEO: P R
Venketrama Raja
CFO: K Ramachandran
Senior VP: Bivek Luthra
bivekluthra@rsc.ramco.com
Chief Marketing Officer: Barbara Angius Saxby
COO: Kamesh Ramamoorthly
Estimated Sales: $20.7 Million
Number Employees: 20-49
Other Locations:
San Jose CA
Frankfurt, Germany
Central Milton, UK
Basel, Switzerland
New Delhi, India
Malaysia, Asia
Singapore, Asia
Durban, South Africa
Dubia, Middle East

28211 Ramondin USA Inc
2557 Napa Vly Corporate Dr # G
Suite G
Napa, CA 94558-6295
707-944-2277
Fax: 707-257-1408 www.ramondin.com
Wine industry capsules
Manager: Steve Galvan
Estimated Sales: $1 - 3 Million
Number Employees: 5-9

28212 Ramoneda Bros Stave Mill
13452 Rixeyville Rd
Culpeper, VA 22701
540-825-9166
Fax: 540-547-3271
Manufacturer and exporter of oak staves
Owner: Vincent Ramoneda
ramonedabros@aol.com
Partner: Vincent Ramoneda
Manager: Vincent Ramoneda
Estimated Sales: $5 - 10 Million
Number Employees: 5-9

28213 Ramsay Signs Inc
9160 SE 74th Ave
Portland, OR 97206-9345
206-623-3100
Fax: 503-777-0220 www.ramsaysigns.com
Neon and electrical indoor and outdoor advertising
signs
Owner: Darryl Paulsen
General Manager: Joe Gibson
VP: John Olds
Estimated Sales: Less Than $500,000
Number Employees: 1-4

28214 Ramsey Winch Co
4707 N Mingo Rd
Tulsa, OK 74117-5904
918-438-2760
Fax: 918-438-6888 info@ramsey.com
www.ramsey.com
Checkweighers, conveyor accesories including belt
tracking, conveyors and metal detecting
CEO: Bruce Barron
Chairman of the Board: Robert Heffron
Estimated Sales: $25-50 Million
Number Employees: 250-499

28215 Rancolio North America
8102 Lemont Rd # 1200
Woodridge, IL 60517-7773
630-427-1703
Fax: 630-493-4265 www.rancilio.com
VP: Glenn Surlet
Contact: Chris Gittens
cgittens@ranciliogroupna.com
Estimated Sales: $300,000-500,000
Number Employees: 1-4

28216 (HQ)Rand-Whitney Group LLC
1 Agrand St
Worcester, MA 01607-1699
508-791-2301
Fax: 508-792-1578 www.randwhitney.com
Paper, wooden and corrugated boxes and wooden
skids and crates; also, plastic foam fabricating and
molding
President: David Walsh
CEO: Edwin Davis
edavis@randwhitney.com
CEO: Peter Hamilton
Estimated Sales: $10 - 20 Million
Number Employees: 500-999

28217 (HQ)Rand-Whitney Group LLC
1 Agrand St
Worcester, MA 01607-1699
508-791-2301
Fax: 508-792-1578 joconnor@randwhitney.com
www.randwhitney.com
Corrugated boxes, containers, displays and protec-
tive packaging
President: Robert Kraft
CEO: Edwin Davis
edavis@randwhitney.com
CEO: Edwin Davis
Sales Manager: Jerry O'Connor
Estimated Sales: $20 - 50 Million
Number Employees: 500-999

28218 Rand-Whitney Group LLC
1 Agrand St
Worcester, MA 01607-1699
508-791-2301
Fax: 508-792-1578 www.randwhitney.com
Folding paper boxes, cartons and containers
President & CEO: Nicholas Smith
Estimated Sales: $50,000,000 - $99,999,999
Number Employees: 500-999
Parent Co: Kraft Group LLC

28219 Rand-Whitney Packaging Corp
166 Corporate Dr
Suite 200
Portsmouth, NH 03801-6815
508-791-2301
Fax: 603-822-7396 www.randwhitney.com
Corugated containers
President/CEO: Edwin Davis
VP (Rand-Whitney): Dwight Hamlin
Contact: Beth Saengsour
beths@randwhitney.com
Operations Manager: Raymond Hey
Estimated Sales: Less Than $500,000
Number Employees: 1-4
Square Footage: 160000
Parent Co: Rand-Whitney Group LLC

28220 Randall Manufacturing Inc
722 N Church Rd
Elmhurst, IL 60126-1402
630-782-0001
Fax: 630-782-0003 800-323-7424
info@randallmfg.com www.randallmfg.com
Manufacturer and exporter of bulkheads for refriger-
ator trailer partitions, plastic strip curtains for cool-
ers and freezers and insulated pallet covers and
curtain walls
President: Fred Jevaney
fjevaney@randallmfg.com
CFO: Philip Pick
VP: Fred Jevaney
Number Employees: 50-99
Square Footage: 80000
Type of Packaging: Food Service, Bulk
Brands:
Conservador
Insul-Wall
Tough One

28221 Randall Printing
707 Centre Street
Brockton, MA 02302-3310
508-588-3830
Fax: 508-588-3830
Labels, forms and booklets
Estimated Sales: Less than $500,000
Number Employees: 1-4

28222 Randell ManufacturingUnified Brands
252 South Coldwater Road
Weidman, MI 48893

Fax: 888-864-7636 888-994-7636
unifiedbrands.net
Stainless steel preparation tables, custom equipment, refrigerators, freezers, precise temperature solutions, equipment stands, and hot food tables.
Estimated Sales: $50 - 100 Million
Number Employees: 250-499
Parent Co: Dover Corporation
Brands:
Rancraft
Randell
Ranserve

28223 Randware Industries
P.O. Box 414
Prospect Heights, IL 60070-0414
847-299-8884
Fax: 847-299-8885 info@randware.com
www.randware.com
Food display items including chafing dishes with logos
Manager: Neal Katz
Estimated Sales: $3 - 5 Million
Number Employees: 1-4
Brands:
Chafer Shield

28224 Ranger Blade Manufacturing Company
PO Box 205
1561 South Main
Traer, IA 50675

Fax: 319-478-8298 800-377-7860
info@rangerblade.com
Household and professional metal cutlery including processing and packaging machinery blades
President: Rex Betts
CFO: Louis Rausch
Quality Control: Matt Devick
Sales Manager: Steve Droste
Estimated Sales: $5 - 10 Million
Number Employees: 20-49
Square Footage: 32000
Parent Co: Clearline Cutlery

28225 Ranger Tool Co Inc
5786 Ferguson Rd
Memphis, TN 38134-4533
901-213-0458
Fax: 901-386-8088 800-737-9999
Manufacturer and exporter of peelers which remove cellulose casing from frankfurters and sausages
President: Eleanor Kiss
Estimated Sales: $2.5-5 Million
Number Employees: 5-9
Brands:
Apollo Peeler

28226 Rankin Delux
3245 Corridor Dr
Mira Loma, CA 91752-1030
951-685-0081
Fax: 951-685-0084 rankinone@aol.com
www.rankindelux.com
Broilers, griddles, hot plates, cheese melters, stock pot and oriental ranges, etc
President/CEO: Dick Jones
Chairman: William Rankin
VP: Peggy Jones
Manager: Virna Alcantara
rankinone@aol.com
Estimated Sales: $2.5-5 Million
Number Employees: 20-49

28227 Ranpak Corp
7990 Auburn Rd
Painesville, OH 44077-9701
440-354-4445
Fax: 440-639-2198 800-726-7257
inquiries@ranpak.com www.ranpak.com
Packaging, cushioning
President: David Gabrielsen
CEO: Dave Gabrielsen
dgabrielsen@ranpak.com
Estimated Sales: $20 - 50 Million
Number Employees: 100-249

28228 Ransco Industries
1655 Mesa Verde Avenue
Suite 250
Ventura, CA 93003-6518
805-487-7777
Fax: 805-486-7024
Industrial refrigeration and freezing equipment; also, design and construction services available
VP Product: Robert Briner
Marketing Manager: Taylor Hobson
Sales Manager: Lou Coppo
Production Manager: Jim Topp
Estimated Sales: $10-20 Million
Number Employees: 50-99

28229 Rapa Products (USA)
1 Depot Lane
Seabrook, NH 03874-4492
603-474-5508
Fax: 603-474-3919
Natural casings
Estimated Sales: $1-5 Million
Number Employees: 8

28230 Rapak
1201 Windham Pkwy # D
Suite D
Romeoville, IL 60446-1699
815-372-3670
Fax: 630-296-2195 www.rapak.com
Bag-in-Box liquid packaging systems for dairy, edible oil, fruits/purees, juices, liquid egg, post mix/syrup, sauces, water, wine
President: Kevin Grogan
kevin.gorgan@rapak.com
SVP: Paul Petriekis
Marketing/Sales Director: Pierre Ferrai
VP Sales: Joe Pranckus
Number Employees: 100-249
Square Footage: 121000
Parent Co: DS Smith Group

28231 Rapat Corp
919 Odonnel St
Hawley, MN 56549-4313
218-483-3344
Fax: 218-483-3535 800-325-6377
www.rapat.com
Manufacturer and exporter of material handling equipment including conveyors and conveyor belting
Owner: Thomas Sparrow
Sales Manager: Greg Deal
tsparrow@rapat.com
Estimated Sales: $10-20 Million
Number Employees: 50-99

28232 (HQ)Rapid Displays Inc
4300 W 47th St
Chicago, IL 60632-4404
773-927-5000
Fax: 773-927-6446 800-356-5775
info@rapiddisplays.com www.rapiddisplays.com
Manufacturer and designer of advertising point of purchase displays
President: David Abramson
dabramson@rapiddisplays.com
President: David Abramson
VP: Brian Mc Cormick
Quality Control: Jim Guadgnola
VP/Sales Manager: Pierre Pype
Estimated Sales: $20 - 50 Million
Number Employees: 100-249
Square Footage: 360000

28233 Rapid Industries Inc
4003 Oaklawn Dr
Louisville, KY 40219-2701
502-968-3645
Fax: 502-968-6331 800-787-4381
info@rapidindustries.com www.rapidi.com
Manufacturer, importer and exporter of conveyors including trolley, enclosed track, power, free and floor
President: Mary Sheets
Controller: Jansen Nally
Marketing Manager: Paul McDonald
Sales Manager: Walt Hiner
Estimated Sales: $20 - 50 Million
Number Employees: 50-99
Type of Packaging: Bulk

28234 Rapid Pallet
100 Chestnut St
Jermyn, PA 18433-1433
570-876-4000
Fax: 570-876-4002
Manufacturer and exporter of lumber pallets
President: John Conrad
conrad@aacr.org
Estimated Sales: $10-20 Million
Number Employees: 50-99

28235 Rapid Rack Industries
14421 Bonelli St
City of Industry, CA 91746
626-333-7225
Fax: 626-333-5265 800-736-7225
www.rapidrack.com
Racks and mobile aisle and mezzanine systems; importer of wire storage racks; exporter of wire and storage rack
CEO: William Marvin
CEO: Vaughn Sucevich
Marketing Director: Clara Banegas
VP Sales: Steve Painter
Contact: Margaret Andrade
m_andrade@haylorfinancial.com
Operations Manager: Rosemarie Kodarte
Production Manager: Alfredo Calderon Kodarte
Plant Manager: Ed Sledge
Purchasing Manager: Dennis Fachler
Estimated Sales: $30 - 50 Million
Number Employees: 250-499
Square Footage: 192000
Parent Co: Hampshire Equity Partners
Type of Packaging: Consumer

28236 Raque Food Systems
11002 Decimal Dr
Louisville, KY 40299-2420
502-267-9641
Fax: 502-267-2352 sales@raque.com
www.raque.com
Food processing equipment
President: Glenn Raque
VP: Ed Robinson
Director Marketing: Tim Kent
IT Executive: David Ross
dcross07@yahoo.com
Estimated Sales: $20 - 50 Million
Number Employees: 50-99

28237 Rasco Industries
730 Tower Drive
Hamel, MN 55340
763-478-5100
Fax: 763-478-5101 800-537-3802
www.rasco.com
Screen sectional loading dock doors used with existing commercial rolling, high, vertical, standard lift and side sliding doors; also, overhead screen door systems and service door screen inserts
VP/Sales Manager: Rick Brown
Inside Sales Manager: Victoria Scully
Estimated Sales: $3-6 Million
Number Employees: 22
Square Footage: 100000
Brands:
The Bug Blocker

28238 Ratcliff Hoist Company
1655 Old County Rd
San Carlos, CA 94070-5205
650-595-3840
Fax: 650-595-5687
Material handling equipment including hoists
President: Bruce Ratcliff
ratcliffhoist@yahoo.com
Chairman: Ralph A Ratcliff
Estimated Sales: $1-2.5 Million
Number Employees: 10-19

28239 Rath Manufacturing Company
P.O. Box 389
Janesville, WI 53547
608-754-2222
Fax: 608-754-0889 800-367-7284
Manufacturer and exporter of stainless steel pipes and tubing
President: Harley Aplan
CEO: Michael G Schwartz
VP Sales: James Coenen
Estimated Sales: $50 - 100 Million
Number Employees: 100-249

28240 Rathe Productions
555 W 23rd Street
New York, NY 10011-1011
212-242-9000
Fax: 212-242-5676
Displays and exhibits
Contact: Ryan Peacock
rpeacock@rathe.com
Estimated Sales: $10 - 20 Million
Number Employees: 50-99

28241 Ratioflo Technologies
1284 Puerta Del Sol
San Clemente, CA 92673
949-369-2425
Fax: 949-369-2429 www.ratioflo.com
Fillers, pail lidders, and denesters
OWNER: Dale Tanner
Estimated Sales: Below $5 Million
Number Employees: 10
Number of Products: 5

28242 Rational Cooking Systems
895 American Lane
Schaumburg, IL 60173-4575
847-755-9583
Fax: 847-755-9584 888-320-7274
info@rationalusa.com
Manufacturer and importer of combination ovens
President: Peter Schon
Marketing Director: Werner Jochem
Sales Director: Robert Bratton
Contact: Gunter Blaschke
g.blaschke@rational-online.com
Estimated Sales: $2.5-5 Million
Number Employees: 20-49
Parent Co: Rational AG
Brands:
Clima Plus Combi
Climaplus Control
Rational Combi-Steamers

28243 Ray C. Sprosty Bag Company
323 E Liberty St
Wooster, OH 44691
330-264-8559
Fax: 330-263-4621
Film and bags including multi-wall, woven poly-
propylene, burlap, cotton and paper
President: Ray C Sprosty Iii
CFO: Pam Farthing
Quality Control: Tom Catamzarite
General Manager: Tom Catanzarite
Estimated Sales: $10 - 20 Million
Number Employees: 10-19
Square Footage: 30000

28244 Ray-Craft
2067 W 41st St
Cleveland, OH 44113
216-651-3330
Fax: 216-651-8714
Manufacturer and exporter of advertising novelties
and promotional materials
President: Thomas Topp
Office Manager: Agnes Milter
Estimated Sales: $500,000-$1 Million
Number Employees: 9

28245 (HQ)Raymond Corp
22 S Canal St
Greene, NY 13778
607-656-2311
Fax: 607-656-9005 800-235-7200
www.raymondcorp.com
Manufacturer and exporter of electric forklift trucks
President/ Operations: Michael G Field
Chief Financial Officer: Edward J Rompala
VP, General Counsel: Lou Callea
EVP Sales & Marketing: Timothy Combs
VP Sales: Gary Kirchner
EVP, Human Resources: Stephen E VanNostrand
Vice President, Distribution Development: Patrick
McManus
Estimated Sales: $130,000
Number Employees: 1000-4999
Square Footage: 1000000

28246 Rayne Sign Co
813 S Adams Ave
Rayne, LA 70578-5626
337-334-4276
Fax: 337-334-4263 www.rayneplasticsigns.com
Plastic signs including illuminated outdoor

President: Hilman Meche
hilman@rayneplasticsigns.com
Secretary: Verline Meche
Manager: Blaine Meche
Estimated Sales: $1-2.5 Million
Number Employees: 5-9

28247 Raypak Inc
2151 Eastman Ave
Oxnard, CA 93030-5194
805-278-5300
Fax: 805-278-5489 www.raypak.com
Manufacturer and exporter of water heating equip-
ment including boosters
Vice President: Michael Sentovich
msentovich@raypak.com
VP: Louis Falzer
Number Employees: 250-499
Square Footage: 235000
Parent Co: Rheem
Other Locations:
Raypak
Victoria

28248 Raypress Corp
380 Riverchase Pkwy E
Hoover, AL 35244-1813
205-989-3731
Fax: 205-989-7203 800-423-3731
sales@raypress.com www.raypress.com
Pressure sensitive labels and tags
President: Thomas Ray
tray@raypress.com
Estimated Sales: $5-10 Million
Number Employees: 20-49

28249 (HQ)Raytek Corporation
P.O. Box 1820
Santa Cruz, CA 95061-1820
831-458-1110
Fax: 831-425-4561 800-866-5478
solutions@raytek.com www.raytek.com
Monitor hot and cold holding, reheating, cooling,
and storage temperature instantly in steam tables,
warming ovens, freezers, display cases and coolers
with the new Raytek Mini Temperature Food Safety
infrared thermometer
President: Carl Pickard
VP: Jim Love
Marketing: Fernando Lisboa
Sales: Bob Bader
Public Relations: Kate McGuire
Estimated Sales: $20-50 Million
Number Employees: 100-249
Number of Brands: 1
Type of Packaging: Private Label

28250 Raytheon Co
870 Winter St
Waltham, MA 02451-1449
781-522-3000
Fax: 781-860-2172 www.raytheon.com
Manufacturer and exporter of dehydration equip-
ment for sugar, minerals, chemicals, corn and grain;
also, evaporators, vacuum pans, dryers, crystallizers,
granulators and coolers; engineering design services
available
Chief Executive Officer: Thomas A. Kennedy
tkennedy@raytheon.com
SVP and Chief Financial Officer: David C. Wajsgras
Senior Vice President: Keith J. Peden
Estimated Sales: Over $1 Billion
Number Employees: 10000+
Square Footage: 1200000
Brands:
Stearns-Roger

28251 Razor Edge Systems
303 N 17th Ave E
Ely, MN 55731-1853
218-365-6419
Fax: 218-365-5360 800-541-1458
sales@razoredgesystems.com
www.razoredgesystems.com
Cutting and boning devices, sharpening machines
and services, general packinghouse equipment,
maintenance, sharpening and overhaul equipment
CEO: Eddie Bravo
eddieb@razoredgesystems.com
Service Technician: Jim Dally
Sales/Service Representative: Robert Sanders
Manager: Joann O'Reilly
Estimated Sales: Less Than $500,000
Number Employees: 1-4

28252 Rea UltraVapor
665 Tradewind Drive
Unit 10
Ancaster, ON L9G 4V5
Canada
905-572-0946
Fax: 905-304-3067 800-323-3865
mail@ultravapor.com www.ultravapor.com
Food equipment sanitation and infection control.

28253 Read Products Inc
3615 15th Ave W
Seattle, WA 98119-1392
206-283-2510
Fax: 206-282-8339 800-445-3416
info@cuttingboards.com
www.sagecuttingsurfaces.com
Manufacturer and exporter of food preparation cut-
ting boards and tools
President: Charles R Read
cread@cuttingboard.com
Marketing Manager: Chuck Read
Inside Sales/Production Manager: Robert Read
Estimated Sales: $5-10 Million
Number Employees: 10-19
Square Footage: 80000
Type of Packaging: Food Service
Brands:
Read Woodfiber Laminate

28254 Readco Kurimoto LLC
460 Grim Ln
York, PA 17406-7949
717-848-2801
Fax: 717-848-2811 800-395-4959
readco@readco.com www.readco.com
Manufacturer and exporter of containerized batch
and continuous processing mixers
President: David Sieglitz
Manager: Ce Tyson
gtyson@readco.com
Estimated Sales: $5-10 Million
Number Employees: 20-49
Brands:
Cbm

28255 Reading Bakery Systems Inc
380 Old West Penn Ave
Robesonia, PA 19551-8903
610-693-5816
Fax: 610-693-5512 info@readingbakery.com
www.readingbakery.com
Manufacturer and exporter of extruders, cookers,
topical seasoning applicators, multifuel ovens, guil-
lotine dough cutters, dough handling systems and
biscuit, cookie and cracker sheeters and laminators
President: Joseph Zaleski
EVP/ CFO: Chip Czulada
Director of Engineering: Tremaine Hartranft
Director, Science & Innovation Center: Ken
Zvoncheck
VP, Sales & Marketing: David Kuipers
VP of Sales: Shawn Moye
Human Resources Manager: Roseann Reinhold
Vice President of Operations: Travis Getz
Estimated Sales: $10-20 Million
Number Employees: 50-99
Square Footage: 62000

28256 (HQ)Reading Box Co Inc
250 Blair Ave
Reading, PA 19601-1906
610-372-7411
Fax: 610-372-2143
Wooden boxes
President: Brent Atkins
Estimated Sales: Below $5 Million
Number Employees: 10-19

28257 Reading Plastic Fabricators
94 Dries Rd # A
Reading, PA 19605-9225
610-926-3245
Fax: 610-926-7026 www.readingplastic.com
Custom fabricated plastic wear materials including
tanks, hoods, covers and guards; also, clear acrylic
and polycarbonate displays and nylon and derlin
conveyor parts
President: Tom Funk
Quality Control Manager: Kenny Williams
National Sales Manager: Patty Alagna
HR Controller: Tracie Smith
General Manager: Tim Long
Office Manager: Susan Laird

Estimated Sales: $2.5-5 Million
Number Employees: 10-19
Square Footage: 20000

28258 Reading Technologies Inc
1031 Macarthur Rd
Reading, PA 19605-9402

610-372-9200
Fax: 610-372-1984   800-521-9200
info@driair.com   www.rti-pbe.com
President: Paul Flynn
paul@briair.com
Estimated Sales: $3 - 5 Million
Number Employees: 10-19

28259 Ready Access
1815 Arthur DriveWest
Chicago, IL 60185

630-876-7766
Fax: 630-876-7767   800-621-5045
ready@ready-access.com   www.ready-access.com
Manufacturer and exporter of pass-thru windows
and air curtain systems for fast food establishments
President: John Radek
CFO: Robert McKeever
R & D: Scott Hammac
Marketing/Sales/Public Relations: Kristy Rivera
Sales Director: Vince Asta
Operations/Production: Bob McKeever
Estimated Sales: $5 - 10 Million
Number Employees: 20-49
Square Footage: 70000

28260 Ready White
532 Main St # 4
Holyoke, MA 01040-5647

413-534-4864
Fax: 413-534-4864
Wiping rags
Owner: Leon E Barlow
Estimated Sales: Less than $500,000
Number Employees: 1-4

28261 Rebel Green
1317 Towne Square Rd
Mequon, WI 53092

262-240-9992
Fax: 262-241-5054   ali@rebelgreen.com
www.rebelgreen.com
Food sanitation equipment
Owner: Melina Marcus
Operations Manager: Kristina Nosbisch
Estimated Sales: Under $500,000
Number Employees: 2-10
Brands:
Rebel Green

28262 Rebel Stamp & Sign Co
307 Choctaw Dr
Baton Rouge, LA 70805-7653

225-387-4634
Fax: 225-344-1218   800-860-5120
orders@rebelstamp.com   www.rebelstamp.com
Marking devices including stamps, daters, etc.; also,
interior and exterior office signage including name
plates, name badges, etc
President: Lewis Roeling
orders@rebelstamp.com
Estimated Sales: $500,000-$1 Million
Number Employees: 5-9
Square Footage: 12000
Brands:
Royal Mark

28263 Recco International
3940 Platt Springs Rd
West Columbia, SC 29170-1606

803-356-4003
Fax: 803-356-4439   800-334-3008
sales@reccointernational.com
www.reccointernational.com
Manufacturer and exporter of printed labels and
tapes
Owner: John W Etters
john@reccointernational.com
General Manager: Craig Hall
Estimated Sales: $20 - 50 Million
Number Employees: 20-49

28264 Rechner Electronics Industries
8651 Buffalo Ave # 3
Niagara Falls, NY 14304-4382

716-283-8744
Fax: 716-283-2127   800-644-1756
service@htmsensors.com   www.htmsensors.com
Supplier of sensing devices
Owner: Ed Figarski
edf@htmsensors.com
Vice President: Arthur Ramsay
Estimated Sales: Less Than $500,000
Number Employees: 1-4

28265 Red Diamond Coffee & Tea
400 Park Ave
Moody, AL 35004

800-292-4651
qcdept@reddiamond.com   www.reddiamond.com
Coffee, tea bags and coffee brewers.
VP, Sales Development: John Padgett
VP, Manufacturing: Joe George
Year Founded: 1906
Estimated Sales: $45.9 Million
Number Employees: 100-249
Number of Brands: 1
Square Footage: 195000
Type of Packaging: Consumer, Food Service, Pri-
vate Label, Bulk
Brands:
Red Diamond

28266 Red Kap Industries
P.O. Box 140995
Nashville, TN 37214-0995

615-565-5000
Fax: 615-565-5284   www.vfc.com
Uniforms
Vice President of Corporate Relations: Cindy
Knoebel
Account Executive: Ray Hoff
Director of Corporate Communications: Carole
Crosslin
Estimated Sales: $20-50 Million
Number Employees: 250-499
Brands:
Red Kap

28267 (HQ)Red Lion Controls Inc
20 Willow Springs Cir
York, PA 17406-8473

717-767-6511
Fax: 717-764-0839   www.redlion.net
A range of control devices that include process mea-
surement and control, and digital measurement and
control
President: Sandy Albright
sandya@redlion-controls.com
Development: Vincent Paolizzi
Sales Director: George Simok
Estimated Sales: $20-$50 Million
Number Employees: 100-249
Square Footage: 100000

28268 Red River Lumber Company
2959 Saint Helena Highway N
Saint Helena, CA 94574-9703

707-963-1251
Fax: 707-963-3142
Manufacturer and exporter of redwood boxes
Estimated Sales: $5-10 Million
Number Employees: 20-49

28269 Red Star BioProducts
433 E Michigan Street
Milwaukee, WI 53202-5104

414-347-3936
Fax: 414-347-3912   800-528-3388
Number Employees: 50-99

28270 Red Valve Co Inc
600 N Bell Ave # 200
Carnegie, PA 15106-4315

412-279-0044
Fax: 412-279-7878   valves@redvalve.com
www.redvalve.com
A complete line of pinch valves and control valves
for use in the food industry; aeration and sparging
products, flexible connectors, and instrument protection devices
President: Chris Raftis
craftis@redvalve.com
Chairman: Spiros G Raftis
Marketing Manager: David Schneider

Estimated Sales: $20 - 50 Million
Number Employees: 100-249
Type of Packaging: Bulk

28271 Red-Ray Manufacturing Co Inc
10 County Line Rd # 22
Suite 22
Branchburg, NJ 08876-6009

908-722-0040
Fax: 908-722-2535   burners@red-ray.com
www.red-ray.com
Gas-fired and infrared process burners
President: Thomas Bannos
toneal@red-ray.com
Chairman of the Board: Robert S Adelson
Vice President, Product & Applications M: Tim
O'Neal
Applications Engineering: Mike Strand
Controller: Jorge Acosta
Estimated Sales: $5 - 10 Million
Number Employees: 10-19

28272 Reddi-Pac
215 W Church Rd
Suite 112
King of Prussia, PA 19406-3203

610-265-1827
Fax: 610-992-1407   www.naturalfertilitycenter.com
Laminated and formed paperboard
Owner: Meredith L Murphy

28273 Redding Pallet Inc
5323 Eastside Rd
Redding, CA 96001-4534

530-241-6321
Fax: 530-241-3475   www.redding.com
Manufacturer and exporter of hardwood and soft-
wood pallets
President: Don Lincoln
Estimated Sales: $1 - 5 Million
Number Employees: 10-19

28274 Redex Packaging Corporation
860 E State Pkwy
Schaumburg, IL 60173-4529

847-882-9500
Fax: 847-882-9570

28275 Redi-Call Inc
5655 Riggins Ct # 22
Reno, NV 89502-6554

775-331-0183
Fax: 775-331-2730   800-648-1849
sales@redi-callusa.com   www.redi-callusa.com
Manufacturer, importer and exporter of stainless
steel cup and lid dispensers, condiment holders for
bars, circular wheel check holders for restaurant
kitchens, stainless steel pump units, squeeze bottles,
waitress/waiter paging/callstations, etc
President: Melinda James
VP: Eric Seltzer
Purchasing Agent: Dave Schankin
Estimated Sales: Less Than $500,000
Number Employees: 1-4
Square Footage: 80000
Brands:
Redi-Call
Speed-Rak
Top O' Cup

28276 Redi-Print
49 Mahan St
Unit B
West Babylon, NY 11704

631-491-6373
Fax: 631-491-6372   rediprint1@aol.com
Manufacturer and exporter of pre-printed menu pa-
per and menu designing software
President: Tom Vlahakis
Estimated Sales: $300,000-500,000
Number Employees: 10
Square Footage: 5000

28277 Redicon Corporation
2824 Woodlawn Ave NW
Canton, OH 44708-1424

330-477-2100
Fax: 330-477-2101
Systems supplier for beverage and food can manufacturers: complete systems for draw, redraw, cans,
shell (lid) systems for beverage cans, end systems
for CWI cans, die sets for existing systems; both low
and high volume requirements
Owner: Tracee Mc Afee-Gates

28278 Redlake Imaging Corporation
11633 Sorrento Valley Road
San Diego, CA 92121-1039
858-481-8182
Fax: 858-792-3179 800-462-4307
Packaging production, manufacturing, inspection
Estimated Sales: $10.5 Million
Number Employees: 20-49

28279 Redlake MASD
6295 Ferris Sq
Suite A
San Diego, CA 92121-3248
858-481-8182
Fax: 858-350-9390 800-462-4307
President: Stephen Ferrell
Contact: Mary Hardison
mhardison@red-lake.com
Estimated Sales: $15 - 20 Million
Number Employees: 100-250

28280 Redwood Vintners
12 Harbor Dr
Novato, CA 94945-3507
415-892-6949
Fax: 415-892-7469 www.vinarium-usa.com
Distribution and marketing of wines
Sales Contact: Charles Daniels
Estimated Sales: $20 - 50 Million
Number Employees: 50-99
Brands:
Redwood Vintners

28281 Reed Ice
Lincolnton, GA
706-359-3127
Fax: 706-359-5465 800-927-9612
reedice@nu-z.net www.reedice.com
Manufacturer, wholesaler and distributor of ice;
serving the food service market.
Owner: Talmadge Reed
Estimated Sales: $20-50 Million
Number Employees: 10-19
Type of Packaging: Private Label, Bulk

28282 Reed Oven Co
1720 Nicholson Ave
Kansas City, MO 64120-1453
816-842-7446
Fax: 816-421-0422 www.reedovenco.com
Manufacturer and exporter of revolving shelf and
rack ovens, proofers, retarders, fermentation rooms
and steam cabinets
President: Kay Davies
reedoven@mindspring.com
Marketing Director/ IT Supervisor: Chris Davies
Operations: Brad Mitchell
Administrative Assistant: Linda Zeller
Plant Manager/ Engineer: Tim Davies
Purchasing Manager: Linda Zeller
Estimated Sales: $2.5-5 Million
Number Employees: 10-19
Square Footage: 72000
Brands:
Reed

28283 Reef Industries Inc
9209 Almeda Genoa Rd
Houston, TX 77075-2339
713-507-4200
Fax: 713-507-4295 800-231-6074
ri@reefindustries.com www.reefindustries.com
Reinforced film laminates and plastics.
Owner: Phillip Cameron
Vice President: Tameka Crawford
tamekacrawford@crossmark.com
Sales Manager: Jeff Garza
Number Employees: 100-249
Brands:
Armorlon
Banner Guard
Griffolyn
Permalon
Roll-A-Sign
Terra Tape

28284 Reelcraft Industries Inc
2842 E Business 30
Columbia City, IN 46725-8451
260-248-8188
Fax: 260-248-2605 800-444-3134
reelcraft@reelcraft.com www.reelcraft.com
Manufacturer and exporter of industrial-grade hose,
cord and cable reels, including stainless steel.

President: Walter Sterneman
wsterneman@reelcraft.com
Estimated Sales: Over $50 Million
Number Employees: 100-249
Square Footage: 130000
Type of Packaging: Consumer, Food Service

28285 Reeno Detergent & Soap Company
9421 Midland Boulevard
Saint Louis, MO 63114-3327
314-429-6078
Fax: 314-429-6078
Manufacturer, importer and exporter of powder and
liquid laundry detergents and industrial cleaners
President: Colleen Trotter
VP Sales: Tim Trotter
VP Purchasing: Brad Trotter
Estimated Sales: $1-2.5 Million
Number Employees: 5-9
Brands:
Borax-Splash
Borax-Sudz
Woolmaster

28286 Rees Inc
405 S Reed Rd
Fremont, IN 46737-2129
260-495-9811
Fax: 260-495-2186 sales@reesinc.com
www.reesinc.com
Manufacturer and exporter of industrial control
switches including cable, palmbutton and stop-start
President: Daniel Breeden
db@reesinc.com
Estimated Sales: $1 - 5 Million
Number Employees: 10-19
Square Footage: 70000

28287 Reese Enterprises Inc
16350 Asher Ave E
Rosemount, MN 55068-6000
651-423-1126
Fax: 651-423-2662 800-328-0953
info@reeseusa.com www.reeseusa.com
Manufacturer, importer and exporter of plastic doors
and door strips, aluminum roll-up mats, aluminum
stair treads, floor mats and grates, weatherstrips and
thresholds
President: Jim Beitzell
beitzell@reeseusa.com
National Sales/Marketing Manager: Edward Green
Estimated Sales: $10-20 Million
Number Employees: 1-4
Number of Products: 4
Square Footage: 160000
Parent Co: Astro Plastics

28288 Reeve Store Equipment Co
9131 Bermudez St
Pico Rivera, CA 90660-4507
562-949-2535
Fax: 562-949-3862 800-927-3383
info@reeveco.com www.reeveco.com
Manufacturer and exporter of point of purchase dis-
plays, tags, card holders and fixtures
President: John Frackelton
COO: Jim Thompson
jthompson@reeve.com
Manager Sales/Marketing: Robert Frackelton
Estimated Sales: $20 - 50 Million
Number Employees: 50-99
Square Footage: 160000

28289 Reeves Enterprises
1350 Palomares St # A
La Verne, CA 91750-5230
909-392-9999
Fax: 909-392-0124 www.californialocker.com
Store fixtures; also, woodworking services available
President and CFO: Dennis Reeves
dennis@dreevesinc.com
Accounting: Michelle Scherer
Vice President: Brad Reeves
Engineering: Al Gonzaga
Sales: Joe Greco
Estimated Sales: Below $5,000,000
Number Employees: 5-9

28290 Refcon
220 Route 70
Medford, NJ 8055
609-714-2330
Fax: 609-714-2331

Manufacturer and exporter of curved display cases
for candy, baked goods, deli meat, fish and poultry
President: Herman Jakubowski
Manager/Manufacturing: Len Pushkantser
Engineer: Rapael Colon
Estimated Sales: $3-5 Million
Number Employees: 20-49
Square Footage: 88000

28291 Refinishing Touch
9350 Industrial Trace
Alpharetta, GA 30004
770-751-7227
Fax: 770-475-4782 800-523-9448
sales@therefinishingtouch.com
www.therefinishingtouch.com
Firm providing refinishing and refurbishing services
for furniture
Founder, President: Mario Insenga
National Sales Manager: Roberta Bernhardt
Contact: Amber Coelho
amberc@therefinishingtouch.com
Estimated Sales: $500,000-$1 Million
Number Employees: 5-9

28292 Reflectronics
3881 Leighton Ln
Lexington, KY 40515
888-415-0441
Fax: 888-415-0442 info@reflectronics.com
www.reflectronics.com
Optical sensors for process monitoring and control
Estimated Sales: Under $500,000
Number Employees: 2
Number of Products: 2

28293 Reflex International
6624 Jimmy Carter Boulevard
Norcross, GA 30071-1727
770-729-8909
Fax: 770-729-8805 800-642-7640
Point of purchase software, touch screen monitors,
peripheral printers, mag card readers, kiosk cabinets,
scanners and rack mounted open and close chassis
displays
Marketing Director: John Dodrill
Sales Manager: Bryan Graves
Estimated Sales: $5-10 Million
Number Employees: 45
Square Footage: 180000
Parent Co: CTX International

28294 Refractron TechnologiesCorp
5750 Stuart Ave
Newark, NY 14513-9798
315-331-6222
Fax: 315-331-7254 sales@refractron.com
www.refractron.com
Manufacturer, importer and exporter of advanced
porous ceramic filters including water, process, gas,
micro, cross-flow, ceramic membrane, air, etc.; also,
diffusers including liquid and gas
Owner: Bob Stanton
CFO: Darrell Johanneman
Director R & D: Gregg Crume
VP, Sales & Marketing: Adam Osekoski
bstanton@refractron.com
Estimated Sales: $10-20 Million
Number Employees: 50-99
Square Footage: 130000
Type of Packaging: Private Label
Brands:
Durasieve
Refractite
Solidome

28295 Refrigerated Design Tech
1808 Fm 66
Waxahachie, TX 75167-5507
972-938-1100
Fax: 972-937-0970 800-736-9518
randall@rdtonline.com
Custom made refrigeration equipment and systems
President: Randall Dyess
randall@rdtonline.com
Quotations: Brent Dyess
Purchasing: Jim Wright
Estimated Sales: $2.5-5 Million
Number Employees: 10-19
Parent Co: RJS Company

28296 Refrigerated Warehouse Marketing Group
PO Box 530
La Verne, CA 91750-0530
909-625-4512
Fax: 909-625-4612

28297 Refrigerated Warehousing
198 High Trail Vista Cir
Jasper, GA 30143
770-894-4012
Fax: 706-692-3749 800-873-2008
dshine@rwizero.com www.rwizero.com
Designer and constructor of refrigeration warehouses and processing facilities
President: Dennis M. Shine
Estimated Sales: $1-2.5 Million
Number Employees: 1-4

28298 Refrigeration Design & Svc
14 Union Hill Rd
Conshohocken, PA 19428-2727
267-316-0800
Fax: 610-834-0807 www.refrigerationdesign.com
President: Micheal Zion
Estimated Sales: $10 - 20 Million
Number Employees: 10-19

28299 Refrigeration Engineering
3123 Wilson Dr NW
Grand Rapids, MI 49534-7565
616-453-2441
Fax: 616-453-0750 800-968-3227
www.hussmann.com
Commercial refrigeration equipment including cases and walk-in coolers; also, sales and services available
Manager: John Atsma
Manager: Dave Mulka
dave_mulka@hussmann.com
Parts Manager: Carl Boltz
Estimated Sales: $10-20 Million
Number Employees: 10-19

28300 (HQ)Refrigeration Research
525 N 5th St
PO Box 869
Brighton, MI 48116-1293
810-227-1151
Fax: 810-227-3700 info@refresearch.com
www.refresearch.com
Manufacturer and exporter of component parts for commercial refrigeration systems
Vice President: Michael Ramalia
mramalia@refresearch.com
Vice President: M Ramalia
Estimated Sales: $5-10 Million
Number Employees: 100-249
Type of Packaging: Bulk

28301 Refrigeration Systems Company
1770 Genessee Ave
Columbus, OH 43211
614-263-0913
Fax: 614-263-6660
President: Robert Appleton
CEO: Tom Leighty
Contact: Keith Agler
k.agler@rsc-gc.com
Estimated Sales: $10 - 20 Million
Number Employees: 50-99

28302 Refrigeration Technology
595 Portal Street
Cotati, CA 94931-3023
707-792-1934
Fax: 707-792-1417 800-834-2232
Wine industry refrigeration units

28303 Refrigerator Manufacturers LLC
17018 Edwards Rd
Cerritos, CA 90703-2422
562-926-2006
Fax: 562-926-2007 sales@rmi-econocold.com
Manufacturer, importer and exporter of walk-in cold storage rooms and environmental chambers
President: Lawrence Jaffe
VP: Leo Lewis
Contact: Tony Bedy
tbedy@airdyne.com
Estimated Sales: $10-20 Million
Number Employees: 5-9
Square Footage: 80000

Brands:
Econocold
Rmi

28304 Refrigiwear Inc
54 Breakstone Dr
Dahlonega, GA 30533-7603
706-973-5000
Fax: 706-864-5898 800-645-3744
keepmewarm@refrigiwear.com
www.refrigiwear.com
Manufacturer and exporter of insulated and protective work clothing, head, hand, and footwear, thermal insulated blankets and carts and pallet covers
President: Ronald Breakstone
rbreakstone@refrigiwear.com
Vice President: Mark Silberman
Quality Control: Kate Bishop
Marketing: Kristy Chrisciaske
VP Sales: Don Byerly
Vice President/Operations: Scotty Depriest
Estimated Sales: $25 Million
Number Employees: 100-249
Square Footage: 80000
Brands:
Iron Tuff
Refrigiwear
Storm Trac
Weatherguard

28305 Refrigiwear Inc
54 Breakstone Dr
Dahlonega, GA 30533-7603
706-973-5000
Fax: 706-864-5898 800-645-3744
customerservice@refrigiwear.com
www.refrigiwear.com
President/CFO: Ronald Breakstone
rbreakstone@refrigiwear.com
Vice President: Scotty Depriest
Marketing Manager: Kate Bishop
Chief Operating Officer: Mark Silberman
Estimated Sales: $10 - 20 Million
Number Employees: 100-249

28306 Refrigue USA
3845 Shopton Rd
Suite 350
Charlotte, NC 28217-3030
704-347-1511
Fax: 704-347-1448
Safety equipment and apparel

28307 Regal Box Corp
923 E Garfield Ave
Milwaukee, WI 53212-3494
414-562-5890
Fax: 414-562-0341
Corrugated boxes
President: John Schwartz
Estimated Sales: Below $5 Million
Number Employees: 1-4

28308 Regal Custom Fixture Company
22 Burrs Rd., Bldg. C
PO Box 446
Westampton, NJ 08060-0446
609-261-3323
Fax: 609-261-4929 800-525-3092
Manufacturer and exporter of display cases including bakery, deli and candy
VP: Mike Rainbolt
National Sales Manager: Shawn Adair
Number Employees: 20-49
Type of Packaging: Food Service
Brands:
Regal

28309 Regal Equipment Inc
4171 State Route 14
Ravenna, OH 44266-8739
330-325-9000
Fax: 330-325-7900 sales@regalequipment.com
www.regalequipment.com
Dealer of used and rebuilt cutters, dicers, blanchers, centrifuges grinders, and other food processing equipment
President: Kenneth Regal
Estimated Sales: $1 - 3 Million
Number Employees: 5-9

28310 Regal Manufacturing Company
5438 W Roosevelt Road
Chicago, IL 60644-1495
773-921-3071
Fax: 773-921-3076
Metal and wooden bar stools and dining chairs
President: Gerald Saviano
Contact: D Lund
d@regalmfg.com
Estimated Sales: $5-10 Million
Number Employees: 20-49
Square Footage: 70000

28311 Regal Pinnacle Integrations
220 Route 70
Medford, NJ 08055-9522
609-714-2330
Fax: 609-714-2331 www.rpiindustries.com
President: Peter C Palko
pcpalko@rpiindustries.com
Estimated Sales: $5-10 Million
Number Employees: 100-249

28312 Regal Plastic Company
5310 Canterbury Road
Mission, KS 66205-2611
816-483-3040
Fax: 816-483-7948 800-852-1556
Thermoformed FDA approved tote boxes and freezer spacers
President: A Bashor
CFO: J Streeter
VP Sales: L Haber
Plant Manager: Doug Meyer
Estimated Sales: $50-100 Million
Number Employees: 50-99

28313 Regal Plastic Supply Co
1500 Burlington St
Kansas City, MO 64116-3815
816-471-6390
Fax: 816-221-5822 800-444-6390
jnorman@regalplastic.com www.regalplastic.com
Acrylic items including food containers, store fixtures, advertising signs and name plates
President: Harry R Greenwald
CEO: Enzo Castelli
Manager: Shawn Slavik
shawn@regalplastic.com
Estimated Sales: $1-2.5 Million
Number Employees: 20-49
Square Footage: 10000

28314 Regal Power Transmission Solutions
7120 New Buffington Rd
Florence, KY 41042
859-342-7900
www.regalpts.com
Conveying products: motorized and traditional conveyor pulleys, conveyor modules, module plastic belts, conveying chain. Bearing products: beverage bearings, high temperature bearings
CEO: Louis Pinkham
CFO: Robert Rehard
Chief Information Officer: John Avampato
Estimated Sales: $164 Million
Number Employees: 1000-4999
Number of Brands: 16

28315 (HQ)Regal Ware Inc
1675 Reigle Dr
Kewaskum, WI 53040-8923
262-626-2121
Fax: 262-626-8565 www.regalware.com
Manufacturer, importer and exporter of frying and sauce pans, coffee makers and urns
President/CEO: Jeffery Reigle
Chairman: James Reigle
SVP/Chief Financial Officer: Gerald Koch
SVP/Chief HR Officer: David Lenz
Sales Director: Jim Dorn
SVP Operations: Joe Swanson
Purchasing: John McCormack
Estimated Sales: $36.8 Million
Number Employees: 500-999
Square Footage: 500000
Other Locations:
Regal Ware
Jacksonville AR
Brands:
Kitchen Pro
La Machine

Poly Perk
Regal

28316 Regency Coffee & Vending
2022 E Spruce Cir
Olathe, KS 66062-5404
913-829-1994
Fax: 913-393-0097 www.regencycoffee.com
Coffees, teas and snacks
Owner: Nancy Robinson
 regency@regencycoffee.com
Estimated Sales: $205 Million
Number Employees: 10-19
Number of Brands: 8
Number of Products: 80
Type of Packaging: Consumer, Food Service, Private Label, Bulk

28317 Regency Label Corporation
217 Berger Street
Wood Ridge, NJ 07075-1802
201-342-2288
Fax: 201-438-3439
Printed labels including pressure sensitive
VP Marketing: Mike Pagano
Estimated Sales: less than $500,000
Number Employees: 1-4

28318 Reggie Balls Cajun Foods
501 Bunker Rd
Lake Charles, LA 70615-3875
337-436-0291
Fax: 337-433-9851 www.ballscajunfoods.com
Cajun seasonings and mixes; Contract packaging and private labeling
Owner/President: Reginald Ball
Estimated Sales: Less Than $500,000
Number Employees: 1-4
Type of Packaging: Private Label

28319 Regina USA
305 E Mahn Ct
Oak Creek, WI 53154-2101
414-571-0032
Fax: 414-571-0225 sales.us@reginachain.net
Manufacturer, of metal and plastic power transmission chains, conveying chains and plastic belts
President: Carlo Garbagnati
VP Sales/Marketing: Michael Hager
Sales: Brian Kelley
IT: Sandy Martino
 smartino@reginausa.com
Estimated Sales: $20 Million
Number Employees: 10-19
Square Footage: 65000
Parent Co: Regina Industria SPA
Brands:
 Regina

28320 Regina-Emerson
1604 S West Avenue
Waukesha, WI 53189-7434
262-521-1790
Fax: 262-521-1790
Belting

28321 Regional Produce
624 16th Ave W
Birmingham, AL 35204-1421
205-324-4569
Fax: 205-252-4434 800-726-0711
 www.regionalproduce.net
Regional foodservice distributor.
Director of Purchasing: Jason Kenwright
Number Employees: 50-99
Square Footage: 30000
Type of Packaging: Consumer, Food Service
Brands:
 Granny's

28322 Rego China Corporation
200 Broadhollow Road
Suite 400
Melville, NY 11747-4806
516-753-3700
Fax: 516-753-3728 800-221-1707
 www.oneida.com
Manufacturer, importer and exporter of chinaware
President, CEO: Foster Sullivan
Sales Manager: Frank Fan
Estimated Sales: $300,000-500,000
Number Employees: 40
Parent Co: Oneida
Type of Packaging: Food Service

28323 Reheis Co
235 Snyder Ave
Berkeley Heights, NJ 07922-1150
908-464-1500
Fax: 908-464-7726
Chemicals and pharmaceuticals
General Manager: Douglas McF+R2441arlend
Plant Manager: Gerry Kirwan
Estimated Sales: Less Than $500,000
Number Employees: 1-4
Parent Co: General Chemicals

28324 Rehrig Pacific Co
4010 E 26th St
Los Angeles, CA 90058
323-262-5145
Fax: 323-269-8506 800-421-6244
info@rehrigpacific.com www.rehrigpacific.com
Plastic injection molding, returnable plastic crates and pallets.
President: William Rehrig
 wrehrig@rehrigpacific.com
Year Founded: 1913
Estimated Sales: $101.4 Million
Number Employees: 1000-4999

28325 Reichert Analytical Instruments
3362 Walden Avenue
Depew, NY 14043
716-686-4500
Fax: 716-686-4545 www.reichertai.com
Hand held digital refractometers.
Contact: Ashley Agnew
 aagnew@reichert.com

28326 Reid Boiler Works
920 10th St
Bellingham, WA 98225
360-714-6157
Fax: 360-734-6660
Canning retorts and pressure vessels
President: Robert Reid
Office Manager: Shirley Maytag
Estimated Sales: Less than $500,000
Number Employees: 1-4

28327 Reid Graphics Inc
7 Connector Rd
Andover, MA 01810-5922
978-474-1930
Fax: 978-474-1931 800-887-7461
 www.reidgraphics.com
Labels and decals
President: Stephen Dunlevy
 reidgrafx@aol.com
General Manager: Robert Stewart
Estimated Sales: $10-20 Million
Number Employees: 20-49

28328 Reidler Decal Corporation
264 Industrial Pk. Road
PO Box 8
Saint Clair, PA 17970
570-429-1528
Fax: 570-429-1528 800-628-7770
 marketing@reidlerdecal.com
 www.reidlerdecal.com
Manufacturer and exporter of decals, plastic safety signs, fleet graphics, reflective markings, reflective striping and roll labels
President: Edward Reidler
Marketing Coordinator: Maralynn Hudock
Estimated Sales: $5 - 10 Million
Number Employees: 20-49
Square Footage: 100000
Brands:
 Ad Vantage
 Fleet Mark

28329 Reilly Foam Corporation
1101 E Hector St # 1
Conshohocken, PA 19428-2382
610-834-1900
Fax: 610-834-0769 www.reillyfoam.com
Plastic foam sheets including die cut, laminated and pressure sensitive
Owner: Charles Reilly
VP Marketing: Stephen Phillips
Estimated Sales: $20-50 Million
Number Employees: 100-249
Square Footage: 249000

28330 Reiner Products
196 Mill St
Waterbury, CT 06706-1208
203-574-2666
Fax: 203-755-8178 800-345-6775
 info@reinerproducts.com
 www.reinerproducts.com
Manufacturer, importer and exporter of salt and pepper shakers
Owner: Patrick Bergin
Estimated Sales: $2.5-5 Million
Number Employees: 10-19

28331 Reinhold Sign Svc Inc
2070 Holmgren Way
Green Bay, WI 54304-4593
920-494-7161
Fax: 920-494-8720 sales@reinholdsigns.com
 www.vehiclewrapsgreenbay.com
Interior and exterior signage, truck and trailer lettering and vinyl letters
President: John Gage
 john@reinholdsign.com
Sales & Service Manager: Robert Ott
Estimated Sales: $1 - 5 Million
Number Employees: 10-19
Square Footage: 32000

28332 Reinke & Schomann
3745 N Richards St
Milwaukee, WI 53212
414-964-1100
Fax: 414-964-1995
 sales@reinkeandschomann.com
 www.reinkeandschomann.com
Manufacturer and exporter of steel and stainless steel screw conveyors and components
President: Frederick Schomann
VP Engineering/Sales: Ken Buchholz
Estimated Sales: Below $5,000,000
Number Employees: 5-9
Square Footage: 30000

28333 Reis Robotics
856 Commerce Pkwy
Carpentersville, IL 60110
847-741-9500
Fax: 847-844-0745 www.kuka.com
Manufacturer and importer of automated robotic material handling and palletizing systems and system integrators
President, KUKA Robotics Corp US: Joseph Gemma

Year Founded: 1957
Estimated Sales: $1,000,000,000+
Number Employees: 10-19
Square Footage: 45000
Parent Co: KUKA Robotics Corporation

28334 (HQ)Reiser
725 Dedham St
Canton, MA 02021-1450
734-821-1290
Fax: 781-821-1316 sales@reiser.com
High-quality food processing and packaging equipment that includes tray sealing, vacuum and form/fill/seal packaging equipment as well as processing machines used for stuffing, portioning, grinding, injecting, extruding and slicing.Equipment can be used as stand-alone machines or as complete systems.
President/CEO: Roger Reiser
Engineering/R&D Technician: Dan Flaherty
Contact: Ahmad Adam
 mhansen@reiser.com
Estimated Sales: $23 Million
Number Employees: 5-9
Brands:
 Amfec
 Fomaco
 Holac
 Ross
 Seydelmann
 Vemag

28335 Reit-Price ManufacturingCompany
532 W Chestnut St
Union City, IN 47390
765-964-3252
Fax: 765-964-5343 800-521-5343
 customerservice@reitprice.com
 www.reitprice.com

Wet and dust mops, squeegees, push brooms, floor brushes and handles
President: Roger Stewart
Sales Manager: R Stewart
Estimated Sales: $10-20 Million
Number Employees: 20-49
Square Footage: 100000
Brands:
  Black Cat

28336 Relco Unisystems Corp
2281 3rd Ave SW
Willmar, MN 56201-2799

320-231-2210
Fax: 320-231-2282
lorencorle@relcounisystems.com
www.relco.net
Provides dairy and food plants with customized cheese, whey, soy, and processing equipment and systems through design, engineering, fabrication, installation, and commissioning. Relco process and control systems are recognized as industry leaders because of their application knowledge, understanding of sanitary and regulatory requirements, and focus on consumer needs
President: Loren Corle
  lcorle@relco.com
VP: M Douglas Rolland
Estimated Sales: $20-50 Million
Number Employees: 50-99

28337 (HQ)Reliable Container Corporation
12029 Regentview Ave
Downey, CA 90241-5517

562-745-0200
Fax: 562-861-3969 www.reliablecontainer.com
Manufacturer and exporter of corrugated boxes and foil-lined, coated, printed and plain cake circles and pads
President: Dan Brough
VP: Andrew Rosen
VP: Robert Schwartz
Estimated Sales: $20 - 50 Million
Number Employees: 100-249
Square Footage: 112500
Other Locations:
  Reliable Container Corp.
  Tijuana, Baja CA

28338 Reliable Fire Equipment
12845 S Cicero Ave
Alsip, IL 60803-3083

708-444-7339
Fax: 708-389-1150 fire@reliablefire.com
www.reliablefire.com
Wholesaler/distributor of restaurant fire supression and security systems, alarm monitoring, fire alarms, portable, industrial and special hazard fire extinguishers, emergency lights, smoke detectors and first aid equipment, serving the food service market.
President: Debra Horvath
Vice President: Barbara Horvath
VP Sales: Robert Marek
Purchasing Manager: Tim Zurek
Estimated Sales: $22 Million
Number Employees: 50-99
Number of Brands: 30
Number of Products: 200
Square Footage: 40000

28339 Reliable Food Service Equipment
Units 5,7,8
Concord, ON L4K 1L3
Canada

416-738-6840
Fax: 416-739-7271
sales@restaurantequipmentdepot.com
www.restaurantequipmentdepot.com
Steam tables, ovens, freezers, sinks, etc
President: Frank Gambino
Number Employees: 8

28340 Reliable Label
1427 Centre Cir
Downers Grove, IL 60515-1045

630-620-8100
Fax: 630-620-8125 800-323-7265
sales@reliablelabel.com www.reliablelabel.com
Labeling services
President: Kevin Callahan
callahan@reliablelabel.com

Estimated Sales: $10 - 20 Million
Number Employees: 20-49

28341 Reliable Tent & Awning Co
501 N 23rd St
Billings, MT 59101-1341

406-252-4689
Fax: 406-252-6508 800-544-1039
sales@reliabletent.com www.reliabletent.com
Commercial awnings
President: Dave Niemer
  dave@reliabletent.com
Estimated Sales: $1-2,500,000
Number Employees: 10-19
Type of Packaging: Private Label

28342 Reliance Product
1093 Sherwin Road
Winnipeg, MB R3H 1A4
Canada

204-633-4403
Fax: 204-633-5193 800-665-0258
www.relianceproducts.com
Shipping containers including HDPE pails and bottles includes Camping lines
President: Charles Schiele
CFO: Arla Ervett
VP General Manager: Linda Lemer
Sales Manager: Peter Harvey
Number Employees: 10
Parent Co: Moll Industries

28343 Reliance-Paragon
2070 Wheatsheaf Lane
Philadelphia, PA 19124-5041

215-743-1231
Fax: 215-742-1584
Packaging products including set-up, paper and folding boxes; also, plastic boxes
VP: Larry Chatzkel
Plant Supervisor: William Scnappor
Estimated Sales: $1 - 5 Million
Number Employees: 50-99
Square Footage: 120000

28344 (HQ)Remco Industries International
PO Box 480008
Fort Lauderdale, FL 33348-0008

954-462-0000
Fax: 954-564-0000 800-987-3626
remco2mill@aol.com www.remcousa.com
Manufacturer and exporter of cooking equipment including wood burning and infrared rotisseries and pizza ovens; also, spit racks, bagel ovens and warming carts; manufacturer and importer of wood burning, infrared and carousel brick pizza ovens; manufacturer of grease free chicken wing roaster the Wing King and BBQ Boy
President/CEO: Romano Moreth
CFO: Susan Test
Vice President: Rob Moreth
R&D/Plant Manager: Remy Moreth
Quality Control: Wayne Wilkenson
Marketing/Public Relations: Pascal Ledesma
Sales Director: Joe Obrien
Operations: David Finch
Production Manager: Vean George
Plant Manager: Sean Harker
Purchasing Manager: Ed Moreth
Estimated Sales: $7-8 Million
Number Employees: 20-49
Number of Brands: 3
Number of Products: 6
Square Footage: 160000
Type of Packaging: Food Service

28345 Remco Products Corp
4735 W 106th St
PO Box 698
Zionsville, IN 46077-8761

317-876-9856
Fax: 317-876-9858 800-585-8619
www.remcoproducts.com
Ice and beverage dispensing products
Founder: Richard Garrison
President: David Garrison
Accounting: Cristal Garrison
Vice President Sales & Marketing: Steve Hawhee
Sales Representative: Paula Pearson
Operations: Mike Garrison
Customer Service: Amye Kersey
Number Employees: 10-19

28346 Remco Products Corp
4735 W 106th St
Zionsville, IN 46077-8761

317-876-9856
Fax: 317-876-9858 800-585-8619
sales@remcoproducts.com
www.remcoproducts.com
Remco Products sells a high quality line of products to the food processing, sanittation, pharmaceutical, safety, and material handling industries. Our tubs and polyropylene shovels have been used in these areas for over 30 years. The Vikan line of cleaning brooms, brushes, and squeegees is specifically designed to meet the stringent hygienic requirements of these different industries. We can also provide you with other hand tools such as scoops, scrapers, mixing paddles, forkkand rakes.
President: David Garrison
Marketing/Sales Support: Richard L. Williams
Director/Sales and Marketing: Chuck Bush
President of Operations: Richard L. Garrison
Estimated Sales: $2.5-5 Million
Number Employees: 10-19
Number of Brands: 2
Number of Products: 737
Square Footage: 96000
Brands:
  Remco

28347 Remcon Plastics Inc
208 Chestnut St
Reading, PA 19602-1809

610-376-2666
Fax: 610-375-4750 800-360-3636
info@remcon.com www.remcon.com
ISO 9001 certified material handling equipment, including bulk bins, liquid shippers, drums, pallets, tanks, aseptic packaging equipment, lockers, tote boxes, safety barriers, hoppers and candy trays. Structural foam molding and rotational molding
President: Antonio Andino
  antonio.andino@remcon.com
Marketing/Inside Sales Manager: Sylvie Mackenzie
Regional Sales Manager: Michael Pierotti
Purchasing Manager: Susan Cook
Estimated Sales: $10-20 Million
Number Employees: 100-249
Square Footage: 280000
Type of Packaging: Private Label, Bulk
Brands:
  Remcon

28348 Remcraft Lighting Products
12870 NW 45th Ave
PO Box 54-1487
Miami, FL 33054

305-687-9031
Fax: 305-687-5069 800-327-6585
customerservice@remcraft.com
www.bacimirrors.com
Manufacturer and exporter of electric and fluorescent lighting fixtures
President: Jeffrey Robboy
CEO: Michell Roboy
Estimated Sales: $1 - 2.5 Million
Number Employees: 20-49
Square Footage: 80000
Type of Packaging: Consumer, Private Label
Brands:
  Baci
  Remcraft

28349 Remel
12076 Santa Fe Dr
P.O. Box 14428
Lenexa, KS 66215

Fax: 800-621-8251 800-255-6730
www.remel.com
Manufacturer and exporter of microbiology products including culture media, dehydrated culture media identification kits, reagents and stains.
President & CEO, Thermo Scientific: Marc Casper
Year Founded: 1973
Estimated Sales: Over $1 Billion
Parent Co: Thermo Fisher Scientific
Brands:
  Chrisope
  Ids
  Remel

28350 Reminox International Corporation
7207 Bay Drive
Apt 13
Miami, FL 33141-5457
305-865-0925
www.creminox.com
Sales Manager: Roberto Garcia
Estimated Sales: $1 - 5 Million

28351 Remmele Engineering
677 Transfer Rd
Saint Paul, MN 55114
651-643-3700
Fax: 651-642-5665 800-854-7742
www.aspectautomation.com
Packaging and filling
President: Terry Johnson
Quality Control: Jim Schaefer
Chairman of the Board: William J Saul
Contact: Florinel Ciubotaru
florinel.ciubotaru@remmele.com
Estimated Sales: $75 - 100 Million
Number Employees: 100-249

28352 Remmey Wood Products
PO Box 1020
Southampton, PA 18966-0720
215-355-3335
Fax: 215-355-3781
Packaging and shipping products including wood
pallets, boxes, skids, crates, etc
VP Marketing: Donald Remmey Jr
Estimated Sales: $2.5-5 Million
Number Employees: 20-49

28353 Remote Equipment Systems
11390 Old Roswell Road
Alpharetta, GA 30004-2058
770-777-2627
Fax: 770-777-2662 800-803-9488
Data loggers for material handling systems
VP Sales: Doug Reed
Estimated Sales: $5-10 Million
Number Employees: 20-49

28354 Rempak Industries
2125 Center Avenue #200
Fort Lee, NJ 07024-5810
201-585-9007
Fax: 201-585-0918
Contract packager of portion control powders, liquids and solids
President: Gene Cohen
Estimated Sales: Less than $500,000
Number Employees: 14
Type of Packaging: Consumer, Food Service, Private Label

28355 Remstar International
41 Eisenhower Dr
Westbrook, ME 04092
207-854-1861
Fax: 207-854-1610 800-639-5805
www.remstar.com
Manufacturer, importer and exporter of automated
storage and retrieval systems
President: Gary Gould
Marketing Director: Ed Romaine
Contact: Brian Baker
brian.baker@kardexremstar.com
Estimated Sales: $20-50 Million
Number Employees: 20-49
Parent Co: Kardex A.G.

28356 Renard Machine Company
PO Box 19005
Green Bay, WI 54307-9005
920-432-8412
Fax: 920-432-8430
Manufacturer and exporter of packaging machinery
including fillers, sealers, labelers, weighers and
wrappers; also, paper converting equipment including folding, cutting, etc
Division Controller: Gary Rossman
Production Manager: Carl Strebel
Plant Manager: Ken Harvey
Estimated Sales: $5-10 Million
Number Employees: 50-99
Square Footage: 300000
Parent Co: Paper Converting Machine Company

28357 Renato Specialty Product
3612 Dividend Drive
Garland, TX 75042
972-272-4800
Fax: 972-272-4848 866-575-6316
renatos@renatos.com www.renatos.com
Manufacturer and exporter of food service equipment including broilers, ovens, griddles, grills and
rotisseries
President, Founder: Renato Riccio
Estimated Sales: $1-2.5 Million
Number Employees: 5-9
Type of Packaging: Consumer, Food Service

28358 Renau Electronic Lab
9309 Deering Ave
Chatsworth, CA 91311-5858
818-341-1994
Fax: 818-341-8063 info@renau.com
www.renau.com
President: Karol Renau
cdomanski@renau.com
Estimated Sales: $10 - 20 Million
Number Employees: 20-49

28359 Render
1800 Elmwood Avenue
Buffalo, NY 14207-2410
716-447-1010
Fax: 716-447-8918 888-446-1010
Bakery display cases with solid wood construction,
rearload options, adjustable shelving and accesory
bins, and an internal lighting system specifically to
enhance bakery products
President: Robert Nehin
Number Employees: 10

28360 Rennco LLC
300 S Elm St
Homer, MI 49245-1337
517-568-4121
Fax: 517-568-4798 800-409-5225
sales@rennco.com www.rennco.com
Manufacturer and exporter of vertical L-Bar sealers
VP/General Manager: Eric Vorm
Marketing Director: Jeanne George
Contact: Teresa Farmer
teresafarmer@rennco.com
Director of Operations: Terry Draper
Number Employees: 70
Parent Co: Pro Mach
Type of Packaging: Consumer, Food Service, Bulk
Brands:
Renwrap

28361 Reno Technology
3310 E 4th Ave
Hutchinson, KS 67501-1962
620-663-2753
Fax: 620-665-5793 800-562-8065
www.megafab.com
President: Mieke Ellwood
mieke@renocountycddo.org
Estimated Sales: $10 - 20 Million
Number Employees: 50-99

28362 Renold Ajax
100 Bourne St # 2
Westfield, NY 14787-9706
716-326-3121
Fax: 716-326-6121 800-879-2529
www.renold.com
Custom design vibratory materials handling equipment: dewatering units, conveyors, feeder, screeners,
bulk bab and box weigh filling systems, bulk bag
unloading stations
President: Adriano Ambos
adriano.ambos@renold.com
Estimated Sales: $20 - 50 Million
Number Employees: 250-499

28363 Renold Products
P.O. Box A
Westfield, NY 14787-0546
716-326-3121
Fax: 716-326-6121 800-879-2529
ainfo@renoldajax.com www.renold.com
Manufacturer and exporter of material handling
equipment including mechanical power transmission
products and packer weigh scales and conveyors.
President: Thomas Murrer
Business Development Director: Alan Dean
Estimated Sales: $20-50 Million
Number Employees: 100-249

Square Footage: 120000
Parent Co: Renold PLC
Brands:
Ajax
Renold

28364 Renovator's Supply
PO Box 2515
Conway, NH 3818
800-659-0203
Fax: 603-447-1717
Manufacturer and exporter of hardware, lighting,
plumbing and gift accessories; also, solid brass, iron,
porcelain and stainless steel sinks and work centers
President: Cindy Harris
Estimated Sales: $10-20 Million
Number Employees: 100-249
Brands:
Renovator's Supply

28365 Reotemp Instrument Corp
10656 Roselle St
San Diego, CA 92121-1524
858-784-0710
Fax: 858-784-0720 800-648-7737
sales@reotemp.com www.reotemp.com
Manufactures temperature and pressure instrumentation. Provide bimetal thermometers, pressure
gauges, diaphragm seals, transmitters, RTD's and
thermocouples and related accessories.
President: Joanne Lin
joanne.lin@intel.com
VP/General Manager: John Sisti
Quality/Engineering Manager: Cora Marsh
Marketing Manager: Nathan O'Connor
Sales Manager, Global Sales: Mark Leonelli
Purchasing Associate: Stacy Munoz
Estimated Sales: $6 Million
Number Employees: 20-49
Square Footage: 15000

28366 Replacements LTD
1089 Knox Rd
Mc Leansville, NC 27301-9228
336-697-3000
Fax: 336-697-3100 800-737-5223
inquire@replacements.com
www.replacements.com
Manufacturer and exporter of household and institutional cutlery
CEO: Robert L Page
robert.page@replacements.com
Director Marketing: Maron Atkins
General Manager: James Robellard
Estimated Sales: $5-10 Million
Number Employees: 500-999
Square Footage: 140000
Parent Co: Syratech

28367 Republic Foil
55 Triangle St
Danbury, CT 06810
203-743-2731
Fax: 203-743-8838 800-722-3645
Manufacturer and exporter of aluminum foil on coils
President: John Jehle
CFO: Fred Wallace
Contact: Joan Garofalo
joan.garofalo@garmcousa.com
Estimated Sales: $20 - 50 Million
Number Employees: 50-99
Square Footage: 100000
Type of Packaging: Bulk
Brands:
Republic High Yield

28368 Republic Refrigeration Inc
2890 Gray Fox Rd
Monroe, NC 28110-8422
704-225-0410
Fax: 704-283-2180
info@republicrefrigeration.com
www.republicrefrigeration.com
Design, install and maintain industrial refrigeeration
systems.

Vice President: Annmarie Greene
greene@carlyle.com
CEO: Walter F. Teeter
Founder: Henry Saye
Vice President: Robert G. Belanger
Director of Process Refrigeration: Joe Ramsey
Director of Business Development: Wayne Donaldson
Regional Manager: Banks Thomas
Insulation Project Manager: Jamie R. Foster
Estimated Sales: Less Than $500,000
Number Employees: 1-4

28369 Republic Sales
5131 Cash Rd
Dallas, TX 75247-5805

469-930-0518
Fax: 214-631-3673 800-847-0380
info@republicsales.com www.republicsales.com
President: George Goff
Vice President/International: Dan Marlett
Marketing: Nicole Taylor
Sheet Metal Sales: Andrew Servais
Contact: Gerardo Alaniz
gerardoalaniz@republic-mfg.com
Production: Raul Maldonado
Estimated Sales: $1 - 5 Million
Number Employees: 10-19

28370 Republic Storage Systems LLC
1038 Belden Ave NE
Canton, OH 44705

330-438-5800
Fax: 330-454-7772 800-477-1255
sales@republicstorage.com
www.republicstorage.com
Steel storage products including lockers, shelving and storage racks. Also shop furniture
President: Chris Carr
CFO: Eric Cook
CEO: James T Anderson
Marketing Director: Cathy Maxin
Sales Director: Ed Meek
Contact: Erin Allen
eallen@sibcycline.com
Estimated Sales: $20 - 50 Million
Number Employees: 500-999
Square Footage: 1300000
Brands:
Mondrian
Wedge Lock

28371 Rer Services
19431 Business Center Dr # 17
Northridge, CA 91324-6408

818-993-1826
Fax: 818-993-0016 rerserv@flash.net
Manufacturer and exporter of packaging machinery
Owner: Rick Ray
Estimated Sales: $2.5-5,000,000
Number Employees: 5-9

28372 Research & Development Packaging Corporation
1221 Us Highway 22
Suite 1
Lebanon, NJ 08833

908-236-2111
Fax: 908-236-7013
President: Donald Bogut
donald.bogut@key-pak.com
Estimated Sales: $1 - 3 Million
Number Employees: 5-9

28373 Research Products Co
1835 E North St
Salina, KS 67401-8567

785-825-2181
Fax: 785-825-8908
Insecticides
President: Monte White
montewhite@researchprod.com
Marketing Coordinator (Flour Division): Edna Richard
Estimated Sales: $20-50 Million
Number Employees: 50-99
Parent Co: McShares

28374 Resina
27455 Bostik Court
Temecula, CA 92590

951-296-6585
Fax: 951-296-5018 800-207-4804
sales@resina.com www.resina.com

Manufacturer and exporter of container capping machines
CEO: Micheal Tom
Director Sales: Andrew May
Sales Director: Tina Tricome
Estimated Sales: $10-20 Million
Number Employees: 1-4
Square Footage: 70000
Brands:
Resina

28375 Resource Equipment
1547 Palos Verdes Mall
Walnut Creek, CA 94597-2228

925-825-5536
Fax: 925-687-5513 800-324-1030
www.reisite.net
President: Jeff Slamal
Owner: Kenneth Gottfried
Contact: Ken Gottfried
specbuilt@aol.com
Estimated Sales: Below $5 Million
Number Employees: 2

28376 Resource One/Resource Two
6900 Canby Ave # 106
Reseda, CA 91335

818-343-3451
Fax: 818-343-3405 info@resourceone.com
www.resourceoneinc.com
Table cloths, napkins and chair covers
Founder/ CEO: Roberta Karsch
Contact: Thomas Patston
tpatston@rocs.com
Estimated Sales: $5-10,000,000
Number Employees: 20-49

28377 Resource Optimization
P.O. Box 2747
Knoxville, TN 37901-2747

865-522-2211
Fax: 865-522-7907
Software for quantification of ingredients in multi-level products
President: T Brient Mayfield
R&D: Bill Walter
Estimated Sales: Below $5 Million
Number Employees: 10-19

28378 Resources in Food & FoodTeam
222 S Central Ave # 202
St Louis, MO 63105-3509

314-727-0002
Fax: 314-727-5590 800-875-1028
www.rifood.com
Professional placement service for the food industry
President: Bonnie Pollock
VP Sales/Marketing: Mike Bray
Marketing Secretary: Marylynn Hayes
Estimated Sales: $300,000-500,000
Number Employees: 1-4
Parent Co: Resources in Food And Food Team

28379 Respirometry Plus, LLC
PO Box 1236
Fond Du Lac, WI 54937-7527

Fax: 920-922-1085 800-328-7518
operations@respirometryplus.com
www.respirometryplus.com
Manufacturer and exporter of bench and on-line respirometer
Owner: Louis Sparagarto
CEO: Robert Arthur
Contact: Tim Keuler
tim@respirometryplus.com
Estimated Sales: $1 - 2,500,000
Number Employees: 10

28380 Restaurant Data
1 Bridge St
Irvington, NY 10533-1560

732-667-5885
Fax: 914-591-5494 800-346-9390
info@netsoftsolutions.com restaurantdata.com
Cashew and other nuts; Co-packing services
President: James Santo
R&D: Paul Mlynar
Contact: Jeff Kydd
jeff@foodservicereport.com
Purchasing Director: Joe Di Donato
Estimated Sales: $1-2 Million
Number Employees: 1-4
Number of Brands: 1

Number of Products: 12
Square Footage: 48000
Type of Packaging: Consumer, Private Label, Bulk
Brands:
Nutsco

28381 Restaurant Development Svc
7404 Helmsdale Rd
Bethesda, MD 20817-4628

301-263-0400
Fax: 301-263-0151
info@restaurantdevelopment.com
www.restaurantdevelopment.com
Consultant specializing in business planning for restaurants
Owner: Paul Fields
pfields@restaurantdevelopment.com
Estimated Sales: less than $500,000
Number Employees: 10-19

28382 Restaurant Partners
1030 N Orange Ave # 200
Orlando, FL 32801-1030

407-839-5070
Fax: 407-839-3388
contact@restaurantpartnersinc.com
www.restaurantpartnersinc.com
Consultant providing strategic and expansion planning services for restaurants
Owner: Dave Manuchia
dmanuchia@restaurantpartnersinc.com
Sr Consultant: George Cheros
VP, Operations: Eric Sheen
Estimated Sales: $500,000-$1 Million
Number Employees: 10-19

28383 Restaurant TechnologiesInc
2250 Pilot Knob Rd # 100
Suite 100
Mendota Heights, MN 55120-1127

651-796-1600
Fax: 651-379-4914 888-796-4997
customercare@rti-inc.com www.rti-inc.com
President: Paul Plooster
CEO: Jeffrey R. Kiesel
CFO: Robert E. Weil
VP: Brad Schoendauer
Vice President, Engineering & Quality As: Bradley J. Schoenbauer
Vice President, Sales/Marketing: Sara Sampson
Vice President, Operations: Leanne E. Branham
Estimated Sales: $1 - 3 Million
Number Employees: 100-249

28384 Restaurant Workshop
PO Box 122
Franklin, AR 72536-0122

734-434-7761
Fax: 734-434-7761 866-434-7761
Restaurant Workshop provides training and educational material to the food service and hospitality industries. Employee and management training
President: Jeff Crawford
VP/Public Relations: Kip Jaros
Type of Packaging: Food Service

28385 Retail Automations Products
45 W 38th Street
New York, NY 10018

Fax: 212-391-0575 800-237-9144
www.alohapos4me.com
Reseller of aloha computer point of sale, inventory tracking, smart card, automated delivery, touch screen and accounting systems; also, catering software, internet security. Also the tri-state area's premiere integrator of foodservice automation technologies. Through Aloha POS software, we serve NYC, Long Island and Southern CT. POS Inventory-tracking, seurity cameras, automated delivery, touch screen and accounting systems.
Contact: Robert Breitenstein
robert.breitenstein@rap-pos.com
Estimated Sales: $500,000 - $1 Million
Number Employees: 10
Square Footage: 12000
Brands:
Aloha
Business Works Accounting
Cater Ease

885

28386 Retail Decor
PO Box 4019
Ironton, OH 45638-4019
740-532-9559
Fax: 740-532-5288 800-726-3402
Decor packages for commercial interiors including aisle directories, end display pricers, check lane signal lights, chalk, menu and bulletin boards, signage, custom wall graphics, etc.; installation services available
Estimated Sales: $500,000-$1,000,000
Number Employees: 6
Square Footage: 20000

28387 Retalix
2490 Technical Dr
Miamisburg, OH 45342
937-445-1936
Fax: 937-384-2280 877-794-7237
www.ncr.com
Manufacturer and exporter of computer software including point of sale backoffice and headquarters systems for supermarkets, grocery stores and convenience stores
President: Ronen Levkovich
CEO: Shuky Sheffer
CFO: Sarit Sagiv
Head Innovation & Portfolio Strategy: Dr,Gill Roth
Marketing: Oren Betzaleli
Sales Director: Rick Cumberland
Contact: Jefferson Alcott
 j.alcott@retalix.com
Operations Manager: Eli Spirer
Estimated Sales: $10 - 20 Million
Number Employees: 50-99
Square Footage: 60000
Parent Co: Retalix, Ltd
Type of Packaging: Consumer
Brands:
 Consumer Scan

28388 Retrotec
W197N7577 F and W Ct
Lannon, WI 53046
262-253-9677
Fax: 262-253-9685
Full line of still and end over end rotating batch retorts, processes and style of hermetically sealed package in full or partial water immersion
President: Henry Cathers
Estimated Sales: $1-2.5 Million
Number Employees: 5-9

28389 Revent Inc
100 Ethel Rd W
Piscataway, NJ 08854-5967
732-777-9433
Fax: 732-777-1187 info@revent.com
www.revent.com
Manufacturer and exporter of ovens including deck, mini and bake and roast rack; also, proof boxes
President: Torvjorn Alm
 t.alm@revent.com
Quality Control: Tom Parker
Estimated Sales: $1 - 3 Million
Number Employees: 5-9
Square Footage: 200000
Parent Co: Revent International
Brands:
 Do-Sys
 Revent

28390 Revere Group
9310 4th Ave S
PO Box 80157
Seattle, WA 98108-4601
206-545-1850
Fax: 206-545-3676
www.customzipperpouches.com
Packaging supplies (accessories, bags, boxes, confectionery supplies, equipment, gift asket supplies, wrapping film, box pads and trays, ribbons, tissue, thermal transfer ribbon and gift wrap)
Vice President: Tom DE Angelo
 tom@rgroup.com
Vice President: Tom DE Angelo
 tom@rgroup.com
Number Employees: 50-99

28391 Revere Group
9310 4th Ave S
Seattle, WA 98108-4601
206-545-1850
Fax: 206-545-3676 info@rgroup.com
www.customzipperpouches.com
Specialty food packaging i.e. gift wrap/boxes/containers.
Vice President: Tom DE Angelo
 tom@rgroup.com
Vice President: Tom DE Angelo
 tom@rgroup.com
Marketing: Bill Revere
Estimated Sales: $190,000
Number Employees: 50-99

28392 Revere Packaging
39 Pearce Industrial Rd
Shelbyville, KY 40065-8125
502-633-1404
Fax: 502-633-9547 800-626-2668
www.reverepackaging.com
Foil containers and polystyrene plastic items
CEO: David Watts
Estimated Sales: $61 Thousand
Number Employees: 50-99
Square Footage: 2178

28393 Reviss Service
175 E Hawthorn Pkwy # 142
Suite 142
Vernon Hills, IL 60061-1493
847-680-4522
Fax: 847-680-5159
Irradiation
Vice President: John Schrader
 john.schrader@reviss.com
Vice President: John Schrader
 john.schrader@reviss.com
Number Employees: 1-4

28394 Rex Art Manufacturing Corp.
655 N Queens Avenue
Lindenhurst, NY 11757-3004
631-884-4600
Fax: 631-884-4611
Point of purchase displays including plastic wood and steel; also, metal specialties and aluminum sheet metal and tubing; custom rack fabrications available
President/General Manager: Robert Santangelo
Number Employees: 50
Square Footage: 80000

28395 Rex Carton Co Inc
4528 W 51st St
Chicago, IL 60632-4597
773-581-4115
Fax: 773-581-4120 info@rexcarton.com
www.rexcarton.com
Corrugated boxes
President: Ronald Lemar
 ron@rexcarton.com
VP/Plant Manager: Sal Arena
Customer Service: Greg Fleck
Plant Manager: Joe Lara
Controller: Diane Green
Estimated Sales: $5-10 Million
Number Employees: 20-49

28396 Rex Chemical Corporation
2270 NW 23rd St
Miami, FL 33142
305-634-2471
Fax: 305-634-5546 877-634-5539
rexchem@bellsouth.net www.rexchemical.com
Liquid and powder cleaners; wholesaler/distributor of janitorial supplies
President: Beatriz Granja
Contact: Mary Meier
 m.meier@sandc.com
Estimated Sales: $10-20 Million
Number Employees: 20-49

28397 Rexam Containers
743 Westgate Road
Deerfield, IL 60015-3136
847-945-2249
Fax: 847-945-4938 carrollpjx@aol.com
Director Sales: Patrick Carroll

28398 Rexcraft Fine Chafers
4139 38th Street
Long Island City, NY 11101-3617
718-361-3052
Fax: 718-361-3054 888-739-2723
rexchafer@aol.com
Manufacturer and exporter of banquetware including chafers, coffee/tea brewers and urns, hollowware, steam table inserts, serving trays and food warmers
President: Ahsan Ullaha
VP: John Berman
Engineer & Designer: David Berman
Number Employees: 40
Square Footage: 36000
Brands:
 Rexcraft

28399 Rexford Paper Company
5802 Washington Ave
Suite 102
Racine, WI 53406-4088
262-886-9100
Fax: 262-886-9130
Manufacturer, wholesaler/distributor and exporter of gummed, and reinforced paper and tapes including plain and printed, heat seal coated, lightweight meat packaging, gummed stay and pressure sensitive carton closure
CFO: Muriel Fincle
Sales Service Manager: James Carse
Sales Manager: Rory Wolf
Estimated Sales: $5 - 10 Million
Number Employees: 10-19
Parent Co: Inland Paperboard & Packaging
Type of Packaging: Consumer, Food Service
Brands:
 Lok-A-Box
 Redcore
 Rexford
 Safe-T-Seal

28400 (HQ)Rexnord Corporation
Corporate Headquarters
511 Freshwater Way
Milwaukee, WI 53204
414-643-3000
866-739-6673
www.rexnord.com
Manufacturer, importer and exporter of belt, bottle and chain conveyors.
President & CEO: Todd Adams
SVP/Chief Financial Officer: Mark Peterson
SVP, Business & Corporate Development: Rodney Jackson
Chief Human Resources Officer: George Powers
Chief Information Officer: Mike Troutman
VP/General Counsel/Secretary: Patty Whaley
Year Founded: 1891
Estimated Sales: $1 Billion
Number Employees: 8,000
Brands:
 Autogard
 Berg
 Cambridge
 Centa
 Duralon
 Euroflex
 Falk
 Highfield
 Link-Belt
 Rex
 Stearns
 Thomas
 Tollok

28401 Rexnord Corporation
Power Transmission Headquarters
4701 W Greenfield Ave.
Milwaukee, WI 53214
866-739-6673
www.rexnord.com
Bearings, couplings, gear drives, PT drive components, conveying solutions (including FlatTop), and industrial chain.
President & CEO: Todd Adams
President, Process & Motion Control: Kevin Zaba

28402 Rexroth Corporation
5150 Prairie Stone Pkwy
Hoffman Estates, IL 60192-3707
847-645-3600
Fax: 847-645-0804 www.boschrexroth-us.com

Manufacturer and importer of servodrives and controls for motion control of processing and packaging machinery
President, Chief Executive Officer: Berend Bracht
VP Sales/Marketing: Richard Huss
Contact: Quentin Gilbert
quentin.gilbert@boschrexroth-us.com
Estimated Sales: $20-50 Million
Number Employees: 1,000-4,999
Square Footage: 50000
Parent Co: Rexroth Corporation
Brands:
  Indramat

28403 Reyco Systems Inc
1704 Industrial Way
Caldwell, ID 83605-6906
208-795-5700
Fax: 208-795-5749 info@reycosys.com
www.reyco.com
Manufacturer and exporter of pneumatic waste conveying, dewatering and fryer oil recovery equipment
General Manager: Rex McArthur
Account Manager: Marilyn McGrew
Design Manager: Jeff Denkers
Sales Director: Kathryn Brown
Manager: Wyland Atkins
awyland@reycosys.com
Plant Manager: Rex McArthur
Purchasing Manager: David Lethcoe
Estimated Sales: $5 - 10,000,000
Number Employees: 5-9
Brands:
  Cornell Pumps and Pumping Systems
  Dynavac and Watervac Water Systems
  Oil Miser Oil Recovery Systems
  Pneumatic Conveying Systems
  Ventilation & Process Air Systems

28404 Reynold Water Conditioning
24545 Hathaway St
Farmington Hills, MI 48335-1549
248-620-1433
Fax: 248-888-5005 800-572-9575
info@reynoldswater.com www.reynoldswater.com
Water softeners, filters and purifiers
President: James Reynolds
jamie@reynoldswater.com
VP: James Reynolds Jr
Estimated Sales: Less Than $500,000
Number Employees: 1-4
Square Footage: 22000
Type of Packaging: Consumer
Brands:
  Clearstream
  Oxy-Catalytic
  Soft-Sensor
  Softstream
  Turbo Sensor
  Twin-Stream

28405 Reynolds Foodservice Packaging
6603 W Broad Street
Richmond, VA 23230-1723
804-281-2525
Fax: 804-281-3289 pnquick@rmc.com
Offers more than 1,000 products designed for the food service industry including foil, film, aluminum and plastic containers and lids, food service bags, catering trays, sandwich bags and wraps, baking cups and trays
General Contact: Paula Quick
Estimated Sales: $3 - 5 Million
Number Employees: 5-9

28406 Rez-Tech Corp
1510 Mogadore Rd
Kent, OH 44240-7531
330-673-4009
Fax: 330-673-2273 800-673-5277
Blow and injection molded clear plastic food containers
Chairman of Board: Tom Podnar
Co-President/CEO: Jack Podnar
CEO: Scott Podnar
VP: Craig Podnar
CEO: Jack Podnar
Purchasing Manager: Martha Sth
Estimated Sales: $2.5 - 5 Million
Number Employees: 20-49
Square Footage: 90000
Type of Packaging: Consumer, Food Service, Private Label

28407 Rhee Brothers
7461 Coca Cola Dr
Hanover, MD 21076
410-799-6656
Fax: 410-381-9080 www.rheebros.com
Asian food products
President: Syng Rhee
CFO: Ha Chang
Contact: Phillip Ahn
phillipahn@rheebros.com
Estimated Sales: $20-50 Million
Number Employees: 100-249
Type of Packaging: Private Label

28408 Rheo-Tech
640 Sanders Ct
Gurnee, IL 60031-3135
847-367-1557
USDA certified pumps and extruders for cheese, licorice candy, ground meat, sausage meat, fillings, peanut butter, etc
President: John Mowli
Estimated Sales: $1-2.5,000,000
Number Employees: 1-4

28409 Rheometric Scientific
109 Lukens Drive
New Castle, DE 19720-2765
732-560-8550
Fax: 732-560-7451
Rheometers, viscometers, thermal analyzers and process controllers
VP: Joseph Musanti
Managing Director: Don Becker
Marketing Manager: Joyce Altauia
Director Sales: Sean Kohl
Sales Manager: Michael Goliner
District Manager of Rheology: Howard Eubanks
Number Employees: 100-249

28410 Rheon
445 Holly Street
Laguna Beach, CA 92651-1746
949-497-3150
Fax: 949-497-3951
Manufacturer, importer and exporter of food processing equipment including automated mass production lines and flexible compact tables

28411 Rheon USA
2 Doppler
Irvine, CA 92618-4306
949-768-1900
Fax: 949-855-1991 us.info@rheon.com
www.rheon.com
Manufacturer, importer and exporter of food processing equipment including automated mass production lines and flexible compact tables
General Manager: Kiyo Kamiyama
Sales Coordinator: Terry Smith
Manager Engineering Sales: Kazu Onuki
Manager: Kazu Onuki
us.info@rheon.com
Estimated Sales: $500,000-$1 Million
Number Employees: 20-49
Brands:
  Cwc System
  Ez Table

28412 Rheon, U.S.A.
9490 Toledo Way
Irvine, CA 92618
949-768-1900
Fax: 949-855-1991 www.rheon.com
Dough sheet & pastry equipment, bread equipment and encrusting machines.
Contact: Hiroshi Kimura
hiroshi.kimura@rheon.com

28413 Rhineland Cutlery
345 Stan Dr
Melbourne, FL 32904-1085
321-725-2101
Fax: 321-253-0737 www.rhinelandcutlery.com
Cooking implements, housewares
Principal: Phillip McMahon
Estimated Sales: Less Than $500,000
Number Employees: 1-4

28414 Rhino Foods Inc
179 Queen City Park Road
Burlington, VT 05401
802-862-0252
Fax: 802-865-4145 info@rhinofoods.com
www.rhinofoods.com
Ice cream, brownies, cookie dough batter, cakes, truffles, pie squares and baking inclusions.
President/Owner: Ted Castle
tcastle@rhinofoods.com
Vice President: Rooney Castle
Director, Sales/Marketing: Rachel Moss
Marketing Manager/Demand Planner: Gillian Bell
Year Founded: 1981
Estimated Sales: $25 Million
Number Employees: 100-249
Number of Brands: 2
Square Footage: 29000
Type of Packaging: Consumer, Food Service, Private Label, Bulk
Brands:
  Chessters
  Vermont Velvet

28415 Rhoades Paper Box Corporation
PO Box 1666
Springfield, OH 45501
937-325-6494
Fax: 937-324-1597 800-441-6494
www.3g-graphics.com
Paper set-up boxes used for fine candies
Owner: Jeanie Lape
Sales Manager: Pat Hays
Estimated Sales: $2.5 - 5 Million
Number Employees: 20-49
Square Footage: 100000
Parent Co: Graphic Paper Products Corporation

28416 Rhode Island Label WorkInc
14 Clyde St
West Warwick, RI 02893-3504
401-828-6400
Fax: 401-828-8884
Seals and labels including UPC/bar code, pressure sensitive, gum, ungummed and transfer
President: William H Cole
rilabel@aol.com
Estimated Sales: Less Than $500,000
Number Employees: 1-4
Square Footage: 10000

28417 Rhodes Bakery Equipment
14330 SW McFarland Boulevard
Portland, OR 97224-2906
503-232-9101
Fax: 503-232-9206 800-426-3813
sales@kook-e-king.com www.kook-e-king.com
Manufacturer and exporter of cookie depositors and cutters
Marketing/Sales: Jan Duncan
Number Employees: 10-19
Square Footage: 120000
Brands:
  Kook-E-King

28418 Rhodes Machinery International
1350 S 15th St
Louisville, KY 40210
502-213-3865
Fax: 502-213-0096 www.rsisystemsinc.net
Manufacturer and exporter of tow line conveyors
President: William Rhodes
Plant Manager: Mark Wolford
Estimated Sales: $1 - 3 Million
Number Employees: 5-9
Parent Co: Rhodes Systems Worldwide
Type of Packaging: Bulk

28419 Ribble Production
1601 Mearns Road
Warminster, PA 18974-1115
215-674-1706
Fax: 215-674-0123
Decorative toppings, nonpareils, jimmies and mixes; custom manufacturing and packaging
VP: Joseph Van Houten
Number Employees: 20-49
Type of Packaging: Consumer, Food Service, Private Label, Bulk

28420 Ricca Chemical Co
1490 Lammers Pike
Batesville, IN 47006-8631
812-932-1160
Fax: 812-932-1254 888-467-4222
www.riccachemical.com
Laboratory chemicals used for quality control
President: Peter J Ricca
Manager: Paul Brandon
pbrandon@riccachemical.com
Estimated Sales: $5-10 Million
Number Employees: 10-19

28421 (HQ)Rice Lake Weighing Systems
230 W Coleman St
Rice Lake, WI 54868-2422
715-234-9171
Fax: 715-234-6967 800-472-6703
prodinfo@ricelake.com www.ricelake.com
Manufacturer and exporter of heavy capacity scales
and computer interface equipment; also, full metal
services available
Cmo: Pat Ranfranz
pranfranz@ricelake.com
VP: Rick Tyree
Regional Sales Director: Matt Crawford
Estimated Sales: $2.5-5 Million
Number Employees: 250-499
Square Footage: 100000

28422 Rice Packaging Inc
356 Somers Rd
Ellington, CT 06029-2628
860-872-8341
Fax: 860-872-0880 800-367-6725
info@ricepackaging.com www.ricepackaging.com
Custom printed folding cartons, stock boxes, point
of purchase displays and pressure sensitive and em-
bossed foil labels
President: Clifford Rice
cliff@ricepackaging.com
Sales Manager: Angelo Salvatore
Estimated Sales: $10-20 Million
Number Employees: 50-99

28423 Rice Paper Box Company
PO Box 62096
1187 East 68th Avenue
Colorado Springs, CO 80962-2096
303-733-1000
Fax: 303-733-6789
Rigid set up, folding and transparent paper boxes
President: Douglas E Miller
CFO: David Rice
VP: Eugene Rice
Sales/Marketing: Michael Porter
Director of Operations: Matt Juhasz
Estimated Sales: Below $5 Million
Number Employees: 45

28424 Rich Xiberta USA Inc
450 Aaron St
Cotati, CA 94931-3068
707-795-1800
Fax: 707-795-1667 www.xiberta.com
Natural, high-end quality cork manufacturers
President: Ferran Botifoll
Contact: Rich Xiberta
r.xiberta@xiberta.com
Estimated Sales: Below $5 Million
Number Employees: 5-9

28425 Richard Read Construction Company
302 North First Avenue Suite #2
Arcadia, CA 91006
626-445-3002
Fax: 626-445-1027 888-450-7343
RRCCO@Pacbell.net
Plastic containers and bottles
Owner: Richard Read
rrcco@pacbell.net
Estimated Sales: $1 - 5 Million
Number Employees: 1-4

28426 Richards Industries Systems
4 Fairfield Cres
West Caldwell, NJ 07006-6296
973-575-7480
Fax: 973-575-6783 www.rifab.com
Bucket Z-type conveyors, dumpers, skip hoists and
material lifts; also, steel fabricators for all shapes
and forms of industrial equipment
Owner: Chuck Wampler
pspina@richardsind.com
VP: Chuck Wampler
Sales: Patricia Spina
Estimated Sales: $5 - 10 Million
Number Employees: 10-19
Square Footage: 50000

28427 Richards Packaging
4721 Burbank Rd
Memphis, TN 38118-6302
901-360-1121
Fax: 901-360-0050 800-583-0327
memphissales@richardspackaging.com
www.richardsmemphis.com
Manufacturer, exporter and importer of glass and
plastic bottles and jars; also, droppers, sprayers and
closures
CEO: Robert Boord
Estimated Sales: $10 Million
Number Employees: 10-19
Number of Brands: 100
Number of Products: 1000
Square Footage: 60000

28428 Richardson International
2800 One Lombard Pl.
Winnipeg, MB R3B 0X8
Canada
204-934-5961
866-217-6211
info@richardson.ca www.richardson.ca
Grains and oilseed.
President/CEO: Curt Vossen
Chief Operations Officer: Darwin Sobkow
Executive Vice President, Finance/CFO: Craig
Sheldon
SVP, Corporate Affairs/General Counsel: Jean-Marc
Ruest
SVP, Processing, Food & Ingredients: Darrell
Sobkow
SVP, Commodity Merchandising: John Peterson
SVP, Agribusiness Operations: Tom Hamilton
Year Founded: 1857
Estimated Sales: $28.6 Billion
Number Employees: 3,000+
Type of Packaging: Consumer, Food Service, Pri-
vate Label, Bulk

28429 Richardson Researches
480 Grandview Drive
South San Francisco, CA 94080
510-653-4385
Fax: 510-785-6857 info@richres.com
www.richres.com
Consultant for new products and process develop-
ment; also, courses available in chocolate and con-
fectionery technology
President: Terence Richardson
CEO: Rose Marie Richardson
VP: RM Richardson
Estimated Sales: $1-2.5 Million
Number Employees: 5-9

28430 Richardson Seating Corp
2545 W Arthington St
Chicago, IL 60612-4107
312-829-4040
Fax: 312-829-8337 800-522-1883
sales@richardsonseating.com
www.richardsonseating.com
Bar and counter stools, logo seating and stack, din-
ing, upholstered and club chairs and consumer furni-
ture
Owner/CEO: Earl Lichtenstein
National Sales Manager: Jim Spatzek
Manager: Mike Liren
mike@richardsonseating.com
Estimated Sales: $10-20 Million
Number Employees: 20-49
Square Footage: 150000

28431 Richardson's Stamp Works
8566 Katy Fwy # 127
Suite 124
Houston, TX 77024-1811
713-973-0314
Fax: 713-973-0314
Stamp pad ink, name plates and badges, signs and
rubber and plastic stamps
President: Marjorie Waltman
Estimated Sales: $300,000-500,000
Number Employees: 5-9

28432 (HQ)Richmond Corrugated BoxCompany
PO Box 7715
Richmond, VA 23231
804-222-1300
Fax: 804-222-4897 www.richbox.com
Corrugated boxes and die cut products
President: Mark Williams
Vice President/General Manager: Chuck White
Structural Design: Wayne Johnson
Quality Control: Walters Spence
Sales: George Bayer
Contact: Brooke Hatcher
brookeh@richbox.com
Sales Manager: Mike Kelly
Production Manager: Mark Lawrence
Estimated Sales: $2.5 - 5 Million
Number Employees: 20-49
Square Footage: 96000
Other Locations:
Richmond Corrugated BoxCo.
Wilmington NC

28433 Richmond Printed Tape &Label
1901 N Penn Road
Hatfield, PA 19440-1961
804-798-4753
Fax: 804-798-0632 800-522-3525
Pressure sensitive tapes and labels
President: Scott Moeller
Quality Control: Kevin Moller
Manager Sales/Marketing: Mark Moeller
Estimated Sales: Below $5 Million
Number Employees: 15

28434 Richway Industries
504 N Maple St
PO Box 508
Janesville, IA 50647-7704
319-987-2976
Fax: 319-987-2251 800-553-2404
Chemicals and equipment
President: R Borglum
rborglum@richwayind.com
Estimated Sales: $5-10 Million
Number Employees: 20-49

28435 Rico Packaging Company
3617 S Ashland Avenue
Chicago, IL 60609-1320
773-523-9190
Fax: 773-523-7965
Manufacturer and exporter of printed flexible pack-
aging
President: William Wrigeyjr
CFO: Carol Riley
Manager: Don Bicking
R & D: William Wrigeyjr
Estimated Sales: $10-20 Million
Number Employees: 10
Parent Co: Wrigley

28436 Ricoh Technologies
1022 Santerre St
Grand Prairie, TX 75050-1937
972-602-0210
Fax: 972-602-3126 800-585-9367
Commercial fryers
President: Mac Shinagawa
Sales Representative: David Coronado
Estimated Sales: $2.5-5,000,000
Number Employees: 20-49
Parent Co: Sivex Corporation
Brands:
Aqua Pro

28437 Ridg-U-Rak
120 S Lake St
North East, PA 16428
866-479-7225
www.ridgurak.com
Racks including storage, flow, pushback, structural
and cold-formed; custom designing available.
VP, Manufacturing: John Pellegrino
National Sales & Marketing Manager: Dave Olson
Estimated Sales: $27 Million
Number Employees: 250-499
Square Footage: 160000

28438 RidgeView Products LLC
2527 East Avenue S
La Crosse, WI 54601-6759
608-781-5946
Fax: 608-781-4408 888-782-1221
www.ridgeproducts.com
Manufacurer of brush and broom products
President: Keith Martin
Marketing/Sales: Roshelle Easterday
Number Employees: 4

28439 Rieke Packaging Systems
500 W 7th St
Auburn, IN 46706-2006
260-925-3700
Fax: 260-925-2493 sales@riekecorp.com
www.riekepackaging.com
Manufacturer and exporter of dispensing equipment
including pumps, pourspouts and faucets
CEO: David M Pritchett
dpritchett@riekecorp.com
CEO: Lynn Brooks
CFO: Chris Baron
VP: Don Laipple
Marketing Director: Wayne Schmidt
Director of Sales: William Heimach
Purchasing Manager: Jim Szink
Estimated Sales: $1 - 5,000,000
Number Employees: 250-499
Type of Packaging: Consumer, Food Service
Brands:
Englass
Flexspout
Flo-King
Flo-Rite
Fnd-30
Hybrid
Maxi
Multi-Meter
R-30

28440 Rietschle
1800 Gardner Expy
Quincy, IL 62305
Fax: 410-712-4148 800-247-2158
Vacuum pumps and compressors
President: Stephen J Lovell
Marketing Manager: Ron Heller
Estimated Sales: $10 - 20 Million
Number Employees: 60

28441 Rig-A-Lite Inc
8500 Hansen Rd
PO Box 12942
Houston, TX 77075-1096
713-378-7800
Fax: 713-943-8354 www.rigalite.com
Innovative and energy efficient lighting solutions for
food processing environments, where rugged light-
ing products are required. Offer a complete line of
high pressure hose down and corrosion resistant
lighting products for severeenvironments suitable
for almost any applications using florescent, HID,
incandescent and LED lamping.
R&D: Syed Hasan
Marketing: Ross Blanford
Sales: Paul Markee
Contact: Maxine Hernandez
lovey1986@gmail.com
Operations: Walter Despain
Purchasing: Gordon Logan
Estimated Sales: $10-25 Million
Number Employees: 100
Parent Co: AZZ incorporated

28442 Rigid Plastics Packaging Institute
1667 K St
NW Suite 1000
Washington, DC 20006
202-974-5200
Fax: 202-296-7005 www.plasticsindustry.org
Plastics
President: William Cartuaex
Number Employees: 100-249

28443 Rigidized Metal Corp
658 Ohio St
Buffalo, NY 14203-3185
716-849-4760
Fax: 716-849-0401 800-836-2580
hr@rigidized.com www.rigidized.com

Manufacturer, importer and exporter of embossed
metal parts for conveyors, packaging machinery and
food processing equipment
Manager: Os Putman
osputman@rigidized.com
VP Sales: Louis Martin
Estimated Sales: $2.5-5,000,000
Number Employees: 50-99
Brands:
Rigid-Tex
Rigidized

28444 Riley & Geehr
2205 Lee Street
Evanston, IL 60202-1559
847-869-8100
Fax: 847-869-4765
Flexible pouches, stand-up pouches, shaped
pouches, zipper pouches
CEO: Tom Riley
Sales Director: Diane Riley
Estimated Sales: $5-10 Million
Number Employees: 80
Type of Packaging: Consumer, Food Service, Pri-
vate Label, Bulk

**28445 Riley Cole
ProfessionalRecruitment**
4110 Redwood Road
Suite 201
Oakland, CA 94619-2370
510-336-2333
Fax: 510-428-2072
Executive search firm
Co-Partner: Donald Cole
Co-Partner: James Riley
Partner: James Riley
Estimated Sales: Below $5 Million
Number Employees: 2

28446 Rimex Metals Inc
2850 Woodbridge Ave
Edison, NJ 08837-3616
732-549-3800
Fax: 732-549-6435 sales@rimexusa.com
www.rimexmetals.com
President: Barbara Brandt
barbara.brandt@rimexmetals.com
Estimated Sales: $10 - 20 Million
Number Employees: 20-49

28447 Rio Syrup Co
2311 Chestnut St
St Louis, MO 63103-2298
314-436-7700
Fax: 314-436-7707 800-325-7666
flavors@riosyrup.com www.riosyrup.com
Syrups, extracts and concentrates, slush flavors and
bases, fountain syrups and liquid food colors
President: Phillip Tomber
phil@riosyrup.com
Estimated Sales: $500,000-$1 Million
Number Employees: 5-9
Number of Products: 1200
Square Footage: 92000
Type of Packaging: Consumer, Food Service, Bulk
Brands:
Rio

28448 Rios, J J
4890 E Acampo Rd
Acampo, CA 95220-9601
209-333-7167
Fax: 209-333-3715
Wine industry vineyard services
Owner: Jose Rios
rios.jose.j@gmail.com
Estimated Sales: Less Than $500,000
Number Employees: 5-9

28449 Ripon Manufacturing Co Inc
652 S Stockton Ave
Ripon, CA 95366-2798
209-599-2148
Fax: 209-599-3114 800-800-1232
sales@riponmfgco.com www.riponmfgco.com
Manufacturer and exporter of edible nut processing
equipment and conveyance systems
President: Glenn Navarro
sales@riponmfgco.com
VP: Ernst Boesch
Sales: Bruce Boyd
Purchasing: Denise Judd

Estimated Sales: $6 Million
Number Employees: 20-49
Square Footage: 126000

28450 Risco USA Corp
60 Bristol Dr
PO Box 198
South Easton, MA 02375-1193
508-230-3336
Fax: 508-230-5345 888-474-7267
info@riscousa.com www.riscousa.com
Equipment manufacturer to the meat and poultry in-
dustry which includes; stuffers, vacuum stuffers and
systems
President: Alan Miller
amiller@riscousa.com
VP: P Kean
Technician: Victor Silva
Estimated Sales: $2.5-$5 Million
Number Employees: 10-19

28451 Ritchie's Foods
527 S West St
Piketon, OH 45661-8042
740-289-4393
Fax: 740-289-4375 800-628-1290
ritchiefoods.com
Foodservice distributor
CEO: James Ritchie
jritchie@ritchiefoods.com
Estimated Sales: $17.4 Million
Number Employees: 20-49
Square Footage: 30000
Type of Packaging: Consumer, Food Service

28452 Rite-Hite
8900 N Arbon Dr
Milwaukee, WI 53223
414-355-2600
Fax: 414-355-9248 800-841-4283
www.ritehite.com
Loading dock equipment, industrial doors, safety
barriers, HVLS fans, industrial curtain walls, and
more.
President & CEO: Kyle Nelson
Chair: Michael White
Year Founded: 1965
Estimated Sales: $100-500 Million
Number Employees: 1000-4999

28453 Ritt-Ritt & Associates
5105 Tollview Drive
Suite 110
Rolling Meadows, IL 60008-3724
847-827-7771
Fax: 847-827-9776
Executive search firm specializing in job placement
for the food and hospitality industries
Chairman: Art Ritt
President: William Morris
Estimated Sales: Less than $500,000
Number Employees: 1-4
Square Footage: 4400

28454 Ritz Packaging Company
54 Knickerbocker Avenue
Brooklyn, NY 11237-1636
718-366-2300
Fax: 631-476-4358
Paper boxes for ravioli, pasta, doughnuts,
breadsticks and candy
*Estimated Sales:*less than $500,000
Number Employees: 1-4

**28455 (HQ)Rival Manufacturing
Company**
800 E 101st Terrace
Suite 100
Kansas City, MO 64131-5308
816-943-4100
Fax: 816-943-4123 www.rivco.com
Manufacturer and exporter of can openers, vegetable
and fruit shredders/slicers, mini choppers, slow
cookers and ice cream freezers
Number Employees: 100-249
Other Locations:
Rival Manufacturing Co.
Kansas City MO
Brands:
Chop 'n Shake
Crock Pot
Dolly Madison

28456 River City Sales & Marketing
11700 Congo Ferndale Rd
Alexander, AR 72002-7007
501-316-3663
Fax: 501-794-0605
Owner: Vick Pannell
vickpannell@vickpannell.com
Estimated Sales: $1 - 5 Million
Number Employees: 1-4

28457 Riverside Industries
PO Box D
St Helens, OR 97051-0280
503-397-1922
Fax: 503-397-1527
Contract packager of liquids, powders, creams and solids
Executive Director: Cindy Stockton
Director Marketing: John Briggs
Number Employees: 50-99
Square Footage: 16000

28458 Riverside ManufacturingCompany
3405 N Arlington Heights Rd
Arlington Hts, IL 60004-1581
847-577-9300
Fax: 847-577-9318 800-877-3349
info@flagmaster.org
www.riversidemedicalsc.com
Manufacturer and exporter of custom made plastic and fluorescent display pennants, flags and banners
VP Marketing: Andy Krupp
Estimated Sales: $1 - 5 Million
Number Employees: 20-49
Square Footage: 80000
Type of Packaging: Food Service
Brands:
    Flagmaster

28459 Riverside Wire & Metal Co.
PO Box 122
Ionia, MI 48846-0122
616-527-3500
Fax: 616-527-8550
Wire racks and baskets
Owner: Don Shephard
Estimated Sales: $500,000-$1 Million
Number Employees: 5-9
Parent Co: Col-Mell
Type of Packaging: Consumer, Food Service

28460 Riverview Foods
1360 Bethleham Road
PO Box 765
Warsaw, KY 41095
859-567-5211
Fax: 859-567-5213
Smoked meats, barbecue and tomato sauces; research and development services
President: Bob Weldon
VP Sales/Marketing: Robert Schroeder
General Manager: Mike Benton
Number Employees: 50-99
Square Footage: 100000
Type of Packaging: Consumer, Food Service, Private Label, Bulk
Brands:
    Riverview Foods Authentic

28461 Riverwood International
814 Livingston Ct SE
Marietta, GA 30067-8940
770-644-3000
Fax: 770-644-2962
investor.relations@graphicpkg.com
Paperboard and paperboard packaging machinery company
President: Thomas H Johnson
CEO: David W Scheible
Marketing Manager: Hous King
Contact: Sylvia Gillenwaters
sylvia.gillenwaters@riverwood.com
Estimated Sales: $50-100 Million
Number Employees: 10,000

28462 Riverwood International
3350 Riverwood Pkwy SE
Atlanta, GA 30339-6401
770-984-5477
Fax: 770-644-2620 www.riverwood.com
Packaging systems and machinery for beverages, produce, etc

CEO: Stephen Humphrey
CFO: Don Baldwin
Estimated Sales: $50 - 100 Million
Number Employees: 100-249

28463 Riviana Foods Inc.
75 Shannon Rd
Suite B
Harrisburg, PA 17112
713-529-3251
Fax: 713-535-8285 info@riviana.com
www.riviana.com
Rice and pasta.
President/CEO: Enrique Zaragoza
Chairman: Antonio Hern ndez Callejas
Senior VP/CFO: Michael Schwartz
Senior VP, Marketing: Sandra Kim
Senior VP, Human Resources: Gerard Ferguson
Year Founded: 1965
Estimated Sales: $500 Million
Number Employees: 1,000-4,999
Number of Brands: 33
Parent Co: Ebro Foods, S.A.
Type of Packaging: Consumer, Food Service, Private Label, Bulk
Other Locations:
    Corporate Office
    Harrisburg PA
    Corporate Office
    Etobicoke, ON, Canada
    Manufacturing Facility
    Brinkley AR
    Manufacturing Facility
    Carlisle AR
    Manufacturing Facility
    Hazen AR
    Manufacturing Facility
    Fresno CA
    Manufacturing Facility
    Crowley LA
    Manufacturing Facility
    Clearbook MN
    Manufacturing Facility
    Memphis TN
    Manufacturing Facility
    Alvin TX
    Manufacturing Facility
    Freeport TX
Brands:
    AA
    AA Brand
    Abu Bint
    Adolphus
    Adolphus
    Blue Ribbon
    Blue Ribbon Rice
    Carolina
    Carolina
    Colusa Rose
    Colusa Rose
    Comet
    Comet Rice
    Gourmet House
    Gourmet House
    Green Peacock
    Mahatma
    Mahatma
    Minute
    Minute
    Pear Blossom
    Pear Blossom
    Rice Select
    RiceSelect
    River
    River Rice
    Sello Rojo
    Sello Rojo
    Success
    Success
    Water Maid
    Water Maid
    Wonder

28464 Rixie Paper Products Inc
10 Quinter St
Pottstown, PA 19464-6514
610-323-9220
Fax: 610-323-6146 800-377-2692
www.sonoco.com
Manufacturer and exporter of disposable paper products including coasters: cellulose, pulpboard, budgetboard, nonwoven, etc.; also, placemats and sanitary caps for drinking glasses

President: Tom Johnson
Chairman: Roger Schrum
roger.schrum@sonoco.com
VP Sales/Marketing: Smitty Thomas
VP Operations: Kent Adicks
Plant Manager: Lee Burg
Estimated Sales: $5 - 10 Million
Number Employees: 10-19
Parent Co: Engraph
Type of Packaging: Food Service
Brands:
    Cupkin
    Rixcaps
    Sof-Ette

28465 Rjo Associates
3645 Cortez Rd W Ste 140
Bradenton, FL 34210
941-756-3001
Fax: 941-756-0027 admin@mriflorida.com
Search consultants for technical product development and marketing in food and food ingredient manufacturing
President: R Rush Oster
Estimated Sales: Less than $500,000
Number Employees: 1-4
Parent Co: Management Recruiters

28466 Rjr Technologies
7875 Edgewater Dr
Oakland, CA 94621-2001
510-638-5901
Fax: 510-638-5958 www.rjrtechnologies.com
Manufacturer and exporter of flexible packaging products including folding foil cartons, barrier films and aluminum foil; also, printing and lamination available
President & CEO: Wil Salhuana
CFO: Tony Bregante
Estimated Sales: $1 - 5 Million
Number Employees: 100-249

28467 Rjs Carter Co Inc
251 5th St NW # D
New Brighton, MN 55112-6864
651-636-8818
Manufacturer and exporter of synthetic rubber balls for sifter and screener cleaning
President: John Galt
Estimated Sales: Less Than $500,000
Number Employees: 1-4
Brands:
    Screwballs

28468 Ro-An Industries Corporation
6420 Admiral Ave
Flushing, NY 11379
718-366-8971
Fax: 718-821-3838 800-255-7626
Plastic bag machinery
President: Angelo Cervera
Contact: Eric Schwarz
schwarz@roan.com
Estimated Sales: $10-20 Million
Number Employees: 100-249

28469 Roaring Brook Dairy
Po Box 753
Chappaqua, NY 10514
646-559-9330
Fax: 866-733-6736 roaringbrookdairy@gmail.com
Cheesemaking kits
Marketing: Leslie Kozupsky
Estimated Sales: $88,000
Number Employees: 2

28470 Robar International Inc
3013 N 114th St
Milwaukee, WI 53222-4289
414-259-1104
Fax: 414-259-0842 800-279-7750
rhoelzl@robarinternational.com
Dispoza-Pak trash compactors.
President: Robert Hoelzl
rhoelzl@robarinternational.com
VP: Daniel Hoelzl
Estimated Sales: Below $5 Million
Number Employees: 5-9
Brands:
    Dispoza-Pak

28471 Robatech USA Inc
1005 Alderman Dr # 108
Suite 108
Alpharetta, GA 30005-3825
770-663-8380
Fax: 770-663-8381 info@robatechusa.com
www.robatech.com
Hot melt and cold adhesive application equipment,
patten controls
CEO: Deon Strauss
Contact: Steve Green
sgreen@robatechusa.com
Estimated Sales: $500,000-$1 Million
Number Employees: 1-4
Parent Co: Robatech Group

28473 Robbie Manufacturing Inc
10810 Mid America Dr
Lenexa, KS 66219-1295
913-492-3400
Fax: 913-492-1543 800-255-6328
Packaging equipment and materials
President/CEO: Irv Robinson
COO: Pepper Stokes
Executive VP Sales/Marketing: Doug Larson
Product Development Director: Jeff Linton
Estimated Sales: $20 - 50 Million
Number Employees: 100-249
Square Footage: 94596
Type of Packaging: Food Service, Private Label

28474 Robby Vapor Systems
10224 NW 47th Street
Sunrise, FL 33351-7970
954-746-3080
Fax: 954-746-0036 800-888-8711
robbyvapor@aol.com
Manufacturer, importer and exporter of stainless
steel vapor cleaning systems and carts
President: Fran Vogt-Strauss
Office Manager: Lisa Skewes
Estimated Sales: $500,000-$1 Million
Number Employees: 9
Square Footage: 22240
Brands:
Robby Vapor Systems
Vapor Dragon

28475 Robecco
99 Park Ave # 7
New York, NY 10016-1506
212-286-8585
Fax: 212-490-8966 sales@robecoinc.com
www.robecoinc.com
Supplier of vinyl sheeting
President: Maurice Rosenthal
Estimated Sales: $10-20 Million
Number Employees: 20-49

28476 Robelan Displays Inc
395 Westbury Blvd
Hempstead, NY 11550-1900
516-564-8600
Fax: 516-564-8077 865-564-8600
main@robelan.net www.robelan.net
Merchandising fixture and food display units; im-
porter of theme props
President: Andrew Abatemarco
CFO: John Didiovanni
HR Executive: Rob Abatemarco
main@robelan.net
VP Sales: Rob Abutemarco
Customer Service: Carol Kirk
Estimated Sales: $5 - 10 Million
Number Employees: 50-99
Type of Packaging: Food Service

28477 Robert Bosch LLC
38000 Hills Tech Dr
Farmington, MI 48331
917-421-7209
www.bosch.us
Filling and sealing equipment
President, North America: Mike Mansuetti
CFO: Maximiliane Straub
Estimated Sales: $80 Billion
Number Employees: 400,100
Parent Co: Robert Bosch GmbH
Brands:
Svk
Trans-Zip

28478 Robert C Vncek Design Assoc
30 Eric Trl
Sussex, NJ 07461-4110
973-702-8553
Fax: 973-702-8553 www.rcvdes.com
Consulting firm providing packaging design, development, engineering, graphics, validation, source reduction, troubleshooting and project management
services
Contact: Robert Vincek
rcvdes@warwick.net
Estimated Sales: Below $500,000
Number Employees: 5

28479 Robert-James Sales
699 Hertel Ave
Buffalo, NY 14207-2341
716-871-0091
Fax: 716-871-0923 800-777-1325
RJSales@RJSales.com www.RJSales.com
Manufacturer and exporter of fittings, pipes, tubing,
hose clamps and sanitary stainless steel valves
Sales Manager: Thomas Callahan
Estimated Sales: $50-100 Million
Number Employees: 100-249

28480 Robertet Group
10 Colonial Dr.
Piscataway, NJ 08854
732-981-8300
Fax: 732-981-1717 www.robertet.com
Flavorings.
Chairman: Philippe Maubert
CEO: Jerome Bruhat
Director, North America: Robert Weinstein
Director, Fragrance Division: Christophe Maubert
Director, Flavor Division: Julien Maubert
Chief Growth Officer: Arthur Le Tourneur D'Ison
Chief Operating Officer: Herve Bellon
General Counsel: Eugenie Cossart
Project Director: Jean-Daniel Dor
Managing Director, Purchasing: Stephanie Groult
CFO: Isabelle Pardies
Year Founded: 1850
Estimated Sales: $524.9 Million
Number Employees: 1,800
Number of Brands: 5
Square Footage: 16805
Parent Co: Robertet SA
Type of Packaging: Food Service
Other Locations:
Robertet Culinary
Schoten, Belgium
Brands:
Accord Flavours
Citra-Next
Flavour Sensations
Natur-Cell
Smart Flavours

28481 Roberts Packaging Equipment
424 Howard Ave
Des Plaines, IL 60018-1910
847-390-9410
Fax: 847-390-6170 888-221-0700
Contract packager and manufacturer of high speed
pouch packaging equipment
President: Robert G Koppe
Director Sales/Marketing: Michael Boyd
Manager: Alex Waterman
axwaterman@cloudps.com
Estimated Sales: $2.5-5 Million
Number Employees: 50-99
Square Footage: 80000

28482 Roberts Pallet Co
607 County Road 500
Ellington, MO 63638-7759
573-663-7877
Fax: 573-663-7873
Wooden pallets
Owner: Phillip Roberts
palletgal6@aol.com
VP: Wes Roberts
Estimated Sales: Less than $500,000
Number Employees: 20-49
Square Footage: 18000

28483 Roberts Poly Pro Inc
5416 Wyoming Ave
Charlotte, NC 28273-8861
704-588-1794
Fax: 704-588-1821 800-269-7409
info@robertspolypro.com
www.robertspolypro.com
Manufacturer and exporter of converting equipment
and systems including folder/gluers, case packers,
prefeeders, turntables, stack turners, etc.; also, plastic packaging components and machinery including
label and pour spoutapplicators, etc
President: Vipul Deshani
vipul.deshani@vvfltd.com
VP Engineering: Claude Monsees
Estimated Sales: $5-10 Million
Number Employees: 50-99
Square Footage: 140000
Parent Co: Pro Mach

28484 Roberts Systems
8506 S Tryon St # A
Charlotte, NC 28273-3549
704-588-5210
Fax: 704-588-8199 800-269-7409
sales@robertssystems.com
Motion cartoner and automatic inserter
Estimated Sales: $.5 - 1 million
Number Employees: 1-4

28485 Roberts Technology Group
120 New Britain Blvd
Chalfont, 18 18936-9637
215-822-0600
Fax: 215-822-0662 info@rtgpkg.com
www.rtgpkg.com
Bandages bundling, shrink

28486 Roberts-Gordon LLC
1250 William St
Buffalo, NY 14206-1885
716-852-4400
Fax: 716-852-0854 800-828-7450
www.robertsgordon.com
Gas-fired infrared heaters and energy management
systems
President: Meredith Christman
christman@rg-inc.com
R & D: Mak Murdlch
Marketing Director: Madonna Courtney
Sales Director: Kevin Mahoney
Plant Manager: Roy Wyzykowski
Purchasing Manager: Judith Cloon
Estimated Sales: $20-50 Million
Number Employees: 100-249

28487 Robertson Furniture Co Inc
890 Elberton St
Toccoa, GA 30577-3479
706-886-1494
Fax: 706-886-8998 800-241-0713
tzirkle@robertson-furniture.com
www.robertson-furniture.com
Manufacturer and importer of chairs, tables, booths,
steel frame seating and casegoods
President: Scott Hodges
tzirkle@robertson-furniture.com
Director Sales/Marketing: Tim Zirkle
Sales Exec: Tim Zirkle
Estimated Sales: $10 - 20 Million
Number Employees: 50-99
Square Footage: 400000
Type of Packaging: Food Service, Private Label

28488 Robin Shepherd Group
1301 Riverplace Blvd.
Suite 1100
Jacksonville, FL 32207
904-359-0981
Fax: 904-359-0808 877-896-8774
trsginfo@shepherdagency.com www.trsg.net
Consultant providing food product development,
point of purchase display design, public relations
and marketing services; importer, exporter and
packager of specialty foods including condiments
and sauces
President: Robin Shepherd
VP Marketing: Tom Nuijens
Contact: Marina Martin
mmartin@shepherdagency.com
Estimated Sales: $5-10 Million
Number Employees: 20-49
Square Footage: 20000

Type of Packaging: Consumer, Food Service, Private Label

28489 Robinett & Assoc
2011 N Collins Blvd # 701
Suite 701
Richardson, TX 75080-2689

972-234-1945

Consultant providing designing and engineering of heating, ventilation, air conditioning, plumbing, electrical, security, fire, smoke detection and alarm and energy management facilities
President: Robert Robinett
Estimated Sales: Less Than $500,000
Number Employees: 1-4
Square Footage: 3200

28490 (HQ)Robinette Co
250 Blackley Rd
Bristol, TN 37620-5028

423-968-7800

Fax: 423-968-7982 www.therobinetteco.com
Printed paper for flour, cornmeal, sugar, construction industry, and food industry
President: Joseph Robinette
CEO: Bill Bouton
bbouton@therobinetteco.com
CFO: Gary Hunt
Vice President: Gary Hunt
Quality Control: Payne Greg
Customer Service: Laura Mann
Estimated Sales: $20-50 Million
Number Employees: 100-249
Square Footage: 200000
Type of Packaging: Consumer, Food Service, Private Label
Other Locations:
  Robinette Co.
  Bristol TN
Brands:
  Shinglgard
  Shinglwrap

28491 Robinson Cold Storage
24415 NE 10th Ave
Ridgefield, WA 98642

360-887-3501

Frozen foods storage
President/CEO: Allen Nirenstein
Chairman: Thomas Klein
Estimated Sales: Less than $500,000
Number Employees: 1-4

28492 Robinson Industries Inc
3051 W Curtis Rd
Coleman, MI 48618-8549

989-465-6111

Fax: 989-465-1217 info@robinsonind.com
www.robinsonind.com
Manufacturer and exporter of thermoformed and injection molded plastic pallets, trays and totes. Also, consumer items. Custom designed.
President: Bin Robinson
CEO: Inez Kaleto
CFO: Kurt Schefka
Research & Development: Jeff Sankler
Quality Control: Rod Crites
Marketing: Ronda Robinson
VP Sales/Sales Manager: Mark Weidner
Production: Tom Roberts
Plant Manager: Melissa Jellum
Purchasing: Jason Pahl
Estimated Sales: $40 Million
Number Employees: 100-249
Square Footage: 152005

28493 Robinson Tape & Label
32 Park Drive East
Branford, CT 6405

203-481-5581

Fax: 203-481-6076 800-433-7102
www.robinsontapeandlabel.com
Pressure sensitive tapes and labels; wholesaler/distributor of tape machines and shipping supplies
President: Edward Pepe
Marketing: Sarah Yale
Sales: Mike Dellavalle
Contact: Timothy Grahm
timothygrahm@robinsontapeandlabel.com
Production: Anthony Martone
Purchasing: Dennis Smith
Estimated Sales: $5-10 Million
Number Employees: 10-19
Square Footage: 22000

Type of Packaging: Consumer, Food Service, Private Label, Bulk

28494 Robinson/Kirshbaum Industries
261 E 157th St
Gardena, CA 90248

310-354-9948
Fax: 310-354-9921 800-929-3812
www.rki-inc.com

Beverage equipment including dispensers, water filtration, etc
VP: Bruce Kirshbaum
Contact: Jon Robinson
jrobinson@rki-inc.com
Estimated Sales: $1-2,500,000
Number Employees: 5-9

28495 Robinson/Kirshbaum Industries
261 E 157th St
Gardena, CA 90248

310-354-9948
Fax: 310-354-9921 support@rki-inc.com
www.rki-inc.com

Beverage equipment including dispensers, water filtration, etc
President: Jon Robinson
jrobinson@rki-inc.com
Executive VP: Bruce Kirshbaum
R&D: Bruce Kirshbaum
Estimated Sales: Below $5 Million
Number Employees: 1-4

28496 Robocom Systems Intl
1111 Broadhollow Rd # 100
#100
Farmingdale, NY 11735-4819

631-753-2180
Fax: 843-881-4893 info@robocom.com
www.robocom.com

Computer software for order processing, inventory control, purchasing and warehouse management
President/Owner: Fred Radcliffe
fradcliffe@robocom.com
VP: Rick Register
VP, Customer Services: Richard Adamo
Number Employees: 1-4
Brands:
  Control Ii
  Csw

28497 Robocom Systems Intl
1111 Broadhollow Rd # 100
Suite 100
Farmingdale, NY 11735-4819

631-753-2180
Fax: 516-795-6933 800-795-5100
info@robocom.com www.robocom.com

Develops and implements logistic warehouse solutions designed to maximize productivity and streamline warehouse operations. Services provide inlcude software development and installation, and support
President/Owner: Fred Radcliffe
fradcliffe@robocom.com
VP, Customer Services: Richard Adamo
Estimated Sales: Below $5 Million
Number Employees: 1-4

28498 Robot Coupe
280 S Perkins St
Ridgeland, MS 39157-2719

601-898-8411
Fax: 601-898-9134 800-824-1646
info@robotcoupeusa.com

Manufactures commercial food processors, vegetable preparation units, and combination processing units.
President: Jay Williams
VP: David Mouck
VP/Controller: C Redding
VP Marketing: David Mouck
National Accounts Manager: David Mouck
Estimated Sales: $10-20 Million
Number Employees: 50-99
Square Footage: 60000
Type of Packaging: Food Service
Brands:
  Robot Coupe

28499 (HQ)Robotic Vision Systems
486 Amherst Street
Nashua, NH 03063-1224

781-821-0830
Fax: 781-828-8942 800-646-6664

Bar code scanners, data collection systems, decoders, machine vision, and scanners
Senior VP: John Agapakis
Estimated Sales: $1 - 5 Million
Number Employees: 100-249

28500 Rocheleau Blow Molding Systems
117 Industrial Road
Fitchburg, MA 01420-4697

978-345-1723
Fax: 978-345-5972 sales@rocheleautool.com
www.rocheleautool.com

Extrusion blow molding and plastic blow molding machinery
President: Steven Rocheleau
Number Employees: 10-19

28501 (HQ)Rochester Midland Corp
155 Paragon Dr
Rochester, NY 14624-1167

585-336-2200
Fax: 585-266-8919 800-535-5053
webmaster@rochestermidland.com
www.rochestermidland.com

Cleaning/sanitary equipment and supplies including dish washing compounds, detergents, disinfectants, floor polish, chemicals, etc.; also, insecticides and insect control systems
CEO: Harlan D Calkins
Estimated Sales: $2.5-5 Million
Number Employees: 500-999

28502 Rochester Midland Corp
155 Paragon Dr
Rochester, NY 14624-1167

585-336-2200
Fax: 585-266-8919 800-387-7174
www.rochestermidland.com

Deli and butcher paper and latex and poly gloves
Chairman/ CEO: H.D. Calkins
key person: Brenda Barr
National Sales Manager: Bob Guberman
Manager: Brenda Barr
National Account Manager: Matt Willoughby
Estimated Sales: $10 - 20 Million
Number Employees: 500-999

28503 Rochester Midland Corp
155 Paragon Dr
Rochester, NY 14624-1167

585-336-2200
Fax: 585-266-8919 800-836-1627
www.rochestermidland.com

Manufacturer and exporter of production cleaning and sanitizing chemicals for food and beverage processing facilities; also, water and wastewater treatment chemicals
CEO: Brad Calkins
Purchasing Manager: Richard Roy
Estimated Sales: $83 Million
Number Employees: 500-999
Square Footage: 190000
Brands:
  Brandguard

28504 Rock Valley Oil & Chemical Co
1911 Windsor Rd
Loves Park, IL 61111-4293

815-654-2401
Fax: 815-654-2428 www.rockvalleyoil.com

'Today, Rock Valley has grown to be recognized as an international manufacturer and supplier of superior quality industrial lubricants, metalworking and hydraulic fluids, as well as reference oils and calibrating fluids tailored to theautomotive and heavy truck industry'. www.rockvalleyoil.com
President: Roger Schramm
sales@rockvalleyoil.com
Estimated Sales: $12.5 Million
Number Employees: 50-99
Brands:
  Sun Oil
  Viscor
  Viscosity

28505 Rock-Tenn Company
504 Tasman St
Norcross, GA 30071

608-223-6272
Fax: 608-246-1145 www.rocktenn.com

Manufacturer and exporter of folding paper cartons, boxes and displays
Owner: Bill Rock
General Manager: Gary Adrian

Estimated Sales: $5-10 Million
Number Employees: 1-4

28506 Rockaway Baking
PO Box 392
Rockaway, NJ 07866-0392
973-625-3003
Fax: 973-625-4271 877-762-5225
rockbake@aol.com
Automatic equipment for baking industry; specializing in English muffin systems, materials handling conveyors, spiral conveyors for freezing, proofing and cooling
Estimated Sales: $1 Million
Number Employees: 2

28507 Rocket Man
2501 Maple St
Louisville, KY 40211-1163
502-775-7502
Fax: 502-775-7519 800-365-6661
sales@rocketman.com www.rocketman.com
Manufacturer, importer and exporter of backpack drink dispensers and portable beverage dispensing equipment
Owner: Mike Hinson
Contact: Mazen Masri
mazenm@rocketman.com
Estimated Sales: $1-3 Million
Number Employees: 10-19
Square Footage: 20000
Brands:
  Rocket Man

28508 Rockford Chemical Co
915 W Perry St
Belvidere, IL 61008-3498
815-544-3476
Fax: 815-544-0532
Boiler compounds
President: Vann W Rossmiller
Estimated Sales: $1-2.5 Million
Number Employees: 1-4

28509 Rockford Sanitary Systems
5159 28th Ave
Rockford, IL 61109-1720
815-229-5077
Fax: 815-229-5108 800-747-5077
www.rkfdseparators.com
Grease, oil, sand and lint separators; also, trench drains
President: Merritt Mott
mjmott@aol.com
CEO: James Griffin
VP Engineering: Bryce Russell
Quality Control: Jim Griffin
Estimated Sales: $5 - 10 Million
Number Employees: 20-49
Square Footage: 68000

28510 Rockford-Midland Corporation
1715 Northrock Ct
Rockford, IL 61103
815-877-0212
Fax: 815-877-0419 800-327-7908
Manufacturer and exporter of fully and semi-automatic case packers and sealers including hot melt, cold glue and tape
President: Adrienne Murphy
Sales Director: Donna Bonetti
Production Manager: Tim Vronch
Purchasing Manager: Karen Steiner
Estimated Sales: $5-10 Million
Number Employees: 20-49
Square Footage: 80000
Brands:
  Casestar
  Sealstar

28511 Rockland Foods
300 Corporate Drive
Suite14
Blauvelt, NY 10913-1162
845-358-8600
Fax: 845-358-9003 800-962-7663
rfi@rfiingredients.com www.rfiingredients.com
Owner: Jeff Wuagneux
Quality Control: Pi-Yu Hsu
Contact: Jennifer Diliddo
jennifer.diliddo@rfiingredients.com
Estimated Sales: $1 - 5 Million
Number Employees: 10-19

28512 Rockland Technology
817 S Mill Street
Suite 104
Lewisville, TX 75057-4637
972-221-6190
Fax: 972-420-0055
President: Thomas Bronson
tbronson@diamondtouchpos.com
Estimated Sales: Below $5 Million
Number Employees: 20

28513 Rockline Industries
4343 S Taylor Dr
Sheboygan, WI 53081
920-453-2769
800-558-7790
customercareteam@rocklineind.com
www.rocklineind.com
Private label consumer products; including coffee filters and baby wipes.
President: Randy Rudolph
Year Founded: 1976
Estimated Sales: $100-500 Million
Brands:
  Bake Fresh
  Brew Rite
  Fresh'n Up
  Natural Brew
  Star

28514 Rockwell Automation Inc
1201 S 2nd St
Milwaukee, WI 53204
414-382-2000
www.rockwellautomation.com
Industrial automation equipment, machinery and components.
Chairman & CEO: Blake Moret
blmoret@ra.rockwell.com
SVP/Chief Technology Officer: Sujeet Chand
SVP, Control Products & Solutions: Ted Crandall
SVP, Corporate Development: Elik Fooks
SVP/Chief Financial Officer: Patrick Goris
SVP/General Counsel/Secretary: Rebecca House
SVP/Global Sales & Marketing: Thomas Donato
SVP, Connected Enterprise Consulting: Bob Murphy
Year Founded: 1903
Estimated Sales: $6.3 Billion
Number Employees: 22,000
Brands:
  Allen-Bradley
  FactoryTalk
  Rockwell Automation

28515 Rocky Shoes & Boots Inc
39 E Canal St
Nelsonville, OH 45764
740-753-3130
866-442-4908
www.rockyboots.com
Nonslip service shoes and boots.
Chairman: Mike Brooks
CEO: Jason Brooks
CFO: Tom Robertson
President, Operations: Richard Simms
President, Manufacturing/Operations: Dave Dixon
Year Founded: 1932
Estimated Sales: $100-500 Million
Number Employees: 1000-4999
Brands:
  4 Way Step

28516 Roddy Products Pkgng CoInc
1 Merion Ter
Aldan, PA 19018-3000
610-623-7040
Fax: 610-623-0521 joearoddy@aol.com
Manufacturer and exporter of wooden shipping crates
President: Joseph Masticola Sr
CFO: Joseph Masticola Sr
IT: Tina Moore
marieroddy@aol.com
Estimated Sales: $1 - 2.5 Million
Number Employees: 10-19

28517 Rodem Inc
5095 Crookshank Rd
Cincinnati, OH 45238-3366
513-922-0096
Fax: 513-922-1680 sales@rodem.com
www.rodem.com
Agitation systems, curd, milk, silo, tank, analyzers/tests, plant operations,chlorine, total solids, chillers, clean rooms and equipment, custom fabrication, deaerators, dispensers, milk, ice equipment, ingredient feeders, laddersvat, margarine process
President: Chris Diener
cdiener@rodem.com
R&D: Stan Pritchart
Chairman of the Board: Robert Diener
Estimated Sales: $30 - 50 Million
Number Employees: 50-99

28518 Rodes Professional Apparel
4938 Brownsboro Road
Louisville, KY 40222
502-584-3112
Fax: 502-584-8840 info@rodes.com
www.rodes.com
Uniforms, aprons and shoes
President: Lawrence Smith
Number Employees: 80
Parent Co: Lithgow Industries

28519 Rodo Industries
44 Meg Drive
London, ON N6E 3R4
Canada
519-668-3711
Fax: 519-668-3257 sales@rodoinc.com
www.rodoinc.com
Stacking and regular chairs, fast food seating, cushions, pads, bar/counter stools, tables including legs, bases and booths
President: Randy Snow
CFO: Gary Forgrade
R&D: Gary Forgrade
Quality Control: Gary Forgrade
Sales: Hugh Crosby
Estimated Sales: $3.5 Million
Number Employees: 45

28520 Roechling Engineered Plastics
PO Box 2729
Gastonia, NC 28053-2729
704-922-7814
Fax: 704-922-7651 800-541-4419
Manufacturer and exporter of conveyor components, industrial plastics, HDPE, PP, UHMW and PVDF; also, sheets, tubes and profiles
President: Lewis Carter
Quality Control: Brychan Griffiths
Marketing: Tim Brown
Sales: Paul Krawczyk
Contact: Kathy Millen
millen@roechling.com
Number Employees: 50-99
Square Footage: 560000
Brands:
  Polystone Cut-Rite
  Sustamid
  Sustarin
  Sustatec

28521 Roechling Machined Plastics
1551 Woodward Drive Ext
Greensburg, PA 15601
724-834-1340
Fax: 724-834-5822 www.roechling-plastics.us
Fiberglass plastic machining
Estimated Sales: $20-50 Million
Number Employees: 20-49

28522 Roesch Inc
100 N 24th St
Belleville, IL 62226-6659
618-233-2760
Fax: 618-233-1186 800-423-6243
sales@roeschinc.com www.roeschinc.com
Enameling of steel and cast iron, stoves, refrigerators and specialty parts, including high temperature ceramic coatings and metal fabricatiors of sheet metal parts
President: Jason Baughman
j.baughman@roeschinc.com
Executive Vice President: Debbie Voges-Schneider
Sales Manager: Debbie Thomas
Estimated Sales: $10-20 Million
Number Employees: 50-99

28523 Roeslein & Assoc Inc
9200 Watson Rd # 200
Suite 200
St Louis, MO 63126-1528
314-729-0055
Fax: 314-729-0070 sales@roeslein.com
www.roesleinae.com
Owner: Dave May
dmay@roeslein.com
CFO: Fritz Dickmann
Estimated Sales: $5 - 10 Million
Number Employees: 100-249

28524 Rofin-Baasel Inc
68 Barnum Rd
Devens, MA 01434-3508
978-635-9100
Fax: 978-635-9199 www.rofin.com
President: Walter Volkmar
Contact: Derrick Brewster
brewster@rofin.com
Number Employees: 1000-4999

28525 Roflan Associates
5314 S Yale Avenue
Suite 1100
Tulsa, OK 74135-6251
978-475-0100
Fax: 978-475-4144
Lighting fixtures
VP/Manager: Mike Lacharite
Number Employees: 22

28526 Roha USA LTD
5015 Manchester Ave
St Louis, MO 63110-2011
314-289-8300
Fax: 314-531-0461 888-533-7642
roha.usa@rohagroup.com www.roha.com
Distributors of synthetic colors, lake pigments and
dye blends. Custom blends. Patent pending, dust free
colors
CEO: Rohit Tibrewala
Research & Development: Mike Chin
Estimated Sales: $2.5-5 Million
Number Employees: 50-99
Number of Brands: 3
Parent Co: Roha Dyechem
Brands:
Dust Free Form of Fd&C Colors

28527 Rohm America Inc.
2 Turner Place
Piscataway, NJ 08855
732-981-5250
Fax: 732-981-5382
Contact: Gerald Bagenski
gerald.bagenski@evonik.com
Estimated Sales: $1 - 5 Million

28528 Rohrer Corp.
717 Seville Rd
PO Box 1009
Wadsworth, OH 44282
800-243-6640
info@rohrer.com www.rohrer.com
Manufacturer and exporter of skin packaging, blister
cards and stretch pack cards
National Sales Director: Jim Price
Year Founded: 1973
Estimated Sales: $50-100 Million
Number Employees: 100-249
Type of Packaging: Bulk

28529 Rolfs @ Boone
1773 219th Ln
P.O. Box 369
Boone, IA 50036
515-432-2010
Fax: 515-432-5262 800-265-2010
info@boonegroup.com www.boonegroup.com
Manufacturer and exporter of dust systems, high and
low bag filters, cyclones, ducting, fittings, bearing
and belt alignment instrumentation and hazard and
motion monitoring controls
President: Kevin Miles
Sales: Greg Knoxx
Dust Control: Delmar Mains
Production Manager: Brian Huffman
Estimated Sales: $5 - 10 Million
Number Employees: 10-19
Square Footage: 112000

28530 Roll Rite Corp
3480 Investment Blvd
Hayward, CA 94545-3811
510-293-1444
Fax: 510-293-1450 800-345-9305
info@rollrite.com www.roll-rite.net
Material handling equipment including factory hand
trucks, wheels, casters, skewing racks and
nonpowered equipment; exporter of wheels and
casters
CEO/President: Mario Sequeira
ms@roll-rite.net
Estimated Sales: $1-2.5 Million
Number Employees: 5-9
Square Footage: 17800
Brands:
Alumiflex
Areo
Bassick
Colson
Dutro
Hamilton
Magliner
Roll Rite Super Caster
Roll-Rite Corp.
Wesco

28531 Roll-O-Sheets Canada
130 Big Bay Point Road
Barrie, ON L4N 9B4
Canada
705-722-5223
Fax: 705-722-7120 888-767-3456
info@roll-o-sheets.com
Manufacturer, importer and exporter of converted
PVC film; wholesaler/distributor of vacuum
pouches, table covers, Cellophane and plastic sand-
wich and ovenable containers
General Manager: Bryce Atkinson
Number Employees: 20
Square Footage: 88000
Brands:
Row L
Row S
Wrap It

28532 Rolland Machining & Fabricating
43 Ventnor Avenue
Moneta, VA 24121-5350
973-827-6911
Fax: 973-827-5699
Custom fabricated plastic materials including ducts,
fittings, tanks, trays, etc.; also, general machining in
soft metals and plastic
President: Mary Rolland
Number Employees: 10
Square Footage: 8000

28533 Rollhaus Seating Products Inc
2109 Borden Ave # 4
Long Island City, NY 11101-4531
718-729-9111
Fax: 718-729-9117 800-822-6684
www.seatingproducts.com
Booths, chairs and folding tables
President: Michael Rollhaus
33mrbb@gmail.com
Estimated Sales: $2.5 - 5,000,000
Number Employees: 20-49

28534 Rollon Corp
30 Wilson Dr # A
Sparta, NJ 07871-4408
973-300-5492
Fax: 973-300-9030 877-976-5566
infocom.usa@rollon.com www.rolloncorp.com
Contact: A Lou
l.woloszyn@rolloncorp.com
Estimated Sales: $5 Million
Number Employees: 1-4

28535 Rollprint Packaging Prods Inc
320 S Stewart Ave
Addison, IL 60101-3310
630-628-1700
Fax: 630-628-8510 800-276-7629
mail@rollprint.com www.rollprint.com
Manufacturer and exporter of flexible food packaging materials including lidding, pouches, peelable
and non-peelable composites. FlexForm and
ClearForm line of forming webs provide tough,
puncture resistant substrates that provideuniform
film draw without snapback for frozen food applica-
tions including: poultry, meat, seafood, bakery,
pizza, vegetables, fruits, and bakery goods.
President: Dhuanne Dodrill
ddodrill@rollprint.com
CFO: David Reed
Marketing Manager: Edward Verkuilen
Estimated Sales: $20-50 Million
Number Employees: 100-249
Square Footage: 198000
Type of Packaging: Consumer, Food Service, Pri-
vate Label, Bulk
Brands:
Allegro
Clearfoil
Flexform
Forte
Multimix
Propapeel
Propaseal

28536 Rollstock Inc
5720 Brighton Ave
Kansas City, MO 64130-4532
816-444-1789
Fax: 616-570-0430 800-295-2949
rollstockkc@aol.com www.rollstock.com
Horizontal form, fill and seal machine, vacuum,
map, cap
Sales: Tom Foley
Plant Manager: Gary Filippone
Estimated Sales: $1 - 5 Million
Number Employees: 5-9

28538 Romaco Inc
6 Frassetto Way # D
Unit D
Lincoln Park, NJ 07035-2055
973-709-0691
Fax: 973-605-1360
Printing and labeling systems for bottles
Estimated Sales: $5-10 Million
Number Employees: 1-4

28539 Romanow Container
346 University Ave
Westwood, MA 02090-2309
781-320-9200
Fax: 781-461-5900 www.romanowcontainer.com
Manufacturer and exporter of corrugated and
wooden boxes, foam converters and fabricators;
also, contract packaging available
Owner: Theodore Romanow
info@romanowcontainer.com
Estimated Sales: $5-10 Million
Number Employees: 100-249

28540 Romanow Container
346 University Ave
Westwood, MA 02090-2309
781-320-9200
Fax: 781-461-5900 www.romanowcontainer.com
Corrugated fiber boxes
President: Theodore Romanow
info@romanowcontainer.com
Executive VP: Richard Romanow
Estimated Sales: $20-50 Million
Number Employees: 100-249
Square Footage: 145000

28541 Romatic Manufacturing Co
1200 Main St S
Southbury, CT 06488-2159
203-264-3442
Fax: 203-264-3442
Metal caps for bottles, cans and jars
President: Roger Hebert
CEO: Rob Pecci
rpecci@romaticmanufacturing.com
CEO: Rob Pecci
Estimated Sales: $20-50 Million
Number Employees: 100-249

28542 Rome LTD
1427 Western Ave
Sheldon, IA 51201
712-324-5391
Fax: 712-324-5394 800-443-0557
www.romegrindingsolutions.com

Processing equipment
President: Craig Jongerius
   craigjongerius@rome-ltd.com
Quality Control: Tim McDonald
Sales Director: Jim Justi
Estimated Sales: $10 - 20 Million
Number Employees: 20-49

28543 Rome Machine & Foundry Co
906 Walnut Ave SW
PO Box 5383
Rome, GA 30161-6166

706-234-6763
Fax: 706-232-0337 800-538-7663
Manufacturer and exporter of custom fabricated conveyors and food processing machinery
President: Albert Berry
   aberry@romemachine.com
Sales/Marketing Manager: Willis Rogers
Chief Engineer: Jay Burnett
Purchasing Manager: Ted Porterfield
Estimated Sales: $1-2.5 Million
Number Employees: 10-19
Square Footage: 129600

28544 Romicon
1300 W Lodi Avenue
Suite 19a
Lodi, CA 95242-3000

209-333-8100
Fax: 209-333-2947
Wine industry filtration equipment
Estimated Sales: $500,000-$1 Million
Number Employees: 5-9

28545 Romme Lag USA Inc
27905 Meadow Dr # 9
Evergreen, CO 80439-2110

303-674-8333
Fax: 303-670-2666 mail@rommelag.com
www.rommelag-engineering.com
Supplier of packaging machinery specializing in blow/fill/seal machines for the aseptic filling of liquids in plastic
Manager: Tim Kram
   tim.kram@rommelag.com
President and General Manager: Anke Henke
Estimated Sales: Less Than $500,000
Number Employees: 1-4

28546 Ron Teed & Assoc
26W325 Menomini Dr
Wheaton, IL 60189-5987

630-462-7662
Fax: 630-462-7669 ronteed@aol.com
Owner: Ronald Teed
   ronteed@aol.com
Estimated Sales: $.5 - 1 million
Number Employees: 1-4

28547 Ron Ungar Engineering Inc
1595 Walter St # 4
Suite 4
Ventura, CA 93003-5613

805-642-3555
Fax: 805-642-0326 800-235-5644
Owner: Ron Ungar
Estimated Sales: $1 - 3 Million
Number Employees: 5-9

28548 Ron Vallort & Associates
502 Forest Mews Dr
Oak Brook, IL 60523

630-734-3821
Fax: 630-734-3822 ronvallort@aol.com
Engineering and building consultants specializing in site planning, facility design, construction management and operational analysis for the food industry including processing, freezing, storage and distribution
President: Ron Vallort

28549 Ron Vallort and Associates, Ltd
2 S. Atrium Way
606
Elmhurst, IL 60126

630-334-3821
Fax: 630-734-3822 ronvallort@aol.com
Engineering and building consultants specializing in site planning, process design, facility design, construction management, expert investigation and building analysis for the food industry including processing, freezingstorage/distribution, sanitation and refrigeration.

President: Ron Vallot
Estimated Sales: Below $5 Million
Number Employees: 10

28550 RonI
8001 Tower Point Dr
Charlotte, NC 28227

704-847-2464
Fax: 866-543-9532 866-543-8635
info@roni.com www.roni.com
Material handling applications including rollhandling, clean room, product pouring and weighing
President: John Hebert
CFO: Lena Melton
Contact: Don Bedel
   don.bedel@roni.com
Estimated Sales: $1 - 2.5 Million
Number Employees: 30
Brands:
   LIFT-O-Flex
   MOBI-Crane
   Movomech
   Voyager

28551 Ronchi America
63 Duncan Cir
Hiram, GA 30141-3237

678-398-7413
Fax: 770-694-6071 info@ronchiamerica.com
www.ronchipackaging.com
Plastic bottle unscramblers, bottle fillers, advanced flowmeter filling technology, pump cappers, case packaging, and integrated lines
VP: Frank Chitg
Contact: Michele Falsini
   m.falsini@ronchiamerica.com
Estimated Sales: $2.5-5 Million
Number Employees: 10-19
Square Footage: 60000
Parent Co: Ronchi Mario

28552 Rondo Inc
51 Joseph St
Moonachie, NJ 07074-1027

201-229-9700
Fax: 201-229-0018 800-882-0633
info@us.rondo-online.com
Manufacturer, importer and wholesaler/distributor of high volume bakery equipment including mixers and sheeters
President: Jerry Murphy
   jerry.murphy@rondo-online.com
VP Sales: Andrea Henderson
Estimated Sales: $2.5-5 Million
Number Employees: 20-49

28553 Rondo of America
209 Great Hill Rd
Naugatuck, CT 6770

203-723-7474
Fax: 203-723-5831
custserv@rondopackaging.com
www.rondopackaging.com
Manufacturer and exporter of protective packaging, automatic packaging machinery and paper boxes
Owner: James Sinkins
Contact: Donna Pendleton
   donna@rondopackaging.com
Estimated Sales: $5-10 Million
Number Employees: 20-49
Parent Co: Interrondo

28554 Ronell Industries
298 Cox St
Roselle, NJ 07203-1798

908-245-5255
Fax: 908-241-4244
Environmental services including cleaning and sanitation
President: Ronald Globerman
VP: John Carroll
Contact: Jim Daley
   jimdaley@ronellmanagedservices.com
Estimated Sales: $5 - 10 Million
Number Employees: 10-19

28555 Roni LLC
8026 Tower Point Dr
Charlotte, NC 28227-7726

704-847-2464
Fax: 704-714-5317 866-543-8635
www.liftoflex.com

Automated ergonomic material handling systems and equipment.
Owner: Gunner Lofgren
Number Employees: 5-9

28556 Ronnie Dowdy
1839 Batesville Blvd
Batesville, AR 72501

870-251-3222
Fax: 870-251-3763 800-743-5611
Transportation firm providing refrigerated trucking services including local, long and short haul
Owner: Ronnie Dowdy
Owner: Sandra Dowdy
Contact: David Bergan
   dbergan@ronniedowdy.com
Number Employees: 250-499

28557 Ronnie's Ceramic Company
5999 3rd St
San Francisco, CA 94124

415-822-8068
Fax: 415-822-8966 800-888-8218
Manufacturer and exporter of tableware, platters, coffee mugs and water pitchers
President: Risly Cheung
Vice President: Risly Chin
Estimated Sales: $3 - 5,000,000
Number Employees: 15
Square Footage: 8500
Brands:
   Ronnie's Ocean
   Terramoto

28558 Roofian
8605 Kewen Ave
Sun Valley, CA 91352-3123

818-768-9945
Fax: 818-768-9285 800-431-3886
roofian@juno.com www.roofian.com
Gift and floral baskets
Owner: Shelia Missaghi
   roofian@juno.com
VP: Shahla Roofian
Estimated Sales: $1.1 Million
Number Employees: 10-19

28559 (HQ)Rooto Corp
3505 W Grand River Ave
Howell, MI 48855-9610

517-546-8330
Fax: 517-548-5162
Manufacturer and exporter of ammonia, liquid soap and chemical cleaners for drains, toilets and septic tanks
Manager: Penny Rulason
National Sales Manager: Roger Sheets
Manager: Roger Sheets
   roger.sheets@rootocorp.com
Plant Manager: Ken Wood
Purchasing Manager: Dennis West
Estimated Sales: $2.5-5 Million
Number Employees: 20-49
Square Footage: 1000000
Type of Packaging: Consumer, Food Service, Private Label
Brands:
   Blue Ribbon
   Rooto

28560 Ropak
1515 W.22nd Street
Suite 550
Oak Brook, IL 60523
Canada

800-527-2267
sales@bwaycorp.com www.ropakcorp.com
Manufacturer and exporter of polyethylene containers
President: Greg Toft
Sales Representative: Ricahrd Harrison
Operations Manager: Nevin McKay
Number Employees: 110
Parent Co: Bway Corporation
Type of Packaging: Food Service, Bulk

28561 Ropak Manufacturing Co Inc
1019 Cedar Lake Rd SE
Decatur, AL 35603-1730

256-350-4241
Fax: 256-350-1611 sales@ropak.com
www.ropak.com

Manufacturer and exporter of form/fill/seal, liquid/dry and vertical/horizontal packagers, stik-pak packager
President/CEO: Ernest Matthews
VP, Electrical Engineer: Richard Matthews
Business Development: Chuck Garrett
VP Operations: Ernest Matthrews
Purchasing Manager: Ken Ray
Estimated Sales: $5-10,000,000
Number Employees: 20-49
Brands:
Expresspak

28562 Roplast Industries Inc
3155 S 5th Ave
Oroville, CA 95965-5858
530-532-9500
Fax: 530-532-9576 800-767-5278
sales@roplast.com www.roplast.com
Integrated domestic manufacturer of plastic (LDPE/LLDPE) film and bags.
President: Robert Bateman

r.bateman@leeassociates-temeculavalley.ccsend.com
COO: Chris Mann
Director of Sales: Roxanne Vaughan
Sales Manager: Erik Johansen

r.bateman@leeassociates-temeculavalley.ccsend.com
Estimated Sales: $20 - 30 Million
Number Employees: 100-249
Square Footage: 130000
Type of Packaging: Food Service, Private Label

28563 (HQ)Rosco Inc
14431 91st Ave
Jamaica, NY 11435-4302
718-526-2652
Fax: 718-297-0323 800-227-2095
www.roscomirrors.com
Manufacturer and exporter of acrylic and glass convex safety mirrors
President: Sol Englander
Quality Control: George Lewandowski
VP and Finance: Danny Englander
VP Engineering and Ops: Ben Englander
National Sales Manager: Dave Mostel
Sales Manager: Joe Liberman
Contact: Amy Ahn
aahn@roscomirrors.com
Estimated Sales: $5 - 10 Million
Number Employees: 5-9
Square Footage: 140000

28564 Rose City Awning Co
2728 NW Nela St
Portland, OR 97210-1714
503-226-2761
Fax: 503-222-5060 800-446-4104
sales@rosecityawning.com
www.rosecityawning.com
Canvas products, vinyl door strips, moving pads, solar screen transparent shades, tarpaulin, awnings, cloth and polythylene taper, polyethylene film and rope including nylon, sisal, manilas, poly, twine, etc
Owner: Pam Butcher
sales@rosecityawning.com
Sales Department: Ida Pfenning
Factory Manager: Mike Pedersen
Estimated Sales: Below $5 Million
Number Employees: 10-19
Square Footage: 4000

28565 Rose City Label
7235 SE Label Ln
Portland, OR 97206-9339
503-777-4711
Fax: 503-777-4799 800-547-9920
info@rclabel.com
Labels including pressure sensitive, flexo, hot stamped, embossed, sheet fed and custom printed
President/ Co-Owner: Scott Pillsbury
scott@tlmi.com
CFO: Whitney Pillsbury
Marketing: Scott Pillsbury
Sales Manager: Walt Ostergard
Estimated Sales: $5-10 Million
Number Employees: 10-19

28566 Rose City Printing & Packaging
900 SE Tech Center Dr
Suite 100
Vancouver, WA 98683
503-241-6486
Fax: 503-241-3604 800-704-8693
info@rcpp.com
Folding cartons, blister cards and beverage carriers
President: Richard L Safranski
CEO: Chuck Parsons
CFO: Chris Farm
Quality Control: Steve Rautenbach
Marketing Director: Kathryn Rautenbach
Sales Director: Dave Wehrman
Contact: Armando Herrera
aherrera@rcpp.com
Operations Manager: Ken Karallis
General Manager: Steve Lobis
Estimated Sales: $5 - 10 Million
Number Employees: 100-249
Square Footage: 124000

28567 Rose Forgrove
1 Illinois St Ste 300
Suite 400
Saint Charles, IL 60174
630-443-1317
Fax: 630-377-3069 www.hayssen.com
Manufacturer and exporter of flow wrappers for food and candy
VP Sales: Liam Buckley
Number Employees: 3
Square Footage: 5000
Parent Co: Howven
Brands:
Flowpak

28568 Rose Forgrove
1 Illinois St
Suite 300
Saint Charles, IL 60174
630-443-1317
Fax: 630-377-3069
Hermatic seals and other high quality wrapping applications

28569 Rose Plastic
525 Technology Dr
Coal Center, PA 15423-1053
724-938-0511
Fax: 724-938-8532 www.rose-plastic.us
President: Ken Donahue
info.us@rose-plastic.us
Executive Vice President Technical and M: Peter Hess
Western Sales Director: Lisa Montgomery
Director of Human Resources: Jen Capozza
Estimated Sales: $300,000-500,000
Number Employees: 50-99

28570 Rosemount Analytical Inc
2400 Barranca Pkwy
Irvine, CA 92606-5018
949-757-8500
Fax: 949-757-3001 800-543-8257
www.emersonprocess.com
Liquid analyzers including pH, conductivity, ORP, residual chlorine, dissolved ozone and oxygen refractometers, water activity measurement systems and gas analyzers and systems
President: Ken Biele
ken.biele@emersonprocess.com
President: Ken Biele
Marketing Manager: John Wright
Sales Manager: Ken Partridge
Estimated Sales: $50 - 100 Million
Number Employees: 100-249
Parent Co: Fisher-Rosemont

28571 Rosenthal ManufacturingCo Inc
1840 Janke Dr
Northbrook, IL 60062-6704
847-714-0404
Fax: 847-714-0440 800-621-1266
411@rosenthalmfg.com www.rosenthalmfg.com
Sheeting machines
Owner: Lorelei Rosenthal
info@rosenthalmfg.com
Estimated Sales: $10-20 Million
Number Employees: 20-49

28572 Rosenwach Tank Co LLC
4025 Crescent St
Long Island City, NY 11101-3897
212-972-4411
Fax: 718-482-0661 info@rosenwachgroup.com
www.rosenwachgroup.com
Manufacturers of wooden and steel water towers, wooden cheese vats, tanks, planters and benches
Owner: Andrew Rosenwach
amr@rosenwachgroup.com
Chairman of the Board: Wallace Rosenwach
Estimated Sales: $5-10 Million
Number Employees: 50-99
Parent Co: Rosenwach Group

28573 Roseville Charcoal & Mfg Co
500 Monroe St
Zanesville, OH 43701-3875
740-452-5473
Fax: 740-452-5474
Manufacturer and exporter of industrial and commercial charcoal briquettes including hardwood, granular and lump
President: Tim R Longstreth
Estimated Sales: $1-2.5 Million
Number Employees: 1-4

28574 Ross & Wallace Inc
204 Old Covington Hwy
Hammond, LA 70403-5121
985-345-1321
Fax: 985-345-1370 800-854-2300
customerservice@rossandwallace.com
www.rossandwallace.com
Manufacturer and exporter of paper and plastic bags and wrappings
President: Ken Ross
Chairman: Albert Ross
Estimated Sales: $10-20 Million
Number Employees: 50-99
Square Footage: 350000
Type of Packaging: Consumer, Bulk

28575 Ross Computer Systems
19 W 44th St
Suite 715
New York, NY 10036
212-221-7677
Fax: 212-221-0362
Software for route accounting and manufacturing, handheld sales tracking-ordering-route settlement systems and host systems including Bakers Dozen and PrepMaster
Owner: Seymour Weiss
Contact: Arlene Davis
arlened@rossusa.com
Estimated Sales: $1-2.5 Million
Number Employees: 10-19

28576 Ross Computer Systems
214 S Peters Rd Ste 208
Knoxville, TN 37923
865-690-3008
Fax: 865-690-1089 www.afsi.com
Manufacturer and exporter of computer hardware and software; also, consulting services available
President: Louis Schumacher
CEO: Jesse Hermann
CFO: Mark Schonau
Executive VP: Louis Schumacher
Chief Technology Officer: Suhas Gudihal
VP Sales: Greg Roberts
Chief Customer Officer: Lisa Whinney
Estimated Sales: Below $5 Million
Number Employees: 10-19

28577 Ross Cook
8630 Fenton Street
Suite 824
Silver Spring, MD 20910
301-565-4035
Fax: 408-929-9944 800-233-7339
lookingforanswers@cookross.com
www.cookross.com
Centrifugal blowers and exhausters and industrial vacuum systems
President: Mike Fisher
Contact: Dwight Anderson
dwighta@cookross.com
VP Operations: Bill Splinder
Estimated Sales: $10-20 Million
Number Employees: 20-49
Square Footage: 88000

28578 Ross Engineering Inc
32 Westgate Blvd
Savannah, GA 31405-1400
912-238-3300
Fax: 912-238-5983 800-524-7677
www.mixers.com
Manufacturer and exporter of food processing
equipment including mixing, blending and disper-
sion machinery
President: Richard Ross
COO: D Hathaway
d_hathaway@rossengineering.net
Vice President: David Hathaway
Estimated Sales: $10-20,000,000
Number Employees: 20-49
Square Footage: 60000
Parent Co: Charles Ross & Son Company

28579 Ross Industries Inc
5321 Midland Rd
Midland, VA 22728
540-439-3271
Fax: 540-439-2740 sales@rossindinc.com
www.rossindinc.com
Food processing and packaging equipment including
pre-formed tray seal machines, tunnel freezers, mechanical tenderizers and meat presses.
Estimated Sales: $20-50 Million
Number Employees: 100-249

28580 Ross Industries Inc
5321 Midland Rd
Midland, VA 22728-2135
540-439-3271
Fax: 540-439-2740 800-336-6010
sales@rossindinc.com www.rossindinc.com
President: Michel Defenbac
mdefencac@rossindinc.com
Estimated Sales: $20 - 50 Million
Number Employees: 100-249

28581 Ross Systems
2 Concourse Pkwy NE # 800
Atlanta, GA 30328-5588
770-351-9600
Fax: 770-351-0036 info@rossinc.com
www.keops.com
Computer software design and programming service
President: J Patrick Tinley
CEO: Peter Yip
Contact: Jay Jordan
jjordan@cdcsoftware.com
Estimated Sales: $30 - 50 Million
Number Employees: 50-99

28582 Ross Systems & ControlsInc
34 Westgate Blvd
Savannah, GA 31405-1400
912-238-5800
Fax: 912-238-1905 866-797-2660
mail@rosssyscon.com www.rosssyscon.com
Owner: Paul Rose
Account Executive: Mike Ellis
Manager: Gary Barber
gbarber@rosssyscon.com
Estimated Sales: $1 - 5 Million
Number Employees: 5-9

28583 Ross Technology Corp
104 N Maple Ave
Leola, PA 17540-9799
717-656-5600
Fax: 717-656-3281 800-345-8170
www.rosstechnology.com
Manufacturer and exporter of storage rack systems
including pallet rack, drive-in, thru-flow and push
back
Owner: Don Spicher
Vice President: Jay Otto
jotto@rosstechnology.com
Sales Manager: Tom Crippen
Estimated Sales: $20-50 Million
Number Employees: 100-249
Square Footage: 54000
Type of Packaging: Bulk

28584 Rosson Sign Co
3071 Broadway
Macon, GA 31206-1551
478-788-3905
Fax: 478-788-8020 jrosson@rossonsign.com
www.rossonsign.com
Electric, neon, painted and plastic signs

President: Jack T Rosson
jrosson@rossonsign.com
Estimated Sales: $1-2.5 Million
Number Employees: 10-19

28585 Roth & Associates PC
554 E Maple Rd # 100
Troy, MI 48083-2805
248-583-1221
Fax: 248-583-3221
President: Robet Roth Jr
Estimated Sales: $5 - 10 Million

28586 Roth Sign Systems
606 Lakeville Street
Petaluma, CA 94952-3324
707-778-0200
Fax: 707-765-6079 800-585-7446
Manufacturer and exporter of menu, black and chalk
boards; also, signs including changeable letter, ad-
vertising, luminous tube, plastic, etc
Owner: Lary Mathews
Estimated Sales: $500,000-$1 Million
Number Employees: 10
Square Footage: 80000
Parent Co: Rothcoast Company

28587 Roth Young Bellevue
PO Box 3306
Bellevue, WA 98009-3306
425-454-0677
Fax: 425-453-4552
Executive search firm
Owner: B K Lee
Division Manager: Robert Richardson
CFO: David Salzberg
VP: C Salzberg
R&D: Bob Richardson
Estimated Sales: Below $5 Million
Number Employees: 5-9

28588 Roth Young Chicago
1100 W Northwest Highway
Suite 106
Mount Prospect, IL 60056
847-797-9211
Fax: 847-797-9303
Employment agency/executive search firm specializ-
ing in permanent selection and placement of food in-
dustry personnel
Number Employees: 10
Square Footage: 3600
Parent Co: Winston Franchise Corporation

28589 Roth Young Farmington Hills
31275 Northwestern Hwy
Farmington Hills, MI 48334-2558
248-539-9242
Fax: 248-626-7079 rydetroit@worldnet.att.net
Executive search firm specializing in the selection
and placement of food industry personnel
President: Samuel Skeegan
Number Employees: 5-9
Square Footage: 6000
Parent Co: Winston Franchise Corporation

28590 Roth Young Hicksville
P.O. Box 7365
Hicksville, NY 11802-7261
516-822-6000
Fax: 516-822-6018
Executive search firm specializing in selection and
placement of food industry personnel
Owner: George Jung
Estimated Sales: Below $500,000
Number Employees: 1-4
Square Footage: 2960
Parent Co: Winston Franchise Corporation

28591 Roth Young Minneapolis
6212 Vernon Court S
Minneapolis, MN 55436-1669
952-932-0769
Fax: 952-831-7413 800-356-6655
Executive search firm specializing in selection and
placement of professional and managerial personnel
in the retail and grocery industries
Estimated Sales: $500,000
Number Employees: 6
Square Footage: 6400
Parent Co: Winston Franchise Corporation

28592 Roth Young Murrysville
3087 Carson Ave
Murrysville, PA 15668-1814
724-733-5900
Fax: 724-733-0183 rothyoungpit@cs.com
Employment agency/executive search firm specializ-
ing in selection and placement of food industry
personnel
President: Leonard Di Naples
Director (Health Care): Ann Marie Panzek
VP: Len DiNaples Jr
Estimated Sales: Below $5 Million
Number Employees: 1-4
Parent Co: Winston Franchise Corporation

28593 Roth Young New York
122 E 42nd Street Room 320
New York, NY 10168-0300
212-557-8181
Employment agency/executive search firm specializ-
ing in selection and placement of food industry per-
sonnel; See our ad on the spine of the print product
VP: David Silver
VP: Eric Kugler
Number Employees: 2
Parent Co: Winston Franchise Corporation

28594 Roth Young Washougal
24 S A Street
Suite A
Washougal, WA 98671-2101
360-835-3136
Fax: 360-835-9383 info@ruthyoung.com
Employment agency/executive search firm specializ-
ing in selection and placement of food industry
personnel
President: David Salzberg
Estimated Sales: Less than $500,000
Number Employees: 4
Parent Co: Winston Franchise Corporation

28595 Roth Young of Tampa Bay
14914 Winding Creek Ct
Tampa, FL 33613-1603
813-269-9889
Fax: 813-269-9919 800-646-1513
Employment agency/executive search firm specializ-
ing in selection and placement of food industry
personnel
President: Barry Cushing
Estimated Sales: $400,000
Number Employees: 1-4
Square Footage: 2000
Parent Co: Winston Franchise Corporation

28596 (HQ)Rothchild Printing Company
7920 Barnwell Ave
Flushing, NY 11373-3727
718-899-6000
Fax: 718-397-1921 800-238-0015
Coupons, tags and labels including multiple page,
paper, foil, flat, rolls and die-cut
VP: Paul Rothchild
Estimated Sales: $10-20 Million
Number Employees: 50-99
Square Footage: 80000

28597 Rotisol France Inc
341 N Oak St
Inglewood, CA 90302-3312
310-671-7254
Fax: 310-671-8171 800-651-5969
info@rotisolusa.com www.rotisolusa.com
Manufacturer, importer and exporter pizza and rotis-
serie ovens; also, grills
Owner: Jim Doar
Head Accounts: Milene Berry
Business Development Manager: Orlane Parsons
Director Sales: Alain Lebret
Sales Coordinator: Cedric Dauphin
Office/Customer Service Manager: Kate Gramcko
jim@rotisolusa.com
Estimated Sales: $2.5 - 5 Million
Number Employees: 5-9
Parent Co: Rotisol S.A.

28598 Roto-Flex Oven Co
135 E Cevallos
San Antonio, TX 78204-1795
210-222-2278
Fax: 210-222-9007 877-859-1463
www.rotoflexoven.com
Manufacturer and exporter of food service equipment and pizza ovens

CEO: Richard Dunfield
service@rotoflexoven.com
CFO: Ed Dunfield
Vice President: Doug Dunfield
Marketing Director: Marijke Carey
Plant Manager: Jose Briano
Estimated Sales: $2 Million
Number Employees: 5-9
Number of Brands: 2
Number of Products: 10
Square Footage: 50000
Type of Packaging: Consumer, Food Service
Brands:
   Dual-Flex
   Js-1
   Roto-Flex Oven
   Roto-Smoker

28599 Roto-Jet Pump
P.O. Box 209
Salt Lake City, UT 84110-0209
801-359-8731
Fax: 801-355-9303 www.rotojet.com
Specialty pumps including high pressure washing,
centrifugal screw impeller and abrasive/corrosive
resistant
CEO: Joseph W Roark
Director Marketing: Steven Osborn
Sales Manager: Sebastien Dumas
Estimated Sales: $1 - 5 Million
Number Employees: 500-999
Brands:
   Ash
   Galigher
   Roto Jet
   Wemco

28600 (HQ)Rotonics Manufacturing
17038 S Figueroa St
Gardena, CA 90248
310-327-5401
Fax: 310-538-5579 corporate@rotonics.com
www.rotonics.com
Manufactures FDA approved containers, bins, totes,
hoppers, pallets for the food industry
Chairman/CEO: Sherman McKinniss
CFO: Doug Russell
VP: Dawn Whitney
Number Employees: 50-99
Other Locations:
   Rotonics Manufacturing
   Bensenville IL
   Rotonics Manufacturing
   Commerce City CO
   Rotonics Manufacturing
   Bartow FL
   Rotonics Manufacturing
   Gardena CA
   Rotonics Manufacturing
   Caldwell ID
   Rotonics Manufacturing
   Gainesville TX
   Rotonics Manufacturing
   N Las Vegas NV
   Rotonics Manufacturing
   Brownwood TX
   Rotonics Manufacturing
   Knoxville TN
   Rotonics Manufacturing
   Miami FL

28601 Rotronic Instrument Corp Inc
135 Engineers Rd # 150
Suite 150
Hauppauge, NY 11788-4018
631-348-6844
Fax: 631-427-3902 800-628-7101
sales@rotronic-usa.com www.rotronic-usa.com
Water activity measuring instrumentation
Manager: David P Love
david@rotronic-usa.com
Vice President: David Love
Marketing Director: Rose Mannarino
Estimated Sales: $2.5-5 Million
Number Employees: 10-19

28602 Rotronics Manufacturing
736 Birginal Dr
Bensenville, IL 60106-1213
630-773-9510
Fax: 630-773-4274 chicago@rotonics.com
www.rotonics.com
Storage containers and systems, tanks, drums
Manager: Jay Rule
Estimated Sales: $20 - 50 Million
Number Employees: 50-99

28603 Round Noon Software
14785 Preston Road
Suite 550
Dallas, TX 75254-7899
972-789-5191
info@roundnoon.com
Restaurant management software
Estimated Sales: $1 - 5 Million

28604 Round Paper Packages Inc
511 Enterprise Dr # 2
Erlanger, KY 41017-1516
859-331-7200
Fax: 859-331-7285 www.roundpaperpackages.com
Fiber and paper cans, tubes and cores
President: James Meier
rppinc@insightbb.com
VP: Linda Meier
Marketing: David Meier
Sales Exec: Linda J Meier
Estimated Sales: $20-50 Million
Number Employees: 20-49

28605 Roundup Food Equip
180 Kehoe Blvd
Carol Stream, IL 60188-1814
630-784-1000
Fax: 630-784-1650 800-253-2991
www.ajantunes.com
Manufacturer and exporter of toasters, steamers and
hot dog grills
President: Glenn Bullock
customerservice@roundupfoodequip.com
Chairman of the Board: Virginia M Antunes
CFO: Bill Nelson
R & D: Tom Goodman
VP Marketing: Thomas Krisch
Estimated Sales: $5 - 10 Million
Number Employees: 100-249
Parent Co: A.J. Antunes & Company

28606 Rovema
650 Hurricane Shoals Rd NW
Lawrenceville, GA 30045-4460
770-513-9604
Fax: 770-513-0814 jnielsen@rovema.com
Vertical form-fill-seal machines, horizontal
form-fill-seal machines, zipper applicators,
cartoners, end-packing machines
President: Klaus Kraemer
Research & Development: Donald Harmon
Sales Director: Charlotte Koellner
Contact: Darlene Crawley
darlene@rovema.com
Operations Manager: Ronald Kahlmann
Purchasing Manager: Dave Henninger
Estimated Sales: $10-20 Million
Number Employees: 50-99

28607 Rowe International
2517 Shadowbrook Drive SE
Grand Rapids, MI 49546-7457
616-246-0483
www.roweinternational.com
Manufacturer and exporter of currency changers, bill
acceptors, under-the-counter safes, jukeboxes and
vending machines including refrigerated food, snack
and popcorn
Estimated Sales: $160 Thousand
Number Employees: 3
Square Footage: 3096
Brands:
   Rowe
   Rowe Ami

28608 Rowland Technologies
320 Barnes Rd
Wallingford, CT 06492-1804
203-269-9500
Fax: 203-265-2768 www.rowlandtechnologies.com
Manufacturer and exporter of decorative plastic and
polycarbonate packaging film
President: Peter Connerton
pconnerton@rowtec.com
Sales Manager: Carl Heflin
Estimated Sales: $5 - 10 Million
Number Employees: 20-49
Square Footage: 120000

28609 Rowlands Sales Company
Butler Industrial Park
PO Box 552
Hazleton, PA 18201-0552
570-455-5813
Fax: 570-454-4790 800-582-6388
rowlands@rowlands.com www.rowlands.com
Aseptic processing equipment, batch control sys-
tems, cheese equipment, blenders, heat exchangers,
plate, scraped surfaces, tubular, homogenizers, ice
equipment, ingredient feeders
President: William Rowlands
CEO: David Rowlands
Contact: Linda James
ljames@rowlands.com
Estimated Sales: $10-20 Million
Number Employees: 20-49

28610 Rownd & Son
PO Box 1495
Dillon, SC 29536-1495
803-774-8264
Vegetable shipping containers
CEO: Annie Dollison
VP Sales: Harry Rownd
Estimated Sales: $2.5-5 Million
Number Employees: 20-49

28611 Rox America
PO Box 5561
Spartanburg, SC 29304-5561
864-463-4352
Fax: 864-463-4670 800-458-3194
info@roxenergy.com www.zimmer-usa.com
Flavor and taste assessment and stability for analyti-
cal services and instrumentation
President: Roland Zimmer
Vice President of Technology: Juergen Merz
National Sales Director: Bob Patterson
Estimated Sales: $1 Million
Square Footage: 3500

28612 (HQ)Roxanne Signs Inc
23413 Woodfield Rd
Gaithersburg, MD 20882-3015
301-428-4911
Fax: 301-253-5833 rox_signs@yahoo.com
www.roxannesigns.com
Custom designed menu signs, menus and advertising
specialty items including logos, banners, neon signs,
window lettering, etc
President: Roxanne Riley
roxannesigns@gmail.com
Estimated Sales: Less Than $500,000
Number Employees: 1-4

28613 (HQ)Roxide International
24 Weaver St
Larchmont, NY 10538
914-630-7700
Fax: 914-235-5328 800-431-5500
roxide@aol.com
Manufacturer and importer of insecticides, repel-
lents, swatters, traps, fly paper, baits and muldicides;
also, graffiti removers, organic cleaners and lubri-
cants; exporter of fly paper and insecticides
President: James Cowen
Estimated Sales: $2.5-5 Million
Number Employees: 10
Type of Packaging: Food Service
Brands:
   Aeroxon
   Revenge
   Roxo

28614 Roy's Folding Box
5140 Richmond Rd
Cleveland, OH 44146-1331
216-464-1191
Fax: 216-464-1562
Paper folding boxes
Owner: Sue Harky
Controller: Jeff Stuteman
Estimated Sales: $1 - 3 Million
Number Employees: 5-9

28615 Royal ACME
3110 Payne Ave
Cleveland, OH 44114-4504
216-241-1477
Fax: 216-241-1479 sales@royalacme.com
www.agwstamps.com
Rubber stamps

Owner: John Enci
johne@royalacme.com
Estimated Sales: $1-2.5 Million
Number Employees: 10-19

28616 Royal Broom & Mop Factory Inc
5717 Plauche Ct
New Orleans, LA 70123-4119
504-818-2244
Fax: 504-818-2266 800-537-6925
sales@royalbroom.com www.royalbroom.com
Brooms and mops; wholesaler/distributor of brushes
and paint sundries
Owner: William Staehle III
CEO: Donald Staehle
donald@royalbroom.com
CFO: Donald Staehle
Estimated Sales: $5 - 10 Million
Number Employees: 5-9
Square Footage: 36000
Type of Packaging: Consumer, Private Label

28617 Royal Chemical Co Inc
204 Memory Ln
Albemarle, NC 28001-5402
704-982-5513
Fax: 704-982-3018 800-650-6346
Janitorial and industrial cleaning compounds
President: Joyce Morton
Sales/Marketing Executive: Madilyn Lampley
Purchasing Agent: Boyce Hill
Estimated Sales: Less Than $500,000
Number Employees: 1-4

28618 Royal Cup Coffee
PO Box 170971
Birmingham, AL 35217-0971
800-366-5836
webjava@royalcupcoffee.com
www.royalcupcoffee.com
Coffee, tea, and coffee equipment.
CEO: Bill Smith

Year Founded: 1896
Estimated Sales: $100-$500 Million
Number Employees: 859
Number of Brands: 4
Square Footage: 260000
Type of Packaging: Food Service
Other Locations:
Royal Cup
Birmingham AL
Brands:
H.C. Valentine
Prideland
ROAR
Royal Cup

28619 Royal Display Corporation
725 Main St
Middletown, CT 6457
860-344-9988
Fax: 860-344-1045 800-569-1295
service@royaldisplay.com
Custom wire display racks, point of purchase dis-
plays and signs and shelves
President: Rick Wright
VP: Laurie Ambrose
Contact: Heather Eyres
heather@royaldisplay.com
Estimated Sales: $2.5-5 Million
Number Employees: 20-49
Square Footage: 100000

28620 Royal Ecoproducts
119 Snow Boulevard
Vaughan, ON L4K 4N9
Canada
905-761-6406
Fax: 905-761-6419 800-465-7670
Manufacturer and exporter of plastic pallets
President: Burno Casciato
President: Maircein Tarascandalo
Director Sales/Marketing: Anthony DiNunzio
Sales Coordinator: Vince Franze
Number Employees: 30

28621 Royal Group
1301 S 47th Ave
Cicero, IL 60804-1516
708-656-2020
Fax: 708-656-2108 www.royalbox.com
Corrugated containers, boxes and crates; also, die
cuts available

President: Jay King
CEO: Kathleen Allen
kallen@royalbox.com
Marketing Director: Doug Holizllan
Sales Manager: Ken Hirsh
Purchasing Manager: Karen Hutinson
Estimated Sales: $5-10 Million
Number Employees: 100-249
Square Footage: 180000

28622 Royal Industries Inc
4100 W Victoria St
Chicago, IL 60646-6727
773-478-6300
Fax: 773-478-4948 800-782-1200
www.royalindustriesinc.com
Wholesaler/distributor of restaurant supplies; serv-
ing the food service market
President: Ervin Naiditch
CFO: Joe Lewis
VP: Jay Johnson
Estimated Sales: $10-20 Million
Number Employees: 20-49
Square Footage: 400000

28623 Royal Label Co
50 Park St
Dorchester, MA 02122-2611
617-825-6050
Fax: 617-825-2678 sales@royallabel.com
www.royallabel.com
Manufacturer and exporter of pressure sensitive la-
bels, price tags, decals, name plates and panels
Owner/President: Paul Clifford Jr.
pdc@royallabel.com
VP: Paul Ryan
Director of QA: Craig DiGiovanni
Business Development: Marychristine Clifford
Operations Manager: Paul Pelletier
Operations & Scheduling: Steve Gefteas
Plant Manager: Paul Pelletier
Controller: Eileen Clifford
Estimated Sales: Below $5 Million
Number Employees: 20-49
Square Footage: 50000

28624 Royal Oak Enterprises
1 Royal Oak Ave
Roswell, GA 30076-7583
678-461-3200
Fax: 678-461-3220 www.royal-oak.com
Manufacturer and exporter of instant light charcoal
briquettes and natural lump charcoal
Owner: James Keeter
jkeeter@royaloakenterprises.com
VP Sales/Marketing: Harold Ovington
Sales Manager: Brian Kerrigan
jkeeter@royaloakenterprises.com
Estimated Sales: $1 - 5 Million
Number Employees: 50-99

28625 Royal Paper Box Co
1105 S Maple Ave
Montebello, CA 90640-6007
323-728-7041
Fax: 323-722-2646 www.royalpaperbox.com
Paper boxes
CEO: James Hodges
Estimated Sales: $50-100 Million
Number Employees: 100-249

28626 Royal Paper Products
PO Box 151
Coatesville, PA 19320
610-384-3400
Fax: 610-384-5106 800-666-6655
www.royalpaper.com
Manufacturer and importer of place mats, coasters,
bibs, napkin bands, chef hats, aprons, gloves, tooth-
picks, sword picks, arrow picks, skewers, coffee stir-
rers, griddle blocks/screens, scouring pads and metal
sponges
President: David Milberg
CEO/CFO: Vince Mazzei
Executive VP: Fred Leibowitz
Quality Control: Debbie Sumka
Marketing Director: Todd Straves
Sales Director: Mark LaRusso
Contact: Candy Warfel
candyw@royalpaper.com
Plant Manager: Ross Glazer
Estimated Sales: $5 - 10 Million
Number Employees: 20-49
Number of Brands: 1

Number of Products: 300
Square Footage: 480
Type of Packaging: Food Service, Private Label,
Bulk
Brands:
Royal Land

28627 Royal Prestige Health Moguls
1025 Old Country Road
Suite 206
Westbury, NY 11590-5654
516-997-1775
Fax: 516-759-1997 888-802-7433
Servicioalcliente@royalprestige.com.mx
www.royalprestige.com
Cookware, water and air purifcation equipment,
china, crystal, tableware and cutlery
President: Steven Pollack
District Manager: Matt Rubin
Estimated Sales: $1 - 3 Million
Number Employees: 10
Square Footage: 800
Parent Co: Royal Prestige Distribution Center
Type of Packaging: Consumer

28628 Royal Range Industries
1768 W 1st Street
Irwindale, CA 91702-3259
626-812-4434
Fax: 626-812-4437
Estimated Sales: $3 - 5 Million
Number Employees: 20-49

28629 Royal Silver Mfg Co Inc
3300 Chesapeake Blvd
Norfolk, VA 23513-4099
757-855-6004
Fax: 757-855-0017 contact@royalsilver.com
Stainless steel flatware
President: Lloyd Gilbert Jr
Secretary and Treasurer: Edward Landreth
President: Alan Gilbert Jr
Estimated Sales: $2.5 - 5 Million
Number Employees: 5-9
Square Footage: 144000

28630 Royal Welding & Fabricating
1000 E Elm Ave
Fullerton, CA 92831-5022
714-680-6669
Fax: 714-680-6646 info@royalwelding.com
www.royalwelding.com
Custom stainless steel process tanks; also, vacuum
chambers, mixers and cookers
President: Wallace Cook
CFO: Sekyung Kim
Vice President/Chief Engineer: Brad Card
Quality Control: Merritt Read
Chief Engineer: Collie Janda
General Manager: Wallace Cook
Estimated Sales: $4.0 Million
Number Employees: 20-49
Square Footage: 116000
Parent Co: Cook & Cook
Brands:
Dimple Plate

28631 Royalton Foodservice Equip Co
9981 York Theta Dr
North Royalton, OH 44133-3545
440-237-0806
Fax: 440-237-1694 800-662-8765
sales@RoyaltonFoodService.com
Food service equipment including baking, roasting
and holding ovens and cabinets
President: Leonard May
Service Engineer: Fred McKinney
CFO: Pat Tatton
Quality Control: David Kinshaw
IT: Hannelore May
hmay@mayind.com
Estimated Sales: $10-20 Million
Number Employees: 20-49

28632 Royce Corp
PO Box 729
Glendale, AZ 85311-0729
Canada
602-256-0006
Fax: 623-435-2030 info@roycemasonry.com
Manufacturer and exporter of wire and metal shelv-
ing, production line trucks, warehouse bins, point of
purchase displays and racks; also, custom designed
for chip, beverage, soups and biscuits

President: George Knowles
General Manager: Glenn Millar
Customer Service: Dave Haywood
Manager Operations: John Fox
Number Employees: 50
Square Footage: 212000
Parent Co: Royce Corporation
Type of Packaging: Consumer, Food Service, Private Label, Bulk
Brands:
 Royce

28633 Royce Rolls Ringer Co
16 Riverview Ter NE
Grand Rapids, MI 49505-6245
      616-361-9266
  Fax: 616-361-5976 800-253-9638
info@roycerolls.net www.roycerolls.net
Manufacturer and exporter of stainless steel mopping equipment, multi and single roll toilet paper dispensers, restroom fixtures and janitorial cleaning carts
President: Charles Royce Jr
VP: Charles Royce
Marketing Director: William Swartz
IT: Angelica Tant
 angel@roycerolls.net
Estimated Sales: $1-3 Million
Number Employees: 20-49
Square Footage: 117200

28634 (HQ)Rqa Product Dynamics
10608 163rd Pl
Orland Park, IL 60467-8858
      708-364-7055
  Fax: 708-364-7061 info@rqa-inc.com
      www.rqa-europe.com
Consultant providing quality assurance evaluations of consumer products and competitive product comparison; also, consumer complaint, domestic and international product retrievals, product recalls, quality consulting services, etc;product development, sensory evaluation and consumer research at new state of the art facility.
President: Lawrence Platt
Executive VP: Mary Ann Platt
Sales: Pamela Vaillancourt
Contact: Cheryl Alesso
 c.alesso@rqa-inc.com
Number Employees: 5-9
Other Locations:
 RQA
 Calabasas CA

28635 Rtech Laboratories
4001 Lexington Ave N
St Paul, MN 55126-2934
      651-481-2207
  Fax: 651-486-0837 800-328-9687
      www.rtechlabs.com
Research laboratory offering focus groups, analytical testing, sensory evaluation, nutrition labeling, pilot plant facilities, etc
Business Development Manager: Carle Shanks
Sales: Annette Sass
Sales: Annette Sass
Estimated Sales: $5 - 10 Million
Number Employees: 100-249
Square Footage: 34000
Parent Co: Land O'Lakes

28636 Rtech Laboratories
4001 Lexington Ave N
St Paul, MN 55126-2934
      651-481-2207
  Fax: 651-486-0837 800-328-9687
  awdotterweich@landolakes.com
      www.rtechlabs.com
Microbiology and chemistry testing, sensory, evaluation and custom processing services for the retail, food service and food development markets
General Manager: Alecia Dotterweich
Sales: Annette Sass
Estimated Sales: $5 - 10 Million
Number Employees: 100-249
Parent Co: Land O'Lakes, Inc.

28637 RubaTex Polymer
PO Box 1050
Middlefield, OH 44062-1050
      440-632-1691
  Fax: 440-632-5761 www.universalpolymer.com
Manufacturer and exporter of plastic straws, can coolers and stoppers

President: Joe Colebank
VP: Andy Cavanagh
Sales/Marketing Manager: Philip Moses
Estimated Sales: $3 - 5 Million
Number Employees: 5-9

28638 Rubbair Door
100 Groton Shirley Rd
Ayer, MA 01432-1050
      978-772-0480
  Fax: 978-772-7114 800-966-7822
info@rubbair.com www.rubbair.com
Vinyl and plastic interior and exterior double impact doors
Manager: Alex Eckel
CEO: Alan Eckel
CFO: Joe Tunneva
Sales Director: Randy Gowld
General Manager: Alex Eckel
Purchasing Manager: John Waldron
Estimated Sales: $1 - 5 Million
Number Employees: 20-49
Number of Products: 12
Parent Co: Eckel Industries

28639 Rubber Fab Molding & Gasket
26 Brookfield Dr
Sparta, NJ 07871-3212
      973-579-2959
  Fax: 973-579-7275 866-442-2959
sales@rubberfab.com www.rubberfab.com
Hygienic seals, sanitary gaskets, hose assemblies, valve, pump and filler machine components in a wide range of high purity elastomer materials
President: Patrick Parisi
Chief Executive Officer: Bob DuPont, Sr.
Chief Financial Officer: Daniel Licini, CPA
Quality Assurance: Allison Luke
Marketing Department: Laura Schnitzer
Sales Manager: Gary Johnson
Materials Manager: Kellie Cash
Estimated Sales: $6.5 Million
Number Employees: 20-49

28640 Rubber Stamp Shop
PO Box 610
Accokeek, MD 20607-610
  Fax: 301-423-2208 800-835-0839
Rubber stamps; also, letter press printing services available
President: Carl Harlow
VP: Carl Harlow
Estimated Sales: less than $500,000
Number Employees: 1-4
Square Footage: 2500
Parent Co: Rubber Stamp Shop

28641 Rubbermaid
4110 Premier Dr.
High Point, NC 27265
      888-895-2110
      www.rubbermaid.com
Ice coolers and chests, thermal jugs and containers, re-freezable ice substitutes and lunch kits, and hummingbird feeders and accessories.
President/CEO, Newell Brands: Michael Polk
Year Founded: 1920
Estimated Sales: $114.70 Million
Number Employees: 1,426
Number of Products: 15
Parent Co: Newell Brands Inc.
Type of Packaging: Food Service
Other Locations:
 Rubbermaid Specialty Products
 Winchester VA
Brands:
 Rubbermaid

28642 Rubbermaid Canada
586 Argus Road
Oakville, ON L6J 3J3
Canada
      905-279-1010
  Fax: 905-279-5254 chpcanada@rubbermaid.com
    www.rubbermaidcommercial.com
Commercial dinnerware
Estimated Sales: $1 - 5,000,000
Parent Co: Rubbermaid Commercial Products
Brands:
 Rubbermaid

28643 (HQ)Rubbermaid Commercial Products
2000 Overhead Bridge Rd NE
Cleveland, TN 37311-4692
      423-476-4544
     Fax: 423-559-9393
    www.rubbermaidcommercial.com
Manufacturer and exporter of mops and cleaning aids
President & CEO: Michael McDermott
Estimated Sales: $50-100 Million
Number Employees: 250-499
Parent Co: Newell Rubbermaid Inc.

28644 Rubbermaid Commercial Products
1400 Laurel Blvd
Pottsville, PA 17901-1427
      570-622-7715
  Fax: 570-622-3817 800-233-0314
    united@unitedrecept.com
   www.rubbermaidcommercial.com
Manufacturer and exporter of fiberglass, steel aluminum, marble and cement waste receptacles; also, smokers' urns, planters and restroom accessories
President/CEO: Richard Weiss
CFO: Rick Piger
 rpiger@unitedrecept.com
Vice President: Layton Dodson
Marketing Director: Tom Palangio
Plant Manager: George Derosa
Purchasing Manager: Margaret Zimmerman
Estimated Sales: $50-100 Million
Number Employees: 100-249
Square Footage: 145000

28645 (HQ)Rubicon Industries
848 E 43rd St
Brooklyn, NY 11210-3500
      718-434-4700
  Fax: 718-434-6174 800-662-6999
sales@rubiconhx.com www.manninglewis.com
Stainless, carbon and high alloy steel and tube heat transfer equipment; also, pressure vessels, stainless steel tanks, reactors and ribbon blenders
President: Michael Rubinberg
 sales@rubiconhx.com
Estimated Sales: $500,000-$1,000,000
Number Employees: 20-49

28646 Ruby Manufacturing & Sales
9853 Alpaca St
South El Monte, CA 91733-3101
      626-443-1171
  Fax: 626-443-0028 info@rubymfg.com
      www.rubymfg.com
Manufacturer and exporter of vegetable juice extractors
Owner: Dan Turner
 info@rubymfg.com
Estimated Sales: $500,000-$1 Million
Number Employees: 5-9
Type of Packaging: Food Service

28647 Rudd Container Corp
4600 S Kolin Ave
Chicago, IL 60632-4497
      773-847-7600
  Fax: 773-847-7930 ruddbox@aol.com
      www.ruddcontainer.com
Corrugated cartons and point of purchase displays
President: Darrell J. Rudd
 ruddbox@aol.com
Vice President: Ted Bihun
Design Manager: Lynna Cavallo
Sales Manager: Errol Dolin
Customer Service: Ann Rudd
Plant Manager: Ken Coyle
Estimated Sales: $15 Million
Number Employees: 20-49
Square Footage: 100000

28648 Rudolph Industries
1176 Cardiff Boulevard
Mississauga, ON L5S 1P6
Canada
      905-564-6160
  Fax: 905-564-6155 info@rudolphind.com
      www.rudolphind.com
Machine knives and injector needles for food processors
President: Bill Rudolph

Number Employees: 10
Square Footage: 80000
Parent Co: W. Rudolph Investments

28649 Rudy's L&R
432 W 38th St
New York, NY 10018-2816
212-245-4966
Fax: 212-262-4815
Suppliers of expresso and capuccino machines
President: Louis Martinez
Estimated Sales: Less than $500,000
Number Employees: 1-4

28650 Rueff Sign Co Inc
1530 E Washington St
Louisville, KY 40206-1831
502-582-1714
Fax: 502-584-6427 www.rueffsigns.com
Signs including electric, plastic, metal and wooden
President: Robert C Rueff
bob@rueffsigns.com
Estimated Sales: Below $5 Million
Number Employees: 20-49

28651 Ruffino Paper Box Co
63 Green St
Hackensack, NJ 07601-4082
201-487-1260
Fax: 201-487-3926 www.ruffinopackaging.com
Folding paper boxes
Owner: Raymond Ruffino
ruffinopkg@aol.com
VP: Raymond Ruffino
Director Sales/Marketing: Rosanne Baleccny
Estimated Sales: $1 - 2.5 Million
Number Employees: 10-19

28652 Ruggles Sign Company
101 Kuhlman Blvd.
Versailles, KY 40383
859-879-1199
Fax: 859-873-1697 www.rugglessign.com
Neon and plastic signs
President: Tim Cambron
CFO: Anna Cambron
Design Development: Jason Elmore
National Sales & Marketing: Elizabeth Pitchford
Sales & Special Projects: Tony Shaw
Office Manager: Lisa Smith
Production Manager: John Ratcliff
Account Manager: Elizabeth Pitchford
Purchasing: Brad Turpin, Jr
Estimated Sales: $5-10 Million
Number Employees: 50-99
Square Footage: 110000

28653 (HQ)Ruiz Flour Tortillas
1200 Marlborough Ave
Riverside, CA 92507
909-947-7811
Fax: 909-947-2338 www.ruizflourtortillas.com
Traditional and specialty, ethnic and gourmet flour tortillas serving food manufacturers, foodservice industry, restaurant distributors, retail food brokers, and specialty retail outlets
Founder: Edward Ruiz
CFO: Uriel Maciaf
Vice President: Vickie Salgado
R&D: David Rodriguez
Manager: Maria Lopez
Contact: Oscar Figari
oscarfigari@ruizflourtortillas.com
Purchasing: Carmen Sandoval
Type of Packaging: Food Service, Private Label, Bulk

28654 Ruland Manufacturing CoInc
6 Hayes Memorial Dr
Marlborough, MA 01752-1830
508-485-1000
Fax: 508-485-9000 800-225-4234
sales@ruland.com www.ruland.com
Owner: Robert Ruland
bob.ruland@ruland.com
Number Employees: 50-99

28655 Rusken Packaging
PO Box 2100
Cullman, AL 35056-2100
256-775-0014
Fax: 256-734-3008 www.rusken.com
Corrugated containers

President: Greg Rusken
Office Manager: Robin Marty
Sales Manager: Joy Jackson
Estimated Sales: $20-50 Million
Number Employees: 20-49

28656 Russel T. Bundy Associates, Inc.
417 E Water St
P.O. Box 150
Urbana, OH 43078
800-652-2151
info@bundybakingsolutions.com
www.bundybakingsolutions.com
Remanufacturer of baking equipment.
President: Tom Bundy
CEO: Gilbert Bundy
Sales Manager: Terry Bauer
tbartsch@shaffermanufacturing.com
Estimated Sales: $10 - 20 Million
Number Employees: 10-19

28657 Russell
201 Thomas French Dr
Scottsboro, AL 35769-7405
800-288-9488
russell.htpg.com
Commercial refrigeration systems
Director of Sales & Marketing: Paul Westbrook
Parent Co: Rheem

28658 Russell Finex Inc
625 Eagleton Downs Dr
Pineville, NC 28134-7424
704-588-9808
Fax: 704-588-0738 800-849-9808
www.russellfinex.com
Sieving, filtering, separation equipment
President: John Edwards
shuan.edwards@russellfinex.com
Managing Director: Ray Singh
Estimated Sales: $1 - 2.5 Million
Number Employees: 20-49
Parent Co: Russell Group

28659 Russell-William
1710 Midway Rd
Odenton, MD 21113-1128
410-551-3602
Fax: 410-551-9076
Store fixtures and point of purchase displays
CEO: Robert Williams
CEO: Robert Williams
Sales Manager: Rick Sauer
Contact: Russell Winter
russell@william-russell.com
Estimated Sales: $20 - 50 Million
Number Employees: 100-249

28660 Rust-Oleum Corp
11 Hawthorn Pkwy
Vernon Hills, IL 60061
847-367-7700
800-367-7700
www.rustoleum.com
Flooring, floor and wall coating materials, paints, enamels and coatings.
President & CEO: Ed Voorhees
Year Founded: 1921
Estimated Sales: $199.80 Million
Number Employees: 100-249

28661 Rutan Poly Industries Inc
39 Siding Pl
Mahwah, NJ 07430-1896
201-529-1474
Fax: 201-529-4440 800-872-1474
sales@rutanpoly.com www.rutanpoly.com
Polyethylene film, bags, tubing and sheeting
President and CEO: Arnold Tanowitz
bagman@rutanpoly.com
Vice President: Esther Tanowitz
Estimated Sales: $5 - 10 Million
Number Employees: 20-49
Square Footage: 92800
Type of Packaging: Food Service

28662 Rutherford Engineering
1731 Apaloosa
Rockford, IL 61107
815-623-2141
Fax: 815-623-7170
Manufacturer and exporter of fillers, valves and packaging equipment
President: Ashwin Patel

Estimated Sales: $950,000
Number Employees: 15
Square Footage: 27000
Brands:
Akra-Pak
Rutherford

28663 Rutler Screen Printing
1000 S. 27th Street
Easton, PA 18045
610-829-2999
Fax: 610-829-2994 orders@rutler.com
www.rutler.com
Garments, point of purchase displays, posters, decals, bumperstickers, T-shirts, etc
Owner: John Shubert
Contact: Ian Frey
ian@rutler.com
Estimated Sales: $1-2.5 Million
Number Employees: 10-19

28664 Ryan Technology Inc.
2705 SE 39th Loop # B
Suite B
Hillsboro, OR 97123-8415
503-648-9967
Fax: 503-640-3846 800-277-2290
info@ryanslicer.com www.ryanslicer.com
Rotary table and in-line horizontal slicers
President: John Ryan
ryanslicer@aol.com
Sales: Sandra Ryan
Estimated Sales: Less Than $500,000
Number Employees: 1-4

28665 (HQ)Ryder System, Inc
11690 NW 105th St
Miami, FL 33178
305-500-3726
800-467-9337
www.ryder.com
Transportation firm providing leasing and transportation management services; also, vehicle maintenance and inventory deployment services available
Chairman & CEO: Robert Sanchez
EVP/Chief Legal Officer/Secretary: Robert Fatovic
EVP/Chief Financial Officer: Scott Parker
EVP/Chief Sales Officer: John Gleason
EVP/Chief Marketing Officer: Karen Jones
SVP/Chief Human Resources Officer: Frank Lopez
SVP/Chief Information Officer: Rajeev Ravindran
SVP/Chief Procurement Officer: Tim Fiore
Estimated Sales: $7.3 Billion
Number Employees: 39,600
Square Footage: 440000
Other Locations:
Ryder Integrated Logistics
Birmingham AL

28666 Ryowa Company America
555 Bonnie Ln
Elk Grove Village, IL 60007
847-952-8363
Fax: 847-952-8309 800-700-9692
contact@ryowaamerica.com
www.ryowaamerica.com
Conveyors, conveyor merge units and accessories for packaging and slicers and slicer applicatiors for processing
President: Hiroshi Hayashi
hiroshi.hayashi@ryowaamerica.com
Technical Sales Manager: Bill Linahan
Estimated Sales: Less than $500,000
Number Employees: 1-4

28667 Ryson International
300 Newsome Dr
Yorktown, VA 23692-5006
757-898-1530
Fax: 757-898-1580 sales@ryson.com
www.ryson.com
Materials handling equipment
President: Scott Christensen
schristensen@ryson.com
CFO: Ragnhild Rygh
Estimated Sales: Below $5 Million
Number Employees: 10-19

28668 Rytec Corporation
780 N Water St
Milwaukee, WI 53202-3512
414-273-3500
Fax: 414-273-5198 888-467-9832
info@rytecdoors.com

Manufacturer and exporter of high-speed, rolling and folding doors including cold storage
Chairman: Donald Grasso
Regional Manager: Jamie Lilly
Marketing Manager: Scott Blue
Estimated Sales: $20-50 Million
Number Employees: 250-499
Brands:
    Bautam
    Clean-Roll
    Fast-Fold
    Fast-Seal
    Preda

28669 Ryter Corporation
32732 730th Avenue
Saint James, MN 56081-5516
                        507-642-8529
        Fax: 507-642-3692 800-643-2184
Bacteria and enzyme products for waste water treatment, drains, grease traps and odor control
President: Terry Etter
Sales Manager: Barb Nelson
Estimated Sales: $1-2.5 Million
Number Employees: 9
Brands:
    Odormute

28670 Ryther-Purdy
174 Elm St
PO Box 622
Old Saybrook, CT 06475-4105
                        860-388-4405
        Fax: 860-388-9401 tpurdy@rytherpurdy.com
                www.rytherpurdy.com
Lighting standards and fixtures
President: Timothy Purdy
    tpurdy@rytherpurdy.com
Estimated Sales: $1-2.5 Million
Number Employees: 5-9

28671 S & G Resources Inc
266 Main St # 23
Olde Medfield Square
Medfield, MA 02052-2056
                        508-359-7771
        Fax: 508-359-7775 877-359-7776
sandg@sandgresources.com www.sgresources.net
President: Michael I Goldman
    sandg@sandgresources.com
Estimated Sales: Below $5 Million
Number Employees: 1-4

28672 S & H Uniform Corp
1 Aqueduct Rd
White Plains, NY 10606-1003
                        914-937-6800
        Fax: 914-937-0741 800-210-5295
                info@sandhuniforms.com
                www.sandhuniforms.com
Uniforms, aprons, smocks, caps and visors
President: Glen Ross
    info@sandhuniforms.com
Vice President: Kevin Ross
Sales Manager: Pat Kraft
Estimated Sales: $35 Million
Number Employees: 50-99
Square Footage: 50000
Type of Packaging: Private Label
Brands:
    S&H Uniforms

28673 S & J Laboratories Inc
4669 Executive Dr
Portage, MI 49002-9389
                        269-324-7383
        Fax: 269-324-7384 info@sandjlab.com
                www.sandjlab.com
Food laboratory service providing chemical, microbiological and physical analysis for food, feed and ingredients
President: Sheree Lin
    shereelin@sandjlab.com
Vice President: James Lin
Estimated Sales: $500,000-$1 Million
Number Employees: 5-9
Square Footage: 16000

28674 S & L Store Fixture
3755 NW 115th Ave
Doral, FL 33178-1857
                        305-599-8906
        Fax: 305-599-8906 800-205-4536
info@slstoredisplays.com www.usahanger.com

Manufacturer and exporter of store fixtures including metal shelving
President: Ronald Maier
VP: Ron Maier
Estimated Sales: $2.5 - 5 Million
Number Employees: 10-19
Square Footage: 128000
Brands:
    Kent Supermatic

28675 S & R Products
765 Oak Rd
Bronson, MI 49028-9353
                        517-369-2351
        Fax: 517-369-2424 800-328-3887
                www.sandrproductsllc.com
Manufacturer and wholesaler/distributor of automatic liquor control pourers
Owner: Scot Kubasiak
    scott.kubasiak@srproducts.com
Sales Manager: Rick Sandvik
Estimated Sales: Less Than $500,000
Number Employees: 1-4
Square Footage: 14000
Parent Co: Kazico
Brands:
    Cheapshot

28676 S & S Metal & Plastics Inc
3740 Morton St
Jacksonville, FL 32217-2276
                        904-730-4655
        Fax: 904-739-1394 c.strickland@ssmetal.com
                www.ssmetal.com
Plastic signs
President: Cindy Strickland
    c.strickland@ssmetal.com
VP: Tim Clifton
Estimated Sales: $5-10 Million
Number Employees: 20-49

28677 S & S Soap Co
815 E 135th St
Bronx, NY 10454-3584
                        718-585-2900
                Fax: 718-585-2902
Powdered, liquid and hand soap; also, detergents
President: David Sebrow
    david@sssoap.com
Estimated Sales: $10 - 20 Million
Number Employees: 10-19
Square Footage: 80000
Brands:
    Pink Magic
    White Magic

28678 S & S Svc Parts
409 Saint Croix Ave
New Richmond, WI 54017-2609
                        715-246-3299
        Fax: 715-246-3212 sales@bagcloser.com
                www.bagcloser.com
Hand sealers, band sealers, bagging scales, conveyors, palletizers and vertical form fill and seal systems
Owner: Mike Preece
    mike@ssserviceparts.com
Sales Director: Tim Tonkson
Estimated Sales: $500,000-$1 Million
Number Employees: 5-9

28679 S & W Pallet Co
2120 Divider And Natchez Trace
Camden, TN 38320-6559
                        731-584-4540
        Fax: 731-584-2664 800-640-0522
        sales@swpallet.com www.swpallets.com
Wooden pallets and skids
President: Jackie Wimberly
    jackiewimberly@swpallets.com
Manager: Jackie Wimberly
Estimated Sales: $5-10 Million
Number Employees: 50-99

28680 S E & M
2660 Perrowville Rd
Forest, VA 24551-1859
                        434-525-7707
        Fax: 434-525-7739 800-488-6055
        info@se-m.com www.se-m.com
President: Jack Balrd
Vice President: Cb Messer
    cbmesser@se-m.com
CFO: Jack Balrd

Estimated Sales: Below $5 Million
Number Employees: 20-49

28681 S Hochman Company
PO Box 1204
Danville, CA 94526-8204
                        925-838-9990
        Fax: 925-743-1234 800-999-9511
Food and beverage industry
Owner: Shayel M Hochman Jr

28682 S I Jacobson Mfg Co
1414 Jacobson Dr
Waukegan, IL 60085-7600
                        847-623-1414
        Fax: 847-623-2556 800-621-5492
        plzang@sij.com www.sij.com
CEO: Seth Greenwald
    sigreenwald@gmail.com
Estimated Sales: $50 - 100 Million
Number Employees: 100-249

28683 S J Controls Inc
2248 Obispo Ave # 203
Suite 203
Signal Hill, CA 90755-4026
                        562-494-1400
        Fax: 562-494-1066 info@sjcontrols.com
                www.sjcontrols.com
Manufacturer and exporter of blending and batching equipment, process control systems, flow meters and level detectors; also, engineering services available
President: Dave Olszewski
CAO: Noel Brown
    nbrown@sjcontrols.com
CFO: Cindy Pawn
Engineer: Steve Czaus
Estimated Sales: Below $5 Million
Number Employees: 5-9

28684 S Kamberg & Co LTD
445 Northern Blvd # 25
Great Neck, NY 11021-4804
                        516-482-4141
        Fax: 516-482-4147 www.skamberg.com
Supplier of Corn Meal, Dairy Products, Fats, Flour, Fruits, Honey, Nut Meats, Seeds, Sprinkles/Chocolate and Tomoato Products.
President: Doreen Tiseo
    dtiseo@skamberg.com
CEO: Mark Kamberg
Sales Manager: Mark Glickman
Estimated Sales: $5 - 10 Million
Number Employees: 5-9

28685 S L Doery & Son Inc
299 Rockaway Tpke
Lawrence, NY 11559-1269
                        516-239-8090
                Fax: 516-239-0696
Commerical awnings
President: Tom Peppe
Estimated Sales: Less than $500,000
Number Employees: 5-9

28686 S L Sanderson & Co
173 Sandy Springs Ln
Berry Creek, CA 95916-9759
                        530-589-3062
        Fax: 530-589-3062 800-763-7845
Manufacturer and exporter of handheld capsule fillers and tampers; wholesaler/distributor of gelatin capsules
President: Cydney Sanderson
    capsulefillers@gmail.com
Estimated Sales: Less Than $500,000
Number Employees: 1-4
Number of Products: 6
Brands:
    Cap. M. Quik

28687 S Walter Packaging Corp
2900 Grant Ave
Philadelphia, PA 19114-2310
                        215-676-8890
        Fax: 215-698-7119 888-429-5673
        shop@swalter.com www.swalter.com
Bags, boxes, ribbons, bows, gift wrap, tissue paper and labels for packaging supplies.

President: John Dowers
  john@swalter.com
Finance Executive: Maury Jaffe
EVP: James Leddy
SVP Marketing/Sales: Paula Wilmer
Human Resources Manager: Barbara Guido
  john@swalter.com
VP Operations: Marc Leventhal
Purhcasing Agent: Beth Lopergola
Estimated Sales: $70 Million
Number Employees: 100-249
Square Footage: 200000

28688 (HQ)S&M Manufacturing Company
PO Box 1637
Cisco, TX 76437-1637
                          254-442-1380
        Fax: 254-442-1643 800-772-8532
Mops and brooms
President: George Owens
Executive VP: Gail Hogan
VP: Sandy Boyett
Estimated Sales: Below $5 Million
Number Employees: 5-9
Brands:
  Sheen Master

28689 S&O Corporation
527 Layton Rd
Gallaway, TN 38036
                          901-867-2223
        Fax: 901-867-3760 800-624-7858
Garbage bags
President: Terry Draughon
VP: Tommy White
Contact: Toi Spearmon
  tois@sandocorporation.com
Estimated Sales: $5-10 Million
Number Employees: 20 to 49

28690 S&P Marketing, Inc.
11100 86th Ave
Maple Grove, MN 55369
                          763-559-0436
              Fax: 763-557-1318
Fruit ingredients including tropical and temperate
fruit juices, purees, dried fruits, powders and more.
Niche products include tamarind, coconut cream,
alphonso mango puree, prickly pear juice, puree,
powder, fiber and oil.
President: Chareonsri Srisangnam
Marketing/R&D: Vinod Padhye
  om@snpmarketing.com
Contact: Om Padhye
  om@snpmarketing.com
Type of Packaging: Food Service, Bulk

28691 S&P USA Ventilation Systems, LLC
6393 Powers Ave
Jacksonville, FL 32217
                          904-731-4711
        Fax: 904-737-8322 800-961-7370
              www.solerpalau-usa.com
Manufacturer and exporter of commercial restaurant
exhaust fans and ventilation equipment
Owner: Patrick M Williams Sr
VP Sales: Mike Wanek
Contact: Karen Antonell
  karen.antonell@healogics.com
Manufacturing/Product Manager: Jim Webster
Estimated Sales: $10-20 Million
Number Employees: 100-249
Square Footage: 150000
Parent Co: Breidert Air Products
Type of Packaging: Consumer, Food Service, Private Label, Bulk
Brands:
  Breidert Air
  Jennfan
  Stanley

28692 S&R Machinery
943 Underwood Rd
Olyphant, PA 18447-2619
                          570-489-1212
        Fax: 570-489-2572 800-229-4896
Manufacturing automated packaging machinery for
your business
President: Brain McCarthy
Sales: Tim McAndrew
Production: Tim Mcandrew
Plant Manager: Tim Mc Andrew

Estimated Sales: $1-2.5 Million
Number Employees: 1-4
Number of Brands: 12
Number of Products: 1
Square Footage: 28000
Type of Packaging: Food Service

28693 S-H-S International of Wilkes
1124 Highway 315 Blvd
Wilkes Barre, PA 18702-6943
                          570-825-3411
              Fax: 570-825-7790
Recruiter of technical and managerial personnel for
the food industry
Owner: Christopher Hackett
President: Chris Hackett
Estimated Sales: $1 - 3 Million
Number Employees: 10-19

28694 S. B. C. Coffee
19529 Vashon Highway SW
Vashon, WA 98070-6029
                          206-463-5050
              Fax: 206-463-5051
Import and retail coffee equipment and supplies
President: J Stewart
Estimated Sales: $500,000-$1 000,000
Number Employees: 5-9
Type of Packaging: Private Label, Bulk

28695 S. Katzman Produce
Hunts Point Market
Row B, Unit 213
Bronx, NY 10474
                          718-991-4700
  Fax: 718-589-3655 info@katzmanproduce.com
                    katzmanproduce.com
Fruits and vegetables
President: Stephen Katzman
VP, Finance: Gary Allen
Director of Operations: Andrew Roy
Manager: Mario Andreani
Estimated Sales: $50-100 Million
Number Employees: 5-9
Type of Packaging: Food Service

28696 S.L. Canada Packaging Machine
1391 Kebet Way
Port Coquitlam, BC V3C 6G1
Canada
                          604-941-6538
        Fax: 604-941-2924 info@marpak.ca
President: George Davis
Number Employees: 20-40

28697 S.S.I. Schaefer System International Limited
140 Nuggett Court
Brampton, ON L6T 5H4
Canada
                          905-458-5399
        Fax: 905-458-7951 sales@ssi-schaefer.ca
Plastic, steel, stacking and nesting storage containers
General Manager: Otto Fasthuber
Number Employees: 25

28698 S.V. Dice Designers
1836 Valencia Street
Rowland Heights, CA 91748-3050
                          909-869-7833
        Fax: 909-869-0515 888-478-3423
Manufacturer and exporter of packaging machinery
including case packers, erectors and sealers
President: Todd Dice
VP: Don Jameson
Engineer: Kent Martins
Estimated Sales: $2.5-5 Million
Number Employees: 1-4
Square Footage: 60000

28699 SA Wald Reconditioners
534 Foothill Road
Bridgewater, NJ 08807-2236
                          908-218-0627
              Fax: 201-433-0098
Tea and coffee industry equipment and machinery
reconditioning
Estimated Sales: $1 - 5 Million
Number Employees: 7

28700 SAF Products
433 E Michigan St
Milwaukee, WI 53202-5104
                          414-221-6333
        Fax: 414-615-4000 800-641-4615
              www.safbankproducts.com
CEO: John Riesch
Estimated Sales: $10-20 Million
Number Employees: 50-99

28701 SASA Demarle
8 Corporate Dr
Cranbury, NJ 08512-3630
                          609-395-0219
        Fax: 609-395-1027 sales@demarleusa.com
              www.demarleusa.com
President: Hatsuo Takeuchi
Finance & Administration Manager: Andrew Rozek
Vice President: Pierre Bonnet
Marketing & Sales Administrator: Brandon
Iacometta
Contact: Pierre Bonnet
  pierre.bonnet@sasademarle.com
Estimated Sales: $5 - 10 Million
Number Employees: 10-19

28702 SASOL North America
900 Threadneedle
Suite 100
Houston, TX 77079
                          281-588-3000
        Fax: 281-588-3144 info@us.sasol.com
              www.sasolnorthamerica.com
Medium chain triglycerides, release agents, emulsifiers, fats
President: Charles Putnik
SNA Finance Manager: Patrick Cain
Vice President, Sasol US Operations: Mike Thomas
Research & Development Manager: Holger Ziehe
Marketing: Barbara Pagliocca
Sales: Barbara Pagliocca
Contact: Kevin Dedeaux
  kdedeaux@energyxxi.com
Manager O&S US Operations: Paul Hippman
Estimated Sales: $5 - 10 Million
Number Employees: 500-999

28703 SBA Software
10460 NW 29th Ter
Doral, FL 33172-2527
                          305-477-7366
        Fax: 305-477-7175 800-222-8324
    sales@restez.com www.pintodesigns.net
Point of sale hospitality and back office software
Owner: Pelia Pinto
Director Development: Roman Teller
Technical Services Director: Brad Sherman
Estimated Sales: $5 - 10 Million
Number Employees: 1-4
Brands:
  Rest Ez

28704 SBB & Associates
4708 S Old Pch Rd Ste 100a
Norcross, GA 30071
                          770-449-7610
        Fax: 770-449-1839 www.eventective.com
Executive personnel search firm
President: Mark Barlow
Estimated Sales: Below $5 Million
Number Employees: 1-4

28705 SBN Associates
5702 Larchmont Drive
Erie, PA 16509-2918
                          814-454-6326
              Fax: 814-459-3359
Computer systems and software for the meat industry

28706 SBS of Financial Industries
28 New Hampton Road
Washington, NJ 07882-4002
                          908-689-5520
              Fax: 908-689-5774
Electronic card processing and check vertification
services for the food service industry
CEO: Joe Kaplan
Director New Business Development: Linda Booth
VP: Tim Jochner
Parent Co: Superior Bankcard Service (SBS)

28707 SCA Hygiene Paper
PO Box 719
San Ramon, CA 94583-5719
925-830-2970
Fax: 925-830-0628 800-992-8675
Industrial food wipes, toilet tissue, towels, polishing
cloths and soaps
EVP: Dan Filippini
Marketing Specialist: Debbie Allyn
Estimated Sales: $1 - 5 Million
Number Employees: 100-250
Brands:
  Mevon
  Tork

28708 SCA Tissue
Cira Centre, Suite 200
2929 Arch Street
Philadelphia, PA 19104
920-725-7031
Fax: 920-727-8801 866-722-8675
www.torkusa.com
Paper products including napkins, table cloths, place
mats, tray covers, towels and toilet and facial tissue
President: Joe Raccuia
Director Marketing: Greg Linnemanstons
Sr. VP Sales/Marketing: Pete Chiericozzi
VP Distribution Sales: Joe Selzer
Estimated Sales: $5-10 Million
Number Employees: 250-499
Parent Co: Chesapeake Corporation
Brands:
  Main Street
  Park Avenue
  Park Avenue Ultra
  Second Nature Plus

28709 SCA Tissue North America
1 River St
S Glens Falls, NY 12803-4768
518-743-0240
Fax: 518-793-2650 www.sca.com
Napkins, paper towels and toilet paper
President: Joe Raccuia
  joe.raccuia@sca.com
Director Marketing/National Accounts: Scott
Milburn
Sr VP Sales/Marketing: Don Lewis
Estimated Sales: $50-100 Million
Number Employees: 250-499
Brands:
  Ovation

28710 SCK Direct Inc
905 Honeyspot Rd
Stratford, CT 06615-7140
203-377-4414
Fax: 203-377-8187 800-327-8766
sales@fastinc.com www.kitchenbrains.com
Manufacturer and exporter of appliance timers and
controls for frying, cooking, roasting, proofing, re-
tarder-proofing, baking, etc.; also, portable shorten-
ing filter machines and software systems for
appliance diagnostics
Chairman: Bernard G Koether
  bkoether@mysck.com
President: George F Koether
CEO: Seth Lukash
Sales Operations Manager: Sherry Kraynak
Estimated Sales: $10 - 20 Million
Number Employees: 50-99
Brands:
  Fastfilter
  Fastimer
  Fastpak
  Fastron
  Sck

28711 SCK Direct Inc
905 Honeyspot Rd
Stratford, CT 06615-7140
203-377-4414
Fax: 203-377-8187 800-327-8766
sales@fastinc.com www.kitchenbrains.com
Food processing appliance controls
Chairman: Bernard G Koether
  bkoether@mysck.com
Sales Operations Manager: Sherry Kraynak
Estimated Sales: $10-20 Million
Number Employees: 50-99

28712 (HQ)SDIX
111 Pencader Dr
Newark, DE 19702-3322
302-456-6789
Fax: 302-456-6770 800-544-8881
sales@sdix.com www.sdix.com
SDIX is a leader in developing accurate, simple, and
rapid tests for pathogens. Our Rapidchek Tests for
E.coli 0157, Listeria and Salmonella Enteritidis give
you confidence in test reslutls, shortened product
hold times and loweroverall testing costs. Rapidchek
is Simply Accurate.
President/CEO: Fran DiNuzzo
R&D: Klaus Linopaintner
Marketing: Tim Lawink
Contact: Anthony Simonetta
  anthony@haydenir.com
Estimated Sales: $30 Million
Number Employees: 5-9
Brands:
  Inquest
  Rapid Assays
  Rapid Prep

28713 SEC
106 N Main St
Plymouth, MI 48170
734-455-4500
Fax: 734-455-1026
Ceiling fan, light fixture and protective wire guards;
also, industrial ceiling-suspended fans
President: Donald Keeth
National Sales Manager: Patricia Keeth
Estimated Sales: $1-2.5 Million
Number Employees: 10-19

28714 SEI Consultants
429 South St
Slidell, LA 70460-8834
985-781-1015
Fax: 985-781-1025 800-738-1000
info@seihq.com www.seihq.com
Software for food processing, packing and distribu-
tion
President: James Stolt
  jim@seihq.com
VP Sales/Marketing: Donald Tyler
Estimated Sales: Less than $500,000
Number Employees: 10-19
Brands:
  Sei

28715 SEMCO
1211 W. Harmony
PO Box 505
Ocala, FL 34478-0505
800-451-3383
Fax: 352-351-3088 800-749-6894
salesatsemco@aol.com
Spinner racks, grid systems, peg hooks, dump bins,
pegboard and slatwall fixtures; also, custom display
items
VP: Adrian Simonet
Marketing: Tammy Robinson
Sales: Tammy Robinson
Public Relations: Fran Smith
Estimated Sales: $1 - 5 Million
Number Employees: 100-250
Square Footage: 540000
Parent Co: Leggett & Platt

28716 SEMCO Systems
6355 Kestrel Road
Mississauga, ON L5T 1Z5
Canada
905-670-9301
Fax: 905-670-9367 800-730-5859

28717 SERCO Laboratories
2817 Anthony Lane South
Suite 104
St. Anthony, MN 55418
612-782-9716
Fax: 612-782-9782 800-388-7173
www.sl-ser.com
Environmental testing laboratory
CEO: David Allen
Project Manager: Diane Anderson
Contact: Dave Allen
  da@sl-ser.com
Estimated Sales: $500,000 - $1 Million
Number Employees: 5-9

28718 SFB Plastics
P.O. Box 533
Wichita, KS 67201-0533
316-262-0409
Fax: 316-712-0112 800-343-8133
sales@sfbplastics.com www.sfbplastics.com
Packaging equipment
President: David Long
CFO: David Long
R&D: David Long
Quality Control: Debbie Stevens
Contact: Cindy Andersen
  candersen@sfbplastics.com
Estimated Sales: $10 - 20 Million
Number Employees: 50-99

**28719 (HQ)SFBC, LLC dba Seaboard
Folding Box**
P.O Box 547
Fitchburg, MA 01420
978-342-8921
Fax: 978-342-1105 800-225-6313
info@seaboardbox.com www.cjfox.com
Boxes, cards, labels and tags
President: Robert Starr
Quality Control: Les Coster
Marketing Manager: Joe Wescott
VP Marketing: Jill Fox-Tabak
Public Relations: Joe Wescott
Estimated Sales: $1 - 2.5 Million
Number Employees: 100-249
Square Footage: 260000
Type of Packaging: Private Label
Other Locations:
  C.J. Fox Co.
  Providence RI

28720 SFK Danfotech, Inc.
8301 N.W. 101st Terrace #7
Kansas City, MO 64153
816-891-7357
Fax: 816-891-0550
Automated cutting, slaughtering, deboning and processing machines for the meat industry.
Contact: Soren Rasmuessen
  sales@sfk.com

28721 SFS intec, Inc
Spring Street & Van Reed Rd
Wyomissing, PA 19610
610-376-5751
Fax: 610-376-8551 610-376-8551
www.sfsintecusa.com
Freezing, material handling, chilling, automated
freezing, automated chilling
Managing Director: R John Smith
Contact: Maryann Joyal
  jmar@sfsintec.biz
Estimated Sales: $5-10 Million
Number Employees: 10-19

28722 SG Frantz Company
PO Box 1138
Trenton, NJ 08606-1138
215-943-2930
Fax: 215-943-2931 800-227-7642
sales@sgfrantz.com www.sgfrantz.com
Magnetic separation equipment and industrial pro-
cessing equipment including dry materials, liquids
and slurries and laboratory equipment
VP: Steve Fortunate
Estimated Sales: $1-5 Million
Number Employees: 1

28723 SGS International
201 State Rt 17 # 2
Rutherford, NJ 07070-2597
201-935-1500
Fax: 201-508-3193 800-747-9047
Environmental and social accountability manage-
ment systems registration; ISO 14001 training in-
cludes IRCA-accredited lead assessor and internal
auditing courses, EMS implementation, environmen-
tal laws and regulations
Chairman of the Board: Ernani Perez
VP: Michael J Brigante
Estimated Sales: $2.5-5 Million
Number Employees: 20-49

28724 SHURflo
3545 Harbor Gateway S
Suite 103
Costa Mesa, CA 92626
714-371-1550
Fax: 714-242-1362 800-854-3218
customer_service@shurflo.com www.pentair.com
Manufacturer and exporter of pumps including gas
operated demand, liquid, electric and dual inlet gas
systems for beverage syrups and condiments.
President & CEO, Pentair: John Staunch
Year Founded: 1968
Estimated Sales: $100-500 Million
Number Employees: 250-499
Parent Co: Pentair Inc.
Type of Packaging: Food Service

28725 SI Systems Inc
101 Larry Holmes Dr # 500
Suite 500
Easton, PA 18042-7723
610-252-7321
Fax: 610-252-3102 800-523-9464
www.sihs.com
Material handling equipment including horizontal
transport, order fulfillment and sortation systems
President/CEO: John C Molloy
molloy@sihs.com
CFO: Deborah Mertz
Director Business Development: Dean Stavraka
Director Marketing: Mary Denvir
VP Marketing & Sales: Ed Romaine
VP Operations: Victor Egberts
Purchasing: Tony Franco
Estimated Sales: $10 - 20 Million
Number Employees: 20-49
Brands:
Sps 3000

28726 SICK Inc
6900 W 110th St
Bloomington, MN 55438-2397
952-946-6800
Fax: 952-941-9287 800-325-7425
www.sickusa.com
A global manufacturer of sensors, safety systems,
machine vision and automatic identification prod-
ucts for industrial applications. Including: 2D and
2D machine vision cameras, Color Vision Sensors
(CVS), and capacitative sensors.
President: Tony Peet
tony.peet@sick.com
Managing Director: Renate Sick-Glaser
Marketing Director: Maria Mueller
Sales Manager: Marion Bentin
Number Employees: 1000-4999
Parent Co: SICK, Inc

28727 SICOM Systems
4434 Summer Meadow Dr
Doylestown, PA 18902
Fax: 215-489-2769 800-547-4266
the SL18, a Linux-based color touch screen, point of
sale ssytem for the quick service restaurant environ-
ment.
President: William Doan
Contact: Wendy Kemmerer
wkemmerer@sicompos.com
Estimated Sales: $10-20,000,000
Number Employees: 50-99

28728 SIG Combibloc
5327 Fisher Road
Columbus, OH 43228-9511
614-347-9971
Fax: 614-876-8678 800-843-2562
www.sigcombibloc.com
Aseptic packaging systems, aseptic filling equip-
ment
President: Stphen Walliser
Estimated Sales: $50 - 100 Million
Number Employees: 25

28729 SIG Combibloc USA, Inc.
2501 Seaport Drive
River Front Suite 100
Chester, PA 19013-9791
610-546-4200
Fax: 610-546-4201 www.sigcombibloc.com
Manufacturer and exporter of aseptic carton filling
and packaging systems for liquid foods and
beverages

President: Yerry Derrico
Director Marketing: Bob Abamson
VP Sales/Marketing: Geoff Campbell
Contact: Kevin Abrams
kevin.abrams@sig.biz
Estimated Sales: $50-100 Million
Number Employees: 100-249
Parent Co: PKL Verpackungssysteme GmbH

28730 SIG Pack Services
2401 Brentwood Rd
Raleigh, NC 27604-3686
919-872-5561
Fax: 919-877-0887 www.sigpack.com
Tea and coffee industry, bag and pouch sealers, bag
filling and sealing machines, brushes, wrapping,
foiling, carton machines: closing, filling, forming,
sealing, closing equipment: bag closure, heat seal,
conveyor accesories
President: Harold Carr
Estimated Sales: Below $5 Million
Number Employees: 20-49

28731 SIG Packaging Technologies
PO Box 5838
Norwalk, CT 06856-5838
203-845-8900
Fax: 203-846-3792
Packaging machinery
Estimated Sales: $1 - 5 Million
Number Employees: 20-50

28732 SIGHTech Vision Systems
2953 Bunker Hill Lane
Suite 400
Santa Clara, CA 95054
408-282-3770
Fax: 408-413-2600 sales@sightech.com
www.sightech.com
Manufacturer and exporter of quality control and as-
surance machinery for visual inspection
Chairman, Chief Executive Officer: Art Gaffin
Director Marketing Communications: Jeanette
Hazelwood
VP Sales/Marketing: Francis Tapon
Contact: Martha Cogan
mcogan@sightech.com
Estimated Sales: $1-2.5 Million
Number Employees: 4
Brands:
Sightech

28733 SIMBA USA
99 Lake Park Drive
Morehead, KY 40351
606-784-2008
Fax: 606-784-0057 info@simbausa.com
www.somaiagroup.com
Personalized towels
Contact: Hiten Somaia
hiten.somaia@simbatex.com.au

28734 SIMS Manufacturing Co Inc
134 N 1st Ave
Yakima, WA 98902-2617
509-453-7690
Fax: 509-457-8606 dau@simsmfg.com
www.simsmfg.com
Manager: Dustin Kissel
dustinkissel@gmail.com
Estimated Sales: $10 - 20 Million
Number Employees: 20-49

28735 SIPROMAC Inc.
240 Industriel Boulevard
Saint-Germain-de-Grantha, QC J0C 1K0
Canada
819-395-5151
Fax: 819-395-5343 855-395-5252
www.sipromac.com
President: Dave Couture
Vice President/Mktg & Sales Mgr.: Andre
Francoevr
Research & Development: Yoann Frechette
Purchasing Manager: Richard Tremblay
Estimated Sales: $1 - 5 Million
Number Employees: 27

28736 SIT Indeva Inc
3630 Green Park Cir
Charlotte, NC 28217-2866
704-357-8811
Fax: 704-357-8866 info@sit-indeva.com
www.sit-indeva.com

Manufacturer and importer of material handling
equipment including balancers
Vice President: Stefania Zanardi
szanardi@sit-indeva.com
VP: Stefania Zanardi
Estimated Sales: $2.5-5 Million
Number Employees: 10-19
Parent Co: Scaglia America
Type of Packaging: Bulk
Brands:
Liftronic Balancer

28737 SIT Indeva Inc
3630 Green Park Cir
Charlotte, NC 28217-2866
704-357-8811
Fax: 704-357-8866 info@sit-indeva.com
www.sit-indeva.com
Lifting devices for payloads
Vice President: Stefania Zanardi
szanardi@sit-indeva.com
VP: Stefania Zanardi
Estimated Sales: Below $5 Million
Number Employees: 10-19

28738 SJ Industries
7217 Lockport Place
Suite 101
Lorton, VA 22079-1596
703-751-5400
Fax: 703-370-3672
inquiry@arrowheadsystems.com
Accumulating conveyors, bottle rinsers, both twist
and positive gripper type, can rinsers using ionized
air and water, bidirectional accumulation tables, can
and bottle warmer, can and bottle pasteurizer and
coolers, plastic casewasher, preheater for ho
Estimated Sales: $5-10 Million
Number Employees: 30

28739 SK Food International
4666 Amber Valley Parkway
Fargo, ND 58104
701-356-4106
Fax: 701-356-4102 skfood@skfood.com
www.skfood.com
Family-owned import/export company and bulk
grain supplier.
Type of Packaging: Bulk
Other Locations:
SK Food Specialty Processing
Moorhead MN

28740 SKF Motion Technologies
1530 Valley Center Pkwy # 180
Bethlehem, PA 18017-2266
610-861-3700
Fax: 610-861-4811
Ball and roller screws for linear drive systems
Manager: Jim Brown
Estimated Sales: $20 - 50 Million
Number Employees: 20-49

28741 SKW Biosystems
2021 Cabot Blvoulevard
Langhorne, PA 19047-1810
215-702-1000
Fax: 215-702-1015
Estimated Sales: $10-20 Million
Number Employees: 50-99

28742 SKW Gelatin & Specialties
PO Box 234
Waukesha, WI 53187-0234
Canada
262-650-8393
Fax: 262-650-8456 800-654-2396
gelatin.usa@rousselot.com www.rousselot.com
Food processing equipment manufacturer specializ-
ing in vacuum packaging machines (table top, sin-
gle/double chamber, automatic and belted chambers)
shring tunnels, tray sealers, thermoforming ma-
chines, injectors, tumblers, massagers
andsmokehouses. Exports internationally to more
than 50 countries.
President: Geoge Masson
CFO: Steve Smith
Estimated Sales: $1,000,000 - $2,499,999
Number Employees: 10

28743 SKW Industrial Flooring
23700 Chagrin Boulevard
Cleveland, OH 44122-5506
216-831-5500
800-537-4722
Polymer flooring systems with exceptional chemical
impact and wear resistance
Estimated Sales: $1 - 5 Million
Number Employees: 250-499

28744 SLT Group
303 Ridge Rd
Dayton, NJ 08810
732-661-1030
Fax: 732-661-1034 www.sltgroup.com
Basmati rice, lentils, beans, flour and spice.
Estimated Sales: $60 Million
Number Employees: 320
Number of Brands: 8
Brands:
Heritage Select
KINGS
Khazana
Khazana Organic
Kings Regal
Nature's Delite
Royal Elephant
TIRUPATI

28745 SLX International
3453 Empresa Drive
Suite A
San Luis Obispo, CA 93401-7328
805-541-8356
Fax: 805-541-8320 800-883-9121
Reusable shipping containers
President and CEO: Edward De Temple
VP Engineering: Thomas DeTemple
Estimated Sales: $5-10 Million
Number Employees: 19

28746 SMC Corp of America
10100 Smc Blvd
Noblesville, IN 46060-8701
317-899-4440
Fax: 317-899-3102 800-726-7621
mrhode@smcusa.com www.smcusa.com
Low to high speed packing machines including
shrink wrappers, multi packers, wrap around case
packers, handle applicators and turn key complete
lines.
Vice President: Linda Abell
labell@smcusa.com
VP: Steve Lefevre
Sales Representative: Mike Rhode
Estimated Sales: $1 - 5 Million
Number Employees: 100-249

28747 SMC Corp of America
10100 Smc Blvd
Noblesville, IN 46060-8701
317-899-4440
Fax: 317-899-3102 800-762-7621
dbrushi@smcusa.com www.smcusa.com
Vice President: Steve Ade
sade@smcusa.com
Vice President: Steve Ade
sade@smcusa.com
Estimated Sales: $1 - 5 Million
Number Employees: 100-249

28748 SMI USA
5500 South Cobb Dr. Building 400
Suite 5
Smyrna, GA 30080
404-799-9929
Fax: 860-688-5577 sales.us@smigroup.net
www.smigroup.it
General Manager: Walter Gallo
Number Employees: 10-19

28749 SMP Display & Design Group
4215 Cromwell Rd
Chattanooga, TN 37421
423-892-3720
Fax: 423-855-1869 800-251-6308
smp-display@smp-display.com
www.smp-display.com
Contact: George Guthrie
gguthrie@smpinstore.com

28750 SOPAKCO Foods
215 S Mullins St
Mullins, SC 29574-3207
843-464-0121
Fax: 423-639-7270 800-276-9678
www.sopakco.com
Pasta sauces; also, retortable pouch manufacturer,
canner and contract packager of poultry, meat, fish,
pasta, vegetable, bean, fruit and dessert products,
flexible, semi-rigid and glass containers
CEO: Al Reitzer
CFO: Steve Keight
R&D: Jim Dukes
Quality Control: Phyllis Calhoun
General Manager: Wynn Pettibone
Plant Manager: Carl Whitmore
Purchasing Director: Beverly Stacey
Estimated Sales: $5-10 Million
Number Employees: 100
Square Footage: 400000
Parent Co: Unaka Corporation
Type of Packaging: Consumer, Food Service, Pri-
vate Label

28751 SP Graphics
PO Box 1591
Santa Rosa, CA 95402-1591
707-542-9492
Fax: 707-542-9492
Wine industry label design

28752 (HQ)SP Industries
2982 Jefferson Rd.
Hopkins, MI 49328
269-793-3232
Fax: 269-793-7451 800-592-5959
info@sp-industries.com www.sp-industries.com
Manufacturer and exporter of hydraulic cart/dump-
ers, vertical balers, recycling equipment and refuse,
precrusher and self-contained compactors
Owner/President: Denny Pool
Vice President: Roger Arndt
Marketing Mgr: David Jackiewicz
Sales Manager: Gene Koelsch
Office Manager: Elise Pool
Production Mgr: Julie Tahaney
Estimated Sales: $10-20 Million
Number Employees: 20-49
Square Footage: 100000

28753 SP Industries Inc
935 Mearns Rd
Warminster, PA 18974-2811
215-672-7800
Fax: 215-672-7807 800-523-2327
cs@spindustries.com www.spindustries.com
Manufactures Wilmad-LabGlass NMR & EPR
tubes, hotpack incubators, chambers and glassware
washers, VirTis Laboratory to production scale
freeze dryers, FTS Smart Freeze Dryers Technology
anf Precision Thermal Control Equipment,
Genevacevaporator systems, and Hull
Luophilization Systems.
CEO: Patrick Addvensky
patrick.addvensky@spindustries.com
CEO: Chuck Grant
CEO: Charles Grant
Marketing Director: Jennifer Colaiacomo
Sales: Robert Hoesly
Number Employees: 50-99
Square Footage: 280000

28754 (HQ)SPG International
11230 Harland Dr NE
Covington, GA 30014-6411
770-787-9830
Fax: 770-787-7432 877-503-4774
info@spgusa.com www.spgusa.com
Manufacturer and exporter of aluminum and stain-
less steel carts, racks and bakery shelving
Owner: Steve Durnell
steve.durnell@leggett.com
President, Chief Executive Officer: Steven DarnelL
VP Mfg.: Jose Lopez
Vice President of Business Development: Dave
Mack
Vice President of Operations: Bob Buehler
Number Employees: 100-249
Square Footage: 320000
Parent Co: Keggerr & Platt Storage Products Group
Type of Packaging: Food Service
Other Locations:
Kelmax Equipment Co.
San Luis Potosi

28755 SPI's Film and Bag Federation
1667 K St., NW
Suite 1000
Washington, DC 20006-1620
202-974-5200
Fax: 202-296-7005 www.plasticsindustry.org
President: William Cartuaex
CFO: John Maguire
R&D: Tommy Fouthall
Contact: Bill Carteaux
bill.carteaux@spi.com
Number Employees: 100-249

28756 (HQ)SPX Corporation
13320-A Ballantyne Corporate Place
Charlotte, NC 28277
980-474-3700
www.spx.com
Manufactures a wide range of food process technol-
ogies from control valves to integrated food process-
ing equipment.
President & CEO: Gene Lowe
Global Operations: J. Randall Data
VP/General Counsel/Secretary: John Nurkin
VP/Treasurer/Chief Financial Officer: Scott Sproule
VP & Chief Human Resources Officer: Tausha
White
Year Founded: 1912
Estimated Sales: $1.6 Billion
Number Employees: 4,500
Square Footage: 10411
Brands:
Anhydro
Apv
Bran+Luebbe
Clydeunion Pumps
Copes-Vulcan
Delair
Deltech
Dollinger
Gd Engineering
Gerstenberg Schroder
Hankison
Jemaco
Johnson Pump
Lightnin
M&J Valve
Plenty
Pneumatic Products
Waukesha Cherry-Burrell

28757 (HQ)SPX Flow Inc
13320 Ballantyne Corporate Pl
Charlotte, NC 28277
704-449-9187
800-252-5200
communications@spxflow.com
www.spxflow.com
Manufacturer, importer and exporter of fat crystalli-
zation machinery for the processing of mayonnaise,
salad dressings, margarine and shortening
President & CEO: Marc Michael
President, Food & Beverage: Dwight Gibson
VP & CFO: Jaime Easley
Chief Strategy Officer: Brian Taylor
Estimated Sales: $1.5 Billion
Number Employees: 5000-9999

28758 SPX Flow Inc
135 Mount Read Blvd
Rochester, NY 14611-1921
585-436-5550
Fax: 585-527-1742 www.spxflow.com
Mixers and impeller systems for industrial water and
wastewater treatment.
Number Employees: 250-499
Parent Co: SPX Flow Inc

28759 SQP
602 Potential Pkwy
Schenectady, NY 12302-1041
518-831-6800
Fax: 518-831-6890 800-724-1129
www.specialtyqualitypackaging.com
Tissue, paper food trays, plastic straws and stirrers,
napkins, chicken boxes and paper hinged takeouts
Owner: Amar Martin
Plant Manager: Barbara Flaming
National Sales Manager: William Gnatek
Sales Manager: Richard Bonaker
rjssbonaker@msn.com
Plant Manager: Larry Meyers
Estimated Sales: $20-50 Million
Number Employees: 100-249

Type of Packaging: Bulk
Brands:
   Valay

28760 SRC Vision
PO Box 1666
Medford, OR 97501
   541-776-9800
   Fax: 541-779-4104
Computerized optical sorting systems for the detection and automatic removal of defects from food processing lines; specialists in vision automated systems
Estimated Sales: $1 - 5 Million
Number Employees: 1-4

28761 SRI
203 Frances Ln
Barrington, IL 60010
   847-382-3877
   Fax: 847-382-3878 abean5452@aol.com
   www.srimatch.com
Owner: Alan Bean
CEO: Allen Bean
Contact: Charlie Garza
   cgarza@sriservices.com
Estimated Sales: $300,000-500,000
Number Employees: 1-4

28762 SSE Software Corporation
P.O. Box 384
Buckner, KY 40010
   502-553-8653
   Fax: 888-866-1931 contact@ssestandards.com
   www.ssesoftware.com
Sanitary CAD/Design software
President: James Wynn
Number Employees: 12

28763 SSOE Group
1001 Madison Ave
Toledo, OH 43604-5585
   419-255-3830
   Fax: 419-255-6101 lslusher@ssoe.com
   www.ssoe.com
Engineering consultant specializing in the design of food plants and food process design
Senior Project Manager: Joe Badalomenti
CEO: Bob Howell
   bhowell@ssoe.com
Executive Vice President: Bob Howell
Senior Vice President: Mike Murphy
Division Manager: Ken Gruenhagen
Estimated Sales: Less Than $500,000
Number Employees: 500-999

28764 SSW Holding Co Inc
1100 W Park Rd
Elizabethtown, KY 42701-3168
   270-769-5526
   Fax: 270-769-0105 info@sswholding.net
   www.sswholding.net
Manufacturer and exporter of wire racks and refrigerator and freezer shelving and baskets
President: Paul Kara
Marketing: Brad Nall
VP Sales/Marketing: Mark Gritton
Marketing Manager: Brad Nall
Contact: Richard Baker
   r.baker@sswholding.net
Product Development Manager: Jeff Ambrose
Number Employees: 1-4
Square Footage: 1120000
Parent Co: SSW Holding Company
Other Locations:
   SSW Holding Co.
   Fort Smith AR

28765 ST Restaurant Supplies
#1 - 1678 Fosters Way
Delta, BC V3M 6S6
Canada
   604-524-0933
   Fax: 604-524-0633 888-448-4244
Manufacturer, importer and wholesaler/distributor of chef hats, hairnets, gloves and aprons; also, woodenware and nylon/metal scrubbers
President: Terry Kuehne
CEO: Sandy Lee
Sales: Sabastien Lachat
Purchasing: Sandy Lee
Number Employees: 21
Number of Products: 220
Square Footage: 160000

Type of Packaging: Food Service, Private Label, Bulk
Other Locations:
   ST Restaurant Supplies
   Dallas TX

28766 STA Packaging Tapes
100 S Puente St
Brea, CA 92821-3813
   714-255-7888
   Fax: 800-235-8273 800-258-8273
Carton sealing tape, hand dispensers, case sealers
President: Ikusuke Shimizu
CEO: Ernest J Wong
CFO: Matt Minami
VP: Stephen Wilson
R&D: Dinesh Shah
Marketing: Melissa Morris
Contact: Pat Hagglof
   phagglof@aptosshoesandapparel.com
Plant Manager: C Fang
Estimated Sales: $20 - 50 Million
Number Employees: 100-249
Square Footage: 185000

28767 STARMIX srl
Via dell'Artigianato, 5
Marano, VI 36035
   044- 57- 659
   Fax: 044- 57- 203 info@starmix.it
Food service equipment including meat slicers
Estimated Sales: $300,000-500,000
Number Employees: 1-4
Brands:
   Fleetwood

28768 STD Precision Gear
318 Manley St # 4
West Bridgewater, MA 02379-1087
   508-580-0035
   Fax: 508-580-0071 888-783-4327
   sales@stdgear.com www.stdgear.com
Manufacturer and exporter of corrosion-proof precision gears, sprockets, ratchets, splines, pulleys, etc
President: James Manning
CFO: Doug Grant
Sales Director: Susan Dauwer
Estimated Sales: $1-2 Million
Number Employees: 20-49
Square Footage: 26000
Brands:
   Std Precision Gear & Instrument

28769 STERIS Corp
5960 Heisley Rd
Mentor, OH 44060-1834
   440-354-2600
   www.steris.com
Laboratory equipment including sterilizers, glassware washers and dryers, detergents, and surface disinfection.
President & Chief Executive Officer: Walter Rosebrough, Jr.
VP, Global Marketing: Tamara Struk
VP, Sales & Marketing: Trey Howard
Year Founded: 1987
Estimated Sales: $2.78 Billion
Number Employees: 12,000

28770 STM Mortgage Co
2626 Cole Ave
Dallas, TX 75204-1083
   214-665-9544
   Fax: 214-634-9219 800-766-7861
Commercial specialty printing: fleet graphics and P.O.P and architectural and digital products
Controller: Terry Thomas
CFO: Robert Schlezier
VP: Tim Allen
Customer Service Manager: Larry Morrow
Plant Manager: Mark Kitzman
Estimated Sales: $5-10 Million
Number Employees: 5-9

28771 STOBER Drives Inc
1781 Downing Dr
Maysville, KY 41056-8683
   606-759-5090
   Fax: 606-759-5045 800-711-3588
   sales@stober.com

President: Peter Feil
   pfeil@stober.com
CFO: Peter Fiel
R&D: Shane Art
Quality Control: Mick Michelle
Estimated Sales: $5 - 10 Million
Number Employees: 100-249

28772 STRAPEX Corporation
2601 Westinghouse Blvd
Charlotte, NC 28273
   704-588-2510
   Fax: 704-588-6838 800-346-1804
Plastic strapping equipment for the security of loads during transport
General Manager: Bill Drake
Controller: Glenn Boyd
Estimated Sales: $10 - 20 Million
Number Employees: 20-49

28773 SUEZ Water Technologies & Solutions
4636 Somerton Rd
Trevose, PA 19053
   866-439-2837
   www.suezwatertechnologies.com
Food and beverage water and wastewater treatment
CEO: Heiner Markhoff
CFO: Mamta Patel
Chief Marketing Officer: Ralph Exton
Other Locations:
   BetzDearborn
   Horsham PA
Brands:
   Aquafloc
   Bio Scan
   Ferroquest
   Polymate
   Polyquest
   Sterisafe

28774 SV Dice Designers
1836 Valencia Street
Rowland Heights, CA 91748-3050
   909-869-7833
   Fax: 909-869-0515 888-478-3423
Bag in box system, case packers, high speed case erectors, case semers
Owner: S Virgil Dice
Estimated Sales: $2.5-5 Million
Number Employees: 1-4

28775 SV Research
7429 Allentown Blvd
Harrisburg, PA 17112-3609
   717-540-0370
   Fax: 717-540-0380
Optical character recognition and optical character verification system designed to provide complete inspection on labeling and packaging lines and fully automatic spray nozzle monitoring system for quick and easy retrofit into mostcoating machines
President: Ron Lawson
Sales Director: Bob Leiby
Contact: Susan Baker
   s.baker@seidenader.com
Estimated Sales: Below $5 Million
Number Employees: 20-49

28776 SWF Co
1949 E Manning Ave
Reedley, CA 93654-9462
   559-638-8484
   Fax: 559-638-7478 800-344-8951
   www.swfcompanies.com
Manufacturer and exporter of automatic case and tray loading machinery
Vice President: Braden Beam
   braden.beam@thieletech.com
VP/ General Manager: Ed Suarez
Director Engineering: Dan Nourian
Sales/Marketing Executive: Gregory Cox
Product Manager: Craig Friesen
Special Project Manager: Dennis Decker
Estimated Sales: $10-20 Million
Number Employees: 100-249
Square Footage: 400000
Parent Co: Thiele Technologies
Brands:
   Sure Way

28777 SWF Co
1949 E Manning Ave
Reedley, CA 93654-9462
559-638-8484
Fax: 559-638-7478 800-344-8951
info@swfcompanies.com
www.swfcompanies.com
Flexible bags, case loaders, horizontal tray formers, lidding equip
Vice President: Roland Parker
rolandp@swfcompanies.com
VP: Ed Suarez
Number Employees: 100-249

28778 SWF Co
1949 E Manning Ave
Reedley, CA 93654-9462
559-638-8484
Fax: 559-638-7478 800-344-8951
cfriesen@swfcompanies.com
www.swfcompanies.com
Vice President: Marc Atoui
matoui@swfcompanies.com
VP: Ed Suarez
VP Sales/Marketing: Bob Williams
Product Manager: Craig Friesen
Number Employees: 100-249

28779 SWF Co
1949 E Manning Ave
Reedley, CA 93654-9462
559-638-8484
Fax: 559-638-7478 800-344-8951
cfriesen@swfcompanies.com
www.swfcompanies.com
Vice President: Braden Beam
braden.beam@thieletech.com
Vice President, General Manager: Ed Suarez
Product Manager: Craig Friesen
Estimated Sales: $1 - 5 Million
Number Employees: 100-249

28780 SWF McDowell
5505 Carder Road
Orlando, FL 32810-4738
407-291-2817
Fax: 407-293-7054 800-877-7971
Manufacturer and exporter of carton forming and packaging systems including case, inverted bottle and drop packers, top sealers and case erectors
Service Manager: David Robertson
Operations Manager: Dennis Ramey
Estimated Sales: $1 - 5 Million
Number Employees: 50-99
Square Footage: 72000
Parent Co: SWF Machinery

28781 SYSPRO USA
959 South Coast Drive
Suite 100
Costa Mesa, CA 92626
714-437-1000
800-369-8649
info@us.syspro.com us.syspro.com
Services: analytics software, packaging, food traceability software.
President: Joey Benadretti
CEO: Brian Stein
Chief Financial Officer: Doug Garnhart
Chief Marketing Officer: Dawna Olsen
PR Manager: Stanley Goodrich
Year Founded: 1978
Estimated Sales: $4.8 Million
Number Employees: 51-200
Brands:
SYSPRO

28782 Saatitech
247 Route 100
Somers, NY 10589-3231
914-767-0100
Fax: 914-767-0109 800-719-7130
Manager: Todd Burt
Number Employees: 50-99

28783 Sabate USA
902 Enterprise Way # M
Napa, CA 94558-6288
707-256-2830
Fax: 707-256-2831 sabateusa@sabate.com
Wine and spirits corks and closures
President: Eric Mertier
CFO: Olivier Poissonnier

Estimated Sales: Below $5 Million
Number Employees: 5-9

28784 Sabel Engineering Corporation
1010 East Lake Street
Villard, MN 56385
320-554-3611
Fax: 320-554-2650 www.massmanllc.com
Manufacturer and exporter of automatic case packers and tiering mechanisms for collating multiple layers
President: Herbert Sabel
Engineering Manager: Stan Lundquist
Sales Director: Gary Ensey
Manager: Dave Rosenburg
General Manager: Noel Barbulesco
Estimated Sales: $5 - 10 Million
Number Employees: 20-49
Square Footage: 28800
Parent Co: Massman Automation Designs, LLC
Brands:
Carousel Caser
Descender

28785 (HQ)Sabert Corp
2288 Main St
Sayreville, NJ 08872-1476
732-721-5546
Fax: 732-721-0622 800-722-3781
sabert@sabert.com www.sabert.com
Plastic disposable plates, platters, containers and bowls; exporter of disposable platters and bowls
President: Katya Connor
kconnor2216@msn.com
Marketing Director: Mark Seckinger
Sales Director: Bob Shemming
Estimated Sales: $5-10 Million
Number Employees: 100-249
Square Footage: 200000
Other Locations:
Sabert Corp.
Brussels
Brands:
Freshpack Bowls
Roma Gold
Roma Marble
Roma Silver
Ultima

28786 Sabert Corp
2288 Main St
Sayreville, NJ 08872-1476
732-721-5546
Fax: 732-721-0622 www.sabert.com
Designs, manufactures and distributes quality, cost-effective solutions for packaging, displaying, serving and storing fine food.
President: Katya Connor
kconnor2216@msn.com
VP: Gary Westrol
VP Sales/Marketing: Robert Shemming
VP Human Resources: Brian Duffy
VP Operations: Mark Fessler
Assistant Product Manager: Cameron McGettigan
Number Employees: 100-249
Type of Packaging: Consumer, Food Service

28787 Sable Technology Solution
1628 Norwood Dr
St Paul, MN 55122-2754
651-994-8441
Fax: 510-293-8553 800-722-5390
info@sabletechnology.com
Manufacturer and exporter of compact point of sale systems for table and quick service restaurants
Executive VP: Adrian Bryan
VP Sales: James Files
Estimated Sales: $1 - 5 Million
Number Employees: 20-50
Square Footage: 16000
Type of Packaging: Food Service

28788 Sackett Systems
1033 Bryn Mawr Ave
Bensenville, IL 60106-1244
630-766-5500
Fax: 630-766-5631 800-323-8332
www.sackettsystems.com
Lift trucks, carriers, racks, etc
President: Leonard Maniscalco
Director of Sales: Chris Lareau
Contact: Mike Borton
mborton@sackett-systems.com
Regional Accounts Manager: Andy Kerrins

Estimated Sales: $5 - 10 Million
Number Employees: 10-19

28789 (HQ)Sacramento Bag Manufacturing
440 N Pioneer Ave
Suite 300
Woodland, CA 95776-1788
530-662-6130
Fax: 530-662-6381 tiffanyj@sacbag.com
www.sacbag.com
Bags including raschel knit, polyethylene, burlap, polypropylene and cotton
Sales: Larry Deman
Customer Service Reps: Kathy Anderson
General Manager/Controller: Paresh Shah
Accounts Receivables: Suvo Lahiri
Plant Manager: Dennis Joost
Estimated Sales: $2.5 - 5 Million
Number Employees: 20-49
Square Footage: 110000
Parent Co: Acme Bag Company
Other Locations:
Sacramento Bag Manufacturing
Vernon CA

28790 (HQ)Sadler Conveyor Systems
1845 William Street
Montreal, QC H3J 1R6
Canada
519-941-4858
Fax: 519-941-7339 888-887-5129
Custom conveying systems for case and pallet handling from horizontal to vertical applications
President: Stephen Sadler
Vice President: Neil Sadler
R & D: Neil Sadler
Marketing Director: Luc Martineau
Sales Director: Chris Morin
Production Manager: Marcel Richard
Engineering: Eric Allard
Estimated Sales: Below $5 Million
Number Employees: 10
Square Footage: 144000
Other Locations:
Sadler Conveyor Systems
Hartford CT
Brands:
Hercules
Ls-Q50
Sadler
Uni-Flo

28791 Saeco
7905 Cochran Rd # 100
Cleveland, OH 44139-5470
440-528-2000
Fax: 440-542-9173 estronic@aol.com
Manufacturer and importer of espresso and cappuccino machines including self-grinding, fully automatic and manual
President: John Mc Cann
Marketing Manager (Commercial Products):
Julianna Benedick
Sales Manager (Housewares): Elizabeth Will
Contact: Kevin Lemaster
k.lemaster@saeco-usa.com
Estimated Sales: $2.5-5 Million
Number Employees: 20-49
Square Footage: 80000
Parent Co: Estro/Saeco
Type of Packaging: Consumer, Food Service
Brands:
Estro Da-Line
Saeco Housewares

28792 Saeplast Canada
PO Box 2087
St John, NB E2L 3T5
Canada
506-633-0101
Fax: 506-658-0227 800-567-3966
saeplast@saeplastcanada.com
www.saeplastcanada.com
Manufacturer and exporter of plastic pallets and insulated containers for transporting fruits, vegetables, frozen foods and fresh fish
President: Torfi Gudmundsson
CFO: Dave Burnan
Number Employees: 50-60
Brands:
Dynoplast

28793 Saf-T-Gard International Inc
205 Huehl Rd
Northbrook, IL 60062-1972
847-291-1600
Fax: 847-291-1610 800-548-4273
safety@saftgard.com www.saftgard.com
Disposable gloves, mesh gloves
President: Richard Rivkin
rrivkin@saftgard.com
Quality Control: Tom Rearer
Chairman of the Board: Norman Rivkin
Estimated Sales: $10 - 20 Million
Number Employees: 50-99

28794 Safe-T-Cut Inc
97 Main St
Monson, MA 01057-1320
413-267-9984
Fax: 413-267-9585 info@safetcut.com
www.safetcut.com
Manufacturer and exporter of safety knives for cutting films, foams and cartons
President: Richard Baer
CEO: Mary Clark
CFO: Debra Baer
Manager: Debbie Baer
info@safetcut.com
Number Employees: 10-19
Number of Products: 10
Brands:
Safe T Cut

28795 Safety Fumigant Co
197 Beal St # 2
Hingham, MA 02043-1599
781-749-1199
Fax: 781-740-4996 800-244-1199
safetyfumigant@aol.com
www.safetyfumigant.com
Insecticides
President: John Hall
safetyfumigant@aol.com
Estimated Sales: Less than $500,000
Number Employees: 10-19

28796 Safety Light Corporation
4150 Old Berwick Rd
Suite A
Bloomsburg, PA 17815
570-784-4344
Fax: 570-784-1402
Self-luminous nonelectric exit and safety signs
President: C Richter White
Contact: Greg Beese
gbeese@safetylight.com
Plant Manager: Larry Harmon
Estimated Sales: $2.5-5 Million
Number Employees: 20-49

28797 Safety Seal Industries
447 Main Street
Catskill, NY 12414-1317
518-943-1300
Fax: 518-943-0873
customer-service@tmi-pvc.com

28798 Safeway Solutions
2804 SE Loop 820
Fort Worth, TX 76140-1012
817-237-6373
Fax: 817-237-2613 info@safewaysolutions.com
Chief Executive Officer: Randall Price

28799 Sage Automation Inc
4925 Fannett Rd
Beaumont, TX 77705-4305
409-842-8040
Fax: 409-842-9141 800-731-9111
rbeller@sagerobot.com www.sagerobot.com
Custom material handling and case packing
President: Don W Cawley
doncawley@sagerobot.com
Applications Engineer: Greg White
Marketing/Technology: Jason Blake
Business Development: Randy Beller
Public Relations: Rodney Gonzalez
Estimated Sales: $10-20 Million
Number Employees: 50-99

28800 Sahara Date Company
8456A Tyco Road
Vienna, VA 22182
703-745-7463
www.saharadate.com
Dates
Co-Founder: Maile Ramzi
Co-Founder: Jean Houpert
Estimated Sales: $6.9 Million
Number Employees: 34
Brands:
Sahara Date Company

28801 Sailor Plastics
08 Main Ave.
PO Box 309
Adrian, MN 56110
507-483-2469
Fax: 507-483-2777 800-380-7429
sales@sailorplastics.com www.sailorplastics.com
Plastic bottles
President & Owner: Lorin Krueger
Estimated Sales: $3 Million
Number Employees: 2-10
Brands:
French Square
Honey Bears
Sailor Plastics

28802 Saint Jimmy's Coffee Services
311 Bowes Road
Main Unit
Vaughan, ON L4K 1J1
Canada
833-546-6971
info@saintjimmyscoffee.ca saintjimmyscoffee.ca
Manufactures and supplies over 20+ flavours in coffee, tea, and hot chocolate.
Year Founded: 2016
Number Employees: 51-200
Number of Brands: 1
Number of Products: 20+
Type of Packaging: Consumer, Food Service
Brands:
Saint Jimmy's

28803 Saint-Gobain Containers
20 Moores Rd
Malvern, PA 19355
www.saint-gobain-northamerica.com
Glass bottles and containers for food, wine, liquor and beer
President & CEO: Bruce Cowgill
Estimated Sales: $50-100 Million
Number Employees: 100
Parent Co: Saint-Gobain

28804 Saint-Gobain Corporation
20 Moores Rd
Malvern, PA 19355
610-893-6000
Fax: 855-639-6629
www.saint-gobain-northamerica.com
Building materials for a variety of industries including commercial construction.
Chairman, Saint-Gobain North America: Tom Kinisky
Senior Manager, Commercial Sales: Heather Whitaker
Commercial Business Development Manager: Brittany Wright
National Accounts Manager: Bernie Shalvey
Year Founded: 1967
Estimated Sales: $6.2 Billion
Number Employees: 15,000
Parent Co: Compagnie de Saint-Gobain S.A.

28805 Saint-Gobain Performance Plastics
31500 Solon Rd
Solon, OH 44139
www.plastics.saint-gobain.com
Products for food and beverage dispensing, food processing, packaging, quick service, and raw milk collection.
Production: Scott Yudkin
Estimated Sales: $10-20 Million
Number Employees: 50-99

28806 (HQ)Salem China Company
1000 S Broadway Avenue
Salem, OH 44460-3773
330-337-8771
Fax: 330-337-8775 salem-urfic@worldnet.att.net
Custom manufacturer and exporter of chinaware, dinner sets, teapots, beer steins, stainless flatware and mugs; importer of dinnerware sets
Secretary: Carolyn Brubaker

Estimated Sales: $500,000-$1 Million
Number Employees: 10-19

28807 Salem-Republic Rubber Co
475 W California Ave
Sebring, OH 44672-1922
330-938-9801
Fax: 330-938-9809 800-425-5079
www.salem-republic.com
Manufacturer, importer and exporter of FDA approved hoses and hose assemblies, rubber tubing and pipes
President: Drew Ney
dney@salem-republic.com
VP Corporate Development: Anthony Kindler
Sales Manager: Raymond Willis
Estimated Sales: $10-20 Million
Number Employees: 50-99
Brands:
Champion
Flexrite
Vol-U-Flex

28808 Sales Building Systems
9325 Progress Pkwy
Mentor, OH 44060
440-639-9100
Fax: 440-639-9190 800-435-7576
Consultant specializing in restaurant chain database marketing
President: Pat White
CFO: Jack Zaback
Founder: Tim McCarthy
VP Sales: Cindy Venable
Contact: Terry Goins
haleyhaddix@justiceretail.com
Operations Manager: Shelly Furness
Estimated Sales: $5 - 10,000,000
Number Employees: 50-99
Number of Products: 2

28809 Sales Partner System
789 S Nova Rd
Ormond Beach, FL 32174
386-672-8434
Fax: 386-673-4730 800-777-2924
www.spsi.com
Computer software for sales automation
CEO: Larry Frank
VP/General Manager: Ken Yontz
President: Jal Belix
Number Employees: 10-19

28810 SalesData Software
6340 San Ignacio Avenue
San Jose, CA 95119-1209
408-281-5811
Fax: 408-281-3736 www.act.com
Computer software for the food service industry including point of sale management systems, cash and sale analysis, menu costing, marketing tools, inventory control and purchase ordering; also, installation and training servicesavailable
President: Binh Nguyen
Parent Co: Aureflam Corporation
Brands:
Restaurant Basics
Retail Basics

28811 Salient Corp
203 Colonial Dr # 101
Horseheads, NY 14845-8602
607-739-4511
Fax: 607-739-4045 info@salient.com
www.salient.com
Developer of strategic sales management solutions for high volume businesses, Windows-based software and sales management software tools for sales data online, service rep productivity and a high-power work-order tracking system
President: Guy Amisano
gamisano@salient.com
Sales Director: Larry Beuter
Marketing Director: John Shannon
Business Development: Mike Dzikowski
Operations Manager: Sandy Houper
Estimated Sales: $5-10 Million
Number Employees: 100-249

28812 Salinas Valley Wax Paper Co
1111 Abbott St
Salinas, CA 93901-4501
831-424-2747
Fax: 831-424-5883

Manufacturer and importer of printed and plain packaging paper including kraft, laminated, waxed, tissue, pads, box liners, etc
President: Chas Nelson
CEO: Charles Nelson
  charles@svwpco.com
VP: Bill Zimmerman
Plant Manager: Richard Johnson
Estimated Sales: $10 - 20 Million
Number Employees: 20-49
Number of Brands: 1
Square Footage: 80000
Type of Packaging: Private Label, Bulk
Brands:
  Ratan
  Salinas Valley Wax Paper Co.

28813 Salonika Imports Inc
3509 Smallman St
Pittsburgh, PA 15201-1936

412-682-2700
800-794-2256
www.salonika.net
Mediterranean culinary products
President/Owner: Chris Balouris
  sales@salonika.net
Number Employees: 5-9

28814 Salvajor Co
4530 E 75th Ter
Kansas City, MO 64132-2081

816-363-1030
Fax: 816-363-4914 800-SAL-AJOR
sales@salvajor.com www.salvajor.com
Manufacturer, importer and exporter of commercial food waste disposal and waste handling systems
President: Timothy Dike
  cadman@modelwarships.com
Vice President: Don Misenhelter
Research & Development: Chris Hohl
National Sales Manager: Dennis Easteria
Purchasing Manager: P Cooper
Estimated Sales: $10 - 20 Million
Number Employees: 50-99
Square Footage: 80000
Brands:
  Scrapmaster
  Troughveyor

28815 Sam Pievac Company
14044 Freeway Dr
Santa Fe Springs, CA 90670

562-404-5590
Fax: 562-404-7566 800-742-8585
mjohnson@spcdisplays.com
www.sampievaccompany.com
Store fixtures and displays
President/COO: Matt Johnson
Chairman/CEO: Scott Pievac
VP: Michael Pievac
VP, Sales: Robin Hess
Contact: Eric Canavan
  ecanavan@pievac.net
Estimated Sales: $10-20 Million
Number Employees: 20-49
Square Footage: 29000

28816 Sambonet USA
1180 Mclester St # 8
Elizabeth, NJ 07201-2931

908-351-4800
Fax: 908-351-3351 www.sambonet.it
Wholesaler/distributor and importer of general merchandise including cutlery, trays, coffee and tea service equipment, chafing dishes, etc.; serving the food service market
President: Pierre Luigi Coppo
CFO: Harish Patel
VP: Andrea Viannello
Quality Control: Harish Patel
Estimated Sales: $2.5 - 5 Million
Number Employees: 5-9
Parent Co: Paderno SpA

28817 Samco Freezerwear
3499 Lexington Ave N # 205
Ste 205
St Paul, MN 55126-7070

651-638-3888
Fax: 651-638-3896 info@polarwear.com
www.freezerwear.com
Insulated industrial clothing including pants, jackets, full suits, hoods, vests, safety boots and light and heavy weight

President: Thomas Bramwell Sr
CEO: Tom Bramwell Jr
CFO: Richard Schuster
VP: Dave Bramwell
Quality Control: David Bramwell
Estimated Sales: $12-18 Million
Number Employees: 1-4
Square Footage: 160000

28818 Samsill Corp
5740 Hartman Rd
Fort Worth, TX 76119-6234

817-536-1906
Fax: 817-535-6900 800-255-1100
www.samsill.com
Presentation and storage products including binders, sheet protectors and menu covers
Executive Director: Michelle McLaughlin
CEO: James Bankes
  jbankes@samsill.com
CFO: Dave Paton
Executive VP Marketing/Sales: Bob Schultz
Number Employees: 100-249
Type of Packaging: Food Service

28819 Samson Controls
4111 Cedar Boulevard
Baytown, TX 77523-8588

281-383-3677
Fax: 281-383-3690 www.samson-usa.com
Manufacturer and exporter of controls and control systems, flow regulators, valves and valve operators
President: Siegfried Hanicke
Contact: Javier Delamora
  jdelamora@aerodynamix.com
Estimated Sales: $2.5-5 Million
Number Employees: 20-49
Parent Co: Samson Controls

28820 Samsung Electronics America, Inc.
85 Challenger Rd.
Ridgefield Park, NJ 07660

201-229-4000
800-726-7864
www.samsungusa.com
Consumer electronics and digital products, including refrigerators, ranges, microwaves and more.
President/Chief Executive Officer: Young Hoon Eom
CFO: Roh Hee-chan
Year Founded: 1978
Estimated Sales: $9.4 Billion
Number Employees: 1,700
Parent Co: Samsung Electronics Co., Ltd.

28821 Samuel P. Harris
55 Pawtucket Avenue
Rumford, RI 2916

401-438-4020
Fax: 401-438-8980
Vacuum formed plastic packaging materials
President: Kenneth Hatch
Treasurer: David Brower
VP Operations: Suzanne Manzak
Estimated Sales: $5-10 Million
Number Employees: 100-249

28822 Samuel Pressure Vessel Group
2121 Cleveland Ave
PO Box 100
Marinette, WI 54143-3711

715-453-5326
Fax: 888-506-4271 spvg@samuel.com
Fabricator of custom designed screw conveyors, heat exchangers, sanitary tanks, pressure vessels from stainless steel and other high alloy metals with sanitary finish
President: Barry Berquist
Quality Control: Gary Anderson
Sales Director: Robert Eaton
Manager: Paul Anderson
  paulanderson@samuelpressurevesselgroup.com
Plant Manager: Lenny Bartz
Purchasing Manager: Ann Kelash
Estimated Sales: $10 Million
Number Employees: 500-999
Square Footage: 130000
Parent Co: the Samuel Pressure Vessel Group

28823 Samuel Strapping Systems Inc
1401 Davey Rd # 300
Woodridge, IL 60517-4991

630-783-8900
Fax: 630-783-8901 800-323-4424
www.samuelstrapping.com
Manufacturer and exporter of steel and plastic straps; also, carton closing machines
President: Robert Hickey
  rhickey@samuelstrapping.com
CFO: Richard Louis
Controller: Dick Louis
Sales/Marketing: Tom Gould
Marketing Manager: Cy Slifka
Purchasing Manager: Joe Capoccio
Estimated Sales: $30 - 50 Million
Number Employees: 20-49
Parent Co: Samuel Manu-Tech

28824 Samuel Strapping Systems
2000 K Boyer S Drive
Fort Mill, SC 29173

803-802-3203
Fax: 803-802-3209 smt@samuelmanutech.com
www.samuelstrapping.com
Plastic strapping
President: Robert Hickey
Quality Control: Donna Shicely
Estimated Sales: $1-5 Million
Number Employees: 10
Parent Co: Samuel Manu-Tech

28825 Samuel Underberg Food Store
1784 Atlantic Ave
Brooklyn, NY 11213-1208

718-363-0787
Fax: 718-363-0786
Wire butter and cheese cutters, electric graters, meat hooks, box openers and fish scalers
CEO: David Chalom
Estimated Sales: $1-2.5 Million
Number Employees: 1-4
Number of Brands: 100
Number of Products: 2100

28826 Samuels Products Inc
9851 Redhill Dr
Blue Ash, OH 45242-5694

513-891-4456
Fax: 513-891-4520 800-543-7155
www.samuelsproducts.com
Computer and pressure sensitive labels and printed bags
Owner: Millard Samuels
  mes@samuelsproducts.com
National Sales Manager: Tim Kroger
Purchasing Manager: Rick Helton
Estimated Sales: $5-10 Million
Number Employees: 20-49
Square Footage: 120000

28827 San Aire Industries
101 W Felix St
Fort Worth, TX 76115

817-924-8105
Fax: 817-921-3963 800-757-1912
sales@san-aire.com www.san-aire.com
Manufacturer and exporter of commercial dish, trayware, pot and pan dryers
President: Hatcher James
  hjames@sanaire.com
VP Sales/Marketing: Bruce Barker
Estimated Sales: $1 - 2.5 Million
Number Employees: 1-4
Brands:
  Powerdry

28828 San Diego Health & Nutrition
PO Box 1318
Bonita, CA 91908-1318

619-470-3345
Fax: 619-470-3822 www.sdhnsclasses.com
Consultant providing food safety and sanitation training
Partner: Jack Ezroj
Estimated Sales: $100,000
Number Employees: 1-4

28829 San Diego Paper Box Company
PO Box 1219
Spring Valley, CA 91979-1219

619-660-9566
Fax: 619-660-9570 www.sdpbc.com
Folding cartons

President: Sidney B Chapman
CFO: Richard Chapman
R&D: Richard Chapman
Vice President of Sales and Marketing: Jeff
Shipman
jeff.shipman@sdpbc.com
Production Manager: Gilbert Bernal
Estimated Sales: $20 - 50 Million
Number Employees: 50-99

28830 San Fab Conveyor
2000 Superior St
Sandusky, OH 44870-1824
419-626-4465
Fax: 419-626-6376
Manufacturer, importer and exporter of package and
bulk conveying components and systems including
stainless, pallet handling and table top conveyors,
carton sealers and stainless case tapers
Owner: Timothy Shenigo
Manager (Packaging Equipment): Don Williams
Engineering Manager: Charles Wheeler
Estimated Sales: $5-10 Million
Number Employees: 10-19
Square Footage: 320000
Brands:
San Fab

28831 San Jamar
555 Koopman Ln
Elkhorn, WI 53121-2012
262-723-6133
Fax: 262-723-4204 800-248-9826
info@sanjamar.com www.sanjamar.com
Manufacturer and exporter of built-in dispensing
units for condiments and disposable paper products
including cups, towels and napkins; also, bar sup-
plies and check management systems
President: Charles Colman
CFO: Andy Skerkowitz
Marketing Manager: Topper Woelfer
Senior Sales Coordinator: Michael Johnson
Estimated Sales: $10 - 20 Million
Number Employees: 100-249
Number of Brands: 3
Number of Products: 600
Type of Packaging: Consumer, Food Service
Brands:
Classic
Gourmet

28832 San Joaquin Pool Svc & Supply
8576 Live Oak Rd
Stockton, CA 95212-9305
209-952-0680
Fax: 209-466-1080
Soaps, disinfectants and sterilizers
VP: Mick Albright
Regional Sales Manager: Mike Valasquez
Estimated Sales: Less Than $500,000
Number Employees: 1-4

28833 San Jose Awnings
755 Chestnut St
San Jose, CA 95110-1832
408-350-7000
Fax: 408-350-7001 800-872-9646
sales@sanjoseawning.com
www.sanjoseawning.com
Commercial awnings
President: Michael Yaholkovsky
sales@sanjoseawning.com
Estimated Sales: $1 - 2.5 Million
Number Employees: 10-19

28834 San Juan Signs Inc
736 E Main St
Farmington, NM 87401-2716
505-326-5511
Fax: 505-326-5513 linda@sanjuansigns.com
www.sanjuansigns.com
Advertising displays and signs
President: Clint L Roper
clint@sanjuansigns.com
VP: Teri Roper
Office Manager: Phyllis Davis
Estimated Sales: $1-2.5 Million
Number Employees: 20-49
Square Footage: 11200

28835 San Marco Coffee, Inc.
3120 Latrobe Dr
Suite 280
Charlotte, NC 28211-2186
704-366-0533
Fax: 704-366-0534 800-715-9298
www.sanmarcocoffee.com
American coffee, espresso, cappuccino
Chief Executive Officer: Marc Decaria
marc@sanmarcocoffee.com
Number Employees: 5-9
Type of Packaging: Consumer, Food Service, Pri-
vate Label
Brands:
San Giorgio

28836 San Miguel Label Manufacturing
PO Box 1401
Ciales, PR 00638-1401
787-871-3120
Fax: 787-871-0443
Labels and plastic bags
Estimated Sales: $1 - 5 Million
Number Employees: 20-50
Square Footage: 40000

28837 San-Rec-Pak
9995 SW Avery St
PO Box 3210
Tualatin, OR 97062-3210
503-692-5552
Fax: 503-692-4477
Manufacturer and exporter of maltsters' machinery
Manager: Karla Mc Combs
Estimated Sales: $3 - 5 Million
Number Employees: 10-19
Parent Co: Kloster Corporation

28838 SanSai North America Franchising, LLC
1365 E. Gladstone Street
Suite 300
Glendale, CA 91203-2678
909-599-9456
Fax: 818-244-2470 800-368-5594
www.sansaiusa.com
Ingredients for chocolate making
Owner: Peter Han
Estimated Sales: $1 - 5 Million
Number Employees: 10-19
Parent Co: Nestle USA

28839 Sanchelima International
1783 NW 93rd Ave
Miami, FL 33172
305-591-4343
Fax: 305-591-3203 sales@sanchelimaint.com
www.sanchelimaint.com
Manufacturer and exporter of dairy and cheese mak-
ing equipment, fillers and sealers, homogenizers,
molds, centrifugal separators, bottle unscramblers,
pasteurizers, tanks and valves; processor and
exporter of cultures
President: Juan A Sanchelima
Technical Director: Jesus Gonzalez
CFO: Maximo Questa
Estimated Sales: $5-10 Million
Number Employees: 10-19

28840 Sanco Products Co Inc
330 Harrison Ave
Greenville, OH 45331-1566
937-548-2225
Fax: 937-548-0132
Disinfectants, insecticides, etc
President: John Saylor
sanco@embarqmail.com
Quality Control: John Saylor
Estimated Sales: Below $5 Million
Number Employees: 5-9

28841 Sancoa International
92 Ark Rd
Lumberton, NJ 08048
609-953-5050
Fax: 856-273-2710
Manufacturer, exporter and importer of pressure sen-
sitive labels and shrink sleeves
President: Joseph Sanski
Controller: Roger Spreen
CFO: Kevin Austin
Quality Assurance Manager: Bob Zimmerman
Contact: Mark Brennan
mbrennan@sancoa.com

Estimated Sales: $20 - 50 Million
Number Employees: 250-499

28842 Sanden Vendo America Inc
10710 Sanden Dr
Dallas, TX 75238
214-765-9066
Fax: 800-541-5684 800-344-7216
www.vendoco.com
Automatic and manual vending machines for bottles
and cans
President: Bernt Voelkel
CEO: Frank Kabei
Contact: Bryce Batchelor
bbatchelor@vendoco.com
Number Employees: 500-999
Parent Co: Sanden Corporation

28843 Sanders Manufacturing Co
1422 Lebanon Pike
Nashville, TN 37210-3159
615-254-6611
Fax: 615-242-3732 866-254-6611
Advertising specialties
President: Julie Sanders
jsanders@samcoline.com
Manager: Paul Cowan
Mngr.: Paul Cowan
Estimated Sales: $10-20 Million
Number Employees: 50-99
Square Footage: 92000
Brands:
Samco

28844 Sanderson Computers
450 W Wilson Bridge Road
Worthington, OH 43085-2237
614-781-2525
Fax: 614-781-2755
Software for the process, food and formulations in-
dustries
Owner: Gary Sanderson
Marketing (US): David Lee
President US Operations: Carl Parker
Parent Co: Sanderson Group PLC
Brands:
Formul8

28845 Sandler Seating
1175 Peachtree Street NE
Suite 1850
Atlanta, GA 30361
404-982-9000
Fax: 404-321-7882 www.sandlerseating.com
Manufacturer and exporter/importer of tables and
chairs for hotels, restaurants, and food courts
U.S. Director of Sales: Rusty Wolf
Chief Executive Officer: Roy Sandler
Sales Manager: Anita Haslett
Estimated Sales: $5 - 10 Million
Number Employees: 5-9
Brands:
Sandler Seating

28846 Sandusky Plastics
400 Broadway Street
Sandusky, OH 44870-2006
419-626-8980
Fax: 419-616-1803 800-234-7587
www.whirley.com
Thermoformed plastic containers
President: Lincoln Sokolski
Administrator: Holly Colvin
Human Resources: DiAnn Savko
Estimated Sales: $50-100 Million
Number Employees: 250-499

28847 Sandvik Process SystemsInc
21 Campus Rd
Totowa, NJ 07512-1211
973-790-1600
Fax: 973-790-9247
Process equipment for drying vegetables, fruits, and
rice, roasters for nuts and beans, freezers for seafood
and slurries for freeze drying, melt solidification
systems, cooling tunnels and dropformers for choco-
late and steam cookingtunnels for meat
Marketing Director: Craig Batsbh
Manager: Paula Benish
paula.benish@sandvik.com
Manager: Craig Bartsch
Estimated Sales: $1 - 5 Million
Number Employees: 50-99

28848 Sandvik Process Systems
30 Stockholm
Box 510, SE-101
Sweden, NJ 7512

973-790-1600
Fax: 973-790-9247 www.sandvik.com
Manufacturer and exporter of food processing
equipment including dryers, coolers, freezers,
drop-formers and steam cookers
President: Olof Faxander
Chairman: Anders Nyr,n
Marketing Manager: Craig Bartsch
Estimated Sales: $1 - 5 Million
Number Employees: 55
Parent Co: Sandvik
Brands:
Roto-Former

28849 Sandy Butler Group
1375 Jackson St
Suite 401
Ft Myers, FL 33901

239-357-6162
Fax: 239-333-0481
jerome@sandybutlergroup.com
www.sandybutlergroup.com
Balsamic, oilve oil, flavored olive oil, pasta, vegetables, wine vinegar and salts

28850 Sanford Redmond
780 E 134th St
Bronx, NY 10454-3527

718-792-7000
Fax: 718-292-0010
Small disposable containers for cream, jams, ect
Estimated Sales: $1-2.5 Million
Number Employees: 10-19

28851 Sanford Redmond Company
65 Harvard Ave
Stamford, CT 06902

203-351-9800
Fax: 718-292-0010
Manufacturer and exporter of wrapping, food pro-
cessing and packaging machinery
President: S Redmond
Contact: Sanford Redmond
ezpaks@sanred.com
Estimated Sales: $1-2,500,000
Number Employees: 5-9

28852 Sangamon Mills
PO Box 467
Cohoes, NY 12047

518-237-5321
Fax: 518-237-6282
Knit wash and dish cloths
President: Ella Fisher
Estimated Sales: Below $5 Million
Number Employees: 10-19
Brands:
Sunflower
White Swan

28853 Sani-Fit
620 S Raymond Avenue
Suite 9
Pasadena, CA 91105-3261

626-395-7895
Fax: 626-395-7899
Manufacturer, importer and exporter of stainless
steel sanitary fittings, diaphragm valves and food
processing fitting components
Estimated Sales: $1 - 5,000,000
Brands:
Bradford Cast Metals
Garitech
Sanifit
Topline

28854 Sani-Matic
P.O. Box 8662
Madison, WI 53708-8662

608-222-1935
Fax: 608-222-5348 800-356-3300
info@sanimatic.com www.sanimatic.com
Cleaning systems for the food and pharmaceutical
industries. Product lines include clean-out-of-place
parts washers, clean-in-place systems,
rinse/foam/sanitize pressure systems, conveyorized
wash tunnels, and a variety of cabinetwashers to
clean vats, racks, pallets, ibc, bin, totes and other
product handling items.

President: Ted Lingard
Marketing: Kelsy Boyd
Sales: Chad Dykstra
Contact: John Leach
johnl@sanimatic.com
Plant Manager: Wayne Huebner
Estimated Sales: $20 Million
Number Employees: 100-249
Number of Products: 10
Square Footage: 40000
Brands:
Sani-Matic
Ultra Flow

28855 Sani-Pure Food Laboratories
178-182 Saddle River Road
Saddle Brook, NJ 07663-4619

201-843-2525
Fax: 201-843-4934 sanipure.labs@verizon.net
www.sanipure.com
Quality control lab testing facility specializing in
microbiological, extraneous matter, packaging mate-
rials, pesticide residue, pharmalogical, water and
effluent testing services
Owner: Ronald Snitcher
Estimated Sales: $1-2.5 Million
Number Employees: 10-19
Square Footage: 15000

28856 Sani-Tech Group
PO Box 1010
Andover, NJ 07821-1010

973-579-1313
Fax: 973-579-3908

28857 Sani-Top Products
PO Box 117
De Leon Springs, FL 32130-0117

386-985-4667
Fax: 386-985-0202 800-874-6094
Manufacturer and exporter of plastic trays, bowls,
servers and food covers; also, acrylic specialty dis-
play cases
President: A David Logan
CEO: Joyce Monaco
Purchasing Manager: Walt Houdeshell
Estimated Sales: $1 - 3 Million
Number Employees: 10-19
Parent Co: Mastercraft Products Corporation

28858 SaniServ
451 E County Line Rd
Mooresville, IN 46158

317-831-7030
Fax: 317-831-7036 800-733-8073
sdowling@saniserv.com www.saniserv.com
Manufacturer and exporter of batch machines, freez-
ers and dispensers for ice cream, shakes, frozen bev-
erages/cocktails, yogurt and custard; processor of
cappuccino; importer of visual slush machines
President: Robert Mc Afee
CFO: Allen McCormick
Contact: Robert Mcafee
rmcafee@saniserv.com
Number Employees: 50-99
Square Footage: 300000
Parent Co: MD Holdings
Type of Packaging: Consumer, Food Service, Pri-
vate Label
Brands:
Saniserv

28859 Sanicrete
24535 Hallwood Ct
Farmington Hills, MI 48335-1667

248-893-1000
Fax: 248-893-1000
Designer of sanitary floor and lining systems for the
food and beverage industries.
Contact: Mike Fortman
mikef@sanicrete.com
Number Employees: 10-19

28860 Sanitary Couplers
275 S Pioneer Boulevard
Springboro, OH 45066-1180

513-743-0144
Fax: 513-743-0146 reseal@compuserve.com
Manufacturer and exporter of high purity sanitary
hoses, fittings and hose assemblies
General Manager: Jeffrey Zornow
Manager: Mark Hess
Sales Manager (Western Region): Jason Parks
Customer Service: Tracy Brandenburg

Estimated Sales: $2.5-5 Million
Number Employees: 9
Square Footage: 80000
Parent Co: Norton Performance Plastics
Brands:
Challenger
Cleargard
Gladiator
Permaseal
Protector
Reseal
Sanigard
Sentry

28861 (HQ)Sanitech Inc
7207 Lockport Pl # H
Lorton, VA 22079-1534

703-339-7001
Fax: 703-339-6848 800-486-4321
www.sanitechcorp.com
Manufacturing sanitation systems for food process-
ing and food service operations
President/CEO: alan weinstein
sumeersharma@sanitech.com
CFO: Pash Bhalla
VP: Bill Hannigan
Director Marketing: Sumeer Sharma
Sales Exec: Sumeer Sharma
Production: Tom Wines
Plant Manager: J R Bhalla
Purchasing Manager: Mike Sherman
Estimated Sales: $5 Million
Number Employees: 5-9
Square Footage: 20000
Brands:
Sanitech Mark Series Systems

28862 (HQ)Sanitek Products Inc
3959 Goodwin Ave
Los Angeles, CA 90039-1187

818-242-1071
Fax: 818-242-1071 818-242-1071
info@sanitek.com www.sanitek.com
Manufacturer and exporter of floor finishes, hand
cleaners and industrial chemicals; also, liquid soap
and specialty chemicals available
President: Robert L Moseley
info@sanitek.com
VP: David Moseley
R&D and QC: Ronald Ostroff
Estimated Sales: $5 - 10 Million
Number Employees: 10-19
Square Footage: 160000
Type of Packaging: Consumer, Private Label

28863 Sanitor Manufacturing Co
1221 W Centre Ave
Portage, MI 49024-5384

269-327-3001
Fax: 269-327-4562 800-379-5314
customerservice@sanitorusa.com
www.sanitorusa.com
Paper toilet seat covers and dispensers
President: David J Dietrich
dave@sanitorusa.com
Director Sales/Marketing: Mike Fawley
Estimated Sales: $5-10 Million
Number Employees: 10-19
Square Footage: 50000
Brands:
Neat Seat

28864 Santa Fe Bag Company
4950 E 49th Street
Vernon, CA 90058-2736

323-585-7225
Fax: 323-585-0313
Multi-wall and paper bags
President: David Sugarman
Estimated Sales: $10-20 Million
Number Employees: 20-49

28865 Santa Ynex Trading Company
500 N 8th Street
Suite B
Lompoc, CA 93436-4946

805-737-7967
Fax: 805-737-1844
Wine industry corks and capsules

28866 Santana Products
801 E Corey St
Scranton, PA 18505-3523
570-343-7921
Fax: 570-348-2959 800-368-5002
Storage systems
Contact: Glenn Fischer
glenn.fischer@wachovia.com
Estimated Sales: $20-50 Million
Number Employees: 100

28867 Sapac International
PO Box 2035
Fond Du Lac, WI 54936-2035
920-921-5060
Fax: 920-921-0822 800-257-2722
Palletizers; importer of bag filling and sealing equipment
Project Manager: Henry Brown
President/National Sales Manager: Bruce McMurry
Controls Manager: Jerome Haser
Number Employees: 1-4
Parent Co: Sapac

28868 Sapat Packaging Industry
PO Box 65723
Albuquerque, NM 87193-5723
505-275-9251
Fax: 505-271-8830
Estimated Sales: $.5 - 1 million
Number Employees: 1-4

28869 Sarasota Restaurant Equipment
2651 Whitfield Ave Ste 101
Sarasota, FL 34243
941-924-1410
Fax: 941-923-1510 800-434-1410
Manufacturer and wholesaler/distributor of restaurant and kitchen equipment
Owner: Marylin Snodell
Project Manager: Thomas Moon
Sales Manager: Joe Todd
Estimated Sales: $2.5-5 Million
Number Employees: 10-19
Square Footage: 20000

28870 Sardee Industries Inc
2211 W Washington St
Orlando, FL 32805-1254
407-297-6362
Fax: 407-297-6362 www.sardee.com
Container and lid conveyor handling systems including air, vacuum, magnetic and mechanical; also, PET bottle palletizers/depalletizers
Manager: Mike Schreiber
mschreiber@sardee.com
Manager: Bill Bryer
Estimated Sales: $1-2.5 Million
Number Employees: 20-49
Square Footage: 200000

28871 Sardee Industries Inc
5100 Academy Dr # 400
Suite 400
Lisle, IL 60532-4208
630-824-4200
Fax: 630-824-4225 sales@sardee.com
www.sardee.com
Manufacturer and exporter of palletizers, depalletizers and pallet, container and end handling equipment
President: Steve Sarovich
ssarovich@sardee.com
Sales Director: Gary Bishop
Estimated Sales: $5 - 10 Million
Number Employees: 10-19
Square Footage: 100000
Parent Co: Sardee Industries

28872 Sargent & Greenleaf
P.O. Box 930
Nicholasville, KY 40340-0930
859-885-9411
Fax: 859-885-3063 800-826-7652
www.sglocks.com
Security products including money safe locks and exit devices with alarms
President: Bill Demtsey
R&D: Mike Clarke
CEO: Jerry A Morgan
Quality Control: Wayne Landa
Director Marketing: Gary Kepler
Customer Services Manager: Brian Costley

Estimated Sales: $20 - 50 Million
Number Employees: 100-249
Brands:
 Arm-A-Dor
 Secure Panic Hardware

28873 (HQ)Sargento Foods Inc
1 Persnickety Pl
Plymouth, WI 53073-3544
920-893-8484
Fax: 920-893-8399 800-243-3737
www.sargento.com
Natural and processed cheese manufacturer.
CEO: Louis Gentine
Executive VP: Karri Neils
karri.neils@sargentocheese.com
Estimated Sales: Over $1 Billion
Number Employees: 1000-4999
Type of Packaging: Consumer, Food Service, Private Label, Bulk
Brands:
 Artisan Blends
 Balanced Breaks
 Chef Blends
 Natural Blends
 Sargento
 Snack Bites
 Ultra Thin

28874 Sartorius Corp
131 Heartland Blvd
Edgewood, NY 11717-8315
631-254-4249
Fax: 631-254-4253 800-635-2906
www.sartorius-omnimark.com
Filtration and weighing products including lab and moisture determination balances and industrial scales
President: Silvano Ghirardi
VP: Maurice Knapp
Director Marketing Communications: Arnold Breisblatt
Estimated Sales: $50-100 Million
Number Employees: 100-249
Square Footage: 35000
Parent Co: Sartorius AG
Other Locations:
 Sartorius Corp.
 Mississauga ON

28875 Sartorius Corp
131 Heartland Blvd
Edgewood, NY 11717-8315
631-254-4249
Fax: 631-254-4253 800-635-2906
www.sartorius-omnimark.com
Wine industry filtration and weighing equipment
President: Silvano Ghirardi
VP: Maurice Knapp
Estimated Sales: $50-100 Million
Number Employees: 100-249

28876 Sasib Beverage & Food North America
808 Stewart Drive
Plano, TX 75074-8101
800-558-3814
Manufacturer and exporter of high speed beverage fillers and processing systems, labelers, bottle washers, rinsers, casers, palletizers and turnkey beverage production facilities
President: Claudia Salvi
VP Manufacturing: Robert Prescott
Estimated Sales: $20-50 Million
Number Employees: 186
Square Footage: 300000
Parent Co: Sasib Beverage
Brands:
 Alfa
 Meyer
 Mojonnier
 Pama
 Sarcmi
 Simonazzi

28877 Sasser Signs
750 Craghead St
Danville, VA 24541
434-792-2696
Fax: 434-793-8964 800-752-6091
Electric signs and billboards including neon
Owner: Cindy Sasser-Hill
VP: Diane Sasser

Estimated Sales: $1-2.5 Million
Number Employees: 10-19
Square Footage: 30000

28878 Satake USA
10905 Cash Rd
Stafford, TX 77477
281-276-3600
Fax: 281-494-1427 cvincent@satake-usa.com
www.satake-usa.com
Manufacturer and exporter of sorters including color, nut meat and tomato; also, rice processing and cereal milling equipment available
President: J J Naoki
VP Marketing: Peter Cawthorne
Marketing Specialist: Sandra Langlois
Contact: Mathew Abraham
mabraham@satake-usa.com
Estimated Sales: $20-50 Million
Number Employees: 100-249
Parent Co: Satake Corporation
Other Locations:
 Satake (USA)
 Cheshire, UK
Brands:
 3vision
 Colorwatch
 Scanmaster
 Shell-Ex
 Summa-6

28879 Saticoy Lemon Association
600 E Third Street
Oxnard, CA 93030
805-654-6543
Fax: 805-654-6510
webmaster@saticoylemon.com
www.saticoylemon.com
Agricultural Cooperative that is owned by the lemon grower members of which the marketing of the fruit is handled through their affiliation with Sunkist Growers, Inc.
President: Glenn Miller
Chief Financial Officer: Mike Dillard
Exchange/Business Development Manager: John Eliot
Field Manager: David Coert
Sales Coordinator: Jose Mendez
MIS Director: Lee Raymond
Personnel Director: Michael Dennington
Production Manager: Ron Davis
Plant Superintendent: Albert Rivera
Shipping Supervisor: Albert Palacio
Type of Packaging: Food Service

28880 Sato America
10350 Nations Ford Rd # A
Charlotte, NC 28273-5824
704-644-1662
Fax: 704-644-1662 888-871-8741
www.satoamerica.com
Manufacturer and exporter of bar code printers
President: Robert Linse
robertlinse@satoamerica.com
Marketing Manager: Nikki Aunn
Number Employees: 50-99
Type of Packaging: Consumer, Food Service, Private Label, Bulk
Brands:
 Sato

28881 Satoris America
1403 Heritage Drive
Suite B
Northfield, MN 55057
507-663-6100
Fax: 507-663-6123 877-663-6100
Company's products and services includes autoclaves and retorts, customer service, sales and replacement parts for German technology food safety systems. sales of new retorts, as well as replacement parts for stock retorts used insterilization of commercial food products. Official supplier of OEM parts for retort brnads stock, satori stocktec, satoris.
CEO: Oliver Barth
Sales: Pam Tidona
Estimated Sales: $4,000,000
Brands:
 Satori Stocktec
 Satoris
 Stock

28882 Saturn Overhead Equipment
100 Apgar Dr
Somerset, NJ 08873-1146
732-560-7210
Fax: 973-465-4219 800-631-4473
sgordon@saturnoe.com www.saturnoe.com
Hoists including overhead electric wire and rope
President: Stephen Gordon
CFO: Debbie Swerdlow
VP: Eugenio Moutela
Quality Control: Gert Martens
Estimated Sales: Below $5 Million
Number Employees: 5-9

28883 Sauereisen
160 Gamma Dr
Pittsburgh, PA 15238
412-963-0303
Fax: 412-963-7620 questions@sauereisen.com
www.sauereisen.com
Corrosion-resistant material of construction, corrosion and skid-resistant flooring
CEO: Eric Sauereisen
Quality Control: Craig Maloney
Number Employees: 40

28884 Saunder Brothers
Bacon Street
Bridgton, ME 4009
207-647-3331
Fax: 207-647-2064
Manufacturer and exporter of wooden candy sticks, skewers and plain dowels
Co-Owner/President/General Manag: Read Grover
Co-Owner/VP: Robert Berry
Sales Manager/Treasurer: Terri Grover
Number Employees: 24

28885 Saunders Manufacturing Co.
PO Box 12539
N Kansas City, MO 64116-0539
816-842-0233
Fax: 816-842-1129 800-821-2792
goldenstar@goldenstar.com www.goldenstar.com
Manufacturer and exporter of regular and dust mops including antimicrobial, cotton wet, disposable and rayon; also, mop handles and frames and carpet mats and mattings
President: Gary Gradinger
National Sales Manager: Ssteve Lewis
VP Manufacturing: Mike Julo
Estimated Sales: $20 - 50 Million
Number Employees: 20-49
Square Footage: 100000
Parent Co: Golden Star
Type of Packaging: Consumer, Food Service, Private Label, Bulk

28886 Saunders West
975 N Todd Ave
Azusa, CA 91702-2226
626-691-1111
Fax: 626-691-0116 888-932-8836
west@saunderscorp.com www.saunderscorp.com
Pressure sensitive and adhesive tapes; also, die cutting of roll stock available
CEO: Robert McCollum
Sales Manager: Mike Hibbard
Contact: Jeff Oyster
joyster@saunderscorp.com
Manager: John Sciacca
Manager: Jon Tarian
General Manager: Wilson Wong
Estimated Sales: $10-20 Million
Number Employees: 1-4
Square Footage: 42000
Parent Co: R.S. Hughes Company

28887 Sauvagnat Inc
12200 Herbert Wayne Court
Suite 180
Huntersville, NC 28078-6396
704-948-0440
Fax: 704-948-0190 800-258-5619
Outdoor furniture including chairs, tables and lounges
President: Bradford Elliot
CEO: John Menas
Marketing Director: Shannon Lowe
Number Employees: 15
Parent Co: Groupe Sauvagnat
Brands:
Allibert
Triconfort

28888 Sauve Company Limited
151 Mill St
Amherst, WI 54406
715-824-2502
Fax: 715-824-2192
Executive recruiters for the food and dairy industry
President: Gordon Sauve
Vice President: Diane Sauve
Estimated Sales: Less than $500,000
Number Employees: 10

28889 Savage Brothers Company
1125 Lunt Ave
Elk Grove Vlg, IL 60007
847-981-3000
Fax: 847-981-3010 800-342-0973
info@savagebros.com www.savagebrothers.com
Supplier of cookers, mixers, stoves, chocolate melting and processing tanks, kettles, mixing bowls and pumps for food depositing, transferring and metering
President: David Floreani
Marketing Manager: Robert Parmley
Contact: John Weeks
john@savagebros.com
Estimated Sales: $2.5-5,000,000
Number Employees: 20-49
Square Footage: 20000
Type of Packaging: Food Service
Brands:
Firemixer
Hi-Speed Cooker
Liftiltruk

28890 Savanna Pallets
805 Tall Pine Ln
Cloquet, MN 55720-3164
218-879-8553
Fax: 218-879-8560 pallets@frontiernet.net
www.savannapallets.com
Pallets
Owner: Al Raushel
chadraushel@savannapallets.com
Manager: Al Raushel
Estimated Sales: $1-2.5 Million
Number Employees: 20-49

28891 Savanna Pallets
106 E 1st Ave
PO Box 308
McGregor, MN 55760
218-768-2077
Fax: 218-768-3112 pallets@frontiernet.net
www.savannapallets.com
Skids and pallets
President: Allen Raushel
VP: Al Raushel
Contact: Craig Joriman
craigjoriman@savannapallets.com
Estimated Sales: $1 - 5 Million
Number Employees: 50-99
Square Footage: 20000

28892 Savasort Inc
6811 Garden Rd
Riviera Beach, FL 33404-5997
561-848-8744
Fax: 561-840-8515 800-255-8744
info@savasort.com www.agilitymats.com
Document sorting equipment
President: Phillip Elmore
savasort@aol.com
Estimated Sales: Less Than $500,000
Number Employees: 1-4
Square Footage: 36000

28893 Save-A-Tree
1338 Berkeley Way
P.O. Box 862
Berkeley, CA 94701
510-843-5233
Fax: 510-843-4906 lolalone@yahoo.com
Organic cotton bags
Proprietor: Penny Marienthal
Contact: Chris Hawkins
chawkins@saveatreeprinting.com
Estimated Sales: Below $5,000,000
Number Employees: 1

28894 Save-O-Seal Corporation
PO Box 553
Elmsford, NY 10523-0553
914-592-3031
Fax: 914-592-4511 800-831-9720

Manufacturer and exporter of bagging machines and heat sealing equipment; also, coated slitting blades
President: Tullio Muscariello
Sales: Anna DeLuca
Estimated Sales: $2.5 - 5 Million
Number Employees: 5-9

28895 Saver Glass Inc
841 Latour Ct # B
Suite B
Napa, CA 94558-7546
707-259-2930
Fax: 707-259-2933 www.saverglass.com
Wine and spirits bottles
CEO: Sally Arnold
sjt@saverglass.com
VP Faiance: Michael Graham
Manager: Mike Graham
Estimated Sales: $500,000-$1 Million
Number Employees: 10-19
Parent Co: Saverglass group

28896 Savogran Co
259 Lenox St
Norwood, MA 02062-3463
781-762-2371
Fax: 781-762-1095 800-225-9872
www.savogran.com
Paint remover and cleaning powder
Contact: Mark Conti
mconti@savogran.com
Estimated Sales: $20-50 Million
Number Employees: 20-49
Brands:
Dirtex

28897 Savoye Packaging
645 Edison Way
Reno, NV 89502-4136
775-351-0501
Fax: 775-857-3601
Wine industry polyaluminum capsules
Owner: Hanna Lasilla
Estimated Sales: $10-20 Million
Number Employees: 5-9

28898 Saxco International LLC
200 Gibraltar Rd # 101
Horsham, PA 19044-2385
215-443-8100
Fax: 215-443-8370 800-245-1016
info@saxcointl.com www.saxco.com
Wine industry packaging materials
President: Herb Sachs
CEO: Matthew Malenfant
matthew@saxcointl.com
Estimated Sales: $5 - 10 Million
Number Employees: 10-19

28899 Saxco International LLC
200 Gibraltar Rd # 101
Horsham, PA 19044-2385
215-443-8100
Fax: 215-443-8370 info@saxcointl.com
www.saxco.com
Wine industry closures
President: Herbert L Sachs
CEO: Matthew Malenfant
matthew@saxcointl.com
Estimated Sales: $5 - 10 Million
Number Employees: 10-19

28900 Sayco Yo-Yo Molding Company
2 Sunset Ave
Cumberland, RI 2864
401-724-5296
Manufacturer and exporter of advertising promotions and novelties including yo-yos, yo-yo promotions
President: Lawrence Sayegh
Plant Manager: Leroy Sayegh
Purchasing Manager: Larry Sayco
Estimated Sales: Under $300,000
Number Employees: 5
Square Footage: 3000
Parent Co: L.J. Sayegh & Company
Type of Packaging: Consumer, Private Label
Brands:
Sayco
Sayco Tournament

28901 Scaltrol Inc
460 Brogdon Rd # 500
P.O. Box 3288
Suwanee, GA 30024-2314
678-541-5138
Fax: 877-769-2751 800-868-0629
rzimmerman@scaltrolinc.com
www.scaltrolinc.com
Manufacturer and exporter of water treatment units for removal of scale and staining
Owner: Austin Hansen
Business Manager: Hilda Epsten
Manager: Rob Zimmerman
rzimmerman@scaltrolinc.com
Operations Manager: Sunday Christopher
Number Employees: 1-4
Square Footage: 10000
Brands:
Scaltrol

28902 Scan Coin
20145 Ashbrook Pl # 110
Ashburn, VA 20147-3375
703-729-8600
Fax: 703-729-8606 800-336-3311
info@scancoin-usa.com www.scancoin-usa.com
Manufacturer and importer of coin and currency handling equipment including counting, sorting and packing
President/Chief Executive Officer: Per Lundin
Contact: Gaaron Gilham
gilham@scancoin-cds.com
Estimated Sales: Below $5 Million
Number Employees: 5-9
Parent Co: Scan Coin AB
Type of Packaging: Consumer

28903 Scan Corporation
110 Lithia Pinecrest Rd Ste G
Brandon, FL 33511
813-653-2877
Fax: 813-654-3949 800-881-7226
sales@scancorporation.com
www.scancorporation.com
Manufacturer and exporter of point of sale systems including touch screen p.c.'s and terminals, membrane keyboards and scanning equipment
President: Frank Harrison
Estimated Sales: $10-20 Million
Number Employees: 10-19

28904 Scan Group
1820 S Mohawk Dr
Appleton, WI 54914-4732
920-730-9150
Fax: 920-730-8991 www.scangroup.net
Paper tableware including plates, cups and napkins
Manager: Steve Mueller
Estimated Sales: $5-10 Million
Number Employees: 1-4

28905 ScanTech Sciences
4940 Peachtree Industrial Blvd.
Ste. 340
Norcross, GA 30071
470-359-3660
info@scantechsciences.com
www.scantechsciences.com
Designs and manufactures E-beam systems for food treatment. Offers services for growers, wholesalers, retailers, and food safety directors.
Co-Founder & Chairman: Dolan Falconer
CEO: Dwayne House
CFO: H. Martin Rice
Co-Founder & COO: Chip Starns
Year Founded: 2009
Number Employees: 35-50

28906 Scandia Packaging Machinery Co
15 Industrial Rd
Fairfield, NJ 07004-3017
973-473-6100
Fax: 973-473-7226 jbrown@scandiapack.com
www.scandiapack.com
Manufacturer and exporter of automatic packaging equipment for overwrapping, bundling, banding, multipacking, cartoning and collating

President: Bill Bronander
wbb@scandiapack.com
Finance: Cecelia G. Bronander
Engineering: Arthur Goldberg
Sales Representative: Carolyn Placentino
Customer Service: Maria Van Ness
Sales Manager: James J. Brown
Parts Department: Lewis D'Allegro
Estimated Sales: $10-20 Million
Number Employees: 20-49
Square Footage: 61200

28907 Scanning Devices Inc
31 Dunham Rd # 2
Unit 1
Billerica, MA 01821-5701
978-362-1123
Fax: 978-362-8693 mail@scanningdevices.com
www.scanningdevicesinc.com
Photoelectric control and optical activated counters, optical sensors and scanners Force Measurement instrumentation,Display devices
Contact: Dave Chanoux
dave.chanoux@scanningdevices.com
Estimated Sales: $2.5 - 5 Million
Number Employees: 1-4

28908 Scattaglia Farm LLC
10400 E Avenue U
Littlerock, CA 93543-3121
661-944-3880
Fax: 661-944-5790
President: Louis Scattaglia
louis.scattaglia@scattagliafarms.com
Estimated Sales: $50 - 100 Million
Number Employees: 50-99

28909 Schaefer Machine Co Inc
200 Commercial Dr
Deep River, CT 06417-1682
860-526-4000
Fax: 860-526-4654 800-243-5143
schaefer@schaeferco.com www.schaeferco.com
Manufacturer and exporter of label gluing and cementing machinery
Owner: Robert Gammons
schaefer01@snet.net
Estimated Sales: $1-3 Million
Number Employees: 5-9
Square Footage: 40000
Brands:
Schaefer Ms Label

28910 Schaefer Technologies Inc
4901 W Raymond St
Indianapolis, IN 46241-4733
317-546-4081
Fax: 317-546-4095 800-435-7174
www.schaefer-technologies.net
Distributor of quality equipment specialized in the fit the needs of the pharmaceutical, health, food and cosmetic industries
President: Steven Schaefer
CEO: Christina Cadwallader
ccadwallader@schaefertech.us
Estimated Sales: $5-10 Million
Number Employees: 50-99
Number of Products: 19

28911 Schaeff
8657 S. Beloit Ave
Bridgeview, IL 60455
Fax: 708-598-1877 888-436-7867
www.schaafequipment.com
Fork lift trucks, tow tractors and electric rider material transport vehicles
Owner: Bill Schaaf
Sales Manager: Melanie Bohle
Estimated Sales: $10-20 Million
Number Employees: 5-9
Square Footage: 288000

28912 Schaeffler Group USA Inc
308 Springhill Farm Rd
Fort Mill, SC 29715-9784
803-548-8500
Fax: 803-548-8599 info.us@schaeffler.com
www.schaeffler.us
CEO: Bruce Warmbold
bruce@ina.com
Estimated Sales: $1 - 5 Million
Number Employees: 500-999

28913 Schaerer USA Corp
15501 Red Hill Ave
Suite 200
Tustin, CA 92780
562-989-3004
Fax: 562-989-3075 888-989-3004
info@schaererusa.com www.schaererusa.com
Supra-automatic espresso machines.
Director of Sales: Jim Crowley
jcrowley@schaererusa.com
Year Founded: 1993
Parent Co: M. Schaerer AG
Brands:
Schaerer

28914 Schaffer Poidometer Company
5421 Claybourne Street
Pittsburgh, PA 15232-1623
412-281-9031
Fax: 412-281-1911
Poidometers for weighing and blending large quantities of raw ingredients
Owner: Joseph Pfenninger
Estimated Sales: Less than $500,000
Number Employees: 4
Square Footage: 20000

28915 Schanno Transportation
837 Apollo Rd
Eagan, MN 55121-2387
651-457-9700
Fax: 651-552-5835 800-544-6172
Estimated Sales: $1 - 5 Million
Number Employees: 100-249

28916 Scheb International
27 Clarington Way
North Barrington, IL 60010-6932
847-381-2573
Fax: 847-381-2573 schebltd@aol.com
www.schebltd.com
Manufacturer and exporter of tote, storage and material handling boxes; also, bulk carbon dioxide storage and delivery systems for beverage use; importer of carbon dioxide bulk delivery systems
Estimated Sales: $1 - 5 Million
Number Employees: 3
Parent Co: Carbo Carbonation Company
Type of Packaging: Food Service
Brands:
Carbo Mizers
Econ-O-Totes

28917 Schebler Co
5665 Fenno Rd
Bettendorf, IA 52722-5711
563-359-0110
Fax: 563-359-8430 www.schebler.com
Conveying and weighing equipment, vibratory feeders and food eqiupment
CEO: Gerald McClure
CFO: Jim Booe
Quality Control: Ron Wildermuth
Marketing Director: Don Gbeault
Sales Director: John Guinta
Production Manager: Larry Jones
Purchasing Manager: Barbara Welsch
Estimated Sales: $20 - 30 Million
Number Employees: 100-249
Square Footage: 190000

28918 Scheidegger
345 Kear St Ste 200
Yorktown Heights, NY 10598
914-245-7850
Fax: 914-243-0976
Manufacturer, importer and exporter of tamper evident sealing and full body sleeving machinery
VP Sales/Marketing: Dipak Modi
Number Employees: 2
Parent Co: Sch. S.A.

28919 Schenck Process
746 E Milwaukee St
Whitewater, WI 53190-2125
262-473-2441
Fax: 262-473-2489 888-742-1249
mktg@accuratefeeders.com
www.schenckaccurate.com
Manufacturing and supplying superior volumetric and gravimetric feeders, weighfeeders, solids flow meters, bulk bag discharging systems, and vibratory feeders to a wide variety of markets throughout the world.

President: Dirk Maroske
CEO: Dennis Hummel
 d.hummel@schenckprocess.com
CFO: Neal Mueller
Number Employees: 100-249
Parent Co: Schenck AccuRate
Brands:
 Mechatron Gravimetric Feeders
 Mechatron Volumetric Feeders
 Sac Master Bulk Bag Dischargers
 Solid Flow Vibratory Feeders
 Tuf-Flex Volumetric Series Feeders

28920 Schenck Process
746 E Milwaukee St
P.O. Box 208
Whitewater, WI 53190-2125
 262-473-2441
 Fax: 262-473-2489 888-742-1249
 mktg@accuratefeeders.com
 www.schenckaccurate.com
Vibratory feeders with loss-in-weight batch control systems and loss-in-weight continuous flow systems; also, portable universal bin and feeder combination, bulk bag discharger, box dumps, weightbelts, and screw feeders
President: Dirk Maroske
CEO: Jay Brown
Research & Development: Bob Stephenson
Marketing Director: Mike Koras
Sales Director: Chris Isom
Regional Sales Manager: Rick Pruden
Plant Manager: Bill Samborski
Purchasing Manager: Angie Adams
Estimated Sales: $3-4 Million
Number Employees: 100-249
Square Footage: 128000
Parent Co: Schenck Process
Brands:
 Accuflow
 Solidsflow

28921 Schenck Process
746 E Milwaukee St
Whitewater, WI 53190-2125
 262-473-2441
 Fax: 262-473-2489 800-558-0184
 www.schenckaccurate.com
Dry material feeders
President: Dirk Maroske
CEO: Christoper Aberle
 c.aberle@schenckprocess.com
Marketing Manager: Gary Kuehneman
Estimated Sales: $20-50 Million
Number Employees: 100-249

28922 Schermerhorn Inc
165 Front St # D12
Chicopee, MA 01013-1270
 413-598-8348
 Fax: 413-594-8439
Paper set-up boxes
President: Nicholas Dobrilla
 nicholas@schermerhorn-realestate.com
Estimated Sales: $20-50 Million
Number Employees: 20-49
Square Footage: 37000

28923 Scherping Systems
PO Box 10
Winsted, MN 55395-0010
 320-485-4401
 Fax: 320-485-2666
Custom stainless steel tanks, cheese making machinery and clean-in-place systems; also, design installation and control services available
President: Tim High
CFO: Cindy Tellinghuisen
Sales Manager: George Schwinghammer
Contact: Ryan Anderson
 ryan.anderson@tetrapak.com
Plant Manager: Harvey Dvorak
Number Employees: 100-249

28924 Schiefer Packaging Corporation
160 Beverly Rd
Syracuse, NY 13207-1302
 315-422-0615
 Fax: 315-478-4140
Boxes for food products
President: Charles Simek
Estimated Sales: $1-2.5 Million
Number Employees: 1-4

28925 Schiff & Co
1120 Bloomfield Ave # 103
Ste 103
West Caldwell, NJ 07006-7131
 973-227-1830
 Fax: 973-227-5330 RSchiff13@aol.com
 www.schiffandcompany.com
Regulatory services for the food and cosmetic industry.
Owner: Robert Schiff
 rschiff13@aol.com
VP: Jack Parker
Business Development: John Round
Estimated Sales: $2.5 - 5 Million
Number Employees: 1-4
Square Footage: 6000

28926 (HQ)Schiffenhaus Industries
2013 McCarter Hwy
Newark, NJ 07104
 973-484-5000
 Fax: 973-484-8628
Corrugated paper boxes and P.O.P. displays
President: J Anton Schiffenhaus
CEO: Steven Grossman
Estimated Sales: $28.7 Million
Number Employees: 100-249

28927 Schiffmayer Plastics Corp.
1201 Armstrong St
Algonquin, IL 60102
 847-658-8140
 Fax: 847-658-0863
Capping and closing supplies
President: Karl F Schiffmayer
Quality Control: Gary Hunt
Estimated Sales: $20 - 30 Million
Number Employees: 70

28928 Schlagel Inc
491 Emerson St N
Cambridge, MN 55008-1316
 763-689-5991
 Fax: 763-689-5310 800-328-8002
 sales@schlagel.com www.schlagel.com
Manufacturer and exporter of feed and grain equipment
CEO: Chris Schlagel
 chris@schlagel.com
Sales Manager: Jeff Schwab
Purchasing Manager: Drew Stoffell
Estimated Sales: $10-20 Million
Number Employees: 50-99

28929 Schleicher & Company ofAmerica
5715 Clyde Rhyne Drive
Sanford, NC 27330
 919-775-7318
 Fax: 919-774-8731 800-775-7570
 soa@interpath.com
Distributor and supplier of compactors and balers, paper shredders
President: Jack Costelloe
VP: John Ulam
Marketing Manager: Libby Nelson
Estimated Sales: $10 - 20 Million
Number Employees: 20
Square Footage: 100000
Brands:
 Intimus
 Olympia
 Schleicher

28930 Schleicher & Schuell MicroSience
800 Centennial Ave # 1
Piscataway, NJ 08854-3911
 973-245-8300
 Fax: 973-245-8301 800-645-2302
 www.whatman.com
Microbiological media, membranes, monitors, HACCP kits, MI agar & broth, Coliform broth, Listeria swabs, E coli media, paper filtration, glass filtration, sample preparation filtration, ultra filtration for pharmaceutical research andproduction, cell counters
President: Keith Jaythaward
Quality Control: Berni Reedes
Senior VP: Richard Dool
VP Marketing: John Perini
VP Sales: Joseph Murdock
Operations Manager: Louis Gugliotta
Estimated Sales: $9 - 12 Million
Number Employees: 10-19

Parent Co: Schleicher & Schuell MicroScience, GmbH
Brands:
 Biopath

28931 Schloss Engineered Equipment
10555 E Dartmouth Ave
Suite 230
Aurora, CO 80014
 303-695-4500
 Fax: 303-695-4507
Drum and bar screens, compactors, grit and sludge collectors, flocculators and conveyors
President: Kristy Schloss
Contact: Charles Snyder
 charles.snyder@swe.org
Estimated Sales: $5-10 Million
Number Employees: 5-9

28932 (HQ)Schlueter Company
310 N. Main Street
Janesville, WI 53545
 608-755-5444
 Fax: 608-755-5440 800-359-1700
 www.schlueterco.com
Manufacturer and exporter of dairy and food plant equipment including process tanks, conveyors, hoppers, sanitizing systems (CIP-COP-HY pressure-foam), liquid/solid separators, strainers, filters, rotary drums, etc.; also, carts andwork tables
President: Brad Losching
VP: H Losching
Marketing Manager: C Benskin
Estimated Sales: $10-20 Million
Number Employees: 50
Square Footage: 200000
Other Locations:
 Schlueter Co.
 Fresno CA
Brands:
 Safgard

28933 Schlueter Company
310 N Main St
Janesville, WI 53545
 608-755-5444
 Fax: 608-755-5440 800-359-1700
 schlueter@socket.net www.schlueterco.com
Custom plastic blow molding, recreational, medical, toys, industrial and others all under the category if custom moulding. also post moulding and resins under the category of plastic moulding
President: Bradley W Losching
Estimated Sales: $5-10 Million
Number Employees: 50-99

28934 Schlueter Company
310 N. Main Street
PO Box 548
Janesville, WI 53545
 608-755-5444
 Fax: 608-755-5440 800-359-1700
 www.schlueterco.com
Clean rooms and equipment, custom fabrication, flow diversion stations
President: Brad Losching
Marketing: Charles Benskin
Plant Manager: Erik Eide
Estimated Sales: $10-20 Million
Number Employees: 35
Square Footage: 80000
Type of Packaging: Food Service

28935 Schmalz
5200 Atlantic Ave
Raleigh, NC 27616-1870
 919-713-0880
 Fax: 919-713-0883 schmalz@schmalz.us
 www.schmalz.com
Supplier of; vacuum lifting equipment, vacuum components & gripping systems
President: Volker Schmitz
 volker.schmitz@schmalz.us
CFO: Kevin Saylor
Estimated Sales: $10 Million
Number Employees: 10-19
Parent Co: Schmalz

28936 Schmersal
660 White Plains Rd # 160
Suite 160
Tarrytown, NY 10591-5185
914-347-4775
Fax: 914-347-1567 888-496-5143
salesusa@schmersal.com www.schmersal.com
Man and machine safeguarding devices
President: Peter Engstrom
CFO: Mario Tucci
Manager: John Monahan
Estimated Sales: $3 - 5 Million
Number Employees: 20-49

28937 Schmidt Progressive
360 Harmon Ave
P.O. Box 380
Lebanon, OH 45036-8801
513-934-2600
Fax: 513-932-8768 800-272-3706
steve@schmidtprogressive.com
Design, engineering and manufacturing display fix-
tures for the supermarket, bakery, concession, food
service and floral industries.
Owner/CEO: Julia Rodenbeck
julia@schmidtprogressive.com
VP Sales/Marketing: Stephen Moore
VP Sales/Marketing: Stephen Moore
VP Administration: Joseph Perdy
VP Manufacturing: Don Blades
Plant Manager: Robert Newton
Purchasing Manager: Don Blades
Estimated Sales: $2-5 Million
Number Employees: 20-49
Square Footage: 240000
Brands:
Food Furniture
Schmidt

28938 Schneider Electric
70 Mechanic St
Foxboro, MA 02035
781-534-7535
www.schneider-electric.us
Manufacturer and exporter of programmable logic
controllers and software.
Chairman & CEO: Jean-Pascal Tricoire
CFO: Hilary Maxson
EVP, Supply Chain, North America: Annette
Clayton
Global Marketing: Chris Leong
Year Founded: 1836
Estimated Sales: $100-500 Million
Number Employees: 500-999
Parent Co: Groupe Schneider
Brands:
Modicom
Square D
Telemechanique

28939 Schneider Packaging Eqpt Co
5370 Guy Young Rd
Brewerton, NY 13029-8706
315-676-3035
Fax: 315-676-2875 sales@schneiderequip.com
www.schneiderequipment.com
Manufacturers case packing and robotic palletizing
equipment and integrates conveyors, case eleva-
tors/lowerators, pallet dispensers, slip sheet dispensers and shuttle transfer cars for full unit loads.
CEO: Alex Naugle
alexnaugle@gmail.com
Estimated Sales: $500,000-$1 Million
Number Employees: 100-249
Square Footage: 400000

28940 Schnuck Markets, Inc.
11420 Lackland Rd.
PO Box 46928
St. Louis, MO 63146
314-994-4400
800-264-4400
nourish.schnucks.com
Grocery, bakery, deli, dairy, seafood, meat, frozen
foods, produce, floral, liquor, and more.
Chairman/CEO: Todd Schnuck
Chief People Officer: Jada Reese
Year Founded: 1939
Estimated Sales: $3.1 Billion
Number Employees: 14,500
Number of Brands: 16
Brands:
Baby Basics
Culinaria

Culinary Circle
Equaline
Everyday Essential
Full Circle Market
Paws Happy Life
Pure Harmony
Schnucks
Shoppers Value
Simply Done
Stone Ridge Creamery
Super Chill
Tippy Toes
TopCare
Wild Harvest

28941 Schober USA Inc
4690 Industry Dr
Fairfield, OH 45014-1923
513-489-7393
Fax: 513-489-7485 800-344-8324
solutions@schoberusa.com www.schoberusa.com
Rotary die cutting equipment
President: Jill Sanner
jsanner@osu.edu
CFO: Marion Hixon
Manager: Marion Hixson
Estimated Sales: $1 - 2.5 Million
Number Employees: 5-9

28942 Schoeneck Containers Inc
2160 S 170th St
New Berlin, WI 53151-2287
262-786-9360
Fax: 262-786-0772 www.schoeneck.com
Plastic bottles
President: Scott Chambers
schambers@schoeneck.com
Chairman: Robert Schoeneck
CFO: Jim Anderson
Estimated Sales: Below $5 Million
Number Employees: 100-249
Square Footage: 240000

28943 Scholle IPN
2500 Cooper Ave
Merced, CA 95348
209-384-3100
Fax: 209-384-3166
NorthAmerica@scholleipn.com
www.scholleipn.com
Supplier of bag-in-box packaging, metallized plas-
tics and paper, flexible shipping containers, industry
leading bag-in-box tap and filling technology, ma-
rine salvage devices and battery electrolyte.
President & CEO: Ross Bushnell
Year Founded: 1947
Estimated Sales: $227.30 Million
Number Employees: 1900
Square Footage: 35000
Brands:
Rhino

28944 Schoneman Inc
4540 Park Ave
Ashtabula, OH 44004-6967
440-998-2273
Fax: 440-998-2285 800-255-4439
steve@schoneman.com
Software for meat, poultry, seafood and produce
companies
President: Steve Schoneman
steve@schoneman.com
Number Employees: 5-9

28945 School Marketing Partners
32302 Camino Capistrano # 207
San Juan Cpstrno, CA 92675-4506
949-487-1515
Fax: 949-661-7778 800-565-7778
www.schoolmenu.com
Menus for school cafeterias
Manager: Lana Huie
Estimated Sales: Below $5 Million
Number Employees: 5-9
Brands:
B.J. Spot
Tooned-In Menus

28946 Schreck Software
1420 Interlachen Cir
Woodbury, MN 55125-8859
651-731-6822
Food costing, inventory and margin management
software

28947 Schreiber Foods Inc.
400 N. Washington St.
Green Bay, WI 54301
920-437-7601
Fax: 920-437-1617 contact@schreiberfoods.com
www.schreiberfoods.com
Dairy products such as cheese, yogurt, milk, milk
powders and more.
President/CEO: Ron Dunford
SVP/CFO: Chip Smoot
SVP, U.S. Operations: Tony Nowak
SVP/Chief Innovation Officer: Vinith Poduval
VP, Global Chain Sales: Shari Antonissen
SVP/Chief Commercial Officer: Trevor Farrell
Year Founded: 1945
Estimated Sales: Over $5 Billion
Number Employees: 9,000
Number of Brands: 10
Type of Packaging: Consumer, Food Service, Pri-
vate Label, Bulk
Other Locations:
Tempe AZ
Gainesville GA
Carthage MO
Clinton MO
Monett MO
Mt Vernon MO
Ravenna NE
Shippensburg PA
Nashville TN
Stephenville TX
Logan UT
Smithfield UT
Wisconsin Rapids WI
Brands:
American Heritage
Clearfield
Cooper
Laferia
Lov-It
Menu
Raskas
Ready-Cut
School Chioce
Schreiber

28948 Schroeder Machine
165 Balboa St # C2
Ste C-2
San Marcos, CA 92069-1347
760-591-9733
Fax: 760-591-4019 sales@ssmci.com
www.schroedermachinetechnologies.com
Manufacturer and exporter of automatic case pack-
ing and erecting machines
Owner: John Schroeder
CFO: Richard Jones
Chief Mechanical Engineer: Patrick Burton
Marketing: Sandy Delepovitz
Sales Manager: Matt Brown
jschroeder@ssmci.com
Public Relations: Sandy Delepovit
Operations: David Barriello
Estimated Sales: $1 Million
Number Employees: 5-9
Square Footage: 160000
Type of Packaging: Private Label
Brands:
Formnumatic
Quadnumatic

28949 Schroter, USA
508 Clinton Street
Defiance, OH 43512-2635
419-782-2430
Fax: 419-784-9717
Air pollution control and environmental services,
drying rooms, ovens, smokehouses, refrigeration
systems, tempering systems and accessories

28950 Schubert Packaging Systems
4505 Excel Pkwy
Addison, TX 75001-5677
972-233-6665
Fax: 972-233-3422 sales@schubertpackaging.com
www.schubertpackaging.com
Casing equipment, packers
Manager: Doug Granowski
Head of Sales: Gerald Grad
Contact: Wolfgang Haas
whaas@schubertpackaging.com
Estimated Sales: $500,000-$1 Million
Number Employees: 10-19

28951 Schurman's Wisconsin Cheese Country
1401 Hwy 23 North
Dodgeville, WI 53533
608-935-5741
Fax: 608-794-2194
dodgeville@schurmanscheese.com
www.schurmanscheese.com
Broker of health foods, natural cheeses, packaging and private label items
President: Lorraine Schurman
CEO: Jim Morgan
CFO: Jim Morgan
R&D: John Schurman
Quality Control: Jim Morgan
Estimated Sales: $10 - 20 Million
Number Employees: 20-49
Type of Packaging: Private Label

28952 Schutte Buffalo Hammermill
61 Depot St
Buffalo, NY 14206-2203
716-855-1555
Fax: 716-855-3417 800-447-4634
info@hammermills.com www.hammermills.com
Hammer mills including crushers, pulverizers, and grinders .
Owner: Tom Warne
warne@hammermills.com
General Manager/Co-Owner: Jim Guarino
Estimated Sales: $5 - 10 Million
Number Employees: 20-49
Square Footage: 100000

28953 Schwaab, Inc
11415 W. Burleigh Street
Milwaukee, WI 53222
Fax: 800-935-9866 800-935-9877
schwaab@schwaab.com www.schwaab.com
Rubber and steel stamps, corporate and notary seals and name plates
President, Chief Executive Officer: Doug Lane
Vice President and Controller: Bill Yentz
Vice President and Controller: Bill Yentz
VP Sales: Sara Wagner
Contact: Pamela Bielmeier
bielmeier@schwaab.com
Chief Operating Officer: Jeremiah McNeal
Estimated Sales: Below $5 Million
Number Employees: 100-249

28954 Schwab Paper Products Co
636 Schwab Cir
Romeoville, IL 60446-1144
815-372-2233
Fax: 815-372-1701 800-837-7225
info@schwabpaper.com www.schwabpaper.com
Manufacturer and exporter of layerboards, wax paper and steak paper for bakery, confectionery, frozen meat, seafood and poultry packaging
President: Kathy Schwab
CEO: Michael Schwab
mike@schwabpaper.com
Estimated Sales: Below $5 Million
Number Employees: 1-4
Square Footage: 120000
Brands:
Econo-Board
Frees-It
Ovenable
Quilon Bakeable Paper

28955 Schwartz Manufacturing Co
1000 School St
PO Box 328
Two Rivers, WI 54241-3533
920-793-1375
Fax: 920-793-2235 service@schwartzmfg.com
www.schwartzmfg.com
Filters and filter systems for the dairy, food, beverage and brewery industries.
Sales Exec: Alessandra Schwartz
Number Employees: 20-49

28956 Schwarz Supply Source
8338 Austin Ave
Morton Grove, IL 60053
800-323-4903
info@schwarz.com www.schwarz.com
Food service packaging including take-out and pizza boxes.

President: Andy McKenna
Vice President: Kevin Pittner
Vice President, Sales: Dan Arkus
Year Founded: 1907
Estimated Sales: $100-500 Million
Number Employees: 250-499

28957 Schwerdtel Corporation
530 van Buren Street
Ridgewood, NJ 7450
201-485-8160
Fax: 201-485- 815 www.schwerdtel.de
Automatic filling machines for sealants and food concentrates
President & CFO: Cay Werner
Senior Sales Manager: Florian Mendheim
Estimated Sales: $1 - 2.5 Million
Number Employees: 1-4

28958 Scienco Systems
3240 N Broadway
Saint Louis, MO 63147-3515
314-621-2536
Fax: 314-621-1952 www.sciencofast.com
Manufacturer and exporter of food and preservative tablets, oil/water separators, grease traps and waste water treatment equipment
General Manager: Jim Predeau
Sales Manager: Gary Wotli
Estimated Sales: $2.5 - 5 Million
Number Employees: 10-19
Parent Co: Smith Loveless

28959 Scientech, Inc
5649 Arapahoe Ave
Boulder, CO 80303-1399
303-444-1361
Fax: 303-444-9229 800-525-0522
inst@scientech-inc.com www.scientech-inc.com
Electronic balances and scales
President: Tom O'Rourke
VP/COO: Tom Campbell
Contact: Mike Brunner
mbrunner@scientech-inc.com
Estimated Sales: $2 Million
Number Employees: 10-19
Number of Brands: 6
Number of Products: 75
Square Footage: 52000
Brands:
Astral Laser Power
Mentor Laser Power
Sa Analytical
Sg General
Sl Laboratory
Sp Precision
Synergy Laser Power
Ultra Laser Power
Vector Laser Power

28960 Scientific Fire Prevention
47-25 34th Street
Suite 203
Long Island City, NY 11101
718-433-3880
Fax: 718-433-0652 sales@scientificfire.com
www.scientificfire.com
Fire prevention and exhaust systems; also, indoor air quality testing services available
President: Roy Leonard
Marketing Director: Jeffrey Schwartz
Contact: Brian Higgins
brian@scientificfire.com

28961 Scientific Process & Research
P.O. Box 5008
Kendall Park, NJ 08824-5008
732-846-3477
Fax: 732-846-3029 800-868-4777
www.spar.com
Manufacturer and exporter of extruder, timing and conveyor screws and extruder barrels; exporter of extruder screws and software
Production Manager: Felicia Cappo
Estimated Sales: $2.5-5 Million
Number Employees: 10-19
Square Footage: 80000

28962 Scope Packaging
PO Box 3768
Orange, CA 92857
714-998-4411
Fax: 714-998-5323
Manufacturer and exporter of corrugated boxes

President: Michael Flinn
VP Marketing: Cindy Baker
Contact: Christine Maple
christinem@scopepackaging.com
Estimated Sales: $20-50 Million
Number Employees: 50-99
Type of Packaging: Bulk

28963 (HQ)Scorpio Apparel
3318 Commercial Avenue
Northbrook, IL 60062-1909
847-559-3100
Fax: 847-559-3103 800-559-3338
Manufacturer and exporter of uniforms
President: Allan L Klein
CEO: Lew Klein
Vice President: Carolyn Philips
Sales Director: Juli Shapiro
Estimated Sales: $2 Million
Number Employees: 34
Square Footage: 14000
Type of Packaging: Private Label
Other Locations:
Scorpio Products
Chicago IL
Brands:
9th Wave
Scorpio
Vespron

28964 Scot Young Research LTD
503 Renick St
St Joseph, MO 64501-3660
816-233-4898
Fax: 816-232-3701 www.syrclean.com
Manufacturer and exporter of ergonomic and color coded mopping systems
General Manager: Myong Stracener
Contact: Jamie Carpentier
jamie.carpentier@syrclean.com
Estimated Sales: Less Than $500,000
Number Employees: 1-4
Brands:
Syr

28965 Scotsman Beverage System
2007 Royal Lane
Suite 100
Dallas, TX 75229-3279
972-488-1030
Fax: 972-243-8075 800-527-7422
Parent Co: ENODIS

28966 Scotsman Ice Systems
101 Corporate Woods Pkwy.
Vernon Hills, IL 60061
847-215-4500
Fax: 847-913-9844 800-726-8762
customer.relations@scotsman-ice.com
www.scotsman-ice.com
Ice machines including flakers and nugget makers and hotel dispensing bins, drink dispensers, water filtration systems, etc.
President: Kevin Clark
CFO: Jo Rendino
Estimated Sales: $92 Million
Number Employees: 800
Square Footage: 36000
Parent Co: Scotsman Industries
Type of Packaging: Consumer, Food Service
Other Locations:
Scotsman Ice Systems
La Verne CA
Brands:
Cm3 Cubers
Dc33 Luxury
Fme Flakers
Nme Nugget
Scotsman
Slim Line Cubers
Tde Dispensers

28967 Scott & Daniells
264 Freestone Ave
Portland, CT 06480-1640
860-342-1932
Fax: 860-342-2436
Folding cartons
VP: Robert Papa
VP Operations: Kevin Robrge
Plant Manager: Robert Papa
Estimated Sales: $10-20 Million
Number Employees: 50-99
Square Footage: 240000

28968 Scott Equipment Co
605 4th Ave NW
New Prague, MN 56071-1121
952-758-2591
Fax: 952-758-4377 800-264-9519
dave.lucas@scottequipment.com
www.scottequipment.com
Mixers, dryers, high speed blenders, size reduction, de-packaging, turbo dominator, and horizontal batch mixers, available in carbon or stainless steel
President: Dave Lucas
CEO: Richard Lucaas
IT: Joshua Lucas
joshua.lucas@gmail.com
Estimated Sales: $20 - 50 Million
Number Employees: 50-99

28969 Scott Group
10801 Corkscrew Rd # 336
Estero, FL 33928-9451
239-949-2252
Fax: 239-949-0346 www.chicos.com
Services and marketing communication
Managing Partner: Stephen Scott
Estimated Sales: $3 - 5 Million
Number Employees: 10-19

28970 Scott Laboratories Inc
2220 Pine View Way
Petaluma, CA 94954-5687
707-765-6666
Fax: 707-765-6674 800-797-2688
info@scottlabsltd.com www.scottlab.com
Wine industry equipment and supplies
President/Owner: Bruce Scott
Senior Vice President: Tom Anders
Sales Representative: Peter Anderson
Vice President of Sales: Bob Fithian
Vice President of Operations: Bruce Edwards
Estimated Sales: $5 - 10 Million
Number Employees: 50-99

28971 Scott Packaging Corporation
340 N 12th St
Philadelphia, PA 19107-1102
215-925-5595
Packaging products including thermoformed trays, blisters and clamshells
Owner: Scott Page
Estimated Sales: $300,000-500,000
Number Employees: 1-4
Square Footage: 24000
Parent Co: Supplies Unlimited

28972 Scott Pallets Inc
8660 Crowder St
Amelia Court Hse, VA 23002
804-561-2514
Fax: 804-561-2664 800-394-2514
www.scottpalletsinc.com
Wooden pallets
President: Joanne Scottwebb
scottpallets@tds.net
Quality Control: Joanne Scott
Manager: Ray Hoerger
Estimated Sales: $2.5 - 5 Million
Number Employees: 10-19
Square Footage: 40000
Brands:
Gma
Gpc

28973 Scott Process Equipment& Controls
15 Southgate Drive
Guelph, ON N1G 3M5
Canada
519-836-6902
Fax: 519-836-3325 888-343-5421
info@scottpec.com www.scottpec.com
Processing equipment and controls.
President: Ladislav Rudik
Estimated Sales: $1.3 Million
Number Employees: 5
Square Footage: 4855

28974 Scott Sign Systems
7525 Pennsylvania Ave # C
PO Box 1047
Sarasota, FL 34243-5065
941-355-5171
Fax: 941-351-1787 800-237-9447
mail@scottsigns.com www.scottsigns.com

Manufactures signs and sign systems including letters, logos, graphics and architectural signs.
President: Steve Evans
Cio/Cto: Maurice Aguinaldo
mauricea@scottsigns.com
Estimated Sales: $1-5 Million
Number Employees: 20-49
Square Footage: 150000
Parent Co: Identity Group
Brands:
Brailldots
Braillplaques
Scotslants
Scott-A.D.A.'s Brailleters
Scott-Elites
Scott-Thins
Scott-Trax
Snap-Ins
Tabbee

28975 Scott Turbon Mixer
9351 Industrial Way
Adelanto, CA 92301-3932
760-246-3430
Fax: 760-246-3505 800-285-8512
sales@scottmixer.com www.haywardgordon.com
Manufacturer and exporter of sanitary mixing equipment for dairy, beverage and meat; also, complete systems including tanks, platforms and piping, lab and pilot plant mixers
Owner: William Scott
bill@scottmixer.com
Sales Director: Tim Moore
Estimated Sales: $1 - 5 Million
Number Employees: 20-49
Square Footage: 50000
Brands:
Scott Turbon

28976 Scott Turbon Mixer
9351 Industrial Way
Adelanto, CA 92301-3932
760-246-3430
Fax: 760-246-3505 800-285-8512
sales@scottmixer.com www.haywardgordon.com
Owner: William Scott
bill@scottmixer.com
Estimated Sales: $5 - 10 Million
Number Employees: 20-49

28977 (HQ)Scott's Liquid Gold-Inc
4880 Havana St # 400
Denver, CO 80239-2432
303-373-4860
Fax: 303-576-6151 800-447-1919
www.scottsliquidgold.com
Household and industrial polishes and air fresheners
Chairman of the Board: Mark Goldstin
CEO: Mark E Goldstein
mgoldstein@slginc.com
R&D and Quality Control: Sharon Moore
CEO: Mark E Goldstein
VP Marketing: Jeff Hinkle
Sales Operations Manager: Linda Melphy
Estimated Sales: $20 - 30 Million
Number Employees: 50-99
Brands:
Touch of Scent

28978 Scranton Lace Company
PO Box 121
Forest City, PA 18421
570-344-1124
Fax: 570-344-1125 800-822-1036
slclace@icontech.com
Cotton and lace tablecloths, window curtains, place mats and accessories
President: Robert Hyne
CEO: Jennifer Herman
VP Sales: Carol Rabe
Office Manager/EDI COOrd: Wendy Yannuzzi
Estimated Sales: $10-20 Million
Number Employees: 50-99
Square Footage: 1200000
Parent Co: Jerry's SportCenter
Brands:
Black Tie Collection
Classic Home Collection

28979 Screen Print Etc
1081 N Shepard St # E
Anaheim, CA 92806-2819
714-630-1100
Fax: 714-630-3719

Display and exhibit boards, decals, flags, pennants, banners and signs; also, commercial printing, graphic design and plastic printing services available
Owner: Ray Lynch
rlynch@screenprintetc.com
Estimated Sales: $530 Million
Number Employees: 5-9
Square Footage: 4000
Type of Packaging: Private Label, Bulk

28980 (HQ)Screw Conveyor Corp
700 Hoffman St
Hammond, IN 46327-1827
219-931-1450
Fax: 219-931-0209 sales@screwconveyor.com
Screw conveyors and accessories, elevator buckets, industrial and grain bucket elevators, hydraulic truck dumpers, screw lifts, tube screws and belt conveyor idlers
Owner: Garry M Abraham
sales@screwconveyor.com
Manager of Engineering & Procurement: Steve Rauhut
VP Marketing/Sales: Randy Block
Sales Manager: Anita Kozlowski
Customer Service Supervisor/Sales Engine: Robert Belko
Senior Applications Engineer: Barry Stacy
Estimated Sales: $10 - 20 Million
Number Employees: 20-49
Other Locations:
SCC Industries
Guadalajara, Jal.
Brands:
Enduro-Flo
Enduro-Roll
Exacta-Flo
Kewanee
Rigid-Flo
Screw-Lift
Super-Flo

28981 Scrivner Equipment Co Inc
1811 Hopoca Rd
Carthage, MS 39051-9449
601-267-7614
Industrial equipment and supplies
Owner: Martin Scrivner
pscrivnerequipco@aol.com
Estimated Sales: $200,000
Number Employees: 1-4
Square Footage: 2625

28982 Scroll Compressors LLC
1675 Campbell Rd
Sidney, OH 45365-2479
937-498-3011
Fax: 937-498-3203 www.emersonclimate.com
Manufacturer and exporter of compressors for air conditioning and refrigeration
President: Tom Bettcher
Number Employees: 10-19
Type of Packaging: Food Service
Brands:
Copeland

28983 Se Kure Controls Inc
3714 Runge St
Franklin Park, IL 60131-1112
847-288-1111
Fax: 847-288-9999 800-250-9260
info@se-kure.com www.se-kure.com
Manufacturer, importer and exporter of safes, vaults, security mirrors and cameras and anti-shoplifting devices
Founder/President/CEO: Roger Leyden
rogerleyden@se-kure.com
Executive VP Administration & Finance: Laura Greenwell
National Sales Manager: John Mangiameli
Estimated Sales: $20-50 Million
Number Employees: 100-249
Number of Products: 500
Square Footage: 200000

28984 Sea Breeze Fruit Flavors
441 Main Road
Towaco, NJ 07082
800-732-2733
info@seabreezesyrups.com
www.seabreezesyrups.com

Syrups including chocolate, pancake and milkshake; sundae toppings, bar mixes, juice concentrates, soda, iced tea, lemonade, fruit juice, flavored water and beverage dispensing equipment.
President: Steve Sanders
Vice President: Josh Sanders
Technical Director: Frank Maranino
Year Founded: 1925
Estimated Sales: $20-50 Million
Number Employees: 50-99
Number of Brands: 6
Type of Packaging: Consumer, Food Service, Private Label
Brands:
Bosco
Joshua Miguel
New York Bash
Sea Breeze
Toshimi
Tropic Beach

28985 Sea Gull Lighting Products, LLC
306 Elizabeth Lane
Corona, CA 92880-2504
951-273-7380
Fax: 800-877-4855 800-347-5483
Info@SeaGullLighting.com
www.seagulllighting.com
Lighting fixtures
Vice President, Marketing: Ace Rosenstein
Estimated Sales: $1-2.5 Million
Number Employees: 5-9

28986 Seaboard Bag Corporation
3412 Moore St
Richmond, VA 23230-4444
Fax: 804-355-9100
Multi-walled and pasted paper valve bags
Owner: Jim Edge
Estimated Sales: $10-20 Million
Number Employees: 50-99
Parent Co: Morgan Brothers Bag Company

28987 Seaboard Carton Company
1140 31st Street
Downers Grove, IL 60515-1212
708-344-0575
Fax: 708-344-4058
Folding cartons
Estimated Sales: $10-20 Million
Number Employees: 50-99
Square Footage: 180000

28988 Seaboard Folding Box Corp
35 Daniels St
Fitchburg, MA 01420-7606
978-342-8921
Fax: 978-342-1105 800-255-6313
info@seaboardbox.com www.seaboardbox.com
Manufacturer and exporter of paper boxes
President: Alan Rabinow
CEO: Allen Rabinow
allen.rabinow@jordanind.com
Number Employees: 100-249

28989 Seaga Manufacturing Inc
700 Seaga Dr
Freeport, IL 61032-9644
815-297-9500
Fax: 815-297-1700 info@seaga.com
www.seaga.com
Vending equipment for cold beverage merchandisers, soda and beverage vendors, e-cigarette vending equipment, custom vending equipment
President: Steven Chesney
schesney@seagamfg.com
Chairman of the Board and Owner: Steven Chesney
Estimated Sales: $30 - 50 Million
Number Employees: 100-249
Parent Co: Seaga Manufacturing

28990 Seajoy
6619 S Dixie Hwy
PO Box 344
Miami, FL 33143
305-669-0108
Fax: 302-663-0312 877-537-1717
www.seajoy.com
Shrimp including raw head-on whole shrimp, raw shell-on tails, raw shell-on E-Z peel meats, raw peeled & deveined tail on or off, uncut, raw peeled, butterfly meat, raw breaded shrimp meat, and raw peeled & deveined meat on skewers

Administrative President: Peder Jacobson
VP Sales & Operations: Brad Price
Estimated Sales: $220 Thousand
Brands:
Bluefield
Cjoy
Seabrook
Seajoy

28991 Seal King North America
21720 Hamburg ave
Lakeville, MN 55044
952-469-6639
Fax: 803-364-5008 800-582-4372
info@sealking.com www.sealking.com
Bag sealing tape, double coated foam tapes, tissue tapes and polyester tape, spooled tapes, fingerlift tapes for plastic and paper envelopes and siliconised release liners
President/Founder: Ben Nelson
Contact: Cheryl Alben
cheryl.alben@medtronic.com
Number Employees: 12

28992 Seal Pac USA
5901 School Ave
Richmond, VA 23228-5447
804-261-0580
Fax: 804-261-0581 info@sealpac-us.com
Distributor of tray sealers
Number Employees: 1-4

28993 Seal Science Inc
17131 Daimler St
Irvine, CA 92614-5508
949-251-1832
Fax: 949-253-3141 800-576-7325
westernsales@sealscience.com
www.sealscience.com
Manufactures gaskets, molded rubber products, engineered seal systems, O-rings, teflon seals, vacuum cups and diaphragms; custom plastic machining
CEO: Rick Tuliper
rickt@sealscience.com
Marketing/Sales: Doug Albin
Purchasing Manager: Christy Seastedt
Estimated Sales: $5-10 Million
Number Employees: 100-249
Square Footage: 25000
Parent Co: Seal Science East

28994 Seal the Seasons
501 W Franklin St
Suite 106
Chapel Hill, NC 27516
919-245-3535
Fax: 919-930-8970 hello@sealtheseasons.com
www.sealtheseasons.com
Frozen produce
Founder & CEO: Patrick Mateer
Controller: Dawn Paffenroth
Chief Sales Officer: Jonathan Mills
COO: Alex Piasecki
Number Employees: 2-10
Brands:
Seal the Seasons

28995 Seal-A-Tron Corp
3815 SE Naef Rd
Portland, OR 97267-5615
503-652-5200
Fax: 503-652-5205 800-487-3257
drehs@seal-a-tron.com www.seal-a-tron.com
Industrial shrink wrap equipment
Owner: Warner Duemmer
wduemmer@seal-a-tron.com
Technical Assistance: Werner Duemmer
Customer Service Officer: John Borich
Estimated Sales: Below $5 Million
Number Employees: 10-19

28996 Seal-O-Matic Corp
2542 Humbug Creek Rd
Jacksonville, OR 97530-9618
541-846-1000
Fax: 541-846-1004 800-631-2072
info@sealomatic.com www.sealomatic.net
Manufacturer, importer and exporter of shrink wrap and packaging equipment including gummed tape dispensers, safety knives, shipping room equipment, price labeling guns, staplers, staples, etc

President: Mel Ortner
Vice President: Janine Ortner
Marketing Director: Greg Sparre
Contact: Janine Ortner
janine@sealomatic.com
Purchasing Manager: Kim Westmoreland
Estimated Sales: $1 - 3 Million
Number Employees: 10-19
Square Footage: 10000
Brands:
Flash
Labelmaster
Lewis
Pricemaster

28997 Seal-Tite Bag Company
4324 Tackawanna St
Philadelphia, PA 19124
717-917-1949
Fax: 215-288-5664
Transparent and flexible packaging, plastic and heat sealed and plastic bags; also, plastic film and poly labels
Estimated Sales: $1-2.5 Million
Number Employees: 8
Brands:
Seal-Tite

28998 Sealed Air Corp
2415 Cascade Pointe Boulevard
Charlotte, NC 28208
980-430-7000
800-391-5645
www.sealedair.com
Flexible plastic packaging materials including film, food packaging and shrink wrap. the inventors of Bubble Wrap.
Chairman/Chief Executive Officer: Ted Doheny
SVP/Chief Supply Chain Officer: Emile Chammas
SVP/Chief Financial Officer: Jim Sullivan
VP/Chief Human Resources Officer: Susan Edwards
SVP/Chief Commercial Officer: Karl Deily
VP/General Counsel/Secretary: Angel Willis
VP/Chief Strategy Officer: Sergio Pupkin
Year Founded: 1960
Estimated Sales: $4.7 Billion
Number Employees: 15,500

28999 Sealeze Inc
8000 Whitepine Rd
N Chesterfield, VA 23237-2263
804-743-0982
Fax: 804-271-3428 800-787-7325
www.sealeze.com
Strip brush for selaing out debris, shielding, guiding on conveyors, positioning products during production and static dissipation.
President: Molly Kent
kentm@jacksonlea.com
Number Employees: 20-49

29000 Sealstrip Corp
103 Industrial Dr
Gilbertsville, PA 19525-8832
610-367-6282
Fax: 610-367-7727 888-658-7997
hhartmann@tearstripsystems.com
www.tearstripsystems.com
Shrinkable teartape, shrink tape applicators, resealable bags and systems
Owner: Harold Forman
hforman@sealstrip.com
Manufacturing Manager: Jacob Greth
Estimated Sales: $2.5-5 Million
Number Employees: 50-99

29001 Sealstrip Corporation
200 N Washington St
Boyertown, PA 19512-1115
610-367-6282
Fax: 610-367-7727 www.sealstrip.com
Manufacturer and exporter of resealable packaging equipment and materials
President: Joanne Forman
Owner: Harold Forman
R&D: Ajrlod Forman
Sales: Heather Hartman
Manufacturing Manager: Jacob Greth
Estimated Sales: Below $5 Million
Number Employees: 20-49
Square Footage: 28000
Brands:
Everfresh
Fresh Pak

Sealstrip
Serv & Seal

29002 SeamTech
24231 Fuhrman Rd
Acampo, CA 95220-9766

209-464-4610
Fax: 209-464-1438 www.seamtechpk.com
Service parts and sales of fillers, seamers and warehouse equipment
President: Pete Saavedra
CFO: Pete Saavedra
Quality Control: Jason Saavedra
Estimated Sales: Below $5 Million
Number Employees: 5

29003 Search West
PO Box 641609
Los Angeles, CA 90064-6609

310-203-9797
Executive search firm recruiting middle to upper level managers, professionals and executives in sales, administrative and technical areas
President: Bob Cowan
Estimated Sales: $500,000-$1 Million
Number Employees: 50-100

29004 Season Harvest Foods
4906 El Camino Real # 206
Suite 206
Los Altos, CA 94022-1444

650-968-2273
Fax: 877-413-3894
sales@seasonharvestfoods.com
www.seasonharvestfoods.com
Organic vegetable and spice supplier.

29005 Seasons 4 Inc
4500 Industrial Access Rd
Douglasville, GA 30134-3949

770-489-5405
Fax: 770-489-2938 jkodobocz@seasons4.net
www.seasons4.net
Manufacturer and exporter of custom engineered HVAC systems for supermarkets
President: Lewis Watford
lwatford@seasons4.net
VP Sales: Todd Smith
Purchasing Manager: Rick Rothschild
Estimated Sales: $50 - 100 Million
Number Employees: 250-499
Square Footage: 145000

29006 Seatex Ltd
445 TX-36
Rosenberg, TX 77471

713-357-5300
Fax: 713-357-5301 800-829-3020
kaimes@seatexcorp.com www.seatexcorp.com
Providers of turn key chemical compounding, toll manufacturing and private label packaging services. Areas of expertise included the food service, food processing, automotive, institutional and industrial laundry, janitorialindustrial and oilfield service markets.
President/CEO: Jim Nattier
CFO: John Nowak
VP: Kelly Aimes
R&D: Don Trepel
Director QA/QC: Don Trepel
Sales/Marketing: Tom Austin
Sales/Marketing: Kelly Aimes
Contact: Deneen Case
dcase@seatexcorp.com
Operations/Production: Dan Boone
Warehouse/Logistics: Jim Dockery
VP Purchasing: Larry Brown
Estimated Sales: $26 Million
Number Employees: 85
Number of Products: 400
Square Footage: 220000
Type of Packaging: Consumer, Food Service, Private Label, Bulk

29007 Seating Concepts Inc
125 Connell Ave
Rockdale, IL 60436-2466

815-730-7980
Fax: 815-730-7969 800-421-2036
sales@seating-concepts.com
www.seating-concepts.com
Manufacturer and exporter of chairs, booths, cafeteria counters, tables and waste receptacles; importer of chairs

Owner: Marianne Dieter
Sales Director: Chris Mazzoni
mdieter@travstor.com
Estimated Sales: $3,000,000
Number Employees: 50-99
Type of Packaging: Food Service

29008 Seattle Boiler Works Inc
500 S Myrtle St
Seattle, WA 98108-3495

206-762-0737
Fax: 206-762-3516 www.seattleboiler.com
Manufacturer and exporter of boilers, heat exchangers and pressure vessels; also, stainless steel fabrication, pipe and tube bending services available
Owner: Craig Hopkins
chopkins@seattleboiler.com
VP: Craig Hopkins
Quality Control: Craig Hopkins
Estimated Sales: $5-10 Million
Number Employees: 20-49
Square Footage: 140000
Type of Packaging: Bulk

29009 Seattle Menu Specialists
5844 South 194th Street
Kent, WA 98032

206-784-2340
Fax: 206-782-7778 800-622-2826
customerservice@seattlemenu.com
www.seattlemenu.com
Manufacturer and designer of menu, wine and guest check covers and placemats; exporter of menu covers
President: Dale Phelps
Operations Manager: Lonnie Axtell
Purchasing Manager: George Rought
Estimated Sales: Below $5 Million
Number Employees: 10
Brands:
Duracrafic

29010 Seattle Plastics
309 S Cloverdale St # E7
#E7
Seattle, WA 98108-4591

206-233-0869
Fax: 206-233-0874 800-441-0679
info@seattleplastics.com www.seattleplastics.com
Display cases, bagel and coffe bins and lid holders; also, custom fabrication available
President: Mike Albanese
info@seattleplastics.com
Estimated Sales: $1-2,500,000
Number Employees: 5-9

29011 Seattle Refrigeration &Manufacturing
1057 S Director St
Seattle, WA 98108

206-762-7740
Fax: 206-762-1730 800-228-8881
Manufacturer and importer of compressors, pressure vessels, belt and spiral freezers, condensers, heat exchangers, ice makers, chillers, freezers, hoses, pumps, etc.; importer of compressors, plate freezers and valves; exporter ofcompressors, and ice makers
President: Tracy Abbott
R&D: Frank Kanpp
Quality Control: Bob Petersen
Service Manager: Don Irons
Estimated Sales: $5 - 10 Million
Number Employees: 10-19
Square Footage: 30600
Parent Co: Seattle Refrigeration
Brands:
Alco
Asme
C.P.
Carrier
Copeland
Dunham-Bush
Eagle Signal
F.E.S.
Frick
Fuller
Grasso
Henry
Howden
Howe
Johnson (Penn)
Paragon
Ranco
Sabroe

Shank
Sporian
Sullair
Tecumseh
Vitter
Wolf Linde
York

29012 Seattle's Best Coffee
18870 103rd Avenue
Vashon, WA 98070-5229

206-463-5050
Fax: 206-463-5764
Tea and coffee industry, bags (brick packs, flexible, and valve packs)
Estimated Sales: $1-5 Million
Number Employees: 6

29013 Seattle-Tacoma Box Co
23400 71st Pl S
Kent, WA 98032-2994

253-854-9700
Fax: 253-852-0891 info@seattlebox.com
www.seattlebox.com
Manufacturer and exporter of wooden produce and corrugated boxes
Vice President: Michael Nist
mike@seattlebox.com
Marketing Director: Rob Nist
Estimated Sales: $30 - 50 Million
Number Employees: 20-49

29014 Seattle-Tacoma Box Co
23400 71st Pl S
Kent, WA 98032-2994

253-854-9700
Fax: 253-852-0891 www.seattlebox.com
Custom designed corrugated boxes and wood boxes. Skids, pallets, wooden containers, plastic bags, styrofoam and other packaging supplies.
Owner: Jacob Nist
Vice President: Michael J Nist
mike@seattlebox.com
Sales: Joseph Nist
Number Employees: 20-49

29015 Sebesta Blomberg & Assoc
2381 Rosegate
Roseville, MN 55113-2625

651-634-0775
877-706-6858
info@sebesta.com www.lionbrand.com
President: James Sebesta
Contact: Rob Costello
rcostello@sebesta.com
Number Employees: 1-4
Square Footage: 160000

29016 Sebring Container Corporation
PO Box 359
Salem, OH 44460

330-332-1533
Fax: 330-332-2205
Flat corrugated containers
President: William Mc Devitt
Sales Manager: John Berlin
Contact: Amy Cannon
a.cannon@sebringcontainer.com
Estimated Sales: $10-20 Million
Number Employees: 20-49

29017 Seco Industries
6858 E Acco St
Commerce, CA 90040-1902

323-726-9721
Fax: 323-726-9776 sales@seco-ind.com
www.gramatech.com
Barrier packaging, heat sealing equipment, and vacuum sealers
CEO: Charles De Heras
randy@seco-ind.com
Vice President: Jerome Druss
Estimated Sales: $5-10 Million
Number Employees: 20-49
Square Footage: 120000

29018 Seco Industries
6858 E Acco St
Commerce, CA 90040-1902

323-726-9721
Fax: 323-726-9776 sales@seco-ind.com
www.gramatech.com
CEO: Charles De Heras
randy@seco-ind.com

Estimated Sales: $1 - 5 Million
Number Employees: 20-49

29019 Security Link
816 N Gilbert Street
Danville, IL 61832
217-446-4871
Fax: 309-685-7161
Alarm systems
General Manager: Deborah Morris
dmorris@adt.com
Estimated Sales: Less than $500,000
Number Employees: 1-4

29020 Security Packaging
PO Box 892
North Bergen, NJ 07047-0892
201-854-1955
Fax: 201-854-1978
Corrugated boxes
President: Norbert Mester
Estimated Sales: $1-2.5 Million
Number Employees: 5-9
Square Footage: 3000

29021 Sedalia Janitorial & Paper Supplies
4211 S 65 Highway
Sedalia, MO 65301
660-826-9899
Janitorial and paper supplies
Estimated Sales: $1 - 5 Million
Number Employees: 1

29022 Sedex Kinkos
PO Box 1198
Tualatin, OR 97062-1198
503-692-3550
Fax: 503-692-1860 800-800-6271
www.fineartsgraphics.com
Wine industry label printing
Estimated Sales: $5-10 Million
Number Employees: 10

29023 Sediment Testing Equipment
7366 N Greenview Ave
Chicago, IL 60626-1924
773-465-3634
Fax: 773-465-4309 800-853-7323
info@sedimenttesting.com
www.sedimenttesting.com
Sediment testing equipment and supplies recommended for scorch-particles testing of reconstituted nonfat dry milk and coffee, determining sediment or extraneous matter in milk products and batch sample testing when quality-controlstandards have been est
President: Kathleen S Fox
Estimated Sales: $.5 - 1 million
Number Employees: 1-4

29024 Seeds of Change
P.O. Box 4908
Rancho Dominguez, CA 90220
888-762-7333
www.seedsofchange.com
Organic, non-GMO seeds of herbs and vegetables.
Co-Founder: Alan Kapuler
CEO: Kafi Dixon
Year Founded: 1989
Estimated Sales: $58 Million
Number Employees: 120
Parent Co: Mars, Inc.

29025 Seepex Inc
511 Speedway Dr
Enon, OH 45323-1057
937-864-7150
Fax: 937-864-7157 800-695-3659
sales@seepex.net www.seepex.com
Designs, manufactures, and sells Progressive Cavity Pumps and Pump accessories.
President: Michael Dillon
CEO: Florencio Alvarez
falvarez@seepex.com
VP: Francis Harris
R&D: Mathew Brown
Quality Control: Robert Mentz
Marketing/Public Relations: Daniel Lakovic
Director, Sales: Mark Murphy
Product Manager: Joe Zinck
Purchasing: Robert Mentz
Estimated Sales: $30 Million
Number Employees: 250-499
Number of Brands: 1

Number of Products: 1000
Square Footage: 40000
Parent Co: Seepex
Brands:
Map
Seepex
Tricam

29026 Sefar
111 Calumet St
Depew, NY 14043-3734
716-683-4050
Fax: 716-683-4053 www.sefar.us
President: David Koebcke
david.koebcke@sefar.us
CEO: Art Alex
R & D: Richard Gaiser
Number Employees: 50-99

29027 Sefi Fabricators Inc
50 Ranick Dr E
PO Box 338
Amityville, NY 11701-2822
631-842-2200
Fax: 631-842-2203 info@sefifabricators.com
www.imcteddy.com
Custom stainless steel food service equipment, countertops, cabinets, floordrains, lab furniture, shelving, grating sinks and tables
President: Asit Majumdar
imcteddy@aol.com
Sales Manager: Louis Stanley
Sales Engineer: Barry Greene
Customer Service: Maria Fernandez
Estimated Sales: $2.5-5 Million
Number Employees: 20-49
Square Footage: 34000
Type of Packaging: Consumer, Food Service, Private Label, Bulk

29028 Seiberling Associates Inc
655 3rd St # 203
Suite 203
Beloit, WI 53511-6269
608-313-1235
Fax: 608-313-1275 craig.guyse@seiberling.com
Consultant providing engineering services and project management; also, installation and start-up services available
Vice President: Don Huett
don.huett@seiberling.com
CFO: Don Hewitt
VP: Don Huett
Estimated Sales: $2.5-5 Million
Number Employees: 20-49

29029 Seidenader Equipment
25 Hanover Rd # 210
Florham Park, NJ 07932-1424
973-301-9800
Fax: 973-301-9090 800-342-6910
www.seidenader.de
Manufacturers of fully automatic inspection machines for parental products, semi-automatic inspection machines, exterior vial washers, and tray loaders
Manager: Eileen Scanlon
Marketing Manager: Sara Savastano
Contact: Ed Chobanoff
echobanoff@svresearch.com
Estimated Sales: $500,000 - $1 Million
Number Employees: 1-4

29030 Seidman Brothers
25 6th St
Chelsea, MA 02150-2422
617-884-8110
Fax: 617-884-4284 800-437-7770
info@seidmanbros.com
Commercial kitchen exhaust systems. custom stainless steel, and distributors of food service equipment.
President: Allen Seidman
General Manager: Jack Seidman
Sales: Gina Venezia
Operations Manager: Rick Seidman
Estimated Sales: $5-10 Million
Number Employees: 10-19

29031 Seiler Plastics
9750 Reavis Park Dr
St Louis, MO 63123-5316
314-685-3267
Fax: 314-815-3025 888-673-4537
rjones@seilerpc.com www.seilerpc.com
Plastic products including tubing profiles, sheets, etc.; die cutting and thermoforming services available
Owner: John Sieler
VP: Paul Benson
Sales Manager: Paul Dyer
Contact: Paul Meyer
p.meyer@seilerpc.com
Estimated Sales: $5-10 Million
Number Employees: 10-19
Square Footage: 48000

29032 Seitz Memtec America Corporation
635 Shannon Corners Rd
Dundee, NY 14837-9158
607-243-7568
Fax: 607-243-5251
Wine industry equipment
Owner: Joe Gibson

29033 Seitz Schenk Filter Systems
2118 Greenspring Drive
Lutherville, MD 21093-3112
443-322-2494
Fax: 443-322-2496 877-716-8778
info@benelogic.com www.benelogic.com
Filters and filtration equipment
CEO: Matthew T Oros
Estimated Sales: $5-10 Million
Number Employees: 250-499

29034 Seitz Stainless Inc
17578 400th St
Avon, MN 56310-9735
320-746-2781
Fax: 320-746-2782 sales@seitzstainless.com
www.seitzstainless.com
Custom fabrication, dryers, spray, heat recovery systems, heat exchangers, pasteurizers, tubular
President: Jeff Haviland
sales@seitzstainless.com
Sales Exec: Nicole Hagman
Estimated Sales: $10-20 Million
Number Employees: 20-49

29035 Seiz Sign Co Inc
1231 Central Ave
Hot Spgs Natl Pk, AR 71901-6037
501-623-3181
Fax: 501-623-4594 david@seizsigns.com
www.seizsigns.com
Advertising signs
President: David Hamilton
VP & Billboard Sales: Tammy Hamilton
Office Manager: Shannon McLean
Estimated Sales: $1-2.5 Million
Number Employees: 10-19

29036 Sekisui TA Industries
100 S Puente St
Brea, CA 92821-3813
714-255-7888
Fax: 800-235-8273 800-258-8273
www.sta-tape.com
Manufacturer and exporter of FDA approved B.O.P.P. pressure sensitive tapes and semi and fully automatic carton sealing machinery
President: Ikusuke Shimizu
CEO: Ernest J Wong
CFO: Matt Minami
VP: Stephen J Wilson
R&D: Dinesh Shan
Marketing Administrator: Melissa Morris
Contact: Alison Barth
barth@cmu.edu
Plant Manager: C P Fang
Estimated Sales: $20 - 50 Million
Number Employees: 100-249
Square Footage: 185000
Parent Co: Sekisui Chemical
Brands:
Sta Series
Sta-Pack
Supreme

29037 Selby Sign Co Inc
2138 Bypass Rd
Pocomoke City, MD 21851-2756

410-742-0095
Fax: 410-957-1074 www.selbysign.com
Exterior and interior illuminated signs including
electronic message centers, time/temperature units,
neon, etc.; also, installation and maintainence
available
Owner: David Selby
  davidselby@selbysign.com
VP: Steve Selby
Production Manager: Doug Dryden
Estimated Sales: $1-2.5 Million
Number Employees: 20-49
Square Footage: 12000

29038 Selby/Ucrete IndustrialFlooring
26383 Broadway Ave
Cleveland, OH 44146-6516

440-232-6644
Fax: 216-839-8822 800-445-6182
Owner: Chuck Slaby
Estimated Sales: $1 - 5 Million
Number Employees: 1-4

29039 Selco Products Company
605 S East St
Anaheim, CA 92805-4842

714-917-1333
Fax: 714-917-1355 800-257-3526
sales@selcoproducts.com
www.selcoproducts.com
Selco offers mechanical and electronic temperature
controls, control knobs, and digital and analog panel
meters
CEO: Tim Wilkinson
Marketing Manager: Michelle Blakeslee
Sales Manager: Russell Kido
Estimated Sales: $5-10 Million
Number Employees: 50-99

29040 Select Appliance Sales,Inc.
159 West Harris Avenue
San Francisco, CA 94080

650-588-9100
Fax: 650-588-9108 888-235-0431
www.selectappliance.com
President: Russell Zipkin
Marketing Manager: Ming Chu
Estimated Sales: 3MM
Number Employees: 4

29041 Select Stainless
11145 Monroe Rd
PO Box 158
Matthews, NC 28105-6564

704-841-1090
Fax: 704-841-1590
generalinfo@selectstainless.com
www.selecthealthcareproducts.com
Owner: Benjamin Williams
Vice President: Mike Auten
President: Ben Williams
National Sales Manager: Doug Joyner
bwilliams@selectstainless.com
Estimated Sales: $3 - 5 Million
Number Employees: 100-249

29042 Select Technologies Inc
8093 Graphic Dr NE
Belmont, MI 49306-9448

616-866-6700
Fax: 616-866-6770 www.select-technologies.com
Designer, builder and installer of plant facility &
utility systems and production lines for processing
and material handling.
Owner: Eric Staley
ericstaley@select-technologies.com
Number Employees: 5-9

29043 Selective Foods
P.O. Box 446
Carnegie, PA 15106

412-458-1930
Fax: 412-458-1932 info@selectivefoods.net
www.selectivefoodmarketing.com
To help food manufacturers, operators and distribu-
tors succeed in the evolving Western Pennsylvania
market.
Partner/Sales: Ken Fisher
Partner/Sales: Susan Battaglia
Customer Service: Paula Sapienza
Square Footage: 3000

29044 Selecto
1400 Market Place Blvd # 109
Cumming, GA 30041-7925

770-205-0800
Fax: 770-448-7021
Tea and coffee industry, filtration equipment
Owner: Kirk Sherrill
Number Employees: 5-9

29045 (HQ)Selecto Scientific
3980 Lakefield Ct
Suwanee, GA 30024

678-475-0799
Fax: 678-475-1595 800-635-4017
Customer-service@selectoinc.com
www.selectoinc.com
Manufacturer and exporter of water filters for scale
reduction, taste and odor and sediment for fountain
dispensing equipment, coffee makers, ice equipment
and steamers
Owner: Terry Libin
Co-founder and CEO: Ehud Levy
Director R&D/QC: Cang Li
VP Sales/Marketing: Terry Libin
Contact: Alisha Kuzma
  alisha_kuzma@mckinsey.com
Purchasing Manager: Kenny Powell
Estimated Sales: $1 - 3 Million
Number Employees: 10-19
Square Footage: 136000
Brands:
  Leadout
  Supraplus
  Uptaste

29046 Selig Chemical Industries
1100 Spring St NW # 550
Atlanta, GA 30309-2848

404-876-5511
Fax: 404-875-2629 www.seligenterprises.com
Disinfectants, insecticides, household cleaners,
soaps, sanitizers and polishes
President: S Stephen Selig
Chief Financial Officer: Ronald J. Stein, CPA
Co-Owner & Senior Vice President: Cathy Selig
Director Marketing: Tom Graves
Estimated Sales: $5-10 Million
Number Employees: 50-99

29047 Sellers Cleaning Systems
420 3rd St
Piqua, OH 45356-3918

937-778-8947
Fax: 937-773-2238 seller@internetMCI.com
Wine industry, sanitation processing unit
Manager: Mike Kemp
Estimated Sales: $500,000-$1 Million
Number Employees: 250-499

29048 Sellers Engineering Division
PO Box 48
Danville, KY 40423-0048

859-236-3181
Fax: 859-236-3184
Manufacturer and exporter of boiler feed systems,
steam and hot water boilers, water heaters and
deaerators
President & Public Relations: G. Miller
CEO/CFO: S Miller
Controller: J. Sizemore
VP Research & Development: Bill Doughty
Quality Control: L Gambrel
Marketing Director: R Larson
Sales Director: R Larson
Production/Plant Manager: R Woolum
Plant Manager: R Woolum
Purchasing Manager: P Coffman
Estimated Sales: $20-50 Million
Number Employees: 78
Square Footage: 64000
Type of Packaging: Food Service
Other Locations:
  Sellers
  Dallas TX
  Weestern Engineering
  Danville KY
Brands:
  Sellers

29049 Selma Wire Products Company
County Road 700 E
Selma, IN 47383

765-282-3532
Fax: 765-282-4428

Wire store display racks
Estimated Sales: $1-2.5 Million
Number Employees: 20-49
Parent Co: Mid-West Metal Products Company

29050 Selo
196 120th Ave # A
Holland, MI 49424-3309

616-392-7849
Fax: 616-392-2262
Equipment for materials handling, processing,
slaughtering and temperature control
Owner: Paul Sale
Estimated Sales: $1 - 5 Million
Number Employees: 5-9

29051 Semanco International
500 Clanton Road
Suite H
Charlotte, NC 28217-1310

704-527-9010
Fax: 704-527-8290
Electronic process evaluation systems for soft drink
bottlers, bottling lines, all blended products, wine
processing, packaging lines and fruit and juices
Number Employees: 20-49

29052 Semco Manufacturing Company
705 E Us Highway 83
PO Box 1686
Pharr, TX 78577

956-787-4203
Fax: 956-781-0620 semcoice.com
Manufacturer and exporter of mobile/portable ice
plants, slush ice makers, hydro coolers, freezers and
vegetable harvesting and packing equipment
President: James Hatton
Sales Director: Jason Hatton
Contact: Raul Mora
  raul@semcomfgco.com
Purchasing Manager: Rod Bradley
Estimated Sales: Below $5 Million
Number Employees: 20-49
Square Footage: 60000
Brands:
  Semco

29053 Semco Plastic Co
5301 Old Baumgartner Rd
St Louis, MO 63129-2944

314-487-4557
www.semcoplastics.com
Manufacturer and exporter of plastic products in-
cluding drinking straws, boxes and advertising
novelties.
President: Chuck Voelkel
  cvoelkel@semcoplastic.com
Year Founded: 1944
Estimated Sales: $100-500 Million
Number Employees: 100-249
Square Footage: 450000

29054 Semi-Bulk Systems Inc
159 Cassens Ct
Fenton, MO 63026-2543

636-343-4500
Fax: 636-343-2822 800-732-8769
info@semi-bulk.com www.semi-bulk.com
Manufacturer and exporter of mixers including
batch and continuous; also, dry ingredient handling
interface systems
President: Jeff Doherty
CEO: Charles Attack
Chief Financial Officer: Al Moresi
Vice President: Ron Bentley
Research/Development: Iris Freidel
Controller: All Moresi
Sales/Marketing: Ronald Bentley
Public Relations: Diana McMahon
Operations/Production/Purchasing: Bernie Klipsch
Estimated Sales: $10 Million
Number Employees: 20-49
Square Footage: 220000
Brands:
  Vacucam

29055 Sencon Inc
6385 W 74th St
Chicago, IL 60638-6128

708-496-3100
Fax: 708-496-3105 www.sencon.com

Specialized control devices, sensors, and quality instruments to the metal packaging industry; tooling protective systems, line control devices and a range of manual and automatic quality gauges
Owner: Winston Shields
Technical Manager: Ian Blackledge
Estimated Sales: $10-20 Million
Number Employees: 50-99

29056 Sencorp White
400 Kidds Hill Rd
Hyannis, MA 02601-1850
508-771-9400
Fax: 508-790-0002 info@sencorpwhite.com
www.sencorpwhite.com
Storage and retrieval systems, vertical and horizontal carousels, transporters, robots and power columns
CEO: Brian Urban
brian.urban@dtindustries.com
VP Operations: John Molloy
VP Marketing: Richard Frye
Estimated Sales: Less than $500,000
Number Employees: 100-249

29057 Seneca Environmental Products
Airport Industrial Park 1685 S. County
PO Box 429
Tiffin, OH 44883
419-447-1282
Fax: 419-448-4048
Manufacturer and exporter of sanitary type dust collectors including stainless steel, carbon steel, reverse jet, cartridge, cyclone, shaker and cylindrical; also, noise pollution control equipment, miscellaneous sanitary and steelfabrication
President: C Harple
Sales Manager: Don Harple
Estimated Sales: $1 - 3 Million
Number Employees: 20-49
Square Footage: 100000

29058 Seneca Tape & Label
13821 Progress Pkwy
Cleveland, OH 44133-4398
440-237-1600
Fax: 440-237-0427 800-251-0514
sales@senecalabel.com www.senecalabel.com
Pressure sensitive labels
Vice President: Paul Macmorob
pmacmurdo@senecalabel.com
VP Finance: John Hoopingarner
Estimated Sales: $2.5-5 Million
Number Employees: 50-99

29059 Senior Flexonics
300 E Devon Ave
Bartlett, IL 60103-4608
630-837-1811
Fax: 630-837-2672 800-473-0474
www.seniorflexonics.com
Deep fryer hoses and filters
President: John Divine
Sales Manager: Gerry Blanchet
Contact: Robert Chambers
robertc@flexonics.com
Estimated Sales: $5-10,000,000
Number Employees: 10-19
Parent Co: Senior Flexonics
Brands:
Filter-Master
Fryer Pro

29060 (HQ)Senior Housing Options Inc
1510 17th St
Denver, CO 80202-1202
303-595-4464
Fax: 303-595-9225 800-659-2656
info@seniorhousingoptions.org
www.seniorhousingoptions.org
Plain and printed plastic bags; also, plastic film
President: James A. Roberts
Controller: Vicky Campbell
Vice-President: Teri Romero
Quality Assurance Director: Jennifer Marcols
Estimated Sales: Less Than $500,000
Number Employees: 5-9

29061 Sensaphone
901 Tryens Rd
Aston, PA 19014-1522
610-558-2700
Fax: 610-558-0222 877-373-2700
sales@sensaphone.com www.sensaphone.com

Wine industry security systems
President: Kenneth E Blanchard
VP Marketing/Sales: Mary Ellen Gomeau
Vice President of Sales and Marketing: Bob Douglass
Manager: Brook Abboud
babboud@sensaphone.com
Estimated Sales: $5 - 10 Million
Number Employees: 1-4
Square Footage: 60000

29062 Sensidyne
1000 112th Circle North
Suite 100
St. Petersburg, FL 33716
727-530-3602
Fax: 727-539-0550 800-451-9444
info@sensidyne.com www.sensidyne.com
Manufacturer and exporter of gas detection and air sampling systems
President: Howie Mills
VP: Glenn Warr
Quality Control: George Mason
Marketing: Mary Slattery
National Sales Manager: Gary Queensberry
Contact: Mabie Eggleston
meggleston@sensidyne.com
Estimated Sales: $10-20 Million
Number Employees: 50-99

29063 Sensient Colors Inc
2515 N Jefferson Ave
St Louis, MO 63106-1939
314-889-7600
Fax: 314-658-7318 800-325-8110
foodcolors.stl@sensient.com
www.sensientfoodcolors.com
Global food and beverage color manufacturer.
President, Color Group: Michael Geraghty
Parent Co: Sensient Technologies Corporation
Type of Packaging: Consumer, Food Service, Private Label, Bulk

29064 Sensient Flavors and Fragrances
Flavors North America
5115 Sedge Boulevard
Hoffman Estates, IL 60192
800-445-0073
Fax: 847-645-7395 800-445-0073
www.sensientflavorsandfragrances.com
Flavoring extracts and syrups.
CEO, Sensient Technologies: Paul Manning
Year Founded: 1882
Estimated Sales: $100-200 Million
Number Employees: 1,000-4,999
Parent Co: Sensient Technologies Corporation

29065 Sensitech
P.O. Box 599
Redmond, WA 98073-0599
425-883-7926
Fax: 425-883-3766 800-999-7926
info@sensitech.com www.sensitech.com
Temperature and humidity measurement in food and beverages
Manager: Mike Hanson
Contact: Andy Englehardt
a.englehardt@sensitech.com
Estimated Sales: $10-25 Million
Number Employees: 50-99
Parent Co: Sensitech

29066 Sensitech Inc
8801 148th Ave NE
P.O. Box 599
Redmond, WA 98052-3492
425-883-7926
Fax: 425-883-3766 800-999-7926
www.sensitech.com
Manufacturer and exporter of time/temperature and humidity monitors for perishable commodities in transit, storage or processing
Manager: Mike Hanson
CFO: Mike Hurton
Senior Director of Quality Assurance: Dave Ray
Director Marketing: Susan Milant
VP Sales: Dan Vache
Estimated Sales: $10-20 Million
Number Employees: 50-99

29067 Sensitech Inc
800 Cummings Ctr
Suite 258X
Beverly, MA 01915
978-927-7033
800-843-8367
info@sensitech.com www.sensitech.com
Temperature monitoring systems and electronic temperature monitors and recorders for perishable products; also, hand-held HACCP compliance systems.
President: Mike Hurton
mike.hurton@sensitech.com
Director of Quality: Dave Ray
VP, Global Marketing & Communications: Elizabeth Darragh
VP, Product Development & Operations: Scott Hubley
Estimated Sales: $100 Million
Number Employees: 1000-4999
Square Footage: 6000
Brands:
Quickcheck
Temptale
Temptale 2
Temptale 3
Temptale 4

29068 Sensor Systems
8929 Fullbright Ave
Chatsworth, CA 91311-6179
818-341-5366
Fax: 818-341-9059 info@sensorantennas.com
www.sensorantennas.com
Moisture measurement and control instrumentation
President: Mayra Alatorre
mayra_alatorre@med3000.com
Director of Sales and Marketing: Mike Crow
Estimated Sales: $1-2.5 Million
Number Employees: 100-249

29069 Sensors Quality Management
156 Duncan Mill Road
Suite 19
Toronto, ON M3B 3N2
Canada
416-444-4491
Fax: 416-444-2422 800-866-2624
sqm@sqm.ca www.sqm.ca
Consultant specializing in the evaluation of company operations including quality assurance, competition analysis, integrity inspections, training programs, research and surveys, marketing, promotions, etc
President: David Lipton
VP: Craig Henry
VP: Craig Henry
Number Employees: 10

29070 Sensory Computer Systems
144 Summit Avenue
Berkeley Heights, NJ 7922
908-665-6464
Fax: 908-665-6493 800-579-7654
johnream@sensorysims.com
www.sensorysims.com
Sensory testing and market research software used for laboratory, central location and point-of-sale testing of consumer survey data
Director: John Ream
Contact: Francois Abiven
f.abiven@reperes.net
Account Manager of Logistics, Chief Oper: Elena Keegan
Estimated Sales: $500,000-$1 Million
Number Employees: 5-9

29071 Sensory Spectrum
554 Central Ave
New Providence, NJ 07974-1555
908-376-7000
Fax: 908-376-7040
spectrum@sensoryspectrum.com
www.sensoryspectrum.com
Consultant specializing in sensory evaluation techniques applied to the understanding of consumer products through descriptive analysis, advanced sensory methodology, qualitative and quantitative consumer research, experimentaldesign, etc
President: Gail Vance-Civille
gvciville@sensoryspectrum.com
Marketing Executive: Emily Engler
Sales Executive: Marie Rudolph
Estimated Sales: $5 - 10 Million
Number Employees: 20-49

29072 Sentinel Lubricants Inc
15755 NW 15th Ave
PO Box 694240
Miami, FL 33169-5651
305-625-6400
Fax: 305-625-6565 800-842-6400
info@sentinelsynthetic.com
www.sentinelsynthetic.com
Manufacturer and exporter of food grade synthetic
lubricants including nontoxic oil and grease
CEO: R Chaban
VP: J C Barroso
Research & Development: Charles Clay
Quality Control: Phil Sauder
Marketing Director: Emile Freidman
Sales: Raul Oquendo
Public Relations: Marta Garcia
Operations Manager: Randye Chaban
Production Manager: Juanillo Barroso
Plant Manager: Philip Sauder
Purchasing Manager: Martha Garcia
Estimated Sales: $18 Million
Number Employees: 10-19
Number of Brands: 200
Number of Products: 400
Square Footage: 50000
Type of Packaging: Consumer, Private Label
Brands:
  Biosyn
  Sentinel
  Sentishield
  Sl Nt

29073 Sentinel Polyolefins
P.O. Box 355
West Hyannisport, MA 02672-0355
508-775-5220
Fax: 508-771-1554 800-457-3234
Crosslinked polyethylene foam and specialty elasto-
mers for packaging applications including
multi-density lamination for end-caps packaging
Estimated Sales: $1 - 3 Million
Number Employees: 1-4

29074 Sentron
7117 Stinson Ave # C
Gig Harbor, WA 98335-4902
253-851-7881
Fax: 253-851-7899 800-472-4361
www.sentron.ca
Nonglass, ion sensitive field effect transistor(ISFET)
and pH measurement equipment
Marketing: Eric Amundson
Technical Sales Manager: Eric Amundson
Number Employees: 5-9
Square Footage: 24000
Other Locations:
  Sentron
  9300 AC Roden
Brands:
  Sentron

29075 Sentry Equipment Corp
966 Blue Ribbon Cir N
Oconomowoc, WI 53066-8666
262-567-7256
Fax: 262-567-4523 sales@sentry-equip.com
www.sentry-equip.com
Manufacturer and exporter of sanitary samplers for
milk, cream, whey, orange juice, viscous food prod-
ucts, wastewater liquids and slurries
President: Michael Farrell
CEO: John Hazlehurst
  john_h@sentryequipment.com
Marketing Director: Lynn Castrodale
Sales Director: Doris Hoeft
Number Employees: 100-249
Brands:
  Isolok

29076 Sentry Equipment/Erectors Inc
13150 E Lynchburg Salem Tpke
Forest, VA 24551-4328
434-525-0769
Fax: 434-525-1701 sales@sentryequipment.com
www.sentryequipment.com
Conveyor belts and equipment
President: Adam Vinoskey
Estimated Sales: $50-100 Million
Number Employees: 250-499

29077 Sentry/Bevcon North America
16630 Koala Road
PO Box 578
Adelanto, CA 92301-0578
800-854-1177
Fax: 760-246-4044 800-661-3003
sales@ici.us www.ici.us
Manufacturer and exporter of portable bars and dis-
pensers including soda, juice, coffee, liquor and beer
President: Joe Suarez
Quality Control: Jerry Wheeler
R & D: Jerry Wheeler
Marketing: Ken Wogberg
Sales: Amber Micham
Public Relations: Ken Wogberg
Technical Support: Jerry Wheeler
President: Joe Suarez
Number Employees: 35
Square Footage: 224000
Parent Co: International Carbonic
Type of Packaging: Consumer, Food Service, Pri-
vate Label
Brands:
  Bevcon
  Ici

29078 Separators Inc
5707 W Minnesota St
Indianapolis, IN 46241-3825
317-484-3745
Fax: 317-484-3755 800-233-9022
separate@sepinc.com www.separatorsinc.com
Leader in the sale and repair of reconditioned centri-
fuges.
President/CEO: Joe Campbell
COO/CFO: Joe Mansfield
Director of Manufacturing: Dan Goss
Estimated Sales: $10-20 Million
Number Employees: 20-49
Square Footage: 60000

29079 Sepragen Corp
1205 San Luis Obispo St
Hayward, CA 94544-7915
510-475-0650
Fax: 510-475-0625 info@sepragen.com
www.sepragen.com
Manufacturer and exporter of process control sys-
tems and instruments and separation machinery for
the dairy industry
CEO/ CTO: Vinit Saxena
CFO: Henry Edmunds
Director Quality & Tech Support: Salah Ahmed
Number Employees: 20-49

29080 Septimatech Group
106 Randall Drive
Waterloo, ON N2V 1K5
Canada
519-746-7463
Fax: 519-746-3464 888-777-6775
sales@septimatech.com www.septimatech.com
Septimatech is the total solution provider in line
changeover products, innovation, services, research
and development. Specializing in Quick Change
Tooling solutions, Customer Container Handling so-
lutions and enhancements, andproviding RXNT,
Unison Guide Rails, and OEM parts.
President & CEO: Sharron Gilbert
VP Engineering/Innovation: Glenn Bell
VP Marketing/Sales/Service: Gord Beaton
VP Manufacturing/Quality: Quinn Martin
Number Employees: 50-99
Number of Brands: 2

29081 Septipack
2313 Benson Mill Rd
Sparks Glencoe, MD 21152-9420
410-472-2575
Fax: 410-771-1528
Aseptic packaging systems
President: Herve Franceschi
Estimated Sales: $300,000-500,000
Number Employees: 1-4

29082 Sequa Can Machinery
6949 S Potomac St
Englewood, CO 80112
Fax: 201-933-9029
Machinery for the 2-piece can industry: cuppers,
rutherford decorators and base coaters, can industry
products tooled, cuppers, shell presses and DRD
systems and FM&S replacement parts

President: Gus Reall
CFO: Bob Mayone
Quality Control: John Agar
Number Employees: 175

29083 Sequoia Pacific
20940 Avenue 296
Exeter, CA 93221-9713
559-562-3726
Fax: 415-442-0563
Wine industry, label printing
Chairman: James Matthews
CEO: Michael Marino
CFO: Ruth Damsker
Estimated Sales: $20-50 Million
Number Employees: 1-4

29084 SerVend International
2100 Future Drive
Sellersburg, IN 47172-1868
812-246-7000
Fax: 812-246-9922 800-367-4233
www.servend.com
Manufacturer and exporter of ice makers, beverage,
cup and ice dispensers, ice storage bins and bever-
age dispensing valves
CEO: Terry Growcock
VP Sales/Marketing: Lonnie Shafer
Director Marketing: Elaine Momson
Contact: Greg Gummere
  greg.gummere@manitowoc.com
Estimated Sales: $20 - 30 Million
Number Employees: 250
Square Footage: 155000
Parent Co: Manitowoc Foodservice Group
Other Locations:
  SerVend International
  Clackamas OR
Brands:
  Flomatic
  Servend

29085 Serac Inc
300 S Westgate Dr
Carol Stream, IL 60188-2243
630-510-9343
Fax: 630-510-9357 serac@serac-usa.com
www.serac-inc.com
Filling and packaging machinery
President: Christopher Lebraun
Manager: Ron Ercolani
  rone@serac-usa.com
Number Employees: 20-49

29086 (HQ)Serfilco
2900 Macarthur Blvd
Northbrook, IL 60062-2007
847-509-2900
Fax: 847-559-1995 800-323-5431
sales@serfilco.com www.serfilco.com
Designs, manufactures and markets a broad line of
corrosion resistant high performance pumps, agita-
tors, filtration systems and instruments.
President: James Berg
  jamesb@serfilco.com
Marketing: Chuck Schultz
Operations: Mike Berg
Production Manager: Jerry Swooda
Estimated Sales: $10 - 20 Million
Number Employees: 20-49
Other Locations:
  Serfilco Ltd.
  Lancaster PA
Brands:
  Guardian
  Space'saver
  Titan '90

29087 Sergeant E M Pulp & Chem Co
66 Brighton Rd
Clifton, NJ 07012-1600
973-472-9111
Fax: 973-472-5686 www.sergeantchem.com
President: A Reisch
Estimated Sales: $10 - 20 Million
Number Employees: 5-9

29088 Sermatech ISPA
12505 Reed Rd., #100
Sugar Land, TX 77478-2876
410-644-4500
Fax: 410-644-1766 800-882-4772
Applicator of nonstick coatings for food processing
and handling equipment including mixers, enrobers,
chutes, dryers, etc

925

Owner: Ron Kaufmann
VP: Scott Vogt
Sales Director: Paul Kellogg
Sales: Rob Aldave
Purchasing Manager: Wes Prince
Estimated Sales: $10-20 Million
Number Employees: 20-49
Square Footage: 140000
Parent Co: Sermatech International
Brands:
  Fluoroshield-Magna
  Teflon

29089 Sermia International
100-742 Boulevard Industrial
Blainville, QC J7C 3V4
Canada
                         450-433-7483
    Fax: 450-433-7484 800-567-7483
    info@sermia.com www.sermia.com
Manufacturer and exporter of filters for liquids
Number Employees: 10
Brands:
  Sermia

29090 Serpa Packaging Solutions
7020 W Sunnyview Ave
Visalia, CA 93291-9639
                         559-651-2339
    Fax: 559-651-2345 800-348-5453
    sales@serpapackaging.com www.serpapkg.com
Manufacturer and exporter of cartoners and case
packers and erectors; also, custom designs and turn-
key applications available
President/CEO: Fernando M Serpa
    fsepra@serpapackaging.com
Director of Marketing: Rich James
Estimated Sales: $10,000,000
Number Employees: 50-99
Square Footage: 92000

29091 Serr-Edge Machine Company
4471 W 160th St
Cleveland, Cl 44135-2625
                         216-267-6333
    Fax: 216-267-2929 800-443-8097
Manufacturer and exporter of industrial and com-
mercial sharpening machines for scissors, knives
and shears
President: Linda Ribar Oakley
Owner: Matthew Oakley
Estimated Sales: Below $5 Million
Number Employees: 5-9
Brands:
  Easisharp
  Keenedge
  Tru-Hone

29092 Sertapak Packaging Corporation
PO Box 1500
Woodstock, ON N4S 8R2
Canada
                         519-539-3330
    Fax: 519-539-4499 800-265-1162
Manufacturer and exporter of returnable and ex-
pandable packaging systems, containers, pallets and
sealed edge plastic corrugated slip sheets
President: C J David Nettleton
CEO: Alison Clarke
CFO: Bruce Orr
Number Employees: 10
Brands:
  Rak Pak
  Sertote

29093 Serti Information Solution
7555, Beclard Street
Montreal, QC H1J 2S5
Canada
                         514-493-1909
    Fax: 514-493-3575 800-361-6615
    info@serti.com www.serti.com
Consulting services providing software and solu-
tions for a solid foundation on completing-achieving
all your information technology projects
President: LOUIS LAPORTE
Vice-President, finance & operations: MAURICE
LANTHIER
Vice-President, IT Consulting Services: ODILE
PATRY
Vice-President, Business Development: FRANCIS
GINGRAS

29094 (HQ)Servco Equipment Co
3189 Jamieson Ave
St Louis, MO 63139-2519
                         314-781-3189
    Fax: 314-645-7003 www.servco-stl.com
Manufacturer and exporter of conveyors and under
and back bar refrigerators
President: Earl Gates Jr
Sales Exec: Helen Gage
Estimated Sales: $5-10 Million
Number Employees: 20-49
Square Footage: 112000
Brands:
  Gates
  Servco

29095 Server Products Inc
3601 Pleasant Hill Rd
PO Box 98
Richfield, WI 53076-9417
                         262-628-5100
    Fax: 262-628-5110 800-558-8722
    spsales@server-products.com
    www.server-products.com
Manufacturer and exporter of small pumps, food dis-
pensers and warmers, bars and accessories, rails and
pizza ovens
President: Chris Falkner
    spsales@server-products.com
VP Sales: Ron Ripple
VP Production: Carol Miller
Estimated Sales: $10 - 20 Million
Number Employees: 50-99
Square Footage: 250000

29096 Service Brass & AluminumFittings
190 N Wiget Lane
Suite 202
Walnut Creek, CA 94598-2440
                         925-977-8320
                    Fax: 925-256-0318
Wine industry, hose fittings
Estimated Sales: Under$500,000
Number Employees: 25-49

29097 Service Ideas
2354 Ventura Dr
Woodbury, MN 55125-4403
                         651-730-8800
    Fax: 651-730-8880 800-328-4493
    sales@serviceideas.com www.serviceideas.com
Manufacturer, importer and exporter of insulated
serving plates, beverage servers, dispensers, pitchers
and buffet bowls
President: Christina Brandt
    laura@serviceideas.com
VP & HR Manager: Megan Blohowiak
Foodservice Sales Director: Andy Krawczyk
Site Manager: Laura Bjorkman
    laura@serviceideas.com
Operations Director: Mark Bolowiak
Estimated Sales: $10 - 20 Million
Number Employees: 20-49
Square Footage: 80000
Brands:
  Aero-Serv
  Brew'n'pour Lid
  Eco-Serv
  Magnetag
  Metallic Luster
  New Generation
  Sculptured Ice
  Thermo-Plate
  Thermo-Serv
  Thermo-Serv Sculptured Ice

29098 Service Manufacturing
1601 Mountain St
Aurora, IL 60505-2402
                         630-898-1394
    Fax: 630-898-7800 888-325-2788
    tvickers@theramp.net www.rocktenn.com
Manufacturer, importer and exporter of custom
packaging products including insulated coolers,
cases and bags
President: Camerina Torres
Vice President: David Goodman
Marketing/Sales: Matthew Sheridan
Plant Manager: Octavio Serrano
Purchasing Manager: Clarence Eisernman
Estimated Sales: $10-20 Million
Number Employees: 10-19
Square Footage: 376000

Type of Packaging: Bulk
Brands:
  Service Manufacturing
  Sun Valley

29099 Service Master Co LLC
150 Peabody Place
Memphis, TN 38103
                         888-937-3783
                www.servicemaster.com
Facilities management, plant operations and mainte-
nance, ground and landscaping management, custo-
dial services, energy management.
Interim CEO & Chair: Naren Gursahaney
SVP & Chief Financial Officer: Anthony DiLucente
SVP & Chief Transformation Officer: Pratip
Dastidar
SVP, Business Development: Dion Persson
Chief Human Resources Officer: David Dart
Year Founded: 1929
Estimated Sales: $2.59 Billion
Number Employees: 13,000

29100 Service Neon Signs
6611 Iron Pl
Springfield, VA 22151
                         703-354-3000
    Fax: 703-354-5810 info@snsigns.org
                www.snsigns.org
Neon, plastic and aluminum on-site identification
signs
CEO: Mark Luxenburg
VP/General Manager: Robert Gray
Sales: George Marino, Jr.
Plant Manager: Jack Evans
Purchasing Manager: Mike Volpe
Estimated Sales: $5 - 10 Million
Number Employees: 50-99
Square Footage: 150000

29101 Service Sales Corporation
390 Richmond St E
South St Paul, MN 55075-5939
                         651-451-2206
    Fax: 651-451-2710 800-225-6128
Wholesaler/distributor of labels, price marking
equipment, bar code printers and thermal supplies
President: Rob Iten
Estimated Sales: $5-10 Million
Number Employees: 10-19
Square Footage: 56000

29102 Service Stamp Works
1227 W Jackson Boulevard
Chicago, IL 60607-2895
                         312-666-8839
    Fax: 312-666-4167 marionk@hsonline.net
Rubber stamps, printing plates and food inks
Operations Manager: Peter Haack
Estimated Sales: $500,000-$1 Million
Number Employees: 5-9

29103 Service Tool International
39 S La Salle St
Suite 1410
Chicago, IL 60603
                         847-439-7000
                    Fax: 847-439-7009
Easy-open conversion systems, shell manufacturing
systems, and integrated manufacturing lines for
ends, shells, or EOE; partial product list: carbide
scroll dies, tab dies, lane dies, single, double and
multi-dies, beader tooling, andcurler tooling
President: Loren Scheel
CEO: John Tensland
R & D: Just Klingel
Quality Control: Mike Fries
Estimated Sales: $10-20 Million
Number Employees: 20-49

29104 Servin Company
51518 Industrial Dr
Suite E
New Baltimore, MI 48047
                         586-725-5571
    Fax: 586-725-5573 800-824-0962
                www.information.com
Reusable coated nylon bags
VP: Charles Clandinen
Sales Manager: Charles Clendinen
Estimated Sales: $.5 - 1 million
Number Employees: 5-9

29105 Servomex
525 Julie Rivers Dr # 185
Sugar Land, TX 77478-2845

281-295-5800
Fax: 281-295-5899 800-862-0200
www.servomex.com
Servomex food pack analyzers offer simple, fast and accurate analysis of oxygen and carbon dioxide in soft packages or rigid containers
VP: Claire Lucarino
Marketing: Jane Hammond
Sales: Susan Harris
Contact: Brian Anderson
   banderson@servomex.com
Plant Manager: Ed Arestie
Purchasing Director: Jon Pryer
Estimated Sales: $10 - 20 Million
Number Employees: 20-49
Brands:
   1450 Food Pack Analyzer
   574 Portable Oxygen Analyzer

29106 Servomex Inc
4 Constitution Way # I
Woburn, MA 01801-1042

281-295-5800
Fax: 781-938-0531 800-433-2552
americas_sales@servomex.com
www.servomex.com
Oxygen and carbondioxide CAP/MAP analyzers
Estimated Sales: $10-20 Million
Number Employees: 20-49

29107 Servpak Corp
5844 Dawson St
Hollywood, FL 33023-1910

954-962-4262
Fax: 954-962-5776 800-782-0840
www.serv-pak.com
Manufacturer and exporter table-topheat seal packaging machinery forrigid and semi rigid trays covered by pre-cut lids or lid film on a roll
Owner: Joel Mahler
Estimated Sales: Less than $500,000
Number Employees: 10-19
Square Footage: 4000

29108 Sesame Label System
1501 Third Ave
New York, NY 10028

212-989-3020
Fax: 212-989-3021 800-551-3020
Labels, decals and name plates; also, custom printing available
Purchasing: Tony Jackson
Estimated Sales: $2.5-5 Million
Number Employees: 10
Square Footage: 4000

29109 Sessions Co Inc
801 N Main St
Enterprise, AL 36330-9108

334-393-0200
Fax: 334-393-0240
CEO: H Moultrie Sessions Jr
CFO: Jeff Outlaw
   sesscom@frost.snowhill.com
Estimated Sales: $2.5-5 Million
Number Employees: 50-99

29110 Set Point Paper Company
31 Oxford Rd
Mansfield, MA 02048-1126

508-339-0700
Fax: 508-339-9929 800-225-0501
Food containers, cups, specialty bags and folding cartons
Manager: Elizabeth Dudley
VP: Michael Keneally
VP: Richard Madigan Jr
Estimated Sales: $300,000-500,000
Number Employees: 1-4
Square Footage: 250000
Brands:
   Smart Cup
   Smart Seal

29111 Setaram/SFIM
210 Lakeview St
Grand Prairie, TX 75051-4998

972-262-4900
Fax: 972-641-3711
sales@stormlawnandgarden.com
www.stormlawnandgarden.com

Thermal analysis instrumentation for fats, liquids, etc
Owner: R L Storm
Estimated Sales: $2.5-5 Million
Number Employees: 5-9

29112 Setco
34 Engelhard Dr
Monroe Twp, NJ 08831

609-655-4600
Fax: 609-655-0225 www.setco.com
Manufacturer and exporter of plastic bottles
VP, Technology & New Product Sales: Brian Schloemer
VP, Service Operations 7 Sales: Bob Schwallie
Estimated Sales: $50-100 Million
Number Employees: 250-500
Parent Co: APL Company

29113 Setco
P.O. Box 68008
Anaheim, CA 92817-0808

714-777-5200
Fax: 714-777-5355
Stock and custom plastic bottles
President: Don Parodi
VP Sales/Marketing: Thomas Dunn
Estimated Sales: $1 - 5 Million
Number Employees: 250-499
Parent Co: McCormick & Company
Other Locations:
   Setco
   Monroe Township NJ

29114 Seton Indentification Products
20 Thompson Rd
PO Box 819
Branford, CT 06405-2842

203-488-8059
Fax: 203-488-5973 800-571-2596
seton_mailroom@seton.com www.seton.com
Signs, tags, labels, identification and safety products
Cmo: Dave Giroux
   dave_giroux@seton.com
Manager: Pascal Deman
Estimated Sales: Less than $500,000
Number Employees: 250-499
Brands:
   Set Mark

29115 Setter, Leach & Lindstrom
730 2nd Ave S # 1100
Minneapolis, MN 55402-2455

612-338-8741
Fax: 612-338-4840 www.leoadaly.com
Consultant specializing in design and project management of food distribution centers
President: Bob Egge
Chairman: Leo Daly
Vice President: Charles Dalluge
Estimated Sales: $20-50 Million
Number Employees: 100-249

29116 Setterstix Corp
261 S Main St
Cattaraugus, NY 14719-1312

716-257-3451
Fax: 716-257-9818 nan@setterstix.com
www.setterstix.com
Manufacturer and exporter of rolled paper sticks for the confectionery industry
President: Paul Elly
   pelly@setterstix.com
CFO: Ron Wasmund
Sales: Nan Mikowicz
Plant Manager: Eric Pritchard
Estimated Sales: $10 - 15 Million
Number Employees: 50-99
Square Footage: 60000
Parent Co: Knox Industries
Brands:
   Setterstix

29117 Seven B Plus
46161 SE Wildcat Mountain Dr
Sandy, OR 97055

503-668-5079
Fax: 503-668-6347
Smokers

29118 Seven Mile Creek Corp
315 S Beech St
Eaton, OH 45320-2311

937-456-3320
Fax: 937-456-3320 800-497-6324
sevenmile@voyager.net
www.sevenmilecreek.com
Industrial and promotional aprons; also, silk screening available
President: William Cressell
   sevenmile@voyager.net
Estimated Sales: Less Than $500,000
Number Employees: 5-9
Square Footage: 80000

29119 Severn Newtrent
2660 Columbia St
Torrance, CA 90503-3802

310-618-9700
Fax: 310-618-1384 800-777-6939
www.severntrentservices.com
Manufactures machines and equipment for use in service industries, water purification systems
President, Chief Executive Officer: Martin Kane
VP: Marwan Nesicolaci
Contact: Chad Dannemann
   cdannemann@severntrentservices.com
Estimated Sales: $10-20 Million
Number Employees: 100-249

29120 Severn Trent Svc
3000 Advance Ln
Colmar, PA 18915-9432

215-822-2901
Fax: 215-997-4062
marketing@capitalcontrols.com
www.severntrentservices.com
Manufacturer and exporter of water treatment systems including chlorinators, ultraviolet sterilization systems, pH/orp monitors and chlorine, ammonia and fluoride residue analyzers
President, Chief Executive Officer: Martin Kane
Marketing Manager: Anne Penkal
Plant Manager: Jeff Dohnam
Estimated Sales: $20-50 Million
Number Employees: 100-249

29121 (HQ)Severn Trent Svc
580 Virginia Dr # 300
Suite 300
Fort Washington, PA 19034-2723

215-646-9201
Fax: 215-283-3487 www.severntrentservices.com
Supplier of water and wastewater treatment solutions
President/CEO: Martin Kane
Senior VP/CFO: Stephane Bouvier
VP Marketing/Business Development: Thomas Mills
Contact: Rick Bacon
   rbacon@severntrentservices.com
Operations Director: Alex Lloyd
Estimated Sales: Less Than $500,000
Number Employees: 1-4

29122 Seville Display Door
27495 Diaz Road
Temecula, CA 92590-3414

951-676-6161
Fax: 951-676-7728 800-634-0412
Glass refrigerator and PVC sliding doors
Owner: Randy Fitzpatrick
Estimated Sales: $2.5-5 Million
Number Employees: 10-19
Square Footage: 120000

29123 (HQ)Seville Flexpack Corp
9905 S Ridgeview Dr
Oak Creek, WI 53154-5556

414-761-2751
Fax: 414-761-3140 www.sevilleflexpack.com
Manufacturer and exporter of flexible packaging materials, stand-up pouches and cold seal coatings
President: Jan Drzewiecki
Director Sales: Jay Yakich
VP Manufacturing: James Yakich
Estimated Sales: $20-50 million
Number Employees: 50-99
Square Footage: 11999999
Other Locations:
   Seville Flexpack Corp.
   Waco TX
Brands:
   Fastseal

Flexfilm
Hide-A-Winner
Up-Right

29124 Seville Flexpack Corp
9905 S Ridgeview Dr
Oak Creek, WI 53154-5556
414-761-2751
Fax: 414-761-3140
Flexible packages, packaging materials
President: Jan Drzewiecki
CFO: Cris Mercener
VP: Jim Yakich
VP Marketing and Sales: Jay Yakich
Marketing Manager: Mark Hoffman
Sales Manager: J Yakich
Operations Manager: Jim Yakich
Production Manager: Dave Gras
Purchasing Manager: Roger Kline
Estimated Sales: $20 - 50 Million
Number Employees: 50-99
Parent Co: Seville Flexpack Corporation

29125 Sew-Eurodrive Inc
1295 Old Spartanburg Hwy
P.O. Box 518
Lyman, SC 29365
864-439-8792
Fax: 864-949-3039 www.seweurodrive.com
Manufacturer and exporter of drives, motors and accessories.
CEO: Juergon Blickle
Year Founded: 1931
Estimated Sales: $100-500 Million
Number Employees: 250-499
Square Footage: 250000
Brands:
Movidrive
Movidyn
Movimot
Movitrac
Snuggler

29126 Sexton Sign
PO Box 5555
Anderson, SC 29623-5555
864-226-6071
Fax: 864-226-4074
Commercial electric signs
Estimated Sales: $1 - 5 Million

29127 Seymour Housewares
885 N Chestnut St
Seymour, IN 47274
812-522-5130
Fax: 812-522-5294 800-457-9881
Shopping carts, ironing tables, pad and cover sets
and laundry products
President: Norman Proulx
Director Marketing: Kurt Tyler
VP Sales: Tony Taggart
Estimated Sales: $20 - 50 Million
Number Employees: 100-249

29128 Seymour Woodenware Company
522 Seymour St
Seymour, WI 54165
920-833-6551
Fax: 920-833-7698 qadamski@new.rr.com
Wooden boxes and baskets including cheese, wine,
coffee, gift, veneer, etc
President: Quintin J Adamski
qadamski@new.rr.com
General Manager: Steven Adamski
Estimated Sales: $1-2.5 Million
Number Employees: 10-19
Square Footage: 50000

29129 Sfb Plastics Inc
1819 W Harry St
P.O. Box 533
Wichita, KS 67213-3243
316-262-0400
Fax: 316-712-0112 800-343-8133
sales@sfbplastics.com www.sfbplastics.com
Manufacturer and exporter of polyethylene air flow
separators, pallets, pallet equipment and industrial
blow molded plastic containers
President: David Long
dlong@sfbplastics.com
Quality Control: Debbie Speven
Marketing: John Fosse
Sales: John Fosse

Estimated Sales: $10 - 20 Million
Number Employees: 50-99
Square Footage: 168000

29130 Shadetree Canopies
6317 Busch Blvd
Columbus, OH 43229-1864
614-844-5990
Fax: 614-844-5991 800-894-3801
www.shadetreecanopies.com
Manufacturer and exporter of retractable awnings
Owner: Colin Leveque
CFO: Richard O Keith
Quality Control: Ken Wagner
VP Marketing: Dwayne Williams
Sales: Don Preston
Estimated Sales: $2.5-5 Million
Number Employees: 10-19
Parent Co: Certain Teed
Brands:
Shade Tree

29131 Shae Industries
PO Box 1268
Healdsburg, CA 95448-1268
707-431-2337
Fax: 707-431-8060
Manufacuring quality stainless steel products for the
winery, microbrewery and dairy industries
Owner: Darrell Beer
Estimated Sales: Less Than $500,000
Number Employees: 1-4

29132 Shafer Commercial Seating
4101 East 48th Ave
Denver, CO 80216
303-322-7792
Fax: 303-393-1836
Manufacturer and exporter of booths, chairs, cush-
ions, pads, stools and tables including legs and bases
President: Randall Shafer
CFO: Dick Gish
CEO: Richard Gish
R & D: Dennis Trutcman
Marketing Director: Richard Howard
Contact: Darren Lingle
dalin@shafer.com
Purchasing Manager: Carla Rembolt
Estimated Sales: $18 Million
Number Employees: 100-249
Type of Packaging: Food Service

29133 Shaffer Sports & Events
601 W 6th Street
Houston, TX 77007
713-699-0088
Fax: 713-426-1672 shaffers@coshocton.com
www.shaffersports.com
Commercial awnings
Manager: Robert Hamilton
Contact: Dion Baccus
baccusd@shaffersports.com
Estimated Sales: $1 - 5 Million
Number Employees: 20-49

29134 Shah Trading Company
3451 McNicoll Avenue
Scarborough, ON M1V 2V3
Canada
416-292-6927
Fax: 416-292-7932 info@shahtrading.com
www.shahtrading.com
Rice, spices, beans, peas, and lentils, specialty flours
and nuts and dried fruits.
Other Locations:
Pulse and Canning Plant
Scarborough ON
Rice Plant
Scarborough ON
Brands:
Dunya Harvest

29135 Shambaugh & Son
7614 Opportunity Dr
Fort Wayne, IN 46825
260-487-7777
Fax: 260-487-7701 www.shambaugh.com
Construction/engineering services for industrial,
commercial and institutional industries.
CEO: Paul Meyers

CFO: Mark Veerkamp
SVP, General Counsel: William Meyer
Year Founded: 1926
Estimated Sales: $100-250 Million

Number Employees: 1000-4999
Square Footage: 100000
Parent Co: EMCOR Group, Inc.

29136 Shammi Industries
390 Meyer Cir # A
Corona, CA 92879-6617
951-340-3419
Fax: 951-340-2716 800-417-9260
info@sammonsequipment.com
www.sammonsequipment.com
Manufacturer, importer and exporter of banquet and
transport equipment including carts, heated cabinets,
racks, tables, dollies and shelving
President: Dani Pollard
traci@curryelectric.com
Estimated Sales: $1-2.5 Million
Number Employees: 10-19
Square Footage: 42000
Brands:
Queen Mary's
Samco

29137 (HQ)Shamrock Foods Co
3900 E. Camelback Rd.
Suite 300
Phoenix, AZ 85018
602-233-6400
877-228-9030
www.shamrockfoodservice.com
General line items, groceries, meats, produce, dairy
products, frozen foods, baked goods, equipment and
fixtures, general merchandise and seafood; serving
the food service market.
CEO: Kent McClelland
CFO: Stephen Down
Year Founded: 1922
Estimated Sales: $3 Billion
Number Employees: 3,500
Number of Brands: 45
Type of Packaging: Food Service
Other Locations:
Phoenix AZ
Commerce City CO
Meridian ID
Albuquerque NM
Brands:
AZAR
B&G Foods, Inc.
BROWN Paper Goods
BUENO
Beautiful Harvest
Brickfire Bakery
Cheese Merchants
Cobblestreet MKT
Coffee Roasters Ridgeline
Custom Culinary
ECOLAB
Fair Meadow
Florida's Natural
Four Leaf Roasters
Gold Canyon Meat Co.
Hormel Foods
Intros Appetizers & hors d'oeuvres
Jenson Foods
Katy's Kitchen
Kellogg's Away From Home
Kraft Heinz
LambWeston
Markon
Michael Foods Inc.
Mission Foodservice
NCCO
Nestl, Professional
Perdue
Pier 22 Seafood Co.
Pier Port Seafood
Prairie Creek
ProClean
ProPak
ProSystem
ProWare
REMA FOODS IMPORTS
RICH'S
Rejuv
Roland
SCHREIBER
Shamrock Farms
Smithfield Culinary
Sugar Foods Corporation
Trescerro Premium Teas
Villa Frizzoni
Vista Verde

29138 Shamrock Foods Co
Boise Foods Branch
1495 N Hickory Ave
Meridian, ID 83642
208-884-8400
www.shamrockfoodservice.com
Serves Idaho, Oregon and Utah.
Parent Co: Shamrock Foods Co

29139 Shamrock Foods Co
Colorado Foods Branch
5199 Ivy St
Commerce City, CO 80022
800-289-3595
coinfo@shamrockfoods.com
www.shamrockfoods.com
Serves Colorado, Western Kansas, Western Nebraska and Wyoming.
Senior VP: Kent Mullison
 kent_mullison@shamrockfoods.com
Number Employees: 500-999
Parent Co: Shamrock Foods Company

29140 Shamrock Foods Co
Arizona Foods Branch
2540 N 29th Ave
Phoenix, AZ 85009
602-233-6400
Fax: 928-537-3428 800-289-3663
azinfo@shamrockfoods.com
www.shamrockfoodservice.com
Estimated Sales: $100+ Million
Number Employees: 10-19
Parent Co: Shamrock Foods Company

29141 Shamrock Foods Co
Southern California Foods Branch
12400 Riverside Dr
Eastvale, CA 91752
855-664-5166
cainfo@shamrockfoods.com
www.shamrockfoodservice.com
Parent Co: Shamrock Foods Company

29142 Shamrock Foods Co
New Mexico Foods Branch
2 Shamrock Way NW
Albuquerque, NM 87120
877-577-1155
nminfo@shamrockfoods.com
www.shamrockfoodservice.com
Serves New Mexico and West Texas.
Parent Co: Shamrock Foods Company

29143 Shamrock Paper Company
1 Convent Street
Saint Louis, MO 63104
314-241-2370
Fax: 314-241-9230 www.shamrockpaper.com
Butcher, locker and kraft wrapping paper
President: William Firestone
Vice President: Rick Bliss
VP Sales: Sally Lippmann
Estimated Sales: $5 - 10Million
Number Employees: 10-19
Square Footage: 100000
Type of Packaging: Consumer, Food Service, Private Label, Bulk
Brands:
 Somethin' Special
 Sun Bright

29144 Shamrock Plastics
633 Howard St
Mt Vernon, OH 43050-3709
740-392-5555
Fax: 740-392-3555 800-765-1611
jay.ruffner@shamrockplastics.com
www.shamrockplastics.com
Plastic packaging and containerizing products including wicketed and bakery bags
Owner: Tom Ruffner
 tom.ruffner@shamrockplastics.com
Account Representative: Susan Orlando
Sales Exec: Tom Ruffner
Estimated Sales: $3 - 5 Million
Number Employees: 10-19
Square Footage: 170000

29145 Shamrock Technologies Newark
255 Pacific St
Newark, NJ 07114-2824
973-242-3859
Fax: 732-242-8074
marketing@shamrocktechnologies.com
www.shamrocktechnologies.com
Manufacturer and exporter of powdered waxes and PTFE (polytetrafluoroethylene); also, dispersions and emulsions including carnauba, PE, PP, paraffin, microcrystalline and blends
Owner: William B Neuberg
President: Bill Neueerg
Marketing Manager: Melanie McCarroll
Estimated Sales: $20 - 50 Million
Number Employees: 5-9

29146 Shanghai Freemen
2035 Route 27
Suite 3005
Edison, NJ 08817
732-981-1288
info@shanghaifreemen.com
shanghaifreemen.com
Dietary supplements and food and beverage ingredients, such as vitamins, stevia, natural beta carotene, energy beverage ingredients, amino acids and joint health products; their collection includes glucosamine, chondroitin, hyaluronicacid, fish gelatin, collagen, ascorbic acid, natural vitamin E, green tea extract, L-Glutamine, L-Valine, melatonin, probiotics, bromelain, vanillin, Sopure Stevia and many more.
President: Hanks Li
Director, Business Development: Paul Niemann
Director, Strategic Development: Lottie Siann
Executive Vice President: Christine Balediata
Year Founded: 1995
Estimated Sales: $100 Million
Number Employees: 51-200
Parent Co: Zhucheng Haotian Pharm Co.
Type of Packaging: Bulk
Other Locations:
 Shanghai Freemen Europe B.V.
 Rijswijk, the Netherlands
 Shanghai Freemen Lifescience Co.
 Shanghai, China
 Shanghai Freemen Americas, LLC.
 Brea CA
 Shanghai Freemen Japan Co., Ltd
 Tokyo, Japan
 Shanghai Freemen Australia
 Melbourne, Australia
 US Warehouse
 Fontana CA
 US Warehouse
 Cranbury NJ
 US Warehouse
 La Mirada CA
 US Warehouse
 Irving TX
 US Warehouse
 Salt Lake City UT

29147 Shanker Industries
301 Suburban Avenue
Deer Park, NY 11729
631-940-9889
Fax: 631-940-9895 877-742-6561
sales@shanko.com www.shanko.com
Manufacturer and exporter of decorative wall and ceiling tiles for hotels and restaurants
President: John Shanker
VP Advertising and Finance: Francine Shanker
VP Sales: David Shanker
Contact: Grace Chai
 grace@shanko.com
Estimated Sales: $500,000 - $1 Million
Number Employees: 5-9
Square Footage: 120000
Type of Packaging: Food Service

29148 Shanzer Grain Dryer
PO Box 2371
Sioux Falls, SD 57101-2371
605-336-0439
Fax: 605-336-9569 800-843-9887
sales@dwindustries.us
Manufacturer and exporter of grain dryers
Owner: Marian Leuning
Secretary/Treasurer: Dave Leuning
VP: Marian Leuning
Estimated Sales: $3 - 5 Million
Number Employees: 20-49
Parent Co: D&W Industries

29149 Shaped Wire
900 Douglas Road
Batavia, IL 60510-2294
630-406-0800
Fax: 630-406-0003 www.shapedwire.com
Packaging materials
President: William Wolford
Contact: Teri Grandt
 tgrandt@leggett.com
Estimated Sales: $20-50 Million
Number Employees: 50-99

29150 Shared Data Systems
P.O. Box 7787
Charlotte, NC 28241-7787
704-588-2233
Fax: 704-588-7154 800-622-2140
Custom-made software for material handling systems
President: Larry Jones
CFO: Doug Yoder
Estimated Sales: $5 - 10 Million
Number Employees: 20-49

29151 Sharon Manufacturing Inc
540 Brook Ave
Deer Park, NY 11729-6802
631-242-8870
Fax: 631-586-6822 800-424-6455
info@sharonmfg.com www.sharonmfg.com
Manufacturer and exporter of replacement parts for gable top and reconditioned fillers for dairy and juice products
President: Robert Stamm
 rob@sharonmfg.com
Number Employees: 5-9

29152 Sharp Brothers
201 Orient St
Bayonne, NJ 7002
201-339-0404
Manufacturer and exporter of yeast extruders and cutters
Owner: Basem Abdelnour
Estimated Sales: $500,000-$1 Million
Number Employees: 1-4
Square Footage: 8750

29153 (HQ)Sharp Electronics Corporation
Sharp Plaza
Mahwah, NJ 7495
201-529-8200
Fax: 201-529-8425 800-237-4277
www.sharpusa.com
Manufacturer and importer of commercial microwave ovens
President: Joel Biterman
CEO: Raymond Philippon
Chairman: Toshiaki Urushisako
Senior VP: Robert Scaglione
Number Employees: 1,000-4,999
Square Footage: 600000
Type of Packaging: Consumer, Food Service, Private Label
Other Locations:
 Sharp Electronics Corp.
 Romeoville IL

29154 Sharp Packaging Systems Inc
N62W22632 Village Dr
Sussex, WI 53089-3972
262-246-8815
Fax: 262-246-8885 800-634-6359
info@sharppackaging.com
www.sharppackaging.com
Pre-opened plastic bags on a roll, specialty films, and automatic bagging machines
President: Mike Menz
 mikem@sharppackaging.com
CEO: Jim Kornfeld
Estimated Sales: $20 - 50 Million
Number Employees: 250-499

29155 Sharpe Measurement Technology
97 West Avenue
Stratford, CT 06615-6112
203-380-1776
Fax: 203-386-0087 info@smt-usa.com
www.smt-usa.com
Continuous thickness gauges and rolling mill control systems
Estimated Sales: $2.5-5 Million
Number Employees: 9

29156 Sharpsville Container Corp
600 W Main St
Sharpsville, PA 16150-2058
724-962-1100
Fax: 724-962-1226 800-645-1248
sales@scacon.com www.sharpsvillecontainer.com
Stainless steel and plastic tanks, stock pots, drums,
hoppers, mixing and steaming kettles, etc.; also,
plastic boxes and stainless steel hand carts; custom
fabrication available
President: Thom Rigsby
Cio/Cto: Beverly Hunkus
bhunkus@scacon.com
Controller: Joe Higgins
Sales/Customer Service: Laura Puskar
Plant Manager: Michel Altenor
Estimated Sales: $10-20 Million
Number Employees: 50-99
Square Footage: 200000
Parent Co: Spartanburg Stainless Products

29157 Sharpsville Container Corp
600 W Main St
Sharpsville, PA 16150-2058
724-962-1100
Fax: 724-962-1226 800-645-1248
sales@scacon.com www.sharpsvillecontainer.com
Stainless steel and rotationally molded plastic vessels
President: Rick Mallat
Cio/Cto: Beverly Hunkus
bhunkus@scacon.com
Controller: Joe Higgins
Plant Manager: Michel Altenor
Estimated Sales: $10-20 Million
Number Employees: 50-99

29158 Shashi Foods
55 Esandar Dr
Toronto, ON M4G 4H2
Canada
416-645-0611
Fax: 416-645-0612 866-748-7441
Spices, herbs, seasoning blends and specialty flours,
also, custom grinding, blending, bottling, and bagging.
President: Sujay Shah
VP: Ajay Shah
Estimated Sales: $7.37 Million
Number Employees: 30
Brands:
Elephant Brand
King of Spice
Patak's
Shashi

29159 Shat R Shield Inc
116 Ryan Patrick Dr
Salisbury, NC 28147-5624
704-633-2100
Fax: 704-633-3420 800-223-0853
ayost@shatrshield.com www.shatrshield.com
Manufacturer and exporter of plastic-coated and
shatter-proof fluorescent lamps and Teflon-coated
125 and 250 watt infrared heat lamps
Owner: Bob Nolan
bnolan@shatrshield.com
Marketing Coordinator: Anita Yost
VP Sales/Marketing: Marty Pint
Marketing/Communications Manager: Bill Hahn
Estimated Sales: Below $5 Million
Number Employees: 50-99
Square Footage: 84000
Type of Packaging: Food Service
Brands:
Shat-R-Shield

29160 (HQ)Shaw & Slavsky Inc
13821 Elmira St
Detroit, MI 48227-3099
313-834-3990
Fax: 313-834-2680 800-521-7527
www.shawppcdesign.com
POP signs for grocery retailers. Also manufacture a
wide variety of metal sign holders, poster floor
stands, large-format graphics and signage, checkout
lights, custom light boxes and custom fixtures.
President: Tom Smith
Estimated Sales: $10 - 20 Million
Number Employees: 50-99
Square Footage: 200000
Other Locations:
Shaw & Slavsky
Detroit MI

29161 Shaw-Clayton Corporation
90 Montecito Road
San Rafael, CA 94901-2378
415-472-1522
Fax: 415-472-1599 800-537-6712
www.shaw-clayton.com
Manufacturer and exporter of small hinged lid containers
President: H Shaw
Sales: L Smith
Public Relations: S Hanson
Estimated Sales: Less than $500,000
Square Footage: 8000
Type of Packaging: Consumer
Brands:
Flex-A-Top

29162 Shawano Specialty Papers
W7575 Poplar Rd
Shawano, WI 54166-6082
715-526-2181
800-543-5554
paper@littlerapids.com www.littlerapids.com
Manufacturer and exporter of paper including
glazed, wet crepe, dry crepe tissue and serim reinforced tissue
Estimated Sales: $50-100 Million
Number Employees: 100-249
Parent Co: Little Rapids Corporation
Type of Packaging: Consumer, Bulk

29163 Sheahan Sanitation Consulting
424 Hazelnut Drive
Oakley, CA 94561-2404
925-625-9683
Fax: 925-625-2310 800-554-4243
Sanitation and food safety consultant providing
training, surface hygiene testing and chemical and
hygiene audits and inspections
Estimated Sales: $500,000-$1 Million
Number Employees: 1

29164 Shear/Kershman Laboratories
701 Crown Industrial Ct # F
Suite F
Chesterfield, MO 63005-1135
636-519-8900
Fax: 636-519-0959 www.shearkershman.com
Research and development consultant for the food
and confectionery industries; also, sourcing for material and co-packing available
Vice President: Alvin Kershman
akershman@shearkershman.com
Executive Vice President & Co-Founder: Al
Kershman
VP Pharmaceuticals Division: Arthur B. Hermelin
Research & Development: Harold Cole
Office Manager: Sue Wagoner
Estimated Sales: $570,000
Number Employees: 5-9
Square Footage: 12000

29165 Sheboygan Paper Box Co
716 Clara Ave
PO BOX 326
Sheboygan, WI 53081-5349
920-458-8373
Fax: 920-458-2901 800-458-8373
www.spbox.com
Folding cartons, displays, blister cards. Specializing
in polycoated and microflute packaging
President: Tom Liebl
Branch Manager: Tom Van De Kreeke
Executive VP: Larry Schneider
Director Sales/Marketing: David Moga
Estimated Sales: $10 - 20 Million
Number Employees: 100-249
Square Footage: 412000
Type of Packaging: Consumer, Food Service, Private Label, Bulk

29166 Sheffield Platers Inc
9850 Waples St
San Diego, CA 92121-2921
858-546-8484
Fax: 858-546-7653 800-227-9242
mwatkins@sheffieldplaters.com
www.sheffieldplaters.com
Coffee urns; wholesaler/distributor of punch bowls,
chaffing sets, trays, etc.; serving the food service
market; repair and replating services available
President: Dale L. Watkins Jr
dwatkins@sheffieldplaters.com
VP: Mark E. Watkins
Director, Business Development: Vincent Noonan
VP, Marketing: Mark Watkins
VP, Sales: Mark Watkins
Estimated Sales: $2.5-5 Million
Number Employees: 20-49
Square Footage: 68000

29167 (HQ)Shelby Co
865 Canterbury Rd
Westlake, OH 44145-1496
440-871-9901
Fax: 440-871-0326 800-842-1650
www.shelbycompany.com
Printed folding cartons and point of purchase advertising signs
President: Richard Rapacz
Controller: Wayne McGan
Executive VP: Sue Hintze
Manager: Kevin Smith
ksmith@shelbycothe.com
Plant Manager: Brian Charlton
Estimated Sales: $5-10 Million
Number Employees: 50-99
Square Footage: 200000
Type of Packaging: Consumer

29168 Shelby Pallet & Box Company
PO Box 27
Shelby, MI 49455-0027
231-861-4214
Fax: 231-861-0054
Pallets and skids
President: Brad Smith
Number Employees: 9

**29169 (HQ)Shelby Williams Industries
Inc**
810 W Highway 25 70
Newport, TN 37821-8044
423-623-0031
Fax: 866-319-9371 800-873-3252
www.shelbywilliams.com
Manufacturer and exporter of seating; importer of
wicker chairs
President: David Morley
Chairman and CEO: Franklin Jacobs
VP Operations: Marty Blaylock
Plant Manager: Bob Drey
Number Employees: 1000-4999
Parent Co: Falcon Industries
Other Locations:
Williams, Shelby, Industries
Statesville NC

29170 Shelby Williams Industries Inc
810 W Highway 25 70
Newport, TN 37821-8044
423-623-0031
Fax: 866-319-9371 800-873-3252
www.shelbywilliams.com
President: David Morley
CFO: Jean Fleetwood
R & D: Terry Roche
Quality Control: Marriane Carter
Plant Manager: Bob Drey
Number Employees: 1000-4999
Parent Co: Falcon Products

29171 Shelcon Inc
2081 S Hellman Ave # J
Suite J
Ontario, CA 91761-8024
909-947-4877
Fax: 909-947-1083 www.shelconveyors.com
Soiled tray, tray assembly and plating conveyors;
also, display rotisseries
President: Jon Clark
CEO: John Silvas
shelconveyors@verizon.net
Estimated Sales: $1-2.5 Million
Number Employees: 5-9
Square Footage: 14800

**29172 (HQ)Shelden, Dickson, & Steven
Company**
6114 Country Club Road
Omaha, NE 68152-2020
402-571-4848
Manufacturer and exporter of vending machines,
fluorescent light fixtures, wall safes, etc
President: Richard Lebron

Estimated Sales: $.5 - 1 million
Number Employees: 16
Square Footage: 200000

29173 Sheldon Wood Products
PO Box 339
Toano, VA 23168-0339

757-566-8880
Fax: 757-566-2230

Wooden pallets and skids
President: S Sheldon
Number Employees: 25

29174 Shell Oil Company
3333 Hwy 6 S
Houston, TX 77082-3101

281-544-9900
855-697-4355
HOU-OSP-Chemicals-CRC-Americas@shell.com
www.shell.us
Oil & chemical manufacturer
Chief Executive Officer: Ben van Beurden
Year Founded: 1890
Estimated Sales: $305 Billion
Number Employees: 92,000
Parent Co: Royal Dutch Shell PLC

29175 Shelley Cabinet Company
1407 N 630 E
Shelley, ID 83274

208-357-3700
Fax: 208-357-7447
Custom cabinets and counter tops
President: Dan Tschikof
Purchasing Manager: Greg Wilklund
Estimated Sales: $500,000-$1 Million
Number Employees: 10-19
Square Footage: 20000

29176 Sheman Tov Corporation
150 Oakwood Ave
Orange, NJ 07050-3912

973-673-2350
President: Lee Saal
Estimated Sales: Below $5 Million
Number Employees: 1-4

29177 (HQ)Shen Manufacturing Co Inc
40 Portland Rd
Conshohocken, PA 19428-2717

610-825-2790
Fax: 610-834-8617
Manufacturer, importer and exporter of placemats, chair pads, pot holders, oven mitts, aprons, bar mops, dish towels and cloths inclduing table, dish, scrub, dusting and polishing
President: Elissa Vogt
e.vogt@johnritz.net
CFO: Robert Steidle
VP Sales/Marketing: Howard Steidle Jr
Estimated Sales: $5-10 Million
Number Employees: 20-49

29178 Shepard Brothers Co
503 S Cypress St
La Habra, CA 90631-6126

562-697-1366
Fax: 562-697-5786 800-645-3594
info@shepardbros.com www.shepardbros.com
Manufacturer and exporter of cleaners, sanitizers and water treatment and waste treatment systems; also, consultant specializing in sanitation
President: Georgia Anglin
georgia@njcost.com
CEO: Ron Shepard
VP Sales: Tony Terranova
Estimated Sales: $15 - 20 Million
Number Employees: 50-99

29179 Shepard Niles Parts
220 N Genesee St
Montour Falls, NY 14865-9646

607-535-7111
Fax: 607-535-7323 800-727-8774
www.shepard-niles.com
Hoists and genuine Shepard Niles replacement parts
Manager: Michael Baker
Number Employees: 10-19
Type of Packaging: Bulk
Brands:
Cleveland Tramrail
Enduro
Liftabout
Safpowrbar

29180 Sheridan Sign Company
124 Wilson St
Salisbury, MD 21801-4100

410-749-7441
Fax: 410-749-4179
Signs including painted, electric and neon
President: Eugene F Trapkin
Manager: Marlynn R Schaeffer
Estimated Sales: Below $5 Million
Number Employees: 10-19

29181 Sherwood Tool
10100 Reisterstown Road
Owings Mills, MD 21117-3815

860-828-4161
Fax: 860-828-5387
Manufacturer and exporter of packaging machinery
President: Paul R Corazzo Sr
Parent Co: Sherwood Industries
Type of Packaging: Food Service, Private Label
Brands:
Shercan

29182 Shibuya International
1070 Reno Avenue
Modesto, CA 95351-1176

209-529-6466
Fax: 209-529-1834
www.shibuya-international.com
Importer of food processing and packaging machinery including aseptic filling systems, cappers, cartoners, unscramblers, casers, uncasers, washers, cleaners, pasteurizers, warmers, coolers, conveyors and labelers
President: Ken Saisho
CEO: Ian Greenland
Estimated Sales: $1 - 3 Million
Number Employees: 4
Square Footage: 66800
Parent Co: Shibuya Kogyo Company

29183 Shick Esteve
4346 Clary Blvd
Kansas City, MO 64130-2329

816-861-7224
Fax: 816-921-1901 877-744-2587
info@shickesteve.com www.shickesteve.com
Ingredient automation systems provider
President & CEO: Tim Cook
Executive VP & CFO: Blake Day
Director, Sales & Marketing: Jason Stricker
Estimated Sales: $40 Million
Number Employees: 100-249

29184 Shields Bag & Printing Co
1009 Rock Ave
Yakima, WA 98902-4629

509-248-7500
Fax: 509-248-6304 800-541-8630
www.shieldsbag.com
Manufacturer and exporter of plain and printed mono and co-extrusion polyethylene, nylon and polypropylene film and bags; also, commercial printing services available.
President: Patrick Shields
Estimated Sales: $50-100 Million
Number Employees: 500-999
Square Footage: 300000

29185 Shields Products Inc
530 Exeter Ave
West Pittston, PA 18643-1755

570-655-4596
Fax: 570-655-0262
Packaging materials including shredded cellophane, tissue, waxed paper and parchment
Owner: Warren Hemmelwright
Estimated Sales: Less Than $500,000
Number Employees: 1-4

29186 Shiffer Industries
41 Moana Ave
Kihei, HI 96753-7170

216-524-6546
800-642-1774
Manufacturer and exporter of assemblers, handlers, formers, feeders, index transferers, sorters, orienters, fillers, meters, markers, cutters, counters, loaders, unloaders, dispatchers, dedimplers, deburrers, labelers, etc.; customdesigning available
Office Manager: L Mangal
President: Stuart Shiffer
Estimated Sales: $2.5-5 Million
Number Employees: 20-49

29187 Shild Company
9 Lispenard St
New York, NY 10013-2290

212-431-7489
Fax: 212-941-1702 866-435-2949
shild1@aol.com www.shieldpress.com
Advertising specialties, wine list covers, manufacturers of corporate executive leather goods
Owner: Steven Shield
VP: Abe Horawitzch
Marketing: Abe Horowitz
Sales: Abe Horowitz
Purchasing: Abe Horowitz
Estimated Sales: $500,000-$1,000,000
Number Employees: 05to10
Number of Products: 75
Type of Packaging: Consumer, Food Service

29188 Shillington Box Co LLC
3501 Tree Court Ind Blvd
St Louis, MO 63122-6683

636-825-6471
Fax: 636-225-5306 info@shillingtonbox.com
www.shillingtonbox.com
Corrugated boxes
Estimated Sales: $18 Million
Number Employees: 50-99
Square Footage: 112000

29189 Shimadzu Scientific Instrs
7102 Riverwood Dr
Columbia, MD 21046-2502

410-381-1227
Fax: 410-381-1222 800-477-1227
www.shimadzu.com
Provides instruments for the food testing industry.
President: Alex Bready
alex.bready@gmail.com
Manager: Will Bankert
Estimated Sales: $1-2.5 Million
Number Employees: 250-499
Parent Co: Shimadzu Corporation

29190 Shingle Belting
420 Drew Ct # A
King of Prussia, PA 19406-2681

610-239-6667
Fax: 610-239-6668 800-345-6294
belting@shinglebelting.com
www.shinglebelting.com
Manufacturer and exporter of flat sheet and profile thermoplastic conveyor belting including PU, PVC and polyester and bakery belts
President/ Owner: Rennie Keating
CFO: Frank Manley
fmanley@shinglebelting.com
Marketing Coordinator: Monica Berry
Sales VP: Bob Frasetto
Operations: Frank Manley
Plant Manager: Bob Bolan
Estimated Sales: $5-10 Million
Number Employees: 20-49
Square Footage: 60000
Brands:
European Monofilements
Polyflex
Rounthane
Veethane

29191 Ship Rite Packaging
161 Woodbine Street
Bergenfield, NJ 07621-2839

201-385-4747
Fax: 201-385-2448 800-721-7447
www.shipritebags.com
Flexible polyethylene film; also, bags including flexible polyethylene, ziplock, rollstock and wicketted; custom printing available
President: Mayer Schlisser
Estimated Sales: $1-2.5 Million
Number Employees: 1-4

29192 Shipley Basket Mfg Co
191 Shipley Ln
Dayton, TN 37321-5589

423-775-2051
Fax: 423-775-2145 800-251-0806
shipleybasket@aol.com www.shipleybasket.com
Manufacturer and exporter of fruit and vegetable baskets
President: Diane Shipley
arthell3@aol.com
Estimated Sales: $5-10 Million
Number Employees: 20-49

29193 Shipmaster Containers Ltd.
380 Esna Park Drive
Markham, ON L3R 1G5
Canada
416-493-9193
Fax: 416-493-6223 info@shipmaster.com
www.shipmaster.com
Corrugated paper containers
Estimated Sales: $10 - 15 Million
Number Employees: 50-99

29194 Shippers Paper ProductsCo
808 Blake Rd
Sheridan, AR 72150-8476
870-942-4043
Fax: 870-942-5933 800-468-1230
inquiry@itwshippers.com
www.shippersproducts.com
Manufacturer and exporter of paper and plastic
dunnage bags
Contact: Jacqueline Garcia
jackie.garcia@shippersproducts.com
Plant Manager: Jeff Maness
Number Employees: 10-19

29195 Shippers Supply
2815A Cleveland Avenue
Saskatoon, SK S7K 8G1
Canada
306-242-6266
Fax: 306-933-4333 800-661-5639
saskatoon@shipperssupply.com
www.shipperssupply.com
Manufacturer and wholesaler/distributor of printed
labels, pressure sensitive tapes, corrugated boxes,
material handling equipment, stretch and shrink film
and shipping supplies
President: Ron Brown
CFO: Miles Jern
Branch Manager: Neil Nutter
Number Employees: Oover 200
Square Footage: 400000

29196 Shippers Supply
2815A Cleveland Avenue
Saskatoon, SK S7K 8G1
Canada
306-242-6266
Fax: 306-933-4333 800-661-5639
saskatoon@shipperssupply.com
www.shipperssupply.com
Manufacturer, wholesaler/distributor and importer of
printed labels, pressure sensitive tapes, corrugated
boxes, material handling equipment, stretch film and
shipping supplies; exporter of labels and printed
tape
President: Ron Brown
Branch Manager: Ken Nordyke
Number Employees: Oover 200
Square Footage: 400000
Brands:
Labelgraphics
Redeman

29197 Shippers Supply
102 King Edward Street E
Winnipeg, NB R3H 0N8
Canada
204-772-9800
Fax: 204-772-9834 800-661-5639
winnipeg@shipperssupply.com
www.shipperssupply.com
Printed labels, pressure sensitive tapes, corrugated
boxes, material handling equipment, stretch film and
shipping supplies
President: Ron Brown
Branch Manager: Bob Letchford
Number Employees: 10
Square Footage: 400000

29198 Shippers Supply, Labelgraphic
8-3401 19 Street NE
Calgary, AB T2E 6S8
Canada
403-291-0450
Fax: 403-291-3641 800-661-5639
airways@shipperssupply.com
www.shipperssupply.com
Manufacturer and wholesaler/distributor of printed
labels, pressure sensitive tapes, corrugated boxes,
material handling equipment, stretch film and shipping supplies

President: Ron Brown
General Manager: Dennis Rhind
Branch Manager: Jerry Pierce
Number Employees: Oover 200
Square Footage: 400000
Parent Co: Shippers Supply

29199 Shivvers
613 W English St
Corydon, IA 50060-1015
641-872-1007
Fax: 641-872-1593 www.shivvers.com
Manufacturer and exporter of continuous flow dry-
ing equipment and computer controls for dryers
President: Carl Shivvers
CFO: Ron Raasch
shivvers@shivvers.com
VP: Carl Shivvers
Assistant Sales Manager: Jim Ratliff
Estimated Sales: $20-50 Million
Number Employees: 100-249
Square Footage: 120000
Parent Co: Shivvers Manufacturing

29200 ShockWatch
5501 Lyndon B Johnson Fwy
Suite 350
Dallas, TX 75240
214-630-9625
Fax: 214-638-4512 800-393-7920
info@shockwatch.com www.shockwatch.com
Damage prevention products for shipping and hand-
ing of fragile and environmentally sensitive goods.
President/CEO: Tony Fonk
Vice President, Chief Financial Officer: Robert
Hutson
VP, Global Marketing & NA Sales: Tyson Stuelpe
Vice President, Operations: Jim Edwards
Estimated Sales: $9 Million
Number Employees: 70
Other Locations:
ShockWatch Manufacturing
Graham TX
Shockwatch Europe, BV
The Netherlands
ShockWatch China
ShangHai
Shockwatch Latin America
Mexico
Brands:
Shock Switch
Shock Watch

29201 Shoes for Crews/Mighty Mat
1400 Centrepark Blvd # 31
West Palm Beach, FL 33401-7402
561-683-5090
Fax: 561-683-3080 800-667-5477
scotts@shoesforcrews.com
www.shoesforcrews.com
Shoes for Crews Slip-Resistant Footwear will
prevent your slips and falls with over 38 styles to
choose from at prices starting at $24.98. We offer
the exclusive $5000 Slip & Fall Warranty: If any
employee slips and falls wearing SHOESFOR
CREWS, we will reimburse your company up to
$5000 on the paid workers comp claim. Call us at
1-877-667-5477 for details
Chairman of the Board: Stanley Smith
Contact: Stan Smith
s.smith@shoesforcrews.com
Estimated Sales: $5 - 10 Million
Number Employees: 1-4
Type of Packaging: Private Label
Brands:
Shoes For Crews

29202 Shook Kelley Design Group
2151 Hawkins St
Suite 400
Charlotte, NC 28203
704-377-0661
www.shookkelley.com
Brand strategy, architecture and design consultancy,
specializing in food retailing and consumption.
Founding Partner & Principal: Terry Shook
Founding Partner & Principal: Kevin Kelley
CFO: Brenda Lally
Founding Principal: Frank Quattrocci
Founding Principal: Stan Rostas
Year Founded: 1992
Estimated Sales: $350 Million

29203 Shoppers Plaza USA
PO Box 450
Dewitt, MI 48820-0450
517-327-9949
Fax: 517-886-9633
Retailer of industrial food equipment
Estimated Sales: Below 1 Million
Number Employees: 5

29204 Shore Distribution Resources
18 Manitoba Way
Marlboro, NJ 07746-1219
732-972-1297
Fax: 732-972-7669 800-876-9727
shordist@aol.com
Wholesaler/distributor of packaging materials and
equipment including plastic containers, polyester
film, cellophane and polypropylene; also, carry out
platters, bowls, disposable thermometers and food
safety products
President: Elaine Shore
CEO: Harvey Shore
shordist@aol.com
Sales: Harvey Shore
Operations: Scott Shore
Estimated Sales: $1-2.5 Million
Number Employees: 5-9
Square Footage: 12000
Type of Packaging: Food Service

29205 Shore Paper Box Co
9821 Riverton Rd
PO BOX 149
Mardela Springs, MD 21837-2164
410-749-7125
Fax: 410-860-2188 office@shorepaperbox.com
www.shorepaperbox.com
Set-up paper boxes; also, die cutting and hot stamp-
ing available. made to order only
President: Sharon Steckman
ssteckman@shorepaperbox.com
Chairman: Vernon Taylor
CFO: Vernon Taylor
Vice President: Mary Thompson
Quality Control: Mary Thompson
Estimated Sales: Below $5 Million
Number Employees: 10-19

29206 Shorewood Engineering Inc
865 Industrial Blvd
Waconia, MN 55387-1045
952-442-2526
Fax: 952-442-4036
sales@shorewoodengineering.com
www.shorewoodengineering.com
Packaging machinery
Owner: Matt Donahoe
matt@shorewoodengineering.com
Estimated Sales: $1-2.5 Million
Number Employees: 5-9

29207 Shorewood Packaging
1 Kero Rd
Carlstadt, NJ 07072-2604
201-933-3203
Fax: 203-754-6020
shorewoodmarketing@ipaper.com
Set-up fancy boxes
President: Mark Shore
Chairman: John Faraci
Senior Vice President of Corporate Devel: Cato Ealy
Contact: Steve Emergen
steve.emergen@ipaper.com
Estimated Sales: $20-50 Million
Number Employees: 100-249

29208 Shouldice Brothers SheetMetal
400 W Dickman Rd
Battle Creek, MI 49037
269-962-5579
Fax: 269-962-8114
shobro@shouldicebrothers.com
www.shouldicebrothers.com
Bins, ovens and material handling equipment includ-
ing conveyors, hoppers and carts
President: Dave Shouldice
Secretary and Treasurer: Dave Shouldice
VP: Dave Middlesworth
Contact: Davi Vanmiddleswort
vanmiddleswort@shouldicebrothers.com
Estimated Sales: $2.5-5 Million
Number Employees: 20-49

29209 Showa
579 Edison St
P.O. Box 8
Menlo, GA 30731-6335
706-862-2302
Fax: 706-862-6000 800-241-0323
usa@showabestglove.com www.showagloves.com
Manufacturer and exporter of protective gloves
President & COO, Americas: Shuji Kondo
Estimated Sales: $50 - 100 Million
Number Employees: 500-999
Brands:
Black Knight
D Flex
Ndex
Ndex Free
Nitri Pro
Nitty Gritty

29210 Showeray Corporation
2028 E 7th St
Brooklyn, NY 11223
718-965-3633
Fax: 718-965-3647
Manufacturer, importer and exporter of tablecloths
Estimated Sales: $1 - 5 Million
Number Employees: 50-99
Square Footage: 120000

29211 Shrinkfast Marketing
460 Sunapee St
Newport, NH 03773-1488
603-863-7719
Fax: 603-863-6225 800-867-4746
www.shrinkfast-998.com
Manufacturer and exporter of portable propane operated heat guns for shrinkwrap and palletizing applications
CFO: Chuck Milliken
cmilliken@ameriforge.com
Manager Sales/Marketing: Douglas Barton Jr
Estimated Sales: $5 - 10 Million
Number Employees: 5-9

29212 Shure-Glue Systems
600 Vine Street
Suite 1004
Cincinnati, OH 45202
513-333-0014
Fax: 513-874-3612 www.suhrelaw.com
Owner: Joe B Suhre Iv
Estimated Sales: Below $5 Million
Number Employees: 1-4

29213 Shurtape Technologies LLC
1712 8th St Dr sE
Hickory, NC 28602
828-322-2700
Fax: 828-322-4029 888-442-8273
custservice@shurtape.com www.shurtape.com
Commodity, industrial grade and specialty adhesive tapes.
Chief Executive Officer: Jim Shuford
Executive Vice President: Stephen Shuford
Vice President, Marketing: Jeff Pierce
Year Founded: 1996
Estimated Sales: $650 Million
Number Employees: 1,500
Parent Co: STM Industries
Brands:
Duck Brand
Frogtape
Kip
Painter's Mate
Shurtape Brand
T-Rex

29214 Shuster Corporation
4 Wright St
New Bedford, MA 02740
508-999-3261
Fax: 508-991-8585 info@shustercorp.com
www.shustercorp.com
Specialty ball and roller bearings including ceramic anticorrosive bearings for harsh applications;
President: Steven Shuster
Quality Control: John Sinlk
Contact: Stephen Anderson
sanderson@shustercorp.com
Estimated Sales: $5-10 Million
Number Employees: 20-49
Parent Co: Genuine Parts Company

29215 Shuster Laboratories
85 John Rd
Canton, MA 02021-2826
781-821-2200
Fax: 781-821-2200 800-444-8705
Consultant and contract research and development firm providing research and development for product development, sensory testing, nutrition analysis/labeling, HACCP, GMP, audits, regulatory liaison, shelf-life studies andmicrobiological and analytical testing
President: Philip Katz
CEO: Roy Lamothe
Director Marketing: Patricia Baressi
Contact: Tina Astore
bettina.astore@strquality.com
Estimated Sales: $10 - 20 Million
Number Employees: 100-249
Square Footage: 126000
Parent Co: Hauser Chemical Research Company
Other Locations:
Shuster Laboratories
Smyrna GA

29216 Shuster Laboratories
85 John Rd
Canton, MA 02021-2826
781-821-2200
Fax: 781-821-2200 800-444-8705
Product development, product formulation, sensory evaluation, market research, quality assurance, analytical and microbiological testing
President: Thil Katz
Manager: Ed Sarcione
CEO: Roy Lamothe
National Sales Manager: Eric Wieland
Contact: Tina Astore
bettina.astore@strquality.com
Estimated Sales: $10 - 20 Million
Number Employees: 100-249
Square Footage: 42000

29217 (HQ)Shuttleworth North America
10 Commercial Rd
Huntington, IN 46750-8805
260-356-8500
Fax: 260-359-7810 800-444-7412
inc@shuttleworth.com
www.collaborativeconveyor.com
Custom engineered solutions, conveyors, devices and material handling systems
President: Carol Shuttleworth
CEO: Steve Bucher
smbucher@gmail.com
Estimated Sales: $10-20 Million
Number Employees: 50-99
Number of Brands: 4
Square Footage: 9200
Parent Co: Shuttleworth
Other Locations:
Shuttleworth
Petaling Jaya
Brands:
Clean Glide
Slip-Torque
Slip-Trak
Zone Control

29218 Si-Lodec
4611 S 134th Place
Tukwila, WA 98168-3202
206-244-6188
Fax: 714-731-2019 800-255-8274
Manufacturer and exporter of scales including mobile, portable axle and force measurement
President: Rick Beets
Director International Sales: Arthur Tyson
Number Employees: 80
Square Footage: 60000

29219 Sicht-Pack Hagner
Musbacher Str. 21-23
Dornstetten/ Hallwangen, QC D-72280
Canada
004- 7-43 2
Fax: 004- 74-3 31 800-454-5269
info@sicht-pack-hagner.de
www.sicht-pack-hagner.de
President: Heirich Hagner
Number Employees: 10

29220 (HQ)Sico Inc
7525 Cahill Rd
Minneapolis, MN 55439-2745
952-941-1700
Fax: 952-941-6688 800-328-6138
sales@sicoinc.com www.sico-wallbeds.com
Manufacturer and exporter of room service carts and mobile folding banquet and buffet tables; also, fuel-powered and electric food warmers. Also manufacture portable dance floors, and portable stages, and bellmans carts and trucks
President: Jerry Danielson
jdanielson@sicoinc.com
President: Ken Steinbauer
CFO: Keith Dahlen
Vice President, Global Sales: Jerry Danielson
Marketing: Joel Mondshane
National Sales Manager: Heidi Niesen
Vice President, Operations: James Kline
Plant Manager: Pam Heller
Estimated Sales: $20-50 Million
Number Employees: 100-249
Type of Packaging: Food Service
Other Locations:
SICO America
Singapore
Brands:
Sico

29221 Sidel Inc
5600 Sun Ct
Norcross, GA 30092-2892
678-221-3000
Fax: 770-447-0084 800-453-7439
www.sidel.com
Sidel is the leading global provider of PET solutions for liquid packaging. We are committed to being an innovative, responsive, and reliable partner, providing sustainable solutions for the beverage industry.
Zone VP: Sebastien Geffrault
CFO: Richard Edwards
richard.edwards@sidel.com
Estimated Sales: $19.60 Million
Number Employees: 100-249

29222 Sidney Manufacturing Co
405 N Main Ave
PO Box 380
Sidney, OH 45365-2345
937-492-4154
Fax: 937-492-0919 800-482-3535
www.sidneymanufacturing.com
Equipment used in handling wet and dry bulk materials with a customer base in industries such as grain, wood byproducts, cellulose fibers, animal feeds, pet foods, flour, pellets, powders, food products and the line. ALso manufacture aline of industrial personnel elevators from 300lbs to 1000lbs capacity four passengers.
President: Steve Baker
sbaker@sidneymfg.com
Executive Vice President: Paul Borders
Engineering Manager: Tom Gross
Design Engineer: Josh Hicks
Sales Engineer/Customer Service: Joe Swartz
Purchasing Agent: Ward Cartwright
Estimated Sales: Below $5 Million
Number Employees: 20-49
Square Footage: 100000
Brands:
Sidney
Smc

29223 Sieberts Engineers
4951 Indiana Ave # 100
Lisle, IL 60532-3818
630-824-1515
Fax: 630-824-1535
john.joanis@siebertengineers.com
www.siebertengineers.com
Consulting engineers for food manufacturers
President: John Joanis
Contact: Jim Delapena
jim.delapena@sei-eng.com
Estimated Sales: $5 - 10 Million
Number Employees: 20-49

29224 Sielt Stone
6965 Union Park Center
Midvale, UT 84047-6008
801-268-9100
Fax: 801-268-9114 800-688-9781
Number Employees: 10

29225 Siemens Dematic
507 Plymouth Ave NE
Grand Rapids, MI 49505
616-913-7700
Fax: 616-913-7701 877-725-7500
usinfo@dematic.com www.dematic.com
Chief Executive Officer: Alan Bradley
CEO: John K Baysore
Contact: James Lindstrom
james.lindstrom@dematic.com
Estimated Sales: $3 - 5 Million
Parent Co: Siemens AG

29226 Siemens Industry Inc
3333 Old Milton Pkwy
Alpharetta, GA 30005-4437
770-751-2000
Fax: 770-751-4333 800-743-6367
AC/DC drives, programmable controllers and industrial systems
CEO: Denis Sadlowski
CFO: Harry Volande
Contact Person in USA: Andreas Klenke
Estimated Sales: Less than $500,000
Number Employees: 250-499
Parent Co: Siemens

29227 Siemens Measurement Systems
1000 Pittsford Victor Rd
Pittsford, NY 14534-3822
585-248-3050
800-568-7721
Data collection and analysis systems and software for statistical process control applications for food and beverage processors
President: Aubert Martin
Senior Vice President, Chief Information: Craig Berry
Executive Vice President of Global Sales: Paul Vogel
Number Employees: 20-49
Square Footage: 24000
Brands:
Focus Plus
Sentinel
Sentry/Sentry Plus

29228 Sierra Converting Corporation
1400 Kleppe Ln
Sparks, NV 89431
775-331-8221
Fax: 775-331-8385 800-332-8221
www.sierraconverting.com
Manufactures, prints and laminates packaging for the food and snack industries; zippered pouches and pouch bags
President: Robert Yarhi
VP: Daniel Yarhi
Quality Control: Victor Seballes
Sales: Jim Harmon
Contact: Chris Back
chrisb@washington.k12.ga.us
Operations: Bill Anglos
Productions: Ron Vurwip
Plant Manager: Otis Wilson
Purchasing: Chris Back
Estimated Sales: $20 - 30 Million
Number Employees: 75
Type of Packaging: Consumer, Food Service, Private Label

29229 Sierra Dawn Products
1814 Empire Industrial Ct # D
Santa Rosa, CA 95403-1946
707-535-0172
Fax: 707-588-0757 www.sierradawn.com
Manufacturer and exporter of liquid soaps, recycled packaging and household cleaning products with vegetable-based ingredients
President: Chris Maurer
chris@sierradawn.com
VP: Janet Jenkins
Estimated Sales: $1-2.5 Million
Number Employees: 1-4
Brands:
Lifetree

29230 Sifter Parts & Svc
29807 State Road 54
Wesley Chapel, FL 33543-4507
813-991-9400
Fax: 813-991-9700 800-367-3591
Info@SifterParts.com

Filters and sifters

Owner: Bob Williams
bob@ourtroopsonline.com
CFO: Tim Robinson
CEO: Bob Williams
Quality Control: Derek Williams
Estimated Sales: $5 - 10 Million
Number Employees: 10-19

29231 Sig Pack
2107 Livingston St
Oakland, CA 94606-5218
510-533-3000
Fax: 510-534-3000 800-824-3245
www.sigpacksystems.com
Manufacturer and exporter of vertical form/fill/seal machinery, linear scales and combination weighers
Regional Sales Manager: Pete Butler
Production Manager: Gary Barlettano
Estimated Sales: $1 - 5 Million
Number Employees: 50-100
Square Footage: 160000
Parent Co: SIG Pack International
Brands:
Golden Eagle
Infinity
Phasor

29232 Sigma Engineering Corporation
39 Westmoreland Ave
White Plains, NY 10606
914-682-1820
Fax: 914-682-0599 info@sigmaus.com
www.sigmaus.com
Manufacturer and exporter of drum pumps and forming extruders
President: Edward Derrico
Estimated Sales: $5 - 10 Million
Number Employees: 5-9
Square Footage: 40000

29233 Sigma Industrial Automation
5450 Fm 1103
Schertz, TX 78108-2110
210-659-5000
Fax: 210-659-3443 800-578-5060
dean@sigma-usa.com
Data collection in washdown environments, washdown computers, food processing-SPC, high speed and manual box labeling
Owner: Kathleen Chinni
kathi@sigma-usa.com
Director - SPC/QA: Dr. Guy Gibson
VP - Systems Engineering: Jeff Chinni
Engineering Manager: Rick Curcio
GM - Sales Director: Dean Chinni
kathi@sigma-usa.com
Applications Development Manager: Doug Lansdowne
Accounts Receivable: Anita Torres
Estimated Sales: $1-2.5 Million
Number Employees: 10-19

29234 Sigma Industries
4905 Hoffman Street
Suite B
Elkhart, IN 46516
574-295-9660
Fax: 574-293-8552 cs@sigma-wire.com
Manufacturer and exporter of material handling equipment including pallets, pallet racks, decking and steel wire mesh containers
President: Stanley Jurasek
CFO: Stanley Jurasek
Sales Director: Jan Richardson
Estimated Sales: $2.5 - 5 Million
Number Employees: 10-19
Brands:
Junior
Palletainer
Rigitainer

29235 Sign Art
6225 Old Concord Rd
Charlotte, NC 28213-6311
704-597-9801
Fax: 704-597-9808 800-929-3521
randy.souther@signartsign.com
www.signartsign.com
Electric signs; installation services available

Owner: Randy Souther
rsouther@signartsign.com
Director Project Management: Sue Prince
CFO: Randy Souther
Sales Leader: Earl Floyd
rsouther@signartsign.com
General Manager: Bill Sundberg
Estimated Sales: $2.5 - 5 Million
Number Employees: 20-49

29236 Sign Classics
1014 Timothy Dr
San Jose, CA 95133-1042
408-298-1600
Fax: 408-298-3177
Manufacturer and exporter of custom signs and designs including restaurant
President: Kenneth Fisher
Sales Manager: Clare Wild
Estimated Sales: $1-2.5 Million
Number Employees: 10-19

29237 Sign Expert
2044 Rose Ln
Pacific, MO 63069-1161
314-968-3565
Fax: 636-257-3566 800-874-9942
www.signexperts.com
Manufacturer and exporter of advertising signs
President: Paul Stojeba
paul@signexperts.com
CFO: Deb Stojeba
Estimated Sales: Less than $500,000
Number Employees: 5-9

29238 Sign Factory
13905 Artesia Blvd
Cerritos, CA 90703-9001
562-809-1443
Fax: 562-809-1435 www.cerritossigns.com
Flags, pennants, banners and signs; lettering service available
Owner: Ernst Dinkel
Manager: Ernie Dinkel
signfactorycerritos@gmail.com
Estimated Sales: Less Than $500,000
Number Employees: 1-4
Square Footage: 8000

29239 Sign Graphics
2317 E Florida St
Evansville, IN 47711
812-476-9151
Fax: 812-479-5147
Signs and custom directory systems; also, vehicle and window lettering engraving and decals
President: Brad Nash
Plant Manager: Kerry Dubuque
Estimated Sales: $500,000-$1 Million
Number Employees: 5-9
Square Footage: 8000

29240 Sign Products
1664 Terra Ave # 1
Sheridan, WY 82801-6135
307-672-3145
Fax: 307-672-9829 800-532-4753
54663signprod@aol.com
www.signproductsinc.com
Restaurant signage including neon and road boards
Manager: Terry Reimers
sales@signproductsinc.com
Sales: Paul Cox
Estimated Sales: Less Than $500,000
Number Employees: 1-4
Parent Co: Billings Neon

29241 Sign Systems, Inc.
23253 Hoover Road
Warren, MI 48089
586-758-1600
www.signsystemsofmichigan.com
Manufacturer and exporter of metal and plastic advertising signs
Manager: Barbara Warren
Contact: Dave Sedlarz
d.sedlarz@signsystemsofmichigan.com
Type of Packaging: Consumer, Food Service, Bulk

29242 Sign Warehouse
2614 Texoma Dr
Denison, TX 75020-1053
903-462-7700
Fax: 800-966-6834 800-699-5512
www.signwarehouse.com
Signs
Owner: Chris Grip
Sales/Design: Gary Gale
chris.grip@signwarehouse.com
Manager: Rhonda Cummings
Estimated Sales: $1-2.5 Million
Number Employees: 100-249

29243 SignArt Advertising
PO Box 2
Van Buren, AR 72957-0002
479-474-8581
Fax: 479-474-4708
Interior and exterior signs
President: Charles Jannen
VP: Gene Jennen
In-House Sales Manager: Linda Jennen
Contact: Chuck Jennen
signart@aol.com
Estimated Sales: Below $5 Million
Number Employees: 10-19
Square Footage: 18000

29244 Signal Equipment
3616 E Marginal Way S
Seattle, WA 98134-1130
206-324-8400
Fax: 206-623-0510 800-542-0884
Fire and security systems and emergency generator
systems
President: Tony Hastings
Estimated Sales: $5-10 Million
Number Employees: 5-9
Square Footage: 16000
Brands:
Edwards
Energy Dynamics
F.G. Wilson
Generac

29245 Signature Foods
73-D Enterprise Drive
Pendergrass, DR 30587
706-693-0098
Co-packer and support manufacturer for food com-
panies
President: Oran B Talkington
Estimated Sales: $3.3 Million
Number Employees: 23

29246 Signature Packaging
18 Dockery Dr
West Orange, NJ 7052
973-324-1838
Fax: 973-884-1909 800-376-2299
Plain and printed polyethylene bags for chicken, potatoes, fruits, etc.; also, paper and turkey tags, closures, packaging machinery, paper wrap, etc.;
wholesaler/distributor of produce and specialty
foods
Estimated Sales: less than $500,000
Number Employees: 1-4
Square Footage: 5000

29247 Signco Inc
3113 Merriam Ln
Kansas City, KS 66106-4615
913-722-1377
Fax: 913-722-3614 signs@signcokc.com
www.signcokc.com
Signs and decals; also, screen printing, vinyl
graphics available
President: Mike Sailer
signs@signcokc.com
Estimated Sales: Less Than $500,000
Number Employees: 5-9

29248 Signco Stylecraft
2611 Crescentville Rd
Cincinnati, OH 45241-1588
513-771-9090
Fax: 513-326-3090 800-733-0045
info@signcoscreenprinting.com
www.inky-tees.com
Printed T-shirts for food service vendors

President/Owner: Craig Howell
craig@signco.net
Vice President: Scott Howell
Head of the Art Department: Steve Diedling
Sales: Mary Beth
Estimated Sales: $1 - 2.5 Million
Number Employees: 10-19

29249 Signet Graphic Products
9037 Saint Charles Rock Rd
St Louis, MO 63114-4253
314-426-0200
Fax: 314-426-3535
Signs, banners and decals; fleet graphics available
Corporate Secretary: Ilene Leichtle
Manager: Bill Jones
Estimated Sales: $10-20 Million
Number Employees: 10-19
Square Footage: 140000

29250 Signet Marking Devices
3121 Red Hill Ave
Costa Mesa, CA 92626-4567
714-549-0341
Fax: 714-549-0972 800-421-5150
sales@signetmarking.com
www.signetmarking.com
Manufacturer and exporter of steel type marking
equipment
Owner: Melba Andrews
m.andrews@signetmarking.com
Operations Manager: Brian McGiffin
Estimated Sales: Below $5,000,000
Number Employees: 10-19

29251 Signets/Menu-Quik
7280 Industrial Park Boulevard
Mentor, OH 44060-5383
440-946-8676
Fax: 440-946-4646 800-775-6368
menuboardsales@signets.com
Menu boards
President: Robert Ledenican
Vice President: Terence Zuik
Marketing/Sales: Brenda Rolf
Number Employees: 25

29252 Signmasters
18421 Gothard St # 300
Huntington Beach, CA 92648-1236
949-364-9128
Fax: 949-364-6743
Banners, signs, flags and pennants
Owner: Mike Suzanski
Estimated Sales: Less than $500,000
Number Employees: 1-4

29253 Signode Industrial Group LLC
3650 W Lake Ave
Glenview, IL 60026-1215
847-724-6100
Fax: 847-657-5323 800-323-2464
www.signodegroup.com
Manufacturer and exporter of protective packaging
systems, equipment and consumables for steel and
plastic strapping, stretch film and tape
CEO: Mark Burgess
mburgess@signodecorp.com
Director National Sales: Jeff Osisek
Manager: George Heller
Estimated Sales: $3 - 5 Million
Number Employees: 5000-9999
Parent Co: Illinois Tool Works
Brands:
Apex
Contrax
Gemini
High Strength Tenex
Magnus
Octopus
Spiral Grip
Tenax

29254 Signode Industrial Group LLC
3650 W Lake Ave
Glenview, IL 60026-1215
847-724-6100
Fax: 847-657-5323 800-323-2464
ccunningham@signode.com
www.signodegroup.com
President: Russell Flaum
CEO: Mark Burgess
mburgess@signodecorp.com
CFO: John Mayfield

Number Employees: 5000-9999

29255 Signs & Designs
620 E Rancho Vista Blvd
Palmdale, CA 93550-4753
661-947-4473
Fax: 661-947-3559 888-480-7446
sales@signsanddesigns.tv
www.signsanddesigns.tv
Wood, metal, plastic, electrical and neon signs
Owner: Craig Mc Nabb
Estimated Sales: $1-2.5 Million
Number Employees: 10-19

29256 Signs & Shapes Intl
2320 Paul St
Omaha, NE 68102-4030
402-331-3181
Fax: 402-331-2729 800-806-6069
www.walkaroundmascots.com
Manufacturer and exporter of standard and custom
cold air-inflated walk-around costumes; also, signs
and character shapes; grand opening packages
available
President: Lee Bowen
lee@walkaround.com
Estimated Sales: Below $5 Million
Number Employees: 20-49
Square Footage: 26000
Type of Packaging: Food Service

29257 Signs O' Life
45 Bodwell St
Avon, MA 2322
800-750-1475
Fax: 508-583-9780
Illuminating and nonilluminating signs and graphics
Owner: Alvin Barber
VP: Steven Supinski
Estimated Sales: $1-2.5 Million
Number Employees: 10-19

29258 Signtech Electrical Advg Inc
4444 Federal Blvd
San Diego, CA 92102-2505
619-527-6100
Fax: 619-527-6111 sales@signtechusa.com
www.signtechus.com
Commercial awnings
President: David Schauer
CEO: Harold Schauer Jr.
hs@signtechusa.com
CFO: Kimra Schauer
VP Sales: Art Navarro
Estimated Sales: Less than $500,000
Number Employees: 50-99

29259 Siko Products Inc
2155 Bishop Cir E
Dexter, MI 48130-1565
734-426-3476
Fax: 734-426-3453 800-447-7456
sales@sikoproducts.com www.siko-global.com
Position, feedback devices
President: Maurizio Masullo
IT / Web Admin: Peter Crist
Sales Engineer: Cary Mulvany
Customer Service/Sales: Jim Schnebelt
Office Manager/Returns: Terry Miller
Shipping: Lisa LaRoe
Estimated Sales: $1 - 2.5 Million
Number Employees: 5-9

**29260 Silent Watchman Security
Services LLC**
P.O. BOX 3017
Danbury, CT 06813
203-743-1876
Fax: 203-743-9814 800-932-3822
Manufacturer and exporter of smoke and infrared in-
trusion detectors, recording door locks, CCTV and
multiplex security systems
President: Vincent Dascano
General Manager: Gary Sherman

29261 Silesia Grill Machines Inc
4770 County Road 16
St Petersburg, FL 33709-3130
727-544-1340
Fax: 727-544-2821 800-237-4766
sales@veloxgrills.us www.veloxgrills.com
Manufacturer and exporter of high speed contact
grills, crepe makers, panini grills and bucket openers

Owner: Silesia Grill
veloxgrills@aol.com
Estimated Sales: Less Than $500,000
Number Employees: 1-4
Type of Packaging: Food Service
Brands:
  Silesia

29262 Silesia Grill Machines Inc
4770 County Road 16
St Petersburg, FL 33709-3130
727-544-1340
Fax: 727-544-2821 800-267-4766
www.veloxgrills.com
Manufacturer and exporter of high speed contact
grills, crepe machines and bucket openers
Owner: Silesia Grill
veloxgrills@aol.com
Estimated Sales: Less Than $500,000
Number Employees: 1-4
Type of Packaging: Food Service

29263 Silgan Containers LLC
21800 Oxnard St # 600
Suite 600
Woodland Hills, CA 91367-3609
818-710-3700
Fax: 818-593-2255 www.silgancontainers.com
Plastic and aluminum closures for bottles and alumi-
num containers, capping machinery and feed
systems
Chair & CEO: Anthony Allott
Estimated Sales: Over $1 Billion
Number Employees: 1000-4999
Type of Packaging: Bulk
Brands:
  Drop-Lok
  Jetflow
  Magna Torq
  Pharma-Lok
  Plasti-Lug
  Ro
  Wing-Lok

29264 Silgan Plastic Closure Sltns
1140 31st St
Downers Grove, IL 60515-1212
630-515-8383
Fax: 724-657-8597 800-727-8652
www.silganpcs.com
Manufacturer and exporter of tamper evident plastic
bottle closures and related capping machinery
President: Tom Blaskow
CEO: Jack Watts
R&D: Borilla
Quality Control: Jee Book
Director: Bill Lauderbaugh
Sales/Marketing Manager: Don Kirk
General Manager: Alex Williams
Estimated Sales: $10 - 20 Million
Number Employees: 1000-4999
Parent Co: Partola Packaging
Other Locations:
  Partola Packaging
  Chino CA

29265 (HQ)Silgan Plastic Closure Sltns
1140 31st St
Downers Grove, IL 60515-1212
630-515-8383
Fax: 630-369-4583 800-767-8652
Manufacturer and exporter of capping equipment
and closures
President: James Taylor
CEO: Kevin Kwilinski
kevin@portpack.com
CFO: Deniss Berk
CEO: Brian Bauerbach
Quality Control: Jo Beni Kisto
VP Sales/Services: Ross Markely
Number Employees: 1000-4999
Other Locations:
  Portola Packaging
  Guadalajara
Brands:
  Cap Snap
  Nepco
  Portola Packaging

29266 (HQ)Silgan Plastic Closure Sltns
185 Northgate Cir
New Castle, PA 16105-5537
724-658-3004
Fax: 724-658-5138 www.ipec.biz

Manufacturer and supplier of plastic closures and
capping equipment
President: Joseph Giordano
jgiordano@ipec.biz
Sales Manager: Robert Harding
Estimated Sales: $8-$10 Million
Number Employees: 50-99
Square Footage: 340000
Other Locations:
  Brewton AL

29267 Silgan Plastics Canada
14515 North Outer Forty
Suite 210
Chesterfield, MO 63017
Canada
416-293-8233
Fax: 314-469-5387 800-274-5426
www.silganplastics.com
Manufacturer and exporter of plastic jars, bottles
and closures including standard screw cap, child re-
sistant and dispensing
National Sales Manager: David Meharg
Contact: Britt Babiarz
britt.babiarz@silganplastics.com
Estimated Sales: $1 - 5 Million
Number Employees: 100
Square Footage: 460000
Parent Co: Silgan Plastics Corporation

29268 Silgan Plastics LLC
14515 North Outer 40 Rd # 210
Suite 210
Chesterfield, MO 63017-5746
314-542-9223
Fax: 314-469-5387 800-274-5426
www.silganplastics.com
HDPE bottles and stock/private containers, closures
and fitments
President: Sarah T Macdonald
sarah.macdonald@silganplastics.com
CEO: Derek Schmidt
Estimated Sales: $61.5 Million
Number Employees: 1000-4999
Square Footage: 265000
Other Locations:
  Silgan Plastics
  Ottawa OH

29269 Silgan White Cap LLC
1140 31st St
Downers Grove, IL 60515-1212
630-515-8383
Fax: 630-515-5326 800-515-1565
www.americas.silganwhitecap.com
Manufacturer and exporter of metal and plastic vac-
uum closures and related sealing equipment includ-
ing cappers
CEO: Anthony J Allott
VP Sales: George Sullivan
Estimated Sales: $10-20 Million
Number Employees: 50-99
Square Footage: 20000
Parent Co: Schmalbach Lubecca
Type of Packaging: Bulk
Brands:
  Plast-Twist
  Twist-Off

29270 (HQ)Sillcocks Plastics International
PO Box 421
Hudson, MA 01749-0421
978-568-9000
Fax: 978-562-7128 800-526-4919
www.428main.com
Manufacturer and exporter of advertising novelties
including plastic credit, debit and photo/ID cards;
also, mag stripe signature panels, holography and se-
curity printing available
CEO and President: John Herslow
VP Sales/Marketing: Michele Logan
Estimated Sales: $3 - 5 Million
Number Employees: 10-19
Square Footage: 244000
Brands:
  Silcard

29271 Silliker Canada Company
90 Gough Road
Markham, ON L3R 5V5
Canada
905-479-5255
Fax: 519-822-0132
customercare@sillikercanada.com
Technical Sales Manager: Greg Forster
Number Employees: 90
Parent Co: MÉRIEUX NUTRISCIENCES COR-
PORATION

29272 Silliker Laboratories of Ga
2169 W Park Ct # G
Stone Mountain, GA 30087-3553
770-469-2701
Fax: 770-469-2883
kurt.westmoreland@silliker.com
www.merieuxnutrisciences.com
Consultant for sanitation, testing, analysis, etc
Manager: Robert Yemm
Regional Manager: Kurt Westmoreland
Manager: Robert Yemm
Estimated Sales: $2.5-5 Million
Number Employees: 20-49
Parent Co: Silliker Laboratories

29273 Silliker Laboratories-Pa Inc
6390 Hedgewood Dr
Allentown, PA 18106-9588
610-366-0264
Fax: 610-366-9357 silliker@silliker.com
www.silliker.com
Food consultant providing plant sanitation, microbi-
ological research and analysis of foods and
infestation
Vice President: Bob Colvin
Microbiology Manager: Kathy Jost-Keating
VP: Bob Colvin
Estimated Sales: $5-10 Million
Number Employees: 50-99
Parent Co: Silliker Laboratories Group

29274 Silliker, Inc
111 E Wacker Dr
Suite 2300
Chicago, IL 60601
312-938-5151
www.silliker.com
Laboratory providing food testing, microbiological
and chemical analysis, technical consulting and au-
dits for HACCP/GMPs employee training services
and custom research
President: James Ondyak
VP: Jim Hayes
Marketing Communications Manager: Jessica
Sawyer-Lueck
Contact: Kristin Carlson
kristyn.j.carlson@rrd.com
Number Employees: 50-99
Parent Co: BioMerieux Alliance

29275 Silver King Refrigeration Inc
1600 Xenium Ln N
Minneapolis, MN 55441-3706
763-923-2441
Fax: 763-553-1209 800-328-3329
info@silverking.com www.silverkingrefrig.com
Refrigerated bulk milk dispensers
President: Corey Kohl
Executive VP: Benjuman Rubin
Marketing Head: Benjuman Rubin
Estimated Sales: $15 - 20 Million
Number Employees: 100-249
Parent Co: Prince Castle
Brands:
  Norris
  Silver King

29276 Silver King Refrigeration Inc
1600 Xenium Ln N
Minneapolis, MN 55441-3706
763-923-2441
Fax: 763-553-1209 800-328-3329
info@silverking.com www.silverkingrefrig.com
Manufacturer and exporter of refrigerators, freezers,
prep tables, ice cream cabinets, bulk milk and salad
dispensers, display cases and fountainettes
President: Corey Kohl
Executive VP: Benjamin Rubin
Estimated Sales: $15 - 20 Million
Number Employees: 100-249
Parent Co: Prince Castle
Type of Packaging: Food Service

Brands:
Silver King

29277 Silver Mountain Vineyards
PO Box 3636
Santa Cruz, CA 95063-3636
408-353-2278
Fax: 408-353-1898 info@silvermtn.com
www.silvermtn.com
Wine
President: Jerold O'Brien
info@silvermtn.com
Estimated Sales: Less Than $500,000
Number Employees: 1-4
Type of Packaging: Private Label
Brands:
Silver Mtn Vineyards

29278 (HQ)Silver Spur Corp
16010 Shoemaker Ave
Cerritos, CA 90703-2239
562-921-6880
Fax: 562-921-7916 vivian@silverspurcorp.com
www.silverspurcorp.com
Manufactures glass bottles, glass containers, HDPE (High Density Polyethlene) Packers, PET (polyethylene terephthalare) containers and closures. 1
President: James Hao
Vice President: Vivian Chu
vivian@silverspurcorp.com
Marketing: Alvin Hao
Operations Manager: Vivian Chu
Plant Manager: James Wilder
Estimated Sales: $9 Million
Number Employees: 100-249
Square Footage: 200000

29279 Silver State Plastics Inc
2626 8th Ave
Greeley, CO 80631-8412
970-346-8667
Fax: 970-346-9191
silverstateplastics@comcast.net
Plain and printed polyethylene bags
Owner: James Cornforth
james.cornforth@silverstateplastics.com
Sales: Vickie Walker
Plant Manager: Richard Dailey
Estimated Sales: $5 - 10 Million
Number Employees: 10-19
Square Footage: 80000
Type of Packaging: Private Label

29280 Silver Weibull
14800 E Moncrieff Place
Aurora, CO 80011-1211
303-373-2311
Fax: 303-373-2319
Manufacturer and exporter of sugar centrifugals, reheaters and crystallizers
Manager Technical Process: Tommy Persson
Business Unit Manager (Worldwide): Derrald Houston
Manager: Randy Copsey
Estimated Sales: Below $5 Million
Number Employees: 3
Square Footage: 200000
Parent Co: Consolidated Process Machinery
Brands:
Silver-Weibull

29281 Silverson Machines Inc
355 Chestnut St
PO Box 589
East Longmeadow, MA 01028-2702
413-525-4825
Fax: 413-525-5804 800-204-6400
fran@silverson.com www.silverson.com
Manufacturer, supplier and exporter of food processing equipment including blending and batching equipment, high shear mixers, colloid mills and homogenizers; also, laboratory equipment and supplies
President: Harold Rothman
Clerk/VP: David Rothman
VP: Anne Rothman
Sales Manager: Brian Martin
IT: Frances Carhart
fran@silverson.com
General Manager: Michael Boyd
Estimated Sales: $2.6 Million
Number Employees: 10-19
Parent Co: Silverson Machines

Brands:
Flashblend
Silverson

29282 Simco
2257 N Penn Rd
Hatfield, PA 19440-1998
215-822-2171
Fax: 215-822-3795 800-203-3419
www.megapathdsl.net
Packaging, static control, electrostatic charging, web cleaning
President: Gary Swink
Sales: Lou Gieleonora
Manager: Michael Oldt
moldt@simcomail.com
Estimated Sales: Less Than $500,000
Number Employees: 1-4

29283 Simco
2257 N Penn Rd
Hatfield, PA 19440-1998
215-822-2171
Fax: 215-822-3795 800-203-3419
www.megapathdsl.net
President: Gary Swink
Manager: Michael Oldt
moldt@simcomail.com
Estimated Sales: Less Than $500,000
Number Employees: 1-4

29284 Simkins Industries Inc
317 Foxon Rd # 3
East Haven, CT 06513-2038
203-787-7171
Fax: 203-782-6324 www.simkinsindustries.com
Folding boxes; also, glassine and greaseproof paper and paperboard
President: Leon Simkins
CFO: Anthony Battaglia
Estimated Sales: Less Than $500,000
Number Employees: 1-4
Square Footage: 1600

29285 (HQ)Simmons Engineering Corporation
1200 Willis Ave
Wheeling, IL 60090
847-419-9800
Fax: 847-419-1500 800-252-3381
sales@simcut.com www.simcut.com
Manufacturer and exporter of cutting knives and blades for bread, cake, fish, fruit, vegetables and meat products
President/Owner: Bruce Gillian
VP/General Manager: Colin Murphy
Customer Service & Marketing Manager: Erin O'Brien
Contact: Lorenzo Barrios
l.barrios@simcut.com
Estimated Sales: $5 - 10 Million
Number Employees: 50-99
Square Footage: 60000
Brands:
Tru-Trak

29286 Simolex Rubber Corp
14505 Keel St
Plymouth, MI 48170-6002
734-453-4500
Fax: 734-453-6120 info@simolex.com
www.simolex.com
Manufacturer and exporter of rubber products including beverage hoses, juice tubing, milk hoses, gaskets, seals and bottle stoppers
President: Bob Dungarani
info@simolexrubber.com
Estimated Sales: $10-20 Million
Number Employees: 20-49
Square Footage: 50000
Type of Packaging: Food Service

29287 Simon S. Jackel Plymouth
684 Hidden Lake Drive
Tarpon Springs, FL 34689-2600
727-942-3991
Consultant specializing in product and ingredient development and improvement for companies supplying baking ingredients and products
Director: Simon Jackel PhD

29288 Simonds International
135 Intervale Rd
PO Box 500
Fitchburg, MA 01420-6519
Canada
978-345-7521
Fax: 978-424-2212
www.simondsinternational.com
Manufacturer, exporter and importer of knives for packaging and food processing equipment, cryovac, etc
President: Roy Erdwins
roy.erdwins@simondsinternational.com
Sales Manager: Fred Adams
Number Employees: 100-249
Square Footage: 60000
Parent Co: IKS International

29289 Simonds International
135 Intervale Rd
P.O. Box 500
Fitchburg, MA 01420-6519
978-345-7521
Fax: 978-424-2212 800-343-1616
www.simondsinternational.com
Manufacturer and exporter of band and hack saws and saw blades, circular machine knives, files and investment castings
President: Roy Erdwins

CFO: Henry Botticello
Estimated Sales: $83 Million
Number Employees: 100-249
Square Footage: 400000

29290 Simoniz USA Inc
201 Boston Tpke
Bolton, CT 06043-7203
860-646-0172
Fax: 860-645-6070 800-227-5536
wgorra@simonizusa.com www.simonizusa.com
Manufacturer and exporter of waterless hand cleaners, soap and specialty chemicals
President: William Gorra
CEO: Mark Kershaw
mkershaw@simonizusa.com
VP Marketing: Michele O'Neal
Estimated Sales: $10,000,000 - $19,999,999
Number Employees: 50-99

29291 Simonson Group
35 Washington Street
Winchester, MA 01890-2927
781-729-8906
Fax: 781-729-5079
Consultant specializing in marketing research and product development; serving food service manufacturers and restaurants
Executive VP: Barbara Simonson
Estimated Sales: $1 - 5 Million
Number Employees: 1-4

29292 Simplex Filler Co
640 Airpark Rd # A
Napa, CA 94558-7569
707-265-6801
Fax: 707-265-6868 800-796-7539
www.simplexfiller.com
Manufacturer and exporter of piston and pressure fillers for bottle, can, jar and bag filling; also, conveyors, unscramblers, lid droppers, accumulators and heated hoppers
CEO: G Donald Murray
Estimated Sales: $1-5 Million
Number Employees: 10-19
Square Footage: 30000
Parent Co: Wild Horse Industrial Corporation
Brands:
Simplex

29293 Simplex Time Recorder Company
1936 E Deere Avenue
Suite 120
Santa Ana, CA 92705-5732
949-724-5000
Fax: 978-630-7856
Manufacturer and exporter of fire alarms and time recorders
General Manager: Russell Stafford
Area/Branch Manager: Gary Holmes
Estimated Sales: $1 - 5 Million
Number Employees: 100
Brands:
Simplex

29294 Simplex Time Recorder Company
1936 E Deere Avenue
Suite 120
Santa Ana, CA 92705-5732
949-724-5000
Fax: 978-630-7856 800-746-7539
Manufacturer and exporter of fire alarm and security systems
General Manager: Russell Stafford
Estimated Sales: $1 - 5 Million
Number Employees: 20

29295 Simplimatic Automation
1046 W London Park Dr
Forest, VA 24551
434-385-9181
Fax: 434-385-7813 800-294-2003
sales@simplimatic.com www.simplimatic.com
Manufacturer and exporter of product handling equipment including tray film packaging systems, palletizers and de-palletizers, rinsers and conveyor systems.
President & CEO: Tom DiNardo
Year Founded: 1965
Estimated Sales: $100+ Million
Number Employees: 51-200
Square Footage: 60000
Brands:
    Simpli-Clean
    Simpli-Flex
    Simpli-Pak
    Simpli-Pal
    Simpli-Snap
    Sure-Grip

29296 Simply Manufacturing
E11259 County Road Pf
Prairie Du Sac, WI 53578
608-643-6656
www.simplymfg.com
Meat processing accessories and replacement parts such as vats, meat sticks, ham press towers, screens, and portable racks.
Contact: Mike Disrud
    mike.disrud@simplymfg.com

29297 Simply Products
RR 5
Box 5299
Kunkletown, PA 18058-9696
610-681-6894
Fax: 610-681-6885
Software for point of sale and back office systems
President: Dave Rottkamp
VP Operations: Allison Ohl
Number Employees: 6
Square Footage: 8000
Brands:
    Simply Food

29298 Simpson Electric
2916 Kelly Dr
Elgin, IL 60124-4349
847-697-2260
Fax: 847-697-2272 cservice@simpsonelectric.com
www.simpsonelectric.com
Process control systems
Founder: Ray Simpson
Estimated Sales: $20-50 Million
Number Employees: 10-19

29299 Sims Machinery Co Inc
3621 45th St SW
PO Box 446
Lanett, AL 36863-6305
334-576-2101
Fax: 334-576-3116 www.simsmachinery.com
Manufacturer and exporter of stainless steel food grade tanks; also, custom stainless steel fabrications available
CEO: Lynn Duncan
Sales Manager: Bryant Hollon
Estimated Sales: $5-10 Million
Number Employees: 10-19
Square Footage: 80000

29300 Sims Superior Seating
6951 Highway 42
Locust Grove, GA 30248-4640
770-957-9667
Fax: 770-954-1935 800-729-9178
simssales@simsseating.com
www.simsseating.com
Restaurant hospitality seating, booths, tabletops and bases, kitchen equipment covers and plantters
Owner: Cathy Sims
CFO: Kathryn Sims
VP: Charles Sims
Sales: T Wonder
    csims@simsseating.com
Plant Manager: T Wonder
Estimated Sales: $5-10 Million
Number Employees: 20-49
Square Footage: 56000

29301 Sinco
3965 Pepin Avenue
Red Wing, MN 55066-1837
860-632-0500
Fax: 860-632-1509 800-243-6753
Manufacturer and exporter of safety netting systems for guarding material handling equipment including conveyors, pallet racks, etc
President: David Denny
Estimated Sales: $10 - 20 Million
Number Employees: 40

29302 Sine Pump
14845 W 64th Ave
Arvada, CO 80007-7523
303-425-0800
Fax: 303-425-0896 888-504-8301
pumps@sundyne.com www.sinepump.com
Manufacturer and exporter of sanitary positive displacement pumps for the food and dairy industries including low-shear, low-pulsation and high-suction. designs, manufactures and supports industrial pump and compressor products for theprocess fluid and gas industries
President: William Taylor
Human Resources: Christine Lopez
Area Sales Manager: Brad Juntunen
After Market Specialist: Chuck Zachrich
Number Employees: 500-999
Parent Co: Sundyne Corporation
Brands:
    Sine Pump

29303 Sinicrope & Sons Inc
1124 Westminster Ave
Alhambra, CA 91803-1294
323-283-5131
Fax: 323-283-3399
Store fixtures
President: Gary Sinicrope
    gary@sinicropeandsons.com
VP: Sandra Sinicrope
Estimated Sales: Below $5,000,000
Number Employees: 20-49

29304 Sioux Corp
1 Sioux Plz
Beresford, SD 57004-1500
605-763-3333
Fax: 605-763-3334 888-763-8833
email@sioux.com www.sioux.com
Manufacturer and exporter of hot, cold and combination pressure washers and steam cleaners; also, all-electric and explosion-proof units available
President/Owner: Jack Finger
CEO: Amanda Cooper
    acooper@sioux.eu
Marketing Manager: Jessica Johnson
Sales Manager: Meg Andersen
Regional Manager - International Sales (: David Nelson
Estimated Sales: $2.5-5 Million
Number Employees: 20-49
Number of Products: 500+
Brands:
    Dakota
    Sioux
    Steam-Flo

29305 Sioux Falls Rbr Stamp Works
212 S Main Ave
Sioux Falls, SD 57104-6310
605-334-5990
Fax: 605-334-0750 855-334-5990
www.sfrubberstamp.com
Rubber stamps
President: Paul Brue
    order.sfrubberstamp@midconetwork.com
Estimated Sales: $1 - 5 Million
Number Employees: 1-4

29306 Sipco
12610 Galveston Road
Webster (Houston), TX 77598
281-480-8711
Fax: 281-480-8656 info@sipco-mls.com
www.sipco-mls.com
Mechanical linkage solutions
Manager: Tom Jones
Accountant: Marissa Reise
Estimated Sales: $10 - 20 Million
Number Employees: 20-49
Parent Co: Standalone
Type of Packaging: Private Label, Bulk

29307 Sipco Products
4301 Prospect Road
Peoria Heights, IL 61616-6537
309-682-5400
Fax: 309-637-5120 terry@sipcoproducts.com
www.pnduniforms.com
Ashtray receptacles, smoking urns, safety related items, wire racks and plastic bag holders; exporter of ashtray receptacles
President: Eileen Grawey
Office Manager: Audrey Wylie
Contact: Sharon Brick
    sharon@sipcoproducts.com
Estimated Sales: $3 - 5 Million
Number Employees: 1-4
Square Footage: 40000
Type of Packaging: Food Service
Brands:
    Rack-A-Bag
    Sipco Dunking Station

29308 Sirco Systems
2828 Messer Airport Highway
Birmingham, AL 35203
205-731-7800
Fax: 205-731-7885
Manufacturer and exporter of food storage equipment including steel drums
VP Sales: Jack Matheson
Estimated Sales: $5-10 Million
Number Employees: 50-99
Parent Co: Jemison Investment Company

29309 Sirman Spa/IFM USA
9490 Franklin Ave
Franklin Park, IL 60131-2833
847-288-9500
Fax: 847-288-9501 www.ifmusa.com
CEO: Alessandro Lorengato
Estimated Sales: $1 - 5 Million
Number Employees: 1-4

29310 Sitka Store Fixtures
PO Box 410247
Kansas City, MO 64141-0247
816-531-8290
Fax: 816-753-5701 800-821-7558
Wooden retail store fixtures including customer service centers and bakery, deli, produce and feature display
President: Patrick Clifford
Sales/Design: Brian Kipper
Project/Production Manager: Dave Sellers
Number Employees: 21
Square Footage: 68000
Parent Co: Cliff-Stan Industries

29311 Sitma USA
Via Vignolese
Spilamberto, MO 41057
390-597-8031
Fax: 390-597-8030 800-728-1254
sitmausa@sitma.com www.sitma.com
Manufacturer and importer of packaging equipment including horizontal form, fill and seal systems and bundle wrappers
President: Aris Ballestrazzi
CEO/Managing Director: Pete Butikis
National Sales Manager: Al Lindsay
Estimated Sales: $2.5 - 5 Million
Number Employees: 10-19
Square Footage: 66000
Parent Co: Sitma Machinery SPA
Other Locations:
    Sitma USA
    BP 28-77013 Melun Cedex

29312 Sitram/Global Marketing
PO Box 5503
Parsippany, NJ 07054-6503
973-515-0085
Fax: 973-515-3467 800-515-8585
Manufactures stainless steel cookware with new surface technology, cybernox
President: Christopher D Boyhan
Vice President: Allan Wolk
Estimated Sales: $1-2.5 Million
Number Employees: 19
Parent Co: Sitram France
Brands:
 Catering
 Cybernox
 Magnum
 Profiserie

29313 Sivetz Coffee
349 SW 4th St
Corvallis, OR 97333-4622
541-753-9713
Fax: 541-757-7644
Roasted coffee beans, extracts, almond kernels, hazelnut kernels, and coffee roasting machines
President: Mike Sivetz
Number Employees: 1-4
Type of Packaging: Consumer, Bulk
Brands:
 Sivetz Coffee Essence

29314 Six Hardy Brush Manufacturing
1172 East St S
Suffield, CT 06078-2410
860-623-8465
Specialty bakers' and confectioners' brushes
President: Steven Pierz
Estimated Sales: $2.5-5 Million
Number Employees: 5 to 9
Square Footage: 6400

29315 Skalar Inc
5012 Bristol Industrial # 107
Suite 107
Buford, GA 30518-1775
770-945-6008
Fax: 770-416-6718 800-782-4994
info@skalar-us.com www.skalar.com
Wine industry lab equipment, flow analyzers, process analyzers, robotic analyzers
President: Lel Seruyzken
CFO: Sjaak Surrer
Quality Control: Jomen Ting
Estimated Sales: Below $5 Million
Number Employees: 10-19

29316 Skc Inc
850 Clark Dr # 2
Budd Lake, NJ 07828-4313
973-347-7000
Fax: 973-347-7775 800-526-2717
jbrown@skcfilms.com www.skcfilms.com
Polyester film
President: Y J Joon
Contact: Chai Chuly
cchai@skcfilms.com
Estimated Sales: Less Than $500,000
Number Employees: 5-9

29317 (HQ)Skd Distribution Corp
13010 180th St
Jamaica, NY 11434-4108
718-525-6000
Fax: 718-276-4595 800-458-8753
rachel@skdparty.com www.biggiftbow.com
Manufacturer and exporter of plastic molders and fabricators, rigid foam fillers, wedges and foam packing inserts for boxes
Manager: Richard Mark
VP: Jack Schnitt
Marketing: Bill Stephan
Contact: Stanley Ast
sast@skdparty.com
Estimated Sales: $5-10 Million
Number Employees: 20-49
Square Footage: 1080000

29318 Skinetta Pac-Systems
55742 Currant Road
Mishawaka, IN 46545-4808
574-254-1950
Fax: 219-254-1955 info@skinetta.com
Packaging machinery: end-of-line machines

Estimated Sales: $2.5-5 Million
Number Employees: 4

29319 Skinner Sheet
3536 Bee Cave Road
Suite 211
West Lake Hills, TX 78746-5474
512-328-7785
Fax: 512-328-7786
Corrugated board products

29320 (HQ)Skrmetta Machinery Corporation
3536 Lowerline Street
New Orleans, LA 70125-1004
504-488-4413
Fax: 504-488-4432
Manufacturer and exporter of shrimp peeling and deveining machinery
President: Eric Skrmetta
VP: Dennis Skrmetta
Estimated Sales: $5,800,000
Number Employees: 55
Square Footage: 40000
Other Locations:
 Skrmetta Machinery Corp.
 New Orleans LA

29321 Slautterback Corporation
11475 Lakefield Drive
Duluth, GA 30097-1511
831-373-3900
Fax: 831-373-0385 800-827-3308
www.slautterback.com
Manufacturer and exporter of hot melt adhesive packaging equipment
President: Fred Erler
President, Chief Executive Officer: Michael Hilton
Marketing Manager: Jim Pagnella
Vice President of Systems: Douglas Bloomfield
Number Employees: 135
Square Footage: 252000
Parent Co: Nordson Corporation

29322 Slicechief Co
3333 Maple St
P.O. Box 80206
Toledo, OH 43608-1147
419-241-7647
Fax: 419-241-3513
Manufacturer and exporter of nonelectric vegetable/fruit slicers and cheese shredders
President: Sue Brown
Estimated Sales: $2.5-5 Million
Number Employees: 1-4
Type of Packaging: Food Service
Brands:
 Chief 900 Series

29323 Slidell
PO Box 39
New Market, MN 55054-0039
507-451-0365
Fax: 507-451-2405 800-328-1769
Packaging equipment for paper or plastic needs
Estimated Sales: $20-50 Million
Number Employees: 100

29324 Slip Not
2545 Beaufait St
Detroit, MI 48207-3467
313-923-0400
Fax: 313-923-4555 800-754-7668
info@slipnot.com www.slipnot.com
SlipNOT manufactures NSF registered stainless steel slip resistant flooring products from floor plates, drain covers, bar grating, ladder rungs/covers, to stair treads/covers, perforated and expanded metal retrofit plates. SlipNOTproducts can withstand the extreme cold of cyrogenics and heat of cookers, as well as caustic cleaning agents.
President: William S Molnar
National Sales Manager: Brian Pelto
Estimated Sales: $.5 - 1 million
Number Employees: 20-49
Parent Co: WS Monar Comapany
Brands:
 Flex-Grip
 Grid-Grip
 Grip-Grate
 Grip-Plate
 Slipnot

29325 Slip-Not Belting Corporation
PO Box 386
Kingsport, TN 37662
423-246-8141
Fax: 423-246-7728
Manufacturer and exporter of leather, plastic and perlon transmission and conveyor belting
President/CEO: David Shivell
CEO: Phill Shivell
Marketing: David Shivell
Estimated Sales: $3 - 5 Million
Number Employees: 5-9

29326 Slm Manufacturing Corp
215 Davidson Ave
Somerset, NJ 08873-4190
732-469-7500
Fax: 732-469-5546 800-526-3708
slminfo@slmcorp.com www.slmcorp.com
Semi-rigid plastic cut to size roll form tubing that can be combined with stock end caps to form complete tooling-free packages
Owner: Thomas Vajtay
tvajtay@slmcorp.com
Estimated Sales: $2.5-5 Million
Number Employees: 5-9

29327 Smalley Manufacturing Co Inc
10640 Dutchtown Rd
Knoxville, TN 37932-3205
865-966-5866
Fax: 865-675-1618 droberto@smalleymfg.com
www.smalleymfg.com
Conveyor, feeder and storage systems
President: Dale Roberto
VP Sales: Mike Green
Sales Engineer: Keith Iddins
Sales: Mark Kipfer
Estimated Sales: $10-20 Million
Number Employees: 50-99
Square Footage: 92000

29328 Smalley Package Company
PO Box 231
Berryville, VA 22611
540-955-2550
Fax: 540-955-4590
Wooden, pallets, pallet boxes, baskets; also, recycled/remanufactured pallets
President: Robert W Smalley Jr
Vice President: James Livengood
Sales Director: William Hair
Estimated Sales: $5-10 Million
Number Employees: 1-4

29329 Smartscan, Inc
33083 Eight Mile Road
Livonia, MI 48152
248-477-2900
Fax: 248-477-7453 ussales@smartscan.com
www.smartscaninc.com
Variable beam spacing, link systems, marshaling boxes, and light curtaining
President: Paul Budesheim
paul.budesheim@smartscaninc.com
CFO: Paul Budesheim
Quality Control: Paul Budesheim
General Manager: Paul Budesheim
Estimated Sales: $20 - 50 Million
Number Employees: 20-49
Number of Products: 4

29330 Smetco
PO Box 560
14633 Ottaway Rd NE
Aurora, OR 97002
503-678-3081
Fax: 503-678-3095 800-253-5400
www.smetco.com
Manufacturer and exporter of pallet handling systems for sorting and repair; also, conveyors, scissor lifts, dispensers, stackers and turn tables
President: John Smet
CFO: Kelly Wick
Vice President: John Smets
Marketing Director: Ken Butler
Contact: Carolyn Herman
carolynh@smetco.com
Estimated Sales: $1-3 Million
Number Employees: 20-49
Square Footage: 116000
Brands:
 Smetco
 Stackers

29331 Smico Manufacturing Co Inc
6101 Camille Ave
Oklahoma City, OK 73149-5036
405-946-1461
Fax: 405-946-1472 800-351-9088
www.smico.com
Manufacturer and exporter of vibrating screens and
gyratory sifters
President: Randall Stoner
smico@smico.com
CEO: Erick Held
VP: Tim Douglass
Sales: Holly Lindsey
Operations: Randall Stoner
Purchasing Director: Jane Wenk
Estimated Sales: $5 - 10 Million
Number Employees: 20-49
Square Footage: 92000

29332 Smith & Loveless Inc
14040 Santa Fe Trail Dr
Lenexa, KS 66215-1284
913-888-5201
Fax: 913-888-2173 800-898-9122
answers@smithandloveless.com
www.smithandloveless.com
Water and wastewater treatment and transfer equip-
ment
President: Frank Rebori
CFO: David Ferbezar
Estimated Sales: $30 - 50 Million
Number Employees: 250-499

29333 Smith & Taylor
1071 Howell Mill Rd NW
Atlanta, GA 30318-5557
404-872-8135
Fax: 404-872-0471 sunlow1@aol.com
Owner: Danny Graham
Sales Director: Jerry Hernnebaul
Estimated Sales: $3 - 5 Million
Number Employees: 10-19

29334 Smith Design Associates
205 Thomas St
Bloomfield, NJ 07003
973-429-2177
Fax: 973-429-7119 laraine@smithdesign.com
www.smithdesign.com
Package design and brand identity
President: Laraine Smith
CFO: James C Smith
Contact: Laraine Blauvelt
laraine@smithdesign.com
Estimated Sales: $5 Million
Number Employees: 10-19
Type of Packaging: Consumer, Private Label

29335 Smith Packaging
6045 Kestrel Road
Mississauga, ON L5T 1Y8
Canada
905-564-6640
Fax: 905-564-5681
Manufacturer and exporter of boxes, cartons and
containers
President: Mervin Hillier
Operations Manager: Gerard Gregoire
Number Employees: 100
Type of Packaging: Consumer, Bulk

29336 Smith Pallet Co Inc
159 Polk Road 29
PO Box 207
Hatfield, AR 71945-7002
870-389-6184
Fax: 870-389-6194 spallet@windstream.net
www.smithpallet.com
Skids, crating, dunnage, boxes and hooked and soft-
wood pallets
President: Jim Wilson
jwilson@smithpallet.com
Sales Manager: Tate Mendoza
Sales: Jim Mabry
General Manager: Lyle Wilson
Controller: Bryan Schoeppey
Plant Manager: Dalton Doughty
Estimated Sales: Below $5 Million
Number Employees: 100-249

29337 Smith, RD, Company
PO Box 186
Eau Claire, WI 54702
715-832-3479
Fax: 715-832-7456 800-826-7336
www.rdsmithco.com
Centrifuges, cheese equipment, flow diversion sta-
tions, heat exchangers, ladders, vats
President: Frederick Smith
Controller: Steve Burk
Vice President of Administration: Joan Bliesener
Vice President of Operations: Bob Kutchera
Estimated Sales: $5 - 10 Million
Number Employees: 10-19

29338 Smith-Berger Marine
7915 10th Ave S
Seattle, WA 98108-4404
206-764-4650
Fax: 206-764-4653 sales@smithberger.com
www.smithberger.com
Processing machinery for pacific salmon prior to
canning; leasing available
President: Bonnie Warrick
CFO: Bonnie Warrick
Sales Exec: Tom Phipps
Estimated Sales: $1 - 2.5 Million
Number Employees: 20-49
Square Footage: 30000
Brands:
Berger
Smith Berger

29339 Smith-Emery Co
781 E Washington Blvd
Los Angeles, CA 90021-3091
213-745-5333
Fax: 213-741-8620 mktla@smithemery.com
www.smithemery.com
Consultant specializing in air pollution analysis
President: James E Partridge
VP Marketing: Fred Partridge
Estimated Sales: $10-20 Million
Number Employees: 100-249

29340 Smith-Lee Company
2920 N Main St.
PO Box 2038
Oshkosh, WI 54901
315-363-2500
Fax: 315-363-9573 800-327-9774
marketing@hoffmaster.com www.hoffmaster.com
Manufacturer and exporter of paper plates, place
mats, napkins, bottle caps and packaged lace and
linen doilies
President: Jonathan M Groat
VP Sales: Thomas Hennessey
VP Manufacturing: Alan Mattei
Estimated Sales: $10-20 Million
Number Employees: 50-99
Parent Co: Hoffmaster Group, Inc
Brands:
Serv-Ease

29341 Smith-Lustig Paper Box Manufacturing
2165 E 31st St
Cleveland, OH 44115
216-621-0454
Fax: 216-621-0483
Manufacturer and exporter of paper boxes
President: Richard Ames
Contact: Jim Di Francesco
jdifrancesco@smithlustigbox.com
Estimated Sales: $5-10 Million
Number Employees: 20-49

29342 Smokaroma
62 Bar-B-Que Avenue
P.O. Box 25
Boley, OK 74829-0025
918-667-3341
Fax: 918-667-3935 800-331-5565
www.smokaroma.com
Manufacturer and exporter of barbecuing, smoking
and cooking equipment for hamburgers, hot dogs,
sausage patties, chicken fillets, etc.; also, spices for
meat and barbecue sauce mix
Owner: Maurice W Lee Iii
CEO: Maurice Lee Jr
Marketing Director: Tonia Guess
Estimated Sales: $5-10 Million
Number Employees: 10-19
Square Footage: 160000

Brands:
Bar B Q Boss Sauce Mix
Bar Bq Boss
Instant Burger
One Step Prep Mix
Red Rub

29343 Smoke Right
4602 S Pulaski Rd
Chicago, IL 60632-4038
647-933-0623
Fax: 312-425-0020 888-375-8885
Smoke-free ashtrays
Owner: Anna Greengurg
Circulation Coordinator: Envija Svanberga
Marketing Director: Roseanna Mazzei
Production Manager: Lynne Campbell
Estimated Sales: $300,000-500,000
Number Employees: 1-4
Brands:
Smoke Right

29344 Smokehouse Limited
4867 NC Highway 22 N
Franklinville, NC 27248
336-824-1424
Fax: 336-824-1026 800-554-8385
info@smokehouselimited.com
www.smokehouselimited.com
Supplies pneumatic seals and foam over door gaskets for smokehouses, brine chillers and other processing equipment.

29345 Smoot Co
1250 Seminary St
Kansas City, KS 66103-2599
913-362-1710
Fax: 913-362-7863 800-748-7000
smootco@aol.com www.magnumsystems.com
President: Gary Saunders
gsaunders@magnumsystems.com
Estimated Sales: $10 - 20 Million
Number Employees: 50-99

29346 Smurfit Kappa
1161 E Walnut St
Carson, CA 90746-1317
310-537-8190
Fax: 310-604-4880
Designer and manufacturer of corrugated packaging
displays, industrial containers, cardboard counter
displays, bulk boxes, cardboard sheets, marketing
displays, pallet display, point of purchase displays,
shipping containers, shippingboxes and custom
consumer packaging.
President: Lewis Eagle
CEO: Brenda Beltran
brenda@empirepackaginganddisplays.com
VP: Norman Eagle
Estimated Sales: $10 - 20 Million
Number Employees: 50-99
Type of Packaging: Consumer, Food Service, Pri-
vate Label, Bulk

29347 Smurfit Stone
504 Thrasher St
Norcross, GA 30071-1967
314-656-5300
Fax: 716-694-9262 www.smurfit.com
Packaging materials including corrugated boxes
Contact: Rod Castor
rcastor@smurfit.com
General Manager: Andrew Giambroni
Estimated Sales: Below $5 Million
Number Employees: 50-99
Parent Co: Jefferson Smurfit

29348 Smurfit Stone
504 Thrasher St
Norcross, GA 30071-1967
314-656-5300
Fax: 408-293-1022 www.smurfit.com
Containerboard and corrugated containers,
point-of-purchase displays, specialty boxes, consumer packaging, recycled materials packaging and
containers and packaging

Executive Secretary: Karen Korienek
Executive Secretary (Carol Stream): Janelle Lenza
VP Sales/Marketing (Carol Stream): James Duncan
Manager E-Commerce: Greg St Laurent
Executive Secretary (Procurement): Ronald Daniels
Contact: Rod Castor
  rcastor@smurfit.com
Manager: Chad Wilson
VP (Procurement): Mark O'Bryan
Estimated Sales: $10 - 20 Million
Number Employees: 20-49
Square Footage: 220000
Parent Co: Jefferson Smurfit Group
Type of Packaging: Consumer, Private Label, Bulk

29349 Smurfit Stone Container
8182 Maryland Ave
Suite 1100
St Louis, MO 63105-3915

314-679-2300
Fax: 314-679-2300
Folding cartons, corrugated containers and labels including printed paper, foil and heat transfer; exporter of linerboard
VP Corporate Sales/Marketing: Jack Straw
Marketing: James P Duncan
Contact: Mary Duda
  mduda@smurfit.com
Estimated Sales: $1 - 5 Million
Number Employees: 20-49
Parent Co: Jefferson Smurfit Group

29350 Smurfit Stone Container
1980 S 7th St
San Jose, CA 95112

408-925-9391
Fax: 408-293-1022 888-801-2579
www.smurfit-stone.com
Valve bag filling systems, force air packers, jet flow impeller packers, easiflow screw packers, gravity fill bags, bulk bag fillers, bag sealer
Manager: Chad Wilson
Estimated Sales: $10 - 20 Million
Number Employees: 20-49

29351 Smurfit-Stone ContainerCorp
13833 Freeway Dr
Santa Fe Springs, CA 90670-5701

714-523-3550
Fax: 562-921-0620 www.westrock.com
Corrugated boxes and displays
CFO: Paul Hailey
Cmo: Tom Vogan
  tvogan@smurfit.com
President: Dale McClurgh
Quality Control: Debra Heyeen
Sales Manager: Morgan Welch
Production Manager: Paul Smith
Estimated Sales: $30 - 50 Million
Number Employees: 100-249
Square Footage: 250000
Parent Co: Stone Container Corporation

29352 Smurfit-Stone ContainerCorporation
4364 SW 34th St
Orlando, FL 32811

407-843-1300
Fax: 407-843-8459 888-254-6696
www.smurfit-stone.com
President: Tom Graham
Contact: Amer Aganovic
  aganovica@transitair.com
Estimated Sales: $20 - 50 Million
Number Employees: 20-49

29353 Smyrna Container Co
4676 S Atlanta Rd SE
Atlanta, GA 30339-1503

404-794-4305
Fax: 404-799-7209 800-868-4305
Paper folding boxes for bakeries, pizza and carry-out
President: Blair Harrell
  bharrell@smyrnacontainer.com
Estimated Sales: $1-2.5 Million
Number Employees: 10-19
Square Footage: 50000

29354 Smyth Co
311 W Depot St
Bedford, VA 24523-1937

540-586-2311
Fax: 540-586-0549 800-950-7011
www.smythco.com

Pressure sensitive, sheeted, in-mold and PET labels; also, graphic design services available
Manager: Ben Witt
  bwitt@smytheco.com
Marketing Communications Manager: Bill Orme
VP Sales/Marketing: Bill Bumgarner
Estimated Sales: $20 - 50 Million
Number Employees: 100-249
Square Footage: 125000

29355 (HQ)Smyth Co LLC
1085 Snelling Ave N
St Paul, MN 55108-2705

651-646-4544
Fax: 651-646-2385 800-473-3464
info@smythco.com www.smythco.com
Manufacturer of sheet-fed and pressure sensitive labels, coupons, and high speed labelers for consumer goods packaging.
Estimated Sales: $41 Million
Number Employees: 10-19
Square Footage: 110000
Parent Co: G.G. McGuiggan Corporation
Other Locations:
  Smyth Companies
  Bedford PA

29356 Snack Food Assn
1600 Wilson Blvd # 650
Arlington, VA 22209-2510

703-836-4500
Fax: 703-836-8262 800-628-1334
www.snacintl.org
International trade association reprsenting snack manaufacturers and suppliers.
President: James Mccarthy
  cmelchert@sfa.org
CEO: Tom Dempsey
Director of Finance and Administration: Paul Downey
Vice President, Meetings & Events: Liz Wells
Manager, Marketing and Member Services: David Walsh
Manager, Meetings & Events: Meegan Smith
Number Employees: 20-49

29357 Snap Drape Inc
2045 Westgate Dr # 100
Carrollton, TX 75006-9478

972-466-1030
Fax: 972-466-1049 800-527-5147
info@snapdrape.com www.snapdrape.com
Manufacturer and exporter of table skirting and drapes
President: Timothy Nealon
  tmengel@msmandf.com
Contact: Daielon Sasser
Sales Manager: Kevin Burns
Estimated Sales: $10-20 Million
Number Employees: 50-99
Type of Packaging: Food Service

29358 Snap Drape International
2045 Westgate Dr
Suite 100
Carrollton, TX 75006

972-466-1030
Fax: 972-466-1049 800-527-5147
info@snapdrape.com www.snapdrape.com
President: Darrin Garlish
CEO: Felton Norris
CFO: John Phillips
Vice President: Ray Belknap
Marketing Manager: Tammy Brazeal
Sales Manager: Kevin Burns
Contact: Tim Nealon
  t.nealon@msmandf.com
Operations Manager: Jose Aguado
Estimated Sales: $10 - 20 Million
Number Employees: 50-99

29359 Snapware
4101 Bonita Place
Fullerton, CA 92835-1007

714-446-9212
Fax: 714-446-9217 800-334-3062
www.snapware.com
Manufacture of Food Service containers, caps, and closures
President: John Lown
VP: Jim Spillane
Marketing: Heidi Slocumb
Sales: George Ghesquiere

Estimated Sales: $20-46 Million
Number Employees: 50-100
Number of Brands: 6
Number of Products: 15
Square Footage: 90000
Brands:
  Living Hinge
  Make a Gift Products
  Sandcap
  Snap'n Stack
  Snap-N-Serve
  Snapware

29360 Snee Chemical Co
5565 Pepsi St
New Orleans, LA 70123-3221

504-734-7633
Fax: 504-734-5221 800-489-7633
www.sneechemical.com
Janitorial supplies including detergents and soaps
President: Mitchell Mark
  mmark@sneechemical.com
Estimated Sales: $5-10 Million
Number Employees: 20-49

29361 Sneezeguard Solutions
2508 Paris Rd
Columbia, MO 65202-2514

573-443-5756
Fax: 573-449-7126 800-569-2056
www.sneezeguardsolutions.com
Manufacturer and exporter of sneeze guards
President: Sydney Baumgartner
  sneezeguard@centurytel.net
CFO: Susan Baumgaltner
Marketing: Bill Pfeiffer
Plant Manager: John Bazzell
Estimated Sales: $1 - 3 Million
Number Employees: 5-9
Number of Brands: 14
Number of Products: 14
Square Footage: 40000
Brands:
  Magic Buss
  Next Generation Magic Buss
  Plexus
  Sampler
  Sneezeguard

29362 Snowden Enterprises Inc
3257 E Central Ave
Fresno, CA 93725-2506

559-237-5546
Fax: 559-237-6383
SO2 dispensers
President: Kirk Snowden Shermer
Contact: Heather Pemble
  heather.pemble@wellsfargo.com
Estimated Sales: $10-20 Million
Number Employees: 10-19

29363 Snyder Crown
602 Industrial St
Marked Tree, AR 72365-1909

870-358-3400
Fax: 870-358-3140
Manufacturer and exporter of custom, rotational-molded plastic transport tanks, storage bins and containers
Director Marketing: David Kelley
Director Operations: Dale Givens
Plant Manager: Ronnie Stone
Estimated Sales: $10-20 Million
Number Employees: 20 to 49

29364 Snyder Industries Inc
736 Birginal Dr
Bensenville, IL 60106-1213

630-773-9510
Fax: 630-773-4274 877-768-6642
www.snydernet.com
Manager: Jay Rule
Estimated Sales: $30 - 50 Million
Number Employees: 50-99

29365 Snyder Industries Inc.
4700 Fremont Street
P.O. Box 4583
Lincoln, NE 68504

Fax: 402-465-1220 800-351-1363
www.snyderplasticsolutions.com
Custom rotational molded plastic containers

President: David Fair
Contact: Marjorie Badousek
  mbadousek@snydernet.com
Production Manager: Claretta Jo Segura
Number Employees: 20-49

29366 SoOPAK
2280 Drew Road
Mississauga, ON L5S 1B8
Canada

855-766-7225
905-677-9666
soopak.com

Cartons and boxes
President: Jiang Yajun
Sales Manager: Tony Li
Year Founded: 2014
Number Employees: 11-50
Type of Packaging: Consumer

29367 Sobel Corrugated Containers
18612 Miles Rd
Cleveland, OH 44128

216-475-2100
Fax: 216-475-2107

Corrugated containers
President: Arthur Sobel
Executive VP: Terry Sobel
Estimated Sales: $20-50 Million
Number Employees: 20-49

29368 Soco System USA
1931 Mac Arthur Rd
Waukesha, WI 53188-5702

262-547-0777
Fax: 262-547-4707 800-535-SOCO
info@socosysteminc.com
www.johnmayecompany.com
End-of-line packing and handling systems, case
sealers and palleters
Owner: John Maye
Service Manager: Tage Peterson
Sales Director: Hans Sondersted
Contact: Paul Bangs
  pb@socosystem.com
Estimated Sales: $5-10 Million
Number Employees: 10-19

29369 Soco System USA
1931 Mac Arthur Rd
Waukesha, WI 53188-5702

262-547-0777
Fax: 262-547-4707 800-441-6293
www.johnmayecompany.com
Owner: John Maye
Accounts: Don Mertins
Sales: Jeff Devorse
Contact: Paul Bangs
  pb@socosystem.com
Operations: John Maye
Estimated Sales: $5 - 10 Million
Number Employees: 10-19
Type of Packaging: Consumer

29370 Sodexo Inc
9801 Washingtonian Blvd
Gaithersburg, MD 20878

301-987-4000
888-763-3967
www.sodexousa.com
Food Service management business.
CEO, Government: Brett Ladd
SVP & CFO: Ramesh Mahal
Year Founded: 1966
Estimated Sales: $9.5 Billion
Number Employees: 133,000
Parent Co: Sodexo

29371 Sohn Manufacturing
PO Box X
Elkhart Lake, WI 53020-0427

920-876-3361
Fax: 920-876-2952
Label printing and die-cutting machines, automatic
label dispensers and paper converters; also, inks,
printing plates, label stocks and printed labels
President: Wallace Beaudry
Estimated Sales: $20-50 Million
Number Employees: 100-249
Square Footage: 100000

29372 Solapak
8219 Saint James Avenue
Elmhurst, NY 11373-3720

718-457-9589
Fax: 718-396-2875
Automatic wrapping machines
President: Wang
Number Employees: 10-19

29373 Solarflo Corp
22901 Aurora Rd
Bedford, OH 44146-1701

440-439-1680
Fax: 440-439-8612 www.solarflo.com
President: Jeff Briggs
  jeffb@solarflo.com
Production & Chief Technician: Dave Frederick
Purchasing: Mike Kane
Estimated Sales: $3 - 5 Million
Number Employees: 10-19

29374 Solazyme Inc
225 Gateway Blvd
South San Francisco, CA 94080-7019

650-589-5883
Fax: 650-989-6700
Microalgae-based healthy food ingredients and oils.
Microalgae-derived lipid, protein and fiber-based
products for nutrition, taste, texture and functional-
ity.
CEO: Jonathan Wolfson
CFO & COO: Tyler Painter
Contact: Annie Chang
  achang@solazyme.com
Estimated Sales: Less Than $500,000
Number Employees: 1-4
Type of Packaging: Bulk
Other Locations:
  Global Headquarters
  San Francisco CA
  Midwestern Operations
  Peoria IL
  South American Operations
  Sao Paulo, Brazil

29375 Solbern Corp
8 Kulick Rd
Fairfield, NJ 07004-3385

973-227-3030
Fax: 973-227-3069 sales@solbern.com
www.solbern.com
Manufacturer and exporter of container filling and
dough folding equipment
President: Gil Foulon
VP: Jorge Espino
VP: Tom Berger
Marketing Director: Jorge Espino
Sales: Jorge Espino
Operations: Tom Berger
Estimated Sales: $5-10,000,000
Number Employees: 20-49
Square Footage: 24000

29376 Solganik & Associates
116 N Jefferson St
Dayton, OH 45402-1385

937-438-1666
Fax: 937-433-2354 800-253-8512
Consultant specializing in retail food service and
product development
VP: Carin Solganik
Estimated Sales: $500,000-$1 Million
Number Employees: 50-99
Square Footage: 20000

29377 Solid Surface Acrylics
800 Walck Rd # 14
North Tonawanda, NY 14120-3500

716-743-1870
Fax: 716-743-0475 888-595-4114
info@ssacrylics.com
www.solid-surface-acrylics.com
Acrylic solid surface tabletops, cutting boards, serv-
ing trays, planters, logo tops
President: Jack Tillotson
  jtillotson@ssacrylics.com
CEO: Robert Barenthaler
Designer: Melissa Aldrich
VP Sales: Allen Vaillancourt
Shipping Manager: Barb Smith
Plant Manager: Mark Lawrence
Estimated Sales: $2.5-5 Million
Number Employees: 20-49
Square Footage: 120000

Brands:
  Dinelle

29378 Solka-Floc
1 Park 80 Plaza W
Saddle Brook, NJ 07663-5808

201-712-1188
Fax: 201-712-1250

29379 Sollas Films & PackagingSystems
146 Keystone Drive
Montgomeryville, PA 18936-9637

215-283-3250
Fax: 215-283-3254 film@rtgpkg.com
www.rtgpkg.com
Acrylic coated, shrinkable, and co-ex polypropylene,
polyethylene films, polyolefin films, and printed,
pearlescent, metallized, barrier, laminations, cellophane, mylar and tear-tape specialty films, wrapping
equipment, bandingequipment and cartostretch

29380 Solo Cup Company
150 Spouth Saunders Rd.
Lake Forest, IL 60045

info@solocup.com
www.solocup.com
Single-use cups, plates, cutlery, take-out contaiers.
CEO, Dart Container Corporation: Jim Lammers
Year Founded: 1936
Estimated Sales: $1.6 Billion
Number Employees: 6,400
Parent Co: Dart Container Corporation
Type of Packaging: Consumer, Food Service, Pri-
  vate Label, Bulk

29381 Solo Foods
5315 Dansher Rd
Countryside, IL 60525

800-328-7656
info@solofoods.com www.solofoods.com
Cake and pastry fillings, almond paste and marzipan.
CEO, Sokol: John Novak
Estimated Sales: $20-50 Million
Number Employees: 100-249
Number of Brands: 1
Parent Co: Sokol Custom Food Ingredients
Type of Packaging: Consumer, Food Service, Pri-
  vate Label
Brands:
  Solo

29382 Solon Manufacturing Company
7 Grasso Ave
North Haven, CT 6473

203-230-5300
Fax: 207-474-7320 800-341-6640
Wooden spoons and sticks for ice cream novelties
President: Steve Clark
CEO/CFO: Larry Feinn
Marketing Director: Jayne Norman
Sales Director: Grover Kilpatrick
Contact: Steve Laack
  steve.laack@solon.com
Estimated Sales: $10-20 Million
Number Employees: 100-249
Type of Packaging: Private Label, Bulk

29383 Solus Industrial Innovations
30152 Aventura
Rcho Sta Marg, CA 92688-2019

949-589-3900
Fax: 949-858-0300 solusteam@solusii.com
www.solusii.com
CEO: Garland Jones
Contact: Sandra Leonard
  solusteam@solusii.com
Estimated Sales: $50 - 100 Million
Number Employees: 100-249

29384 Solutions By Design
451 Clovis Ave # 130
Suite #130
Clovis, CA 93612-1338

559-326-7899
Fax: 559-436-5263 800-888-4084
support@solutionsbydesign.com
www.solutionsbydesign.com
Wine industry research
Owner: Rhoads Donald
  rhoads.donald@solutionsbydesign.com
Marketing Director: Sherry Netto
Estimated Sales: $2.5-5 Million
Number Employees: 10-19

29385 Solutions Plus
2275 Cassens Drive
Suite 147
Fenton, MO 63026-2574
636-349-4922
Fax: 636-349-8027
Analytical standards and testing reagents
President: Nancy Brinner
Partner: Peter Ricca
Estimated Sales: $1-5 Million
Number Employees: 15
Square Footage: 8500

29386 Solvay Specialty Polymers LLC
4500 Mcginnis Ferry Rd
Alpharetta, GA 30005-2203
770-772-8200
Fax: 770-772-8454 www.solvayplastics.com
Research for industrial carbon fibers and engineering polymers
Number Employees: 100-249

29387 Solvay Specialty Polymers LLC
4500 Mcginnis Ferry Rd
Alpharetta, GA 30005-2203
770-772-8200
Fax: 770-772-8454 888-765-3378
www.solvayplastics.com
Polyvinylidene choloride extrusion resins,
polyvinylidene chloride soluble resins, and
polyvinylidene chloride aqueous dispensions
President: Roger Kurne
CEO: George Corbin
Number Employees: 100-249
Parent Co: Solvay Group

29388 Solve Needs International
10204 Highland Rd
White Lake, MI 48386
248-698-3200
Fax: 248-698-3070 800-783-2462
sales@solveneeds.com
Manufacturer, importer and exporter of corrugated
bins, boxes, dividers, drawers, shelving, cantilever
and pallet racks, hydraulic and scissor lifts, pallet
jacks, stairways, rolling ladders, casters, wheels,
carts, platform andutility trucks, new equipment and
repair parts, etc
President: Don Burski
Estimated Sales: $3 - 5 Million
Number Employees: 5-9
Square Footage: 200000
Brands:
  Ecoa
  Equipment Company of America

29389 Solvit
7001 Raywood Rd
Monona, WI 53713-2299
608-222-8624
Fax: 608-222-8733 888-314-1072
www.solvitnow.com
Solvit all-purpose pine cleaner including window,
toilet bowl cleaner, warewashing compounds, de-
greasers and rat and mouse bait stations
President: J H Kelly
solvit1@aol.com
Estimated Sales: $550,000
Number Employees: 1-4
Square Footage: 20000
Type of Packaging: Consumer, Food Service, Pri-
  vate Label
Brands:
  Solvit

29390 Solvox Manufacturing Company
PO Box 26506
Milwaukee, WI 53226
414-774-5664
Fax: 414-774-0888
Food grade defoamers including kosher; manufac-
turer of food grade cleaning compounds, sanitizers,
food ingredients commoditites, processing aids and
waste water tratment
VP: Glen Polzin
Marketing: Bill McCoy
Sales: Kim Ireland
Operations: Shane Ireland
Purchasing: Shane Ireland
Estimated Sales: $20-50 Million
Number Employees: 10
Number of Products: 100
Square Footage: 58000
Parent Co: Hydrite Chemical Company

29391 Somat Company
3200 Lakeville Hwy
Petaluma, CA 94954-5675
707-762-0071
Fax: 707-762-5036 www.stero.com
Director of Operations: Terry Goodfellow
General Manager: Lin Sensening
Parts Department: Wendy Grado
Director of Operations: Terry Goodfellow
Estimated Sales: $2,500,000 - $4,999,999
Number Employees: 10,000

29392 Somerset Food Service
910 Highway 461
Somerset, KY 42503-0799
606-274-4858
Fax: 606-274-5141 800-264-2633
www.somersetfoods.com
Food distributor
President/CEO: Tim Williams
Co-Owner: Mac Goodby
Estimated Sales: $20 - 50 Million
Number Employees: 100-249

29393 Somerset Industries
1 Esquire Rd
Billerica, MA 1862
978-667-3355
Fax: 978-671-9466 800-772-4404
somerset@smrset.com www.smrset.com
Manufacturer and exporter of bakery equipment in-
cluding dough sheeters, rollers, fillers, depositors,
bread molders and croissant machines
CEO: Andrew Voyatzakis
Estimated Sales: $2.5-5 Million
Number Employees: 10
Brands:
  Cdr
  Gpf-1
  Somerset
  Spm-45

29394 Somerville Packaging
7830 Tranmere Drive
Mississauga, ON L5S 1L9
Canada
905-678-8211
Fax: 905-678-7462 info@cascades.com
Aluminum foil and cartons for milk, frozen foods,
juice and cereal
Estimated Sales: $1 - 5 Million
Number Employees: 1800
Parent Co: Paperboard Industries Corporation

29395 Somerville Packaging
5760 Finch Ave. East
Toronto, ON M1B 5J9
Canada
416-754-7228
Fax: 416-754-9574
Folding cartons and packaging systems
Customer Service Manager: D Hayes
Plant Manager: K Mucha
Estimated Sales: $1 - 5 Million
Number Employees: 100-250
Parent Co: Paperboard Industries Corporation

29396 Something Different Linen
474 Getty Ave
Clifton, NJ 07011
973-772-8019
Fax: 973-772-6519 800-422-2180
Manufacturer and exporter of tablecloths, skirting
and napkins; custom sizes available
President: Mitchell Smith
Quality Control: Micheal Gates
Sales Manager: Wally Rachmaciej
Contact: Aricelis Baiz
  abaez@somethingdifferentlinen.com
Estimated Sales: $20 - 50 Million
Number Employees: 50-99
Parent Co: Something Different Linen

29397 Sommer Awning Company
1160 W 16th Street
Indianapolis, IN 46202
317-257-4300
Fax: 317-257-1973 855-257-4301
www.sommerawning.com
Commercial awnings
President/ Sales: Steve Sommer
CFO/ COO: Moises Lopez
Contact: Kent King
  kent@apsigngroup.com

Estimated Sales: $300,000-500,000
Number Employees: 1-4

29398 Sommers Plastic ProductCo Inc
31 Styertowne Rd
Clifton, NJ 07012-1713
973-777-7888
Fax: 973-777-7890 800-225-7677
sales@sommers.com www.sommers.com
Manufacturer and exporter of plastic packaging
products including sheeting, fabrics, cloths and film
President: Ed Schecter
  eschecter@aol.com
VP: Fred Schecter
R&D: Fred Schecter
Estimated Sales: $5 - 10 Million
Number Employees: 20-49

29399 Sonderen Packaging
2906 N Crestline St
PO Box 7369
Spokane, WA 99207-4809
509-487-1632
Fax: 509-483-2964 800-727-9139
www.sonderen.com
Paper folding boxes
President: Andrea Anger
  andrea.anger@sonderen.com
Sales Manager: Steve Agen
Estimated Sales: $5-10 Million
Number Employees: 100-249
Square Footage: 170000

29400 Sonic Air Systems Inc
1050 Beacon St
Brea, CA 92821-2938
714-255-0124
Fax: 714-255-8366 800-827-6642
asksonic@sonicairsystems.com
www.sonicairsystems.com
Drying systems, air knives, blowers
Owner: Mary Hsu
  yanina@pacificclinics.org
Estimated Sales: $5-10 Million
Number Employees: 20-49

29401 Sonic Corp
1 Research Dr
Stratford, CT 06615-7184
203-375-0063
Fax: 203-378-4079 866-493-1378
kurt.limbacher@sonicmixing.com
www.sonicmixing.com
Manufacturer and exporter of food processing ma-
chinery including propeller mixers, agitators, contin-
uous inline multiple-feed liquid blending systems,
colloid mills and homogenizing systems.
President: Robert Brakeman
  rob.brakeman@sonicmixing.com
Sales Manager: Kurt Limbacher
Estimated Sales: $2.5-5 Million
Number Employees: 10-19
Square Footage: 26000
Brands:
  Sonolator
  Tri-Homo
  Typhoon
  Wizard

29402 Sonicor
82 Otis St
West Babylon, NY 11704-1406
631-920-6555
Fax: 631-920-6080 800-864-5022
customerservice@sonicor.com www.sonicor.com
Ultrasonic and nonultrasonic cleaning equipment for
processing machinery
President: Mike Parker
Marketing Manager: Gary Levanti
VP Sales: Ed Parker
Contact: Augusto D'Agostino
  augusto@sonicor.com
Estimated Sales: $2.5 - 5 Million
Number Employees: 10-19

29403 Sonics & Materials Inc
53 Church Hill Rd # 2
Newtown, CT 06470-1699
203-270-4600
Fax: 203-270-4610 800-745-1105
info@sonics.com www.sonicsandmaterials.com
Manufacturer and exporter of liquid processing systems, food processing equipment, and food cutting
equipment.

President/CEO: Robert Soloff
CEO: Thomas Bennetti
tbennetti@sonics.com
Quality Control: Dan Grise
Sales Manager: Lois Baiad
Biotechnology Manager: Mike Donaty
North Am. Sales Mngr., Welding Products: Brian Gourley
Estimated Sales: $10-20 Million
Number Employees: 50-99
Square Footage: 90000
Brands:
  Vibra-Cell

29404 Sonoco Alloyd
1500 Paramount Pkwy
Batavia, IL 60510-1468
630-879-0121
www.alloyd.com
Blister card packaging and insert cards
Vice President: Jim Lassiter
Estimated Sales: $10 - 20 000,000
Number Employees: 50-99
Parent Co: Sonoco Products Co

29405 Sonoco Paperboard Specialties
3150 Clinton Ct
Norcross, GA 30071
770-476-9088
Fax: 770-476-0765 800-264-7494
www.sonocospecialties.com
Manufacturer and exporter of biodegradable and recyclable paperboard glassware caps used in the lodging, food and hospital industries for sanitary purposes
General Manager: Jeff Burgner
Division Controller: Gus Copeletti
gus.copeletti@sonoco.com
Plant Manager: Kelly Mowen
Plant Manager: Bill Janda
Estimated Sales: $5 - 10 Million
Number Employees: 20-49
Square Footage: 132000
Parent Co: Sonoco Products Co
Type of Packaging: Consumer, Food Service, Private Label, Bulk

29406 Sonoco Products Co
1 N 2nd St
Hartsville, SC 29550-3305
843-383-7000
800-377-2692
corporate.communications@sonoco.com
www.sonoco.com
Global manufacturer of consumer and industrial packing products and provider of packaging services.
President & CEO: R. Howard Coker
VP & CFO: Julie Albrecht
EVP: Rodger Fuller
Corporate VP & CIO: Rick Johnson
VP, Marketing & Innovation: Marcy Thompson
Year Founded: 1899
Estimated Sales: $5 Billion
Number Employees: 21,000

29407 Sonoco ThermoSafe
3930 N Ventura Dr
Suite 450
Arlington Heights, IL 60004
800-323-7442
www.thermosafe.com
Insulated containers
Estimated Sales: $5-10 Million
Number Employees: 50-99
Square Footage: 92000
Parent Co: Sonoco Products Co

29408 Sonofresco
1365 Pacific Dr
Burlington, WA 98233
360-757-2800
Fax: 360-757-8172 office@sonofresco.com
sonofresco.com
Coffee roasting equipment.
Chief Operating Officer: Robert Penrose
Year Founded: 2000
Number Employees: 5-9
Parent Co: Coffee Holding Company, Inc.
Type of Packaging: Food Service

29409 Sonoma Pacific Company
1540 S Greenwood Avenue
Montebello, CA 90640-6536
323-838-4374
Fax: 323-838-4381
Manufacturer and recycler of pallets and skids including hardwood, softwood and plywood
Regional Manager: Tony Serge
District Manager: Len Spitzer
Number Employees: 60
Square Footage: 500000
Parent Co: Palex

29410 Sonoma Signatures
4381 17th Street
San Francisco, CA 94114-1804
415-864-2582
Fax: 415-864-2582
Tea and coffee industry jars (glass)

29411 Soodhalter Plastics
PO Box 21276
Los Angeles, CA 90021
213-747-0231
Fax: 213-746-8125
soodhalterplastics@yahoo.com
Manufacturer, importer and exporter of party and bar accessories including plastic cocktail forks, stirrers and picks
President: Jackie Wolfson
CFO: Jackie Wolfson
Estimated Sales: $5-10 Million
Number Employees: 10-19

29412 Sooner Scientific
1501 Riverbluff Rd
PO Box 180
Idabel, OK 74745
405-237-0302
Fax: 580-286-4268 800-991-1974
DNA electrophoresis products
Estimated Sales: $1-2.5 Million
Number Employees: 1-4

29413 Sophia Foods
480 Wortman Ave
Brooklyn, NY 11208
718-272-1110
Fax: 718-272-1230 www.sophiafoods.com
Oil, vinegar, salt, vegetables, rice and grains, sauces and spreads, pasta, crackers, grissini, cakes and cookies, preserves and juices.
CEO: Candace Abitbul
candace@sophiafoods.com
Director of Sales & Business Development: Paul Berger
Year Founded: 1991
Estimated Sales: $2.4 Million
Number Employees: 11-50
Type of Packaging: Consumer, Food Service
Brands:
  Sophia

29414 Sopralco
6991 W Broward Blvd
Plantation, FL 33317-2907
954-584-2225
Fax: 954-584-3271 sopralco@aol.com
Ready-to-drink espresso
Owner: Peter Marciante
VP: Arcelia De Battisti
Marketing: Ana Ordaz
Estimated Sales: $1,500,000
Number Employees: 1-4
Square Footage: 1250
Parent Co: Sopralco
Type of Packaging: Consumer, Food Service
Brands:
  Espre
  Espre-Cart
  Espre-Matic

29415 Sorensen Associates
999 NW Frontage Rd
Suite 190
Troutdale, OR 97060
503-665-0123
Fax: 503-666-5113 800-542-4321
www.tns.com
Market research consultant specializing in in-store shopper surveys and new product development for the packaged goods industry

President: Herb Sorensen
CFO: Jack Birnbach
Sr. VP: James Sorensen
VP Marketing: Bill Hruby
Contact: Don Sorensen
d.sorensen@sorensenvance.com
Estimated Sales: $2.5-5 Million
Number Employees: 20-49
Square Footage: 10000

29416 Sorenson
632 NW California Street
Chehalis, WA 98532
360-748-8877
Fax: 360-748-1288 800-332-3213
www.sorensontransport.com
Owner: Darrell E Sorensen
Estimated Sales: $5 - 10 Million
Number Employees: 10-19

29417 Sorg Paper Company
901 Manchester Avenue
Middletown, OH 45042
513-420-5300
Fax: 513-420-5324
Paper products: abrasive coating, bactericides, cotton furnish, deeptone colors, fiberglass pulp matrix, flame retardant, latex, moisture barrier, recycled/post consumer, wet strength resin, specialty pulps, u.v. coatings and watermarking
VP Sales/Marketing: Joe Piela
Production Manager (Tissue): Carl Eisenmenger
Production Manager (Decorative): Bill Huggins
Number Employees: 200

29418 Sortex
39161 Farwell Dr
Fremont, CA 94538-1050
510-797-5000
Fax: 510-797-0555 sales@sortex.com
www.sortex.com
Manufacturer and exporter of color sorters and vision systems
VP Sales: Mike Evans
Sales Director of Product: Christoph Naef
Head of Corporate Communications: Corina Atzli
Number Employees: 20-49
Square Footage: 80000
Parent Co: Buhler
Brands:
  Sortex

29419 Sortie/Kohlhaas
PO Box 534
Monee, IL 60449-0534
708-534-3940
Fax: 708-534-8013
Sorting devices

29420 Sossner Steel Stamps
180 Judge Don Lewis Blvd
Elizabethton, TN 37643-6006
423-543-4001
Fax: 423-543-8546 800-828-9515
info@sossnerstamps.com
www.sossnerstamps.com
Manufacturer and exporter of marking stamps
President: Neil Friedman
International Sales: Vianney Cabrera
General Manager: Russel Lacy
Estimated Sales: $5 - 10 Million
Number Employees: 20-49
Square Footage: 94000
Parent Co: Sossner Steel Stamps
Brands:
  2-In-1 Time-Saver
  Roll-A-Matic
  Shal-O-Groove
  True-Sharp

29421 Soten
21572 Surveyor Cir
Huntington Beach, CA 92646-7067
714-969-9510
Fax: 714-969-9520

29422 Soudal Accumetric
350 Ring Rd
Elizabethtown, KY 42701-6777
270-769-3386
Fax: 270-765-2412 800-928-2677
www.accumetricinc.com
USDA approved silicone sealant used for packaging

CEO: James V Hartlage Jr
CFO: Charlie Casper
　ccasper@accumetricinc.com
VP: Alan Hartlage
VP Domestic Sales/Marketing: Ed Linz
Operations: Joe Fowler
Purchasing: Tim Patterson
Estimated Sales: $50-100 Million
Number Employees: 100-249
Square Footage: 75000
Brands:
　Boss

29423 Sould Manufacturing
PO Box 21064
Winnepeg, NB　R3R 3R2
Canada
　　　　　　　　　　　　204-339-3499
　　　　　　　　Fax: 204-334-6844
Concession carts
Number Employees: 9

29424 Source Distribution Logistics
2s700 Horseshoe Dr
Batavia, IL　60510
　　　　　　　　　　　　630-761-1231
　　　　　　　　Fax: 630-761-2974
Sales and marketing consultant for the warehousing
industry
President: Thomas Peters
Estimated Sales: $300,000-500,000
Number Employees: 1-4

29425 Source Marketing
761 Main Ave # 2
Norwalk, CT　06851-1080
　　　　　　　　　　　　203-291-4000
　　　　　Fax: 203-291-4010　800-536-1235
info@source-marketing.com　www.sourcecxm.com
Textile screen printing
President: Janie Goldberg
CEO: Paul Antonevich
　antonevich@source-marketing.com
Estimated Sales: $1-5 Million
Number Employees: 50-99
Type of Packaging: Bulk

29426 Source Packaging Inc
215 Island Rd
Mahwah, NJ　07430-2130
　　　　　　　　　　　　201-831-0005
　　　　Fax: 201-831-0009　888-665-9768
　　　　　　　　www.casesbysource.biz
Manufacturer of custom and stock carrying cases
and transport care.
President: Alan Alder
Sales Director: Veronica Knipping
　veronica@sourcepac.com
Estimated Sales: $5 - 10 Million
Number Employees: 10-19
Square Footage: 80000

29427 Source for Packaging
227 E 45th Street
New York, NY　10017-3306
　　　　　　　　　　　　212-687-4700
　　　　Fax: 212-687-4725　800-223-2527
Manufacturer and exporter of shopping bags, pro-
motional items, labels, foil, pressure sensitive tapes;
also, packaging design services available
President: Jay Raskin
VP Sales/Operations: Louis Cruz
Estimated Sales: $50-100 Million
Number Employees: 250-499

29428 South Akron Awning Co
763 Kenmore Blvd
Akron, OH　44314-2196
　　　　　　　　　　　　330-848-7611
　　　Fax: 330-753-4224　info@southakronawning.com
　　　　　　　www.southakronawning.com
Commercial awnings and renter of tents and party
supplies.
President: Ranell Minear
　jack@southakronawning.com
Vice President: Mike Halgaga
Sales: Jack Carroll
Estimated Sales: $1-2.5 Million
Number Employees: 10-19

29429 South Jersey Awning
101 Oak Avenue
Egg Harbor Township, NJ　08234-2211
　　　　　　　　　　　　609-646-2002
　　　　　　　　Fax: 609-646-2656
Commercial awnings
President: Steve Alberts
Estimated Sales: $500,000-$1,000,000
Number Employees: 5-9

29430 South Jersey Store Fixtures Co
773 Kaighn Ave
Camden, NJ　08103-2405
　　　　　　　　　　　　856-365-6664
　　　Fax: 856-365-9010　www.infoaroundphilly.com
Wholesaler/distributor of food service equipment in-
cluding broilers, bar equipment, barbecues, chairs,
beverage coolers, dishwashers, freezers, shelving,
slicers, stools, toasters, kitchen ventilating systems,
etc.; serving the foodservice market
President: George Fatlowitz
CEO: Edward Fatlowitz
Manager: Ismel Eema
Estimated Sales: Below $5 Million
Number Employees: 1-4
Square Footage: 200000

29431 South River Machine
115 S River Street
Hackensack, NJ　07601-6909
　　　　　　　　　　　　201-487-1736
　　　　　　　　Fax: 201-487-1508
Mixing/kneading mixers and pasta machinery for
ravioli, cavatelli, manicotti, noodles, etc
Estimated Sales: $500,000-$1 Million
Number Employees: 4

29432 South Shore Controls Inc
4485 N Ridge Rd
Perry, OH　44081-9760
　　　　　　　　　　　　440-259-2500
　　　Fax: 440-259-5015　mail@southshorecontrols.com
　　　　　　　www.southshorecontrols.com
Manufacturer and exporter of controls and control
panels for food processing equipment, material han-
dling equipment, freezers, etc
President: Rick Stark
　rjs@southshorecontrols.com
Sales Director: John Sauto, Jr.
Estimated Sales: $6 Million
Number Employees: 20-49
Square Footage: 58000

29433 South Valley Citrus Packers
9600 Road 256
Terra Bella, CA　93270
　　　　　　　　　　　　559-906-1033
　　　　Fax: 559-525-4206　vcpg@vcpg.com
Packinghouse and licensed shipper of Sunkist Grow-
ers Inc. citrus products.
Manager: Cliff Martin
Grower Service Representative: Maribel Nenna
General Manager Visalia Citrus Packing: Bob
Walters
Parent Co: Visalia Citrus Packing Group
Type of Packaging: Food Service

29434 South Valley Mfg Inc
9665 New Ave
Gilroy, CA　95020-9135
　　　　　　　　　　　　408-842-5457
　　　　　　　　Fax: 408-842-1097
Food processing equipment including brine tanks,
kettles, steam blanchers, atmospheric can cookers,
coolers, deaerators, sterilizers, tubular heat
exchangers
President: Paul L Jennings
Estimated Sales: Below $5 Million
Number Employees: 5-9
Square Footage: 18000
Brands:
　South Valley Manufacturing

29435 South Well Co
928 N Alamo St
San Antonio, TX　78215-1576
　　　　　　　　　　　　210-223-1831
　　　Fax: 210-223-8517　sales@southwellco.com
　　　　　　　www.southwellco.com
Pre-inked rubber stamps for check endorsement
Owner: Wilson P Southwell Jr
　scott@southwellco.com
CEO: Wilson P Southwell Jr
Sales Exec: Scott Southwell

Estimated Sales: $2.5 - 5 Million
Number Employees: 10-19
Brands:
　Super-Stamp

29436 Southeast Asia Market
52 15th St
Brooklyn, NY　11215
　　　　　　　　　　　　718-965-6500
　　　　　　　　info@seamarketny.com
　　　　　　　www.seamarketny.com
Asian foods and produce
Operations Manager: Cathy Chow
General Manager: Kevin Liang
Bilingual Purchasing Agent: Dan Josephson
Estimated Sales: $6.6 Million
Number Employees: 11-50
Brands:
　Eton Dumplings

29437 Southeastern FiltrationSysts
158 Railroad St
Canton, GA　30114-3060
　　　　　　　　　　　　770-720-2800
　　　Fax: 770-720-2900　800-935-8500
　　　　gerhard@sfes.com　www.sfes.com
Water treatment systems for high and low tempera-
ture applications
Owner: John Brandreth Iii
　j.brandreth@sfes.com
VP Marketing: Gerhard Zamorano
Estimated Sales: $1-2,500,000
Number Employees: 10-19
Square Footage: 22000
Brands:
　Hydroblend
　Microlene
　Scalestick

29438 Southeastern Fisheries Assn
1118 Thomasville Rd # B
Tallahassee, FL　32303-6238
　　　　　　　　　　　　850-224-0612
　　　Fax: 850-222-3663　bobfish@aol.com
　　　　　　　www.sfaonline.org
Hot sauces, fisheries
Executive Director: Robert P Jones
Chairman: Dennis Henderson
Executive Director: Robert Jones
Number Employees: 1-4

29439 Southend Janitorial Supply
11422 S Broadway
Los Angeles, CA　90061-1898
　　　　　　　　　　　　323-754-2842
　　　Fax: 323-779-5457　leday@aol.com
　　　　　　　www.triple-s.com
Janitorial supplies and equipment
President: John Leday
　leday@aol.com
Estimated Sales: $5-10 Million
Number Employees: 5-9

29440 Southern Ag Co Inc
942 N Main St
PO Drawer 546
Blakely, GA　39823-2029
　　　　　　　　　　　　229-723-4262
　　　Fax: 229-723-3223　souagcom@windstream.net
Manufacturer and exporter of conveyors, elevators,
sizers and separators for peanuts; also, grain bins
Owner: Harold Still
Estimated Sales: $2.5-5 Million
Number Employees: 10-19

29441 Southern Atlantic LabelCo
1300 Cavalier Blvd
Chesapeake, VA　23323-1528
　　　　　　　　　　　　757-485-0508
　　　Fax: 757-487-9712　800-456-5999
　　info@salinc.com　www.multicolorcorp.com
Pressure sensitive roll labels, coupons, tags, polysty-
rene inserts, 4 color process, 9 color in line printing,
16-inch web capacity, static cling and screen printed
point of purchase, foil stamping and bar codes
CEO: Chil Daper
CEO: Phillip W Draper
President: James Cumming
CEO: Phillip W Draper
Sales Manager: Kurt Webber
Estimated Sales: $20 - 50 Million
Number Employees: 100-249
Square Footage: 33000

29442 Southern Automatics
2845 Brooks Street
Lakeland, FL 33803-7379
863-665-1633
Fax: 863-665-2500 800-441-4604
Manufacturer, importer and exporter of high-volume fruit and vegetable packing machinery; also, compact optic sorters and sizers
President: Hugh Oglesby
VP: Scott Oglesby
Estimated Sales: $1 - 3 Million
Number Employees: 20
Square Footage: 40000
Parent Co: Future Alloys

29443 Southern Awning & Sign Company
532 Industrial Drive
Woodstock, GA 30189-7214
770-516-8652
Fax: 770-516-3940
Commercial awnings
President: Ron Dinsmore
Number Employees: 5

29444 Southern California Packaging
4102 Valley Blvd
Walnut, CA 91789-1404
909-598-3198
Fax: 909-598-1363 info@scpe.com
www.scpe.com
Packaging supplies
CEO: David Byrne
dbyrne@scpe.com
Estimated Sales: $3 - 5 Million
Number Employees: 10-19
Brands:
Ruby Kist

29445 (HQ)Southern Champion Tray LP
220 Compress St
PO Box 4066
Chattanooga, TN 37405-3724
423-756-5121
Fax: 423-756-0223 800-468-2222
Manufacturer and exporter of paperboard folding cartons
President & CEO: John Zeiser
CEO: Mark Lonqnecker
Vice President: Bruce Zeiser
National Sales Manager: Paul Powell
Operations Manager: Jim Skidmore
Number Employees: 250-499
Square Footage: 650000
Type of Packaging: Consumer, Food Service, Private Label, Bulk
Other Locations:
Southern Champion Tray L.P.
Chattanooga TN

29446 Southern Container Corporation
140 W Industry Ct
Deer Park, NY 11729
631-586-6006
Fax: 631-586-6068
Corrugated packaging including die cut, pre-print and hi-graphic; also, point-of-purchase displays
CEO: Steven M Grossman
Sales Manager: Barry Kolevzon
Contact: Noelle Pastore
noelle.pastore@southerncontainer.com
Estimated Sales: $20-50 Million
Number Employees: 100-249

29447 Southern Express
2305 N Broadway
Saint Louis, MO 63102-1405
770-662-0220
800-444-9157
Manufacturer and designer of restaurant kiosks, mobile merchandisers and mobile carts
Manager: Michael Samborn
Number Employees: 20
Parent Co: Duke Manufacturing Company

29448 Southern Film Extruders
2327 English Road
High Point, NC 27262
336-885-8091
Fax: 336-885-1221 800-334-6101
www.southernfilm.com
FDA polyethylene packaging films
Estimated Sales: $24 Million
Number Employees: 145

Square Footage: 115000
Parent Co: Sigma Plastics
Type of Packaging: Private Label

29449 Southern Gardens Citrus
1820 County Road 833
Clewiston, FL 33440-9222
863-983-3030
Fax: 863-983-3060 800-339-6025
www.ussugar.com
Citrus juices, not-from-concentrate and concentrated citrus by-products
Finance Executive: Ginny Pena
Contact: Dan Casper
dcasper@southerngardens.com
Estimated Sales: $25-50 Million
Number Employees: 100-249

29450 Southern Imperial Inc
1400 Eddy Ave
Rockford, IL 61103-3198
815-310-9120
Fax: 815-877-7454 800-747-4665
grothmeyer@southernimperial.com
www.southernimperial.com
Manufacturer and exporter of scanning hooks, display hooks, wire racks and baskets, clip strips, J-hooks, paper and adhesive labels and merchandising accessories
President: Stan C Valiulis
ekuehl@southernimperial.com
CFO: Dean Zanseil
Quality Control: Denise Bermingham
R&D: Tom Zeliulis
Marketing Manager: Tom Valiulis
Estimated Sales: $20 - 30 Million
Number Employees: 100-249
Square Footage: 320000

29451 Southern Metal Fabricators Inc
1215 Frazier Rd
Albertville, AL 35950-0719
256-891-4343
Fax: 256-891-0922 800-989-1330
sales@southernmetalfab.com
www.southernmetalfab.com
Manufacturer and exporter of ventilating systems, ducts, hoods, blowpipes, fittings, tanks, hoppers, railings, funnels, racks, boxes, vats and conveyors
President/CEO: Charles Bailey
charles.bailey@southernmetalfab.com
CFO: Teresa Hammett
Vice President: Regenia Bailey
Quality Control: Donnie Buchanan
Sales Manager: Bud Weed
Operations Manager: Danny Murray
Estimated Sales: $5 Million
Number Employees: 20-49
Square Footage: 189000

29452 (HQ)Southern Missouri Containers
900 N Belcrest Ave
Springfield, MO 65802-2513
417-831-2685
Fax: 417-831-7912 800-999-7666
www.smcpackaging.com
Corrugated boxes
President: Rich Bachus
Chairman/CEO: Kevin Ausburn
Director, Finance: Matt Ausburn
SVP, General Manager: Mark McNay
Manager, Operations: Matthew Massey
Estimated Sales: $63 Million
Number Employees: 100-249
Square Footage: 153000
Other Locations:
Southern Missouri Containers
Kansas City MO

29453 Southern Packaging Machinery
PO Box 112
Athens, GA 30603-0112
706-208-0814
Fax: 706-208-0815 sales@southernpackaging.com
www.benchmarkautomation.net
Corrugated paper containers
CEO: Don Evans
Director of Sales: Vince Tamborello
Estimated Sales: $2.5-5 Million
Number Employees: 5-9

29454 Southern Packaging Machinery
PO Box 112
Athens, GA 30603-0112
706-208-0814
Fax: 706-208-0815 sales@southernpackaging.com
www.benchmarkautomation.net
Horizontal form/fill/seal pouch packaging machinery
Owner: Roy Miller
Engineering Manager: Mike Rupert
Director, Sales: Vince Tamborello
Estimated Sales: $5-10 Million
Number Employees: 5-9
Type of Packaging: Food Service

29455 Southern Packaging Machinery
PO Box 112
Athens, GA 30603-0112
706-208-0814
Fax: 706-208-0815 800-922-8030
sales@southernpackaging.com
www.benchmarkautomation.net
Owner: Roy Miller
Engineering Manager: Mike Rupert
Regional Sales Manager: Jay Cavanaugh
Contact: Billy Barrick
billy@benchmarkautomation.net
Number Employees: 5-9

29456 Southern Pallet
24 Produce Place
P O Box 11075,
Christchurch, NZ 38101
901-942-4603
Fax: 901-942-4613
enquiries@southernpallet.co.nz
southernpallet.co.nz
Wooden shipping crates and pallets
Manager: Verna Frye
Production Manager: Louis Ratchford
Estimated Sales: $500,000-$1 Million
Number Employees: 5-9

29457 Southern Perfection Fab
232 GA Highway 49 S
Byron, GA 31008-6937
478-956-5441
Fax: 478-956-4001 800-237-4726
www.southernperfection.com
President/CFO: Gordon Hale
ghale@southernperfection.com
Estimated Sales: Below $5 Million
Number Employees: 20-49

29458 Southern Pride Distributing
401 S Mill St
Alamo, TN 38001-1913
731-696-3175
Fax: 731-696-3180 800-851-8180
parts@sopride.com www.southernpride.com
Manufacturer and exporter of ovens including mobile, revolving and warming; also, commercial barbecue equipment, smokers and rotisseries
President/CEO: Mike Robertson
VP: Jared Robertson
Quality Control: Bret Robertson
Marketing Director: Jack Griggs
Operations Manager: Jerry Cadle
Plant Manager: Marty Degrini
Purchasing: Rich Rowell
Estimated Sales: $10 Millions
Number Employees: 5-9
Square Footage: 130000
Type of Packaging: Food Service
Brands:
Southern Pride

29459 Southern Rubber Stamp
2637 E Marshall St
Tulsa, OK 74110-4757
918-587-3818
Fax: 918-587-3819 888-826-4304
sales@southernmark.com www.southernmark.com
Manufacturer and exporter of rubber stamps, seals, numbering machines, embossers, special inks, etc
President: Mike Forehand
mike@perfectseal.net
VP: David Parnell
Estimated Sales: Less Than $500,000
Number Employees: 5-9
Type of Packaging: Consumer, Food Service, Bulk
Brands:
Perfect Seal

29460 (HQ)Southern Store FixturesInc
275 Drexel Rd SE
Bessemer, AL 35022-6416
205-428-4800
Fax: 205-428-2552 800-552-6283
chughes@southerncasearts.com
Manufacturer, exporter and designer of mobile and
modular refrigerated cases for deli, bakery, salads,
produce and floral; store and fixture design and in-
stallation services available
President: Gene Cary
Cmo: Dan Mcmurray
dmcmurray@southernstorefixtures.com
National Sales Manager: Joe Moore
Estimated Sales: $10 - 20 Million
Number Employees: 250-499
Square Footage: 216000

29461 Southern Tailors Flag &Banner
1862 Marietta Blvd NW
Atlanta, GA 30318-2803
404-367-8660
Fax: 404-367-8654 877-655-2321
www.southerntailors.com
Custom flags, banners, ribbons, buttons and other
advertising specialties; also, engraving available
Owner: Neal Zucker
nzucker@southerntailors.com
Estimated Sales: $1 - 2.5 Million
Number Employees: 10-19
Square Footage: 14000
Parent Co: Southern Tailors

29462 Southern Tool
738 Well Road
West Monroe, LA 71292-0138
786-866-9865
Fax: 318-387-5372 800-458-3687
www.southern-tool.com
Manufacturer and exporter of packaging equipment
President: Dale Doty
Plant Manager: Buck Carlisle
Number Employees: 65
Square Footage: 200000
Parent Co: Southern Tool

**29463 Southern United States Trade
Association**
701 Poydras Street
Suite 3845
New Orleans, LA 70139
504-568-5986
Fax: 504-568-6010 susta@susta.org
www.susta.org
Marketing services
Executive Director: Bernadette Wiltz
Deputy & Financial Director: Troy Rosamond
Director, Marketing & Communications: Danielle
Viguerie
Office Manager: Sondleta B. Johnson
Year Founded: 1973
Number Employees: 11-50

29464 Southland Packaging
303 E Alondra Boulevard
Gardena, CA 90248-2809
213-532-3720
Estimated Sales: $2.5-5 Million
Number Employees: 10-19

29465 Southline Equipment Company
P.O. Box 8867
Houston, TX 77249
713-869-6801
Fax: 713-869-2875 800-444-1173
www.eqdepot.com
Wholesaler/distributor of material handling equip-
ment including new and used forklift trucks, parts,
service and rental in addition to industrial sweep-
ers/scrubbers.
Manager: Jeff Jones
Finance: F Rigell
Marketing Director: Bob McClelland
Sales Manager: M Zinda
Operations Manager: M Gunter
Estimated Sales: $20 Million
Number Employees: 50-99
Square Footage: 60000

29466 Southpack LLC
1 Hartford Sq # 19
New Britain, CT 06052-1174
860-224-2242
Fax: 860-224-2445 spc@southpack.com
www.southpack.com
Custom thermoforming and contract packaging
Owner: Lynn Mogielnicki
lynn@southpack.com
VP: Kurt Mogielnicks
Number Employees: 20-49
Square Footage: 60000
Type of Packaging: Food Service, Private Label,
Bulk

29467 Southwest Endseals
4323 South Drive
Houston, TX 77053-4820
832-399-3900
Fax: 832-399-3903 866-832-1454
info@swformseal.com www.swformseal.com
Ceiling jaws for packaging machines
President: John Deterling
Number Employees: 10-19

29468 Southwest Fixture
8909 Chancellor Row
Dallas, TX 75247-5324
214-634-2800
Fax: 214-634-2847
Store fixtures
Owner: Dan Thor
danthor@comcast.net
VP: A Winkler
Estimated Sales: $2.5-5 Million
Number Employees: 5-9

**29469 Southwest Indiana and American
Cold Storage**
P.O. Box 875
Newburgh, IN 47629-0875
812-858-3555
Fax: 812-858-3558
Manager: Larry Taylor
Number Employees: 1-4

29470 Southwest Neon Signs
7208 South W.W. White Rd
San Antonio, TX 78222-5204
210-648-3221
Fax: 210-648-4709 800-927-3221
www.southwestsigns.com
Indoor and outdoor advertising and electric signs
President: Chad Jones
Sales Manager: Greg Burkette
Estimated Sales: $10-20 Million
Number Employees: 50-99
Square Footage: 100000

29471 Southwest Vault Builders
596 Bennett Ln
Lewisville, TX 75057-4806
469-671-5800
Fax: 469-671-5812 800-749-1431
Specializes in cold storage construction
President: Larry Nolan
lnolan@southwestvault.com
Number Employees: 50-99

**29472 Southwestern Electric Power
Company**
428 Travis St
Shreveport, LA 71101
888-216-3523
www.swepco.com
Electric utility systems.
President & COO: Albert Smoak
VP, Regulatory & Finance: Thomas Brice, Jr
VP, External Affairs: Brian Bond
Estimated Sales: $1,000,000,000+
Parent Co: American Electric Power

29473 (HQ)Southwestern Porcelain Steel
201 E Morrow Road
Sand Springs, OK 74063-6531
918-245-1375
Fax: 918-241-7339
Porcelain enamel tops for steel tables, counters and
signs; importer of cast iron stove top grates; also,
silk screen porcelain graphics available
Vice President: Jim Bigelow
Plant Superintendent: Don Bushnell

Estimated Sales: $5-10 Million
Number Employees: 20-50
Square Footage: 512000

29474 Southworth Products Corp
11 Gray Rd
Falmouth, ME 04105-2027
207-878-0700
Fax: 207-797-4734 800-743-1000
www.southworthproducts.com
Material handling equipment including lift tables,
dock lifts, container tilters, vertical conveyors, man-
ual palletizers, elevating transporters, rotators,
upenders and adjustable workstations
Owner: Lewis P Cabot
lcabot@southworthproducts.com
CFO: Mike Nordman
Marketing Program Manager: Meredith Herzog
Sales Manager: Randy Moore
Director Product Support: James Galante
Estimated Sales: $5 - 10 Million
Number Employees: 50-99
Parent Co: Southworth International Group

29475 Soyatech Inc
1369 State Highway 102
Bar Harbor, ME 04609-7019
207-288-4969
Fax: 207-288-5264 800-424-7692
www.soyatech.com
Consultant specializing in soybean processing and
product development services
President: Peter Golbitz
Chief Executive Officer: Chris Erickson
cerickson@highquestpartners.com
Publisher & Operations Director: Keri Hayes
Marketing/Sales: Susan Bradley
Regional Sales Manager: Mark Phillips
Publisher & Operations Director: Keri Hayes
Estimated Sales: Less Than $500,000
Number Employees: 5-9

29476 Soynut Butter Co
4220 Commercial Way
Glenview, IL 60025-3597
847-635-9960
Fax: 847-635-6801 800-288-1012
www.soynutbutter.com
Peanut free peanut butter, made from roasted soy.
President: Steve Grubb
s.grubb@soynutbutter.com
Estimated Sales: Below $5 Million
Number Employees: 5-9

29477 Spaceguard Products
711 S Commerce Dr
Seymour, IN 47274-4023
812-523-3044
Fax: 812-523-3362 800-841-0680
www.spaceguardproducts.com
Woven wire partitions
President: Eddie Murphy
eddie@fedsource.com
VP Sales: Gary Myers
Estimated Sales: $5-10 Million
Number Employees: 20-49
Brands:
Ford Logan Wire
Space Guard 2000

29478 Spacekraft Packaging
1811 W Oak Pkwy
Marietta, GA 30062-2216
770-429-3500
Fax: 770-429-3535 800-483-1168
www.spacekraft.com
Manufacture of laminated panels.
Estimated Sales: $1 - 5 Million
Number Employees: 10-19
Square Footage: 20000

29479 Spacekraft Packaging
4901 W. 79th Street
Indianapolis, IN 46268
317-871-6999
Fax: 317-871-6993 800-599-8943
www.spacekraft.com
Packaging containers for liquid, semi-bulk products
Contact: Jeffery Alexander
jeffery@weyerhaeuser.com
Estimated Sales: $5-10 Million
Number Employees: 20-50

29480 Spacesaver Corp
1450 Janesville Ave
Fort Atkinson, WI 53538-2798
920-563-6362
Fax: 920-563-2702 800-492-3434
ssc@spacesaver.com www.spacesaver.com
Manufacturer and exporter of mobile high-density
storage systems
President: Paul Olsen
R&D: David Klumb
Vice President: Bill Wettstein
CFO: Ryan Bittner
Marketing Director: Christopher Batterman
Sales Director: Kevin Carmody
Public Relations: Karen King
Operations Manager: Jim Muth
Purchasing Manager: Patricia Cropp
Estimated Sales: $75 - 100 Million
Number Employees: 250-499
Parent Co: KI
Type of Packaging: Bulk

29481 Span Tech LLC
1115 Cleveland Ave
Glasgow, KY 42141-1011
270-651-9166
Fax: 270-651-7533 billy_miller@spantechllc.com
www.spantechllc.com
USDA and BISSC approved modular side flexing
conveyor systems with plastic belting
CEO: James Layne
james_layne@spantechllc.com
Engineering Director: Lavon Riegel
Quality Control: Paul Chambers
Marketing/Sales: Genia Johnson
Operations: Jimmy Wiley
Production/Plant Manager: Phillip Coleman
Purchasing: Alf McDougal
Estimated Sales: $20 - 50 Million
Number Employees: 50-99
Square Footage: 50000
Brands:
    Designer System
    Maxispan
    Minispam
    Monospan
    Multispan

**29482 Spanco Crane & Monorail
Systems**
604 Hemlock Rd
Morgantown, PA 19543-9710
610-286-7781
Fax: 610-286-0085 800-869-2080
www.spanco.com
Manufacturer and exporter of stainless steel material
handling equipment including cranes and conveyor
systems and components
Vice President: George Nolan
gnolan@spanco.com
VP: George Nolan
Sales Manager: George Nolan
Estimated Sales: $20 - 50 Million
Number Employees: 50-99

29483 Spann Sign Company
PO Box 546
Kenosha, WI 53141-0546
262-658-1288
Fax: 262-658-1878
Electric, neon and plastic signs
President: Duane Laska
Number Employees: 6
Brands:
    Spann Signs

29484 Sparkler Filters Inc
101 N Loop 336 E
Conroe, TX 77301-1446
936-756-4471
Fax: 936-756-4519 sales@sparklerfilters.com
www.sparklerfilters.com
Manufacturer and exporter of filter systems including fryer oil and liquid; also, manual and automatic

President: J T Reneau
jim@sparklerfilters.com
CFO: Robert Thompson
VP: Jose Sentmanat
Quality Control: James Dunklin
Marketing: Jose Sentmanat
Sales: Tom Buttera
Public Relations: Norm Hofer
Operations/General Manager: Link Reneau
Plant Manager: Alan Powell
Purchasing: Phil Lawson
Estimated Sales: $5-5.5 Million
Number Employees: 20-49
Number of Brands: 2
Square Footage: 140000
Type of Packaging: Food Service
Brands:
    Sparklaid
    Sparkler

29485 Sparks Belting Co
3800 Stahl Dr SE
Grand Rapids, MI 49546-6148
616-949-2750
Fax: 616-949-8518 800-451-4537
sbcinfo@sparksbelting.com
www.sparksbelting.com
Wholesaler/distributor of food-approved and pack-
age handling conveyor belting; manufacturer of mo-
torized pulleys; importer of thermoplastic belting,
motorized pulleys and rollers
President: Steven Swanson
CFO: Martha Vrias
VP: Steven Bayus
Quality Control: Dave Vanderwood
Marketing: Frank Kennedy
Contact: Andy Balog
ajbalog@sparksbelting.com
Operations: Bruce Dielema
Production: Joe Graver
Plant Manager: John Grasmeyer
Purchasing Director: Mark White
Estimated Sales: $20 - 50 Million
Number Employees: 100-249
Square Footage: 52000
Brands:
    Dura-Drive Plus
    Microrollers

29486 Sparks Companies
P.O. Box 17339
Memphis, TN 38187
901-766-4600
Fax: 901-766-4462 info@informaecon.com
Agriculture research and consulting company
Chairman of the Board: Willard Sparks
Estimated Sales: $10 - 15 Million
Number Employees: 100-249

29487 Spartan Flag Co
323 S Shabwasung St
Northport, MI 49670
231-386-5150
Fax: 231-386-5904
Flags, pennants and banners
President: Cheryl Feipke
VP: Milt Seipke
Estimated Sales: Below $5 Million
Number Employees: 10-19

29488 Spartan Showcase
702 Spartan Showcase Drive
P.O. Box 470
Union, MO 63084
636-583-4050
Fax: 636-583-4067 800-325-0775
Manufacturer and exporter of bakery and deli
wallcases, merchandising and self-serve display
cases and dry and refrigerated showcases; also, cus-
tom glass and wood fixtures
CEO: Mike Lause
VP Marketing: Steve Lause
Sales Director: Royce Buehrlen
Manager: Greg Hall
Estimated Sales: $14 Million
Number Employees: 120
Square Footage: 400000
Parent Co: Leggett & Platt Inc

29489 Spartan Tool LLC
1506 Division St
Mendota, IL 61342-2426
815-539-7411
Fax: 815-539-9786 800-435-3866
customerservice@spartantool.com
www.spartantool.com
Drain and sewer cleaning equipment
Member of the Board: Tom Pranka
tpranka@spartantool.com
Advertising Manager: Nancy Dessing
Sales Manager: Bill Madden
Estimated Sales: $10 - 20 Million
Number Employees: 10-19

29490 Spartanburg Steel Products Inc
121 Broadcast Dr
Spartanburg, SC 29303-4711
864-699-3200
Fax: 864-699-3250 800-974-7500
www.ssprod.com
Pressurizable stainless steel beverage, beer, and
chemical containers
President: Richard Dye
CEO: Dick Dye
CFO: Barry Whipple
Quality Control: Daniel Ahein
VP Sales/Marketing: Del Strandburg
Operations: Buck Wiggins
Production: Chuck Manahan
Purchasing: Tyler Evans
Estimated Sales: $3 - 5 Million
Number Employees: 100-249
Square Footage: 800000
Parent Co: Reserve Group

29491 Spartanics
3605 Edison Pl
Rolling Meadows, IL 60008-1077
847-394-5700
Fax: 847-394-0409 sales@spartanics.com
www.spartanics.com
Blanking and die-cutting systems, optical and me-
chanical counters, laser cutting machines, digital
printing equipment, converting systems, finishing
equipment, material handling machinery, screen
printing systems.
President: Thomas Ohara
tohara@spartanics.com
Vice President of Sales & Marketing/Inte: Mike
Bacon
Marketing Coordinator: Jeanette DesJardins
National Sales Manager - US: Rick Roberts
Estimated Sales: $5,000,000 - $9,999,999
Number Employees: 20-49
Type of Packaging: Food Service

29492 Spartec Plastics
PO Box 620
Conneaut, OH 44030-0620
440-599-8175
Fax: 440-593-2003 800-325-5176
Manufacturer and exporter of extruded low and high
density polyethylene and polypropylene products in-
cluding thermoplastic and rolled sheets, rods, tex-
tured cutting boards and sanitary paneling systems
with antibacterial additives
Operations Manager: Ernie Szydlowski
Estimated Sales: $2.5-5 Million
Number Employees: 19
Square Footage: 190000
Brands:
    Arp
    Permaclean
    Resinol

29493 Spartech Plastics
1444 S Tyler Rd
Wichita, KS 67209
316-722-8621
Fax: 316-722-4875 www.spartech.com
Sheet and roll plastics and plastic film
Contact: Patricia Asher
patricia.asher@spartech.com
Plant Manager: Steve Zubke
Estimated Sales: $20-50 Million
Number Employees: 100-249
Square Footage: 60000
Parent Co: Atlas Alchem
Type of Packaging: Bulk

29494 Spartech Plastics
1325 Adams St
Portage, WI 53901

608-742-7123
Fax: 608-745-1703 800-998-7123
www.spartech.com
Extruder of plastic sheet and rollstock
VP: Steven J Ploeger
Quality Control: Tim Hofp
Marketing: Kurt Kassner
Sales: Scott Eaton
Contact: Jay Eggleston
eggleston@spartech.com
Operations: Don Asch
Plant Manager: Don Asch
Purchasing: Jay Eggleston
Estimated Sales: $20-50 Million
Number Employees: 100-249
Square Footage: 170000
Parent Co: Spartech Plastics

29495 Spartech Poly Com
120 South Central Avenue
Suite 1700
Clayton, MI 63105-1705

314-721-4242
Fax: 314-721-1447 888-721-4242
mark.garretson@spartech.com www.spartech.com
Compounder of PVC for tubing & other applications
Manager: Nate Sofer
CEO: Natehen Sofer
Marketing/Sales: Mark Garretson
Contact: Matt Sweeney
matt.sweeney@spartech.com
Estimated Sales: $10-20 Million
Number Employees: 20-49
Number of Products: 250
Parent Co: Spartech Corporation

29496 Spear Packing
25 Home News Row
New Brunswick, NJ 08901-3645

732-247-4212
Beverages
President: John Ciullo
Estimated Sales: $50-100 Million
Number Employees: 50

29497 Special Events Supply Company
P.O. Box 12415
Hauppauge, NY 11788

Fax: 631-436-7715 specialevt@aol.com
Promotional goods including display equipment,
banners and pennants
Estimated Sales: $300,000-500,000
Number Employees: 1-4

29498 Special Products
1526 South Enterprise
Springfield, MO 65804

417-881-6114
Fax: 417-881-7314 cs@fhfoodequipment.com
www.fhfoodequipment.com
Brushes, centrifuge parts and fittings, flow meters,
homogenizers, pumps, thermometers and valves
Owner: Wilbur Feagan
Manager: Dennis Wiggins
Inside Sales Manager: Stacy Toal
Purchasing Manager: Bob Collins
Estimated Sales: Below $5 Million
Number Employees: 1-4
Parent Co: Mid-America Dairymen

29499 Specialities Importers & Distributers
85 Division Avenue
PO Box 409
Millington, NJ 07946

908-647-6485
Fax: 908-647-8305 800-899-6689
www.specialitiesinc.com
Deli: cheeses, cured meats and hams.
President: Ron Schinbeckler
r.schinbeckler@specialitiesinc.com
Vice President, Sales & Marketing: Richard Kessler
Year Founded: 1991
Type of Packaging: Food Service
Brands:
Bayonne Ham
Bellentani
Carpuela
Ermitage
Solera
leBistro

29500 Specialized Packaging London
5 Cuddy Boulevard
London, ON N5W 5R6
Canada

519-659-7011
Fax: 519-452-3197 www.spgroup.com
Litho-printed cutter boxes and folding cartons for
food, beverage, paper and personal care products
President: Carlton Highsmith
Site Manager: Don Gray
CFO: Lamaemig Rosekrans
Quality Control: Scott Laking
Director Operations: Robert Gariepy
Number Employees: 200
Parent Co: Lawson Mardon Group
Brands:
Pakastrip

29501 Specialty Blades
9 Technology Drive
PO Box 3166
Staunton, VA 24402-3166

540-248-2200
Fax: 540-248-4400
Manufacturer and exporter of custom made indus-
trial-duty food blades including stainless, high-speed
and tool steel or carbide; also, prototyping available
President & CEO: Peter Harris
Contact: Dan Andrew
dan@specialtyblades.com
Estimated Sales: $8.5 Million
Number Employees: 50-99
Square Footage: 160000
Type of Packaging: Consumer, Food Service, Pri-
vate Label, Bulk

29502 Specialty Box & Packaging
1040 Broadway
Menands, NY 12204-2590

518-465-7344
Fax: 518-465-7347 800-283-2247
wrapit@acmenet.net
Packaging
President: Eric Fialkoff
efialkoff@specialtybox.com
Vice President: Jason Fialkoff
Graphic Design/Print Media: Jessica L. Jones
Business Office Manager: Daphne Playotes
Estimated Sales: $5-10 Million
Number Employees: 5-9

29503 Specialty Cheese Group Limited
24 King Street
Apt 4
New York, NY 10014-4937

212-243-7274
Fax: 212-243-0807 cheesenyc@aol.com
Consultant specializing in new product development
for cheese; also, retail buying, training and merchan-
dising services for supermarkets, wholesalers and
manufacturers available
President: Lynne Edelson
Number Employees: 1

29504 Specialty Commodities Inc
1530 47th St N
Fargo, ND 58102-2858

701-282-8222
Fax: 701-264-5744
www.specialtycommodities.com
Manufacturer and importer of specialty ingredients
for snack food, dairy, bakery, cereal, energy bar and
confectionary. Products include dehydrated, dried
fruit, legumes, nuts, seeds, spices and grains.
President: Ken Campbell
Vice President: Kevin Andreson
Number Employees: 10-19
Parent Co: Archer Daniels Midland Company
Type of Packaging: Private Label, Bulk
Other Locations:
Corporate Office
Fargo ND
Processing Plant
Lodi CA
Processing Plant
Stockton CA
Processing Plant
Modesto CA

29505 Specialty Equipment Company
1415 Mendota Heights Rd
Mendota Heights, MN 55120

651-452-7909
Fax: 651-452-0681
Manufacturer, importer and exporter of high pres-
sure washing equipment
CEO: Sheldon Russell
President: Bryan Russell
Estimated Sales: $20-50 Million
Number Employees: 20-49
Square Footage: 70000
Type of Packaging: Consumer, Bulk

29506 Specialty Equipment Company
1221 Adkins Rd
Houston, TX 77055

713-467-1818
Fax: 713-467-9130 www.specialtyequipment.com
Manufacturer of packaging machinery and material
handling systems, including liquid fillers, custom
dry solids fillers, drum and pallet conveyors, and
palletizers.
Year Founded: 1969
Estimated Sales: $257 Million
Type of Packaging: Food Service
Other Locations:
Specialty Equipment Cos.
Etten-leur
Brands:
Beverage Air
Bloomfield Industries
Carter Hoffmann
Gamko
Nova
Taylor Company
Wells Manufacturing
World Dryer

29507 Specialty Films & Associates
2000 Arbor Tech Dr
Hebron, KY 41048

859-647-4100
Fax: 859-647-4105 800-984-3346
Plastic flexible packaging products including vac-
uum, zipper and stand-up pouches; also, forming
and nonforming film including vertical form/fill/seal
President: Jane Dirr-Cherot
CEO: Tony Cherot
Estimated Sales: $20 - 50 Million
Number Employees: 50
Square Footage: 40000
Brands:
Spec-Bar
Spec-Flex
Spec-Plus
Spec-Up
Spec-Vac
Spec-Zip

29508 Specialty Food America Inc
5055 Huffman Mill Rd
Hopkinsville, KY 42240-9162

270-889-0017
888-881-1633
www.specialtyfoodamerica.com
Herbs and spices; cooking related supplies and con-
tract packaging
Owner: Thomas L Marshall
specialtyfoodtom@gmail.com
Estimated Sales: Less Than $500,000
Number Employees: 1-4
Square Footage: 4800
Type of Packaging: Consumer, Private Label
Brands:
Lucini Honestete
Sonoma Syrups

29509 Specialty Lubricants
8300 Corporate Park Dr
Macedonia, OH 44056-2300

330-425-2567
Fax: 330-425-9637 800-238-5823
steve@speclubes.com www.speclubes.com
Food grade lubricants; contract packaging for pri-
vate labeling
Manager: Kathy Turner
COO: Sherry Bugenske
R&D: Stve Bugenske
Quality Control: Keith Lahrmer
Marketing Director: Steve Bugenske
Sales Director: Rick Beichner
Plant Manager: Chuck Turner
Purchasing Manager: Marge Bugenske

Estimated Sales: $10 - 20 Million
Number Employees: 20-49
Number of Brands: 1
Number of Products: 8
Square Footage: 69040
Type of Packaging: Private Label
Brands:
   Huskey Specialty Lubricants

29510 Specialty Packaging Inc
3250 W Seminary Dr # A
Fort Worth, TX 76133-1145
                817-922-9727
     Fax: 817-922-8262 800-284-7722
Food service paper bags and wrap
President: H Dorris
spac@earthlink.net
R&D: Herman Chenezert
Estimated Sales: $10 - 20 Million
Number Employees: 50-99

29511 Specialty Paper Bag Company
17625 East Railroad St.
PO Box 8445
City of Industry, CA 91748-0445
                718-893-8888
     Fax: 718-893-5662 800-962-2247
Plain and printed bags including bread, food, kraft
paper and plastic
Foreman: Brian Birchall
Number Employees: 18
Square Footage: 95000

29512 Specialty Saw Inc
30 Wolcott Rd
Simsbury, CT 06070-1445
                860-658-4419
     Fax: 860-651-5358 800-225-0772
info@specialtysaw.com www.specialtysaw.com
Band saws, carbide-tipped saw and high speed steel
blades, saw machinery and coolants
Owner: Anthony Scearce
anthony@scearcelaser.com
Estimated Sales: $3 Million
Number Employees: 10-19

29513 (HQ)Specialty Wood Products
900 Lumac Rd
Clanton, AL 35045-9610
                205-755-6016
     Fax: 205-755-3678 800-322-5343
info@specwood.com www.specwood.com
Store fixtures and gift baskets
President: Bonny Smith
info@specwood.com
Sales Exec: K Smith
Estimated Sales: Below $5 Million
Number Employees: 20-49
Type of Packaging: Food Service

29514 Specific Mechanical Systems
6848 Kirkpatrick Crescent
Victoria, BC V8M 1Z9
Canada
                250-652-2111
   Fax: 250-652-6010 info@specific.net
      www.specificmechanical.com
Manufacturer and exporter of stainless steel process
and storage tanks, pressure vessels and mixers
President and CEO: Phil Zacharias
CFO: Bill Cumming
Engineering Manager: Tom Goldbach
Quality Control: Darren Combs
Sales Director: Blaine Clouston
Plant Manager: Bill Cummings
Estimated Sales: Below $5 Million
Number Employees: 40
Square Footage: 72000

29515 Spectape Inc
2771 Circleport Dr
Erlanger, KY 41018-1083
                859-283-2044
     Fax: 859-283-2068 www.spectape.com
Pressure sensitive tape
President: Maurice J Halpin Iv
mohalpin@spectape.com
Quality Control: Maury Halpin Jr
Production Manager: Leo Henrichs
Estimated Sales: Below $5 Million
Number Employees: 10-19
Square Footage: 120000

29516 Spectratek TechnologiesInc
5405 Jandy Pl
Los Angeles, CA 90066-7005
                310-822-2400
   Fax: 310-822-2660 888-442-6567
mkelem@spectratek.net www.spectratek.net
Holographic film and glitter
President: Michael Wanlass
CEO: Michael Dedonato
mjdcgb@hotmail.com
CFO: Michael Dedonaco
Estimated Sales: $10 - 20 Million
Number Employees: 20-49

29517 Spectro
1515 Us Highway 281
Marble Falls, TX 78654-4507
                830-798-8786
   Fax: 830-798-8467 800-580-6608
          www.spectro.com
Manufacturer and exporter of X-ray fluorescent ele-
mental analyzers
Manager: Robert Bartek
Marketing Communications Manager: Gisela Becker
VP Sales/Marketing: Phil Almquist
Contact: Andreas Eerden
aeerden@spectro.com
Estimated Sales: $3 - 5 Million
Number Employees: 5-9
Square Footage: 120000

29518 Spectronics Corp
956 Brush Hollow Rd
Westbury, NY 11590-1714
                516-333-4840
   Fax: 516-333-4859 800-274-8888
        www.spectroline.com
Manufactures a variety of ultraviolet lamps useful to
the foodand beverage industry
President: Jonathan Cooper
jcooper@spectroline.com
Estimated Sales: $30 Million
Number Employees: 100-249

29519 Spectrum Ascona
1305 Fraser St
Suite D2
Bellingham, WA 98229-5800
                360-647-0877
   Fax: 360-734-8106 800-356-1473
Bags, boxes, ribbons, cups, gift basket supplies,
shrink wrapping equiment, and films
Owner: Bruce Maynard
Estimated Sales: $1-2.5 Million
Number Employees: 1-4

29520 Spectrum Enterprises
3220 Kratzville Road
Evansville, IN 47710-3357
                812-425-1771
            Fax: 812-425-1637
Rubber stamps and pads
General Manager: Thomas Evans
Estimated Sales: Less than $500,000
Number Employees: 4

29521 Spectrum Plastics
3311 S Jones Boulevard
Suite 209
Las Vegas, NV 89146-6775
                702-876-8650
            Fax: 702-876-8260
Custom and standard plastic bags

29522 Spee-Dee Packaging Machinery
P.O. Box 656
1360 Grandview Parkway
Sturtevant, WI 53177
                262-886-4402
   Fax: 262-886-5502 877-375-2121
info@spee-dee.com www.spee-dee.com
Manufacturer and exporter of volumetric cup-type
and auger filling equipment for powders, granulars
and pastes
President: James P Navin
Vice President: Timm Johnson
Operations Manager: Paul Navin
Estimated Sales: Below $5 Million
Number Employees: 20-49
Square Footage: 20000
Brands:
   Digitronic
   Spee-Dee

29523 Speedrack Products Group LTD
7903 Venture Ave NW
Sparta, MI 49345-9427
                616-887-0002
   Fax: 616-887-2693 www.speedrack.net
Storage racks including adjustable tubular and struc-
tural steel
Owner: Ron Ducharme
sales@speedrack.net
CFO: H W Baird
CEO: Ron Ducharme
Marketing Director: Butch Newland
Estimated Sales: $30 - 50 Million
Number Employees: 20-49
Square Footage: 280000

29524 Speedways Conveyors
PO Box 9
Lancaster, NY 14086-0009
                716-893-2222
   Fax: 716-893-3067 800-800-1022
Aluminum conveyors including gravity, powered,
pallet flow and line shaft; exporter of pallet flow
systems
Executive VP: John Jacobowitz
VP Sales: Daniel Buckley
Estimated Sales: $5-10 Million
Number Employees: 50-99
Square Footage: 440000
Type of Packaging: Consumer, Food Service
Brands:
   C-Square
   Clean Wheel
   Q-50

29525 Spencer Business Form Company
PO Box 229
Spencer, WV 25276
                304-372-8877
            Fax: 304-372-8902
Rubber stamps and office supplies
President: Milton S Griffith
Estimated Sales: $300,000-500,000
Number Employees: 5

29526 Spencer Packing Company
PO Box 753
Washington, NC 27889-0753
                252-946-4161
            Fax: 252-946-4162
Processor and packer of pork
President: Harold Spencer
Estimated Sales: $1,250,000
Number Employees: 10-19

29527 Spencer Research Inc
1290 Grandview Ave
Columbus, OH 43212-3439
                614-488-3123
   Fax: 614-421-1154 800-488-3242
       www.spencer-research.com
Consultant specializing in consumer testing for tech-
nical product development providing sensory test-
ing, statistical experimental design and analysis
Owner: George Maynard
spencerresearch1@aol.com
President: Betty Spencer
Estimated Sales: $5 - 10 Million
Number Employees: 20-49
Square Footage: 30000

29528 Spencer Strainer Systems
6205 Gheens Mill Rd
Jeffersonville, IN 47130
                812-282-6300
   Fax: 812-282-7272 800-801-4977
      spencer@spencerstrainer.com
       www.spencerstrainer.com
MIG and TIG welding, general machining, drilling,
boring, cutting, surface grinding, mill and lathe
work; stainless steel filtration systems; Spencer
strainer system
President: Glenn Spencer
Contact: Paul Deaver
pdeaver@spencerstrainer.com
Number Employees: 5-9

29529 Spencer Turbine Co
600 Day Hill Rd
Windsor, CT 06095-4706
                860-688-8361
   Fax: 860-688-0098 800-232-4321
       marketing@spencer-air.com
        www.spencerturbine.com

Manufacturer and exporter of central vacuum systems, tubing, fittings and centrifugal blowers; also, air and gas handling equipment, air knives and pressure fans
President/CEO: Mike Walther
mwalther@spencer-air.com
VP: Paul Burdick
Marketing Manager: Janis Cayne
Sales: Jim Yablonski
Estimated Sales: $20 - 50 Million
Number Employees: 100-249
Square Footage: 200000
Brands:
    Dirt Eraser
    Fume Eraser
    Industravac
    Jet-Clean
    Power Mizer
    Sump-Vac
    Top Hat
    Vortex

29530 Sperling Boss
51 Station Street
Box 100
Sperling, MB R0G 2M0
Canada

    204-626-3401
Fax: 204-626-3252 877-626-3401
sperling@sperlingind.com www.sperlingind.com
Designs, manufactures, and installs equipment and building for the beef and hog processing industry.
Manager: Jeff Nicolajsen

29531 (HQ)Sperling Industries
2420 Z St
Omaha, NE 68107-4430

    402-556-4070
Fax: 402-556-2927 sperlingboss@aol.com
Manufacturer and exporter of meat processing equipment including sausage makers, cookers, renderers, cutters, presses and grinders, as well as food processing machinery. Also material handlers and conveyors
President: Craig Ellett
Executive VP: C Schmidt
Manager: Allen Tegtmneier
Estimated Sales: $3 - 5 Million
Number Employees: 10-19
Square Footage: 400000
Other Locations:
    Cincinnati Boss Co.
    Bellevue NE
Brands:
    Boss
    Chop Cut
    Excoriator
    Permeator

29532 Sperling Industries
2420 Z St
Omaha, NE 68107-4430

    402-556-4070
Fax: 402-556-2927 800-647-5062
sperling@sperlingind.com
Meat and food processing equipment; exporter of meat packing house equipment
President: Craig Ellett
Manager: Jim Adrian
adrian@sperlingind.com
Manager: Jeff Nicolajsen
Estimated Sales: $3 - 5 Million
Number Employees: 10-19
Square Footage: 7000
Parent Co: Cincinnati-Boss Company

29533 Sperling Industries
2420 Z St
Omaha, NE 68107-4430

    402-556-4070
Fax: 402-556-2927 800-647-5062
ronb@sperlingomaha.com
Meat rail equipment and accessories, conveyor systems and accessories, architects and engineers, consultants, on-rail kill systems and accessories
President: Craig Ellett
CFO: Craig Ellett
R & D: Russel Nicolajsen
Manager: Brock Pappas
pappas@sperlingind.com
Estimated Sales: $3 - 5 Million
Number Employees: 10-19

29534 Spicetec Flavors & Seasonings
11 Conagra Drive
Omaha, NE 68102

    402-240-4005
800-921-7502
jaime.emanuel@conagrafoods.com
President/Consumer Foods: Andr, Hawaux
CEO: Gary Rodkin
EVP/CFO: John Gehring
EVP: Colleen Batcheler
EVP, Research, Quality & Innovation: Al Bolles
President/Commercial Foods: Paul Maass
EVP/Chief Marketing Officer: Joan Chow
President/ConAgra Foods Sales: Doug Knudsen
SVP/Human Resources: Nicole Theophilus
Plant Manager: Liam Doherty
Number Employees: 10-19
Parent Co: Conagra Brands

29535 Spin-Tech Corporation
1024 Adams St
Suite A
Hoboken, NJ 7030

    201-659-6110
Fax: 201-963-7674 800-977-4692
Beverage fountains, candelabra, serving trays and liquid fuel candles; exporter of beverage fountains, table candles and floral holders
Owner: Frank Pasquale
Estimated Sales: $1-2.5 Million
Number Employees: 5-9
Square Footage: 50000

29536 Spinco Metal Products Inc
1 Country Club Dr
Newark, NY 14513-1250

    315-331-6285
Fax: 315-331-9535 cthayer@spincometal.com
www.spincometal.com
Manufacturer and exporter of copper refrigeration components, brass flow metering devices and stainless steel beverage lines, welded and brazed assemblies, cut to length tubing
President: Robert C Straubing
crstraubing@spincometal.com
Engineering/Quality Manager: David Gardner
Quality Assurance Coordinator: Craig Thayer
Inside Sales: Connie Rios
Estimated Sales: $10-20 Million
Number Employees: 50-99
Square Footage: 120000

29537 Spinzer
799 Roosevelt Road
Bldg 6
Glen Ellyn, IL 60137-5908

    630-469-7184
Fax: 630-469-7185 www.spinzer.us/
Stirrers for hot and cold beverages, drinking straws
Estimated Sales: 100000
Number of Brands: 1
Number of Products: 2
Parent Co: SPINZER OFFICE SUPPLIES
Type of Packaging: Consumer, Bulk

29538 Spir-It/Zoo Piks
200 Brickstone Sq # G05
Andover, MA 01810-1439

    978-964-1551
Fax: 978-964-1552 800-343-0996
Manufacturer and exporter of plastic cutlery, picks, sticks, stirrers, straws and other food service accessories; importer of wooden stirrers and toothpicks
President: Donald McCann
CFO: Peter Maki
VP Sales/Marketing: Joe Pierro
Sales/Marketing Manager: Marva White
Number Employees: 100-249
Square Footage: 320000
Type of Packaging: Food Service
Other Locations:
    Spir-It/Zoo Piks
    Dallas TX
Brands:
    Glassips
    Hob Nob
    Oakhill
    Spir-It

29539 Spiral Biotech Inc
2 Technology Way
Norwood, MA 02062-2680

    781-320-9000
Fax: 781-320-8181 800-554-1620
mail@aicompanies.com
Manufacturer and exporter of laboratory equipment including fast sample dilutors, spiral platers, automated plate counters and colony counting systems; importer of microbial air samplers and filter bags; wholesaler/distributor ofmicrobial air samplers
President: John Coughlin
VP Operations: P Emond
Estimated Sales: $10 - 20 Million
Number Employees: 50-99
Square Footage: 6000
Parent Co: Advanced Instruments
Brands:
    Autoplate 4000
    Casba Ii
    Casba Iv
    Labpro Gravimetric

29540 Spiral Manufacturing CoInc
11419 Yellow Pine St NW
Minneapolis, MN 55448-3158

    763-392-2336
Fax: 763-755-6184 800-426-3643
info@spiralmfg.com www.spiralmfg.com
Manufacturer and exporter of commercial and industrial HVAC, ventilation, air conditioning and pneumatic conveying, dust and fume collection distribution systems
President: Tom Menth
Contact: Jesiah Durene
jdurene@spiralmfg.com
Estimated Sales: $5 - 10 Million
Number Employees: 1-4

29541 Spiral Slices Ham Market
1930 Division St
Detroit, MI 48207-2153

    313-259-6262
Fax: 313-259-4219
Manufacturer and distributor of vertical ham slicing machines
Owner: Don Bonanno
Estimated Sales: Below $5 Million
Number Employees: 1-4

29542 Spiral Systems
8630 Farley Way
Fair Oaks, CA 95668

    916-852-0177
Fax: 916-966-7771 800-998-6111
info@spiralsystems.com www.spiralsystems.com

29543 Spiral-Matic Corp
7772 Park Pl
Brighton, MI 48116-8387

    248-486-5080
Fax: 248-486-5081 contact@spiralmatic.com
www.spiralmatic.com
Slicing blades, slicers
President: Dan Mcphail
dan@spiralmatic.com
Manager: Bill Mc Phail
Estimated Sales: $1-2.5 Million
Number Employees: 10-19
Square Footage: 20

29544 Spirax Sarco Inc
1150 Northpoint Blvd
Blythewood, SC 29016-8873

    803-714-2000
Fax: 803-714-2222 800-575-0394
insidesalesleads@spirax.com
www.spiraxsarco.com/us
Air eliminators
President: Lorraine Wiseman
lwiseman@spirax.com
Regional Manager: Ed Beedle
Branch Manager: Steve Williams
Estimated Sales: Below $5 Million
Number Employees: 1000-4999
Number of Products: 12
Square Footage: 103000
Type of Packaging: Private Label

29545 Spirit Foodservice, Inc.
200 Brickstone Square
Suite G-05
Andover, MA 01810
978-964-1551
Fax: 978-964-1552 800-343-0996
www.spiritfoodservice.com
Manufacturer and exporter of plastic swizzle sticks, picks, napkin holders, tip trays, napkins, drinking straws and disposable drinkware; also, custom imprinting available
Contact: Peter Maki
maki@spir-it.com
Estimated Sales: $5-10 Million
Number Employees: 100-249
Brands:
Zoo

29546 Spiro-Cut Equipment Co
3005 Bledsoe St
Fort Worth, TX 76107-2905
817-877-3266
Fax: 817-877-3742 888-887-4267
www.spirocut.com
Meat slicers
President: Tom Misfeldt
info@spirocut.com
Estimated Sales: $1 Million
Number Employees: 5-9
Square Footage: 2200

29547 Spiroflow Systems Inc
1609 Airport Rd
Monroe, NC 28110-7393
704-291-9595
Fax: 704-291-9594 info@spiroflowsystems.com
www.spiroflow.com
CEO: Jeff Dudas
jeffdudas@spiroflowsystems.com
Manager: Marline Carlisle
Estimated Sales: Below $5 Million
Number Employees: 100-249

29548 Spokane House of Hose Inc
5520 E Sprague Ave
Spokane Valley, WA 99212-0880
509-535-3638
Fax: 509-535-3670 800-541-6351
sales@spokanehose.com www.spokanehose.com
Full color menu cards
Owner: Larry Hayden
sales@spokanehose.com
Estimated Sales: $1-2.5 Million
Number Employees: 20-49

29549 Spontex
100 Spontex Dr
Columbia, TN 38401
931-388-5632
Fax: 931-490-2105 800-251-4222
sales@mapaglove.com
www.spontexindustrial.com
Cellulose sponges, scrubbers, and rubber gloves
Estimated Sales: $50 - 75 Million
Number Employees: 100-249
Square Footage: 193000
Parent Co: Hutchinson SA
Brands:
Spontex

29550 Sportsmen's Cannery & Smokehouse
182 Bayfront Loop
Winchester Bay, OR 97467
541-271-3293
Fax: 541-271-9381 800-457-8048
karch@presys.com www.sportsmenscannery.com
Processor and canner of salmon, albacore tuna, sturgeon and shellfish
Manager: Brandy Roelle
Owner: Mikayle Karcher
Number Employees: 1-4
Type of Packaging: Consumer, Private Label
Brands:
Winchester

29551 Spot Wire Works Company
413 Green St
Philadelphia, PA 19123
215-627-6124
Fax: 215-627-0950
Stainless steel and wire shelves, trays and display racks; also, wire parts and guards
President: Eli Brownstein

Estimated Sales: $10-20 Million
Number Employees: 10-19
Square Footage: 20000

29552 Spray Drying
5320 Enterprise St # J
Sykesville, MD 21784-9354
410-549-8090
Fax: 410-549-8091 sales@spraydrysys.com
www.spraydrysys.com
Manufacturer and exporter of spray dryers
President: Jeff Bayliss
bayliss@spraydrysys.com
Quality Control: Jess Bayliss
Vice President: Jeff Bayliss
Estimated Sales: Below $5 Million
Number Employees: 5-9
Square Footage: 7000

29553 Spray Dynamics LTD
108 Bolte Ln
St Clair, MO 63077-3218
636-629-7366
Fax: 636-629-7455 800-260-7366
spraydynamics@heatandcontrol.com
www.spraydynamics.com
Manufacturer and exporter of liquid and dry ingredient applicators and dispensers for food processing machinery.
Owner: Dave Holmeyer
Accounts Payable: Melanie Booher
Marketing Coordinator: Stephanie Butenhoff
Sales Representative: George Wipperfurth
Service Manager: Craig Booher
Estimated Sales: $2.5-5 Million
Number Employees: 20-49
Brands:
Clog-Free Slurry Spray Encoater
Delta Dry
Delta Liquid
Econoflo
Enhancer
Master Series
Meter Master
Micro-Meter Airless
Powder Xpress
Soft Flight
Unispense

29554 Spray Tek Inc
344 Cedar Ave
Middlesex, NJ 08846-2433
732-469-0050
Fax: 732-302-0866 www.spray-tek.com
Spray drying
Vice President: David Brand
david.brand@spray-tek.net
VP: David Brand
Estimated Sales: $20 - 50 Million
Number Employees: 50-99

29555 Spraying Systems Company
North Avenueand Schmale Road
PO Box 7900
Wheaton, IL 60187
630-655-5000
Fax: 630-260-0842 info@spray.com
www.spray.com
Manufacturer and exporter of nozzles, spray guns, portable spray systems and spray nozzle accessories including connectors, ball fittings, valves, regulators, etc
President/CEO: James Bramsen
VP Manufacturing: Don Fox
VP/COO: Dave Smith
Sr Applications Engineer: Wes Bartell

29556 Spraymation Inc
5320 NW 35th Ave
Fort Lauderdale, FL 33309-7014
954-484-9700
Fax: 954-484-9778 800-327-4985
sales@spraymation.com www.spraymation.com
Standard and Custom designed hot melt, cold adesive and fluid dispensing equipment, featuring Electromatic Applicator Heads for the application of beads, dots, spray patterns and slot coating; DC Pattern Controllers, Pumping Systemsand Temperature Control Units
President: Eric J Cocks Sr
R&D: David Kerzel
Quality Control: Ken Jones
Estimated Sales: Below $5 Million
Number Employees: 20-49

29557 Sprayway Inc
1005 S Westgate St
Addison, IL 60101-5021
630-628-3000
Fax: 630-543-7797 800-332-9000
info@spraywayinc.com
Manufacturer and exporter of aerosol products including all purpose and glass cleaners, dust control sprays and insecticides
President: Michael Rohl
CFO: Roger Hayes
rhayes@spraywayinc.com
VP Sales/Marketing: Bob Potvin
Estimated Sales: $10 - 20 Million
Number Employees: 100-249
Number of Brands: 1
Square Footage: 160000
Type of Packaging: Private Label
Brands:
Crazy Clean
Dust Up
Sprayway
Tru-Nox

29558 Spring Air Systems
1464 Cornwall Road
Unit 9
Oakville, ON L6J 7W5
Canada
905-338-2999
Fax: 905-338-0179 866-874-4505
www.springairsystems.com
Specializes in kitchen ventilation systems
Number Employees: 10

29559 Spring Cove Container Div
301 Cove Lane Rd
Roaring Spring, PA 16673-1619
814-224-5141
Fax: 814-224-5783 scc@roaringspring.com
www.springcove.com
Corrugated cartons
President: Daniel B Hoover
dhoover@roaringsprint.com
Sales: P Adams
Plant Manager: Johnathen Sneed
Estimated Sales: $20-50 Million
Number Employees: 20-49
Parent Co: Roaring Spring Blank Book Company

29560 Spring USA Corp
127 Ambassador Dr # 147
Naperville, IL 60540-4079
630-527-8600
Fax: 630-527-8677 800-535-8974
springusa@springusa.com
Products range from chafing dishes to professional cookware, from induction ranges to coffee urns.
President: Tom Brija
springusa@springusa.com
Sales/Marketing Supervisor: Kelly Boyle
Estimated Sales: $2.5-5,000,000
Number Employees: 5-9
Parent Co: Spring Switzerland
Brands:
Blackline
Brigade
Brigade +
Endurance
Flix
Mr. Induction
Vulcano

29561 Spring Wood Products
4267 Austin Rd
Geneva, OH 44041
440-466-1135
Fax: 440-466-1138
Wooden pallets and shipping containers
CEO: Jacob Castrilla
VP: Gregory Castrilla
VP: Thomas Castrilla
Estimated Sales: $2.5-5 Million
Number Employees: 20-49

29562 (HQ)Springer-Penguin
PO Box 199
Mount Vernon, NY 10552-0199
914-699-3200
Fax: 914-699-3231 800-835-8500
Manufacturer and exporter of refrigerators, file cabinets and wood office furniture including conference tables, bookcases, etc.; importer of wooden bookcases

Number Employees: 10
Square Footage: 80000
Brands:
  Penguin

29563 Springfield Metal Products Co
8 Commerce St
Springfield, NJ 07081-2903
973-379-4600
Fax: 973-379-7314
jd.sommer@springfieldmetalproducts.com
www.springfieldmetalproducts.com
Sheet metal and structural fabrications in stainless
steel and aluminum
President: John Sommer
  jd.sommer@verizon.net
VP/Secretary: Irene Powell
Estimated Sales: Below $5 Million
Number Employees: 10-19
Square Footage: 12000

29564 Springport Steel Wire Products
4906 Hoffman Street
Suite B
Elkhart, IN 46516
574-295-9660
Fax: 574-293-8552 cs@sigma-wire.com
www.sigmawire.com
Manufacturer and exporter of handling equipment
including containers, pallets, wire and mesh shelv-
ing and conveyor guards
Estimated Sales: $2.5-5 Million
Number Employees: 20-50
Brands:
  Wire Dek
  Wiretainer

29565 Springprint Medallion
1431 Marvin Griffin Road
Augusta, GA 30906-3852
800-543-5990
Fax: 800-982-6434
Custom printed place mats, napkins, coasters and
tray covers
VP Sales/Marketing: Layne Allen
VP Converting Operations: Eric Simmons
Number Employees: 2
Parent Co: Marcal Paper Mills

29566 Sprinkman Corporation
PO Box 390
Franksville, WI 53126-0390
262-835-2390
Fax: 262-835-4325 800-816-1610
www.sprinkman.com
Wholesaler/distributor of dairy and food processing
equipment and supplies; consultant specializing in
the design processing systems; also, installation and
reconditioning services available
Chief Operating Officer: Robert Sprinkman
CFO: Dale Metcoff
President: Brian Sprinkman
Vice President: Merlin Winchell
Contact: Jimmi Sukys
  j.sukys@sprinkman.com
Estimated Sales: $30 Million
Number Employees: 100
Square Footage: 35000
Parent Co: W.M. Sprinkman Corporation

29567 Sprinter Marking Inc
1805 Chandlersville Rd
Zanesville, OH 43701-4644
740-453-1000
Fax: 740-453-6750 sales@sprintermarking.com
www.sprintermarking.com
Automatic ink code dating and marking machinery
for cups
CEO: Bob Bishop
Estimated Sales: $1-5 Million
Number Employees: 10-19
Square Footage: 12000
Brands:
  Sprinter

29568 Sprouts Farmers Market Inc.
5455 E. High St.
Suite 111
Phoenix, AZ 85054
www.sprouts.com
National grocery store chain specializing in fresh
foods and health foods.

Chief Executive Officer: Jack Sinclair
Chief Financial Officer: Lawrence "Chip" Molloy
Chief Legal Officer: Brandon Lombardi
SVP/Chief Marketing Officer: Alisa Gmelich
President/Chief Operating Officer: Nick Konat
Year Founded: 2002
Estimated Sales: $6.1 Billion
Number Employees: 33,000
Number of Brands: 4
Brands:
  Country Kitchen Meals
  Henry's Heritage Bread
  Sprouts
  Sunflower

29569 Spudnik Equipment Co
584 W 100 N
PO Box 1045
Blackfoot, ID 83221-5518
208-684-4120
Fax: 208-785-1497 www.spudnik.com
Manufacturer and exporter of potato handling equip-
ment and parts including pliers, scoopers, convey-
ors, sorters, bins, bulk beds, van unloaders,
semi-trailers, etc
CEO: Rolf Geier
Sales Manager: Dennis Schumacker
Engineering Manager: Andrew Blight
Estimated Sales: $10-20 Million
Number Employees: 100-249
Square Footage: 200000

29570 Spurgeon Co
1330 Hilton Rd
Ferndale, MI 48220-2837
248-547-3805
Fax: 248-547-8344 800-396-2554
Manufacturer and exporter of conveyors, unscram-
blers, aluminum casting and stacking equipment;
importer of aluminum casting and stacking
equipment
CEO: Andy Willermet
  awillermet@yoplait.fr
VP: Thomas Woodbeck
VP: Bernie Makie
Estimated Sales: $10-20 Million
Number Employees: 50-99
Square Footage: 200000
Parent Co: Overhead Conveyor Company

29571 (HQ)Spurrier Chemical Companies
PO BOX 16297
Atlanta, GA 30321
770-968-9222
Fax: 770-968-7281 800-795-9222
www.spurrierchemical.com
Cleaning products including institutional and indus-
trial chemicals and detergents
CEO: Robin Spurrier
CFO: Tony DiStefano
Vice President: Donald Ryel
Research & Development: Bruce Lavery
Quality Control: Karen Rowe
VP Distribution Sales & Kansas/Missouri: Marshall
Ryel
Sales Director: Kurt Luhmann
Operations Manager: Marcia Ryel
Production Manager: Marcia Ryel
Plant Manager: Todd Hardesty
Purchasing Manager: Jeff Alfaro
Estimated Sales: $10 - 20 Million
Number Employees: 50-99
Square Footage: 120000
Type of Packaging: Food Service, Private Label
Other Locations:
  Spurrier Chemical Companies
  Clwyd, North Wales

29572 Squar-Buff
1000 45th Street
Oakland, CA 94608-3314
510-655-2470
Fax: 510-652-0969 800-525-6955
Manufacturer and exporter of floor and rug cleaning
machinery
Number Employees: 5

29573 Squid Ink Mfg Inc
7041 Boone Ave N
Minneapolis, MN 55428-1504
763-795-8856
Fax: 763-795-8867 800-877-5658
info@squidink.com www.squidink.com

Ink jet coding and inks, coding and marking equip-
ment, and date codes batch numbers product identi-
fication
Owner: Kevin Blair
  kblair@engagetechnologies.net
Vice President: Loyd Tarver
Engineering: Chris Miller
Marketing Manager: Chad Carney
Estimated Sales: $5 - 10 Million
Number Employees: 20-49

29574 (HQ)Squire Corrugated Container Company
PO Box 405
South Plainfield, NJ 7080
908-561-8550
Fax: 908-561-2791 info@squirebox.com
Corrugated packaging
President: James Beneroff
Sales Manager: James Benneroth
Contact: Seymour Beneroff
  beneroff@squirebox.com
Estimated Sales: $10-20 Million
Number Employees: 100-249

29575 Squirrel Systems
3157 Grandview Highway
Vancouver, BC V5M 2E9
Canada
604-412-3300
Fax: 604-434-9888 800-388-6824
www.squirrelsystems.com
Manufacturer and exporter of electronic point of sale
terminals
Vice President of Research and Developme: Joe
Cortese
Vice President of Corporate Sales: David Atkinson
Estimated Sales: $20 - 30 Million
Number Employees: 100-250
Brands:
  Squirrel

29576 St Joseph Packaging Inc
PO Box 579
St Joseph, MO 64502-0579
816-233-3181
Fax: 816-233-2475 800-383-3000
Custom industrial packaging offset/flexo printing,
diecut/cello windowing, laminating and direct print
on mini-flute corrigated
President: C Hamilton Jr
CFO: Patty Waitkoss
CEO: Brad Keller
Quality Control: Don Kragel
Marketing: Pam Hurley
Plant Manager: Josh Hamilton
Purchasing: Kenny Hayter
Estimated Sales: $15 Million
Square Footage: 220000
Type of Packaging: Consumer, Food Service, Pri-
vate Label

29577 St Onge Ruff & Associates
2400 Pershing Road
Ste 400
Kansas City, MO 64108
816-329-8700
Fax: 816-329-8701 800-800-5261
marketing@transystems.com
Engineering firm specializing in the planning, design and construction of processing and distribution
facilities
Number Employees: 5-9

29578 St. Clair Pakwell
120 25th Ave
Bellwood, IL 60104-1201
708-547-7500
Fax: 708-547-9052 800-323-1922
Manufacturer and exporter of decorative packaging
including wrapping paper
Estimated Sales: $20-50 Million
Number Employees: 100-249
Parent Co: Field Container Corporation
Type of Packaging: Food Service, Bulk

29579 St. Elizabeth Street Display Corporation
21 Main Street
West Wing, Suite 349
Hackensack, NJ 07601

201-883-0333
Fax: 201-883-1333 bill@stelizdisp.com
www.stelizdisp.com
Point of sale displays
President: William Talaia
Estimated Sales: Below $5 Million
Number Employees: 20-49

29580 St. George Crystal
1101 William Flynn Hwy
Glenshaw, PA 15116-2637

724-523-6501
Fax: 724-523-0707 800-677-0261
Wine industry glassware
President: Richard Rifenburgh
Estimated Sales: $50 - 100 Million
Number Employees: 275

29581 St. Louis Carton Company
1620 N Jefferson Ave
Saint Louis, MO 63106

314-241-0990
Fax: 314-241-0991 www.stlcarton.com
Folding paper boxes
President: Bonnie Green
Estimated Sales: $1-2.5 Million
Number Employees: 1-4

29582 St. Louis Stainless Service
2305 N Broadway
St Louis, MO 63102

636-343-3000
Fax: 314-231-5074 800-735-3853
www.dukemfg.com
Tables, cabinets, counters, sinks and floor troughs
President: Don Durham
Estimated Sales: $5-10,000,000
Number Employees: 5-9

29583 St. Pierre Box & LumberCompany
66 Lovely St
Canton, CT 6019

860-693-2089
Fax: 860-693-6155
Wooden boxes, pallets and steel skids
President: John St Pierre
Estimated Sales: $500,000-$1 Million
Number Employees: 5-9

29584 St. Simons Trading
PO Box 5511
Hilton Head Island, SC 29938

843-757-9889
800-621-9935
Estimated Sales: $.5 - 1 million
Number Employees: 1-4

29585 Sta-Rite Ginnie Lou Inc
245 E South 1st St
PO Box 435
Shelbyville, IL 62565-2332

217-774-3921
Fax: 217-774-5234 800-782-7483
www.sta-riteginnielou.com
Manufacturer, importer and exporter of nylon hair nets, hairpins, bobbypins and haircare accessories.
Chairman: Robert Bolinger
CEO: Noel Bolinger
  noelbolinger@consulated.net
Sales Director: Linda Stewardson
Estimated Sales: $1 Million
Number Employees: 5-9
Number of Brands: 10
Number of Products: 1300
Square Footage: 32000
Type of Packaging: Consumer, Food Service, Private Label, Bulk
Brands:
  Ginnie Lou
  Sta-Rite

29586 Staban Engineering Corp
65 N Plains Industrial Rd # 5
PO Box 8
Wallingford, CT 06492-5832

203-294-1997
Fax: 203-294-0583 888-782-2261
sales@staban.com www.staban.com
Packaging machinery
President: Dennis Bandecchi
Estimated Sales: $2.5-5 Million
Number Employees: 10-19

29587 Stablized Products
1832 W Square Drive
High Ridge, MO 63049-1968

636-677-5764
Fax: 636-376-5811 800-546-7349

29588 Stackbin Corp
29 Powder Hill Rd
Lincoln, RI 02865-4424

401-333-1600
Fax: 401-333-1952 800-333-1603
www.stackbin.com
Stackable storage systems for small parts
President: William A Shaw
  wshaw@stackbin.com
Quality Control and VP: Scott Shaw
Sales Supervisor: Andrew Porter
Estimated Sales: $10 - 20 Million
Number Employees: 10-19

29589 Stadia Corporation
691 Corporate Cir
Golden, CO 80401-5622

303-273-0336
Fax: 303-273-1414 800-765-6600
sales@cognitive.com www.cogsol.com
Print and apply labeling equipment
President: Patrick Frinat
Marketing Manager: Vic Barczyk
Number Employees: 100-249

29590 (HQ)Stafford-Smith Inc
3414 S Burdick St
Kalamazoo, MI 49001-4888

269-343-1240
Fax: 269-343-2509 800-968-2442
djs@staffordsmith.com www.staffordsmith.com
Freezers, dishwashers, ranges, slicers, fryers, refrigeration equipment, etc
President: David J Stafford Sr
Cio/Cto: Randy Clark
  rclark@staffordsmith.com
Estimated Sales: $50 - 75 Million
Number Employees: 100-249
Other Locations:
  Stafford - Smith
  Lansing MI

29591 Stage Coach Sauces
3829 Reid St
Palatka, FL 32177-2509

386-328-6330
Fax: 386-328-6330 info@stagecoachsauces.com
www.stagecoachsauces.com
Contract packager and exporter of sauces and condiments including steak, barbecue, pepper, chicken wing and seafood; also, contract packaging of wet and dry products available.
President: Terry Geck
VP Marketing: Lisa Marie Geck
Plant Manager: Terry Geck
Estimated Sales: $3 - 5 Million
Number Employees: 5-9
Square Footage: 20000
Type of Packaging: Consumer, Food Service, Private Label
Brands:
  Stage Coach Sauces

29592 Stainless
305 Tech Park Drive
Suite 115
La Vergne, TN 37086-3633

954-421-4290
Fax: 954-421-4464 800-877-5177
www.stainless.com
Manufacturer and exporter of stainless steel kitchen and dining room equipment including tables and sinks
VP/General Manager: Edward Umphlette
VP Sales: Tom Kassab

Estimated Sales: Less than $500,000
Number Employees: 4
Square Footage: 920000
Parent Co: Franke USA Holding
Other Locations:
  Stainless
  Holland MI

29593 Stainless Equipment Manufacturing
5950 Cedar Springs Road
Suite 125
Dallas, TX 75235-6816

214-357-9600
Fax: 214-358-4959 800-736-2038
Metal sinks, counters and work tables for hotels and restaurants
Shop Foreman: Rex Riddle
Plant Manager: Bill Cross
Purchasing Agent: Patricia Corder
Estimated Sales: $5 - 10 Million
Number Employees: 35
Parent Co: White Swan

29594 Stainless Fabricating Company
860 Navajo St
Denver, CO 80204-4317

303-573-1700
Fax: 303-573-3776 800-525-8966
Stainless steel counters, tabletops, dish tables, shelving and sinks
President: Jeff Manion
Estimated Sales: $5-10 Million
Number Employees: 20-49

29595 Stainless Fabrication Inc
4455 W Kearney St
PO Box 1127
Springfield, MO 65803-8705

417-865-5696
Fax: 417-865-7863 800-397-8265
sfi-info@stainlessfab.com www.stainlessfab.com
Design and manufacture high quality, custom, shop and field fabricated stainless steel processing equipment including tanks, dryers, reaactors, columns, sanitary processing tunnels and other vessels
President: Sherry Miller
  jeff.harris@trivantis.com
Estimated Sales: $16 Million
Number Employees: 100-249
Square Footage: 90000

29596 Stainless International
2650 Mercantile Dr Ste C
Rancho Cordova, CA 95742

916-638-7370
Fax: 916-638-1172 888-300-6196
www.all-stainless.com
Stainless steel hoods, under counter bar equipment, sinks, dish tables and counters; also, custom fabrication services available
President: Ted Lambertson
CFO: Monica Lambertson
Estimated Sales: $2.5-5 Million
Number Employees: 20-49

29597 Stainless Motors Inc
7601 Nita Pl NE
Rio Rancho, NM 87144-8707

505-867-0224
Fax: 505-867-0225 info@stainlessmotors.com
www.stainlessmotors.com
Stainless steel power transmission equipment
Owner: John Oleson
  john@stainlessmotors.com
Engineering: John Oleson
Sales/Customer Service: Gene Filion
  john@stainlessmotors.com
Marketing/Human Resources: Lori Costa
Estimated Sales: $1.2 Million
Number Employees: 20-49
Square Footage: 22000

29598 Stainless One DispensingSystem
790 Eubanks Drive
Vacaville, CA 95688-9470

800-722-6738
Fax: 707-448-1521 888-723-3827
autobar@aol.com
Manufacturer and exporter of beer dispensing equipment
VP: Clark Smith
Number Employees: 3

Brands:
  Perfect Pour
  Stainless One

29599 Stainless Products
1649 72nd Ave
P O Box 169
Somers, WC 53171
262-859-2826
Fax: 262-859-2871 800-558-9446
sales@stainless-products.com
www.stainless-products.com
Manufacturer and exporter of stainless steel fabrications including O-rings, pumps, gauges, welding and valves; also, clean-in-place systems
President: Cindy Gross
  jerickson@stainless-products.com
President: Cindy Gross
Sales/Purchasing: Mike Shoop
Estimated Sales: $1 - 5 Million
Number Employees: 20-49
Type of Packaging: Bulk

29600 Stainless Specialists Inc
T7441 Steel Ln
Wausau, WI 54403-8732
715-675-4155
Fax: 715-675-9096 800-236-4155
www.ssi-wis.com
Manufacturer installation and exporter of stainless steel food processing and equipment, conveyors, tanks and work platforms
President: Roger Prochnow
CFO: Paul Kinate
Sr VP Sales: Mike Slattery
R&D: Steve Radant
Quality Control: Brian Stoffel
Marketing/Sales/Public Relations: Roger Prochnow
Operations: Keith Christian
Production: Shannon Herdt
Plant Manager: Keith Christian
Purchasing: Corey Eimmer
Estimated Sales: $20 Million
Number Employees: 100-249
Square Footage: 15000

29601 Stainless Steel
800 Aviation Parkway
Smyrna, TN 37167
888-437-2653
Fax: 954-421-4464 800-877-5177
www.stainless.com
Manufacturer and distributor of french fry dispensers and food service equipment
Parent Co: Franke
Brands:
  Robofry

29602 Stainless Steel Coatings
835 Sterling Road
P.O. Box 1145
South Lancaster, MA 01561-1145
978-365-9828
Fax: 978-365-9874 info@steel-it.com
www.steel-it.com
Manufacturer and exporter of anti-corrosion and stainless steel pigmented paint coatings
President: Michael Faigen
Estimated Sales: $1-2,500,000
Number Employees: 10-19
Number of Brands: 2
Number of Products: 14
Square Footage: 20000
Brands:
  Steel It
  Steel It Lite

29603 Stainless Steel Fabricator Inc
15120 Desman Rd
La Mirada, CA 90638-5737
714-739-9904
Fax: 714-739-0502 info@cookking.net
www.ssfab.net
Ovens, broilers, deep fat fryers, continuous oil filters and conveyor systems
President: Craig Miller
  craig@cookking.net
Executive VP: Dick Naess
Marketing Director: Coby Naess
Number Employees: 50-99
Square Footage: 110000

29604 Stainless Steel Fabricators
11967 State Highway 64 W
Tyler, TX 75704-6939
903-595-6625
Fax: 903-592-8819 info@ssftexas.com
www.ssftexas.com
Stainless steel, corrugated, copper and brass vent hood systems, countertops, sinks, tables and shelving
President/ Owner: Greg King
Sales & Marketing: Ryan King
Estimated Sales: $5-10,000,000
Number Employees: 10-19

29605 (HQ)Stainless Steel Fabricator Inc
15120 Desman Rd
La Mirada, CA 90638-5737
714-739-9904
Fax: 714-739-0502 info@ssfab.net
www.ssfab.net
Food processing machinery
President: Phil Benoit
  phil@ssfab.net
Sales Representative: Dick Naess
Estimated Sales: $20-50 Million
Number Employees: 50-99

29606 StainlessDrains.com
PO Box 1278
Greenville, TX 75403
888-785-2345
Fax: 877-785-2342
Manufactures a full line of stainless steel drains and drain products, from roof drains to sanitary floor drains.

29607 Stamfag Cutting Dies
2 Braley Point Road
Po Box 1249
Bolton Landing, NY 12814-1249
518-644-2054
Fax: 518-644-2546 www.stamfag-usa.com
Manufacturing and cutting dies for label printers and lithographers
Type of Packaging: Consumer, Food Service, Private Label, Bulk

29608 Stampede Meat, Inc.
7351 S 78th Ave
Bridgeview, IL 60455
Fax: 888-376-9349 800-353-0933
stampedemeat.com
Beef, pork and chicken products.
CEO/President: Brock Furlong
COO: Vito Giustino
CFO: Vito Tamburello
VP, Technical Innovation/Culinary Dev.: Dennis Gruber
VP, Food Safety/Quality Assurance: Adam Miller
Sr. VP, Sales/Marketing: Ray McKiernan
Director, Human Resources: Christina Hackney
VP, Production: Krys Harbut
Year Founded: 1995
Estimated Sales: $133 Million
Number Employees: 501-1,00
Number of Brands: 5
Square Footage: 285000
Type of Packaging: Consumer, Food Service
Other Locations:
  Cook Processing Facility
  Oak Lawn IL
Brands:
  Cro-Mag
  Cro-Magnon
  Cro-Man
  Mission Hill Bistro
  Stampede

29609 Stampendous
1122 N Kraemer Pl
Anaheim, CA 92806-1922
714-688-0288
Fax: 714-688-0297 800-869-0474
stamp@markenterprises.com
www.stampendous.com
Manufacturer and exporter of stain and spot removers
Owner: Fran Sieford
  stamp@stampendous.com
General Manager: Mark Bruhns
Product Manager: Regina Ashbaugh

Estimated Sales: $5 - 10 Million
Number Employees: 50-99
Square Footage: 40000
Brands:
  Spoto

29610 Stancase Equipment Company
165 Chubb Ave
Suite 3
Lyndhurst, NJ 07071
201-434-6300
Fax: 201-434-1508
Cheese equipment, agitators, cutters, forks, knives
President: Michael Koss
Executive: Joel Koss
Estimated Sales: $5 - 10 Million
Number Employees: 50-99

29611 Stand Fast Pkgng Prods Inc
350 S Church St
Addison, IL 60101-3750
630-543-6390
Fax: 630-543-6390 scott@standfastpkg.com
www.standfastpkg.com
Corrugated boxes and dispaly packaging
Owner: John Carman Sr
CEO: John Carmen
HR Executive: Tracy Miller
  tracy@standfastpkg.com
Research & Development: Keith Carman
Quality Control: John Carman
Sales Manager: Scott Carmen
Plant Manager: Jon Clair
Purchasing Manager: Phil Lynch
Estimated Sales: $20-25 Million
Number Employees: 100-249
Square Footage: 90000
Type of Packaging: Consumer

29612 (HQ)Standard Casing Company
165 Chubb Ave
Lyndhurst, NJ 07071-3503
201-434-6300
Fax: 201-434-1508 800-847-4141
Manufacturer, importer and exporter of sausage processing equipment including stuffers as well as sausage casings
President: Michael Koss
Executive VP: Joel Koss
Manager Sales: Richard Theise
Contact: Patricia Wisniewski
  patriciaw@standardcasing.com
Estimated Sales: $10-20 Million
Number Employees: 50-99
Square Footage: 70000
Type of Packaging: Bulk
Brands:
  Gold Hog Casings
  Platinum Hog Casings
  Stancase
  Standard

29613 Standard Folding Cartons Inc
7520 Astoria Blvd # 100
Flushing, NY 11370-1645
718-396-4522
Fax: 718-507-6430 stanfold@aol.com
www.thestandardgroup.com
Manufacturer and exporter of folding cartons
President: Louis Cortes
Manager: Tanya Borges
  tanyab@thestandardgroup.com
Estimated Sales: $20-50 Million
Number Employees: 20-49

29614 Standard Paper Box MachCo Inc
347 Coster St # 2
Bronx, NY 10474-6813
718-328-3300
Fax: 718-842-7772 800-367-8755
SPBM@prodigy.net 800-367-8755
Manufacturer and exporter of box making machinery
President: Bruce Adams
Sales: Ronnie Nadel
Estimated Sales: $5 - 10 Million
Number Employees: 10-19
Square Footage: 200000
Brands:
  Standard Econocut Die Cutters
  Standard Excalibur Die Cutters
  Standard Folder Gluers

29615 Standard Pump
1540 University Dr
Auburn, GA 30011

770-307-1003
Fax: 770-307-1009 866-558-8611
info@standardpump.com www.standardpump.com
Barrel and container pumps and flow control systems are commonly used through out the food processing, cosmetics, pharmaceutical, bio-tech, chemical processing, waste water treatment, plating, medical, semi-conductor, agriculture andpetroleum industries.
President: Don Murphy
Vice President: Christopher Murphy
Contact: Jacob Berg
  jacobberg@standardpump.com
Estimated Sales: $2-$3 Million
Number Employees: 5-9
Square Footage: 80000

29616 Standard Rate Review
PO Box 23415
San Antonio, TX 78223

210-532-6000
Fax: 210-532-6200 info@standardratereview.com
www.standardratereview.com
President: Alan Ziperstein

29617 Standard Refrigeration Co
321 Foster Ave
Wood Dale, IL 60191-1432

708-345-5400
Fax: 708-345-3513
stanref.customerservice@alfalaval.com
www.alfalaval.us
Manufacturer and exporter of heat exchangers for refrigeration applications
CEO: Tom Erixon
Estimated Sales: $50-100 Million
Number Employees: 100-249

29618 Standard Terry Mills
38 Green St
Souderton, PA 18964-1702

215-723-8121
Fax: 215-723-3651
Manufacturer and exporter of knitted and woven dish cloths, kitchen towels, oven mitts, aprons, food covers and pot holders; importer of kitchen towels
President: Kerry Gingrich
VP Production: G Nam
Estimated Sales: $10-20 Million
Number Employees: 1-4
Square Footage: 200000

29619 Standard-Knapp Inc
63 Pickering St
Portland, CT 06480-1987

860-342-1100
Fax: 860-342-1557 800-628-9565
info@standard-knapp.com
www.standard-knapp.com
Automated packaging machinery including vertical case, continuous motion tray, shrink and bottle packers
President: Arthur Tanner
CEO: Michael Weaver
  mweaver@standard-knapp.com
CFO: Michael Montano
CEO: Robert Reynolds
R&D: Mike Weaver
Quality Control: David Lou
VP Marketing: Kristofer Kolstad
Estimated Sales: $5 - 10 Million
Number Employees: 100-249

29620 Standex International Corp.
11 Keewaydin Dr.
Salem, NH 03079

603-893-9701
Fax: 603-893-7324 www.standex.com
Food service equipment, air distribution products, casters, supermarket cart wheels, pumps, point of purchase displays, hydraulic cylinders, etc.
President/Chief Executive Officer: David Dunbar
VP/Chief Financial Officer: Thomas DeByle
VP/Chief Legal Officer/Secretary: Alan Glass
Year Founded: 1955
Estimated Sales: $635 Million
Number Employees: 5,400
Brands:
  APW Wyott
  BKI Worldwide
  Bakers Pride

Federal Industries
Master-Bilt
Nor-Lake
Procon Products
Tri-Star Manufacturing
Ultrafryer

29621 Stanford Chemicals
12640 E Northwest Hwy # 411
Dallas, TX 75228-8091

972-682-5600
Fax: 972-682-9553
Industrial cleaning compounds
President: Ted Egerton
Customer Service: Lynnette Ladd
Chemist: Kenn Gretz PhD
Estimated Sales: $1 - 3 Million
Number Employees: 5-9
Square Footage: 40000

29622 Stanfos
3908 69th Avenue NW
Edmonton, AB T6B 2V2
Canada

780-468-2165
Fax: 780-465-4890 800-661-5648
info@stanfos.com www.stanfos.com
Manufacturer, exporter and wholesaler/distributor of dairy, food and meat processing equipment including pasteurizers
President: Lang Jameson
Sales Manager: Shawna Bungax
Number Employees: 10-19

29623 Stanley Access Technologies
65 Scott Swamp Rd
Farmington, CT 06032-2803

717-597-6958
Fax: 877-339-7923 800-722-2377
S-SAT-SatInfo@sbdinc.com
www.stanleyaccess.com
Manufacturer and exporter of automatic doors including fireproof, sliding, swinging and electrical; also, access control systems and door operating devices
President: Justin Boswell
International Sales/Marketing: Jennifer Loranger
Customer Service: Susan Martin
Administrative Assistant: Jennifer Almeida House
Estimated Sales: Below $500,000
Number Employees: 5-9
Parent Co: Stanley Works
Brands:
  Dura-Glide
  Magic-Access
  Magic-Swing
  Sentrex
  Stan-Ray

29624 Stanley Black & Decker Inc
1000 Stanley Dr
New Britain, CT 06053-1675

860-225-5111
CorporateRequest@sbdinc.com
www.stanleyblackanddecker.com
Fastening equipment and hand tools manufacturer.
President & CEO: James Loree
  jloree@stanleyworks.com
EVP & Chief Financial Officer: Donald Allan, Jr.
VP, Corporate Tax & Treasurer: Michael Bartone
VP & Chief Accounting Officer: Jocelyn Belisle
VP & Chief Information Officer: Rhonda Gass
VP, Investor Relations: Dennis Lange
Chief Communications Officer: Shannon Lapierre
SVP/General Counsel/Secretary: Janet Link
Chief Technology Officer: Mark Maybury
Chief Human Resources Officer: Joseph Voelker
Year Founded: 1843
Estimated Sales: $12.74 Billion
Number Employees: 60,767
Number of Brands: 22
Type of Packaging: Private Label, Bulk
Brands:
  AEROSCOUT
  BLACK + DECKER
  BOSTITCH
  CAM
  CRAFTSMAN
  CRIBMASTER
  DeWALT
  FACOM
  IRWIN
  LENOX
  LISTA

MAC TOOLS
PORTER-CABLE
PROTO
SONITROL
STANLEY
VIDMAR

29625 Stanley Roberts
501 Hoes Ln Ste 108
Piscataway, NJ 08854

973-778-5900
Fax: 973-778-8542
Flatware
President: Edward Pomeranz
Estimated Sales: $20-50 Million
Number Employees: 20-49

29626 Stanly Fixtures Co Inc
11635 NC 138 Hwy
Norwood, NC 28128-7509

704-474-3184
Fax: 704-474-3011 sandeel@cvnc.net
www.stanlyfixtures.com
Store fixtures
President: Todd Curlee
  ronnyaldridge@stanlyfixtures.com
Quality Control/CFO: Boyce Thompson
Sales Exec: Ronald Aldridge
Manager: Kenny Bowers
Senior Project Manager/Estimator: Harold Thompson
Estimated Sales: $10 - 20 Million
Number Employees: 50-99

29627 Stanpac, Inc.
Spring Creek Road
R.R. # 3
Smithville, ON L0R 2AO
Canada

905-957-3326
Fax: 905-957-3616 www.stanpacnet.com
Ice cream packaging, refillable glass milk bottles and closures, and glass bottles for the beverage and wine industries.
President: Steve Witt
Vice President, Marketing: Murray Bain
Vice President, Sales: Andrew Witt
Vice President, Operations: Ian Killins
Purchasing: Barry Kirk

29628 (HQ)Staplex Co Inc
777 5th Ave
Brooklyn, NY 11232-1695

718-768-3333
Fax: 718-965-0750 800-221-0822
info@staplex.com www.staplex.com
Electric staplers for packaging applications. Made in the U.S.A.
President: Doug Butler
  info@staplex.com
CEO: Phil Reed
Estimated Sales: $5 - 10 Million
Number Employees: 20-49
Brands:
  Accuslitter
  Staplex
  Tabster

29629 Stapling Machines Co
41 Pine St # 30
Rockaway, NJ 07866-3139

973-627-4400
Fax: 973-627-5355 800-432-5909
sales@smcllc.com www.package-testing.com
Manufacturer and exporter of packaging machinery for wirebound containers
President: Norbert Weissburg
  n.weissberg@package-testing.com
Estimated Sales: $10 - 20 Million
Number Employees: 10-19
Parent Co: Stapling Machines Company

29630 Star Container Company
2635 E Magnolia St
Phoenix, AZ 85034

480-281-4200
Fax: 480-281-4201
Biaxillary-oriented PET containers including wide mouth, narrow neck, custom and stock
VP and General Manager: Paul Ellis
Project Engineer: Phil Blank
Purchasing Agent: Earnest LaFrance

Estimated Sales: $20-50 Million
Number Employees: 1-4
Parent Co: Tech Group

29631 Star Container Corporation
175 Pioneer Dr
Leominster, MA 01453

978-537-1676
Fax: 978-537-9119

Corrugated boxes
President: Nick Campagna
General Manager: Bill Ferzoco
Human Resources: Marlene Nazare
Estimated Sales: $20-50 Million
Number Employees: 100-249
Square Footage: 180000

29632 Star Filters
PO Box 518
Timmonsville, SC 29161-0518

843-346-3101
Fax: 843-346-3736 800-845-5381
www.hilliard.com
Manufacturer and exporter of disposable filters and
stainless steel plate and frame filter presses for pro-
cess filtration applications; also, polypropylene
dewatering presses for wastewater applications
Regional Sales Manager: Scott Thomas
Regional Sales Manager: Frank Reid
Sales/Marketing Executive: Howard Reed
Estimated Sales: $2.5-5 Million
Number Employees: 20-49
Square Footage: 140000
Parent Co: Hillard Corporation
Brands:
Carbon Comet
Easy Earth
Star

29633 Star Glove Company
106 S Oak St
Odon, IN 47562

812-636-7395
Fax: 812-636-8038 800-832-7101
starglov@dmrtc.net www.starglove.com
Gloves including industrial knitted, canton flannel,
hot mill, double palm and cut resistant
VP: Eric Moll
Sales: Marc Gebhart
Contact: Akane Suzuki
asuzuki@tri-starglove.com
Estimated Sales: $10-20 Million
Number Employees: 50-99
Parent Co: Star Glove Company

29634 Star Industries, Inc.
P.O. Box 178
La Grange, IL 60525

708-240-4862
Fax: 708-240-4915 bob@starhydrodyne.com
www.starhydrodyne.com
Manufacturer and exporter of automatic floor scrub-
bing systems
Executive Director: Susan Frassato
Regional Sales Manager: Scott O'Brien
Estimated Sales: $2.5-5 Million
Number Employees: 50-100
Square Footage: 160000
Brands:
Star Hydrodyne

29635 Star Label Products Inc
42 Newbold Rd
Fairless Hills, PA 19030-4308

215-295-3441
Fax: 215-295-1994 800-394-6900
info@starlabel.com www.starlabel.com
Owner: Shev Okumus
shev@starlabel.com
CFO: Sevket Okumus
Estimated Sales: $2.5 - 5 Million
Number Employees: 20-49

29636 Star Manufacturing IntlInc
10 Sunnen Dr
PO Box 430129
St Louis, MO 63143-3800

314-678-6303
Fax: 314-781-4344 800-264-7827
technical@star-mfg.com www.star-mfg.com

Manufacturer and exporter of food service equip-
ment including gas and electric cooking equipment,
sandwich grills, toasters/waffle bakers, hot dog
equipment, condiment dispensers, popcorn equip-
ment, specialty warmers, dispensing
anddisplay/merchandising equipment
President/CEO: Frank Ricchio
VP Sales/Marketing: Tim Gaskill
VP Engineering: Doug Vogt
VP: Mike Barber
Marketing Director: Cindi Benz
Sales Director: Phil Kister
Contact: Ibrahim Nestor
nibrahim@star-mfg.com
Estimated Sales: $1 - 3 Million
Number Employees: 50-99
Square Footage: 380000
Type of Packaging: Food Service
Brands:
Chromemax
Galaxy
Jetstar
Starmax

29637 Star Micronics
1150 King Georges Post Rd
Edison, NJ 08837-3731

732-623-5500
Fax: 732-623-5590 800-782-7636
sales@starmicronics.com www.starmicronics.com
Miniature electronic buzzers, audio transducers and
dot matrix, thermal and P.O.S. printers utilized in re-
tail and restaurant applications
President: Takayuki Aoki
Marketing Manager: Patty McCarthy
Number Employees: 1,000-4,999
Parent Co: Star Micronics Company

29638 Star Pacific Inc
1205 Atlantic St
Union City, CA 94587-2002

510-471-6555
Fax: 510-471-4339 800-227-0760
starpac7@aol.com
Manufacturer and exporter of cleaning compounds
including household/consumer detergents
Chairman of the Board: Joon Moon
Manager: Ed Kubiak
starpacnew@aol.com
Estimated Sales: $5 - 10 Million
Number Employees: 10-19
Square Footage: 114000
Type of Packaging: Consumer
Brands:
Blue Ribbon
Blue Ribbon Classic

29639 Star Poly Bag Inc
200 Liberty Ave
Brooklyn, NY 11207-2904

718-384-7034
Fax: 718-384-2342 rachel@starpoly.com
www.starpoly.com
Manufacturer and exporter of plastic bags including
shopping, food, confectioners', heat sealed, etc.;
also, packaging materials including cellulose acetate
film and garbage and ice cream can liners
President: Rachel Posen
Contact: Rivkah Ffe
rivkah@starpoly.com
Production: Hershy Rosenfeld
Estimated Sales: Below $5 Million
Number Employees: 1-4
Square Footage: 100000

29640 Star Restaurant Equipment & Supply Company
18430 Pacific St
Fountain Valley, CA 92708

714-683-2658
Fax: 818-782-8179 www.chefstoys.com
Wholesaler/distributor of food service equipment
and supplies; serving the food service market
President/Owner: Les Birken
Purchasing: Lee Siegel
Estimated Sales: $5 -10 Million
Number Employees: 10-19
Square Footage: 30000

29641 Star-K Kosher Certification
122 Slade Avenue
Suite 300
Baltimore, MD 21208

410-484-4110
Fax: 410-653-9294 star-k@star-k.org
www.star-k.org
International Kosher certification service
President: Dr. Avrom Pollak
Executive Vice President: Patricia (Pesi) Herskovitz
Contact: Patricia Herskovitz
patricia.herskovitz@starkosher.com
Development Director: Steve Sichel
Estimated Sales: $3.5 Million
Number Employees: 250

29642 Starbrook Industries Inc
325 S Hyatt St
Tipp City, OH 45371-1241

937-473-8135
Fax: 937-473-0331 www.starbrookind.com/
Product line includes forming and non-forming food
packaging films designed for Bi-Vac, Dixie Pak and
Multi Vac machines.
Sales Manager: Richard Anderson

29643 Starflex Corporation
204 Turner Rd
Jonesboro, GA 30236

770-471-2111
Fax: 770-478-1304
Poultry packing and processing
Chairman of the Board: Ollie Wilson Jr
VP: Bob Polkinghorne
Estimated Sales: $5-10 Million
Number Employees: 20-49

29644 Starkey Chemical Process Company
PO Box 10
La Grange, IL 60525

708-352-2565
Fax: 708-352-2573 800-323-3040
Rubber cement, duplicating fluids, printing chemi-
cals, hand cleaners, toners and gelled alcohol cook-
ing and heating fuels; exporter of ink marking and
duplicating fluids
President: Linda Yates
Estimated Sales: $1-2.5 Million
Number Employees: 20-49
Square Footage: 54000
Brands:
Bantam
Perf
Starkey
Super Key

29645 Starlite Food Service Equipment
9200 Conner St
Detroit, MI 48213-1238

313-521-6600
Fax: 313-521-2400 888-521-6603
Stainless steel food service equipment including
work tables, refrigerators, freezers, canopies, hoods,
shelving, storage units, sinks, etc
Owner: Rodney Gullett
VP Operations: Ettore Commisso
Controller: Maria Kraft
Estimated Sales: Below $5 Million
Number Employees: 5-9
Square Footage: 32000

29646 Start International
4270 Airborn Dr
Addison, TX 75001-5182

972-248-1999
Fax: 972-248-1991 800-259-1986
info@startinternational.com
www.startinternational.com
Tape and label dispensers, hand-held label applica-
tors, semi-automatic bottle labeler
President: Dan Sternberg
dan@startinternational.com
Vice President: Todd Sternberg
Marketing Director: Melanie Riddick
Production Manager: Mike Pfattenberger
Estimated Sales: $1-2.5 Million
Number Employees: 5-9
Brands:
The Label Dispenser
The Tape Dispenser

29647 Starview Packaging Machinery
1840 St Regis Blvd
Dorval, QC H9P 1H6
Canada

514-920-0100
Fax: 514-920-0092 888-278-5555
info@starview.net www.starview.net
Plastic packaging machinery.
Technical Director: Iwan Heynen
Number Employees: 15
Square Footage: 36216
Type of Packaging: Private Label
Brands:
  Starview

29648 (HQ)Statco Engineering
7595 Reynolds Cir
Huntington Beach, CA 92647-6752

714-375-6300
Fax: 714-375-6314 800-421-0362
www.statco-engineering.com
Distributor and systems integrators for the sanitary
processing marketing in North America. Products
include pumps, valves, heat exchangers, homogeniz-
ers, separators, fillers, conveyor systems, instrumen-
tation/controls and otherpackaging and processing
equipment
Manager: Kathleen Hall
CFO: James Statham
Vice President: David Statham
Marketing Director: Randy Smith
Sales Director: Eric Perkins
Estimated Sales: $50 Million
Number Employees: 20-49

**29649 (HQ)State Industrial Products
Corp**
5915 Landerbrook Dr # 300
Suite 300
Mayfield Heights, OH 44124-4034

216-861-7114
Fax: 216-861-5213 877-747-6986
www.stateindustrial.com
Disinfectants and soap
CEO: Seth Uhrman
Estimated Sales: $96 Million
Number Employees: 500-999
Square Footage: 240000

29650 State Products
4485 California Avenue
Long Beach, CA 90807-2417

562-495-3688
Fax: 562-495-5788 800-730-5150
Manufacturer and exporter of standard baking pans,
cookie sheets, French bread frames and fiberglass
fabric liners coated with silicon rubber
Chairman: Arthur Haskell
Estimated Sales: $1-2.5 Million appx.
Number Employees: 20
Square Footage: 106000

29651 Statex
3947 Street Hubert
Montreal, QC H2L 4A6
Canada

514-527-6039
Fax: 514-524-0343
Wholesaler/distributor of sensory analysis software;
consultant offering training, technical support and
quality control services
Vice President: Michel Guillet
Estimated Sales: $1 - 5,000,000

29652 Stavin Inc
358 Blodgett St
Cotati, CA 94931

707-285-2050
Fax: 415-331-0516 info@stavin.com
www.stavin.com
Wine industry oak infusion systems
President: Allan Sullivan
Manager: Michael Bittner
mbittner@stavin.com
General Manager: Jemie Zenk
Estimated Sales: $500,000 - $1 Million
Number Employees: 20-49
Type of Packaging: Private Label

29653 Stay Tuned Industries
8 W Main St
Clinton, NJ 08809-1290

908-730-8455
Fax: 908-735-8180

Wholesaler/distributor and exporter of steel and alu-
minum cans and easy-open ends; also, consultant for
can manufacturers
Owner: Ray Slocum
Estimated Sales: $500,000-$1 Million
Number Employees: 1-4
Square Footage: 1800

29654 Steamway Corporation
2128 S Leslie Ln
Scottsburg, IN 47170

812-889-0896
Fax: 812-889-2269 800-259-8171
hopkins@scottsburg.com
Microwavable food containers
President/CEO: Gary Hopkins Sr
CFO: Drusilla Hopkins
VP: Gary Hopkins
R&D: Gary Hopkins Sr
Quality Control: Gary Hopkins
Marketing/Sales: Tim Barrett
Estimated Sales: $50 Million
Number Employees: 5-9
Number of Brands: 1
Number of Products: 15
Square Footage: 100000
Type of Packaging: Food Service, Private Label

29655 Stearns Packaging Corp
4200 Sycamore Ave
Madison, WI 53714-1330

608-246-5150
Fax: 608-246-5149 www.stearnspkg.com
Cleaning supplies including detergents
President: John Everitt
  bill.bestman@stearnspkg.com
Controller: Dennis Stuart
Product Manager: Darla Steinborn
Sales Exec: Bill Bestmann
Purchasing Manager: Jeff Hanson
Estimated Sales: $20-50 Million
Number Employees: 20-49
Square Footage: 500000
Brands:
  Stearns
  Vallley View

**29656 Stearns Technical Textiles
Company**
100 Williams Street
Cincinnati, OH 45215-4602

513-948-5292
Fax: 513-948-5281 800-543-7173
Manufacturer and exporter of hot oil filters for deep
fryers and medium and heavy duty nonabrasive
scrub pads; manufacturer of milk filters
Director Sales: Kevin Finn
Customer Service Manager: Joanne Heidotting
Estimated Sales: $20-50 Million
Number Employees: 100-249
Square Footage: 50000
Brands:
  Ffc
  Scrubbe
  Stearns

29657 Stearnswood Inc
320 3rd Ave NW
PO Box 50
Hutchinson, MN 55350-1625

320-587-2137
Fax: 320-587-7646 800-657-0144
info@stearnswood.com www.stearnswood.com
Manufacturer and exporter of corrugated cartons,
wooden boxes, crates, plastic pallets and bulk ship-
ping cartons and bins
Owner: Paul Stearns
Sales Director: Paul Stearns
  paul@stearnswood.com
Operational Manager: Mark Stearns
Plant Manager: Corey Stearns
Purchase Agent: Steve Fitzloff
Estimated Sales: 100000
Number Employees: 20-49
Square Footage: 60000
Type of Packaging: Bulk
Brands:
  Flow Max
  Ultra Bin

29658 Steel Art Co
189 Dean St
Norwood, MA 02062-4542

617-566-4079
Fax: 617-566-0618 800-322-2828
info@steelartco.com www.steelartco.com
Manufacturer and exporter of metal signs, letters and
plaques
President: John Borell
Director of Sales/Marketing: Charles Blanchard
CFO: Stew Dobson
Vice President: Stewart Dobson
Manager of Design & Engineering: Ciaran Dalton
Vice President of Sales: Charles Blanchard
Customer Service Manager: Kindra Jones
Vice President of Operations: Ashley Borell
Lead Production Manager: Jorge Aguirre
A/R-Credit Manager: Robert Smith
Estimated Sales: $5 - 10 Million
Number Employees: 100-249

29659 Steel Art Signs
37 Esna Park Drive
Markham, ON L3R 1O9
Canada

905-474-1678
Fax: 905-474-0515 800-771-6971
thrivnak@steelart.com www.steelart.com
Electric signs
President: Tom Hrivnak
Sales Manager: Gene Mordaunt
Operations Manager: Jorge Dasilva
Number Employees: 90
Square Footage: 348000

29660 (HQ)Steel City Corporation
PO Box 1227
Youngstown, OH 44501-1227

330-792-7663
Fax: 330-792-7951 800-321-0350
jsmith@scity.com www.scity.com
Manufacturer, wholesaler/distributor, importer and
exporter of plastic bags, plastic and wire racks and
coin operated vending machines; manufacturer and
importer of rubber bands
President: C Kenneth Fibus
CFO: Mike Janak
Quality Control: Steve Speece
National Sales Manager: Jim Smith
VP Sales: Lee Rouse
Sales Department: Erika Flaherty
Estimated Sales: $30 - 50 Million
Number Employees: 100-249
Square Footage: 150000

29661 Steel Craft FluorescentCompany
191 Murray St
Newark, NJ 07114-2751

973-349-1614
Fax: 973-824-0825
Manufacturer and exporter of fluorescent lighting
fixtures

Estimated Sales: $1 - 3 Million
Number Employees: 10-19

29662 Steel King Industries
2700 Chamber St
Stevens Point, WI 54481

715-341-3120
Fax: 715-341-8792 800-553-3096
info@steelking.com www.steelking.com
Manufacturer and exporter of racks including pallet,
pushback, flow, cantilever and portable. Products
also inclucde steel containers and guard railing
President: Jay Anderson
Marketing Director: Don Heemstra
National Sales Manager: Skip Eastman
Contact: Chrissy Christenson
  c.christenson@renters-choice-inc.com
Plant Manager: Ralph Gagas
Estimated Sales: $20-50 Million
Number Employees: 100-249
Parent Co: VCI
Brands:
  Sk 2000
  Sk 2500
  Sk 3000
  Sk 3400
  Sk 3600 Rock

29663 Steel Products
750 44th Street
Marion, IA 52302-3841
319-377-1527
Fax: 319-377-4580 800-333-9451
www.marioniron.com
Hot chocolate and cappuccino dispensers; exporter
of hot chocolate dispensers and parts
Customer Service: Lori Pickart
Operations Manager: Bryce Sandell
Estimated Sales: $1-2.5 Million
Number Employees: 5-9
Square Footage: 66000
Parent Co: Conagra Brands

29664 Steel Storage Systems Inc
6301 Dexter St
Commerce City, CO 80022-3128
303-287-0291
Fax: 303-287-0159 800-442-0291
info@steelstorage.com
Manufacturer and exporter of material handling
equipment including roller conveyors, sheet racks
and drawers
President: Brian Mc Callin
Estimated Sales: $5-10 Million
Number Employees: 20-49
Type of Packaging: Bulk
Brands:
Spacesaver

29665 Steelite International USA
4041 Hadley Rd
South Plainfield, NJ 07080-1111
908-755-0357
Fax: 908-755-7185 800-367-3493
usa@steelite.com www.steelite.com
Importer of ceramic commercial china
CEO: R J Chadwick
Marketing Director: Karen Gowarty
Contact: Kimberly Faloon
kfaloon@steeliteusa.com
Estimated Sales: $5-10 Million
Number Employees: 10-19
Parent Co: Steelite International
Type of Packaging: Food Service

29666 Steelmaster Material Handling
503 Commerce Park Drive SE
Suite B
Marietta, GA 30060-2745
770-425-7244
Fax: 770-423-7545 800-875-9900
Manufacturer and exporter of new and used ware-
house equipment including pallet racks and shelving
President: Mike Miller
CEO: Deborah Molley
Plant Manager: James Young
Estimated Sales: $1-2.5 Million
Number Employees: 5-9
Square Footage: 40000
Brands:
Bilt

29667 Steep & Brew
855 E Broadway
Monona, WI 53716-4012
608-223-0707
Fax: 608-223-0355 www.steepandbrewcoffee.com
Espresso machines and accessories, grinders,roast
coffees, wholesale and resale of coffee
Owner: Mark Ballering
mb@steepnbrew.com
Vice President: Mark Mullee
Estimated Sales: $10 - 20 Million
Number Employees: 10-19

29668 Stefanich & Company
1933 N Farris Avenue
Fresno, CA 93704-5912
559-237-2295
Fax: 559-237-2299 stefanich@aol.com
Stainless steel fittings
President: Steven Stefanich

29669 (HQ)Stegall Mechanical INC
2800 5th Ave S
Birmingham, AL 35233-2820
205-251-0330
Fax: 205-328-1988 800-633-4373
www.stegallmechanical.com

Manufacturer and exporter of food service ventilation equipment including ventilation/exhaust hoods
and fans; also, custom fabrications in stainless steel
and wood available
President: Vince Chiarella
vchiarella@stegallmechanical.com
Estimated Sales: $10 - 15 Million
Number Employees: 20-49
Type of Packaging: Food Service

29670 Stein-DSI
PO Box 98
Northfield, MN 55057-0098
507-645-9546
Fax: 507-645-6148
Supplier of food processing solutions
Estimated Sales: $10 - 20 Million
Number Employees: 50-99

29671 Steiner Company
401 W Taft Drive
Holland, IL 60473-2015
708-333-2003
Fax: 800-578-2507 800-222-4638
Manufacturer and exporter of waterless hand and
skin soaps; also, soap dispensers
President: Guy Marchesi
Director OEM Sales: Craig Brown
Marketing Director: Karen Siravo
VP Sales: Greg Fachet
Contact: Brent Stack
bstack@stnr.com
Estimated Sales: $10-20 Million
Number Employees: 50-99
Parent Co: Steiner Company
Type of Packaging: Private Label
Brands:
Bulkmaster
Change-O-Matic
Economaster
Handmaster
Papermaster
Swiss Air
Wesco

29672 Steiner Industries Inc
5801 N Tripp Ave
Chicago, IL 60646-6013
773-588-3444
Fax: 773-588-3450 800-621-4515
info@steinerindustries.com
www.steinerindustries.com
Manufacturer and exporter of air freshener and soap
dispensers; also, garment lockers, soaps, lotions and
hand cleaners
President: Raefel Krammer
rk@steinerindustries.com
Marketing: Karen Siravo
Sales Director: Greg Fachet
Estimated Sales: $10 - 20 Million
Number Employees: 50-99
Parent Co: Steiner Corporation
Type of Packaging: Consumer, Food Service, Bulk
Brands:
Bulkmaster
Change-O-Matic
Economaster
Handmaster
Papermaster
Swiss Air
Wesco

29673 Steingart Associates Inc
5211 Main St
South Fallsburg, NY 12779-5422
845-434-4321
Fax: 845-436-8609 www.steingartprinting.com
Advertising specialties, envelopes, brochures, letter-
heads, business cards, posters, etc
President: Ira Steingart
isteingart@steingartprinting.com
VP: Cindy Perlmutter
Estimated Sales: $1-2,500,000
Number Employees: 5-9

29674 Steinmetz Machine WorksInc
44 Homestead Ave
Stamford, CT 06902-7213
203-327-0118
Fax: 203-327-4942 smwct@aol.com
Machinery for the baking industry
President: Sharon Walsh
smwct@aol.com

Estimated Sales: $3 - 5 Million
Number Employees: 5-9

29675 (HQ)Stellar Group
2900 Hartley Rd
Jacksonville, FL 32257
904-260-2900
800-488-2900
info@stellar.net www.stellar.net
Provides design, engineering, construction and mechanical services on design/build, general contracting and construction management projects.
Chairman: Ronald Foster

CEO: Michael Santarone
CFO: Clint Pyle
SVP, General Counsel: Michael Wodrich
President & COO: Brian Kappele
Estimated Sales: $500 Million
Number Employees: 639

29676 Stellar Steam
276 E Allen St
Suite 5
Winooski, VT 05404
802-654-8603
Fax: 802-654-8618
Boilerless steamers
President: Michael G Colburn
Quality Control: Steven Bogner
Estimated Sales: Below $5 Million
Number Employees: 20-49

29677 Stello Products Inc
840 W Hillside Ave
PO Box 89
Spencer, IN 47460-1117
812-829-2246
Fax: 812-829-6053 800-878-2246
www.stelloproducts.com
Signs including metal and silk screen
President: Todd Zellers
todd.zellers@stelloproducts.com
Foreman: John Summerlot
Estimated Sales: $500,000-$1 Million
Number Employees: 10-19
Square Footage: 36000

29678 (HQ)Stelray Plastic Products Inc
50 Westfield Ave
Ansonia, CT 06401-1121
203-735-9412
Fax: 203-735-9412 800-735-2331
www.stelray.com
Plastic injection molded products
President: Lawrence D Saffran
General Manager: John Therriaelt
Contact: Les Alderich
lalderich@stelray.com
Estimated Sales: Less Than $500,000
Number Employees: 1-4

29679 Step Products
1500 Chisholm Trail
Round Rock, TX 78681
512-255-0888
Fax: 815-646-4896 800-777-7837
www.stepproducts.com
Fluorinated HDPE containers and plastic compo-
nents
General Manager: Jim Niemeyer
Sales: Scott Ellison
Sales: Diane Sherin
Number Employees: 35
Square Footage: 40000

29680 Stephan Machinery GmbH
1385 Armour Blvd.
Mandelein, IL 60060
847-247-0182
Fax: 847-247-0184
Processing lines and machines for the food, dairy,
meat, confectionary and convenience food industries.
Contact: Rolf Heinze
heinze@stephan-machinery.com

29681 Stephan Machinery, Inc.
1385 Armour Blvd
Mundelein, IL 60060
224-360-6206
Fax: 847-247-0184 800-783-7426
weirich@stephan-machinery.com
www.stephan-machinery.com

Designs, engineers and builds the finest food processing equipment available.
CEO: Olaf Pehmoller
CFO: Gunter Dahling
Sales Manager: Eric Weirich
Contact: Rolf Heinze
  heinze@stephan-machinery.com
Operations Director: Dirk Kuhnel
Estimated Sales: $7 -10 Million
Number Employees: 5-9
Square Footage: 28000
Brands:
  Microcut
  Stephan

29682 Steri Technologies Inc
857 Lincoln Ave
Bohemia, NY 11716-4100

631-563-8300
Fax: 631-563-8378 800-253-7140
steri@steri.com www.steri.com
Manufacturer, importer and exporter of dryers including vacuum shelf, lab and band; also, pressure leaf and vacuum filters
President: Clemens Nigg
  steri@steri.com
Estimated Sales: $10 - 20 Million
Number Employees: 10-19
Square Footage: 30000
Type of Packaging: Private Label
Brands:
  Funda
  Zwag Nutsche

29683 Steri Technologies Inc
857 Lincoln Ave
Bohemia, NY 11716-4100

631-563-8300
Fax: 631-563-8378 800-253-7140
www.steri.com
Stainless steel motors and worm reducers for sanitary applications, continuous vacuum band dryers, pressure extractors and Aseptomag aseptic valves
President: Clemens Nigg
  steri@steri.com
Estimated Sales: $10-20 Million
Number Employees: 10-19

29684 Sterigenics International
2015 Spring Rd
Suite 650
Oak Brook, IL 60523

630-928-1700
800-472-4508
info@sterigenics.com www.sterigenics.com
Irradiator of spices, dried herbs, food packaging, closures with seals, filaments, bottle closures, pouches, plastic bottles, and liquid poly-liners.
President: Phil MacNabb
Contact: Amy Edwards
  aedwards@sterigenics.com
Number Employees: 20-49
Brands:
  Sterigenics

29685 Steril-Sil Company
PO Box 495
Bowmansville, PA 17507

717-405-2258
Fax: 617-739-5063 800-784-5537
orders@sterilsil.com www.sterilsil.com
Manufacturer and exporter of condiment and silverware dispensers, containers and covers
President: David Stiller
CFO: Laura McEachern
VP: Bernard Chiccariello
Sales: Brian Schilling
  brian@sterilsil.com
Estimated Sales: $500,000-$1 Million
Number Employees: 1-4
Parent Co: Stiller Equipment Corporation

29686 Steritech Food Safety &Environmental Hygiene
7600 Little Avenue
Charlotte, NC 28226

704-971-4725
Fax: 704-544-8705 800-868-0089
contact@steritech.com www.steritech.com
Consultant providing food safety audits, pest prevention and food safety training to the food processing and hospitality industries

Executive Chairman, Founder: John Whitley
Chief Executing Officer: Rich Ennis
Chief Financial Officer: Mike Lynch
Vice President of HR: Jennifer Courtney-Trice
Board Member: Mark Jarvis
VP Pesticides (Mid-Atlantic Region): Eric Eicher
Contact: Mitch Anderson
  mitch.anderson@steritech.com
Chief Operating Officer: Rich Ennis
Number Employees: 30

29687 Sterling Ball & Jewel
2900 S 160th St
New Berlin, WI 53151-3606

262-641-8610
Fax: 262-641-8653 800-423-3183
dazarello@corpemail.com www.sterlco.com
Manufacturer and exporter of temperature control units & other heating & cooling equipment
President: Jeff Ackerberg
  jeff.ackerberg@kohler.com
VP: Mike Zvolanek
Marketing: Bill Desrosiers
Sales: Wayne Lange
Public Relations: Nichole Saccomonto
Operations Manager: Rich Cramer
Number Employees: 100-249
Parent Co: Sterling
Type of Packaging: Private Label

29688 Sterling China Company
511 12th Street
Wellsville, OH 43968-1303

330-532-1609
Fax: 330-532-4587 800-682-7628
Vitrified china
Vice President: Bruce Hill
National Sales Manager: Brian Lewis
Estimated Sales: $10-20 Million
Number Employees: 250-500
Square Footage: 250000

29689 Sterling Corp
2001 E Gladstone St # B
Glendora, CA 91740-5381

909-305-0968
Fax: 909-981-1441 800-932-9561
www.stercorp.com
Manufacturer and importer of security equipment including fire and burglar alarms and systems; also, installation services available
Manager: Bill Jones
  bill@stercorp.com
Estimated Sales: $2.5-5,000,000
Number Employees: 1-4

29690 (HQ)Sterling Electric Inc
7973 Allison Ave
Indianapolis, IN 46268-1613

317-872-0471
Fax: 800-474-0543 800-654-6220
websales@sterlingelectric.com
www.sterlingelectric.com
Production of customized/standard AC induction motors along with drive products such as; AC adjustable frequency controls, DC permanent magnet motors and controls, mechanical adjustable speed transmissions, shaft mounts and screwconveyors, and cycloidal reducers and gearmotors
President: Walter Mashburn
  walter@sterlingelectric.com
Sales: Roman Wiggins
Manager: Walter Mashburn
Number Employees: 20-49
Other Locations:
  Sterling Distribution Center
  Indianapolis IN
  Sterling Power Systems
  Hamilton, ON

29691 Sterling Net & Twine Company
P.O. Box 411
Cedar Knolls, NJ 07927

973-783-9800
Fax: 973-783-9808 800-342-0316
Manufacturer and exporter of nets and netting, conveyors, pallets and custom bags for produce and customer packaging
President: James Van Loon
Sales Manager: Jerry Eick
Estimated Sales: $5 - 10,000,000
Number Employees: 20-49
Square Footage: 32000

29692 Sterling Novelty Products
1940 Raymond Dr
Northbrook, IL 60062-6715

847-291-0070
Fax: 847-291-0120
Manufacturer and exporter of U.S. flag sets, nylon mesh scouring cloths and plastic food bags
President: Marvin Glasser
Secretary/Treasurer: Michael Glasser
Estimated Sales: $1 - 3 Million
Number Employees: 10-19
Square Footage: 10000
Parent Co: Sterling Novelty

29693 Sterling Paper Company
1845 Progress Avenue Columbus
Ohio, PA 19134-2799

215-744-5350
Fax: 215-533-9577 800-282-1124
www.sterling-paper.com
Manufacturer, exporter and importer of paper plates, Chinese food pails and food trays; also, boxes including cake, pizza, doughnuts, sausage, steak, pastry, etc
President: Martin Stein
Secretary: John Paul
VP: Suzy Faigen
Estimated Sales: $10-20 Million
Number Employees: 50-99
Square Footage: 650000
Brands:
  Aristocrat

29694 Sterling Process Engineering
333 Mccormick Blvd
Columbus, OH 43213-1526

614-868-5151
Fax: 614-868-5152 800-783-7875
sales@sterlingpe.com www.sterlingpe.com
Stainless steel process tanks, pipe/tubing, clean-in-place systems, stainless steel conveyor, platforms, skid mounted process equipment, design, fabrication and installation of food and beverage process system
President: Jerry Martin
  jmartin@sterlingpe.com
Sales Director: Jack Selvages
Operations Manager: Russ Flax
Estimated Sales: $10-20 Million
Number Employees: 20-49
Square Footage: 70000

29695 Sterling Rubber
675 Woodside Street
Fergus, ON N1M 2M4
Canada

519-843-4032
Fax: 519-843-6587
Manufacturer and exporter of rubber gloves
President: Robert Joyce
Manager Quality Assurance: Norma Ford
Number Employees: 30
Square Footage: 54000

29696 (HQ)Sterling Scale Co
20950 Boening Dr
Southfield, MI 48075-5737

248-358-0590
Fax: 248-358-2275 800-331-9931
sales@sterlingscale.com www.sterlingscale.com
Manufacturer, importer, exporter and wholesaler/distributor of industrial scales; manufacturer of engineering software for weighing equipment
President: E Donald Dixon
CFO: J Dixon
Vice President: Tom Ulicny
Research & Development: T Klauinger
Quality Control: Jeff Shultz
Marketing Director: Tom Ulicny
Plant Manager: J Holcomb
Purchasing Manager: S Latucca
Estimated Sales: $2-3 Million
Number Employees: 20-49
Number of Brands: 5
Number of Products: 100
Square Footage: 112000
Brands:
  Sterling
  Sterling Eliminator

29697 Sterling Systems & Controls
24711 Emerson Rd
Sterling, IL 61081-9171
815-625-0852
Fax: 815-625-3103 800-257-7214
sci@sterlingcontrols.com
www.prater-sterling.com
Manufacturer, importer and exporter of batching and
weighing process controls for dry and liquid prod-
ucts; also, weighing systems for poultry and meat
President: Don Goshert
VP/General Manager: Don Goshert
Western Sales: Bob Rogan
South/Southeastern Sales: Dean Considine
Northeastern Sales: Marty Gustafson
Estimated Sales: $2.5-5 Million
Number Employees: 10-19
Square Footage: 21000
Parent Co: Prater Industries

29698 Sterling Truck Corporation
4747 N Channel Ave
Portland, OR 97217-7613
Fax: 440-269-5979 800-785-4357
www.sterlingtrucks.com
Senior VP: John Merrifield
Sales: Richard Saward
Contact: Vaughn Burrell
vburrell@sterlingtrucks.com
Estimated Sales: $20 - 30 Million
Number Employees: 100-249

29699 Sterner Lighting Systems
701 Millennium Blvd
Greenville, SC 29607-5251
864-678-1000
Fax: 320-485-2881 866-898-0131
www.sternerlighting.com
Manufacturer and exporter of indoor and outdoor
lighting equipment
General Manager: Mike Naylor
Marketing Manager: Sherry Thomson
Plt Mgr: Ken Lehner
Estimated Sales: $10 - 20 Million
Number Employees: 20-49
Parent Co: Hubbel Lighting
Type of Packaging: Food Service
Brands:
Softform

29700 Sterno
1064 Garfield Street
Lombard, IL 60148
630-792-0080
Fax: 630-792-9914
Manufacturer and exporter of candles, including ta-
ble, birthday, tapers, and table lamps
President: Richard T Browning
Number Employees: 50-99
Parent Co: Sterno
Type of Packaging: Food Service
Brands:
Chafing Fuels
Handy Fuel Brand
Tabie Lamps & Stereo Brand

29701 Stero Co
3200 Lakeville Hwy
Petaluma, CA 94954-5903
707-762-0071
Fax: 707-762-5036 800-762-7600
www.stero.com
Commercial dish, glass, pot/pan and tray washers
Manager: Terry Goodfellow
VP Sales/Marketing: Lars Noren
Contact: Dan Ancheta
danancheta@stero.com
Estimated Sales: Less Than $500,000
Number Employees: 1-4
Square Footage: 66000
Parent Co: PMI
Brands:
Stero

29702 Stertil Alm Corp
200 Benchmark Industrial Dr
Streator, IL 61364-9400
815-673-5546
Fax: 815-673-2292 800-544-5438
info@stertil-ALM.com www.stertil-alm.com
US manufacturer of bulkbag discharge and fill lifts,
welding and assembly positioner. ALM specializes
in custom heavy duty lifting equipment.

President: Doug Grunnet
grunnet@almcorp.com
Sales Director: Patricia Galick
Estimated Sales: $10 - 20 Million
Number Employees: 20-49
Square Footage: 110000
Brands:
Ibc

29703 Steven Label Corp
11926 Burke St
Santa Fe Springs, CA 90670-2546
562-698-9971
Fax: 562-698-1507 800-752-4968
slc4you@stevenlabel.com www.stevenlabel.com
Labels including bar code and pressure sensitive;
also, decals
President: Steve Stong
steve.stong@stevenlabel.com
Estimated Sales: $20-50 Million
Number Employees: 100-249

29704 Stevens Linen Association
137 Schofield Ave
Suite 5
Dudley, MA 1571
508-943-0813
Fax: 508-949-1847 800-772-9269
www.co-store.com/stevenslinen
Manufacturer and exporter of linen goods, pot hold-
ers and place mats
President: Gregory Kline
VP Sales/Marketing: Nancy Dalrymple
Contact: Timothy Barnardo
timothyb@stevenslinen.com
Estimated Sales: $10-20 Million
Number Employees: 100-249
Square Footage: 150000

29705 Stevens Transport
9757 Military Pkwy
Dallas, TX 75227-4805
972-216-9254
Fax: 972-289-8545 800-823-9369
www.stevenstransport.com
Transportation firm providing refrigerated and dry
rail and long haul TL and LTL services
President: Clay Aaron
Chairman and CEO: Steven Aaron
Executive Vice President: Michael Richey
mrichey@stevenstransport.com
Estimated Sales: Over $1 Billion
Number Employees: 5000-9999

29706 Stevenson-Cooper Inc
1039 W Venango St
PO Box 46345
Philadelphia, PA 19140-4391
215-223-2600
Fax: 215-223-3597 waxcooper@aol.com
Manufacturer and exporter of oils including cotton-
seed and palm oils; also, manufacturer of paraffin
and sealing wax
President: Dennis Cooper
dcooper@stevensonseeley.com
R&D: Tammy Pullins
Estimated Sales: Below $5 Million
Number Employees: 5-9

29707 (HQ)Stewart Assembly & Machining
7234 Blue Ash Rd
Cincinnati, OH 45236-3660
513-891-9000
Fax: 513-891-0449 sales@stewartam.com
www.stewartam.com
Manufacturer and exporter of packaging machinery
President: Jim Weckenbrock
VP Sales: Ray Meyer
Estimated Sales: $5-10 Million
Number Employees: 10-19
Type of Packaging: Bulk

29708 Stewart Laboratories
21639 Route 322
Strattanville, PA 16258
814-379-3663
Fax: 814-379-3601 800-640-7869
Laboratory glassware detergents
Owner: Stanley Segelbaum
National Sales Manager: Stanley Stewart
Customer Service Manager: Joyce Berk

Estimated Sales: $2.5-5 Million
Number Employees: 1-4
Square Footage: 10000
Brands:
Labkol
Labkolax
Labkolite

29709 Stewart Marketing Services
11122 NE 41st Drive
Apt 31
Kirkland, WA 98033-7725
425-889-2455
Fax: 425-889-8786
Consultant specializing in sales and advertising for
the frozen food market in the Pacific Northwest
President: Bill Stewart

29710 Stewart Mechanical Seals
3600 Pegasus Dr # 10
Suite #10
Bakersfield, CA 93308-7090
661-391-9332
Fax: 661-391-9336 bill@stewartseals.com
www.gatorgaskets.com
Supplier of sealing and packing parts for machinery
used in the foodservice packing industry
Contact: Bill Stewart
bill@stewartseals.com
Estimated Sales: $450,000
Number Employees: 5-9
Square Footage: 8800
Type of Packaging: Consumer, Private Label, Bulk
Brands:
Four Aces
M&R

29711 Stewart Sutherland Inc
5411 E V Ave
Vicksburg, MI 49097-8387
269-649-0530
Fax: 269-649-3961 www.ssbags.com
Sandwich wraps and bags including bakery, french
bread, candy, doggie, foil insulated, french fry, sand-
wich, pizza, etc
President: John Stewart
CEO/VP/Pub Relations & Operations: Tom Farrell
tomf@ssbags.com
Quality Control: Anna Liggett
Research & Devel/Marketing & Sales: Shelley Averill
Quality Control: Irene Carroll
VP Sales: Jack Bailey
VP Production: William Moran
Plant Manager: Dick Vandrestradten
Purchasing: Loretta Johnson
Estimated Sales: $42 Million
Number Employees: 100-249

29712 Stewart Systems Baking LLC
808 Stewart Dr
Plano, TX 75074-8197
972-422-5808
Fax: 972-509-8734 www.stewart-systems.com
Conveyors, ovens and proofers
Vice President: Jim Makins
Sales: Bill Camp
Estimated Sales: $20-50 Million
Number Employees: 100-249
Parent Co: Sasi B. Baking

29713 Stewart Systems Baking LLC
808 Stewart Dr
Plano, TX 75074-8197
972-422-5808
Fax: 972-509-8734 800-558-3814
www.stewart-systems.com
Designs and manufactures a wide variety of packaging and processing equipment for all industries, with
a particular emphasis on fruits and vegetables, beer
and softdrinks, consumer foodstuffs, household
goods, and petroleum products
Sales: Bill Camp
Estimated Sales: $20 - 30 Million
Number Employees: 100-249

29714 StickerYou
Toronto, ON
Canada
416-532-7373
support@stickeryou.com
www.stickeryou.com
Custom stickers and labels

President: Andrew Witkin
Business Development: Barry Witkin
Director of Marketing: Ana Caracaleanu
Sales Manager: Stephen Fields
Social Content & Community Manager: Cy Svendson
Director of Production: Bret Simpson
Year Founded: 2008
Estimated Sales: Under $500,000
Number Employees: 51-200

29715 Stickney Hill Dairy Inc

15371 County Road 48
Kimball, MN 55353-9771

320-398-5360
Fax: 320-398-5361 sales@stickneydairy.com
www.stickneydairy.com
Goat cheeses
General Manager: Cheryl Willenbring
Quality Assurance Manager: Kathy Ratka
Manager: Frankie Lenzmeier
flenzmeier@stickneydairy.com
Estimated Sales: $2 Million
Number Employees: 10-19

29716 Stiles Enterprises Inc

114 Beach St # 1w
PO Box 92
Rockaway, NJ 07866-3529

973-625-9660
Fax: 973-625-9346 800-325-4232
www.stilesenterprises.com
Packaging machine replacement parts-rubber parts, conveyor belts, drive belts, fabricated belts, resurface rubber rollers, parts for cappers, fillers, labelers, bottle unscramblers, case tapers, form/fill/seal baggers , heattunnels.
Owner: Rich Stiles
CFO: Nancy Stiles
R&D: John Dubowchik
Sales: Ken Stiles
info@stilesenterprises.com
Estimated Sales: $5-10 Million
Number Employees: 10-19

29717 (HQ)Stock America Inc

900 Cheyenne Ave # 700
Suite 700
Grafton, WI 53024-1653

262-375-4100
Fax: 262-375-4101 michaelg@stockamerica.com
www.stockpackaging.com
Wholesaler/distributor of full-water and steam retorts, temperature and pressure monitoring equipment, fillers, packaging containers and sealing equipment.
President: Michael Galvin
Vice President: Victoria Schlegger
CEO: Michael Galvin
Vice President: Tim Schurr
Marketing: Donette Lambert
Sales Manager: Rick Eleew
Contact: Jay Brunner
jayb@stockamerica.com
Estimated Sales: $5 - 10 Million
Number Employees: 10-19
Number of Brands: 8
Number of Products: 5
Square Footage: 72000
Type of Packaging: Consumer
Other Locations:
Stock America
Montreal PQ
Stock America
Cary NC

29718 Stocker & Son Inc

34 Suydam Ln
Bayport, NY 11705-2198

631-472-1881
Fax: 631-472-8069 www.stockerandsons.com
German made slicing blades and chopping knives for the food processing industry
Owner: Lee Stocker
Estimated Sales: $1-2.5 Million
Number Employees: 1-4

29719 Stoffel Seals Corp

36 Stoffel Dr
Tallapoosa, GA 30176

770-574-2696
Fax: 770-574-7937 800-422-8247
www.stoffel.com

Stoffel Seals is a key supplier for product identification and branding systems, packaging enhancements, advertising premiums/promotional products, employee identification badges, tamper evident security seals and many other custommanufactured products. Our specialty items for the food and beverage industry include ham bone guards, trussing loops, rotisserie tags, tray pack inserts, pricing/shellfish tags, metal seals, string
Quality Control: Henry Bosshard
Marketing: Valerie Cates
Sales: Mark Swan
Production: Mike Brown
Plant Manager: Norbert Falk
Purchasing: James Westmoreland
Estimated Sales: $40 Million
Number Employees: 250-499
Square Footage: 180000
Parent Co: Stoffel Seals
Type of Packaging: Consumer, Food Service, Private Label, Bulk
Brands:
Prestige

29720 Stoffel Seals Corp

36 Stoffel Dr
Tallapoosa, GA 30176

770-574-2696
Fax: 770-574-7937 800-422-8247
www.stoffel.com
We are the supplier of choice for product identification and branding systems, packaging enhancements, advertising premiums/promotional products, employee identification badges, tamper evident security seals and many other custommanufactured products. Our specialty include ham bone guards, trussing loops, rotisserie tags, turkey lifters, tray pack inserts, pricing/shellfish tags, metal seals for kosher foods, elastic string tags, bottle neckers and cohes
President and CEO: Charles Fuehrer
Executive VP: Norbert Falk
Vice President: Joe Williams
Marketing Director: Pat Renz
Sales Director: Joe Cusack
Plant Manager: Norbert Falk
Estimated Sales: $50 - 100 Million
Number Employees: 250-499
Square Footage: 40000
Type of Packaging: Consumer, Private Label, Bulk
Brands:
Prestige

29721 Stogsdill Tile Co

14604 Harmony Rd
Huntley, IL 60142-9201

847-669-1255
Fax: 847-669-1278 800-323-7504
info@stogsdilltile.com www.stogsdilltile.com
Manufacturer and exporter of stainless steel floor drains; also, acid brick and monolithic flooring installation services available
President: Gloria Stogsdill
gstogsdill@stogsdilltile.com
Operations Manager: Ivan Gonzalez
Estimated Sales: $1 - 5 Million
Number Employees: 1-4
Square Footage: 32000

29722 Stokes

400 Kitts Hillroad
Hyannis, MA 02601

215-788-3500
Fax: 215-781-1122 800-635-0036
www.stokesdti.com
Tablet presses, tabletting dedusters, tooling, granulators, metal detectors, automated control systems, encapsulation equipment and size reduction equipment
President: Brayan Urban
Marketing: Barb McPeditt
Number Employees: 100

29723 Stokes Material Handling Systs

1000 Crosskeys Dr
Doylestown, PA 18902-1019

215-340-2200
Fax: 215-230-9280 nwfeigles@stokesmhs.com
www.stokesmhs.com
Conveyor systems; custom designing available - specializing in USDA/FDA approved systems

Owner: Jonathan Doughty
doughty@stokesmhs.com
Marketing Director: Steve Heinel
VP Operations: Neal Feigles
Estimated Sales: $8,500,000
Number Employees: 10-19
Square Footage: 12000

29724 Stolle Machinery Co LLC

6949 S Potomac St
Centennial, CO 80112-4036

303-708-9044
Fax: 303-708-9045 www.stollemachinery.com
High-speed wide and narrow coil and sheet-fed shell systems for D-I and D-R-D cans, complete draw-redraw can systems and air cup conveyors; other services include complete rebuilds, speed-ups and retolling of shell and cuppingpresses
President: Ralph P Stodd
CEO: Bob Eisaman
robert.eisaman@stollemachinery.com
VP: David Bolek
CFO: Jimm Miceli
Estimated Sales: $2.5 - 5 Million
Number Employees: 100-249

29725 Stone Container

12112 Greens Ferry Road
Moss Point, MS 39562-8836

502-491-4870
Fax: 502-491-7283
Corrugated boxes
General Manager: Michael Cash
Estimated Sales: $5-10 Million
Number Employees: 20-49

29726 Stone Container

150 N Michigan Ave # 1700
Chicago, IL 60601-7597

312-346-6600
Fax: 312-580-2299 www.smurfit-stone.com
Manufacturer and exporter of envelopes, plastic film and bags: multi-wall, paper and plastic
President: Pat Moore
Estimated Sales: $10 - 20 Million
Number Employees: 10,000
Parent Co: Stone Container

29727 Stone Enterprises Inc.

10011 J St
Suite 3
Omaha, NE 68127

402-753-0500
Fax: 402-502-8102 877-653-0500
sales@stoneent.net www.stoneent.net
Designer and manufacturer of custom built machinery, refurbished machines and replacement parts.
Contact: Kim Banat
kbanat@24hourfitness.com

29728 Stone Soap Co Inc

2000 Pontiac Dr
Sylvan Lake, MI 48320-1758

248-706-1000
Fax: 248-706-1001 800-952-7627
sales@stonesoap.com www.stonesoap.com
Manufacturer, importer and exporter of cleaning products including hand cleaners, detergents and soaps
President: Ken Stone
stonesoap@stonesoap.com
National Sales Manager: Patty Muskat
Purchasing Agent: Jacqueline ElChemmas
Estimated Sales: $5-10 Million
Number Employees: 10-19
Square Footage: 200000
Brands:
Sport Mate

29729 Stoner

PO Box 65
Quarryville, PA 17566

717-786-7355
Fax: 717-786-9088 800-227-5538
timesaver@stonersolutions.com
www.stonersolutions.com
FDA approved specialty lubricants
President: Rob Ecklin
Owner: John H Stoner
Sales Manager: Tim Bupp
Contact: Jon Farrel
timesaver@stonersolutions.com
Estimated Sales: $5 - 10 Million
Number Employees: 1-4

Brands:
Food Grade

29730 Stoneway Carton Company
3047 78th Ave SE # 203
Mercer Island, WA 98040-2847
206-232-2645
Fax: 206-232-2725 800-498-2185
Manufacturer and exporter of cartons, pads, and parts. Also graphic and structural design
President: Charles E Farrell
General Manager: Russ Salger
Sr. Account Executive Sales: Art Wical
Purchasing Manager: Troy Giesinger
Estimated Sales: $2.5-5 Million
Number Employees: 1-4
Square Footage: 240000

29731 Stonhard
1000 E Park Ave
Maple Shade, NJ 08052
800-257-7953
info@stonhard.com www.stonhard.com
Manufacturer and installer of polymer floors, high performance epoxy floors.
CEO: David Dennsteadt
Year Founded: 1922
Estimated Sales: $260 Million
Number Employees: 1000-4999

29732 Stor-Loc
880 N Washington Ave
Kankakee, IL 60901-2004
815-936-0774
Fax: 815-936-0767 800-786-7562
sales@storloc.com www.stor-loc.com
High density storage equipment, drawer cabinets and workstations
President: Michael J Ryan
mryan@stor-loc.com
Quality Control: Ed Ryan
Estimated Sales: Below $5 Million
Number Employees: 20-49
Parent Co: Ryan Metal Products
Brands:
Stor-Frame

29733 Stor-Rite Freezer Storage
215 N Mill Rd
Vineland, NJ 08360-3433
856-696-1451
Fax: 856-696-1451
Manager: Bob Bradway
Estimated Sales: $1 - 5 Million
Number Employees: 5-9

29734 Storad Tape Company
126 Blaine Ave
Marion, OH 43301-0493
740-382-6440
Fax: 740-383-3241 sales@storadlabel.com
www.storadlabel.com
Pressure sensitive labels
President: Bob Hord
Estimated Sales: $5-10 Million
Number Employees: 10-19

29735 Storage Unlimited
1001 N Kenneth Street
Nixa, MO 65714-8401
417-725-3014
Fax: 417-725-5750 800-478-6642
Manufacturer and exporter of racks including can, storage, dunnage, pan, tray; also, dish mobiles
President: Glenn Scott
Secretary: Mary Van Noy
Office Manager: Lisa Lewellen
Estimated Sales: 700000
Number Employees: 5-9
Square Footage: 24000
Brands:
Always Can

29736 Storax
72 Sherwood Road
Bromsgrove, UK B60 3DR
845-130-3090
Fax: 152-757-6144 info@storaxsystems.com
Mobile rack systems
VP Operations: Jim McLain
Number Employees: 10
Parent Co: Barpro Group

29737 Stork Fabricators Inc
525 Vossbrink Dr
Washington, MO 63090-1046
636-239-7424
Fax: 636-239-7322 sales@texwrap.com
www.storkfab.com
Fully automatic shrink wrap machinery including; horizontal side seals, tunnels, L-sealers, belted and flighted conveyors and high speed wrappers, our machines are touchscreen operated for easy set-up
President: Robert Stork
CFO: David Hood
VP & R&D: Brian Stork
Quality Control: Steve Angell
Marketing: Tom Dickman
Estimated Sales: $10 - 20 Million
Number Employees: 50-99
Square Footage: 72000

29738 Stork Food Dairy Systems
P.O. Box 1258
Gainesville, GA 30503-1258
770-535-1875
Fax: 770-536-0841 jan.kuiper@stork.com
www.sfds.com
Sales and service of various integrated processing and packaging systems for food, dairy, juice and beverage industry
CEO: Bath Dowdy
VP: Jan Lucas-Kuiper
Executive VP: Ben Hamer
Quality Control: Robert Terhaar
Contact: Andr Haket
andr.haket@stork.com
Estimated Sales: Below $5 Million
Number Employees: 10-19

29739 Stork Food Machinery
3525 W Peterson Ave
Suite 611
Chicago, IL 60659-3318
773-583-7793
Fax: 773-583-8155 800-81S-TORK
Automatic warehouse systems, aseptic packaging systems and aseptic processing equipment
Manager: Nicole Stack
Estimated Sales: $.5 - 1 million
Number Employees: 1-4

29740 Stork Townsend Inc.
PO Box 1433
Des Moines, IA 50306-1433
515-265-8181
Fax: 515-263-3333 800-247-8609
info.townsendusa@stork.com
www.townsendeng.com
Manufacturer and exporter of meat processing machinery including pork, fish and poultry skinners, sausage stuffers, linkers, bacon injectors, sausage coextrusion, sausage loaders and meat harvesting systems.
President: Theo Bruinsma
Regional Sales Manager: David Bertelsen
Contact: Janet Bergeron
janet.bergeron@marel.com
Estimated Sales: $20-50 Million
Number Employees: 100-249
Type of Packaging: Food Service
Brands:
Townsend

29741 Storm Industrial
PO Box 14666
Shawnee Mission, KS 66285-4666
913-599-3650
Fax: 559-277-9580 800-745-7483
Manufacturer and exporter of plastic and brass valves including pilot mini, automatic drain, speed control exhaust, solenoid, hydraulic nonelectric, slip, pressure regulating, electric and barbed drain; also, wire connectors
Number Employees: 50
Square Footage: 80000
Parent Co: Imperial Valve Company
Brands:
Imperial

29742 Stormax International
90 Manchester St
Concord, NH 03301-5129
603-223-2333
Fax: 603-223-2330 800-874-7629

Manufacturer, importer and exporter of filling, sealing and lidding machinery for cups, trays, tubs and paper containers
President: Earl Gestewitz
Estimated Sales: Below $5 Million
Number Employees: 1-4
Parent Co: Stormax International A/S

29743 Storopack Packaging Systs USA
12007 Woodruff Ave
Downey, CA 90241-5603
562-803-5582
Fax: 562-803-4462 800-827-7225
www.storopack.com
Manufacturer, converter and recycler of EPS (Expanded Polystyrene) with primary activities that include the conversion of EPS, natural starch, paper and plastic cushioning materials
Manager: John Melat
VP Marketing: Paul Deis
Estimated Sales: $20-50 Million
Number Employees: 50-99
Type of Packaging: Private Label, Bulk

29744 Storsack Inc
7111 Perimeter Park Dr # 300
Houston, TX 77041-4048
713-461-0840
Fax: 713-461-0654 800-841-4982
info@storsack.com
Global manufacturer of flexible intermdiate bulk bags
CEO: Bruce Boyd
Sales Director of Public Relations: Sonja GrAger
Estimated Sales: $10-25 Million
Number Employees: 20-49
Brands:
Cleanmaster
Guardmaster
Safemaster
Spacemaster
Tripmaster

29745 Stout Sign Company
6425 W Florissant Ave
Saint Louis, MO 63136-3622
314-385-4600
Fax: 314-385-9412 800-325-8530
www.stoutsign.com
Manufacturer and exporter of point of purchase signs and displays; silk screening available
President: Patrick Conners
Sales Manager: Randall Simonian
Contact: Redmond Egart
regart@stoutsign.com
VP Operations: Lee Witt
Estimated Sales: $15 - 20 Million
Number Employees: 100-249
Square Footage: 140000
Parent Co: Stout Industries of Delaware

29746 Strahl & Pitsch Inc
230 Great East Neck Rd
West Babylon, NY 11704-7602
631-669-0175
Fax: 631-587-9120 www.strahlpitsch.com
Confectionery waxes, custom blending
President: Brian Ardito
bardito@spwax.com
Marketing Manager: Dan Damico
Estimated Sales: $20-50 Million
Number Employees: 20-49

29747 Strahman Valves Inc
2801 Baglyos Cir
Lehigh Valley Industrial Park VI
Bethlehem, PA 18020-8033
484-893-5080
Fax: 484-893-5099 877-787-2462
strahman@strahman.com
Manufacturer and exporter of cleaning products, hoses and valves
President/CEO: August Percoco
apercoco@strahman.com
CFO: Dan Eckel
VP: Kevin Carroll
Director of IT: Eric Hays
Director Quality Control: Arthur Pultz
Marketing Manager: Vanessa Reagle
VP Sales: Jan Willem Savelkoel
Customer Service Manager: Rosalind Bowens
VP Operations: William Doll
Purchasing & Inventory Control M: Chris Lipinski

Estimated Sales: $10-20 Million
Number Employees: 100-249
Type of Packaging: Bulk

29748 Straight Line Filters
701 Christiana Ave
Wilmington, DE 19801-5842
302-654-8805
Fax: 302-655-5038
Food-processing vacuum belt filters
Manager: Kenneth Seibert
Estimated Sales: $1-2.5 Million
Number Employees: 10-19

29749 Straits Steel & Wire Co
902 N Rowe St # 100
Ludington, MI 49431-1495
231-843-3416
Fax: 231-843-8096 www.sswholding.net
Wire shelves, racks, fruit and vegetable baskets and
displays
Vice President: Steve Koss
VP: James Boals
Estimated Sales: $20 - 50 Million
Number Employees: 100-249

29750 Strand Lighting
10911 Petal St
Dallas, TX 75238-2424
214-647-7880
Fax: 714-899-0042 www.strandlighting.com
Manufacturer and exporter of electric and incandes-
cent lighting fixtures
President: Tim Burnham
peter.rogers@philips.com
VP Marketing: Peter Rogers
Sales Exec: Pete Borchetta
Estimated Sales: $20 - 30 Million
Number Employees: 20-49
Parent Co: Rank Industries America
Type of Packaging: Food Service

29751 Strapack
30860 San Clemente St
Hayward, CA 94544-7135
510-475-6000
Fax: 510-475-6090 800-475-5006
www.strapack.com
Strapping machines, corrugated converting machine
Owner: Keisho Yamamoto
Contact: Asami Cillo
anc@strapack.com
Estimated Sales: $10-20 Million
Number Employees: 10-19

29752 Strapex Corporation
2601 Westinghouse Blvd
Charlotte, NC 28273
704-588-2510
Fax: 704-588-6838 800-346-1804
Bottle and can containers
Estimated Sales: $10-20 Million
Number Employees: 20-49

29753 Strasburger & Siegel
7249 National Dr Ste 2
Hanover, MD 21076
410-712-7373
Fax: 410-712-7378 888-726-3753
www.eurofinsus.com
Consultant to food technologists for product formu-
lation, evaluation, analysis, etc
President: Rick Gjesdal
Director: Tom Light
Contact: Wendy Bowie
wendybowie@eurofinsus.com
Estimated Sales: $1-2.5 Million
Number Employees: 20-49

29754 Stratecon
5215 Mountain View Road
Winston Salem, NC 27104-5117
336-768-6808
Fax: 336-765-5149 cbeckstc@bellsouth.net
www.stratecon-intl.com
Consultant specializing in strategic planning,
start-up feasibility, marketing research, technology
assessment, project management, etc. for the food
industry
Estimated Sales: Below $500,000
Number Employees: 2
Square Footage: 4000

**29755 Stratecon
InternationalConsultants**
5215 Mountain View Road
Winston Salem, NC 27104-5117
336-768-6808
Fax: 336-765-5149 www.stratecon-intl.com
We combine the experience of twelve seasoned food
industry professionals who work together to fulfill
client needs. Members have skills in processed
foods and ingredients. Specialties: business development, coffee manufacturingdietary fibers, due dili-
gence, food safety, fortification, process and
equipment development, product introduction, strategic planning, and training. See website for
individual consultant locations
Coordinator: Catherine Side
Estimated Sales: Below $500,000
Number Employees: 2

29756 Strategic Equipment & Supply
8360 E Via De Ventura
Scottsdale, AZ 85258-3172
480-905-5530
Food service equipment
Estimated Sales: Less than $500,000
Number Employees: 1-4

29757 Stratis Plastic Pallets
5677 W 73rd St
Indianapolis, IN 46278
317-328-8000
Fax: 317-328-8080 800-725-5387
sales@pallets.com www.pallets.com
Plastic pallets
President: Andrew Elder
Contact: Reed Elder
relder@pallets.com
Estimated Sales: $300,000-500,000
Number Employees: 1-4

29758 (HQ)Stratix Corp
4920 Avalon Ridge Pkwy
Peachtree Cor, GA 30071-1572
770-326-7580
Fax: 770-326-7591 800-883-8300
info@stratixcorp.com www.stratixcorp.com
Bar code generation software, bar code verification
equipment, bar code pressure sensitive labels, verifi-
cation/label printing systems and thermal transfer/di-
rect thermal printers
President & CEO: Gina Gallo
gina.gallo@ipaper.com
CEO: Bonney Shuman
CFO: John Pumpelly
Marketing Director: Kathryn Fraas
SVP, of Sales: Brian Burkett
VP, Operation: Ross Homans
Estimated Sales: $10 - 20 Million
Number Employees: 100-249
Other Locations:
Stratix Corporation
St. Leonards
Brands:
Bar Code Creator
Symart Systems
Xaminer

29759 Straub Designs Co
2238 Florida Ave S # A
Suite A
St Louis Park, MN 55426-2880
952-546-6686
Fax: 763-546-3056 800-959-3708
parts@straubdesign.com www.straubdesign.com
Manufacturer and exporter of packaging and taping
machinery
President: Dennis Schuette
dschuette@straubdesign.com
Sales: Mark Baillie
Sales: Glenn Baillie
Estimated Sales: $2.5-5 Million
Number Employees: 20-49
Square Footage: 40000

29760 Straub Designs Co
2238 Florida Ave S # A
St Louis Park, MN 55426-2880
952-546-6686
Fax: 763-546-3056 parts@straubdesign.com
Manufacturer and exporter of hand and electric
grinding mills for dry and oily materials including
beans, nuts and herbs and for preparing laboratory
samples for analysis

President: Dennis Schuette
dschuette@straubdesign.com
Office Manager: Judy Haag
Number Employees: 20-49
Parent Co: Clinton Separators, Inc.
Brands:
Quaker City

29761 Straubel Company
1891 Commerce Drive
De Pere, WI 54115
920-336-1412
Fax: 920-336-1308 888-336-1412
Disposable plastic and paper products including ta-
ble covers; also, plastic banquet tables, drop cloths,
and laminations
President: Thomas Tess
Vice President: Craig Nothstine
VP Sales: Jay McDowell
Contact: Duane Bashell
duane@straubelcompany.com
VP Operations: Paul Piikila
Production Planning: Brenda Scray
Plant Manager: John Westcott
Supply Chain Management: Shari Linksens
Estimated Sales: Below $5 Million
Number Employees: 10-19
Square Footage: 80000
Brands:
Breez Proof
Picnic Time
Table Mate

29762 Streamfeeder
315 27th Ave NE
Minneapolis, MN 55418
763-502-0000
Fax: 763-502-0100 info@streamfeeder.com
www.streamfeeder.com
Electromechanical products and friction feeders for
inserting, feeding and collating
President: Mitch Speicher
Contact: Emily Lang
emily.lang@streamfeeder.com
Estimated Sales: $10-20 Million
Number Employees: 20-49

29763 Streater Inc
411 S 1st Ave
Albert Lea, MN 56007-1794
507-373-0611
Fax: 507-373-7630 800-527-4197
salesinfo@streater.com www.streater.com
Store fixtures including gondolas and wall cases
President: Thomas Stensrude
Cmo: Peter Nelson
peter@streater.com
Finance Executive: Dan Juntunen
Marketing: Dan Heckmann
Sales: Dave Sprunt
Estimated Sales: $1 - 3 Million
Number Employees: 100-249
Square Footage: 2240000
Parent Co: Joyce International

29764 Streator Dependable Mfg
1705 N Shabbona St
Streator, IL 61364-2100
815-672-0551
Fax: 815-672-7631 800-798-0551
sales@streatordependable.com
www.streatordependable.com
Manufacturer and importer of material handling
equipment including containers, pallets, stacking
racks, skids and spools
President: Paul A Walker
pwalker@streatordependable.com
Marketing: Bill Bontemps
Sales Manager: Nathan Hovious
Number Employees: 100-249
Square Footage: 200000

29765 Stretch-Vent Packaging System
PO Box 51462
Ontario, CA 91761-1062
909-947-3993
Fax: 909-947-0579 800-822-8368
Manufacturer, importer and exporter of vented pro-
duce wrap
VP Sales/Marketing: T Lasker
Director Sales/Operations: Phil Beach
Estimated Sales: $10-20 Million
Number Employees: 50-99
Type of Packaging: Consumer, Bulk

Brands:
Stretch-Vent
Vex-Cap

29766 Stretchtape
18460 Syracuse Ave
Cleveland, OH 44110
216-486-9400
Fax: 216-486-9444 888-486-9400
info@stretchtape.com www.stretchtape.com
President: Sean Mc Donald
Estimated Sales: $1 - 5 Million
Number Employees: 20-49

29767 Stribbons
2921 W Cypress Creek Rd
Suite 101
Fort Lauderdale, FL 33309
305-628-4000
Fax: 305-621-6109 info@mncstribbons.com
www.stribbons.com
Decorative packaging services: giftwrap, labels,
boxes and containers.
Marketing: Michael Flynn
Contact: Harold Tepper
htepper@mncstribbons.com

29768 Stricker & Co
500 Kent Ave
La Plata, MD 20646
301-934-8346
Fax: 301-870-3112
Signs, printed labels and point of purchase displays
Owner: Susan Stiles
Estimated Sales: Less Than $500,000
Number Employees: 1-4
Square Footage: 10000

29769 Stricklin Co
1901 W Commerce St
Dallas, TX 75208-8104
214-637-1030
Fax: 214-747-7872 www.stricklincompany.com
Manufacturer and exporter of blenders, cookers and
mixers; also, repair services available
President: Tom Johnson
tom.johnson@baldwinmetals.com
Controller: Don Smith
Engineer: Mitch Withem
Estimated Sales: Below $5 Million
Number Employees: 20-49
Square Footage: 120000
Parent Co: Baldwin Metals
Brands:
Stricklin
Strico

29770 Stripper Bags
121 Quail Run Road
Henderson, NV 89014-2129
800-354-2247
Fax: 702-898-9938
Manufacturer and exporter of preprinted poly bags
for food portioning and rotation; also, labels including peel/stick and disposable for food rotation
President: Mark Tenner

29771 Strohmeyer & Arpe Co Inc
106 Allen Rd # 203
Basking Ridge, NJ 07920-3851
908-580-9100
Fax: 908-580-9300 800-628-2374
sales@strohmeyer.com www.strohmeyer.com
Natural waxes including beeswax, carnauba,
candelilla, ouricouri and Japan wax, bulk honey, private label canned fruits, vegetables and seafood
President: Charles Kocot
ckocot@strohmeyer.com
Estimated Sales: $5 - 10 Million
Number Employees: 5-9

29772 Strong Hold Products
6333 Strawberry Ln
Louisville, KY 40214-2930
502-363-4175
Fax: 502-363-3827 800-880-2625
info@strong-hold.com
www.strongholdindustrial.com
Industrial welded storage cabinets and shelving
President: Thomas Diebold
VP: Tina Gillenwoater
Vice President: Tom Diebold
Sales Director: Peggy Drake
Plant Manager: Dannis Hughbanks

Estimated Sales: $10-20 Million
Number Employees: 100-249
Square Footage: 216000
Parent Co: Fabricated Metals

29773 Strongarm
425 Caredean Drive
Horsham, PA 19044
215-443-3400
Fax: 215-443-3002 sales@strongarm.com
www.strongarm.com
Operator interface mountings and systems
President: Tom Holden
Sales Manager: Bill Flemming

29774 Stronghaven Containers Co
11135 Monroe Rd
Matthews, NC 28105-6564
704-847-7743
Fax: 704-847-5871 800-222-7919
info@stronghaven.com www.stronghaven.com
Manufacturer and exporter of corrugated boxes
Estimated Sales: $1 - 5 Million
Number Employees: 20-49
Square Footage: 500000

29775 Stroter Inc
PO Box 892
Freeport, IL 61053
815-616-2506
Fax: 815-244-2102 www.stroter.com
Spare parts, electric motors and complete replace-
ment units

29776 Structural Transport
888 E Porter Rd
Norton Shores, MI 49441-5848
231-798-6342
Fax: 231-798-0198 www.structuralconcept.com
President: David P Geerts
Quality Control: Jeff Cimnes
Chairman: James Doss
Manager: John Bell
johnbell@structuralconcept.com
Estimated Sales: $30 - 50 Million
Number Employees: 5-9

29777 Structure
3000 E 1st Ave Ste 126
Denver, CO 80206
303-329-9560
Fax: 303-329-0833
President: Tom Noto
Vice President: Todd McAtee
Estimated Sales: $2.5-5 Million
Number Employees: 20-49

29778 (HQ)Structure Probe
PO Box 656
West Chester, PA 19381-0656
610-436-5400
Fax: 610-436-5755 800-242-4774
spi3spi@2spi.com www.2spi.com
Independent laboratory offering problem solving
and analysis
President and Chairman of the Board: Violet Garber
Corporate Secretary and Vice President: Kim
Murray
Vice President: Eugene Rodek
Vice President, Technical: Andrew W. Blackwood,
Ph.D.
Quality Officer: Andrew W. Blackwood, Ph. D.
Office Manager: Nancy Blackwood
Estimated Sales: $1 - 2.5 Million
Number Employees: 10-19
Square Footage: 80000
Other Locations:
Structure Probe
Fairfield CT

29779 Stryco Wire Products
1110 Flint Road
North York, ON M3J 2J5
Canada
416-663-7000
Fax: 416-663-7001
Wire baskets and shelving, cooler shelves, slide
guards and barbecue grills
President: Calford Robinson
CFO: Jana Bonder
Quality Control: Ken Duffney
R&D: Ede Zendai
Number Employees: 30-40

29780 Stuart W Johnson & Co
1002 Mobile St
Lake Geneva, WI 53147-2449
262-248-8851
Fax: 262-248-0277 800-558-5904
sales@stuartjohnsonco.com
Aseptic processing equipment, centrifuges, cheese
equipment, filtration equipment, clean rooms and
equipment, cutting equipment, fillers, pin, milk,
steam, flow diversion stations, heat exchangers,
plate, tubular, homogenizersladders, vat, meters,
flow
President: Eric Behling
eric.behling@stuartjohnsonco.com
Estimated Sales: $5-10 Million
Number Employees: 10-19

29781 Studd & Whipple Company
PO Box 17
Conewango Valley, NY 14726-0017
716-287-3791
Fax: 716-287-3309
Wooden pallets and pre-cut pallet materials
Estimated Sales: $10 - 20 Million
Number Employees: 8
Parent Co: Crawford Manufacturing Company

**29782 (HQ)Sturdi-Bilt Restaurant
Equipment**
7150 Nollar Rd
Whitmore Lake, MI 48189
313-231-4911
Fax: 800-444-2895 800-521-2895
sbrei@juno.com www.sturdibilt.com
Kitchen equipment and ventilation systems
Chairman: Arnold H Robinson
Secretary: Ruth Ann Robinson
Sales Director: Shirley Van Reuter
Estimated Sales: $2.5-5 Million
Number Employees: 5-9

29783 Stutz Products Corp
606 S Walnut St
Hartford City, IN 47348-2627
765-348-2510
Fax: 765-348-1001 info@stutzproducts.com
Food processing machine knives
President: Bill Musselman
bill@stutzproducts.com
Estimated Sales: Less Than $500,000
Number Employees: 5-9
Square Footage: 12000

29784 Stylmark Inc
6536 Main St NE
PO Box 32008
Minneapolis, MN 55432-4314
763-574-7474
Fax: 763-574-1415 800-328-2495
info@stylmark.com www.stylmark.com
Manufacturer and exporter of back-lit, edge-lit and
nonlit graphic display products; also, static graphic
display products, sequential image, programmable
multi-image and scrolling units available.
President: Andy Steinfeldt
CEO: Javier Barral Amil
jbarralamil@stylmark.com
Number Employees: 100-249
Brands:
A-Frame
Edgelite
Graphic Revolutions
Impact Island
Litewall
Luminaire
Luminaire Ultra
Luminaire Ultra Ii
Movingpix
Neon Plus E
Print Frame
Stretchframe
Triad

29785 Suan Farma
17 Zink Place
Suite 9
Fair Lawn, NJ 07410
201-343-1188
info@suanfarma.com
suanfarmausa.com
Distributor of ingredients for the pharma- and
nutraceutical industries.
Other Locations:
Fair Lawn NJ

Tempe AZ
Bogota, Colombia
Juarez, Mexico
Caracas, Venezuela
Sao Paulo, Brasil
Madrid, Spain
Barcelona, Spain
Fribourg, Switzerland
Shenyang, China
Mumbai, India
Dubai, UAE

29786 Suburban Corrugated BoxCompany
6363 Keokuk Rd
Indianhead Park, IL 60525-4341
630-920-1230
Fax: 630-920-1353 subcorr1@aol.com
Corrugated boxes
VP: Gene Mazurek
Estimated Sales: $2.5-5 Million
Number Employees: 10-19

29787 Suburban Laboratories Inc
1950 S Batavia Ave # 150
Suite 150
Geneva, IL 60134-3330
708-544-3260
Fax: 708-544-8587 800-783-5227
dan@suburbanlabs.com www.suburbanlabs.com
Consultant and analyst for the food and sanitation industries providing analytical, enviromental and microbiological testing, nutritional assays and water and sterility testing
President: Jarrett Thomas
jarrett@suburbanlabs.com
Business Dev. Manager: Shane Clarke
VP, Sales: Dan Galehar
Estimated Sales: $2.5-5 Million
Number Employees: 20-49

29788 Suburban Sign Company
19611 Jasper Street NW
Anoka, MN 55303-9642
763-753-8849
Fax: 763-753-8225
Signs including advertising, plastic, painted and wooden
Owner: Burt Pfeifer
Number Employees: 2

29789 Suburban Signs
5051 Greenbelt Rd
College Park, MD 20740
301-474-5051
Fax: 301-345-1196 www.suburbansigns.com
Signs
President: Robert Wells
VP: Joel Hurst
Estimated Sales: Below $5 Million
Number Employees: 1-4
Square Footage: 4200

29790 Success Systems
45 Church St P.O. Box 2457
st. 106
Stamford, GA 06906
404-252-6002
Fax: 203-921-1660 800-653-3345
mkt@success-systems.com
www.success-systems.com
Computer systems and software
VP: Howard Spiller
Estimated Sales: $1 - 5 Million
Number Employees: 20-49
Square Footage: 40000

29791 Sudmo North America, Inc
1330 Anvil Road
Machesney Park, IL 61115
815-639-0322
Fax: 815-639-1135 800-218-3915
www.sudmona.com
Supplier of valves and components to the food, dairy, beverage and pharmaceutical industries
Director of Sales: Jim Banks
Contact: Deb Baggs
dbaggs@sudmona.com
Estimated Sales: $5-10 Million
Number Employees: 10-19
Parent Co: Pentair

29792 Suffolk Iron Works Inc
418 E Washington St
PO Box 1943
Suffolk, VA 23434-4518
757-539-2353
Fax: 757-539-1520 info@suffolkironworks.com
www.suffolkironworks.com
Manufacturer and exporter of peanut machinery and bulk material handling systems
Owner: John C Harrell
charrell@suffolkironworks.com
VP: Jenny Winslow
Senior Project Engineer: John Harrell
Estimated Sales: $5-10 Million
Number Employees: 20-49

29793 Sugar Plum LLC
5756 W Main St
Houma, LA 70360-1745
985-872-9524
Fax: 985-872-9664
Designer cakes, wedding cakes, holiday cakes, confectionary, and various other desserts
Owner: Cindy Dugas
thesugarplum1@comcast.net
Number Employees: 10-19
Square Footage: 10000

29794 (HQ)SugarCreek
2101 Kenskill Ave
Washington Ct Hs, OH 43160-9404
740-335-7440
Fax: 740-335-7443 800-848-8205
www.sugarcreek.com
Manufacturer of bacon and turkey bacon.
Chairman: John Richardson
Prsident: Michael Richardson
CFO: Tom Bollinger
tbollinger@sugar-creek.com
EVP, Operations: Mike Rozzano
Year Founded: 1966
Estimated Sales: $20 Million
Number Employees: 2,000+
Number of Brands: 1
Type of Packaging: Consumer, Food Service, Bulk
Other Locations:
  Dayton OH
  Hamilton OH
  Fairfield OH
  Cambridge City IN
  Frontenac KS
Brands:
  Sugar Creek

29795 Sugarplum Desserts
20381 62nd Avenue
Building 5
Langley, BC V3A SE6
Canada
604-534-2282
Fax: 604-534-2280 info@sugarplumdesserts.com
www.sugarplumdesserts.com
Thaw and serve cheesecakes and thaw and bake cookies
President: Leslie Goodman
Number Employees: 15
Square Footage: 32000

29796 Suhner Manufacturing
S Suhner Drive
Rome, GA 30162
706-235-8046
Fax: 706-235-8045
Chairman of the Board: Otto Suhner
Estimated Sales: $20 - 30 Million
Number Employees: 100-250

29797 Sultan Linen Inc
313 5th Ave
New York, NY 10016-6518
212-689-8900
Fax: 212-689-8965
Manufacturer and exporter of decorative linens, towels, table cloths, place mats and aprons
President: Daniel Sultan
daniel@sultanslinens.com
Sales Manager: Daniel Sultan
Estimated Sales: $500,000 - $1 Million
Number Employees: 1-4
Parent Co: SLI Home Fashions

29798 Sumitomo Machinery Corp
4200 Holland Blvd
Chesapeake, VA 23323-1529
757-485-3355
Fax: 757-485-0643 800-SMC-YCLO
www.sumitomodrive.com
Mechanical and electrical adjustable speed drives, parallel shaft and right angle reducers, shaft mounted gear motors, and helical, planetary, spiral bevel, gear reducers
President: Ron Smith
Executive VP: James Magee
CFO: Nobuhiao Kawamusa
Estimated Sales: $50 - 75 Million
Number Employees: 250-499

29799 Summit Commercial
770 Garrison Ave
Bronx, NY 10474-5603
718-893-3900
Fax: 718-842-3093 800-932-4267
info@summitappliance.com
www.summitappliance.com
Equipment
President: Felix Storch
Vice President: Paul Storch
Estimated Sales: $40-50 Million
Number Employees: 100
Number of Brands: 1
Number of Products: 170
Square Footage: 150000
Brands:
  Summit

29800 Summit Industrial Equipment
930 Riverside Pkwy # 30
Broderick, CA 95605-1511
916-372-5890
Fax: 916-372-1973 www.summitindustrial.com
Air compressors
Manager: Mark Kabnick
Communications Director: Chris Fisher
Vice President of Corporate Communicatio: Annika Berglund
Estimated Sales: $5-10 Million
Number Employees: 5-9

29801 Summit Machine Builders Corporation
550 W 53rd Place
Denver, CO 80216-1612
303-294-9949
Fax: 303-294-9622 800-274-6741
Manufacturer and exporter of automation and automated assembly equipment including dry and fibrous product feeding, filling and dispensing systems; also, ingredients dispensing and automatic micro weighing equipment
President: Scott Harris
Director Sales: Mike Schmehl
Estimated Sales: $5-10 Million
Number Employees: 85
Square Footage: 200000
Brands:
  Sro Feeder
  Vibra-Meter Feeder

29802 Summit Premium Tree Nuts
8680 Greenback Lane
Suite 250
Orangevale, CA 95662
916-988-1081
Fax: 916-988-1089 www.summittreenuts.com
Premium tree nuts
President: Dale Darling

29803 Summitville Tiles Inc
15364 State Route 644
Summitville, OH 43962
330-223-1511
Fax: 330-223-1414 info@summitville.com
www.summitville.com
Ceramic tiles
President: David Johnson
dwjohnson@summitville.com
CFO: Rich Finnicun
Estimated Sales: $20-50 Million
Number Employees: 100-249

29804 Sun Industries
16115 S 450 E
Goodland, IN 47948
219-297-3195
Fax: 219-297-3010 www.sunind.com

Packaging machinery and equipment
President: Carl Potsch
  cpotsch@aol.com
Estimated Sales: $1-2.5 Million
Number Employees: 10-19

29805 Sun Paints & Coatings
4701 East 7th Avenue
PO Box 75070
Tampa, FL 33605
                        813-367-4444
        Fax: 813-367-0263 800-247-9691
                        www.suncoatings.com
Manufacturer and exporter of window, tile and mildew cleaners
President: Barton Malina
Contact: Tom Crosier
  tcrosier@sunpaintsandcoatings.com
Estimated Sales: $5-10 Million
Number Employees: 20-49
Square Footage: 200000

29806 Sun Plastics
PO Box 37
Clearwater, MN 55320-0037
                        320-558-6130
        Fax: 320-558-6119 800-862-1673
Thermoformed plastic packaging for food
President: Paul Amundson
Plant Manager: Ken Doble
Estimated Sales: $2.5-5 Million
Number Employees: 20-49
Square Footage: 48000

29807 Sun Ray Sign Group Inc
376 Roost Ave
Holland, MI 49424-2032
                        616-392-2824
        Fax: 616-392-5797
Signs
Owner: Scott Tardiff
  scott.tardiff@itworld.com
Estimated Sales: Less Than $500,000
Number Employees: 1-4

29808 Sunbeam Products Co LLC
623 Main St
Toledo, OH 43605-1745
                        419-691-1551
Soap and detergents
Owner: Todd Lincoln
  sunbeamtodd@bex.net
Estimated Sales: $1-2.5 Million
Number Employees: 1-4

29809 Sunco & Frenchie
489 Getty Avenue
Clifton, NJ 07011
        Fax: 973-478-1063 973-478-1011
                        www.sunconatural.com
Dried fruits, nuts, granola, raw sugar, quick oats, corn meal, and juice.
Co-Owner: Joel Ammar
Year Founded: 2009
Estimated Sales: $1-5 Million
Number Employees: 15
Brands:
  Frenchie
  Sunbest
  Sunco

29810 Sundance Architectural Prod
4249 L B Mcleod Rd
Orlando, FL 32811-5600
                        407-297-1337
        Fax: 407-296-4330 800-940-1337
                info@sdap.com www.sdap.com
Commercial awnings and fabric structures
Owner: Paula Toot
  paula.toot@sdap.com
Estimated Sales: $5 - 10 Million
Number Employees: 50-99

29811 (HQ)Sundyne Corp
14845 W 64th Ave
Arvada, CO 80007-7523
                        303-425-0800
        Fax: 303-425-0896
Air/gas compressor pumps and pumping equipment

President: Jeff Wiemelt
  jwiemelt@sundyne.com
CFO: John O'Toole
VP/General Manager: Jeff Wiemelt
Human Resources Director: Marie Weiss-Rich
Estimated Sales: $41.8 Million
Number Employees: 250-499

29812 Sunflower Packaging
8952 NW 24th Ave
Miami, FL 33147
                        305-591-3388
        Fax: 305-591-9356 lungmeng@lung-meng.com
                        www.lung-meng.com
Packaging machinery
Manager: Allen Tsai
General Manager: Allen Tsai
Estimated Sales: $5-10 Million
Number Employees: 10-19

29813 Sungjae Corporation
Po Box 6525
Irvine, CA 92616
                        949-757-1727
        Fax: 949-757-1723
Printed flexible packaging,packing materials, films, wrap, wrapping zipper bag,stand up bag and shrink film.
President: Kim Eunhee
Marketing Director: Vin Eun Hee
Estimated Sales: $5 - 10,000,000
Number Employees: 8
Parent Co: Sungjae Corporation

29814 Sungjae Corporation
27 Highpoint
Irvine, CA 92603
                        949-757-1727
        Fax: 949-757-1723
Rotogravure printed flexible packaging, packaging materials, bags, film, wrap, wrapping, printers, printing
Owner: Minhee Kim
Marketing Head: Min Hee
Estimated Sales: Less than $500,000
Number Employees: 1-4

29815 Sunkist Growers
27770 Entertainment Dr.
Valencia, CA 91355
                        661-290-8900
                        www.sunkist.com
Fruit juices, fruit drinks, healthy snacks, baking mixes, carbonated beverages, confections, vitamins, frozen novelties, salad toppings, freshly peeled citrus, chilled jellies and nonfood products.
Chief Executive Officer: Jim Phillips
Chief Operating Officer: Christian Harris
Year Founded: 1893
Estimated Sales: $1 Billion
Number Employees: 6,000
Type of Packaging: Food Service, Private Label
Other Locations:
  Sunkist Growers
  Toronto Canada ON
  Sunkist Growers
  Cary NC
  Sunkist Growers
  Pittsburgh PA
  Sunkist Growers
  Buffalo NY
  Sunkist Growers
  Stafford TX
  Sunkist Growers
  Visalia CA
  Sunkist Growers
  Cherry Hill NJ
  Sunkist Growers
  West Chester OH
  Sunkist Growers
  Detroit MI
  Sunkist Growers
  Long Valley NJ
  Sunkist Growers
  Phoenix AZ
  Sunkist Growers
  Clackamas OR
  Sunkist Growers
  Anjou Canada QC

29816 Sunland Manufacturing Company
1658 93rd Ln NE
Minneapolis, MN 55449
                        763-785-2247
        Fax: 763-785-9667 800-790-1905
                        www.sunlandmfg.com

Polyethylene bags
Owner: Pat Haley
Estimated Sales: $2.5-5 Million
Number Employees: 10-19
Square Footage: 16000

29817 Sunmark Special Markets
10820 Sunset Office Dr
St Louis, MO 63127-1016
                        314-822-2800
        Fax: 314-984-9433
Hard and soft candy
President: L Delicandro
Sales Director: Charles Dodson
Number Employees: 100-249
Parent Co: Nestle USA

29818 Sunmaster of Naples Inc
900 Industrial Blvd
Naples, FL 34104-3612
                        239-261-3581
        Fax: 239-261-7499 info@sunmasterinc.com
                        www.titanscreen.com
Commercial awnings
President: John Wilkinson
  john@sunmasterinc.com
Vice President: David Rinker
Estimated Sales: $2.5-5,000,000
Number Employees: 20-49

29819 Sunny Cove Citrus LLC
1315 E Curtis Ave
Reedley, CA 93654-9317
        Fax: 559-626-7210
Packinghouse and licensed shipper of citrus products for Sunkist Growers Inc.
President: Tom Clark
Field Manager: Justin Kulikov
Controller: Warren Lee
Office Manager: Vera Fast
Square Footage: 340000
Type of Packaging: Food Service

29820 Sunpoint Products
PO Box 567
Lawrence, MA 01842-1267
                        978-794-3100
        Fax: 978-685-7840
Disinfectants, anti-bacterial soaps, etc
President: Brooks O Kane
Sales Manager: Bob Monroe
Number Employees: 3
Brands:
  Red Cross Nurse

29821 (HQ)Sunroc Corporation
PO Box 13150
Columbus, OH 43213-0150
                        302-678-7800
        Fax: 302-678-7809 800-478-6762
                        www.sunroc.com
Manufacturer and exporter of electric and bottled water coolers,drinking fountains and point-of-use coolers
President: Anthony Salamone
CFO: Mark Whitaker
Director Engineering: Ronald Greenwald
Quality Control: Tom Huber
VP Sales/Marketing: John Ott
Contact: Mel Sloan
  msloan@sunroc.com
Estimated Sales: $20-50 Million
Number Employees: 100-249
Square Footage: 250000
Brands:
  Softtouch

29822 Sunset Paper Products
3148 Divernon Avenue
Simi Valley, CA 93063-1611
                        323-587-4488
        Fax: 323-587-1313 800-228-7882
Manufactures baking and candy cups
President: Alan Newman
Estimated Sales: $20-50 Million
Number Employees: 50-99

29823 Sunset Sales
PO Box 446
Hurricane, UT 84737-0446
                        435-635-3199
        Fax: 435-635-0205

Commercial food packaging and processing machinery
Estimated Sales: $1-5 Million
Number Employees: 9

29824 Sup Herb Farms
300 Dianne Dr
Turlock, CA 95380-9523
          209-633-3600
    Fax: 209-633-3644 800-787-4372
      www.supherbfarms.com
Processors and marketers of culinary herbs and specialty products the selection of which includes fresh, frozen and freeze-dried varieties.
President: Mike Brem
EVP/Strategic Planning & CFO: Francis Contino
SVP/General Counsel & Secretary: Robert Skelton
VP/Human Relations: Cecile Perich
Number Employees: 100-249
Parent Co: McCormick & Company Inc

29825 Supelco Inc
595 N Harrison Rd
Bellefonte, PA 16823-6217
          814-359-3441
    Fax: 814-359-5459 800-247-6628
Chromatography products for analysis and purification
Estimated Sales: $50 - 75 Million
Number Employees: 250-499
Parent Co: Sigma-Aldrich Corporation

29826 Super Beta Glucan
5 Holland # 109
Irvine, CA 92618-2570
          949-305-2599
    Fax: 626-203-0655 service@superbetaglucan.com
      www.superbetaglucan.com
Mushroom Beta Glucan (Immulink MBG)
Founder: Dr. S.N. Chen
Vice President: Sherwin Chen
Number Employees: 5-9

29827 Super Cooker
6049 Peterson Rd
Lake Park, GA 31636-4003
          229-559-1662
    Fax: 229-559-1611 800-841-7452
Manufacturer and exporter of portable barbecue grills and smokers including charcoal, wood and gas
Owner: Ben Futch
  ben@supercooker.com
Estimated Sales: $3 - 5,000,000
Number Employees: 10-19

29828 Super Radiator Coils
451 Southlake Blvd
N Chesterfield, VA 23236-3091
          804-794-2887
    Fax: 804-379-2118 800-229-2645
vainfo@superradiatorcoils.com www.srcoils.com
Coils and heat exchangers; exporter of coils, evaporators and condensors
Cmo: John Perez
  john.perez@superradiatorcoils.com
Estimated Sales: $30+ Million
Number Employees: 100-249
Square Footage: 112000
Parent Co: Super Radiator Coils
Other Locations:
  Super Radiator Coils
  Phoenix AZ
Brands:
  Super

29829 Super Seal ManufacturingLimited
670 Rowntree Dairy Road
Woodbridge, ON L4L 5T8
Canada
          905-850-2929
    Fax: 905-850-4440 800-337-3239
info@supersealmfg.com www.supersealmfg.com
Manufacturer and exporter of energy saving devices, retail and industrial impact traffic, P.V.C. and bi-folding doors, dock seals, truck shelters and inflatable seals and shelters
President: Renato Torchetti
Director Sales (USA): Paul Ricci
Number Employees: 10
Square Footage: 160000
Brands:
  Atmo

29830 (HQ)Super Steel
7900 W Tower Ave
Milwaukee, WI 53223-3253
          414-355-4800
    Fax: 414-355-0372 www.supersteel.com
Fabricated metal parts
President & General Manager: Jason Gaare
VP, Engineering: Dan Brook
Estimated Sales: $50-100 Million
Number Employees: 250-499
Square Footage: 650000
Other Locations:
  Super Steel Products Corp.
  Troy OH

29831 Super Sturdy
200 Rock Fish Drive
Weldon, NC 27890-2106
          252-536-4833
    Fax: 252-536-2118 800-253-4833
Custom stainless steel mobile carts, sinks, tables and cabinets
VP: Salvatore Pirruccio
Estimated Sales: $2.5-5 Million
Number Employees: 17
Square Footage: 66000
Parent Co: Marlo Manufacturing Company

29832 Super Vision International
9400 Southridge Park Ct # 200
Orlando, FL 32819-8643
          407-857-9900
    Fax: 407-857-0050
Manufacturer and exporter of signs, lighting and lighting fixtures
President: Mike Bauer
Chairman of the Board: Brett M Kingstone
Sales (USA): Rick Hunter
International Sales: Paula Vega
Number Employees: 50-99
Square Footage: 320000
Brands:
  Endglow
  Sideglow
  Supervision

29833 Super-Chef Manufacturing Company
9235 Bissonnet Street
Houston, TX 77074
          713-729-9660
    Fax: 713-729-8404 800-231-3478
Manufacturer and exporter of broilers, fryers, griddles, warming units, ovens, hoods, ranges, hot plates, food concession trailers and compact kitchens with recirculating filter hoods
President: Chris Pappas
CEO: Regina Seale
CFO: Isabel Repka
VP: Ed Seale
R&D: Chris Pappas
Quality Control: Ed Seale
Marketing: Regina Seale
Sales: Isabel Repka
Public Relations: Regina Seale
Operations: Chris Pappas
Production: Barry Berg
Plant Manager: Barry Berg
Purchasing: Ed Seale
Number Employees: 20-49
Number of Brands: 2
Square Footage: 160000
Brands:
  Fat Mizer
  Kompact Kitchen
  Super Chef

29834 Superflex Limited
152 44th St
Brooklyn, NY 11232-3310
          718-768-1400
    Fax: 718-768-5065 800-394-3665
sales@superflex.com www.seal-proof.com
Manufacturer and exporter of P.V.C. flexible suction and discharge reinforced hoses, liquid tight conduit and electrical tubing used for pumps, refrigerators, dairy equipment, beverage dispensers, etc
President: Yigal Elbaz
  yelbaz@superflex.com
VP: Y Elbaz
Estimated Sales: Less Than $500,000
Number Employees: 1-4
Brands:
  Rollerflex

Sealproof
Superflex

29835 Superfos Packaging Inc
11301 Superfos Dr SE
2630 Taastrup
Cumberland, MD 21502-8772
          301-759-3145
    Fax: 301-759-4905 800-537-9242
superfos@superfos.com www.superfos.com
Rigid open top plastic containers
President: Mike Bosley
  bmichael@rpc-superfos.com
CEO: Rene Valentin
CFO: Lars Hoeyer Tindbaek
Executive VP: Soren Marcussen
Quality Manager: Michal Kaminski
Sales Manager: Stephen Towl
Estimated Sales: $10-$20 Million
Number Employees: 100-249
Parent Co: Superfos Emballagelas
Brands:
  Flex Off
  Ring Lock
  Vapor Lock

29836 Superior Belting
6 Andrews St
PO Box 8678
Greenville, SC 29601-3902
          864-605-0076
    Fax: 864-269-9754
salesdepartment@superiorbelt.com
      www.superiorbelt.com
Conveyor belting for the food processing industry
President: Leonard Sandy Chace
  sales@superiorbelting.com
CFO: Allan Thompson
R&D: Sandy Chace
Estimated Sales: Below $5 Million
Number Employees: 10-19

29837 (HQ)Superior Brush Company
3455 W 140th St
Cleveland, OH 44111
          216-941-6987
    Fax: 216-252-8838
Manufacturer and exporter of metal strip brushes; also, custom design services available
VP Sales/Marketing: Richard Mertes
Estimated Sales: $10-20 Million
Number Employees: 20-49
Square Footage: 22000

29838 Superior Distributing Co
103 N 32nd St
Louisville, KY 40212
          502-778-6661
    Fax: 502-775-7519 800-365-6661
      www.superiordisplayboards.com
Manufacturer and exporter of FDA approved wiping cloths, polyethylene bags, hairnets, beard guards, gloves and butchers' paper
Owner: Michael Hinson
Sales Manager: Susan Thrapp
Manager: Robert Mc Roberts
Estimated Sales: $5-10 Million
Number Employees: 1-4

29839 Superior Food MachineryInc
7635 Serapis Ave
Pico Rivera, CA 90660-4516
          562-949-0396
    Fax: 562-949-0180 800-944-0396
info@Superiorinc.com www.superiorinc.com
Manufacturer, importer, exporter and designer of tortilla and tortilla chip processing equipment; also, corn feeders, ovens and washers
Owner: Maria Castro
General Sales Manager: Rick Rangel
Customer Service Manager: Mark Reyes
  maria@superiorinc.com
Estimated Sales: $5-10 Million
Number Employees: 20-49
Square Footage: 7000

29840 Superior Imaging Group Inc
22710 72nd Ave S
Kent, WA 98032-1926
          253-872-7200
    Fax: 253-872-7202 888-872-7200
sales@superiorimaging.com
      www.superiorimaging.com
Commercial screen printing on nontextiles

Owner: Eric Richards
CFO: Michelle McKenzie
Contact: Jerry Blaha
blaha@superiorimaging.com
Estimated Sales: Less Than $500,000
Number Employees: 1-4

29841 Superior Industries
315 State Highway 28
Morris, MN 56267-4699
320-589-2406
Fax: 320-589-3892 800-321-1558
info@superior-ind.com www.superior-ind.com
Manufacturer and exporter idlers and portable conveying equipment
President: Riley Arndt
rarndt@supind.com
Estimated Sales: $15 - 20 Million
Number Employees: 500-999

29842 Superior Label Company
625 Gotham Pkwy
Carlstadt, NJ 07072-2403
201-438-4500
Fax: 201-438-8126 800-877-3795
superior95@aol.com
Pressure sensitive label application equipment including primary labeler or bar code printer and applicator

29843 Superior Linen & Work Wear
3001 Cherry St
Kansas City, MO 64108-3124
816-931-4477
Fax: 816-931-0504 800-798-7987
sales@superiorlinen.com www.superiorstyle.com
Table covers, uniforms, aprons,towels, table cloths, table skirts, chef wear, oxford shirts, and polo shirts
Chairman of the Board: William G Kartsonis
wgk@superiorline.net
Estimated Sales: $20-50 Million
Number Employees: 50-99
Type of Packaging: Consumer, Private Label

29844 Superior Menus
PO Box 6
Mankato, MN 56002-8465
800-464-2182
Fax: 800-842-9371
customerservice@superiormenus.com
www.superiormenus.com
Supplier of hospitality mints, various menus covers, laminators and laminating products, table tents, menu inserts, gift certificates, placemats, chef apparel and aprons, napkin bands, name badges, menu display racks, window messageboards, guest checks, server pads
Parent Co: Thayer

29845 Superior Neon Signs Inc
2515 N Oklahoma Ave
Oklahoma City, OK 73105-3094
405-528-5515
Fax: 405-528-5535 www.superiorneon.com
Sign manufacturer
President: Dan Lorant
dan.lorant@superiorneon.com
Estimated Sales: $1-2.5 Million
Number Employees: 20-49

29846 Superior Packaging Equipment Corporation
3 Edison Pl
Suite 4
Fairfield, NJ 7004
973-575-8818
Fax: 973-890-7295 www.superiorpack.com
Manufacturer and exporter of cartoning machinery including forming, gluing, inserting, closing, sealing and opening
President: Glenn Rice
Executive VP: Russell Rice
Estimated Sales: $5 - 10 Million
Number Employees: 10
Square Footage: 76000

29847 Superior Product PickupServices
5707 W Howard Street
Niles, IL 60714-4012
847-647-4720
Fax: 847-647-4739 www.productpickup.com
Consultant offering market research on consumer products

Estimated Sales: $1 - 5 Million
Number Employees: 20
Square Footage: 10000

29848 Superior Products Company
P.O. Box 64177
Saint Paul, MN 55164
651-636-1110
800-328-9800
Wholesale Distributor of foodservice equipment and supplies
Contact: Charlette Edwards
charlette_edwards@ndgstp.com
Number Employees: 1-4
Type of Packaging: Food Service
Other Locations:
  Alexandria VA
  Anaheim CA
  Atlanta GA
  Baltimore MD
  Boston MA
  Charlotte NC
  Cleveland OH
  Dallas TX
  Hartford CT
  Orlando FL
  Pennsauken NJ
  Reno NV
  San Diego CA
Brands:
  Next Day Gourmet
  Superior Monogram

29849 Superior Tank
11415 Erie Ave SW
Beach City, OH 44608-9589
330-756-2030
Fax: 330-756-2015 superiortank@yahoo.com
www.superiortankinc.com
Wine industry stainless steel tanks
Owner: Thomas Burkey
superiortank@yahoo.com
VP: Byron Kovalaske
VP Sales: Byron Kovalaske
Estimated Sales: $20-50 Million
Number Employees: 20-49

29850 Superior Uniform Group
10055 Seminole Blvd
Seminole, FL 33772
800-727-8643
info@superioruniformgroup.com
www.superioruniformgroup.com
Manufacturer and exporter of aprons, restaurant smocks, sheeting, knit shirts, hats and cloth bags.
Chief Executive Officer: Michael Benstock
Executive Vice President: Peter Benstock
COO/CFO/Treasurer: Andrew Demott, Jr.
VP/General Counsel/Secretary: Jordan Alpert
Year Founded: 1920
Estimated Sales: $100-$500 Million
Square Footage: 60000

29851 Superior-Studio Specialties
2239 Yates Ave
Commerce, CA 90040-1913
323-278-0100
Fax: 323-278-0111 800-354-3049
jake@superiorstudio.com
www.superiorstudio.com
Decorative items, lighting and theme props
Manager: Erin Allen
erin@superiorstudio.com
Estimated Sales: $1 - 5 Million
Number Employees: 5-9
Parent Co: Superior Specialties LLC

29852 Superklean Washdown Products
1550 Bryant Street
Suite 750
San Francisco, CA 94103-4877
415-252-2861
Fax: 415-255-2032 superkln@aol.com
Spray nozzles, hot and cold water mixer-hose stations, steam and cold water mixer-hose stations, swivel fittings, 3-piece fittings, and accessories

29853 Supermarket Associates
4209 Pin Oak Drive
Durham, NC 27707-5270
919-493-0994
Fax: 919-493-0994
Consultant specializing in advertising, marketing and management services for the food retailing industry

President: Sheldon Sosna
VP: Charles Ebner
Estimated Sales: $500,000-$1 Million
Number Employees: 1-4
Square Footage: 2000

29854 SuppliesForLess
905 G St
Hampton, VA 23661
757-245-7675
Fax: 757-244-4819 800-235-2201
Floating advertising balloons and blimps and flexible neon rope lights
Estimated Sales: $1 - 3 Million
Number Employees: 10-19
Square Footage: 243000
Brands:
  Bend-A-Lite
  Blimpy
  Giant

29855 Supply Corp
1351 Elkhorn Rd
Lake Geneva, WI 53147-1078
262-248-8837
Fax: 262-248-9530 800-558-2455
supplies@supplycorp.com www.supplycorp.com
Industrial safety, sanitation supplies, lubricants and tools for maintence, food processing supplies, cleaning supplies, brushes, mops, gloves, containers and material handling products
President: Rex Anderson
CEO: Roland Johnson
Sales: Rex Anderson
Number Employees: 5-9
Parent Co: Stand Alone Company

29856 Supply One Inc
12322 E 55th St
Tulsa, OK 74146
www.supplyone.com
Wholesaler/distributor of paper and plastic products, janitorial chemicalsand equipment; serving the food service market.
President & CEO: Bill Leith

29857 Supramatic
3313 Lakeshore Boulevard West
Toronto, ON M8W 1M8
Canada
416-251-3266
Fax: 416-251-1433 877-465-2883
info@supramatic.com www.supramatic.com
Manufacturer and importer of espresso, coffee and cappuccino machines; importer of coffee beans
President: Rene Peterson
Estimated Sales: Below $5 Million
Number Employees: 3

29858 Supreme Corporation
2572 East Kercher Road
Goshen, IN 46528
574-533-0331
Fax: 574-642-4729 800-642-4889
info@supremecorp.com
Manufacturer and exporter of refrigerators, freezers and refrigerated truck cars
CEO: Herbert M Gardner
VP Marketing/Sales: Rick Horn
Contact: David Allen
dallen@supre.com
Estimated Sales: $10 - 20 Million
Number Employees: 2
Type of Packaging: Bulk

29859 Supreme Corporation
5901 S 226th St
Kent, WA 98032-4861
253-395-8712
Fax: 253-395-8713
Synthetic wine closures, synthetic closures for specialty food bottles
President: Robert Anderson
CEO: Bob De Monte
Contact: Bob Anderson
banderson@supremecorq.com
Estimated Sales: $5 - 10 Million
Number Employees: 50-99

29860 Supreme Fabricators
19127 Pioneer Blvd Spc 18
Artesia, CA 90701
323-583-8944
Fax: 323-583-8946

Stainless steel tanks and automatic storage and handling systems
President: Dean Graves
Estimated Sales: $500,000-$1,000,000
Number Employees: 1-4

29861 Supreme Metal
3125 Trotters Parkway
Alpharetta, GA 30004-7746

Fax: 770-740-6010 800-645-2526
Manufacturer and exporter of stainless steel hot food tables, sinks, ice storage equipment and wait stations; also, bars, bins and glass racks
President: Rick Schwartz
VP Sales: Lisa Finegan
National Sales Manager: Sandy Hill
Contact: Talisha Hardy
talishahardy@gmail.com
Type of Packaging: Food Service

29862 Supreme Murphy Truck Bodies
4000 Airport Dr NW
Wilson, NC 27896

252-291-2191
Fax: 252-291-9183 800-334-2298
Refrigerated truck, trailer and van bodies
Estimated Sales: $10-25 Million
Number Employees: 100

29863 Supreme Products
PO Box 154308
Waco, TX 76715-4308

254-799-4941
Fax: 254-799-4943 sales@supremeproducts.com
Food and beverage concession trailers and vending carts.
President: Pat Hood
VP: Hugh Hood
Number Employees: 10
Square Footage: 70000
Brands:
    Supreme

29864 (HQ)Surco Products
290 Alpha Dr
RIDC Industrial Park
Pittsburgh, PA 15238

412-252-7000
Fax: 412-252-1005 800-556-0111
www.surcopt.com
Manufacturer and exporter of air fresheners, deodorants and insecticides
President: Arnold Zlotnik
CEO: Bernard Surloff
Estimated Sales: $10 - 20 Million
Number Employees: 50-99
Square Footage: 114000
Type of Packaging: Consumer, Private Label, Bulk
Brands:
    2-In-One Deodorizer
    24 Hour Odor Absorber
    Air-Savers
    Air-Scent
    Ban-O-Dor
    End Smoke
    Fresh As a Baby
    Garb-O-Flakes
    Odomaster
    Oh No!
    Potty Fresh
    Round the Clock
    Rug Aroma
    Sani-Aire
    Sani-Flakes
    Sani-Scent
    Scatter
    Scent-Flo
    So-Fresh
    Sta-Fresh
    Surco
    Surcota
    Zorb-It-All

29865 Sure Beam Corporation
9276 Scranton Rd Ste 600
San Diego, CA 92121

858-795-6300
Fax: 858-552-9973
Provider of electronic pasteurization systems and services
President: Terrance Bruggeman
Contact: Laura Peschel
lpeschel@surebeam.com

Number Employees: 50-99

29866 Sure Clean Corporation
PO Box 1
Two Rivers, WI 54241-0001

920-793-3838
Fax: 920-793-1555
Detergent, soap, household cleaners, etc
Estimated Sales: $1 - 5 Million

29867 Sure Kol Refrigerator
490 Flushing Ave
Brooklyn, NY 11205-1615

718-625-0601
Fax: 718-624-1719 surekol@hughes.net
www.surekol.com
Walk-in refrigerators
Owner: Jack Waslin
jwaslin@surekol.com
Estimated Sales: $2.5 - 5 Million
Number Employees: 10-19
Square Footage: 32000
Brands:
    Sure-Kol

29868 Sure Shot Dispensing Systems
100 Dispensing Way
Lower Sackville, NS B4C 4H2
Canada

902-865-9602
Fax: 902-865-9604 888-777-4990
sales@sureshotdispensing.com
www.sureshotdispensing.com
President: Michael Duck
VP: David Macaulay
R&D: Ian Maclean
Quality Control: Peter Black
Marketing: Chad Wiesner
Sales: William Morris
Operations: Garth I
Production: Dennis Dickinson
Plant Manager: Ken Lawrence
Purchasing Director: Tracey S
Number Employees: 90
Square Footage: 260000

29869 Sure Torque
12100 West 6th Avenue
Lakewood, CO 80228

303-987-8000
Fax: 303-987-8989 800-387-6572
spearson@suretorque.com www.suretorque.com
Manufacturer and exporter of container closure torque measurement instruments including near and on-line, automatic and electronic
Owner: Michelle Bergeron
R&D: Steve Pearson
Technical Engineer: Tibor Szenti
Sales/Technical: Gloria LaCroix
Director Operations: Jeff Dubrow
Estimated Sales: Below $5 Million
Number Employees: 1-4
Square Footage: 5000
Brands:
    Torque Tester

29870 Sure-Feed Engineering
12050 49th St N
Clearwater, FL 33762

727-571-3330
Fax: 727-571-3443 www.pb.com
Feeders, attaching systems
Sales/Marketing: Abe Mammau
Contact: Ron Kinney
ron.kinney@pb.com
Manager: Joe Springer
Estimated Sales: $1-2.5 Million
Number Employees: 100-249

29871 Surekap Inc
579 Barrow Park Dr
Winder, GA 30680-3417

770-867-5793
Fax: 770-867-5799 support@surekap.com
www.surekap.com
Manufacturer and exporter of liquid filling and bottle and capping equipment including plastic, metal, tamper evident, CRC, etc
President: John Antoine
john@surekap.com
Estimated Sales: $10-20 Million
Number Employees: 5-9

29872 Surface Measurement Systems
2125 28th St SW # 1
Suite 1
Allentown, PA 18103-7380

610-798-8299
Fax: 610-798-0334 sales@smsna.com
www.smsna.com
Automated laboratory systems measuring all materials for food industry
Manager: Joe Domingue
Director Sales/Marketing: Joe Domingue
Manager: Andrea Gimbar
agimbar@smsna.com
Estimated Sales: $1 - 5 Million
Number Employees: 10-19

29873 Surface Skil Corporation
3270 Homeward Way
Fairfield, OH 45014-4236

724-935-9020
Fax: 724-935-9010 800-228-5400
wjr@sgi.net
We clean concrete, install seamless resinous flooring systems for all types of food facilities
CFO: Phil Buda
Sales Director: Bill Esau

29874 Surfine Central Corporation
PO Box 5698
Pine Bluff, AR 71611-5698

870-247-2387
Fax: 870-247-9830
Paper bags
President: Bob Ratchford
Number Employees: 45

29875 Surtec Inc
1880 N Macarthur Dr
Tracy, CA 95376-2841

209-820-3700
Fax: 209-820-3793 800-877-6330
orderdesk@surtecsystem.com
www.surtecsystem.com
Manufacturer, importer and exporter of floor cleaning systems, chemicals and high-speed buffing machines
Owner: William Fields
CFO: Bill Haag
VP/Director Reaserch/Development: Don Fromm
Manager Sales: Kurt Grannis
william.fields@surtecsystem.com
Estimated Sales: $5 - 10 Million
Number Employees: 50-99
Square Footage: 140000

29876 Sus-Rap Protective Packaging
4010 Suburban Drive
Danville, VA 24540-6116

434-836-1666
Fax: 434-836-7606 800-558-7078
www.multiwall.com
Supplier of paper products
Manager: Melvin Shumate

29877 Sussman Electric Boilers
4320 34th St
Long Island City, NY 11101

718-937-4500
Fax: 718-937-4676 800-238-3535
seb@sussmancorp.com www.sussmanboilers.com
Manufacturer and exporter of electric boilers including steam, hot water, stainless steel and humidification, also, steam superheaters and steam-to-steam generators
President: Charles Monteverdi
Marketing: Louise Mound
Sales: Louise Mound
Production: Ben Cavanna
bcavanna@sussmancorp.com
Plant Manager: Ben Cavanna
Purchasing Manager: Arthur Perlman
Estimated Sales: $10 - 20 Million
Number Employees: 50-99
Parent Co: Sussman-Automatic Corporation
Brands:
    Sussman

29878 Sutherland Stamp Company
PO Box 151319
San Diego, CA 92175-1319

858-233-7784
Fax: 858-233-0105
Badges, medals, plastic signs and rubber stamps
Owner: Richard Branch

Number Employees: 3

29879 Sutter Process Equipment
P.O. Box 5459
Walnut Creek, CA 94596-1459
925-937-1405
Fax: 707-642-2288 888-254-2060
Wine presses
Owner: Jerry Denham
Number Employees: 10-19
Square Footage: 88000
Parent Co: S.A. Juvenal
Type of Packaging: Private Label

29880 (HQ)Sutton Designs
215 N Cayuga Street
Ithaca, NY 14850-4329
607-277-4301
Fax: 607-277-6983 800-326-8119
Plexiglass counter cards, menu holders and displays
CFO: L Karro
VP Marketing: Dan Steele
Sales Director: Mark Miller
Purchasing Manager: Ned Ficher
Estimated Sales: $7.5 Million
Number Employees: 42
Number of Products: 350
Square Footage: 20000

29881 Suzhou-Chem, Inc.
396 Washington St
Suite 318
Wellesley, MA 02481
781-433-8618
Fax: 781-433-8619 info@suzhouchem.com
www.suzhouchem.com
Food and beverage ingredients including ascorbic
acid, sodium ascorbate, calcium ascorbate, sodium
saccharin granular, sodium saccharin dehydrate, so-
dium saccharin powder, calcium saccharin, insoluble
saccharin, acesulfame-kaspartame, caffeine,
potassium, sorbic acid, etc.
President: Joan Ni
Year Founded: 1999
Estimated Sales: $302 Million
Number Employees: 5-10
Type of Packaging: Bulk
Other Locations:
Distribution Center
Bayonne NJ
Distribution Center
Newark NJ
Distribution Center
St. Louis MO
Distribution Center
Dallas TX
Distribution Center
Salt Lake City UT
Distribution Center
Los Angeles CA
Distribution Center
Toronto, Ontario, Canada

29882 Svedala Industries
621 S Sierra Madre St
Colorado Springs, CO 80903-4016
719-471-3443
Fax: 719-471-4469 denversala@aol.com
www.metso.com
Manufacturer and exporter of thermal heat
exchangers
Manager: Kirk Smith
Production Manager (Thermal Equipment):
Siegfried Nierenz
Estimated Sales: $20 - 50 Million
Number Employees: 20-49
Brands:
Holo Flite

29883 Svedala Industries
621 S Sierra Madre St
Colorado Springs, CO 80903-4016
719-471-3443
Fax: 719-471-4469 denversala@aol.com
www.metso.com
Manufacturer and exporter of belt conveyor compo-
nents for bulk material handling systems
Manager: Kirk Smith
Manager: Rick Pummell
Manager Sales Administration: Jim Danielson
Estimated Sales: $20 - 50 Million
Number Employees: 20-49
Parent Co: Svedala Industries

29884 Sverdrup Facilities
222 S Riverside Plz # 1400
Chicago, IL 60606-6001
312-416-0990
Fax: 312-416-1700 800-337-3239
Engineers, architects, planners, food technologists,
sanitation specialists and construction experts, pro-
cessing plants and productions systems
Contact: Jacob Prizer
jprizer@devereux.org
Estimated Sales: $5 - 10 Million
Number Employees: 20-49

29885 Sverdrup Facilities
801 N 11th Blvd
Saint Louis, MO 63102-1815
314-552-8339
Fax: 314-552-8453 800-325-7910
Consultant specializing in architecture, construction
and engineering design services for sanitary processing facilities, etc
VP: Bill Vicary

29886 Svresearch
7429 Allentown Blvd
Harrisburg, PA 17112-3609
717-540-0370
Fax: 717-540-0380
President: Ron Lawson
Contact: Susan Baker
s.baker@seidenader.com
Estimated Sales: $3 - 5 Million
Number Employees: 20-49

29887 Swan Label & Tag Co
929 2nd Ave # A
PO Box 308
Coraopolis, PA 15108-1434
412-264-9000
Fax: 412-264-7259 info@swanlabel.com
Manufacturer and exporter of pressure sensitive la-
bels and tags
President: Jill Clendenning
jill@swanlabel.com
Art/Graphic Department: Justin Kevish
Sales: Jill Clendening
Customer Service: Gilda Clendenning
General Manager: Mike Chieski
Estimated Sales: $10-20 Million
Number Employees: 5-9

29888 Swancock Designworks
755 Sherri Court
Bosque Farms, NM 87068-9770
603-465-2015
Fax: 603-465-2015
Wine industry label design

29889 Swander Pace & Company
101 Mission Street
Suite 1900
San Francisco, CA 94105-1529
415-477-8500
Fax: 415-477-8510 info@spcap.com
www.spcap.com
Consultant offering strategy development, acquisi-
tions and divestitures, market and competitive as-
sessments, category management, salesforce
optimization, etc
President: Bill Tace
Managing Director: Bill Pace
Managing Director: Todd Hooper
VP: Pete Boylan
Contact: Peter Boylan
peter@spcap.com
Estimated Sales: $5-10 Million
Number Employees: 20-49

29890 Swanson Wire Works Industries, Inc.
4229 Forney Rd
Mesquite, TX 75149
972-288-7465
Fax: 972-285-3030 swwind@prodigy.net
Powder coated and regular wire shelves, display
racks and barbecue grills
President: David J Burroughs
VP: Ken Brunson
Estimated Sales: $5-10 Million
Number Employees: 20-49
Square Footage: 200000

29891 Sweco Inc
8029 Dixie Hwy
PO Box 1509
Florence, KY 41042-2941
859-371-4360
Fax: 859-283-8469 800-807-9326
info@sweco.com www.sweco.com
Manufacturer and exporter of FDA approved separa-
tion/screening equipment
President: David M Sorter
davidsorter@sweco.com
VP Engineering: Brad Jones
Marketing Manager: Jeff Dierig
Number Employees: 250-499
Parent Co: M-I LLC
Brands:
Supertaut Plus Ii
Vibro-Energy

29892 Sweet Manufacturing Co
2000 E Leffel Ln
PO Box 1086
Springfield, OH 45505-4625
937-325-1511
Fax: 937-322-1963 800-334-7254
sales@sweetmfg.com www.sweetmfg.com
Specialize in bulk material handling, conveying and
processing equipment.
President/CEO: Alicia Sweet Hupp
Vice President: Julio Contreras
sales@sweetmfg.com
VP Marketing: Mike Gannon
VP Sales: Julio Contreras
Number Employees: 50-99
Square Footage: 140000
Brands:
Calormatic
Filte-Veyor
Gollath
Quick-Key
Silver-Grip
Silver-Span
Silver-Sweet

29893 Sweet New England, Co.
600 Highland Drive
Suite #618
Westampton, NJ 08060
860-436-2560
orders@sweetne.com www.sweetnewengland.com
Sugar (organic and non-organic) manufacturer.
President: Rafael Carmelo
Year Founded: 2011
Estimated Sales: #3.2 Million
Square Footage: 14000
Type of Packaging: Food Service, Bulk

29894 Sweetener Supply Corp
9501 Southview Ave
Brookfield, IL 60513-1529
708-588-8400
Fax: 708-588-8460 888-784-2799
sweetenersupply.com
Manufacturer and distributor of sweeteners for the
food, beverage and confectionery industries.
Number Employees: 20-49
Number of Brands: 5
Brands:
Ambersweet
Delicious
Ridgeland
Sur Sweet
Ultraclear

29895 Sweeteners Plus Inc
5768 Sweeteners Blvd
Lakeville, NY 14480-9741
585-346-3193
Fax: 585-346-2310 www.sweetenersplus.com
Manufacturer and distributor of liquid and dry
sweeteners including white and brown sugar, or-
ganic and kosher products, fructose, maltitol, corn
syrup, and invert syrups. Also bottling, custom
blending, and liquid fondants. Shippedregionally
long haul by rail and short haul by trucks and na-
tionally by distribution products
President & CEO: Carlton Myers
Quality Assurance Manager: Mark Rudolph
VP Sales: Mark Whitford
Operation Manager: Bill Devine
Estimated Sales: $14.7 Million
Number Employees: 1-4
Type of Packaging: Food Service, Bulk

29896 Sweetware
2821 Chapman St # A
Oakland, CA 94601-2133
510-436-8600
Fax: 510-436-8601 800-526-7900
inquiries@sweetware.com www.sweetware.com
Manufacturer and exporter of inventory control, order entry, invoicing, accounts receivable, recipe formula costing and nutrition analysis software
Owner: David Dunetz
info@sweetware.com
Estimated Sales: $500,000-$1 Million
Number Employees: 1-4
Brands:
Nutra Coster
Smallpics
Stock Coster

29897 Swift Creek Forest Products
20200 Patrick Henry Hwy
Jetersville, VA 23083-2118
804-561-4498
Fax: 804-561-6137
Pallets and skids
President: Scott Long
swftcreek@aol.com
Estimated Sales: $2.5-5 Million
Number Employees: 20-49

29898 (HQ)Swing-A-Way Manufacturing Company
4100 Beck Ave
St Louis, MO 63116-2694
314-773-1488
Fax: 314-773-5187
Manufacturer, importer and exporter of corkscrews, ice crushers and can and jar openers
President: Dorothy Rhodes
Estimated Sales: $10-20 Million
Number Employees: 50-99
Square Footage: 250000
Type of Packaging: Consumer
Other Locations:
Swing-A-Way Manufacturing Co.
Saint Louis MO
Brands:
Swing-A-Way

29899 Swirl Freeze Corp
1261 S Redwood Rd # H
Salt Lake City, UT 84104-3705
801-886-1196
Fax: 801-973-7620 800-262-4275
sales@swirlfreeze.com www.swirlfreeze.com
Manufacturer and exporter of ice cream and frozen yogurt blending machinery
President: D Heinhold
Vice President: K Heinhold
Marketing Director: D Savage
Estimated Sales: $1 Million
Number Employees: 1-4
Number of Brands: 1
Number of Products: 6
Square Footage: 30000
Type of Packaging: Consumer
Brands:
Swirl Freeze

29900 Swirl Freeze Corp
1261 S Redwood Rd # H
Unit H
Salt Lake City, UT 84104-3705
801-886-1196
Fax: 801-973-7620 800-262-4275
sales@swirlfreeze.com www.swirlfreeze.com
Supplier of ice cream and frozen yogurt blending machinery
President: Duane Heinhold
VP: Ken Heinhold
Estimated Sales: $.5 - 1 million
Number Employees: 1-4
Square Footage: 30000

29901 Swisher Hygiene
4725 Piedmont Row Drive
Suite 400
Charlotte, NC 28210
908-353-8500
Fax: 908-353-6752 800-444-4138
contact@swsh.com www.swsh.com
Manufacturer and exporter of dishwashing and laundry products

President: Norman Lubin
Vice President: Mark Sherman
Contact: Bill Ainsley
bainsley@swsh.com
Estimated Sales: $10-20 Million
Number Employees: 50-99
Type of Packaging: Food Service
Brands:
Sanolite

29902 Swissh Commercial Equipment
5520 Chabot 203
Montreal, QC H2H 2S7
Canada
514-524-6005
Fax: 514-524-3305 888-794-7749
info@swissh.ca www.swissh.com
Technologically advanced dishwashers.
President: Bruno O Frank
Marketing: Elyse Pastor
Production: Miguel Viche
Number Employees: 7
Number of Brands: 4
Number of Products: 50
Square Footage: 16000
Brands:
Swissh

29903 Swisslog Logistics Inc
161 Enterprise Dr
Newport News, VA 23603-1369
757-887-8080
Fax: 757-887-5588 800-777-6862
www.swisslog.com
Manufacturer and exporter of integrated and automated material handling software and equipment
President: Karl Puehringer
Chief Executive Officer: Remo Brunschwiler
Sr. VP Marketing: Brad Moore
Estimated Sales: $20-50 Million
Number Employees: 50-99
Square Footage: 50000
Parent Co: Swisslog

29904 Swisslog Logistics Inc
161 Enterprise Dr
Newport News, VA 23603-1369
757-887-8080
Fax: 757-887-5588 800-783-9840
wds.us@swisslog.com www.swisslog.com
President: Karl Puehringer
Chairman: Hans Ziegler
CFO: Christian M„der
Estimated Sales: $5 - 10 Million
Number Employees: 50-99

29905 Swivelier Co Inc
600 Bradley Hill Rd # 3
Blauvelt, NY 10913-1171
845-353-1455
Fax: 845-353-1512 info@swivelier.com
www.swivelier.com
Lighting, including track, low-voltage display, clamp-on, display and accent, lighting fixtures, light converters and extenders
President: I Schucker
is@swive.com
VP Manufacturing: Gerard Phelan
Estimated Sales: $5 - 10 Million
Number Employees: 1-4
Square Footage: 480000
Brands:
Convert-A-Lite
Cozy-Lite
Litestrip
Star Track
Swivelier

29906 Sybo Composites LLC
404 Riberia St
St Augustine, FL 32084-5108
904-599-7093
Fax: 937-746-9706 800-874-4088
Manager: Martin South
Sales Director: Pam South
Estimated Sales: $5,000,000 - $9,999,999
Number Employees: 1-4
Square Footage: 20000

29907 Sycamore Containers
215 Fair St
Sycamore, IL 60178
815-895-2343
Fax: 815-895-5555 www.landsberg.com

President: Lawrence Kendzora
Contact: Craig Bates
cbates@landsberg.com
Manufacturing Executive: Marvin Barnes
Estimated Sales: $10 - 15 Million
Number Employees: 20-49

29908 (HQ)Syfan USA Corporation
PO Box 203
Everetts, NC 27825-0212
877-792-2547
Fax: 252-792-3185 www.syfanusa.com
Packaging, shrink films, over wrap, bread bags, skin films
Executive V.P: Ramy Diga
President: Frank Marrowitz
Product Development Manager: Alan Castle
Regional Manager: Bruce Paster
Contact: Alaine Chesson
alaine@syfanmfg.com
Estimated Sales: $1 - 2.5 Million
Number Employees: 10
Type of Packaging: Consumer, Food Service, Private Label

29909 Symmetry Products Group
55 Industrial Cir
Lincoln, RI 02865-2643
401-365-6272
Fax: 401-365-6273 www.symmetryproducts.com
Manufacturer and exporter of signs; also, theme and architectural designing available
President: Steven Lancia
Marketing Director: Justine Ruizzo
Sales Director: Rich Dowd
Plant Manager: Tony Chernasky
Estimated Sales: $20 - 50 Million
Number Employees: 100-249
Square Footage: 150000
Parent Co: Lance Industries

29910 Sympak, Inc.
1385 Armour Blvd.
Mundelein, IL 60060
847-247-0182
Fax: 847-247-0184 sympak-usa@sympak.com
www.sympak-usa.com
Processing and packaging equipment for the dairy, confectionery/baking industries and convenience stores.
Contact: Erich Weirich
eric.weirich-usa@sympak.com
Number Employees: 600

29911 Symtech,Inc
P.O. Box 2627
Spartanburg, SC 29304-2627
219-477-4554
Fax: 219-464-3352 www.strayfieldfastran.co.uk
Contact: Alberto Beani
abeani@symtech-usa.com

29912 Synchro-Systems Technology
4563 Nance Road
Stanfield, NC 28163-8630
704-888-6407
Fax: 704-888-5080
Indexing, collating, and accumulating machinery, auto-loaders

29913 Syngenta
P.O. Box 18300
Greensboro, NC 27419
800-334-9481
www.syngenta-us.com
Offers products and services for growers concerning crop protection, seed treatments, planting, pest solutions, and sustainability.
CEO: J. Erik Fyrwald
Year Founded: 2000
Number Employees: 28,000

29914 Synthron Inc.
420 W Fleming Drive
Suite C
Morganton, NC 28655-3966
828-437-8611
Fax: 828-437-4126
Processor and exporter of detergents and oil and wax emulsifying agents
President: Raymond Pinard
Estimated Sales: $5-10 Million
Number Employees: 10-19
Type of Packaging: Bulk

29915 Syracuse China Company
2801 Court St
Syracuse, NY 13208-3241
315-455-5671
Fax: 315-455-6763 800-448-5711
www.libbey.com
China
President: Charles S Goodman
Contact: Christopher Novak
chris.novak@libbey.com
Estimated Sales: Below $500,000
Number Employees: 500-999
Parent Co: Libbey

29916 Syracuse Label Co
110 Luther Ave
Liverpool, NY 13088-6726
315-422-1037
Fax: 315-422-6763 www.syrlabel.com
Pressure sensitive labels
President: Kathy Alamio
kathy@syrlabel.com
Estimated Sales: $20-50 Million
Number Employees: 100-249

29917 (HQ)Sysco Corp
1390 Enclave Pkwy
Houston, TX 77077
281-584-1390
Fax: 281-584-1737 800-337-9726
www.sysco.com
Food products, equipment and supplies for the food
service industry
President/CEO: Tom Ben,
Chairman: Jackie Ward
EVP/Chief Financial Officer: Joel Grade
SVP/Chief Accounting Officer: Anita Zielinski
SVP/Merchandising: Brian Todd
SVP/Sysco Labs & Customer Experience: Brian
Beach
EVP/Supply Chain: Scott Charlton
SVP/Sales & Marketing: Bill Goetz
EVP/Administration & Corp. Secretary: Russell
Libby
SVP/US Foodservice Operations: Greg Bertrand
Year Founded: 1969
Estimated Sales: $59 Billion
Number Employees: 67,000
Type of Packaging: Food Service

29918 Sysco Corp
1 Sysco Dr
Lincoln, IL 62656-0620
217-735-6100
Food products, equipment and supplies for the food
service industry
Type of Packaging: Food Service

29919 Sysco Corp
1 Liebich Ln
Halfmoon, NY 12065-1421
518-877-3200
Food products, equipment and supplies for the food
service industry
Type of Packaging: Food Service

29920 Sysco Corp
601 Comanche Rd NE
Albuquerque, NM 87107
505-761-1200
Food products, equipment and supplies for the food
service industry
Type of Packaging: Food Service

29921 Sysco Corp
4500 Corporate Dr NW
Concord, NC 28027
704-786-4500
Food products, equipment and supplies for the food
service industry
Type of Packaging: Food Service

29922 Sysco Corp
4000 W 62nd St
Indianapolis, IN 46268-2518
317-291-2020
Food products, equipment and supplies for the food
service industry
Type of Packaging: Food Service

29923 Sysco Corp
1509 Monad Rd
Billings, MT 59107
406-247-1100

Food products, equipment and supplies for the food
service industry
Type of Packaging: Food Service

29924 Sysco Corp
7705 National Tpke
Louisville, KY 40214
502-364-4300
Food products, equipment and supplies for the food
service industry
Type of Packaging: Food Service

29925 Sysco Corp
136 S Mariposa Rd
Modesto, CA 95354
209-527-7700
Food products, equipment and supplies for the food
service industry
Type of Packaging: Food Service

29926 Sysco Corp
1951 E Kansas City Rd
Olathe, KS 66061
913-829-5555
Food products, equipment and supplies for the food
service industry
Type of Packaging: Food Service

29927 Sysco Corp
600 Packer Ave
Philadelphia, PA 19148
215-463-8200
Food products, equipment and supplies for the food
service industry
Type of Packaging: Food Service

29928 Sysco Corp
900 Kingbird Rd
Lincoln, NE 68521
402-423-1031
Food products, equipment and supplies for the food
service industry
Type of Packaging: Food Service

29929 Sysco Corp
250 Wieboldt Dr
Des Plaines, IL 60016-3192
847-699-5400
Food products, equipment and supplies for the food
service industry
Type of Packaging: Food Service

29930 Sysco Corp
20 Theodore Conrad Dr
Jersey City, NJ 07305
201-433-2000
Food products, equipment and supplies for the food
service industry
Type of Packaging: Food Service

29931 Sysco Corp
9494 S Prosperity Rd
West Jordan, UT 84081
801-563-6300
Food products, equipment and supplies for the food
service industry
Type of Packaging: Food Service

29932 Sysco Corp
10710 Greens Crossing Blvd
Houston, TX 77038
713-672-8080
Food products, equipment and supplies for the food
service industry
Type of Packaging: Food Service

29933 Sysco Corp
10510 Evendale Dr
Cincinnati, OH 45241
513-563-6300
Food products, equipment and supplies for the food
service industry
Type of Packaging: Food Service

29934 Sysco Corp
714 2nd Pl
Lubbock, TX 79401
806-747-2678
Food products, equipment and supplies for the food
service industry
Type of Packaging: Food Service

29935 Sysco Corp
2400 County Road J
St Paul, MN 55112
763-785-9000
Food products, equipment and supplies for the food
service industry
Type of Packaging: Food Service

29936 Sysco Corp
6601 Changepoint Dr
Anchorage, AK 99518
907-565-5567
Food products, equipment and supplies for the food
service industry
Type of Packaging: Food Service

29937 Sysco Corp
3700 Sysco Ct SE
Grand Rapids, MI 49512-2083
616-949-3700
Food products, equipment and supplies for the food
service industry
Type of Packaging: Food Service

29938 Sysco Corp
5000 Beeler St
Denver, CO 80238
303-585-2000
Food products, equipment and supplies for the food
service industry
Type of Packaging: Food Service

29939 Sysco Corp
99 Spring St
Plympton, MA 02367
781-422-2300
Food products, equipment and supplies for the food
service industry
Type of Packaging: Food Service

29940 Sysco Corp
1451 River Oaks Rd W
Harahan, LA 70123
504-731-1015
Food products, equipment and supplies for the food
service industry
Type of Packaging: Food Service

29941 Sysco Corp
3905 Corey Rd
Harrisburg, PA 17109
717-561-4000
Food products, equipment and supplies for the food
service industry
Type of Packaging: Food Service

29942 Sysco Corp
1000 Sysco Dr
Calera, AL 35040
205-668-0001
Food products, equipment and supplies for the food
service industry
Type of Packaging: Food Service

29943 Sysco Corp
One Whitney Drive
Harmony, PA 16037
724-452-2100
Food products, equipment and supplies for the food
service industry
Type of Packaging: Food Service

29944 Sysco Corp
8000 Dorsey Run Rd
Jessup, MD 20794
410-799-7000
Food products, equipment and supplies for the food
service industry
Type of Packaging: Food Service

29945 Sysco Corp
4400 Milwaukee St
Jackson, MS 39209-2636
601-354-1701
Food products, equipment and supplies for the food
service industry
Type of Packaging: Food Service

29946 Sysco Corp
4359 B.F. Goodrich Blvd
Memphis, TN 38118-7306
901-795-2300
Food products, equipment and supplies for the food
service industry

Type of Packaging: Food Service

29947 Sysco Corp
2225 Riverdale Rd
College Park, GA 30337
404-765-9900
Food products, equipment and supplies for the food service industry
Type of Packaging: Food Service

29948 Sysco Corp
33300 Peach Orchard Rd
Pocomoke, MD 21851
410-677-5555
Food products, equipment and supplies for the food service industry
Type of Packaging: Food Service

29949 Sysco Corp
1350 W Tecumseh Rd
Norman, OK 73069-8200
405-717-2700
Food products, equipment and supplies for the food service industry
Type of Packaging: Food Service

29950 Sysco Corp
5710 Pan Am Ave
Boise, ID 83716
208-345-9500
Food products, equipment and supplies for the food service industry
Type of Packaging: Food Service

29951 Sysco Corp
20701 E Currier Rd
Walnut, CA 91789
909-595-9595
Food products, equipment and supplies for the food service industry
Type of Packaging: Food Service

29952 Sysco Corp
22820 54th Ave S
Kent, WA 98032-4898
206-622-2261
Food products, equipment and supplies for the food service industry
Type of Packaging: Food Service

29953 Sysco Corp
26250 SW Parkway Center Dr
Wilsonville, OR 97070
503-682-8700
Food products, equipment and supplies for the food service industry
Type of Packaging: Food Service

29954 Sysco Corp
611 S 80th Ave
Tolleson, AZ 85353
623-936-9920
Food products, equipment and supplies for the food service industry
Type of Packaging: Food Service

29955 Sysco Corp
131 Sysco Ct
Columbia, SC 29209
803-239-4000
Food products, equipment and supplies for the food service industry
Type of Packaging: Food Service

29956 Sysco Corp
100 Inwood Rd
Rocky Hill, CT 06067-3422
860-571-5600
Food products, equipment and supplies for the food service industry
Type of Packaging: Food Service

29957 Sysco Corp
800 Trinity Drive
Lewisville, TX 75056
769-384-6000
Food products, equipment and supplies for the food service industry
Type of Packaging: Food Service

29958 Sysco Corp
4577 Estes Pkwy
Longview, TX 75603-0900
903-252-6100

Food products, equipment and supplies for the food service industry
Type of Packaging: Food Service

29959 Sysco Corp
1 Sysco Dr
Jackson, WI 53037
262-677-1100
Food products, equipment and supplies for the food service industry
Type of Packaging: Food Service

29960 Sysco Corp
2001 W Magnolia Ave
Geneva, AL 36340
334-684-4000
Food products, equipment and supplies for the food service industry
Type of Packaging: Food Service

29961 Sysco Corp
7000 Harbour View Blvd
Suffolk, VA 23435
757-673-4000
Food products, equipment and supplies for the food service industry
Type of Packaging: Food Service

29962 Sysco Corp
1501 Lewis Industrial Dr
Jacksonville, FL 32254
904-786-2600
Food products, equipment and supplies for the food service industry
Type of Packaging: Food Service

29963 Sysco Corp
900 Tennessee Ave
Knoxville, TN 37921-2630
865-545-5600
Food products, equipment and supplies for the food service industry
Type of Packaging: Food Service

29964 Sysco Corp
1 Hermitage Plz
Nashville, TN 37209
615-350-7100
Food products, equipment and supplies for the food service industry
Type of Packaging: Food Service

29965 Sysco Corp
3225 12th Ave N
Fargo, ND 58102
701-293-8900
Food products, equipment and supplies for the food service industry
Type of Packaging: Food Service

29966 Sysco Corp
1032 Baugh Rd
Selma, NC 27576
919-755-2455
Food products, equipment and supplies for the food service industry
Type of Packaging: Food Service

29967 Sysco Corp
7062 Pacific Ave
Pleasant Grove, CA 95668
916-569-7000
Food products, equipment and supplies for the food service industry
Type of Packaging: Food Service

29968 Sysco Corp
12180 Kirkham Rd
Poway, CA 92064
858-513-7300
Food products, equipment and supplies for the food service industry
Type of Packaging: Food Service

29969 Sysco Corp
1999 Dr Martin Luther King Jr Blvd
Riviera Beach, FL 33404
561-842-1999
Food products, equipment and supplies for the food service industry
Type of Packaging: Food Service

29970 Sysco Corp
300 N Baugh Way
Post Falls, ID 83854
208-777-9511
Food products, equipment and supplies for the food service industry
Type of Packaging: Food Service

29971 Sysco Corp
3100 Sturgis Rd
Oxnard, CA 93030
877-205-9800
Food products, equipment and supplies for the food service industry
Type of Packaging: Food Service

29972 Sysco Corp
5900 Stewart Ave
Fremont, CA 94538
510-226-3000
Food products, equipment and supplies for the food service industry
Type of Packaging: Food Service

29973 Sysco Corp
910 South Blvd
Baraboo, WI 53913-2793
608-356-8711
Food products, equipment and supplies for the food service industry
Type of Packaging: Food Service

29974 Sysco Corp
4747 Grayton Rd
Cleveland, OH 44135
216-201-3000
Food products, equipment and supplies for the food service industry
Type of Packaging: Food Service

29975 Sysco Corp
41600 Van Born Rd
Canton, MI 48188-2797
734-397-7990
Food products, equipment and supplies for the food service industry
Type of Packaging: Food Service

29976 Sysco Corp
5800 Frozen Rd
Little Rock, AR 72209
501-562-4111
Food products, equipment and supplies for the food service industry
Type of Packaging: Food Service

29977 Sysco Corp
1260 Schwab Rd
New Braunfels, TX 78132
830-730-1000
Food products, equipment and supplies for the food service industry
Type of Packaging: Food Service

29978 Sysco Corp
12500 NW 112th Ave
Medley, FL 33178
305-651-5421
Food products, equipment and supplies for the food service industry
Type of Packaging: Food Service

29979 Sysco Corp
1 Sysco Pl
Ankeny, IA 50021
515-289-5300
Food products, equipment and supplies for the food service industry
Type of Packaging: Food Service

29980 Sysco Corp
200 Story Rd
Ocoee, FL 34761
407-877-8500
Food products, equipment and supplies for the food service industry
Type of Packaging: Food Service

29981 Sysco Corp
2508 Warners Rd
Warners, NY 13164
315-672-7000
800-736-6000

Food products, equipment and supplies for the food service industry
Type of Packaging: Food Service

29982 Sysco Corp
5081 S Valley Pike
Harrisonburg, VA 22801
540-434-0761
Food products, equipment and supplies for the food service industry
Type of Packaging: Food Service

29983 Sysco Corp
36 Thomas Dr
Westbrook, ME 04092
207-871-0700
Food products, equipment and supplies for the food service industry
Type of Packaging: Food Service

29984 Sysco Corp
3850 Mueller Rd
St Charles, MO 63301
636-940-9230
Food products, equipment and supplies for the food service industry
Type of Packaging: Food Service

29985 Sysco Corp
15750 Meridian Pkwy
Riverside, CA 92518
951-601-5300
Food products, equipment and supplies for the food service industry
Type of Packaging: Food Service

29986 Sysco Corp
199 Lowell Ave
Central Islip, NY 11722
631-342-7400
Food products, equipment and supplies for the food service industry
Type of Packaging: Food Service

29987 Sysco Corp
900 Hwy 10 S
St Cloud, MN 56304
320-251-3200
Food products, equipment and supplies for the food service industry
Type of Packaging: Food Service

29988 Sysco Corp
3000 69th St E
Palmetto, FL 34221
941-721-1450
Food products, equipment and supplies for the food service industry
Type of Packaging: Food Service

29989 Sysco Corp
6201 E Centennial Pkwy
Las Vegas, NV 89115
702-632-1800
Food products, equipment and supplies for the food service industry
Type of Packaging: Food Service

29990 Systech Illinois
2401 Hiller Rdg
Suite A
Johnsburg, IL 60051
815-344-6212
Fax: 815-344-6332
illinstr@illinoisinstruments.com
www.systechillinois.com
President: Brian Cummings
Contact: Donna Palmer
d.palmer@systechillinois.com
Estimated Sales: $5 - 10 Million
Number Employees: 20-49

29991 Systech International
2540 US Highway 130
Suit 128
Cranbury, NJ 08512-3519
609-235-0004
Fax: 609-395-0064 800-847-7123
www.systech-tips.com
President: Robert Dejean
CFO: Kenith Kirktatrick
Director of Sales: Paulo Machado
Contact: Joseph Costa
joseph@systech.com

Number Employees: 1-4

29992 System Concepts Inc
15900 N 78th St # 201
Scottsdale, AZ 85260-1215
480-951-8011
Fax: 480-951-2807 800-553-2438
ftsales@foodtrak.com www.foodtrak.com
SCI's FOOD-TRAK System is a food & beverage management system that enables foodservice operations to increase purchasing and accounting efficiencies; reduce cost of goods and increase asset security.
President/Founder: William Schwartz
CEO: Bill Schwartz
bills@foodtrak.com
Estimated Sales: Below $5 Million
Number Employees: 20-49
Brands:
Food-Trak

29993 System Graphics Inc
1530 S Kingshighway Blvd
St Louis, MO 63110-2228
314-773-4151
Fax: 314-773-3338 800-221-7858
labels@systemsgraphics.com
www.systemsgraphics.com
Pressure sensitive and paper labels for food products
President: Martin Daly
martindaly@systemsgraphics.com
Estimated Sales: $2.5-5 Million
Number Employees: 20-49

29994 System Packaging
28905 Glenwood Rd
PO Box 109
Perrysburg, OH 43551-3020
419-666-9712
Fax: 419-666-1549 sales@systempackaging.com
www.systempackaging.com
Owner: Tom Ziems
tsz@glassline.com
Estimated Sales: $1 - 5 Million
Number Employees: 5-9

29995 System Plast
130 Wicker St
Suite B
Sanford, NC 27330-4265
919-775-5716
Fax: 919-775-5720 800-726-2630
info@systemplast.com www.solusii.com
CEO: Garland Jones
Estimated Sales: $1 - 5 Million
Number Employees: 10-19

29996 System-Plast
2000 Boone Trail Rd
Sanford, NC 27330
919-775-5716
Fax: 919-775-5720 info@systemplast.com
www.systemplast.com
Conveyor components
Member: Sergio Marcitti
CEO: Garland Jones
Vice President - Finance: Marco Manzoni
Director of Engineering: Ted Van Der Hoeven
VP Marketing & Sales: Dick Overtoom
Procurement Manager: Stephan Petzold
Estimated Sales: $5-10 Million
Number Employees: 10-19

29997 Systemate Numafa
6390 Hickory Flat Hwy
Canton, GA 30115-9224
770-345-1055
Fax: 770-345-5926 800-240-3770
www.carnetts.com
Industrial washing systems, tote washers, pallet washers, tray washers, rack washers, drum washers, vat washers
Manager: Michael Warren
National Sales Manager: Scott Hazenbroek
Number Employees: 20-49

29998 Systems Comtrex
101 Foster Rd # B
Moorestown, NJ 08057-1118
856-778-9322
Fax: 856-778-9322 800-220-2669
Sales@Comtrex.com www.comtrex.co.uk
Manufacturer and exporter of point of sale terminals, peripherals and software

CEO: Duane Reed
duane.reed@comtrex.co.uk
CEO: Jefferey C Rice
Estimated Sales: $1 - 3,000,000
Number Employees: 10-19
Type of Packaging: Food Service
Brands:
Comtrex
Pcs5000 System

29999 Systems IV
6641 W Frye Rd
Chandler, AZ 85226
Fax: 480-961-1247 800-852-4221
sales@systemsiv.com www.systemsiv.com
Manufacturer and exporter of food service water treatment systems for ice makers, steamers, coffee machines, proofers, misters and post mix systems
President: Leroy Terry
Quality Control: Dave Terry
Manager Sales/Marketing: Sean Terry
Contact: David Terry
davecterry@gmail.com
Number Employees: 20-49
Brands:
System Iv

30000 Systems Modeling Corporation
504 Beaver St
Sewickley, PA 15143
412-741-3727
Fax: 412-741-5635 www.rockwell.com
Simulation and scheduling software
President: Keith Bush
Estimated Sales: $20-50 Million
Number Employees: 10

30001 Systems Online
1001 NW 62nd St
Fort Lauderdale, FL 33309-1900
954-840-3467
Fax: 954-376-3338 support@sysonline.com
www.sysonline.com
EZ Trade, the ultimate forms based e-trading solution/distribution management software DiMan for Windows95/98,2000; e-commerce, inventory, sales, purchasing, accounting
Estimated Sales: $1-2.5 Million
Number Employees: 1-4

30002 Systems Technology Inc
1351 Riverview Dr
San Bernardino, CA 92408-2945
909-799-9950
Fax: 909-796-8297
info@systems-technology-inc.com
www.systems-technology-inc.com
Manufacturer and exporter of packaging machinery
President: John G St John
johnstjohn@systems-technology-inc.com
CFO: Steve Fox
Estimated Sales: $10 - 20 Million
Number Employees: 20-49
Square Footage: 80000
Parent Co: Baldwin Technology Corporation

30003 Systems Technology Inc
1351 Riverview Dr
San Bernardino, CA 92408-2945
909-799-9950
Fax: 909-796-8297
info@systems-technology-inc.com
www.systems-technology-inc.com
STI, Systems Technology has been a worldwide leader in packing machinery for over 30 years. Our high-speed wraparound cartoning technology for the automated packaging of books, CDs, DVD's videos, and a variety of other products in arange of protective corrugated carton blanks has made us a preferred supplier in the fulfillment industry
President: John G St John
johnstjohn@systems-technology-inc.com
Controller: Steve Fox
Estimated Sales: $20 - 50 Million
Number Employees: 20-49

30004 T & A Metal Products Inc
1671 Hurffville Rd
Deptford, NJ 8096
856-227-1700
Fax: 856-227-1805
Stainless steel kitchen equipment
Owner: Nicholas Demarco

Estimated Sales: $5-10 Million
Number Employees: 5-9

30005 T & C Stainless
1016 Progress Rd
Mt Vernon, MO 65712-1057
417-466-4704
Fax: 417-466-4705 Sales@TC-Stainless.com
www.tcstainless.com
President: Terry L Cook
terryc@tc-stainless.com
Estimated Sales: $5-10 Million
Number Employees: 20-49

30006 T & M Distributing Co
12 Sunset Way
Henderson, NV 89014-2003
702-458-1962
Fax: 702-458-1160 www.rallyshirts.com
Flags, pennants and banners
Owner: Mitchell Patton
m.patton@rallyshirts.com
Estimated Sales: Less Than $500,000
Number Employees: 1-4

30007 (HQ)T & S Brass & Bronze Work
2 Saddleback Cv
Travelers Rest, SC 29690-2232
864-834-4102
Fax: 864-834-3518 800-476-4103
tsbrass@tsbrass.com www.tsbrass.com
T&S produces a full line of faucets, fittings, and
specialty products for the food service, industrial,
commercial plumbing, and laboratory markets all
across the world.
President: I Claude Theisen
CEO: Claude Theisen
claudetheisen@tsbrass.com
Vice President: Craig Ashton
Research & Development: Jeff Baldwin
Quality Control: Gary Cole
Marketing Director: Eva Fox
Sales Director: Ken Gallagher
Public Relations: Mary Alice Bowers
Operations Manager: Bob Clemment
Assembly Supervisor: David Whitlock
Purchasing Manager: Steve Abercrombie
Estimated Sales: $20-50 Million
Number Employees: 250-499
Type of Packaging: Consumer, Food Service, Private Label, Bulk
Brands:
Sage
T&S Brass and Bronze

30008 T & S Brass & Bronze Work
2 Saddleback Cv
PO Box 1088
Travelers Rest, SC 29690-2232
864-834-4102
Fax: 864-834-3518 800-476-4103
www.tsbrass.com
T&S produces a full line of faucets, fittings and specialty products for the foodservice, industrial, commercial plumbing, and laboratory markets.
President: Claude Theisen
claudetheisen@tsbrass.com
Number Employees: 250-499
Type of Packaging: Consumer, Food Service, Private Label, Bulk

30009 T & S Perfection Chain Prods
301 Goodwin Rd
Cullman, AL 35058-0307
256-734-6538
Fax: 256-734-1610 888-856-4864
info@tsperfection.com www.tsperfection.com
Manufacturers welded and weldless chains and
chain accessories. Also, upholstery nails, furniture
glides, escutcheon pins and commercial can openers
President: Tom Pretak
VP Human Resources: Carol Soliani
CFO: Ken Rizzi
Chairman of the Board: Allen M Sperry Sr
VP Sales: Frank Silano
Estimated Sales: $10 - 20 Million
Number Employees: 50-99
Square Footage: 200000
Type of Packaging: Food Service

30010 T & T Industries Inc
5070 S Highway 95
Fort Mohave, AZ 86426-7200
928-768-4511
Fax: 928-768-4766 800-437-6246
tandtinc@pacbell.net www.twistems.com
Manufactures paper, foil & plastic twist ties
President: John Vaughan
COO: John Mayberry
CFO: John Mayberry
R&D: Pat Clemmons
Quality Control: Art Vigil
Director Sales/Marketing: Jim Doherty
Number Employees: 20-49
Brands:
Twis-Tags
Twist-Ems

30011 T & T Valve & Instrument Inc
1181 Quarry Ln # 150
Suite 150
Pleasanton, CA 94566-8458
925-484-4898
Fax: 925-484-4727 sales@tt-valve.com
www.tt-valve.com
Wine industry valves
President: Sanford B Wolfe
Engineering Support, Design & Major Proj: Sanford
Wolfe
Sales Manager: Delain Murphy
Office Manager: Terri Stark
tstark@willisseafood.net
Inventory Control, Purchasing: Javier Cendejas
Estimated Sales: $1 - 5 Million
Number Employees: 5-9

30012 T D Sawvel Co
5775 Highway 12
Maple Plain, MN 55359-9777
763-479-4322
Fax: 763-479-3517 877-488-1816
www.sawvelautomation.com
Manufacturer and exporter of denesters, fillers, sealers and lidders for plastic and paper containers for
dairy and nondairy products; also, blenders,
variegators, inline and rotary machines; custom design services available
President: Troy Sawvel
troy@tdsawvel.com
Estimated Sales: $1-3 Million
Number Employees: 10-19
Square Footage: 32000
Brands:
Bottomup

30013 T E Ibberson Co
828 5th St S
Hopkins, MN 55343-7785
952-938-7007
Fax: 952-939-0451 tei@ibberson.com
www.ibberson.com
Consultant specializing in design, engineering and
construction services for new or expanding food and
oil seed processing plants
President: Mark Geitzenauer
mark.geitzenauer@ibberson.com
Vice President: Gerry Leukam
Marketing: Glenn Higgins
Estimated Sales: $1 - 5 Million
Number Employees: 100-249
Square Footage: 90000
Parent Co: the Industrial Company

30014 T E Ibberson Co
828 5th St S
Hopkins, MN 55343-7785
952-938-7007
Fax: 952-939-0451 tei@ibberson.com
www.ibberson.com
Design, engineering and construction services
President: Mark Geitzenauer
mark.geitzenauer@ibberson.com
Estimated Sales: $1 - 3 Million
Number Employees: 100-249

30015 T J Smith Box Co
515 S I St
PO Box 1643
Fort Smith, AR 72901-4323
479-782-8275
Fax: 479-782-8276 877-540-7933
Folding and set-up paper boxes
Owner: Chris Hahn
tjsmithboxcompany@gmail.com

Estimated Sales: $2.5-5 Million
Number Employees: 20-49
Type of Packaging: Consumer, Food Service, Private Label, Bulk

30016 T Q Constructors
911 2nd Ave
Dayton, KY 41074-1203
859-655-6700
Fax: 859-655-6704 888-655-0300
mail@tqconstructors.com
www.tqconstructors.com
TQ provides total quality mechanical process system
fabrication and installation for the food, beverage,
cosmetic, and pharmaceutical industries.
Project Director: Kent Fennell
kfennell@tqconstructors.com
National Account Manager: David Cauley
Vice President: John Bardo
Project Engineer: Greg Dennis
Local Account Manager: Larry Schuler
Regional Account Manager: Tom Burkhart
Operations Manager: Bill Sharkey
Number Employees: 50-99

30017 T&G Machinery
Unit 5
Orangeville, ON L9W 4N6
Canada
519-940-3527
Fax: 519-940-4558

30018 T&S Blow Molding
117 Simott Road
Scarborough, ON M1P 4S6
Canada
416-752-8330
Fax: 416-752-1909
Manufacturer and exporter of plastic bottles and jars
President: Donald Seaton
CEO: Peter Barker
CFO: Eric Lakien
Sales: Donna Strong
Plant Manager: Grant Ross
Estimated Sales: $14 Million
Number Employees: 10
Number of Brands: 5
Number of Products: 300
Square Footage: 136000
Type of Packaging: Consumer, Food Service, Private Label, Bulk

30019 T-Drill Industries Inc
1740 Corporate Dr # 820
Norcross, GA 30093-2934
770-381-4460
Fax: 770-925-3912 800-554-2730
sales@t-drill.com www.t-drill.fi
Pipe and tube fabricating equipment
President: Kenny Dockins
rperez@aflac.com
Vice President: Mark Sanders
Industrial Sales: John Hodges
Estimated Sales: $2.8 Million
Number Employees: 10-19

30020 T.D. Rowe Company
18890 S Susana Road
Compton, CA 90221-5706
310-639-6710
Fax: 310-604-3227
Vending machines
VP Sales: John Hulick
Estimated Sales: $2.5-5 Million
Number Employees: 20-49

30021 T.J. Topper Company
2734 Spring St
Redwood City, CA 94063
650-365-6962
Fax: 650-368-4547
Institutional and antique coffee makers; also, urns
including coffee, hot chocolate, iced tea, tea and hot
water
President: Willard Dann
Estimated Sales: $2.5-5 Million
Number Employees: 20-49
Parent Co: Tilley Manufacturing Company

30022 T.K. Designs
2551 State Street
Carlsbad, CA 92008
760-434-6225
Fax: 760-434-0058

Indoor-outdoor countertops, wall and easel, chalk-crayon boards

30023 T.K. Products
1565 N Harmony Cir
Anaheim, CA 92807-6003
714-621-0267
Fax: 714-693-3762
Manufacturer, importer and exporter of high speed and high shear mixers, dispersers and kneaders
President: Hisashi Furuichi
Marketing Director: Masaki Mori
Estimated Sales: $1-2,500,000
Number Employees: 4
Parent Co: T.K. Japan

30024 T.O. Plastics
1325 American Boulevard E
Suite 6
Minneapolis, MN 55425-1152
952-854-2131
Fax: 952-854-2154 www.toplastics.com
Manufacturer and exporter of plastic sheeting and thermoformed and foam packaging materials
CFO: Doug Cundell
National Sales Manager: Jeff Smesmo
Contact: Karen Bohn
karen@toplastics.com
Estimated Sales: $20-50 Million
Number Employees: 10
Type of Packaging: Bulk

30025 TA Instruments Inc
159 Lukens Dr
New Castle, DE 19720-2795
302-427-4000
Fax: 302-427-4001 www.tainstruments.com
Thermal analysis and rheology instruments
President: Terrence P Kelly
tkelly@tainstruments.com
CFO: Randy Mercner
Vice President: Terry Kelly
R&D: Jan Wenstrut
Quality Control: John Gaito
Marketing Director: George Dallas
Estimated Sales: $75 - 100 Million
Number Employees: 100-249
Brands:
Ar Series Rheometers
Q Series Thermal Analysis

30026 TAC-PAD
1370 Reynolds Avenue
Irvine, CA 92614
949-851-4337
Fax: 949-252-8079 800-947-1609
Pressure sensitive labels and warehouse and bin tags
Estimated Sales: $1 - 5 Million
Number Employees: 5-9

30027 TAWI-USA Inc
683 Executive Dr
Willowbrook, IL 60527-5603
630-655-2905
Fax: 630-655-2907 sales@tawiusa.com
www.tawi.com
Vacumove lifting device
Manager: Mike Lee
mlee@tawiusa.com
Estimated Sales: $2 Million
Number Employees: 5-9

30028 TC/American Monorail
12070 43rd St NE
Saint Michael, MN 55376
763-497-7000
Fax: 763-497-7001 www.tcamerican.com
Manufacturer and exporter of cranes and monorail systems
President: Paul Lague
Sales/Marketing: Beth Keene
Sales Administration Manager: Bill Swanson
Contact: Jami Brown
jbrown@andersencorp.com
Number Employees: 100-249
Square Footage: 180000

30029 TCC Enterprises
16310 Arthur Street
Cerritos, CA 90703-2129
562-802-0998
Fax: 562-802-5069 800-725-8233
Heat sealers, product bag sealers and reclosable bags

Estimated Sales: $10-25 Million
Number Employees: 46

30030 TCG Technologies
1050 Thomas Jefferson Stree
NW-Suite 2300
Washington, DC 20007
972-820-4759
Fax: 703-847-5041 800-226-9999
info@domin-8.com
Rotary cappers, retorquers, torque release chucks
Owner: Tim Flachman
CEO: Bob Franseth
Number Employees: 5-9
Square Footage: 8000

30031 TCT&A Industries
308 E Anthony Drive
Urbana, IL 61802
217-328-5749
Fax: 217-328-5759 800-252-1355
info@awning-tent.com
Commercial awnings
President: Byron Yonce
CEO: Kevin Yonce
Vice President, Chief Financial Officer: Wanda Yonce
Chairman: Wayne Yonce
Vice President of Sales: Ron Crick
Office Administrator: Mary Crider
Production Manager: Byron Yonce
Director of Installations: Matthew Steinkruger
Estimated Sales: $3 - 5 Million
Number Employees: 20-49

30032 (HQ)TDF Automation
PO Box 816
Cedar Falls, IA 50613-0040
319-277-3110
Fax: 319-277-7023 800-553-1777
sales@doerfer.com
Manufacturer and exporter of display cartoning and casepacking systems; also, collaters/loaders and product handling machinery; consultant specializing in designing automated systems; custom fabricating services available
President: David Takes
Chairman: Sunder Subbaroyan
Plant Manager: Curt Barfels
Estimated Sales: $1-2.5 Million
Number Employees: 10
Square Footage: 320000
Type of Packaging: Consumer, Food Service
Other Locations:
Doerfer Engineering
Eagan MN

30033 TDH
20520 W Wekiwa Rd
Sand Springs, OK 74063-8192
918-241-8800
Fax: 918-241-8884 888-251-7961
www.tdhmfginc.com
Manufacturer and exporter of mixers, presses, pumps and automation equipment
Owner: John Owens
tdhmfginc@earthlink.net
VP: J Owens
VP: R Owens
Estimated Sales: Less Than $500,000
Number Employees: 1-4
Square Footage: 16000

30034 TEC
P.O. Box 1086
Gualala, CA 95445-1086
707-884-9655
Fax: 707-884-9656 vickitec@aol.com
www.kirkdenson.com
Winery equipment
Owner: Anthony Agliolo
Partner: Vicki Mastbaum
Estimated Sales: Less than $500,000
Number Employees: 1-4

30035 TEI Analytical Svc Inc
7177 N Austin Ave
Niles, IL 60714-4617
847-647-1345
Fax: 847-647-0844 gayle@teianalytical.com
www.teiasi.com
Laboratory offering chemical testing
President: Gayle O'Neill
gayle@teianalytical.com

Estimated Sales: $500,000-$1 Million
Number Employees: 1-4

30036 TEMP-TECH Company
PO Box 2941
Springfield, MA 01101-2941
413-783-2355
Fax: 413-782-7220 800-343-5579
sales@temp-tech.com
Heatstones, thermal bags, tray totes and plastic smallwares including trays, plates and covers; exporter of trays
President: Jack Anderson
VP: Chuck Attridge
Contact: Greg Schurch
greg@temp-tech.com
Purchasing Agent: Layla O'Shea
Estimated Sales: $2 Million
Number Employees: 5-9
Square Footage: 24000
Type of Packaging: Food Service
Brands:
Temp-Tech

30037 TEQ
11320 Main St
Po Box 68
Huntley, IL 60142-7396
847-669-5291
Fax: 847-669-2720 800-874-7113
info@teqnow.com www.teqnow.com
Plastic containers and blister skin packaging materials
President: Randall Loga
CAO: Paul Sepe
psepe@tekpackaging.com
VP, Finance & Administration: Paul Sepe
Director of Sales & Marketing: Todd McDonald
Director of Operations: Peter Jasinski
Estimated Sales: $10 - 20 Million
Number Employees: 50-99
Parent Co: ESCO Technologies
Brands:
Combo/Combo

30038 TES-Clean Air Systems
2021 Las Positas Ct Ste 119
Livermore, CA 94551
510-656-5333
Fax: 510-656-5335 sales@paçaids.com
www.tesinc.com
President: James Harris

30039 TESTO
P.O. Box 1030
Sparta, NJ 07871-5030
973-579-3400
Fax: 973-579-3222 800-227-0729
info@testo.com www.ita.cc
Manufacturer and importer of thermometers, probes and data loggers
Manager: Melissa Curro
VP: Andrew Kuezkuda
Marketing/Sales: John Bickers
Estimated Sales: $3 - 5 Million
Number Employees: 10-19
Square Footage: 20000
Parent Co: TESTO GMBH
Type of Packaging: Consumer, Food Service
Brands:
Testoterm

30040 TGI Texas
8700 Clay Road
Suite 100
Houston, TX 77080-8104
909-772-6658
Fax: 626-574-8123

30041 TGR Container Sales
2374 Davis Street
San Leandro, CA 94577-2206
510-562-2251
Fax: 510-562-3226 800-273-6887
Storage containers; also, leasing services available
Manager: Nelio Fernandes

30042 TGW International
5 Spiral Dr Ste 3
Florence, KY 41042
859-647-7383
Fax: 859-647-7877 800-407-0173
sales@tgwint.com

Circular and straight machine knives and cutters for food processing and packaging equipment
President: Jeff Littmer
Vice President: Jeff Litmer
Marketing Director: Debbie Busching
Estimated Sales: Below $5 Million
Number Employees: 5-9
Parent Co: Wolstenholme Machine Knives

30043 (HQ)THARCO
2222 Grant Ave
San Lorenzo, CA 94580-1804
510-276-8600
Fax: 510-317-2728 800-772-2332
sales-slz@tharco.com www.tharco.com
Corrugated boxes, packaging materials and displays; exporter of corrugated boxes and foam cushion packaging
President: Oscar Fears
Marketing Manager: Steve Malmquist
Sales Manager: Don Godshall
Estimated Sales: $20-50 Million
Number Employees: 1000-4999
Square Footage: 550000
Other Locations:
THARCO
Algona WA

30044 THARCO
2222 Grant Ave
San Lorenzo, CA 94580-1804
510-276-8600
Fax: 510-317-2728 800-446-6676
sales-slz@tharco.com www.tharco.com
Shipping containers
President: Oscar Fears
Estimated Sales: $20-50 Million
Number Employees: 1000-4999

30045 THE Corporation
PO Box 445
Terre Haute, IN 47808-0445
812-232-2151
Fax: 800-783-2534 800-783-2151
corpies@thecorp.org
Graphic design, prepress, printing plates for packaging primary foods
CEO: Kenneth Williams
Sales Director: Dave Bryan
Estimated Sales: $3 Million
Number Employees: 31
Square Footage: 128000

30046 TKF Inc
726 Mehring Way
Cincinnati, OH 45203-1809
513-241-5910
Fax: 513-651-2792 www.tkf.com
Manufacturer, designer and exporter of custom vertical conveyor systems, including continuous vertical lift conveyors, reciprocating vertical lift conveyors, pallet handling conveyors, zero-pressure accumulating conveyors, and overheadmonorail conveyors
Owner: Ronald Eubanks
VP Sales: Jim Walsh
reubanks@tkf.com
Estimated Sales: $20 - 50 Million
Number Employees: 50-99

30047 TKO Doors
N56w24701 N Crporate Cir Ste A
Sussex, WI 53089
262-820-1217
Fax: 262-820-1273 800-575-3366
www.tkodoors.com
Automatic doors and accessories, loading dock equipment
Manager: Wayne Strauss
Marketing Manager: Rob Innps
Estimated Sales: $5 - 10 000,000
Number Employees: 50-99

30048 (HQ)TLB Corporation
150 Willard Avenue
PO Box 6954
Ellicott, MD 21042
410-773-9443
Fax: 203-233-1268
Manufacturer, importer and exporter of pre-fabricated waste water treatment plants and pumping stations; also, effluent can be sanitized for reuse
President/Chief Engineer: Thomas Bond
Finance: Russell Correll
Production Manager: Thomas Farrell

Number Employees: 20-49
Square Footage: 60000
Brands:
Hart Boost
Hart Treat
Hartlift
Oxy Tower

30049 TLC & Associates
5600 Bell Street
Suite 105, PMB 167
Amarillo, TX 79109
806-353-1517
Fax: 806-335-4321
Management consulting in the food service industry.
President: Charles King

30050 TMB Baking Equipment
480 Grandview Drive
South San Francisco, CA 94080
650-589-5724
Fax: 650-589-5729 contact@tmbbaking.com
www.tmbbaking.com
President: Michel Suas
Estimated Sales: $3 - 5 Million
Number Employees: 10-19

30051 TMCo Inc.
10801 Hammerly Blvd.
Suite 232
Houston, TX 77043
713-465-3255
Fax: 713-465-3237 gwyn.childress@tmcousa.com
www.tmco-usa.com
Cereal chemists' laboratory equipment
President/CFO: Roland Temme
Quality Control/R&D: John Alberf
Manager: John Albers
Estimated Sales: $10 - 20 Million
Number Employees: 50-99
Parent Co: TMCO
Brands:
Mixograph

30052 TMCo Inc.
10801 Hammerly Blvd.
Suite 232
Houston, TX 77043
713-465-3255
Fax: 713-465-3237 gwyn.childress@tmcousa.com
www.tmco-usa.com
Manufacturer and exporter of displays
President: Roland Temme
VP Manufacturing: Joe Smith
Estimated Sales: $10-20 Million
Number Employees: 50-99

30053 TMF Corporation
850 West Chester Pike
Suite 303
Havertown, PA 19083
610-853-3080
Fax: 610-789-5168 info@tmfcorporation.com
www.tmfcorporation.com
Pallets
Contact: Debbie Bergen
d_bergen@tmfcorporation.com
Number Employees: 4
Square Footage: 3016

30054 TMI-USA
11491 Sunset Hills Rd # 310
Suite 310
Reston, VA 20190-5244
703-668-0114
Fax: 703-668-0118 qi.xiangyu@tmigi.com
www.tmi-orion.com
Manufacturers of data loggers for sterilization processors
President: Guillaume Favre
CEO: Jean-Luc Favre
jeanlucfavre@tmigi.com
VP: Guillaume Favre
Sales Manager: Emmanuel Cisternino
Operations Manager: Myriam Vidal
Estimated Sales: Less Than $500,000
Number Employees: 1-4

30055 TMS
2 Lombard Street
San Francisco, CA 94111-6206
415-665-2565
Fax: 415-362-1756 800-447-7223

Refrigerated and nonrefrigerated cargo and storage containers
President: Robert Skinner
General Manager: Scott Weiser
Estimated Sales: $300,000-500,000
Number Employees: 1-4

30056 TMT Software Company
Eastpoint 1
6085 Parkland Blvd
Mayfield Heights, OH 44124
216-831-6606
Fax: 216-831-3606 800-401-6682
solutions@tmwsystems.com
Manufacturer and developer of fleet and equipment maintenance management software including PM scheduling, fuel, parts, tire, warranty, bar coding, shop planner, mechanics workstation and accounting programs; software operates on LANWAN, PCs and IBM AS/400
President: David Wangler
EVP, Finance: Jeffery Ritter
Vice President: Renaldo Adler
EVP, Marketing: Scott Vanselous
SVP, Sales: Dave Schildmeyer
EVP, Operations: Rod Strata
Estimated Sales: $3 - 5 Million
Number Employees: 20-49
Number of Products: 3
Square Footage: 14000
Brands:
Tmt Transman

30057 TMT Vacuum Filters
407 S. College
Danville, IL 61832
217-446-0742
Fax: 217-446-0744
www.modernmachinebaggers.com
Bag filling machinery; also, industrial maintenance and repair available
President: Manny Mechalas
CFO: Manny Mechalas
Estimated Sales: $1 - 2.5 Million
Number Employees: 10-19

30058 TNA Packaging Solutions
702 S Royal Lane
Suite 100
Coppell, TX 75019-3800
972-462-6500
Fax: 972-462-6599
mark.lozano@tnasolutions.com
www.tnasolutions.com
Manufacturer and exporter of packaging systems including vertical form/fill/seal machinery; importer of multi-head scales and metal detectors
Founder & Director: Nadia Taylor
Founder & CEO: Alf Taylor
Group Finance Manager: Peter Calopedis
VP - Americas: Alfredo Blanco
Group Marketing Manager: Shayne De la Force
Group Sales Manager: Patrick Avelange
Group Operations Manager: Natasha Avelange
Group Manufacturing Manager: Andrew Smith
Estimated Sales: $3.5 Million
Number Employees: 240
Square Footage: 192000
Brands:
Robag

30059 TNN-Jeros, Inc.
P.O. Box 12
Byron, IL 61010
815-978-2210
Fax: 815-234-5915 www.tnn-jeros.com
Cleaning and washing equipment for the baking and food service industries.

30060 TNT Container Logistics
10751 Deerwood Park Blvd # 200
Jacksonville, FL 32256-4836
904-928-1400
Fax: 904-928-1410 800-272-3129
www.tntlogistics.com
Dairy industry packaging containers
Senior VP: Mark Johnson
Director: Joseph Keller
Number Employees: 100-249

30061 TNT Container Logistics
10751 Deerwood Park Blvd # 200
Jacksonville, FL 32256-4836
904-928-1400
Fax: 904-928-1410 800-272-2129
mal_perry@tnt.com.au
Senior VP: Mark Johnson
Director: Joseph Keller
Number Employees: 100-249

30062 TOPS Software Corporation
275 W Campbell Rd
Suite 600
Richardson, TX 75080
972-739-8677
Fax: 972-739-9478 800-889-2441
info@topseng.com www.topseng.com
Offers packaging software and truck loading soft-
ware for packaging and distribution professionals.
President: Bill Rehring
Contact: Erika Ledesma
eledesma@topseng.com
Manager: Reet Randhawa
Estimated Sales: $1-2.5 Million
Number Employees: 10-19

30063 TPS International
7650 Binnacle Lane
Owings, MD 20736-3102
301-855-3541
Fax: 301-855-0474
Forming tubes and shoulders for form full seal bag-
ging machines
Founder: Don Wooldridge
Estimated Sales: $2.5-5 Million
Number Employees: 19

30064 (HQ)TRC
15005 Enterprise Way
Middlefield, OH 44062
440-834-0078
Fax: 440-834-0083
Manufacturer and exporter of staple set brushes;
also, custom injection molding of thermoplastic
materials
Owner: Terry Ross
terry.martinez@apparelnews.net
VP Sales/Marketing: Dan Armstrong
Plant Manager: William O'Donnell
Estimated Sales: $10-20 Million
Number Employees: 100-249
Square Footage: 80000

30065 TRFG Inc
300 E Auburn Ave
Springfield, OH 45505-4703
937-322-2040
Fax: 937-322-2254
Sales and sales management; representing a wide
range of packaged goods like confections, salted
snacks, natural foods
President: Jeff Kreidenweis
jkreidenweis@aol.com
Estimated Sales: $3 - 5 Million
Number Employees: 1-4
Type of Packaging: Food Service, Private Label

30066 TRITEN Corporation
3657 Briarpark
Houston, TX 77042
713-690-9050
Fax: 713-690-9080 832-214-5000
info@triten.com www.triten.com
Manufacturer and exporter of plunger pumps, water
blasting equipment and accessories
Chairman/President/ CEO: John Scott Arnoldy
President/Chief Executive Officer: Thomas Amonet
Executive Vice President/Chief Financial: Donald
O. Bainter
Executive Vice President and Chief Opera: Gary J.
Baumgartner
Contact: Jack Adams
j.adams@triten.com
Product Manager: John Matlock
Estimated Sales: $1-2.5 Million
Number Employees: 100-249
Square Footage: 50000
Brands:
Hydro-Laser

30067 TSA Griddle Systems
395 Penno Road
Suite 100
Kelowna, BC VIX 7W5
Canada
250-491-9025
Fax: 250-491-9045 info@griddlesystems.com
www.griddlesystems.com
Manufacturer and exporter of food processing
equipment including pancake, waffle, french toast,
egg patty and baked goods; also, mixers, blenders,
depositors and cooling systems
President: Kevin Forrest
Estimated Sales: Below $5 Million
Number Employees: 10
Square Footage: 40000

30068 TSE Industries Inc
4370 112th Ter N
Clearwater, FL 33762-4902
727-573-7676
Fax: 727-572-0487 800-237-7634
www.tse-rubber.com
Custom rubber molding
Owner: Rob Clingle
Vice Chairman/Director: Helen Klingel
Director: Diane Klingel
CEO: Robert R Klingel Sr
VP Rubber Products Division: Louis Mirra
VP Speciality Chemicals Division: William
Stephens
VP Plastics/Machine Shop Division: Gary Reese
VP Materials: Mark Neuman
robclingle@tse-industries.com
Estimated Sales: $10 - 20 Million
Number Employees: 100-249
Square Footage: 150000

30069 TSG Merchandising
410 E Walnut Street
Perkasie, PA 18944-1618
215-453-9220
Fax: 215-453-7710
Designer of point of purchase displays, store fix-
tures, etc
President: Paul Schmidt
Number Employees: 10-19

30070 TTS Technologies
160 Farm Hill Cir
Roswell, GA 30075-4263
770-640-7808
Fax: 770-622-9183

30071 TULSACK
10405b E 55th Pl
Tulsa, OK 74146-6502
918-664-0664
Fax: 918-664-0849 800-228-1936
www.tulsack.com
Handled paper bags
President: Jarrod Dyess
HR Executive: Tina Schroeder
tina@tulsack.com
Estimated Sales: $10-20 Million
Number Employees: 100-249
Parent Co: Denmar Products

30072 TURBOCHEF Technologies
2801 Trade Center Drive
Carrollton, TX 75007
214-379-6000
Fax: 214-340-6073 800-908-8726
www.turbochef.com
Designs, develops, manufactures and markets speed
cooking solutions
President: James K. Pool III
CEO: James Price
CFO: Al Cochran
COO: Paul Lehr
VP Marketing: David Shave
Sr VP Global Sales/Business Development: Peter
Ashcraft
Contact: Max Abbott
max.abbott@turbochef.com
Plant Manager: Jeanean Weaver
Vice President Procurement: Rusty Rose
Estimated Sales: $10 - 20 Million
Number Employees: 10
Square Footage: 22000
Brands:
Turbochef

30073 (HQ)TVC Systems
284 Constitution Ave
Portsmouth, NH 03801-5616
603-431-5251
Fax: 603-431-8909 888-431-5251
info@tvcsystems.com www.tvcsystems.com
Turnkey process control and information systems
President: Jim Fradsham
fradsham@tvcsystems.com
CEO: Nels Tyring
Operations Manager: Linda Tyring
Estimated Sales: $5 - 10 Million
Number Employees: 10-19
Square Footage: 14000

30074 TVT Trade Brands
18503 Pines Blvd.
Suite 308
Pembroke Pines, FL 33029
954-353-9003
Fax: 954-507-5933 info@tvttrade.com
www.tvttrade.com
Ethnic foods: Mediterranean, European, Asian,
Latin-American, Middle Eastern, African and Aus-
tralian; spices, superfoods and delicatessen.
Global Business Development Manager: Rubert
Velasquez
Estimated Sales: $1-5 Million
Number Employees: 10-20
Type of Packaging: Food Service
Other Locations:
Warehouse
Miami FL
Brands:
Mystik Spices
Origin Foods
Powerbite

30075 TW Metals Inc
760 Constitution Dr
Suite 204
Exton, PA 19341
610-458-1300
www.twmetals.com
Steel, nickel alloys, aluminum, copper, brass, carbon
alloys in all metal configurations. Processing equipment services for cutting, shearing, leveling, and
slitting, distributor of fittings and flanges.
President & CEO: Kirk Moore *Year Founded:* 1907

30076 TWM Manufacturing
1960 Concession 3
Leamington, ON N9Y 2E5
Canada
519-326-0014
Fax: 519-326-7746 888-495-4831
sales@tugweld.com
Premium quality custom made food processing ma-
chinery and automated mechanical systems/special-
ists in stainless steel
President: John Friesen
VP: Jake Friesen
Estimated Sales: $2-3 Million
Number Employees: 13
Square Footage: 88000
Brands:
Cluster Buster
Tugweld
Twm

30077 TXS
124 Commercial Avenue
B
Rogers, AR 72757
501-631-1363
Fax: 501-631-1294 800-562-6552

30078 Table De France: North America
390 George St
Suite 404-407
New Brunswick, NJ 8901
732-565-0820
Fax: 732-565-0828 888-680-4616
JFagan390@cs.com www.tabledefrance.net
Silver utensils and tabletop supplies
VP: James Fagan
Parent Co: Christoff Silver
Brands:
Christoff

30079 Table Talk Pies Inc
120 Washington St
Worcester, MA 01610
508-798-8811
Fax: 508-798-0848 info@tabletalkpie.com
www.tabletalkpie.com
4, 6, 8, 9, and 10 inch pies in a variety of dessert and
fruit flavors.
Director of Sales/Marketing: Timothy Mulcahy
Brand Manager: Tara Tula
Logistics: Valdemar Siqueira
Year Founded: 1924
Estimated Sales: $40 Million
Number Employees: 50-99
Number of Brands: 1
Square Footage: 30000
Brands:
    Table Talk

30080 Tablecheck Technologies, Inc
13276 Research Blvd # 103
Austin, TX 78750
512-219-9711
Fax: 512-219-6964 800-522-1347
info@tablecheck.com www.tablecheck.com
Manufacturer and exporter of electronic seating sys-
tems
President: Barbara Horan
Estimated Sales: $1 - 5 Million
Number Employees: 5-9
Number of Brands: 1
Number of Products: 1
Square Footage: 3200
Brands:
    Tablecheck

30081 Tablecraft Products Co Inc
801 Lakeside Dr
Gurnee, IL 60031-2489
847-855-9000
Fax: 847-855-9012 800-323-8321
info@tablecraft.com
Manufacturer, importer and exporter of smallwares,
salt and pepper shakers, condiment and beverage
dispensers, bar supplies, kitchen utensils, coffee
equipment, baskets, salad bowls, rangettes, etc
President: Dave Burnside
    dburnside@tablecraft.com
CFO: Ron Kostrewa
Vice President: Larry Davis
General Manager: Ted Rutkowski
Marketing Director: Amy Garrard
Sales Director: Dave Burnside
Plant Manager: Ted Rotkowski
Purchasing Manager: Larry Davis
Number Employees: 5-9
Square Footage: 400000
Parent Co: Hunter Manufacturing Company
Brands:
    Kenket
    Seattle Series
    Superlevel
    Tablecraft

30082 Tables Cubed
2305 Manor Ridge Drive
Chesterfield, MO 63017
314-843-3001
Fax: 314-843-2127 800-878-3001
Occasional tables for hospitality environment.
President: Don Depke
Sales: Seth Lieberman
Estimated Sales: $1,000,000 - $2,499,999
Number Employees: 5-9

30083 Tablet & Ticket Co
1120 Atlantic Dr
West Chicago, IL 60185-5103
630-231-6611
Fax: 630-231-0211 800-438-4959
sales@tabletandticket.com
www.tabletandticket.com
Custom menu display boards including stainless
steel, brass, aluminum, illuminated and
nonilluminated; also, matching bulletin boards
available
President: Brian Blair
    brianb@tabletandticket.com
CFO: Tom Evans
Estimated Sales: $5 - 10 Million
Number Employees: 10-19
Square Footage: 30000

30084 Taconic
P.O. Box 69
Petersburg, NY 12138
518-658-3202
Fax: 518-658-3988 800-833-1805
info@4taconic.com www.4taconic.com
Manufacturer, importer and exporter of PTFE and
silicone coated fiberglass fabrics and tapes; also, re-
usable and nonstick coated cake rings and liners for
trays, bagel boards, ovens, roasting and proofing
Executive: Philippe Heffley
Sales: Al Hepp
Contact: Jeffrey Browne
    jeffrey.browne@taconic.com
Estimated Sales: $20 - 50 Million
Number Employees: 100-249
Brands:
    Tefbake

30085 Tafco Inc
PO Box 269
Hyde, PA 16843-0269
814-765-5378
Fax: 814-765-5410 800-233-1954
bridgettwhite@walkins.com www.walkins.com
Walk-in coolers and freezers
President/CEO: William Carr
VP: Gary Brannon
Vice President of Sales: Bridgett White
Contact: Chris Aughenbaugh
    caughenbaugh@walkins.com
Estimated Sales: $20-50 Million
Number Employees: 100-249

30086 Tag-Trade Associated Group
1730 W Wrightwood Ave
Chicago, IL 60614-1972
773-871-1300
Fax: 773-871-8432 800-621-8350
www.tagltd.com
Napkins, place mats, tablecloths, wine racks and
buckets and candles
National Sales Manager: Nancy Mathyer
Estimated Sales: $20-50 Million
Number Employees: 50-99

30087 (HQ)Taisei Lamick USA, Inc.
2416 Estes Ave.
Elk Grove Village, IL 60007
847-258-3283
Fax: 847-258-3284 www.taiseilamick.com
Packaging and containers manufacturing. Taisei
Lamick's plastic film is suitable for filling packets of
liquid, gel, paste, and syrup.
President: Taka Asai
Estimated Sales: $228.1 Million
Number Employees: 11-50

30088 Taisei Lamick USA, Inc.
20775 S. Western Ave.
#102
Torrance, CA 90501
424-376-5001
Fax: 424-376-5004 www.taiseilamick.com
Packaging and containers manufacturing.

30089 Taisei Lamick USA, Inc.
145 Industrial Ave
Business Park Unit N
Little Ferry, NJ 07643
908-388-1352
www.taiseilamick.com
Packaging and containers manufacturing.

30090 Talbert Display
5713 Hart St
Fort Worth, TX 76112-6918
817-429-4504
Fax: 817-457-4066
Store fixtures and cabinets
Owner: Mark Talbert
Estimated Sales: Less than $500,000
Number Employees: 1-4
Square Footage: 24000

30091 (HQ)Talbot Industries
1211 W Harmony St
Neosho, MO 64850-1636
417-451-5900
Fax: 417-451-7830
Point of purchase displays, store displays and steel
wire products
President: Jerral Downs
VP (National Accounts): Mike Howley
Quality Control: Greg Harris
Human Resources: Beth Foust
VP Sales: Jeff Talbot
Manager: Laurie Borland
    laurie.borland@leggett.com
Number Employees: 250-499
Square Footage: 800000
Other Locations:
    Talbot Industries
    Point TX

30092 Tallygenicom
15345 Barranca Pkwy
Irvine, CA 92618-2216
714-368-2300
800-665-6210
tallygenicom.com
Manufacturer and provider of industrial and
back-office enterprise printing solutions for of-
fice/industrial marketplace and distribution supply
chain.
CEO: Werner Heid
SVP, EMEA Sales & Marketing: Rosemarie Zito
SVP, Operations: Wui Kian Tay
Estimated Sales: $50-100 Million
Number Employees: 500-999
Square Footage: 140000
Parent Co: Printronix
Brands:
    Computer Printers
    Tally Printer Corporation

30093 Tamanet (USA) Inc
16541 Gothard St
Suite 112
Huntington Beach, CA 92647
714-698-0990
Fax: 714-842-5600 800-441-8262
jeff@tamanetusa.com www.tamanetusa.com
Knited net for wrapping pallets
President: Nackem Dorou
Contact: Bobbie Smith-Cruz
    bobbie@tamanetusa.com
Estimated Sales: $5-10 Million
Number Employees: 1-4
Parent Co: TAMA Plastic Industry

30094 Tamarack Products Inc
1071 N Old Rand Rd
Wauconda, IL 60084-1239
847-526-9333
Fax: 847-526-9353 info@tamarackproducts.com
www.tamarackproducts.com
Manufacturer and exporter of printing, labeling and
die cutting equipment
President: David Steidinger
    dsteidinger@tamarackproducts.com
Estimated Sales: $2.5-5 Million
Number Employees: 20-49

30095 Tampa Bay Copack
15052 Ronnie Dr # 100
Dade City, FL 33523-6011
352-567-7400
Fax: 352-567-2257
Contract manufacturing beverage bottling,
pastuerizer, formulation, private label, product
development.
President: Scot Ballantyne
Research & Development: Vince Curetto
Contact: Valerie Hval
    vhval@tampabaycopack.com
Number Employees: 5-9
Square Footage: 34000
Type of Packaging: Private Label

30096 Tampa Corrugated CartonCompany
3517 N 40th Street
Tampa, FL 33605-1641
813-623-5115
Fax: 813-626-2153
Manufacturer and exporter of custom and stock
boxes including corrugated, paper and paper fold-
ing; also, cartons
General Manager: Ron Pollard
Estimated Sales: $10-20 Million
Number Employees: 50-99

30097 Tampa Pallet Co
2402 S 54th St
Tampa, FL 33619-5364

813-626-5700
Fax: 813-623-5180
TAMPAPALLET@AOL.COM
www.tampapallet.com
Manufacturer and exporter of wooden pallets, crates and boxes
Owner, President: Fred Haman
tampapallet@aol.com
Estimated Sales: $5-10 Million
Number Employees: 5-9

30098 Tampa Sheet Metal Co
1402 W Kennedy Blvd
Tampa, FL 33606-1847

813-251-1845
Fax: 813-254-7399 sales@tampasheetmetal.com
www.tampasheetmetal.com
Aluminum, steel and stainless steel cabinets, hoppers, pipes, tanks, etc
President: John L Jiretz
president@tampasheetmetal.com
General Manager: J Jiretz
Estimated Sales: $1 - 2,500,000
Number Employees: 10-19

30099 Tanaco Products
3465 Bonnie Hill Dr
Los Angeles, CA 90068-1325

360-332-6010
Fax: 360-332-0936
Manufactures conventional Tanaco plastic plug valves and rebuilding of all types of plug valves, also manufacturers tanaco in-line automatic and hand actuated plug valves
Owner: Annelie Hoyer
Estimated Sales: Less than $500,000
Number Employees: 1-4
Other Locations:
Tanaco Products
Vancouver, B.C., Canada

30100 Tangent Systems
8030 England Street
B
Charlotte, NC 28273-5978

704-554-0830
Fax: 704-554-0820 800-992-7577
www.versid.com
Manufacturer and exporter of temperature measurement and data logging instruments
Sales Manager: Mary Lynn Rogers
Estimated Sales: $1-2.5 Million
Number Employees: 10
Brands:
Tempest
Versid

30101 Tangerine Promotion
900 Skokie Blvd # 275
Suite 275
Northbrook, IL 60062-4034

847-313-6000
Fax: 847-313-6092
info@tangerinepromotions.com
www.tangerinepromotions.com
Promotional products and marketing agency
President/CEO: Steve Friedman
CFO/COO: Adam Rosenbaum
Sales Director: Michael Gertz
Manager: Jon Lavarre
jlavarre@tangerineme.com
Director of Production: Carolyn Boehm
Estimated Sales: $2.8 Million
Number Employees: 10-19
Square Footage: 28000

30102 Tangible Vision
320 Billingsly Ct # 50
Suite 50
Franklin, TN 37067-4707

615-771-7177
Fax: 630-969-7523 800-763-8634
www.tangiblevision.net
Software for customer service, accounting, manufacturing, etc
Owner: Paul Reeves
paul@tangiblevision.net
VP Marketing: Kathy Harmon
Estimated Sales: $2.5-5 Million
Number Employees: 5-9

30103 Tango Shatterproof Drinkware
P.O. Box 737
Walpole, MA 02081

888-898-2646
Fax: 508-668-0543 Kpicchi@IslandOasis.com
www.tango-shatterproof.com
Shatterproof glasses, tumblers and pitchers
General Manager: Paul Shilo
Sales: Marie Sandre
Parent Co: Island Oasis
Brands:
Tango Shatterproof

30104 Tank Temp Control
23275 NE Dayton Ave
Newberg, OR 97132-6816

503-538-8267
Fax: 503-538-1837 888-960-9090
www.tanktemp.com
Wine industry temperature monitoring
Owner: Curtis Jungwirth
Estimated Sales: Less than $500,000
Number Employees: 1-4

30105 Tantec
630 Estes Avenue
Schaumburg, IL 60193-4403

847-524-5506
Fax: 847-524-6956 mrtantec@aol.com
Industrial equipment including static control, corona treating and surface measuring
President: Waltraud Legat
Contact: Jeff Gradus
jeff@tantec.com
Estimated Sales: $2.5 - 5 Million
Number Employees: 20

30106 Tap Packaging Solutions
2160 Superior Ave. E
Cleveland, OH 44114

800-827-5679
Fax: 800-276-2572 contact@tap-usa.com
tap-usa.com
Packaging containers: consumer brand, photography, confections, paperboard
Chairman: David Chilcote
President & CEO: J. Anthony Hyland
Quality Manager: Kamal Haddad
Vice President, Sales & Marketing: Jordana Revella
Manager, Human Resources: Christina Balint
Vice President, Operations: Matthew Moir
Year Founded: 1906
Estimated Sales: $50-70 Million
Number Employees: 51-200
Type of Packaging: Consumer

30107 Tape & Label Converters
8231 Allport Ave
Santa Fe Springs, CA 90670-2105

562-945-3486
Fax: 562-696-8198 888-285-2462
www.stickybiz.com
Printer of high quality short run digital and large run flexographic pressure sensitive lavels. 35+ years of experience with food and beverage labels. Customers are small family owned companies to Fortune 500.
CEO: Robert Varela Sr.
Research & Development: Robert Varela Jr.
Quality Control: Roger Varela
Marketing: Mas Crawford
Sales: Mas Crawford
Public Relations: Mas Crawford
Operations: Robert Varela Sr.
Production: Roger Varela
Plant Manager: Randy Varela
Purchasing: Robert Varela Jr.
Estimated Sales: $1-2.5 Million
Number Employees: 10-19
Square Footage: 24000
Type of Packaging: Consumer, Food Service, Private Label

30108 Tape & Label Engineering
2950 47th Avenue N
St Petersburg, FL 33714-3132

727-527-6686
Fax: 727-526-0163 800-237-8955
Die-cut cloth, foil, mylar, paper and pressure-sensitive labels; wholesaler/distributor of pressure sensitive application equipment

Manager: Bob White
Marketing Director: Chuck Pullich
Sales Director: Charlie Goldson
Production Manager: Tom Bowers
tom.bowers@tle.net
Purchasing Manager: Michael Summers
Estimated Sales: $10-20 Million
Number Employees: 50-100
Square Footage: 168000
Parent Co: Weber Marking Systems
Type of Packaging: Consumer, Private Label

30109 Tapesolutions
1217 Rabas Street
Algoma, WI 54201-1985

847-776-8880
Fax: 847-776-8890 800-323-6026
Manufacturers of security tapes and labels
CEO: Terrence Fulwiler
Estimated Sales: $5-10 Million
Number Employees: 5-9
Square Footage: 10000
Parent Co: W.S Packaging

30110 Taprite-Fassco Mfg Inc
3248 Northwestern
San Antonio, TX 78238-4043

210-523-0800
Fax: 210-520-3035 800-779-8488
sales@taprite.com www.taprite.com
CO2 regulators, BIB packs, portable bars, and asessory items for the beverage industry
President: David Lease
dlease@taprite.com
CFO: Scott Cary
Estimated Sales: $20 - 50 Million
Number Employees: 50-99

30111 Tar-Hong MELAMINE USA
780 Nogales St
City of Industry, CA 91748-1306

626-935-1612
Fax: 626-585-1609 cservice@tarhong.com
www.tarhong.com
Plastic dinnerware, stainless steel flatware and tumblers
Owner: Eddie Liu
Manager: Ralph Liu
Manager: Joe Wen
Estimated Sales: $5 - 10 Million
Number Employees: 5-9

30112 Tara Communications
698 Litchfield Lane
Dunedin, FL 34698-7429

303-417-9602
Fax: 303-413-1869
Consultant specializing in sales and advertising for the natural products industry
Partner: Joel Packman
Partner: Tish Packman
Number Employees: 1-4

30113 Tara Foods LLC
1900 Cowles Ln
Albany, GA 31705-1514

229-431-1330
Fax: 229-439-1458 www.thekrogerco.com
Sauces, peanut butter, food color
Sales Manager: Marilyne Moore
Plant Manager: Jesse Turner
Estimated Sales: $25-49.9 Million
Number Employees: 100-249
Parent Co: Kroger Company

30114 Tara Linens
PO Box 1350
Sanford, NC 27331-1350

919-774-1300
Fax: 919-774-3525 800-476-8272
Manufacturer and exporter of table linens including cloths, napkins, place mats, skirting, runners, aprons and tray and chair covers; importer of table aprons
President: Brooks Pomeranz
Number Employees: 100-249
Square Footage: 480000
Parent Co: Cascade Fibers Company
Brands:
Checkmate
Classic
Nouveau
Queens Linen
Windsor

30115 Tara Tape
250 Canal Rd
Fairless Hills, PA 19030
215-736-3644
Fax: 215-428-4510 800-366-8272
sales@taratape.com
Filament tape, strapping tape, tearstrip tape, printed
tape, overlaminate, laminated label stocks
President: Tom Dodd
Estimated Sales: $2.5-5 Million
Number Employees: 50-99

30116 Tarason Packaging, LLC.
1101 Keisler Road
Conover, NC 28613
828-464-4743
Fax: 828-465-5517
Pressure sensitive labels, hang tags and cloth printed
labels
President: Kevin McKenna
Operations Manager: Ronnie A. Caldwell
Estimated Sales: Below $5 Million
Number Employees: 10-19

30117 Target Industries
95 S River Bend Way
North Salt Lake, UT 84054
866-617-2253
Fax: 801-383-3251 info@targetlabel.com
www.targetlabel.com
Extruded plastic bags, sheetings, discs, liners and
tubings; also, converter of polyamide/plastic casings
for processed meat, cheese and poultry; importer of
plastic casings
President: Tom Fox
CFO: Warren Greenberg
Sales Manager: Guy Eric
Estimated Sales: $10-20 Million
Number Employees: 50-99
Square Footage: 106000

30118 Tartaric Chemicals Corporation
515 Madison Ave Rm 1902
New York, NY 10022
212-752-0727
Fax: 212-207-8037 www.tartarics.com
President: Alessandro Bonecchi
Estimated Sales: $2.5-5 Million
Number Employees: 5-9

30119 Task Footwear
1251 1st Ave
Chippewa Falls, WI 54729-1408
715-723-1871
Fax: 715-720-4260 800-962-0166
Steel toe, nonsteel and slip resistant shoes
Wholesale Manager: Linda Jackson
CEO: Daniel Hunt
VP Marketing: Herb Steinmetz
Estimated Sales: $1 - 5,000,000
Number Employees: 250-499
Brands:
Mason

30120 Tasler Inc
1804 Tasler Dr
Webster City, IA 50595-7625
515-832-5200
Fax: 515-832-2721 www.tasler.com
Wooden pallets
President: Greg Tasler
gtasler@tasler.com
Estimated Sales: $20-50 Million
Number Employees: 100-249

30121 Tate Western
36 Aero Camino
Goleta, CA 93117-3105
805-685-5544
Fax: 805-685-3695 800-903-0200
Manufacturer, importer and exporter of automatic
chemical dispensers including warewash, laundry
and metering pumps
President: Russ Kovacevich
Sales Manager: Glen Kent
Estimated Sales: $5-10 Million
Number Employees: 25
Square Footage: 34000
Parent Co: Shurflo Pump Manufacturing
Brands:
Gorilla Bowl
Tate Western
Versa Pro

30122 Taylor Box Co
293 Child St
PO Box 343
Warren, RI 02885-1907
401-245-5900
Fax: 401-245-0450 800-304-6361
info@taylorbox.com www.taylorbox.com
Manufacturer and exporter of specialty paper and
metal boxes for consumer goods and confectionery
items
President: Dan Shedd
Design/Engineering: Julie Passey
Sales/Marketing: Daniel Shedd
Administration: Martha Lemoi
Production: Donna Costa
Estimated Sales: $10 - 20 Million
Number Employees: 20-49

30123 Taylor Made Custom Products
66 Kingsboro Ave
Gloversville, NY 12078-3415
518-725-0681
Fax: 518-725-4335
tmginfo@taylormadegroup.com
www.taylormadecustomproducts.com
Commercial awnings
President/CEO: Andy Jobbins
CFO: Robert Khalife
Secretary: John Taylor
Contact: Emory Lyons
elyons@taylormadesystems.com
Estimated Sales: $1 - 3,000,000
Number Employees: 5-9
Parent Co: Taylor Made Group

30124 Taylor Manufacturing Co
128 Talmadge Dr
PO Box 625
Moultrie, GA 31768-5049
229-985-5445
Fax: 229-890-9090 www.peasheller.com
Manufacturer and exporter of motor driven shelling
machinery for peas and beans
President/CFO: Terry Taylor Sr
VP: Terry Taylor
Estimated Sales: Below $5 Million
Number Employees: 5-9

30125 Taylor Precision Products
2311 West 22nd St
Suite 200
Oak Brook, IL 60523
info@taylorusa.com
www.tayloruds.com
Thermometers including digital and mechanical, in-
stant read, pocket and hand-held; for meat, candy,
jelly, scales, portion control, receiving and utility
CEO: Rob Kay
Estimated Sales: $50 Million
Number Employees: 20-49
Square Footage: 85000
Parent Co: Filament
Other Locations:
Taylor Precision Products
Juarez, Mexico
Taylor Precision Products
Las Cruces NM
Brands:
Bi-Therm
Taylor
Tru-Temp

30126 Taylor Precision Products
2311 W 22nd St # 200
Oak Brook, IL 60523-5625
630-954-1250
Fax: 630-954-1275 866-843-3905
info@taylorusa.com www.taylorusa.com
Manufactures thermometers, scales and related mea-
surement devices.
CFO: Donald Robinson
VP: Donald Robinson
Director Sales/Marketing: Kent Beaverson
Contact: Elvira Abate
eabate@taylorusa.com
Estimated Sales: $1-2,500,000
Number Employees: 10-19
Type of Packaging: Consumer, Food Service, Pri-
vate Label, Bulk

30127 (HQ)Taylor Products Co
2205 Jothi Ave
Parsons, KS 67357-8477
620-421-5550
Fax: 620-421-5586 888-882-9567
www.magnumsystems.com
Manufacturer and exporter of bag filling and unload-
ing bagging scales, applicable for open mouth,
valve, drum/box and bulk bags
CEO: Gary Saunders
CFO: Debra Weidert
Sales Manager: Brad Schultz
Estimated Sales: $20-50 Million
Number Employees: 20-49
Square Footage: 208000
Other Locations:
Taylor Products Co.
Decatur AL
Brands:
Avatar
Weigh Trac

30128 Taylor-Made Labels Inc
17252 Pilkington Rd # A
Lake Oswego, OR 97035-5393
503-699-5000
Fax: 503-699-0408 800-878-8654
dtaylor@taylormadelabels.com
www.taylormadelabels.com
Manufacture of custom pressure sensitive labels and
tags. Distributor of label application equipment.
President: Paul Taylor
ptaylor@taylormadelabels.com
Vice President: Dan Taylor
Plant Manager: Mike Summers
Estimated Sales: $20 - 50 Million
Number Employees: 50-99

30129 Taymar Industries
4-151 Monterey Ave
Palm Desert, CA 92201-2388
760-775-2424
Fax: 760-775-2420 800-624-1972
Plastic product display cases; also, stock and custom
pieces available
VP: Bob Stevens
Marketing: Dave Parkinson
Sales Manager: Bonnie Miller
Estimated Sales: $1-2.5 Million
Number Employees: 30

30130 Teaco
5800 Monroe Rd
Charlotte, NC 28212-6104
704-535-5305
Fax: 704-531-5801 globaoco2K@cs.com
Teabag wire, threads
President: Steven Cropp
Estimated Sales: $1-2.5 Million
Number Employees: 5-9

30131 Teamwork Technology
7700 Riverside Drive
Dublin, OH 43016-9044
419-782-4990
Fax: 419-782-3577 www.fessmann.com
Continuous and batch smokehouses, smoke genera-
tors and chill equipment
Number Employees: 2

30132 Tec Art Industries Inc
28059 Center Oaks Court
Wixom, MI 48393
248-624-8880
Fax: 248-624-8066 800-886-6615
www.tecartinc.com
Back lit signs, banners, poster and banner stands,
metal tackers, counter stools, custom floor mats and
neon. Over 300 in stock - Title Signs available.
CEO: Steve Bolin
COO/CFO: Kimberly Perrigan
VP Sales/Marketing: Michele Wehr
Contact: Jeffrey Dunstan
jdunstan@tecartinc.com
Estimated Sales: $5 Million +
Number Employees: 20-49
Square Footage: 64000
Brands:
Alumitec Elite
Alumtec
Tec Frames
Tecneon
Tectwo

30133 Tec-Era Engineering Corporation
1860 Altamont Dr
Felton, CA 95018
831-438-1930
Fax: 831-438-1939
Water treatment equipment
President: Gerald G Green
Estimated Sales: Less than $500,000
Number Employees: 5-9

30134 Tec5USA
80 Skyline Dr
Plainview, NY 11803
516-653-2000
quality control and food safety equipment.
General Manager: Dan Fields
Number Employees: 11 - 50

30135 Tech Development
6800 Poe Ave
Dayton, OH 45414
937-898-9600
Fax: 937-898-8431 www.tdi-turbotwin.com
Turbo machinery, propulsion simulators, pumps, in-
dustrial air motors and engine air starters
Manager: Tom Jacobs
Field Service Engineer: Mike Briscoe
Marketing Coordinator: Anita Hamilton
Northern Regional Sales Manager: Bob Englet
Customer Service: Deanne Hartman
General Manager: William Nordby
Estimated Sales: $10 - 20 Million
Number Employees: 100-249

30136 (HQ)Tech Lighting LLC
7400 Linder Ave
Skokie, IL 60077-3219
847-410-4400
Fax: 847-410-4500 800-323-3226
lblcseast@lbllighting.com
Manufacturer, importer and exporter of lighting fix-
tures
President/Owner: Steve Harriott
Vice President: Dennis Beard
dbeard@lbllighting.com
Sales: Krista Fischer
Plant Manager: Don Clark
Purchasing Director: Cathy Santiago
Number Employees: 100-249
Square Footage: 140000
Parent Co: Encompass Lighting

30137 Tech Pak Solutions
85 Bradley Drive
Westbrook, ME 04092-2013
207-878-6667
Fax: 425-883-9455
Temperature controlled management for food prod-
ucts.
Vice President: Richard Brown

30138 Tech-Roll Inc
PO Box 959
Blaine, WA 98231-0959
360-371-4321
Fax: 360-371-0752 888-946-3929
www.hydraulicdrummotors.com
Hyrdaulic motorized pulleys for the meat, poultry
and food processing equipment industries.
Number Employees: 1-4

30139 Techform
PO Box 270
Mount Airy, NC 27030
336-789-2115
Fax: 336-789-2118
www.plasticingenuity.com/techform/
Custom thermoformed plastic products including
blisters, clamshells, trays, cups, lids, etc.; also, con-
tract packaging services available
President: Richard Wimbish
Quality Control: Allan Hick
Sales/Administrative: Shannon Branch
Estimated Sales: $5 - 10 Million
Number Employees: 10-19
Square Footage: 114000
Type of Packaging: Consumer, Food Service, Pri-
vate Label, Bulk

30140 Technetics Industries
1201 N Birch Lake Boulevard
St. Paul, MN 55110-5246
651-777-4780
Fax: 651-777-5582 800-536-4880
www.tecweigh.com
Weighing systems and equipment
President: Jon Madgett
CFO: Dteven Fiank
Service Manager: Chuck Svoboda
Marketing Director: Andrew Holloway
Regional Manager: Jeff Desjardin
Estimated Sales: $1 - 5 Million
Number Employees: 20-49
Type of Packaging: Private Label

30141 Techni-Chem
1 N Maple Grove Rd
Boise, ID 83704-8265
800-635-8930
Fax: 208-376-3605 800-635-8930
brian@technichemcorp.com
Liquid and dry cleaning compounds for restaurant
stove hoods
President: Brian Rencher
brian@technichemcorp.com
Estimated Sales: $750,000
Number Employees: 1-4
Number of Brands: 200
Number of Products: 1
Square Footage: 20000
Brands:
Technichem

30142 TechniStar Corporation
7825 Fay Avenue
Suite 200
La Jolla, CA 92037
858-454-1400
Fax: 858-300-5118 www.technistar.com
Robotic carton loaders, casing equipment, packers,
conveyor or accessories, belt tracking

30143 Technibilt/Cari-All
700 E P St
Newton, NC 28658
828-464-7388
Fax: 828-464-7603 800-233-3972
custserv@technibilt.com www.technibilt.com
Manufacturer and exporter of wire shelves, carts,
stacking baskets, dunnage and display racks, secu-
rity units, stock trucks, containers, utility/shopping
carts and high density storage sytems
President: Pierre Lafleur
General Manager: Marcel Bourgeoys
Sales Manager: Charles Nicely
Estimated Sales: $20-50 Million
Number Employees: 250-499
Square Footage: 260000
Parent Co: Cari-All Products
Type of Packaging: Food Service
Brands:
Adapta-Flex
Adapta-Plus

30144 Technical Inc
3445 N Causeway Blvd # 1001
Suite 1001
Metairie, LA 70002-3721
504-733-0300
Fax: 504-733-0345 support@tcal.com
Owner: Lee Cabes
lcabes@tcal.com
Founder/CEO: Leon Cabes
Estimated Sales: $.5 - 1 million
Number Employees: 5-9

**30145 Technical Instrument
SanFrancisco**
7545 Carroll Rd
San Diego, CA 92121-2401
858-578-1860
Fax: 858-578-2344 800-765-1860
www.tsystemsinternational.com
Wine industry laboratory equipment
President: David Everitt
Chairman, Chief Executive Officer: Samuel Allen
Vice President: Aaron Wetzel
Manager of Marketing: Brett Bedard
Vice President of Sales and Marketing: Christoph
Wigger
Vice President of Public Affairs: Charles Stamp
Senior Vice President of Operations: Lawrence
Sidwell

Estimated Sales: $50 - 100 Million
Number Employees: 100-249

30146 Technical Tool Solutions Inc.
766 Oakwood Ave
Lake Forest, IL 60045
847-235-5551
Fax: 847-574-2506 sales@techtoolsolutions.com
www.techtoolsolutions.com
Portable machining and welding equipment.
Manager: Carl Middelegge
carl@techtoolsolutions.com
Number Employees: 1-4

30147 TechnipFMC
11740 Katy Freeway
Energy Tower 3
Houston, TX 77079
218-591-4000
www.technipfmc.com
Manufacturer and exporter of flow and level control
equipment, environmental analyzers and process
control instrumentations including flow meters,
level controls, valves, oil detectors, etc.
Chairman & CEO: Douglas Pferdehirt
EVP & Chief Financial Officer: Maryann Mannen
EVP & Chief Legal Officer: Dianne Ralston
EVP/Chief Technology Officer: Justin Rounce
EVP, People & Culture: Agnieszka Kmieciak
Estimated Sales: $13 Billion
Number Employees: 37,000
Square Footage: 268000
Brands:
Envirolert
Leveltronic

30148 Technipac
31515 Cambria Ave
Le Sueur, MN 56058-4509
Canada
507-665-6658
Fax: 507-665-2870 www.custompouches.com
Wooden boxes, containers, skids and pallets
President: Mark Steele
VP, Sales & Development: Greg Melchoir
Manager: Bonnie Dahn
Estimated Sales: Below $5 Million
Number Employees: 50-99

30149 Techniquip
530 Boulder Ct # 103
Suite 103
Pleasanton, CA 94566-8318
925-523-3421
Fax: 925-251-0704 888-414-0789
blue@techniquip.com www.techniquip.com
Digital refractometers
Owner: George Grauer
gg@techniquip.com
Estimated Sales: $2.5-5 Million
Number Employees: 10-19

30150 Technistar Corporation
1725 Gaylord Street
100
Denver, CO 80206-1208
303-651-0188
Fax: 303-651-5600 support@ew3.com
www.technistar.com
Manufacturer and exporter of flexible robotic pack-
aging equipment including carton loaders, case
packers, palletizers, kit assembly, vision inspection
and system integration
Chief Engineer: Rick Tallian
Sales Manager: Mike Weinstein
Number Employees: 85
Square Footage: 172000
Brands:
Galileo
Standard Systems

30151 Technium
68 Stacy Haines Road
Medford, NJ 08055
609-702-5910
Fax: 609-702-5915
Manufacturer, exporter and importer of juice ma-
chines
Chief Executive Officer: Ian Bell
Vice President of Product Development: Jeronimo
Barrera
Chief Technical Officer: Dan Gaul
Vice President of Sales: Sean Cullinane

Estimated Sales: $1-3 Million
Number Employees: 10
Square Footage: 32000
Brands:
   Power Glide
   Technium

30152 Techno-Design
1664 Frogtown Rd #203
Union, KY 41091

844-615-7281
Fax: 859-534-0939 800-641-1822
https://bdtechnodesigns.com

Machinery for frozen pasta products including manicotti, lasagna, ravioli, stuffed rigatoni, etc.; also, blanchers
Owner: Ruben Diaz
Estimated Sales: $500,000-$1 Million
Number Employees: 1-4
Square Footage: 16000

30153 Technomic Inc
300 S Riverside Plz # 1200
Suite 1200
Chicago, IL 60606-6637

312-876-0004
Fax: 312-876-1158 foodinfo@technomic.com
www.technomic.com

Research and consulting firm specializing in emerging channel/segment analyses, new product research, strategic planning, acquisition studies and local market planning
President: Ron Paul
VP: Alan Hyatt
IT: Chris Urban
   curban@technomic.com
Estimated Sales: $5-10 Million
Number Employees: 50-99

30154 Technoquip Co
19515 Wied Rd # A
Suite A
Spring, TX 77388-4590

281-350-1970
Fax: 281-350-4239 sales@technoquip.com
www.technoquip.com

Filtration systems
President: Angel Santiago
sales@technoquip.com
Number Employees: 5-9

30155 Tecnocap
1701 Wheeling Ave
Glen Dale, WV 26038

304-845-3402
Fax: 304-843-5475 800-999-2567
sales@tecnocapclosures.com
www.tecnocapclosures.com

Metal closures for glass jars and bottles for the food, beverage and cosmetics industries
President/Owner: Paolo Ghigo
Number Employees: 850+

30156 Tecogen Inc
45 1st Ave
Waltham, MA 02451-1105

781-466-6400
Fax: 781-466-6466 800-678-0550
products@tecogen.com www.tecogen.com

Natural gas engine-driven refrigeration systems
Chairperson: Angelina M. Galiteva
Chief Executive Officer: Dr. John N. Hatsopoulos
Chief Financial Officer: Bonnie Brown
Principal Engineer: Joseph Gehret
Vice President of Sales: Jeffrey Glick
Estimated Sales: $5-10 Million
Number Employees: 50-99

30157 Tectonics
62 Old Route 12 N
Westmoreland, NH 3467

603-352-8894
Fax: 603-352-8897

Plastic sheets and boxes
President: Kenneth Bergmann
Estimated Sales: Less Than $500,000
Number Employees: 1-4
Square Footage: 20000

30158 Tecumseh Products Co.
5683 Hines Dr.
Ann Arbor, MI 48108

734-585-9500
Fax: 734-352-3700 www.tecumseh.com

Refrigeration compressors, condensing units and gasoline engines, power train components and centrifugal pumps; exporter of ice making, refrigerating and cooling machinery.
CEO: Douglas Murdock
   douglas.murdock@tecumseh.com
Executive VP/CFO: Michael Baursfeld
General Counsel: Carrie Williamson
Year Founded: 1934
Estimated Sales: $854 Million
Number Employees: 5,800
Square Footage: 7176000
Other Locations:
   Tecumseh Products Co.
   Paris
Brands:
   Tecumseh

30159 Tecweigh
1201 N Birch Lake Blvd
St Paul, MN 55110-6709

651-777-4780
Fax: 651-777-5582 800-536-4880
info@tecweigh.com www.tecweigh.com

Manufacturer and exporter of volumetric and gravimetric feeders, weigh belts, belt scales, batching systems and bulk bag dischargers
CFO: John Madgett Jr
Quality Control: Steve Frank
President: John P Madgett Sr
Regional Manager: Jeff Desjardin
Estimated Sales: $10 - 20 Million
Number Employees: 20-49
Square Footage: 60000
Brands:
   Flex-Feed
   Multi-Weigh
   Tec Line
   Tecweigh

30160 Tedea-Huntliegh
20630 Plummer street
Chatsworth, CA 91311

818-701-2750
Fax: 818-701-2799 800-423-5483
info@celesco.com www.celesco.com

Load cells and indicators
President: Michael Katz
Quality Control: Tony Roblen
Marketing: Mark Armstrong
Sales: Mark Armstrong
Estimated Sales: $2.5 - 5 Million
Number Employees: 35

30161 Tee-Jay Corporation
415 Howe Ave
Suite 202
Shelton, CT 6484

203-924-4767
Fax: 203-924-2967

Manufacturer and exporter of industrial sponge rubber products
Owner: Thomas J Mc Queeney Jr
Estimated Sales: Less than $500,000
Number Employees: 1-4

30162 (HQ)Teepak LLC
1011 Warrenville Rd # 255
Lisle, IL 60532-0910

630-493-9080
Fax: 630-719-3805 800-621-0264
www.viscofan.com

Meat casings and plastic films
President/CEO: Paul Murphy
Sales Director: Joseph Wallner
Estimated Sales: $2 Million
Number Employees: 20-49

30163 Teilhaber ManufacturingCorp
2360 Industrial Ln
Broomfield, CO 80020-1612

303-466-2323
Fax: 303-466-2366 800-358-7225
www.teilhaber.com

Manufacturer and exporter of pallet racks, shelving and storage accessories
President: Norm Ooms
   nooms@teilhaber.com
VP Sales: Don Rutkowski
Estimated Sales: $.5 - 1 million
Number Employees: 50-99
Square Footage: 140000
Brands:
   C.U.E.

30164 Tek Visions
40970 Anza Rd
Temecula, CA 92592-9368

951-506-9709
Fax: 951-506-4035 800-466-8005
tekv@primenet.com www.tekvisions.com

Manufacturer, importer and exporter of touch monitors, PCs and POS systems. TechVisions specializes in fast-loading, quickly-developed and memorable Web sites that are within any budget!
Owner: Tom Cramer
VP, Sales: Nick Christie
Tech Support Engineer: Fred Meyerhofer
VP, Sales: Tom Cramer
   tom@tekvisions.com
Estimated Sales: $5-10 Million
Number Employees: 5-9

30165 Teknor Apex Co
420 S 6th Ave
City of Industry, CA 91746-3128

626-968-4656
Fax: 626-968-4040 800-556-3864
www.teknorapex.com

PVC film
VP Marketing: Wayne Small
Plant Manager: Bill Boseman
Number Employees: 100-249

30166 Teksem LLC
19 Wayne Street
Jersey City, NJ 07302-3614

646-552-5807
Fax: 503-213-9627

President: Burak Arikan
   burak@burakarikan.com
VP Marketing: Burak Arikan
Estimated Sales: $5 Million
Type of Packaging: Private Label, Bulk
Other Locations:
   Fruit Acres Farm Market
   Coloma MI

30167 Tel-Tru Manufacturing Co
408 Saint Paul St
Rochester, NY 14605-1734

585-232-1440
Fax: 585-232-3857 800-232-5335
info@teltru.com

Manufactures and distributes instrumentation products such as Bimetal Thermometers, Digital Thermometers, Temperature and Pressure Transmitters, pressure gauges, and accessory products that are designed and manufactured for worldwidedistribution to sanitary, industrial OEM, HVAC, and food service markets.
President: Andy Germanow
Cmo: Kati Chenot
   kchenot@teltru.com
Marketing Manager: Kati Chenot
Sales Manager: Yvonne O Brien
Estimated Sales: $20-50 Million
Number Employees: 100-249
Square Footage: 100000
Brands:
   Check-Temp Ii
   Tel-Tru

30168 TeleTech Label Company
113 Commerce Dr
Fort Collins, CO 80524-2764

970-221-2275
Fax: 970-221-2530 888-403-8253
www.teletech.com

Manufacturer and exporter of pressure sensitive and extended format promotional labels and weather and ultra-violet resistant tags; also, digital printing on films and hot stamping available
President: Carol Hargadine
Director Sales/Marketing: Lindsay Woods
Estimated Sales: $3 - 5 Million
Number Employees: 5-9
Brands:
   Polytech

30169 Telechem Corp
6477 Peachtree Industrial # D
Atlanta, GA 30360-2126

770-451-7117
Fax: 770-451-7758 800-637-0495
carson@telechem.com www.telechem.com

Water treatment chemicals, hand cleaners, detergents and sanitation chemicals; also, project services available

CEO/Founder: Les Washington
Director: Les Washington
Marketing: Dena Stacks
Sales Exec: Donny Mize
Estimated Sales: $2.5-5 Million
Number Employees: 10-19
Square Footage: 18000
Parent Co: Sun Mar

30170 Teledyne Benthos Inc
49 Edgerton Dr
North Falmouth, MA 02556-2826
508-563-1000
Fax: 508-563-6444 taptone@teledyne.com
www.taptone.com
Manufacturer and exporter of package inspection
equipment and leak detectors
General Manager: Francois Leroy
CFO: Franke Dunne
Director of Research: Bob Melvin
Director of QC/QA: Andrew Bonacker
Marketing Manager: Melissa Rossi
Sales/Marketing Director: Doug McGowen
Director of Production: Rick Martin
Estimated Sales: $5-10 Million
Number Employees: 100-249
Parent Co: Teledyne Technologies
Type of Packaging: Bulk

30171 Teledyne Benthos Inc
49 Edgerton Dr
North Falmouth, MA 02556-2826
508-563-1000
Fax: 508-563-6444 800-223-4044
www.benthos.com
President: Ronald Marsiglio
CMO: Doug Mcgowen
dmcgowen@benthos.com
CFO: Frank Dunne
Vice President: Richard Martin
Estimated Sales: $10,000,000 - $19,999,999
Number Employees: 100-249

30172 Teledyne ISCO
4700 Superior St
Lincoln, NE 68504-1328
402-464-0231
Fax: 402-465-3064 800-228-4373
www.isco.com
Instruments for rapid fat/oil analysis, wastewater
monitoring
Cmo: Vikas V Padhye
vpadhye@teledyne.com
VP: Vikas V Padhye
Estimated Sales: $50 Million
Number Employees: 250-499

30173 Teledyne TEKMAR
4736 Socialville Foster Rd
Mason, OH 45040-8265
513-229-7042
Fax: 513-229-7050 800-874-2004
tekmarinfo@teledyne.com
www.teledynetekmar.com
Manufacturer and exporter of equipment used for
flavors and fragrance analysis, bacterial count analy-
sis and food packaging material studies
Manager: Charlie Fulmer
Cio/Cto: Kym Silber
kym_silber@teledyne.com
CFO: Cindy Reed
Chairman of the Board: Robert Mehrabian
Director Operations: Ron Uchtman
Estimated Sales: $20-50 Million
Number Employees: 50-99
Parent Co: Rosemount
Brands:
  3100 Sample Concentrator
  7000 Ht High Temperature Headspace
  Vector Chns/O Analyzer

30174 Telesonic Packaging
805 E 13th St
Wilmington, DE 19802-5000
302-658-6945
Fax: 302-658-6946 telesonics@aol.com
www.telesoniconline.com
Manufacturer and exporter of flexible and shrink
packaging equipment, form/fill/seal and bagging
machinery and horizontal flow wrappers
Owner: Bernard Katz
telesonics@aol.com

Estimated Sales: $1 - 5,000,000
Number Employees: 5-9
Square Footage: 20000
Brands:
  Versapak

30175 (HQ)Televend
111 Croydon Rd
Baltimore, MD 21212
410-532-7818
Fax: 410-532-7818
Manufacturer and exporter of computer terminal
systems and custom application software including
supermarket incentive gaming; importer of computer
software
President: Stephen R Krause
CEO: Nat Miller
CFO: Sam Katz
VP: George Panda
R&D: SR Krause
Quality Control: Earl Davis
Marketing/Sales: Nat Miller
Contact: Sam Katz
sktv@comcast.net
Operations: RM Martin
Production: Charles Caplan
Plant Manager: Earl Davis
Purchasing: Geroge Panda
Estimated Sales: $1-3 Million
Number Employees: 50-99
Number of Brands: 12
Number of Products: 11
Square Footage: 5000
Type of Packaging: Bulk
Brands:
  Chain-Data
  Prize Box

30176 Tema Systems Inc
7806 Redsky Dr
Cincinnati, OH 45249-1632
513-792-2840
Fax: 513-489-4817 www.tema.net
Centrifuge parts, filtration and recycling equipment,
separators, clarifiers and whey processing equip-
ment; exporter of centrifuges and separators
President: Mike Mullins
changar.glori@lexisnexis.com
Technical Manager: Mike Vastola
Estimated Sales: $10-20 Million
Number Employees: 20-49
Square Footage: 30000
Parent Co: Siebtechnik
Brands:
  Conidur
  Conturbex

30177 Temco
2100 Dennison St
Oakland, CA 94606
707-746-5966
Fax: 707-746-5965 www.temcoscales.com
Manufacturer and exporter of packaging machinery
including weighers, bag openers, fillers, sealers and
case and can fillers
President: David Travis
Engineer: Rob Vincent
Equipment Sales: Jeff Reed
Plant Manager: Bob Breitenstein
Estimated Sales: Below $5 Million
Number Employees: 10
Square Footage: 36000

30178 Temkin International
213 Temkin Way
Payson, UT 84651
800-235-5263
info@temkininternational.com
www.temkininternational.com
Flexible film packaging (zipper pouches, wicketed
bags, sandwich bags) and digital printing services
Owner: Danny Temkin
Sales Manager: Eric Hopkins
Production Manager: Marcelo Menjivar
Year Founded: 1980
Number Employees: 200-500
Brands:
  Cello Wrap
  Hyper Clear
  Loft 213
  Party Bags

30179 (HQ)Temp Air Inc
3700 W Preserve Blvd
Burnsville, MN 55337-7746
952-894-3000
Fax: 952-707-5104 800-836-7432
www.temp-air.com
Chemical-free pest control, environmental air sys-
tems and air cleaners
CEO: Jim Korn
jkorn@temp-air.com
Product Manager: Mimoun Abaraw
Technical Field Representative: Warren Barich
Marketing Manager: Jessica Anderson
National Sales Manager: Tom Danley
Estimated Sales: $20 - 50 Million
Number Employees: 50-99

30180 Temp Air Inc
3700 W Preserve Blvd
Burnsville, MN 55337-7746
952-894-3000
Fax: 952-707-5104 800-836-7432
info@temp-air.com www.temp-air.com
Provide chemical pest management for milling oper-
ations and processors
Chairman of the Board: Ruth E Rupp
CEO: Jim Korn
jkorn@temp-air.com
Sales Director: Mimoum Abaraw
Number Employees: 50-99
Square Footage: 140
Parent Co: Rupp Industries

**30181 Tempco Electric Heater
Corporation**
607 N Central Ave
Wood Dale, IL 60191-1452
630-350-2252
Fax: 630-350-0232 888-268-6396
info@tempco.com www.tempco.com
Manufacturer and exporter of industrial and com-
mercial electric heating elements including air, band,
bolt and cartridge heaters; temperature sensors and
controls, including thermocouples and RTDs.
President: Fermin Adames
faadames@tempco.com
Quality Control: Tony Ocosta
Estimated Sales: $30 Million
Number Employees: 400
Square Footage: 260000

30182 Tempera/Sol
74 Hightland Cir
Suite 126
Wayland, MA 01778-1731
508-358-0090
Fax: 978-358-0099
Industrial equipment to temper, thaw, chill, crust,
freeze, or cook food
President: Ronald Snider

30183 Temple-Inland
6400 Poplar Avenue
Memphis, TN 38197
901-419-9000
internationalpaper.comm@ipaper.com
www.templeinland.com
Shipping containers
Estimated Sales: $50-100 Million
Number Employees: 100-249
Parent Co: International Paper

30184 Templock Corporation
the Vercal Building 170
Santa Barbara, CA 93130
805-962-3100
Fax: 805-962-3110 800-777-1715
sales@templock.com www.templock.com
Manufacturer and exporter of PVC heat shrinkable
tubing for tamper-evident seal, label and sleeve ap-
plications
President: William Spargur
Executive VP: Paul Montgomery
Sales Manager: Kristine Hille
Estimated Sales: $5-10 Million
Number Employees: 20-49
Square Footage: 60000
Brands:
  Templock

30185 Tenchy Machinery Corporation
P.O. Box 284
Eastpointe, MI 48015
586-773-8822
Fax: 586-445-1358 sales@techmachinery.com
Manufacturer and distributor of twistwrapping,
pillowpack and overwrap packaging machinery
Brands:
Tenchi

30186 Tenent Laboratories
6555 Quince Road
Suite 202
Memphis, TN 38119-8214
901-272-7511
Fax: 901-272-2926 800-880-1038
Analytical chemistry services for food industry, nu-
trition labeling, microbiology, lipid analysis, fatty
acid profiles, proximate chemistry, vitamin and
mineral
Estimated Sales: $1 - 5 Million
Number Employees: 100-250

30187 Tenka Flexible Packaging
5418 Schaefer Ave
Chino, CA 91710
909-628-2788
Fax: 909-902-0097 888-836-5255
info@tenkapack.com www.tenkapack.com
Coffee bags; bags for snack foods, pet foods, gourmet items, specialty foods and various other products; stand up pouches, flat pouches, foil bags and
paper bags
Sales Executive: Angie Ramirez
Contact: Dawn Aubry
dawn@tenkapack.com
Regional Manager: Corrine Douglas

30188 Tennant Co.
701 N. Lilac Dr.
P.O. Box 1452
Minneapolis, MN 55422
Fax: 763-513-2142 800-553-8033
info@tennantco.com www.tennantco.com
Clean room and sanitation equipment and supplies,
power sweeper/scrubbers, floor coatings and floor-
ing.
President/CEO/Director: Chris Killingstad
Managing Director: Junzo Tsuda
Vice President/Chief Financial Officer: Thomas
Paulson
Vice President, Global Operations: Don Westman
Vice President, Technology: Thomas Bruce
Director, Public Relations: Michael Buckley
Vice President, Operations: Steven Weeks
Year Founded: 1870
Estimated Sales: $739 Million
Number Employees: 1000-4999
Number of Brands: 4
Type of Packaging: Bulk
Brands:
Alfa
Nobles
Orbio Technologies
Tennant

30189 Tenneco Inc
500 N Field Dr
Lake Forest, IL 60045-2595
847-482-5000
Fax: 847-482-5940 800-403-3393
www.tenneco.com
Manufacturer and exporter of dual oven pressed pa-
perboard trays
Chairman: Gregg Sherrill
gsherrill@tenneco.com
CEO: Hari N Nair
CFO/EVP: Kenneth R Trammell
SVP, General Counsel & Corp. Secretary: James
Harrington
Marketing Administration: Carly Rhoads
VP Sales North America: William Read
SVP, Global HR & Administration: Gregg A Bolt
Estimated Sales: Over $1 Billion
Number Employees: 10000+
Square Footage: 1172000
Parent Co: Tenneco Packaging
Type of Packaging: Food Service
Brands:
Pressware

30190 Tenneco Packaging
777 Oakmont Lane
Westmont, IL 60559-5511
630-850-7034
Fax: 303-452-0430
Corrugated boxes and interior cushion packaging
Sales Manager: Michael Farmer
Contact: Karen Mcgill
karen_mcgill@packagingcorp.com
Estimated Sales: $1 - 5 Million
Parent Co: Tenneco Packaging

30191 Tenneco Specialty Packaging
2907 Log Cabin Drive SE
Smyrna, GA 30080-7013
404-350-1300
Fax: 404-350-1489 800-241-4402
Manufacturer and exporter of foam and barrier mod-
ified atmosphere packaging trays, disposable table-
ware, plastic utensils and foam cups
Manager: Ross Eckerman
Number Employees: 1500
Parent Co: Tenneco
Type of Packaging: Consumer, Food Service

30192 Tennessee Mills
5546 Clay County Highway
Red Boiling Springs, TN 37150-5265
615-699-2253
Fax: 615-699-2033
Wooden pallets
Owner: W White
VP Marketing/Sales: David White
Estimated Sales: $2.5-5 Million
Number Employees: 20-49

30193 Tennessee Packaging
1500 Elizabeth Lee Pkwy
PO Box 418
Loudon, TN 37774-5687
865-458-3567
Fax: 423-337-0881 800-968-6894
swinfield@tnpkg.com
www.buckeyecorrugated.com
Corrugated boxes
Division President: Scott Winfield
Cio/Cto: Terri Wall
twall@tnpkg.com
Sales Manager: Scott Barnett
Administrative Operations Manager: Terri Wall
Production Manager: Don Laurie
Estimated Sales: $10-20 Million
Number Employees: 50-99
Parent Co: BCI Companies

30194 Tennsco Corp
201 Tennsco Dr
Dickson, TN 37055-3014
615-446-8000
Fax: 615-446-7224 800-251-8184
info@tennsco.com www.tennsco.com
Manufacturer and exporter of wire shelving systems,
lockers and cabinets
CEO: Lester Speyer
VP Sales: Hal McCalla
Plant Manager: Johnnie Morris
Purchasing Manager: Mickey Self
Estimated Sales: $80 Million
Number Employees: 500-999
Square Footage: 1400000
Type of Packaging: Food Service
Brands:
Logic

30195 Tenor Controls Company
2120 S Calhoun Rd
New Berlin, WI 53151-2218
262-782-3800
Fax: 262-782-3880 800-468-4494
tenor@execpc.com
Timers, relays and controls
Estimated Sales: $1-5 Million
Number Employees: 5-9

30196 Tente Casters Inc
2266 S Park Dr
Hebron, KY 41048-9537
859-586-5558
Fax: 859-586-5859 800-783-2470
info@tente-us.com www.tente.us
NSF listed casters; importer of casters

President: Brad Hood
Vice President: Renne Beltramo
Marketing Director: Sabine Batsche
Sales Director: Aaron Romer
Production Manager: Sue Dinkel
Estimated Sales: $10 - 20 Million
Number Employees: 100-249
Square Footage: 130000
Parent Co: TENTE-ROLLEN Gmbh

30197 Tente Casters Inc
2266 S Park Dr
Hebron, KY 41048-9537
859-586-5558
Fax: 859-586-5859 800-783-2470
info@tente-us.com www.tente.us
NSF certified casters and wheels.
CEO: Brad Hood
Marketing: Sabine Batsche
Sales: Aaron Romer
Plant Manager: Sue Dinkel
Estimated Sales: $20 Million
Number Employees: 100-249
Square Footage: 65000

30198 Tente Casters Inc
2266 S Park Dr
Hebron, KY 41048-9537
859-586-5558
Fax: 859-586-5859 800-783-2470
info@tente-us.com www.tente.us
Company is a manufacturer of NSF Certified casters
and wheels.
CEO: Brad Hood
Marketing/Public Relations: Sabine Batasche
Sales Director: Aaron Romer
Plant Manager: Sue Dinkel
Estimated Sales: $20 Million
Number Employees: 100-249
Square Footage: 65000

30199 Tepromark International
249 5th Avenue SE
Osseo, MN 55369
763-273-8484
Fax: 763-273-8486 800-645-2622
www.tepromark.com
Floor mats, corner guards and railings
VP: Harold Klein
Sales Associate: Diane Mazuelerich
Manager: Alvin Templeton
Estimated Sales: $10 - 20 Million
Number Employees: 10-19

30200 Terkelsen Machine Company
Airport Road
Hyannis, MA 2601
508-775-6229
Fax: 508-778-4441
Manufacturer and exporter of baling wire for bulk
packaging
President: Russell Terkelsen
Number Employees: 4

30201 Terlet USA
520 Sharptown Rd
Swedesboro, NJ 08085
856-241-9970
Fax: 856-241-9975
Aseptic and sterile process equipment and systems.
Founder: J.W. Terlet
CEO: Philip Stibbe
Contact: Bart Brouwer
b.brouwer@jongia.com
Estimated Sales: $1-2 Million
Parent Co: Stibbe Management Group

30202 Terminix
3050 Whitestone Expy # 303
Flushing, NY 11354-1995
516-671-2411
Fax: 718-939-4161 866-319-6528
www.terminix.com
Manufacturer and exporter of waste disposal and
pest control systems
Owner: Anthony Tabacco
Chief Operating Officer: Larry Pruitt
VP, Customer Experience: Phil Barber
Chief Marketing Officer: Kevin Kovalski
Vice President of Sales: Steve Good
VP, Communications: Valerie Middleton
Vice President of Operations: Larry Pruitt

Estimated Sales: $2.5-5 Million
Number Employees: 20-49
Parent Co: Terminix Commercial Services
Brands:
Terminix

30203 Terphane Inc
2754 W Park Dr
Bloomfield, NY 14469-9385
585-657-5800
Fax: 585-657-5838 800-724-3456
mail@terphane.com www.terphane.com
Manufacturer, importer and exporter of polyester
film
General Manager: Dan Roy
Sales/Marketing Manager: Brian Ochsner
Human Resources Manager: Karen VanDerEems
Plant Manager: Chuck Mac Cary
Estimated Sales: $10-20 Million
Number Employees: 50-99
Square Footage: 320000
Brands:
Terphane

30204 Terracon Corp
1376 W Central St # 130
Suite 130
Franklin, MA 02038-7100
508-429-8737
Fax: 508-429-8737 sales@terracon-solutions.com
www.terracon-solutions.com
Wine industry plastic tanks. These tanks are also
used in water/waste treatment, biotech, pharmaceuti-
cal, plating/etching, food, medical, ceramics,
aquaculture and semiconductor markets
President: Rob Jewett
Technical Sales: Joe Bolandrino
Sales Manager: Bernie Lanaham
Contact: Joe Bolandrina
jbolandrina@tricatgroup.com
Operations Manager: Rob Jewett
Estimated Sales: $5-10 Million
Number Employees: 10-19

30205 Terriss Consolidate
807 Summerfield Ave
Asbury Park, NJ 07712-6970
732-988-2044
Fax: 732-502-0526 800-342-1611
terriss@terriss.com www.terriss.com
Laboratory equipment: testing equipment, stainless
steel fabricators, mixing tanks, tables, and sinks
Owner: Judy Bodnobich
Research and Development: Marc Epstein
Sales: Edward DellaZanna
terriss@terriss.com
Estimated Sales: $1.8 Million
Number Employees: 10-19
Square Footage: 25000

30206 Terry Manufacturing Company
PO Box 130041
Birmingham, AL 35213-0041
205-250-0062
Fax: 334-863-8835
Manufacturer and exporter of uniforms
President: Roy Terry
Estimated Sales: $1-2.5 Million
Number Employees: 1-4
Type of Packaging: Food Service

30207 Tesa Tape Inc
5825 Carnegie Blvd
Charlotte, NC 28209-4633
704-554-0707
Fax: 704-553-5677 800-429-8273
customercare@tesatape.com www.tesatape.com
Manufacturer and exporter of pressure sensitive ad-
hesive tape
CEO: Norman Goldberg
CFO: Jorg Diesfeld
Estimated Sales: $50,000,000 - $99,999,999
Number Employees: 50-99
Parent Co: tesa AG
Type of Packaging: Consumer, Food Service, Pri-
vate Label, Bulk
Brands:
Nopi
Tesa
Tuck

30208 Testing Machines Inc
40 Mccullough Dr
New Castle, DE 19720-2066
302-613-5619
Fax: 302-613-5019 800-678-3221
info@testingmachines.com
www.testingmachines.com
Manufacturer and exporter of crush, permeation, hu-
midity, thickness and printability testing machinery
CEO: John Sullivan
Vice President: Richard Young
Marketing Director: Dave Muchorski
Sales Director: Richard Young
Estimated Sales: $10-20,000,000
Number Employees: 100-249
Brands:
Lab Master

30209 Testo
P.O. Box 1606
Berlin, MA 21811
410-777-8555
Fax: 973-579-3222 800-227-0729
info@testo.com www.ita.cc
Digital thermometers, data loggers, portable instru-
ments for humidity, air velocity and water quality
Manager: Melissa Curro
VP: Andrew Kuczkuda
Quality Control: Cate Mariott
Marketing Manager: Lori Lyonn
Estimated Sales: Below $5 Million
Number Employees: 10-19

30210 (HQ)Tetra Pak
Communications
3300 Airport Rd
Denton, TX 76207
940-380-4630
www.tetrapak.com
Components and systems for processing, packaging
and distribution of liquid foods; serving the dairy
and beverage industries.
President & CEO: Adolfo Orive
EVP, Supply Chain Operations: Eric Baudier
SVP, Corporate Communications: Nicholas Bloch
SVP, Finance: Bruce Burrows
EVP, Processing Solutions & Equipment: Ola
Elmqvist
EVP, Services: Roberto Franchitti
Cluster VP, Americas: Tatiana Liceti
SVP, Legal Affairs & General Counsel: Pal Lunning
SVP, Human Resources: Phil Read
Year Founded: 1943
Estimated Sales: $11.5 Billion
Number Employees: 24,800
Brands:
Tetra Brik Aseptic
Tetra Rex

30211 Tetra Pak
600 Bunker Ct
Vernon Hills, IL 60061
847-955-6000
Fax: 847-955-6500 www.tetrapak.com
Components and systems for processing, packaging
and distribution of liquid foods; serving the dairy
and beverage industries.
Parent Co: Tetra Laval Group

30212 Tetra Pak
12255 Ensign Avenue N
Champlin, MN 55316
763-421-2721
www.tetrapak.com
Components and systems for processing, packaging
and distribution of liquid foods; serving the dairy
and beverage industries.
Type of Packaging: Consumer, Food Service, Pri-
vate Label
Brands:
Tetra Alblend
Tetra Albrix
Tetra Alcarb Spark
Tetra Alcip
Tetra Alcross
Tetra Aldose
Tetra Alvac
Tetra Alvap
Tetra Alwin
Tetra Brik Aseptic
Tetra Centri
Tetra Classic
Tetra Fino
Tetra Plantcare
Tetra Plantmaster
Tetra Plantopt
Tetra Plex
Tetra Prisma
Tetra Rex
Tetra Spiraflo
Tetra Tebel
Tetra Therm
Tetra Top
Tetra Wedge
Treta Alex
Treta Alfast
Treta Almix
Treta Alrox
Treta Alsafe
Treta Alscreen

30213 Tetra Pak
423 Arlington Ave
Fond Du Lac, WI 54935
www.tetrapak.com
Components and systems for processing, packaging
and distribution of liquid foods; serving the dairy
and beverage industries.

30214 Tew Manufacturing Corp
470 Whitney Rd
PO Box 87
Penfield, NY 14526-2326
585-586-6120
Fax: 585-586-6083 800-380-5839
info@tewmfg.com www.tewmfg.com
Manufacturer and exporter of fruit and vegetable
cleaning equipment
Owner: William H Tew
tewmfg@aol.com
Estimated Sales: Less Than $500,000
Number Employees: 1-4
Square Footage: 16000

30215 Texas Baket Company
100 Myrtle Drive
Jacksonville, TX 75766-1110
903-586-8014
Fax: 903-586-0988 800-657-2200
sales@texasbasket.com www.texasbasket.com
Wooden baskets, display racks and hand-painted
baskets
President: Mardin Swanson
CFO and R&D: Troy Parker
Quality Control: David Habberle
Estimated Sales: Below $5 Million
Number Employees: 100-249

30216 Texas Corn Roasters
3300 X A Meyer Rd
Granbury, TX 76049-2306
817-573-7313
Fax: 817-561-5006 800-772-4345
cornroaster@live.com
Mobile corn roasters and concession trailers
Owner: Ken O'Keefe
Number Employees: 1-4

30217 Texas Hill Country Barbacue
919 State Highway 46 E
Boerne, TX 78006-5758
830-336-2858
Fax: 830-336-2991 866-302-7289
Barbacued foods and smoked meats, product line of
which includes smoked beef brisket, smoked sausage, chopped beef BBQ with sauce, pulled pork
with sauce, whole smoked chicken, whole smoked
turkey, spiral cut ham and smoked BBQsauce.
CEO: Jesse Tindall
Sales & Marketing: Hal McCall
Type of Packaging: Food Service

30218 Texas Neon Advertising Inc
245 W Josephine St
San Antonio, TX 78212-4153
210-734-6694
Fax: 210-734-6697
Indoor and outdoor signs including neon
President: George Ryan
gryan@texasneonadv.com
Estimated Sales: $1 - 2.5 Million
Number Employees: 10-19

30219 (HQ)Texas Refinery Corp
840 N Main St
Fort Worth, TX 76164-9486

817-332-1161
Fax: 817-332-6110 trc711@texasrefinery.com
www.texasrefinery.com
Food machinery lubricants
President: Jerry Hopkins
CEO: A M Pate III
CFO: Chuck Adamson
VP: Jim Peel
R&D: Seth Davis
Sales: Dennis Parks
Purchasing: Barbara Main
Estimated Sales: $20-50 Million
Number Employees: 50-99

30220 Texas Spice Co
2709 Sam Bass Rd
Round Rock, TX 78681-1811

512-255-8816
Fax: 512-255-4189 800-880-8007
contact@texas-spice.net www.texas-spice.net
Wholesale and retail custom blending, spices, sea-
soning blends, bases, extracts, flavors, coffee & tea
Owner: Beckie Forsyth
Contact: Jason Spangler
spangler@texas-spice.net
Estimated Sales: Less Than $500,000
Number Employees: 1-4
Type of Packaging: Food Service
Brands:
Texas Spice

30221 Texican Specialty Products
10900 Brittmoore Park Dr Ste H
Houston, TX 77041

713-896-9924
Fax: 713-896-9925 800-869-5918
www.texicanspecialty.com
Tostada dispensers and warming cabinets
President: Donald J Spilger
Vice President: V Spilger
Contact: Jb Spilger
generalsales@texicanspecialty.com
Estimated Sales: $500,000
Number Employees: 1-4
Number of Brands: 1
Number of Products: 2
Square Footage: 7600

30222 Texpak Inc
892 Route 73 N
Suite 1
Marlton, NJ 08053-1228

856-988-5533
Fax: 856-988-5524 texpak@bellatlantic.net
Roasters (machines), bin silo systems and storage,
blending and mixing equipment (coffee), computer
systems, grinders
Estimated Sales: $1 - 5 Million

30223 Textile Buff & Wheel
511 Medford St # 1
Charlestown, MA 02129-1495

617-241-8100
Fax: 617-241-7280 www.textilebuff.com
Manufacturer and exporter of wiping cloths, mill
remnants, cheesecloths and cotton gloves
Owner: Jerold Wise
Partner: Andrew Wise
Estimated Sales: $5-10 Million
Number Employees: 20-49
Square Footage: 200000

30224 Textile Products Company
2512-2520 W Woodland Drive
Anaheim, CA 92801-2636

714-761-0401
Fax: 714-761-2928
Manufacturer and exporter of cheesecloth wiping
rags and disposable rags
Marketing Director: Pearl Seratelli
Estimated Sales: $1 - 5 Million
Parent Co: Textile Products

30225 Texture Technologies Corporation
18 Fairview Rd
Scarsdale, NY 10583

914-472-0531
Fax: 914-472-0532
marcj@texturetechnologies.com
www.texturetechnologies.com
Manufacturer, importer and exporter of measure-
ment instrumentation and software for testing food
texture; also, bloom gel testers
President: Boine Johnson
CEO: Marc Johnson
CFO: Sue Perko
Quality Control: Joseph Piperis
Contact: James Fabry
jimf@texturetechnologies.com
Estimated Sales: $5 Million
Brands:
Ta-Xt2
Texture Expert For Windows

30226 Thamesville Metal Products Ltd
2 London Road
Thamesville, ON N0P 2K0
Canada

519-692-3963
Fax: 519-692-5213 bulldogsteelwool@kent.net
www.bulldogsteelwool.ca
Steel wool scouring pads
President: Robert Schieman
CFO: Greg Schieman
Estimated Sales: Below $5 Million
Number Employees: 10
Square Footage: 240000
Brands:
Bulldog

30227 Tharo Systems Inc
2866 Nationwide Pkwy
PO Box 798
Brunswick, OH 44212-2362

330-273-4408
Fax: 330-225-0099 800-878-6833
info@easylabel.fr www.tharo.com
Manufacturer and exporter of computer software for
custom designing and printing bar code, RFID and
food ingredient labels, printers and printer/applica-
tors, ribbons, labels, label rewinds, unwinds, and
dispensers
President: Michelle Lyngoe
m_lyngoe@aimforsafety.com
VP Marketing: Lauren Shaarda
Sales Director: James Danko
Operations: Randy Thatcher
Estimated Sales: $5 - 10 Million
Number Employees: 10-19
Number of Brands: 1000
Number of Products: 4
Brands:
Cab Produkttechnik
Datamax Corporation
Dispensa-Matic
Easylabel
Sony Chemicals
Tharo

30228 the Canvas Exchange Inc
2324 Dennison Avenue
Cleveland, OH 44109

216-749-2233
Fax: 216-749-0987 ceiawning@sbcglobal.net
www.ceiawning.com
Manufacturer of commercial awnings.
President: Hank Proctor
Contact: Kevin Potoczak
kevin@ceiawning.net
Account Rep.: Kevin Potoczak
Year Founded: 1984
Estimated Sales: $500,000-$1 Million
Number Employees: 5-9

30229 the Carriage Works
1877 Mallard Ln
Klamath Falls, OR 97601-5522

541-882-0700
Fax: 541-882-9661 sales@carriageworks.com
www.carriageworks.com
Manufacturer, importer and exporter of food service
and retail merchandising carts, in-line concepts, ki-
osks and machines including espresso, hot dog, ice
cream and beverage
President & CEO: Brian Dunham
VP, Sales & Marketing: Lori Butler
Estimated Sales: $5 - 10 Million
Number Employees: 20-49

30230 the Consumer Goods Forum
8455 Colesville Rd # 705
Silver Spring, MD 20910

301-563-3383
Fax: 301-563-3386
washington@theconsumergoodsforum.com
www.theconsumergoodsforum.com/index.aspx
Bringing together consumer goods manufacturers
and retailers for efficiency and positve change.
Co-Chairman: Dick Boer
Co-Chairman: Paul Bulcke
Contact: Thomas Bailey
t.bailey@theconsumergoodsforum.com
Number Employees: 20-49

30231 the Good Food Institute
1380 Monroe St. NW
Ste. 229
Washington, DC 20010

866-849-4457
www.gfi.org
Offers marketing, design, legal, business, and media
consultations.
Co-Founder & Executive Director: Bruce Friedrich
Director of Finance & General Counsel: Sarah
David
Director of Development: Susan Halteman
Director of Communications: Annie Gull *Year
Founded:* 2015

30232 the Lobster Place
75 Ninth Avenue
Chelsea Market
New York, NY 10011

212-255-5672
info@lobsterplace.com
lobsterplace.com
Lobster, seafood
President: Brendan Hayes
CEO: Ian MacGregor
Lead Sales Executive: Joe Cooper
Contact: Renee Alevras
ralevras@lobsterplace.com
Operations Manager: Christian Quintana
Purchasing Manager: Mark Grobman

30233 the National Provisioner
155 N. Pfingsten Rd.
Suite 205
Deerfield, IL 60015

847-763-9534
Fax: 847-763-9538 www.provisioneronline.com
Manufacturer and exporter of material handling
products including conveyors and laser guided auto-
mated vehicle systems
Owner: Elmer Hartford
COO: Kevin Donahue
Engineer Manager: Todd Frandsen
Vice President of Services: Tom Egan
Sales Manager: Diana Rotman
Contact: Andy Hanacek
hanaceka@bnpmedia.com
Number Employees: 100-249
Square Footage: 300000
Brands:
Pulverlaser

30234 the Procter & Gamble Company
2 P&G Plaza
Cincinnati, OH 45202

513-983-1100
Fax: 513-983-9369 800-692-0132
us.pg.com
Baby diapers, fabric care, feminine products, sham-
poos, paper towels, toilet paper, tissues, condition-
ers, dishwashing detergent, home cleaning products,
razors, shaving gels, supplements, pregnancy tests,
cough syrup, and more.
Executive Chairman: David Taylor
President/CEO: Jon Moeller
CFO: Andre Schulten
COO: Shailesh Jejurikar
Estimated Sales: $80.2 Billion
Number Employees: 97,000
Number of Brands: 70
Type of Packaging: Consumer
Brands:
ARC
Align
All Good
Always
Always Discreet
Aria
Aussie

Being Girl
Bodewell
Bounce
Bounty
Braun
Burt's Bees
Cascade
Charlie Banana
Charmin
Cresr
Dawn
DermaGeek
Downy
Dreft
EC30
EraÆ
Fairy
Febreze
Fixodent
Gain
Gillette
Gillette Baldly
Gleem-DTC
Good Skin MD
Hair Biology
HairFood
Head & Shoulders
Herbal Essences
HomeMadeSimple
Ivory
Joy
Just
L.
LumibyPampers
Luvs
Metamucil
Microban 24
Mr Clean
MyBlackIsBeautiful
NBD
NOU
Native
Nervive
Ninjamas
Olay
Old Spice
Oral B
Pampers
Pantene
Pepto-Bismol
Puffs
SK-II
Scope
Secret
Spring & Vine
Swiffer
Tampax
The Art of Shaving
Theory
Tide
The Art of Shaving
Theory
Tide
Venus
kiwi
thisisl

30235 the Pub Brewing Company
EAST COAST
185 Route 17 North
Mahwah, NJ 07430

201-512-0387
Fax: 201-512-1459 www.pubbrewing.com
President: Erwin Eibert
Estimated Sales: $5 - 10 Million
Number Employees: 10-19

30236 the Pub Brewing Company
WEST COAST
3600 C Standish Avenue
Santa Rosa, CA 95407

Fax: 201-512-1459 www.pubbrewing.com
President: Erwin Eibert
Estimated Sales: $5 - 10 Million
Number Employees: 10-19

30237 the Rubin Family of Wines
5220 Ross Rd
Sebastopol, CA 95472-2158

707-887-8130
Fax: 707-887-8160
wine@rubinfamilyofwines.com
rubinfamilyofwines.com
Wines
Founder: Ron Rubin
Winemaker: Joe Freeman
Estimated Sales: Under $500,000
Number Employees: 1-4
Type of Packaging: Private Label
Brands:
River Road Vineyards

30238 the Tombras Group
830 Concord Street
Knoxville, TN 37919

865-524-5376
Fax: 865-524-5667 jwelsch@tombras.com
www.tombras.com
President: Charles P Tombras Jr
Estimated Sales: $5 - 10 Million
Number Employees: 100+

30239 Theimeg
58 W Shenango St
Sharpsville, PA 16150-1154

724-962-3571
Fax: 724-962-4310 www.cattron.com
Remote control systems for cranes, locomotives and
other industrial machinery
President: John Paul
Estimated Sales: $10 - 15 Million
Number Employees: 10-19
Parent Co: Theimeg

30240 Theingredienthouse
120 Applecross Rd # 2
2nd Fl
Pinehurst, NC 28374-8520

910-693-0037
Fax: 877-542-4844 info@theingredienthouse.com
www.theingredienthouse.com
Supplier of food ingredients to food manufacturers
such as high intensity sweeteners, soluble fibers, hy-
drocolloids, agave syrup, polyols, insoluble fibers,
sugar alcohols, cooling compounds
President, COO: Rudi Van
CEO: Graham Hall
graham.hall@theingredienthouse.com
Vice President Quality Assurance: Jeff Lewis
VP Marketing: Peter Brown
VP Sales: Janet Timko
Customer Service Director: Ann Hall
VP Operations: Kevin Lovett
Estimated Sales: $300 Thousand
Number Employees: 5-9

30241 (HQ)Theochem Laboratories Inc
7373 Rowlett Park Dr
Tampa, FL 33610-1101

813-237-6463
Fax: 813-237-2059 800-237-2591
www.theochem.com
Manufacturer and exporter of chemical cleaners and
inorganic cleaning compounds
COO and President: John Theofilos
Director Operations: Lenny Wydotis
Estimated Sales: $20-50 Million
Number Employees: 5-9
Square Footage: 250000
Brands:
Solutions For a Cleaner World

30242 Theos Foods
119 N Duke St
Hummelstown, PA 17036-1310

717-566-5622
Fax: 717-566-5592 800-755-8436
Cost effective bulk packaged items such as Theo's
Stromboli, pre-baked sandwiches also available
President and CFO: Ted Atanasoff
theosfoods@verizon.net
Manager: Barry Broadwater
Estimated Sales: $5 - 10 Million
Number Employees: 20-49

30243 Therm L Tec Building Systems
15115 Chestnut St
Basehor, KS 66007-9207

913-728-2662
Fax: 913-724-1446 www.thermltec.com

Insulated commercial cold storage panels, partitions,
doors and liners
Sales: Dennis Bixby
Contact: Joshua Cole
jcole@thermltec.com
Estimated Sales: $5-10 Million
Number Employees: 1-4
Square Footage: 300000
Brands:
Therm-L-Bond

30244 Therm-Tec Inc
20525 SW Cipole Rd
Sherwood, OR 97140-8339

503-625-7575
Fax: 503-625-6161 800-292-9163
www.thermtec.com
Manufacturer and exporter of solid, animal and hu-
man crematories, and hospital waste incinerators;
also air pollution control equipment
Owner: Dean Robbins
thermtec@earthlink.net
Estimated Sales: Below $5 Million
Number Employees: 10-19
Square Footage: 160000
Brands:
Therm-Tec

30245 Therma Kleen
10212 S Mandel St # A
Plainfield, IL 60585-5374

630-820-6700
Fax: 630-305-8696 800-999-3120
steamtk@aol.com www.therma-kleen.com
Manufacturer and exporter of steam cleaners and
pressure washers
President: Andy Heller
VP: Linda Heller
IT: Linda Hubbell
steamtk@aol.com
Estimated Sales: $500,000-$1 Million
Number Employees: 5-9
Square Footage: 5600
Brands:
Therma-Kleen

30246 Thermaco Inc
646 Greensboro St
PO Box 2548
Asheboro, NC 27203-4739

336-629-4651
Fax: 336-626-5739 800-633-4204
info@thermaco.com www.thermaco.com
Manufacturer and exporter of pre-treatments and au-
tomatic solid and grease/oil removal units for restau-
rants and food processing plants
President: William Batten
info@thermaco.com
Estimated Sales: $1-2.5 Million
Number Employees: 10-19
Square Footage: 12000
Brands:
Big Dipper
Big Flipper
Superceptor

30247 Thermafreeze
776 Lakeside Drive
Mobile, AL 36693-5114

251-666-2011
Fax: 251-666-5660
Solutions for the safe shipment of temperature-criti-
cal media
President: J Murray
Contact: Joseph Murray
joseph.murray@thermafreeze.com

30248 Thermal Bags By Ingrid Inc
131 Sola Dr
Gilberts, IL 60136-9748

847-836-4400
Fax: 847-836-4408 800-622-5560
Mary@ThermalBags.com www.thermalbags.com
Manufacturer and exporter of thermal food bags,
racks, thermal hoods, insulated carrying bags, pizza
delivery pouches and catering bags. Also light-
weight insulated bags for the carry-out market and
advertising specialites
Inventor & CEO: Ingrid Kosar
ingrid@thermalbags.com
Marketing Director: Fred Kosar
Estimated Sales: $2.5-5 Million
Number Employees: 5-9
Type of Packaging: Food Service

Brands:
Food Carriers
Thermal Bags By Ingrid

30249 Thermal Engineering Corp
2741 the Blvd
Columbia, SC 29209-3527

803-783-0750
Fax: 803-783-0756 800-331-0097
www.tecinfrared.com
Under-fired infrared gas charbroilers and griddles
for the consumer and food service industry
President: Bill Best
CEO: W H Best
wh.best@tecinfrared.com
CFO: Tony Stihom
Sales/Marketing Executive: Johnny Johnson
Sales Manager: Jack Whitten
Public Relations: Renee Pecks
Estimated Sales: $20-50 Million
Number Employees: 100-249
Parent Co: Thermal Engineering Corporation
Type of Packaging: Food Service

30250 Thermal Package TestingLaboratory
41 Pine Street
Rockaway, NJ 07866-3139

973-627-4405
Fax: 973-627-5355 800-432-5909
info@package-testing.com
www.package-testing.com
Testing: ASTM, ISTA, Unidot, vibration, drop;
inafine impact, compression, environmental cham-
bers, pallet loads, supersacks, drums
President: David Dixon
Estimated Sales: $.5 - 1 million
Number Employees: 5-9

30251 Thermal Technologies
630 Park Way
Broomall, PA 19008-4209

610-353-8887
Fax: 610-353-8663
Produce repening systems for the fruit industry. Also
design, engineering and construction of cold rooms
Estimated Sales: $.5 - 1 million
Number Employees: 1-4

30252 Thermaline Inc
1531 14th St NW # 1
Auburn, WA 98001-3518

253-833-7118
Fax: 253-833-7168 800-767-6720
info@thermaline.com www.thermaline.com
Plate heat exchangers, tubular heat exchangers, skid
mounted pasteurization systems, boiler packages and
CIP systems
President: Jerry Sanders
jsanders@thermaline.com
Estimated Sales: $1-2.5 Million
Number Employees: 5-9

30253 Thermalogic Corp
22 Kane Industrial Dr
Hudson, MA 01749-2922

978-562-5974
Fax: 978-562-6753 sales@thlogic.com
www.thermalogic.com
Temperature control systems including analog, digi-
tal indicating and microprocessor based
Owner: Lou Grein
CEO: John Dubois
john@thlogic.com
Estimated Sales: $20 - 50 Million
Number Employees: 20-49

30254 Thermedics Detection
220 Mill Road
Suite 1
Chelmsford, MA 01824-4127

978-251-2002
Fax: 978-251-2010 888-846-7226
Sorting systems, soft rejectors, moisture analysis and
inspection equipment including fill level, net content, package integrity, foreign particle and chemical

Chairman, President, Chief Executive Off: James
Hambrick
Corporate Vice President of Human Resour: Andrew
Panega
Corporate Vice President of Research and: Robert
Graf
Director Sales (North America): Ron Pokraka
Corporate Vice President of Operations: Mike
Vaughn
Production Manager: George McNeil
Parent Co: Thermedics

30255 Thermex Thermatron
10501 Bunsen Way # 102
Suite 102
Louisville, KY 40299-2563

502-493-1299
Fax: 502-493-4013
sales@thermex-thermatron.com
www.thermex-thermatron.com
Industrial microwave equipment and RF heat sealing
equipment.
Owner: Ray Lund
VP Marketing: John Hokanson
Sales Director: Robert Dachert
ray@thermex-thermatron.com
Sales: Mark Isgrigg
Operations Manager: Zoly Bogdan
Estimated Sales: $7 Million
Number Employees: 20-49
Number of Brands: 2
Square Footage: 144000
Brands:
Thermatron
Thermex

30256 Thermo BLH
75 Shawmut Rd
Canton, MA 02021-1408

781-821-2000
Fax: 781-828-1451 sales@blh.com
www.blh.com
Weighing system, scales, and web tension measure-
ment systems
President: Robert Murphy
CEO: Bob Murphy
Vice President: Rainer Halmberg
Quality Control: Jay Bailey
Marketing Director: Art Koehler
Estimated Sales: $16 Million
Number Employees: 1-4
Parent Co: Thermo Electron

30257 Thermo Detection
27 Forge Pkwy
Franklin, MA 02038-3135

508-520-0430
Fax: 508-520-1732 866-269-0070
www.thermo.
Manufacturer and exporter of moisture and other
consistent process analyzers and monitors
Administrator: Michael Nemergut
VP Sales/Marketing: Terry Rose
National Sales Manager: Don Piatt
Inside Sales: Jill Holman
Number Employees: 50-99
Square Footage: 80000
Parent Co: Thermedics Detection
Brands:
Micro Lab
Micro Quad
Quadra Beam 6600

30258 Thermo Fisher Scientific
168 Third Ave
Waltham, MA 02451

781-622-1000
800-678-5599
www.thermofisher.com
Laboratory equipment including quality control sup-
plies/machinery.
President & CEO: Marc Casper
SVP & General Counsel: Michael Boxer
SVP & Chief Financial Officer: Stephen Williamson
EVP & Chief Operating Officer: Mark Stevenson
SVP/President, Customer Channels: Gregory
Herrema
SVP/President, Specialty Diagnostics: Gianluca
Pettiti
SVP/President, Regions: Syed Jafry
SVP, Integrations: Shiraz Ladiwala
Estimated Sales: $25 Billion
Number Employees: 75,000

Brands:
APPLIED BIOSYSTEMS
FISHER SCIENTIFIC
INVITROGEN
THERMO SCIENTIFIC
UNITY LAB SERVICES

30259 Thermo Instruments
84 Horseblock Rd
Unit D
Yaphank, NY 11980

631-924-0880
Fax: 631-924-0923
Hydrometers and thermometers
President: Michael Charzuk
Estimated Sales: $500,000-$1 Million
Number Employees: 1-4
Brands:
Thermo

30260 Thermo Jarrell Ash Corporation
27 Forge Pkwy
Franklin, MA 02038-3135

508-520-1880
Fax: 508-520-1732 www.thermo.com
Instruments used to analyze water, oil and metal
content
General Manager: Mark Whiteman
Contact: John Bowman
john.bowman@thermo.com
Number Employees: 400

30261 Thermo King Corp
314 W 90th St
Bloomington, MN 55420-3693

952-887-2200
Fax: 952-887-2615 888-887-2202
bridgeton_contact_center@irco.com
www.thermoking.com
Freezers, heaters, refrigeration equipment, tempera-
ture indicators and controllers, and refrigeration
trucks
President: Donald Ashton
donald_ashton@thermoking.com
VP: John Cobb
Number Employees: 10000+
Parent Co: Westinghouse

30262 Thermo Pac LLC
1609 Stone Ridge Dr
Stone Mountain, GA 30083-1109

770-934-3200
www.thermopacllc.com
Wide range of thin-to-thick viscosity liquids includ-
ing processed cheese sauces, tomato-based sauces
and other savory or sweet sauces. Also peanut but-
ter, in pouches, single serve cups and dried powder
sticks.
Manager: Dave Barnes
Controller/Director: Leticia Simbach
IS Manager: Glenn Corbin
Administrative Assistant: Jean Williams
Plant Manager: John Stevens
Purchasing Manager: Buddy Wilson
Estimated Sales: $12.4 Million
Number Employees: 100-249
Square Footage: 120000
Parent Co: AmeriQual Group LLC
Type of Packaging: Consumer, Food Service, Pri-
vate Label, Bulk

30263 Thermo Service
3901 Pipestone Rd
Dallas, TX 75212-6017

214-631-0307
Fax: 214-631-0566 800-635-5559
www.thermoserv.com
Molded plastic servingware and insulated beverage
ware and speciality cups and mugs
President: Joe Betras
CEO: Jay Rigby
Marketing Director: Peggy Hock
National Sales Director: Jon Hock
COO: Tom Morris
Purchasing: Beverly Robbins
Estimated Sales: $40 Million
Number Employees: 100-249
Parent Co: New Thermo Serv, Ltd.

30264 Thermo Wisconsin
PO Box 5030
De Pere, WI 54115-5030

920-766-7200
Fax: 920-766-5211 www.thermo.com

Stainless steel tanks and vessels
Manager Custom Fabrication: Jeff Loker
Designer: Scott Brauer
Estimated Sales: Less than $500,000
Number Employees: 1-4
Square Footage: 560000
Parent Co: Thermo Electron Corporation

30265 Thermo-KOOL/Mid-South Ind Inc
723 E 21st St
Laurel, MS 39440-2457

601-649-4600
Fax: 601-649-0558 sales@thermokool.com
www.thermokool.com
Manufacturer and exporter of self-contained, remote, quick connect and walk-in refrigeration equipment
President: Randolph McLaughlin
CEO: Patricia McLaughlin
VP: Randplph McLaughlin
Sales: Gary Crocker
Plant Manager: Duane Eldridge
Purchasing: Lee Thames
Estimated Sales: $20-50 Million
Number Employees: 100-249
Square Footage: 123000
Brands:
    Thermo-Kool

30266 ThermoWorks
1762 W 20 S
Suite 100
Lindon, UT 84042

801-756-7705
Fax: 801-756-8948 800-393-6434
www.thermoworks.com
President: Randy Owen
Contact: Tricia Buss
    tricia.buss@thermoworks.com
Estimated Sales: Below $5 Million
Number Employees: 5-9

30267 Thermodynamics
6780 Brighton Blvd
Commerce City, CO 80022

Fax: 918-251-2826 800-627-9037
www.okpallets.com
Reusable plastic pallets, bins, boxes, containers and trays including standard and custom; exporter of plastic pallets
CEO: Sheri Orlowitz
General Manager: Robert Lux
Production Manager: Shawn Harley
Plant Manager: Robert Luxtwood
Purchasing Manager: Ray Carr
Estimated Sales: $5 - 10 Million
Number Employees: 20-49
Square Footage: 70000
Parent Co: Shan Industries

30268 Thermodyne Foodservice Prods
4418 New Haven Ave
Fort Wayne, IN 46803-1650

260-428-2535
Fax: 260-428-2533 800-526-9182
www.tdyne.com
Manufacturer and exporter of conduction ovens
President: Vincent Tippmann Sr
General Manager: Sue Brown
IT: Dave Schenkel
    dave.schenkel@polarking.com
Number Employees: 1-4
Square Footage: 600000
Parent Co: Polar King International

30269 Thermodyne International LTD
1841 S Business Pkwy
Ontario, CA 91761-8537

909-923-9945
Fax: 909-923-7505 sales@thermodyne.com
www.thermodyne.com
Manufacturer and exporter of reusable plastic containers and instrument shipping and carrying cases; also, custom vacuum forming services available
President: Gary Ackerman
    gackerman@thermodyne-online.com
Sr. VP: Gary Ackerman
Chairman of the Board: Gary S Ackerman
Estimated Sales: $10 - 20 Million
Number Employees: 50-99

Brands:
    Rack-Pack
    Shok-Stop

30270 Thermoil Corporation
7 Franklin Avenue
Brooklyn, NY 11211-7801

718-855-0544
Fax: 718-643-6691
Manufacturer and exporter of industrial oils and greases
Estimated Sales: $10-20 Million
Number Employees: 10-19

30271 Thermolok Packaging Systems
5050 Prince George Drive
Prince George, VA 23875-2623

452-001- 001
Fax: 804-452-2011 thermolok7@aol.com
www.strapmc.com
Manufacturers of plastic strapping equipment, stretch film machines and tape machines
Estimated Sales: $1-2.5 Million
Number Employees: 1-4

30272 Thermomass
1000 Technology Dr
PO Box 950
Boone, IA 50036-4457

515-433-6088
Fax: 515-433-6088 800-232-1748
www.thermomass.com
Composite sandwich walls used for cold or frozen storage units, also wineries
President: Tom Stecker
R&D: Rex Donahey
Contact: Rich Brownrigg
    rbrownrigg@thermomass.com
Estimated Sales: $5 - 10 Million
Number Employees: 10-19

30273 Thermoquest
3661 Interstate Park Road N
Suite 100
Riviera Beach, FL 33404-5906

561-383-2000
Fax: 561-383-2043 888-383-2025
www.palmbeachschools.org
Manufacturer and exporter of stainless steel pots and pans
General Manager: Ralph Kearney
Number Employees: 50
Parent Co: Floaire
Type of Packaging: Food Service
Brands:
    Floware

30274 Thermos Company
475 N Martingale Road
Suite 1100
Schaumburg, IL 60173

847-439-7821
Fax: 847-593-5570 800-243-0745
customer@grilllovers.com www.thermos.com
Vacuum insulated bottles and carafes, stainless steel thermal cookware, ice buckets, coffee presses and airpot coffee dispensers
Chairman: Shouji Toida
Executive VP: Rick Dias
Director Special Marketing Division: Nedda Glenn
Contact: Praveen Amudala
    amudala@thermos.com
Estimated Sales: $1-2,500,000
Number Employees: 500-999
Brands:
    Thermos

30275 Thermoseal
1310 Highway 287 S
Suite 105
Mansfield, TX 76063-5705

817-453-0813
Fax: 817-453-0594
Sealers
President: Shawn Kennedy

30276 Theta Sciences
11835 Carmel Mountain Road
Suite 1304
San Diego, CA 92128-4609

760-745-3311
Fax: 760-745-5519

Manufacturer, importer and exporter of electronic instruments specializing in food process control and personnel hazard monitoring
President: Hal Buscher
VP: Bob LeClair
VP: Dave Furuno
Estimated Sales: $1-2.5 Million
Number Employees: 9
Square Footage: 19200
Brands:
    Theta Sciences

30277 Thiel Cheese & Ingredients
N7630 County Hwy BB
Attn: Kathy Pitzen
Hilbert, WI 54129

920-989-1440
Fax: 920-989-1288 www.thielcheese.com
Manufacturer and custom formulator of processed cheeses that are used primarily as ingredients in other food products
President: Steven Thiel
Sales: Kathy Pitzen
Number Employees: 50-99
Type of Packaging: Consumer, Food Service, Private Label, Bulk
Brands:
    Thiel

30278 Thiele Engineering Company
810 Industrial Park Boulevard
Fergus Falls, MN 56537

218-739-3321
Fax: 218-739-9370 info@swfcompanies.com
www.thieletech.com
Manufacturer and exporter of cartoners and case packers
VP Sales: Wayne Slaton
Number Employees: 260
Square Footage: 173900
Parent Co: Barry-Wehmiller Company

30279 Thiele Technologies Inc
315 27th Ave NE
Minneapolis, MN 55418-2715

612-782-1200
Fax: 612-782-1203 www.thieletech.com
Packaging and palletizing equipment
CEO: Laurence P Smith
    laurence.smith@thieletech.com
Sales/Marketing Manager: Todd Sandell
Estimated Sales: $20-50 Million
Number Employees: 500-999

30280 Thiele Technologies Inc
315 27th Ave NE
Minneapolis, MN 55418-2715

612-782-1200
Fax: 612-782-1203 800-542-3647
www.thieletech.com
Conveying, insulation converting and bagging equipment, conveyors
CEO: Laurence P Smith
    laurence.smith@thieletech.com
CFO: Keith Skerrett
R&D: Bob Odom
Marketing/Sales Manager: Todd Sandell
Estimated Sales: $20 - 30 Million
Number Employees: 500-999

30281 Thiele Technologies-Reedley
1949 E Manning Ave
Reedley, CA 93654-9462

559-638-8484
Fax: 559-638-7478 800-344-8951
Sales@ThieleTech.com www.thieletech.com
Manufacturer and exporter of corrugated box forming and sealing machinery, case erectors, automatic case packers, case openers/positioners, cartoners and robotics automation.
President: Larry Smith
VP: Ed Suarez
Sales Director: Craig Friesen
Contact: Stephen Akins
    stephen.akins@thieletech.com
Number Employees: 250-499
Square Footage: 400000
Parent Co: Barry-Wehmiller
Other Locations:
    SWF Machinery
    Orlando FL

30282 Thielmann Container Systems
6301 Gravel Ave
Alexandria, VA 22310

703-836-4003
Fax: 703-836-4070

Cylindrical and cubic containers
Estimated Sales: $1 - 3 Million
Number Employees: 5-9

30283 Thinque Systems Corporation
4130 Cahuenga Boulevard
Suite 128
Toluca Lake, CA 91602-2847

818-752-1350
Fax: 818-752-1355 sales@thinque.com
www.thinque.com

President: George Bayz
VP Business Development: Rich Love
VP Marketing: Ellen Libenson
Estimated Sales: $27 Million
Number Employees: 150

30284 Thirstenders International
11518 Bedford St
Houston, TX 77031-2108

713-664-8050
Fax: 713-559-8449 www.thirstenders.com

Manufacturers proprietary, mobile delivery systems for food, beverages and consumer products.
President: Fred Ash
info@thirstenders.com
Quality Control: Lee Grover
R&D: Fred Ash
Estimated Sales: Below $5 Million
Number Employees: 1-4

30285 Thirty Two North Corporation
32north Corporation16 Pomerleau Street
Biddeford, ME 04005

800-782-2423
Fax: 207-284-5015 800-782-2423
info@32north.com

Safety shoes, detachable anti-slip soles
Owner: Anne Gould
Estimated Sales: Below $5 Million
Number Employees: 10

30286 Thomas J Payne Market Devmnt
865 Woodside Way
San Mateo, CA 94401-1611

650-340-8311
Fax: 650-340-8568 tpayne@tjpmd.com
www.tjpmd.com

Consultant specializing in marketing development and food technology
President: Tom Payne
CEO: Thomas J Payne
tpayne@tjpmd.com
Market Development Activities: Edith Nagy
Estimated Sales: $500,000-$1 Million
Number Employees: 1-4

30287 Thomas L. Green & Company
380 Old West Penn Ave
Robenosia, PA 19551

610-693-5816
Fax: 610-693-5512 info@readingbakery.com
www.readingbakery.com

Manufacturer and exporter of bakery machinery including automatic band ovens, dough mixers, conveyors for crackers and cookies, biscuit cutters, dough formers and dough sheeters
Chairman: Thomas Lugar
EVP & CFO: Chip Czulada
CEO: Terry Groff
CFO: Charles Czulada
Quality Control: Mike Johnson
VP, Sales and Marketing: David Kuipers
VP of Sales, Americas: Shawn Moye
VP, Operations: Travis Getz
Estimated Sales: $5 - 10 Million
Number Employees: 10-19

30288 Thomas Lighting Residential
10275 W Higgins Rd, 8th Floor
Rosemont, IL 60018

Fax: 800-288-4329 800-825-5844
info@thomaslighting.com
www.thomaslighting.com

Manufacturer and exporter of outdoor lighting fixtures
Sales Manager: Sheryl Fraga
Number Employees: 350

30289 Thomas Precision, Inc.
3278 S Main St
Rice Lake, WI 54868-8793

715-234-8827
Fax: 715-234-6737 800-657-4808
sales@tpm-inc.com www.tpm-inc.com

Manufacturer and exporter of stainless steel and alloy replacement parts for food processing equipment including grinder plates, blades and screens; also, build and rebuild separating machines and augers
CEO: Roger Norberg
Sales: Jerry Klasen
Plant Manager: Kevin Nyra
Purchasing Agent: Rod Stoyke
Estimated Sales: $10 Million
Number Employees: 60
Square Footage: 48000
Brands:
Tpm

30290 Thomas Pump & Machinery
120 Industrial Dr
Slidell, LA 70460-4650

985-649-4300
Fax: 985-649-4300 www.thomaspump.com

Cleaning and washing equipment, pressure washers, heaters-water, heat reclaiming systems, automobile products
President: Jim Thomas
tpump@thomaspump.com
VP of Finances: Rebecca Rhoto
VP of Inside Sales: Craig Robinson
VP of Operations: Joe Galey
Estimated Sales: $1 - 3 Million
Number Employees: 20-49

30291 Thomas Pump & Machinery
120 Industrial Dr
Slidell, LA 70460-4650

985-649-4300
Fax: 985-649-4300 tpump@thomaspump.com
www.thomaspump.com

Owner: Jim Thomas
tpump@thomaspump.com
Estimated Sales: $2.5-5 Million
Number Employees: 20-49

30292 Thomas Tape & Supply CoInc
1713 Sheridan Ave
Springfield, OH 45505-2263

937-325-6414
Fax: 937-325-2850 www.thomastape.com

Manufacturer and exporter of sealing tape including paper, cloth, reinforced glass fiber, gummed, and pressure sensitive tape
President: David Simonton
dave11@thomastape.com
Sales/Marketing Executive: Kevin Amidon
Estimated Sales: $300,000-500,000
Number Employees: 5-9
Square Footage: 120000
Brands:
Paxrite
Raycord

30293 Thomas Technical Svc
W4780 US Highway 10
Neillsville, WI 54456-6213

715-743-4666
Fax: 715-743-2062

Ultrafiltration and reverse osmosis systems for the dairy industry; wholesaler/distributor of replacement parts
Owner: Randy L Thomas
CEO: Theresa Thomas
CFO: Randy Thomas
Estimated Sales: Below $5 Million
Number Employees: 1-4
Square Footage: 18000
Brands:
Thomas Fractioner

30294 Thomas Technical Svc
W4780 US Highway 10
Neillsville, WI 54456-6213

715-743-4666
Fax: 715-743-2062

Ultra filtration, reverse osmosis, membrane systems
Owner: Randy L Thomas
randy@thomastechnical.com
Estimated Sales: less than $500,000
Number Employees: 1-4

30295 Thomasen
1303 43rd St
Kenosha, WI 53140

262-652-3662
Fax: 262-652-3526 sales@lcthomsen.com

Custom fabrication, filters, milk, flow diversion stations
President: Wayne Borne
Sales: Joyce Saftig
Estimated Sales: $1-5 Million
Number Employees: 20-49

30296 Thombert
P.O. Box 1123
316 E. 7th Street N.
Newton, IA 50208-1123

641-792-4449
Fax: 641-792-2390 800-433-3572
thombert@thombert.com www.thombert.com

Polyurethane wheels and tires for forklift trucks
Chairman of the Board: Walter Smith
President: Dick Davidson
Sales Marketing Manager: Reggie Collette
Sales Representative: Brandon Mastin
Contact: Paul Ellis
pellis@thombert.com
VP Manufacturing: Terry Beckham
Estimated Sales: $10-20 Million
Number Employees: 50-99
Brands:
Dyalon
Vulkollan

30297 (HQ)Thompson Bagel Machine Mfg
8945 Ellis Ave
Los Angeles, CA 90034-3380

310-836-0900
Fax: 310-836-0156 sales@bagelproducts.com
www.bagelproducts.com

Manufacturer and exporter of one and two bank bagel machines including horizontal and vertical; also, two and four row rotary dividers.
President: Steve Thompson
sales@bagelproducts.com
Research & Development: Dan Thompson
Marketing/Sales: Charles Ducat
Operations Manager: Craig Thompson
Estimated Sales: $1-5 Million
Number Employees: 5-9
Number of Products: 10
Type of Packaging: Private Label
Brands:
Thompson Bagel Machines

30298 Thompson Scale Co
9000 Jameel Rd # 190
Suite 190
Houston, TX 77040-5061

713-932-9071
Fax: 713-932-9379 info@thompsonscale.com
www.thompsonscale.com

Weighing systems and packaging machinery controls
President: Bobbie Thompson
bobbie.thompson@thompsonscale.com
Estimated Sales: $2 Million
Number Employees: 10-19
Square Footage: 9000

30299 Thomsen Group LLC
1303 43rd St
Kenosha, WI 53140-2738

262-652-3662
Fax: 262-652-3526 800-558-4018
sales@lcthomsen.com www.lcthomsen.com

Wine industry pumps and valves
President: Wayne Borne
Sales: Joyce Saftig
Manager: Jon Huges
j.huges@lcthomsen.com
Number Employees: 10-19

30300 (HQ)Thomson-Leeds Company
450 Park Avenue S
2nd Floor
New York, NY 10016-7320

914-428-7255
Fax: 914-428-7047 800-535-9361

Manufacturer, importer and exporter of displays, fixtures, package designs and point of purchase merchandising materials. Broker of specialty displays

President: Vince Esposito
CEO: Douglas Leeds
Director Marketing: Peter Weiller
Estimated Sales: $2.5-5 Million
Number Employees: 50-99
Square Footage: 80000
Brands:
  Fiberpoptics
  Freelight
  Greenpop
  Security Peg Hook
  Stockpop

30301 Thor Inc
1280 W 2550 S
Ogden, UT 84401-3238

801-393-3312
Fax: 801-621-3298 888-846-7462
Custom formulating and contract packaging for vitamins and supplements in liquids, capsules and powders
Owner: Whittle Allen
  whittle.allen@thor.com
Estimated Sales: $10-20 Million
Number Employees: 10-19
Type of Packaging: Private Label

30302 Thorco Industries LLC
1300 E 12th St
Lamar, MO 64759

417-682-3375
Fax: 417-682-1326 800-445-3375
Manufacturer and exporter of point of purchase displays, wire grids, store fixtures, bag holders and baskets
President: John Kuhahl
CFO: Jeff Gardener
Quality Control: Rodney Walters
Contact: Sarah Dorris
  sdorris@lauracookseymusic.com
Estimated Sales: $5,000,000 - $9,999,999
Number Employees: 500-999
Parent Co: Marmon Corporation

30303 Thoreson Mc Cosh Inc
1885 Thunderbird
Troy, MI 48084-5472

248-362-0960
Fax: 248-362-5270 800-959-0805
  sales@thoresonmccosh.com
  www.thoresonmccosh.com
Manufacturer and exporter of dryers, hoppers, loaders and loading systems, tilters and bulk handling systems
President: David Klatt
  sales@thoresonmccosh.com
Sales Exec: Steven Taugher
Estimated Sales: $10-20 Million
Number Employees: 20-49
Type of Packaging: Bulk

30304 Thorn Smith Laboratories
7755 Narrow Gauge Rd
Beulah, MI 49617-9792

231-882-4672
Fax: 231-882-4804 auric@thornsmithlabs.com
  www.thornsmithlabs.com
Manufacturer and exporter of temperature specific sterilizer controls for use in quality assurance programs
President: Robert Brown
Plant Manager: Melanie Cederholm
Estimated Sales: Below $5 Million
Number Employees: 1-4
Square Footage: 17200
Brands:
  Diack
  Vac

30305 Thornton Plastics
745 W Pacific Ave
Salt Lake City, UT 84104-1022

801-322-3413
Fax: 801-359-2800 800-248-3434
  sales@thorntonplastics.com
  www.thorntonplastics.com
Transparent plastic snap-cap vials
President: Briton C Mc Conkie
  briton@thorntonplastics.com
VP: Jean Eastham
Estimated Sales: Below $5 Million
Number Employees: 5-9
Square Footage: 34000

30306 Thorpe & Associates
227 N Chatnam Ave
Siler City, NC 27344-3443

919-742-5516
Fax: 919-742-4657
Manufacturer and importer of chairs and tables
President: Bill Thorpe
VP Design: William Thorpe
VP Sales: Van Thorpe
Estimated Sales: Less than $500,000
Number Employees: 500
Square Footage: 400000

30307 Thorpe Rolling Pin Co
336 Putnam Ave
Hamden, CT 06517-2744

203-787-0281
Fax: 203-230-2753 800-344-6966
Rolling and pizza pins
President: Timothy Pagnam
Estimated Sales: $1-2.5 Million
Number Employees: 20-49

30308 Three P
333 Andrew Ave
Salt Lake City, UT 84115-5113

801-486-7407
Fax: 801-571-4896
Manufacturer and exporter of custom printed and pressure sensitive decals, labels, tags, signs, etc
Owner: Edd Lancaster
Quality Control: Ernie Ashcroft
Marketing: Denise Lancaster
Sales: Edd Lancaster
Estimated Sales: $500,000-$1 Million
Number Employees: 5-9
Type of Packaging: Private Label, Bulk

30309 Three-A Sanitary Standards Symbol
6888 Elm Street
Suite 2D
McLean, VA 22101

703-790-0295
Fax: 703-761-6284 3-AINFO@3-A.org
  www.3-a.org
To enhance product safety for consumers of food, beverages, and pharmaceutical products.
Executive Director: Timothy Rugh
Contact: Angus Abels
  aabels@3-a.org

30310 Threshold Rehabilitation Svc
1000 Lancaster Ave
Reading, PA 19607-1699

610-777-7691
Fax: 610-777-1295 www.trsinc.org
Contract packagers
President: Ronald Williams
  tdesanto@trsinc.org
Sales/Marketing: Nancy Benjamin
VP Program Operations: Tom McNelis
Year Founded: 1973
Estimated Sales: $20 - 50 Million
Number Employees: 250-499
Square Footage: 20000

30311 Thunder Pallet Inc
625 Menomonee St
Theresa, WI 53091-9805

920-488-4211
Fax: 920-488-4306 800-354-0643
Wooden pallets, skids, boxes, crates, etc
President: Ben Mahsem
  ben@thinderpallet.com
Estimated Sales: Below $5 Million
Number Employees: 50-99

30312 Thunderbird Food Machinery
P.O. BOX 4768
4602 Brass Way
Blaine, WA 98231

214-331-3000
Fax: 214-331-3581 866-875-6868
  tbfm@tbfm.com www.thunderbirdfm.com
Importer and wholesaler/distributor of food processing equipment including mixers, dough sheeters, vegetable and bread slicers, meat grinders, etc
Owner: Ky Lin
Marketing Director: Kara M
Estimated Sales: $1-2.5 Million
Number Employees: 5-9

30313 Thunderbird Label Corportion
70 Clinton Road
Fairfield, NJ 07004-2928

973-575-6677
Fax: 973-575-4970
Pressure sensitive labels including prime, coupon, tamper-evident and four color process
President: Karl Beierle
VP Sales: George Coughlin
Estimated Sales: $2.5-5 Million
Number Employees: 19
Square Footage: 48000

30314 Thurman Scale
4025 Lakeview Crossing
Groveport, OH 43125

614-221-9077
Fax: 614-221-8879 800-688-9741
  thurmanscales@fancor.com
  www.thurmanscale.com
Weighing equipment
Contact: Neil Copley
  ncopley@thurmanscale.com
Estimated Sales: $.5 - 1 million
Number Employees: 1-4
Parent Co: Fancor

30315 Thwing-Albert Instrument Co
14 W Collings Ave
West Berlin, NJ 08091-9134

856-767-1000
Fax: 856-767-2615 info@thwingalbert.com
  www.thwingalbert.com
Thwing-Albert Instrument Company provides a complete offering of tensile testers and other materials testing instruments for quality control, research & development and process control applications worldwide.
President: Joseph Raab
  jraab@thwingalbert.com
VP/Sales/Marketing: Steven Berg
Estimated Sales: $5 - 10 Million
Number Employees: 50-99

30316 Tiax LLC
35 Hartwell Ave
Lexington, MA 02421-3102

781-879-1200
Fax: 617-498-7200 800-677-3000
  www.tiaxllc.com
Consultant specializing in technology, product and marketing services, health, safety, product formulation, and research and development.
President: Nadine Andon
  andon.n@tiaxllc.com
VP: Arthur Schwope
VP Sales: Bernard Lupien
VP Operations: Boyd Boucher
Purchasing Manager: Jose Bairos
Estimated Sales: $20 - 50 Million
Number Employees: 1-4
Square Footage: 120000
Other Locations:
  Cupertino CA
  Irvine CA

30317 Tibersoft
2200 W Park Dr # 430
Westborough, MA 01581-3961

508-898-9555
Fax: 508-898-1820 888-888-1969
  info@tibersoft.com www.tibersoft.com
Founder: Christopher Martin
CEO: Tom Beninghof
  tom.beninghof@tibersoft.com
Vice President, Founder: Mary Wilson
Estimated Sales: $1 - 5 Million
Number Employees: 20-49

30318 Tidland Corp
2305 SE 8th Ave
Camas, WA 98607-2261

360-834-2345
Fax: 360-834-5865 800-426-1000
Manufactures air expanding shafts, chucks, air brakes, slitting knife holders and electronic slitting positioning machines
President: Quino Lorente
Cmo: Stephanie Tuggle
  stuggle@tidland.com
Director International Marketing: John Rupp
Estimated Sales: Below $5 Million
Number Employees: 100-249

30319 Tieco-Unadilla Corporation
22 Depot Street
Unadilla, NY 13838
607-369-3236
Fax: 607-369-2011 877-889-6540
tieco@tyups.com www.tyups.com
Manufacturer and exporter of tying devices for securing bundles and pallets
President: Scott McLean
Estimated Sales: Below $500,000
Number Employees: 5-9
Brands:
Ty-Up

30320 Tiefenthaler Machinery Co, Inc
W227 N913 Westmound Dr
Waukesha, WI 53186
262-513-1111
Fax: 262-513-1113
President: James Tiefenthaler
Estimated Sales: $5 - 10 Million
Number Employees: 5-9

30321 Tier-Rack Corp
425 Sovereign Ct
Ballwin, MO 63011-4432
636-527-0700
Fax: 636-256-4901 800-325-7869
info@tier-rack.com www.tier-rack.com
Manufacturer and exporter of portable storage racks
Owner: Scott Ten Eyck
steneyck@tier-rack.com
General Manager: George Willis
Controller: Ward Wilson
Estimated Sales: $1 - 2.5 Million
Number Employees: 10-19
Square Footage: 150000
Brands:
Tier-Rack

30322 Tifa (CI)
109 Stryker Lane
Building 3, Suite 4&5
Millington, NJ 8844
908-829-3230
Fax: 908-829-3240 www.tifausa.com
Manufacturing of aeorsol fogging equipment for public health
President: Gamel Osman
Chairman: Vladimir Alexanyan
Vice President: Deirdre Cerciello
Estimated Sales: $1-2.5 Million
Number Employees: 10-19

30323 Tiffin Metal Products Co
450 Wall St
Tiffin, OH 44883-1366
419-447-8414
Fax: 419-447-8512 800-537-0983
www.tiffinmetal.com
Stainless steel lockers and special sheet metal fabrication, ergonomic seating, stainless, plated polyurethane seats for washdown areas, adjustable work tables, packing stands and anti-fatigue matting
President/CEO: Will Heddles
CEO: Willard P Heddles
wheddles@tiffinmetal.com
Chief Financial Officer: Timothy Demith
VP Outdoor/Custom & OEM Products: Ron Myers
VP Security Products & Marketing: Andrew Beebe
Marketing Manager: Mike Wittman
National Sales Manager Custom/OEM: Rodney Osmena
Estimated Sales: $5 - 10 Million
Number Employees: 50-99

30324 Tiger-Vac
73 SW 12th Ave # 107
Dania, FL 33004-3523
954-925-3625
Fax: 954-925-3626 800-668-4437
sales@tiger-vac.com www.tiger-vac.com
Industrial vacuum cleaners, specializes in systems for clean manufacturing areas and contamination controlled environments, foodgrade vacuums, continuous duty vacuums, vacuums with high efficiency
President: Rocco Mariani
rmariani@tiger-vac.com
Estimated Sales: $1 - 2.5 Million
Number Employees: 50-99
Number of Products: 15

30325 Tilly Industries
4210 Blvd Poirier
St Laurent, QC H4R 2C5
Canada
514-331-4922
Fax: 514-331-4924 www.tillyindustries.com
Manufacturer and exporter of aluminum foil dies for pie plates and containers
VP: Dagmar Tilly
Estimated Sales: $1 - 5 Million
Number Employees: 8
Square Footage: 36000
Parent Co: Maven Engineering Corporation

30326 Timberline Consulting
3333 S Bannock St # 600
Suite 800
Englewood, CO 80110-2450
303-781-3977
Fax: 303-781-4305
Owner: Daniel David
ddaniel@timberlineconsulting.com
Estimated Sales: $810,000
Number Employees: 10-19

30327 Timbertech Company
1055 White Mountain Highway
Milton, NH 03851-4443
603-669-7743
Fax: 603-669-2024 800-572-5538
Pallets including new and rebuilt 48 x 40 grocery; also, disposal
Owner and President: Rod Van Sciver
Office Manager: Nancy Boudreau
Estimated Sales: $2.5-5 Million
Number Employees: 20-49
Square Footage: 50000

30328 Timco Inc
2 Greentown Rd
Buchanan, NY 10511-1007
914-736-0206
Fax: 914-736-0395 800-792-0030
sales@timco-eng.com www.timco-eng.com
Rigging gear, hardware, jacks and rollers: sheaves, chain guides
Owner: Marc Walter
Sales: Joe Yaniv
marc@licharzmail.com
Plant Manager: Barry Volaski
Estimated Sales: $6 Million
Number Employees: 20-49
Number of Brands: 3
Number of Products: 30

30329 Time Products
3780 Browns Mill Rd SE
Atlanta, GA 30354
404-767-7526
Fax: 404-767-7010 800-241-6681
tymebill@aol.com
Cleaning compounds
VP and General Manager: Bill Drew
CEO: John Theophilis
Chairman of the Board: Steve Theofilos
Marketing Director: Stan Lanch
Production Manager: Rod Abrahansen
Estimated Sales: $20-50 Million
Number Employees: 20-49
Square Footage: 100000
Parent Co: Theochem Laboratories
Brands:
Time-Saver

30330 Timely Signs Inc
2135 Linden Blvd
Elmont, NY 11003-3901
516-285-5339
Fax: 516-285-9637 800-457-4467
sales@timelysigns.net
Manufacturer and exporter of labels, marketing signs and banners; wholesaler/distributor of computerized sign making equipment
President: Gene Goldsmith
signs11003@aol.com
Estimated Sales: $1-2.5 Million
Number Employees: 5-9
Square Footage: 4000
Brands:
Duracast
Timely Signs
Ulta Mag

30331 Timemed Labeling Systems
27770 N Entertainment Drive
Suite 200
Valencia, CA 91355
818-897-1111
Fax: 818-686-9317 intl@pdcorp.com
www.pdchealthcare.com
Manufacturer and exporter of pressure-sensitive labels, embossed seals and printed gummed tapes
President: Jerry Nerad
General Manager: Lee Smith
Contact: Tima Fanning
tima.fanning@phoenix.edu
Plant Manager: Dave Luther
Estimated Sales: $10 - 20 Million
Number Employees: 20-49
Parent Co: Timemed Labeling Systems

30332 (HQ)Tin Box Co of America Inc
216 Sherwood Ave
Farmingdale, NY 11735-1718
631-845-1600
Fax: 631-845-1610 800-888-8467
info@tinboxco.com www.tinboxco.com
Decorative metal boxes
Owner: Lloyd Roth
Director of Sales: Andy Siegel
Sales Manager: Richard Spitz
rothl@tinboxco.com
Estimated Sales: $5 - 10 Million
Number Employees: 20-49
Square Footage: 80000

30333 Tinadre Inc
15310 Amberly Dr # 180
Tampa, FL 33647-1640
813-866-0333
Fax: 813-866-0462 tinadre@gte.net
www.tinadre.net
Turnkey customer frequency pre-paid private label cards, electronic gift certificates and payment processing services for food service operators; also, POS software and hardware
Owner: Michael Crochet
VP: Mike Crochot
VP: Zachary Tapp
Production: Steven Malcanas
Estimated Sales: $500,000-$1 Million
Number Employees: 5-9

30334 Tindall Packaging
1150 E U Ave
Vicksburg, MI 49097
269-649-1163
Fax: 616-649-1163
Manufacturer and exporter of filling equipment for dairy, deli and cultured products; also, single and two-flavor variegators
President: Marianne Tindall
marianne@tindallpackaging.com
VP: Marianne Tindall
Quality Control: Frank Tindall
Number Employees: 5

30335 Tinwerks Packaging Co
1237 W Capitol Dr
Addison, IL 60101-3116
630-628-8600
Fax: 630-628-0330 www.tinwerks.com
Tins
Vice President: Joseph Marlovits
sales@tinwerks.com
VP: Peter Goschi
Sales: Joseph Marlovits
Number Employees: 5-9

30336 Tiny Drumsticks
43-66 11th St.
New York, NY 11101
917-526-3263
info@tinydrumsticks.com
www.tinydrumsticks.com
Supplies kitchens and kitchen designs.
President & CEO: Benjamin Sloan
Year Founded: 2013
Square Footage: 5000
Type of Packaging: Food Service

30337 Tipper Tie Inc
2000 Lufkin Rd
Apex, NC 27539-7068
919-362-8811
Fax: 919-362-4839 www.tippertie.com

Clippers, aluminum clips, aluminum wire products, electric fence supplies and netting
Estimated Sales: $35 Million
Number Employees: 100-249
Square Footage: 130000
Parent Co: JBT
Brands:
Tipper Clippers

30338 (HQ)Tippmann Group
9009 Coldwater Rd # 300
Fort Wayne, IN 46825-2072
260-490-3000
Fax: 260-490-1362
tippsales@tippmanngroup.com
www.tippmanngroup.com
Design and building construction of refrigerated warehouses/facilities
CEO: John V Tippmann Sr
Contact: Kyle Angelet
kangelet@tippmanngroup.com
Number Employees: 50-99

30339 Tisma Machinery Corporation
1099 Estes Avenue
Elk Grove Village, IL 60007-4907
847-427-9525
Fax: 847-427-9550
bwilliams@swfcompanies.com
Manufacturer and exporter of automatic cartoning machinery and systems
Estimated Sales: $10-20 Million
Number Employees: 50-99
Square Footage: 176000

30340 Titan Corporation
3033 Science Park Rd
San Diego, CA 92121
858-552-9565
Fax: 858-535-3609
Markets technology for the electronic irradiation of food products
President: Andy Ivers
Contact: Matt Armato
m.armato@titanandco.com
Number Employees: 250-499
Brands:
Surebean

30341 Titan Industries Inc
735 Industrial Loop Rd
New London, WI 54961-2600
920-982-6600
Fax: 920-982-7750 800-558-3616
www.titanconveyors.com
Manufacturer and exporter of conveyors
President: Dan Baumbach
dbaumbach@titansystems.com
Estimated Sales: $5-10 Million
Number Employees: 20-49
Square Footage: 84000

30342 Titan Plastics
433 Murray Hill Pkwy
East Rutherford, NJ 7073
201-935-7700
Fax: 201-935-1584
Plastic containers
President: Rich Probinsky
Contact: Carol Vail
carolv@pennbottle.com
Estimated Sales: $10-20 Million
Number Employees: 10-19
Square Footage: 200000
Parent Co: Penn Bottle & Supply Company

30343 Titan Ventures International, Inc
170 Millennium Blvd
Moncton, NB E1E 2G8
Canada
506-858-8990
Fax: 506-859-6929 800-565-2253
sales@bakemax.com www.bakemax.com
Wholesaler/distributor of Planetary Mixers, Hot Dog Roller Grills, Slicers, Spiral Mixers, Water Meters, Bakery Equipment, Countertop Pizza or Pie Sheeter, Electric Display Food Warmers, Deli or Meat Equipment, Bread SlicersReversible Sheeters, Bun Dividers and more
Chief Financial Officer: Cathy Flanagan
Sales: Shawn Melanson
Estimated Sales: $3-5 Million
Number Employees: 5
Square Footage: 48000

Type of Packaging: Bulk

30344 Tlf Graphics Inc
235 Metro Park
Rochester, NY 14623-2618
800-356-2701
Fax: 585-272-5525 800-356-2701
www.tlfgraphics.com
Label printing
Owner: Ronald Le Blanc
Contact: Tod Bitter
tod@staples.com
Estimated Sales: $10-20 Million
Number Employees: 5-9

30345 Tnemec Co Inc
123 W 23rd Ave
N Kansas City, MO 64116-3094
952-746-1909
Fax: 816-842-3904 800-TNE-MEC1
www.tnemec.com
High performance paints, coatings and floor toppings, industrial steel maintenance paints and primers, concrete, brick and masonry waterproofing materials, chemical resistant coatings for steel
President & COO: Chase Bean
Marketing Director: Mark Thomas
Manager: Melanie Watt
Estimated Sales: $50,000,000 - $99,999,999
Number Employees: 100-249

30346 Tni Packaging Inc
333 Charles Ct # 101
West Chicago, IL 60185-2604
630-293-3030
Fax: 630-293-5303 800-383-0990
www.tnipackaging.com
Manufacturer and exporter of open mesh netting bags, pre-tied elastic poultry trusses and mechanical meat tenderizers
President: Jerry J Marchese
jmarchese@tnipackaging.com
Marketing Director: Ana Tirado
Sales Director: Jane Larsen
Plant Manager: Victor Castijelo
Estimated Sales: $3-5 Million
Number Employees: 5-9
Number of Brands: 7
Number of Products: 4
Square Footage: 48000
Type of Packaging: Consumer, Food Service, Private Label, Bulk
Brands:
Chicken-Tuckers
Mister Tenderizer
Net-All
Tie-Net

30347 Tnn-Jeros Inc
697 N Colfax St
PO Box 12
Byron, IL 61010-1439
312-261-6004
jens_hedegaard@tnn-jeros.com
www.tnn-jeros.com
Supplier of cleaning and washing equipment for food manufacturers
Partner: Jens Hedegaard
jeros@jeros.us
Number Employees: 10-19

30348 Toastmaster
1400 Toastmaster Drive
Elgin, IL 60120-9274
847-741-3300
Fax: 847-741-0015 mww@middleby.com
www.toastmastercorp.com
Manufacturer and exporter of broilers, fryers, griddles, grills, hot plates, ovens, ranges, rotisseries and toasters
President: Mark Sieron
Estimated Sales: $1 - 5 Million
Number Employees: 5-9
Parent Co: Middleby Corporation

30349 Todd Construction Services
1206 Price Ave
Pomona, CA 91767-5840
909-469-6242
Fax: 909-469-6241
Designers, engineers and planners for the food production and cold storage industry

President: Glenn Todd
Contact: Carrie Todd
carrie@toddconstructionservices.com
Estimated Sales: $5-10 Million
Number Employees: 5-9

30350 Todd Uniform
PO Box 29107
Saint Louis, MO 63126-0107
800-458-3402
Fax: 800-231-8633
Uniforms
Sales: Robin Berry

30351 Todd's
PO Box 4821
Des Moines, IA 50305
515-266-2276
Fax: 515-266-1669 800-247-5363
Variety of food products, wet and dry, kosher and organic certified.
President/CEO: Alan Niedermeier
Quality Control: Diana Burzloff
Public Relations: Alissa Douglas
Operations: Duane Hettkamp
Production: Jeff Sullivan
Plant Manager: John Routh
Purchasing: Danielle Robinson
Estimated Sales: $1 - 3 Million
Number Employees: 30
Number of Brands: 40
Number of Products: 200
Square Footage: 320000
Type of Packaging: Consumer, Food Service, Private Label, Bulk
Brands:
Butcher's Friend
Papa Joe's Specialty Food

30352 Token Factory
2131 South Ave
La Crosse, WI 54601
608-785-2439
888-486-5367
custserv@tokenfactory.com
www.tokenfactory.com
Manufacturer and exporter of plastic tokens and swizzle sticks
President: Dale Stevens
Sales Manager: Rosie Hundt
Estimated Sales: $1-2.5 Million
Number Employees: 11

30353 Tokheim Co
560 31st St
Marion, IA 52302-3724
319-362-4847
Fax: 319-377-7953 800-747-3442
info@tokheimco.com www.tokheimco.com
Manufacturer and exporter of liquid level gauges for large storage tanks
President: Vicky Barnes
Quality Control: Chris Peyton
VP: Thomas Barnes
Sales: Barb Riffey
Manager: Tom Barnes
tom.barnes@tokheimco.com
Estimated Sales: Less Than $500,000
Number Employees: 1-4
Square Footage: 40000

30354 (HQ)Tolan Machinery Company
PO Box 695
164 Franklin Ave.
Rockaway, NJ 7866
973-983-7212
Fax: 973-983-7217 www.tolanmachinery.com
Manufacturer and exporter of tanks, reactors, hoppers, bins, heat exchangers, storage vessels and fermentors
President: John Tolpa
VP, General Manager: Stephen Tolpa
Chief Engineer: Bill Ebbinghouser
VP Sales/Marketing: Thomas Spencer
Operations Manager: Brian T. Gill
Estimated Sales: $10 - 20 Million
Number Employees: 20-49
Square Footage: 80000

30355 Tolas Health Care Packaging
905 Pennsylvania Blvd
Feasterville Trevose, PA 19053
215-322-7900
Fax: 215-322-9034 marketing@tolas.com
www.tolas.com
Printed and converted paper, foil and plastics for
packaging; exporter of paper, barrier films and foils
President: Carl D Marotta
CFO: Chuck Klink
Quality Control: Skip Peacock
R & D: Chris Perry
Marketing Team Leader: Denise Dilissio
Sales Director: Leslie Love
 l.love@ciprianopi.com
Operations Manager: Dave Preikszas
Purchasing Manager: Jim McNally
Estimated Sales: $20 Million
Number Employees: 100-249
Square Footage: 50000

30356 Tolco Corp
1920 Linwood Ave
Toledo, OH 43604-5293
419-241-1113
Fax: 419-241-3035 800-537-4786
tolco@tolcocorp.com www.tolcocorporation.com
Funnels, soap dispensers, spouts, containers, scoops,
pumps and trigger spray and plastic bottles
President: Robert Jones
 r.jones@tol-co.com
VP Sales/Marketing: George Notarianni
VP Operations: W Spengler
Purchasing Agent: T Denker
Estimated Sales: $5-10 Million
Number Employees: 50-99
Square Footage: 100000
Brands:
 Spraymist

30357 Toledo Sign Co Inc
2021 Adams St
Toledo, OH 43604-5431
419-244-4444
Fax: 419-244-6546 tsigns@toledosign.com
www.toledosign.com
Changeable, letter, electric, luminous tube, inter-
changeable, point of purchase and plastic signs
President: Brad Heil
 bradheil@toledosign.com
Estimated Sales: $2.5-5 Million
Number Employees: 20-49

30358 Toledo Ticket Co
3963 Catawba St
PO Box 6876
Toledo, OH 43612-1492
419-476-5424
Fax: 419-476-6801 800-533-6620
www.toledoticket.com
Manufacturer and exporter of labels and coupons
President: Roy Carter
VP Sales and Marketing: Tom Carter
Estimated Sales: $5-10 Million
Number Employees: 20-49

30359 Toledo Wire Products
3601 Expressway Dr S
Toledo, OH 43608
419-729-5446
Fax: 419-729-0241 888-430-7445
Wire display racks
President: Ann Obertacz
 anno@toledowire.com
Contact: Ken Obertacz
VP Sales: Rick Breivik
Production Manager: Ken Obertacz
Estimated Sales: $2.5-5 Million
Number Employees: 10-19

30360 Tom Lockerbie
1023 County Highway 20
Edmeston, NY 13335-2524
315-737-5612
Fax: 315-737-5183
Air agitated ice builders
Estimated Sales: $500,000-$1 Million
Number Employees: 3

30361 Tom McCall & Associates
6 Nanticoke Crossing Plaza
Millsboro, DE 19966-9511
410-539-0700
Fax: 212-689-5761

Recruiting and placement agency specializing in
sales and management personnel
Manager: Charley Greene
Assistant Manager: Emma Jean Smith
Estimated Sales: $500,000-$1 Million
Number Employees: 10-19
Square Footage: 1400

30362 (HQ)Tomac Packaging
271 Salem Street
Unit G
Woburn, MA 01801-2004
781-938-1500
Fax: 781-938-7536 800-641-3100
Automatic weighing and bagging equipment for the
produce industry; also, repairing and operating ser-
vices available
President: Richard Gold
VP: Thomas Gold
VP: Hans Van Der Sande
Estimated Sales: $.5 - 1 million
Number Employees: 40
Square Footage: 8000
Other Locations:
 Tomac Packaging
 Idaho Falls ID

30363 Tomco2 Systems
3340 Rosebud Rd
Loganville, GA 30052-7341
770-979-8000
Fax: 770-978-5861 800-832-4262
tomco@tomcoequipment.com
www.tomcosystems.com
Tomco equipment company has developed products
and services to suit all phases of co2 usage with
storage. delivery and co2 application-driven equip-
ment.tomco2's full range of products matches any
carbon dioxcide requirements. EPAcertified professional parts and service technicians are availible
24hrs a day 7 days a week. the company has supplied co2 storage and applications equipment since
1970.
President: John Toepke
CEO: Jack Toepke
 jacktoepke@tomcoequipment.com
Cfo: Lynn Brown
Quality Control: Louis Pittaluga
Vice President Sales: Dan Tenpleton
Operations: Ken Mercer
Purchasing: Rayna Hewitt
Estimated Sales: $20-50 Million
Number Employees: 100-249

30364 Tomlinson Industries
13700 Broadway Ave
Cleveland, OH 44125-1945
216-587-3400
Fax: 216-587-0733 800-945-4589
jengle@tomlinsonind.com
www.tomlinsonind.com
Manufacturer and exporter of faucets and fittings,
kettles, warmers and dispensers for cups, cones, lids,
straws, napkins and condiments; also, table top orga-
nizers, thermal platters and cook and serve skil-
lets;foodservice glovescutting boards and
anti-fatigue mats.
President: Michael Figas
CEO: H Meyer
CFO: Donald Calkins
VP: Louis Castro
Quality Control: John Silcox
Marketing: Jeanne Engle
Operations: Kenneth Sidoti
Purchasing: Michael Ritley
Estimated Sales: $20 - 50 Million
Number Employees: 100-249
Square Footage: 120000
Parent Co: Meyer Company
Brands:
 Frontier Kettle
 Glenray
 Melco
 Modular Dispensing Systems
 No-Drip
 Tomlinson

30365 Tomric Systems Inc
85 River Rock Dr # 202
Suite 202
Buffalo, NY 14207-2170
716-854-6050
Fax: 716-854-7363 www.tomric.com

Custom molds, supplies, equipment and packaging
for chocolate
President: Timothy M Thill
 tthill@tomric.com
Estimated Sales: $1-5 Million
Number Employees: 50-99

30366 Tomsed Corporation
420 McKinney Pkwy
Lillington, NC 27546
910-814-3800
Fax: 910-814-3899 800-334-5552
Manufacturer and exporter of access control equip-
ment including high security and waist-high turn-
stiles, handicapped gates, portable posts and sign
holders; wholesaler/distributor of portable and fixed
crowd railing
President: Robert Sedivy
CEO: Thomas Sedivy
CFO: Karin Sedivy
Sales: Russell Socles
Estimated Sales: $15 Million
Number Employees: 100-249
Number of Brands: 9
Number of Products: 100
Square Footage: 220000
Brands:
 Entry Gard
 Lawrence Model 88
 Roto Gard
 Round Nose
 Safesec
 Tomsed
 Tut-50e
 Tut-50r

30367 Tonnellerie Mercier
171 Spring Grove Avenue
San Anselmo, CA 94960-2410
415-453-2069
Fax: 650-463-5485 www.tonnellerie-mercier.com
Wine industry cooperage
Partner: Ken Deis

30368 Tonnellerie Montross
139 Jenkins Point Road
Montross, VA 22520-3524
804-493-9186
Fax: 804-493-0435 lilreeht@aol.com
www.tonnellerie-mercier.com
Wine industry cooperage and French oak barrels of
all sizes
President: Jackqus Reche
Number Employees: 10

30369 Tonnellerie Radoux USA Inc
480 Aviation Blvd
Santa Rosa, CA 95403-1069
707-284-2888
Fax: 707-284-2894 800-755-4393
www.tonnellerieradoux.com
Wine industry cooperage
Manager: Norm Leighty
Quality Control: Lee Iller
President, Chief Executive Officer, Pres: Michel
Tapol
Manager: Lee Iller
 rx.usa@radoux-usa.com
Estimated Sales: $5 - 10 Million
Number Employees: 10-19
Square Footage: 100000
Parent Co: Radoux

30370 Tonnellerie Remond
793 Broadway
Sonoma, CA 95476-7010
707-935-2176
Fax: 707-935-4774 remondsonona@aol.com
Wine industry cooperage
Manager: Todd Stanfield
 remondsonona@aol.com
Manager: Todd Stanfield
Estimated Sales: $1 - 3 Million
Number Employees: 1-4

30371 Tooterville Trolley Company
5422 Bice Lane
Newburgh, IN 47630-8815
812-858-8585
Fax: 812-858-8580
Manufacturer and exporter of mobile carts including
shaved ice, fruit and salad bar; also, soda vending
machines
Owner: Thomas Rennels

Number Employees: 1
Square Footage: 2400
Brands:
 Jolly Trolley
 Tooterville Express

30372 (HQ)Top Line Process Equipment Company
PO Box 264
Bradford, PA 16701
814-362-4626
Fax: 814-362-4453 800-458-6095
topline@toplineonline.com
www.toplineonline.com
Supplier of hygienic stainless steel process equipment
CEO: Dan McCone
VP: Kevin O'Donnell
Marketing: Debra Fowler
Sales: John Quteri
Contact: Thomas Nicola
 tnicola@toplineonline.com
Operations: Tom Wilson
Plant Manager: Tim Fox
Purchasing: Marlene Raszmann
Number Employees: 5-9
Brands:
 Top Flo

30373 Top Source Industries
503 S Westgate St # C
PO Box 1246
Addison, IL 60101-4531
630-543-1886
Fax: 630-543-2076 800-362-9625
Clear acrylic display cases, floor, counter and wall displays, trade show displays, counters, cabinets and custom plastic products
President: Viola Wycislak
VP Sales: Gene Wycislak
Estimated Sales: $350,000
Number Employees: 1-4
Square Footage: 20000

30374 Topco Associates LLC
150 Northwest Point Blvd.
Elk Grove Village, IL 60007
847-676-3030
Fax: 847-676-4949 consumerservices@topco.com
www.topco.com
Grocery, frozen, dairy, and bakery, branded meat, equipment and supplies, business services, world brands and diverting.
President/CEO: Randall Skoda
 rskoda@topco.com
Executive VP/CFO, IT: Thomas Frey
Senior VP/General Counsel: Andy Broccolo
Senior VP, Member Development: Scott Caro
Year Founded: 1944
Estimated Sales: $15 Billion
Number Employees: 600+
Number of Brands: 20
Type of Packaging: Consumer, Food Service, Private Label
Other Locations:
 Produce
 Visalia CA
 Produce
 West Palm Beach FL
 Indirect Spend
 Quincy MA
Brands:
 Basket & Bushel
 Bloom'n Co.
 Cape Covelle Seafood Market
 CharKing
 Cornershop Cuts Delicatessen
 Cow Belle Creamery's
 Crav'n Flavor
 Culinary Tours
 Flock's Finest
 Food Club
 Full Circle Market
 Over the Top
 Paws Happy Life
 Pure Harmony
 Simply Done
 Sweet P's Bake Shop
 That's Smart!
 Tippy Toes
 TopCare
 Wide Awake Coffee Co.

30375 Topflight Grain Co-Op
400 E Bodman St
Bement, IL 61813-1299
217-678-2261
Fax: 217-678-8113 www.topflightgrain.com
Stores and distributes corn and grains
Manager: Derrick Bruhn
Manager: Yoshi Hatanaka
 hatanaka@us.astellas.com
Estimated Sales: $10 - 20 000,000
Number Employees: 50-99

30376 Topos Mondial Corp
600 Queen St
Pottstown, PA 19464-6031
610-970-2270
Fax: 610-970-1619 Sales@toposmondial.com
www.toposmondial.com
Owner: Louis Doleac
 ldoleac@verizon.net
Vice President: Damian Morabito
Estimated Sales: $5 - 10 Million
Number Employees: 20-49

30377 Tops Business Forms
1001 Rialto Rd
Covington, TN 38019-4242
901-476-4094
Fax: 785-233-4291 800-762-7283
www.tops-products.com
Business forms
President: Rodney Olson
Estimated Sales: Less Than $500,000
Number Employees: 1-4

30378 Tops Manufacturing Co
83 Salisbury Rd
Darien, CT 06820-2225
203-655-9367
Coffee and tea equipment including percolators, knobs, handles, carafes, coffee makers and filters, tea infusers, liquid coffee flavors, glass cups, instant and ground coffee dispensers, measuring spoons, etc
President: Michael Davies
 michael@endeavourpartners.net
VP: Pat Himmel
Sales Manager: Ernie Hurlbut
Estimated Sales: Less than $500,000
Number Employees: 1-4
Square Footage: 31400
Type of Packaging: Consumer, Food Service
Brands:
 Brick-Pack Clip
 Fitz-All
 Flav-A-Brrew
 Kaf-Tan
 Measure Fresh
 Perma-Brew
 Rapid Brew
 Tops

30379 Tor Rey Refrigeration Inc
3741 Yale St
Houston, TX 77018-6563
713-884-1988
Fax: 281-564-3246 888-265-3462
www.tor-rey-refrigeration.com
Wholesaler/distributor of meat grinders and parts, saws, slicers, scales and bandsaw blades
Owner: Jesus Iglecis
 gmanager@tor-rey.com
Estimated Sales: $10-20 Million
Number Employees: 5-9

30380 Tor Rey USA
3737 Yale St
Houston, TX 77018
713-884-1988
Fax: 713-564-3246
Chopper plates and knives, choppers, grinder plates and knives, grinders and scales
Owner: Jesus Iglecis
Contact: Patricio Bacco
 latinexport@tor-rey.com
Estimated Sales: $10 - 20 Million
Number Employees: 5-9

30381 Toray Plastics America Inc
50 Belver Ave
North Kingstown, RI 02852
Fax: 401-294-2154 800-453-6866
www.toraytpa.com

Biaxially oriented film, polyprolylene film, metallized.
President & CEO: Michael Brandmeier
Year Founded: 1926
Estimated Sales: $18 Billion
Number Employees: 46,000
Parent Co: Toray Industries Inc

30382 Torbeck Industries
355 Industrial Dr
Harrison, OH 45030-1483
513-367-0080
Fax: 513-367-0081 800-333-0080
Producer of material handling and safety equipment used inmanufacturing, distribution and warehousing facilities throughout North America.
President: R L Torbeck Jr
Estimated Sales: $10,000,000 - $49,900,000
Number Employees: 50-99
Square Footage: 80000
Brands:
 Astrodeck
 Quik-Space
 Saf-T-Rail

30383 Toroid Corp
225 Wynn Dr NW
Huntsville, AL 35805-1958
256-837-7510
Fax: 256-837-7512 toroidcorp@hotmail.com
www.toroidcorp.com
Custom weighing equipment, load cells and repairing load cells.
President: Anne Paelian
 toroidcorp@hotmail.com
Vice President/Sales Manager: Paul Paelian
Estimated Sales: $1 Million
Number Employees: 10-19
Square Footage: 80000
Brands:
 Lowboy
 Omniflex

30384 Toromont Process Systems
395 W 1100 N
North Salt Lake, UT 84054-2621
801-292-1747
Fax: 801-292-9908
www.toromontpowersystems.com
Manufacturer and exporter of custom designed industrial and chemical refrigeration systems
President: Hugo Sorenson
CFO: Jerry Frailec
Manager: Jim Shepherd
Contact: Vladimir Kratser
 vkratser@toromontsystems.com
Estimated Sales: $30-50 Million
Number Employees: 10
Square Footage: 70000
Parent Co: Toromont Industries
Other Locations:
 Toromont Process Systems
 Malden MA

30385 Toronto Fabricating & Manufacturing
1021 Rangeview Road
Mississauga, ON L5E 1H2
Canada
905-891-2516
Fax: 905-891-7446 sales@tfmc.com
www.tfmc.com
Manufacturer and exporter of tables, chairs, table tops and bases, benches, barstools and decorative lighting sconces and fixtures
Manager: Allan Farnum

30386 Toronto Kitchen Equipment
1150 Barmac Drive
North York, ON M9L 1X5
Canada
416-745-4944
Fax: 416-745-3217
Stoves, ovens, hoods, mixers, slicers and grills
General Manager: Paul Antolin
Number Employees: 20-49

30387 Torpac Capsules
333 Route 46
Fairfield, NJ 07004
973-244-1125
Fax: 973-244-1365 www.torpac.com

Processor, importer and exporter of gelatin capsules; manufacturer and exporter of capsule filling machinery
President: Raj Tahil
Quality Control: Ajay Varma
Estimated Sales: Below $5 Million
Number Employees: 10
Square Footage: 40000
Type of Packaging: Consumer
Brands:
  Torpac

30388 Tortilla Industry Associ
8300 Douglas Ave Ste 800
Dallas, TX 75225
   214-706-9193
   Fax: 214-706-9194
This Association was created to serve the emerging tortilla industry.
Number Employees: 1-4

30389 Tosca Ltd
1032 Bay Beach Road
Green Bay, WI 54302
   920-617-4000
   Fax: 920-465-9198 info@toscaltd.com
   www.toscaltd.com
Plastic containers for food storage
President: John Frey
Business Development: Robin Last
VP: Michael Fechter
Contact: Sarah Conway
  sconway@toscaltd.com
VP Operations: Greg Gorske
Plant Manager: Curt Dhein
Estimated Sales: $40 Million
Number Employees: 180
Square Footage: 21000

30390 Toscarora
2901 W Monroe Street
Sandusky, OH 44870-1810
   419-625-7343
   Fax: 419-625-1171
Manufacturer and exporter of custom designed plastic thermoformed food trays; also, custom designed cookie trays
Operations Manager: Joe Knight
Plant Manager: Mike LaFond
Estimated Sales: $10-20 Million
Number Employees: 50-99
Square Footage: 200000

30391 Toska Foodservice Systems
W197n7577 Fw Court
Lannon, WI 53046
   262-253-4782
   Fax: 262-253-9685
Designer and manufacturer of commercial modular combination kitchens serveries. Supplier of customer operated order and payment system. Supplier of prepaid card systems
President: Guenter Toska
Sales Manager: Thomas Conlan
Estimated Sales: Below $5 Million
Number Employees: 10

30392 Toss Machine Components
539 S Main St # 1
Nazareth, PA 18064-2795
   610-759-8883
   Fax: 610-759-1766 info@tossheatseal.com
   www.tossheatseal.com
Heatsealing plastic materials, temperature controllers, dataloggers, heatseal bands, transformers, back-up materials, heatseal bars
President: Charles Trillich
  ctrillich@packworldusa.com
Vice-President: Helma Young
Sales Manager: Andy Becan
Estimated Sales: $5-10 Million
Number Employees: 10-19
Square Footage: 400000
Type of Packaging: Consumer, Food Service

30393 Total Control Products
2001 Janice Avenue
Melrose Park, IL 60160-1010
   708-345-5500
   Fax: 708-345-5670
Electronic controls
Estimated Sales: $10-20 Million
Number Employees: 50-99

30394 Total Foods Corporation
6018 W Maple Rd
West Bloomfield, MI 48322-4404
   248-851-2611
   Fax: 248-737-2035
Manager: Dave Owens
Estimated Sales: $50-100 Million
Number Employees: 5-9

30395 (HQ)Total Identity Group
255 Pinebush Road
Cambridge, ON N1T 1B9
Canada
   519-622-4040
   Fax: 519-622-4031 877-551-5529
   info@pridesigns.com www.pridesigns.com
Custom signs and awnings
Manager: David Kurty
CFO: Dan Cass
Marketing Director: Lara Fedele
Operations Manager: Joel Shenton
Purchasing Manager: Denise Carroll
Number Employees: 100-249

30396 Total Lubricants
5 N Stiles St
Linden, NJ 07036-4208
   908-862-9300
   Fax: 908-862-1647 IBU-CSR@total-us.com
   http://keystonelubricants.com/keystone/index.htm
Product lines includes food machinery lubricants; air compressor fluids; metalworking lubricants; and maintenance lubricants.
Human Resources: Steve Daubert
Food Industry Sales Specialist: Jim Cancila
Food Industry Sales Specialist: Bruce Wolfe
Contact: Mark Catano
  mark.catano@total-us.com
International Food Industry Specialist: Christine Richard
Estimated Sales: $50,000,000 - $99,999,999
Number Employees: 10,000

30397 Total Quality Corp
320 Soundview Rd
Guilford, CT 06437-2973
   203-689-5435
   Fax: 203-483-7449 800-453-9729
   tqcinfo@totalqualitycorp.com
   www.totalqualitycorp.com
Off-line inspection for contamination, container equipment, inspection and systems division
Marketing Director: Kimberly Seneco
Contact: Stephen Evon
  s.evon@totalqualitycorp.com
Estimated Sales: $1-2.5 Million
Number Employees: 1-4

30398 Total Quality Corporation
PO Box 723
Branford, CT 06405-0723
   203-483-7447
   Fax: 203-483-7449 800-453-9729
   tqcinfo@totalqualitycorp.com
   www.totalqualitycorp.com
X-ray inspection service for raw and finished products
Office Manager: Kymberly Seneco
Estimated Sales: $1-2.5 Million
Number Employees: 4
Square Footage: 20000

30399 Total Scale Systems
1040 N Dutton Avenue
Santa Rosa, CA 95401-5042
   707-526-2221
   Fax: 707-526-0644
Wine industry scales
Estimated Sales: $1 - 5 Million
Number Employees: 6

30400 Toter Inc
841 Meacham Rd
Statesville, NC 28677-2983
   704-872-8171
   Fax: 704-878-0734 800-772-0071
   toter@toter.com www.toter.com
Manufacturer and exporter of carts and lifter systems
President: Jeff Gilliam
  jgilliam@wastequip.com
VP Sales: Rick Hoffman
Estimated Sales: $50-100 Million
Number Employees: 50-99

Brands:
  Toter Worksaver

30401 Touch Controls
520 Industrial Way
Fallbrook, CA 92028
   760-723-7900
   Fax: 760-723-7910 800-848-4385
Rugged sized touch screens, industrial computers, industrial enclosures, fiberoptic transmission systems
Estimated Sales: $5-10 Million
Number Employees: 20-49

30402 Touch Menus
1601 116th Ave NE # 111
Bellevue, WA 98004-3010
   425-881-3100
   Fax: 425-881-2980 800-688-6368
Manufacturer and exporter of touch screen point of sale systems and software; also, credit card services available
VP: Darrin Howell
Marketing Manager: Gill Gilman
Estimated Sales: $5-10 Million
Number Employees: 5-9
Square Footage: 8000
Type of Packaging: Private Label
Brands:
  Cats
  Editpro
  Touch Menus
  Trapr

30403 Tourtellot & Co
99 Colorado Ave
Warwick, RI 02888
   401-734-4200
Wholesaler/distributor of produce; serving the food service market; also, retail consultation services available.
Vice President: Jamie Manville
Vice President & Part Owner: Steve Sigal
Year Founded: 1898
Estimated Sales: $20-50 Million
Number Employees: 20-49
Square Footage: 65000

30404 Tower Pallet Co Inc
5211 County Road X
PO Box 5006
De Pere, WI 54115-9798
   920-336-3495
   Fax: 920-336-3025
Pallets and skids
President: William Koltz
  tpc@towerpallet.net
VP/Treasurer: Randy Koltz
Estimated Sales: $2.5-5 Million
Number Employees: 20-49

30405 Town & Country Uniforms, Inc.
1975 Bd Dagenais West
Laval, QC H7L 5V1
Canada
   450-622-5107
   Fax: 450-622-4632 800-361-0388
   www.tcuniforms.com
Manufacturer of uniforms for the food service industry.
Year Founded: 1957
Estimated Sales: $6.4 Million
Number Employees: 11-50

30406 Townfood Equipment Corp
72 Beadel St
Brooklyn, NY 11222-5232
   718-388-5650
   Fax: 718-388-5860 800-221-5032
   customerservice@townfood.com
   www.townfood.com
Asian barbecue equipment, cooking utensils, china, soup stoves, ovens, ranges, smokers and electric rice cookers; importer of hand hammered woks and gas rice cookers; exporter of rice cookers, ranges and smokers

President: Charles Suss
Founder: Morris Suss
VP: Sada Nair
R&D/Quality Control: Ken Trosterman
Marketing Executive: Marianne Suss
Sales: Mary Ann Balk
Equipment Specialists: Sincere Chan
Production: Ken Tosterman
Purchasing Director: Sada Nair
Estimated Sales: $5-10 Million
Number Employees: 10-19
Square Footage: 100000
Type of Packaging: Consumer, Private Label
Brands:
   Rice Master
   York & Masterrange

30407 Townsend Research Laboratories, Inc
1339 Sadlier Circle W Drive
Indianapolis, IN 46239
                    317-375-0893
          Fax: 317-375-1046
Food microbiology and consulting
President: Lou Townsend
Lab Director: Rick Ehrhardt
Quality Manager: Raymond Leiber
Sales Manager: Susan Hughes

30408 Townsend-Piller Packing
719 19 4th Avenue
Cumberland, WI 54829
          715-822-4910
Packing supplies and equipment
President: Robert Townsend

30409 Toyo Seikan Kaisha
707 Skokie Blvd # 670
Northbrook, IL 60062-2857
                    847-509-3080
          Fax: 847-509-3088
Total packaging system, from material to processing
Owner: Masa Morotomi
Estimated Sales: $1 - 5 Million
Number Employees: 1-4

30410 Toyota Tsusho America Inc.
805 3rd Ave.
17th Floor
New York, NY 10022
                    212-355-3600
          www.taiamerica.com
International trading, supply-chain services, and intermediate goods processing. Engages in business opportunities related to industrial and consumer products and services.
President/CEO: Ichiro Kashitani
Chairman: Jun Karube
CFO: Hideyuki Iwamoto
Year Founded: 1960
Estimated Sales: $5.3 Billion
Number Employees: 100-249
Square Footage: 16234
Parent Co: Toyota Tshusho Corporation

30411 Traco Manufacturing Inc
620 S 1325 W
Orem, UT 84058-4987
                    801-225-8040
   Fax: 801-226-1509 866-516-1205
          www.tracopackaging.com
Shrink film, tamper-resistant packaging, heat sealer machines
President: John Palica
CFO: John Hiatt
HR Executive: Scott Goodman
   sgoodman@traco-mfg.co
Quality Control: Craig Johnson
VP Sales: Ron Moore
Purchasing Manager: Craig Johnson
Estimated Sales: Below $5 Million
Number Employees: 50-99
Square Footage: 40000
Brands:
   Impulse Heat Sealer
   Shrink Bags
   Shrink Bands & Preforms

30412 Trade Fixtures
1501 Westpark Dr # 5
Little Rock, AR 72204-2457
                    501-664-1318
   Fax: 501-664-9253 800-872-3490
cservice@tradefixtures.com www.h2optimized.net

Manufacturer and exporter of molded displays for bulk food items including gravity and scoop bins
Manager: Scott Johnson
   sjohnson@tradefixtures.com
Quality Control: Walter Baumgarten
President: Scott Johnson
VP Sales: Clay Odom
VP Sales: Doug Holland
General Manager: Joe Herrmann
Purchasing Manager: Roy Jackson
Estimated Sales: $5 - 10 Million
Number Employees: 50-99
Square Footage: 112000
Parent Co: Display Technologies

30413 Trade Wings
4929 Wyaconda Rd
Rockville, MD 20852-2443
                    301-770-8770
          Fax: 301-770-8771
Owner: Nader Dibiglari
Estimated Sales: Under$500,000
Number Employees: 5-9

30414 Tradeco International Corp
1107 S Westwood Ave
PO Box 1155
Addison, IL 60101-4920
                    630-628-1112
   Fax: 630-628-6616 800-628-3738
ventura@tradecointl.com www.tradecointl.com
Manufacturer and importer of chinaware including plates, cups, saucers and holloware
President: Leslie D Plass
   lplass@tradecointl.com
Estimated Sales: $1 - 3,000,000
Number Employees: 10-19
Type of Packaging: Consumer
Brands:
   Ventura China

30415 Trademarx Inc
1443 E Washington Blvd.,
Pasadena, CA 94110
                    626-795-0587
   Fax: 626-795-0548 sales@trademarx.net
          www.trademarx.net
Manufacture disposable plastic and paper products for the foodservice industry.
President/CEO: Scott James
CFO/Public Relations: Jenny Wang
VP/R&D: Peter Song
Quality Control: Shelly Lu
Marketing/Sales: Scott James
Estimated Sales: $5 Million
Number Employees: 250-499
Number of Brands: 3
Number of Products: 100
Square Footage: 680000
Type of Packaging: Consumer, Food Service, Private Label, Bulk
Brands:
   Jay
   Purex
   Trademarx

30416 Tradepaq Corporation
30 Montgomery Street
Jersey City, NJ 07302
                    201-716-2665
   Fax: 201-435-9916 www.tradepaq.com
Supplier of commodity trading software
CFO: Charles Griffs
Sales: Deborah Laska
Contact: David Janay
   djanay@tradepaq.com
Estimated Sales: $5-10 Million
Number Employees: 10-19

30417 Traeger Industries
10450 SW Nimbus Ave
Building R, Suite A
Portland, OR 97223
                    503-845-9234
   Fax: 503-94 -155 800-872-3437
   traeger@traegerindustries.com
          www.traegergrills.com
Manufacturer and exporter of wood pellet smokers and cooking appliances
President: Joseph Traeger
VP Sales/Marketing: Randy Traeger
VP Production: Mark Traeger

Estimated Sales: $5 - 10 Million
Number Employees: 50-99
Square Footage: 108000
Brands:
   Traeger

30418 Traex
101 Traex Dr
Dane, WI 53529
                    608-849-2500
   Fax: 608-849-2580 800-356-8006
          www.libbey.com
Manufacturer, importer and exporter of food trays, straw dispensers, portion control and napkin dispensers, bus boxes, dishracks and tabletop accessories
Marketing: Lori Barger
Contact: Allen Byers
   allen.byers@libbey.com
Plant Manager: Steve Boeder
Purchasing Agent: Rose Ohlert
Estimated Sales: $10-20 Million
Number Employees: 100-249
Square Footage: 30000
Parent Co: Menasha Corporation
Brands:
   Barkeep
   Batter Boss
   Cupro
   Dripcut
   Kondi-Keeper
   Lidpro Lid Dispenser
   Quik-Pik
   Rackmaster
   Sauce Boss
   Self Service System
   Straw Boss
   T-Rex

30419 (HQ)Tragon Corp
350 Bridge Pkwy
Redwood City, CA 94065-1061
                    650-412-2100
   Fax: 650-412-2001 800-841-1177
   info@tragon.com www.tragon.com
Consultant specializing in product testing, market research and management consultation services. Quantitative and qualitative market research
President/CEO: Douglas Vort
Co-Founder: Herbert Stone
   hstone@tragon.com
VP: Rebecca Bleibaum
Marketing: Joseph Salerno
Chief Operating Officer: Brian Adkins
Estimated Sales: $2.5-5 Million
Number Employees: 20-49
Square Footage: 21000
Other Locations:
   Tragon Corporation
   Buffalo Grove IL
Brands:
   Prop
   Prop Plus
   Qda
   Qda Software

30420 Traitech Industries
100 Four Valley Drive
Unit C
Vaughan, ON L4K 4T9
Canada
                    905-695-2800
   Fax: 905-695-0737 877-872-4835
   info@traitech.com www.traitech.com
Manufacturer and exporter of ventilated merchandising trays, baskets and displays custom manufacturer
President: Tom Penton
VP: Ryan Slight
Type of Packaging: Consumer, Food Service, Private Label, Bulk
Brands:
   California
   California Trays

30421 Trak-Air/Rair
555 Quivas St
Denver, CO 80204-4915
                    303-779-9888
   Fax: 303-694-3575 800-688-8725
   sales@trak-air.com www.trak-air.com
Manufacturer and exporter of hot air and greaseless countertop fryers; also, pizza ovens
President: Dale Terry
   dterry@coloradosalesinc.com

Estimated Sales: $1 - 2 Million
Number Employees: 20-49
Square Footage: 64000
Type of Packaging: Food Service
Brands:
  Rair 2000
  Rair 7000
  Trak-Air Ii
  Trak-Air V

30422 Traker Systems
43460 Ridge Park Dr # 250
Suite 250
Temecula, CA 92590-3736
951-693-1376
Fax: 951-693-1386 800-314-6863
www.itracker.net
Traker Systems is an inventory management and inventory software application that enables manufacturing and transportation industries the power to regulate, dominate, or manipulate services and products, purchasing, receivinginvoicing, pricing, product allocation, bar coding, forms and shipping into one, convenient package.
Owner: Kuba Fandl
  kubaf@trakersystems.com
Number Employees: 10-19

30423 Tramontina USA
12955 W Airport Blvd
Sugar Land, TX 77478-6119
281-340-8400
Fax: 281-340-8410 800-221-7809
tusa@tramontina-usa.com
www.tramontina-usa.com
Cutlery, cookware and servingware
President: Antonio Galafassi
Manager Food Service Sales: Steve Kozicki
Sales Assistant (Food Service): Debbie Rademacher
Contact: Rawan Abdeljaber
  rabdeljaber@sizzlingplatter.com
Estimated Sales: $10-20,000,000
Number Employees: 250-499

30424 Trane Inc
800-E Beaty St
Davidson, NC 28036
704-655-4000
www.trane.com
Manufacturer and exporter of roof top and self-contained air conditioner; also, heat pumps including water-source.
President, Commercial HVAC Americas: Donald Simmons
President, Residential HVAC & Supply: Jason Bingham
Year Founded: 1913
Estimated Sales: $10 Billion
Number Employees: 29,000
Parent Co: Ingersoll Rand
Brands:
  Aire Systems
  Centravac
  Earthwise Systems
  Integrated Comfort Systems
  Intellipack
  Service First
  Tracer Summit
  Tracker
  Trag
  Trane
  Unit Trane
  Varitrac
  Varitrane

30425 Trans Flex Packagers Inc
34 Burnham Ave
PO Box 127
Unionville, CT 06085-1263
860-673-2531
Fax: 860-673-6238 www.tfpackagers.com
Flexible plastic bags including cellulose, polyethylene and polypropylene
Owner: Mike Kaplan
  mike@tfpackagers.com
Estimated Sales: $5-10 Million
Number Employees: 20-49
Square Footage: 50000

30426 Trans World Services
72 Stone Pl
Melrose, MA 02176-6016
781-665-9200
Fax: 781-665-6649 800-882-2105
twsinc@gis.net
Manufacturer and exporter of thermometers and sandwich packaging materials including crystal wrap and cellophane; also, packaging machinery. Consumer, institution and processor packaging of T-shirts, USDA/FSIS partner
President: Thomas E Ford
CFO: Thomas Foid
Vice President: Dan Tuono
R&D: Thomas Foid
Quality Control: Thomas Foid
Sales/Marketing: Ira Siegal
Estimated Sales: $10 - 20 Million
Number Employees: 10-19
Square Footage: 208000
Type of Packaging: Food Service

30427 (HQ)Trans-Chemco Inc
19235 84th St
PO Box 9
Bristol, WI 53104-9184
262-857-2363
Fax: 262-857-9127 800-880-2498
info@trans-chemco.com www.trans-chemco.com
Manufacturer, importer and exporter of chemicals including defoamers and antifoamers; also, laboratory research and development for products and special needs
President: Susanne Gardiner
CFO: Irene Swan
VP/Director: Merle Gardiner
VP R&D: Merle Gardiner
Operations Manager: Sheila Cleveland
Estimated Sales: $1 - 3 Million
Number Employees: 10-19
Square Footage: 60000
Brands:
  Trans-10
  Trans-100
  Trans-30

30428 Transbotics Corp
3400 Latrobe Dr
Charlotte, NC 28211-4847
704-362-1115
Fax: 704-364-4039 www.transbotics.com
Design, development, support and installation of Automatic Guided Vehicles, or transportation robots, with an emphasis on complete customer satisfaction. Supplier of Automatic Guide Vehicle Systems, AGV controls technology, engineeringservices, AGV batteries, charges and other related products
CEO: Claude Imbleau
EVP: Neville Croft
Service/ Quality System Manager: Robert Stiteler
Marketing & Aftermarket Sales: Jayesh Mehta
Sales: Chuck Rossell
Public Relations: Ryan Willis
Operations: Mark Ramsey
Purchasing Manager: David Melton
Estimated Sales: $1 - 5,000,000
Number Employees: 20-49
Parent Co: NDC Automation
Type of Packaging: Bulk

30429 Transition Equipment Company
444 Laguna Vista Road
Santa Rosa, CA 95401
707-537-7787
Fax: 707-537-7174 vickitec@aol.com
www.transitionequipment.com
Used equipment, winery, packaging and beverage
Fiscal Operations Manager: Eileen Paul
Director of Sales: Vicki Mastbaum
  vicki@transitionequipment.com
Estimated Sales: Below $500,000
Number Employees: 3

30430 Transnorm System Inc
1906 S Great Southwest Pkwy
Grand Prairie, TX 75051-3580
972-606-0303
Fax: 972-606-0768 800-259-2303
sales@transnorm.com www.transnorm.com
Manufacturer and exporter of belt curve conveyors including mini edge, power, spiral, straight, etc
President: Kay L Wolfe
VP: Rick Lee

Estimated Sales: $20-50 Million
Number Employees: 10
Square Footage: 80000
Parent Co: Transnorm System GmBH
Brands:
  F.R.P.
  Safeglide

30431 Transparent Container Co
325 S Lombard Rd
Addison, IL 60101-3023
630-458-9031
Fax: 312-666-3163
marketing@transparentcontainer.com
Containers
President: Dan Greiwe
  dgreiwe@transparentcontainer.com
CFO: Ron Pranger
VP/Sales: Dan Wyss
General Manager: Steve Fifer
Estimated Sales: $5-10 Million
Number Employees: 50-99

30432 Tranter INC
1900 Old Burk Hwy
Wichita Falls, TX 76306-5904
940-723-7125
Fax: 940-723-5131 sales@tranter.com
www.tranter.com
Surface and plate heat exchangers, cabinet liners for walk-in refrigerator/freezing rooms, freezing storage units, cold and hot food displays; exporter of heat exchangers
President: Charles Monachello
CEO: Roy Mason
CFO: Arnold Downes
VP: Roy Mason
Research & Development: Jeff Mathur
Marketing Director: Ronald Stonecipher
Sales Director: Frank Kierzkowski
Purchasing Manager: Czeech Richardson
Number Employees: 100-249
Square Footage: 480000
Parent Co: Tranter
Brands:
  Colbank
  Freeztand
  Maxchanger
  Platecoil
  Snobanc
  Snopan
  Steempan
  Superchanger

30433 Trap-Zap Environmental
255 Braen Ave
Wyckoff, NJ 07481-2948
201-251-9970
Fax: 201-251-0903 800-282-8727
Biological products for greasetraps, drains and septic systems, septic system additives and floor and surface cleaners; also, consultant providing wastewater management, turnkey programs and greasetrap maintenance
President: Robert Belle
  rbelle@trapzap.com
National Accounts Manager: Rick Albano
Estimated Sales: $2.5-5 Million
Number Employees: 10-19
Square Footage: 10000
Brands:
  Bio-Zap
  D-Grade
  Trap-Zap Plus

30434 Traub Container Corporation
22475 Aurora Road
Cleveland, OH 44146-1270
216-475-5100
Fax: 216-475-5015
Corrugated displays, shipping containers and fiberboard sheets
Sales Manager: Bob Mavity
General Manager: Donald Colombo
Plant Manager: Dale Kiaski
Estimated Sales: $10 - 20 Million
Number Employees: 135
Square Footage: 250000
Parent Co: MacMillan Bloedel Packaging

30435 Traulsen & Co
4401 Blue Mound Rd
Fort Worth, TX 76106-1928
817-625-1168
Fax: 817-624-4302 800-825-8220
Manufacturer and exporter of commercial refrigerators and freezers including display, stainless steel, anodized aluminum, vinyl, reach-in, roll-in and pass-through
Manager: Gary Hoying
Vice President: Pepe Griffo
Marketing Director: Mark Kauffman
Operations: Gary Hoying
Purchasing: John Hebert
Estimated Sales: $20-50 Million
Number Employees: 10-19
Square Footage: 300000
Parent Co: ITW
Other Locations:
  Traulsen & Co.
  New Troy MI
Brands:
  Show-Off
  Traulsen
  Ultima
  Ultra

30436 Travaini Pumps USA
200 Newsome Dr
Yorktown, VA 23692-5002
757-988-3930
Fax: 757-988-3975 800-535-4243
customerservice@travaini.com www.travaini.com
Liquid ring vacuum pumps
President: Dominic Gemmiti
Vice President: Federico Colagrande
Estimated Sales: $10-20 Million
Number Employees: 20-49

30437 Travelon
700 Touhy Ave
Elk Grove Vlg, IL 60007-4916
847-621-7000
Fax: 847-621-7001 800-537-5544
www.travelonbags.com
Manufacturer, importer and exporter of metal displays and carts
Owner: Don Godshaw
  dong@travelonbags.com
VP Marketing: Kathy Novak
Estimated Sales: $1 - 5 Million
Number Employees: 100-249
Square Footage: 100000
Type of Packaging: Consumer

30438 Travis Manufacturing Corp
13231 Salem Church St NE
Alliance, OH 44601-9441
330-875-1661
Fax: 330-875-4240
Custom fabricated stainless steel tables, shelving
President: Roger W Oberlin
VP: Brian Taranto
Estimated Sales: Less Than $500,000
Number Employees: 1-4
Square Footage: 17000

30439 Tray-Pak Corp
251 Tuckerton Rd
Reading, PA 19605-1154
610-926-5800
Fax: 610-926-9140 info@traypak.com
www.traypak.com
Thermoformed plastic trays
President: John Rusnock
CEO: William Barrick
  bbarrick@traypak.com
CEO: Randy Simcox
Marketing: William Mosier
Estimated Sales: $20-50 Million
Number Employees: 250-499

30440 Traycon Manufacturing Co
555 Barell Ave
Carlstadt, NJ 07072-2891
201-939-5555
Fax: 201-939-4180 info@traycon.com
www.traycon.com
Manufacturer and exporter of conveyors and carts for dish and tray handling systems
CEO: Nicholas Pisto
VP: Candice Pisto

Estimated Sales: $5-10 Million
Number Employees: 20-49
Square Footage: 40000
Brands:
  Dw
  Ra
  Rdb
  Rdl
  Sdb
  Sdl
  Ssw
  Traycon

30441 Tree Saver
2830 S Shoshone Street
Englewood, CO 80110-1204
303-781-2646
Fax: 303-762-8616 800-676-7741
www.savers.com
Reusable bags including cloth grocery, trash liner and produce
Operations Manager: Carol Sweet
Estimated Sales: $500,000-$1 Million
Number Employees: 19
Brands:
  Tree Saver Bags

30442 TreeHouse Foods, Inc.
2021 Spring Rd.
Suite 600
Oak Brook, IL 60523
708-483-1300
info@treehousefoods.com
www.treehousefoods.com
Cereals, snack foods, condiments, frozen baked goods and frozen prepared meals.
President/CEO: Steven Oakland
Year Founded: 2005
Estimated Sales: $6.3 Billion
Number Employees: 13,489
Number of Brands: 4
Type of Packaging: Consumer, Private Label
Brands:
  Bay Valley Foods
  E.D. Smith
  Flagstone Foods
  TreeHouse Private Brands

30443 Treen Box & Pallet Inc
1950 Street Rd # 400
Bensalem, PA 19020-3752
215-639-5100
Fax: 215-639-8530 www.treenpallet.com
Wooden boxes, pallets and skids
President: George Geiges
  ggeiges@comcast.net
VP: A Geiges
Estimated Sales: $30 Million
Number Employees: 20-49
Square Footage: 30000

30444 Treier Popcorn Farms
16793 County Line Rd
Bloomdale, OH 44817
419-454-2811
Fax: 419-454-3983 ptreier@wcnet.org
Popcorn including natural, buttered and microwaveable; wholesaler/distributor of commercial popcorn poppers and other concession supply equipment; serving the food service market
President: Don Treier
Secretary/Treasurer: Peggy Treier
Estimated Sales: $500,000-$1 Million
Number Employees: 15
Number of Brands: 2
Number of Products: 6
Square Footage: 12000
Parent Co: Treier Family Farms
Type of Packaging: Consumer, Food Service, Bulk
Brands:
  Lake Plains
  Pelton's Hybrid Popcorn

30445 Treif USA
230 Long Hill Cross Rd
Shelton, CT 06484-6160
203-929-9930
Fax: 203-849-8517 treifusa@treif.com
www.treif.com
High speed, high-output slicing and dicing equipment
President: Robert Linke
Contact: Alicia Clayton
  aclayton@treif.com

Estimated Sales: $1-2.5 Million
Number Employees: 5-9

30446 Treif USA Inc
50 Waterview Dr # 130
Suite 130
Shelton, CT 06484-4377
203-929-9930
Fax: 203-929-9949 info@treif.com
www.treif.de
High-speed slicing machines, bone in or boneless high volume dicing machines
President: Terry Albrecht
  terry.albrecht@treif.com
Vice President: Bill Render
Marketing Director: Alicia Kidd
  terry.albrecht@treif.com
Estimated Sales: $6.0 Million
Number Employees: 5-9
Parent Co: Treif Machinery GmbH

30447 Trent Corp
1384 Yardville Hamilton Squ Rd
Trenton, NJ 08691-3343
609-587-7515
Fax: 609-586-9710 trentboxmfgco@aol.com
www.trentbox.com
Packaging materials including bikini packs, box lids and corrugated containers
President: Carl A Angelini
Quality Control: Bob Campbell
Sales/Marketing Executive: Charles Baumann
Purchasing Agent: Lynda Saganowski
Estimated Sales: $10 - 20 Million
Number Employees: 10-19
Brands:
  Kwik-Pak
  Twin-Pak

30448 Trenton Mills Inc
400 Factory St
PO Box 107
Trenton, TN 38382-2012
731-855-1323
Fax: 731-855-9000 sales@trentonmills.com
www.trentonmills.com
Stockinette knit for meat packing and filters
Owner: Bobby Blakely
  blakely@trentonmills.com
Operations: Bubby Blakely
Estimated Sales: $3 - 5 Million
Number Employees: 20-49
Square Footage: 520000
Parent Co: Dyersburg Fabrics

30449 Treofan America LLC
6001 Gun Club Rd
Winston Salem, NC 27103-9727
336-766-9448
Fax: 336-766-8260 800-424-6273
www.treofan.com
Packaging films and labels
Manager: Grant Gustason
  grant.gustason@treofan.com
Number Employees: 20-49

30450 (HQ)Trepte's Wire & Metal Works
14822 Lakewood Boulevard
Bellflower, CA 90706-2857
562-630-6798
Fax: 562-630-5901 800-828-6217
rontrepte@hotmail.com
Skewers, hot pan grips, spoons and racks including roasting, baking and broiling
President and CEO: A Ron Trepte Sr
Secretary: E Trepte
Number Employees: 10
Square Footage: 48000
Brands:
  E-Z-V

30451 Trevor Industries
8698 S Main St
Eden, NY 14057
716-992-4775
Fax: 716-992-4788
Manufacturer, importer and exporter of plastic drinking straws and cocktail stirrers
Owner: Gary Ballowe
VP Administration: Karen Amico
Plant Manager: Robert Martin

Estimated Sales: $5 - 10 Million
Number Employees: 20-49
Square Footage: 150000

30452 Trevor Owen Limited
80 Barbados Boulevard
Unit 5
Scarborough, ON M1J 1K9
Canada

416-267-8231
Fax: 416-267-1035 866-487-2224
sales@trevorowenltd.com
www.trevorowenltd.com
Manufacturer and exporter of banners and insulated food delivery bags
President: Pierre Barcik
Sales Executive: Trevor Owen
Number Employees: 10
Square Footage: 40000

30453 Tri County Citrus Packers
12143 Avenue 456
Orange Cove, CA 93646-9504

559-626-5010
Fax: 559-626-7951 vcpg@vcpg.com
Packinghouse and licensed shipper of citrus products for Sunkist Growers, Inc.
Manager: John Kalendar
Assistant Manager: Eric Fultz
Manager: John Clower
jclower@vcpg.com
Number Employees: 50-99
Parent Co: Visalia Citrus Packing Group

30454 Tri Tool Inc
3041 Sunrise Blvd
Rancho Cordova, CA 95742-6502

916-288-6100
Fax: 916-288-6160 800-345-5015
customer.service@tritool.com www.tritool.com
Manufactures pipe cutting and welding preparation equipment
President: Jennifer Arsenault
jennifer.a.arsenault@wellsfargo.com
CEO: Jerry VanDer Pol
Chairman: George J Wernette
CFO: Tom Meyer
R & D: Dale Flood
Sales: Daryl Anderson
Production: Jim Bergstrand
Purchasing: Barbara Porter
Estimated Sales: $20-50 Million
Number Employees: 100-249
Type of Packaging: Bulk

30455 Tri-Boro Shelving & Partition
300 Dominion Dr
Farmville, VA 23901-2371

434-315-5600
Fax: 434-315-0139 800-633-3070
sales@triboroshelving.com
www.triboroshelving.com
Shelving, bin units, mobile shelf trucks and service carts
Owner: Fred Demaio
fdemaio@triboroshelving.com
CFO: Tony De Maio
Estimated Sales: $2.5 - 5 Million
Number Employees: 20-49
Square Footage: 400000
Brands:
    Boxer
    Rivet Rak
    Stor-It
    Sturdi-Frame

30456 Tri-Clover
PO Box 7731
Richmond, VA 23231-0231

804-545-8120
Fax: 804-545-0194 800-558-4060
Pumps, valves, fittings, blenders, filter, batch control systems, cheese equipment, fillers, gravity, milk, flow diversion stations
Marketing Director: Chip Bresette
Public Relations: Joyce Bergh
Estimated Sales: $1 - 5 Million
Number Employees: 250-499

30457 Tri-Connect
111 Frank Lloyd Wright Lane
Oak Park, IL 60302-2644

708-660-8190
Fax: 312-951-6243 triconnect@aol.com

Wholesaler of England Farmhouse Biscuits packaged in gift tins and boxes, d'Orsay Chocolatier featuring imported Belgian chocolate and petit four desserts. Private labeling available
President: Tony Birbeck
CEO: Linda Murphy
CFO: Anthony Cioffi
Estimated Sales: Below $5 Million
Number Employees: 5
Type of Packaging: Private Label, Bulk
Brands:
    Farmhouse Biscuits

30458 Tri-K Industries Inc
2 Stewart Ct
PO Box 10
Denville, NJ 07834-1028

973-298-8850
Fax: 201-750-9785 rebecca.morton@tri-k.com
www.tri-k.com
Owner: Manoj Agarwal
manoj.agarwal@galaxysurfactants.com
Number Employees: 20-49

30459 Tri-Pak Machinery Inc
1102 N Commerce St
Harlingen, TX 78550-4814

956-423-5140
Fax: 956-423-9362
dfitzgerald@tri-pakmachinery.com
www.tri-pak.com
Manufacturer and exporter of fruit and vegetable processing machinery including belt and chain conveyors, graders, sizers, cleaners, packers and wax coaters; also, graders for shrimp
President: David A Fitzgerald
VP: Charles M. Kilbourn
Director of Sales and Marketing: James W. Fitzgerald
Sales: Robert E. Fitzgerald
Director of Operations: Daniel J. Groves
Purchasing: Chuck Kilbourn
Estimated Sales: $5 - 10 Million
Number Employees: 20-49
Square Footage: 516000

30460 Tri-Seal
900 Bradley Hill Rd
Blauvelt, NY 10913-1196

845-353-3300
Fax: 845-353-3376
LinersNorthAmer@tekni-plex.com
tri-seal.tekni-plex.com
Manufacturer and exporter of coextruded thermoplastic bottle cap liners and extruded rigid and flexible PVC tubing and profiles
CEO: F Smith
President: Bruce Burus
VP Sales/Marketing: Walter Burgess
Estimated Sales: $5 - 10 Million
Number Employees: 50-99
Square Footage: 440000
Brands:
    Tri-Foil
    Tri-Gard
    Tri-Lam
    Tri-Seal

30461 (HQ)Tri-State Plastics
PO Box 337
Henderson, KY 42419-0337

270-826-8361
Fax: 270-826-8362
Manufacturer and exporter of injection molded food containers
Owner: Mike Walden
VP/Secretary/Treasurer: Mike Walden
Estimated Sales: less than $500,000
Number Employees: 1-4
Square Footage: 70000
Type of Packaging: Private Label, Bulk

30462 Tri-State Plastics
PO Box 496
Glenwillard, PA 15046-0496

724-457-6900
Fax: 724-457-6901 www.crightonplastics.com
Manufacturer and exporter of vacuum formed plastic products including trays, covers, guards, material handling components, etc.
President/ Sales: Chris Crighton
General Manager: Michael Lopez
Production Manager: Charles Goetz

30463 Tri-Sterling
1050 Miller Dr
Altamonte Spgs, FL 32701-7505

407-260-0330
Fax: 407-260-7096
Manufacturer and exporter of packaging equipment and shrink wrappers
VP: Ken Schilling
Marketing: Thomas Jimenez
Estimated Sales: $20-50 Million
Number Employees: 100-249
Brands:
    Genesis Ii

30464 Tri-Tronics
7705 Cheri Ct
PO Box 25135
Tampa, FL 33634-2419

813-886-4000
Fax: 813-884-8818 800-237-0946
info@ttco.com www.ttco.com
Manufacturer and exporter of material handling and automation application controls including photoelectric sensors, registration scanners, photoelectric eyes and flexible plastic/glass fiber optic light guides
President: Scott Seehawer
scotts@ttco.com
VP/Sales Manager: Dennis Henderson
Estimated Sales: $10-20 Million
Number Employees: 50-99
Square Footage: 56000
Brands:
    Color Mark
    D.C. Eye
    Mity-Eye
    Smarteye
    Tiny-Eye
    U.S. Eye
    Visioneye

30465 Triad Pallet Co Inc
4910 Bartlett St
Greensboro, NC 27409-2802

336-292-8175
Fax: 336-292-8175
Wooden skids and pallets
President/CFO: B Bare
Manager: B M Bare
Estimated Sales: Less Than $500,000
Number Employees: 1-4
Square Footage: 8000

30466 Triad Products Company
1913 Commerce Circle
Springfield, OH 45504-2011

937-323-9422
Fax: 937-328-6463
Aprons
President: Louis Jung
Number Employees: 20

30467 Triad Scientific
6 Stockton Lake Blvd
Manasquan, NJ 08736-3024

732-292-1994
Fax: 732-292-1961 800-867-6690
triadscientific@gmail.com www.triadsci.com
Manufacturer and exporter of laboratory equipment including balances, analysis instrumentation, filtration, incubators, lamps, microscopes, monitoring systems, ovens, sterilizers, spectrophotometers, etc.; also, analysis, designservice and repair available
VP: Tom Leskow
Estimated Sales: $3 - 5 Million
Number Employees: 1-4
Square Footage: 20000
Type of Packaging: Food Service, Bulk

30468 Triad Scientific
6 Stockton Lake Blvd
Manasquan, NJ 08736-3024

732-292-1994
Fax: 732-292-1961 800-867-6690
triadscientific@gmail.com www.triadsci.com
President: Tom Leskow
Vice-President: Bill Aronoff
Number Employees: 1-4

30469 Triangle Package Machinery Co
6655 W Diversey Ave
Chicago, IL 60707-2293
773-889-0201
Fax: 773-889-4221 800-621-4170
wcray@trianglepackage.com
www.trianglepackage.com
Manufacturer and exporter of bag and carton making, closing, filling, packing, weighing and sealing machinery
President: Bryan Muskat
bmuskat@trianglepackage.com
R&D: Jerone Lasky
Quality Control: Roger Gaw
Director Sales: John Michalson
Purchasing Agent: John Musso
Estimated Sales: $20 - 50 Million
Number Employees: 100-249
Square Footage: 10000000
Brands:
Acceleron Advantage
Proline
Selectacom
Selectech 32 Controls

30470 Triangle Sign & Svc
11 Azar Ct
Halethorpe, MD 21227-1504
410-247-5300
Fax: 410-247-1944 info@trianglesign.com
www.trianglesign.com
Neon and plastic signs
President: Robert Altshuler
robert.altshuler@trianglesign.com
Estimated Sales: $10 - 20 Million
Number Employees: 100-249

30471 Tribology Tech Lube
35 Old Dock Rd
Yaphank, NY 11980-9702
631-345-3000
Fax: 631-345-3001 800-569-1757
info@tribology.com www.tribology.com
Manufacturer and exporter of synthetic and specialty lubricants
President: William Krause
Sales: Paul Anderson
Manager: T Tierney
Operations/General Manager: Terence Tierney
Purchasing: Gail Moore
Estimated Sales: $50-100 Million
Number Employees: 10-19
Number of Products: 300
Square Footage: 35000
Type of Packaging: Private Label, Bulk

30472 Trico Converting Inc
1801 Via Burton
Suite A
Fullerton, CA 92831-5319
714-563-0701
Fax: 714-772-7528 www.printaccess.com
Manufacturer and exporter of flexible packaging; also, printing and laminating available
President: Larry Schow
lschow@goarmy.com
VP: Tim Love
Estimated Sales: $10 - 20 Million
Number Employees: 5-9
Square Footage: 40000
Type of Packaging: Consumer, Food Service, Private Label, Bulk

30473 Tricor Systems Inc
1650 Todd Farm Dr
Elgin, IL 60123-1145
847-742-5542
Fax: 847-742-5574 800-575-0161
info@tricor-systems.com www.tricor-systems.com
Specialized test instruments including gloss, color and texture analysis systems aand chocolate temper meters
President: Tim Allen
mail@tricor-systems.com
Sales Director: Thomas Allen
Estimated Sales: $5 - 10 Million
Number Employees: 20-49
Square Footage: 37000

30474 Tricor Systems Inc
1650 Todd Farm Dr
Elgin, IL 60123-1145
847-742-5542
Fax: 847-742-5574 800-575-0161
info@tricor-systems.com www.tricor-systems.com
TRICOR is ISO 90001-2008 Certified, ISO 13485:2003 Certified, Mil Spec Certified and FDA registered manufacturer. TRICOR also offers products designed and manufactured by TRICOR which include: DOI/Haze Meter, gloss meters, videophotometers, imaging spectrophotometers, switch testers, life cycle tester and chocolate temper meters.
President: Tim Allen
mail@tricor-systems.com
VP of Sales: Thomas Allen
Estimated Sales: $5 - 10 Million
Number Employees: 20-49
Square Footage: 96000

30475 Tricore AEA
6921 Mariner Dr
Mt Pleasant, WI 53406-3946
262-880-3630
Fax: 262-886-1676 www.tricore.com
Software engineering for the food, dairy, beverage industries
President: David Mc Carthy
President, Chief Executive Officer: David McCarthy
Engineering/Business Development VP: Steve Reiter
IT: Chris Edwards
cedwardswi@yahoo.com
Number Employees: 20-49

30476 Trident
1114 Federal Rd
Brookfield, CT 06804-1140
203-740-9333
Fax: 203-775-9660 www.trident-itw.com
Print heads and inks for industrial applications
Manager: Juan Lopez
General Manager: Jean-Marie Gutierrez
Marketing/Sales: Robert Donofrio
Manager: Edward Broadhurst
edward.broadhurst@tridentamericas.com
Estimated Sales: $1 - 5,000,000
Number Employees: 50-99
Parent Co: ITW
Brands:
A 3000
Allwrite
Hi-Def
Jetwrite
Microcoder
Pixeljet
Ultrajet
Versaprint

30477 Trident Plastics
1009 Pulinski Rd
Ivyland, PA 18974
215-672-5225
Fax: 215-672-5582 800-222-2318
sales@tridentplastics.com
www.tridentplastics.com
Manufacturer and exporter of plastic tubes, sheets, rods, ducts, films, slabs and signs
President: Ronald Cadic
Sales Manager: Michael Peroni
Contact: William Thomas
vasales@tridentplastics.com
Estimated Sales: $1-2.5 Million
Number Employees: 10-19

30478 Tridyne Process Systems
80 Allen Rd
South Burlington, VT 05403-7801
802-863-6873
Fax: 802-860-1591 sales@tridyne.com
www.tridyne.com
Manufacturer and exporter of automatic weighing and counting systems including net weighers and weigh counters; also, baggers, cartoners, conveyors, etc
President: Susith Wijetunga
Estimated Sales: $1 - 5 Million
Number Employees: 5-9
Square Footage: 44000
Parent Co: Tridyne Process Systems, Inc
Type of Packaging: Consumer, Food Service, Private Label, Bulk

Brands:
Tridyne

30479 Trilla Steel Drum Corporation
2959 W 47th St
Chicago, IL 60632-1998
773-847-7588
Fax: 773-847-5550
Steel shipping barrels and drums
Owner: Lester Trilla
CFO: Andy Perpetual
Quality Control: Chris Racawski
Sales Manager: Robert Craven
Estimated Sales: $20-50 Million
Number Employees: 5-9

30480 Trilogy Essential Ingredients
1304 Continental Dr
Abingdon, MD 21009-2334
410-612-0691
Fax: 410-612-9401 info@trilogyei.com
www.trilogyei.com
Flavors, seasonings, liquid spice extracts, proprietary delivery systems and functional ingredients.
Contact: Amy Ashcraft
aashcraft@trilogyei.com
Number Employees: 10-19
Number of Brands: 3
Type of Packaging: Bulk
Brands:
CitraSense
NextWave
Tril-Clear

30481 Trimble Agriculture
10368 N Westmoor Dr.
Westminster, CO 80021
agriculture.trimble.com
Provides solutions for a number of agriculture phases, including land preperation, guidance and steering, planting and seeding, water management, harvest, and data management.
President & CEO: Robert Painter
SVP & CFO: David Barnes

30482 Trimen Foodservice Equipment
1240 Ormont Drive
North York, ON M9L 2V4
Canada
416-744-3313
Fax: 416-744-3347 877-437-1422
paul_cesario@trimen.net www.trimen.net
Manufacturer and exporter of ovens, broilers, tables, booths and refrigeration equipment
President: Paul Cesario
Finance Manager: Grace Giulano
Head Operations: Mario Dipiede
Purchasing Manager: Mario Dipiede
Estimated Sales: $50-75 Million
Number Employees: 10
Type of Packaging: Food Service

30483 Trimline Corp
500 Industrial Dr
Elkhart Lake, WI 53020-1972
920-876-3611
Fax: 920-876-3527 800-555-5895
www.plyco.com
Insulated utility doors including food service and plastic
Plant Manager: Blend Luedtk
CEO: Gary Matz
CFO: Tom Matz
Estimated Sales: $10 - 20 Million
Number Employees: 20-49
Brands:
Plyco

30484 Trine Rolled Moulding Corp
1421 Ferris Pl
Bronx, NY 10461-3610
718-828-5200
Fax: 718-828-4052 800-223-8075
info@trinecorp.com www.trinecorp.com
OEM manufacturer of factory direct original F-series baffle grease filters, aluminum, galvanized, stainless steel, all sizes-large inventory,
UL/MEA/USA
President: Frank Rella
info@trinecorp.com
Plant Manager: James Lange
Estimated Sales: $5-10 Million
Number Employees: 50-99
Square Footage: 264000

Type of Packaging: Private Label
Brands:
  Trine Baffle

30485 Triner Scale & Mfg Co
8411 Hacks Cross Rd
Olive Branch, MS 38654-4010

662-890-2385
Fax: 901-363-3114 800-238-0152
info@trinerscale.com www.trinerscale.com
Manufacturer and exporter of scales including electronic, postage and platform; stainless steel, washdown and USDA approved
Owner: Arthur Wendt
  awendt@trinerscale.com
Estimated Sales: $1 - 2.5 Million
Number Employees: 10-19
Square Footage: 120000
Brands:
  Triner

30486 Trinidad Benham Corporation
3650 S Yosemite, Suite 300
P.O. Box 378007
Denver, CO 80237

303-220-1400
Fax: 303-220-1490 info@trinidadbenham.com
www.trinidadbenham.com
Dry beans, rice, popcorn and peas.
President: Linda Walmsley
Vice President: Steve Dipasquale
Chief Operating Officer: Jeff Bornmann
Year Founded: 1917
Estimated Sales: $36.3 Million
Number Employees: 500-1,000
Number of Brands: 12
Square Footage: 35000
Type of Packaging: Consumer, Food Service, Private Label, Bulk
Other Locations:
  Food Packaging
  Chino CA
  Food Packaging
  City of Industry CA
  Food Packaging
  Dallas TX
  Food Packaging
  LaVergne TN
  Food Packaging
  Mineola TX
  Food Packaging
  Sterling CO
  Food Packaging
  Vernalis CA
  Non-Food Packaging
  LaGrange CA
  Receiving
  Alliance NE
  Receiving
  Courtenay ND
  Receiving
  Gering NE
  Receiving
  Pillsbury ND
  Bean Processing
  Bayard NE
Brands:
  Budget Buy
  Cookquik Ranch Wagon
  Diamond
  Everyday Chef
  Green Earth Organics
  Jack Rabbit
  Master Wrap
  Peak
  Sabor Del Campo
  Siler's
  Solfresco
  Wonder Foil

30487 Trinity Packaging
55 Innsbruck Dr
Cheektowaga, NY 14227-2703

716-668-3111
Fax: 716-668-3816 800-778-3111
Flexible packaging, process printing and film laminations; exporter of printed laminated rollstock; also, slitting and bag making available
President: Richard Gioia
Chairman: Tony Gioia
  tgioia@cello-pack.com
VP: Sam Brown
Operations: Compton Plummer
Purchasing Director: Tim Shiley

Estimated Sales: $20 - 50 Million
Number Employees: 100-249
Square Footage: 100000
Type of Packaging: Consumer, Food Service, Private Label, Bulk

30488 Trinkle Sign & Display
24 5th Ave
Youngstown, OH 44503-1191

330-747-9712
Fax: 330-747-9712
Manufacturer and exporter of signs and displays
Owner: Robert Page
Estimated Sales: Less Than $500,000
Number Employees: 1-4

30489 (HQ)Trio Packaging Corp
90 13th Ave # 11
Ronkonkoma, NY 11779-6819

631-588-0800
Fax: 631-467-4690 800-331-0492
sales@triopackaging.com
www.triopackaging.com
Manufacturer, importer and exporter of form/fill/seal packaging equipment and films
President: John Bolla
  john@triopackaging.com
Vice President: Frederick Kramer
Sales Director: Anthony Carris
Estimated Sales: $20 - 50 Million
Number Employees: 20-49
Square Footage: 20000
Other Locations:
  Trio Packaging Corp.
  Ronkonkoma NY

30490 Trio Products
250 Warden Ave
Elyria, OH 44035

440-323-5457
Fax: 440-323-3247
Manufacturer and exporter of plastic food packaging materials including regular and thermoforming sheets and bacon boards
National Sales Representative: C Derringer
Contact: Christine Hood
  christineh@trioproducts.com
Engineering/Technical: Mike Linner
Estimated Sales: $10-20 Million
Number Employees: 10-19
Type of Packaging: Consumer, Private Label, Bulk

30491 Triple A Containers
16069 Shoemaker Ave
Buena Park, CA 90621

714-521-2820
Fax: 714-521-8781 bruce@tripla.com
www.tripla.com
Corrugated shipping containers
Owner: Brad McCroskey
Purchasing: Bob Ryan
Estimated Sales: $20-50 Million
Number Employees: 100-249

30492 Triple A Neon Company
12325 Califa Street
Valley Village, CA 91607-1106

323-877-5381
Fax: 818-763-6255
Neon signs
President: Todd Showalter
Estimated Sales: Less than $500,000
Number Employees: 4

30493 Triple Dot Corp
3302 S Susan St
Santa Ana, CA 92704-6841

714-241-0888
Fax: 714-241-9888 info@triple-dot.com
www.triple-dot.com
Plastic containers, dessicant packages and neck bands; importer of glass containers
Owner: Tony Tsai
  tytsai@aol.com
VP: Jason Tsai
Estimated Sales: $5-10 Million
Number Employees: 20-49
Square Footage: 140000
Brands:
  Seca-Pax
  Tdc

30494 Triple S Dynamics Inc
2467 E US Highway 180
Breckenridge, TX 76424-4956

254-559-8266
Fax: 254-559-8057 800-527-2116
sales@sssdynamics.com www.sssdynamics.com
Manufacturer and exporter of conveyors, separators and vibrating screens
Marketing: Jim Tatum
Estimated Sales: $10-20,000,000
Number Employees: 10-19
Square Footage: 125000
Brands:
  Slipstick

30495 Triple-A Manufacturing Company
44 Milner Avenue
Toronto, ON M1S 3P8
Canada

416-291-4451
Fax: 416-291-1292 800-786-2238
Manufacturer and exporter of storage systems, shelving, steel work benches, modular storage drawers, plastic and corrugated bins, welded wire partitions and mezzanines; also, racks including bottle, can, cold storage room, palletwine, wire, barrel, drum, etc
President: Joe Harnest
VP Finance: A Lerman
VP Sales: R Gasner
Buyer: T Kelly
Estimated Sales: $10 - 20 Million
Number Employees: 35
Square Footage: 240000
Other Locations:
  Triple-A Manufacturing Co. Lt
  Exeter NH

30496 Trisep Corporation
95 S La Patera Ln
Goleta, CA 93117

805-964-8003
Fax: 805-964-1235 sales@trisep.com
www.trisep.com
Manufactures membrane filters and separators, spiral wound reverse osmosis elements
President: James Bartlett Jr
Sr. Vice President -Commercial: Jon Goodman
SpiraSep UF Marketing Mgr.: Mike Snodgrass
International Sales Director: John Waring
Contact: Steve Spicer
  steves@provisio.net
Estimated Sales: $8 Million
Number Employees: 50-99

30497 Triune Enterprises
13711 S Normandie Ave
Gardena, CA 90249-2609

310-719-1600
Fax: 310-719-1800 www.triuneent.com
Films, polypropylene, polyester, gas packaging materials, shrink packaging materials, vacuum packaging materials
President: Jerry Christman
  jerry@triuneent.com
CFO: John Jerry Christman
Estimated Sales: $4 Million
Number Employees: 20-49

30498 (HQ)Trojan Commercial Furniture Inc.
163 Van Horne
Montereal, QC H2T 2J2
Canada

514-271-3878
Fax: 514-271-8960 877-271-3878
Manufacturer and exporter of wooden restaurant furniture including tables, chairs, booths and counters
President: Dennis Petsinis
Co-President: Chris Petsinis
Number Employees: 10
Square Footage: 24000
Type of Packaging: Food Service, Bulk
Brands:
  Trojan Commercial

30499 (HQ)Trojan Inc
198 Trojan St
Mt Sterling, KY 40353-8000

859-498-0526
Fax: 859-498-0528 800-264-0526
sales@trojaninc.com www.trojaninc.com

Manufacturer and exporter of lighting including long life, energy-efficient incandescent, fluorescent, HID, NSF approved, shatter-resistant, lamps, etc.; also, adapters and plate and exit sign retrofit kits
President: Edward Duzyk
CEO: Dennis Duzyk
sales@trojaninc.com
Estimated Sales: $3 - 5 Million
Number Employees: 10-19
Square Footage: 340000
Type of Packaging: Food Service
Other Locations:
 Trojan
 Meadville PA
Brands:
 Hytron
 Hytronics
 Powersaver
 Saf-T-Cote

30500 Trola Industries Inc
2360 N George St
York, PA 17406-3202
717-848-3700
Fax: 717-848-6993 tbarton@trolaindustries.com
www.trolaindustries.com
Design, build, install control systems and panels (UL508A)
President: Thomas Barton
Vice President: Steve Halweski
Sales Director: Jim Schneider
customer Service: Shiellyn Hutson
General Manager: Mike Miller
Estimated Sales: $10-20 Million
Number Employees: 10-19
Square Footage: 46000

30501 Tronex Industries
1 Tronex Centre
Denville, NJ 07834
800-833-1181
Fax: 973-625-7630 800-833-1181
information@tronexcompany.com
Manufacturer and distributor of disposable gloves and apparel including bouffant cups, aprons, beard and sleeve covers
CFO: John Prail
Executive VP: Poyee Tai
Marketing Director: Carol Fletcher
Sales Director: Robert Larsen
Operations Manager: Mike Rowe
Number Employees: 20
Square Footage: 320000
Parent Co: Tronex International
Brands:
 Choice
 Tronex

30502 Tronics America
1430 E 86th Pl
Merrillville, IN 46410-6342
219-769-0876
Fax: 219-769-0962 sales@TronicsAmerica.com
www.tronicsamerica.com
Pressure sensitive labeling machines and heat transfer decorators
Manager: Richard Dew
rdew@tronicsamerica.com
Estimated Sales: $1-2.5 Million
Number Employees: 5-9

30503 Tropic KOOL
1232 Donegan Rd
Largo, FL 33771-2904
727-581-2824
Fax: 727-587-7973 www.tropickool.com
Metal parts for vents and air conditioning systems
President: Kenneth W. Bray
General Manager: Ken Bray
Estimated Sales: $5-10 Million
Number Employees: 10-19
Square Footage: 72000

30504 Tropical Soap Company
1512 Silverleaf Dr.
PO Box 112220
Carrollton, TX 75011-2220
972-492-7939
Fax: 972-233-1955 800-527-2368
Coconut oil soap including liquid and bar
Brands:
 Sirena

30505 Trout Lake Farm Company
PO Box 181
Trout Lake, WA 98650
509-395-2025
Fax: 509-395-2749 800-655-6988
www.troutlakefarm.com
Quality Control: Angie Brackhahn
Sales Manager: Martha Jane Hylton
Contact: Sharon Frazey
 sharon.frazey@troutlakefarm.com
Operations Supervisor: Danielle Hawkins
General Manager: Lloyd Scott
Number Employees: 50

30506 Trowelon
973 Haven Place
Green Bay, WI 54313-5207
920-499-8778
Fax: 920-499-9065 800-975-8778
Floor and wall coating materials
CEO: Lewis Krueger
Estimated Sales: $5-10 Million
Number Employees: 50-99

30507 (HQ)Troxler Electronic Lab Inc
3008 Cornwallis Rd
PO Box 12057
Durham, NC 27709-0129
919-549-8661
Fax: 919-549-0761 877-876-9537
troxsale@troxlerlabs.com www.troxlerlabs.com
Moisture and density testing equipment
President: Stephen Browne
 sbrowne@troxlerlabs.com
Director Product Service: Bill Worrell
Estimated Sales: $10-20 Million
Number Employees: 100-249
Square Footage: 250000

30508 (HQ)Troy Lighting
14508 Nelson Ave
City of Industry, CA 91744-3514
626-336-4511
Fax: 626-330-4266 800-533-8769
Manufacturer, exporter and importer of electric lighting fixtures including decorative interior, track and recessed; also, exterior including wall, hanging, flush and post lanterns
Owner: Carol Coffey
VP Sales/Marketing: Steve Nadell
 carolc@troycsl.com
Estimated Sales: $20-50 Million
Number Employees: 5-9
Square Footage: 100000

30509 Tru Form Plastics
17809 S Broadway
Gardena, CA 90248-3541
310-327-9444
Fax: 310-878-1107 800-510-7999
www.tru-formplastics.com
Food processing/service equipment and supplies, air conditioning and vents, lighting fixtures, point of purchase displays, uniform hats and caps, refrigeration equipment, sinks, etc
President: Douglas Sahm
CEO: Mario Guzman
National Sales Manager: Doug Sahm
Customer Service: Yolanda Cardenas
VP Operations: Mario Guzman
Estimated Sales: $1-2,500,000
Number Employees: 20-49

30510 Tru Hone Corp
1721 NE 19th Ave
Ocala, FL 34470-4701
352-622-1213
Fax: 352-622-9180 800-237-4663
www.truhone.com
Manufacturer and exporter of knife sharpeners
President: James Gangelhoff
 truhone@truhone.com
CEO: Fred R Gangelhoff
Estimated Sales: $1-2.5 Million
Number Employees: 10-19
Square Footage: 13200
Brands:
 Tru Hone

30511 Tru Hone Corp
1721 NE 19th Ave
Ocala, FL 34470-4701
352-622-1213
Fax: 352-622-9180 800-237-4663
www.truhone.com
Knife sharpeners and accessories for industrial operations, meat, fish, poultry and produce plants.
President: James Gangelhoff
 truhone@truhone.com
Number Employees: 10-19

30512 TruHeat Corporation
P.O. Box 190
Allegan, MI 49010-0190
269-673-2145
Fax: 269-673-7219 800-879-6199
www.truheat.com
Manufacturer and exporter of electric heating elements and assemblies for warming, broiling, frying, steaming and defrosting
President: Larry Nameche
Marketing/Sales: Jim Jennings
Estimated Sales: $10-20 Million
Number Employees: 100-249
Square Footage: 104000

30513 True Food Service Equipment, Inc.
2001 E Terra Ln
O Fallon, MO 63366-4434
636-240-2400
Fax: 636-272-2408 800-325-6152
truefood@truemfg.com www.truemfg.com
Manufacturer and exporter of commercial refrigeration equipment including deli cases, refrigerators, freezers and coolers; also, beer dispensers and pizza prep tables
President: Robert J Trulaske
Contact: Randy Bates
 rbates@truemfg.com
Estimated Sales: $.5 - 1 million
Number Employees: 1-4
Brands:
 True

30514 True Manufacturing
2525 Lakeview Rd
Mexico, MO 65265
636-240-2400
Fax: 636-272-2408 truefoodservice@truemfg.com
www.truemfg.com
President: Robert Trulaske
Contact: Charles Hon
 chon@truemfg.com
Estimated Sales: $.5 - 1 million
Number Employees: 1-4

30515 True Pac
420 Churchmans Rd
New Castle, DE 19720-3157
302-326-2222
Fax: 302-326-9330 800-825-7890
info@truepack.com www.truepack.com
Manufacturer and exporter of insulated shipping containers
Owner: Steve Nam
 steve@truepack.co.kr
Manager: Joan Carter
Estimated Sales: $1 - 5 Million
Number Employees: 20-49

30516 Truesdail Laboratories
14201 Franklin Avenue
Tustin, CA 92780-7008
714-730-6239
Fax: 714-730-6462 rgates@truesdail.com
www.truesdail.com
Consultant offering laboratory testing and sanitary analysis
Owner: John Hill
Chief Scientist: Steve Roesch
Quality Assurance: Michael Ngo
Contact: Paymon Abri
 paymon@truesdail.com
Chief Operating Officer: Randy Gates
Estimated Sales: $10-20 Million
Number Employees: 50-99
Square Footage: 120000

30517 Truitt Bros, Inc.
1105 Front St NE
PO Box 309
Salem, OR 97301-1034
503-362-3674
Fax: 503-581-5912 800-547-8712
truittbros@truittbros.com www.truittbros.com
Canned green beans, cherries, pears and plums; also,
shelf stable entrees.
Owner: David Truitt
davidt@truittbros.com
Year Founded: 1971
Estimated Sales: $20-50 Million
Number Employees: 500-999
Parent Co: Baxters Food Group
Type of Packaging: Consumer, Food Service, Private Label
Brands:
Truitt Bros.

30518 Truly Nolen Pest Control
3636 E Speedway Blvd
Tucson, AZ 85716-4018
520-327-3447
Fax: 52-32-400 877-977-1553
www.trulynolen.com
Pest control systems
President: Truly Nolen
trulynolencaguas@trulynolen.net
Estimated Sales: $1-2.5 Million
Number Employees: 50-99

30519 Trumbull Nameplates
1101 Sugar Mill Dr
New Smyrna Beach, FL 32168
386-423-1105
Signs and pressure sensitive labels
General Manager: Frank Tisler
Number Employees: 1-4
Square Footage: 3600

30520 Try Coffee Group
320 Carlisle Street
Harrisburg, PA 17104-1226
717-238-8381
Fax: 717-238-9173 www.trycoffee.com
Brewers, grinders
Estimated Sales: $5-10 Million
Number Employees: 10

30521 Tryco Coffee Service Annex Warehouse
3146 Corporate Place
Hayward, CA 94545-3916
510-293-9199
Fax: 510-293-0971 annextryco@aol.com
www.annextryco.net
Blending and mixing equipment (coffee), cleaners
(green coffee), reconditioners, samplers, weighers,
storage, consolidations, and packaging
CEO: Terry Sloat
Number Employees: 40

30522 Tubesales QRT
800 Roosevelt Road
suite 410
Glen Ellyn, IL 60137-5839
800-545-5000
Fax: 800-545-5883
www.plumbingnet.com/listt.html

30523 Tucel Industries, Inc.
2014 Forestdale Rd.
Forestdale, VT 05745-0146
802-247-6824
Fax: 802-247-6826 800-558-8235
Manufacturer and exporter of produce sponges and
food preparation brushes including pastry; also, janitorial supplies including brushes, brooms, scours
and squeegees
President: John Lewis Jr
CEO: Joanne Raleigh
Estimated Sales: $3 - 5 Million
Number Employees: 20-49
Square Footage: 180000
Type of Packaging: Consumer, Food Service, Private Label, Bulk
Brands:
Cycle Line
Fused
Hygienic Fusedware
Sponge 'n Brush
Tu-Scrub
Tucel

30524 Tuchenhagen
6716 Alexander Bell Drive
Suite 125
Columbia, MD 21046-2186
410-910-6000
Fax: 410-910-7000
Manufacturer and exporter of compact modular
skid-mounted processing units and systems including blending, mixing, yeast pitching, etc.; also,
valves, in-line flow measuring instruments and sanitary fittings, etc.; also, consultationservices available
Marketing Coordinator: Mads Michael Skaarenborg
Sales Director: Dave Medlar
Estimated Sales: $2.5-5 Million
Number Employees: 20-49
Parent Co: Tuchenhagen North America

30525 Tuchenhagen North America
90 Evergreen Dr
Portland, ME 04103-1066
207-797-9500
Fax: 207-878-7914 info.TNA@geagroup.com
Process components for the milk processing and
beverage industries.
President: David Medlar
COO: Tim Jenneman
tim.jennemen@geagroup.com
Sales Manager: Ulf Thiessen
Number Employees: 10-19

30526 Tuchenhagen-Zajac
90 Evergreen Dr
Portland, ME 04103-1066
207-797-9500
Fax: 207-878-7914
Liquid processing
President: Dave Metler
CFO: Ralf Brockman
COO: David Harding
Estimated Sales: $5 - 10 Million
Number Employees: 5-9

30527 Tuckahoe Manufacturing Co
327 Tuckahoe Rd
Vineland, NJ 08360-9243
856-696-4100
Fax: 856-691-7312 800-220-3368
Strip doors; wholesaler/distributor of vinyl strip,
sheet and panel materials and soft impact doors
President/Owner: John Tombleson
Estimated Sales: Less Than $500,000
Number Employees: 1-4
Square Footage: 3600

30528 Tucker Industries
2835 Janitell Road
Colorado Springs, CO 80906-4104
719-527-4848
Fax: 719-527-1499 800-786-7287
www.burnguard.com
Manufacturer and exporter of burn protective garments including oven mitts, aprons and hot pads
President: Vincent A. Tucker
Safety Director: Les Burns
CFO: Hathy Tucker
Quality Control: Hathy Tucker
VP Marketing: Paul Weklinski
Contact: Andrea Mabe
andrea@burnguard.com
Estimated Sales: Below $5 Million
Number Employees: 20-49
Square Footage: 172000
Brands:
Burnguard
Safestep
Vaporguard

30529 (HQ)Tucson Container Corp
6601 S Palo Verde Rd
Tucson, AZ 85756-5044
520-746-3171
Fax: 520-741-0962 www.tucsoncontainer.com
Manufacturer and exporter of fiber and corrugated
boxes; also, packaging materials and foam products
Estimated Sales: $16 Million
Number Employees: 50-99
Square Footage: 160000
Other Locations:
Tucson Container Corp.
El Paso TX

30530 Tudor Pulp & Paper Corporation
17 White Oak Dr
Prospect, CT 6712
203-758-4494
Fax: 203-758-4498
Manufacturer and importer of specialty paper for
packaging including grease resistant, oil resistant,
industrial and electric
VP Sales: Stephen Hansen
Manager: Brad Russell
Estimated Sales: $1 - 5 Million
Number Employees: 10-19

30531 Tufco International
P.O. Box 456
Gentry, AR 72734-0456
479-736-2201
Fax: 479-736-2947 800-364-0836
info@tufcoflooring.com www.tufcoflooring.com
Flooring
President: Brent Mills
VP Sales: Russell Cox
Estimated Sales: Below $5 Million
Number Employees: 50-99

30532 Tufty Ceramics Inc
47 S Main St
PO Box 785
Andover, NY 14806
607-478-5150
www.tuftyceramics.com
Manufacturer and exporter of terracotta bakeware
including nonstick, microwaveable and dishwasher
safe
President: Karen Tufty
Estimated Sales: Below $500,000
Number Employees: 1-4
Brands:
Alfred Bakeware

30533 Tulip Molded Plastics Corp
714 E Keefe Ave
Milwaukee, WI 53212-1668
414-963-3120
Fax: 414-962-1825 tulip@tulipcorp.com
www.tulipcorp.com
President: Fred Teshinsky
fteshinsky@phi-tulip.com
Principal: Courtland Hientze
Senior VP: Alan Schmidt
Estimated Sales: $20-50 Million
Number Employees: 20-49

30534 Tully's Coffee
3100 Airport Way S
Seattle, WA 98134
206-233-2070
Fax: 206-233-2077 www.tullys.com
Retailer, wholesaler, and distributor of coffee and
coffee products
President: Carl Pennigton Sr
Contact: Kerry Carlson
kc@tullys.com
Estimated Sales: $50,000,000 - $99,999,999
Number Employees: 1,000-4,999
Brands:
Tullys

30535 Tulox Plastics Corporation
P.O. Box 984
Marion, IN 46952
765-664-5155
Fax: 765-664-0257 800-234-1118
www.tulox.com
Tubes and toppers that are available in rounds,
squares, rectangulars, triangulars, and custom
shapes, transparent, opaque, colored, or striped
President: John Sciaudone
Vice President: Bill Patuzzi
National Sales Director: Christopher Sciaudone
Contact: Christopher Sciaudone
sales@tulox.com
Type of Packaging: Consumer

30536 Tulsa Plastics Co
6112 E 32nd Pl
Tulsa, OK 74135-5406
918-664-0931
Fax: 918-622-2943 888-273-5303
sales@tulsaplastics.com www.tulsaplastics.com
Store fixtures, sky lights, plastic sheet materials,
plastic signs and displays

President: Raleigh Blakemore
 rblakemore@tulsaplastics.com
CFO: Jim Blakemore
Estimated Sales: Below $5 Million
Number Employees: 10-19

30537 Tupperware Brands Corporation
14901 South Orange Blossom Trail
Orlando, FL 32837
800-366-3800
comments@tupperware.com
www.tupperwarebrands.com
Plastic storage containers and cookware.
Interim CEO: Christopher O'Leary
Executive Vice Chairman: Richard Goudis
VP/Controller: Madeline Otero
EVP/CFO: Cassandra Harris
EVP/Chief Legal Officer: Karen Sheeran
EVP/Chief Strategy & Marketing Officer: Asha Gupta
EVP/Chief Talent & Engagement Officer: Lillian Garcia
EVP, Product Innovation & Supply Chain: William Wright
Year Founded: 1946
Estimated Sales: $2.3 Billion
Number Employees: 13,500
Brands:
 Tupperware

30538 Turbo Refrigerating Company
P.O. Box 396
Denton, TX 76202-0396
940-387-4301
Fax: 940-382-0364 info@turboice.com
Manufacturer and exporter of ice making, storage and distribution systems; processor of ice
President: El Beard
CFO: Chris Worghington
VP: Dan Aiken
VP Sales/Marketing: T Baker
Estimated Sales: $20 - 50 Million
Number Employees: 20-49
Parent Co: Henry Vogt Machine Company
Other Locations:
 Turbo Refrigerating Co.
 Louisville KY

30539 Turbo Systems
4 Glenberry Ct
Phoenix, MD 21131-1400
410-527-2800
Fax: 954-925-4190 rubosysfl@aol.com
www.turbosystemsusa.com
Aerators, bar formers, bottomers, chocolate equipment, vermicelli machines, coaters, conveyors, cookers
Vice President: Joost DE Koomen
 sales@turbosystemsusa.com
Sr. Vice President: Joost J. de Koomen
Estimated Sales: $.5 - 1 million
Number Employees: 1-4

30540 Turck
3000 Campus Dr
Minneapolis, MN 55441-2656
763-694-2300
Fax: 763-553-0708 888-546-5880
www.turck.us
Leader in providong bus network products. Providing smart stations, junctions, connectorized cable and accessories for unique plug-and-play concept to distributed process control and automation solutions. These plug-and-play componentsallow for quick installation of new plant layouts and easy retrofits to existing plants
President: Murray Death
CEO: David Lagerstrom
 david.lagerstrom@turck.com
Number Employees: 250-499
Brands:
 Busstop

30541 Turck
3000 Campus Dr
Minneapolis, MN 55441-2656
763-694-2300
Fax: 763-553-0708 800-544-7769
www.turck.us
Provides sensing solutions and related components by manufacturing and marketing proximity sensors, cordsets, connection products and automation devices. the company's products are primaly used in manufacturing automationapplications

President: William Scheneider
CEO: David Lagerstrom
 david.lagerstrom@turck.com
CFO: Bill Chrisianson
CEO: David Lagerstrom
R&D: Boss
Quality Control: Bamian Pike
Marketing Director: Grant Bistram
Production Manager: Hanz Ziesch
Estimated Sales: $50 - 100 Million
Number Employees: 250-499

30542 Turkana Food
555 N Michigan Avenue
Kenilworth, NJ 07033
908-810-8800
Fax: 908-810-8820 info@turkanafood.com
www.turkanafood.com
Ethnic foods: European, Mediterranean and Middle Eastern.
Business Development: Furkan Bugra Er
Admisnitrative Service Manager: Tuncay Yalim
Estimated Sales: $9-11 Million
Number Employees: 11-50
Type of Packaging: Food Service

30543 Turtle Wax
PO Box 247
Westmont, IL 60559-0247
905-470-6665
Fax: 708-563-4302
distributorinfo@turtlewax.com
www.turtlewax.com
Manufacturer and exporter household cleaners, dressings and polishes
CEO: Denis J Healy
Chairman: Sondra A Healy
Contact: Huntington Beach
 hbeach@turtlewax.com
Estimated Sales: $5 - 10 Million
Number Employees: 1,000-4,999

30544 Tuthill Vacuum & BlowerSystems
P.O. Box 2877
Springfield, MO 65801-2877
417-865-8715
Fax: 417-865-2950 800-825-6937
vacuum@tuthill.com www.tuthillvacuum.com
Manufacturer and exporter of positive displacement rotary lobe blowers mechanical vacuum boosters, rotary piston vacuum pumps, liquid ring vacuum pumps and complete systems
President: John Ermold
Controller: James Ashcraft
Sales/Marketing Director: Mike Branstetter
Contact: Henry Mateja
 hmateja@tuthill.com
Estimated Sales: $10-20 Million
Number Employees: 250-499
Number of Brands: 10
Number of Products: 6
Square Footage: 130000
Parent Co: Tuthill Corporation
Brands:
 Acousticair
 Competitor Plus
 Equalizer
 Pd Plus

30545 Tuway American Group
191 E Pearl St
Rockford, OH 45882
419-363-3191
Fax: 419-363-2129 800-537-3750
www.tuwaymops.com
Manufacturer, importer and exporter of dust cloths and mops, carpet cleaning pads and bonnets, scouring pads, wall washing supplies and handles
President: Trudy Koster
Director Sales: M Healy
National Sales Manager: Steve Grimes
Manager: John Feeney
Plant Manager: John Feeney
Estimated Sales: $20 - 50 Million
Number Employees: 50-99
Parent Co: Tu-Way Products Company
Brands:
 Dustmaster
 Dustroyer
 Speed Trek
 Wide Track

30546 Tuxton China
21011 Commerce Point Drive
Walnut, CA 91789-3052
909-595-2510
Fax: 909-595-5353 info@tuxton.com
www.tuxton.com

30547 Twelve Baskets Sales & Market
5200 Phillip Lee Dr SW
Atlanta, GA 30336
404-696-9922
Fax: 404-696-9099 800-420-8840
Wholesaler/distributer of general line items; also, packer of edible oils
Owner: Ken Mc Millan
 ken@twelvebaskets.net
President: Kirk McMillen
Sales: Bob Quinet
Estimated Sales: $20 - 50 Million
Number Employees: 20-49
Square Footage: 15000

30548 Twenty First Century Design
1008 Madison Ave
Albany, NY 12208-2600
518-446-0939
www.manta.com
Designer of restaurant interiors, mechanical and electrical systems; also, architectural and engineering services available
Owner: Menglin Liu
Estimated Sales: $500,000-$1 Million
Number Employees: 6
Square Footage: 10000

30549 Twenty/Twenty Graphics
7895 Cessna Ave # S
Gaithersburg, MD 20879
240-243-0511
Fax: 240-243-0512
Signs, displays and decals; screen printing available
President: Luclere Lee
Estimated Sales: $2.5-5 Million
Number Employees: 10-19

30550 Twi Laq
1345 Seneca Ave
Bronx, NY 10474-4611
718-638-5860
Fax: 718-789-0993 800-950-7627
customerservice@twi-laq.com www.twi-laq.com
Manufacturer and exporter of cleaning chemicals including soaps, degreasers, detergents, marble care chemicals and floor finishes
Vice President: Shanelle Acabeo
 sacabeo@twi-laq.com
VP: Robert Wels
VP Operations: Michael Wels
Estimated Sales: $5-10 Million
Number Employees: 10-19
Brands:
 Stone Glo
 Sun-Glo
 Top-Guard
 Welsite

30551 Twin City Bottle
1227 E Hennepin Ave
Minneapolis, MN 55414
612-331-8880
Fax: 612-379-5118 800-697-0607
sales@kaufmancontainer.com
Major supplier of all types of containers
CEO: Roger Seid
Estimated Sales: $20-50 Million
Number Employees: 50-99

30552 Twin City Pricing & Label
744 Kasota Cir SE
Minneapolis, MN 55414-2883
612-378-1055
Fax: 612-379-0112 800-328-5076
www.twincityproduce.com
Custom printed labels
President: John Rotondo
Production Manager: Curtis James
Estimated Sales: $10 - 20 Million
Number Employees: 20-49
Square Footage: 26000

30553 Twin City Wholesale
519 Walker St
Opelika, AL 36801-5999
334-745-4564
Fax: 334-749-5125 800-344-6935
Wholesaler and distributor of products and supplies for convenience stores and grocery chains; offers business floor plan design services.
Owner: Johanna Bottoms
twincity@mindspring.com
Estimated Sales: $76 Million
Number Employees: 50-99

30554 Twin State Signs
14 Gauthier Dr
Essex Junction, VT 05452-2825
802-872-8949
Fax: 802-878-0200 twinsign@together.net
www.twinstatesigns.com
Signs including neon, electric, indoor, outdoor, wooden, etc.; also, signage repair and installation services available
President: Mary Denault
twinsign@together.net
CFO/R&D: Ray Denault
Sales Manager: Suzanne Denault
Estimated Sales: Below $5 Million
Number Employees: 5-9
Brands:
Gerber Edge
Scotch Print

30555 Twinkle Baker Decor USA
285 Westlake Couter
Daly City, CA 94015
707-364-2740
Baking decorations and decorating tools
Operations Manager: Karen Tang
Brands:
Twinkle Baker Decor

30556 Two Rivers Enterprises
490 River St W
Holdingford, MN 56340-4519
320-746-3156
Fax: 320-746-3158 joeh@stainlesskings.com
www.tworiversstainlesskings.com
Restaurant and food service equipment; also provides renovations of processing plants and on-site equipment.
President: Robert Warzecha
bobw@stainlesskings.com
Midwest Regional Sales: Joe Herges
Sales Engineer: Jeff Jones
Midwest Regional Sales: Steve Bairett
Number Employees: 20-49

30557 Tyco Fire Protection Products
1400 Pennbrook Pkwy
Lansdale, PA 19446-3840
215-362-0700
Fax: 215-362-5385 800-558-5236
sales@starsprinkler.com
Manufacturer and exporter of automatic self-adjusting fire sprinkler systems including concealed and recessed
President: Colleen Repplier
colleen.repplier@tycofp.com
Marketing Manager: John Corcoran
International Sales Manager: Patti Kowalski
Number Employees: 500-999
Parent Co: Tyco Corporation
Brands:
Quasar
Starmist

30558 Tyco Fire Protection Products
1 Stanton St
Marinette, WI 54143-2542
715-732-3465
Fax: 715-732-3471 800-862-6785
www.ansul.com
Manufacturer and exporter of fire protection products includes fire extinguishers and hand line units; pre-engineered restaurant, vehicle, and industrial systems; sophisticated fire detection/suppression systems and a complete line of dry chemical, foam, and gaseoue extinguishing agents.

President: Colleen Repplier
Cmo: David A Pelton
dpelton@tycoint.com
CFO: Dennis Moraros
Operations: Sally Falkenberg
Director, R&D: Jay Thomas
Director, Global Marketing: David Pelton
VP Sales: William Smith
Number Employees: 10-19
Parent Co: Tyco International
Brands:
Ansul Automan
Ansulex
Foray
K-Guard
Piranha
Plus-50
R-102
Sentry

30559 Tyco Plastics
8235 220th St W
Lakeville, MN 55044-8059
952-469-8771
Fax: 952-469-5337 800-328-4080
Manufacturer and exporter of packaging supplies including barrier bags, films and pouches for meats, cheeses, etc
Sales/Marketing: Mike Baarts
Business Unit Manager (Food): Dennis Leisten
Business Unit Manager (Industrial): Tom Lundborg
Purchasing Manager: Gordon Raway
Estimated Sales: $20-50 Million
Number Employees: 100-249
Brands:
Rexfit
Rextape
Startex
Starvac
Starvac Ii
Starvac Iii

30560 Tycodalves & Controls
1010 N Edward Ct
Anaheim, CA 92806-2601
714-575-9201
Fax: 714-575-9206 800-972-8926
Wine industry valves
Manager: Eddie Kim
Contact: Larry Taft
ltaff@tycovalves.com
Estimated Sales: $10 - 20 Million
Number Employees: 10-19

30561 Typecraft Wood & Jones
2040 E Walnut St
Pasadena, CA 91107-5804
626-795-8093
Fax: 626-795-2423 info@typecraft.com
www.typecraft.com
Labels; also, printing available
Estimated Sales: $1 - 5 Million
Number Employees: 50-99

30562 U B KLEM Furniture Co Inc
3861 E Schnellville Rd
St Anthony, IN 47575-9633
812-326-2236
Fax: 812-326-2525 800-264-1995
info@ubklem.com www.ubklem.com
Chairs, barstools, booths, tables, pedestals and trash receptacles
President: Wes Graman
wgraman@ubklem.com
CEO: U Butch Klen
Estimated Sales: $10-20 Million
Number Employees: 100-249
Square Footage: 150000

30563 U L Wholesale Lighting Fixture
3443 10th St
Long Island City, NY 11106-5107
718-726-7500
Fax: 718-626-8812 www.ullighting.net
Manufacturer and importer of lighting fixtures
Owner: Charlie Papastylianou
Estimated Sales: $2.5 - 5,000,000
Number Employees: 10-19
Square Footage: 10000

30564 U Roast Em Inc
16778 W US Highway 63
Hayward, WI 54843-7214
715-634-6255
Fax: 715-934-3221 info@u-roast-em.com
Supplier of green coffee beans, bulk teas, home roasting supplies and coffee flavorings
Manager: Terry Wall
info@u-roast-em.com
Number Employees: 1-4
Type of Packaging: Consumer
Brands:
Bodum
Fresh Beans

30565 U-Line Corporation
8900 N 55th St
Milwaukee, WI 53223
414-354-0300
Fax: 414-354-0349 800-779-2547
sales@u-line.com www.u-line.com
Ice making machinery, compact freezers and compact, built-in and under-counter refrigerators
VP: Jennifer Seraszewski
CEO: Jennifer U Straszewski
Quality Control: Dean Bycnski
Sales/Marketing Manager: Henry Uline
Contact: Roland Marciniak
roland.marciniak@u-line.com
Vice President of Operations: Andrew Doberstein
Estimated Sales: $20 - 50 Million
Number Employees: 250-499

30566 U.S. Range
1177 Kamato Rd
Mississauga, ON L4W IX4
Canada
905-624-0260
800-424-2411
www.garland-group.com
Manufacturer of cooking systems.

30567 UAA
2561 N Greenview Avenue
Chicago, IL 60614-2028
773-755-4545
Fax: 773-755-4555 800-813-1711
Paging and surveillance systems including two-way radios; consulting services available
President: Joe Grody

30568 UBC Food Distributors
12812 Prospect St
Dearborn, MI 48126-3652
877-846-8117
Fax: 313-846-8118 info@wellmadefood.com
www.wellmadefood.com
Honey, chocolates, cookies, juices, and snacks
Sales Manager: Hassan Houssami
Estimated Sales: $10-12 Million
Number Employees: 10
Other Locations:
East Coast NJ
West Coast CA
Brands:
Wellmade Honey

30569 UCB Inc
1950 Lake Park Dr SE
Smyrna, GA 30080
770-970-8338
www.ucb-usa.com
Cellulose and polypropylene specialty films that are supplied into packaging, industrial and label markets.
President & Head of Operations: Duane Barnes
Chief Ethics/Compliance Officer: Anisa Dhalla
Head of Corporate Affairs: Patty Fritz
Year Founded: 1928
Estimated Sales: $100+ Million
Number Employees: 7,500
Parent Co: UCB Worldwide
Type of Packaging: Consumer, Food Service, Private Label
Brands:
Cellophane
Celloplus
Cellotherm
Natureflex
Optitwist
Propafilm
Propafiol
Proparearm

Ratoface
Startwist

30570 UDEC Corp
271 Salem St # A
Woburn, MA 01801-2004
781-933-7770
Fax: 781-933-5366 800-990-8332
Manufacturer and exporter of solid-state fluorescent emergency, exit and night lights; also, electronic ballasts for back lighting
President: Eugene P. Brandeis
e.brandeis@udeccorp.com
CFO: Janice Ferro
Purchasing Manager: J Ferro
Estimated Sales: Below $5 Million
Number Employees: 5-9
Square Footage: 9200
Type of Packaging: Food Service, Private Label

30571 UDY Corp
201 Rome Ct
Fort Collins, CO 80524-1427
970-482-2060
Fax: 970-482-2067 www.udyone.com
Manufacturer and distributor of protein analyzers, shakers, sample mills, hay samplers and other general lab equipment. Also custom plastic fabrication for science and general industries.
President: William Lear
bill@udycorp.com
CFO: William Lear
Estimated Sales: Below $5 Million
Number Employees: 5-9
Number of Brands: 3
Number of Products: 20
Brands:
Colorado Hay Products
Cuclone Sample Mills
Dairy Tester Ii
Plastic Fabrication
Protein Color Meter
React-R-Mill

30572 UFE
520 Industrial Way
Fallbrook, CA 92028-2244
760-723-7900
Fax: 760-723-7910
Ruggedized solutions for harsh conditions, clean rooms and NEMA4X, power touch displays and workstations feature enhanced infrared
Marketing Manager: Christopher McDonald
VP Sales: Tony Faint
Manager Information Systems: Michael McGinley
Estimated Sales: $1 - 5 Million
Number Employees: 100-250

30573 UFE Incorporated
1850 Greeley St S
Stillwater, MN 55082
651-351-4273
Fax: 651-351-4272
Caps and closures specializing in custom thermoplastic injection molds and molding
President: Martin N Kellogg
CEO: Greg Willis
Estimated Sales: $20 - 50 Million
Number Employees: 100-249

30574 UFP Technologies
1521 Windsor Dr
Clinton, IA 52732-6611
563-242-2444
Fax: 563-242-0444 888-638-3456
info@ufpt.com www.ufpt.com
Design, prototyping, tooling, testing and manufacturing of protective packaging made from 100% recycled paper
CFO: Ron Latiaille
Manager: Susan Waters
swaters@ufpt.com
Estimated Sales: $500,000-$1 Million
Number Employees: 100-249

30575 UNEX Manufacturing
50 Progress Pl
Jackson, NJ 08527
732-928-2800
Fax: 732-928-2828 800-695-7726
span@unex.com www.unex.com
Carton flow track and carton flow accumulating conveyors

President: Brian Neuwirth
CEO: Mark Newrith
CEO: Frank Neuwirth
Vice President Sales: Mark Neuwirth
Marketing Manager: Mike Levine
Southern Regional Sales Manager: Bill McKenzie
Contact: Maria Bird
m.bird@unex.com
Product Manager: David Scelfo
Estimated Sales: $10-25 Million
Number Employees: 50-99

30576 UPACO Adhesives
4105 Castlewood Rd
Richmond, VA 23234-2707
804-275-9231
Fax: 804-743-8366 800-446-9984
info@worthenind.com
www.worthenindustries.com
Water-based, solvent-based and hot melt adhesives and coatings
President/CEO: Robert Worthen
Quality Control: Ralph Roane
Marketing/Sales: Steven Adams
Plant Manager: Dave Smith
Estimated Sales: $20-30 Million
Number Employees: 20-49
Square Footage: 40000
Parent Co: Worthen Industries

30577 UPM Raflatac
400 Broadpointe Dr
Mills River, NC 28759
800-992-3882
www.upmraflatac.com
Supplier of self-adhesive label materials and producer of HF and UHF radio frequency identification (RFID) tags and inlays.
Vice President: Dan O'Connell
Year Founded: 1975
Estimated Sales: $1.4 Billion
Number Employees: 3,000

30578 UPN Pallet Company
305 N Virginia Ave
Penns Grove, NJ 8069
856-299-1192
Fax: 856-299-5824
Wooden pallets
Office Manager: Mano Massari
Estimated Sales: $500,000-$1 Million
Number Employees: 5-9
Square Footage: 16000

30579 UPS Logistics Technologies
849 Fairmount Ave # 400
Towson, MD 21286-2601
410-823-0189
Fax: 410-847-6246 800-762-3638
market@upslogistics.com
Street routing and scheduling software, wireless dispatch software
COO: Len Kennedy
Director Customer Services: George Evans
Vice President of Product Management: Cyndi Brandt
Sales Director: Charlie Virden
Public Relations: Lisa Beck
Purchasing Manager: Donna Blizzard
Estimated Sales: $20 - 50 Million
Number Employees: 100-249
Number of Products: 5
Parent Co: United Parcel Service

30580 US Apple Assn
8233 Old Courthouse Rd # 200
Vienna, VA 22182-3816
703-442-8850
Fax: 703-790-0845 info@usapple.org
www.usapple.org
Provides consumers with information on the health benefits of apples and apple products.
CEO: Jim Bair
jbair@usapple.org
Vice President of Public Affairs: Diane Kurrle
Director Consumer Health & PR: Wendy Brannen
Office Manager: Laura Stephens
Number Employees: 5-9

30581 (HQ)US Can Company
1101 Todds Lane
Rosedale, MD 21237-2905
410-686-6363
Fax: 410-391-9323 800-436-8021

Manufacturer and exporter of aluminum and tin cans
VP Sales/Marketing: David West
Sales Director: Jack Finnell
Estimated Sales: $20-50 Million
Number Employees: 20-49
Type of Packaging: Consumer, Food Service, Private Label, Bulk

30582 US Cap Systems Corporation
111 Elm St
Suite 204
Worcester, MA 01609-1967
508-754-7283
Fax: 508-752-5546 800-727-5555
President: Emanuel Wohlgemuta
Estimated Sales: $1 - 5 Million
Number Employees: 1-4

30583 US Chemical
316 Hart St
Watertown, WI 53094-6631
920-261-3453
Fax: 920-206-3979 800-558-9566
www.uschemical.com
Specialty chemicals including warewashing, laundry, maintenance, carpet and floor care chemicals; exporter of cleaning products and dispensing systems
General Manager: Bill Moody
Technical Manager: Cheryl Maas
QC Lab: Brian Truman
Sales Leader: David Kohnke
Contact: Eric Losey
eric.losey@uschemical.com
Plant Manager: Dennis Bollhurst
Estimated Sales: $30-50 Million
Number Employees: 100-130
Square Footage: 150000
Parent Co: Diversey, Inc

30584 US Coexcell Inc
400 W Dussel Dr # C
Maumee, OH 43537-1636
419-897-9110
Fax: 419-897-9112 info@uscoxl.com
www.uscoxl.com
Owner: Bob Huebner
bhuebner@uscoxl.com
President, Chief Executive Officer: Harley Cramer
VP: Mark Woltell
Estimated Sales: $2.5-5 Million
Number Employees: 20-49

30585 US Cooler Company
401 Delaware St
Quincy, IL 62301
217-228-2421
Fax: 217-228-2424 800-521-2665
www.uscooler.com
Walk-in coolers and freezers
President/Owner: Allen Craig
Marketing Director: Kristin Peters
Contact: Tia Albers
tia@uscooler.com
Number Employees: 50-99
Square Footage: 80000
Parent Co: Craig Industries

30586 US Filter
40004 Cook Street
Palm Desert, CA 92211-3299
760-340-0098
Fax: 760-341-9368 www.usfilter.com
Water and wastewater treatment systems and equipment
President: Richard Heckmann
President, Chief Executive Officer: Eric Spiegel
Vice President: Alison Taylor
Corporate Marketing Manager: Mike Markovsky
Executive Vice President of Global Sales: Paul Vogel
Estimated Sales: $1 - 5 Million
Number Employees: 50-99
Square Footage: 4000000

30587 US Filter
40004 Cook Street
Palm Desert, CA 92211-3299
760-340-0098
Fax: 760-341-9368 www.usfilter.com
Water purification equipment

President: Richard Heckmann
President, Chief Executive Officer: Eric Spiegel
Vice President: Alison Taylor
Executive Vice President of Global Sales: Paul
Vogel
Estimated Sales: $50-100 Million
Number Employees: 100-249

30588 US Filter Corporation
2330 Scenic Highway
P.O. Box is 871329
Snellville, GA 30078

518-758-2179
Fax: 518-758-2182
President, Chief Executive Officer: Eric Spiegel
Vice President: Alison Taylor
Executive Vice President of Global Sales: Paul
Vogel
Estimated Sales: $1 - 5 Million

30589 US Filter Dewatering Systems
2155 112th Ave
Holland, MI 49424-9609

616-772-9011
Fax: 616-772-4516 800-245-3006
Manufacturer and exporter of filter presses and other
dewatering equipment for processing and waste
treatment
President: Ken Hollidge
President, Chief Executive Officer: Eric Spiegel
CEO: Chuck Gordon
Executive Vice President of Global Sales: Paul
Vogel
Estimated Sales: $20 - 50 Million
Number Employees: 100-249
Square Footage: 140800
Brands:
J-Press

30590 US Filter/Continental Water
5413 Bandera Road
Suite 405
San Antonio, TX 78238-1955

210-523-8181
Fax: 210-523-8393 800-426-3426
www.usfilter.com
Water purification equipment
President, Chief Executive Officer: Eric Spiegel
Vice President: Alison Taylor
Executive Vice President of Global Sales: Paul
Vogel
Estimated Sales: Less than $500,000
Number Employees: 1-4
Parent Co: US Filter/Continental Water

30591 US Industrial Lubricants
3330 Beekman St
Cincinnati, OH 45223-2424

513-541-2225
Fax: 513-541-2293 800-562-5454
www.usindustriallubricants.com
Manufacturer and exporter of vegetable oil and liq-
uid soap, synthetic liquid detergent and lubricants
including petroleum and synthetic
Co-Owner: Don Mattcheck
dmattcheck@usindustriallubricants.com
R & D: Ted Korzep
Facilities Engineer: Adam Freeman
Inside Sales: Jenny Anderson
USIL National Sales Manager: Dave Darling
Controller: Shannon Schlichte
Estimated Sales: $5-10 Million
Number Employees: 10-19
Number of Brands: 3
Number of Products: 250
Square Footage: 70000
Brands:
Nusheen
Oilkraft
Usil

30592 (HQ)US Label Corporation
2118 Enterprise Rd
Greensboro, NC 27408-7004

336-332-7000
Fax: 336-275-7674
Manufacturer and exporter of printed cloth, woven
and paper labels; also, label tape
CFO: Charlie Davis
VP Marketing: Phil Koch
Sales Manager: James Grant
Contact: Edward Tidaback
edward@uslabelcorp.com
Number Employees: 250-499

30593 US Line Company
16 Union Avenue
Westfield, MA 01085-2497

413-562-3629
Fax: 413-562-7328
Manufacturer and exporter of specialized industrial
braided synthetics
President: Brad Gage
CFO: Brad Gage
Quality Control: Brad Gage
R&D: Brad Gage
Marketing Director: Bradley Gage
Estimated Sales: Below $5 Million
Number Employees: 15

30594 US Magnetix
7140 Madison Ave W
Minneapolis, MN 55427-3602

763-540-9497
Fax: 763-540-0142 sales@usmagnetix.com
www.usmagnetix.com
Magnetic products; specializing in promotional
magnetic products. the company's core competen-
cies include printing, die cutting, assembly, packag-
ing, promotional marketing and graphic design
President: John Condon
john@usmagnetix.com
Sales Business Development Director: Chris Ryder
Art Director: Dean Vaccaro
Lead Production Operator: Neil Deonarain
Production Manager: Keith Johnson
Estimated Sales: $1-2.5 Million
Number Employees: 10-19

30595 US Plastic Corporation
PO Box 104
Swampscott, MA 01907-0104

781-595-1030
Fax: 781-593-6440
Polyethylene and plastic film bags
Estimated Sales: $20-50 Million
Number Employees: 100-249

30596 US Product
1101 Todds Ln
Baltimore, MD 21237-2905

410-686-6364
Fax: 410-687-6741 www.ball.com
Custom and stock decorated tins, cups and closures
President: Bernie Salles
Estimated Sales: $50 - 100 Million
Number Employees: 100-249

30597 US Seating Products
707 S W 20th Street
Ocala, FL 34471

Fax: 352-629-2860 800-999-2589
info@admiralfurniture.com
www.admiralfurnitureonline.com
Manufacturer and exporter of aluminum and vinyl
benches, chairs, cushions and pads, tray stands, ta-
bles and booths including legs and bases
President: Peter Villella
Estimated Sales: $10-20 Million
Number Employees: 10
Type of Packaging: Food Service

30598 US Standard Sign
11400 Addison Ave
Franklin Park, IL 60131-1124

847-455-7446
Fax: 847-455-3330 800-537-4790
sales@usstandardsign.com
www.usstandardsign.com
Aluminum sign blanks
President: Rick Mandel
CFO: Steve Fallon
Estimated Sales: $1 - 2.5 Million
Number Employees: 50-99
Parent Co: Mandel Metals

30599 US Tag & Label
2208 Aisquith St
Baltimore, MD 21218

410-962-2676
Fax: 410-889-1227 800-638-1018
72723.1042@compuserve.com
Labels
Estimated Sales: $1-5 Million
Number Employees: 50-99

30600 US Tsubaki Holdings Inc
301 E Marquardt Dr
Wheeling, IL 60090

847-459-9500
Fax: 847-459-9515 800-323-7790
sales@ustsubaki.com www.ustsubaki.com
Precision roller chains.
Year Founded: 1917
Estimated Sales: $290 Million
Number Employees: 500-1000

30601 USA Canvas Shoppe
2435 Glenda Lane
Dallas, TX 75229

972-484-7633
Fax: 972-620-0364 877-626-8468
awnings@usacanvas.com www.usacanvas.com
Commercial awnings and back-lit awnings
President: Gary Cozart
Contact: Ellen Cozart
ellen.cozart@usacanvas.com
Estimated Sales: $1-2.5 Million
Number Employees: 10-19
Parent Co: Four Seasons Patio and Awning
Company

30602 USC Consulting Group
3000 Bayport Drive
Suite 1010
Tampa, FL 33607

813-636-4004
Fax: 813-636-5099 800-888-8872
www.usccg.com
Consulting services
President: George Coffey
Chairman/CEO: Ronald Walker
President: James Ostrosky
Marketing Director: Gary Brown
Contact: Michelle Maloni
mmaloni@hklaw.com
VP/Senior Operations Manager: Terence Maher
Estimated Sales: $45 Million
Number Employees: 150
Square Footage: 3000

30603 (HQ)USDA-NASS
1400 Independence Ave SW
Washington, DC 20250-0002

202-690-8122
Fax: 202-720-9013 800-727-9540
nass@nass.usda.gov www.nass.usda.gov
the mission is to research and develop knowledge
and technology needed to solve technical agricultural problems of broad scope in order to ensure ade-
quate production of high quality food and
agricultural products
Administrator: Cynthia Clark
Director of Research and Development: Mark Harris
Contact: Art Fairson
art.fairson@ars.usda.gov
Director of Operations: Kevin Barnes
Number Employees: 250-499

30604 USECO
P.O. Box 20428
Murfreesboro, TN 37129-0428

615-893-4820
Fax: 615-893-8705 info@useco.com
www.useco.com
Manufacturer and exporter of stainless steel and alu-
minum food service equipment including hot and
cold food service carts, tray line refrigerators, blast
chillers, tray lifters, pellet heaters, etc
President: John Westbrook
VP (Food Service Systems Tech.): Sara Hurt
VP Sales/Marketing (USECO): Paul Murphy
Estimated Sales: $20-50 Million
Number Employees: 50-99
Square Footage: 100000
Parent Co: Standex International Corporation
Type of Packaging: Food Service
Brands:
Catr
Remotaire
Rota-Chill
Unitray
Unitron
Useco

30605 Udi's Food
101 East 70th Ave
Denver, CO 80221

303-657-1600
Fax: 303-657-1615

Prepared foods
Owner: Udi Baron
General Manager & Partner Udis Granola: Eric Clayman
CFO: Jason Kashman
Vice President: Etai Baron
Director of Foodservice: Jared Josleyn
Manager Quality Assurance: Natasha Phipps
Marketing Communications Manager: Heather Collins
Sales Executive/Manager: Cynthia Drennan
Contact: Jim Heilman
  jheilman@udisfood.com
VP Operations/Production Manager: Yosi Lutwak
Human Resources Director: Rosa Woods
Vice President Foodservice: Dana Spaeth

30606 Uhrden
750 Edelweiss Dr.
PO Box 705
Sugarcreek, OH 44681
330-852-2411
Fax: 330-852-2415 800-852-2411
Bulk dumping equipment and vertical reciprocating conveyors
Chairman of the Board: Kenneth L Cook
General Manager: Mike Sigma
Sales: Rod Synder
Purchasing Agent: Lois Harig
Estimated Sales: Below $5 Million
Number Employees: 20-49
Square Footage: 130000
Brands:
  Tubar

30607 Uhtamaki Foods Services
242 College Ave
Waterville, ME 04901-6226
207-873-3351
Fax: 207-877-6504 www.chinet.com
Biodegradable disposable tableware; serving the food service industry
Manager: Steve Bosse
CEO: Mark Staton
Contact: Peter Deane
  peter.deane@us.huhtamaki.com
Estimated Sales: $1 - 5 Million
Number Employees: 500-999
Parent Co: Royal Packaging Industries

30608 Ulcra Dynamics
3000 Advance Lane
Colmar, PA 18915-9432
201-489-0044
Fax: 201-489-9229 800-727-6931
Manufacturer and exporter of water treatment systems
Estimated Sales: $500,000-$1 Million
Number Employees: 10-19
Parent Co: Severn Trent Services

30609 Ullman, Shapiro & UllmanLLP
425 Park Ave 27th Floor
New York, NY 10022
212-755-0299
www.usulaw.com
Manufacturer and exporter of platters, plates, bowls, tumblers and pitchers
Partner: Marc Ullman
Chief Executive Officer: Zev Weiss
Executive VP: Marvin Lipkind
Estimated Sales: $10-20 Million
Number Employees: 1-4
Square Footage: 300000

30610 Ulmer Pharmacal
1614 Industrial Ave W
Park Rapids, MN 56470-3510
218-732-2656
Fax: 218-732-5300 800-848-5637
www.lobanaproducts.com
Vitamins, disinfectants, chemical detergents and soaps
President: Al Trudeau
  ulmer@unitelc.com
National Sales Manager: Rick Dressler
Estimated Sales: $1-2.5 Million
Number Employees: 5-9
Parent Co: Ulmer Pharmacal Company
Brands:
  Derm Ade
  Lobana
  Peri Garde

30611 Ultimate Textile
18 Market St
Paterson, NJ 07501-1721
973-523-5866
Fax: 973-523-5460 www.ultimatetextile.com
Tabletop accessories including napkins, table cloths and skirting
President: Roger Glicman
  rglicman@pecata.com
Estimated Sales: $20-50 Million
Number Employees: 100-249

30612 Ultra Cool International
PO Box 57844
Sherman Oaks, CA 91413-2844
818-908-9208
Fax: 818-908-4058

30613 Ultra Industries Inc
2801 Carlisle Ave
Racine, WI 53404-1888
262-633-5102
Fax: 262-633-5102 800-358-5872
info@ultradustcollectors.com
www.ultradustcollectors.com
Dust collection equipment, cartridge collectors and pneumatic filter receivers
President: Ko Kryger
CFO: Evone Hagerman
General Manager: Dave Cleveland
Sales and Marketing Manager: Tom Meyer
Application/Sales Engineer: Daniel Hahn
Contact: Mike Blair
  mblair@ultradustcollectors.com
Product Manager: Norman Pratt
Estimated Sales: $2.5-5 Million
Number Employees: 10-19
Square Footage: 2000

30614 Ultra Lift Corp
475 Stockton Ave # E
San Jose, CA 95126-2435
408-287-9400
Fax: 408-297-1199 800-346-3057
info@ultralift.com www.ultralift.com
Powdered material handling equipment products are specially designed for food and beverage equipment movers and installers
President: George Dabb
  info@ultralift.com
VP: Charae Hewphill
Estimated Sales: $1-2.5 Million
Number Employees: 5-9
Brands:
  Kegmaster
  Ultra Lift

30615 Ultra Packaging Inc
534 N York Rd
Bensenville, IL 60106-1607
630-595-9820
Fax: 630-595-9710 ultrapkg@aol.com
www.ultrapackaging.com
Cartoning machines
Owner: Bob Stockus
  ultrapkg@aol.com
Estimated Sales: $1-2.5 Million
Number Employees: 10-19

30616 Ultra Process Systems
733 Emory Valley Road
Oak Ridge, TN 37830-7017
865-483-2772
Fax: 865-483-2979
High temperature process equipment and services to the dairy and food processors

30617 Ultrafilter
3560 Engineering Drive
Norcross, GA 30092-2819
770-942-5322
Fax: 770-448-3854 800-543-3634
Worldwide supplier of compressed gas, steam and liquid purification equipment. Process filtration: culinary steam filters, sterile gas filters, process liquid filters, tank vent filters, 3-A approved sanitary filter housings, microfiltration cartridges. Compressed air filters and dryers, on-site compressed air quality testing: ultra-survey programs
President: Keith Hayward
Sales/Marketing: Jeff Touo
Number Employees: 20-49
Square Footage: 132000
Parent Co: Ultrafilter GmBH

Other Locations:
  Ultrafilter
  Scarborough ON
Brands:
  Boreas
  Buran
  Ufmt
  Ultrafilter
  Ultrair
  Ultrapac
  Ultraqua
  Ultrasep
  Ultratoc
  Ultrex

30618 Ultrafryer Systems Inc
302 Spencer Ln
San Antonio, TX 78201-2018
210-731-5000
Fax: 210-731-5099 800-545-9189
ultrafryersales@ultrafryer.com
www.ultrafryer.com
Manufacturer and exporter of gas and electric fryers, filters, breading tables, warmers, cookers and hoods
President: Ed Odmark
CEO: Edward T Odmark
  eodmark@ultrafryer.com
National Manager Sales: Steve Ricketson
General Manager: William Collins
Estimated Sales: $10-20 Million
Number Employees: 50-99
Square Footage: 150000
Type of Packaging: Consumer, Food Service
Brands:
  Ultrafryer

30619 Ultrak
6252 W 91st Avenue
Westminster, CO 80031-2909
303-428-9480
Fax: 303-429-6609
Closed-circuit surveillance equipment
Managing Director: Tom Verzuh
Marketing Coordinator: Linda Pohl
Sales Manager: Chris Staniforth
Number Employees: 24
Square Footage: 14000

30620 Ultralight Plastic
6700 E Rogers Cir
Boca Raton, FL 33487
561-988-1676
Fax: 561-988-0928 palletbox@hotmail.com
Plastic pallets, pallet bases
CEO: Geoffrey Bourne
Estimated Sales: $12 Million
Number Employees: 5
Parent Co: Ultralight Plastic

30621 Ultrapak
134 Franklin Ave
Dunkirk, NY 14048-2806
716-366-3654
Fax: 716-366-0041 800-228-6030
www.ultrapak.us
Decorative labels, tamper evident bands, and unitizing sleeves for multipacks
President: Khalid Khan
  khalid@ultrapak.us
CFO: William Cook
Marketing Director: Jackie Patterson
Sales Director: Gracie Bane
Production Manager: Dan Lentz
Estimated Sales: $2.5-5 Million
Number Employees: 20-49
Type of Packaging: Food Service

30622 Ultrapar Inc.
13 Flintlock Dr
Warren, NJ 07059-5014
908-647-6650
Fax: 908-647-1281 chrisparkinson@ultrapar.com
www.ultrapar.com
Wholesaler/distributor of steam filters, culinary steam filtration systems, air sterilizing filters and liquid sterilizing filtration systems.
President: Chris Parkinson
Vice President: Nancy Siconolfi
Estimated Sales: $1 - 1.5 Million
Number Employees: 3
Square Footage: 7200

30623 Ultratainer
910 Industrial Boulevard
St Jean-Sur-Richelie, QC J3B 8J4
Canada
514-359-3651
Fax: 514-359-3653 ultra@ultratainer.com
www.ultratainer.com
Collapsible, reusable, stackable, stainless steel and
wire mesh containers
CEO: Bert Gaumond
Plant Manager: Dave Lapierre
Purchasing Manager: Lina Levert
Estimated Sales: $10 Million
Number Employees: 30
Square Footage: 50000
Type of Packaging: Bulk

30624 Umec Solar Inc
548 Claire St
Hayward, CA 94541-6412
510-537-4744
Fax: 510-537-9564 800-933-8632
www.umec.net
Elevators, loaders, lifters and dumpers, belt convey-
ors, blenders, chup separators, massagers and tum-
blers, mixers, screw conveyors
President: Barry Brescia
CEO: Benny Brescia
CEO: Ralph Creech
Sales Director: Dennis Dennings
Manager: Cecilia Hewett
Estimated Sales: $2.5 - 5 Million
Number Employees: 20-49
Type of Packaging: Food Service, Private Label

30625 Unarco Industries LLC
400 SE 15th St
Wagoner, OK 74467-7900
918-485-9531
Fax: 918-485-2131 800-654-4100
www.unarco.com
Manufacturer and exporter of shopping carts, retail
display fixtures, stainless steel tables and accesso-
ries, food service containers and carts and warehous-
ing and stocking carts
President: Randy Garvin
CFO: Misty Allen
 misty.allen@unarco.com
Sales: Richard Wilkinson
VP International Sales: David Warneke
VP Sales: Richard Wilkinson
Estimated Sales: $50-100 Million
Number Employees: 250-499
Square Footage: 650000
Type of Packaging: Food Service

30626 Unarco Material Handling Inc
407 E Washington St
Pandora, OH 45877
419-384-3211
Fax: 419-384-7239 800-448-0784
www.unarcorack.com
Manufacturer and exporter of roll-formed pallet rack
systems
National Sales Manager: David Johnstone
Manager: Mike Burris
 mikeb@clymer-rack.com
Estimated Sales: $10-20 Million
Number Employees: 50-99
Parent Co: Unarco Material Handling, Inc.
Type of Packaging: Bulk

30627 Underwriters Laboratories Inc
2600 NW Lake Rd
Camas, WA 98607-8542
360-817-5500
Fax: 360-817-6000 877-854-3577
www.ul.com
Testing and certification service for product, envi-
ronmental and public safety of appliances and
equipment
Vice President: Ralph Parker
 ralph.j.parker@us.ul.com
CFO: Michael Saltzmen
CEO: Keith E Williams
VP Sales/Marketing: Stuart Paul
Number Employees: 250-499

30628 Uneco Systems
8412 Autumn Drive
Woodridge, IL 60517
630-910-0505
Fax: 630-910-0558 800-700-6894
junewitz@att.net

President: John Unewitz
 junewitz@att.net
Estimated Sales: $1-2.5 Million
Number Employees: 1-4

30629 Unette Corp
1578 Sussex Tpke # 5
Building #5
Randolph, NJ 07869-1833
973-328-6800
Fax: 973-537-1010 info@unette.com
www.unette.com
Contract packager of food colors, condiments, gro-
ceries, etc
President: Joseph R Hark
Sales Service Coordinator: Dawn Stone
Estimated Sales: $4400000
Number Employees: 50-99
Square Footage: 240000

30630 Unex Manufacturing Inc
691 New Hampshire Ave
Lakewood, NJ 08701-5452
732-928-2800
Fax: 732-928-2828 800-334-8639
span@unex.com www.unex.com
Carton flow truck and storage products
President: Brian Neuwirth
CEO: Frank Neuwirth
CFO: Eilean Brant
VP Sales: Mark Neuwrith
R&D: Haward McIbaine
Marketing Director: Carolann Neuwirth
Northwest Sales Manager: Bill Link
Contact: Deena Brown
 dbrown@unix.com
Estimated Sales: Less Than $500,000
Number Employees: 5-9
Brands:
 Pathline
 Spantrack

30631 Unger Co
12401 Berea Rd
Cleveland, OH 44111-1607
216-252-1400
Fax: 216-252-1427 800-321-1418
info@ungerco.com www.ungerco.com
Supplier of packaging for bakery and deli products.
Importer of polyethylene, polyprop and plastic shop-
ping bags, and boxes. Consulting services available
President/CEO: Gerald Unger
 info@ungerco.com
Controller: Scott Smith
VP: Diane Tracy
Estimated Sales: $5-10 Million
Number Employees: 10-19
Type of Packaging: Food Service
Brands:
 Bake'n Show
 Deleez
 Ungermatic

30632 Uni Carriers Americas Corp
240 N Prospect St
Marengo, IL 60152-3235
815-568-0061
Fax: 815-568-0179 800-871-5438
nfcsales@nfcna.com
Industrial gas, lp and electric forklift, walkie and
reach trucks
President: Jan Aten
 atenjan@unicarriersamericas.com
Director Marketing: Keith Allmandinger
Manager Media Marketing: Tim Haley
 atenjan@unicarriersamericas.com
Number Employees: 500-999
Square Footage: 1400000
Parent Co: Nissan Motor Company

30633 Uni First Corp
68 Jonspin Rd
Wilmington, MA 01887-1086
978-658-8888
Fax: 978-657-5663 800-455-7654
ufirst@unifirst.com www.unifirst.com
Supplier of workwear and textile services. Rent,
lease, and sell uniforms, protective clothing, custom
corporate workwear, floorcare, and other facility services products to all kinds of businesses.
President/CEO: Roland Croatti
CEO: Ronald D Croatti
 ronald_croatti@unifirst.com

Estimated Sales: Over $1 Billion
Number Employees: 10000+

30634 Uni-Chains Manufacturing
Hjulmagervej 21
Vejle, DK 7100
457-572-3100
Fax: 457-572-3348 800-937-2864
admin@unichains.com www.unichains.com
Manufactures a comprehensive programs for inter-
nal transport offering chains in both steel and plas-
tic, modular plastic belt and conveyor accessories.
President: Soren Pedersen
Number Employees: 10-19
Parent Co: Uni Chains

30635 UniChem Enterprises
1905 S Lynx Place
Ontario, CA 91761
909-321-1000
Fax: 425-696-3568 sales@unichemsupply.com
Raw materials and ingredients supplier to the food,
feed, nutraceutical, supplement and cosmetics industries.
Contact: Tony Hang
 thang@unichemsupply.com

30636 UniPro Foodservice, Inc.
2500 Cumberland Pkwy. SE
Suite 600
Atlanta, GA 30339
770-952-0871
Fax: 770-952-0872 info@uniprofoodservice.com
www.uniprofoodservice.com
Coffee, tea, cappucino, sugar packets, non-dairy
creamer, and coffee bowls, cutlery, foodservice
film, paper goods, dry pastas, frozen filled pastas,
Italian cheeses, soups, olive oil, sausage and meat-
balls, tomato products, pizzacrusts and pizza top-
pings. Pork, produce, dairy, oils/grains, beef, veal,
lamb, seafood, and poultry.
CEO: Bob Stewart
CFO: Tracy Britton
Executive VP of Marketing: Keith Durnell
Executive VP, Sales: Scott Strull
Year Founded: 1997
Estimated Sales: $987 Million
Number Employees: 1000-4999
Square Footage: 9303
Brands:
 Code
 Companions
 Comsource
 Cortona
 Nifda
 Nugget
 Reflections

30637 (HQ)UniTrak Corporation
299 Ward Street
PO Box 330
Port Hope, ON L1A 3W4
Canada
905-885-8168
Fax: 905-885-2614 866-883-5749
info@unitrak.com www.unitrak.com
Manufacturer and exporter of bucket elevators,
packaging machinery and conveyors
President: W Gorsline
Engineering Team Leader: Keith Douglas
Scheduling and Special Project: D Snoddon
Marketing Team Leader: Marie Lytle
Operations Manager: D Snoddon
Plant Manager: Ivan Patton
Number Employees: 10
Square Footage: 40000
Other Locations:
 UniTrak Corp. Ltd.
 Furness Vale, High Peak
Brands:
 Bagstarder
 Efficia
 Tiptrak

30638 Unibloc-Pump Inc
1701 Ashborough Rd SE
Marietta, GA 30067-8925
770-218-8900
Fax: 770-218-8442 info@uniblocpump.com
www.uniblocpump.com
Aseptic processing equipment
Owner: Harry Soderstrom
 harry@flowtechdiv.com
Number Employees: 10-19

30639 Unibloc-Pump Inc
1701 Ashborough Rd SE
Marietta, GA 30067-8925
770-218-8900
Fax: 770-218-8442 info@flowtechdiv.com
www.uniblocpump.com
Sanitary lobe pumps and valves
President/Owner: Harry Soderstrom
harry@flowtechdiv.com
Estimated Sales: $4-8 Million
Number Employees: 10-19
Square Footage: 25000

30640 Unichema North America
4650 S Racine Ave
Chicago, IL 60609-3321
773-650-7600
Fax: 773-376-0095
Industrial chemicals, oleic, stearic and fatty acids,
lubricating oils and greases
Estimated Sales: $50 - 100 Million
Number Employees: 100-249

30641 Unidex
2416 North Main Street
Warsaw, NY 14569
585-786-3170
Fax: 585-786-3223 800-724-1302
sales@unidex-inc.com www.unidex-inc.com
Lifting, positioning and manipulating devices in-
cluding pallet lifting tables, adjustable height work
benches, stainless steel lifts and carts, roll handling
President: Arthur Crater
CFO: Tom Baldwin
Quality Control: Don Cunningham
Sales: Sue Gardner
Estimated Sales: $2.5-5 Million

30642 Unifiller Systems
7621 MacDonald Road
Delta, BC V4G 1N3
Canada
604-940-2233
Fax: 604-940-2195 888-733-8444
www.unifiller.com
Manufacturs of stainless steel food grade filling and
portioning systems for the baking and food service
industries. Extensive line of bakery depositors,
pumps/depositors and fully automated cake assem-
bly/finishing lines
President: Kuno Kurschner
CEO: Mark Soares
CFO: Ballard Client
Vice President: Benno Bucher
R&D: Andy Fillers
Quality Control: Chris Moora
VP Marketing: Stewart MacPherson
Sales Director: Nick Frost
Number Employees: 50
Brands:
Deco-Mate
Handi-Matic
Uni-Versal

30643 Unifoil Corp
12 Daniel Rd
Fairfield, NJ 07004-2536
973-244-9990
Fax: 973-244-5555 www.unifoil.com
Manufacturer and exporter of laminated and coated
aluminum foil; also, metallized and holographic pa-
per and boards
President: Joseph Funicelli
CEO: Milica Bubalo
mbubalo@unifoil.com
CFO: William Mulooney
Quality Control: Robert Galloino
Sales Director: Robert Rumer
Plant Manager: Dwight Penrell
Estimated Sales: $20-50 Million
Number Employees: 50-99

30644 Uniforms To You
9525 S. Cicero Avenue
Oak Lawn, IL 60453
708-424-4747
800-889-6072
www.uniformstoyou.com
Uniforms, work gear and career apparel.
Estimated Sales: $20 - 50 Million
Number Employees: 500-999
Parent Co: Cintas Corp
Brands:
Cintas

Dickies
Fabian International
Segal
Uncommon Threads

30645 Uniforms To You & Co
5600 W 73rd St
Chicago, IL 60638-6273
708-563-0108
Fax: 708-563-5003 800-864-3676
Uniforms and special clothing
Sr. VP Sales/Marketing: Michael DiMino
Contact: Michael Dimino
michaeldimino@uty.com
General Manager: Keith Nacker
Number Employees: 5-9

30646 Uniloy Milacron
5550 Occidental Hwy
Suite B
Tecumseh, MI 49286
517-424-8900
Fax: 517-423-6827 www.milacron.com
Blowmolding and structural foam machinery. In-
cluded are stretch blowmolding systems for PET.
Molds, tooling, parts, training and technical support.
Chief Executive Officer: Tom Goeke
Chief Financial Officer: Bruce Chalmers
VP/General Counsel/Secretary: Hugh O'Donnell
Chief Human Resources Officer: Mark Miller
Year Founded: 1860
Estimated Sales: $74.5 Million
Number Employees: 5,368

30647 Unimar Inc
3195 Vickery Rd
Syracuse, NY 13212-4574
315-699-4400
Fax: 315-699-3700 800-739-9169
www.unimar.com
Refrigerators, freezers, beverage dispensers, snack
bars, C-stoves, and heaters
Owner: Michael Marley
mike@unimar.com
Estimated Sales: $2.5-5 Million
Number Employees: 10-19

30648 Unimove LLC
1145 Little Gap Rd # C
Palmerton, PA 18071-5027
610-826-7855
Fax: 610-826-8422 unimove@ptd.net
www.unimove.com
Manufacturer and exporter of vacuum tube lifting
systems
Director: Robert Shannon
unitech@ptd.net
VP: Vincent Julian Jr
Director Marketing: Ken Kasick
Operations: Alan Zimmermann
Purchasing: Charles Kistler
Estimated Sales: 1,000,000
Number Employees: 5-9
Number of Brands: 1
Square Footage: 140000
Brands:
Unimove

30649 Union Camp Corporation
5050 Ironton Street
Denver, CO 80239-2412
303-371-0760
Fax: 303-375-0718
Inner packaging materials including fiber corrugated
boxes; also, enhanced graphics and pre-print
available
Sales Manager: Ron Wise
General Manager: Paul Areson
Number Employees: 130
Square Footage: 260000
Parent Co: Union Camp Corporation

30650 Union Cord Products Company
425 N Martingdale Road
Schaumburg, IL 60173
847-240-1500
Fax: 847-240-1576 info@unionleasing.com
www.unionleasing.com
Manufacturer and exporter of gaskets including
braided, knitted, rubber insert and poly-jacketed
cellulose
CEO: Warren Benis
Estimated Sales: $1 - 5,000,000
Parent Co: Sasser Family Holdings Inc.

30651 Union Industries
10 Admiral St
Providence, RI 02908
401-274-7000
Fax: 401-331-1910 800-556-6454
Manufacturer and exporter of flexible packaging
President: Harley Frank
Chairman: H Alan Frank
CFO: John Wilbur
Sales Director: Michael Kauffman
Contact: Anne Delany
adelany@unionpaperco.com
Estimated Sales: $23.5 Million
Number Employees: 125
Square Footage: 125000
Type of Packaging: Food Service, Private Label

30652 Union Plastics Co
132 E Union St
Marshville, NC 28103-1141
704-624-2112
Fax: 704-624-6119
Plastic and vinyl hose and tubing
President: Sandra Osborn
Plant Manager: C Osborn
Estimated Sales: Below $5 Million
Number Employees: 5-9

30653 Union Process
1925 Akron Peninsula Rd
Akron, OH 44313
330-929-3333
Fax: 330-929-3034 eli@unionprocess.com
www.unionprocess.com
Manufacturers a broad line of wet and dry milling
attritors and small media mills. Also offer a wide as-
sortment of grinding media and provide toll milling
and refurbishing services. Also the meading manu-
facturer of rubber inks forballoons, swim caps and
other rubber products.
President: Arno Szegvari
R & D Lab: Margaret Yang
National Sales Manager: Robert Schilling
Production: Craig McCaulley
Plant Manager: Ron Sloan
Estimated Sales: $5 - 10 Million
Number Employees: 20-49
Square Footage: 56000
Brands:
Attritor

30654 Unipac Shipping
18216 147th Ave # 2
2nd. Floor
Jamaica, NY 11413-3704
718-995-8168
Fax: 718-995-8169 800-586-2711
info@unipacshippinginc.com
www.unipacshipping.com
Absorbent pads for pre-packaging meats, poultry,
fish, sprouts, asparagus, apples, pizza, etc
President: Richard Engel
Number Employees: 20-49
Square Footage: 120000

30655 Unipak Inc
715 E Washington St
West Chester, PA 19380-4595
610-436-6600
Fax: 610-436-6069 info@unipakinc.com
www.unipakinc.com
Paper boxes; also, printing services available
President: Tim Craig
tcraig@unipakinc.com
Structural / Graphic Design: Nicole Dana
Sales/Marketing: Teddy Frain
Customer Service: Angela Marchetti
Operations: Mike Golas
Supply Chain and Operations: Zak Allen
Purchasing/Estimating: Jenn Correa
Estimated Sales: $5 - 10 Million
Number Employees: 50-99

30656 Uniplast Films
1017 Wilson Street
Palmer, MA 01069-1137
413-283-8365
Fax: 413-283-8278 800-343-1295
Film laminates and plastic and coextended film; ex-
porter of plastic film
VP: Fredy Steng
Customer Service: Diane Fihal
Estimated Sales: $1 - 5 Million
Number Employees: 100

Square Footage: 160000
Parent Co: Uniplast Industries

30657 Unique Boxes
6548 N Glenwood Ave
Chicago, IL 60626

773-743-6617
Fax: 773-254-1023 800-281-1670
rrchagin@aol.com
Box partitions, set-up paper boxes and folding cartons
President: R Chagin
CFO: Rafael Chagin
Contact: Rafael Chagin
rrchagin@aol.com
Estimated Sales: Below $5 Million
Number Employees: 5

30658 Unique Manufacturing
1920 W Princeton Ave Ste 17
Visalia, CA 93277

559-739-1007
Fax: 559-739-7725 888-737-1007
Manufacturer and importer of silverware sleeves,
paper napkin bands, beverage coasters, menu covers,
chopsticks, flag food picks and paper parasols
President: Irwin Smith
Marketing: Paul Smith
Sales: Erwin Smith
Number Employees: 5-9
Square Footage: 4000

30659 Unique Manufacturing Company
1050 Corporate Ave
Suite 108
North Port, FL 34289

941-429-6600
Fax: 253-669-7645 sales@uniquemanuf.com
www.uniquemanuf.com
Importers and manufacturing of hospitality items.
Custom printed stock flag food picks, beverage stirs,
paper/foil parasols, napkins bands, silverware
sleeves, chenille and foil decorator picks, plastic
food picks, chop stickscoasters, paper glass covers,
placemats, tray covers, and menu covers and binders
Owner: Michael Jakubowski
Estimated Sales: Below $5 Million
Number Employees: 1-4
Number of Products: 500
Square Footage: 2000
Type of Packaging: Consumer, Private Label
Brands:
    American Ingredients
    Dole Packaged Foods
    Nakand
    Nutrin Corp
    Qa Products
    Quick Dry Foods
    Vita Foods

30660 Unique Plastics
372 Rio Rico Drive
Rio Rico, AZ 85648-3517

520-377-0595
Fax: 520-377-0696 800-658-5946
Round plastic trays
Estimated Sales: $1 - 5,000,000
Number Employees: 20-50
Square Footage: 28000

30661 Unique Solutions
2836 Corporate Pkwy
Algonquin, IL 60102-2564

847-960-1110
Fax: 847-540-1431 info@unique-solutions.com
www.unique-solutions.com
Product line includes inserting and labeling equipment produced in a continuous, perforated bandolier
format in addition to that of two or three-dimensional premiums and labels that are inserted
(In-Pakrs) or attached to the outside ofprimary
packaging (On-Pakrs).
President: Mark Ulan
Chairman/CEO: Joyce Witt
    info@unique-solutions.com
Business Development Manager: Brian Dawson
VP Sales: Walter Peterson
COO: Jason Raasch
Production Manager: Norman Hendle
    info@unique-solutions.com
Customer Service Representative: Christie Haack
Estimated Sales: $2.5-5 Million
Number Employees: 5-9

Square Footage: 52000
Parent Co: Unique Coupons

30662 Unirak Storage Systems
7620 Telegraph Rd
Taylor, MI 48180-2237

313-291-7600
Fax: 313-291-7605 800-348-7225
sales@unirak.com www.unirak.com
Manufacturer and exporter of racks including adjustable storage, pallet, galvanized, refrigerated, selective, drive-in/thru, deck, pallet flow, push-back and
carton flow
Vice President: Eric Gonda
    sales@unarak.com
Sales Director: Eric Gonda
Estimated Sales: $3 - 5 Million
Number Employees: 10-19
Number of Brands: 4
Number of Products: 110
Square Footage: 400000
Type of Packaging: Bulk
Brands:
    Unirack Drive-In Rack
    Unirak Pallet Rack

30663 Unisoft Systems Associates
4890 Trailpath Drive
Dublin, OH 43016

614-791-1592
Fax: 614-791-1592 800-448-1574
www.unisoft-systems.com
Food management software including inventory, recipe, invoicing, forecasting, nutrient, diet office management, bid list and daily activity
Technical Support: Robert Davis
Research & Development: Diane Clapp
Contact: Diane Bruce
    dianebruce@unisoft-systems.com
Estimated Sales: $2.5-5 Million
Number Employees: 19
Square Footage: 4800
Brands:
    Food System 4 Windows

30664 (HQ)Unisource ManufacturingInc
8040 NE 33rd Dr
Portland, OR 97211-2016

503-281-4673
Fax: 503-281-5845 800-234-2566
info@unisource-mfg.com
www.unisource-mfg.com
Manufacturer and engineering of industrial hoses
and related products
President: Joseph Thompson
CEO: Joe Thompson
    jthompson@unisource-mfg.com
Quality Mgr.: Blu Matsell
National Sales Mgr.: Joseph Thompson
General/Human Resources Mgr: Dan Christiansen
Operations/Purchasing Mgr.: Ron Bateman
Purchasing Manager: Ralph Lorusso
Number Employees: 50-99

30665 Unitech Scientific
12026 Centralia Rd # H
Hawaiian Gardens, CA 90716-1067

562-924-5155
Fax: 562-809-3140 info@unitechscientific.com
www.unitechscientific.com
Glucose, fructose, L-malic acid, acetic acid, primary
amino nitrogen and other food testkits
President: Geoffrey Anderson
    geoff@unitechscientific.com
CEO: Lee Anderson
R & D: Ted Chou
Quality Control: Jim Sisowth
Estimated Sales: Below $5 Million
Number Employees: 5-9

30666 United Ad Label
3075 Highland Parkway
Suite 400
Downers Grove, IL 60515-5560

714-990-2700
Fax: 800-962-0658 800-423-4643
Manufacturer and exporter of pressure sensitive labels
President: Cal Laird
VP Marketing: Brad Baylies
New Markets Manager: Cheryl Hall
    cheryl.hall@rrd.com
Estimated Sales: $1 - 5 Million
Number Employees: 100-250

Type of Packaging: Consumer, Bulk

30667 (HQ)United Air Specialists Inc
4440 Creek Rd
Blue Ash, OH 45242-2832

513-891-0400
Fax: 513-891-4171 800-992-4422
www.uasinc.com
Manufacturer and exporter of air filtration media including electrostatic precipitators, liquid coating and
dust collection systems
President: Rich Larson
    riclar@uasinc.com
VP Marketing: Lynne Laake
Estimated Sales: $20,000,000 - $49,999,999
Number Employees: 250-499
Square Footage: 152500
Other Locations:
    United Air Specialists
    Cincinnati OH
Brands:
    Crystal-Aire
    Dust-Cat
    Dust-Hog
    Smog-Hog
    Smokeeter
    Total-Stat

30668 United Bags Inc
1355 N Warson Rd
St Louis, MO 63132-1598

314-421-3700
Fax: 314-421-0969 800-550-2247
custserv@unitedbags.com www.unitedbags.com
Manufacturer and importer of bags including bulk,
burlap, multi-wall, polypropylene, paper and cotton
President: Todd Greenberg
    unitedbags@aol.com
CEO: Herbert Greenberg
CFO: Ruth Allen
VP: Todd Greenberg
Estimated Sales: $2.5-5 Million
Number Employees: 20-49
Square Footage: 600000

30669 United Bakery Equipment
19216 S Laurel Park Rd
Rancho Dominguez, CA 90220-6008

310-635-8121
Fax: 310-635-8171 www.ubeusa.com
VP: Mike Bastasch
Director of Domestic/international Sales: Tom
Sheffield
Manager: Mike Bastasch
Estimated Sales: $10 - 20 Million
Number Employees: 20-49

30670 United Bakery EquipmentCompany
15815 W 110th St
Shawnee Mission, KS 66219

913-541-8700
Fax: 913-541-0781 www.ubeusa.com
Manufacturer and exporter of slicers and baggers for
breads, buns, tortillas, muffins, bagels, etc
President: Frank Bastasch
Vice President: Paul Bastasch
Sales Director: Bob Plourde
Contact: Levent Gokkaya
    lgokkaya@untek.com.tr
Estimated Sales: $20 - 50 Million
Number Employees: 50-99
Square Footage: 32000
Parent Co: United Bakery Equipment Company
Type of Packaging: Food Service, Private Label

30671 United Barrels
1303 Jefferson Street no. 210a
Napa, CA 94559-2470

707-258-0795
Fax: 707-259-5324
Wine barrels, French oak wine barrels
President: Scott Harrop
Estimated Sales: Below $5 Million
Number Employees: 1-4

30672 United Basket Co Inc
5801 Grand Ave
Maspeth, NY 11378-3216

718-894-5454
Fax: 718-326-3378 ubsales@verizon.net
www.unitedbasketco.com
Baskets and gift basket supplies and packaging supplies

Founder: Max Hanfling
CEO: Phil Hanfling
  ubsales@verizon.net
Number Employees: 5-9
Square Footage: 56

30673 United Commercial Corporation
20 Avenue At the Cmn
Shrewsbury, NJ 07702-4801

732-935-0025
Fax: 732-935-0022 800-498-7147
wpearl@verizon.net
We supply plastic fabrication for dispensing hot and cold food merchandising equipment and menu systems
President: Wade Pearlman
Estimated Sales: $2 Million

30674 United Desiccants
985 Damonte Ranch Parkway
Suite #320
Reno, NE 89521

505-864-6691
Fax: 505-864-9296 888-659-1377
insidesale@desiccare.com www.desiccare.com
Manufacturer and exporter of desiccant absorption packs; also, humidity indicators for packaging
President: William Monin
General Manager: George Klett
Business Unit Manager: Richard Greenlaw
Number Employees: 300
Parent Co: United Catalysts
Brands:
  Adsormat
  Container Dri
  Desi Pak
  Desi View
  Sorb Pak
  Sorb-It
  Tri-Sorb

30675 United Electric Controls Co
180 Dexter Ave
Watertown, MA 02472-4200

617-926-1000
Fax: 617-926-4354 support@ueonline.com
www.ueonline.com
Manufacturer and exporter of temperature control and detection devices including thermostats, pressure and temperature switches, transducers and sensors for general purpose and sanitary service.
President & CEO: Dave Reis
Director of Materials: Cheryl O'Connell
Year Founded: 1931
Estimated Sales: $100+ Million
Number Employees: 100-249
Other Locations:
  United Electric Controls Co.
  Milford CT

30676 United Fabricators
1110 Carnall Avenue
Fort Smith, AR 72901-3756

479-782-9169
Fax: 479-783-5901 800-235-4101
Custom stainless steel food service equipment including chef's counters, canopies, sinks, work tables, etc
EVP: Jerry Bollin Jr
Sales Manager: Greg Donald
Contact: Kathy Griffin
  griffinkathya@hotmail.com
Office Manager: Jeanne Emery
Estimated Sales: $3.6 Million
Number Employees: 35
Square Footage: 160000
Type of Packaging: Food Service
Brands:
  Unifab

30677 United Filters Intl
901 S Grant St
Amarillo, TX 79101-3625

806-373-8386
Fax: 806-371-7783 info@unitedfilters.com
www.unitedfilters.com
Manufacturer and exporter of string wound filter cartridges and vessels
Manager: David Otwell
Sales Manager (South): David Otwell
Sales Manager (North): Lynn Love
Estimated Sales: $500,000-$1 Million
Number Employees: 10-19

Square Footage: 100000
Parent Co: Perry Equipment Corporation
Brands:
  United Filters

30678 United Fire & Safety Service
979 Saw Mill River Rd,
PO Box 53
Yonkers, NY 10710-0053

914-968-4459
Fax: 914-747-3983
Safety equipment, exhaust hoods and fans and fire suppression systems
President: Maureen Ulley
Estimated Sales: $1-2.5 Million
Number Employees: 5-9

30679 United Flexible
900 Merchants Concourse
Westbury, NY 11590-5142

516-222-2150
Fax: 516-222-2168 captivepackaging@aol.com
Manufacturer and exporter of plastic bags, printed roll stock and shrink packaging and lamination
President/CEO: Aldel Englander
Marketing Head: Elen Blonett
Estimated Sales: $5-10,000,000
Number Employees: 1-4

30680 United Floor Machine Co
7715 S South Chicago Ave # 1
Chicago, IL 60619-2797

773-734-0874
Fax: 773-734-0874 800-288-0848
unico1946@aol.com
Manufacturer and exporter of burnishers, heavy duty floor polishers and scrubbers, carpet shampooers
President/Owner: Richard Leitelt
  unico1946@aol.com
VP: David Leitelt
Estimated Sales: Below $5 Million
Number Employees: 1-4
Square Footage: 6000
Brands:
  Aero
  Floor Magic
  Floorite
  Glo-Pro
  Uni-Vac
  Unico

30681 United Industries GroupInc
11 Rancho Cir # 1100
Lake Forest, CA 92630-8324

949-759-3200
Fax: 949-759-3425 info@unitedind.com
www.unitedind.com
Manufacturer and exporter of storage tanks and wastewater treatment and water purification systems; also, designer of water bottling and water purification package plants
Manager: Jim Mansour
Quality Control: John Mansell
VP: M Mulvaney
IT: James P Mansour
  info@unitedind.com
Estimated Sales: $20-30 Million
Number Employees: 20-49

30682 United Industries Inc
1546 Henry Ave
Beloit, WI 53511-3668

608-365-8891
Fax: 608-365-1259 www.unitedindustries.com
Stainless steel sanitary finishing and welding equipment; also, tubing and pipe
President: Greg Sturicz
  gregsturicz@unitedindustries.com
Estimated Sales: $50-100 Million
Number Employees: 100-249

30683 United Insulated Structures
5430 Saint Charles Rd
Berkeley, IL 60163-1291

708-544-8200
Fax: 708-544-8274 800-821-5538
office@unitedinsulated.com
www.unitedinsulated.com
Design build firm specializing in architecture, engineering and contruction for the food industry

President: Sally Baldwin
  sallyb@unitedinsulated.com
EVP: Frank Maratea
SVP: Rich Maleczka
Marketing Director: Connie Maratea
Public Relations: Frank Maratea
Estimated Sales: $10-20 Million
Number Employees: 20-49
Square Footage: 140000

30684 United Label Corp
65 Chambers St
Newark, NJ 07105-2893

973-589-6500
Fax: 973-589-4465 800-252-0917
info@unitedlabelcorp.com
www.unitedlabelcorp.com
Labels
President: Joe Cic
Vice President: John Connor
  joconnor@unitedlabelcorp.com
Sales Manager: Harry Stillman
Estimated Sales: $2.5-5 Million
Number Employees: 5-9

30685 United Mc Gill Corp
1 Mission Park
Groveport, OH 43125-1100

614-829-1200
Fax: 614-829-1291 personnel@unitedmcgill.com
www.unitedmcgill.com
Vacuum drying equipment
Owner: James D Mc Gill
Sales Manager: Don Crockett
  james.mcgill@unitedmcgill.com
Number Employees: 500-999

30686 United Olive Oil Import
139 Fulton St
Suite 314
New York, NY 10038-2537

212-346-0942
Fax: 212-504-3297 scott@unitedoliveoil.com
www.unitedoliveoil.com
Italian food: olive oils, pasta and tomatoes, beans and grains, vegetables, condiments, coffee, cookies, fish, cheese and spices.
President & CEO: Tommaso Asaro
Business Development Manager: Cristina Ile
Director of Operations: Zach Casso
Estimated Sales: $5.3 Million
Number Employees: 30
Other Locations:
  National Distribution Centers
  Edison NJ
  Southern Warehousing & Distribution
  San Antonio TX

30687 United Pentek
8502 Brookville Road
Indianapolis, IN 46239-9427

317-359-3858
Fax: 317-353-9845 800-357-9299
Conveyor systems
Sales Manager: Jeffrey Smeathers
Estimated Sales: $10,000,000 - $25,000,000
Number Employees: 100-249

30688 United Performance Metals
3045 Commercial Ave
Northbrook, IL 60062-1912

847-498-3111
Fax: 847-498-2810 888-922-0040
www.upmet.com
Manufacturer and exporter of titanium caustic food processing equipment and machine parts including scrapper, tubing and pipe coils
President: Richard Leopold
Senior VP: Jerry St Clair
Marketing Director: Joanie Leopold
Sales: Steve Gerzel
Operations: Adelberto Cordova
Estimated Sales: $9000000
Number Employees: 20-49
Parent Co: United Performance Metals

30689 United Products & InstrInc
182 Ridge Rd # E
Dayton, NJ 08810-1594

732-274-1155
Fax: 732-274-1151
Spectrophotometers for food and beverage labs
Owner: Albert Chang
  achang@unicosci.com

Estimated Sales: $3 - 5 Million
Number Employees: 20-49

30690 United Ribtype Co
1319 Production Rd
Fort Wayne, IN 46808-1164
260-424-8973
Fax: 260-426-5502 800-473-4039
sales@ribtype.com www.ribtype.com
Manufacturer and exporter of rubber stamps
Owner: Tom Beaver
sales@ribtype.com
VP Sales: John Peirce
Estimated Sales: $3,000,000
Number Employees: 20-49
Square Footage: 40000
Parent Co: Indiana Stamp Company
Brands:
Ribtype

30691 United Seal & Tag Corporation
1544 Market Cir
Building 8
Port Charlotte, FL 33953
941-625-6799
Fax: 941-625-3644 800-211-9552
www.unitedsealandtag.com
Manufacturer and exporter of pressure sensitive, embossed, hot stamp, acetate and vinyl foil labels; also, foil tags
Owner: Robert Freda
Estimated Sales: $500,000-$1 Million
Number Employees: 10-19
Square Footage: 20000

30692 United Showcase Company
PO Box 145
Wood Ridge, NJ 07075-0145
201-438-4100
Fax: 201-438-2630 800-526-6382
Manufacturer and exporter of stainless steel and brass showcases, nonrefrigerated salad cooler cases, collapsible cutting board brackets, pot and pan racks, sneeze guards, guide rails, tray slides, tray slide brackets and salad barshields
President/CEO: Robert Cline
CFO: Doris Cline
VP: Robert Cline
R&D: Robert Cline
Quality Control: William Stevick
Marketing: Robert Cline
Sales/Public Relations: Robert Cline
Operations/Production/Plant Manager: William Stevick
Plant Manager: Bill Stevick
Estimated Sales: $1-2.5 Million
Number Employees: 20-49
Square Footage: 60000

30693 United Sign Corp
4900 Lister Ave
Kansas City, MO 64130-2838
816-923-9512
Fax: 816-923-9512 unitsignkc@aol.com
www.unitedsign.com
Signs including metal, plastic and neon
President: David Pickett
unitsignkc@att.net
Owner: Dave Pickett
Estimated Sales: $2.5-5 Million
Number Employees: 10-19

30694 United Specialty Flavors
999 Willow Grove Street
Suite 2-12e
Hackettstown, NJ 07840-5001
908-850-1118
Fax: 908-850-6099
Flavors and custom flavor delivery systems
President/CEO: William May
Number Employees: 30

30695 United States Systems Inc
1028 Scott Ave
Kansas City, KS 66105-1222
913-281-1010
Fax: 913-281-2901 888-281-2454
gregahawkins@aol.com
www.unitedstatessystems.com
Manufacturer and exporter of portable and stationary pneumatic conveyor systems for dry bulk goods including railcar unloading systems and in-plant transfers; also, storage silos, dust filters and bulk bag/box filling machines

President: Greg Hawkins
gregahawkins@aol.com
General Manager: Mark Aron
Sales Manager: Greg Hawkins
Estimated Sales: $2.5-5 Million
Number Employees: 5-9
Square Footage: 10000
Brands:
A/F Pot
Fwp - 7000
P/D Pot
Uss In-Tank Filter System
Vactank
Venturi 25 Air Conveyor
Venturi 30
Vibracone

30696 United Steel Products Company
P.O. Box 407
East Stroudsburg, PA 18301-0407
570-476-1010
Fax: 570-476-4358 www.usprack.com
Manufacturer and exporter of roll-formed and structural steel storage rack systems
President: Martin A Skulnik
Sales: Mary Petronio
Plant Manager: Bob Micco
Purchasing Manager: Maria Sosa
Estimated Sales: $50-100 Million
Number Employees: 100-249
Square Footage: 390000
Parent Co: United Steel Enterprises
Brands:
Storage Rack-Steel-Clad

30697 United Textile Distribution
350 Shipwash Dr
Garner, NC 27529-6890
919-779-4151
Fax: 919-779-6065 800-262-7624
www.unitedtextiledistribution.com
Manufacturer and exporter of disposable food service wipers including cloth and paper; also, towels and absorbent traffic mats; importer of towels
Owner: Rick EtheridgeGradin
ricketheridge@aol.com
Sales Representatives: Dave Shelton
Estimated Sales: $1 - 5 Million
Number Employees: 5-9
Number of Brands: 20
Number of Products: 4000
Brands:
Absorbant Rugs & Pads
Envirotex
Industrial Traffic Mats

30698 Unitherm Food System
502 Industrial Rd
Bristow, OK 74010-9763
918-367-0197
Fax: 918-367-5440
unitherm@unithermfoodsystems.com
www.unithermfoodsystems.com
Manufactures a full range of stainless steel cooking, chilling, and pasteurizing systems, including spiral ovens, impingement ovens, continuous water cookers, vertical crusters, branders, and infra-red surface pasteurization, waterpasteurization and combination pasteurization systems, as well as a full range of clean room equipment, inclusing hands-free sinks, automatic bootwashers and drains.
President: David Howard
unitherm@unithermfoodsystems.com
Marketing Director: Tom Van Doorn
Estimated Sales: Below $5 Million
Number Employees: 20-49

30699 Unitherm Food System
502 Industrial Rd
Bristow, OK 74010-9763
918-367-0197
Fax: 918-367-5440
www.unithermfoodsystems.com
Steamers & spiral ovens, roasters, smokehouses and grilling systems, pasteurizing equipment and chillers.
President: David Howard
unitherm@unithermfoodsystems.com
Number Employees: 20-49

30700 Unity Brands Group
319 W Town Pl
Suite 28
Saint Augustine, FL 32092-3103
904-940-8975
Fax: 866-878-9306 info@unitybrandsgroup.com
unitybrandsgroup.com
Marketing services
President: Praful Mehta
Marketing Executive: William Edwards
Estimated Sales: $1-2.5 Million
Number Employees: 1-10
Type of Packaging: Food Service

30701 Univar USA
2256 Junction Ave
San Jose, CA 95131-1216
408-435-8700
Fax: 408-435-1735 www.univar.com
Chemical compounding and manufacturing, coatings, inks and adhesives, electronics and precision cleaning, food and pharmaceutical, forest products, mining, oil, gas and CPI, professional pest control, waste management and watertreatment
General Manager: Jamie Hanks
President, Chief Executive Officer: Erik Fyrwald
Branch manager: Bob Crandall
Executive Vice President, General Counse: Amy Weaver
Manager: Sara Stewart
sara.stewart@univarusa.com
Number Employees: 50-99

30702 Universal Aqua Technologies
2660 Columbia St
Torrance, CA 90503
310-618-9700
Fax: 310-618-1384 800-777-6939
www.severntrentservices.com
CFO: Howard Halem
VP: Marwan Nesicolaci
Quality Control Manager: Mark Wright
Contact: Fernando Guerrero
fguerrero@severntrentservices.com
Estimated Sales: $10 - 20 Million
Number Employees: 100-249

30703 Universal Beverage Equipment
100 Leland Ct # B
Bensenville, IL 60106-1603
630-227-0250
Fax: 630-227-0253 800-627-0026
Owner: Ed Moriarty
ubeusa@aol.com
Engineering/Technical: Gino Notardonato
Purchasing Executive: Joy Claffey
Estimated Sales: $5-10 Million
Number Employees: 10-19

30704 Universal Coatings
8511 Tower Dr
Twinsburg, OH 44087-2088
330-963-6776
Fax: 330-963-6743
Manufacturer and applicator of electrostatic powder paints, fluid bed, plastic dip, corrosion resistant and F.D.A. approved coatings
Owner: John Palik
VP Sales: Ken Palik
japuniv@aol.com
VP Operations: John Palik
Estimated Sales: $20-50 Million
Number Employees: 10-19
Square Footage: 40000

30705 Universal Container Corporation
11805 State Road 54
Odessa, FL 33556-3469
727-376-0036
Fax: 727-372-1957 800-582-7477
Plastic drink containers
President: Kent Bissell
VP: Chip Williams
Estimated Sales: $2.5-5 Million
Number Employees: 18

30706 (HQ)Universal Die & Stampings
735 15th St
Prairie Du Sac, WI 53578-9618
608-643-2477
Fax: 608-643-2024 breunigb@unidie.com
www.unidie.com

Manufacturer and exporter of stainless steel conveyor belts for tab conversion systems: for food, beer and beverage
Owner: Carol Baier
  cbaier@unidie.com
Research & Development: Bryan Jaedike
Quality Control: Steve Heyn
Sales Director: Gene Everson
Plant Manager: Karl Anderson
Estimated Sales: $5-10 Million
Number Employees: 20-49
Square Footage: 80000

30707 Universal Dynamics Technologies
100-13700 International Place
Richmond, BC V6V 2X8
Canada

  604-214-3456
Fax: 604-214-3457 888-912-7246
Manufacturer and exporter of software for automation process control equipment
Sales/Marketing Executive: Steve Crotty
Product Manager: Bill Gough

30708 Universal Folding Box
181 S 18th Street
East Orange, NJ 07018-3902

  973-482-4300
Fax: 973-676-3628
Folding paper display boxes
President: Frank Pauza
General Manager: Steve Carretero
Estimated Sales: $20 - 30 Million
Number Employees: 100-250

30709 Universal Folding Box Company
555 13th Street
Hoboken, NJ 07030-6414

  201-659-7373
Fax: 201-798-4126
Folding paperboard cartons
VP Manufacturing: Richard Berkey
Number Employees: 100-249
Square Footage: 520000

30710 Universal Handling Equipment
PO Box 3488, Station C
Hamilton, ON L8H 7L5
Canada

  905-547-0161
Fax: 905-549-6922 877-843-1122
www.universalhandling.com
Waste disposal units and refuse compactors
President: David Gerard
CFO: James Hreljac
Director Sales/Marketing: Richard Kool
Estimated Sales: $20-50 Million
Number Employees: 10
Square Footage: 80000
Type of Packaging: Food Service

30711 Universal Impex Corporation
780 Fenmar Drive
Toronto, ON M9L 2T9
Canada

  416-743-7778
info@universalimpexcorp.com
www.universalimpexcorp.com
Seasonings and spices, sugars, baking products, flavors, fruit jams, condiments, sauces, marinades and dips, sweeteners, drinks (sodas, nectars, energy drink), coconut oil, coconut milk and plantain chips.
Operations Manager: Paul Bridgemohan
Estimated Sales: $5.7 Million
Number Employees: 15
Brands:
  British Class
  Cool Runnings
  Mekong

30712 Universal Industries Inc
5800 Nordic Dr
Cedar Falls, IA 50613-6942

  319-277-7501
Fax: 319-277-2318 800-553-4446
sales@universalindustries.com
www.universalindustries.com
Manufacturer and exporter of bucket elevators and belt conveyors
President: Dean Bierschenk
Marketing: Drew McConnell
Sales: Mike Giaaratmnd
Operations: Carolyn Peterson
Purchasing: Gail Snyder

Estimated Sales: $9 Million
Number Employees: 50-99
Square Footage: 240000

30713 Universal Jet Industries
PO Box 70
Hialeah, FL 33011

  305-887-4378
Fax: 305-887-4370
Manufacturer and exporter of air curtains
Chairman: L Bass
General Manager: B Warshaw
Number Employees: 12
Square Footage: 36000
Brands:
  Uji

30714 Universal Labeling Systems Inc
3501 8th Ave S
St Petersburg, FL 33711-2201

  727-327-2123
Fax: 727-323-4403 877-236-0266
sales@universal1.com www.ulsdistributors.com
A complete line of pressure sensitive labeling equipment
President: L Douglas Hall
Director Business Development: Michael Bieda
  deidre@walmart.com
CFO: Ivan Campbell
Estimated Sales: $5 - 10 Million
Number Employees: 20-49
Square Footage: 80000

30715 Universal Machine Co
645 Old Reading Pike
Pottstown, PA 19464-3733

  610-323-1810
Fax: 610-323-9343 800-862-1810
www.umc-oscar.com
Custom built machinery, general and CNC machining, drilling, boring, cutting, honing, welding, lathe and mill work
President: Richard Francis
  rfrancis@umc-oscar.com
Estimated Sales: $10-20 Million
Number Employees: 50-99

30716 Universal Marketing
1647 Pilgrim Ave
Bronx, NY 10461-4807

  914-576-5383
Fax: 914-576-1711 800-225-3114
Wholesaler/distributor, importer and exporter of commercial kitchen equipment including freezers, refrigerators, coolers and fast food cooking equipment; serving the food service market
President: James Deluca
VP: Henry Muench
Estimated Sales: Below $5 Million
Number Employees: 7
Square Footage: 12000

30717 Universal Overall
1060 W Van Buren St
Chicago, IL 60607-2988

  312-226-3336
Fax: 312-226-1986 800-621-3344
email@universaloverall.com
www.universaloverall.com
Food handlers' shirts, butchers' frocks and beef luggers
President: Sanford Eckerling
  email@universaloverall.com
Estimated Sales: $10-20 Million
Number Employees: 100-249
Brands:
  Stone-Cutter
  Universal

30718 Universal Packaging Inc
1308 Upland Dr
Houston, TX 77043-4719

  713-461-2610
Fax: 713-461-1459 800-324-2610
Manufacturer and exporter of vertical form/fill/seal machinery, conveyors, flexible packaging equipment, augers, coders and indexers
Owner: Patricia Wylie
R & D: Bill Huhn
Sales: Jim Hooper
Estimated Sales: Below $5 Million
Number Employees: 10-19

Brands:
  Mark Ii
  Mark Iii

30719 Universal Packaging Mchry Corp
965 Shadick Dr
Orange City, FL 32763-8904

  386-775-2969
Fax: 386-774-4900 800-351-8263
www.universal-ultraspeed.com
Industrial bottling machinery soft drink filling valves
President: Elisha Bethany
Quality Control: Michael Purvis
Sales: Elihu Rivera
Purchasing/Shipping: Thomas Neff
Estimated Sales: $1-2 Million
Number Employees: 10-19

30720 Universal Paper Box
644 NW 44th St
Seattle, WA 98107-4431

  206-782-7105
Fax: 206-782-3817 800-228-1045
www.paperboxco.com
Manufacturer and exporter of boxes including rigid, set-up and die-cut; also, PVC lids and bases
Owner: Greg Donald
  paperbox@paperboxco.com
Estimated Sales: Below $5 Million
Number Employees: 10-19
Square Footage: 72000
Type of Packaging: Consumer, Food Service, Private Label

30721 Universal Plastics
75 Whiting Farms Rd
Holyoke, MA 01040-2831

  413-592-4791
Fax: 413-592-6876 800-553-0120
info@universalplastics.com
www.universalplastics.com
Plastic bags
President: Jay Kumar
  kumarj@universalplastics.com
Estimated Sales: $2.5-5 Million
Number Employees: 100-249

30722 Universal Sanitizers & Supplies
2491 Stock Creek Blvd
Rockford, TN 37853

  865-573-7296
Fax: 865-573-7298 888-634-3196
info@universalsanitizers.com
Consulting services including sanitation testing and analysis, employee training and vendor audits; wholesaler/distributor of industrial cleaners and sanitizers, water treatment products and conveyor lubricant/santizer systems
President: Amy Rigo
VP: Emilia Rico
Contact: Emilia Rico
  emilia.rico@universalsanitizers.com
Estimated Sales: $5 - 10 Million
Number Employees: 5-9
Square Footage: 16000

30723 Universal Sign Company and Manufacturing Company
PO Box 62032
Lafayette, LA 70596

  337-234-1466
Fax: 337-234-2180 unisign@aol.com
www.unisignco.com
Neon and illuminated plastic signs
Owner: Dewey Boudreaux
Marketing Director: Michael Taylor
Estimated Sales: $1 - 3 Million
Number Employees: 10-19
Square Footage: 30000

30724 Universal Sign Company and Manufacturing Company
PO Box 62032
Lafayette, LA 70596

  337-234-1466
Fax: 337-234-2180 unisign@aol.com
www.unisignco.com
Signs including neon, plastic and electric
Owner: Dewey Boudreaux
Marketing Director: Michael Taylor

Estimated Sales: $1 - 3 Million
Number Employees: 10-19
Square Footage: 30000

30725 Universal Stainless
14002 E 33rd Pl
Aurora, CO 80011

303-375-1511
Fax: 303-375-1626 800-223-8332
info@lpstorage.com
Stainless steel sinks, utlity cabinets, counters, racks, tables and shelving
Manager: Robert Buehler
Contact: Robert Beuhler
robert.beuhler@leggett.com
Number Employees: 50-99
Square Footage: 80000
Parent Co: Leggett & Platt Storage Products Group
Brands:
Universal Stainless

30726 Universal Stainless & Alloy
121 Caldwell St
Titusville, PA 16354-2055

814-827-9723
Fax: 814-827-2766 800-295-1909
www.univstainless.com
Stainless steel sinks, shelving, utility cabinets, counters, tables and racks
Manager: Robert Buehler
Manager: Skip Peak
s.peak@univstainless.com
Number Employees: 50-99
Square Footage: 60000
Parent Co: Leggett & Platt

30727 Universal Strapping
630 Corporate Way
Valley Cottage, NY 10989-2002

845-268-2500
Fax: 845-268-7999 800-872-1680
info@universalstrapping.com
www.universalstrapping.com
Manufacturer and sells a complete line of non-metallic and steel strapping. This includes everything from hand grade, all the way up to machine grade strapping, which runs on the most sophisticated strapping machinery availabletoday.
President: Joe Grodz
joe@universalstrapping.com
Number Employees: 1-4

30728 Universal Tag Inc
36 Hall Rd
PO Box 1518
Dudley, MA 01571-5964

508-949-2411
Fax: 508-943-0185 800-332-8247
www.universaltag.com
Printed labels and tags including pressure sensitive and nonpressure sensitive; also, printed specialties available
President: Armand Mandeville
Sales Director: Robert Meyers
Manager: Carol Poirier
carol@universaltag.com
VP Operations: Paul Mandeville
Estimated Sales: $3 - 5 Million
Number Employees: 20-49
Square Footage: 80000

30729 (HQ)University Products
517 Main St
Holyoke, MA 01040-5514

413-532-3372
Fax: 413-532-9281 800-628-9281
www.universityproducts.com
Pressure sensitive labels
President: John Magoon
Chairman: D Magoon
dlmagoon@universityproducts.com
CFO: Bruce Riggott
Assistant Marketing Manager: Linda McInerney
Advertising Sales Manager: John Dunphy
President, Chief Operating Officer: Scott Magoon
Estimated Sales: $20 - 50 Million
Number Employees: 50-99

30730 University-Brink
131 Morse Street
Foxboro, MA 02035-5220

617-926-4400
Fax: 617-924-7965
Electric, neon and plastic signs

Estimated Sales: $1 - 5 Million
Number Employees: 10

30731 Univex Corp
3 Old Rockingham Rd
Salem, NH 03079-2140

603-893-6191
Fax: 603-893-1249 800-258-6358
info@univexcorp.com www.univexcorp.com
Manufacturer and exporter of food preparation machines including ground beef fat analyzers, vertical, electric bench and floor model mixers, electric bench model vegetable peelers, slicers and shredders and gravity feed electric meatslicers
President: John Tsiakos
john@univexcorp.com
VP Marketing: Richard McIntosh
National Sales Manager: John Tsiakos
Estimated Sales: $10-20 Million
Number Employees: 50-99
Type of Packaging: Food Service
Brands:
Perfect Peeler

30732 Uniweb Inc
222 S Promenade Ave
Corona, CA 92879-1743

951-279-7999
Fax: 951-279-7989 800-486-4932
www.uniwebinc.com
Metal store fixtures and displays
CEO: Karl Weber
CEO: Karl F Weber
kweber@uniwebinc.com
Estimated Sales: $20-50 Million
Number Employees: 100-249
Square Footage: 45000

30733 Update International
5801 S Boyle Ave
Vernon, CA 90058-3926

323-585-0616
Fax: 323-585-4021 800-747-7124
stephen@update-international.com
www.update-international.com
Manufacturer, importer and exporter of stainless steel kitchenware and utensils; also, air pots and steam table pans
President: Alec Chung
alec@update-international.com
Controller: Herman Yu
VP: Andrew Lazar
Marketing: Charles Arjavac
Vice President of Sales and Marketing: Steven Linzy
Operations: Jose Aleman
Estimated Sales: $5 - 10 Million
Number Employees: 50-99
Square Footage: 320000

30734 Upham & Walsh Lumber
2155 Stonington Ave # 209
Hoffman Estates, IL 60169-2058

847-519-1010
Fax: 847-519-3434
Manufacturer and importer of wooden, steel and plastic pallets; also, skids and watermelon and onion bins
Partner: Chris Hayden
c_hayden@uphamwalshlumber.com
Office Manager: Lauren Kowalski
Sales Manager: Sean Hayden
Estimated Sales: $7 Million
Number Employees: 1-4

30735 Upper Limits EngineeringCompany
5662 La Ribera Street
Suite F
Livermore, CA 94550-2528

510-538-8500
Fax: 510-538-8533 888-700-0717
orenm@aol.com
Net weight filler, bag filler sealer
Estimated Sales: $5-10 Million
Number Employees: 10-19

30736 Upright
10715 Kahlmeyer Dr
St Louis, MO 63132-1621

314-426-4347
Fax: 314-426-0145 800-248-7007
www.wyksorbents.com

Manufacturer and exporter of sorbents, anti-slip compounds and spill response products
President: James Dunn
Sales Manager: James Meador
Production: James Callaham
Estimated Sales: $1-3 Million
Number Employees: 10-19
Square Footage: 80000
Brands:
Upright
Wyk

30737 Urania Engineering Co Inc
198 S Poplar St
Hazleton, PA 18201-7198

570-455-7531
Fax: 570-455-0776 800-533-1985
info@uraniaeng.com
www.medicalheatsealing.com
Pouch handling system, heat sealer
President/CEO: Joe Zoba
CEO: Andrew Postupack
apostupack@uraniaengineer.com
Estimated Sales: $5-10 Million
Number Employees: 20-49

30738 Urnex Brands Inc
700 Executive Blvd
Elmsford, NY 10523-1208

914-345-6080
Fax: 914-963-2145 800-222-2826
info@urnex.com www.urnex.com
Manufacturer and exporter of coffee and tea equipment cleaning compounds, urn brushes, lemon covers, lemon wedge bags and shellfish steamer bags
President: Kofi Amoako
kofi.amoako@urnex.com
R & D: Jason Dick
Quality Control: Bill Colter
Sales Manager: Joshua Dick
General Manager: Jay Lazarin
Assist. Mngr: Frankie Dominiquez
Estimated Sales: Less Than $500,000
Number Employees: 1-4
Square Footage: 30000
Brands:
Urnex

30739 Urschel Laboratories
2503 Calumet Avenue
Valparaiso, IN 46384-2200

219-464-4811
Fax: 219-462-3879 info@urschel.com
www.urschel.com
Manufacturer and supplier of high capacity food cutting equipment
President: Robert Urschel
CFO: Dan Marchetti
VP Sales: Tim O'Brien
Contact: Jen Abatie
jabatie@urschel.com
Regional Manager: Alan Major
Plant Manager: Dave Whitenack
Number Employees: 250-499
Square Footage: 500000
Type of Packaging: Food Service
Brands:
Comitrol
Urschalloy
Urschel

30740 Ursini Plastics
RR 2 High Falls Road
Bracebridge, ON P1L 1W9
Canada

705-646-2701
Swizzle sticks
Owner: John Ursini
Number Employees: 1-4

30741 Us Bottlers Machinery Co Inc
11911 Steele Creek Rd
Charlotte, NC 28273-3773

704-588-4750
Fax: 704-588-3808 sales@usbottlers.com
www.usbottlers.com
Manufacturer and exporter of bottling machinery including liquid filling, bottle rinsing, container cleaning and capping equipment
President: Thomas Risser
julie.kimbrell@usbottlers.com
Sales: Julie Kimbrell
Estimated Sales: $10-20 Million
Number Employees: 50-99

30742 Us Flag & Signal
802 Fifth St
Portsmouth, VA 23704-6762
757-497-8947
Fax: 757-497-1819 flagmaker@flagmaker.com
www.flagmaker.com
Flags, pennants and banners
Owner: Dory Wilgus
Number Employees: 20-49

30743 Us Rubber
238 N 9th St # 1
Brooklyn, NY 11211-2160
718-782-7888
Fax: 718-782-8788
Manufacturer and exporter of food hoses, tubing and
conveyor belts
Owner: Ken Auster
kauster@usrubbersupply.com
Estimated Sales: $10-20 Million
Number Employees: 20-49

30744 Useco/Epco Products
P.O. Box 20428
Murfreesboro, TN 37129-0428
615-893-8432
Fax: 615-890-3196 800-251-1429
info@useco.com www.useco.com
Number Employees: 10-19
Parent Co: Standex International

30745 Utah PaperBox Company
920 South 700 West
Salt Lake City, UT 84104
801-363-0093
Fax: 801-363-9212 www.upbslc.com
Folding carton, rigid box and litho lam packaging.
President: Steve Keyser
Vice President: Teri Jensen
Sales Service: Tom Harrison
Human Resource Manager: Ben Misik
Controller: Richard Severson
Estimated Sales: $20 - 50 Million
Number Employees: 200 - 500
Type of Packaging: Food Service

30746 (HQ)Utica Cutlery Co
820 Noyes St
PO Box 10527
Utica, NY 13502-5053
315-733-4663
Fax: 315-733-6602 800-879-2526
info@uticacutlery.com www.walcostainless.com
Manufacturers of pocket knives and importers of
stainless steel cutlery
President: David Allen
davidallen@uticacutlery.com
CFO: Jess Gouger
VP (Walco): Kathleen Allen
International Sales Manager: Dave Meislin
Estimated Sales: $10 - 20 Million
Number Employees: 100-249

30747 Utility Refrigerator Company
7355 E Slauson Avenue
Los Angeles, CA 90040-3626
323-267-0700
Fax: 323-728-2318 800-884-5233
www.utilityrefrigerator.com
Manufacturer and exporter of commercial cooking
equipment, refrigerators and freezers
Customer Service: Larry Gomez
Customer Service: Mark Parra
Customer Service: Martha Gonzalez
General Manager: Mark Champaigne
Estimated Sales: $.5 - 1 million
Number Employees: 160
Square Footage: 800000
Parent Co: Stery Manufacturing Company
Brands:
Dynasty
Jade Range
Utility

30748 V C 999 Packaging Systems
419 E 11th Ave
Kansas City, MO 64116-4162
816-472-8999
Fax: 816-472-1999 800-728-2999
www.shrinkbagpackaging.com

Vacuum packaging machines, vacuum chamber machines, shrink systems, dryers, vacuum skin pack
machines, automatic rollstock machines, preformed
tray sealing machines, packaging accessories, packaging material and equipment related topackaging
Owner: Silvio Weder
silvio.weder@vc999.com
Number Employees: 20-49

30749 V C 999 Packaging Systems
419 E 11th Ave
Kansas City, MO 64116-4162
816-472-8999
Fax: 816-472-1999 800-728-2999
www.shrinkbagpackaging.com
Manufacturer and supplier of packaging equipment,
materials and supplies such as trays, bags/pouches,
containers and film.
President: Silvio Weder
silvio.weder@vc999.com
Number Employees: 20-49

30750 V R Food Equipment Inc
5801 County Rd 41
P.O. Box 25428
Farmington, NY 14425-9998
315-531-8133
Fax: 315-531-8134 800-929-9367
info@vrfoodequipment.com
www.vrfoodequipment.com
Processing and packaging equipment for packaging
equipment; fruit, vegetable, aseptic processes.
President: Steven Von Rhedey
steve@vrfoodequipment.com
Controller: Fran Seager
Marketing & Sales Manager: Matthew Moroz
Sales Manager: Steve Casey
Shipping & Receiving Manager: Peter Von Rhedey
Warehouse & Shipping Specialist: Robert
Novakowski
Year Founded: 1986
Estimated Sales: $1-2.5 Million
Number Employees: 5-9

30751 V&R Metal Enterprises
272 39th St
Brooklyn, NY 11232-2820
718-768-8142
Fax: 718-768-0921
Lighting fixtures and metal fabrications including
pizza pans
Owner: Hon Ng
Estimated Sales: $1 - 3,000,000
Number Employees: 1-4
Square Footage: 3000

30752 V-Ram Solids
620 S Broadway Ave
PO Box 289
Albert Lea, MN 56007-4526
507-373-3996
Fax: 507-373-5937 888-373-3996
sales@vram.com
Manufacturer, importer and exporter of solids han-
dling pumps for waste/rendering
President: David A Olson
Sales Director: Jeff Hall
Purchasing Manager: Rose Modderman
Estimated Sales: $3 - 5 Million
Number Employees: 10-19
Brands:
V-Ram

30753 V-Ram Solids
620 S Broadway Ave
Albert Lea, MN 56007-4526
507-373-3996
Fax: 507-373-5937 888-373-3996
sales@vram.com
Pumps designed for the meat industry.
Number Employees: 10-19
Parent Co: Olson Manufacturing Company

30754 VC Menus
P.O. Box 71
Eastland, TX 76448-0071
254-629-2626
Fax: 254-629-1134 800-826-3687
www.vcmenus.com
Manufacturer and exporter of menus and covers
President: Cary Meeks
Secretary and Treasurer: Donald Eaves
Corporate Sales/Marketing: Trent Smith

Estimated Sales: $5-10 Million
Number Employees: 20-49
Brands:
Euro-Menu
Poly-Menu

30755 VCF Films Inc
1100 Sutton St
Howell, MI 48843-1799
517-546-2300
Fax: 517-546-2984 888-823-4141
www.vcffilms.com
Manufacturer and marketer of plastic flexible packaging materials to industrial manufacturers, packagers, distributors, and retailers in North America and
internationally
Owner: Reva Kamins
rkamins@vcffilms.com
Estimated Sales: $5-10 Million
Number Employees: 20-49

30756 VCG Uniform
5050 Weat Irving Park Road
Chicago, IL 60641
773-545-3676
Fax: 773-545-0876 800-447-6502
info@vcguniform.com www.vcguniform.com
In-stock and custom uniforms
CEO: Vince Gerage
Estimated Sales: $1-2.5 Million
Number Employees: 10-19
Parent Co: VCG
Other Locations:
Carlson-Murray
Chicago IL

30757 VEGCHEESE
Toronto, ON M9M 2X5
Canada
416-727-0589
hello@vegcheese.com
www.vegcheese.com
Dairy-free, nut-free, gluten-free, plant-based
cheeses. Cheeses are handcrafted in Toronto, On-
tario, in small batches, with a base of organic soy
milk and organic coconut oil.
Founder & President: Lori Sroujian
Head, Sales & Operations: Aren Sroujian
Number Employees: 2-10
Number of Brands: 1
Number of Products: 4
Type of Packaging: Food Service
Brands:
VEGCHEESE

30758 VICAM
34 Maple St
Milford, MA 01757-3604
617-926-7045
Fax: 617-923-8055 800-338-4381
vicam@vicam.com www.vicam.com
Mycotoxin testing equipment
President: Hike Hutchens
eejmike_hutchens@waters.com
Estimated Sales: $2.5-5 Million
Number Employees: 1000-4999
Type of Packaging: Bulk

30759 VIFAN Canada
1 Rue Vifan
Lanoraie, QC J0K 1E0
Canada
514-640-1599
Fax: 514-640-1577 800-557-0192
www.vifan.com
Packaging products for the food industry
VP, Sales: Ezra Bowen
Estimated Sales: $185 Million
Number Employees: 245
Number of Brands: 78
Number of Products: 78
Square Footage: 130000
Parent Co: Vibac S.p.A.
Type of Packaging: Food Service
Brands:
Vifan Bt
Vifan Cl/Cls
Vifan Cz

30760 VINITECH
1611 N Kent St
Suite 903
Arlington, VA 22209
703-522-5000
Fax: 703-522-5005 888-522-5001
usa@promosalons.com
Viticulture, viniculture, bottling equipment
Owner: Philippe Bazin
Number Employees: 1-4

30761 VIP Real Estate LTD
3945 S Archer Ave
Chicago, IL 60632-1157
773-376-5000
Fax: 773-376-5091 www.viprealestateltd.com
Manufacturer and exporter of folding boxes, printed
folding cartons, point of purchase displays and
polylined, freezer-coated boxes for frozen foods.
Items manufactured to order
Owner: Sammy Cruz
sammy@viprealestateltd.com
VP: Ray Maza
Marketing: James Coen
Estimated Sales: $5-10 Million
Number Employees: 10-19
Square Footage: 212000
Type of Packaging: Consumer, Food Service, Private Label

30762 (HQ)VMC Signs
102 E Mockingbird Ln
Victoria, TX 77904-2046
361-575-0548
Fax: 361-575-8464 vmcsigns@txcr.net
www.2vmcsigns.com
Interior and exterior neon signs and menus; also,
water filtration and air filtration systems
Owner: Tom Willis
tom@vmcsigns.com
General Manager: Aibie McLeroy
Estimated Sales: $1-2.5 Million
Number Employees: 10-19
Square Footage: 100000
Other Locations:
VMC Signs
Victoria TX
Brands:
Vmc-Nsa

30763 VPC Gordon Sign
2930 W 9th Ave
Denver, CO 80204-3713
303-629-6121
Fax: 303-629-1024 sales@gordonsign.com
www.gordonsign.com
Electrical advertising displays, signs and menu
boards
President: James Skagen
CFO: Lee Prevost
lprevost@gordonsign.com
Director Sales/Marketing: Harry Grass
Estimated Sales: $10-20 Million
Number Employees: 50-99
Square Footage: 200000
Parent Co: C.G. Industries

30764 VPI
P.O. Box 138
Sheboygan Falls, WI 53085-0138
920-467-6422
Fax: 920-467-2692 vpi@vpicorp.com
www.spartech.com
Plastic film and sheet
President: P Gregory Mickelson
Senior Vice President - Human Resources: Robert
Lorah
Estimated Sales: $10-20 Million
Number Employees: 100-249

30765 VPI Manufacturing
11814 S. Election Rd
Ste 200
Draper, UT 84020
801-495-2310
Fax: 866-307-0033 www.vpimanufacturing.com
Manufacturer and exporter of heat shrinkable polyethylene cook-in bags for meat, poultry, etc
President: Aron Perlman
VP: Hessa Tary
Estimated Sales: $4114713
Number Employees: 20-49

30766 (HQ)VT Industries Inc
1000 Industrial Park
P.O. Box 490
Holstein, IA 51025-7730
712-368-4381
Fax: 712-368-4111 800-827-1615
www.vtindustries.com
Manufacturer and exporter of post-formed laminated
and solid surface countertops; also, laminated
multi-use components
President: Jason Farver
CFO: Wayne Terry
Plant Manager: Gary Henry
Estimated Sales: $32 Million
Number Employees: 250-499
Square Footage: 300000
Brands:
Casemate
Curvflo
Durallure

30767 VT Kidron
911 W 5th St
P.O. Box 880
Washington, NC 27889-4205
252-946-6521
Fax: 330-857-8451 800-763-0700
ksales@kidron.com www.kidron.com
Manufacturer and exporter of refrigerated truck bodies and trailers
President: Mike Tucker
Executive VP: John Sommer
Estimated Sales: $5-10 Million
Number Employees: 5-9
Parent Co: TTI
Type of Packaging: Food Service
Brands:
Glacieruan
Hackney Ultimate
Polauan
Ultra

30768 VWR Scientific
3745 Bayshore Blvd
Brisbane, CA 94005
415-468-7150
Fax: 415-468-1105 800-932-5000
solutions@vwr.com www.vwr.com
Distributors of scientific equipment, supplies, chemicals and furniture
President: Walter Zywottek
VP: Arne Brandon
Contact: Sandy Antalis
sandy.antalis@vwr.com
Number Employees: 250-499

30769 Vac Air Inc
5254 N 124th St
Milwaukee, WI 53225-2902
414-466-1852
Fax: 414-353-5289 www.vac-airinc.com
Cutting and boning devices, vacuum systems,
slaughtering equipment, dehairing machines and
equipment, hock cutters
President: Chuck Air
cair@vac-air.com
CFO: Mary Baertlein
Quality Control: Lee Baertlein
Estimated Sales: $1 - 2.5 Million
Number Employees: 5-9
Brands:
Vac Airr

30770 Vac-U-Max
69 William St
Belleville, NJ 07109-3040
973-759-4600
Fax: 973-759-6449 800-822-8629
info@vac-u-max.com www.vac-u-max.com
Manufacturer, importer and exporter of pneumatic
conveying systems and ingredient storage systems;
also, handling and batching systems
President: Stevens Pendelton
CEO: H Kadel
VP: Doan Pendleton
IT: Stevens Pendleton
info@vac-u-max.com
Estimated Sales: $10 - 20 Million
Number Employees: 50-99
Square Footage: 200000
Brands:
Vac-U-Max

30771 Vacuform Inc.
500 Courtney Road
PO Box 117
Sebring, OH 44672
330-938-9674
Fax: 330-938-9676 www.vacuforminc.com
Manufacturer and importer of interior and exterior
signs, menus and image products including point of
purchase displays
President: Kenneth Galloway
CEO: Dennis Kaufman
Contact: Catherine Hubbs
c_hubbs@vacuforminc.com
Estimated Sales: $10-20 Million
Number Employees: 100-249
Square Footage: 400000
Type of Packaging: Food Service

30772 Vacumet Corp
20 Edison Dr
Wayne, NJ 07470-4713
973-628-1067
Fax: 973-628-0491 bfoley@vacumet.com
Manufacturer and exporter of metallized and holographic films and papers; also microwave susceptor
and barrier films for flexible packaging, label stock
available.
President: Robert Korowicki
Estimated Sales: $20,000,000 - $49,999,999
Number Employees: 10-19
Parent Co: Scholle Corporation
Brands:
Barrier-Met

30773 Vacumet Corporation
7929 Troon Cir
Austell, GA 30168-7759
404-432-6300
Fax: 404-505-8984 800-776-0865
Plain and metallized flexible packaging films and
microwaveable interactive packaging
President: Raymond Woody
Manager: Steve Eulieno
Executive VP: Andy Terakawa
VP Staff/Marketing: Dave McKae
Contact: Anthony Threat
athreat@gadoe.org
Plant Manager: Steve Euliano
Estimated Sales: $10 - 20 Million
Number Employees: 20-49
Square Footage: 82000
Parent Co: Marubeni America Corporation
Brands:
Himac
Himet

30774 Vacuum Barrier Corp
4 Barten Ln
Woburn, MA 01801-5601
781-933-3570
Fax: 781-932-9428 sales@vacuumbarrier.com
www.vacuumbarrier.com
Manufacturer, importer and exporter of cryogenic
pipe systems including liquid nitrogen injection
equipment for pressurizing hot filled beverages,
food, etc
President: Bart Limpens
bart@vbseurope.com
CFO: Leonard Gardner
Vice President: David Gorham
Quality Control and R&d: David Tucker
VP Sales: Edward Hanlon Jr
Purchasing Manager: Douglas Vanaruem
Estimated Sales: $5 - 10 Million
Number Employees: 20-49
Square Footage: 84000
Brands:
Linerter
Linjector
Semiflex

30775 Vacuum Depositing Inc
1294 Old Fern Valley Rd
Louisville, KY 40219-1903
502-969-4227
Fax: 502-969-3378 sales@vdi-llc.com
www.vdi-llc.com
Sputter and vapor metallized film for solar control,
microwave and anti-static products
President: David Bryant
dbryant@vdi-llc.com
Sales Manager: Teeny Lee

Estimated Sales: $5-10 Million
Number Employees: 20-49
Square Footage: 140000

30776 Vaisala Inc
10 Gill St # D
Woburn, MA 01801-1721

781-933-4500
Fax: 781-933-8029 888-824-7252
www.vaisala.com
Supplier of humidity measurement instrumentation for process and environmental monitoring. In addition to relative humidity and dewpoint, offers innovative measurement solutions for carbon dioxide, ammonia, and barometric pressure.Global organization that is ISO9002 certified and committed to excellence in all facets of the business
CEO: Steve Chansky
Marketing Director: Elizabeth Mann
Sales Director: Gerry Ducharme
Estimated Sales: $20 - 30 Million
Number Employees: 50-99

30777 Val-Pak Direct Market Systems
8605 Largo Lakes Dr
Largo, FL 33773-4912

727-393-1270
Fax: 727-399-3061 pat_fridley@coxtarget.com
www.valpak.com
Supplier and exporter of coupons
President: Joe Bourdow
Contact: Juliane Abudi
juliane_abudi@valpak.com
Number Employees: 1,000-4,999
Parent Co: Cox Industries
Type of Packaging: Consumer, Bulk

30778 Valad Electric Heating Corporation
PO Box 577
160 Wildey Street
Tarrytown, NY 10591

914-631-4927
Fax: 914-631-4395 info@valadelectric.com
www.valadelectric.com
Manufacturer and exporter of food warming ovens, hot plates and food warming cabinets
President: Dante Cecchini
VP: Arthur Cecchini
Sales: Mike Sona
Estimated Sales: Below $5 Million
Number Employees: 10-19
Square Footage: 70000
Type of Packaging: Consumer, Food Service

30779 Valco Melton
411 Circle Freeway Dr
West Chester, OH 45246-1213

513-874-6550
Fax: 513-874-3612 sales@valcocincinnatiinc.com
www.valcomelton.com
Manufacturer and exporter of hot melt and cold glue dispensers
President: Karla Bridges
karla.bridges@valcomelton.com
CFO: Scott Soutar
CEO: Gregory Amend
Purchase: Jim Epp
Sales Manager: Paul Chambers
Estimated Sales: $5 - 10 Million
Number Employees: 100-249
Square Footage: 200000

30780 Valeo
555 taxter Road
Suite 210
Elmsford, Ny 10523

800-634-2704
Fax: 800-831-9642 800-634-2704
www.valeoinc.com
Manufacturer and exporter of safety accessories including back support belts, wrist supports, knee supports, elbow support, and material handling gloves
President: Lisa Yewer
Estimated Sales: $5 - 10 Million
Number Employees: 20-49
Square Footage: 240000

30781 Valesco Trading
1 Terminal Road
Lyndhurst, NJ 07071

201-729-1414
Fax: 201-729-1515 aos@valescofoods.com
www.valescofoods.com

Mediterranean olives, sun dried tomatoes, dried figs and apricots.
President: Ali Sozer
Estimated Sales: $3.6 Million
Number Employees: 12
Type of Packaging: Food Service

30782 Valley City Sign Co
5009 West River Dr NE
Comstock Park, MI 49321-8961

616-784-5711
Fax: 616-784-8280 www.valleycitysign.com
Plastic and illuminated signs
Owner: Kim Finley
CEO: Judson Kovalak Jr
CFO: Sam Kovalak
Sales Representative: Jack Vos
Sales Representative: Jean Hughes
kim.finley@xerox.com
Sales Representative: Jeff Surman
Estimated Sales: $5 - 10 Million
Number Employees: 50-99
Square Footage: 150000

30783 Valley Container Corporation
858 Kingsland Avenue
Saint Louis, MO 63130-3112

314-652-8050
Fax: 314-652-2719
Corrugated boxes
General Manager: John Clark Sr
Estimated Sales: $5-10 Million
Number Employees: 20-49

30784 (HQ)Valley Container Inc
850 Union Ave
Bridgeport, CT 06607-1137

203-368-6546
Fax: 203-367-5266 flutedpartition@aol.com
www.valleycontainer.com
Manufacturer and exporter of corrugated shipping containers
President: Arthur Vietze Jr
CEO: Rudy Niederneier
rudy.niederneier@valleycontainer.com
VP Sales: Richard Jackson
Estimated Sales: $20 - 50 Million
Number Employees: 50-99

30785 Valley Craft Inc
2001 S Highway 61
Lake City, MN 55041-9557

651-345-3386
Fax: 651-345-3606 800-328-1480
customer@valleycraft.com www.valleycraft.com
Manufacturer and exporter of hand and delivery trucks, trailers and forklift attachments, and storage equipment, custom-designed manufacturing and production equipment.
Owner: Dennis Campbell
Manager: Roger Goff
R&D: Josh Rodewald
Marketing: Daria Dalager
Sales: Dave Minck
Production: Tom Balow
tombalow@valleycraft.com
Plant Manager: Roger Goff
Estimated Sales: $10-20,000,000
Number Employees: 1-4
Number of Brands: 6
Number of Products: 300+
Square Footage: 332000
Parent Co: Liberty Diversified International
Type of Packaging: Consumer, Private Label, Bulk
Brands:
Dura-Lite
Proline
Viking

30786 Valley Fixtures
171 Coney Island Drive
Sparks, NV 89431-6317

775-331-1050
Manufacturer and exporter of cabinet fixtures for bars, restaurants, casinos, hotels and stores
Sales Manager: Dillon Moore
Estimated Sales: $10-20 Million
Number Employees: 100-249
Square Footage: 100000

30787 Valley Lea LaboratoriesInc
4609 Grape Rd # D4
D4
Mishawaka, IN 46545-8259

574-272-8484
Fax: 574-273-0370 800-822-1283
Laboratory offering quality assurance and microbiological testing for food, dairy and water
Owner: Bob Coffee
Number Employees: 5-9

30788 Valley Packaging SupplyCo
3181 Commodity Ln
Green Bay, WI 54304-5671

920-336-9012
Fax: 920-336-3935
general@valleypackagingsupply.com
www.valleypackagingsupply.com
Manufacturer and exporter of pouches and bags for food and industry
President: Lance Czachor
lance@valleypackagingsupply.com
Treasurer: Richard Czachor
Sales Director: Lance Czachor
Operations Manager: Ty Parsons
Purchasing Manager: Jean Rottier
Estimated Sales: $5 Million
Number Employees: 100-249
Square Footage: 272000
Type of Packaging: Bulk
Brands:
Valley

30789 Valmont Composite Structures
19845 US Highway 76
Newberry, SC 29108-8407

803-276-5504
Fax: 803-276-8940 800-800-9008
www.skp-cs.com
Fiberglass lighting poles including breakaway, ornamental and transmission
Director Sales/Marketing: Bill Griffin
HR Executive: Alice Moore
amoore@skp-cs.com
Operations-Production: Ray Jeffords
Plant Manager: Scott Burriss
Estimated Sales: $1 - 5 Million
Number Employees: 250-499
Parent Co: K 2

30790 Valspar Corp
P.O. Box 1461
Minneapolis, MN 55440-1461

612-851-7000
valspar.com
Provides coatings and metal decorating inks for food cans, beverage cans, aerosol, paint cans and paper, film and foil markets.
Chief Executive Officer: Gary Hendrickson
gary.h@valspar.com
Executive Vice President: Steven Erdahl
VP, Global Consumer Sales & Marketing: Steven Person
Year Founded: 1866
Estimated Sales: $4.19 Billion
Number Employees: 11,000
Parent Co: Sherwin-Williams Co.

30791 Valspar Paint
101 Prospect Ave
Cleveland, OH 44115

800-845-9061
877-825-7727
www.valsparpaint.com
Industrial and commercial floor coatings including solvent and water based epoxies and urethanes.
Chief Executive Officer: Gary Hendrickson
Executive Vice President: Steven Erdahl
Product Manager: Suzette Bojarski
sbojarski@valspar.com
Square Footage: 328000
Parent Co: Sherwin-Williams Co.

30792 Valu Guide & Engineering
1a Morgan
Irvine, CA 92618-1917

949-472-7336
Fax: 949-837-3481 800-825-8364
www.firstteam.com
Packaging equipment components
President: Joe Duenas
Number Employees: 100

30793 Valvinox
650 1st Rue
Iberville, QC J2X 3B8
Canada
450-346-1981
Fax: 450-346-1067 www.valvinox.it
Manufacturer and exporter of fittings, pumps, stainless steel valves, tubing and pipe
Administrator: Chantal Allard
Number Employees: 10,000
Parent Co: SQRM
Type of Packaging: Bulk

30794 Van Air Systems
2950 Mechanic St
Lake City, PA 16423-2095
814-774-2631
Fax: 814-774-0778 800-840-9906
www.vanairsystems.com
Manufacturer and exporter of compressed air dryers, condensation drain valves, after coolers, filters, oil/water separators, etc.; importer of filters
President: Mark Sunseri
 msunseri@vanairinc.com
CEO: J Currie
CFO: Mark Sunseri
VP: Jeff Mace
Sales: W J Ulrich
Estimated Sales: $20 Million
Number Employees: 20-49
Number of Brands: 8
Square Footage: 65000
Brands:
 Dry-O-Lite

30795 Van Blarcom Closures Inc
156 Sandford St
Brooklyn, NY 11205-3985
718-855-3810
Fax: 718-935-9855 www.vbcpkg.com
Manufacturer and exporter of metal and plastic caps
Chairman of the Board: Vincent Scuderi Jr
VP Sales/Marketing: John Scuderi
Estimated Sales: $20-50 Million
Number Employees: 500-999

30796 Van Dam Machine Corp
81b Walsh Dr
Parsippany, NJ 07054-5708
973-257-7050
Fax: 973-257-7398 info@vandammachine.com
www.vandamusa.com
Printer
President: Andy Stobb
CFO: Kim Filippone
 kfilippone@vandamusa.com
Estimated Sales: $5 - 10 Million
Number Employees: 10-19

30797 Van Der Graaf Corporation
1481 Trae Lane
Lithia Springs, GA 30122
770-819-6650
Fax: 770-819-6675 www.vandergraaf.com
Drum motors for conveyor belts.
Contact: Jason Kanaris
 jkanaris@vandergraaf.com

30798 Van Dereems Mfg Co
40 Schoon Ave
Hawthorne, NJ 07506-1408
973-427-2355
Fax: 973-427-2356
Wooden store fixtures including skids, boxes and laminated workbenches
President: John Vandereems
Estimated Sales: Below $5 Million
Number Employees: 5-9
Square Footage: 20000

30799 Van Leer Flexibles
9505 Bamboo Rd
Houston, TX 77041
713-462-6111
Fax: 713-690-2746 800-825-3766
info@valeron.com www.valeron.com
High density polyethylene film for packaging
Contact: Kevin Clothier
 kevin_clothier@valic.com
Estimated Sales: $25-50 Million
Number Employees: 250-499

30800 Van Lock Co
6834 Center St
Cincinnati, OH 45244-3404
513-561-9692
Fax: 513-561-0314 800-878-1826
vanlock@excite.com www.vanlock.com
Locks, padlocks, cam locks and alarm systems
Owner: James S Padjen
 jpadjen@vanlock.com
Owner: Chris Padjen
CFO: John Sali
Estimated Sales: $1-2.5 Million
Number Employees: 20-49

30801 Van Nuys Awning Co
5661 Sepulveda Blvd
Van Nuys, CA 91411-2916
818-345-4926
Fax: 818-782-6837
awnings@vannuysawning.com
www.vannuysawning.com
Commercial awnings
President: James Powell
Manager: Roy Megahan
 vna5661@earthlink.net
Estimated Sales: $5 - 10 Million
Number Employees: 20-49

30802 Van Pak Corporation
1188 Walters Way Lane
Saint Louis, MO 63132-2200
314-432-2224
Fax: 314-432-2227 800-811-7710
All types of conveyors, palletizers/depalletizers
President: Jon Vaninger
Estimated Sales: $5-10 Million
Number Employees: 10

30803 Van der Pol Muller International
4801 Harbor Pointe Dr.
Suite 1305
North Myrtle Beach, SC 29582
803-691-8941
Fax: 803-240-1384
benmuller@mullerinternational.com
www.mullerinternational.com
Engineering and consulting company for the food industry, specializing in the baking industry
President: Ben Muller
Estimated Sales: Below $5 Million
Number Employees: 2

30804 VanSan Corporation
16735 E Johnson Dr
City of Industry, CA 91745-2469
626-961-7211
Fax: 626-369-9510
President: Mark E Vanlandingham
Estimated Sales: $1 - 5 Million
Number Employees: 10-19

30805 Vance Metal FabricatorsInc
251 Gambee Rd
Geneva, NY 14456-1025
315-789-5626
Fax: 315-789-1848 800-234-6752
sales@vancemetal.com www.vancemetal.com
Stainless, structural and aluminum steel tanks
President: Joseph Hennessy
CEO: Joe Hennessy
 jhennessy@vancemetal.com
Vice President of Sales: Chris Jennings
Quality and Safety Manager: Brian Mott
Business Development Specialist - Sales: Wade Woodworth
Operations Manager: Len Visco
Purchasing Associate: Laura Gute
Estimated Sales: $10-25 Million
Number Employees: 50-99
Square Footage: 70000

30806 Vanco Products Company
1269 Massachusetts Avenue
Dorchester, MA 2125
617-265-3400
Bakery supplies
President: Chris Anton
Production Manager: Carl Hogenda
Estimated Sales: $5 - 10 Million
Number Employees: 10-19
Square Footage: 45000
Parent Co: Johnson's Food Products Corporation
Type of Packaging: Consumer

30807 Vancouver Manufacturing
765 S 32nd Street
Washougal, WA 98671-2519
360-835-8519
Fax: 360-835-8521
Wooden pallets
Owner: Al Ely
General Manager: Rob Burnett
Estimated Sales: $20-50 Million
Number Employees: 20-49

30808 Vande Berg SCALES/Vbs Inc
770 7th St NW
Sioux Center, IA 51250-1918
712-722-1181
Fax: 712-722-0900 info@vbssys.com
www.vbssys.com
Conveyor scales, meat/produce sortation systems
Owner: Dave Vande Berg
 vbs@mtcnet.net
Office Manager: Diane Vande Berg
Estimated Sales: $5 Million
Number Employees: 20-49
Brands:
 Bicerba
 Duran
 Gse
 Vande Berg Scales
 Weigh-Tranix

30809 Vanguard Packaging Film
9970 Lakeview Ave
Shawnee Mission, KS 66219-2502
913-599-1111
Fax: 913-599-0096 800-772-1187
President: John Campbell
Estimated Sales: $1 - 3 Million
Number Employees: 5-9

30810 Vanguard Technology Inc
29495 Airport Rd
Eugene, OR 97402-9524
541-461-6020
Fax: 541-461-6023 800-624-4809
info@vanguardtechnologyinc.com
www.vanguardtechnologyinc.com
High-efficiency gas fired domestic hot water heaters, gas fired booster water heaters
President: S Kujawa
 vti1999@aol.com
Estimated Sales: $1 Million
Number Employees: 1-4
Square Footage: 20000
Type of Packaging: Food Service
Brands:
 Firepower
 Powermax
 Powerpac

30811 Vanmark Equipment
300 Industrial Pkwy
Creston, IA 50801-8102
641-782-6575
Fax: 641-782-9209 800-523-6261
www.vanmarkequipment.com
Manufacturer of industrial food processing for a wide range of produce products.
Manager: Tom Mathues
Sales: Tom Jones
Manager: Jason Davis
Operations: Rich Shafar
Estimated Sales: $5-10 Million
Number Employees: 20-49
Square Footage: 120000
Brands:
 Vanmark

30812 Vanmark Equipment LLC
4252 S Eagleson Rd
Boise, ID 83705
208-362-5588
Fax: 208-362-3171 800-523-6261
sales@vanmarkequipment.com
www.vanmarkequipment.com
Manufacturer and exporter of food processing equipment for produce including tension blades and wedge, square and rectangular tension cutters
Owner: George Mendenhall
Estimated Sales: $2.5-5 Million
Number Employees: 10-19

30813 Vansco Products
2652 Lashbrook Avenue
South El Monte, CA 91733-1598
626-448-7611
Fax: 626-448-0221 www.vansco.com
Manufactures adhesive application systems, cold
glue, hot glue, hand and automatic and carton
sealing
President/CEO: Gregory Amend
CFO: Scott Soutar
Vice President: Fred Van Loben Sels
R & D: Eric Sueyoshi
Sales Manager: Richard Goennier
Contact: Grek Ameg
ameg@vansco.com
Plant Manager: Grek Ameg
Estimated Sales: Below $5 Million
Number Employees: 10-19
Square Footage: 32000

30814 Vantage Pak International
221 South St
New Britain, CT 06051-3650
860-832-8766
Fax: 860-832-8766 800-839-9030
Packaging equipment: high speed, multi-size tray
packer of cans and bottles, wrap around tray/case
packers, integrated tray, shrink wrapping systems
Estimated Sales: $5 Million
Number Employees: 20-49

**30815 (HQ)Vantage Performance
Materials**
3938 Porett Dr
Gurnee, IL 60031-1244
847-244-3410
Fax: 847-249-6790 aronson@ppg.com
www.petroferm.com
Manufacturer and exporter of precipitated silica for
anticaking and carrier applications
President: Michael Horton
Vice President: Anup Jain
Vice President of Research and Developme: Charles
Kahle
Marketing Manager: Paul Brown
Manager: Steve Korzeniewski
steve.korzeniewski@polyonics.com
Vice President of Operations: John Richter
Vice President of Purchasing: Stephen Lampe
Estimated Sales: $20-50 Million
Number Employees: 100-249
Type of Packaging: Food Service, Bulk
Brands:
Flo-Gard

30816 Vantage Performance Materials
3938 Porett Dr
Gurnee, IL 60031-1244
847-244-3410
Fax: 847-249-6790 aronson@ppg.com
www.petroferm.com
Organic surfactants, defoamers, emulsifiers, sili-
cones and silicone emulsions
President: Michael Horton
Vice President: Anup Jain
Vice President of Research and Developme: Charles
Kahle
Manager: Steve Korzeniewski
steve.korzeniewski@polyonics.com
Vice President of Operations: John Richter
Vice President of Purchasing: Stephen Lampe
Estimated Sales: $50-100 Million
Number Employees: 100-249

30817 Vantage USA
4740 S Whipple St
Chicago, IL 60632
773-247-1086
Fax: 708-401-1565 www.VantageUSA.net
Organic/natural & commodity wholesaler consolida-
tor/supplier and logistics provider. Specializing in
natural and private label products planning &
development.
Owner: Dan Gash
dan@vantageusa.net
Type of Packaging: Food Service, Private Label,
Bulk
Brands:
Applegate Farms
Cargill
Colavita
Cucina Viva
Eberly
Excalibur

Excel
Gotham
Great Plains
Honeysuckle
Norbest
Prairie Grove
Reichert
Roma
Smart Choice
Taste It
Turano

30818 Vapor Power Intl LLC
551 S County Line Rd
Franklin Park, IL 60131-1013
630-694-5500
Fax: 630-694-2230 888-874-9020
info@vaporpower.com www.vaporpower.com
Manufacturer and exporter of steam generators and
liquid phase heaters
President: Curt Diedrick
CEO: Bob Forslund
Sales Manager: B Corrigan
Number Employees: 20-49
Parent Co: Westinghouse Air Brake Company

30819 Varco Products
PO Box 915
Chardon, OH 44024-0915
216-481-6895
Fax: 216-481-6897
Fluorescent light fixtures and signs
President: Edward Vlack
VP: Norman Arnos
Number Employees: 8
Square Footage: 28000

30820 (HQ)Variant
7169 Shady Oak Road
Eden Prairie, MN 55344-3516
612-927-8611
Fax: 612-927-4624 info@variantinc.com
Manufacturer, importer and exporter of advertising
products
President: Jerry Gruggen
Operations: Jan Davis
Controller: Tom Fournelle
Plant Manager: Ted Fors
Square Footage: 30000
Other Locations:
Variant
Minneapolis MN

30821 Varick Enterprises
P.O. Box 84
Winchester, MA 01890-0184
781-729-9140
Fax: 781-729-9143 800-882-7425
sales@euromachines.com
www.euromachines.com
Bar formers, bar take-off machines, batch kneaders,
batch spinners, belting, cooling tunnel, plastic, steel,
wire mesh, conveying, bars, hard candy, cookers,
cooking equipment, cooling equipment
Contact: Fred Hintlian
varick@euromachines.com
Estimated Sales: Below 1 Million
Number Employees: 3

30822 Variety Glass Inc
201 Foster Ave
Cambridge, OH 43725-1219
740-432-3643
Fax: 740-432-8693 www.mosserglass.com
Manufacturer and exporter of drug and laboratory
glassware
President: Thomas Mosser
VP: Tim Mosser
Estimated Sales: $2.5 - 5,000,000
Number Employees: 10-19

30823 Varimixer North America
14240 S Lakes Dr
Charlotte, NC 28273-6793
980-333-0032
Fax: 704-583-1703 800-221-1138
mixer@varimixer.com www.varimixer.com
Commercial mixers and food preparation equipment
President: Richard Aversa
Sales Manager: Gerald McGuffin
Operations: Charlie Strate
Plant Manager: Charlie Strate

Number Employees: 5-9
Square Footage: 400000
Parent Co: ENODIS
Type of Packaging: Food Service

30824 Varitronic Systems
6835 Winnetka Cir
Brooklyn Park, MN 55428
763-536-6400
Fax: 763-536-0769
Manufacturer and exporter of electronic lettering
systems and labels
Manager: David Grey
President: Cathy Hudson
Estimated Sales: $20 - 30 Million
Number Employees: 5-9
Parent Co: W.H. Brady

30825 Vasconia Housewares
6391 De Zavala Rd # 301
San Antonio, TX 78249-2159
210-545-4241
Fax: 210-558-9568 800-377-6723
Aluminum cookware including pots, pans and pres-
sure cookers
Manager: Jack Nimmo
President: Olivia Lozano
Estimated Sales: Less than $500,000
Number Employees: 1-4
Brands:
Vasconia

30826 Vasinee Food Corporation
1247 Grand Street
Brooklyn, NY 11211
718-349-6911
Fax: 718-349-7002 800-878-5996
info@vasinee.com vasineefoodcorp.com
Thai and Asian food: bamboo, juices, coconut milk,
fruits and vegetables, curry and paste, noodles, pre-
serves, rice, beans, sauces and spices.
Director of Business Development: Valaya
Dipongam
Logistics & Orders Coordinator: Daniel Lee
Year Founded: 1978
Estimated Sales: $14.3 Million
Number Employees: 15
Type of Packaging: Food Service, Private Label,
Bulk

30827 Vaughan Co Inc
364 Monte Elma Rd
Montesano, WA 98563-9798
360-249-4042
Fax: 360-249-6155 888-249-2467
info@chopperpumps.com
www.chopperpumps.com
Heavy duty chopper pumps for chopping and pump-
ing solids in wastewater without plugging
President: Kevin Hauser
kevin@hausers.com
President: Dale Vaughan
CFO: Pattcornwell Cornwell
Sales Manager: Bob Simonetti
Chief Engineer: Glenn Dorsch
Estimated Sales: $10 - 20 Million
Number Employees: 50-99

30828 Vaughan-Chopper Pumps
1989 Peabody Road
Suite 235
Vacaville, CA 95687-6286
707-447-6300
Fax: 707-447-6400
info@rockwellengineering.com
www.rockwellengineering.com
Wine industry chopping pumps

30829 Vaughn Belting Co-Main Acct
200 Northeast Dr
PO Box 5505
Spartanburg, SC 29303-6616
864-574-0234
Fax: 864-574-4258 800-533-9086
sales@vaughnbelting.com
www.vaughnbelting.com
Hoses and belts including conveyor, food grade, tim-
ing, nylon core, etc
VP: Brian Schachner
Manager: Amanda Hash
vaughnbe@bellsouth.net
Manager: Amanda Hash
Estimated Sales: $5 - 10 Million
Number Employees: 10-19

30830 (HQ)Vector Corp
675 44th St
Marion, IA 52302-3800
319-377-8263
Fax: 319-377-5574
vector.sales@vectorcorporation.com
www.freund-vector.com
Designs, manufactures, and markets processing
equipment for the processing of solid dosage form
materials.
President: Max Kubota
max.kubota@vectorcorporation.com
CFO: Tatsuo Matsugaki
VP Marketing: Greg Smith
Sales: Greg Smith
Production: Mike Douglas
Purchasing Director: Keith Wenndt
Estimated Sales: $25-50 Million
Number Employees: 100-249
Square Footage: 75000
Other Locations:
Vector Corp.
Huxley IA

30831 (HQ)Vector Packaging
2021 Midwest Rd # 307
Suite 307
Oak Brook, IL 60523-4349
630-968-9040
Fax: 630-434-9650   800-435-9100
www.vectorpackaging.com
Packaging materials
President/CEO: Brian Samuels
VP Sales/Marketing: Dave McCaffrey
Sales Director: Dave Hugg
Contact: Cyndi Draski
cyndi.draski@vectorpackaging.com
VP Operations: David Fiedler
Operations Director: Cyndi Christel
Number Employees: 20-49

30832 Vector Technologies
6820 N 43rd St
Milwaukee, WI 53209
414-247-7100
Fax: 414-247-7110   800-832-4010
sales@vector-vacuums.com
Manufacturer and exporter of dust collectors and
vacuum cleaners and conveying systems
President: Stebe Schonberger
CFO: Chris Koe
Contact: Matthew Benson
mbenson@vector-vacuums.com
Operations Manager: Bruce Kolb
Estimated Sales: $5 - 10 Million
Number Employees: 20-49
Square Footage: 90000
Parent Co: Vector Technologies
Brands:
Hepavac
Invader
Klean Scrub
Mdc
Rapid Response
Spartan
Titan
Vec Loader

30833 Vee Gee Scientific Inc
13600 NE 126th Pl # A
Kirkland, WA 98034-8720
425-823-4518
Fax: 425-820-9826   800-423-8842
sales@veegee.com   www.veegee.com
Manufacturer and importer of laboratory products
including refractometers, volumetric glassware, por-
celain and microscopes
Owner: Guy Mc Farland
gmac@veegee.net
Chairman of the Board: Guy McFarland
Estimated Sales: $5-10,000,000
Number Employees: 10-19

30834 Vega Americas Inc
4241 Allendorf Dr
Cincinnati, OH 45209-1501
513-272-0131
Fax: 513-272-0133   800-367-5383
www.vega-americas.com
Manufacturer and exporter of sensors and gauges

President: Ron Hegyesi
r.hegyesi@vega.com
CFO: Ken Seldmenn
Quality Control: Matt Phomas
Advertising Manager: Patrick Schreiber
r.hegyesi@vega.com
Estimated Sales: $20 - 50 Million
Number Employees: 100-249
Type of Packaging: Bulk
Brands:
Densart
Levelart
Moistart
Weighart

30835 Vega Mfg Ltd.
Unit 112-1647 Broadway Street
Port Coquitlam, BC V3C 6P8
Canada
604-941-0761
Fax: 604-941-0781   800-224-8342
sales@vegacases.com   www.vegacases.com
Bakery Showcases
President: Walter Kollenberg

30836 Vegware
Pierside Pavilion
300 Pacific Coast Hwy. # 110
Huntington Beach, CA 92648
949-543-0422
844-610-0915
us.info@vegware.com   www.vegwareus.com
Compostable packaging: hot and cold drink cups,
food containers, takeout boxes
Founder: Bob Bond

30837 Velcro USA
95 Sundial Ave
Manchester, NH 03103
Fax: 603-669-9271   800-225-0180
marketing@velcro.com   www.velcro.com
Hook and loop industrial fasteners.
President & CEO: Fraser Cameron
Year Founded: 1941
Estimated Sales: $100-500 Million
Number Employees: 2,500

30838 Vendome Copper & Brass Works
729 Franklin St
Louisville, KY 40202-6007
502-587-1930
Fax: 502-589-0639   888-384-5161
office@vendomecopper.com
Manufacturer and exporter of copper and confec-
tioners' kettles, distilling apparatus, vacuum pans,
evaporators, coils, etc
President: Patricia Seale
pseale@cleansolutionspro.com
Estimated Sales: $5-10 Million
Number Employees: 50-99
Type of Packaging: Food Service

30839 Vent Master
1021 Brevik Place
Mississauga, ON L4W 3R7
Canada
905-624-0301
Fax: 800-665-2438   800-565-2981
Manufacturer and exporter of exhaust fans, air fil-
ters, fire safety equipment, heat recovery units,
hoods and utility distribution and ventilating
systems
Vice President: Mark Meulenbeck
Sales Director: Dan O'Brien
Operations Manager: Barry Carter
Estimated Sales: $1 - 5 Million
Parent Co: ENODIS
Type of Packaging: Food Service

30840 (HQ)Vent-A-Hood Co
1000 N Greenville Ave
Richardson, TX 75081-2799
972-235-5201
Fax: 972-231-0663   800-331-2492
www.vahdistributing.com
Manufacturer and exporter of hoods

President: Miles Woodall Iii
CEO: Mileas Woodall
Quality Control: David Stiles
sjacobs@ventahood.com
HR Executive: Stewart Jacobs
sjacobs@ventahood.com
Limited Partner: Miles Woodall III
National Sales Manager: Ed Gober
Estimated Sales: $10 - 20 Million
Number Employees: 100-249

30841 (HQ)Venture Measurement Co LLC
150 Venture Blvd
Spartanburg, SC 29306-3805
864-574-8960
Fax: 864-574-8063 www.venturemeasurement.com
Manufacturer and exporter of level sensors
President: Mark Earl
CFO: Michael Hallinan
R&D: Roy Zielinski
Sales Manager: Rick Ayers
Contact: Russ Barnett
rbarnett@venturemeas.com
Estimated Sales: $30-50 Million
Number Employees: 50-99
Square Footage: 42000
Brands:
Bin-Dicators
Cap Level Iia
Pulse Point
Roto-Bin-Dicator

30842 Venture Measurement Co LLC
150 Venture Blvd
Spartanburg, SC 29306-3805
864-574-8960
Fax: 864-574-8063   800-426-9010
sales@venturemeas.com
www.venturemeasurement.com
Manufacturer and exporter of level measurement,
weight and batching instrumentation for tanks, silos
and hoppers; also, PC based bulk inventory monitor-
ing software
President: Mark Earl
Quality Control: Bennett Connvlly
R&D: Joe Dejuzman
CFO: Mick Hallinan
Marketing: Jamie Ives
Contact: Jeff Baker
jeff.baker@kistlermorse.com
Estimated Sales: $5 - 10 Million
Number Employees: 50-99
Brands:
Ld Blous
Ldbxi
Load Disk Ii
Microcell
Multi-Vessel System
Orb
Ou
Rope
Sonocell
Ultracell
Ultrasonic Sensor
Ultraware

30843 Venture Packaging Inc
311 Monroe St
Monroeville, OH 44847-9406
419-465-2912
Fax: 419-465-2702 www.berryplastics.com
Plastics containers
Manager: Howard Weatherwax
Marketing Manager (Container Division): Brent
Beeler
Contact: Wendy Schultz
chawkins@gapageants.com
Estimated Sales: Less Than $500,000
Number Employees: 1-4

30844 Venturetech Corporation
10720 Lexington Dr
Knoxville, TN 37932
865-966-2532
Fax: 865-675-2532   800-826-4095
venturet@aol.com
www.venturetechcorporation.com
Soap, detergents, bleaches, etc.; also, insecticides
and insect control systems

President: Richards Wills
VP/GM: Brandon Wills
Graphics Manager/Web Development: Justin Marion
Contact: Brandon Wills
venturetech@tds.net
Estimated Sales: $2.5-5 Million
Number Employees: 10-19

30845 Venus Corp
302 Industrial Dr
Blytheville, AR 72315-6892

870-763-3830
Fax: 870-763-4529
Custom fabricated sheet metal including full CNC punching, forming and laser cutting
CEO: Clifford Carver Sr
ccarver@venus.com
Engineer: Chris Carver
Plant Manager: Clifford Carver Jr
Estimated Sales: $2.5-5 Million
Number Employees: 10-19

30846 (HQ)Verax Chemical Co
20102 Broadway Ave
Snohomish, WA 98296-7937

360-668-2431
Fax: 360-668-5186 800-637-7771
info@veraxproducts.com
www.veraxproducts.com
Maintenance chemicals and supplies including hand and toilet bowl cleaners, disinfectants, mops, soap and floor polish; importer of cocoa mats
President: Julie Curkendall
Secretary/Treasurer: Sue Copeland
Contact: Brent Casteel
brent@veraxproducts.com
Estimated Sales: Less Than $500,000
Number Employees: 1-4
Square Footage: 30000

30847 Veri Fone Inc
11700 Great Oaks Way # 210
Alpharetta, GA 30022-2463

770-663-0196
Fax: 770-754-3422 www.verifone.com
Payment processing/transaction automation systems
Manager: Robbie Lopez
Director Marketing: Mike Matthis
Industry Marketing Manager: Kathy LeNoir
Product Marketing Manager: Ida Wu
Estimated Sales: $20-50 Million
Number Employees: 100-249

30848 Verify Brand Inc
7277 Boone Ave N
Brooklyn Park, MN 55428

763-235-1400
Fax: 763-235-1401 888-896-7882
www.verifybrand.com/
Verify Brand, Inc. provides product authentication system based on mass serialization. Verify Brand works with brand owners to design, construct, install and support turnkey product serialization and data formation, supply chainauthentication, unauthorized event management and product tracking, and reporting solutions based on the concept of mass serialization.
President: Kevin Erdman
Director Project Management: Curt Tomhave
Contact: Laurie Aukland
laurie.aukland@verifybrand.com

30849 Verilon Products Co
452 Diens Dr
Wheeling, IL 60090-2641

847-541-1920
Fax: 847-541-4525 800-323-1056
sales@verilonvinyl.com www.verilonvinyl.com
Vinyl strips for freezers and coolers
Vice President: Kim Pullen
VP: Kim Pullen
Marketing Director: Linda Mallon
VP Sales: Dorine Hanson
Estimated Sales: Below $5 Million
Number Employees: 10-19
Brands:
   Verilon

30850 Vermillion Flooring
1207 S Scenic Ave
Springfield, MO 65802-5199

417-862-3785
Fax: 417-862-3789 www.vermillion-flooring.com

Manufacturer and exporter of serving trays, pantryware, wood-chopping blocks, cedar accessories and wall decor; also, racks including wine, cookbook and mug trees
President: Art Thomas
VP: Gary Robinson
Special Markets Manager: Steve Baker
Estimated Sales: Less Than $500,000
Number Employees: 1-4
Square Footage: 160000
Brands:
   10th St. Bakery
   Chef's Select
   Classic Images

30851 Vermont Bag & Film
PO Box 135
Bennington, VT 05201-0135

802-442-3166
Fax: 802-442-3167
Plastic bags including sandwich, shopping, etc
Sales Manager: James Comi
Estimated Sales: $1 - 5 Million
Number Employees: 12

30852 Vermont Container Corp
473 Bowen Rd
Bennington, VT 05201-5020

802-442-5455
Fax: 802-442-6910 www.unicorr.com
Corrugated boxes
VP: Gerald Lambert
Contact: Besen Berry
bbesen@unicorr.com
Estimated Sales: $5 - 10 Million
Number Employees: 20-49
Parent Co: Unicorr Packaging Group

30853 Vermont Tent Co
14 Berard Dr
South Burlington, VT 05403-5809

802-863-6107
Fax: 802-863-6735 800-696-8368
www.vttent.com
Event rental and manufacturer of commercial gas convection ovens
President: John Crabbe Jr.
jcrabbe@vttent.com
CFO: Lon Finkelstein
VP Marketing & Sales: Michael Lubas
VP Operations: Michael Solomon
Estimated Sales: $5-10,000,000
Number Employees: 50-99

30854 Vermont Tissue Paper Company
RR 67a
North Bennington, VT 5257

802-447-7558
Fax: 802-447-8673
Tissue paper
President: Edward Woodard
Estimated Sales: $5 - 10 Million
Number Employees: 6

30855 Vern's Cheese
312 W Main St
Chilton, WI 53014-1312

920-849-7717
Fax: 920-849-7883 info@vernscheese.com
www.vernscheese.com
Cheeses.
President: Vern Knoespel
info@verncheese.com
Year Founded: 1964
Estimated Sales: $20-50 Million
Number Employees: 20-49

30856 Vernon Plastics
25 Shelley Road
Haverhill, MA 01835-8033

978-373-1551
Fax: 978-373-6562
Commercial awnings, plastic materials
President: Blair McIntosh
CFO: Joe Juliano
R&D: Dave Morse
VP: Mark Delaney
Marketing Manager: Steve Giaquinta
Estimated Sales: $50 - 100 Million
Number Employees: 25
Parent Co: Bordon

30857 Veronica's Treats
31 W Grove St # C
Middleboro, MA 02346-1859

508-946-4438
Fax: 508-946-4460 866-576-1122
info@veronicastreats.com
www.veronicastreats.com
Personalized cookies, brownies, and cupcakes
Owner: Hilary Souza
veronicastreats@gmail.com
Number Employees: 10-19
Square Footage: 24000
Type of Packaging: Private Label

30858 Versa Conveyor
PO Box 899
London, OH 43140-0899

740-852-5609
Fax: 740-869-2839 www.versaconveyor.com
Manufacturer and exporter of gravity and power conveyor
President: Andrew Petitt
Chief Executive Officer: Chris Cole
Vice President of Project Management: Alfred Rebello
Chief Technical Officer: Ray Neiser
Senior Vice President of Sales and Marke: Jim McKnight
Vice President of Operations: Chris Arnold
Estimated Sales: $20-50 Million
Number Employees: 100-249
Parent Co: Tomkins Industries

30859 Versa-Matic Pump Company
800 North Main Street
Mansfield, OH 44902

419-526-7296
Fax: 419-526-7289 800-843-8210
customerservice.versamatic@idexcorp.com
www.versamatic.com
Line of air-operated, double diaphragm pumps and replacement parts, air decompression pumps, 3A sanitary pumps, and food processing pumps
Estimated Sales: $5-10 Million
Number Employees: 20-49

30860 (HQ)Versailles Lighting
1305 Poinsettia Dr Ste 6
Delray Beach, FL 33444

561-278-8758
Fax: 561-278-8759 888-564-0240
Manufacturer, importer and exporter of lighting fixtures and metal tables
President: Max Guedj
CEO: Maurine Locke
CFO: Tung Nguyen
Quality Control: Rajendrauth James
Sales: Samantha Basdeo
Estimated Sales: $3 - 5 Million
Number Employees: 10-19
Square Footage: 40000
Other Locations:
   Versailles Lighting
   Delnay FL

30861 Versatile Mobile Systems
19105 36th Ave W
Lynnwood, WA 98036

425-778-8577
Fax: 425-712-0326 800-262-1633
info@versatilemobile.com versatilemobile.com
Mobile and barcode scanner solutions
EVP, Sales: Oliver Poppenberg
Year Founded: 1993

30862 Vertex China
1793 W 2nd St
Pomona, CA 91766-1253

909-594-4800
Fax: 909-595-1993 800-483-7839
info@vertexchina.com www.vertexchina.com
Manufacturer, importer and exporter of dinnerware, chinaware and tableware including lead-free, microwave/dishwasher safe, cups, saucers, bowls, dishes, platters and mugs; custom decoration available
President: Hoi Shum
info@vertexchina.com
Sales: Ken Joyce
Estimated Sales: $10-20 Million
Number Employees: 10-19
Square Footage: 50000
Brands:
   Alpine
   City Square

Crystal Bay
Kentfield
Market Buffet
Rubicon
Sausalito
Vertex

30863 Vertex Interactive
23 Carol Street
Clifton, NJ 07014-1490

973-777-3500
Fax: 973-472-0814

Manufacturer and exporter of balances, weights, bar code and magnetic strip card readers, industrial scales and data collection software
Chairman: James Maloy
CEO/President: Ron Byer
Number Employees: 60
Parent Co: Vertex Industries
Brands:
Torbal

30864 Vertical Systems Intl
2126 Chamber Center Dr
Lakeside Park, KY 41017-1669

859-485-9650
Fax: 859-485-9654 sales@vsilift.com
www.vsilift.com

Manufacturer and exporter of vertical lifts, stackers, conveyors, dumpers, and autostore units
President: Daniel Quinn
dan.quinn@vsilift.com
Member: Daniel Quinn
VP Sales: Steve Templeton
Estimated Sales: $5 - 10 Million
Number Employees: 5-9
Square Footage: 88000

30865 Vertique Inc
115 Vista Blvd
Arden, NC 28704-9457

828-654-8900
Fax: 828-654-8908

Vertique specializes in warehouse distribution equipment (Vertique systems and VPS picking and loading software) for the beverage and food industry, providing complete product services specifically designed to meet any manufacturing and distribution need.
Owner: Jay Stingel
VP: John Stingel
Senior Engineer: James Smith
Vice President Sales: Jeff Stingel
Manager: Tom Algai
toma@vertique.com
Estimated Sales: $20-50 Million
Number Employees: 50-99
Type of Packaging: Bulk

30866 Vescom America
2289 Ross Mill Rd
Henderson, NC 27537-5966

252-436-9067
Fax: 252-436-9069 usacanada@vescom.com

Manufacturer, importer and exporter of recycling systems for food wastes including feeders, shredders, weight controllers, screeners, conveyors, packers and dust collection systems
Owner: Robert Vrabel
Contact: Lisa Brooks
l.brooks@vescom.com
Estimated Sales: $300,000-500,000
Number Employees: 1-4
Square Footage: 1000

30867 Vetrerie Bruni
3101 W Mcnab Rd
Pompano Beach, FL 33069

954-590-3990
Fax: 954-590-3991 800-432-4825

Glass containers for wine, champagne and food
Estimated Sales: $10-20 Million
Number Employees: 10-19

30868 Vetter Vineyards Winery
8005 Prospect Station Rd
Westfield, NY 14787-9630

716-326-3100
Fax: 716-326-3100

Wines
Owner: Mark Lancaster
wine@fairpoint.net
Co-Owner: Barbara Lancaster

Estimated Sales: Less Than $500,000
Number Employees: 1-4
Type of Packaging: Private Label
Brands:
Vetter Vineyards

30869 Viacam
313 Pleasant Street
Watertown, MA 02472-2418

617-926-7045
Fax: 617-923-8055 800-338-4381
viacom@viacom.com www.viacom.com

Rapid myocotoxin testing kits, tests for the detection of DON, fumonisin, ochratoxin and zearalenone and tests for the detection of listeria, salmonella and salmonella enteritidis
President and Chief Executive Officer: Philippe Dauman
CFO: Wade Davis
Senior Vice President of Investor Relati: James Bombassei
CFO: Majoire Radlo
Contact: Jim Cary
jim@radlo.com
Estimated Sales: $2.5 - 5 Million
Number Employees: 20-49

30870 Viatec
777 Fort Street
Victoria, BC V8W 1G9
Canada

250-483-3214
Fax: 269-945-2357 800-942-4702
sales@viatec.ca www.viatec.ca

Manufacturer and exporter of dairy processors, cookers, coolers, stainless and fiberglass tanks, mixers and valves
CEO: Dan Gunn
Marketing & Communications Coordinator: Robbie Aylesworth
Sales (Stainless): Bob Johnson
Manager of Operations & Finance: Michelle Gaetz
Estimated Sales: $10-20 Million
Number Employees: 50-99
Square Footage: 104000
Brands:
Chemtek
Duratek
Permasan
Resinfab

30871 Viatec Process Storage System
500 Reed St
PO Box 99
Belding, MI 48809-1532

616-794-1230
Fax: 616-794-2487 klk@viatec.com

Manufacturer and exporter of dairy processors, cookers, coolers, stainless and fiberglass tanks, mixers and valves
Sales Director: Bob Johnson
Plant Manager: Ron Timmer
Estimated Sales: $5,000,000 - $9,900,000
Number Employees: 20-49
Square Footage: 52000
Parent Co: Viatec
Brands:
Chemtek
Duratek
Permasan
Resinfab

30872 Viatran Corporation
3829 Forest Park Way
Suite 500
North Tonawanda, NY 14120

716-773-1700
Fax: 716-773-2488 800-688-0030
solutions@viatran.com www.viatran.com

Sanitary, flush/CIP, solid state pressure, level and flow transmitters
Contact: Matt Carrara
carrara@viatran.com
Number Employees: 50-99

30873 Vibrac LLC-Fax
19 Columbia Dr
Amherst, NH 03031-2305

603-886-3857
Fax: 603-886-3857 www.vibrac.com

Cap torque testing laboratory and on-line

President: Tom Rogers
CEO: Quentin Searle
Vice President of Engineering: Bob Searle
Contact: Ken Diegel
kdiegel@vibrac.com
VP of Operations: Lisa Rogers
Production Manager: Scott Whipple
Plant Manager: Richard Brams
Estimated Sales: $3 Million
Number Employees: 1-4
Number of Brands: 2
Number of Products: 6
Square Footage: 15000
Brands:
Gold Bottle
Torgo

30874 VibroFloors World
1415 Highway 85 N
Suite 310-361
Fayetteville, GA 30214

770-632-9701
Fax: 770-632-9710 info@vibrofloorswg.com
www.vibrofloorsworldgroup.com

High performance and maintenance free flooring for commercial and industrial work facilities
President: Jackie Smith Jr
CEO: Dejana Gavrilovic
Project Manager: T Freddy Venos
Parent Co: VibroFloors WorldGroup, LLC

30875 Vicksburg Chemical Company
5100 Poplar Ave Fl 24
Memphis, TN 38137-4000

901-747-0234
Fax: 901-747-4031 800-227-2798
jhreeves@aol.com

Processor, importer and exporter of potassium nitrates, potassium carbonates, monammonium phosphates and monopotassium phosphates
Sales Manager/Distributor: John Reeves
Estimated Sales: $1 - 5 Million
Number Employees: 100-250
Type of Packaging: Private Label

30876 Vicmore Manufacturing Company
20 Grand Avenue
Brooklyn, NY 11205-1317

718-855-7758
Fax: 718-852-3768 800-458-8663

Manufacturer and exporter of double polished clear tablecloths, and vinyl and chemical aprons
President: Morris Steinberg
Estimated Sales: $5-10 Million
Number Employees: 50-99

30877 Victone Manufacturing Company
726 W 19th St
Chicago, IL 60616-1024

312-738-3211
Fax: 312-738-3214

Wire racks and stands
President: Joe Di Monte
Plant Manager: Raymond Di Monte
Estimated Sales: $2.5-5 Million
Number Employees: 10-19

30878 Victor Associates
514 Creekside Ct
Golden, CO 80403-1903

720-379-6850
Fax: 303-526-5069

Food consulting
C.E.O: Michael S Victor
mvictor@fralo.com
Estimated Sales: $1 - 5 Million
Number Employees: 1

30879 Victoria Porcelain
7790 NW 67th St
Miami, FL 33166-2702

305-593-2353
Fax: 305-593-8363 888-593-2353
sales@victoriaporcelain.com
www.victoriaporcelain.com

Porcelain cups, bowls, plates, gravy boats, saucers, mugs, ovenware, teapots, etc.; importer and exporter of flatware and knives
President: Jose Espejo
jespejo@victoriaporcelain.com
VP Sales: David Yablin
Customer Service Manager: Phyllis Halpern

Estimated Sales: $2.5 - 5 Million
Number Employees: 1-4
Square Footage: 40000

30880 Victory Box Corp
645 W 1st Ave
Roselle, NJ 07203-1049

908-245-5100
Fax: 908-245-5670 www.victoryboxcorp.com
Corrugated boxes
President: Alex Landy
VP Sales: Paul Bell
Estimated Sales: $20 - 50 Million
Number Employees: 100-249

30881 Victory Packaging, Inc.
3555 Timmons Lane
Suite 144
Houston, TX 77027

713-961-3299
Fax: 800-778-7210 800-486-5606
www.victorypackaging.com
Custom and stock corrugated boxes
CEO: Benjamin Samuels
CFO: Carol Black
Estimated Sales: $62 Million
Number Employees: 900

30882 Victory Refrigeration
110 Woodcrest Rd
Cherry Hill, NJ 08003

856-428-4200
Fax: 856-428-7299 victory@victory-refrig.com
www.victory-refrig.com
Commercial refrigerators and freezers
President: Mark Whalen
CFO: Eileen Kurskin
R&D and Quality Control: Robert Hettinger
Director Sales Marketing: Jim Hurston
Contact: Jeff Yates
jim@informzone.net
Estimated Sales: $30 - 50 Million
Number Employees: 1-4
Square Footage: 240000
Parent Co: Middleby Corporation
Brands:
    Victory

30883 Videojet Technologies Inc
1500 N Mittel Blvd
Wood Dale, IL 60191-1073

800-843-3610
vti.domesticcs@videojet.com www.videojet.com
Manufacturer and exporter of coding and labeling
equipment, printing inks and printing equipment;
also, material handling equipment.
Chief Technology Officer/VP of R&D: John Folkers
Principal Software Engineer: Eric Amy
Mechanical Engineer Manager: Kevin Kuester
Number Employees: 4,000
Parent Co: Donaher Corporation
Brands:
    Cheshire
    Excel
    Inksource
    Maxum
    Sigmark
    Totalsource
    Triumph
    Videojet

30884 Videojet Technologies Inc
1500 N Mittel Blvd
Wood Dale, IL 60191-1072

630-860-7300
Fax: 630-616-3623 800-843-3610
www.videojet.com
President: Matt Trerotola
Contact: Jay Buckley
jay.buckley@videojet.com
Estimated Sales: $1 - 5 Million
Number Employees: 1000-4999

30885 Videx Inc
1105 NE Circle Blvd
Corvallis, OR 97330-4285

541-738-5500
Fax: 541-752-5285 support@videx.com
Manufacture portable bar code scanners and ibutton
readers in addition to access control and security
products, electronic locks

President: Steve Braaten
steveb@videx.com
Marketing Director: Stephanie Ulrich
Sales Director: Tish Phillips
Number Employees: 50-99
Number of Brands: 25
Number of Products: 226
Brands:
    Authorizer
    Barcode Labeler
    Cyber Key
    Cyber Lock
    Cyber Point
    Duratrax
    Duraward
    Laserlite Mx
    Laserlite Pro
    Omni Wand
    Pulse Star
    Time Wand I
    Time Wand Ii
    Touch Access
    Touch Alert
    Touchprobe

30886 View-Rite Manufacturing
455 Allan St
Daly City, CA 94014-1627

415-468-3856
Fax: 415-468-4784
Manufacturer and exporter of store fixtures
President: Nha Nguyen
nnguyen@viewrite.com
VP: Nha Nguyen
Number Employees: 20-49
Square Footage: 160000

30887 Vifan USA
1 Vifan Dr
Morristown, TN 37814

423-581-6990
Fax: 423-581-9998 866-843-2668
www.vifan.com
Bi-axially polypropylene films, film for industrial
and flexible packaging applications
President: Pietro Battista
CFO: Thomas Mohr
Executive VP: Vittoriano Di Luzio
Contact: F Massey
f.massey@vibac.com
Estimated Sales: $10 - 20 Million
Number Employees: 100-249
Number of Products: 4
Square Footage: 280000

30888 Viking Corp
210 Industrial Park Dr
Hastings, MI 49058-9631

269-945-9501
Fax: 269-945-4495 800-968-9501
techsvcs@vikingcorp.com
Manufacturer and exporter of fire protection systems
including wet and dry pipe, deluge and fire cycle;
also, valves, sprinklers, spray nozzles and alarm
devices
CEO: Tomdra Groos
CEO: Kevin Ortyl
Marketing Director: Sandra Wake
Sales Director: Bill Phair
Contact: Will Allgood
wallgood@supplynet.com
Purchasing Manager: Jerry Dinges
Estimated Sales: $20 - 30 Million
Number Employees: 100-249
Parent Co: Tyden Seal Company

30889 Viking Identification Product
8964 Excelsior Blvd
Hopkins, MN 55343

952-935-5245
Fax: 952-935-3764
Pressure sensitive, foil and silk-screened labels
Owner: Tim Paulson
Estimated Sales: Below $5 Million
Number Employees: 5-9

30890 Viking Industries
489 Tumbull Bay Rd
New Smyma Beach, FL 32168

386-428-9800
Fax: 386-409-0360 888-605-5560

Manfacturer and exporter of hot melt adhesive appli-
cation equipment for carton and case sealings; also,
hot wax dispensing systems for wine bottle seals,
cheese products and hot candy
Owner: Walter Warning Jr
VP Sales/Marketing: Douglas White
Estimated Sales: $2.5-5,000,000
Number Employees: 10-19
Square Footage: 40000
Brands:
    Sys-Clean
    Titan

30891 Viking Label Inc
5652 Lakers Ln
PO Box 10
Nisswa, MN 56468-4701

218-963-2575
Fax: 218-963-4849 800-247-6573
info@vikinglabel.com www.vikinglabel.com
Labels
Owner: Tammie Barry
Sales Manager: Kim Larson
tbarry@vikinglabel.com
Estimated Sales: $5-10 Million
Number Employees: 20-49

30892 Viking Machine & DesignInc
1408 Viking Ln
De Pere, WI 54115-9265

920-336-1190
Fax: 920-336-2970 888-286-2116
Cheese processing equipment for processing of moz-
zarella, provolone, and blue cheese
President, Founder: Don Lindgren Sr
Engineer and CFO: Dan Lindgren
Founder: Don Lindgren
Quality Control: Rick Felchlin
Sales Director: Rick Felchlin
Plant Manager: Rick Felchlin
Shop Foreman / Project Coordinator / Pur: Rick
Felchlin
Estimated Sales: $1 - 2.5 Million
Number Employees: 1-4
Square Footage: 128640
Brands:
    Hydra Form
    Hydra Mold

30893 Viking Packaging & Display
620 Quinn Avenue
San Jose, CA 95112-2604

408-998-1000
Fax: 408-293-8162
Corrugated containers, protective foam packaging
and point of purchase displays
President: Peter Keady
Production: Ed Hirle
Estimated Sales: $20-50 Million
Number Employees: 20-49
Square Footage: 80000

30894 Viking Pallet Corp
9188 Cottonwood Ln N
PO Box 167
Maple Grove, MN 55369-3902

763-425-6707
Fax: 763-425-4400 sales@vikingpallet.com
www.vikingpallet.com
Wooden pallets
Owner/ General Manager: Tim Logan
sales@vikingpallet.com
Office Manager: Kathy Plocharski
Plant Foreman: Mark Aanenson
Estimated Sales: Below $5 Million
Number Employees: 20-49

30895 Viking Pump Inc
406 State St
Cedar Falls, IA 50613-3343

319-266-1741
Fax: 319-273-8157 www.vikingpump.com
Stainless steel rotary pumps and equipment
President: Paul Schwar
CEO: Jason Struthrs
CFO: Steve Huan
Vice President: Joe Michaels
joemichaels@idexcorp.com
Sales Director: Kevin Rhodes
Number Employees: 500-999
Square Footage: 154
Parent Co: IDEX Corp.
Brands:
    Acculube

Classic Rotary Lobe Pumps
Concept Sq
Duralobe
Sterilobe

30896 Vikkor, Inc.
90 Nolan Court
Unit 37
Markham, ON L3R 4L9
Canada

647-792-7891

Bakery equipment, including convection ovens,
mixers, dough dividers, and pasta/pizza making.

30897 Vilter Manufacturing Corporation
5555 S Packard Ave
Cudahy, WI 53110

414-744-0111

Fax: 414-744-3483 www.vilter.com
Compressors, condensors, air untis and custom
packaged systems
President/CEO/COO: Ron Prebish
VP Business Development: Wayne Wehber
VP Sales/Marketing: Mark Stencel
Contact: Mark Stencel
mark.stencel@emersonclimate.com
VP Operations: John Barry
Estimated Sales: $43 Million
Number Employees: 100-249
Number of Brands: 4
Number of Products: 7
Square Footage: 400000
Brands:
450xl
Econ-O-Mizer
Power Pincher
Steady-Mount
Super Separator
Tri-Micro
V-Plus
Vilter
Vmc

30898 Vimco
300 Hansen Access Rd # A
King of Prussia, PA 19406-2440

610-768-0500

Fax: 610-768-0586 www.vimcoinc.com
Lighting and lamp fixtures including food heating,
industrial task, bench and assembly
President: Vic Maggitti, Jr
vic@vimcoinc.com
Sales Manager: Dave Gyuris
Administration: Brandon O'Brien
Plant Manager: Max DiRado
Estimated Sales: $1 - 3 Million
Number Employees: 50-99

30899 Vin-Tex
1 Mount Forest Drive
Ontario, CA N0G-2L2

519-323-0300
Fax: 519-323-4777 800-846-8399
sales@vintex.com

Reusable packaging bags
Estimated Sales: $5-10 Million
Number Employees: 20-49

30900 Vincent Commodities Corporation
7182 US Highway 14
Middleton, WI 53562

608-831-4447
Fax: 608-833-0555 800-279-4447
vcc20@msn.com

President: Ronald Vincent
Estimated Sales: $2.5-5 Million
Number Employees: 5-9

30901 Vincent Corp
2810 E 5th Ave
Tampa, FL 33605-5638

813-248-2650
Fax: 813-247-7557 vincent@vincentcorp.com
www.vincentcorp.com

Manufacturer and exporter of screw presses for
dewatering; also, pectin peel and citrus by-product
machinery for liquids separation/solids concentra-
tion
President: Robert Johnston
spj110@msn.com
Project Engineer: Bob Johnston
Estimated Sales: $2.5-5 Million
Number Employees: 50-99
Square Footage: 160000

Brands:
Vincent

30902 Vine Solutions
200 Tamal Plaza
Suite 100
Corte Madera, CA 94925-1172

415-927-3308

Fax: 415-485-6011 tnikaidoh@vinesolutions.com
Consultant specializing in accounting services, stra-
tegic market planning, restructuring and restaurant
start-up
Owner: Edward Vine
Chief Executive Officer: Edward Levine
Executive Vice President: John Priest
Contact: Janina Bandi
jbandi@vinesolutions.com
Director, Accounting: Takashi Nikaidoh
Estimated Sales: Below $5 Million
Number Employees: 1-4
Square Footage: 3600

30903 Vineco International Products
27 Scott Street W
St Catharines, ON L2R 1E1
Canada

905-685-9342
Fax: 905-685-9551

Manufacturer and wholesaler/distributor of wine and
beer making kits
President: Rob Van Wely
CFO: Jason Hough
R&D: Sandra Sartor
Quality Control: Sandra Sartor
Marketing: Michael Hind
Estimated Sales: $5 - 10 Million
Number Employees: 45
Parent Co: Andres Wines
Type of Packaging: Consumer
Brands:
Bin 49
Brew Canada
California Connoisseur
European Select
Kendall
Lagacy
Ridge Classic
Ridge Showcase
V.I.P. Series

30904 Vintage
225 Clay Street
P.O. Box 231
Jasper, IN 47547

812-482-3204
Fax: 812-936-9979 800-992-3491
humanresources@jaspergroup.us.com
www.jaspergroup.us.com

Bar stools, tables, chairs and benches
President: Mike Elliott
Technical Services Manager: Amilcar Ubiera
Marketing Director: Lisa Kieffner
Sales Territory Manager: Jimi Barreiro
Operations Manager: Ronald Beck
Plant Manager: Mark Kluemper
Purchasing Manager: Dan Herman
Number Employees: 100-249
Parent Co: Jasper Seating Company

30905 Virgin Cola USA
3600 Wilshire Blvd
Los Angeles, CA 90010-2603

213-380-3433
Fax: 213-487-3631

Owner: Virgil Sy

30906 Virginia Artesian Bottling Company
4300 Spring Run Rd
Mechanicsville, VA 23116-6639

804-779-7500
Fax: 866-291-9504 sales@virginiaartesian.com
virginiaartesian.com

Bottled water
Owner: Steven Brown
Sales Manager: Frank Atwood
Production Manager: Nick Brown
Year Founded: 2003
Estimated Sales: Under $500,000
Number Employees: 1-10
Type of Packaging: Food Service
Brands:
Virginia Artesian

30907 Virginia Department of Agriculture & Consumer Services
102 Governor Street
Richmond, VA 23219

804-786-3520
webmaster.vdacs@vdacs.virginia.gov
www.vdacs.virginia.gov

Information services for food industry: food safety,
lab services, marketing.
Agribusiness Development: Bill Scruggs
Director, Marketing: Keith Long
Public Relations & Marketing: Marshall Payne
Year Founded: 1877
Number Employees: 200-500
Brands:
Virginia Grown
Virginia's Finest

30908 Virginia Industrial Services
P.O. Box 532
Waynesboro, VA 22980-391

Fax: 540-943-7192 800-825-3050
Manufacturer and exporter of food processing
equipment; also, repair and modification available
President: William Merrill
Estimated Sales: Below $5,000,000
Number Employees: 10-19
Square Footage: 20000

30909 Virginia Plastics Co
3453 Aerial Way Dr SW
Roanoke, VA 24018-1503

540-981-9700
Fax: 540-375-0135 800-777-8541
sales@vaplastics.com www.vaplastics.com

Manufacturer and exporter of packaging materials
including polyethylene film and tubing
President: Mike Callister
Estimated Sales: $5-10 Million
Number Employees: 20-49

30910 Virtual Packaging
530 S Nolen Dr
Southlake, TX 76092-9165

817-328-3945
Fax: 817-328-3901 888-868-7848
sales@virtualpackaging.com
www.virtualpackaging.com

Mock-ups, full-color bags, boxes, cans, labels,
shrink film and wrappers
President: Monty Patterson
Marketing Manager: Paul Ferreris
Manager: Rafael Guerra
rafael@virtualpackaging.com
Estimated Sales: Less than $500,000
Number Employees: 20-49

30911 Visalia Citrus Packing Group
19743 Avenue 344
Woodlake, CA 93286

559-564-3351
Fax: 559-564-3865 vcpg@vcpg.com

Golden State Citrus Packers is a licensed commer-
cial shipper of citrus products for Sunkist Growers,
Inc.
President: George Lambeth
Manager: John Kalendar
johnkalendar@vcpg.com
Office Manager: Judith Jenkins
Plant Manager: Raul Gamez
Number Employees: 100-249
Parent Co: Visalia Citrus Packing Group
Type of Packaging: Food Service

30912 Viscofan USA Inc
50 County Ct
Montgomery, AL 36105-5506

334-396-0092
Fax: 334-396-0094 800-521-3577
www.viscofan.com

Manufacturer and distributor of artifical casings for
the meat industry
President: Jose Maria Fernandez
CEO: Jose Fernandez
fernandezj@usa2.viscofan.com
Sales VP: David Hambert
Product Manager: Tripp Ferguson
Estimated Sales: $1.2 Million
Number Employees: 100-249
Type of Packaging: Consumer, Food Service, Bulk

30913 Visionary Design
620 Wolfs Hollow Dr
Atglen, PA 19310
610-408-0540
Fax: 610-408-0541 vdi@epix.net
Out of the box innovative creativity for the food industry
President: Eugene Gadlardi
Quality Control: Frank Oas
Estimated Sales: Below $5 Million
Number Employees: 3

30914 Visions Espresso Svc
2737 1st Ave S
Seattle, WA 98134-1823
206-623-6709
Fax: 206-623-6710 800-277-7277
info@visionsespresso.com
www.visionsespresso.com
Espresso machine cleaners, espresso machines/accessories, filtration equipment, service espresso machines
Owner: Dawn Loraas
dawn@visions.com
Manager: Bethanie Fritz
Estimated Sales: $500,000-$1 Million
Number Employees: 20-49

30915 Visipak
209 N Kirkwood Rd
St Louis, MO 63122-4029
314-984-8100
Fax: 314-984-0021 800-949-1171
www.visipak.com
Clear plastic tubing
Manager: Mike Boysen
Estimated Sales: $20-50 Million
Number Employees: 100-249

30916 Viskase Co Inc
8205 Cass Ave # 115
Darien, IL 60561-5319
630-874-0700
Fax: 630-874-0178 800-323-8562
www.viskase.com
Manufacturer and exporter of nonedible, fibrous and cellulosic food casings and film including barrier, polypropylene and cook-in
President/CEO: Robert Weisman
VP/COO: Henry Palacci
VP/CFO/Secretary/Treasurer: Charles Pullin
VP Sales, North America: Maurice Ryan
Contact: Eric Wynveen
eric.wynveen@viskase.com
VP Worldwide Operations: Bernard Lemoine
Estimated Sales: $20 Million
Number Employees: 1,000-4,999
Other Locations:
Viskase Manufacturing Plant
Kentland IN
Viskase Manufacturing Plant
Loudon TN
Viskase Manufacturing Plant
Osceola AR
Viskase Manufacturing Plant
Escobedo, Mexico
Viskase Manufacturing Plant
Sao Paulo, Brazil

30917 Vista International Packaging
1126 88th Pl
Kenosha, WI 53143-6538
262-697-6520
Fax: 262-694-4824 800-558-4058
www.vistapackaging.com
Custom food packaging for meat, poultry and cheese
President/CEO: David Hagman
CFO: Paul Schulz
VP Sales and Marketing: Ron Ramsey
R & D: Lloyd Wallenslager
Quality Control: Marie McMahon
VP Marketing: David Jaeger
VP Sales: Paul Walter
Contact: Anne Eichstedt
aeichstedt@vistapackaging.com
Operations Manager: Mike Schultz
Plant Manager: Steve Vanzeeland
Estimated Sales: $10-20 Million
Number Employees: 5-9
Type of Packaging: Consumer, Food Service, Private Label, Bulk

30918 Vista International Packaging
1126 88th Pl
Kenosha, WI 53143-6538
262-697-6520
Fax: 262-694-4824 800-558-4058
Forming and non-forming films, shrink bags, and tubular plastics for the poultry, meat and cheese industries.
Contact: Anne Eichstedt
aeichstedt@vistapackaging.com
Number Employees: 5-9

30919 Visual Marketing Assoc
9560 Pathway St # 6
Santee, CA 92071-4181
619-258-0393
Fax: 619-258-0790
Backlit and nonbacklit menu display systems and retro-fit menu systems; also, transparency illuminators
President: Dale R Godfrey
Estimated Sales: Below $5 Million
Number Employees: 1-4
Square Footage: 34000
Brands:
Broadway Menu
Light Hawk

30920 Visual Packaging Corp
91 4th Ave
Haskell, NJ 07420-1141
973-835-7055
Fax: 973-835-0445
visualpackaging@optimum.net
www.visualpackagingcorp.com
Transparent plastic candy containers and boxes
President: Don Stackhouse
sales@visualpackaging.com
Estimated Sales: $500,000-$1 Million
Number Employees: 5-9

30921 Visual Planning Corp
1320 Route 9 #3314
Champlain, NY 12919
518-298-8404
Fax: 518-298-2368 800-361-1192
info@visualplanning.com
www.visualplanning.com
Scheduling boards-magnetic, perforated, T-card, boardmaster, fixed, rotating, planner sheets, PC software & accessories, AV equipment & supplies-easels, pads, lecterns, bulletin boards, conference cabinets, electronic boardsprojectors, screens, markers, Graphic Arts materials-templates, portfolios, filing systems, precision knives; Signs-labels, badges, nameplates, directory boards, magnetic, etc; office supplies.
President: Joseph Josephson
Marketing: Boris Polanski
Plant Manager: Stefan Neciorek
Purchasing Manager: Paul Harrison
Estimated Sales: $1 - 3 Million
Number Employees: 20-49
Type of Packaging: Private Label
Brands:
All Ways
Kling
Lecturers' Marker
Liquid Chalk
Magnetically Aligned
Overlay/Underlay
Triple Erasability System
Visitint
Visutate
Visutype

30922 Vita Craft Corp
11100 W 58th St
Shawnee, KS 66203-2299
913-631-6265
Fax: 913-631-1143 800-359-3444
info@vitacraft.com
Manufacturer and exporter of stainless steel and multi-ply cooking utensils
President: Gary Martin
garymartin@vitacraft.com
CEO: Mamoru Imura
VP: John Ratigan
Estimated Sales: $10-20 Million
Number Employees: 20-49
Parent Co: Rena-Ware Distributors
Type of Packaging: Consumer, Food Service

30923 Vita Juice Corporation
10725 Sutter Ave
Pacoima, CA 91331-2553
818-899-1195
President: Fred Farago
Estimated Sales: $1 - 5 Million
Number Employees: 1-4

30924 Vita Key Packaging
6975 Arlington Ave
Riverside, CA 92503
909-355-1023
Fax: 909-355-1070
Full service contract packaging, custom formulation and overflow packaging for the food and nutritional supplement industries
Owner: Douglas Delia
Director Operations: Robert Lockovich
Estimated Sales: $2.5-5,000,000
Number Employees: 20-49
Type of Packaging: Private Label, Bulk

30925 VitaMinder Company
23 Acorn St
Providence, RI 02903-1066
401-273-0444
Fax: 401-273-0630 800-858-8840
sales@vitaminder.com www.medportllc.com
Manufacturer and exporter of multi-compartment vitamin containers, portable blenders for powdered drink mixes and food scales; importer of scales, tablet splitters/crushers and blenders
President: Larry Wesson
CFO: Larry Weffon
Quality Control: Vanessa Honwybhan
VP Sales: James Shuster
Sales Manager: Ken Michaels
Number Employees: 10-19
Parent Co: Ocean Group
Brands:
Vitaminder

30926 Vitakem Neutraceutical Inc
811 West Jericho Turnpike
Smithtown, NY 11787
855-837-0430
www.vitakem.com
Vitamins and supplements
President/CEO: Bret Hoyt Sr
Contact: Aaron Berkman
aaron@vitakem.com

30927 Vitamix
8615 Usher Rd
Olmsted Twp, OH 44138-2199
440-235-4840
Fax: 440-235-3726 800-437-4654
foodservice@vitamix.com www.vitamix.com
Manufactures highly engineered, high performance commercial food blenders and drink mixers built for outstanding durability and versatility
President: John Barnard
CEO: Jodi Berg
international@vitamix.com
Marketing Director: D Scott Hinckley
Estimated Sales: $20 - 50 Million
Number Employees: 250-499
Brands:
Bar Boss
Blending Station
Mix'n Machine
Rinse-O-Latic
Touch and Go Blending Station
Vita-Mix Drink Machine
Vita-Prep
Vita-Pro

30928 Vitatech Nutritional Sciences
2802 Dow Ave
Tustin, CA 92780-7212
714-832-9700
Fax: 714-731-8482 info@vit-best.com
www.vit-best.com
Vitamins.
CEO: Thomas Mooy
VP Supply Chain: Katie Watts
Director of Technical Services: David Jiang
Estimated Sales: $20-50 Million
Number Employees: 100-249
Type of Packaging: Private Label

30929 Vitex Packaging Group
1137 Progress Rd
Suffolk, VA 23434-2301
757-538-3115
Fax: 757-538-3120
Paper based flexible packaging tea tags and envelopes
President: Sandy Arulf
sarulf@vitexpackaging.com
Estimated Sales: $20 Million
Number Employees: 100-249

30930 Vitro Packaging
5200 Tennyson Pkwy Ste 100
Plano, TX 75024
469-443-1100
Fax: 469-443-1258 800-766-0600
www.vitro.com/vitro_packaging/ingles/
Stock and private design glass containers.
President: John Shaddox
Vice President Finance: Kevin Jackson
Vice President Sales & Marketing: Doug Hesche
Contact: Jose Alonso
jalonso@vitro.com
Estimated Sales: $20-50 Million
Number Employees: 50-99
Parent Co: Vitro S.A.

30931 Vitro Packaging
3700 Preston Rd
Plano, TX 75093-7440
972-596-6483
Fax: 972-960-1076 800-766-0600
www.vto.com
Glass bottles in all shapes, sizes and colors
Estimated Sales: $20-50 Million
Number Employees: 50-99

30932 Vitro Seating Products
201 Madison St
St Louis, MO 63102-1329
314-241-2265
Fax: 314-241-8723 800-325-7093
mail@vitroseating.com www.vitroseating.com
Manufacturer and exporter of hotel, restaurant and bar furniture including fountain and bar stools, booths, chairs and tables
CEO: Rose Crofford
rcrofford@ccstl.org
CEO: Stephen Scott
VP of Administration: Mike Scott
Senior Designer: Kim Luce
National Sales Manager: Matt Schliecher
Accounts Receivable Manager: Lauren Rush
VP of Manufacturing: Steve Scott Jr.
Purchasing Mngr./CSR: Matt Schleicher
Estimated Sales: $5-10 Million
Number Employees: 50-99
Square Footage: 450000
Type of Packaging: Food Service

30933 Vivolac Cultures Corp
6108 W Stoner Dr
Greenfield, IN 46140-7383
317-866-9528
Fax: 317-356-8450 800-848-6522
www.vivolac.com
Laboratory specializing in dairy and food microbiological testing, consultation and sanitation
Owner: David Jaramillo
Chief Marketing Officer: Philip Reinhardt
Technical Sales Manager: Rossana Reyes
djaramillo@vivolac.com
Estimated Sales: $1-2.5 Million
Number Employees: 5-9

30934 Vogel Lubrication Systems
1008 Jefferson Ave
Newport News, VA 23607-6122
757-380-0164
Fax: 757-380-0709
Centralized lubrication systems and liquid pumps for industry
President: Robert Amen
Quality Control: Thomas Steinhoff
Contact: Joe Ahrens
jahrens@vogel-lube.com
Estimated Sales: $10 - 20 Million
Number Employees: 10-19

30935 Vogt Tube Ice
1000 W Ormsby Ave # 19
Louisville, KY 40210-1549
502-635-3000
Fax: 502-634-0479 800-853-8648
info@vogtice.com www.vogtice.com
Manufacturer and exporter ice machines including cubers and crushers
Chairman/ Managing Member: J.T. Sims
President: Tobi Ferguson
CEO: Mark Barter
VP, Business Development & Engineering: Charles Holwerk
Manager of Quality & Manufacturing: Vince Stewart
Commercial Marketing Manager: Tim Burke
International Sales Manager: Ivan Villalba
Estimated Sales: $5 - 10 Million
Number Employees: 50-99
Type of Packaging: Food Service
Brands:
Vogt Tube-Ice

30936 Voigt Lighting Industries Inc.
79 Commerce St
Garfield, NJ 7026
973-928-2252
Fax: 973-478- 015 paul@voightlighting.com
www.voightlighting.com
FDA compliant lighting fixtures for food processing areas and warehouses
President: Paul Goldberg
CFO: Frank Stein
Contact: Benny Benyamini
bbb@voigtlighting.com
Estimated Sales: Below $5 Million
Number Employees: 4
Brands:
Asym-A-Lyte
Frugalume
Korode-Not

30937 Volckening Inc
6700 3rd Ave
Brooklyn, NY 11220-5296
718-836-4000
Fax: 718-748-2811 800-221-0276
info@volckening.com www.volckening.com
Manufacturer and exporter of replacement parts for beverage filling machinery; also, industrial brushes
Chairman: William Schneider
wschneider@volckeninginc.com
CEO: F Schneider
Estimated Sales: $10-20 Million
Number Employees: 20-49
Square Footage: 50000

30938 (HQ)Volk Corp
23936 Industrial Park Dr
Farmington Hills, MI 48335-2861
248-477-6700
Fax: 248-478-6884 800-521-6799
sales@volkcorp.com www.volkcorp.com
Manufacturer and exporter of signs, rubber stamps, markers, name badges, envelopes, tapes, tape dispensers, advertising novelties, printing dies, zinc plates, steel stamps, ink cartridges, etc
President: Bill Woolfall
billw@volkcorp.com
Marketing Director: Todd Cruthfield
Sales Director: Ron Harper
Plant Manager: Donald Schultz
Purchasing Manager: Scott Szumanski
Estimated Sales: $5-10 Million
Number Employees: 50-99
Other Locations:
Volk Corp.
Grand Rapids MI

30939 Volk Enterprises Inc
1335 Ridgeland Pkwy # 120
Suite 120
Alpharetta, GA 30004-0728
770-663-5400
Fax: 770-663-5411 sales@volkenterprises.com
www.volkenterprises.com
President: Ken Bragg
k.bragg@volkprotectiveproducts.com
Vice President: Daniel J. Volk (DAN)
Regional Sales Manager: Burt Hewitt
Estimated Sales: $500,000-$1 Million
Number Employees: 50-99

30940 Volk Packaging Corp
11 Morin St
Biddeford, ME 04005
207-282-6151
Fax: 207-283-1165 vpc@volkboxes.com
www.volkboxes.com
Manufacturer and exporter of packaging and containerizing supplies including corrugated, fiber and wooden boxes, cartons and containers.
President/Owner: Derek Volk
Chief Executive Officer: Douglas Volk
Chief Financial Officer: Douglas Hellsfrom
Production Manager: Richard Wills
Purchasing Manager: Glorijane Winslow
Estimated Sales: $25-35 Million
Number Employees: 85
Square Footage: 140000

30941 Vollrath Co LLC
1236 N 18th St
Sheboygan, WI 53081-3201
920-457-4851
800-624-2051
vollrathcompany.com
Frozen treat equipment, contract manufacturing, industrial washers and electronic cleaning equipment, and wholesale/retail consumer cookware and bakeware.
President & CEO: Paul Bartlet
VP, Human Resources: Jeff Madson
Marketing & Communications Director: Cathy Fitzgerald
SVP, Operations: Dennis Heaney
Year Founded: 1874
Estimated Sales: $100-500 Million
Number Employees: 1000-4999
Type of Packaging: Food Service
Brands:
Impressions
New York, New York
Super Pan Ii

30942 Volta Belting Technology, Inc.
11 Chapin Road
Pine Brook, NJ 07058
973-276-7905
Fax: 973-276-7908 sales@voltabelting.com
www.voltabelting.com
Food conveyor belts, power transmission & timing belts and belt welding tools.
Contact: Denise Buongiorno
denise@voltabelting.com

30943 Volumetric Technologies
401 Cannon Industrial Blvd #1
Cannon Falls, MN 55009
507-263-0034
www.volumetrictechnologies.com
Filling and packaging equipment including conveyors, cup machines, piston fillers/depositors, complete turn key filling lines, dispensing nozzles and net weight filling lines. Applications include meats, soups, dipstaco/burrito/tamale filling, chili, pizzas, bakery items, dairy products, condiments/sauces, precooked dinners, deli products and creamed meats.
President: Timothy Piper
VP: Keith Piper
VP/Secretary: Bruce Piper
Number Employees: 6
Type of Packaging: Bulk

30944 Vomela/Harbor Graphics
444 Fillmore Avenue East
St Paul, MN 55107
651-228-2200
Fax: 651-228-2295 800-645-1012
sales@vomela.com www.vomela.com
Screen and digital printing of graphics and signage for retail , fleet, P.O.P., vehicle, tradeshow and event marketing
President: Thomas Auth
President: Mark Auth
Marketing/Sales: Jeff Noren
Plant Manager: Mark Gillen
Estimated Sales: $1 - 3 Million
Number Employees: 5-9

30945 Von Gal Corp
3101 Hayneville Rd
Montgomery, AL 36108-3900
334-261-2700
Fax: 334-261-2801 800-542-6570
www.ptchronos.com

Palletizers for baking, bottling and brewing industries
Manager: Paul Probst
Sales Manager: Jason Bennett
Number Employees: 20-49

30946 Vonco Products LLC
201 Park Ave
Lake Villa, IL 60046-8999
847-356-2323
Fax: 847-356-8630 800-323-9077
sales@vonco.com www.vonarma.com
Poly and laminated bags
President: L Lawrence Laske
Chairman: Les Laske
les@vonco.com
VP Sales: Les Laske
Sales Representative: Gary Link
Estimated Sales: $10-20 Million
Number Employees: 100-249
Square Footage: 76000

30947 Voorhees Rubber Mfg Co
6846 Basket Switch Rd
Newark, MD 21841-2214
410-632-1582
Fax: 410-632-1522 info@voorheesrubber.com
www.voorheesrubber.com
Manufacturer, exporter and wholesaler/distributor of
rubber candy molds
President: Richard Jackson
info@voorheesrubber.com
Vice President: Teresa Jackson
Estimated Sales: Below $5 Million
Number Employees: 5-9
Brands:
Voorhees

30948 Vorti-Siv
36165 Salem Ganga Road
PO Box 720
Salem, OH 44460-0720
330-332-4958
Fax: 330-332-1543 800-227-7487
info@vorti-siv.com www.vorti-siv.com
Manufacturer and exporter of gyrating sieves and
tanks; self-cleaning filters
President: Barbara Maroscher
CFO: Barb Groppe
VP: Vic Maroscher
Sales: Dennis Ulrich
Plant Manager: Kevin Penner
Estimated Sales: $3 - 5,000,000
Number Employees: 10-19
Square Footage: 35000
Parent Co: MM Industries
Brands:
Vorti-Siv

30949 Vortron Smokehouse/Ovens
120 South Main Street
Iron Ridge, WI 53035
608-362-0862
Fax: 608-362-9012 800-874-1949
sales@vortronsmokehouses.com
www.vortronsmokehouses.com
Manufacturer and exporter of food processing machinery, ovens, smokehouses, drying rooms and
smoke generators
VP: Dan Mertes
Plant Manager: Dan Mertes
Estimated Sales: $2.5-5 Million
Number Employees: 10-19
Parent Co: Apache Stainless Equipment
Other Locations:
Vortron Smokehouse/Ovens
Beaver Dam WI

30950 Vorwerk
3255 E. Thousand Oaks Blvd.
Thousand Oaks, CA 91362
888-867-9375
service@thermomix.us thermomix.com
Thermomix cooking equipment.
Managing Partner: Reiner Strecker
Managing Partner: Frank Van Oers
Managing Partner: Rainer Christian Genes
Year Founded: 1883
Estimated Sales: $1-2 Billion
Number Employees: 10,000+
Brands:
Thermomix

30951 Voss Belting & Specialty Co
6965 N Hamlin Ave # 1
Lincolnwood, IL 60712-2598
847-673-8900
Fax: 847-673-1408 info@vossbelting.com
www.vossbelting.com
Rubber and thermoplastic conveyor belting; neoprene and urethane timing belts; high temperature
silicone/teflon conveyor belting
President: Richard A Voss
rvoss@vossbelt.com
Estimated Sales: $5-10 Million
Number Employees: 20-49

30952 Vrymeer Commodities
PO Box 545
St Charles, IL 60174-0545
630-377-2584

30953 Vulcan Electric Co
28 Endfield St
Porter, ME 04068-3502
207-625-3231
Fax: 207-625-8938 800-922-3027
sales@vulcanelectric.com
www.vulcanelectric.com
Manufacturer and exporter of heaters including immersion, strip and fin strip, radiant cartridge, band
and flexible; also, tubular elements, thermocouples,
programmable/mechanical temperature controls and
sensors
President: Michael Quick
General Manager: Stan Haupt
CFO: Jenet Floyd
Quality Control: Bob Doglus
Estimated Sales: $20 - 30 Million
Number Employees: 50-99
Square Footage: 50000
Brands:
Cal-Stat

30954 Vulcan Food Equipment Group
3600 North Point Blvd
Baltimore, MD 21222-2726
410-284-0662
Fax: 410-288-3662 800-814-2028
www.vulcanequipment.com
Manufacturer and exporter of broilers, steam cookers, ranges, fryers and warmers; also, bakery, food
processing, hotel, restaurant and pizza ovens
Vice President: Wally Beal
beal@vulcanequipment.com
VP Sales National Accounts: Tom Cassin
VP: Jim Cullinane
Director Sales: Dennis Ball
National Accounts Manager: Jim Thompson
Estimated Sales: $10 - 20 Million
Number Employees: 250-499
Parent Co: ITW Food Equipment Group LLC
Type of Packaging: Food Service

30955 Vulcan Industries
300 Display Dr
Moody, AL 35004-2100
205-640-2400
Fax: 205-640-2412 888-444-4417
hello@vulcanind.com www.vulcanind.com
Manufacturer and exporter of point of purchase display fixtures and products including tubular, sheet
metal, hard board, plastic and wire
VP: J Whitley
Quality Control: Steve Brugge
Manager Sales/Marketing: Douglas Stockham
Accountant: Virgil Wells
Plant Manager: James Raynor
Number Employees: 10-19
Square Footage: 330000
Parent Co: Ebsco Industries

30956 Vulcan Materials Co
1200 Urban Center Dr
P.O. Box 385014
Vestavia, AL 35242-2545
205-298-3000
Fax: 205-298-2960 www.vulcanmaterials.com
Foam cleaner, sanitizer, hard surface disinfectants,
chlorine dioxide water treatment and odor control
agents

President: David P Clement
clementd@vmcmail.com
Chairman, Chief Executive Officer: Don James
EVP, Chief Financial Officer: John R. McPherson
VP, Marketing Support Services: Sidney F. Mays
National Sales Director: Richard Higby
EVP, Chief Operating Officer: J. Thomas Hill
Estimated Sales: Over $1 Billion
Number Employees: 5000-9999
Square Footage: 240000
Brands:
Absorb
Akta Klor
Bioslide
Dura Klor
Rio Klor

30957 Vynatex
7 Carey Pl
Suite 2
Port Washington, NY 11050
516-944-6130
Fax: 516-767-7056
Custom menu covers, wine books, check presentation folders, guest service directories and in-room
hotel products including ice buckets, promotional
items, etc.
President: Angela Lamagna
angie@vynatex.com
Sales Manager: Alexander Juarez
Estimated Sales: $1-2.5 Million
Number Employees: 5-9
Square Footage: 60000
Brands:
Compu-Check
Dynahyde
Sculptathane
Scultahyde

30958 V,g,gourmet
375 Boul Roland-Therrien
Bureau 240
Longueuil, QC J4H 4A6
Canada
450-651-0777
Fax: 450-651-0775 info@vegegourmet.com
www.vegegourmet.com
Vegan and lactose-free cheeses.
Number of Products: 8
Type of Packaging: Food Service

30959 (HQ)W A Powers Co
125 S Main St
Fort Worth, TX 76104-1293
817-332-7151
Fax: 817-334-0855 800-792-1243
info@wapowers.com www.wapowers.com
Conveyor systems including gravity, wheel and
roller powered
President: Doyle Powers
dpowers@wapowers.com
Estimated Sales: $2.5-5 Million
Number Employees: 10-19
Other Locations:
Powers, W.A., Co.
Fort Worth TX

30960 W H Cooke & Co Inc
6868 York Rd
P.O. Box 893
Hanover, PA 17331-6814
717-630-2222
Fax: 717-637-9999 800-772-5151
sales@whcooke.com www.whcooke.com
Temperature and RH sensors, temperature and RH
controls, dough temperature boxes, proofer control
systems
President: Shawn Beck
shawnb@whcooke.com
Estimated Sales: Below $5 Million
Number Employees: 10-19

30961 W H Wildman Company
25956 U.S. Route 33
P.O. Box 42
New Hampshire, OH 45870
419-568-7531
Fax: 419-568-7531 scott@wildmanspice.com
www.wildmanspice.com
Wholesale packager; general groceries
Owner: Scott Gray
Estimated Sales: Less than $300,000
Number Employees: 1-4

Type of Packaging: Consumer, Food Service, Private Label, Bulk
Brands:
  Wildman's

30962 W J Egli & Co
205 E Columbia St
Alliance, OH 44601-2563
330-823-3666
Fax: 330-823-0011 info@wjegli.com
Manufacturer and exporter of wire, wood and tube display racks
President: Jeff Egli
VP: Mike Egli
Marketing Director: Jeff Egli
Estimated Sales: $2.5 - 5 Million
Number Employees: 20-49
Square Footage: 200000

30963 W L Jenkins Co
1445 Whipple Ave SW
Canton, OH 44710-1321
330-477-3407
Fax: 330-477-8404 info@wljenkinsco.com
www.wljenkinsco.com
Manufacturer and exporter of mechanically operated fire alarm systems; also, bells and gongs
Owner: Susan Jenkins
  info@wljenkinsco.com
Estimated Sales: $2.5-5 Million
Number Employees: 5-9
Parent Co: W.L. Jenkins Company

30964 W R Grace & Co
7500 Grace Dr
Columbia, MD 21044
410-531-4000
Fax: 410-531-4367 www.grace.com
Processor and exporter of silica gel absorbents; also, clarifying and anticaking agents.
President & Chief Executive Officer: Hudson La Force
Senior VP & Chief Financial Officer: William Dockman
Senior VP, Human Resources: Elizabeth Brown
Year Founded: 1832
Estimated Sales: $1.72 Billion
Number Employees: 3,900
Brands:
  Condensation Gard
  Sycoid
  Trisyl

30965 W&H Systems
120 Asia Pl
Carlstadt, NJ 07072
201-933-9849
Fax: 201-933-2144 www.whsystems.com
Provider of distribution logistics service emphasizing conveyor and computer system and integration including visual control, manifesting and paperless picking
President: Don Betman
Executive VP: Ron Quackenbush
CFO: Frank Artizone
VP: Ken Knapp
Contact: Thomas Annunziato
  gary.ciolorito@siemens.com
Estimated Sales: $20-50 Million
Number Employees: 100-249
Square Footage: 31000
Brands:
  Buschman
  Promech

30966 W.A. Golomski & Associates
N9690 County Road U
Algoma, WI 54201-9528
920-487-9864
Fax: 920-487-7249
Consultant specializing in product introductions, motivation programs and total quality management programs
President: William Golomski
Estimated Sales: Less than $500,000
Number Employees: 4

30967 W.A. Schmidt Company
99 Brower Ave
Oaks, PA 19456
215-721-8300
Fax: 215-721-5890 800-523-6719
www.pencoproducts.com

Manufacturer and exporter of storage systems and racks
President: Greg Grogan
Estimated Sales: $20-50 Million
Number Employees: 100-249
Square Footage: 246000
Brands:
  H.F. Cradle System

30968 W.G. Durant Corporation
9825 Painter Ave # A-E
Whittier, CA 90605-2700
562-946-5555
Fax: 562-946-5577
Manufacturer and exporter of palletizers, bag packers, conveyors and system electrical controls
Owner: Zara Badalian
Sales Manager: Jack Schreyer
Estimated Sales: $3 - 5 Million
Number Employees: 5-9
Square Footage: 600000
Parent Co: Westmont Industries
Brands:
  Hy-Ac Iv

30969 W.M. Barr & Co Inc.
8000 Centerview Pkwy.
Suite 400
Memphis, TN 38106
901-775-0100
Fax: 901-775-5468 wmbarr.com
Aerosols and liquid cleaners including glass and hand cleaners.
CEO: Richard Loomis
Year Founded: 1946
Estimated Sales: $100-500 Million
Number Employees: 250-499
Parent Co: W.M. Barr & Company
Brands:
  Citrus Solvent
  Klean Hand
  P&D
  Pane Relief

30970 W.M. Sprinkman Corporation
1002 Academy Street
P.O. Box 57
Elroy, WI 53929-0057
608-462-8456
Fax: 608-462-8774 800-816-1610
sales@sprinkman.com www.sprinkman.com
Agitation systems, milk, silo, tank, agitators, cutters, drainers, fines savers, forks, presses, manual, tanks, starter, custom fabrication, flow diversion stations, and ladders
General Manager: Larry Willer
Contact: Dennis Kuchel
  kucheld@sprinkman.com
Estimated Sales: $1 - 2.5 Million
Number Employees: 10-19

30971 W.Y. International
2000 S. Garfield Ave.
Los Angeles, CA 90040
323-726-8733
Fax: 323-726-9409 info@wyintl.com
www.wyintl.com
Asian sauces, canned goods, grains, and snacks; European and Californian wine and oils; machinery & tools.
President: David N. Wong
Vice President: Henry P. Wong
Year Founded: 1982
Estimated Sales: $2-5 Million
Number Employees: 2-10

30972 WA Brown & Son
209 Long Meadow Dr
Salisbury, NC 28147
704-636-5131
Fax: 704-637-0919
Manufacturer, importer and exporter of walk-in coolers, freezers, and structural insulated panels
President: Ed Brown
Vice President: Paul Brown
Sales Director: Dave Morris
Contact: Frank Preolette
  kellerrd@appstate.edu
Operations Manager: Deric Skeen
Estimated Sales: $25-50 Million
Number Employees: 100-249
Square Footage: 250000
Type of Packaging: Food Service, Private Label

Brands:
  W.A. Brown

30973 WAKO Chemicals USA Inc
1600 Bellwood Rd
N Chesterfield, VA 23237-1326
804-271-7677
Fax: 804-271-7791 labchem@wakousa.com
www.wakousa.com
Specialty chemicals
Manager: Ed Sata
R&D: Hiramatsu Max
CFO: Ed Sata
Manager: William Chang
  chang.william@wako-chem.co.jp
Estimated Sales: $20 - 50 Million
Number Employees: 20-49

30974 WCB Ice Cream
1108 Frankford Ave
Philadelphia, PA 19125-4118
215-425-4320
Fax: 215-426-2034 www.gram-equipment.com
Manufacturer and exporter of fillers, sealers, fittings, freezers, homogenizers, pumps, tanks and frozen novelty equipment
Manager: John Dorety
  jdorety@wcbicecream.com
Office Manager: Susie Margolis
Plant Manager: Vince Somers
Estimated Sales: $2.5-5 Million
Number Employees: 10-19

30975 WCB Ice Cream
267 Livingston Street
Northvale, NJ 7647
201-784-1101
Fax: 201-784-1116 800-252-5200
wcbice@wcbicecream.com
Cheese equipment, firesavers, heat exchangers, scraped surface, ice cream equipment, ingredient feeders
President: Ken Rodi
CFO: Ken Rodi
Quality Control: Harry Colber
Contact: Mick Arnold
  marnold@wcbicecream.com
Number Employees: 10,000

30976 WCB Ice Cream USA
267 Livingston Street
Northvale, NJ 07647
215-425-4320
Fax: 215-426-2034 800-644-4320
www.wcbicecream.dk
Dairy equipment and food processing machinery repair and rebuilding
Manager: John Dorety
Contact: Mick Arnold
  marnold@wcbicecream.com
Estimated Sales: $1-5 Million
Number Employees: 20-49
Parent Co: Udi And Spx.

30977 WCR
221 Crane St
Dayton, OH 45403
937-223-0703
Fax: 937-223-2818 800-421-4927
info@wcr-regasketing.com
www.wcr-regasketing.com
Plate heat exchangers
Owner: Brad Stevens
Applications Engineer: Heather Comer
Director of Sales and Technical Support: Jeremy Foley
Contact: Edward Aring
  earing@wcr-heatexchangers.com
Production Coordinator: Jenna Grigsby
Estimated Sales: $5-10 Million
Number Employees: 20-49

30978 WCS Corp
2498 American Ave
Hayward, CA 94545-1810
510-782-8727
Fax: 510-783-6843 www.royalchemical.com
Cleaning compounds, liquids and powders
Executive VP: Jeanette Conde
Estimated Sales: $20-50 Million
Number Employees: 10-19
Parent Co: Royal Chemical Company

30979 WE Killam Enterprises
PO Box 741
Waterford, ON N0E 1Y0
Canada

519-443-7421
Fax: 519-443-6922
Manufacturer, importer and exporter of packaging equipment including inkjet printers, case coding, full wrap and spot labelers, case and tray packing and sealing machinery and can ejectors, standard knapp, burt, fmc, ace/kore, ualcosystems.
President: Roger Elliott
Number Employees: 1-4
Square Footage: 5000
Brands:
  Ace & Icore
  Labellett
  Mateer-Burt
  Sauven
  Standard Knapp
  Valco

30980 WE Lyons Contruction
1301 Ygnacio Valley Rd
Walnut Creek, CA 94598

925-658-1600
Fax: 925-658-1604 800-493-5966
info@welyons.com www.welyons.com
Design-build construction; manufacturing, food service, food processing, distribution, and USDA design and construction
President: Greg Lyon
CFO: Debora Allan
Estimated Sales: $10 - 20 Million
Number Employees: 50-99

30981 (HQ)WEBB-Stiles Co
675 Liverpool Dr
PO Box 464
Valley City, OH 44280-9717

330-273-9222
Fax: 330-225-5532 webb-stiles@webb-stiles.com
www.webb-stiles.com
Manufacturer and exporter of custom designed conveyor systems for custom package and pallet handling
CEO: Donald Stiles Jr
Vice President: Larry Birchler
Sales Director: Matthew Weisman
Estimated Sales: $10-20 Million
Number Employees: 100-249
Square Footage: 600000
Other Locations:
  Webb-Stiles Co.
  Gadsden AL

30982 WEI Equipment
207 Evergreen Ave
Haddon Township, NJ 08108-3508

856-863-9577
Fax: 856-863-9641
Materials handling equipment, elevators, loaders, lifters and dumpers, used and rebuilt equipment, frozen meat slicers, flakers and breakers, grinders, mixers, screw conveyors
President: John Camp
Estimated Sales: $1-2.5 Million
Number Employees: 9

30983 WEI Equipment
4312 Jade Avenue
Cypress, CA 90630

714-827-9510
Fax: 714-209-0023 800-934-4934
Used food processing equipment for the red meat industry
Estimated Sales: $1-2.5 Million
Number Employees: 9

30984 WEIS Markets Inc.
1000 S. 2nd St.
PO Box 471
Sunbury, PA 17801

570-286-4571
866-999-9347
www.weismarkets.com
Grocery, bakery, deli, produce, floral, seafood, and more.
Chair/President/CEO: Jonathan Weis
jweis@weismarkets.com
Year Founded: 1912
Estimated Sales: $4 Billion
Number Employees: 23,000
Number of Brands: 9

Other Locations:
  Manufacturing Facility - Market St
  Sunbury PA
  Manufacturing Facility - N 4th St
  Sunbury PA
Brands:
  Full Circle
  Paws Premium
  TopCare
  Weis 360
  Weis Organic
  Weis Quality
  Weis Quality Premium Meats
  Weis Signature
  Weis Simply Great

30985 WES Plastics
561 Edward Avenue
Richmond Hill, ON L4C 9W6
Canada

905-508-1546
Displays, boxes, stands; also, custom fabrication available for acrylic items
Owner: Wayne Simpson
Number Employees: 1-4

30986 WGN Flag & Decorating Co
7984 S South Chicago Ave
Chicago, IL 60617-1096

773-768-8076
Fax: 773-768-3138 sales@wgnflag.com
www.wgnflag.com
Flags, pennants, banners and signs
President: Carl Gus Porter III
VP: Gus Porter
Estimated Sales: $1-2.5 Million
Number Employees: 10-19

30987 WITT Industries Inc
4600 N Mason Montgomery Rd
Mason, OH 45040-9176

513-923-5821
Fax: 877-891-8200 800-543-7417
sales@witt.com www.witt.com
Manufacturer and exporter of wastebaskets and firesafe steel, outside, torpedo and fiberglass waste receptacles; importer of structural foam lockers
President: Tim Harris
Chairman: Marcy Wydman
Director Sales/Marketing: Chris Adams
Purchasing Manager: Rick Royce
Estimated Sales: $10-20 Million
Number Employees: 20-49
Square Footage: 150000
Type of Packaging: Food Service

30988 WMF/USA
85 Price Parkway
Farmingdale, NY 11735-1305

704-882-3898
Fax: 631-694-0820 800-999-6347
consumer@WMFAmericas.com
Wholesaler/distributor of flatware, holloware, cookware, china and crystal
President: Stefan Nisi
VP Sales and Marketing: Peter Braley
National Sales Manager: Emma Popolow
Contact: Markus Glueck
  markus.glueck@wmf-usa.com
Parent Co: WMF/AG

30989 WNA
2155 W Longhorn Dr
Lancaster, TX 75134-2916

Fax: 972-224-3067 800-334-2877
www.wna.biz
Manufacturer and importer of plastic fabrications, containers and cups.
Number Employees: 100-249
Brands:
  Celebrity Cups

30990 WNA
5930 Quintus Loop
Chattanooga, TN 37421-2216

Fax: 800-762-4753 800-404-9318
www.wna.biz
Manufacturer and exporter of injection molded plastic disposables including platters, bowls, utensils and specialty items.
Number Employees: 100-249

30991 WNA
50 E River Center Blvd
Suite 650
Covington, KY 41011-1656

Fax: 978-256-1614 888-962-2877
Manufacturer and exporter of injection molded plastic disposables including platters, bowls, utensils and specialty items.
Estimated Sales: $50-100 Million
Number Employees: 100-249

30992 WNA Hopple Plastics
7430 Empire Drive
Florence, KY 41042-2924

859-283-1570
Fax: 859-283-0061 800-446-4622
Extruded and thermoformed custom plastic packaging including food trays and containers; also, design consultation services available
VP Sales: Brett York
Contact: Mike Evans
  mike@hopple.com
Estimated Sales: $20-50 Million
Number Employees: 250-499
Square Footage: 185000
Parent Co: John Waddington

30993 WORC Slitting & Mfg Co
50 Suffolk St # 1
Worcester, MA 01604-3792

508-754-9112
Fax: 508-754-9117 800-356-2961
info@coverallcovers.com
www.coverallcovers.com
Duty vinyl Rack Covers, Velcro Strip Doors, PVC Display Rack, Quality Controlled Anti-Bacterial Covers for Health Care Industry, Carts, Transport Bins, Racks & Equipment, Food Service Equipment, Covers for Slicers, Utility Carts, DishDollies, Mixers
CEO: George Najemy
  najemy@aol.com
Estimated Sales: $1 Million
Number Employees: 10-19
Square Footage: 60000
Type of Packaging: Bulk

30994 WOW! Factor Desserts
3508 56th Avenue
Sherwood Park, AB T8A 3X8
Canada

780-464-0303
Fax: 780-467-3604 800-604-2253
info@wowfactordesserts.com
www.wowfactordesserts.com
Canadian frozen dessert manufacturer of cheesecakes, cakes, flans, and sheet cakes. Products are hand-made, gluten-free, and vegan.
President & Owner: Debbie Gust
VP, General Manager: Colin Ruttle
EVP, Market Development: Ron Kent
National Sales Manager: Brenda Palsson
Operations Manager: Joe Swiston
Controller: Arthur Schilling
Year Founded: 1982
Estimated Sales: $10 Million
Number Employees: 51-200
Type of Packaging: Consumer, Food Service
Other Locations:
  Bakery & Retail Outlet
  Sherwood Park AB
  Distribution Centre & Bakery Outlet
  Etobicoke ON

30995 WP Bakery Group
3 Enterprise Drive
Suite 108
Shelton, CT 06484

203-929-6530
Fax: 203-929-7089 www.kemperusa.com
Bakery equipment
President: Patricia Kennedy
Controller: Karen Smith
VP Marketing/Mixer Product Manager: Shawna Goldfarb
Vice President of Sales: Bruce Gingrich
Estimated Sales: $5 Million
Number Employees: 5-9

30996 WR Key
4770 Sheppard Avenue E
Scarborough, ON M1S 3V6
Canada
416-291-6246
Fax: 416-291-4882 www.wrkey.com
Manufacturer and exporter of stainless steel serving
carts, cash boxes, desk trays and card cabinets
President and CEO: Gw Key
R&D and QC: Lisa Key
Sales Manager: Lisa Key
Estimated Sales: $5 - 10 Million
Number Employees: 40
Type of Packaging: Consumer, Food Service, Private Label

30997 (HQ)WS Packaging Group Inc
2571 S Hemlock Rd
Green Bay, WI 54229
877-977-5177
info@wspackaging.com
www.wspackaging.com
Manufacturer and exporter of labels, tags, folded
cartons, instant redeemable coupons, F.D.A. packaging and tape; also, offset printing available.
CEO: Dean Wimer
Year Founded: 1966
Estimated Sales: $400 Million
Number Employees: 1000-4999
Square Footage: 110000
Type of Packaging: Private Label
Other Locations:
  WL Group-Wisconsin Label
  Tulsa OK
Brands:
  Xl

30998 WS Packaging Group Inc
950 Breezewood Ln
Neenah, WI 54956
888-532-3334
www.wspackaging.com
Manufacturer and exporter of labels, tags, folded
cartons, instant redeemable coupons, F.D.A. packaging and tape; also, offset printing available.

30999 WS Packaging Group Inc
1102 Jefferson St
Algoma, WI 54201
800-236-3424
www.wspackaging.com
Manufacturer and exporter of labels, tags, folded
cartons, instant redeemable coupons, F.D.A. packaging and tape; also, offset printing available.

31000 WS Packaging Group Inc
3530 Pipestone Rd
Dallas, TX 75212
214-330-7770
www.wspackaging.com
Manufacturer and exporter of labels, tags, folded
cartons, instant redeemable coupons, F.D.A. packaging and tape; also, offset printing available.

31001 WS Packaging Group Inc
303 W Marquette Ave
Oak Creek, WI 53154
800-837-3838
www.wspackaging.com
Manufacturer and exporter of labels, tags, folded
cartons, instant redeemable coupons, F.D.A. packaging and tape; also, offset printing available.
Square Footage: 84000

31002 WS Packaging Group Inc
29 Jet View Dr
Rochester, NY 14624
800-836-8186
www.wspackaging.com
Manufacturer and exporter of labels, tags, folded
cartons, instant redeemable coupons, F.D.A. packaging and tape; also, offset printing available.
Type of Packaging: Consumer, Food Service, Private Label
Brands:
  Accorista
  Genisis
  Roll Tax 200
  Supergard

31003 WS Packaging Group Inc
1217 Rabas St
Algoma, WI 54201
800-323-6026
www.wspackaging.com
Labeling solutions, ranging from prime label and
equipment to promotional coupons, screen labels
and unsupported film labels for the beverage
industry

31004 WS Packaging Group Inc
1642 DeBence Dr
Franklin, PA 16323
800-372-1313
www.wspackaging.com
Manufacturer and exporter of labels, tags, folded
cartons, instant redeemable coupons, F.D.A. packaging and tape; also, offset printing available.

31005 WS Packaging Group Inc
7400 Industrial Row Dr
Mason, OH 45040-1302
800-877-9596
www.wspackaging.com
Manufacturer and exporter of labels, tags, folded
cartons, instant redeemable coupons, F.D.A. packaging and tape; also, offset printing available.

31006 WS Packaging Group Inc
2222 Beebee St
San Luis Obispo, CA 93401
800-234-3320
www.wspackaging.com
Manufacturer and exporter of labels, tags, folded
cartons, instant redeemable coupons, F.D.A. packaging and tape; also, offset printing available.

31007 WS Packaging Group Inc
7500 Industrial Row Dr
Mason, OH 45040-1302
800-877-3795
www.wspackaging.com
Manufacturer and exporter of labels, tags, folded
cartons, instant redeemable coupons, F.D.A. packaging and tape; also, offset printing available.

31008 WS Packaging Group Inc
1720 James Pkwy
Heath, OH 43056
740-929-2210
www.wspackaging.com
Manufacturer and exporter of labels, tags, folded
cartons, instant redeemable coupons, F.D.A. packaging and tape; also, offset printing available.

31009 WS Packaging Group Inc
202 Galewski Dr
Winona, MN 55987
507-452-2315
www.wspackaging.com
Manufacturer and exporter of labels, tags, folded
cartons, instant redeemable coupons, F.D.A. packaging and tape; also, offset printing available.

31010 WS Packaging Group Inc
1 Riverside Way
Wilton, NH 03086
800-258-1050
www.wspackaging.com
Manufacturer and exporter of labels, tags, folded
cartons, instant redeemable coupons, F.D.A. packaging and tape; also, offset printing available.

31011 WS Packaging Group Inc
10215 Caneel Dr
Knoxville, TN 37931
865-437-3400
www.wspackaging.com
Manufacturer and exporter of labels, tags, folded
cartons, instant redeemable coupons, F.D.A. packaging and tape; also, offset printing available.

31012 WS Packaging Group Inc
531 Airpark Dr
Fullerton, CA 92833
714-992-2574
www.wspackaging.com
Manufacturer and exporter of labels, tags, folded
cartons, instant redeemable coupons, F.D.A. packaging and tape; also, offset printing available.

31013 WS Packaging Group Inc
11 Col. La Leona
Garcia, NL
Mexico
www.wspackaging.com
Manufacturer and exporter of labels, tags, folded
cartons, instant redeemable coupons, F.D.A. packaging and tape; also, offset printing available.

31014 Wabash Power Equipment Co
444 Carpenter Ave
Wheeling, IL 60090-6081
847-541-5600
Fax: 847-541-1279 800-704-2002
info@wabashpower.com www.wabashpower.com
Deaerators, boilers, power generation equipment and
technical energy services
President: Pete Wilberscheid
  pete.wilberscheid@ubid.com
Estimated Sales: $10-20 Million
Number Employees: 20-49

31015 Waco Broom & Mop Factory
PO Box 1656
Waco, TX 76703-1656
254-753-3581
Fax: 254-753-3595 800-548-7716
msimon7760@aol.com
Mops, brooms and handles
President: Mark Simon
Number Employees: 15
Square Footage: 36000
Brands:
  Crown

31016 Waddington North America
6 Stuart Rd
Chelmsford, MA 01824-4108
978-256-6553
Fax: 978-256-1614 888-962-2877
Manufacturer and exporter of disposable plastic dinnerware, drinkware, servingware, cutlery, cutlery
packets, straws and stirrers
President: Mike Evans
CEO: Dave Gordon
CFO: Steve Morehouse
Quality Control: Tom Whitcumb
Marketing Director: Al Madonna
Contact: Russell Allen
  rallen@mswalker.com
Operations Manager: Jim Messeder
Estimated Sales: $25-100 Million
Number Employees: 250-499
Square Footage: 12000
Parent Co: Waddington PLC
Brands:
  Classic Crystal
  Classicware
  Comet
  Crystal Flex
  Designerware
  Frost Flex

31017 Wade Manufacturing Company
PO Box 23666
Tigard, OR 97281-3666
503-692-5353
Fax: 503-692-5358 800-222-7246
sales@waderain.com www.waderain.com
Manufacturer and exporter of agricultural irrigation
systems including handrove, poweroll and center
pivot; also, micro irrigation products and aluminum
casters
President: Ed Newbegin
VP: Cliff Warner
Contact: Pierre Lameh
  plameh@waderain.com
Estimated Sales: $20-50 Million
Number Employees: 50-99
Parent Co: R.M. Wade & Company
Brands:
  Wade Rain

31018 WaffleWaffle
43 River Rd
Nutley, NJ 07110-3411
201-559-1286
info@mywafflewaffle.com
mywafflewaffle.com
Waffles: Belgian-style, cones, doughs, mixes, and
waffle irons.

Co-Founder: Justin Samuels
Co-Founder: Samuel Rockwell
Vice President, Business Development: Brian Samuels
Chief Marketing Officer: David Song
Vice President, Sales: Bracken Abrams
Director of Operations: Grant Ramsey
Estimated Sales: $2 Million
Number Employees: 12
Type of Packaging: Consumer, Food Service, Private Label
Brands:
  WaffleWaffle

31019 Wag Industries
4117 Grove Street
Skokie, IL 60076-1713
773-638-7007
Fax: 773-533-6951 800-621-3305
blunt232@aol.com
Manufacturer and exporter of mobile catering truck units including bar and hot dog carts
President: Gail Gilbert
CEO: Doris Gilbert
CFO: George Gilbert
Quality Control: Gavin London
Purchasing Manager: Gavin Lendan
Estimated Sales: $5-10 Million
Number Employees: 10

31020 Wagner Brothers Containers
4101 Ashland Ave
Baltimore, MD 21205-2924
410-354-0044
Fax: 410-354-3125
Corrugated boxes
President: Lawrence K Wagner
VP: Lawrence Wagner Jr
Contact: Bill Hampton
bhampton@commercialwagner.com
Estimated Sales: $10 - 20 Million
Number Employees: 50-99

31021 Wahlstrom Manufacturing
15235 Boyle Ave
Fontana, CA 92337-7254
909-822-4677
Fax: 909-822-1675
Wire point-of-purchase display racks
Owner: Zach Fener
Estimated Sales: 700000
Number Employees: 5-9
Square Footage: 16000

31022 Wal-Vac
900 47th St SW # A
Suite A
Wyoming, MI 49509-5142
616-241-6717
Fax: 616-241-1771 info@walvac.com
www.walvac.com
Manufacturer and exporter of built-in central vacuum cleaning systems
President: David Mol
walvac@walvac.com
VP Operations: David Mol
Estimated Sales: Less Than $500,000
Number Employees: 1-4
Square Footage: 19200
Brands:
  Wal-Vac

31023 Walco
820 Noyes St
PO Box 10527
Utica, NY 13502-5053
315-733-4663
Fax: 315-733-6602 800-879-2526
sales@walcostainless.com
www.walcostainless.com
Manufacturer, importer and exporter of stainless steel flatware, steak knives, hollow ware, buffetware, and chafers
President: David S Allen
Sales/Marketing: Philip Benbenek
Contact: Phil Bembenek
phil@walcostainless.com
Estimated Sales: $10 - 20 Million
Number Employees: 100-249
Square Footage: 225000
Parent Co: Utica Cutlery Company
Type of Packaging: Food Service
Brands:
  Walco

31024 Walco-Linck Company
PO Box 5643
Bellingham, WA 98227-5643
845-353-7600
Fax: 845-353-8056 800-338-2329
Manufacturer and exporter of aerosol insecticides, ant and roach baits and fly paper
President: William Burge
Executive VP: Richard Bozzo
CFO and QC: Richard Bozzo
Estimated Sales: $5 - 10 Million
Number Employees: 15
Brands:
  Tat

31025 Wald Imports
11200 Kirkland Way
Suite 300
Kirkland, WA 98033
425-822-0500
Fax: 425-828-4201 800-426-2822
alsnel@waldimports.com www.waldimports.com
Decorative containers for gift baskets and floral
President: Lou Wald
Controller: Greg Best
VP: Martin Sippy
Sales Coordinator: Andria Blizzard
Contact: Gregory Best
gregorybest@waldimports.com
Order Entry & Invoicing: Gwen McClellan
Estimated Sales: $3.8 Million
Number Employees: 23

31026 Wald Wire & Mfg Co
846 Witzel Ave
Oshkosh, WI 54902-5796
920-231-5590
Fax: 920-231-2212 800-236-0053
waldwire@waldwire.com www.waldwire.com
Wire racks for refrigerators and displays, wire forms, shelving, guards
President: Bob Mueller
rmueller@waldwire.com
Estimated Sales: Below $10 Million
Number Employees: 20-49

31027 Waldon Manufacturing LLC
201 W Oklahoma Ave
Fairview, OK 73737-9602
580-227-3711
Fax: 580-227-2165 800-486-0023
www.waldonequipment.com
Forklift trucks, lift truck attachments and compact wheel loaders
Owner: Greg Wickert
CEO: Don Collins Jr
Sales Director: Tim Carroll
Public Relations: Kent Tyler
Operations Manager: Ricky Heflin
Number Employees: 10-19
Brands:
  Lay-Mor
  Waldon

31028 Walker Bag Mfg Co
11198 Ampere Ct
Louisville, KY 40299-3879
502-266-5696
Fax: 502-266-9823 800-642-4949
bagmann@aol.com www.printex-usa.com
Custom designed burlap, canvas, cotton, jute, paper, tote and polypropylene bags; importer of polypropylene bags
CEO: Steve Dutton
steved@printex-usa.com
VP: Steve Dutton
Estimated Sales: $5-10 Million
Number Employees: 20-49

31029 Walker Brush Inc
82 E Main St # 4
Webster, NY 14580-3243
585-545-4748
Fax: 585-342-2264 pgtaft@frontiernet.net
www.brushmfg.com
Brushes
Owner: Tom Erb
Sales Director: Timothy Mura
tom@brushmfg.com
Estimated Sales: $500,000-$1 Million
Number Employees: 5-9

31030 Walker Co
121 NW 6th St
Oklahoma City, OK 73102-6026
405-235-5319
Fax: 405-235-1698 800-522-3015
info@walkercompanies.com
www.walkercompanies.com
Signs, banners and marking devices including rubber stamps
Manager: Sue Stephens
Quality Control: Sue Steven
VP: Kenny Walker
Manager: Melissa Rust
Estimated Sales: Below $5 Million
Number Employees: 20-49

31031 Walker Engineering Inc
9255 San Fernando Rd
Sun Valley, CA 91352-1416
818-252-7788
Fax: 818-252-7785 www.walkerairsep.com
Signs, awnings, canopies, flags, pennants and banners
Owner: Robert Walker
sales@airsep.com
Estimated Sales: Below $5 Million
Number Employees: 20-49
Type of Packaging: Bulk

31032 Walker Magnetics Group Inc
20 Rockdale St
Worcester, MA 01606-1922
508-853-3232
Fax: 508-852-8649 800-962-4638
sales@walkermagnet.com
www.walkermagnet.com
Designer and manufacturer of magnetic workholding chucks, lifting, material handling, and separation applications.
Owner: Eric Englested
Plant Manager: Dick Isabell
Estimated Sales: Below $5 Million
Number Employees: 100-249

31033 Walker Magnetics Group Inc
20 Rockdale St
Worcester, MA 01606-1922
508-853-3232
Fax: 508-852-8649 800-962-4638
info@walkermagnet.com www.walkermagnet.com
Suppliers of conveying systems tailored to the canmaking and can filling industries, magnetic cable conveyors, elevators, loverators, palletizing heads, magnetic twist conveyors, end handling conveyors, magnetic rails, rollers andcomplete turnkey systems
Owner: Eric Englested
Estimated Sales: $10 - 20 Million
Number Employees: 100-249

31034 Walker Stainless Equipment Co
625 W State St
New Lisbon, WI 53950
608-562-7500
www.walkerep.com
Manufacturer and exporter of stainless steel transportation and plant equipment tanks for the dairy industry.
Year Founded: 1943
Estimated Sales: $250-500 Million
Number Employees: 1000-4999
Square Footage: 200000
Parent Co: Wabash National Corporation
Brands:
  Norman Machinery
  Walker

31035 Wall Conveyor & Manufacturing
PO Box 7664
Huntington, WV 25778-7664
304-429-1335
Fax: 304-429-1337 800-456-1335
Package handling conveyors including rebuilt; also, accessories
Owner: Jim Fankhanel
Office Manager: Liz Rexroad
Estimated Sales: $1-2.5 Million
Number Employees: 1-4
Square Footage: 12000

31036 Wallace & Hinz
100 Taylor Way
P.O. Box 708
Blue Lake, CA 95525
707-668-1825
Fax: 707-826-0224 800-831-8282
info@wallaceandhinz.com
www.wallaceandhinz.com
Manufacturer and exporter of bars including portable and modular
Owner: Tom Tellez
Sales Manager: Richard Cook
Estimated Sales: $10-20 Million
Number Employees: 20-49
Square Footage: 30000

31037 Wallace Computer Services
111 South Wacker Drive
Chicago, IL 60606
312-326-8000
Fax: 312-326-8001 888-925-8324
www.wallace.com
Prime, pressure sensitive and linerless labels, bar code and ingredient labeling software and printers including automatic label applicators and dispensers and bar code
Owner: Tushar Pandya
President, Chief Executive Officer: Thomas Quinlan
VP: David Jones
General Sales Manager: Chuck Wilson
Senior Vice President of Public Affairs: Gian-Carlo Peressutti
Estimated Sales: $10-20 Million
Number Employees: 1-4
Parent Co: Wallace Computer Services
Other Locations:
Wallace Computer Services
Hinsdale IL
Brands:
Label-Aire
Printware

31038 Wallace Computer Services
2275 Cabot Dr
Lisle, IL 60532
630-588-5000
Fax: 630-588-5115 800-323-8447
www.wallace.com
Printed business forms, packaging labels, automatic applicators and bar coding software, direct mail, point of purchase products and product collateral
President: Mike Duffield
Estimated Sales: $50-100 Million
Number Employees: 250-499

31039 Walle Corp
600 Elmwood Park Blvd
New Orleans, LA 70123-3350
504-734-8000
Fax: 504-733-2513 800-942-6761
www.walle.com
Manufacturer and exporter of labels for cans, bottles, plastics, etc.; also, lithographic and flexographic printing available
Vice President: Allen Dummitt
allen_dummitt@walle.com
Vice Chairman/CEO: Michael Keeney
VP: Colleen Rottmann
Estimated Sales: $20-50 Million
Number Employees: 100-249
Square Footage: 300000

31040 Walnut Packaging Inc
450 Smith St
Farmingdale, NY 11735-1105
631-293-3836
Fax: 631-293-3878 info@wpiplasticbags.com
www.wpiplasticbags.com
Manufacturer and exporter of polyethylene bags; also, print designers
Owner: Jose Alvarado
Estimated Sales: $2.5-5 Million
Number Employees: 10-19

31041 Walong Marketing
6281 Regio Ave.
Buena Park, CA 90620-1040
714-670-8899
Fax: 714-670-6668 www.asianfoodsonline.com
Asian foods: rice, cereal and grains, baking mixes, soups, vegetables, fruits, snacks, confections, condiments, sauces, drinks, deli, seafood, meats, kitchenware and canned foods.

Merchandiser: Tony Chiu
Chief Operating Officer: Coo Chen
Product Manager: Nancy Hsu
Estimated Sales: $73.2 Million
Number Employees: 130
Other Locations:
Beuena Park CA
Bolingbrook IL
Duluth GA
Jersey City NJ
Stafford TX

31042 Walsh & Simmons Seating
2511 Iowa Ave
Saint Louis, MO 63104
314-664-1215
Fax: 314-664-0703 800-727-0364
sales@walshsimmons.com
www.walshsimmons.com
Manufacturer and exporter of benches, booths, chairs and cushion pads, stools and tables including legs and bases
President: Bill Simmons
Contact: Tony Pezzo
tonyp@walshsimmons.com
Estimated Sales: $10 - 20 Million
Number Employees: 100-249
Square Footage: 400000
Type of Packaging: Food Service

31043 Walsroder Packaging
7330 South Madison Street
Willowbrook, IL 60527-5588
Fax: 630-789-8489 800-882-9987
sales@walsroder.com
www.walsroderpackaging.com
Plastic and fibrous food casings for sausages and deli meats.
Contact: Gregg Alex
greggalex@walsroderpackaging.com

31044 Waltco Truck Equipment Company
285 Northeast Ave
Tallmadge, OH 44278
330-633-9191
Fax: 330-633-1418 800-211-3074
sales@waltco.com
Truck and hydraulic cylinder electrohydraulic tailgate lifts
CEO: Rod Robinson
Director Marketing/Sales: Ray Thompson
Contact: Chris Adkins
christopher.adkins@waltco.com
Estimated Sales: $30 - 50 Million
Number Employees: 100-249

31045 Walter Molzahn & Company
1050 W Fullerton Avenue
Chicago, IL 60614
312-528-0550
Cake ornaments and decorations
Type of Packaging: Private Label

31046 Walters Brothers
10489 W State Road 27 70
Radisson, WI 54867-7084
715-945-2646
Fax: 715-945-2878
Brite stack pallets
President: Tim Walters
tim.walters@waltersbrotherslumber.com
Vice President: Timothy Walters
Estimated Sales: $7 Million
Number Employees: 20-49
Square Footage: 20000

31047 Waltham Fruit Company
105 2nd St
Chelsea, MA 02150-1803
617-354-1994
Fax: 617-354-8423 www.baldor.com
Owner: Pat Pizzuto
Chief Executive Officer: Ronald Tucker
Vice President of Materials: Amy Lakin
Vice President of International Sales: Joe Maloney
Estimated Sales: $10-20 Million
Number Employees: 20-49

31048 Walton's Inc
3639 N Comotara St
Wichita, KS 67226-1304
316-262-0651
Fax: 316-262-5136 800-835-2832
www.waltonsinc.com
Manufacturer and exporter of brine pumps; wholesaler/distributor of meat processing equipment and butchers' supplies including saws, slicers and tenderizers, vacuum machines and bags and smokehouses
Owner: Don Walton
CEO: Brett Walton
brett@waltonsinc.com
Sales Director: Kurt Carter
Sales: Mark Schrag
Operations Manager: Brett Walton
Production Manager: Tim Fox
Purchasing Manager: Brett Walton
Estimated Sales: $1.8 Million
Number Employees: 20-49
Number of Brands: 25
Number of Products: 200
Square Footage: 71000
Type of Packaging: Food Service
Brands:
Double J

31049 Wang Cheong CorporationUSA
193 6th Street
Brooklyn, NY 11215-3104
718-222-0880
Fax: 718-222-9037
Adhesive, stationary and printed tape

31050 Ward Ironworks
2 Broadway Avenue
Welland, ON L3B 5G4
Canada
905-732-7591
Fax: 905-732-3310 888-441-9273
Manufacturer, importer and exporter of material handling machinery including bucket elevators, regular and vibrating conveyors, empty bag compactors, vibrating feeders and screens
President: Guy Nelson
Estimated Sales: $5-10 Million
Number Employees: 10
Square Footage: 200000
Parent Co: Ward Automation

31051 Wardcraft Conveyor & Quick Die
1 Wardcraft Dr
Spring Arbor, MI 49283-9757
517-750-9100
Fax: 517-750-2244 800-782-2779
info@wardcraft.net www.wardcraftconveyor.com
Manufacturer and exporter of pneumatic conveyors and quick die change systems
President: Pat Sprague
psprague@wardcraft.net
VP: Pat Sprague
National Sales: Paul Miner
Estimated Sales: $5 - 10 Million
Number Employees: 20-49
Square Footage: 72000

31052 Waring Products
314 Ella Grasso Ave
Torrington, CT 06790-2345
860-496-3100
Fax: 860-496-9008 800-492-7464
waring@conair.com www.waringproducts.com
Manufacturer, exporter and importer of commercial food processors, blenders, juice extractors, bar glass washers, rod mixers, food choppers, slicers, ice crushers and glass and can crushers
Manager: Richard Dombroski
HR Executive: James Mc Closkey
james_mccloskey@conair.com
CFO: James McCooskey
Consultant: Larry Casalino
Estimated Sales: $5 - 10 Million
Number Employees: 50-99
Parent Co: Dynamics Corporation of America
Type of Packaging: Food Service
Brands:
Acme
Qualheim
Waring

31053 Warner Electric Inc
449 Gardner St
South Beloit, IL 61080-1397
815-389-3771
Fax: 815-389-6425 800-234-3369
info@warnerelectric.com
www.warnerelectric.com
the Colfax Power Transmission Group is a leading
supplier of mechanical and electrical power transmission products to the food processing and packaging industries. With hundreds of years of industry
experience, Colfax PT has developedsome of the
premier products, delivery programs and services
available today.
Marketing VP: Craig Schuele
Sales Manager: Jan Dixon
Contact: Warner Ab
hakan.persson@tollo.com
Number Employees: 1000-4999
Type of Packaging: Bulk

31054 Warren Analytical Laboratory
650 O St
Greeley, CO 80631
970-475-0252
Fax: 970-475-0280 800-945-6669
info@warrenlab.com www.warrenlab.com
Analytical food testing laboratory offering services
for nutritional labeling, microbiological testing,
chemistry and residue analysis
President: Rob Yemm
Vice President: Michael Aaronson
Sales Director: Kristen Peter
Contact: Michael Aaronson
amichael@warrenlab.com
Estimated Sales: $2.5-5 Million
Number Employees: 20-49
Square Footage: 24000
Parent Co: ConAgra Foods

31055 Warren E. Conley Corporation
1099 3rd Ave SW
Carmel, IN 46032-2564
317-846-5890
Fax: 317-846-5899 800-367-7875
Manufacturer and wholesaler/distributor of mainte-
nance and cleaning products including brooms,
brushes, cleaning polish and concentrates, hand
soap, window cleaners, insecticides, kitchen de-
greasers, lime/rust remover, bowl cleansersdrain
openers and squeegees
President: Kevin Conley
Estimated Sales: $1-2.5 Million
Number Employees: 1 to 4
Brands:
Blue Satin
Butter Better
Butter Up
Cut-Off
Dapper Actor
Dapper Duster
Drain Warden
Kleenitol
Kleenzup
Leplus Ultra
Lime Lite
Miss Kriss
One-For-All
Pastry Pal
Power Quota
Reveal
Satin Doll
Satin Fan
Showtime
Softasilk
Sparkle 'n' Glo
Sqyer
Star Guard
Swab 'n' Smile
Terminator
Tyle Style
W C Insect Finish One
Warcon Out

31056 Warren Packaging
879 East Rialto Avenue
San Bernardino, CA 92408
909-888-7008
Fax: 714-690-2905 phil@warrenpkg.com
Folding cartons, marketing displays and packaging
solutions
Estimated Sales: $300,000-500,000
Number Employees: 1-4

31057 Warren Pallet Co Inc
601 County Road 627
Bloomsbury, NJ 08804-3426
908-995-7172
Fax: 908-995-4146
Reconditioned wooden pallets; various sizes avail-
able
Owner: Donald Tigar Sr
warrenpalletco@ptd.net
VP Marketing (Special Projects): J Bernard Noll Jr
Estimated Sales: $10-20 Million
Number Employees: 20-49

31058 (HQ)Warren Rupp Inc
800 N Main St
Mansfield, OH 44902-4209
419-524-8388
Fax: 419-522-7867 www.warrenruppinc.com
Air-operated, double-diaphragm pumps and accesso-
ries
President: John Carter
Co-Founder: Charles Young Jr
District Manager: Tim Zetzman
Estimated Sales: $2,500,000 - $4,999,999
Number Employees: 100-249
Parent Co: IDEX Corporation
Brands:
Sandpiper

31059 Warrenton Products
1410 E Old Us Highway 40
Warrenton, MO 63383-1316
636-456-3492
Fax: 636-456-3422
Contract packaging
Estimated Sales: $50-100 Million
Number Employees: 100-249

31060 Warsaw Chemical Co Inc
390 Argonne Rd
Warsaw, IN 46580-3884
574-267-3251
Fax: 574-267-3884 800-548-3396
wcc@warsaw-chem.com www.warsaw-chem.com
Manufacturer and exporter of sanitary chemicals and
compounds
President: Ken Bucher
ken-bucher@warsaw-chem.com
R & D: Jeff Rufner
Quality Control: Scott Ware
Estimated Sales: $10-20 Million
Number Employees: 50-99

31061 Warther Museum
331 Karl Ave
Dover, OH 44622-2767
330-343-7513
Fax: 330-343-1443 info@warthers.com
www.warthercutlery.com
Cutlery
President: Mark Warther
markw@warthers.com
CFO: Juanne Warther
Quality Control: Dale Warther
Estimated Sales: $1 - 3 Million
Number Employees: 10-19
Square Footage: 10000
Brands:
Warther Handcrafted Cutlery

31062 Warwick Manufacturing &Equip
1112 12th St
North Brunswick, NJ 08902-1869
732-729-0400
Fax: 732-729-1235
sales@warwickequipment.com
Manufacturer and exporter of new, used and rebuilt
packaging and bakery food processing equipment
Managing Director: Gregory Pantchenko
Estimated Sales: Below $500,000
Number Employees: 1-4
Square Footage: 25000

31063 Warwick Products
5350 Tradex Pkwy
Cleveland, OH 44102-5887
216-334-1200
Fax: 216-334-1201 800-535-4404
info@warwickproducts.com
www.warwickproducts.com
Bulk food and bakery displays, barrels, store fixtures
and bins including bagel, bulk and candy

Owner: Matt Beverstock
info@warwickproducts.com
General Manager: John Heim
Sales Manager: Jon Murray
info@warwickproducts.com
Estimated Sales: $1-2.5 Million
Number Employees: 50-99

31064 Washing Systems
167 Commerce Dr
Loveland, OH 45140-7727
513-870-4830
Fax: 513-870-4850 800-272-1974
sales@washingsystems.com
www.washingsystems.com
Pallet and tote washers
Owner: Robert Fisher
rfisher@washingsystems.com
VP: Gary Turnbull
Sales Manager: James Smylie
rfisher@washingsystems.com
Estimated Sales: $1 - 3 Million
Number Employees: 50-99
Brands:
The Eliminator

31065 Washington Frontier
PO Box 249
Grandview, WA 98930-0249
509-469-7662
Fax: 509-469-7739
Used process equipment sales and fruit and vegeta-
ble juice sales
Manager General Operations: Joe Stoops
Estimated Sales: $10 - 15 Million
Number Employees: 50-100

31066 Washington Group International
600 Montgomery Street
26th Floor
San Francisco, CA 94111-2728
205-995-7878
Fax: 205-995-7777 800-877-0980
www.urs.com
Design consultant providing engineering, procure-
ment, construction and environmental services
VP: Charles Dietz
Marketing/Sales: Bill Lott
Contact: Scott Wilson
scott.wilson@wgint.com
Estimated Sales: $1 - 5 Million
Number Employees: 500-999
Square Footage: 2000000
Parent Co: Washington Group International

31067 Washington Group International
1020 31st St # 300
Downers Grove, IL 60515-5578
630-829-3000
Fax: 630-829-3513
Worldwide design and construction of manufactur-
ing plants for: processed/packaged foods, beverages,
agro-industrial
Manager: Robert Nickel
Marketing: Paul Kervan
Sales Director: Gail Luttinen
Contact: John Lasota
john.lasota@wgint.com
Estimated Sales: $50-100 Million
Number Employees: 250-499

31068 Washington State Juice
10725 Sutter Ave
Pacoima, CA 91331-2553
818-899-1195
Fax: 818-899-6042
Manufactures and processes fruit concentrates,
blends and natural flavors. Custom blending is
available
President: Fred Farago
Estimated Sales: $.5 - 1 million
Number Employees: 100-249
Type of Packaging: Food Service, Private Label,
Bulk

31069 Wasserman Bag Company
26 Frowein Road
Center Moriches, NY 11934
631-909-8656
Fax: 631-878-1569 www.wassermanbag.com
Master distributor of bags including paper, burlap,
mesh, polyethylene and polyproylene; also, tapes,
wire and waxed and dry boxes as well as packaging
equipment

President: Karen Wasserman
Operations Manager: Charlie Greco
Estimated Sales: $2.5 - 5 Million
Number Employees: 10-19
Type of Packaging: Consumer, Food Service, Bulk

31070 Waste Away Systems
132 S 30th St # B
Newark, OH 43055-1994
                    740-349-2783
   Fax: 813-222-0220   800-223-4741
        www.wasteawaysystems.com
Compactors, balers and waste reduction and recycling equipment for hospitals, schools and restaurants
President: Dennis Calnan
VP Sales: David Fagan
Office Manager: Glenda O'Hara
Estimated Sales: $1-2.5 Million
Number Employees: 10-19
Square Footage: 80000
Brands:
    Advance 2000
    Convenience Pac 1000
    Custom Pac 2000
    Twin Chamber 3002
    Twin Pac 2203
    Twin Pac 2204
    Twin Pac 2205

31071 Waste King Commercial
PO Box 4146
Anaheim, CA 92803-4146
                    714-524-7770
   Fax: 714-996-7073   800-767-6293
        www.anaheimmfg.com
President: Thomas P Dugan
Number Employees: 100-249

31072 Waste Minimization/Containment
2140 Scranton Rd
Cleveland, OH 44113-3544
                    216-696-8797
 Fax: 216-696-8794 jbecker@cryogenesis-usa.com
        www.cryogenesis-usa.com
Manufacturer and exporter of dry ice blast cleaning equipment
President: Jim Becker
   jbecker@cryogenesis-usa.com
Sales Manager: John Whalen
Estimated Sales: Less Than $500,000
Number Employees: 1-4
Brands:
    Cryogenesis

31073 Wastequip Inc
6525 Morrison Blvd # 300
Suite 300
Charlotte, NC 28211-0500
                    704-366-7140
        sales@wastequip.com
        www.wastequip.com
Manufacturer and exporter of waste handling equipment including compactors, hoists, balers, etc
Manager: Bram Chappell
CEO: Christine Anastasio
   canastasio@wastequip.com
VP Sales/Marketing: Donald Sharp
Owner: Roy Holt
Estimated Sales: $5 - 10 Million
Number Employees: 1000-4999
Square Footage: 308000
Type of Packaging: Bulk

31074 Wastequip Teem
6526 Morrison Blvd
Suite 300
Charlotte, NC 28211
                    605-336-1333
   Fax: 605-334-8704 877-468-9278
   sales@wastequip.com www.wastequip.com
Manufacturer and exporter of rear-end loading refuse containers
Manager: Val Bochenek
Estimated Sales: $2.5-5 Million
Number Employees: 20-49
Parent Co: Wastequip

31075 Water & Oil Technologies Inc
52 Eastfield Rd
Montgomery, IL 60538-2402
                    630-892-2007
   Fax: 630-892-7472   800-841-6580
        fuelalternatives@sbcglobal.net

Waste treatment and by-product use equipment including natural florculents, systhetic cationic, nonionic florculents and equipment and by-product recovery and marketing assistance
President: Ed Laurent
Estimated Sales: $500,000-$1 Million
Number Employees: 1-4

31076 (HQ)Water & Power Technologies
P.O. Box 27836
Salt Lake City, UT 84127
                    801-974-5500
   Fax: 801-973-9733 888-271-3295
Manufacturer and exporter of custom designed skid-mounted and mobile water purification systems including reverse osmosis, demineralization, electrodeionization, ultrafiltration, manganese, greensand filters, softners, carbon towersand in-line filtration, etc.
General Manager: Jim Laraway
Controller: Tom Kirkland
Sales: Bryan Schillar
Purchase Manager: Chuck Gendre
Sales/Marketing: James Laraway
Contact: Alan Acker
   alan.acker@a-wpt.com
Operations: Fred Farmer
Plant/Production Manager: Emma Anderson
Purchasing: Lee Courtney
Estimated Sales: $10 - 20 Million
Number Employees: 50-99
Square Footage: 84000
Type of Packaging: Consumer
Other Locations:
    Water & Power Technologies
    Portland OR
    Water & Power Technologies
    Denver CO
    Water & Power Technologies
    Dallas TX
    Water & Power Technologies
    Columbia SC
    Water & Power Technologies
    Houston TX
    Water & Power Technologies
    Ontario, Canada
Brands:
    Smart-Ro
    Superskids
    Waterpro

31077 Water Equipment Svc
818 Cattlemen Rd
Sarasota, FL 34232-2811
                    941-371-4995
   Fax: 941-377-2649 www.wesinc.com
Water treatment aeration and degassing equipment; gravity filters
Owner: Anthony DE Loach
   tonyd@wesinc.com
VP: Laurie Deloach
Estimated Sales: $2.5 - 5 Million
Number Employees: 10-19

31078 Water Furnace RenewableEnergy
9000 Conservation Way
Fort Wayne, IN 46809-9794
                    260-478-5667
   Fax: 260-747-2828 www.waterfurnace.com
Manufacturer and exporter of geothermal heating and cooling systems
CEO: Tom Huntington
CEO: Bruce Ritchey
Director Sales: Mike Murphy
Estimated Sales: $20,000,000 - $49,999,999
Number Employees: 500-999
Type of Packaging: Food Service

31079 Water Management Resources
PO Box 219
Overton, NV 89040-0219
                    706-743-0870
   Fax: 702-397-8450 800-552-5797
        www.watermr.com
Providing food safety and water conservation
Design & Engineering: Terry Griffiths
Field Sales: Greg Bilyeu
General Manager: Larry Griffiths
Number Employees: 1-4

31080 Water Savers Worldwide
PO Box 1101
Santa Barbara, CA 93102
                    916-354-0718
Wine industry water treatment

Owner: Bill Wampler
Owner: Lori Wampler

31081 Water Sciences Services, Inc.
280 Emmans Road
PO Box 5000-364
Jackson, TN 38302
                    973-584-4131
        Fax: 731-660-4115
Manufacturer and exporter of ice cubing/bagging machinery, bottled water sanitizers, bottled spring water, descaling equipment and water filters
President: Elizabeth Reed
Vice President: Paul Reed
Estimated Sales: $1-2.5 Million
Number Employees: 15
Square Footage: 36000
Brands:
    Crystal Clean

31082 Water System Group
27737 Bouquet Canyon Rd # 126
Santa Clarita, CA 91350-3743
                    661-297-6294
   Fax: 818-597-9923 800-350-9283
Reverse osmosis, carbon filtration and water softening systems
Owner: Miguel Alvarez
VP: Martin Swanson
Estimated Sales: $1 - 5,000,000
Number Employees: 1-4

31083 Waterlink Technologies
3610 Quantum Blvd
Boynton Beach, FL 33426-8637
                    561-684-6300
   Fax: 561-697-3342 800-684-4844
        www.wetpurewater.com
Water purification systems, filters
General Manager: Audrey Pinkerton
Engineering Manager: Mike Mudrick
Operations Manager: Jason Gallegly
Estimated Sales: $10-25 Million
Number Employees: 50-99

31084 Waterlink/Sanborn Technologies
4100 Holiday Street NW
Canton, OH 44718-2556
                    330-649-4000
   Fax: 330-649-4008 800-343-3381
        www.waterlink.com
Manufacturer and exporter of liquid/solid separation equipment and systems, wastewater pretreatment and food waste dewatering systems
VP Operations: Steve Friedman
Estimated Sales: Below $500,000
Number Employees: 4
Square Footage: 180000

31085 Waterloo Container
2311 State Route 414
Waterloo, NY 13165-9440
                    315-539-3922
   Fax: 315-539-9380 888-539-3922
   wcbottles@flare.net www.fastfromstock.com
Wine industry bottles and packaging
Owner: Ben Ahner
CFO: William Lutz
Sales: Mike Shaffer
   ben@waterloocontainer.com
Chief Operating Officer: John Dixon
Estimated Sales: $1 - 2.5 Million
Number Employees: 10-19

31086 Waters Corp
34 Maple St
Milford, MA 01757-3696
                    508-478-2000
   Fax: 508-872-1990 800-252-4752
   customerservice@waters.com www.waters.com
Liquid chromatography, mass spectrometry, and thermal analysis.
President & CEO: Christopher O'Connell
Chairman: Flemming Ornskov
Year Founded: 1959
Estimated Sales: $2.3 Billion
Number Employees: 7,200
Brands:
    Andrew Alliance
    ERA
    Nonlinear Dynamics
    TA Instruments
    VICAM

31087 Watershed Foods
202 N Ford St
Gridley, IL 61744-3902
309-747-3000
Fax: 309-747-4647
jill.legner@watershedfoods.com
Contract processor of yogurt, purees, fruits and other healthy snacks. Services include freeze drying and pumpable liquids and R&D test drying.
President & COO: Jeremy Zobrist
jeremy.zobrist@watershedfoods.com
CFO: Lynette Schick
Director of Food Quality & Safety: Craig Hammond
VP Sales & Marketing: Brandon Rinkenberger
VP & Director Operations: Marc Johnson
Manager: Jill Legner
Estimated Sales: $4.3 Million
Number Employees: 5-9

31088 (HQ)Watlow Electric
12001 Lackland Rd
St Louis, MO 63146
314-878-4600
Fax: 314-878-6814 info@watlow.com
www.watlow.com
Designer and manufacturer of heaters, sensors, controllers and software.
CEO: Peter Desloge
SVP & CFO: Steve Desloge
Year Founded: 1922
Estimated Sales: $330 Million
Number Employees: 2,000
Type of Packaging: Food Service

31089 Watlow Electric
5710 Kenosha St
Richmond, IL 60071
info@watlow.com
www.watlow.com
Designer and manufacturer of heaters, sensors, controllers and software.
Estimated Sales: $330 Million
Number Employees: 2,000
Parent Co: Watlow
Type of Packaging: Food Service
Other Locations:
    Watlow
    Columbia MO
    Watlow
    Winona MN
Brands:
    Xactpak

31090 Watlow Electric
6781 Via Del Oro
San Jose, CA 95119
www.watlow.com
Designer and manufacturer of heaters, sensors, controllers and software.
Estimated Sales: $330 Million
Number Employees: 2,000

31091 Watts Premier Inc
8716 W Ludlow Dr # 1
Peoria, AZ 85381-4918
480-675-7995
Fax: 602-866-5666 800-752-5582
mail@premierh2o.com www.premierh2o.com
Manufacturer and exporter of water purification equipment
Vice President: Shannon Murphy
VP: Shannon Murphy
Estimated Sales: $5-10 Million
Number Employees: 20-49
Parent Co: Watts Water Technologies Co.

31092 Watts Radiant Inc
4500 E Progress Pl
Springfield, MO 65803-8816
417-864-6108
Fax: 417-864-8161 800-255-1996
www.wattsradiant.com
President: Mike Chiles
CEO: John Kolson
kolsonj@watts.com
Estimated Sales: $1 - 5 Million
Number Employees: 100-249

31093 Watts Regulator Co
815 Chestnut St
North Andover, MA 01845-6098
978-688-1811
Fax: 978-794-1848 www.wattswater.com
Valves, grease interceptors and drains.

President & CEO: Robert Pagano, Jr.
Year Founded: 1874
Estimated Sales: $224 Million
Number Employees: 100-249
Parent Co: Watts Industries
Type of Packaging: Food Service, Private Label

31094 Waukesha Cherry-Burrell
2025 S Hurstbourne Pkwy
Louisville, KY 40220-1623
502-491-4310
Fax: 502-491-4312 800-252-5200
www.halfpricebooks.com
Fluid handling and process equipment including PD pumps, centrifugal pumps, valves, heat exchangers, and ice cream equipment
Manager: Jeff Comara
VFO and VP Finance: Ken Rod
Estimated Sales: $1 - 3 Million
Number Employees: 10-19
Number of Brands: 10
Number of Products: 50
Parent Co: SPX
Brands:
    Heat Exhangers
    Positive Displacement Pumps
    Universal
    Votatr

31095 Waukesha Cherry-Burrell
2025 S Hurstbourne Pkwy
Louisville, KY 40220-1623
502-491-4310
Fax: 502-491-4312 www.gowcb.com
Manufacturer and exporter of aseptic processing equipment, colloid mills, coopers/kettles, fittings, freezers, ingredient feeders, pumps and tanks
Manager: Jeff Comara
National Sales Manager: Tony Mazza
Sales Manager (Process Prod.): Paul Duddleson
Estimated Sales: $20-50 Million
Number Employees: 10-19
Parent Co: United Dominion Company

31096 Waukesha Foundry Inc
1300 Lincoln Ave
Waukesha, WI 53186-5389
262-542-0741
Fax: 262-549-8440 800-727-0741
www.waukeshafoundry.com
Anti-galling alloys and stainless steel castings
President: Ken Kurek
kkurek@waukeshafoundry.com
VP Sales/Marketing: Gary Evans
Manager Sales/Advertising: Thomas Kerwin
Estimated Sales: $10-20 Million
Number Employees: 250-499

31097 Waukesha Specialty Company
N3355 Us Highway 14
PO Box 160
Darien, WI 53114-5014
262-724-3700
Fax: 262-724-5120
Manufacturer and exporter of fittings, stainless steel hinges and sanitary valves
President: Stephen Miller
VP: Malcom Miller
Estimated Sales: $1 - 2.5 Million
Number Employees: 2

31098 Wausau Paper Corp.
100 Paper Place
Mosinee, WI 54455
866-722-8675
torkusaessity.com
www.wausaupaper.com
Towels, tissue, soap, wipers and dispensing system.
President, Professional Hygiene - Essity: Michael Burandt
Year Founded: 1899
Estimated Sales: $822 Million
Number Employees: 870
Number of Brands: 14
Parent Co: Essity
Type of Packaging: Food Service
Other Locations:
    Warehouse & Slitting Facility
    Roopville GA
    Warehouse & Slitting Facility
    Irving TX
    Warehouse & Slitting Facility
    Las Vegas NV
    Warehouse & Slitting Facility
    Kent WA

    Warehouse & Slitting Facility
    Iztapalapa, Mexico
Brands:
    Alliance
    Artisan
    Dubl-tough
    DublNature
    DublServe
    DublSoft
    EcoSoft
    OptiSource Convertible
    Optiserv
    Optiserv Hybrid
    Optiserv accent
    Revolution
    Silhouette
    Wave'n Dry

31099 Wausau Tile/Textura Designs
9001 Business Hwy 51
Rothschild, WI 54474
715-359-3121
Fax: 715-355-4627 800-388-8728
wtile@wausautile.com www.wausautile.com
Manufacturer of architectural products including pavers, site furnishings, custom precast concrete, custom precast terrazzo and terrazzo tile.
Vice President: Rob Geurink
rgeurink@wausautile.com
Year Founded: 1953
Estimated Sales: $50-100 Million
Number Employees: 250-499
Square Footage: 550000

31100 Wave Chemical Company
350 5th Avenue
Suite 1806
New York, NY 10118-1806
973-243-5852
Fax: 973-243-5853
Cleaning chemicals and dishwashing detergents
Assistant Manager: Mark Lim
VP: Charles Lim

31101 Waxine
65 River Rd
Suite A
Bow, NH 3304
603-228-8241
Fax: 603-228-2324 mrsrptng@aol.com
Dustless sweeping compounds
President: Richard Seymour
VP/Treasurer: Richard Seymour
Estimated Sales: less than $500,000
Number Employees: 1-4
Square Footage: 4000

31102 Waymar Industries
14400 Southcross Dr W
Burnsville, MN 55306
952-435-7100
Fax: 952-435-2900 888-474-1112
www.plymold.com
Manufacturer and exporter of restaurant, cafeteria and industrial seating, table tops and trash containers
President: Dick Koehring
CFO: Greg Klingler
Director Manufacturing: Bill Smith
Marketing/Sales: Bill Ziegler
Contact: Jodie Anderson
j.anderson@waymar.com
Operations Manager: Bob Haugen
Plant Manager: Mike Boegeman
Purchasing Manager: Doug Schultz
Estimated Sales: $10 - 20 Million
Number Employees: 50-99
Square Footage: 280000
Parent Co: Foldcraft Co
Brands:
    Waymar

31103 Wayne Automation Corp
605 General Washington Ave
Eagleville, PA 19403-3695
610-630-8900
Fax: 610-630-6116 www.wayneautomation.com
Automatic packaging equipment including partition inserters, case erectors, case packers and tray formers; exporter of partition inserters and case erectors

President: Jay L Bachman, Jr.
CFO: Dorothy Schlosser
  dschlosser@wayneautomation.com
VP & General Manager: Jay L Bachman, III
VP, Sales and Marketing: Harry M. Dudley
Estimated Sales: $5-10 Million
Number Employees: 50-99
Square Footage: 60000
Brands:
  Ce-15/22
  Cpt-25
  Sf-400
  Wr-25

31104 Wayne Combustion Systems

801 Glasgow Ave
Fort Wayne, IN 46803-1344
                      260-425-9200
    Fax: 260-424-0904 800-443-4625
          clagemann@waynecs.com
Manufacturer and exporter of custom gas and oil
burners; also, oven, fryer and griddle design analysis
available
Manager: Karen Myrice
R & D: Dan Voorhis
Marketing: Karen Wygant
Sales: Dennis Parda
Manager: Paul Wert
  pwert@waynecs.com
Purchasing: Phil Fenker
Estimated Sales: $10 - 20 Million
Number Employees: 50-99
Square Footage: 560000
Parent Co: Scott Fetzer Company
Brands:
  Blue Angel
  Premix Technology
  Wayne

31105 Wayne Engineering

701 Performance Dr
Cedar Falls, IA 50613-6952
                      319-266-1721
    Fax: 319-266-8207 info@wayneusa.com
Manufacturer and exporter of mobile material han-
dling equipment and refuse equipment
CEO: Jim Marks
  jimmarks@wayneusa.com
CEO: Kevin Watje
Sales Manager: Dave Severson
Sales Coordinator: Sherry Berak
Estimated Sales: $20-50 Million
Number Employees: 100-249
Square Footage: 60000
Brands:
  Cargomaster

31106 Wayne Group LTD

110 Sutter St
San Francisco, CA 94104-4002
                      415-421-2010
    Fax: 415-421-2060 jjw@waynegroup.com
                      www.waynegroup.com
Executive search firm
Contact: Dwayne Eason
  dde@waynegroup.com
Estimated Sales: less than $500,000
Number Employees: 5-9
Parent Co: Wayne Group

31107 Wayne Industries

1400 8th St N
Clanton, AL 35045
                      205-755-2365
    Fax: 205-755-1516 800-225-3148
Indoor and outdoor signs and displays; also, lighted
and nonlighted menu boards
National Sales: Bill Weston
Sales Manager: Monte Easterling
Operations Manager: Mike Cooper
Manager: Steve Hill
Manager: Stevde Hill
Estimated Sales: Below $5 Million
Number Employees: 50-99
Square Footage: 250000
Parent Co: Ebsco Industries

31108 Waypoint Analytical Inc

2790 Whitten Rd
Memphis, TN 38133-4753
                      901-213-2400
    Fax: 901-213-2440 support@allabs.com
          www.waypointanalytical.com
Fat testing, water treatment systems

President: Scott Mckee
  smckee@allabs.com
Estimated Sales: $1 - 3 000,000
Number Employees: 50-99

31109 WePackItAll

2745 Huntington Dr.
Duarte, CA 91010
                      626-301-9214
    Fax: 626-301-9216 www.wepackitall.com
Contract packager of food supplement tablets and
powders in pakettes and blister cards
President: Jack Bershtel
General Manager: Sharla Hughes
Contact: Daisy Acevedo
  daisya@wepackitall.com
Plant Manager: Sharla Hughes
Estimated Sales: $5-10 Million
Number Employees: 20-49
Square Footage: 120000

31110 Wearwell/Tennessee Mat Company

P.O. Box 100186
Nashville, TN 37224-0186
                      615-254-8381
    Fax: 615-255-4428 info@wearwell.com
                      www.wearwell.com
Safety and ergonomic matting
President: Elliot Greenberg
CEO: Steve Goldsmith
National Sales Manager: Nick Mead
Contact: Michael Franklin
  michael.franklin@wearwell.com
Estimated Sales: $20 - 50 Million
Number Employees: 100-249

31111 Weavewood, Inc.

7520 Wayzata Blvd
Golden Valley, MN 55426-1622
                      763-544-3136
    Fax: 763-544-3137 800-367-6460
Manufacturer and exporter of woodenware including
bowls, plates, trays, coasters, tongs, susans, fork,
spoon and magnetic server sets, etc.; also, aluminum
and stainless steel steak platters
President: Howard Thompson
Quality Control: Tim Zanor
R&D: Tim Zanor
CFO: Howard Thompson Jr
Marketing Director: Peter Meyer
Estimated Sales: Below $5 Million
Number Employees: 20-49
Square Footage: 120000
Type of Packaging: Consumer, Food Service, Pri-
  vate Label, Bulk
Brands:
  Weavewood

31112 Web Industries

377 Simarano Drive
Suite 220
Marlborough, MA 01752
                      508-898-2988
    Fax: 508-898-3329 800-932-3212
          askus@webindustries.com
                      www.webindustries.com
Suppliers of precision slitting, rewinding, spooling,
sheeting, coating/printing, spooling
President: Don Romine
Chief Financial Officer: Carl Rubin
Executive Vice President: Dennis Latimer
Contact: Jeffrey Allen
  jallen@webindustries.com
Chief Operations Officer: Mark Pihl
Number Employees: 10

31113 Web Industries Inc

3925 Ardmore Ave
Fort Wayne, IN 46802-4237
                      260-432-0027
    Fax: 260-436-2195 800-366-4584
                      www.webindustries.com
Insulating tape and textile converting
Manager: Dan Alt
  d.alt@ktindustriesinc.com
CEO: Don Romine
Chief Financial Officer: Carl Rubin
Executive Vice President: Dennis Latimer
Vice President Sales And Marketing: Tom Burns
Manager: Dan Alt
  d.alt@ktindustriesinc.com

Estimated Sales: $20-50 Million
Number Employees: 50-99
Square Footage: 110000

31114 Web Label

600 Hoover St NE
Suite 500
Minneapolis, MN 55413
                      612-588-0737
    Fax: 612-706-3757 www.weblabel.com
Manufacturer and exporter of pressure sensitive la-
bels
Owner: John Coldwell
Sales Manager: Dave Olson
Contact: James Bullert
  jim.bullert@liesch.com
Estimated Sales: $5 - 10 Million
Number Employees: 20-49
Type of Packaging: Consumer, Bulk

31115 Webb's Machine Design

2251 Montclair Rd
Clearwater, FL 33763-4325
                      727-799-1768
    Fax: 727-791-1639 www.contrast-design.com
Citrus processing equipment
Owner: John D Webb
  john@webbsmachinedesign.com
CFO: Jon Weber
R&D: Jon Weber
Quality Control: Jon Weber
Estimated Sales: Below $5,000,000
Number Employees: 5-9

31116 Webb-Triax Company

34375 W 12 Mile Rd
Farmington Hills, MI 48331
                      248-553-1000
    Fax: 440-285-1878 info@jerviswebb.com
Manufacturer and exporter of automated storage and
retrieval systems, including cooler and freezer stor-
age systems and deep lane flow rack systems
Sales Director: Fred Cirino
Estimated Sales: $1 - 5,000,000
Number Employees: 20-49
Parent Co: Jervis B. Webb Company
Type of Packaging: Bulk
Brands:
  Ms/Rv
  Retriever

31117 (HQ)Webber Smith Assoc

1857 William Penn Way # 200
Lancaster, PA 17601-6713
                      717-291-2266
    Fax: 717-291-4401 800-231-0392
          gsmith@webbersmith.com
                      www.webbersmith.com
Engineering design firm specializing in the design
and construction of food processing, storage and dis-
tribution facilities throughout the usa.
President: Keith Shollenberger
Chairman: Garry Smith
VP: Joe Shaffer
Marketing & Public Relations Manager: Don Landis
Contact: Ed Bianchi
  ed.bianchi@webbersmith.com
Estimated Sales: Less Than $500,000
Number Employees: 1-4

31118 Webber Smith Assoc

1857 William Penn Way # 200
Suite 201
Lancaster, PA 17601-6713
                      717-291-2266
    Fax: 717-291-4401 info@webbersmith.com
                      www.webbersmith.com
A multi-discipline planning, engineering firm which
specializes in bakery, meat, poultry, seafood, bever-
age, prepared foods, fruits and vegetables, confec-
tion, grocery distribution, foodservice distribution
and public cold storagefacilities.
Contact: Doettner Alice
  doettner.alice@webbersmith.com
Estimated Sales: Less Than $500,000
Number Employees: 1-4

31119 Weber Display & Packaging Inc

3500 Richmond St
Philadelphia, PA 19134-6102
                      215-426-3500
    Fax: 215-634-3073 www.weberdisplay-pkg.com
Corrugated shipping boxes

President: Jim Doherty
jimd@weberdisplay-pkg.com
Estimated Sales: $20-50 Million
Number Employees: 100-249

31120 Weber Inc
10701 N Ambassador Dr
Kansas City, MO 64153-1216

816-891-8397
Fax: 816-891-0074 www.weberslicer.com
Manufacturer and supplier of slicing machines for
the meat and cheese industry
President: Scott Scariven
HR Executive: Jason Miera
jmiera@weberslicer.com
Estimated Sales: $2.5-5 Million
Number Employees: 20-49

31121 Weber Inc
10701 N Ambassador Dr
Kansas City, MO 64153-1216

816-891-8397
Fax: 816-891-0074 800-505-9591
www.weberslicer.com
Slicers for the meat, pork, poultry and cheese pro-
cessing industries.
HR Executive: Jason Miera
jmiera@weberslicer.com
Number Employees: 20-49

31122 Weber Packaging Solutions Inc
711 W Algonquin Rd
Arlington Heights, IL 60005-4457

800-843-4242
www.webermarking.com
Manufacturer and exporter of pressure-sensitive la-
bels, labeling systems and continuous ink jet
systems.
President & CEO: Doug Weber
Vice President, Finance & CFO: Chris Shealy
Year Founded: 1932
Estimated Sales: $100-500 Million
Number Employees: 200-500
Square Footage: 320000
Type of Packaging: Consumer, Food Service, Pri-
vate Label, Bulk
Other Locations:
Tape & Label Engineering
St. Petersburg FL
Brands:
Legijet
Legitronic

31123 Weber Scientific Inc
2732 Kuser Rd
Trenton, NJ 08691-1806

609-584-7677
Fax: 609-584-8388 800-328-8378
info@weberscientific.com
www.weberscientific.com
Products for dairy, food and water testing.
President: Nancy Silvester
nsilvester@weberscientific.com
VP: Joyce Arcarese
Account Manager: MaryBeth Karczynski
National Accounts Manager: Sharon Wilson
Account Manager: Nancy Silvester
Purchasing Manager: John Santillo
Estimated Sales: $1-2.5 Million
Number Employees: 5-9
Square Footage: 100000

31124 Weber-Stephen Products Company
200 E Daniels Rd
Palatine, IL 60067

847-934-5700
Fax: 847-407-8900 800-446-1071
support@weberstephen.com www.weber.com
Gas, charcoal, and electric grills. Useful for smoked
products or grilled foods in restaurants or events.
President & CEO: James Stephen
Executive VP & CFO: Leonard Gryn
Quality Control Manager: Steve Butirro
Quality Control Manager: Dave Lohbauer
Marketing Manager: Brooke Jones
Media Contact: Melanie Hill
Executive VP Sales, Americas: Dale Wytiaz
Director of Public Relations: Sherry Bale
Operations Manager: Ken Stephen
Product Manager: Trace Weskamp
Plant Manager: Stan Gucwa
Director of Purchasing: Christoher Stephen
Square Footage: 1200000

Brands:
Weber

31125 Webster Packaging Corporation
715 S Riverside Ave
Loveland, OH 45140

513-683-5666
Fax: 513-683-0535
Corrugated products including shipping containers
and displays
President: Denny Philips
Sales Manager: Susan Terlau
Estimated Sales: $20-50 Million
Number Employees: 50-99

31126 Wedgwood USA
1330 Campus Pkwy
Wall Township, NJ 07753-6811

732-938-5800
Fax: 732-938-7108 800-999-9936
Manufacturer and importer of fine bone china table-
ware
Sales Manager: Michael Durao
Director Hotel/Restaurant Sales: Kathy Santangelo
Estimated Sales: $20-50 Million
Number Employees: 250-499
Square Footage: 368000
Parent Co: Waterford Wedgwood USA
Brands:
Johnson Brothers
Mason's Ironstone
Waterford Crystal
Wedgwood

31127 Wedlock Paper ConvertersLtd.
2327 Stanfield Road
Mississauga, ON L4Y 1R6
Canada

905-277-9461
Fax: 905-272-1108 800-388-0447
info@wedlockpaper.com www.wedlockpaper.com
Manufacturer and exporter of paper bags
Customer Service: Scott Wedlock
Number Employees: 100
Type of Packaging: Consumer

31128 Wega USA
524 North York Road
Bensenville, IL 60106-1607

630-350-0066
Fax: 630-350-0005 info@expressoshoppe.com
www.expressoshoppe.com
Manufacturer, exporter and importer of coffee grind-
ers and espresso equipment
President: David Dimbert
Estimated Sales: $500,000-$1 Million
Number Employees: 1-4
Square Footage: 20000
Type of Packaging: Food Service
Brands:
Bunn
Carioca
Jura
Pavoni
Ranulio
Saeco
Wega

31129 Weigh Right Automatic Scale Co
612 Mills Rd # A
Joliet, IL 60433-2843

815-726-4626
Fax: 815-726-7638 800-571-0249
mikep@weighright.com www.weighright.com
Net weigh scales, volumetric fillers, wiegh/count
scales. Industries serviced: fresh cut produce, IQF
foods, confectionery, coffee, petfood, meat, spice,
pharmaceutica, hardware, snack food, nuts, and
more
President: Steve Almberg
Marketing Director: Mike Phillips
Estimated Sales: Below $5 Million
Number Employees: 10-19
Square Footage: 20000

31130 WeighPack Systems/Paxiom Group
2525 Louis Amos
Montreal, QC H8T 1C3
Canada

514-422-0808
Fax: 514-932-8118 888-934-4472
info@weighpack.com www.weighpack.com

Manufacturer and exporter of net-weighing systems;
also, micro-processors and bagging systems
National Sales Manager: Anthony Delviscio
Number Employees: 30
Square Footage: 400000
Brands:
Aef-1
Aef-25
Aef-7
B-1
Bbf
Multi-Trix
Vs Bagger
Weigh Pack Systems
Zippy Bagger

31131 Weighpack Systems
2525 Louis Amos
Montreal, QC H8T 1C3
Canada

514-422-0808
Fax: 514-422-0834 888-934-4472
info@weighpack.com www.weighpack.com
Packaging machinery and conveying systems
President: Louis Taraborelli
Sales/Marketing Coordinator: John Brown
Sales Director: Nicholas Taraborelli

31132 (HQ)Weiler & Company
1116 E Main St
Whitewater, WI 53190

262-473-5254
Fax: 262-473-5867 800-558-9507
weilerinfo@provisur.com www.provisur.com
Manufacturer and exporter of meat, poultry and sea-
food processing equipment including grinders, mix-
ers, screw and belt conveyors, portioning systems,
meat/bone separtators and mixers/grinders; also,
special equipment and designservices available
CEO: Nick Lesar
Corporate Director Equipment Sales: Jim
Schumacher
International Sales Manager: Dave Schumacher
Contact: Walter Jackson
wjackson@idcnet.com
General Manager: John Allred
Estimated Sales: $10-20 Million
Number Employees: 100-249
Square Footage: 144000
Other Locations:
Weiler & Co.
Sandy UT
Brands:
Beehive
Weiler

31133 Weiler Equipment
1116 E Main Street
Whitewater, WI 53190

262-473-5254
Fax: 262-473-5867 800-558-9507
Premier meat grinders and integrated food process-
ing systems
President/CEO: Mel Cohen
VP Sales/Marketing: Kevin Howard
Contact: Walter Jackson
wjackson@idcnet.com

31134 Weinbrenner Shoe Co
108 S Polk St
Merrill, WI 54452-2348

715-536-5521
Fax: 715-536-1172 800-826-0002
www.weinbrennerusa.com
Manufacturer, importer and exporter of slip resisting
safety shoes
President: L Nienow
CFO: David Giffleman
VP Sales/Marketing: Fred Girsky
Manager Sales: Shane Baganz
Manager: John Chezel
jschenzel@weinbrennerusa.com
Estimated Sales: $20 - 50 Million
Number Employees: 50-99
Parent Co: Weinbrenner Shoe Company
Brands:
Mainstream
Thorogard
Thorogood

31135 Weiss Instruments Inc
905 Waverly Ave
Holtsville, NY 11742-1109
631-207-1200
Fax: 631-207-0900 sales@weissinstruments.com
www.weissinstrument.com
Manufacturer and exporter of thermometers and
pressure gauges
President: John Weiss
johnw@weissinstruments.com
OEM Sales Manager: Stephen Weiss
Industrial Sales Manager: Thomas Keefe
Number Employees: 100-249
Square Footage: 200000

31136 Weiss Sheet Metal Inc
105 Bodwell St
Avon, MA 02322-1112
508-583-8300
Fax: 508-588-5690
stainlessfab@weiss-sheetmetal.com
www.weiss-sheetmetal.com
Custom stainless steel work tables, counters, sinks
and wall mounted stacked shelves
President: Wayne G DE Lano
wdelano@weiss-sheetmetal.com
Vice President: Brian De Lano
Shop Foreman: James Warfield
Estimator: Al Quieto
Estimated Sales: $3 Million
Number Employees: 10-19
Square Footage: 52000
Type of Packaging: Food Service

31137 (HQ)Welbilt Corporation
500 Summer St # 4
Stamford, CT 06901-4301
203-325-8300
Fax: 203-323-4550 www.aquent.com
Manufacturer and exporter of ventilators, ice ma-
chines and commercial cooking, warming and refrig-
eration equipment including broilers, fryers, ovens,
toasters, rotisseries, mixers, etc
Manager: Maggie Patterson
Vice President of Services: Deb McCusker
Account Director: Damien Rocherolle
Estimated Sales: $5 - 10 Million
Number Employees: 1-4
Square Footage: 7200000
Other Locations:
  Welbilt Corp.
  Shreveport LA
Brands:
  Belshaw
  Clark
  Cleveland
  Contempo
  Dean
  Euro
  Frymaster
  Garland
  Ice-O-Matic
  Lincoln
  Merco
  Mercury
  Panorama
  Savory
  Titan
  Us Range
  Varimixer

31138 Welbilt Inc.
2227 Welbilt Blvd.
New Port Richey, FL 34655
727-375-7010
Fax: 727-375-0472 877-375-9300
Food and beverage equipment for commercial
foodservice, including refrigerators, freezers, ovens,
grills, fryers and more.
President/CEO: William Johnson
Executive VP/CFO: Martin Agard
Executive VP/General Counsel: Joel Horn
Executive VP/COO: Josef Matosevic
Year Founded: 1902
Estimated Sales: $138 Million
Number Employees: 5,500
Number of Brands: 13
Square Footage: 14120
Other Locations:
  Manitowoc Ice
  Franklin TN
  Manitowoc Company
  Manitowoc WI

Brands:
  Cleveland
  Convotherm
  Crem International
  Delfield
  Frymaster
  Garland
  Kolpak
  Lincoln
  Manitowoc
  Merco
  Merrychef
  Multiplex
  Welbilt

31139 (HQ)Welch Brothers
9N325 Rt. 25
Bartlett, IL 60103
847-741-6134
Fax: 847-697-0123 www.welchbrothers.com
Packer of steaks and portion-controlled meats; also,
slaughtering and locker services available
President and CEO: Ron Hards
VP: Robert Welch
Sales: Bob Jones
Estimated Sales: $2.5-5 Million
Number Employees: 5-9
Square Footage: 36000
Type of Packaging: Consumer, Food Service

31140 Welch Packaging Group Inc
1020 Herman St
Elkhart, IN 46516-9028
574-295-2460
Fax: 574-295-1527 www.welchpkg.com
Corrugated cartons and pallets
President: Austin Adams
adamsat@welchpkg.com
Estimated Sales: $20-50 Million
Number Employees: 100-249

31141 Welch Stencil Company
7 Lincoln Ave.
Scarborough, ME 04074
207-883-6200
Fax: 207-883-8588 800-635-3506
Rubber stamps and engraved signs
President: Terry Davis
VP: Kathy Davis
Estimated Sales: $3 - 5 Million
Number Employees: 10-19

**31142 WellSet Tableware Manufacturing
Company**
201 Water Street
Brooklyn, NY 11201-1111
718-624-4490
Fax: 718-596-3959

**31143 Welliver Metal Products
Corporation**
672 Murlark Ave NW
Salem, OR 97304
503-362-1568
Fax: 503-585-3374
Manufacturer and exporter of case packagers, size
graders, steam kettles, tanks, size sorters, etc
President: Glenn Welliver
CEO/General Manager: Del Starr
Engineer Manager: Gray Johnson
Quality Control: John Hell
CEO: Del Starr
Estimated Sales: $3 - 5 Million
Number Employees: 20-49
Square Footage: 54000

31144 Wells Lamont
6640 W Touhy Ave
Niles, IL 60714-4587
847-647-8200
Fax: 847-647-6943 800-323-2830
www.wellslamont.com
Vinyl impregnated gloves
President: Jack Akin
jakin@ccfc.com
CFO: Tom Palzer
VP: William Trainer
VP: R Stoller
Marketing Director: Jace Suttner
Estimated Sales: $5 - 10 Million
Number Employees: 1000-4999
Parent Co: A Marmon Group / Berkshire Hathaway
Company

Brands:
  Golden Gripper
  Grips
  Handy Andy
  No Sweat
  Nob Nob
  Sure Gard
  Tuff Guys
  Wells Lamont
  White Mule

31145 Wells Lamont
6640 W Touhy Ave
Niles, IL 60714-4587
847-647-8200
Fax: 847-647-6943 800-323-2830
kmeger@wellslamont.com www.wellslamont.com
Hand protection including cut-resistant heat resis-
tant, leather and general purpose. Products include
cut-resistant gloves, bakers pad, terry gloves, leather
gloves, jersey gloves, canvas gloves, cut-resistant
and heat resistantsleeves
President: Jack Akin
jakin@ccfc.com
VP: William Trainer
Marketing Coordinator: Michelle Kurtz
Sales Director: Jim Buckingham
Public Relations: Michelle Kurtz
Operations Manager: Bruce Smith
Estimated Sales: Below $500,000
Number Employees: 1000-4999
Type of Packaging: Private Label, Bulk

31146 Wells Lamont
6640 W Touhy Ave
Niles, IL 60714-4587
847-647-8200
Fax: 847-647-6943 800-247-3295
wligcs@wellslamont.com www.wellslamont.com
Hand protection including cut resistant, heat resis-
tant, general purpose, liquid/chemical resistant,
leather gloves and more.
President: Mark Premarathna
mpremarathna@wellslamontindustrial.com
Marketing Coordinator: Dena Riccio
VP Human Resources: Lawrence Rist
Operations Executive: Heat Mathias
Number Employees: 1000-4999
Square Footage: 82000

31147 Wells Manufacturing Company
P.O. Box 280
Verdi, NV 89439
775-345-0444
Fax: 775-345-8220 www.wellsbloomfield.com
Contact: Jeanine Blue
blue@launchtower.com
Estimated Sales: $30 - 50 Million
Number Employees: 250-499
Parent Co: Carrier Commercial Refrigeration

31148 Wells Manufacturing Company
10 Sunnen Drive
P.O. Box 280
St. Louis, MO 63143-3800
775-345-0444
Fax: 314-781-5445 888-356-5362
www.wellsbloomfield.com
Manufacturer and exporter of commercial griddles,
fryers, broilers, warmers, coffee and tea brewers,
espresso machines and accessories, dispensers,
decanters, etc
President: Paul Angrick
Quality Control: Terry Mees
Sales Manager: Jeanine Blue
Number Employees: 250-499
Square Footage: 308000
Parent Co: Specialty Equipment Companies
Type of Packaging: Food Service

31149 Welltep International Inc
138 Palm Coast Pkwy NE # 192
Palm Coast, FL 32137-8241
386-437-5545
Fax: 386-437-5546
Broker of grocery related products
President: Luis Lopez
Estimated Sales: $1 - 3 Million
Number Employees: 1-4

31150 Wemas Metal Products
636 36th Avenue NE
Calgary, AB T2E 2L7
Canada
403-276-4451
Fax: 403-277-0725 sales@wemas.com
Manufacturer and exporter of custom stainless steel,
aluminum and exotic metal food processing
machinery
General Manager: Dave Swedak
Sales: Enno Ziemann
Sales: Joanne McCaughey
Number Employees: 44
Square Footage: 180000

31151 Wemco Pumps
P.O. Box 209
Salt Lake City, UT 84110-0209
801-359-8731
Fax: 801-355-9303 www.wemcopump.com
Wine industry pumps
CEO: Joseph W Roark
Marketing Director: Dave Borrowman
Production Manager: Gary Pearson
Estimated Sales: $50-100 Million
Number Employees: 500-999

31152 Wenda America Inc
1811 High Grove Ln
Unit 167
Naperville, IL 60540
844-999-3632
sales@wendaingredients.com
www.wendaingredients.com
Global meat and poultry ingredients manufacturer
and processor.
President: Xiong Wei
Year Founded: 1995
Estimated Sales: $200 Million
Number Employees: 200-500
Number of Brands: 2
Type of Packaging: Bulk
Brands:
    NatureBind
    SafePlate

31153 Wendell August Forge
1605 South Center Street
PO Box 109
Grove City, PA 16127
724-450-8700
Fax: 724-458-0906 800-923-1390
info@wendell.com www.wendellaugust.com
Hand-hammered aluminum, bronze, pewter and ster-
ling silver advertising specialties, collector's items
and gifts
CEO: F W Knecht Iii
Marketing Director: George Kenyon
Sales Director: Erin Pisano
Sales: Carol Snyder
Estimated Sales: $10-20 Million
Number Employees: 100-249
Number of Brands: 1
Number of Products: 100

31154 Wenglor
2280 Grange Hall Rd
Beavercreek, OH 45431
937-320-0011
Fax: 937-320-0033 877-936-4567
info.us@wenglor.com www.wenglor.com
Analog sensors, laser sensors, color sensors, line and
optical sensors, reflex sensors and proximity sensors
General Manager: Tobiaf Schmitt
Estimated Sales: $500,000 - $1 Million
Number Employees: 5

31155 Wepackit
1-16 Tideman Drive
Orangeville, ON L9W 4N6
Canada
519-942-1700
Fax: 519-942-1702
Manufacturer and exporter of case packers, erectors,
sealers, de-casers and tray formers
President: David Wiggins
Number Employees: 55-60
Number of Products: 7
Square Footage: 80000

31156 Wes Inc
6389 Tower Ln
Sarasota, FL 34240-8810
941-371-7617
Fax: 941-378-5218 800-881-9374
info@wesinc.com www.wesinc.com
Water treatment equipment
Owner: Anthony DE Loach
    tonyd@wesinc.com
Estimated Sales: $10-20 Million
Number Employees: 50-99

31157 Wes Tech Engineering Inc
3625 S West Temple
Salt Lake City, UT 84115
801-265-1000
Fax: 801-265-1080 info@westech-inc.com
www.westech-inc.com
Wastewater and water treatment systems; solid and
liquid separators
President: Rex Plaizier
    rplaizier@westech-inc.com
VP: Rex Plaizier
Marketing Manager: Marshall Palm
Sales Director: Jeff Easton
Estimated Sales: $30 - 50 Million
Number Employees: 250-499
Brands:
    Cop
    Simarotor

31158 Wesco Industrial Products
1250 Welsh Rd
North Wales, PA 19454-1820
215-699-7031
Fax: 215-699-3836 800-445-5681
bmunion@wescomfg.com www.wescomfg.com
Material handling products
President: Allen Apter
President: Jamie Johnson
Vice President: Mike Esris
    mesris@ra-industries.com
Director of Sales: Mike Esris
Estimated Sales: $10-25 Million
Number Employees: 1-4

31159 Wescor
370 W 1700 S
Logan, UT 84321-5294
435-752-6011
Fax: 435-752-4127 800-453-2725
biomed@wescor.com
Manufacturer and exporter of osmometers and ther-
mometers
President: Wayne K Barlow
Estimated Sales: $5-10,000,000
Number Employees: 50-99

31160 Wesley International Corp
3680 Chestnut St
Scottdale, GA 30079-1206
404-792-7441
Fax: 404-292-8469 800-241-8649
sales@wesleyintl.com
Manufacturer and exporter of electric vehicles, bur-
den and personnel carriers and trucks including hand
hydraulic pallets, skids and straddles
Sales/Marketing: Lee Gatins
Manager: Jeremy Driver
    jeremy.driver@wesleyintl.com
Manager: Vanessa Holiday
Estimated Sales: $5 - 10 Million
Number Employees: 50-99
Square Footage: 50000
Brands:
    Pack Mule
    Pallet Mule

31161 Wesley-Kind Associates
200 Old Country Rd
Suite 364
Mineola, NY 11501-4240
516-747-3434
Fax: 516-248-2728
Management consultant specializing in plant and
warehouse layouts and operating systems for the
movement, storage and control of materials and
products
Executive Director: Daniel Kind
Director Engineer: Oliver Wesley
Marketing Director: Daniel Kind
Estimated Sales: Less than $500,000
Number Employees: 1-4

31162 West Agro
11100 N Congress Ave
Kansas City, MO 64153
816-891-7700
Fax: 816-891-1606 www.universaldairy.com
Manufacturer and exporter of cleaning and sanita-
tion supplies including clean-in-place systems; also,
sanitation control system consultant
President: Walt Maharay
VP: Thomas Fahey
Contact: Mark Curtis
    dan.brookhart@delaval.com
Number Employees: 100-249
Parent Co: Tetra Laval Group

31163 (HQ)West Carrollton Parchment Company
PO Box 49098
West Carrollton, OH 45449
937-859-3621
Fax: 937-859-7610
Manufacturer and exporter of paper including print-
ing, rewinding, sheeting, die cutting, creping and
coating
President: Cameron Lonergan
CEO: Pierce Lonergan
VP Finance: Alan Berens
Quality Control: Brandon Carpenter
Sales/Marketing: Larry Teague
Operations: Bob Scancella
Production: Tom Bray
Purchasing Director: Jerry Lienesch
Estimated Sales: $30 Million
Number Employees: 100-249
Number of Products: 150
Square Footage: 260000
Parent Co: Friend Group
Type of Packaging: Food Service
Brands:
    Gvp-100

31164 (HQ)West Chemical Products
1000 Herrontown Rd Ste 2
Princeton, NJ 08540
609-921-0501
Fax: 609-924-4308
Manufacturer and exporter of sanitizing agents in-
cluding detergents and disinfectants; also, insecti-
cides including liquid and fly killing
President: Elwood Phares
CEO: Elwood W Phares Ii
Contact: Bruce Muretta
    bmuretta@westchemicalproducts.com
Estimated Sales: $20,000,000 - $49,999,999
Number Employees: 100-249
Other Locations:
    West Chemical Products
    Tenefly NJ

31165 West Coast Industries Inc
750 Battery St # 100
Suite 100
San Francisco, CA 94111-1543
580-259-6267
Fax: 415-552-5368 800-243-3150
info@westcoastindustries.com
www.westcoastindustries.com
Restaurant and contract furniture including counters,
tables, etc
President: Rob Liss
Secretary/Treasurer: Ron Liss
VP: Norman Sobel
Estimated Sales: $5-10 Million
Number Employees: 10-19

31166 West Coast Specialty Coffee
71 Lost Lake Lane
Campbell, CA 95008
650-259-9308
Fax: 650-259-8024 rh@specialtycoffee.com
www.specialtycoffee.com
Coffee and coffee equipment and supplies
President: Robert Hensley
    rh@specialtycoffee.com
Estimated Sales: $500,000
Number Employees: 2
Type of Packaging: Consumer, Food Service, Bulk

31167 West Hawk Industries
1717 S State St Frnt
Ann Arbor, MI 48104-4684

734-761-3100
Fax: 734-761-8430 800-678-1286
sales@westhawkpromo.com
www.westhawkind.com
Manufacturer and exporter of advertising novelties, decals, signs, banners, calendars, imprinted matches, bags and custom printed cups; also, imprinted mints and chocolates
President: Jan Hawkins
CEO: Harry Hawkins
Vice President: Sarah Spratt
Sales Director: Harry Hawkins
Estimated Sales: $2.5-5 Million
Number Employees: 5-9
Number of Products: 800
Square Footage: 30000
Type of Packaging: Private Label

31168 West Louisiana Ice Svc
1707 Smart St
Leesville, LA 71446-5061

337-239-4530
Fax: 337-238-5095 www.siceco.com
Owner: James S Shapkoff Jr
IT: Salina Johnson
westlaice@bellsouth.net
Estimated Sales: Less Than $500,000
Number Employees: 1-4

31169 West Metals
463 Nightingale Avenue
London, ON N5W 4C4
Canada

519-457-0603
Fax: 519-457-7960 800-300-6667
sales@westmetals.com www.westmetals.com
Glass display cases, cocktail mix and beverage units, sinks, prep and steam tables, work centers, exhaust hoods and fans
Number Employees: 10

31170 West Oregon Wood Products Inc
2305 2nd St
Columbia City, OR 97018-9504

503-397-6707
Fax: 503-397-6887
A manufacturer of premium wood fuel pellet, all 100 percent wood fire logs, animal bedding, firestarter, and BBQ pellets. the quality products combined with a strong value proposition has provided us the platform to build categoryleading products. We continue to lead the industry in innovation, product development, and service.
Owner: Christopher Sharron
csharron@wowpellets.com
General Manager: Mike Knobel
Director Marketing/Sales: Mark Ross
Estimated Sales: $1-2.5 Million
Number Employees: 20-49
Square Footage: 560000
Brands:
Blazers
Lil' Devils

31171 West Penn Oil Co Inc
2305 Market St
Warren, PA 16365

814-723-9000
www.westpenn.com
Contract packager of lubricating oils.
President: Larry Lang
lalang@westpenn.com
Year Founded: 1921
Estimated Sales: $20-50 Million
Number Employees: 50-99
Square Footage: 60000
Brands:
Emblem

31172 West Rock
1000 Abernathy Road NE
Atlanta, GA 30328

770-448-2193
www.westrock.com
Produces containerboard and paperboard packaging for food, hardware, apparel and other consumer goods.

Chief Executive Officer: Steven Voohees
EVP/Chief Financial Officer: Ward Dickson
President, Business Development: Jim Porter
President, Consumer Packaging: Patrick Lindner
President, Corrugated Packaging: Jeff Chalovich
President, Multi Packaging Solutions: Marc Shore
Chief Transformation Officer: Shan Cooper
EVP/General Counsel/Secretary: Bob McIntosh
Chief Human Resources Officer: Vicki Lostetter
Chief Environmental Officer: Nina Butler
Chief Communications Officer: Donna Owens Cox
Year Founded: 2015
Estimated Sales: $14.8 Billion
Number Employees: 45,000
Type of Packaging: Consumer, Food Service, Private Label, Bulk

31173 West Star Industries
4445 E Fremont St
Stockton, CA 95215-4007

209-955-8220
Fax: 209-955-8250 800-326-2288
wsi@weststarindustries.com
www.weststarindustries.com
Stainless steel products including sinks, tables, exhaust hoods and refrigeration equipment
President: Michelle Focke
mfocke@weststarindustries.com
VP: William George
Estimated Sales: $5-10 Million
Number Employees: 20-49
Square Footage: 60000
Brands:
West Star

31174 West-Pak
PO Box 763847
Dallas, TX 75376

214-337-8984
Fax: 214-337-8988
Protective packaging
President: Edwin Monroe
Estimated Sales: $10 - 20 Million
Number Employees: 20-49

31175 Westec Tank & Equipment
1402 Grove St
Healdsburg, CA 95448-4700

707-431-9342
Fax: 707-431-8809 joe@westectank.com
www.westectank.com
Wine industry valves and fittings
President: Wanda Alary
Vice President: Jim Belli
jim@westectank.com
Estimated Sales: $5 - 10 Million
Number Employees: 20-49

31176 Westeel
PO Box 1370
Saskatoon, SK S7K 3P5
Canada

306-931-2855
Fax: 306-931-2786 www.westeel.com
Storage bins
President: Robert Skull
CFO: Ray Anderson
Quality Control: Linda Thurston
R & D: Bruce Allen
Operations Manager: Bruce Allen
Number Employees: 10
Parent Co: Jenisys

31177 Westerbeke Fishing GearCo Inc
400 Border St
Boston, MA 02128-2402

617-561-9967
Fax: 617-561-3752 800-536-6387
westerbekecompany@gmail.com wfg1.com
Wholesaler/distributor of boots, clothing, cutlery, shovels, netting, forks, containers, gloves, etc.; serving the seafood industry; liferaft annual inspections and netting & vinyl products.
Owner: Elaine Halligan
Sales Director: Ed Creamer
westerbekecompany@gmail.com
Purchasing Manager: Ed Creamer
Estimated Sales: $1 Million
Number Employees: 5-9
Square Footage: 24000

31178 Western Carriers
2220 91st Street
North Bergen, NJ 07047-4713

800-631-7776
201-869-3300
wine@westerncarriers.com
www.westerncarriers.com
Warehouse providing storage for wines and spirits, and the alcoholic beverage industry.
President: Michael Hodes
Contact: Rick Albee
walter@itoasys.com
Estimated Sales: $5-10 Million
Number Employees: 50-99
Square Footage: 3600000
Other Locations:
Vallejo 1,000,000 Sq Ft CA

31179 Western Combustion Engineering
640 E Realty St
Carson, CA 90745-6016

310-834-9389
Fax: 310-834-4795 info@westerncombustion.com
www.westerncombustion.com
Manufacturer, exporter of ovens, oil fryers and food processing equipment
President: Marcia Paul
mpaul@westerncombustion.com
Vice President: Marcia Paul
Estimated Sales: $1-2,500,000
Number Employees: 10-19
Square Footage: 10000

31180 (HQ)Western Container Company
4323 Clary Blvd
Kansas City, MO 64130

816-924-5700
Fax: 816-924-7032
Manufacturer and exporter of cartons including folding, cellophane window and plastic coated
President: Richard Horton
CFO: Allen Booe
Quality Control: Charlie Palmer
Contact: Kyle Adams
kylea@westerncontainer.com
Estimated Sales: $20 - 50 Million
Number Employees: 100-249

31181 Western Exterminator Co
1732 Kaiser Ave
Irvine, CA 92614-5706

949-954-8023
Fax: 949-474-7767 mlawton@west-ext.com
www.westernexterminator.com
Pest control systems
Founder: Carl Strom
Vice President of Administration: Debbie Byrne
Vice President of Sales: Michael Britt
Contact: Todd Frantz
tfrantz@west-ext.com
Estimated Sales: $2.5-5 Million
Number Employees: 20-49

31182 Western Laminates
431 S 91st Cir
Omaha, NE 68114

402-556-4600
Fax: 402-556-4601
Laminated doors, cabinets and counter tops
President: Bennett Wagner
bwwesternlam@qwestoffice.net
Estimated Sales: Below $5 Million
Number Employees: 10-19

31183 Western Lighting Inc
2349 17th St
Franklin Park, IL 60131-3432

847-451-7200
Fax: 847-451-7275
westernlighting@sbcglobal.net
www.westernlightinginc.com
Light fixtures and illuminated signs
Owner: Norma Heen
vheen@westernlighting.com
Site Manager: Victor Heen
vheen@westernlighting.com
Number Employees: 10-19

31184 Western Pacific Oils, Inc.
201 S Anderson St
Los Angeles, CA 90033

213-232-5117
Fax: 213-232-5102 www.westpacoils.com
Palm oils and coconut oil.

Manager: Y Neman
Contact: Suraj Bhojwani
 suraj@westpacoils.com
Estimated Sales: $900 Thousand
Type of Packaging: Food Service, Bulk
Brands:
 Golden Coconut Oil
 Golden Joma Palm Oil
 Golden Palm Cake & Icing
 Golden Palm Margarine
 Golden Palm Shortening

31185 Western Pacific Stge Solutions
300 E Arrow Hwy
San Dimas, CA 91773-3339
                          909-305-9526
       Fax: 909-451-0311 800-888-5707
                          trogers@wpss.com
Manufacturer and exporter of steel and boltless
shelving, carton flow racks and mezzanine systems
President: Tom Rogers
 trogers@wpss.com
Marketing Manager: Diane Gowgill
Estimated Sales: $5-10,000,000
Number Employees: 100-249
Brands:
 Deluxe
 Industrial Structures
 Pacific
 Quik Pik
 Rivetier

31186 Western Plastics
105 Western Dr
Portland, TN 37148-2018
                          615-325-7331
                  Fax: 615-325-4924
Manufacturer, importer and exporter of aluminum
foil rolls, PVC film cutter-boxes, pallet stretch wrap,
perforated food wrap and shrink film
President: Tommy Mcclean
 tommy@westernplastics.ie
VP: Gene Ketter
Sales Manager: David Sullender
Estimated Sales: $5-10 Million
Number Employees: 100-249
Square Footage: 120000
Brands:
 Air Flow
 Eco Wrap
 Ez Bander
 Indenti-Film
 Securi Seal
 Strong Bow
 Wp
 Wp Foodfilm
 Wp Handywrap
 Wrapnet

31187 (HQ)Western Plastics
2399 Highway 41 South SW
Calhoun, GA 30701-3346
                          706-625-5260
       Fax: 706-625-0003 800-752-4106
       calhoun@wplastics.com www.wplastics.com
Manufacturer and exporter of packaging materials
including plastic film and aluminum foil
President: Tom Cunningham
 tcunningham@wplastics.com
CEO: Frederick Young
CFO: George Schultz
Vice President: Frederick Young
Marketing Director: Paul O'Loghlen
Operations Manager: Bobby Hyde
Purchasing Manager: Jeff Silvers
Estimated Sales: $40 Million
Number Employees: 50-99
Square Footage: 100000
Type of Packaging: Food Service, Private Label,
 Bulk
Other Locations:
Brands:
 Eldorado

31188 Western Plastics
2399 US 41 SW
Calhoun, GA 30701
                          706-625-5260
       Fax: 706-625-0003 800-752-4106
       calhoun@wplastics.com www.wplastics.com
Foil, foodfilm, pallet stretch film, meat and produce
film
President: Tom Cunningham

Estimated Sales: $10-20 Million
Number Employees: 1-4

31189 Western Polymer Corp
32 Road R SE
Moses Lake, WA 98837-9303
                          509-765-1803
       Fax: 509-765-0327 800-362-6845
                  www.westernpolymer.com
Processor, exporter and importer of starch; manufac-
turer of starch recovery systems
CEO: Sheldon Townsend
Marketing: Mike Markillie
Estimated Sales: $20-50 Million
Number Employees: 50-99
Parent Co: Moses Lake
Type of Packaging: Bulk

31190 Western Precooling
43990 Fremont Blvd
Fremont, CA 94538-6057
                          510-656-2220
       Fax: 510-656-1137 www.westernprecooling.com
Wine industry refrigeration
President: Maeve Austin
 maeve_austin@toyota.com
CFO: Jerry Nopis
Estimated Sales: Below $5 Million
Number Employees: 20-49

31191 Western Pulp Products Co
5025 SW Hout St
Corvallis, OR 97333-9540
                          541-757-1151
       Fax: 541-757-8613 800-547-3407
       sales@westernpulp.com www.westernpulp.com
Wine industry pulp byproducts
President: Mel Kelsey
 melk@westernpulp.com
CFO: Brad McIntyre
Estimated Sales: $10 - 25 Million
Number Employees: 50-99

**31192 Western Refrigerated Freight
Systems**
8238 W Harrison Street
Phoenix, AZ 85043
                          602-254-9922
                  www.westernrefrigerated.com
Handles all temperature sensitive shipping and dis-
tribution needs throughout California, Arizona &
Nevada
President: Jeff Boley
Estimated Sales: $6 Million
Number Employees: 50
Other Locations:
 Las Vegas NV

31193 Western Square Industries
1621 N Broadway Ave
Stockton, CA 95205-3046
                          209-944-0921
       Fax: 209-944-0934 800-367-8383
                  info@westernsquare.com
                  www.westernsquare.com
Racks to hold bottled water
President: Trygve Mikkelsen
 tmikkelson@westernsquare.com
Accounts Payable / Receivables: Joan Mikkelsen
Chief Engineer: Larry Bartko
Southern Coast Sales: Bobby Fox
Plant Manager: Robert Craven
Purchasing Agent: Russell Danero
Estimated Sales: $6 Million
Number Employees: 20-49
Square Footage: 44000

31194 Western Stoneware
521 W 6th Ave
Monmouth, IL 61462
                          309-734-2161
       Fax: 309-734-5942 www.westernstoneware.com
Manufacturer and exporter of stoneware bean pots,
cheese crocks, canister sets, cups, mugs, soup bowls
and steins
Owner: Jack Horner
CFO: Jean Wiseman
VP: Gene Wiseman
Estimated Sales: Below $5 Million
Number Employees: 20-49

**31195 (HQ)Western Textile &
Manufacturing Inc.**
1750 Bridgeaway
Suite B207
Sausalito, CA 94965
                          415-431-1458
       Fax: 415-431-5980 800-734-8683
       westex@bagmakers.com www.bagmakers.com
Manufacturer and exporter of leather goods includ-
ing menu covers
Owner: Craig Storek
Contact: David Hanson
 david@bagmakers.com
Office Manager: Lorraine Storek
Estimated Sales: $2.5-5 Million
Number Employees: 1-4

31196 (HQ)Westervelt Co Inc
1400 Jack Warner Pkwy NE
Tuscaloosa, AL 35404-1002
                          205-562-5000
       Fax: 205-562-5010 www.westervelt.com
Custom printed, die-cut and glued folding cartons,
solid bleached sulphate paperboard for food contact
use and line of dual paperboard packaging
President/CEO: Brian Luoma
VP, Finance & CFO: Mark Tobin
VP, General Counsel: Ray Robbins
Estimated Sales: $67 Million
Number Employees: 1000-4999
Square Footage: 90000
Brands:
 E-Z Serve
 Heritage

31197 Westfalia Separator
100 Fairway Ct
Northvale, NJ 07647
                          201-767-3900
       Fax: 201-784-4313 800-722-6622
Equipment for clarifying suspensions, separating
liquids with removal of solids, separating liquid
mixtures of differing densities of viscosities, extract-
ing of active substances, classifying substances, and
concentrating anddewatering of solids.
President: Michael Vick
COO: Hanno Lehmann
CFO: Norbert Breuer
Lab Director: Pete Malanchuk
Quality Control Director: Bill Taylor
Marketing Manager: Frank Kennedy
Sales: Michael Rohr
Contact: Samuel Barcenas
 samuel.barcenas@gea.com
VP Operations: Joseph Pavlosky
Purchasing Manager: John Nayancsik
Estimated Sales: $36.7 Million
Number Employees: 530
Square Footage: 105000
Brands:
 Westfalia

31198 Westfield Sheet Metal Works
North 8th St & Monror Ave
PO Box 128
Kenilworth, NJ 7033
                          908-276-5500
Fax: 908-276-6808 info@westfieldsheetmetal.com
                  www.westfieldsheetmetal.com
Stainless steel belt guards, bins, booths, cabinets,
canopies, gloves boxes, consoles, carts, casings,
chutes, conveyors, cooling towers, cornices, damp-
ers, ducts, dust collectors, exhaust systems, flues,
guardrails, hoods, hoppersOSHA machine guards,
pressure vessels, U&R racks, skids, tanks. Also a
consultant for engineering, fabrication, and
installation
President: C Johnstone
CEO: Tom Johnstone
CFO: Gregg Wheatley
VP/Office Manager: Lorraine Carine
Quality Control/R&D: William Nicolson
Marketing: Walter Basilone
Sales Director: Hubert Plungis
Chief Engineer: William Nicolson
VP/Manager Production: Thomas Johnstone
Plant Manager: Mike McElroy
Purchasing Manager: Stanley Guididas
Estimated Sales: $10-20 Million
Number Employees: 50-99
Square Footage: 100000

1045

31199 Weston Emergency Light Co
10 Sibley Rd
Weston, MA 02493-2550
781-894-1585
Fax: 781-894-1590 800-649-3756
sales@westonemergencylights.com
www.westonemergencylights.com
Manufacturer and importer of exit signs, lamps and lighting fixtures; also, emergency light batteries, portable rechargeable hand lights and flashlights
President: Michelle Flynn
Manager: Thomas Silveira
Clerk: Paul Amsden
Estimated Sales: $5-10 Million
Number Employees: 1-4
Square Footage: 10000

31200 Weston Solutions Inc
1400 Weston Way
PO Box 2653
West Chester, PA 19380-1492
610-701-3000
Fax: 610-701-3186
contactweston@westonsolutions.com,
www.westonsolutions.com
Infrastructure redevelopment firm providing integrated, sustainable solutions
Manager: Richard H Mehl
CEO: William L Robertson
william.robertson@westonsolutions.com
Estimated Sales: $5 - 10 Million
Number Employees: 1000-4999

31201 Westra Construction
1263 12th Ave E
Palmetto, FL 34221
941-723-1611
Fax: 920-324-5957 800-388-3545
info@westraconst.com www.westraconst.com
Building and construction contractor, design/builder, construction management and consultants
President and CEO: Don Thayer Jr
CFO: Patrick Flynn
Vice President: Peter Roehrig
VP Operations: Scott Heaze
Marketing Director: Gena Herwig
Sales Director: Scott Clark
Contact: Donald Anderson
donaldanderson@westraconst.com
Operations Manager: Rick Bickert
Estimated Sales: $1.7 Million
Number Employees: 240

31202 Westrick Paper Co
3011 Mercury Rd S
Jacksonville, FL 32207-7981
904-737-2122
Fax: 904-737-9129 info@westrickpaper.com
www.westrickpaper.com
Envelopes, writing tablets and other paper specialties
President: Jack Lamb
jack.lamb@westrickpaper.com
Estimated Sales: $5-10 Million
Number Employees: 1-4

31203 Westvaco Corporation
2000 Ogletown Road
Newark, DE 19711-5439
302-453-7200
Fax: 302-453-7280
Folding cartons and MAP packaging; exporter of ovenware packaging
Business Development Manager: Rufus Miller
Manager (Frozen Foods): Shelly Dicken
National Account Manager: Richard De Ruiter
Estimated Sales: $1-2.5 Million
Number Employees: 9
Square Footage: 120000

31204 Westvaco Corporation
320 Hull St
Richmond, VA 23224
804-233-9205
Fax: 804-232-3975 www.meadwestvaco.com
Contract packager of microwaveable entrees, baked goods, etc
Sales Manager: John McInerney
Sales: Bob London
Estimated Sales: $20 - 50 Million
Number Employees: 250-499
Parent Co: Westvaco Corporation

31205 Wetterau Wood Products
10 Corporate Drive
Burlington, MA 1803
602-267-3600
Fax: 715-623-4399 800-986-0958
wetterauwood@yahoo.com www.homestead.com
Pallets and skids
President: Michael Wetterau
VP: Deborah Wetterau
Number Employees: 10

31206 Wexler Packaging Products
777 Schwab Rd # M
Hatfield, PA 19440-3272
215-631-9700
Fax: 215-631-9705 800-878-3878
sales@wexlerpackaging.com
www.wexlerpackaging.com
Paper/poly banding machines
Owner: Kelley Detweiler
kdetweiler@wexlerpackaging.com
Marketing Manager: Joseph Ambrose
Estimated Sales: $5-10 Million
Number Employees: 10-19

31207 Wexxar Corporation
3851 W Devon Avenue
Chicago, IL 60659-1024
630-983-6666
Fax: 630-983-6948 sales@wexxar.com
www.wexxar.com
Manufacturer and exporter of packaging equipment including tray and case formers and sealers
Vice President of Sales: Jim Stoddard
Estimated Sales: Less than $500,000
Number Employees: 4
Square Footage: 200000
Parent Co: Wexxar Packaging Machinery
Brands:
  Wexxar

31208 Wexxar Packaging Inc
13471 Vulcan Way
Richmond, BC V6V 1K4
Canada
604-930-9500
Fax: 604-930-9368 888-565-3219
sales@wexxar.com www.wexxar.com
Case forming, case sealing by hot glue, cold glue, tape. Poly bag insertors stainless steel wash down corrosion resistant machinery
President: William Chu
Marketing Director: Melissa Montague
Parent Co: ProMach Inc
Type of Packaging: Food Service
Brands:
  Bel Line

31209 Weyauwega Star Dairy
109 N Mill St
P.O. Box 658
Weyauwega, WI 54983
920-867-2870
888-813-9720
www.wegastardairy.com
Cheese manufacturer, specializing in Parmesan, Asiago and Romanao; sting cheeses and curds; meat products; spreadable cheeses. Provide private label, shredding and packing services.
President: James Knaus
Contact: Gerard Knaus
gknaus@wegastardairy.com
Estimated Sales: $12.5 Million
Number Employees: 75
Number of Brands: 7
Type of Packaging: Consumer, Food Service, Private Label, Bulk
Brands:
  Alacreme
  Fontina Cheese
  Lakeside's
  Rose Cottage
  Scott's
  Star Dairy
  Weyauwega

31210 Weyerhaeuser Co
220 Occidental Ave S # 7
Seattle, WA 98104-3120
253-924-3215
800-525-5440
www.weyerhaeuser.com
Corrugated boxes
President & CEO: Devin Stockfish
SVP/CFO: Nancy Loewe
SVP, General Counsel: Kristy Harlan
SVP, Chief Development Officer: Russell Hagen
Estimated Sales: Less Than $500,000
Number Employees: 1-4
Square Footage: 14672
Parent Co: Wayerhaeuser Company

31211 Whallon Machinery Inc
205 N Chicago St
PO Box 429
Royal Center, IN 46978-2101
574-643-9561
Fax: 574-643-9218 info@whallon.com
www.whallon.net
Manufacturer and exporter of palletizers and depalletizers for cans, cases and pails
Owner: Leslie Smith
Engineering Manager: Jeff Tevis
Sales Manager: Bruce Ide
lsmith1@whallon.com
Purchasing Manager: Judy Roudebush
Estimated Sales: $10-20 Million
Number Employees: 50-99
Square Footage: 70000

31212 Whatman
800 Centennial Ave # 1
Piscataway, NJ 08854-3911
973-245-8300
Fax: 973-245-8301 www.whatman.com
Provides separations technology and in known throughout the scientific community for providing innovative products and solutions.
CEO: Bob Thein
Senior VP: Richard Dool
Contact: Giles Barton
giles.barton@whatman.com
Product Manager: Tiana Gorham
Estimated Sales: $7 Million
Number Employees: 50-99
Other Locations:
  Sanford ME
Brands:
  Whatman

31213 Whatman
PO Box 8223
Haverhill, MA 01835-0723
978-374-7400
Fax: 978-374-7070
Manufacturer and exporter of filters, analytical instruments and laboratory equipment and supplies
VP Sales/Marketing: David Largesse
Estimated Sales: $500,000-$1 Million
Number Employees: 50-99
Type of Packaging: Bulk

31214 Wheaton Plastic Containers
1101 Wheaton Ave
Millville, NJ 08332-2003
856-825-1400
Fax: 856-825-1368 wheaton.com
Plastic and glass containers, plastic bottles, caps and closures
President, Chief Executive Officer: Stephen Drozdow
Vice President of Global Marketing: Michael Blazes
Vice President of Quality: Nicholas DeBello
Regional Manager: Al Lancto
Vice President of Operations: Gregory Bianco
Number Employees: 250-499

31215 Wheel Tough Company
1597 E Industrial Drive
Terre Haute, IN 47802-9265
812-298-8606
Fax: 812-298-1166 888-765-8833
Manufacturer and exporter of aluminum bar and restaurant furniture including stools, chairs and tables; also, gas and charcoal grills, deep fryers and steamers
President: Rudolph J Stakeman Jr
Estimated Sales: $1 Million
Number Employees: 5
Square Footage: 272000
Brands:
  Driver's Seat, The
  Trackside Cookery

31216 Whey Systems
PO Box 1689
Willmar, MN 56201-1689
320-905-4122
Fax: 320-231-2282
Provides edible whey processing equipment and systems to the dairy industry. Each system and component is specifically designed to efficiently process the desired whey fraction. Recognized as the world leader in providing lactosedrying systems, with the lowest capital and operating cost to produce high quality edible powder. Providing systems for whey, WPC, lactose, permeate, demineralization, and ammonium lactate.
President: Loren Corle
Product Manager: Jay Gilbert
Number Employees: 20-49

31217 Whirl Air Flow
20055 177th St NW
Big Lake, MN 55309-8015
763-262-1200
Fax: 763-262-1212 800-373-3461
whirlair@whirlair.com www.whirlair.com
Dense and dilute phase pneumatic conveyors including pressure and vacuum
President: E Mueller
emueller@whirlair.com
Marketing Director: Gregg Hedtke
Sales Director: Gregg Hedtke
Plant Manager: Ken Hanley
Purchasing Manager: Wendy Holland
Estimated Sales: $6-7 Million
Number Employees: 20-49
Number of Brands: 45
Square Footage: 100000

31218 Whirley Industries Inc
140 W Harmar St
Warren, PA 16365-2184
814-723-8696
Fax: 814-723-3245 800-825-5575
klabarbera@whirley.com
www.whirleydrinkworks.com
As the world's leading manufacturer of plastic promotional drink containers, Whirley Industries offers a diverse line of products ranging from 12-128 oz
Owner/CEO: Lincoln Sokolski
CFO: Greg Aross
Marketing: Andrew Solkoski
Sales: William Turner
Manager: Kitty Cerra
kcerra@whirleydrinkworks.com
Estimated Sales: $20-50 Million
Number Employees: 250-499
Type of Packaging: Bulk

31219 (HQ)Whisk Products Inc
130 Enterprise Dr
Wentzville, MO 63385-5544
636-327-6262
Fax: 636-327-6288 800-204-7627
whisk@whiskproducts.com
www.whiskproducts.com
Manufacturer and exporter of hand cleaners, germicidal hand soap and dishwashing detergents; also, soap dispensers
Owner: Raymond Lamantia
Sales: Brad LaMantia
ray@whiskproducts.com
Plant Manager: Scott Berg
Purchasing: Lisa Thess
Estimated Sales: $3 - 5 Million
Number Employees: 10-19
Number of Brands: 1
Number of Products: 32
Square Footage: 46000
Brands:
Metalife
Sir
Whisk
Xcel

31220 Whit-Log Trailers Inc
PO Box 668
Wilbur, OR 97494
541-673-0651
Fax: 541-673-1166 800-452-1234
brett@whitlogtrailers.com
www.whitlogtrailers.com
Manufacturer and exporter of hydraulic material handling equipment including truck mounted and pedestal electric stationary cranes

Owner: Gene Whitaker
gene@whitlogtrailers.com
Sales Manager: Jim Davidson
Estimated Sales: $300,000-500,000
Number Employees: 1-4

31221 White Mop Wringer Company
P.O. Box 16647
Tampa, FL 33687-6647
813-971-2223
Fax: 813-971-6090 800-237-7582
Manufacturer and exporter of janitorial equipment including burnishers, carts, floor and carpet care products and waste baskets and receptacles
Chief Financial Officer: Thomas Halluska
Estimated Sales: $50 - 100 Million
Number Employees: 100-249
Type of Packaging: Food Service
Brands:
Gator
Microscrub
Mipro
Propak
Pullman-Holt Gansow
Rugboss
Smartbasket

31222 White Mountain Freezer
800 E 101st Terrace
Kansas City, MO 64131-5322
816-943-4100
Fax: 816-943-4123
Manufacturer and exporter of ice cream and fruit processing machinery including freezers, parers and pitters
VP Marketing: Phil Gyori
Marketing Manager: Lori Baker
Production Manager: Melea Burghart
Parent Co: Rival Company

31223 White Mountain Lumber Co
30 E Milan Rd
PO Box 7
Berlin, NH 03570-3566
603-752-1000
Fax: 603-752-1400 www.whitemtnlumber.com
Wooden pallets
President: Barry J Kelley
barry@whitemtnlumber.com
Treasurer: Mark Kelley
Sales Director: Phil Bedard
General Manager/Wholesale Manager: Barry Kelley
Estimated Sales: $10-20 Million
Number Employees: 50-99
Square Footage: 50000

31224 White Oaks Frozen Foods
2525 Cooper Ave
Merced, CA 95348-4313
209-725-9492
Fax: 209-725-9441
www.whiteoakfrozenfoods.com
Reduced Moisture (RM) vegetable ingredients processor.
President: Jack Sollazzo
CEO: Suvan Sharma
Vice President, Sales: Dan Wilkinson
Number Employees: 1-4
Parent Co: Cascade Specialties, Inc.

31225 White Rabbit Dye Inc
4265 Meramec St
St Louis, MO 63116-2615
314-664-6563
Fax: 314-664-5563 800-466-6588
info@whiterabbitdye.com
www.whiterabbitdye.com
Easter egg dyes, kits and food colors; also, wire dippers; exporter of dry food colors
Co-Owner: Julie Consolino
Co-Owner: Jeff Petroski
Estimated Sales: $5-10 Million
Number Employees: 10-19
Square Footage: 32000
Parent Co: Premier Packaging
Type of Packaging: Consumer
Brands:
White Rabbit

31226 White Stokes International
3615 South Jasper Place
Chicago, IL 60609
773-523-7540
Fax: 773-523-0767 800-978-6537

Quality ingredients for bakery, confectionary, and ice cream. Founded in 1906.
President: Nicholas Tzakis
Vice President: George Tzakis
Number Employees: 26

31227 White Way Sign & Maintenance
451 Kingston Ct
Mt Prospect, IL 60056
847-391-0200
Fax: 847-642-0272 866-621-4122
Manufacturer and exporter of electronic message displays
President: Robert B Flannery Jr
VP of Sales: Robert Flannery
kcooper@amfam.net
Contact: Keisha Cooper
kcooper@amfam.net
Plant Mgr: Pete Tomaselli
Estimated Sales: $20 - 50 Million
Number Employees: 100-249

31228 Whiteshell Chairs Ltd.
Provincial Rd 408
River Hills, MA R0E 1T0
Canada
204-348-2770
Fax: 204-348-2548 866-959-4247
sales@whiteshellchairs.com
www.whiteshellchairs.com
Furniture manufacturer for the hospitality and food service industry. Products include bar stools, dining chairs, banquet chairs, table bases & tops, and outdoor furniture.
Production Manager - Powder Coating: Mark Gross

31229 (HQ)Whitford Corporation
33 Sproul Rd
Frazer, PA 19355
610-296-3200
Fax: 610-647-4849 sales@whitfordww.com
www.whitfordww.com
Manufacturer and exporter of nonstick coatings designed for food contact and food associated applications
President: David Willis Jr
Chief Administrative Officer: Joan Eberhardt
CFO: Brian Kilty
Marketing Director: John Badner
Contact: Daniel Brim
daniel.brim@whitfordww.com
Plant Manager: Scott De Bourke
Purchasing Manager: Jill Schultz
Estimated Sales: $30 - 50 Million
Number Employees: 100
Square Footage: 60000
Brands:
Excalibur
Quantanium
Quantum
Ultralon
Xylac
Xylan
Xylan Eterna
Xylan Plus

31230 Whiting & Davis
PO Box 1270
Attleboro Falls, MA 02763-0270
508-699-0214
Fax: 508-643-9303 800-876-6374
www.whitinganddavis.com/
Manufacturer, exporter and importer of stainless steel ring mesh safety protective clothing including gloves, aprons, arm and body gear
Director Sales/Marketing: Ron DiMarzio
Contact: David Youngerman
david.youngerman@whitingdavis.com
Estimated Sales: $5-10 Million
Number Employees: 100
Square Footage: 400000
Parent Co: WDC Holdings
Brands:
3-Step
Aegis
Ultra Guard
Whiting & Davis

31231 Whitley Manufacturing Company
PO Box 112
Midland, NC 28107
704-888-2625
Fax: 704-888-3023 www.whitleyhandle.com
Mop, broom and shovel handles; importer of dowels

President: Arlene Whitley
CEO: A Whitley
Quality Control: Arlene Whitley
Estimated Sales: $20 - 50 Million
Number Employees: 20-49
Square Footage: 35000

31232 (HQ)Whitlock Packaging Corp
1701 S Lee St
Fort Gibson, OK 74434-8419

918-478-4300
Fax: 918-478-7360 www.whitlockpkg.com
Contract packager providing glass, steel, aluminum
can, PET and plastic packaging services for
noncarbonated beverages
President: David Moller
CEO: Bruce Outland
b.outland@compsourceok.com
Vice President: Keith Bishop
VP Marketing/Sales: Terry Milan
VP Sales & Private Label: Bill Towler
VP Human Resource: Ted Smith
VP Manufacturing: Abraham Jospeh
Plant Manager: Joe Tomaskovic
Purchasing Manager: Tammy Sanders
Number Employees: 100-249
Square Footage: 562

31233 Whitmire Microgen Research Lab
3568 Tree Court Industrial Blv
St Louis, MO 63122-6682

636-825-9775
Fax: 636-225-3739 800-777-8570
www.basf.com
Pest control equipment and chemicals
CEO: Tony Accurso
National Sales Manager: Larry Sharp
Director Manufacturing/Logistics: Chuck Sutton
IT Executive: S Sims
steve.sims@wmmg.com
Estimated Sales: $15 Million
Number Employees: 50-99
Parent Co: S.C. Johnson & Son
Brands:
    Advance
    Allure
    Ascend
    Avert
    Mouse Master
    Vector

31234 Whittle & Mutch Inc
712 Fellowship Rd
Mt Laurel, NJ 08054-1004

856-235-1165
Fax: 856-235-0902 jmutch3d@wamiflavor.com
www.wamiflavor.com
President: John C Mutch Jr
Estimated Sales: $10-20 Million
Number Employees: 10-19

31235 WholesalePortal.com
6135 Seaview Avenue NW
Suite 3a
Seattle, WA 98107-2628

206-782-7040
Fax: 206-782-9641
Wholesaler

31236 Wichita Stamp & Seal Inc
807 N Main St
Wichita, KS 67203-3606

316-263-4223
Fax: 316-263-9738
Notary and corporate seals, rubber stamps, interior
signs, etc.; also, ink jet printers, coders and FDA ap-
proved inks
Owner: Lynne Bird
CFO: Linne Bird
Marketing Director: Martha Hays
Estimated Sales: Less Than $500,000
Number Employees: 5-9

31237 Wick's Packaging Service
7545 S State Road 75
Cutler, IN 46920

574-967-3104
Fax: 765-268-2729 info@wickspackaging.com
www.wickspackaging.com
Manufacturer and exporter of rebuilt vertical
form/fill/seal packaging machinery. Distribute plastic pouch making machinery: T-shirt, standup zip
lock pouch, and wicketed bags

Owner: Steven Wickersham
Vice President: Barb Wickersham
Research & Development: Craig Wickersham
Contact: Shawn Wickersham
shawn@wickspackaging.com
Packaging Engineer: Shawn Wickersham
Production Manager: Jerry Reef Jr
Estimated Sales: $2.5-5 Million
Number Employees: 1-4
Square Footage: 28000
Type of Packaging: Consumer, Food Service, Pri-
vate Label, Bulk

31238 Wick's Packaging Service
7545 South State Road 75
Cutler, IN 46920-9670

574-967-3104
Fax: 765-268-2729 info@wickspackaging.com
www.wickspackaging.com
Vertical form seal bag makers
President: Steve Wickersham
Contact: Shawn Wickersham
shawn@wickspackaging.com
Estimated Sales: Below $5 Million
Number Employees: 1-4

31239 (HQ)Wico Corporation
7847 N Caldwell Avenue
Niles, IL 60714-3375

847-583-1320
Fax: 847-583-1043 800-367-9426
Parts and supplies for coin-operated vending and
amusement equipment

31240 Wiegmann & Rose
Thermxchanger
9131 San Leandro St # 220
Oakland, CA 94603-1208

510-632-8828
Fax: 510-632-8920
jlogan@wiegmannandrose.com
www.wiegmannandrose.com
Designer and manufacturer of ammonia flooded,
spray shell and tube chillers for food and wine pro-
cessing
CEO: Scott E. Logan
Executive VP: R Trent
VP Quality: Jon E. Hammons
Sales: Scott E. Logan
Sales: K Gardner
Administration, Personnel: Suzette I. Logan
Plant Manager: Gary D. Keeler
Purchasing: Will O' Bryant
Estimated Sales: $2.5-5 Million
Number Employees: 20-49
Square Footage: 212000
Parent Co: Xchanger Manufacturing Corporation
Brands:
    Thermxchanger
    Wiegmann & Rose

31241 Wifag Group Polytype America
Corp
10 Industrial Ave
Mahwah, NJ 07430-2205

201-995-1000
Fax: 201-995-1080
Dry offset printing on plastic containers
President: Pieter S. van der Griendt
VP Sales: Thomas Stuart
Sales Manager: Felix Gomez
Operations Manager: Jim Dominico
Estimated Sales: $1-5 Million
Number Employees: 25
Parent Co: wifag//polytype

31242 Wiginton Corp
699 Aero Ln
Sanford, FL 32771-6699

407-585-3200
Fax: 407-592-9099 www.wiginton.net
Automatic fire sprinkler systems
President: Pete Aziz
pxa@wiginton.net
Sr. Project Manager: Bob Lyle
Manager of Sales: Kenny Trevino
Estimated Sales: $20-50 Million
Number Employees: 20-49

31243 Wika Instrument LP
1000 Wiegand Blvd
Lawrenceville, GA 30043-5868

770-513-8200
Fax: 770-338-5118 800-645-0606
info@wika.com www.wika.us
Full line of mechanical and electronic pressure in-
struments, temperature instruments and diaphram
seals manufactured to stric ISO 9001 standards
President: Dave Wannamaker
Estimated Sales: $20 - 50 Million
Number Employees: 500-999
Square Footage: 225000
Parent Co: Wika Instrument Corporation
Brands:
    Trend

31244 Wika Instrument LP
1000 Wiegand Blvd
Lawrenceville, GA 30043-5868

770-513-8200
Fax: 770-338-5118 888-945-2872
info@wika.com www.wika.us
President: Bill Anderson
banderson@wika.com
Chief Financial Officer: Steve McCullough
Chief Revenue Officer: Drew Firestone
Quality Control: Bernett Bigts
Estimated Sales: $5 - 10 Million
Number Employees: 500-999

31245 Wilbur Curtis Co
6913 W Acco St
Montebello, CA 90640-5403

323-837-2300
Fax: 323-837-2406 800-421-6150
info@wilburcurtis.com www.wilburcurtis.com
Manufacturer and exporter of coffee and tea brewing
equipment
CEO: Kevin Curtis
krcurtis@wilburcurtis.com
COO: Joe Laws
Estimated Sales: $30 - 50 Million
Number Employees: 100-249
Square Footage: 105000
Brands:
    Advanced Digital System
    Alpha
    Curtis
    Gemini
    Mercury
    Polaris
    Primo Cappaccino
    Thermologic

31246 Wilch Manufacturing
1345 SW 42nd Street
Topeka, KS 66609-1267

785-267-2762
Fax: 785-267-6825
Manufacturer and exporter of ice cream blenders,
cooking grills, freezers and dispensers including
slush, cocktail, yogurt and soft serve
President: Bill Young
Sales: Dave White
Purchasing Manager: Dee Kuhn
Number Employees: 45
Square Footage: 102000
Brands:
    Wilch

31247 Wilco Distributors Inc
1200 W Laurel Ave
Lompoc, CA 93436-5158

805-735-2476
Fax: 805-735-3629 800-769-5040
williewilc@aol.com www.wilcodistributors.com
Manufacture and distributor of rodenticides in ther
Western portion of the United States and Canada.
President: Blake Hazen
jbhazen@aol.com
Chief Executive Officer, Founder: Donald Willis
VP: Blake Hazen
Estimated Sales: $3 - 5 Million
Number Employees: 10-19

31248 Wilco Precision Testers
145 Main St
Tuckahoe, NY 10707-2906

914-337-2005
Fax: 914-337-8519 info@ptiusa.com
www.ptipacktech.com

Specialty packaging and inspection machinery for the pharmaceutical, food, container and automotive industries including total container inspection, package integrity testing, e-z open peelable can ends, and filling and heat sealing
Member of the Board: Anton Stauffer
Estimated Sales: $10 - 20 Million
Number Employees: 20-49

31249 Wilco, USA
181 Woodland Valley Drive
Woodland Park, CO 80863-9314
719-686-0074
Fax: 719-686-0112
gc-schramm@compuserve.com
Leak inspection equipment for all products

31250 Wilden Pump & Engineering LLC
22069 Van Buren St
Grand Terrace, CA 92313-5651
909-422-1700
Fax: 909-783-3440 wilden@psgdover.com
www.psgdover.com
Air operated double diaphragm pumps.
President: Monique Cisneros
mcisneros@nissanriverside.com
VP Finance: William Barton
VP Sales/Marketing: Martino Valela
Director Business Development: Greg Duncan
Director Operations: Dwane Lamb
VP Engineering: Gary Lent
Estimated Sales: $2,4,000,000
Number Employees: 250-499
Brands:
Pro-Flow

31251 Wilder Manufacturing Company
41 Mechanic St
Port Jervis, NY 12771
845-856-5188
Fax: 845-856-1950 800-832-1319
Manufacturer and exporter of holding, warming and transporting equipment including proofing cabinets, bins, racks, utility tables, etc
VP Sales/Marketing: Ray Addington
Estimated Sales: $1 - 5 Million
Parent Co: Win-Holt Equipment Group
Type of Packaging: Food Service
Brands:
Wilder

31252 Wildes Printing Co Inc
4321 Charles Crossing Dr
4321 Charles Crossing Drive
White Plains, MD 20695-3027
301-870-4141
Fax: 301-932-7495 info@wildes-spirit.com
www.wildes-spirit.com
General commercial markers and stamps
CEO: Katie Stickel
kstickel@wilde-spirit.com
Owner: Katie Stickel
Estimated Sales: $2.5 - 5 Million
Number Employees: 20-49
Brands:
Crown Marketing

31253 Wilen Professional Cleaning Products
3760 Southside Industrial Pkwy
Atlanta, GA 30354-3219
404-366-2111
Fax: 404-361-8832 800-241-7371
www.wilen.com
Manufacturer and exporter of cleaning equipment and supplies including brushes, scouring and hand pads and floor/carpet products
President: Vance Perry
Quality Control: Rachael Alexander
VP Marketing/Customer Relations: Rhonda Lassiter
Production Manager: John Akin
Purchasing Manager: Norris Minnis
Estimated Sales: $75 - 100 Million
Number Employees: 100-249
Square Footage: 150000

31254 Wilevco Inc
10 Fortune Dr
Billerica, MA 01821-3996
978-667-0400
Fax: 978-670-9191 sales@wilevco.com
www.wilevco.com

Manufacturer and exporter of automatic batter control systems, rotary atomization spray applicators and swept surface heat exchangers for process chilling systems
President: Leverett P Flint
Chairman/Founder: Putnam Flint
Vice President: John Whitmore
Estimated Sales: Below $5 Million
Number Employees: 10-19
Square Footage: 32000
Brands:
Cryolator
Wilevco

31255 Wilheit Packaging LLC
1527 May Dr
Gainesville, GA 30507-8464
770-532-4421
Fax: 770-532-8956 www.wilheit.com
Corrugated boxes
President and CFO: Philip Wilheit
pwilheit@wilheit.com
Marketing: Barbara Edwards
Estimated Sales: $20 - 50 Million
Number Employees: 50-99

31256 Wilhelmsen Consulting
455 Falcato Dr
Milpitas, CA 95035-6113
408-946-4525
Fax: 413-235-0121 ewilhel@klarify.com
Consultant providing analytical and business development services; also, food safety and training available
Owner: Eric Wilhelmsen
ewilhel@klarify.com
Estimated Sales: Less Than $500,000
Number Employees: 1-4

31257 Wilhite Sign Company
201 N Joplin
Joplin, MO 66762
417-623-1411
Fax: 417-623-2223
Signs including neon, plastic and painted
President: Jeplin Hipple
Estimated Sales: $500,000-$1 Million
Number Employees: 5-9

31258 Wilkens-Anderson Co
4525 W Division St
Chicago, IL 60651-1674
773-384-4433
Fax: 773-384-6260 800-847-2222
waco@wacolab.com www.wacolab.com
Laboratory and quality control equipment, supplies instruments and chemicals can testing equipment, can seam evaluation equipment
President/CEO: Bruce Wilkens
info@waco-lab-supply.com
Marketing Director: Peter Thomases
Sales Director: Don Hartman
Operations Manager: Eric Jensen
Production Manager: Don Lamonica
Estimated Sales: $6-8 Million
Number Employees: 20-49
Square Footage: 220000
Brands:
Waco

31259 (HQ)Wilkie Brothers Conveyor Inc
1765 Michigan Ave # 2
PO Box 219
Marysville, MI 48040-2046
810-364-4820
Fax: 810-364-4824 www.wilkiebros.com
Manufacturer and exporter of new and reconditioned overhead conveyor systems and equipment including chains, trolleys, attachments and structural components
Owner: Paul Naz
pnaz@wilkiebros.com
Sales Manager: Robert Wilkie
Sales: John Moews
Estimated Sales: $2.5-5 Million
Number Employees: 20-49
Square Footage: 240000
Type of Packaging: Bulk
Brands:
Bluewater Mfg., Inc.
J.B. Webb Co.
R.W. Zig Zag
Unibuilt

31260 Wilkinson Baking Company
2465 Old Milton Highway
Walla Walla, WA 99362
info@wilkinsonbaking.com
www.wilkinsonbaking.com
Manufacturer of fully-automated bread-making machines.
Co-Founder & President: Ron Wilkinson
Chairman: Randall Wilkinson
Chief Executive Officer: Paul Rhynard
Vice President, Operations: Christian Bell
Year Founded: 1998
Estimated Sales: $3 Million
Number Employees: 2-10

31261 (HQ)Wilkinson ManufacturingCompany
PO Box 490
Fort Calhoun, NE 68023
402-468-5511
Fax: 402-468-5521 info@wilkmfg.com
Manufacturer and exporter of aluminum foil pans
President: Bob Dalziel
R&D: Ray Massey Jr
Quality Control: Claude Weimcr
Director Marketing: Ray Salinas
Contact: Joseph Richardson
j.richardson@wilkinsonindustries.com
Estimated Sales: $30 - 50 Million
Number Employees: 250-499
Type of Packaging: Consumer, Food Service

31262 Wilks Precision Instr Co Inc
4800 Green Valley Rd
Union Bridge, MD 21791-9157
410-775-7917
Fax: 410-775-7919
Custom plastic injection molded boxes, trays and funnels
President: Tom Wilks
tbwilks@verizon.net
Estimated Sales: $1-2.5 Million
Number Employees: 5-9

31263 Will & Baumer
PO Box 2992
Syracuse, NY 13220
315-451-1000
Fax: 315-451-0120 info@willbaumer.com
www.willbaumer.com
Manufacturer, importer and exporter of candles, processed beeswax and candlelamps
President: Marshall Ciccone
Sales Director: John Dowd
Contact: Jeff Field
jefff@willbaumer.com
Estimated Sales: $5-10 Million
Number Employees: 50-99
Square Footage: 400000
Type of Packaging: Food Service
Brands:
Brite-Lite
Mood Lite

31264 Will-Pemco Inc
3333 Crocker Ave
Sheboygan, WI 53081-6425
920-458-2500
Fax: 920-458-1265 www.pemco-solutions.com
Sheeting and packaging
President: Mark Maertz
CFO: Jim Wanalstine
CEO: Lee Sleiter
Estimated Sales: $50 - 100 Million
Number Employees: 100-249

31265 Willamette Industries
PO Box 666
Beaverton, OR 97075-0666
503-641-1131
Fax: 503-526-8830 www.weyerhaeuser.com
Corrugated shipping containers
President: Michael Miller
General Manager: Richard Knapton
Sales Manager: Larry Brill
Estimated Sales: $20-50 Million
Number Employees: 100-249
Square Footage: 240000
Parent Co: Willamette Industries

31266 Willamette Industries
PO Box 666
Beaverton, OR 97075-0666
503-641-1131
Fax: 503-526-8830 www.weyerhaeuser.com
Manufacturer and exporter of corrugated boxes and
folding cartons
Plant Manager: David Dickey
Sales Manager: Brent Wagner
Estimated Sales: $20-50 Million
Number Employees: 100-249
Parent Co: Willamette Industries

31267 Willamette Industries
P.O. Box 666
Beaverton, OR 97075-0666
503-641-1131
Fax: 503-526-8830 www.weyerhaeuser.com
Custom shipping containers and full color
floor/counter displays
Sales Manager: Rick Lantello
Assistant Sales Manager: Jim Weiks
Plant Manager: David Dickey
Estimated Sales: $20-50 Million
Number Employees: 100-249
Square Footage: 300000
Parent Co: Willamette Industries

31268 Willamette Industries
2300 Greene Way
Louisville, KY 40220-4040
502-753-0264
Fax: 502-753-0276 800-465-3065
Manufacturer and exporter of liquid bulk one-way
disposable containers
Manager: Jim Woolums
General Manager: Larry Ogle
Sales Manager (Liquid Systems): H Edwin Cross
Estimated Sales: $50-100 Million
Number Employees: 5-9
Brands:
Willpak Liquid Systems

31269 Willard Packaging Co
18940 Woodfield Rd
Gaithersburg, MD 20879-4717
301-948-7700
Fax: 301-963-2375 www.willardpackaging.com
Corrugated boxes, foam parts and packaging sup-
plies
President: Dale Salkeld
Chairman of the Board: Raymond W Salkeld Jr
Sales Manager: H Harper
Estimated Sales: $20 - 50 Million
Number Employees: 50-99
Square Footage: 86000

31270 Willett America
1500 N Mittel Boulevard
Wood Dale, IL 60191-1072
817-222-2233
Fax: 817-222-0466 800-259-2600
Ink jet coding systems
President: Wes Lansford
VP Sales: Wayne Moore
Marketing Manager: Terri Carruth
Contact: Derrick Varnell
derrick_varnell@msn.com

31271 William Brown Co Inc
6429 Hegerman St
Philadelphia, PA 19135-3315
215-331-2776
Fax: 215-333-4231 800-962-7696
www.wmbrownco.com
Cutting systems for food processing
President: William Black
Vice President: Kevin Beck
Sales Director: Benjamin Rickards
Estimated Sales: $2.5 - 5 Million
Number Employees: 5-9

31272 William Hecht
508 Bainbridge Street
Philadelphia, PA 19147
215-925-6223
Fax: 215-923-6798
Display cases and store fixtures; also, architectural
millwork and casework available
President: Stuart Hecht
Number Employees: 49
Square Footage: 100000

31273 William J. Mills & Company
74100 W Front St
P.O. Box 2126
Greenport, NY 11944
631-477-1500
Fax: 631-477-1504 800-477-1535
www.millscanvas.com
Commercial awnings
Owner: William Willets
Estimated Sales: Below 1 Million
Number Employees: 20-49

31274 William Willis Worldwide
310 W Lyon Farm Drive
PO Box 4444
Greenwich, CT 06831-0408
Fax: 203-532-9292 203-532-1919
Executive search firm
President: William H. Willis
wwwinc@aol.com
Estimated Sales: $1-2.5 Million
Number Employees: 3
Square Footage: 3000

31275 Williams & Mettle Company
14309 Sommermeyer Street
Houston, TX 77041-6204
713-939-1830
Fax: 713-939-1337 800-526-4954
Filters and extruder pack screens
President and COO: Alan Arterbury
Chairman/CEO: Ken Howard
VP Finance: Allan Goertz
Number Employees: 140
Square Footage: 190000
Parent Co: WMW Industries

31276 Williams Pallet
9154 Port Union Rialto Rd
West Chester, OH 45069
513-874-4014
Fax: 513-874-5438
Wooden pallets and skids
Estimated Sales: $10-20 Million
Number Employees: 10

31277 Williams Refrigeration
65 Park Ave
Hillsdale, NJ 07642-2109
201-358-6005
Fax: 201-358-0401 800-445-9979
williamsref@msn.com
www.williams-refrigeration.co.uk
Manufacturer and exporter of commercial refrigera-
tion equipment including blast chillers and reach-in,
roll-in and counter refrigerators
Owner: William Gesner
william@williams-refrigeration.co.uk
VP: Nicholas Williams
Engineering Director: Steve Bernard
Marketing Director: Malcolm Harling
Sales Manager: Andy Ward
Purchasing Manager: Lynette Wixey
Number Employees: 250-499
Square Footage: 1400000
Parent Co: Williams Refrigeration
Type of Packaging: Food Service
Brands:
Williams

**31278 Williams Shade &
AwningCompany**
4834 Hickory Hill Rd
Memphis, TN 38116-3252
901-368-5055
Fax: 901-396-2327
Commercial awnings
President: R Allen Gray
Number Employees: 20

31279 Williamsburg Metal Spinning
263 Kent Ave
Brooklyn, NY 11249-4189
718-782-7040
Fax: 718-384-7424 888-535-5402
williamsburgmetal@hotmail.com
www.williamsburgmetal.com
Round baking pans, heat lamp reflectors and alumi-
num cooking items
President: Thomas Desanti
Estimated Sales: $1-2.5 Million
Number Employees: 10-19
Square Footage: 20000

31280 Williamsburg Millwork
29155 Richmond Tpke
Ruther Glen, VA 22546
804-994-2151
Fax: 804-994-5371
Wooden pallets
President: M R Piland Iii
VP: M Piland
Estimated Sales: $20 - 50 Million
Number Employees: 20-49
Square Footage: 40000

31281 Williamson & Co
9 Shelter Dr
Greer, SC 29650-4818
864-848-1011
Fax: 864-848-4310 800-849-3263
www.williamsonandcompany.com
Manufacturer and exporter of automated packaging,
data collection and material handling systems, trans-
port trucks and jacks.
President: Dan Williamson
dwilliamson@williamsonandcompany.com
Chief Financial Officer: Larry Williamson
VP: Lester Collins
Operations: Gene Settles
Estimated Sales: $5 - 10 Million
Number Employees: 50-99

31282 Willow Specialties
34 Clinton St
Batavia, NY 14020-2899
585-344-2900
Fax: 585-344-0044 800-724-7300
info@willowspecialties.com
www.willowgroupltd.com
Baskets and packaging supplies
Owner: Bernie Skalny
bskalny@willowgroupltd.com
Number Employees: 50-99

31283 Willson Industries
1003 Tuckahoe Road
P.O. Box 8
Marmora, NJ 08223
609-390-0756
Fax: 609-390-0757 800-894-4169
Point-of-purchase displays and custom advertising
specialties
President: Edward Willson
Estimated Sales: $1 - 2.5 Million
Number Employees: 4
Square Footage: 16000

31284 (HQ)Wilson AL Chemical Co
1050 Harrison Ave
Kearny, NJ 07032-5941
201-997-3300
Fax: 201-997-5122 800-526-1188
help@alwilson.com www.alwilson.com
Manufacturer and exporter of laundry and dry clean-
ing stain removers
President: Bob Edwards
bob@alwilson.com
Estimated Sales: $10 - 20 Million
Number Employees: 10-19

31285 Wilson Steel Products Company
PO Box 70214
Memphis, TN 38107
901-527-8742
Fax: 901-527-8779
Structural steel bins, chutes, hoppers and bucket ele-
vators
President: Robert Wilson
Estimated Sales: $2.5-5 Million
Number Employees: 10-19

31286 Wiltec
P.O. Box 367
Leominster, MA 01453-0367
978-537-1497
Fax: 978-537-7806
Plastic tabletop, partyware and food service products
including cafeteria bowls, ladles, trays, cups, tum-
blers, utensils, tongs, plates, etc
President: Amy Ullman
Sales/Marketing: Diane Holloway
Estimated Sales: $3 - 5 Million
Number Employees: 10-19
Number of Brands: 2
Number of Products: 100
Type of Packaging: Consumer, Food Service, Pri-
vate Label, Bulk

Brands:
Galaware
Wiltec

31287 Wilton Armetale
903 Square St
Mt Joy, PA 17552-1911
717-653-4444
Fax: 717-653-6573 800-779-4586
www.armetale.com
Manufacturer and exporter of metal tabletop ware
and salad bar accessories
President: Ed Leibensperger
eleibensperger@armetale.com
Estimated Sales: $1 - 5 Million
Number Employees: 50-99
Brands:
Armetale

31288 (HQ)Wilton Brands LLC
2240 75th St
Woodridge, IL 60517-2333
630-963-7100
Fax: 630-810-2712 info@wilton.com
www.wilton.com
Manufacturer and exporter of kitchenware including
bakeware, cake decorating supplies, tools and gad-
gets; also, picture frames
CEO: Sue Buchta
Estimated Sales: $50 Million
Number Employees: 500-999
Square Footage: 1000000
Brands:
Copco
Rowoco
Weston Gallery
Wilton

31289 Wilton Industries CanadaLtd.
98 Carrier Drive
Etobicoke, ON M9W 5R1
Canada
416-679-0790
Fax: 416-679-0798 800-387-3300
canadasales@wilton.ca www.wilton.com
Cake, candy and cookie decorating and making sup-
plies
President: Jeff McLaughlin
General Manager: Steve Curtis
Number Employees: 45
Square Footage: 90000
Parent Co: Towerbrook Capital Partners

31290 Win-Holt Equipment Group
141 Eileen Way
Syosset, NY 11791
516-222-0335
Fax: 516-921-0538 800-444-3595
sales@winholt.com www.winholt.com
Material and food handling equipment, food service
equipment and heating, holding and transporting
equipment
President/ COO: Dominic Scarfogliero
Chairman, Chief Executive Officer: Jonathan J
Holtz
R&D: Nancy Korista
Marketing Director: Bruce Schwartz
Sales Director: Jeff Herbert
Sales: Tim Sullivan
President, Chief Operating Officer: Dominick
Scarfogliero
VP Operations: John Jameson
Purchasing Manager: Glen Stein
Estimated Sales: $10 - 20 Million
Number Employees: 300-500
Number of Brands: 4
Number of Products: 200

31291 Winchester Carton
P.O. Box 597
Eutaw, AL 35462-0597
205-372-3337
Fax: 205-372-9226 www.rocktenn.com
Boxes including recycled paper
President: Ben Williams
Plant Manager: Willie Carpenter
Estimated Sales: $20 - 50 Million
Number Employees: 100-249
Parent Co: Rock Tenn Company

31292 Wincup Holdings
4640 Lewis Rd
Stone Mountain, GA 30083
770-771-5861
www.wincup.com
Styrofoam bowls, cups and food containers; also,
custom design and printing available.
President/Chief Revenue Officer: Michael Winters
CEO: Brad Laporte
VP, Accounting: Jay Dahlquist
Chief Information Officer: Matthew Marrazza
Year Founded: 1962
Estimated Sales: $101.8 Million
Number Employees: 1,000+
Brands:
Compac
Profit Pals
Simplicity
Styrocups

31293 (HQ)Wind River Environmental
163 Western Ave
Gloucester, MA 01930-4042
978-281-4443
Fax: 978-281-6321 800-332-6025
custsvc@strong-holster.com
www.wrenvironmental.com
Custom made leather menu covers, wine lists, check
presenters and ID badges
Owner: Don Strong
CEO: Rich Cutter
Marketing Director: Larry Angello
Operations Manager: Steve Kaity
Purchasing Manager: Brian Cutter
Estimated Sales: $5 Million
Number Employees: 1-4
Number of Products: 250
Square Footage: 232000
Type of Packaging: Bulk

31294 Windhorst Blowmold
P.O. Box 696
Euless, TX 76039-0696
817-540-6639
Fax: 817-540-0271
Retrofitter and installer of electrical and mechanical
components for the blowmolding industry
Owner: Michael Windhorst
Vice President: Gerry Trainque
Estimated Sales: $500,000-$1 Million
Number Employees: 20-49

31295 Windmill Electrastatic Sprayers
PO Box 220
Hughson, CA 95326-1490
209-883-4405
Fax: 209-883-9565 800-426-5615
www.vrisimo.com
Wine industry sprayers
President and Owner: Fred Brenda
Estimated Sales: $1 - 3 Million
Number Employees: 5-9

31296 Windmoeller & HoelscherCorporation
23 New England Way
Lincoln, RI 02865
401-334-0965
Fax: 401-333-6491 800-854-8702
info@whcorp.com www.whcorp.com
A supplier of flexographic and gravure printing
press, blown and cast film extrusion systems,
multiwall equipment, plastic sack and bag making
machines, as well as form-fill-seal machinery for the
converting and packaging industry.
President: Hans Deamer
Corporate Controller: Walter Kaehler
Vice President: Andrew Wheeler
Contact: Tom Apple
t.apple@whcorp.com
Estimated Sales: $50 - 75 Million
Number Employees: 20-49

31297 Windrush Estate Winery
3100 Concession Road
3 Adjala
Palgrave, ON L0N 1P0
Canada
905-729-0060
windrushestatewinery.com
Wines.
Co-Founder & General Partner: J.C. Pennie
Co-Founder & General Partner: Marilyn Field

Year Founded: 2017
Number of Brands: 1
Number of Products: 9
Type of Packaging: Food Service
Brands:
Windrush

31298 (HQ)Windsor Wax Co Inc
510 Carolina Back Rd
Charlestown, RI 02813-3809
401-364-5941
Fax: 401-364-3729 800-243-8929
Manufacturer and exporter of floor care products in-
cluding wax, polymer finishes, cleaning compounds,
carpet cleaner and concrete coatings; importer of
natural wax and paraffin
Office Manager: M Wojcik
CEO: D Kahn
CEO: David Kahn
Number Employees: 1-4
Brands:
Konkrete
Wincoat
Windsor
Woodee

31299 Wine Analyst
23230 Ravensbury Avenue
Los Altos Hills, CA 94024-6429
650-949-5929
Fax: 650-941-1892
Wine industry analyst software
President: Ray Smith
Number Employees: 10

31300 Wine Appreciation Guild
360 Swift Ave # 34
South San Francisco, CA 94080-6220
650-866-3020
Fax: 650-866-3029 info@wineappreciation.com
Wine industry tasting room supplies
Manager: James Mackey
Vice President: Elliott Mackey
info@wineappreciation.com
Estimated Sales: $10 Million
Number Employees: 20-49

31301 Wine Cap Company
PO Box 1784
Santa Rosa, CA 95402-1784
707-535-1950
Fax: 707-939-3934 pstaehle@winecap.com
Wax Cap and B-Cap bottle closure systems
CEO: Dwight Pate
Estimated Sales: $500,000-$1 Million
Number Employees: 4

31302 Wine Chillers of California
1104 E 17th St Ste F
Santa Ana, CA 92701
714-541-5795
Fax: 714-541-3139 800-331-4274
Custom builder and provider of wine chilling equip-
ment.
President: Robert Sizemore
CEO: D Sizemore
Estimated Sales: $.5 - 1,000,000
Number Employees: 1-4
Square Footage: 4000000
Brands:
Cruvinet
Vimo Cave
Vino Temp
Vinotheque
Wine Well
Winekeeper

31303 Wine Concepts
135 Mason Cir
Suite K
Concord, CA 94520
925-521-9001
Fax: 925-521-9006 800-560-0105
Wine industry tasting room supplies
Owner: Gerry Dodd
Estimated Sales: $1-2.5 Million
Number Employees: 10-19

31304 Wine Country Cases
995 Vintage Ave # 100
St Helena, CA 94574-1409
707-967-4805
Fax: 707-967-4807 info@winecountrycases.com
www.winecountrycases.com

Wine industry wooden wine boxes
President: Dan Pina
  dan@winecountrycases.com
Owner: Ignacio Delgadillo
Estimated Sales: $2 Million
Number Employees: 50-99

31305 Wine Things Unlimited
PO Box 1349
Sonoma, CA 95476
707-935-1277
Fax: 707-935-3403 800-447-3983
www.winethings.com
Wine industry tasting room supplies
President: David Liberstein
Estimated Sales: $1 - 5 Million
Number Employees: 5-9

31306 Wine Things
1006 S. Milpitas Blvd.
Milpitas, CA 95035
408-262-1898
Fax: 408-262-1890 800-796-7797
www.winethings.com
Wine racks
President: David Lieberstein
Estimated Sales: $1 - 5 Million
Number Employees: 5-9

31307 Wine Well Chiller Co
301 Brewster Rd # 3c
Milford, CT 06460-3700
203-878-2465
Fax: 203-878-2466 winewellchiller@aol.com
www.epichead.com
Manufacturer and exporter of high-speed beverage
chillers including wine
Owner: Tyrone Petr
CEO/President: Anabel Fisher
Sales: Melissa Lawless
  winewellchiller@aol.com
Production: Tyrone P
Estimated Sales: $1 - 3 Million
Number Employees: 5-9
Square Footage: 4000
Brands:
  Microchiller
  Wine Well

31308 WineAndHospitalityJobs.com
640 Michael Drive
Sonoma, CA 95476
707-933-0687
Online job board for the wine and hospitality industry.

31309 WineEmotion Canada
14 Automatic Road
Unit #33
Brampton, ON L6S 5N5
Canada
647-910-9463
customerservice@wineemotion.ca
www.wineemotion.ca
Liquor dispenser and wine preserving machines.
Founder, WineEmotion: Riccardo Gosi
President, WineEmotion Canada: Tony Francis

31310 Winekeeper
625 E Haley St
Santa Barbara, CA 93103
805-963-3451
Fax: 805-965-5393 www.winekeeper.com
Wome dispensing and wine cellaring equipment
President: Norman Grant
Contact: Connie Grant
  connie@winaire.com
Number Employees: 5-9
Parent Co: Winekeeper
Brands:
  Cruvinet
  Winekeeper

31311 Wineracks by Marcus
PO Box 2713
Costa Mesa, CA 92628-2713
714-546-4922
Fax: 714-549-8238
Wineracks By Marcus; a strong, accessible,
space-efficient aluminum racks with a sharp, clean
look for restaurants, serious collectors and retail.
Manufactured to order, custom sizes and layout
drawings available
President: Steve Marcus

Estimated Sales: $300,000-500,000
Number Employees: 1-4

31312 Winkler USA LLC
88 S State St
Hackensack, NJ 07601-3920
201-488-9291
Fax: 201-525-0771 www.winklerusa.com
Sales Director: Cindy Chananie
Contact: Mattia Fiorilli
  mfiorilli@winklerusa.com
Number Employees: 100-249

31313 Winmark Stamp & Sign
2284 S West Temple
Salt Lake City, UT 84115-2659
801-486-2011
Fax: 801-467-6265 800-438-0480
sales@winmarkinc.com www.winmarkinc.com
Signage, badges, name plates, notary seals, marking
devices and rubber stamps including pre-inked and
self-inking
Owner: Traci Szwedko
  traci@winmarkinc.com
CFO: Traci Szwedko
Estimated Sales: Less Than $500,000
Number Employees: 5-9
Square Footage: 16000

31314 Winn-Sol Products
PO Box 978
Oshkosh, WI 54903-0978
920-231-2031
Lime, rust, scale and milkstone solvents and remov-
ers used in dishwashers
President: James Driessen Sr
Secretary: Jenece Driessen
VP: Connie Hart
Estimated Sales: $300,000-500,000
Number Employees: 1-4
Brands:
  Dairi-Sol
  Industri-Sol
  Lime-Elim

31315 Winnebago Sign Company
PO Box 662
Fond Du Lac, WI 54936-0662
920-922-5930
Fax: 920-922-5930
Luminous tube and plastic signs; also, servicing of
signs available
Owner: Donald E Gross
Sign Installer: Bob Samp
Office Manager: Laura Leichtfuss
Estimated Sales: Less than $500,000
Number Employees: 1-4
Parent Co: Barber Graphix

31316 Winpak Lane Inc
998 S Sierra Way
San Bernardino, CA 92408-2122
909-885-0715
Fax: 909-381-1934 800-804-4224
info@wli.winpak.com www.winpak.com
Manufatures vertical-form-fill-seal packaging for
flexible pouches and cups through innovative machine building and design. Our expertise in liuid filling (ranges 1.5m-19ml and hot-fill capabilities up to
90 degrees excelsiors)mbinedwith a commitment to
never compromise on quality makes Winpak equipment one of the standards in the industry
President: David Stacey
  david.stacey@winpak.com
Marketing/Sales: John Schcfer
Estimated Sales: $10-20 Million
Number Employees: 100-249
Parent Co: Wipak Group

31317 Winpak Portion Packaging
998 South Sierra Way
San Bernardino, CA 92408
909-885-0715
Fax: 909-381-1934 800-804-4224
www.winpak.com
Manufacturer and exporter of pre-formed portion
controlled plastic packaging. Diecut for lidding and
filling equipment
President: Thomas Herlihy
Vice President: Jim McMacken
Marketing Director: Debbie Calvarese
Contact: Kathy Boynton
  kathy.boynton@winpak.com

Number Employees: 225
Parent Co: Winpak
Type of Packaging: Consumer, Food Service, Pri-
vate Label

31318 Winpak Technologies
85 Laird Drive
Toronto, ON M4G 3T8
Canada
416-421-1700
Fax: 416-421-7957
Packaging
Director Sales & Marketing: L de Bellefeuille
Manufacturing: J Millwrad
Estimated Sales: $1 - 5 Million
Number Employees: 250
Square Footage: 600000
Parent Co: Winpak

31319 Wins Paper Products
321 Murray Road
Springtown, TX 76082-6520
817-281-6550
Fax: 817-281-0560 800-733-2420
Manufacturer and wholesaler/distributor of paper
bags; serving the food service market
President: Douglas Wiley
Chairman: Gordon Wiley
Estimated Sales: Below $5 Million
Number Employees: 10
Square Footage: 156000

31320 Winston Industries
2345 Carton Dr
Louisville, KY 40299-2513
502-495-5500
Fax: 502-495-5458 800-234-5286
information@winstonind.com
www.winstonind.com
Manufacturer and exporter of stainless steel ovens,
pressure cookers and holding cabinets
President/ CEO: Valerie Shelton
  vshelton@winstonind.com
Quality Control: Tina Thompson
CFO: Bob Leavitt
VP Global Sales: Shaun Tanner
COO: Paul Haviland
VP Manufacturing: Leo Gutgsell
Estimated Sales: $10 - 20 Million
Number Employees: 100-249
Type of Packaging: Food Service
Brands:
  C-Vap
  C-Vat
  Collettramatic

31321 Winston Laboratories Inc
100 N Fairway Dr # 134
Suite 134
Vernon Hills, IL 60061-1859
847-362-8200
Fax: 847-362-8394 800-946-5229
Consultant specializing in nutritional and laboratory
testing for food additives, pesticide residues, MSG,
sulfites, etc.; also, FDA liaison service, HACCP
plans, food plant inspections and certification of
acidified foods and thermalprocesses available
President: Marvin Winston
CEO: Joel E Bernstein
CFO: Barry Hollingsworth
Senior Scientist: Porus Aria PhD
Contact: Ronald Abrahams
  ron@winstonlabs.com
Vice President, Operations: David A Henninger
Estimated Sales: $500,000-$1 Million
Number Employees: 10-19
Square Footage: 19500

31322 Winzen Film
P.O. Box 677
407 West 2nd Street
Taylor, TX 76574
903-885-7595
Fax: 903-885-4702 800-779-7595
www.winzen.com
Manufacturer and exporter of plastic container mate-
rials
Manager: Frank Neidhart
CEO: Robert Williamson
Estimated Sales: $10 - 20 Million
Number Employees: 20-49
Parent Co: BAG Corporation

31323 Wipe-Tex International Corp
110 E 153rd St # 2
Bronx, NY 10451-5230
718-665-0013
Fax: 718-665-0787 800-643-9607
Washed and sterilized cloths including wiping rags, cotton cleaning remnants, kitchen and new hemmed towels; also, cheesecloth
Owner: Alex Fudder
wiperrags@msn.com
VP Sales Marketing: Richard Chesney
Number Employees: 20-49
Square Footage: 200000

31324 (HQ)Wipeco Inc
250 N Mannheim Rd
Hillside, IL 60162-1835
708-544-7247
Fax: 708-544-7248 info@wipeco.com
www.wipeco.com
Wiping rags and nonwoven wipers
President: Jeff Shanken
Chief Executive Officer: Sandy Woycke
Manager: Justin Woycke
jwoycke@wipeco.com
Estimated Sales: $370,000
Number Employees: 5-9

31325 Wire Belt Co of America
154 Harvey Rd
Londonderry, NH 03053-7473
603-644-2500
Fax: 603-644-3600 sales@wirebelt.com
Stainless steel open-mesh conveyor belting
President: David Greer
dgreer@wirebelt.com
Marketing Director: Richard Spiak
Sales: Richard Spiak
Operations: Scott Monk
Estimated Sales: $20-50 Million
Number Employees: 100-249
Brands:
Eye-Flex
Flat-Flex
Flat-Flex El
Flat-Flex Xt
Flex-Turn

31326 Wire Products Mfg
1000 Mathews St
Merrill, WI 54452-2837
715-536-7884
Fax: 715-536-1476
Manufacturer and exporter of wire racks including display and fryer
President: Roger C Dupke
Manager: Jim Dupke
Estimated Sales: $20-50 Million
Number Employees: 20-49
Type of Packaging: Consumer, Food Service, Bulk

31327 Wirefab Inc
75 Blackstone River Rd
Worcester, MA 01607-1493
508-754-5359
Fax: 508-797-3620 877-877-4445
info@wirefab.com www.wirefab.com
Manufacturer and exporter of wire baskets, shelving and racks including doughnut and bagel baskets and deep-fry crumb screens
Owner: A B Zakarian
wirefab@gis.net
CEO: A Zakarian
VP: M M Zakarian
R & D: Larry Clough
Sales: William Binson
wirefab@gis.net
Public Relations: Michael Murdock
Operations: John Michaels
Production: Christopher Bousbouras
Plant Manager: James Hall
Purchasing: Barbara Vasdagalis
Estimated Sales: $5-10 Million
Number Employees: 50-99
Square Footage: 160000
Type of Packaging: Bulk

31328 Wiremaid Products Div
11711 W Sample Rd
Coral Springs, FL 33065-3155
954-545-9000
Fax: 954-545-9011 800-770-4700
www.vutec.com
Manufacturer and exporter of wire and metal products including displays, racks, shelves, etc
Manager: Bryan Sciullo
CEO: Howard L Sinkoff
howardsinkoff@vutec.com
CFO: Jeff Chanoff
VP: Allen Axman
R&D: Hai Nguyen
Marketing: John Cavanaugh
Sales: Allen Axman
Production: Raul Passalaqua
Plant Manager: Raul Passalaqua
Purchasing: Robert Ciarletto
Estimated Sales: $20-50 Million
Number Employees: 1-4
Square Footage: 100000
Parent Co: Vutec Corporation
Brands:
Vutec Usa
Wiremaid Usa

31329 Wireway Husky Corp
6146 Denver Industrial Park Rd
Denver, NC 28037-7805
704-483-1900
Fax: 704-483-1911 800-438-5629
productinfo@wirewayhusky.com
www.wirewayhusky.com
Material handling equipment including pallet racks and cable reel racks
President: Ron Young
ryoung@wirewayhusky.com
VP: Gregory Young
Estimated Sales: $10 - 20 Million
Number Employees: 100-249
Parent Co: Husky Systems

31330 Wisco Industries Assembly
955 Market St
Oregon, WI 53575-1009
608-835-3300
Fax: 608-835-7399 800-999-4726
info@wiscoind.com www.wiscoind.com
Counter top ovens and warmers for pizza, pretzels and cookies; exporter of pizza ovens, food warmers, toasters and sandwich grills
CEO: Elving Kjellstrom
Marketing Director: Donald Porkner
Sales Director: Randy Kjellstrom
Estimated Sales: $20 - 30 Million
Number Employees: 5-9
Square Footage: 200000

31331 Wisconsin Aluminum Foundry Co
838 S 16th St
Manitowoc, WI 54220-5004
920-682-8286
Fax: 920-682-7285 inquiries@wafco.com
Manufacturer and exporter of griddles,grills, can sealers, sterilizers, pressure cookers, cookware, etc... importer of cookware.
President: Jim Hatt
jhatt@wafco.com
CEO: Philip Jacobs
Quality Control: Don Noworatsky
Estimated Sales: $5 - 10 Million
Number Employees: 250-499
Number of Brands: 1
Type of Packaging: Consumer
Brands:
Chef's Design
Chef-Way

31332 Wisconsin Bakers Assn Inc
2514 S 102nd St # 100
Milwaukee, WI 53227-2154
414-258-5552
Fax: 414-258-5582 www.wibakers.com
Serves as the catalyst for bringing bakers together through special events such as workshops, conferences, conventions, and member events.
Executive Director: David Schmidt
dave@wibakers.com
Number Employees: 1-4

31333 Wisconsin Bench Mfg
507 E Grant St
Thorp, WI 54771-9662
715-669-5360
Fax: 715-669-5929 800-242-2303
www.wibenchmfg.com
Bench tops

General Manager: Steve Burgess
steve@wibench.com
CEO: Phillip Jeska
Estimated Sales: $5-10 Million
Number Employees: 100-249
Square Footage: 70000

31334 Wisconsin Box Co
929 Townline Rd
PO Box 718
Wausau, WI 54403-6681
715-842-2248
Fax: 715-842-2240 www.wisconsinbox.com
Manufacturer and exporter of wooden shipping containers and crates
Owner: Jeff Davis
CFO: Michael Shipway
Vice President of Sales: Gene Davis
jdavis@wisconsinbox.com
Customer Service: Jim Geise
Plant Manager: Bob Schultz
Plant Manager: Charley Ewell
Estimated Sales: $5 - 10 Million
Number Employees: 20-49
Type of Packaging: Bulk

31335 Wisconsin Box Co
929 Townline Rd
PO Box 718
Wausau, WI 54403-6681
715-842-2248
Fax: 715-842-2240 800-876-6658
garyl@tcrllc.com www.wisconsinbox.com
Manufacturer and exporter of wirebound and collapsible pallet boxes and crates
Owner: Jeff Davis
jdavis@wisconsinbox.com
CEO: Gary LeMaster
Sales Manager: Dennis Maxson
jdavis@wisconsinbox.com
Controller / Human Resources: Michael Shipway
Estimated Sales: $10 - 20 Million
Number Employees: 20-49
Square Footage: 150000

31336 Wisconsin Converting Inc
1689 Morrow St
Green Bay, WI 54302-2605
920-437-6400
Fax: 920-436-4964 800-544-1935
sc@wisconsinconverting.com
www.wisconsinconverting.com
Mailers and bags including paper, lined, candy and nut bags and self opening food sacks
President: John Brogan
jbrogan@wisconsinconverting.com
CEO: Charles Johns
Marketing Director: Jill Walschinski
VP Operations: Bob McGee
Estimated Sales: $10 - 20,000,000
Number Employees: 20-49

31337 Wisconsin Film & Bag Inc
3100 E Richmond St
Shawano, WI 54166-3845
715-524-2565
Fax: 715-524-3527 800-765-9224
greggreene@wifb.com www.wifb.com
Polyethylene sheeting and bundling films and bags
Vice President: Mohammad Bashir
bashir.mohammad@wolterskluwer.com
Director of Sales Operations: Leann Gueths
CFO: Al Johnson
V.P. of Major Accounts: Greg Greene
VP: Ian Anderson
Inside Sales Representative: Kristin Gehm
Regional Sales Manager: Tony Hindley
Estimated Sales: Below $5 Million
Number Employees: 100-249
Square Footage: 118000
Brands:
Atlas
Inflation Fighter

31338 Wisconsin Precision Casting
W405 County Road L
East Troy, WI 53120-2406
262-642-7307
Fax: 262-642-4115 866-642-7307
www.wisconsinprecision.com

Owner: Clyde Klemowits
cpk@wisconsinprecision.com
VP - Manufacturing: Cliff Fischer
VP - Engineering: Claude Klemowits
Sales and Marketing Manager: Dean Kirschner
Estimated Sales: $10-20 Million
Number Employees: 50-99
Square Footage: 40

31339 Wisdom Adhesives Worldwide

1575 Executive Drive
Elgin, IL 60123

847-841-7002

Fax: 847-841-7009 www.wisdomadhesives.com
Water-based adhesives, animal glue, hot melts and
custom adhesives
Chief Executive Officer: Jeff Wisdom
Vice President of Technologies: Tom Rolando
Vice President of Sales: Paul Preston
Contact: Ed Marzano
edmarzano@wisdomadhesives.com
Vice President of Operations: Linda Wisdom
Estimated Sales: $1-5 Million
Number Employees: 12

31340 Wishbone Utensil Tableware Line

15 Paramount Pkwy
Wheat Ridge, CO 80215-6615

303-238-8088

Fax: 253-595-7673 866-266-5928
Forever replaces chopsticks. One piece tong, skewer
& ergonomic utensil. Child safe. Dishwasher
friendly. Assisted living compatible. Solution for the
chopstick challenged. Popular among hotel/resorts,
restaurateur and occupationalhealth. Ten mo-
tif-friendly colors. FDA approved. Stylish, durable,
reusable, fun. Sanitized and individually wrapped.
Gourmet quality Feng Shui tableware
CEO: R Farlan Krieger Sr
Estimated Sales: Under $300,000
Number Employees: 9
Number of Brands: 4
Number of Products: 8
Square Footage: 50000
Parent Co: RF Krieger, LLC
Type of Packaging: Consumer, Food Service, Pri-
vate Label, Bulk
Brands:
   Wishbone Utensil Tableware Line

31341 Witt Plastics

P.O. Box 808
Greenville, OH 45331-0808

937-548-7272

Fax: 937-547-6046 800-227-9181
www.wittplastics.com
Roll and sheet high impact polystyrene and poly-
propylene for container and lid stock thermoforming
President: Bob Kramer
Owner/CEO: John Witt
Purchasing Manager: Bill Simmons
Estimated Sales: $10 - 20 Million
Number Employees: 50-99
Square Footage: 100000

31342 Wittco Foodservice Equipment

7737 N 81st St
Milwaukee, WI 53223-3839

414-365-4400

Fax: 414-354-2821 800-821-3912
www.wittco.com
Manufacturer and exporter of carts including
hot/cold food delivery and insulated tray; also,
cook/chill equipment
Cmo: Jim Sherman
jsherman@wittco.com
Estimated Sales: $5 Million
Number Employees: 20-49
Square Footage: 180000
Parent Co: Nichols Industries
Type of Packaging: Food Service
Brands:
   Meals-On-Wheels

31343 Wittco Foodservice Equipment

7737 N 81st St
Milwaukee, WI 53223-3839

414-365-4400

Fax: 414-354-2821 800-367-8413
www.wittco.com
Manufacturer and exporter of heated food holding
equipment and cook/hold ovens

General Manager: Steve Jensen
CEO: Tim Murray
VP: Jeff Smith
Marketing: Joe Burns
Operations Manager: Dave Braun
Estimated Sales: $5-10 Million
Number Employees: 20-49

31344 Witte Brothers ExchangeInc

575 Witte Industrial
Troy, MO 63379-3964

636-462-8402

Fax: 636-528-6139 800-325-8151
info@wittebros.com www.wittebros.com
Warehousing, transportation and distribution for refrigerated and frozen products including LTL, TL
(also dry), consolidation, freight pooling, rail service, and full freight management capabilities. Full
in ventory management. Temprange to -15°F
2,000,000 cubic feet warehouse with 34 doors and
20,000 square feet refrigerated cross dock.
President: Brent Witte
Sr. Director of Business Development: Laura Wort
Director of Operations: Shane Carter
Number Employees: 100-249

31345 Witte Co Inc

507 Route 31 S
Washington, NJ 7882

908-689-6500

Fax: 908-537-6806 info@witte.com
www.witte.com
Manufacturer and exporter of vibrating screens, con-
veyors, fluid bed dryers and coolers
President: Tyson Witte
Sales/Marketing: Jim Schak
Engineering Manager: Larry Stoma
Purchasing Manager: Marilyn March
Estimated Sales: $10 - 20,000,000
Number Employees: 1-4
Square Footage: 60000
Type of Packaging: Private Label
Brands:
   Witte

31346 Wittemann Company

1 Industry Dr
Palm Coast, FL 32137

386-445-4200

Fax: 386-445-7042 us@union.dk
www.wittemann.com
Manufacturer and exporter of carbon dioxide gener-
ation and recovery systems; also, dryers, cylinder
filling units and dry ice systems
President: William Geiger
General Manager: Bill Gieyer
CFO: Cara Brammer
Sales Manager: Gabreil Dominguez
Regional Sales Manager: Daniel Gruber
Contact: Donna Grabowski
donnag@wittemann.com
Product Manager: Jay Soto
Estimated Sales: $3 - 5 Million
Number Employees: 10-19
Square Footage: 120000

31347 (HQ)Wittern Group

8040 University Blvd
Clive, IA 50325-1171

515-274-3641

Fax: 515-271-8530 855-712-8729
contact@vending.com www.wittern.com
Manufacturer and exporter of vending machines for
snacks, canned and hot beverages, refrigerated and
frozen foods, desserts, etc
Chairman of the Board: Francis Wittern
CEO: Heidi Chico
Purchasing Manager: Ron Harter
Estimated Sales: $9 Million
Number Employees: 250-499
Square Footage: 420000
Parent Co: 8040 Holdings, Inc.
Brands:
   Servomatic

31348 Wna Comet West Inc

1135 Samuelson St
City of Industry, CA 91748-1222

626-913-4022

Fax: 626-913-1776 800-225-0939
www.olympuspartners.com
Disposable plastic dinnerware including cutlery,
tumblers, plates, bowls, etc

manager: Kurt Rogstad
Executive VP: R Greer
Sales Manager: Michael Sharpe
Manager: Curt Heverly
curt@wna-inc.com
Estimated Sales: $20-50 Million
Number Employees: 250-499
Square Footage: 200000
Parent Co: WNA-Waddington North America

31349 Wnc Pallet & Forest Pdts Co

1414 Smoky Park Hwy
Candler, NC 28715-8237

828-667-5426

Fax: 828-665-4759
Wooden and recycled pallets, skids and boxes; also,
pallet recycling
President: Tom Orr
torr@wncpallet.com
VP: T Orr
Sales: Cyndi Commozi
Manager: Brent Orr
Estimated Sales: $10 - 20 Million
Number Employees: 100-249

31350 Woerner Wire Works

3008 Evans St
PO Box 11449
Omaha, NE 68111-3272

402-451-5414

Fax: 402-451-5415
Established in 1892. Structural Steel Manufacturer,
ornamental metal work, wholesale wire, fabricated
wire, manufacturers, metal fabricator.
President: Daniel Scanlan
dan@woernerwire.com
VP: Sandor Horvath
Project Manager: Rick Weitkemper
Vice President: Daniel J Scanlan
dan@woernerwire.com
Estimated Sales: Below $5 Million
Number Employees: 10-19
Square Footage: 40000

31351 Wohl Associates Inc

50 Floyds Run
Bohemia, NY 11716-2154

631-244-7979

Fax: 631-244-6987 info@wohlassociates.com
www.wohlassociates.com
Dealer of used and rebuilt scrubbers, blanchers,
steamers, labelers, and other food processing equipment
Owner: Andrew Wohl
info@wohlassociates.com
Estimated Sales: $5 - 10 Million
Number Employees: 10-19

31352 Wohl Associates Inc

50 Floyds Run
Bohemia, NY 11716-2154

631-244-7979

Fax: 631-244-6987 info@wohlassociates.com
www.wohlassociates.com
Buyer and seller of surplus equipment including
blanchers, dicers, mixers, dryers and coolers
Owner: Andrew Wohl
info@wohlassociates.com
CFO: Anndy Wohl
Estimated Sales: $5 - 10 Million
Number Employees: 10-19

31353 Wohlt Cheese Corp

1005 Orville Dr
P.O. Box 203
New London, WI 54961-9398

920-982-9000

Fax: 920-982-6288
Manufacturer of processed cheeses (including
American cheese, cheese food, cheese spread and
other cheese products); available in loaves and
blocks, flavoured varities, custom blends and vari-
ous melts. Offer shredding and dicingservices.
President: Marilyn Taylor
Quality Manager: Frederick Ladenburger
Production Manager: Mark Gelhausen
Estimated Sales: $19.6 Million
Number Employees: 50-99
Square Footage: 20000
Type of Packaging: Consumer, Food Service, Pri-
vate Label, Bulk

31354 Wolens Company
PO Box 560964
Dallas, TX 75356-0964

214-634-0800
Fax: 214-634-0880
Manufacturer and exporter of plastic letters and signs
President: Steve Schwartz
Estimated Sales: $1-2.5 Million
Number Employees: 1-4

31355 Wolf Company
3101 S 2nd St
Louisville, KY 40208-1446

800-814-2028
www.wolfequipment.com
Manufacturer and exporter of commercial gas broilers, fryers, griddles, ranges and ovens; also, household ranges and slide-ins.
Chairman & CEO, ITW: E. Scott Santi
Estimated Sales: $100-500 Million
Parent Co: ITW Food Equipment

31356 Wolf Packaging Machines
9310 SW 100th Avenue Road
Miami, FL 33176-1724

305-274-3641
Fax: 305-274-3685
Packaging machines, such as vertical f/f/s machines
Estimated Sales: $1 - 5 Million

31357 Wolf Works
167 Vard Loomis Court
Arroyo Grande, CA 93420-2919

805-489-2920
Fax: 805-239-1787 800-549-3806
wolfworkswood@hotmail.com
Wine industry wine gift boxes/crates/tasting room items
President: Mark Wolf
Co-Owner: Christina Wolf
Estimated Sales: less than $500,000
Number Employees: 2
Square Footage: 1200

31358 Wolfkiny
PO Box 30970
Columbus, OH 43230-0970

614-863-3144
Fax: 614-863-3296 800-292-3144
Analyzing fat testing, continuous sausage processing systems, emulsifiers, accessories, grinders, massagers and tumblers, pickle injectors, belt and screw conveyors, handling systems for ground meats, dry sausages, hams, pizzatoppings, patties and poultry
Estimated Sales: $5-10 Million
Number Employees: 50-99

31359 Womack International Inc
451 Azuar Ave
Vallejo, CA 94592-1148

707-647-2370
Fax: 707-562-1010 www.womack.com
Manufacturer and exporter of food processing filters including multiple plate, vertical stack and pressure
President: Thomas H. Womack
CEO: Michael Oakes
  oakes@womack.com
VP Engineer: Michael Oakes
VP Sales: Stanley Jennings
Estimated Sales: $3 - 5 Million
Number Employees: 20-49
Square Footage: 100000
Brands:
  Filter-Max
  Micron One

31360 Wonderware Corp
26561 Rancho Pkwy S
Lake Forest, CA 92630-8301

949-727-3200
Fax: 949-727-3270 press@wonderware.com
www.wonderware.com
Industrial automation software, enterprise asset management and maintenance software and enterprise resource planning (ERP) software
President: Sudipta Bhattacharya
Branch Manager: Roy Slavin
Contact: Deon Aardt
  deon.aardt@wonderware.com
Estimated Sales: $43.4 Million
Number Employees: 500-999

31361 Wood & Laminates
102 Route 46 E
Lodi, NJ 7644

973-773-7475
Fax: 973-773-8344 gabriels@wlbars.com
www.wlbars.com
Custom-made bars
Owner: Gabriel Salacar
Estimated Sales: $2.5 - 5 Million
Number Employees: 10-19

31362 Wood Goods Industries
407 S Duncan St
Luck, WI 54853-9082

715-472-2226
Fax: 715-472-8708 info@woodgoods.com
www.woodgoods.com
Table tops and bases for the contract, hospitality and institutional trades
President: Brad Johnson
  brad@woodgoods.com
CFO: Brad Johnson
Quality Control: Brad Johnson
Customer Service/Purchasing: David Corredato
Estimated Sales: $5 - 10 Million
Number Employees: 100-249
Square Footage: 120000

31363 Wood Stone Corp
1801 W Bakerview Rd
Bellingham, WA 98226-9105

360-650-1111
Fax: 360-650-1166 800-988-8103
info@woodstone.net www.woodstone-corp.com
Manufacturer and exporter of broilers, stone hearth ovens, pizza equipment and rotisseries; cast ceramic available
President: Kurt Eickmeyer
  kurte@woodstone.net
CEO: Keith R. Carpenter
COO: Harry E. Hegarty
VP Sales: K Carpneter
President Manufacturing: Harry Hegarty
Estimated Sales: $5 - 10 Million
Number Employees: 100-249
Square Footage: 100000

31364 Wood Stone Corp
1801 W Bakerview Rd
Bellingham, WA 98226-9105

360-650-1111
Fax: 360-650-1166 800-988-8103
info@woodstone-corp.com
www.woodstone-corp.com
Stone-health cooking equipment
President: Kurt Eickmeyer
  kurte@woodstone.net
CEO: Kurt I. Eickmeyer
VP - Finance: Justin Mitchell
Marketing Director: Tamra Nelson
VP - Sales: Phil Eaton
VP Client Relations: Kurt Eickmeyer
Chief Operating Officer: Harry E. Hegarty
Purchasing Agent: Matt Laninga
Estimated Sales: $10 - 20 Million
Number Employees: 100-249

31365 Woodard
222 Merchandise Mart Plaza
PO Box 1037
Coppell, TX 75019-1037

989-725-4500
Fax: 989-725-4221 800-877-2290
retail3@woodard-furniture.com
www.woodard-furniture.com
Restaurant furnishings including wrought iron and cast and extruded aluminum
President: Dean Engelage
VP Contract Sales/International Sales: Eric Parsons
Estimated Sales: $10-20 Million
Number Employees: 3
Square Footage: 2000000

31366 Woodfold-Marco Manufacturing
1811 18th Ave
PO Box 346
Forest Grove, OR 97116

503-357-7181
Fax: 503-357-7185 info@woodfold.com
www.woodfold.com
Manufacturer and exporter of wood roll up and accordion doors and custom shutters; also, laminated kitchen and machined hardwood products

President: Mark Lewis
Vice President: Randall Roedl
Estimated Sales: $10-20 Million
Number Employees: 100-249
Square Footage: 320000

31367 Woodhead
3411 Woodhead Drive
Northbrook, IL 60062-1812

847-272-7990
Fax: 847-272-8133 888-456-1990
www.danielwoodhead.com
Wiring devices, portable lighting, portable power, cable reels, cord grips, push buttoms, and pendants
President: Terry Spandet
Contact: Joseph Nogal
  joseph.nogal@connector.com
Estimated Sales: $2.5-5 Million
Number Employees: 100-249

31368 Woods Fabrication
2759 Old State Highway 113
P.O. Box 167
Taylorsville, GA 30178-1706

770-684-5377
Fax: 770-684-0858 www.woodsfab.com
Cooling tunnels and conveyors
Owner/ President: Rickey Woods
  info@woodsfab.com
Engineering Manager: Nevin Harne
Safety Manager: Henry Mathews
Sales Manager: John Dodson
Office Manager: Allen Wilson
Procurement: Tim McGinnis
Number Employees: 20-49

31369 Woodson
7 Wynfield Drive
Lititz, PA 17543-8001

717-627-6990
Fax: 717-627-6920 888-627-6990
www.woodsoninc.com
Automatic storage and retrieval systems (AS/RS) specifically designed for high density, deep lane storage warehouses. the AS/RS accommodate pallet and palletless applications and include a fully functional automated warehousemanagement system. For frozen food, dairy and bakery applications
President: J Thomas Woodson
Vice President: Richard Troy
Sales Director: Mark Linesay
Estimated Sales: $5-10 Million
Number Employees: 10-19
Number of Products: 4
Square Footage: 30000

31370 Woodson Pallet Co
165 Pallet St
Anmoore, WV 26323

304-623-2858
Fax: 304-623-2865
Pallets and corrugated boxes
Owner: John Wilt
CFO: William T Woodson
Estimated Sales: Below $5 Million
Number Employees: 5-9

31371 Woodson-Tenent Laboratories
5659 Brentlinger Dr
Dayton, OH 45414

937-236-5756
Fax: 937-236-5756 www.eurofinsus.com
Laboratory specializing in nutritional analysis with amino acid, dietary fiber, microbiological, proximate and vitamin analyses; pesticide and residue testing and mycotoxin screening
Manager: Michael Muse
  michaelmuse@eurofinsus.com
Vice President of Corporate Development: Joseph Dunham
Operations Manager, Director of Client S: Jules Skamarak
Estimated Sales: $1-2.5 Million
Number Employees: 1-4
Parent Co: Woodson-Tenent Laboratories

31372 Woodson-Tenent Laboratories
1331 Union Ave
Ste 1500
Memphis, TN 38104-7512

515-280-8378
Fax: 770-536-6909 www.eurofins.com

Laboratory specializing in nutritional analysis with amino acid, dietary fiber, microbiological, proximate and vitamin analyses; pesticide and residue testing and mycotoxin screening available
Manager: Robert W Brooks
Contact: Lars Reimann
lreimann@warrenlab.com
Estimated Sales: $500,000-$1 Million
Number Employees: 100-250
Parent Co: Woodson-Tenent Laboratories

31373 Woodson-Tenent Laboratories
P.O. Box 1292
Des Moines, IA 50306-1292
515-265-1461
Fax: 515-266-5453 www.eurofinsus.com
Laboratory specializing in nutritional analysis of amino acids, dietary fibers, microbiologicals, proximates and vitamins; also, mycotoxin screening
Manager: Ardin Backous
Branch Manager: Cecil Bogy
Vice President of Corporate Development: Joseph Dunham
Operations Manager, Director of Client S: Jules Skamarak
Estimated Sales: $1-2.5 Million
Number Employees: 50-99
Parent Co: Woodson-Tenent Laboratories

31374 Woodson-Tenent Laboratories
P.O. Box 1292
Des Moines, IA 50306-1292
515-265-1461
Fax: 515-266-5453 www.eurofinsus.com
Laboratory specializing in nutritional analyses including amino acids, dietary fibers, microbiological proximates and vitamins; also, pesticide and residue testing and mycotoxin screening
Manager: Ardin Backous
Vice President of Corporate Development: Joseph Dunham
Operations Manager, Director of Client S: Jules Skamarak
Estimated Sales: $2.5 - 5 Million
Number Employees: 50-99
Parent Co: Woodson-Tenent Laboratories

31375 Woodstock Line Co
83 Canal St
Putnam, CT 06260-1909
860-928-6557
Fax: 860-928-1096 info@woodstockline.com
www.woodstockline.com
Manufacturer and exporter of braided cordage and twine
Owner: Burney Phaneuf
info@woodstockline.com
Estimated Sales: $2.5-5 Million
Number Employees: 10-19
Square Footage: 50000

31376 Woodstock Plastics Co Inc
22511 W Grant Hwy
Marengo, IL 60152-9660
815-568-5281
Fax: 815-568-5339 sales@woodstockplastics.com
www.woodstockplastics.com
Manufacturer and exporter of fabricated plastic displays, dump bins, containers, clamshell and vinyl pouches including sealed, vacuum formed, molded and blow molded
Owner: Brian Jenkner
brianj@woodstockplastics.com
CFO: Matthew Jenkner
Vice President: John Jenkner
Quality Control: Jude Jons
Estimated Sales: $10 - 20 Million
Number Employees: 20-49
Square Footage: 90000

31377 Woodward Manufacturing
299 Forest Ave
Suite F
Paramus, NJ 7652
201-262-6700
Fax: 201-262-1322
Packaging machinery
President: Cyril H T Woodward
VP: Joseph Giorgio
National Sales Director: Louis Cannizzaro
Estimated Sales: $1-2.5 Million
Number Employees: 10
Brands:
Vac-U-Pac

31378 Woody Associates Inc
844 E South St
York, PA 17403-2849
717-843-3975
Fax: 717-843-5829 info@woody-decorators.com
www.woody-decorators.com
Manufacturer and exporter of automatic confectionery and bakery decorating machinery
President: Harry Reinke
woody@woody-decorators.com
VP: Kerrie Reinke
Sales: Harry Reinke
Estimated Sales: $1 - 3 Million
Number Employees: 5-9
Square Footage: 2000
Brands:
Woody Stringer

31379 Wooster Novelty Company
45 Washington Street
Floor 6a
Brooklyn, NY 11201-1029
718-852-8934
Fax: 718-624-6925
Cutting board underliners for hot plates
President: Stephen Winaker
Partner: Scott Kail
Estimated Sales: $500,000-$1 Million
Number Employees: 9

31380 Worcester Envelope Co
22 Millbury St
Auburn, MA 01501-3200
508-832-5397
Fax: 508-832-5870 www.worcesterenvelope.com
Commercial and official envelopes
President: Eldon D Pond Iii
epond@worcester-envelope.com
Estimated Sales: $20-50 Million
Number Employees: 250-499

31381 Worcester Industrial Products
7 Brookfield St
Worcester, MA 01605-3901
508-757-5161
Fax: 508-831-9990 800-533-5711
sales@shortening-shuttle.com
www.howardproducts.info
Waste oil transfer systems used to transport waste shortening from fryers to grease dumpsters
President: Martha Hawley
CEO: David Hawley
sales@shortening-shuttle.com
Marketing: Elaine Liad
Vice President of Sales: Jeremiah Hawley
Estimated Sales: $2.5-5 Million
Number Employees: 10-19
Number of Products: 5
Type of Packaging: Food Service
Brands:
Shortening Shuttle

31382 Work Well Company
861 Taylor Road
Unit C
Gahanna, OH 43230-6275
614-759-8003
Fax: 614-759-8013
Manufacturer and exporter of safety gloves and oven mitts
Contact: Bill Balentine
bbalentine@workwell.com
Estimated Sales: $1 - 5 Million

31383 Workman Packaging Inc.
345 Montee de Liesse
Saint-Laurent, QC H4T 1P5
Canada
514-344-7227
Fax: 514-737-4288 800-252-5208
info@multisac.com www.multisac.com
Manufacturer and exporter of woven and laminated polyethylene and polypropylene bags, covers and wraps
President: Mark Kraminer
CFO: Luc Dumont
Quality Control: Bryan Morton
Director Marketing: Mark Kraminer
Number Employees: 100
Brands:
Multisac
Plastex
Stretch-Tite
Toss 'n' Tote

31384 Worksafe Industries
130t W 10th Street
Huntington Station, NY 11746-1616
516-427-1802
Fax: 516-427-1840 800-929-9000
Manufacturer and exporter of protective clothing including gloves, respirators, goggles and industrial safety equipment
President: Larry Densen
Number Employees: 300

31385 Worksman 800 Buy Cart
9415 100th St
Ozone Park, NY 11416-1707
718-322-2003
Fax: 718-529-4803 800-289-2278
vending@worksman.com www.worksman.com
Manufacturer and exporter of vending carts, trucks, trailers and kiosks.
President: Wayne Sosin
Mobile Food Equity, VP: Jack Beller
Estimated Sales: $5-10 Million
Number Employees: 50-99
Square Footage: 360000
Type of Packaging: Food Service
Brands:
Admar
Worksman Cycles

31386 World Division
12023 Denton Dr
Dallas, TX 75234
972-241-2612
Fax: 972-247-8807 903-339-9843
info@worlddivision.com www.worlddivision.com
Manufacturer and exporter of banners, pennants, streamers and signs
President: John Adams
Sr. VP: Francois Louis
Operations Director: David Fry
Estimated Sales: $5-10,000,000
Number Employees: 1-4

31387 World Dryer Corp
5700 Mcdermott Dr
Berkeley, IL 60163-1196
708-449-6950
Fax: 708-449-6958 800-323-0701
sales@worlddryer.com www.worlddryer.com
Warm air push button and automatic hand dryers, baby changing tables, automatic soap dispensers, 3-in-1 towel dispenser/hand dryer systems and ADA compliant/handicapped approved hand dryers.
President: Tom Vic
CFO: Tom Bic
Vice President: Chris Berl
Marketing Director: Stacey Hefford
Sales Director: Erin Eddy
Estimated Sales: $10 - 20 Million
Number Employees: 20-49
Square Footage: 100000
Parent Co: Specialty Equipment Companies
Brands:
Airspeed
Electric Aire
Sensamatic
World

31388 World Finer Foods
1455 Broadacres Dr Ste 100
Bloomfield, NJ 07003
973-338-0300
Fax: 973-338-0382 www.worldfiner.com
Specialty food distributor.
President: Frank Muchel
CFO: Jon Beer
Estimated Sales: Less than $500,000
Number Employees: 1-4

31389 World Food Processing LLC
4301 World Food Ave
Oskaloosa, IA 52577-9313
641-672-9651
Fax: 641-672-9596
www.worldfoodprocessing.com
Soybean and soy-based products supplier.
President: Jerry Lorenzen
jlorenzen@worldfoodp.com
Number Employees: 10-19
Other Locations:
Headquarters
Oskaloosa IA
Processing
Randolph MN

Processing
Turtle Lake WI

31390 World Food Tech Services
153 Cherry St
Malden, MA 02148-1603
781-321-3750
Fax: 781-321-3750
Aids in developing the import/export and product
development of spruce in the US market
President: Daniel Casper
VP: Jane Casper
Sales: Jersy Moytasch

31391 World Kitchen
PO Box 1555
Elmira, NY 14902-1555
607-377-8000
Fax: 607-377-8962 800-999-3436
www.worldkitchen.com
Manufacturer and exporter of glassware including
bottles, jars, cookware, trays, urns, etc
President/ CEO: Carl Warschausky
CFO: Stephen Earhart
SVP, Human Resources & Chief Legal Offic: Ed
Flowers
VP Marketing: Clark Kinlin
Contact: David Livingston
  livingstond@worldkitchen.com
SVP/ General Manager, Global Business: Lee Mui
Estimated Sales: $5 - 10 Million
Number Employees: 10-19
Brands:
  Corningware
  Pyrex
  Visions

31392 World Kitchen
5500 Pearl St Ste 400
Rosemont, IL 60018
847-678-8600
Fax: 847-678-9424
Manufacturer and exporter of plastic containers;
wholesaler/distributor and exporter of bakery racks
and food trays; serving the food service market
President: Jim Sharman
CEO: Joe Mallof
Contact: Michael Cwiertniakm
  cwiertniakm@worldkitchen.com
Estimated Sales: $20 - 50 Million
Number Employees: 100-249
Parent Co: Borden Inc.
Type of Packaging: Food Service
Brands:
  Bakers Secret
  Chicago Cutlery
  Corelle
  Corningware
  Cuisinart
  Ekco
  Farberware
  Grilla Gear
  Olfa
  Oxo
  Pyrex
  Regent Sheffield
  Revere
  Visions

31393 World Pride
PO Box 41463
St Petersburg, FL 33743-1463
727-522-5020
Fax: 727-522-2317 800-533-2433
Kitchen apparel including aprons, chef coats and
hats; also, ice carvers
President: Douglas S Fyvolent
VP Marketing: Douglas Fyvolent
Estimated Sales: $1-2.5 Million
Number Employees: 4
Brands:
  Kitchen Wise
  Laural
  Noble
  Pro-Icer
  Progold
  Provell
  Sterling

31394 World Tableware Inc
300 Madison Ave
Toledo, OH 43604-1561
419-325-2608
Fax: 419-325-2749 800-678-9849
stock@libbey.com www.libbey.com
Importer, exporter and wholesaler/distributor of tab-
letop supplies including flatware, dinnerware and
holloware; serving the food service market
President: John Myer
CEO: Jay Achenbach
  achenbachj@libbey.com
Quality Control: Allwyn Cahoun
CEO: John Meier
R & D: Bill Herp
Number Employees: 5-9
Parent Co: Libbey
Type of Packaging: Food Service

31395 World Technitrade
PO Box 72
Villanova, PA 19085-0072
610-525-1600
Fax: 610-525-1600
Confectionery, bakery, and pressure and vacuum
vessels import and export
President: Erwin Von Allmen
Estimated Sales: $1 - 5 Million

31396 World Trade Center Harrisburg
1000 North Cameron St
Harrisburg, PA 17103
717-843-1090
Fax: 717-854-0087 info@wtccentralpa.org
wtccentralpa.org
Education, informational services, consulting, networking; connects manufacturers and trade service
providers
Executive Director: Tina Weyant
  tina@wtccentralpa.org
Event & Membership Coordinator: Jan Kreidler
Number Employees: 2-10

31397 World Variety Produce
Po Box 514599
Los Angeles, CA 90021
323-588-0151
Fax: 323-588-9774 800-588-0151
www.melissas.com
Importer and distributor of specialty produce
President & CEO: Joe Hernandez
CFO: Lee Zeller
Director of Marketing: Bill Schneider
VP Sales: Peter Steinbrick
Director Public Relations: Robert Schueller
Estimated Sales: $20.4 Million
Number Employees: 325
Type of Packaging: Consumer, Food Service, Bulk
Brands:
  Don Enrique
  Jo San
  Melissas

31398 World Water Works
4000 SW 113th St
Oklahoma City, OK 73173-8322
405-943-9000
Fax: 405-943-9006 800-607-7973
Wastewater treatment.
Contact: Kyle Booth
  kyle.booth@worldwaterworks.com
Number Employees: 50-99

31399 World Water Works
4 Vernon Lane
Elmsford, NY
800-607-7873
sales@worldwaterworks.com
www.worldwaterworks.com
Designs, builds and installs a line of wastewater
treatment systems
President: Mark Fosshage
Vice President of Technology: Greg Parks
Director of Sales and Marketing: John Schnecker
Contact: Scott Poe
  poe@worldwaterworks.com
Estimated Sales: $10 Million
Number Employees: 4

31400 World Wide Beverage
P.O. Box 191
Glencoe, IL 60022-0191
847-835-3444
Fax: 847-835-3434

Manufacturers of accumulating table conveyors,
bag-in-box filling equipment, bag-in-box dispensers,
bottle, can warmers, bottle rinsers and washers
President: Howard Buckner
Estimated Sales: $1-2.5 Million
Number Employees: 1-4
Type of Packaging: Bulk

31401 World Wide Fitting Corp
600 Corporate Woods Pkwy
Vernon Hills, IL 60061-3113
847-793-8456
Fax: 847-588-2212 800-393-9894
sales@worldwidefittings.com
Pneumatic and hydraulic fittings for food processing
machinery
Chairman of the Board: Joseph D Mc Carthy
  sales@worldwidefittings.com
VP Sales: Mike Casey
VP Production: Sean McCarthy
Estimated Sales: $5-10,000,000
Number Employees: 100-249

31402 World Wide Hospitality Furn
7311 Madison St # D
Paramount, CA 90723-4038
562-630-2700
Fax: 562-630-2227 800-728-8262
wrldwideh@aol.com www.wwhfurniture.com
Manufacturer and importer of tables, chairs and
booths
CEO: Isaac Gonshor
  wrldwideh@aol.com
Estimated Sales: $1 - 5,000,000
Number Employees: 10-19
Type of Packaging: Food Service
Brands:
  World Wide

31403 World Wide Safe Brokers
112 Cromwell Court
Woodbury, NJ 08096
856-863-1225
Fax: 856-845-2266 800-593-2893
www.worldwidesafebrokers.com
Fire safes, electronic safes, gun safes, safe deposit
boxes, hotel room safes, insulated files, burglary
safe, vaults, vault doors, in-floor safes, depository
safes, custom designed and manufactured safes.
President: Edward Dornisch
VP: Mildred Dornisch
Estimated Sales: $.5 - 1 million
Number Employees: 3
Square Footage: 16000

31404 Worldwide Dispensers
1201 Windham Parkway
Suite D
Romeoville, IL 60446
630-296-2000
Fax: 630-296-2195 www.dssmith.com
Fun, fabulous ceramic products. All are bright and
bold with witty sentiments, all designed by artist
Lorrie Veasey. Lead free ceramic, dishwasher and
microwave safe
Estimated Sales: $2,500,000 - $4,999,999
Number Employees: 250-499
Number of Products: 200
Type of Packaging: Consumer

31405 Wornick Company
PO Box 55
McAllen, TX 78505-0055
561-227-0765
Fax: 956-631-0857
Meals Ready to Eat (MRE). Humanitarian Daily Ra-
tions (HDR)

31406 (HQ)Worthen Industries Inc
3 E Spit Brook Rd
Nashua, NH 03060-5783
603-888-5443
Fax: 603-888-7945 info@worthenind.com
www.upacofootwear.com
Manufacturer and exporter of labels and adhesive
tapes
President: Robert Worthen
CEO: Eileen Morin
  emorin@worthenind.com
CEO: Eileen Morin
Estimated Sales: $1 - 3 Million
Number Employees: 100-249

31407 Wrap Pack
1728 Presson Pl
Yakima, WA 98903-2238
509-248-6774
Fax: 509-453-3653 800-879-9727
www.fruitwrap.com
Fruit wrappers and packing needle holders
President: Lance Braden
CFO: Ted Smith
General Manager: G Lance Braden
Plant Manager: Shane May
Estimated Sales: $2.5 - 5 Million
Number Employees: 20-49

31408 Wrapade Packaging Systems
27 Law Dr # B
Suite B/C
Fairfield, NJ 07004-3206
973-787-1788
Fax: 973-773-6010 888-815-8564
sales@wrapade.com www.wrapade.com
Manufacturer and exporter of vertical, horizontal
and stand-up pouch packaging machinery
President: Bill Beattie
bill.b@wrapade.com
Estimated Sales: $2.5-5 Million
Number Employees: 10-19
Square Footage: 88000

31409 Wraps
810 Springdale Avenue
East Orange, NJ 07017-1298
973-673-7873
Fax: 973-673-2240
Manufacturer and exporter of flexible packaging
materials, heat sealers and packaging machinery
President: Ralph Barone
General Manager: Michael Mikulis
Sales Manager: Brian Guidera
Contact: Chad Carpenter
chad.carpenter@wrapsforless.com
Estimated Sales: $2.5-5 Million
Number Employees: 20-49
Square Footage: 192000
Brands:
Clamco

**31410 Wright Brothers Paper Box
Company**
800 Morris St
Fond Du Lac, WI 54935
920-921-8270
Fax: 920-921-8384 info@wbpaperbox.com
www.wbpaperbox.com
Rigid set-up paper boxes and folding cartons
President: Joan Pennau
President: Victor Pupo
Chairman: Frank Erdman
Sales / Customer Service: Diane Seibel
Contact: Barb Bogart
bbogart@wbpaperbox.com
Operations: Mary Vandermolen
Estimated Sales: $5-10 Million
Number Employees: 50-99

31411 Wright Global Graphic Solutions
5115 Prospect St
Thomasville, NC 27360
800-678-9019
Fax: 336-476-8554 800-678-9019
www.wrightglobalgraphics.com
Labels and labeling materials
President/CEO: Greg Wright
Vice President of Marketing: Vicki Fishman
Vice President of Sales: Carol Phillips
Contact: Jason Collett
jcollett@wrightglobalgraphics.com
Estimated Sales: Under $500,000
Number Employees: 200

**31412 (HQ)Wright Metal Products
Crates**
100 Ben Hamby Dr
Greenville, SC 29615-5700
864-297-6610
Fax: 864-281-0594 www.wrightmetalproducts.com
Machine parts for food handling equipment
Vice President: Marty Hyatt
mhyatt@wrightmetalsinc.com
VP: Jim Camden
General Manager: Jim Camden

Estimated Sales: $10-20 Million
Number Employees: 20-49
Square Footage: 80000
Other Locations:
Wright Metal Products
Greenville SC

31413 Wright Plastics Company
1107 Doster Road
Prattville, AL 36067-4329
334-365-9494
Fax: 334-365-9559 800-874-7659
Polyethylene bags and film
Estimated Sales: $10-20 Million
Number Employees: 19

31414 Wt Nickell Co
4360 Winding Creek Blvd
Batavia, OH 45103-1729
513-752-2191
Fax: 513-752-2354 888-899-1991
labels@wtnickell.com www.wtnickell.com
Custom pressure sensitive labels, printer ribbons and
stock labels.
President: Rick Meyer
rlmeyer@wtnickell.com
Vice President: Jaime Kinkade
Estimated Sales: Under $1 Million
Number Employees: 5-9
Type of Packaging: Private Label

31415 Wylie Systems
1190 Fewster Drive
Mississauga, ON L4W 1A1
Canada
905-238-1619
Fax: 905-238-5623 800-525-6609
info@wyliemetals.com www.wyliemetals.com
Manufacturer and exporter of railings and partitions
for hotels, restaurants, etc.; also, sneeze guards
President: Michael Wylie
Brands:
Decorail

31416 Wynn's Grain and Spice
2750 B Gunter Park Drive West
Montgomery, AL 36109
334-270-9180
800-792-2216
wynnsgrainandspice.com
Wholesale fried chicken blends and seasoning spices
supplier.
Chief Executive Officer: Ted Giles
Vice President, Sales & Operations: Cody Stevens
Year Founded: 1952
Estimated Sales: $5.3 Million
Number Employees: 11-50

31417 Wyssmont Co Inc
1470 Bergen Blvd
Fort Lee, NJ 07024-2197
201-947-4600
Fax: 201-947-0324 www.wyssmont.com
Manufacturer, designer and exporter of food pro-
cessing equipment including rotating tray dryers,
lumpbreakers, fixed and rotating bars and self-clean-
ing airlock feeders; also, solid handling equipment
President: Edward Weisselberg
ebw@wyssmont.com
VP: Joseph Bevacqua
R&D: J Ulrich
VP Sales: Joseph Henderson
Estimated Sales: $2.5-5 Million
Number Employees: 20-49
Square Footage: 40000
Brands:
Turbo-Dryer

31418 X-Press Manufacturing
271 Fm 306
New Braunfels, TX 78130-2557
830-629-2651
Fax: 830-620-4727 800-365-9440
sales@x-pressmfg.com www.x-pressmfg.com
Display tortilla cookers, pressers and warmers
Owner: Charles Smith
President/Owner: Rex Wilson
Customer Service: Anne Sowell
Shop Manager: Charlie Smith
Estimated Sales: $.5 - 1 million
Number Employees: 1-4
Square Footage: 7500
Parent Co: Copprex

Brands:
X-Press

31419 X-R-I Testing Inc
1961 Thunderbird
Troy, MI 48084-5467
248-362-5050
Fax: 248-362-4422 800-973-4800
foodx@aol.com www.xritesting.com
Manufacturer and exporter of in-line and off-line
X-ray inspection equipment; also, X-ray inspection
services available
President: Scott Thams
Manager: Kurt Andrews
kurta@xrayindustries.com
Estimated Sales: $30 - 50 Million
Number Employees: 50-99
Square Footage: 30000
Parent Co: X-Ray Industries

31420 X-Rite Inc
4300 44th St SE
Grand Rapids, MI 49512-4009
616-803-2100
888-800-9580
www.xrite.com
Portable hand-held spectrophotometers and
colorimeters with supporting computer software for
color control applications and color formulation.
President: Tom Vacchiano
Year Founded: 1958
Estimated Sales: $261.5 Million
Number Employees: 500-999
Parent Co: Danaher Corporation
Brands:
Qa-Master
Sp68

31421 XL Corporate & ResearchServices
62 White Street
New York, NY 10013-3593
212-431-5000
Fax: 212-431-5111 800-221-2972
Consultant providing product, company or industry
research including trademark research on product
names, company names and logos, preparation and
filing of trademarks and credit reports
President: Robert Blumerang
Counsel: Marc Moel
General Counsel: Arthur McGuire
Estimated Sales: $20 - 50 Million
Number Employees: 30
Square Footage: 5000
Parent Co: Julius Blumberg

31422 Xango LLC
2889 W Ashton Blvd # 1
Lehi, UT 84043-4968
801-766-3050
Fax: 801-816-8001 877-469-2646
Markets daily dietary supplemental juice beverage
made from the mangosteen fruit.
President/Chief Executive Officer: Aaron Garrity
Chairman: Gary Hollister
President Intnl Distributor Relations: Joe Morton
EVP International Relations: Bryan Davis
Quality Assurance Manufacturing: Wayne Davis
Chief Marketing Officer: Gordon Morton
President Operations: Ken Wood
Number Employees: 500-999

31423 Xcel Tower Controls
1600 W 6th St
PO Box 187
Gilbertsville, NY 13776
574-259-7804
Fax: 574-259-5769 800-288-7362
info@xcel.com www.xcel.com
Manufacturer and exporter of control and process
control systems, universal programmers, program-
mable control systems and industrial computers,
tower light controllers and monitoring systems
President: Bruce Shepard
CEO: John Brickley
Sales Director: Bruce Shepard
Estimated Sales: $2.5-5 Million
Number Employees: 10-19
Square Footage: 30000

31424 Xcell International
16400 Est 103rd Street
Lemont, IL 60439
630-323-0107
Fax: 630-323-0217 800-722-7751
info@xcellint.com www.xcellint.com
Spice blends, confectionery dessert toppings, coffee flavors and creamers, teas and coffee and tea accessories.
CEO: Raymond Henning
Estimated Sales: $20-50 Million
Number Employees: 50-99

31425 Xela Pack Inc
8300 Boettner Rd
Saline, MI 48176-9642
734-944-1300
Fax: 734-429-4714 800-742-7225
info@xelapack.com www.xelapack.com
Single and multi-dose packaging alternative to bottles and tubes
Owner: Al Gentile
algentile@mac.com
Estimated Sales: $2.5 - 5Million
Number Employees: 50-99

31426 Xiaoping Design
73 Hudson Street
New York, NY 10013-2870
212-962-4080
Fax: 212-962-4071 800-891-9896
Custom furniture including tables and chairs also designs for custom furniture
President: Xiaoping Zao
VP/Marketing/Sales/Operations: David Chang
Estimated Sales: $1 Million
Number Employees: 2
Number of Brands: 1
Number of Products: 45

31427 Xpander Pak
1045 Technology Park Drive
Glen Allen, VA 23059-4500
804-266-5000
Fax: 804-266-4474 800-720-1777
sales@xpander.com www.xpander.com
Projective packaging: Xpander Pak super protective shippers, Safe-T Shipper, Safe-T Shipper ESD
CEO: Joseph Sullivan
Estimated Sales: $1-2.5 Million
Number Employees: 9

31428 Xtreme Beverages, LLC
32565-B Golden Lantern
#282
Dana Point, CA 92629
Canada
949-495-7929
Fax: 949-495-8015 xtremebeverages@cox.net
Wood and bamboo box; wood and bamboo tea chest; wine box; baskets; tea and coffee accessories; wine accessories; MDF box; cardboard box; wooded tea dispenser; wrought iron tea can rack; wood and bamboo products, candles; candleholders; gourmet gift packaging and food and beverage gift packaging
President: William Quinley
VP: James Moffitt
Estimated Sales: $5 Million
Number Employees: 4
Type of Packaging: Consumer, Food Service, Private Label, Bulk

31429 Xylem Inc
1 International Dr
Rye Brook, NY 10573
914-323-5700
www.xylem.com
Field, portable, online and laboratory analytical instrumentation.
President & Chief Executive Officer: Patrick Decker
SVP/Chief Innovation/Technology Officer: David Flinton
SVP & Chief Financial Officer: Mark Rajkowski
SVP/President, Measurement & Control: Colin Sabol
SVP/Chief Human Resources Officer: Kairus Tarapore
SVP/General Counsel/Corporate Secretary: Claudia Toussaint
SVP/Chief Marketing Officer: Joseph Vesey
Year Founded: 2011
Estimated Sales: $5.2 Billion
Number Employees: 17,000
Type of Packaging: Bulk

31430 Y-Pers Inc
5622 Tulip St
PO Box 9559
Philadelphia, PA 19124-1698
215-743-1500
Fax: 215-289-6811 800-421-0242
www.ypers.com
Manufacturer and exporter of cheesecloths and uniforms including disposable clothing, hairnets and gloves
President: David Blum
ypers@aol.com
CFO: David Blum
R&D: David Blum
Estimated Sales: Below $5 Million
Number Employees: 10-19

31431 Y-Z Sponge & Foam Products
811 Cundy Avenue
Annacis Island
Delta, BC V3M 5P6
Canada
604-525-1665
Fax: 604-525-1081 info@a-zfoam.com
www.a-zfoam.com
Polyurethane foam

31432 YAAX International
3111 Tieton Dr # 300
Yakima, WA 98902-3628
509-249-5555
Fax: 509-469-2133 info@yaax.com
www.yaax.com
Wholesaler & distributor of fruit juice concentrates flavors, purees, dehydrated fruit and dairy products, glass and plastic packaged juices. Supplier of processed vegetable products.
President: Bruce Simpson
Marketing: Jennifer Tilley
Number Employees: 2 - 10
Type of Packaging: Private Label, Bulk

31433 YCU Air/York International
1519 Highway 13 E
Burnsville, MN 55337-2917
952-707-1286
Fax: 952-707-0914 www.york.com
Clean rooms and equipment
Estimated Sales: $1 - 5 Million

31434 YESCO
1605 S Gramercy Rd
Salt Lake City, UT 84104-4888
801-487-8481
Fax: 801-762-0036 800-444-3847
info@yesco.com www.yesco.com
Manufacturer and exporter of electric signs
President: Michael Young
Cmo: Wes Van Dyke
wvandyke@yesco.com
CFO: Duane Wardle
Sales Manager: Susan Ward
Estimated Sales: $30 - 50 Million
Number Employees: 250-499

31435 YSI Inc
1725 Brannum Ln
Yellow Springs, OH 45387-1107
937-767-7241
Fax: 937-767-9353 800-765-4974
support@ysi.com www.ysi.com
Instrumentation for the analysis of carbohydrates, organic acids, sugars, dissolved oxygen, etc.; also, conductivity meters and temperature devices
President: Richard Omlor
rfielder@ysi.com
CFO: Lee Erdman
VP: Jim Smith
Quality Control: Marek Jezior
Sales Exec: Rick Fielder
Estimated Sales: $50-75 Million
Number Employees: 250-499

31436 YW Yacht Basin
8341 Black Dog Alley
Easton, MD 21601-6329
410-822-0414
Fax: 410-822-1090
Material handling conveyors; also, custom metal, structural and steel fabrications of stairs and handrails available
President: Douglas Weinmann
VP Sales: David Weinmann

Number Employees: 6
Square Footage: 50000

31437 Yakima Wire Works
1949 E. Manning Avenue
Reedley, CA 93654
559-638-8484
Fax: 559-638-7478 800-344-8951
info@swfcompanies.com
www.swfcompanies.com
Manufacturer and exporter of fully and semi-automatic bagging, weighing and batching, modular net dispensers, check-weighers, dual-belt conveyors and blowers
President: Gary Germunson
Chairman/VP: Tim Main
Estimated Sales: $.5 - 1 million
Number Employees: 1-4

31438 Yamada America
1575 Highpoint Drive
Elgin, IL 60123-9303
847-697-1878
Fax: 847-697-2794 800-990-7867
sales@yamadapump.com www.yamadapump.com
Air-operated, double diaphragm pump
President: Steve Kameyama
Estimated Sales: Below $500,000
Number Employees: 3

31439 Yamato Corporation
1775 S. Murray Blvd.
Colorado Springs, CO 80916-4513
719-591-1500
Fax: 719-591-1045 800-538-1762
www.yamatocorp.com
Manufacturer and exporter of electronic and mechanical scales, electronic weight printers and computerized weighing systems
President: Sadao Nakamura
CEO: Sado Nakamura
Marketing Director: Gary Mendenhall
Sales Director: Prague Mehta
Contact: Lula Babb
babb@yamatocorp.com
Estimated Sales: $2.5 - 5 Million
Number Employees: 20-49
Square Footage: 96000
Brands:
Accuweigh
Yamato

31440 Yardney Water Management Syst
6666 Box Springs Blvd
Riverside, CA 92507-0736
951-656-6716
Fax: 951-656-3867 800-854-4788
www.yardneyfilters.com
Manufacturer and exporter of water quality improvement and filtration systems
President: Kenneth Phillips
kennethphillips@yardneyfilters.com
CFO: Kenneth Phillips
Quality Control: Janie Weissberg
Industrial Field Sales Manager: Ron Gamble
Estimated Sales: $5 - 10 Million
Number Employees: 20-49
Square Footage: 200000
Brands:
Yardney

31441 Yargus Manufacturing Inc
12285 E Main St
Marshall, IL 62441-4127
217-826-8059
Fax: 217-826-8551 layco@yargus.com
www.laycoproautomation.com
Stainless steel equipment including conveyors, hopper scales, blenders and bucket elevators; exporter of conveyor and blender systems
Owner: Jose Aguayo
Vice President US Sales: Mark Anderson
Sales: Lyle Yargus
jaguayo@bigwsales.com
Estimated Sales: $5-10 Million
Number Employees: 100-249
Square Footage: 102000
Brands:
Layco

31442 Yates Industries Inc
23050 E Industrial Dr
St Clair Shores, MI 48080-1177
586-778-7680
Fax: 586-778-6565 sales@yatesind.com
www.yatesind.com
Pneumatic and hydraulic cylinders including stainless steel, food grade and epoxy paint
President: Jennifer Adams
jadams@yatesind.com
Sales/Marketing Manager: Fred Cormier
Estimated Sales: $10+ Million
Number Employees: 20-49
Square Footage: 120
Parent Co: Yates Cylinder

31443 Yeager Wire Works
620 Broad St
Berwick, PA 18603-1418
570-752-2769
Fax: 570-752-2934
Display racks including wire and sheet-metal
President: David Ungemach
VP: Robert Ungemach
Estimated Sales: Less Than $500,000
Number Employees: 1-4

31444 Yerecic Label Co
701 Hunt Valley Rd
New Kensington, PA 15068-7076
724-334-3300
Fax: 724-335-8872 experts@yereciclabel.com
Pressure sensitive labels; printing services available
President: Arthur Yerecic
yerecica@yereciclabel.com
VP: Arthur Yerecic Jr
Estimated Sales: $2.5 - 5 Million
Number Employees: 5-9
Square Footage: 15000

31445 Yerger Wood Products
3090 Wentling Schoolhouse Road
East Greenville, PA 18041-2313
215-679-4413
Fax: 215-679-8797
Wooden pallets
President: James Yerger Jr
CEO/Sales: Susan Klolz
Estimated Sales: Below $5 Million
Number Employees: 10

31446 Yeuell Name Plate & Label
8 Adele Rd
Woburn, MA 01801-1911
781-933-2984
Fax: 781-933-3569 tbarry@yeuell.com
www.yeuell.com
Nameplates and labels; also, metal etching services available
President: Andrew F Hall Iii
Estimated Sales: $2.5-5 Million
Number Employees: 20-49

31447 (HQ)Yohay Baking Co
146 Albany Ave
Lindenhurst, NY 11757-3628
631-225-0300
Fax: 631-225-4277
Processor, importer and exporter of wafer rolls, specialty cookies, biscotti, and fudge mix, kosher and all natural products. Retail packaging available
Owner: Michael Soloman
solomanyohay@aol.com
Number Employees: 20-49
Type of Packaging: Consumer, Food Service, Private Label, Bulk
Brands:
Fudge Gourmet
Gourmet Cookie Place
Sweetheart Fudge

31448 York Container Co
138 Mount Zion Rd
York, PA 17402-8985
717-757-7611
Fax: 717-755-8090 www.yorkcontainer.com
Corrugated shipping containers
President: Chuck Wolf
CFO: William C Ludwig
wludwig@yorkcontainer.com
Executive VP: Charles Wolf Jr
Estimated Sales: $20 - 50 Million
Number Employees: 250-499
Square Footage: 200000

31449 York Refrigeration Marine US
5005 York Drive
Norman, OK 73069
206-285-0904
Fax: 206-285-0965 877-874-7378
www.york.com
Reciprocating and screw compressors and customized LT pump recirculation packages; also, freezers
President: Thomas Berfenfeldt
Director Sales and Marketing: Jack Barney
Sales: Slawonir Tabaczynski
Estimated Sales: $10-20 Million
Number Employees: 20-49
Parent Co: York Refrigeration A/S
Brands:
Sabroe
Unisab
Unisafe

31450 York River Pallet Corporation
PO Box 191
Shacklefords, VA 23156
804-785-5811
Fax: 804-785-3702
Wooden pallets and pallet materials
President/CEO: James Potts
Estimated Sales: Below $5 Million
Number Employees: 5-9

31451 York Saw & Knife
295 Emig Rd
P.O. Box 733
York, PA 17406-9734
717-767-6402
Fax: 717-764-2768 800-233-1969
info@yorksaw.com www.yorksaw.com
Manufacturer and exporter of circular and straight knives for food processing; custom and standard specifications available
President: Mike Pickard
mpickard@yorksaw.com
CFO: Todd Gladfeltzer
Quality Control: Tim Wentz
Estimated Sales: $10 Million
Number Employees: 50-99
Square Footage: 130000

31452 York Tape & Label Company
P.O. Box 1309
York, PA 17405-1309
717-266-9675
Fax: 717-266-9837 yorkwebsite@yorklabel.com
www.yorklabel.com
Labels and tags, nameplates, commercial printing and bar coding
President: Timothy Hare
CFO: Dennis Cole
Sales: Karen S Chavez
Quality Control: Tom Walko
VP Sales: John Attayek
Estimated Sales: $50 - 100 Million
Number Employees: 250-499

31453 York Tent & Awning
7 E 7th Ave
York, PA 17404-2199
717-230-8837
Fax: 717-843-6555 800-864-3510
sales@yorktentandawning.net
www.yorktentandawning.com
Commercial awnings
President: John Musti
yorktent@aol.com
Estimated Sales: $1-2,500,000
Number Employees: 10-19

31454 Yorkraft
2675a Eastern Boulevard
York, PA 17402-2905
717-845-3666
Fax: 717-846-3213 800-872-2044
Food service equipment including cabinetry products, salad bars, buffet lines and merchandising carts; also, decorative lighting panels available
President: David Imhoff
dimhoff@yorkraft.com
VP Operations: Jack Smith
VP: William Imhoff
Estimated Sales: $5-10 Million
Number Employees: 10
Square Footage: 360000

31455 YottaMark
203 Redwood Shores Parkway
Suite 100
Redwood City, CA 94065
650-264-6200
Fax: 650-264-6220 866-768-7878
info@yottamark.com www.yottamark.com
Product fingerprint solution detects and deters counterfeiting, diversion and fraud and allows manufacturers, brand protection personnel, law enforcement officials-even consumers- to authenticate individual products anytimeanywhere.
President/CEO: J Scott Carr
President, Chief Executive Officer: Scott Carr
Engineering VP: Matthew Self
Founder, Chief Marketing Officer: Elliott Grant
Senior Vice President of Sales: Michael Bromme
Chief Operating Officer: Paul Gifford

31456 Young & Associates
8915 58th Pl
Kenosha, WI 53144-7802
262-657-6394
Fax: 262-657-4306
Manufacturer and supplier of food product machinery
President: William B Young
CEO: Bill Young
Public Relations: Nancy Beck

31457 Young & Swartz Inc
39 Cherry St
Buffalo, NY 14204-1298
716-852-2171
Fax: 716-852-5652 800-466-7682
info@youngandswartz.com
Brushes, brooms and janitorial supplies
President: Paul Winzig
paul@buffalobrushworks.com
Estimated Sales: Less Than $500,000
Number Employees: 1-4
Square Footage: 30000

31458 Young Industries Inc
16 Painter St
Muncy, PA 17756-1423
570-546-1826
Fax: 570-546-1888 www.younginds.com
Tea blending equipment, conveying equipment (elevators, machines and buckets), blending and mixing equipment, portioning equipment, bin silo systems and storage, safety/occupational health/environment, listing of equipment, fieldservice, quality assurance, manufacturing, technical information
Owner: John Young
jmyoung@younginds.com
R&D: John Pfeiffer
Estimated Sales: $10 - 20 Million
Number Employees: 20-49

31459 Young's Lobster Shore Pound
2 Fairview St
Belfast, ME 04915-7208
207-338-1160
Fax: 207-338-1656
Sea food supplier
Owner: Raymond Young
raymond@youngslobsterpound.com
CEO: Katrina Young
Vice President: Diane Young
Quality Control: Joe Young
Estimated Sales: $500,000-$1 Million
Number Employees: 20-49
Type of Packaging: Consumer, Food Service, Private Label, Bulk

31460 Your Place Menu Systems
2600 Lockheed Way
Carson City, NV 89706-0717
775-882-7834
Fax: 775-882-5210 800-321-8105
Manufacturer and exporter of outdoor and indoor illuminated and nonilluminated menu boards
President, Sales Manager: John O Neil
Operations Manager, Product Design: Matt Stutsman
Number Employees: 20-49
Square Footage: 280000
Parent Co: Impact International

31461 Yuan Fa Can-Making
PO Box 14016
Torrance, CA 90503-8016
310-532-5829
Fax: 310-536-4216
Tea and coffee cans

31462 Yumenomori USA
133 Maple Street
Stoughton, MA 02072
781-573-4135
yumenomoriusa@gmail.com
www.yumenomoriusa.com
Supplier of bubble tea equipment, sealing machines, shaking machines, steamer machines, and syrup dispensers.
President: Keisuke Takemae *Year Founded:* 2018
Type of Packaging: Food Service

31463 Z 2000 the Pick of the Millenium
819 S Madison Boulevard
Bartlesville, OK 74006-8534
918-335-2030
Fax: 918-335-1789 800-654-7311
Manufacturer and exporter of 45 degree angled dental cleaners
President: Mack Blevins
VP: Pamela Blevins
Estimated Sales: $1 - 5 Million
Number Employees: 1-4
Square Footage: 15000
Parent Co: Mack Blevins Enterprises
Type of Packaging: Consumer, Food Service, Private Label, Bulk
Brands:
  Angled Pro Picks

31464 Z-Loda Systems Engineering Inc
1010 Summer St # 101
Suite 101
Stamford, CT 06905-5533
203-325-8001
Fax: 203-978-0104 www.zahhnagel.com
Manufacturer and exporter of vertical lift systems
President: Clifford Mollo
Estimated Sales: Less Than $500,000
Number Employees: 1-4

31465 Z-Trim Holdings, Inc
1101 Campus Drive
Mundelein, IL 60060
847-549-6002
Fax: 847-549-6028
Ingredients
Sales Director: Rick Harris
VP Sales/Applications: Lynda Carroll
Applications Project Manager: Aili Young
Research Chef: Erin Ryan

31466 Zacmi USA
2391 Zanker Road
Suite 320
San Jose, CA 95131-1145
408-433-0100
Fax: 408-433-0224 zacmiUS@aol.com
Processing machinery sales, fillers for all products
President: Charles Hoffman
Estimated Sales: $500,000-$1 Million
Number Employees: 4

31467 Zahm & Nagel Co
210 Vermont St
PO.Box 400
Holland, NY 14080-9735
716-537-2110
Fax: 716-537-2106 800-216-1542
info@zahmnagel.com
Quality control equipment: CO2 and air testers, pilot plants, carbonating equipment, batch tester filter
President: Dave Koch
sales@zahmnagel.com
Estimated Sales: $5 - 10 Million
Number Employees: 5-9

31468 Zaloom Marketing Corp
51 James St
South Hackensack, NJ 07606-1438
201-488-3535
Fax: 201-488-8056 800-878-7609
jzzmc@aol.com www.zaloommarketing.com
Consultant specializing in marketing, promotion and food technology; importer of seafood products including imitation crab meat

President: Roy Zaloom
jzzmc@aol.com
Estimated Sales: $10-20 Million
Number Employees: 10-19

31469 Zanasi USA
8601 73rd Ave No. # 38
Brooklyn Park, MN 55428
763-593-1907
Fax: 763-593-1941 800-627-2633
info@zanasiusa.com www.zanasiusa.com
Coding and marking equipment
President: Gianni Zanasi
CFO: Dana Paige
Marketing Director: Jenny Worre
National Sales Manager: Mark Koethe
Estimated Sales: Below $5 Million
Number Employees: 5-9
Square Footage: 8000
Brands:
  Jet 2000
  Modul Print
  Z Jet

31470 Zander Insurance Group
212 Oceola Ave
Nashville, TN 37209-3116
615-356-1700
Fax: 615-352-2850 info@zanderins.com
www.zanderinsurancetips.com
Compressed air and industrial gas purification products
Owner: Bud Zander
jaz@zanderins.com
Estimated Sales: $2.5 - 5 Million
Number Employees: 50-99

31471 Zapata Industries
2699 S Bayshore Drive
Miami, FL 33133
305-856-8804
Fax: 305-856-3046
Metal crowns, aluminum closures, plastic closures, lining compounds
President: Claudio Zapata
Estimated Sales: $1-2.5 Million
Number Employees: 1-4

31472 Zast Foods Corporation
222 Islington Avenue
Suite 6C
Toronto, ON M8V 3W7
Canada
416-539-9278
Fax: 416-539-9299 info@zastfoods.com
zast-foods.com
Wines, soups, tea, cereals, popcorn, Mexican snacks, seasonings, sweeteners, and frozen fruits.
President & CEO: Ryan Pennie
Director, Retail Sales: Chris Sanderson-Kirby
VP, Operations: Jayne Hughes
Number of Brands: 11
Type of Packaging: Food Service
Brands:
  Big Screen Snax
  Cineplex Big Screen Snax
  Cookin' Greens
  Cream of Wheat
  El Rabioso
  Mrs Dash
  Nourishtea
  Nudefruit
  Nudesoup
  Sugar Twin
  Windrush

31473 Zealco Industries
PO Box 809
Calvert City, KY 42029-0809
800-759-5531
Fax: 270-395-9522
Manufacturer and exporter of high pressure commercial and industrial washing equipment
Parent Co: Purlanco

31474 Zebra Technologies Corporation
3 Overlook Point
Lincolnshire, IL 60069
847-634-6700
Fax: 847-913-8766 866-230-9494
www.zebra.com
Bar code equipment including printers, supplies and software for point-of-application labeling and performance thermal transferring.

Chairman: Michael Smith
Chief Executive Officer: Anders Gustafsson
Chief Financial Officer: Nathan Winters
Chief Legal Officer: Cristen Kogl
Chief Marketing Officer: Jeff Schmitz
Chief of Global Operations & Services: Stephen Williams
Year Founded: 1969
Estimated Sales: $5.6 Billion
Number Employees: 9,800
Square Footage: 167600
Other Locations:
  Holstville NY
  Agoura Hills CA
  Alpharetta GA
  Austin TX
  Bentonville AR
  Buffalo Grove IL
  Burlingotn MA
  Eden Prairie MN
  Flowery Branch GA
  Germantown MD
  Greenville WI
  Hauppauge NY
  Kennesaw GA
Brands:
  Zebra
  Zebra Value-Line
  Zebra Xii

31475 Zed Industries
3580 Lightner Rd
PO Box 458
Vandalia, OH 45377-9735
937-667-8407
Fax: 937-667-3340 info@zedindustries.com
www.zedindustries.com
Manufacturer and exporter of vacuum and pressure thermoforming equipment, heat sealers, formers/fillers/sealers, blister packers and custom engineered plastic packaging systems
President: Mark Zelnick
dzelnick@zedindustries.com
CFO: Helen Zelnick
VP: Peter Zelnick
Sales: Leonard Loomis
Estimated Sales: $10-20 Million
Number Employees: 50-99
Type of Packaging: Consumer, Food Service, Bulk

31476 Zeeco Inc
22151 E 91st St S
Broken Arrow, OK 74014-3250
918-258-8551
Fax: 918-251-5519 sales@zeeco.com
www.zeeco.com
Manufacturer and exporter of gas and oil food burners used for heating and drying; also, fume/liquid incinerators used for hazardous waste disposal
President: Jason Abbott
jason.abbott@zeeco.com
Chairman: John Zink
Sales Manager: D Caho
Purchasing Manager: D Updike
Estimated Sales: Less Than $500,000
Number Employees: 1-4
Square Footage: 42000

31477 Zeier Plastic & Mfg Inc
2203 Leo Cir
Madison, WI 53704-2615
608-244-5782
Fax: 608-244-1810 DZ@Zeierplastic.com
Manufacturer and exporter of thermoplastic injection molded trays and funnels; also, custom injection molded parts available
Owner: Dennis Zeier
dz@zeierplastic.com
VP: Dennis Zeier
Estimated Sales: $2.5-5 Million
Number Employees: 10-19

31478 Zelco Industries
110 Haven Ave
Mount Vernon, NY 10553
914-699-6230
Fax: 914-699-7082 800-431-2486
office@zelco.com
Lighting fixtures, cooking and barbecuing utensils, stainless steel cutlery and coffee brewers

Chairman of the Board: Noel E Zeller
CEO: Noel Zeller
CFO: Mike Ronan
Vice President: Nicole Zeller
Marketing Director: Terri Manganelli
Sales Director: Mike Boylan
Operations Manager: Robert Jacobs
Estimated Sales: $2.5-5,000,000
Number Employees: 20-49
Square Footage: 55000
Type of Packaging: Consumer, Private Label

31479 Zeltex
130 Western Maryland Parkway
Hagerstown, MD 21740
301-791-7080
Fax: 301-733-9398 800-732-1950
canders@zeltex.com www.zeltex.com
Manufacturer and exporter of near-infrared analyzers for the food, grain and patrochemical industries
President: Todd Rosenthal
Director of Sales: Chris Anders
Number Employees: 20
Brands:
  Zeltex

31480 Zeltex
130 Western Maryland Pkwy
Hagerstown, MD 21740-5116
301-791-7080
Fax: 301-733-9398 800-732-1950
canders@zeltex.com www.zeltex.com
Near infrared instrumentation for moisture and product constituents
President: Todd Rosenthal
Director of Sales: Chris Anders
Estimated Sales: $1-5 Million
Number Employees: 24

31481 Zenar Corp
7301 S 6th St
Oak Creek, WI 53154-2047
414-764-1800
Fax: 414-764-1267 mail@zenarcrane.com
www.zenarcrane.com
Manufacturer and exporter of electric overhead cranes and hoist units
President: John Maiwald
CEO: John A Maiwald
jmaiwald@zenarcrane.com
Estimated Sales: $10 - 20 Million
Number Employees: 100-249

31482 Zenith Cutter
5200 Zenith Pkwy
Loves Park, IL 61111-2735
815-282-5200
Fax: 815-282-5232 800-223-5202
toddg@zenithcutter.com www.zenithcutter.com
Manufacturer and exporter of machine knives and cutters; also, custom manufacturing and duplicating available
President: Cedric Blazer
cedricb@zenithcutter.com
Personnel: Bob Yocum
VP: Robert Yocum
Quality Control: Tim Greve
Director Sales/Marketing: Tim Schoenecker
Production Manager: Terry Willis
Estimated Sales: $20 - 50 Million
Number Employees: 100-249
Square Footage: 140000
Type of Packaging: Bulk

31483 Zenith Specialty Bag Co
17625 Railroad St
PO Box 8445
City of Industry, CA 91748-1195
626-912-2481
Fax: 626-810-5136 800-962-2247
cust.serv@zenithbag.com www.zbags.com
Manufacturer and exporter of paper products including custom print, pan liners, wax paper bags and grease resistant sheets
President: Marco Alcala
m.alcala@zenithbag.com
CEO: Betty Anderson
CFO: Jack Grave
Vice President: Ron Anderson
VP: Ron Anderson
Marketing Director: Susan Washle
Sales Director: Scott Apperson
Operations Manager: Jeff Behrends

Estimated Sales: $10 - 20 Million
Number Employees: 100-249
Square Footage: 170000
Brands:
  Sta-Fresh
  The Cubby
  Thermal Gard

31484 Zep Superior Solutions
1310 Seaboard Industrial Dr
Atlanta, GA 30318
404-352-1680
Fax: 404-350-2742 www.zepmfg.com
Owner: Marty Zappa
CFO: John Ehrie
Quality Control: Bruce Dunkley
Estimated Sales: $300,000-500,000
Number Employees: 1-4

31485 Zepf Technologies
5320 140th Ave N
Clearwater, FL 33760-3743
727-535-4100
Fax: 727-539-8944 sales@zepf.com
www.pneumaticscale.com
Manufacturer and exporter of shrink wrappers, case packers, bundlers, tray formers, straw applicators, rotary uncasers, combiners and laners
President: Michael Mc Laughlin
Contact: Doug Dougherty
  doug.dougherty@hayssen.com
Estimated Sales: $20-50 Million
Number Employees: 50-99
Square Footage: 45000
Brands:
  Akron
  Akron Hawk
  Akron Spartan
  Flex-Packer
  Flexwrap
  Iac 2000
  Pilot Divider
  Tampco
  Universal

31486 Zephyr Manufacturing Co
200 Mitchell Rd
Sedalia, MO 65301-2114
660-827-0352
Fax: 660-827-0713 info@zephyrmfg.com
www.zephyrmfg.com
Processor and exporter of brushes, floor and carpet cleaners, wet mops, handles, mopsticks, sponges, frames, squeegees
President: Charles Close
cclose@zephyrtool.com
Estimated Sales: $20-50 Million
Number Employees: 50-99
Brands:
  Dover Grill Scraper
  Zephyr

31487 Zephyrhills Bottled Water Company
6403 Harney Rd
Tampa, FL 33610-9349
813-630-5763
Fax: 813-620-6862 800-950-9398
Bottled water
President: Kim Jeffery
Marketing Director: John Bryan
Sales Manager: Monica Kelley
Operations Manager: Eddie Edmunds
Estimated Sales: $.5 - 1 million
Number Employees: 1-4
Parent Co: Perrier Group of America
Type of Packaging: Private Label

31488 Zerand Corp
15800 W Overland Dr
New Berlin, WI 53151-2882
262-827-3800
Fax: 262-827-3911 www.zerand.com
Manufacturer and exporter of paper board printing and packaging machinery
VP: Paul Capper
Director Sales/Marketing/Administration: Bill Dennis
Estimated Sales: $10 - 20 Million
Number Employees: 50-99

31489 Zero Manufacturing Inc
500 W 200 N
North Salt Lake, UT 84054-2734
801-298-5900
Fax: 801-299-7389 800-959-5050
sales@apwi.com www.zerocases.com
Vacuum and thermoformed plastic reusable shipping containers and closures; also, aluminum and steel modular electronic cabinets and racks
CEO: Ryan Ramsey
  ryan.ramsey@zerocases.com
Estimated Sales: $10-20 Million
Number Employees: 250-499
Parent Co: Zero Corporation

31490 Zero Temp
2510 N Grand Ave # 112
Suite 112
Santa Ana, CA 92705-8753
714-538-3177
Fax: 714-538-1531 gflassoc@aol.com
www.zerotempcoldstorage.com
Manufacturer and exporter of turn key refrigerated warehouses, walk-in freezers, walk-in coolers, controlled environment rooms and clean rooms
Owner: Gary F Lyons
  gflassoc@aol.com
CEO: Michael Lyons
CFO: Donna Lyons
R&D: David Pinillos
Operations: Pat McBride
Production: Gary Lyons
Estimated Sales: $6 Million
Number Employees: 10-19
Square Footage: 6000
Parent Co: Garry F Lyons & Associates

31491 Zero-Max Inc
13200 6th Ave N
Minneapolis, MN 55441-5509
763-546-4300
Fax: 763-546-8260 800-533-1731
www.zeromax.com
Servoclass couplings, composite disk couplings, torque limiters
President: Doug Moore
  dmoore@zero-max.com
Estimated Sales: $20-50 Million
Number Employees: 50-99

31492 Zeroll Company
PO Box 999
Fort Pierce, FL 34954
772-461-3811
Fax: 772-461-1061 800-872-5000
sales@zeroll.com www.zeroll.com
Manufacturer and exporter of scoops, dishers and spades
Plant Manager: Thomas Funka Sr
General Manager/CEO: Lenny Van Valkenburg
Plant Manager: Thomas Funka, Jr.
Estimated Sales: $10 Million
Number Employees: 20-49
Number of Brands: 5
Number of Products: 40
Square Footage: 60000
Type of Packaging: Consumer, Food Service, Private Label, Bulk
Brands:
  Nuroll
  Roldip
  Universal
  Zeroll
  Zerolon

31493 Zeroloc
9757 NE Juanita Dr # 119
Kirkland, WA 98034-8966
425-823-4888
Fax: 425-820-9749 www.zeroloc.com
Insulated panel and door systems
Number Employees: 1-4
Other Locations:
  Zeroloc Manufacturing Plant
  Brantford, ON
  Zeroloc Manufacturing Plant
  Langley, BC

31494 Zesto Food Equipment Manufacturing
6450 Hutchison Street
Montreal, QC H2V 4C8
Canada

514-278-4621
Fax: 514-278-4622 info@zesto.ca
President: George Moshonas
Number Employees: 20

31495 Zimmer Custom-Made Packaging
1450 E 20th St
Indianapolis, IN 46218

317-263-3436
Fax: 317-263-3427
A leading supplier in the worldwide flexible packaging industry. ZCMP has focused on frozen novelty, butter/margarine, candy, confectionary and other food markets and is currently beginning to supply die cut cone sleeves and die cutlids.
President: Mark Lastovich
CFO: Chuck Bollard
Quality Assurance Manager: Herbert Henson
VP Marketing/Sales: Mike DoBosh
Contact: Mark Murphy
mmurphy@zcmp.com
VP Operations: David Brown
Estimated Sales: $20-50 Million
Number Employees: 20-49
Square Footage: 60000
Other Locations:
Zimmer Custom-Made Packaging
Indianapolis IN

31496 Zimmerman Handling Systems
29555 Stephenson Hwy
Madison Heights, MI 48071-2332
248-398-6200
Fax: 248-398-1374 800-347-7047
seekinfo@irco.com www.irhoist.com
Manufacturer and exporter of ergonomic lifting systems
President: Gerard Geraghty
National Accounts Manager: Stephen Klostermeyer
Estimated Sales: $10 Million
Number Employees: 20-49
Parent Co: Ingersol-Rand

31497 Ziniz
3955 E Blue Lick Road
Louisville, KY 40229-6047
502-955-6573
Fax: 502-955-6960
Manufacturer and exporter of package handling conveyors including chain, gravity belt live roller and overhead trolley; also, installation available
President: Ronny Grant
Marketing/Sales: Paul McDonald
Estimated Sales: $50-100 Million
Number Employees: 250-499
Square Footage: 50000

31498 Zip-Net Inc
801 William Ln
Reading, PA 19604-1523
610-929-9426
Fax: 610-921-1588 www.zip-net.com
President: Andrew Wicklow
Estimated Sales: $20 - 50 Million
Number Employees: 50-99

31499 Zip-Pak
1800 W Sycamore Rd
Manteno, IL 60950-9369
815-468-6500
Fax: 815-468-6550 800-488-6973
info@zippak.com www.zippak.com
Reclosable and reusable polyethylene bags with plastic zippers
Vice President: Dave Atkinson
Finance Executive/Controller: Roger Geckner
Vice President: Dave Atkinson
Boniness Unit Manager: Stephen Schaller
Estimated Sales: $10 - 20 Million
Number Employees: 250-499
Parent Co: Illinois Tool Works

31500 Zip-Pak
1800 W Sycamore Rd
Manteno, IL 60950-9369
815-468-6500
Fax: 815-468-6550 800-488-6973
info@zippak.com www.zippak.com
Resealable zippered packaging

Vice President: Dave Atkinson
Finance Executive: Roger Geckner
Estimated Sales: $10 - 20 Million
Number Employees: 250-499

31501 Zip-Pak
1800 W Sycamore Rd
Manteno, IL 60950-9369
815-468-6500
Fax: 815-468-6550 info@zippak.com
www.zippak.com
Recloseable zipper products that can be used for storing a variety of products within the food industry.
Vice President: Dave Anzini
davea@zippak.com
VP/Investor Relations: John Brooklier
SVP/Chief Financial Officer: Ronald Kropp
Finance Executive: Roger Geckner
VP/Research and Development: Lee Sheridan
Senior Vice President: Allan Sutherland
SVP/General Counsel & Secretary: James Wooten
Senior Vice President Human Resources: Sharon Brady
Vice President Patents & Technology: Mark Croll
Number Employees: 250-499
Parent Co: Illinois Tool Works
Type of Packaging: Consumer

31502 Zip-Pak
4250 NE Expressway
Atlanta, GA 30340
888-866-8091
Fax: 770-454-7350 800-241-1833
www.zippak.com
Recloseable plastic zipper on the top and short side of the package in-line with any vertical f/f/s machine, in-line sealing of webless zipper for recloseable overwrap operations
Vice President: Howie Johnson
Sales/Marketing Manager: Geoff Griffin
Contact: Buddy Linton
buddyl@zippak.com
Estimated Sales: $5-10 Million
Number Employees: 50-99
Square Footage: 228000

31503 Zipskin
3108 Baker Rd
Dexter, MI 48130-1119
734-426-5559
Fax: 734-426-0899
Sanitary hand coverings
President: Gary Gochanour
Estimated Sales: $1 - 5,000,000
Number Employees: 1-4
Brands:
Zipkin

31504 Zitropack Limited
240 S LA Londe Ave
Addison, IL 60101-3307
630-543-1016
Fax: 630-543-7216 info@zitropack.com
Remanufactured and repaired food processing equipment, fillers, filling equipment and sealers
Vice President: Rafael Ortiz
rafael@zitropack.com
VP: Rafael Ortiz
Number Employees: 20-49

31505 Zmd International
600 W 15th St
Long Beach, CA 90813-1508
562-628-0071
Fax: 562-628-0080 800-222-9674
Temperature controlling and trimming equipment
President: Yosi Cohen
VP Marketing: Jacob Horev
Manager Sales: David Maciel
Estimated Sales: $5-10,000,000
Number Employees: 20-49
Number of Products: 7
Square Footage: 92000

31506 Zoia Banquetier Co
4700 Lorain Ave
Cleveland, OH 44102-3443
216-631-6414
Fax: 216-961-5119
www.artisticmetalspinning.com
Food banquet covers, brushes, dollies and carts; exporter of food banquet covers

Owner: Lorraine Hangauer
artistic1@ameritech.net
Secretary: Donald Hangauer
Estimated Sales: $500,000-$1 Million
Number Employees: 1-4
Square Footage: 50000

31507 Zojirushi America Corporation
1149 W., 190th Street
Suite 1000
Gardena, CA 90248
310-769-1900
Fax: 310-323-5522 800-264-6270
www.zojirushi.com
Zojirushi offers a complete line of quality NSF approved vacuum insulated coffee, serving products and a wide variety of restaurant equipment including commerical grade rice cookers and warmers, vacuum insulated carafes, Air Potbeverage dispensers, Gravity Pot beverage dispensers, vacuum insulated creamers and electric soup warmers.
President: Norio Ichikawa
Contact: Jun Mikuchi
j.mikuchi@zojirushi.com

31508 Zol-Mark Industries
470 Logan Avenue
Winnipeg, NB R3A 0R8
Canada
204-943-7393
Fax: 204-943-9803
Commercial steel furniture including chairs, tables and bar stools for the hospitality industry
Marketing: Hart Goldman
Sales: Aaron Goldman
Plant Manager: Aaron Goldman
Number Employees: 20-49

31509 Zollman's Dark Canyon Coffee
428 S Main Street
Pendleton, OR 97801-2248
541-276-2242
Fax: 541-276-2242 888-548-8555
Coffee roasting; wholesale/retail
President: Garry Zollman
CEO/Owner: Kathi Zollman
Vice President: Shaina Zollman
Estimated Sales: Under $500,000
Number Employees: 1-4
Type of Packaging: Private Label
Brands:
Dark Canyon Coffee & Tea
Leter Buck Coffee Co.

31510 Zumbiel Packaging
2100 Gateway Blvd
Hebron, KY 41048
513-531-3600
Fax: 859-689-0763 sales@zumbiel.com
www.zumbiel.com
Boxes, cartons, beverage carriers, transparent plastic lids and tubes.
Owner: Thomas Zumbiel
VP, Sales & Marketing: Charles Mace
Year Founded: 1843
Estimated Sales: $250-500 Million
Number Employees: 200-499
Square Footage: 500000

31511 Zume
250 Polaris Ave.
Mountain View, CA 94043
zume.com
Offers data analysis services to help businesses manage and reduce food waste based on a supply and demand formula.
Chairman & CEO: Alex Garden
COO: Mike McMahon
Year Founded: 2018
Number Employees: 350-500

31512 Zume Manufacturing
250 Polaris Ave.
Mountain View, CA 94043
zume.com
Offers packaging options that are manufactured from agricultural waste. Packaging is 100% compostable and provides customizable products.
Chairman & CEO: Alex Garden
EVP, Source Packaging: Annette Groenink
COO: Mike McMahon
Year Founded: 2018
Number Employees: 350-500
Parent Co: Zume

31513 Zumtobel Staff Lighting
3300 US Highway 9w
Highland, NY 12528-2630
845-691-6262
Fax: 973-340-9898 www.zumtobelstaff.com
Manufacturer, importer and exporter of lighting fixtures
President: Wolfgang Egger
Sales: Allison Craig

Estimated Sales: $50 - 100 Million
Number Employees: 5-9

31514 Zurn Industries LLC
1801 Pittsburgh Ave
Erie, PA 16502-1998
814-455-0921
Fax: 814-875-1402 855-663-9876
www.zurn.com

Commercial, institutional and industrial building products
President: Alex Marini
Vice President: Craig Wehr
Sales/Marketing Manager: Jerry Dill
Number Employees: 1000-4999

Numeric

101, 24536
10th St. Bakery, 30850
1450 Food Pack Analyzer, 29105
1911 Originals, 27330
2-Flap, 19926
2-In-1 Time-Saver, 29420
2-In-One Deodorizer, 29864
2000 Plus, 21219
2001, 22378
21c, 20135
22 K Gold Finish, 20849
24 Hour Odor Absorber, 29864
2404, 18645
2point, 21679
3-36, 21070
3-Cup Measurer, 20011
3-D Degreaser, 20849
3-Step, 31230
302 Hawk Labelers, 20119
3100 Sample Concentrator, 30173
3m, 18287, 18600, 22238, 23918, 27619
3m Littman, 18004
3vision, 28878
4 Way Step, 28515
450xl, 30897
574 Portable Oxygen Analyzer, 29105
5th Avenue, 23786
7000 Ht High Temperature Headspace, 30173
7up, 24840
80wheyusa, 25820
815 Mx, 19923
9000 Series, 23993
9th Wave, 28963

A

A 3000, 30476
A Gage, 19436
A Sign of Good Taste, 18089
A World of Good Fortune, 21078
A&B, 18044
A&W Root Beer, 24840
A-1, 18060, 24536
A-Frame, 29784
A. Thomas Meats, 22527
A.B. Curry's, 22742
A.L. Cook Technology, 20615
A/F Pot, 30695
A2000, 18901
A30, 25256
Aa, 28463
Aa Brand, 28463
Aae Series, 18628
Aaladin, 18248
Aantek, 18068
Aastro, 25059
Ab Sealers, 18885
Abanaki Concentrators, 18255
Abanaki Mighty Minn, 18255
Abanaki Oil Grabber, 18255
Abanaki Petro Extractor, 18255
Abanaki Tote-Its, 18255
Abbe, 25617
Abbey Farms, 18260
Abbey Farms England, 18260
Abbey Farms Holland, 18260
Abc Carrier, 24262
Abco, 18094, 18267
Abco International, 18266
Abel, 18269
Abell-Howe, 20771
Ablex, 18355
Abm, 18101
Abm's Safemark, 18101
Absorb, 30956
Absorbant Rugs & Pads, 30697
Abu Bint, 28463
Abundant, 18280
Ac Slit & Trim, 18023
Acca, 20827
Acceleron Advantage, 30469
Accent, 18283
Accents Frp, 25810
Accord Flavours, 28480
Accorista, 31002
Accu-Clear, 18301
Accu-Flo, 18301
Accu-Poly, 18301
Accu-Spray, 21063
Accu-Therm, 27394

Accucap, 18306
Accucapper, 18306
Accuflow, 28920
Accugard, 27543
Acculobe, 30895
Accupour, 21430
Accurol, 22284
Accuseal, 27543
Accusharp, 22815
Accuslitter, 29628
Accutest, 18056
Accuvac, 18306
Accuvue, 20121
Accuweigh, 31439
Ace, 18004, 18276, 18314
Ace & Icore, 30979
Ace-Tuf, 23577
Acid Free, 27086
Acme, 31052
Acorto, 18337
Acousticair, 30544
Acr Jr., 18114
Acr Powerwatch, 18114
Acrason, 18342
Acrawatt, 18340
Acri Lok, 18342
Acrison, 18342
Across-The-Line, 22531
Acs Industries, Inc. Scrubble, 18115
Act Ii, 20840, 20841
Action Ade, 23410
Activate Drinks, 26708
Active Magnetics, 28194
Actron, 18358
Acu-Rite, 20447
Acumedia, 24106
Ad Vantage, 28328
Ad-Lite, 26806
Ad-Touch, 22152
Adagio, 24840
Adamatic, 27104
Adamation, 18366
Adams McClure, 22217
Adapta-Flex, 30143
Adapta-Plus, 30143
Adex, 18375
Adez, 20703
Adi-Anmbr, 18126
Adi-Bvf Digester, 18126
Adi-Hybrid, 18126
Adi-Mbr, 18126
Adi-Sbr, 18126
Adjust-A-Fit, 25133
Admar, 31385
Admatch, 18384
Admiral, 23294, 25929
Admire, 19754
Admixer, 18128
Admore, 22217
Adnaps, 23193
Adolphus, 18463
Adr, 22736, 24850
Ads Laminaire, 21873
Adsormat, 30674
Advance, 27590, 31233
Advance 2000, 31070
Advance Aroma System, 18200
Advance Tabco, 18401
Advanced, 18417
Advanced Digital System, 31245
Advanced Equipment, 18410
Advanced Polybagger, 18426
Advantage, 18622, 19987
Advantage Rak, 24751
Advantra Z, 24281
Adventra, 23490
Adver-Tie, 27175
Adverteaser, 25460
Aearo/Peltor, 22238
Aef-1, 31130
Aef-25, 31130
Aef-7, 31130
Aegis, 31230
Aep Institutional Products, 18031
Aero, 21219, 30680
Aero Heat Exchanger, 26669
Aero-Counter, 18521
Aero-Serv, 29097
Aerolator, 18454
Aerolux, 27335
Aeromat, 19689
Aeroscout, 29624

Aerospec, 18447
Aerotec, 19689
Aerowhip, 19116
Aeroxon, 28613
Aew, 18138
Afc, 22468
Afco, 18559
Afta, 23470
Agricap, 26300
Agricare, 23606
Agrobotic Technology, 25588
Ags 100, 24979
Agtron, 18486
Agua Jane, 20673
Aie, 21154
Aim, 20577
Aimia Foods, 27838
Air Cush'n, 20667
Air Deck, 21650
Air Flow, 22645, 31186
Air Pro, 18554
Air Repair, 21546
Air Solution, 22042
Air Tech, 21520
Air Therapy, 26091
Air-Lec, 18506
Air-Ply, 18225
Air-Savers, 29864
Air-Scent, 18507, 29864
Air-Trax, 25416
Aire Systems, 30424
Aire-02, 18442
Aire-02 Triton, 18442
Airector, 24556
Airflex, 18554
Airform, 19932
Airlite, 22378
Airmaster, 18518, 24975
Airmatic Lube, 19664
Airomat, 18519
Airport Network Solutions, 24028
Airsan, 18522
Airserv, 24046
Airspeed, 31387
Airswitch, 24046
Airway, 24081
Airx, 20513
Aisle Pro, 19776
Ajax, 20739, 28363
Ajilys, 18523
Ajipro-L, 18523
Akra-Pak, 28662
Akro-Bins, 19939
Akro-Mils, 19921, 19940
Akron, 31485
Akron Hawk, 31485
Akron Spartan, 31485
Akta Klor, 30956
Alabama Rag, 26810
Alacreme, 31209
Aladdin Products, 23987
Alan Bradley, 27323
Alar, 18533
Alarmwork Multimedia, 24086
Alaskan Brewing Company, 26708
Albany, 21219
Albi, 22629
Albin, 24640
Alcan, 26791
Alcatel, 27771
Alco, 29011
Alco Tabs, 18548
Alcohol Prep Pads 100's, 26671
Alcojet, 18548
Alcon Plus, 20641
Alconox, 18548
Aleco, 19921
Alegacy, 18028
Alesco, 24516
Alewel's Country Meats, 18557
Alexander Grappa, 27277
Alexanderwerk, 27404
Alexco, 18560
Alexia, 20840, 20841
Alfa, 24112, 28876, 30188
Alfa-Kortogleu, 22329
Alfred Bakeware, 30532
Algarve, 20983
Algene, 18567
Alhambra, 27838
Align, 30234
Aline, 18573

Alkaline, 18580
Alkazone, 18580
Alkazone Alkaline Booster Drops, 18580
Alkazone Antioxidant Water Ionizer, 18580
Alkazone Vitamins & Herbs, 18580
Alkota, 18581
All a Cart, 18582
All American, 18586
All Good, 30234
All Out, 24423
All Packaging Machinery, 18885
All Plastic Belting, 19119
All Sorts, 18593
All Star, 27281
All Ways, 30921
All-Bottle, 19589
Allan, 23786
Allegro, 28535
Allen, 27751
Allen Bradley, 22511
Allen-Bailey, 22217
Allen-Bradley, 28514
Aller-Snap Protein Residue Test, 24006
Alliance, 18621, 18622, 21238, 31098
Allibert, 28887
Alligator, 22657
Alljuice, 26388
Allstrong, 18650
Alltec, 20771
Allure, 31233
Allvia, 26825
Allwrite, 30476
Alm, 19921
Almond Breeze, 19755
Almond Joy, 23786
Almond Toppers, 19755
Almondina, 25825
Alo, 19647
Aloe Jell Water Less, 23566
Aloha, 28385
Alox, 23511
Alpaire, 22931
Alpha, 27753, 31245
Alpha Laval Flo, 19409
Alpha-Media, 22287
Alpine, 19584, 30862
Alpine/Xpd, 26373
Alps Model 7385, 18499
Alps Smart Test Module, 18499
Alps Sx-Flex, 18499
Alps Vision Plus, 18499
Alta Dena Dairy, 21443
Alumaworks, 18693
Alumicube, 18796
Alumiflex, 28530
Alumin-Nu, 18695
Alumitec Elite, 30132
Alumtec, 30132
Always, 30234
Always Can, 29735
Always Discreet, 30234
Amana, 18339
Amano Jenbrana, 18699
Amano Ocumare, 18699
Amark/Simionato, 18701
Amazon, 28198
Ambassador, 26223
Ambec 10, 22645
Ambec 10r, 22645
Ambersweet, 29894
Ambrose, 18707
Amcel, 18708
Amco, 18700, 18710
Amcoat, 18710
Amcoll, 18710
Ameri-Kart, 19939
American, 23845
American Bulk Conveyors, 27355
American Eagle, 18754
American Extrusion International, 18764
American Greetings, 19619
American Heritage, 28947
American Ingredients, 30659
American Led-Gible, Inc., 18793
American Metal Ware, 23454
American Metalcraft, 18803
American Optical, 24009
American Panel, 18813
American Range, 18822
American Sanders Technology, 20615
American Savory, 26110
American Solving, 18829

Brand Name Index

Brix 50, 25272
Brix 65hp, 25272
Brix 90, 25272
Brix 90hp, 25272
Bro-Tisserie, 18995
Broadway Menu, 30919
Broaster, 19895
Broaster Chicken, 19895
Broaster Foods, 19895
Broaster Recipe, 19895
Broiler Master, 20272
Brooklace, 19898
Brooklyn, 21219, 21891
Brooks, 19901, 20840, 20841, 27584
Brookshire's, 19902
Brookside, 23786
Broussard, 27931
Brower, 19907
Brown, 19912
Brown Brothers, 27277
Brown Paper Goods, 29137
Bruner, 21165
Bruner-Matic, 21165
Brush-Rite, 23232
Brute, 21198
Brute Rack, 19928
Bsp901, 26298
Bubba's Yams, 28134
Bubble Yum, 23786
Bubly, 27476
Buck, 19936
Buck Ice, 19935
Buckeye, 18287
Buckhoen, 19940
Buckpower, 26825
Buckskin Bill, 21833
Budget Buy, 30486
Budgetware, 23845
Budgit, 20771
Budweiser, 26708
Bueno, 29137
Bufalo, 23897
Buffalo, 21793, 24262, 26972
Buffalo Grill, 22297
Buflovak, 19943
Built Rite, 20027
Bulkatilt, 28159
Bulkitank, 28159
Bulklift, 19949
Bulkmaster, 29671, 29672
Bulksonics, 26319
Bulldog, 30226
Bullet, 24218
Bullet Guard, 19953
Bullet Lure, 24310
Bunker Boxes, 19056
Bunn, 19300, 19955, 31128
Bunn-O-Matic, 19955
Buran, 30617
Burg'r Tend'r, 21333
Burgess, 19964
Burkay, 18076
Burke, 23897
Burkle, 21873
Burn Energy Drink, 20703
Burnguard, 30528
Burpee, 25583
Burrows Packaging, 26796
Burt's Bees, 20673, 30234
Burtek, 18881
Burtex, 18882
Busboy, 24034
Busch, 26708, 27771
Buschman, 30965
Business Works Accounting, 28385
Busstop, 30540
Bustops, 26126
Butcher Buddy, 25548
Butcher's Friend, 30351
Butler, 19989
Butter Better, 31055
Butter Kernel Vegetables, 22494
Butter Up, 31055
Button-On, 24556
Bvl, 19356
Bx-100, 19891

C

C-Square, 29524
C-Vap, 31320
C-Vat, 31320

C.G Sargent's Sons, 19948
C.P., 29011
C.U.E., 30163
C/Z, 20728
Cab Produktechnik, 30227
Cab-O-Sil, 20127
Cabana Lemonade, 27134
Cabin Air Filters, 21888
Caboo, 20126
Cache Valley, 21443
Cacti-Nea, 26665
Cactus Cooler, 24840
Cactus Kid, 20134
Cadbury, 23786
Caddy, 18198, 20135
Caddy Cold, 20135
Caddy Connections, 20135
Caddy-All, 26721
Caddy-Flex, 20135
Caddy-Veyor, 20135
Caddymagic, 20135
Cadie, 20136
Cady, 20771
Cae Profile, 18144
Cae Select, 18144
Café Escapes, 24840
Café Punta Del Cielo, 24840
Cafe, 22992
Cafe Amore, 19456
Cafe Del Mundo, 20141
Cafe Elite, 19750
Cafe H, 23897
Cafe-Matic, 24764
Cafe.Com, 24028
Cafiesa, 22590
Cake Comb, 20011
Cake-Mix, 27318
Cal, 20144
Cal Tuf, 19050
Cal Vac, 21154
Cal-Cu-Dri, 21289
Cal-Stat, 30953
Calc-U-Dryer, 21289
Calcomms, 20144
Caldwell Manufacturing, 20541
Calf-Tel, 25023
Calgrafix, 20144
Calhoun Bend Mill, 20152
Calibrated, 22217
Calibration Columns, 24735
Calico Cottage Fudge Mix, 20154
California, 30420
California Connoisseur, 30903
California Crisps, 18388
California Golden Pop, 24589
California Nuts, 19755
California Pantry, 23914
California Rag, 26810
California Trays, 30420
Calistoga Water, 26708
Calla, 21233
Calling Card, 21078
Calogix, 20144
Calormatic, 29892
Calp, 26972
Calsaw, 20161
Calypso, 19647
Cam, 29624
Cam Frequent Diners, 20825
Cam Spray, 20168
Cam Tron, 20169
Cam-Grid, 20171
Camagsolv, 20201
Cambri-Link, 20171
Cambridge, 20172, 28400
Cambro, 20173
Camelot, 27131
Cameo, 19379
Camillus Classic Cartridge, 18024
Camoco, 20293
Can Jet, 22645
Canada Dry, 24840
Canadian Springs, 27838
Canalyzer, 20258
Canco, 18692
Candido, 27277
Cando, 20188
Candy Bracelets, 22949
Canguard, 20194
Cannon, 19619, 23150
Cantech, 20208
Canty, 24461

Cap Level Iia, 30841
Cap Snap, 29265
Cap'n Crunch, 27476
Cap-O-Mat, 27570
Cap. M. Quik, 28686
Capaciagage, 21122
Capamatic, 26519
Cape Covelle Seafood Market, 30374
Cape May, 25037
Capitani, 22173
Capitol Hardware, 20227
Capn Clean, 19754
Capolac, 19057
Capone Foods, 20231
Capri-Sun, 20703
Capsylite, 27031
Captain, 24920
Capture Jet, 23571
Capture Rey, 23571
Capway, 20235
Car Chem, 20700
Car Hartt, 26915
Cara, 25494
Caramelizer, 20023
Carapelli, 25825
Carbo Mizers, 28916
Carbon Comet, 29632
Carbona Cleanit! Oven Cleaner, 21531
Carbone, 20246
Carbonetor Pumps, 24004
Carcos Splutting Saw, 26560
Cardinal, 21598
Care Bears, 20965
Careware, 18334
Cargill, 30817
Cargomaster, 31105
Caribbean Shade Market Umbrellas, 26441
Caribou Coffee, 24840
Carioca, 31128
Carmi Flavors, 20283
Carmine, 18102
Carminic Acid, 18102
Carolina, 28463
Carolina Rag, 26810
Carousel Caser, 28784
Carpet Guard, 23470
Carpet Gun, 22502
Carpet Master, 21373
Carpet Scent, 19754
Carpet Wizard, 21531
Carpuela, 29499
Carr's, 25825
Carrabind, 20303
Carrafat, 20303
Carralite, 20303
Carralizer, 20303
Carraloc, 20303
Carravis, 20303
Carrera 1000 M, 24112
Carrera 1000 Pc, 24112
Carrera 2000 Pc, 24112
Carrera 500 M, 24112
Carrier, 20304, 29011
Carrier Select, 25446
Carrigaline, 18260
Carroll, 20311
Carroll Chair, 20308
Carter, 20319
Carter Hoffmann, 29506
Carter-Hoffmann, 20321, 27497
Carthage, 20323
Cartier, 27250
Cartridge, 18024
Carts, 19824
Carts of Colorado, 20329
Cartwashable, 21373
Carver Aid, 25339
Casa Verde, 20808
Casablanca, 25695
Casba Ii, 29539
Casba Iv, 29539
Cascade, 21959, 30234
Cascades, 18031
Cascades Ifc Disposables, 18031
Casella, 20339
Casemate, 25789, 30766
Casestar, 28510
Casettraypackers, 23752
Cash Caddy, 20340
Cash Handler, 25946
Casing-Net, 24600
Cass Clay, 21443

Cassette Feu, 24445
Cassida Fluids and Greasers, 22261
Castered Safety, 25368
Castillo Espanol, 18260
Castle, 20835
Castle Bag, 20350
Cat Pumps, 20353
Catania-Spagna, 20032
Catarcooler, 20270
Cater Ease, 28385
Catering, 29312
Catermate, 20040
Catertec, 22016
Caterware, 26056
Caterwrap, 23847
Catr, 30604
Cats, 30402
Cattron, 20362
Cavit, 27277
Cbm, 28254
Cbs Baking Band, 19119
Cbs-B, 19811
Cbs-Ch, 19811
Ccbreeze, 26654
Ccc Burners, 25226
Cci, 20055
Ccl, 24844
Ccl Label, 18290
Cd-3 Vendor Cart, 19221
Cdr, 29393
Ce Airestream Hoods, 23758
Ce-15/22, 31103
Cea 266, 20059
Cecor, 20371
Cedar's Premium Beverages, 20678
Celebrate Line, 25003
Celebration, 20270, 21842
Celebrity Cups, 30989
Celebrity Stars, 20374
Celeste, 27584
Celeste Pizza For One, 20840, 20841
Celestial, 25825
Cell-O-Core, 20376
Cell-O-Matic, 23338
Cello Foam, 20379
Cello Wrap, 30178
Cellophane, 30569
Celloplus, 30569
Cellotherm, 30569
Cellscale, 25976
Cellu Flo, 23482
Cellu Pore, 23482
Cellu Stacks, 23482
Cellulose Gum, 19116
Celographics, 20609
Cenprem, 20411
Centa, 28400
Central Volky, 27024
Centravac, 30424
Centri-Matic Iii, 18129
Centrie Clutch, 19822
Centrified, 22234
Centrifuges, 24394
Centrimaster, 18327
Centrimil, 22234
Centrisys, 20406
Centrivap, 25080
Centurion, 25360, 25605
Century Line, 26866
Cera-Q, 24281
Ceramicor, 21519
Cerelose, 24262
Certipack, 24920
Ces, 20771
Cesco, 20429
Cetus Textile Fabrics, 21888
Cf, 22680
Cf Chefs, 20062
Cfc Dunouy Tensiometer, 20105
Cfc Us Standard, 20105
Ch, 18507
Cha's Organics, 20430
Chafer Shield, 28223
Chafermate, 23278
Chaffee, 20432
Chafing Fuels, 29700
Chain-Data, 30175
Chain-In-Channel, 24614
Challenger, 18710, 26396, 28860
Chambir, 27366
Champ, 23606
Champ Awards, 20367

Defrost Controllers, 28063
Deiorio's, 21431
Deja Blue, 24840
Del Fuerte, 23897
Del Monte Fresh, 21482
Del Verde, 25825
Delair, 28756
Delco, 21519
Delco Buffalo, 26973
Delco Technology, 20615
Deleez, 30631
Delfield, 31138
Deli Buddy, 25548
Deli Meats, 23897
Delicious, 29894
Deligraphics, 20609
Delivers, 20270
Dell Amore's, 25825
Delouis, 25825
Delphi, 26654
Delphi 7.0, 26654
Delrin, 21873
Delroyd Worm Gear, 18686
Delta, 21063, 23443, 24112, 26012
Delta 3000 D-Cam, 24112
Delta 3000 Ld, 24112
Delta 3000 Sb, 24112
Delta Dry, 29553
Delta Liquid, 29553
Delta Pure, 21541
Delta Security Solutions, 20304
Deltamat, 22329
Deltech, 28756
Deluxe, 21551, 31185
Delwrap, 26720
Dematic, 21558
Demitasse After Dinner Tea, 23328
Denali, 26373
Denester, 23752
Denmar, 21563
Dennison's, 20840, 20841
Densart, 30834
Denta Brite, 21978
Depend, 24876
Depotpac, 27721
Derm Ade, 30610
Derma-Pro, 23023
Dermageek, 30234
Dermal, 23185
Descender, 28784
Desco, 20545, 21578
Desi Pak, 30674
Desi View, 30674
Desi-Pak, 26438
Design Master, 24666
Design Series Counters, 18310
Designbags, 21586
Designer Displpayer, 20270
Designer System, 29481
Designer's Choice, 18157
Designerware, 31016
Designs By Anthony, 22642
Dessvilie, 25825
Destiny Plastics, 18031
Det-O-Jet, 18548
Det-Tronics, 20304
Detecto, 18333, 21598
Detergent 8, 18548
Dewalt, 29624
Dewater Equipment, 24394
Dewied, 21610
Dexter Russell, 21613
Df 5000, 18097
Dft Series, 21662
Di-Tech, 24908
Diablo, 21615, 25230
Diack, 19050, 30304
Dial Taper, 25824
Dial-A-Fill, 26519
Dialog, 24782
Diamond, 21198, 21622, 21624, 21972, 24554, 30486
Diamond 49 Series, 19040
Diamond 52 Series, 19040
Diamond Brite, 21978
Diamond Clear, 21995
Diamond Grip, 21978
Diamond Wipes, 21630
Dickies, 26915, 30644
Dickinson, 25825
Diedrich Coffee, 24840
Diet Coke, 20703

Diet Rite, 24840
Digestive Care, 24543
Digi, 20535
Digi-Drive, 24702
Digi-Link, 24782
Digi-Stem, 27281
Digibar, 21737
Digisort, 23957
Digispense 2000, 24078
Digispense 700, 24078
Digispense 800, 24078
Digistrip, 24782
Digital (Appliance) Thermometers, 28063
Digital Dining, 21646
Digital Moisture Balance, 20105
Digital Thermostats, 28063
Digitronic, 29522
Digitronic, 23523
Dilusso Deli Company, 23897
Dimple Plate, 28630
Dine Aglow, 25230
Dine-A-Wipe, 23193
Dine-A-Wipe Plus, 23193
Dinelle, 29377
Diner Mug, 25702
Dinner Check, 20340
Dinnerware, 23533
Dinty Moore, 23897
Diosna, 19575, 19576
Dipix Vision Inspection Systems, 21660
Diposables, 27685
Dippy Donuts, 20678
Dipwell, 21661
Direct Fire Technical, Inc., 21662
Direct It, 21558
Dirt Eraser, 29529
Dirt Killer, 21664
Dirtex, 28896
Discovery Plastics, 19050
Discovery System, 24301
Dishwasher Glisten, 19850
Disintegrator, 19584
Disney, 20965
Dispatch, 20673
Dispax Reactor, 24110
Dispensa-Matic, 30227
Dispense Rite, 21669
Dispense-Rite, 21692
Displawall, 25810
Dispomed, 18375
Dispos-A-Way, 20010
Disposable Products Company, 18031
Disposawrapper, 25569
Dispose a Scrub, 24867
Disposer Saver, 24739
Disposertrol, 27801
Disposo-Treet, 23294
Dispoza-Pak, 28470
Dissolve-A-Way, 21421
Distillata, 21680
Ditrac, 19552
Ditting, 21685
Div-10, 22736
Diversified (DCE), 21687
Dixie, 18600, 21700
Dixie Brand, 27324
Dme, 21690
DoA Mar¡A, 23897
Do Haccp, 26706
Do Sop, 26706
Do-It, 21712
Do-Sys, 28389
Dock Xpress, 25416
Doctor's, 21078
Doering, 21714
Dogflex, 21787
Dogsters, 20965
Dole Food Products, 20032
Dole Packaged Foods, 30659
Dole Soft Serve, 24823
Dollarwise, 23845
Dollinger, 28756
Dolly Madison, 28455
Dominion, 26708
Don Enrique, 31397
Don Miguel, 23897
Don's Salads, 21726
Doncella Chocolates, 22590
Donut House Collection, 24840
Door Spy, 26116
Doors, 18801
Doorware, 24773

Dopaco, 18031
Dor-Blend, 21744
Dor-Mixer, 21744
Dor-Opener, 21744
Dorden, 26109
Dorell, 21740
Doritos, 27476
Dormont, 27497
Dorton, 21744
Dositainer, 18245
Dotmark, 21334
Double Cut System, 19154
Double Density Miniroller, 22645
Double J, 31048
Double Planetary, 20462
Doubletalk, 20609
Doughcart, 27935
Doughpro, 27935
Douglas, 21760
Dove, 20649
Dover Grill Scraper, 31486
Dover Phos Foods, 21764
Dow, 18600
Dowd & Rogers, 26825
Downy, 30234
Dowsport America, 21771
Dox Expander, 18928
Doyen, 22139
Doyon, 21780, 27497
Dp, 20076
Dr. Pepper, 24840
Drain Out, 24423
Drain Power, 27086
Drain Warden, 31055
Draino, 21781
Drainthru, 24493
Dratco, 21574
Dre (Direct Reading Echelle Icp), 25256
Dreaco, 21786
Dreft, 30234
Dri-Sheet, 27301
Drink-Master, 24764
Drip Catchers, 20011
Dripcut, 30418
Driver's Seat, The, 31215
Driveroll, 24403
Drize, 23193
Drop-Lok, 29263
Droste, 25825
Drum-Mate, 21801
Drum-Plex, 25265
Drumplex, 25468
Dry-O-Lite, 30794
Drynites, 24876
Ds Special, 20135
Dsi Escort, 25446
Du-Good, 21807
Dual Jet, 23729
Dual-Flex, 28598
Dual-Tex, 19891
Dubl-Fresh, 19379
Dubl-Tough, 31098
Dubl-View, 19379
Dubl-Wax, 19379
Dublnature, 31098
Dublserve, 31098
Dublsoft, 31098
Ducane, 18440
Duck Brand, 29213
Duct Axial, 23678
Duff Norton, 20771
Duke's, 20840, 20841
Dulux, 27031
Dumor, 20655
Dump Clean, 19220
Dump Trap, 23487
Duncan Hies Wilderness, 20840, 20841
Duncan Hines, 20840, 20841, 27584
Duncan Hines Comstock, 20840, 20841
Dunham-Bush, 29011
Dunhill, 21829
Dunkin' Donuts, 21830
Dunkmaster, 27564
Dunya Harvest, 29134
Duo Shield, 21383
Duo-Stress Place Mats, 25486
Duo-Touch, 19436
Duplux, 22069
Dupont, 18600
Dur-A-Edge, 27655
Dura, 21839
Dura Klor, 30956

Dura-Base, 23893
Dura-Drive Plus, 29485
Dura-Glide, 29623
Dura-Kote, 20830
Dura-Lite, 30785
Dura-Max, 18076
Dura-Pak, 18701
Dura-Plate, 24025
Dura-San Belt, 20135
Dura-Tool, 18024
Dura-Ware, 21842
Durabit, 22203
Durabrite, 22302
Duracast, 30330
Durachrome, 18144
Duraclamp, 23484
Duracool, 23643
Duracor, 20373
Duracrafic, 29009
Durajet, 19029
Duralast, 23577
Duraliner, 26465
Durallure, 30766
Duralobe, 30895
Duralon, 28400
Duralux, 21588
Duran, 30808
Durascan, 25587
Durasieve, 28294
Durastrap, 21884
Duratech, 19029
Duratek, 30870, 30871
Duratrax, 22539, 30885
Duratuf, 23145
Duraward, 30885
Durelco, 21839
Duro, 18334
Duro Bag, 26796
Durobor, 24674
Durt Howg, 25842
Durt Tracker, 25842
Dus-Trol, 23294
Dust 'n Clean, 23193
Dust Free Form of Fd&C Colors, 28526
Dust Up, 20607, 29557
Dust-Cat, 30667
Dust-Hog, 30667
Dustalarm, 26319
Duster, 25936
Dusterz, 24034
Dustkop, 18149
Dustmaster, 30545
Dustroyer, 30545
Dutch Gold, 25825
Dutchess, 21856
Dutro, 20157, 28530
Dw, 30440
Dyalon, 30296
Dymo, 21221
Dyna-Link, 25976
Dynablast, 21869
Dynac, 23676
Dynaflex, 26085
Dynagro, 25977
Dynahyde, 30957
Dynalyser, 18239
Dynamaster, 18327
Dynapac, 25972
Dynaplas, 26465
Dynarap, 20120
Dynaric, 21884
Dynashear, 18128
Dynastrap, 21884
Dynasty, 24532, 30747
Dynatred, 22509
Dynavac, 25876
Dynavac and Watervac Water Systems, 28403
Dynestene, 18189
Dynoplast, 28792
Dynynstyl, 21889

E

E-Binder, 23694
E-P Plus, 27443
E-Z Access, 25814
E-Z Dip, 21907
E-Z Fit Barbecue, 23029
E-Z Lift, 21910
E-Z Rak-Clip, 27619
E-Z Seal, 19283
E-Z Serve, 31196

Grillit 12x12, 19446
Grillmaster, 19138
Grills To Go, 23452
Grime Grabber, 21792
Grindmaster, 23454
Grip Clip, 27619
Grip Clips, 21032
Grip Rock, 25901
Grip Top, 19776
Grip-Grate, 29324
Grip-Plate, 29324
Gripper, 25936, 26145, 28159
Grips, 31144
Griptite, 20270
Grizzly, 26326
Grocery Grip, 24605
Groeb Farms, 23459
Groen, 26513
Grosfillex, 23463
Grote, 23465
Gsa, 26271
Gse, 30808
Gst, 20304
Gt Uni-Clip, 27619
Guardcraft, 27335
Guardian, 24309, 29086
Guardian Couplings, 18686
Guardmaster, 29744
Guardsboy, 20901
Guardsmen, 20901
Guardswitch, 22993
Gubiani Maple Espesso Anice, 26676
Guerlain, 27250
Guida's Dairy, 21443
Guidall, 20319
Guideline, 22654
Guidemaker, 24249
Guildware, 21383
Guiloriver, 22624
Guiltless Gourmet, 25825
Gulden's, 20840, 20841
Gump, 19943
Gun Powder Pearl Pinhead Green Tea, 23328
Gvp-100, 31163
Gyrocompact, 22905
Gyrostack, 22905

H

H&T, 23963
H-F 201, 23501
H-F 211, 23501
H-S 410, 23501
H.B. Fuller, 23490
H.C. Duke & Son, 23492
H.C. Valentine, 28618
H.F. Cradle System, 30967
H.K. Anderson, 20840, 20841
H.K. Systems, 18998
H.M. Quackenbush, 25583
H.O.P., 23694
Haagen-Dazs, 20032
Habco, 23516
Haccp, 18358
Hackney, 23549
Hackney Champion, 23549
Hackney Classic, 23549
Hackney Ultimate, 30767
Haco Industries, 21266
Hagerty Foods, 23552
Hahg, 27554
Haier, 22992
Hail Queen, 20623
Hair Biology, 30234
Hairfood, 30234
Hallde, 27404
Hallmark, 27430
Halloween, 21078
Halo, 23523
Halo Heat, 18685
Halton, 23572
Hamer, 25907
Hamilton, 19921, 28530
Hamilton Beach, 23576
Hammar, 23581
Han-D, 21099
Hanco, 23588
Handgards, 23590
Handi Wipes, 20673
Handi-Foil of America, 18031
Handi-Matic, 30642
Handifold, 23193

Handlair, 20565
Handle Capper, 18306
Handmaster, 29671, 29672
Hands, 21447
Handy A&C, 24095
Handy Andy, 31144
Handy Blade, 23597
Handy Fuel Brand, 29700
Handy Wacks, 23598
Handy-Cart, 19616
Handy-Home Helpers, 22609
Hanel Lean-Lift, 23599
Hanel Vertical Carousels, 23599
Hangars, 27814
Hank's, 23602
Hankison, 28756
Hanson Brass, 23616
Hard Cookies, 23861
Hard-Edge, 23139
Hard-Tac, 21462
Hardi-Tainer, 23633
Hardware, 18801
Hardwick, 25929
Harford Duracool, 23642
Harley Activated Pine, 20849
Harmonic, 22475
Harris, 25997
Harris Bug Free, 27072
Harris Famous, 27072
Hart, 23670
Hart Boost, 30048
Hart Treat, 30048
Hartlift, 30048
Hartstone, 23677
Harvest of the Sea, 27006
Harvestove, 20769
Harvestvac, 21833
Hatc, 26513
Hatco, 23687
Haug, 23690
Haul-All, 19502
Havana Cappuccino, 22055
Hawaiian, 27584
Hawaiian Punch, 24840
Hawaiian Snacks, 20840, 20841
Hawaiice, 19369
Hayes Graphics, 22217
Haynes, 23702
Hayon Select-A-Spray, 23703
Haz Mat, 20501
Haze-Out, 21336
Hazel's, 19679
Hazmax Enclosures, 23758
Hd Barcode, 23522
Hd Secureid, 23522
Hd Smartcode, 23522
Hd-900, 19811
Hdc Ii, 27265
Hde, 22934
Head & Shoulders, 30234
Healthcare, 23294
Healthy Choice, 20840, 20841
Healthy Sleep, 24543
Hearthbake, 26326
Heartland, 25339
Heat Exhangers, 31094
Heat on Demand, 18531
Heat Prober, 27281
Heat Spy, 27281
Heat-It, 23727
Heat-Pro, 25307
Heatcraft, 24958
Heath, 23786
Heatmaker Uvm, 25338
Heatzone, 23734
Heavenly Fresh, 24605
Heavy Metal, 22509
Hebrew National, 20840, 20841
Hedliner, 23744
Hedpak, 23744
Hef-T-Clean, 26152
Heinicke, 23740
Heiress, 21447
Hela, 23783
Helical, 26737
Helix, 23622
Henri Hutin, 18260
Henry, 29011
Henry & Henry, 20108
Henry's Heritage Bread, 29568
Hepavac, 30832
Herbal Essences, 30234

Herbox, 23897
Herbs For Kids, 26825
Hercules, 18371, 20272, 28790
Hercules Tables, 19616
Herd King, 20624
Herdez, 23897
Heritage, 31196
Heritage Bag, 26796
Heritage By Orbon, 27434
Heritage Select, 28744
Hermitex, 21437
Hero, 25825
Hershey's, 23786
Hershey's Bliss, 23786
Hershey's Kisses, 23786
Hettich, 27877
Hhp, 22800
Hi - Lo, 20270
Hi Roller, 23794
Hi Shrink, 26144
Hi-Cap, 21289, 26933
Hi-Cone, 24075
Hi-Def, 30476
Hi-Drum, 24556
Hi-Heat, 23533
Hi-Line, 21882
Hi-Lites, 20158
Hi-Lo, 20272, 23577
Hi-Performance, 27448
Hi-Psi-Flex (Water), 21741
Hi-Rise Lls Liquid Separator, 18350
Hi-Speed, 22511
Hi-Speed Cooker, 28889
Hi-Tempir, 27366
Hi-Vi, 22282
Hiac Royco, 27154
Hickory, 23799
Hickory Creek Bar-B-Q Cooker, 24524
Hid-Tuff, 26465
Hidden Temple, 26676
Hidden Valley, 20673
Hide-A-Winner, 29123
High Brew Coffee, 24840
High K, 19426
High Strength Tenex, 29253
Highfield, 28400
Highland Sugar Vermont, 25825
Highland Sugarworks, 23805
Highlight Stretch Rappers, 18885
Hilco, 23812
Hilex 6-40, 23810
Hilex Poly, 26796
Hill-Tween Farms, 22055
Hilliard, 23814
Hillware, 23816
Himac, 30773
Himet, 30773
Hinckley Springs, 27838
Hipir Kart, 21882
Hires, 24840
His-470, 28049
Hisaka Works Ltd, 20564
Hivex Expander, 18928
Hmr Merchandiser, 20311
Hms, 23587
Hob Nob, 29538
Hobart, 24074, 27104
Hodag, 19102
Hoegaarden, 26708
Hoffer, 23841
Hoffer Flow Controls Inc., 20856
Hoffmaster, 23845
Hoge, 23849
Hohberger Products, 25056
Holac, 28334
Holdit, 25307
Holgrain, 25825
Holiday, 20323
Holiday Greetings, 21078
Hollymatic, 23866
Hollys Coffee, 24840
Holo Flite, 29882
Hom-Pik, 27564
Home Commercial, 22952
Home Toter, 27175
Home-Style, 25803
Homemadesimple, 30234
Homeopathy For Kids, 26825
Homs, 18333
Honest, 20703
Honey Bears, 28801
Honey Gardens, 26825

Honeysuckle, 30817
Hoosier Data Forms, 22217
Hop-Syn, 23694
Hoppmann, 19228
Horizon, 24850, 26487
Hormel, 23897
Hormel Chili, 23897
Hormel Foods, 29137
Hormel Health Labs, 23897
Hormel Pepperoni, 23897
Hormel Side Dishes, 23897
Hormel Taco Meats, 23897
Hoshizaki, 27497
Hoshizaki America, 23904
Hosokawa, 19584
Hospitality Suite, 20832
Hostaphan, 26264
Hot Buffet To Go, 19337
Hot N' Tender, 23765
Hot Pops, 19114
Hot Sauce, 21357
Hot Tray, 27646
Hot Water Extract, 20985
Hotel America, 21519
Hotel Bar Butter, 21443
Hotpack, 26518
Hotpan'zers, 23293
Hotpoint, 22992
Hotslot, 27935
House of Raeford, 20113
House of Tsang, 23897
Housewarming, 21078
Howden, 29011
Howe, 20796, 29011
Hs, 23394
Ht-1001, 27009
Ht-500, 27009
Ht80, 24095
Hub Pen, 23942
Hubbell, 23943
Hubort, 26513
Huco, 18686
Hudson's Total Control For Windows, 23950
Huggies, 24876
Hughes, 23957
Humitran, 18901
Humitran-C, 18901
Humitran-Dp, 18901
Humitran-T, 18901
Hungerford & Terry, 23963
Hungry-Man, 20840, 20841
Hunt's, 20840, 20841
Hunter Filtrator Hf Series, 28093
Hunter Oil Skimmer, 18350
Huntingcastle, 22928
Hurri-Kleen, 23974
Hurricane, 18456, 26708
Hurricane Systems, 26165
Huskee, 20901
Huskey, 23978
Huskey Specialty Lubricants, 29509
Husky Master, 18504
Husman's, 20840, 20841, 27584
Hvac, 20913
Hww, 23920
Hy-Ac Iv, 30968
Hy-Drive Systems, 23342
Hy-Tex, 23193
Hy-Trous Plant Foods, 23985
Hybri Flex, 19119
Hybri Grio, 19119
Hybrid, 28439
Hybrute, 20660
Hycom Contact Slides, 19703
Hycor Screening & Dewatering Equip., 27355
Hydra Form, 30892
Hydra Mold, 30892
Hydra-Supreme, 23501
Hydrafeed, 23154
Hydrasieve, 18189
Hydrasperse, 19116
Hydraucuber Super Slicer, 23150
Hydrauflakers, 23150
Hydro-Fil, 23501
Hydro-Laser, 30066
Hydro-Miser, 19005
Hydroblend, 29437
Hydrocheck, 23606
Hydroclear, 20772
Hydroforce, 21070
Hydroheater, 23999

Hydrohelix, 23999
Hydropure Pumps, 24004
Hydroscrubs, 25699
Hydrostatics, 22171
Hydrovane, 23065
Hydrowype, 25699
Hyfroydol, 22742
Hygeaire, 19160
Hygeia Dairy, 21443
Hygenius, 20818
Hygienic Fusedware, 30523
Hygrol, 26669
Hynap, 23193
Hynes, 24051
Hypak, 23993
Hyper Clear, 30178
Hypersoft, 21009
Hypor, 21447
Hyster, 24012
Hytamatic, 23893
Hytrol, 19921
Hytron, 30499
Hytronics, 22171, 30499

I

I-Rap, 27197
Iac 2000, 31485
Ibc, 20866, 24840, 29702
Ice Breakers, 23786
Ice Chiller, 19426
Ice Logic, 19426
Ice Master, 26349
Ice Sculptures, 20270
Ice-Foe, 21781
Ice-O-Matic, 31137
Ice-O-Matic Ice Machines, 24084
Ice-Stir-Cools, 25702
Iceas, 18099
Icelandic Glacial Water, 26708
Icelandic Spring Water, 26708
Iceman, 27805
Ici, 29077
Ics, 22345
Id-Alg, 26665
Ideal, 18282, 24099, 27992
Ideal Mark, 24095
Idealfold, 21437
Ideco, 24095
Identity, 18786
Idockusa, 24028
Ids, 28349
Igloo, 24108
Igloo 2go, 24108
Igloo Stralth, 24108
Iii, 24166
Ikamag, 24110
Il Caffe, 20712
Ile, 24214
Illinois Rag, 26810
Illy, 25825
Illy Chilled Coffee, 26708
Imag!Ne, 27476
Imagex, 24949
Imaje 7s, 24129
Imar, 24133
Imeta, 20887
Impacdoors, 18554
Impacdor, 18553
Impact, 23979
Impact Island, 29784
Impco, 24155
Imperial, 26758, 27497, 29741
Impinger, 25360
Impinger a La Carte, 25360
Impress, 21383
Impressions, 30941
Imprintz, 21219
Impulse, 21383, 24156, 24850
Impulse Heat Sealer, 30411
In-Shear, 24516
In-Sink-Erator, 24159
Ina, 24050
Inc, 24246
Incredible Blue, 20985
Indent-A-Mark, 25906
Indenti-Film, 31186
Independant Folders, 22217
Indiana Rag, 26810
Indiana Wire, 24188
Indiana Woven Wire, 19347
Indicoder, 22934

Indo, 25186
Indramat, 28402
Industravac, 29529
Industri-Sol, 31314
Industrial, 18358, 24234, 24235
Industrial Air, 27455
Industrial Clutch, 18686
Industrial Structures, 31185
Industrial Traffic Mats, 30697
Industrialeveline, 25526
Indy, 24112
Inertia Dynamics, 18686
Inferno, 23635
Infinity, 19589, 24471, 27753, 29231
Infinity Twist, 23294
Infit, 26076
Infitec, 24246
Inflation Fighter, 31337
Info Board, 22152
Infogenesis Gsa, 18470
Infogenesis Hospitality, 18470
Infogenesis Iqs, 18470
Infogenesis Its, 18470
Infogenesis Ticketing, 18470
Infraseal, 24073
Infratech, 18440
Ingersoll Rand, 24256
Inglett, 22611
Ingo-Man, 24007
Ingo-Top, 24007
Ingold, 26076
Ingredion, 24373
Inharvest, 24165
Inhibidor, 21410
Inhibit, 21447
Injectamatic, 24945
Injection Quills, 24735
Ink Stik, 26145
Ink-Koder, 19712
Ink-Stik 'n' Holder, 26145
Inksource, 30883
Inline Fill-To-Level Filler, 21052
Inline Piston Filler, 21052
Inpro, 26076
Inquest, 28712
Insect Inn Iv, 27320
Insect-O-Cutor, 24309
Insight, 20589
Insignia Pops, 24313
Inspecto-Light, 20319
Inspector, 18905
Insta-Balance, 19437
Insta-Pro, 24316
Insta-Tie, 27175
Instabowl, 21046
Instamark, 22045
Instamark Script, 19492
Instamark Signature, 19492
Instamark Stylus, 19492
Instant Burger, 29342
Instant Dip, 20332
Instant Recovery Fryer, 24783
Instant-Ice, 22632
Instantgum, 26665
Instaprep, 27299
Insti-Mash, 24764
Instoematic, 23577
Instore, 23388
Insul-Air, 20941
Insul-Glare, 20941
Insul-Plus, 18531
Insul-Wall, 28220
Insulair, 24323
Insulrock, 18419
Intact, 24945
Intedge, 24326
Integra, 20773
Integra Cm, 20773
Integra T, 20773
Integrated Comfort Systems, 30424
Integrity, 19750
Intelijet, 19554
Intelli Pack, 18345
Intellipack, 30424
Intellorol, 22284
Interactive Sales Manager, 24344
Intercept, 26416
Interchange, 27286
Interlake, 24354, 24848
Interlogix, 20304
International Baler Corp., 20866
International Converter, 26796

International Press & Shear, 20866
International Tank & Pipe, 24397
Intimus, 28929
Intrac, 26076
Intralox, Inc., 24412
Intros Appetizers & Hors D'Oeuvres, 29137
Intrustor, 25023
Invader, 30832
Invercab, 23963
Invert-A-Bin, 21206
Invertose Hfcs, 24262
Inview, 18360
Invisi-Bowl, 27318
Invisible Packaging, 27318
Invitrogen, 30258
Involvo, 18084
Iobio, 19426
Ipm, 24387
Ips, 20866
Iq120 Minilab, 24058
Iq125 Minilab, 24058
Iq150, 24058
Iq240, 24058
Iqs/3, 21165
Iridescents, 21670
Iris, 27929
Irish, 21078
Irish Spring, 20739
Iron Tuff, 28304
Irwin, 29624
Island Diaz, 26676
Island Oasis, 24834
Iso-Flo, 24850
Isobox, 21438
Isolok, 29075
Isometric, 22645
Isowall, 18419
It's a Baby!, 21078
Italian, 21078
Iti, 24128
Ivex, 24080
Ivis, 20258
Ivory, 30234
Iws, 20373
Izze, 27476

J

J Cup, 21383
J-Press, 30589
J-Series, 19811
J.B. Webb Co., 31259
J.C. Ford Co., 24454
Jac-O-Net, 23557
Jack Rabbit, 30486
Jack's Pumpkin Spice, 26708
Jackson Wws, 27497
Jacky Apple Jack, 26676
Jacobs Vehicle Systems, 18686
Jade Range, 24532, 30747
Jade Refrigeration, 24532
Jagenberg Diana, 24533
Jahabow, 19050
Jahbo Showcases, 24039
Jalea De Jalapeño, 19114
James Remind-O-Timer, 18839
Jamy's Three Dragon, 18899
Janus, 26076
Japan Food Canada/Kikkoman, 20032
Jardin Savon, 27319
Jarvis, 24559
Java Jacket, 24562
Javarama, 27838
Jax, 19537
Jax Lubricants, 24563
Jay, 30415
Jay Bee, 24567
Jayhawk Mills, 24569
Jayone, 24570
Jazz, 22629
Jemaco, 28756
Jennair, 25929
Jennfan, 28691
Jennie-O Turkey, 23897
Jenson Foods, 29137
Jered, 27124
Jerome, 19049
Jesco, 27315
Jess Jones Farms, 24589
Jet 2000, 31469
Jet Air, 21780

Jet Cleaner, 23308
Jet Cut, 25339
Jet Set, 26721
Jet Sifter, 26776
Jet Spray, 20802, 20994
Jet Streamer, 25917
Jet White, 27086
Jet-A-Mark, 25906
Jet-A-Mark/Linx, 25906
Jet-Clean, 29529
Jet-O-Mizer, 22692
Jetaway, 18843
Jetflow, 29263
Jetstar, 29636
Jetwrite, 30476
Jetzone, 20097
Jewish, 21078
Jif-Pak, 24600
Jif-Y-Clean, 26152
Jiffy Pop, 20840, 20841
Jiffy Roll, 21437
Jigg-All, 20010, 20011
Jilbert Dairy, 21443
Jo San, 31397
Jo-Lock, 25423
Job-Built, 23577
Jobhandler, 24432
Jobmaster, 25756
John Foster Green, 20808
John Morrell, 24621
Johnson (Penn), 29011
Johnson Brothers, 31126
Johnson Pump, 28756
Johnsondiversey, 18031
Joker's Wild Energy, 21787
Joki, 24403
Jolly Rancher, 23786
Jolly Trolley, 30371
Jomar, 24649
Jones Zylon, 24656
Jordon, 22707, 24661
Jordon Scientific, 22707
Joshua Miguel, 28984
Joy, 20178, 30234
Joyce Farms, 22527
Jr Buffalos, 24471
Jrs, 21221
Js-1, 28598
Judel, 24674
Juice Out, 20985
Juice Tree, 24677
Juice-It, 23306
Juice-Master, 24764
Juicy Whip, 24678
Jumbo Bin, 20622
Jumbo Straws, 20011
Junior, 29234
Jura, 31128
Just, 30234
Just 'n Time, 19441
Just Juice, 21482
Just-Rite, 18282
Justin's, 23897
Justrite, 25735

K

K Box, 20885
K Line, 25003
K-14, 24760
K-Commander, 24702
K-Flex Systems, 18461
K-Guard, 30558
K-Link, 24702
K-Mars, 24739
K-Modular, 24702
K-Products, 18786
K-Tron Soder, 24702
K-Way, 24703
K-Wheel, 22509
K10s, 24702
K2-Modular, 24702
Kaak, 19575
Kaboom, 20577
Kady, 24747
Kadyzolvers, 24747
Kaf-Tan, 30378
Kahl£A, 24840
Kairak, 24074
Kaktus, 20134
Kakuhunter, 23242
Kal, 26825

Lehigh Valley Dairy Farms, 21443
Leica, 25272
Leister Heat Guns, 25277
Leland, 25279
Leland Southwest, 25278
Lemon Glo, 24071
Lemon Kleen 32, 27260
Lemonee-8, 20849
Lender's, 20840, 20841, 27584
Lenel-S2, 20304
Lenox, 29624
Lepakjr Capsealing System, 25293
Leplus Ultra, 31055
Lestoil, 20673
Leter Buck Coffee Co., 31509
Letica, 25301
Letter-Lites, 25130
Level Star Ls Level Sensing Fillers, 23713
Levelair, 21679
Levelart, 30834
Levelhead 2, 24271
Levelmatic, 19174
Leveltronic, 30147
Lewa Ecodos, 18791
Lewa Lab, 18791
Lewa Modular, 18791
Lewa Triplex, 18791
Lewis, 28996
Lewis Iqf, 22905
Lexington, 20270
Lexmark Carpet, 21583
Leybold, 27771
Lfc, 21467
Libbey, 25322
Libby's, 20840, 20841
Libertyware, 25330
Libitalia, 22173
Libman, 25331
Lid Placers, 23752
Lid Press, 23752
Lid-Off Pail Opener, 20011
Lidd Off, 20010
Lidpro Lid Dispenser, 30418
Life, 27476, 28026
Life Extension, 19696
Life Wtr, 27476
Lifemount, 22171
Lifestore, 21977
Lifestyle, 26487
Lifetime, 26338
Lifetree, 29229
Lift Apfel Schorle, 20703
Lift Products, 18885
Lift-N-Weigh, 27153
Lift-O-Flex, 28550
Lift-Rite, 19921
Liftabout, 29179
Liftiltruk, 28889
Liftronic Balancer, 28736
Light Forms, 25524
Light Hawk, 30919
Lighthouse, 25345
Lightjet, 24129
Lightjet Vector, 24129
Lightnin, 19409, 28756
Lightning, 24106
Lightning Wrap, 26720
Lightwaves, 25344
Lil Wunder-Miniature Scrub, 24867
Lil' Devils, 31170
Lil' Orbits, 25349
Lily, 21382
Lime Lite, 31055
Lime-Elim, 31314
Limpido, 20673
Linablue A, 21285
Linbin's, 25376
Linc, 20929
Lincoln, 31137, 31138
Lincoln Ovens, 25562
Linde, 27762
Lindt, 25825
Linear, 18132, 24171
Linear Separator, 26933
Lineir, 27366
Linen-Like, 23845, 23847
Linen-Like Natural, 23847
Linen-Like Select, 23847
Linen-Like Supreme, 23847
Linen-Saver, 24739
Linerter, 30774
Lingot Stainless & Hardwood Floors, 26441

Linjector, 30774
Link N Load, 27609
Link-Belt, 28400
Linkerlube, 25371
Linkspot, 24028
Linshelf, 25376
Liposofast, 19263
Lipton, 27476
Liquavision, 21679
Liqui-Nox, 18548
Liquid Chalk, 30921
Liquid Freeze, 22632
Liquid Scale, 25388
Liquid-Plumr, 20673
Liquiplex, 25468
Liquitote, 23886
Lista, 29624
Listo, 25393
Lite Touch, 22645
Lite Writer, 24391
Lite-N-Tuff, 23577
Litestrip, 29905
Litewall, 29784
Little David, 25492
Little Giant, 22111
Little Mule, 20771
Little Red Smokehouse, 24451
Little Sizzlers, 23897
Little Squirt, 25404, 26982
Little Swimmers, 24876
Live Brine, 23487
Live Link, 23902
Live Real Farms, 21443
Living Hinge, 29359
Lloyd, 25410
Lloyds Barbeque Co, 23897
Llsa, 19138
Lmc, 25310
Lo-Density, 27901
Load Disk Ii, 30842
Load Locker, 25318
Loadbank, 25416
Loadmaster, 26662
Lobana, 30610
Lobster Call, 25460
Locktile, 24493
Loctite, 23762
Loeffler, 23707
Loft 213, 30178
Loftware, 22988
Log Cabin, 20840, 20841, 27584
Logic, 30194
Logix, 24403, 25447
Logo River, 26595
Logotop, 25523
Lok-A-Box, 28399
Lok-Tight Handle, 24867
Long Reach, 20272
Loon, 26559
Loop Plus, 22532
Lost Energy, 26708
Losuds, 19442
Lotech, 25414
Louisiana Rag, 26810
Lov-It, 28947
Love My Popper, 23289
Low Boy, 22111
Low Profile E-Z Wrap, 18504
Low Temp, 25494
Lowboy, 30383
Lowerraters, 18219
Lowery's Coffee, 25498
Loyal, 25501
Lozier, 19050, 24039
Lozier Reeve, 20016
Lr01 Laboratory Refractometer, 25856
Ls-Q50, 28790
Lsc Model 614, 25390
Lsc Model 725, 25390
Lube-Gard, 23577
Lubest, 26312
Lubriplate, 22620
Lucini Honestete, 29508
Luck's, 22494
Lucky Dutch, 23443
Luetzow, 25517
Luke's Almond Acres, 25519
Lumaco, 25522
Lumalier, 20798
Lumalux, 27031
Lumibypampers, 30234
Luminaire, 29784

Luminaire Ultra, 29784
Luminaire Ultra Ii, 29784
Luminate Ultra, 20641
Lumisolve, 19102
Lumisorb, 19102
Lumulse, 19102
Lunita, 25322
Luseaux, 25531
Lusterator, 18366
Lustre Rail, 19859
Luvs, 30234
Lw Private Reserve, 25143
Lx, 21383
Lyco, 25538
Lye Cross, 18260
Lynnply, 25544
Lyrica, 23878
Lytegress, 25265

M

M, 27124
M Logic, 19426
M&J Valve, 28756
M&R, 24080, 29710
M-8 Slitter, 23150
M-Bond, 26331
M-Cut, 20921
M-D-G Formula-2, 26201
M-Drive, 20921
M-Line, 21383
M-Purity Ring, 26331
M-Purity Seal, 26331
M-Rotary, 20921
M-Shuttle, 20921
M-Track, 20921
M-Traverse, 20921
M-Trim, 20921
M-Ware, 18226
M.O.-Lift, 25568
M074, 24095
M30, 25844
M850 Series, 19040
Mac Tools, 29624
Mac-Copy, 25587
Mac-Gloss, 25587
Mac-Jet, 25587
Machine Detergent Ii, 19205
Machine Mochers, 26036
Machine-Guard, 19436
Macrowave, 28191
Mactac, 23918
Maestro, 20077
Mag Melon, 21482
Mag Slide, 19957
Magic, 25668
Magic Buss, 29361
Magic Chef, 25929
Magic Disk, 21346
Magic Line, 27359
Magic Master, 24666
Magic Melt, 18381
Magic Mist, 27359
Magic Mold, 27359
Magic Pepper Sauce, 25669
Magic Sauce & Marinades, 25669
Magic Wall, 18710
Magic Wash, 25047
Magic-Access, 29623
Magic-Flo, 20010
Magic-Mesh, 20010, 20011
Magic-Mounts, 26218
Magic-Swing, 29623
Magicater, 25667
Magictrol, 27801
Magikitch'n, 19746, 25667
Magline, 19921, 20157, 26599
Magliner, 28530
Magna Torq, 29263
Magna-Bar, 20205
Magnaclamp, 27619
Magnamight, 19756
Magneflex, 26085
Magneroll, 23115
Magnesol, 21336
Magnet Source, The, 18064
Magnetag, 29097
Magnetek, 20771
Magnetic Menumaster, 24391
Magnetic Scrap Board, 24739
Magnetically Aligned, 30921
Magnum, 19160, 25682, 29312

Magnum Alert, 26486
Magnupeeler, 19177
Magnus, 29253
Magnuwasher, 19177
Magpowr, 25687
Magsys, 25688
Mahatma, 28463
Maille, 25825
Main Street, 28708
Mainstream, 31134
Mainstreet, 25700
Maitakegold, 24281
Major Business Systems, 22217
Make a Gift Products, 29359
Maker, 27476
Mal-X, 20985
Malaxator, 22624
Mali's, 25711
Malo, 25714
Malpotane, 23712
Malthus System V, 25719
Maltopure, 25820
Mamor, 23886
Mancini, 25727
Manitowoc, 31138
Mann's, 21482
Mannhardt, 25907
Mannhart, 25737
Mansi, 18546
Manta, 24850
Manwich, 20840, 20841
Map, 29025
Map-Fresh, 24588
Map-Seal, 24588
Mapimpianti, 27400
Maple Leaf, 25751
Mar-Con, 25753
Marga-Ezy, 20011
Margarita Made Easy, 20010
Margaritaville, 24840
Margaritaville Paradise Key Teas, 26708
Margin Minder Software, 19449
Mari-Net, 25843
Marie Callender's, 20840, 20841
Marioff, 20304
Marion, 25779
Mark, 23523
Mark Cal, 23018
Mark Ii, 21940, 25272, 30718
Mark Ii Plus, 25272
Mark Iii, 30718
Mark Royal, 27434
Mark V, 21520
Mark-300a, 25795
Mark-Time, 25584
Market Buffet, 30862
Market Forecaster, 25239
Market Master, 24945
Marking Methods, Inc., 25795
Marko, 25797
Marko Intl., 25798
Markoated, 25798
Markon, 29137
Marksman, 24128
Markwell, 25799
Marland Clutch, 18686
Marlate, 24878
Marlen, 25806
Marlite, 19050, 25810
Marlite Brand Frp, 25810
Marlite Modules, 25810
Marmalade, 25339
Marmite, 25825
Marprene, 25812
Marque Uncle Bob's Brand, 26980
Marquis Fountains, 19945
Marriott Walker, 25819
Mars, 25821, 27497
Mars 5, 20060
Mars-X, 20060
Marshall Blue, 25831
Marshall Pink Under the Sink, 25831
Marshallan, 24781
Mart Cart, 19127
Martin, 25842
Martin/Baron, 25847
Mary Kitchen, 23897
Marzetti, 25159
Mas-7000, 20060
Mash, 27134
Mason, 30119
Mason's Ironstone, 31126

Master, 18886, 24074
Master Chef Ltd., 18602
Master Fit, 18076
Master Jet, 22933
Master Rigger, 20291
Master Series, 29553
Master Turf, 27923
Master Wrap, 30486
Master-Bilt, 29620
Mastercraft International, 25877
Mastermark, 25879
Mastertech, 19029, 25864
Mastertech Direct Fired, 25864
Matador, 27476
Match Light, 20673
Match Pay, 25446
Mate-Lock, 23048
Mateer Burt, 18290
Mateer-Burt, 30979
Matrix, 18686, 25901
Matrix 916, 25903
Matrix Sneezegaurd, 22210
Matrix1000, 25903
Matthiesen, 25907
Maui Cup, 25301
Maui Style, 27476
Maurer, 25910
Maxbullet, 18554
Maxchanger, 30432
Maxi, 28439
Maxi Marketeer, 19645
Maxi-Amo, 19436
Maxi-Beam, 19436
Maxi-Bins, 19939
Maxi-Cap, 26933
Maxi-Con, 20953
Maxi-Duty, 23577
Maxi-Lift, 20942
Maxima, 18886, 27645
Maxima Series, 19040
Maximice, 27394
Maximicer, 25918
Maximizer, 23306
Maximount, 24774
Maxipor, 21447
Maxispan, 29481
Maxon, 20744
Maxslide, 18554
Maxum, 30883
Mayer Hook N' Loop, 20461
Mayer Magna, 20461
Maytag, 25929
Mbi, 25847
Mbt (Lubeca), 20887
Mc2, 25609
Mc3, 25609
McCann's, 25825
McI Group, 21583
McIlhenny Company Tabasco, 20032
McKnit, 25942
McMillin Wire, 25948
McNarin Packaging, 18031
McP, 24129
McP Barcode, 24129
McP Series, 24129
Md-16, 20059
Md-Ii, 18342
Md-Ii-200, 18342
Mdc, 30832
Meadow Gold Dairy, 21443
Meadows, 25974
Meals-On-Wheels, 31342
Measure Fresh, 30378
Measurex, 25977
Meat Magic, 25669
Meat Marking, 24095
Meat Pak, 26720
Mec, 27124
Mechanix Orange, 21070
Mechatron Gravimetric Feeders, 28919
Mechatron Volumetric Feeders, 28919
Med Flo, 24369
Med-I-San, 24540
Medalist, 21940
Mediclean, 27889
Medifast, 21810
Meese, 20157
Mega Cal, 24543
Mega Warheads, 22786
Mega-Con, 20953
Mega-Mill, 27755
Mega-Slicer, 25803

Mega-Temp, 20135
Mega/Fill, 26892
Megachar, 19016
Megacrunch, 24471
Megatron, 19160
Meguiar's, 25992
Meguiar's Mirror Glaze, 25992
Mekong, 30711
Melanie's Medleys, 21726
Melba, 25825
Melco, 30364
Melind, 21221
Melissas, 31397
Melitta, 25825, 25999
Mem-Pure, 26147
Memco, 25877
Memmert, 27877
Mentor Laser Power, 28959
Menu, 28947
Menu Master, 24391
Menulink, 26024
Menumaster, 18339
Mepsco, 26025
Mer, 20703
Merchant & Moli-Shields, 26305
Merco, 31137, 31138
Mercury, 26031, 31137, 31245
Merix, 26038
Merlin, 27840
Merrychef, 31138
Metal Polish Scrubs, 24071
Metalarc, 27031
Metalarm, 22282
Metaledge, 27993
Metalife, 31219
Metalix, 18590
Metallic Luster, 29097
Metaloom, 22406
Metalphoto, 27552
Metalwash, 24326
Metamucil, 30234
Meteor, 20270, 20272
Meter Master, 29553
Meto, 22301
Meto/Primark, 22301
Metrak, 19567
Metromax, 24341, 26067
Metromax Q, 26067
Mevon, 28707
Meyer, 28876
Mezzo Mix, 20703
Mgr, 25907
Mgv, 22045
Mh Press Systems, 20887
Mibco, 26109
Mibrush, 26109
Mica Wax, 26720
Michael Foods Inc., 29137
Michelob Light, 26708
Michigan Dessert, 26110
Michigan Rag, 26810
Microduct, 26144
Micro Flex, 26139
Micro Lab, 30257
Micro Phep, 23606
Micro Quad, 30257
Micro Raves, 18916
Micro-Amp, 19436
Micro-Brush, 26123
Micro-Con, 20953
Micro-Deck, 22287
Micro-Jet, 22692
Micro-Media, 22287
Micro-Meter Airless, 29553
Micro-Mini, 26145
Micro-Oxymax, 20770
Micro-Petter, 22694
Micro-Precision, 20319
Micro-Pure, 26147
Micro-Recharger, 27478
Micro-Screen, 19436
Microban, 27889
Microban 24, 30234
Microbest, Inc., 26133
Microcell, 30842
Microchiller, 31307
Microcoder, 30476
Microcut, 29681
Microduction, 26153
Microfloat, 18442
Microfluidizer Pro.Equipment, 26140
Microgourmet, 21383

Microgreen, 21383
Microklear, 18533
Microlacer, 20670
Microleak, 21423
Microlene, 29437
Microlog, 19693
Micron One, 31359
Micronair, 22897
Microplate, 19693
Micropower, 23646
Micropower Ac, 23646
Microproof, 23533
Micropub, 26146
Microrollers, 29485
Micros, 26994
Microscan, 26148
Microscrub, 31221
Microspense Ap, 24078
Microstar, 21438
Microstat, 26144
Microtouch, 26151
Microtronic, 19811
Microware, 23533
Mid-Trak, 27619
Middlebe Marshal, 26167
Middleby Marshall, 26168
Middleby Marshall Ovens, 25562
Midland, 21065
Midwest, 26180
Midwest Marko, 25798
Mieloguard, 20076
Mies, 26196
Mifab, 25615
Mighty Blade, 26901
Mighty Mini, 18255
Mighty Pine, 19754
Mighty Wipe, 18279
Mighty-Pure, 19160
Mikrodyne, 27895
Mikropul, 19584
Mil-E-Qual, 20953
Milford, 23878
Miljoco, 26207
Milk Duds, 23786
Milk-Stor, 22882
Milkadamia, 19647
Milkman, 25820
Milko, 24257
Millenium Message, 21078
Millennuim, 21023
Miller Lite, 24711
Milsek, 26227
Miltex, 23193
Mimi Foods, 20032
Mimi's Muffins, 24425
Mini Brute, 26737
Mini Max Iii, 28093
Mini Rx Hone, 28106
Mini Scents, 19135
Mini Sdx, 21517
Mini Tubs, 23861
Mini-6, 18306
Mini-Array, 19436
Mini-Beam, 19436
Mini-Con, 20953
Mini-Gas Series, 18628
Mini-Mark, 25824
Mini-Module, 24556
Mini-Mornap, 23193
Mini-Pak, 20728
Mini-Pinch, 18306
Mini-Pro, 22148
Mini-Punch, 18306
Mini-Screen, 19436
Mini-Sip, 22214
Mini-Vac, 23622
Mini-Wedge Press, 19508
Mini-Wheel, 24979
Minikeeper, 22538
Minilab, 24058
Minilab Micro Compouuder, 23537
Minimint, 27514
Minipax, 26418
Minipure, 19160
Minispam, 29481
Minitree, 24556
Miniveil, 19605
Miniworks, 26373
Minnesota Automation, 26242
Minnesota Rag, 26810
Minute, 28463
Minute Glow, 25226

Minute Maid, 20703
Mione W P-1, 26248
Mipro, 31221
Miprodan, 19057
Miraclean Griddle, 24783
Miracryl, 20270
Mirage, 23557, 28066
Miroil, 26250
Mirro Foley, 26252
Miss Kriss, 31055
Miss Vickies, 27476
Mission, 21482
Mission Foods, 20032
Mission Foodservice, 29137
Mission Hill Bistro, 29608
Mississippi Rag, 26810
Missouri Rag, 26810
Mister Fudge, 20154
Mister Jinx, 20607
Mister Tenderizer, 30346
Mistkup, 18149
Mistolin, 20673
Mity-Eye, 30464
Mitydrive, 18953
Mityflex, 18953
Mitzi, 21447
Mix Master, 24907
Mix'n Machine, 30927
Mix-Mill, 18037
Mixograph, 30051
Mixpap, 18547
Miztique, 26825
Mm710, 26458
Mobi-Crane, 28550
Mobile Merchandising Systems, 20329
Mochem, 26312
Mod-A-Flex, 18710
Mod-Plex, 25265
Mod-U-Beam, 25265
Model #10, 25936
Model Am, 20524
Model Cf, 23138
Model Sam, 27906
Modern Chef, 27434
Modern Mill, 18036
Modicom, 28938
Modul Print, 31469
Modular Dispensing Systems, 30364
Modular Kt, 26286
Modular Pouch Machine, 20082
Modular Tile, 19159
Modulator, 26290
Moduline, 28023
Moistart, 30834
Moisturlok, 18416
Mojonnier, 28876
Moli-Tron, 26308
Moline, 26306
Moly-Xl, 26311
Molyube, 19543
Momarket, 26312
Monarch, 22988, 25705, 27697
Monarch Can Crushers, 18036
Monarch-Mclaren, 26316
Mondrian, 28370
Monitor, 18645
Monkey, 26676
Monnini, 25825
Monogram, 22992
Monolyn, 25574
Monorail, 20609
Monospan, 29481
Monster, 27471
Monster Energy, 20703, 26708
Montana Big Sky, 26825
Monterey, 20134
Mood Lite, 31263
Mop Pac, 27721
Mop Paclite, 27721
Mopac, 26382
Mor-Fruit, 27324
Morgro, 18031
Mori-Nu, 21810
Mornap, 23193
Morning Tide, 24446
Morrison Farms, 26565
Morse, 26988
Mortimer, 20673
Morton Kaciff, 20157
Mosaica, 21233
Mosar Design Displayware, 20270
Mother's Day, 21078

Motoman, 26366
Mott's, 24840
Mouli, 26367
Mounds, 23786
Mount Vernon Mantel Company, 24711
Mountain Country, 20714
Mountain Dew, 27476
Mountain Mats' Apples, 28134
Mountain White, 20007
Mountain-Grown Fancy Ceylon, 23328
Mouse Master, 31233
Movidrive, 29125
Movidyn, 29125
Movie Trivia, 21078
Movimot, 29125
Movincool, 26380
Moving Pix, 20641
Movingpix, 29784
Movitrac, 29125
Movomech, 28550
Moyer Diebel, 18571, 20442
Moyno, 26383
Mp Series, 19633
Mpi 90, 25629
Mpi-L, 25629
Mr Clean, 30234
Mr Pure, 19647
Mr. Doodler, 21793
Mr. Fizz, 25279
Mr. Food, 25583
Mr. Ice Bucket, 26386
Mr. Induction, 29560
Mr. John, 19754
Mr. Neat, 23176
Mr. P'S, 22925
Mr. Scrapy, 24651
Mr.Goodbar, 23786
Mr16, 22045
Mrs Dash, 31472
Mrs. Butterworth's, 27584
Mrs. Grimes, 22494
Mrs. Paul's, 27584
Mrs. Richardson Toppings, 19412
Mrs. Smith's, 26389
Mrs.Butterworth's, 20840, 20841
Mrs.Paul's, 20840, 20841
Ms-1400, 24588
Ms-25, 24588
Ms-55, 24588
Ms-700, 24588
Ms/Rv, 31116
Msi-6000, 25976
Msi-9000, 25976
Msr, 26373
Msr Carabiners, 26373
Mt. Rainbow Series, 24446
Mt20, 18247
Mtj Seating, 21583
Mucon, 24805
Muffin Monster, 24687
Mug Root Beer, 27476
Multi Mixer, 27840
Multi-Beam, 19436
Multi-Con, 20953
Multi-Meter, 28439
Multi-Scale, 24214
Multi-Screen, 19436
Multi-Trix, 31130
Multi-Vessel System, 30842
Multi-Weigh, 30159
Multibulk, 26411
Multichlor, 20504
Multichrome, 22045
Multifoods, 20108
Multimix, 28535
Multipack, 23847
Multiplex, 24078, 26214, 31138
Multipurpose, 22069
Multisac, 31383
Multislicer, 23150
Multispan, 29481
Multispense, 24078
Multitech, 19029
Multivac, 21154
Munchie, 20270
Munchos, 27476
Muro, 26430
Murphy Oil Soap, 20739
Muscle Milk, 23897
Mustang, 19811, 26145
Mustang Iv, 19811
Mutual Graphics, 22217

My-T-Lite, 25265
Myblackisbeautiful, 30234
Myers Ice Co., 26446
Mylanbox Ibc, 26202
Mynap, 23193
Mystik Spices, 30074
Myti Host Chair, 26265
Myti Lite Tables, 26265
Myti Taff Chair, 26265

N

N'Ice Ties, 24739
N.E.M., 26619
N.F. Peeler, 19177
Nair, 20577
Nakand, 30659
Naked, 27476
Nalley, 20840, 20841, 27584
Naltex, 26477
Nalu Fruity Energizer, 20703
Nam Power, 19926
Namco, 26479
Nance's Mustards, 19412
Nantucker Nectars, 24840
Napkin Deli, 20270
Napoleon, 26487
Nassco, 26543
National, 24889
National Drying Wachinery, 19948
National Importers/Twinnings, 20032
National Imprint Corporation, 22217
National Labortory Products, 26518
National Poultry Company, 21482
National Tank & Pipe, 24397
Native, 30234
Natrabio, 26825
Natrasorb, 26418
Natur-Cell, 28480
Natural Balance, 26825
Natural Blends, 28873
Natural Brew, 28513
Natural Choice, 23897, 26839
Natural Light, 26708
Natural Lite, 18851
Natural Pure, 20865
Natural Solutions, 24871
Natural Sport, 26825
Natural Vitality, 20673
Naturalcare, 26825
Naturalcrisp, 24471
Nature Scent, 18507
Nature's Best Liquid Live, 18718
Nature's Candy, 20158
Nature's Choice, 26388
Nature's Delite, 28744
Nature's Herbs, 26825
Nature's Orange, 20513
Nature's Own, 26559
Naturebind, 31152
Natureflex, 30569
Naturemost Labs, 26557
Natures Plumber, 27279
Naughty But Nice!, 21078
Nbd, 30234
Nbr 2000, 26836
Nbs Sorter, 22284
Ncc, 18181
Ncco, 29137
Nci, 19262
Ndex, 29209
Ndex Free, 29209
Ne-On the Wall, 26596
Near East, 27476
Neat Seat, 28863
Neatgards, 23590
Nebraska Rag, 26810
Negus Octapak, 27548
Negus Square Pak, 27548
Nehi Cola, 24840
Nelson, 21233
Nem, 24543
Neo-Image, 26591
Neocell, 20673
Neon Design-A-Sign, 26595
Neon Light Pegs, 26595
Neon Plus E, 29784
Neoneon, 21670
Neonetics, 26596
Neopuntia, 26665
Neosyl, 21113
Nepco, 29265

Nervive, 30234
Nestea, 20703
Nestier, 19939
Nestl, Professional, 29137
Nestle, 19252
Nestle Ice Cream, 20032
Nestle Nesquick, 26708
Net-All, 30346
Net-Rap, 24171
Net/Mass, 26892
Netpac, 24782
Neuro, 24840
Neurosome, 24543
Neutraclean, 20504
Neutrapac, 27721
Nevamar, 25971
Never Scale, 20908
Nevlen, 26606
Nevr-Dull Polish, 23183
New Age, 27923
New Generation, 29097
New Jersey Machine, 26464
New London Eng, 18885
New London Engineering, 25954
New Mexico Rag, 26810
New York Bash, 28984
New York Brand Bakery, 25159
New York Brand Texas Toast, 25159
New York Flatbread, 25825
New York, New York, 30941
New-Glass, 26615
Newly Weds, 26651
Newman, 26653
Newmann's Own Organics, 24840
Newport Coffee Traders, 22594
Nexcare, 18004
Nexel, 26662
Nexelite, 26662
Nexelon, 26662
Next Day Gourmet, 29848
Next Generation Magic Buss, 29361
Nextwave, 30480
Ni9, 26676
Nice N Easy, 18695
Nice-N-Clean, 26671
Nifda, 30636
Nimbus Cs, 26688
Nimbus Fs, 26688
Nimbus N, 26688
Nimbus Sierra, 26688
Nimbus Watermaker, 26688
Ninjamas, 30234
Nishibe, 27112
Nita Crisp, 26693
Nitri Pro, 29209
Nitro-Flush, 24588
Nitty Gritty, 29209
Nme Nugget, 28966
No Frost, 26669
No Name, 22952
No Pudge, 20965
No Survivor, 24310
No Sweat, 31144
No-Drip, 30364
No-Tox, 19543
Nob Nob, 31144
Noble, 31393
Nobles, 30188
Nonlinear Dynamics, 31086
Nopi, 30207
Nor-Lake, 29620
Nordic Mist, 20703
Nordson, 22511
Nordstrom, 27250
Noresco, 20304
Noritake, 26972
Norman Machinery, 31034
Norman Rockwell, 19619
Nornap Jr., 23193
Norpac, 20032
Norrbox, 26722
Norris, 29275
Norseman, 20700, 27000
Northern Pride, 23556
Northern Temple, 26676
Northstar, 22217
Northwest Co, 22952
Noryl, 21873
Not So Sloppy Joe, 23897
Note Minder, 22350
Nou, 30234

Nourishtea, 31472
Nouveau, 30114
Nova, 18518, 21233, 23138, 26785, 29506
Nova Ii, 26702
Novexx, 18290
Novitool, 22657
Novus Plastic, 26797
Now, 19754
Nr, 27124
Nu-Flex, 23577
Nu-Last, 23577
Nu-Nap, 23193
Nu-Pak Performance F-Series, 25803
Nu-Pak Portion, 25803
Nu-Wipes, 18838
Nuco2, 26804
Nudefruit, 31472
Nudesoup, 31472
Nugget, 30636
Numeri-Tech, 18829
Nuova Simonelli, 26819
Nuparch, 26720
Nuroll, 31492
Nusheen, 30591
Nut Harvest, 27476
Nut Thins, 19755
Nutec, 26821
Nutra Biogenesis, 26825
Nutra Coster, 29896
Nutra Naturally Essentials, 18095
Nutri Source, 19369
Nutrifaster N-350, 26827
Nutriform, 26832
Nutrilac, 19057
Nutripure, 19160
Nutrisentials, 24543
Nutrition Service Suite, 20040
Nutritionist Iv, 22607
Nutrivail, 27591
Nutsco, 28380
Nuttall Gear, 18686
Nutty Bavarian, 26836

O

O'Doul's, 26708
O-Tex, 27034
O.N.E, 27476
Oak Draw, 26874
Oak Farms Dairy, 21443
Oak Kleen, 26874
Oak Kool, 26874
Oak Kote, 26874
Oak Mor, 23482
Oak Protect, 26874
Oakhill, 29538
Oakhurst Dairy, 21443
Oakmont Labs, 26825
Oakton, 26881
Oasis, 19680, 20703
Oberdorfer, 19356
Obfs, 25855
Objective, 20673
Oc Guide Bearing, 18012
Ocean 7, 27009
Ocean Spray, 22055
Octaview, 21438
Octopus, 29253
Octron, 27031
Oddy, 19575
Odom's Tennessee Pride, 20840, 20841
Odomaster, 29864
Odorid, 19677
Odormute, 28669
Odyssey, 19578, 22378
Oe200, 25272
Oem Products, 26518
Off the Eaten Path, 27476
Oh No!, 29864
Ohaus, 18333, 24214, 26902
Ohio, 26907
Ohio Rag, 26810
Ohmega, 19949
Oil Concentrator, 18255
Oil Grabber, 18255
Oil Grabber Multi-Belt, 18255
Oil Miser Oil Recovery Systems, 28403
Oil Rids, 26911
Oil-Dri, 26911
Oilkraft, 30591
Ok, 26841

Printxcel, 22217
Prismalier, 25265
Pristine, 23878
Pritikin, 25825
Private Label, 20132
Prize Box, 30175
Prize Taker, 23443
Prl, 27554
Prm-Ii (Prime Rib Master), 22762
Pro, 27753, 27877
Pro Bowl, 24613
Pro Chef, 24613
Pro Floc, 27944
Pro Seris, 22952
Pro Soap, 26123
Pro-Clean Hygiene Surface Test, 24006
Pro-Cut, 27370
Pro-Flo, 26147
Pro-Flo Pourer, 20011
Pro-Flow, 31250
Pro-Icer, 31393
Pro-Lims, 25113
Pro-Magic, 20700
Pro-Pal, 27861
Pro-Zorb, 27645
Pro/Fill, 26892
Pro/Matic, 26892
Pro/Star, 25339
Proces-Data, 20856
Proclean, 29137
Procol, 27698
Procon Products, 29620
Procount Salt Counter, 24329
Proctor, 20097
Proctor Silex, 23576
Prodigy, 27753
Product Vision, 18430
Profat 2, 20060
Proferm, 24262
Professional, 21878
Profile Ii Plus, 27265
Profiler, 26271
Profire, 18440
Profiserie, 29312
Profit Pals, 31292
Progold, 31393
Progress, 25644
Progum, 27698
Proline, 21230, 30469, 30785
Prolon Products, 27934
Promaster, 18024
Promech, 30965
Promo Assist, 24301
Promolux, 22045
Promotissues, 18384
Pronto, 22236
Prop, 30419
Prop Plus, 30419
Propafilm, 30569
Propafiol, 30569
Propak, 29137, 31221
Propapeel, 28535
Propaream, 30569
Propaseal, 28535
Propel, 27476
Propmaster, 18327
Proscan, 19270
Prostease, 24543
Prosystem, 29137
Protape, 18622
Protech, 23269
Protecta, 19552
Protecting Wear, 27685
Protecto-Freeze, 24990
Protecto-Temp, 24990
Protector, 25080, 28860
Protectowire, 27951
Protein Color Meter, 30571
Protexo, 23947
Proto, 29624
Protochill, 23979
Protocol, 23979
Proud Source, 27134
Provatec, 26821
Provell, 31393
Proview, 18360
Provitamina, 24543
Proware, 29137
Prowler, 26246
Pru Lites, 27963
Psgjme, 27112
Psglee, 27112

Ptl-Condos Systems, 19221
Puck, 18433
Puffs, 30234
Pul-A-Nap, 23193
Pull-Ups, 24876
Pullman, 18282
Pullman-Holt Gansow, 31221
Pullulan, 24756
Pulsar, 22934, 24129
Pulsarr, 19450
Pulse Point, 30841
Pulse Star, 30885
Pulseprint, 27973
Pulverlaser, 30233
Pumice Jell, 23566
Pumicizied Advantage Plus, 21792
Pumpsaver, 22654
Pura, 27120
Pure & Simple, 18851
Pure Assam Irish Breakfast, 23328
Pure Chem, 27099
Pure Harmony, 28940, 30374
Pure Leaf, 27476
Pure Water, 27979
Pure-Life, 20386
Pure-Pak, 22153
Purecop, 23713
Purefil, 23713
Pureliner, 26445
Purestack, 26445
Purevac, 26445
Purex, 30415
Purifier, 25080
Purifry, 23436
Puritan, 23637, 27988
Puritron, 18840
Purity, 27992
Purity Dairy, 21443
Purity Pat, 23175
Purity Wrap, 18916
Purogene, 19677
Purswab, 23637
Push-Pac, 20565
Push-Pops, 19064
Pushback, 18400
Pushbak Cart, 22203
Put-Ons U.S.A., 27995
Pw 800, 24349
Pw 850, 24349
Pyrex, 21000, 31391, 31392
Pyrex Plus, 21000
Pyro, 28001
Pyropure, 27394
Pyrorey, 25322

Q

Q Series Thermal Analysis, 30025
Q-50, 29524
Q-Ber, 25803
Q-Can, 21558
Q-Matic, 28008
Q-Swab Environmental Collection, 24006
Q31, 28023
Q32, 28023
Qa Products, 30659
Qa-Master, 31420
Qbd, 28010
Qc Assistant, 25239
Qc Database Manager, 25239
Qd-Loop Rapid Dilution Devices, 24006
Qda, 30419
Qda Software, 30419
Qic, 23707
Qlam, 28066
Qmi, 28013
Qmi Safe Septum, 28013
Qpet, 28066
Qu995, 24281
Quad-Steer, 27480
Quadnumatic, 28948
Quadra Beam 6600, 30257
Quadro, 28024
Quaker, 24781, 27476, 28026
Quaker City, 29760
Qualheim, 31052
Quality, 23294
Quality Chekd Dairy Products, 28036
Quality Espresso, 18562
Quality Paper Products, 18031
Quantanium, 31229
Quantum, 20258, 22378, 31229

Quarrymaster, 25876
Quartz Collection, 27318
Quartzone, 23734
Quasar, 30557
Quat Clean Sanitizer, 19923
Quat E-2, 26036
Quat F-5, 26036
Queen Anne, 20270
Queen Mary's, 29136
Queen O Mat, 18042
Queens Linen, 30114
Qugg, 25825
Quic-Cheese, 28052
Quic-Flavor, 28052
Quick 'n Easy, 19836
Quick Drop, 25946
Quick Dry Foods, 30659
Quick Shift, 21447
Quick Step...The Produce Manager, 26003
Quick-Fit, 26568
Quick-Key, 29892
Quick-Step Stair Systems, 26949
Quickcheck, 23523, 29067
Quickchiller, 18685
Quickset, 23847
Quicksilver, 22350
Quickstop, 19003
Quiet Classic, 21383
Quiet Thunder, 23255
Quiet' Slide, 20546
Quik, 21219
Quik 'n Crispy, 28015
Quik - Go, 22538
Quik Flo, 24369
Quik Lock Ii, 21005
Quik Lok, 19836
Quik Pik, 31185
Quik-Change, 23294
Quik-Fence, 22714
Quik-Pik, 21066, 30418
Quik-Space, 30382
Quik-Wipes, 18838
Quikmix, 21801
Quikserv, 28017
Quikstik, 28020
Quiktree, 24556
Quikwater, 28082
Quilon Bakeable Paper, 28954
Qwik Pack Systems, 28086
Qwik Pak, 19836

R

R&M, 26383
R-102, 30558
R-30, 28439
R.W. Zig Zag, 31259
Ra, 30440
Rack & Pour, 27772
Rack & Roll, 20157
Rack-A-Bag, 29307
Rack-Pack, 30269
Rack-The-Knife, 25339
Rackmaster, 30418
Rada, 19067
Radarange, 18339
Radarline, 18339
Radiant Ray, 18022
Radiant Wrap, 21151
Radio Pack, 22004
Raid, 21781
Railex, 28197
Railtite, 23484
Rain Sweet, 28134
Rainbow Agar, 19693
Rainbow Delight, 21807
Rainbow Light, 20673
Rainbow of New Colors, 18276
Rair 2000, 30421
Rair 7000, 30421
Rak Pak, 29092
Ralphs, 28204
Ram Center, 28124
Ram-Jet, 25756
Rama, 23656
Rampro, 25756
Ranch Style Beans, 20840, 20841
Ranco, 29011
Rancraft, 28222
Randell, 28222
Ranserve, 28222
Ranulio, 31128

Rao's, 25825
Rap-In-Wax, 20644
Rap-Up 90, 20807
Rapi-Kool, 24739
Rapid Assays, 28712
Rapid Brew, 30378
Rapid Fire, 26373
Rapid Flex, 25954
Rapid Freeze, 23929
Rapid Prep, 28712
Rapid Rack, 18998, 24848
Rapid Response, 30832
Rapid Sort, 21558
Rapidvap, 25080
Rapiscan, 24949
Rapistan, 21558
Rapplon, 18881, 18882
Rapptex, 18881, 18882
Rare, 25186
Raskas, 28947
Ratan, 28812
Rational Combi-Steamers, 28242
Ratoface, 30569
Raven, 20077
Ravifruit, 24834
Ray-O-Matic, 18022
Raycord, 30292
Rcci, 27838
Rcs Air Samplers, 19703
Rdb, 30440
Rdl, 30440
Re-Fresh, 26416
Rea-A-Matic, 23308
React-R-Mill, 30571
Reaction Arm, 27727
Read Woodfiber Laminate, 28253
Ready Cheese, 20411
Ready Made, 24666
Ready Mop, 20673
Ready Roll, 21383
Ready-Cut, 28947
Real Bacon Toppings, 23897
Real Medleys, 28026
Realemon, 24840
Really Cookin' Chef Gear, 24124
Rebel Green, 28261
Record Haccp, 26706
Recotech, 25635
Red - Go, 22538
Red Cross Nurse, 29820
Red Diamond, 28265
Red Dragon, 24543
Red Goat, 24074
Red Jim, 24440
Red Kap, 26915, 28266
Red Label, 23861
Red Line, 22040
Red Rock Deli, 27476
Red Rub, 29342
Red X, 27099
Redbridge, 26708
Redco, 25360
Redcore, 28399
Reddi-Wip, 20840, 20841
Redeman, 29196
Redhook Esb, 26708
Redi-Call, 28275
Redi-Grill, 27840
Redi-Prime, 20997
Redington, 19997
Redirail, 28022
Redwood Vintners, 28280
Reed, 28282
Reese's, 23786
Reese's Pieces, 23786
Refillo, 23468
Reflections, 24080, 30636
Refractance Window, 25597
Refractite, 28294
Refrigerated Entre,S, 23897
Refrigerator Fresh, 26825
Refrigiwear, 28304
Regal, 20557, 21383, 21940, 28308, 28315
Regent, 18419
Regent Sheffield, 31392
Regina, 28319
Regional Delphi, 26654
Rego, 26972, 26973
Reichert, 30817
Reign Total Body Fuel, 20703
Reineveld, 21467

Sas Super 90, 19701
Sat-T-Ice, 24739
Sat-T-Mop, 24739
Sateline, 18939
Satin Doll, 31055
Satin Fan, 31055
Sato, 18290, 28880
Satori Stocktec, 28881
Satoris, 28881
Saturn Series, 18628
Sauce Boss, 30418
Sausalito, 30862
Sauven, 30979
Sava-Klip, 25473
Save - All, 20270
Save-A-Nail, 20010
Save-T, 27917
Savetime, 20929
Savlin, 22288
Savory, 31137
Saxon, 22611
Sayco, 28900
Sayco Tournament, 28900
Scalestick, 29437
Scaltrol, 28901
Scan-A-Plate, 19090
Scanmaster, 28878
Scannable Bar Code Hologram, 25629
Scanvision, 24949
Scatter, 29864
Scent Flo, 18507
Scent Sation, 19754
Scent-Flo, 29864
Sceptre, 21447
Schaefer Ms Label, 28909
Schaerer, 28913
Schleicher, 28929
Schmidt, 28937
Schnucks, 28940
Scholar, 21000
Schonwald, 26972, 26973
School Chioce, 28947
Schott, 26972
Schott Zwiesel, 26973
Schreiber, 28947, 29137
Schugi, 19584
Schuss, 20703
Schweppes, 20703, 24840
Schwepps, 20703
Sck, 28710
Scoop Away, 20673
Scoop It, 22742
Scoop-N-Bake, 20108
Scope, 30234
Scorpio, 28963
Scotch, 18004
Scotch Painter's Tape, 18004
Scotch Print, 30554
Scotch-Brite, 18004
Scotslants, 28974
Scotsman, 28966
Scott, 24877
Scott Turbon, 28975
Scott's, 31209
Scott-A.D.A.'s Brailleters, 28974
Scott-Elites, 28974
Scott-Thins, 28974
Scott-Trax, 28974
Scottex, 24876
Scotts, 24711
Scotty Ii, 19811
Scourlite, 19061
Scout 20, 27086
Scrapmaster, 28814
Scratch-Guard, 18554
Screen-Flo, 23893
Screeners, 24394
Screw-Lift, 28980
Screwballs, 28467
Screwloose, 21070
Scrollware, 23533
Scrub 'n Shine, 18393
Scrub Pac, 27721
Scrub-Vactor, 21110
Scrubbe, 29656
Scrubs In-A-Bucket, 24071
Sculptathane, 30957
Sculptured Ice, 29097
Scultahyde, 30957
Sdb, 30440
Sdl, 30440
Sdx, 21517

Sdx Iii, 21517
Sea Bag, 19949
Sea Breeze, 28984
Sea Mist, 25205
Sea Watch International, 20032
Sea's Gift, 24570
Sea-View, 24984
Seabrook, 28990
Seabulk Powerliner, 27748
Seacure, 27944
Seafood Magic, 25669
Seaglass, 25702
Seagram's, 20703
Seajoy, 28990
Seal N' Serve, 23412
Seal the Seasons, 28994
Seal Weld, 20769
Seal-Tite, 28997
Seal-Top, 24893
Sealcup, 23175
Sealed Air, 27697
Sealgard, 27543
Sealproof, 29834
Sealstar, 28510
Sealstrip, 29001
Sealtest, 24257
Seasonedcrisp, 24471
Seasonmaster, 22196
Seattle Series, 30081
Seca-Pax, 30493
Second Nature Plus, 28708
Secret, 30234
Securcode Ii, 20929
Secure Panic Hardware, 28872
Securely Yours, 27301
Securi Seal, 31186
Security, 18630
Security Peg Hook, 30300
Securlume, 25265
Seedpak, 25113
Seepex, 29025
Segal, 30644
Segma-Flo, 26147
Segma-Pure, 26147
Sei, 28714
Select Recipe, 24471
Select Wax, 23864
Select-A-Horn/Strobe, 18187
Select-A-Strobe, 18187
Selectacom, 30469
Selectech 32 Controls, 30469
Selectrak, 22203
Selectware, 24080
Self Service System, 30418
Selford, 23193
Sell Strip, 22502
Sella & Mosca, 27277
Sellers, 29048
Sello Rojo, 28463
Selton, 20673
Semco, 29052
Semiflex, 30774
Sensamatic, 31387
Sensas, 25186
Sensation, 19754
Sensations, 23845
Sensibly Indulgent Cupcakes, 20108
Sensitech, 20304
Sentinel, 27697, 29072, 29227
Sentio, 21023
Sentishield, 29072
Sentrex, 29623
Sentrol 3l, 27407
Sentrol Em3, 27407
Sentron, 29074
Sentry, 23947, 28860, 30558
Sentry Ii, 23947, 27394
Sentry Seal, 27010
Sentry/Sentry Plus, 29227
Separators, 24394
Sepr, 23242
Sepro Flow, 19752
Sepro Kleen, 19752
Sepro Pure, 19752
Septic Clean, 19372
Serco, 24645
Sergeant, 19191
Series 9000, 18068
Series S, 26361
Series U, 20059
Series100, 18198
Series4000, 18198

Series6000c, 18198
Sermia, 29089
Serrico, 24310
Sertote, 29092
Serv & Seal, 29001
Serv 'n Express, 25133
Serv 'r Call, 26470
Serv-A-Car, 18425
Serv-Ease, 29340
Servco, 29094
Serve-N-Seal, 21046
Servend, 29084
Servi-Shelf, 20135
Service First, 30424
Service Manufacturing, 29098
Service Solutions Series, 22350
Serving Stone, 23321
Servo Ii, 23704
Servo-Pak, 27609
Servo/Fill, 26892
Servomatic, 31347
Servotronic, 19811
Set Mark, 29114
Set-N-Serve, 19174
Set-O-Swiv, 23294
Setterstix, 29116
Seville, 23878
Sew 400, 18129
Sew 800, 18129
Seydelmann, 28334
Sf-400, 31103
Sg General, 28959
Shade Tree, 29130
Shadow, 18187
Shakers Prepackaged Accessories, 20011
Shal-O-Groove, 29420
Shamrock Farms, 29137
Shank, 29011
Sharp 'n' Easy, 22815
Sharples, 18564
Sharpshooter, 18225
Shashi, 29158
Shat-R-Shield, 29159
Shaw-Box, 20771
Shear Flow, 26958
Shear Pak, 21088
Shear Sharp, 22815
Sheen Master, 28688
Shelby Williams, 20796
Shelf Clean A-1, 26036
Shelfnet, 21956
Shell Fm Fluids and Greasers, 22261
Shell-Ex, 28878
Shelleyglass, 21520
Shelleymatic, 21520
Shelly Williams Seating, 21583
Shelving By the Inch, 18710
Sherbrooke Oem, 26000
Shercan, 29181
Shields, 26796
Shimmer, 26235
Shimp, 25388
Shine-Off, 18393
Shinglgard, 28490
Shinglwrap, 28490
Shiny Sinks Plus, 19441
Ship 'n Shop, 20205
Ship Wise, 25446
Shire Gate, 22527
Sho-Bowls, 24080
Sho-Me, 27863
Shock Switch, 29200
Shock Top Belgian White, 26708
Shock Watch, 29200
Shockmaster, 18538
Shoes For Crews, 29201
Shok-Stop, 30269
Shooters Made Easy, 20010
Shop Master, 22952
Shoppers Value, 28940
Short Stop, 23549
Short-Stop, 19090
Shortening Shuttle, 31381
Shotskies Gelatin Mixes, 20011
Shove-It Rods, 25855
Show Patrol, 20513
Show-Off, 30435
Shower Patrol Plus, 20513
Showtime, 31055
Shrimp Magic, 25669
Shrimperfect, 27760
Shrink Bags, 30411

Shrink Bands & Preforms, 30411
Shuckman's Fish Co. & Smokery, Inc., 22527
Shufflo, 19177
Shur-Grip, 26477
Shur-Wipe, 23193
Shurtape Brand, 29213
Sicli, 20304
Sico, 29220
Side Swipe Spatula, 24739
Sideglow, 29832
Sidewinders, 24471
Sidney, 29222
Siebler, 22329
Sierra Mist, 27476
Sierra Nevada, 26708
Sierra Springs, 27838
Siesta Shade Market Umbrellas, 26441
Sight Line, 22069
Sightech, 28732
Sigma, 20712
Sigma Plates, 18200
Sigmark, 30883
Sigmastar, 18200
Sigmatec, 18200
Sigmatherm, 18200
Signature, 21842, 26487, 27753
Signature Select, 20270
Signature Series, 23516
Signet, 21940
Signette, 27257
Silcard, 29270
Silent Service, 21383
Siler's, 30486
Silesia, 29261
Silform, 21555
Silhouette, 22302, 31098
Silpat, 21555
Silver King, 29275, 29276
Silver Mtn Vineyards, 29277
Silver Shield, 20624
Silver Sonic, 23255
Silver Streak, 24673
Silver Sword, 18024
Silver-Grip, 29892
Silver-Span, 29892
Silver-Sweet, 29892
Silver-Weibull, 29280
Silverpak, 18304
Silverson, 29281
Silverstone, 22968
Simarotor, 31157
Similac Toddler's Best, 18262
Simonazzi, 28876
Simor, 22618
Simplate, 24106
Simple Solutions, 19158
Simplex, 19643, 20135, 21563, 26085, 29292, 29293
Simpli-Clean, 29295
Simpli-Flex, 29295
Simpli-Pak, 29295
Simpli-Pal, 29295
Simpli-Snap, 29295
Simplicity, 31292
Simplot Classic, 24471
Simplot Daily Pick, 24471
Simplot Good Grains, 24471
Simplot Harvest Fresh Avocados, 24471
Simplot Simple Goodness, 24471
Simplot Sweets, 24471
Simplot Thunder Crunch, 24471
Simplux, 22069
Simply Done, 28940, 30374
Simply Food, 29297
Simply Gold, 24471
Simply Saline, 20577
Simply Sensational 100% Coffee, 20677
Simpson Technology, 20615
Sin Fill, 26110
Sine Pump, 29302
Sinkmaster, 18900
Sintra, 21873
Sioux, 29304
Sipco Dunking Station, 29307
Siplace, 21558
Sir, 31219
Sir Dust-A-Lot, 25705
Sir Flip Flop, 25517
Sirco, 23390
Sirena, 30504
Sirius Ttr, 21888
Sirnap, 23193

Stakker, 23770
Stallion, 24613
Stampede, 29608
Stan-Pak, 24762
Stan-Ray, 29623
Stancase, 29612
Standard, 29612
Standard Coffee, 27838
Standard Econocut Die Cutters, 29614
Standard Excalibur Die Cutters, 29614
Standard Folder Gluers, 29614
Standard Knapp, 30979
Standard Systems, 30150
Standard-Keil, 20819
Stanislaus Food Products, 20032
Stanley, 28691, 29624
Staplex, 29628
Star, 19816, 25257, 27497, 28513, 29632
Star Award Ribbon Co., 22217
Star Brite, 26201
Star Controls, 23987
Star Dairy, 31209
Star Guard, 31055
Star Hydrodyne, 29634
Star Pager, 25460
Star Plus, 20270
Star Systems, 20060
Star Track, 29905
Starborne, 23294
Starbucks Frappacino, 27476
Starkey, 29644
Starline, 20649
Starlite, 23549
Starmax, 29636
Starmist, 30557
Starr, 19915
Starr Hill Amber Ale, 26708
Starrett, 25257
Stars, 18857
Startex, 30559
Startwist, 30569
Starvac, 30559
Starvac Ii, 30559
Starvac Iii, 30559
Starview, 29647
Static Mixers, 24735
Staylock, 21383
Staynap, 23193
Stb Stahlhammer Bommern, 20771
Std Precision Gear & Instrument, 28768
Steady-Mount, 30897
Steak Sauce, 21357
Steakmarkers, 20011
Stealth Fries, 25143
Steam 'n' Hold, 18294
Steam Pac, 27721
Steam-Flo, 29304
Steamcraft, 20658
Steamflo, 21639
Steamix, 19067
Steamscrubber, 25080
Stearns, 26904, 28400, 29655, 29656
Stearns-Roger, 28250
Steclite, 20270
Sted Stock Ii, 20270
Steel It, 29602
Steel It Lite, 29602
Steelcraft, 21054
Steeline, 20901
Steeltest, 23577
Steeltite, 23484
Steeltree, 24556
Steeluminum, 20270
Steempan, 30432
Steer Clear, 27388
Steffens, 21908
Stein/Checker, 20489
Steinco Casters, 24602
Stella, 21233
Stella Artois, 26708
Steller Steam, 24101
Stephan, 29681
Steri-Flo, 22588
Sterigenics, 24023, 29684
Sterileware, 19542
Sterilin, 21873
Sterilobe, 30895
Sterisafe, 28773
Sterling, 18622, 23877, 29696, 31393
Sterling Eliminator, 29696
Sterno, 24886
Stero, 24074, 27104, 29701

Stewart Sutherland, 18031
Stewart's, 24840
Stick 'n Stay, 23820
Stieber, 18686
Stiffel, 25695
Stillpax, 18645
Stirator, 21289
Stock, 28881
Stock Coster, 29896
Stockmaster, 20942
Stockpop, 30300
Stone Burr Mills, 25974
Stone Glo, 30550
Stone Ridge Creamery, 28940
Stone-Cutter, 30717
Stop Aging Now, 20673
Stor-Frame, 29732
Stor-It, 30455
Storage Rack-Steel-Clad, 30696
Storage Wall, 25392
Store'n Pour, 20270
Storeworks, 25603
Storgard, 24310
Storm Trac, 28304
Stouffers, 19252
Stow Away, 23533
Stowaway, 25073
Strahman, 19409
Straight Up Tea, 24840
Strainomatic, 23707
Strapping, 20264
Strapslicer System, 18307
Stratagraph, 23388
Straw Boss, 30418
Streamlight, 26494
Stressease, 24543
Stresstech, 18239
Stretch Frame, 20641
Stretch-Tite, 31383
Stretch-Vent, 29765
Stretchframe, 29784
Stricklin, 29769
Strico, 29769
Strip Pac, 27721
Stripir, 27366
Striplok, 24743
Stromag, 18686
Strong Bow, 31186
Strong Scott, 19584
Strong-Scott, 23907
Structolene, 20901
Strypel, 27474
Stuart, 21873
Stubborn Soda, 27476
Stubby Clear-Vue, 26359
Stubby Less Crush, 26359
Studio Colors, 23193
Stumptown Coffee, 27134
Sturdi-Frame, 30455
Sturdystyle, 23847
Stylene, 23193
Stylus, 24313
Styprint, 27474
Styrocups, 31292
Stysorb, 27474
Sublime, 25186
Success, 28463
Suds - Pail, 20270
Sugar Creek, 29794
Sugar Foods Corporation, 29137
Sugar Free Cookies, 23861
Sugar Plum, 25339
Sugar Twin, 31472
Sugardale, 22891
Sullair, 29011
Summa-6, 28878
Summerripe, 22488
Summit, 22533, 29799
Summit Lectern, 26265
Sump-Vac, 29529
Sun Bright, 29143
Sun Chips, 27476
Sun Drop, 24840
Sun Oil, 28504
Sun Valley, 29098
Sun-Glo, 30550
Sunbeam, 28034
Sunbest, 29809
Sunbrand, 25825
Sunburst, 28025
Sunco, 29809
Sunflower, 28852, 29568

Sunglo, 18440, 23393
Sunkist, 24840
Sunlite, 23993
Sunmalt, 24756
Sunny Fresh, 20260
Sunny Green, 26825
Sunnyd, 24840
Sunpak, 18440
Sunripe, 21469, 27324
Sunrise, 25762
Sunvista, 22494
Sup-Ex, 25047
Super, 21070, 29828
Super Adjustable, 24341
Super Adjustable Super Erecta, 26067
Super Bar, 22811
Super Carrot Cutter, 19177
Super Cart, 26721
Super Chef, 18819, 23029, 29833
Super Chill, 28940
Super Cutter, 19177
Super Drive Sifter, 26776
Super Erecta, 24341, 26067
Super G, 25901
Super H, 19811
Super Hook, 19090
Super Hot, 18628
Super Iron Out, 24423
Super Iron Out Dignio, 24423
Super Key, 29644
Super Links, 19776
Super Marker, 26145
Super Moderna, 24666
Super Mustang, 19811
Super Pack-Man, 23046
Super Pan Ii, 30941
Super Pik, 19907
Super Power, 20136
Super Sack, 19315
Super Scald, 19907
Super Separator, 30897
Super Sheath, 20379
Super Slicer, 20011
Super Strip, 21099
Super Systems, 27598
Super-Flex, 23577
Super-Flo, 28980
Super-Stamp, 29435
Super-Trete, 21099
Super-Trol, 19911
Superbag, 20905
Superbag Jr., 20905
Superbase, 22302
Superbridge, 25609
Superceptor, 30246
Superchanger, 30432
Superflex, 29834
Superfly, 26373
Superformer, 18097
Supergard, 31002
Supergotcha, 28162
Supergrain, 27430
Superguard, 18630
Superior Monogram, 29848
Superior Rex, 18503
Superior Systems, 23249
Superior's Brand, 22891
Superlast, 23577
Superlevel, 24527, 30081
Supermix, 18183
Superportable, 20565
Supershield, 18187
Superskids, 31076
Supersnap High Sensitivity Atp Test, 24006
Supersorb, 22584
Superstar Strawberry, 23410
Supertaut Plus Ii, 29891
Supertilt, 18183
Supertower, 20565
Supervision, 29832
Superwear, 28025
Superwheel, 24979
Supr Swivel, 21741
Supr-Safe (Gas), 21741
Supra, 20304
Supraplus, 29045
Suprega, 21447
Supreme, 20270, 20684, 24637, 27455, 29036, 29863
Sur Sweet, 29894
Surco, 29864
Surcota, 29864

Surcotta, 18507
Sure Chef, 23765
Sure Chef Climaplus Combi, 23765
Sure Gard, 31144
Sure Sak, 20271
Sure Shot, 27772
Sure Way, 28776
Sure-Bake, 21247
Sure-Bake & Glaze, 21247
Sure-Grip, 29295
Sure-Kol, 29867
Sure-Stik, 23164
Surebean, 30340
Surebond, 24262
Suredrain, 23886
Sureflow, 21282
Sureseal, 27543
Sureshot, 18103
Surety Pwd Hand Soap, 23566
Surface Systems, 25810
Surge, 22999, 23113
Susan Winget, 24425
Suspentec, 21050
Sussman, 29877
Sustamid, 28520
Sustarin, 28520
Sustatec, 28520
Svendborg Brakes, 18686
Svk, 28477
Sw, 22494
Swab 'n' Smile, 31055
Sweeping Beauty, 25705
Sweet Moose, 26825
Sweet P'S Bake Shop, 30374
Sweet Things, 25143
Sweetfree Magic, 25669
Sweetheart Fudge, 31447
Swiffer, 30234
Swift Set Folding Chairs, 26265
Swift Tooth Bands, 19154
Swifty, 19836
Swing Arm Diverter, 22284
Swing Top, 20901
Swing-A-Way, 29898
Swingster, 18786
Swirl, 23533
Swirl Freeze, 29899
Swiss Air, 29671, 29672
Swiss Castle, 18260
Swiss Colony Foods, 20751
Swiss Premium Dairy, 21443
Swissh, 29902
Swivelier, 29905
Sword, 18024
Sycoid, 30964
Symart Systems, 29758
Symbol, 22800
Symbol Jet, 25824
Symetix, 24850
Symmetrix Frp, 25810
Symphony, 20270, 21842, 23786
Symtec, 23646
Synchromat, 26519
Syncrospense, 24078
Synergy, 23807
Synergy Laser Power, 28959
Syr, 28964
Syracuse, 19362, 25323
Syracuse China, 25322
Syrelec, 21118
Sys-Clean, 30890
Syspro, 28781
System 7, 27443
System Iv, 29999
System Master, 22838
System Sensor, 23268
Systemaker, 24249
Systemsure Plus Atp Hygiene, 24006

T

T&S Brass and Bronze, 30007
T-Line, 23771
T-Rex, 29213, 30418
T.G. Lee Dairy, 21443
Ta Instruments, 31086
Ta-3, 19270
Ta-Xt2, 30225
Tab X-Tra, 20703
Tabbee, 28974
Tabie Lamps & Stereo Brand, 29700
Table De France, 21519

Touch Access, 30885
Touch Alert, 30885
Touch and Go Blending Station, 30927
Touch in a Box, 22152
Touch Menus, 30402
Touch of Scent, 28977
Touch Taper, 25824
Touchprobe, 30885
Touchseal, 18818
Tough Guy Totes, 23296
Tough Guy's, 21357
Tough One, 28220
Townsend, 29740
Toyo Jidoki, 20564
Tpa, 25853
Tpm, 30289
Tpro, 26706
Tr, 27124
Tr 1000-2000, 25475
Trace, 25113
Tracer Summit, 30424
Tracker, 30424
Trackside Cookery, 31215
Trade Envelopes, 22217
Trademarx, 30415
Tradex International, 18031
Traditional, 24471
Traditionalware, 25360
Traeger, 30417
Traffic Graffic, 23147
Trag, 30424
Trak Clip, 27619
Trak-Air Ii, 30421
Trak-Air V, 30421
Trak-Shield, 26949
Trakstat, 27258
Trampak, 27119
Trane, 30424
Trans Label, 25587
Trans-10, 30427
Trans-100, 30427
Trans-30, 30427
Trans-Zip, 28477
Transaction Drawer, 21895
Transafe, 21001
Transback, 19567
Transchem, 21206
Transilon, 22785, 26037
Transitainer, 21206
Transitions, 25702
Transitray, 19649
Transmart, 20108
Transporter, 20311
Transtex, 22785
Transtore, 21206
Transwheel, 24979
Trantorque, 22538
Trap-Zap Plus, 30433
Trapper, 19552, 24773
Trapr, 30402
Trashpacker, 20538
Traulsen, 24074, 26513, 30435
Travel-Jon, 20409
Traveler, 19059, 21383
Tray Star, 19077
Traycon, 30440
Traysaver, 24739
Traytrak, 22203
Trc, 27322
Tred-Ties Adjustable Railroad Ties, 18350
Tree Saver Bags, 30441
Treehouse Private Brands, 30442
Treestock, 26559
Trehalose, 24756
Trench Former System, 18020
Trend, 31243
Trendreader, 18114
Trenet, 20673
Trescerro Premium Teas, 29137
Treta Alex, 30212
Treta Alfast, 30212
Treta Almix, 30212
Treta Alrox, 30212
Treta Alsafe, 30212
Treta Alscreen, 30212
Trewax Hardware, 20513
Trewax Industrial, 20513
Trewax Janitorial, 20513
Tri-Arc Manufacturing, 25368
Tri-C Business Forms, 22217
Tri-Clover, 19409
Tri-Drum, 24556

Tri-Flex, 19629
Tri-Flex Loop, 22654
Tri-Flow, 22882
Tri-Foil, 30460
Tri-Gard, 30460
Tri-Homo, 29401
Tri-Lam, 30460
Tri-Micro, 30897
Tri-Seal, 30460
Tri-Sorb, 30674
Tri-Stacker, 22882
Tri-Star Manufacturing, 29620
Tri-Tray, 22882
Tri-Wall, 26438
Triad, 20641, 29784
Triarc Beverages, 26183
Tricam, 29025
Triconfort, 28887
Tridyne, 30478
Trigo Labs, 26557
Tril-Clear, 30480
Trim-Line, 18628
Trimlina, 20270
Trimlume, 25265
Trimma, 21787
Trine Baffle, 30484
Trine Labeling, 18290
Triner, 30485
Triola, 20641
Trion Indoor Air Quality, 18503
Trionix, 18538
Triple Erasability System, 30921
Triples, 22069
Tripmaster, 29744
Tristar, 25339
Trisyl, 30964
Tritab, 27543
Triumph, 21219, 21908, 30883
Trivia, 21078
Trix, 20965
Trodat, 26338
Trojan Brands, 20577
Trojan Commercial, 30498
Trolly-Freeze, 23108
Tronex, 30501
Trophy, 21383, 23637
Tropic Beach, 28984
Tropical Bee, 25825
Tropical Coffee, 19826
Tropical Royal, 23410
Tropicana, 20965, 27476
Tropico, 20703
Trouble Shooter, 18700
Troughveyor, 28814
Tru Balance, 23394
Tru Blue Blueberries, 28134
Tru Brew, 18936
Tru Hone, 30510
Tru-Hone, 29091
Tru-Nox, 29557
Tru-Temp, 30125
Tru-Test, 23113
Tru-Trak, 29285
Truckstop, 26126
True, 30513
True Flow, 19220
True Health, 20673
True Measure, 19356
True Pine, 19754
True Recipe, 24471
True Tracker, 22030
True-Sharp, 29420
Truitt Bros., 30517
Trust, 22302
Ts Conveyor, 24979
Tu-Scrub, 30523
Tu-Way, 23150
Tubar, 30606
Tube Mastervent, 18327
Tube-Lok, 29160
Tubular Sonics, 26198
Tucel, 30523
Tuck, 30207
Tucker, 28148
Tuf'n Ega, 21447
Tuf-Flex Volumetric Series Feeders, 28919
Tuf-N-Low, 27153
Tuff Grip (Gloves), 19819
Tuff Guys, 31144
Tuff Stuff, 25644
Tuff-Coder, 22934
Tuff-Cut, 24739

Tuff-Dot, 20291
Tuffgards, 23590
Tufkote, 26866
Tuftboard, 25118
Tugweld, 30076
Tulip Deli, 20270
Tully's Coffe, 24840
Tullys, 30534
Tupperware, 30537
Turano, 30817
Turbo, 18442, 19987, 23704, 25907
Turbo Sensor, 28404
Turbo-Dryer, 31417
Turbo-Flo, 24850
Turbochef, 30072
Turbodisc, 20506
Turbofan, 26294
Turbula, 23242
Turn-O-Matic, 22301
Tuscan Dairy Farms, 21443
Tut-50e, 30366
Tut-50r, 30366
Tuttle & Bailey, 18503
Twiflex, 18686
Twin Abs Poucher, 18274
Twin Chamber 3002, 31070
Twin Pac 2203, 31070
Twin Pac 2204, 31070
Twin Pac 2205, 31070
Twin Taper, 25824
Twin-Pak, 30447
Twin-Shell, 27389
Twin-Stream, 28404
Twin-Tex, 23193
Twinings, 25825
Twinkle Baker Decor, 30555
Twintower, 28082
Twis-Tags, 30010
Twist-Ems, 30010
Twist-Off, 29269
Twizzlers, 23786
Twm, 30076
Two-Can, 19801
Twoview, 21679
Ty-Linker, 25371
Ty-Peeler, 25371
Ty-Up, 30319
Tyle Style, 31055
Tyme Chef, 19100
Type 1, 18628
Typhoon, 29401
Tyson, 19252, 20113

U

U-Fry-It, 22931
U.N.L.O.C.C., 23741
U.S. Bag, 18528
U.S. Eye, 30464
U.S. Gauge, 18872
Udi's, 27584
Udisco, 20311
Uf Feeder, 23115
Ufmt, 30617
Ufo, 24440
Uji, 30713
Ul, 24436
Ulma, 23654
Ulta Mag, 30330
Ultem, 21873
Ultima, 23704, 27979, 28785, 30435
Ultimate Comfort, 19159
Ultipleat, 27265
Ultipor Gf/Gf Plus, 27265
Ultipor Gf, 27265
Ultra, 19754, 23704, 30435, 30767
Ultra Bar, 27887
Ultra Bin, 29657
Ultra Cruvinet, 21145
Ultra Density, 18710
Ultra Flow, 28854
Ultra Glide, 27805
Ultra Guard, 31230
Ultra Laser Power, 28959
Ultra Lift, 30614
Ultra Pac, 24080
Ultra Pumps, 24799
Ultra Siever, 23218
Ultra Taper, 25824
Ultra Thin, 28873
Ultra Wash, 24938
Ultra Wipe, 23193

Ultra Wrap, 18916
Ultra-Beam, 19436
Ultra-Cool, 18840
Ultra-Fil, 23893
Ultra-Gog, 18840
Ultra-Lite, 23577
Ultra-Spec, 18840
Ultra-Turrax, 24110
Ultrablister, 20475
Ultrabond, 24262
Ultracell, 30842
Ultrachef, 26487
Ultraclear, 29894
Ultrafilter, 30617
Ultrafryer, 29620, 30618
Ultrair, 30617
Ultrajet, 30476
Ultralon, 31229
Ultramist, 21009
Ultrapac, 30617
Ultraqua, 30617
Ultrascan, 25587
Ultrasealer, 20475
Ultrasep, 30617
Ultrashine, 18393
Ultraslik, 21247
Ultrasnap Atp Test Devices, 24006
Ultrasonic Equipment, 21823
Ultrasonic Sensor, 30842
Ultratoc, 30617
Ultravac, 24945
Ultravert, 24130
Ultraware, 30842
Ultrefiner, 28198
Ultrex, 30617
Unarco, 18998
Unbelievable Green, 20985
Unbelievable!, 20985
Unbound Energy, 26708
Uncle Sam, 19186
Uncommon Threads, 30644
Underbar, 19211
Ungermatic, 30631
Uni-Badge, 27619
Uni-Band, 26504
Uni-Cart, 20938
Uni-Flo, 28790
Uni-Freeze, 23108
Uni-Lift, 20938
Uni-Matic, 25349
Uni-Mod, 21063
Uni-Pac, 21063
Uni-Pak, 20728
Uni-Steel Lockers, 20368
Uni-Strap, 27619
Uni-Tension, 24387
Uni-Vac, 30680
Uni-Versal, 30642
Unibagger, 27130
Unibar, 20670
Unibuilt, 31259
Unico, 30680
Unicorn, 25824
Unidex, 24262
Unifab, 30676
Unified Industries, 20771
Unifill, 22153
Unifit, 22584
Uniflo, 18432
Uniflow Fume Hoods, 23758
Uniflow Se, 23758
Unikleen, 27889
Unilast, 23577
Uniline Casework, 23758
Unimark, 26145
Unimax Large Floor Mount Hoods, 23758
Unimix, 21933
Unimove, 30648
Uniplace, 19098
Unirack Drive-In Rack, 30662
Unirak Pallet Rack, 30662
Uniroyal Ensolite, 27697
Unisab, 31449
Unisafe, 31449
Unispense, 29553
Unisystem, 18442
Unit Trane, 30424
United Filters, 30677
Unitray, 30604
Unitron, 30604
Unity Lab Services, 30258

Colorado

Connecticut

Delaware

Georgia

MGF.com, 25610
Micromeritics, 26141
Microplas Industries, 26144
Mitec, 26259
Miura Boilers, 26266
Modern Packaging, 26278
Momar, 26312
Mp Equip. Co., 26384
MSK Covertech, 25635
Murzan Inc, 26434
National Discount Textile, 26506
NCR Corp, 26456
NCR Counterpoint, 26457
New Centennial, 26613
Newell Brands, 26649
Nitta Corp of America, 26696
Nomafa, 26700
Nordson Corp, 26712
North American Container Corp, 26725
Novelis Foil Products, 26791
NTN Wireless, 26470
NTS, 26471
OCS Checkweighers Inc, 26853
Ocs Checkweighers, Inc., 26890
Oliver Bentleys, 26932
Omni Apparel, 26954
Omni International, 26958
Orbisphere Laboratories, 27001
Original Wood Seating, 27015
Orkin LLC, 27018
P & L System, 27067
P.F. Harris Manufacturing Company, 27072
Packaging Machine Service Company, 27203
Panamerican Logistics, 27290
Peter Drive Components, 27509
Phoenix Wholesale Foodservice, 27551
Plastech Corp, 27617
Plicon Corporation, 27651
Polar Bear, 27666
Polymercia, 27694
Pratt Industries, 27757
Premier Brass, 27786
Prentiss, 27799
Prince Industries Inc, 27841
Printpack Inc., 27853
Prism, 27864
Processors Co-Op, 27907
Production Packaging & Processing
    Equipment Company, 27913
Production Systems, 27914
Proffitt Manufacturing Company, 27923
Puritan/Churchill Chemical Company, 27989
R.N.C. Industries, 28119
Reed Ice, 28281
Refinishing Touch, 28291
Reflex International, 28293
Refrigerated Warehousing, 28297
Refrigiwear Inc, 28304, 28305
Remote Equipment Systems, 28353
Riverwood International, 28461, 28462
Robatech USA Inc, 28471, 28472
Robertson Furniture Co Inc, 28487
Rock-Tenn Company, 28505
Rome Machine & Foundry Co, 28543
Ronchi America, 28551
Ross Engineering Inc, 28578
Ross Systems, 28581
Ross Systems & Controls Inc, 28582
Rosson Sign Co, 28584
Rovema, 28606
Royal Oak Enterprises, 28624
RTI Inc, 28165
RWI Resources, 28175
Sandler Seating, 28845
SBB & Associates, 28704
Scaltrol Inc, 28901
ScanTech Sciences, 28905
Seasons 4 Inc, 29005
Selecto, 29044
Selecto Scientific, 29045
Selig Chemical Industries, 29046
Showa, 29209
Sidel Inc, 29221
Siemens Industry Inc, 29226
Silliker Laboratories of Ga, 29272
Sims Superior Seating, 29300
Skalar Inc, 29315
Slautterback Corporation, 29321
SMI USA, 28748
Smith & Taylor, 29333
Smurfit Stone, 29347, 29348
Smyrna Container Co, 29353

Solvay Specialty Polymers LLC, 29386,
    29387
Sonoco Paperboard Specialties, 29405
Southeastern Filtration Systs, 29437
Southern Ag Co Inc, 29440
Southern Awning & Sign Company, 29443
Southern Packaging Machinery, 29453,
    29454, 29455
Southern Perfection Fab, 29457
Southern Tailors Flag & Banner, 29461
Spacekraft Packaging, 29478
SPG International, 28754
Springprint Medallion, 29565
Spurrier Chemical Companies, 29571
Standard Pump, 29615
Starflex Corporation, 29643
Steelmaster Material Handling, 29666
Stoffel Seals Corp, 29719, 29720
Stork Food Dairy Systems, 29738
Stratix Corp, 29758
Success Systems, 29790
Suhner Manufacturing, 29796
Super Cooker, 29827
Supreme Metal, 29861
Surekap Inc, 29871
Sysco Corp, 29947
Systemate Numafa, 29997
T-Drill Industries Inc, 30019
Tara Foods LLC, 30113
Taylor Manufacturing Co, 30124
Telechem Corp, 30169
Tenneco Specialty Packaging, 30191
Thermo Pac LLC, 30262
Time Products, 30329
Tomco2 Systems, 30363
TTS Technologies, 30070
Twelve Baskets Sales & Market, 30547
UCB Inc, 30569
Ultrafilter, 30617
Uniblock-Pump Inc, 30638, 30639
UniPro Foodservice, Inc., 30636
US Filter Corporation, 30588
Vacumet Corporation, 30773
Van Der Graaf Corporation, 30797
Veri Fone Inc, 30847
VibroFloors World, 30874
Volk Enterprises Inc, 30939
Wesley International Corp, 31160
West Rock, 31172
Western Plastics, 31187, 31188
Wika Instrument LP, 31243, 31244
Wilen Professional Cleaning Products, 31253
Wilheit Packaging LLC, 31255
Wincup Holdings, 31292
Woods Fabrication, 31368
Zep Superior Solutions, 31484
Zip-Pak, 31502

Hawaii

American Hawaiian Soy Company, 18782
Daga Restaurant Ware, 21314
EBM Technology, 21919
Peter Dudgeon International, 27510
Peterson Sign Co, 27518
Shiffer Industries, 29186

Idaho

A-1 Booth Manufacturing, 18058
ABC Stamp Signs & Awards, 18092
Ace Co Precision Mfg, 18307, 18308
American Forms & Labels, 18772
Analytical Labs, 18906
Boise Cascade Co, 19788
Boise Cascade Corporation, 19789
Boise Cold Storage Co, 19790
Brose Chemical Company, 19903
Buck Knives, 19936
Challenger Pallet & Supply Inc, 20436
Dependable Machine, Inc., 21575
Development Workshop Inc, 21606
Equipment Outlet, 22271
Fabreeka International, 22455
Idaho Beverages Inc, 24089
Idaho Steel Products Inc, 24090
Image National Inc, 24126
Irresistible Cookie Jar, 24425
J. R. Simplot Co., 24471
King Electric Sign Co, 24890
Kuest Enterprise, 25004
Lamb Weston Holdings, Inc., 25143

Lewis & Clark Company, 25308
Lignetics Inc, 25348
Line-Master Products, 25365
Miles Willard Technologies, 26205
Mountain Pacific Machinery, 26371
Mountain Pride, 26372
Nhs Labs Inc, 26667
Pasco Poly Inc, 27371
Pioneer Sign Company, 27596
ProTeam, 27890
Quintex Corp, 28083
Reyco Systems Inc, 28403
Shamrock Foods Co, 29138
Shelley Cabinet Company, 29175
Spudnik Equipment Co, 29569
Sysco Corp, 29950, 29970
Techni-Chem, 30141
Vanmark Equipment LLC, 30812

Illinois

7 Seas Submarine, 18008
A & G Foods, 18015
A J Antunes & Co, 18025
A J Funk & Co, 18026
A La Carte, 18027
A-Z Factory Supply, 18065
A.M. Manufacturing, 18075
Aabbitt Adhesives, 18246
Aaron Equipment Co Div Areco, 18250
Abbott Plastics & Supply Co, 18263
ABM Marking, 18101
Absolute Process Instruments, 18278
Accu-Ray Inspection Services, 18297
Accura Tool & Mold, 18303
Acme Control Svc Inc, 18325
ADE Inc, 18124
Adheron Coatings Corporation, 18376
ADM/Matsutani LLC, 18127
Advance Adhesives, 18391
Advance Lifts Inc, 18399
Advanced Packaging Techniques
    Corporation, 18424
Aero-Motive Company, 18449
AEW Thurne, 18138
Afeco, 18464
Affiliated Resource Inc, 18465
Airfloat LLC, 18512, 18513
Ajinomoto Heartland Inc, 18523
Alar Engineering Corp, 18533
Aldon Co Inc, 18552
Alfacel, 18566
Algus Packaging Inc, 18570
All Spun Metal Products, 18595
Alloyd Brands, 18643
AllPoints Foodservice, 18606
Alnor Instrument Company, 18654
Alpha Gear Drives Inc, 18663
Amber Glo, 18704
Ambitech Engineering Corp, 18706
AME Engineering, 18175
American Autogard Corporation, 18731
American Broom Co, 18736
American Cylinder Co, 18749
American Eagle Food Machinery, 18754
American Environmental International,
    18758
American Extrusion Intl, 18764
American Gasket & Rubber Co, 18778
American Identification Industries, 18785
American Labelmark Co, 18792
American Louver Co, 18796
American Metalcraft Inc, 18803
American Packaging Machinery, 18808,
    18809
American Store Fixtures, 18833
AMETEK National Controls Corp, 18181
Ammeraal Beltech Inc, 18881, 18882
Amstat Industries, 18893
Amtab Manufacturing Corp, 18896
Amwell, 18898
Anderson Snow Corp, 18931
Andfel Corporation, 18938
ANGUS Chemical Co, 18190
Anhydro Inc, 18950
Anixter Inc, 18951
Anritsu Industrial Solutions, 18961
Antunes Controls, 18967
Aoki Laboratory America, 18970
Apco/Valve & Primer Corporation, 18975
Apex Tool Works Inc, 18980

Applegate Chemical Company, 18991
Applexion, 18993
APV Systems, 18217
Aqua Tec Inc, 19012
Aqua-Aerobic Systems Inc, 19013
Arbee Transparent Inc, 19020
Arcar Graphics, 19022
Archer Daniels Midland Company, 19023
Archer Wire Intl Corp, 19024
Architectural Specialty Products, 19028
Ardagh Group, 19041
Ari Industries Inc, 19048
Armato & Associates, 19063
Armbrust Paper Tubes Inc, 19064
ARPAC Group, 18222
Arpac LP, 19077, 19078
Arro Corp, 19080, 19081
Arrow Plastic Mfg Co, 19082
Art Wire Works Co, 19088
Artex International, 19095
Artistic Carton Co, 19105
Asap Automation, 19109
Ascaso, 19110
Association-Nutri, 19137
Astro Machine Corp, 19142
ATK, 18234
Atkinson Dynamics, 19152
Aurora Air Products Inc, 19199
Automated Feeding & Alignment, 19219
Automatic Feeder, 19228
Automatic Liquid Packaging Solutions,
    19231
Automotion Inc, 19246
Awmco Inc, 19273
Awnings Plus, 19276
B R Machinery, 19303
B&G Machine Company, 19309
Baden Baden Food Equipment, 19373
Bagcraft Papercon, 19379
Bakery Machinery & Fabrication, 19397
Baldewein Company, 19409
Baldwin Richardson Foods, 19412
Banner Equipment Co, 19437
Bar NA, Inc., 19443
Barliant & Company, 19461
Barnant Company, 19464
Bauermeister, 19493
Bayer/Wolff Walsrode, 19501
Beacon Inc, 19511
Becker Brothers Graphite Co, 19520
Beehive- Provisur, 19530
Beehive/Provisur Technologies, 19531
Bell & Howell Company, 19548
Bell Flavors & Fragrances, 19550
Belson Outdoors Inc, 19565
Bernard Wolnak & Associates, 19603
Berndorf Belt Technology USA, 19604
Bessco Tube Bending & Pipe Fabricating,
    19616
Bethel Grain Company, 19635
Bettendorf Stanford Inc, 19640
Better Bilt Products, 19641
Beverage Flavors Intl, 19646
Bevistar, 19648
Bevstar, 19651
BG Industries, 19337
Big Beam Emergency Systems Inc, 19659
Bimba Manufacturing Co, 19671
Binks Industries Inc, 19675
Biomist Inc, 19699
BioVittoria USA, 19687
Bismarck Caterers, 19713
Bison Gear & Engineering Corp., 19714
Black Brothers, 19722
Blackhawk Molding Co Inc, 19727
Blackwing Ostrich Meats Inc., 19729
Blakeslee, Inc., 19732
Blommer Chocolate Co, 19749
Bodine Electric Co, 19777
Bodycote Materials Testing, 19779
Bolzoni Auramo, 19796, 19797
Bonar Plastics, 19800
Boss Manufacturing Co, 19819
Boyer Corporation, 19839
BPH Pump & Equipment, 19351
Bradley Industries, 19846
Bran & Luebbe, 19853
Branford Vibrator Company, 19857
Brown Paper Goods Co, 19916
Bruske Products, 19927
Bulk Lift International, LLC, 19949
Bunn-O-Matic Corp, 19955

Royal Group, 28621
Royal Industries Inc, 28622
Rqa Product Dynamics, 28634
RTS Packaging, 28168, 28170
Rudd Container Corp, 28647
Rust-Oleum Corp, 28660
Rutherford Engineering, 28662
Ryowa Company America, 28666
S I Jacobson Mfg Co, 28682
Sackett Systems, 28788
Saf-T-Gard International Inc, 28793
Samuel Strapping Systems Inc, 28823
Sardee Industries Inc, 28871
Savage Brothers Company, 28889
Schaeff, 28911
Scheb International, 28916
Schiffmayer Plastics Corp., 28927
Schwab Paper Products Co, 28954
Schwarz Supply Source, 28956
Scorpio Apparel, 28963
Scotsman Ice Systems, 28966
Se Kure Controls Inc, 28983
Seaboard Carton Company, 28987
Seaga Manufacturing Inc, 28989
Seating Concepts Inc, 29007
Security Link, 29019
Sediment Testing Equipment, 29023
Sencon Inc, 29055
Senior Flexonics, 29059
Sensient Flavors and Fragrances, 29064
Serac Inc, 29085
Serfilco, 29086
Service Manufacturing, 29098
Service Stamp Works, 29102
Service Tool International, 29103
Shaped Wire, 29149
Sieberts Engineers, 29223
Signode Industrial Group LLC, 29253, 29254
Silgan Plastic Closure Sltns, 29264, 29265
Silgan White Cap LLC, 29269
Silliker, Inc, 29274
Simmons Engineering Corporation, 29285
Simpson Electric, 29298
Sipco Products, 29307
Sirman Spa/IFM USA, 29309
Smoke Right, 29343
Snyder Industries Inc, 29364
Solo Cup Company, 29380
Solo Foods, 29381
Sonoco Alloyd, 29404
Sonoco ThermoSafe, 29407
Sortie/Kohlhaas, 29419
Source Distribution Logistics, 29424
Southern Imperial Inc, 29450
Soynut Butter Co, 29476
Spartan Tool LLC, 29489
Spartanics, 29491
Spinzer, 29537
Spraying Systems Company, 29555
Sprayway Inc, 29557
Spring USA Corp, 29560
SRI, 28761
St. Clair Pakwell, 29578
Sta-Rite Ginnie Lou Inc, 29585
Stampede Meat, Inc., 29608
Stand Fast Pkgng Prods Inc, 29611
Standard Refrigeration Co, 29617
Star Industries, Inc., 29634
Starkey Chemical Process Company, 29644
Steiner Company, 29671
Steiner Industries Inc, 29672
Stephan Machinery GmbH, 29680
Stephan Machinery, Inc., 29681
Sterigenics International, 29684
Sterling Novelty Products, 29692
Sterling Systems & Controls, 29697
Sterno, 29700
Stertil Alm Corp, 29702
Stogsdill Tile Co, 29721
Stone Container, 29726
Stor-Loc, 29732
Stork Food Machinery, 29739
Streator Dependable Mfg, 29764
Stroter Inc, 29775
Suburban Corrugated Box Company, 29786
Suburban Laboratories Inc, 29787
Sudmo North America, Inc, 29791
Superior Product Pickup Services, 29847
Sverdrup Facilities, 29884
Sweetener Supply Corp, 29894
Sycamore Containers, 29907
Sympak, Inc., 29910

Sysco Corp, 29918, 29929
Systech Illinois, 29990
Tablecraft Products Co Inc, 30081
Tablet & Ticket Co, 30083
Tag-Trade Associated Group, 30086
Taisei Lamick USA, Inc., 30087
Tamarack Products Inc, 30094
Tangerine Promotion, 30101
Tantec, 30105
TAWI-USA Inc, 30027
Taylor Precision Products, 30125, 30126
TCT&A Industries, 30031
Tech Lighting LLC, 30136
Technical Tool Solutions Inc., 30146
Technomic Inc, 30153
Teepak LLC, 30162
TEI Analytical Svc Inc, 30035
Tempco Electric Heater Corporation, 30181
Tenneco Inc, 30189
Tenneco Packaging, 30190
TEQ, 30037
Tetra Pak, 30211
The National Provisioner, 30233
Therma Kleen, 30245
Thermal Bags By Ingrid Inc, 30248
Thermos Company, 30274
Thomas Lighting Residential, 30288
Tinwerks Packaging Co, 30335
Tisma Machinery Corporation, 30339
TMT Vacuum Filters, 30057
Tni Packaging Inc, 30346
Tnn-Jeros Inc, 30347
TNN-Jeros, Inc., 30059
Toastmaster, 30348
Top Source Industries, 30373
Topco Associates LLC, 30374
Topflight Grain Co-Op, 30375
Total Control Products, 30393
Toyo Seikan Kaisha, 30409
Tradeco International Corp, 30414
Transparent Container Co, 30431
Travelon, 30437
TreeHouse Foods, Inc., 30442
Tri-Connect, 30457
Triangle Package Machinery Co, 30469
Tricor Systems Inc, 30473, 30474
Trilla Steel Drum Corporation, 30479
Tubesales QRT, 30522
Turtle Wax, 30543
UAA, 30567
Ultra Packaging Inc, 30615
Uneco Systems, 30628
Uni Carriers Americas Corp, 30632
Unichema North America, 30640
Uniforms To You, 30644
Uniforms To You & Co, 30645
Union Cord Products Company, 30650
Unique Boxes, 30657
Unique Solutions, 30661
United Ad Label, 30666
United Floor Machine Co, 30680
United Insulated Structures, 30683
United Performance Metals, 30688
Universal Beverage Equipment, 30703
Universal Overall, 30717
Upham & Walsh Lumber, 30734
US Cooler Company, 30585
US Standard Sign, 30598
US Tsubaki Holdings Inc, 30600
Vantage Performance Materials, 30815, 30816
Vantage USA, 30817
Vapor Power Intl LLC, 30818
VCG Uniform, 30756
Vector Packaging, 30831
Verilon Products Co, 30849
Victone Manufacturing Company, 30877
Videojet Technologies Inc, 30883, 30884
VIP Real Estate LTD, 30761
Viskase Co Inc, 30916
Vonco Products LLC, 30946
Voss Belting & Specialty Co, 30951
Vrymeer Commodities, 30952
Wabash Power Equipment Co, 31014
Wag Industries, 31019
Wallace Computer Services, 31037, 31038
Walsroder Packaging, 31043
Walter Molzahn & Company, 31045
Warner Electric Inc, 31053
Washington Group International, 31067
Water & Oil Technologies Inc, 31075
Watershed Foods, 31087

Watlow Electric, 31089
Weber Packaging Solutions Inc, 31122
Weber-Stephen Products Company, 31124
Wega USA, 31128
Weigh Right Automatic Scale Co, 31129
Welch Brothers, 31139
Wells Lamont, 31144, 31145, 31146
Wenda America Inc, 31152
Western Lighting Inc, 31183
Western Stoneware, 31194
Wexxar Corporation, 31207
WGN Flag & Decorating Co, 30986
White Stokes International, 31226
White Way Sign & Maintenance, 31227
Wico Corporation, 31239
Wilkens-Anderson Co, 31258
Willett America, 31270
Wilton Brands LLC, 31288
Winston Laboratories Inc, 31321
Wipeco Inc, 31324
Wisdom Adhesives Worldwide, 31339
Woodhead, 31367
Woodstock Plastics Co Inc, 31376
World Dryer Corp, 31387
World Kitchen, 31392
World Wide Beverage, 31400
World Wide Fitting Corp, 31401
Worldwide Dispensers, 31404
Xcell International, 31424
Yamada America, 31438
Yargus Manufacturing Inc, 31441
Z-Trim Holdings, Inc, 31465
Zebra Technologies Corporation, 31474
Zenith Cutter, 31482
Zip-Pak, 31499, 31500, 31501
Zitropack Limited, 31504

Indiana

A T C Inc, 18035
A T Ferrell Co Inc, 18036, 18037
Abresist Kalenborn Corp, 18275
Accu Temp Products Inc, 18294
Advanced Control Technologies, 18406
Advanced Process Solutions, 18427
Aire-Mate, 18510
Airomat Corp, 18519
Alcoa - Warrick Operations, 18545
American Containers Inc, 18742
American Electronic Components, 18756
American Griddle Corp., 18781
American Metal Door Company, 18801
American Ultraviolet Co, 18840
American-Newlong Inc, 18849
AmeriQual Foods, 18719
Ameristamp/Sign-A-Rama, 18863
Anchor Industries, 18915
Anderson Tool & Engineering Company, 18932
Aqua Blast Corp Mfg, 19009
Archibald Frozen Desserts, 19025
Ardagh Group, 19042
Artistic Carton, 19104
Assmann Corp of America, 19130
Atlas Restaurant Supply, 19179
Balemaster, 19415
Bar Keepers Friend Cleanser, 19441
Basiloid Products Corp, 19486
Bell Packaging Corporation, 19553
Berry Global, 19606
Bluffton Motor Works, 19771
BNW Industries, 19347
Brulin & Company, 19923
Bryan Boilers, 19930
Butler Winery, 19989
Caloritech, 20166
Capitol City Container Corp, 20226
Capitol Hardware, Inc.,, 20227
Cardinal Container Corp, 20251
Cardinal Packaging, 20253
Carico Systems, 20263
Carman Industries Inc, 20279, 20280
Carmel Engineering, 20281, 20282
Central Fine Pack Inc, 20396
Century Chemical Corp, 20409
Century Industries Inc, 20413
Chicago Automated Labeling Inc, 20531
Chore-Boy Corporation, 20563
CK Products, 20073
CLARCOR Air Filtration Prods, 20076
Classico Seating, 20618
Closure Systems Intl Inc, 20674

Color Box, 20753
Command Belt Cleaning Systems, 20786
Cornerstone, 20998
Cosco Home & Office Products, 21022
Crawford Packaging, 21068
Creative Industries Inc, 21084
Cummins Power Generation Inc., 21173
Custom Machining Inc, 21205
Custom Poly Packaging, 21216
CXR Co, 20121, 20122
D M Sales & Engineering Co, 21255
Diamond Chain, 21620
Diskey Architectural Signs, 21667
Dolco Packaging Co, 21717
Dometic Mini Bar, 21720
Doughmakers, LLC, 21754
Dow Agro Sciences LLC, 21770
Driall Inc, 21794
Dwyer Instruments Inc, 21861
E-Pak Machinery, 21904
E-Z Dip, 21907
Eash Industries, 21995
EFP Corp, 21926
Ehrgott Rubber Stamp Company, 22081
Elanco Food Solutions, 22093
Electronic Liquid Fillers, 22117
ELF Machinery, 21936
Elliott-Williams Company, 22143
Endress & Hauser, 22191
Environmental Consultants, 22243
Faultless Caster, 22509
FDL/Flair Designs, 22414
Fibertech Inc, 22562, 22563
Flashfold Carton Inc, 22638
Flavor Burst, 22641
Flexible Foam Products, 22660
Flomatic International, 22678
Flow Aerospace, 22686
Fonda Group, 22719
Formflex, 22755
Fort Wayne Awning, 22808
Foster Forbes Glass, 22820
G W Berkheimer Co, 22976
G.V. Aikman Company, 22983
Galbreath LLC, 23046
Garver Manufacturing Inc, 23076
Gary Sign Co, 23085
General Cage, 23135
Genflex Roofing Systems, 23174
Grasso, 23367
Harsco Industrial IKG, 23669
Helmer, 23757
Hewitt Manufacturing Co, 23790
Hodge Design Assoc PC, 23836
Hot Food Boxes, 23910
Howden Group, 23928
Hydro Life, 23995
Indco, 24170
Indiana Bottle Co, 24182
Indiana Carton Co Inc, 24183
Indiana Michigan Power, 24185
Indiana Vac Form Inc, 24186
Indiana Wiping Cloth, 24187
Indiana Wire Company, 24188
Indianapolis Container Company, 24189
Indy Lighting, 24242
Innovative Energy, 24291
Inscale, 24308
Insects Limited Inc, 24310
Iron Out, 24423
Jarden Home Brands, 24554
Jasper Seating Company, 24561
Jeco Plastic Products LLC, 24572
Jessup Paper Box, 24591
JH Display & Fixture, 24499
Johnson Brothers Sign Co Inc, 24632
Josam Co, 24663
JVC Rubber Stamp Company, 24510
KCL Corporation, 24713
Kelly Box & Packaging Corp, 24797
Kenray Associates, 24817
KTR Corp, 24740
Kuepper Favor Company, Celebrate Line, 25003
Lafayette Tent & Awning Co, 25120
Laidig Inc, 25123
Langsenkamp Manufacturing, 25175
LDI Manufacturing Co, 25047
Lillsun Manufacturing Co, 25350, 25351
Lincoln Coders Corp, 25359
Little Giant Pump Company, 25400
Locknetics, 25424

Iowa

Kansas

Kentucky

A C Tool & Machine Co, 18023
Ad Mart Identity Group, 18362
Advance Distribution Svc, 18394
Advanced Insulation Concepts, 18419
Ahlstrom Filtration LLC, 18488
Alltech Inc, 18651
American Fuji Seal, 18775
American Wire Products, 18847
Anderson Wood Products, 18933
Aquionics Inc, 19017
Aventics Corp, 19258
AWP Butcher Block Inc, 18244
Ayr King Corp, 19288
B & W Awning Co, 19296
Balluff Inc, 19422
BEC International, 19325
Blaze Products Corp, 19738
Blendex Co, 19740
Bluegrass Packaging Industries, 19768
Camco Chemicals, 20174
Caraustar, 20239
Carrier Vibrating Equip Inc, 20307
Catalent Pharma Solutions Inc, 20354
CCL Label Inc, 20047
Cello Bag Company, 20378
Central Pallet Mills Inc, 20401
Clayton & Lambert Manufacturing, 20624
Compact Mold, 20809
Corman & Assoc Inc, 20990
Cusham Enterprises, 21186
D D Williamson & Co Inc, 21252
Daniel Boone Lumber Industries, 21358
Engraph Label Group, 22211
F N Sheppard & Co, 22396
Feed the Party, 22527
Foodservice Consultants Society
    International, 22773
Foodworks, 22779
Freudenberg Nonwovens, 22897
Gch Internatonal, 23108
GCJ Mattei Company, 22989
GE Appliances, 22992
Germantown Milling Company, 23199
Graham Pallet Co Inc, 23337
Greensburg Manufacturing Company, 23422
Grindmaster-Cecilware Corp, 23454
Halton Company, 23571
Hoegger Alpina, 23839
Horton Fruit Co Inc, 23900
Ideas Etc Inc, 24100
International Inflight Food Service
    Association, 24378
J.V. Reed & Company, 24485
Jackson Msc LLC, 24523
January & Wood Company, 24549
Ken Coat, 24807
Kentucky Grocers Assn Inc, 24827
Kentucky Power, 24828
Kinergy Corp, 24881
L ChemCo Distribution, 25020
LANTECH.COM, 25041
Lasco Composites, 25190
Legacy Plastics, 25258
Lesco Design & Mfg Co, 25299
Littleford Day, 25405
Louisville Bedding Co Inc., 25488
Louisville Dryer Company, 25490
Louisville Lamp Co, 25491
Martin Laboratories, 25844
Mathews Conveyor, 25897
MDH Packaging Corporation, 25602
Microdry, 26138
Midwest Paper Products Company, 26187
Neff Packaging, 26575
Nemeth Engineering Assoc, 26590
NST Metals, 26469
Oates Flag Co Inc, 26882
Palintest USA, 27261
Parallel Products Inc, 27334
Phoenix Process Equipment, 27549
Pioneer Plastics Inc, 27595
Plastic Printing LLC, 27630
Porcelain Metals Corporation, 27712
Premium Foil Products Company, 27795
Professional Engineering Assoc, 27920
ProMach, 27888
Psion Teklogix, 27967
Quality Natural Casing, 28054
R A Jones & Co Inc, 28089
Rapid Industries Inc, 28233

Raque Food Systems, 28236
Reflectronics, 28292
Regal Power Transmission Solutions, 28314
Revere Packaging, 28392
Rhodes Machinery International, 28418
Riverview Foods, 28460
Rocket Man, 28507
Rodes Professional Apparel, 28518
Round Paper Packages Inc, 28604
Rueff Sign Co Inc, 28650
Ruggles Sign Company, 28652
Sargent & Greenleaf, 28872
Sellers Engineering Division, 29048
SIMBA USA, 28733
Somerset Food Service, 29392
Soudal Accumetric, 29422
Span Tech LLC, 29481
Specialty Films & Associates, 29507
Specialty Food America Inc, 29508
Spectape Inc, 29515
SSE Software Corporation, 28762
SSW Holding Co Inc, 28764
STOBER Drives Inc, 28771
Strong Hold Products, 29772
Superior Distributing Co, 29838
Sweco Inc, 29891
Sysco Corp, 29924
T Q Constructors, 30016
Techno-Design, 30152
Tente Casters Inc, 30196, 30197, 30198
TGW International, 30042
Thermex Thermatron, 30255
Tri-State Plastics, 30461
Trojan Inc, 30499
Vacuum Depositing Inc, 30775
Vendome Copper & Brass Works, 30838
Vertical Systems Intl, 30864
Vogt Tube Ice, 30935
Walker Bag Mfg Co, 31028
Waukesha Cherry-Burrell, 31094, 31095
Willamette Industries, 31268
Winston Industries, 31320
WNA, 30991
WNA Hopple Plastics, 30992
Wolf Company, 31355
Zealco Industries, 31473
Ziniz, 31497
Zumbiel Packaging, 31510

Louisiana

Alcoa - Lake Charles Carbon Plant, 18543
Allpax Products, 18645
Ameriglobe LLC, 18858
Backwoods Smoker Inc, 19371
Bancroft Bag Inc, 19433
Bell Foods, 19551
Bulk Pack, 19950
Calhoun Bend Mill, 20152
Chill Rite Mfg, 20545
Containment Technology, 20894
Cord Tex, 20984
CTI Celtek Electronics, 20115
Delta Container Corporation, 21533
Delta Machine & Maufacturing, 21539
Dixie Maid Ice Cream Company, 21703
Dupuy Storage & Forwarding LLC, 21837
Dynasty Transportation, 21885
Ed Smith's Stencil Works LTD, 22056
Entech Systems Corp, 22225
Entergy's Teamwork Louisiana, 22226
Frosty Factory of America Inc, 22924
Frymaster, 22933
Greig Filters Inc, 23436
H A Sparke Co, 23488
Hart Designs LLC, 23671
Honiron Corp, 23882
IdentaBadge, 24104
Industrial Signs, 24231
Intralox LLC, 24412, 24413
J & M Industries Inc, 24450
Jefferson Packing Company, 24575
Kentwood Spring Water Company, 24829
Laitram LLC, 25125
Lamar Advertising Co, 25140
Layflat Products, 25224
Lengsfield Brothers, 25281
Lighthouse for the Blindin New Orleans,
    25345
Magic Seasoning Blends, 25669
Martin Brothers Inc, 25838
Modern Electronics Inc, 26275

National Tape Corporation, 26545
Ouachita Machine Works, 27042
Pallet Reefer International LLC, 27272
Patio Center Inc, 27380
Paxon Polymer Company, 27403
Pelican Marine Supply LLC, 27439
Pellerin Milnor Corporation, 27443
Pensacola Rope Company, 27463
Pepper Source Inc, 27472
PPI, 27110
Pratt Industries, 27758
Procell Polymers, 27896
Progressive Tractor & Implement Co.,
    27931
Quetzal Foods International Company, 28073
Quick Stamp & Sign Mfg, 28078
Rayne Sign Co, 28246
Rebel Stamp & Sign Co, 28262
Reggie Balls Cajun Foods, 28318
REX Pure Foods, 28143
Ross & Wallace Inc, 28574
Royal Broom & Mop Factory Inc, 28616
SEI Consultants, 28714
Skrmetta Machinery Corporation, 29320
Snee Chemical Co, 29360
Southern Tool, 29462
Southern United States Trade Association,
    29463
Southwestern Electric Power Company,
    29472
Sugar Plum LLC, 29793
Sysco Corp, 29940
Technical Inc, 30144
Thomas Pump & Machinery, 30290, 30291
Universal Sign Company and Manufacturing
    Company, 30723, 30724
Walle Corp, 31039
West Louisiana Ice Svc, 31168

Maine

Belleco Inc, 19557
Coastal Products Company, 20691
Corinth Products, 20988
Diamond Pheonix Corporation, 21626
Display Concepts, 21670
Downeast Chemical, 21776
Eam, 21990
EGW Bradbury Enterprises, 21930
F.E. Wood & Sons, 22404
Fluid Imaging Technologies Inc, 22693
Food Business Associates, 22723
Fox Brush Company, 22833
Gardiner Paperboard, 23064
Geiger Bros, 23120
Gerrity Industries, 23200
Goodman Wiper & Paper Co, 23305
H A Stiles, 23489
Hardwood Products Co LP, 23637
Harold F Haines Manufacturing Inc, 23649
Hauser Packaging, 23692
Haven's Candies, 23695
Idexx Laboratories Inc, 24106
Ingredients Solutions Inc, 24261
Intelligent Controls, 24332
J.A. Thurston Company, 24473
Kady International, 24747
Leavitt & Parris Inc, 25242
Lobsters Alive Company, 25417
Lyman-Morse Fabrication, 25540
Maine Industrial Plastics & Rubber
    Corporation, 25697
Maine Poly Aquisition, 25698
Market Sign Systems, 25789
Neokraft Signs Inc, 26594
Net Pack Systems, 26600
Northeast Laboratory Svc, 26746
Northeast Packaging Co, 26747
Penley Corporation, 27453
Pine Point Fisherman's Co-Op, 27581
Quality Containers of New England, 28039
Remstar International, 28355
RTS Packaging, 28171
Saunder Brothers, 28884
Southworth Products Corp, 29474
Soyatech Inc, 29475
Sysco Corp, 29983
Tech Pak Solutions, 30137
Thirty Two North Corporation, 30285
Tuchenhagen North America, 30525
Tuchenhagen-Zajac, 30526
Uhtamaki Foods Services, 30607

Volk Packaging Corp, 30940
Vulcan Electric Co, 30953
Welch Stencil Company, 31141
Young's Lobster Shore Pound, 31459

Manitoba

Arctic Glacier Premium Ice, 19036
Besco Grain Ltd, 19614
Best Cooking Pulses, Inc., 19621
Legumex Walker, Inc., 25266
Reliance Product, 28342
Richardson International, 28428
Sperling Boss, 29530

Maryland

3Greenmoms LLC, 18003
A O A C Intl, 18032
A.K. Robins, 18073
Abicor Binzel, 18271
AD Products, 18117
AK Robbins, 18158
Alpha MOS America, 18664
American Equipment Co, 18759
American Wood Fibers, 18848
Analyticon Discovery LLC, 18909
Artcraft Badge & Sign Company, 19093
ASI/Restaurant Manager, 18231
Awb Engineers, 19272
Awning Enterprises, 19275
Bakeware Coatings, 19401
Baltimore Aircoil Co, 19426, 19427
Baltimore Sign Company, 19428
Baltimore Spice Inc, 19429
Baltimore Tape Products Inc, 19430
Barcoding Inc, 19452
Batching Systems, 19489
Bertels Can Company, 19610
Bioscience International Inc, 19701
Born Printing Company, 19808
Brimrose Corporation of America, 19884
Brooks Barrel Company, 19900
BYK Gardner Inc, 19360
C R Daniels Inc, 20009
Cambridge Intl. Inc., 20171
Cantwell-Cleary Co Inc, 20213
Charles Engineering & Service, 20457
Charles Tirschman Pallet Co, 20464
Claude Neon Signs, 20620
Clyde Bergemann Eec, 20679
Coddington Lumber Co, 20705
Commercial Corrugated Co Inc, 20792
Compliance Control Inc, 20818
Comus Restaurant Systems, 20838
Control Systems Design, 20932
Creative Cookie, 21078
Creative Signage System,, 21090
Crown-Simplimatic, 21141
Cumberland Box & Mill Co, 21168
Cynter Con Technology Adviser, 21236
Cyntergy Corporation, 21237
Dade Canvas Products Company, 21311
Day Basket Factory, 21414
Daystar, 21423
Del Monte Fresh Produce Inc., 21495
Delta Chemical Corporation, 21532
Dirt Killer Pressure Washer, 21664
Display Craft Mfg Co, 21671
Dixie Printing & Packaging, 21706
DomainMarket, 21719
Dryomatic, 21803
Dsr Enterprises, 21805
Dutter's Food, 21858
Eastern Cap & Closure Company, 22003
Elite Spice Inc, 22130
Ellenco, 22136
EVAPCO Inc, 21969
Exquis Confections, 22384
F & F and A. Jacobs & Sons, Inc., 22391
Felco Packaging Specialist, 22530
FFI Corporation, 22420
Fleet Wood Goldco Wyard, 22645
Food Instrument Corp, 22736
Foss Nirsystems, 22818
Franklin Uniform Corporation, 22862
Frazier Precision Instr Co, 22871
G K & L Inc, 22972
Galvinell Meat Co Inc, 23051
Gamse Lithographing Co Inc, 23055
Gann Manufacturing, 23057
Gardenville Signs, 23063

GEA Evaporation Technologies LLC, 22995
Gea Process Engineering Inc, 23111
Gerstel Inc, 23201
Goodwrappers Inc, 23311
H & M Bay Inc, 23486
H H Franz Co, 23496, 23497
Haas Tailoring Company, 23539
Harford Duracool LLC, 23642
Harford Systems Inc, 23643
Harvey W Hottel Inc, 23680
Hedwin Division, 23744
Hill Brush, Inc., 23811
Howard Overman & Sons, 23925
Hub Labels Inc, 23941
Hydromax Inc, 24002
IGEN, 24037
IGEN International, 24038
Independent Can Co, 24173
Insight Distribution Systems, 24311
Integrated Restaurant Software/RMS Touch, 24330
International Meat Inspection Consultants, 24383
Intralytix, 24414
Jack Stone Lighting & Electrical, 24519
Jamison Door Co, 24544
JM Huber Chemical Corpo ration, 24503
KANE Bag Supply Co, 24706
LA Motte Co, 25038
Landsman Foodservice Net, 25169
Le Smoker, 25232
Lido Roasters, 25336
Light Technology Ind, 25343
M S Willett Inc, 25570, 25571
Mail-Well Label, 25693
Marlin Steel Wire Products, 25809
Maryland Packaging Corporation, 25853
Maryland Plastics Inc, 25854
Materials Handling Systems, 25892
Mathason Industries, 25896
Memor/Memtec America Corporation, 26011
Microbiology International, 26135
Mobern Electric Corporation, 26269
Modern Stamp Company, 26283
Morris Industries, 26350
Mulholland-Harper Company, 26400
National Instruments, 26519
Nelson Co, 26583
Neonetics Inc, 26596
North American Deer Farmers Association, 26726
Olson Wire Products Co, 26939
Onguard Industries LLC, 26975, 26976
Ottenheimer Equipment Company, 27037
Outotec USA Inc, 27046
Paramount Packing & Rubber Inc, 27338
Patrick Signs, 27385
PEAK Technologies, Inc., 27091
Pearson Signs Service, 27414
Permaloc Security Devices, 27496
Polytemp Corp, 27704
Precision Plastics Inc, 27770
Quantis Secure Systems, 28064
Quick Judith & Assoc, 28074
Ralph L. Mason,, 28203
RBA-Retailer's Bakers A ssociation, 28129
Restaurant Development Svc, 28381
Rhee Brothers, 28407
Ross Cook, 28577
Roxanne Signs Inc, 28612
Rubber Stamp Shop, 28640
Russell-William, 28659
RVS, 28172
Seitz Schenk Filter Systems, 29033
Selby Sign Co Inc, 29037
Septipack, 29081
Sheridan Sign Company, 29180
Sherwood Tool, 29181
Shimadzu Scientific Instrs, 29189
Shore Paper Box Co, 29205
Sodexo Inc, 29370
Spray Drying, 29552
Star-K Kosher Certification, 29641
Strasburger & Siegel, 29753
Stricker & Co, 29768
Suburban Signs, 29789
Superfos Packaging Inc, 29835
Sysco Corp, 29944, 29948
Televend, 30175
The Consumer Goods Forum, 30230
TLB Corporation, 30048
TPS International, 30063

Trade Wings, 30413
Triangle Sign & Svc, 30470
Trilogy Essential Ingredients, 30480
Tuchenhagen, 30524
Turbo Systems, 30539
Twenty/Twenty Graphics, 30549
UPS Logistics Technologies, 30579
US Can Company, 30581
US Product, 30596
US Tag & Label, 30599
Voorhees Rubber Mfg Co, 30947
Vulcan Food Equipment Group, 30954
W R Grace & Co, 30964
Wagner Brothers Containers, 31020
Wildes Printing Co Inc, 31252
Wilks Precision Instr Co Inc, 31262
Willard Packaging Co, 31269
YW Yacht Basin, 31436
Zeltex, 31479, 31480

Massachusetts

Acebright Inc., 18318
ACME Sign Corp, 18110
Acryline, 18347
Acumen Data Systems Inc, 18360
Adhesive Applications, 18377
Advanced Instruments Inc, 18417, 18418
Aeration Technologies Inc, 18443
Aero Company, 18445
AERTEC, 18135
All Star Dairy Foods, 18597
Altra Industrial Motion Corp, 18686
Amcel, 18708
American Apron Inc., 18726
American Bag & Burlap Company, 18732
American Holt Corp, 18783
American Insulated Panel Co, 18788
American LEWA, 18791
AMETEK Brookfield, 18177
Analog Devices Inc, 18902
Analogic Corp., 18904
ANVER Corporation, 18194
Anver Corporation, 18968
Applied Analytics, 18995
Arlin Manufacturing Co, 19058
Arthur D Little Inc., 19097
Artisan Industries, 19101
Atlantic Rubber Products, 19159
Auburn Systems LLC, 19189, 19190
Autofry, 19214
Automatic Specialties Inc, 19234
Avon Tape, 19266
Avtec Industries, 19268
Ayer Sales Inc, 19287
Azonix Corporation, 19291
Baird & Bartlett Company, 19384
Batch, 19488
Belt Technologies Inc, 19567
Bematek Systems Inc, 19571
Bete Fog Nozzle Inc, 19633
Blanche P. Field, LLC, 19736
BLH Electronics, 19343
Bostik Inc, 19821
Boston Gear, 19822
Boston Rack, 19823
Boston Retail, 19824
Boston's Best Coffee Roasters, 19826
Brady Enterprises Inc, 19850
Brown Plastics & Equipment, 19917
Bryant Glass, 19931
C & K Machine Co, 19997
C H Babb Co Inc, 20002
Cab Technology Inc, 20125
Cabot Corp, 20127
Cambridge Viscosity, Inc., 20172
Capone Foods, 20231
Caravan Company, 20241
Carman And Company, 20278
CDF Corp, 20056
Cellier Corporation, 20377
Century Products, 20414
Chapman Manufacturing Co Inc, 20451
Charles H Baldwin & Sons, 20459
Charm Sciences Inc, 20468
Chemex Division/International Housewares Corporation, 20509
Chemi-Graphic Inc, 20511
Chilson's Shops Inc, 20547
Cluster Goods Inc, 20678
CMT, 20087
Cold Chain Technologies, 20725

Coleman Manufacturing Co Inc, 20735
Consolidated Thread Mills, Inc., 20876
Control Technology Corp, 20934
Convectronics, 20936
Cooper Decoration Company, 20968
Corning Life Sciences, 21000
Cotter Brothers Corp, 21031
Cove Woodworking, 21044
Covestro LLC, 21047
Craft Corrugated Box Inc, 21053
Crown Uniform & Linen Service, 21139
Crunch Time Information Systems, 21144
CSPI, 20110
Cumberland Farms, 21170
Custom Metalcraft, Architectural Lighting, 21208
Cyborg Equipment Corporation, 21232
D & S Mfg, 21246
Dalton Electric Heating Co, 21341
Danafilms Inc, 21352
Datapaq, 21394
Day Lumber Company, 21415
Decorated Products Company, 21465
Defreeze Corporation, 21470
Del Monte Fresh Produce Inc., 21496
Delta Engineering Corporation, 21536
Delta F Corporation, 21537
Den Mar Corp, 21563
Dennis Engineering Group, 21568
Dennsi Group, 21569
Design Technology Corporation, 21590, 21591
Design-Mark Industries, 21592
Dexter Russell Inc, 21613
Diamond Machining Technology, 21624
Dietzco, 21643
Dimensional Insight, 21654
Dipwell Co, 21661
Double E Co LLC, 21747, 21748
Dow Industries, 21772
Dresco Belting Co Inc, 21791
DSA Software, 21296
DT Packaging Systems, 21305
Dunkin' Brands, Inc., 21830
Durastill Export Inc, 21852
Dusobox Company, 21855
Dynabilt Products, 21868
Eastern Container Corporation, 22004
Econocorp Inc, 22046
Edge Resources, 22063
Energy Sciences Inc, 22195
Erving Industries, 22288
ESI Qual Intl, 21963
Eurosicma, 22330
Extech Instruments, 22385
Fabreeka International Inc, 22456
Fay Paper Products, 22513
Fibre Leather Manufacturing Company, 22566
Firematic Sprinkler Devices, 22602
First Plastics Co Inc, 22609
FLEXcon Company, 22425
Flow of Solids, 22690
Foam Concepts Inc, 22699
Foilmark Inc, 22710
Food Management Search, 22740
Foodmark, Inc., 22770
Foods Research Laboratories, 22772
Foodservice East, 22775
Formation Systems, 22791
FORT Hill Sign Products Inc, 22434
Forte Technology, 22809
Foster Miller Inc, 22821
Frem Corporation, 22884
Friend Box Co, 22901
Frost Manufacturing Corp, 22923
Fuller Box Co, 22940
Fuller Flag Company, 22941
Fygir Logistic Information Systems, 22962
Gamewell Corporation, 23054
General Electric Company, 23142
GHM Industries Inc, 23015
Giltron Inc, 23219
Ginseng Up Corp, 23221
Global Organics, 23259
Gloucester Engineering, 23275
Good Idea, 23300
Grace Tea Co, 23328
Greenfield Paper Box Co, 23420
Greerco High Shear Mixers, 23426
Grinnell Fire ProtectionSystems Company, 23456

Group One Partners, 23467
Gruenewald ManufacturingCompany, 23468
Halmark Systems Inc, 23569
Hampden Papers Inc, 23584
Hano Business Forms, 23610
Hanson Box & Lumber Company, 23615
Hardi-Tainer, 23633
Harpak-Ulma, 23656
Harpak-ULMA Packaging LLC, 23654
Harvard Folding Box Company, 23679
Hazen Paper Co, 23708
Health Star, 23713
Healthstar Inc, 23716
Healthy Truth, LLC, 23719
HH Controls Company, 23525
HI-TECH Filter, 23527
Hillards Chocolate System, 23814
Hodge Manufacturing Company, 23837
Holland Co Inc, 23858
Hot Mama's Foods, 23911
Hoyt Corporation, 23936
Hub Folding Box Co, 23940
Hub Pen Company, 23942
Hudson Belting & Svc Co Inc, 23949
Hudson Poly Bag Inc, 23951
Hy-Trous/Flash Sales, 23985
Hyer Industries, 24005
I M A North America, 24016
Iconics Inc, 24086
IGS Store Fixtures, 24039
Imsco Technology, 24157
Infinity Tapes LLC, 24245
International Smoking Systems, 24396
International Thermal Dispensers, 24398
Intertek USA, 24411
ISS/GEBA/AFOS, 24061
J&J Corrugated Box Corporation, 24467
Janedy Sign Company, 24546
Jarisch Paper Box Company, 24555
Jarvis-Cutter Company, 24560
Jedwards International Inc, 24573
Jen-Coat, Inc., 24578
Jenike & Johanson Inc, 24580
Jim Did It Sign Company, 24603
John E. Ruggles & Company, 24616
John J. Adams Die Corporation, 24618
JP Plastics, Inc., 24506
Kaye Instruments, 24782
Keena Corporation, 24786
Kelley Wood Products, 24796
KEMCO, 24715
Kerrigan Paper Products Inc, 24833
Keurig Dr Pepper, 24840
Kidde-Fenwal Inc, 24865
Kimball Companies, 24875
KLEEN Line Corp, 24728
Knott Slicers, 24943
Koch Membrane Systems Inc, 24947
Krueger Food Laboratories, 24996
Labelprint America, 25103
Laboratory Devices, 25109
Lambeth Band Corporation, 25147
Lamco Chemical Co Inc, 25148
Laminated Papers, 25152
Lamson & Goodnow, 25158
Larien Products, 25183
Legal Sea Foods, 25259
Lenze Americas, 25289
LEWA Inc, 25053
Lifoam Industries LLC, 25340
Lightolier, 25346
LineSource, 25366
Lion Labels Inc, 25380
Liquid Solids Control Inc, 25390
LIST, 25055
Lista International Corp, 25392
Litecontrol, 25397
Lock Inspection Systems, 25420, 25421
Lockwood Packaging, 25437
Lynn Sign Inc, 25544
M D Stetson Co, 25561
M&L Plastics, 25573
Magnetic Technologies LTD, 25679
Mainline Industries Inc, 25699
Management Insight, 25723
Market Forge Industries Inc, 25787
Market Sales Company, 25788
Markwell Manufacturing Company, 25799
Marlow Watson Co, 25812
Mclaughlin Paper Co Inc, 25966
Mcnairn Packaging, 25968
Metcalf & Eddy, 26061

Minnesota

Mississippi

Missouri

New Mexico

New York

Wastequip Teem, 31074
Whitley Manufacturing Company, 31231
Wireway Husky Corp, 31329
Wnc Pallet & Forest Pdts Co, 31349
Wright Global Graphic Solutions, 31411

North Dakota

Adams Inc, 18367
Century Sign Company, 20417
Conviron, 20949
Fargo Automation, 22493
Firebird Artisan Mills, 22601
Great Plains Software, 23389
Integrated Barcode Solutions, 24327
Kerian Machines Inc, 24832
National Sunflower Assn, 26544
SK Food International, 28739
Specialty Commodities Inc, 29504
Sysco Corp, 29965

Nova Scotia

ABCO Industries Limited, 18094
AC Dispensing Equipment, 18103
Chester Plastics, 20525
Day Nite Neon Signs, 21417
Farnell Packaging, 22498
GN Thermoforming Equipment, 23020
IMO Foods, 24048
JDG Consulting, 24495
Sure Shot Dispensing Systems, 29868

Ohio

Abanaki Corp, 18255
ABC Scales, 18091
Accra Laboratory, 18289
Accu-Pak, 18296
AccuLife, 18299
Ace Manufacturing, 18311
ACO Polymer Products, 18113
Acoustical Systems Inc, 18338
Acro Plastics, 18344
Ad Art Litho., 18361
Adam Electric Signs, 18364
Adpro, 18387
Advance Weight Systems Inc, 18403
Advanced Food Equipment LLC, 18412
Advanced Food Systems, 18414
Advanced Organics, 18423
Advanced Poly-Packaging Inc, 18426
Aerotech Enterprise Inc, 18457
AFCO Manufacturing, 18141
AGA Gas, 18146
Agrana Fruit US Inc, 18471
AgriTech, 18477
AIDCO International, 18153
Aidco International, 18491
Air Locke Dock Seal, 18498
Air Technical Industries, 18504
Air-Knife Systems/PaxtonProducts Corporation, 18505
Airflex, 18511
AK Steel Corp, 18159
Akro-Mils, 18526
Akron Cotton Products, 18527
All A Cart Custom Mfg, 18582
All Foils Inc, 18590
Alliance Knife Inc, 18620
Allstate Manufacturing Company, 18649
Alumin-Nu Corporation, 18695
American Box Corporation, 18735
American Cut Edge Inc, 18748
American Electric Power, 18755
American Glass Research, 18779
American Led-Gible, 18793
American Manufacturing-Engrng, 18798
American Pan Co, 18812
American Solving Inc., 18829
American Ventilation Company, 18842
Americana Wholesale Equipment, 18846
Americana Art China Company, 18850
Ametco Manufacturing Corp, 18870
Ametek Technical & Industrial Products, 18874
Ampac Packaging, LLC, 18885
Ampak, 18886
Ample Industries, 18888
Amster-Kirtz Co, 18894
Amtekco, 18897
Anchor Hocking Operating Co, 18914
Anderson International Corp, 18928

Apex Welding Inc, 18981
Applied Industrial Tech Inc, 18999
Architectural Sheet Metals LLC, 19027
Armco, 19065
Arnold Equipment Co, 19072
Arthur Corporation, 19096
Arthur Products Co, 19099
Artx Limited, 19108
ASC Industries Inc, 18224
Aspect Engineering, 19122
Audsam Printing, 19193
Austin Brown Co, 19201
Austin Co, 19202
Automated Container Corp, 19217
Automated Packaging Systems, 19223
Avalon Foodservice, 19252
Avery Dennison Corporation, 19259
Avure Technologies Svc & Sales, 19269
B&J Machinery, 19312
B.E.S.T., 19318
Babcock & Wilcox Power Generation Group, 19364
Baker Concrete Construction, 19388
Bakery Crafts, 19395
Barrette Outdoor Living, 19472
Beech Engineering, 19529
Bel-Terr China, 19544
Belcan Corp, 19545
Benko Products, 19577
Berghausen E Cheml Co, 19592
Berlekamp Plastics Inc, 19596
Berlin Fruit Box Company, 19598
Bessamaire Sales Inc, 19615
Best, 19617
Best & Donovan, 19618
Best Restaurant Equip & Design, 19627
Bethel Engineering & Equipment Inc, 19634
Bettcher Industries Inc, 19638, 19639
Biro Manufacturing Co, 19710
Bishop Machine Shop, 19712
Blako Industries, 19733
Bluffton Slaw Cutter Company, 19772
Boardman Molded Products Inc, 19776
Bolling Oven & Machine Company, 19793
Bonneau Company, 19802
Bonnot Co, 19803
Brand Castle, 19854
Brechbuhler Scales, 19863
Bril-Tech, 19982
Broadway Companies, 19894
Broughton Foods LLC, 19906
Brown Fired Heater, 19911
Bry-Air Inc, 19929
Buckeye Group, 19937
Buckhorn Inc, 19940
Burns Chemical Systems, 19973
C & R Inc, 19999
C Nelson Mfg Co, 20005, 20006
C S Bell Co, 20012
Canton Sign Co, 20211
Canton Sterilized Wiping Cloth, 20212
Capital Plastics, 20223
Caravan Packaging Inc, 20242
Card Pak Inc, 20249
Carhoff Company, 20262
Carnegie Textile Co, 20287
Caron Products & Svc Inc, 20296
Carton Service Co, 20325
Cast Nylons LTD, 20346
CB Mfg. & Sales Co., 20038
CC Custom Technology Corporation, 20044
CCP Industries, Inc., 20050
Ceilcote Air Pollution Control, 20373
Cell-O-Core Company, 20376
Central Coated Products Inc, 20392
Central Fabricators Inc, 20395
Central Ohio Bag & Burlap, 20399
Charles Mayer Studios, 20461
Chart Industries Inc, 20471
Chase Doors, 20473, 20474
Chase Industries Inc, 20475
Chase-Doors, 20476
Chatelain Plastics, 20479
Chatfield & Woods Sack Company, 20480
Chem Pack Inc, 20499
Chemineer, 20515
Chester Hoist, 20524
Chocolate Concepts, 20558
Christy Machine Co, 20568
Cimino Box & Pallet Co, 20581
Cincinnati Convertors Inc, 20583
Cincinnati Foam Products, 20584

Cincinnati Industrial Machry, 20585, 20586
Cintas Corp, 20588
Clamco Corporation, 20608
Cleveland Canvas Goods Mfg Co, 20652
Cleveland Menu Printing, 20653
Cleveland Metal Stamping Company, 20654
Cleveland Mop Manufacturing Company, 20655
Cleveland Motion Controls, 20656
Cleveland Plastic Films, 20657
Cleveland Specialties Co, 20659
Cleveland Vibrator Co, 20660
Cleveland Wire Cloth & Mfg Co, 20661
Climax Packaging Machinery, 20667
Clippard Instrument Lab Inc, 20669
Coblentz Brothers Inc, 20701
Cold Jet, LLC, 20726
Collins & Aikman, 20743
Columbus Instruments, 20770
Columbus Paperbox Company, 20772
Combi Packaging Systems LLC, 20780
Comstar Printing Solutions, 20834
Congent Technologies, 20857
Consolidated Plastics Co Inc, 20875
Continental-Fremont, 20916
Conveyance Technologies LLC, 20938
Convoy, 20950
Corbox-Meyers Inc, 20982
Cornish Containers, 21001
COW Industries Inc, 20092
Crane Pumps & Systems, 21065
Crayex Corp, 21069
Creegan Animation Company, 21093
Cres Cor, 21096
Cresset Chemical Company, 21099
Crown Battery Mfg, 21119
Crown Closures Machinery, 21121
Crown Equipment Corp., 21125
Crystal Creative Products, 21151
CSC Worldwide, 20106
Culinart Inc, 21161
Custom Quality Products, 21218
Custom Tarpaulin Products Inc, 21225
Cutler-Hammer, 21229
Cutrite Company, 21230
D. Picking & Company, 21265
Dairy Specialties, 21326
Damon Industries, 21344
Darcy Group, 21374
Darfill, 21375
Daymark Safety Systems, 21421, 21422
Dayton Bag & Burlap Co, 21425
Dayton Marking Devices Company, 21426
Dayton Reliable Tool, 21427
Dayton Wire Products, 21428
DCS Sanitation Management, 21275
Decko Products Inc, 21461
Degussa Flavors, 21472
Del Monte Fresh Produce Inc., 21484
Demag Cranes & Components Corp, 21554
Desco Equipment Corporation, 21578
Diamond Electronics, 21623
Diamond Roll-Up Door, 21627
Dicks Packing Plant, 21634
Diehl Food Ingredients, 21640
Dillin Automation Systems Corp, 21650, 21651
Dinovo Produce Company, 21659
Distaview Corp, 21679
Distillata, 21680
Distribution Results, 21683
Diversified Capping Equipment, 21687
Dorpak, 21743
Dover Chemical Corp, 21764
Drackett Professional, 21781
Dreaco Products, 21786
DT Industrials, 21303
Du Bois Chemicals, 21806
Dualite Sales & Svc Inc, 21812
DuBois Chemicals, 21808
Duplex Mill & Mfg Co, 21835
Dupps Co, 21836
Durable Corp, 21843
Durashield USA, 21850
E C Shaw Co, 21894
E F Bavis & Assoc Inc, 21895
Eagle Wire Works, 21985
Eaton Corporation, 22018
Ebel Tape & Label, 22025
Eclipse Innovative Thermal Solutions, 22034
Edgerton Corporation, 22066
Edwards Products, 22077

Electro Alarms, 22103
Embro Manufacturing Company, 22161
Emc Solutions, 22162
EMCO, 22175
En-Hanced Products Inc, 22184
Enerfab Inc., 22194
Enting Water Conditioning Inc, 22233
Erie Container, 22279
Esterle Mold & Machine Co Inc, 22306
Eurofins Scientific Inc., 22326
Evans Adhesive Corp LTD, 22334
Executive Match Inc, 22369
Fabohio Inc, 22453
Fair Publishing House, 22471
Fairborn USA Inc, 22473
Falls Filtration Technologies, 22482
Fasson Employee FCU, 22500
FCI Inc, 22412
FECO/MOCO, 22415
Fedco Systems, 22515
Femc, 22535
Ferro Corporation, 22550
FFR Merchandising Inc, 22421
FIB-R-DOR, 22422
Filmco Inc, 22578
Finn & Son's Metal Spinning Specialists, 22595
Fioriware, 22598
Fishers Investment, 22617
Flavorseal, 22643
Food Equipment Manufacturing Company, 22729
Food Industry Equipment, 22733
Food Plant Engineering, 22745
Forest Manufacturing Co, 22789
France Personalized Signs, 22848
Fred D Pfening Co, 22874
Fredrick Ramond Company, 22876
Freely Display, 22879
Freeman Co, 22880
Fremont Die Cut Products, 22885
French Oil Mill Machinery Co, 22887
Fresh Mark Inc., 22891
Frozen Specialties, Inc., 22925
Fuller Weighing Systems, 22945
Funke Filters, 22950
G & S Metal Products Co Inc, 22968
G.F. Frank & Sons, 22981
Gabriella Imports, 23035
Gafco-Worldwide, 23038
Garland Floor Company, 23069
Garvey Products, 23078, 23079
Gasser Chair Co Inc, 23087
Gbs, 23107
GE Lighting, 22994
General Bag Corporation, 23134
General Cutlery Co, 23139
General Data Co Inc, 23140
General Films Inc, 23145
Gilson Co Inc, 23218
Glassline Corp, 23234
Glawe Manufacturing Company, 23239
Glo-Quartz Electric Heater, 23250
Globe Food Equipment Co, 23269
GOJO Industries Inc, 23023
Gold Medal Products Co, 23289
Golden Eagle Extrusions Inc, 23292
Golden Needles Knitting & Glove Company, 23293
Goodyear Tire & Rubber Company, 23312
Goshen Dairy Company, 23317
Gralab Instruments, 23339
Grayline Housewares Inc, 23374
Great Lakes Cold Storage, 23381
Greenbridge, 23413
Greif Brothers Corporation, 23431
Greif Inc, 23432, 23433, 23434
Gross & Co Licensed Bus Pro, 23464
Grote Co, 23465
H P Mfg Co, 23498
Hall China Co, 23560
Hall Safety Apparel, 23563
Hamilton Caster, 23577
Hamilton Manufacturing Corp, 23579
Hamrick Manufacturing & Svc, 23587
Haney, Inc., 23600
Hapco Inc, 23620, 23621
Hardware Components Inc, 23636
Harold M. Lincoln Company, 23652
Harris & Company, 23662
Hartstone Pottery Inc, 23677
Hartzell Fan Inc, 23678

Tema Systems Inc, 30176
Tharo Systems Inc, 30227
The Canvas Exchange Inc, 30228
The Procter & Gamble Company, 30234
Thomas Tape & Supply Co Inc, 30292
Thurman Scale, 30314
Tiffin Metal Products Co, 30323
TKF Inc, 30046
TMT Software Company, 30056
Tolco Corp, 30356
Toledo Sign Co Inc, 30357
Toledo Ticket Co, 30358
Toledo Wire Products, 30359
Tomlinson Industries, 30364
Torbeck Industries, 30382
Toscarora, 30390
Traub Container Corporation, 30434
Travis Manufacturing Corp, 30438
TRC, 30064
Treier Popcorn Farms, 30444
TRFG Inc, 30065
Triad Products Company, 30466
Trinkle Sign & Display, 30488
Trio Products, 30490
Tuway American Group, 30545
Uhrden, 30606
Unarco Material Handling Inc, 30626
Unger Co, 30631
Union Process, 30653
Unisoft Systems Associates, 30663
United Air Specialists Inc, 30667
United Mc Gill Corp, 30685
Universal Coatings, 30704
US Coexcell Inc, 30584
US Industrial Lubricants, 30591
Vacuform Inc., 30771
Valco Melton, 30779
Valspar Paint, 30791
Van Lock Co, 30800
Varco Products, 30819
Variety Glass Inc, 30822
Vega Americas Inc, 30834
Venture Packaging Inc, 30843
Versa Conveyor, 30858
Versa-Matic Pump Company, 30859
Vitamix, 30927
Vorti-Siv, 30948
W H Wildman Company, 30961
W J Egli & Co, 30962
W L Jenkins Co, 30963
Waltco Truck Equipment Company, 31044
Warren Rupp Inc, 31058
Warther Museum, 31061
Warwick Products, 31063
Washing Systems, 31064
Waste Away Systems, 31070
Waste Minimization/Containment, 31072
Waterlink/Sanborn Technologies, 31084
WCR, 30977
WEBB-Stiles Co, 30981
Webster Packaging Corporation, 31125
Wenglor, 31154
West Carrollton Parchment Company, 31163
Williams Pallet, 31276
WITT Industries Inc, 30987
Witt Plastics, 31341
Wolfkiny, 31358
Woodson-Tenent Laboratories, 31371
Work Well Company, 31382
World Tableware Inc, 31394
WS Packaging Group Inc, 31005, 31007,
   31008
Wt Nickell Co, 31414
YSI Inc, 31435
Zed Industries, 31475
Zoia Banquetier Co, 31506

Oklahoma

Acme Engineering & Mfg Corp, 18327
ACO, 18112
Acra Electric Corporation, 18340
ADSI Inc, 18129
American Lifts, 18794
API Industries, 18201
Apigent Solutions, 18982
Atlantis Plastics Linear Film, 19163
Autoquip Corp, 19304
B S & B Safety Systems LLC, 19304
Ball Foster Glass Container Company, 19418
Bio Cide Intl Inc, 19677
Burford Corp, 19962

Burgess Mfg. - Oklahoma, 19965
C & D Valve Mfg Co, 19996
Carlisle Food Svc Products Inc, 20270
Carlisle Sanitary Mntnc Prods, 20272
Century Refrigeration, 20415
Climate Master Inc, 20665
Cookshack, 20960
Cooling Products Inc, 20966
Dinex International, 21656
Dura-Ware Company of America, 21842
Durant Box Factory, 21849
Eaton Quade Plastics & Sign Co, 22023
Excell Products Inc, 22363
Falcon Belting, 22478
Fife Corp, 22571
FMB Company, 22426
Forster & Son, 22804
Gavco Plastics Inc, 23100
Georg Fischer Central Plastics, 23181
Governair Corp, 23325
Green Bay Packaging Inc., 23401
Griffin Food Co, 23443
Gulf Systems, 23480
H S Inc, 23500
Hasty Bake Charcoal Grills, 23686
Hectronic, 23739
Kleen Products Inc, 24917
Lockhee Martin Postal Tech Inc, 25422
Malo Inc, 25714, 25715
Mid-Southwest Marketing, 26160
Montello Inc, 26332
Muskogee Rubber Stamp & Seal Company,
   26437
OK Stamp & Seal Company, 26855
Oklabs, 26916
Oklahoma Neon, 26917
Order-Matic Corporation, 27005
Paragon Films Inc, 27328
Professional Image, 27921
Public Service Company of Oklahoma, 27969
Quikwater Inc, 28082
Ramsey Winch Co, 28214
Roflan Associates, 28525
Smico Manufacturing Co Inc, 29331
Smokaroma, 29342
Sooner Scientific, 29412
Southern Rubber Stamp, 29459
Southwestern Porcelain Steel, 29473
Superior Neon Signs Inc, 29845
Supply One Inc, 29856
Sysco Corp, 29949
TDH, 30033
Tulsa Plastics Co, 30536
TULSACK, 30071
Unarco Industries LLC, 30625
Unitherm Food System, 30698, 30699
Waldon Manufacturing LLC, 31027
Walker Co, 31030
Whitlock Packaging Corp, 31232
World Water Works, 31398
York Refrigeration Marine US, 31449
Z 2000 the Pick of the Millenium, 31463
Zeeco Inc, 31476

Ontario

A&J Mixing International, 18050
A&K Automation, 18051
A&M Process Equipment, 18055
ABI Limited, 18097
Accraply/Trine, 18290
Aco Container Systems, 18336
Aerowerks, 18461
Alcan Foil Products, 18541
Alcon Packaging, 18547
Alfa Food Service, 18562
ALPI Food Preparation Equipment, 18167
Amsler Equipment Inc, 18892
Annette's Donuts Ltd., 18956
APIUM Apparel, 18203
ARBO Engineering, 18220
Arctica Showcase Company, 19040
Armstrong Manufacturing, 19069
Arpeco Engineering Ltd, 19079
Artel Packaging Systems Limited, 19094
Associated Packaging Equipment
   Corporation, 19134
Atlas Corporation, 19168
Atlas Match Company, 19172
Avestin, 19263
B W Cooney & Associates, 19307
Beer Magic Devices, 19533

Beka Furniture, 19540
Belly Treats, Inc., 19563
Berg Chilling Systems, 19587, 19588
Bericap North America, Inc., 19594
Beverage World Inc., 19647
BFB Consultants, 19333
BioExx Specialty Proteins, 19684
Blue Giant Equipment Corporation, 19757
Bluewater Environmental, 19769
BluMetric Environmental Inc., 19752
Bowers Process Equipment, 19831
Britt Food Equipment, 19889
Browne & Company, 19920
Buckhorn Canada, 19939
Bunn-O-Matic Corporation, 19956
C.F.F. Stainless Steels, 20025
C.W. Shasky & Associates Ltd., 20032
Cache Cuisine, Inc., 20133
Camerons Brewing Co., 20179
Can-Am Instruments, 20193
Canada Coaster, 20195
Canada Goose Wood Produc, 20196
Canada Pure Water Company Ltd, 20197
Canadian Display Systems, 20198
Canarm, Ltd., 20199
Cantol, 20210
Cardinal Kitchens, 20252
CCL Container, 20046
CCS Creative, Inc., 20053
Celplast Metallized Products Limited, 20383
Chain Restaurant Resolutions, 20433
Chil-Con Products, 20542
Cinelli Esperia, 20587
Cleveland Range, 20658
Club Coffee, 20677
Cog-Veyor Systems, Inc., 20719
Coldmatic Building Systems, 20730
Coldmatic Refrigeration, 20731
Colgate-Palmolive Professional Products
   Group, 20739
Compass Group Canada, 20811
Compusense Inc., 20823
Conflow Technologies, Inc., 20856
Control & Metering, 20922
Cousins Packaging, 21041
Criveller East, 21109
Crown Chemical Products, 21120
Crown Custom Metal Spinning, 21124
Crown Verity, 21140
Cube Plastics, 21155
Culinary Papers, 21164
Darcor Casters, 21373
Dart Canada Inc., 21382
Dashco, 21384
David Roberts Food Corp., 21404
Daytech Limited, 21424
DBE Inc, 21270
Deb Canada, 21447
Decartes Systems Group, 21455
Deco Labels & Tags, 21462
Del Monte Fresh Produce Inc., 21513
Delta Wire And Mfg., 21547
DIPIX Technologies, 21286
Dipix Technologies, 21660
Divine Menu Covers Ltd., 21698
Dominion Regala, 21722
Dover Hospitality Consulting, 21765
Dynablast Manufacturing, 21869
E & E Process Instrumentation, 21891
EB Box Company, 21916
Ecolo Odor Control Systems Worldwide,
   22042
Edge Food Equipment, 22060, 22061, 22062
Edson Packaging Machinery, 22073
Enhance Packaging Technologies, 22214
ENJAY Converters Limited, 21945
Enjay Converters Ltd., 22215
Envirolights Manufacturing, 22241
Equipment Express, 22269
Erb International, 22274
Fiedler Technology, 22569
Food Machinery of America, 22738
Food Resources International, 22750
Fort James Canada, 22806
Fortress Technology, 22812, 22813
Francis Restaurant Industry Equipment
   Services (F.R.I.E.S.), 22850
Future Care Packaging Inc., 22958
Garland Commercial Ranges, 23068
Garland Commercial Ranges Ltd., 23067
GBS Foodservice Equipment, Inc., 22987
General Conveyor Company, 23137

Genpak, 23175
Grande Chef Company, 23348
Graphic Apparel, 23355
Gridpath, Inc., 23440
H.J. Jones & Sons, 23512
Habasit Canada Limited, 23544
HABCO Beverage Systems, 23516
Halton Packaging Systems, 23572
Harco Enterprises, 23631
Have Our Plastic Inc, 23694
Hayward Gordon, 23706
Hercules Food Equipment, 23776
Hermann Laue Spice Company, 23783
Hogtown Brewing Company, 23851
Hohner Corporation, 23853
Holland Chemicals Company, 23857
Hollandia Bakeries Limited, 23861
Hollingsworth Custom Wood Products,
   23862
Hood Packaging, 23884
Horizon Plastics, 23894
Hygiene-Technik, 24007
Impulse Signs, 24156
Instacomm Canada, 24318
Inter-Access, 24337
International Cooling Systems, 24367
ITC Systems, 24063, 24064
J.S. Ferraro, 24484
James River Canada, 24537
Jamieson Wellness Inc., 24543
JMC Packaging Equipment, 24505
Kennedy's Specialty Sewing, 24816
KIK Custom Products, 24723
Kildon Manufacturing, 24870
King Products, 24894
Kitchener Plastics, 24912
KL Products, Ltd., 24727
Knight Equipment Canada, 24937
Kord Products Inc., 24978
Label Systems, 25092
Langen Packaging, 25172
Lasertechnics Marking Corporation, 25193
Legge & Associates, 25260
Libby Canada, 25323
Lift Rite, 25341
Little Squirt, 25404
Longford Equipment International, 25463
Lorenz Couplings, 25477
MacDonald Steel Ltd, 25640
Malpack Polybag, 25716
Marquis Products, 25818
Masternet, Ltd, 25880
Maves International Software Corp., 25914
MDS Nordion, 25605
MeGa Industries, 25972
Melitta Canada, 25998
Micro-Chem Laboratory, 26124
Milvan Food Equipment Manufacturing,
   26231
Monarch-McLaren, 26316
Montebello Packaging, 26331
Morphy Container Company, 26348
Mountain View Estates Coffee, 26376
Napoleon Appliance Corporation, 26487
Nature Knows, Inc., 26556
Nella Cutlery Toronto, Inc., 26578, 26579,
   26580
Neo-Image Candle Light, 26591
Nickel 9 Distillery, 26676
Northland Consultants, 26757
Omcan Inc., 26945
Omcan Manufacturing & Distributing
   Company, 26946
Ontario Glove and Safety Products, 26979
Ontario Popping Corn Co., 26980
OnTrack Automation Inc, 26971
Opal Manufacturing Ltd, 26982
Orbis Corp., 27000
OSF, 26866
Oxoid, 27058
P&H Milling Group, 27071
Packaging & Processing Equipment, 27185
Packaging Group, 27202
Patterson Industries, 27387
Pecora Nera, Inc., 27420
Pemberton & Associates, 27445
Permul Ltd., 27497
Petro-Canada Lubricants, 27521
PFM Packaging Machinery Corporation,
   27093
PlexPack Corp, 27650
Polar Process, 27673

Polyair, 27687
Polytainers, 27702
Polytarp Products, 27703
Priority One Packaging, 27861
ProBar Systems Inc., 27887
Propak, 27948
QMS International, Inc., 28014
Quadro Engineering, 28024
Quality Containers, 28038
Radcliffe System, 28185
Rea UltraVapor, 28252
Reliable Food Service Equipment, 28339
Rodo Industries, 28519
Roll-O-Sheets Canada, 28531
Royal Ecoproducts, 28620
Rubbermaid Canada, 28642
Rudolph Industries, 28648
S.S.I. Schaefer System International Limited, 28697
Saint Jimmy's Coffee Services, 28802
Scott Process Equipment & Controls, 28973
SEMCO Systems, 28716
Sensors Quality Management, 29069
Septimatech Group, 29080
Sertapak Packaging Corporation, 29092
Shah Trading Company, 29134
Shashi Foods, 29158
Shipmaster Containers Ltd., 29193
Silliker Canada Company, 29271
Smith Packaging, 29335
Somerville Packaging, 29394, 29395
SoOPAK, 29366
Specialized Packaging London, 29500
Spring Air Systems, 29558
Stanpac, Inc., 29627
Steel Art Signs, 29659
Sterling Rubber, 29695
StickerYou, 29714
Stryco Wire Products, 29779
Super Seal ManufacturingLimited, 29829
Supramatic, 29857
T&G Machinery, 30017
T&S Blow Molding, 30018
Thamesville Metal Products Ltd, 30226
Toronto Fabricating & Manufacturing, 30385
Toronto Kitchen Equipment, 30386
Total Identity Group, 30395
Traitech Industries, 30420
Trevor Owen Limited, 30452
Trimen Foodservice Equipment, 30482
Triple-A Manufacturing Company, 30495
TWM Manufacturing, 30076
U.S. Range, 30566
UniTrak Corporation, 30637
Universal Handling Equipment, 30710
Universal Impex Corporation, 30711
Ursini Plastics, 30740
VEGCHEESE, 30757
Vent Master, 30839
Vikkor, Inc., 30896
Vineco International Products, 30903
Ward Ironworks, 31050
WE Killam Enterprises, 30979
Wedlock Paper ConvertersLtd., 31127
Wepackit, 31155
WES Plastics, 30985
West Metals, 31169
Wilton Industries CanadaLtd., 31289
Windrush Estate Winery, 31297
WineEmotion Canada, 31309
Winpak Technologies, 31318
WR Key, 30996
Wylie Systems, 31415
Zast Foods Corporation, 31472

Oregon

A & K Development Co, 18016
AB McLauchlan Company, 18085
Abundant Earth Corporation, 18280
AGC Engineering Portland, 18148
Amax Nutrasource Inc, 18702
American Brush Company, 18737
Anton Kimball Design, 18964
ATW Manufacturing Company, 18240
Autio Co, 19204
Best Manufacturers, 19624
Bi-O-Kleen Industries, 19652
Blue Feather Products Inc, 19756
Boyd's Coffee Co, 19838
Bridgewell Resources LLC, 19878
Can & Bottle Systems, Inc., 20188

Cascade Earth Sciences, 20333
Cascade Signs & Neon, 20334
Cascade Wood Components, 20335
Chaucer Foods, Inc., 20485
CIDA, 20070
City Grafx, 20601
Clean Water Systems, 20631
Clock Associates, 20671
Coffee Sock Company, 20717
Commercial Dehydrator Systems, 20794
Confection Art Inc, 20853
Contact Industries, 20884
Container Services Company, 20889
Cornell Pump Company, 20997
Crate Ideas by Wilderness House, 21067
Crossroads Espresso, 21114
CRS Marking Systems, 20102
Curtis Restaurant Equipment, 21182
Custom Stamping & Manufacturing, 21222
Dana Labels, 21350
Datalogic ADC, 21393
De Leone Corp, 21433, 21434, 21435
De Paul Industries, 21436
Del Monte Fresh Produce Inc., 21500
Dewatering Equipment Company, 21608
DH/Sureflow, 21282
Dynic USA Corp, 21888
Easybar Corp, 22014
Engineered Food Systems, 22199
Enviro-Pak, 22237
ERO/Goodrich Forest Products, 21955
Esha Research, 22296
Eutek Systems, 22332
Exhibitron Co, 22373
Faulkenberg Inc, 22508
Food Handling Systems, 22731
Food Products Lab, 22749
Fooddesign Machinery & Systems, 22768, 22769
FOODesign from tna, 22433
Fruition Northwest LLC, 22929
G & D Chillers Inc, 22965
Gage Industries, 23039
Gaylord Industries, 23104
GE Interlogix Industrial, 22993
GEM Equipment of Oregon Inc, 23008, 23009
Gerber Legendary Blades, 23198
Glass Tech, 23233
Grande Ronde Sign Company, 23349
Great Western Chemical Company, 23392
Grecon, 23395
Griffin Bros Inc, 23442
Grigsby Brothers Paper Box Manufacturers, 23448
Hanset Stainless Inc, 23614
Hewlett-Packard, 23792
Industrial Design Corporation, 24203
Industrial Labsales, 24215
Integrated Systems, 24331
International Tank & Pipe Co, 24397
Java Jacket, 24562
JVNW, 24512
Kysor/Kalt, 25013
L G I Intl Inc, 25022
LaCrosse Safety and Industrial, 25079
Lewis Packing Company, 25311
Longview Fibre Company, 25468
Luhr Jensen & Sons Inc, 25518
M & D Specialties Inc, 25547
Marble Manor, 25759
Marlen International, 25803, 25804
McCormack Manufacturing Company, 25940
Molded Container Corporation, 26301
Monastary Mustard, 26317
Mountain-Pacific Machinery, 26377
Northwest Analytical Inc, 26766
Northwest Food Processors Assn, 26769
Oregon Pacific Bottling, 27008
Pacific Scale Company, 27153
Pacific Scientific Instrument, 27154
Package Containers Inc, 27175
Paradigm Technologies, 27323
Permacold Engineering Inc, 27495
Pike Awning Co, 27573
Plastic Fantastics/Buck Signs, 27627
Pneucon, 27657
Portland Paper Box Company, 27722
Ppm Technologies LLC, 27751, 27752
Pro-Ad-Co Inc, 27879
Purity Laboratories, 27991
Ramsay Signs Inc, 28213

Rhodes Bakery Equipment, 28417
Riverside Industries, 28457
Rose City Awning Co, 28564
Rose City Label, 28565
Ryan Technology Inc., 28664
San-Rec-Pak, 28837
Seal-A-Tron Corp, 28995
Seal-O-Matic Corp, 28996
Sedex Kinkos, 29022
Seven B Plus, 29117
Sivetz Coffee, 29313
Smetco, 29330
Sorensen Associates, 29415
Sportsmen's Cannery & Smokehouse, 29550
SRC Vision, 28760
Sterling Truck Corporation, 29698
Sysco Corp, 29953
Tank Temp Control, 30104
Taylor-Made Labels Inc, 30128
The Carriage Works, 30229
Therm-Tec Inc, 30244
Traeger Industries, 30417
Truitt Bros, Inc., 30517
Unisource Manufacturing Inc, 30664
Vanguard Technology Inc, 30810
Videx Inc, 30885
Wade Manufacturing Company, 31017
Welliver Metal Products Corporation, 31143
West Oregon Wood Products Inc, 31170
Western Pulp Products Co, 31191
Whit-Log Trailers Inc, 31220
Willamette Industries, 31265, 31266, 31267
Woodfold-Marco Manufacturing, 31366
Zollman's Dark Canyon Coffee, 31509

Pennsylvania

A A Label Co, 18018
A M S Filling Systems, 18030
A Tec Technologic, 18040
A.A. Pesce Glass Company, 18067
Abel Pumps, 18269
Accommodation Mollen, 18287
Accu-Sort Systems, 18298
ACLAUSA Inc, 18108
Acme International Limited, 18331
Action Technology, 18355
Adhesives Research, 18382
Adhesives Research Inc, 18383
Advantage Puck Technologies, 18433, 18434
Aerocon, 18452
Aerzen USA Corp, 18462
AFCO, 18140
AgroFresh, 18483
AIM, 18154
Air Products & Chemicals Inc, 18501
Air-Scent International, 18507
Air/Tak Inc, 18508
Alcoa Corp, 18546
Alef Custom Packaging, 18555
Alex E Fergusson Co Inc, 18559
All Fill Inc, 18588, 18589
All-Clad METALCRAFTERS LLC, 18602
ALLCAMS Machine Company, 18164
Allegheny Bradford Corp, 18608
Allegheny Technologies Inc, 18609
Allen Gauge & Tool Co, 18611
Allflex Packaging Products, 18617
Alpha Checkweigher, 18662
Alphabet Signs, 18670
American Association-Meat, 18728
American Auger & Accesories, 18729
American Crane & Equip Corp, 18745
American Glass Research, 18780
American Olean Tile Company, 18806
American Packaging Corporation, 18807
American Pallets, 18811
Ameripak Packaging Equipment, 18860, 18861
Ametek, 18871, 18872
Ametek Drexelbrook, 18873
AMETEK, 18178, 18180
Ametek Us Gauge, 18875
Anderson Products, 18930
Andrew H Lawson Co, 18942
Andrew W Nissly Inc, 18943
ANDRITZ Inc, 18189
Apex Fountain Sales Inc, 18977
Arbocaleno Pasta Machines, 19033
Armstrong Engineering Associates, 19066
Asgco Manufacturing Inc, 19113
Associated Products Inc, 19135

ATD-American Co, 18233
Athena Controls Inc, 19149
ATL-East Tag & Label Inc, 18235
Atlas Minerals & Chemicals Inc, 19175, 19176
Atlas Rubber Stamp & Printing, 19180
ATOFINA Chemicals, 18237
Audubon Sales & Svc, 19194
Auger Fab, 19195, 19196
Auger Manufacturing Spec, 19197
Automated Production Systems Corporation, 19224
Automation Devices Inc, 19236
Ay Machine Company, 19286
B T Engineering Inc, 19306
Bacharach Inc, 19367
Backus USA, 19370
Bal/Foster Glass Container Company, 19407
Bally Block Co, 19423
Ballymore Company, 19425
BAW Plastics Inc, 19321
Beach Filter Products, 19509
Beistle Co, 19539
Bennington Furniture Corporation, 19582
Bermar America, 19601
Berner International Corp, 19605
Best Buy Uniforms, 19620
Betz Entec, 19644
Big John Corp, 19661
Bower's Awning & Shade, 19830
Brad's Raw Foods, 19841
Bradley Lifting, 19847
Brewers Outlet-Chestnut Hill, 19875
Brooks Instrument LLC, 19901
BSI Instruments, 19353
Burns Industries, 19975
C Palmer Mfg Co Inc, 20008
C-P Flexible Packaging, 20019, 20020, 20021
C.B. Dombach & Son, 20024
Calcium Chloride Sales Inc, 20148
Calgon Carbon, 20151
Can Corp of America Inc, 20189
Capway Conveyor Systems Inc, 20235
Carbon Clean Industries Inc, 20245
Carl Strutz & Company, 20265
Carleton Helical Technologies, 20266, 20267
Carton Closing Company, 20324
Cattron Group International, 20362
CCL Container, 20045
Cellucap Manufacturing Co, 20382
Centi Mark Corp, 20390
Century Crane & Hoist, 20410
Ceramic Color & Chemical Mfg, 20420
Chalmur Bag Company, LLC, 20437
Charles Beck Machine Corporation, 20453
Charles Beseler Company, 20454
Charles Gratz Fire Protection, 20458
Chaucer Press Inc, 20486
Chef Specialties, 20494
Chesmont Engineering Co Inc, 20523
Chester-Jensen Co., Inc., 20526
China Lenox Incorporated, 20551
CHL Systems, 20068
Chop-Rite Two Inc, 20561
Chroma Tone, 20570
Chromalox Inc, 20571
Clarkson Supply, 20616
Clayton L. Hagy & Son, 20627
Collegeville Flag & Manufacturing Company, 20741
Colorcon Inc, 20759
Computer Aid Inc, 20824
Conpac, 20864
Consolidated Container Co, 20869
Constantia Colmar, 20878, 20879
Consumer Cap Corporation, 20882
Consumers Packing Company, 20883
Continental Refrigeration, 20912
Continental Refrigerator, 20913, 20914
Contour Packaging, 20917
Control Chief Holdings Inc, 20924
Copper Clad, 20976
Corp Somat, 21003
Corrections Dept, 21008
Corrugated Inner-Pak Corporation, 21012
CPM Wolverine Proctor LLC, 20098
Crane Environmental, 21063
Crc Industries Inc, 21070
Crisci Food Equipment Company, 21106
Crown Cork & Seal Co Inc, 21123
Crown Holdings, Inc., 21126

Prince Edward Island

Puerto Rico

Quebec

Rhode Island

Saskatchewan

South Carolina

Bamco Belting, 19432
BE&K Building Group, 19324
Best Value Textiles, 19629
BKI Worldwide, 19342
BlueKey Inc, 19766
Bradman Lake Inc, 19849
Carbis Inc, 20243
Carolina Mop, 20293
Chef Revival, 20493
Columbia Lighting, 20766
Compactors Inc, 20810
Contec, Inc., 20895
Corson Rubber Products Inc, 21019
Crucible Chemical Co, 21143
Davis & Small Decor, 21407
De Royal Textiles, 21437
DEL-Tec Packaging Inc, 21279
Delavan Spray Technologies, 21516
DEMACO, 21280
Dispoz-O Plastics, 21678
Dixie Poly Packaging, 21705
Driam USA Inc, 21795
Dubor GmbH, 21814
Electric City Signs & Neon Inc., 22100
Engineered Products Corp, 22203
Environmental Express, 22244
Filtration Solutions, 22585
Gamecock Chemical Co Inc, 23053
Greenville Awning Company, 23423
Greenwood Mop & Broom Inc, 23424
Hahn Laboratories, 23553
Hartness International, 23676
Hayssen Flexible Systems, 23704, 23705
Hersey Measurement Company, 23785
High-Purity Standards, 23803
Hubbell Lighting, Inc, 23945
In-Line Labeling Equipment, 24161
Industrial Test Systems Inc, 24233
Inland Paperboard & Packaging, 24268
Intedge Manufacturing, 24326
Intermold Corporation, 24359
International Knife & Saw, 24380
InterXchange Market Network, 24343
JW Aluminum, 24514
KION North America, 24724
Kold-Hold, 24960
Kontane, 24972
LA Graphics, 25035
Long Food Industries, 25458
Ltg Inc, 25503
Makat, 25706
MAP Tech Packaging Inc, 25591, 25592
MapFresh, 25749
Marko Inc, 25797, 25798
Marley Engineered Products LLC, 25808
Martech Research, 25837
Mcclancy Seasonings Co, 25958
Metal, 26052
Midwest Industrial Packaging, 26182
Milliken & Co, 26223
Mister Label, Inc, 26258
Mitsubishi Polyester Film, Inc., 26264
Mrs. Smith's Bakeries, 26389
National Computer Corporation, 26501
Northview Laboratories, 26763
Novolex, 26796
O'Dell Corp, 26845
Ojeda USA, 26912
Pace Labels Inc, 27127
Package Concepts & Materials Inc, 27174
Package Supply Equipment, 27182
Palmetto Packaging, 27283
Patterson Fan Co Inc, 27386
Pioneer Packaging Machinery, 27594
Progress Lighting, 27925
Purico USA, 27987
Quaker Chemical Company, 28025
R C Molding Inc, 28090
Recco International, 28263
Rownd & Son, 28610
Rox America, 28611
Samuel Strapping Systems, 28824
Schaeffler Group USA Inc, 28912
Sew-Eurodrive Inc, 29125
Sexton Sign, 29126
Sonoco Products Co, 29406
SOPAKCO Foods, 28750
Spartanburg Steel Products Inc, 29490
Spirax Sarco Inc, 29544
St. Simons Trading, 29584
Star Filters, 29632
Sterner Lighting Systems, 29699

Superior Belting, 29836
Symtech,Inc, 29911
Sysco Corp, 29955
T & S Brass & Bronze Work, 30007, 30008
Thermal Engineering Corp, 30249
Valmont Composite Structures, 30789
Van der Pol Muller International, 30803
Vaughn Belting Co-Main Acct, 30829
Venture Measurement Co LLC, 30841, 30842
Williamson & Co, 31281
Wright Metal Products Crates, 31412

South Dakota

A&M Industries, 18054
Aaladin Industries Inc, 18248
Alkota Cleaning Systems Inc, 18581
Dakota Corrugated Box, 21329
Dakota Valley Products, Inc., 21330
Esco Manufacturing Inc, 22293, 22294
Hi Roller Enclosed Belt Conveyors, 23794
Imperial Signs & Manufacturing, 24150
International Molded Packaging Corporation, 24385
Pride Neon Inc, 27824
Shanzer Grain Dryer, 29148
Sioux Corp, 29304
Sioux Falls Rbr Stamp Works, 29305

Tennessee

A.M. Loveman Lumber & Box Company, 18074
Access Solutions, 18284
Accurate Paper Box Co Inc, 18305
ACH Rice Specialties, 18106
Acraloc Corp, 18341
Advanced Coating & Converting, 18404, 18405
Advanced Labelworx Inc, 18421
Agri-Sales Assoc Inc, 18475
Aladdin Temp-Rite, LLC, 18531
Alburt Labeling Systems, 18540
Allen Signs Co, 18613
Alliance Products LLC, 18621
Allied Uniking Corp Inc, 18634
American Engineering Corporation, 18757
American Services Group, 18827
American Style Foods, 18834
APR Associates Inc, 18208
Auto Chlor Systems, 19205
AZO Food, 18245
Bacon Products Corp, 19372
Barrow-Agee Laboratories Inc, 19475, 19476
BCN Research Laboratories, 19323
Berryhill Signs, 19607
Berthold Technologies, 19611
Big Basket Company, 19658
BK Graphics, 19340
Black Horse Mfg Co, 19723
Bren Instruments, 19868
Brower Equipment Co, 19908
Bryce Corp, 19933
Camel Canvas Shop, 20176
Cantech Industries Inc, 20208
Cantley-Ellis Manufacturing Company, 20209
Chattanooga Labeling Systems, 20482
Chattanooga Rubber Stamp & Stencil Works, 20483
Chuppa Knife Manufacturing, 20576
City Signs LLC, 20604
Commercial Furniture Group Inc, 20796
Commercial Lighting Design, 20798
Cook Neon Signs, 20956
CRT Custom Products Inc, 20103
CSS Inc, 20111
Cumberland Container Corp, 21169
Cummings, 21171
Daido Corp, 21318
Damp Rid, 21346
Davron Technologies Inc, 21411
Dehyco Company, 21473
Den Ray Sign Company, 21564
Denman Equipment, 21567
Dixie Graphics, 21702
Dole Refrigerating Co, 21718
East Memphis Rubber Stamp Company, 21999
EG&G Instruments, 21927
Elm Packaging Company, 22145
Elmeco SRL, 22149

EPCO, 21949
Evergreen Packaging, 22344
Exact Mixing Systems Inc, 22353, 22354
Fabrication Specialties, 22460
Falcon Fabricators Inc, 22479
Fell & Co Intl Inc, 22534
Fitec International Inc, 22621
Fixtur World, 22628
Flexible Tape & Label Co, 22662
Floor Master Inc, 22679
Fortenberry Mini-Storage, 22810
Francis & Lusky Company, 22849
Galbraith Laboratories Inc, 23045
Gold Bond Inc, 23288
Great Southern Corp, 23390
Hanco Manufacturing Company, 23588
Heatec, 23730
Heimann Systems Corporation, 23748
Hickory Zesti Smoked Specialties, 23800
Hubbell Lenoir City Inc, 23944
Hunter Fan Co, 23965
IBA Food Safety, 24023
Ideal Supply & Rubber Stamp Company, 24091
IFC Disposables Inc, 24034
Imaging Technologies, 24128
Industrial Information Systems, 24211
Inman Foodservices Group LLC, 24275
International Paper Co., 24390
Interstate Packaging, 24406
It's A Corker, 24435
ITW Dynatec, 24072
Jackson Restaurant Supply, 24524
Jacob Tubing LP, 24528
Jarvis Caster Company, 24558
Jones Packaging Machinery, 24654
KM International Corp, 24730
KNOX Stove Works Inc, 24733
Kolpak, 24964
Kolpak Walk-ins, 24964
Langston Co Inc, 25176
Larry B Newman Printing, 25187
Lewisburg Printing, 25314
Lockwood Greene Engineers, 25429, 25430, 25431, 25432
Lodge Manufacturing Company, 25439
M & M Industries Inc, 25553
Mc Call Co, 25933
McDowell Industries, 25942
Memphis Delta Tent & Awning, 26012
MicroFlo Company, 26127
Mid South Graphics, 26157
Milan Box Corporation, 26202
Music City Metals Inc, 26435
Nashville Display Manufacturing Company, 26491
Nashville Wire Products, 26492
Nashville Wraps LLC, 26493
Omar Awnings & Signs, 26944
Oreck Manufacturing Co, 27007
Pallet Pro, 27271
Panhandler, Inc., 27292
Parasol Awnings, 27339
Petoskey Plastics, 27519
Phytotherapy Research Laboratory, 27554
Plasti-Line, 27620
Plastics Industries, 27639
Precision Printing & Packaging, 27773
Precit, 27780
PROCON Products, 27114
Quality Industries Inc, 28051
Ram Industries, 28207
Ranger Tool Co Inc, 28225
RAPAC Inc, 28127
Red Kap Industries, 28266
Resource Optimization, 28377
Richards Packaging, 28427
Robinette Co, 28490
ROI Software, LLC, 28161
Ross Computer Systems, 28576
Rubbermaid Commercial Products, 28643
S & W Pallet Co, 28679
S&O Corporation, 28689
Sanders Manufacturing Co, 28843
Service Master Co LLC, 29099
Shelby Williams Industries Inc, 29169, 29170
Shipley Basket Mfg Co, 29192
Slip-Not Belting Corporation, 29325
Smalley Manufacturing Co Inc, 29327
SMP Display & Design Group, 28749
Sossner Steel Stamps, 29420
Southern Champion Tray LP, 29445

Southern Pride Distributing, 29458
Sparks Companies, 29486
Spontex, 29549
Stainless, 29592
Stainless Steel, 29601
Sysco Corp, 29946, 29963, 29964
Tangible Vision, 30102
Temple-Inland, 30183
Tenent Laboratories, 30186
Tennessee Mills, 30192
Tennessee Packaging, 30193
Tennsco Corp, 30194
The Tombras Group, 30238
Tops Business Forms, 30377
Trenton Mills Inc, 30448
Ultra Process Systems, 30616
Universal Sanitizers & Supplies, 30722
USECO, 30604
Useco/Epco Products, 30744
Venturetech Corporation, 30844
Vicksburg Chemical Company, 30875
Vifan USA, 30887
W.M. Barr & Co Inc., 30969
Water Sciences Services, Inc., 31081
Waypoint Analytical Inc, 31108
Wearwell/Tennessee Mat Company, 31110
Western Plastics, 31186
Williams Shade & Awning Company, 31278
Wilson Steel Products Company, 31285
WNA, 30990
Woodson-Tenent Laboratories, 31372
WS Packaging Group Inc, 31011
Zander Insurance Group, 31470

Texas

4front Entrematic, 18005
A A A Awning Co Inc, 18017
A C Horn & Co Sheet Metal, 18022
A.O. Smith Water Products Company, 18076
AAA Electrical Signs, 18080
AAA Mill, 18082
AB6, 18086
ABCO Industries, 18093
ABLOY Security Inc, 18100
Ace Engineering Company, 18309
Advance Grower Solutions, 18398
Advanced Ergonomics Inc, 18411
AEP Texas, 18133
Aggreko Rental, 18469
Air Liquide USA, LLC, 18497
Air System Components Inc, 18503
Alfa Laval Ashbrook Simon-Hartley, 18563
All States Caster/F.I.R, 18599
Allergen Air Filter Corp, 18616
Allmark Impressions LTD, 18637
Allpac, 18644
Alphasonics, 18671
Amarillo Mop & Broom Company, 18700
Ambaflex, 18703
Amco Mechanical, 18709
American Excelsior Co, 18762, 18763
American Resin Corp, 18824
Americode LLC, 18854
AMISTCO Separation Products, 18186
Amri Inc, 18890
Amy Food Inc, 18899
Anchor Crane & Hoist Service Company, 18912
Andritz Separation Inc, 18945
Antek Industrial Instruments, 18963
Apt-Li Specialty Brushes, 19006
Arctic Star, 19039
Arrow-Magnolia Intl Inc, 19085
ASI Electronics Inc, 18227
Astro/Polymetron Zellweger, 19146
Atlantic Group Inc, 19157
Atlas Match Corporation, 19173
Audion Automation, 19191
Authentic Biocode Corp, 19203
Autobox NA/Jit Box Machines, 19212
Automated Food Systems, 19221
Automation Equipment, 19237
Automation Group, 19238
Automation Products, 19243
Avalon Canvas & Upholstery Inc, 19251
Aztec Grill, 19291
Azz/R-A-L, 19293
B&B Neon Sign Company, 19308
B.A.G. Corporation, 19315
Bacchus Wine Cellars, 19366
Baker Hughes, 19390

Wyoming

Titles from Grey House

Visit www.GreyHouse.com for Product Information, Table of Contents, and Sample Pages.

Opinions Throughout History

Opinions Throughout History: Church & State
Opinions Throughout History: Conspiracy Theories
Opinions Throughout History: The Death Penalty
Opinions Throughout History: Diseases & Epidemics
Opinions Throughout History: Drug Use & Abuse
Opinions Throughout History: The Environment
Opinions Throughout History: Free Speech & Censorship
Opinions Throughout History: Gender: Roles & Rights
Opinions Throughout History: Globalization
Opinions Throughout History: Guns in America
Opinions Throughout History: Immigration
Opinions Throughout History: Law Enforcement in America
Opinions Throughout History: Mental Health
Opinions Throughout History: Nat'l Security vs. Civil & Privacy Rights
Opinions Throughout History: Presidential Authority
Opinions Throughout History: Robotics & Artificial Intelligence
Opinions Throughout History: Social Media Issues
Opinions Throughout History: The Supreme Court
Opinions Throughout History: Voters' Rights
Opinions Throughout History: War & the Military
Opinions Throughout History: Workers Rights & Wages

This is Who We Were

This is Who We Were: Colonial America (1492-1775)
This is Who We Were: 1880-1899
This is Who We Were: In the 1900s
This is Who We Were: In the 1910s
This is Who We Were: In the 1920s
This is Who We Were: A Companion to the 1940 Census
This is Who We Were: In the 1940s (1940-1949)
This is Who We Were: In the 1950s
This is Who We Were: In the 1960s
This is Who We Were: In the 1970s
This is Who We Were: In the 1980s
This is Who We Were: In the 1990s
This is Who We Were: In the 2000s
This is Who We Were: In the 2010s

Working Americans

Working Americans—Vol. 1: The Working Class
Working Americans—Vol. 2: The Middle Class
Working Americans—Vol. 3: The Upper Class
Working Americans—Vol. 4: Children
Working Americans—Vol. 5: At War
Working Americans—Vol. 6: Working Women
Working Americans—Vol. 7: Social Movements
Working Americans—Vol. 8: Immigrants
Working Americans—Vol. 9: Revolutionary War to the Civil War
Working Americans—Vol. 10: Sports & Recreation
Working Americans—Vol. 11: Inventors & Entrepreneurs
Working Americans—Vol. 12: Our History through Music
Working Americans—Vol. 13: Education & Educators
Working Americans—Vol. 14: African Americans
Working Americans—Vol. 15: Politics & Politicians
Working Americans—Vol. 16: Farming & Ranching
Working Americans—Vol. 17: Teens in America
Working Americans—Vol. 18: Health Care Workers
Working Americans—Vol. 19: The Performing Arts

Grey House Health & Wellness Guides

Addiction Handbook & Resource Guide
The Autism Spectrum Handbook & Resource Guide
Autoimmune Disorders Handbook & Resource Guide
Cardiovascular Disease Handbook & Resource Guide
Dementia Handbook & Resource Guide
Depression Handbook & Resource Guide
Diabetes Handbook & Resource Guide
Nutrition, Obesity & Eating Disorders Handbook & Resource Guide

Consumer Health

Complete Mental Health Resource Guide
Complete Resource Guide for Pediatric Disorders
Complete Resource Guide for People with Chronic Illness
Complete Resource Guide for People with Disabilities
Older Americans Information Resource
Parenting: Styles & Strategies
Teens: Growing Up, Skills & Strategies

General Reference

American Environmental Leaders
Constitutional Amendments
Encyclopedia of African-American Writing
Encyclopedia of Invasions & Conquests
Encyclopedia of Prisoners of War & Internment
Encyclopedia of the Continental Congresses
Encyclopedia of the United States Cabinet
Encyclopedia of War Journalism
The Environmental Debate
Financial Literacy Starter Kit
From Suffrage to the Senate
The Gun Debate: Gun Rights & Gun Control in the U.S.
Historical Warrior Peoples & Modern Fighting Groups
Human Rights and the United States
Political Corruption in America
Privacy Rights in the Digital Age
The Religious Right and American Politics
Speakers of the House of Representatives, 1789-2021
US Land & Natural Resources Policy
The Value of a Dollar 1600-1865 Colonial to Civil War
The Value of a Dollar 1860-2019

Business Information

Business Information Resources
Complete Broadcasting Industry Guide: TV, Radio, Cable & Streaming
Directory of Mail Order Catalogs
Environmental Resource Handbook
Food & Beverage Market Place
The Grey House Guide to Homeland Security Resources
The Grey House Performing Arts Industry Guide
Guide to Healthcare Group Purchasing Organizations
Guide to U.S. HMOs and PPOs
Guide to Venture Capital & Private Equity Firms
Hudson's Washington News Media Contacts Guide
New York State Directory
Sports Market Place

Grey House Publishing | Salem Press | H.W. Wilson | 4919 Route, 22 PO Box 56, Amenia NY 12501-0056

Grey House Imprints

Visit www.GreyHouse.com for Product Information, Table of Contents, and Sample Pages.

Grey House Titles, continued

Education
Complete Learning Disabilities Resource Guide
Digital Literacy: Skills & Strategies
Educators Resource Guide
The Comparative Guide to Elem. & Secondary Schools
Special Education: Policy & Curriculum Development

Statistics & Demographics
America's Top-Rated Cities
America's Top-Rated Smaller Cities
The Comparative Guide to American Suburbs
Profiles of America
Profiles of California
Profiles of Florida
Profiles of Illinois
Profiles of Indiana
Profiles of Massachusetts
Profiles of Michigan
Profiles of New Jersey
Profiles of New York
Profiles of North Carolina & South Carolina
Profiles of Ohio
Profiles of Pennsylvania
Profiles of Texas
Profiles of Virginia
Profiles of Wisconsin

Canadian Resources
Associations Canada
Canadian Almanac & Directory
Canadian Environmental Resource Guide
Canadian Parliamentary Guide
Canadian Venture Capital & Private Equity Firms
Canadian Who's Who
Cannabis Canada
Careers & Employment Canada
Financial Post: Directory of Directors
Financial Services Canada
FP Bonds: Corporate
FP Bonds: Government
FP Equities: Preferreds & Derivatives
FP Survey: Industrials
FP Survey: Mines & Energy
FP Survey: Predecessor & Defunct
Health Guide Canada
Libraries Canada

Weiss Financial Ratings
Financial Literacy Basics
Financial Literacy: How to Become an Investor
Financial Literacy: Planning for the Future
Weiss Ratings Consumer Guides
Weiss Ratings Guide to Banks
Weiss Ratings Guide to Credit Unions
Weiss Ratings Guide to Health Insurers
Weiss Ratings Guide to Life & Annuity Insurers
Weiss Ratings Guide to Property & Casualty Insurers
Weiss Ratings Investment Research Guide to Bond & Money Market
    Mutual Funds
Weiss Ratings Investment Research Guide to Exchange-Traded Funds
Weiss Ratings Investment Research Guide to Stock Mutual Funds
Weiss Ratings Investment Research Guide to Stocks

Books in Print Series
American Book Publishing Record® Annual
American Book Publishing Record® Monthly
Books In Print®
Books In Print® Supplement
Books Out Loud™
Bowker's Complete Video Directory™
Children's Books In Print®
El-Hi Textbooks & Serials In Print®
Forthcoming Books®
Law Books & Serials In Print™
Medical & Health Care Books In Print™
Publishers, Distributors & Wholesalers of the US™
Subject Guide to Books In Print®
Subject Guide to Children's Books In Print®

Grey House Publishing | Salem Press | H.W. Wilson | 4919 Route, 22 PO Box 56, Amenia NY 12501-0056

Titles from Salem Press

Visit www.SalemPress.com for Product Information, Table of Contents, and Sample Pages.

LITERATURE

Critical Insights: Authors

Louisa May Alcott
Sherman Alexie
Isabel Allende
Maya Angelou
Isaac Asimov
Margaret Atwood
Jane Austen
James Baldwin
Saul Bellow
Roberto Bolano
Ray Bradbury
The Brontë Sisters
Gwendolyn Brooks
Albert Camus
Raymond Carver
Willa Cather
Geoffrey Chaucer
John Cheever
Joseph Conrad
Charles Dickens
Emily Dickinson
Frederick Douglass
T. S. Eliot
George Eliot
Harlan Ellison
Ralph Waldo Emerson
Louise Erdrich
William Faulkner
F. Scott Fitzgerald
Gustave Flaubert
Horton Foote
Benjamin Franklin
Robert Frost
Neil Gaiman
Gabriel Garcia Marquez
Thomas Hardy
Nathaniel Hawthorne
Robert A. Heinlein
Lillian Hellman
Ernest Hemingway
Langston Hughes
Zora Neale Hurston
Henry James
Thomas Jefferson
James Joyce
Jamaica Kincaid
Stephen King
Martin Luther King, Jr.
Barbara Kingsolver
Abraham Lincoln
C.S. Lewis
Mario Vargas Llosa
Jack London
James McBride
Cormac McCarthy
Herman Melville
Arthur Miller
Toni Morrison
Alice Munro
Tim O'Brien
Flannery O'Connor
Eugene O'Neill
George Orwell
Sylvia Plath
Edgar Allan Poe
Philip Roth
Salman Rushdie
J.D. Salinger
Mary Shelley
John Steinbeck
Amy Tan
Leo Tolstoy
Mark Twain
John Updike
Kurt Vonnegut
Alice Walker
David Foster Wallace
Edith Wharton
Walt Whitman
Oscar Wilde
Tennessee Williams
Virginia Woolf
Richard Wright
Malcolm X

Critical Insights: Works

Absalom, Absalom!
Adventures of Huckleberry Finn
The Adventures of Tom Sawyer
Aeneid
All Quiet on the Western Front
All the Pretty Horses
Animal Farm
Anna Karenina
The Awakening
The Bell Jar
Beloved
Billy Budd, Sailor
The Book Thief
Brave New World
The Canterbury Tales
Catch-22
The Catcher in the Rye
The Color Purple
The Crucible
Death of a Salesman
The Diary of a Young Girl
Dracula
Fahrenheit 451
The Grapes of Wrath
Great Expectations
The Great Gatsby
Hamlet
The Handmaid's Tale
Harry Potter Series
Heart of Darkness
The Hobbit
The House on Mango Street
How the Garcia Girls Lost Their Accents
The Hunger Games Trilogy
I Know Why the Caged Bird Sings
In Cold Blood
The Inferno
Invisible Man
Jane Eyre
The Joy Luck Club
Julius Caesar
King Lear

The Kite Runner
Life of Pi
Little Women
Lolita
Lord of the Flies
The Lord of the Rings
Macbeth
The Merchant of Venice
The Metamorphosis
Midnight's Children
A Midsummer Night's Dream
Moby-Dick
Mrs. Dalloway
Nineteen Eighty-Four
The Odyssey
Of Mice and Men
The Old Man and the Sea
On the Road
One Flew Over the Cuckoo's Nest
One Hundred Years of Solitude
Othello
The Outsiders
Paradise Lost
The Pearl
The Plague
The Poetry of Baudelaire
The Poetry of Edgar Allan Poe
A Portrait of the Artist as a Young Man
Pride and Prejudice
A Raisin in the Sun
The Red Badge of Courage
Romeo and Juliet
The Scarlet Letter
Sense and Sensibility
Short Fiction of Flannery O'Connor
Slaughterhouse-Five
The Sound and the Fury
A Streetcar Named Desire
The Sun Also Rises
A Tale of Two Cities
The Tales of Edgar Allan Poe
Their Eyes Were Watching God
Things Fall Apart
To Kill a Mockingbird
War and Peace
The Woman Warrior

Critical Insights: Themes

The American Comic Book
American Creative Non-Fiction
The American Dream
American Multicultural Identity
American Road Literature
American Short Story
American Sports Fiction
The American Thriller
American Writers in Exile
Censored & Banned Literature
Civil Rights Literature, Past & Present
Coming of Age
Conspiracies
Contemporary Canadian Fiction
Contemporary Immigrant Short Fiction
Contemporary Latin American Fiction
Contemporary Speculative Fiction

Titles from Salem Press

Visit www.SalemPress.com for Product Information, Table of Contents, and Sample Pages.

HISTORY

The Decades
The 1910s in America
The Twenties in America
The Thirties in America
The Forties in America
The Fifties in America
The Sixties in America
The Seventies in America
The Eighties in America
The Nineties in America
The 2000s in America
The 2010s in America

Defining Documents in American History
Defining Documents: The 1900s
Defining Documents: The 1910s
Defining Documents: The 1920s
Defining Documents: The 1930s
Defining Documents: The 1950s
Defining Documents: The 1960s
Defining Documents: The 1970s
Defining Documents: The 1980s
Defining Documents: American Citizenship
Defining Documents: The American Economy
Defining Documents: The American Revolution
Defining Documents: The American West
Defining Documents: Business Ethics
Defining Documents: Capital Punishment
Defining Documents: Civil Rights
Defining Documents: Civil War
Defining Documents: The Constitution
Defining Documents: The Cold War
Defining Documents: Dissent & Protest
Defining Documents: Domestic Terrorism & Extremism
Defining Documents: Drug Policy
Defining Documents: The Emergence of Modern America
Defining Documents: Environment & Conservation
Defining Documents: Espionage & Intrigue
Defining Documents: Exploration and Colonial America
Defining Documents: The First Amendment
Defining Documents: The Free Press
Defining Documents: The Great Depression
Defining Documents: The Great Migration
Defining Documents: The Gun Debate
Defining Documents: Immigration & Immigrant Communities
Defining Documents: The Legacy of 9/11
Defining Documents: LGBTQ+
Defining Documents: Manifest Destiny and the New Nation
Defining Documents: Native Americans
Defining Documents: Political Campaigns, Candidates & Discourse
Defining Documents: Postwar 1940s
Defining Documents: Prison Reform
Defining Documents: Secrets, Leaks & Scandals
Defining Documents: Slavery
Defining Documents: Supreme Court Decisions
Defining Documents: Reconstruction Era
Defining Documents: The Vietnam War
Defining Documents: U.S. Involvement in the Middle East
Defining Documents: Workers' Rights
Defining Documents: World War I
Defining Documents: World War II

Defining Documents in World History
Defining Documents: The 17th Century
Defining Documents: The 18th Century
Defining Documents: The 19th Century
Defining Documents: The 20th Century (1900-1950)
Defining Documents: The Ancient World
Defining Documents: Asia
Defining Documents: Genocide & the Holocaust
Defining Documents: Human Rights
Defining Documents: The Middle Ages
Defining Documents: The Middle East
Defining Documents: Nationalism & Populism
Defining Documents: The Nuclear Age
Defining Documents: Pandemics, Plagues & Public Health
Defining Documents: Renaissance & Early Modern Era
Defining Documents: Revolutions
Defining Documents: Women's Rights

Great Events from History
Great Events from History: American History, Exploration to the
    Colonial Era, 1492-1775
Great Events from History: The Ancient World
Great Events from History: The Middle Ages
Great Events from History: The Renaissance & Early Modern Era
Great Events from History: The 17th Century
Great Events from History: The 18th Century
Great Events from History: The 19th Century
Great Events from History: The 20th Century, 1901-1940
Great Events from History: The 20th Century, 1941-1970
Great Events from History: The 20th Century, 1971-2000
Great Events from History: Modern Scandals
Great Events from History: African American History
Great Events from History: The 21st Century, 2000-2016
Great Events from History: LGBTQ Events
Great Events from History: Human Rights
Great Events from History: Women's History

Great Lives from History
Great Athletes
Great Athletes of the Twenty-First Century
Great Lives from History: The 17th Century
Great Lives from History: The 18th Century
Great Lives from History: The 19th Century
Great Lives from History: The 20th Century
Great Lives from History: The 21st Century, 2000-2017
Great Lives from History: African Americans
Great Lives from History: The Ancient World
Great Lives from History: American Heroes
Great Lives from History: American Women
Great Lives from History: Asian and Pacific Islander Americans
Great Lives from History: Autocrats & Dictators
Great Lives from History: The Incredibly Wealthy
Great Lives from History: Inventors & Inventions
Great Lives from History: Jewish Americans
Great Lives from History: Latinos
Great Lives from History: The Middle Ages
Great Lives from History: The Renaissance & Early Modern Era
Great Lives from History: Scientists and Science

Grey House Publishing | Salem Press | H.W. Wilson | 4919 Route, 22 PO Box 56, Amenia NY 12501-0056

Titles from Salem Press

Visit www.SalemPress.com for Product Information, Table of Contents, and Sample Pages.

CAREERS

BUSINESS

Grey House Publishing | Salem Press | H.W. Wilson | 4919 Route, 22 PO Box 56, Amenia NY 12501-0056

Titles from H.W. Wilson

Visit www.HWWilsonInPrint.com for Product Information, Table of Contents, and Sample Pages.

The Reference Shelf

Affordable Housing
Aging in America
Alternative Facts, Post-Truth and the Information War
The American Dream
Artificial Intelligence
The Business of Food
Campaign Trends & Election Law
College Sports
Democracy Evolving
The Digital Age
Embracing New Paradigms in Education
Food Insecurity & Hunger in the United States
Future of U.S. Economic Relations: Mexico, Cuba, & Venezuela
Gene Editing & Genetic Engineering
Global Climate Change
Guns in America
Hacktivism
Hate Crimes
Immigration
Income Inequality
Internet Abuses & Privacy Rights
Internet Law
LGBTQ in the 21st Century
Marijuana Reform
Mental Health Awareness
Money in Politics
National Debate Topic 2014/2015: The Ocean
National Debate Topic 2015/2016: Surveillance
National Debate Topic 2016/2017: US/China Relations
National Debate Topic 2017/2018: Education Reform
National Debate Topic 2018/2019: Immigration
National Debate Topic 2019/2021: Arms Sales
National Debate Topic 2020/2021: Criminal Justice Reform
National Debate Topic 2021/2022: Water Resources
National Debate Topic 2022/2023: Emerging Technologies &
    International Security
National Debate Topic 2023/2024: Economic Inequality
New Frontiers in Space
Policing in 2020
Pollution
Prescription Drug Abuse
Propaganda and Misinformation
Racial Tension in a Postracial Age
Reality Television
Renewable Energy
Representative American Speeches, Annual Editions
Rethinking Work
Revisiting Gender
The South China Sea Conflict
Sports in America
The Supreme Court
The Transformation of American Cities
The Two Koreas
UFOs
Vaccinations
Voting Rights
Whistleblowers

Core Collections

Children's Core Collection
Fiction Core Collection
Graphic Novels Core Collection
Middle & Junior High School Core
Public Library Core Collection: Nonfiction
Senior High Core Collection
Young Adult Fiction Core Collection

Current Biography

Current Biography Cumulative Index 1946-2021
Current Biography Monthly Magazine
Current Biography Yearbook

Readers' Guide to Periodical Literature

Abridged Readers' Guide to Periodical Literature
Readers' Guide to Periodical Literature

Indexes

Index to Legal Periodicals & Books
Short Story Index
Book Review Digest

Sears List

Sears List of Subject Headings
Sears List of Subject Headings, Online Database
Sears: Lista de Encabezamientos de Materia

History

American Game Changers: Invention, Innovation & Transformation
American Reformers
Speeches of the American Presidents

Facts About Series

Facts About the 20th Century
Facts About American Immigration
Facts About China
Facts About the Presidents
Facts About the World's Languages

Nobel Prize Winners

Nobel Prize Winners: 1901-1986
Nobel Prize Winners: 1987-1991
Nobel Prize Winners: 1992-1996
Nobel Prize Winners: 1997-2001
Nobel Prize Winners: 2002-2018

Famous First Facts

Famous First Facts
Famous First Facts About American Politics
Famous First Facts About Sports
Famous First Facts About the Environment
Famous First Facts: International Edition

American Book of Days

The American Book of Days
The International Book of Days

Grey House Publishing | Salem Press | H.W. Wilson | 4919 Route, 22 PO Box 56, Amenia NY 12501-0056